PSYCHOLOGY

PSYCHOLOGY

Second Edition

Saul Kassin
Williams College

PRENTICE HALL, UPPER SADDLE RIVER, NEW JERSEY 07458

Library of Congress Cataloging-in-Publication Data
Kassin, Saul M.
Psychology / Saul Kassin.—2nd ed.
p. cm.
Includes bibliographical references and indexes.
ISBN 0-13-863887-X (alk. paper)
1. Psychology. I. Title
BF121.K34 1997
150—dc21 97-23212
CIP

Editorial director: Charlyce Jones Owen
Editor-in-chief, Social Sciences: Nancy Roberts
Executive editor: Bill Webber
Development editor: Jean Smith
Editorial assistant: Tamsen Adams
Director of production: Barbara Kittle
Managing editor: Bonnie Biller
Production liaison: Shelly Kupperman
Project manager: York Production Services
Creative design director: Leslie Osher
Art director: Carole Anson
Art coordinator: Michele Giusti
Interior designer: Ximena Piedra Tamvakopoulous
Cover designer: Ximena Piedra Tamvakopoulous
Manufacturing manager: Nick Sklitsis
Manufacturing buyer: Tricia Kenny
Image resource director: Lorinda Morris-Nantz
Image permission assistant: Carolyn Gaunt
Image researcher: Eloise Donnelly
Director of marketing: Gina Sluss
Marketing manager: Michael Alread

This book was set in 10/13 Sabon by York Graphic Services, Inc. and printed and bound by Von Hoffman Press, Inc. The cover was printed by Lehigh Press, Inc.

Acknowledgments appear on page C-1, which constitutes a continuation of this copyright page.

Printed in the United States of America
10 9 8 7 6 5 4 3 2

ISBN 0-13-863887-X

Prentice Hall International (UK) Limited, *London*
Prentice-Hall of Australia Pty. Limited, *Sydney*
Prentice-Hall Canada Inc., *Toronto*
Prentice-Hall Hispanoamericana, S.A., *Mexico*
Prentice-Hall of India Private Limited, *New Delhi*
Prentice-Hall of Japan, Inc., *Tokyo*
Simon & Schuster Asia Pte. Ltd., *Singapore*
Editora Prentice-Hall do Brasil, Ltda., *Rio de Janeiro*

I dedicate this book to Carol, Briana, and Marc.

About the Author

Saul Kassin is Professor of Psychology at Williams College in Williamstown, Massachusetts. Born and raised in New York City, he graduated with a B.S. from Brooklyn College in 1974. He received his Ph.D. in personality and social psychology from the University of Connecticut in 1978. He then spent one year at the University of Kansas and two at Purdue University. In 1984 he was awarded a prestigious U.S. Supreme Court Judicial Fellowship in Washington, D.C., and in 1985 he worked as a postdoctoral fellow in the Psychology and Law Program at Stanford University.

Kassin is coauthor of *Social Psychology,* now in its third edition. He has also authored or edited six other books and has written numerous articles on the topics of attribution theory, social and cognitive development, and applications of psychology to jury decision-making, eyewitness testimony, confession evidence, and other aspects of law. He has served on the editorial boards of several major journals.

Away from work, Kassin has managed youth baseball teams. He enjoys quiet nights at home and has an insatiable appetite for sports, politics, rock 'n' roll, and ethnic food.

Brief Contents

Contents

6 *Memory* 206

7 *Thought and Language* 254

8 *Motivation* 292

Preface

Some of my best friends are psychologists. They have different backgrounds and interests, but to a person they're excited about their work, the field, and the contributions being made by this intelligent and useful discipline.

I had three goals in writing this textbook. *My first goal is to spark in students the same hunger, passion, and excitement that psychologists have for their work.* Toward this end, I have tried to write a book that is not only "readable" but also warm, personal, engaging, and newsy. I have not ducked the hot and sticky issues. The ethics of animal research, the biological roots of homosexuality, and the recovery of repressed childhood memories are just a few of the current controversies that I have confronted head-on by reviewing available research. I have also made it a point to illustrate the principles of psychology with vivid events from the worlds of sports, entertainment, literature, medicine, politics, law, and current events. As a result, I never, ever, resort to "John and Mary in the dorm" hypotheticals to illustrate a point. The examples I use thus reflect my conviction that students have a deep and vested interest in a world that extends past the borders of the college campus.

My second goal is to teach students that psychology is not a mere laundry list of names, dates, theories, and terms, but is an active and dynamic process of discovery—and that the state of our knowledge evolves over time. Every psychology textbook presents the discipline as a science. Indeed, many authors devote a whole second chapter to research methods. I have taken a somewhat more integrated approach. Since research methods are central to psychology's identity and development, this topic is introduced fully and comprehensively in Chapter 1, along with the field itself. In learning about research methods, from the use of case studies to experiments and meta-analysis, students are encouraged to see science as a process that is slow, cumulative, and dynamic.

My third goal—which is the hardest to achieve but is also the most important—is to get students thinking like psychologists. I believe that an author cannot invoke critical thinking in students the way a parent spoonfeeds a baby. Rather, critical thinking is a frame of mind, an attitude that emerges naturally in response to information that is engaging and personally relevant—which leads me to the special features of this book. Determined to get the student reader thinking like a psychologist, and to do so without gimmicks, I have integrated the following features into this textbook.

Special Features

"What's Your Prediction?" Studies

To orient students to the material in each chapter—and to get them thinking in operational terms—I open each chapter with a detailed account of an actual study. Some are classics in the field; others are new. Some are laboratory experiments; others are field studies, archival studies, or surveys. In some, students are asked to imagine being a subject in an experiment. In others, they are cast into the role of the researcher or observer. In all cases, I set the stage with a vivid account of the procedures used. After students have read about the situation and have imagined being part of it, they are asked to predict the results. The actual findings are then revealed, followed by a discussion of what it all means.

I have used this technique in the classroom for many years and have found that it works like a charm. After students become personally committed to a prediction, they sit at the edge of their seats, eager to know what happened. Then when the results are revealed, they think long and hard about the study and its methods—particularly when the results contradict their predictions. Now *that's* critical thinking.

Intersection Boxes

A second feature designed to get the student thinking like a psychologist is highlighted in material called *Intersections.* I use this term to refer to the various connections between *basic theory and research,* on the one hand, and various *real-world applications,* on the other. Of the many fertile domains of application that animate psychologists, I have chosen to present, systematically throughout the text, the areas I think of as the "Big Five Applications": *health, education, business, law,* and the *environment.* Thus, featured in special, high-interest boxes are such topics as subliminal advertising, being left-handed in a right-handed world, attention-deficit disorder in the classroom, personality testing in the workplace, population density and architectural design, the insanity defense, and jury decision making. There are one or two Intersections in each chapter, enabling students to see psychology from an important and enticing other perspective—"out there," in action, and in the public forum.

In the Field Resources

For the interested and motivated student, every chapter contains a list of resources for learning more about its subject matter. Many texts provide lists of readings for this purpose, but in today's multimedia-oriented world, there are other rich educational sources available. Students who use these resources will find themselves seeking information as psychologists do—inside the classroom and out, when they're reading this book and when they're not. To make it easy for students to explore psychology on their own, these "In the Field" resources include trade books, scientific journals, films and videos, telephone information services and mailing addresses, and the Internet. I am particularly excited about the ways in which the Internet can bring psychology to life. Many of the sites presented in this text offer brochures, newsletters, demonstrations, opportunities to participate in ongoing research—and links to still other sites.

Coverage of Human Diversity

Psychologists have always been fascinated by differences—among cultures, among racial and ethnic groups within cultures, and between men and women. As we approach the twenty-first century, this topic is generating a great deal of scientific interest and controversy. These topics are addressed, as appropriate, throughout this text. Similarities and differences are thus noted in perception, emotion, reasoning, intelligence, development and aging, social behavior, the structure of personality, and psychopathology.

In order to bring together the most important new work in the area of human diversity, I have also dedicated an entire chapter to this subject. Chapter 14, entitled

"Social and Cultural Groups," examines such topics as cultural differences between East and West, stereotyping, prejudice, racism in America, and gender similarities and differences. As this chapter reveals, everyone is basically the same, yet no two people are alike.

A Capstone Chapter

All introductory psychology texts that I've seen come to an end on whatever happens to be the final word of the last substantive chapter. Typically, no effort is made to integrate the material or to provide students with a sense of closure. A feature unique to this text is a closing "capstone" chapter that brings together the various areas of psychology on a hot topic that is dear to everyone's heart: health and well-being. Following an initial discussion of "mind over matter," Chapter 18 presents the latest research on the self, the health implications of self-awareness and self-deception, the processes of stress and coping, and the exciting new work in the area of psychoneuroimmunology. As noted in this final chapter, "The mind is a powerful tool. The more we know about how to use it, the better off we'll be."

Pedagogical Aids

In addition to the features just described, the following pedagogical devices are included to help students navigate their way through the material.

- **Chapter outline** at the beginning of each chapter
- **Focusing questions** before each major section
- **Narrative summary** at the end of each chapter
- **Key terms boldfaced** in the text, defined in the margin, and reprinted in a comprehensive end-of-book glossary
- **Abundant graphic presentations**—tables, figures, photographs, hands-on exercises, cartoons, and quotations—carefully selected to illustrate and evoke important principles
- **Detailed subject and author indexes**
- **References:** A complete list of more than 2,400 text citations

Statistical Appendix

For those who wish to analyze research results using descriptive and inferential statistics, this appendix clearly leads students, step by step, through methods of describing data, measures of central tendency and variability, the normal distribution, correlations, *t* tests, and the analysis of variance.

What's New

- ***Flexible Organization.*** This is a comprehensive and mainstream textbook and contains eighteen chapters. In the first edition, the chapters were divided into five parts—biological, cognitive, developmental, social, and clinical. To give instructors greater flexibility (to skip topics or vary the order), this edition presents each chapter on its own, independent of the others. As a result, the biological perspectives are now considered across the whole range of topics—as are cognitive, developmental, social, and clinical perspectives.

- *Motivation Chapter.* Those familiar with the first edition will notice the presence of a new chapter—on motivation. This is a noteworthy addition to this book because it paved the way for new or expanded coverage of such important topics as obesity, eating disorders, the evolution of desire, sexual orientation, and motivation in the workplace.
- *Most Recent Research.* From one area to the next, this book is remarkably up to date. I have taken a fresh look at the latest research developments within each and every chapter. In doing so, I have tried to strike a balance between the "classics" from psychology's historical warehouse and new studies hot off the presses. But my main goal is to describe the state of psychology *today*—and to do so in a way that is responsible. As in any text, the scholarship must be accurate. Therefore, the more than 800 new references rely most heavily on research that is reported in high-quality peer-reviewed journals.

The Supplements Package

For the Instructor

An ***Instructor's Resource Manual,*** prepared by Alan Swinkels of St. Edward's University and Traci Giuliano of Southwestern University, contains an overview, detailed lecture suggestions and outlines, learning objectives, demonstrations and activities, teaching tips, suggested student projects, transparency suggestions, and video resources for each chapter.

For new instructors, adjuncts, or teaching assistants, Fred W. Whitford's, ***Teaching Psychology, Second Edition*** serves as a guide to manage the myriad complex tasks required to teach effectively from the start. The *Second Edition* has been updated to include coverage of the regional teaching of psychology conferences and organizations, and a new section on using the Internet and online services to enhance teaching.

A ***Test Item File*** prepared by John Caruso of the University of Massachusetts at Dartmouth contains an average of 140 multiple-choice, 15 short-answer, and 5 essay questions per chapter. All test questions are available on disk on the ***Custom Test*** test-generating software for IBM (DOS and Windows) and Macintosh. The test generator contains a gradebook, a tutoring system, a graphics package, and a special on-line network testing program.

For those instructors who would like customized tests ready at the touch of a dial, ***Prentice Hall's 800-Number Telephone Test Preparation Service*** is at the ready at 1-800-842-2958. This telephone test preparation service allows instructors to call a special toll-free number and select up to 200 questions from the printed Test Item File. The test and an alternate version (if requested), and answer key are mailed within 48 hours, ready for duplication.

Prentice Hall's ***Introductory Psychology Series IV Color Transparencies*** and a special auxiliary set prepared especially for *Psychology, Second Edition,* are available to adopting schools.

Two ***laserdiscs*** are available for adopters. ***LaserPsych*** contains over 500 full-color frames of figures, charts, graphs, definitions, photographs and demonstrations and

60 minutes of exclusive ABC News programming on current issues in psychology and segments on classic research studies. An ***Auxiliary Laserdisc*** for Introductory Psychology contains video clips from psychology experiments and lecture segments from a variety of sources.

Instructors who want to build their own computer-generated lecture presentations may use Prentice Hall's ***Digital Resource Library for Introductory Psychology Release 2.0*** on CD-ROM. This software helps instructors build their own computer-based lectures by compiling and sequencing material contained on the CD-ROM, video segments found on our two laserdiscs, and material created by the instructors on MicroSoft's popular PowerPoint© presentation software. The same CD-ROM disk can be used on both IBM and Macintosh platforms.

A wealth of video material that can serve as "guest lecturers" is available to adopters of *Psychology, Second Edition:*

ABC News/Prentice Hall Video Library: Prentice Hall has assembled a collection of feature segments from award-winning news programs. The following libraries are currently available to qualified adopters:

ABCNEWS

Themes in Psychology (0-13-735101-1); (73510-0) consists of segments from such programs as *ABC Nightly News* with Peter Jennings, *Nightline, 20/20, Prime Time Live,* and *The Health Show.* A summary and questions, designed to stimulate critical thinking for each segment, are included in the Instructor's Resource Manual.

Issues in Psychology (0-13-736026-6); (73602-5) presents additional segments from ABC News programs, providing a contemporary look at stress, therapy, depression, prejudice and discrimination, violence and aggression, and gender.

The Alliance Series: The Annenberg/CPB Collection. The Alliance Series is the most extensive collection of professionally produced videos available with any introductory psychology textbook. Selections include videos in the following Annenberg series: *The Brain, The Brain Teaching Modules, Discovering Psychology, The Mind,* and *The Mind Teaching Modules.*

Prentice Hall's new ***College Newslink Service*** is a dynamic Web news service, offering professors who assign this book daily delivery of clippings from the world's leading newspapers such as *The New York Times, The International Herald Tribune, The South China Morning Post, The Toronto Globe and Mail, The Medical Tribune News Service,* and *The Independent* (London). Clippings can be customized upon request for up to 100 different courses areas.

Prentice Hall's ***Critical Thinking Resource Manual*** offers intriguing questions, exercises, and activities for each of the major topics of the introductory course. It is divided into three types of resources: questions, exercises, and extended activities, presenting scenarios from the student perspective. The format facilitates copying and use as class handouts.

PSYCHActivities Software. PSYCHActivities offers brief and entertaining activities and demonstrations through which students can participate in recreating psychological principles and concepts.

For the Student

An accompanying ***Study Guide,*** prepared by Pamela Regan of California State University at Los Angeles, is available to help students focus on the essential elements of each chapter. This student workbook presents a highly visual approach, incorporating key graphics and illustrations from the book. Every chapter contains an overview and outline, learning objectives, key terms, matching or labeling exercises, practice multiple-choice and true-false questions, and practice essay questions with brief guidelines for correct answers.

In addition, an exciting new ***Psychology on CD-ROM multimedia companion*** version of the text is available for use as a supplemental learning aid for students. It features an interactive study guide and a wealth of multimedia teaching and learning devices, including the full narrative content of the textbook to help students review and understand the correct responses to study guide questions. The CD-ROM runs on both PCs and Macintosh computers.

An Interactive Website prepared specifically for student readers of *Psychology, Second Edition* can be accessed at http://www.prenhall.com/kassin. Visitors will find a range of interactive resources, including the following:

- a **free** interactive Study Guide
- provocative interesting summaries of psychology in the news
- virtual discussion group/chat area
- related links and resources

Psychology on the Internet 1997–1998: A Student's Guide, by Andrew Stull, Xiangen Hu and Charles Long of the University of Memphis is a "hands-on" Internet tutorial featuring Web sites related to psychology. This supplement is available in a package with the text and helps students capitalize on all the resources that the Internet and World Wide Web have to offer.

"Themes of the Times," a sixteen-page ***New York Times Supplement*** containing recent articles pertinent to introductory psychology from the nation's most respected newspaper augments the text material and provides real-world examples. This timely, high-interest supplement is designed to look like a real newspaper and is updated twice a year.

The following workbooks and supplementary textbooks are available in specially discounted packages with the textbook or as stand-alone supplements:

Guide to the Brain: A Graphic Workbook (0-13-365982-8); (36598-1) by Mark B. Kristal of the State University of New York at Buffalo. This study aid helps students learn the names and locations of the most important structures and functions of the brain and nervous system.

How to Think Like a Psychologist: Critical Thinking in Psychology by Donald McBurney of the University of Pittsburgh is a 128-page paperback that uses a question-and-answer format to explore some of the most common questions students ask about psychology.

Forty Studies that Changed Psychology, Second Edition by Roger Hock of New England College presents forty seminal research studies that have shaped modern psychological study. This paperback supplement provides an overview of each ground-breaking study, its findings, the impact these findings have had on current thinking in the discipline, and the most notable extensions and follow-up studies.

The World of Sidney Slug and His Friends is a behavior modification computer simulation of games designed to teach students basic behavioral principles and techniques and help them understand how behavior can be managed and modified effectively. The program allows students to actually modify the behavior of Sidney Slug and his friends while it offers on-line advice, periodic evaluation of input, and feedback.

Acknowledgments

I am deeply indebted to Jean Smith, my developmental editor, who knows better than anyone I've met how to take a good book and make it better. With an uncanny ability to see through the eyes of a student, instructor, and author, all at the same time, Jean was my guide in this edition. I also want to thank Susanna Lesan and others at Prentice Hall for their commitment to excellence. Examine the pages of this book, and you'll see why I am grateful to those responsible for the design, photography, artwork, and other aspects of production.

I also want to thank Pamela C. Regan (California State University, Los Angeles) for writing the excellent *Study Guide* that accompanies this book, Alan Swinkels (St. Edwards University) and Traci Giuliano (Southwestern University) for writing the *Instructor's Manual,* and John Caruso (University of Massachusetts-Dartmouth) for his work on the *Test Bank*.

Finally, I could never have written this textbook without the many thoughtful reviews provided by friends and colleagues at other institutions. Through the various stages of the first and second editions, these teachers and scholars gave me invaluable insights, corrections, references, examples, and alternative points of view—all of which helped make me a better author and this a better book. For their expertise and generosity, I thank:

Lewis R. Aiken, *Pepperdine University*
Tony Albiniak, *University of South Carolina—Coastal Carolina College*
Larry M. Anderson, *Kwantlen College*
Virginia Andreoli Mathie, *James Madison University*
James R. Averill, *University of Massachusetts—Amherst*
Gregory F. Ball, *Johns Hopkins University*
Marie Banich, *University of Illinois at Urbana-Champaign*
Judith Barker, *Cuyahoga Community College*
Patricia Barker, *Schenectady Community College*
Carol M. Batt, *Sacred Heart University*
Robert C. Beck, *Wake Forest University*
Charles Blaich, *Wabash College*
Marc Bornstein, *National Institute of Child Health and Human Development*
John J. Boswell, *University of Missouri—St. Louis*
Jack H. Brennecke, *Mt. San Antonia College*
Robert C. Brown, *Georgia State University*
Danuta Bukatko, *College of the Holy Cross*
David W. Carroll, *University of Wisconsin—Superior*
John L. Caruso, *University of Massachusetts—Dartmouth*
John C. Cavanaugh, *University of Delaware*
John S. Childers, *East Carolina University*
Larry Christensen, *Texas A&M University*
Charles E. Collyer, *University of Rhode Island*

John Colombo, *University of Kansas*
Marla Colvin, *Cuyahoga Community College Metro*
Joseph G. Cunningham, *Brandeis University*
John P. Davis, *University of Washington*
Robin DiMatteo, *University of California—Riverside*
V. Mark Durand, *State University of New York—Albany*
Robert A. Emmons, *University of California—Davis*
Martha Ewing, *Collin County Community College*
Morton P. Friedman, *University of California—Los Angeles*
Mauricio Gaborit, *Saint Louis University*
William Peter Gaeddert, *State University of New York—Plattsburgh*
Grace Galliano, *Kennesaw State College*
Rod Gillis, *University of Miami*
David Goldstein, *Duke University*
Mary Alice Gordon, *Southern Methodist University*
Robert L. Gossette, *Hofstra University*
Peter Gram, *Pensacola Junior College*
Richard A. Griggs, *University of Florida*
Jim Hail, *McLennan Community College*
Lynn Halpern, *Brandeis University*
Elaine Hatfield, *University of Hawaii—Honolulu*
Holly Hillary, *Nassau Community College*
Cynthia Holland, *Cuyahoga Community College West*
John C. Jahnke, *Miami University*
Patricia A. Jarvis, *Illinois State University*
John Jonides, *University of Michigan—Ann Arbor*
Cindy Kennedy, *Sinclair Community College*
Frederick L. Kitterle, *Stephen F. Austin State University*
Stephen B. Klein, *Mississippi State University*
Mike Knight, *University of Central Oklahoma*
Richard S. Lehman, *Franklin & Marshall College*
Paul E. Levy, *University of Akron*
Robert M. Levy, *Indiana State University*
Richard Lewis, *Pomona College*
Dan Lipscomb, *Collin County Community College*
Charles A. Lowe, *University of Connecticut*
Mark Marschark, *University of North Carolina—Greensboro*
Louis D. Matzel, *State University of New Jersey—Rutgers*
Joan K. McDermott, *Towson State University*
David McDonald, *University of Missouri—Columbia*
Susanne W. McKenzie, *Dawson College*
Steven E. Meier, *University of Idaho*
Rick Mitchell, *Hartford Community College*
Steven O. Moldin, *Washington University School of Medicine*
Timothy H. Monk, *University of Pittsburgh School of Medicine*
Douglas Moore, *Temple University*
Joel Morgovsky, *Brookdale Community College*
James H. Nelson, *Parkland College*
Michael Numan, *Boston College*
Richard Panman, *State University of New York—New Paltz*
Fred Patrizi, *East Central University*
David G. Payne, *State University of New York—Binghamton*
Roger D. Phillips, *Lehigh University*
Cornelius P. Rea, *Douglas College*
Judith C. Reiff, *University of Georgia*
Daniel Rosenbaum, *Detroit College of Business*
Laurie Rotando, *Westchester Community College*
Timothy A. Salthouse, *Georgia Institute of Technology*
Edwin A. Schwartz, *College of San Mateo*
Barry D. Smith, *University of Maryland—College Park*
William P. Smotherman, *Binghamton University*
Thomas Spencer, *San Francisco State University*
Patricia N. Taylor, *Sumter Area Technical College*
David G. Thomas, *Oklahoma State University*
Arthur Tomie, *State University of New Jersey—Rutgers*
Lori R. Van Wallendael, *University of North Carolina—Charlotte*
Scott R. Vrana, *Purdue University—West Lafayette*
Paul J. Wellman, *Texas A&M University*
Bernard E. Whitley, Jr., *Ball State University*
Paul Whitney, *Washington State University*
Gordon Whitman, *Sandhills Community College*
Gail M. Williamson, *University of Georgia*
Sharon B. Zeitlin, *University of Toronto—Scarborough*
Betty Zimmerberg, *Williams College*

PSYCHOLOGY

1 Introducing Psychology and Its Methods

WHAT IS PSYCHOLOGY?

Historical Roots
Expansion of Psychology's Horizons

SCIENTIFIC METHODS

Research Settings
Psychological Measurements
Research Designs
Ethical Dilemmas

PSYCHOLOGY TODAY

Biological Perspectives
Sociocultural Perspectives

THINKING LIKE A PSYCHOLOGIST

What's Your Prediction?

Thinking like a psychologist

The situation When you first signed up to take Introductory Psychology, you weren't really sure what you were in for. You may have read about Sigmund Freud or B. F. Skinner, you may have seen a child psychologist on a TV talk show, or you may have heard a therapist giving personal advice on the radio. You may even have taken a psychology course in high school, had exposure to psychology in other classes, or done some reading on your own. Whatever your background may be, it's important to realize that you come into this course with many intuitive or commonsense theories about people. Everyone does. What are some of *your* theories? And are they correct in light of what psychologists know on the basis of scientific research?

Make a prediction Let's stop and evaluate some of your intuitive beliefs about people. The ten statements below concern topics in psychology that are found in this book (the chapters in which they appear are shown in parentheses). Read each statement carefully and write down whether you think it is generally TRUE or FALSE. When you've finished, try to estimate the number of answers you got correct.

___ 1. Although 90 percent of Americans are right-handed, left-handedness is common in many nonindustrialized cultures. (2)

___ 2. Some people dream; others do not. (4)

___ 3. Behaviorists often use punishment to eliminate unwanted behaviors. (5)

___ 4. Human memory capacity is limited and cannot truly be increased through the use of memory "tricks." (6)

___ 5. A smile has different meanings in different cultures. (9)

___ 6. Contrary to popular belief, the ability to memorize new material does *not* decline in old age. (11)

___ 7. Children's IQ scores are *not* predictive of their grades in school. (12)

___ 8. If you're assaulted on the street, you are more likely to get help if there are three onlookers than if there's only one. (13)

___ 9. A schizophrenic is someone with a multiple or split personality. (16)

___ 10. People who think about themselves a lot are healthier and happier than those who do not. (18)

The results Assuming that you have completed the commonsense psychology quiz, you are now ready to read this section on how to score it. In fact, the scoring is easy: All ten statements are false. So how well did you do? This is a true-false quiz, so you could expect to get about five answers correct just by guessing or flipping a coin. Did you do any better than that?

What does it all mean? Look back at the statements in this quiz and you'll notice that they cover a broad spectrum of topics, including sleep and dreams, intelligence and education, memory, aging, helping in emergencies, and mental health. These topics represent psychology today—a remarkably diverse discipline with many areas of specialization.

If you did not get a perfect score on the test, you'll also have noticed that at least some of the answers are not obvious as a matter of common sense. For example, later in this book we'll see that right-handedness predominates in all human cultures and across all generations. We'll also see that everyone dreams, that behaviorists advise against the use of punishment, that a smile has the same meaning all over the world, that there are ways to powerfully boost memory, and that people are less likely to help in an emergency when others are present—contrary to the belief that there is safety in numbers. And there's lots more. But for now, let's step back and define what psychology is and look at its history and its methods.

As you prepare for the challenges of the twenty-first century, there are many directions you can take. In the future, as in the past, it will be essential to be equipped with the most basic tools of literacy: reading, writing, arithmetic, an awareness of geography, a sense of history, and some knowledge of general science. Knowing a second or third language will be helpful, too. You may be especially intrigued by the world of high technology. Lightning-fast computers, CD-ROM players, modems that offer instant access to the Internet, giant space telescopes that transmit crisp images of distant planets, new advances in genetic engineering, and the use of laser beams to repair delicate tissue are just a few of the jewels found in this brave new world.

But tomorrow, as well as yesterday and today, the key to success will be understanding people—yourself, your friends, adversaries, coworkers, and others. The questions we ask ourselves about what makes people tick are numerous: How do we make important life decisions? Can people accurately bring back memories repressed from childhood? What motivates us to work hard or slack off, or to pursue one career instead of another? Why are some men and women homosexual and others heterosexual? Why do some teenagers get so depressed that they commit suicide, and what can be done to prevent it? What is intelligence, and how can it be measured? Why do some athletes choke under pressure? What causes prejudice, and why is it so widespread? If you find these questions interesting and important, and if you think the answers should be sought in a serious manner, then psychology should be part of your future.

What Is Psychology?

Based on what you know, how would you define psychology? Is it the study of the human mind, or is the focus on behavior? How has the field changed over the years? And what do you see as important issues and areas of specialization?

[Drawing by Cline; 1993, The New York Magazine, Inc.]

"Maybe you love too much."

Each of us has intuitive theories about people and their behavior.

Psychology is the scientific study of behavior and the mind. If you dissect this definition, you'll see that it contains three elements. First, psychology is a *scientific enterprise*. At an intuitive level, everyone is a psychologist—you, me, Ann Landers, the bartender who listens to one drunken sob story after another, and the novelist who paints exquisite verbal portraits of fictional characters. Unlike those who rely on their personal experience, however, psychologists employ systematic, objective methods of observation.

The second key element in the definition of psychology is that it is the study of behavior. The term *behavior* refers to any activity that can be observed, recorded, and measured. It may be as simple as the blink of an eye or as complex as making the decision to get married.

Third, psychology is the study of the *mind*. For many years, researchers flinched at the mere use of the term. It was like talking about spirits or souls or ghosts in the human machine. Today, the term *mind* is used to refer to all conscious and unconscious mental states. These states cannot actually be seen, but psychologists try to infer them from observable behavior.

Historical Roots

Psychology has been said to have a long past but a short history. There is truth in this statement. The Greek philosopher Socrates (470–399 BCE) and his followers Plato and Aristotle wrote extensively about human nature. They wrote about pleasure and pain, the five senses, imagination, desire, and other aspects of the "psyche." They also speculated about whether human beings were innately good or evil, rational or irrational, and capable of free will or controlled by outside forces. At about the same time, Hippocrates (460–377 BCE), the "father of modern medicine," referred to the human brain as an "interpreter of consciousness." Years later, Roman physician Galen (130–200 CE) theorized that every individual is born with one of four personality types or "temperaments."

Many other men and women have planted more recent seeds. French mathematician and philosopher René Descartes (1596–1650) theorized that the body is a physical structure, that the mind is a spiritual entity, and that the two interact only through a tiny structure in the brain. This position, known as **dualism**, implied that although the body could be studied scientifically, the mind—as the product of a willful "soul"—could not. Thomas Hobbes (1588–1679) disagreed. He and other English philosophers argued that the entire human experience, including our conscious thoughts and feelings, are physical processes emanating from the brain—and therefore are subject to study.

psychology The scientific study of behavior and the mind.

dualism The assumption that the body and mind are separate, though perhaps interacting, entities.

Wilhelm Wundt

Psychology also has its origins in physiology (a branch of biology that deals with living organisms) and medicine. In the nineteenth century, physiologists began studying the brain and other psychologically relevant structures. For example, Hermann von Helmholtz (1821–1894) studied sensory receptors in the eye and ear, and Gustav Fechner (1801–1887) developed a technique to measure subjective perceptions by varying physical sensations. Within the medical community, there were two particularly notable developments. In an influential textbook, German psychiatrist Emil Kraepelin (1856–1926) likened mental disorders to physical illness and devised the first comprehensive system for classifying the various disorders. In Paris, neurologist Jean Charcot (1825–1893) discovered that patients suffering from nervous disorders could sometimes be cured through hypnosis, a psychological form of intervention. From philosophy, physiology, and medicine, then, psychology is deeply rooted in the past (Hilgard, 1987; Watson & Evans, 1991).

Pioneers in the Study of the Mind Historians tell us that modern experimental psychology was born in 1879, in Germany, at the University of Leipzig. It was there that physiologist Wilhelm Wundt (1832–1920) founded the first laboratory dedicated to the scientific study of the mind. At the time, no courses in psychology were being taught because the discipline did not exist on its own. Yet many students from Europe and the United States were drawn to Wundt's laboratory, comprising the first generation of scholars to call themselves psychologists. In this group were G. Stanley Hall (who in 1891 founded the American Psychological Association [APA], with twenty-six members), James McKeen Cattell (the first to study individual differences), and Hugo Münsterberg (among the first to apply psychology to industry and the law). Overall, 186 students were awarded doctoral degrees under Wundt's supervision, including 33 from the United States (Benjamin et al., 1992). Over the course of his career, Wundt published 54,000 pages of material, edited psychology's first journal, and wrote its first book. His goal, as stated in the book's preface, was ambitious: "to mark out a new domain of science."

William James

Wundt's approach to the study of mind was a far cry from the "armchair speculation" of the philosophers of his time. He used methods of intensive **introspection**, in which trained observers reported on their moment-to-moment reactions to tones, visual displays, and other stimuli presented to them. In this way, Wundt studied such topics as attention span, reaction time, color vision, and time perception. In one study, for example, he had an observer look at a block of twelve letters for a fraction of a second, then immediately report as many as he could remember. Six letters seemed to be his limit. What would happen if the number of letters in the array were varied? How would others do if given the same task? By recruiting people to serve as subjects, varying stimulus conditions, and demanding that all observations be repeated, Wundt was laying the foundation for today's psychology experiment.

In the United States, this budding new field was hearing a second voice. That voice belonged to William James (1842–1910)—a graduate of medical school who went on to become a professor at Harvard University. In 1875, James (whose brother Henry was the famous novelist) offered his first course in psychology. He was very different from Wundt, but he too was influential. While Wundt was establishing psychology as a rigorous new laboratory science, James was arousing interest in the subject matter through rich ideas and eloquent prose. Those who studied with James described him as an "artist" (Leary, 1992). This group included G. Stanley Hall (who had also worked with Wundt), Mary Whiton Calkins (a memory researcher who became the first female president of

introspection Wundt's method of having trained observers report on their conscious, moment-to-moment reactions.

the American Psychological Association), and Edward Thorndike (known for his work on animal learning).

In 1890, James published a brilliant two-volume text entitled *Principles of Psychology*, and in 1892 he followed it with a condensed version. In twenty-eight chapters, James wrote about habit formation, the stream of consciousness, individuality, the link between mind and body, emotions, the self, and other deep and challenging topics. The original text was referred to as "James"; the brief version was nicknamed "Jimmy." For American psychology students of many generations, at least one of these books was required reading. Now, more than a hundred years later, psychologists continue to cite these classics. The brief version can still be found in the paperback section of many bookstores.

Sigmund Freud

A third prominent leader of the new psychology was Sigmund Freud (1856–1939), a Viennese neurologist. Quite far removed from the laboratory, Freud was developing a very different approach to psychology through clinical practice. After graduating from medical school, he saw patients who seemed to be suffering from ailments that had no physical basis. These patients were not consciously faking, and they could often be "cured" under hypnosis. Based on his observations, Freud formulated **psychoanalysis**—a theory of personality, a form of psychotherapy, and one of the most influential schools of thought in modern history. Freud and his early followers (most notably, Carl Jung and Alfred Adler) left a permanent mark on psychology.

Freud (1900) introduced his theory in *The Interpretation of Dreams*, the first of twenty-four books he would write. In sharp contrast to Wundt and James, who were defining psychology as the study of conscious experience, Freud argued that people are driven largely by *un*conscious forces. Indeed, he likened the human mind to an iceberg: The small tip above the water is the conscious part, and the vast region submerged beneath the surface is the unconscious. Based on this assumption, Freud and his followers developed personality tests and therapy techniques designed to penetrate this hidden but important part of the human mind (see Chapters 15 and 17).

Despite the differences in their approaches, Wundt, James, and Freud were the pioneers of modern psychology. Indeed, they were recently ranked by twenty-nine prominent historians as the first, second, and third most important psychologists of all time (Korn et al., 1991). There were many others who also helped shape this new discipline (see Table 1.1). In 1885, the German philosopher Hermann Ebbinghaus published the results of classic experiments on memory and forgetting, using himself as a subject. In 1886, American Lightner Witmer opened the first psychological clinic. He later established the first journal and training program in a new helping profession that he would call "clinical psychology" (McReynolds, 1996). In 1905, French psychologist Alfred Binet devised the first major intelligence test in order to assess the academic potential of schoolchildren in Paris. And in 1912, Max Wertheimer discovered that people see two stationary lights flashing in succession as a single light moving back and forth. This illusion paved the way for Gestalt psychology, a theoretical approach based on the idea that what people perceive is greater than the sum of isolated sensations. In the emergence of psychology as the study of mental processes, there were many, many heroes.

The Behaviorist Alternative The first generation of psychologists were just beginning to explore conscious and unconscious mental processes when they were struck by controversy about the direction they were taking: Can a science really be based on introspective reports of subjective experience? Should understanding how the mind works be the goal of this new science? There were those who did not think so.

psychoanalysis Freud's theory of personality and method of psychotherapy, both of which assume the importance of unconscious processes.

Table 1.1 Pioneers of Modern Psychology

Wilhelm Wundt	At the University of Leipzig, Germany, established the first psychology laboratory (1879).
William James	At Harvard University, published *The Principles of Psychology* (1890).
Sigmund Freud	In Vienna, introduced psychoanalysis in *The Interpretation of Dreams* (1900).
Hermann Ebbinghaus	In Germany, conducted classic experiments on memory and forgetting (1885).
Lightner Witmer	In the United States, established the first psychological clinic (1886).
G. Stanley Hall	Founded the American Psychological Association (1892).
Edward Thorndike	In the United States, reported on the first experiments on animal learning (1898).
Alfred Binet	In Paris, developed the first modern intelligence test for assessing schoolchildren (1905).
Mary Whiton Calkins	Became the first female president of the American Psychological Association (1905).
Ivan Pavlov	In Leningrad, discovered classical conditioning in research with dogs (1906).
Max Wertheimer	In Germany, discovered the illusion of apparent movement, which launched Gestalt psychology (1912).
John Watson	Defined psychology as the study of behavior, sparking behaviorism in the United States (1913).

In 1898, Edward Thorndike conducted a series of experiments on "animal intelligence." In one study, he put cats into a cage, put food outside a door, and timed how long it took for them to learn how to escape. After several trials, Thorndike found that the cats, by repeating behaviors that "worked," became quicker with practice. Then in 1906, Russian physiologist Ivan Pavlov made another discovery. Pavlov was studying the digestive system in dogs by putting food in their mouths and measuring the flow of saliva. After repeated testing, he found that the dogs would salivate in anticipation, before the food was in the mouth. At first, Pavlov saw this "psychic secretion" as a nuisance. But soon he realized what it revealed: that a very basic form of learning had taken place.

Interesting. But what do puzzle-solving cats and salivating dogs have to do with psychology? Indeed, what's the relevance to people of *any* animal research? To answer these questions, John Watson—an American psychologist who experimented with dogs, cats, monkeys, frogs, fish, rats, and chickens—redefined psychology as the study of observable behavior, not of the invisible and elusive mind. Said Watson, "Psychology as the behaviorist views it is a purely objective experimental branch of natural science. Its theoretical goal is the prediction and control of behavior" (1913, p. 158). Sensations, thoughts, feelings, and motivations may fuel speculation for the curious philosopher, but if it can't be seen, then it has no place in psychology. Psychoanalysis, barked Watson, is "voodooism" (1927, p. 502). As for using animals, Watson—like others who were influenced by Darwin's theory of evolution—saw no reason to believe that the principles of behavior would be any different from one species to the next.

behaviorism A school of thought that defines psychology as the scientific study of observable behavior.

American psychologists were immediately drawn to the hard-boiled approach of **behaviorism.** The behaviorist's research goals were clear: vary a *stimulus* in the environment and observe the organism's *response*. There were no fuzzy ideas about mental processes inside the head, just stimulus-response connections. It was all neat, clean, and objective. Watson himself was forced out of academic psychology in 1920 when it became public that he had fallen in love with his research assistant. He divorced his wife, married the assistant, and was fired as a result of this incident. (Watson then went into advertising, where he applied the new principles of conditioning and became a leading figure in the industry.) But behaviorism was alive and well. Psychology was defined as the scientific study of behavior, and animal laboratories were springing up all over the United States.

Behaviorism had many proponents and was popular for many years. After Watson, another leader emerged: B. F. Skinner, the psychologist who coined the term *reinforcement*, invented an apparatus for use in testing animals, and demonstrated in numerous experiments with rats and pigeons that behavior is controlled by reward contingencies in the environment. Skinner first reported on his experiments in 1938. Later, he and others used his findings to modify behavior in the workplace, the classroom, the clinic, and other settings. To the day he died, Skinner (1990) maintained that psychology could never be a science of mind.

The "Cognitive Revolution" Behaviorism dominated psychology in the United States from the 1920s through the 1960s. Ultimately, however, psychologists were unwilling to limit their scope to the study of observable behavior. There was too much happening inside the organism that was interesting and hard to ignore. Physiology researchers were locating new pathways in the brain that regulate thoughts, feelings, and behavior. Animal researchers were finding that inborn biological instincts often interfere with learning. Child development researchers were noticing that children pass through a series of cognitive stages in the way they think about the world. Those interested in social relations were finding that our interactions with people are influenced by the way we perceive and interpret their actions. Those studying psychoanalysis were coming to appreciate more and more the powerful influences of unconscious motivation. And psychologists who called themselves humanists argued that people strive not only for reward but also to achieve "self-actualization," a higher state of fulfillment. There were many, many voices in the wilderness waiting to be heard.

The most dramatic change that took place in psychology was (and still is) the "cognitive revolution." The term **cognition** refers to the mental processes that intervene between a stimulus and response—including images, memories, expectations, and abstract concepts. At least in the United States, the cognitive psychologies of Wundt and James were swept under the proverbial rug for years with the rise of behaviorism. The subject matter was considered "soft" and nonscientific. Then the pendulum swung back and cognitive psychology reemerged, stronger than ever. Looking back, many researchers view the cognitive revolution as sudden and dramatic (Sperry, 1993); others argue that the change was gradual rather than abrupt (Leahey, 1992). Either way, many eminent psychologists admit that they were stunned by the power and dominance of this perspective (Boneau, 1992).

What rekindled this interest in mental processes? One source of inspiration was the invention of the computer. Designed for information-processing purposes, computers provided a new and intriguing model of the human mind. The computer receives input in the form of symbols, converts the symbols into a special code, stores the information, then retrieves it from memory when directed to do so. Computer hardware was likened to the brain, and computer programs provided a step-by-step flowchart model of how information about a stimulus is processed to

cognition A general term that refers to mental processes such as thinking, knowing, and remembering.

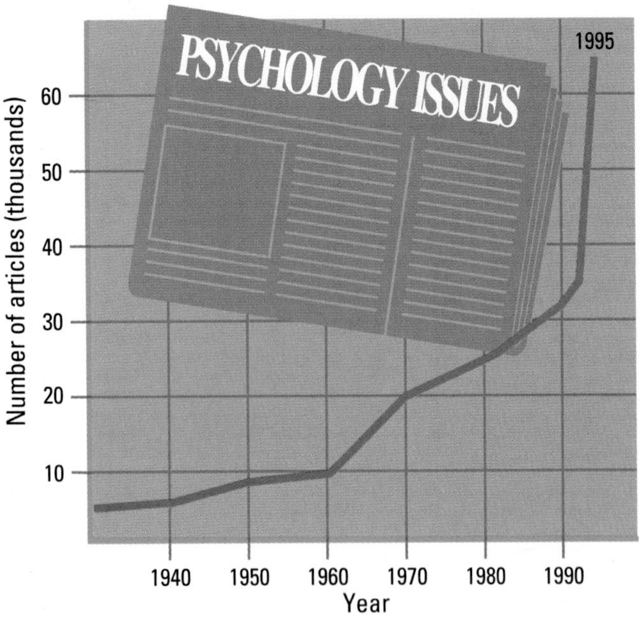

Figure 1.1 Growth of psychology As measured by the number of articles published, psychology has flourished over the years and is currently in the midst of an enormous growth spurt.

produce a response. Computers were at the cutting edge of science, so the metaphor was readily accepted (Neisser, 1967; Newell et al., 1958).

A second source of inspiration came from the work of Swiss psychologist Jean Piaget. Beginning in the 1920s, Piaget studied the way children think. He developed various tasks that revealed how children of various ages reason about people, objects, time, nature, morality, and other aspects of the world. From dozens of studies described in his more than forty books, Piaget theorized that from infancy to adolescence, all children advance through a series of cognitive stages. Despite the dominance of behaviorism in the United States, Piaget had a large following in Europe, and his writings—which were being translated into English in the 1950s and 1960s—were ultimately deemed too important to ignore.

The cognitive revolution was also fueled by developments in the study of language. B. F. Skinner (1957) had argued that the laws of learning control the acquisition of language in much the same way that they control the bar-pressing response of a rat. However, linguist Noam Chomsky (1959) was quick to charge that such an account was naive. Chomsky noted that children all over the world start to speak at roughly the same age and proceed at approximately the same rate without explicit training or reinforcement. Indeed, he argued convincingly that our capacity for language is innate and that specialized cognitive structures are "hard-wired" into the human brain as a product of evolution. Chomsky's theory dealt a serious blow to behaviorism and stimulated a great deal of interest in psycholinguistics—a topic that has played a key role in the cognitive revolution.

Today, very few psychologists identify themselves as strict behaviorists. Free to probe beneath the surface, researchers have made some interesting discoveries. Psychologists now know, for example, that people all over the world smile when they're happy; that a memory can be altered by misinformation; that our views of one another are biased by first impressions; that intelligence, creativity, and personality are partly inherited; and that drugs can be used to treat mental disorders. Behaviorism has had a profound, lasting, and positive impact, but psychology's horizons have expanded in exciting ways.

Expansion of Psychology's Horizons

Just one hundred years ago, psychology was in its infancy. Since that time, it has grown taller, wider, and stronger than it used to be (see Figure 1.1). Psychology has developed in three important ways. First, there are many more areas of **basic research** than in the past. The goals of basic research are to test theories, study processes, discover general principles, and build a factual foundation of knowledge for the field. There are now many subfields of psychology, and each focuses on mind and behavior from a different angle.

Second, psychology has expanded in the area of **applied research**. Although some psychologists believe that the discipline should remain a pure and basic laboratory science, others want to study people in real-world settings and to use the results to

basic research "Pure science" research that tests theories and builds a foundation of knowledge.

applied research Research that aims to solve practical human problems.

Psychology is a diverse discipline. Its interests include the social behavior in large crowds (above, left) and the study of the human brain (below).

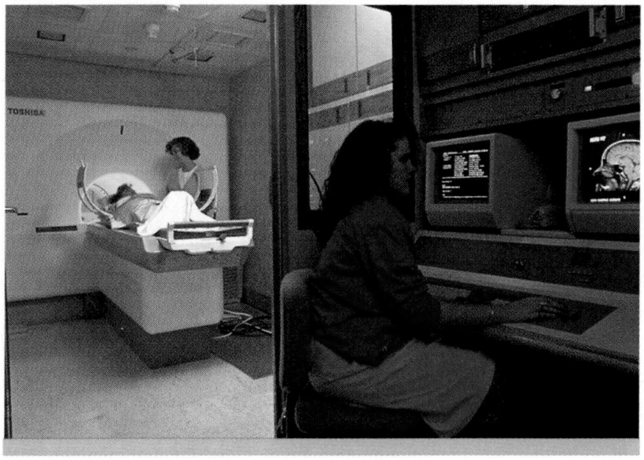

solve practical problems. There are numerous specific areas of applied research—such as health, education, business, law, the environment, religion, politics, engineering, and sports.

Third, psychology has been strengthened over the years by refining its research methods. Human beings are complex and difficult to study. As individuals, we differ in our biological makeup, age, experience, and cultural background. The way we behave in one setting may differ from the way we behave in another. The inner workings of the mind can never actually be "seen." In fact, we often lack insight into ourselves. To meet these challenges, researchers use personality and IQ tests, mazes, inkblots, optical illusions, shock-generating devices, computerized perception tasks, brain scans, and sophisticated instruments that record physiological states. Most important, as we'll soon see, psychology stands high on the shoulders of the scientific method.

Basic Areas of Specialization Psychology has become a highly specialized discipline. To provide a comprehensive look at the field as a whole, this textbook covers all the basic areas and the important questions they raise concerning human nature.

Biological Roots First, we will examine the biological areas of psychology and the intricate links between the body and the mind. Chapter 2, on behavioral neuroscience, builds the foundation for this approach by describing the structures and functions of the human brain and nervous system. In all subsequent chapters of the text, we'll also see important biological perspectives provided by researchers who study animal behavior, the evolutionary origins of human behavior, behavioral genetics, hormonal influences, and drugs.

Cognitive and Affective Processes We will also examine major cognitive and affective processes. With the computer serving as a model of the human mind, we consider the extent to which people are competent and objective in the way they process information about the world. We will look at the topics of sensation and perception, consciousness, learning, memory, thought, and language. Then, we consider the ways in which we warm-blooded humans are driven by motivations and emotions.

Human Development Developmental psychology examines the ways in which people develop over the lifespan. Central to this area is the "nature–nurture" debate, concerning genetic and environmental influences. As we'll see, some developmental psychologists study prenatal development, infants, young children, or adolescents. Others specialize in adults, the elderly, or the process of dying. Still others are interested in intelligence, testing, and education.

Social Psychology Next we look at *social* psychology. Drawn together by the belief that situations often cause us to behave in ways that are "out of character," social psychologists focus on the influences of other people on the individual. By observing people in carefully staged social settings, researchers in this area study the way we perceive, influence, and relate to one another. They also study cultural influences on behavior.

Clinical Psychology Finally, we look at clinical psychology, the largest branch of the discipline (see Figure 1.5). Based on the study of human personality and on the belief that people have a capacity for change and renewal, clinical psychologists and other mental-health workers seek to diagnose and treat mental disorders such as anxiety, depression, and schizophrenia. In a related pursuit, counseling psychologists provide marriage, family, career, and guidance counseling to people with less severe problems.

Practical Applications Many Olympic teams hire sports psychologists to work with their athletes. Corporations, advertising agencies, law firms, and school systems hire psychologists for research and consulting purposes. And psychologists teach in schools of medicine, law, business, and education. Like other basic sciences, psychology has strayed from the laboratories of the ivory tower into the real world. The secret is out.

The application of psychology—or any other science, for that matter—raises hard questions about values, professional ethics, and social responsibility. For example, should research be suppressed if it yields socially sensitive results? It's easy in the abstract for psychologists to assert that they must seek the truth regardless of where it may lead, but what about the policy implications? Should IQ-test scores of different racial and ethnic groups be compared? And if some groups score lower than others, should the disparity be reported? What about studies suggesting that the testimony of young children—often essential to the prosecution of sex abusers—cannot be trusted? Additional questions confront those who apply psychology. Is it ethical to dispense mental health advice on television or over the radio? Should psychologists use their scientific credentials to promote drug company products or to lobby for abortion rights, handgun control, and other political causes? Should psychologists testify as experts in trials involving the insanity defense? Working in a discipline that addresses many delicate topics, psychologists must face these important questions.

> *"There are no such things as applied sciences, only applications of science."*
>
> —LOUIS PASTEUR

To illustrate some of the fascinating links between basic and applied psychology, every chapter of this text contains at least one special "intersection"—highlighted material that presents relevant research in one of the following major domains of application: health, education, business, law, and the environment.

Health Psychology is applied in many ways to the study of health and medicine. How does stress affect the body, and what coping mechanisms are most adaptive? Is it healthier to have an accurate perception of reality or a bias toward optimism? Are people with certain personalities prone to disease? Why do cancer patients live longer if they are socially connected than if they are alone? Answers to these questions appear throughout the text and are the focus of the final chapter.

Education In 1993, the U.S. Department of Education estimated that 90 million American adults are incompetent at practical tasks such as reading a bus schedule and calculating the cost of carpeting a room. Clearly, psychology has a lot to say about education—about IQ tests, creativity, bilingualism, a child's motivation to learn, ways to improve memory, and so on. Researchers are now seeking answers to important practical questions, which are discussed throughout the book.

Business There are two ways in which psychologists are involved in business. *Industrial/organizational (I/O) psychology* focuses on human behavior in the workplace and other organizations. I/O researchers study personnel selection and training, leadership, and worker motivation and productivity. In contrast, *consumer psychology* focuses on behavior in the marketplace. Researchers in this area study consumer attitudes, advertising, and economic decision making. As we'll see, psychology's involvements in the world of business are numerous.

Law Today, many psychologists are at work in the legal system consulting with attorneys and judges, testifying in court, teaching in law schools, and conducting research on justice-related issues. Those studying psychology in law are involved in a wide range of topics, including jury selection and decision making, eyewitness testimony, lie-detector tests, prison reform, and the insanity defense.

The Environment Why are some cities healthier to live in than others? Can the architectural design of a building or neighborhood affect the crime rate? *Environmental psychologists* study the relations between people and their physical surroundings—including the effects of street noise, heat, and population density. In a related field, *human-factors psychologists* design furniture, tools, and other human-made aspects of the environment in order to maximize comfort, safety, and convenience.

To summarize, psychology's horizons have expanded both in the study of basic processes and in the domains of application. In the coming chapters, all of the basic areas will be discussed, and all five areas of applications will be featured in special sections called Intersections. As we'll see, this two-dimensional growth has given rise to some exciting new research connections.

Scientific Methods

What are scientific methods, and why are they important? Is it better to study people in a laboratory or in natural settings? Why do psychologists devise subtle measures of behavior when they can just ask people about themselves? What ethical concerns have been raised about using human subjects in research? What about the use of animals?

It happens all the time. I'll see a report on the evening news, a magazine story, or an ad for a new product, and I'll react with a mixture of curiosity and skepticism. For example, I've heard that students can raise SAT scores 150 points by taking a test-preparation course, that a full moon triggers bizarre behavior, that workaholics drive themselves to an early grave, that pornography incites rape, and that girls start talking before boys do. Some of these claims are true; others are not. My reaction is always the same: "Hmm. Interesting," I'll say to myself. "But prove it!"

Many of us are drawn to psychology because people are fascinating and the subject matter is important. What unifies psychology as a discipline, however, is its commitment to scientific methods. A basic goal in science is one that should be modeled by everyone: critical thinking. Critical thinking is a skill, and it's also an attitude. The objective of scientific inquiry is to generate creative ideas and entertain these ideas with an open mind—but, at the same time, to be cautious, to demand that all claims be tested, and to scrutinize the results. The "art" in science is to achieve a balance between these competing objectives. It's good to be creative but not intellectually sloppy. Similarly, it's good to be critical, even skeptical, but not close minded. The key to thinking like a psychologist is learning how to walk these fine lines. And that means knowing something about psychology's methods of research.

> *"At the heart of science is an essential tension between two seemingly contradictory attitudes—an openness to new ideas, no matter how bizarre or counterintuitive they may be, and the most ruthless skeptical scrutiny of all ideas, old and new."*
>
> —CARL SAGAN

The first important step in research is to formulate a hypothesis to be tested. As discussed earlier, you already have many intuitive theories on psychological issues. Everyone does. When I was choosing a graduate school, I had to decide whether or not to leave town to go to the best possible program—which meant leaving behind a girlfriend. What should I do? What effect would distance have on our relationship? One friend was certain he knew the answer: "Absence makes the heart grow fonder." Those words of encouragement made sense to me until a second friend said with equal certainty, "Out of sight, out of mind." Just what I needed. Two contradictory theories, both derived from common sense.

Psychological theories are more formal than the hunches we come up with in everyday conversation. A **theory** is an organized set of principles that describes, predicts, and explains a phenomenon. One can derive a theory from logic, a world event, a personal experience or observation, another theory, a research finding, or an accidental discovery. Some theories are broad and encompassing; others account for only a thin slice of behavior. Some are simple; others contain a large number of interrelated propositions. In all cases, a theory should provide specific testable predictions, or **hypotheses**, about the relation between two or more variables. Researchers can then test these hypotheses to evaluate the theory as a whole.

There is no magic formula for determining how to test a hypothesis. In fact, as we'll see, studies vary along at least three dimensions: (1) the setting in which observations are made, (2) the ways in which psychological variables are measured, and (3) the types of conclusions that can be drawn. Let's separately examine each of these dimensions.

theory An organized set of principles that describes, predicts, and explains some phenomenon.

hypothesis A specific testable prediction, often derived from a theory.

laboratory research Research conducted in an environment that can be regulated and in which subjects can be carefully observed.

Research Settings

There are two types of settings in which people can be studied. Sometimes, data are collected in a laboratory, usually located at a university, so that the environment can be regulated and the subject carefully observed. **Laboratory research** offers control, precision, and an opportunity to keep conditions uniform for different subjects. For example, bringing volunteers into a sleep lab enables the psychologist to monitor their eye movements and brain-wave activity, record the exact time they fall asleep, and get dream reports the moment they awaken. Likewise, bringing a parent and child into a special playroom equipped with hand-picked toys, two-way mirrors, a hidden camera, and a microphone enables the psychologist to record every word uttered and analyze every nuance of their interaction. To study the way juries make decisions, I recruit people to serve on mock juries so that I can videotape and later analyze their deliberations.

Laboratory research is common in science. NASA physicists construct special chambers to simulate weightlessness in space; chemists generate chemical reactions in the test tube; botanists study plant growth in the greenhouse; and meteorologists use wind tunnels to mimic atmospheric conditions. Similarly, psychologists often find it necessary to simulate events in a laboratory. There is, however, a drawback. Can someone sleep normally in a strange bed with metal electrodes pasted to the scalp? Will a parent and child interact in the playroom the way they do at home? Do mock juries reach verdicts the same way real juries do? Possibly not. Being an artificially constructed world, the laboratory may elicit atypical behavior.

The alternative is **field research** conducted in real-world locations. The psychologist interested in sleep and dreams may have subjects report back periodically on their experiences. The parent and child could be visited in their own home. And jurors could be questioned about their decision-making process after a trial is over. The setting chosen depends on the behavior to be measured. Indeed, psychologists have observed people in city streets, classrooms, factories, offices, singles bars, subways, dormitories, elevators, and even public restrooms. To understand behavior in real-world settings, there is no substitute for field research. Unfortunately, the psychologist "out there" cannot control what happens to his or her subjects or measure with precision all aspects of their experiences. That's why the most fruitful approach is to use both laboratory and field settings.

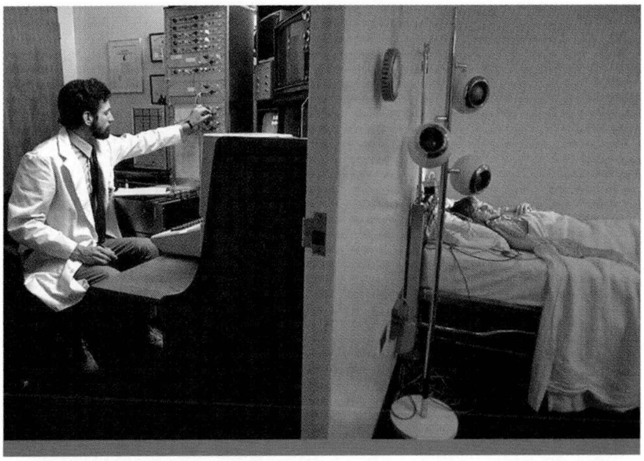

There are two types of research settings. In a laboratory study, behavior is observed in a controlled environment—such as a sleep laboratory (above). In field studies, people are observed in the street and in real-world settings (below).

Psychological Measurements

Regardless of where observations are made, many different types of measurements can be taken. These types fall into three categories: self-reports, behavioral observations, and archival records. These three types of observations, and the advantages and disadvantages of each, are summarized in Table 1.2.

field research Research that is conducted in real-world locations.

Table 1.2 Three Ways to "Observe" People

METHOD	DESCRIPTION	ADVANTAGES	DISADVANTAGES
Self-reports	Ask people to report on themselves in interviews, surveys, or questionnaires.	People often reveal inner states that cannot be "seen" by others.	People distort self-reports to present themselves in a favorable light. People are not always aware of their own inner states.
Behavioral observations	Observe behavior firsthand, openly or covertly, sometimes using special tasks or instruments.	Behavior can be measured objectively.	Inner states can only be inferred from behavior, not actually seen. People may behave differently if they know they are being observed.
Archival records	Observe behavior secondhand, using available records of past activities.	The behavior occurs without the biasing presence of an observer	Records of past activities are not always complete or accurate.

Self-Reports One way to assess a person's thoughts, feelings, or behavior is to go right to the source and ask. This is the method of **self-report**. Through interviews, questionnaires, or diaries, people are asked to report on their behavior, perceptions, beliefs, attitudes, and emotions. Self-reports are quick and easy to get. The information, however, can be inaccurate and misleading.

There are two problems with self-reports. First, people sometimes distort their responses in order to present themselves in a favorable light. It's hard to get anyone to admit to failures, mistakes, and shortcomings. Studies show, for example, that people tend to overestimate their own contributions to a joint effort (Ross & Sicoly, 1979), report after the occurrence of an event that they knew all along it would happen (Hawkins & Hastie, 1990), hide their feelings of prejudice (Crosby et al., 1980), and overestimate the accuracy of their own predictions (Dunning et al., 1990). Thus, when James Shepperd (1993) asked college students about their SAT scores and then checked their academic records, he discovered that they overestimated their actual scores by an average of seventeen points.

A second problem with self-report data is that even when respondents try to be accurate, they are often limited in their ability to do so. Long ago, Freud noted that people block certain thoughts and wishes from awareness. And studies show that people often lack insight into the causes of their own behavior (Nisbett & Wilson, 1977). In a surprising illustration of the limits of self-reports, Stanley Coren (1993), an expert on left-handedness, notes that when he asks people if they're right- or left-handed, 7 percent answer incorrectly. "One man who confidently reported that he was a right-hander, when tested to see which hand he used to throw a ball, aim a dart, cut with scissors, and the like, performed every single action with his left hand. His only detectable right-handed activity was writing" (p. 34).

Self-report measures are common in psychology, sometimes even essential. As you read through this book, however, you'll see that researchers often go out of their way to collect data in more subtle, indirect ways. Now you know the reason: The source is not always the best source.

self-report A method of observation that involves asking people to describe their own thoughts, feelings, or behavior.

Behavioral Observations It is said that actions speak louder than words—and many researchers would agree. Many years ago, the Nielsen ratings of TV shows (which determine the cost of advertising and success of programs) were derived from the results of surveys and diary forms mailed to viewers. Realizing that these self-reports are flawed, however, Nielsen Media Research recently installed "People Meters" in 5,000 sample households across the country to electronically record what viewers are watching, when, and for how long.

In psychology as well, the major alternative to self reports is firsthand **behavioral observation.** To animal researchers, the pressing of a bar, the running of a maze, and the consumption of food pellets are important behaviors. Sucking, smiling, crying, moving the eyes, and turning the head are significant sources of information for those who study infants. As for those who study adults, psychologically relevant behaviors range from the blink of an eye to the choice of a career. Even changes in internal states (such as respiration, heart rate, eye movements, brain waves, hormone levels, muscle contractions, and white blood-cell activity) can be monitored with the use of special instruments.

Behavioral observation is critical to psychology. In this study, a four-month-old baby is tested to see if she knows that an object in motion will not stop in midair.

Behavioral observation plays a particularly important role in the study of subjective experience. One cannot crawl under a subject's skin and see what's on his or her mind. But researchers can try to infer various internal states from behavior. It is usually (though not always) safe to assume, for example, that recognition reveals the presence of a memory, that solving difficult problems reveals intelligence, and that the person who breaks into a cold sweat and runs at the sight of a snake has a fear of snakes.

Archival Records A third way to collect information about people is to conduct **archival research** that involves examining records of past activities instead of ongoing behavior. Archival measures used in psychology include medical records, birth rates, literacy rates, newspaper stories, sports statistics, photographs, absenteeism rates at work, personal ads, marriages, and divorce. A major advantage of these kinds of measures is that by observing behavior secondhand, researchers can be sure that they did not influence the subjects by their presence. An obvious limitation is that existing and available records of human activity are not always complete or detailed enough to be useful.

Archival measures are particularly valuable for examining cultural or historical trends. For example, Coren (1993) wanted to know if right-handedness was always dominant among humans (today, roughly 90 percent of the population is right-handed). So he went through a collection of art books and analyzed 1,180 drawings, paintings, and engravings that depicted an individual using a tool or a weapon. The drawings ranged from Stone Age sketches dated 15,000 BCE to paintings from the year 1950 CE. Yet Coren found that 90 percent of all characters were portrayed as right-handers—and that this percentage was the same thousands of years ago as in the twentieth century.

behavioral observation A form of research that is based on the firsthand observation of a subject's behavior.

archival research A form of research that relies on existing records of past behavior.

Research Designs

Regardless of how and where the information is obtained, researchers use **statistics** to summarize and then analyze the results. In some cases, statistical tests are used simply to describe what happened in terms of averages, percentages, frequencies, and other quantitative measures. In other cases, analyses are used to test inferences about people in general and their behavior. More about the use of statistics in psychological research is available in the Appendix of this book. For now, it is important to note that the types of conclusions that are drawn are limited by the way a study is designed. In particular, three types of research are used: descriptive studies, correlational studies, and experiments.

Descriptive Research

The first purpose of research is simply to *describe* a person, group, or psychological phenomenon through systematic observation. This goal can be achieved through case studies, surveys, and naturalistic observations.

Case Studies Sometimes it is useful to study one or more individuals in great detail. Information about a person can be obtained through tests, interviews, first-hand observation, and biographical material such as diaries and letters written. **Case studies** are conducted in the hope that an in-depth look at one individual will reveal something important about people in general. The problem with case studies is that they are time consuming and often are limited in their generality. To the extent that a subject is atypical, the results may say little about the rest of us.

Nevertheless, case studies have played an influential role in psychology. Sigmund Freud based his theory of personality on a handful of patients. Behaviorist John Watson used a case study to try to debunk psychoanalysis. Swiss psychologist Jean Piaget formulated a theory of intellectual development by questioning his own children. Neuroscientists gain insights into the workings of the brain by testing patients who have suffered brain damage. Cognitive psychologists learn about memory from rare individuals who can retain enormous amounts of information. Psycholinguists study language development by recording the speech utterances of their own children over time. Intelligence researchers learn about human intellectual powers by studying child prodigies, chess masters, and other gifted individuals. Social psychologists pick up clues about leadership by analyzing biographies of great leaders. And clinical psychologists refine the techniques of psychotherapy through their shared experiences with individual patients. When an individual comes along who is exceptional in some way or when a psychological hypothesis can be answered only through systematic, long-term observation, the case study provides a valuable starting point.

Surveys In contrast to the in-depth study of one person, **surveys** describe an entire population by looking at many cases. In a survey—which can be conducted in person, over the phone, or through the mail—people can be asked various questions about themselves. Surveys have become very popular in recent years and tell us, for example, that 95 percent of all American men and women have sexual fantasies (Leitenberg & Henning, 1995), that 96 percent believe in God (Golay & Rollyson, 1996), that 49 percent daydream about being rich (Roper Reports, 1989), and that 75 to 80 percent are generally happy (Diener & Diener, 1996). In case you've been wondering, 37 percent of women and 18 percent of men squeeze the toothpaste tube from the bottom (Weiss, 1991).

Surveys are sometimes necessary for the purpose of describing psychological states that are difficult to observe directly. For example, this method is an important

statistics A branch of mathematics that is used for analyzing research data.

case studies A type of research that involves making in-depth observations of individual persons.

survey A research method that involves interviewing or giving questionnaires to a large number of people.

tool in **epidemiology**—the study of the distribution of illnesses in a population. How many children are awakened by nightmares? What percentage of college students are plagued by test anxiety? How common are depression, alcoholism, and suicide? These kinds of questions are vital for determining the extent of a problem and knowing how to allocate health-care resources. Surveys are also useful for describing sexual practices. With AIDS spreading at an alarming rate, it's important to know how sexually active people are, whether they use condoms, and whether some segments of the population are more at risk than others. Today, surveys are so common, and the results have such significant implications, that the method (which, after all, relies on self-report) should be carefully scrutinized. Two factors are particularly important: who the respondents are and how the questions are asked.

In 1948, newspapers projected that Dewey defeated Truman for president. As Truman basked in his victory, pollsters realized that their pre-election predictions were based on nonrandom samples of voters. Most polls were conducted by phone—and more Republicans than Democrats had phones.

To describe a group, any group—males, females, college students, redheads, homeowners, Americans, or all registered voters—researchers select a subset of individuals. The entire group is called the *population*; the subset of those questioned constitutes a *sample*. For a survey to be accurate, the sample must be similar to or representative of the population on key characteristics such as sex, race, age, region, income, and cultural background. Short of questioning everyone in the population, the best way to ensure representativeness is to use a **random sample**, a method of selection in which everyone has an equal chance of being chosen. Survey researchers usually pick names arbitrarily from a phone book or some other list. This seems like a reasonable strategy (and the larger the sample, the smaller the margin of error), but no sample is perfect. Not everyone has a telephone, some people have unlisted numbers, and some people who are called may not be home or may refuse to participate. In the 1948 U.S. presidential election, pollsters nationwide predicted that Thomas Dewey would defeat Harry Truman by a wide margin. Yet Truman won. The problem was that most polls were conducted by phone—and at the time, more Republicans than Democrats had phones. For a sample to accurately reflect its parent population, it must be selected in a manner that is random, not biased.

A second factor to consider is the wording of questions and the context in which they are asked (Tourangeau et al., 1991). The following examples illustrate the point.

- When survey respondents were asked about "assisting the poor," only 23 percent said that too much money was being spent. Yet among those asked about "welfare," 53 percent gave this negative response (*Time*, 1994).
- College students tried to estimate the distance from New York City to San Francisco (3,200 miles). Among those who were first asked if the distance is more or less than 1,500 miles, the average estimate was 2,600. Yet among those first asked if the distance was more or less than 6,000 miles, the average estimate was 4,000 (Jacowitz & Kahneman, 1995).
- Subjects who were asked whether "People should have the freedom to express their opinions publicly" were more likely to say *yes* when the previous question was about the Catholic Church than after a question about Nazis (Ottati et al., 1989).
- Eighty-eight percent of subjects thought condoms were effective in stopping AIDS when condoms were said to have a "95 percent success rate." However, when condoms were said to have a "5 percent failure rate," only 42 percent of the subjects were similarly optimistic (Linville et al., 1992).

Naturalistic Observations A third descriptive approach is to observe behavior as it occurs in the real world. **Naturalistic observations** are common in anthropology,

epidemiology The study of the distribution of illnesses in a population.

random sample A method of selection in which everyone in a population has an equal chance of being chosen.

naturalistic observation The observation of behavior as it occurs naturally in real-world settings.

Naturalistic observation is a common form of descriptive research. For many years, Jane Goodall has observed chimpanzees in the wild.

where field workers seek to describe a culture by living in it for long periods of time. Psychologists use this method as well to study parents and their children, corporate executives, factory workers, nursing-home residents, and others.

Naturalistic observation is particularly common among ethologists, who study the behavior of animals in their natural habitats. For example, Jane Goodall has spent more than thirty-five years watching chimpanzees in African jungles (Goodall, 1986; Peterson & Goodall, 1993). She has observed their social structure, courting rituals, struggles for dominance, and child-rearing practices. She also saw the chimps strip leaves from twigs and use the twigs to fish termites out of nests—a finding that disproved the widely held assumption that only humans are capable of making tools. In another program of research, Dorothy Cheney and Robert Seyfarth (1990) observed vervet monkeys in Kenya and discovered that these monkeys behave as if they know the kinship bonds within their group, use deception to outsmart rivals, and use vocal calls in ways that are more sophisticated than was previously expected. To truly understand primates, and perhaps their similarities to humans, one has to observe their behavior in the wild—not captive in a zoo or laboratory.

Correlational Studies Description is a nice first step, but science demands much more. A second goal is to find connections, or correlations, between variables so that one factor can be used to predict another. Correlational research is reported in psychology—and in the news—with remarkable frequency. Consider a few examples: The more violence children watch on TV, the more aggressive they are. Men with high testosterone levels are more prone to crime and violence. College graduates earn more money than nongraduates. The more optimistic people are, the less often they get sick. Adults who exercise regularly live longer than those who do not. People who are shy have fewer friends than those who are outgoing. So what do these statements of correlation *really* prove? And what do they not prove?

A **correlation** is a statistical measure of the extent to which two factors are associated. Expressed in numerical terms, *correlation coefficients* range from +1 to −1. A positive correlation exists when the two variables increase or decrease together, in the same direction. The link between TV violence and aggression is positive—more of one means more of the other; so are the correlations between testosterone and aggression, education and income, exercise and longevity. In contrast, a negative correlation exists when an increase in one variable is accompanied by a decrease in the other, and vice versa. The link between optimism and illness is in a negative direction, as is the one between shyness and friendships.

Correlation coefficients vary not only in direction but also in strength. The higher a correlation is, regardless of whether it is positive or negative, the stronger the link is between variables. Correlations that are very low—near zero—indicate that two variables are independent. Contrary to popular opinion, research shows, for example, that there is no correlation between phases of the moon and criminal activity, between an eyewitness's confidence and accuracy, or between intelligence-test scores in infancy and adulthood. In short, full moons, confident witnesses, and infant

correlation A statistical measure of the extent to which two variables are associated.

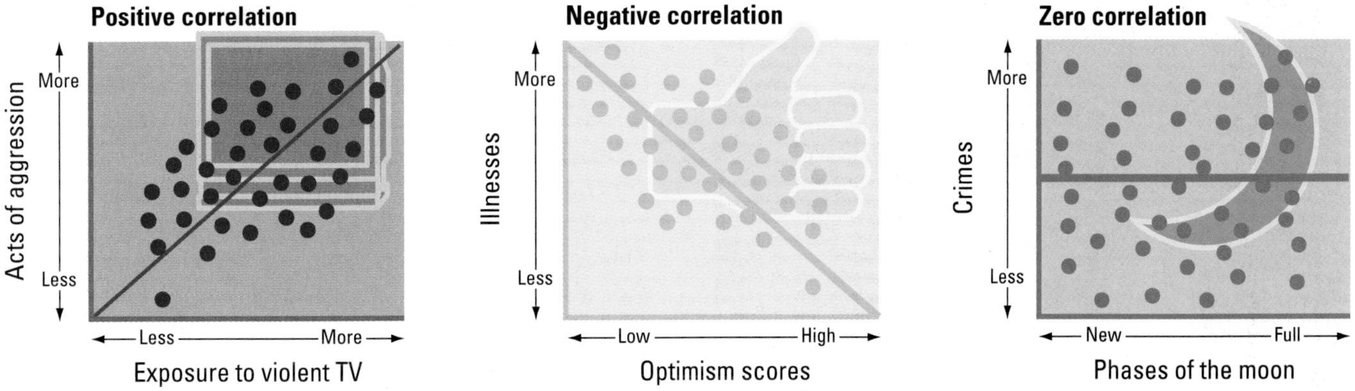

Figure 1.2 Visualizing correlations Scatterplots provide a graphic representation of the observed relationship between two variables. The graphs above illustrate a positive correlation (left), a negative correlation (center), and a zero correlation (right). Each point locates the position of a single subject on the two variables. The solid straight lines show what the correlations would look like if they were perfect.

test scores cannot be used to predict crime, accuracy, or adult IQ. As shown in Figure 1.2, the direction and strength of a correlation can be represented in a **scatterplot.**

Correlational studies serve an important function: Based on existing associations, researchers can use one variable (or more) to make *predictions* about another variable. Before interpreting correlations, however, two important limitations should guide the cautious scientist. First, correlations between psychological variables are seldom perfect. Human beings are complex and their behavior is multidetermined. If you know a boy who spends twenty hours a week watching war movies, professional wrestling, or MTV's heavy-metal cartoon, *Beavis and Butt-Head*, you might predict that he gets into fights at school. But the positive correlation between TV violence exposure and aggressiveness is far from perfect, and you may well be wrong. Similarly, not every optimist is healthy and not every college graduate brings home a hefty paycheck. Unless a correlation is close to 1, it can be used only to make general statements of probability, not predictions about specific individuals.

There is also a limit to the types of conclusions that can be drawn from correlational evidence. It's tempting to assume that because one variable predicts another, the first must have caused the second. Not true. This interpretation is an error frequently committed by laypeople, college students, the news media, and sometimes even researchers themselves. Think about the correlations described earlier. Now, admit it: Didn't you assume that exposure to TV violence *causes* aggression, that testosterone fuels violence, that a college diploma brings financial reward, that optimism fosters health, that exercise prolongs life, and that shyness inhibits friendships? Regardless of how intuitive or accurate these conclusions may be, there's a cardinal rule of statistics: *Correlation does not prove causation.*

It's important to know and understand this rule. It does not mean that correlated variables are never causally related, only that the link may or may not be causal. Think again about our examples, and you'll see there are other ways to interpret these correlations. Sure, it's possible that TV violence (X) triggers aggression (Y). But based solely on the observation that these two variables go hand in hand, it's also possible that the causal arrow points in the opposite direction—that children who are aggressive (Y) are naturally drawn to violent TV shows (X). Or perhaps both variables are caused by a third factor (Z), such as the absence of involved parents at home.

scatterplot A graph in which paired scores (X, Y) for many subjects are plotted as single points to reveal the direction and strength of their correlation.

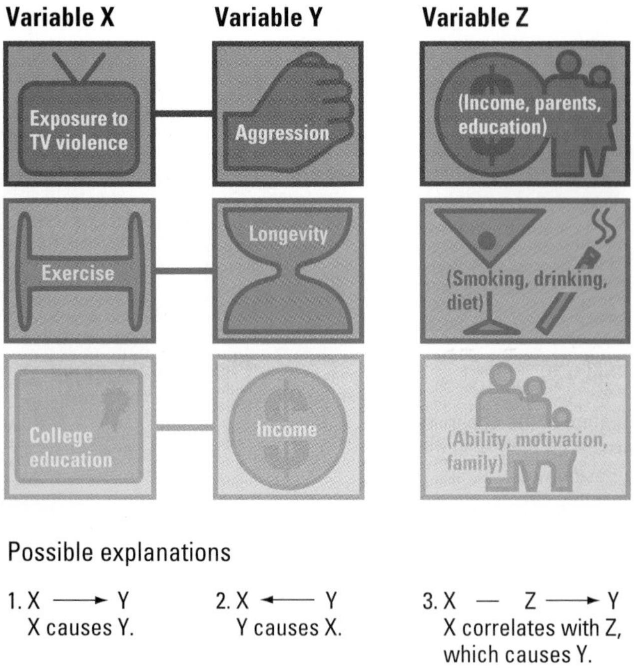

Figure 1.3 Explaining correlations There are three possible ways to explain the association between two variables, X and Y. Look at the examples above and consider possible alternatives (Z refers to extraneous variables).

Reconsider our other examples, and you'll further appreciate the point. Perhaps people become optimistic because they are healthy or are shy because they lack friends. As for the fact that college graduates earn more money than nongraduates, being smart or coming from an upper-middle-class family (Z) may both propel a student through college (X) and lead to financial success (Y). In a similar vein, maybe adults who exercise live longer because they also tend to smoke less, drink less, and eat healthier foods (see Figure 1.3).

Experiments Correlation allows prediction, but to *explain* a relationship between variables, one needs a more exacting method of research: the scientific experiment. In an **experiment**, the psychologist seeks to establish causal connections by actively controlling the variables in a situation and measuring the subject's behavior. The factor an experimenter manipulates (the proposed cause) is called the **independent variable**, so named because it can be varied on its own—"independent" of any other factors. The behavior that is being measured (the proposed effect) is called the **dependent variable** because it is said to "depend" on the experimental situation. If you were to test the hypothesis that exposure to TV violence causes aggression, TV violence would be the independent variable, and aggression would be the dependent variable.

The purpose of an experiment is to focus on a causal hypothesis—by manipulating the independent variable, keeping other aspects of the situation constant, and observing behavior. A true experiment contains two essential sets of ingredients. The first is control over the independent variable and use of a comparison group. Second is the random assignment of subjects to conditions. By means of these ingredients, any differences in behavior can logically be traced back to the independent variable (see Figure 1.4).

Control and Comparison I heard a report on the radio recently that half of all couples who live together before marriage later get divorced. "Wow, that's high," I said to a friend. "I wonder why." Then it hit me. "Wait a second. Isn't there a 50 percent divorce rate in the United States?"

In order to evaluate the significance of a number, you have to ask the question "Compared to what?" In its most basic form, a typical experiment compares subjects who are exposed to the independent variable with others, similarly treated, who are not. Subjects who receive the treatment make up the **experimental group**; the others constitute the **control group**. To the extent that the two groups differ in behavior, the difference can then be attributed, with varying degrees of certainty, to the independent variable. The key is to *vary one factor, keep other aspects of the situation constant, and measure the effect.* To test the hypothesis that TV violence triggers aggression, for example, researchers bring children into the laboratory, show rock'em–sock'em films to half of them (the others would watch nonviolent films or else nothing at all), and measure subsequent aggression in a laboratory or field setting (Wood et al., 1991).

The comparison between an experimental and a control group provides the building blocks for more complex experiments. There are three ways to expand upon this

experiment A type of research in which the investigator varies some factors, keeps others constant, and measures the effects on randomly assigned subjects.

independent variable Any variable that the researcher manipulates in an experiment (the proposed cause).

dependent variable A variable that is being measured in an experiment (the proposed effect).

experimental group Any condition of an experiment in which subjects are exposed to an independent variable.

control group The condition of an experiment in which subjects are not exposed to the independent variable.

basic two-group design. The first is to create more than two levels of the independent variable. Instead of comparing the presence and absence of TV violence, for example, one might form three groups by varying the amount, or "dosage," of exposure (high, medium, low). Second, researchers can manipulate more than one independent variable in the same experiment. For example, they might vary not only the amount of exposure but also the context in which the violence is portrayed (cartoons, films, or sports). The separate and joint effects of these variables can then be evaluated. The third way to increase the complexity of an experiment is to use more than one dependent variable, or to measure the dependent variable on more than one occasion. In our example, aggression could be measured both before and after subjects watch TV.

[Drawing by Donnelly; 1994, The New Yorker Magazine, Inc.]

"I'm down to two hundred and sixty-three packs a day."

Random Assignment The second essential ingredient of an experiment is that subjects be assigned to conditions in an arbitrary manner. **Random assignment** ensures that all participants in a study have an equal chance of being put into an experimental or control group. If I were to show *Beavis and Butt-Head* to children in one school and *Free Willy* to those in another school, it would later be impossible to know whether observed differences in aggression were produced by this exposure or whether they reflect instead differences that exist between the schools. Similarly, if I were to let the children pick their own condition ("Which show would you rather see?"), observed differences might mean that those who chose the violent show were more aggressive to begin with.

By flipping a coin to determine which children in a sample are in the experimental and control groups, a researcher can neutralize individual differences. Assuming that enough subjects are recruited, the two conditions would contain roughly equal numbers of male and female children as well as rich and poor, active and passive, and bright and dull. To similarly evaluate the health benefits of exercise, one might recruit volunteers and assign half of them randomly to take part in an experimental aerobics program. Chances are that both the exercise and the no-exercise groups would then have an equal mixture of men, women, smokers, health-food eaters, couch potatoes, and so on. Then if exercisers turn out to be healthier, the reason would be clear.

> *"No amount of experimentation can ever prove me right; a single experiment can prove me wrong."*
>
> —ALBERT EINSTEIN

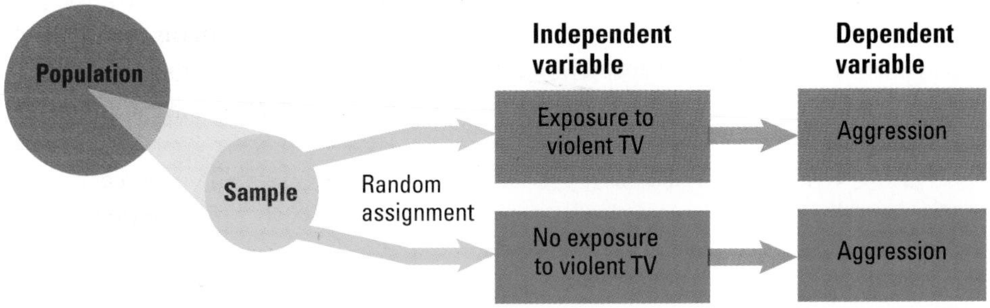

Figure 1.4 Basic model of an experiment To test the hypothesis that TV violence triggers aggression, researchers select a subset of the population, randomly assign these subjects to an experimental (exposure) or control (no-exposure) group, and measure subsequent behavior.

random assignment The procedure of assigning subjects to conditions of an experiment in an arbitrary manner.

Literature Reviews Seeking to describe, predict, and explain psychological phenomena, researchers use a diverse assortment of investigative tools, including single case studies, large-scale surveys, naturalistic observations, correlational studies, and experiments in laboratory and field settings. Yet regardless of the method used, there is a humbling lesson in this scientific enterprise. It is that knowledge accumulates slowly, in increments, one small step at a time. There are no "critical" experiments, and no single study can literally "prove" a hypothesis.

There *are* exciting new discoveries destined to become research classics. But each raises questions, the most important being: Will a finding replicate? **Replication** is an essential property of science. It refers to the process of conducting a second, nearly identical study to see if the initial findings can be repeated. If the result does not replicate, the cautious scientist concludes that the findings may not be reliable enough to pursue further. If the result does replicate—in other words, if the result is consistent enough to stand the test of time—then attention shifts to a second important question, that of **generalizability**: Is a finding limited to one narrow set of conditions, or does it apply across a broad range of circumstances? Just how generalizable is the result? Suppose I find that TV violence causes aggression. Would the result be the same if the study were conducted in another culture or if children of a different age group were used? What if subjects were shown different materials or if aggression were measured in a different way? Once replication is achieved, the next step is to establish the boundaries of the phenomenon. As with some fine wines, good science takes time.

Science demands replication and generalizability, but it is often difficult to make sense of the growing bodies of evidence. One study may show that exposure to TV violence causes aggression in children, but another study may produce contradictory or ambiguous results. Why the disparity? Sometimes many studies are needed before clear patterns begin to emerge. There are two ways to discern these patterns. One is to conduct a review of the research literature, noting the strengths or weaknesses of various studies, making comparisons, and arguing for certain conclusions. In contrast to the interpretive, somewhat subjective style of a review, the second method is to use a recently developed quantitative technique known as **meta-analysis**. Meta-analysis is a set of statistical procedures that is used to review a body of evidence by combining the data and results from multiple studies (Cook et al., 1992; Rosenthal, 1991; Schmidt, 1992). By "meta-analyzing" a sample of *studies* the way researchers "analyze" individual *subjects*, reviewers can sometimes draw precise conclusions concerning the strength and breadth of support for a hypothesis. Many of the conclusions drawn in this textbook were informed by the reviews and meta-analyses published by others.

To summarize, advances in psychological knowledge are made through primary research in the form of descriptive studies, correlational studies, and experiments. As the data from these efforts accumulate in the published literature, patterns begin to emerge. These patterns are revealed in reviews and statistical meta-analyses. The various tools of discovery discussed here are summarized in Table 1.3.

replication The process of repeating a study to see if the results are reliable enough to be duplicated.

generalizability The extent to which a finding applies to a broad range of subject populations and circumstances.

meta-analysis A set of statistical procedures used to review a body of evidence by combining the results of individual studies.

Ethical Dilemmas

All professions wrestle with ethical questions, and psychology is no exception. Regardless of whether a psychologist teaches for a living, administers tests, offers counseling

Table 1.3 The Tools of Discovery

METHOD	PURPOSE
Descriptive research	To *describe* the thoughts, feelings, and behaviors of an individual or group using case studies, surveys, and naturalistic observations
Correlational studies	To uncover links, or "correlations," between variables so that one factor can be used to *predict* another
Experiments	To test hypotheses about cause and effect in order to establish that one factor can *cause* another
Literature reviews	To *summarize* an existing body of research in a narrative review or in a statistical meta-analysis of studies previously conducted

and psychotherapy, conducts research, writes books, consults with the news media or professionals in other areas, or testifies in the courts, ethical dilemmas abound (Bersoff, 1995; Kendler, 1993; Pope & Vetter, 1992). For the scientists of psychology, questions arise most often concerning the use and treatment of research subjects.

Ethics Considerations in Human Research When I took introductory psychology in my first year of college, I signed up for all sorts of experiments. In one, other students and I were preparing to fill out questionnaires when our experimenter—a young female graduate student—was mugged by an intruder, right there in front of us, in the classroom! Soon after the commotion subsided, a security officer walked in and asked us to describe what happened and to pick the culprit from a set of photographs. Apparently, the crime was staged and we were unsuspecting subjects in a study of eyewitness testimony. Years later, I came to realize that this experiment was a classic. It was an awesome experience.

That same semester, I spent an hour trying to memorize 100 strings of letters (I still see them in my dreams: *PTVPS, PVV, TSSSXS*), only to be tested afterward for whether I had discerned the rules that were used to generate these items (I didn't even know there were rules). The session was harmless but boring. Then three years later, I heard more about the research (the task was designed to simulate the way people learn grammar, by mere exposure) and was so intrigued by it (people seem to "learn" the grammar without even realizing there is one) that I seized upon an opportunity to serve as an experimenter. That experience was my *real* introduction to psychology.

I was also in a third experiment I'll never forget. I was given an IQ test containing SAT-like analogies and math questions and was told afterward that my score was very low, in the 25th percentile. I don't remember exactly how badly I felt, but after I left and walked down the hall, I was approached by a student conducting a survey. Would I answer some questions? Not being in the mood, I said no. Suddenly my experimenter reappeared to tell me that there was no survey and that the feedback I was given earlier was false. The purpose was to see if having a positive or negative experience in one situation (some subjects were told they scored high on the IQ test) influences whether people are then willing to help someone in an unrelated situation (the student with the survey).

My encounters as a psychology subject were, I think, quite typical. In most experiments, subjects fill out questionnaires; work on learning, problem-solving, perception, or memory tasks; or interact socially with other subjects. Physiological functions may be recorded, responses may be made on a computer keyboard, or behavior may be videotaped. Some experiments are interesting and fun; others are tedious and relatively boring. Most of them are inoffensive. But sometimes subjects are asked personal questions or are stressed, saddened, or put into a bad mood—or are deceived about the true purposes of the experiment. Witnessing a crime and being told I had failed an IQ test were upsetting experiences. Trying to memorize letter strings was not. In all cases, I was misled about what was being tested.

What ethical issues are raised by research involving human subjects, and how are these issues resolved? There are three specific concerns: the subject's right to privacy, the possible harm or discomfort caused by experimental procedures, and the use of **deception**. In response to these concerns, researchers follow guidelines established by professional organizations, university ethics committees, and granting agencies. For example, the American Psychological Association (1992) urges its members to (1) tell prospective subjects what they will encounter so they can give their **informed consent** to participate, (2) instruct subjects that they're free to withdraw from the experiment at any time, (3) minimize all harm and discomfort, (4) keep the data obtained from subjects confidential, and (5) if deception is necessary, "debrief" subjects afterward by fully explaining the research.

The principles contained in these guidelines are important, and all investigators are responsible for the well-being of those who participate in their research. Some psychologists argue that these rules should be followed without exception. Others point out that many important issues could not then be investigated. In practice, ethical decisions are seldom clear-cut. For example, informed consent is necessary, and everyone agrees that deception is undesirable, but it's often impossible to test a hypothesis on a fully informed subject. Think about my own experiences. If I had known in advance that I would witness a staged crime, if I had known that I was supposed to look for patterns while memorizing letters, and if I had known that the IQ test I took was phony, I would have behaved in ways that were unnatural, not spontaneous. As a compromise, therefore, many researchers describe to subjects the procedures they may encounter but withhold complete disclosure of the key variables and hypothesis until later, when subjects are debriefed.

Other types of judgment calls also must be made from time to time. For example, is it ethical to put subjects under stress—perhaps by presenting impossible problems to solve, showing a pornographic film, sharing the negative results of a test they took, or leading them to think temporarily that they inflicted harm on another person? Is it ethical to study pain tolerance or to ask subjects to recount a traumatic episode? When the polio vaccine was tested in 1954, 2 million children were selected for study, but many received a placebo (a dummy medication that contains no active ingredients) instead of the real vaccine. Was that ethical? Similarly, is it ethical for psychologists testing a new remedy for anxiety to randomly assign half the subjects to a no-treatment control group? In making these kinds of decisions, researchers weigh the costs to the subject against the benefits to science and humanity. In weighing these outcomes, however, there is widespread disagreement among psychologists of differing values (Kimmel, 1991; Rosnow et al., 1993).

deception A research procedure used to mislead subjects about the true purposes of a study.

informed consent The ethical requirement that prospective subjects receive enough information to permit them to decide freely whether to participate in a study.

Ethics Considerations in Animal Research

When Charles Darwin (1859) presented his theory of evolution in *The Origin of Species*, he set the stage for the use of animals in research. Human beings, said Darwin, are biologically related to other

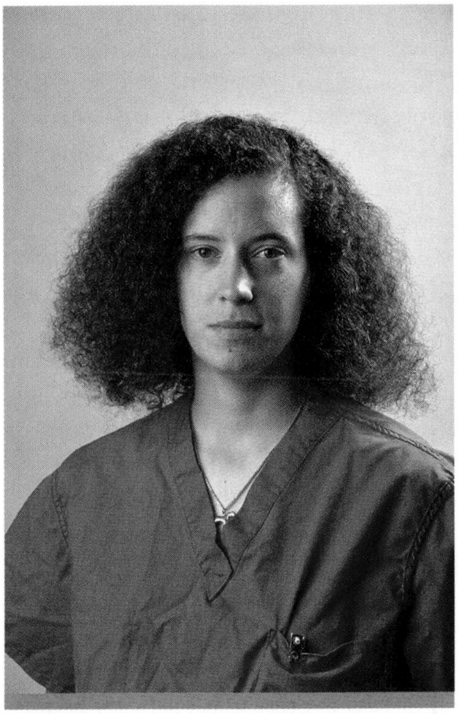

Animal researcher Jessica Szymczyk (left) writes: "I've been a vegetarian since I was 13 years old . . . I don't buy or wear fur. I refuse to wear or use leather if at all possible. And I absolutely love animals . . . So why am I working in a biomedical research lab that uses animals in its experiments?. . . The work we do is crucial. It's important to me as a woman, as a human, and as an animal lover . . . My love for animals matches anyone's, but there's no question in my mind as to who would come first." Animal rights activists protest the use of animals for research purposes (right).

creatures on the planet. Hence, the study of animals has relevance for understanding people. Does it ever. Over the years, psychology has made great strides using animals to study the brain and nervous system, vision and other senses, learning, reasoning, social behavior, anxiety and psychological disorders, and the impact of various drugs. Mice, rats, rabbits, cats, dogs, apes, monkeys, and even birds, fish, insects, and sea slugs have proved valuable in this endeavor.

There are three reasons for using animals in research: to learn more about certain kinds of animals, to evaluate the cross-species generality of the principles of behavior, and to examine variables that cannot ethically be imposed on human subjects. Many years ago, for example, medical researchers noted a correlation between cigarette smoking and lung cancer, but they could not determine if there was a causal link by forcing randomly selected people to smoke. Similarly, psychologists cannot inject human subjects with steroids in order to test the hypothesis that testosterone fuels aggression. For questions such as these, animal research is the only alternative.

Is it ethical to experiment on animals? Many animal-rights activists say no—and are vocal in their opposition (Langley, 1989). A few years ago, at a psychology convention in Washington, D.C., a hundred or so demonstrators waved posters that contained pictures of mutilated dogs and cats. Their claim was that research animals are routinely shocked senseless, starved to death, locked in isolation chambers, and injected with painful mind-altering drugs. Animals are entitled to the same rights as humans, they say, and besides, the research is trivial. On a number of occasions, militants have broken into laboratories, vandalized the equipment and records, and stolen experimental animals. In one incident, the words *ANIMAL KILLER* were spray-painted in black across the garage door of a National Institutes of Health researcher.

To understand how psychologists respond to these charges, it helps to know what the animal-rights groups stand for. Everyone, including those in the research community, consider themselves to be advocates for animal *welfare*—and support the establishment of shelters for lost pets, inoculation programs, the prevention of cruelty to animals, and the protection of endangered species (Johnson, 1990). Indeed, researchers argue that although food deprivation, mild shock, drugs, and surgery are often performed, the allegations of mistreatment are grossly exaggerated. Caroline Coile and Neil Miller (1984) analyzed 608 animal-based research articles published in the preceding five years and found that the charges were not supported in a single instance.

As formalized in the American Psychological Association's Code of Ethics (1992), researchers have a moral obligation to treat animals humanely and minimize their pain and suffering. However, many researchers and activists part company over the issue of animal *rights*. In the eyes of many activists, it is wrong to kill chickens for food, cows for leather, insects to save crops, or rats for research purposes because humans and other living beings should be treated equally. A poster held up at an animal-rights march scorned the Amish use of horses to plow cornfields as a form of animal exploitation. In a survey of more than 400 activists, a majority said they were strict vegetarians, did not use leather products, and placed an equal or greater value on nonhuman life. Overall, 85 percent endorsed the statement "If it were up to me, I would eliminate all research using animals"—and 60 percent favored laboratory break-ins to achieve that goal (Plous, 1991). According to one researcher, "The animal rights movement is not about achieving humane treatment for animals. It is about ending all human uses of animals" (Johnson, 1990).

Psychologists and medical researchers defend their practices by pointing to the many ways in which their work has helped to improve the quality of human life and arguing that it would be immoral *not* to use animals for our most serious problems (Miller, 1985). Animal studies were instrumental in the development of a rabies vaccine, in organ transplants, and in understanding diseases such as cancer and diabetes. Animal studies have contributed to the treatment of anxiety, depression, and other mental disorders, and they have shed light on what is currently known about neuromuscular disorders, Alzheimer's disease, alcoholism, headaches, aggression, and obesity. Indeed, important new research on the links between psychology and the immune system relies heavily on the use of animals (Moynihan & Ader, 1996).

Should animals be sacrificed to spare, prolong, or enhance the quality of human life? Should scientists seeking a cure for AIDS or a biochemical treatment for schizophrenia use mice to test new drugs? Animal activists say no; researchers say yes. What do *you* think? In general, do you support or oppose the use of animals in psychological research? S. Plous (1996) recently posed this question to 1,188 psychology majors attending 42 colleges and universities. The result: 72 percent supported, 18 percent opposed, and 10 percent were not sure. This generally positive response closely paralleled the results of a national survey of professional psychologists—and is interesting in light of the fact that the contributions of animal research are often not explicitly noted in introductory psychology textbooks (Domjan & Purdy, 1995).

Psychology Today

In what ways is psychology strongly influenced by biological perspectives? Why are more and more researchers studying people from different cultures and ethnic groups?

Before psychology became established in science, it was popularly associated with astrology, numerology, handwriting analysis, and psychic experiences. In fact, the phenomena of "parapsychology" continue to fascinate people. Yet you are in no way influenced by the movements of planets and stars (I'm a Taurus and, yes, often I'm stubborn, but who isn't?); your personality cannot be judged by the size of your nose, the bumps on your head, or the way you curve your *S* when you write; and nobody can predict the future by analyzing your dreams or reading your palm. The problem with these claims is that despite their widespread appeal (according to a recent Gallup poll, more Americans believe in ESP than in evolution) and despite thousands of experiments, there is not a shred of convincing empirical support for them (Marks, 1986).

Grounded in the older disciplines of philosophy, biology, and medicine, and firmly rooted in the conviction that mind and behavior can be studied using scientific methods, psychology has made enormous progress as a field of study. From the first subject to be tested in Wundt's original Leipzig laboratory, to the first patient to lie on Freud's couch, to the first psychologist ever to work in an applied setting, to the barrage of new discoveries concerning the links among mind, body, and health, psychology has come a long, long way.

Although psychologists study basic processes, they often touch upon some of the most important and socially sensitive topics of our generation. The similarities and differences between men and women; racial and ethnic diversity; sexuality; AIDS; abortion; adoption; IQ testing; obesity; dieting; and the effects of Ritalin, Prozac, and other drugs are among the topics now being addressed. If you're interested in the possibility of a future career in psychology, refer to the list of major subfields (what psychologists do) and employment settings (where they do it) presented in Figure 1.5.

In recent years, psychology has grown by leaps and bounds. At the college level, psychology's popularity is unprecedented. According to the U.S. Department of Education, it is currently the second largest college major, behind only business administration (Murray, 1996). There are more women in the field than ever before, more African Americans, Hispanics, Asians, and other minorities, more articles being published, and more topics being studied. The American Psychological Association now has more than 82,000 members and 49 divisions—each dedicated to a particular area of specialization (in 1980 there were only 56,000 members and 38 divisions). In addition, a group of scientists recently established a rival organization dedicated solely to basic research (the APA also addresses the concerns of practicing clinical and counseling psychologists). This new organization, which was founded in 1988, is called the American Psychological Society, or APS. Already it has 16,000 members. Both APA and APS have Internet web sites (which are listed in the In the Field Resources section at the end of this chapter), where you can check on the latest advances in psychology.

Biological Perspectives

Increasingly, all branches of psychology are being influenced by two broad perspectives: biological and sociocultural. At the heart of a biological perspective is the

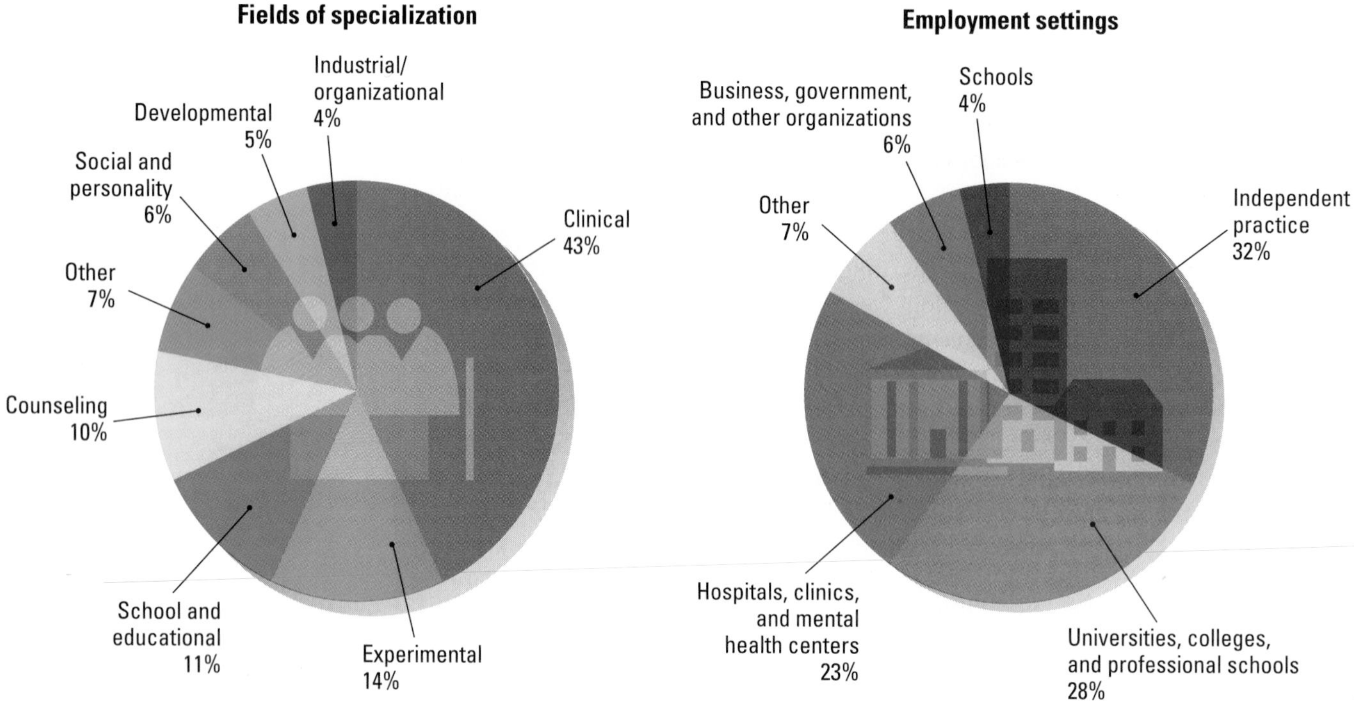

Figure 1.5 Psychology as a profession At the start of 1997, the American Psychological Association had more than 82,000 members. This graphic shows what these members do for a living (their fields of specialization, *left*) and where they do it (employment settings, *right*).

notion that we humans, like other species, have an evolutionary history that predisposes us to behave in certain adaptive ways to survive and reproduce. As we'll see in later discussions of attraction, jealousy, aggression, and altruism, **evolutionary psychology** is a growing force and has a great deal to say about the possible innate and universal tendencies in human behavior.

Related to this interest in evolution is an increasing interest in the study of **behavioral genetics**—a subfield that examines the effects of genes on behavior. Nobody disputes the claim that there is a genetic basis for height, weight, skin color, and other physical attributes. But can the same also be said of our psychological makeup? Is musical talent an inherited trait? What about athletic ability, shyness, or the tendency to commit suicide? We'll see in Chapter 10 that researchers try to estimate the contribution of genetic factors by looking at the similarities between pairs of individuals who vary in terms of their genetic relatedness. We'll also see that this method has been used to estimate the genetic bases of sexual orientation, infant temperament, intelligence, personality, and psychological disorders such as schizophrenia.

A third important biological perspective is provided by a large and growing body of research in **behavioral neuroscience**, the study of the links between the brain and behavior. Triggered by recent breakthroughs in biomedical technology, which enable researchers to observe the living brain in action, this area is generating a great deal of excitement. So is the related area of **cognitive neuroscience**, where researchers are now able to record physical activity in different parts of the brain as a subject reads, speaks, looks at pictures, listens to music, or solves math problems. In this way, researchers are hopeful that they can pinpoint the activities in the brain that correspond to different operations of the mind.

evolutionary psychology A subfield that uses the principles of evolution to understand human social behavior.

behavioral genetics A subfield that examines the role of genetic factors on behavior.

behavioral neuroscience A subfield that studies the links among the brain, nervous system, and behavior.

cognitive neuroscience A subfield that studies the links among the brain, nervous system, and various mental activities.

Sociocultural Perspectives

Just as the biological perspectives are prominent today, so too are sociocultural perspectives. As we approach the twenty-first century, high-speed jumbo jets, communication satellites, and computers are bringing together people from vastly different cultures—and raising questions about the ways in which we are all similar and different.

Increasing numbers of psychologists are conducting **cross-cultural research** in an effort to evaluate the global generality of their theories and to compare people from different regions of the world who have lived very different lives. Do people all over the world prefer sweet foods to bitter? Do children all over the world start to walk and talk at roughly the same age? Do people in all cultures conform to groups? Is depression a universal affliction? Cultural similarities and differences in such areas are discussed throughout the text and are highlighted in Chapter 14, "Social and Cultural Groups."

In 1920, Francis Sumner became the first black person to earn a PhD in psychology. Today there are several hundred African American psychologists.

In addition to comparing people from different parts of the world, psychologists are also conducting **multicultural research**, the study of racial and ethnic groups within cultures. As in most countries, the population of the United States is heterogeneous and diverse—and is becoming more so with time (according to the 1990 census, 22 million Americans alive that year were born in another country). Are there racial and ethnic differences in intelligence-test scores? If so, what do they mean? How do immigrants torn between two cultures form a new identity, and what special problems do they face? Why are racism and other forms of prejudice so pervasive, and what can be done about it? These topics are discussed throughout the text, particularly in Chapter 14.

Thinking Like a Psychologist

It is important to realize that there are so many recent developments in theory, technology, and research, and so many new areas of specialization, that it is impossible to cover all of psychology in a single textbook. It is also important to realize that because psychology is a dynamic discipline, its knowledge evolves somewhat over time. To be sure, at least some of the conclusions drawn in this book may differ from those appearing in textbooks of the 1980s—and some may require further revision in the year 2001. To the extent possible, I have presented in this book the state of psychology *today*.

As described earlier, this book addresses the biological roots of experience, cognitive and affective processes, human development, social psychology, and clinical psychology. Drawing on each of these areas, we then close with a "capstone" chapter on fascinating new discoveries in the area of health and well-being. As we'll see, the theme of this chapter is: "The mind is a powerful tool. The more we know about how to use it, the better off we'll be."

I had three goals in writing this textbook. My first was to inform you about the different areas of psychology and to give you a sense of the field as a whole. My second goal was to spark in you the hunger, the passion, and the excitement that energize those of us who work in psychology for a living. My third goal—which may be the hardest to achieve but also the most important—is to get you thinking like a psychologist.

I will try to get you thinking like a psychologist in a number of ways. First, every chapter opens with an activity entitled *What's Your Prediction?* In some, you'll be

cross-cultural research A body of studies designed to compare and contrast people of different cultures.

multicultural research A body of studies designed to compare and contrast racial and ethnic minority groups within cultures.

[© 1997 by Sidney Harris]

"In this field, Dudley, you miss a few hours and you're no longer on the cutting edge."

asked to imagine being a subject in an experiment. In others, you'll be cast into the role of the researcher, or an observer. Either way, I'll state the research question and then set the stage by giving you a vivid, step-by-step account of the procedures used in an actual experiment. After you've read about the experimental situation and imagined being part of it, you'll be asked to predict how the subjects behaved. The results are then revealed, followed by a discussion of what it all means. I urge you to make use of these activities. I have used this technique in the classroom, and I find that it leads students to think carefully about the research process when challenged to make a prediction—and afterward, as well, particularly if the results prove to be surprising.

A second feature that I hope will get you thinking like a psychologist is called *Intersections*. I use this term to refer to connections between basic research and real world applications. Within each and every chapter, I present one or two boxes that describe recent work on socially relevant problems in the areas of health, education, business, law, or the environment—the kind of topics that animate psychology. I think you'll enjoy them. What's more, I am hopeful that they will help you to see psychology from an important other perspective—"out there," in action, and in the public forum.

Third, each major section of every chapter opens with the kinds of *focusing questions* that psychologists always ask. These questions are designed to both preview and guide you through the section to come. You will also be asked, throughout the text, to consider the relevance of your own experiences and observations as well as stories you read about in the news.

Fourth, at the end of every chapter, you'll see a list of **In the Field Resources.** These are suggestions for where you can go to learn more about the chapter topic from books, films and videos, professional journals, the Internet, and telephone information services, and mailing addresses. Use these resources and you may find yourself approaching the world as a psychologist would—inside the classroom and out, when you're reading this book and when you're not.

Summary and Key Terms

In tomorrow's world, the key to success in life will be the same as it is today: understanding people. Psychology is a serious means of pursuing this understanding.

What Is Psychology?

Psychology can be defined as the scientific study of behavior and the mind.

Historical Roots

Psychology's origins can be traced to ancient Greek philosophers and physicians. During the Renaissance, Descartes developed **dualism**, a theory that the mind is spiritual and the body physical. This theory implied that the mind could not be studied scientifically. Thomas Hobbes and others disagreed, arguing that thoughts and feelings are physical processes.

Modern experimental psychology began in 1879 when Wilhelm Wundt established his laboratory in Germany. Wundt used a method of **introspection**, in which trained observers described their reactions to stimuli. In the United States, William James wrote his classic *Principles of Psychology*; and in Vienna, Sigmund Freud developed **psychoanalysis** to examine the unconscious mind.

The emerging discipline faced a major controversy: Should psychologists speculate about the invisible mind, as Freud and Wundt did, or should they confine themselves to observable behavior? **Behaviorism**, as defined by John Watson, held that psychology should concentrate on what can be seen and measured. Studying the way organisms respond to stimuli, behaviorists such as B. F. Skinner refused to speculate about mental processes.

Behaviorism dominated American psychology from the 1920s through the 1960s. Then the focus shifted to **cognition**, the mental processes that intervene between a stimulus and response. The computer, which offers a model of the human mind, helped inspire this "cognitive revolution." So did the child development theories of Jean Piaget and the linguistic theories of Noam Chomsky.

Expansion of Psychology's Horizons

Since its early days, psychology has expanded considerably. It now includes specialized areas of both **basic research** and **applied research**, and it relies on sophisticated research methods.

The main parts of this textbook reflect broad subfields of basic research. The biological subfield focuses on the links between the mind and body. The cognitive subfield considers whether human beings are generally competent and objective in the way they process information. The study of human development tackles the nature-nurture controversy. Social psychology considers the extent to which social situations overpower individuals. And clinical psychology deals with personality, disorders, and the question of whether people have the capacity for change.

Throughout this text, the areas of basic research are linked to five major areas of applied psychology—health, education, business, law, and the environment—to demonstrate psychology's many real-world implications.

Scientific Methods

Connecting all strands of psychology is an emphasis on critical thinking and scientific methods. A **theory** is an organized set of principles that describes, predicts, and explains an aspect of human behavior, and provides testable propositions known as **hypotheses**. Psychological studies vary in their settings, their ways of measuring variables, and the types of conclusions the research is designed to reach.

Research Settings

There are two types of research settings: **laboratory research**, valuable for its control and precision; and **field research**, conducted in real-world environments.

Psychological Measurements

Self-reports are interviews or questionnaires in which people report on their own thoughts, feelings, or behavior. These are easy to administer but are sometimes misleading. The alternatives are direct **behavioral observation** and the **archival research** that uses records of past behavior such as medical files and public documents.

Research Designs

No matter how the information is collected, researchers use **statistics** to analyze it and draw conclusions. The types of conclusions they reach depend on the research design.

There are three types of descriptive studies designed simply to describe a person, group, or phenomenon. **Case studies** collect detailed information about a particular person. **Surveys** use interviews or questionnaires to draw conclusions about an entire population. To make a survey as accurate as possible, researchers study a **random sample**, so that each individual in the group has an equal chance of being chosen. **Epidemiology**, the study of the distribution of illnesses in a population, is a particularly important form of survey research. The third type of descriptive study, **naturalistic observation**, involves the measurement of behavior in natural settings.

When description is not enough, researchers often employ correlational studies. A **correlation** is a statistical measure of the extent to which two factors are associated. In numerical terms, correlation coefficients range from +1 to −1 and can be shown on a **scatterplot**. Researchers use correlational studies to make predictions about one variable based on what they know about another variable. Correlation, however, does not prove causation.

To study causal links, researchers turn to the **experiment**, where the investigator manipulates an **independent variable** (the proposed cause) and measures a **dependent variable** (the proposed effect). Then the researcher compares the **experimental group** of subjects to a **control group** that was not exposed to the independent variable. An effective experiment requires **random assignment** of subjects, so that each participant has an equal chance of being in either group.

Finally, psychological research often includes reviews of the existing evidence. By summarizing the current state of knowledge, research reviews can help resolve the questions of **replication** (Would a new study produce the same results?) and **generalizability** (Is the finding applicable under other sets of conditions?). Various studies can be summarized through literature reviews and through **meta-analysis**, a set of statistical procedures for combining the results of individual studies.

Ethical Dilemmas

Like other professions, psychology faces ethical questions, for example, about the use and treatment of research subjects. For human subjects, concerns include the subject's right to privacy, the harm or discomfort that may be caused, and the use of **deception**. Research guidelines stress the need to obtain **informed consent** from participants, to let them know they can withdraw at any time, to minimize discomfort, to keep data confidential, and to debrief subjects afterward. When the experimental subjects are animals, researchers must treat them humanely and minimize their suffering.

Psychology Today

Because of the richness of psychological research and its many applications, there are more people in psychology today than ever before, and their work touches on many vital public policy topics.

Biological Perspectives

Triggered by advances in biomedical technology, biological perspectives are prominent. **Evolutionary psychology** considers possible ways in which evolutionary forces predispose us to behave in certain ways. **Behavioral genetics** examines the effects of genes on psychological makeup and behavior. **Behavioral neuroscience** examines the links between neural activity in the brain and behavior. And **cognitive neuroscience** examines the links between the brain and mental activities.

Sociocultural Perspectives

Increasingly, psychologists are testing the universality of their principles in **cross-cultural research** all over the world. With increasing diversity in the populations in many countries, there is also an increase in **multicultural research**, studies of racial and ethnic groups within cultures.

Thinking Like a Psychologist

This book is designed in four ways to get you thinking like a psychologist. First, each chapter opens with *What's Your Prediction?*, an activity in which you'll be asked to read the details of an actual experiment and predict the results. Second, a feature called *Intersections* focuses on the connections between basic research and applications. Third, all major sections within chapters open with the kinds of *focusing questions* that psychologists ask. Fourth, every chapter provides a list of *In the Field Resources* where you can go to learn more about the chapter topic.

In the Field Resources

Books

Hunt, Morton (1993). *The story of psychology*. New York: Doubleday.

Intended for the nonprofessional, this book is an informally written and interesting historical overview of psychology.

Paulos, J. A. (1988). *Innumeracy*. New York: Hill & Wang.

Written by a mathematician, this paperback describes how our faulty intuitions about coincidence, probability, and other statistical concepts can lead us into making bad decisions.

Stanovich, K. E. (1992). *Thinking straight about psychology* (3rd ed.). New York: HarperCollins.

This book is about faulty uses of evidence and how they lead to popular misconceptions about psychological phenomena. The goal is to foster critical thinking in psychology.

Internet

American Psychological Society (http://psych.hanover.edu/APS/)

Provides the *APS Observer*, links to other psychology sites, online studies, and a feature called "Today in Psychology's History."

American Psychological Association (http://www.apa.org/)

Provides the *APA Monitor*, mental-health help center, Psych Crawler for topical searches, and access to psychological resources on the Web.

Canadian Psychological Association (http://www.cpa.ca/)

Provides a gateway to online psychology sites in Canada and access to CPA's newspaper, and psychology discussion groups.

Web Psychological Club (http://www.queendom.com/psyclub.html)

For people interested in psychology, this nonprofessional site offers online tests, counseling resources, and live chats.

Journals and Periodicals

American Psychologist
APA Monitor
APS Observer
Psychological Bulletin
Psychological Science

2 *Behavioral Neuroscience*

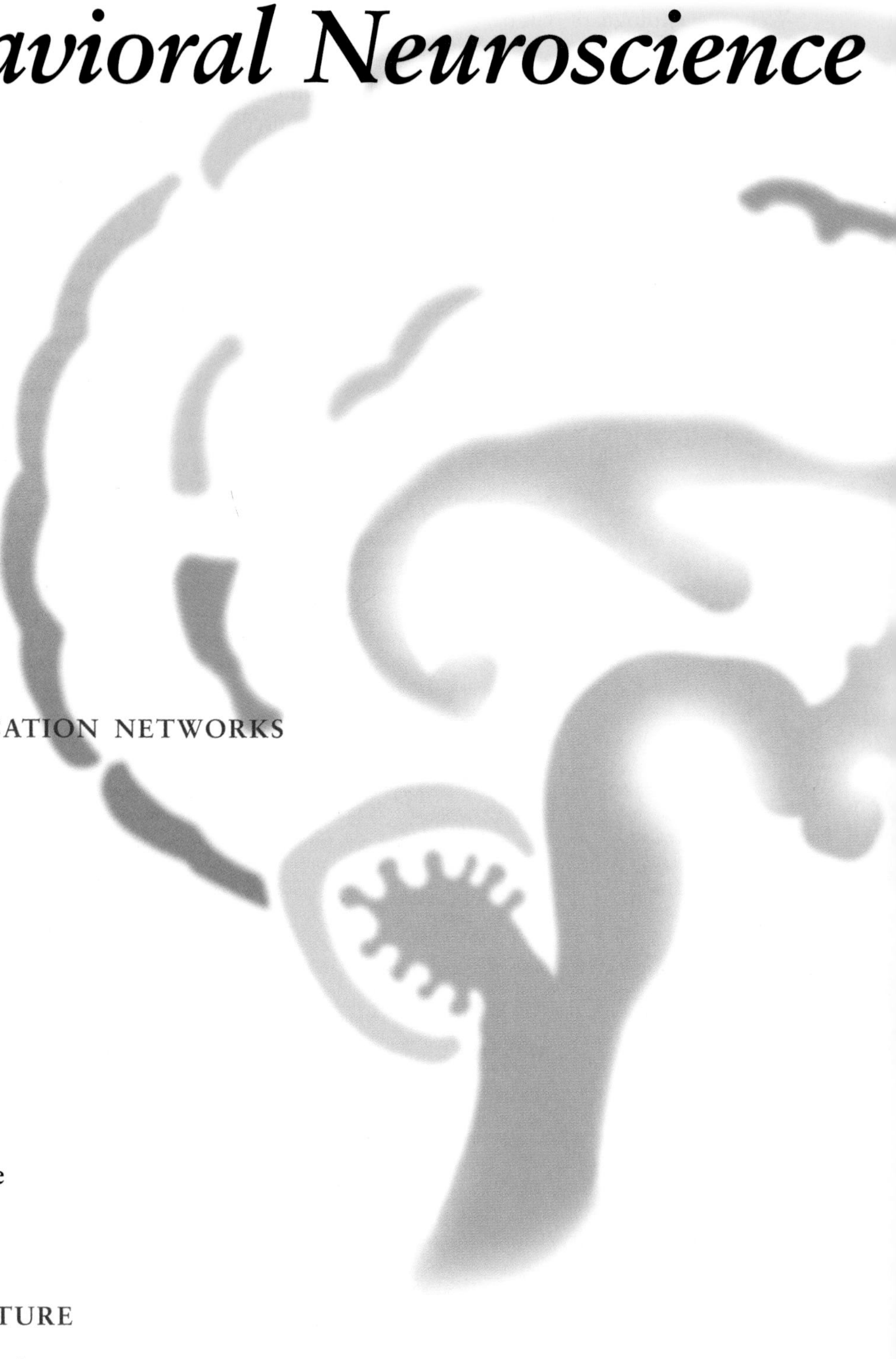

What's Your Prediction?

One brain or two?

The situation You've seen pictures of the human brain, so you have a fairly good sense of what it looks like. You know that the whole brain works together, but you've also read that the right and left sides (or "hemispheres") have different strengths—that the left side handles reading and other verbal processes, while the right side is involved more in visual and spatial tasks. And you've read that each hemisphere controls the opposite side of the body.

You're only mildly interested. But wait. What if the two halves of a person's brain were to become physically separated from each other? Would each side compensate for the loss and function on its own, or would the person flounder? This sounds like one of those hypothetical problems that philosophers like to ponder, but it's real. On rare occasions, people who suffer life-threatening seizures undergo a radical form of surgery in which the cable of nerves that connect the brain's right and left hemispheres is completely severed. In these "split-brain" patients, the two sides of the brain can no longer communicate. The question is: What is the effect?

Now imagine the following situation. The year is 1961 and a split-brain patient by the name of W.J. agrees to take part in a psychological experiment in which you are assisting. After introductions, you show W.J. a series of cards, each containing a red-and-white geometrical pattern, and a set of cubes—each containing two red sides, two white sides, and two mixed sides divided along the diagonal. His task is to arrange the blocks in squares that match the patterns on the cards (see Figure 2.1). Oh, there's one hitch. You tell W.J. that he can use only one hand to assemble the blocks. On some cards, you tell him to use his right hand and keep the left one tucked under the table. On other cards, you tell him to use only his left hand. Can W.J. match the patterns? Does it matter which hand he uses?

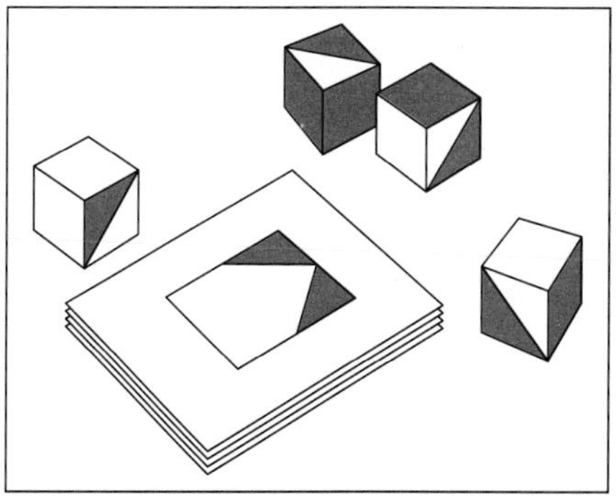

Figure 2.1 The block-design task given to W.J.

Make a prediction Reread the situation and examine the clues given earlier about the human brain, the type of surgery that W.J. had, and the nature of the task he is being asked to complete. Also keep in mind that W.J. is a normal and intelligent man—at least he was before the surgery. Putting all these pieces together, do you think he is able to complete the task with his right hand? What about with his left hand? Make two predictions, one for each hand.

	YES	NO
left-hand success	_______	_______
right-hand success	_______	_______

The results Before W.J. was tested, researchers Michael Gazzaniga and Roger Sperry were not sure what to expect. W.J. seemed normal in conversation, but perhaps both sides of an integrated brain are needed for complex mental activities. Or perhaps one side is sufficient if it's the one that specializes in the task at hand. The result was dramatic: W.J. could assemble the block patterns with his left hand—but not with his right hand. In fact, as his right hand struggled, the left hand occasionally sneaked up from under the table to help out!

What does it all mean? W.J. was the first split-brain patient ever tested, but others later confirmed the basic result. The left hand succeeded at the spatial block-design task because the left hand is controlled by the "spatial" right hemisphere. Yet his right hand—because it is controlled by the left hemisphere and is unable, after the surgery, to receive signals from the right side—was clueless. This case study involving W.J. shows that the brain's two hemispheres specialize in different types of mental activities—something we normally don't notice because the hemispheres are connected and both sides are involved in everything we do. More important, this study shows that when the two halves are disconnected, they act as two separate brains. Reflecting on the implications, Gazzaniga (1992) notes that "each half brain seemed to work and function outside of the conscious realm of the other" (p. 122).

Case studies such as this one have played a major role in our understanding of the human brain and its links to the body and the mind. The brain is a complex anatomical structure, and researchers today have many tools at their disposal to study how it works. In this chapter, we'll examine the human brain, how it's built, its place in the nervous sytem, and the psychological functions that it serves.

At twenty-five years of age, Phineas Gage was a supervisor for the Rutland & Burlington Railroad in Vermont. He was bright, well liked, and energetic. On the afternoon of September 13, 1848, Gage and his coworkers were blasting rock to pave the way for new railroad tracks. To do this, they drilled holes in the rock and packed the holes with gunpowder and sand, using a three-foot-long rod called a tamping iron. All of a sudden, a spark ignited the powder, causing an explosion that propelled the rod upward like a missile. As shown in Figure 2.2, the rod (which was an inch and a quarter in diameter) pierced Gage's left cheek, exited the front-top part of his skull, flew fifty feet into the air, and landed in a pile of dirt, covered with blood.

Gage's body was catapulted backward to the ground, where he began to shake uncontrollably. To everyone's amazement, he was still alive. Minutes later, he was sitting up, moving about, and talking to those around him. Doctors soon stopped the bleeding, cleaned out the loose bits of bone and brain tissue, and packed the wound. Within a few months, Gage was back at work. He showed no loss of intellectual ability. But the front part of his brain, the area known as the frontal lobes, was badly damaged. As a result, this normally soft-spoken, controlled, and considerate young man had become irritable, demanding, and unrestrained—and at times he engaged in gross profanity. According to his doctor, the change in his personality was so profound that his friends said he was "no longer Gage." To complete the sad story: Gage lost his job, traveled with P. T. Barnum's circus, and exhibited his skull and tamping iron at circuses all over the country. Twelve years after the accident, at the age of thirty-seven, he died (Harlow, 1868; Macmillan, 1986).

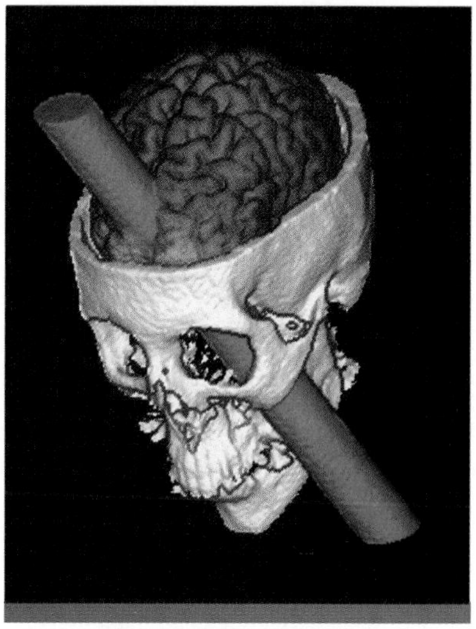

Figure 2.2 Phineas Gage's skull Using photographs and measurements of Gage's skull, as well as computerized images of normal brains, Hanna Damasio and her colleagues (1994) plotted the possible paths of the tamping iron and produced this computerized reconstruction of the damage to Gage's skull. A cast of Gage's head is on display at Harvard Medical School.

Psychologists now know that the frontal lobes are involved in thinking, planning, setting goals, and inhibiting impulses (Fuster, 1989). But the case of Phineas Gage told us much more. It told us that the human brain and nervous system are not a single or simple entity but rather an integrated "system" consisting of different specialized parts. And it told us that the links among the brain, the mind, and behavior can be revealed by the effects of damage to specific structures. These points set the stage as we begin to explore the biological roots of the human experience. As we'll see, all aspects of our existence—every sight, sound, taste, and smell, every twitch, every movement, every feeling of pleasure or pain, all our dreams, learned associations, memories, thoughts, emotions, and even our personalities and social interactions—are biological events. The subfields of psychology that focus on these links are behavioral and cognitive neuroscience.

The Body's Communication Networks

How do the sensory organs, muscles, and other parts of the body prepare for action? What are the body's communication networks, and how does the brain act as a central command center?

The human brain weighs only 3 pounds and, with its gnarled mass of cells, feels like a lump of jelly and looks like an oversized, wrinkled gray walnut. It may not sound appetizing, but the brain is an extraordinary organ—capable of great feats and more complex than any computer. It is one of those "miracles" of life that inspire philosophers and scientists alike. Perhaps that is why the U.S. Congress declared the 1990s to be the "decade of the brain."

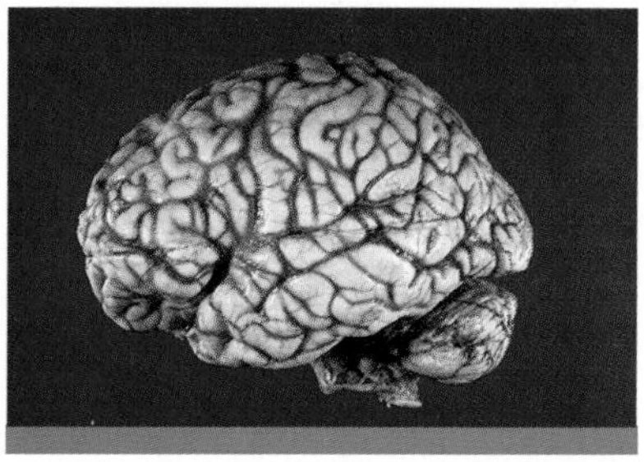

A lateral view of the human brain.

The Nervous System

The human brain is the centerpiece of the body's nervous system, an elaborate electrochemical communication network that connects the brain and spinal cord to all sensory organs, muscles, and glands. The nervous system is divided into two major parts: central and peripheral. The **central nervous system** (CNS) consists of the brain

central nervous system (CNS) The network of nerves contained within the brain and spinal cord.

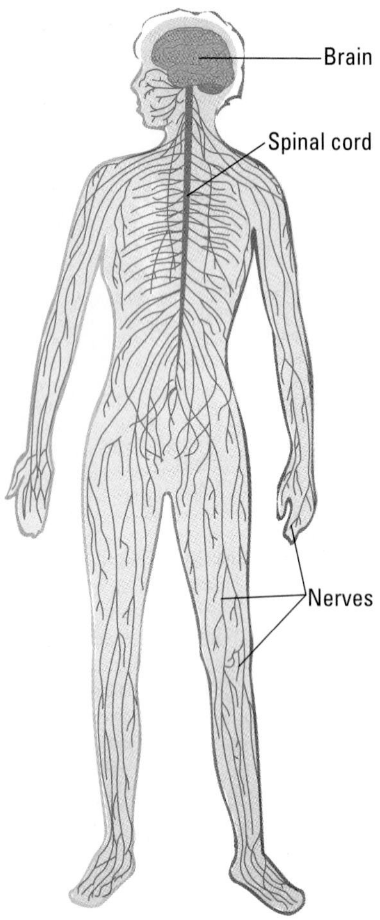

Figure 2.3 Divisions of the nervous system

peripheral nervous system (PNS) The network of nerves that radiate from the central nervous system to the rest of the body. The PNS comprises the somatic and autonomic nervous systems.

somatic nervous system The branch of the peripheral nervous system that transmits signals from the sensory organs to the CNS, and from the CNS to the skeletal muscles.

autonomic nervous system The branch of the peripheral nervous system that connects the CNS to the involuntary muscles, organs, and glands.

sympathetic nervous system The division of the autonomic nervous system that heightens arousal and energizes the body for action.

parasympathetic nervous system The division of the autonomic nervous system that reduces arousal and restores the body to its pre-energized state.

and the spinal cord. The spinal cord is a long tubular column of neural tissue surrounded by a ring of bone that runs from the lower back up to the base of the skull. Basically, it is a transmission cable filled with nerve fibers and pathways—and it serves as an "information superhighway." Later in this chapter, we'll see that the spinal cord transmits signals from sense organs and muscles below the head up to the brain and funnels signals from the brain to the rest of the body. Injury to the spinal cord can cause partial or complete paralysis.

The **peripheral nervous system (PNS)** consists of all the nerves that radiate from the CNS to the rest of the body—from the top of the head to the fingers, toes, and skin. The peripheral nervous system is divided into two components: somatic and autonomic. The nerves of the **somatic nervous system** transmit signals (such as sights, sounds, tastes, smells, and pain) from the sensory organs and skin to the CNS. They also relay motor commands from the CNS to the skeletal muscles of the arms, legs, torso, and head, thus directing the body's voluntary movements. The nerves in the **autonomic nervous system** connect the CNS to all of the smooth *in*voluntary muscles and organs (such as the heart, stomach, and liver) and to the body's many glands, which secrete hormones (see below). As the term *autonomic* implies, this system automatically regulates internal states such as heartbeat, blood pressure, body temperature, digestion, hormone levels, and glucose levels in the blood. As we'll see later in this book, people can learn to use yoga and other techniques to exert some control over these bodily functions.

The autonomic nervous system itself has two parts: sympathetic and parasympathetic. In light of the functions served by these subsystems, they may be thought of as the body's "departments of war and peace." The **sympathetic** division energizes the body for action. In times of stress, it directs the adrenal glands, which rest atop the kidneys, to secrete more of the hormones epinephrine and norepinephrine (more commonly known as *adrenaline* and *noradrenaline*)—thereby increasing the heart rate and heightening physiological arousal. The pupils dilate to let in more light, breathing speeds up to bring in more oxygen, and perspiration increases to cool down the body. When action is no longer necessary, as when the stress subsides, the **parasympathetic** division takes over and restores the body to its pre-energized state. The heart stops racing, the pupils contract, breathing slows down, and energy is conserved. The blood levels of epinephrine and norepinephrine slowly diminish, and the body relaxes, cools down, and returns to normal. As we'll see in Chapter 9, these systems play a vital role in the experience of emotion.

To summarize, the brain is a member of the nervous system, which has two parts, central and peripheral. The CNS contains the brain and spinal cord. The PNS is subdivided into the somatic (voluntary) and autonomic (involuntary) systems. In turn, the autonomic system contains both sympathetic (arousing) and parasympathetic (calming) divisions. This overview of the nervous system is presented in Figure 2.3.

The Endocrine System

Closely linked to the nervous system is the body's second communication system. The **endocrine system** is a collection of ductless glands that regulate our growth, sexual development, reproduction, metabolism, mood, and certain aspects of behavior by secreting chemical messengers called **hormones** (the word *hormone* means to "set in motion"). Hormones are produced in tissue and secreted into the bloodstream, which then carries them to "target organs" throughout the body. Compared to the speedy transmission of impulses through the nervous system, hormonal messages may take several seconds, hours, or even days to take effect. Once they do, however, the impact is often long lasting. Dozens of hormones are produced by the body. Some of the major glands, along with their locations and their functions, are illustrated in Figure 2.4.

As we'll see later, a small but important structure in the brain called the hypothalamus controls the endocrine system through the **pituitary gland,** a pea-size gland that sits at the base of the brain. The pituitary can be thought of as the master gland of the endocrine system. Upon command from the control center in the brain, the pituitary releases a hormone that then stimulates the production of hormones in other endocrine glands. In turn, many hormones flow from the bloodstream back to the brain—which sends a signal to the hypothalamus that more or less additional secretion is needed. The importance of hormone regulation for the maintenance of the body is apparent when an endocrine gland malfunctions in some way. For example, when a thyroid gland produces too little hormone, people become easily tired and sensitive to cold. When the thyroid produces too much of the hormone, people tend to get nervous and irritable and lose weight.

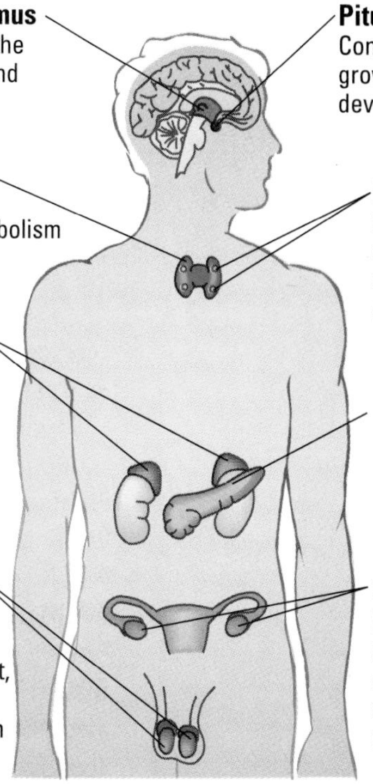

Figure 2.4 Major endocrine glands Taking commands from the hypothalamus, the glands of the endocrine system regulate growth, reproduction, metabolism, and behavior by secreting hormones into the bloodstream. These hormones are carried to certain "target organs" throughout the body.

Notice that there is a constant flow of communication between the nervous system and the endocrine system. Indeed, the brain regulates the release of hormones the same way that a thermostat maintains the temperature of a room. If you set a thermostat at 70 degrees and the temperature dips below that level, the heat comes on until the room tops 70, at which point it shuts itself off. Similarly, if a hormone drops below a certain level, the hypothalamus signals the pituitary and other glands that more is needed. Then once the hormone levels are sufficient, the hypothalamus signals the pituitary gland to stop the additional release of hormones. With the brain in command, the nervous system and endocrine system work together.

The Neuron

What are neurons, how are they constructed, and how do they transmit information throughout the body? What are neurotransmitters, and what do they contribute to the process?

Now that we have drawn a sketch of the nervous system let's fill in the textures and fine details. We begin with the tiny but numerous building blocks and the electrical and chemical impulses that fire throughout the body. In humans and other animals, the nervous system consists of two main types of cells: nerve cells and glial cells.

Playing the lead role are the nerve cells, or **neurons.** Neurons send and receive information throughout the body in the form of electrochemical signals. There are three types of neurons. **Sensory neurons** send signals from the senses, skin, muscles, and internal organs to the CNS. When you see an awesome sunset, scrape your knee,

endocrine system A collection of ductless glands that regulate aspects of growth, reproduction, metabolism, and behavior by secreting hormones.

hormones Chemical messengers secreted from endocrine glands, into the bloodstream, to various organs throughout the body.

pituitary gland A tiny gland in the brain that regulates growth and stimulates hormones in other endocrine glands at the command of the hypothalamus.

or enjoy the flavor of a gourmet meal, messages fire from the eyes, knee, and taste buds; these messages are then relayed up to the brain. **Motor** (motion-producing) **neurons** transmit commands the other way around—from the CNS to the muscles, glands, and organs. Once the sunset, injured knee, and delicious food "register," you and your body act accordingly. Finally, **interneurons** serve as neural connectors within the central nervous system. Among their functions is that of linking input signals from the sensory neurons to output signals from the motor neurons.

> *"Living threads more numerous than stars frame the universe of my mind."*
>
> —DANIEL P. KIMBLE

No one knows for sure how many neurons there are in a brain, but researchers estimate that the number is between 100 and 200 billion—as many as the number of stars in our galaxy. To give you an idea of how much that is, consider this: If you were to count one neuron every second, it would take you up to 6,000 years to count them all. Even more mind-boggling is the fact that each neuron is linked to more than a thousand other neurons, thus providing each of us with literally trillions of connections among the neurons in the brain.

The nervous system also has a supporting cast of smaller cells called **glial cells,** or neuroglia. The word *neuroglia* is derived from the Latin and Greek words meaning "nerve glue." These cells are so named because they provide structural support, insulation, and nutrients to the neurons, thereby "gluing" the system together. They also play a role in the development and repair of neurons and the speed of the neural signals throughout the system. Glial cells are much smaller than the neurons they support. But because they outnumber neurons ten to one, they constitute about half of the brain's total mass (Nicholls et al., 1992; Travis, 1994).

To appreciate how various neurons work together within the nervous system, let's trace the neural pathway of a simple **reflex,** defined as an automatic response to external sensory stimulation. If you've ever had a medical checkup, you are probably familiar with the "knee jerk" reflex. Using a rubber mallet, the doctor taps your patellar tendon, located just below the knee, and this causes your leg to kick forward. You don't have to think about it; the reaction is immediate, and there's nothing you can do to stop it. The tap triggers the kick automatically. How? As shown in Figure 2.5, the knee stretches your thigh muscle, which sends a sensory signal to the spinal cord, which sends a motor signal right back to the thigh muscle. Tap, kick! This two-step chain of events takes only 50 milliseconds because it does not involve higher mental processes in the brain. Reflexes like this are very adaptive. When your hand touches a hot iron or the thorn of a rose bush, a sensory neuron sends a quick message to the spinal cord, which activates a motor neuron and causes you to pull your hand away. The entire reaction takes place in the spinal cord—before you and your brain feel the pain and before too much damage is done.

In the case of more complex forms of behavior—say, driving, working on a math problem, playing a musical instrument, talking to a friend, or reading this sentence—more extensive activity is needed than is possible within the spinal cord. Sensory inputs travel toward the spinal cord (via the somatic nervous system), but they are then forwarded up to the brain and "processed" before a behavioral "decision" is reached. This decision is sent back down through the spinal cord and out to the muscles, which results in behavior. Most of the behaviors that interest psychologists are of this sort.

neurons Nerve cells that serve as the building blocks of the nervous system.

sensory neurons Neurons that send signals from the senses, skin, muscles, and internal organs to the central nervous system.

motor neurons Motion-producing neurons that transmit commands from the central nervous system to the muscles, glands, and organs.

interneurons Central nervous system neurons that connect sensory inputs and motor outputs.

glial cells Nervous system cells, also called neuroglia, that provide structural support, insulation, and nutrients to the neurons.

reflex An inborn automatic response to a sensory stimulus.

Structure of the Neuron

The neuron is a lot like other cells in the body. It is surrounded by a membrane and has a nucleus that contains genetic material. What makes the neuron so special is its

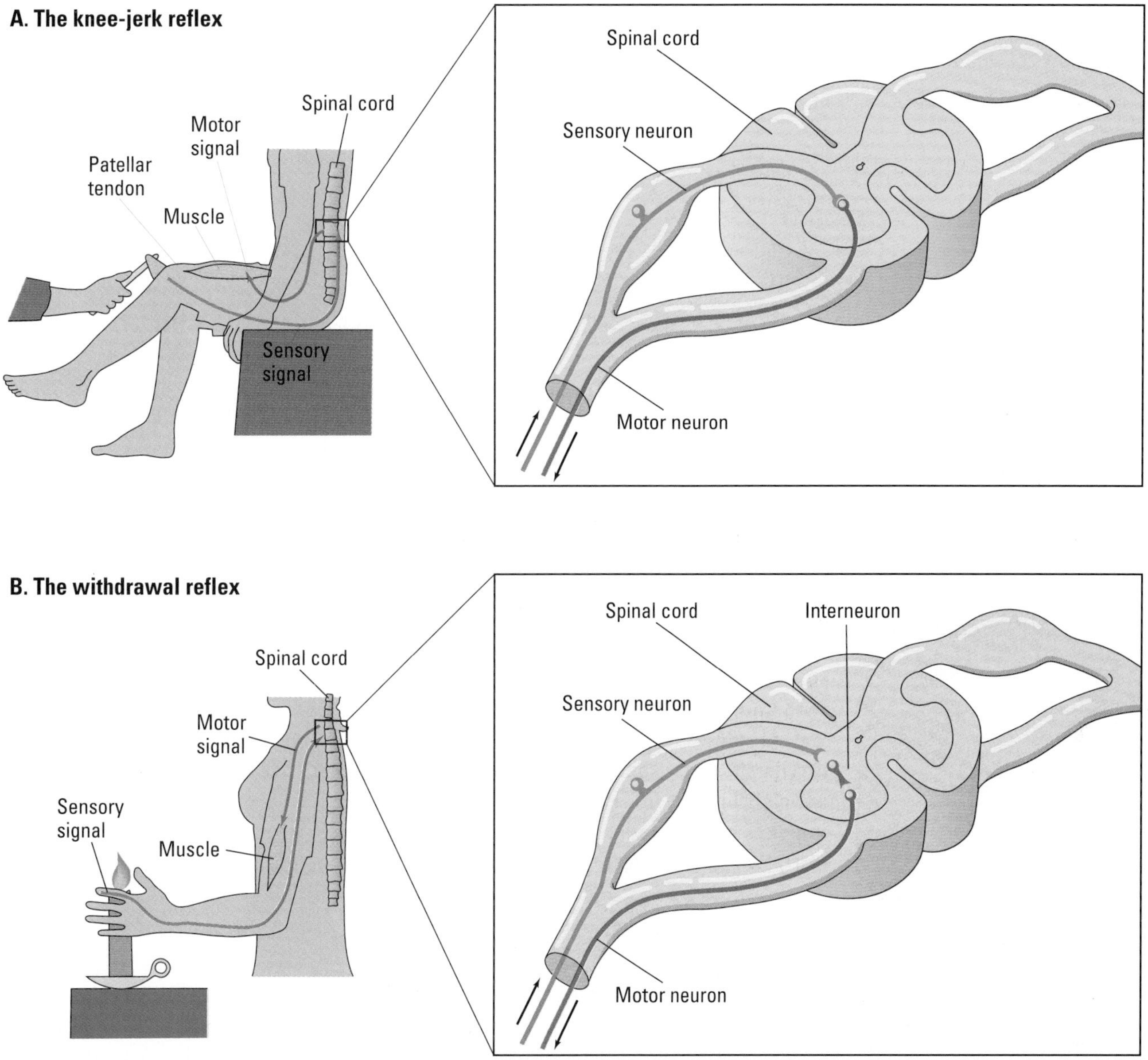

Figure 2.5 **(A) The knee-jerk reflex** A tap on the knee sends a sensory signal to the spinal cord, which sends a motor signal back to the muscle. Tap, kick! **(B) The withdrawal reflex** Touch a hot object, and your hand will immediately pull away. In this case, sensory and motor neurons are linked by an interneuron.

ability to communicate. Everything that we do and all that we know depend on the transfer of signals from one neuron to another.

It's hard to describe the dimensions of a "typical" neuron because these cells come in hundreds of different shapes and sizes, depending on their specific function. But the various neurons do have certain structural features in common. As illustrated in Figure 2.6, every neuron has a roundish **soma,** or cell body, which stores the nucleus of the cell and maintains a chemical balance. Connected to the cell body are two types of branched fibers, or tentacles. The **dendrites** (derived from the Greek word for "tree") *receive* impulses from sensory organs or other neurons. The more dendrites there are, the more information can be received. The **axon** (so named because of its

soma The cell body of a neuron.

dendrites Extensions from the cell body of a neuron that receive incoming impulses.

axon Extension of the cell body of a neuron that sends impulses to other neurons.

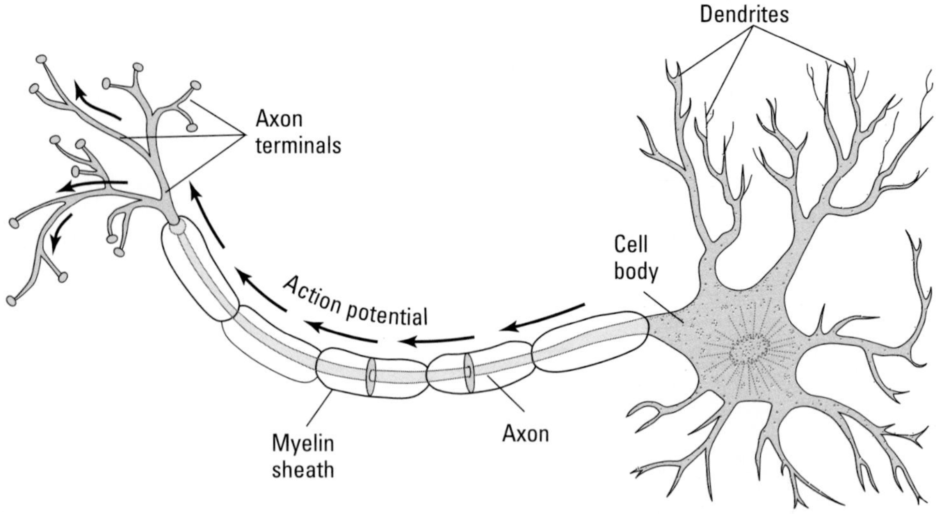

Figure 2.6 Structure of the neuron Every neuron consists of a soma, or cell body, and two types of branched fibers. Dendrites receive electrical impulses from sensory organs or other neurons and the axon relays these impulses to other neurons or muscles. As shown, many axons are insulated with myelin sheath, a fatty layer that speeds the movement of the impulses.

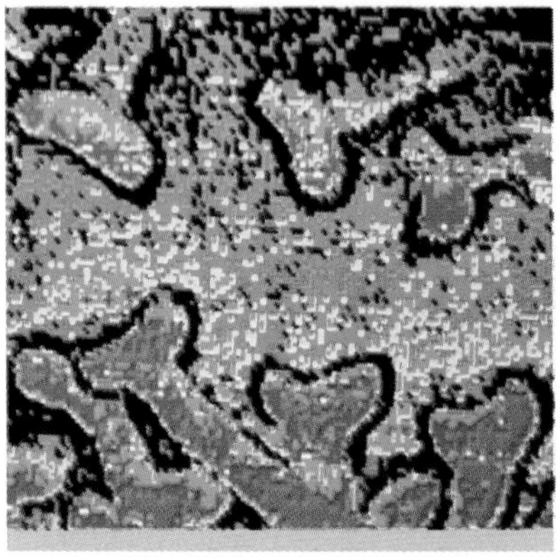

Microscopic photograph of the knoblike axon terminals.

axlelike shape) *sends* the impulse through the neuron to other neurons. Some axons are short and stubby; others are several feet long and slender (some run from the spine down to the muscles of your big toe). At the end of each axon are branches with knoblike tips called axon terminals. As we'll see, these tips contain vital chemical substances to be released onto other cells. Many axons are also covered with the **myelin sheath,** a shiny white layer of fatty cells that is tightly wrapped around the axon to insulate it. This insulation helps to speed up the movement of electrical impulses by preventing leakage. To summarize, neural signals travel from the dendrites, through the (cell body) soma, down the axon, and into the axon terminals.

The Neuron in Action

To understand how messages are transmitted from the axon of one neuron to the dendrites of another, you need to know that these messages occur in the form of electrical impulses. So here is a quick lesson in the electricity of the nervous system.

Every neuron is covered by a membrane, a semipermeable skin that permits some chemicals to pass through more easily than others. Dissolved in fluid on both sides of the membrane are electrically charged particles called ions. Three kinds of ions are present: sodium (positively charged ions that do not pass easily through the membrane, so remain concentrated outside the cell), potassium (positively charged ions that cross easily and are concentrated inside the cell), and negatively charged ions that are trapped permanently inside the cell. When a neuron is at rest, the inside of the cell has a negative charge relative to the outside, making it a store of potential energy—much like a tiny battery.

When the dendrites of a neuron are stimulated, usually by other neurons, this delicate balance is suddenly altered. The semipermeable membrane breaks down, permitting the positively charged sodium ions outside the cell to rush in. For an instant, the charge inside the cell becomes less negative and, as a result, may trigger an **action potential**—a quick burst of electrical energy that surges through the axon like a spark along a trail of gunpowder. Depending on the neuron, most impulses travel at speeds ranging from 2 miles an hour up to 200 miles an hour—faster than a car but 3 million times slower than the speed of electric current passing through a wire. At top

myelin sheath A layer of fatty cells that is tightly wrapped around the axon to insulate it and speed the movement of electrical impulses.

action potential An electrical impulse that surges through an axon, caused by an influx of positive ions in the neuron.

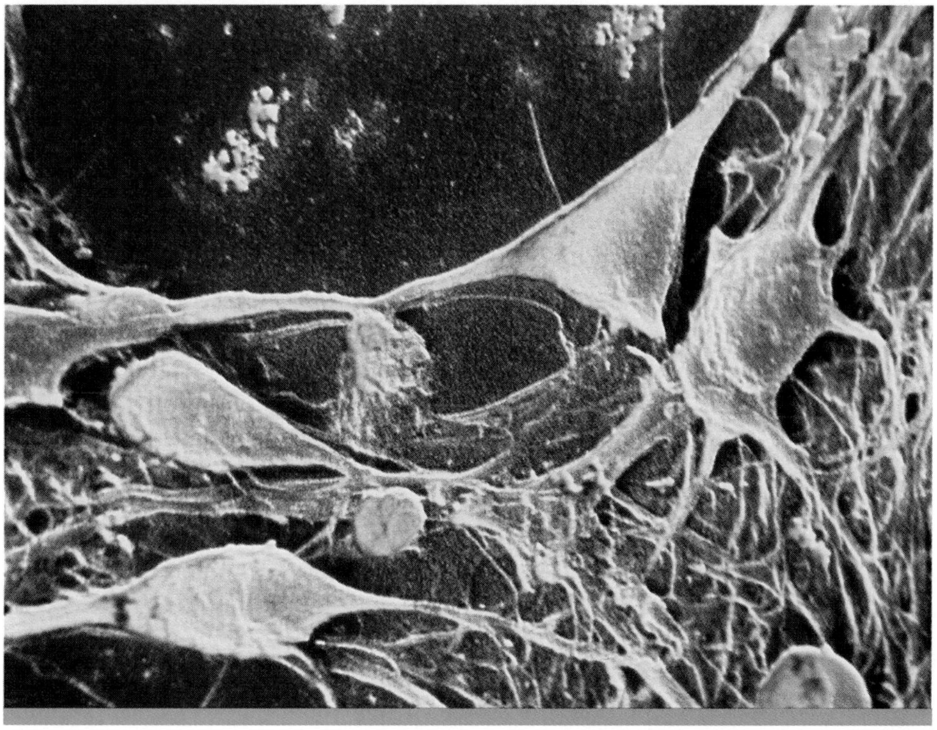

As shown, neurons transmit electrochemical signals throughout the body.

speed, then, it takes an action potential one-hundredth of a second to run along an axon from the spinal cord to a muscle in the finger or toe. Then after an impulse has passed, the positive ions inside the cell are pumped back to the outside of the membrane. The neuron returns to its resting state and is once again ready for action.

The stimulation of a neuron does not always trigger the firing of an electrical impulse. At any given moment, a neuron may be receiving signals on its dendrites from very few or from hundreds, even thousands, of other neurons. Whether the neuron fires depends on the sum total of signals impinging upon it. Only if the combined signals exceed a certain minimum intensity, or **threshold,** does the neuron's membrane break down and begin to transmit an electrical impulse. If it does not, then nothing changes. In other words, the action potential is an *all-or-none response*. Either it fires or it does not. This effect is like the shooting of a gun. If you squeeze the trigger past a certain point (the threshold), bang! If not, nothing is fired. You can't half-shoot, and you can't vary the intensity of the shot. Or it's like turning on a lamp. Unless you have a special dimmer switch, the light is either on or off.

The firing of an electrical impulse is as quick as the blink of an eye, but it has profound significance. Information in the nervous system is made up of action potentials. Every thought you have, every dream, every emotion, every action you take, and every decision you make is coded in the form of action potentials. For behavioral neuroscientists, cracking the action potential code is a key to understanding the language of the nervous system and unlocking new discoveries about the biology of our minds and behavior.

How Neurons Communicate

Imagine that you are watching a neural impulse racing from the receiving dendrites (the starting line), through the cell body, and down the axon. What happens when the signal reaches the axon terminals? And how does it then get to the dendrites of

threshold The level of stimulation needed to trigger a neural impulse.

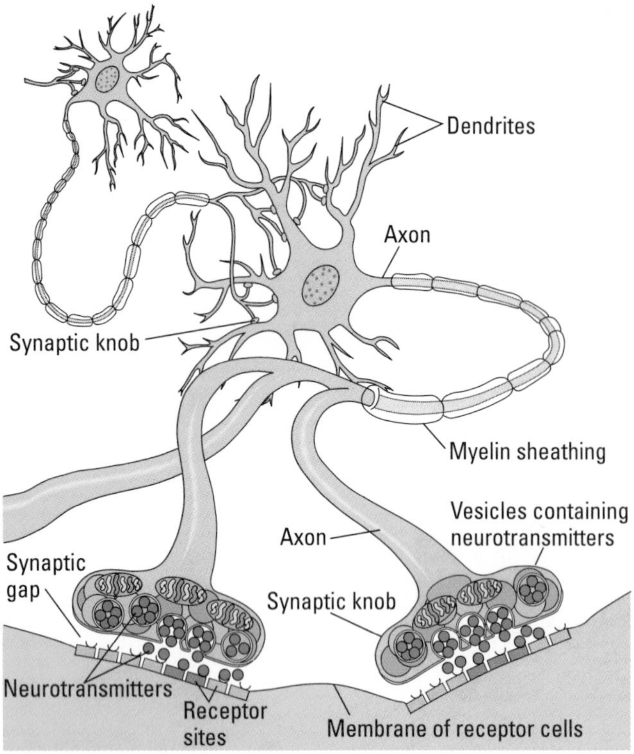

Figure 2.7 How neurons communicate When an impulse reaches the axon terminal, it forces the release of neurotransmitters, which are stored in tiny vesicles. These chemicals squirt across the synaptic gap and bind to receptors on the receiving neuron. There are different neurotransmitters. Each fits only certain receptors the way a key fits only one lock.

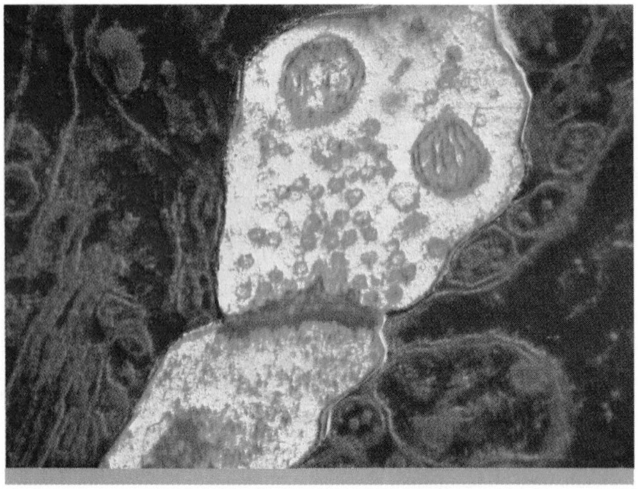

Micrograph of neurotransmitters in synaptic vesicles (top) *squirting across the synaptic gap* (center) *to a receiving neuron* (bottom).

the next neuron? The transmission of messages through the nervous system is like a relay race. When the impulse reaches the end of one cell, it passes the electrochemical baton to the next cell or to a muscle or gland. How is this accomplished? Scientists used to think that the branching axons and dendrites of adjacent neurons always touched, thus enabling impulses to travel seamlessly, the way an electrical current crosses two extension cords that are plugged together. We now know that this is not the main way it works. Rather, there is a narrow gap between neurons that is roughly one-millionth of an inch wide. This gap is called a **synapse,** from a Greek word meaning "point of contact." The question is: How does the impulse cross this synaptic gap to the next neuron?

The answer has to do with the action of **neurotransmitters.** When an electrical impulse reaches the knoblike axon terminal, it forces the release of chemical messengers called neurotransmitters—so named because they aid in the *transmission* of information from one *neuron* to another. These chemical substances are manufactured by the neuron and stored in tiny round packets called synaptic vesicles. Upon their release, the neurotransmitters literally squirt across the synapse and bind to specialized **receptors** on the dendrites of the receiving neuron. There are different types of neurotransmitters. Some will excite (fire) an action potential in the next neuron, while others will inhibit (restrain the firing of) the next action potential. It's a truly remarkable process. There are many different neurotransmitters and many different types of receptors—and each has its own shape. This fact is significant because a neurotransmitter binds snugly only to certain receptors the way a key fits only one lock. The entire electrochemical process is illustrated in Figure 2.7.

Neurotransmitters

Anxiety, feelings of calm, sadness and depression, pain and relief, memory disorders, drowsiness, hallucinations, paralysis, tremors and seizures—all have something in common: a link to the activity of neurotransmitters. Neuroscientists used to think that just a few substances were involved in neural transmission. But thanks to recent technological advances, some of which will be discussed later, we now know that the human nervous system is a prolific chemical factory. To date, researchers have identified about 75 neurotransmitters—and have further suggested the possibility of up to 300 in all. Indeed, a recent and surprising discovery was that the gases nitric oxide and carbon monoxide serve as neurotransmitters (Snyder, 1992; Verma et al., 1993).

synapse The junction between the axon terminal of one neuron and the dendrites of another.

The activities of certain neurotransmitters—where in the body they're produced, their effects on mind and behavior, and their responsiveness to drugs—are well

Table 2.1 Major Neurotransmitters

NEUROTRANSMITTER	FUNCTION	CHAPTER
Acetylcholine (ACh)	Links motor neurons and muscles. Also facilitates learning and memory. Alzheimer's patients have an undersupply of ACh.	11
Dopamine	Concentrated in the brain, it is linked to muscle activity. A shortage a can cause Parkinson's disease; an excess of dopamine receptors is linked to symptoms of schizophrenia.	16, 17
Endorphins	Distributed throughout the CNS, these natural opiates relieve pain.	3
Norepinephrine	Widely distributed in the CNS, it increases arousal. Too much may produce a manic state; too little may lead to depression.	9, 16, 17
Serotonin	Produced in the brain, it lowers activity level and causes sleep. Too little is linked to depression.	4, 16, 17
GABA (gamma aminobutyric acid)	Produced in the brain, it lowers arousal and reduces anxiety. It is the main inhibitory neurotransmitter in the nervous system.	17

understood. (See Table 2.1, which summarizes the functions of some of the more important neurotransmitters and the chapters in which they are discussed.)

The first substance identified as a neurotransmitter was **acetylcholine (ACh)**, which is found throughout the nervous system and is most concentrated in the parts of the brain that control motor behavior. Using powerful electron microscopes, researchers can see the sacs that store and release ACh molecules—and have found that ACh is the chemical key that links the motor neurons and muscles. Thus, it is released whenever you walk, talk, ride a bike, throw a ball, or take a breath. So what would happen if you somehow blocked the release of all ACh in the system? Think about the link that would be severed, and you'll have the answer. Curare—a poison that some South American Indians put on the tips of their hunting arrows—blocks the ACh receptors and causes complete paralysis of the skeletal muscles. And what about the opposite condition? What would happen if you were to flood the synapses between motor neurons and muscles with ACh? The toxic bite of a black widow spider does just that, resulting in violent muscle contractions, sometimes even death. ACh may also play a role in the formation of new memories. As we will see in Chapter 11, people who have been struck by Alzheimer's disease, a degenerative brain disorder that destroys memory, have abnormally low levels of ACh.

Another neurotransmitter that plays an important role in the regulation of movement is **dopamine.** For example, Parkinson's disease—a motor disorder that is characterized by hand tremors, stooped posture, and a loss of control over one's voluntary movements—is caused by the death of neurons that produce dopamine. For people with this disease, the symptoms can often be eased with L-dopa, a chemical substance that the neurons convert into dopamine, which replenishes the supply (we'll see later that another promising new

neurotransmitters Chemical messengers in the nervous system that transmit information by crossing the synapse from one neuron to another.

receptors Specialized neural cells that receive neurotransmitters.

acetylcholine (ACh) A neurotransmitter found throughout the nervous system that links the motor neurons and muscles.

dopamine A neurotransmitter that functions as an inhibitor and is involved in the control of voluntary movements.

approach is to implant healthy tissue containing dopamine into the brains of Parkinsonian patients). As we'll see in Chapters 16 and 17 on psychological disorders and treatment, researchers have also found that many schizophrenia sufferers have an oversupply of dopamine receptors in the brain and that their symptoms can often be treated with drugs that block the activity of dopamine (Resnick, 1992).

Another exciting discovery is that the brain produces it own morphine, a painkiller. Several years ago, Candace Pert and Solomon Snyder (1973) injected laboratory animals with morphine, a powerful and addictive painkilling drug derived from opium. To their surprise, they found that the morphine binded to certain receptors in the brain the way neurotransmitters do. This discovery is only mildly interesting, you may think. But wait. Why would the brain have receptors for a chemical produced outside the body? If there's a special receptor for morphine, doesn't it mean that the brain produces its own morphinelike substance? The answer is yes—and the neurotransmitter is called an **endorphin** (from the words *endogenous,* which means "internal," and *morphine*). Researchers soon found that endorphins and their receptors, and other similar substances, are distributed throughout the central nervous system (Hughes et al., 1975).

What triggers the release of endorphins? Sensations of pain and discomfort. For example, the exhilarating "runner's high" so often described by long-distance runners might be caused by the release of endorphins (Farrell et al., 1982). So might the pain-relieving effects of acupuncture, the traditional Chinese medical procedure in which needles are inserted into certain parts of the body (He, 1987). Still other researchers have suggested that the release of endorphins is triggered by physical injury and by the labor pains that precede childbirth (Akil, 1982). Although the causes and effects of endorphins are not yet clearly understood, it does appear that the human body comes equipped with a natural, built-in pharmacy for pain relief.

The Brain

How do psychologists study activity in the human brain? Do different parts specialize in certain functions or operate as an integrated system? Does each side of the brain have its own "mind"? How could such a hypothesis be tested, and what do you think would be the results?

Encased in a hard protective skull, the brain is the crown jewel of the nervous system. It weighs only 3 pounds and constitutes only 1/45th of the human body's average weight. But, as we saw earlier, it contains billions of neurons and trillions of synaptic connections. For those interested only in anatomy, it was easy to determine the physical *structure* of the brain by dissecting brains removed from dead animals and from humans who had donated their bodies to science. For behavioral neuroscientists, however, the task is more challenging: to determine the *functions* of the living brain and to understand its influences on the way we think, feel, and behave.

Tools of Behavioral Neuroscience

Before the term *neuroscience* had ever been uttered, Viennese physician Franz Gall (1758–1828) founded **phrenology,** the pseudoscientific theory that psychological

endorphin A morphinelike neurotransmitter that is produced in the brain and is linked to pain control and pleasure.

phrenology The pseudoscientific theory that psychological characteristics are revealed by bumps on the skull.

characteristics are revealed by bumps on the skull. Apparently, as a young boy, Gall "noticed" that his friends who had the best memories also had protruding, large eyes. In believing that speech, math ability, aggression, and other characteristics are "localized" in certain regions of the brain, Gall was on the right track. However, in using bumps on the skull to find these links, he was very much on the wrong track (Zola-Morgan, 1995).

To fully understand and evaluate what researchers currently know about the brain, it helps to be aware of *how* they arrive at that knowledge—the methods they use and why they use them. Thanks in part to advances in technology, today's behavioral neuroscientists are like explorers on a new frontier. As we'll see, four types of research methods are commonly used: clinical case studies, experimental interventions, electrical recordings, and imaging techniques.

In the nineteenth century, Franz Gall tried to map the human brain by measuring bumps on the skull.

Clinical Case Studies One approach is the clinical case study, in which researchers observe people with brain damage resulting from tumors, diseases, head injuries, or exposure to toxic substances. In the case of Phineas Gage, massive damage to the frontal lobes was followed by changes in his personality (specifically, an inability to control impulses), yet his intellectual abilities remained the same as before. Thus, this case suggested that the frontal lobes are involved in the control of behavior. Other case studies, too, have proved invaluable. Neurologist Oliver Sacks tells many colorful and provocative stories about brain-damaged patients who exhibited specific deficits in speech, memory, motor behavior, sleep, and even their self-concept. In *An Anthropologist from Mars* (1995), for example, Sacks described an artist who suffers brain damage from a car accident. He lost all color vision but eventually gained more sensitivity to forms, textures, and patterns. As a result, he became a more productive painter than ever—in black and white.

Clinical evidence is tantalizing and often enlightening, but it cannot provide the sole basis for behavioral neuroscience. One drawback is that when part of the brain is damaged, nearby neurons sometimes sprout new branches, and other structures sometimes pick up the slack. These forms of compensation are wonderfully adaptive, but they may mask the effects of damage. Another drawback is that natural injuries are seldom localized, so the resulting deficit may not really be traceable to a single structure. In the Phineas Gage case, for example, the skull was pierced by a long rod that was over an inch in diameter—hardly a surgical incision.

Experimental Interventions A second common method is to "invade" the brain through an experimental intervention and then measure the effects on behavior. One technique, often used by animal researchers, is to purposely disable, or "lesion," a part of the brain by surgically destroying it. Often this is done by anesthetizing an animal, implanting an electrode into a specific site in the brain, and passing a high-voltage current through it to burn the tissue.

A second technique is to administer drugs that are suspected of having effects on neurotransmitters and other activity in the brain. Over the years, the effects of many substances on the brain and behavior have been tested in this manner—substances including alcohol, caffeine, adrenaline, nicotine, and the sex hormones testosterone and androgen.

A third form of intervention is through electrical brain stimulation. In these studies, a microelectrode is inserted in the brain and a mild electrical current is used to "activate" the neurons in a particular site. Most of these experiments are conducted with animals, but on occasion clues are derived from human brain-surgery patients. How does this occur? Since no two brains are exactly alike, brain surgeons often must "map" the patient's brain so they don't accidentally destroy key functions. Toward this end, the patient is given a local anesthetic and kept awake for the procedure. While treating epilepsy patients, for example, neurosurgeon Wilder Penfield stimulated different areas along the surface of the brain and found that, depending on the region he stimulated, the patients would report visual images, tingling sensations, muscular twitches, and other reactions (Penfield & Roberts, 1959).

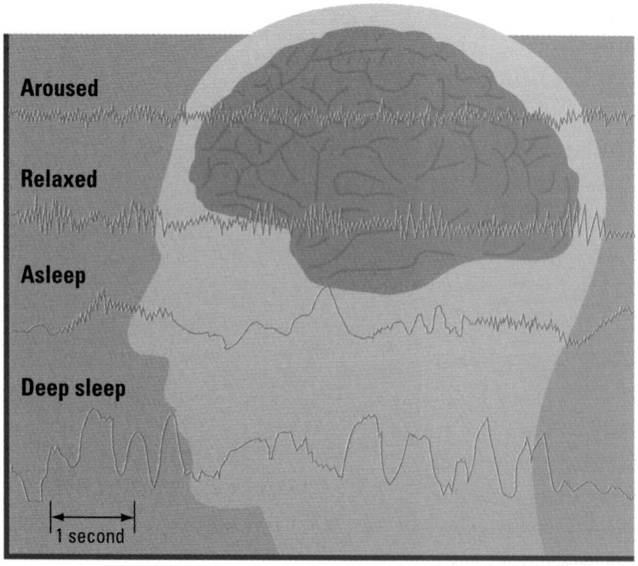

Figure 2.8 The EEG Through electrodes on a subject's scalp, the electroencephalogram records electrical activity in the brain and displays the output in line tracings called brain waves. Varying in their frequency (cycles per second) and amplitude (voltage), EEG patterns differ according to a person's mental state.

Electrical Recordings The most exciting advances in behavioral neuroscience arise from techniques that are not invasive to the human subject. In 1929, German psychiatrist Hans Burger invented a machine that could detect, amplify, and record waves of electrical activity in the brain using metal electrodes pasted to the surface of the scalp. The instrument is called an **electroencephalograph (EEG)**, and the information it provides is in the form of line tracings called *brain waves* (see Figure 2.8).

As we'll see in later chapters, researchers using the EEG have found that brain waves differ depending on whether a person is excited, relaxed, pensive, drowsy, or asleep. It's also used for diagnosing brain damage and various neurological disorders. For example, people with epilepsy have seizures because a certain portion of the brain is overexcitable and prone to fire in a wild manner—which sets off electrical spikes, or "explosions." The EEG may even be useful for diagnosing pathological conditions such as depression and alcoholism (John et al., 1988). There are limits, however, to what EEG recordings can tell us. The problem is that the EEG merely summarizes all the electrical activity of billions of neurons firing along the brain's surface. Thus, as one group of researchers put it, "we are like blind men trying to understand the workings of a factory by listening outside the walls" (quoted by Hassett, 1978). For greater precision, animal researchers sometimes use microelectrodes, wires with tips so tiny that they can stimulate or record the activity of a single cell.

Brain-Imaging Techniques When people think about the wonders of high technology, what comes to mind are global communication satellites and giant-size telescopes that can spy on the distant galaxies of the universe. But recent advances in technology have also enabled us to turn the scientific eye on ourselves, to inner recesses of the human brain never previously seen. Designed to provide visual images of the live human brain, without ever having to lift a scalpel, this new technology uses computers to combine thousands of still "snapshots" into models of the brain in action. As described in *Images of Mind* (Posner & Raichle, 1994), there are three basic types of imaging techniques, all popularly known by their initials: CAT, PET, and MRI.

First introduced to medicine in the 1970s, the **computerized axial tomography (CAT) scan** is a computer-enhanced X ray of the brain. In this technique, X-ray beams are passed through the head at 1-degree intervals over a 180-degree arc, and a computer is used to convert this information into an image that depicts a horizontal slice of the brain. This technique takes advantage of the fact that when a highly focused beam of X rays is passed through the body, the beam is affected by

electroencephalograph (EEG) An instrument used to measure electrical activity in the brain through electrodes placed on the scalp.

CAT (computerized axial tomography) scan A series of X rays taken from different angles and converted by computer into an image that depicts a horizontal slice of brain.

the relative density of the tissue through which it passes. CAT scans are invaluable for diagnosing tumors and strokes and for identifying brain abnormalities in people who suffer from schizophrenia and other psychological disorders.

A second revolutionary imaging technique, one that can be used to map activity of the brain over time, is the **positron emission tomography (PET) scan.** Based on the fact that glucose supplies the brain with energy, the level of activity in a given region of the brain can be measured by the amount of glucose it burns. After a tiny amount of radioactive glucose is injected into the brain, the scanner measures the amount of it consumed in different regions. The results are then fed to a computer, which produces an enhanced color picture (Martin et al., 1991). Can the PET scan actually spy on our thought processes? In a way, yes. Look at Figure 2.9, and you'll see the PET scans of a person with his eyes and ears open or closed. (In these scans, "hot" colors such as red, orange, and yellow indicate more activity, whereas cool colors such as violet, blue, and green mean less activity.) Research also shows that PET scans can often distinguish among different types of psychological disorders (Andreasen, 1988; Resnick, 1992). In one interesting study, researchers had schizophrenia patients relax with their eyes closed and press a button whenever they started to hear imaginary voices and when they stopped hearing these voices. The result: On PET scans, hallucinating lit up certain areas of the brain more than others (Silbersweig et al., 1995).

A "new and improved" technique is **magnetic resonance imaging (MRI).** MRI is similar to a CAT scan, but instead of using an X ray, it passes the subject's head

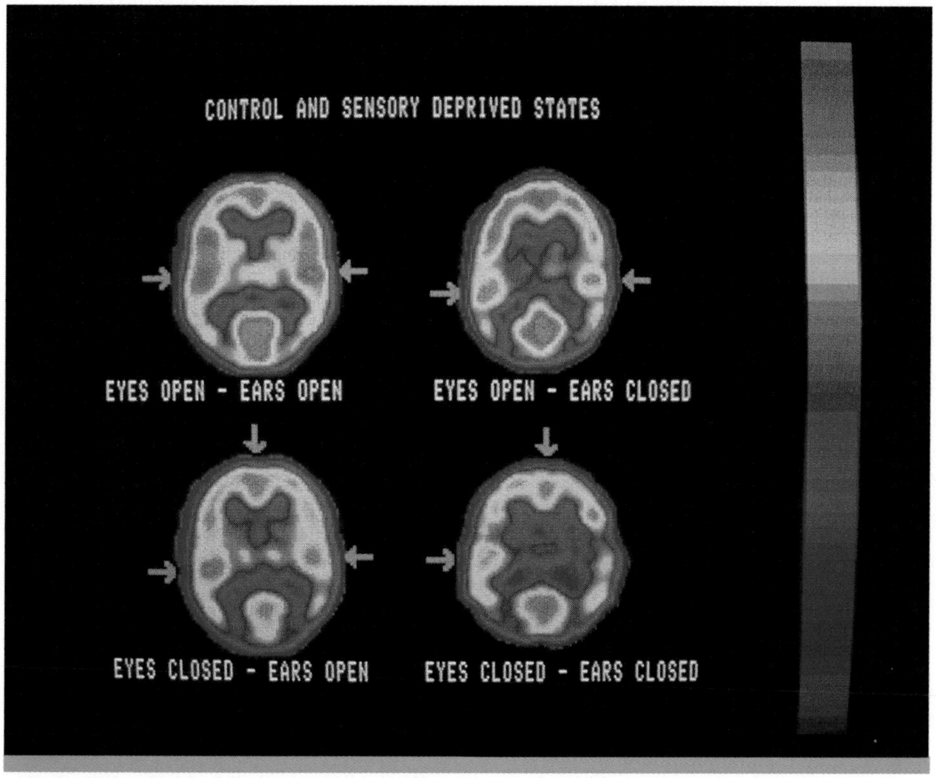

Figure 2.9 PET scans After radioactive glucose has been injected into the brain, a scanner measures how much glucose is consumed in different regions. The results are displayed in a computer-enhanced picture in which hotter colors (red, orange, yellow) indicate more activity. In these images, visual areas of the brain "lit up" when the subject's eyes were open, as did auditory areas when the subject's ears were stimulated with sound.

PET (positron emission tomography) scan A visual display of brain activity, as measured by the amount of glucose being used.

magnetic resonance imaging (MRI) A brain-scanning technique that uses magnetic fields and radio waves to produce clear, three-dimensional images.

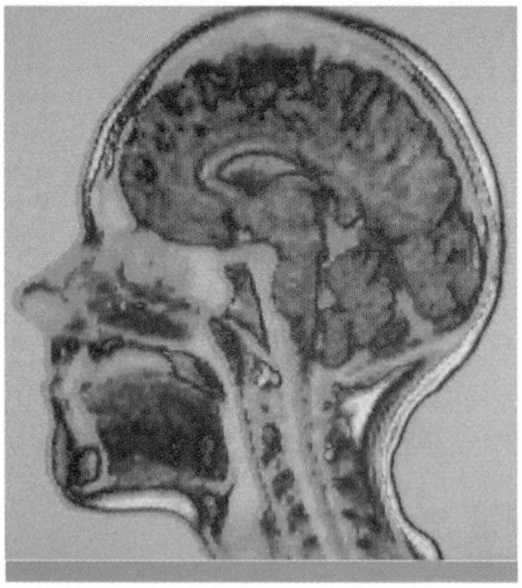

Figure 2.10 The MRI Magnetic resonance imaging yields the best resolution for visualizing brain structures.

through a strong but harmless magnetic field to align the brain's atoms. A quick pulse of radio waves is then used to disorient the atoms, which give off detectable signals as they return to normal. The MRI can produce clear and detailed pictures of the brain's soft tissues. In fact, a high-speed version of MRI known as *functional MRI* can be used to take moving pictures of the brain in action (see Figure 2.10).

Still other techniques are being developed as you read this book. As shown in Figure 2.11, one new method combines EEG and MRI. The researcher first uses electrodes to record electrical signals from 124 points on the scalp, and a new reading is taken every few milliseconds as the subject receives some stimulus or engages in a specific task. A computer is then used to create an ongoing videolike record of electrical activity at the surface of a three-dimensional MR image of the brain (Gevins et al., 1996).

This new technology is generating tremendous excitement. Indeed, researchers are now saying, "This is the wonder technique we've all been waiting for," and calling it "the most exciting thing to happen in the realm of cognitive neuroscience in my lifetime" (Blakeslee, 1993). Does the brain respond differently to music than to words? Is there something different about the brain of an artist than that of a physicist? Some psychologists are concerned that these techniques will invite researchers to mistakenly assume that certain complex mental functions occur exclusively in local regions of the brain (Sarter et al., 1996). Others are eager to use MRI and other new imaging technologies to explore these new frontiers (Raichle, 1994).

Regions of the Brain

The human brain is a unique product of evolution. In some ways it is similar to the brains of "lower" animals; in other ways it is quite different. Salmon, caribou, and migrating birds have navigational abilities unparalleled in our own species. Dogs, cats, and many other mammals have senses of hearing and smell that are downright superhuman. Yet no other animal on the planet can solve problems, think about itself and the future, or communicate as we do. As we'll see, these relative strengths and weaknesses can be traced to the unique structure of the human brain.

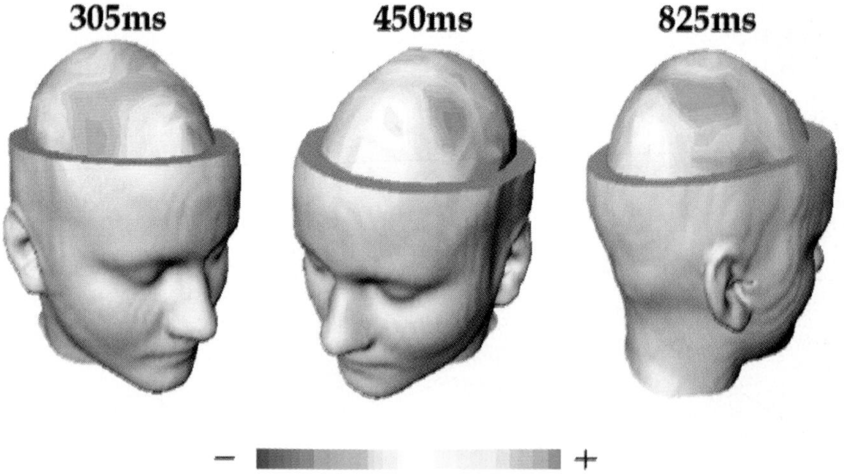

Figure 2.11 Recording activity in a three-dimensional brain By recording electrical signals all over the scalp, measuring changes per milliseconds, and using a computer to create ongoing MR images, researchers can generate a videolike record of activity in a three-dimensional model of the brain.

Although the brain is a single organ containing interconnected pathways of nerve fibers, neuroscientists have found that there are really three mini-brains rolled into one. The *brainstem* is the old "inner core" that rests atop the spinal cord and helps to regulate primitive life-support functions such as breathing, heartbeat, and muscle movements. Surrounding the brainstem, the *limbic system* provides an increased capacity for motivation, emotional responses, and basic forms of learning and memory. And in the *cerebral cortex*, which features the wrinkled outer layer of the brain, "higher" mental processes enable more complex forms of learning, memory, thought, and language. The cerebral cortex is the last part to develop—both within the individual and in the species as a whole (see Figure 2.12).

The Brainstem As the spinal cord enters the skull, it enlarges into the **brainstem,** a primitive inner core. As illustrated in Figure 2.13, the brainstem contains three key structures: the medulla, the pons, and the reticular formation. Located just above the spinal cord, the **medulla** controls some of our most vital, involuntary functions—swallowing, breathing, heart rate, and muscle control. As we'll soon see, it's also a "crossover" point where nerves from one side of the brain connect to the opposite side of the body. There's nothing particularly exotic about the medulla, but if it were severed, blood pressure would drop to zero, breathing would stop, and death would soon follow. Just above the medulla is a bulbous structure called the

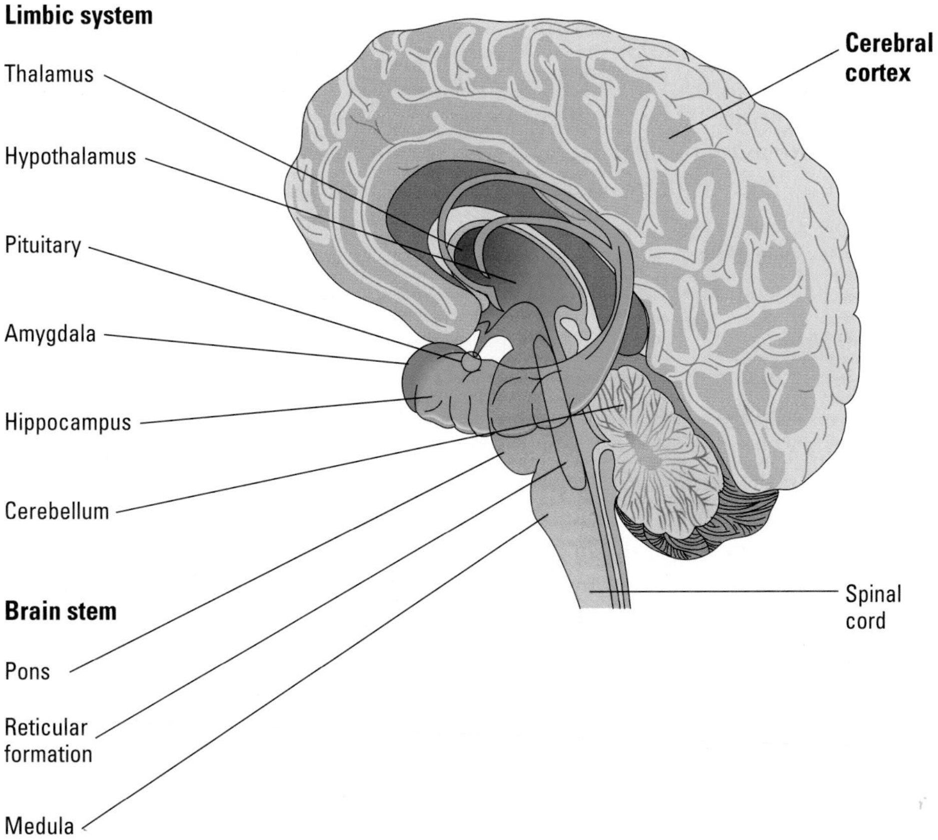

Figure 2.12 The human brain There are three main regions of the human brain. The *brainstem* is the old "inner core" that controls life support functions. The *limbic system* regulates motivation, emotion, and basic forms of learning and memory. The *cerebral cortex,* which features the wrinkled outer layer of the brain, controls "higher" mental processes that enhance learning, memory, thought, and language.

brainstem The inner core of the brain that connects to the spinal cord and contains the medulla, pons, and reticular formation.

medulla A brainstem structure that controls vital involuntary functions.

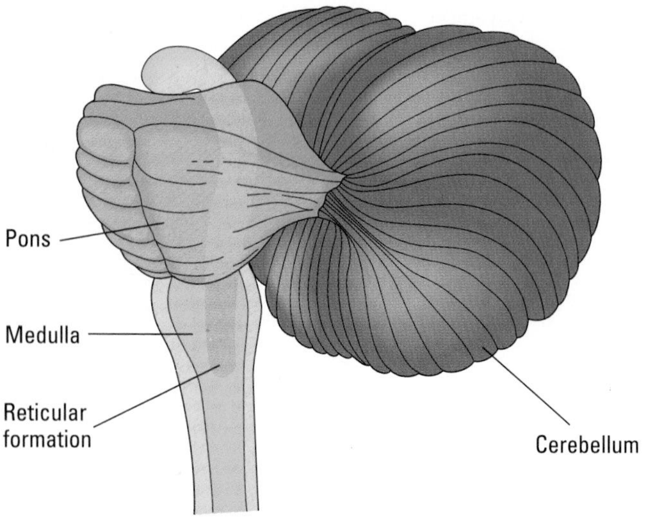

Figure 2.13 The brainstem The brainstem is the most primitive structure of the brain. Resting atop the spinal cord, it contains the medulla, pons, and reticular formation and is attached to the cerebellum.

pons (meaning "bridge"), which helps to connect the lower and higher regions of the brain. The pons also has neurons that play a role in sleep and arousal. Damage to this area can put a person into a coma. Finally, the **reticular formation** is a netlike group of nerve cells and axons that project throughout the brain and help to control sleep, arousal, and attention. It is here that sensory information is filtered in or out of our consciousness.

Also attached to the back of the brainstem is the **cerebellum,** which means "little brain." Look again at Figure 2.13, and you'll see that the cerebellum resembles a miniature brain within the brain, wrinkles and all. This structure is one of the oldest in the nervous system and is highly developed in fish, birds, and lower mammals. It plays a role in learning and memory, but its primary function (like that of certain other structures distributed throughout the brain) is balance and the coordination of voluntary movements (Thach et al., 1992). Damage to the cerebellum makes it difficult to coordinate movements such as walking, kicking, typing, or throwing a ball. The reason that drunken drivers can't pass the roadside test given by the police ("Close your eyes, put out your arms, and touch your nose with the index finger") is that alcohol affects the cerebellum.

The Limbic System Continuing upward from the brainstem is a ring of loosely connected structures collectively known as the **limbic system.** Just above the inner core, yet surrounded by the cerebral cortex, the limbic system contains several structures that play a role in the regulation of motivation, emotion, and memory. Brain researchers disagree as to which structures actually qualify as "limbic" and whether they really form a unified "system." Still, the key structures here include the thalamus, the amygdala, the hippocampus, and the hypothalamus (see Figure 2.14).

The Thalamus Directly atop the brainstem, and buried like the pit inside a peach, is the **thalamus** ("inner chamber"). The thalamus is a sensory relay station that directs neural traffic between the senses and the cerebral cortex. All input from what you see, hear, taste, and touch is received in the thalamus and then sent for processing to the appropriate region of the cortex. For example, there's a special nucleus located in the thalamus that receives visual input from the optic nerve behind the eye and sends the information to the visual cortex. It's interesting that the sense of smell completely bypasses the thalamus because it has its own private relay station that directs input from the nose to the olfactory bulb, which sits near areas that control emotion. This may explain why perfume, meat sizzling on the grill, freshly cut grass, and other scents often arouse powerful emotions in us.

The Amygdala The **amygdala** is an almond-shape bulge that has been called an "aggression center." This phrase oversimplifies both the behavioral functions of the amygdala and the biological roots of aggression. But there is a link, and experiments have shown that stimulation of the amygdala can produce anger and violence, as well as fear and anxiety (Davis, 1992).

In 1937, psychologist Heinrich Kluver and neurosurgeon Paul Bucy found that lesions of the amygdala calmed ferocious rhesus monkeys. Later experiments on other wild animals revealed the same mellowing effect. Can amygdala lesions be

pons A portion of the brainstem that plays a role in sleep and arousal.

reticular formation A group of nerve cells in the brainstem that help to control sleep, arousal, and attention.

cerebellum A primitive brainstem structure that controls balance and coordinates complex voluntary movements.

limbic system A set of loosely connected structures in the brain that help to regulate motivation, emotion, and memory.

thalamus A limbic structure that relays neural messages between the senses and areas of the cerebral cortex.

amygdala A limbic structure that controls fear, anger, and aggression.

used to treat people who are uncontrollably violent? In one case, Julia, a twenty-one-year-old woman, had suffered from epilepsy since childhood. Every now and then, she would have seizures accompanied by fits of rage, temper tantrums, and violent outbursts. Julia was dangerous to herself and others. Four times she tried to commit suicide. In one incident, she plunged a dinner knife into the chest of a woman who had accidentally bumped into her. Eventually Julia's father called neurosurgeon Vernon Mark for help. Mark implanted electrodes in Julia's brain to record electrical activity, and he detected abnormal discharges in the amygdala. Next, he tried electrical stimulation. In most sites, nothing happened. But activating the amygdala triggered explosive attacks. At one point, Mark stimulated the amygdala while Julia was playing the guitar. Suddenly she stopped, stared into space, and smashed the guitar against the wall, just missing the doctor's head. Mark treated Julia by destroying part of her amygdala, and her fits of rage eventually, over time, subsided (Mark & Ervin, 1970). Apparently, there is a relationship between the amygdala and aggression. We'll see in Chapter 17, however, that the use of psychosurgery—operating on the brain as a way to alter behavior—raises profound ethical questions (Valenstein, 1986).

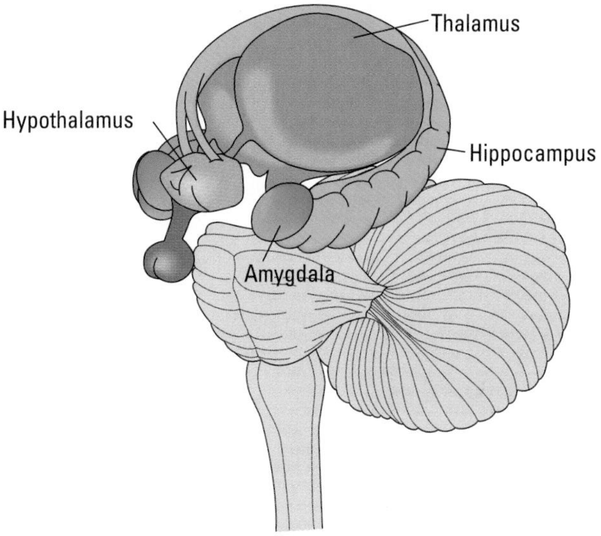

Figure 2.14 The limbic system Just above the inner core, yet surrounded by the cerebral cortex, the limbic system plays a role in motivation, emotion, and memory. As shown, this system is composed of many structures, including the thalamus, amygdala, hippocampus, and hypothalamus.

The Hippocampus The largest structure in the limbic system is the **hippocampus,** which is Greek for "seahorse," whose shape it roughly resembles. Research reveals that the hippocampus plays a key role in the formation of new memories. In rats, monkeys, and other animals, hippocampal lesions cause deficits in memory. In fact, when this structure is removed from black-capped chickadees—food-storing birds that have an unusually large hippocampus, compared to nonstoring birds—they lose the natural ability to recover food they had previously stored (Hampton & Shettleworth, 1996). In humans, brain scans reveal that the hippocampal area is shrunken in people with severe memory loss, even while surrounding areas of the brain are intact (Squire, 1992). As we'll see in Chapter 6, long-term memories are not necessarily stored in the hippocampus, but they may well be formed there.

The Hypothalamus At the base of the brain, there is a tiny yet extraordinary limbic structure called the **hypothalamus** (which means "below the thalamus"). The hypothalamus is the size of a kidney bean, weighs only about half an ounce, and constitutes less than 1 percent of the brain's total volume. Yet it regulates the body's temperature and the activities of the autonomic nervous system, controls the endocrine system by triggering the release of hormones into the bloodstream, helps regulate basic emotions such as fear and rage, and is involved in basic drives such as hunger, thirst, sleep, and sex. The hypothalamus is also home to one of the brain's "pleasure centers"—an area that is highly rewarding when stimulated (Wise, 1996). If you had to sacrifice an ounce of brain tissue, you wouldn't want to take it from the hypothalamus.

The Cerebral Cortex

The **cerebral cortex** is the outermost covering of the brain. Its name is derived from the words *cerebrum* (which is Latin for "brain") and *cortex* (which means "bark"). It is the newest product of evolution, overlaid upon the older structures. If you were to examine the cerebral cortex of various species, you would

hippocampus A limbic structure that plays a key role in the formation of new memories.

hypothalamus A tiny limbic structure in the brain that helps regulate the autonomic nervous system, endocrine glands, emotions, and basic drives.

cerebral cortex The outermost covering of the brain, largely responsible for higher order mental processes.

see that the more complex the animal, the bigger the cerebral cortex is relative to the rest of the brain. You would also notice that in complex animals, the cortex is wrinkled rather than smooth and is lined with ridges and valleys. This wrinkling allows more tissue to fit compactly inside the skull (much like crumpling up a piece of paper allows one to squeeze it into a small space). As shown in Figure 2.15, the cerebral cortex is virtually absent in all fish, reptiles, and birds. But it is present in mammals (particularly in primates, dolphins, and whales) and is the most highly developed in humans. In volume, it constitutes 80 percent of the human brain (Kolb & Whishaw, 1990). Whenever you read, write, count, speak, reflect on the past or think about the future, plot your next move on the chessboard, or daydream about being rich and famous, neurons are firing by the billions in the cerebral cortex.

The cortex is divided into left and right hemispheres, and each hemisphere is further divided along deep grooves, which are called fissures, into four sections called lobes. These are the *frontal lobes* (in front, just behind the forehead), the *temporal lobes* (at the temple, above the ear), the parietal lobes (in the back, at the top of the skull), and the *occipital lobes* (in the back, at the base of the skull). Although these regions describe the anatomy of the cerebral cortex, most psychologists prefer to divide the areas of the brain according to the functions they serve. As shown in Figure 2.16, the functional regions include the sensory areas of the cortex, the motor cortex, the association cortex, and two special areas where language is processed and produced.

Sensory and Motor Areas While operating on his hundreds of epilepsy patients, Wilder Penfield, in 1947, stimulated exposed parts of the cortex with a tiny electric

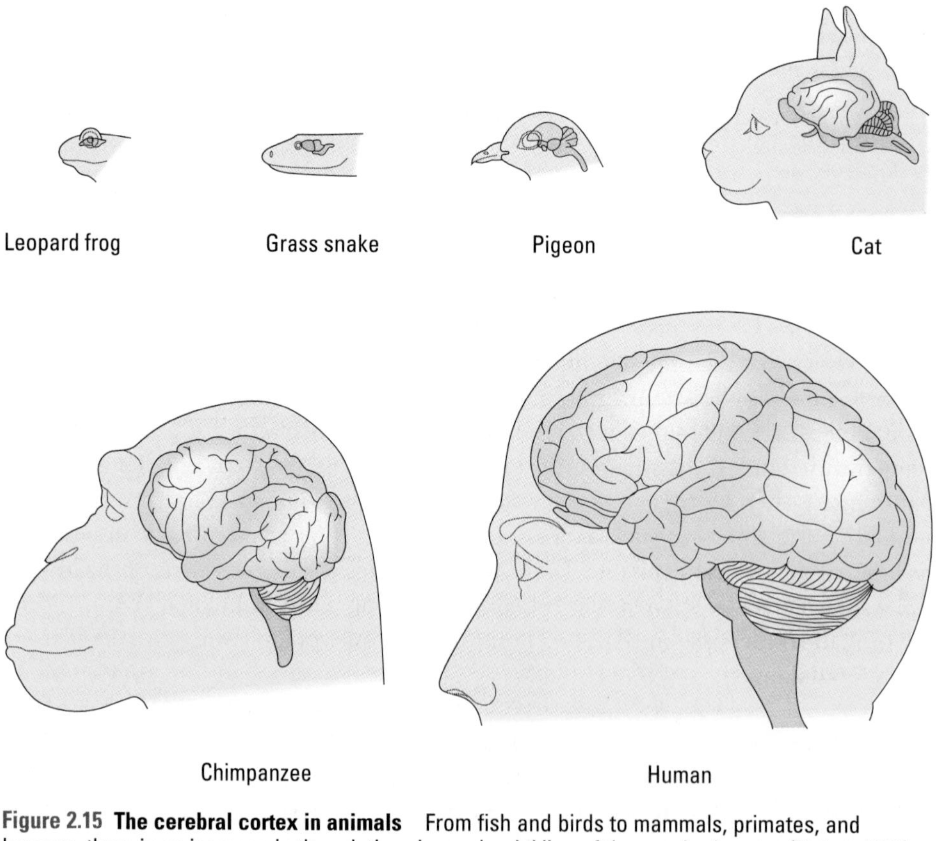

Figure 2.15 The cerebral cortex in animals From fish and birds to mammals, primates, and humans, there is an increase in the relative size and wrinkling of the cerebral cortex (Hubel, 1979).

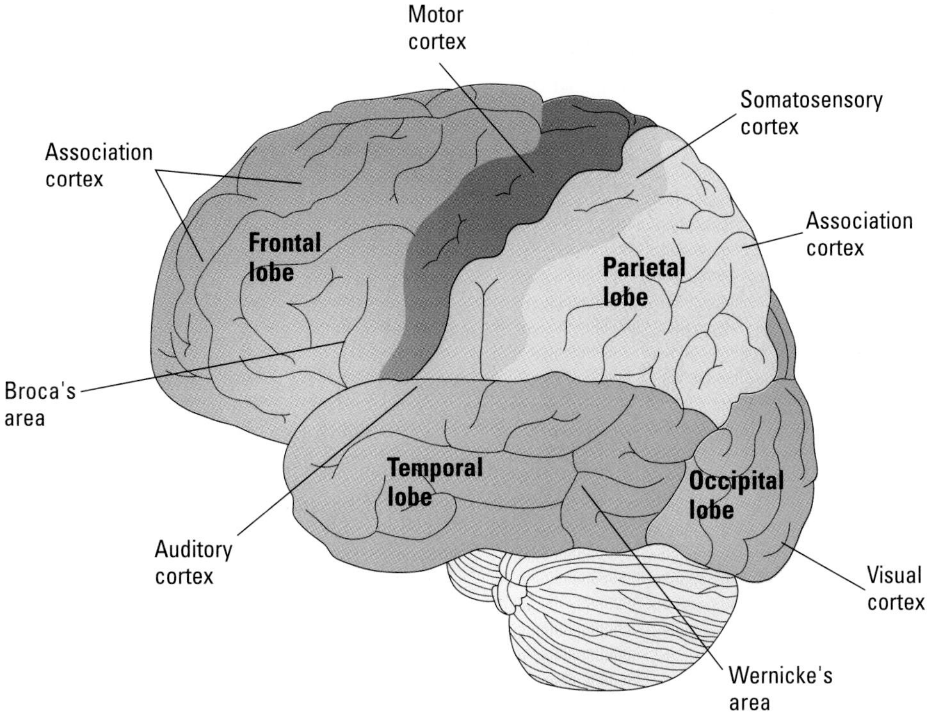

Figure 2.16 The cerebral cortex The cortex is divided along deep grooves, or fissures, into four lobes. Within these lobes, areas are further distinguished by their functions. These include the sensory areas (visual, auditory and somatosensory), the motor area, the association areas, and two special areas found in the left hemisphere—Broca's area and Wernicke's area—where language is processed and produced.

probe and thereby "mapped" the human cortex. One of Penfield's discoveries was that certain areas specialize in receiving sensory information. When he touched the occipital lobe in the back of the brain, patients would "see" flickering lights, colors, stars, spots, wheels, and other visual displays. This area is the primary visual cortex—and damage to it can leave a person blind. Or damage to a specific part of it may result in a more specific visual deficit. For example, in *The Man Who Mistook His Wife for a Hat* (1985), Oliver Sacks (1985) tells a story about a patient who suffered occipital lobe damage. As this patient looked for his hat while preparing to leave Sacks's office, he grabbed his wife's head and tried to lift it. Suffering from visual agnosia—an inability to recognize familiar objects—this patient had apparently mistaken his own wife for a hat.

Penfield discovered other sensory areas in the cortex as well. When he stimulated a small area of the temporal lobe, now called the auditory cortex, the patients would "hear" doorbells, engines, and other sounds. Indeed, damage in this area can cause deafness. And when he stimulated a narrow strip in the parietal lobe, the **somatosensory cortex,** patients would "feel" a tingling of the leg, hand, cheek, or some other part of the body. In general, the more sensitive to touch a body part is, the larger is the cortical area devoted to it (see Figure 2.17).

Mirroring the somatosensory cortex is another narrow strip that specializes in the control of motor functions. Once again, much of what is currently known came from Penfield's work. Stimulating different parts of this strip triggers movement in different parts of the body. Stimulate the top, and a leg twitches; stimulate the bottom, and the tongue or jaw moves. All 600 muscles of the human body are represented in what is now called the **motor cortex.** As in the somatosensory cortex,

somatosensory cortex The area of the cortex that receives sensory information from the touch receptors in the skin.

motor cortex The area of the cortex that sends impulses to voluntary muscles.

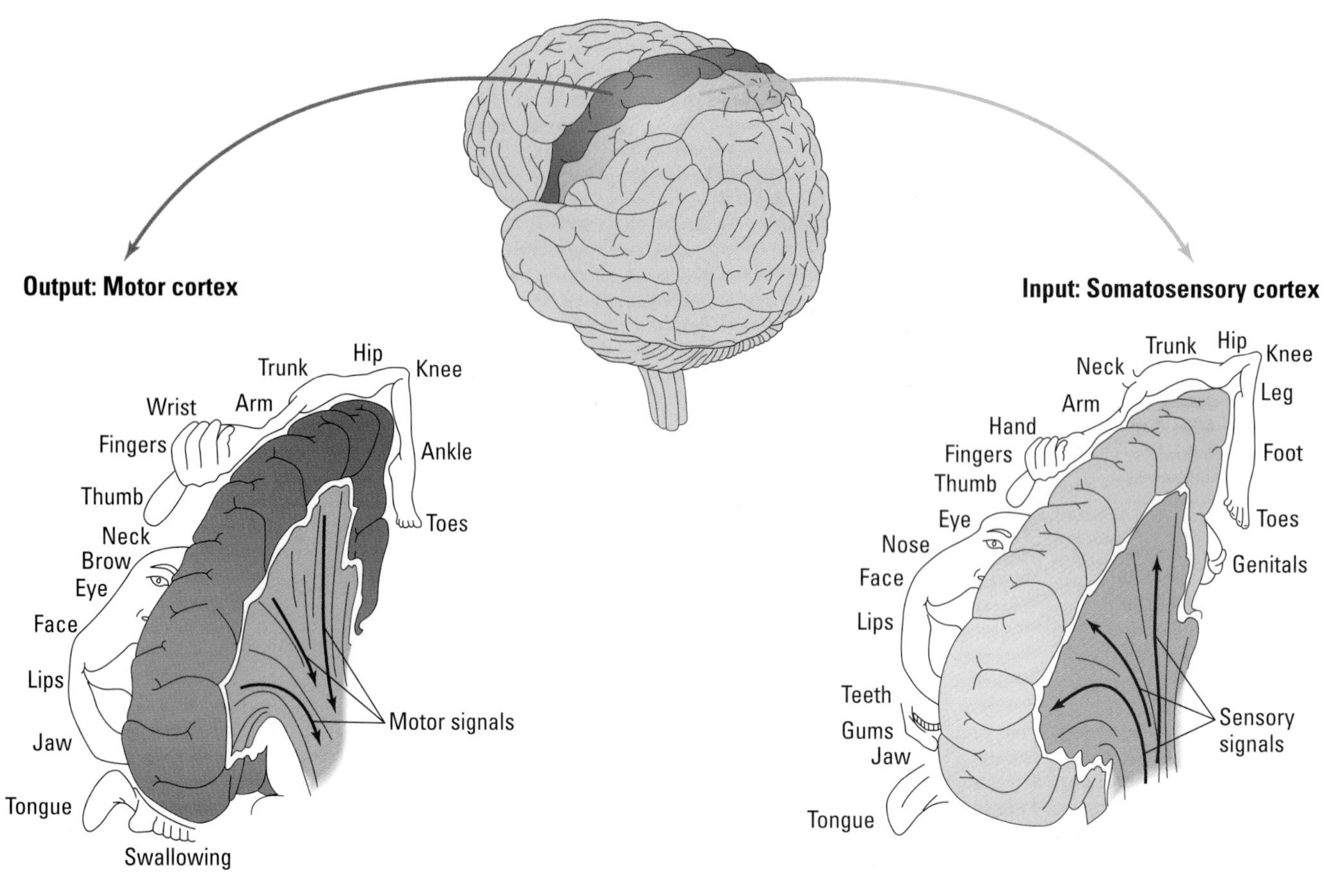

Figure 2.17 The somatosensory and motor areas Each part of the body is represented in the somatosensory (*right*) and motor (*left*) cortex. Note that the amount of tissue devoted to a body part does not correspond to its actual size. Rather, more area is devoted to parts that are most sensitive to touch (such as the lips) and in need of fine motor control (such as the thumbs).

the greater the need for precise control over a body part, the larger is its area in the motor cortex. Thus, Figure 2.17 shows more surface area devoted to the face, hands, and fingers than to the arms and legs.

Association Areas The cerebral cortex does more than just process sensory information and direct motor responses. There are also vast areas that collectively make up the **association cortex.** These areas communicate with both the sensory and the motor areas and house the brain's higher mental processes. Electrical stimulation of these sites does not elicit specific sensations or motor twitches in specific parts of the body, so it's hard to pin these areas down. But damage to the association cortex can have rather devastating results. In the frontal lobes, such damage can change someone's personality, as in the case of Phineas Gage. In other association areas, damage can impair specific kinds of memories, distort our spatial awareness, or cause odd speech deficits. For the most part, our ability to adapt to life's demands through learning, memory, and thought processes is spread throughout the regions of the cortex. But language—a complex activity for which humans, and in some ways only humans, are uniquely prepared—is different. Carved within the cortex are two special areas dedicated to language.

association cortex Areas of the cortex that communicate with the sensory and motor areas and house the brain's higher mental processes.

Language Areas There are two special regions of the cortex dedicated to language. One controls the production of speech; the other, comprehension. In 1861, French physician Paul Broca observed that people who have incurred damage in an area of the frontal lobe of the left hemisphere lose the ability to form words to *produce* fluent speech. The words sputter out slowly, and what is said is often not grammatical ("Buy milk store"). This region of the brain is called **Broca's area** (Schiller, 1992).

A few years later, German neurologist Carl Wernicke (1874) found that people with damage to part of the left temporal lobe lose their ability to *comprehend* speech. As you might expect, this region is called **Wernicke's area.** In short, people with language disorders, or aphasias, demonstrate that there are at least two distinct cortical centers for language. People with Broca's aphasia can comprehend speech but have trouble producing it. Those with Wernicke's aphasia can speak, but their comprehension is impaired. Interestingly, these two areas are connected by a neural pathway, thus forming part of a language circuit within the brain (Geschwind, 1979).

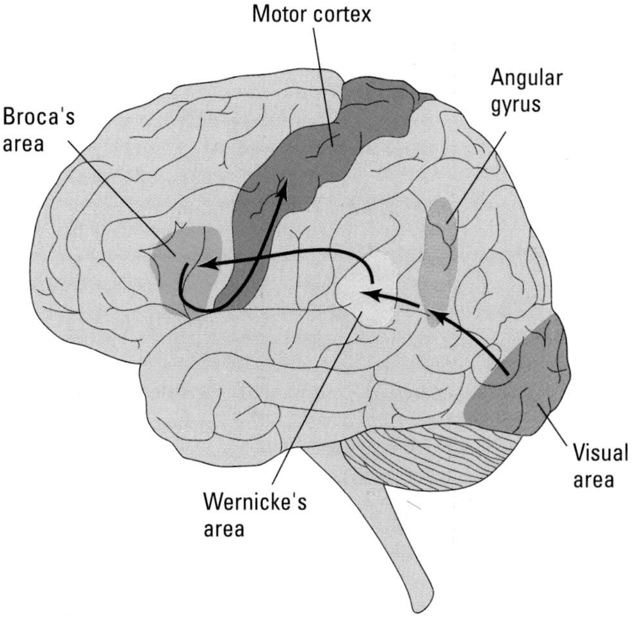

Figure 2.18 Language processing Although different regions specialize in certain functions, the brain operates as an integrated system. The "simple" act of speaking a written word, for example, requires a coordinated effort of the eyes, the visual cortex, the angular gyrus, Wernicke's area, Broca's area, and the motor cortex.

Before concluding our overview of the cortex, let's stop for a moment and ponder the contention that different functions, or behaviors, are "localized" in certain areas. As noted earlier, Penfield was able to pinpoint or "map" various locations in the cortex that house sensory and motor functions. However, it is important not to overstate the case for localization. It's clear that different cortical regions *specialize* in certain functions, but it's also clear that the healthy human brain operates as an *integrated* system. This point is illustrated by the role of the brain in language, whereby different cortical areas are activated depending on whether a word is spoken, written, or presented in music, or even whether it is a verb or a noun (Caramazza & Hillis, 1991). Consider what it takes simply to repeat the written word *ball.* From the eyes, the stimulus must travel for processing to the visual cortex. The input must then pass through the angular gyrus to be recorded, to Wernicke's area to be understood, and then to Broca's area, where signals are sent to the motor cortex, which drives the muscles of your lips, tongue, and larynx so that you can repeat the word (see Figure 2.18).

It's also important to note that this model may not accurately describe the ways in which the different brain regions interact to produce language. Figure 2.18 suggests that the neural events related to language occur in *serial* fashion, one step at a time. In fact, there is evidence to suggest that language and other complex mental processes may be more accurately represented by *parallel* models in which neural signals move along several routes at once and are processed simultaneously (Peterson et al., 1989). As in an orchestra, it takes the coordinated work of many instruments—often playing together—to make music.

The Split Brain

Before the first psychology laboratory was founded, in 1879, scientists interested in the nervous system and intrigued by the relationship between the body and the mind debated an old question concerning the brain. The "traditional" view was that the left and right hemispheres were symmetrical, mirror images of each other. Just as the body has two eyes, two ears, two legs, and two hands, the brain has two identical

Broca's area A region in the left hemisphere of the brain that directs the muscle movements in the production of speech.

Wernicke's area A region in the left hemisphere of the brain that is involved in the comprehension of language.

"I felt a cleavage in my mind
As if my brain had split;
I tried to match it, seam by seam
But could not make them fit."

—EMILY DICKINSON

hemispheres. The symmetry argument seemed self-evident. If you open up a skull, you'll see that the brain looks just like the two identical halves of a walnut packed together inside a shell.

Others argued that things are not always as they seem on the surface. Portrait artists know fully well that the human face is not perfectly symmetrical—for example, one eye may be larger than the other, or one cheek may have a dimple that the other does not. The same asymmetry is true of the brain. As we saw, Broca (1861) and Wernicke (1874) both found key language centers only in the left hemisphere. From the start, this finding gave rise to the notion that the left hemisphere is "dominant" (Jackson, 1958)—a notion also used to explain why most people are right-handed. Indeed, nearly all right-handers and a majority of left-handers process language mainly in the left hemisphere. It also suggested that the two hemispheres are specialized for different functions. Carrying this idea a giant step further, German physicist Gustav Fechner (1860) proposed that each side of the brain has its own mind. If your brain could be divided in half, he speculated, you would have two separate streams of consciousness. What a fascinating concept for an experiment. At the time, Fechner had no idea that such an experiment would one day come to pass.

INTERSECTION

BEHAVIORAL NEUROSCIENCE AND HEALTH

Lefties in a Right-Handed World

When Bill Clinton, George Bush, and Ross Perot faced each other in the 1992 presidential election, they had something beside the election in common: All are left-handers. With which hand do *you* write or draw? Which hand do you use to throw a ball? In which hand do you hold your toothbrush or a knife? In which hand do you hold a match to strike it? In short, are you mostly right-handed or left-handed?

Roughly 90 percent of the human population is right-handed. This percentage (though somewhat higher among women and lower among men) is highly consistent over time and place. In a study cited in Chapter 1, Stanley Coren (1993) found that 90 percent of all the human characters portrayed in works of art have been right-handers—and that this was as true thousands of years ago as it is today. In fact, archaeological records of prehistoric stone tools yield fossil evidence for right-handedness as far back as 2 or 3 million years ago—long before the evolution of *Homo sapiens* (Corballis, 1989). This asymmetry is not the product of culture. Studies show that right-hand predominance is universal and that most thumb-sucking fetuses suck the right thumb rather than the left (Hepper et al., 1990). It's interesting that a similar bias is not found in cats, rats, monkeys (Annett, 1985), or even our closest relative, the chimpanzee (Hopkins, 1996). It's also interesting that although nine out of ten humans are right-handed, only eight out of ten show a preference for the right foot, seven out of ten for the right eye, and six out of ten for the right ear (Coren, 1993). Yet some situations do appear to favor left-handedness. For example, since the start of major league baseball more than 100 years ago, the number of left-handed batters and pitchers steadily increased before stabilizing at about 30 percent (Goldstein & Young, 1996).

Lefties, righties, what's the difference? Does it really matter? Perhaps. Research shows that left-handers are more likely to emerge as gifted athletes, mathematicians, and artists. But they're also more likely to have allergies, insomnia, reading disabilities, and certain other disorders. Investigating the links between cerebral lateralization and behavior, Clare Porac and Stanley Coren (1981) surveyed 5,147 men and women of all ages in the United States and Canada. To their surprise, the percentage of left-handers in the population showed a steady decline across the life span. As illustrated in Figure 2.19, 15 percent of the ten-year-olds were left-handed, compared to only 5 percent of fifty-year-olds and less than 1 percent of eighty-year-olds. By age eighty-five, right-handers out-

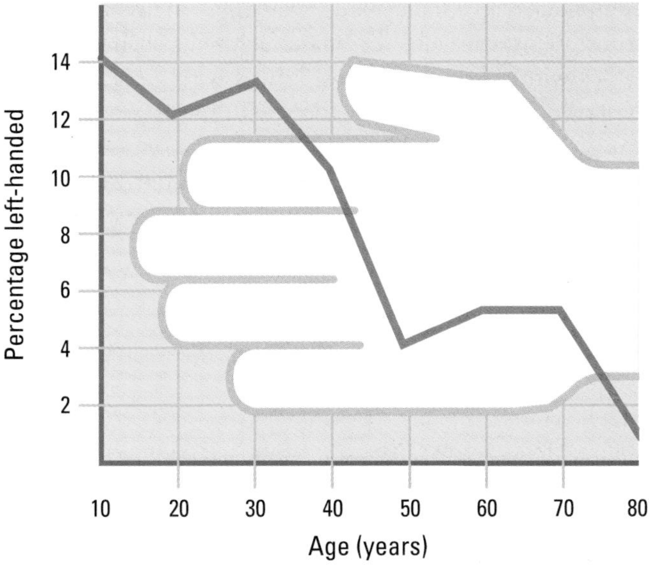

Figure 2.19 Left-handedness across the life span In a study of 5,147 individuals, the percentage of left-handers in the sample declined with age (Coren, 1993).

numbered left-handers by 200 to 1. Other researchers have since replicated this puzzling finding (Halpern & Coren, 1993). For some reason, the population of lefties dwindles with age. The question for the psychologist detective is, why?

There are two possible explanations. One is the *longevity hypothesis,* which states that left-handers simply have a shorter life span. In support of this hypothesis, Coren and Halpern (1991) examined 987 death certificates and found that the average age of death was higher for right-handers than for left-handers. Other researchers have argued that this disparity is small. Instead, they propose the *modification hypothesis,* which states that the number of left-handers diminishes with age because many natural lefties switch to the right hand—due, perhaps, to pressures from parents, teachers, or an environment that is far better suited to right-handedness. According to Lauren Harris (1993), modification is the more plausible explanation. It turns out, for example, that the decline in left-handedness is matched by an increased number of right-handers who say they had switched when younger (Hugdahl et al., 1993).

Researchers may disagree about the reason that left-handers do not appear in the elderly population, but they agree completely that the physical environment is designed more for the comfort and safety of right-handers. Scissors and pruning shears have handles shaped so that one hole is angled correctly for the right thumb and the other hole is for the other fingers of the right hand. In schools, spiral notebooks, chairs with built-in desktops on the right, and even rulers are designed for the right hand. In the workplace, computer keyboards, portable power saws, and certain types of heavy machinery create problems as well. Indeed, on-off and safety switches are almost always on the right side for quick use in an emergency. It's no wonder, says Coren (1993), that lefties are so often stereotyped as clumsy and awkward (see Figure 2.20).

These inconveniences are like booby traps and may well prove hazardous to the health of all left-handers. For example, Coren asked nearly 2,000 college students to fill out a handedness questionnaire and to report on any accidents they had experienced in the past two years. Responses showed that left-handers were 89 percent more likely to have accident-related injuries requiring medical attention—in sports, at work, at home, and, most of all, driving a car. Why is driving so risky? Coren notes that driving on the right side of the road puts the steering wheel on the left and the gear shifting on the right, a design that favors right-handers. What's more, he finds that when startled (which causes us to put our hands up to protect the body), lefties are more likely to raise the right hand higher than the left. In an emergency, this reflexive response could cause them to veer left, swerving the car into traffic rather than to the right side of the road. Consistent with this speculation, Coren finds that traffic accidents are less

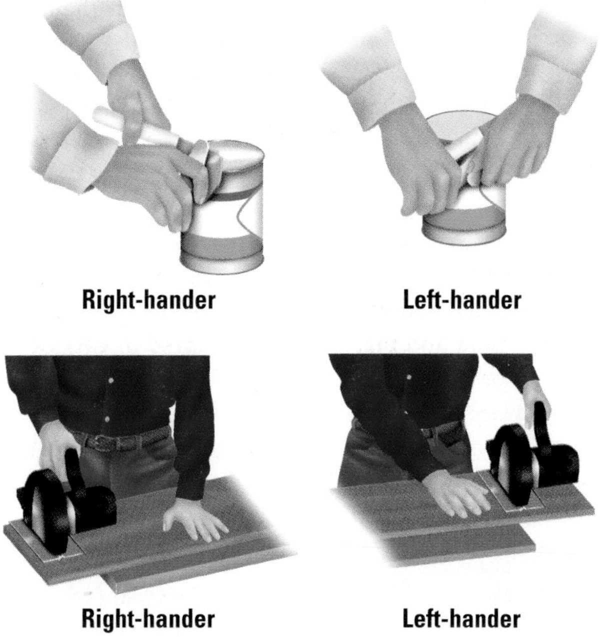

Figure 2.20 Right-handed objects Many common items are designed for right-handers. As shown, left-handers have to hold their hands in an awkward position while using a can opener and stand dangerously close to the blade while using a portable power saw (Coren, 1993).

frequent in the United Kingdom and Ireland, where motorists drive on the left side of the road, than in other European countries.

Can anything be done to improve matters for the average left-hander? Yes. The physical environment can be made more "user friendly." Tool grips can be designed for lefties at no extra cost, on-off and safety switches can be placed on both sides of an instrument, and left-handed kitchen utensils, power tools, school supplies, and office equipment can all be made available. Many ambidextrous items can also be manufactured—such as soup ladles with two pouring lips, knives with serrated edges on both sides of the blade, tools with finger grooves that can accommodate either hand, and instrument panels with controls that are more centered. Solutions would be easy to implement. The key is to recognize first that the problem exists.

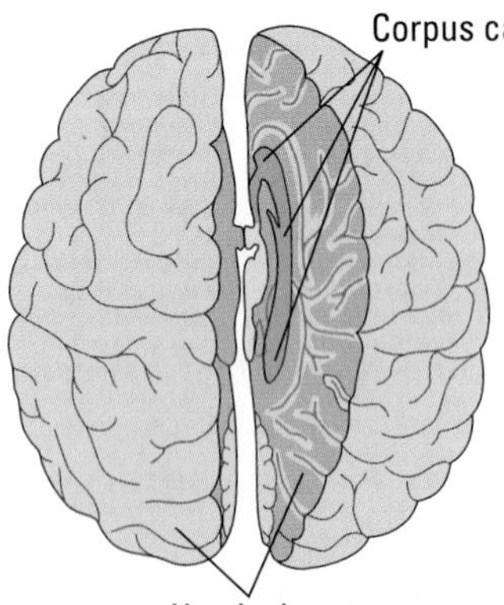

Figure 2.21 The corpus callosum Containing millions of nerve fibers, the corpus callosum joins the left and right hemispheres.

Split-Brain Studies For people with severe epilepsy, seizures are the brain's equivalent of thunder-and-lightning storms. A seizure usually starts in one small area, but it quickly spreads across the brain from one side to the other. The experience can be terrifying, and at times life-threatening. In the past, neurosurgeons tried to control the problem by removing the overactive area, but these operations had only limited success. To prevent the seizures from spreading, a more radical approach was needed. The goal was to separate the two hemispheres. The method was to cut the **corpus callosum,** a four-inch-long, quarter-inch-thick bundle consisting of millions of white nerve fibers that join the two hemispheres (see Figure 2.21). This **split-brain** surgery often eliminates the epileptic seizures, as hoped. But are there psychological side effects? Was Fechner right in proposing that a split brain, in which the link between the two hemispheres is severed, contains two minds?

Before we examine the effects of split-brain surgery, it's important to know more about the divisions of labor within the brain. As we've noted before, the left hemisphere receives sensory input from, and sends motor commands to, the right side of the body (hands, legs, arms, and so on), whereas the right hemisphere communicates with the left side of the body. Processing visual and auditory input is somewhat more complex. Both eyes send information to both hemispheres, but images in the right half of the visual field are sent to the left hemisphere, and images in the left half of the visual field are sent to the right hemisphere. In other words, if you're looking straight ahead at someone, images on the left are sent by both eyes to the right hemisphere, and images on the right are sent by both eyes to the left hemisphere (see Figure 2.22). Auditory inputs are also sent to both hemispheres, but sounds received in one ear register in the opposite hemisphere first.

If your brain is intact, then this odd crossover arrangement poses no problem because information received by each hemisphere is quickly sent to the other side through the corpus callosum. By sharing information in this manner, the two sides of the brain work as a team. But what happens when the neuron-filled highway that connects the hemispheres is severed? In 1963, two neurosurgeons, Philip Vogel and Joseph Bogen, described the case of a forty-eight-year-old man who had severe epileptic seizures following a head injury. A split-brain operation was performed (the corpus callosum was cut), and it was successful. As for side effects, the man's behavior, like that of other split-brain patients, seemed normal (tests generally show that perceptual abilities, intelligence, memory, and personality are unaffected). But when researchers probe beneath surface appearances, some unusual effects are revealed (Iaccino, 1993; Nebes, 1990; Springer & Deutsch, 1989).

Roger Sperry (who was awarded a Nobel prize in 1981 and died in 1994), Michael Gazzaniga (his student), and others have helped bring this picture into focus

corpus callosum A bundle of nerve fibers that connects the left and right hemispheres.

split brain A surgically produced condition in which the corpus callosum is severed, thus cutting the link between the left and right hemispheres of the brain.

through an ingenious series of studies, such as the one cited at the beginning of this chapter. Involving split-brain patients, the basic procedure was to present information to one hemisphere or the other, and then to measure what the subject "knew" by testing each hemisphere separately.

In one study, Sperry (1968) asked a female patient, identified as N.G., to stare at a black dot in the center of a screen. Then, for only a fraction of a second, he flashed a picture of a spoon either to the right or to the left of the dot and asked, "What do you see?" The result was fascinating. When the image was shown in the right visual field, and thus sent to the left hemisphere, N.G. was quick to reply that she saw a spoon. But when the image was presented on the left side and sent to the right hemisphere, she could not say what she saw. Why? As noted earlier, speech is controlled by the left hemisphere. If an image in the right side of the brain cannot cross over to the left side, then the person cannot transform what is seen into words. But wait. How do we know that N.G. actually saw the spoon? Maybe the right hemisphere is just stupid. To probe further, Sperry asked N.G. to reach behind a screen and feel an assortment of objects, such as a pencil, an eraser, a key, and a piece of paper. "Which of these did you see before?" Easy. Touching the objects with her left hand (which sent the sensations to the right hemisphere), she selected the spoon. The right side knew all along it had seen a spoon, but only the left side could say so (see Figure 2.23).

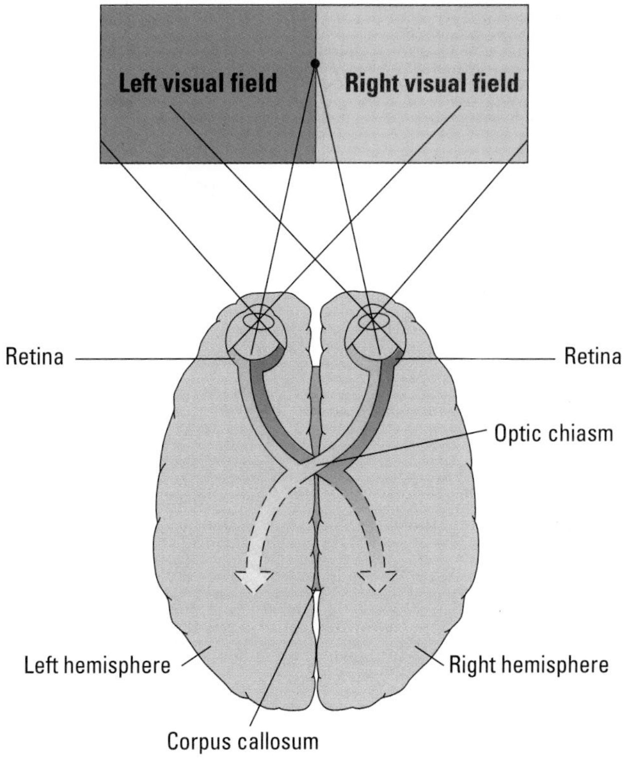

Figure 2.22 Visual processing Both eyes send information to both hemispheres, but images in the right half of the visual field are sent to the left hemisphere, and images in the left half of the visual field are sent to the right hemisphere. Each image is instantly sent to the other side through the corpus callosum.

In a second similar study, Gazzaniga (1967) had split-brain patients stare at a black dot and flashed the word *teacup* on the screen. The letters *tea* were presented to the left visual field (the right hemisphere), and *cup* was presented to the right visual field (the left hemisphere). If you were the subject—and if your corpus callosum was intact—you would see the full word, *teacup*. But the split-brain patients reported seeing only *cup*, the portion of the word that was

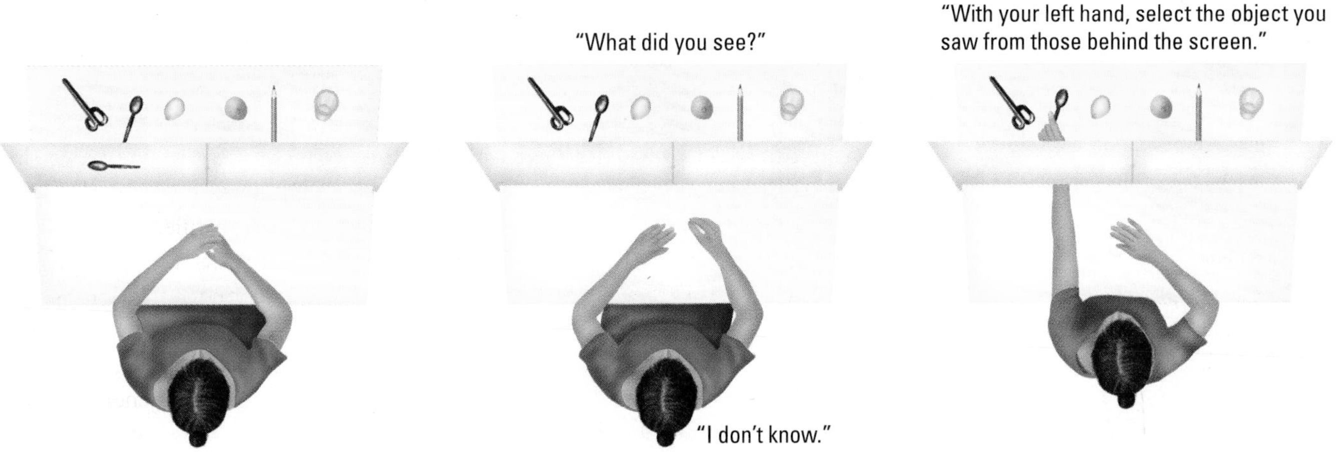

Figure 2.23 Sperry's split-brain experiment When the image of a spoon was projected to the right hemisphere, the split-brain patient could not say what she saw. Yet when she felt various objects with her left hand, she selected the spoon. The right side knew all along that it saw the spoon, but only the left side could say so (Sperry, 1968).

flashed to the left hemisphere. Again, how do we know they actually saw the second part of the word? When told to choose between the two parts by pointing with the left hand, they pointed to *tea,* the letters sent to the right hemisphere. As in the spoon study, each hemisphere was in touch with only half of the total input. Under normal circumstances, stimuli reaching both hemispheres are blended to form a unified experience. Disconnected, each hemisphere has a mind of its own.

In a third study, Jerre Levy and others (1972) took pictures of various faces, cut them vertically in half, and pasted different right and left halves together. These composite photographs were then presented rapidly on slides. As in other studies, subjects stared at a center dot so that half of the image fell on either side. Look at the stimulus presented in Figure 2.24. When asked what they saw, subjects said it was a child. Because they were forced to respond in words, the left hemisphere dominated, causing them to name the image in the right visual field. But when subjects were told to point to the face with the left hand, they pointed to the woman wearing glasses, whose image was projected on the left side. Remarkably, split-brain patients did not seem to know that the composite face was unusual.

Split-brain patients exhibit so much "disconnection" in laboratory tests that one wonders how they manage to get along in their everyday affairs. To be sure, some instances of bizarre behavior have been observed. One patient had trouble dressing because he would pull his pants up with one hand and pull them down with the other. Another couldn't decide what to wear one morning because she would pick one item of clothing from the closet with her right hand and a different item with her left hand. In instances like these, one hand literally does not know what the other hand is doing.

Although there are plenty of stories like these to be told, disconnection experiences are not all that common. Why not? One possibility is that some input reaches both hemispheres through "subcortical" (below the cortex) structures that remain connected after the corpus callosum is cut. Justine Sergent (1990) explored this issue

Figure 2.24 Levy's split-brain experiment Split-brain subjects stared at a dot and viewed a composite of two faces (A). When asked what they saw, subjects chose the child—the image sent to the verbal left hemisphere (B). But when subjects pointed to the face with the left hand, they chose the woman with glasses—whose image was received by the right hemisphere (C) (Levy et al., 1968).

in a split-brain study in which she flashed pictures of celebrities to the left or right hemisphere and asked a series of probing questions. At one point, she presented a picture of Robert Redford to the patient's right hemisphere and asked, "Is this a man or a woman?" The patient responded, "I am not sure . . . a man." Let's eavesdrop on part of the interview:

Q: Does this man look familiar to you?
A: I think so.
Q: Where have you seen him?
A: I don't know.
Q: What does he do for a living?
A: Is he a movie actor? . . . Yes, an actor.
Q: What kind of character does he play?
A: A playboy.
Q: What do you mean?
A: He is quite handsome, don't you think?
Q: How do you know he is handsome?
A: Well, I know.
Q: Can you picture him? Can you describe his face?
A: No, I can't say what he looks like but I think he's handsome.
Q: Can you recall some movies of his you saw?
A: I know I have seen him play, but I can't tell any movie.
Q: Do you know his name?
A: No.

Now notice what happened when the same picture was presented to the patient's left hemisphere.

Q: Did I show this face before?
A: No.
Q: Does he look like the one you just saw?
A: No. I don't know.
Q: Do you know who he is?
A: Yes. He is quite handsome too . . . Robert Redford.

These scripts are typical of the split-brain syndrome: the patient's right hemisphere could not identify or describe Robert Redford's picture when it was presented in the left visual field. And when it appeared in the right visual field, the patient did not know that she had seen it before. But notice that even though she could not identify the picture through the right hemisphere, she knew, somehow, that it depicted a handsome male actor. Sergent speculates that the disconnection in split-brain patients is only partial, not complete—and that some information may have slipped into the right hemisphere through subcortical structures (Banich, 1995; Hoptman & Davidson, 1994).

Cerebral Lateralization Split-brain research has generated tremendous excitement in behavioral neuroscience. When the corpus callosum is severed, input to one hemisphere is trapped, unable to pass to the other side. As a result, neither hemisphere knows what the other is doing. But what about the day-to-day operations of a normal and healthy brain, corpus callosum and all? We know that speech is usually located in the left hemisphere, but are there other asymmetries in the human brain? Are other functions similarly **lateralized?** Does one side or the other control math, music, or the ability to recognize faces?

cerebral lateralization The tendency for each hemisphere of the brain to specialize in different functions.

Several different methods are used to determine if there are hemispheric differences in the "connected" brain. One method is to compare people with damage to the right or left hemisphere. A second method is to present various tasks and then measure activity in both sides of the brain using EEG recordings, measures of cerebral blood flow, or imaging techniques. To the extent that a given task is processed in one hemisphere more than in the other, that hemisphere should be relatively more active. A third method is to present a stimulus to either the right or left hemisphere and measure the speed with which subjects act on the information. If the input has to be relayed through the corpus callosum to the other side, it will take the subject up to 20 milliseconds longer to make a response. A fourth method is to briefly sedate the right or left hemisphere and then test for disruptive effects.

Using an array of tools, researchers have uncovered many strands of evidence for hemispheric lateralization in the human brain (Davidson & Hugdahl, 1995; Iaccino, 1993; Springer & Deutsch, 1989). As we saw, the left hemisphere largely controls verbal activities—including reading, writing, speaking, and other aspects of language. It has long been known that damage to Broca's and Wernicke's areas, which reside in the left hemisphere, produces various types of aphasias, or speech disorders. Studies also show that people recognize words, letters, and other verbal stimuli faster when these stimuli are sent directly to the left hemisphere. Deaf people also seem to rely on the left hemisphere more than the right for reading sign language (Corina et al., 1992). Finally, PET scans show that different regions of the left hemisphere (and some areas of the right hemisphere as well) "light up" depending on whether subjects are listening to words that are spoken (hearing), reading words on a screen (seeing), saying words aloud (speaking), or coming up with related words (thinking). A sample PET scan appears in Figure 2.25 (Peterson & Fiez, 1993).

Whereas the left hemisphere is a verbal specialist, there is converging evidence that the right hemisphere plays a vital role in nonverbal activities such as visual-spatial tasks, music, and face recognition. Clinical case studies illustrate this point. Gazzaniga (1985) instructed a split-brain patient to draw a cube and found that he produced a better drawing with the left hand than with the right—even though he was right-handed. Other case studies reveal that various nonverbal deficits—such as an impaired ability to recognize faces—are more likely to result from damage to the right hemisphere than from damage to the left. For example, right hemisphere damage may cause people to lose their sense of direction while driving, get lost in their own homes, or have trouble locating items in a familiar supermarket (Newcombe & Ratcliff, 1990). In some cases, right hemisphere damage caused by a stroke or accident triggers a disruption of spatial awareness called "neglect." People with neglect syndrome lose all awareness of the left side of space, including the left side of their own bodies. As a result, they may comb their hair only on the right side of the head, shave only the right side of the face, or eat food only if it's on the right side of the plate (see Figure 2.26). Finally, laboratory studies show that people are usually faster at locating dots, drawing three-dimensional objects, and recognizing faces when the material is presented to the right hemisphere than to the left (Bradshaw & Nettleton, 1981).

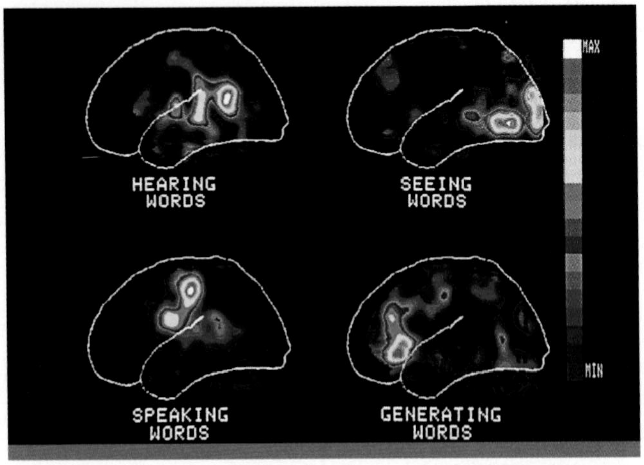

Figure 2.25 The talking left hemisphere PET scans show that a single word activated different left-hemisphere areas depending on whether it was heard, seen, spoken, or thought about. Notice that these "lit-up" areas are in the visual cortex, auditory cortex, Broca's area, and frontal lobes, respectively.

There is no simple way to summarize all the research on hemispheric differences. The evidence clearly suggests that there is specialization, with the left side more verbal and the right side more spatial. As we'll see in Chapter 9, research also shows that positive emotions evoke more electrical activity in the left hemisphere, while negative emotions elicit more activity in the right (Davidson, 1993). But some researchers believe that the key difference between hemispheres is not in *what* kind of input is processed but in *how* that input is processed. In essence, a good deal of research now suggests that the left hemisphere processes information in analytical, piecemeal style—as in word analogies, arithmetic, and logical problem solving; and that the right hemisphere processes information in a more global, holistic style—as used in music, art, and various forms of creative expression (Ornstein, 1978). Either way, it's important not to overstate the case for lateralization, because neither hemisphere has exclusive control over functions. Indeed, both sides of the brain are capable of processing various kinds of information (Efron, 1990).

Figure 2.26 Neglect syndrome A patient with a stroke in the right hemisphere was asked to copy model pictures. As with many neglect syndrome patients, he almost completely overlooked the left side of each drawing.

One Mind or Two? Let us now step back for a moment and reflect on the big picture: Does splitting the brain in half produce two separate minds, as Fechner had proposed? From the start, Sperry (1966) argued that severing the corpus callosum leaves the split-brain patient with two separate minds and that "what is experienced in the right hemisphere seems to lie entirely outside the realm of experience of the left hemisphere." Sir John Eccles (1965), who won a Nobel prize in physiology, disagreed. According to Eccles, the right hemisphere cannot think without the speech capabilities of the left side.

Clearly, the research supports Sperry's claim. At one point, researchers encountered a split-brain patient, known as P.S., who had the unique ability to communicate with the right hemisphere by arranging Scrabble letters with the left hand in response to questions. To put the dual-mind hypothesis to the test, Joseph Ledoux and his colleagues (1977) questioned each hemisphere separately—and found that the two sides often disagreed. For example, when P.S. was asked what job he would like, his left hemisphere said he wanted to be a "draftsman," but his right hemisphere spelled out "automobile racer."

Although split-brain patients seem to have two independent streams of consciousness, it's important to keep in mind that their behavior is reasonably well integrated. It's also important to be cautious in generalizing to individuals whose brains are intact. The fact that our right and left hemispheres are specialized in no way implies that they function independently. Through the corpus callosum, information between the hemispheres is exchanged with such speed that we enjoy a seamless, well-synchronized experience.

Prospects for the Future

Is the adult brain fixed in its structure, or does it have a capacity to change as a result of experience? Is it possible for people to recover functions lost to brain damage? What about the fanciful idea that healthy tissue can be transplanted from one brain into another?

Enriching the Brain through Experience

The human brain is an impressive organ. Encased in a hard, protective skull, it is not only complex, but it also has flexibility, or **plasticity** (from the word "plastic")—a capacity to change as a result of usage, practice, and experience (Spear et al., 1995).

Psychologists used to believe that the neural circuits of the adult brain and nervous system were fully developed and no longer subject to change. Then a series

plasticity A capacity to change as a result of experience.

BEHAVIORAL NEUROSCIENCE AND EDUCATION

Right-Brain Education—Science or Science Fiction?

A recent magazine article advised parents to have their children tested to see whether they are "right-brained" or "left-brained" thinkers, so that teachers can customize their lessons and methods to suit each child's style. Similar claims are often made about people in different occupations. Do artists use the right hemisphere more than lawyers do? What about chemists and poets? Are there hemispheric differences between cultures? And what about commercial products such as books, tapes, and seminars that are designed to unleash your "untapped" brain resources? Browse through the shelves of your local bookstore, and you'll see recent paperback titles such as *Whole-Brain Thinking, Educating the Right Brain,* and *The Other Side of the Mind.* So, what advice is contained in these books? What are the educational implications of the split-brain studies discussed in this chapter?

Based on research findings that the left hemisphere largely controls verbal skills (such as reading, writing, arithmetic, and logical problem solving) while the right hemisphere plays a major role in various nonverbal activities (such as spatial tasks, music, art, and face recognition), Robert Ornstein (1972) argued that Westerners use only the left side of the brain and neglect the "intuitive" right side. Some educators complained that American schools, because they focused on reading, writing, and arithmetic, did not enable children to develop their right-brain potential in visualization, music, art, and other forms of creative expression.

This view inspired educational reformists critical of a conventional curriculum that relies heavily on reading, speaking, listening, and writing. The proposed alternatives vary. They include increased exposure to music and art; a greater use of drawings, charts, and other illustrative material; and right-brain mental exercises such as mirror drawing, charades, fantasy, meditation, and photography. In a bestseller entitled *Drawing on the Right Side of the Brain,* for example, art teacher Betty Edwards (1979) claimed that although the right hemisphere has the ability to draw, many people find it difficult to copy familiar scenes or objects because they tend to label and analyze the material. To reduce this interference from the left hemisphere, she recommended that students view the pictures to be copied upside down so the pictures cannot be recognized and labeled. According to Edwards, this exercise improves the quality of drawings that are rendered.

Although discussions of right-brain education have sparked excitement, there is little scientific evidence to support this application of the split-brain research (Hellige, 1990; Springer & Deutsch, 1989). Lauren Harris (1988) notes two related problems. First, this application is based on the incorrect assumption that various functions are completely localized within the right or left hemispheres. In reality, as we saw, both hemispheres are involved at least to some extent in language, music, art, and other mental activities. Except in split-brain patients, information between the two hemispheres flows quickly and seamlessly through the corpus callosum.

Second, the call for right-brain education springs from the complaint that schools do not sufficiently encourage children to use the right hemisphere—and that this lack of exercise prevents them from realizing their full potential in nontraditional domains. Granted, the school curriculum may be flawed, and perhaps a greater emphasis should be placed on music, the visual arts, and other "nonacademic" subjects. As Harris (1988) warns, however, "educators who are displeased with the educational curriculum should present the case for change on its own merits and not seek to win scientific respectability for their arguments by dressing them in neuropsychological jargon" (p. 226). The concern here is that the call for right-brain education is founded on an exaggerated and overly simplistic view of the brain. Thus, as two researchers put it, "the duplex house that Sperry built grew into the K-mart of brain science" (Hooper & Teresi, 1986, p. 223).

of provocative experiments showed that this is not so. Mark Rosenzweig (1984) built an "amusement park" for rats to examine the effects of an enriched environment on neural development. Some rats lived together in a cage filled with ladders, platforms, boxes, and other toys, while others lived in solitary confinement. The enriched rats developed heavier, thicker brains with more dendrites and synapses than those who were deprived. In fact, the growth can be quite specific. Rats flooded with visual stimulation formed 20 percent more synaptic connections per neuron in the visual cortex than those who were raised in darkness (Greenough et al., 1987). And "acrobatic" rats trained to run between pylons on elevated runways formed new synaptic connections in the cerebellum, the structure involved in balance and motor coordination (Greenough et al., 1990). Similar results with birds, mice, squirrels, and monkeys of different ages have confirmed a basic point: Experiences can spark the growth of new synaptic connections and mold the brain's neural architecture (Rosenzweig, 1996).

Plasticity has profound and practical implications for human development and adaptation. In an interesting study, Avi Karni and Leslie Ungerleider (1996) considered the proposition that repeated stimulation of a body part would cause corresponding changes in the human brain. Every day, these researchers had six men perform one of two finger-tapping sequences for 10 to 20 minutes. After five weeks, they brought the men into the laboratory and had them tap out both the practiced and nonpracticed sequences. Using functional MRI, they found that tapping the practiced sequence lit up a larger portion of the primary motor cortex. Interestingly, other researchers have found that, when their often-used fingers are stimulated, blind braille readers and string musicians exhibit more activity in the somatosensory cortex than the average person (Pascual-Leone et al., 1993; Elbert et al., 1995). "Practice may not always make perfect, but it is likely to make a lasting impression on your brain" (Azar, 1996).

Recent studies indicate that the brain's plasticity can also be a burden, as in the case of amputation. Psychologists have long been puzzled by phantom pain—the fact that amputees often feel excruciating pain in the area of their lost limb. In the past, some interpreted the sensation as a form of denial, and others saw it as a cry of protest from the truncated nerve endings in the stump. It now appears that phantom pain results, ironically, from the brain's capacity for growth. This possibility was first raised when Michael Merzenich (1984) severed the nerve of the middle finger in an adult monkey and found that the area of the somatosensory cortex dedicated to that finger did not wither away. Rather, nearby neurons activated by other fingers filled in the dormant region. The sensations produced by these neurons might thus fool the brain into thinking that the limb is still there. Indeed, a recent study with human amputees revealed that the more cortical "reorganization" that had occurred, as detected in brain scans, the more phantom pain the patients felt (Flor et al., 1995).

Repairing the Damaged Brain

The brain has great capacity for enrichment, but alas, we are mortal and our brains are fallible. Strokes, spinal cord injuries, diseases that strike at the core of the nervous system, exposure to toxic substances, and addictions to alcohol and other drugs are among the possible causes of brain damage. The varying effects include paralysis, motor disorders, thought and speech disorders, blunted emotion, changes in personality, and a loss of sensory capabilities, consciousness, and memory (see Figure 2.27).

One of the sad realities of brain damage is its permanence. If you get an ulcer, break a finger, or scrape your knee, new cells will be produced to heal the wound. But the brain does not have this capacity to completely repair itself. Once a neuron is damaged, it is forever disabled. And once the brain is developed, it does not produce more neurons. Yet every now and then, we hear stories about "miraculous"

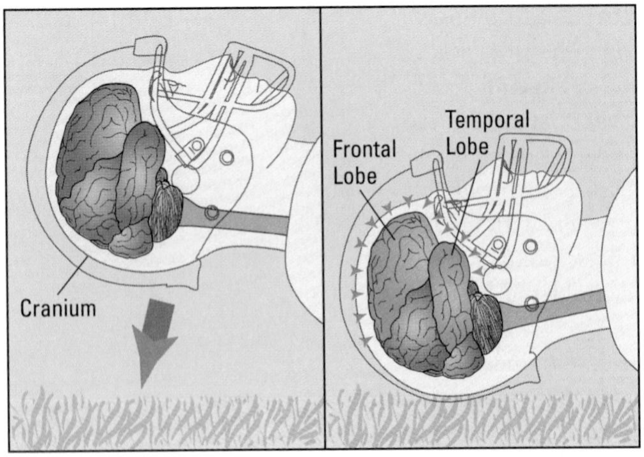

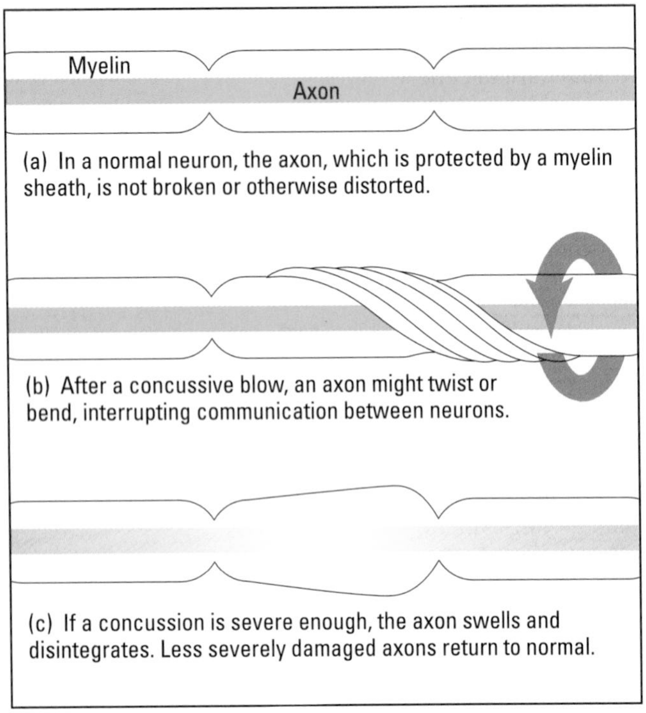

(a) In a normal neuron, the axon, which is protected by a myelin sheath, is not broken or otherwise distorted.

(b) After a concussive blow, an axon might twist or bend, interrupting communication between neurons.

(c) If a concussion is severe enough, the axon swells and disintegrates. Less severely damaged axons return to normal.

Figure 2.27 Anatomy of a concussion How often have you seen an athlete take a crushing blow to the head, go down, and leave the game? Featured NFL quarterbacks such as Troy Aikman, Steve Young, Jim Kelly, and Bret Favre, have all suffered repeated concussions. So do thousands of other athletes each year. But with what effect?

A concussion occurs when axons are stretched, twisted, or sheared by a blow to the head, which interrupts signals between neurons. A mild concussion ("dingers") may cause headaches, blurred speech, a ringing in the ears, and a momentary loss of consciousness. A severe concussion can also damage the brainstem and disrupt heart rate and breathing. The long-term toll is unknown, but doctors fear that players who suffer repeated concussions may face lasting cognitive declines.

Can anything be done to lessen the damage? In pro football, the standard helmet contains an inflatable sack to cushion blows, but most players don't inflate it because it makes the helmet too tight. There is also ProCap, a helmet that has a shock-absorbing polyurethane cushion attached to the exterior, but most players find this device bulky. Perhaps what is needed, at this point, is greater awareness of the possible risks.

recoveries from brain damage. What makes this possible is that we have that adaptive capacity to compensate for loss by strengthening old synaptic connections and sprouting new axons and dendrites to form new connections. Also, healthy brain tissue will sometimes pick up lost functions. Thus, children who have substantial damage to the left hemisphere early in life can still learn to speak, and adults who suffer strokes are often able to recover their speech and motor abilities.

Is it possible to further restore the brain through medical intervention? For the millions of people each year who are struck by Parkinson's disease, Alzheimer's disease, and other degenerative nerve disorders, can the damaged brain be repaired? What about the damage to *Superman* actor Christopher Reeve, who compressed his spinal cord and is now paralyzed from the neck down as a result of a horseback-riding accident? Reeve, who is in his forties, has one goal: to stand up on his fiftieth birthday. Will this be possible?

Actor Christopher Reeve was paralyzed from the neck down in a horseback riding accident, in which his spinal cord was compressed.

As wild and as fanciful as these ideas seemed just a few years ago, progress is being made on a number of fronts. One particularly exciting development is that researchers have been busy trying to transplant healthy tissue from the central nervous system of one animal into that of another animal in a surgical procedure known as a **neural graft.** Using amphibians and fish, researchers long ago demonstrated that it was possible to transplant neurons in cold-blooded animals. In a classic series of experiments conducted in the 1940s, Sperry transplanted eyeballs in frogs and found that these grafts formed new pathways to the brain and restored vision.

Would neural grafting work as well in warm-blooded mammals? To find out, a team of researchers destroyed a dopamine-producing area of the brainstem called the substantia nigra in laboratory rats. As anticipated, the lack of dopamine caused severe tremors and other symptoms that mimicked Parkinson's disease. Next, they implanted healthy tissue from brains taken from rat fetuses. The result: After four weeks, there was a 70 percent decline in symptoms (Perlow et al., 1979). And in more recent experiments involving rats, mice, and primates, researchers also used neural grafting successfully in other regions of the brain to reverse cognitive learning deficits, spatial deficits, and alcohol-induced memory loss (Kimble, 1990; Sinden et al., 1995).

News from animal laboratories is encouraging. But is it possible to use brain grafts in treating people who suffer from degenerative nerve disorders? In March 1982, a male Parkinson's patient in Stockholm, Sweden, agreed to serve as a human guinea pig. Barely able to move without medication, he underwent an experimental operation. The neurosurgeons removed part of his adrenal gland, which produces dopamine, and injected the tissue directly into his brain (Parkinson's disease results from a shortage of dopamine). But the result was disappointing. The patient showed some minor improvement during the first couple of weeks, but he soon reverted to

neural graft A technique of transplanting healthy tissue from the nervous system of one animal into that of another.

his presurgery state (Backlund et al., 1985). Undiscouraged, others pursued the use of brain grafts with Parkinson's patients with varying degrees of success. In 1987, a group of Mexican researchers stirred up a good deal of excitement when they reported that transplanted dopamine-producing tissue produced remarkable improvement in two patients (Madrazo et al., 1987). Additional clinical studies were then conducted. The results were not nearly as dramatic, but they too revealed at least modest improvement in many patients (Gage, 1993). To date, the most encouraging news comes from Sweden, where researchers implanting tissue from human fetuses have found that patients are exhibiting improvement (Lindvall et al., 1992).

As we approach the twenty-first century, neuroscientists are poised at the edge of an exciting new frontier: using fetal tissue to repair the damaged brain. As with many scientific discoveries, however, controversy surrounds progress. Is it ethical to use medical procedures that generate a need for fetal tissue? It's doubtful that anyone would object to using miscarried fetuses to save lives, but what about the use of aborted fetuses? Would such use encourage women to conceive children and have abortions in order to help ailing family members, or to make a profit? As neural grafting becomes more effective, this debate is sure to heat up (Hoffer & Olson, 1991). Another question concerns whether the procedure is ready for use with human beings. Some researchers "call for patience rather than patients" (Sladek & Shoulson, 1988) and warn about the possible medical risks involved in the procedure (Stein & Glasier, 1995). Others are eager to realize the clinical possibilities of using neural grafting to treat people suffering from various cognitive and motor disorders (Bjorklund, 1991; Sinden et al., 1995).

The human brain remains one of the great frontiers in science. From the nervous system's trillions of tiny building blocks, consisting of axons, dendrites, synapses, and neurotransmitters, to the structures of the brain stem, limbic system, and cerebral cortex, there is a solid biological foundation for the study of mind and behavior. The goal, as we'll see in later chapters, is to understand the links between the human body and psychological processes—processes that range far and wide, from visual perception and mind-altering drugs to moral development, social aggression, and the benefits of psychotherapy.

Summary and Key Terms

Phineas Gage's dramatic brain injury showed that the human brain and nervous system form a complex, integrated system—the concern of *behavioral neuroscience.*

The Body's Communication Networks

The body has two communication networks: the nervous system and the endocrine system.

The Nervous System

The human nervous system has two basic parts. The **central nervous system (CNS)** includes the brain and the spinal cord. The **peripheral nervous system (PNS)** consists of the nerves that radiate from the CNS to the rest of the body.

The PNS is further divided into two components. The **somatic nervous system** transmits signals from the sensory organs and skin to the CNS. It also relays motor commands from the CNS to the skeletal muscles. The **autonomic nervous system** connects the CNS to the involuntary muscles, organs, and glands, thus regulating such functions as heartbeat and temperature. The autonomic nervous system has two parts: the **sympathetic nervous system,** which energizes the body for action and the **parasympathetic nervous system,** which returns the body to its normal state.

The Endocrine System

The **endocrine system** is a collection of ductless glands that regulate growth, metabolism, and other functions by secreting **hormones** into the bloodstream. These secretions are controlled in the brain by the hypothalamus, which signals the **pituitary gland.**

The Neuron

Neurons, or nerve cells, transmit and receive information throughout the nervous system. **Sensory neurons** transmit information from the senses, skin, muscles, and internal organs to the CNS. **Motor neurons** send commands from the CNS to the muscles, glands, and organs. **Interneurons** serve as connectors within the CNS. **Glial cells** help support, insulate, and nourish the neurons. A simple **reflex** like the knee jerk illustrates the speed of neural signals.

Structure of the Neuron

Each neuron has a rounded body, called the **soma,** and two types of branched fibers: **dendrites,** which receive impulses, and an **axon,** which sends impulses through its terminals. Many axons are covered with **myelin sheath,** a fatty insulating layer that speeds impulses.

The Neuron in Action

A neuron transmits messages by means of an electrical process. When dendrites receive signals of sufficient strength, the cell's membrane breaks down. Positively charged sodium ions rush in, altering the charge inside in such a way that a burst of electrical energy known as an **action potential** surges through the axon as soon as a certain necessary level of stimulation, or **threshold,** is reached.

How Neurons Communicate

To transmit a signal across the **synapse,** the tiny gap between two neurons, the sending neuron releases chemical **neurotransmitters** from vesicles in its axon terminals. These chemicals bind to **receptors** on the dendrites of the receiving neuron. There are many neurotransmitters, and each fits only certain receptors.

Neurotransmitters

Acetylcholine (ACh) is a neurotransmitter that links motor neurons and muscles. ACh has an excitatory effect on muscles. **Dopamine,** in contrast, inhibits muscles and helps control voluntary movements. Alzheimer's disease, Parkinson's disease, and schizophrenia have all been linked to problems with these chemical messengers. Other neurotransmitters called **endorphins** serve as the body's own pain relievers.

The Brain

The basic anatomy of the brain has long been known, but behavioral neuroscientists face the more difficult task of understanding how it functions.

Tools of Behavioral Neuroscience

Although **phrenology** was misguided in linking psychological characteristics to bumps on the skull, it correctly supposed that functions are localized in particular parts of the brain.

Today, neuroscientists use four methods to study brain functions: (1) clinical case studies of people with brain damage; (2) invasion of the brain through surgery, drugs, or electrical stimulation; (3) electrical recordings of activity using the **electroencephalograph (EEG);** and (4) new brain-imaging techniques, such as **computerized axial tomography (CAT), positron emission tomography (PET),** and **magnetic resonance imaging (MRI).**

Regions of the Brain

The brain consists of three main parts: the brainstem, the limbic system, and the cerebral cortex. Each of these comprises several important structures.

The **brainstem** is the inner core. It contains the **medulla,** which controls vital involuntary functions such as breathing; the **pons,** involved in sleep and arousal; and the **reticular formation,** a netlike group of cells that filter sensory information and help control sleep, arousal, and attention. Nearby is the **cerebellum,** which plays an important role in balance and coordination.

Above the brainstem is the **limbic system,** which helps govern motivation, emotion, and memory. It includes the **thalamus,** a relay station for sensory information; the **amygdala,** linked to fear, anger, and aggression; the **hippocampus,** which performs a key function in memory formation; and the **hypothalamus,** which helps regulate the autonomic nervous system, emotions, and basic drives.

The outermost 80 percent of the brain, the wrinkled **cerebral cortex,** controls higher-order mental processes. Anatomically, it consists of two hemispheres and four lobes. It can also be divided into areas based on function: (1) Sensory areas specialize in receiving sensory information. For example, the **somatosensory cortex** receives information from the touch receptors in the skin. (2) The **motor cortex** controls the voluntary muscles. (3) The

association cortex areas communicate with the sensory and motor areas and house higher mental processes. Within the association cortex, two areas specialize in language. **Broca's area** directs the production of speech, and **Wernicke's area** is involved in language comprehension.

The Split Brain

Researchers have investigated Fechner's idea that each side of the brain has its own mind. The studies rely on the fact that the left hemisphere communicates with the right side of the body, and the right hemisphere with the left side. The hemispheres are connected by, and share information through, the **corpus callosum.** Experiments with **split-brain** patients, in whom the corpus callosum has been severed, show that each hemisphere has a somewhat different version of experience.

Other research has tried to determine which functions are **lateralized,** or controlled by a single side of the brain. The key language centers are in the left hemisphere. The right hemisphere plays a crucial role in nonverbal functions. But the most important distinction may be the style of processing. The left hemisphere seems to rely on analytical processing, while the right hemisphere is more holistic.

Research supports the notion that the two hemispheres, when their links are cut, produce separate streams of consciousness. But in the healthy brain, they exchange information so quickly that our experience is a seamless whole.

Prospects for the Future

Recent advances in the study of the brain have addressed two questions: Does the adult brain have a capacity to change and adapt as a result of experience, and is it possible to repair a damaged brain?

Enriching the Brain through Experience

Research shows that the brain has **plasticity,** a capacity to change. Specifically, certain experiences can spark the branching of new dendrites and the growth of new synaptic connections.

Repairing the Damaged Brain

Advances in understanding the brain have led to attempts at brain repair. With the **neural graft** procedure, researchers have transplanted brain tissue from one animal to another in an effort to reduce deficits in brain function. Among human beings, the greatest hope may lie in transplantation of fetal tissue, a highly controversial procedure.

In the Field Resources

Books

Gazzaniga, M. S. (1992). *Nature's mind.* New York: Basic Books

Written by a leading neuroscientist, this book provides an insider's view of the breakthroughs in split-brain research and what it tells us about the human mind.

Posner, M. I., & Raichle, M. E. (1994). *Images of mind.* New York: Scientific American Library.

Written by cognitive neuroscientists, this book describes how PET and other brain imaging techniques are being used to "see" the live brain in action.

Sacks, O. (1985). *The man who mistook his wife for a hat.* New York: Summit Books.

As in his many other books, Sacks presents fascinating, often amusing, case studies of people with certain types of brain damage—and the consequences for their behavior.

Springer, S. P., & Deutsch, G. (1994). *Left brain, right brain* (4th ed.). New York: W. H. Freeman.

This book describes studies on the workings of the right and left hemispheres in brain-damaged, split-brain, and normal people, and what they mean for theories of consciousness.

Films and Videos

Awakenings (1990, 121 min.)

Based on cases described by Oliver Sacks, the film is about sleeping-sickness patients "awakened" but only temporarily cured by L-dopa. (Robin Williams, Robert De Niro, Julie Kavner, Ruth Nelson, John Heard, Penelope Ann Miller.)

Internet

Society for Neuroscience (http://www.sfn.org/)

This organization for brain researchers offers brochures and newsletters for educational purposes.

Gallery of Neuro-Links (http://www.brainnet.org/links.htm)

Provides links to sites on Alzheimer's disease, headaches, epilepsy, and other topics pertaining to the human brain.

Journals and Periodicals

Behavioral and Brain Sciences
Behavioral Neuroscience
Journal of Cognitive Neuroscience
Nature
Science

3 *Sensation and Perception*

What's Your Prediction?

Perceiving depth and distance

The situation You have always assumed that when it comes to vision, hearing, and other biological senses, all people are basically the same. But you also suspect that the way each of us perceives the world is influenced by our life experiences and cultural backgrounds. So which is it? Thinking about the problem, you realize that one possible way to tease apart biological and cultural influences is to select an important aspect of perception, create a task to measure it, and then compare people from different parts of the world.

In reading up on the visual system, you learn that images projected on the eye's retina are flat and two dimensional. So, you wonder, how do people judge depth and distance? How do people know that one object in the visual field is closer than another? Is depth perception innate among humans, or are certain types of life experience necessary? To examine these questions, you create the drawings shown in Figure 3.1 and ask the following question: Which animal is nearer the hunter: the antelope or the elephant? The task seems easy. To you, the elephant looks farther away because its image is so small and because it stands either on a hill that is partly blocked (*top*) or at the top of a road with converging lines that form an upside-down **V** (*bottom*).

Figure 3.1 Which animal is closer to the hunter?

Make a prediction Determined to test people from very different backgrounds and cultural experiences, you show the drawings to English-speaking men and women. Then you travel to southern Africa and present the same pictures to both illiterate and educated Bantu inhabitants living in a rural area. What will you find? Will everyone, as you do, see the pictures in three-dimensional terms and see the antelope as nearer than the elephant?

Using the table below, put a check mark next to the group(s) in which you think most participants will see the antelope as closer than the elephant:

Educated Western	_______
Educated Bantus	_______
Illiterate Bantus	_______

The results This study, conducted by W. Hudson (1960), was one of the first to examine perception from a cross-cultural perspective. Using drawings like those shown on the previous page, Hudson found that compared to Western adults, illiterate Bantu participants saw the pictures as flat and the elephant as closer to the hunter. And what about the school-educated Bantus? It's interesting that in this group, most participants saw the antelope as closer. Apparently, seeing three-dimensional depth in two-dimensional displays is a skill that develops—probably from exposure to books, photographs, artwork, and other flat visual representations of reality.

What does it all mean? Among researchers who study vision and other senses, certain aspects of perception—such as our ability to perceive depth and distance—seem biologically "hard-wired" and universal. From the two eyes to the neural pathways that carry visual signals to the brain, most humans are similarly equipped. Yet other researchers, such as those who study people from different cultures, have come to realize that in some ways our perceptions are influenced by our experiences. It's interesting, for example, that people living in urban environments that contain many edges and right angles are more likely than those living in open spaces to fall prey to certain line-based optical illusions (Deregowski, 1989). So are the processes of perception biologically based or learned? As we'll see in this chapter, both views are correct.

Before you were born, you spent nine months floating in a warm, wet, mostly dark sac of fluid. You swished around a bit from all the movement, and you could hear the drumlike beat of your mother's heart, but none of this quite prepared you for the sensations that later make life so worth living. The thunderous noise of ocean waves crashing into the shore, the haunting vision of a bright full moon against the black night sky, the colors of a rainbow splashed over a canvas, the rich sweet flavor of chocolate ice cream sliding down a cold throat, and the warm tingly feeling inside that comes with a lover's embrace—the world out there has lots to offer, and our sensory systems bring some of it into the brain with radarlike sensitivity.

"How sense-luscious the world is."

— DIANE ACKERMAN

In this chapter, we will examine the psychology of sensation and perception. These terms are used to describe different stages in the process by which we acquire information about the world. In **sensation**, raw physical energy is absorbed by our eyes, ears, and other sensory receptors. Through the process of **transduction**, this

sensation The processes by which our sense organs receive information from the environment.

transduction The process by which physical energy is converted into sensory neural impulses.

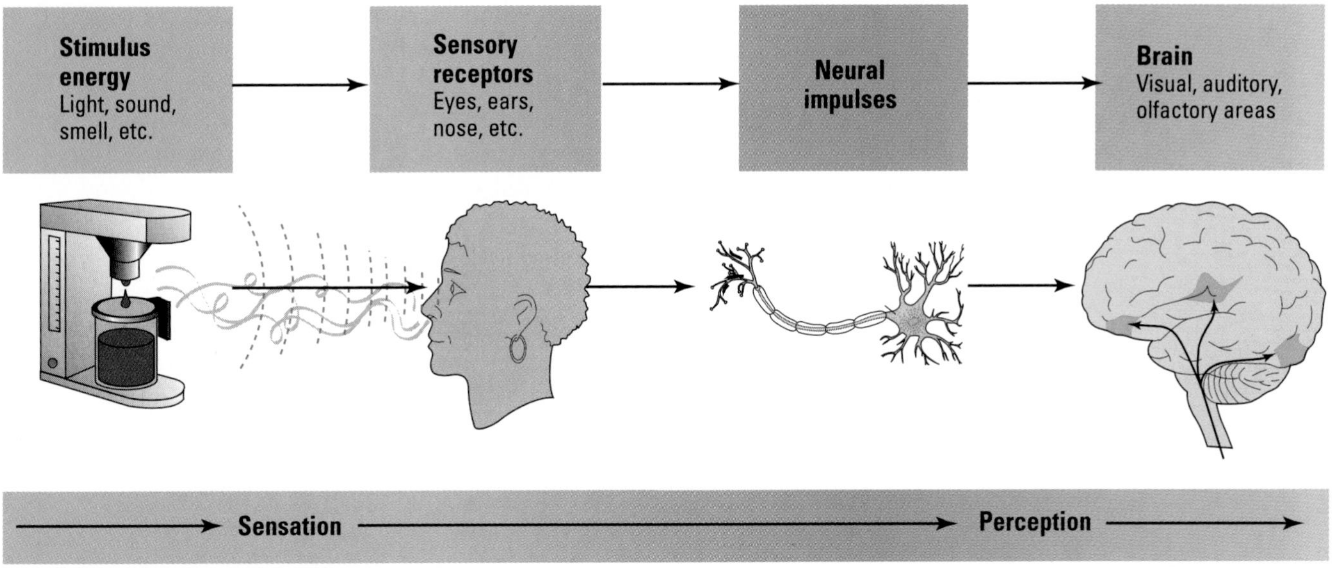

Figure 3.2 Processes of sensation and perception

energy is converted into neural signals that are sent to the brain. In **perception**, these signals are then selected, organized, and interpreted (see Figure 3.2).

Psychologists used to treat sensation and perception as separate. Sensation was considered a strictly physiological process involving the various sense organs, receptors, neural pathways, and regions of the brain. Perception was considered a purely psychological process by which we derive meaning from these sensations. In this view, the body supplied the raw material, then the mind made sense of that material. We now know, however, that in this continuous stream of events, there is no bright line dividing sensation and perception. As we'll see, the interaction between the body and the mind is seamless. There are different processes at work, however, so psychologists still find it useful to make the distinction.

This distinction comes to life in a poignant story told by neurologist Oliver Sacks (1995). The story was about Virgil, a fifty-year-old Oklahoma man who had been blind since the age of six. Based on the fact that Virgil could see light and faint shadows, a local ophthalmologist suggested that it might be possible to restore his eyesight through surgery. Starting with the right eye, the doctor removed a thick cataract that blanketed the retina, inserted a new lens implant, and bandaged the eye for twenty-four hours. The next day, the bandage was removed. It was the moment of truth. But Virgil did not cry out with joy or react in any other way. Instead, he stared blankly at the surgeon, silent and bewildered. As Sacks put it, "The dramatic moment stayed vacant, grew longer, sagged." Was the operation a success? Could Virgil see? In a manner of speaking, yes. He said he could detect light, forms, movement, and color, all mixed up in a confusing and cluttered blur. But only when the doctor started to speak did Virgil realize that he was staring at a face. His retina was alive and well, but his brain could not make sense of the information. There was sensation, but no perception.

Even as the weeks passed, Virgil remained disoriented. In the supermarket, he was overwhelmed, even stressed, by all the visual stimulation—the bright lights, the shelves lined with cans and jars, the fruits and vegetables, and the people wheeling carts up and down the aisles. "Everything ran together," he said. Virgil could not identify by sight common objects such as chairs and tables that he recognized easily

perception The processes by which people select, organize, and interpret sensations.

by touching. He also lacked the ability to perceive depth. He was confused by shadows, often stopping to step over one. Yet he saw a staircase as a flat surface of parallel and crossing lines rather than as a three-dimensional solid object. Movement posed additional problems. He would recognize his dog one moment, but then wonder if it was the same animal when he saw it from a different angle.

For reasons that are unclear, Virgil suddenly became ill, collapsed, and almost died. He had a respiratory illness and needed a constant supply of oxygen. By the time he returned home from the hospital, he had to carry an oxygen tank wherever he went. Unable to work, Virgil lost his job, his house, and, once again, his eyesight. Extensive tests showed that there was no response to light whatsoever—and no electrical activity in the visual cortex. He was totally blind. But all was not lost. As Sacks (1995) put it, "Now, at last, Virgil is allowed to not see, allowed to escape from the glaring, confusing world of sight and space, and to return to his own true being, the intimate, concentrated world of the other senses that had been his home for almost fifty years" (p. 152).

This chapter will begin with the study of sensation, the raw material that transforms the brain into a mind. We will examine the physiology of vision, hearing, smell, taste, touch, and other sensory systems. Then we will examine the psychological processes of perception that enable us to comprehend and interpret this raw material. As we'll see, the world "out there" comes to us through an interaction of physical energy, the body, and the mind.

Measuring the Sensory Experience

How does physical energy become a psychological experience? What's the minimum amount of stimulation needed to register on our senses, and how can this be measured? What is the smallest *change* in stimulation that people can detect, and how can this be measured?

Light, vibration, odor-filled molecules, cold winds, warm breezes, and the collision of bodies. Whatever the stimulus, the first generation of psychologists, including Wilhelm Wundt, and others trained in physiology raised the most basic of questions: How does physical energy become a psychological experience? How much light is necessary to see? Can you hear a pin drop or detect minute variations in pitch well enough to tune a musical instrument? How different must two wines be for a wine taster to tell them apart? Inspired by the work of Gustav Fechner (1860), questions of this nature gave birth to **psychophysics**, psychology's first subfield.

The key to psychophysics is measurement. Because sensation is subjective, it cannot be measured using objective instruments the way you assess height, weight, or time. There are no yardsticks, or scales, or stopwatches—only the subject and his or her self-report. New procedures thus had to be devised to maximize the accuracy of these reports (Bolanowski & Gescheider, 1991; Gescheider, 1985). Much of the material discussed in this chapter was derived from these psychophysical procedures.

Absolute Thresholds

psychophysics The study of the relationship between physical stimulation and subjective sensations.

What is the minimum amount of light that can be seen, the weakest vibration that can be heard, or the faintest odor that can be smelled? How much sugar needs to be added to a food for it to taste sweeter? What is the slightest amount of skin pressure that can be felt? Just how sensitive are our sensory systems? Researchers interested in a sensation begin by trying to determine an **absolute threshold**, the minimum level of stimulation that an organism can detect.

There are different ways to derive an absolute threshold. One method is simply to ask a subject to adjust the intensity of a stimulus until it is barely detectable. A second method is to gradually increase the intensity level and ask the subject from one trial to the next if he or she detects the stimulus. A third method is to vary the stimulus presentation randomly, again checking with the subject on each trial. Over the years, research has shown that absolute thresholds are not "absolute." There is no single point on the intensity scale at which people suddenly detect a stimulus. Rather, detection rates increase gradually. Psychophysics researchers thus define the absolute threshold as the point at which a stimulus can be detected 50 percent of the time. Defined in this way, some of our absolute thresholds are highly impressive (see Table 3.1).

Signal-Detection Theory

Imagine you're a subject in a classical psychophysics experiment. You're sitting in a darkened room staring at a blank wall, and the experimenter presents a series of flashes varying in brightness. Did you see it? What about the next one? On some trials, the flashes are clear, well above threshold, so you say *yes*. But on other trials, you're just not sure. With the experimenter waiting for a response, what do you say? Confronted with this dilemma, some subjects prefer to say *yes* (when in doubt, go for it). Others, more cautious, say *no* (unless it's clear, don't go out on a limb). These tendencies to respond *yes* and *no* in uncertain situations are individual response biases—and they have little to do with sensation. The problem for the researcher, then, is that a subject's responses are influenced not only by the strength of the signal but also by background factors such as his or her personality, motivation, and expectations.

Enter signal-detection theory. Based on the assumption that performance is jointly determined by the strength of a signal and the subject's response criterion (his or her willingness to say *yes* rather than *no*), **signal-detection theory** gave rise to a more sophisticated method. On some trials, a weak stimulus is presented. On others, no stimulus is presented. By comparing a subject's "hit" versus "miss" rate on stimulus trials to his or her tendency to commit "false alarms" by saying *yes* in blank trials, the researcher can mathematically separate the subject's detection performance from the response bias (Green & Swets, 1966). The method of establishing absolute

Table 3.1 Some Absolute Thresholds

SENSORY SYSTEM	ABSOLUTE THRESHOLD
Vision	A lit candle 30 miles away on a dark, clear night
Hearing	The tick of a watch 20 feet away in total quiet
Smell	1 drop of perfume dispersed throughout a 6-room apartment
Taste	1 teaspoon of sugar in 2 gallons of water
Touch	The wing of a bee falling on your cheek from a height of 1 centimeter

absolute threshold The smallest amount of stimulation that can be detected.

signal-detection theory The theory that detecting a stimulus is jointly determined by the signal and the subject's response criterion.

thresholds was based on the assumption that a threshold is determined solely by the stimulus. But signal-detection theory recognizes that response biases are also at work. This approach provides the psychologist with a valuable tool for analyzing why air-traffic controllers are so quick to detect danger signals on the radar screen, why overeager witnesses identify innocent suspects in police lineups, or why doctors over-diagnose certain diseases from available test results (Swets, 1996).

Difference Thresholds

Sensory capacities are measured not only by our ability to detect low levels of stimulation but also by the extent to which we can detect subtle differences. This ability is determined by asking subjects to compare the brightness of two light bulbs, the loudness of two tones, the weight of two blocks, and so on. Given one stimulus, the subject is asked to adjust the level of another stimulus so that the two are the same. Or subjects are given two stimuli and asked to report whether they are the same or different. Either way, it is possible to pinpoint the smallest change in stimulation that subjects can detect 50 percent of the time. This point is called the difference threshold, or **just noticeable difference (JND)**.

While measuring difference thresholds, Ernst Weber (1834) quickly noticed that JNDs increase with the size or intensity of the stimulus—and that the magnitude of a JND is a constant *proportion* of the original stimulus. This general principle is known as **Weber's law**. To illustrate, the JND for weight is 1/50, or 2 percent. In other words, if you lift a 50-ounce object, and then a 51-ounce object, you will probably notice that the second one is heavier than the first. However, you would not feel a difference between one object that weighs 50 pounds and another that weighs 50 pounds, 1 ounce. Again, there is an absolute difference of 1 ounce; but a JND of 2 percent means that if your reference point is a 50-pound object, you would not detect a difference unless the second object is equal to or greater than

Tuning a piano requires a heightened ability to detect subtle differences among tones.

just noticeable difference (JND) The smallest amount of change in a stimulus that can be detected.

Weber's law The principle that the just noticeable difference of a stimulus is a constant proportion despite variations in intensity.

51 pounds. Except at the extremes, Weber's law provides a good estimate of our difference thresholds. It can also be applied to other senses—though each has a different threshold. For example, the JND is 2 percent for brightness, 10 percent for loudness, and 20 percent for the taste of salt.

Sensation

How does the human visual system convert light into meaningful color images? How does the auditory system convert vibrating air molecules into meaningful sounds? What about the chemical senses of smell and taste, or the ability to feel pressure, warmth, cold, pain, and balance?

Back in school, I was taught that there are five senses: vision, hearing, taste, smell, and touch. This notion can be traced to Aristotle (384–322 BCE). Even today, people who believe in "extrasensory" perception, or ESP, call it the "sixth sense." In fact, there are more than five sensory modalities. Vision has two subsystems, one for daylight and one for nighttime conditions. The chemical senses of taste and smell are easily distinguished, but touch is really a mixture of several skin senses—including pressure, pain, warmth, and cold. We also have a keen sense of balance and of the position and movement of body parts. Combined, these various systems bring in a steady stream of information from the world around us.

> *"From a swirling sea of energies, each sense selects its own."*
>
> — DANIEL P. KIMBLE

Vision

You and I are visual creatures. How many times have you said, "Show me." "I'll believe it when I see it." "I saw it with my own eyes." "Out of sight, out of mind." "See?" "My eyes are playing tricks on me." As with other aspects of human anatomy, our visual system is a brilliantly molded product of evolution. The earliest forms of life could "see" in the sea through faint patches of membrane that were sensitive to light. They could tell brightness from dark and even turn in the direction of the light source. In contrast, other features—such as shapes, textures, motion, and color—could be detected only later, by more advanced forms of life (Land & Fernald, 1992).

Light Every sensory system uses physical energy as its source of stimulation. The stimulus input for vision is light—a form of energy known as electromagnetic radiation that travels through empty space in oscillating waves. As illustrated in Figure 3.3, what we see as light comes from a narrow band in the spectrum of electromagnetic radiation. All matter gives off electromagnetic radiation of different wavelengths (a wavelength is measured by the distance between waves). The sun and other stars give off radiation that includes light. So do fires and electric lamps. Visible wavelengths range from about 380 to 760 nanometers (a nanometer is one billionth of a meter). Thus, some waves (such as X rays, ultraviolet rays, and gamma rays) are too short for us to see and fall below our visible range. Others (such as infrared rays, TV signals, radio waves, and radar) are too long for us to see, so they exceed our visible range. In both cases, the wavelengths are invisible to the human

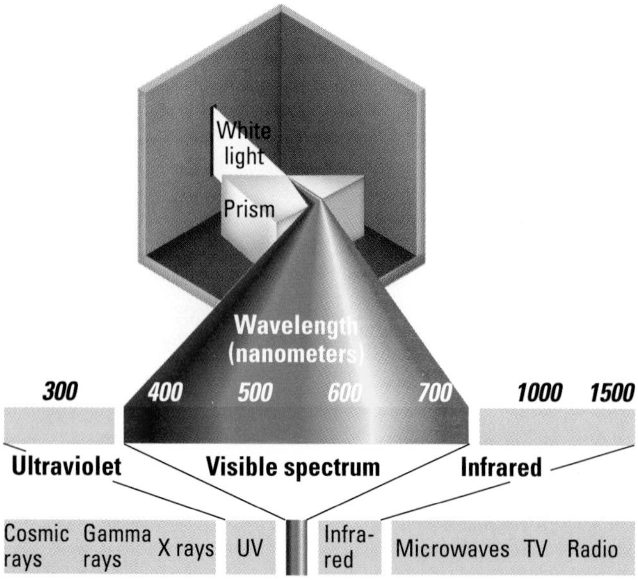

Figure 3.3 The electromagnetic spectrum The human eye is sensitive to only a narrow band of electromagnetic radiation. As shown, visible wavelengths range from 380 to 760 nanometers.

eye. Other organisms have sensory capabilities that are different from ours. For example, most insects can see shorter wavelengths in the ultraviolet spectrum, and most fish and reptiles can see longer wavelengths in the infrared spectrum.

The *length* of a light wave determines its hue, or perceived *color*. To the human eye, white light is made up of all visible wavelengths combined. Short wavelengths look bluish, medium wavelengths look greenish, and long wavelengths look reddish. The picturesque colors of the visible wavelengths can be seen in a rainbow or in the spectrum of colors produced when white light passes through a glass prism. A second property of light is its intensity, or *amplitude*, as measured by the height of the peaks in the wave. As wavelength determines color, amplitude determines *brightness*. The higher the amplitude, the brighter the light appears to be. A third physical property of light is its *purity*, as measured by the number of wavelengths that make up the light. Purity influences the *saturation*, or richness, of colors. The fewer wavelengths there are in a light (the purer it is), the richer or more saturated is the color. A pure red light made up of only a narrow band of wavelengths would give off a rich fire-engine or tomatolike color. In contrast, white light—which contains all visible wavelengths—is completely unsaturated and lacking in color.

The Visual System

Light waves provide the stimulus input for vision, but what is actually seen depends on the capabilities of the visual system that's in place. Accordingly, different species see the world in different ways. Eagles can spot a tiny field mouse moving in the grass a mile away. Owls have binocularlike eyes that enable them to see prey in the dark of night. Cows and sheep have eyes on the sides of their heads so they can spot predators sneaking up from behind. And bees can judge the angle at which light strikes the eye, so they know the sun's position in the sky—even on a gray, overcast day. Nature provides us with visual systems uniquely suited to our ways of life.

The Eye

The fantastic journey of neural impulses through the human visual system begins with the eye—an extension of the brain and the most exposed part of the central nervous system. Lying in a protective bony socket within the skull, the eye transforms, or transduces, light waves into electrochemical neural impulses. The major structures of the human eye are presented in Figure 3.4.

cornea The clear outer membrane that bends light so that it is sharply focused in the eye.

iris The ring of muscle tissue that gives eyes their color and controls the size of the pupil.

pupil The small round hole in the iris of the eye through which light passes.

lens A transparent structure in the eye that focuses light on the retina.

Light rays from the outside world first pass through the **cornea**, a clear, curved membrane, or "window." The cornea bends light so that it is sharply focused within the eye. Abnormalities in the shape of the cornea cause astigmatism, usually experienced as a selective blurring of parts of the image at a particular orientation, such as horizontal. Next, there is the ring-shaped **iris**, which gives the eye its color. The iris is a muscle that is controlled by the autonomic nervous system. Its function is to regulate the size of the **pupil**—the small, round hole in the iris through which light passes. The iris causes the pupil to dilate (enlarge) under dim viewing conditions to let in more light and to contract (shrink) under brightness to let in less light.

Behind the pupil, light continues through the **lens**, another transparent structure whose function is to fine-tune the focusing of the light. The lens brings an image into

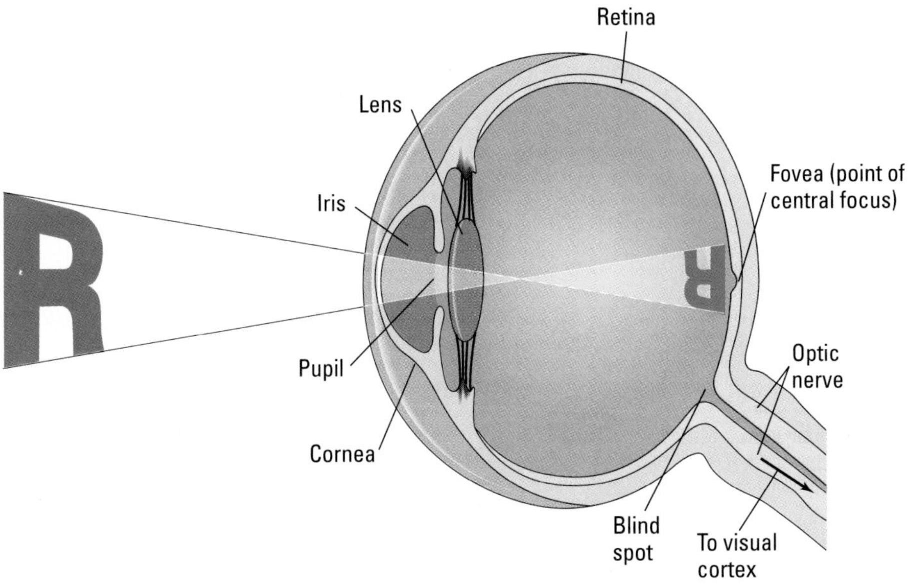

Figure 3.4 Structures of the human eye

focus by changing its shape, in a process called **accommodation**. Specifically, the lens becomes more rounded for focusing on nearby objects and flatter for more distant objects (the cornea, which has a fixed shape, cannot make these adjustments for different distances). With age, the lens loses much of its elasticity and keeps the flatter shape appropriate for viewing at a distance. As a result, many middle-aged people start to need glasses for reading or bifocals with a near-vision portion in the lower part of the glass.

Filling the central part of the eyeball is a clear jellylike substance called the vitreous humor. Light passes through this fluid before it reaches the retina. The **retina** is a multilayered screen of cells that lines the back inside surface of the eyeball. It is one of the most fascinating tissues in the body—both because of its function, which is to transform patterns of light into images that the brain can use, and because of its structure, which illustrates many basic principles of neural organization (see Figure 3.5). In an odd twist of nature, the image projected on the retina is upside down. That is, light from the top part of the visual field stimulates photoreceptor cells in the bottom part of the retina, and vice versa.

The retina has aptly been called an extension of the brain (Gregory, 1990). It has several relatively transparent layers and contains 130 million photoreceptor cells that convert light energy into neural activity. The bottom layer, closest to the back of the eyeball, is lined with two specialized types of nerve cells called rods and cones (again, see Figure 3.5). **Rods** are long, thin, cylindrical cells that are highly sensitive to light. They are concentrated in the sides of the retina and are active for black-and-white vision in dim light. Under impossibly ideal conditions, rods have the capacity to detect the light produced by one ten-billionth of a watt. On a perfectly clear, pitch-dark night, that's like seeing the light of a match struck thirty miles away. **Cones** are shorter, thicker, more-tapered cells that are sensitive to color under high levels of illumination. Cones are densely clustered in the center of the **fovea**, the pinhead-size center of the retina. The fovea contains only cones, and the ratio of rods to cones increases in the outer edges of the retina.

In owls and other nocturnal (active only at night) animals, the retina contains only rods. Thus, they can see at night but their vision is in black and white. In

accommodation The visual process by which lenses become rounded for viewing nearby objects and flatter for viewing remote objects.

retina The rear multilayer part of the eye where rods and cones convert light into neural impulses.

rods Rod-shaped photoreceptor cells in the retina that are highly sensitive to light.

cones Cone-shaped photoreceptor cells in the retina that are sensitive to color.

fovea The center of the retina, where cones are clustered.

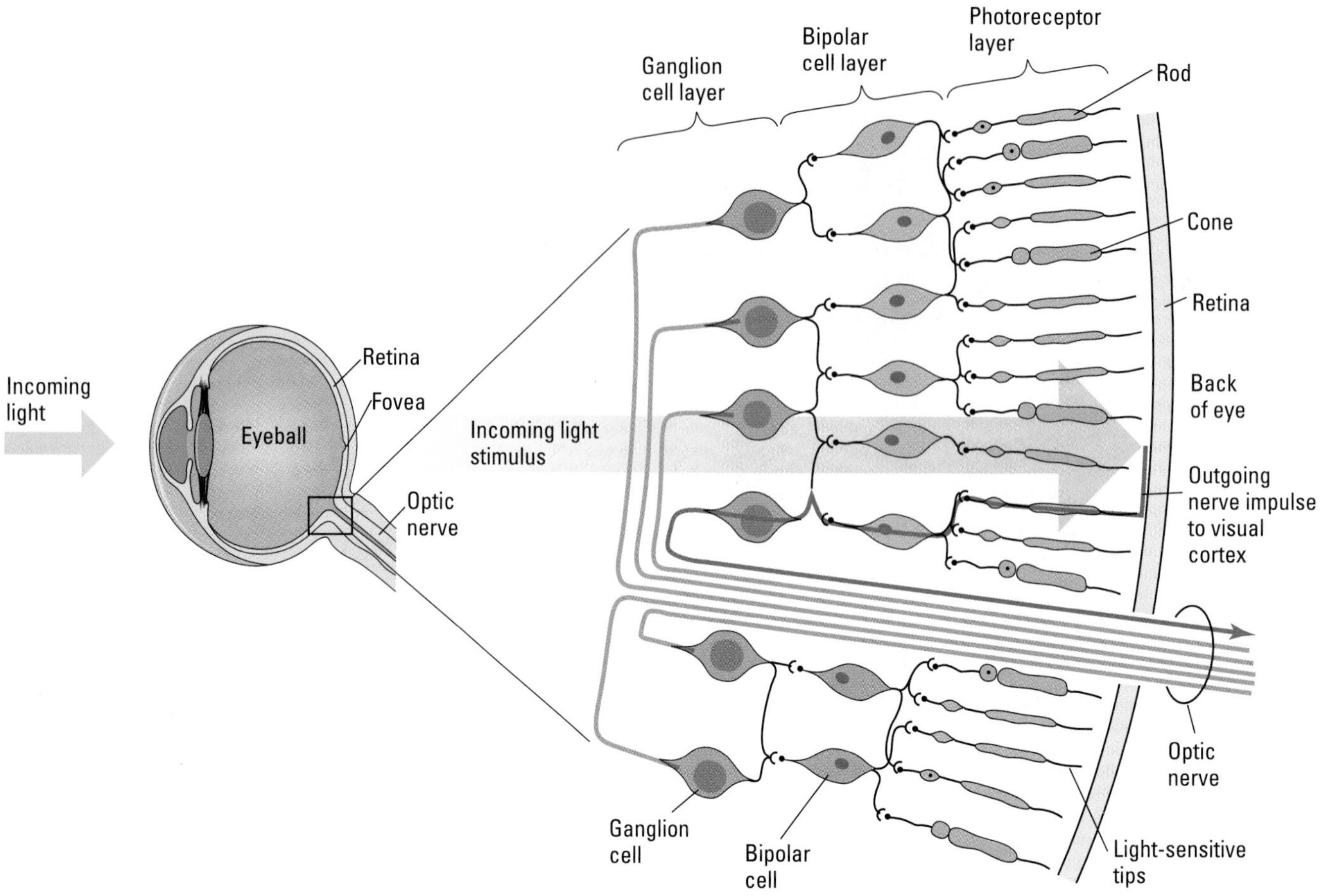

Figure 3.5 The retina The back wall of the retina has three major layers containing 130 million photoreceptor cells. Light-sensitive rods are concentrated in the sides of the retina, and color-sensitive cones are clustered in the center.

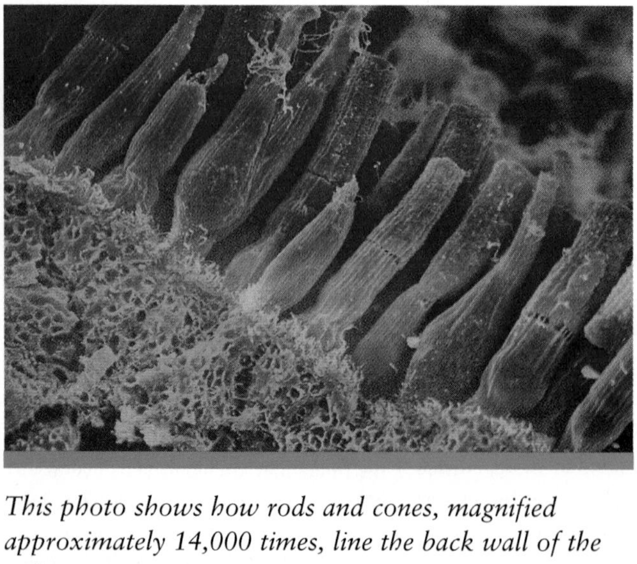

This photo shows how rods and cones, magnified approximately 14,000 times, line the back wall of the retina.

chipmunks, pigeons, and other diurnal (active only during the day) animals, the retina contains only cones. Thus, they are virtually blind at night. In animals that are active both day and night, the retina has a mixture of rods and cones. For example, the human retina has about 120 million rods and 6 million cones, enabling us to see colors under normal lighting and to make out forms under low levels of illumination. Individuals whose retinas contain no rods suffer from night blindness; those without cones lack all color vision.

Often, we need to adjust to radical changes in illumination. It's happened to me, and I'm sure it has happened to you, too. You step inside a darkened movie theater on a sunny day. As you start walking down the aisle, however, you have to put your arms out and inch slowly forward, stumbling around as if you were blind. After a few minutes, you can see again. This experience illustrates **dark adaptation**, the process by which eyes become more sensitive to light in a dark environment. It takes about thirty minutes for you to fully adapt to the dark—at which point the eyes become 10,000 times more sensitive. It also takes time to adjust to bright light. That's why,

dark adaptation A process of adjustment by which the eyes become more sensitive to light in a dark environment.

when you emerge from a movie theater during the day, everything seems so "washed out" that you have to squint initially to keep out the glare. This is an instance of **light adaptation**, the process by which our eyes become less sensitive to light under high levels of illumination.

Figure 3.6 How to find your blind spot The optic nerve area has no rods or cones, so it is "blind." To find your blind spot, hold this book at arm's length, cover your left eye and stare at the left button with your right eye. Now slowly move the book toward you until the right button disappears. To test your left eye, simply reverse the procedure.

When light strikes the rods and cones, it sparks a chain of events within a network of interconnected neurons that results in vision. Rods and cones contain photopigments, chemicals that break down in response to light, thus triggering neural impulses. These impulses activate bipolar cells, which, in turn, activate nearby ganglion cells. The axons of the ganglion cells form the **optic nerve**, a pathway that carries visual information from each eyeball to the brain. The area where the optic nerve enters the eye has no rods or cones, only axons. So each eye has a **blind spot**. You don't normally notice it because your eyes are always moving, but you can find your blind spot through a simple exercise (see Figure 3.6).

Psychologists used to think that electrical impulses were delivered from the retina to the brain, as on an assembly line. It was as if there was a simple division of labor, whereby retinal neurons "received" sensory information and passed it along on a conveyer belt to the visual cortex for perceptual "processing." We now know that the mechanisms of vision are more complex. Ultimately, signals from 130 million rods and cones are funneled through a mere 1 million axons in the optic nerve. Think for a moment about these numbers, and you'll realize what they mean: that the bipolar and ganglion cells must be integrating and compressing signals from multiple receptors. The retina is a "smart" optical instrument. Not only does it receive light, but it also processes visual information.

Any ganglion cell that represents a cluster of neighboring rods and cones receives input from a sizable portion of the retina. This region is called a receptive field. By recording the activity of individual ganglion cells, researchers have found that there are many different types of receptive fields (Kuffler, 1953). The most common are circular "center-surround" fields in which light falling in the center has the opposite effect of light in the surrounding area. Some cells are activated by light in the center and inhibited by light in the surrounding area (center-on cells), while others work the opposite way, inhibited by light in the center and activated by light in the surrounding area (center-off cells). This arrangement makes the human eye particularly attuned to brightness-and-darkness contrasts in the visual field—contrasts that indicate corners, borders, and edges. There's an old joke about an art dealer who tries to sell a blank canvas. "What is it?" asks the prospective buyer. "A white cow in a snowstorm," says the dealer. Funny or not, this joke clearly underestimates our visual acuity. A white cow would differ in brightness from white snow, and its body would differ in texture, thus forming a subtle but discernible outline against the background.

Visual Pathways Axon fibers of ganglion cells form the optic nerve, which is the first part of the visual pathway that links each eyeball to the brain. The two optic nerves meet at the optic chiasm, where axons from the inside half of each eye cross over to the opposite half of the brain. This arrangement means that the left visual field of both eyes is projected to the right side of the brain, while the right visual field of both eyes is projected to the left side of the brain. After reaching the optic chiasm, the nerve fibers travel along two tracts, through the thalamus, the relay station where sensory signals are directed to appropriate areas of the **visual cortex**. Located in the back of the brain, the visual cortex is the main information-processing center for visual information (see Figure 3.7).

light adaptation The process of adjustment by which the eyes become less sensitive to light in a bright environment.

optic nerve The pathway that carries visual information from the eyeball to the brain.

blind spot A part of the retina through which the optic nerve passes. Lacking rods and cones, this spot is not responsive to light.

visual cortex Located in the back of the brain, it is the main information-processing center for visual information.

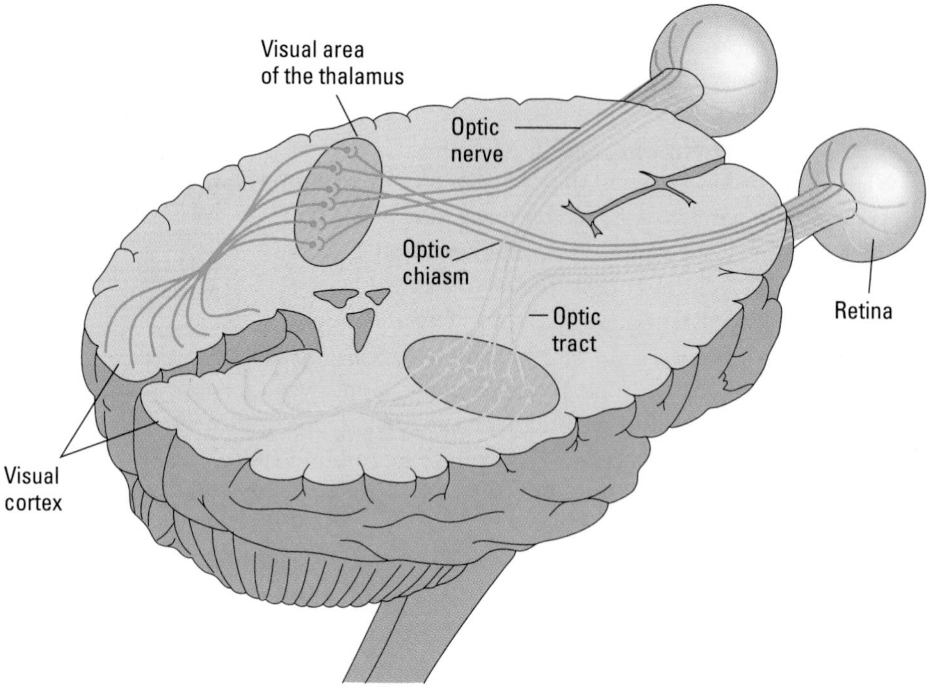

Figure 3.7 Visual pathways From both eyes, the optic nerves meet at the optic chiasm, where the signals cross to the opposite half of the brain. The nerve fibers travel in two tracks through the thalamus, where they are directed to the visual cortex.

The Visual Cortex Once information from the ganglion cells reaches the visual cortex, it is processed by **feature detectors**—neurons that are sensitive only to certain aspects of a visual image. This phenomenon was first revealed by David Hubel and Torsten Wiesel (1962), who implanted microelectrodes in the visual cortexes of cats (and later monkeys), projected different types of visual stimuli on a screen, and measured the electrical activity of single cells. Do different neurons specialize in certain types of information? If so, the goal was to map or "decode" the visual cortex (see Figure 3.8).

In 1981, Hubel and Wiesel were awarded a Nobel prize for their work. In a painstaking series of studies, they discovered that three types of neurons service the visual cortex and that each type has its own specialists at work (Hubel & Wiesel, 1979; Hubel, 1988). *Simple cells* are activated by highly particular images. For example, some simple cells fire in response to a vertical line in the middle of the screen but not to a line that is off-center or tilted at a different angle. Other simple cells fire in response to horizontal lines, wider lines, or lines tilted at a 45-degree angle. The stimulus-response connection is that specific. *Complex cells* receive input from many simple cells. Although they specialize in certain types of images, they react to those images anywhere in the receptive field—center, bottom, side, and so on. Finally, *hypercomplex cells* receive input from complex cells and respond to stimulus patterns. If one simple cell is activated by /, a second by \, and a third by —, the hypercomplex cell might react to a combination of these features, as in the letter *A*. When you consider the complexity of words, faces, landscapes, three-dimensional objects, skylines, and other images that enrich our lives, it's no wonder that the visual cortex is tightly packed with more than 100 million neurons.

feature detectors Neurons in the visual cortex that respond to specific aspects of a visual stimulus (such as lines or angles).

In the years since Hubel and Wiesel's discovery of feature detectors in the visual cortex, others have identified neurons that fire primarily in response to highly spe-

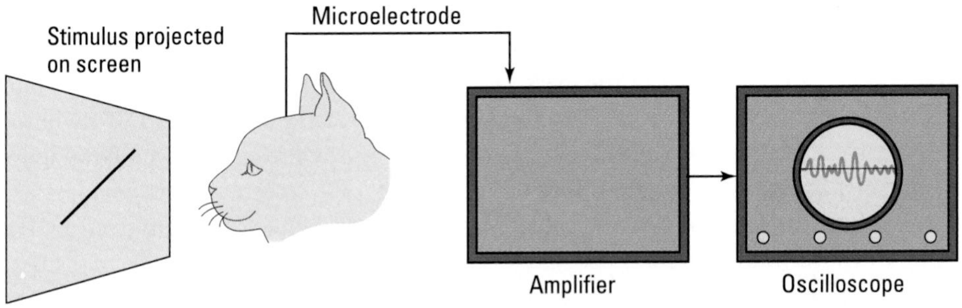

Figure 3.8 Hubel and Wiesel's apparatus Hubel and Wiesel implanted microelectrodes in a cat's visual cortex, projected visual stimuli, and measured single-cell activity. These signals were amplified and displayed on an oscilloscope.

cific features such as color, form, movement, and the depth of a visual stimulus (Livingstone & Hubel, 1988). Certain areas of the visual cortex also specialize in complex patterns, or configurations. For example, experiments with monkeys indicate that some cells are activated by the image of a hand (Gross et al., 1972), while others fire in response to faces (Bayliss et al., 1985) and upward or downward movements (Logothetis & Schall, 1989). Some neurons are most responsive to bull's-eyes, concentric circles, and spiral patterns (Gallant et al., 1993), while others are responsive to starlike shapes (Sary et al., 1993). It seems that the visual system is uniquely prepared to detect biologically adaptive types of visual stimulation. Indeed, damage to certain areas of the visual cortex produces very specific deficits—such as a complete or partial loss of color vision, face recognition, or an ability to see stationary or moving objects (Zeki, 1992).

Color Vision Ruby-red apples. Yellow taxi cabs. Lush green grass. Navy-blue uniforms. Purple mountains at sunset. Although some animals see the world in pale shades (including the bull, which is supposedly enraged by the sight of a matador's bright-red cape), all mammals have some form of color vision (Jacobs, 1993). For human beings, color is a particularly vital part of the visual experience. It is also linked in interesting ways to emotion. Thus, sadness feels blue, anger makes us see red, death is mourned in black, and jealousy brings a visit from the green-eyed monster.

People think that color is an objective property of objects. In fact, it is a property of organisms. When sunlight shines on a red rose, only the long red rays in the spectrum are reflected into our eyes. All other wavelengths are absorbed in the flower's surface. (If no wavelengths were absorbed, the rose would appear white.) Ironically, then, the rose holds everything but red. Most people can discriminate among 200 different colors and thousands of different shades. How do we do it? There are two major theories of color vision: the trichromatic theory and the opponent-process theory (Boynton, 1988).

Early in the nineteenth century, physiologists Thomas Young (1802) and Hermann von Helmholtz (1852) argued that the human eye is receptive to three primary colors—red, blue, and green—and that all other colors are derived from combinations of these primaries. By recording the neural responses of individual cones to different wavelengths of light, twentieth-century researchers later confirmed the Young-Helmholtz **trichromatic theory** (Schnapf et al., 1987; Wald, 1964). Specifically, there are three types of cones, each having a different photochemical that produces a particular response to light. One type fires most when struck by short wavelengths, so it picks up the color blue. The second type is most sensitive to the middle wavelengths,

trichromatic theory A theory of color vision stating that the retina contains three types of color receptors—for red, blue, and green—and that these combine to produce all other colors.

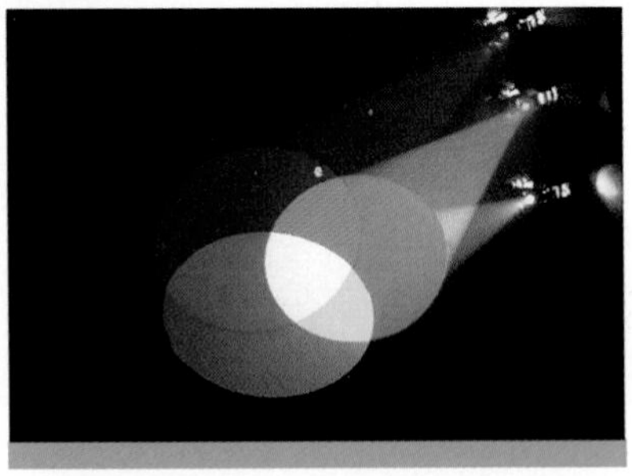

Figure 3.9 Trichromatic theory As shown, any color can be produced by mixing blue, green, and red light waves. When all three colors are combined, white is produced.

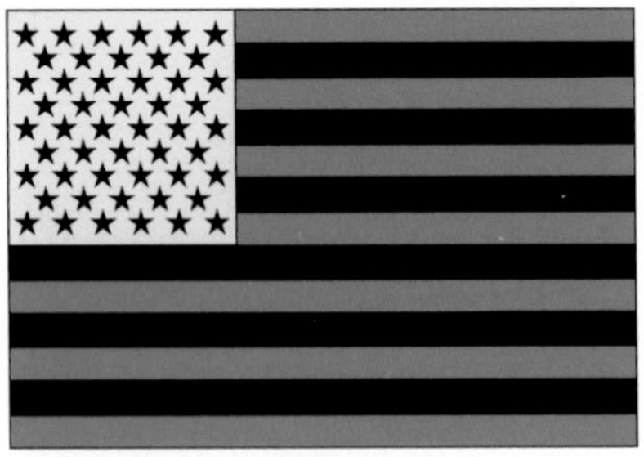

Figure 3.10 Afterimages Stare at this flag for 60 seconds, then look at a white sheet of paper. According to the opponent-process theory, you should see a negative afterimage that converts green to red, yellow to blue, and black to white. If you don't see an afterimage right away, blink and look again.

afterimage A visual sensation that persists after prolonged exposure and removal of a stimulus.

opponent-process theory The theory that color vision is derived from three pairs of opposing receptors. The opponent colors are blue and yellow, red and green, and black and white.

for the color green. The third type is most sensitive to long wavelengths, for the color red. In short, blue cones, green cones, and red cones serve as the building blocks for color vision. Other colors in the eye's "palette" are produced by the different combinations of cones. Activate both red and green cones, for example, and you will see the color yellow. Activate all three types of cones, and white is produced (see Figure 3.9). This, by the way, is what happens on a color TV screen—where pictures are formed from tiny red, green, and blue dots (hence the name *Trinitron* given by the Sony Corporation to its color TVs).

German physiologist Ewald Hering (1878) was not completely satisfied with the trichromatic theory. As he saw it, yellow was a primary color, not a derivative of red and green. He also noticed that certain color combinations just don't seem to exist. A mix of red and blue gives rise to varying shades of purple, but what is reddish green? Another puzzling phenomenon that didn't fit was the occurrence of negative **afterimages.** An afterimage is a sensation that persists after prolonged exposure to a stimulus. Stare at the image presented in Figure 3.10 for sixty seconds and in good lighting. Then look at a blank white sheet of paper. What do you see? In situations such as this one, staring at a green image leaves a red afterimage, yellow leaves a trace of blue, and black leaves white.

Putting the pieces together, Hering proposed the **opponent-process theory** of color vision. According to this theory, there are three types of visual receptors, and each is sensitive to a pair of complementary or "opponent" colors. One type reacts to the colors blue and yellow, a second type detects red and green, and a third type detects variations in brightness ranging from black to white. The color wheel in Figure 3.11 illustrates how these primary colors and their "companions" line up on nearly opposite sides of the circle. Notice that red and green are opponent colors, as are blue and yellow. Within each pair of red-green, blue-yellow, and black-white receptors, some parts fire more to one color whereas other parts react to its opposite. That's why we never see bluish yellow or reddish green, but we might see bluish green and reddish yellow. While seeing one color at a specific spot on the retina, you cannot also see its opposite on the same spot (Shapley, 1990).

The opponent-process theory can explain two aspects of color vision that its predecessor theory could not. First, it explains afterimages. Staring at the green stripes in Figure 3.10 causes the green-seeing cells to fire. Then, when the green color is removed from view, these parts of the cells become temporarily fatigued, leaving only the red parts to fire normally (Vimal et al., 1987). This process tips the neural balance to red, which produces a brief "rebound" effect (staring at yellow and black triggers a similar rebounding of blue and white).

Second, opponent-process theory can explain color blindness, a genetic disorder. In actuality, only about 1 in 100,000 people are color "blind," seeing the world in only black, white, and shades of gray (Nathans, 1989). Rather, color-deficient people tend to confuse certain colors. The most common problem, particularly among men, is red-green color blindness, in which there is an inability to distinguish between red and green because both appear gray (how ironic that these are the universal traffic colors for stop and go!). Though very rare, a second form of color blindness is the inability to distinguish between—you guessed it—blue and yellow (see Figure 3.12).

For many years, researchers debated the relative merits of the trichromatic and opponent-process theories of color vision. As often happens in either-or debates, it now appears that both theories are correct—and that both are necessary to fully understand the way we sense color. The human retina contains red, blue, and green cones, as suggested by the trichromatic theory. But in the thalamus—where these signals are sent en route to the visual cortex—single-cell recordings reveal that neurons operate in accordance with the opponent-process theory. That is, some cells are excited by red and inhibited by green, and vice versa. Other cells react to blue and yellow (DeValois & DeValois, 1975). Color vision is thus a complex process and is still not fully understood (Abramov & Gordon, 1994).

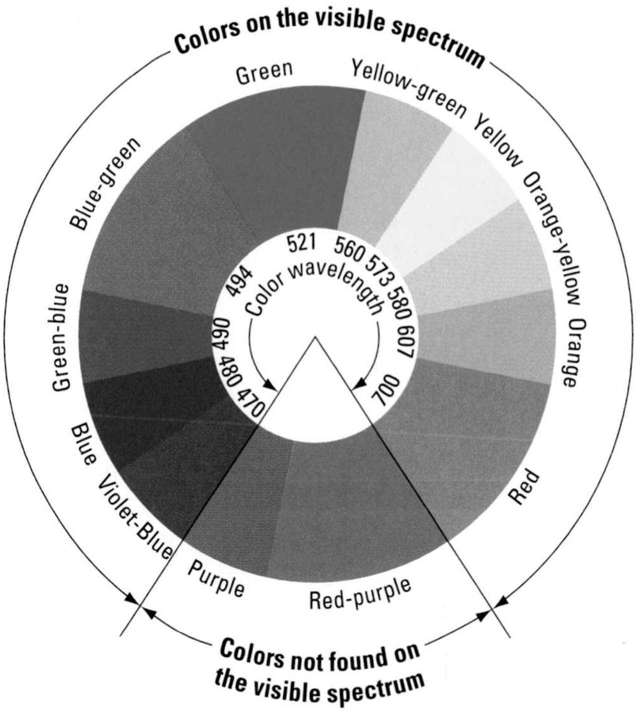

Figure 3.11 The color wheel As shown, opponent colors are directly across from each other in the circle (red is across from green, blue is across from yellow). The numbers on the spokes are wavelengths, expressed in nanometers.

Hearing

If you had to suffer one fate—to be blind or to be deaf—which would you choose? It's a morbid question, I know. Ask around, however, and you'll find that most people would rather lose their hearing than their eyesight. Yet Helen Keller, like many others who are both blind and deaf, wrote that deafness was by far the greater handicap.

It's easy to take the sounds of everyday life for granted—and, indeed, we often say that "silence is golden." But auditory sensations surround us and inform us. The chatter of voices, the clanging of dinner dishes, music throbbing from stereo speakers, birds chirping, babies crying, horns honking, a creaking old floor breaking the silence of night, the trickling of water over pebbles, the whisper of a secret, the crunching of potato chips, the sound of a figure skater's blade scraping the ice, the steady hum of a fluorescent lamp, the crack of a wooden bat against a baseball, the clinking of champagne glasses on New Year's Eve, the screeching of a train roaring into the station, the snap-crackle-pop of breakfast

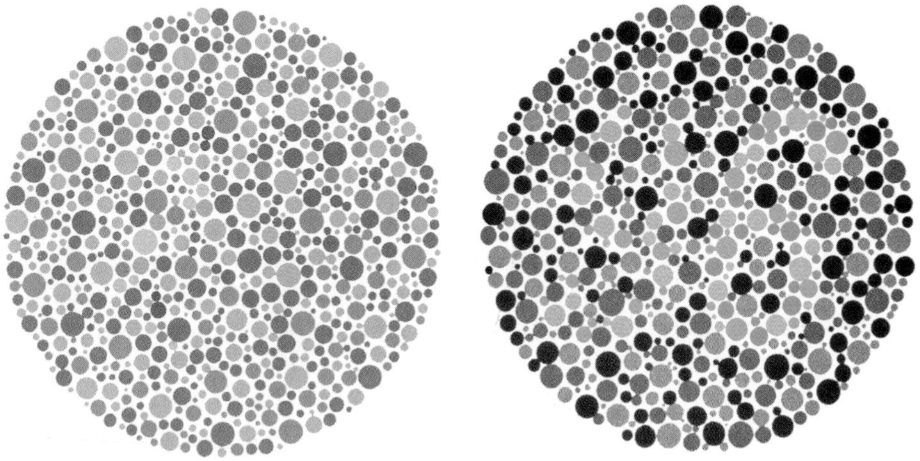

Figure 3.12 Test of color deficiency In items like these, people with red-green color blind-ness have difficulty perceiving the numbers embedded in the pattern. The inability to distinguish between red and green, as in this pattern or in traffic signals, caused a 1996 train crash near Hoboken, New Jersey. According to the National Transportation Safety Board, the engineer, who had failed a color-vision test, failed to detect the red signal. New Jersey Transit now requires all of its engineers to pass a color-vision test consisting of fourteen circular plates of polka dots in which numbers are formed by slightly contrasting colors. (Ishihara, "Test for Color Deficiency". (Courtesy Kanehara Shuppan Co., Ltd. Offered Exclusively in The USA by Graham-Field, Inc., Hauppauge, New York)

cereal, and the one I've become the most accustomed to—the woodpeckerlike tapping of fingers on a computer keyboard. These are just some of the familiar sounds of life. But what is sound, and how do we hear it?

Sound Waves Every sensation is born of energy. For vision, or seeing, the stimulus is light. For **audition**, or hearing, the stimulus is sound. As in light, sound travels in waves. Physically, sound is *vibration*, a pattern of rapid wavelike movement in molecules of air. First, something has to move—an engine, vocal cords, violin strings, or clapping hands. The movement jolts the surrounding molecules of air, and these collide with other air molecules. As in the ocean, sound ripples in waves that ebb and flow in all directions. It loses energy from one ripple to the next, however, which is the reason sound fades at a distance. Sound travels through air at 750 miles per hour—much slower than the speed of light, which is 186,000 miles per second. That's why, in thunderstorms, you see lightning before you hear the accompanying thunder.

As with light, sound waves can be distinguished by three major properties. The first is wavelength, or *frequency*. As molecules of air push outward from a source, they expand and compress in cycles. Frequency, measured by the number of cycles completed per second, is expressed as hertz (Hz). One cycle per second equals one Hz. Subjectively, the frequency of a sound wave determines its *pitch* (the highness or lowness of a sound). The higher the frequency, the higher the pitch. Humans can hear frequencies ranging from about 20 Hz to 20,000 Hz—in music, the equivalent of almost ten octaves. Homing pigeons and elephants can hear lower frequencies. Bats, dogs, and dolphins hear at higher frequencies (dogs can hear at 50,000 Hz, which is why a "silent" dog whistle is not silent to a dog). Most of the sounds we need to hear, and certainly those we enjoy hearing, are well within this range (the lowest note on a piano is 27.5 Hz, the highest note is 4,180 Hz, and the voices of conversation range from 200 to 800 Hz). When all frequencies of the sound spectrum are combined, they produce a hissing sound. This hissing is called **white noise**—named by analogy to the white light that results from the combination of all wavelengths in the visible light spectrum.

The second property of sound is *amplitude*. Amplitude refers to the intensity, or height, of each sound wave. Psychologically, the amplitude of a wave determines its *loudness*. The greater the amplitude, the louder the sound. We may not be able to hear a pin drop, but our ears are responsive to a remarkably wide range of amplitudes. Indeed, the loudest sound we can tolerate without pain is billions of times greater in amplitude than the softest sound we can hear. For variations within this range, amplitude is measured in decibels (dB). The Intersection box on page 96 provides examples of the loudness of various sounds at different dB levels. As you look at Figure 3.15, note that dB levels over 120 are painful—and can cause permanent damage to the ears (Henry, 1984; Kryter, 1994).

A third property of sound is purity, or *complexity*. Strike a tuning fork, and you'll produce something rare: a pure tone consisting of a single frequency of vibration. In reality, most sounds are complex mixtures of waves of different frequencies. Speech, music, a ringing bell, and a breaking window are some common examples (Bregman, 1990; Krumhansl, 1991). Psychologically, the complexity of a sound determines its *timbre*, or tonal quality. Play the same note at the same loudness on a piano, trumpet, saxophone, tuba, and violin, and what you'll hear are differences in timbre.

audition The sense of hearing.

white noise A hissing sound that results from a combination of all frequencies of the sound spectrum.

The Auditory System Philosophers like to ponder the age-old question, "If a tree falls in a forest, but no one is around to hear it, does it make a sound?" This really

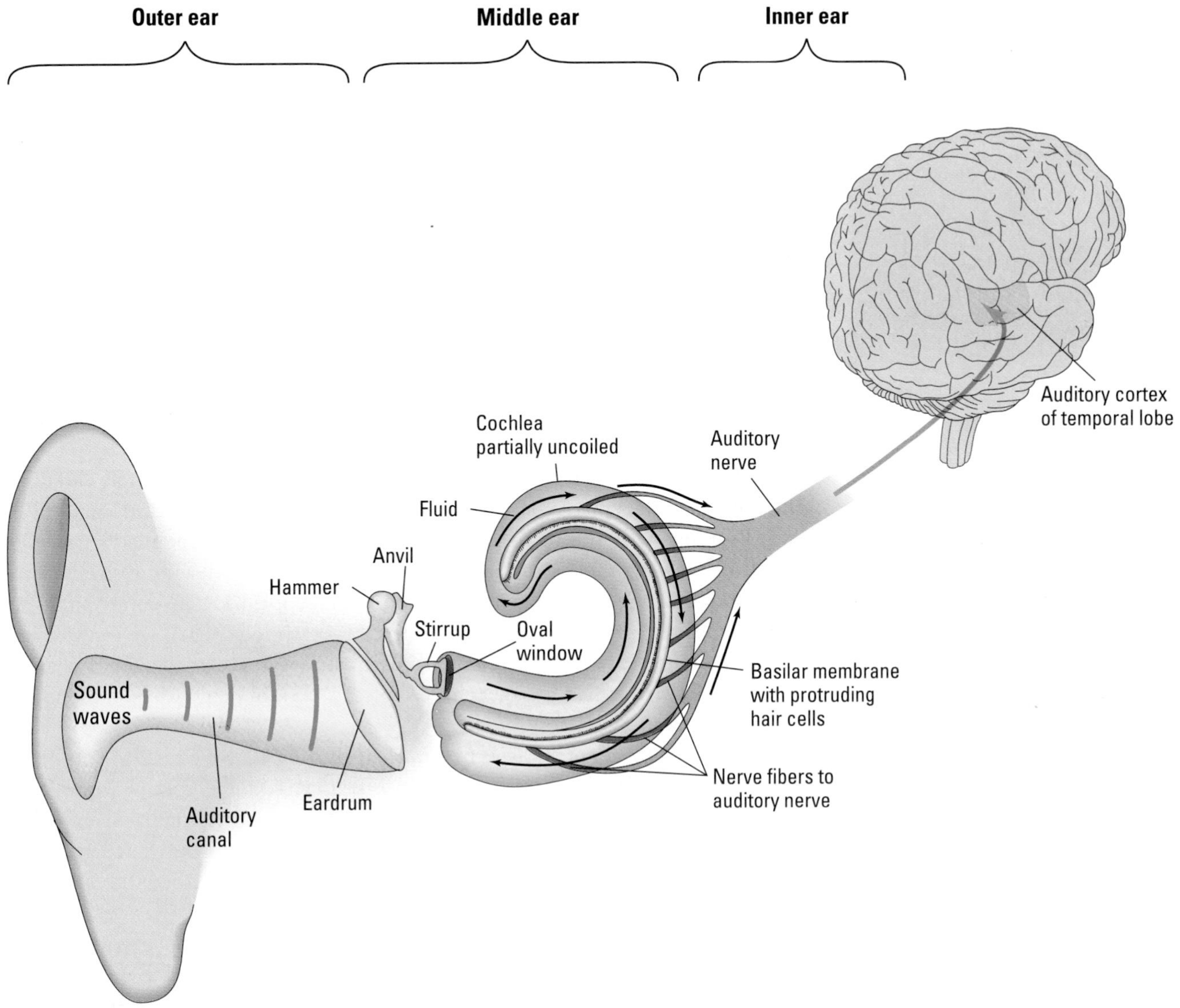

Figure 3.13 The human ear As shown, the process of hearing begins in the three-part (outer, middle, and inner) structure of the ear. From the auditory nerve, signals are relayed to the auditory cortex.

is a profound question. We know that the fall of a tree sends waves of molecules blasting through the air, but we also know that without an auditory system to catch these molecules—well, you make the call. As in vision, hearing requires that energy be detected, converted into neural impulses, and relayed to the brain. As shown in Figure 3.13, this complex process begins in the three-part (outer, middle, and inner) structure of the human ear.

Sound waves are collected in the *outer ear*, beginning with the fleshy pinna. Some animals, such as dogs, cats, and deer, can wiggle this structure like a radar dish to maximize the reception of sound (humans cannot). The sound waves are then funneled through the auditory canal to the eardrum, a tightly stretched membrane that separates the outer and middle portions of the ear. The eardrum vibrates back and forth to the waves, thereby setting into motion a series of tiny connecting bones in the *middle ear*—the hammer, the anvil, and the stirrup (for you trivia buffs, these are the three smallest bones in the body). This middle-ear activity amplifies sound by a factor of 30. The last of these bones, the stirrup, then vibrates against a soft

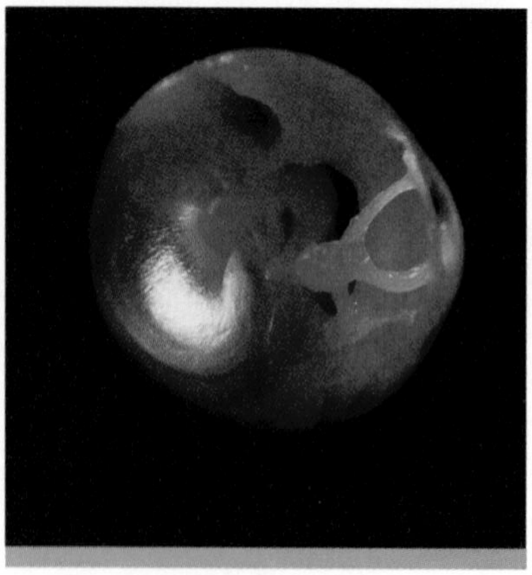

In this photograph of the middle ear, you can see the eardrum (left), hammer (top) anvil (center), and stirrup (right).

inner-ear membrane called the oval window. This, in turn, vibrates the fluid that fills the canals of the cochlea, a snail-shape tube—and the resulting motion presses up against a membrane, which brushes up against about a million sensitive hair cells (Hudspeth, 1985). These hair cells bend, exciting fibers in the auditory nerve—a bundle of 35,000 axons that link to auditory centers of the brain. Also in the inner ear are the semicircular canals, which, as we'll see later, play a critical role in balance (Teas, 1989).

To summarize, the "plumbing" and "wiring" that turn sound waves into meaningful input are fairly intricate. Air collected in the outer ear is transformed first into a salt-watery fluid and then into electrical impulses in the inner ear. From the auditory nerve, signals then cross to the other side of the brain. Next, they get routed to the thalamus, where they're relayed to areas of the auditory cortex. Once there, the signals are processed by cells that specialize in high, middle, or low frequencies of sound (Hirsh & Watson, 1996; Moore, 1995).

Hearing Abilities Hearing is not one sensory ability but many. People can detect sound, understand spoken language, and appreciate the acoustical qualities of music. Everyone with normal hearing can distinguish between sounds that are loud and soft or between those produced by horns and those produced by string instruments. And although fewer than one in a thousand people have "absolute pitch" (an ability to identify a musical note as middle C, F-sharp, or B-flat), we can all make judgments of "relative pitch"—enabling us to know, for example, that a child's voice is higher than a man's (Takeuchi & Hulse, 1993). In many ways, our auditory competence is impressive.

One particularly adaptive aspect of normal hearing that we take for granted is **auditory localization**—the ability to tell the *direction* a sound is coming from. Localization is needed to determine if the blaring siren you hear is coming from behind you on the road, or if the approaching footsteps are coming from your left or your right. This skill was vital to the survival of our primitive ancestors and is a matter of life and death to all animals of prey.

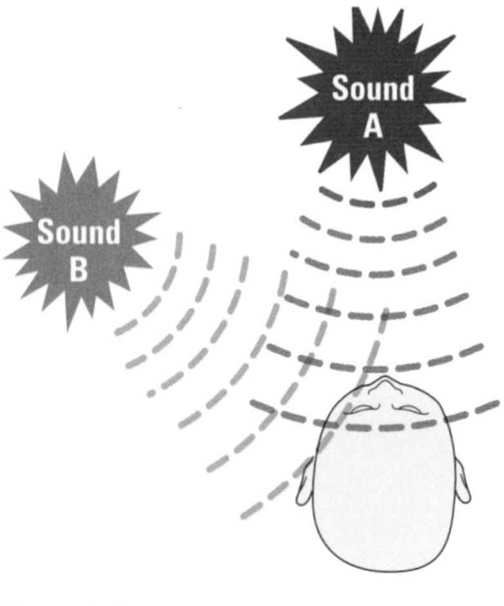

Figure 3.14 Auditory localization The brain is able to detect small differences in the timing and intensity of sound between the two ears—and can use these differences to localize the source.

Unless you're being fooled by the visual manipulations of a ventriloquist, it's usually easy to tell if a sound is coming from your left or your right. Have you ever heard children in a swimming pool screaming, "Marco—Polo—Marco—Polo"? Most kids love the game, while most adults trying to enjoy a relaxing day at the pool find it irritating. Basically, it's a game of tag in which one player, with eyes closed, screams, "Marco," prompting the others to reply by yelling, "Polo." The first player then tries to find the others by tracking their voices. The key skill here is auditory localization, and children of all ages are good at it. In fact, if you stand to the left or right of an infant and shake a rattle, it will often turn its head in your direction, as if locating the source (see Chapter 10).

What makes auditory localization possible is that we hear in stereo, using two ears spaced about six inches apart. If you're at a noisy gathering and someone on your left calls your name, your left ear receives the signal before the right ear does (it's closer to the source) and more intensely (your head is a barrier to the more distant ear). The six inches of brain tissue and skull that separate your ears may seem too little to matter, but our auditory system is sensitive. Unless a sound is directly above, below, in front of, or behind us, the brain can detect small differences in timing and intensity between the two ears—and use these differences to locate the source (Middlebrooks & Green, 1991; Konishi, 1993). This process is shown in Figure 3.14.

auditory localization The ability to judge the direction a sound is coming from.

Auditory localization is not always so easy. If you're at the same noisy gathering and someone directly behind you calls your name, both ears will receive the input at the same time and at the same intensity. What then? Lacking physical cues to locate the source, you will turn your head as if it were a radar dish in an effort to produce controlled differences in the timing and intensity of the signals to the two ears. The objective in such circumstances is to "fine-tune" the reception of information.

Hearing Disabilities It's natural to take your sensory competence for granted—until you don't have it. In fact, millions of people have hearing impairments that range from a partial loss to profound deafness. There are two kinds of hearing impairment. The symptoms are the same, but the causes and treatment are very different. One type is **conduction deafness**, in which damage to the eardrum or to the bones in the middle ear diminishes their ability to conduct sound waves. Fortunately, hearing can be partially restored through surgery or by means of a hearing aid that amplifies sound waves—provided that the inner-ear structures are intact. A far more serious problem is **nerve deafness**, in which there is inner-ear damage to the cochlea, hair cells, or auditory nerve. Nerve deafness can be caused by certain diseases, by biological changes due to old age, or by exposure to intensely loud noises. Researchers have long believed that once neural tissue is destroyed, it cannot be repaired or replaced. Recent studies have shown that hair cells taken from guinea pigs, rats, and humans can be regenerated—but the newly regenerated cells are not functional (Lefebvre et al., 1993; Warchol et al., 1993).

Although it is not currently possible to regenerate damaged auditory hair cells in humans and although conventional hearing aids do not restore hearing in nerve deafness, researchers are now developing artificial cochlea implants, or "bionic ears." Intended for people with damaged hair cells, this device has a tiny microphone in the outer ear that sends sound to a miniature electrode implanted in the cochlea. This electrode stimulates the auditory nerve—and an impulse is fired to the brain. Cochlea implants may enable many people who are profoundly deaf to detect

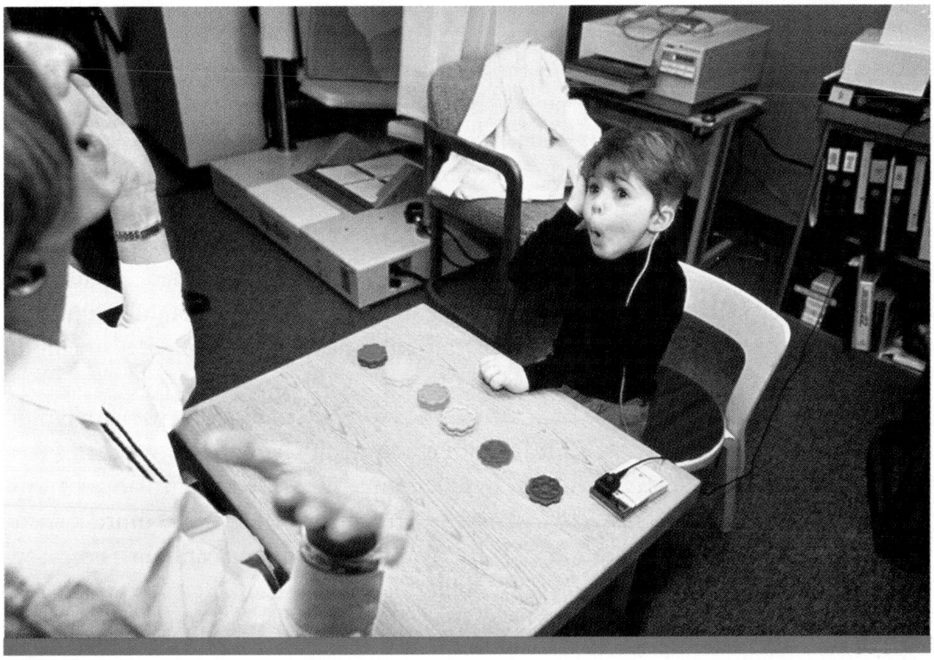

With the help of a surgical implant that stimulates the auditory nerve, this four-year-old boy—who has been deaf since birth—is hearing sound for the first time in his life.

conduction deafness Hearing loss caused by damage to the eardrum or bones in the middle ear.

nerve deafness Hearing loss caused by damage to the structures of the inner ear.

the presence of sound, perhaps for the first time in their lives. To be sure, the sensations produced by these devices are crude, as wearers can detect changes in volume and pitch but cannot make out distinct words (Mulder et al., 1992; Townsend et al., 1987). But deafened adults who use cochlea implants, after a few years, become more proficient lipreaders and better at word recognition (Tyler et al., 1995). Clearly, this approach is a promising one.

INTERSECTION

SENSATION AND PERCEPTION AND THE ENVIRONMENT

Noise and Your Hearing

When I was a teenager, my parents would warn me that the constant blaring of my stereo and the Grateful Dead marathons I went to would hurt my ears. "Parents," I muttered to myself, "what do they know?" Sure, my ears would be ringing after a rock concert, and sure, voices would seem muffled for a while, but my ears were back to normal the next day. Or were they?

It is estimated that 28 million Americans, which is more than 10 percent of the population, suffer serious hearing loss. Often this loss is due to exposure to loud noise, and often the victims are adolescents and children. Researchers are now convinced that exposure to intense noise can cause such violent vibrations in the inner ear that it can damage hair cells and permanently impair hearing. When does "sound" become "noise?" When does "loud" become "too loud?" The amplitude of a sound, which determines its loudness to the human ear, is measured in decibels (dB). To understand this scale, it's important to know that loudness doubles with every increase of 10 dB (an increase from 0 to 100 dB thus produces a 10 billion-fold increase in loudness). Constant daily exposure to sounds of over 85 dB (heavy street traffic, jackhammers, subways, and machinery) can flatten the inner-ear hair cells over time and cause a gradual loss of hearing. Even a brief assault by an ear-shattering sound that exceeds 140 dB (a gunshot, explosion, or rocket launch) can tear the delicate inner ear tissues and cause permanent hearing loss. Look at Figure 3.15, and you'll see that danger to the ear is all around us.

Most current research on sound exposure addresses the occupational hazards of noise in factories, airports, construction sites, and other work settings (Kryter, 1994). But there's also a lot of concern about exposures to amplified music vibrating from huge speakers. Spend two hours at a rock concert or turn the stereo volume up to full blast, and you may be putting your ears at risk (West & Evans, 1990). Many experts claim that if your Walkman can be heard by someone near you, then you're damaging your ears. And the loss can be irreversible. In 1986, The Who entered the *Guinness Book of World Records* for the loudest rock concert ever when they blasted sounds that measured 120 dB at a distance of 164 feet from the speakers. Unless their ears were protected, everyone within a 164-foot radius probably suffered irreversible hearing loss. The Who's Peter Townshend (as well as Jeff Baxter of the Doobie Brothers and other rock musicians) is now partially deaf. He also complains of a constant ringing in his ears. According to audiologist Dean Garstecki, director of a hearing impairment program, "We've got 21-year-olds walking around with hearing loss patterns of people 40 years their senior" (Toufexis, 1991).

Much of the noise that surrounds us is unavoidable. But too often people don't realize how harmful it is. Baggage handlers and others who work on airport runways wear ear protectors, which can muffle noise by about 35 dB. You too can do the same if necessary. Just as you wouldn't stare at the sun's penetrating rays, you should not expose the delicate structures of your ears to piercing, high-volume sound waves. As my parents used to say, "Can't you just turn the volume down a little?".

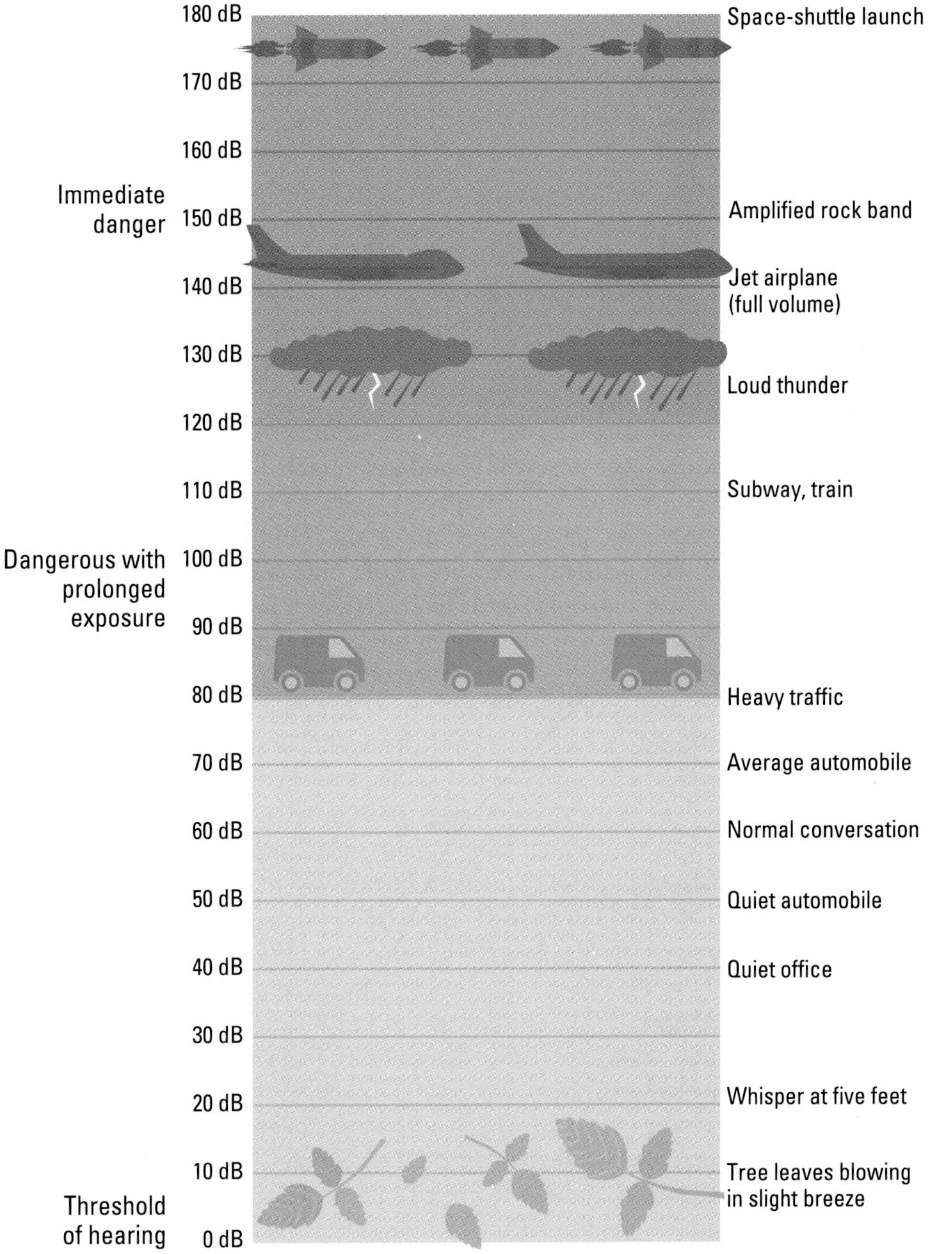

Figure 3.15 Common sounds and the amounts of noise they produce, in decibels

Other Senses

Psychologists know more about seeing and hearing than about other sensory systems, but these other systems are also essential to the adaptive human package. You can't see or hear the heat of a fire, the sting of a bee, the stench of a gas leak, or the bitter taste of a poisonous plant. Nor can you see or hear the sensuous pleasures of a scent-filled rose, creamy chocolate, or a soothing massage. To get along, human beings have developed the ability to detect, process, and integrate information from many sources.

Because of their acute sense of smell, trained dogs are being used in airports to sniff out terrorist explosives.

When airborne odor molecules dissolve in the nose, they are trapped by the hairlike olfactory receptors shown in this picture.

olfactory system The structures responsible for the sense of smell.

Smell Dogs are known for their ability to sniff out faint scents and to track down animals, criminals, and illegal drugs over time and long distances. In fact, the U.S. government now uses trained dogs in airports to help detect terrorist explosives (Buckley, 1996). In a contest of smelling ability, we humans would have little to brag about compared to our canine buddies—who may well have the keenest noses in the whole animal kingdom (Marshall & Moulton, 1981). But our own sense of smell, which is the product of the body's **olfactory system**, is more sensitive than you may realize—and more important.

All smells have a chemical origin (Bartoshuk & Beauchamp, 1994). Depending on their molecular structure, substances emit odor-causing molecules into the air. Some objects, such as glass and metal, have no smell (any scent these objects may emit comes from impurities on the surface). Other objects, like the musk oil extracted from animal sweat glands, produce overpowering odors. By breathing through the nose and mouth, we inhale these airborne odorant molecules—which dissolve and become trapped by *olfactory receptors* in the moist yellow lining of the upper nasal passages just above the roof of the mouth. There are about 10 million of these hairlike receptors in the human nose (the average dog has 200 million). Certain molecules seem to fit certain types of receptors the way a key fits a lock. Once activated, they trigger an action potential in the *olfactory nerve* (Firestein & Werblin, 1989). This nerve connects the nose to the *olfactory bulb*, a bean-size organ that distributes information throughout the cortex and to the nearby limbic-system structures that control memory and emotion. It's interesting that smell is the only sensation that is not routed to the cortex through the thalamus. The olfactory bulb is its own private relay station (see Figure 3.16).

Unlike other animals, humans do not need a sense of smell to mark territory, signal danger, establish dominance hierarchies, or attract a mate. Furthermore, because language does not provide an adequate supply of olfaction words, it's hard for people to describe smells (Richardson & Zucco, 1989). Yet the millions of olfactory receptors in the nose do enable us to distinguish among 10,000 different odor molecules (Buck & Axel, 1991)—including the proposed "primary" odors of vinegar, roses, mint, rotten egg, mothballs, dry-cleaning fluid, and musk (Amoore et al., 1964). Many smells have powerful effects on people—which, perhaps, is why so much money is spent on mint-flavored mouthwashes, deodorants, pine- and lemon-scented air fresheners, herbal shampoos, and perfumes. The olfactory bulbs extend some of their axons directly into the brain's limbic system, so it's not that surprising that certain familiar smells—such as a whiff of cologne, a musty attic, or holiday food cooking in the oven—often bring on a rush of memories and emotions (Engen, 1982).

Our sense of smell is influenced by many factors. To begin with, individuals differ in their sensitivity. Helen Keller, who was blind and deaf from infancy, called smell "the fallen angel of the senses." She had a prodigious olfactory sense and wrote that she could often smell storms brewing. Professional perfumers and whiskey blenders can also distinguish odors better than the average person. At the other end of the spectrum are people who suffer from "anosmia," or odor blindness that can be caused by a serious head injury, viral infection, or toxic exposure. It's ironic that Ben Cohen, the co-founder of Ben & Jerry's Ice Cream, is anosmic—which is why, he says, his ice cream is rich and smooth in its texture.

For reasons yet unknown, women outperform men at identifying odors (Doty et al., 1985). Odor sensitivity also changes with age. Young babies cannot talk, but they do respond nonverbally to odor. Put a swab of honey under a baby's nose, and you may well see a smile. Put a swab of rotten egg under the nose, and the baby will grimace (Steiner, 1979). Even at the tender age of two weeks, nursing infants are

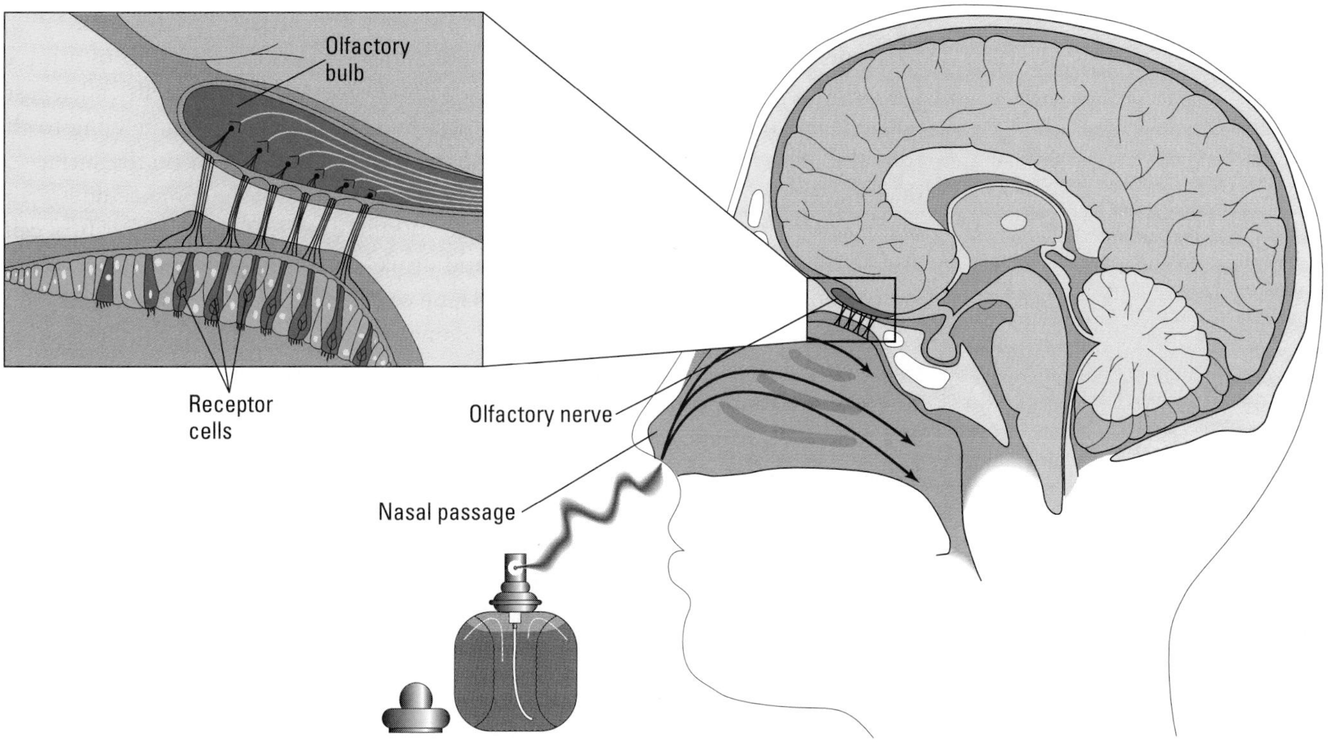

Figure 3.16 The olfactory system Once in the nose, odorant molecules are trapped by olfactory receptors. These receptors send signals through the olfactory nerve to the olfactory bulb, which communicates with various parts of the brain.

more attracted to their own mothers' body odor than to that of other women (Cernoch & Porter, 1985). Among adults, olfactory sensitivity peaks in middle age and declines as people reach their seventies and eighties. This age trend was revealed in a *National Geographic* survey of 1.42 million subscribers who responded to a scratch-and-sniff odor recognition test (Gilbert & Wysocki, 1987).

Smell is a primitive sense—yet so successful, suggests Diane Ackerman (1990), "that in time the small lump of olfactory tissue atop the nerve cord grew into a brain" (p. 20). Given this view, it's hardly surprising that researchers have tried to identify pheromones in human beings. **Pheromones** are chemicals secreted by animals that transmit signals to others, usually of the same species. Ants, bees, termites, and other insects secrete chemicals that attract mates and "release" other behaviors. Many mammals are also sexually excited by scent; for example, a female dog in heat sends neighboring male dogs into a state of frenzy. Are humans similarly aroused? If so, could the scent be bottled and manufactured? For perfumists, the potential is easy to imagine.

Studies show that people can recognize others by their body odor. In this research, various subjects would shower using the same soap and then wear a T-shirt for at least twenty-four hours. After the shirts were collected, subjects would sniff them and try to identify the wearer. The result: College students can usually recognize their own shirts, mothers can pick out the shirts worn by their own children, and people in general can discriminate by odor between the shirts worn by men and women (Russell, 1976). Is there any evidence for a *sexual* attractant in humans? Some perfumes currently found in stores contain *alpha androstenol*, a sexual pheromone secreted by male pigs (and also found in human underarm secretions). To date, there's no evidence from which to draw a conclusion. It's clear, however, that human sexuality is too complex to be chemically "controlled" by scent.

It seems hard to believe, but if you slice an apple and an onion into small cubes, hold your nose, and conduct a blind taste test, you'll have trouble telling the two foods apart.

pheromones Chemicals secreted by animals that transmit signals—usually to other animals of the same species.

Taste Taste is a product of the body's **gustatory system** (Simon & Roper, 1993). Like smell, taste is a chemical sensation. Put a morsel of food or a squirt of drink in the mouth, and it will come into contact with clusters of receptor cells called **taste buds**. There are about 10,000 hairlike taste buds in the mouth. Some cling to the roof and back of the throat, but most line the trenches and bumps on the surface of the tongue. Taste buds are most densely packed on the tip of the tongue and are virtually absent from the center of the tongue. Within each taste bud, about fifty cells absorb the chemical molecules of food and drink—and trigger neural impulses that are routed to the thalamus and cortex. These cells are replaced every ten days, so if you burn your tongue on hot soup, the damage to your receptors will be repaired (see Figure 3.17).

There are four primary tastes: sweet, salty, sour, and bitter. However, the *flavor* of a food is determined not only by taste but by other factors as well. You may have noticed that after you've brushed your teeth in the morning, orange juice tastes bitter. And after you've eaten artichokes, water tastes sweet. Chemical residues from the substance already eaten mix with what you're currently eating to produce a new taste sensation. Temperature, texture, and appearance are also important factors, which is why no one likes warm soda or soggy potato chips and why the great chefs prepare dishes for the eye as well as for the palate. By far the most important determinant of flavor is odor. When I have a cold and my nose is all stuffed up, I lose my appetite. For me, there is no joy to chewing on food without flavor. Indeed, research shows that people lose their ability to identify common flavors—such as chocolate, vanilla, coffee, wine, and even onion and garlic—when they're prevented from smelling the food (Mozell et al., 1969).

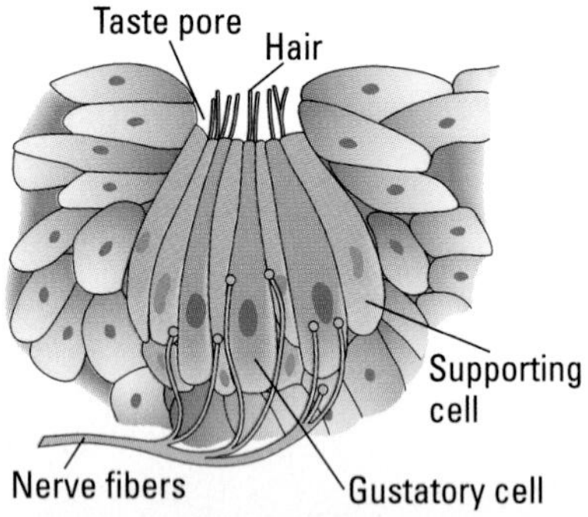

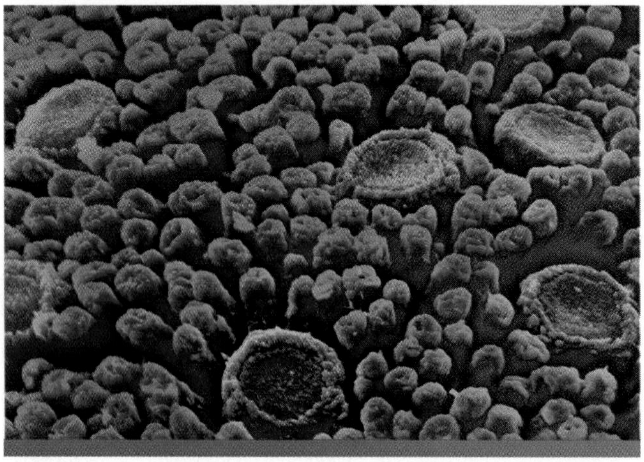

Figure 3.17 Taste buds This photograph is of the surface of a human tongue, magnified seventy-five times. As shown in the sketch, the taste buds are located in the large round areas called papillae.

The more taste buds that dot your tongue, the more sensitive you're likely to be to various tastes. Children have more taste buds than adults do, for example, which may explain why they are often so picky about eating "grown-up" foods. Even among adults, individuals differ in the number of taste buds they have—and in their sensitivity to taste. Indeed, recent studies have shown that people can be divided into one of three groups: nontasters, medium tasters, and supertasters. At one extreme, nontasters (25 percent of the population) are unable to detect certain sweet and bitter compounds and are less sensitive in general to taste. At the other extreme, supertasters (also about 25 percent of the population) react strongly to certain sweet and bitter compounds. Compared to most, supertasters use only half as much sugar or saccharin in their coffee or tea. They also suffer more oral burn from eating the active ingredient in chili peppers. These differences in taste sensitivity correspond nicely to our physiological makeup. Using videomicroscopy to count the number of taste buds on the tongue, researchers have found that nontasters have an average of 96 taste buds per square centimeter, medium tasters have 184, and supertasters have 425. Put differently, the number of taste buds on the human tongue can range from a low of 500 to a high of 10,000 (Bartoshuk & Beauchamp, 1994; Miller & Reedy, 1990).

gustatory system The structures responsible for the sense of taste.

taste buds Nets of taste-receptor cells.

Touch Every organism has a sense of touch. Sea snails withdraw their gills at the slightest pressure. Sponges sense an intruder by feeling the water around them quiver. As for humans, often feeling is believing. Put up a "wet paint" sign, and you'll find, paradoxically, that it seems to invite touching rather than inhibit it. Tactile sensations are unique in many ways. To begin with, touch is the only sensation with receptors that are not localized in a single region of the body. We need eyes to see, ears to hear, a nose to smell, and a tongue to taste. But the organ of touch, and the site of its sensory receptors, is *skin*.

Skin is by far the largest organ of the body. It covers two square yards and weighs six to ten pounds. It is multilayered, waterproof, elastic, and filled with hair follicles, sweat-gland ducts, and nerve endings that connect to the central nervous system. When you consider all the sensations that emanate from your skin—feeling hot, cold, wet, dry, sore, itchy, scratchy, sticky, gooey, greasy, tingly, numb, and sharp pain—you can see that touch involves not one sensory system but many (Heller & Schiff, 1991).

Smells can influence us in subtle but interesting ways.

The sensations of touch are vital for survival. Without it, you would not know that you're in danger of becoming frostbitten or burned; you would not know if you've been stung by a bee; you would be unable to swallow food. When other sensory systems fail, touch takes on even more importance. All of us can feel the differences between leather, sandpaper, brick, cork, velvet, and other textures (Hollins et al., 1993). But for Virgil, the blind man whose eyesight was temporarily restored, shapes and textures are particularly important for recognizing objects. When passed a bowl of fruit, he could easily distinguish among a slick plum, a soft fuzzy peach, a smooth nectarine, and a rough, dimpled orange. He was even able to "see" through the disguise of an artificial wax pear that had fooled everyone else. "It's a candle," he said, "shaped like a bell or a pear" (Sacks, 1995, p. 149).

It's important to distinguish between passive and active touch. In passive touch, a person's skin is contacted by another object, as when a cat rubs up against your leg. In active touch, it is the person who initiates the contact, as when you pet your cat. Psychologically, the effects are different. For example, James Gibson (1962) tested subjects for their ability to identify shapes from cookie cutters shaped like stars, triangles, circles, and so on. When the objects were pressed lightly onto the hand (passive), they were identified correctly 29 percent of the time. When subjects actively explored the shapes with their fingers, the accuracy rate increased to 95 percent. Other research, too, shows that people can make fine discriminations among common objects when they explore them by grasping, lifting, holding, squeezing, rubbing, and tracing the edges (Klatsky & Lederman, 1992).

Active touch is what allows Virgil to feel the differences among plums, peaches, oranges, and nectarines. It is also the key to *braille*, the alphanumeric system that allows many blind people to read. Braille letters and numbers consist of coded patterns of raised dots on a page that readers scan with their fingertips. Some braille readers can achieve a reading rate as high as 200 words per minute—which is remarkable considering that the average rate among sighted readers is 250 words per minute (Foulke, 1991). In a recent experiment, blind people using their braille-reading fingers outperformed blindfolded sighted adults by 20 percent in the ability to discriminate different shapes by touch (Stevens et al., 1996).

Using braille, blind people learn to read by running their fingers over coded patterns of raised dots.

Most psychologists agree that the sense of touch consists of four basic types of sensations: pressure, warmth, cold, and pain. Researchers initially thought that there was a separate receptor in the skin for each of these four sensations, but it now appears that only *pressure* sensations have unique and specialized nerve endings dispersed throughout the body. One of the most striking aspects of touch is that sensitivity to pressure or vibration is different from one part of the body to another. To determine the thresholds for touch (how much force it takes before a subject reports

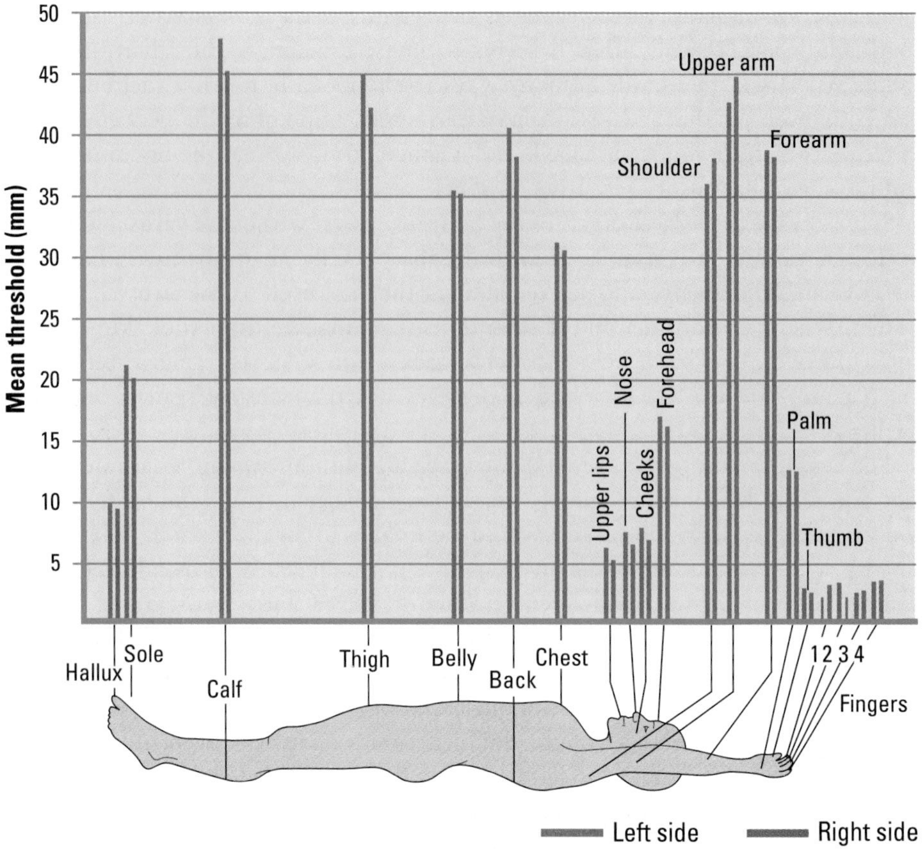

Figure 3.18 **Sensitivity to touch** Thresholds for touch are estimated by applying varying degrees of pressure to the skin (a lower threshold means greater sensitivity). Below are the average thresholds for male subjects (the relative values for females are similar but slightly lower overall). The genital areas, which are likely to contain the lowest thresholds, were not tested.

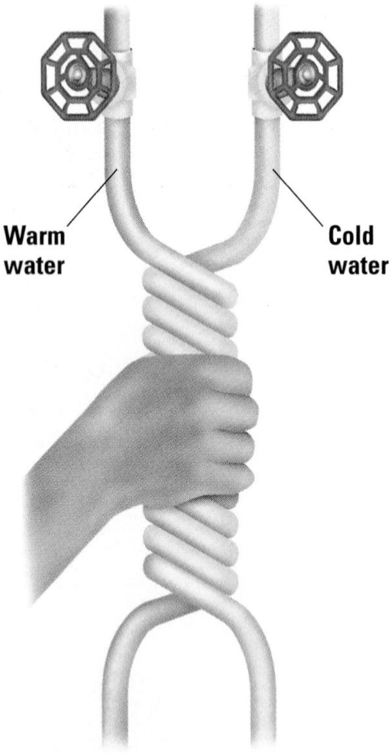

Figure 3.19 **The heat grill** When people grasp two braided pipes—one with cold water running through it, the other with warm water—the sensation is "very hot."

a feeling), researchers would apply a thin rod or wire to different areas of skin and would vary the pressure (Weinstein, 1968). Figure 3.18 shows that the hands, fingers, and face are the most sensitive areas, while the calves, thighs, and arms are the least sensitive. In all cases, pressure causes the nerve endings to fire messages through the spinal cord, brainstem, and thalamus en route to the somatosensory cortex (Burton & Sinclair, 1996; Greenspan & Bolanowski, 1996).

Temperature Normal human body temperature is 98.6 degrees Fahrenheit, or 37 degrees Celsius (temperatures at the surface of the skin are slightly lower). There are two striking facts about the sensation of temperature. First is that it is, to a large extent, *relative* to your current state. To demonstrate, fill three buckets with tap water—one cold, one hot, and one at room temperature. Place your right hand into the cold water and your left hand into the hot water, and leave them there for a minute. Then place both hands together into the third bucket. You can probably predict the amusing result: Both hands are now in the same water, yet your right hand feels warm and your left hand feels cool. If you ever plunged into a cold pool or eased yourself into a hot tub, you know that the sensations are triggered by temperatures that are well above or below your own current "adaptation level" (Hensel, 1981).

The second fact about temperature is that there are really two separate sensory systems—one for signaling warmth, the other for signaling cold. Early studies showed that some spots on the skin respond more to warming and others to cooling (Dallenbach, 1927). "Hot" is a particularly intriguing sensation in that it is triggered when these warm and cold spots are simultaneously stimulated. Thus, when people grasp two braided pipes—one with cold water running through it, the other with warm water—they will pull away, complaining that the device is literally too hot to handle (see Figure 3.19). Apparently, the brain interprets the dual firing of both types of temperature receptors as being caused by a burning hot stimulus.

Pain Pain is a dentist's drill boring through a tooth. Pain is stepping on a thumbtack. Pain is a pulled muscle, a splitting headache, a backache, sunburn blisters, and leg cramps. Ouch! Whatever the source, people are understandably motivated to avoid and escape from pain. Yet pain is crucial to survival because it serves as a red flag, a warning system that signals danger and the risk of tissue damage. Life without pain may sound great, but it would be a life that is not likely to last very long. The case of a seven-year-old girl named Sarah illustrates the point. Born with a congenital indifference to pain, she often injures herself without realizing it. As a result, her body is scarred by burns, cuts, scrapes, and bruises (Restak, 1988).

When asked by his dentist, "Where does it hurt?" philosopher Bertrand Russell replied: "In my mind, of course."

Pain is a subjective, emotionally charged sensation. No single stimulus triggers pain the way that light does vision, no nerve endings in the skin are specially dedicated to pain over other sensations, and people with similar injuries often experience different degrees of pain. Clearly, the conditions that lead us to report pain include not only the threat of bodily harm but also culture, personality, expectations, and other factors. Theories of pain must take all of these factors into account (Fernandez & Turk, 1992; Kruger, 1996).

In the 1996 Olympics, gymnast Kerri Strug fell hard and sprained her ankle on a vault. Strug was in intense pain, but she managed to block it from her mind, focus on her second jump, and land it perfectly on one foot—clinching the first-ever gold medal for the U.S. women's gymnastic team.

Gate-Control Theory If you have a sore leg muscle or if you scrape your knee, nerve endings in the skin send messages to the spinal cord through one of two types of nerve fibers. Dull, chronic aches and pains—as in a sore muscle—are carried to the spinal cord by "slow" thin nerve fibers that also respond to nonpainful touch. Sharp, acute, piercing sensations—as when you scrape your knee—are relayed through "fast" myelinated fibers. In short, an express lane to the spinal cord is reserved for acute, emergencylike sensations. But how are these signals then sent from the spinal cord to the brain? And can they be blocked when the pain is too intense to bear?

In answer to these questions, Ronald Melzack and Patrick Wall (1965, 1982) proposed the **gate-control theory** of pain. According to this theory, the nervous system can process only a limited number of sensory signals at once. When the system is full, a neural "gate" in the spinal cord either blocks or allows the upward passage of additional signals to the brain (the gate is not an actual structure but a pattern of inhibitory neural activity). Research shows that although Melzack and Wall were wrong about the physiological details of their theory, they were generally right about the key point: that pain signals to the brain can be blocked (Humphries et al., 1996; Jessell & Kelly, 1991).

This theory has a valuable practical implication: that you can partially shut the gate on pain by creating competing sensations. If you fall and hurt your knee, rubbing it hard will send new impulses into the spinal cord—and inhibit other pain signals. That's one reason it often helps to put ice on a bruise or to scratch the skin near a mosquito bite. For chronic pain, such interventions as deep massage, electrical stimulation, and acupuncture may provide temporary relief in the same way. It seems paradoxical, but as the theory correctly suggests, you can ease the pain by causing additional pain.

gate-control theory The theory that the spinal cord contains a neurological "gate" that blocks pain signals from the brain when flooded by competing signals.

What's nice about gate-control theory is the idea that our sensory system enables us to partially regulate how much pain we have to endure. To further help matters, our bodies send in reinforcements in the form of *endorphins*, neurotransmitters that are distributed throughout the central nervous system and are released in response to pain or discomfort (see Chapter 2). Studies show that endorphin-rich areas are also involved in the "gating" of pain signals—and that pain can be reduced by electrically stimulating these areas (Watkins & Mayer, 1982; Barbaro, 1988).

Psychological Control One psychological approach people often use is to block the pain from awareness. Just try not to think about it, okay? This advice sounds great, but beware: The strategy can backfire. Research shows that the more we try to suppress a particular thought, the more readily that thought pops to mind. Try not to think about the itch you're not supposed to scratch, and the harder you try, the less likely you are to succeed (Wegner, 1989).

Fortunately, there's a happy solution: focused self-distraction (McCaul & Malott, 1984). In a study of pain tolerance, Delia Cioffi and James Holloway (1993) had subjects put one hand into a bucket of ice-cold water and keep it there until they could no longer bear it. One group was instructed to avoid thinking about the sensations in the hand (suppression), while a second group was told to form a vivid mental picture of their room at home (distraction). Regardless of which strategy was used, most subjects kept their hand in the water for a little over two minutes. Afterward, however, subjects who had coped through suppression were slower to recover from the pain than those who had used distraction. To manage the effects of intense physical discomfort, you'd do better to focus on something specific ("think about the layout of your room") than try to suppress the thought ("don't think about the ice-cold water"). In prepared-childbirth classes, women are encouraged to cope with labor pains by staring at a "focal point" (it could be a key chain, a wall hanging, a door knob, or anything else) and concentrating on special breathing techniques. As we'll see in Chapter 4, hypnosis can also be used to combat pain, in part through a refocusing of attention. Mind over sensation.

Fencing requires quickness, agility, and the coordination of movements that is provided by the kinesthetic system.

Coordination

The five traditional senses and their subdivisions are vital adaptive mechanisms, but by themselves they do not enable us to regulate sensory input through movement. To bend, lean, stretch, climb, turn the head, maintain an upright posture, and run from danger, we need to sense the parts of our bodies as well as our orientation in space. The **kinesthetic system** monitors the positions of various body parts in relation to each other. Just as vision comes to us through sensory receptors in the eye, coordination of movement is provided by receptors in the joints, tendons, and muscles. These receptors are linked to motor areas of the brain. Without this system, an acrobat could not turn somersaults and cartwheels. Nor could gymnasts, dancers, and athletes perform their feats of bodily magic. Nor, for that matter, could you and I walk upright, deliver a firm handshake, aim food into our mouths, or touch our noses with the tip of the index finger.

kinesthetic system The structures distributed throughout the body that give us a sense of position and movement of body parts.

vestibular system The inner ear and brain structures that give us a sense of equilibrium.

A related sensory mechanism is provided by the **vestibular system**, which monitors head tilt and location in space. Situated in the inner ear, this system has two parts: (1) the *semicircular canals*, three fluid-filled tubes that are set at right angles to one another, and (2) two *vestibular sacs*, which are also filled with fluid. Whenever you move about, the movement rotates and tilts your head, causing the fluid to slosh back and forth, which pushes tiny hair cells. In turn, these hair cells send impulses to the cerebellum, which signals from moment to moment whether you are sitting, lying down, or standing on your head. The vestibular system provides us with the sense of equilibrium, or balance. But sometimes this delicate sense is disrupted by an excess of fluid or by certain types of motion. The result may be car sickness, sea sickness, or the dizzying aftereffects of twirling in circles (Howard, 1986).

Sensation: Keeping the Signals Straight

In a world filled with lights and colors, voices and musical tones, smells and tastes, and feelings of cold, warmth, pressure, pain, and other sensations, our sensory ability seems marvelously adaptive. How do we bring in so much information without becoming overwhelmed? With neural impulses flooding the brain from an array of different receptors throughout the body, it's amazing that we don't get our signals crossed. Why is it that we see light and hear sound rather than the other way around?

In a very rare condition known as **synesthesia** ("joining the senses"), some people say they experience sensory "crossovers"—and thus report that bright lights are loud, that the sound of a jazz trumpet is hot, that colors can be felt through touch, or that they can "enjoy the sweet smell of purple" or "taste the sound of raindrops" (Stein & Meredith, 1993). As described in Richard Cytowic's (1993) *The Man Who Tasted Shapes*, a number of fascinating cases have been reported over the years. Recent studies indicate that the condition is found in only 1 out of 2,000 people—and that most are women (Baron-Cohen et al., 1996). Can the self-reports of those claiming to have synesthesia be trusted? Although there is reason to be skeptical, two recent studies provide intriguing evidence. In one study, nine women with word-color synesthesia and nine controls were asked to report on the color sensations triggered by 130 letters, words, and phrases. When retested one year later, without warning, the synesthetic women reported the identical sensations 92 percent of the time—compared to only 38 percent in the control group. In a second study, six synesthetic women and six controls listened to words while blindfolded. PET scans revealed that this auditory stimulation activated the language areas of the brain in both groups. But among the synesthetic women, it also activated certain areas of the *visual* cortex (Paulesu et al., 1995).

As a general rule, our sensory systems do not cross. After all, different receptors are sensitive only to certain types of energy and stimulate only certain nerve pathways to the brain. Rods are responsive to light, not sound, and they transmit impulses through the optic nerve, not the auditory nerve. There may be some exceptions—as when pressing on a closed eyelid stimulates the optic nerve and causes you to "see" a flash of light—but each sensory system operates independent of the others (Martin, 1991).

There are two other aspects of sensation that enable us to respond to volumes of information without confusion. First, all of our sensory systems are designed to detect novelty, contrast, and change—not sameness. After constant exposure to a stimulus, sensation fades. This decline in sensitivity is known as **sensory adaptation**. We saw earlier that the eyes gradually adapt to bright light and darkness. The same is true of the other senses. After a while, you simply get used to the new contact lenses in your eyes, the new watchband on your wrist, the noise level at work, or the coldness of winter. To those sensitive to the musty odor that often pervades the hallway of apartment buildings, it is comforting to know that people also adjust to

synesthesia A rare condition in which stimulation in one sensory modality triggers sensations in another sensory modality.

sensory adaptation A decline in sensitivity to a stimulus as a result of constant exposure.

chronic odors (Dalton & Wysocki, 1996). By adapting to repeated stimulation, you are free to detect important changes in the environment.

A second adaptive mechanism is selective attention. As we will discover in Chapter 4, people can choose to focus on some sensory input and block out the rest. This selective attention enables us to pick out a face or a voice in a crowded room or to find distractions from pain and discomfort. Parents thus can hear their baby cry over the sounds of a TV, traders on the floor of the stock exchange can hear orders to buy and sell amid all the noise, and commuters in a city can spot yellow cabs in the street through all the commotion of rush-hour traffic. People are not passive sensation-recording devices. We have a way of "zooming in" on sensations that are personally important.

Perception

In what ways is perception an active mental process? How do we manage to identify objects despite apparent changes in their size, shape, and other features? How do we perceive depth in three-dimensional space? Are these skills inborn or learned from experience? And why, with all our impressive abilities, do we fall prey to perceptual illusions?

Our sensory systems convert physical energy from a multitude of sources into neural signals that are transmitted to the brain. But we do not see inverted retinal images, hear the bending and swaying of hair cells in the cochlea, or smell the absorption of odorant molecules in the nose. These and other sensations must be further processed to make sense. Perception is not a mere "copying" process, and the brain does more than just serve as a sensory Xerox machine. As perceivers, we must select, organize, and interpret input from the world in ways that are adaptive. Putting the sensory pieces together is a "constructive" mental process.

Figure 3.20 Reversible figures What do you see—a young woman or an older woman? Visual input can be perceived in different ways.

To illustrate this point, look at the picture in Figure 3.20. What do you see? When I first saw it, I didn't hesitate to say it was an elegant young woman. Then I read the caption, which revealed that the picture is a **reversible figure** that could also be seen as an "old hag." Huh? I stared and stared, but I just could not see it. All of a sudden, I did a double take. There it was! The lines and shading had not changed, yet now I saw the woman's chin as a nose. I took another look a few minutes later, and once again all I could see was a young woman. The point is, visual input can be processed in different ways. The sensation may be the same, but the perception can vary (see also Figure 3.21).

When Virgil's eyesight was restored at the age of fifty, he was able to detect lights, shadows, colors, shapes, and textures, but he could not separate one figure from another or identify common objects just by looking at them. In busy settings such as a supermarket, he was so overwhelmed by sensory information that "everything ran together." In this section, we examine the ways in which the brain organizes and interprets sensory input. As in much of the research, we will focus on visual perception.

Perceptual Organization

reversible figure A drawing that one can perceive in different ways by reversing figure and ground.

In 1912, Max Wertheimer discovered that people perceive two stationary lights flashing in rapid succession as a single light moving back and forth. This illusion of apparent motion paved the way for **Gestalt psychology**—a school of thought arising in Germany that was founded on the premise that the whole (perception) is greater than the sum of its parts (sensation). The word *gestalt* is German for "pattern" or "whole," and Gestalt psychologists believed that humans have an inborn tendency to construct meaningful perceptions from fragments of sensory input. A classic example is the way people listen to music. A melody has a form that is different from the individual notes that make it up. So if the melody is transposed to another key, even if that means changing every note, listeners would still recognize the music because the form of the melody would be the same. The perception of music is based on a gestalt, not on a particular set of notes (Koffka, 1935; Kohler, 1947; Rock & Palmer, 1990).

Figure 3.21 "It may take a magician to pull a rabbit out of a hat, but we all possess sufficient magic to pull a duck out of a rabbit." (Shepard, 1990).

Figure and Ground The first gestalt principle of perceptual organization is that people automatically focus on some objects in the perceptual field to the exclusion of others. What we focus on is called the *figure*. Everything else fades into the *ground*. A teacher in front of a blackboard, an airplane in the sky, the printed black words on this page, the neon light that burns bright on a dark highway, a scream in the night, and the lead singer's voice in a rock band—all are common figures and grounds. Gestalt psychologists were quick to point out that these perceptions are in the eyes of the beholder—but also that people are prone to "figurize" objects that are novel, intense, loud, and moving rather than still. As in the reversible figure shown earlier, however, the image in Figure 3.22 shows that you can mentally flip-flop the figure and ground from one moment to the next. It's as if each of us is shining a spotlight on a portion of the sensory field—and can move that spotlight if necessary.

Figure 3.22 Figure and ground Depending on whether you see the white or black areas as figural, this drawing may be perceived as a vase or as two people facing each other.

Gestalt Laws of Grouping Another principle of perceptual organization is that we tend to group collections of shapes, sizes, colors, and other features into perceptual wholes. These natural grouping tendencies are not arbitrary; on the contrary, they follow rules like those shown in Figure 3.23. The Gestalt psychologists maintained that these tendencies are inborn, and they may have been right. Research shows that even infants "group" stimulus objects in the predicted ways (Kellman & Spelke, 1983; Quinn et al., 1993; Van Giffen & Haith, 1984). These laws of grouping are:

- *Proximity.* The closer objects are to one another, the more likely they are to be perceived as a unit. The lines in Figure 3.23(A) are thus seen as rows rather than as columns because they are nearer to one another horizontally than vertically.
- *Similarity.* Objects that are similar in shape, size, color, or any other feature tend to be grouped together. The dots in Figure 3.23(B) form perceptual columns rather than rows because of similarities in color.
- *Continuity.* People perceive the contours of straight and curved lines as continuous flowing patterns. In Figure 3.23(C), we see points 1 and 2 as belonging to one line, and points 3 and 4 as belonging to another. The same pattern could be seen as two **V** shapes, but instead we perceive two smooth lines that form a cross in the center.
- *Closure.* When there are gaps in a pattern that resembles a familiar form, as in Figure 3.23(D), people mentally "close" the gaps and perceive the object as a whole. This tendency enables us to recognize imperfect representations in hand drawings, written material, and so on.
- *Common fate.* Extending upon the static grouping principles of proximity and similarity, we find that objects moving together in the same direction, or

Gestalt psychology A school of thought rooted in the idea that the whole (perception) is greater than the sum of its parts (sensation).

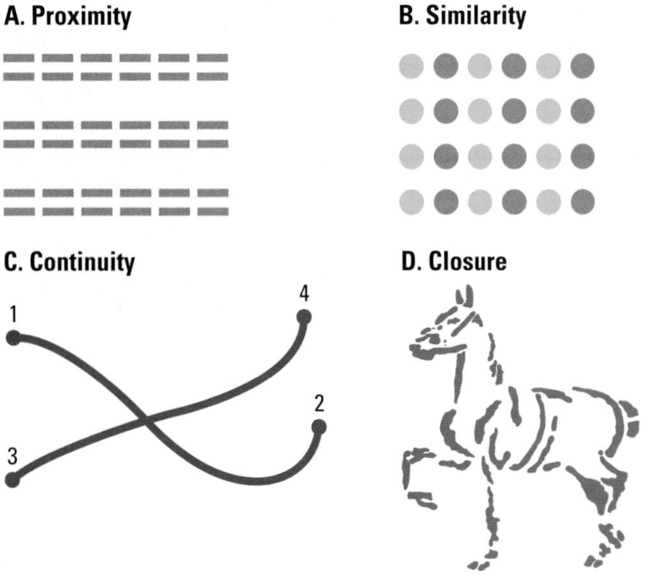

Figure 3.23 Gestalt laws of grouping

sharing a "common fate," are perceived as belonging to a single group. Examples include marching bands, schools of fish, flocks of birds, and sports fans sending the "wave" around a stadium.

The principles of Gestalt psychology describe how people transform raw visual input—lights, shadows, lines, points, shapes, and colors—into meaningful displays. Indeed, the same principles explain the confusion that results when figures are concealed from view through camouflage. But what happens to our perception of an object when its retinal image changes from one moment to the next? How do we know that objects have depth when the images projected on the retina are flat and two-dimensional? How are interpretations of input influenced by characteristics of the perceiver? As we'll see, people are highly adept, yet often fooled, by disparities between sensation and perception.

Perceptual Constancies

Unlike a camera or microphone stationed on a tripod, the human perceiver is active and mobile. And unlike the portrait or landscape hanging on a wall, many of the objects of our perception are likewise active and mobile. As the perceiver and perceived move about, the image projected on the retina may change in size, shape, brightness, color, and other properties. But this is not a problem. Thanks to perceptual constancies, perceptions remain stable despite radical changes in sensory input (Rock, 1997).

While surfing the Internet, I encountered this odd survey question: "Is a zebra a white horse with black stripes or a black horse with white stripes?" What would you say? Neither color is figural in gestalt terms, and survey responses were split.

Size Constancy

Size constancy is the tendency to view an object as constant despite changes in the size of its image on the retina. You've noticed this phenomenon countless times. You'll be watching from the ground as an airplane pokes its nose through a cloud to descend for a landing. Or a friend will walk away and eventually fade into the distance. Visualize these moving pictures. As the plane approaches, its image looms larger and larger. And as your friend walks away, the image gets smaller. If you didn't know better, the changing sensations might lead you to think that the airplane was growing and that your friend was shrinking right before your eyes.

But we do know better—for two reasons. One has to do with experience and familiarity. You know that airplanes are bigger than people and that people are bigger than insects, so your perceptions remain stable despite variations in retinal image size. Distance cues provide a second source of information. As objects move around in space, we perceive the change in distance and adjust our size perceptions accordingly. In other words, we know that the closer an object is, the larger the image it casts on the retina, so we make the adjustment.

size constancy The tendency to view an object as constant in size despite changes in the size of the retinal image.

This skill is so basic that it can be observed in infants, shortly after birth. Alan Slater and his colleagues (1990) showed newborns in a maternity ward a large or small black-and-white block. After they became familiarized to it, they were shown either the same block at a different distance or a different-sized (larger or smaller) block. Did the babies recognize the familiar block when distance was varied? Infants are visually attracted to novel objects, so the researchers recorded their eye movements as the blocks were shown. The result: They spent more time looking at a new block than at an old block presented at a different distance. Through size constancy, they "recognized" the original blocks despite the change in distance.

The capacity for size constancy may be present in infancy, but cultural and environmental experiences also play a role. In 1961, anthropologist Colin Turnbull studied Pygmies who lived in a densely wooded central African forest. At one point, he took a native named Kenge for a Jeep ride out of the forest. It was Kenge's first trip away from home—and he was disoriented. Standing on a mountain overlooking miles of open plain, Kenge saw buffaloes and thought they were insects. Then

By blending into the lily, this white-lipped green tree frog is concealed from predators by a natural form of camouflage.

Note how these Buddhist monks in Thailand appear to be the same size even though the images they project on your retina shrink with distance. Belgian artist René Magritte's The Human Condition *(1933) depicts an ambiguous boundary between reality and illusion created by the lack of contrast. (Copyright 1998 C. Herscovici, Brussels/Artists Rights Society (ARS), New York. Magritte, Rene (Belgian, 1898–1967), "La condition humaine," 1933, Canvas/oil on canvas, 1.000 x .810 x .016 (39-3/8 x 31-7/8 x 5/8), Copyright 1997 Board of Trustees, National Gallery of Art, Washington, Gift of the Collectors Committee, 1933.)*

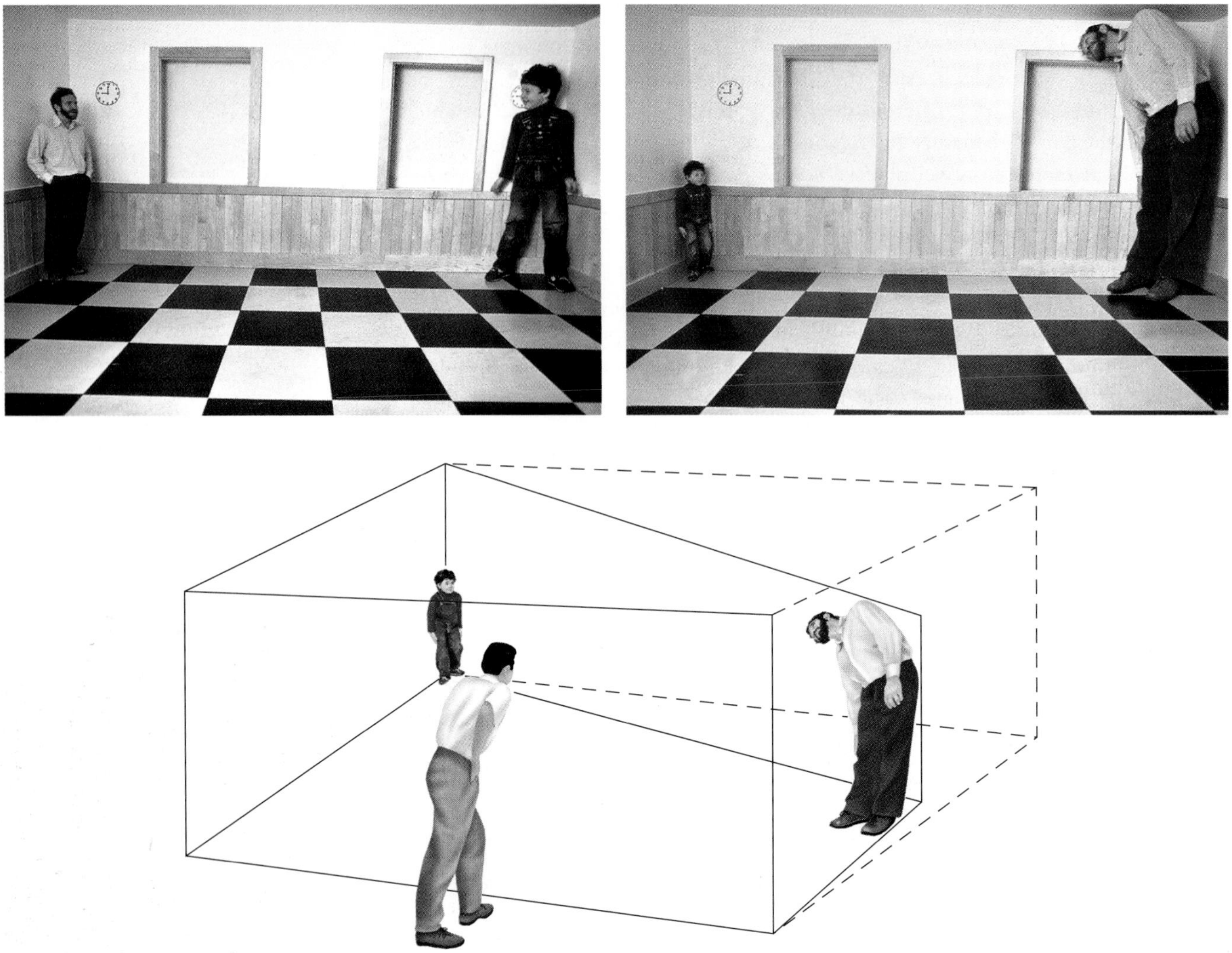

Figure 3.24 The Ames room Adelbert Ames designed this room to distort perceptions of size. The room seems rectangular, which makes the two figures look equally distant. But the right corner is closer to the peephole (and has a lower ceiling) than the left. The person on the right is thus perceived as bigger because distance cues are masked.

he saw a fishing boat in the middle of a lake and thought it was a floating piece of wood. The problem? Turnbull came to realize that "in the forest the range of vision is so limited that there is no great need to make an automatic allowance for distance when judging size" (1961, p. 252). As for the rest of us, the perceived link between size and distance makes us vulnerable to some striking illusions (see Figure 3.24).

shape constancy The tendency to see an object as retaining its form despite changes in orientation.

Shape Constancy Also important is **shape constancy**, the tendency to see an object as retaining its form despite changes in its orientation. Take a coin, hold it up at eye level so that the "head" side faces you, and it will reveal a circular appearance. Rotate it 45 degrees, and it casts an elliptical, egg-shape image on the retina. Turn it another 45 degrees, and it looks like a straight line. The changes in orientation are dramatic, yet you still see the coin as a flat, circular object (see Figure 3.25). As with size, shape constancy is inborn. But it may also require visual experience. Indeed, you may recall that Virgil found it difficult to recognize moving objects—including his own pet dog—when seen from another angle of view (Sacks, 1995).

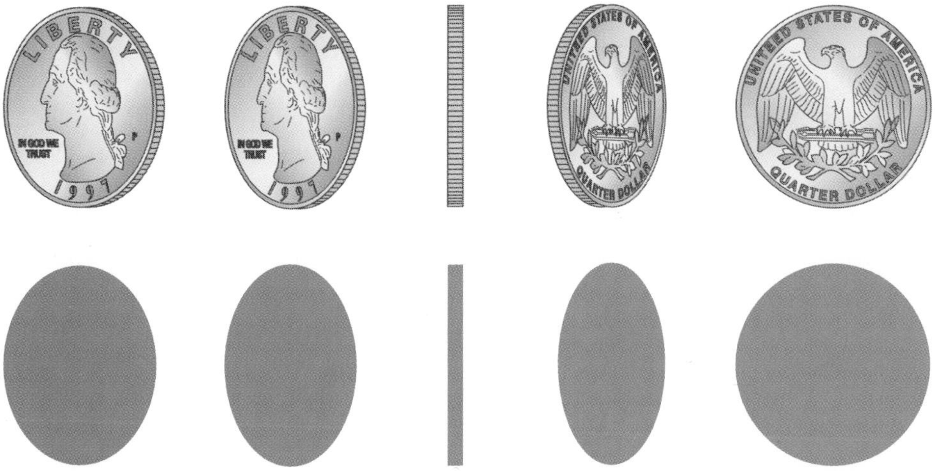

Figure 3.25 Shape constancy People see objects as retaining their form despite changes in their orientation.

Depth and Dimension

Perceptual constancies enable us to identify objects despite changes in sensory input. But there's another problem: How do we know that objects in three-dimensional space have depth, and how do we perceive distance when images projected on each retina are flat and two-dimensional? Two types of information are used in **depth perception:** binocular cues and monocular cues.

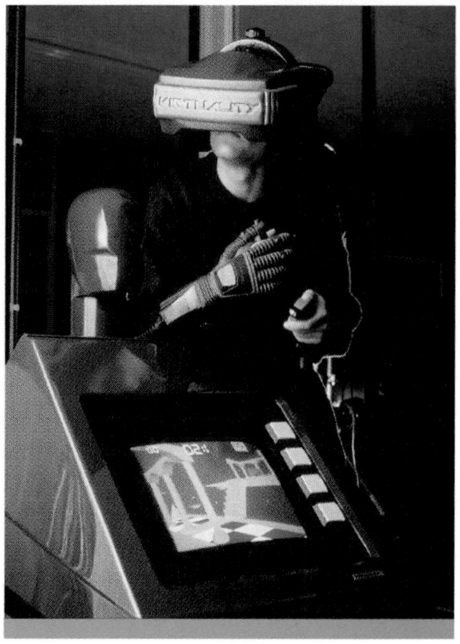

In simulating reality, virtual reality headsets are most realistic at short distances when they display separate but overlapping images to each eye.

depth perception The use of visual cues to estimate the depth and distance of objects.

convergence A binocular cue for depth perception involving the turning inward of the eyes as an object gets closer.

binocular disparity A binocular cue for depth perception whereby the closer an object is to a perceiver, the more different the image is in each retina.

Binocular Depth Cues

Deer, sheep, and other prey have eyes on the sides of their heads so they can use peripheral vision to see predators sneaking up from behind. By contrast, lions, owls, and other predators have eyes squarely at the front of their heads, an arrangement that maximizes depth perception and enables them to track their prey. Look into the mirror, and you'll see that human eyes are the eyes of a predator. Thus, we are provided with binocular (two-eyed) vision, which in turn allows us to use two binocular depth cues: convergence and binocular disparity.

Convergence refers to the fact that the eyes turn in toward the nose or "converge" as an object gets closer, and move outward or "diverge" to focus on objects farther away. Hold your finger up at arm's length and slowly move it toward your nose. As you refocus, you can actually feel your eye muscles contracting. This signals the brain about the object's distance from the eyes. The second cue is **binocular disparity**. With our eyes set about $2\frac{1}{2}$ inches apart on the face, each retina receives a slightly different image of the world. To demonstrate, hold your finger about 4 inches from your nose and shut your right eye. Then shut only your left eye and look at the finger. Right. Left. As you switch back and forth, you'll see that each eye picks up the image from a slightly different vantage point. Now hold up your finger farther away, say at arm's length, and repeat the routine. This time you'll see less image shifting. The reason: Binocular disparity decreases with distance. Special neurons located in the visual cortex use this retinal information to "calculate" depth, distance, and dimensionality (Mustillo, 1985).

If two eyes combine to give us a three-dimensional look at the world, can flat pictures do the same? In the nineteenth century, British physicist Charles Wheatstone invented the first stereoscope—an optical instrument that brought two-dimensional pictures to life. To create the illusion, Wheatstone photographed a scene twice, using

Texture gradient.

Linear perspective.

two cameras spaced inches apart. He then mounted both pictures side by side on the device, using mirrors to overlap the images. This technique underlies the "Viewmaster"—a toy that shows 3-D scenes in double-view cardboard slides. It is also now being used in the development of virtual reality (VR) systems in which simulated environments are projected on a screen mounted inside a helmet. A head tracker on the top of the helmet and computerized gloves sense head and body movements and signal the computer generating the image to change the scene according to the viewer's changing position. The U.S. military is using VR to train fighter pilots and ground troops. Of relevance to depth perception, studies conducted at the Army Research Institute have shown that the experience feels most realistic at short distances when the VR displays stereoscopic images—that is, separate but overlapping images to each eye.

Monocular Depth Cues Binocular depth cues are useful at short distances. But for objects that are farther away, convergence and binocular disparity are uninformative. At such times, we can utilize **monocular depth cues**, which enable us to perceive depth, quite literally with one eye closed. These are cues that many artists use to bring a flat canvas to life. What are they? Look at the pictures accompanying each description, and see for yourself.

- *Relative image size.* We saw earlier that as the distance of an object increases, the size of its retinal image shrinks—and vice versa. Object size can thus be used to judge depth.
- *Texture gradient.* As a collection of objects recedes into the horizon, they appear to be spaced more closely together, which makes the surface texture appear to become denser.
- *Linear perspective.* With distance, the parallel contours of highways, rivers, railroad tracks, and other rowlike structures perceptually converge—and eventually reach a vanishing point. The more the lines converge, the greater the perceived distance.
- *Interposition.* As most objects are not transparent, those nearer to us will partly or completely block our view of more distant objects. This overlap provides a quick and easy way to judge relative distances.
- *Atmospheric perspective.* The air contains a haze of dust particles and moisture that blurs images at a distance. This blurring, or atmospheric perspective, makes duller and less detailed objects appear farther away.
- *Relative elevation.* Below the horizon line, objects that are lower in our field of vision are seen as nearer than those that are higher. Above the horizon line, however, objects that are lower are perceived as farther away.
- *Motion parallax.* As we move forward or backward, objects in the environment appear to move as well (anyone who has looked out the window of a

monocular depth cues Distance cues, such as linear perspective, that enable us to perceive depth with one eye.

moving car knows this). But the nature of this perceived movement depends on distance. Compared to what we're gazing at, closer objects seem to speed by in the opposite direction, while remote objects appear to move more slowly and in the same direction. Relative distances are thus revealed by the speed and direction of apparent movement (see Figure 3.26).

Familiarity. Experience provides familiar reference points for judging distance. We know the approximate size of houses, people, cars, and other objects, and this knowledge helps us judge their distance. In fact, the presence of a familiar object in a scene helps us judge the sizes and distances of everything around it.

Interposition.

Atmospheric perspective.

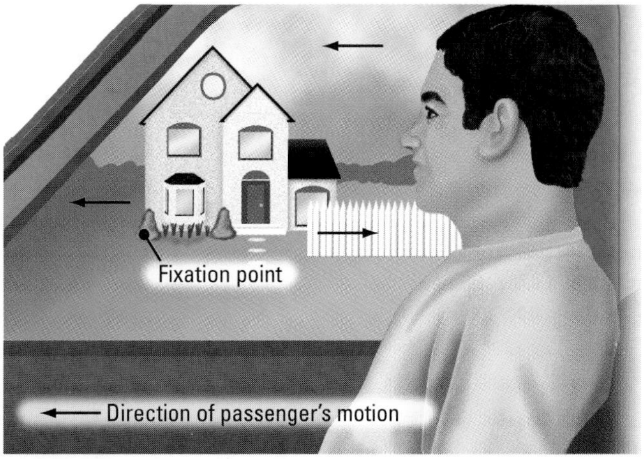

Figure 3.26 Motion parallax

Origins of Depth Perception With normal vision, interpreting the layout of objects in an environment is easy and requires no conscious thought or effort. Why is depth perception so easy? Clearly, a rich array of depth cues are available to one or both eyes—especially when we're moving about (Gibson, 1979). But how do we know how to interpret these cues? Assuming you're not a visual artist or mathematician, how do you effortlessly interpret angles of convergence, linear perspective, texture gradients, relative elevations, and other "geometric" types of information? How do you know that railroad tracks are parallel even though they seem to converge? You may think this is an odd question because, well, "you just know." But were you born with these skills, or did you learn them from experience?

Perceptual Experience The average person has an enormous amount of experience with depth perception. Is this experience necessary? Case studies of blind people who had their eyesight surgically restored during adulthood suggest that experience is critical to depth perception. Sacks (1995) observed that Virgil sometimes stepped over shadows so he would not trip or failed to step up on a staircase that, for all he knew, was a flat surface consisting of parallel and crossing lines. Richard Gregory (1990) studied a similar patient by the name of S.B. and described his perception of depth as "peculiar." At one point, S.B. thought he could touch the ground below his hospital window with his feet—even though his window was on the fourth floor.

Cross-cultural evidence also highlights the importance of perceptual experience and learning. We saw earlier that when a Pygmy named Kenge was taken from his dense forest home to the open plain, he saw distant buffaloes as insects and a large boat as a floating log. And as we saw at the start of this chapter, people lacking exposure to three-dimensional representations in artwork have difficulty judging relative distance from pictures (Deregowski, 1989).

Figure 3.27 **The visual cliff** This apparatus is used to test depth perception in infants and animals.

Depth Perception as Inborn Experience may seem necessary, but studies of infants suggest otherwise. Infants cannot tell us what they see, so Eleanor Gibson and Richard Walk (1960) devised the **visual cliff,** a clever nonverbal test of depth perception. As shown in Figure 3.27, the apparatus consists of a glass-covered table top, with a shallow one-inch drop on one end and a steep "cliff" on the other end. Infants six to fourteen months of age were placed in the middle of the table, and their mothers tried to lure them into crawling to one side or the other. The entire surface was covered by sturdy transparent glass, so there was no real danger. The result: Six month-old babies would crawl to their mothers at the shallow end. But despite all the calling, clapping, waving, and encouragement, most did not crawl out over the cliff. Clearly, they had perceived the steepness of the drop.

Does the visual cliff experiment prove that depth perception is innate? Not necessarily, argued critics. Perceptual learning begins at birth, so by the tender age of six months an infant has already experienced over a thousand waking hours—and has had lots of perceptual practice. What about younger babies? They may not be able to crawl, but their bodies can communicate to an astute researcher. Accordingly, Joseph Campos and his colleagues (1970) moved two-month-old infants from one side of the glass top to the other and found that the infants exhibited a change in heart rate when placed over the deep side but not over the shallow side. These infants were too young to fear the situation as you and I would, but they "noticed" the difference. Additional studies have shown that most newborn lambs, chicks, ducklings, pigs, cats, rats, and other animals that can walk the day they're born also avoid the deep end of the visual cliff (Walk, 1981).

Is depth perception innate or is it the product of visual experience? As the pieces of the puzzle have come together, it seems that both factors are at work. Using binocular cues—and, later, monocular cues—infants are capable of perceiving depth and dimension. But early experience is necessary for this skill to emerge. Thus, newborn rats and cats that are initially reared in a dark laboratory step over the visual cliff when first tested—and formerly blind humans have trouble making judgments of depth when their eyesight is surgically restored. As the saying goes, you have to "use it or lose it."

visual cliff An apparatus used to test depth perception in infants and animals.

perceptual set The effects of prior experience and expectations on interpretations of sensory input.

Perceptual Set

At any given moment, your interpretation of sensory input can be influenced by prior experiences and expectations, which create a **perceptual set.** To illustrate, look

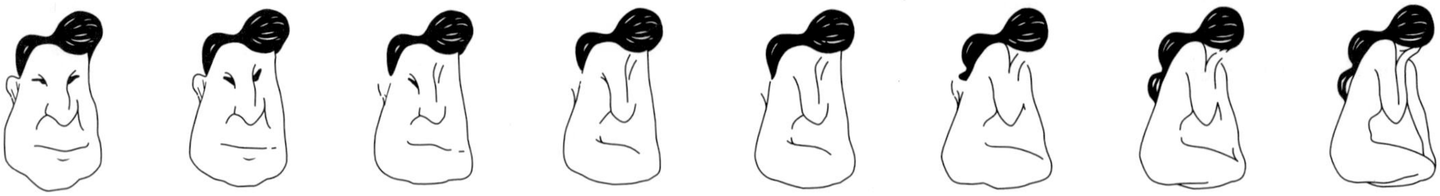

Figure 3.28 **Perceptual set** What you see in the middle drawings depends on the order in which you look at the pictures. Subjects who start at the far left see the drawings in the middle as a man's face; those who start at the far right see a woman's figure.

at Figure 3.28. The middle drawings in this series are ambiguous: They can be seen as either a man's face or the figure of a kneeling young woman. Which do you see? It turns out that interpretations are biased by prior experience. Subjects who were first shown the drawing on the far left saw the middle pictures as a man's face, while those who were first shown the drawing on the far right saw the same pictures as a kneeling woman (Fisher, 1968). This finding highlights an important point about perception: At times, we see what we expect to see.

Perceptual sets are established not only by past experience but also by the context in which a stimulus is perceived. In Figure 3.29, for example, the same physical pattern of black and white is used for the letter *B* as for the number *13*. Look closely and you'll see that the *B* and *13* are physically identical. Which of the two you "see" thus depends on whether the surrounding context consists of letters or numbers. The same phenomenon can influence our perceptions of others. In one study, for example, subjects were shown photographs of people, each with neutral expressions on the face. When the target person was supposedly being threatened by a vicious dog at the time, subjects saw his or her facial expression as fearful; when told that he or she had just won money in a TV game show, subjects interpreted the very *same* expression as a sign of happiness (Trope, 1986).

Sometimes perception is influenced not only by what we *expect* to see but by what we *want* to see.

By leading us to see what we expect to see, perceptual sets can lead us astray. Imagine that you're looking at a slide that is completely out of focus. Gradually, it is focused so that the image becomes less blurry. At each step, you're asked, "Can you recognize the picture?" The response you're likely to make is interesting. Subjects have more trouble identifying the picture if they watch the gradual focusing procedure than if they simply view the final image. In trying to interpret the initially blurry image, subjects exposed to gradual focusing formed perceptual sets that later interfered with their ability to "see straight" once presented with improved evidence (Bruner & Potter, 1964). Similarly, people are slower to identify common objects such as toothbrushes and fire hydrants when these objects are presented "out of context" (Biederman, 1987).

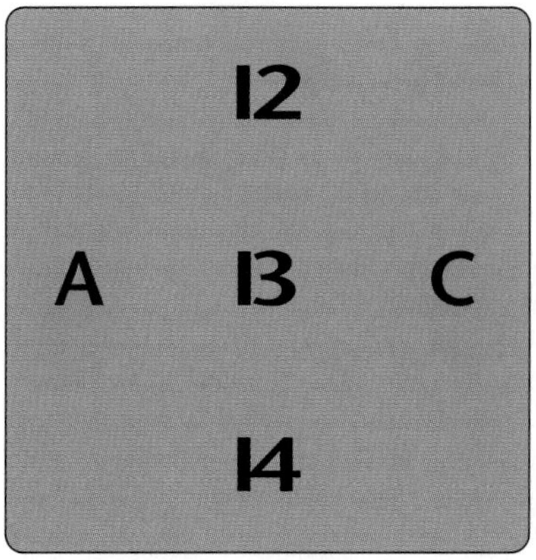

Figure 3.29 Context effects Indicating the effects of context on perception, people see the middle item as *B* or *13* depending on whether it is surrounded by letters or numbers.

The World of Illusions

The brain's capacity to transform sensations into accurate perceptions of reality is impressive. Without conscious thought, effort, or instruction, we often manage to perceive size, shape, depth, and other properties in an accurate manner. But the mind also plays tricks on us. Magicians, ventriloquists, and artists count on it. So do perception psychologists. Over the years, researchers have learned a good deal about how people perceive the world by probing the systematic ways in which we *mis*perceive the world. **Perceptual illusions** are all around us (Block & Yuker, 1989; Wade, 1990). A few examples illustrate the point.

> *"The eye, or really the mind behind the eye, can be tricked into interpretive flips or mental somersaults."*
>
> — ROGER N. SHEPARD

A puddle glistens on the highway in front of you. It seems about a mile away. But as you drive, the road stays dry and the wet spot remains out of

perceptual illusions Patterns of sensory input that give rise to misperceptions.

Figure 3.30 The horizontal-vertical illusion The horizontal-vertical illusion can be seen in the St. Louis Gateway Arch and in the perpendicular lines drawn to the right.

reach. There is no puddle, of course, just a "mirage"—an illusion caused by a layer of hot air sitting below cooler air and casting a reflection from the sky onto the road.

- Baseball players claim that many pitchers throw a "rising fastball." The laws of physics state that this is impossible. So why do players insist that they can see the fastball rise? Apparently, it's an illusion that occurs when the batter underestimates the speed of a fast pitch (Bahill & Karnavas, 1993).
- If you've ever driven through St. Louis, then you've seen the towering Gateway Arch. Look at Figure 3.30. Is the arch taller than it is wide? Most people say *yes*—and this illustrates the common "horizontal-vertical illusion." In fact, the height and width of the Gateway Arch are both 630 feet.

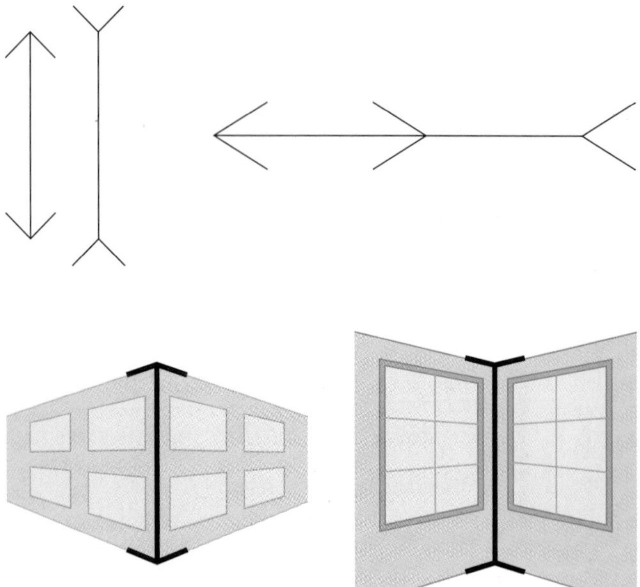

Figure 3.31 The Müller-Lyer illusion

What's interesting about perceptual illusions is that they often stem from the overapplication of rules that normally serve us well. Look at the two vertical lines with the arrowed tips in Figure 3.31. Which is longer? Most people see the line on the right as slightly longer than the one on the left. Measure them, however, and you'll see that they are of the same length. Now compare the two sides of the horizontal line. Again, which is longer? Most people see these lines as equal. Wrong. In this case, the line on the left is longer than the one on the right. As devised by Franz Müller-Lyer, in 1889, these comparisons illustrate the classic **Müller-Lyer illusion.**

Why is the Müller-Lyer illusion so compelling? There are several possible explanations (Nijhawan, 1991). One is that the arrowed tips trick us into overapplying linear-perspective depth cues and the principle of size constancy. As also shown in Figure 3.31, the vertical configuration on the left side resembles the near outside corner of a room or building, while that on the right resembles a far inside corner. Since both lines cast equal-size retinal images, we assume that the farther one must be larger. Part of the problem, then, is that people mistakenly apply a rational rule of three-dimensional depth perception—that distance decreases image size—to a flat two-dimensional figure (Gregory, 1990).

Look at the horizontal lines in Figure 3.32, and you'll see a second illusion. The tendency to view the horizontal line on top as longer than the one on the bottom is called the **Ponzo illusion.** Can you see why this misperception is so common? Think again about depth perception, and you may notice that the linear perspective that provides the context for these lines makes the top one seem farther away. As in the Müller-Lyer illusion, the two lines cast the same-size retinal image, so the one that seems more distant is perceived to be larger. In fact, the more depth-perception cues there are in the background, the stronger is the illusion (Leibowitz et al., 1969). Consistent with this explanation is the fact that people from certain African cultures who live in rural "noncarpentered" environments—without right angles, corners, squares, and hard edges—are less likely to be fooled by the Müller-Lyer and Ponzo illusions (Deregowski, 1989; Segall et al., 1966).

A third illusion that seems to stem from depth-related cues is the most spectacular but also the most puzzling. Have you ever noticed how a full moon looks larger when it's low on the horizon than when it's high in the sky? The moon is the moon, of course. It does not change in size or in its distance from the earth. So, what causes this **moon illusion**?

Throughout history, scholars have tried to understand this phenomenon. Then, in 1962, Lloyd Kaufman and Irvin Rock brought it to the attention of perception psychologists, stimulating numerous theories and explanations. Some psychologists claimed that the increased perceived size is caused by buildings, trees, and other

Müller-Lyer illusion An illusion in which the perceived length of a line is altered by the position of other lines that enclose it.

Ponzo illusion An illusion in which the perceived length of a line is affected by linear perspective cues.

moon illusion The tendency for people to see the moon as larger when it's low on the horizon than when it's overhead.

Figure 3.32 The Ponzo illusion

The Moon Illusion. *Viewed low over the San Francisco skyline* (right), *the moon seems larger than when it is seen higher in the sky* (left).

earth-bound depth cues that make the moon seem farther away and thus trick us into "seeing" a larger object. Indeed, if you peer at the low moon through a tube, apart from surrounding cues, it will appear smaller. But others have found that people sometimes perceive the horizon moon as closer, not more distant (Coren & Aks, 1990), that the illusion does not occur when the target object is a star instead of the moon (Reed & Krupinski, 1992), and that the illusion persists even when the moon is projected at different angles without depth cues, as in the total darkness of an indoor planetarium (Suzuki, 1991). To this day, the moon illusion remains a perceptual mystery (Hershenson, 1989).

Extrasensory Perception

Is it possible to perceive something in the absence of a physical stimulus? What is ESP, and what types of extrasensory powers do psychics claim to have? What is the evidence for and against these claims? And where do you stand: Are you a believer or a skeptic?

Every New Year's Eve, "psychics" make predictions for the year to come. From political fortunes to natural disasters, the soothsayers claim they can see the future the way you and I see the sun rise and set. Can they really? With varying degrees of accuracy, scientists make predictions all the time. Astronomers tell us when we'll see the next solar eclipse, economists forecast inflation rates, and meteorologists warn us about upcoming storms. But there's a difference between these forms of prediction and psychic fortune-telling. Scientists base their predictions on sensory input, whereas psychics claim to have **extrasensory perception**, or ESP—an ability to perceive in the absence of ordinary sensory information.

Psychologists as a group have long been skeptical, if not downright cynical, about these claims. Indeed, this entire chapter is dedicated to the proposition that perception is the product of *physical* energy received by *sensory* receptors and interpreted by the *brain*. Yet, as we've noted before, pollsters consistently find that more than half of all Americans believe in ESP. So what is the basis for this belief? Are there people who can read your mind, levitate or move objects without contact, have "out of body" experiences, communicate with ghosts, see the future in dreams, or identify serial killers for the police? In order to evaluate the evidence, we must first make some distinctions.

The Case for ESP

The claims vary far and wide, but **parapsychologists**—who study psychic phenomena through case studies and experiments—distinguish among three types of extrasensory power (Broughton, 1991). The first is telepathy, or mind-to-mind communication, an ability to receive thoughts transmitted by another person without the usual sensory contact. The second type is clairvoyance, the ability to perceive remote events via "extra" sensory channels or contact with another person. The third type is precognition, the ability to see future events, also without direct contact with another person. Whatever the details, these phenomena are all thought to involve perception without sensation (some psychics also claim to have telekinesis, the ability to move objects or influence events without material contact).

These are the claims. Why are there so many believers? And what's the evidence? According to Thomas Gilovich (1991), the reason so many people believe in ESP is that the evidence "seems" overwhelming. Stage magicians, TV psychics, paperbacks that make millions of dollars from tales of the occult, coincidences that seem to defy explanation, and the friend who has a premonition come true—all conspire to leave an impression that where there's smoke, there must be fire. So, where's the fire?

In the 1930s, Duke University professor J. B. Rhine sought for the first time to document ESP through rigorous laboratory experiments. Considered by many the founder of parapsychology, Rhine devised a special set of ESP cards, each designated by a distinct, easy-to-recall symbol on one side (see Figure 3.33). Subjects were asked to guess the symbol on each card, and the number of "hits" was compared to "chance" performance (for 25 cards, subjects can be expected by guesswork to make 5 correct responses). This procedure was used to test for telepathy (a "sender" looked at the cards and the subject tried to read his or her mind), clairvoyance (the cards were placed face down), and precognition (the subject predicted the sequence of cards before the deck was shuffled). In many hours of painstaking research, Rhine obtained close to 100,000 responses from various subjects. Then in 1934, he reported the results: using a 25-card deck, his subjects averaged 7.1 correct identifications—a statistically significant and large improvement over pure chance performance. The skeptics were baffled. Had they been too close-minded, like those who laughed at Galileo, Edison, and the Wright brothers, or like those who once used the term *impossible* to describe space travel and the splitting of the atom?

extrasensory perception (ESP) The alleged ability to perceive something without ordinary sensory information.

parapsychology The study of ESP and other claims that cannot be explained by existing principles of science.

Figure 3.33 ESP cards As devised by Rhine (1934), these five arbitrary symbols have been used in many hundreds of ESP experiments.

The Case against ESP

In many ways, Rhine's (1934) studies were like much of parapsychology's history—promising high points, inevitably followed by disappointment. Researchers scrutinized Rhine's methods and found that many subjects had been allowed to handle the cards, which made it possible to cheat; that the cards could be identified by warped edges, spots, and other physical marks; and that faint images of the symbols could be seen when held up to light. Worst of all, Rhine's most impressive subject could not replicate his performance for outside experimenters.

Over the years, hundreds more experiments were performed. Some provided what seemed to be clear and compelling "evidence" of psychic powers. But typically the findings obtained in one laboratory could not be reproduced in another. And often hoaxes were exposed. If you've ever watched a live stage psychic, you know how compelling the performance can be. Some mind readers have associates who circulate through a crowd before the show and spy on conversations, picking up personal information that can later be used. Another strategy is to use "multiple outs"—statements that apply to almost anyone ("sometimes you're shy, yet at other times you're outgoing"). A third strategy is the "one-ahead" ploy in which audience members submit questions in sealed envelopes to be "read" without opening. Secretly, the psychic opens one envelope and memorizes its contents. Then he or she begins the performance by holding up and "reading" a second envelope. In fact, the first remembered message is recited. He or she then opens the second envelope, supposedly to confirm the prediction, and uses its contents to "read" a third envelope. This procedure can be repeated indefinitely, with the psychic always one step ahead of the mystified audience.

Is this a UFO? Many people are quick to believe what they see with their own eyes. Look at the full picture on the next page, however, and you'll appreciate that things are not always as they seem.

It's important to realize that many parapsychologists are exacting in their methods and honorably motivated to seek the truth. But it's also important to realize that many so-called psychics are frauds who rely on magic and illusion. In 1974, physician Andrew Weil investigated an Israeli psychic named Uri Geller, who claimed that he could bend metal without touching it, start broken watches, and guess the contents of sealed envelopes. Apparently true to his word, Geller performed these remarkable feats and convinced Weil of his psychic powers. Then Weil met James Randi, a famous magician. Amazingly, Randi duplicated many of Geller's feats—through trickery. Illustrating the power of perceptual sets, Weil marveled at how the mind (in this case, his own) "sees what it expects to see." For his part, Randi (1980) offered $10,000 to anyone who could perform a single paranormal feat in his presence. Although the offer stands to this day, he has yet to part with his money (Yam, 1995).

The Continuing Controversy

In the book *Practical Intuition*, Laura Day (1996) claims that everyone is gifted with intuitive powers that would enable them to divine future events. Preferring the term "practicing intuitive" rather than "psychic," Day presents exercises that she says would enable all of us to bring out our innate capacities. For example, one exercise invites readers to guess which horse won a past race. How? Get centered. Record your thoughts for thirty seconds. Visualize colors, forms, and other images. Then examine the list of horses for connections. The book was an instant best-seller.

So what are we to conclude about extrasensory perception? Some forms of ESP, such as the ability to "will" the movement of objects, openly defy the laws of physics. But parapsychologists argue for the possibility that people can receive messages from others through a sensory medium that simply has yet to be identified—and they point to rigorous new studies as evidence of this phenomenon (Broughton, 1991). Most recently, Daryl Bem and Charles Honorton (1994) used the *ganzfield procedure* in which a "receiver" sits in a reclining chair in a soundproof chamber. A red floodlight is shined at the eyes, which are covered by ping-pong ball halves. Headphones placed over the ears play continuous white noise. In a separate room, a "sender" spends thirty minutes concentrating on a visual stimulus—a drawing, picture, or film. The receivers talk aloud about what they are thinking. Afterward, they are given four stimuli and asked to rate the extent to which each one matches their earlier thoughts. Despite their lack of access to sensory information, the receivers in these studies are reported to have achieved a 32 percent "hit" rate—which is statistically higher than the 25 percent expected by chance.

Do these new studies prove that ESP exists? It depends on who you ask. Some critics point out that the research methods are still flawed in important ways, so

These objects may look like spaceships, but they are actually lenticular (lens-shape) clouds. This picture was taken in Santos, Brazil.

they take a skeptical wait-and-see attitude (Hyman, 1994). They note that the history of ESP research is filled with initial demonstrations that later failed to replicate. Indeed, despite thousands of studies, there is no sound empirical support, nor is there a single individual who can demonstrate psychic powers to independent investigators (Marks, 1986). Chairing a committee that spent two years studying ESP for the U.S. Army, John Swets concluded that "the committee finds no scientific justification from research conducted over a period of 130 years for the existence of para-psychological phenomena" (Swets & Bjork, 1990). So, what are we to conclude? With several research teams now trying to replicate the most recent results, the one safe prediction I can make is that we have not heard the last of this perennial debate.

Summary and Key Terms

Through **sensation** we absorb raw energy with our sense organs. **Transduction** converts this energy into neural signals to the brain, and then we select, organize, and interpret the signals through **perception**. Sensation and perception are interconnected. But as the story of Virgil demonstrates, they involve different processes.

Measuring the Sensory Experience

Psychophysics uses special measuring procedures to study the link between physical stimuli and the sensations they arouse.

Absolute Thresholds

The **absolute threshold** is defined as the smallest amount of stimulation an organism can detect 50 percent of the time.

Signal-Detection Theory

The original work on absolute thresholds assumed that the stimulus alone determined the threshold. But **signal-detection theory** takes the subject's response bias into account as well.

Difference Thresholds

Researchers also measure the ability to detect differences between two levels of a stimulus. The smallest detectable change is called the difference threshold, or **just-noticeable difference (JND)**. According to **Weber's law**, the JND is a constant proportion of the stimulus, so it increases as the stimulus increases.

Sensation

Humans have several distinct sensory modalities—more than the so-called five senses.

Vision

The light we see is only a small band in the spectrum of electromagnetic radiation. The physical properties of light waves—length, amplitude, and purity—correspond, respectively, to our sensations of color, brightness, and saturation.

The human eye translates light waves into neural impulses. Light passes through the **cornea**, which bends the light to focus it. Behind the cornea, the ring-shape **iris** controls the size of the **pupil**, the hole through which light enters the eye. The **lens** continues the task of focusing the light, becoming rounder for nearby objects and flatter for remote ones—a process called **accommodation**. After passing through the vitreous humor, the light hits the **retina**, a multilayer screen of photoreceptor cells. The **rods** in the retina are responsible for black-and-white vision in dim surroundings. The **cones**, which provide for color vision, are concentrated in the **fovea**, the center of the retina. With millions of photoreceptors, the eye can adjust to lighting changes through **dark adaptation** and **light adaptation**.

The rods and cones stimulate bipolar and ganglion cells that integrate the information they receive and pass it on to the **optic nerve**, composed of the axon fibers of the ganglion cells. Since the area where the optic nerve enters the eye has no rods or cones, each eye has a **blind spot**.

The two optic nerves meet at the optic chiasm, where the axons split up so that fibers from inside half of each eye cross to the opposite side of the brain. The fibers travel through the thalamus to the **visual cortex**. There the image is processed by specialized neurons called **feature detectors**.

There are two theories of color vision. According to the **trichromatic theory**, the human eye has three types of cones, sensitive to red, green, and blue. However, this theory cannot explain **afterimages**, the visual sensations that linger after prolonged exposure to a stimulus. The **opponent-process theory** also assumes that there are three types of photoreceptors, but it contends that each kind responds to a pair of "opponent" colors. Both theories are correct. The retina contains the types of cones described by the trichromatic theory, but neurons in the thalamus operate in accordance with the opponent-process theory.

Hearing

The stimulus for **audition**, or hearing, is sound—vibrations in air molecules caused by movement of an object. Our sensations of pitch, loudness, and timbre derive from the frequency, amplitude, and complexity of sound waves. **White noise** is the hissing sound we hear when all frequencies of the sound spectrum are combined.

Collected by the outer ear, sound waves travel through the auditory canal to vibrate the eardrum. The vibration continues through the bones in the middle ear, the oval window of the inner ear, the fluid of the cochlea, and a membrane that excites hair cells that activate the auditory nerve. As with visual impulses, signals cross to the opposite side of the brain and pass through the thalamus before reaching the auditory cortex.

The remarkable faculties of human hearing include **auditory localization**, our ability to judge a sound's direction. There are two types of hearing impairment: **conduction deafness** (caused by damage to the eardrum or middle-ear bones) and **nerve deafness** (resulting from damage to the inner ear).

Other Senses

Our sense of smell derives from the **olfactory system**. Odor-causing molecules dissolve and become trapped by receptors in the upper nasal passages, triggering the olfactory nerve. Instead of passing through the thalamus like other sensory information, the impulse goes straight to the olfactory bulb, which distributes the information to the cerebral cortex and to limbic structures. Researchers are investigating whether humans secrete **pheromones**, chemicals that transmit signals to other humans.

Like smell, taste is a chemical sensation. The **gustatory system** begins with **taste buds** in the mouth, which absorb molecules in food or drink and trigger neural impulses to the thalamus and cortex. There are four primary tastes: sweet, salty, sour, and bitter. The flavor of food depends in part on the number of taste buds that dot the tongue and in part on other factors such as odor.

Touch is based in the skin, the body's largest organ. Touch involves many sensory systems and the sensations of pressure, warmth, cold, and pain. Active touch, as used by braille readers, provides much more information than passive touch.

Temperature is a sensation with two unusual aspects: It is generally relative to a person's current state, and it entails two separate sensory systems—one for signaling warmth and the other for signaling cold.

Pain is a subjective sensation with no single stimulus. The **gate-control theory** suggests that pain signals to the brain can be blocked when they become too intense. This theory explains why pain can often be eased by a competing sensation. Endorphins, the body's natural pain relievers, can also help control pain, as does the psychological technique of distraction.

Our sense of coordination derives from the **kinesthetic system**. Receptors in the joints, tendons, and muscles, linked to motor areas of the brain, help us register the body's position and movements. The related **vestibular system** includes structures in the inner ear that monitor the head's tilt and location in space, giving us our sense of equilibrium.

Sensation: Keeping the Signals Straight

In the welter of sensations that confront us, three factors help us keep our signals straight. First, the different senses have different receptors—though some people have **synesthesia**, a very rare condition in which one sensory modality triggers sensations in another sensory modality. Second, our senses are built to detect novelty rather than sameness. As a result of **sensory adaptation**, our sensitivity to a stimulus declines as a result of constant exposure. Third, selective attention allows us to focus on one input and to block out the rest.

Perception

Perception is an active, "constructive" process. As simple **reversible figures** demonstrate, perception involves selecting, organizing, and interpreting sensory information.

Perceptual Organization

Based on the idea that the whole (perception) is greater than the sum of its parts (sensation), **Gestalt psychology** studies the way we construct meaningful perceptions. In any perceptual field, we focus on the figure rather than the background. We also group features into perceptual wholes according to the rules of proximity, similarity, continuity, closure, and common fate.

Perceptual Constancies

Although sensory inputs are always changing, perceptual constancies keep our perceptions stable. Because of **size constancy**, we see an object as retaining its size even when its retinal image grows or diminishes. Because of **shape constancy**, we see an object's form as remaining the same when its orientation varies.

Depth and Dimension

Through **depth perception**, flat images on the retina are used to perceive distances in three-dimensional space. One binocular depth cue is **convergence**, the turning inward of the eyes when objects get closer. Another cue is **binocular disparity**, the difference in retinal image between the two eyes. The closer the object is, the greater the disparity. There are also **monocular depth cues** that enable depth perception, including relative image size, linear perspective, and motion parallax.

Experiments with the **visual cliff** indicate that the capacity for depth perception may be inborn. But case studies of blind people whose eyesight was restored and cross-cultural evidence suggest as well that experience is needed to interpret depth cues correctly.

Perceptual Set

Our prior experience and expectations often create a **perceptual set** that leads us to see what we expect to see.

The World of Illusions

Despite the brain's astonishing feats of perception, it falls prey to various **perceptual illusions**. In the **Müller-Lyer illusion**, the perceived length of a line is changed by the position of other lines that enclose it. The **Ponzo illusion** makes the length of two equal lines seem different if they appear to be at different distances. And in the **moon illusion**, the full moon looks larger when it's close to the horizon than when it's high in the sky.

Extrasensory Perception

More than half of all Americans believe in **extrasensory perception (ESP)**. But is it possible to perceive something in the absence of sensory input?

The Case for ESP

Parapsychologists distinguish three types of extrasensory power: telepathy, clairvoyance, and precognition. Rhine's studies suggested that all three types exist.

The Case against ESP

Critics pointed out flaws in Rhine's methods, and similar problems were revealed by later experiments. Findings could not be reproduced, and many hoaxes have been exposed.

The Continuing Controversy

The debate continues. There appears to be new, more rigorous evidence for ESP, but skeptics are still critical of the methods. As yet, there is no sound empirical support for the existence of ESP.

In the Field Resources

Books

Ackerman, D. (1990). *The natural history of the senses*. New York: Random House.

Written by a nonpsychologist, this book describes in vivid detail sights, sounds, smells, and other sensations—and how we perceive them.

Shepard, R. (1990). *Mind sights*. New York: W. H. Freeman.

The author, a cognitive psychologist and artist, presents drawings that use visual illusions that illustrate points about perception and art.

Internet

American Speech-Language Hearing Association (http://asha.org/)

Provides news, career information, educational programs, and information on noise, hearing loss, and related topics.

Exploratorium Exhibits (http://www.exploratorium.edu/imagery/exhibits.html)

Straight from a science museum in San Francisco, various visual tests and illusions are presented online.

Vision Research Links (http://socsci.uci.edu/cogsci/vision.html)

Provides links to vision-research labs all over the world.

WWW Sites for Experimental Psychology (http://www.psychologie.unibonn.de/allgm/links.htm#mue)

Contains links to demonstrations and sites relevant to sensation and perception.

Journals and Periodicals

Journal of Experimental Psychology: Human Perception and Performance
Perception
Perception and Psychophysics
Science
Scientific American

4 Consciousness

What's Your Prediction?

Do subliminal self-help tapes work?

The situation You saw a newspaper ad seeking volunteers for a study of subliminal tapes, and you could not resist. No money is offered for participating, but you've heard about the power of subliminal (outside of conscious awareness) messages, so you sign up. During your first session, an experimenter hands you a cassette tape made by a company that specializes in subliminal materials. He asks you to listen to the tape once a day, every day, for five weeks. But first, you fill out some questionnaires, including some self-esteem scales and memory tests. When you've finished, you are handed a cassette tape labeled either "Subliminal Building Self-Esteem" or "Subliminal Memory Improvement."

With tape in hand, you go home and try it. All you can hear is classical music, but you know that the tape contains faint messages you cannot consciously detect, such as "I have high self-worth" or "My ability to remember is increasing daily." The tape is now part of your daily routine, and after five weeks, you return to the lab for testing. As before, you fill out some self-esteem scales and memory tests. Then depending on the group you're in, the experimenter asks, "Do you feel that the tape has improved your self-esteem (memory)?"

The procedure in this study is simple. Participants are exposed to positive subliminal messages concerning their self-esteem or memory. After five weeks, the experimenter measures both actual improvement on objective tests and self-rated improvement. There's just one hitch. Although half the participants receive tapes that are correctly labeled, the other half have tapes with the labels reversed (the self-esteem tapes have the memory label, and vice versa).

What's your prediction? So what do you think happens? Let's focus on the potential for improvement in memory. To some extent, objective-test scores should increase across the board simply because participants had practice taking such tests in the first session. But what about the added benefit to those who listened to the tape? In the first row of the table below, put an *X* in those conditions in which you think the tape produced an *actual* increase in memory-test scores. Then in the second row, put an *X* where you think the participants *perceived* an improvement in their memory.

	MEMORY TAPE		SELF-ESTEEM TAPE	
	M Label	*SE Label*	*M Label*	*SE Label*
ACTUAL	______	______	______	______
PERCEIVED	______	______	______	______

The results When Anthony Greenwald and his colleagues (1991) conducted this study, they asked two questions: (1) Did the memory tapes *actually* work? and (2) Did participants *perceive* that they worked? The key results are presented in the table below. First, scores on the objective memory test were no higher for those who listened to the subliminal memory tape than for those given the self-esteem tape. Second, participants perceived that their memory had improved—but based on which label was on the tape, not on which message the tape actually contained. People may believe in the power of the hidden message, but the tapes themselves had no real effect. Other research has shown that subliminal weight-loss tapes too are ineffective (Merikle & Skanes, 1992).

	MEMORY TAPE		SELF-ESTEEM TAPE	
	M Label	*SE Label*	*M Label*	*SE Label*
ACTUAL	______	______	______	______
PERCEIVED	*X*		*X*	

What does it all mean? Ever since psychology was born as a discipline, questions have been raised about consciousness and the extent to which we are influenced by information that is not in awareness. If you predicted that the subjects in this study did not benefit from subliminal self-help messages, you were right (you were also right if you predicted that they believed the tapes to be effective, illustrating the power of suggestion). If you think, however, that people are not in other ways subject to influence without awareness, stay tuned to the rest of this chapter. To fully understand the human organism, one must account for both what we attend to in our normal waking lives and the effects of sleep, dreams, hypnosis, and other less conscious processes.

Have you ever been offered "a penny for your thoughts"? As strange as it sounds, it's not always that easy to respond. From one moment to the next, there is an endless stream of new sights and sounds to absorb, new odors, internal sensations pressing for attention, thoughts, daydreams, and memories that pop to mind, problems that need to be solved, and other intrusions on what we call consciousness.

When psychology was born as a discipline, it was defined primarily as the study of consciousness. Wilhelm Wundt trained subjects to report on their own rapidly changing reactions to tones, visual displays, and other stimulus cues. William James wrote extensively about the functions and contents of "normal waking consciousness," and Sigmund Freud argued that people are driven by *un*conscious forces that stir beneath the surface. Despite this initial interest, however, the rise of behaviorism led many researchers to focus on observable behavior, not on the mind. It wasn't until the decline of behaviorism that interest in conscious and unconscious processes returned. Equipped with electrical recording devices, brain-imaging techniques, computers, and perceptual and cognitive tests, researchers made important new discoveries. In this chapter, we'll see that human consciousness ranges on a continuum from an alert waking state of attention to varying depths of sleep, dreams, hypnosis, and the "altered" states produced by psychoactive drugs. We'll also see that the more we know about consciousness, the more able we will be to regulate our own states of mind.

Attentional Processes

In what ways is consciousness like a spotlight? Can people attend selectively to one stimulus among many, and do the stimuli we try to block out still register on the mind? How do people divide their attention in a way that permits them to simultaneously engage in more than one activity? And are we influenced by stimuli that never register in our awareness?

The word **consciousness** has many different meanings (Baruss, 1987), but most psychologists define it in terms of **attention**—a state of awareness consisting of the sensations, thoughts, and feelings that one is focused on at a given moment. As implied by this definition, consciousness has a limited capacity. Whether you are mentally focused on a memory, a conversation, a foul odor, this sentence, or your growling stomach, consciousness is like a spotlight. It can shift rapidly from one stimulus to another, but it can shine on only one stimulus at a time. Try free associating into a tape recorder sometime, and you'll find yourself mentally straying in what William James (1890) called the stream of consciousness.

Consciousness may be limited and the mind may wander, but there are three important and adaptive processes at work. First, attention is selective—so, to some extent, people can control consciousness the way they control the channels of a television set. Second, for tasks that require little conscious effort, people can divide their attention and simultaneously engage in more than one activity. Third, even when people are conscious of one stimulus, they are also capable of reacting to other stimuli in the environment—which suggests that we can process information outside of awareness. As we'll see, these features enable us to widen, narrow, and move the spotlight of consciousness as needed.

consciousness An awareness of the sensations, thoughts, and feelings that one is attending to at a given moment.

attention A state of awareness consisting of the sensations, thoughts, and feelings that one is focused on at a given moment.

Selective Attention

Picture this scene in your mind. You're standing at a cocktail party with a drink in one hand and a drumstick in the other. In the background, there's music playing, as well as the chatter of voices. You're in the middle of a conversation with a friend when suddenly you overhear two other people talking about someone you know.

Can you tune into the gossip and still carry on a conversation? How easy is it to selectively attend to one stimulus among many?

In a classic test of this **cocktail party phenomenon,** Colin Cherry (1953) presented subjects wearing headphones with two different messages, played simultaneously, one to each ear. In this dichotic listening task, subjects were told to "shadow"—that is, follow and repeat aloud, word for word—only one of the two messages. Were they able to do it? Yes, especially when the competing messages were different, as when one featured the voice of a man and the other the voice of a woman. But what happened to the message that subjects had filtered out and ignored? Later, subjects could not recall any of it. Even when they were stopped in the middle of the presentation and asked to repeat the unattended message, their ability to do so was limited. Through a process of **selective attention,** people can zoom in on a single auditory stimulus, but then they lose track of competing auditory stimuli.

To examine selective attention in another sensory modality, Ulric Neisser and Robert Becklen (1975) devised a visual analog of the dichotic listening task. They simultaneously showed subjects two videotapes, one superimposed over the other. One tape showed three people passing a basketball, and the other showed two people playing a hand-slapping game (see Figure 4.1). The task was to keep track of one game or the other. As in the shadowing study, subjects could attend to only one stimulus at a time. In fact, the filtering process was so complete that out of twenty-four subjects who were focused on the basketball players, all but one failed to notice that the hand slappers had stopped their game at one point to shake hands. When the experimenter later replayed this segment, these subjects were shocked at what they had missed. This result illustrates that information may be included or excluded from consciousness through a process of selective attention. (To test your own ability at visual shadowing, see Figure 4.2.)

cocktail party phenomenon The ability to attend selectively to one person's speech in the midst of competing conversations.

selective attention The ability to focus awareness on a single stimulus to the exclusion of other stimuli, as in the cocktail party phenomenon.

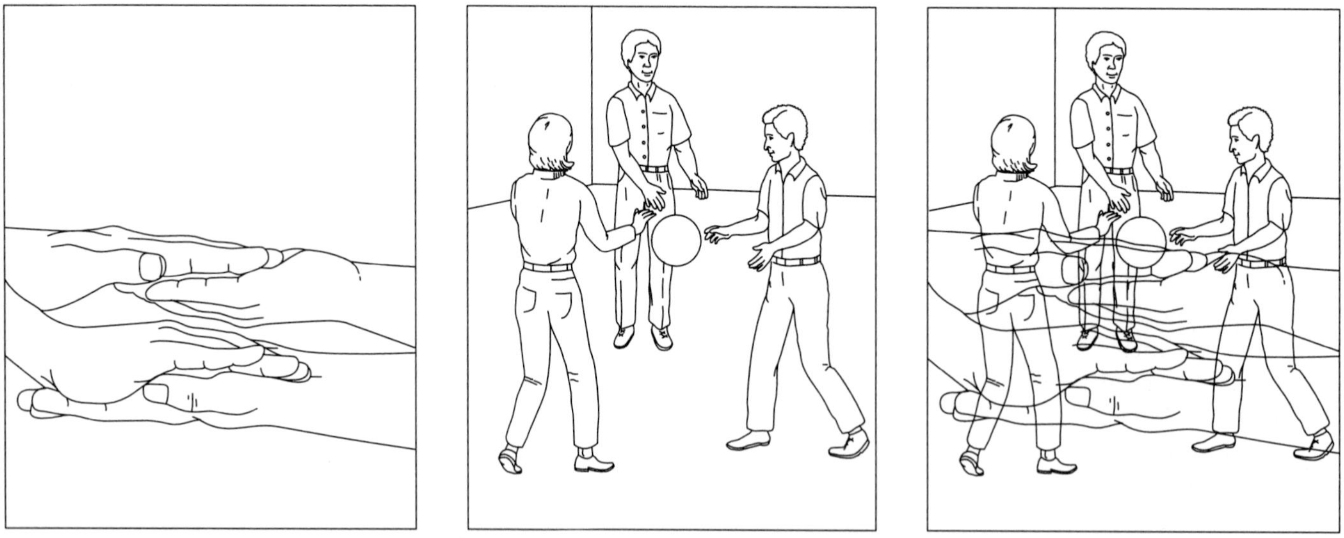

Figure 4.1 Selective attention Shown here are drawings of the two videotapes (*left and center*) and the resulting superimposed image (*right*). Subjects who were focused on the basketball players did not see the hand slappers, and vice versa (Neisser & Becklen, 1975).

In performing an experiment like this one on man attention car it house is boy critically hat important shoe that candy the old material horse that tree is pen being phone read cow by book the hot subject tape for pin the stand relevant view task sky be red cohesive man and car grammatically house complete boy but hat without shoe either candy being horse so tree easy pen that phone full cow attention book is hot not tape required pin in stand order view to sky read red it nor too difficult

Figure 4.2 Visual shadowing The passage above contains two messages—one in red ink, the other in blue. Read only the red-ink message aloud as quickly as possible. Now, without looking back, write down all the blue-ink words you can remember. The result? As in the dichotic listening studies, you probably did not recall many unshadowed words—even though the same words appeared over and over again.

Divided Attention

Consciousness may be limited, but the filtering process does not immediately or completely block out all of the extraneous information. In dichotic listening experiments, for example, most subjects do manage to hear the mention of their own names (Moray, 1959), sexually explicit words (Nielson & Sarason, 1981), and words they had learned to associate with electric shock (Dawson & Schell, 1982)—even when these are irrelevant stimuli spoken in the unattended ear. Many subjects in this situation could even tell that something odd had occurred in the unattended ear when the speech in that ear was switched from ordinary English to English played backward (Wood & Cowan, 1995).

Is it safe to talk on the phone while driving? In a study published in a 1997 issue of the New England Journal of Medicine, *researchers examined the phone records of 699 motorists who were in accidents and who had cellular telephones. They found that the accident rate was four times higher when drivers were on the phone than when not—even with speakerphones that did not require use of a hand. Driving may be a largely automatic process, but people need to stay alert to traffic and other changing conditions (Redelmeier & Tibshirani, 1997).*

Is it possible, despite our selective tendencies, to divide attention among competing stimuli? Can you simultaneously watch TV and read a book or else drive a car, listen to the radio, and carry on a conversation? It depends on how much conscious effort is needed for the various tasks (Damos, 1992). Consider driving. When first learning to drive, you have to concentrate on how to operate the steering wheel, accelerator, and brake and on how to monitor traffic and watch for pedestrians, signs, and lights. At that point, driving is so *effortful* an activity that even the radio is distracting. As you gain more experience behind the wheel, however, driving becomes an *automatic* process that does not require high levels of effort or awareness or your undivided attention. As a result, you can drive, listen, and talk all at the same time (Logan, 1992; Schneider & Shiffrin, 1977; Treisman et al., 1992).

The distinction between effortful and automatic processing explains how people are able to exhibit **divided attention** when at least one competing task is "on automatic." It's easy to walk, talk, and chew gum simultaneously, but for most of us it is difficult to play chess while watching TV. To demonstrate the automatic nature of highly practiced activities, look at the patches of color in Figure 4.3. Beginning in the top left-hand column, try to name all the colors as

divided attention The ability to distribute one's attention and simultaneously engage in two or more activities.

Despite the jokes often made about us humans, it is easy to engage in two—or more—automatic activities at once.

fast as you can—and time yourself. Ready, set, go! That was easy, right? Now look at the list of color-printed words, and this time ignore the word and name the colors of the ink in which each word is printed. Again, do it as fast as you can and time yourself.

If you followed these instructions, then you have just taken the **Stroop test,** which was devised in 1935 by John Stroop. As for the result, you probably found that the second task was much more difficult than the first and took almost twice as long. When Stroop first presented subjects with 100 items, he found that the first task took an average of 63 seconds, and the second took 110 seconds—a 74 percent slowdown in performance time. I took this test as an undergraduate and thought it would be easy. But I repeatedly paused, stammered, and got all tongue-tied, and I had to admit that the words, which contradicted the colors, kept getting in the way.

Researchers have now used the Stroop test in more than 700 experiments, and they continue to debate the reasons for the effect (MacLeod, 1991). However, one conclusion is clear: Experienced readers process word meanings automatically, without effort or awareness. It just happens. And since the test words contradict the colors (when they don't, performance is quicker), reading interferes with the color-naming task. Recent studies also show that personally relevant and emotionally provocative words interfere with color naming more than neutral words do. Thus, people diagnosed as having a fear of spiders are highly disrupted by words such as *crawl* and *hairy,* while those overly concerned about their health are disrupted more by *cancer* and *blood* (Williams et al., 1996).

Influence without Awareness

Whereas Wundt and James pioneered the study of conscious processes, Sigmund Freud theorized that people are driven more by *un*conscious forces. Freud argued that there are three levels of awareness in the human mind: (1) *conscious* sensations, thoughts, and feelings that are currently in the spotlight of attention; (2) *preconscious* material that is temporarily out of awareness but is easy to bring to mind; and (3) an *unconscious* reservoir of material that is suppressed, banned from awareness. According to Freud, people are influenced by material that resides outside of awareness. Was he right?

Figure 4.3 The Stroop test In the left-hand task, name each color as fast as you can. In the right-hand task, name the color of ink in which each word is printed as fast as you can.

Stroop test A color-naming task that demonstrates the automatic nature of highly practiced activities such as reading.

For years, many researchers were skeptical of this claim. But an outpouring of new studies brought unconscious processes to the forefront of modern psychology. These studies suggest that people can be influenced in subtle ways by **subliminal messages**—information that is presented so faintly or so rapidly that it is perceived "below" our threshold of awareness (Bornstein & Pittman, 1992). Let's consider some examples that illustrate the point.

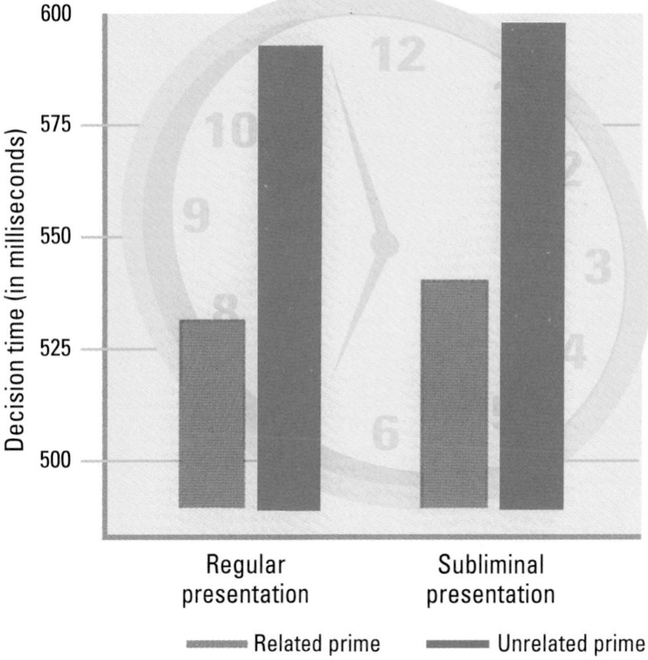

Figure 4.4 Subliminal priming Subjects took less time to decide if a target item was an actual word after exposure to a related rather than unrelated prime word (*left*). This priming effect also occurred when the first words were subliminally presented (*right*). This result demonstrates influence without awareness (Marcel, 1983).

Mere Exposure

We'll see in Chapter 13 that there is a powerful principle of attraction called the mere exposure effect: The more often you see a stimulus—whether it's a word, an object, a melody, or a face—the more you come to like it (Zajonc, 1968). But must you be aware of the prior exposures for this effect to occur? Not necessarily. In a typical study, subjects are shown pictures of geometrical objects, each for only one to five milliseconds, which is too quick to register in awareness—and too quick for anyone to realize that some objects appear more often than others. After the presentation, subjects are shown each of the objects and asked two questions: Do you like it? Have you ever seen it before? Perhaps you can predict the result. The more frequently presented the object, the more subjects like it. And when asked if they've ever seen the liked objects before, they say *no*. This pattern of results demonstrates the mere exposure effect, a form of influence without awareness (Kuntz-Wilson & Zajonc, 1980; Bornstein, 1992).

Priming

Have you ever noticed that whenever a novel word slips into conversation, it gets repeated over and over again? If so, then you have observed **priming,** the tendency for a recently presented concept to "prime" responses to a subsequent "target" question. Thus, when subjects are asked to decide if the letters D-O-C-T-O-R form a word, they are quicker to say *yes* if the previous item was *N-U-R-S-E* than if it was *A-P-P-L-E* (Meyer & Schvaneveldt, 1971). What if the prime word is presented subliminally, below our threshold of awareness? As shown in Figure 4.4, the result is the same—even when the prime word is presented so quickly that subjects could only recall seeing a flash of light (Marcel, 1983; Merikle & Reingold, 1992).

In a provocative series of experiments, John Bargh and his colleagues (1996) found that human social behavior may also be subject to automatic influence without awareness. In one study, for example, subjects were given thirty sets of words presented in scrambled order ("he it hides finds instantly") and were told to use some of the words in each set to form grammatical sentences. After explaining the test, which would take about five minutes, the experimenter told subjects to locate him down the hall when they'd finished so that he could administer a second task. So far so good. But when subjects found the experimenter, he was standing in the hallway having a conversation—and he stayed in that conversation for ten full minutes without acknowledging the subjects' presence. What's a person to do, wait patiently or interrupt? The subjects didn't know it, but some had worked on a

subliminal message A stimulus that is presented below the threshold for awareness.

priming The tendency for a recently presented word or concept to facilitate, or "prime," responses in a subsequent situation.

scrambled word test that contained many "politeness" words *(yield, respect, considerate, courteous),* while others were exposed to many words related to "rudeness" *(bold, disturb, intrude, bluntly).* Would these test words secretly prime subjects, a few minutes later, to behave in one way or the other? Yes. Compared to subjects given neutral words to unscramble, those primed for rudeness were more likely—and those primed for politeness were less likely—to interrupt the experimenter (see Figure 4.5).

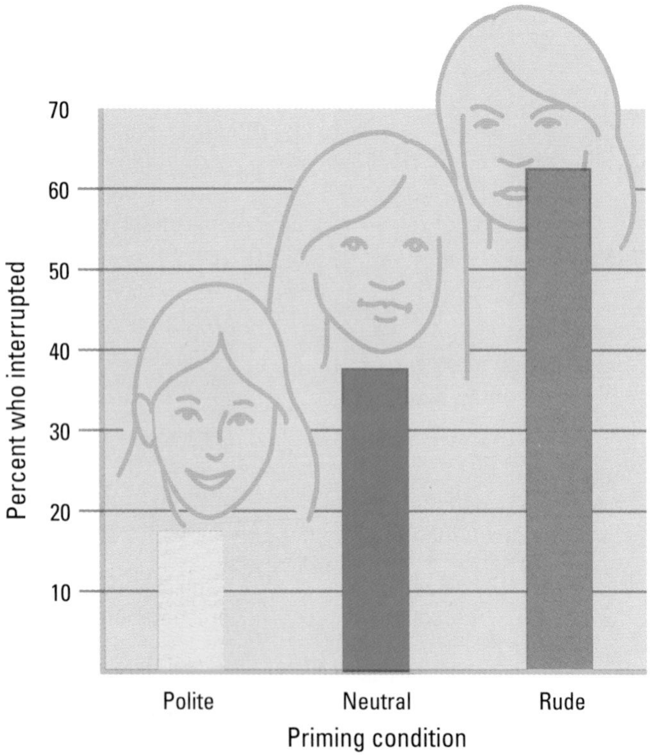

Figure 4.5 Would waiting subjects interrupt the experimenter? Compared to subjects previously given neutral words to unscramble (*center*), those primed for politeness were less likely to cut in (*left*) and those primed for rudeness were more likely to cut in (*right*). These results demonstrate influence without awareness.

Prosopagnosia Influence without awareness can also be seen in people with **prosopagnosia**—a rare condition, often resulting from damage to the temporal lobes, that impairs the ability to recognize family members, friends, celebrities, and other familiar faces, including one's own. Or does it? Although prosopagnosics cannot identify known faces, research shows that they exhibit unique patterns of eye movements, electrical activity in the brain, and increased autonomic arousal when presented with faces that are familiar rather than unfamiliar (Renault et al., 1989; Tranel & Damasio, 1985). And when asked to determine if two faces are the same or different, they make the judgments more quickly when one of the faces is familiar (Young & DeHaan, 1992). In short, it appears that prosopagnosics exhibit glimmers of "recognition"—they just don't realize it. We will revisit this phenomenon, and others like it, in Chapter 6, on memory.

Blindsight Another rare condition is **blindsight,** a form of "vision" without awareness. When people suffer damage that is limited to the primary visual cortex, optic nerve fibers from the eyes may still be connected to other regions of the brain that process visual information. In such cases, the patient is consciously blind yet is able to locate and reach for objects, identify colors in flashing lights, and track moving stimuli (Cowey & Stoerig, 1991; Weiskrantz, 1995). Thus, the person can react to certain visual cues without awareness. As noted, people may be conscious of one stimulus yet also react to other stimuli—and process information outside of awareness.

Although consciousness is limited by selective attention, people can perform certain tasks automatically and react to stimuli that are not "in the spotlight." This capacity of ours to simultaneously process information from many sources—and to do so outside of awareness—is highly adaptive. But can it be used against us? Are there limits to influence without awareness, or are we at the mercy of subliminal messages designed to shape our beliefs, tastes, attitudes, and behavior? Can consumers be lured into purchasing certain products by subliminal messages embedded in advertisements? Can teenagers be provoked into violence by subliminal rock-music lyrics? There are those who believe that subliminal stimuli are more powerful than ordinary "supraliminal" (above-threshold) stimuli because they bypass our conscious defenses. Is this fear well founded? The answer is provided by recent research on the so-called hidden persuaders (see the Intersection on the next page).

prosopagnosia A condition stemming from damage to the temporal lobes that disrupts the ability to recognize familiar faces.

blindsight A condition caused by damage to the visual cortex in which a person encodes visual information without awareness.

CONSCIOUSNESS AND BUSINESS

What Is the Power of Subliminal Advertising?

In 1957, Vance Packard published *The Hidden Persuaders,* an exposé of Madison Avenue. The book climbed to the top of the bestseller list and awakened in the public a deep fear of being manipulated by forces that could not be seen or heard. What had Packard uncovered? In the 1950s, amid growing fears of communism and the birth of rock 'n' roll, a group of advertisers reported that they used *subliminal advertising*—the presentation of commercial messages below the level of conscious awareness. It started in a drive-in movie theater in New Jersey, where the words *Drink Coca-Cola* and *Eat popcorn* were supposedly flashed on the screen during the film for a third of a millisecond. Although the audience never noticed the messages, Coke sales were said to have increased 18 percent and popcorn sales 58 percent over a six-week period of intermissions (Brean, 1958).

This incident was followed by many others. A Seattle radio station presented subaudible antitelevision messages during its programs ("TV is a bore"); department stores played music tapes over public-address systems that contained subaudible antitheft statements ("If you steal, you'll get caught"); and in what has become a multimillion-dollar industry, companies offer consumers audiotapes with subliminal self-help messages embedded in the music. In books entitled *Subliminal Seduction* (1973) and *The Age of Manipulation* (1989), William Bryan Key charged that advertisers routinely sneak faint sexual images in visual ads to heighten the appeal of their products. And recently, concerns have been raised about rock music. In one case, the families of two young men who had committed suicide blamed the British rock group Judas Priest for subliminal lyrics on their *Stained Glass* album ("do it") that promoted satanism and suicide (*National Law Journal,* 1990). It is clear that many people believe in the power of hidden persuaders.

At the time of the New Jersey movie-theater scandal, research on the topic was so sketchy, and the public was so outraged by the sinister implications, that the matter was quickly dropped. But today there is renewed interest and continued controversy. Can subliminal messages really induce us, without our awareness, to drink Coke, eat popcorn, purchase a particular product, or commit a violent act? In 1982, Timothy Moore reviewed all the existing research and concluded that "what you see is what you get"—nothing, "complete scams." Moore may have been right. The original Coke-and-popcorn study was never published. It was later exposed as a publicity stunt, a hoax (Pratkanis, 1992). Indeed, there is no solid evidence of this covert form of influence. As in the study described at the start of this chapter, controlled experiments continue to show that although consumers may believe in the power of hidden messages, subliminal self-help tapes that promise to raise your self-esteem or to help you stop smoking, lose weight, and improve your sex life do not work (Pratkanis et al., 1994).

So why, you may be wondering, is there strong evidence for influence without awareness in studies of mere exposure, priming, prosopagnosia, and blindsight but not in studies of subliminal persuasion? There seems to be a contradiction here. But if you think about the differences, you'll see that this contradiction is more apparent than real. In laboratory settings, subliminal exposures have a short-term effect on simple judgments and actions. But in subliminal persuasion, the exposure is presumed to have long-term effects on consumer purchases, on health, and even on the most profound of violent acts, suicide. Psychologists now agree that we can process a great deal of information at an unconscious level, but they're also quick to point out that this processing is "analytically limited" (Greenwald, 1992).

Sleep and Dreams

Are people, like animals, influenced by biological rhythms, or are we flexible in our sleeping schedules? How do researchers study sleep in the laboratory? What is REM sleep, and what makes it so special? What are dreams, why do we have them, and what do they mean? What are some ways in which sleeping can become impaired and then be repaired?

It may start with a deep yawn. Then the eyelids begin to fall. Then your head drops and you get that drowsy sense of calm before nodding off, tuning out, and calling it a day. For most people, falling asleep is a pleasurable experience. Why? What is sleep? Why do we need to have it? And what about dreams—what purposes do they serve and what, if anything, do they mean? The average person spends about eight hours a day sleeping and ninety minutes dreaming. Given an average life expectancy of seventy-five years, that amounts to about twenty-five years of sleep and five years of dreaming in a lifetime. Yet until recently, we knew very little about this important aspect of our lives. Shakespeare once referred to sleep as "the death of each day's life." Others, too, think of sleep as a state of complete dormancy. They are wrong. As we'll see, the sleeping brain is humming with activity (Carskadon, 1993).

The Sleep-Wake Cycle

Many birds migrate south for the winter. Bears and raccoons hibernate. Certain plants open their leaves during the day and close them at night—even if kept in a dark closet. As biological organisms, humans are also sensitive to seasonal changes, the twenty-eight-day lunar cycle, the twenty-four-hour day, and the ninety-minute activity-rest cycle that is linked to variations in alertness and daydreaming. These and other regular fluctuations are forms of **biological rhythms** (Aschoff, 1981).

From a psychological standpoint, there is one particularly important internal clock: Every twenty-four hours, we undergo a single sleep-wake cycle. This cycle and others that take roughly a day to complete are referred to as a **circadian rhythm.** Humans tend to be most active and alert during the middle of the day, when body temperature peaks, and least active and alert at night, when body temperature drops to its low point. The circadian rhythm is also evident in fluctuations in blood pressure, pulse rate, blood-sugar level, potassium level, growth-hormone secretions, cell growth, and other physiological functions.

Everyone is influenced by circadian rhythms, but everyone's inner clock is set somewhat differently. Think about yourself. Are you a morning person or a night person, a lark or an owl? If you had a choice, would you rather wake up at 6, 8, or 10 o'clock in the morning? How easy is it for you to work late into the night? During what time of day are you most productive? These kinds of questions can be used to determine your circadian rhythm (Smith et al., 1989). Although research shows that morning types fall asleep eighty-eight minutes earlier at night and awaken seventy-two minutes earlier in the morning (Kerkhof, 1985), very few people are extreme in their preference. Most fall somewhere in the middle and adapt as needed to the schedules they must keep. Still, it helps to know when you're likely to be at your best. When subjects were tested for memory at 9 AM, 2 PM, and 8 PM, the larks performed worse as the day wore on, while the owls performed better (Anderson et al., 1991). In a study of college students, larks were more likely than owls to take early morning classes—and they earned higher grades in those classes (Guthrie et al., 1995).

Is the circadian rhythm endogenous (set by an inner clock), or is the human body responsive to outside patterns of lightness and darkness? Ask Stefania Follini, an

"Larks see owls as lazy; owls see larks as party poopers."

— RICHARD M. COLEMAN

biological rhythm Any periodic, more or less regular, fluctuation in a biological organism.

circadian rhythm A biological cycle, such as sleeping and waking, that occurs approximately every twenty-four hours.

Italian interior designer. In January 1989, she descended into a Plexiglas bunker buried in a cave in New Mexico. Sealed off from sunlight, outside noises, changes in temperature, schedules, and clocks, she lived alone in this underground home for 131 days—a "free-running" period of time that allowed her body to establish its own rhythm. Her only link to the world was a personal computer. When Follini emerged from her isolation in May, she thought it was only March. Her "day" had extended to twenty-five hours, then to forty-eight. As time went on, she slept and woke up later and later. She stopped menstruating, ate fewer meals, and lost seventeen pounds.

Other volunteers have similarly been isolated for extended periods of time. Some naturally settled into a "short" day, but most free-ran on a longer cycle that averaged twenty-five hours. With each successive cycle, these subjects tended to go to sleep a little later and to wake up a little later (see Figure 4.6). Body temperature and hormone levels tended to follow the same rhythm. Like Follini, these subjects drifted toward a longer day—and then underestimated the amount of time they had been isolated. When reexposed to sunlight, the subjects readjusted their biological clocks.

So where is this timing device? Animal experiments have shown that the circadian rhythm is controlled in the brain by a cluster of neurons in the suprachiasmatic nucleus (SCN) of the hypothalamus. How does the SCN function? You may recall from Chapter 3 that light passing through the eye is converted to neural signals and sent to the cortex through the optic nerve. Apparently, some of these optic nerve axons—and the information they convey about light—are diverted to the SCN (Ginty et al., 1993; Ralph et al., 1990). Nestled in the center of the brain, the pea-shape pineal gland also plays an important role. As darkness falls, the pineal gland produces melatonin—a hormone that facilitates sleep. When light strikes the retina, melatonin secretion is slowed down. Spurred by a rash of books with titles like *The Melatonin Miracle* and *Melatonin: Nature's Sleeping Pill,* melatonin has been in the news a lot

Stefani Follini emerges into daylight after 131 days in an underground Plexiglas bunker in New Mexico.

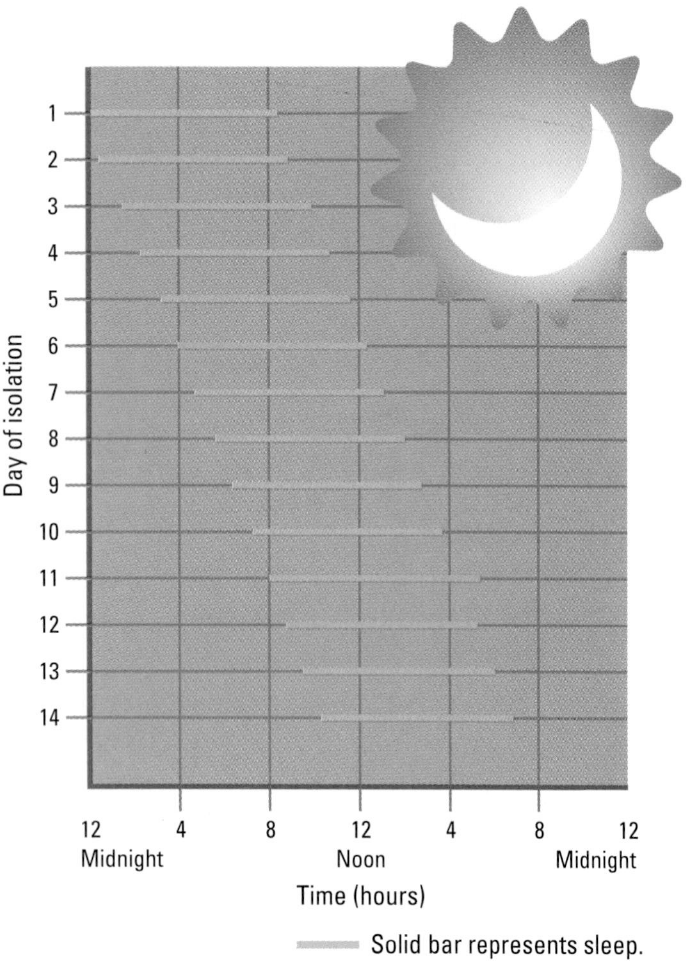

Figure 4.6 The inner clock When people are placed in a "free-running" environment, isolated from all day and night cues, they typically drift toward a twenty-five-hour day. With each cycle, subjects sleep and wake up a little later.

lately. As we'll see later, it is currently being used to treat people who suffer from chronic insomnia.

The circadian rhythm is synchronized like a fine watch by interactions between environmental cues and the brain. But what happens when one's rhythm is disrupted? One common source of disruption is air travel—specifically, flying across time zones, which throws your body out of sync with the new time of day and causes you to sleep at the wrong time. If you've ever flown from one coast to the other or overseas, then you may have suffered jet lag, a condition that makes you feel tired, sluggish, and grumpy. Most people find it easier to fly west, which lengthens the day, than to fly east, which shortens it. Because the body naturally drifts to a longer day, this makes sense. Flying westward goes "with the flow" rather than against it. Consistent with this analysis, research shows that long-distance travel within a time zone does not cause jet lag (Coleman, 1986).

In recent years, researchers have tested various strategies that long-distance travelers can use to combat jet lag (Czeisler et al., 1989). In *How to Beat Jet Lag,* Dan Oren and others (1995) offer a number of behavioral tips for the weary long-distance traveler (the book comes plastic-wrapped with an eye mask and dark glasses). Always get a full night's sleep before a long trip. Anticipate your new time zone. Drink lots of liquids to avoid dehydration, but avoid alcohol, which disrupts later sleep. If you plan to travel east—say, from Los Angeles to New York—you can facilitate the adjustment process by sleeping earlier than normal before you leave so that you more closely "fit" the light-dark cycle of the new time zone. As soon as you board the plane, set your watch to your destination's time zone and eat and sleep accordingly. Based on studies indicating that bright-light exposure at night speeds the resetting of the inner clock, researchers also advise that, upon arrival, you spend the first day outdoors.

Night Work, Sleeping, and Health

We humans are diurnal creatures—active during the day and asleep at night. Thus, we like to work from 9 to 5 and then play, sleep, and awaken to the light of a new day. Yet an estimated 25 percent of all Americans—including emergency-room doctors and nurses, police officers, telephone operators, security guards, factory workers, and truckers—are often forced to work late-night shifts. The question is, What is the effect? Do people adapt over time to shift work and other late-night activity, or does it compromise their health and safety?

Both biological and social clocks set the body for activity during the daytime and sleep at night, so it's no surprise that many shift workers struggle to stay alert. People who choose night work fare better than those assigned on a rotating-shift basis (Barton, 1994). Still, shift workers in general get fewer hours of sleep per week than day workers, complain that their sleep is disrupted, and report being drowsy on the job. Often they blame their lack of sleep on ringing phones, crying babies, honking horns, and other daytime noises. But part of the problem too is that the body's internal alarm clock tries to awaken the day sleeper. Either way, the adverse effects can be seen at work, where night-time energy levels are low, reaction times are slow, and productivity is diminished. In a survey of 1,000 locomotive engineers, 59 percent admitted to having dozed off at the controls on several night trips (Akerstedt, 1988). About 75 percent of other workers as well complain of sleepiness during the night shift (Leger, 1994).

As measured by the amount of time it takes to fall asleep, research shows that people are the sleepiest between 1 and 4 AM—and then again, twelve hours later, between 1 and 4 PM. If you find yourself getting drowsy in midafternoon, you're not alone. This circadian low point—not daytime heat or a full lunch—may be the reason why people in many countries take a siesta, or afternoon nap.

Can anything be done to lessen the dangers posed by shift work? Richard Coleman (1986) recommends that when rotating shifts are necessary, employers should maximize the number of days between shift *changes* (adjustment is easier in three-week cycles than in one-week cycles) and assign workers to successively later shifts rather than earlier shifts (a person who is rotated from the 4 PM shift to the midnight shift will adjust more quickly than one who is rotated in the opposite direction). In addition, it seems to take two days of rest, not one, for workers to fully recover from their nocturnal routine (Totterdell et al., 1995). Charles Czeisler and his colleagues (1990) have found that the realignment of the circadian rhythm can also be speeded up by exposing shift workers to bright levels of light in the workplace and to eight hours of total darkness at home during the day. Within a week, the body's biological clock can be reset and the health risks of night work reduced. It takes only four hours of bright-light exposure one night to improve performance the next night (Thessing et al., 1994).

"Damn! I keep waking up in the middle of the day."

The National Highway Transportation Safety Administration estimates that up to 200,000 traffic accidents a year are sleep related—and that 20 percent of all drivers have dozed off at least once while behind the wheel. To avoid rush-hour traffic, interstate truckers often drive late at night. As shown in Figure 4.7, however, drivers are five to ten times more likely to have an accident late at night than during the daytime hours (Mitler et al., 1988). Indeed, monitoring of their EEG activity levels showed that those who drove in the middle of the night often took quick, two- to three-second **microsleeps,** which increases the risk of accident (Kecklund & Akerstedt, 1993). There are times when a person just can't avoid the situation. Often when I'm out of town and have to return for an early-morning class, I'll find myself driving late at night and fighting to keep my eyes open. I've also had the jolting—and scary—experience of realizing that I'm nodding off and drifting off the road. Is there any way to counteract this tendency?

James Horne and L. Reyner (1996) recently evaluated the possible benefits of two coping strategies: a brief nap and a cup of coffee. Ten subjects, tested in the afternoon, were restricted to five hours of sleep the nights before the study and then placed into a simulated car. On the windshield was an interactive computer-generated screen that projected a four-lane highway, with a shoulder to the side and two audible "rumble strips" between lanes. The route itself was monotonous, but subjects had to steer along gentle curves and occasionally pass a slow-moving car. To measure subjects' driving performance, a computer kept track of the number of incidents in which they drifted from their lane or went off the side of the road. On three

microsleep A brief episode of sleep that occurs in the midst of a wakeful activity.

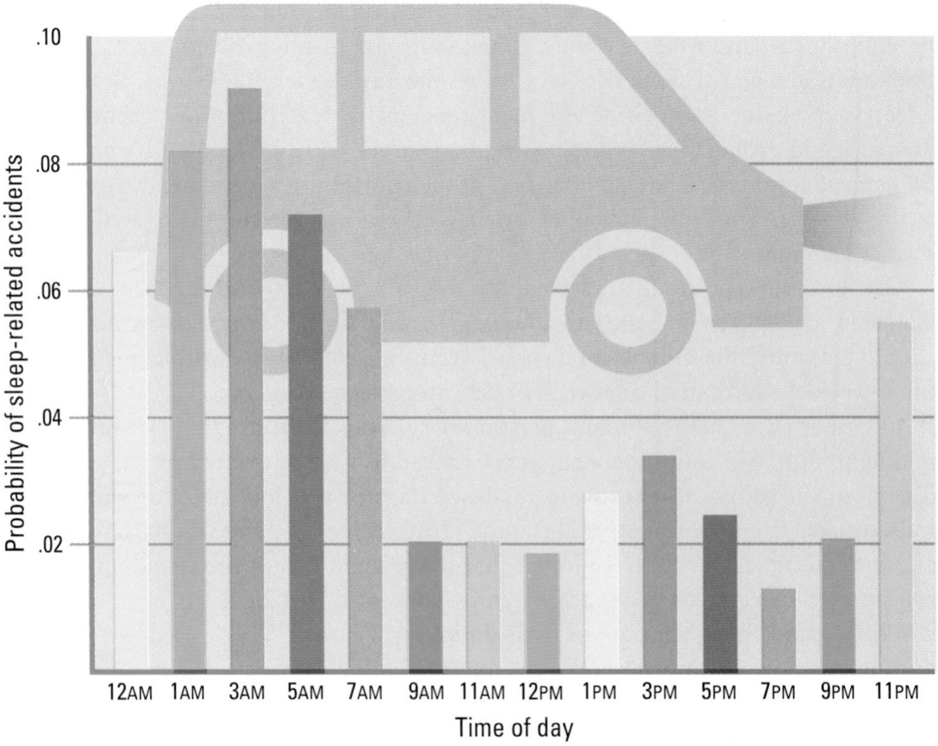

Figure 4.7 Probability of sleep-related accidents throughout the day By looking at traffic statistics, researchers have found that sleep-related accidents are unequally distributed across the day. Such accidents are most likely to occur between 1 and 4 AM. Note also that there's a second "mini-peak" between 1 and 4 PM—which is a time when alertness levels decline (Mitler et al., 1988).

To avoid traffic, many truckers drive at night. Due to drowsiness, however, they are more likely to have an accident during these hours than in the daytime.

separate occasions, subjects drove for an hour, took a thirty-minute break, and then drove for another hour. Would subjects become sleepy—and sloppy—during the second hour? It depended on whether they were assigned, during the break, to drink a regular cup of coffee, to drink a placebo (decaffeinated) cup of coffee, or to take a fifteen-minute nap. Look at the results in Figure 4.8, and you'll see that although the incident rate rose in the placebo group, it dropped in the coffee and nap conditions. Horne and Reyner thus concluded that "many vehicle accidents due to the driver falling asleep at the wheel could be avoided if the driver recognized the dangers beforehand and used the countermeasures investigated here" (p. 309).

The Stages of Sleep

Just as activity levels follow a rhythm, so too does sleep. Every night, humans cycle through five distinct stages of sleep. Much of what is known about these stages first came to light in the 1950s, thanks to the pioneering collaborative work of Nathaniel Kleitman, Eugene Aserinksy, and William Dement.

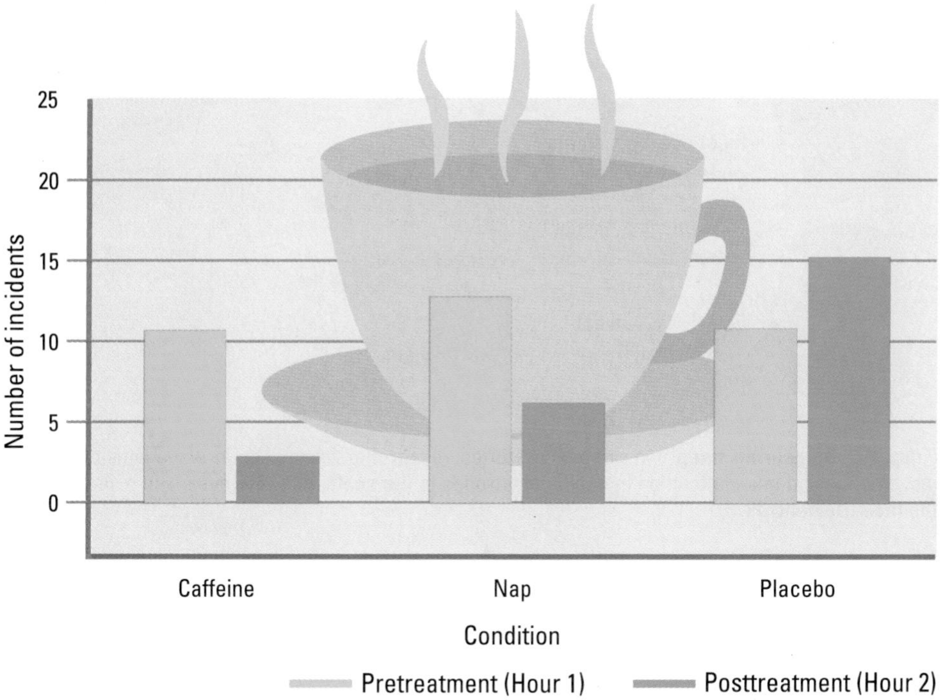

Figure 4.8 How to keep from falling asleep at the wheel Subjects drove for two hours in a simulated car, with a break during which they drank a regular cup of coffee or a placebo cup of decaffeinated coffee, or took a fifteen-minute nap. As measured by the number of traffic incidents they had in the second hour compared to the first, the incident rate increased in the placebo group but was reduced in the coffee and nap conditions (Horne & Reyner, 1996).

To appreciate how these discoveries were made, imagine that you're a subject in a sleep study. As you enter the sleep lab, you meet an experimenter, who gives you some questionnaires to fill out, prepares you for the experience, and takes you to a carpeted, tastefully decorated, soundproof "bedroom." Electrodes are then taped to your scalp to record brain-wave activity, near your eyes to measure eye movements, and under your neck and chin to record muscle tension (see Figure 4.9). Other devices may also be used to measure your breathing, heart rate, and even genital arousal. The pillow is fluffy, the bed is okay, and the blanket is warm. But you know you're being watched, and you can feel the electrodes and wires on your skin, so you wonder how you'll ever manage to fall asleep. The experimenter reassures you that it may take a couple of nights to adapt to the situation.

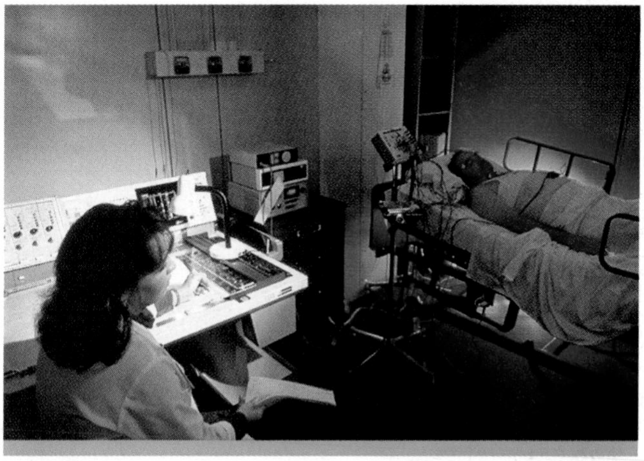

When a subject spends the night in the "bedroom" of a sleep lab, an experimenter in an adjacent room records brain-wave activity, eye movements, muscle tension, and other physiological functions.

Presleep The experimenter departs, shuts off the lights, and leaves you alone. As you try to settle down, EEG recordings reveal that all is well (see Figure 4.10). Typical of a person who is awake and alert, your EEG shows short, quick *beta waves*. This pattern indicates that different parts of your brain are producing small bursts of electrical activity at different times—a sure sign of mental activity. Your eyes move rapidly up and down and from side to side, and there is tension in many of your muscles.

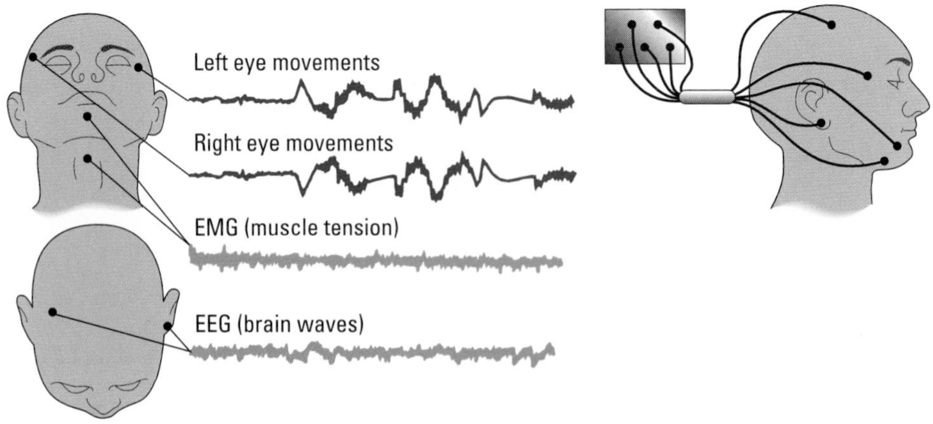

Figure 4.9 **Measuring sleep** In sleep laboratories, researchers record brain-wave activity, eye movements, and muscle tension by taping electrodes to the scalp, near the eyes, and elsewhere on the face (Dement, 1978).

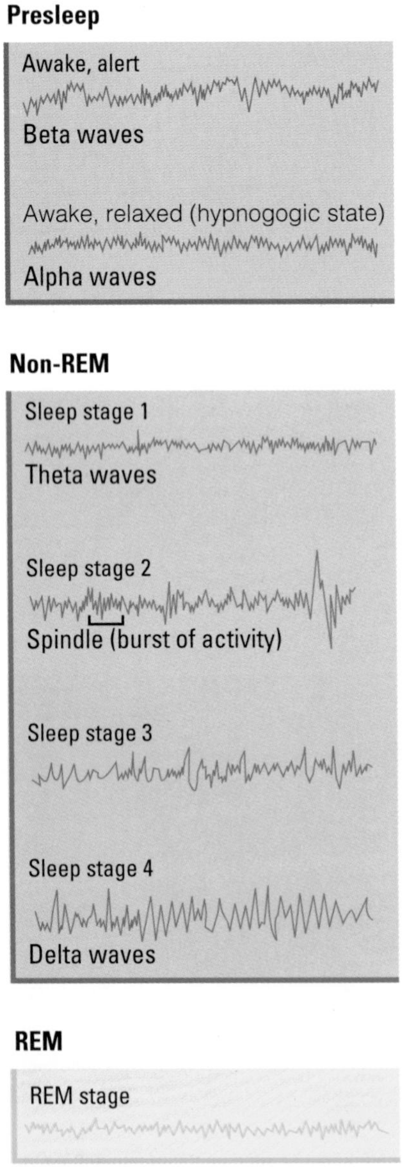

Figure 4.10 **The stages of sleep** As recorded by the EEG, brain waves get larger and slower as sleep deepens from stages 1 to 4. You can see that REM sleep waves closely resemble those of the presleep state.

Stages 1 to 4 You start to become drowsy. Your breathing slows down, your mind stops racing, your muscles relax, your eyes move less, and EEG recordings show a slower, larger, and somewhat more regular pattern of *alpha waves* (alpha waves appear to occur when people are relaxed but not focused on something specific). For a minute or two, you drift into a "hypnogogic state" in which you may imagine seeing flashes of color or light, and perhaps you jerk your leg abruptly as you sense yourself falling. You are entering stage 1 sleep. Electrical activity in the brain slows down some more. Your breathing becomes more regular, your heart rate slows, and your blood pressure drops. This is a period of very light sleep. No one makes a sound or calls your name, however, so you do not wake up.

After about ten minutes in stage 1 sleep, your EEG pattern shows waves that are even slower and larger. As you slip into stage 2 sleep, you become progressively more relaxed, the rolling eye movements stop, and you become less easily disturbed. On the EEG, stage 2 is marked by periodic short bursts of activity called sleep spindles. If the experimenter in the next room makes a noise, your brain will register a response—but you probably will not wake up.

After about twenty minutes in stage 2, you fall into the deepest stages of sleep. Stages 3 and 4 are hard to distinguish because they differ only in degree. Both are marked by the onset of very slow waves with large peaks, called *delta waves,* which last for about thirty minutes (delta waves seem to indicate that increasing numbers of neurons are firing together, in synchrony). At this point, you are "out like a light" or "sleeping like a rock." If the phone rings, you may not hear it. If you do answer the call, you'll sound dazed and confused. It is during the very deep sleep of stages 3 and 4 when young children may wet the bed or when you may walk or talk in your sleep. It's this stage that Mark Twain had in mind when he said, "There ain't no way to find out why a snorer can't hear himself snore." Yet, in keeping with the adaptive and selective nature of attention, certain noises will penetrate consciousness. New parents may be oblivious to the sounds of traffic outside, for example, but they're quick to hear the baby cry.

REM Sleep After an hour of deepening sleep, something odd happens—something first discovered in Kleitman's lab (Aserinksy & Kleitman, 1953; Dement & Kleitman, 1957; Kleitman, 1963). Rather than maintain your deep sleep, you begin to cycle backward to stage 3, then to stage 2. But then instead of returning to stage 1, you enter a new, fifth stage, marked by two dramatic types of changes. On the one hand, the EEG reveals a surge of short, high-frequency beta waves like those found when you were awake. Also indicating an increased level of activity, blood flow to the brain increases, your breathing and pulse rates speed up, and your genitals become aroused—even without sexual thoughts or dreams. On the other hand, you have lost skeletal muscle tone throughout the body. In fact, your arms, legs, and trunk are so totally relaxed that, except for an occasional twitch, you are completely paralyzed. You're also hard to awaken at this stage. This odd combination—of being internally active but externally immobile—has led some researchers to refer to this stage of sleep as paradoxical.

The most prominent change occurs in the eyes. The eyelids are shut, but underneath, your eyeballs are darting frantically back and forth as if you were watching a world-class ping-pong match. These *r*apid *e*ye *m*ovements are so pronounced that this stage has been named **REM sleep**—and it is contrasted with stages 1 through 4, which are lumped together as non-REM or **NREM sleep.** What makes rapid eye movements so special is what they betray about the state of your mind. When experimenters awaken sleeping subjects during non-REM stages, the subjects report on dreams 14 percent of the time. Yet when subjects are awakened during REM, they report on dreams 78 percent of the time—and that includes those subjects who came into the lab saying they don't ever dream (Dement, 1992). Compared to the fleeting thoughts and images reported during stages 1 through 4, REM dreams are more visual, vivid, detailed, and storylike. In the mind's late-night theater, the production of dreams can be seen in the resurgence of activity within the eyes and brain.

In all cultures of the world, beds are designed for sleep in a horizontal position. This universal aspect of human behavior is highly adaptive. EEG recordings show that when people sleep in an upright position (even if in a comfortable chair), they get very little of the slow-wave sleep needed to feel refreshed.

From the time you fall asleep, it takes about ninety minutes to complete one cycle. The contrasts within this cycle are striking. Richard Coleman (1986) describes NREM sleep as "an idling brain in a moveable body" and REM as "an active brain in a paralyzed body." In a full night's sleep, you are likely to recycle through the stages four to six times. The first time through the cycle, you spend only about ten minutes in REM sleep. As the night wears on, however, you spend less time in the deeper NREM periods and more time in REM sleep. During the last hour before you awaken in the morning, the REM period is thirty to sixty minutes long. This explains why people are so often in the middle of a dream when the mechanical tyrant we call an alarm clock rings. The sleep cycles and the progression of stages within each cycle are illustrated in Figure 4.11.

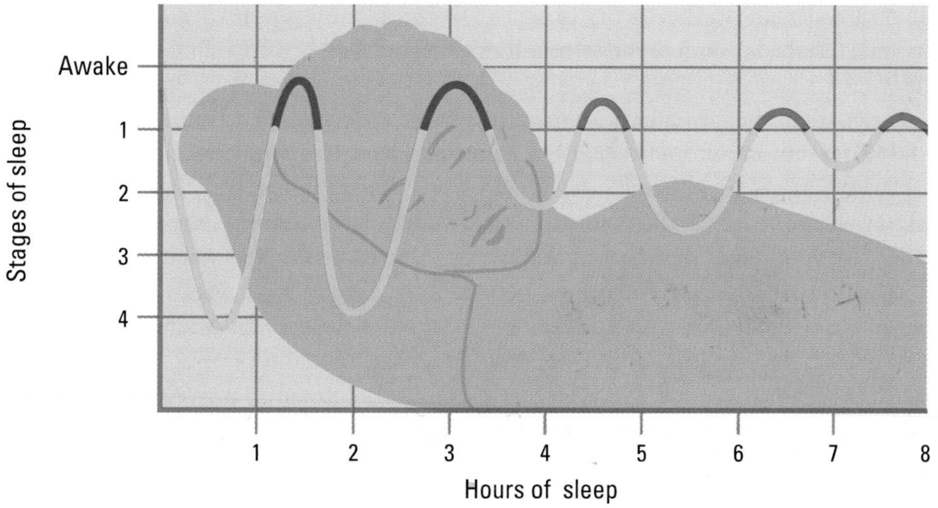

Figure 4.11 A typical night's sleep People pass through four to six ninety-minute sleep cycles per night. As shown, progressively more time is spent in REM sleep and progressively less is spent in the deeper stages.

REM sleep The rapid-eye-movement stage of sleep associated with dreaming.

NREM sleep The stages of sleep not accompanied by rapid eye movements.

Why Do We Sleep?

Because humans spend a third of their lives in this state, it's natural to wonder: Why do we sleep? When we are tired, the urge to doze is overwhelming and very hard to fight, regardless of what we're doing or where we are. And if we are still tired when the alarm clock rings, we might shut it off, clutch our pillows to our ears, or pretend we didn't hear it—even if we have a schedule to keep. Our need for sleep is powerful and irresistible. But why?

One way to investigate this question is to deprive people of sleep and see what happens. I pulled a few "all-nighters" when I was younger and "burned the midnight oil." You may have done so as well, but probably not for periods of time that are long enough to push the limits. A unique opportunity to observe the effects of sleep deprivation presented itself in New York City in 1959. As part of a fund-raising drive, disc jockey Peter Tripp forced himself to stay awake and on the air for 200 hours. By the fifth day, Tripp's speech was slurred, and he was hallucinating and showing signs of paranoia (he believed that "enemies" were trying to drug his coffee). It seemed that sleep was essential to his mental health. But after sleeping for 13 hours, Tripp had completely recovered.

A second highly publicized case came about in 1964, when seventeen-year-old Randy Gardner sought fame in the *Guinness Book of World Records.* As part of a high-school science project, and with the help of two friends, Gardner stayed awake for 264 hours—that's eleven straight days, a world record (which was later broken). When it was over, he held a news conference, during which he said "it's just mind over matter." He went to sleep for 15 hours, woke up feeling fine, and resumed his normal schedule. Follow-up tests confirmed that Gardner suffered no long-term ill effects (Dement, 1992). For many years, the Gardner story was surrounded by the myth that he experienced no ill effects during the episode. But daily tests administered to Gardner showed that his thinking was fragmented, his speech was slurred, he couldn't concentrate, he had memory lapses, and toward the end, he was hallucinating (Coren, 1996).

On the basis of these episodes and numerous studies, sleep researchers have concluded that sleep is a necessary function. There are two types of explanations for why this is so (Hobson, 1989). One comes from restoration theory, which states that sleep recharges the battery, enabling us to recover from the day's physical, cognitive, and emotional demands. This theory explains why people feel run-down as the day wears on and refreshed after a night's sleep. It's also supported by research on the effects of prolonged sleep deprivation in laboratory rats. In a series of experiments, Allan Rechtschaffen and his colleagues placed rats on a circular platform surrounded by cold water and monitored their EEG patterns. There was ample food, and the temperature was set at a suitable level. Whenever the EEG showed that the rat was falling asleep, however, the platform would slowly rotate, causing the rat to move in order to avoid being pushed into the water (control rats were similarly treated but were permitted to sleep). The results were striking: Two to three weeks of sleep deprivation resulted in a lowered body temperature, increased food intake, increased metabolism, weight loss, and a breakdown of the immune system, inevitably followed by death (Everson, 1995; Rechtschaffen & Bergmann, 1995; Everson, 1995).

A second type of explanation for why we sleep comes from the circadian theory, which focuses on the evolutionary significance of sleep. All animals sleep or go through regular intervals of inactivity. According to this view, sleep is a neural mechanism that has evolved over time so that animals can conserve energy and minimize their exposure to predators when they are not foraging for food or seeking a mate. Circadian theory correctly predicts that there are species-specific differences in sleep

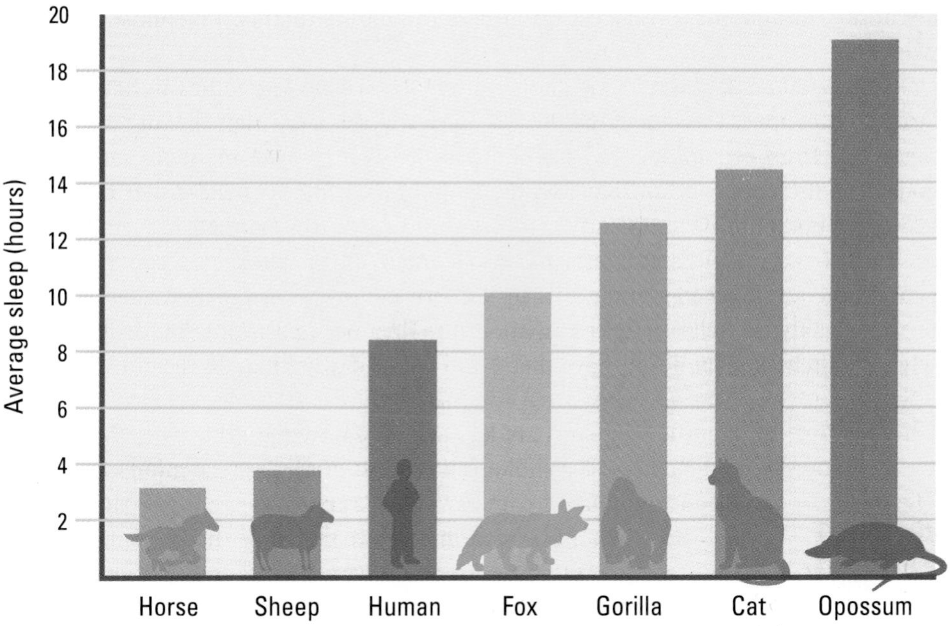

Figure 4.12 Daily hours of sleep: cross-species comparisons

patterns. As shown in Figure 4.12, animals that sleep the longest find food easily and are well hidden from predators while sleeping. In contrast, animals that sleep the shortest amount of time spend more hours foraging and can defend themselves only by running away. Seen from this perspective, we humans sleep at night because we're not very well adapted to searching for food in the dark or protecting ourselves from nocturnal predators (Allison & Cicchetti, 1976; Horne, 1988).

The question of why humans sleep is still something of an unsolved mystery. Restoration and circadian theories do not contradict one another, and many researchers believe that both mechanisms are at work (Borbely, 1986; Webb, 1992). A second important question is: How much sleep do we need in order to function during the day and stay healthy? Clearly, individuals differ in this regard. Thomas Edison, inventor of the modern lightbulb, required only about 4 hours each night. This fact is interesting given that Edison's 1913 lightbulb contributed to a sharp decline in the amount of sleep people get—from 9 hours a night, as measured in 1910, to the current average of less than 7.5 (Coren, 1996). Is this enough? How much sleep do *you* need? Do you sometimes sleep through the alarm? Is getting out of bed a struggle? Do you ever fall asleep when you don't want to? Sleep expert William Dement (1992) believes that Americans suffer from a "national sleep deficit."

Dreams

Between the ages of twelve and eighteen, I had a strange recurring dream. At eye level, I would be looking across a straight, smooth, waxed-wood surface. Then from a distance, a silver ball would start to roll toward me. It started slowly at first but picked up speed as it came closer. As the ball rolled toward my nose, a voice inside it would repeat my name—and get louder as the ball got closer. I could never understand why the ball rolled, because, as the dreamer, I "knew" that the surface was perfectly horizontal. But roll it did, and I would always wake up just as the ball was about to hit

> *"Dreaming permits each and every one of us to be quietly and safely insane every night of our lives."*
>
> — CHARLES FISHER

my nose. Though not a scary dream, it had a haunting quality. Like most people, I wondered, "What does it mean?"

As Robert Van de Castle (1994) notes in *Our Dreaming Mind,* dreams have always fascinated people. The Assyrians, 8,000 years ago, believed that dreams were messages sent from evil spirits. The Egyptians believed they were messages sent by the gods. The Inuits of Hudson Bay and the Pantani of Malaysia believe that one's soul leaves the body during sleep and enters another world. Among the Kurds and Zulus, dreaming of adultery is an offense, and if you dream of receiving a gift, you must compensate the gift giver in waking life. In Western cultures, we assume that dreams, if properly analyzed, tell us something about the dreamer's past, present, or future. So what are dreams, why do we have them, and what, if anything, do they mean?

The Nature of Dreams Dreams are less puzzling now than they were before the 1953 discovery of REM sleep. Psychologists used to think that the mind was idling in sleep and that dreaming was a rare, and therefore significant, event. But then EEG recordings revealed that the sleeping human brain is active and that everyone dreams, without exception, several times a night. We now know that dreams are electrochemical events involving the brainstem and areas of the cortex and that the eyes flutter back and forth. What more is known about this mysterious state of consciousness, a state in which the mind is active but the sleeper is immobilized and hard to awaken?

> *"From the conservative assumptions of three REM periods per night and two dream stories within each period there is a resultant 150,000 dreams per person over a life span of 70 years."*
>
> — WILSE B. WEBB

Researchers now believe that REM sleep and the dreaming that accompanies it are biologically adaptive. This belief arises from three sources of evidence. The first is that all mammals have REM sleep (most birds do too, but reptiles, amphibians, and fish do not). Second, the amount of REM sleep is greatest early in life, while the brain is developing—and there is evidence to suggest that REM sleep is necessary for brain maturation (Marks et al., 1995). Among premature infants, 60 to 80 percent of all sleep time is spent in the REM stage. That number drops to 50 percent in full-term newborns, 30 percent at six months, 25 percent at two years, and 20 percent in early childhood, before diminishing later in life. Third, when subjects are deprived of REM sleep one night, they exhibit a "rebound effect" by taking extra REM time the next night (Brunner et al., 1990).

Is there a linkage between a sleeper's eye movements and dreams? This is a tricky question. Research shows that the longer a REM episode is, the more words an awakened subject uses to describe the dream—and the more elaborate the story. Similarly, the more active the brain is during REM, the more eventful are the dreams that are later reported. But patterns of eye movements do not seem to correspond to the images and actions of a dream—as when we follow characters in a film (Chase & Morales, 1983).

What Do People Dream About? What do people dream about? What do *you* dream about? Over the years, analyses of dream content have shown that certain themes seem to arise with remarkable frequency. Can you guess the three most commonly reported dreams? The first is of falling. The second is of being chased or attacked. The third is of trying repeatedly but failing to do something. Also common are dreams of flying, being unprepared or late for a big event, being rejected, and appearing naked in public (Stark, 1984).

Cataloging more than 10,000 dream reports, Calvin Hall and Robert Van de Castle (1966) found that 64 percent were associated with sadness, fear, or anger (falling

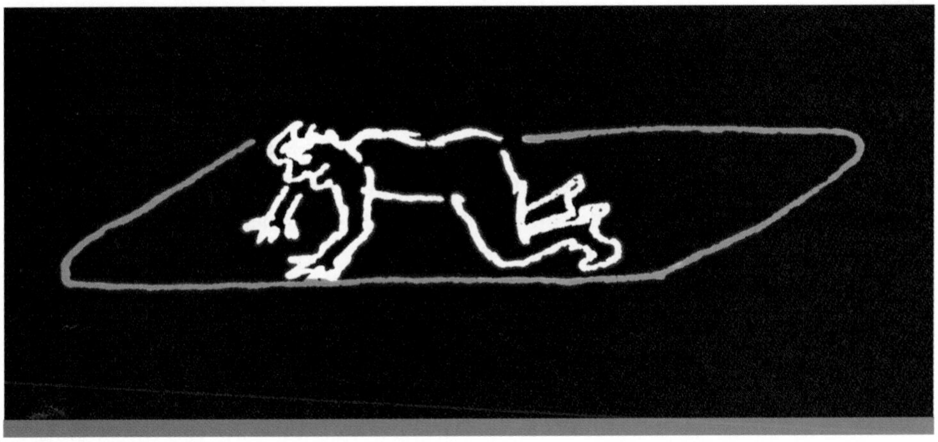

Research shows that dreams of flying are very common. This "flying carpet" image was created by a man who reports his dreams through drawing.

Can you become a lucid dreamer? Stephen LaBerge has invented a number of facilitating instruments, including DreamLight: a mask that picks up eye movements with an infrared detection device and transmits the data to an attached minicomputer. When the computer counts enough eye movements to determine that a REM period is underway, red lights flash inside the mask, signaling the sleeper, who can use the information to achieve lucidity. LaBerge tried using as a signal the tape-recorded phrase "This is a dream!" But he found that sounds tend to wake people up.

dreams, which are reported by 80 percent of college students, usually cause people to awaken abruptly before crashing to the ground), and only 18 percent were happy or exciting (flying dreams, which are reported by one third of people, are almost always seen as fun and exhilarating). Acts of aggression outnumbered acts of friendship by more than 2 to 1. And 29 percent of all dreams were in color. Women are more likely than men to have dreams that take place indoors, often at home, and often with others who are familiar to them. Men are more likely to dream about having sex and about physical activities outside the home, often with strangers in unfamiliar surroundings. About 30 percent of the dreams reported by young children contain threatening wild animals, but only 8 percent of adult dreams include animals—and these are mostly of dogs, horses, and other domesticated species (Van de Castle, 1994).

What influences the contents of our dreams? There are two documented sources. One is the concerns of daily life. If you're struggling financially, if you've had a death in the family, or if you're studying for a big exam or are involved in an exciting new relationship, these issues may well slip into your dreams—and thus provide an opportunity for creative problem solving (Cartwright, 1977). External stimuli are a second source of influence. Have you ever heard the radio alarm go off but slept through the music and dreamed you were at a concert? William Dement (1992) sprayed water on subjects' hands during REM sleep, awakened them a short time later, and found that 42 percent—far more than normal—reported dreaming of rainfalls, leaking roofs, swimming pools, and the like. Similarly, 56 percent incorporated into their dreams the taped sounds of dogs, trains, bells, and other stimuli.

For some dreamers, there is a third source of influence that, in some ways, is the most interesting: themselves. As a general rule, people are not aware that they are dreaming *while* they are dreaming. But have you ever had the odd sensation of dreaming—and knowing that you were in a dream? This "half in–half out" state of consciousness is called **lucid dreaming.** Most people have experienced this state on only an occasional basis—as when a dream takes on such a bizarre quality that they know it cannot be real. But some people are frequent lucid dreamers, and it appears to be a skill that can be developed. In some studies, for example, lucid dreamers have been trained to signal the onset of a dream to an experimenter by moving their eyes and clenching their fists. Lucid dreamers also report that sometimes they can actually control the contents—and outcomes—of their own dreams. In this manner,

lucid dreaming A semiconscious dream state in which a sleeper is aware that he or she is dreaming.

"I wouldn't be too concerned with this dream. Sometimes a 35-foot-tall singing pirate juggling bowling balls is just a 35-foot-tall singing pirate juggling bowling balls."

lucid dreaming can be used to resolve conflicts and tame the monsters in our nightmares (Gackenbach & Bosveld, 1989; LaBerge, 1992).

Our dreams may be influenced by inner concerns and external stimuli, and even by our own will. And most dreams are fairly mundane (Cipolli et al., 1993). But sometimes our dreams have a bizarre, magical quality—whereby time seems to stand still or speed forward, shadowy figures appear and vanish on cue, or we fall into bottomless pits, soar like Superman, and float in utter defiance of gravity. How can these qualities be explained? And what do they tell us about why we dream? No one really knows for sure, but there are two major theories.

Freud's Interpretation In 1900, Sigmund Freud published a classic book entitled *The Interpretation of Dreams.* According to Freud, all people are unconsciously motivated to satisfy sexual and aggressive urges. These ideas are too threatening to express or even to recognize, so we keep them from awareness through the use of defense mechanisms. So far, so good. During sleep, however, our defensive guard is down, and pent-up drives can no longer be suppressed. It would be psychologically shattering to come face to face with our deepest, darkest urges. Such realizations would also disrupt our sleep. The solution: We construct dreams that express the fulfillment of these drives—but in ways that are too indirect and confusing to recognize. In short, the dream we remember in the morning is a disguised, scrambled expression of unconscious wishes. The drive is fulfilled, but in such a way that the psyche—and sleep—are protected.

With his theory of psychoanalysis to guide him (see Chapter 15), Freud saw dreams as a "royal road" to the unconscious. He called the dream we remember in the morning the **manifest content.** The underlying thoughts, urges, conflicts, and needs that give rise to that dream constitute its **latent content.** According to Freud, the only way to uncover this unconscious latent material (which, after all, is the "true meaning") is to decode the dream and the symbols that disguise it. In the language of dreams, he said, kings and queens symbolize parents; small animals symbolize children; a house symbolizes the human body; and flying is the mental equivalent of having sex.

Activation-Synthesis Theory Freud's theory is hard to prove or disprove, and many psychologists worry that it encourages us to "overinterpret" dreams. Recent theories take a different, more neuropsychological approach. The most influential is the **activation-synthesis theory** of J. Allan Hobson and Robert McCarley (1977), which was later revised by Hobson (1988). According to this two-process theory, random neural signals firing in the brainstem spread up to the cortex (activation). Drawing on past experiences stored in memory, the brain then constructs images and stories in an effort to make sense out of these random signals (synthesis). According to this account, the brightness, color, and clarity of dream images are triggered by the firing of sensory neurons during REM sleep (Antrobus, 1991). Similarly, the physical-motion dreams that Freud had described as typical (flying, climbing, falling) are triggered by the activity of motor neurons during REM sleep (Porte & Hobson, 1996).

Both Freud's account and activation-synthesis theory agree that the dream's manifest content is not meaningful. But they differ in two respects. The first concerns the interpretation of the manifest content. For Freud, the mind constructs bizarre dreams to disguise its true meaning from the dreamer. For Hobson and McCarley, the brain constructs bizarre dreams because it has only limited information and operates on short notice. In other words, "the manifest content is the dream. There is no other dream" (Hobson, 1988, p. 258). The second key difference concerns the

manifest content According to Freud, the conscious dream content that is remembered in the morning.

latent content According to Freud, the unconscious, censored meaning of a dream.

activation-synthesis theory The theory that dreams result from the brain's attempt to make sense of random neural signals that fire during sleep.

significance attached to the so-called latent content. Freud believed that dreams spring from deep unconscious wishes. Hobson and McCarley argue that dreams are the incidental by-product of neural overactivity. At this point, there is not enough research to declare a winner between these two approaches. What is clear, however, is that through an interaction of physiological and psychological processes, the mind is remarkably active during sleep.

Sleep Disturbances

At some point in life, nearly everyone suffers from a sleep-related problem. You lie in bed, tossing and turning, brooding over something that happened or worrying about something that might. Or you keep nodding off in class or at work or in other embarrassing situations. Or you leap up in a cold sweat, with your heart pounding, from a realistic and terrifying nightmare. In general, there are three types of disturbances: sleeping too little (insomnia), sleeping too much (hypersomnia), and having disturbed or troubled sleep (parasomnia).

Insomnia

The sleep disturbance known as **insomnia** is characterized by a recurring inability to fall asleep, stay asleep, or get the amount of sleep needed to function during the day. Very few of us adhere to the daily "ideal" of eight hours for work, eight for play, and eight for sleep. On the contrary, people differ in the amount of sleep they want. Some are at their most alert after six hours a night, while others need nine or ten hours to get along. How much time is sufficient depends on who you are.

> *"It is extremely rare to find an animal with insomnia. . . . Insomnia is a human disorder."*
>
> — RICHARD M. COLEMAN

> *"The only thing wrong with insomniacs is that they don't get enough sleep."*
>
> — W. C. FIELDS

About 30 percent of the population complain of insomnia—and half of these people consider the problem to be serious (American Psychiatric Association, 1994). It's not that easy to know when someone has insomnia based on self-report, however. In a study that illustrates the point, Mary Carskadon brought 122 insomniacs into the laboratory and compared their self-perceptions to EEG measures of sleep. The next morning, the subjects estimated that it took them an hour to fall asleep and that they slept for $4\frac{1}{2}$ hours. But EEG tracings revealed that it took them only 15 minutes to fall asleep, which is average, and that they slept for $6\frac{1}{2}$ hours. More than 10 percent of all complaints are from "pseudoinsomniacs" who sleep normally but don't realize it (Kelly, 1991).

Among people who do have trouble falling or staying asleep, insomnia is not a disease but a symptom with many causes. Studies show that psychiatric patients get less sleep than do people without mental disorders (Benca et al., 1992). Medical ailments, pain, life stresses, depression, jet lag, night work, shifting work schedules, old age, and alcohol and drug abuse are also linked to insomnia. In some cases, the only "problem" is that people who think they should sleep eight hours a night go to bed before they're really tired. The use of medications poses a particularly ironic danger. Over-the-counter sleeping pills such as Sominex and Sleep-eze are not effective. Prescription drugs will, at first, put the insomniac to sleep and prevent rude awakenings during the night. But these sedatives will also inhibit certain stages of sleep and cause restlessness after the drug is terminated—if it is terminated. The habit of popping sleeping pills can be addictive and should be avoided. Numerous studies have shown that most people can successfully overcome insomnia by altering their behavior—but that the benefits are smaller for those who take sleeping pills (Morin et al., 1994; Murtagh & Greenwood, 1995). Some helpful tips are presented in Table 4.1.

insomnia An inability to fall asleep, stay asleep, or get the amount of sleep needed to function during the day.

Table 4.1 How to Overcome Insomnia

- Record how much sleep you *actually* get in a night, and set that total as a goal. If you sleep four or five hours, aim for a four-hour schedule.
- Do not take naps during the day.
- Avoid all alcohol, caffeine, and cigarettes within five hours of bedtime; avoid exercise within two hours of bedtime; relax.
- Make sure the bedroom is completely dark when you go to bed. When you awaken, turn on the lights and raise the shades.
- Keep a rigid schedule. Get into bed at 1 AM, not earlier. Set the alarm for 5 AM—and get out of bed no matter what.
- If you're awake but relaxed, stay in bed.
- If you're awake and anxious, get out of bed and return when you are sleepy. Keep the alarm set, and get up when it rings.
- If you stick to this schedule, you should see results in three to five weeks. If you want, you can then add thirty to sixty minutes to your schedule.
- Rest assured that you can get by on less sleep than you want and that a temporary loss of sleep will not cause harm.

Hypersomnia Studies in different countries show that about 5 percent of people complain of hypersomnia—being sleepy during the day and sleeping too much at night (Guilleminault & Roth, 1993). The most profound and most dangerous problem of this type is **narcolepsy** (which means "sleep seizure"), an uncommon disorder characterized by sudden, irresistible attacks of drowsiness and REM sleep during the day (American Psychiatric Association, 1994).

A narcolepsy attack may strike without warning at any time—while playing basketball, eating a meal, having a conversation, working in an office, or having sex. The attack lasts from five to thirty minutes and plunges its victim into REM sleep. The narcoleptic's jaw will sag, the head will fall forward, the arms will drop, and the knees will buckle. This collapse is often accompanied by the hypnogogic hallucinations that usher in the onset of sleep. As you might imagine, people with narcolepsy have problems at work and in their social lives. They are often unfairly perceived as lazy and disinterested. Narcolepsy can also be life-threatening. In one study, 40 percent of the narcoleptics who were questioned admitted they had fallen asleep while driving (Siegel et al., 1991). Although there is no cure, daytime sleep attacks can be minimized through the use of stimulant drugs (Mitler et al., 1994) and regularly scheduled naps (Mullington & Broughton, 1993).

There is an old saying, "Laugh and the world laughs with you, snore and you sleep alone!"

narcolepsy A sleep disorder characterized by irresistible and sudden attacks of REM sleep during the day.

sleep apnea A disorder in which a person repeatedly stops breathing during sleep and awakens gasping for air.

Parasomnias For some people, falling asleep at night and staying awake during the day are not a problem—but too often their sleep is disturbed. There are several specific disorders of this type. One particularly troublesome disturbance is **sleep apnea** (*apnea* means "to stop breathing"), which afflicts between 1 and 4 percent of Americans—mostly obese men. A person with sleep apnea will fall asleep normally but then stop breathing and awaken snorting like a buzz saw, choking, and gasping for air. Sleep-laboratory studies show that a person with sleep apnea will fall asleep again right away, but these partial awakenings can recur 400 times during the night, thus preventing slow-wave sleep and making the person excessively tired and irritable during the day (Langevin et al., 1992). With some success, the problem can be treated with continuous positive airways pressure (CPAP), a plastic mask that gently pumps air into the nose. The air holds the person's throat open and prevents snoring

(Sullivan et al., 1981; Wittig, 1993). Of course, many people without apnea also snore while they sleep—much to the chagrin of roommates and bed partners.

Nightmares are vivid, anxiety-provoking dreams that sometimes haunt us during REM sleep. They are common and should seldom be a source of concern. Children are more likely than adults to have nightmares, and it becomes a problem only if they persist for long periods of time. Nightmares are not dangerous, except for people who have **REM sleep behavior disorder (RBD)**—a very rare condition in which the skeletal muscles do not become paralyzed, as they should, during REM sleep. People with RBD have mobility to act on their nightmares and often do so in violent ways. As a result, 85 percent of sufferers have injured themselves and 44 percent have hurt their bed partners, sometimes seriously (Mahowald & Schenck, 1989; Schenck, 1993).

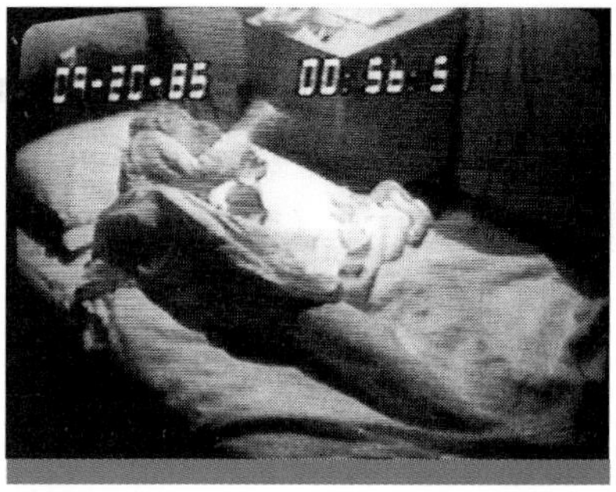

Taken in a sleep lab, this photograph shows a man with REM sleep behavior disorder. While dreaming, he throws a punch at the bed—one of twelve punches he throws in this particular sequence. Fortunately, at this time, he is sleeping alone.

There are also NREM sleep disruptions. In *night terrors,* the person jolts abruptly from a deep sleep, in a state of panic, and gives off a loud, bloodcurdling scream. As with nightmares, this problem is more common among children than adults. It's also more frightening, particularly for others in the household. Because it occurs during NREM sleep, however, the night-terror victim will usually not recall a dream and by morning will have forgotten the whole episode. Another NREM experience is *sleepwalking,* in which the sleeper quietly sits up, climbs out of bed, and walks about with eyes open and a blank expression. Sleepwalkers may start slowly, but soon they're going to the bathroom, dressing, eating, and opening doors. They are prone to accidents such as falling down stairs, so it is safer to gently awaken a sleepwalker than to allow the person to wander about. People used to think that sleepwalkers were acting out dreams. But that's not the case. These episodes occur early in the night, during the deep, slow-wave stages of sleep. Sometimes sleepwalkers will wake up and be disoriented, but most often they just go back to bed. As with night-terror victims, sleepwalkers seldom recall their travels in the morning. This finding reinforces the point that the brain is active even during sleep—and that consciousness is complex and multilayered (Kelly, 1991).

Hypnosis

What is hypnosis, and why has it always been controversial? Are some individuals more susceptible than others to hypnosis? Can people be hypnotized against their will and then coerced to behave in certain ways? Is hypnosis useful in therapy? And is it an "altered" state of mind?

If you worry that you talk in your sleep and might reveal something embarrassing, relax. Sleep talkers seldom reply to questions, and they tend to mumble only senseless words and phrases.

About twenty-five years ago, Ernest Hilgard was demonstrating hypnosis in his psychology class. The student who volunteered to serve as a subject happened to be blind, so Hilgard hypnotized him and said that on the count of three he would become deaf—and would stay that way until touched on the right shoulder. One, two, three! Hilgard then banged blocks together and fired a starter's pistol that made everyone else leap from their seats. But the subject did not respond. His classmates shouted questions and taunted him, but still he did not respond. Then a hand went up. A student wanted to know if any part of the subject knew what was happening, because, after all, there was nothing really wrong with his ears.

It was a fascinating question. Hilgard said to the subject, "Perhaps there is some part of your mind that is hearing my voice and processing the information. If there is, I should like the index finger of your right hand to rise as a sign that this is the

REM sleep behavior disorder (RBD) A condition in which the skeletal muscles are not paralyzed during REM sleep, enabling a sleeper to act upon his or her nightmares, often violently.

case." To everyone's surprise, even Hilgard's, the young man raised his finger and said, "Please restore my hearing so that you can tell me what you did." Hilgard then put his hand on the subject's shoulder and asked, "Can you hear me now?" The subject did. "I remember your telling me that I would be deaf at the count of three and have my hearing restored when you placed your hand on my shoulder. Then everything was quiet for a while. It was a little boring just sitting here so I busied myself with a statistical problem that I had been working on. I was still doing that when I felt my finger lift; that is what I want you to explain to me."

Next, Hilgard asked to speak with "that part of your mind that listened to me before, while you were hypnotically deaf." "Do you remember what happened?" The subject remembered it all—the count to three, the banging blocks, the starter pistol, and the questions from the class to which he did not respond. "Then one of them asked if I might really be hearing, and you told me to raise my finger if I did. This part of me responded by raising my finger, so it's all clear now." Hilgard lifted his hand from the subject's arm to restore the hypnotic state and said, "Please tell me what happened in the last few minutes." The subject replied, "You said . . . some part of me would talk to you. Did I talk?" The young man was assured that he would later recall everything, and the session was terminated (Hilgard, 1992). Hilgard called the aware part of this subject's mind a "hidden observer." This concept is controversial—and, as we'll see, it has profound implications for the study of consciousness. But first things first. What is hypnosis, how is it induced, and what are its effects?

The Seeds of Controversy

Hypnosis is a set of attention-focusing procedures in which changes in a person's behavior or state of mind are suggested. In one form or another, hypnosis has been

Hypnosis is important in the history of psychology and has profound implications for our understanding of consciousness. As shown here, hypnosis is also performed for entertainment purposes.

hypnosis Attention-focusing procedures in which changes in a person's behavior or mental state are suggested.

around for centuries. But the earliest known reference to it is traced to Franz Anton Mesmer (1734–1815), a Viennese physician. Mesmer believed that illness was caused by an imbalance of magnetic fluids in the body—and could be cured by restoring the proper balance. Working in Paris, he would pass his hands across the patient's body and wave a magnetic wand over the infected area. Many patients would descend into a trance and then awaken feeling better. The medical community, however, viewed this treatment with skepticism, and in 1784 a French commission chaired by Benjamin Franklin found that there was no scientific basis for the "animal magnetism" theory, only "mere imagination." Mesmer was labelled a quack and run out of town. When he died, he was penniless. Yet to this day, we acknowledge his work whenever we describe ourselves as being mesmerized.

In the nineteenth century, the trancelike state Mesmer had created was called hypnotism, from the Greek word for "sleep." From that point on, hypnosis has had a rocky relationship with science. On the one hand, stage hypnotists who swing pocket watches back and forth and try to make audience members cluck like chickens associate hypnosis with parlor games, carnivals, and magic acts. On the other hand, psychoanalysis originated with Freud's use of hypnosis to treat patients with various nervous disorders. And today, many health-care specialists use hypnosis with reasonable success to control pain and help patients break bad habits. For researchers interested in consciousness, hypnosis is a useful and provocative phenomenon—one that is still not completely understood (Fromm & Nash, 1992; Rhue et al., 1993; Kirsch & Lynn, 1995).

The Hypnotic Induction

Hypnosis consists of two stages: an *induction,* which guides the subject into a pliable, suggestible frame of mind; then a specific *suggestion.* The induction process is not like casting a spell. There are no magical words or incantations to be uttered, and there is no single technique. But there is one essential ingredient: a focusing of attention.

Speaking in a slow, soft, and monotonous tone of voice, the hypnotist asks the subject to concentrate on something. It can be anything. Hypnotists used to have subjects stare at a flame, a shiny object, or a swinging pendulum, but a spot on the wall will work just as well. So will the subject's imagination. "Imagine that you're lying on a quiet beach. You are so warm and relaxed on the soft white sand, under the sun. You're very tired, and your eyes are closed. You can hear the ocean waves crashing on the shore and the gulls flying overhead. And you can smell the warm, salt air. It's so sunny. Your skin is so warm. And you're so relaxed. Your eyes are growing tired. Very tired. Your eyelids are getting heavy. Heavy. They're starting to close." Whatever technique is used, the purpose is to help the subject filter out all distractions and focus his or her mental spotlight.

Once the subject is in a state of "relaxed alertness," he or she is ripe for stage 2, suggestion. The hypnotist may begin with a quick test by suggesting that "your eyes are closed and your eyelids are shut so tight that you cannot open them no matter how hard you try." Sure enough, the subject's eyes remain closed. At that point, the subject is ready for more. The hypnotist may note that the subject's arm is filling with air like a balloon and that it's feeling lighter and lighter—and is rising in the air. The subject does not know why, but the arm rises, as if being pulled up on a string. The hypnotist may even invite the subject to enjoy the scent of "perfume"—and watch as he or she inhales the fumes from a jar of ammonia. Assuming the subject "passes" these preliminary tests, additional suggestions depend on the reasons for the hypnosis. Thus, a subject may be encouraged to block out pain, recall a traumatic past event, forget a past event, or break a bad habit when the session is over.

Hypnotic Responsiveness

Contrary to popular belief, you cannot be hypnotized against your will. Nobody can. People also differ. Several years ago, Hilgard (1965) developed the Stanford Hypnotic Susceptibility Scale (SHSS), a twelve-item behavioral test that measures one's **hypnotic susceptibility**, or responsiveness, to hypnosis. In this test, a brief induction is followed by suggestions for the subject to close his or her eyes, sway back and forth, stiffen an arm, lower a hand, see an imaginary person, and so on. Over the years, Hilgard has found that some people are highly susceptible to hypnosis and that others are invulnerable to hypnosis but that most fall somewhere between these extremes (Hilgard, 1982). In short, some types of people are more susceptible, and others are less susceptible, to hypnosis (Oakman & Woody, 1996).

What accounts for these individual differences? Research has shown that college students who scored high or low in the early 1960s obtained similar scores when they were retested twenty-five years later (Piccione et al., 1989). This result tells us that there are stable personality differences between the highs and lows. But how are these differences to be interpreted? It has always been interesting to me that in discussions of hypnosis, students often seem eager if not proud to proclaim that they are too "independent" or too "strong-willed" to be hypnotized. But hypnotic responsiveness is not a sign of weakness. High scorers are not generally weaker or more conforming, compliant, or obedient. However, they are more open to experience, have more vivid imaginations, and have an ability to become deeply absorbed in books, movies, and other activities (J. Hilgard, 1979; Nadon et al., 1991). High scorers also have a more sustained attention span and a greater ability to filter out distractions (Crawford et al., 1993). In one study, individuals highly responsive to hypnosis—often referred to as "virtuosos"—were actually led under hypnosis to experience themselves as members of the opposite sex (Noble & McConkey, 1995).

The Myths and Realities

Can a stage hypnotist make you strip naked in front of an audience, clap your hands together, and bark like a seal? Popular portrayals of hypnosis are sometimes accurate, but often they are not. Based on the results of controlled research, let us examine the effects of hypnosis and try to separate the myths from the realities.

Coercion As noted earlier, people cannot be hypnotized against their will. But can subjects, once under hypnosis, be coerced into committing acts that violate their conscience? Are they at the mercy of a skilled hypnotist? For the sake of those who stand to benefit from the therapeutic uses of hypnosis, one would hope not. In response to the idea that the subject is under the hypnotist's control, Karen Olness (1993), a pediatrician and hypnotherapist, says, "Nonsense. All hypnosis is self-hypnosis" (p. 280). Many psychologists share this view. And as a general rule, hypnotized subjects reject immoral commands, knowing fully well that they are in control.

But there is evidence to suggest that hypnotic coercion can lead people to shed inhibitions. In one experiment, Martin Orne and Frederick Evans (1965) convinced

hypnotic susceptibility The extent to which an individual is characteristically responsive to hypnosis.

hypnotized subjects to throw what they thought to be nitric acid into a research assistant's face. To see if this result proved that hypnosis can overpower the will, Orne and Evans told a second group of subjects only to pretend they were hypnotized, issued the same command, and found that they too threw the "acid." Additional studies as well suggest that subjects in hypnosis experiments are well aware of what they are doing—and are confident that they would not be asked to harm themselves or someone else (Gibson, 1991). As we'll see later, these results may say more about obedience to authority than about hypnosis.

Pain Relief "On the operating table, I put myself into a deeply relaxed state. I then concentrated on a favorite memory: living on a farm as a child. In my mind, I felt what it was like to lie on the grass, gaze up at the heavens, and see a bit of the barn out of the corner of my eye. As the surgeon cut into the base of my thumb, I reassured him that I felt no pain. . . . Although I was perfectly aware that I was undergoing surgery, I just wasn't very interested in it." This story, as described by Olness (1993, p. 277), embodies a real benefit of hypnosis: to serve as a psychological anesthetic.

In the classic test of this hypothesis, Hilgard and his colleagues (1975) instructed two groups of subjects to immerse one hand in a tank of ice water for almost a minute. Every ten seconds, they rated how much pain they felt on a 10-point scale. In one group, subjects were hypnotized and given the suggestion that they would feel no pain. In the second group, there was no hypnosis and no suggestion. The result was that the hypnotized subjects reported less pain than did the controls. We'll return to this study shortly to see what it implies about consciousness. What it implies about pain, however, is clear. Today, studies continue to show that for people high in hypnotic responsiveness, hypnosis can be used to reduce pain (Miller & Bowers, 1993) and that this effect can be achieved with or without the use of counterpain images—such as suggestions that the hand is made of wood or is encased in a heavy protective glove (Hargadon et al., 1995). Not everyone can be hypnotized, and not all who are hypnotized will gain relief from pain. But for some, hypnosis can help in coping with dental work, childbirth, and the chronic pain of headaches, backaches, and arthritis (Kihlstrom, 1985).

Posthypnotic Suggestion In the situations described thus far, the subject acts upon the hypnotist's suggestions during the session. In a procedure known as **posthypnotic suggestion,** the subject carries out the hypnotist's suggestion *after* the session is terminated. You've probably seen this procedure depicted on TV shows. With a snap of the finger, the subject would emerge from his or her "trance" and reflexively perform a specific behavior in response to a preset cue. In reality, posthypnotic suggestion lacks dramatic flair. But in conjunction with psychological therapy, it has been used effectively to help people with insomnia, obesity, hypertension, and other problems (Kirsch et al., 1995). It can also help speed the healing of warts and other skin conditions that are affected by psychological factors—though positive suggestions without hypnosis have the same therapeutic effect (Spanos et al., 1988).

posthypnotic suggestion A suggestion made to a subject in hypnosis to be carried out *after* the induction session is over.

Memory Enhancement As in Hilgard's classroom demonstration, hypnosis subjects very often exhibit **posthypnotic amnesia,** an inability to recall events that occurred during the session. It's important to note that these memories have not

posthypnotic amnesia A reported tendency for hypnosis subjects to forget events that occurred during the induction.

been permanently erased. In response to a prearranged signal ("When I snap my fingers you'll recall everything that took place"), subjects can usually retrieve the lost events. Still, research suggests that hypnosis subjects do often exhibit temporary amnesia—and do so without effort or intention (Bowers & Woody, 1996).

At the other end of the hypnosis-memory spectrum, many hypnotists claim that the highly focused and relaxed state of mind produced by hypnosis *enhances* memory—a phenomenon known as **hypermnesia.** This claim has its roots in psychoanalysis—from when Freud reported that hypnotized patients sometimes relived repressed traumas from childhood—and has resurfaced in a rash of recent cases in which hypnosis was used to dredge up "memories" of child sex abuse (Loftus, 1993). This use of hypnosis within the legal system has recently come under scrutiny (see Intersection: Can Hypnosis Enhance Eyewitness Testimony?).

hypermnesia A term referring to the unsubstantiated claim that hypnosis can be used to facilitate the retrieval of past memories.

I N T E R S E C T I O N

CONSCIOUSNESS AND LAW

Can Hypnosis Enhance Eyewitness Testimony?

In 1976, in Chowchilla, California, a busload of twenty-six schoolchildren and the driver were abducted at gunpoint by three masked kidnappers and held for ransom in an underground tomb. Somehow, they managed to escape. The driver had tried to memorize the license plate number of the van the kidnappers used, but he could not recall the number. He was then hypnotized by the police and was mentally transported back to the scene of the crime. All of a sudden, he blurted out all but one digit of the license plate—which led to the arrest and later conviction of the abductors (Smith, 1983).

This case and others like it raise an intriguing question: Can hypnosis be used to refresh a witness's memory? Many police officers seem to think so and use hypnosis to help eyewitnesses recall details of violent crimes they seem to have forgotten. In one popular technique, devised by Martin Reiser (1980), subjects under hypnosis are asked to imagine that they are calmly watching a TV documentary about the event to be recalled and that they can rewind it, stop it, play it back, slow it down, speed it up, zoom in for closeups, and turn the sound volume up or down to improve hearing. Using this technique, police investigators have made some impressive claims about the memory-enhancing power of hypnosis (Reiser & Nielson, 1980).

The success stories are fascinating, but serious questions remain. When a hypnotized witness reports a memory, how do we know that the report is accurate? And if the recollection is later corroborated, how do we know that it was retrieved because of the hypnosis? To answer these questions, some researchers have studied actual cases. Others have conducted experiments in which subjects witness a staged event, report their memory, and then try to

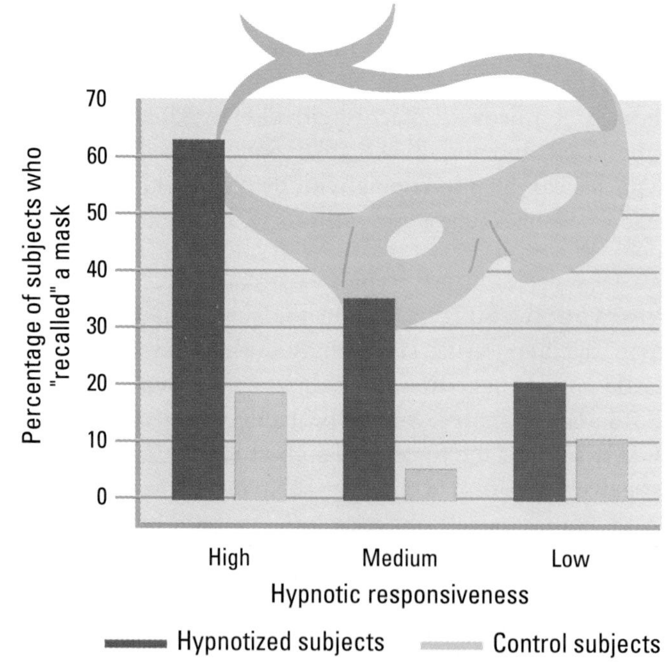

Figure 4.13 Hypnosis and the suggestible eyewitness After seeing a staged crime, subjects were questioned in a hypnotized or waking state by an examiner who suggested that the culprit had worn a mask. Under hypnosis, many subjects—particularly those of high responsiveness—later incorporated this false suggestion into memory.

recall additional details—either under hypnosis or in a normal waking state. Consistently, the research has shown that although people report more and more information with repeated testing, they also inadvertently produce more distorted and false "memories" (Dywan & Bowers, 1983; Dinges et al., 1992; McConkey & Sheehan, 1995).

Another disturbing outcome of hypnosis is that it places the witness in a state of heightened suggestibility. In one study, for example, Peter Sheehan and his colleagues (1991) showed 168 subjects a videotape of a staged bank robbery. In it, a man entered a bank, waved a pistol, warned the tellers not to press an alarm, ordered them to put the money on the counter, put the money in a bag, and ran out. Subjects were immediately questioned about the incident. Half were then hypnotized; the others were not. Moments later, everyone was requestioned by an examiner who "suggested" that the robber wore a mask over his face, which he did not. The hypnotized subjects were then dehypnotized, and everyone was questioned again, this time by a new examiner. Did anyone "recall" the robber wearing a mask? If so, how often did this occur? As illustrated in Figure 4.13 on page 156, the results were quite striking—and sobering. Subjects were more likely to incorporate the false suggestion into memory when they were under hypnosis, and this was particularly true of those who had high or medium scores on a test of hypnotic susceptibility. Among the most vulnerable subjects—those who were both highly susceptible and were exposed to a hypnotic suggestion—false memories were created 63 percent of the time.

Today, some states will allow a witness to testify about memories brought out under hypnosis. In light of recent research findings, however, a majority of American courts have reasonably decided to ban or at least to limit the testimony of witnesses who had earlier been hypnotized (Scheflin & Shapiro. 1989).

Is Hypnosis an "Altered" State?

Since the time Mesmer first used hypnotism to treat medical ailments, there has been widespread interest in the phenomenon. Freud used hypnosis to unlock the unconscious. Others have used it to relieve pain, to treat psychological problems, to uncover repressed memories, and to entertain audiences around the world. Using hypnosis is easy. The tougher question is: What is it? Does hypnosis produce an out-of-the-ordinary, trancelike, "altered" state of consciousness?

Psychologists are not in agreement on this question. Some say *yes,* others say *no.* As a general rule, *special-process* theorists maintain that hypnosis induces a unique state of consciousness and that people are more responsive to suggestion while under hypnosis than in other states (Hilgard, 1986; Bowers, 1992). In contrast, a growing number of *social-psychological* theorists maintain that hypnosis is not a distinct physiological state and that the same phenomena can often be produced through relaxation, role playing, positive expectations, or mere suggestion—without a hypnotic induction (Barber, 1969; Lynn et al., 1990; Spanos, 1986; Wagstaff, 1981).

Special-Process Theories

According to Ernest Hilgard (1986), hypnosis can induce a state of **dissociation**—a division of consciousness in which one part of the person operates independently of another. To some extent, dissociation is a common experience—as when you drive somewhere, only to realize afterward that you "spaced out" and do not recall the route you took or the traffic signals you obeyed. One part of you drove, while another part daydreamed about fame and fortune. In many people, says Hilgard, hypnosis produces a similar split in which one part of the mind goes along with hypnotic suggestions, while the other part—a "hidden observer"—knows what's happening but does not participate.

dissociation A division of consciousness that permits one part of the mind to operate independently of another part.

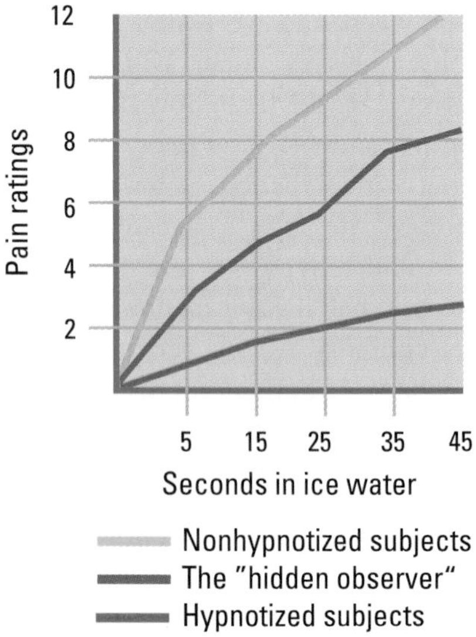

Figure 4.14 Hypnosis, pain, and the "hidden observer" Subjects immersed a hand in ice water and rated the pain they felt. Those under hypnosis reported less pain than did controls. But by pressing a key, they also indicated that a part of them—a "hidden observer"—was aware of the pain (Hilgard et al., 1975).

To illustrate this concept, let's return to the pain-tolerance experiment described earlier, where subjects immersed a hand in ice water and periodically rated how much pain they were in (Hilgard et al., 1975). Look at Figure 4.14, and you'll see that subjects reported far less pain when they were hypnotized to "feel no pain" than when they were not. Compared to control subjects, who reached a pain level of 10 within twenty-five seconds, the average pain rating of hypnotized subjects never exceeded a 2 on the scale. In a fascinating variation on this study, hypnotized subjects were told to press a key with their free hand if "some part" of them was in pain. Look again at Figure 4.14, and you'll see what happened. Even though the hypnotized subjects reported low pain levels, their hidden observer was passively aware of the pain. Because these subjects reported two different experiences at once, reasoned Hilgard, the hypnosis must have induced a state of dissociation. Well, perhaps.

Social-Psychological Theories The skeptics differ in their emphases, but all agree that the impressive effects of hypnosis stem from the power of social influence, not from any special process or trancelike state of altered consciousness. Perhaps highly responsive subjects are motivated to comply. Or perhaps they simply become so absorbed by the situation that they get caught up in their role the way dramatic actors often do. In support of this view, research shows that control subjects in the waking state often exhibit the same remarkable behaviors—when they are sufficiently motivated and believe they can succeed. Thus, pain tolerance in the ice-water test can be increased without a hypnotic induction (Spanos & Katsanis, 1989).

It's important to note that, although there are exceptions, most social-psychological theorists do not believe that hypnosis subjects consciously fake their compliance with the hypnotist's suggestions (Kirsch & Lynn, 1995). Is it possible to test this hypothesis? Yes. If subjects are merely playing along, they might respond to suggestions in the hypnotist's presence—but certainly not in his or her absence. In fact, however, the hypnotic effects carry over. Irving Kirsch and others (1989) hypnotized highly responsive subjects but instructed low-responsive subjects to simulate the hypnosis. The hypnotic test was twice administered over a tape recorder—once in front of the examiner and once when the subject was left alone. As shown in Figure 4.15, the results were clear: In front of the examiner, both hypnotized subjects and simulators complied equally with suggestions. But in the alone condition, a hidden camera revealed that highly responsive hypnosis subjects continued to respond to the test suggestions even while the simulators did not (in some cases, the simulators actually opened their eyes and read a magazine). Additional studies too have indicated that hypnotized subjects are not merely deceiving the experimenter (Spanos et al., 1993; Kinnunen et al., 1994; Reed et al., 1996). Hypnosis may not constitute a "special" process, but the subject's behavior reflects more than mere compliance.

At this point, there are many ways to view hypnosis. It is entirely possible, for example, that highly responsive individuals in hypnosis become so highly focused in their attention and so absorbed that the process feels "special." When college students were interviewed about their behavior in a campus-wide hypnotism show, 28 percent of those who took part thought the hypnotist had complete control over their actions and that they could not resist the suggestions (Crawford et al., 1992). In addition, new evidence from EEG recordings shows that alpha-wave activity—which typically accompanies a drowsy, presleep state—increases during hypnosis, particularly among subjects who are high in hypnotic responsiveness (Graffin et al., 1995). On the other hand, it seems clear that some people succumb to hypnosis and comply with suggestions through the normal channels of social influence, without a change in the state of their consciousness—which explains why subjects' expectations, motivations, and rapport with the hypnotist play an important role (Sarbin, 1992). In short, there may be two roads, both leading to the treasure.

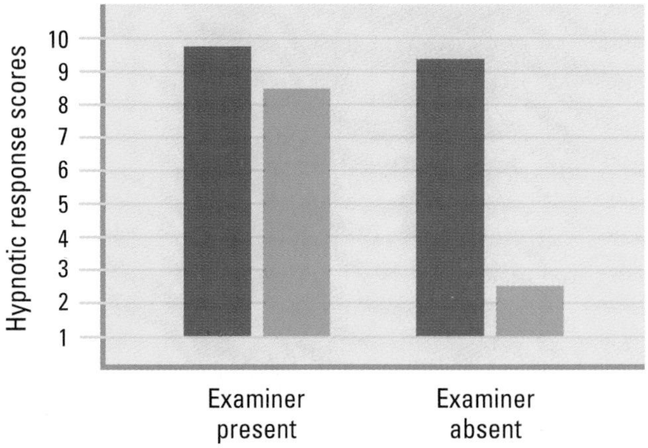

Figure 4.15 Hypnosis: more than mere compliance Subjects who were hypnotized or told to simulate hypnosis were twice given a tape-recorded hypnotic induction—once in the presence of the examiner and once alone. As shown, both groups followed the suggestions in front of the examiner (*left*), but only the hypnotized subjects continued to do so when alone (*right*) (Kirsch et al., 1989).

Consciousness-Altering Drugs

What drugs are considered "psychoactive," and why? When is a drug considered addictive? What are the effects on consciousness of alcohol and tobacco? What about illicit drugs such as marijuana, cocaine, and LSD? What are the long-term health effects?

Throughout history, people all over the world have sought new ways to achieve altered states of consciousness. Dancing, chanting, twirling in circles, repetitive prayer, yoga, ritualized fasting, meditation, sensory isolation, and intoxicants such as opium, alcohol, marijuana, and cocaine are a few examples. The historical and cross-cultural consistency of these behaviors is so compelling that some researchers believe there is an inborn human need to experience altered states of mind (Siegel, 1989; Weil & Rosen, 1993).

Alcohol, probably the first "mind-altering" substance used by humans, goes back about 10,000 years. Opium was used 6,000 years ago, and hallucinogenic mushrooms and weeds go back about 4,000 years (Palfai & Jankiewicz, 1991). More recently, Native Americans smoked tobacco as a goodwill offering. South Pacific islanders drink kava, a calming drink that is made from dried roots. And Europeans celebrate special occasions with wine and champagne. Instances of drug use have even been observed in animals. Baboons eat tobacco, rabbits eat intoxicating mushrooms, and elephants seek out fermented fruit.

People have used psychoactive drugs throughout history. In this Egyptian painting, dated 1350 BCE, the man on the left is sipping beer through a cane.

A quick but often dangerous way to alter consciousness is to use a **psychoactive drug,** a chemical that influences perceptions, moods, thoughts, or behavior. Depending on where in the world you are, a psychoactive substance may be legal or illegal. In most countries, caffeine, tobacco, alcohol, tranquilizers, and sleeping pills are legal. Marijuana, cocaine, crack, heroin, and LSD are illegal and are referred to as illicit drugs. As in our ancient past, humans are also in hot pursuit of the perfect aphrodisiac—a drug that will enhance sexual desire, pleasure, and performance (Rosen & Ashton, 1993).

Psychoactive drugs can become physically or psychologically addictive. **Physical dependence** is a physiological state in which continued drug use is needed to satisfy an intense craving and to prevent the dreaded onset of *withdrawal* symptoms such as shaking, sweating, and vomiting. Continued use of psychoactive drugs also produces *tolerance,* a condition in which larger and larger doses are needed to experience the same effect. Even without a physical addiction, people can also develop a **psychological dependence,** in which continued drug use is needed to maintain a sense of well-

psychoactive drug A chemical that alters perceptions, thoughts, moods, or behavior.

physical dependence A physiological addiction in which a drug is needed to prevent symptoms of withdrawal.

psychological dependence A condition in which drugs are needed to maintain a sense of well-being or relief from negative emotions.

People all over the world behave in ways that alter states of consciousness. As shown, football players do relaxation exercises, Haitian men and women dance in a ritual voodoo ceremony, and Chinese girls sip wine through bamboo straws.

being. As described in the coming pages and as summarized in Table 4.2, there are four major classes of psychoactive drugs: sedatives, stimulants, hallucinogens, and opiates. Drug use is a problem in general but is of greatest concern among youths. The drugs most commonly used by high school seniors in the United States are presented in Figure 4.16. The trends in drug use from 1975 through 1996 are presented in Figure 4.17 on page 162.

Sedatives

Sedatives, or depressants, slow down activity in the central nervous system and produce calmness, drowsiness, and, in large doses, a loss of consciousness. The most commonly used sedatives are alcohol, barbiturates, and benzodiazepines. The last two are used for anesthetic purposes and in the treatment of anxiety and insomnia. As a rule, these drugs are highly addictive (Snyder, 1996).

Alcohol is one of the most widely used drugs in the world. In 1995, the National Household Survey on Drug Abuse revealed—on the basis of 18,000 interviews—that 53 percent of Americans age twelve and older use alcohol on an occasional basis, 16 percent engage in occasional binge drinking (five or more drinks in one sitting), and 5.5 percent are regular heavy drinkers. The question is, what are the effects? Regardless of whether it comes from a six-pack, a bottle of wine, or a glass of whiskey, gin, or vodka, alcohol is something of a paradox. It's known as a party drug that lifts spirits and lowers inhibitions, yet it has a sedative, depressant effect on the body. The symptoms include decreased visual acuity; diminished attention; lowered sensitivity to taste, smell, and pain; slowed reaction times; a loss of balance; slurred speech; and lowered performance on intelligence tests. Alcohol hastens the onset of sleep (as do most depressants) but does not increase the overall amount of time one sleeps in a night. In fact, it suppresses REM sleep—which has a disruptive effect once the alcohol wears off.

"First you take a drink, then the drink takes a drink, then the drink takes you."

— F. SCOTT FITZGERALD

sedatives A class of depressant drugs that slow down activity in the central nervous system.

Anyone who has had a few too many drinks knows that alcohol alters awareness and behavior. As we'll see later in this book, alcohol has two effects in this regard.

Table 4.2 Consciousness-Altering Drugs

TYPE	SUBSTANCE	RANGE OF EFFECTS
Sedatives	Alcohol, barbiturates, benzodiazepines	Slowdown of body functions, relaxation, drowsiness, possibly depression and loss of consciousness
Stimulants	Caffeine, nicotine, amphetamines, cocaine	Speed up of body functions, alertness, energy, elation, jitteriness, loss of appetite
Hallucinogens	LSD, marijuana	Heightened sensory awareness, distorted perceptions of time and space, hallucinations
Opiates	Heroin, morphine, codeine	Suppressed pain, depressed neural activity, relaxation, drowsiness, euphoria

First, people often drown their sorrows in a bottle in order to escape from failure and its harsh implications for their self-esteem. Many of us expect alcohol to provide this type of "relief" (Leigh & Stacy, 1993) and to help us manage our emotional highs and lows (Cooper et al., 1995). Second, people take more risks when drunk than when sober. The reason is that alcohol leads us to become shortsighted about the consequences of our actions—and evokes a state of "drunken excess" (Steele & Josephs, 1990). Statistics consistently link drinking to highway fatalities, murders, stabbings, child abuse, and other acts of recklessness and violence. In laboratory experiments,

"Drunkenness reveals what soberness conceals."

— ENGLISH PROVERB

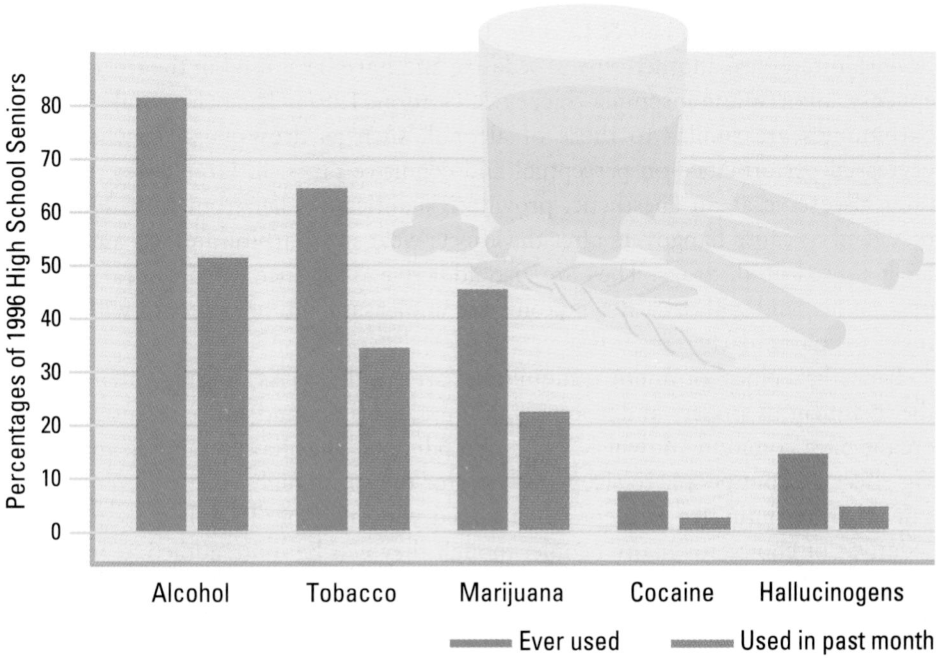

Figure 4.16 The five most commonly used drugs Shown here are the percentages of high school seniors in the Class of 1996 who tried and regularly used various drugs—not for medical purposes (National Institute on Drug Abuse, 1996).

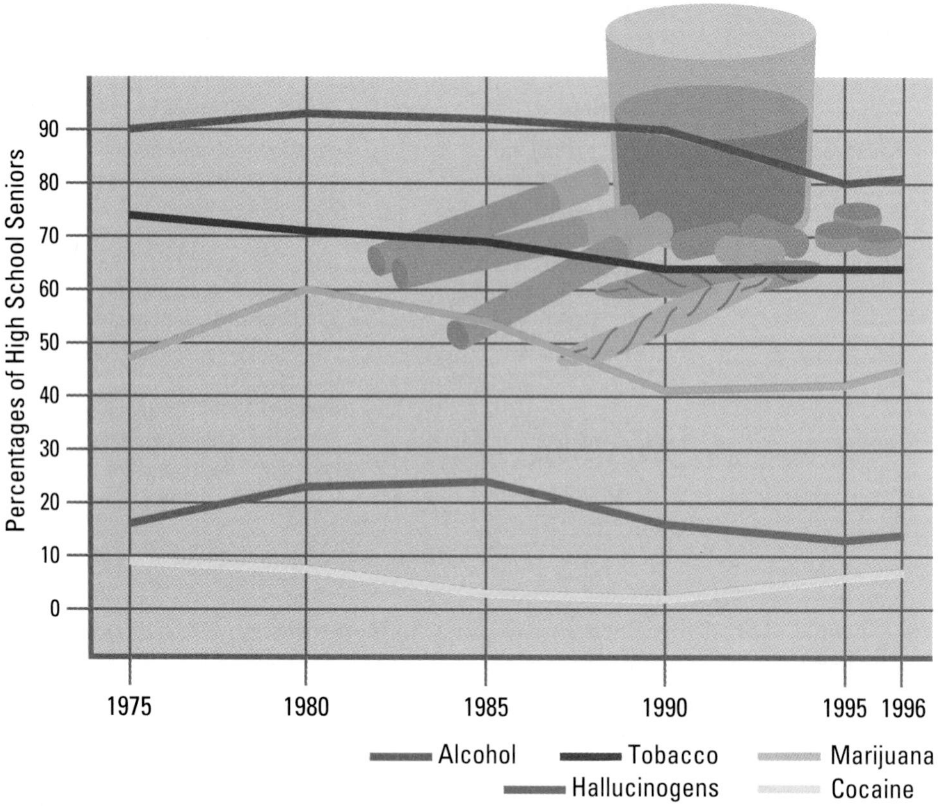

Figure 4.17 Changing patterns of drug use, 1975–1996 The U.S. government has been tracking the use of various drugs by high school seniors since 1975. You can see that although usage rates dropped through the 1980s, the downward trend is reversing somewhat (National Institute on Drug Abuse, 1996). Where will these numbers be in the year 2000?

subjects are more aggressive when given alcohol to drink than when given a nonalcoholic beverage (Bushman & Cooper, 1990).

Barbiturates are another type of sedative and have been used in the treatment of epilepsy, anxiety, and insomnia (Lickey & Gordon, 1991). The behavioral effects of barbiturates are similar to those of alcohol, such as drowsiness, slowness, and decreased performance on perceptual and cognitive tasks. In large doses, barbiturates also serve as an anesthetic, providing significant relief from pain. However, they tend to cause hangovers after the effects wear off. Barbiturates are among the most abused of all drugs. They are also addictive. Tolerance to barbiturates develops rapidly, and withdrawal symptoms are unpleasant. Mixing alcohol with barbiturates is particularly dangerous.

Benzodiazepines, or minor tranquilizers, are another class of drugs often used in the treatment of anxiety and insomnia. Valium, Librium, and, more recently, Xanax are the most common "downers." Taken in pill form, they have a calming and relaxing effect and put people to sleep—usually for the entire night. Benzodiazepines are safer than barbiturates—except when mixed with alcohol. They have become the sedatives of choice for many people, though they can be quite addictive with prolonged use (see Chapter 17).

Stimulants

stimulants A class of drugs that excite the central nervous system and energize behavior.

Stimulants excite the central nervous system and stimulate behavior (Leccese, 1991). Caffeine and nicotine are common mild stimulants. Amphetamines and cocaine have much stronger effects. These drugs speed up body functions (which is why amphetamines are known as speed or uppers), increase breathing and heart rates, heighten alertness, suppress appetite, and produce feelings of excitement, self-confidence, and even elation. For these reasons, stimulants have been used to stay awake, lose weight, and elevate mood. In large amounts, they can make a person anxious, jittery, and hyperalert. As is often the case with psychoactive drugs, the user may come down from the high in a "crash" and feel tired, downbeat, and irritable. As with sedatives, stimulants, including coffee, can be addictive (Silverman et al., 1992).

Amphetamines are synthetic drugs, often taken in pill form, for the treatment of asthma, narcolepsy, depression, and obesity (Palfai & Jankiewicz, 1991). In low doses, amphetamines increase alertness and arousal, boost energy, relieve fatigue, and suppress appetite. In higher doses, these drugs cause confusion, manic behavior, and aggression. Chronic amphetamine use can even trigger schizophrenialike symptoms. Recently, amphetamine modifications have been synthesized in the pharmaceutical laboratory. One of these "designer drugs" is MDMA, or Ecstasy. In addition to its stimulant properties, MDMA is said to evoke a sense of well-being, particularly in relation to others (Shulgin, 1986). One powerful methamphetamine commonly known as "speed" comes in a smokable form ("ice") that is highly addictive and can be fatal.

Cocaine ("coke") is a natural drug derived from the leaves of the coca plant, a shrub native to South America. Its use as a stimulant was discovered hundreds of years ago by Peruvian Indians, who chewed coca leaves to overcome fatigue and increase stamina. Taken in this manner, small amounts of cocaine gradually enter the bloodstream. Today, cocaine in white powder form is usually inhaled through the nose ("snorted"), resulting in a quick and intense *rush* of euphoria. Its consciousness-altering effects, which last up to thirty minutes, are predictably followed by a *crash* caused by a temporary depletion in the supply of dopamine and norepinephrine. A highly potent form of cocaine known as "crack" is smoked in a pipe or injected directly into the bloodstream. Crack gives a higher high but is followed by a lower low—and a craving for another "hit." It is dangerous and highly addictive (Gawin, 1991).

Hallucinogens

Hallucinogens are the psychoactive drugs that cause the most dramatic alterations in consciousness. These drugs (which are also called psychedelics, from the Greek words meaning "mind expanding") distort perceptions of time and space and cause hallucinations—sensations without sensory input. The best-known hallucinogens are LSD and PCP. The latter (also called "angel dust") is a potent but dangerous pain killer. Marijuana, which has mixed sedative and stimulant effects, also acts as a mild hallucinogen.

LSD (lysergic acid diethylamide) is a synthetic drug that was first discovered in 1938 by Albert Hofmann, a Swiss chemist. At one point, Hofmann experimented on himself. He took what he thought to be a small dose of LSD and found himself in a world he would never forget: "Everything in my field of vision was distorted as if seen in a curved mirror. . . . Familiar objects and furniture assumed grotesque, threatening forms . . . opening and closing themselves in circles and spirals, exploding in colored fountains" (Hofmann, 1980). Drug companies, researchers, and intelligence agencies in search of a truth serum soon went on to experiment with LSD. Even when it is taken at low doses, acid "trippers" report that objects shimmer, colors become more vivid, their perception of time is slowed, old memories surface,

hallucinogens Psychedelic drugs that distort perceptions and cause hallucinations.

and emotions range from euphoria to panic. Often, too, there is an eerie feeling of separation from one's own body, panic, and suicidal thoughts and actions (Miller & Gold, 1994). Many researchers believe that LSD and the other hallucinogens produce these effects by blocking activity of the neurotransmitter serotonin.

Marijuana is a milder and less potent hallucinogen. Derived from the leaves and flowering tops of the hemp plant, *Cannabis sativa,* marijuana has been cultivated for 5,000 years in many parts of the world. Its major active ingredient is called THC (delta-9-tetrahydrocannabinol), but it contains other chemicals that also have psychoactive effects. Marijuana is most often smoked in hand-rolled "joints" or pipes, but it may also be mixed into foods such as brownies. At low doses, marijuana may act like a sedative, producing a relaxed state and possibly a mild euphoria. It may also heighten awareness of colors, sounds, tastes, smells, and other sensations. At higher doses, it may distort perceptions of time and space. An estimated 10 million Americans use marijuana at least on occasion, making it the most commonly used illicit drug in the United States. Most alarming, according to the National Household Survey on Drug Abuse (1995), is that the rate of its usage is on the rise among youths twelve to seventeen years old.

Today, marijuana is a subject of raging controversy. In 1996, California and Arizona voters passed bills legalizing its use for medical purposes. In response, the U.S. federal government said it would continue to enforce laws prohibiting marijuana possession and prosecute physicians who dispense marijuana to their patients.

Proponents claim that marijuana has medical benefits, but opponents argue that it poses serious health risks. So what is the evidence? On the positive side, marijuana may have certain clinical uses. Research shows that it helps combat nausea and weight loss in people with cancer and AIDS and helps to reduce pressure in the eyes of glaucoma patients. Thus, in a nationwide survey of cancer specialists, 48 percent said they would prescribe marijuana if it were legal, and 44 percent said they had already recommended marijuana to at least one patient—even though it's illegal (Doblin & Kleiman, 1991). On the negative side, it is clear that smoking marijuana, like smoking tobacco, can cause lung damage. It also slows reaction time and impairs motor coordination—hence the danger of driving or operating machinery while "stoned." Depending on the person and situation, it may also magnify feelings of anxiety, paranoia, or depression. Marijuana can also interfere with learning and the ability to form new memories. Unlike alcohol, which the body eliminates within hours, THC and its by-products linger in the body for a month or more.

Opiates

Opiates are a class of drugs that are related to opium, and they include morphine, codeine, and heroin (McKim, 1991). Their most prominent effect is to produce euphoria and analgesia (they also cause constipation). Because opiates depress neural activity, they are widely prescribed for the alleviation of pain. The user becomes drowsy and lethargic, yet happy and euphoric. Changes in consciousness are not particularly striking. These drugs are highly addictive, as the user quickly develops an insatiable need for more and larger doses. Heroin can be injected, smoked, or inhaled. Heroin users risk death through overdose, contaminated drugs, and AIDS contracted by sharing drug-injection needles.

opiates A class of highly addictive drugs that depress neural activity and provide temporary relief from pain and anxiety.

People all over the world have sought to alter their states of consciousness, often by the consumption of psychoactive drugs. Whatever the reasons for this desire, it is clear that drug use often turns to abuse and that social factors—such as poverty, peer pressure, work stress, and a lack of personal fulfillment—play a role. In the United States, the number of people who use psychoactive drugs, which had declined over the past few years, is now on the rise for the first time in well over a decade. It is not clear, as a matter of public policy, how the problem can be solved. Thus, as policymakers debate the perennial question of whether to legalize the illicit drugs, psychologists concede that they cannot confidently predict the impact of such a policy (MacCoun, 1993).

Consciousness and Control

Can people exert control over the contents of their awareness? When is it possible to do so, and why is it often so difficult?

"A penny for your thoughts?" Over the years, psychologists have equated consciousness with attention and have examined varying states of awareness, ranging from sleep and dreams to hypnosis and the effects of mind-altering drugs. We have seen in this chapter that people can sometimes control the contents of consciousness. Research on selective attention shows that as we focus the spotlight of awareness on one stimulus, we can screen out irrelevant competing information. At times, we can divide our attention, simultaneously engage in two or more activities, and process information without awareness.

Our ability to exert control over the contents of awareness is more impressive than most people realize. We saw earlier, for example, that lucid dreamers can sometimes control their dreams—and that almost anyone who is motivated can be trained to become a lucid dreamer. And we saw that although some of us can be hypnotized easily (a trait that requires the ability to focus attention and become absorbed), people cannot be hypnotized against their will—and those who are normally low in hypnotic susceptibility can learn to become more responsive to induction. Of course, when it comes to drug-induced altered states of consciousness, the choice is yours.

One particularly important way of controlling consciousness—meditation—attracted great interest in the West in the 1950s when "beat generation" heroes like Jack Kerouac and Allen Ginsberg embraced Zen Buddhism. The interest broadened in the 1960s when the Beatles went to India to meditate. In the 1990s, the number of people turning to meditation has grown so dramatically that some meditation centers have had to establish lotteries as a way of accommodating the applicants for retreats. Many are drawn by expectations of stress reduction, equanimity, and even euphoria. But for experienced meditators, while acknowledging these "side effects," the rewards are based on the analogy—more than 3,000 years old—that disciplining the mind is like taming an elephant to make it useful. For them, the value of meditation lies not in some kind of bliss trip but rather in the heightened awareness—consciousness—of their everyday lives.

Despite these impressive abilities, there are times when the control of consciousness seems out of reach. The mind may wander, you may slip into a daydream, you may become distracted despite your efforts at concentration. People who become dependent upon a psychoactive drug may lose the ability to control their states of consciousness. And those who suffer from various anxiety-related disorders may become literally obsessed with certain thoughts (see Chapter 16). Studying what he calls "ironic processes" in mental control, Daniel Wegner (1994) has found that, at times, the harder you try to control your own thoughts, the less likely you are to succeed. Try not to think about a white bear for the next thirty seconds, and chances are that very image will intrude upon your consciousness with remarkable frequency. Tell a jury to disregard an item of inadmissible testimony, and that censored material is sure to pop to mind as they deliberate on a verdict. Try not to worry about how long it's taking to fall asleep, and you'll stay awake. Try not to think about an itch—well, you get the idea. According to Wegner, every conscious effort to control a thought is met by a concern about the failure to do so. For psychologists, and everyone else for that matter, the key is to learn how to minimize these ironic effects.

Summary and Key Terms

Attentional Processes

Psychologists generally define **consciousness** in terms of **attention**—an awareness of the sensations, thoughts, and feelings that one is attending to at a given moment.

Selective Attention

Studies of the **cocktail party phenomenon** demonstrate that people can use **selective attention** to focus on one stimulus and virtually exclude other stimuli from consciousness. Many of these studies use a dichotic listening task in which subjects hear competing messages over headphones and must follow what is said in one ear while ignoring the other.

Divided Attention

Other listening experiments show that **divided attention** is possible: Some stimuli penetrate consciousness even when we are focused on something else. Moreover, if we are so experienced at a particular process that it becomes automatic, we can do other things at the same time. The **Stroop test** demonstrates that experienced readers process word meanings automatically, without effort or awareness.

Influence without Awareness

Research shows that people can be influenced by **subliminal messages**—information that is presented "below" our threshold of awareness. Mere exposure to a stimulus increases liking, even when the exposure is subliminal. This is shown in studies on **priming,** where subliminally presented concepts appear to facilitate, or "prime," responses in a subsequent situation. People with **prosopagnosia,** who cannot recognize familiar faces, show glimmers of recognition without knowing they are doing so. And people with **blindsight** react to certain visual cues without awareness. There is no strong evidence, however, that subliminal persuasion can change our long-term behavior.

Sleep and Dreams

Until recently, there were many myths about sleep and dreams, but little was actually known about these processes.

The Sleep-Wake Cycle

As biological organisms, humans experience regular fluctuations known as **biological rhythms.** Our day-long **circadian rhythm,** such as the sleep-wake cycle, is controlled by the suprachiasmatic nucleus of the hypothalamus, which detects light via the retina. Cut off from sunlight, humans tend to drift toward longer daily cycles. When our rhythms are disrupted, we may experience reactions such as jet lag.

Night Work, Sleeping, and Health

Both biological and social clocks set the body for activity during the daytime and sleep at night, so shift workers struggle to stay alert and experience problems on the job. Many traffic accidents occur at night, as drivers sometimes take brief **microsleeps** while driving. A brief nap or a cup of coffee can help drivers stay awake.

The Stages of Sleep

Sleep follows a cycle of distinct stages: presleep; stages 1 to 4 of deepening sleep, as the body relaxes and brain waves become larger and slower; and REM sleep, characterized by rapid eye movements, increased pulse rate, brain waves like those of presleep, and totally relaxed muscles. It is during **REM sleep** that vivid dreams occur. Each night, as we pass through several cycles, we gradually spend more time in REM sleep and less time in non-REM, or **NREM, sleep.**

Why Do We Sleep?

Sleep is so necessary that when people try to stay awake for long periods, they fall into short microsleeps, a few seconds at a time. According to restoration theory, sleep helps us recover from the day's demands. Circadian theory offers an evolutionary explanation: Sleep helps animals conserve energy and avoid predators when not searching for food or seeking a mate. Individuals differ in the amount of sleep they require.

Dreams

Dreams, too, serve an adaptive function. As shown by studies that measure REM sleep, people do most of their dreaming early in life when the brain is still developing. Common themes include falling and being chased or attacked. Both daily concerns and external stimuli also influence dream content. Some people experience **lucid dreaming,** a semiconscious state in which they are aware of—and can control—their own dreams.

Freud accounted for the bizarreness of dreams by theorizing that they are disguised expressions of unconscious wishes. To interpret dreams, he said, one has to go beyond the **manifest content** to uncover the unconscious meaning, or **latent content.** A more recent hypothesis, the **activation-synthesis theory,** contends that dreams begin with random neural signals in the brainstem. These signals spread up to the cortex, and the brain tries to make sense of them by constructing images and stories.

Sleep Disturbances

Sleep disturbances are common. **Insomnia—**the inability to fall asleep, stay asleep, or get enough sleep—has many causes and can be cured through behavioral means. Hypersomnia (sleeping too much) is less frequent but more dangerous, particularly among those with **narcolepsy,** a disorder that causes sudden attacks of REM sleep during the day. There are other serious sleep disturbances, or parasomnias. People with **sleep apnea** snore loudly and repeatedly stop breathing during sleep and awaken gasping for air. **REM sleep behavior disorder (RBD)** is a condition in which the skeletal muscles are not paralyzed during REM sleep, enabling sleepers to act upon their nightmares, often violently. Other problems include night terrors and sleepwalking.

Hypnosis

The Seeds of Controversy

Hypnosis is a set of attention-focusing procedures in which changes in a subject's behavior or mental state are suggested. It has a long and controversial history in psychology.

The Hypnotic Induction

In the first stage of hypnosis, induction, the subject's attention is focused. In the second stage, suggestion, the subject responds to the hypnotist's cues.

Hypnotic Responsiveness

People differ in their degree of **hypnotic susceptibility,** or responsiveness. Those who are most responsive tend to have vivid imaginations and long attention spans.

The Myths and Realities

Contrary to myth, people cannot be hypnotized against their will or be coerced into violating their consciences. Evidence suggests, however, that hypnotized subjects may shed their inhibitions. Hypnosis can reduce pain. Through **posthypnotic suggestion,** the hypnotist can influence a subject's behavior even after the session ends. **Posthypnotic amnesia** is also common, though not permanent. But **hypermnesia,** the supposed enhancement of a witness's memory by hypnosis, has not been confirmed in experiments. Rather, hypnosis makes witnesses more vulnerable to false memories.

Is Hypnosis an "Altered" State?

Special-process theories maintain that hypnosis induces a unique state of suggestibility. According to one theory, the hypnosis subject experiences **dissociation,** a division of consciousness in which one part of the mind operates independent of another. Social-psychological theories see hypnosis as an ordinary state in which changes are produced by conscious faking or by processes of social influence. To some extent, both theories may be true.

Consciousness-Altering Drugs

Throughout history, people have sought altered states of consciousness, often by using consciousness-altering **psychoactive drugs,** chemicals that change perceptions, moods, thoughts, or behavior. Such drugs are addictive, creating either **physical dependence** or **psychological dependence.**

Sedatives

Among psychoactive drugs, **sedatives** such as alcohol, barbiturates, and benzodiazepines slow activity in the central nervous system. Alcohol was the first and is one of the most widely used drugs in the world.

Stimulants

Stimulants, including caffeine, nicotine, amphetamines, and cocaine, excite the central nervous system and energize behavior. They can be addictive.

Hallucinogens

Hallucinogens, or psychedelic drugs, such as LSD and marijuana, distort perceptions and can cause hallucinations. There is now controversy over the possible medical uses of marijuana and the health risks that it poses.

Opiates

The highly addictive **opiates,** such as heroin, morphine, and codeine, depress neural activity, relieve pain, and produce euphoria.

Consciousness and Control

As studies of attention and hypnosis illustrate, people have a great deal of command over their own consciousness. Yet there are times when our minds wander and we cannot control the distractions. Often we must contend with an irony: The harder we try to manage our thoughts, the less likely we are to succeed.

In the Field Resources

Books

Coren, S. (1996). *Sleep thieves.* New York: Free Press.

Anyone interested in sleep will be fascinated by this easy-to-read book about research on this topic.

Snyder, S. H. (1996). *Drugs and the brain* (2nd ed.). New York: Scientific American Library.

This book provides a complete, well-illustrated description of how marijuana, cocaine, and other drugs affect the brain.

Van de Castle, R. L. (1994). *Our dreaming mind.* New York: Ballantine Books.

Written by a leading researcher, this book opens the "treasure chest of dreams" by looking at views of dreams throughout history, psychological theories, and research.

Wegner, D. M. (1989). *White bears and other unwanted thoughts.* New York: Viking.

Drawing on his own research, the author makes the ironic but compelling case that the harder we try to inhibit a thought, the more likely it is to intrude on consciousness.

Internet

National Institute on Drug Abuse (http://www.nida.nih.gov/)

Provides comprehensive information and national statistics on drug use and links to other relevant sites.

Sleep Net (http://www.sleepnet.com/)

Provides all you need to know about sleep, sleep disorders, dreams, the names and addresses of 280+ sleep labs, and links to other sites.

Journals and Periodicals

International Journal of Clinical and Experimental Hypnosis

Journal of Abnormal Psychology

Journal of Experimental Psychology: General

Sleep

Telephone and Mail

Association for the Study of Dreams (ASD, P.O. Box 1600, Vienna, VA 22183)

A nonprofit international organization promoting an awareness and appreciation of dreams.

5 *Learning*

What's Your Prediction?

Implicit learning

The situation As you enter the laboratory reception area, you are met by an experimenter, taken to a small room, and told that you will be taking part in a study of human memory. Next you're told that you'll have seven minutes to examine the following strings of letters and that you should simply try to "learn and remember as much as you can." Ready, begin:

PVV TSSSXXVV TSXXTVPS PVPXTVPS TSSXXVV TSXS PTVPXVV TXXTVPS TXXTTTVV PVPXXVV TSSXXVPS TXXVPXVV PTVPS PTTTVPS PTVPXV

You look at these meaningless items one by one, trying to memorize. *P–V–V. T–S–X–S.* You just keep repeating them under your breath. After seven minutes, the experimenter stops you. Time's up. You can't wait to write down what you remember before you lose it—but the experimenter has other plans. He or she now reveals that the items were formed according to a set of rules, an "artificial grammar" if you will, and that he or she is interested in whether you know what the rules are. As the experimenter explains the test you're about to take, you get a sinking feeling in the pit of your stomach. "Uh-oh. There were rules? I wasn't looking for rules!"

The test is straightforward. On slides, you'll see 100 new items made up of the same letters as before, one item per slide. Half the items will be grammatical (according to the rules); half will not. For each one, you are to press a button marked *YES* if you think the item is grammatical or *NO* if you think it's not. You should also rate your confidence in each judgment on a scale marked from 1 to 5. Oh, one more thing: Your responses will be timed.

The slide projector is turned on, the overhead lights are shut off, and you've got your fingers on the buttons ready to fire. First item: *PTTTVPVS.* It looks okay, as it contains the usual letters, and all. But are these letters ordered in a way that fits the grammar? "If I don't know," you ask, "should I just guess?" Instructed to respond to every item, you press a button and state your confidence. The next one is *PVTW.* Same routine. *PVPS. SVPXTW. SXXVPS.* Sometimes you answer quickly; at other times you stare at the screen for a while before making a response. By the hundredth slide, you're ready for a cool drink and a nap.

Make a prediction How well do you think people fare in this task? Having been in this experiment myself, I can tell you that many subjects shrug their shoulders in confusion. Based on what you've read, what do you think is the average test score? If all you did was guess, you would get roughly a 50 percent accuracy rate. If you came up with rules that were wrong, your score could be lower. If you knew the right rules, you would do better. So, what is your estimate, 10 percent? 30? 55? 90? Circle your prediction:

0 5 10 15 20 25 30 35 40 45 50 55 60 65 70 75 80 85 90 95 100%

The results For thirty years, cognitive psychologist Arthur Reber (1993) has used experiments like this one to study "implicit learning"—the tendency for people to acquire complex, abstract concepts without awareness or intention. Consistently, Reber finds that subjects cannot describe the grammar they use to form the letter strings, nor can they explain the reasons for their YES and NO judgments. Yet in the study just described, subjects made the correct response 77 percent of the time—and usually did so quickly.

What does it all mean? Implicit learning, which occurs without our awareness, is a primitive but powerful form of adaptation. Indeed, people learn this grammar not by actively searching for rules or by receiving explicit instruction but simply through exposure to properly formed letter strings. Without really trying, subjects learn the grammar the way we learn to speak in our native tongue, figure out how to behave properly in a new setting, or "calculate" the trajectory of a ball in flight in order to make the catch. To learn from experience, as the subjects did in this study, people must be attuned to associations between the stimuli in their environment and between behavior and its consequences. As we'll see in this chapter, association is the basic building block for all learning.

Programmed by instinct, bees build honeycombs and spiders weave webs.

Every spring, a tiny freshwater fish called the stickleback performs an intriguing reproductive ritual. As the male's belly turns from dull gray to a bright red, he builds a nest and does a zigzag courtship "dance" to attract a female, sometimes brushing her belly with his stickles. He then escorts her to the nest, prods her tail to induce spawning, fertilizes her eggs, aerates the eggs by fanning the water, and vigorously attacks all red-bellied male intruders. Once the eggs hatch a week later, he guards the young and keeps them close by until they are ready to leave the nest.

Many land animals also exhibit adaptive, complex forms of behavior. When the herring-gull mother returns to the nest with food, newly hatched chicks will peck at her bright yellow bill, causing her to regurgitate the food for their consumption. The honeybee uses a wax it secretes to build hives in which each comb consists of hexagonal cells that form a mathematically efficient, perfect design. The indigo bunting, a small bird, navigates south every winter, using as a guide the bright North Star, the only star in the Northern Hemisphere that maintains a fixed compass position through the night. Similarly prepared by instinct, the canary sings, the spider weaves its web, the beaver builds dams, and the newly hatched duckling follows the first moving object it sees, usually its mother. How do the stickleback and others know what to do? Simple. In many animal species, certain behaviors are programmed by instinct.

Inspired by Darwin's theory of evolution and led by Nobel prizewinners Konrad Lorenz and Nikolaas Tinbergen, **ethologists** study the behavior of animals in their natural habitat (Dewsbury, 1992; Eibl-Eibesfeldt, 1989). Based on their observations, these researchers refer to the instinctual behaviors as **fixed action patterns.** A fixed action pattern is a species-wide sequence of movements that is built into the nervous system and triggered or "released" by a specific stimulus. The response to the stimulus is automatic, like a reflex—no ifs, ands, or buts. Thus, the stickleback male attacks all red-bellied forms, even those that do not resemble a fish (see Figure 5.1). Similarly, the herring-gull chick pecks at all moving red dots, even if they do not resemble another bird (see Figure 5.2).

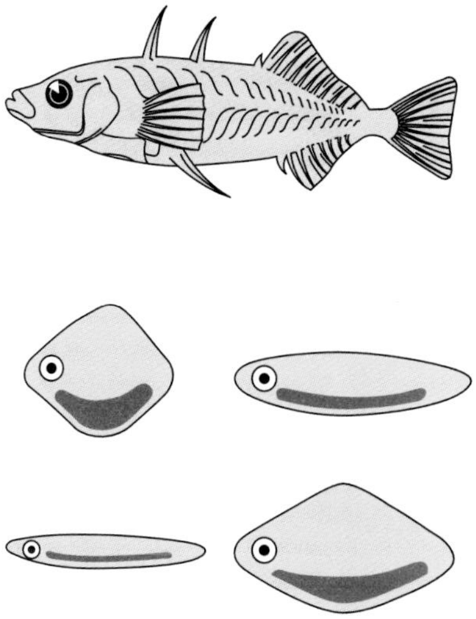

Figure 5.1 Stickleback models Research shows that various red-bellied objects trigger male attack, yet a replica of another male stickleback without a red belly does not. The red belly is the stimulus that releases this fixed action pattern (Tinbergen, 1951).

Do people exhibit fixed action patterns? Are we instinctual creatures? We'll see later that human newborns are equipped with adaptive, instinctlike behaviors in the form of reflexes. Upon birth, an infant will clutch anything that touches the palm of the hand, turn with an open mouth toward any object that grazes the cheek, start sucking when the lips are touched, and swallow when the back of the mouth is stimulated. These reflexes are not within the infant's control, and some disappear in a few months, never to return. Why are we less equipped with inborn, reflexlike rituals than the stickleback? Because we adapt to life's demands not by instinct but through learning.

When psychologists talk about **learning,** they are referring to a relatively permanent change in knowledge or behavior that comes as a result of *experience*. Experience is necessary for us to speak, read, write, add and subtract, ride a bicycle, swim, play a saxophone or trumpet, or know how to charm a romantic partner. The topic of learning is near and dear to the heart of all psychologists—regardless of whether they study biological, cognitive, developmental, social, or clinical processes. Often what we learn makes us happier, healthier, and more successful; sometimes it does not. The beauty of adaptation by learning is that it is flexible, not rigidly preset like a stickleback's dance-and-attack ritual. In principle, this means that each of us can learn to behave in ways that benefit rather than harm ourselves and others. The question is: How does this learning take place?

The simplest form of learning is **habituation**—the tendency to become familiar with a stimulus merely as a result of repeated exposure. The first time it happens, a sudden loud noise as a blast of cold air has a startling effect on us and triggers an "orienting reflex." Among humans, the eyes widen, the eyebrows raise, muscles tighten, the heart beats faster, skin resistance drops, and brain-wave patterns indicate

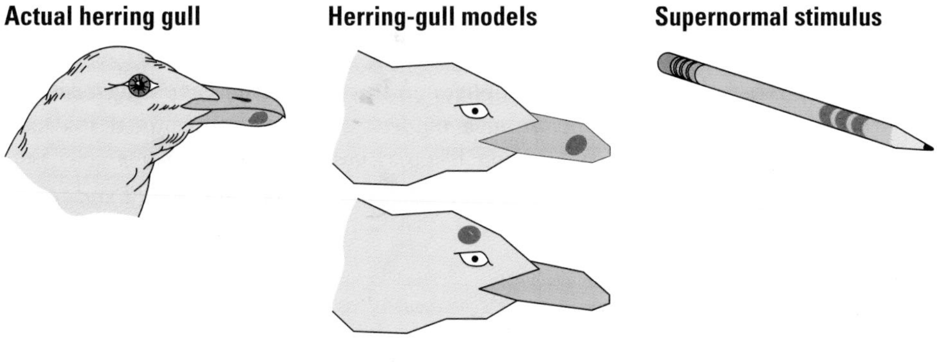

Figure 5.2 Herring-gull models Research shows that pecking is released by the movement of any red dot—even on objects, such as a pencil, that do not resemble the gull's beak (Hailman, 1969).

ethology The study of the behavior of animals in their natural habitat.

fixed action pattern A species-specific behavior that is built into an animal's nervous system and triggered by a specific stimulus.

learning A relatively permanent change in knowledge or behavior that results from experience.

habituation The tendency of an organism to become familiar with a stimulus as a result of repeated exposure.

a heightened level of physiological arousal (Sokolov, 1963). On the second and third exposures to the stimulus, the effect is weakened. Then as we become acclimated or "habituated" to the stimulus, the novelty wears off, the startle reaction disappears, and boredom sets in.

Habituation is a primitive form of learning and is found among mammals, birds, fish, insects, and all other organisms. For example, sea snails reflexively withdraw their gills at the slightest touch. Then after repeated tactile stimulation, the response disappears (Kandel, 1979). Habituation also occurs in human infants. If a picture or sound is presented over and over again, an infant will eventually get bored, lose interest, look away, and exhibit a lower heart rate (Bornstein, 1989). Think about everyday life, and numerous examples of habituation will come to mind. People who move from a large city to the country or from a region of the world that is hot to one that is cold often need time to adjust to the sudden change in stimulation. Once they do, the new environment seems less noisy, quiet, hot, or cold. In habituation, an organism learns from exposure that a stimulus is familiar. Over the years, however, psychologists have focused more on the ways in which we learn relationships between events. In this chapter, three such processes are discussed: classical conditioning, operant conditioning, and observational learning.

Classical Conditioning

What did Pavlov learn from his experiments with salivating dogs? What is classical conditioning, and does it have any relevance to human behavior? Is it possible to condition people to develop new fears or attitudes? Can bodily functions similarly be "trained"?

I will always remember the summer of 1969 on the beach—the body surfing, bikinis, Frisbees, rock 'n' roll, the feel of hot sand between the toes, low-flying gulls, and warm air blowing the scent of salt water and coconut-oil suntan lotion. To this day, these memories flood my mind whenever I hear a song that was a radio hit at the time.

In stark contrast, I will never forget a cold, dark night in January 1976. I was in graduate school and had eaten dinner with a friend. Driving back to campus, I hit a patch of ice and skidded. Before I knew it, the car had scraped the wall of a brick building, turned on its side, and stalled. My friend and I were shaken but not hurt. Yet I vividly recall the red lights flashing on the dashboard, the smell of burned rubber, and the blast of cold air that hit my face when we climbed out through the door. I can also recall the song that played on the radio as we tried to escape. I still flinch whenever I hear it.

Following Aristotle, modern philosophers and psychologists have long believed that the key to learning is *association,* a tendency to connect events that occur together in space or time. Can learning by association be studied in a scientific manner? With the arrival of the twentieth century, psychology was poised and ready for one of its most important discoveries.

Pavlov's Discovery

Enter Ivan Pavlov, a Russian physiologist. After receiving his medical degree in 1882, he spent twenty years studying the digestive system and won a Nobel prize

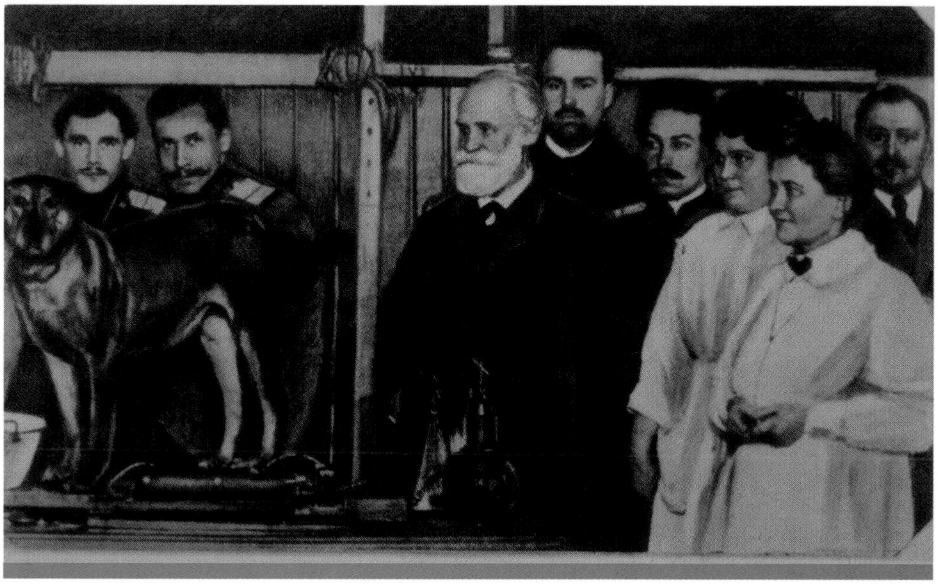

Ivan Pavlov and some of the 200 other scientists who worked with him during his illustrious career.

for that research in 1904. Pavlov was the complete dedicated scientist. Rumor has it that he once reprimanded a lab assistant who was ten minutes late for an experiment because of street riots stemming from the Russian Revolution: "Next time there's a revolution," he said, "get up earlier!" (Hothersall, 1990).

Ironically, Pavlov's most important contribution was the result of an incidental discovery. In studying the digestive system, he strapped dogs in a harness, placed different types of food in their mouths, and measured the flow of saliva through a tube surgically inserted in the cheek (see Figure 5.3). But there was a "problem": After

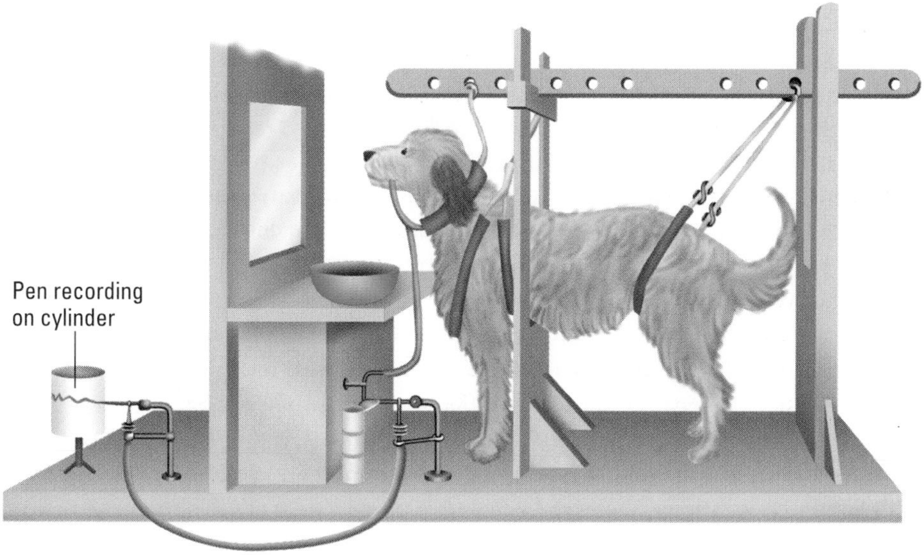

Figure 5.3 Pavlov's classical-conditioning apparatus Strapped into an apparatus like the one shown here, Pavlov's dogs were conditioned to salivate. Through a tube surgically inserted into each dog's cheek, saliva was recorded by a pen attached to a slowly rotating cylinder of paper.

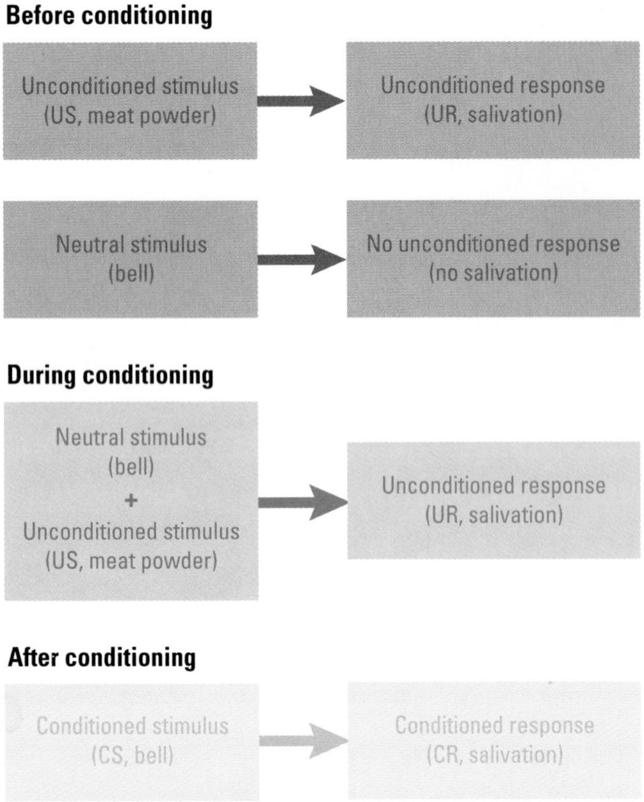

Figure 5.4 Classical conditioning Note the sequence of events before, during, and after Pavlov's study. At first, only the US (meat) elicits a UR (salivation). After a neutral stimulus (bell) repeatedly precedes the US, however, it becomes a CS and can elicit a CR (salivation) on its own.

repeated sessions, the dogs would begin to salivate *before* the food was actually put in their mouths. In fact, they would drool at the mere sight of food, the dish it was placed in, the assistant who brought it, or even the sound of the assistant's approaching footsteps. Pavlov saw these "psychic secretions" as a nuisance, so he tried to eliminate the problem by sneaking up on the dogs without warning. He soon realized, however, that he had stumbled on a very basic form of learning. This phenomenon was **classical conditioning,** and Pavlov devoted the rest of his life to studying it.

To examine the classical conditioning systematically, Pavlov needed to control the delivery of food, often a dry meat powder, as well as the events that preceded it. The animals did not have to be trained or "conditioned" to salivate. The salivary reflex is an innate **unconditioned response (UR)** that is naturally set off by food in the mouth, an **unconditioned stimulus (US).** There are numerous unconditioned stimulus-response connections. Tap your knee with a rubber mallet and your leg will jerk. Blow a puff of air into your eye and you'll blink. Turn the volume up on an alarm clock and, when it rings, your muscles will tighten. In each case, the stimulus automatically elicits the response. No experience is necessary.

Using the salivary reflex as a starting point, Pavlov (1927) sought to determine whether dogs could be trained by association to respond to a "neutral" stimulus—one that does not naturally elicit a response. To find out, he conducted an experiment in which he repeatedly rang a bell before placing food in the dog's mouth. Bell, food. Bell, food. After a series of these paired events, the dog started to salivate to the sound alone. Because the bell, which was initially a neutral stimulus, came to elicit the response through its association with food, it became a **conditioned stimulus (CS),** and salivation, a **conditioned response (CR).** With this experiment as a model, Pavlov and others trained dogs to salivate in response to buzzers, ticking metronomes, tuning forks, odors, lights, colored objects, and a touch on the leg. Similarly, researchers have trained animals to react with fear to such stimuli when they are paired with an unpleasant US, such as an electric shock or bright light. In one study, rhesus monkeys reacted with an accelerated heart rate to a simple tone that had been paired with a loud noise and a blast of air to the face (Kalin et al., 1996). In another study, rats froze and did not move whenever they were put into a cage in which they had previously been exposed to high concentrations of carbon dioxide (Mongeluzi et al., 1996). The basic classical conditioning procedure is diagrammed in Figure 5.4.

As we'll see, classical conditioning affects us all in ways that we're often not aware of. We learn to salivate (CR) to lunch bells, menus, the smell of food cooking, and the sight of a refrigerator (CS) because these stimuli are often followed by eating (US). Similarly, we cringe at the screeching sound of a dentist's drill because of past associations between that sound and pain. And we tremble at the sight of a flashing blue light in the rearview mirror because of its association with speeding tickets. For me, the beach—which was the site of so many good times of the past—is a conditioned stimulus that fills me with peaceful, easy feelings.

classical conditioning A type of learning in which an organism comes to associate one stimulus with another (also called Pavlovian conditioning).

unconditioned response (UR) An unlearned response (salivation) to an unconditioned stimulus (food).

unconditioned stimulus (US) A stimulus (food) that triggers an unconditioned response (salivation).

conditioned stimulus (CS) A neutral stimulus (bell) that comes to evoke a classically conditioned response (salivation).

conditioned response (CR) A learned response (salivation) to a classically conditioned stimulus (bell).

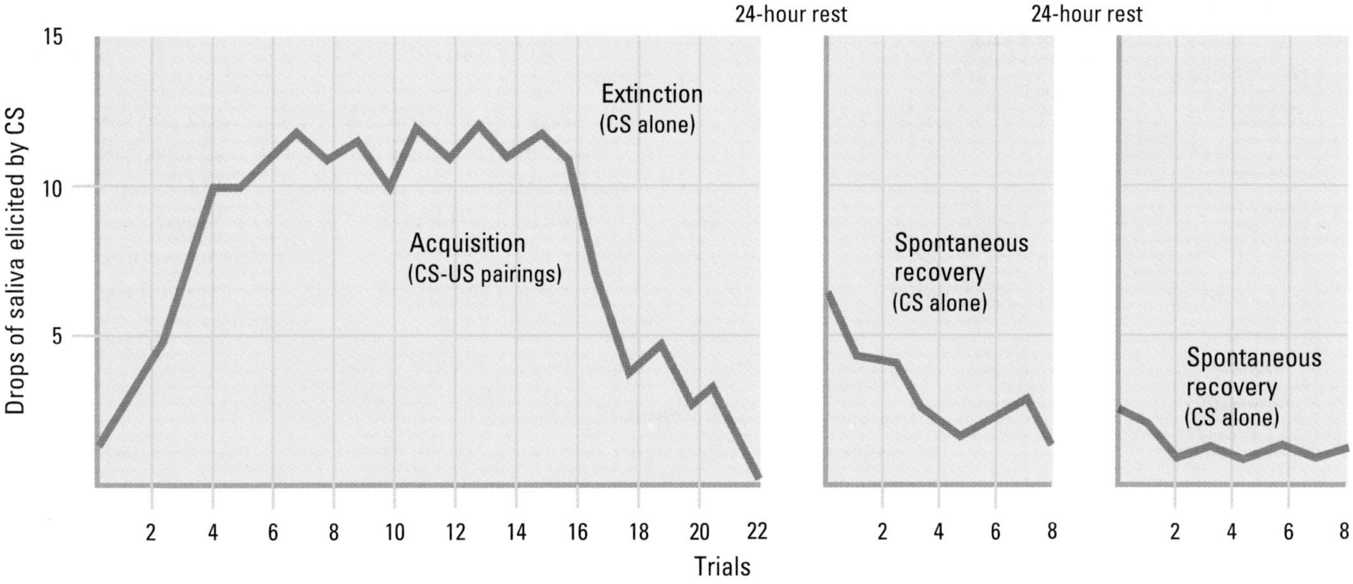

Figure 5.5 The rise and fall of a conditioned response In classical conditioning, the CS does not evoke a CR on the first trial, but over time it increases rapidly until leveling off. During extinction, the CR gradually declines. After a brief delay, however, there is usually a spontaneous recovery, or "rebounding," of the CR—until it is completely extinguished.

Basic Principles

Inspired by his initial discovery, Pavlov spent more than thirty years examining the factors that influence classical conditioning. Other researchers throughout the world also became involved. As a result, we now know that various species can be conditioned to blink when they hear a click that is paired with a puff of air to the eye, to fear colored lights that signal the onset of painful electric shocks, and to develop a distaste for foods they ate before becoming sick to the stomach (Schwartz & Reisberg, 1991). We also know that there are four very basic principles of learning: acquisition, extinction, generalization, and discrimination.

[Cartoon by John Chase]

Acquisition Classical conditioning seldom springs full blown after a single pairing of the CS and US. Usually, it takes some number of paired trials for the initial learning, or **acquisition,** of a CR. In Pavlov's experiments, the dogs did not salivate the first time they heard the bell. As shown in the left panel of Figure 5.5, however, the CR increases rapidly over the next few pairings—until the "learning curve" peaks and levels off.

The acquisition of a classically conditioned response is influenced by various factors. The most critical are the order and timing of the presentation. In general, conditioning is quickest when the CS (the bell) precedes the onset of the US (food)—a procedure known as *forward* conditioning. Ideally, the CS should precede the US by about half a second and the two should overlap somewhat in time. When the onset of the US is delayed, conditioning takes longer and the conditioned response is weaker. When the CS and US are *simultaneous,* it takes even longer. And when the US is presented before the CS (a procedure referred to as *backward* conditioning), learning often does not occur at all (see Figure 5.6).

acquisition The formation of a learned response to a stimulus through the presentation of an unconditioned stimulus (classical conditioning) or reinforcement (operant conditioning).

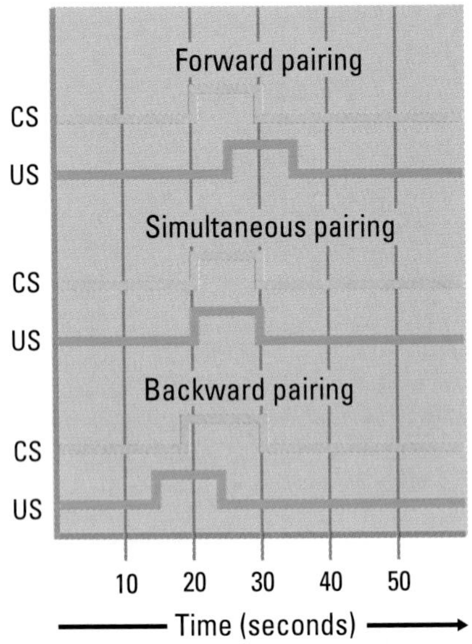

Figure 5.6 Temporal relations in classical conditioning A key factor in classical conditioning is the timing of the CS and US. The three temporal patterns illustrated here are presented in order—from the most to least effective.

Once a buzzer, light, or other neutral stimulus gains the power to elicit a conditioned response, it becomes a CS—and can serve as though it were the US for yet another neutral stimulus. In one experiment, for example, Pavlov trained a dog to salivate to the sound of a bell, using meat powder as the US. After the CS–US link was established, he presented a second neutral stimulus, a black square, followed by the bell—but no food. The result: After repeated pairings, the black square on its own elicited small amounts of salivation. Through a process of "higher-order" conditioning, as illustrated in Figure 5.7, one CS was used to create another CS. In effect, the black square came to signal the bell, which, in turn, signaled the appearance of food (Rescorla, 1980).

Extinction In the acquisition phase of classical conditioning, a conditioned response is elicited by a neutral stimulus that is paired with a US. But what happens to the CR when the US is removed? Would a dog continue to salivate to a bell if the bell is no longer followed by food? Would the screeching of the dentist's drill continue to send chills up the spine if it is no longer followed by pain? No. If the CS is presented often enough without the US, it eventually loses its response-eliciting power. This apparent reversal of learning is called **extinction** (look again at the middle panel of Figure 5.5).

Extinction is a gradual process. Indeed, Pavlov found that when the same dog was returned for testing a day or two after extinction, it once again salivated to the bell—a rebound effect known as **spontaneous recovery** (depicted in the right panel of Figure 5.5). Often the dogs were easily reconditioned after just one repairing of the CS and US. Apparently, extinction does not *erase* what was previously learned—it only *suppresses* it.

Generalization After an animal is conditioned to respond to a particular CS, other similar stimuli will often evoke the same response. In Pavlov's experiments, the dogs salivated not only to the original tone but also to other tones that were similar but not identical to the CS. Other researchers have made the same observation. In one study, for example, rabbits were conditioned to blink to a tone of 1,200 Hz (a pitch that is roughly two octaves higher than middle C) that was followed by a puff of air to the eye. Later, they blinked to other tones ranging from 400 Hz to 2,000 Hz. The result: The more similar the tone was to the CS, the more likely it was to evoke a conditioned response. This tendency to respond to stimuli other than the original CS is called **stimulus generalization** (Pearce, 1987).

Discrimination Stimulus generalization can be useful because it enables us to apply what we learn to new, similar situations. But there are drawbacks. As illustrated by the child who is terrified of all animals because of one bad encounter with a barking dog, or the racist who assumes that "they" are all alike, generalization is not always adaptive. Sometimes we need to distinguish between objects that are similar—a process of **discrimination.** Again, Pavlov was the first to demonstrate this process. He conditioned a dog to salivate in the presence of a black square (a CS) and then noticed that the response generalized to a gray-colored square. Next, he conducted a series of conditioning trials in which the black square was followed by food while the gray one was not. The result: The dog continued to salivate only to the original CS. In a similar manner, the dog eventually learned to discriminate between the color black and darker shades of gray.

extinction The elimination of a learned response by removal of the unconditioned stimulus (classical conditioning) or reinforcement (operant conditioning).

spontaneous recovery The reemergence of an extinguished conditioned response after a rest period.

stimulus generalization The tendency to respond to a stimulus that is similar to the conditioned stimulus.

discrimination In classical and operant conditioning, the ability to distinguish between different stimuli.

Pavlov's Legacy

Classical conditioning is so powerful and so basic that it occurs in animals as primitive as the sea slug, the fruitfly, and even the flatworm (the body of the flatworm contracts in response to electric shock; if the shock is repeatedly paired with light, the flatworm's body eventually contracts to the light alone) and as sophisticated as us humans (Turkkan, 1989; Krasne & Glanzman, 1995). In recent years, psychologists have taken classical conditioning in two directions: Some want to better *understand* the phenomenon—how, when, and why it works—while others are eager to *apply* it to different aspects of the human experience.

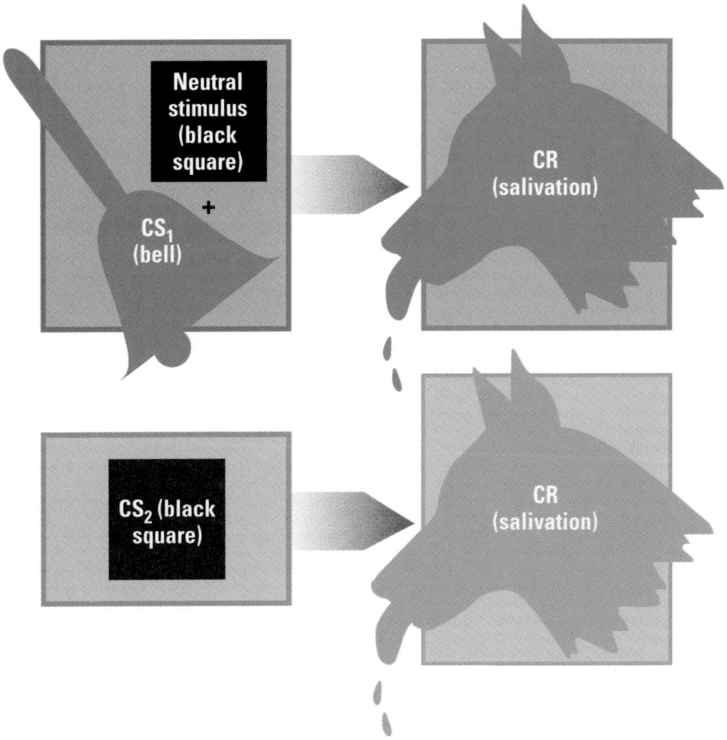

Figure 5.7 Higher-order conditioning After Pavlov trained a dog to salivate (CR) to a bell (CS), he preceded the bell with another neutral stimulus, a black square. After repeated pairings, the dog would salivate to the square itself. In effect, one CS was used to create another CS.

Theoretical Advances

Inspired by their initial successes and by the Darwinian assumption that all animals share a common evolutionary past, Pavlov and other early behaviorists made a bold claim: That any organism can be conditioned to any stimulus. It does not matter if the subject is a dog, cat, rat, pigeon, or person. Nor does it matter if the conditioned stimulus is a bell, light, buzzer, or odor. Whenever an initially neutral stimulus is paired with an unconditioned stimulus, the result is classical conditioning.

The early behaviorists also insisted that a science of human behavior must focus only on external, objective, quantifiable events. A *stimulus* can be observed and measured. So can its effect on an overt *response*. Together, these form the basis for what is known as S–R psychology. As far as the organism itself is concerned—its instincts, drives, perceptions, thoughts, and feelings—the behaviorists refused to speculate. In fact, Pavlov was said to have fined laboratory assistants who slipped into using soft "mentalistic" language. So where does the *organism* fit in? In recent years, researchers have come to appreciate some of the ways in which the "O" bridges the S and R—giving rise to a more flexible S–O–R brand of behaviorism. Two factors within the organism are particularly important: biological preparedness and cognitive representations.

Biological Preparedness All animals are biologically programmed, for survival purposes, to learn some associations more easily than others. This phenomenon was first discovered by John Garcia and Robert Koelling (1966). While studying the effects of radiation exposure on laboratory rats, they noticed that the animals would not drink from the plastic water bottles inside the radiation chambers. Since the radiation (US) was causing nausea (UR), they reasoned, perhaps the rats had acquired an aversion (CR) to the "plastic" taste of the water (CS).

To test this hypothesis, these investigators rigged an apparatus that worked as follows: When a rat licked a plastic drinking tube, it tasted sweetened water, saw a flash of light, and heard a loud clicking noise—all at the same time. The rats were then exposed to a high dose of X rays, which caused poisoning and nausea. The result: The rats later came to avoid the sweetened water after radiation poisoning, but they did not also learn to avoid the light or noise. The link between taste (CS) and poison (US) was so easily learned that it took only one pairing—even though the rats did not get sick until hours later (a far cry from the split-second CS–US interval that is usually necessary). Garcia and Koelling (1966) next found that when the US was a painful electric shock to the feet instead of X-ray poisoning, the rats continued to drink the water, but this time they avoided the audiovisual stimuli instead. In other words, although the rats were exposed to all stimuli, they proceeded to avoid only the flavored water after X-ray poisoning and only the light and noise after shock. Why was taste such a powerful CS when it was paired with poison but not with shock? And why were light and noise conditioned to the shock but not to the poison? Think about these associations for a moment, and one word will come to mind: *adaptiveness.* In nature, food is more likely to produce stomach poisoning than a pain in the foot, and an external stimulus is more likely to cause a pain in the foot than stomach illness. If you get sick after eating dinner in a new restaurant, you are likely to blame your illness on something you ate, not on the decor or the music that played. Clearly, we are "prepared" by nature to learn some CS–US associations more easily than others.

It is important to note that people acquire taste aversions, too—often with important practical implications. Consider, for example, an unfortunate side effect of chemotherapy treatments for cancer. These drugs tend to cause nausea and vomiting. As a result, patients often become conditioned to react with disgust and a loss of appetite to foods they had eaten hours before the treatment (Bovbjerg et al., 1992). Thankfully, the principles of classical conditioning offer a solution to this problem. When cancer patients are fed a distinctive maple-flavored ice cream before each treatment, they acquire a taste aversion to that ice cream—which becomes a "scapegoat" and protects the other foods in the patient's diet (Bernstein & Borson, 1986).

Research on the classical conditioning of fear reactions also illustrates the point that organisms are biologically predisposed to learn certain stimulus-response connections more than others. As we'll see in Chapter 16, people all over the world share many of the same fears. Particularly common are fears of darkness, height, snakes, and insects—relatively harmless objects, some of which are never encountered. Yet very few of us are as terrified of automobiles, electrical outlets, appliances, and other objects that can be dangerous. Why? Martin Seligman (1971) speculated that the reason for this disparity is that humans are predisposed by evolution to be wary of stimuli and situations that posed a threat to our prehistoric ancestors.

Not everyone agrees with this analysis (Davey, 1995). However, it is supported by various strands of research. Susan Mineka and Michael Cook (1993) found that when laboratory-raised rhesus monkeys saw a wild-reared monkey of the same species exhibit fear in the presence of a toy snake, they acquired an intense fear of snakes. But when they saw the other monkey show fear in the presence of a toy rabbit, they did not similarly acquire a fear of rabbits (Cook & Mineka, 1990). Similar results are found in research with humans. When subjects are conditioned to fear an object that is paired with electric shock, their reaction—as measured by physiological arousal—is acquired faster and lasts longer when the object is a snake, a spider, or an angry face than when it is a "neutral" stimulus such as a flower, a house, or a happy face (Ohman, 1986; McNally, 1987). This differential response to fear-relevant objects is so basic that it occurs even when they are presented subliminally, outside of conscious awareness (Esteves et al., 1994).

Cognitive Representations According to Pavlov, classical conditioning occurs whenever a neutral stimulus is paired with an unconditioned stimulus. With dogs salivating to bells, it all seemed passive, mindless, and automatic—a mechanical process in which the control of a reflex is simply passed from one stimulus to another. But is the process really that passive? Laboratory animals do not have to be geniuses to acquire a conditioned response, but they may be cognitively more active than Pavlov was willing to admit. Perhaps Pavlov's dogs salivated to his bells and tones because prior experience led them to *expect* food.

Based on years of research, Robert Rescorla (1988) concluded that classical conditioning is the process by which an organism learns that one event (CS) *predicts* another event (US). In other words, says Rescorla, a simple pairing of two stimuli is often not sufficient for conditioning. Rather, the organism must also learn that one event signals the coming onset of another. To demonstrate, Rescorla (1968) exposed rats to an electric shock (US) that was always paired with a tone (CS). In one condition, every shock was accompanied by the tone—so the CS reliably predicted the US. In a second condition, the rat experienced the same tone-shock pairs but was occasionally shocked without the tone as well. In other words, although the two events were paired, the CS did not reliably predict the US (see Figure 5.8). As Rescorla expected, the rats acquired a fear of the tone in the first condition but not in the second. Apparently, classical conditioning requires more than a simple pairing of a CS and US. It requires that there be a reliable predictive relationship.

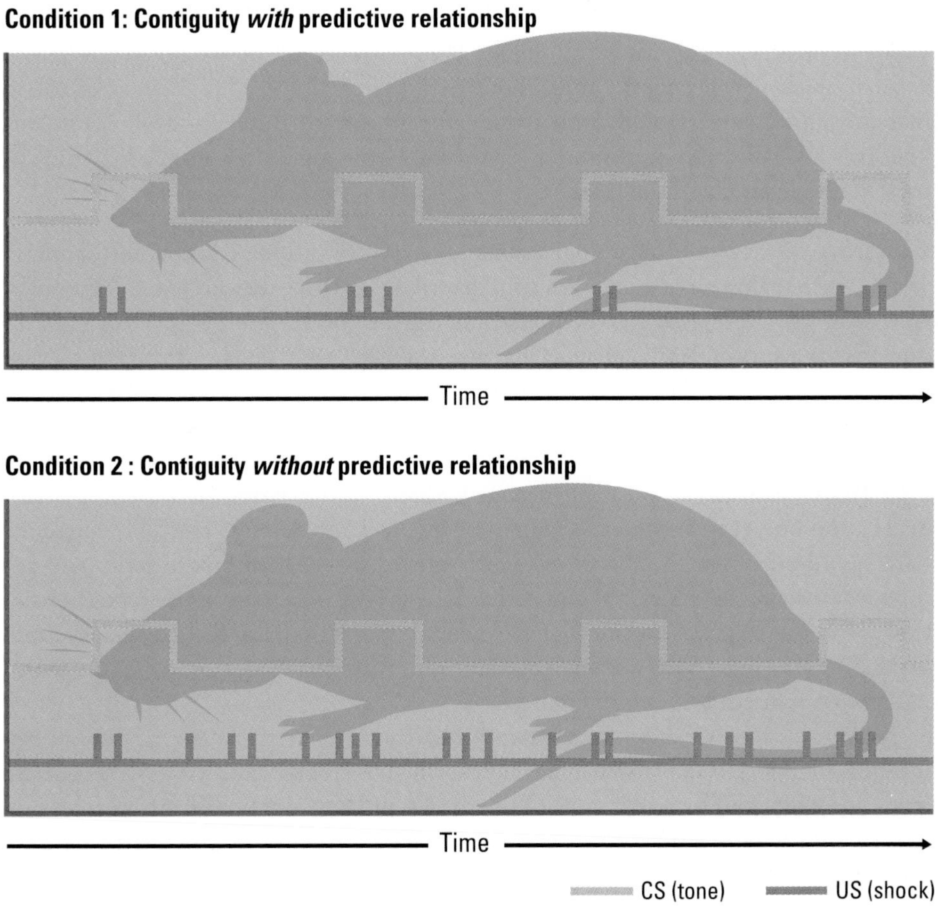

Figure 5.8 Classical conditioning: when the CS predicts the US Rescorla (1968) exposed rats to a shock (US) paired with a tone (CS). In one condition, every US was paired by the CS (*top*). In a second condition, shocks were sometimes administered without a tone—so the CS did not predict the US (*bottom*). Indicating that a predictive relationship is required, rats learned to fear the tone in the first condition but not in the second.

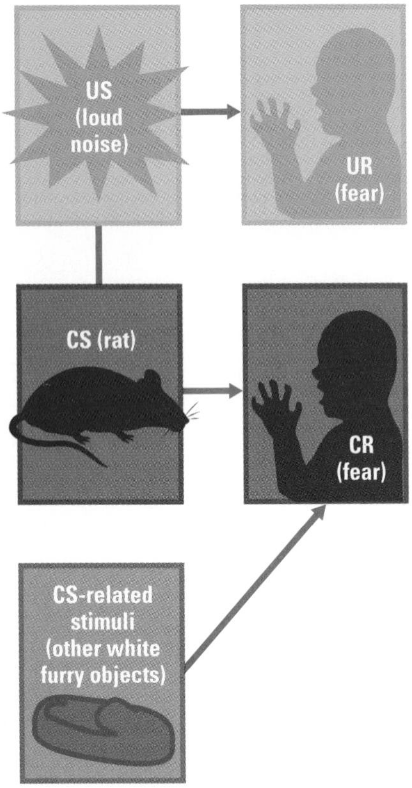

Figure 5.9 The conditioning of Little Albert By linking a harmless white rat to an aversive loud noise, Watson conditioned a baby boy to react with terror to the rat. In fact, the fear spread, or "generalized," to other, superficially similar objects.

There is a great deal of research support for Rescorla's cognitive redefinition of the process of classical conditioning (Miller et al., 1995). This point of view is significant because it helps to explain various aspects of classical conditioning. For example, it explains why a conditioned response is hard to produce through a backward conditioning procedure in which the CS *follows* the US. The two stimuli co-occur, as in forward and simultaneous conditioning, but the CS cannot predict the US when it comes second in the sequence of events. Rescorla's model also explains why certain associations are learned more easily than others. You may recall that in the taste-aversion study described earlier, rats quickly learned to avoid food that was paired with stomach poisoning, and lights and noise that were paired with electric shock. But they did not similarly link food to external pain, or lights and noise to stomach poisoning. Why? As Rescorla (1988) put it, "Conditioning is not a stupid process by which an organism willy-nilly forms associations between any two stimuli that happen to co-occur. Rather the organism is better seen as an information seeker using logical and perceptual relations among events and its own preconceptions to form a sophisticated representation of its world" (p. 154).

Practical Applications When Pavlov first found that he could train Russian dogs to drool to the sound of a dinner bell, nobody cared. In fact, E. B. Twitmyer, an American graduate student, had reported similar results at a psychology conference in 1904—the same year that Pavlov won the Nobel prize. At the time, Twitmyer was studying the knee-jerk reflex in humans. Before each trial, he would ring a bell to warn subjects that a hammer was about to strike the knee. Like Pavlov, he found that the subject's leg would soon twitch in response to the bell—even before the knee was hit. Was this a profound development? You might think so, but Twitmyer's presentation attracted little interest.

Conditioned Fears Psychologists finally took notice of classical conditioning in 1914, when behaviorist John Watson described Pavlov's research to a group of American psychologists. To demonstrate the relevance of the phenomenon to humans, Watson and his assistant Rosalie Rayner (1920) conditioned an eleven-month-old boy named Albert to fear a white laboratory rat. "Little Albert" was a normal, healthy, well-developed infant. Like others his age, he was scared by loud noises but enjoyed playing with furry little animals. Enter John Watson. Modeled after Pavlov's research, Watson presented Albert with a harmless white rat. Then just as the boy reached for the animal, Watson made a loud, crashing sound by banging a steel bar with a hammer, which caused the startled boy to jump and fall forward, burying his head in the mattress he was lying on. After seven repetitions of this event, the boy was terrified of the animal. What's worse, his fear generalized, leading him to burst into tears at the sight of a rabbit, a dog, a Santa Claus mask, and even a white fur coat (see Figure 5.9).

From an ethical standpoint, Watson and Rayner's study was shameful. They infected an innocent baby with a fear that seemed to spread like a contagious disease from one white and furry stimulus to the next—and they did not "decondition" him (in case you're wondering, ethics committees would not approve this study today). Watson said that the boy was taken away before he had a chance to do so, but others believe that he may have known in advance that Albert's mother was going to remove her son from the research project (Harris, 1979). On the positive side, Little Albert's fear is a legend in the history of psychology because it established for the first time a link between Pavlov's dogs and an important aspect of the human experience. We now know that people can come to fear objects or places because they happened to be associated with aversive experiences. As we'll see in Chapter 17, classical conditioning spawned a revolutionary and effective method of treating these irrational fears and other anxiety-related disorders.

It is also important to note that babies can be conditioned to form positive *preferences* as well—for example, toward stimuli that are associated with maternal care. In one study, Regina Sullivan and her associates (1991) exposed newborns to a neutral odor. After each presentation, some were gently touched, an inherently pleasurable experience, while others were not. The next day, all the infants were returned to the lab and tested. As predicted, those for whom the odor was paired with the tactile stimulation were more likely to turn their heads toward that odor rather than away from it. This effect occurs not only in human infants but also in young rats, mice, hamsters, deer, guinea pigs, squirrel monkeys, and other species (Leon, 1992).

Social Attitudes and Behavior Not everyone was happy about the possible uses of classical conditioning. In *Brave New World,* novelist Aldous Huxley (1932) warned us of a future in which diabolical leaders use Pavlov's methods to control followers. These concerns are unfounded. However, classical conditioning does affect our lives in many ways. Think about the movie *Jaws.* Early in the film, pulsating bass music is followed by the sight of a shark's fin and the bloody underwater mutilation of a young swimmer. Then it happens again. And again. Before you know it, the music alone (CS)—even without the great white shark (US)—has the audience trembling and ducking for cover. Many other examples illustrate this point. Based on powerful associations, American politicians wrap themselves in stars and stripes, the swastika strikes terror in the hearts of Jewish people, and the burning cross arouses fear among African Americans. In the words of Shelby Steele (1990), a black English professor, "there are objective correlatives everywhere that

Through classical conditioning, people often react with strong emotions to once neutral objects such as national flags, yellow ribbons, and other symbols.

evoke a painful thicket of emotions...covering everything from Confederate flags and pickup trucks with gun racks to black lawn jockeys" (p. 154).

These examples suggest that people form strong positive and negative *attitudes* toward neutral objects by virtue of their links to emotionally charged stimuli. Arthur and Carolyn Staats (1958) thus presented college students with a list of national names (German, Swedish, Dutch, Italian, French, and Greek), each repeatedly paired with words that had pleasant (*happy, gift, sacred*) or unpleasant (*bitter, ugly, failure*) connotations. When subjects later evaluated the nationalities by name, they were more positive in their ratings of those that had been paired with pleasant words rather than with unpleasant words. Other researchers have altered people's reactions to neutral strings of letters by pairing their presentation with electric shock (Cacioppo et al., 1992). Recognizing the power of this effect, advertisers try to link their products to positive emotional symbols: sexy models, happy tunes, and nostalgic images—a strategy that seems to work by drawing attention to the product (Janiszewski & Warlop, 1993).

It's also possible to influence social *behavior* through classical conditioning. Consider the blue-and-yellow stripes on a VISA card, or the orange-and-yellow circles on a MasterCard. Through past associations, these logos may serve as visual cues that lead us to spend money. In one study, college students who were asked to estimate how much money they would be willing to spend on various consumer products gave higher estimates when there was a credit card lying on a table in the testing room than when there was not (Feinberg, 1986). In a second study, which was conducted in a restaurant, diners were randomly given tip trays for payment that were either blank or had a major credit card logo on it. With sixty-six cash-paying customers in the sample, the credit-card tray elicited an increase in tipping from 15.6 percent of the bill to 20.2 percent (McCall & Belmont, 1996).

The Immune System One of the most exciting new research developments is the finding that just as animal reflexes and human emotional reactions can be classically conditioned, so can the body's immune system (Ader & Cohen, 1993). Consisting of more than a trillion white blood cells, the immune system guards our health by warding off bacteria, viruses, and other foreign substances that invade the body. When this system fails, as it does when it is ravaged by the AIDS virus, disease and death are the certain outcome (see Chapter 18). With that in mind, you can appreciate the following striking discovery. Psychologist Robert Ader had been using classical-conditioning procedures with rats in which he paired sweetened water with cyclophosphamide, a drug that causes nausea. Water, drug. Water, drug. As expected, the rats developed a taste aversion to the sweetened water. Unexpectedly, however, many of the animals died because the drug Ader used weakened the immune system by destroying certain types of white blood cells. To further explore this phenomenon, Ader joined with immunologist Nicholas Cohen (1985) in a series of experiments. They repeatedly fed the rats sweetened water, which is harmless, followed by the cyclophosphamide (US), which weakens the immune response (UR). The result: After several pairings, the sweetened water on its own (CS) caused a weakening of the immune response, followed by sickness and sometimes death (CR).

In light of this result, Dana Bovjberg and others (1990) wondered about cancer patients who take chemotherapy drugs. These drugs are designed to inhibit the growth of new cancer cells, but they also inhibit the growth of immune cells. With chemotherapy drugs always being given in the same room in the same hospital, is it possible, over time, that a patient's immune system would be conditioned to react in advance to cues in the surrounding environment? Yes. In a study of women who had undergone a number of chemotherapy treatments for ovarian cancer, these researchers found that their immune systems were weakened as soon as they were brought to the hospital—before they were treated. As with Pavlov's bell, the hospital setting had become a conditioned stimulus, thus triggering a maladaptive change in cellular activity.

These discoveries raise an exciting question: If the immune system can be weakened by conditioning, can it similarly be strengthened? Might it be possible some day to use classical conditioning to help people fight AIDS? Research on this question is still in its early stages, but positive results with animals have been reported (MacQueen et al., 1989; Shurin et al., 1995; Alvarez-Borda et al., 1995). And in recent studies with humans, researchers found that after repeatedly pairing sweet sherbet or other neutral stimuli with shots of adrenaline (which has the unconditioned effect of increasing activity in certain types of immune cells), the sherbet flavor alone eventually triggered an increase in the immune response (Buske-Kirschbaum et al., 1992, 1994).

Operant Conditioning

What is operant conditioning? How does it differ from classical conditioning? What is a reinforcement, and how does it differ from punishment? How do behaviorists explain the persistence of such maladaptive behaviors as gambling? Why are biological and cognitive perspectives on operant conditioning important?

I'll never forget the first time I took my children to Sea World. After watching a dazzling show that featured killer whales jumping through hoops, sea lions playing volleyball, and dolphins dancing on the water, my son, who was only three years old at the time, asked, "How did the animals learn to do these tricks?...Did they go to college?"

Classical conditioning may explain why people salivate at the smell of food, cringe at the sound of a dentist's drill, run when someone yells, "Fire," or tremble at the sight of a flashing blue light in the rearview mirror. But it cannot explain how animals learn to perform complex acrobatics. Nor can it explain how we learn to solve equations, make people laugh, or behave in ways that earn love, praise, sympathy, or the respect of others. As we will see, the acquisition of voluntary, complex, and goal-directed behaviors such as these involves a second form of learning.

The Law of Effect

Before Pavlov had begun his research, an American psychology student named Edward L. Thorndike (1898) was blazing another trail. Interested in animal intelligence, Thorndike built a "puzzle box" from wooden shipping crates so he could observe how different animals learn to solve problems. In one study, he put hungry cats into a cage, one at a time, with a door that could be lifted by stepping on a lever. He then placed a tantalizing chunk of raw fish outside the cage—and beyond reach. You can imagine what happened next. After sniffing around the box, the cat tried to escape by reaching with its paws, scratching the bars, and pushing at the ceiling. At one point, the cat accidentally banged on the lever. The door opened and the cat

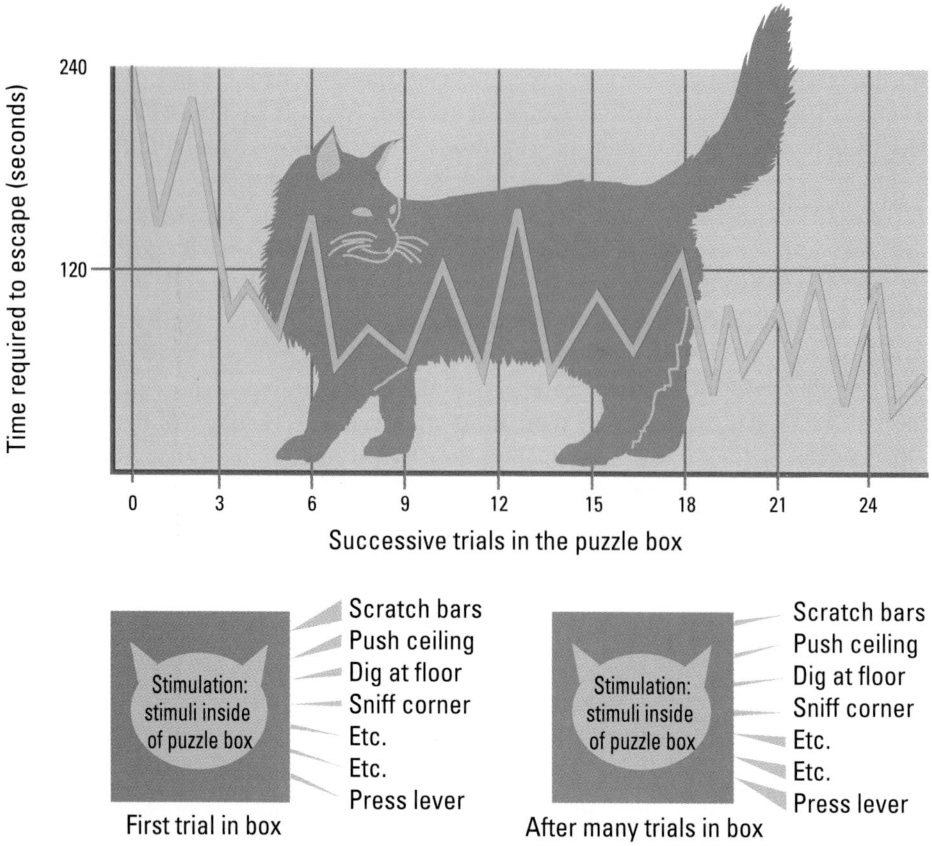

Figure 5.10 Thorndike's law of effect Thorndike's hungry cats initially engaged in various behaviors—sniffing, pawing, scratching the bars, pushing the ceiling, and pressing the lever that opened the escape hatch. Over a series of trials, the cats took less and less time to press the lever (*top*). Accordingly, Thorndike proposed that behaviors followed by a reward are "stamped in," while others fade away (*bottom*).

scampered out to devour the food. Thorndike repeated the procedure again. The cat went through its previous sequence of movements and eventually found the one that caused the latch to open. After a series of trials, Thorndike's cats became more efficient: They went straight to the latch, stepped on the lever, and ate the food (see Figure 5.10).

Based on studies like this one, Thorndike (1911) proposed the **law of effect:** Behaviors that are followed closely in time by a satisfying outcome are "stamped in" or repeated, while those followed by a negative outcome or none at all are extinguished. In the puzzle box, cats spent progressively more time stepping on the latch and less time poking at the bars and ceiling. In the case of humans, Thorndike's law of effect was used to describe the process of socialization. By using rewards and punishments, parents train their children to eat with a utensil, and not to fling their mashed potatoes across the table. To the extent that we learn how to produce desirable outcomes, the process is adaptive.

law of effect A law stating that responses followed by positive outcomes are repeated while those followed by negative outcomes are not.

The Principles of Reinforcement

Following in Thorndike's footsteps, behaviorist B. F. Skinner transformed the landscape of modern psychology. But first things first. To study learning systematically,

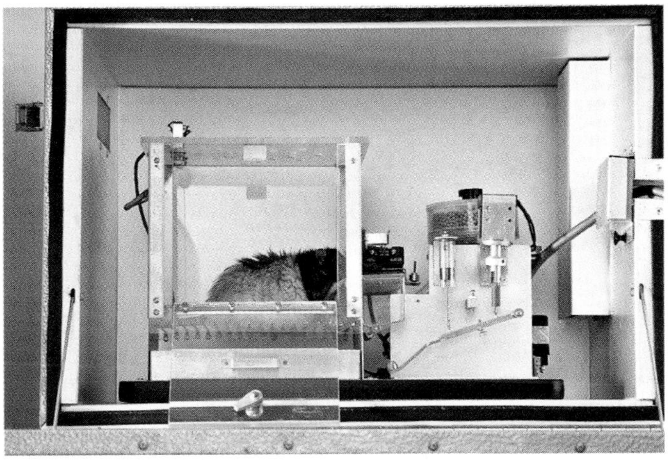

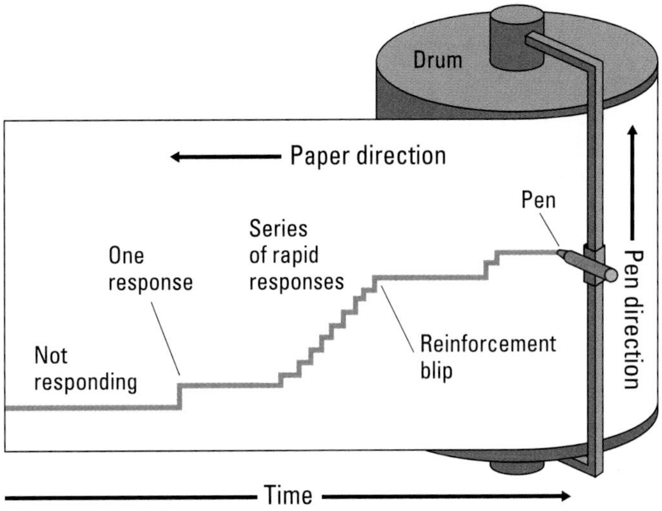

Figure 5.11 The Skinner box

Skinner knew that he had to design an environment in which he controlled the organism's response-outcome contingencies. So as a graduate student in 1930, he used an old ice chest to build a soundproof chamber equipped with a stimulus light, a response bar (for rats) or pecking key (for pigeons), a device that dispenses dry food pellets or water, metal floor grids for the delivery of electric shock, and an instrument outside the chamber that automatically records and tabulates the responses. This apparatus came to be known as the **Skinner box** (see Figure 5.11).

Next, Skinner introduced a new vocabulary. To distinguish between the active type of learning that Thorndike had studied (whereby the organism operates on the environment) and Pavlov's classical conditioning (whereby the organism is a more passive respondent), Skinner coined the term *operant conditioning*. **Operant conditioning** is the process by which organisms learn to behave in ways that produce desirable outcomes. The behavior itself is called an "operant" because it is designed to operate on the environment. In other words, in contrast to classical conditioning—which involves the learning of associations between stimuli, resulting in a passive response—operant conditioning involves the learning of an association between a spontaneously emitted action and its consequences (Rescorla, 1987).

To avoid speculating about an organism's internal state, Skinner also used the term **reinforcement** instead of *reward* or *satisfaction*. Objectively defined, a reinforcer is any stimulus that increases the likelihood of a prior response. There are two types of reinforcers: positive and negative. A *positive reinforcer* strengthens a prior response through the presentation of a positive stimulus. In the Skinner box, the food that follows a bar press is a positive reinforcer. For humans, so are money, grades, hugs, kisses, and a pat on the back. Even mild electrical stimulation to certain "pleasure centers" of the brain, which releases the neurotransmitter dopamine, has a satisfying effect and serves as a positive reinforcer (Olds & Milner, 1954; White & Milner, 1992; Wise & Rompre, 1989). In contrast, a *negative reinforcer* strengthens a response through the removal of an aversive stimulus. In a Skinner box, the termination of a painful electric shock is a negative reinforcer. Similarly, we learn to take aspirins to soften a headache, fasten our seatbelts to turn off the seatbelt buzzer, and rock babies to sleep to stop them from crying.

Skinner box An apparatus, invented by B. F. Skinner, used to study the effects of reinforcement on the behavior of laboratory animals.

operant conditioning The process by which organisms learn to behave in ways that produce reinforcement.

reinforcement In operant conditioning, any stimulus that increases the likelihood of a prior response.

[Jester of Columbia]

"Boy, do we have this guy conditioned. Every time I press the bar down he drops a pellet in."

It is important to keep straight the fact that positive and negative reinforcers both have the same effect: to strengthen a prior response. Skinner was quick to point out that punishment is not a form of negative reinforcement. Although the two are often confused, **punishment** has the opposite effect: It decreases, not increases, the likelihood of a prior response. There are two types of punishment. A *positive punisher* weakens a response through the presentation of an aversive stimulus. Shocking a lab rat for pressing the response lever, scolding a child, locking a criminal behind bars, and boycotting a product are examples of this form of punishment designed to weaken specific behaviors. In contrast, a *negative punisher* weakens behavior by the removal of a stimulus typically characterized as positive. Taking food away from a hungry rat and grounding a teenager by suspending driving privileges are two examples. The different types of reinforcement and punishment are summarized in Table 5.1. Notice that a reinforcement is a stimulus that strengthens a response through (1) the presentation of a positive stimulus, or (2) the removal of a negative stimulus. In contrast, punishment is a stimulus that weakens a response through (1) the presentation of a negative stimulus, or (2) the removal of a positive stimulus.

Shaping and Extinction Modeled after the law of effect, Skinner's basic principle seemed straightforward. Responses that produce a reinforcement are repeated. But wait—if organisms learn by the consequences of their behavior, where does the very first response come from? Before the first food pellet, how does the animal come to press the bar? As demonstrated by Thorndike, one possibility is that the response occurs naturally as the animal explores the cage. Skinner pointed to a second possibility: that the behavior is gradually **shaped,** or guided, by the reinforcement of responses that come closer and closer to the desired behavior.

Imagine that you are trying to get a hungry white rat to press the bar in a Skinner box. Where do you begin? The rat has never been in this situation before, so it sniffs around, pokes its nose through the air holes, grooms itself, rears its hind legs, and so on. At this point, you can wait for the target behavior to appear on its own, or you can speed up the process. If the rat turns toward the bar, you drop a food pellet into the cage. Reinforcement. If it steps toward the bar, you deliver another pellet. Reinforcement. If the rat moves closer or touches the bar, you deliver yet another one. Once the rat is hovering near the bar and pawing at it, you withhold the next pellet until it presses down, which triggers the feeder. Before long, your subject is pressing the bar at a rapid pace. By reinforcing "successive approximations" of the target response, you will have shaped a whole new behavior.

Shaping is the procedure that animal trainers use to get circus elephants to walk on their hind legs, bears to ride bicycles, chickens to play a piano, squirrels to water-ski,

Table 5.1 Types of Reinforcement and Punishment

	EFFECT ON BEHAVIOR	
PROCEDURE	***Increases***	***Decreases***
Presentation of stimulus	Positive reinforcement (feed the rat)	Positive punishment (shock the rat)
Removal of stimulus	Negative reinforcement (stop the shock)	Negative punishment (stop the food)

punishment In operant conditioning, any stimulus that decreases the likelihood of a prior response.

shaping A procedure in which reinforcements are used to gradually guide an animal or person toward a specific behavior.

Using operant conditioning, Sea World animal trainers can get these orca whales to jump on cue.

B. F. Skinner was born in 1904 and received his psychology degree from Harvard in 1931. Skinner's behavioral approach was so influential that it spawned a separate division of the APA, an independent professional organization, and several journals (Lattal, 1992). Skinner is consistently ranked by his peers as one of the most important psychologists of all time (Korn et al., 1991).

On August 10, 1990, Skinner made his final public appearance in Boston at the APA's annual convention and he received an award for Outstanding Lifetime Contribution to Psychology. I was there—and so, it seemed, was everyone else I knew. Upon his introduction, Skinner was greeted with a thunderous standing ovation. Everyone in the audience knew they were watching a living legend. They also knew he was dying. The talk itself was vintage Skinner. For twenty minutes, and without notes, he insisted, as always, that psychology could never be a science of the mind, only a science of behavior.

On August 17, 1990, Skinner completed his last article, for the American Psychologist. *He died the next day.*

and dolphins to jump through hoops—which brings me back to Sea World. The dolphin trainer begins by throwing the dolphin a fish for turning toward a hoop, then for swimming toward it, swimming through it underwater, and finally jumping through a hoop that is many feet up in the air. The process applies to people as well. Young children are toilet trained, socialized to behave properly, and taught to read through step-by-step reinforcement. Similarly, political candidates repeat statements that draw loud applause and abandon those that are met with silence—thereby creating messages that are shaped by what voters want to hear. Rumor has it that a group of college students once conspired to shape the behavior of their good-natured psychology professor. Using eye contact as a reinforcer, the students trained this professor to lecture from a certain corner of the room. Whenever he moved in that direction, they looked up at him; otherwise, they looked down. Before long, he was lecturing from the corner of the classroom, not quite realizing that he had been "shaped."

In classical conditioning, repeated presentation of the CS without the US causes the CR to gradually weaken and disappear. Extinction also occurs in operant conditioning. If you return your newly shaped rat to the Skinner box but disconnect the feeder from the response bar, you'll find that after the rat presses the bar a few times without reinforcement, this behavior will fade and become extinguished. By the same token, people stop smiling at those who don't smile back, stop helping those who never reciprocate, and stop working when their efforts meet with continued failure.

Schedules of Reinforcement Every now and then, scientists stumble into their greatest discoveries. Pavlov was a classic example. So was Skinner. Early in his research career, Skinner would reinforce his animals on a continuous basis: Every bar press produced a food pellet. Then something happened. At the time, Skinner had to make his own pellets by squeezing food paste through a pill machine and then waiting for them to dry. The process was time consuming. "One pleasant Saturday afternoon," Skinner recalled, "I surveyed my supply of dry pellets and, appealing to certain elemental theorems in arithmetic, deduced that unless I spent the rest of the afternoon and evening at the pill machine, the supply would be exhausted by 10:30 Monday morning" (1959, p. 368). Not wanting to spend the whole weekend in the lab, Skinner rationalized to himself that not *every* response had to be reinforced. He adjusted his apparatus so that the bar-press response would be reinforced on a partial basis—only once per minute. Upon his return the next week, however, he found rolls of graph paper with response patterns that were different from anything he had seen before. From this experience, Skinner came to realize the powerful effects of "partial reinforcement." Indeed, he and others went on to identify four schedules of reinforcement (see Figure 5.12), each having different effects on behavior (Ferster & Skinner, 1957).

Fixed-Interval (FI) Schedule In the situation just described, reinforcement followed the first response made after a fixed interval of *time* had elapsed. In an FI-1 schedule, the response produces food after each new minute; or it may be made available only after every two (FI-2), ten (FI-10), or fifteen (FI-15) minutes. The schedule is fixed by time, and it tends to produce a slow, "scalloped" response pattern. After the animal learns that a certain amount of time must elapse, it pauses after each reinforcer and then responds at an accelerating rate until it nears the end

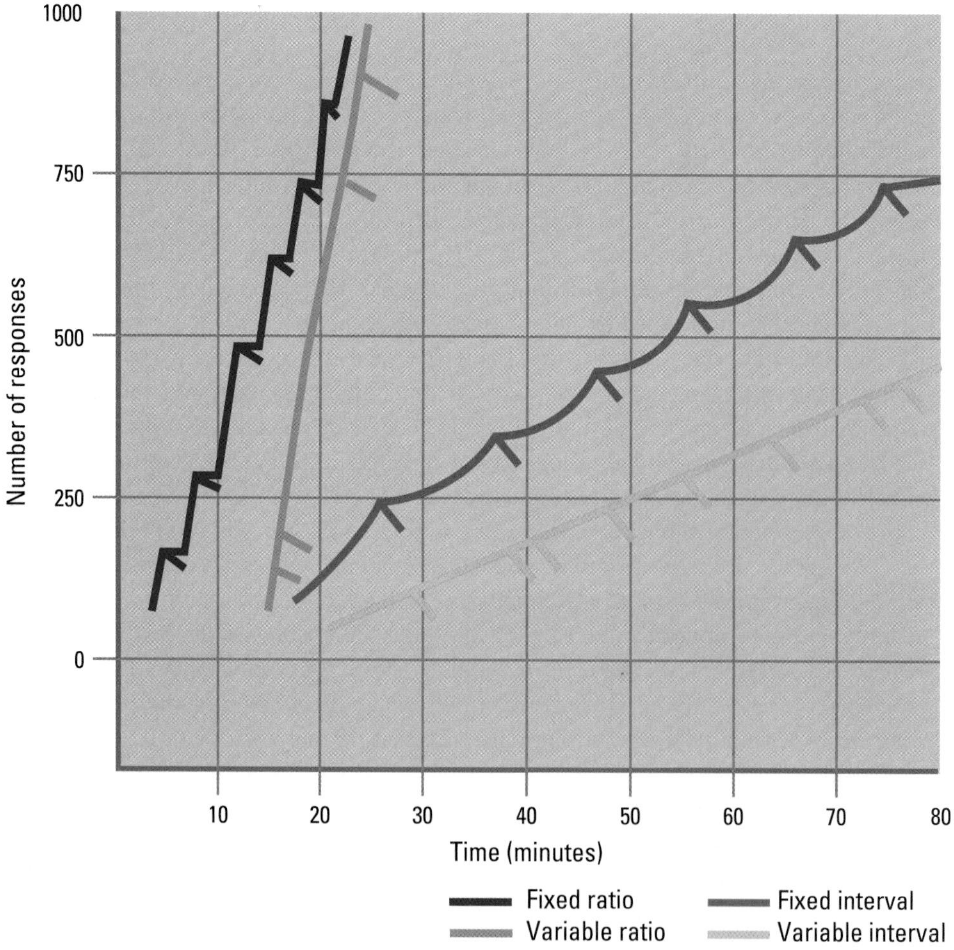

Figure 5.12 Schedules of reinforcement These curves show the response patterns typically produced by different schedules of reinforcement. The steeper the curve, the higher the response rate (the slash marks on each curve indicate the delivery of a reinforcement). As you can see, the rate of responding is higher under ratio than interval schedules.

of the cycle—which signals that the next reinforcement is available. The student whose rate of studying starts slow, increases before midterms, trails off, and picks up again before finals illustrates this reaction to an FI schedule.

Variable-Interval (VI) Schedule Once animals learn what the fixed pattern is, they press the bar only as they near the end of each interval. To counter this lazy response pattern, Skinner tried varying the interval around an average. In other words, an interval may average one minute in length (a VI-1 schedule), but the actual timing of a reinforcement is unpredictable from one interval to the next—say, after fifty seconds, then two minutes, ten seconds, and one minute. The result is a slow but steady, not scalloped, pattern of responses. In effect, teachers who give pop quizzes are using a VI schedule to ensure that their students keep up with the reading rather than cram at the last minute.

Fixed-Ratio (FR) Schedule In this situation, a reinforcer is administered after a fixed number of *responses*—say, every third response, or every fifth, tenth, or fiftieth. In an FR-10 schedule, it takes ten bar presses to get food. If thirty responses are needed, it is an FR-30 schedule. The response-to-reinforcement ratio thus remains constant. In a Skinner box, animals on an FR schedule exhibit a burst of bar presses until the food appears, pause briefly, then produce another burst. The result is a fast, steplike response pattern. Frequent-flier programs, where you can earn a free flight after 25,000 miles of air travel, CD clubs that offer a free CD after every fifth purchase, and the employer who pays workers after they produce a certain number of products all operate on a fixed-ratio schedule.

Variable-Ratio (VR) Schedule In this situation, the reinforcement appears after some average number of responses is made—a number that varies randomly from one reinforcement to the next. On a VR-15 schedule, a rat would have to press the bar an average of fifteen times, but the food may appear on the fifth response, then the twentieth, fourteenth, twenty-first response, and so on. Unable to predict which response will produce a food pellet, animals on a VR schedule respond at a constant high rate. In one case, Skinner trained pigeons to peck a disk 10,000 times for a single food pellet! Slot machines and lotteries are rigged to pay off on a VR schedule, leading gamblers to deposit coins and purchase tickets at a furious, addictive pace. If you've ever tried to access the Internet only to receive a busy signal, chances are you too kept trying with dogged persistence. The reason: When it comes to getting online, our efforts are reinforced, as with slot machines, on a variable-ratio schedule.

Reinforcement schedules affect extinction rates as well as learning. Specifically, the operant response is more enduring and, later, more resistant to extinction when the organism is reinforced on a partial basis rather than on a continuous, 100 percent schedule. This phenomenon is called the **partial-reinforcement effect.** The rat that is fed after every bar press is quick to realize once the feeder is disconnected that the contingency has changed. But the rat that is fed on only an occasional basis persists more before realizing that a reinforcement is no longer forthcoming. If you drop coins into a Coke machine and do not get the drink you ordered, you walk away. Because vending machines are supposed to operate on a continuous-reinforcement basis, it would be immediately apparent that this one is out of order. Deposit coins into a broken slot machine, however, and you may go on to lose hundreds more. After all, you expect slot machines to pay off on an irregular basis. The partial-reinforcement effect has ironic implications. For example, parents who only sometimes give in to a child's temper tantrums and try to tough it out on other occasions create "little monsters" with more tenacious, hard-to-eliminate outbursts than do parents who always give in.

partial-reinforcement effect The tendency for a schedule of partial reinforcement to strengthen later resistance to extinction.

[Drawing by Mankoff; © 1996 The New Yorker Magazine,

"I think I should warn you that the flip side of our generous bonus-incentive program is capital punishment."

Punishment In 1948, Skinner wrote *Walden Two,* a novel about a fictional society in which socially adaptive behaviors were maintained by various schedules of reinforcement. The book was a blueprint for the use of "behavioral engineering" to design a happy, healthy, and productive community. Skinner never hesitated to preach the use of reinforcement. Yet he just as adamantly opposed the use of punishment, even though it is a common form of behavior control. Think about it. Parents scold their children, police officers fine motorists for speeding, referees penalize athletes for committing fouls, and employers fire workers who are lazy. So what's the problem? Aren't these forms of punishment effective?

Research shows that punishment has mixed effects (Axelrod & Apsche, 1983). When it is strong, immediate, consistent, and inescapable, punishment clearly does suppress unwanted behaviors. Shock a rat for pressing the response bar and it will quickly stop making the response. Yell, "No!" at the top of your lungs to a child playing with matches, and it is unlikely to happen again. There is an episode of the old TV show *Cheers* in which Cliff Claivin—an obnoxious, know-it-all postal worker—hires a behaviorist to shape his social skills so that he will be better liked. The two men enter the bar, and each time Claivin makes an offensive or boastful remark, the behaviorist jolts him with a remote-controlled electric-shock device. This scene is hilarious, and it illustrates that punishment can be an effective deterrent.

It is important to know, however, that punishment can also have unwanted side effects. There are four specific problems in this regard. First, a behavior that is met with punishment may be temporarily inhibited or hidden from the punishing agent—but it is not necessarily extinguished. The child who lights matches and the teenager who smokes cigarettes may both continue to do so at school, at a friend's house, or at home when the parent is at work. Second, even when punishment does suppress an unwanted behavior, it does not replace that behavior with one that is more adaptive. It's okay to lock up the convicted criminal, but to change his or her future behavior, some form of rehabilitation program is necessary. Third, punishment can sometimes backfire because a stimulus thought to be aversive may, in fact, prove rewarding. The neglected child who acts up and is scolded by his or her busy parents may actually "enjoy" the attention and make trouble again in the future. Fourth, punishment (especially if it is severe) can arouse fear, anger, frustration, and other negative emotions—leading the person to strike back, retaliate, tune out, or run away.

Properly administered, punishment can be used to suppress an unwanted behavior. As we have seen, however, it can also create more problems than it solves. It is better, advised Skinner, to use a combination of reinforcement (to increase the frequency of alternative desirable behaviors) and extinction (to extinguish the undesirable behaviors) in order to shape a new, more adaptive way of life.

Stimulus Control In operant conditioning, organisms learn to respond in ways that are reinforced. But there is more to the story. A pigeon trained in a Skinner box learns to peck a key for food, but it may also learn that the response produces reinforcement only in the presence of certain cues. Since reinforcements are often available in one situation but not in another, it is adaptive to learn not only *what* response to make but *when* to make it. If pecking a key produces food only when a green disk is lit, a pigeon may learn to discriminate and to respond on a selective basis. The green light is a **discriminative stimulus** that "sets the occasion" for the behavior to be reinforced (Ross & LoLordo, 1987).

When people learn to respond in some situations and not others, their behavior is said to be under "stimulus control." In human terms, this is often important for treating behavioral disorders. Consider the problem of insomnia. Research shows that insomniacs too often use the bed for nonsleeping activities such as watching TV, listening to the radio, reading magazines, and worrying about personal problems. In other words, the bed is a discriminative stimulus for so many activities that it becomes a source of arousal, not relaxation. To counter this problem, insomniacs are advised, frequently with successful results, to lie in bed only for the purpose of sleeping (Morawetz, 1989).

In recent years, the Chinese government has ordered the execution of hundreds of prisoners—a form of punishment designed to deter crime.

An operant response may spread from one situation to another through the process of stimulus generalization. As in classical conditioning, the more similar a new stimulus is to the original discriminative stimulus, the more likely it is to trigger the response. In one study, for example, pigeons were reinforced for pecking a key that was illuminated with yellow light. They were then tested with lights of different colors. The more similar the test lights were to the yellow discriminative stimulus—for example, green and orange as opposed to red and blue—the more likely the pigeons were to peck at it (Guttman & Kalish, 1956). In another study, horses were trained to press a lever that was placed in their stalls, a response that released oats and hay into a feed tray. The animals were conditioned in the presence of an illuminated black circle 2.5 inches in diameter. They were then tested in the presence of circles that varied in size from this original. The closer the resemblance, the more likely the horses were to press the lever. The results for two horses, named Lady Bay and Bud Dark, are illustrated in Figure 5.13 (Dougherty & Lewis, 1991).

Discrimination and generalization are important aspects of human operant conditioning. From experience, a child might learn that temper tantrums bring results from busy parents but not from teachers, that studying increases grades in social studies but not math, that lewd remarks elicit laughter in the locker room but not in the classroom, and that aggression wins praise on the football field but not in other settings. As adults, we routinely regulate our behavior according to situational cues.

Practical Applications of Operant Conditioning

From the start, Skinner was interested in the practical applications of operant conditioning. In World War II, he worked for the United States government on a top-secret project in which he shaped pigeons to guide missiles toward enemy ships. Based on this work, the U.S. Navy recently trained dolphins and sea lions to locate explosive mines in the Persian Gulf and perform other dangerous underwater missions (Morrison, 1988). Similarly, the Coast Guard now uses pigeons to search for people lost at sea. The birds are strapped under the belly of a rescue helicopter and trained to spot floating orange objects in the water (orange is the international color of life jackets). In response to this stimulus, the birds are conditioned to peck a key that buzzes the pilot (Simmons, 1981).

discriminative stimulus A stimulus that signals the availability of reinforcement.

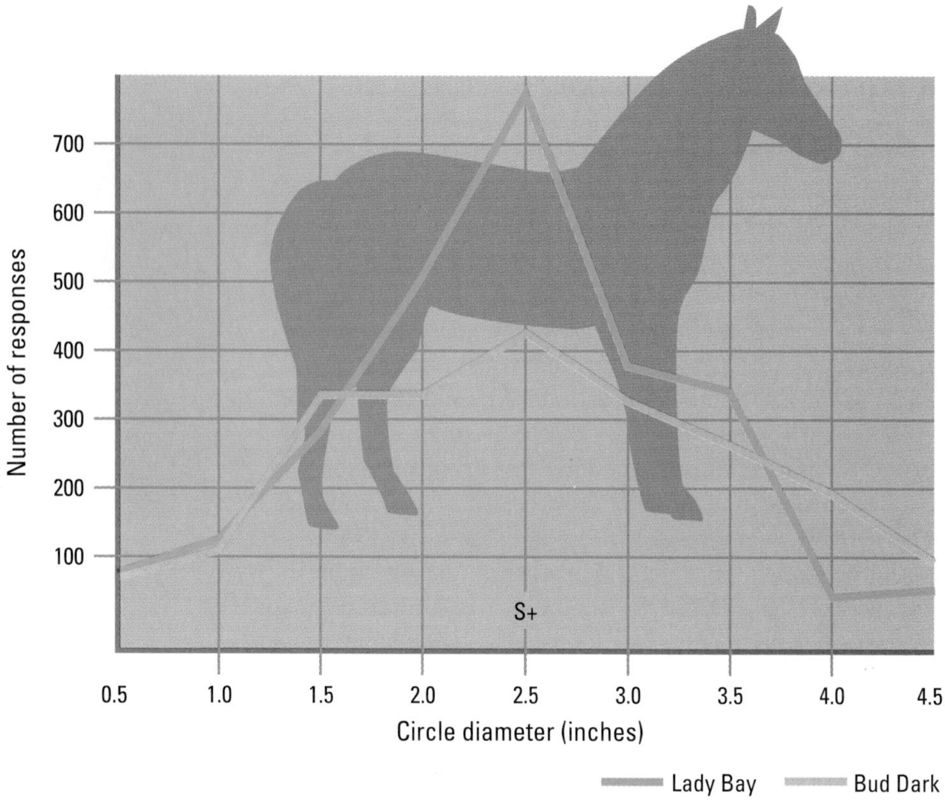

Figure 5.13 Stimulus generalization The more similar a new stimulus is to a discriminative stimulus, the more likely it is to trigger the operant response. In this study, two horses trained to press a lever in the presence of a 2.5-inch circle later responded to new circles based on their level of similarity to the original (Dougherty & Lewis, 1991).

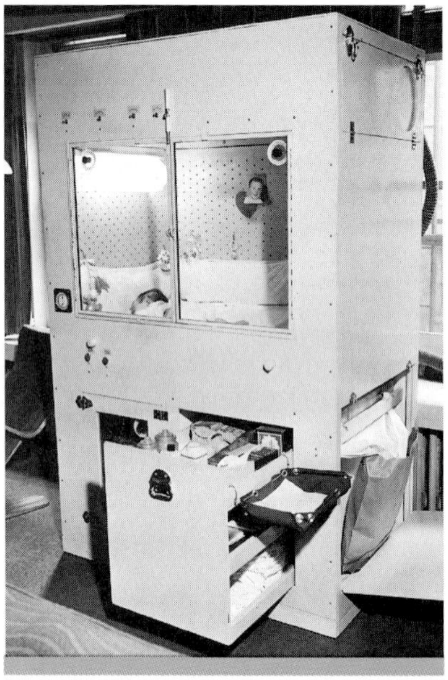

Skinner's daughter in the air crib he invented. Contrary to popular misconceptions, he did not put her in a Skinner box to shape her behavior.

Skinner was eager to use operant conditioning in other ways as well, but his efforts were sometimes misunderstood. In 1945, he constructed an "air crib" for his infant daughter, Deborah. This crib, which he called a "baby tender," was a temperature-controlled enclosed space equipped with an air filter, sound-absorbing walls, a stretched canvas floor, a safety glass window with a curtain, and a roll of diapers. The goal was to provide the infant with an environment that was comfortable, safe, and stimulating. Skinner tried to market his new invention and wrote about it for *Ladies' Home Journal* in an article he titled "Baby Care Can Be Modernized." Unfortunately, the *Journal* editor changed the title to "Baby in a Box"—which led the public to think that he was experimenting on his daughter the way he did with rats and pigeons. Rumors later spread about his daughter's mental health. Indeed, to this day, many people think that she suffered a nervous breakdown and committed suicide. In fact, she is very much alive and well (Bjork, 1993).

"I am not trying to change people. All I want to do is change the world in which they live"

— B. F. SKINNER

Over the years, Skinner advised parents on how to raise children with the use of reinforcement rather than punishment. He also invented a "teaching machine" that would enable students to learn at their own individualized pace by solving a graded series of problems and receiving immediate feedback on their answers. Today, computer-assisted instruction in schools is based on this early work (Benjamin, 1988). In fact, personal computers are now being used just as Skinner had envisioned to train students to type, play the piano, or practice their academic skills. Inspired by Skinner, other behaviorists have applied the principles of operant conditioning to get people to use safety belts, recycle wastes, conserve energy, or simply help themselves (Martin & Pear, 1992).

The use of operant conditioning is now commonplace in the health clinic, the workplace, the classroom, and other settings. For clinical purposes, it laid an important foundation for the techniques of behavior modification, in which reinforcement is used to change maladaptive thoughts, feelings, and behaviors (see Chapter 17). It also forms the basis for biofeedback—an operant procedure in which electronic instruments are used to provide people with continuous information, or "feedback," about their own physiological states. With the aid of electronic sensors to the body and an instrument that amplifies the signals, people can monitor—and then learn to regulate—their own heart rate, blood pressure, and muscular tension. Biofeedback can thus be used in the treatment of migraine headaches, chronic back pain, and other health problems (Schwartz et al., 1995).

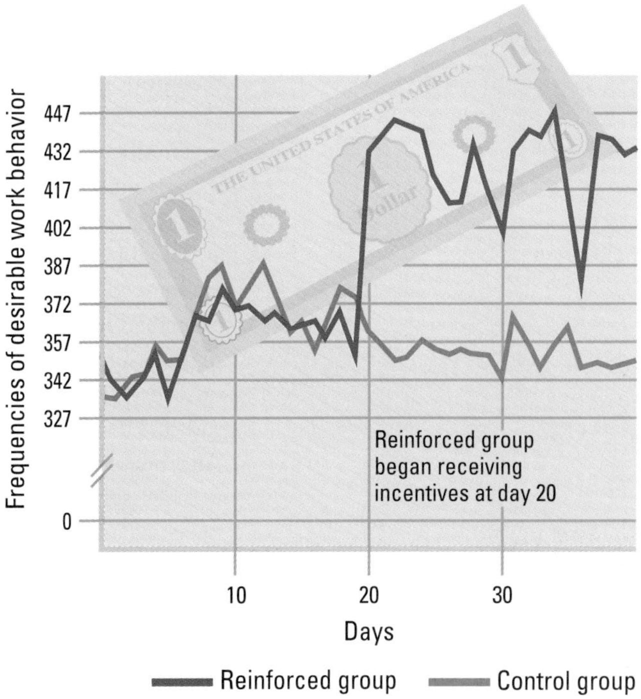

Figure 5.14 Using reinforcement to boost job performance As observed in many studies, department-store salesclerks who were offered incentives improved their job performance while those in the control group did not (Luthans et al., 1981).

Operant conditioning has also been extensively used in the workplace. In a study conducted within a large department store, Fred Luthans and his colleagues (1981) observed sales clerks from sixteen departments for a period of four weeks. The employees in half of these departments were then reinforced for productive performance with cash, time off, or a chance to win a company-paid vacation. The other half were not offered added incentives. As shown in Figure 5.14, the two groups were equivalent in their performance during the first phase of the study. In the second phase, however, the reinforced group improved dramatically, even after the reinforcement period, but the control group did not. Similar effects have been produced in work-incentive programs involving waiters and waitresses (George & Hopkins, 1989), electric-utility-company employees (Petty et al., 1992), and others

There are many practical applications of operant conditioning. In the workplace, organizations recognize employees for their performance. In the classroom, computer games reward children for correct answers through colorful animated displays.

in workplace settings (Pritchard et al., 1988). It is no wonder that so many business organizations now use profit-sharing plans, bonuses, and employee-recognition programs to increase worker satisfaction, motivation, and productivity (Horn, 1987).

Finally, operant conditioning is regularly used in the classroom. Skinner's teaching machine was one application, but there are others as well. For example, many teachers establish large-scale reinforcement programs in which children earn gold stars, ribbons, or "tokens" for engaging in desired behaviors—tokens that can be exchanged for toys, extra recess time, and other privileges. Skinner (1988) himself described how a sixth-grade teacher gave her students a card every time they handed in an assignment. The students put their cards into a jar and, at the end of the week, one card was randomly drawn, with the winner receiving a prize—say, a portable radio. The result: a dramatic improvement in the number of assignments completed. Another use of operant techniques is "precision teaching." In this approach, the teacher, serving as a coach, organizes material for students and shows them how to measure and chart their progress to receive immediate feedback. Students are thus trained to teach themselves and each other (Lindsley, 1992).

I N T E R S E C T I O N

LEARNING AND HEALTH

Self-Help through Operant Conditioning

Do you need to diet or exercise in order to lose weight? Would you like to stop smoking? Do you have trouble falling asleep at night? Are you painfully shy in groups? Do you spend too much time watching TV? If you answered *yes* to any of these questions, then you can help yourself with an individualized program of operant conditioning, or "behavior modification." In a "how to" book on using behavior modification for personal adjustment, David Watson and Roland Tharp (1989) outline the specific steps people must take in order to reach their own behavioral goals:

1. ***Identify the target behavior*** you want to change. Make sure you define the problem in precise terms ("I eat too much junk" or "I don't exercise enough"), not in terms that are more general and harder to pin down ("I am overweight").
2. ***Record your baseline.*** First, measure your current behavior level to get a baseline. If overeating is the problem, count the number of calories you consume in a seven-day period. If smoking is the problem, write down how many cigarettes you smoke each day. Keep written records so you can chart your progress, say on a graph. Also notice the stimulus conditions in which the target behavior occurs (where you are, what you are doing, and who you're with) and the effects it has (so you can see how it is being reinforced).
3. ***Formulate your plan.***

   (a) To *increase* a *wanted* behavior, use positive reinforcement. The reinforcer can be anything: a

day at the mall, a new CD, a long-distance call to an old friend. Make the plan challenging but realistic—for example, "If I run three miles a day for ten days, I earn a trip to the mall." If you are not yet able to make the desired target response, shape your behavior using Skinner's method of successive approximations. If you cannot run a full three miles, for example, start by rewarding yourself for one mile a day for the first week, two miles a day for the next week, and so on.

(b) To *extinguish* an *unwanted* behavior, you should either avoid the situations in which it occurs or remove the reinforcements that sustain it. If, for example, you tend to overeat while talking on the kitchen telephone or watching TV, it would help to spend less time in these situations. To ensure that you follow through, the punishment should not be too severe.

4. ***Implement the plan.*** Once you start, keep a log of the frequency of the target behavior. If you see no improvement, reexamine the program (the reinforcer may be too weak, or you may have set goals that are too high or too easy to reach). If you need to boost your commitment, make a behavioral "contract" in front of friends.
5. ***Maintain the change.*** Once you reach your goal, the key is to stay there. It's better to phase the program out gradually rather than all at once. You can do this by lowering the reinforcement-to-behavior ratio until, eventually, the reinforcement is no longer necessary.

New Developments in Operant Conditioning

Believing that a science of behavior must restrict its focus to observable stimulus-response relationships, Pavlov overlooked aspects of the organism that influenced classical conditioning. In the realm of operant behavior, Skinner took the same narrow view, leaving others to study the impact of inborn biological predispositions and cognitive processes.

Biological Constraints Behaviorists used to think that animals and humans alike could be trained to emit any response that they were physically capable of making. We now realize, however, that there are biological limits to what an animal can learn. In 1947, Keller and Marian Breland, former students of Skinner, founded Animal Behavior Enterprises in Hot Springs, Arkansas. The Brelands were in the business of training animals to do tricks in county fairs, zoos, circuses, movies, and TV commercials. Indeed, they trained thousands of animals belonging to thirty-eight different species—including bears, whales, chickens, pigs, goats, and reindeer.

Despite their professional successes, the Brelands had to concede that biological predispositions often interfered with the shaping of a new behavior. At one point, for example, they tried to train a raccoon to pick up a wooden coin and deposit it into a piggy bank. But instead, the raccoon would clutch the coin or rub two coins together, dip them into the container, pull them out, and rub them again—rather than make the deposit that was reinforced with food. The Brelands also sought to train a pig in the same routine, but after a while the pig would drop the coin, push it with its snout, toss it in the air, and drop it again. What was the problem? In an article entitled "The Misbehavior of Organisms," Breland and Breland (1961) concluded that animals revert to species-specific behavior patterns, a powerful tendency they called *instinctive drift*. In the wild, raccoons manipulate food objects and dunk or "wash" them, while pigs "root" for food in the ground—foraging instincts that inhibit the learning of new operant responses.

Biological predispositions may also constrain an animal's ability to learn how to escape from danger. For example, rats are easily conditioned to freeze, run from one place to another, or attack another rat—if these responses are reinforced by the termination of a painful electric shock. Yet they are slow to learn to escape by pressing a lever, a response they easily learn to make for food and water. According to Robert Bolles (1970), an animal's innate defensive reactions compete with the learning of a new escape response. All this serves to remind us that behavior is guided not just by personal experience but also by an organism's evolutionary past. As with classical conditioning, in which some associations are more easily learned than others, operant learning is limited by an organism's own adaptive ways (Gould & Marler, 1987).

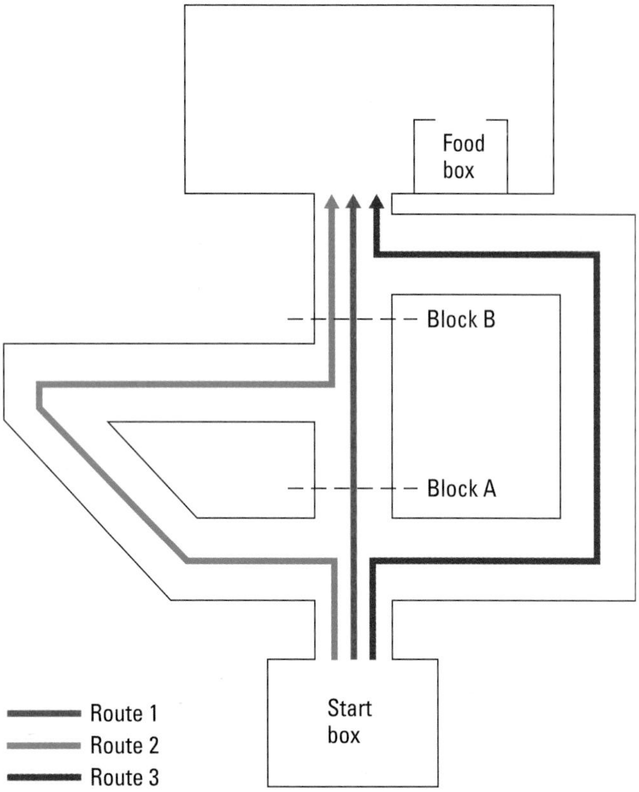

Figure 5.15 Rats in a maze: evidence for a cognitive map Tolman trained rats to run a maze like the one shown here, but he then blocked the most-direct routes to the goal box. Operating as if they had a cognitive map, the animals took the best available detours.

Cognitive Perspectives Up to the day he died, Skinner (1990) steadfastly refused to speculate about internal mental processes. Although this radical position still has its share of proponents (Poling et al., 1990), most psychologists now believe that it is important to understand internal cognitive processes—not only in humans but in animals as well (Ristau, 1991; Vauclair, 1996).

Latent Learning The first prominent theorist to adopt a cognitive position was Edward Tolman. According to Tolman (1948), animals in their natural habitat learn more than just a series of stimulus-and-response connections. They also acquire a "cognitive map," which is a mental spatial model of the layout—and they do so regardless of whether their explorations are reinforced. Thus, when Tolman trained rats to run a maze but then changed the starting place or blocked the most-direct routes, the animals behaved as if they were using a street map of their surroundings: They took the best available detours (see Figure 5.15).

To examine whether spatial learning required that the rats be reinforced for their exploratory behavior, Tolman and Honzik (1930) conducted a classic experiment. Once a day for two weeks, they put three groups of rats into a complex maze and measured their speed in reaching the "goal box." One group was rewarded with food and improved considerably over time. A second group was not rewarded and did not improve much over time. From an operant standpoint, neither of these results is surprising. The third group, however, was the key to this experiment. In this group, the rats were not rewarded during the first ten days, but they received food beginning on the eleventh. The result: They showed immediate and dramatic improvement. On the eleventh day, before realizing that there was food in the goal box, they were just as slow as the no-reward group. But on the twelfth day, after one reinforcement, they were just as fast as the group that had been rewarded all along (see Figure 5.16).

This result was significant because it demonstrated what Tolman called **latent learning,** learning that is not exhibited in overt performance until there is an incentive to do so. By making this distinction between "learning" and "performance," Tolman was able to demonstrate that animals learn from experience—with or without rein-

latent learning Learning that occurs but is not exhibited in performance until there is an incentive to do so.

forcement. More recent research provides additional support for this phenomenon (Keith & McVety, 1988).

Locus of Control Strict behaviorists claim that people are controlled by objective reinforcement contingencies. In contrast, a cognitive perspective holds that behavior is influenced more by our subjective interpretations of reinforcement. To illustrate the point, consider the following two incidents. The first was a demonstration by Skinner (1948) in which he dropped food pellets into a pigeon's cage on a random basis, leading the animal to repeat whatever it happened to be doing at the time. Soon this "superstitious" pigeon was busy turning, hopping on one leg, bowing, scraping, and raising its head. This pigeon—like most humans, says Skinner—was under the illusion that it had control, even though it did not. The second story concerns a young male psychotherapy patient named Karl S. who was depressed because he felt incompetent to find a job, friends, or a woman. E. Jerry Phares (1976), Karl's therapist, tried to raise his expectancy for success through a series of small achievements—submitting a job application, striking up a conversation with a woman, and so on. Karl succeeded in these efforts but remained passive and pessimistic. The problem? He did not see the link between his actions and successful outcomes. In contrast to the superstitious pigeon, Karl had control but didn't realize it. So he didn't try.

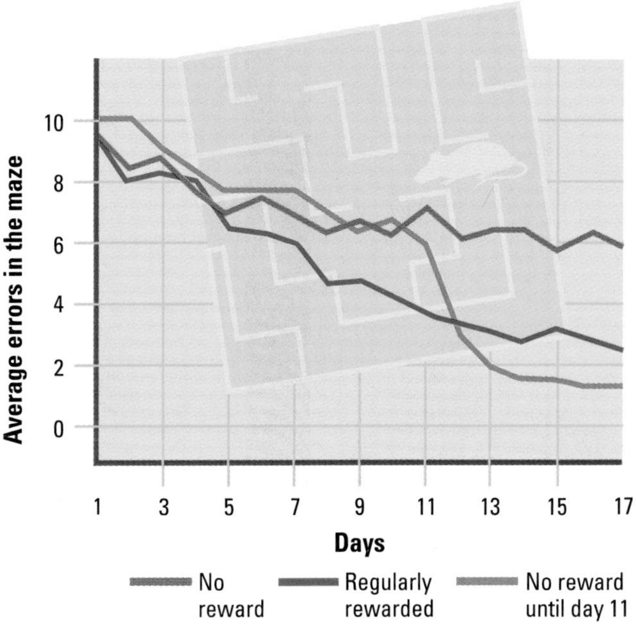

Figure 5.16 Latent learning Tolman and Honzik (1930) put rats into a maze and measured how quickly they reached the goal box. Those rewarded with food improved; those without reward did not. A third group received no food until the eleventh day. Note that the rats in this last group showed a marked improvement from the eleventh day (before they knew there was food in the goal box) to the twelfth (after the first reward). These animals had exhibited latent learning, learning without reinforcement.

According to Julian Rotter (1966), reinforcement influences behavior only if we perceive the two as causally connected. For students who believe that studying increases their grades, for workers who think that hard work will be rewarded, and for citizens who believe that they can influence government policy, reinforcement strengthens behavior. But for students who believe that grades are arbitrarily determined, for workers who think that getting ahead requires more luck than effort, and for citizens who feel that they're at the mercy of powerful leaders, reinforcement does not strengthen behavior. Research shows that people differ in their "generalized expectancies" for personal control and in their responsiveness to reinforcement. Those who have a relatively *internal* locus of control tend to believe that they determine their own destiny. Those with an *external* locus of control believe that luck, fate, and powerful others determine their reinforcements. Compared to externals, internals get higher grades in school, persist longer at laboratory tasks, and play a more active role in political and social affairs (Strickland, 1989; Rotter, 1990).

Hidden Costs of Reward By focusing on how people interpret reinforcement, the cognitive perspective raises a second issue. After someone is rewarded for an enjoyable task, what happens to his or her interest and motivation once that reward is no longer available? Does reinforcement enhance motivation or detract from it? We'll address this issue in Chapter 8 when we discuss worker motivation. But for now, let's consider the implications for education, a topic close to Skinner's heart.

In a study conducted in a preschool classroom, Mark Lepper and his colleagues (1973) gave children a chance to play with colorful felt-tipped markers—a chance most could not resist. By observing how much time the children spent on the activity, the researchers were able to measure their initial level of interest in it. Two weeks

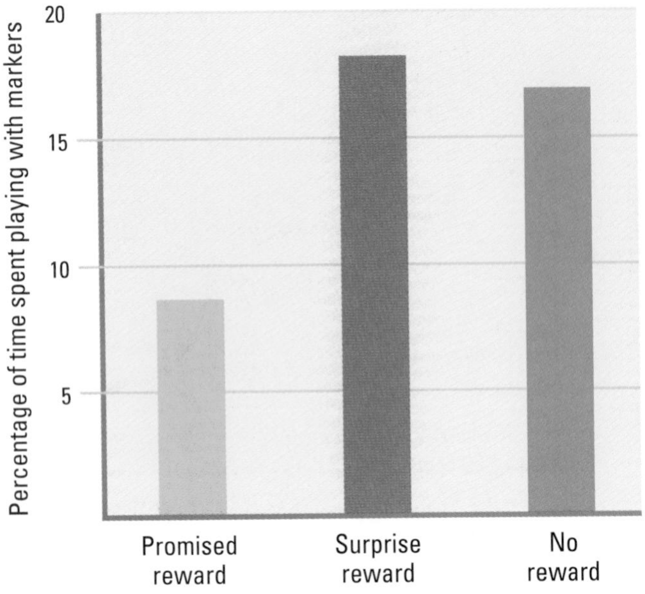

Figure 5.17 The hidden cost of reward Preschool children received a promised reward, a surprise reward, or no reward to draw pictures with magic markers. One week later, researchers recorded the amount of classroom time these children spent with the markers. As shown, children who had drawn pictures to get a reward were later the least interested in the activity when the reward was no longer available.

later, the children were randomly divided into three groups. In one, they were simply asked if they would draw some pictures with the markers. In the second, they were told that if they used the markers they would receive a "Good Player Award," a certificate with a gold star and a red ribbon. In the third group, the children were not offered a reward for drawing pictures, but then—like those in the second group—they received a reward when they were finished.

About a week later, the teachers placed the markers and paper on a table in the classroom while the experimenters hid behind a one-way mirror. This time, without a hint of reward, the amount of free time the children spent playing with the markers was once again recorded. The results are shown in Figure 5.17. Note that children who had previously drawn pictures for the promise of a reward were now less interested in the markers. Yet children who were not rewarded or had received a surprise reward (so they did not feel as if they played with the markers in order to get it)—were not adversely affected. In follow-up research, Teresa Amabile found that subjects who were offered payment for drawing pictures also produced less creative work.

This hidden cost of reward can have serious implications in the classroom. Take a child who loves to read and a teacher who awards gold stars for books completed. During the year, the child continues to read at a lively pace. But what will happen later on, when there are no gold stars? Will the child then begin to wonder if it is still worth the effort? And does this mean that reinforcement should never be used? No, not at all. If a child is not engaged in the wanted behavior to start with, offering reward can help. For the child who doesn't normally read, gold stars provide a necessary incentive in much the same way food pellets increase bar pressing in the Skinner box. Also, reward can be used to send different messages. When presented as a bonus (for superior performance) rather than as a bribe (for just doing it), reward will enhance rather than diminish a child's future motivation (Boggiano et al., 1985; Cameron & Pierce, 1994).

"Children have never been very good at listening to their elders, but they have never failed to imitate them."

— JAMES BALDWIN

To summarize, the lessons of a cognitive perspective are clear: People do not mindlessly repeat behaviors that happened to be followed by reinforcement but instead are influenced by their perceptions, beliefs, and expectations.

Observational Learning

Is learning by imitation a uniquely human form of learning? What kinds of behaviors can be learned by observation, and what is the process like?

Classical and operant conditioning are two ways in which organisms adapt and learn from experience. But something is missing. Forget the dogs, cats, rats, and pigeons that drool, press bars, peck keys, jump from shocks, and run in mazes. What about the human learning of complex behavior? Don't we sometimes learn without direct experience? Think about the first time you danced, drove a car, or programmed a VCR. Now imagine how slow and inefficient you would have been if the skills had to be acquired from scratch—"shaped," as Skinner would say, through trial and error.

Complex new behaviors can also be learned by watching and imitating others. This form of learning occurs not only among humans but in many types of animals (Heyes & Galef, 1996). In one experiment, for example, golden hamster pups were put in a cage with their mothers. Some of the mothers, but not others, had been specifically pretrained to use their teeth and front paws to get sunflower seeds that dangled from a chain. The question was whether the young hamster pups learn to do the same just by watching—and the answer was *yes*. Although fewer than 20 percent were able to retrieve seeds in the presence of the naive mother, that number was up to 73 percent in the trained-mother group (Previde & Poli, 1996). In a second experiment, naive pigeons watched through a window others of their species who were trained to get food from a feeder either by stepping on a bar or by pecking at it. When later given access to the same bar and feeder, the pigeons were more likely to use the technique they had previously seen used (Zentall et al., 1996).

> *"Behavioral psychology is the science of pulling habits out of rats."*
>
> — DOUGLAS BUSCH

Human infants also exhibit rudimentary forms of imitation. Research shows that they copy adults who stick out their tongues (Anisfeld, 1991); use a particular hand to reach, point, wave, and make other gestures (Harkins & Uzgiris, 1991); or utter sounds such as *meh, dah,* and *bee* (Poulson et al., 1991). Similarly, toddlers imitate others of their own age grasping, pulling, pushing, and poking at various toys (Hanna & Meltzoff, 1993). It is clear that imitation is adaptive: By observing their peers and elders, young members of a species learn to interact and develop the skills of past generations.

Based on studies showing that exposure to violent models increases aggression in children, a storm of controversy has surrounded MTV's heavy-metal cartoon, Beavis and Butt-Head.

Studies of Modeling

According to Albert Bandura (1986), people learn by watching others. These others are called models, and the process is known as **observational learning.** In a classic experiment to demonstrate the point, nursery-school children were exposed to a live adult model who behaved aggressively (Bandura et al., 1961). In a typical session, the child would be sitting quietly, drawing a picture. From another part of the room, an adult approached a Bobo doll, an inflatable clownlike toy that is weighted on the bottom so that it pops back up whenever it is knocked down. For the next ten minutes, the adult repeatedly abused the doll—sitting on it, pounding it with a hammer, kicking it, throwing balls at it, and yelling, "Sock him in the nose…Kick him!"

After the outburst, the child was taken to a room filled with attractive toys but told that these toys were being saved "for the other children." Frustrated, the child was then taken to a third room containing additional toys, including—you guessed it—a Bobo doll. At that point, the child was left alone and observed through a one-way mirror. What happened? Compared to children exposed to a nonviolent model or to no model at all, those who witnessed the aggressive display were far more likely to assault the doll. In fact, they often copied the model's attack, action for action, and repeated the same abusive remarks, word for word. The children had acquired a whole new repertoire of aggressive behavior. More recent research confirms the point: Among children and adolescents, exposure to aggressive models on TV and in the movies triggers aggression—not just in the laboratory but in the classroom, the playground, and other settings as well (Wood et al., 1991).

observational learning Learning that takes place when one observes and models the behavior of others.

Observational learning can also have beneficial effects. In one study, snake phobics gained the courage to approach a live snake by first watching someone else do so—which is why models are often used in the treatment of phobias (Bandura et al., 1969). In a second study, bystanders were more likely to help a stranded motorist or donate money to charity, two acts of generosity, if they had earlier observed someone else do the same (Bryan & Test, 1967). And in a third study, elementary-school children learned by watching others how to sharpen their logical skills in the game of "twenty questions"—indicating that exposure to models can be used to facilitate the learning of new concepts and strategies (Johnson et al., 1991).

The Process of Modeling

According to Bandura (1977, 1986), observational learning is not a simple, automatic, reflexlike reaction to models. Rather, it consists of two-stages: acquisition and performance. You may recall that Edward Tolman had earlier made this distinction by noting that a newly acquired response often remains "latent" until the organism is motivated to perform it. Building on Tolman's work, Bandura described observational learning as a chain of events involving four steps: attention, retention, reproduction, and motivation.

- ***Attention.*** To learn by observation, one must pay attention to the model's behavior and to the consequences of that behavior. Due to their ability to command our attention, parents, teachers, political leaders, and TV celebrities are potentially effective models.
- ***Retention.*** In order to model someone else's behavior minutes, days, weeks, months, or even years later, one must recall what was observed. Accordingly, modeling is likely to occur when the behavior is memorable or when the observer thinks about or rehearses the behavior.
- ***Reproduction.*** Attention and memory are necessary conditions, but observers must also have the motor ability to reproduce the modeled behavior. As closely as I watch, and as hard as I try, I will never be able to copy Michael Jordan's graceful flight to the basket.
- ***Motivation.*** People may pay attention to a model, recall the behavior, and have the ability to reproduce it—all laying a necessary foundation for modeling. Whether an observer takes action, however, is determined by his or her expectations for reinforcement—expectations that are based not only on personal experience but also on the experiences of others. This last point is important because it illustrates "vicarious" reinforcement: that people are more likely to imitate models who are rewarded for their behavior and less likely to imitate those who are punished. Apparently, learning can occur without direct, firsthand experience.

Perspectives on Learning

- Thinking back over the material presented in this chapter, why were Pavlov and Skinner considered S–R behaviorists? And why is it often said that today's learning researchers adhere more to an S–O–R model?

For about a century now, psychologists have studied with remarkable intensity the basic laws of classical conditioning, operant conditioning, and observational learning. To a large extent, the knowledge gained from this research has had far-reaching implications for a wide range of animal and human behaviors. Inspired by Pavlov and Skinner, the psychology of learning is grounded in hard-nosed S–R behaviorism. Today, however, a vast majority of researchers recognize that biological dispositions, cognitive processes, and other factors residing within the person play a critical role. Thus, we now know that all organisms are genetically prepared to learn some associations more easily than others, that beliefs about reinforcement can have a greater impact on behavior than the reinforcement itself, and that learning is also achieved by observing others.

In the upcoming chapters, we'll see that psychologists today are systematically exploring the inner workings of the human mind. Some are exploring the ways in which we can bolster our body's immune systems through classical-conditioning procedures (Ader et al., 1991). Others are newly focused on the ways in which learning can alter the neural connections in the brain (Rosenzweig, 1996). Still others focus on memory, thought and language, motivation, and emotion. Clearly, there is tremendous interest in the "O" part of S–O–R psychology. Learning theorists are also studying the acquisition of complex human skills—such as how we learn to read, speak, understand stories, solve math problems, recognize music, play chess, use a computer, and drive a car (Holding, 1989). And they are interested in the way people learn complex material without really trying—through the kinds of unconscious or "implicit" processes described at the start of this chapter (Reber, 1993). Finally, there's a great deal of interest in applications of learning theory to instructional issues, education, and the acquisition of knowledge (Glaser, 1990).

Summary and Key Terms

As in the case of the stickleback, **ethologists** have found that many aspects of animal behavior are programmed by inborn **fixed action patterns.** In contrast, human beings adapt primarily through **learning,** a relatively permanent change in knowledge or behavior that comes from experience. The simplest form of learning, found in lower organisms, is **habituation,** the tendency for an organism to become familiar with a stimulus as a result of repeated exposure.

Classical Conditioning

The key to learning is association, a tendency to connect events that occur together in space or time.

Pavlov's Discovery

Studying the digestive system in dogs, Pavlov stumbled upon **classical conditioning.** In his experiments, the salivary reflex was the **unconditioned response (UR),** and it was elicited by food, an **unconditioned stimulus (US).** Through pairing of a bell with the food, the bell became a **conditioned stimulus (CS)** that on its own could elicit salivation, a **conditioned response (CR).** This experiment serves as a model of classical conditioning in humans.

Basic Principles

After Pavlov's initial experiment, he and others discovered four basic principles of learning: (1) the **acquisition** of a CR is influenced by the order and timing of the CS–US pairing; (2) in **extinction,** repeated presentation of the CS without the US causes the CR to lose its power, though there is an occasional rebound effect known as **spontaneous recovery;** (3) after an organism is conditioned to a CS, similar stimuli will often evoke the CR through **stimulus generalization;** and (4) **discrimination** is the opposite process, one of learning to distinguish between stimuli.

Pavlov's Legacy

As demonstrated by taste-aversion studies, research shows that animals are biologically prepared to learn some associations more easily than others. The process involves learning that one event (CS) predicts another event (US). There are many applications of classical conditioning. For example, people can be conditioned to develop fears or preferences and positive or negative social attitudes. Recent studies show that the body's immune cells can be classically conditioned as well.

Operant Conditioning

The learning of voluntary, complex, goal-directed behaviors is achieved by a different form of learning, one that involves the link between an action and its consequences.

The Law of Effect

Using animals, Thorndike studied the **law of effect:** that actions followed by a positive outcome are repeated, while those followed by a negative outcome or no outcome are not.

The Principles of Reinforcement

By testing animals in a controlled environment called a **Skinner box,** Skinner systematically examined **operant conditioning,** the process by which we learn to behave in ways that produce reinforcement. A **reinforcement** is any stimulus that strengthens a prior response. There are two types of reinforcers: positive (the presentation of a desirable stimulus) and negative (the withdrawal of an aversive stimulus). In contrast, **punishment** has the opposite effect of weakening, not strengthening, a prior response. Punishers may be positive (presentation of an aversive stimulus) or negative (withdrawal of a desirable stimulus).

Skinner found that complex new behaviors can be **shaped** through reinforcement of successive responses that come closer and closer to the target behavior. Skinner discovered the **partial-reinforcement effect,** that partial reinforcement increases resistance to extinction. He and others went on to identify four types of reinforcement schedules (fixed-interval, variable-interval, fixed-ratio, variable-ratio), each having different effects on learning and extinction. In addition, animals can be trained to respond only in the presence of a **discriminative stimulus** that signals the availability of reinforcement. Although punishment can often be used to suppress unwanted behavior, it has undesirable side effects and should be used cautiously. As in classical conditioning, generalization and discrimination are important aspects of operant learning.

Practical Applications of Operant Conditioning

Skinner was interested in practical applications. Following in his footsteps, many behaviorists use the principles of operant conditioning to solve practical problems in clinical settings, the workplace, and the classroom.

New Developments in Operant Conditioning

Although operant conditioning is broadly applicable, animal studies have shown that species-specific biological dispositions often interfere with the shaping of a new behavior. And although Skinner refused to speculate about mental processes, others have not. Thus, researchers have found that animals exhibit **latent learning** (learning without reinforcement), that people are more influenced by the perception of control over reinforcement than by objective contingencies, and that rewards sometimes undermine our intrinsic motivation.

Observational Learning

Complex new behaviors are often learned not through direct experience but through the observation and imitation of others.

Studies of Modeling

According to Bandura, we learn by watching others. These others are called models, and the process is called **observational learning.** Studies indicate that both desirable (helping) and undesirable (aggressive) behaviors may be learned in this manner.

The Process of Modeling

Observational learning involves not simple, reflexlike imitation but a four-step process that requires attention, retention, reproduction, and motivation. Through a process of vicarious reinforcement, people are most likely to imitate models who are rewarded for their behavior.

Perspectives on Learning

Inspired by Pavlov and Skinner, the psychology of learning is grounded in S–R behaviorism. Today, however, researchers are also interested in evolutionary dispositions, links to the brain and immune system, cognitive processes, and other factors residing within the organism.

In the Field Resources

Books

Bjork, D. W. (1993). *B. F. Skinner: A life*. New York: Basic Books.

This book provides a warm, sensitive, balanced, and insightful portrait of one of psychology's giants.

Martin, G., & Pear, J. (1992). *Behavior modification: What it is and how to do it*. Englewood Cliffs, NJ: Prentice Hall.

This is an easy-to-read introduction to basic principles of conditioning and their application in schools, businesses, hospitals, and other settings.

Films and Videos

A Clockwork Orange (1971, 137 min.)

This is a surrealistic film about a violent gang of youths who brutalize others for the fun of it. When captured, aversive-conditioning techniques are used to modify their behavior. (Malcom McDowell.)

Journals and Periodicals

Journal of Applied Behavior Analysis
Journal of Experimental Psychology: Learning, Memory, and Cognition
Quarterly Journal of Experimental Psychology

6 *Memory*

The situation You sign up for a study of memory, and when you appear for the session, the experimenter says that you'll hear several lists of words over a tape recorder. Listen carefully. After each list, you will hear either a tone or a knocking sound to signal whether you should spend the next two minutes writing down the words in that list or working on some arithmetic problems. After the first list, you'll hear a second list, a third list, and so on, until you're finished. You have no questions, so the session begins.

The experimenter turns on the tape recorder and you hear a male voice reciting a word every 1.5 seconds. Try it: *bed, rest, awake, tired, dream, wake, night, blanket, doze, slumber, snore, pillow, peace, yawn, drowsy.* Got it? Now look away, take out a sheet of paper, and take two minutes to write down as many of these words as you can. Okay, time's up. Here's the next list: *note, sound, piano, sing, radio, band, melody, horn, concert, instrument, jazz, symphony, orchestra, art, rhythm.* Again try to recall as many words as you can.

What's Your Prediction?

How to create a false memory

After completing all the lists, you are told that your ability to recognize the original words will now be tested. You'll receive a set of ninety-six words, some of which appeared earlier. For each word, you should indicate whether it is *new* (never presented before) or *old* (presented earlier on tape). Next, for each word you recognize as old, you're asked: Are you sure you vividly recall hearing the speaker say that word on tape? Try it. Cover the last paragraph and circle each of the following words that you recognize from before: *tooth, beach, sleep, art, traffic, pillow, kitten, music.*

As a participant in this experiment, you know that some of the test items are new, others old. What you don't know is that some of the new items were meaningfully related to words that did appear in the original lists. The experimenters referred to these as "lures." The question is, how easy was it to tell the difference?

Make a prediction Think about the recognition test. Participants were reshown some of the same words they had seen just minutes earlier. So how well can they recognize these items? And will they ever "remember" hearing the lure words *not* on the list? To get you started, the percentage of old items correctly seen as old is presented below. As you can see, participants recognized 79 percent of these words—57 percent of which they were absolutely sure about. Using these numbers as a guideline and the table below, predict how often (0–100 percent) the participants falsely recognized and were sure about the lures that were never actually presented.

RECOGNIZE?	OLD WORDS	NEW "LURES"
Yes	79%	________ %
Sure	57%	________ %

The results In this study, Henry Roediger and Kathleen McDermott (1995) were curious to see if they could get people to create "false memories" of words not previously heard. So what did you predict? Compared to the percentage of old items correctly and confidently recognized, how often did participants "recognize" lure words? The results were striking. As shown below, participants could not tell the difference between words that were on the list and those that were not.

RECOGNIZE?	OLD WORDS	NEW "LURES"
Yes	79%	81%
Sure	57%	58%

What does it all mean? To appreciate what happened in this experiment, take another look at the test materials and your own responses. After hearing sleep-related words such as *bed* and *yawn* and music-related words such as *jazz* and *instrument,* didn't you think that you had also heard *sleep* and *music*—words that fit but were not actually on the list? Most people do. I was at a conference where Henry Roediger, in a talk entitled "Creating False Memories in the Classroom," reproduced this result with an audience of psychology professors, including myself. Other researchers, too, have obtained this result (Read, 1996).

Psychologists often liken human memory to a computer that faithfully records information for later use. This study reveals, however, that there is much more to the story. As we'll see in this chapter, remembering is an active process, and we sometimes *construct* memories in light of our own beliefs, wishes, needs, contextual factors, and information received from outside sources.

On November 22, 1963, thousands of Dallas residents watched one of the most tragic events in modern American history: the assassination of President John F. Kennedy. What happened? Some witnesses said they saw a lone gunman in the sixth-floor window of a nearby building. Others recalled the presence of two or three men in the same window. Still others insisted that they saw shooting from a grassy knoll. To add to the confusion, some witnesses recalled hearing three shots fired; others swore they heard five or six.

Twenty-eight years later, in 1991, John Demjanjuk was identified by four survivors of a World War II concentration camp as "Ivan the Terrible," a Nazi guard who killed thousands of Jews. After forty-five years, these witnesses identified the elderly man as Ivan. Based on their testimony, Demjanjuk was convicted and sentenced to death in a Jerusalem courtroom—only to be released two years later when he was exonerated by evidence that was previously withheld.

It was also in 1991 that TV viewers watched in astonishment as law professor Anita Hill accused Supreme Court nominee Clarence Thomas of sexual harassment. Word for word, she repeated lewd remarks he had allegedly made ten years earlier. Thomas adamantly denied all the charges.

These three cases have little in common, but they raise the same basic question: Can remembrances of the past be trusted? Human memory is often the subject of controversy. Sometimes we seem able to recall a face, a voice, the contents of a lecture, a foreign language, a news event, a first date, the birth of a child, or the death of a loved one with precision and certainty. At other times, however, memory is limited, flawed, and biased—as when we forget a phone number we just looked up, the items on the grocery list left at home, coursework from last semester, or the

After the 1963 assassination of John F. Kennedy, many eyewitnesses came forward. Some reported seeing one gunman in a sixth-floor window of a nearby building; others recalled two or three gunmen in the same building; still others thought the shots were fired from the ground. Such are the pitfalls of eyewitness memory.

name of someone we recently met. How are our experiences stored in the brain and later retrieved? What causes us to preserve some events but not others? How accurate are our recollections of the past? To answer these questions, cognitive psychologists study **memory,** the process by which information is retained for later use (Bjork & Bjork, 1996; Schacter, 1996).

An Information-Processing Model

In what ways can human memory be likened to the working of a computer? What are the differences between sensory, short-term, and long-term memory?

According to Aristotle and Plato, memory is like stamping an impression into a block of wax. Over the years, others have likened memory to a switchboard, storage box, workbench, library, layered stack, and tape recorder. Today, cognitive psychologists like to compare the human mind to a computer and memory to an information-processing system. If you have ever worked on a computer, you will appreciate the analogy. Your PC *receives* input from a keyboard, joystick, or mouse; it *converts* the symbols into a special numeric code; it *saves* the information on a hard or floppy disk; it then *retrieves* the data from the disk by displaying it on the screen or sending it to a printer. If the computer crashes, if there's not enough space on the disk, if the file was deleted, or if you type in the wrong retrieval command, then the information becomes inaccessible, or "forgotten."

Using the computer as a model, memory researchers seek to trace the flow of information as it is mentally processed. In this **information-processing model,** a stimulus that registers on our senses is remembered only if it (1) draws *attention,* which brings it into consciousness; (2) is *encoded,* or transferred to *storage* sites in the brain; and (3) is *retrieved* for use at a later time (Atkinson & Shiffrin, 1968).

Within this information-processing approach, three types of memory have been distinguished: sensory, short-term, and long-term. **Sensory memory** stores all stimuli that register on the senses, holding literal copies for a brief moment ranging from a fraction of a second to three seconds. Sensations that do not draw attention tend to vanish, but those we "notice" are transferred to **short-term memory (STM),** another temporary storage system that can hold seven or so items of information for about twenty seconds. Although STM fades quickly, information can be held for a longer period of time through repetition and rehearsal. When people talk about attention span, they are referring to short-term memory. Finally, **long-term memory (LTM)** is a somewhat permanent storage system that can hold vast quantities of information for many years. Science writer Isaac Asimov once estimated that LTM takes in a quadrillion separate bits of information in the course of a lifetime. And mathematician John Griffith estimated that, from birth to death, the average person stores 500 times more information than the *Encyclopedia Britannica.* When people talk about memory, long-term memory is typically what they have in mind.

As depicted in the flowchart in Figure 6.1, this information-processing model is used to structure the present chapter. Note, however, that it is only a model and does *not* necessarily mean that there are three separate storage bins in the brain. This is only one view of how memory works. There is a radically different view. Most computers process instructions sequentially, one linear step at a time. In contrast, the human brain performs many operations simultaneously, "in parallel." Thus, some cognitive psychologists have rejected the information-processing model in favor of

memory The process by which information is retained for later use.

information-processing model A model of memory in which information must pass through discrete stages via the processes of attention, encoding, storage, and retrieval.

sensory memory A memory storage system that records information from the senses for up to three seconds.

short-term memory (STM) A memory storage system that holds about seven items for up to twenty seconds before the material is transferred to long-term memory or is forgotten.

long-term memory (LTM) A relatively permanent memory storage system that can hold vast amounts of information for many years.

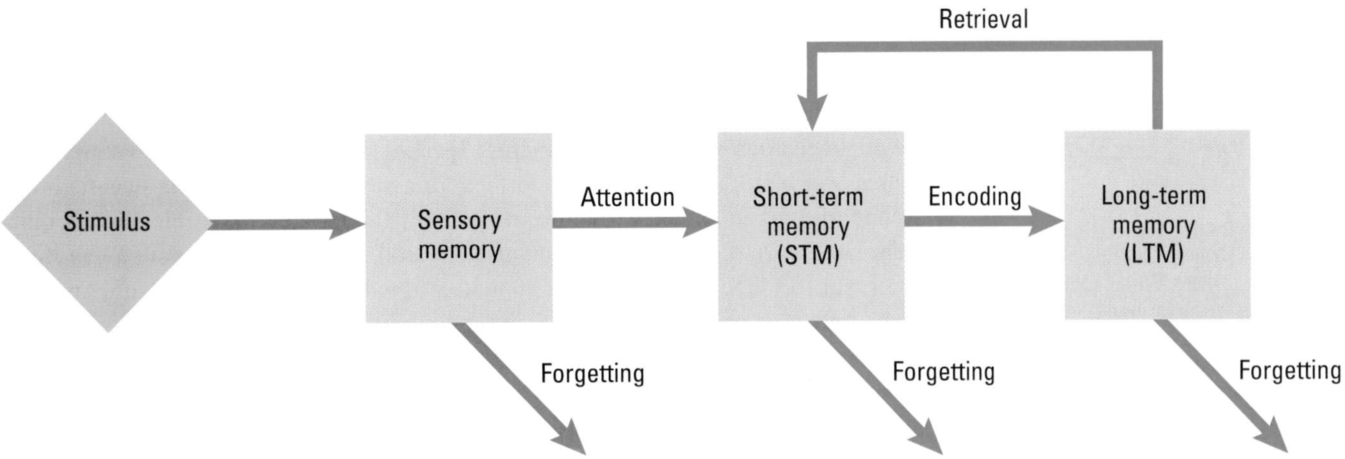

Figure 6.1 An information-processing model of memory Many stimuli register in sensory memory. Those that are noticed are briefly stored in short-term memory, and those that are encoded are transferred to a more permanent facility. As shown, forgetting may be caused by failures of attention, encoding, or retrieval.

parallel processing models in which knowledge is represented in a weblike network of connections among thousands of interacting "processing units"—all active at once (Rumelhart et al., 1986).

As you read through this chapter, you'll notice that memory researchers ask two types of questions (Koriat & Goldsmith, 1996). First, how are memories stored? Is there a single unitary system, as some believe, or are there multiple memory systems, each uniquely dedicated to storing certain types of information? Second, what is the degree of correspondence between our memories of the past and reality? We'll see that researchers have exposed some serious flaws and biases in human memory. Thus, you'll notice a recurring theme in cognitive psychology: Human beings are both competent and incompetent—and both objective and subjective—in their processing of information.

In this collage, entitled The Color of Memory, *artist Richard Schaffer portrays his view of using the computer* (left) *as a model for human memory* (right). *Interpreting this work of art, researcher Daniel Schacter (1996) states: "Schaffer's piece suggests—and I strongly concur—that the computer is a retriever of information but not a rememberer of experiences" (p. 37).*

The Sensory Register

Do fleeting traces of sensation linger in the mind even after a stimulus is removed? What is iconic memory, what is echoic memory, and how do they differ?

Take a flashlight into a dark room, turn it on, shine it on a wall, and wave it quickly in a circular motion. What do you see? If you twirl it fast enough, the light will appear to leave a glowing trail, and you'll see a continuous circle. The reason: Even though the light illuminates only one point in the circle at a time, your visual system stores a "snapshot" of each point as you watch the next point. The visual image is called an icon, and the snapshot it stores is called **iconic memory** (Neisser, 1967).

iconic memory A fleeting sensory memory for visual images that lasts only a fraction of a second.

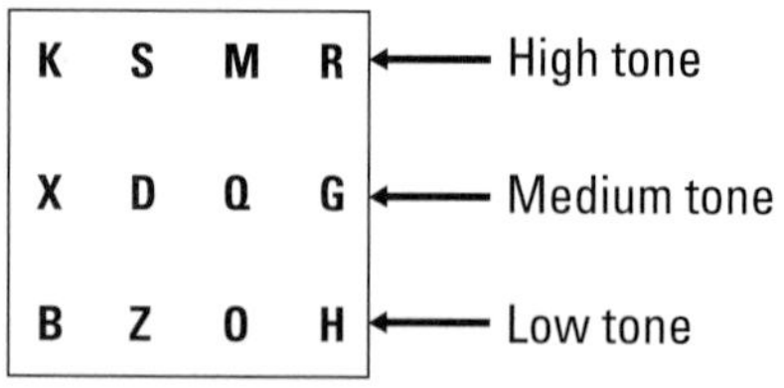

Figure 6.2 Testing for iconic memory Here is an array of letters like that used by Sperling (1960). When subjects viewed this array for one-twentieth of a second and tried to name all the letters, they could recall only four or five. But when signaled after the items to recall only one row, they were able to recall three or four per line—for an average of ten letters.

Iconic Memory

People typically don't realize that a fleeting mental trace lingers after a stimulus is removed from view. Nor did cognitive psychologists realize it until George Sperling's (1960) ingenious series of experiments. Sperling instructed subjects to stare at the center of a blank screen. Then he flashed an array of letters for one-twentieth of a second and asked subjects to name as many of the letters as possible. Take a quick glance at Figure 6.2, and try it for yourself. You'll probably recall about a handful of letters. In fact, Sperling found that no matter how large the array was, subjects could name only four or five items. Why? One possibility is that people can register just so much visual input in a single glance—that twelve letters is too much to see in so little time. A second possibility is that all letters registered but the image faded before subjects could report them all. Indeed, many subjects insisted they were able to "see" the whole array but then forgot some of the letters before they could name them.

Did the information that was lost leave a momentary trace, as subjects had claimed, or did it never register in the first place? To test these alternative hypotheses, Sperling devised the "partial-report technique." Instead of asking subjects to list all the letters, he asked them to name only one row in each array—a row that was not determined until *after* the array was shown. In this procedure, each presentation was immediately followed by a tone signaling which letters to name: A high-pitch tone indicated the top line; a medium pitch, the middle line; a low pitch, the bottom line. If the entire array was seen, subjects should have been able to report all the letters in a prompted row correctly—regardless of which row was prompted. Sperling was right: subjects correctly recalled 3.3 letters per row. In other words, 10 letters (9.9), not 4 or 5, were instantly registered in consciousness before fading, held briefly in iconic memory. To determine how long this type of memory lasts, Sperling next varied the time between the letters and the tone that signaled the row to be recalled. As depicted in Figure 6.3, the visual image started to fade as the interval was increased to one-third of a second and had almost completely vanished two-thirds of a second later. Iconic memory lasts for just a fraction of a second (Coltheart, 1980; G. Loftus et al., 1992).

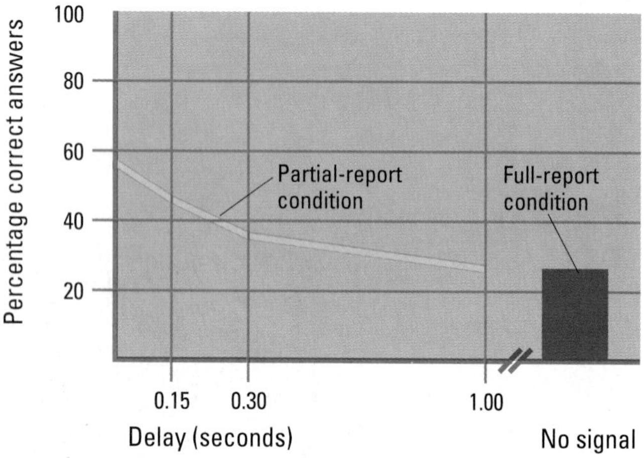

Figure 6.3 Duration of iconic memory How long does an iconic memory last? Sperling (1960) varied the time between the letters and the tone signaling the row to be recalled. The iconic image started to fade after one-third of a second and vanished completely after one full second.

Echoic Memory

A similar phenomenon exists for auditory stimuli. The next time you listen to the radio, notice after you turn it off how an "echo" of the sound seems to reverberate in your head. This auditory sensory register is called **echoic memory.** Just how much auditory input is stored in echoic memory, and for how long? In a study modeled after Sperling's, Christopher Darwin and others (1972) put headphones on subjects and all at once played three sets of spoken letters—in the right ear, in the left ear, and in both ears at once. Subjects then received a visual signal indicating which set to report. Based on this study and others, researchers have found that echoic memory holds only a few items but lasts for two or three seconds, and perhaps even longer, before activation in the auditory cortex fades (Cowan, 1988; Lu et al., 1992; Sams et al., 1993).

echoic memory A brief sensory memory for auditory input that lasts only two to three seconds.

Whether a sensory memory system stores information for one-third of a second or for three seconds, one wonders: What's the point of having a "memory" that is so quick to decay? To answer this question, try to imagine what your perceptions of the world would be like without sensory memories. Without the visual icon, for instance, you would lose track of what you see with every blink of the eye—as if you were viewing the world through a series of snapshots rather than on a continuous film. Similarly, it would be hard to understand spoken language without the persistent traces of echoic memory. Speech would be heard as a series of staccato sounds rather than as connected words and phrases. In fact, we have other sensory memories as well—for tactile (touch), olfactory (smell), and gustatory (taste) stimuli.

Short-Term Memory

What's the limit in the amount of information that can be stored in short-term memory? Is there also a time limit? What functions are served by short-term memory, and can this memory be expanded? What is the serial-position curve and why does it occur?

I recently traveled by Amtrak to New York City. As I climbed the stairs of Penn Station onto Eighth Avenue, I was bombarded by sensations: the vibration under my feet from a train rumbling into the station; the sound of horns honking, a siren blaring, and a bus screeching to a stop; a faint aroma of freshly brewed coffee being overwhelmed by the smell of exhaust fumes; and the sight of skyscrapers, traffic lights, street vendors, cars bouncing over bumps in the road, and white steam billowing through a hole in the ground.

I'm sure more stimuli reached my sensory registers than I can write about, but most never reached consciousness and were quickly "forgotten." The key is *attention.* As noted earlier, sensations that do not capture our attention quickly tend to evaporate, while those we notice are transferred to short-term memory—a somewhat more lasting but limited storage facility. As we saw in Chapter 4 on consciousness, people are selective in their perceptions and can instantly direct their attention to stimuli that are interesting, adaptive, or important. During my visit to New York, I was so busy searching for a taxicab going uptown that I zoomed in on moving yellow objects to the exclusion of everything else.

The information-processing model of memory regards attention as a necessary first step. In tennis and other tasks, people selectively tune in to stimuli that are adaptive, interesting, and important.

From the sensory register, information is encoded—that is, converted into a form that can be stored in short-term memory. A stimulus may be encoded in different ways. After you read this sentence, for example, you might recall a picture of the letters and their placement on the page (visual encoding), the sounds of the words themselves (acoustic encoding), or the meaning of the sentence as a whole (semantic encoding). Research shows that people typically encode this type of information in acoustic terms. Thus, when subjects are presented a string of letters and immediately asked to recall them, they make more "sound-alike" errors than "look-alike" errors. For example, subjects misrecall an *F* as an *S* or *X*, but not as an *E* or *B* (Conrad, 1964). Subjects are also more likely to confuse words that sound alike (*man, can*) than words that are similar in meaning (*big, huge*)—further indicating that we tend to encode verbal information in acoustic terms rather than in semantic terms (Baddeley, 1966).

Capacity

Attention limits what information comes under the spotlight of STM at any given time. To the extent that one stimulus captures our attention, others may be ignored—sometimes with startling effects on memory. For example, research on eyewitness testimony shows that when a criminal displays a weapon, witnesses are less able to identify that culprit than if no weapon is present (Steblay, 1992). Why? One reason is that the witness's eyes fixate on the weapon, thereby drawing attention away from the face. To demonstrate, Elizabeth Loftus and her colleagues (1987) showed subjects slides of a customer who walked up to a bank teller and pulled out either a gun or a checkbook. By recording eye movements, these researchers found that subjects spent more time looking at the gun than at the checkbook. The result: an impairment in their ability to identify the criminal in a lineup.

Limited by attentional resources, short-term memory can hold only a small number of items. How small a number? To appreciate the limited capacity of STM, try the *memory-span task* in Figure 6.4, or test a friend. By presenting increasingly long lists of items, researchers seek to identify the point at which subjects can no longer recall without error. In tasks like this one, the average person can store seven or so list items (usually between five and nine)—regardless of whether they are numbers, letters, words, or names. This limit is so consistent that George Miller (1956) described the human STM capacity by the phrase "the magical number seven, plus or minus two."

Once short-term memory is filled to capacity, the storage of new information requires that existing contents be discarded or "displaced." Thus, if you're trying to memorize historical dates, chemical elements, or a list of vocabulary words, you may find that the eighth or ninth item pushes out those earlier on the list. It's like the view you get on a computer screen. As you fill the screen with more and more new information, old material scrolls out of view. This limited capacity seems awfully disabling. But is it absolutely fixed, or can we overcome the magical number seven?

According to Miller, STM can accommodate only seven items, but there's a hitch: Although an item may consist of one letter or digit, these can be grouped into chunks of words, sentences, and large numbers—thus enabling us to use our storage capacity more efficiently. To see the effects of chunking on short-term memory, read the following letters, pausing at each space; then look up and name as many of the letters as you can in correct order: *CN NIB MMT VU SA.* Since this list contains twelve discrete letters, you probably found the task quite frustrating. Now try this next list, again pausing between spaces: *CNN IBM MTV USA.* Better, right? This list contains the same twelve letters. But because the letters are "repackaged" in familiar groups, you had to store only four chunks, not twelve—well within the "magical" capacity (Bower, 1970).

Chunking enables us to improve our short-term-memory span by using our capacity in a more efficient manner. You may be limited to seven or so chunks, but you can learn to increase the size of those chunks. To demonstrate, a group of researchers trained two male college students, both long-distance runners and of average intelligence, for several months. For an hour a day, three or four days a week, these students were asked to recall random strings of numbers. If they recalled a sequence correctly,

5	7	3									
9	0	7	6								
8	5	4	0	2							
0	9	1	3	5	6						
8	6	0	4	8	7	2					
1	7	5	4	2	4	1	9				
9	6	5	8	3	0	8	0	1			
5	7	3	5	1	2	0	2	8	5		
3	1	7	9	2	1	5	0	6	4	2	
2	1	0	1	6	7	4	1	9	8	3	5

Figure 6.4 Memory-span test Try this memory-span task. Read the top row of digits, one per second, then look away and repeat them back in order. Next, try the second row, the third row, and so on, until you make a mistake. The average person's memory span can hold seven items of information.

another digit was added to the next sequence and the task was repeated. If they made a mistake, the number of digits in the next sequence was reduced by one. As shown in Figure 6.5, the improvement was astonishing. Before practicing, their memory span was the usual seven digits. After six months, they were up to eighty items (Ericsson & Chase, 1982; Ericsson et al., 1980). In one session, for example, the experimenter read the following numbers in order:

8931944349250215784166850612094888856877273141861054629748012949749659228

After two minutes of concentration, the subject repeated all seventy-three digits, in groups of three and four. How did he do it? Given no special instruction, the subject developed his own elaborate strategy: He converted the random numbers into ages ("89.3 years, a very old person"), dates (1944 was "near the end of World War II"), and cross-country racing times for various distances (3492 was "3 minutes and 49.2 seconds, nearly a world's record for the mile").

The value of chunking is evidenced by the way people retain information in their areas of expertise. Study the arrangement of pieces on the chessboard shown in Figure 6.6, and in five seconds memorize as much of it as you can. Chances are, you'll be able to reproduce approximately seven items. Yet after looking at the same arrangement for five seconds, chess masters can reproduce all the pieces and their row-and-column positions almost without error. It's not that chess masters are born with computerlike minds. When chess pieces are placed randomly on the board, they are no more proficient than the rest of us. But when the arrangement is taken from an actual game between good players, they naturally chunk the configurations of individual pieces into familiar patterns such as the "Romanian Pawn Defense" and "Casablanca Bishop's Gambit" (De Groot, 1965; Chase & Simon, 1973). Remarkably, researchers estimate that chess masters store up to 50,000 such chunks in memory (Gobet & Simon, 1996). Indeed, from years of experience, experts in all domains—including computer programmers, sports fans, waiters, bartenders, and professional actors—chunk information to boost their short-term-memory capacity (Cohen, 1989).

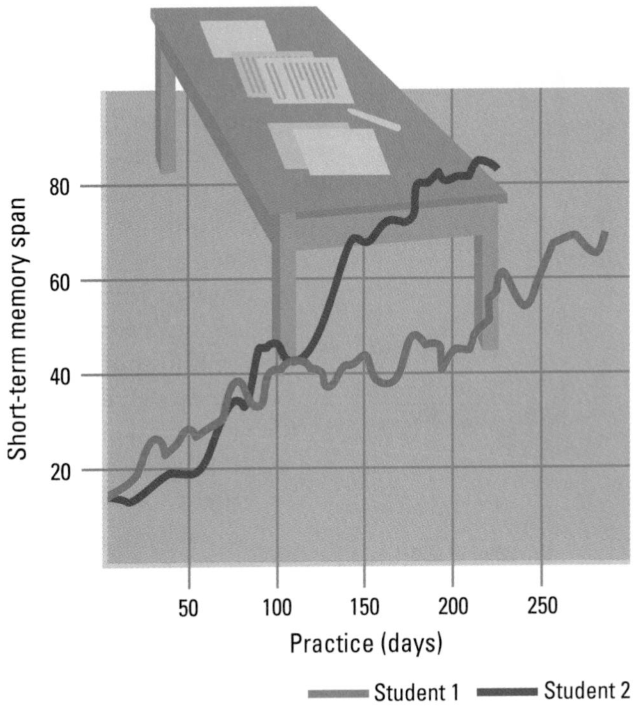

Figure 6.5 Increased memory span Two students practiced memory-span tasks for an hour a day, three to four days a week, for six months Remarkably, their short-term memory span increased from seven digits to eighty (Ericsson & Chase 1982). One subject soon had a memory span that exceeded one hundred digits (Staszewski 1988).

Duration

It has happened to me, and I'll bet it has happened to you too. You look up a telephone number, repeat it to yourself, put away the directory, and start dialing. Then you stop. You hit the first three numbers without a hitch, but then you go blank, get confused (was that a 5 or a 9?), and hang up in frustration. After just a few seconds, the phone number is gone, like it evaporated, and is no longer in memory. Then there is the matter of names. I'll be at a party or social gathering and meet someone for the first time. We'll talk for a while, then I'll turn to introduce my wife—only to realize with embarrassment that I have already forgotten the name of my new acquaintance.

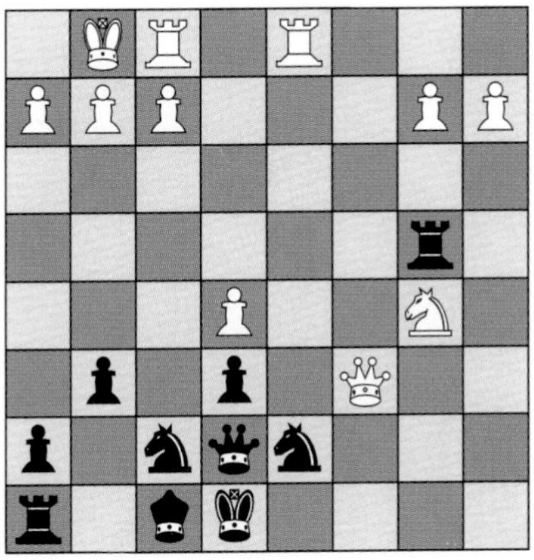

Figure 6.6 The value of chunking Study this arrangement of chess pieces for five seconds. Then turn to the empty board on page 217 and try to reproduce the arrangement as best you can. Unless you are a highly experienced chess player, the number of pieces you can place in the correct squares should approximate the magical number seven.

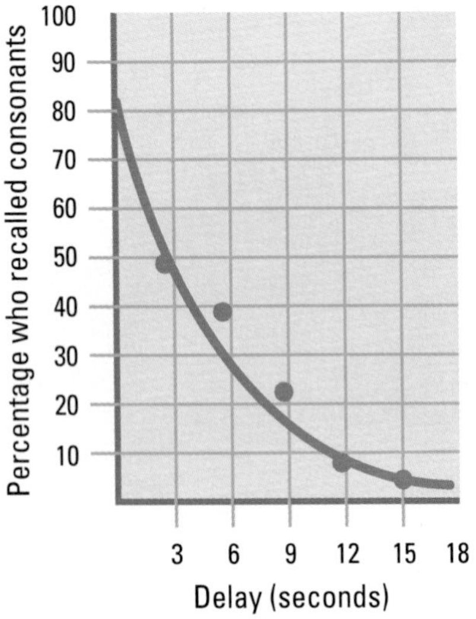

Figure 6.7 Duration of short-term memory What is the duration of short-term memory? When subjects are kept from rehearsing material they are trying to recall, their short-term memory vanishes within twenty seconds (Peterson & Peterson, 1959).

These types of experiences are common because short-term memory is limited not only in the *amount* of information it can store but also in the length of *time* it can hold that information. What is the duration of short-term memory? That is, how long does a memory trace last if a person does not actively rehearse or repeat it? To measure how rapidly information is forgotten, Lloyd and Margaret Peterson (1959) asked subjects to recall a set of unrelated consonants such as *MJK*. So that subjects could not rehearse the material, they were given a number and instructed to count backward from that number by 3s: *564, 561, 558, 555,* and so on. After varying lengths of time, subjects were cued to recall the consonants. After eighteen seconds, performance plummeted to below 10 percent (see Figure 6.7).

Knowing the fleeting nature of short-term memory, one can prevent forgetting by repeating information silently or aloud. That's why, if I do not have a pen and paper handy, I will repeat a phone number over and over again until I have dialed it. And that's why I try to silently repeat the person's name while being introduced. Repetition extends the twenty-second duration of STM in the same way that chunking expands its seven-item capacity.

The retention benefits of sheer repetition, or **maintenance rehearsal,** were first demonstrated by Hermann Ebbinghaus (1885; reprinted in 1913), a German philosopher who was a pioneer in memory research. Using himself as a subject, Ebbinghaus created a list of all possible nonsense syllables consisting of a vowel inserted between two consonants. Syllables that formed words were then eliminated—which left a list of unfamiliar items (*RUX, VOM, QEL, MIF*), each written

In a neighborhood park in Geneva, Switzerland, residents socialize over a giant outdoor chessboard. Do you think chess masters could recall the configurations on this giant board as they can from their perspective on a table? This question has never been put to test.

maintenance rehearsal The use of sheer repetition to keep information in short-term memory.

on a separate card. To study the effects of rehearsal, Ebbinghaus would turn over the cards, one at a time, and say each syllable aloud to the ticking rhythm of a metronome. Then, after reading the items once, he would start again and go through the cards in the same order. This procedure was repeated until he could anticipate each syllable before turning over the card. Ebbinghaus found that he could recall a list of seven syllables after a single reading (there's that magical number again) but that he needed more practice for longer lists. The more often he repeated the items, the more he could recall. Numerous other studies confirm the point: "Rehearsal" can be used to "maintain" an item in short-term memory for an indefinite period of time.

"Hi. I'm, I'm, I'm . . . You'll have to forgive me, I'm terrible with names."

Functions of Short-Term Memory

Short-term memory's limitations may seem to be a handicap, but in fact they are economic and adaptive. As with clearing outdated papers off a desk or purging old files from a computer disk, it is convenient to forget what is no longer useful. Otherwise, your mind would be cluttered with every sensation, every name, phone number, ZIP code, and morsel of trivia that ever entered the stream of your consciousness. If STM had unlimited capacity, you would constantly be distracted—possibly with devastating results. In Chapter 16, for example, we'll see that people who suffer from schizophrenia are often incoherent, jumping from one topic to the next as they speak, in part because they cannot filter out distractions.

In the computer we call the human mind, STM is like the screen. On a computer, material displayed on the monitor may be entered on a keyboard or retrieved from previously saved files. Similarly, STM contains both new sensory input and material that is pulled from long-term storage. All cognitive psychologists agree that people have fleeting memories that are limited in capacity and duration (Shiffrin, 1993). It is important to note, however, that many researchers are now critical of the traditional view that STM is a passive storage depot where information is held until it either fades or is transferred to a permanent warehouse (Crowder, 1993).

To conceptualize STM as an active mental workspace where information is processed, Alan Baddeley (1992) and others now prefer to use the term **working memory.** According to Baddeley, our working memory consists of a "central executive" processor and two specialized storage-and-rehearsal systems—one for auditory input, the other for visual and spatial images (see Figure 6.8). This working-memory system is critical for intelligent functioning. In order to interpret spoken or written language, for example, you have to remember the early part of a statement after it has receded into the past. And to solve an arithmetic problem, you have to keep track of the different steps you take—as in remembering to carry the *1* when adding *45* and *55* together. Research supports the notion that working memory contains separate systems for auditory and visual input (Shah & Miyake, 1996)—and that the system as a whole is highly adaptive. Thus, the more words or sentences that adults can hold for brief periods of time, the higher scores they are likely to get on the verbal SAT and other measures of language and reading comprehension (Engle et al., 1992; Just & Carpenter, 1992). Among children, too, the more rhymes, numbers, stories, map directions, pictures, and other items they can hold in working memory, the higher their scores are on measures of intelligence and achievement (Swanson, 1996).

working memory Term used to describe short-term memory as an active workspace where information is accessible for current use.

Research also suggests that it may be useful to distinguish between short-term and long-term memory. Whenever people try to memorize a list, they inevitably recall items from the beginning and end of the list better than those sandwiched in

Working memory

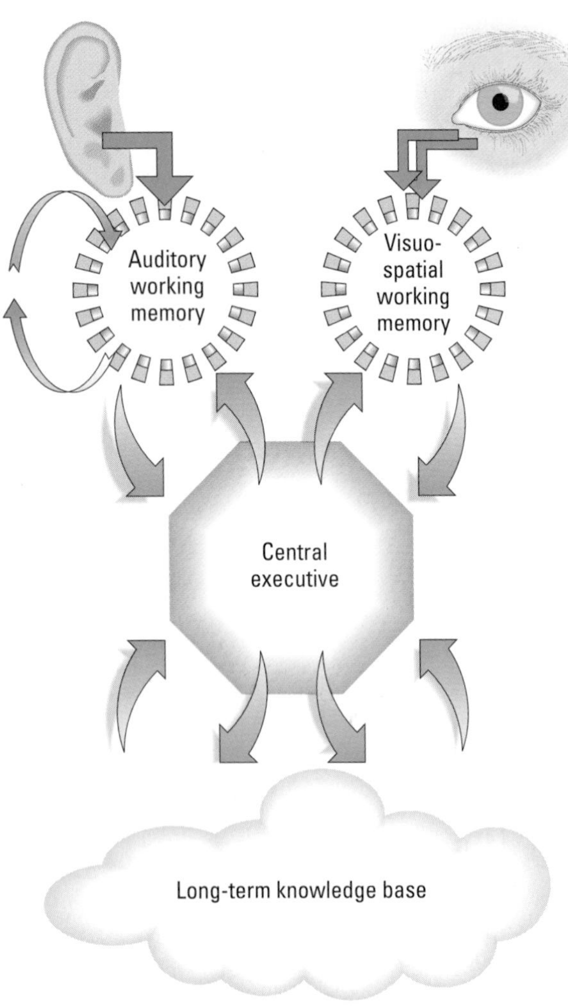

Figure 6.8 Working memory According to Baddeley, STM is a "working memory" that contains a "central executive" processor and two specialized systems—one for auditory input, the other for visual and spatial input. Note that material can enter the conscious workspace from your senses or from your long-term store of knowledge. Also note that information can be held in this area through rehearsal—by saying it to yourself over and over or by visualizing it in a mental image.

the middle. The enhanced recall of early items is called *primacy*, the advantage for the later items is called *recency*, and the combined pattern is known as the **serial-position curve.** This result was first discovered in the 1890s by Mary Whiton Calkins, the first woman to serve as president of the American Psychological Association (Madigan & O'Hara, 1992). Since that time, researchers have consistently observed the same effects.

The serial-position curve is pervasive and is observed not only in human memory subjects but also in monkeys, pigeons, rabbits, and rats. In one study, for example, rats were put into different paths of a radial maze, one path at a time, where they were rewarded with food pellets. Later, the rats were given a series of choices between paths previously visited and new ones they had never seen before. As measured by their choices, the rats were more likely to "recognize" paths they had previously visited early and late in the sequence than those sandwiched in the middle. The rats recognized the middle paths only when they encountered a highly distinctive stimulus there (Reed & Richards, 1996).

What explains the serial-position effect? It appears that different factors are responsible for primacy and recency. Primacy is easy to understand. Imagine receiving a list of words and trying hard to recall them for a test: *chair, artichoke, bicycle, frame, teacher,* and so on. Chances are, you'll later recall the first word because you repeated it to yourself over and over again. You must divide your attention in half for the second word as you try to hold two in memory, divide your attention into thirds for the third item, and so on, through the list. In other words, primacy occurs because the first few words receive more attention and rehearsal than later ones—and are more likely to be transferred into long-term memory.

Explaining the recency effect is trickier. On the basis of the information-processing model described earlier, researchers argued that the last items in a list are recalled better because they are still fresh in short-term storage when the test begins. Initially, several studies supported this explanation. For example, Murray Glanzer and Anita Cunitz (1966) presented two groups of subjects with fifteen words to memorize. One group was tested right after the presentation; the second was distracted for thirty seconds and then tested. Look at Figure 6.9, and you'll see that subjects who were immediately tested exhibited the usual effect: The first items were recalled by rehearsal, the last ones had not yet faded, and those in the middle slipped through the cracks. But notice that there was no recency effect in the delayed-testing group—only primacy. After thirty seconds and no opportunity for rehearsal, the last few items vanished from short-term memory.

serial-position curve A U-shape pattern indicating the tendency to recall more items from the beginning and end of a list than from the middle.

This explanation of the serial-position curve seems convincing, but there's a problem with it: Recency effects are often found in tasks that do not involve short-term memory. For example, take a blank piece of paper and write down as many

U.S. presidents as you can name in the correct order. What do you come up with? Robert Crowder (1993) asked college students to complete this task, and he found primacy, recency, and the usual decline in the middle (see Figure 6.10). Let's see: Washington, Adams, Jefferson,...Lincoln,...Carter, Reagan, Bush, Clinton. Notice that the one exception to the U-shape pattern is that Lincoln was recalled more frequently than would be expected from his middle position—a performance "spike" that is common when a distinctive item is embedded in an otherwise homogeneous list (Wallace, 1965; Schmidt, 1991).

At this point, it's clear that the serial-position curve is a common and pervasive phenomenon in memory. It's also clear, however, that other mechanisms are needed to explain it (Cowan et al., 1994; Thapar & Greene, 1993). For example, recent studies suggest the possibility that the first and last few items in a series are easier to recall because they are distinctive (Reisberg, 1997). Indeed, we'll see later in this chapter that people tend to retain information that is bizarre, emotional, or, in other ways, out of the ordinary.

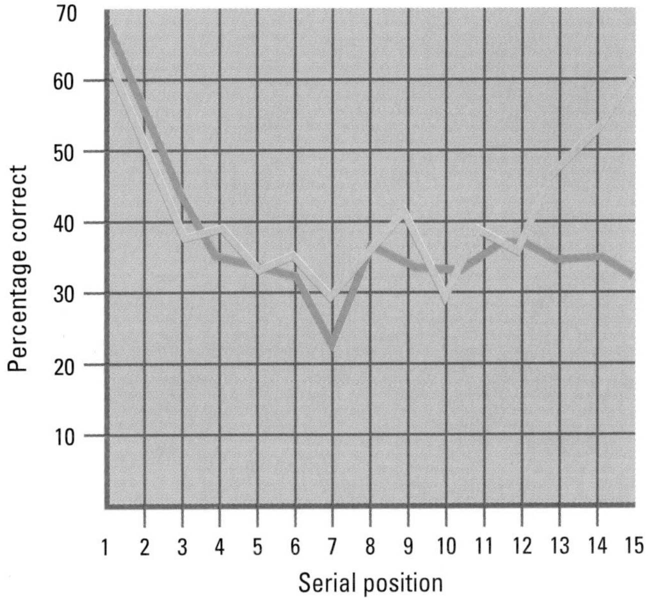

Figure 6.9 The serial-position effect Subjects trying to memorize a list of words were tested immediately or after thirty seconds of distraction. In the first group, subjects recalled the first and last few items the best, yielding the U-shape serial-position curve. In the delay group, however, there was no recency effect. After thirty seconds without rehearsal, subjects forgot the later items (Glanzer & Cunitz, 1966).

Long-Term Memory

What input is transferred from short-term memory into long-term memory? Where in the brain are these memories stored, how are they retrieved, and why are they often forgotten? Who is H.M., and why is this amnesia patient so important? Why is it said that memory is reconstructive, and what are the implications?

Do you remember your fourth birthday, the name of your first-grade teacher, or the smell of floor wax in the corridors of your elementary school? Can you describe a dream you had last night or recite the words of the national anthem? To answer these questions, you would have to retrieve information from the mental warehouse of long-term memory. Long-term memory is a relatively enduring storage system that has the capacity to retain vast amounts of information for long periods of time. This section examines long-term memories of the recent and remote past—how they are encoded, stored, retrieved, forgotten, and even reconstructed in the course of a lifetime.

Encoding

Information can be kept alive in STM by rote repetition, or maintenance rehearsal. But to transfer something into long-term memory, you would find it much more effective to use **elaborative rehearsal**—a strategy that involves thinking about the material in a more meaningful way and associating it with other knowledge that is already in long-term memory. The more deeply you process something, the more likely you are to recall it at a later time.

elaborative rehearsal A technique for transferring information into long-term memory by thinking about it in a deeper way.

To demonstrate, Fergus Craik and Endel Tulving (1975) showed subjects a list of words, one at a time, and for each asked them for (1) a simple visual judgment that

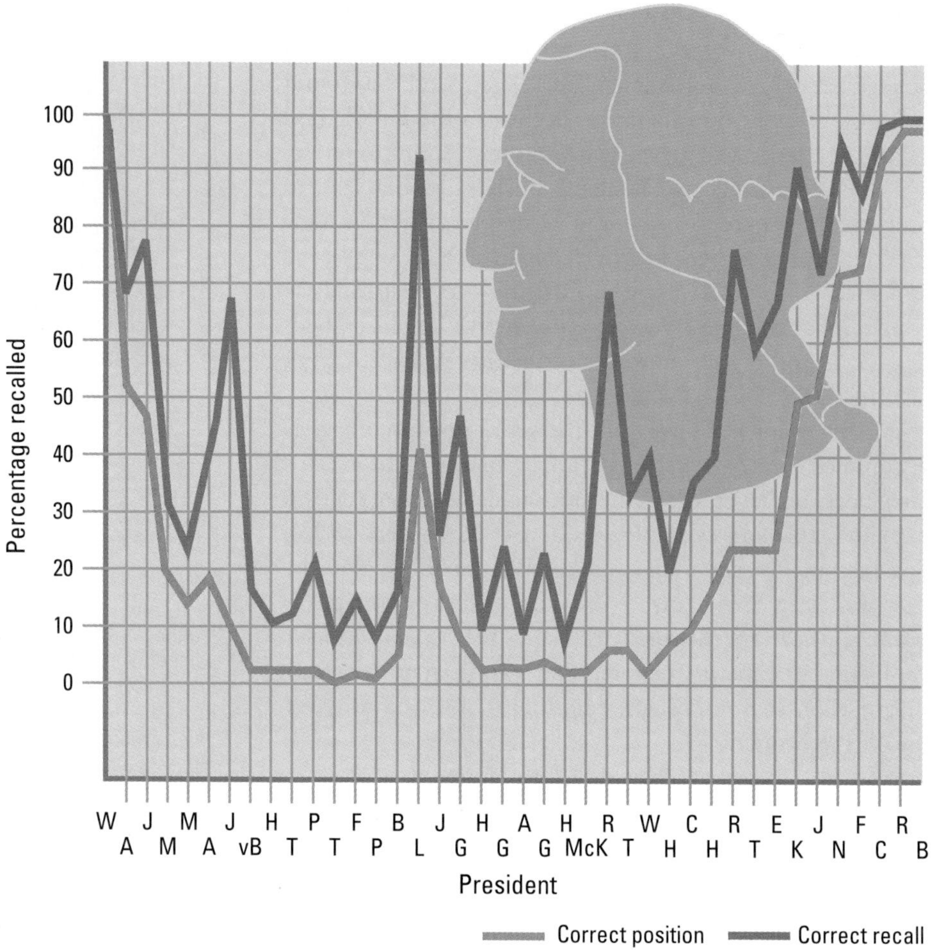

Figure 6.10 The long-term serial-position effect When subjects tried to list U.S. presidents in correct order, the typical serial-position curve was found—except that Lincoln was often recalled. Note that although subjects performed better when they could recall the presidents in any order (the two Roosevelts and Kennedy were frequently recalled in this situation), primacy and recency effects were still evident (Crowder, 1993).

required no thought about the words themselves ("Is ___ printed in capital letters?"); (2) an acoustic judgment that required subjects to at least pronounce the letters as words ("Does ___ rhyme with *small?*"); or (3) a more complex semantic judgment that compelled subjects to think about the meaning of the words ("Does the word fit the sentence 'I saw a ___ in the pond'?"). Subjects did not realize that their memory would be tested later. Yet words that were processed at a "deep" level, in terms of meaning, were more easily recognized than those processed at a "shallow" level (see Figure 6.11). Deep processing can also enhance our ability to recognize faces. Lance Bloom and Samuel Mudd (1991) displayed a series of faces and asked subjects to make judgments that were superficial ("Is the face male or female?") or more complex ("Is the face honest or dishonest?"). Those who had to process the pictures at a deep level spent more time looking, made more eye movements, and were more likely to recognize the faces later.

Does making complex semantic judgments, compared to simple perceptual judgments, activate different regions of the brain? Is it possible to see the physical traces of deep processing? Using functional MRI technology, John Gabrieli and others (1996) devised a study similar to Craik and Tulving's in which subjects were shown stimulus words on a computer and were instructed to determine whether the words were concrete or abstract (a semantic judgment) or simply whether they were printed in uppercase or lowercase letters (a perceptual judgment). As in past research, subjects later recalled more words for which they had made semantic rather than perceptual judgments. In addition, however, the brain-imaging measures showed that processing the words in semantic terms triggered more activity in a part of the frontal cortex of the language-dominant left hemisphere.

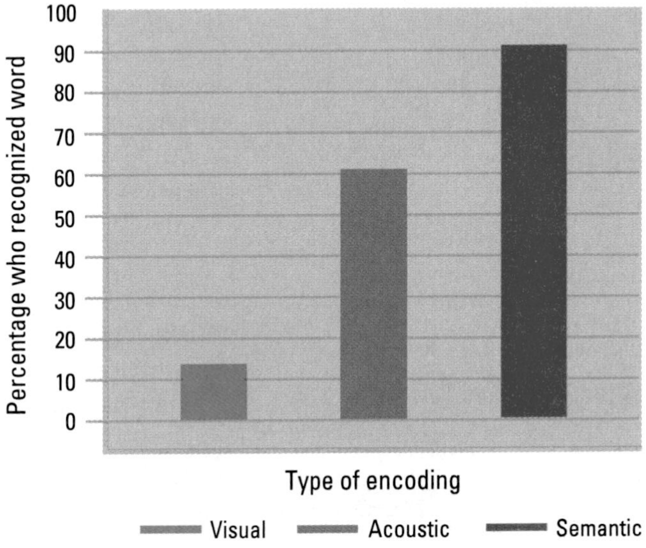

Figure 6.11 Elaborative rehearsal Subjects read a long list of words and for each one judged how it was printed (visual), how it sounded (acoustic), or what it meant (semantic). The more thought required to process the words, the easier they were to recognize later (Craik & Tulving, 1975).

Perhaps the most effective form of elaborative rehearsal is the linking of new information to the self. In one study, subjects sat in front of a microcomputer and looked at forty trait words (for example, *shy, friendly, ambitious*). In some cases, they were told to judge whether the words were self-descriptive; in others, they judged the words' length, sound, or meaning. When asked to list as many of the words as they could, the subjects remembered more when they had thought about the words in reference to themselves than for other purposes (Rogers et al., 1977). Apparently, the self can be used as a memory aid: By viewing new information as relevant to our own experience, we consider that information more fully and organize it around common themes. The result is an improvement in recall (Greenwald & Banaji, 1989).

Memorizing—definitions, mathematical formulas, poems, or historical dates—usually requires conscious effort. When I teach a large class, I pass out index cards on the first day and ask students to write down their names and a vivid personal detail that will help me remember who they are. Then I locate each student's photograph in the college "face book," match the face to the name, and run through the cards until I can identify each student. With tasks like this one, practice makes perfect. In 1885, Ebbinghaus read through a list of nonsense syllables 0, 8, 16, 24, 32, 42, 53, or 64 times and checked his memory for the items twenty-four hours later. As predicted, the more learning time he spent the first day, the better his memory was on the second day.

But there's more. Ebbinghaus and others found that retention is increased through "overlearning"—that is, continued rehearsal even after the material seems to have been mastered (Driskell et al., 1992; Semb et al., 1993). Researchers also discovered that long-term memory is better when the practice is spread over a long period of time than when it is crammed in all at once, a phenomenon known as the "spacing effect" (Dempster, 1988). Harry Bahrick and Lynda Hall (1991) thus found that adults retained more of their high-school math skills when they had later practiced the math in college—and when that practice was extended over semesters rather than condensed into a single year. When you think about it, this spacing effect makes adaptive sense. Names, faces, and events that recur over long intervals of time rather than in concentrated brief periods are probably, in real life, more important to remember (Anderson & Schooler, 1991).

Although the transfer of information to LTM often requires a great deal of thought and effort, certain types of information are encoded automatically and without conscious control. When I meet someone for the first time, I always have to work on recalling that person's name but I can easily and without rehearsal remember the face. It just happens. Similarly, we encode information about time, spatial locations, and event frequencies. In a study that provides evidence of this automatic processing, Lynn Hasher and Rose Zacks (1984) showed subjects a long list of words. Some subjects were warned in advance that they would be asked to recall how many times a certain word was presented. Yet others who were not similarly prepared were still just as accurate in their later estimates. Evidently, numerical frequencies are encoded without conscious effort.

Storage

Whether the encoding process is effortful or automatic, cognitive psychologists have long been interested in the *format,* the *content,* and the *neural bases* of long-term memory as it is represented in the brain.

Formats of Long-Term Memory In long-term memory, information is stored in two forms or "codes": one semantic, the other visual. Semantic coding is easy to demonstrate. When we process verbal information—such as a spoken phrase, a speech, a written sentence, or a story—what we store is the meaning of the information, not specific words. In a demonstration of this phenomenon, Jacqueline Sachs (1967) had subjects listen to a tape-recorded passage. She then presented a series of sentences (for example, "He sent a letter about it to Galileo, the great Italian scientist") and asked if they were the same as or different from those of the original passage. Subjects correctly rejected sentences that changed the meaning ("Galileo, the great Italian scientist, sent him a letter about it"), but they did not reject sentences with the same meaning that were worded differently ("A letter about it was sent by him to Galileo, the great Italian scientist"). The reason: They had stored the semantic content of the passage—not an exact, word-for-word representation. In fact, people often read "between the lines" and recall hearing not just what was said but what was *implied.* For example, subjects who heard that a paratrooper "leaped out the door" often recalled later that he "jumped out of the plane." And mock jurors who heard a witness testify that "I ran up to the alarm" later assumed the witness had said, "I rang the alarm" (Harris & Monaco, 1978).

Although verbal information is stored in a semantic form, visual inputs and many long-term memories (including some of our most cherished childhood recollections) are stored as visual images. In visual coding, a mental picture is generated of an object or scene—a process that has implications for how people retrieve the information. To demonstrate, Stephen Kosslyn (1980) showed subjects some drawings like the boat in Figure 6.12. Later, he asked the subjects to visualize each drawing, to focus on the right or left side of it, and then, as quickly as possible, to indicate whether or not a specific object was present by pressing a YES or NO button that stopped a clock. If the drawing is stored in a visual manner, reasoned Kosslyn, then it should take longer for subjects to "scan" their image for an answer when the object is located away from the subject's focus of attention. That is exactly what happened. When subjects were mentally focused on the left rather than the right side of the drawing, for example, it took them longer to determine that a flag was present on the right side of the boat.

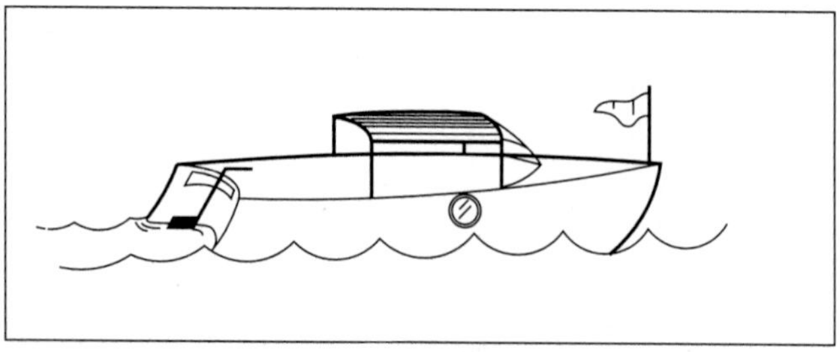

Figure 6.12 Visual coding When subjects visualized the left rather than right side of this drawing, it took them longer to recall the flag. This result suggests that subjects "scanned" a mental image for the answer (Kosslyn, 1980).

Mental images play an important role in long-term memory. Popular books on how to improve your memory advise people to use imagery, and research shows that this advice is well founded. As an illustration, try to memorize the following list of word pairs so that the first word triggers your memory of the second: *lawyer-chair, snowflake-mountain, shoes-milk, dog-bicycle, chef-pickle, student-sandwich, boy-flag*. You might try to master the list by silently repeating the items over and over. But now take a different approach: For each item, form an image in your "mind's eye" that contains the two words of each pair interacting in some way. For example, imagine a brown *dog* chasing a *bicycle* or a *student* eating a foot-long *sandwich*. This method should improve performance (Bower & Winzenz, 1970; Paivio, 1969).

Consistent with the notion that imagery facilitates memory, concrete words that are easy to visualize (*fire, tent, statue, zebra*) are recalled better than abstract words that are difficult to represent in a picture (*infinite, freedom, process, future*). To remember something, it's better to encode it in *both* semantic and visual forms than in either alone (Paivio, 1986). Also, certain types of images are better memory aids than others. For example, it is better to imagine the items-to-be-recalled as interactive, not as separate and static objects. And bizarre images are more memorable than common ones—provided they are distinctive relative to other stimuli to be recalled (McDaniel et al., 1995). Look again at the word pairs presented in the preceding paragraph and try to form images that are not only interactive but also bizarre. For example, you might imagine a scene of a *dog* riding a *bicycle,* or a *student* stabbing a *sandwich*. Using items like those presented in Table 6.1, the recall of word pairs improves more when subjects hear sentences that describe images that are bizarre rather than common (Einstein et al., 1989; Riefer & Rouder, 1992).

Contents of Long-Term Memory

Increasingly it is clear that there is more than one type of long-term memory. Following Endel Tulving (1985), researchers now commonly distinguish two types. One is **procedural memory,** which consists of our stored knowledge of learned habits and skills—such as how to drive, swim, type, ride a bike, and tie shoelaces. The second type is **declarative memory,** which consists of both *semantic* memories for facts about the world (such as who O.J. Simpson is, what a dollar is worth, what you need to access the World Wide Web, and what the word *gravity* means) and *episodic* memories that we have about ourselves (such as who our parents are, where we went to school, and what football team we root for). This distinction is important, as we'll see later, because people with amnesia are often unable to recall facts and events (declarative memory) yet still retain many of the skills they had previously learned (procedural memory).

With all that's stored in long-term memory—habits, skills, verbal information, and knowledge of words, names, dates, faces, pictures, personal experiences, and

Table 6.1 Imagery and Recall

COMMON	BIZARRE
1. The *chef* sliced the *pickle.*	1. The *chef* smoked the *pickle.*
2. The *lawyer* sat on the *chair.*	2. The *lawyer* argued with the *chair.*
3. The *snowflake* fell on the *mountain.*	3. The *snowflake* climbed the *mountain.*
4. The *shoes* were placed by the *milk.*	4. The *shoes* were filled with *milk.*
5. The *maid* spilled the *ammonia.*	5. The *maid* drank the *ammonia.*

procedural memory Stored long-term knowledge of learned habits and skills.

declarative memory Stored long-term knowledge of facts about ourselves and the world.

the like—it's amazing that anything can ever be retrieved from this vast warehouse. Surely our knowledge must be organized in memory, perhaps the way books are filed in a library. One popular view is that memories are stored in a complex web of associations, or **semantic networks.** According to proponents of this view, items in memory are linked together by semantic relationships (see Figure 6.13). When one item is brought to mind, the pathways leading to meaningfully related items are *primed*—thus increasing the likelihood that they too will be retrieved (Collins & Loftus, 1975; Anderson, 1983).

A good deal of research supports the notion that memories are stored in semantic networks. When subjects are given a list of sixty words that fall into four categories (animals, professions, names, fruits)—even if the words are presented in a mixed order—subjects later tend to recall them in clusters. In other words, retriev-

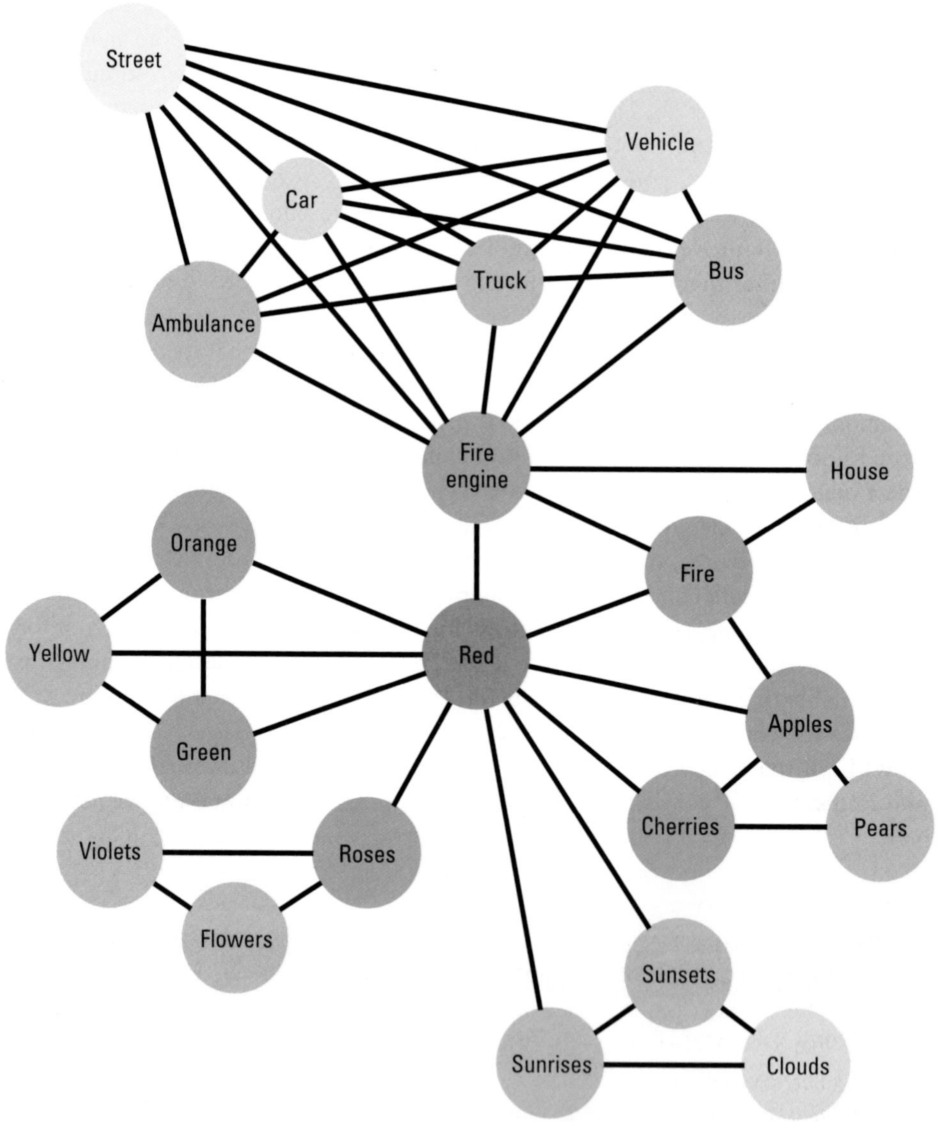

semantic network A complex web of semantic associations that link items in memory such that retrieving one item triggers the retrieval of others as well.

Figure 6.13 **Semantic networks** According to semantic-network theories, memories are linked in a complex web of associations. The shorter the link between items, the more likely it is that the retrieval of one item will trigger that of the other (Collins & Loftus, 1975).

There are two types of long-term memory. Procedural memory contains our knowledge of various skills—such as how to swim. Declarative memory contains our knowledge of facts—for example, what a pyramid is or where it can be found.

ing *tiger* is more likely to trigger one's memory for *baboon* than for *dentist, Jason,* or *banana* (Bousfield, 1953; Romney et al., 1993). Research on "lexical decision making" also illustrates the point. In these studies, people are given a string of letters (*nart, wire, bent, tise*) and must decide as quickly as possible if the letters form a word. Consistently, people make these decisions more quickly when the letter string comes after a semantically related word than after an unrelated word. Thus, subjects are quicker to decide on *fire* when the preceding word was *red* than when it was *clouds.* Subjects are even quicker in their decision making when given two target-related primes rather than only one (Balota & Paul, 1996). To sum up, researchers use lexical decision-making response times to map our underlying networks of associations—memory's filing system (McNamara, 1992).

Neural Bases of Long-Term Memory Is it possible to pinpoint a site in the brain that houses these associations? Do memories leave a physical trace that can be "seen"? Are there drugs that we can take to improve our memory? Neuroscientists have long been intrigued by such possibilities—but have also been led astray by some exciting developments.

In 1959, James McConnell and others reported that they had chemically transferred the memory of one flatworm to another. Specifically, they conditioned worms to contract to light, cut them in half, and found that the worms that regenerated from both the head and the tail ends were quicker to condition than new worms—suggesting that they had inherited a "memory." This result captured the imagination, and indeed, McConnell himself speculated in a *Newsweek* article that "It may be that in the schools of the future students will facilitate the ability to retain information with chemical injections" (can you picture taking a memory pill to feed you a knowledge of this entire textbook?). But researchers could not replicate the finding, and interest in memory transfer faded. In a sad postscript to the story, James McConnell, in 1985, was the victim of an attempted assassination when he received a letter bomb sent by the now infamous Unabomber. Fortunately, McConnell was not killed (Rilling, 1996).

In another promising development, neurosurgeon Wilder Penfield reported that he had triggered long-forgotten memories in humans through brain stimulation. In the 1940s, Penfield was treating epileptics by removing portions of their brains. To locate the damage, he stimulated different cortical areas with a painless electrical current. Sometimes, his patients—who were awake during the procedure—would "relive" long-lost events from the past. For example, one woman said she heard a mother calling her child when a certain spot was stimulated. From reports like this, Penfield concluded that experience leaves a permanent "imprint" that can be played back years later as though there was a tape recorder in the brain (Penfield & Perot, 1963). This observation sparked a great deal of excitement until cognitive psychologists scrutinized the data and made two sobering discoveries. First, the phenomenon itself was very rare, reported by only a handful of Penfield's 1,100 patients. Second, the "flashbacks" were probably dreamlike illusions, not actual memories (Loftus & Loftus, 1980; Neisser, 1967).

Despite these dead ends, today's researchers continue in hot pursuit of the *engram*—a term used to describe the physical trace of memory. There are two objectives in this endeavor: (1) to locate the anatomical structures in the brain where memories are stored, and (2) to understand the neural and biochemical changes that accompany these memories. Along these lines, let us examine some recent developments.

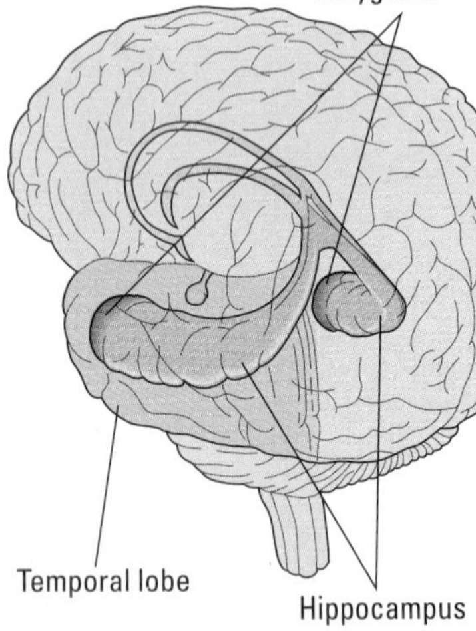

Figure 6.14 The hippocampal region As shown here, the hippocampus is located under the temporal lobe of the cerebral cortex. This structure is necessary for encoding and transferring new information into long-term memory.

Where Is the Engram? The search for memory traces in the brain was pioneered by Karl Lashley (1950). For thirty years, Lashley trained rats to run a maze, removed different structures from their brains, then returned the rats to the maze to test their memory. No matter what structures he removed, however, the rats recalled at least some of what they had learned. Eventually, Lashley was forced to conclude that memories do not reside in any specific location.

Then along came H.M., a twenty-seven-year-old man who underwent brain surgery in 1953 for severe epileptic seizures. Two holes were drilled into the patient's skull above the eyes, and through a silver straw the surgeon removed parts of both temporal lobes and sucked out the entire *hippocampus*—a curved pinkish-gray structure in the limbic system (see Figure 6.14). The operation proceeded uneventfully and succeeded in controlling the man's seizures. But something was terribly wrong. What made H.M. one of the most famous neurology cases of all time is that the surgery had an unexpected side effect: It produced **anterograde amnesia,** an inability to form new long-term memories. (This should not be confused with **retrograde amnesia,** which is an inability to retrieve long-term memories from the past.) H.M. still recalled the people, places, and events from before the surgery. He also performed as well as before on IQ tests and could still read, write, and solve problems so long as he stayed focused on the task. But he could not retain new information. He would meet someone new but then forget the person; or he would read an article without realizing that he had read it before; or he would not know what he ate for his last meal. At one point, H.M.'s family moved. Yet one year later, he still did not know the new address. It was as if new information "went in one ear, out the next" (Scoville & Milner, 1957; Milner et al., 1968). Now in his seventies, H.M. is the subject of *Memory's Ghost,* a book by Philip Hilts (1995). Hilts, who spent a great deal of time with H.M., tells of a remarkable experience. For H.M., he says, "Each moment is a surprise, a new puzzle to be worked out from a quick glance at the paltry evidence at hand as it comes rapidly upon him" (p. 139).

anterograde amnesia A memory disorder characterized by an inability to store new information in long-term memory.

retrograde amnesia A memory disorder characterized by an inability to retrieve long-term memories from the past.

H.M.'s case is important for two reasons. First, he exhibited a very specific information-processing deficit. H.M. could bring new information into short-term memory, and he could retrieve long-term memories previously stored. But he could not form new long-term memories. Second, H.M.'s case was the first to prove what Lashley could not—that localized lesions in the brain can have disruptive effects on memory. In fact, this case revealed that the hippocampus—and perhaps other areas of the limbic system as well (notably, the amygdala and thalamus)—play key roles.

Recent research with animals and humans has confirmed this point: The hippocampus is essential for the explicit recollection of newly acquired information (Cohen & Eichenbaum, 1993; Squire, 1992). Hippocampal lesions that mimic H.M.'s surgery thus produce a similar impairment in rats, monkeys, and other animals. Consider, for example, black-capped chickadees and other food-storing birds. In a remarkable feat of memory, they can locate up to 6,000 caches of food that they have buried weeks earlier in scattered locations—and they do not revisit old sites previously depleted. Anatomical studies have shown that food-storing birds are endowed with a larger hippocampus than is found in nonstoring birds—and that they lose their natural ability to recover food when this hippocampus is removed (Sherry, 1992; Hampton & Shettleworth, 1996).

Is all of memory stored in the hippocampus? No. When this structure is surgically removed from monkeys, they lose most of their recall for events of the preceding month, but their more distant memories remain intact (Squire & Zola-Morgan, 1991). And among humans, older adults with a shrunken hippocampus are impaired in their ability to recall new words and pictures, but they can still revisit past events (Golomb et al., 1993). Together, the various strands of evidence point to the conclusion that the hippocampus plays a role in the initial encoding of information and serves as a way station from which information is sent for long-term storage to neural circuits in the cerebral cortex (Squire, 1992; Fuster, 1995; McClelland et al., 1995).

Clearly, not all aspects of memory require the hippocampus. As we'll see later, amnesics like H.M. do exhibit memory, but in indirect ways. They can be conditioned to blink to a tone that has been paired with a puff of air to the eye, and they can remember how to work a maze they have practiced—but they cannot recall the training sessions. Similarly, they form preferences for new music they hear but do not recognize the melodies in a test situation. And they retain their procedural memories of how to read, write, and use other previously learned skills. For these types of memory tasks, different structures are involved. For example, David McCormick and Richard Thompson (1984) located a microscopic spot in the *cerebellum* that controls the classical conditioning of the eyeblink reflex. Certain areas of the brain may specialize in certain types of input, but for something as complex as memory, many areas are needed (Desimone, 1992).

This black-capped chickadee has a remarkable memory. During winter and early spring, this food-storing bird can locate many hundreds of caches of buried pine seeds.

Biochemistry: What Is the Engram? As some researchers try to locate where memories are stored, others seek to identify the accompanying biochemical changes that take place in the neural circuits. Most of these changes are likely to be found at the synapses, the tiny gaps between neurons that are linked together by the release of neurotransmitters (Lynch & Baudry, 1984).

One neurotransmitter that seems to play an important role in memory is *acetylcholine*. Research shows that people who suffer from Alzheimer's disease—a degenerative brain disorder characterized by a striking loss of memory for new information (see Chapter 11)—have lowered levels of acetylcholine in the brain, a link supported by animal studies as well. This finding suggests the possibility that Alzheimer's patients can be treated by boosting their levels of acetylcholine. Unfortunately, positive results have not been obtained—in part because Alzheimer's disease, and human memory in general, involves more than one neurotransmitter (Thal, 1992).

Certain hormones are also involved in memory. James McGaugh (1990) has found, in experiments with rats, that moderate postlearning increases in *epinephrine*—a hormone that is released in states of arousal—improve retention. Hormones do not enter the brain directly, so what explains their memory-enhancing power? One possibility is that epinephrine triggers the release of the sugar glucose into the bloodstream. Once in the brain, glucose may then work directly or through its effects on neurotransmitters (Gold, 1992). This discovery has exciting implications. One is that certain drugs may impair memory by blocking the activity of certain neurotransmitters. For example, alcohol disrupts the activity of serotonin, which could explain why eyewitnesses are less accurate in their crime reports when slightly drunk than when sober (Yuille & Tollestrup, 1990). Another implication is that glucose treatments can be used to facilitate the formation of long-term memories, especially for people with memory disorders. Paul Gold (1993) had twenty-two healthy senior citizens listen to a taped passage and then drink lemonade sweetened with either glucose or saccharine, the sugar substitute. When tested the next day, those who had taken the glucose recalled 53 percent more information from the passage. Memory pills may seem like futuristic science fiction, but it has been suggested that a glucose-based "cognitive enhancer" may not be far off (Wenk, 1989).

Retrieval

Once information is stored, how do you know it exists? Because people can openly report on their recollections, this seems like a silly question. In fact, however, it is one of the thorniest questions confronting cognitive psychologists. Hermann Ebbinghaus (1885; reprinted in 1913) was not only the first person to study memory systematically but also the first to realize that a memory may exist without awareness. In his words, "These experiences remain concealed from consciousness and yet produce an effect which is significant and which authenticates their previous experience" (p. 2).

Memory without awareness illustrates how human beings can be both competent and incompetent at the same time, and it poses a profound challenge to the researcher: If people have memories they cannot report, how can we ever know these memories exist? To his credit, Ebbinghaus devised a simple but clever technique. He tested memory by its effect on performance. Acting as his own subject, he would learn a set of nonsense syllables and then count the number of trials it later took him to *relearn* the same list. If it took fewer trials the second time around than the first, then he must have retained some of the material—even if he could not consciously recite it.

explicit memory The types of memory elicited through the conscious retrieval of recollections in response to direct questions.

implicit memory A nonconscious recollection of a prior experience that is revealed indirectly, by its effects on performance.

In recent years, other techniques have been devised. Basically, there are two types of tests, and each assesses a different type of memory: one explicit, the other implicit. **Explicit memory** is a term used to describe the recollections of facts and events that people *try* to retrieve in response to *direct* questions. In contrast, **implicit memory** is a term used to describe the retention of information without awareness, as measured by its *indirect* effects on a person's performance (Jacoby et al., 1993; Rajaram & Roediger, 1993). Why is this distinction important? The reason, as we'll see, is that people often exhibit dissociations between the two types of tasks. That is, people will consciously forget (have no explicit memory of) an experience but at the same time show the effects (have an implicit memory) of that experience. There are two ways to look at this pattern. Some theorists believe that explicit and implicit memory are separate systems controlled by different parts of the brain (Squire, 1992; Schacter, 1992; Tulving & Schacter, 1990). Others believe that the dissociations merely indicate that there are differences in the encoding and retrieval of information (Jacoby et al., 1992; Roediger, 1990). Either way, it's important to consider these two aspects of memory separately (see Table 6.2).

Can you name the Seven Dwarfs? The answer appears on page 230. [© The Walt Disney Company.]

Explicit Memory Can you name all of Walt Disney's Seven Dwarfs? Try it. When I was put to the test, I could list only six. As hard as I tried, I could not come up with the seventh. This type of task, in which a person is asked to reproduce information without the benefit of external cues, is an example of a **free-recall** test of explicit memory. Other examples include taking an essay exam, describing a criminal's face to the police, and struggling to recall a childhood experience. Now try a different task. Consider the following names, and circle only those of the Seven Dwarfs: Grouchy, Gabby, Sleepy, Smiley, Happy, Jumpy, Droopy, Dopey, Sneezy, Goofy, Grumpy, Bashful, Cheerful, Wishful, Doc, and Pop. This task, in which a person must select a remembered item from a list of alternatives, is a form of **recognition** test. So are taking a multiple-choice exam and picking a criminal from a lineup or photograph.

Research shows that recall and recognition are both forms of explicit memory in that people are consciously trying to retrieve the information (Haist et al., 1992). There is, however, a key difference: People tend to perform better at recognition. The Seven Dwarfs task illustrates the point. When college students were asked to recall the characters on their own, they correctly produced an average of 69 percent of the names. When they made selections from a list, however, the accuracy rate increased to 86 percent (Meyer & Hilterbrand, 1984). Even I was able to recognize the name that I could not recall (it was Bashful). Bahrick and others (1975) reported the same difference in a study of long-term memory. They showed people pictures of classmates taken from their high-school yearbooks. Seven years after they graduated, subjects were able to correctly *recall* only 60 percent of the names belonging to each face. But those who only had to *recognize* the right names from a list of possible alternatives were 90 percent accurate—even when tested fourteen years after graduation.

Table 6.2 Differences between Explicit and Implicit Memory

EXPLICIT MEMORY	IMPLICIT MEMORY
Conscious retention	Nonconscious retention
Direct tests	Indirect tests
Disrupted by amnesia	Intact with amnesia
Encoded in the hippocampus	Encoded elsewhere

free recall A type of explicit-memory task in which a person must reproduce information without the benefit of external cues (e.g., an essay exam).

recognition A form of explicit-memory retrieval in which items are represented to a person who must determine if they were previously encountered.

From left to right, Snow White's Seven Dwarfs are Sneezy, Doc, Grumpy, Bashful, Happy (front row), and Sleepy and Dopey (back row).

With the names of American soldiers killed in action etched in black marble, the Vietnam Veterans Memorial in Washington, D.C., serves as a powerful retrieval cue for the veterans who survived and the loved ones of those who did not.

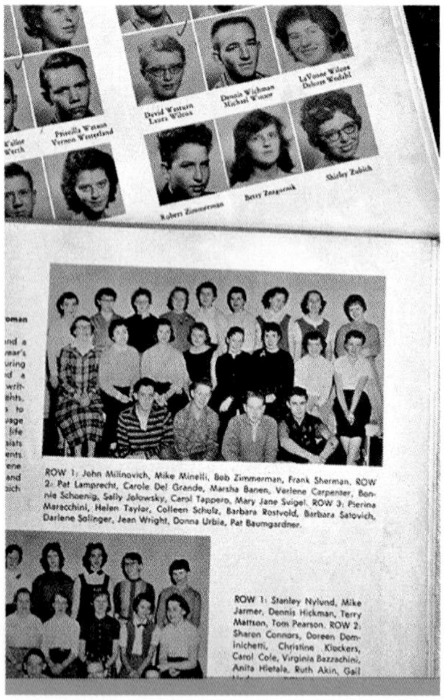

When shown old high-school yearbook photos, people find it easier to recognize the names of their classmates from a list than to recall the names on their own. In this album was a student named Robert Zimmerman—better known as Bob Dylan.

encoding specificity The principle that any stimulus encoded along with an experience can later jog one's memory of that experience.

The fact that recognition is easier than recall suggests that forgetting sometimes occurs not because memory has decayed but because the information is difficult to reclaim from storage. Retrieval failure is a common experience. Have you ever felt as though a word or a name was just out of reach—on the tip of your tongue? In a classic study of the tip-of-the-tongue phenomenon, Roger Brown and David McNeill (1966) prompted this experience by giving students definitions of uncommon words and asking them to produce the words themselves. For example, what is "the green-colored matter found in plants"? And what is "the art of speaking in such a way that the voice seems to come from another place"? Most often, subjects either knew the word immediately or were certain that they did not know it. But at times, subjects knew they knew the word but could not recall it—a frustrating state that Brown and McNeill likened to being on the brink of a sneeze.

The experience is an interesting one. When a word is on the tip of the tongue, subjects often come up with other words that are similar in sound or meaning. Groping for *chlorophyll,* subjects might say *chlorine* or *cholesterol.* For *ventriloquism,* they produce words such as *ventilate* and *vernacular.* In fact, a surprising number of people will guess the correct first letter, last letter, and number of syllables contained in the missing word. These cases indicate that the information is in memory but that subjects need additional retrieval cues to dislodge it (A. Brown, 1991).

Recognition is often easier than recall because recognition tasks contain *retrieval cues,* or reminders. A retrieval cue is a stimulus that helps us to access information in long-term memory. According to Tulving's (1983) principle of **encoding specificity,** any stimulus that is encoded along with an experience can later trigger one's memory of that experience. The retrieval cue may be a picture, a location, a word, a song, another person, or even a fragrance or the mood we're in.

Context-Dependent Memory Tulving's principle gave rise to the interesting notion that memory is "context-dependent"—that people would find it easier to retrieve information from memory when they're in the same situation in which the information was obtained in the first place. In an unusual test of this hypothesis, Duncan Godden and Alan Baddeley (1975) presented scuba divers with a list of words in one of two settings: fifteen feet underwater or on the beach. Then they tested the divers in the same setting or in the other setting. Illustrating context-dependent memory, the divers recalled 40 percent more words when the material was learned and retrieved in the same context (see Figure 6.15).

Other research has reinforced the point. In one experiment, subjects reported on sixteen events from their own past while sitting indoors in a dimly lit cubicle or outdoors in a scenic garden. As in the scuba-diver study, those who were returned, two days later, to the same setting recalled more of the events from the previous session than those who were taken to the other setting (Eich, 1995). In a second study, subjects learned a list of words while fast- or slow-tempo music played in the background. They were then tested with music playing faster, slower, or at the same tempo. Again, subjects retrieved more items when the music in the learning and test-taking situations was the same than when it was different (Balch & Lewis, 1996).

When you stop to think about it, even smells can be remarkably potent and nostalgic reminders of the past (Schab & Crowder, 1995). A whiff of perfume, the top of a baby's head, freshly cut grass, a locker room, the musty odor of a basement, the smell of mothballs in the attic, and the leathery scent of a new car—each may trigger what Diane Ackerman (1990) has called "aromatic memories." Frank Schab (1990) tested this hypothesis in a series of experiments. In one, subjects were given a list of

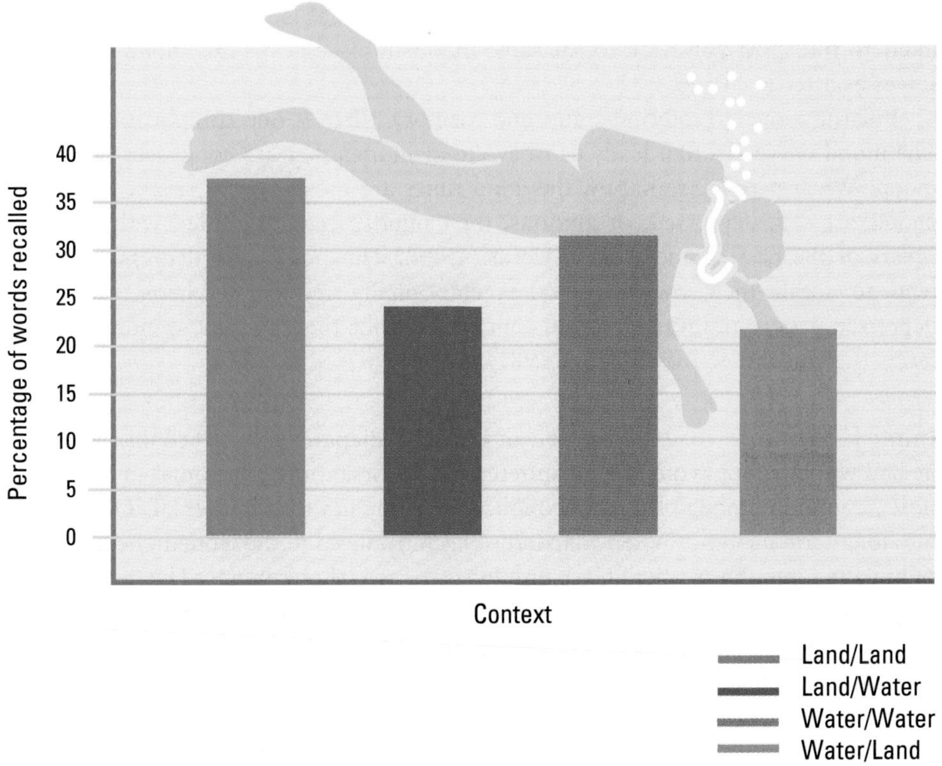

Figure 6.15 Context-dependent memory Whether on land or at sea, deep-sea divers recalled more words when learning and retrieval took place in the same setting. This result illustrates the context dependence of memory (Godden & Baddeley, 1975).

adjectives and instructed to write an antonym for each one. In half of the sessions, the sweet smell of chocolate was blown into the room. The next day, subjects were asked to list as many of the antonyms as they could—again, in the presence or absence of the chocolate aroma. As it turned out, the most words were recalled when the smell of chocolate was present at both the learning and the recall sessions. Demonstrating further the influence of context on memory, the aroma was encoded along with the words, so it later served as a retrieval cue.

Context seems to activate memory even in three-month-old infants. In a series of studies, Carolyn Rovee-Collier and her colleagues (1992) trained infants to shake an overhead mobile equipped with colorful blocks and bells by kicking a leg that was attached to the mobile by a ribbon. The infants were later more likely to recall what they learned (in other words, to kick) when tested in the same crib with the same visual cues than when there were differences. Apparently, it is possible to jog your memory by reinstating the initial context of an experience. This explains why I'll often march with determination to my secretary's office only to go blank, forget why I am there, return in defeat to my desk, look around, and ZAP! suddenly recall what it was I needed.

State-Dependent Memory Internal cues that become associated with an event may also spark the retrieval of explicit memories. Illustrating the phenomenon of "state-dependent" memory, studies reveal that it is often easier to recall something when our state of mind is the same at testing as it was during encoding. If you have an experience when you are intensely happy or sad, drunk or sober, calm or aroused, that experience is more likely to pop to mind or be free-recalled when your internal state later is the same than when it's different (Bower, 1981; Eich et al., 1994). In fact, Eric Eich (1995) has found that the reason it helps to be memory-tested in the same place where you learned the material is that the environment is likely to transport you back to the same mood state—and it's this mood state that serves as a retrieval cue.

When it comes to internal states and memory, there is one complicating factor: The mood we're in often leads us to evoke memories that are congruent with that mood. When people are happy, the good times are most easy to recall. But when people are sad, depressed, or anxious, their minds become flooded with negative events of the past (Blaney, 1986; Ucros, 1989). Thus, currently depressed people tend to recall their own parents as emotionally rejecting, whereas formerly depressed people and nondepressed controls describe their parents in more positive terms (Lewinsohn & Rosenbaum, 1987).

Implicit Memory

In 1911, physician Edouard Claparède described an encounter he had with a young woman who suffered from Korsakoff's syndrome—a brain disorder, common among chronic alcoholics, that impairs the transfer of information into long-term memory. When Claparède was introduced to the woman, he hid in his right palm a pin that pricked her painfully as the two shook hands. The next day, he returned to the hospital. Due to her memory disorder, the patient did not recognize the doctor and could not answer questions about their prior interaction. Yet when he reached out to shake her hand, she pulled back abruptly. Why did she refuse? After some confusion, all she could say was "Sometimes pins are hidden in people's hands" (Schwartz & Reisberg, 1991).

Implicit Memory in Amnesia Patients Did Claparède's patient remember him or not? On the one hand, she knew enough to be afraid. On the other hand, she did not know why. It was as if she had a memory but didn't know it. As unusual as this story may seem, we now know that there are many others like it. As in the case of H.M., cognitive psychologists are keenly interested in people with amnesia. It used to be believed that amnesics lack the ability to encode or store information in long-term memory. They could still perform "skills"—but could not keep new "information" in memory.

Or could they? In 1970, Elizabeth Warrington and Lawrence Weiskrantz published an article in *Nature* that challenged the prevailing view. These researchers gave a list of words to four amnesics and sixteen normal control subjects. Four memory tests were then administered. Two were standard measures of explicit memory—one a recall task, the second involving recognition. The other tests were indirect measures of implicit memory in which the subjects were asked merely to complete word fragments (such as *k---ht, c-l---e,* and *t---v-s---on*) and stems (for example, *kni---, col----,* and *tele------*) with the first "guess" that came to mind. The results are shown in Figure 6.16. As was expected, the control subjects scored higher than the amnesics on the explicit-memory tests. But on the incomplete-word tasks, the amnesics were just as likely to form words that appeared on the original list. Like Claparède's Korsakoff's patient, they retained the information enough to use it. They just didn't realize it.

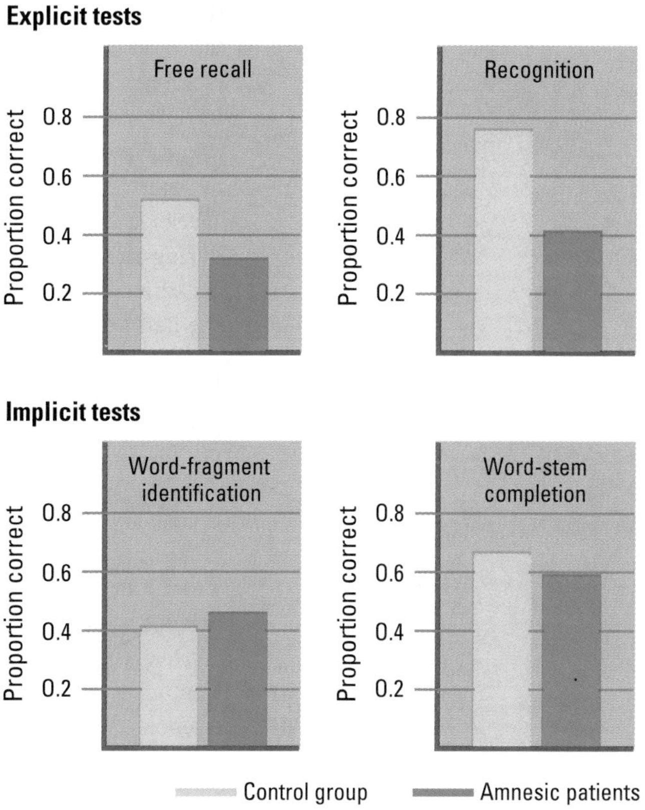

Figure 6.16 Retention without awareness Amnesic patients and normal controls were tested for their memory of words previously learned. As you can see, the amnesics performed poorly on the measures of explicit memory (recall and recognition) but not on indirect measures of implicit memory (word-fragment and word-stem completion tasks). The amnesics retained the information but didn't know it (Warrington & Weiskrantz, 1970).

Today, there are many case studies indicating that amnesics know more than they realize. Consider H.M., the most celebrated amnesia patient of them all. At one point, *Memory's Ghost* author Philip Hilts (1995) visited H.M. in the hospital to interview him in the testing room, a place where as a patient he had spent many long hours. H.M. said he did not know where that room was—but then he stood up and reflexively turned his body in the right direction.

This dissociation—the tendency for amnesics to show signs of long-term retention of information without awareness—has now been amply observed in studies involving different types of amnesia and different implicit-memory tests (Schacter, 1987; Shimamura, 1986; Squire & Butters, 1992). For example, patients with prosopagnosia (a brain disorder that impairs one's ability to recognize faces) could not match names to famous faces in a multiple-choice test, but they became physiologically more aroused when the faces were named correctly than incorrectly (Bauer & Verfaellie, 1992; Bruyer, 1991). In another case, researchers tried to classically condition an anterograde-amnesia patient by pairing a harmless tone with electric shock. Although he could not recall these sessions, he reacted with an increased level of arousal whenever the tone was presented (Bechara et al., 1995). Once again, there was an implicit memory—or, as Henry Roediger (1990) puts it, "retention without awareness."

Finally, there's an interesting new line of research on what surgery patients can recall about events that took place in the operating room (Sebel et al., 1993). If you've ever had major surgery, you're probably scratching your head at this point. Yet in one study, twenty-five surgery patients were read a list of word-pairs during their operations—after they were rendered "unconscious" by general anesthesia. Later on in the recovery room, and again after two weeks, these patients could not recall or recognize the items. But they frequently came up with the correct "guess" in response to the first word of each pair (Kihlstrom et al., 1990). This phenomenon can explain what happened to a woman who underwent a successful operation to remove a cyst but became deeply depressed afterward without knowing why. Weeks later, while in hypnosis, she recalled hearing the muffled voice of the surgeon during the operation utter the word *cancer,* and she was terrified. Although fully anesthetized, she had heard something that led her to become depressed even though she had no explicit memory of it (Coren, 1996).

Implicit Memory in Everyday Life You don't have to suffer from brain damage to exhibit a dissociation between memory and awareness. Have you ever had the eerie feeling that you've been in a situation before, even though you had not? This is called *déjà vu,* and it is defined as the illusion that a new situation is familiar (the term is French for "already seen"). In a way, déjà vu is the opposite of amnesia. Whereas amnesics have memory without awareness or familiarity, the person with déjà vu has a sense of familiarity but no real memory. Estimates vary, but between 30 and 96 percent of people report having had such an episode (Sno & Linszen, 1990).

Déjà vu is not the only type of dissociation that is commonly experienced. Retention without awareness occurs in all of us—sometimes with interesting consequences. We now consider four of these consequences: false fame, the illusion of truth, eyewitness transference, and cryptomnesia.

1. ***The false-fame effect.*** Is Sebastian Weisdorf famous? He is not. But Larry Jacoby and his colleagues (1989) found a way to make him and other no-names famous overnight. They had subjects read aloud a long list of made-up names, supposedly to test the speed and accuracy of their pronunciation. Some of the names appeared repeatedly, but others were read only once. The next day, subjects received a new list of names—some famous, some nonfamous, and some from the first list that were nonfamous. Their task was to decide for each one whether it was the name of a famous person. This seems easy enough, and, for the most part, it was. Subjects distinguished with little difficulty between names that were truly famous and those that were not, and they were sure that the names repeatedly presented the day before were not famous. But they misjudged as famous many of the names that were previously presented only once. Why? These names were familiar, but subjects did not know why. Not realizing that these names were from the first list, subjects made an assumption: If a name rings a bell, the person must be famous.
2. ***The illusion of truth.*** A second consequence of retention without awareness is the illusion of truth. Subjects in one study listened to a series of statements and were instructed to determine how interesting they found each one. Some of the statements were true ("Henry Ford forgot to put a reverse gear in his first car"); others were false ("The average person in Switzerland eats about twenty-five pounds of cheese each year"). Afterward, subjects rated the credibility of additional statements on a scale that ranged from "certainly true" to "certainly false." Subjects didn't realize it, but some of the statements in the second task were repeats from the earlier task, and others were new. The result: Sentences that were repeated—regardless of whether they were true or false—were more likely to be believed (Begg et al., 1992). Additional studies, in which subjects were retested after three months, have shown that these illusions are long-

lasting (Brown & Nix, 1996). As demonstrated by the use of sheer repetition for persuasion purposes in politics and advertising, say something often enough and people will believe it.

3. ***Eyewitness transference.*** False fame and the illusion of truth may seem amusing, but retention without awareness can also have serious consequences. A few years ago, I received a call from a San Francisco lawyer whose client was being tried for murder based on an eyewitness identification. In this case, a witness saw someone, late at night and from a distance, throw a road flare into a window of an apartment building. The building caught fire and a resident was killed. Due to the circumstances, the witness could give the police only a general description of the man (which did not match the defendant's appearance). One week later, the witness looked through a book of mug shots that included a picture of the defendant, but he could not make a selection. Weeks later, that same witness viewed a six-person lineup, recognized the defendant, and made an identification. Was the defendant familiar to the witness? Probably he was. But from the crime or the mug shots?

   The problem illustrated by this case is that people often remember a face but forget the circumstances in which they saw it. In one study, for example, subjects witnessed a staged crime and then looked through mug shots (Brown et al., 1977). A few days later, they were asked to view a lineup. The result was startling: Subjects were just as likely to identify an innocent person whose photograph was in the mug shots as they were to pick the actual criminal. This familiarity effect gives rise to the phenomenon of eyewitness transference, whereby a person seen in one situation is later confused in memory with a person seen in a second situation (Loftus, 1979). Incidentally, the defendant I described was found guilty and sentenced to life in prison—based primarily on the eyewitness's identification.

4. ***Unintentional plagiarism.*** False fame, the illusion of truth, and unconscious transference occur when we are aware that something is familiar but cannot pinpoint the correct source of that familiarity (Johnson et al., 1993; Mandler, 1980). In other words, the experience has an impact on behavior, but without our conscious awareness. There is another possible repercussion of implicit memory: cryptomnesia, or unintentional plagiarism. Several years ago, former Beatle George Harrison was sued for recording "My Sweet Lord"—a song that bore a striking resemblance to "He's So Fine," recorded in 1962 by the Chiffons. At trial, Harrison admitted that he'd heard the earlier song but denied that he copied it. The judge ruled against him, however, and concluded that he was influenced by what was in his unconscious memory.

   Have you ever had an insight you thought was original, only later to realize or be told that it was "borrowed" from another source? Are people who write, compose music, solve problems, or come up with creative ideas vulnerable to cryptomnesia? Alan Brown and Dana Murphy (1989) had subjects in groups take turns generating items that fit a particular category (sports, four-legged animals, musical instruments, and clothing). After four rounds, they asked subjects individually to recall the items that they personally had generated and to come up with new ones from the same categories. As it turned out, 75 percent of the subjects took credit for at least one item of someone else's, and 71 percent came up with a "new" item that was given earlier. Some subjects inadvertently plagiarized their own ideas, but most often they "stole" from others in the group. Additional research shows that the incidence of cryptomnesia increases with time, task difficulty, and the memorability of the ideas that are taken (Marsh & Bower, 1993; Marsh & Landau, 1995). As in other research on implicit memory, these studies show that there is a bit of amnesia in us all.

Forgetting

Before we celebrate the virtues of memory and outline the techniques that we can use to improve it, let's stop for a moment and ponder the wisdom of William James (1890), who said, "If we remembered everything, we should on most occasions be as ill off as if we remembered nothing" (p. 680). James was right. Many years ago, Russian psychologist Alexander Luria (1968) described his observations of Solomon Shereshevskii, a man he called S., who had a truly exceptional memory. After one brief presentation, S. would remember lists containing dozens of items, recite them forward or backward, and still retain the information fifteen years later. But there was a drawback: No matter how hard S. tried, he could not forget. Images of letters, numbers, and other items of trivia were so distracting that he had to quit his job and support himself by entertaining audiences with his feats of memory. Sometimes it is better to forget.

"Memory is the thing you forget with."

— ALEXANDER CHASE

The Forgetting Curve Memory failure is a common experience in everyday life (see Table 6.3). I wish I had a dollar for every time I left something I needed at home, neglected to bring up a point in conversation, or forgot the name of someone I met. To measure the rate at which information is forgotten, Ebbinghaus (1885; reprinted

Table 6.3 Forgetting in Everyday Life

How's your memory? Read the statements below and think about how often you've had each experience. The numbers in parentheses are the ratings given by the average person (Baddeley, 1990).

_______ 1. Forgetting where you have put something; losing things around the house (5)

_______ 2. Having to go back to check whether you have done something that you meant to do (4)

_______ 3. Failing to recognize, by sight, close relatives or friends that you meet frequently (1)

_______ 4. Telling friends a story or joke that you have told them once already (2)

_______ 5. Forgetting where things are normally kept, or looking for them in the wrong place (2)

_______ 6. Finding that a word is on the "tip of your tongue"; you know what it is but cannot quite find it (4)

_______ 7. Forgetting important details of what you did or what happened to you the day before (1)

_______ 8. Forgetting important details about yourself, such as your birthday or where you live (1)

_______ 9. Completely forgetting to take things with you, or leaving things behind and having to go back and fetch them (3)

_______ 10. Finding that the faces of famous people, seen on TV or in photographs, look unfamiliar (2)

Note: Subjects responded on the following scale: 1 = never in the last six months, 2 = once in six months, 4 = once a month, 5 = more than once a month,...9 = more than once a day.

in 1913) tested his own memory for nonsense syllables after intervals ranging from twenty minutes to thirty-one days. As shown in the **forgetting curve** plotted in Figure 6.17, Ebbinghaus found that there was a steep loss of retention within the first hour, that he forgot more than 60 percent of the items within nine hours, and that the rate of forgetting leveled off after that. How quickly we forget.

The Ebbinghaus forgetting curve shows a rapid loss of memory for meaningless nonsense syllables. Does it apply to real-life memories as well? Bahrick (1984) tested nearly 800 English-speaking adults who took Spanish in high school. Depending on the subject, the interval between learning and being tested ranged from zero to fifty years. Compared to students who had just taken the course, those who were tested two to three years later had forgotten much of what they learned. After that, however, scores on vocabulary, grammar, and reading-comprehension tests stabilized—even among people who had not used Spanish for forty or fifty years (see Figure 6.18 on page 238). A similar pattern was also found for the retention, for up to twelve years, of material learned in a college psychology course (Conway et al., 1991). These impressive results have led Bahrick to argue that such knowledge may enter a *permastore*—a term he coined to describe permanent, very-long-term memory for well-learned material. It's interesting that although this very-long-term curve is not identical to that reported by Ebbinghaus, there are similarities. Based on a summary analysis of 210 post-Ebbinghaus studies, David Rubin and Amy Wenzel (1996) concluded that his classic forgetting curve describes a consistent and lawful pattern of human retention and forgetting.

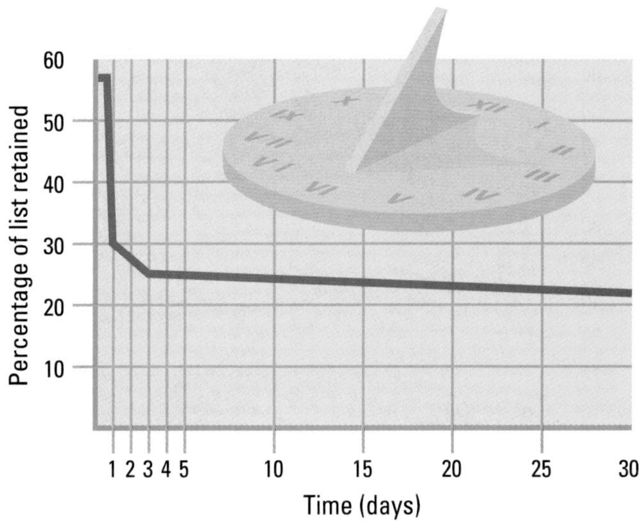

Figure 6.17 The Ebbinghaus forgetting curve Ebbinghaus's forgetting curve indicates the rate at which nonsense syllables were forgotten. You can see that there was a steep decline in performance within the first day and that the rate of forgetting leveled off over time.

Why Do People Forget?

Knowing the rate at which information is lost is just the first step. The next important question is: Why? Do memory traces fade with time? Are they displaced by new memories? Or do memories get buried, perhaps blocked by unconscious forces? As we'll see, forgetting can result from one of four processes: a lack of encoding, decay, interference, or repression. In the first two, the forgotten information is simply not in long-term-memory storage. In the second two, the memory may exist, but it is difficult, if not impossible, to retrieve.

Encoding Do you know what a penny looks like? Would you recognize one if you saw it? If you live in the United States, you have undoubtedly looked at, held, and counted thousands of copper pennies in your life. Yet many people cannot accurately draw one from memory, name its features, or distinguish between a real penny and a fake. Look at the coins in Figure 6.19. Do you know which is the real one? Raymond Nickerson and Marilyn Adams (1979) presented this task to college students and found that 58 percent did *not* identify the right coin. The reason for this result is not that the subjects forgot what a penny looks like—it's that the features were never encoded into long-term memory in the first place. And why should they be? So long as you can tell the difference between pennies and other objects, there is no need to attend to the fine details. Similarly, you may have difficulty recalling the features of a dollar bill, a telephone dial, the front-page layout of your favorite newspaper, and other common objects.

forgetting curve A consistent pattern in which the rate of memory loss for input is steepest right after it is received and levels off over time.

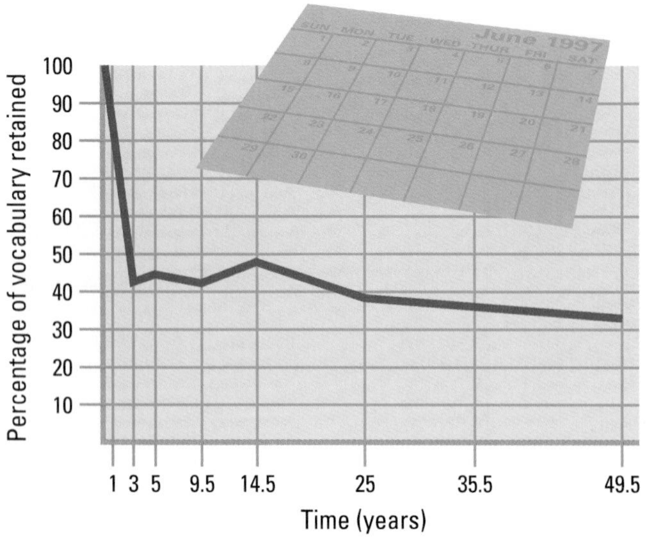

Figure 6.18 Long-term forgetting curve This forgetting curve indicates the rate at which adults forgot the Spanish they took in high school. Compared to new graduates, those tested two to three years later forgot much of what they learned. After that, however, test scores stabilized (Bahrick, 1984).

Decay The oldest theory of forgetting is that memory traces erode with the passage of time. But there are two problems with this simple explanation. One is that there is no physiological evidence of decay that corresponds to the fading of memory. The second is that time alone is not the most critical factor. As we saw earlier, memory for newly learned nonsense syllables fades in a matter of hours, but the foreign language learned in high school is retained for many years.

The key blow to the decay theory of forgetting was landed in 1924 by John Jenkins and Karl Dallenbach. Day after day, these researchers presented nonsense syllables to two subjects and then tested their memory after one, two, four, or eight hours. On some days, the subjects went to sleep between learning and testing; on other days, they stayed awake and kept busy. As shown in Figure 6.20, the subjects recalled more items after they had slept than when they were awake and involved in other activities. Jenkins and Dallenbach concluded that "forgetting is not so much a matter of the decay of old impressions and associations as it is a matter of interference, inhibition, or obliteration of the old by the new" (p. 612). To minimize forgetting, students may find it helpful to go to sleep shortly after studying, thus avoiding "new information" (Fowler et al., 1973).

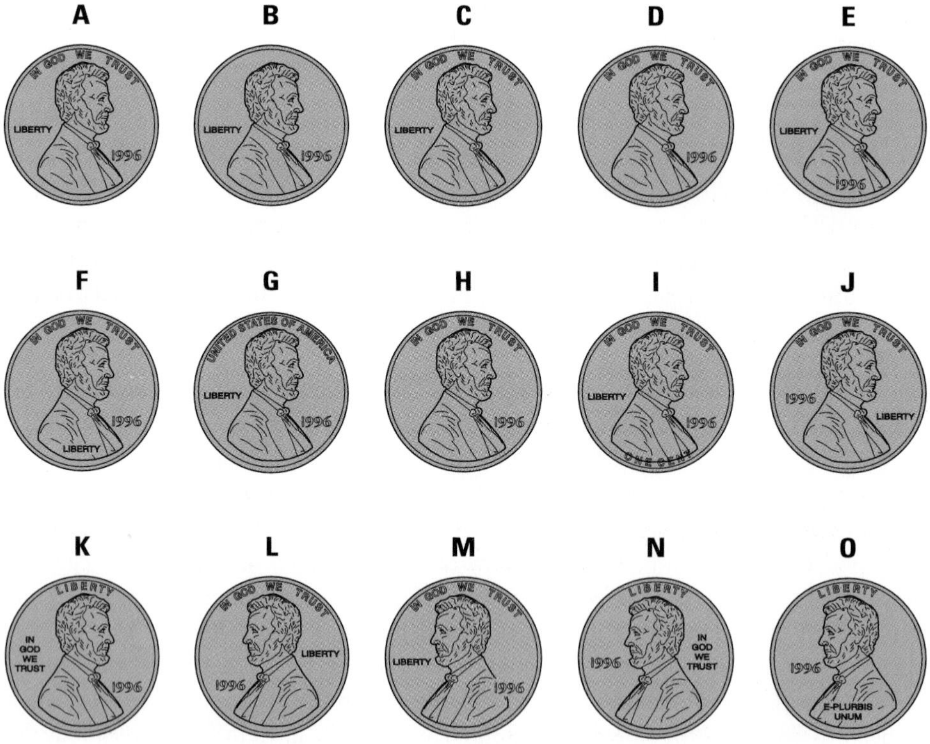

Figure 6.19 Can you recognize a penny? Which of these pennies is the real thing? The answer appears on page 240 (Nickerson & Adams, 1979).

Interference By showing that memory loss may be caused by mental activity that takes place when we are awake, Jenkins and Dallenbach's study suggested a third explanation of forgetting—that something learned may be forgotten due to interference from other information. As summarized in Figure 6.21, there are two kinds of interference. In **proactive interference,** prior information inhibits one's ability to recall something new. If you try to learn a set of names, formulas, phone numbers, or vocabulary words, you will find it more difficult if you had earlier studied a similar set of items. Many years ago, Benton Underwood (1957) found that the more nonsense-syllable experiments subjects had taken part in, the more forgetting they exhibited in a brand-new study. A related problem is **retroactive interference,** whereby new material disrupts memory for previously learned information. Thus, subjects in various experiments were at least temporarily less likely to recognize previously seen pictures of nature scenes, faces, and common objects if they were then exposed to similar photographs before being tested (Chandler, 1991; Wheeler, 1995; Windschitl, 1996). Clearly, one learning experience can displace—or at least inhibit—the retrieval of another.

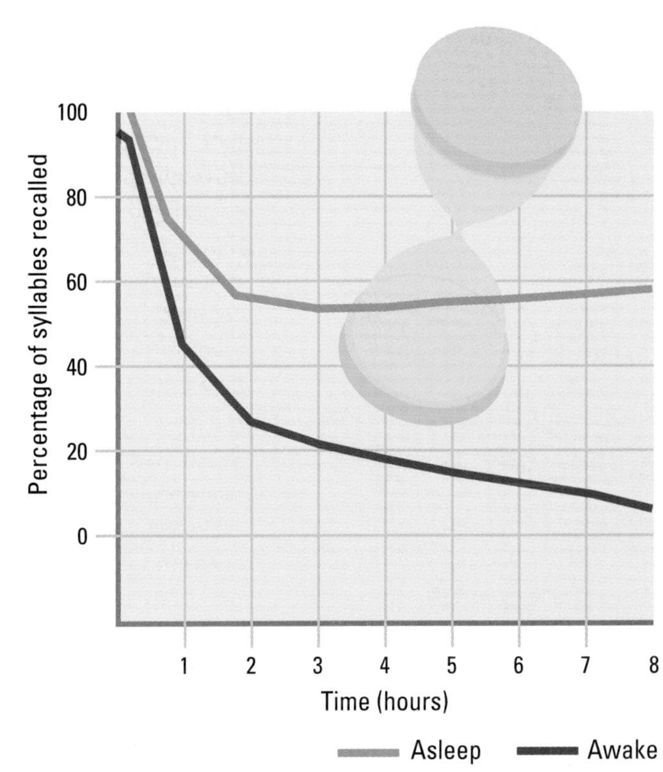

Figure 6.20 Using sleep to minimize forgetting Subjects who studied nonsense syllables recalled more items after one, two, four, or eight hours when they slept than when they stayed awake between the learning and test sessions. This result suggests that forgetting is caused by retroactive interference, not by the mere passage of time (Jenkins & Dallenbach, 1924).

Repression In 1990, a young woman jogging in New York City's Central Park was raped, beaten unconscious, and left for dead by a gang of teenagers. After many months of recovery, the victim said she remembered running that day but could not recall anything about the attack itself. Her amnesia for the event may well have been caused by head injuries she had sustained—or it may have been due to repression, a form of motivated forgetting.

Many years ago, Sigmund Freud, the founder of psychoanalysis, observed that his patients often could not recall unpleasant past events in their own lives. In fact,

	Time 1	Time 2	Retrieval
Proactive interference	**A disrupts B**		
Experimental	Study A	Study B	Test B
Control		Study B	Test B
Retroactive interference	**B disrupts A**		
Experimental	Study A	Study B	Test A
Control	Study A		Test A

Figure 6.21 Interference and forgetting As shown, proactive interference occurs when information acquired at Time 1 inhibits memory for material learned later. Retroactive interference occurs when information learned at Time 2 inhibits memory for material learned earlier. The more similar the two sets of items are, the greater is the interference.

proactive interference The tendency for previously learned material to disrupt the recall of new information.

retroactive interference The tendency for new information to disrupt the memory of previously learned material.

The correctly drawn penny is shown in (A).

they would sometimes stop, pull back, and lose their train of thought just as they seemed on the brink of an insight. Freud called this repression, and he said it was an unconscious defense mechanism that keeps painful personal memories under lock and key—and out of awareness. We'll see in Chapter 16 that people who suffer through childhood traumas such as war, abuse, and rape sometimes develop "dissociative disorders" characterized by large gaps in their explicit memory. Although repression is not easily demonstrated in the laboratory, clinical case studies suggest that repressed memories can be recovered in psychotherapy. As we'll see later in this chapter, it can be difficult in cases such as these to distinguish between dormant memories of actual past events and falsely constructed memories of experiences that never occurred (Loftus, 1993a).

Ways to Prevent Forgetting

Before taking office, President Clinton invited 500 business leaders to an economic summit in Little Rock. When it was over, many of the guests marveled at Clinton's ability to address them all by name. I have always been impressed by stories like this one—by stories of stage actors who memorize hundreds of lines in a week of rehearsal, of people who fluently speak five languages, and of waiters who take large dinner orders without a note pad. How can these accomplishments be explained?

Over the years, psychologists have stumbled upon a few rare individuals who seemed equipped with extraordinary "hardware" for memory. But often the actors, waiters, multilinguists, and others we encounter use memory tricks called **mnemonics**—in other words, they vary their memory's "software." Can you boost your recall capacity through the use of mnemonics? Can you improve your study skills as a result? At this point, let's step back, consider the educational implications, and draw concrete advice from this chapter.

[Drawing by Levin; © 1996 The New Yorker Magazine, Inc.]

"As I get older, I find I rely more and more on these sticky notes to remind me."

Practice Time To learn names, dates, vocabulary words, formulas, or the concepts in a textbook, you'll find that practice makes perfect. In general, the more time spent studying, the better. Skimming or speedreading will not promote long-term retention. In fact, it pays to *over*learn—that is, to review the material even after you think you have it mastered. It also helps to distribute your studying over time rather than cram all at once. You will retain more information from four two-hour sessions than from one eight-hour marathon.

Depth of Processing The sheer amount of practice time is important, but only if it's "quality time." Mindless drills may help maintain information in short-term memory, but, as noted in our discussion of elaborative rehearsal, long-term retention requires that you think actively and deeply about material—about what it means and how it is linked to what you already know. There are many ways to increase your depth of processing. Ask yourself critical questions about the material. Think about it in ways that relate to your own experiences. Talk about the material to a friend, thus forcing yourself to organize it in terms that can be understood.

Hierarchical Organization When you have information to be learned, organize it hierarchically—as in an outline. Start with a few broad categories, then divide them into subcategories and subsubcategories. This is how many experts chunk new information, and it works. When Andrea Halpern (1986) presented subjects with fifty-four popular song titles, she found that recall was greater when the titles were organized hierarchically than when they were scrambled. The implication for studying is clear: Organize the material in your notes, preferably in the form of an outline—and be sure to review these notes later (Kiewra et al., 1991).

mnemonics Memory aids designed to facilitate the recall of new information.

Table 6.4 Advertising Slogans

MATCH	SLOGAN TO	ADVERTISED PRODUCT
________ 1.	Like a good neighbor	(a) General Electric
________ 2.	Be all that you can be	(b) State Farm
________ 3.	You deserve a break today	(c) Busch Beer
________ 4.	Head for the mountains	(d) Allstate
________ 5.	We bring good things to life	(e) McDonald's
________ 6.	You've got the right one, baby	(f) Diet Pepsi
________ 7.	You're in good hands	(g) U.S. Army

Answers: 1(b), 2(g), 3(e), 4(c), 5(a), 6(f), 7(d)

Verbal Mnemonics Sometimes the easiest way to remember a list of items is to use verbal mnemonics, or "memory tricks." Chances are that you have already used popular methods such as *rhymes* ("*I* before *E* except after *C*" is my favorite; "Thirty days hath September, April, June, and November" is another) and *acronyms* that reduce the amount of information to be stored (for example, *ROY G BIV* can be used to recall the colors of the light spectrum: *R*ed, *O*range, *Y*ellow, *G*reen, *B*lue, *I*ndigo, and *V*iolet). Relying on verbal mnemonics, advertisers create slogans, such as those shown in Table 6.4, to make their products memorable. How many of the slogans can you correctly match to the advertised products?

Method of Loci Virtually all books on how to improve memory recommend that verbal information be represented as visual images, and research shows that this advice is well founded. One popular use of imagery is the method of loci, in which items to be recalled are mentally placed in familiar locations. This method is easy to use. First you memorize a series of objects along a familiar route. For example, you might imagine your morning walk from the bedroom, to the bathroom, to the kitchen, and out the door. As you follow this path, visualize some of the objects you pass: your bed, then the bathroom door, shower, stairs, kitchen counter, and so on. These places become pigeonholes for items to be recalled. To memorize a shopping list, for example, you could picture a dozen eggs splattered on the bed, a bag of red apples hanging on the bathroom door, and butter in the soap dish of the shower. When you take a mental stroll through the house, the items on this list should pop to mind. The trick is to link new items to others already in memory.

Peg-Word Method Another powerful imagery mnemonic is the peg-word method, in which a list of words serves as memory "pegs" for the material to be recalled. The first step is to learn a list of peg words that correspond to numbers. An example you may have heard of is this: "one is a bun, two is a shoe, three is a tree," and so on. Next you hang each item to be recalled on each of the pegs by forming a mental image of the two interacting. As illustrated in Table 6.5, the images of an egg being laid on a hamburger bun, a shoe stuffed with apples, and trees made from sticks of butter are easier to recall than words on a page. The more bizarre and interactive the image, the better. Try it and you'll see how easily it works. Most people are able to memorize ten new items in order with the peg-word mnemonic.

Interference Because one learning experience can disrupt memory for another, it is wise to guard against the effects of interference. This problem is particularly

Table 6.5 The Peg-Word Mnemonic

STEP 1 MEMORIZE THESE PEG WORDS IN ORDER.	STEP 2 HANG NEW ITEMS ON THE PEG WORDS.	STEP 3 FORM A BIZARRE, INTERACTIVE IMAGE.
One is a bun	Bun—egg	
Two is a shoe	Shoe—apple	
Three is a tree	Tree—butter	
Four is a door	Door—cola	
Five is a hive	Hive—pasta	
Six is sticks	Sticks—tuna	
Seven is heaven	Heaven—steak	
Eight is a gate	Gate—sugar	
Nine is wine	Wine—chips	
Ten is a hen	Hen—lettuce	

common among students, as material learned in one course can make it harder to retain that learned in another. To minimize the problem, follow two simple suggestions. First, study right before sleeping and review all the material right before the exam. Second, allocate an uninterrupted chunk of time to one course, then do the same for the others. If you study psychology for a while, then move to biology, then go on to math and back to psychology, each course will disrupt your memory of the others—especially if the material is similar.

Context Reinstatement Information is easier to recall when people are in the physical setting in which it was acquired—and in the same frame of mind. The setting and the mood it evokes can serve as cues that trigger the retrieval of the to-be-remembered information. That's why actors like to rehearse on the stage where they will later perform. So the next time you have an important exam to take, it may help to study in the room where the test will be administered.

Reconstruction

Up to now, human memory has been likened to a computer that faithfully encodes, stores, and retrieves information from the recent and distant past. Clearly, however, there is more to the story. As we'll see, remembering is an active process in which we reconstruct memories according to our beliefs, wishes, needs, and information received from outside sources.

In 1932, Frederick Bartlett asked subjects to recall stories taken from the folklore of other cultures and found that although they correctly recalled the gist of these stories, they changed, exaggerated, added, and omitted certain details—resulting in passages that were more coherent to them. Without realizing it, subjects had reconstructed the material to fit their own **schemas,** a term that Bartlett used to describe the preconceptions that people have about persons and situations. Schemas distort memory, often by leading us to fill in missing pieces. After people look at close-ups of various scenes, for example, they mentally extend the borders by reporting details that are not in the picture but might plausibly exist outside the camera's field of view (Intraub et al., 1992).

schemas Preconceptions about persons, objects, or events that bias the way new information is interpreted and recalled.

There are many other examples as well. In one study, subjects were left waiting alone in a small cluttered room that the experimenter called an "office." (Before reading the next sentence, try the demonstration in Figure 6.22.) After thirty-five seconds, subjects were taken out and asked to recall what was in the room. What happened? Nearly everyone remembered the desk, chair, and shelves—objects typically found in an office. But many of the subjects also mistakenly recalled seeing books—an item that fit the setting but was not actually present (Brewer & Treyens, 1981). Our schemas are sometimes so strong that an object that does not belong becomes particularly memorable. After spending time in an office, subjects were quick to remember the presence of a toy truck, blocks, and finger paints. But if that time was spent in a preschool classroom, they were more likely to recall the presence of textbooks, a typewriter, and an ashtray (Pezdek et al., 1989).

Figure 6.22 "Office" schema Look at this picture of an office for thirty seconds. Then list all the objects you recall as being in the room.

The Misinformation Effect Memory is an active construction of the past—a construction that alters reality in ways that are consistent not only with prior expectations but also with postevent information. Consider the plight of those in Atlanta who witnessed firsthand the bombing at the 1996 Olympics. Afterward, they talked about the tragedy, read about it, heard other witnesses being interviewed on TV, and knew what government officials were saying. By the time these witnesses were questioned, one wonders if their original memory was still "pure," uncontaminated by postevent information.

According to Elizabeth Loftus (1979), it probably was not. Based on her studies of eyewitness testimony, Loftus proposed a theory of reconstructive memory. After people observe an event, she said, later information about the event—whether it's true or not—becomes integrated into the fabric of their memory. A classic study by Loftus and her colleagues (1978) illustrates what has been called the **misinformation effect.** In that study, they presented subjects with a slide show in which a red car hits a pedestrian after turning at an intersection. Subjects saw either a STOP sign or a YIELD sign in the slides, but then embedded in a series of questions they were asked was one that implied the presence of the other sign ("Did another car pass the Datsun as it reached the ___ sign?"). The result: The number of subjects who later "recognized" the slide with the wrong traffic sign increased from 25 percent to 59 percent. Other studies soon confirmed the effect. Researchers thus misled subjects into recalling hammers as screwdrivers, Coke cans as cans of peanuts, *Vogue* magazine as *Mademoiselle,* breakfast cereal as eggs, a green object as yellow, a clean-shaven man as having a mustache, and a bare-handed man as wearing gloves. To make matters worse, subjects are often quick to respond and confident in the accuracy of these false memories (Loftus et al., 1989).

This provocative theory has aroused a lot of controversy. Does misinformation permanently impair a witness's real memory, never to be retrieved again (Belli et al., 1994; Weingardt et al., 1995)? Or do subjects merely follow the experimenter's "suggestion," leaving a true memory intact for retrieval under other conditions (Dodson & Reisberg, 1991; McCloskey & Zaragoza, 1985)? Although the debate rages on, an important practical lesson remains: Whether memory is truly altered or

misinformation effect The tendency to incorporate false postevent information into one's memory of the event itself.

[Harris/Cartoonists & Writers Syndicate]

"Do you swear to tell your version of the truth as you perceive it, clouded perhaps by the passage of time and preconceived notions?"

not, our *reports* of what we remember are hopelessly biased by postevent information. As you can imagine, this finding—and others like it—has serious implications for our legal system.

The Creation of Illusory Memories The misinformation effect has led some cognitive psychologists to argue that at times people create memories that are completely false. At the start of this chapter, we saw that subjects who heard a list of sleep-related words (*bed, yawn*) or music-related words (*jazz, instrument*) were often convinced just minutes later that they had also heard *sleep* and *music*—words that fit but were not actually on the list (Roediger & McDermott, 1995; Read, 1996). In another study, subjects who were instructed to imagine certain childhood events (such as getting stuck up in a tree or putting a hand through a window) later became less certain that these events did not *actually* happen to them as children (Garry et al., 1997). And in a third study, college students were repeatedly asked about childhood events. Some were true, according to their parents, and others were fabricated—such as having a birthday party with pizza and a clown or spilling punch at a wedding. The students did not recall any of the fictitious events at first, but after several interviews, 20 to 30 percent of them generated false recollections (Hyman et al., 1995). In Chapter 17, we'll see that these studies are controversial and unsettling for what they imply about the memories of childhood abuse that adults sometimes "recover" while in therapy.

With people being at risk to create "illusory" memories, is there a way to distinguish between these and true recollections? So far, the answer is no. But in a recent study modeled after Roediger and McDermott's (1995) research, Daniel Schacter and others (1996) took a serious first step. These investigators had twelve subjects listen to lists of semantically related words (*thread, pin, prick, haystack, eye, injection, knitting*). With their brains being PET-scanned, these subjects then saw other words on a computer screen—some that were on the original list, others that were not on the list but clearly fit the semantic category (*needle*). For each word, subjects indicated whether they recognized it from the list. Were true recognitions of old

Subjects saw a slide show in which this car turns at a corner that has either a STOP *sign* (left) *or a* YIELD *sign* (right). *Illustrating the misinformation effect, subjects who were later asked questions that implied the presence of the other sign were more likely to "recognize" the wrong slide (Loftus et al., 1978).*

words and false recognitions of new words accompanied by different activity in the brain? The results were fascinating. Blood flow in a specific region near the hippocampus increased equally during both true and false recognitions—which may account for why false memories can seem so real. In contrast, the part of the left hemisphere behind the ear where sounds are processed lit up only when subjects

INTERSECTION

MEMORY AND LAW

Eyewitness Identification Biases

I'll never forget that face!" When these words are uttered, police officers, judges, and juries all take notice. Sometimes, however, eyewitnesses make mistakes. Consider the sad story of William Jackson, identified by two crime victims, convicted, and sent to prison. Five years later, Jackson was proven innocent and released. But the damage had been done. "They took away part of my life, part of my youth," he said.

An estimated 77,000 people a year are charged with crimes solely on the basis of eyewitness identifications (Goldstein et al, 1989). Many of these are accurate, but some are not. What factors influence a witness's testimony? Common sense tells us that brief exposure, long distance, poor lighting, and facial disguise limit our perceptions and that a lineup has to be fair. Several years ago, a TV skit featured comedian Richard Pryor in a police lineup alongside a nun, a refrigerator, and a duck. Sure enough, the witness picked Pryor. You don't have to be a cognitive psychologist to see what's wrong with this situation. But researchers have identified many less obvious problems as well (Ross et al., 1994; Cutler & Penrod, 1995). Before reading this chapter, did you know that the presence of a weapon reduces one's ability to recognize a criminal? Or that your memory of a crime can be altered by your expectations or by the way the questions are worded? The following factors are particularly important:

1. ***Emotional arousal.*** Often witnesses are asked to recall a bloody shooting, accident, or assault—emotional events that arouse high levels of stress. Arousal has a complex effect on memory. Realizing the importance of what they are seeing, highly aroused witnesses zoom in on the central features of an event—perhaps the culprit, the victim, or a weapon. As a direct result of this narrowed attention, arousal impairs a witness's memory for other details (Burke et al., 1992; Christianson, 1992).
2. ***Race.*** By varying the racial makeup of subjects and target persons, eyewitness researchers have discovered that people find it relatively difficult to recognize members of a race other than their own. This cross-race bias is found among subjects who are white, African American, Asian, and Hispanic. Although the reason for the bias is not clear, it appears that when people have little experience or contact with other racial and ethnic groups, "they all look alike" (Brigham & Malpass, 1985).
3. ***Lineup composition.*** In a live lineup, the police present their suspect to the witness along with five or six "foils" who are similar in their appearance. There are many structural and procedural aspects of the lineup that can lead witnesses to make false identifications (Buckhout, 1974; Wells, 1993). In this multiple-choice task, research shows, for example, that anything that makes one lineup member more distinctive than the others increases his or her chance of being selected. This may explain the case of Steve Titus, a man falsely accused of rape when a victim picked his photograph from a set of six. The other men generally resembled Titus, but his picture was smaller and was the only one without a border. He was also the only man in the group with a smile on his face (Loftus & Ketcham, 1991).
4. ***Lineup instructions.*** The instructions that the police give to the witness are also critical. In a study by Roy Malpass and Patricia Devine (1981), students saw a staged act of vandalism and then attended a lineup. Half of the students were led to believe that the culprit was in the lineup; the others were informed that he may or may not be present. The result: Subjects given the first, more suggestive instruction felt

compelled to pick *someone*—so many identified an innocent person.

5. *Eyewitness confidence.* What makes the imperfections of an eyewitness so damaging is that his or her testimony is highly persuasive in court. In a series of experiments, Gary Wells, Rod Lindsay, and their colleagues staged a crime in front of unwary subjects who underwent cross-examination after trying to pick the culprit from mug shots. Other subjects, serving as jurors, watched the questioning and evaluated the witnesses. Time and again, jurors overestimated witness accuracy and could not tell the difference between those who made correct versus incorrect identifications (Lindsay et al., 1989; Wells et al., 1979). Why? The problem is that jurors tend to base their judgments on a witness's statement of self-confidence. Yet research has revealed that confidence does not reliably predict accuracy. The witness who declares, "I am absolutely certain," is no more likely to be correct than the one who hems and haws (Wells & Murray, 1984).

Psychologists who study human memory are sometimes called to testify at trials involving eyewitness testimony. So what do they say to the judge and jury? A survey of sixty-three eyewitness experts reveals that in addition to testifying on the effects of emotional arousal, race, lineup composition, lineup instructions, and confidence, they describe the following other memory phenomena as well—many of which are discussed in this chapter (Kassin, et al., 1989).

Memory Phenomena in Eyewitness Testimony

Wording of questions	An eyewitnesses testimony about an event can be affected by how questions put to that witness are worded.
Misinformation	Eyewitness testimony about an event often reflects not only what the witness actually saw but also information obtained later.
Transference	Eyewitnesses sometimes identify as a culprit someone they saw in another situation or context.
Forgetting curve	The rate of memory loss for an event is greatest right after the event and then levels off over time.
Weapon focus	The presence of a weapon impairs an eyewitness's ability to accurately identify the perpetrator's face.
Schemas	An eyewitness's perception and memory for an event may be affected by his or her attitudes and expectations.

recognized words they had *actually* heard—not when they made false recognitions of words they only *thought* they had heard (see Figure 6.23).

Autobiographical Memory

What autobiographical memories are people most likely to preserve? What makes some experiences particularly vivid and enduring? What is childhood amnesia, and why does it occur? How are our personal memories shaped by our sense of self?

Suppose you were to sit down to write your autobiography. What would you say? What experiences stand out in your mind? Would your reports of the past be accurate or distorted in some way? To answer these kinds of questions, psychologist Marigold Linton (1982) kept an extensive diary and later used it to test her memory for the events of her life. Every day for six years, she wrote the date on one side of an index card and a description of something that happened to her. In all, the diary contained 5,000 entries—some important, others trivial. Once a month, Linton pulled 150 cards at random from her file and tried to recall the events and date them correctly. Like Ebbinghaus, she found that as time passed, her personal memories took longer to recall, were harder to date, and were less detailed—but that, right from the start, this fading occurred at a slower rate. More recently, two psychologists kept personal diaries for seven months and were then tested by colleagues who asked about events that were in the diaries and nonevents that seemed plausible but did not occur. Although the subjects knew in advance that items would be fabricated for the test, they still made several false recollections (Conway et al., 1996).

Many cognitive psychologists have traded in their nonsense syllables to study **autobiographical memory**—the recollections people have of the experiences that have touched their lives (Rubin, 1996). There are two key questions about these memories: (1) What aspects of our own past do we tend to preserve—and what are we likely to forget? (2) Are we generally accurate in our mental time travel, or does memory change as we get older?

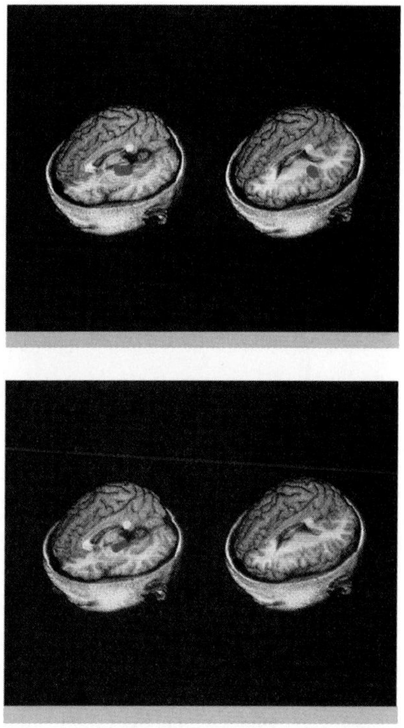

Figure 6.23 Do true and false memories leave different traces on the brain? In this study, subjects made true and false recognitions of words. PET scans revealed that whereas blood flow near the hippocampus increased equally during both true and false recognitions (*top*), the part of the left hemisphere where sounds are processed was more active when subjects exhibited true recognitions of words they had actually heard than false recognitions of words they only thought they had heard (*bottom*) (Schacter et al., 1996).

What Events Do People Remember?

When people are prompted to recall their own experiences, they typically report more events that are recent than are from the distant past. There are, however, two consistent exceptions to this rule. The first is that older adults retrieve a large number of personal memories from their adolescence and early adulthood years (Fitzgerald, 1988; Jansari & Parkin, 1996). This "reminiscence peak" may occur because these early years are busy and formative in one's life. Thus, William Mackavey and others (1991) analyzed the autobiographies written by forty-nine eminent psychologists and found that their most important life experiences tended to be concentrated between the ages of eighteen and thirty-five (see Figure 6.24).

A second exception to the recency rule is that people tend to remember transitional "firsts." Think for a moment about your college career. What events immediately pop to mind—and when did these events occur? Did you come up with the day you arrived on campus or the first time you met your closest friend? What about notable classes, exams, parties, or sports events? When David Pillemer and his colleagues (1996) asked juniors and seniors to recount the most memorable experiences of their first year, 32 percent of all their recollections were from the transitional month of September. And when college alumnae who had graduated one to twenty years earlier were given the same task, they too cited a disproportionate number of events from the opening two months of their first year—followed, interestingly, by the next major transitional period, the last month of their graduating senior year. These patterns are presented in Figure 6.25.

Obviously, not all experiences leave the same impression, and some dates are etched in memory for a lifetime. Marigold Linton (1982) found that unique events were easy to recall but that routines were quickly forgotten. More specifically, David Rubin and Marc Kozin (1984) asked college students to describe their clearest memories and found that births, deaths, weddings, accidents, injuries, sports events, romantic encounters, and vacations were among the highlights that topped the list. Some events in our lives are so vivid that they seem to occupy a particularly special status in memory. Ask people who are old enough to remember November 22, 1963, and the chances are they can tell you exactly what was happening, where they were, and with whom the moment they heard the news that John F. Kennedy had been shot. I, for one, will never forget that day—returning to my fifth-grade classroom after lunch, hearing the principal's voice crack over the loudspeaker, watching my teacher gasp, the silence of the bus ride home, the TV blaring as I walked through the door, and the tears streaming down my mother's face.

autobiographical memory The recollections people have of their own personal experiences and observations.

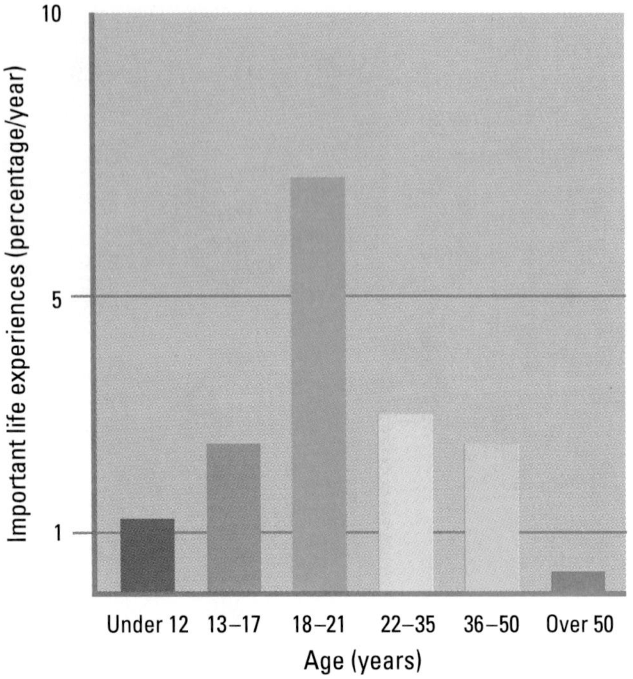

Figure 6.24 The reminiscence peak Illustrating a reminiscence peak, an analysis of autobiographies of forty-nine eminent psychologists revealed that most of their important experiences occurred between the ages of eighteen and thirty-five (Mackavey et al, 1991).

Roger Brown and James Kulik (1977) questioned adults about that day and found that everyone had a memory that was as bold and vivid as a snapshot—not just of the assassination but of their own circumstances upon hearing the news. Brown and Kulik coined the term ***flashbulb memories*** to describe these very enduring, detailed, "high resolution" recollections and speculated that humans are biologically equipped for survival purposes to "print" the most dramatic events in memory (as you may recall, physiological arousal releases hormones that can enhance memory). Indeed, research shows that flashbulb memories are triggered by events that are new to a person, important, surprising, and emotional (Conway, 1995). Does this mean that information that is linked to emotional events is immune to forgetting? Not necessarily. Some of these memories are remarkably accurate, but others are not (McCloskey et al., 1988). As time passes, people do gain more and more confidence in these recollections (Weaver, 1993). Accurate or not, then, flashbulb memories "feel" special and serve as prominent landmarks in the biographies we write about ourselves.

In contrast, there is a period of life that seems entirely lost to us. Think back to your earliest memory. It probably was not the sight of the doctor's hands in the delivery room, or the first time you waved, or even the first real step you took as a toddler. An intriguing aspect of autobiographical memory is that most people cannot recall anything that happened before the age of three or four (Dudycha & Dudycha, 1941; Rubin, 1986). In one study, for example, Pillemer and others (1994) interviewed preadolescent children about a fire-drill evacuation they had experienced in preschool. Those who were four and five years old when the incident occurred were able to recall it seven years later; those who were three years old at the time could not. This memory gap, which is common, is known as **childhood amnesia.**

Why should this be? One possibility is that the forgetting is caused simply by the passage of time and by interference from later experiences. The problem with this explanation is that a college student may be unable to recall events from eighteen years ago, but a thirty-five-year-old can easily recall his or her college days after the same amount of time. Other explanations include the notion that young children lack the conceptual framework or self-concept for organizing information to be stored, as well as the Freudian hypothesis that the early years are repressed because they are filled with trauma (Howe & Courage, 1993).

Do early memories exist? It's hard to say. Some researchers have found that adults can recall certain critical events—moving, the birth of a sibling, being hospitalized, the death of a family member—from the age of two, suggesting that there are exceptions to the rule (Usher & Neisser, 1993). Others caution that these reports may not be memories at all but, rather, educated guesses or stories told by parents (Loftus, 1993b). Still others maintain that people have partial, implicit memories of the early years. Nora Newcombe and Nathan Fox (1994) found that ten-year-old children sometimes reacted physiologically to slides of preschool classmates—even while failing to "recognize" those classmates. This finding is consistent with the fact that the hippocampus is not completely developed in the first few years of life and that infants and young children have memories that are *pre-explicit* (Nelson, 1995). It's also consistent with the fact that one- and two-year-olds can imitate people they

flashbulb memories Highly vivid and enduring memories, typically for events that are dramatic and emotional.

childhood amnesia The inability of most people to recall events from before the age of three or four.

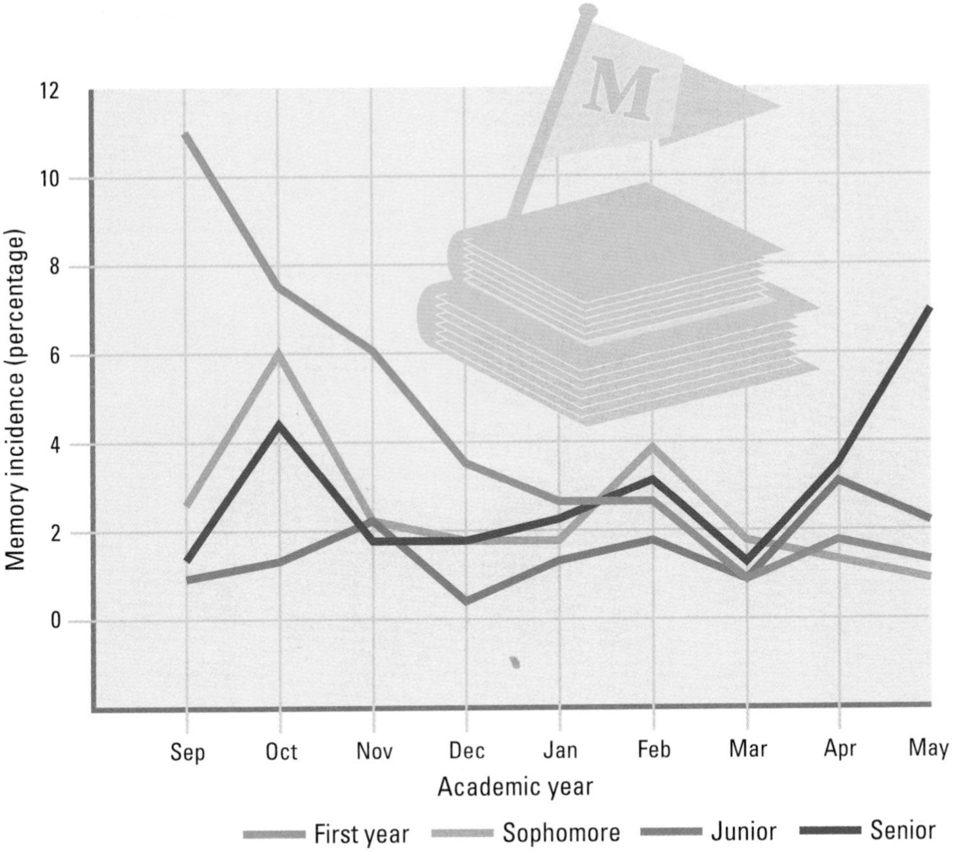

Figure 6.25 Memorable transitions College graduates of varying ages were asked to recount their most memorable experiences while in college. You can see that among the memories that could be pinpointed in time, there was a large number from the first two months of their first year and a large number from the other major transitional period—the last month of their senior year.

see after long periods of time and show the long-term effects of other types of experience (Bauer, 1996). At some level, young children do remember the past. But these recollections are implicit—and not likely to become part of the autobiographical memories that form later in their childhood.

The Self as Personal Historian

By linking the present to the past and providing us with a sense of inner continuity, autobiographical memory is a vital part of a person's identity. Think about it. Who would you be if you could not remember your parents or childhood playmates, your successes and failures, the places you lived, the schools you attended, the books you read, and the experiences you had? It's clear that memories shape the self-concept. What's interesting is that the self-concept shapes our memory as well.

> *"The nice thing about having memories is that you can choose."*
>
> — WILLIAM TREVOR

There are two ways in which memory is shaped by the self. First, people are motivated to distort the past in a manner that is self-inflated, or *egocentric.* According to Anthony Greenwald (1980), "The past is remembered as if it were a drama in which the self was the leading player." To illustrate, let's turn the clock back to a momentous event in American history: the Watergate hearings of 1973. The witness was John Dean, former counsel to President Nixon. Dean had submitted a 245-page statement in which he recounted word for word the details of conversations. Dean's memory seemed so flawless that he was dubbed "the human tape

Do you recall where you were and what you were doing on January 28, 1986, when you learned about the explosion of the space shuttle Challenger? *Many people say that this tragic event triggered a flashbulb memory.*

[Drawing by Lorenz; © 1992 The New Yorker Magazine, Inc.]

"Needless to say, in the course of redefining myself I've taken certain liberties with the factual record."

recorder." In an ironic twist of fate, it turned out that Nixon had actually taped the meetings Dean had recalled. Was Dean accurate? A comparison of his testimony with the tapes revealed that he correctly remembered the gist of his White House conversations, but he exaggerated his own role in these events—leading Ulric Neisser (1981), the cognitive psychologist who analyzed Dean's testimony, to wonder, "Are we all like this? Is everyone's memory constructed, staged, self-centered?" Research shows that the answer is *yes*—there is a bit of John Dean in all of us.

A second important feature of autobiographical memory is the **hindsight bias,** the tendency to think after an event that we knew in advance what was going to happen. Historians are sometimes criticized for making the past seem inevitable in hindsight. We all do. After learning a new fact or an outcome—whether it's the result of a political election, an earthquake, the invasion of one country by another, or the winner of the last Super Bowl—people are quick to claim, "I knew it all along" (Fischhoff, 1975; Hawkins & Hastie, 1990).

hindsight bias The tendency to think after an event that we knew in advance what was going to happen.

When it comes to autobiographical memory, 20/20 hindsight leads people to revise their fading personal histories in ways that reflect favorably on the self. For example, George Goethals and Richard Reckman (1973) found that subjects whose attitudes about school busing were changed by a persuasive speaker later assumed that they had held their new attitude all along. Similarly, Michael Ross (1989) found that after subjects were persuaded by an expert that frequent toothbrushing was desirable, they reported in the context of a subsequent experiment having brushed more often in the previous two weeks. Illustrating that memory can be biased rather than objective, the subjects "updated" the past in light of their new attitude. Most

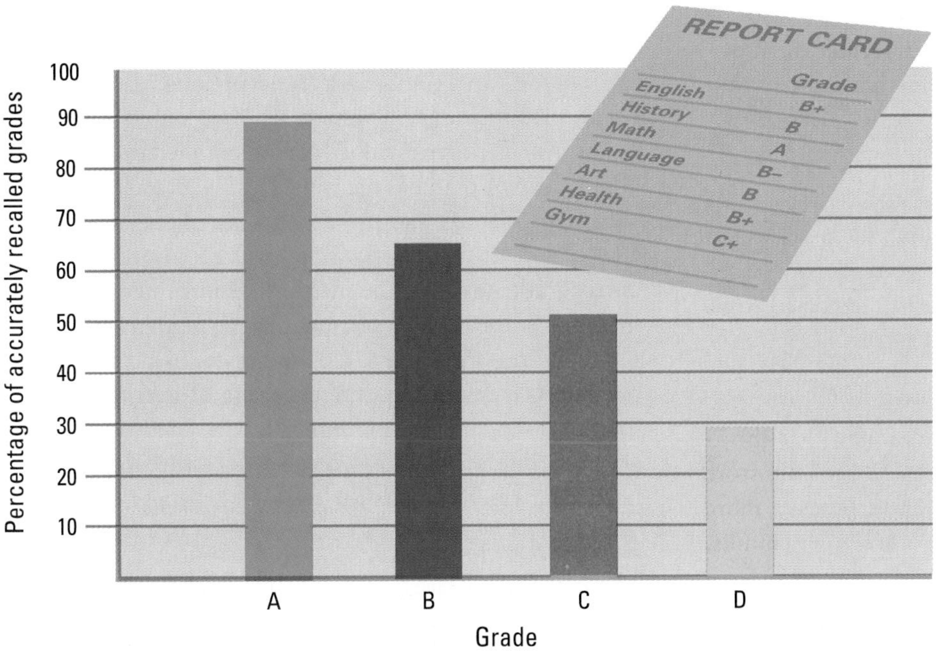

Figure 6.26 Distortions in memory of high-school grades Students were asked to recall their high-school grades, which were then checked against the actual transcripts. These comparisons revealed that most errors in memory were grade inflations. Also as shown, lower grades were recalled with the least accuracy (and the most inflation). It appears that people sometimes revise their own past to suit their current self-image (Bahrick et al., 1996).

recently, Bahrick and others (1996) had ninety-nine college students recall all of their high-school grades and then checked the accuracy of these reports against the actual transcripts. Overall, most grades were recalled correctly. But most of the errors in memory were grade *inflations*—and most of these were made when the actual grades were *low* (see Figure 6.26).

Contemplating the social implications, Ross (1989) suggested that our revisionist tendencies may account for why all generations of parents seem to complain that today's children are not equal to those who grew up in the good old days. According to Ross, adults wrongly assume that they used to be as they are in the present—which makes the next generation seem deficient by comparison. From studies of adult development, George Vaillant (1977) drew a similar conclusion: "It is common for caterpillars to become butterflies and then to maintain that in their youth they had been little butterflies. Maturation makes liars of us all" (p. 197).

Summary and Key Terms

An Information-Processing Model

Cognitive psychologists view **memory** as an **information-processing** system. **Sensory memory** stores sensations for a brief moment. Those that draw attention are transferred to **short-term memory (STM)**, and those that are further encoded are stored in **long-term memory (LTM)**.

The Sensory Register

The sensory register is the first step in the information-processing system.

Iconic Memory

The visual system stores images called icons in **iconic memory.** Using the partial-report technique, Sperling found that many items initially register in consciousness but that most last for only a fraction of a second before fading.

Echoic Memory

The auditory system stores sounds in **echoic memory.** Echoic memory holds only a few items but lasts two or three seconds, sometimes longer.

Short-Term Memory

Sensations that do not capture attention fade quickly, but those we notice are encoded (in visual, acoustic, or semantic terms) and transferred to short-term memory. People usually encode information in acoustic terms.

Capacity

Using a memory-span task, researchers found that short-term memory has a limited capacity. People can store seven items, plus or minus two. STM can be used more efficiently, however, if we group items into larger chunks.

Duration

STM is also limited in the length of time it can hold information. Studies show that items are held in STM for up to twenty seconds. Through repetition or **maintenance rehearsal,** however, input can be held for an indefinite period of time.

Functions of Short-Term Memory

STM contains new sensory input and material from long-term memory. The limits of STM are adaptive, enabling us to discard information that is no longer useful. STM is not just a passive storage depot but an active workspace referred to as a **working memory.** When people memorize a list of items, they exhibit the **serial-position curve,** whereby items from the beginning and end are recalled better than those in the middle.

Long-Term Memory

LTM is a relatively enduring storage system that can hold vast amounts of information for long periods of time.

Encoding

To transfer input to LTM, it is best to use **elaborative rehearsal**—specifically, engaging in "deep" processing and associating the input with information already in LTM. Retention is also increased through overlearning (continued rehearsal after the material is mastered) and through practice spaced over time rather than crammed in all at once.

Storage

In LTM, information may be stored in semantic or visual form. In semantic coding, people store the meaning of verbal information, not just specific words. In fact, memories are stored in complex webs of association called **semantic networks.** In visual coding, people store input as mental pictures. Thus, the use of imagery, particularly when it is interactive and bizarre, improves memory.

There is more than one type of long-term memory. **Procedural memory** consists of learned habits and skills, whereas **declarative memory** consists of memories for facts about the world and about ourselves. Neuroscientists have sought to identify the physical traces of memory. In the case of H.M., the hippocampus was removed, producing **anterograde amnesia,** the inability to form new long-term memories (not **retrograde amnesia,** the inability to retrieve old memories from the past). Studies confirm that the hippocampus is involved in the encoding of information into long-term memory. Biochemically, the neurotransmitter acetylcholine plays a key role. So does the hormone epinephrine, which triggers the release of glucose.

Retrieval

There are two basic techniques by which retrieval can be tested, and each assesses a different aspect of memory: explicit and implicit. **Explicit memories** are the recollections consciously retrieved in response to direct questions. **Implicit memories** are nonconscious recollections that are indirectly measured by their effects on performance. This distinction is important because people may "forget" (have no explicit memory of) an experience and yet show the effects (have an implicit memory) of that experience.

In tests of explicit memory, people find it more difficult to produce a recollection in the form of **free recall** than **recognition.** Apparently, forgetting often occurs not because memory has faded but because the information is difficult to retrieve. Retrieval failure is indicated by the tip-of-the-tongue phenomenon and by the fact that memory is aided by retrieval cues. Research on **encoding specificity** indicates that any stimulus that is encoded along with an experience—including locations (which accounts for context-dependent memory) and internal states (which accounts for state-dependent memory)—can later jog memory of that experience.

Implicit tests uncover memories of which people are not aware by measuring their effects on performance. Many amnesia patients use material they cannot explicitly recall. As shown by the false-fame effect, the illusion of truth, unconscious transference in eyewitness testimony, and unconscious plagiarism, implicit memory is also common in everyday life.

Forgetting

Beginning with Ebbinghaus, researchers have found evidence for a specific **forgetting curve** in which there is an initial steep loss of retention, with the loss rate leveling off over time. Forgetting can result from a lack of encoding, physical decay, interference, or repression. There are two kinds of interference. In **proactive interference,** prior information inhibits one's ability to recall something new. In **retroactive interference,** new material disrupts memory for previously learned information. People can use various techniques, called **mnemonics,** to improve memorization ability.

Reconstruction

Remembering is an active process in which people construct memories based on **schemas,** or preconceptions, and information from outside sources. Experiments by Loftus and others reveal that memory is also "reconstructive"—that after one observes an event, postevent input becomes integrated into the memory. When that information is false, the result is known as the **misinformation effect.** In other ways as well, false or illusory memories can be created.

Autobiographical Memory

Autobiographical memory consists of the recollections people have of their own personal experiences. What aspects of our own past do we preserve? Are these memories accurate?

What Events Do People Remember?

People can best recall events from the recent rather than the distant past, though older adults report many memories from adolescence and early adulthood and people in general tend to recall transitional periods in their lives. For events that are particularly dramatic, people form **flashbulb memories** that are highly vivid and enduring—though not always accurate. Most people cannot recall events from before the age or three or four, a memory gap called **childhood amnesia.**

The Self as Personal Historian

Autobiographical memory is vital to one's identity. Accordingly, our memories are shaped by our need for self-esteem. People thus distort the past in a manner that is egocentric and self-promoting, and they often think afterward that they knew all along what would happen, a phenomenon known as the **hindsight bias.**

In the Field Resources

Books

Hilts, P. (1995). *Memory's ghost: The strange tale of Mr. M. and the nature of memory*. New York: Simon & Schuster.

Based on recent visits, the author provides an up-close and personal look at H.M.—arguably the most important patient in the neuroscience of memory.

Schacter, D. L. (1996). *Searching for memory*. New York: Basic Books.

This is a scientific yet beautifully written book by a leading researcher who takes the lay reader on a journey through fascinating studies of human memory—and what they mean.

Films and Videos

Total Recall (1990, 110 min.)

In this futurist tale, a construction worker takes a "fantasy vacation" to Mars via an implanted memory chip. This film shows how hard it can be to distinguish reality and fantasy. (Arnold Schwarzenegger, Sharon Stone.)

Internet

WWW Sites for Experimental Psychology (http://www.psychologie.unibonn.de/allgm/links.htm#mue)

Contains links to various topics, demonstrations, studies being conducted on the internet of relevance to human memory.

Memory Techniques and Mnemonics (http://www.gasou.edu/psychweb/mtsite/memory.html)

Provided by Mind Tools, this site provides articles on various mnemonics for remembering names, dates, phone numbers, foreign language words, playing cards, and so on.

Journals and Periodicals

Applied Cognitive Psychology
Journal of Experimental Psychology: General
Journal of Experimental Psychology: Learning, Memory, and Cognition
Memory and Cognition

7 Thought and Language

The situation Along with other students who signed up for this laboratory experiment, you are told that you'll be seeing a series of films, each depicting a traffic accident. In fact, the segments you'll see were taken from driver-education films, and each will last five to thirty seconds. Pay close attention, you are told, because later you'll be asked specific questions about these events.

Over the next hour or so, you watch seven films. After each one, you are asked to write down what happened in your own words and then fill out a questionnaire containing specific questions, including the following question about speed: "About how fast were the cars going when they hit each other?" The experiment seems straightforward and to the point. The scenes are not that hard to watch, and the questions are relatively easy. What you don't know is that other students watching the same films are being asked a slightly different form of the speed question. For these other students, the verb *hit* has been replaced with the verbs *contacted* or *smashed*.

What's Your Prediction?

Using words to shape thoughts

Make a prediction Judging the speed of a moving object—like judging time and distance—is not as easy as it seems, which is why witnesses to automobile accidents often vary in their estimates. But consider this particular situation. The participants in this study knew they would be watching accident films, were focused on the films in a quiet and calm laboratory, and knew they would be questioned afterward. In the films that were shown, the collisions actually took place at 20, 30, and 40 mph. How were these events judged? When asked the basic *hit* question, the students estimated, on average, that the cars had been traveling at 34 mph. Do you think that estimates were higher, lower, or similar in response to the other forms of the question? On the mph scale below, circle your prediction of the speed estimates in the other conditions.

HIT	28	29	30	31	(32)	33	34	35	36	37	38	39	40	41
CONTACTED	28	29	30	31	32	33	34	35	36	37	38	39	40	41
SMASHED	28	29	30	31	32	33	34	35	36	37	38	39	40	41

The results In this experiment, Elizabeth Loftus and John Palmer (1974) found that although everyone watched the same accident films, the wording of the speed question significantly affected how they saw these events. Compared to a mean of 32 mph in response to the *hit* question, the estimates were *32* mph in response to the *contacted* question and *41* mph in response to the *smashed* question. In fact, the simple wording of the question completely altered the way these events were interpreted. When students were brought back one week later and asked if there was broken glass in the accident they had seen, one-third of those who initially were asked the *smashed* question said there was. In fact, there was not.

What does it all mean? More and more, psychologists who study the way people think and those interested in the way people communicate have come to realize that thought and language are seamlessly interconnected. In this chapter, we'll see that language is a tool we humans use for articulating concepts, solutions to problems, and other thoughts. But there's more to the story. As we'll see later in this chapter, the classic *hit-smash* study by Loftus and Palmer (1974) shows that the words we use to describe events can, to some extent, shape the way we think.

We humans are a funny species. As a civilization, we have invented the wheel, kept historical records to guide present and future generations, landed space ships on the moon, unlocked the atom, cracked the genetic code, and revolutionized the face of all we do with the development of the computer. When you stop to think about it, our list of triumphs is long and very impressive. Yet at the same time, we massacre each other in war, wreak havoc on the environment, discriminate against other racial and ethnic groups, mistreat our partners in marriage, take drugs that make us sick, and deceive ourselves into believing in witches, ghosts, and alien abductions.

What is it about the way we humans think that leads us to be both rational and irrational? How do we solve difficult problems and then evaluate the solutions, and what kinds of errors are we prone to make along the way? Are we logical in our reasoning, or are the judgments and decisions we make infected with bias? And what role does language have to play in the way we think? What is language, and is it this capacity that most clearly separates humans from other animal species? In the coming pages, we will examine some of the basic processes of thought and language, then address the question of how they are related. But first, let's examine *concepts*—the basic building blocks of abstract thought and language.

Concepts

What are concepts, and how are they stored in memory? What is a prototype, and how does it explain why a robin is considered "birdier" than a chicken?

Freedom. Sports. Cancer. Animals. Education. Furniture. Sex. Peace. Music. Heroes. Triangles. Happiness. Each of these words represents a distinct **concept**—a mental grouping of persons, places, ideas, events, or objects that share common properties. In Chapter 6, we saw that our long-term store of knowledge can be pictured as a complex but orderly network of semantic concepts. So when one concept in the network is activated, other closely related concepts pop to mind,

concept A mental grouping of persons, ideas, events, or objects that share common properties.

or are *primed*. Look at the semantic network depicted in Figure 7.1. Note that the fact that a robin is a type of bird is illustrated by its linkage, and this linkage in itself is a concept that is stored in memory. What's interesting about semantic networks is that one concept can be used to bring others to mind. Thus, hearing the word *bird* makes it easier to pull *robin, chicken,* and *animal* from memory.

To demonstrate priming of this sort, David Meyer and Roger Schvaneveldt (1971) presented subjects with pairs of letter strings and asked them to decide as quickly as possible if both letter strings formed words. On some trials, the two items in a pair were semantically related words (*nurse-doctor*). On other trials, the pairs included unrelated words (*bread-doctor*) or nonwords (*marb-doctor*). As it turned out, subjects were quickest to decide that the items were both words when they were related. Reading the first word of the pair primed semantically related words—thus giving the *nurse-doctor* subjects a "head start" on the second item and speeding up their decisions. Over the years, many researchers have replicated this result (McNamara, 1994).

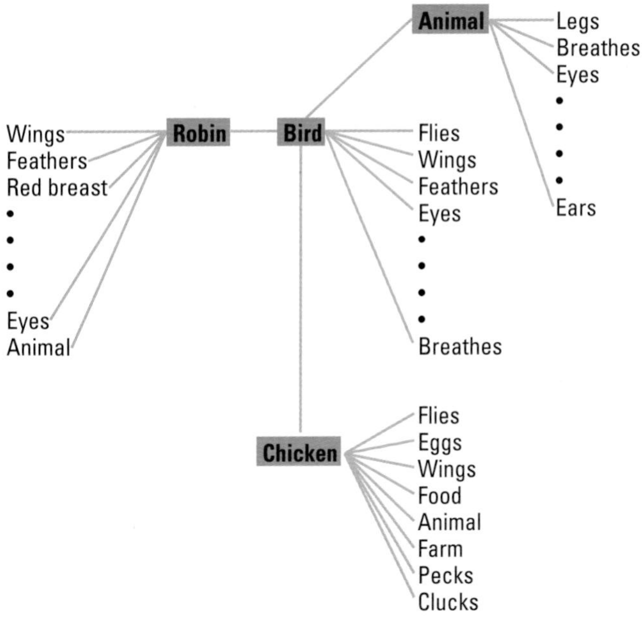

Figure 7.1 A semantic network Long-term memory can be pictured as a complex web of concepts, some of which are cognitively closer than others. When one concept is "activated," others nearby in the network are primed.

Another important aspect of semantic networks is that some concepts are more closely related than others. As shown in Figure 7.1, *chicken* is farther from *bird* than *robin* is—even though both are members of the same category. Assuming that it takes longer to reveal connections between concepts that are distant than between those that are closely related, reaction-time tasks are used to plot the psychological distances between concepts. If I were to time how long it takes you to verify that "a chicken is a bird" and then compare that to the amount of time it takes you to verify that "a robin is a bird," you would probably respond more quickly to the second statement (Collins & Loftus, 1975).

Some members of a category are perceived to be more typical than others. Thus, to most people, a robin is a "birdier" bird than a chicken, an ostrich, or a penguin—which all have wings and feathers and hatch from eggs but do not fly. What makes a category member more or less typical? Look again at Figure 7.1 and notice the partial list of characteristics that are linked to the concepts *bird, robin,* and *chicken.* When people are asked to list properties of different concepts, the most typical members, called **prototypes,** have more of these properties (Smith et al., 1974; Rosch, 1975). Consider the categories listed in Table 7.1. The more prototypical an

Table 7.1 Typicality of Members in Three Categories

CATEGORY	TYPICALITY		
	High	***Moderate***	***Low***
Furniture	Chair	Lamp	Vase
Fruit	Apple	Lemon	Coconut
Vehicle	Car	Boat	Blimp

prototype A "typical" member of a category, one that has most of the defining features of that category.

When you hear the word pet, *what image comes to mind? For this particular concept, some animals (golden retrievers) are more prototypical of the category than others (rabbits or iguanas).*

item is, the more easily we recognize that it is a member of the group and use it to make judgments about the group as a whole (Whitney, 1986).

The use of prototypes is illustrated in many studies. For example, Lance Rips (1975) had subjects read a story about an island that was inhabited by sparrows, robins, eagles, hawks, ducks, geese, and ostriches. Some subjects were informed that a disease had infected the robins, while others were told that the disease had infected the ducks. Subjects were then asked, "What other species would be infected?" Based on what you've just read about prototypes, can you anticipate the result? Subjects in the robin-infected group predicted that the disease would spread to all other bird species on the island. In contrast, the duck group predicted that only the geese, a "related" species, would be infected. Evidently, robins serve as a prototype for the birds, but ducks do not. Other research demonstrates the importance of prototypes in important decision making. In one study, Vicki Smith (1991) found that mock jurors were more likely to vote a defendant guilty of robbery when the crime was prototypical (money taken from the apartment of an elderly person, at night, by a man carrying a gun) than when it was nonprototypical (money taken from the driver of a car, during the day, by an unarmed man on a street corner).

Solving Problems

What are algorithms and heuristics, and how are they more efficient as problem-solving methods than trial and error? What's an analogy, and what makes it a powerful tool? Why do some psychologists believe in problem solving by insight—and why do others think insight is just an illusion? What are some of the "blind spots" that impair our ability to solve problems?

When you lock your keys in the car, play Scrabble, mediate a dispute betweenfriends, or struggle to figure out a function on your computer, the solution you're looking for requires that you combine and manipulate concepts, often in new ways, to solve the problem or to make the necessary judgment. When a solution cannot simply be pulled from memory, it takes effort to obtain. As we'll see, it helps to view problem solving as a process that involves defining and representing the problem, then generating and evaluating possible solutions (Glass & Holyoak, 1986; Ellis & Hunt, 1989). These steps are not a fixed series of stages but rather are mental activities that are used in cycles. So if you're stuck on a problem and realize that you have not represented it correctly in the first place, you might start the process over again.

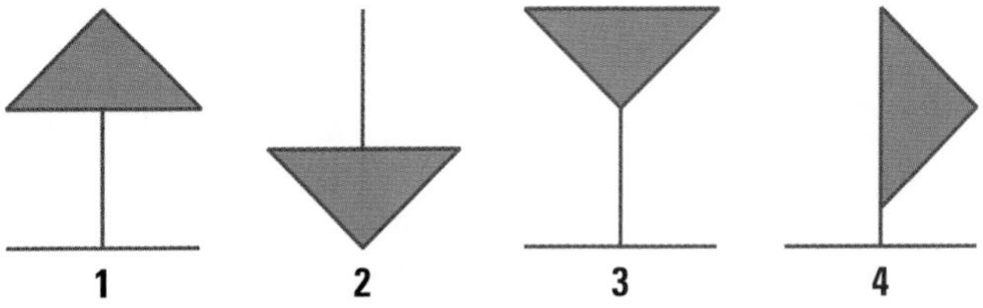

Figure 7.2 Mental-rotation tasks Imagine a capital letter *T*. Rotate it 90 degrees to the right. Put a triangle directly to the left of the figure so that it is pointing to the right. Now rotate the figure 90 degrees to the right. Got it? Now look at the images above and pick the correct one. You can check your answer by drawing the figure on paper or looking on page 261.

Representing the Problem

Many problems we encounter come to us in the form of words and concepts activated from semantic networks. Playing the TV game *Jeopardy!*, trying to recite the lyrics of an old song, and working on a crossword puzzle are some examples. But there are other ways as well to depict problems.

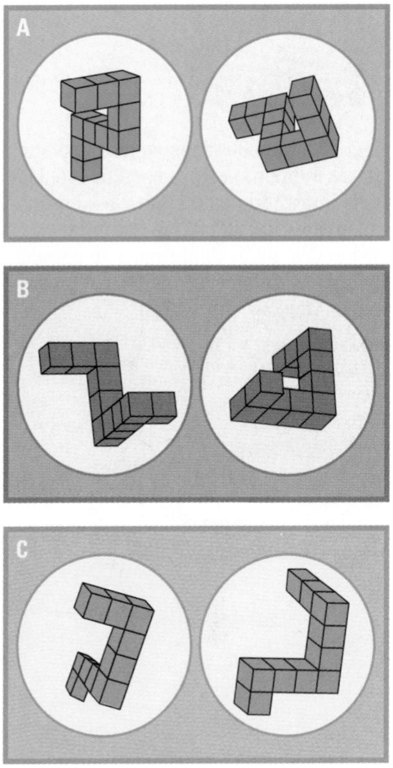

Figure 7.3 3-D mental-rotation tasks Look at the pairs of objects and try to determine whether the two objects in each pair are the same shape or different. Suggesting that people make these judgments by forming images, research shows that the more mental rotation is required to align two objects, the more time it takes people to make the judgment (Shepard & Cooper, 1982).

Mental Images

Often people represent information through **images,** or mental pictures. To turn on the ignition of your car, do you turn the key to the right or to the left? What about the cold-water faucet in your kitchen sink? Which way do the hands of a clock move? (Yes, it's clockwise, but describe what that means.) What's the color of your psychology professor's eyes? And if you can picture a map of the world, which city is farther north, London or New York? To answer these questions, people generate visual images.

In the past, psychologists had to take people at their word when they said they had formed mental pictures. Today, there are more objective ways to study the "mind's eye"—and these new methods have confirmed that imagery is a pervasive aspect of human thought. Consider some specific examples. In one study, Margaret Intons-Peterson (1993) gave people verbal descriptions of simple line drawings, like the one in Figure 7.2, and found that the more rotations that were involved, the longer it took subjects to generate the image. This result suggests that people solve this problem by manipulating mental pictures of the described forms. In fact, the images we form are often like three-dimensional sculptures. Look at the pairs of objects shown in Figure 7.3. When people are asked to judge whether the paired objects are the same shape or different, they try to solve the problem by imagining one of the forms rotating into alignment with the other. The more mental rotation required to align the objects, the more time it takes people to make the judgment (Shepard & Cooper, 1982). Additional evidence concerning the nature of imagery comes from recent brain-scanning studies, where researchers have found that when subjects engage in tasks that require mental imagery, their brains become active in the same areas of the occipital cortex that are involved in vision (Farah, 1989; Isha & Sagi, 1995).

To the cognitive psychologist, it's now clear that mental images play a key role in human problem solving (Kosslyn, 1994). But is imagery a uniquely human thought process? Research in a newly developing area of animal cognition suggests not. In

image A mental representation of visual information.

an intruiging experiment, depicted in Figure 7.4, Jacques Vauclair and others (1993) trained six wild baboons to move a cursor on a computer with the use of a joystick. In a series of trials, each subject then saw a sample stimulus flashed briefly on the screen (the letter *P* or *F*). This presentation was followed by two "comparison stimuli" that were rotated at varying degrees—one always matched the sample; the other was its mirror image. Using the joystick, the subject's task was to select the comparison stimulus that matched the original sample. Each correct response was rewarded with food. Could the baboons perform the necessary mental rotation to achieve this task? Yes. In contrast to what many psychologists would have predicted, the accuracy rate was 70 percent. And, as in humans, their performance varied according to the degree of rotation that was needed to make the comparison.

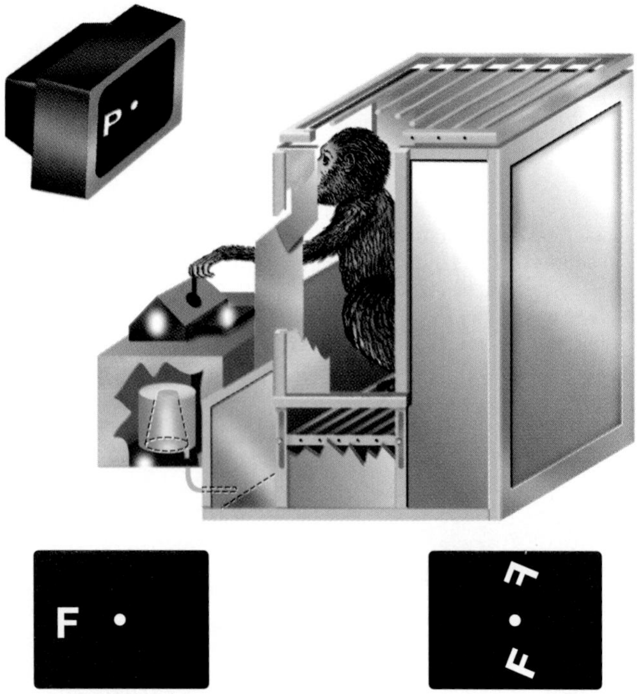

Figure 7.4 Can baboons mentally rotate objects? In this apparatus, six baboons were trained to use a joystick to move a cursor. The sample form on the left would be shown and then subjects would have to choose the rotated form on the right that matched the sample. As evident from a 70 percent accuracy rate, these baboons were able to mentally align objects to make these judgments (Vauclair et al., 1993).

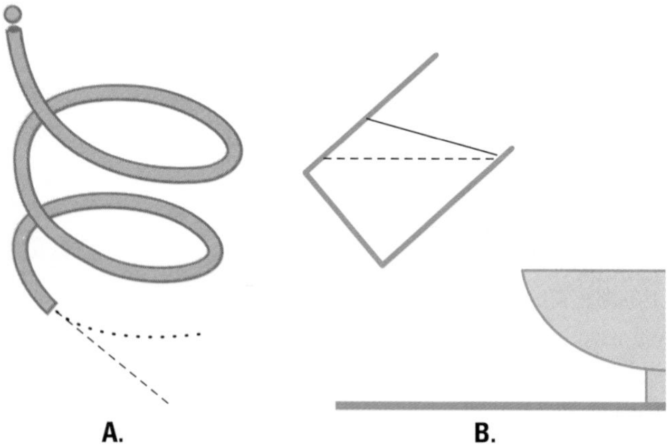

Figure 7.5 Intuitive physics A. Subjects were asked to draw the path that a marble would take as it exited this curved tube. Most subjects incorrectly drew a curved path (*dotted line*) rather than the correct straight path (*dashed line*). Our mental models of motion are often wrong. B. In this task, subjects were asked to draw a line to illustrate the surface of water in the tilted container. Although the line should be depicted as perfectly horizontal to the ground, many people placed it at the titled angle shown below.

Mental Models Do you understand how a virus spreads from one computer to another? Can you describe how an engine works? What about the economy: Do you know how the inflation and unemployment rates interact? At times, the problems that confront us can be best represented in the form of **mental models,** which are intuitive theories of the way things work. When accurate, these theories can be powerful tools for reasoning. By having specific mental models of how human beings, organizations, machines, and other things work, we can diagnose problems and then adapt accordingly (Gentner & Stevens, 1983).

Unfortunately, our mental models are often in error. Before reading on, try the problems in Figure 7.5. These problems are used to study *intuitive physics*—the mental models people have about the laws of motion. Research shows that people are poor intuitive physicists. Consider three common errors. First, many people wrongly believe in the "impetus principle" that an object set in motion acquires its own internal force, which keeps it in motion. So when asked to predict the path of a metal ball rolling through a spiral tube, a majority of subjects predicted that the ball would follow a curved path even after it exits the tube (McCloskey & Kuhl, 1983). A second error is the "straight-down belief" that something dropped from a moving object will fall in a straight vertical line. So when asked to predict the path of a ball dropped at shoulder height by a walking adult, most subjects wrongly assumed that the ball would fall straight down rather than in a forward trajectory (McCloskey et al., 1983). A third error is made in the "water-level task" shown in Figure 7.5. When shown a tilted glass or container filled with liquid, some subjects—including many bartenders and waitresses—harbor the belief that the water surface tilts as well rather than remains horizontal to the ground (Hecht & Proffitt, 1995). Interestingly, physics students don't always perform better on

mental models Intuitive theories about the way things work.

these types of problems, suggesting that mental models can be difficult to change (Donley & Ashcraft, 1992).

Solution to Figure 7.2: The answer is (3).

Generating Solutions

Once a problem is represented through words, static images, or mental models, we try out possible solutions and test to see if they work. If the problem is solved, life goes on. If not, we return to the proverbial drawing board to come up with new ideas. There are many different ways to find solutions, but there are four basic problem-solving processes: trial and error, algorithms, heuristics, and insight.

Trial and Error

Trial and error is the simplest problem-solving strategy there is, and it's often effective. You may recall from Chapter 5 that Edward Thorndike, in 1898, studied animal intelligence by putting cats in a "puzzle box," placing food outside a door, and timing how long it took for them to figure out how to escape. At first, the cats tried various ineffective behaviors. They tried reaching with their paws, but the food was too far away. They scratched at the bars, but that did not work. They pushed at the ceiling, but that did not work either. Then they would literally stumble upon the solution (which was to step on a lever, which opened the door) and repeat that solution whenever they were in the box. The cats solved the problem by trial and error.

As you can imagine, this aimless, hit-or-miss approach is not the most efficient way to proceed. Yet I must confess that when I tinker with my computer and run into problems, I often start pecking furiously at the keyboard or probing and clicking with the mouse, hoping that something I do will effect a change. Sometimes this strategy proves enlightening. For example, Thomas Edison—the most prolific inventor in American history—tested thousands of lightbulb filaments before stumbling upon the one that worked. The problem is that this strategy often takes too long or fails completely. If possible, it's better to take a more systematic, planned approach.

Algorithms and Heuristics

An **algorithm** is a step-by-step procedure that is guaranteed, eventually, to produce a solution. When you were taught in school how to solve two-digit addition problems or long division, you learned an algorithm. An alternative is to use **heuristics,** mental shortcuts, or rules of thumb, that may or may not lead to the correct solution. The "*I* before *E*" heuristic for spelling *I-E* words is a good example. To appreciate the difference between algorithms and heuristics, consider the following anagram problem: Unscramble the letters *L K C C O* to make a word. One strategy is to use an algorithm—to try all possible combinations by systematically varying the letters in each position. Sooner or later, you will form the correct word. An alternative is to use a heuristic. For example, you could try the most familiar letter combinations. A common ending for English words is *CK* so you might start with this combination and arrive quickly at the solution: *CLOCK.*

If algorithms are guaranteed to produce solutions, why not use them all the time? The reason is that algorithms are not always available, and sometimes they take too much time to be practical. Thus, chess experts do not consider all the possible moves on the board, because there are simply too many of them. This strategy is fine for high-speed computers such as "Deep Blue"—an IBM computerized chess master equipped with 512 processors acting in parallel to analyze millions of positions and moves per second. But great players must rely instead on heuristics, such as "Get control of the center of the board."

trial and error A problem-solving strategy in which several solutions are attempted until one is found that works.

algorithm A systematic problem-solving strategy that is guaranteed to produce a solution.

heuristic A rule of thumb that allows one to make judgments that are quick but often in error.

In February 1996, Garry Kasparov, the world chess champion from Azerbaijan, defeated IBM's chess master, Deep Blue. In a rematch played in May 1997, however, Kasparov lost to an even more powerful version of Deep Blue. Equipped with 512 microprocessors working in parallel, IBM's chess master was able to analyze two hundred million positions per second.

Figure 7.6 Tower of Hanoi problem Your mission is to move three rings from peg A to peg C. You may move only the top ring on a peg and may not place a larger ring above a smaller one. See solution on page 263.

Some heuristics are general, in that they can be used to solve a wide range of problems. One important general heuristic is the **means-end analysis** (Newell & Simon, 1972). This involves breaking a larger problem into a series of subgoals. For example, let's say you are starting a new job Monday and have to get to work on time. You could solve this problem by driving your car to work, but your car needs repair. So you set a subgoal of getting your car repaired. But this might require other subgoals, such as finding a mechanic. For some problems, the nested subgoals can get quite complex and involved. In fact, unless people carefully evaluate whether each step brings them closer to the endpoint, it is possible to lose track of what part of the problem is actually being solved (Simon, 1975). The benefits of formulating subgoals can be seen in the *Tower of Hanoi problem,* shown in Figure 7.6.

Another powerful problem-solving heuristic is the use of **analogies.** If you have previously solved some problem that seems similar to a new one, you can use the old solution as a model. The trick is to recognize that the second problem resembles the first. By way of illustration, take a few minutes to try to solve the following "tumor-and-radiation problem" (Gick & Holyoak, 1980):

> Suppose you are a doctor faced with a patient who has a malignant tumor in his stomach. To operate on the patient is impossible, but unless the tumor is destroyed the patient will die. A certain kind of ray, at a sufficiently high intensity, can be used to destroy the tumor. Unfortunately, at this intensity the healthy tissue that the rays pass through on the way to the tumor will also be destroyed. At lower intensities, the rays are harmless to healthy tissue, but they will not affect the tumor. What type of procedure might be used to destroy the tumor using the rays without injuring healthy tissue?

means-end analysis A problem-solving heuristic that involves breaking down a larger problem into a series of subgoals.

analogy A problem-solving heuristic that involves using an old solution as a model for a new, similar problem.

Do you have the answer? If not, read the following "general-and-fortress" story:

> A small country was ruled from a strong fortress by a dictator. The fortress was in the middle of the country, surrounded by farms and villages. Many roads led outward from the fortress like spokes in a wheel. A rebel general vowed to capture the fortress. The general knew that an attack by his entire army would capture the fortress. He gathered his troops at the head of one of the roads, ready to attack the fortress. However, the general learned that the dictator had planted mines on each of the roads. The mines were set so that small bodies of men could pass over them safely, but any large force would detonate the mines. Not only would this blow up the road, but it would also destroy nearby villages. It seemed impossible to capture the fortress. But the the general devised a plan. He divided his army up into small groups and dispatched each group to the head of a different road. When all were ready he gave the signal, and each group marched down a different road. Each group continued down its road to the fortress, so that the entire army finally arrived together at the same time. In this way, the general captured the fortress and overthrew the dictator.

Solution to the Tower of Hanoi Problem: To complete this mission, it helps to break the task into subgoals. The first is to get ring 3 to the bottom of peg C (move ring 1 to peg C, ring 2 to peg B, and ring 1 from peg C to peg B; then put ring 3 at the bottom of peg C). Your second subgoal is to get ring 2 to peg C (move ring 1 to peg A and ring 2 to C). The third subgoal is now easy: just move ring 1 over to peg C—and you're finished.

Okay, now return to the radiation problem and try again. If you're still drawing a blank, here's a hint: Think of the general-and-fortress story as an analogy for the radiation-and-tumor problem. Look beneath the surface differences in the stories. Can you see the relevance of the general's strategy for the surgeon? The radiation solution is to use a low-intensity ray that can be aimed at the tumor from several directions. When all the rays reach the tumor, their effects will add up to that of a single high-intensity beam at the site of the tumor, and healthy tissue will not be destroyed. Demonstrating the usefulness of problem solving by analogy, Gick and Holyoak (1980) found that only 8 percent of naive subjects solved the radiation problem on their own, but among those who had first read the general-and-fortress story, the solution rate increased to 76 percent.

Analogical thinking plays a central role in science, where the heart has been likened to a pump, the brain to a computer, the eye to a camera, molecules to billiard balls, the telephone to an ear, and the spinning earth to a slowing toy top. Indeed, research shows that people are quicker to grasp and use new scientific concepts when these concepts are taught by analogy than when they are explained in literal terms (Donnelly & McDaniel, 1993). In general, the shorter the "mental leap" is between problems, the more effective is the analogy (Holyoak & Thagard, 1997).

[Drawing by Lorenz; © 1992 The New Yorker Magazine, Inc.]

"Now I see your problem—linear thought."

Insight When people struggle with a problem, they usually try to monitor their progress to evaluate whether they're closing in on a solution (Kotovsky et al., 1985). But have you ever puzzled over something, felt as if you were stumped, and then come up with the answer abruptly, out of the blue, as if a lightbulb flashed inside your head? Aha! If so, then you have experienced problem solving by **insight,** a process in which the solution pops to mind all of a sudden—and in which the problem solver doesn't realize the solution is coming and cannot describe what he or she was thinking at the time (Kaplan & Simon, 1990; Sternberg & Davidson, 1995).

Insight is an experience that seems to arise whenever people switch from one strategy to another, reframe the problem, remove a mental block, or identify an analogy from a prior experience (Simon, 1989). Some researchers claim that these apparent flashes of insight actually result from a gradual, step-by-step process—that sometimes we're just not aware of the progress we are making (Weisberg, 1992). Others find that certain types of tasks do seem to promote a special form of problem

insight A form of problem solving in which the solution seems to pop to mind all of a sudden.

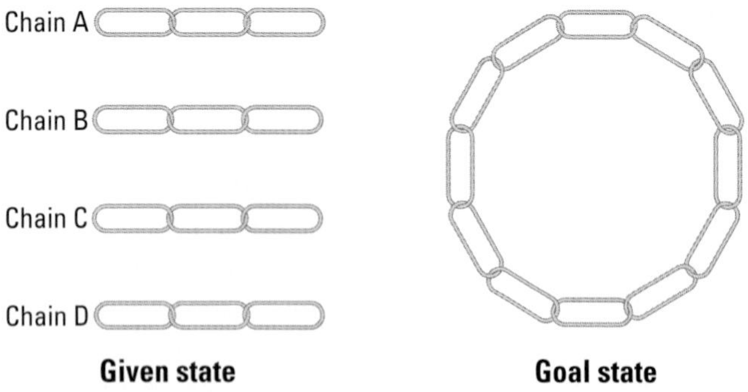

Figure 7.7 **The cheap-necklace problem** Make a necklace out of the four separate chains. It costs two cents to open a link and three cents to close a link. You must make your necklace for fifteen cents or less. The solution can be found in Figure 7.9 on page 267.

solving that has a sudden, all-or-none quality (Smith & Kounios, 1996). Is insight gradual but nonconscious, or is it truly sudden? It's hard to know for sure. Janet Metcalfe and David Wiebe (1987) had subjects work on different types of problems and periodically rate how "warm" they were getting on a seven-point scale. On multistep algebra problems, the ratings increased steadily as subjects neared a solution. On insight problems, however, the warmth ratings remained flat and low, then rose at the moment subjects encountered a solution. It's interesting that when people working on insight problems are asked to describe their thinking along the way, which brings the process into consciousness, their performance deteriorates (Schooler et al., 1993).

People often report that they tried unsuccessfully for hours to solve a problem and then, after taking a break, came back and it "clicked": An insight quickly converted into a solution. The improved ability to solve a problem after taking a break from it is called the incubation effect. One puzzle that psychologists have used to investigate incubation effects in the laboratory is the "cheap-necklace problem," shown in Figure 7.7. Try it for five minutes before reading on. Using this problem, J. Silveira (1971) tested three groups of subjects. All groups worked on the same task for a total of thirty minutes. One group worked without a break. After fifteen minutes, however, the second group took a half-hour break and the third group took a four-hour break. During these rest periods, subjects were kept busy with other activities that kept them from continuing to work on the necklace problem. The results provided strong evidence for incubation: Subjects who took a break were more likely to solve the problem than those who did not. In fact, the longer the interlude was, the better the performance. The practical implication of this effect is clear. Sometimes it helps to take a break while trying to solve problems that require a single critical insight—as in the cheap-necklace problem, where the key is to realize that you can't link all four chains (Anderson, 1990).

The history of science is filled with stories of discovery by insight. But is insight necessarily the product of great minds? Many psychologists believe that other animals too are capable of insight, not just of trial-and-error problem solving. Many years ago, Wolfgang Köhler (1925) claimed that a chimpanzee named Sultan displayed insight in problem solving. Köhler put bananas and a long stick outside the chimp's cage, both out of reach, and put a short stick inside the cage. Sultan poked at the banana with the short stick, but it was too short to reach the fruit. After trying repeatedly, he gave up, dropped the stick, and walked away. Then all of a sudden, Sultan jumped up, picked up the short stick, and used it to get the longer stick—which he used to get the banana. Did this episode reveal insight? Many researchers are skeptical of such a claim and suggest that the apparent insight may be no more than an accumulation of learned behaviors (Epstein et al., 1984). Yet others agree with Köhler. Sociobiologist Edward O. Wilson tells a Sultan-like story of a chimp trying to reach some leaves: "He sat and looked at the tree for a long time, and went over to a log. He dragged it over to the tree, propped it against the trunk, then stood back and charged his ramp. It's extremely difficult to explain that, other than to say the chimp was consciously thinking" (Begley & Ramo, 1993).

This brings us back to questions about animal cognition and whether problem solving is uniquely human. Do other animals have insight or use heuristics? Are they

"'Jeopardy!' is on."

capable of conscious thought? Many comparative psychologists (researchers who study and compare different species) are convinced that those who study thought and language have long underestimated the cognitive capabilities of nonhuman animals (Vauclair, 1996)—particularly the great apes (Russon et al., 1996). This issue is difficult to resolve and is currently the source of lively debate (Timberlake, 1993). As we'll see later in this chapter, there is tantalizing evidence to suggest that chimpanzees and other apes can learn to solve problems that require the use of abstract symbols. We will take a closer look at this research when we discuss attempts to teach language to nonhuman primates.

Figure 7.8(A) The nine-dot problem Connect all nine dots with four straight lines without lifting your pencil from the paper. The solution is revealed in Figure 7.10 (p. 267).

"Blind Spots" in Problem Solving

Using trial and error, algorithms, heuristics, and insight, people often exhibit a remarkable capacity to solve problems. As we have seen time and again, however, our competencies are often compromised by certain "blind spots." To appreciate some of these shortcomings, try the problems in Figure 7.8 before reading on. The solutions are revealed in the upcoming paragraphs and then illustrated on pages 267 and 268.

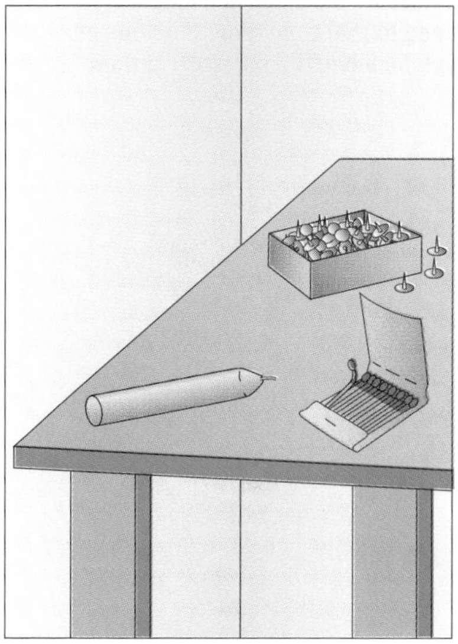

Figure 7.8(B) Duncker's candle problem Using just the objects shown, how could you mount the candle on a wall? The solution appears in Figure 7.11 (p. 268).

Representation Failures

The difficulty of the "nine-dot problem" in Figure 7.8(A) illustrates that failure often results from an incorrect problem representation. Even though the instructions say nothing about staying inside an imaginary square formed from the dots, almost everyone behaves as though the outside dots form a boundary that cannot be crossed (to understand why, think back to the gestalt principles of perceptual grouping in Chapter 3). If you don't mentally handicap yourself in this way, the solution is simple. But people do, which is what makes the problem

Problems	Jar A capacity	Jar B capacity	Jar C capacity	Desired quantity
1	21	127	3	100
2	14	163	25	99
3	18	43	10	5
4	9	42	6	21
5	20	59	4	31
6	23	49	3	20
7	15	39	3	18
8	28	76	3	25
9	18	48	4	14
10	14	36	8	6

Figure 7.8(C) Luchin's water-jar problem Try to solve the following ten problems. In each case, use Jars A, B, and C, with the capacities indicated, to pour out the desired quantities of water (*far-right column*). For example, if Jar A has a capacity of 27 cups, B has 20 cups, and C has 4 cups, you could measure out 50 cups of water by using the formula 2A − C, or 54 − 4.

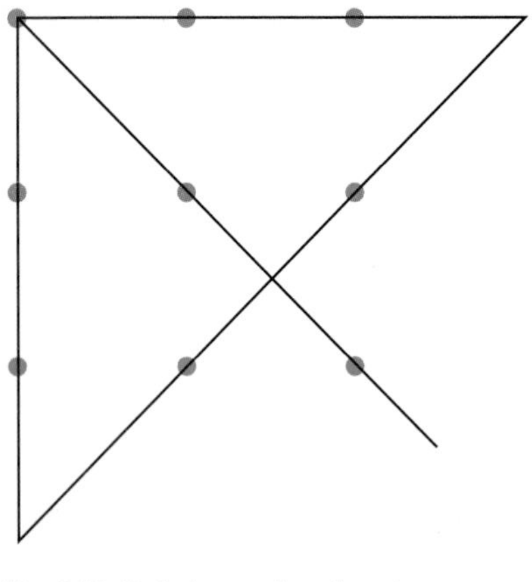

Fig. 7.10 Solution to the nine-dot problem To solve this problem, you need to realize that all four lines must extend beyond the square of dots.

so difficult. Is this tendency to represent problems narrowly limited to clever laboratory puzzles and brainteasers? Sadly, no. As we'll see in Chapter 16, many clinical psychologists find that people suffer needlessly because they conceptualize problems in ways that make them seem insurmountable (Beck, 1985; Ellis, 1962).

Functional Fixedness The "candle problem" in Figure 7.8(B) illustrates a more specific type of representation failure. The difficulty in this case is one of **functional fixedness,** a tendency to think of objects only in terms of their usual functions. In the candle problem, for example, you would struggle for as long as you see the matchbox as only a container, not as a possible shelf. A brick is a brick, but it can also be used as a paperweight. Finding new and creative solutions to practical problems often requires the kind of open-mindedness that enables us to see unusual uses for common objects (Sternberg & Lubart, 1991; Weisberg, 1986).

Mental Sets The "water-jar problem" in Figure 7.8(C) illustrates another related blind spot, the inability due to past experience to view the problem from a new perspective. If you haven't tried this one yet, please do, then come back. How was it? Were you able to solve the first water-jar problem? If so, then you figured out the algorithm: B (127) − A (21) − 2C (6) = 100. Chances are that you also found problems 2 through 7 easy and whizzed through them by using the same formula. But what about problems 8, 9, and 10, which required a new formula? If you're like most students, you probably struggled on these—even though the solution (A − C) is simple. Why? The first few problems lead people to form a **mental set,** a tendency to use a strategy that has worked in the past. As with the use of analogy to solve problems, mental sets are not all bad. After all, carrying over the B − A − 2C formula helped you with items 2 through 7. The drawback is that we often are slow to shed our mental sets when we need to. As I said, students tend to slow down on problems 8, 9, and 10—unless they work on these first, so that no mental set is formed. For an amusing look at mental sets in action, play hide-and-seek with young children, and you'll notice that they always go right back to the last place you hid.

The Confirmation Bias The nine-dot, candle, and water-jar problems are tricky not because they are intellectually demanding but because people tend to be overly rigid in their thinking. But there's more. Once we think we have a solution, we fall prey to the **confirmation bias,** the tendency to look only for evidence that will verify our beliefs—which can prevent us from realizing that we are in error. To demonstrate, Peter Wason (1960) gave students a three-number sequence, *2-4-6,* and challenged them to figure out the rule he had used to generate this set. How should they proceed? By making up their own sequences and asking the experimenter to indicate whether or not they fit the rule. Subjects were told they could test as many sequences as they wanted and to state the rule only if they felt certain that they knew it. The task was straightforward and the rule behind *2-4-6* was easy: any three increasing numbers. Yet out of twenty-nine subjects, only six discovered the correct rule without first seizing upon one that was incorrect. What happened was this: Subjects would start with an initial hypothesis (adding by 2s, even numbers, skipping numbers) and then search only for confirming evidence. Thinking that the rule was "adding by 2s," a subject might test *6-8-10, 50-52-54, 21-23-25,* and so on, yet never try disconfirming sets such as *6-8-4* or *3-2-1.* When all the sequences fit, the subject would proudly and with confidence announce the wrong rule.

functional fixedness The tendency to think of objects only in terms of their usual functions, a limitation that disrupts problem solving.

mental set The tendency to return to a problem-solving strategy that worked in the past.

confirmation bias The inclination to search only for evidence that will verify one's beliefs.

Belief Perseverance As noted, people search for evidence that verifies their beliefs. But what happens when we confront information that plainly contradicts our beliefs? Do we revise our views, as logic would dictate? Not necessarily. In a series of studies, Craig Anderson and his colleagues (1980) found that our beliefs are often highly resistant to change. For example, subjects read case studies suggesting that the best firefighters are either risk takers or cautious types. Next, subjects were asked to come up with a theory for the suggested link. The possibilities are easy to imagine: "He who hesitates is lost" supports risk taking, and "You have to look before you leap" supports caution. Finally, when the experiment was supposedly over, subjects were told that the information they had received was totally false, manufactured for the sake of the experiment. Did this discrediting evidence erase subjects' newly formed beliefs? No, it was too late. Many subjects exhibited **belief perseverance,** clinging to their initial beliefs even after those beliefs had been discredited. Though hardly rational, it seems that our beliefs often outlive the evidence from which they sprung.

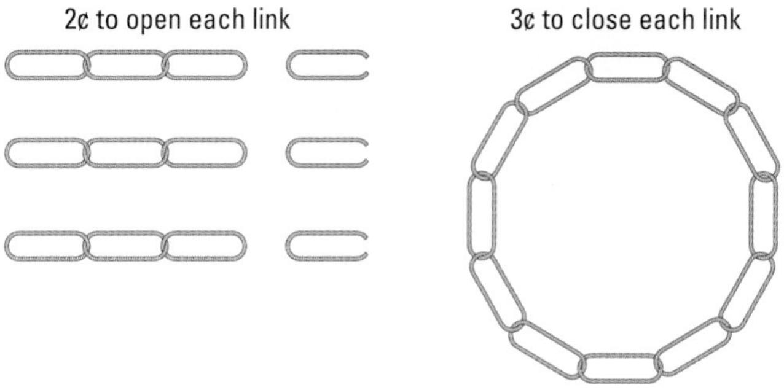

Figure 7.9 Solution to the cheap-necklace problem The key is to realize that you can't link all four chains. To solve the problem, open every link on one chain (this costs six cents), then use these open links to join the three remaining chains (which costs nine cents).

Many currently popular books on how to improve your problem-solving skills provide advice on how to eliminate blind spots (Bransford & Stein, 1984; Zechmeister & Johnson, 1992). We now know that people have to learn to be more flexible in the way they represent problems, the strategies they use, the way they evaluate their initial beliefs, and their responsiveness to discrediting information. At each stage, then, the key is to think flexibly and with an open mind.

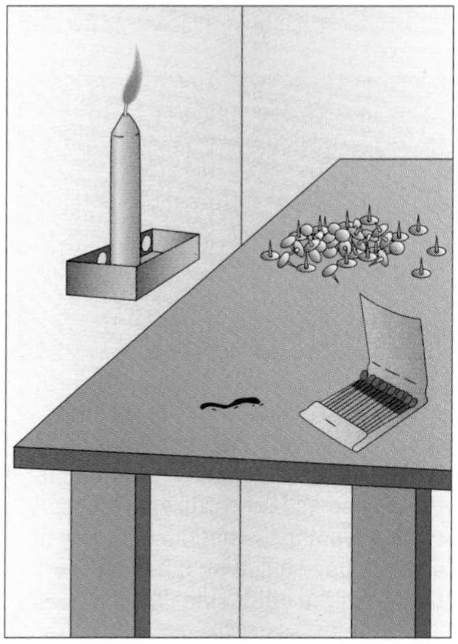

Figure 7.11 Solution to Duncker's candle problem To solve this problem, you need to realize that the box can be used not only as a container but also as a shelf.

Making Judgments

What is syllogistic reasoning, what's conditional reasoning, and how good are we at using these formal rules of logic? What are judgmental heuristics, and how do they illustrate that we often sacrifice accuracy in making speedy decisions? Why do so many people gamble against the odds, an irrational activity, and then persist in the face of defeat?

People have to make decisions every day. Occasionally we are faced with choices that have a major impact on the rest of our lives. Where should I go to school? Should I get married? Should I save my money, spend it, or invest it in stocks? We all like to think of ourselves as thoughtful and logical decision makers who weigh costs and benefits, calculate the probabilities, and act accordingly. But are we that logical, really? Researchers study human decision making in tasks ranging from formal logic to everyday reasoning. The results have given rise to some rather surprising discoveries about *Homo sapiens,* the "rational animal."

The Rules of Formal Logic

Throughout history, philosophers, psychologists, economists, and others have assumed that our natural way of thinking followed the laws of formal logic. One way to test this assumption is to examine the ways in which people solve strictly logical problems.

belief perseverance The tendency to cling to beliefs even after they have been discredited.

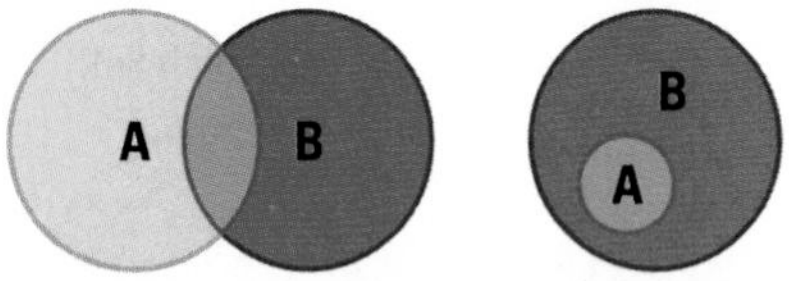

Figure 7.12 Different representations of the same premise "Some *A*s are *B*s."

Syllogistic Reasoning One aspect of formal logic that is studied extensively in psychology is syllogistic reasoning. A **syllogism** is a logical problem in which you are given premises that you must assume are true, then decide whether a certain conclusion can be drawn from these premises. For example, given the premises "All *A*s are *B*s" and "All *B*s are *C*s," is the conclusion "All *A*s are *C*s" a valid one? The answer is *yes*—given the premises, the conclusion must be true. Try the syllogisms in Table 7.2, and try to figure out why some seem so much harder to solve than others. For each set of premises, decide if the conclusion is valid. The answers appear below.

As a general rule, most people find syllogisms easier when they are stated concretely rather than in the abstract "All *A*s are *B*s" format. In fact, one strategy that people naturally use to solve abstract syllogisms is to rephrase them as concrete problems. The problem with this strategy is that it can lead us to make mistakes when we fail to see that there can be more than one way to represent a given premise. Consider the proposition that "Some *A*s are *B*s." The diagrams in Figure 7.12 can be used to make this syllogism more concrete. But note that although the left diagram seems more natural, the right one is also a valid way to show the premise because whenever it's true that "All *A*s are *B*s," it's also true that "Some *A*s are *B*s." After drawing conclusions, people often don't double-check to see if their conclusions would be valid for *all* the different ways of representing the premises (Johnson-Laird, 1983).

A second disadvantage of making syllogisms more concrete is illustrated by the last item in Table 7.2. It's easy to make a logical mistake on this type of problem precisely because the conclusion is true based on general world knowledge. But the actual truth of the matter has nothing to do with whether the conclusion follows logically from the premises. To be sure, some bananas are yellow, as stated in the sample item, but that conclusion does not follow logically from the premises that are provided.

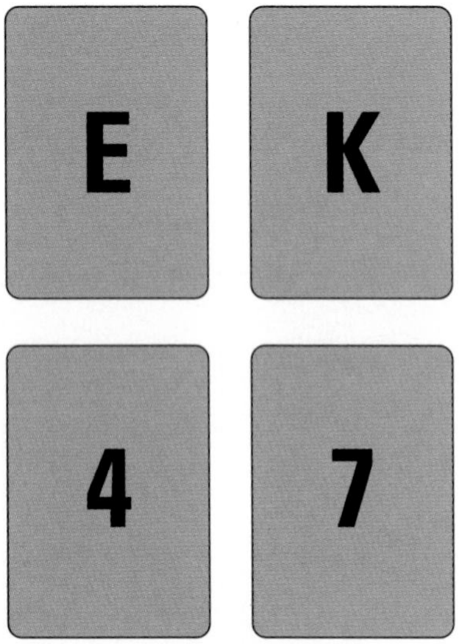

Figure 7.13 A conditional-reasoning problem Each of the four cards has a number on one side and a letter on the other. Using as few cards as necessary, test the hypothesis that if a card has a vowel on one side, then it has an even number on the other side (Wason, 1960).

Conditional Reasoning Another common type of problem derived from formal logic is that of *conditional reasoning,* which takes the form of "if-then" statements. To see what's involved in conditional reasoning, look at the problem shown in Figure 7.13. You're told that each of the four cards has a number on one side and a letter on the other. Your goal is to test the hypothesis that "*if* a card has a vowel on one side, *then* it has an even number on the other side." Using as few cards as necessary, which cards would you need to turn over in order to adequately test this hypothesis? Think about it. What's your answer? Most people realize that the *E* has to be turned over. But another card is needed as well. Is it the one with the 4 showing? No, this card doesn't really help. If there's a vowel on the other side, the

Table 7.2 Syllogism Problems

1. Some *A*s are *B*s. All *B*s are *C*s. Therefore, some *A*s are *C*s.	3. All robins are birds. All birds are animals. Therefore, all robins are animals.
2. All *A*s are *B*s. Some *B*s are *C*s. Therefore, some *A*s are *C*s.	4. All bananas are fruit. Some fruits are yellow. Therefore, some bananas are yellow.

Answers: (1) valid, (2) invalid, (3) valid, (4) invalid

syllogism A logical problem in which the goal is to determine the validity of a conclusion given two or more premises.

rule could still be invalidated by another card. If there's a consonant, the rule is not invalidated (the rule does not state that a card with a consonant cannot have an even number on the other side). The correct choices are *E* and *7*. A vowel on the other side of the 7 would invalidate the rule. In studies with college students, only 4 percent got the right answer. Most picked the *E* and the *4*, probing only for evidence that was consistent with their hypothesis (Wason, 1960). So if you missed it, you are not alone.

This manifestation of the confirmation bias appears in a wide range of reasoning problems. For example, Deanna Kuhn (1991) interviewed people as to how they would evaluate their beliefs on important real issues (such as the causes of criminal behavior and school failure) and found that very few subjects realized that to truly evaluate their beliefs, they would need to consider disconfirming evidence. Everyone is vulnerable—sometimes even motivated—to confirm their initial beliefs. Indeed, case studies in "pathological science" reveal that scientists have been known to test their pet theories in ways that do not allow for disconfirmation (Rousseau, 1992).

Is the confirmation bias an inevitable, fatal flaw in the way human beings reason? Patricia Cheng and her colleagues (1986) found that, compared to people with no formal training in logic, those who had completed a full-semester course in this discipline performed only 3 percent better. There is hope, however. Research shows that people perform well on conditional-reasoning tests using more familiar content. For instance, suppose you're trying to test this rule: "If a person is drinking beer, then he or she must be over twenty-one." In front of you are four cards, each with an age written on one side and what he or she is drinking written on the other. The four cards read *16, 25, cola,* and *beer.* Look at the problem presented in Figure 7.14. Now which cards would you turn over? In an actual experiment, 74 percent of the subjects chose *16* and *beer*—which is correct (Griggs & Cox, 1982). Why was there such vast improvement compared to the last experiment? It may be that because subjects are accustomed to thinking about drinking-age violations they were reminded in this case to search for disconfirming evidence.

What are the educational implications of this result? Can people be trained in the logic of conditional reasoning? To some extent, yes. But the key may be to teach this form of reasoning through the use of concrete problems, the way psychologists do—not through the presentation of abstract rules, as in philosophy. To test this hypothesis, Michael Morris and Richard Nisbett (1993) assessed the conditional-reasoning performance of first- and third-year graduate students enrolled in psychology or philosophy at Michigan, Chicago, and Brown universities. The results were quite striking. As shown in Figure 7.15, philosophy students did not improve from the first year to the third. But the psychology students performed 33 percent better in their third year of study than in their first. After being trained to conduct experiments that test causal hypotheses, the psychology students had learned how to reason in "if-then" terms.

Figure 7.14 A conditional-reasoning problem with familiar context Each of the four cards has an age on one side and a drink on the other. Using as few cards as necessary, test the hypothesis that if a person is drinking beer, then he or she must be over twenty-one.

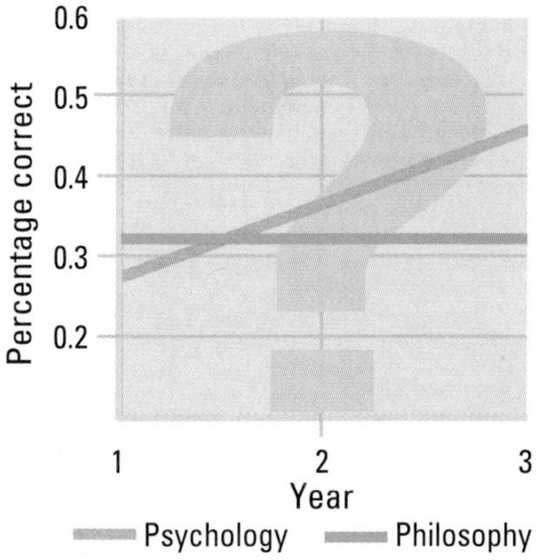

Figure 7.15 Can conditional reasoning be taught? In this study, graduate students in psychology and philosophy were tested for conditional reasoning. As shown, psychology students improved from their first to their third year but those in philosophy did not (Morris & Nisbett, 1993).

Biases in Judgment

Should I buy a Toyota 4-Runner or a Ford Taurus, an IBM PC or a Mac? Should women over forty have routine mammograms? Should you pour money into the stock market, or is it due for a fall? These are the kinds of decisions that people make every day—decisions that are based on intuitive judgments of probability, estimates we make of the likelihood of good and bad outcomes. How do we go about making these judgments? Do the decisions we make match those we *should* have made based on the actual, objective probabilities? In a series of studies,

Daniel Kahneman, Amos Tversky, and others (1982) have found that people consistently use two heuristics in making various judgments: representativeness and availability.

The Representativeness Heuristic A rule of thumb that people often use to make probability estimates is the **representativeness heuristic**—the tendency to judge the likelihood of an event's occurring by how typical it seems (Kahneman & Tversky, 1973). Like other heuristics, this one enables us to make quick judgments. With speed, however, comes bias and a possible loss of accuracy. For example, which sequence of boys (B) and girls (G) would you say is more likely to occur in a family with six children: (1) B,G,B,G,B,G; (2) B,B,B,G,G,G; or (3) G,B,B,G,G,B? In actuality, these sequences are all equally likely. Yet most people say that the third is more likely than the others because it looks typical of a random sequence. As we'll soon discuss (see the Intersection on irrational thinking in the gambling casino, pages 271–272), this use of the representativeness heuristic gives rise to a "gambler's fallacy" in games of chance.

The problem with this heuristic is that it often leads us to ignore numerical probabilities, or "base rates." Suppose I tell you that there's a group of thirty engineers and seventy lawyers. In that group, I randomly select a conservative man named Jack, who enjoys mathematical puzzles and has no interest in social or political issues. Question: Is Jack a lawyer or an engineer? When Kahneman and Tversky (1973) presented this item to subjects, most guessed that Jack was an engineer (because he seemed to fit the stereotyped image of an engineer)—even though he came from a group containing a 70 percent majority of lawyers. In this instance, representativeness overwhelmed the more predictive base rate.

The Availability Heuristic A second mental shortcut that people use is the **availability heuristic,** the tendency to estimate the likelihood of an event based on how easily instances of that event come to mind. To demonstrate, Tversky and Kahneman (1973) asked subjects to judge whether there are more words in English that begin with the letter *K* or the letter *T.* To answer this question, subjects tried to think of words that started with each letter. More words came to mind that started with *T,* so most subjects correctly chose *T* as the answer. In this case, the availability heuristic was useful. It sure beat counting up all the relevant words in the dictionary.

As demonstrated, the availability heuristic enables us to make judgments that are quick and easy. But often, these judgments are in error. For example, Tversky and Kahneman asked some subjects the following question: Which is more common, words that start with the letter *K* or words that contain *K* as the third letter? In actuality, the English language contains many more words with *K* as the third letter than as the first. Yet out of 152 subjects, 105 guessed it to be the other way around. The reason for this disparity is that it's easier to bring to mind words that start with *K,* so these are judged more common.

The letter-estimation bias may seem cute and harmless, but the availability heuristic can lead us astray in important ways—as when uncommon events pop easily to mind because they are very recent or highly emotional. One possible consequence concerns the perception of risk. Which is a more likely cause of death in the United States: being killed by falling airplane parts or being attacked by a shark? Shark attacks get more publicity, and most people say it is a more likely cause of death. Yet the odds of being struck by falling airplane parts are thirty times greater ("Death Odds," 1990). People who are asked to guess the major causes of death thus tend to overestimate the number of those who die in shootings, fires, floods,

representativeness heuristic A tendency to estimate the likelihood of an event in terms of how typical it seems.

availability heuristic A tendency to estimate the likelihood of an event in terms of how easily instances of it can be recalled.

THOUGHT AND LANGUAGE AND BUSINESS

Irrational Thinking in the Gambling Casino

"I hope to break even today," said one gambler to another. "Why is that?" "I really need the money." Anyone who has played poker for money, dropped coins into a slot machine, bet on a sports event, or bought lottery tickets knows how seductive gambling can be. Every year, people from all walks of life spend hard-earned money at casinos, racetracks, and off-track betting parlors and in state lotteries and numbers games. Americans spend hundreds of billions of dollars a year in legal and illegal gambling activities, and they predictably lose between 5 and 20 percent of that figure (Popkin, 1994).

Gambling is a truly puzzling phenomenon. Ordinarily, people do not like to take large financial risks. Offered a hypothetical choice between receiving a certain $1,000 or a 50:50 shot at $2,500, most people choose the smaller, guaranteed alternative (Kahneman & Tversky, 1984). So why do so many people gamble and persist in the face of defeat? There are different theories. From a cognitive perspective, there are three problems: (1) people harbor the illusion that they can exert control over chance events, (2) they do not completely understand the laws of probability, and (3) they come up with biased explanations for their wins and losses.

With the odds always favoring the house, casinos want to keep you gambling for long periods of time—and at a fast rate. Thus, the lighting is good, the air is cool, the stools have back supports, the drinks are free, beautiful women called "starters" are hired to attract the "high rollers," and blackjack dealers are required to deal 60–75 hands per hour.

In a series of experiments on the **illusion of control,** Ellen Langer (1975) found that people delude themselves into believing they can control the outcome in games of chance that mimic skill situations. When subjects cut cards against a competitor in a game of high-card, they bet more money when their opponent seemed nervous rather than confident. When subjects played a lottery, they were more reluctant to sell their tickets after choosing a number themselves than after getting an assigned number. This hardly seems rational. But don't many of us fall prey to these same illusions? Watch people playing slot machines, and you'll see that they try to influence their luck by moving from one machine to another with coins in hand. Or watch players throwing dice in craps, backgammon, or Monopoly, and you'll notice that they often roll hard for high numbers and soft for low numbers (Henslin, 1967).

The effects on gambling are clear. To exploit our tendency to infuse games of chance with an illusion of control, states provide an element of choice in their lotteries by having players pick number combinations themselves. Go to the racetrack, and you will find bettors sizing up the horses and studying the racing forms. In casinos, the dealers are instructed not to intimidate players by shuffling the cards in fancy ways. Why are people so easily fooled? According to Langer, we need to feel that we can control the important events in our lives. Additional research suggests that the more people need to win, the more deluded they become. In one study, for example, subjects took part in a random card drawing with a chance to win a McDonald's Big Mac hamburger. Those who were food-deprived and hungry at the time saw the task as more skill-based and were more confident of success than those who had just eaten (Biner et al., 1995). Thankfully, people think more critically and are less vulnerable when the stakes are high (Dunn & Wilson, 1990).

Gambling also stems from misguided notions about *probability* and the predictions people make about chance events (Wagenaar, 1988). Suppose you flipped a coin six times. Which sequence of heads (H) and tails (T) would you be most likely to get: HHHTTT or HTTHTH? When asked this question, most subjects pick the second alternative. In fact, the two patterns are equally likely. Now suppose you could purchase a lottery ticket containing six numbers out of forty. Would you rather have the numbers *4-33-29-10-2-16,* or *2-2-2-3-3-3?* Given a choice, most people prefer the first ticket over the second (Holtgraves & Skeel, 1992). Yet out of the 3,838,380 possible winning combinations, both are equally likely. In the Pennsylvania Daily Number game, a number between *000* and *999* is randomly drawn every day, and the payoff is always 500 to 1—regardless of how many winners there are. It is not possible to strategically influence one's chances. Yet a study of number selections showed that ticket purchasers shy away from numbers that have won in the recent past (Halpern & Deveraux, 1989). Why?

Kahneman and Tversky (1972) find that the *representativeness heuristic* leads people to falsely assume that any sequence of events, if the result of a truly random process, should "look" random. Since a large number of coin flips will produce roughly a 50:50 split, people expect this ratio to emerge even in a small sample of flips. This assumption gives rise to the *gambler's fallacy*—the belief that random processes are self-correcting so that temporary deviations in one direction will be matched by later deviations in the opposite direction. That's why, after a string of heads, people are likely to predict that the next coin will land on its tail or why, after a long run of red numbers on the roulette wheel, people rush to bet on black numbers. The gambler's fallacy is also the reason many slot-machine addicts say that a machine is "hot" if it has not surrendered a jackpot for a long period of time.

Another problem with the way we judge probabilities stems from the *availability heuristic,* the tendency to overestimate the likelihood of dramatic, memorable events (Tversky & Kahneman, 1973). Think about it. One reason people buy lottery tickets despite the dreadfully low odds of winning is that they are so influenced by the sight of multimillion-dollar winners on TV. The same is true of casinos. The last time I visited one, I had to fight the sense that everyone was coming up a winner. All around me, people were shrieking with joy, bells and sirens were blaring, lights were flashing, and coins were jingling loudly into metal coin trays. What about all those who were losing? They were invisible, a silent majority, nowhere to be seen or heard. If I didn't know any better, I would have thought that everyone was lucky except me. Winning was "available" and easy to overestimate.

The fact that we often bet money on the basis of defective prediction strategies explains part of the gambler's dilemma. But it doesn't explain why people persist after losing. To understand this problem, it is important to know that gamblers generate *biased explanations* for outcomes. Research shows that people are quick to take credit for success and to explain away failure. For example, Thomas Gilovich (1983) questioned subjects one week after they had bet on a series of pro football games. He found that although they accepted winning without scrutiny, they tended to cite fluke events to explain away losses—a fumble on the goal line, an injury to a key player, or a close call by the referee—all to suggest that victory was otherwise close at hand. Can this bias inspire persistent gambling? In basketball, the shot that circles the rim and falls out may bolster the belief that a player is hot, but it may also be used to maintain the belief that another player is cold. Likewise, according to Gilovich, the gambler's ace in the hole is to recall a point in time when he or she was winning and should have quit. We have all heard those regretful last words: "I was close; I could have won if..." Well, maybe next time.

---

terrorist bombings, accidents, and other dramatic events—and to underestimate the number of deaths caused by strokes, heart attacks, diabetes, and other mundane and less memorable events (Slovic et al., 1982). Similarly, research shows that the more often a foreign country is in the news, the more people say they know about it—and the higher are their estimates of its population (Brown & Siegler, 1992).

Another consequence of the availability heuristic is that people are influenced more by one vivid life story than by hard statistical facts. Have you ever wondered why so many people buy lottery tickets despite the low odds, or why so many travelers are afraid to fly even though they're more likely to perish in a car accident? These behaviors are symptomatic of the fact that people are relatively insensitive to numerical probabilities and, instead, are overly influenced by graphic and memorable

illusion of control The tendency for people to believe that they can control chance events that mimics skill situations.

events—such as the sight of a multimillion-dollar lottery winner rejoicing on TV or a photograph of bodies being pulled from the wreckage of a plane crash (Bar-Hillel, 1980). It may not be logical, but one memorable image is worth a thousand numbers.

Dramatic airline disasters, such as the 1996 midair explosion of TWA Flight 800, are so memorable that people overestimate the risks of flying. In fact, mile for mile, travelers are far more likely to die in a car crash than on a commercial flight.

Anchoring Effects Using the availability heuristic, people are heavily influenced in their judgments by the facts that are most available in memory—and they fail to make adjustments to compensate for that bias. A related phenomenon is the **anchoring effect,** the tendency to use one stimulus as an "anchor," or reference point, in judging a second stimulus. Imagine being asked, "What proportion of African nations are in the United Nations?" Think about it. What would be your estimate? Now suppose that before answering this question, the experimenter spun a roulette wheel marked with numbers from *1* to *100*. You think the outcome of the spin is random, but actually the wheel is rigged to stop either at *10* or at *65*. At that point, the experimenter asks, "Is the proportion of African nations in the United Nations above or below the wheel number? Then what, specifically, is your estimate?" The result of this procedure is that subjects vary their estimates according to the numerical reference point provided by the wheel number. Those for whom *10* was the initial anchor estimated that 25 percent of African nations were in the UN. Among those given *65* as an anchor, the estimate was 45 percent. Even though subjects assumed the wheel number to be arbitrary, it served as a starting point for their numerical estimates (Kahneman et al., 1982).

Additional studies have confirmed that anchoring effects are common and that numerical reference points can bias judgments of new events even when subjects are offered a prize to be accurate and even when they say afterward that they were not influenced by the anchor (Wilson et al., 1996). It's no wonder that fund-raisers typically precede their request for a donation by stating a high initial figure.

Framing Effects Overall, research shows that human beings have some powerful reasoning tools but that the process is flawed in serious ways. This theme repeats itself as we explore a topic that bridges thought and language. In a classic series of studies, Tversky and Kahneman (1981) found that decisions are shaped by the language used to describe a dilemma. This tendency to be influenced by the way an issue is worded, or "framed," is called the **framing effect.** To test for this effect, researchers present two versions of the same problem that are worded differently but are logically equivalent. According to reason, preferences should be unaffected by wording. But that's not what happens.

In one study, a vast majority of subjects thought condoms were effective in stopping AIDS when condoms were said to have a "95 percent success rate" but not when they were presented as having a "5 percent failure rate" (Linville et al., 1992). In a second study, consumers preferred ground beef that was labeled "75 percent lean" rather than "25 percent fat" (Levin & Gaeth, 1988). Framing effects such as these seem to indicate that human judgments are not always well reasoned—which is why we often make poor decisions that we later come to regret. But with people often having to make quick judgments on the basis of very little information, psychologists disagree on the extent of the problem (Payne et al., 1992). It's also helpful to know that people can be taught in college and other educational settings to reason in more logical ways (Kosonen & Winne, 1995; Lehman & Nisbett, 1990; Nisbett et al., 1987).

There is, finally, another lesson to be drawn from framing effects. At the beginning of this chapter, we briefly considered the relationship between thought and language. In that context, framing effects suggest that thinking may be shaped by

anchoring effect The tendency to use an initial value as an "anchor," or reference point, in making a new numerical estimate.

framing effect The biasing effects on decision making of the way in which a choice is worded, or "framed."

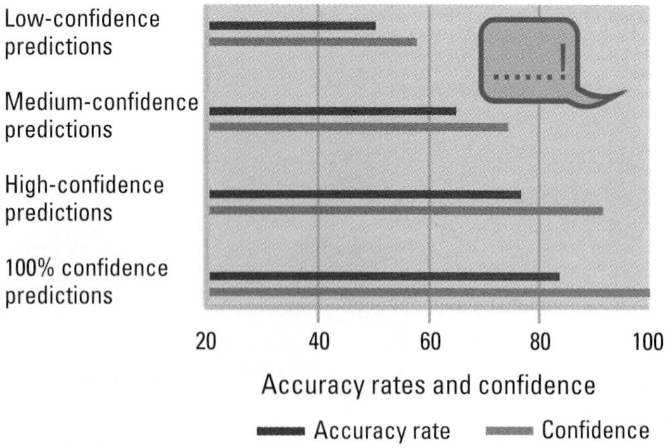

Figure 7.16 The overconfidence effect Students made 2,760 predictions about others that were later verified. Regardless of whether confidence was low, medium, high, or 100 percent, confidence levels consistently exceeded accuracy rates.

language. We'll take up this issue again, after surveying what is known about the nature of language.

Overconfidence Sometimes our judgments are correct; sometimes they are subject to bias. Nobody's perfect. But are we sufficiently aware of our own limitations? Many years ago, Baruch Fischhoff and his colleagues (1977) had people answer hundreds of general-knowledge questions and estimate the odds that each answer was correct. Consistently, the subjects were overly confident. Other studies soon revealed the same pattern. Regardless of whether people are given factual questions ("Which river is longer, the Amazon or the Nile?") or asked to predict future world events ("Who will win the Superbowl?"), confidence exceeds performance (Kahneman & Tversky, 1996).

In a study that illustrates this point, David Dunning and others (1990) asked students to make judgments of a more social nature—to predict how a target person would react in different situations. Some of the subjects made predictions about a fellow student whom they had just met and interviewed, and others made predictions about their roommates. In both cases, the subjects reported their confidence in each prediction, and accuracy was determined by the responses of the target persons themselves. The results were clear: Regardless of whether they judged a stranger or their own roommate, subjects consistently overestimated the accuracy of their predictions. These results are illustrated in Figure 7.16.

People even overestimate their ability to predict their own future behavior. When ninety-eight first-year students made 3,800 self-predictions about the upcoming academic year—predictions that were later verified ("Will you decide on a major?" "Will you have a steady boy/girlfriend?")—they estimated that they would be accurate 82 percent of the time but actually had an accuracy rate of only 68 percent (Vallone et al., 1990). In later chapters, we will see that, as a general rule, self-confidence is a virtue that promotes health, happiness, and success. The key is to avoid becoming so overconfident that we take foolish risks and make hasty decisions—as people often do when they place bets in the gambling casino.

Language

With 4,000 to 6,000 languages spoken, why is it often said that all humans speak in the same tongue? What are the universal properties of all languages, and why don't even the most elaborate animal communication systems qualify? Can apes be taught language, and why is this notion so controversial?

A colleague's friend, who is a psychology professor, had a frightening experience a few years ago. While in his office talking to a graduate student, he found himself suddenly unable to recall words that are basic to his work, like *data* and *experiment*. These words were not on the tip of his tongue, waiting to be retrieved.

Instead, he was suffering from anomia, an inability to recall familiar words. While in this state, he knew what concepts he wanted to express but could not come up with the right labels. Fortunately, the experience lasted for only forty-five minutes. It was caused by a temporary reduction of blood flow to part of the left hemisphere. With surgery, doctors were able to prevent a relapse. If the anomia had resulted from brain damage—due to a stroke, for example—the effects would have been more lasting.

Two lessons relevant to the study of language can be drawn from this episode (Ashcraft, 1993). First, anomia suggests that there is an important distinction between concepts and the words used to represent them. Even when our semantic networks are intact, we can lose the connections between concepts and their verbal representations. The implication is that thought and language are separate. The second lesson is that in trying to understand the psychology of language, it helps to study people with language disturbances, or **aphasias** (Caplan, 1992). Anomia is one type of aphasia. Two other types are Broca's aphasia and Wernicke's aphasia. A person with Broca's aphasia can comprehend language but has difficulty producing fluent speech. In contrast, a person with Wernicke's aphasia can speak fluently but suffers in comprehension.

People who lose part of the capacity for language find the experience devastating. This is not terribly surprising. Language is essential to social living and is the defining milestone in human evolution. Indeed, human beings acquired the capacity for speech despite some of the physical limitations that came with this capacity. For example, the human vocal tract is ideal for the production of many sounds, but the arrangement of the larynx and tongue make it unnervingly easy for humans, compared to other animals, to choke while swallowing their food (Lieberman, 1984). Cognitive scientist Steven Pinker (1994) argues that the ability to learn, speak, and understand language is thus a powerful human instinct—"so tightly woven into the human experience that it is scarcely possible to imagine life without it" (p. 17).

Arguing that the capacity for language is innate, Steven Pinker (1994) states, "Language is no more a cultural invention than is upright posture" (p. 18).

Communication in the Animal World

Among humans, language is a primary means of communication. Other animal species have complex forms of communication as well. Ants send chemical signals secreted from glands in order to share information about food and enemies with other members of the colony. When honeybees discover a source of nectar, they return to the hive and communicate its location to the other worker bees through an intricate dance that signals both direction and distance. Male songbirds of various species sing in the spring to attract female mates and also to warn other males to stay away from their territory to avoid a fight. Dolphins talk to each other at great depths of the ocean by making a combination of clicking, whistling, and barking sounds. Vervet monkeys grunt quietly in relaxed social situations but give off loud alarm calls that differ in sound according to whether the predator they see is a snake, eagle, or leopard.

There is no doubt that animals communicate in ways that benefit their survival. When the honeybee locates nectar and performs its dance, other bees leave the hive and buzz straight to the source—even if the one that discovered it is detained (von Frisch, 1974). And when a monkey produces an alarm call, other members of the group take action. Among East African vervets, for example, a distinctive snake alarm leads others in the group to stand tall and peer into the grass, an eagle call leads them to look up and duck into bushes, and a leopard call leads them to run

aphasia The loss or impairment of language abilities following brain damage, often to the left hemisphere.

The spring song of the male bluebird and the howling of the desert coyote are two of the many adaptive forms of communication found in the animal world.

up into a tree (Cheney & Seyfarth, 1992). There are many other marvelous examples of adaptations that serve species well. So why do some scientists claim that "language" is a uniquely human capacity? To answer this question, we need to know more about what language is and the properties that are used to define it.

Characteristics of Human Language

According to *The Universal Almanac* of 1997, there are between 4,000 and 6,000 languages worldwide, to say nothing of the different dialects within each language. When all the dialects are taken into account, tens of thousands of variations can be distinguished. It's amazing how different the many languages seem on the surface. To appreciate this point, consider the principal languages, ranked in order of usage in the world's population: Chinese, English, Hindi, Spanish, Russian, Arabic, Malay, Bengali, Portuguese, French, German, Japanese, Urdu, and Javanese. Despite the differences, however, linguists are quick to note that from a Martian's perspective, all humans speak a single tongue. The reason is that all languages share three universal properties: semanticity, generativity, and displacement.

semanticity The property of language that accounts for the communication of meaning.

morphemes In language, the smallest units that carry meaning (e.g., prefixes, root words, suffixes).

phonemes The basic, distinct sounds of a spoken language.

Semanticity

Semanticity refers to the fact that there are separate units in a language and that these units have *meaning*. The smallest unit that carries meaning is called a **morpheme.** Every word has one or more morphemes. Simple words like *dog, run,* and *think* contain one. The word *unthinkable* has three morphemes—the prefix *un-,* the root word *think,* and the suffix *-able*—and each adds to the total meaning of the word.

In all spoken languages, morphemes are composed of **phonemes,** the basic *sounds* of a language. Each separate sound you hear when you pronounce the word *unthinkable* is one phoneme. English has twenty-six letters, but forty to forty-five

At a produce market in Beijing, this man and woman converse in Chinese—the most widely spoken language in the world.

phonemes. The word *tip* has three phonemes: *t, i,* and *p*. So do the words *ship* (*sh, i,* and *p*) and *chip* (*ch, i,* and *p*). Linguists estimate that human beings are physiologically capable of producing one hundred basic sounds. No one language uses all of them, however. Most contain between twenty and eighty phonemes. English speakers say *s* and *z* differently. In Spanish, they're one and the same. As a result of such differences in vocal experience, people sometimes struggle to pronounce the phonemes of other languages. For example, many Americans struggle to roll the German *r* or cough up the guttural *ch* sound of Arabic.

The average American high-school graduate knows about 45,000 different words, and the average college graduate has a vocabulary that is nearly twice that size (Miller, 1991). It is really quite remarkable that human beings are able to master a full language vocabulary so well, and so quickly, given that most word sounds are unrelated to meaning. There is no reason why a cat is called a *c-a-t* as opposed to a *d-o-g*. It just happens to be that way. There are some exceptions to this rule, as some words do resemble the sounds they signify (examples include the words *bang* and *crack*). Incidentally, some animal communication signals also seem arbitrary. For example, the East African vervet monkey makes a "chutter" sound to signify the presence of snakes, a two-syllable cough for eagles, and a loud bark for leopards (Cheney & Seyfarth, 1992).

Generativity A second property of language is **generativity,** the capacity to use a finite number of words and rules for combining words to produce an infinite variety of novel expressions. Think about it. When I listened to the news one recent night, I heard the network commentator say, "Well, Tom, it's been quite a night, with both the President's State of the Union and the verdict in the O.J. Simpson trial." It was a pretty mundane sentence. But I'll bet no one in history had ever uttered it before.

generativity The property of language that accounts for the capacity to use a limited number of words to produce an infinite variety of expressions.

Generativity gives language virtually unlimited flexibility as a communication system. There are two features of human language that enable this flexibility: iteration and recursion. *Iteration* means that a phrase can always be added to the end of a sentence in order to form an entirely new sentence. Through iteration, you could go from the sentence "I like psychology" to "I like psychology this semester" to "I like psychology this semester, thanks to the professor," and so on. *Recursion* refers to a related fact of language: One expression can always be inserted inside another. This makes possible the construction of long, embedded sentences.

People usually understand iterative and recursive sentences quite easily. But they can become mentally taxing. If you have ever sat on a jury, you know exactly what I mean. At the end of every trial, the judge instructs the jury on the law that should guide their decision making. Jurors are ordinary folks, not law-school graduates. Yet the instructions they receive are often so filled with iterations and recursions that they're practically impossible to understand. The following instruction on the term *negligence,* commonly used by judges, illustrates the point:

> One test that is helpful in determining whether or not a person was negligent is to ask and answer whether or not, if a person of ordinary prudence had been in the same situation and possessed the same knowledge, he would have foreseen or anticipated that someone might have been injured by or as a result of his action or inaction (Kassin & Wrightsman, 1988, p. 150).

Most English sentences contain twenty words or fewer. According to the Guinness Book of World Records, *however, the longest sentence ever printed contains 1,300 words.*

If language is so generative that we can produce limitless numbers of novel sentences, how are we able to comprehend each other as competently as we do? The key to managing generativity is **syntax,** rules of grammar that govern how words can be arranged in a sentence. Expressions are not random strings of unrelated sounds but rather words that are combined in familiar and orderly ways. Every language has a unique syntax. For example, adjectives usually come *before* the noun in English (*white wine*) but *after* the noun in Spanish (*vino blanca*). We'll see in Chapter 10 that children learn to speak correctly by the age of five, and they do so without explicit instruction. Hardly anyone can explain the rules of grammar, yet most of us can instantly spot a statement that violates these rules. Which us brings another point to...

This brings us to another point about the generativity of language: Any one thought can be expressed in different ways. Regardless of whether I say, "The Bulls won the championship," "The championship was won by the Bulls," or "What the Bulls won was the championship," you grasp the underlying meaning. Linguist Noam Chomsky (1957) explained this phenomenon by making a distinction between the deep structure and surface structure of language. The *deep structure* refers to the underlying meaning of a statement, apart from the particular way that it is expressed. The *surface structure* consists of the words that are actually used to communicate that meaning. According to Chomsky, syntax provides us with a set of "transformational" rules for how to (1) put meaning into words when we speak and (2) derive meaning from words when we are spoken to (see Figure 7.17).

According to the Arts and Humanities Citation Index, *Noam Chomsky is the eighth most cited writer in all the humanities—behind only Marx, Lenin, Shakespeare, the Bible, Aristotle, Plato, and Freud. (He's the only living member of this group.)*

Some transformations are easier to process than others. For example, Daniel Slobin (1966) asked people to read either active sentences ("The dog is chasing the cat") or passive sentences ("The cat is being chased by the dog") and to decide which of two pictures (a dog chasing a cat or a cat chasing a dog) depicted the sentence. He found that both children and adults were faster at choosing the correct picture when the sentence was active. Apparently, passively constructed sentences require additional transformations, and therefore take more time, to get to the deep

syntax Rules of grammar that govern the arrangement of words in a sentence.

structure. The nature of the rules of transformation are not completely understood, and psychologists disagree over how such rules are implemented in the brain (Pinker, 1994; Rumelhart & McClelland, 1986). Still, the evidence suggests that we are on the right track in considering syntax to be separate from, but interacting with, meaning.

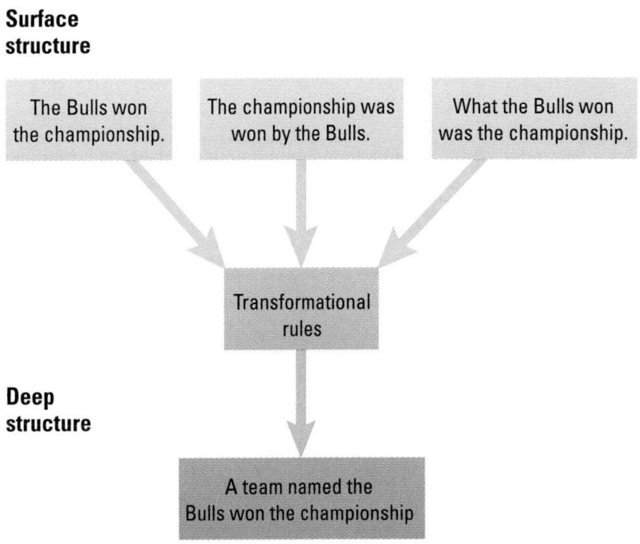

Figure 7.17 Relationship between deep structure and surface structure According to Chomsky, syntax provides a set of rules for transforming meaning (the underlying deep structure) into words (surface structure), and vice versa. As shown, transformational rules enable us to express the same idea in different ways.

Displacement A third property of language is displacement. **Displacement** refers to the fact that language can be used to communicate about things that are not in our immediate surroundings, matters that extend beyond the limits of the here-and-now. Thus, we reminisce about the good old days, we talk about our hopes and dreams for the future, we gossip about others behind their backs, and we discuss abstract ideas concerning God, politics, social justice, and love.

As a means of communication, language is a social activity—and displacement enables us to tell others what we're thinking, how we're feeling, or what we plan to do next. These are complex messages, however, and social interaction is just that, a two-way interaction. To converse with others effectively, therefore, we need more tools than just an extensive vocabulary and an arcane knowledge of the rules of grammar. We must also have a sense of the *pragmatics,* or social context, of language and an understanding of how to use it (Hilton, 1995; Kumon-Nakamura et al., 1995). In the words of Herbert Clark (1985), "Language is a social instrument. When we talk, we direct our words not to the air but to other people" (p. 179). Accordingly, says Clark, intricate rules guide the way speakers and listeners position themselves physically from each other, take turns in conversation, and communicate through the face, voice, body, and other nonverbal channels. We also tailor what we say to suit our audience and the situation we're in. People tend to take language pragmatics for granted. But tension frequently arises when these pragmatics break down—as when natives of very different cultures neglect to realize that the person they're trying to communicate with does not know their local expressions, jargon, and buzzwords (Axtell, 1993). In *You Just Don't Understand,* sociolinguist Deborah Tannen (1990) claims that conflicts between men and women often arise because of gender differences in their communication style, or pragmatics.

To illustrate the importance of pragmatics, consider the story of an early attempt to use computers to translate text from one language to another. After programming a computer to convert material from English to Russian, researchers gave the computer the task of decoding "The spirit is willing, but the flesh is weak." As the story goes, the Russian translation came out "The vodka is fine, but the meat is tasteless." So much for machines. Without pragmatic knowledge, ironic or metaphoric expressions are likely to be interpreted in rather bizarre ways (Simpson, 1989).

Can Animals Learn Language?

Philosophers and scientists have long regarded the capacity for language and abstract thought as uniquely human—the dividing line between us and other animals. Is this still considered to be true, or has a new breed of comparative

displacement The property of language that accounts for the capacity to communicate about matters that are not in the here-and-now.

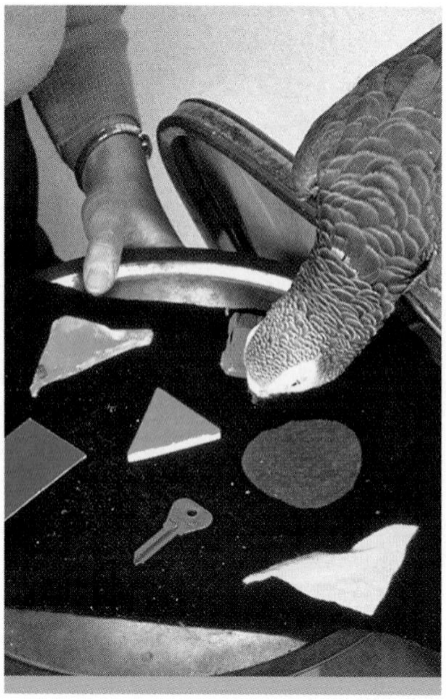

Alex, the African gray parrot, prepares to answer the question "What toy is blue and triangular?"

psychologists studying the once-taboo topic of animal thinking and awareness (Griffin, 1992; Ristau, 1991; Wasserman, 1993) discovered something new?

The Talking Parrot At center stage in this emerging area are research projects aimed at teaching rudimentary language to nonhuman animals. In one such project, Irene Pepperberg (1991) spent nearly twenty years teaching English to Alex, a one-pound African gray parrot. Everyone knows that these birds can "parrot" what people say, but do they understand the words that they use? Pepperberg makes a compelling case. She'll pick up an object from a crowded tray and ask, "What toy?" In response, Alex will name the object ("block") and respond at an 80 percent level of accuracy to questions about its color ("red"), shape ("square"), and substance ("wood"). Overall, Alex can use seventy-one words to name more than thirty objects, seven colors, five shapes, five numbers, actions, and materials. More often than not, he can also tell whether an object is the same as or different from, or bigger or smaller than, something else. He can even count how many items there are in a collection of items ranging from one to six (Pepperberg, 1994).

To bring Alex to this level of competence, Pepperberg had two human trainers vocally and physically interact with the various objects. With Alex watching, one would point to an object and ask a question about it. The other, serving as a model, would then give a programmed answer. If incorrect, the trainer would scold the model and remove the object from view. If the answer was correct, the model was praised and rewarded with the object. The learning process is thus a highly social experience that involves making eye contact with the parrot and pointing to the object while making reference to it. In training sessions with two new gray parrots, Pepperberg and McLaughlin (1996) found that social interaction—specifically, eye contact—was necessary for learning.

The Bottle-nosed Dolphins In Hawaii, Louis Herman and his colleagues (1993) have been studying the language capabilities of two bottle-nosed dolphins, Phoenix and Akeakamai. In this project, researchers communicate with one dolphin through the use of hand gestures and with the other dolphin through electronic whistlelike sounds transmitted through an underwater speaker system. In both cases, the distinct gestures or sounds refer to objects that are in the tank, the relationships between objects, actions to be taken, and location. The behavior of these sea mammals is astonishing in many ways. For example, when given commands consisting of two- to five-word sentences such as "Right water left Frisbee fetch"—which means "Take the Frisbee on your left to the stream of water on your right"—the dolphins perform to specification. They are even responsive to changes in syntax. The dolphins were trained in a system in which modifiers precede objects ("left Frisbee") and objects precede actions ("Frisbee fetch"). So when a command violates these rules of grammar, they do not obey. Just how impressive are these dolphins? "If you accept that semantics and syntax are core attributes of human language," says Herman, "then we have shown that dolphins also account for these two features within the limits of this language" (Linden, 1993, p. 58).

What do these projects tell us about the capacity of animals for language? Many animal-cognition researchers believe they are shattering old assumptions and breaking new ground. In contrast, skeptics make a convincing claim that these studies

"Although humans make sounds with their mouths and occasionally look at each other, there is no solid evidence that they actually communicate with each other."

show little more than mimicry and rote learning—like rats pressing a food bar in a Skinner box. Before addressing the controversy, however, let's first examine the most impressive evidence for the claim—evidence derived from our closest animal relatives, the great apes.

The Great Apes By today's standards, early attempts to teach language to apes were misguided. In 1933, psychologists Winthrop and Luella Kellogg raised a baby chimpanzee alongside their own son and tried to treat them in the same way. Their son learned to coo, babble, and speak on schedule; the chimp did not. A similar attempt was later made by Cathy Hayes (1951), who found that her chimp could recognize pictures, categorize objects, and imitate behaviors but could not speak more than a few rudimentary words. After six years of intensive training, the only words the chimp could say were *cup, up, mama,* and *papa.* Conclusion: Apes do not have the cognitive capacity for language.

The problem with these studies is that chimps may not have the vocal musculature for uttering human phonemes, but is speech a necessary criterion for language? Of course not. What about the symbols on this page, the characters found in other alphabets, the printed characters in braille that enable blind people to read, and the sign languages used by those who are deaf? To overcome the vocalization constraint, psychologists had to take creative new approaches, and they did. David Premack (1971) taught a chimp named Sarah to communicate by placing colored plastic chips, symbolizing words, on a magnetic board. Duane Rumbaugh (1977) then taught a chimp named Lana to communicate by pressing keys on a specially designed computer. Some of the more impressive projects involved the use of American Sign Language (ASL). Allen and Beatrice Gardner (1969) taught sign language to Washoe and four other chimps. Within four years, Washoe had a vocabulary of

Kanzi, the chimpanzee with the most advanced language skills, can "talk" by making hand signals and by pointing to symbols on a special board.

132 words and the ability to combine signs to form simple sentences. In fact, Washoe and her friends communicated in sign language—and she even taught her adopted young son 68 different signs (Fouts et al., 1989). Also using sign language, Herbert Terrace (1986) trained a chimp he called Nim Chimpsky (after linguist Noam Chomsky), and Francine Patterson and Eugene Linden (1981) trained a gorilla named Koko, whose 600-word vocabulary is the largest recorded so far.

Combining the various techniques, Sue Savage-Rumbaugh (1993) and her colleagues taught a young pygmy chimp named Kanzi to talk by making hand signals, pointing to geometric symbols on a laminated board, and punching these symbols on a keyboard. Kanzi also understands spoken English. What sets this project apart from the others is that Kanzi learned the language the way human children do: not by explicit instruction but by mere exposure. The researchers had trained Kanzi's mother, and he learned by watching. As Savage-Rumbaugh put it, "If Kanzi could learn without instruction, I wondered, why teach?" (Linden, 1993, p. 57).

The Controversy The feats of Sarah, Lana, Washoe, Nim, Koko, Kanzi, and others are impressive, even to the critics. Clearly, these are smart animals capable of learning. But is what they learned "language"? Some say yes; others say no. What do *you* think? To address this question, let's stop for a moment and focus on whether these evolutionary relatives of ours show the properties of semanticity, generativity, and displacement in their "language" behavior.

Semanticity Just about everyone agrees that the various language apes satisfy this criterion. With vocabularies ranging from 130 to 600 words, these apes can produce words for concrete objects (*me, chair*), action verbs (*tickle, eat*), and even adjectives (*big, happy*). And they may know more than simple rote associations between signs or symbols and objects. Sherman, a chimp trained by Savage-Rumbaugh, pointed to the symbol "food" when shown a real banana or the symbol for banana. Koko the gorilla signed "finger bracelet" to describe a ring and "eye hat" to describe a mask (Patterson & Linden, 1981). And Kanzi, the chimpanzee with the most advanced skills, reacted appropriately to slightly different requests, such as "Show me the light," "Bring me the light," and "Turn the light on" (Savage-Rumbaugh, 1990).

Generativity Can the apes combine words in lawful ways to produce novel expressions? Some researchers find that their apes do not distinguish—and perhaps cannot distinguish—between word combinations based on how they are ordered (Terrace, 1986). But others claim that their apes do use syntax to combine words they have never heard before. Syntax? Yes, that's the claim. When Washoe wanted to be tickled, she would sign "You tickle Washoe." When she wanted to do the tickling, it was "Washoe tickle you" (Gardner & Gardner, 1978). Kanzi may also understand sentences he never heard before. Once, with his back to the speaker, Kanzi heard "Jeanie hid the pine needles in her shirt." He then turned around, walked up to Jeanie, and searched her shirt (Savage-Rumbaugh, 1990).

Displacement The most demanding criterion for language is displacement, the use of words to talk about matters that are not in the immediate surroundings. People do it all the time, but what about the language apes? Florence Patterson believes that Koko the gorilla used signs to make statements about past events and to express feelings—such as sadness over the death of her pet kitten (Patterson & Linden, 1981). Savage-Rumbaugh (1990) reports that Kanzi also refers to past events. When a trainer asked Kanzi about a wound on his body, he replied, "Matata hurt"—presumably to say that Matata, his mother, had bitten him more than an hour earlier. These types of stories are not common, but they have captured the imagination.

Conclusion The evidence is tantalizing, but skeptics insist that it's open to interpretation. Herbert Terrace (1985) argues that many of the "spontaneous" signs may simply be imitations of or conditioned responses to subtle cues provided by the trainers. Further, he notes, researchers who work with the apes sometimes lose their objectivity and see in an animal's behavior what they are hoping to see—like children seeing pictures in the clouds.

Recently, Savage-Rumbaugh and her colleagues (1993) compared Kanzi's comprehension abilities to those of a two-year-old girl named Alia. In Chapter 10, we'll see that children all over the world develop quickly the ability to form sounds, words, phrases, and finally sentences. Clearly, no ape can *produce* language the way a normal human child can, but how much do they *know?* Research with aphasia patients indicates that language *production* and *comprehension* are based in different parts of the brain, and research with toddlers indicates that they understand more than they're able to say, so there is reason to believe that this is an important distinction to make. In an extensive series of tests, which took nine months to complete, Kanzi and Alia were compared for their responses to 660 commands that were made in spoken English. The sentences were new to both subjects, they were structured in several different ways, and they often combined objects in ways that had never been encountered before ("Put the melon in the potty," "Go get the carrot in the microwave"). To ensure that the subjects could not pick up subtle clues from the experimenters' nonverbal behavior, the commands were given by one experimenter over an intercom, and each subject's behavior was recorded by a second experimenter from behind a one-way mirror. As it turned out, Kanzi responded correctly to 74 percent of the sentences, Alia to 65 percent. Both exhibited comprehension of spoken language, semantics, and syntax. It appears that Kanzi, and presumably other language apes as well, know far more than they can tell. Table 7.3

Table 7.3 Kanzi's Knowledge of English

SENTENCE	KANZI'S RESPONSE	SCORING
"Throw the orange to Rose."	Kanzi picks up the orange, turns, and hands it to Rose.	PC
"Make the snake bite the doggie."	He picks up the toy snake and puts it on top of the toy dog.	C
"Make the doggie bite the snake."	He picks up the toy dog and puts it on top of the snake.	C
"Can you pour the ice water in the potty?"	He picks up the bowl of ice water, heads to the potty, and carefully pours it in.	C
"Take the telephone to the colony room."	He goes to the colony room, but takes nothing with him.	PC
"Put the raisins in the yogurt."	He pours the yogurt on the raisins.	N
"Put the monster mask on your head."	He drops the orange he is eating into the monster mask and puts it on his head.	C
"Give the lighter and the shoe to Rose"	He hands Rose the lighter, then points to some food in a bowl that he would like to eat.	PC
"Hide the toy gorilla, hide him."	He tries to push the toy gorilla under the fence.	C

presents a sample of the 660 requests made to Kanzi. Words and syntax were varied, and comprehension was measured by the correctness of his behavioral response, where C = correct, PC = partially correct, and N = incorrect (Savage-Rumbaugh et al., 1993).

So what are we to conclude? It is clear that apes can be taught words and can understand sentences in which these words are combined according to rules of grammar. It is equally clear, however, that the apes have a small vocabulary and a simple syntax compared to that found in young children. There's also no hard evidence to suggest that they can talk about abstract matters, such as whether humans can master language.

A recent *New York Times* article about this debate reveals the extent of the disagreement (Johnson, 1995). As a result of the research, it's clear that many scientists believe that the bright line separating "us" and "them" is not as bright as was once thought. Thus, in response to those who maintain that Kanzi's feats do not meet the criteria for language, philosopher Stuart Shanker complains that "linguists keep moving the goal post." For other scientists, nothing has changed. Steven Pinker said, "In my mind this kind of research is more analogous to the bears in the Moscow circus who are trained to ride unicycles." Equally adamant, Noam Chomsky likened the ape language experiments to trying to teach people to flap their arms and fly. "Humans can fly about 30 feet—that's what they do in the Olympics. Is that flying?" At this point, it is safest to conclude that what these apes have learned is a "protolanguage"—a form of communication that is cruder and more rudimentary than ours. Again, what do *you* think?

The Relationship between Thought and Language

Everyone assumes that thought gives rise to language, but is the reverse sequence also true? Do words we speak determine, constrain, or shape the way we conceptualize the world? In this regard, what is the impact of using sexist language—and what about the use of euphemisms? Finally, what is "critical thinking," and how can it be put into action?

This chapter has shown that thought and language are separate but interrelated cognitive activities. Having now examined them separately, we are faced with the question "What is the nature of their interrelationship?"

The Linguistic-Relativity Hypothesis

The traditional, intuitive position is that language is a tool for expressing thought, that thought → language. Consistent with this view, child-development researchers often find that young children understand concepts before they have the words to explain them (Flavell et al., 1993). But what about the reverse sequence, that language → thought? Does language have the power to shape thought? In the fifth century BCE, Herodotus, a Greek historian, argued that Greeks and Egyptians thought differently because the Greeks wrote from left to right and Egyptians from right to left. Inspired by anthropologist Edward Sapir, Benjamin Lee Whorf (1956), a self-educated linguist, theo-

> *"The mystery of language was revealed to me...Everything had a name, and each name gave birth to a new thought."*
>
> — HELEN KELLER

rized that the language we speak—the words, syntax, and so on—shapes the way we conceptualize the world. This notion, that our thoughts are "relative" to our linguistic heritage, is known as the **linguistic-relativity hypothesis.**

In an article entitled "Eskimo Words for Snow," anthropologist Laura Martin (1986) debunked the myth that the Eskimo people have 400 words for snow. Where did this myth come from? In 1911, Franz Boas said there were 4 words. Whorf expanded the count to 7 and implied there were more. His article was then cited in popular books, and in the same way that rumors spread, the number grew with each successive telling of the story. The result, said linguist Geoffrey Pullum (1991), was "The great Eskimo vocabulary hoax."

Whorf's hypothesis gave rise to a profound prediction: that people of different cultures must think in different ways (Lucy, 1992). To illustrate, Whorf pointed to cultural differences in the use of words to represent reality. He noted, for example, that although English has only one word for *snow,* Eskimos have several words and that this enables them to make distinctions that others may miss between "falling snow, snow on the ground, snow packed hard like ice, slushy snow, wind-driven flying snow—whatever the situation may be" (p. 216). Even grammar shapes thought, claimed Whorf. For example, he compared English to the language of the Hopis. In English, you can use the same numerical modifier for units of time ("five days") as for concrete objects ("five pebbles"). In the Hopi language, by contrast, different numerical modifiers are used in each case. Whorf argued that this feature causes the speakers of each language to perceive time differently.

Evaluating the linguistic-relativity hypothesis is not easy because people who speak different languages differ in other ways as well. Many bilingual people claim that Whorf is right, citing as personal evidence the odd sense that they think differently in each language—and sometimes get "lost in translation" (Hoffman, 1989; Wierzbicka, 1985). However, there are flaws in both the theory and the research. First, even if members of two cultures did think differently, who's to say that the difference in their language came first? Second, Eskimos may have several words for snow, but does that mean they think about snow differently? Besides, people from other regions of North America distinguish between slush, fresh powder, packed powder, hail, wet snow, and the "loose granular" substance often found on ski slopes. The same is true of color. Eleanor Rosch (1973) studied the Dani, an aboriginal people living in Papua New Guinea. Compared to English, which has eleven basic color words, the Dani language has only two basic color words, one for light hues and one for dark. Can Dani speakers make fine discriminations among colors? Yes. They recognize differences among colors of the same name the way non-Eskimos distinguish between types of snow.

Skiers make distinctions between fresh powder, packed powder, loose granular, and other types of snow.

Today, nobody believes that language *determines* thought the way genes determine a person's height. But most psychologists do agree with a less radical claim: that language *influences* the way we think (Bloom, 1981; Hardin & Banaji, 1993; Hunt & Agnoli, 1991; Lucy, 1992). The experiment described at the start of this chapter—in which estimates of automobile speeds were influenced by the wording of the speed question (Loftus & Palmer, 1974)—clearly illustrates this point. Many others do as well. In one study, researchers showed subjects line drawings and varied the label that accompanied each one (see Figure 7.18). Afterward, subjects redrew these figures from memory in ways that were distorted by the labels (Carmichael et al., 1932). In a second study, subjects were presented with pictures of faces or color chips, and half were asked to describe them. Those who had put what they saw into words later had more difficulty recognizing the original faces and colors. Did

linguistic-relativity hypothesis The hypothesis that language determines, or at least influences, the way we think.

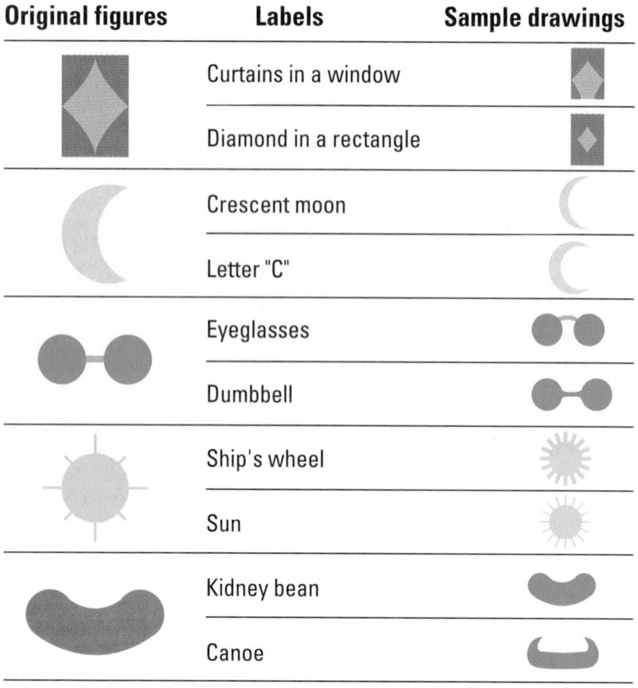

Figure 7.18 Words that distort memory for images Subjects who saw figures like those shown (*left*) later redrew these figures from memory in ways that fit the different labels they had been given (*right*).

language in this case disrupt thought? Yes, according to the investigators, "some things are better left unsaid" (Schooler & Engstler-Schooler, 1990).

Bringing linguistic relativity back to the cultural domain, Curt Hoffman and his colleagues (1986) studied bilingual Chinese-English speakers. These investigators presented descriptions of fictional characters whose personalities could be summarized easily by a single label in either Chinese or English but not in both. For example, English has the stereotypic term *artistic* for someone who paints, lives an unconventional lifestyle, and is imaginative, moody, and intense (the Chinese language has a word for people who are talented in art, but this same word implies nothing about temperament or lifestyle). In contrast, Chinese has the term *shi gu* to describe someone who is worldly, experienced, socially skilled, devoted to family, and somewhat reserved (English does not have one word for this particular collection of traits). Does having an economical term for a type of person make it easier to process certain types of information about others? By random assignment, some of the bilingual subjects took the experiment in English, others took it in Chinese. Consistent with the linguistic-relativity hypothesis, subjects formed quicker, more stereotyped impressions of artistic types when they "thought" in English and of *shi gu* types when they "thought" in Chinese.

If language can influence thought, then words are tools that can be used to socialize our children, sell products, mold public opinion, and stir the masses. People in power are aware of this connection, so they choose their words carefully. As colorfully documented by William Lutz (1989), the result is "doublespeak"—language that is designed to mislead, conceal, inflate, confuse, and distort meaning. Thus, we are told that the new tax is just a "user's fee," that acid rain is "poorly buffered precipitation," that a recession is "negative economic growth," that a bomb is a "vertically deployed antipersonnel device," that civilian war deaths are "collateral damage," and that plastic handbags are made of "genuine imitation leather."

Psychological Impact of Sexist Language

During the 1993–1994 academic year, Williams College celebrated its bicentennial and rewrote its catalog. Despite 200 years of tradition, the term *freshman* was replaced by *first-year student*. In that same year, controversy erupted at the University of Massachusetts over whether to keep or change the name of its sports teams, called the Minutemen (they kept it). In both cases, the existing terms were labeled sexist for using the generic masculine form.

Whatever the political arguments, the psychological question is: "Does sexist language influence the way we think about men and women?" What do you think? Is the term *mail carrier* rather than *mailman* silly and awkward, or does the change help break down gender stereotypes? Does it seem harmless or sexist to talk about "the evolution of *man*," our "fore*fathers*," "*brother*hood," and the "chair*man* of the board"? And what about the generic use of the masculine pronoun *he* to refer to all human beings? Is it okay to say that "a doctor must be trained if *he* is to be competent?" Drawing on the linguistic-relativity hypothesis, many people feel strongly about this issue.

For psychologists, the task is to determine whether the use of generic masculine nouns and pronouns triggers images of men to the exclusion of women. Consistently, the results of this research support the hypothesis that *man, he,* and other masculine words, even when used generically, lead people to think of men. In one study, for example, male and female college students were asked to make up stories based on a topic sentence: "In a large co-ed institution, the average student will feel isolated in ____ courses." Into the blank, the researchers inserted the pronoun *his, his or her,* or *their.* Did the pronoun in the topic sentence make a difference? Yes, when *his* rather than a neutral term was used, 65 percent of the stories written were about men (Moulton et al., 1978). Similar results have been found in both adults and school-age children (Hamilton, 1988; McConnell & Fazio, 1996; Switzer, 1990).

Table 7.4 Guidelines for Nonsexist Language

COMMON SEXIST TERMS	NONSEXIST ALTERNATIVES
Man, mankind	People, humanity, human beings
Manpower	Work force, personnel
Freshman	First-year student
Chairman	Head, chair, chairperson
Foreman	Supervisor
Policeman	Police officer
He, his, him	He or she, his or her, him or her, *or* they, their, them
Mothering	Parenting, nurturing, caregiving
Female doctor	Doctor
Male nurse	Nurse

In a study with unsettling implications, John Briere and Cheryl Lanktree (1983) had one group of college students read a passage from a 1972 version of the American Psychological Association's statement of ethical standards (the statement has since been revised). Part of the passage read: "The psychologist believes in the dignity and worth of the individual human being. He is committed to increasing man's understanding of himself and others." Another group of students read the same passage, but rewritten in gender-neutral language. Subjects in both groups were asked to rate the attractiveness of a career in psychology for males and females. The result: Those given the original wording rated a career in psychology as less attractive for women than did subjects given the neutral wording. Evidently, the use of generic masculine terms is seen as exclusive, not inclusive, of women. Some alternatives to common sexist terms are presented in Table 7.4.

Whorf's original hypothesis—that we can think only in terms provided for in language—was undoubtedly overstated. But this should not blind us to the fact that language does make it easier to conceptualize the world in some ways rather than others. The use of sexist words is one practical implication of linguistic relativity, but there are other implications, too. In the global village, translating ideas from one language to another is tricky and sometimes results in misunderstanding. We need to recognize that the people of the world do not just speak differently but also interpret events through different lenses. Certainly more research is needed to explore this link between language and thought and what it means for intercultural relations.

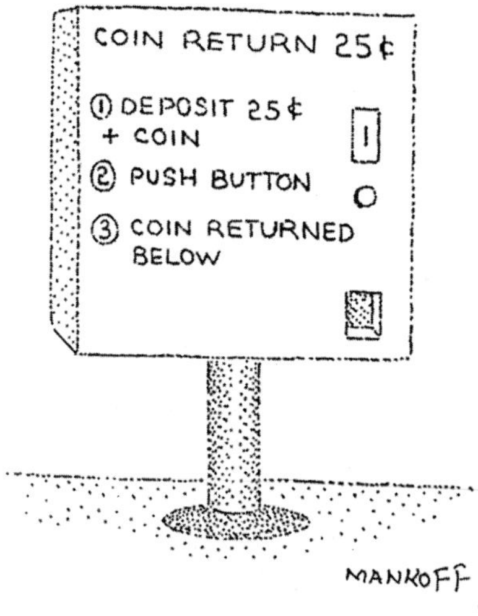

Con artists prosper from people who do not think critically.

Learning to Think Critically

Psychologists who study thought and language—like those who study learning and memory—have come to realize that people are complex, "two-headed" creatures, competent in some ways, flawed in others. Often we solve difficult problems

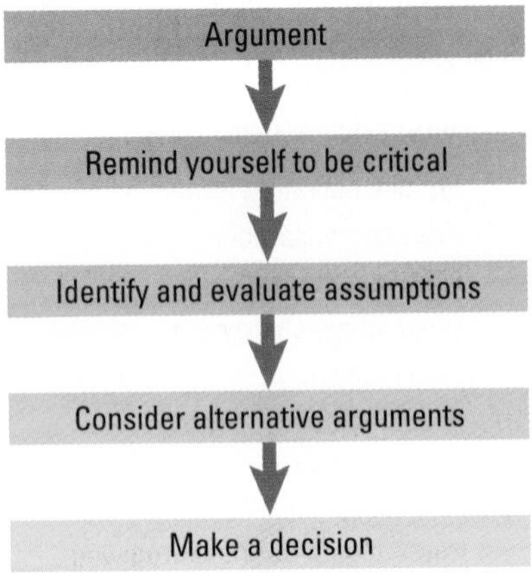

Figure 7.19 Steps in critical thinking

through trial and error, algorithms, heuristics, and a great capacity for creative insight. Yet often we get stuck mentally and fail to find obvious solutions because of functional fixedness, mental sets, and confirmation biases that keep us from fully testing out our ideas. The same dual portrait characterizes the way people make decisions. Sometimes, we're capable of performing feats of formal logic, as in problems involving syllogistic and conditional reasoning. Yet often we put our minds on "autopilot" and allow ourselves to be misled by availability, representativeness, anchoring effects, framing effects, and other heuristics. Then there's language. Despite recent successes in teaching apes to communicate, it is clear that the human capacity for language—whether measured by semanticity, generativity, or displacement—is impressive and unmatched. Yet it is also clear that words can be used to shape, and sometimes distort, the way we think. People are complicated creatures, both competent and flawed at the same time.

The good news is that we have the capacity to improve on the way we think and, therefore, on our ability to adapt to changing circumstances. Earlier, we saw that even when we feel we're stumped on a problem, it is possible to find the insight we need by representing it in a different way, opening our minds to alternative approaches, or perhaps just taking a break. We also saw that people can be taught to reason in more logical ways. There are many ways for us to maximize the use of our cognitive abilities.

The keys to success can be summarized by the term **critical thinking.** Critical thinking means solving problems and making decisions through a careful evaluation of evidence. When faced with important issues, forget old rules of thumb. Scrutinize what others say, consider their motives and emotions, probe beneath the surface of words, and consider the logic of the arguments. And if you can, don't rush to judgment; take your time. Thinking critically about arguments that others make, or that you make to yourself, can improve the quality of your decision making (Kuhn, 1991). See Figure 7.19 for a summary of the steps involved in critical thinking.

The first step is to adopt an attitude of healthy skepticism. Most of us are not in the habit of probing for logical flaws in arguments, especially in the claims we make to ourselves—as shown by the research on the confirmation bias. So thinking critically requires conscious effort. The next step is to identify the assumptions that are quietly made in an argument and consider whether or not they should be challenged. Sometimes a speaker's assumptions are clear from his or her use of facts. But people often present as "facts" mere assumptions that have not been verified. It's also important to avoid being too heavily influenced by smooth talking and jargon. A set of arguments may sound compelling and leave you nodding your head, but are they, really? Next, open your mind, step out of your "mental set," and try to imagine and evaluate alternative arguments. Is it possible that these alternatives are better than the ones being proposed? This step is especially hard when you're trying to imagine alternatives to your own assertions (Kuhn, 1991; Zechmeister & Johnson, 1992). Still, with practice it can be done.

> *"Many people would sooner die than think. In fact they do."*
>
> — BERTRAND RUSSELL

Critical thinking is as much an attitude as it is a skill. As you learn new material in psychology and in other courses, stop to think about the assumptions being made and evaluate the logic and plausibility of the material. Remember: You can't decide if you believe an argument until you understand it.

critical thinking The process of solving problems and making decisions through a careful evaluation of evidence.

Summary and Key Terms

People are both rational and irrational at the same time. Why is this so?

Concepts

Research shows that when a **concept** is activated in a person's mind, other related concepts in the semantic network are primed and emerge more readily from memory. **Prototypes,** concepts that seem "typical" of a particular category because they have most of its defining properties, come most readily to mind and have the strongest influence on our judgments.

Solving Problems

When we cannot find a solution by retrieving the answer from memory, we go through three steps: representing the problem, generating possible solutions, and evaluating those solutions.

Representing the Problem

Representing the problem often involves activating concepts from our semantic memory. It can also involve mental **images** of visual information and intuitive **mental models** of how things work. Our mental models, though useful, are sometimes inaccurate.

Generating Solutions

Once we have represented a problem, we generally choose from four basic problem-solving strategies: trial and error, algorithms and heuristics, and insight. **Trial and error** entails trying various solutions until one works. In contrast, an **algorithm** is a step-by-step procedure guaranteed to produce a solution eventually. **Heuristics** are rules of thumb that lead to quicker but not always accurate solutions. One general heuristic is **means-end analysis,** the breaking down of a problem into subgoals. Another is the use of **analogies,** which involve taking an old solution as a model for a new problem. Sometimes, in a flash of **insight,** a solution pops to mind. In long problem-solving sessions, people often exhibit the incubation effect, whereby sudden insight occurs after they take a break.

"Blind Spots" in Problem Solving

Our "blind spots" in problem solving can result from a number of factors. A problem may be represented incorrectly. Or we may fall into **functional fixedness,** thinking of objects only in terms of their usual functions. A **mental set,** taking us back to a strategy that worked in the past, can also be a hindrance. **Confirmation biases** dispose us to look only for evidence that supports our intial beliefs. And **belief perseverance** leads us to stick to our beliefs even when they have been discredited.

Making Judgments

Studies of decision making have brought further discoveries about the rationality of human beings.

The Rules of Formal Logic

In solving logical **syllogisms,** people often restate the problem in concrete terms to make it easier, but doing so can cause mistakes. In conditional-reasoning problems, people often err because of the confirmation bias.

Biases in Judgment

In making everyday decisions, we consistently rely on judgmental heuristics. The **representativeness heuristic** leads us to judge an event's likelihood by its apparent typicality, so that we ignore numerical probabilities. The **availability heuristic** is the tendency for estimates of event likelihood to be influenced by how easily instances come to mind. The **anchoring effect** is the tendency for an initial value to serve as a reference point in making a new judgment. And studies of the **framing effect** demonstrate that decisions can be biased by the way an issue is worded. Despite the various biases, people are consistently overconfident about their judgment abilities.

Gambling is an irrational but popular activity. There are many explanations for why people gamble, including the **illusion of control,** the tendency for people to believe that they can control chance situations that mimic skill situations, and various heuristics that produce misconceptions about the laws of probability.

Language

Studies of language disturbances known as **aphasias** shed light on the distinction between thought and language. People with anomia, for instance, can remember concepts but forget the corresponding verbal labels.

Communication in the Animal World

Animals such as honeybees and dolphins communicate in ways that are crucial to their survival. Yet scientists have maintained that "language" itself is uniquely human.

Characteristics of Human Language

All languages share the properties of semanticity, generativity, and displacement. **Semanticity** refers to the fact that language has separate units of meaning. The smallest meaningful units are **morphemes.** In all spoken languages, morphemes are made up of basic sounds called **phonemes.**

Through the property of **generativity,** language can turn a finite number of words into an infinite variety of expressions using the processes of iteration and recursion. **Syntax,** the formal grammar, provides the rules for transforming the deep structure of a statement into various possible surface structures.

Finally, all languages are capable of **displacement,** or communication about things beyond the here-and-now. Such communication also involves pragmatics, our knowledge of the social context of language.

Can Animals Learn Language?

Animals as different as parrots, dolphins, and apes have been trained to exhibit some features of language. In experiments, apes have clearly met the semanticity criterion and they may at times exhibit generativity, but there is little hard evidence for displacement. Thus, there is controversy about whether the apes are producing language per se.

The Relationship between Thought and Language

It is assumed that thought gives rise to language, but does language also shape thought? What is the relationship between these cognitive activities?

The Linguistic-Relativity Hypothesis

Going beyond the traditional view that thought shapes language, Whorf's **linguistic-relativity hypothesis** predicts that language can shape the way we think. Some research indicates that people with different cultures do think differently, but investigators disagree about the interpretation. Today, research suggests that language influences but does not completely determine thought.

Psychological Impact of Sexist Language

Consistent with the linguistic-relativity hypothesis, research indicates that sexist language influences the way children and adults conceptualize the roles of men and women.

Learning to Think Critically

Human thought and language are impressive, but they are also prone to illogic and distortion. Through careful evaluation of evidence, **critical thinking** can help us improve our problem solving and decision making. Thinking critically involves having a skeptical attitude, probing underlying assumptions, and considering alternative arguments.

In the Field Resources

Books

Gilovich, T. (1991). *How we know what isn't so.* New York: Free Press.

This book describes many irrational beliefs that people hold—and, more importantly, why they hold them.

Pinker, S. (1994). *The language instinct.* New York: Morrow.

Written by a cognitive neuroscientist, this engaging and witty book is destined to become a classic on human language—and on what all languages have in common.

Internet

On-line dictionaries (http://www.bucknell.edu/~rbeard/diction.html)

Provides dictionaries to many languages of the world as well as specialized dictionaries for medical, legal, banking, computing, and other terms.

WWW Sites for Experimental Psychology (http://www.psychologie.unibonn.de/aalgm/ links.htm#mue)

Contains links to demonstrations and various sites relevant to thinking and problem solving.

Journals and Periodicals

Cognitive Psychology
Journal of Experimental Psychology: General
Psychological Science
Memory and Cognition
Journal of Experimental Psychology: Learning, Memory, and Cognition

8 Motivation

What's Your Prediction?

Motivating people at work

The situation The year was 1927. Calvin Coolidge was president, Babe Ruth hit sixty home runs, Charles Lindbergh flew across the Atlantic for the first time, and the American economy seemed sound, though it would soon become depressed. Just outside Chicago, the Hawthorne plant of the Western Electric Company employed close to 30,000 men and women in the manufacture of telephones, wires, cables, and office equipment. As in other large companies, management wanted to boost the motivation, morale, and productivity of its employees. The bottom line was important.

At first, the Industrial Relations Branch of Western Electric thought that they could make workers at the plant more productive by altering the illumination levels in their factory. Proceeding in logical fashion, they increased the lighting for one group of workers in a special *test room,* kept the same lighting in a *control room,* and compared the effects on their productivity. Western Electric then brought in a team of experts to vary other conditions in the factory. Over the next five years, groups of employees from various departments were selected to do their work in a test room where, at different times, they were given additional rest periods, coffee breaks, a free midmorning lunch, shorter workdays, shorter weeks, a new location, overtime payments, personal financial incentives, dimmer lights, or just a different method of payment. At one point, the researchers even went back and merely reinstated the original prestudy conditions inside the test room.

Make a prediction The researchers involved in this project wanted to know how to increase the motivation and productivity of workers, as measured by their hourly output. Using existing performance levels at the plant as a basis for comparison, they asked what changes in the workplace would have a positive impact. Consider the conditions listed below and check off those that, in your opinion, increased worker productivity.

Brighter lighting	______
Dimmer lighting	______
Two 5-minute rest periods	______
1-hour-shorter workday	______
$\frac{1}{2}$-day-shorter week	______
15-minute rest period + free lunch	______
Financial incentives	______
Reinstating original conditions	______

The results If you thought that adding financial incentives boosted worker productivity, you were right. This change was accompanied by a 12.6 percent increase in hourly output. If you thought that a shorter workday or a shorter workweek or a free lunch had positive effects, you were right again. Brighter lighting? Yes. Dimmer lighting? Yes again. In fact, productivity rates increased no matter what the researchers did—even when they dimmed the lights and even when they merely reinstated the original prestudy conditions. So the correct prediction was to check off *all* conditions.

What does it all mean? The Hawthorne project, described in a book entitled *Management and the Worker* (Roethlisberger & Dickson, 1939), has had a profound influence on the study of motivation in the workplace. At first, the researchers were puzzled and discouraged. With positive effects being observed among all test-room workers (even when the original pretest conditions were in place), it seemed that the project had failed. Think for a moment about the results, however, and you'll see why these studies are important. With striking consistency, workers became more motivated and more productive not because of the specific changes made but because they had been singled out for special assignment. Workers assigned to the test rooms knew they were being studied, and they enjoyed the added attention. This phenomenon, known as the **Hawthorne effect,** laid a foundation for the study of behavior in the workplace and the realization that people are motivated not only by money and other objective states but also by their own needs and social relationships. The Hawthorne plant no longer exists, but the study conducted there has helped psychologists to understand an important practical side of human motivation.

When the news story broke, in April 1996, I was dumbfounded. Seven-year-old Jessica Dubroff was at the controls of a single-engine Cessna, trying to become the youngest pilot ever to cross the United States. Sitting in a red booster seat so that she could see over the dashboard, and using "extenders" so that she could reach the controls, Jessica departed from California with her father and flight instructor aboard. But in an icy rainstorm in Wyoming, the plane crashed into a suburban driveway, and all three were killed. Afterward, everyone who talked about the incident asked the same questions: Why was a seven-year-old girl determined to break a flying record while her peers were happily playing with toys? And what motivated her parents, who not only allowed Jessica to fly but encouraged her to take the risk?

Just three months later in Atlanta, another remarkable story unfolded in front of a worldwide TV audience. Eighteen-year-old Kerri Strug could clinch the first Olympic gold medal ever for the United States women's gymnastics team if she could land a strong vault. She would have two opportunities, so the odds looked good, but on her first vault she fell hard and sprained her left ankle. Visibly hurt, she hobbled back to the starting line, paused, took a deep breath, and sprinted to her final vault. With millions watching, Strug catapulted into the air, landed per-

Hawthorne effect The finding that workers who were put in a special experimental room became more productive regardless of what changes were made.

Seven-year-old Jessica Dubroff gives the "thumbs up" at the controls of a single-engine plane. After she was killed in a crash while at the controls, everyone wondered: What motivated her desire to fly?

fectly on one foot, and earned a gold medal score of 9.712. She winced in pain and fell to the mat. In a moment that no one would soon forget, viewers wondered: What propelled this young athlete? Did she attempt the second jump on her own or at the urging of her coach? Was she driven by a burning desire for personal fame and glory, or was she dedicated instead to her team and country?

To answer the questions raised about Jessica Dubroff and Kerri Strug, and about other human endeavors that result in triumph or defeat, we need to understand the psychology of human motivation. **Motivation** is an inner state that *energizes* an individual toward the fulfillment of a *goal*. In this chapter, we will explore various domains of human motivation, including hunger and eating; sex and sexuality; the social needs for affiliation, intimacy, achievement, and power; and behavior in the workplace. As we'll see, words such as *want, wish, urge, intent, desire, drive, goal, energy,* and *ambition* provide the language used to describe motivation.

After spraining her ankle moments earlier, Kerri Strug landed a jump, favoring her good foot. She then fell to the mat in pain, cried, and had to be carried off by her trainer. All over the world, viewers wondered: What motivated her quest for the gold?

What Motivates Us?

Are there general principles that explain what motivates us? Are people driven by instincts, a need to achieve a certain level of bodily tension, or a desire for attractive rewards? Do all people want to satisfy the same basic needs, and, if so, what are these needs?

motivation An inner state that energizes people toward the fulfillment of a goal.

"You want only happiness, Douglas. I want fame *and* happiness."

Individuals differ in the strength of their various motives.

Over the years, psychologists have approached the subject of motivation in two ways. Some have proposed general theories to explain what all human motives have in common. Others have focused on specific motives such as hunger, sex, affiliation and belonging, and achievement. Let's begin with the first approach.

General Theories of Motivation

Early in this century, as Darwin's theory of evolution gained prominence, many psychologists believed that human behavior, like the behavior of animals, was biologically rooted in instincts. As we saw in Chapter 5 on Learning, an **instinct** is a fixed pattern of behavior that is unlearned, universal within a species, and "released" by a specific set of conditions. Thus, canaries sing, spiders weave webs, and beavers build dams—specific actions that are "hard-wired" by evolution. But is complex human behavior similarly programmed? In 1908, motivation theorist William McDougall argued that a whole range of human behaviors are instinctually based. He went on to compile a long list of human instincts, including those for acquisition, jealousy, mating, parenting, pugnacity, greed, curiosity, cleanliness, and self-assertion.

Instinct theories of human motivation were soon rejected. One problem was that they explained human behavior through a flawed process of circular reasoning: "Why are people aggressive? Because human beings possess a powerful instinct to aggress. How do we know humans have this instinct? Because there is so much aggression." Notice the circularity in the logic: Behavior is attributed to an instinct that, in turn, is inferred from the behavior. A second problem with instinct theory is that many so-called instinctual behaviors are learned, shaped by experience, subject to individual differences, and influenced by culture.

Drive Theory With the demise of instinct-based accounts, psychologists turned to **drive theory** of human motivation. According to drive theory, physiological needs that arise within the body create an unpleasant state of tension, which motivates or *drives* the organism to behave in ways that reduce the need and return the body to a balanced, less tense state (Hull, 1943). In its original form, drive theory was used to explain various biological functions such as eating, drinking, sleeping, and having sex. The hunger-eating cycle illustrates a presumed chain of events: food deprivation → hunger (drive) → seeking food and eating → drive reduction. Clearly, drive theory can be used to explain certain biologically driven behaviors. But today, psychologists agree that it cannot also explain what motivates the compulsive overeater, the late-night workaholic, or the power-starved politician. In particular, drive theory cannot explain why people often engage in activities that *increase* rather than reduce tension—as when we explore new surroundings just to satisfy our curiosity, skip a snack to save our appetite for dinner, or run miles with our hearts pounding in order to stay in shape. Nor can drive theory explain the popularity of ice climbing, extreme skiing, skydiving, bungee jumping, and other high-risk activities.

instinct A fixed pattern of behavior that is unlearned, universal in a species, and "released" by specific stimuli.

drive theory The notion that physiological needs arouse tension that motivates people to satisfy the need.

arousal theory The notion that people are motivated to achieve and maintain an optimum level of bodily arousal.

Arousal Theory To account for the fact that people often seek to increase rather than reduce tension, many psychologists turned to **arousal theory** of motivation. According to arousal theory, human beings are motivated to achieve and maintain an *optimum* level of bodily arousal—not too little, not too much (Fiske & Maddi, 1961). Studies show that people who are put into a state of sensory restriction (blindfolded, ears plugged, and unable to move) or into a monotonous situation quickly become bored and crave stimulation. Studies also show that when people are bombarded with bright lights, blaring music, and other intense stimuli, they soon withdraw in an effort to lower their level of arousal. In Chapter 15, we'll see that individuals differ in the amount of stimulation they find "optimal" (Eysenck & Eysenck, 1985; Zuckerman, 1979). We'll also see, however, that as a general rule people are happier and more motivated when engaged in activities that are challenging in relation to their ability—not too easy, which is boring, and not too difficult, which triggers anxiety (Csikszentmihalyi, 1990; Moneta & Csikszentmihalyi, 1996).

Incentive Theory In contrast to the notion that people are "pushed" into action by internal need states, many motivation psychologists believe that people are often "pulled" by external goals, or incentives. According to the **incentive theory** of motivation, any stimulus that people have learned to associate with positive or negative outcomes can serve as an incentive—grades, money, ice cream, respect, a romantic night out, or relief from pain. People are motivated to behave in certain ways when they *expect* that they can gain the incentive through their efforts and when they *value* that incentive. Recognizing that human beings set goals, make plans, and think about the outcomes they produce, motivation theorists today believe that there is a strong cognitive component to many of our aspirations (Atkinson, 1964; McClelland, 1985; Weiner, 1989).

The Pyramid of Human Motivations

Now that we have considered general theories of motivation, let us examine some of the specific motives that direct and energize our behavior. In other words, what is it that we want most in life? In response to this question, Abraham Maslow (1954) proposed that all human beings are motivated to fulfill a **hierarchy of needs,** from those that are basic for survival up to those that promote growth and self-enhancement (see Figure 8.1).

At the base of the hierarchy are the physiological needs for food, water, oxygen, sleep, and sex. Once these needs are met, people seek safety, steady work, financial security, stability at home, and a predictable environment. Next on the ladder are the social needs for affiliation, belongingness and love, affection, close relations, family ties, and group membership (if these needs are not met, we feel lonely and alienated). Next are the esteem needs, which include our desires for status, respect, recognition, achievement, and power (failing to satisfy this need, we feel inferior and unimportant). In short, everyone strives in their own way to satisfy all the needs on the hierarchy. Once these needs are met, said Maslow, we become ready, willing, and able to strive for self-actualization—a distinctly human need to fulfill one's potential. As Maslow (1968) put it, "A musician must make music, an artist must paint, a poet must write, if he is ultimately to be at peace with himself. What a man *can* be, he *must* be" (p. 46).

By arranging human needs in the shape of a pyramid, Maslow was claiming that the needs at the base take priority over those at the top. In other words, the higher needs become important to us only after more basic needs are satisfied. Research generally confirms Maslow's prediction that those motives lower in the pyramid take precedence, though there are occasional exceptions, as when people starve themselves to death in order to make a political statement. Research also shows that not everyone climbs Maslow's hierarchy in the same prescribed order. Some people seek love and romance before fulfilling their esteem motives, but others who are more achievement-oriented may try to establish a career before a family (Goebel & Brown, 1981).

When snow falls, children in all parts of the world make snowballs. Instinct theorists of the past would attribute this universal behavior to an instinct for play. In an interesting parallel to humans, young Japanese macaques also make snowballs, carry them around as play objects, and even roll them along the ground. But here's where the similarity ends: No one has ever seen a macaque throw a snowball.

incentive theory The notion that people are motivated to behave in ways that produce a valued inducement.

hierarchy of needs Maslow's list of basic needs that have to be satisfied before people can become self-actualized.

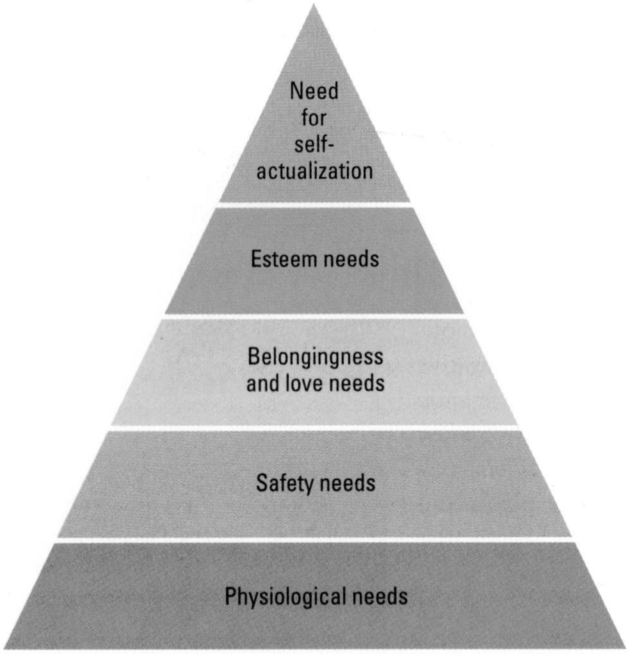

Figure 8.1 Maslow's pyramid of needs Maslow theorized that everyone is motivated to fulfill a hierarchy of needs ranging from those most basic to survival up to those that promote self-enhancement.

Maslow's theory may not accurately describe the motivational path all people take, but his distinctions and the notion that the various needs form a hierarchy provide a convenient framework for the study of motivation. In the coming pages, we'll begin at the base of Maslow's pyramid with hunger and sexuality, then we'll work our way up to the needs for affiliation, intimacy, achievement, and power. Finally, we'll put the psychology of motivation to work, literally, in a discussion of what motivates people on the job.

Basic Human Motives

How do we regulate eating? Is hunger a strictly biological state, or is it influenced by psychological factors? What causes obesity and eating disorders, and what can be done to correct these problems? Turning to the study of sexual and reproductive behavior, are men and women similarly motivated? What influences sexual orientation?

Hunger and Eating

It has been said that "a hungry stomach has no ears" (Jean de La Fontaine), that "Nobody wants a kiss when they are hungry" (Dorothea Dix), and that "Even God cannot speak to a hungry man except in terms of bread" (Mahatma Gandhi). It seems that when it's time to eat, all other urges, desires, and ambitions fade into the background.

Hunger is a powerful sensation that sets in motion the search for and consumption of food. It's interesting that our commonsense notions about hunger are often incorrect. Sometimes, after working nonstop for several hours, I'll hold my stomach, feel the growling, and just know that I'm hungry. On empty. Time to eat. Breakfast, lunch, dinner, a morning coffee break, an afternoon snack, even a late-night raid on the refrigerator are part of the daily routine. At other times, after a big meal, I'll put my hand over my stomach, feel bloated and stuffed, and complain that I'm full. Time to stop. It's as if sensations from the belly were sending "eat" and "stop" messages straight to the brain. But is this the way hunger works?

[Drawing by Cline; © 1996 The New Yorker Magazine, Inc.]

"Your clock may be telling you to get married, but mine's telling me to have lunch."

When it's time to eat, other motives take a back seat.

The Biological Component The biological mechanisms underlying hunger are complex. Following their common sense, early researchers believed that hunger was triggered by sensations in the stomach. In an initial experiment, researcher A. L. Washburn, working with Walter Cannon, swallowed a long tube with a balloon that was then partially inflated and specially designed to rest in his stomach. Whenever the stomach contracted, the balloon compressed. At the same time, Washburn pressed a key each time he felt hungry. Using this device, and testing other subjects, Cannon and Washburn (1912) observed a link between stomach contractions and reports of hunger. In fact, the subjects reported feeling hungry at the height of a contraction, not at the beginning—thus suggesting that the contractions had caused the hunger and not the other way around (see Figure 8.2). Indeed, more recent research shows that people begin to feel hungry when the stomach is about 60 percent empty (Sepple & Read, 1989).

There may be a correlation between stomach contractions and hunger, but additional observations soon discredited Cannon and Washburn's theory. The fatal blow came when studies revealed that even after people had had cancerous or ulcerated stomachs surgically removed, they continued to feel hungry. Clearly, if hunger can be felt without a stomach, then stomach contractions cannot be the cause of hunger. Confronted with this realization, researchers turned their attention to the brain and central nervous system.

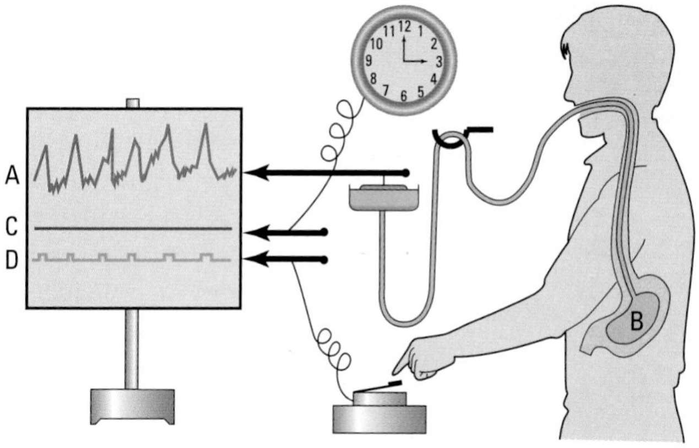

Figure 8.2 Cannon and Washburn's hunger experiment In this study, subjects swallowed a balloon, which rested in the stomach. Recorded over time (A) is the volume of the balloon (B) in minutes (C). Subjects pressed a key whenever they felt hungry (D). Subjects reported feeling hungry at the height of their stomach contractions.

According to one theory, the brain monitors fluctuating levels of glucose (a simple sugar that provides energy) and other nutrients circulating in the bloodstream. When glucose drops below a certain level, people become hungry and eat. When the glucose level in the blood exceeds a certain point, they feel satiated and stop eating (see Figure 8.3). How and where in the body is blood glucose monitored? Although different regions of the brain may be involved in the process, two distinct areas of the *hypothalamus* play a key role (as we saw in Chapter 2, the hypothalamus is a tiny brain structure that regulates body temperature, the autonomic nervous system, and the release of hormones).

Initially, researchers saw the *lateral hypothalamus* (LH) as the "hunger center": when its neurons are stimulated, an animal will eat, and eat, and eat—even if it's full. And when the LH is destroyed, the animal will not eat and may even starve to death unless it is force-fed (Anand & Brobeck, 1951; Teitelbaum & Epstein, 1962). Similarly, researchers identified the *ventromedial hypothalamus* (VH) as a "satiation center": When it is stimulated, an animal will not eat, even if it has been deprived of food. When this area is destroyed, an animal will consume larger quantities than usual and eventually triple its own body weight (Hetherington & Ranson, 1942; Wyrwicka & Dobrzecka, 1960).

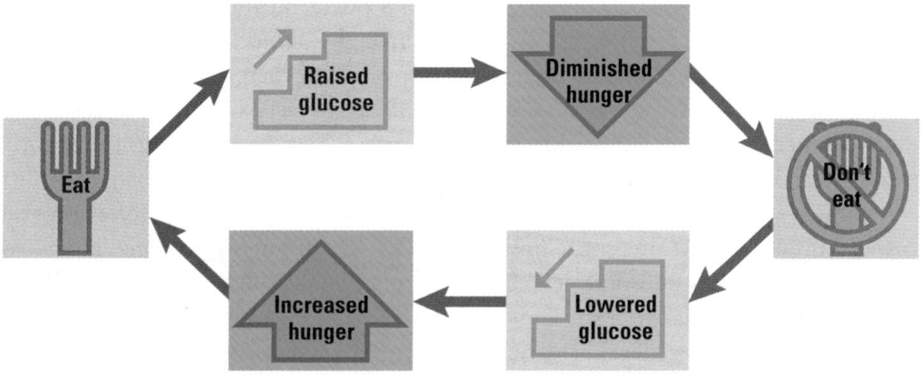

Figure 8.3 The hunger-regulation cycle When blood glucose levels are low, people become hungry and eat. The food then raises glucose levels, which lessens hunger and eating. The "thermostat" that monitors glucose levels is in or near the hypothalamus. Other factors as well control hunger and eating.

A bilateral lesion of the ventromedial part of the hypothalamus caused this rat to triple its body weight over a short period of time. Think about this result. How much would you weigh if your body weight were to triple?

At first, these findings suggested that the hypothalamus monitors blood glucose levels and has an on-off switch for eating (Stellar, 1954). But more recent studies show that the mechanism is far more complicated. It turns out, for example, that certain nerves form a tract that runs up from the brainstem through the lateral hypothalamus—and that these nerves are somehow involved. In fact, such areas may be part of a more general motor-activation system that, when stimulated, motivates an animal to "Do something!" This general command triggers eating if food is present, drinking if water is present, or running if neither food nor water is present (Berridge et al., 1989). Research also shows that other factors control hunger and eating as well—including levels of protein, fat, and insulin and other hormonal activities associated with the liver, pancreas, and intestines. In short, the body is equipped with a complex biochemical system for the regulation of hunger and eating (Logue, 1991; Stricker, 1990; Winn, 1995).

Psychological Influences Hunger may be biologically driven, but researchers have learned that other factors such as taste, smell, and visual cues also play an important role—and that eating patterns, which are learned, can also be unlearned (Capaldi, 1996). Among the psychological influences on eating is taste. In Chapter 3, we saw that there are four primary tastes: sweet, sour, salty, and bitter. It turns out that infants and adults all over the world seek out sweet-tasting foods such as cookies, ice cream, soda, ripe fruit, and candy, as well as salty foods such as pretzels and potato chips. These preferences are innate and universal. Yet in other ways, our tastes in food are shaped by personal and cultural experience. In China, food is flavored primarily with soy sauce, rice wine, and ginger root; in Greece, olive oil, lemon juice, and oregano are used; Moroccan food is seasoned with coriander, cumin, cinnamon, onion, and fruit; and in Mexico, tomatoes and hot chilies are common ingredients (Rozin, 1983). Consistently, people tend to prefer foods that are familiar rather than exotic, which is why most Americans react with disgust to such culinary "treats" from other parts of the world as sheep's eyes, dog meat, snakes, sea urchins, and grasshoppers. Interestingly, taste preferences and aversions that are learned can also be unlearned through repeated exposure to new foods and food-eating models (Hobden & Pliner, 1995; Pliner et al., 1993).

External food cues can also entice us into eating. If you've ever inhaled the floury aroma of pastries in a bakery, popcorn in a movie theater, or garlic in an Italian restaurant, or if you've ever had a sudden urge for beer and a hot dog while sitting in a ball park, you know that sometimes we're drawn into eating by external cues, or incentives. The time of day is also a powerful food cue. For example, Stanley Schachter and Larry Gross (1968) brought subjects into a laboratory, rigged the clock on the wall so that it ran fast or slow, then offered crackers as a snack. Not wanting to spoil their appetite, most subjects of normal weight ate fewer crackers when they thought it was late than when they thought it was early in the afternoon.

Finally, it's important to realize that eating is a social activity and is often subject to social influences. At times, the presence of others can inhibit us from eating—as when young women consume less food in front of men than alone in order to present themselves as appropriately "feminine" (Mori et al., 1987; Pliner & Chaiken, 1990). As a general rule, however, people eat more rather than less in the company of others. Eating-diary studies show that the more people we're with, the longer time we spend at the table and the more food we are likely to consume (de Castro & Brewer, 1992). This effect is particularly pronounced when the people we're with are family and friends (de Castro, 1994).

Obesity With all the talk that surrounds us about dieting and exercise, one would think that Americans are obsessed with their weight. Yet the National Institutes of Health (1992) estimates that one-fourth to one-third of all Americans are overweight, or **obese.** Definitions of obesity vary somewhat, but individuals are generally classified as obese when they carry a surplus of body fat that causes them to exceed their optimum weight by 20 percent.

Being slightly overweight does not pose a health risk. But statistically, obese individuals are more likely to suffer from diabetes, high blood pressure, heart disease, arthritis, respiratory problems, gallstones, and certain forms of cancer (Bray, 1986). To make matters worse, obese people are also subject to stereotyping, ridicule, and discrimination. Research shows that obese people are assumed to be slow, lazy, sloppy, and lacking in willpower (Ryckman et al., 1989). And in a study of long-term social and economic consequences, researchers followed a group of overweight sixteen- to twenty-four-year-old women and found that those who were still obese after seven years made less money than their peers and were less likely to be married (Gortmaker et al., 1993).

What causes obesity? Why do some people but not others fight a chronic battle against gaining weight? As with other aspects of hunger and eating, both biological and psychological factors play a role. Physiologically speaking, getting fat is easy to explain. People gain weight when they *consume* more calories than their body can *metabolize,* or burn up. The excess calories are stored as fat. Evidence for the role of biological factors begins with the finding that obesity runs in families and is influenced by genetics. In one study, Albert Stunkard and others (1990) compared the "Body Mass Index," or BMI (a measure of obesity that controls for height), of genetically identical twins and fraternal twins who were raised together or apart. As illustrated in Figure 8.4, two results provided strong evidence for the role of genetics: (1) The identical twins were more similar in their BMI than were the fraternal twins, and (2) identical twins were similar in this regard even when raised apart, in separate homes. The same conclusion emerges from adoption studies, which show that, when it comes to body weight, adoptees resemble their biological parents more than their adoptive parents (Grilo & Pogue-Geile, 1991).

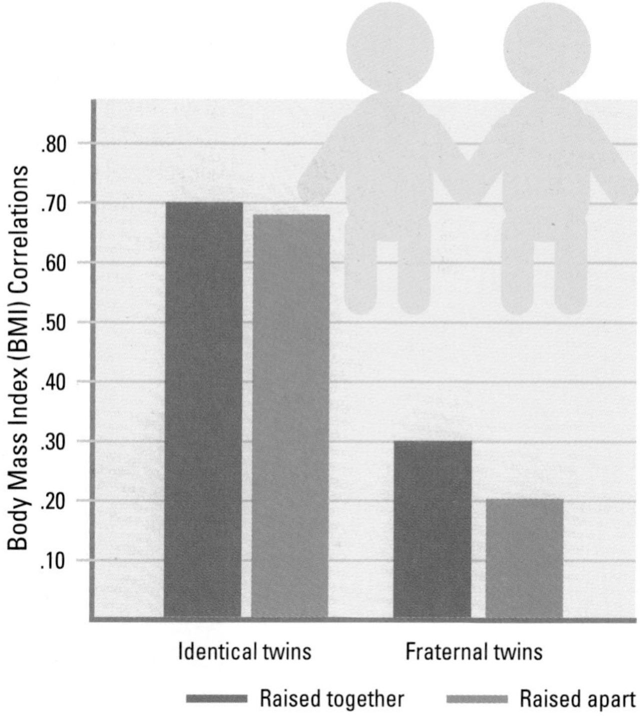

Figure 8.4 Body weight of identical and fraternal twins Indicating the role of genetic factors in body weight, you can see that identical twins (*left*) had more similar body weights than did fraternal twins (*right*). Note also that this same pattern was found regardless of whether the twins were raised together or apart (Stunkard et al., 1990).

So what, specifically, is inherited? Do obese people inherit a tendency to consume large quantities of food, or are they born with a slow metabolism, making it more difficult for them to burn up calories? Research shows that most obese individuals have normal metabolism rates, a finding that suggests that they must eat more than the average person. Why? According to one theory, each of us has a **set point,** a level of weight toward which our body gravitates, and obese people are programmed to maintain a high set-point weight (Keesey, 1995). The set point itself may be genetic or stem from eating habits established early in life. Either way, set points are relatively stable—which explains why it's hard to lose massive quantities of weight and why, after dieting, it's so hard to maintain the loss over time (Garner & Wooley, 1991).

obesity The state of having a surplus of body fat that causes a person to exceed his or her optimum weight by 20 percent.

set point A level of weight toward which a person's body gravitates.

Thankfully, it is not impossible to achieve long-term weight loss. Some people resort to high-risk medical procedures such as gastric-restriction surgery to shrink the stomach and diet drugs that suppress appetite or increase energy expenditure. For most, however, weight reduction can be achieved through alterations in behavior. In this regard, the key to success is to realize that a change in diet must be permanent and that it must be accompanied by a steady regimen of physical exercise (Brownell & Wadden, 1992). Two factors must be present for someone to sustain this effort: information and motivation. First, a person must have an accurate sense of his or her caloric intake and exercise. This sounds easy, but Steven Lichtman and his colleagues (1992) had a group of failed dieters keep a diary and discovered that they unwittingly underreported the amount of food they consumed and overestimated their daily exercise. Second, one's motivation for losing weight is also critical. Research shows that people are more likely to succeed in a long-term weight-reduction program when motivated by their own desires than when motivated by external incentives such as the wishes of a spouse (Williams et al., 1996).

Eating Disorders Psychological influences on hunger and eating are most evident when it comes to serious eating disorders. **Anorexia nervosa** is a disorder in which the person, typically an adolescent girl or young woman, becomes so fearful of gaining weight that she ignores her hunger pangs, limits her eating, becomes emaciated, and sometimes even starves to death. Approximately 95 percent of anorexics are female, and anorexia's worldwide incidence has risen sharply in recent decades. Closely related is **bulimia nervosa,** an eating disorder also found among young women that is marked by cycles of extreme binge eating followed by self-induced vomiting and the overuse of laxatives. A woman with bulimia may eat a whole pizza, a box of cookies, a bucket of fried chicken, or a half-gallon of ice cream—all in one sitting—then purge the food. These binge-and-purge episodes may occur two

Ken and Barbie are the most popular selling dolls in the world. Yet both are unrealistically thin compared to the average young adult.

anorexia nervosa An eating disorder in which the person, usually an adolescent girl or young woman, limits her eating and becomes emaciated.

bulimia nervosa An eating disorder found usually among young women that is marked by cycles of binge eating followed by purging.

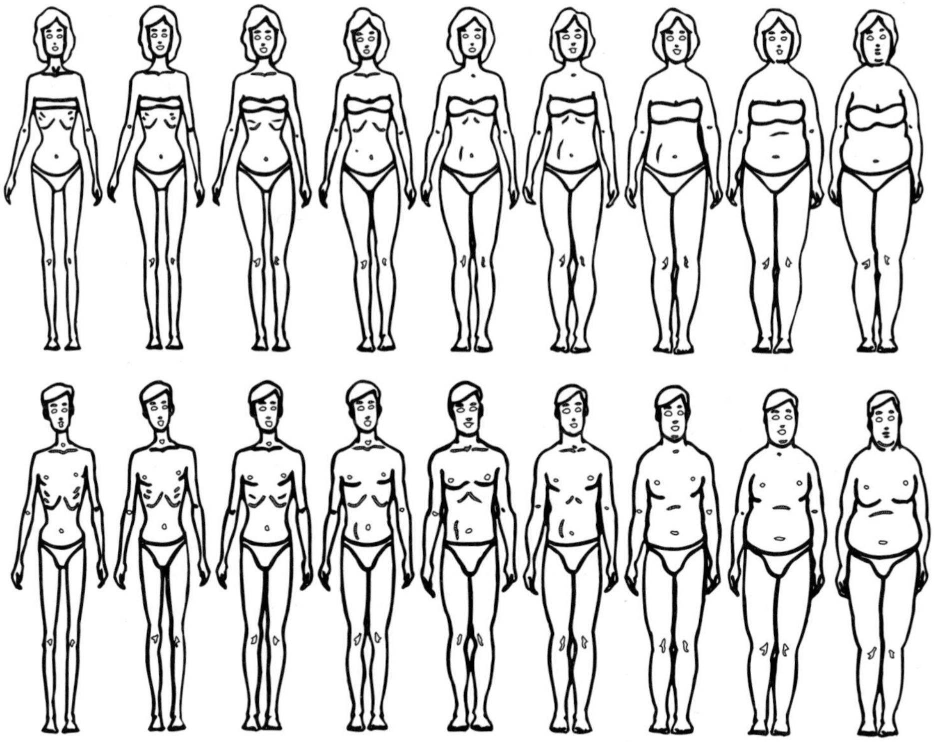

Figure 8.5 Ideal body image Which image do you think is ideal for your sex? And which comes closest to your body? This task is commonly used to assess whether a person has a positive or negative body image.

to fourteen times a week. Bulimia is seldom life-threatening (most sufferers are normal in weight, which makes it easy for them to hide the condition), but the repeated vomiting can cause erosion of tooth enamel, dehydration, damage to intestines, nutritional imbalances, and other medical problems (Brownell & Fairburn, 1995).

How common are eating disorders? Although estimates vary, recent studies indicate that fewer than 1 percent of women suffer from anorexia, that 2 or 3 percent have bulimia, and that these rates are higher among female college students than nonstudents (American Psychiatric Association, 1994). As to the possible causes of eating disorders, psychologists have speculated about genetics, hormone imbalances, low set points, overly demanding parents, and traumas such as sexual abuse. At this point, two findings are clear. First, the problem is most prevalent in weight-conscious cultures in which diet centers, health spas, exercise videos, and shapely supermodels make aspiring women feel pressured to have a slender appearance (Brumberg, 1988; Ruderman & Besbeas, 1992). Second, women with eating disorders have negatively distorted images of their own bodies, often seeing themselves as overweight (Thompson, 1996). Look at the drawings in Figure 8.5. Which do you think is ideal for your sex? And which do you think represents *your* body type? Using this task and others like it, researchers have found that girls with a negative body image (as measured by the discrepancy between their self-image and ideal body types) are most at risk to develop an eating disorder (Attie & Brooks-Gunn, 1989). As for the role of cultural ideals, a recent study showed that college women who were shown TV commercials featuring slender female models (others saw neutral ads) later reported feeling less satisfied with their own appearance (Heinberg & Thompson, 1995). Trying to measure up to the multimillion-dollar supermodel can only prove frustrating to most. The cultural ideal for thinness may even be set early in childhood. Kevin Norton and his colleagues (1996) recently projected the life-size dimensions of the world-popular Ken and Barbie dolls and found that both were unrealistically thin compared to the average young adult. In fact, the estimated odds of a young woman having Barbie's shape is about 1 in 100,000.

Sexual Motivation

One hundred years ago, Sigmund Freud shocked the scientific community by proposing psychoanalysis, a theory that placed great emphasis on sexual gratification as a driving force in human development. As we'll see in Chapter 15, many of Freud's closest colleagues rejected his focus on sexual motivation. But was he wrong? Although sex is essential to the survival of a *species,* it is not—like hunger, thirst, or the need for sleep—vital to the survival of an *individual.* Yet the sexual motive is a force to be reckoned with. Sexual images and themes appear, literally, in our dreams, in the "dirty" jokes we tell, in the TV shows we watch, in the novels we read, and in the music we hear. It's no wonder that public figures are so often mired in sex scandals. It's also no wonder that advertisers use sex to sell everything from mouthwash to jeans, cars, soft drinks, and shaving cream.

Surveys of Sexual Practices With sex being the most private and intimate aspect of human relations, it is difficult to study systematically. During the 1940s, biologist Alfred Kinsey and his colleagues (1948, 1953) conducted the first large-scale survey of sexual practices in the United States. Based on extensive confidential interviews of more than 17,000 men and women, these researchers sought to describe what nobody would openly talk about: patterns of sexual activity. Kinsey's goal was to uncover the hidden norms for all aspects of sexual behavior, including masturbation, homosexuality, and premarital and extramarital sex. Some of Kinsey's results were shocking, as he revealed that sexual activity was more frequent and more varied than expected. Among Kinsey's findings: 90 percent of all men and nearly half of all women had premarital sex, virtually all men and a majority of women masturbated, 50 percent of married men and 26 percent of married women had extramarital affairs, and 40 percent of all college-educated couples said they engaged in oral sex. Kinsey's books became instant best sellers. Although his methods were flawed (for example, most subjects were young, white, urban, and middle class), his findings are still often used as a basis for comparison.

Since Kinsey's groundbreaking study, numerous sex surveys have been conducted. Although one can never know for sure how accurate these self-report results are, it seems that societal norms have changed over time. For example, sexual activity levels peaked during the "sexual revolution" of the 1960s and 1970s, but these numbers appear to have declined since that time (Robinson et al., 1991). Indeed, recent studies suggest that sexual practices today, at least in the United States, are relatively tame (Leigh et al., 1993). In one national survey of more than 3,000 Americans, age eighteen to fifty-nine, researchers found that husbands and wives were sexually more faithful to each other than expected—and that the vast majority preferred "traditional" vaginal sex over oral, anal, and group sex, bondage, and other "kinky" activities (Laumann et al., 1994).

One consistent finding to emerge from all surveys is that men and women differ in certain aspects of their sexual motivation. When subjects were asked to select ten private wishes from a list, most men and women similarly wanted love, health, peace

"Marry me Virginia. My genes are excellent and, as yet, unpatented."

on earth, unlimited ability, wealth, and recognition. There was one major difference: More men than women wanted "to have sex with anyone I choose" (Ehrlichman & Eichenstein, 1992). This finding is rather common. Surveys consistently show that men are sexually more promiscuous than women. They are more likely to enjoy sex without emotional commitment (Laumann et al., 1994), are more permissive in their attitudes toward casual sex (Oliver & Hyde, 1993), and are more likely to fantasize about having sex with multiple partners at once (Leitenberg & Henning, 1995).

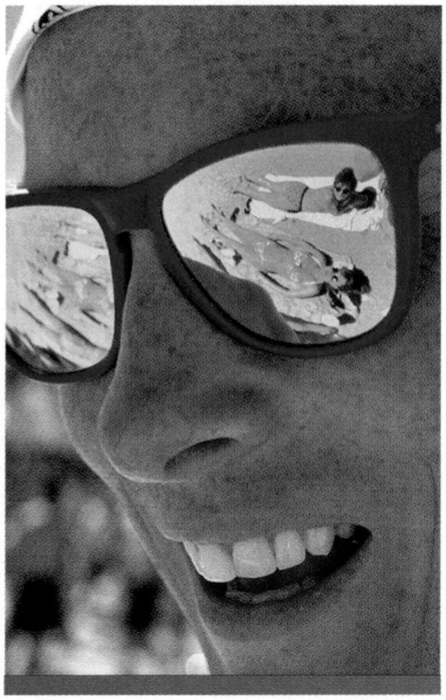

This young man spies through his sunglasses at women lying on the beach. According to the evolutionary perspective in psychology, his attraction is biologically motivated by the search for a fertile reproductive partner.

The Evolution of Desire Why are the differences between sexes so prevalent, and what do they mean? In a book entitled *The Evolution of Desire,* David Buss (1994) argues that the answer can be derived from evolutionary psychology, the subdiscipline that uses the principles of evolution to understand human social behavior. According to this perspective, human beings all over the world exhibit mate-selection patterns that favor the conception, birth, and survival of their offspring—and women and men employ different strategies to achieve that common goal.

According to Buss, a woman must be highly selective because she is biologically limited in the number of children she can bear and raise in a lifetime. Thus, a woman must search for a mate who possesses (or who has the potential to possess) economic resources and a willingness to commit those resources to support her offspring. The strategic result is that women in general should be attracted to men who are older and financially secure or who have intelligence, ambition, stability, and other traits predictive of future success.

In contrast, a man can father an unlimited number of children. He is restricted, however, by his ability to attract a reproductively capable partner and by his uncertainty as to whether the children born are actually his own. With these motives springing from their evolutionary past, men desire women who are young and physically attractive (having smooth skin, full lips, lustrous hair, good muscle tone, and other youthful features)—attributes that signal reproductive fertility. To minimize paternal uncertainty, they should also seek women who are likely to be sexually faithful rather than promiscuous.

To test his theory of sexual motivation, Buss (1989) recruited a team of researchers to survey 10,047 men and women in thirty-seven cultures within North and South America, Asia, Africa, Eastern and Western Europe, and the Pacific. All respondents were asked to rate the importance of various attributes in choosing a mate. The results were consistent with predictions. Both men and women gave equally high ratings to certain characteristics, such as "having a pleasant disposition." But in the vast majority of countries, "good looks" and "no previous experience in sexual intercourse" were valued more highly by men, whereas "good financial prospect" and "ambitious and industrious" were more important to women. Interestingly, personal ads appearing in magazines and newspapers also reveal that women tend to offer beauty and seek wealth, while men seek beauty and offer wealth (Rajecki et al., 1991).

Also consistent with the evolutionary perspective is a universal tendency for men to seek younger women (who are most likely to be fertile) and for women to desire older men (who are most likely to have financial resources). Buss (1989) found this age preference discrepancy in all the cultures he studied, with men on average wanting to marry women who were 2.7 years younger, and women wanting men who were 3.4 years older. Based on an analysis of personal ads, Douglas Kenrick and Richard Keefe (1992) found that men in their twenties are equally interested in younger women and slightly older women still of fertile age. But men in their thirties seek women who are five years younger, while men in their fifties prefer women

With the development of genetic testing, paternity disputes that have plagued men and women throughout human history can now be resolved. Today, 200,000 paternity tests a year are conducted at a cost of a few hundred dollars per test. The DNA samples are taken within seconds from saliva, and the test results are 99.9 percent accurate. Among the clients: "Moms involved in court custody cases, fathers fighting to establish paternal relationships with their children, and black-haired dads who wonder why their kids sport carrot tops" (Cohen, 1997).

ten to twenty years younger. In contrast, women of all ages sought older men. Such a pattern can also be seen in marriage statistics collected from different cultures and historical generations (see Figure 8.6).

A third line of research consistent with evolutionary theory concerns *sexual jealousy,* a negative emotional state arising from a perceived threat to one's sexual relationship (Salovey, 1991; White & Mullen, 1990). Although jealousy is a common and normal human reaction, men and women are aroused by different triggering events. According to the theory, men should be particularly upset by *sexual* infidelity because the woman who has an extramarital affair increases the risk that the children he supports are not his own. In contrast, women should feel threatened more by *emotional* infidelity because the husband who falls in love with another woman might withdraw his financial support.

Two studies support this hypothesis. In one study, male and female college students were asked whether they would be more upset if their romantic partner had formed a deep emotional attachment or had sexual intercourse with another person. Think for a moment about this awful choice. Which situation would *you* find the more distressing? The results revealed a striking sex difference: 60% of the men said they would be more upset by a partner's

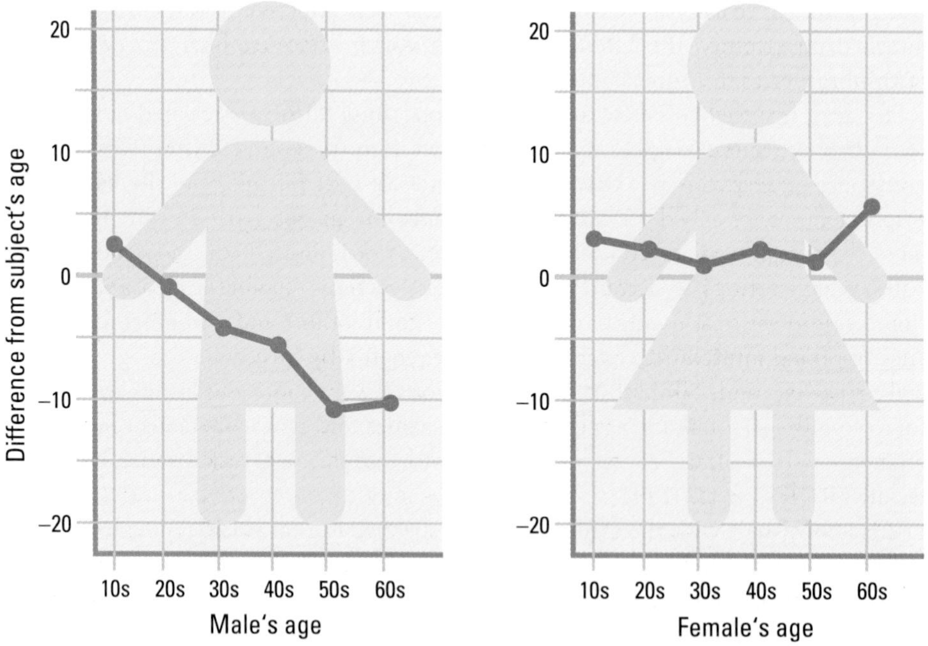

Figure 8.6 Sex differences in age at marriage These marriage statistics collected in the 1980s from the United States show that men marry women who are younger than they are, an age difference that is greater for men who are older. Women, in contrast, consistently marry men who are slightly older than they are (Kenrick & Keefe, 1992). According to evolutionary psychologists, this pattern reflects a male desire for fertile women and a female desire for men with resources. But are there other possible explanations?

sexual infidelity, but 83% of women felt that emotional infidelity was worse (Buss et al., 1992). This difference has been found not only in the United States but also in the Netherlands and Germany (Buunk et al., 1996). In a second study, newly married husbands and wives were interviewed about how they would react if they were to suspect their partner of cheating. Interestingly, the men were most likely to say that they would use various "mate-retention" tactics (concealing or threatening the wife; taking violent action against the male rival) when their wives were young and relatively attractive. In contrast, women were more likely to say they would use mate-retention tactics (being more watchful, or enhancing their appearance) when the men they were married to strived for status and had a higher income (Buss & Shackelford, 1997). In short, men and women may differ in their sexual motives, as the evolutionary psychologist predicts, but both react strongly when these motives are threatened.

The differences between sexes are intriguing, and increasing numbers of researchers are adopting an evolutionary perspective (Simpson & Kenrick, 1997). However, critics of this approach argue that the results can be interpreted in terms that are more "psychological" than "evolutionary." One argument is that women trade youth and beauty for money not for reproductive purposes but rather because they often lack *direct* access to economic power. Another argument is that men are more upset over sexual infidelity not because of uncertain paternity but because they assume that the married woman having a sexual affair is also likely to be forming intimate feelings for her extramarital partner (DeSteno & Salovey, 1996; Harris & Christenfeld, 1996). A third argument is that despite the observed differences, men and women are similar in many ways. For example, women want physical attractiveness as much as men do—in a short-term sexual partner (Regan & Berscheid, 1997). And in Buss's (1989) cross-cultural study, both men and women gave their highest ratings to such traits as kindness, dependability, and a pleasant disposition. To sum up, evolutionary psychology offers a provocative but controversial new perspective on human sexual motivation.

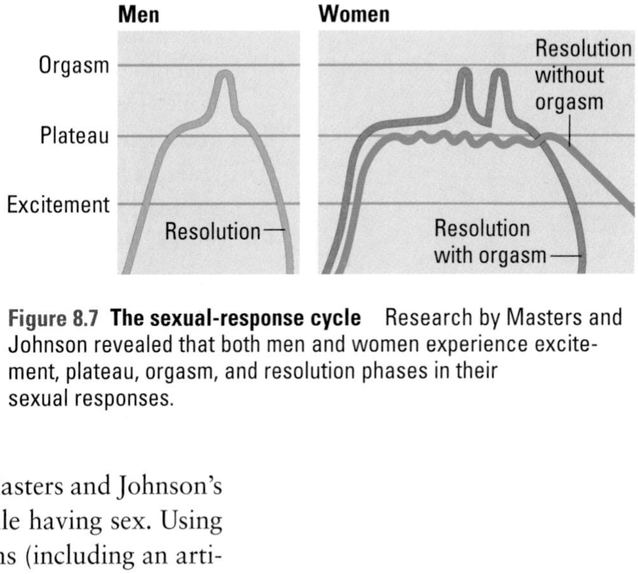

Figure 8.7 The sexual-response cycle Research by Masters and Johnson revealed that both men and women experience excitement, plateau, orgasm, and resolution phases in their sexual responses.

The Sexual-Response Cycle

Survey-based population statistics, questionnaires, personal ads, and laboratory experiments provide only a glimpse into sexual behavior, so more intensive research is also needed. Enter sex researchers William Masters and Virginia Johnson. As reported in their 1966 book *Human Sexual Response,* Masters and Johnson filmed and measured physiological activity in hundreds of male and female volunteers while they masturbated or had sexual intercourse in the laboratory. Masters and Johnson's goal was to understand what happens to people *physically* while having sex. Using various recording devices to monitor changes in bodily functions (including an artificial penis with a camera designed to record physiological reactions in the vagina), they found that despite sex differences in anatomy, evolutionary heritage, socialization, and attitudes, there are striking physiological *similarities* in male and female sexual responses.

There are four stages in the **sexual-response cycle,** and they are much the same for men and women (see Figure 8.7). In the *excitement* stage, a stimulus sparks sexual arousal marked by increased blood flow to the pelvic region, which then causes the genitals to become engorged with blood. During this phase, the man's penis becomes partially erect, while the woman's vagina secretes a lubricant and her

sexual-response cycle The four physiological stages of sexual responding: excitement, plateau, orgasm, and resolution.

nipples harden and become erect. This phase lasts from a few minutes to well over an hour.

The excitement then builds to a *plateau* phase, when breathing and heart rates increase. The man's penis fills with a fluid that may contain live sperm, some of which may appear at the tip of the penis, his erection becomes firmer, the woman's vagina becomes wetter, her breasts become engorged with blood, and a "climax" feels moments away.

During the *orgasm,* rhythmic genital contractions give rise to an intensely pleasurable feeling of sexual release, accompanied in men by the ejaculation of semen. For both men and women, the contractions are spaced at about 8/10 of a second, with the first five or six being the most intense. The feeling seems to be the same for both sexes.

Afterward, the body slowly returns to its normal pre-aroused state and enters the *resolution* phase. In men, this is accompanied by a refractory period, during which another orgasm is impossible. This "downtime" can last from just a few minutes to more than a day. Women do not have a lengthy refractory period and so are capable of experiencing a succession of orgasms if restimulated.

Sexual Orientation Every human motive is directed toward a goal object, and sex is no exception. Everyone is energized to fulfill sexual desires, but individuals differ in the object toward which that energy is directed. Indeed, no discussion of human sexual motivation is complete without a consideration of individual differences in **sexual orientation**—defined as one's sexual preference for members of the same sex (homosexuality), opposite sex (heterosexuality), or both sexes (bisexuality).

The Numbers Game As national leaders, policy makers, and the public debate such issues as gay marriage, political and emotional rhetoric often substitutes for scientific information. How common is homosexuality, and where does it come from? Throughout human history, and in all cultures, a vast majority of people have been heterosexual in orientation. But just how vast a majority is this? For many years, researchers have tried to determine the number of gay men and lesbians in the population, and for many years the surveys have produced a range of results—and a great deal of controversy. Debate over the numbers may not seem to be an emotionally charged issue, but gay-rights activists and their opponents believe that the more homosexuals there are perceived to be, the more political clout they will have (Rogers, 1993).

Seizing upon certain combinations of numbers in Kinsey's original sex surveys, the popular media sometimes claim that 10 percent of the population is homosexual. But recent studies have consistently yielded much smaller estimates. A 1970 survey funded by the Kinsey Institute revealed that 3.3 percent of American men sampled said that they had frequent or occasional homosexual sex (Fay et al., 1989). Then between 1989 and 1992, the National Opinion Research Center reported that only 2.8 percent of American men and 2.5 percent of women had exclusive homosexual activity. Although the number of adults who say they've had at least one homosexual experience is much higher, large-scale surveys conducted in the United States, Europe, Asia, and the Pacific collectively suggest that the size of the exclusively homosexual population in the world is about 4 percent among men and half that number among women (Diamond, 1993).

sexual orientation A sexual preference for members of the same sex (homosexuality), opposite sex (heterosexuality), or both sexes (bisexuality).

Origins of Homosexuality What are the roots of homosexuality? As you might expect, both biological and psychological theories have been proposed. Aristotle believed that homosexuality was inborn but was strengthened by habit, psychoanalysts argue that it stems from a disturbed family environment and the child's over-attachment to a parent of the same or opposite sex, and learning theorists point to reinforcing sexual experiences with same-sex peers in childhood. There is little evidence, however, to support these claims. In a comprehensive study, Alan Bell and others (1981) intensively interviewed 1,500 homosexual and heterosexual adults about their lives. There were no differences in their family backgrounds, numbers of brothers and sisters, absence of a male or female parent, relationship with parents, sexual abuse by someone of the same or opposite sex, age of onset of puberty, or high-school dating patterns. Except for the fact that homosexual adults described themselves as less conforming as children, the two groups could not be distinguished by their past experiences. In fact, both groups strongly felt that their sexual orientation was set long before it became "official."

Increasingly, researchers are finding evidence of a biological disposition. In one highly publicized study, neurobiologist Simon LeVay (1991) autopsied the brains of nineteen homosexual men who had died of AIDS, sixteen heterosexual men (some of whom had died of AIDS), and six heterosexual women. LeVay examined a tiny nucleus in the hypothalamus known to be involved in regulating sexual behavior and known to be larger in heterosexual men than in women. The specimens were numerically coded, so LeVay did not know whether the donor he was examining was male or female, straight or gay. The result: In the male-homosexual brains he studied, the nucleus was half the size as in male-heterosexual brains and was comparable to those found in the female-heterosexual brains. This research is fully described in LeVay's (1993) book *The Sexual Brain.*

Let's stop for a moment and ponder the implications. When LeVay's study was published in *Science,* a storm of controversy erupted. Emerging from the laboratory,

Although some men and women are openly gay, as shown in this wedding announcement for a lesbian couple, researchers can only estimate the prevalence of homosexuality in the population.

LeVay soon found himself in the spotlight—on TV news shows, on talk shows, and in magazines. Within the gay community, reactions were polarized. Some worried that the findings would somehow be used to discriminate against gays, called LeVay homophobic, and referred to his work as antihomosexual. But wait. LeVay himself is openly gay. Still, "one critic said that I wanted to prove that it's not my fault I'm gay" (quoted in Nimmons, 1994, p. 68). The more common reaction was to enthusiastically embrace the notion that sexual orientation is a biological condition so that people would be tolerant rather than judgmental. Thus, LeVay reported that "many gay men sent my study to their parents...and parents, in turn, wrote to say the study helped them understand their kids."

It's important to recognize that LeVay's study reveals only a correlation between sexual orientation and the size of this hypothalamic nucleus and cannot be used to draw conclusions about cause and effect. LeVay himself notes that "I didn't show that gay men are born that way" and that "since I looked at adult brains, we don't know if the differences I found were there at birth or if they appeared later" (Nimmons, 1994, p. 66). Indeed, researchers studying the effects of prenatal hormone levels had previously found that men whose mothers were under severe stress during pregnancy (stress lowers prenatal testosterone levels) were somewhat more likely to become gay (Ellis & Ames, 1987) and that women exposed to high levels of prenatal testosterone were more likely to become lesbians (Dittman et al., 1992).

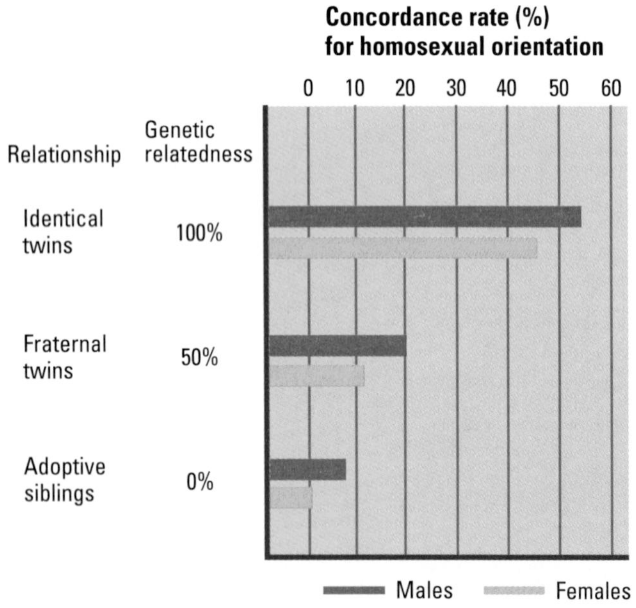

Figure 8.8 Genetic links to sexual orientation As measured by concordance (similarity) rates, the probability that a same-sex sibling of a homosexual man or woman is also homosexual is greater among identical twins than fraternal twins or adoptive siblings. These results suggest that there may be a genetic basis for homosexuality (Bailey & Pillar, 1991; Bailey et al., 1993).

Currently, the strongest support for the biological roots of sexual orientation comes from twin studies suggesting that there is a genetic predisposition. Michael Bailey and Richard Pillard (1991) surveyed 167 gay men and their twins and adopted brothers. Overall, 52 percent of the identical twins were gay, compared to only 22 percent of fraternal twins and 11 percent of adoptive brothers. Two years later, Bailey and his colleagues (1993) conducted a companion study of lesbians with similar results (see Figure 8.8).

The origins of homosexuality are complex. Clearly, there is evidence for a biological disposition, but does that mean there's a "gay gene"? Not necessarily. Daryl Bem (1996) believes that the development of homosexuality is a truly *psycho*biological—and developmental—process. According to Bem, genes determine an individual's temperament at birth, leading some infants and young children to be naturally more active, energetic, and aggressive than others. These differences in temperament will draw some children toward male playmates and "masculine" activities (rough-and-tumble play, contact sports) and others toward female playmates and more "feminine" activities (playing house, hopscotch). Bem refers to children who prefer same-sex playmates as gender-conformists and to those who prefer opposite-sex playmates as gender-nonconformists ("sissies" and "tomboys").

Activity preferences in childhood may be biologically rooted, but what happens next is the psychological part. According to Bem, gender-conforming children will come to see members of the opposite sex as different, unfamiliar, and arousing, even "exotic." Gender-nonconforming children, in contrast, will come to see same-sex peers as different, unfamiliar, arousing, and exotic. Then at puberty, as children become physically and sexually mature, they become attracted to members of the same or opposite sex—depending on which is the more exotic. Bem describes his proposed chain of events as the "exotic becomes erotic" theory of sexual orientation (see Figure 8.9).

At present, there is only sketchy evidence to support this interesting theory. It's true that genetic makeup can influence temperament and predispose a child to favor certain kinds of activities over others (Kagan, 1994). It's also true that gay men are more likely to have been "sissies" and that lesbians are more likely to have been "tomboys" as children (Bell et al., 1981; Bailey & Zucker, 1995). But do peer preferences in childhood influence adult sexual orientation, as Bem suggests, because exotic becomes erotic? Or is there a "gay gene" that fosters both gender nonconformity in childhood and homosexuality in adolescence and adulthood? At this point, additional research is needed to tease apart these biological and psychological influences.

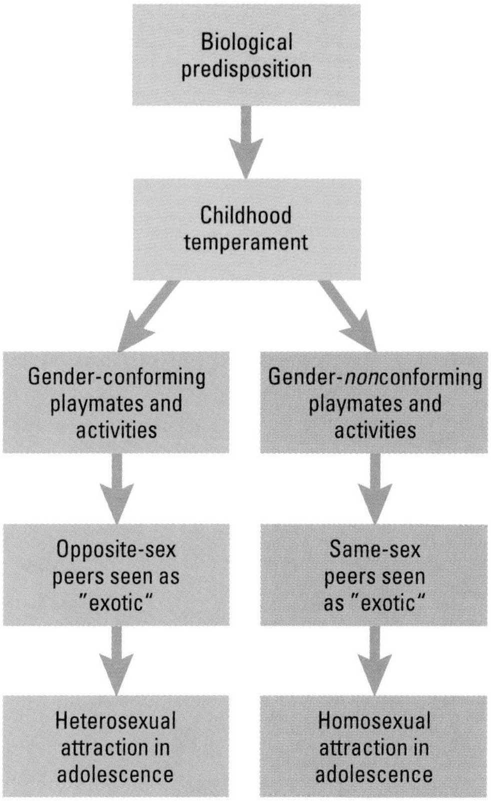

Figure 8.9 Bem's developmental theory of homosexuality According to Bem, genes determine gender-relevant behaviors in childhood. Later, adolescents become attracted to the sex that is different. Thus, childhood "tomboys" and "sissies" are prone to seek members of the same sex.

Social Motives

After biological needs are satisfied, what do we strive for? Do people actually *need* other people? Is the desire for social relationships a fundamental human motivation? What drives individuals who are highly motivated to achieve? What about the need for power—does it promote good leadership or bad?

Satisfying the body's appetite for food or the urge for sex helps propel the biological human engine. But people are not content merely to survive. Most of us want more out of life, much more. In varying degrees, we want to be part of a community, to love and be loved, and to achieve recognition, status, fame, wealth, and power. Whether one's goal is to raise a family, travel the world, earn a million dollars, climb the highest mountain, care for those in need, or paint a masterpiece, to be human is to strive for more than a mere satisfaction of basic drives. Using Maslow's motivational pyramid as a framework, we'll examine two broad classes of motives: belongingness needs and esteem needs.

Belongingness Motives

Although born helpless, human infants are equipped at birth with reflexes that orient them toward people. They are responsive to faces, turn their head toward voices, and are prepared to mimic certain facial gestures on cue. Much to the delight of parents, the newborn seems an inherently social animal. If you reflect on the amount of time you spend talking to, being with, pining for, or worrying about other people, you'll realize that we all are. People need people.

Recognizing the power of our social impulses, Maslow ranked belongingness and love needs third in his hierarchy. Being part of a family or community, playing on a sports team, joining a social or religious or professional group, making friends, falling in love, and having children—all service this important motive. So just how important is it? Do people really *need* other people?

According to Roy Baumeister and Mark Leary (1996), the need to belong is a fundamental human motivation. As they put it, "human beings have a pervasive drive to form and maintain at least a minimum quantity of lasting, positive, and significant interpersonal relationships" (p. 497). This conclusion is supported by a great deal of research. All over the world, people experience joy when they form new social attachments and react with anxiety, loneliness, and grief when these bonds are broken—as when separated from a loved one by distance, divorce, or death. The need to belong runs deep. As we'll see in Chapter 18, people who have a network of close social contacts—in the form of lovers, friends, and relatives—tend to be happier and more satisfied with life than those who are more isolated (Myers and Diener, 1995). In fact, we'll see that people who are more socially connected are also physically healthier and less likely to die a premature death (House et al., 1988; Uchino et al., 1996).

Dan McAdams (1989) notes that Maslow's belongingness motive is actually composed of two distinct needs. The first is the **need for affiliation,** which is defined as a desire to establish and maintain social contacts. The second is the **need for intimacy,** defined as a further desire for close relationships characterized by an openness of communication. Let's consider each of these needs in turn.

The Need for Affiliation Do you ever crave the company of others? Do you ever enjoy being alone? Chances are that you answered *yes* to both questions. Research shows that individuals differ in the strength of their need for affiliation. As you might expect, people with a high need for affiliation are socially more active than lows. They prefer to be in contact with others more often and are more likely to visit friends or even make phone calls and write letters as a way to maintain social contact at a distance (McAdams & Constantian, 1983).

Although individuals differ, even the most gregarious among us wants to be alone at times. In fact, it seems that people are motivated to establish and maintain an *optimum* balance of social contact (not too much, not too little) the way the body maintains a certain level of caloric intake. In an interesting study, Bibb Latané and Carol Werner (1978) found that laboratory rats were more likely to approach others of their species after a period of isolation and were less likely after prolonged social contact. These researchers suggested that rats, like many other animals, have a built-in "sociostat" (a social thermostat) to regulate their affiliative tendencies. Is there any evidence of a similar mechanism in humans? Shawn O'Connor and Lorne Rosenblood (1996) recently had college students carry portable beepers for four days. Whenever the beeper went off (on average, every hour), the students wrote down whether, at the time, they were *actually* alone or in the company of other people, and whether, at the time, they *wanted* to be alone or with others. The results showed that the students were in the state they desired two-thirds of the time—and that the situation they wished they were in on one occasion predicted their actual situation the next time they were signaled. Whether it was solitude or social contact that the students were craving, they successfully managed to regulate their own personal needs for affiliation.

People may differ in the strength of their affiliative needs and in the overall amount of social contact they find satisfying, but there are times when we would all rather be with other people. I'll never forget being with my son at Yankee Stadium in October 1996, the night the New York Yankees won the World Series. There were more than 60,000 fans at the game, and when it ended, nobody wanted to go home. Nobody rushed for the parking lot or raced to the subway. For nearly half an hour, nobody even left their seat. Out in the street, jubilant pedestrians exchanged high-

need for affiliation The desire to establish and maintain social contacts.

need for intimacy The desire for close relationships characterized by open and intimate communication.

fives, slaps on the back, hugs, and kisses. It was clear, even in the big city of strangers, that people wanted to celebrate together rather than alone. Affiliating can be satisfying for other reasons as well. From others, we get energy, attention, stimulation, information, and emotional support (Hill, 1987).

One condition that strongly arouses our need for affiliation is stress. It's always amazing to see how neighbors who otherwise never stop to say hello come together in snowstorms, hurricanes, power failures, and other major crises. Many years ago, Stanley Schachter (1959) theorized that external threat triggers fear and motivates us to affiliate—particularly with others who are facing a similar threat. In a laboratory experiment, Schachter found that subjects expecting to receive painful electric shocks chose to wait with other nervous subjects rather than alone.

[Drawing by Mankoff, © 1996 The New Yorker Magazine, Inc.]

"At this point, my privacy needs are interfering with my intimacy goals."

People are motivated to establish and maintain an optimum level of social contact.

Why do we affiliate in times of stress? Recent research suggests that people under stress seek each other out in order to gain *cognitive clarity* about the danger they are in. In one study, James Kulik and Heike Mahler (1989) found that hospital patients awaiting open-heart surgery preferred to have roommates who were postoperative rather than preoperative, presumably because they were in a position to provide information about the experience. Indeed, patients in a second study who were assigned postoperative rather than preoperative roommates became less anxious about the experience and were later quicker to recover from the surgery (Kulik et al., 1996). Even in a laboratory setting, Kulik and his colleagues (1994) found that subjects awaiting the painful task of soaking a hand in ice-cold water (compared to those told that the task would not be painful) also preferred to wait with someone who had completed the task than with one who had not—and they asked more questions of these experienced peers. Under stress, we adaptively become motivated to affiliate—not with just anybody but with others who can help us cope with an impending threat.

The Need for Intimacy

Affiliating with other people, even superficially, satisfies part of our need for social contact. But in varying degrees, people also have a need for close and intimate relationships. Research shows that individuals who score high rather than low on measures of the need for intimacy are seen by peers as warm, sincere, and loving. They also look at others more, smile more, laugh more, and confide more in their friends. People who score high rather than low on intimacy may also be happier and healthier (McAdams, 1989).

In looking at close relationships and the deep affection that grows between friends or lovers, psychologists have observed that the key ingredient is **self-disclosure,** the sharing of intimate, often confidential details about oneself with another person (Jourard, 1971; Derlega et al., 1993). Self-disclosure tends to follow three predictable patterns. The first is that we typically reciprocate another person's self-disclosure with one of our own—and at a comparable level of intimacy. Bare your soul to someone, and that person is likely to react by doing the same (Berg, 1987). Second, there are sex differences in openness of communication. Compared to men, women tend to self-disclose more than men *to* others (both male and female), and, in turn, they elicit more self-disclosure *from* others (Dindia & Allen, 1992). Third, individuals reveal more and more to each other as relationships grow over time. In the early stages, people give relatively little of themselves to others and receive comparably little in return. If these encounters are rewarding, however, the communication becomes more frequent and more intimate (Altman & Taylor, 1973). Self-disclosure is the glue that binds our most intimate relations. The more of it there is among friends, dating partners, and married couples, the more they like each other, the happier they are in the rela-

self-disclosure The sharing of intimate details about oneself with another person.

tionship, and the more inclined they are to stay together (Hendrick, 1981; Collins & Miller, 1994).

On January 1, 1997, Microsoft's Bill Gates was worth $23.9 billion, making him the richest person in the world, by far. What motivates Gates? Looking back on Bill as a child, his father recently said, "The play was serious. Winning mattered" (Isaacson, 1997).

Esteem Motives

Have you ever met someone so single-mindedly driven to succeed that you couldn't help but wonder why? One individual who pops to mind is Bill Gates—cofounder and chair of Microsoft. Gates is now the richest man in the world and seems to have an insatiable appetite for more. By his own admission, Gates wants to gain worldwide domination of the computer industry. Other images that come to mind are that of the politician who runs for president, the workaholic scientist who spends weekends in the laboratory, and athletes like Kerri Strug, the 1996 Olympic gymnast. What fuels the drive we often have to succeed, excel, and advance in our work? Over the years, psychologists have examined two motives that play a role in this regard: the need for achievement and the need for power.

The Need for Achievement In a classic book entitled *The Achievement Motive*, David McClelland and his colleagues (1953) sought to identify people with high levels of **achievement motivation**—defined as a strong desire to accomplish difficult tasks, outperform others, and excel. There was no question that individuals differ in the intensity of their achievement strivings. The question was how this important and perhaps unconscious motive could be measured. Seeking what he would later call a "psychic X ray," McClelland believed that our motives are revealed in our fantasies. To bring these fantasies out, he asked subjects to make up stories about a series of ambiguous pictures. Look at the sample photo in Figure 8.10. What's your interpretation? Who is the boy, what is he thinking about, and what will happen to him? Assuming that subjects will naturally identify with the main character (some are male, others female), pictures like this provide a screen on which people can project their own needs. Based on a scoring system devised by McClelland and his colleagues, you would be classified as high in the need for achievement if you say that the boy in Figure 8.10 is recalling with pride an exam he aced, thinking about how to win a scholarship, or dreaming of becoming a doctor—and if these types of concerns are a recurring theme in your stories.

From the start, this fantasy measure proved intriguing. For example, it proved to be a reasonably sensitive measure of the need for achievement. To demonstrate this, McClelland and his colleagues (1953) had subjects solve word puzzles before responding to the pictures. Some subjects were told that the puzzles were not that important; others were told that the puzzles tested intelligence and leadership ability—an instruction used to arouse performance concerns. Sure enough, subjects who were induced into a heightened state of achievement need told more achievement-relevant stories. Yet research soon showed that scores from this fantasy measure of achievement do not correlate with the way subjects described their own achievement needs on questionnaires. The reason? It appears that the story-based measure uncovers deeply ingrained, enduring, unconscious motives that predict a person's behavior over long periods of time, while questionnaires measure only conscious, self-attributed motives relevant to the way a person is likely to behave in the immediate situation (McClelland et al., 1989).

achievement motivation A strong desire to accomplish difficult tasks, outperform others, and excel.

As you might expect, there are strong links among a person's motivation, behavior, and level of accomplishment. Those who score high rather than low in the need for achievement work harder and are more persistent, innovative, and future-oriented. They also crave success more than they fear failure (Atkinson, 1964) and then credit success to their own abilities and efforts rather than to external factors (Weiner, 1989). One particularly interesting difference between the highs and lows concerns their level of aspiration. You might think that individuals driven by a need to achieve would take on exceedingly difficult tasks. Not so. When college students playing a ring-toss game could choose where to stand, those high rather than low in the need for achievement stood a moderate distance from the peg—not so close that success would come easy but not so far that they would fail (Atkinson & Litwin, 1960). People who are truly motivated to succeed set goals that are challenging but realistic (McClelland & Koestner, 1992). Indeed, they are more interested in mastering a task than they are fearful of failure (Elliot & Church, 1997).

Figure 8.10 Fantasy measure of achievement Who is the boy, what is he thinking about, and what will happen to him? Using ambiguous pictures like this one, researchers get people to tell stories and then code the stories for achievement imagery.

Clearly, hard work and realistic goal setting pay off in life. Individuals high in the need for achievement get better grades in school, are more successful in their careers, and are more upwardly mobile. In fact, McClelland (1985) and others have found that there is often a positive correlation between the achievement orientation of a whole society (which they measure by analyzing magazine articles and other popular writings) and overall levels of economic growth, scientific progress, and productivity. For example, changing levels of achievement motivation in the United States—as derived from children's readers in the years 1800 and 1950—closely paralleled inventiveness as measured by the per capita number of patents issued during those same years (deCharms & Moeller, 1962). Although these correlations are open to interpretation with regard to cause and effect, it's clear that the more achievement-oriented a society is at a given point in time, the more productive it is likely to be.

The Need for Power

Related but not identical to achievement motivation is the **need for power,** a strong desire to acquire prestige and influence over other people (Winter, 1973). As you might expect, men and women who are high rather than low in the need for power are more likely to run for public office and strive for other positions of authority. In a study that followed women for fourteen years after they graduated from college, those who had scored high in the need for power as seniors were later more likely to plan on, enter, and remain in careers that involved the exercise of power (Jenkins, 1994).

The need for power provides the fuel for great leadership. To be effective, however, leaders must also exercise self-control and use their power for social goals rather than for personal gain. William Spangler and Robert House (1991) analyzed the inaugural speeches written by thirty-three U.S. presidents, from George Washington to Ronald Reagan, in order to determine their need for power and other motives. Using complex measures of presidential effectiveness (which took into account their record on war, peaceful solutions to crises, and other decisions made), they discovered that more effective presidents had higher needs for power and more motivation to use that power for social rather than personal objectives. Can a leader's power motivation influence the course of world events? Perhaps. In a series of studies, David Winter (1993) analyzed 400 years of British history, the outbreak of World War I, and the 1962 Cuban Missile Crisis involving the United States and the former Soviet Union. In each study, Winter derived power-motivation scores for the leaders involved by using government documents and speeches given before, during, and after each conflict. The result: The leaders' need for power was statistically predictive of war and peace. As Winter put it, "When it rises, war is likely; when it falls, war is less likely and ongoing wars are likely to end" (p. 542).

need for power A strong desire to acquire prestige and influence over other people.

MOTIVATION AND EDUCATION

Using Fantasy Play to Motivate Achievement in the Classroom

It is no coincidence that Part I of the recently published *Handbook of Educational Psychology* (Berliner & Calfee, 1996) is devoted not to educational theory, school curricula, teaching methods, classroom management, testing and evaluation, or child development, but to the topic of *motivation.* Educators have long known that learning requires a student's active participation and that some children enter the classroom with a higher level of achievement motivation than others. The tough question is: What can teachers, parents, and others do to motivate students in their schoolwork?

Over the years, psychologists have approached the subject from different perspectives. Behaviorally oriented psychologists seek to influence the student's motivation through the use of rewards (praise, high grades, gold stars, smiley faces, pats on the back, and special privileges) and punishments (criticism, low grades, detention, suspension, letters home, and time in the principal's office). Practically, those who adopt this approach advise teachers to state instructional goals clearly, present tasks that start simple and build in complexity, develop assessment tools to monitor student progress, and provide students with clear and immediate feedback about their performance. Virtually all psychologists agree that reinforcement can be used to raise levels of achievement behavior in the classroom. As we saw in Chapter 5, some who are more cognitively oriented focus as well on how students think about and interpret these reinforcements. As Deborah Stipek (1996) put it, "What is important is not whether one has been rewarded in the past for the behavior but whether one *expects* to be rewarded in the future" (p. 85).

But there is another approach completely to the question of motivation. Try to recall your most memorable learning experiences from elementary school, and chances are that what comes to mind are the kinds of activities that converted work into play. Examples include having students prepare a Renaissance banquet complete with food and music, perform rather than just read a Shakespearian play, and use logical reasoning to solve a crime. Anyone who has ever watched a child spend hours at problem solving in the computer game *Myst* knows the motivational power of fantasy play. But do these techniques really make academic pursuits more interesting and promote better learning, or do they merely "sugarcoat" efforts at serious instruction?

Guided by the assumption that children learn best when they are motivated by interest, not just by grades, Mark Lepper and his colleagues have sought, experimentally, to evaluate the effects of presenting standard academic tasks within the context of a rich fantasy. In one study, Parker and Lepper (1992) developed a lesson plan for teaching third- and fourth-grade children the use of computer-graphic commands in the programming language Logo. On one occasion, the children were presented with a standard lesson on how to draw simple lines, navigate mazes, and construct geometric shapes on the screen. On three other occasions, these same tasks were embedded in fantasy-pretend games in which the students were encouraged to think of themselves as pirates in search of buried treasure, as detectives hunting down criminals, or as astronauts exploring space for new planets.

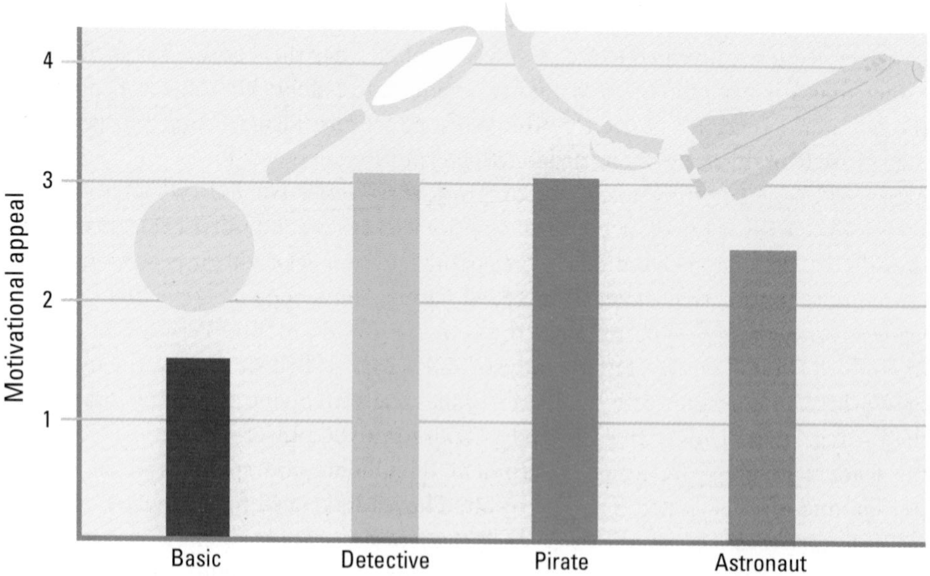

Figure 8.11 Motivational appeal of learning situations

So what were the effects? When the lessons were over, the experimenters asked the students to rank-order the motivational appeal of the different tasks. As shown in Figure 8.11, they preferred all the activities more in the fantasy situation than in the standard situation. In fact, when brought back two days later, they were more likely to choose the fantasy versions of these Logo tasks. Clearly, the children found the tasks more interesting in the game-like situation. But did this simple modification make for better education? Does it make a difference if the learning is fun? The answer is *yes*. In a follow-up study, Parker and Lepper presented either the basic or a fantasy version of the same graphics lesson and then tested the children in writing to measure their knowledge of the material. As shown in Figure 8.12, those who learned within a fantasy-rich context performed better—right after the lesson and again when retested two weeks later. Other experiments too have confirmed the point (Lepper & Cordova, 1992): When instructional material makes work feel like play, students become more engaged, more concentrated, and more likely to achieve.

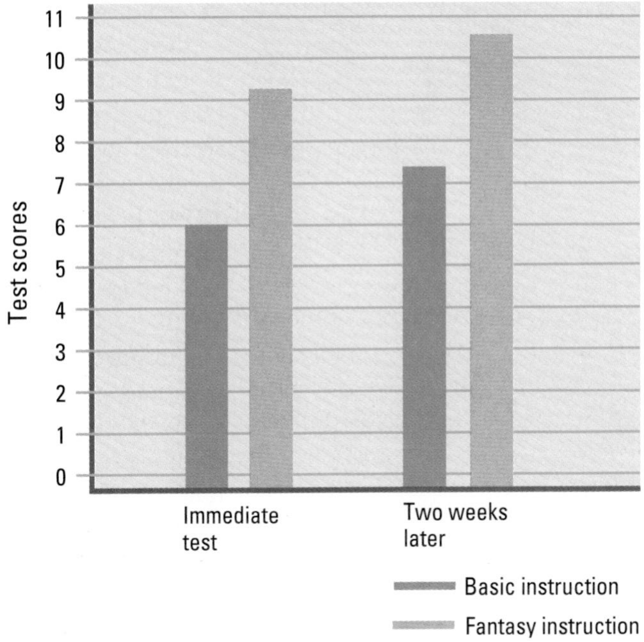

Figure 8.12 Test scores of basic and fantasy instruction situations

Motivating People at Work

What motivates us on the job? Are we driven by strictly economic costs and benefits? Does offering rewards for performance, as in corporate incentive programs, increase or undermine a worker's intrinsic motivation? How do people react when they feel overpaid or underpaid for their work?

In any organization—from Microsoft and Sony to your school and library—one of the critical challenges for industrial/organizational (I/O) psychologists is to determine what motivates individuals to work hard and to work well. Think about it. What drives *your* on-the-job performance? Are your concerns strictly economic, or do you have other personal needs to fulfill? There is no single answer. At work, as in the rest of life, our behavior often stems from the convergence of multiple motives.

Reward-Based Motivation

Out of necessity, people work for money and other economic benefits such as vacation time, sick leave, health insurance, and retirement pensions (Heneman & Schwab, 1985; Judge & Welbourne, 1994). Some of the rewards people get at work are not monetary but symbolic—for example, titles, large offices, windows, and access to parking (Becker, 1981; Sundstrom, 1986). The most popular theory of worker motivation is Victor Vroom's (1964) expectancy theory. According to

Vroom, people are rational decision makers who analyze the benefits and the costs of their possible courses of action. Specifically, he states, people are motivated to work hard whenever they expect that their efforts will improve performance, believe that good performance will be rewarded, and value the rewards they expect to receive. Over the years, expectancy theory has been used with some success to predict worker attendance, productivity, and other job-related behaviors (Mitchell, 1974). In addition, research has shown that people perform better at work and are more productive when they're given specific goals and a clear standard for success and failure than when they're simply told to "do your best" (Locke & Latham, 1990).

Consider a practical application of expectancy theory. In recent years, many corporations have devised and implemented innovative incentive-based programs to motivate workers. A survey of 1,600 American companies revealed that many of them used: (1) individual incentive programs that provide an opportunity to earn time off or extra pay, (2) small-group incentive plans that offer bonuses to members of a work unit for reaching specified goals, (3) profit-sharing plans in which workers earn money from company profits, (4) recognition programs that single out "employees of the month" for trophies and gifts, and (5) pay-for-knowledge plans that raise salaries for workers who are flexible and can perform different jobs within a work unit (Horn, 1987).

Intrinsic Motivation

Although people strive for tangible reward, there's more to money than just economics and more to motivation than just the size of a paycheck. Novelist Mark Twain (1876) seemed to realize this in *The Adventures of Tom Sawyer,* where he quipped, "There are wealthy gentlemen in England who drive four-horse passenger coaches twenty or thirty miles on a daily line, in the summer, because the privilege costs them considerable money; but if they were offered wages for the service that would turn it into work then they would resign." Twain's hypothesis—that reward for an enjoyable activity can undermine interest in that activity—seems to defy intuition and a great deal of psychological research. After all, aren't we all motivated by reward, as declared by B. F. Skinner and other behaviorists? The answer depends on how "motivation" is defined.

As a keen observer of human behavior, Twain anticipated a key distinction between intrinsic and extrinsic motivation. **Intrinsic motivation** originates in factors within a person. People are said to be intrinsically motivated when they engage in an activity for the sake of their own interest, the challenge, or sheer enjoyment. Eating a fine meal, listening to music, and working on a hobby are among the activities you might find intrinsically motivating. In contrast, **extrinsic motivation** originates in factors outside the person. People are said to be extrinsically motivated when they engage in an activity for money, recognition, or other tangible benefits. As the behaviorists have always said, people do strive for reward. The question is: What happens to *intrinsic* motivation once that reward is no longer available? It's clear that business leaders want their employees to be intrinsically motivated, loyal, satisfied, and committed to their work. So where does money fit in? Is tangible reward the bottom line or not?

Research shows that when people start getting paid for a task they already enjoy, they sometimes lose interest in it. In the first demonstration of this effect, Edward Deci (1971) recruited college students to work for three one-hour sessions on some fun block-building puzzles. During the first and third sessions, all subjects were

intrinsic motivation An inner drive that motivates people in the absence of external reward or punishment.

extrinsic motivation The desire to engage in an activity for money, recognition, or other tangible benefits.

treated in the same manner. In the second session, however, half the subjects were paid for each puzzle that they completed. To measure intrinsic motivation, Deci left subjects alone during breaks and secretly recorded the amount of free time they spent on the puzzles when other fun activities were available. Compared to subjects in the no-reward group, those paid in the second session later exhibited less interest in the puzzles when the payment was no longer available (see Figure 8.13). The moral: Receive money for a leisure activity, and, before you know it, what used to be "play" comes to feel like "work."

This paradoxical effect—that rewards can undermine intrinsic motivation—has been observed in many studies using rewards and other extrinsic incentives such as deadlines, competition, and evaluation (Deci & Ryan, 1985; Lepper & Greene, 1978; Tang & Hall, 1995). In the long run, rewards may even have adverse effects on performance. In one study, for example, Teresa Amabile found that subjects who were paid for artistic activities, compared to others who were not paid, produced work that was later judged to be less creative by independent raters. To be maximally productive, people should feel internally driven, not compelled by outside forces.

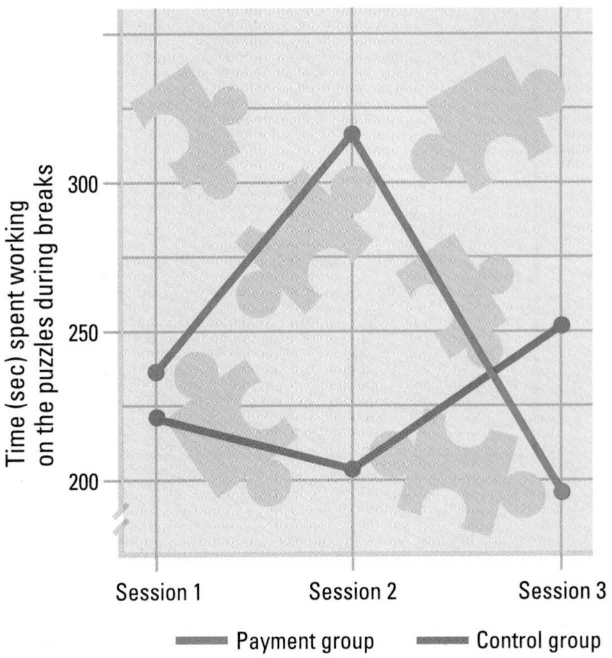

Figure 8.13 Effects of payment on intrinsic motivation In this study, subjects worked three times on fun puzzles. Half were paid for completing puzzles during session 2, the others were not. As measured by the amount of free time spent on the puzzles after each session, those who had been paid later had less interest in the puzzles when the money was no longer available (Deci, 1971).

But wait. If money undermines intrinsic motivation, should employers *not* use monetary incentives? Are pay-for-performance programs often used in the workplace doomed to fail, as some have suggested (Kohn, 1993)? Not necessarily. To answer this question, it's important to realize that a reward can be interpreted in two ways, depending on how it is presented. On the one hand, being offered payment can make a person feel bribed, bought off, and *controlled,* which can result in the detrimental effects just described. On the other hand, rewards often provide people with positive *information* about the quality of their performance—as when people earn bonuses, scholarships, and verbal praise from others they respect. Research now shows that just as controlling rewards can lower intrinsic motivation, informational rewards can have the opposite, positive effect (Eisenberger, 1992; Eisenberger & Cameron, 1996; Cameron & Pierce, 1994). Studying an office-machine company, Deci and his colleagues (1989) found that the less controlling the managers were, the more satisfied workers were with the company as a whole. Many years ago, Studs Terkel (1972) interviewed secretaries, stockbrokers, baseball players, garbage collectors, and workers in other occupations. Over and over again, he heard two complaints: being too closely watched, or "spied on," and getting too little positive feedback—in other words, too much control and not enough strokes.

"Productivity is up nine percent since I made everyone a vice president."

[Drawing by Ed Fisher; © 1995 The New Yorker Magazine, Inc.]

Equity Motivation

A second aspect of payment that influences motivation is the perception that it is *fair.* According to **equity theory,** people want rewards to be equitable, meaning that the ratio between inputs and outcomes should be roughly the same for ourselves as for others. Relative to coworkers, then, the better your performance is,

equity theory The notion that people want the ratio between input and outcome to be roughly the same for themselves as for others.

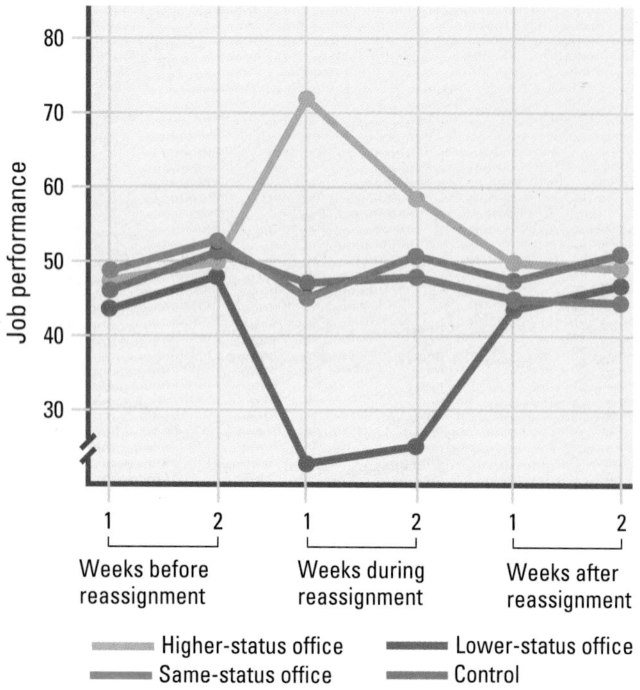

Figure 8.14 Equity motivation in the workplace Insurance company workers were moved temporarily to offices that were higher, lower, or equal in status to their rank. Supporting equity theory, those assigned to higher-status offices increased their job performance, while those sent to lower-status offices exhibited a decrease. When the workers were reassigned to their original offices, their productivity levels returned to normal (Greenberg, 1988).

the more money you think you should earn. If you think you're being overpaid or underpaid, however, you'll feel distressed and try to relieve that unhappy state either by restoring actual equity—say, through working less or seeking a raise—or by convincing yourself that equity already exists (Cropanzano, 1993; Greenberg, 1982).

Equity theory has some fascinating implications for behavior in the workplace. Consider Jerald Greenberg's (1988) study of workers in a large insurance firm. To allow for refurbishing, some 200 employees had to be moved temporarily from one office to another. Randomly, they were assigned to offices that belonged to others who were higher, lower, or equal in rank (the higher the rank, the more spacious the office). Would the random assignments influence job performance? By keeping track of the number of cases processed and the quality of the decisions made, Greenberg measured each worker's job performance before, during, and after the office switch. To restore equity, he reasoned, the workers given higher-status offices would feel overcompensated and improve their performance, while those sent to lower-status offices would feel undercompensated and lower their performance. As shown in Figure 8.14, that is exactly what happened. In a later study, Greenberg (1993) found that many subjects who were underpaid for their participation in an experiment went on to restore equity by stealing from the experimenter.

When we stop to reflect on our own motivations, we see just how varied they are. From the constant short-term need to stuff our face with food or satisfy the urge to have sex, to the desire to be with others or form close relationships, to the burning ambition to achieve excellence or gain power over others, it's clear that we are energized in many ways and toward many goal objects. Is there any more that we want from life? Is there some "ultimate" motivation? Perhaps. If you've ever met someone who seems to have it all—money, a successful career, good friends, a loving partner, and wonderful children—and yet yearns for more, you'll appreciate what's at the very top of Maslow's pyramid. As we'll see in Chapter 15, Maslow theorized that once our biological and social needs are met, we strive to fulfill all of our potential—toward a state he called self-actualization.

Summary and Key Terms

Displaying the **Hawthorne effect,** workers who were put into a special experimental room became more productive regardless of what changes were made.

Motivation is an inner state that energizes people toward the fulfillment of a goal. The question psychologists ask is: What motivates us?

What Motivates Us?

Over the years, some psychologists have proposed general theories to account for commonalities among all human motives. Others have studied specific motives such as hunger, sex, affiliation, and achievement.

General Theories of Motivation

Instinct theories of motivation used to be common but were soon rejected. According to **drive theory,** physiological needs that arise within the body create tension, which motivates us toward its reduction. To account for the fact that people often seek to increase tension, **arousal theory** posits that people are driven to maintain an optimum level of arousal—not too low, not too high. And in **incentive theory,** people behave in ways that they expect will gain a valued external incentive.

The Pyramid of Human Motivations

According to Maslow, all human beings are motivated to fulfill a **hierarchy of needs.** At the base are physiological needs for food, water, and so on. Next, in order, are safety and security needs, the need for belonging, and esteem needs. Once all needs are met, people strive for self-actualization.

Basic Human Motives

Among the basic human needs at the base of Maslow's pyramid are hunger and sexual motivation.

Hunger and Eating

Hunger is a sensation that motivates food search and consumption. The brain monitors glucose in the blood. When glucose drops below a certain level, people experience hunger. Eating then raises the glucose and reduces the motivation to eat. The glucose levels are monitored in or near the hypothalamus. Psychological factors such as personal and cultural tastes, and external food cues such as time and the company of other people also play a role in hunger and eating.

People are considered **obese** when they have a surplus of body fat that causes them to exceed their optimum weight by 20 percent. There is a strong genetic component to obesity, which may determine **set point,** a level of weight toward which our body gravitates. Most people can achieve long-term weight loss through changes in diet and exercise. Psychological influences on eating are most evident in the disorders **anorexia nervosa** and **bulimia nervosa.** Both are most common among adolescent girls and young women, particularly in weight-conscious cultures and in women with negative body images.

Sexual Motivation

Surveys show that men and women differ in aspects of their sexual motivations. From an evolutionary perspective, women are highly selective in mate selection and seek men with economic resources or traits predictive of future earnings. Men seek women who are young and attractive—attributes that signal fertility. Men also seek women who are not promiscuous. Cross-cultural studies, marriage statistics, and personal ads support these and related hypotheses. Still, many researchers argue that the results can be explained by factors that are psychological, not evolutionary.

Despite gender differences, there are striking similarities in the **sexual-response cycles** of men and women. Among both men and women, this cycle is characterized by excitement, plateau, orgasm, and resolution phases.

With regard to **sexual orientation,** about 5 percent of men and 2 to 3 percent of women are homosexual in their orientation. A tiny nucleus in the hypothalamus is larger in heterosexual men than in women and homosexual men. Twin studies involving gay men and lesbians reveal that there is a genetic component. It is not clear, however, whether genes predispose sexual orientation per se or gender-typed behavior in childhood that later gives rise to a sexual orientation.

Social Motives

People are not content merely to satisfy biological needs. In addition, there are social motives for belongingness and esteem.

Belongingness Motives

Maslow's belongingness motives are composed of two distinct needs. In varying degrees, people enjoy being with others, a **need for affiliation.** Research shows that we seek an optimum balance of social contact but that we affiliate more under stress in order to gain cognitive clarity about the situation we're in. People also have a **need for intimacy,** for close relationships that are characterized by open and confidential communication known as **self-disclosure.**

Esteem Motives

People differ in their level of **achievement motivation,** which is defined as the desire to accomplish difficult tasks and to excel. To assess the strength of this motive, researchers use a fantasy measure in which subjects tell stories about the characters in ambiguous pictures and code these stories for achievement themes. Research has shown that people who score high rather than low on this measure work harder, set more realistic goals, and achieve more. Related to this motive is the **need for power,** a desire to gain prestige and influence over others. There are links between the strength of this need and various indexes of leadership.

Motivating People at Work

I/O psychologists seek to determine what motivates people to work hard and well.

Reward-Based Motivation

According to expectancy theory, people work hard when they expect their efforts to improve performance and produce a value reward. Thus, many corporations use incentive-based programs to motivate workers.

Intrinsic Motivation

Psychologists have distinguished between two types of motivation. **Intrinsic motivation** originates within a person out of interest, challenge, and sheer enjoyment. **Extrinsic motivation** originates in factors outside the person (reward, recognition). Research shows that although reward increases extrinsic motivation, it can lower intrinsic motivation, which becomes evident once the reward is no longer available. Reward has this effect when it is seen as a bribe, but it has the opposite effect when presented as positive feedback.

Equity Motivation

Equity theory maintains that people want rewards to be linked in a fair way to performance relative to others. Thus, when people feel overpaid, they work harder to restore equity. Feelings of underpayment lead people to slack off.

In the Field Resources

Books

Buss, D. M. (1994). *The evolution of desire.* New York: Basic Books.

This easy-to-read paperback offers a fascinating introduction to evolutionary psychology as it applies to attraction, mating, and sexual desire.

Logue, A. W. (1993). *The psychology of eating and drinking* (2nd ed.). New York: W. H. Freeman.

This fascinating book provides clear, research-based answers to common questions about food, hunger, taste, obesity, and other aspects of eating and drinking.

Films and Videos

Eating (1990, 110 min.)

This is an odd but interesting film about a group of women who talk openly about eating, dieting, and the importance of food in their lives. (Lisa Richards, Mary Crosby, Gwen Welles, Nely Alard, Frances Bergen, Daphna Kastner.)

Internet

Academy of Management Online (http://www.aom.pace.edu/)

This professional organization offers information about I/O psychology and other business-related fields.

Anorexia Nervosa and Bulimia Association (http://qlink.queensu.ca/ ~ 4map/anabhome.htm)

ANAB provides lots of information about eating disorders as well as other resources and access to support services.

Darwin's Cafe (http://psych.imu.edu/darwin.htm)

An informal discussion board for topics related to evolution and human behavior.

Journals and Periodicals

Appetite
Archives of Sexual Behavior
Journal of Personality
Journal of Personality and Social Psychology
Journal of Sex Research
Motivation and Emotion
Psychological Science

9 *Emotion*

What's Your Prediction?
Cultural influences on emotion

The situation Imagine that you are working as part of a research team that is studying cultural influences. The goal of the project is to examine the effects of culture on the way people interpret facial expressions. Do human beings all over the world show joy, sadness, and other emotions in the same way, or are there differences in facial expressions as there are in the languages we speak?

To answer this question, you collect portrait photographs of adult men and women smiling, frowning, pouting, and expressing other emotions on the face. Your goal is to get pictures of people experiencing, or pretending to experience, six emotional states: happiness, sadness, anger, fear, surprise, and disgust. Then you contact colleagues from other countries and arrange for them to translate the words and show the pictures to natives of their culture. In all, you're able to test more than 500 people from Estonia, Germany, Greece, Hong Kong, Italy, Japan, Scotland, Sumatra, Turkey, and the United States.

The testing procedure is straightforward. Your experimenters schedule "observers" for group sessions. In total, eighteen pictures are shown on slides, for ten seconds each and in random order, and each slide depicts one of the six emotions. Participants are given a response sheet on which they are asked to check off the emotion being displayed in each picture.

Make a prediction The data that you collect in this study are interesting in two ways. The first question you want to answer is: Are emotions universally recognized, or are there cultural differences? In other words, to what extent do people in general (as represented in the ten cultures) *agree* on the emotions displayed by various facial expressions? Second, do some expressions elicit a higher agreement rate across cultures than others? As you prepare to analyze the results, what are your hypotheses? The table below lists the six emotions represented in this study. On a scale of 0 to 100 percent, what percentage of the participants, across all the ten cultures, do you think recognized each type of emotion?

Happiness	_____%	Sadness	_____%	Anger	_____%
Fear	_____%	Surprise	_____%	Disgust	_____%

The results You receive a total of 547 response forms in the mail, tally the results, and notice two interesting findings. Look at the table below and you'll see, first, that a clear majority of observers in *all* cultures interpreted facial expressions in the same way. The total agreement rate was far from perfect, but over all cultures and emotions it was quite high, at 82 percent. The second finding is that some emotions elicited more agreement than others. As you can see, people in general were most likely to agree on expressions of happiness and surprise and least likely to agree on anger and disgust.

Happiness	90%
Sadness	85%
Anger	74%
Fear	80%
Surprise	90%
Disgust	73%

What does it all mean? When Paul Ekman and others (1987) conducted the study just described, they were addressing a recurring debate in psychology concerning the "universality" of emotional states. On the one hand, emotion is so basic to the human experience that one would expect people all over the world to express their feelings in similar ways. On the other hand, there are cultural differences in the way people think about and interpret each other's behavior. Both positions are partly correct. Ekman's cross-cultural study showed that certain facial expressions are similarly interpreted by people all over the world. But what about other aspects of emotion? There is no simple answer. We'll see in this chapter that our emotions are a product of physiological, behavioral, and cognitive factors and that although some aspects are universal, others are shaped by cultural forces.

Scream. Basic Instinct. The English Patient. Mission Impossible. Fargo. Contact. Air Force One. Go to the movies on a Saturday night, and you will witness firsthand the power of human emotion. In darkened theaters all over the world, audiences laugh hysterically, cry in sorrow, gasp in fear, clench their jaws in anger, and tingle with sexual delight. Cheers, tears, sweaty palms, tense muscles, and a pounding heart are a vital part of the entertainment experience.

When scientists compare human beings and other animals, they are quick to point to our superior intellect; to the cognitive processes of learning, memory, thought, and language; and to the ability to formulate plans in order to satisfy our motivations. It is important to realize, however, that we humans are also intensely emotional, warm-blooded creatures. Love, hate, joy, sadness, pride, shame, hope, fear, lust, boredom, surprise, embarrassment, guilt, jealousy, and disgust are among the powerful feelings that color and animate our daily lives.

Emotion is a difficult concept to define, in part because there are so many different emotions in the repertoire of human feelings. Some are universal; others are found only in certain cultures. Some are intense; others are mild. Some are positive; others are negative. Some motivate us to take action; others do not. Despite these vast differences, however, psychologists agree that emotions in general consist of three interacting components: (1) internal physiological arousal, (2) expressive behavior in the face and body, and (3) a cognitive appraisal (see Figure 9.1). This chapter examines each of these components as well as various theories on how they combine to produce the conscious sensations we call emotions.

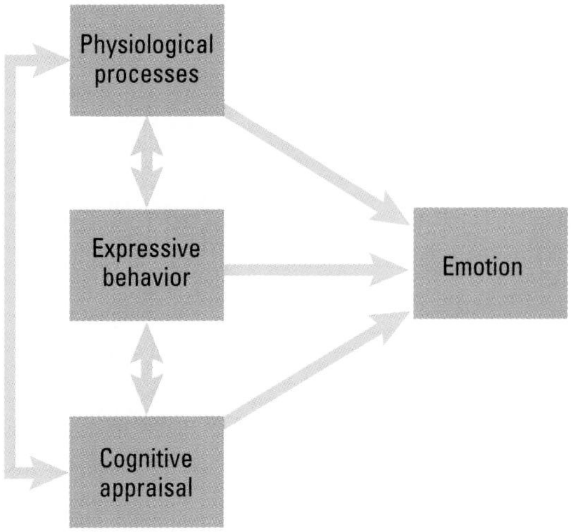

Figure 9.1 Three components of emotion Based on many years of research, psychologists agree that emotions are triggered by a combination of factors.

The Physiological Component

Why is emotion considered a physiological event, and what roles are played by the brain and nervous system? Are all emotions accompanied by a state of general arousal, or does each emotion have its own unique set of symptoms? What is a polygraph, how can it be used as a lie-detector test, and is it accurate?

The first time I gave a talk at a professional conference, I was more nervous than I thought I would be. The symptoms were unmistakable. As I stepped to the podium and looked up at the audience, I had a knot in the pit of my stomach. My heart pounded, my hands shook, cold sweat dripped down my arms, and my mouth was bone dry. If that wasn't bad enough, my voice quivered the moment I started to speak. My body was sending me a message I did not want to hear and could not control. Was this a rare and unique experience? Not at all. Imagine what it feels like to fall head-over-heels in love, to be stranded on a dangerous street at night, to suffer the death of a loved one, or to get cheated out of something you desperately wanted and felt you deserved. The physical sensations may vary, but the body is intimately involved in feelings of intense emotion.

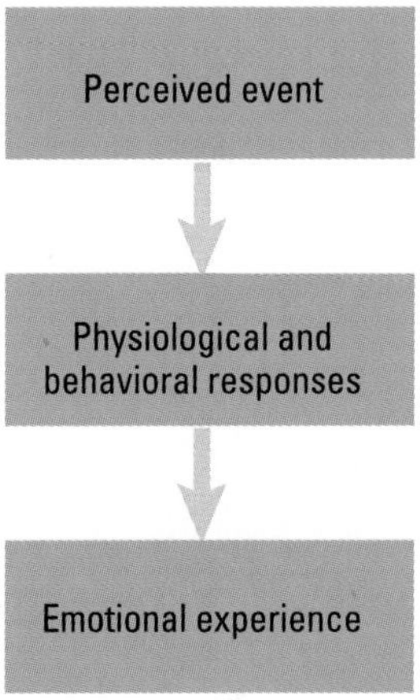

Figure 9.2 The James-Lange theory of emotion

A Historical Perspective

William James was the first psychologist to theorize about the role of bodily functions in emotion. Common sense tells us that we smile because we're happy, cry because we're sad, clench our fists because we're angry, and tremble because we're afraid. Thus, if you are crossing the street and see a car speeding at you, that stimulus will trigger fear, which in turn will cause your heart to pound as you try to escape. This seems reasonable, but in 1884, James turned common sense on its head by proposing what he thought to be a radical new idea (in fact, philosopher René Descartes had made a similar proposal in the seventeenth century): that people feel happy because they smile, sad because they cry, angry because they clench their fists, and afraid because they tremble. In other words, the perception of danger causes your heart to pound as you run for cover—and it's these physiological and behavioral reactions that cause you to become afraid. This proposed chain of events, which was also suggested by a Danish physician named Carl Lange, is known as the **James-Lange theory** of emotion (see Figure 9.2).

emotion A feeling state characterized by physiological arousal, expressive behaviors, and a cognitive interpretation.

James-Lange theory The theory that emotion stems from the physiological arousal that is triggered by an emotion-eliciting stimulus.

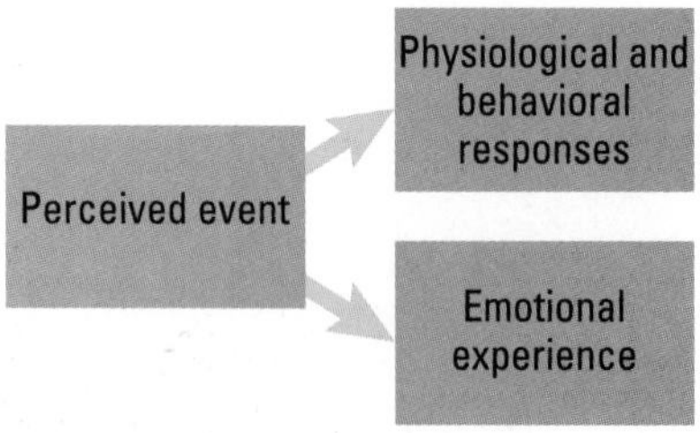

Figure 9.3 The Cannon-Bard theory of emotion

In 1927, physiologist Walter Cannon challenged the James-Lange theory on three grounds. First, said Cannon, bodily sensations alone cannot produce emotion. Indeed, when people are injected with epinephrine—a hormone that energizes the body—they report feeling "pumped up" and aroused but do not experience any specific emotion. Second, said Cannon, we sometimes feel fear, anger, and other emotions instantly, before all the systems of the body have had time to react. Third, the physical changes that do occur are often too general for us to distinguish between different emotions. Fear may make the heart beat faster, but so do anger and love.

As an alternative to the James-Lange theory, Cannon and a colleague named Philip Bard proposed that emotion originates in the thalamus, the part of the brain that simultaneously relays messages from the sensory organs to the autonomic nervous system (arousal), skeletal muscles (motor behavior), and cerebral cortex (conscious thought). According to the **Cannon-Bard theory**, the body and "mind" are activated independently in the experience of emotion. Thus, if you see a car swerving in your direction, your heart will start to pound, you'll run, and you'll become afraid—all at the same time (see Figure 9.3).

The debate between the James-Lange and Cannon-Bard theories was never resolved, and emotion researchers today are not quite as focused on the precise timing and sequence of the internal stream of events (Ellsworth, 1994). Equipped with sophisticated new measurement devices, many physiologically oriented researchers seek instead to understand the role in emotion played by different brain structures, neural pathways, and autonomic arousal. We now consider each of these topics.

Brain Centers of Emotion

What role does the brain play in the experience of emotion? To begin with, research shows that some emotions are regulated by the *limbic system*—an evolutionarily primitive set of neural structures (including the thalamus, hypothalamus, hippocampus, and amygdala) that surrounds the brainstem and is found in lower mammals (see Figure 2.14). Stimulate one part of the limbic system in a cat, and the cat will withdraw in fear; stimulate an adjacent area, and the cat will become enraged—snarling, hissing, and ready to pounce. Electronic stimulation of limbic structures in humans, as is sometimes used in the treatment of epilepsy, has similar effects (Panskepp, 1986).

Recent research points directly to the *amygdala* as a center for fear responses. In a case described by Joseph LeDoux (1996), Antonio Damasio and his colleagues recently encountered a patient who had a rare brain disorder in which excessive amounts of calcium were deposited in her amygdala. This structure was damaged, but other parts of her brain were unaffected. The deficits she exhibited were strikingly specific. When shown pictures of people with different facial expressions, she could identify most emotions, but she could not recognize fear. When asked to show fear on her own face, she could not. This case study parallels recent findings in animal research. In a series of experiments with rats, LeDoux (1996) found that when the amygdala was destroyed, the rats lost the ability to react to harmful stimuli with fear—which they typically do by freezing in place. In other experiments, he chemically traced the pathways in the brain that are activated in threatening situations and found that fear cut a path from the thalamus, where sensory input is sent, straight to the amygdala—without any involvement of the "thinking" cerebral cortex. As we'll see later, this research indicates that fear, and perhaps other raw emotions as well, are triggered instantly—before information reaches the cortex and before we have had time to appraise the situation and formulate a response.

Cannon-Bard theory The theory that an emotion-eliciting stimulus simultaneously triggers physiological arousal and the experience of emotion.

Certain emotions may be quick and automatic, but others appear to involve the *cerebral cortex*—the seat of human intellect. One cannot pinpoint a single region of the cortex that regulates all feelings, because different emotions involve distinct patterns of activity. But there are hemispheric differences in the brain. In a series of experiments, Richard Davidson, Nathan Fox, and others have found that positive emotions evoke more electrical activity in the left cerebral hemisphere, while negative emotions elicit more activity in the right. In one study, Davidson and his colleagues (1990) had subjects watch films that evoked either pleasure (a puppy playing with flowers, a gorilla taking a bath in a zoo) or disgust (a third-degree-burn victim, a gruesome leg amputation), videotaped their facial expressions with a hidden camera, and took EEG recordings in the brain. The result was that pleasure films increased activity in the left hemisphere, and disgust films did so in the right hemisphere. Very similar results have been found in infants. When newborn babies taste sugared water or when ten-month-olds are approached by mom, the left hemisphere is primarily activated. When the taste is sour, however, or when the approaching adult is a stranger, there is greater activity in the right hemisphere (Fox, 1991).

If approach and withdrawal *behaviors* are associated with the left and right hemispheres, respectively, could there be a link between brain activity and *temperament*? Is it possible, using EEG measures, to distinguish between people who are characteristically outgoing and those who are shy and withdrawn? Yes, it appears so. In one study, four-year-old children interacted in play groups, and then, two weeks later, their EEGs were recorded as they attended to a visual stimulus. Those who were sociable in their playgroups later exhibited more relative activity in the left hemisphere, while those who were more isolated and withdrawn exhibited more relative activity in the right hemisphere (Fox et al., 1995). Other research, too, shows that children and adults with a more active left hemisphere tend to be interested, joyful, and enthusiastic, whereas those with a more active right hemisphere tend to be more timid, fearful, nervous, avoidant, and depressed (Davidson, 1993; Tomarken et al., 1992). This asymmetry is illustrated in Figure 9.4.

Emotions evoke specific patterns of EEG activity. In the experiment depicted here, researcher Nathan Fox records brain waves in a four-month-old infant stimulated by toys.

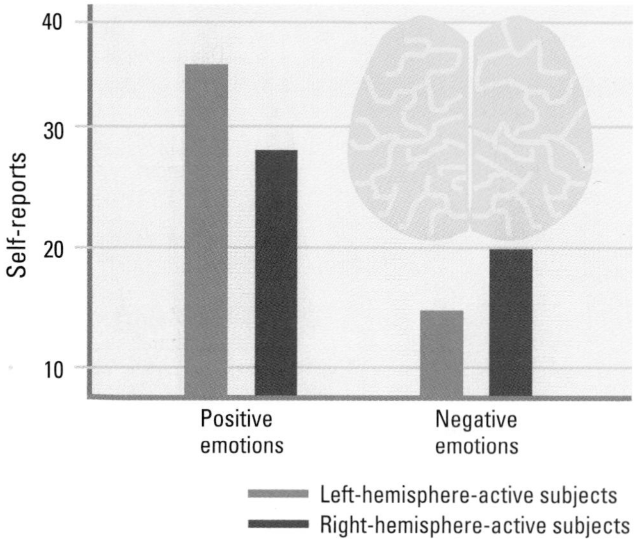

Figure 9.4 Brain centers of emotion Compared to subjects who exhibited greater EEG activity in the right hemisphere, those with a more active left hemisphere had emotions that were more positive (*left*) and less negative (*right*) (Tomarken et al., 1992).

Generalized Autonomic Arousal

When an event prompts an emotional response, the human body prepares for action (Thompson, 1988). To mobilize us for "fight" or "flight," the hypothalamus activates the **sympathetic nervous system**—the branch of the autonomic nervous system (ANS) that controls involuntary activities of the heart, lungs, and other organs. Specifically, the adrenal glands secrete more of the hormones epinephrine and norepinephrine (more commonly known as adrenaline and noradrenalin), which

sympathetic nervous system A branch of the autonomic nervous system that controls the involuntary activities of various organs and mobilizes the body for fight or flight.

Riding a roller coaster activates the sympathetic nervous system. When the ride is over, the parasympathetic nervous system restores the body to its calm state.

increase the heart rate and blood pressure and heighten physiological arousal. Then all at once, the liver pours extra sugar into the bloodstream for energy, the pupils dilate to let in more light, the breathing rate speeds up for more oxygen, perspiration increases to cool down the body, blood clots faster to heal wounds, saliva flow is inhibited, and digestion slows down to divert blood to the brain and skeletal muscles. Epinephrine and norepinephrine supply the physiological fuel for our many passions.

After an emotional event, the **parasympathetic nervous system** takes over and restores the body to its premobilized calm state. The heart stops racing, blood pressure is lowered, the pupils contract, breathing slows down, saliva flows again, the digestive system resumes its normal functions, and energy is conserved. As the levels of epinephrine and norepinephrine in the bloodstream slowly diminish, there is a gradual lowering in the intensity of our feelings, enabling us to relax, cool down, and get on with our normal functions. This aspect of emotion is illustrated in Figure 9.5.

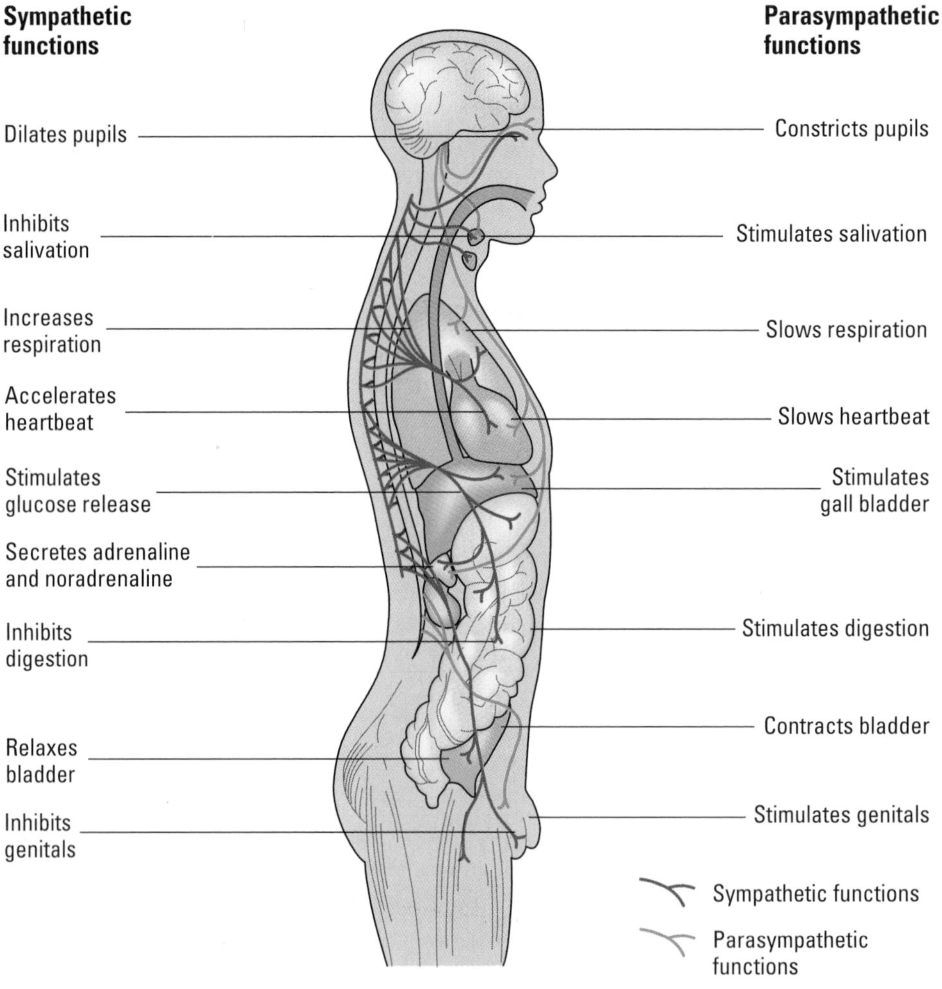

Figure 9.5 The autonomic nervous system Note the differing functions of the sympathetic (arousing) and parasympathetic (calming) divisions of the autonomic nervous system.

parasympathetic nervous system A branch of the autonomic nervous system that calms the body and conserves energy.

Specific Patterns of Arousal

Clearly, physiological arousal intensifies an emotional experience. But are all emotions accompanied by the same general state of arousal, or does each emotion have its own unique set of symptoms? Scholars have been debating this question for many years. William James (1884) and others have argued that each emotion feels different inside because each is associated with its own specific pattern of autonomic activity. Noting that love, rage, and fear all make the heart beat faster, however, Walter Cannon (1927) and, later, others have maintained that all emotions spark the same physiological arousal. Who is right? Does each emotion have its own autonomic "fingerprint," or do they all feel basically the same?

Research suggests there is a bit of truth to both positions. In one study, Paul Ekman and his colleagues (1983) trained subjects (many of whom were actors) to tense up the facial muscles that express happiness, anger, surprise, fear, sadness, or disgust. Aided by a mirror, subjects held each face for ten seconds and the researchers took various measures of autonomic arousal. As it turned out, the posed expressions produced physiological differences. For example, heart rate increased for both anger and fear, but anger increased skin temperature, while fear had the opposite effect. Other studies have since confirmed this point (Levenson, 1992): Many emotions make the heart beat faster, but this similarity masks important differences—differences that are betrayed in the language we use to describe our feelings. Thus, in anger, we say that we're "hot under the collar," that our "blood is boiling," and that we need to "cool off" and "simmer down." In contrast, we describe fear as a "bone-chilling" emotion in which we "freeze" or get "cold feet" (Kovecses, 1990). Even more distinctive is the all-too-familiar pattern of arousal that signals embarrassment, a highly social emotion. When people feel ashamed or embarrassed in front of others, they blush—an involuntary reflex characterized by redness in the cheeks and ears and a rise in body temperature (Shearn et al., 1990).

> *"Man is the only animal that blushes. Or needs to."*
>
> — MARK TWAIN

Clearly, autonomic-nervous-system activity is biologically programmed into the human organism—regardless of whether one lives in North America, South America, Europe, Asia, Africa, or the Pacific Islands. But are the *specific* patterns of arousal similarly universal? Is anger associated with increased heart rate and skin temperature in all cultures? What about the link between fear and cooled skin temperature? To test the cross-cultural generality of Ekman's results, Robert Levenson and his colleagues (1992) studied the Minangkabau culture of West Sumatra, an island of Indonesia. This culture is very different from ours in many ways. Its members are Muslims and farmers, live in extended matrilineal families, and forbid the public display of negative emotions. Yet despite these differences, the Levenson team found that the Minangkabau exhibited patterns of autonomic arousal similar to those of American subjects.

In fact, people all over the world seem to know intuitively how the body reacts in different emotions. Klaus Scherer and Harald Walbott (1994) asked 3,000 students from thirty-seven countries (including the United States, Brazil, France, Norway, Greece, Poland, Botswana, Malawi, Israel, India, Hong Kong, and New Zealand) to describe various emotional experiences and found that there was widespread agreement about the primary sensations. To be sure, there were some cultural differences as well. For example, Japanese subjects reported fewer symptoms than did American and European subjects—perhaps because they are less self-focused and less likely to attend to their own inner states. Still, the sensations that

Japanese subjects did report were very similar to those described by other cultural groups. Table 9.1 shows the most frequently reported bodily symptoms of the various emotions.

The Lie-Detector Test

For centuries, people have known that lying is stressful and that the stress is revealed in involuntary physiological changes. The Bedouins of Arabia used to make crime suspects lick a hot iron. In India and China, the suspects were forced to chew rice powder and then spit it out. Based on the assumption that lying produces a dryness in the mouth, those who burned their tongues or spit out dried powder were judged to be dishonest (Kleinmuntz & Szucko, 1984).

The modern lie-detector test is also based on the assumption that lying heightens autonomic arousal. Because this activity is not observable, law-enforcement officials use the **polygraph**—an electronic instrument that can simultaneously record multiple channels of arousal. The physiological signals are picked up by sensors that are attached to different parts of the body. For example, rubber tubes are strapped around the subject's torso to measure breathing, or respiration; blood pressure cuffs are wrapped around the upper arm to measure pulse rate and other cardiovascular activity; and electrodes on the hand are used to monitor changes in sweat-gland activity, or perspiration. These signals are then boosted by amplifiers and converted into a visual display.

Table 9.1 Cross-Cultural Emotional Experiences

EMOTIONS	SYMPTOMS	PERCENTAGE REPORTED
Joy	Feeling warm	63
	Fast heartbeat	40
	Relaxed muscles	29
Fear	Fast heartbeat	65
	Tense muscles	52
	Rapid breathing	47
	Perspiration	37
	Feeling cold	36
	Lump in throat	29
	Stomach trouble	22
Anger	Fast heartbeat	50
	Tense muscles	43
	Rapid breathing	37
	Feeling hot	32
	Lump in throat	25
Sadness	Lump in throat	56
	Crying	55
	Tense muscles	27
	Fast heartbeat	27
	Feeling cold	22
Shame	Feeling hot	40
	Fast heartbeat	35
	Perspiration	26
Guilt	Lump in throat	28
	Fast heartbeat	27
Disgust	Tense muscles	25
	Fast heartbeat	23
	Stomach trouble	21

polygraph An electronic device that records multiple channels of autonomic arousal and is often used as a lie-detector test.

It is important to keep in mind that the polygraph itself is merely a physiological recording device. It becomes a lie-detector test only when combined with an oral examination. Here's how it usually works. First, the examiner conducts a pretest interview to establish the subject's baseline level of arousal and convince the subject that the polygraph works. Next, the examiner compares the subject's reaction to arousing *crime-relevant* questions ("Did you steal the car last night?") and *control questions* that are arousing but not relevant to the crime ("Did you steal anything when you were younger?"). In theory, crime-relevant questions should evoke more arousal than the control questions among subjects who are lying but not among those who are telling the truth (see Figure 9.6).

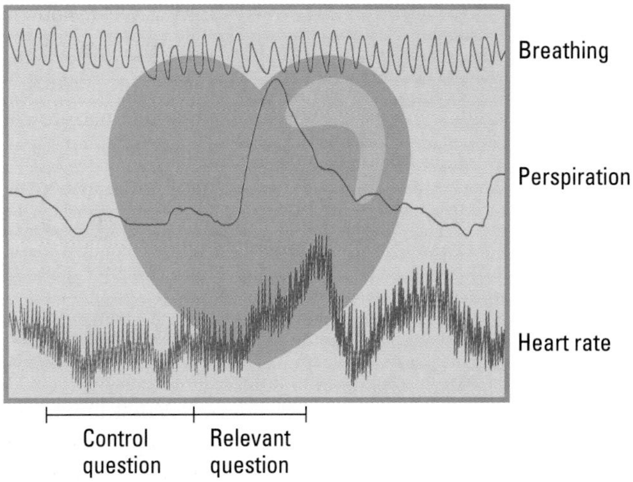

Figure 9.6 Lie-detector test This polygraph recording depicts the physiological reactions of a crime suspect judged guilty. Note that heart rate and perspiration increased more in response to a crime-relevant question than to a control question (Raskin, 1982).

Does the lie-detector test work? Many people think it is foolproof, but professional opinion is split. Some researchers report accuracy rates of about 90 percent (Horvath, 1984; Raskin, 1986). Others say that these claims are exaggerated and that the test is fraught with serious problems (Lykken, 1981). One well-documented problem is that truthful persons too often "fail" the test. For example, a study of polygraph records obtained from police files revealed that although 98 percent of suspects later known to be guilty were correctly identified as such, 45 percent of those who were eventually found innocent were also judged as deceptive (Patrick & Iacono, 1991). A second problem is that the test can be passed through faking. Studies show that you can beat the polygraph by distracting yourself or by tensing your muscles, biting your tongue, or squeezing your toes while answering the *control* questions. Think through the logic of this strategy. By artificially inflating our responses to these "innocent" questions, we can mask the stress that is aroused by lying to the crime-relevant questions (Honts et al., 1994).

What, then, are we to conclude? After carefully reviewing all of the polygraph research for the Congressional Office of Technology Assessment, Leonard Saxe and others (1985) concluded that there is no simple answer. Under certain conditions—for example, when the suspect is naive and the examiner is well trained—it is possible for polygraphers to make accurate and discriminating judgments of truth and deception. The problems just described, however, remain hard to overcome—which is why many states refuse to allow polygraph-test results into evidence. As an alternative, researchers are now trying to develop tests that distinguish between truth-telling and deception by measuring involuntary electrical activity in the brain (Bashore & Rapp, 1993) and pupil dilation when the subject is visually reexposed to an object related to the crime (Lubow & Fein, 1996). At this point, it's too early to tell whether these types of tests will prove to be any more accurate (Rosenfeld, 1995).

Until recently, many companies used the polygraph to screen employees and uncover theft in the workplace. Those who use it argue that it sharpens one's ability to hire employees who are honest. Opponents, however, argue that the test is an invasion of an individual's privacy, that it is often misused, and that the results are not sufficiently accurate. In light of the problems, the U.S. government in 1988 passed a law that prohibits the use of the lie-detector test except for jobs that involve matters of security and public safety. In its place, many companies now require job applicants to take *integrity tests*—questionnaires designed to assess a person's character by asking direct, pointed questions about drug use, drinking, shoplifting, petty theft, and other transgressions. If such a test rings a familiar bell, it's because you may have taken one. Integrity tests have already been administered to millions of job applicants. At this point, the jury is still out on the value of these instruments. On the one hand, research suggests that at least some of these tests are easy to fake and that people can be coached on how to pass them (Alliger et al., 1996). On the other hand, the scores appear to be predictive of absenteeism rates, theft, discipline problems, and other counterproductive on-the-job behaviors (Camara & Schneider, 1994; Ones et al., 1993).

The Expressive Component

What functions are served by our outward expressions of emotion? Are some emotions "basic," and if so, which ones? What is the evidence that facial expressions are inborn and universal? What's the facial-feedback hypothesis, and why does it predict that smiling can make you happy?

Emotion may be an internal, purely subjective experience, but it also has an observable behavioral component. The links between our inner feelings and outward expressions are numerous: We smile when we're happy, cry when we're sad, blush when we're embarrassed, stand tall when we feel proud, drag our feet when we're down, press our lips in anger, bow our heads in shame, and wrinkle our faces in disgust.

> *"Our faces, together with our language, are social tools that help us navigate the social encounters that define our 'selves' and fashion our lives."*
>
> — ALAN J. FRIDLUND

These behavioral expressions of emotion serve two functions. First, they provide us with a means of *nonverbal communication*. People often use words to tell others how they're feeling. But by smiling, frowning, turning bright red in the face, shrugging the shoulders, and winking an eye, we also communicate our feelings nonverbally. Alan Fridlund (1994) thus argues that our expressive behaviors serve more as *signals* to others than as *symptoms* of how we feel—and that the display of emotion is an inherently social experience (see Figure 9.7). The second effect of behavioral expression is to provide us with *sensory feedback*. In 1872, Darwin theorized that the expressions that we make clarify and intensify emotional experiences by providing us with bodily feedback about how we feel. In short, the expressive component of emotion has two audiences: other people and ourselves.

Wink	Smirk	Said smiling	Said frowning	Sardonic incredulity
'-)	:-,	:-)	:-(	;-)
:-|	:-X	:*)	|-(	:-J
Disgusted	Kiss, kiss	Clowning around	Said late at night	Said tongue-in-cheek

Figure 9.7 Some common e-mail "emoticons" The social value of the face is evident to those who communicate online. When e-mail first became popular, the written word was often misinterpreted (especially when the writer was trying to be funny) because it lacked the expressions that normally animate and clarify live interactions. To fill in the facial gap, e-mailers created smiley faces and other "emoticons" (emotion icons) from standard keyboard characters. Meant to be viewed with one's head tilted 90 degrees to the left, some routinely used emoticons are shown above (Sanderson, 1993).

Nonverbal Communication

Knowing how another person is feeling can be tricky because people sometimes try to hide their true emotions. Think about it. Have you ever had to suppress your rage toward someone, mask your disappointment after failure, feign surprise, or pretend to like something just to be polite? Sometimes we come right out and tell people how we feel. But often we actively try to conceal our true feelings. In instances like these, observers tune into a silent language—the language of nonverbal behavior.

Facial Expression What kinds of nonverbal cues do people use to judge how someone is feeling? In *The Expression of the Emotions in Man and Animals*, Charles Darwin

(1872) argued that the *face* communicates emotion in ways that are innate and are understood by people all over the world. Contemporary research provides strong support for this notion. For example, Ekman & Friesen (1974) showed thirty photographs like those appearing below to subjects from New York to New Guinea—including Argentina, Borneo, Brazil, and Japan—and asked them to guess the emotion being portrayed in each photo. The results of this study, and of many others like it, indicate that people can reliably identify six emotions: joy, fear, anger, sadness, surprise, and disgust. In the experiment described at the start of this chapter, for example, subjects from ten different countries exhibited high levels of agreement in their recognition of these same emotions (Ekman et al., 1987). Not everyone agrees that the results are strong enough to support the claim that basic emotions are "universally" recognized in the face (Russell, 1994). Indeed, sometimes we determine how someone is feeling not from their expression but by inferring it from the situation they're in (Carroll & Russell, 1996). It is clear, however, that from one end of the world to the other, a smile is a smile and a frown is a frown, and just about everyone knows what they mean—even when the expressions are "put on" by actors and not genuinely felt (Gosselin et al., 1995).

Chelsey Thomas was known as the little girl who could not smile. She was born with Moebius syndrome, a rare neurological disorder that impairs activity in the facial muscles. "She always smiled, really, on the inside," said her mother. But with the face playing a vital role in communication, one can only imagine what a social price she paid for her outward blank expression. So Chelsey had corrective surgery and then had to learn how—and when—to smile. On June 19, 1996, at the age of seven, she smiled for the first time.

Further supporting the view that certain expressions are inborn is the fact that even humans who are too young to speak and have yet to fully learn the lessons of their culture make faces that are associated with basic emotions. Thus, when Carroll Izard and his colleagues (1980) analyzed the facial expressions of young infants, they were able to identify various basic emotions, each necessary for nonverbal infants to "communicate" from birth with their adult caretakers. More recently, these investigators have found that in pleasant and nonpleasant interactions with their mothers, infants as young as ten weeks old made facial expressions that signaled joy, interest, sadness, and anger (Izard et al., 1995).

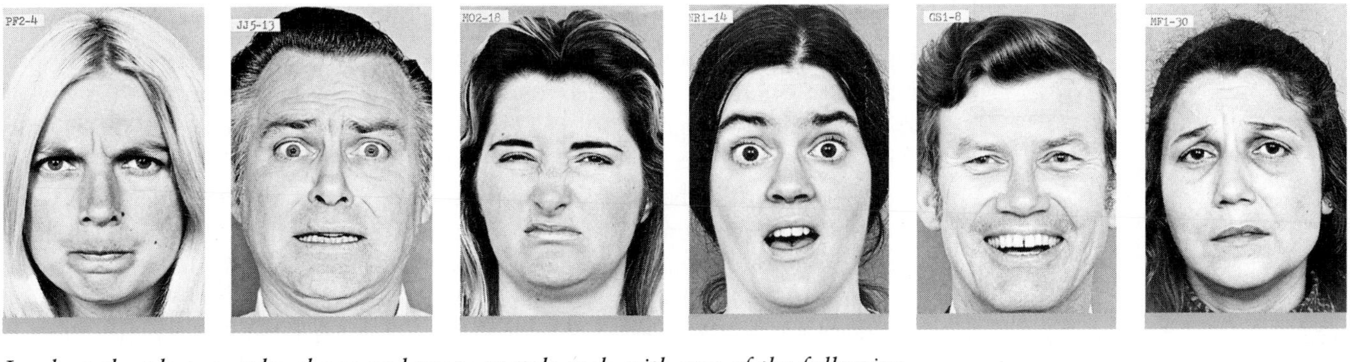

Look at the photographs above and try to match each with one of the following emotions: (1) joy, (2) fear, (3) anger, (4) sadness, (5) surprise, and (6) disgust. People from a diversity of cultures exhibit high levels of agreement on this task.

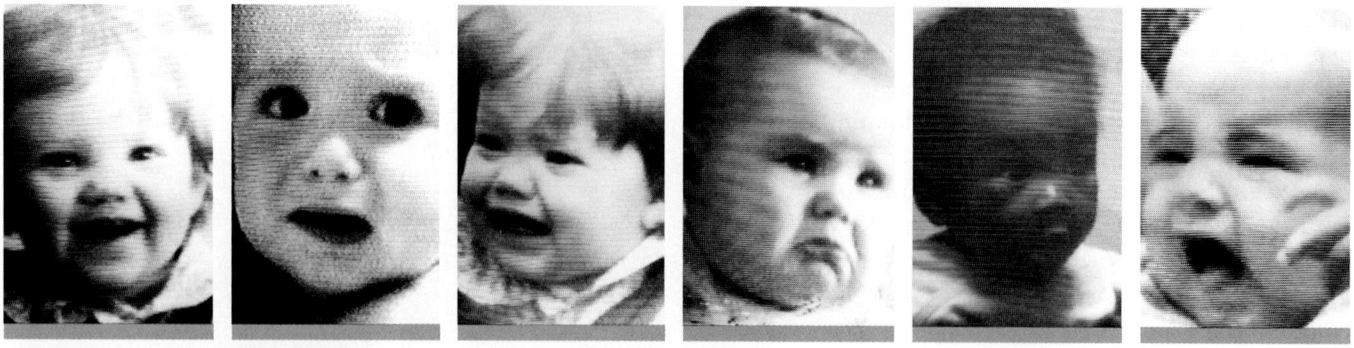

According to Izard (1991), the basic emotional expressions are present at birth. These pictures depict young infants in moments of (1) joy, (2) fear, (3) anger, (4) sadness, (5) surprise, and (6) disgust.

Figure 9.8 The face of anger Anger is universally recognized by geometric patterns on the face. In the examples shown, the left form in each pair seems "angrier" than the one on the right (Aronoff et al., 1992).

Darwin argued that the ability to recognize emotion in others has survival value for all members of a species. This evolutionary hypothesis suggests that some emotions may be more important to identify than others. It is probably more adaptive, for example, to know when someone is angry (and prone to lash out in violence) than to know when someone is happy, a nonthreatening emotion (see Figure 9.8). Are people more sensitive to signs of anger than of happiness? Christine and Ranald Hansen (1988) asked subjects to find discrepant facial expressions in pictures of large crowds, each crowd filled with happy, neutral, or angry faces. In some pictures, all characters wore the same expression; in others, one was discrepant. As Darwin would have predicted, subjects were quicker to spot discrepant angry faces than they were to locate discrepant faces that were happy or neutral. Other studies have shown that angry faces are arousing to people even when subliminally presented (Dimberg & Ohman, 1996).

Emotion is accompanied by changes in facial expression—even when these changes are subtle and cannot be seen with the naked eye. It is estimated that the eighty muscles in the human face can create more than 7,000 different expressions. To measure the spontaneous activity of these muscles and their links to emotion, many researchers use a physiological device known as the **facial electromyograph (EMG)**. In facial EMG studies, subjects are shown images that evoke positive or negative emotions, while electrodes attached to the face record the activity of various muscles (see Figure 9.9). The results of this research indicate that images that elicit positive emotions such as joy, interest, and attraction increase activity in the cheek muscles; those that arouse negative emotions such as anger, distress, and fear spark activity in the forehead and brow area. Evidently, the muscles in the human face reveal smiles, frowns, and other expressions that are otherwise hidden from view (Dimberg, 1990; Tassinary & Cacioppo, 1992).

facial electromyograph (EMG) An electronic instrument used by emotion researchers to record activity in the facial muscles.

Using the facial EMG, researchers have also discovered that there are two distinct types of smiles—one more genuine than the other. In a series of experiments, Ekman and his colleagues found that when people experience real joy, they beam smiles that raise the cheeks high enough to wrinkle up the skin around the eyes and exhibit increased electrical activity in the left hemisphere of the brain. However, when people wear false, "unfelt" smiles—say, to be polite or to pose for a photograph—the muscle activity in the lips and lower cheeks does not extend up to the eyes or trigger a predominance of left-hemisphere activity in the brain (Ekman & Davidson, 1993; Ekman et al., 1990; Frank et al., 1993).

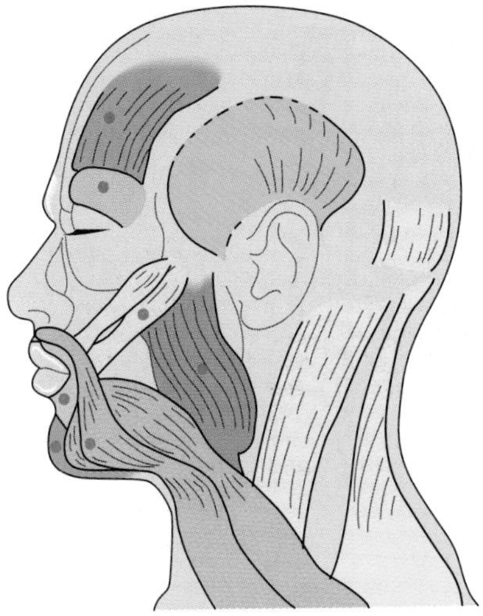

Figure 9.9 The facial electromyograph (EMG) Electrodes placed on the face record activity in various muscles. These recordings reveal that positive emotions increase activity in the cheek muscles, while negative emotions increase activity in the forehead and brow areas (Cacioppo & Petty, 1981).

Body Language Other nonverbal behaviors also communicate emotion, enabling us to make quick, sometimes accurate judgments of how others are feeling (Ambady & Rosenthal, 1992). One common form of expression is *body language*—the way people stand, sit, walk, and gesture. For example, people who have a youthful walking style—who sway their hips, bend their knees, pick up their feet, and swing their arms in a bouncy rhythm—are seen as happier and more powerful than those who walk slowly, take shorter steps, and stiffly drag their feet (Montepare & McArthur, 1988).

Gaze, or eye contact, is also a common and powerful form of communication. The eyes have been called windows of the soul. In many cultures, people assume that someone who avoids looking them in the eye is evasive, cold, fearful, shy, or apathetic; that frequent gazing signals intimacy, sincerity, and confidence; and that the person who stares is tense, angry, and unfriendly. In fact, eye contact is often interpreted in light of preexisting relationships. Among friends and lovers, frequent gaze means warmth and affection. Among enemies, it signals cold hostility (Kleinke, 1986; Patterson, 1983). Thus, it has been said that if two people lock eyes for more than a few seconds, they are either going to make love or kill each other.

Another nonverbal cue is *touch*—a congratulatory high-five, a sympathetic pat on the back, a joking elbow in the ribs, and a warm loving embrace are just a few examples. Physical touch is generally considered an expression of friendship, caring, and sexual interest. But it may also serve other functions. Nancy Henley (1977) observed that men, older persons, and those of high status are more likely to touch women, younger persons, and others of lower status than the other way around. Why? According to Henley, touching is an expression not only of intimacy but also of dominance and control. Researchers are particularly intrigued by the sex differences reported by Henley. In one study, Brenda Major and her colleagues (1990) watched people in city streets, shopping malls, college campuses, airports, and other public settings. Sure enough, men were more likely to touch women than women were to touch men—though this difference was not observed in places where friends ritually greet each other. In another study, Judith Hall and Ellen Veccia (1990) observed 4,500 pairs and found that although men in mixed-sex situations were more likely to initiate contact with the hand, the difference was complicated. For example, men are more likely to put their arms around women, but women are more likely to link arms with men.

Featuring hard, downward, and angular lines, masks worn by many National Hockey League goalies are visually designed to intimidate opponents.

Sensory Feedback

Draw the corners of your mouth back and up and wrinkle your eye muscles. Relax. Now raise your eyebrows, open your eyes wide, and let your mouth drop open slightly. Relax. Now pull your brows down and together and

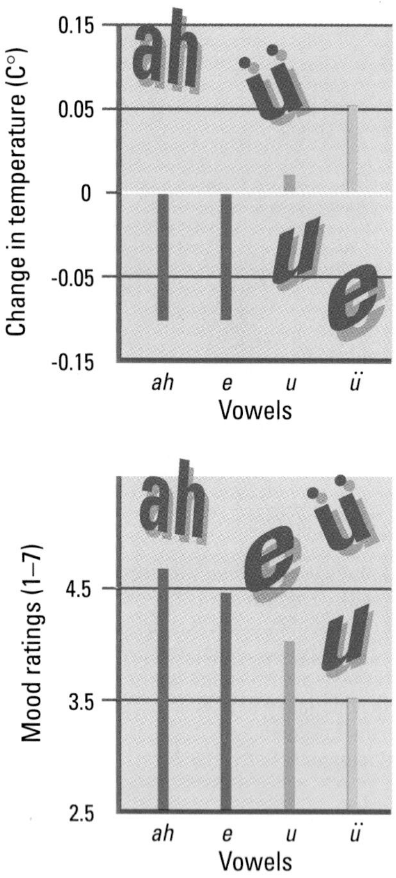

Figure 9.10 Facial feedback In a study by Zajonc et al. (1989), subjects repeated certain vowel sounds. As shown, *ah* and *e*—sounds that cause speakers to smile—lowered brain temperature (*left*) and elevated mood (*right*). In contrast, *u* and *ü*—sounds that cause us to frown—raised brain temperature (*left*) and dampened mood (*right*).

clench your teeth. Relax. If you followed each of these directions, you would have appeared to others to be feeling first happy, then fearful, and finally angry. The question is, do these expressions affect how you actually feel?

According to the **facial-feedback hypothesis**, an expression does more than simply reflect one's emotion—it actually triggers an emotional experience. In an interesting first test of this hypothesis, James Laird (1974) told college students that they would take part in an experiment on the activity of the facial muscles. After attaching electrodes to the face, he showed the subjects a series of cartoons and asked them before each one to contract certain facial muscles in ways that made them smile or frown. The result: Subjects thought the material was funnier and reported feeling happier when they wore a smile than a frown. Similarly, other posed-expression studies show that people can also be induced to experience fear, anger, sadness, and disgust (Duclos et al., 1989). Together, this research suggests that facial expressions—though not *necessary* for the experience of emotion—can evoke and magnify certain emotional states (McIntosh, 1996). Why?

According to Laird, facial expressions activate emotion through a process of self-perception: "If I'm smiling, I must be happy." But there is a second possible reason for this effect. Perhaps expressions trigger an emotional experience by eliciting physiological changes in the brain (Izard, 1990). According to Robert Zajonc (1993), for example, smiling causes facial muscles to increase the flow of air-cooled blood to the brain, which has a pleasant effect by lowering the brain's temperature. Conversely, frowning decreases blood flow, which produces an unpleasant state by raising brain temperature. To demonstrate this mechanism, Zajonc and his colleagues (1989) asked subjects to repeat certain vowels twenty times each, including the sounds *ah*, *e*, *u*, and the German vowel *ü*. As subjects uttered these sounds, temperature in the forehead was measured and subjects reported on how they felt. As shown in Figure 9.10, *ah* and *e* (vowel sounds that cause speakers to mimic smiling) lowered forehead temperature and elevated mood, while *u* and *ü* (vowels that cause speakers to mimic frowning) raised temperature and dampened mood. In other words, movement of the facial muscles influenced emotion even though subjects did not realize that they were wearing a particular expression. The lesson: If you want an emotional lift, just put on a happy face.

Other expressive behaviors such as body posture can also provide us with sensory feedback and influence how we feel. When people feel proud, they stand erect with their shoulders raised, chest expanded, and head held high (*expansion*). When people feel sad and dejected, however, they slump over with their shoulders drooping and head bowed (*contraction*). Clearly, your emotional state is revealed in the way you carry yourself. Is it also possible that the way you carry yourself affects your emotional state? Can people lift their spirits by expanding their posture or lower their spirits through contraction? Yes. Sabine Stepper and Fritz Strack (1993) arranged for subjects to sit in a slumped or upright position by varying the height of the table they had to write on. Those who were forced to sit upright reported feeling more pride after succeeding at a task than did those who were put into a slumped position. In another study, subjects who were instructed to lean forward with their fists clenched during the experiment reported feeling anger, while those who sat slumped with their heads down said they felt sadness (Duclos et al., 1989).

"Refuse to express a passion and it dies."

— WILLIAM JAMES

Emotional states can even be influenced by vocal behavior. Research shows that people tend to speak quickly and raise their voice when fearful or anxious but to slow down and lower the voice when sad or depressed. To examine whether the way people speak can affect the way they feel, Aron Siegman and Stephen Boyle (1993)

facial-feedback hypothesis The hypothesis that changes in facial expression can produce corresponding changes in emotion.

had subjects talk about experiences that had made them anxious or sad. For some events, subjects spoke at a normal rate; for others, they were instructed to speak either fast and loudly or slowly and softly. As predicted, speech style amplified the experience. Talking about anxiety-related events made subjects more anxious when they spoke fast and loudly, and talking about sad events made them feel sadder when they spoke slowly and softly. Apparently, our emotions can be influenced by sensory feedback from the voice as well as from the body and the face.

[Drawing by Mankoff; © 1993 The New Yorker Magazine, Inc.]

"Let's do it, let's fall in love."

Many researchers emphasize the role of cognitive factors in the experience of love and other emotions.

The Cognitive Component

What are the two factors in the two-factor theory of emotion? What role does thought play in the experience of emotion? Which Olympic athlete feels better—the silver medalist or the bronze medalist—and why? What evidence is there to suggest that cognition is *not a* necessary ingredient of emotion?

There is much more to emotion than physiological sensations and expressive behaviors. After all, the heart pounds in fear, but it also pounds in anger. We cry out in grief over the death of a loved one, but we also shed tears of joy at weddings and other happy occasions. We laugh when we're amused, but sometimes we laugh out of nervousness. In other words, there has to be more to grief, joy, amusement, and nervousness than arousal and expression. The missing link is cognitive appraisal.

Psychologists have long been embroiled in debate over the role of cognitive factors in emotion. Are your feelings, like inborn reflexes, triggered by stimuli without conscious thought or awareness, or does the way you feel depend largely on how you perceive, interpret, and evaluate the situation you're in? Do you think first and feel second, or is it the other way around? Theories of emotion suggest different answers to these questions.

Schachter's Two-Factor Theory of Emotion

When I was nineteen, my girlfriend and I were sitting upstairs in her home late at night. Her parents were away for the weekend and nobody else was in the house. The TV was on and we were on the verge of falling asleep. Then suddenly we heard scraping, clicking, the front door opening, and footsteps downstairs. There was an intruder in the house, and we were terrified. My heart pounded so hard that I could feel my chest throb with every beat. Except for the trembling, I was frozen in place like a statue. The emotion we experienced that night was raw fear, plain and simple. How did I "know" that I was feeling afraid and not sad, angry, disgusted, or ill?

According to Stanley Schachter (1964), two factors are necessary to have a specific emotion. First, the person must experience a heightened state of *physiological arousal*, such as a racing heart, sweaty palms, tightening of the stomach, rapid breathing, and so on—the kind of jitteriness you might feel after drinking too much coffee. Second, the person must find a *cognitive label* or attribution to explain the source of that arousal. The night that my girlfriend and I heard an intruder, I had such an obvious explanation for my symptoms that labeling the emotion as fear was easy. In fact, I was shaky for quite some time afterward. (We called the police, and they arrived minutes later to find the front door wide open. They searched the house with flashlights, but it was too late; the intruder had left.) The same is true when people watch intensely emotional films. When moviegoers saw *Silence of the Lambs*, they

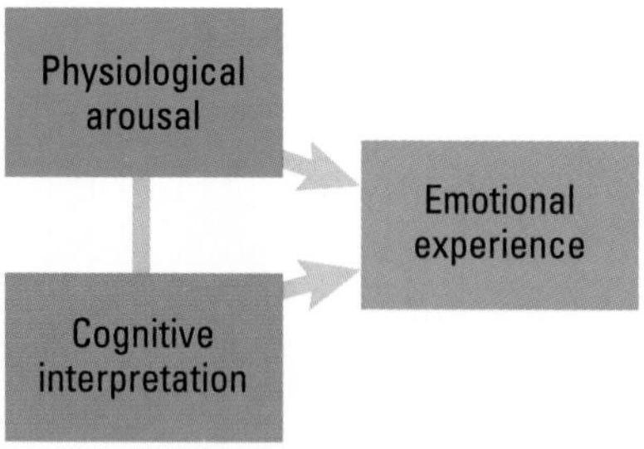

Figure 9.11 Two-factor theory of emotion

knew they were feeling disgusted rather than ashamed, angry, or sad, because the stimulus itself was unambiguous. At times, however, people become generally excited without knowing why—and must examine their surroundings in order to identify the emotion (see Figure 9.11).

To test this **two-factor theory of emotion**, Schachter and Jerome Singer (1962) injected male subjects with epinephrine, the hormone that produces physiological arousal. The subjects in one group were warned in advance about the side effects (they were drug-informed), but those in a second group were not (they were drug-uninformed). In a third group, the subjects were injected with a harmless placebo (this was the placebo control group). Before the drug—which was described as a vitamin supplement—actually took effect, subjects were left alone with a male confederate introduced as another subject who had received the same injection. In some cases, the confederate's behavior was euphoric: He bounced around happily, doodled on paper, sank jump shots into the waste basket, flew paper airplanes across the room, and swung his hips in a hula hoop. In the presence of other subjects, the same confederate behaved angrily. At one point, for example, he ridiculed a questionnaire they were filling out and, in a fit of rage, ripped it up and hurled it into the wastebasket.

Think for a moment about these various situations. In the *drug-informed* group, subjects began to feel their hearts pound, their hands shake, and their faces flush. Told to expect these side effects, however, they did not have to search very far for an explanation. In the *placebo* group, the subjects did not become aroused in the first place, so they had no symptoms to explain. But now consider the predicament of the subjects in the *drug-uninformed* group, who suddenly became aroused without knowing why. Trying to identify the sensations, these subjects—according to the theory—would take their cues from others who are in the same situation, namely the confederate. The results generally supported this prediction. Drug-uninformed subjects reported that they felt more happy or angry depending on the confederate's actions. In some cases, they even displayed similar behavior. For example, one subject "threw open the window and, laughing, hurled paper basketballs at passersby." Subjects in the drug-informed group, who attributed their arousal to the epinephrine, were not as influenced by these social cues. Neither were subjects in the no-drug placebo group—who, after all, were not physiologically aroused.

Schachter's (1964) two-factor theory has attracted a good deal of attention. Not all the research has confirmed the result, but one general conclusion can be drawn: When people are aroused and do not know why, they try to identify their own emotions by observing the situation they're in and making an attribution for their arousal (Reisenzein, 1983). This conclusion has interesting implications. One is that if people attribute their arousal to a nonemotional source, they will experience less emotion (this is what happened in the drug-informed group, where subjects blamed their autonomic symptoms on the epinephrine). Another is that if people attribute their arousal to an emotional source, they will experience more of that emotion (which was the experience of those in the drug-uninformed group). In short, once people are stimulated, they can cognitively intensify, diminish, and alter their own emotions.

One particularly intriguing implication of this theory is that the arousal produced by one source can be "misattributed" or "transferred" to another source. Suppose you had just run two miles, spent a full hour playing basketball, or danced hard at a party. Chances are that you would be sweating and gasping for breath. You would realize, of course, that these symptoms had been caused by physical exertion. But what if you went on to another activity? Because it takes time for the autonomic functions to return to normal, you might later attribute the residual arousal to a new source.

two-factor theory of emotion The theory that emotion is based both on physiological arousal and a cognitive interpretation of that arousal.

Research supports this misattribution hypothesis. Studies have shown that after strenuous physical exercise, subjects are angrier when provoked by an insult and more sexually aroused when they meet someone of the opposite sex. Autonomic arousal from one event thus spills over and enhances feelings toward another event (White et al., 1981; Zillman, 1983; Allen et al., 1989). Donald Dutton and Arthur Aron (1974) demonstrated this spillover effect in a field study conducted on two bridges above British Columbia's Capilano River. One was a narrow, wobbly suspension bridge with a low rail that sways 230 feet above rocky rapids. The other was wide, sturdy, and only 10 feet from the ground. As young men walked over these bridges, they were met by a young woman who introduced herself as a research assistant, asked them to fill out a questionnaire, and gave her phone number in case they wanted more information on the project. As predicted, subjects who walked over the scary bridge—a highly stressful experience that could be misattributed to the research assistant—were more likely than those who crossed the stable bridge to call the woman later. Perhaps terror can fan the hot flames of romance.

If it is possible to intensify an emotion by the transfer of arousal, it should also be possible to diminish emotion in the same way. Consider stage fright, or public-speaking anxiety—an unwanted emotion that claims many victims. As if the dry throat and quivering voice are not embarrassing enough, those who suffer from this common problem get even more anxious because they are anxious. But what if they had an alternative explanation for the symptoms? Is it possible to calm people with speech anxiety by providing face-saving attributions for their arousal? Using the technique of **misattribution**, James Olson (1988) led some subjects but not others to believe that a "subliminal noise" would make them feel anxious while speaking. The result: Those who thought that a noise made them more anxious gave smoother, more fluent speeches. By prompting these subjects to attribute their arousal to an external event rather than to their own anxiety, Olson was able to calm them down and improve their performance. "What, me nervous? My heart may be racing, but thank goodness it's not me—it's just the noise."

Dimensions of Appraisal

According to cognitively oriented theorists, the emotions we experience are determined by the way we appraise the situation we're in—and certain types of appraisals are particularly important in this regard. To appreciate the cognitive approach, think about the last time you experienced a particular emotion—say, joy. Picture the scene in your mind and answer the following questions. Why were you happy? How pleasant was the experience? Did you feel as if you were in control? Were you responsible for what happened? How well did you understand the situation you were in? Did you know how things would turn out? Were you thinking about how you felt, or were you trying to shut your feelings out? Was the situation important to you? By asking people to answer questions like these about their emotion experiences, researchers have found that there are some clear links between our cognitive appraisals and emotional reactions (Frijda, 1986; Roseman et al., 1990; Smith et al., 1993; Weiner, 1985). Even emotions that seem similar on the surface—such as embarrassment, shame, and guilt—can be distinguished upon reflection (Tangney et al., 1996).

The cognitive dimensions of appraisal that are most closely linked to emotion are the *pleasantness* of the situation (whether it's enjoyable), *attention* (whether one is

misattribution An explanation that shifts the perceived cause of arousal from the true source to another one.

focused on what's happening), *agency* (the belief that one is in control), and *certainty* (the clarity of the situation and whether the outcome is predictable). Research thus shows that various emotions can be distinguished by the cognitive appraisals people make on these types of dimensions (Smith & Ellsworth, 1985)—and that these dimensions are relevant not only in the United States but in many other countries as well (Mauro et al., 1992; Mesquita & Frijda, 1992). Consider the following examples:

- ***Happiness*** is a pleasant state that involves high levels of attention, control, and certainty (partying with friends, attending a graduation ceremony).
- ***Surprise*** is a pleasant, effortless state characterized by a high level of attention but low certainty and control (getting an A in a course when a C was expected, getting an unannounced visit from an old friend).
- ***Shame*** is an unpleasant state characterized by a desire to avoid thinking about the situation, by moderate levels of certainty, and by a high level of personal control in the form of self-blame (getting caught cheating, gossiping about someone).
- ***Anger*** is an intensely unpleasant state that involves moderate levels of certainty and attention. Its most prominent aspect is the belief that one's misfortune is controlled by others (having a car stolen, being insulted in public).
- ***Sadness*** is a highly unpleasant state of uncertainty coupled with a desire to minimize attention to the situation. Unlike situations that spark anger, sadness events are usually blamed on circumstances rather than on other people (illness, divorce, the death of a loved one).
- ***Fear*** is also a highly aversive state. Like surprise, it is associated with high levels of uncertainty and low levels of personal control, particularly about one's ability to escape or avoid a dreaded outcome (being held at knife point, skidding on an icy winter road).

Counterfactual Thinking

As thoughtful and curious beings, we often are not content to accept the outcomes in our lives without wondering, at least in private, "What if . . . ?" According to Daniel Kahneman and Dale Miller (1986), people's emotional reactions to events are often colored by **counterfactual thinking**, the tendency to imagine alternative outcomes that might have occurred but did not. If the imagined result is better than the actual result, we're likely to experience feelings of disappointment, frustration, and regret. If the imagined result is worse, then we may react with emotions that range from mild relief and satisfaction to elation. True to the cognitive perspective, then, the emotional impact of positive and negative events depends on the way we think about "what might have been" (Roese & Olson, 1995).

People don't immerse themselves in counterfactual thought after every experience, obviously. But according to Victoria Medvec and Kenneth Savitsky (1997), certain situations—such as being on the *verge* of a better or worse outcome, just above or below some cutoff point—make it easy to conjure up images of what might have happened. The implications are intriguing. Imagine, for example, that you are an Olympic athlete and have just won a silver medal—a remarkable feat. Now imagine that you have just won the bronze medal. Which situation would make you feel better? Rationally, it seems that you should feel more pride and satisfaction with the silver medal. But what if your achievement had prompted you to engage in coun-

counterfactual thinking Imagining alternative scenarios and outcomes that might have happened but did not.

terfactual thinking? What alternative would preoccupy your mind if you had finished in second place? And where would your focus be if you had placed third? Is it possible that the athlete who is better off objectively will feel worse?

To examine this question, Medvec and her colleagues (1995) videotaped forty-one athletes in the 1992 summer Olympic Games the moment they realized that they had won a silver or bronze medal and again later, during the medal ceremony. Then they showed these tapes, without sound, to subjects who did not know the order of finish. The subjects were asked to watch the medalists and rate their emotional states on a scale ranging from "agony" to "ecstasy." The intriguing result, as you might expect, was that the bronze medalists, on average, looked happier than the silver medalists. Was there any more direct evidence of counterfactual thinking? In a second study, subjects who watched interviews with many of these same athletes rated the silver medalists as more negatively focused on finishing second rather than first and the bronze medalists as more positively focused on finishing third rather than fourth. For these great athletes, feelings of satisfaction were based more on their thoughts of what might have been than on the reality of what was.

Is Cognition Necessary?

Schachter's two-factor theory as well as the theories of excitation transfer and cognitive appraisal are all based on the assumption that emotion requires thought. Cognitive-emotion theorists would tell my intruder story as follows: I heard a noise (stimulus) and attributed that noise to someone in the house (cognition), thereby causing me to feel scared (emotion) and to freeze (behavior). We've seen that many psychologists believe that cognition plays a vital role in the experience of emotion. This claim is a source of controversy, however, and was the topic of a spirited exchange between Robert Zajonc (1984), who wrote an article on "the primacy of affect," and Richard Lazarus (1984), who countered with one on "the primacy of cognition."

According to Zajonc, people sometimes react with emotion instantly and without prior appraisal. In other words, sometimes we feel before we think. If you've ever banged your toe into a table, only to explode in anger and pound your fist, you know that the link between pain and rage seems automatic—that you reacted with an angry outburst before realizing just how ridiculous it is to be mad at a piece of furniture. If you've ever drunk milk that was old and curdled, only to gag and spit it out, you likewise know that the link between aversive tastes and disgust may also be automatic. This primacy of affect may help to explain why people develop intense, irrational, persistent fears of objects that are not inherently dangerous. It may also help to explain why infants make reflexlike facial expressions of pain, interest, joy, distress, disgust, and anger before they have the brain capacity to make the proposed cognitive appraisals (Izard, 1990).

Zajonc (1984) argued that human emotions and thoughts are controlled by separate anatomical structures within the brain. In support of this argument, as we saw earlier, animal research shows that certain emotions are triggered instantly—before it is even possible to appraise the situation and formulate a response. From studies described earlier that were aimed at tracing the neural pathways of emotion, Joseph LeDoux (1996) has found in rats that conditioned fear is aroused in a primitive, subcortical pathway within the limbic system—a pathway that connects the eyes and ears through the thalamus directly to the amygdala. This result is significant because it shows that the fear response does not involve the cerebral cortex—which means it need not entail an initial processing of information. According to LeDoux

(1996), this primitive pathway serves as an "early warning system," so that the amygdala can be activated quickly. When we're confronted with pain, noxious food substances, and other threats, this direct pipeline between sensation and emotion enables us to make a rapid-fire defensive motor response without having to stop for a cognitive appraisal (see Figure 9.12).

Representing the cognitive approach, Richard Lazarus (1991) agrees that emotions can spring up quickly and without awareness, but he maintains that it is not possible to have emotion without some kind of thought—even a thought that is quick, effortless, and unconscious. "Without cognitive activity to guide us," says Lazarus, "we could not grasp the significance of what's happening in our adaptational encounters with the environment, nor could we choose among alternative values and courses of action" (p. 353). According to Lazarus, emotion is an individual's response to the perceived harms and benefits of a given situation. Accordingly, Lazarus (1993) presents a list of fifteen emotions and the "core relational

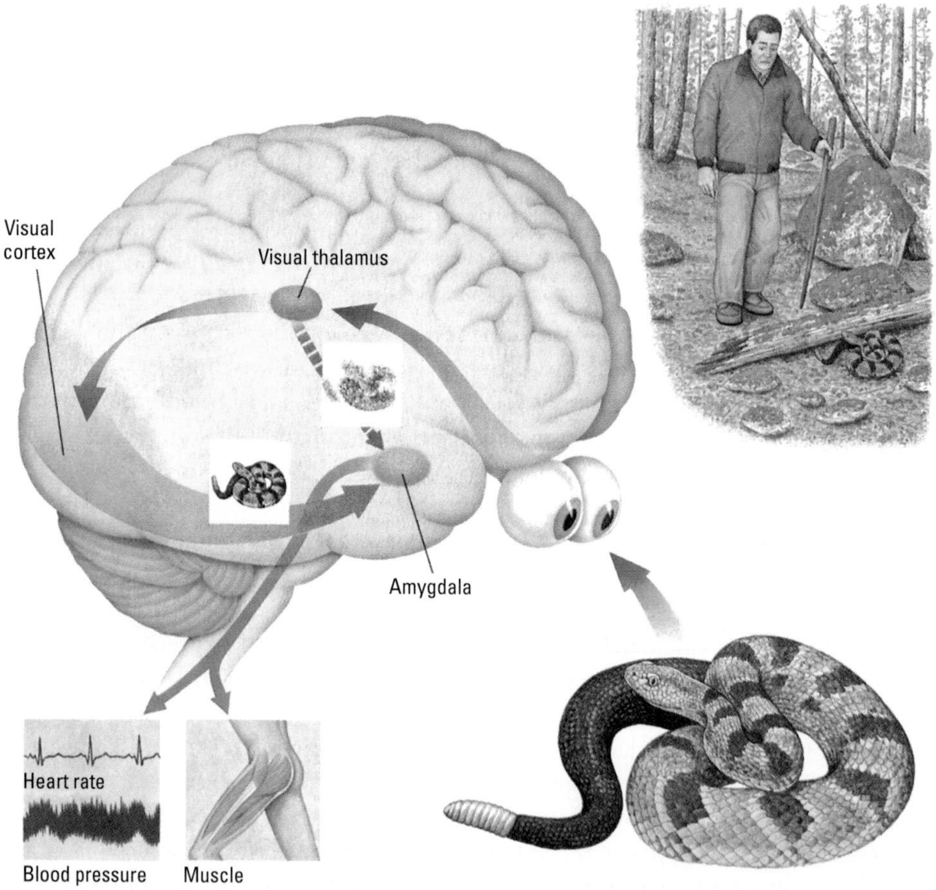

Figure 9.12 Pathway of fear without "thought" According to LeDoux (1996), the sensation of a threat can reach the amygdala by way of direct pathways from the thalamus (a quick "low road") or from the thalamus through the cerebral cortex (a slow "high road"). The direct path permits an instantaneous reaction to danger. This initial response may be overridden after the threat is more fully appraised in the cortex, but "the time saved by the amygdala . . . may be the difference between life and death" (p. 166).

Table 9.2 Emotions and Their "Core Relational Themes"

EMOTION	CORE RELATIONAL THEME
Anger	A demeaning offense against me and mine
Anxiety	Facing an uncertain, existential threat
Fright	An immediate, concrete, overwhelming danger
Guilt	Having transgressed a moral imperative
Shame	Failing to live up to an ego-ideal
Sadness	Having experienced an irrevocable loss
Envy	Wanting what someone else has
Jealousy	Resenting a third party for the threat of losing another's affection or favor
Disgust	Taking in or being close to a repulsive object, person, or idea
Happiness	Making progress toward the realization of a goal
Pride	Ego-enhancement by taking credit for one's own achievement or that of someone identified with
Relief	A distressing condition that has changed for the better
Hope	Fearing the worst but wanting better
Love	Desiring affection that is often but not always reciprocated
Compassion	Being moved by another's suffering and wanting to help

themes" (perceived harms and benefits) that set each of them off (see Table 9.2). Is cognition *necessary* to emotion? The debate rages on.

Human Emotion: Putting the Pieces Together

Can the range of human emotions be categorized into a small number of types? Is there any evidence for the notion that every emotional state triggers its opposite? Are joy, grief, and other emotions universally felt or subject to cultural definition? Are women more emotional than men? Last but not least, who is happy—and why?

Knowing that emotions stem from physiological sensations, expressive behaviors, and cognitive activities is only a first step. The next step is to determine how the different pieces of this puzzle fit together to produce an emotional experience.

Types of Emotions

The English language contains more than 2,000 words for categories of emotions. Are some of these universal, felt by people in all cultures? Over the years, psychologists have tried to classify the human emotions in various ways. Today, as we have seen, there is widespread agreement that fear, anger, joy, disgust, surprise, and sadness are "basic": Each is accompanied by a distinct facial expression, each is displayed by infants and very young children, and each is found in the words that people of diverse cultures use to describe their feelings. Some researchers believe that interest, acceptance, contempt, pride, shame, and guilt should be added to the list.

Certain emotions such as intense joy and grief are "basic" to the human experience. Here, the New York Yankees rejoice after winning the 1996 World Series, while family members lament the death of loved ones who were killed in the Oklahoma City bombing.

If there are only a few basic emotions, what accounts for the vast array of other feelings we so often experience? One possibility suggested by Robert Plutchik (1980) is that basic emotions provide the building blocks for more complex emotions in the same way that the three primary colors combine to form the hues of the color wheel. According to Plutchik, the richness of human emotions is accounted for in three ways. First, there are eight basic types of emotions (he adds interest and acceptance to the original six). Second, each type comes in varying "shades," or levels of intensity (for example, intense disgust may be felt as hatred or loathing, and mild disgust as boredom). Third, new emotions are formed through mixtures of the eight basic ones (for example, love blends joy and acceptance, contempt blends disgust and anger, and nostalgia blends joy and sadness).

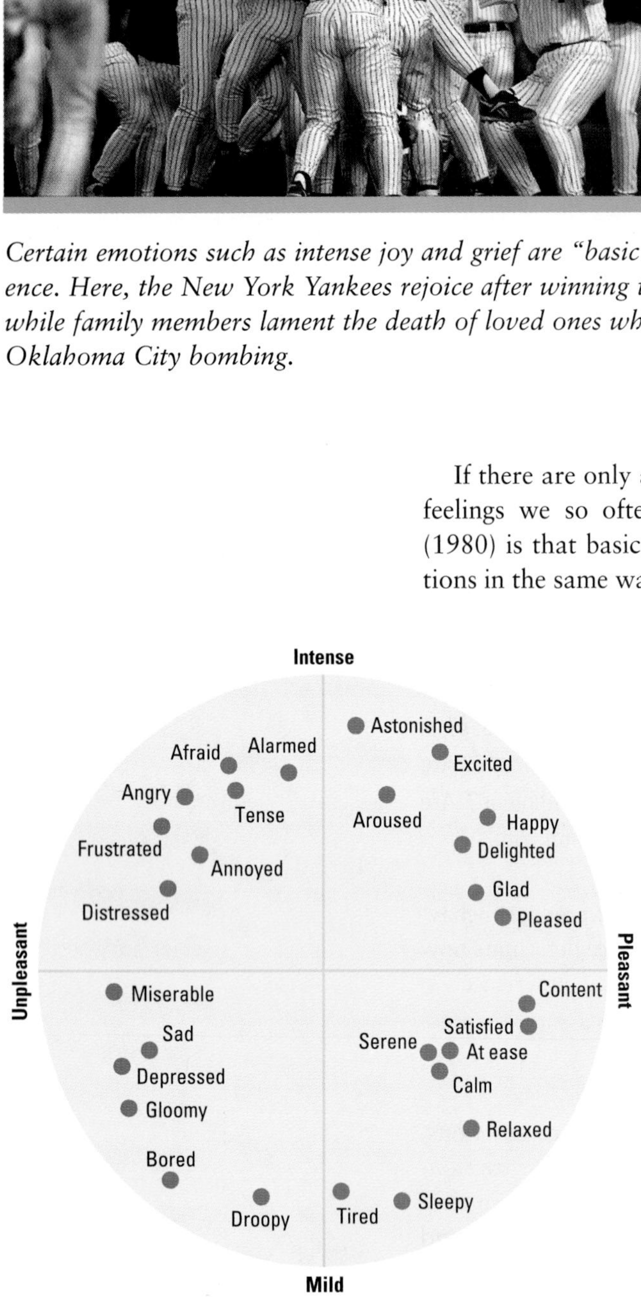

Figure 9.13 Russell's circumplex model According to this circumplex model, there are four types of emotions: pleasant-intense, pleasant-mild, unpleasant-intense, and unpleasant-mild (Russell et al., 1980).

It's easy to generate a list of emotions. The trick is to classify and compare the emotions along a small number of common dimensions. The most popular taxonomy is the circumplex model, in which all emotions are divided along two independent dimensions: pleasantness and intensity. According to James Russell (1980), emotions are either (1) pleasant or unpleasant, and (2) mild or intense. As illustrated in Figure 9.13, the result is a fourfold circle of emotions that are pleasant-and-intense ("delighted"), pleasant-and-mild ("relaxed"), unpleasant-and-mild ("bored"), and unpleasant-and-intense ("alarmed"). Research shows that when people are asked to rate emotion words or sort them into piles, this circular ordering consistently appears—not only in English but also in Chinese, Croatian, Estonian, Greek, Gujarati, Hebrew, Japanese, Polish, Swedish, and German (Larsen & Diener, 1992; Reisenzein, 1994). As illustrated in Figure 9.14, people's ratings of the emotions triggered by images of other human beings, animals, nature, objects, scenes, and events, can similarly be classified (Lang, 1995).

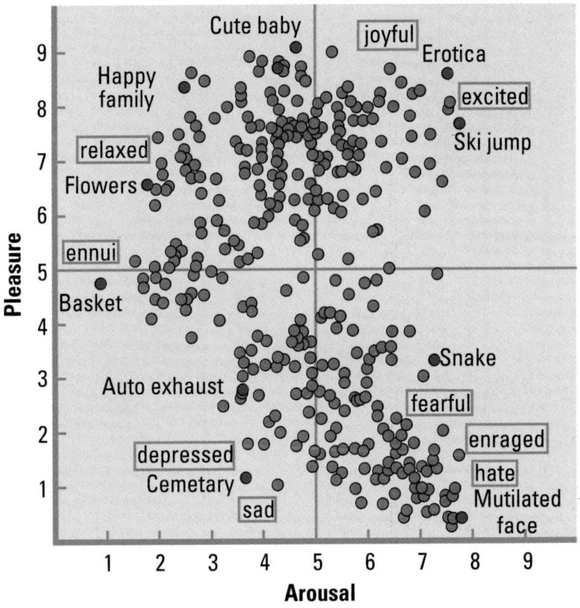

Figure 9.14 Emotion-evoking images On the basis of extensive testing of hundreds of photographic and digitized images, the following items were categorized into the four quadrants of the circumplex model (Lang, 1995).

Dynamics of Emotion

I have always loved roller coasters. I find the speed and sharp turns frightening, the loops make me dizzy, and my neck muscles are often strained after tensing up for so long. But the feeling of relief that rushes through me when the terror-filled experience has ended is alone worth the price of admission. The scarier the ride, the greater the pleasure.

This common paradoxical experience illustrates an important point about emotion: It is dynamic, complex, and ever changing—not easily captured in a snapshot. To explain this type of paradox, Richard Solomon (1980) proposed the *opponent-process theory* of emotion. According to Solomon, an event triggers (1) a "primary state"—an unlearned, automatic response, which in turn triggers (2) an "opponent state"—a learned response that is the emotional opposite of the primary state. Thus, danger activates fear followed by relief, while happy events activate joy followed by sadness. The key difference between the two reactions is that the opponent state, compared to the primary state, starts later and lasts longer. It also gets stronger with repetition and experience. Thus, every positive emotional state is balanced in time by its negative counterpart—and vice versa (see Figure 9.15).

Solomon cites various animal and human studies that support this point. One such study concerned the emotional reactions of skydivers. Right before their first jump, they were terrified: Their bodies stiffened, their pupils dilated, their eyes bulged, and their breathing became irregular. Then, after their feet hit the ground, there was an initial stunned silence followed by relief, chatter, laughter, even a sense of exhilaration. From their normal baseline state, fear had turned to elation. Research on the effects of mind-altering drugs also supports this point. At first, opiate drugs (if the dosage is not excessive) produce a pleasurable "high," followed by a less intense state of euphoria. As the drug wears off, however, the user suffers through an agonizing state of withdrawal that is far less pleasant than his or her predrug state. Skydivers thus find that their fear subsides after several jumps, and drug users find that they must increase their dosage to get high.

The opponent-process theory offers some interesting insights into our changing emotional states. The notion that every emotion triggers its opposite, perhaps to keep us emotionally balanced, may help to explain why women sometimes experience a "letdown" after the joy of childbirth or why health enthusiasts enjoy hard physical exercise, hot and dry saunas, and other types of "good pain." Contemplating the implications, Solomon is quick to note that the opponent-process theory is a puritan's theory: Pleasure will enlarge the appetite for reward and make joy more elusive, while pain and suffering will enhance one's later sense of well-being. Pleasure has its costs; pain its benefits.

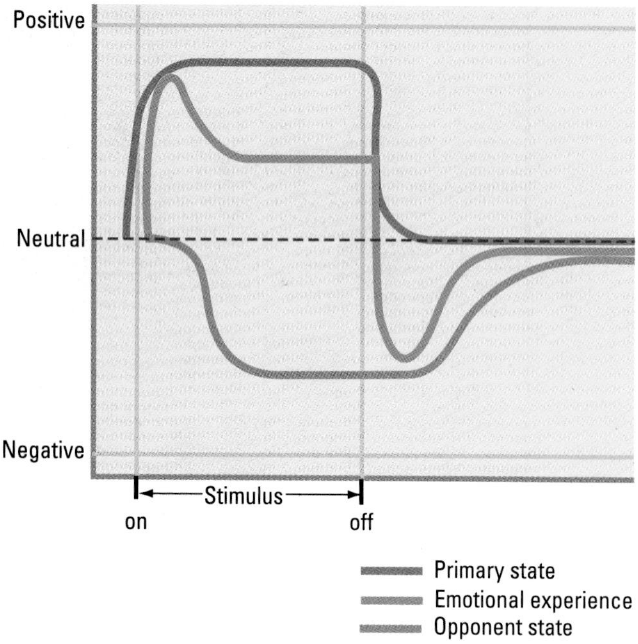

Figure 9.15 Opponent-process theory of emotion According to this theory, every primary emotional state triggers its opposite. The result is a more balanced experience in which a positive state is soon followed by a negative state, and vice versa.

The Cultural Context

Inspired by Darwin's writings, researchers have discovered several "universals" in human emotion. We saw earlier, for example, that people from diverse cultures react to emotion-filled events with similar arousal symptoms and widely recognized facial expressions. To some extent, people of different cultures and languages also categorize human emotions in similar ways. The following passage illustrates the point. "What are the feelings of men? They are joy, anger, sadness, fear, love, disliking, and liking. These seven feelings belong to men without their learning them." This statement may seem to have appeared earlier in this chapter. In fact, it is taken from *Li Chi*, a Chinese encyclopedia that was compiled in the first century BCE.

The physiological and expressive components of human emotion may be inborn and universal, and they may be related in important ways to environmental factors. But there are also some cultural differences in the types of antecedent events that stir our various passions. Batja Mesquita and Nico Frijda (1992) note that certain events reliably trigger certain emotions. In all cultures, for example, friendships and achievement elicit joy; insults and injustice elicit anger; novel experiences and risk taking elicit fear; death, rejection, and the breakup of relationships elicit sadness. The situations that awaken jealousy are also universal. In a cross-cultural study of the "green-eyed monster," college students from seven countries all said they would feel jealous if their boyfriend or girlfriend were to flirt with, kiss, or have sex with another person (Buunk & Hupka, 1987). Yet despite these similarities, the antecedents of emotion differ as a result of culturally specific living conditions. Among the Utku Eskimos, fear is triggered by thin ice, rough seas, dangerous animals, and evil spirits. Yet among Israelis—for whom terrorism, the threat of war, and border clashes are constant—fear is awakened most often by interactions with strangers.

Culture also influences the way people categorize their feelings. Consider the words we use to describe various emotions. Based on ethnographies and cross-cultural studies of language, James Russell (1991) uncovered some striking differences between cultures. As noted earlier, the English language contains more than 2,000 words for categories of emotion. Yet there are only 1,501 emotion words in Dutch, 750 in Taiwanese, 230 in Malay, 58 among the Ifalukian of Micronesia, and 7 among the Chewong of Malaysia.

According to Russell, differences like these provide insight into a culture's folk theories of emotion. Among the Ilongot, a head-hunting people of the Philippines, the word *liget* is used to describe both anger and grief—intense feelings for which head-hunting is an accepted form of release. Among the Gidjingali aborigines of Australia, the word *gurakadj* combines shame and fear; in Samoa, the word *alofa* is used to describe a combination of love, sympathy, and feelings of pity. Japanese lacks a word for "disappointed," Tahitian lacks a word for "sadness," and Gujarati, a language spoken in India, lacks a word for "excited."

In some cultures, emotion words are used that have no clear counterpart in the English language. For example, the German word *schadenfreude* specifically refers to the pleasure derived from another person's suffering. In Indonesia, a distinction is made between *malu*, a feeling of shame brought on by one's own actions, and *dipermalukan*, a feeling of shame caused by someone else's deeds. Among the Baining of Papua New Guinea, *awumbuk* is an emotion that combines sadness, tiredness, and boredom that is brought on specifically by the departure of visiting friends or relatives. Among the Utku Eskimos, *naklik* refers to the love of babies, sick people, and others in need of protection, while *niviuq* is a form of love felt toward those who are charming or admired.

In Japan, it is more important that children learn to fit into the community than to stand out as individuals.

The language of emotion provides clues about the emotional life of a culture. Consider, for example, comparisons often made between the United States and Japan. In the United States, parents teach their children to be independent, self-reliant, and assertive—a "cut above the rest." But in Japan, children are raised to fit into the community because "the nail that stands out gets pounded down." According to Hazel Markus and Shonobu Kitayama (1991), these cultures foster different conceptions of the individual in relation to others. In the United States—and in many other Western countries, too—people have an *independent* conception of themselves as distinct, autonomous, and self-contained. In much of Asia, Africa, and Latin America, however, people hold a more collective or *interdependent* view of themselves as part of a larger group in which social connections are more important than individual self-expression. These different outlooks are evident in the language of emotion (Matsumoto et al., 1988). So although Americans are quick to express jealousy, anger, pride, and other "ego-focused" emotions, non-Westerners are more likely to feel sympathy, shame, respect, and embarrassment—"other-focused" emotions that promote social harmony rather than conflict. Thus, the Japanese describe emotions such as *amae* (a pleasant feeling of trust and dependence), *oime* (feelings of indebtedness), *haji* (shame caused by immodest behavior), and *itoshii* (longing for an absent loved one). To some extent, culture shapes our emotional lives (Kitayama & Markus, 1994).

Finally, there are some striking cultural differences in the **display rules** that determine when it is appropriate for people to express their feelings. The release of anger sparked by insult, jealousy, frustration, or a physical attack is a prime example. People all over the world exhibit similar patterns of autonomic arousal, but cultures teach us whether to manage that arousal by exploding or by suppressing our rage. Among the Kung Bushmen of the Kalahari Desert, nomadic hunters and gatherers who forage as a group and share food, people must control their rage in order to survive. Japanese people also practice restraint, often masking their anger with a polite smile. In Japan, an angry outburst is seen as a shameful loss of control, so it is better to publicly "grin and bear it" (Matsumoto & Ekman, 1989). Yet among the Yanomamo of the Amazon jungle, loud public displays of anger are common. As anthropologists have observed, Yanomamo who are angry sometimes scream at the top of their lungs and launch into a barrage of personal and public insults: "You scaly ass, you bucktooth, you protruding fang, you caiman skin!" (Good & Chanoff, 1991, p. 71).

Are There Sex Differences in Emotion?

When people are asked to compare the typical man and woman, they consistently say that women are more emotional (or, to put it another way, that men are less emotional). This belief is found among children and adults from many different cultures (Fabes & Martin, 1991; Williams & Best, 1982). In a study that illustrates just how deeply ingrained this stereotype is, adult subjects were shown a videotape of a nine-month-old baby. Half were told that they were watching a boy; the other half thought the baby was a girl. In fact, everyone saw the same tape. Yet when the baby burst into tears over a jack-in-the-box, subjects were gender-biased in the way that

display rules Social norms that regulate when, where, and how a person may express certain emotions.

EMOTION AND ENVIRONMENT

Seasonal Affective Disorder—The Winter Blues

Anyone who lives in a four-season climate has a sense that their emotional states can be influenced by the weather. Have you ever had a case of the "blues" after a succession of overcast days, only to be rejuvenated by a cheerful dose of sunshine? After a dreary winter, have you ever caught "spring fever" the first time the sun and air were warm enough for you to shed your coat? If so, you have company. And lots of it.

Psychologists and psychiatrists have recently discovered that although everyone is affected to a greater or lesser extent, some people suffer from **seasonal affective disorder**, or SAD—a form of depression that strikes during the dark days of autumn and winter (see Figure 9.16). Every year, people with SAD who live in relatively cold regions of the world fall into a lethargic emotional state that resembles hibernation. They become listless, drowsy, and withdrawn. They also sleep more, eat more, crave carbohydrates, gain weight, lose interest in sex, and falter at work and in their social relationships. Consistent with the hypothesis that SAD is related to climate, surveys show that both SAD sufferers and people in general report feeling worse during the winter months (Kasper & Rosenthal, 1989)—and that the prevalence of SAD increases with a region's distance north of the equator (see Table 9.3, which combines severe and mild cases). SAD is more commonly found, for example, in Alaska and New Hampshire than in Maryland and Florida (Booker & Hellekson, 1992).

It's not yet clear why the winter months cause SAD or why some people are affected more than others. One theory traces the problem to the pineal gland—a tiny structure in the brain that secretes melatonin, the hormone that causes drowsiness (light inhibits its secretion). Another theory is that the circadian rhythms of SAD sufferers, their internal biological clocks, are disrupted by the relative lack of sunshine. Whatever the specific cause, there is, for many sufferers, a simple and often effective solution: light therapy.

Based on a number of research studies (Blehar & Rosenthal, 1989; Sack et al., 1990; Terman et al., 1989),

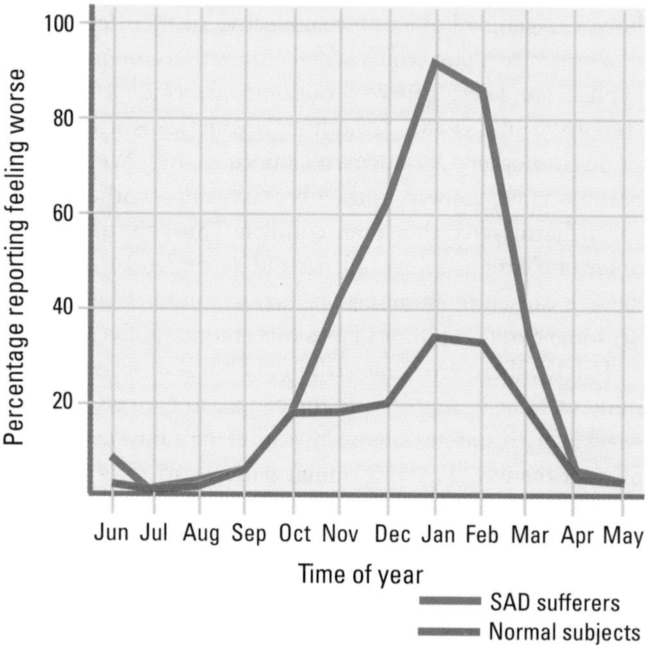

Figure 9.16 Seasonal differences in SAD This graph depicts the percentage of sufferers and "normal" subjects who report feeling blue each month of the year. Most people feel worse in winter, a pattern that is exaggerated among those with SAD (Kasper & Rosenthal, 1989).

Table 9.3 Regional Differences in SAD

SAMPLING AREA	LATITUDE	SAD CASES (ESTIMATED %)
Alaska	65°	28.3
New Hampshire	43°	20.7
New York City	41°	17.1
Maryland	39°	16.7
Florida	27°	4.0

seasonal affective disorder (SAD) A form of depression that strikes during the late autumn and winter months.

Normal Rosenthal (1993) recommends about one to two hours a day, at a time that is convenient, in front of intensely bright fluorescent lights—with your eyes open. After one to two weeks, the clouds of gloom should begin to lift and you should feel more energetic. This treatment should be repeated until spring season brings in an abundance of natural sunshine. Then put the lights away until the autumn leaves start to fall (a portable head-mounted light visor is also now available). Researchers from the National Institute of Mental Health recently conducted a long-term follow-up study of fifty-nine former patients who had been treated with light therapy. They found, after an average of eight years, that many continued to suffer from SAD. Overall, 41 percent continued to use the light treatment with positive results, but for others with more severe cases, the light treatment alone was often not sufficient (Schwartz et al., 1996).

---

they interpreted the child's emotional state: *he* was *angry*, but *she* was *frightened* (Condry & Condry, 1976).

Are there sex differences in emotion, or is this perception a mere illusion? The research is mixed, but certain differences do seem to emerge with regularity (Brody & Hall, 1993; Grossman & Wood, 1993; LaFrance & Banaji, 1992). On the one hand, women describe themselves as more emotional—or men as less emotional—when asked direct questions about their emotionality. On the other hand, there is little support for the conclusion that the sexes differ in their actual feelings. Both men and women become happy when they achieve something that they have strived for. Similarly, both sexes become saddened by the loss of a loved one, angry when frustrated, fearful when in danger, and embarrassed when they slip up in front of others. Men and women also exhibit similar facial expressions and autonomic reactions to emotion-triggering events. People surely differ in their propensity for certain types of feelings, but these differences say more about us as individuals than as men or women.

So in what ways are women more emotional than men? One clear finding is that regardless of how men and women actually feel, they often differ in their public expressions of emotion. Based on a review of 205 studies involving more than 23,000 subjects, Kathryn Dindia and Mike Allen (1992) concluded that women disclose their feelings to others more than men do. Women also exhibit more emotion on the face and more muscle activity on the facial EMG (Dimberg, 1990). The result is that people in general can "read" women better than they can men. In one study, for example, male and female subjects saw slides that evoked emotions ranging from joy to disgust. As they watched, their faces were recorded with a hidden camera. Observers who later watched these tapes were better at judging the emotions felt by the expressive female subjects (Wagner et al., 1986).

Why are women more open and expressive than men? One easy explanation is that girls more than boys are socialized at an early age to talk about their feelings. Researchers who analyze parent-child conversations in the home find that parents talk more about the emotional aspect of events with their daughters than with their sons ("That music was scary, wasn't it?" "You were happy, weren't you?")—even when the children are only two or three years old (Dunn et al., 1987; Kuebli & Fivush, 1992). Another reason, at least in American culture, is that

To combat SAD during the polar nights of winter, teenage girls in Tromso, Norway, receive a daily dose of light therapy.

although women are permitted to be expressive (except when it comes to rage and anger, emotions that men are allowed to express and women are supposed to contain), men are taught to be stoic—to fulfill the ideal of the strong, silent type. Masculinity norms demand that men publicly suppress their own fears and sorrows. As the saying goes, "Big boys don't cry" (Tavris, 1992).

Pleasure and the Pursuit of Happiness

Long before psychology was born into science, philosophers regarded happiness to be the ultimate state of being. In the Declaration of Independence, Thomas Jefferson thus cited life, liberty, and "the pursuit of happiness" as the most cherished of human rights. But what is happiness, and how is it achieved? Aristotle said it was the reward of an active life. Freud pointed to work and love. Others have suggested that happiness requires money and power, health and fitness, religion, beauty, the satisfaction of basic needs, and an ability to derive pleasure from the events of everyday life.

To study happiness—or as many psychologists now call it, "subjective well-being"—one must be able to measure it. How do researchers know if someone is happy? Simple: They ask. Better yet, they use such brief questionnaires as the Satisfaction with Life Scale, in which subjects respond to statements such as "If I could live my life over, I would change almost nothing" (Diener et al., 1984; Pavot & Diener, 1993). As Marcus Aurelius said, "No man is happy who does not think himself so."

Consistently, surveys show that 75 percent of the American population describe themselves as happy—and that in 86 percent of all nations sampled, the mean ratings are more positive than neutral (Diener & Diener, 1996). In general, people who are happy also have cheerful moods, high self-esteem, physical and mental health, a sense of personal control, more memories for positive than negative events, and optimism about the future (Myers & Diener, 1995). It's no secret that our outlook on life becomes rosy right after we win a game, fall in love, land a great job, or make money. Nor is it a secret that the world seems gloomy right after we lose, fall out of love, or suffer a personal tragedy or financial setback. Predictably, the events of our everyday lives trigger fluctuations in mood. For example, people are most happy on Fridays and Saturdays and are least happy on Mondays and Tuesdays (Larsen & Kasimatis, 1990). But what determines our long-term satisfaction, and why are some people happier in general than others?

Seeking the roots of happiness, Ed Diener (1984) and others (Strack et al., 1991) reviewed many years of research and found that subjective well-being is not meaningfully related to such demographic factors as age, sex, race, ethnic background, IQ, education level, or physical attractiveness. Contrary to popular belief, people are not less happy during the so-called crisis years of midlife or in old age than in their "peak" young-adult years. Men and women do not differ, and in the United States African Americans are as happy as white Americans. However, there are three key predictors: (1) *social relationships* (people with an active social life, close friends, and a happy marriage are more satisfied than those who lack these intimate connections), (2) *employment status* (employed people are happier than those who are out of work—regardless of income), and (3) *health* (people who are physically healthy are happier than those who are not). Reflecting the impact of these factors, research shows that happiness levels vary from one country to the next. As shown in Table 9.4, national happiness is highest in Iceland and lowest in the Dominican Republic. Canada ranked fifth and the United States seventh. This rank ordering was based on surveys of more than 100,000 respondents in fifty-five countries (Diener et al., 1995; Veenhoven, 1993).

Table 9.4 National Happiness Rankings

1. Iceland	29. Mexico
2. Sweden	30. Bangladesh
3. Australia	31. France
4. Denmark	32. Spain
5. Canada	33. Portugal
6. Switzerland	34. Italy
7. USA	35. Hungary
8. Colombia	36. Puerto Rico
9. Luxembourg	37. Thailand
10. New Zealand	38. S. Africa
11. N. Ireland	39. Jordan
12. Norway	40. Egypt
13. Finland	41. Yugoslavia
14. Britain	42. Japan
15. Netherlands	43. Greece
16. Ireland	44. Poland
17. Brazil	45. Kenya
18. Tanzania	46. Turkey
19. Belgium	47. India
20. Singapore	48. S. Korea
21. Bahrain	49. Nigeria
22. W. Germany	50. Panama
23. Austria	51. E. Germany
24. Chile	52. USSR
25. Philippines	53. China
26. Malaysia	54. Cameroon
27. Cuba	55. Dominican Republic
28. Israel	

Perhaps the most interesting relationship is between *income* and subjective well-being. Everyone knows the saying "Money can't buy happiness." But personally, I know very few people—particularly among those who are financially strapped—who truly believe it. Is wealth a key to happiness? As reviewed by Myers and Diener (1995), the evidence thus far is mixed. Cross-national studies have revealed that there is a strong positive association between a nation's wealth and the subjective well-being of its people. There are some exceptions, but as a general rule the more money a country has, the happier its citizens are. Within a given country, however, the differences between wealthy and middle-income people are modest. In one survey, for example, a group of the richest Americans said they were happy 77 percent of the time—which was only moderately higher than the 62 percent figure given by those of average income. And when intraculture comparisons are made over time, there is no association between affluence and happiness. Americans on average are twice as rich now as they were forty years ago—before we had personal computers, thirty-inch color TVs, microwave ovens, and answering machines. Yet during that same period of time, the number who said they were "very happy" was 35 percent in 1957 and only 32 percent in 1993. So what are we to conclude? Myers and Diener speculate that having food, shelter, and safety are essential for subjective

[Drawing by Handelsman; © 1996 The New Yorker Magazine, Inc.]

"I could cry when I think of the years I wasted accumulating money, only to learn that my cheerful disposition is genetic."

well-being—but that once these basic needs are met, increasing affluence does not appreciably raise levels of happiness.

Why doesn't money contribute more to happiness? One reason is that our perceptions of wealth are not absolute but relative to a *standard* (Parducci, 1995). For example, according to **social-comparison theory**, people tend to compare themselves to others and feel content or deprived depending on how they fare in this comparison. To demonstrate, Ladd Wheeler and Kunitate Miyake (1992) asked college students to keep for two weeks a written record of every time they mentally compared their grades, appearance, abilities, possessions, or personality to someone else's. Consistently, these diaries revealed that "upward comparisons" (to others who are better off) triggered negative feelings, while "downward comparisons" (to others who are worse off) triggered positive feelings. This result may shed light on why there's only a modest relationship between income and happiness. The middle-class worker whose friends and neighbors can't pay their bills feels successful. Yet the upper-class social climber who moves into an affluent suburb and rubs elbows with the rich and famous feels relatively deprived. The key is to avoid looking to the top of the ladder at others who are better off.

It is also natural for people to use their own recent past as a basis of comparison. According to **adaptation-level theory**, our satisfaction with the present depends on the level of success to which we are accustomed. Get married, buy a new house, or make a killing in the stock market, and you will surely enjoy a wave of euphoria. Before long, however, the glitter will wear off, and you will adapt to your better situation and raise your standard of comparison. Thus, Philip Brickman and others (1978) interviewed twenty-two people who had won between $50,000 and $1 million in a lottery, and they found that these people did not rate themselves as happier than in the past. Compared to others from similar backgrounds, the winners said that they now derived less pleasure from routine activities such as shopping, reading a magazine, watching TV, eating breakfast, and talking to a friend. Perhaps the more money you have, the more you need to stay happy. This may explain why, as Mihaly Csikszentmihalyi (1990) put it, "Waiting rooms of psychiatrists are filled with rich successful patients who, in their forties or fifties, suddenly wake up to the fact that a plush suburban home, expensive cars, and even an Ivy League education are not enough to bring peace of mind" (p. 44).

> *"It matters little whether one is rich or poor, successful or unsuccessful, beautiful or plain: Happiness is completely relative . . . the pleasantness of any particular experience depends on its relationship to a context of other experiences, real or imagined."*
>
> — ALLEN PARDUCCI

There's one other possible explanation for why wealth is not more predictive of happiness: Perhaps each of us, as a result of biological and environmental factors, has a set baseline level of happiness toward which we gravitate. This notion is supported by two recent findings. The first is that ratings of happiness were higher among pairs of identical twins than among fraternal twins—leading David Lykken and Auke Tellegen (1996) to suggest that there may be a genetic basis for being happy and content. The second finding is that the fluctuations in mood that accompany positive and negative life events wear off over time. Eunkook Suh and others (1996) studied subjects for two years and found that only experiences occurring within the last three months correlated with subjective well-being. Although getting engaged or married, breaking up, starting a new job, and being hospitalized were high-impact experiences, their impacts were only temporary. Among these subjects, happiness levels, like their personalities, remained relatively stable over time.

Now that we have explored the psychology of emotion, let us step back and reflect on what it contributes to our understanding of human competence and ratio-

social-comparison theory The theory that people evaluate themselves by making comparisons with others.

adaptation-level theory The theory that people evaluate experiences in relation to current levels to which they have become accustomed.

nality. You will recall that many cognitive psychologists liken human beings to computers, noting the ease with which we are able to learn, recall, reason, and communicate our knowledge. At the same time, however, research shows that performance often falls short of competence. Sometimes people fail to learn (or, instead, learn to behave in maladaptive ways), forget or distort their memories of past events, and use cognitive heuristics that steer them into making poor judgments. This two-headed portrait seems to characterize our emotional lives as well. In this chapter, for example, we saw that although emotion often follows from a rational interpretation of events, it also arises instantly and without conscious thought, perhaps leading us to feel before we think. In addition, we sometimes attribute our arousal sensations to the wrong source, causing us to mislabel our own emotions. In matters of the heart and mind, human beings are not entirely competent or incompetent but a complex and fascinating mixture of both.

Summary and Key Terms

Although **emotion** is a difficult concept to define, most psychologists agree that emotions consist of three interacting components: (1) physiological arousal, (2) expressive behavior, and (3) a cognitive appraisal.

The Physiological Component

The body is intimately involved in feelings of joy, fear, anger, and other emotions. The question is, in what capacity?

A Historical Perspective

According to the **James-Lange theory**, emotion follows from one's reactions to an emotion-eliciting stimulus (you're afraid because you are trembling). In contrast, the **Cannon-Bard theory** states that a stimulus elicits various reactions and emotion at the same time (perceiving a danger causes you to tremble and feel afraid). Today, physiologically oriented emotion researchers seek to understand the role played by different brain structures, neural pathways, and autonomic arousal.

Brain Centers of Emotion

Many emotions are regulated by the limbic system—an evolutionarily primitive set of neural structures. Certain emotional reactions are automatic (triggered instantly by the amygdala); others involve the processing of information in the cerebral cortex. One cannot pinpoint a single region of the cortex that regulates all feelings, but research shows that positive emotions evoke higher levels of EEG activity in the left hemisphere, whereas negative emotions elicit more activity in the right.

Generalized Autonomic Arousal

When an event prompts an emotional response, the **sympathetic nervous system** mobilizes the body for an adaptive "fight or flight" response. Afterward, the **parasympathetic nervous system** restores the body to its premobilized calm state.

Specific Patterns of Arousal

Are all emotions associated with the same state of arousal, or does each emotion have unique symptoms? Research supports the latter alternative. For example, heart rate increases for both anger and fear, but anger increases skin temperature, while fear has the opposite effect.

The Lie-Detector Test

Based on the assumption that lying increases stress, law-enforcement officials often use the **polygraph**, an instrument that records multiple channels of arousal. Subjects who exhibit more arousal to crime-relevant questions than to control questions are judged to be lying. Many professionals claim that lie-detector tests work, but researchers have uncovered some serious problems with such tests.

The Expressive Component

Behavioral expressions of emotion serve two functions. They provide us not only with a means of nonverbal communication to others but also with sensory feedback for the self.

Nonverbal Communication

The face communicates emotion in ways that are understood by people from different countries of the world. Further suggesting that these expressions are innate is the fact that even young infants make the faces that are associated with basic emotions. To measure the activity of facial muscles and their links to emotion, researchers use the **facial electromyograph (EMG)**. This device has revealed that there are two distinct types of smiles, one more genuine than the other. Additional nonverbal behaviors that communicate emotion are body language, gaze, and touch.

Sensory Feedback
According to the **facial-feedback hypothesis**, an expression not only reflects one's emotion but triggers an emotional state as well. Although psychologists disagree over the reason for this effect, research indicates that it does occur.

The Cognitive Component
Psychologists have long debated the role of cognitive factors in emotion. Different theories of emotion provide different points of view.

Schachter's Two-Factor Theory of Emotion
According to the **two-factor theory of emotion**, two factors are necessary to have a specific emotion: (1) a heightened state of arousal and (2) a cognitive label. When people are aroused and do not know why, they determine their emotions by scanning the situation and making an attribution. Through a process of **misattribution**, arousal from one event can spill over and fuel our emotional reaction to another event. Sometimes our emotional reactions to outcomes are influenced by **counterfactual thinking**—as when bronze medalists feel better by imagining a fourth-place finish, while silver medalists feel worse by imagining a first-place finish.

Dimensions of Appraisal
According to cognitive theorists, the emotions we experience are determined by our appraisals of the situation we are in.

Is Cognition Necessary?
Some psychologists argue that people sometimes react with emotion instantly and without cognitive appraisal and that our emotions and thoughts are controlled by separate anatomical structures within the brain. Others maintain that it is not possible to have emotion without thought, even thought that is quick, effortless, and unconscious. This debate remains unresolved.

Human Emotion: Putting the Pieces Together
Knowing that emotions stem from physiological, expressive, and cognitive activities is only a first step. The next step is to determine how these elements combine to produce an emotional experience.

Types of Emotions
There is widespread agreement that fear, anger, disgust, joy, surprise, and sadness are basic human emotions. Some researchers speculate that other emotions are derived from mixtures of these or that all emotions can be classified along two independent dimensions: pleasantness and intensity.

Dynamics of Emotion
According to the opponent-process theory of emotion, an event triggers a "primary state" (an unlearned response), which in turn activates an "opponent state" (a learned response that is the emotional opposite of the primary state). The opponent state starts later, lasts longer, and gets stronger with repetition. Every positive emotional state is thus balanced in time by its negative counterpart, and vice versa.

The Cultural Context
Certain physiological and expressive components of emotion may be inborn and universal, but culture influences the types of events that arouse various emotions, the way we think about and describe emotions, and the **display rules** that determine when it's suitable to express certain feelings.

Are There Sex Differences in Emotion?
Many people believe that women are more emotional than men, and certain differences do emerge. Women describe themselves as more emotional (or men as less emotional), are more self-disclosing to others, and are more facially expressive. Socialization practices may well account for these sex differences.

Pleasure and the Pursuit of Happiness
Most people report being relatively happy, but there are marked individual differences. Three important factors are having social relationships, being employed, and being healthy. Although more affluent nations are happier, the evidence for an association between income level and happiness is mixed. As suggested by **social-comparison theory** and **adaptation-level theory**, one reason is that our perceptions of wealth are relative—to what others have and to what we are accustomed to. It has also been suggested that people have a certain dispositional level of happiness toward which they gravitate over time.

In the Field Resources

Books

Darwin, C. (1872/1965). *The expression of the emotions in man and animals*. Chicago: University of Chicago Press.

In this classic, Darwin presents his theory of emotional expressions and the adaptive functions they serve.

Ekman, P. (1985). *Telling lies: Clues to deceit in the marketplace, politics, and marriage.* New York: Norton.

This is a fascinating book about lying, and about how the face and body often betray our true feelings.

LeDoux, J. (1996). *The emotional brain: The mysterious underpinnings of emotional life.* New York: Simon & Schuster.

This book describes research showing that fear, and perhaps other raw emotions, are triggered instantly—without thought.

Myers, D. G. (1993). *The pursuit of happiness.* New York: Avon Books.

This easy-to-read paperback describes recent research on happiness—what it is, who has it, and why.

Internet

American Polygraph Association (http://www.polygraph.org:83/)

This organization provides publication lists and answers to frequently asked questions about polygraphic lie detection.

Journals and Periodicals

Journal of Applied Psychology
Journal of Nonverbal Behavior
Journal of Personality and Social Psychology
Motivation and Emotion
Psychophysiology

10 *Infancy and Childhood*

BASIC DEVELOPMENTAL QUESTIONS

The Nature–Nurture Debate
Developmental-Research Strategies

THE UNBORN CHILD

Genetic Building Blocks
Prenatal Development
Infancy and Childhood and Health
Drugs and the Fetus
The Birth Experience

THE REMARKABLE NEWBORN

Reflexes
Sensory Capacities

THE INFANT AND GROWING CHILD

Biological Development
Cognitive Development
Social Development

THE MANY FACETS OF DEVELOPMENT

The situation You know from past research that about 15 to 20 percent of all healthy babies are inhibited, timid, and wary of strangers. You also know that 25 to 30 percent are outgoing, fearless, and eager to approach new people. These differences are apparent early in life and remain stable through childhood. But where does this trait come from? Are some infants just born that way, as parents often assume, or does temperament arise from early experiences?

What's Your Prediction?

Nature or nurture?

To tease apart these dual effects, you decide to conduct a twin study. From monthly birth records, you contact all parents of recently born twins. Many agree to take part in your study, and you go on to recruit 178 pairs. About half are genetically identical, or monozygotic (MZ), twins; the other half are genetically nonidentical, fraternal, or dizygotic (DZ), twins. All sets of twins live together. You make appointments so that a mother and her children come to the laboratory when the twins are fourteen months old. Then they return for follow-up visits at twenty and twenty-four months old.

Along with two assistants, you meet the mother and her twins in a reception room. You explain the procedure and place a bib with an identifying letter on each child. One child is randomly selected to join the mother and a second assistant in a playroom, while the other stays in the reception area. Once the testing is complete, the children switch places.

The floor of the playroom is covered with toys. The mother sits on a sofa on the side and is asked not to pay attention to the child unless needed. At this point, the child is free to play. With the entire session being videotaped, two events are then staged to provide additional opportunities to observe the child's behavior. First, a new assistant, a stranger, enters the room holding a toy truck. Soon, she invites the child to play with her (if the child has not already done so). Next, the assistant who brought the mother and child into the playroom opens a cabinet and pulls out an unfamiliar object—a blue stuffed toy monster or a robot made of tin cans and colored lights. After two minutes, the child is encouraged to approach the object (if he or she has not already done so).

To determine each child's level of inhibition, you review the session tapes and record how long it took the child to approach the toys, the stranger, and the unfamiliar object. You also record the percentage of time spent near the mother during these three phases. These standardized behavioral measures are then combined and the child is given an overall inhibition score.

Once all the sessions are scored, the data are ready to be analyzed. The question: What is the *correlation* between pairs of twins? If one twin is inhibited, what is the likelihood that the other is inhibited as well? If you paired unrelated children at random, the correlation would be 0 (remember, a correlation coefficient can range from 0 to +1 or −1). At the other extreme, the behaviors of the identical twin pairs—who have the same genes and live in the same home—should be highly correlated. But what about the comparison group of fraternal twins? If variations in temperament are genetically determined, their correlation should be much lower, even though they live in the same home. But if temperament stems from experience, the correlations should be about the same for the identical and the fraternal twins. It would also be interesting to know whether the correlations remain stable from the first time the children are tested, at fourteen months old, to the third time, after ten months of additional life experience.

Make a prediction You have two groups of twins, identical and fraternal, and for each group you have inhibition scores at fourteen, twenty, and twenty-four months. To get you started, the correlation observed between fourteen-month-old identical twins is presented below: .57. Using that number as a guideline, predict what you would expect for fraternal twins at the same age. Remember, a number between 0 and .57 would indicate a greater role for genetics, while a number similar to .57 would indicate a greater role for experience. Make this prediction and fill in the correlations you'd expect in the follow-up sessions:

AGE	IDENTICAL	FRATERNAL
14 mo	.56	______
20 mo	______	______
24 mo	______	______

The results The research just described is based on a series of studies of infant and child temperament reported by Jerome Kagan (1994). In this study, JoAnn Robinson, along with Kagan and others (1992), sought to determine the extent to which individual differences in inhibition are the product of genetic heritage or the environment. What did you predict? As shown below, the actual results provide two types of support for genetic influences: (1) at fourteen months, the correlation is higher between identical twins than fraternal twins of the same sex, and (2) differences are also found at twenty and twenty-four months—despite the added exposure to environmental influences.

AGE	IDENTICAL	FRATERNAL
14 mo	.56	.24
20 mo	.46	.17
24 mo	.58	.32

What does it all mean? As we'll see shortly, it's now clear that both genetic and environmental influences are important. In this study of one- and two-year-olds, differences in temperament were attributable in part to genetic factors. But the correlations were far from perfect, even among identical twins raised in the same home—which means that other factors were also at work. It's important to realize, too, that not all differences in behavior are rooted in genetics to the same degree. In an unrelated study of the same twins, for example, the twin-pair correlations on verbal and memory tasks were much lower (Plomin et al., 1993). What does it mean? We'll see in this chapter that when it comes to infancy and child development, there are many interacting factors at work.

Like most parents, my wife and I will never forget the birth of our daughter and then, three years later, our son. After nine long months of excitement and anticipation, the moment of truth had arrived. The "baby's room" was furnished and freshly painted, our work schedules were rearranged, anxious grandparents were called, the car was filled with gas, the hospital's birthing room was on reserve, and our obstetrician was ready for action. With these logistical pieces in place, every ounce of our attention turned to what was about to happen and what it would mean for our lives. My head was spinning with questions. How long will the birthing process take? Will it go smoothly? Will the baby be okay? Will it be a boy or a girl? What will the baby look like? Will he or she grow up to be happy, loving, smart, and successful? What will the future hold?

Basic Developmental Questions

How important are genetic and environmental factors in human development? Can the extent of these influences be quantified? Why do so many researchers study twins and adoptees? And what strategies are used to measure the changes due to age?

The study of **developmental psychology** examines the kinds of questions that parents often ask about their offspring and that all of us ask about ourselves:

developmental psychology The study of how people grow, mature, and change over the life span.

How do individuals *change* as they get older? Developmental psychologists study how people grow, mature, and change across the entire life span, from conception through birth, infancy, and childhood; from adolescence through adulthood and old age. Focusing on the first few years of life, this chapter explores biological, cognitive, and social aspects of development. But first, let's step back and examine in greater depth two basic questions, both of which were raised in the study just described: the influences of nature and nurture, and the extent to which development is characterized by stability or change.

The Nature–Nurture Debate

Joseph P. Kennedy, a member of Congress from Massachusetts, is the son of the late senator Robert Kennedy. Folksinger Arlo Guthrie is the son of Woody Guthrie, the folksinger who wrote "This Land Is Your Land." Singer Liza Minnelli is the daughter of Judy Garland, the singer who starred as a child in *The Wizard of Oz*. Baseball stars Ken Griffey, Jr., and Barry Bonds are among the best in the game. A few years ago, so were their fathers. At first glance, these resemblances seem striking. But do they illustrate a rule or exceptions to the rule? What do they tell us about human development? One possible conclusion is that the similarities are built into nature and that these famous sons and daughters are chips off the old block because of genetic similarity to their parents. But wait—these celebrities also were raised by their parents, observed their parents' careers, and learned from the experience.

The **nature–nurture debate** is a classic in psychology. The strict biological (nature) position states that just as you are programmed to grow to a certain height, you are predisposed to become shy, sociable, smart, athletic, cheerful, or depressed—according to a genetic blueprint. In contrast, the extreme environmental (nurture) position says that your fate is shaped by life experience the way clay is molded by the hands of a sculptor. Psychologists who favor this side of the debate trumpet the effects of learning, culture, family background, peer groups, and critical life events.

All psychologists agree that the nature-nurture question should not be framed in either-or terms. Asking whether behavior is caused by genes or by the environment is like asking whether life is sustained by air or by water. Both are essential. The real questions are: How much does each factor contribute, in what ways do they interact, and how can their combined influences be teased apart? To answer these questions, consider the logic of scientific experiments, as described in Chapter 1. You may recall that in order to determine the effect of any given factor on behavior, researchers try to vary that factor and keep all other variables constant. This principle suggests two logically possible ways to examine the relative contributions of nature and nurture: (1) compare individuals who vary in their genetic backgrounds but share a constant environment, and (2) compare individuals who vary in their environment but share the same genetic heritage.

Many years ago, Robert Tyron (1940) took the first approach in an animal study. Tyron identified white rats as "bright" or "dull" based on their performance in a maze. He then mated the bright males with bright females, mated the dull males with dull females, and tested the maze performance of their offspring. He then bred the "brightest of the bright" and the "dullest of the dull" and tested their offspring. After repeating this procedure for twenty-one generations, Tyron had two groups of rats so different from each other that even the lowest bright animals performed better than the highest dull animals. These results are no surprise to animal breed-

nature–nurture debate The debate over the extent to which human behavior is determined by genetics and the environment.

ers. Whenever horses are bred for speed, dogs for hunting, or cows for milk production, the genetic influences on behavior are evident.

Obviously, researchers cannot selectively breed humans. But sometimes life provides a natural laboratory in which conditions can approximate the desired experiment. As depicted in Figure 10.1, two methods have proven particularly useful in the nature-nurture debate. The first is the **twin-study method.** To estimate the role of genetics on individuals who share the same environment, researchers examine the similarities between pairs of twins who are *identical*, or *monozygotic (MZ)*—which means they were born of one sperm fertilizing one egg and are 100 percent genetic replicas of each other. The researchers also examine the similarities within pairs of same-sex twins who are *fraternal*, or *dizygotic (DZ)*—which means they were born of separate sperm fertilizing two eggs and, like other siblings, share only about 50 percent of the same genes. The similarities between groups of identical and fraternal twins are then compared. To the extent that heredity is an important factor in development, identical twins should grow up to be more similar to each other than the same-sex fraternal twins.

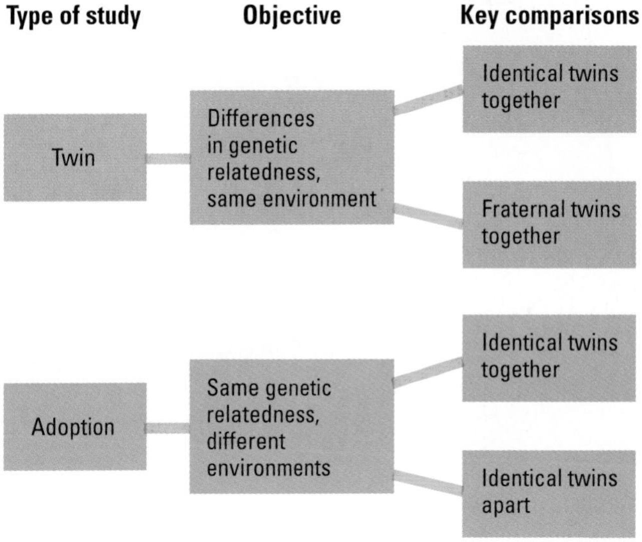

Figure 10.1 Measuring the effects of nature and nurture

Reversing the logic of using twins who live under the same roof, a second method capitalizes on natural variations in the environment but not in the genetics. To estimate the role of the environment on persons who are genetically related, researchers conduct **adoption studies**, in which they compare identical twins who were *raised together* in the same home to those who, for one reason or another, were separated after birth and were *raised apart* by different parents. The contribution of the environment is thus measurable by the extent to which the twins raised together are more similar to each other than those brought up in different homes. In a variation of this design, researchers sometimes test the extent to which adopted children, in general, resemble more closely their *biological* parents, siblings, and other blood relatives (evidence for the role of genetics) or their *adoptive* parents, siblings, and relatives (evidence for the role of environment).

Genetic Influences In 1979, Jim Springer and his identical twin brother, Jim Lewis, were reunited after thirty-nine years apart. Separated five weeks after birth, they were adopted by different families in Ohio. When University of Minnesota psychologist Thomas Bouchard, Jr., heard the story, he invited the "Jim twins" to take part in the ongoing research program dubbed the Minnesota twin studies. What Bouchard and his colleagues (1990) found was astonishing. Not only did both Jims have the same first name, but they both married women named Linda, divorced, and married women named Betty. Springer named his oldest son James Allan; Lewis named his James Alan. In their childhood, both had dogs named Toy, and both liked math but hated spelling. As adults, both men were deputy sheriffs, pumped gas, and worked for McDonald's. Both drank Miller Lite beer, chain-smoked Salem cigarettes, chewed their fingernails, spent vacations on the same Florida beach, and enjoyed stock-car racing and woodworking. In fact, Springer and Lewis had even built similar white benches in their backyards. Additional similarities were revealed in their medical histories. Both men gained and lost ten pounds at about the same age, both started to experience severe headaches at eighteen, and both suffered what seemed like a heart attack (Holden, 1980).

twin-study method A method of testing nature and nurture by comparing pairs of identical and fraternal twins of the same sex.

adoption studies A method of testing nature and nurture by comparing twins and other siblings reared together with those separated by adoption.

Separated a few weeks after birth in 1940, the Jim twins were reunited in 1979.

By administering various tests and collecting biographical data from pairs of identical twins reared apart, Bouchard and his colleagues (1990) found other odd similarities in mannerisms, abilities, tastes, habits, and the like. These stories are fascinating, but what do they prove about the role of genetics in human development? In his book *Innumeracy*, mathematician John Allen Paulos (1988) pointed out that fluke similarities and coincidences like these are not as improbable as we might think. After all, there are so many dimensions on which we could compare ourselves to others that at least some "striking" resemblances are bound by chance to be discovered. Taking a more systematic approach, behavioral geneticists and developmental psychologists search instead for correlations used to calculate **heritability**—a statistical estimate, for a given trait, of the percentage of variation within a group that is due to genetic factors.

Is 5 percent, 50 percent, or 90 percent of the variability in a personality trait attributable to genetic differences? What about intelligence, mental health, and other characteristics? In the temperament study described at the start of this chapter, the observed correlations enabled the investigators to estimate that roughly 57 percent of the variation in shyness among one- and two-year-old children was due to genetic influences (Robinson et al., 1992). In one of the Minnesota studies—which examined 217 pairs of MZ twins raised together, 114 DZ pairs raised together, 44 MZ pairs raised apart, and 27 DZ pairs raised apart—heritability estimates averaged 48 percent. (This is not to say that genes control 48 percent of your personality—only that genetic factors account for that much of the variation within a group.) On a wide range of personality measures, the evidence was clear: (1) When raised together, MZ twins were more similar than DZ twins, and (2) twins raised apart were almost as similar to each other as those living in the same home (Bouchard & McGue, 1990; Tellegen et al., 1988). Additional studies of twins and adoptees have further shown that genetic factors account for some of the differences found in intelligence, verbal and spatial abilities, alcoholism, criminality, vocational interests, aggressiveness, helpfulness, happiness, and various forms of mental illness (Loehlin et al., 1988; Lykken et al., 1993; Plomin & McClearn, 1993; Lykken & Tellegen, 1996).

heritability A statistical estimate of the percentage of the variability of a trait within a group that is attributable to genetic factors.

Environmental Influences Does this wave of support for the forces of nature mean that our home lives, social and cultural backgrounds, and physical environment are unimportant? Are the sons and daughters of shy parents doomed to become wallflowers? Are young schoolchildren genetically programmed for high or low math grades? Are violent criminals born, not made? No, not at all. Robert Plomin (1989) notes that studies of twins and adoptees contain a second clear message that should not be drowned out: "that these same data provide the best available evidence for the importance of the environment" (p. 108).

"It's a shame you missed the eighties."

[Drawing by W. Miller; © 1990 The New Yorker Magazine, Inc.]

Even while growing up in the same home, siblings live in different, "nonshared" environments.

This pro-nurture conclusion is based on two observations. First, even among identical twins, genetic differences usually account for less than 50 percent of the variation in personality (heritability estimates are higher in intellectual domains)—which means that environmental factors are responsible for the rest. Second, children growing up in the same home are remarkably different from each other, regardless of whether they're related by blood or adoption. The reason for these differences is that no two siblings live in exactly the same environment even when they grow up together in the same home (Loehlin et al., 1987; Scarr & Weinberg, 1983). True, there is a *shared environment.* Siblings may have the same parents, attend the same school, take the same vacations, and celebrate the same holidays. But brothers and sisters also experience unique *nonshared environments.* Born at separate times, they are treated differently by their parents, occupy different niches within the family, have different friends and teachers, play on different sports teams, and so on. One sibling may even fall victim to illness or have an accident that another does not. The point is that the forces of nurture are vital to development and can steer us in different directions—both between families and within a family as well (Dunn & Plomin, 1990; Hetherington et al., 1994).

What aspects of the nonshared environment make siblings so different from one another? Do siblings differ because they are treated differently by parents and others within the home, or do the differences stem more from the environment outside the home? In a book entitled *The Limits of Family Influence,* David Rowe (1994) reviewed the behavioral-genetic research and concluded that the effects of the home environment are short-lived and have surprisingly little impact on our adult personalities. Consistent with this proposition, Judith Harris (1995) concluded, "Whether a child resides at 42 Oak Street or at 56 Oak Street is a variable that has no long-term consequences" (p. 482). Rather, the most important aspects of the nonshared environment come from peer groups, friends, and others *outside* the home. Hillary Rodham Clinton often quotes an African saying that "It takes a village to raise a child." As Harris noted, that village has many people, including peers, who exert a strong and lasting influence on development.

Interactive Influences As researchers have struggled to separate the contributions of nature and nurture, they have come to realize that there is another complicating factor: Genetic and environmental influences are not independent. Studies have shown that identical twins receive more similar treatment from parents than fraternal twins do. In fact, the more genetically similar any two siblings are, the more similar their experience is in the home. To some extent, then, our genetic makeup influences the way others treat us, the kind of environment that we live in,

In February 1997, biologists in Scotland successfully cloned a sheep. Dolly, shown here at seven months old, is genetically identical to an adult sheep from which a cell containing DNA was removed and inserted into an unfertilized egg that was stripped of its DNA. The egg was "jump-started" by electric current to grow and divide like a fertilized cell. The resulting embryo was then implanted into a surrogate mother. When news of this experiment broke, some expressed fear that humans would replicate themselves. Others were quick to note that being genetically identical does not mean being the same person. As studies have shown, people are shaped in important ways by their environment.

and the ways in which we perceive and recall the details of that environment (Scarr & McCartney, 1983; Plomin et al., 1994; Hur & Bouchard, 1995).

Urie Bronfenbrenner and Stephen Ceci (1994) presented what they termed a "bioecological" model of development to account for the interaction of nature and nurture. According to this model, infants at birth are endowed with genetic predispositions, but these potentials will ultimately influence them as adults only to the extent that life experiences foster rather than inhibit their expression. There may be a genetic component to intelligence, but children raised in poverty and under stress may not realize their potential, while those who grow up in intellectually stimulating homes are more likely to achieve. Even with height, a highly heritable characteristic, children who are malnourished may not grow to be as tall as they could be.

Developmental-Research Strategies

Before we discuss infancy and childhood, let's consider the major strategies used in developmental research. As illustrated in Figure 10.2, there are basically two approaches for studying developmental processes. In **cross-sectional studies**, people of different ages are examined at the same time and their responses are compared. For example, when intelligence researchers test people in their twenties through seventies, they typically find that older adults obtain lower scores than younger adults.

cross-sectional study A method of developmental research in which people of different ages are tested and compared.

This method of comparison is quick and is easy to implement, but the results should be interpreted with caution. In cross-sectional intelligence studies, for example, the pattern of decline apparently caused by age might instead result from a "cohort effect"—a difference between generations. Today's twenty-year-olds spend more years in school than did their grandparents, who grew up during World War II. Lower scores among the older adults may stem from a relative lack of educational opportunity, not from the effects of chronological age.

A second method is to conduct **longitudinal studies**, in which the same subjects are retested at different times in their lives in order to measure truly age-related changes. Using this method, researchers might observe people at one point in their lives, then collect follow-up data from those same people days, weeks, months, or years later. In the research on age and intelligence, this strategy has revealed that there is less of a decline in performance as the same people grow older. The cross-sectional study may reveal *differences* between groups, but only the longitudinal study measures *change* as a function of age. The main drawback of the longitudinal approach is logistical. These long-term studies take a great deal of time—and require patience from researchers and cooperation from their subjects.

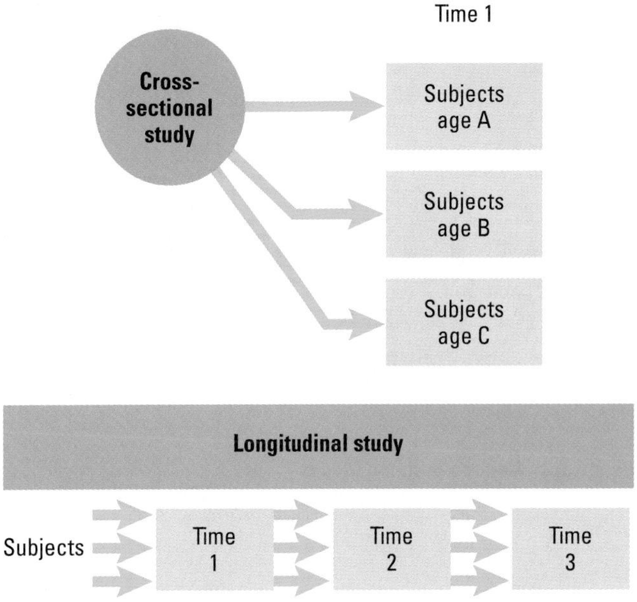

Figure 10.2 Developmental research strategies In cross-sectional studies, subjects of different ages are examined at the same time and compared for differences. In longitudinal studies, the same subjects are tested at different times in order to measure change.

The Unborn Child

What are the three stages of prenatal development? How do alcohol, cigarettes, and cocaine affect the process? What is the womb like as a sensory environment? And can expectant parents "teach" the unborn child by reading stories or playing music?

Recognizing that the passage from the womb into the outside world is a profound one, Westerners celebrate the birthday as the starting point in a person's development. In fact, birth is not so much a beginning as it is a transition. The real beginning occurs nine months earlier, at the moment of conception. That is why the Chinese calculate age from that moment and consider the baby to be a one-year-old at birth.

Genetic Building Blocks

Life begins when a male's *sperm* cell—one of hundreds of millions released into the Fallopian tube during intercourse—is united with a female's *ovum*, or egg cell. The fertilized ovum then forms a barrier that blocks the entry of other sperm. In the meantime, the nucleus of the male and female cells move toward each other, fusing within hours into a single, brand-new cell. This fusion marks the beginning of a new life, genetically endowed by a mother and father. Right from the start, this single cell has a full genetic heritage contained within twenty-three pairs of rodlike structures called **chromosomes**—half carried in the mother's ovum, and half in the father's

longitudinal study A method of developmental research in which the same people are tested at different times to track changes related to age.

chromosomes Rodlike structures, found in all biological cells, that contain DNA molecules in the form of genes.

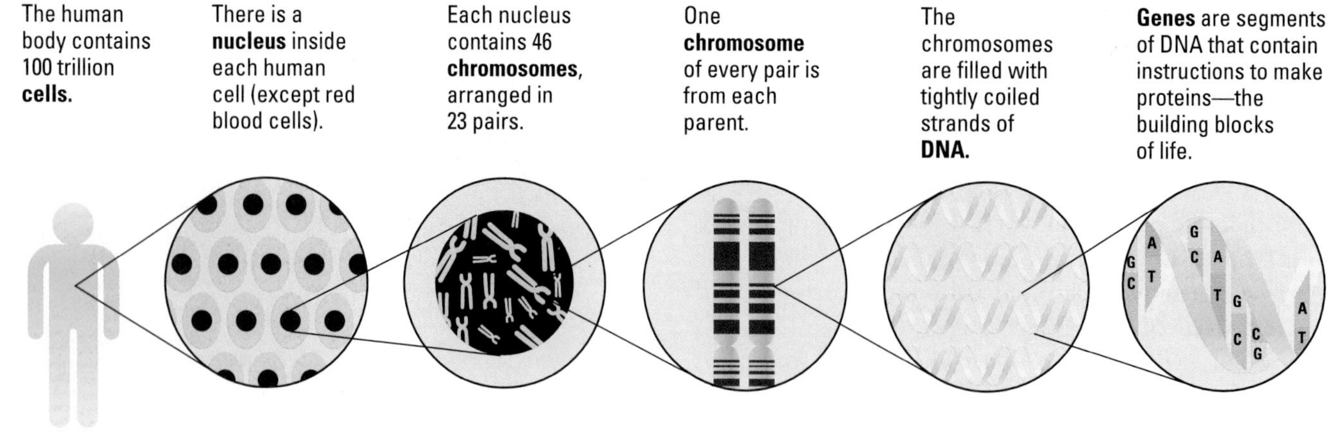

Figure 10.3 Genetic building blocks

sperm. Each of the forty-six chromosomes contains strands of the molecule **deoxyribonucleic acid,** commonly known as **DNA.** In turn, each DNA molecule is made up of many thousands of segments called **genes**—the biochemical building blocks of an individual life (see Figure 10.3).

Like a photograph that has already been taken but has not yet been developed, genes determine our skin color, height, weight, blood type, certain behavioral dispositions, as well as medical and psychological disorders. All humans have certain genes in common, which is why we can all can walk and talk—but not fly, bark, or breathe underwater. At the same time, unless you are one of two identical twins or one of three triplets, you have a distinct combination of genes that makes you unique among all past, present, and future human beings. The twenty-third pair of chromosomes controls your sex. Whereas everyone receives an X chromosome from the mother, there is an equal chance that the father will donate an X or Y chromosome to the pair. If it is X, the offspring will be female (XX); if it is Y, it will be male (XY). The sex of a child thus depends on the father's contribution.

Prenatal Development

Prenatal development during the nine months of pregnancy is divided into three stages: *germinal* (the first two weeks after conception), *embryonic* (third to ninth weeks), and *fetal* (ninth week to birth). From one stage to the next, dramatic biological and behavioral changes take place—and environmental influences are plentiful. These developments are illustrated in Figure 10.4.

First, there is the germinal stage. Thanks to conception, life begins with one remarkable new cell called a **zygote**—about the size of the period at the end of this sentence, yet fully equipped with a rich genetic heritage. Very quickly, a process of cell division takes place: The first cell splits into two, four, eight, and so on. After two and a half days, there are twelve to sixteen cells. By the fourth day, there are more than a hundred cells clustered together in a ball, traveling from the Fallopian tube into the uterus and increasing in both their number and their diversity. Some cells will form muscles and bone; others will form the stomach, liver, and so on. At two weeks, the ball of cells attaches to the uterine wall, braced and ready for eight and a half months in a new home. By the time this zygote is born, it will consist of hundreds of trillions of cells.

deoxyribonucleic acid (DNA) The complex molecular structure of a chromosome that carries genetic information.

genes The biochemical units of heredity that govern the development of an individual life.

zygote A fertilized egg that undergoes a two-week period of rapid cell division and develops into an embryo.

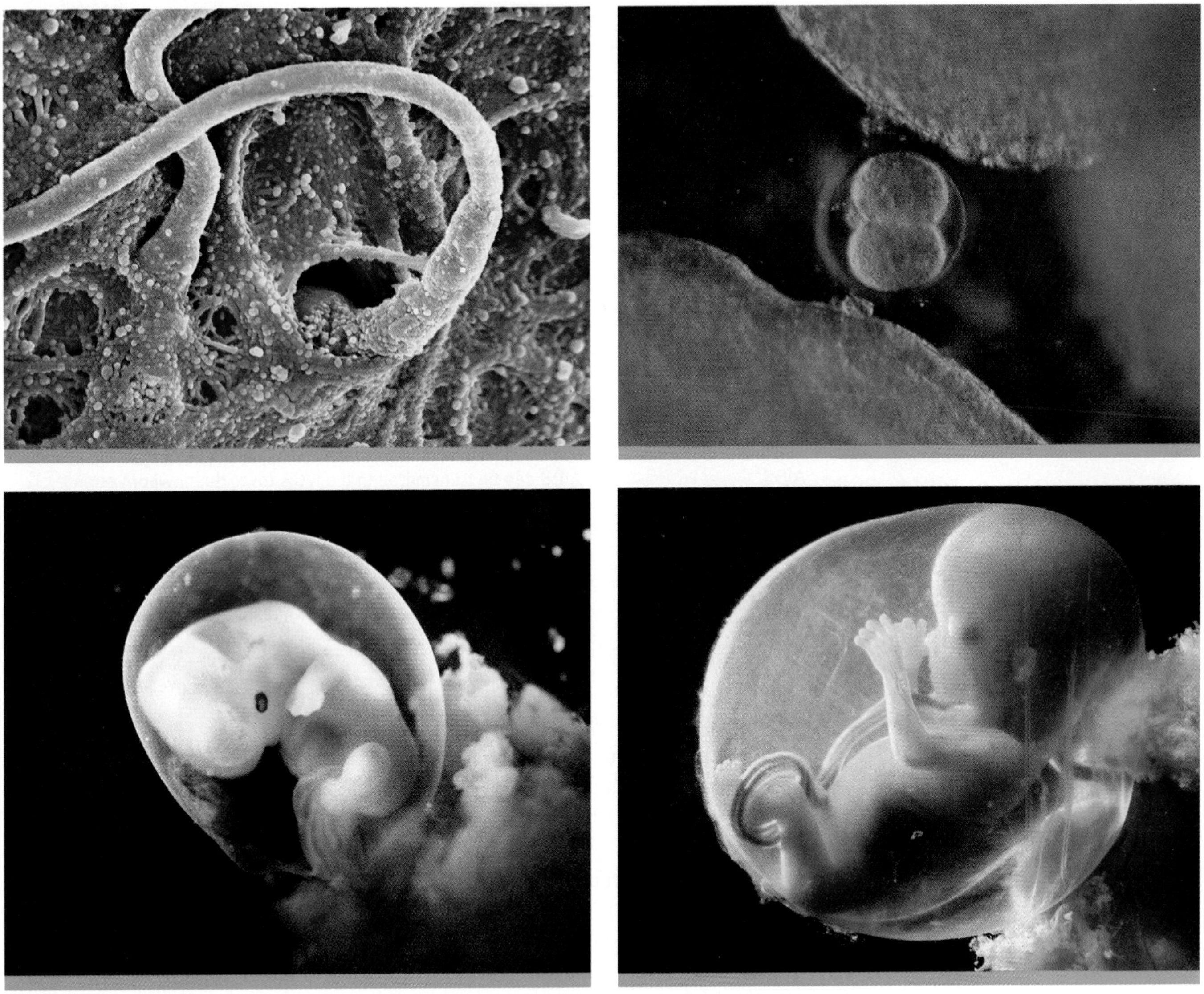

Figure 10.4 Prenatal development Just prior to conception, a sperm penetrates the ovum wall (*top left*). After thirty hours, the fertilized ovum divides for the first time and each cell contains genes from both the mother and the father (*top right*). After six weeks, parts of the embryo's body have formed and the heart beats (*bottom left*). At four months, the fetus is two to four inches long and has a conspicuously human appearance (*bottom right*).

Once the zygote is firmly attached to the uterine wall, the germinal stage is over, and the zygote is called an **embryo**. It is at this point that all parts of the body begin to form—an oversize head with a primitive brain and central nervous system, eyes, ears, a nose, and a mouth with lips and teeth, a heart and circulatory system, arms, legs, fingers, toes, and a tail. During this stage, organs start to function, including a heart that pumps blood and beats, quickly, for the first time. Also during this stage, the male hormone testosterone is secreted in embryos that are genetically male, but not in those destined to become female. The embryo is an astonishing creature: All the pieces of an individual are in place, yet at eight weeks of age it is only an inch long and weighs a tenth of an ounce. You could hold one in the palm of your hand.

From the ninth week on, the embryo becomes a conspicuously human **fetus**. At first, the cartilage in the bones starts to harden and there is rapid growth of the

embryo The developing human organism, from two weeks to two months after conception.

fetus The developing human organism, from nine weeks after conception to birth.

Table 10.1 Some Hazards to the Developing Embryo and Fetus

SUBSTANCE	POSSIBLE DANGER
Alcohol	Excessive use can produce fetal alcohol syndrome. Even one or two drinks a day can cause problems, especially in the early stages of pregnancy.
Cigarettes	Smoking is linked to miscarriages, premature births, and low birth weight. Effects on later behavior and cognitive functioning are harder to pinpoint.
Cocaine	Cocaine use results in lower birth weight and later cognitive and social learning deficits.
Aspirin	Taken in large quantities, aspirin can cause prenatal bleeding, intestinal discomfort, respiratory problems, and low birth weight.
Marijuana	Heavy use can lead to premature birth and to babies with abnormal reactions to stimulation.
AIDS	AIDS can be transmitted to the fetus (or to the newborn during birth). AIDS babies are often born small and with facial deformities.
Rubella	Before the eleventh week, rubella, or German measles, can cause heart problems, mental retardation, cataracts, and deafness.
X rays	Heavy exposure can cause malformation of organs.

brain, heart, lungs, genitals, and other internal organs and body parts. Depending on its age, the fetus can squirm, open its eyes, suck its thumb, kick its legs, curl its toes, and turn somersaults. By the seventh month, the key life-support systems are sufficiently developed so that the fetus can breathe, circulate blood, digest nutrients, and dispose of wastes. At this point, the two-pound fetus has a fighting chance to survive if delivered prematurely. If born on schedule, it will weigh an average of seven pounds.

Although fetal development follows a set biological clock, it is also influenced by environmental factors. Depending on the biological stage of development, exposure to harmful substances called **teratogens** (from the Greek word *teras*, meaning "monster") can have devastating effects on the growing fetus. Obstetricians warn expectant mothers that malnutrition, stress, X rays, AIDS, German measles and other viral infections, certain antibiotics, painkillers, large doses of aspirin, heavy exposure to paint fumes, and a long list of drugs can all prove dangerous in this regard (see Table 10.1). Some teratogens cannot be avoided—and some problems will arise without exposure to toxic substances. There are no guarantees. But expectant mothers can minimize the risks by controlling their intake of certain foods and drugs (see pages 372–373).

Just as a fetus's body changes according to a biological schedule and is subject to environmental influences, so too does its behavior. In a study of fetal neurobehavioral development, Janet DiPietro and others (1996) tested the healthy fetuses of thirty-four pregnant women on six occasions at twenty and thirty-nine weeks of gestation. During each session, they used a "fetal actocardiograph" to record the fetus's heart rate, physical movements, and sleep state. To determine a fetus's responsiveness to stimulation, they also presented a three-second vibration to the mother's abdomen and recorded changes in the fetus's heart rate. As shown in Figure 10.5, certain aspects of fetal behavior from twenty weeks to birth followed a predictable course as the heart rate slowed, physical activity diminished, the fetuses spent more time in active REM sleep, and they became increasingly responsive to stimulation.

teratogens Toxic substances that can harm the embryo or fetus during prenatal development.

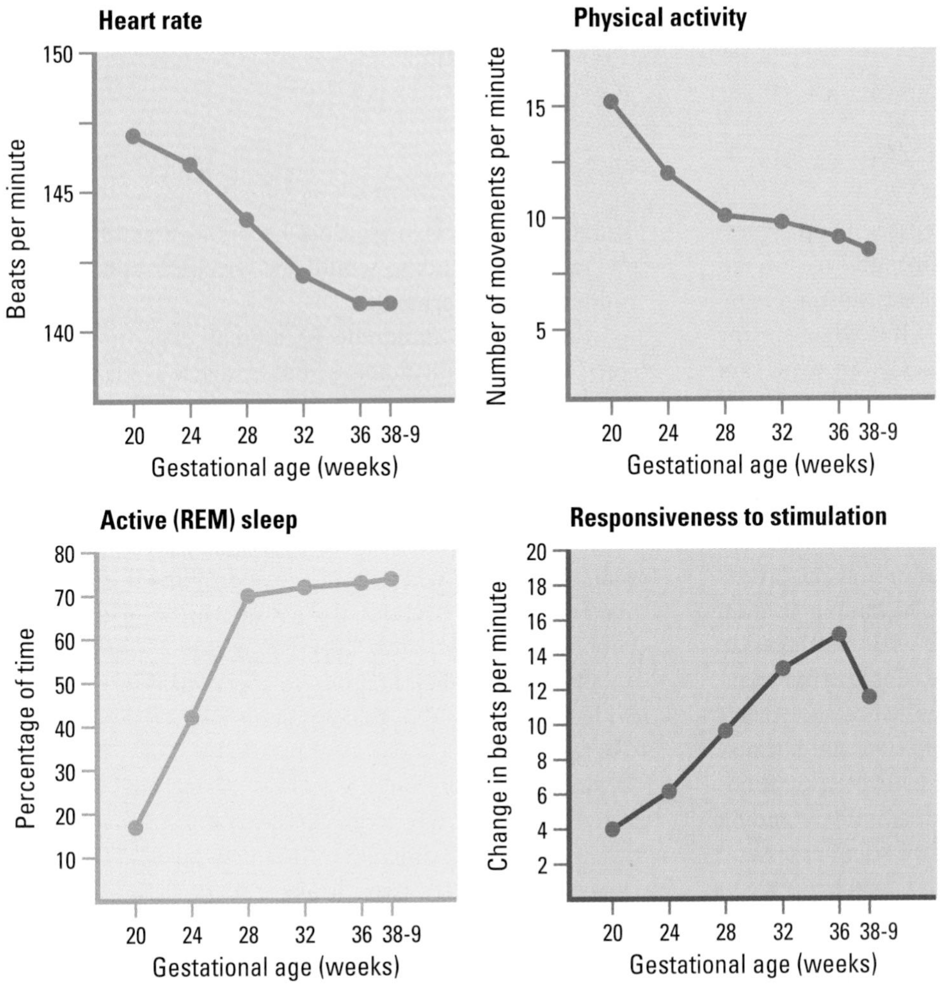

Figure 10.5 Neurobehavioral development in the fetus From twenty weeks to birth, fetuses were monitored through a fetal actocardiograph. As shown, heart rate slowed, physical activity diminished, and there was an increase, at least up to thirty-six weeks, in responsiveness to stimulation (DiPietro et al., 1996).

It's also clear from other research that at varying ages, fetuses move their eyes, stretch, yawn, put their hands to the mouth, and have increasingly regular cycles of rest and activity. The mature fetus can also detect not only mechanical vibration but also specific sounds as well as tastes and odors that pass into the amniotic fluid (Lecanuet et al., 1995; Smotherman & Robinson, 1996).

Let's stop for a moment and ponder a fascinating prospect for parents. During the final three months of pregnancy, a fetus is developed enough to hear and distinguish among sounds from the outside world. Is it possible that the fetus can recognize mom's voice? Can expectant parents soothe—or even teach—their unborn child by reading stories or playing music? Could I have pretrained my daughter and son to appreciate suspense novels and rock 'n' roll? In a fascinating series of experiments, Anthony DeCasper, William Fifer, Chris Moon, and their colleagues have sought to answer these questions. In one

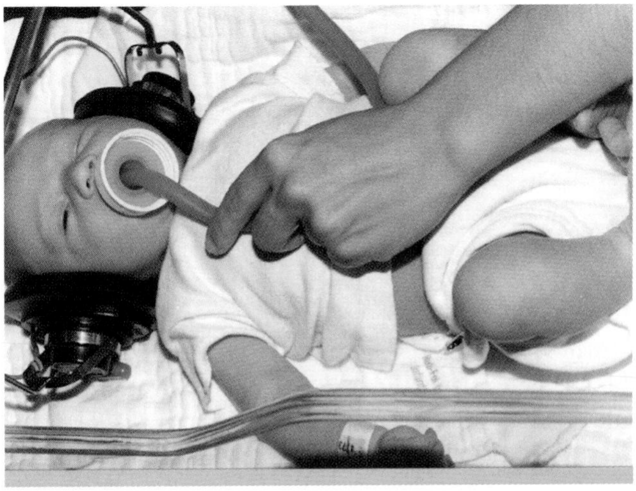

In this study, infants sucked on a nipple more vigorously to hear the sound of their mother's voice rather than that of an unfamiliar male (DeCasper & Fifer, 1980).

INFANCY AND CHILDHOOD AND HEALTH

Drugs and the Fetus

Legally and illegally, people have used drugs throughout human history. The psychoactive effects of various substances on the user were described in Chapter 4. But what are the health risks to the fetus when the user is an expectant mother? Is the fetus more vulnerable in some stages of pregnancy than others? In the emerging area of "behavioral toxicology," researchers are now examining the effects of various substances, including alcohol, tobacco, and cocaine. In animal studies, pregnant mothers are randomly injected with a toxic substance and the effects on their offspring are later measured. In human studies, researchers seek correlations between what mothers say they consumed while pregnant and the subsequent behavior of their children. Because women who take drugs differ in other ways from those who do not, and because the long-term effects of exposure can be subtle, the findings should be taken seriously but with an understanding that the effects may be overestimated in some cases and underestimated in others (Jacobson & Jacobson, 1996).

Alcohol. In 1899, English doctor William Sullivan studied the babies born to women in prison. He compared the children of heavy-drinking mothers with those of nondrinkers and discovered that the rate of stillbirths and infant mortality was two and a half times higher among the children of drinking mothers. This discovery lay dormant for many years. Then in 1973, Kenneth Jones and others noticed that eleven babies of alcoholic mothers were born with a pattern of defects that included stunted growth, facial deformities (widely spaced eyes, a flattened nose, and a thin upper lip), and mental retardation. They called this pattern **fetal alcohol syndrome (FAS).**

The devastating impact of alcohol is not all that surprising in light of the immediate effects it has on the fetus. Soon after a mother takes a drink—whether it's beer, wine, or hard liquor—the alcohol enters her bloodstream. It then passes through the placenta into the fetus's blood, flows to the brain, and impairs breathing. Using ultrasound, researchers observed that fetuses breathed less often after their mothers drank a "screwdriver"—a drink consisting of orange juice and vodka—than when they had just a glass of orange juice (Lewis & Boylan, 1979). It seems that when an expectant mother gets drunk, to some extent so does her unborn child. Indeed, no researcher today would be granted approval to conduct this experiment.

From many hundreds of animal experiments and recent studies with humans, the evidence is clear: Alcoholic mothers are likely to have a "multihandicapped child"—one who suffers from brain damage, intellectual impairments, attentional disorders, speech problems, hyperactivity, and motor problems such as trembling, slow reflexes, lack of coordination, and a weak grip (Hill et al., 1989). But what about social drinking during pregnancy? Does an occasional glass of wine over dinner or bubbly champagne on New Year's Eve damage the unborn child? When it comes to social drinking, too, the evidence suggests that the expectant mother should exercise restraint.

In one study, Sandra Jacobson and others (1993) tested infants born to women who drank varying degrees of alcohol during pregnancy. Infants whose mothers had consumed at least two drinks a day were slower to process information and less likely to engage in playful imitation. In other research, Ann Streissguth and her colleagues interviewed more than 1,500 pregnant women in Seattle—most of whom were white, married, and middle class—and asked about their consumption of alcohol and other substances before and after they knew they were pregnant. Four and a half years later, 457 of these women's children were brought in for testing. Results revealed that the more alcohol consumed by the mother, the more serious the child's problems were later on. Two findings were especially alarming. First, even small doses of alcohol proved harmful. Children of mothers who consumed only one drink a day while pregnant lacked balance, manual dexterity, and a steady hand. At three drinks a day, IQ scores were an average of five points lower. Second, damage was greatest when mothers drank during the third and fourth weeks of pregnancy, a time when the embryo's head was starting to take shape—but before many women realized they were pregnant. There seemed to be no safe level of drinking, and the timing couldn't be worse (Streissguth et al., 1993).

Cigarettes. A second common teratogen is tobacco. When a woman smokes a cigarette, she inhales many chemicals—including nicotine, cyanide, and the same carbon monoxide that spews from the exhaust pipe of a car. How does all this affect the fetus? For starters, as soon as a pregnant woman lights up, oxygen is restricted and the fetus breathes less. It's not surprising, then, that women who smoke are more likely to have miscarriages, premature babies, and full-term babies who are born underweight (Neiberg et al., 1985). The long-term effects are not as easy to pinpoint. A few years ago, several published studies showed a relationship between prenatal tobacco exposure and a host of behavioral problems, including deficits in academic achievement, IQ, and social adjustment. It now appears, however, that women who smoke also tend to be younger, not well educated, less likely to eat a balanced diet, and more likely to drink large amounts of alcohol. Once these other factors are accounted for, it's no longer clear what kind of long-term damage is caused by smoking per se (Streissguth et al., 1989).

Cocaine. Cocaine is a harmful substance whose effects on the developing fetus are clear (Lewis & Bendersky, 1995). Infants exposed in utero to cocaine are smaller at birth than comparable infants who were not exposed. They also have cognitive and social difficulties. In one study, cocaine-exposed infants learned less, had less interest, and derived less pleasure from an enjoyable task (Alessandri et al., 1993). In another study, they were more irritable, more difficult to console, and less likely to smile (Phillips et al., 1996). These results are merely correlational, but animal researchers have found that when randomly assigned rats are injected with cocaine, they become less nurturing in their parental behavior (Zimmerberg and Gray, 1992)—and the pups exhibit learning deficits that persist into their adulthood (Heyser et al., 1993).

study, sixteen women—twice a day in the last six weeks of pregnancy—read passages either from Dr. Seuss's *The Cat in the Hat* or from *The King, the Mice, and the Cheese*, a children's story with a very different cadence. Three days after birth, the babies were brought to the laboratory, where they wore headphones and sucked an electronic pacifier that activated a tape recording of one of these two stories, depending on the rate at which the nipple was sucked. As it turned out, thirteen of the sixteen babies "chose" by sucking faster or slower to hear the story that the mother had read before birth (DeCasper & Spence, 1986). Further demonstrating that late-term fetuses can make auditory discriminations, research has shown that newborn infants "prefer" (as measured by sucking rate) the familiar rhythms of their own mother's voice—particularly when it is muffled, as in the womb—or the sound of a heartbeat to an unfamiliar male voice (DeCasper & Fifer, 1980; DeCasper & Sigafoos, 1983). And newborns whose parents are Spanish- or English-speaking are more responsive at birth to the language they had heard in utero (Fifer and Moon, 1995).

fetal alcohol syndrome (FAS) A specific pattern of birth defects (stunted growth, facial deformity, and mental retardation) often found in the offspring of alcoholic mothers.

The Birth Experience

Few transitions in life are as dramatic as one's emergence from the birth canal into the world. After spending nine months curled up inside a dimly lit, warm sack of amniotic fluid, the baby is pulled out, poked, prodded, and exposed for the first time to cold dry air, bright lights, and high-pitched sounds. As an adult, you would probably feel rather dazed by this rude awakening. But what is it like for a newborn?

Research on the newborn's sensory experience right before and after birth has yielded some surprising findings. In the first place, the mother's womb is not a perfectly tranquil home free from stimulation. Amniotic fluid contains urine, sugars, cholesterol, and fatty acids, so the fetus can taste a mixture of sweet, sour, salty, and

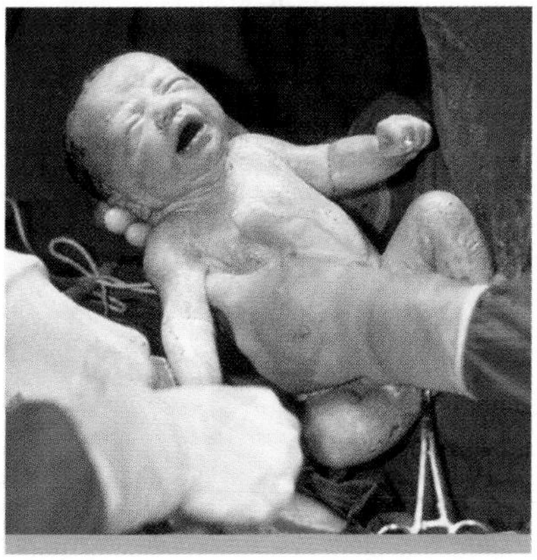

At birth, the newborn is thrust into a world that is brighter, louder, and colder than in the womb.

Infant researchers have recorded facial expressions, head and eye movements, and other behaviors to measure what newborns know but cannot put into words.

bitter flavors in the mouth. There is also a good deal of movement. Although cushioned from many of life's jolts, the early fetus tumbles around, and the more advanced fetus—which is too cramped for gymnastics—fidgets and kicks. Finally, there is noise, and lots of it. Near the fetus, the mother's organs beat, rumble, and growl. And when the mother speaks, her voice travels like thunder down her lungs. As we saw earlier, the fetus is equipped to detect these sounds beginning in the seventh month. So what is the prenatal experience like? Daphne and Charles Maurer (1988) put it this way: "To the adult, withdrawing into the womb would resemble flying cramped inside a light airplane, through turbulent weather, with the taste of air-sickness in your mouth" (p. 7).

Despite this in-utero stimulation, the first few moments after birth are different, to say the least. The typical delivery room is brightly lit. Many parents don't realize that newborns can see right away and can follow moving objects with their eyes. The reason most babies are born with their eyes shut is that the delivery room is so bright. By using invisible, infrared light to photograph eye movements, researchers found that in total darkness newborn babies will open their eyes wide and scan back and forth and that even dim light causes them to squint (Haith, 1980). Think about how it feels to catch a glimpse of the morning sun after a night's sleep, and then imagine that you had slept for nine months. As we saw in Chapter 3, the eye that is adapted to the dark becomes hypersensitive to light.

Upon birth, sounds are not necessarily louder, but they are different. When a baby is born, his or her ears are plugged up with amniotic fluid, which muffles sound. It's just as well, too, because the delivery room is filled with shrieks of pain, joy, and relief and other noises. There is also a change in outside temperature. From constant warmth, the newborn emerges soaking wet and naked into a relatively cold room. Like anyone who steps out of a hot bath, the infant is chilled. Because newborns have a higher proportion of surface area from which to lose heat and less insulation in the form of fat, their body temperature drops sharply right after birth.

The Remarkable Newborn

Why has it been said that babies are a lot smarter than they look? How can newborn infants "communicate" what they know to researchers? What kinds of sights and sounds most attract the newborn, and what's the adaptive significance of these preferences?

In 1890, William James described the newborn's experience of the world as "one great booming, buzzing confusion." Some eighty years later, Lewis Lipsitt (1971) signaled the dawn of a new era in an article entitled "Babies: They're a Lot Smarter than They Look." Why is there such a discrepancy between James and Lipsitt? Babies are not more capable today than in the past—they still sleep sixteen to twenty hours a day, shut their eyes in bright sun, dirty their diapers, and cry a lot. The difference is that developmental psychologists now have high-tech equipment and more sophisticated methods to measure what the newborn cannot tell us in words.

One particularly valuable research technique is based on the measurement of **habituation**, the tendency for attention to a novel stimulus to wane over time. If a picture or a sound is presented over and over again, an infant will eventually get bored, lose interest, look away, and exhibit a change in heart rate—a sure sign that it has "learned" the stimulus and "remembered" the previous exposures (Bornstein, 1989). If the infant then perks up, regains interest, and spends more time looking when a new stimulus is presented, this **recovery** response suggests that it has noticed a difference between the old and new. Using this technique, researchers can determine the age at which infants begin to distinguish among faces, voices, musical notes, speech sounds, colors, geometric shapes, and rudimentary concepts.

Other techniques are also used. To determine what infants find interesting or surprising, researchers put different objects in front of them—dots, lines, balls, whatever—and use an eye-tracking device to record the amount of time spent looking at each object. Or, as in the Dr. Seuss study described earlier, an electronic pacifier can be used to allow infants to express their preferences by sucking on the nipple at a faster or slower rate. As we'll see, there are many subtle ways for a newborn to "communicate" to researchers. Body and head movements, facial expressions, and measured changes in brain waves, heart rate, and respiration are just a few of the possibilities. When it comes to infants, says researcher Mark Strauss, "you can tell the wheels are turning. They're paying attention to the world in incredibly subtle ways" (cited in Grunwald & Goldberg, 1993).

The results of all the recent research are informative—and sometimes startling. For example, Karen Wynn (1992) showed five-month-old infants one or two Mickey Mouse dolls being put on a puppet stage and covered by a screen (see Figure 10.6). Next, they saw her either add a doll to the one behind the screen (1 + 1) or take one away (2 − 1). The screen was then lowered so the babies could see how many dolls were now on stage. Sometimes, the number was correct (2 in addition, 1 in subtraction); at other times, it was incorrect (1 in addition, 2 in subtraction). Can infants add and subtract? If so, reasoned Wynn, they would "expect" correct outcomes and be surprised by incorrect outcomes. That is what happened. By recording their looking time, Wynn found that the babies looked longer at the incorrect—and apparently unexpected—outcomes. Using similar methods, Wynn and others have discovered that five-month-olds have a rudimentary ability not only to add and subtract but also to tell the difference between two objects or event sequences and three (Canfield & Smith, 1996; Wynn, 1996).

Figure 10.6 Can infants add and subtract? Five-month-olds saw a sequence of events that illustrated the addition (1 + 1 = 2) or subtraction (2 − 1 = 1) of Mickey Mouse dolls. In each case, a correct or incorrect outcome was revealed. The infants looked longer at outcomes that were incorrect and, apparently, unexpected (Wynn, 1992).

Reflexes

In light of recent research, developmental psychologists now have a profound respect for the newborn's capacities. To begin with, babies are prepared at birth with many adaptive reflexes—automatic, unlearned reactions to certain types of stimulation. Press into a newborn's palm, and you will stimulate a **grasping reflex** that causes the baby to clutch your hand so hard that it can support its own weight. Touch the newborn's right or left cheek with a nipple, or even a finger, and you will stimulate a **rooting reflex**, causing the baby automatically to turn in that direction and open its mouth. Touch the newborn's lips, and it will try to squeeze your finger between its tongue and palate, breathe through the nose, and begin to *suck*. Move your finger to the back of the baby's mouth, and it will try to *swallow*. None of these reflexes is intentional or within an infant's control, and most disappear within three or four months, never to return. But while they last, grasping, turning, opening the mouth, sucking, and swallowing are important parts of the newborn's adaptive machinery.

habituation The tendency for attention to a stimulus to wane over time (often used to determine whether an infant has "learned" a stimulus).

recovery Following habituation to one stimulus, the tendency for a second stimulus to arouse new interest (often used to test whether infants can discriminate between stimuli).

grasping reflex In infants, an automatic tendency to grasp an object that stimulates the palm.

rooting reflex In response to contact on the cheek, an infant's tendency to turn toward the stimulus and open its mouth.

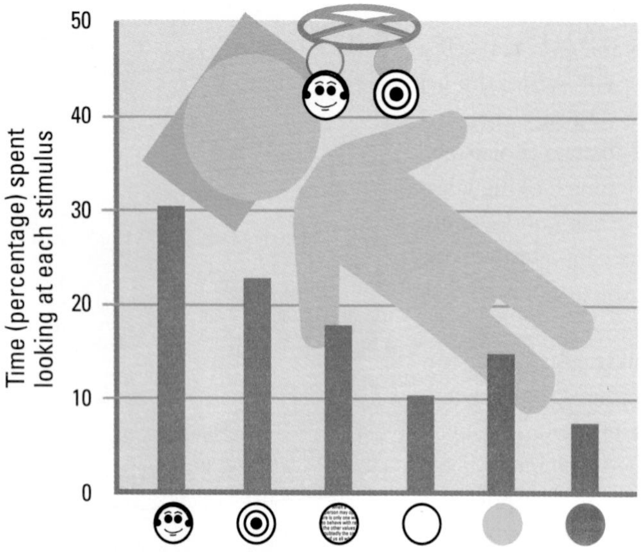

Figure 10.7 Visual preferences in newborns Fantz (1961) recorded the amount of time newborns spent gazing at various disks. As shown, they looked more at the patterns than at solids, and they looked most of all at the human face.

Sensory Capacities

Contrary to what maternity doctors and nurses used to tell new mothers, the newborn has the capacity to see, hear, taste, smell, and feel pain. The question is not whether newborns have these senses, but, rather, what their limitations are and what kinds of stimulation they prefer.

Vision and Visual Preferences

At birth, parts of the eye and the visual cortex are not fully developed, and the newborn is nearsighted. In fact, to see an object as would an adult with 20/20 vision, the newborn needs to be twenty to thirty times closer—with the best distance being about eight inches from the eyes (Banks & Salapatek, 1983). The problem is that the newborn's lenses do not focus on objects at a distance. They also cannot detect subtle differences in light, shading, or color. For that reason, soft pastel colors in the crib or on the wall do not arouse as much interest as a newspaper with bold print or a checkerboard that has stark black-on-white contrast (Adams & Maurer, 1984). What would it be like to see through the eyes of a newborn baby? As Daphne and Charles Maurer (1988) described it, the world would look like "a badly focused snapshot that has been fading in the sun for so many years that you can barely identify the subject" (p. 127).

Newborns may be limited in their vision, but their sensory abilities develop quickly, and they have marked preferences for certain kinds of stimulation. Just a few hours after birth, for example, infants distinguish between light and dark, stare at objects that show contrast, and track slow movement with their eyes. Especially intriguing is a study in which Robert Fantz (1961) recorded the amount of time that two- to five-day-old infants spent gazing at each of the six disks illustrated in Figure 10.7—a human face, a bull's-eye, newsprint, and three solids colored red, white, and yellow. As shown, the infants preferred to look at the patterns over solids. Lo and behold, their favorite pattern was the human face. This finding raised an intriguing question: Do faces just happen to provide the right kind of visual stimulation, or is the human nervous system primed to pay special attention to social stimuli? Is the attraction a mere happy coincidence or the clever design of evolution?

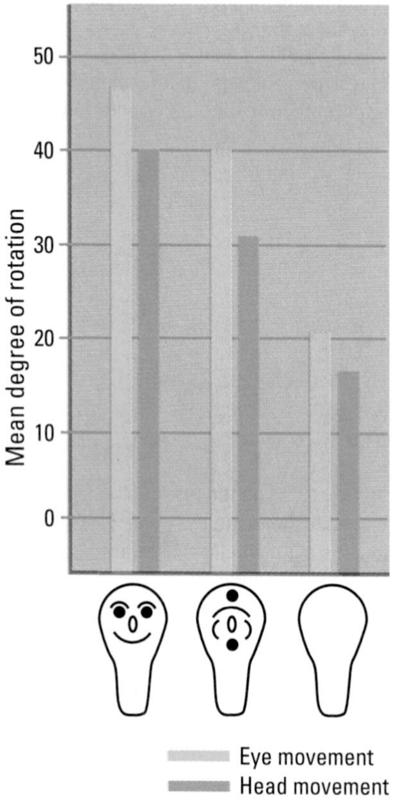

Figure 10.8 Newborn orientation toward the face In this study, a face, a scrambled pattern, or a blank form was moved slowly past each infant's field of view. As you can see, the infants tracked the face more than they did the other patterns (Johnson et al., 1991).

Research supports the evolutionary interpretation. To be sure, newborns look at any object that has complexity, contrast, and a symmetrical pattern of eyelike dots in an outline—whether that object resembles a face or not (Kleiner, 1987). But infants tested within an hour or two of birth exhibit a unique level of interest in facelike stimuli. To demonstrate, Mark Johnson and others (1991) presented newborns with white head-shape forms that depict a properly featured face, a scrambled face, or a blank, featureless face. The experimenter moved each pattern slowly across each infant's field of view and recorded the extent to which the infants rotated their head and eyes to follow the visual stimulus. As shown in Figure 10.8, the infants tracked the facelike pattern more than they did the scrambled and blank patterns. This study and others like it suggest that humans are born with a special orientation toward the face (Morton & Johnson, 1991; Valenza et al., 1996). They can even distinguish, shortly after birth, between the faces of their own mothers and those of female strangers (Walton et al., 1992; Pascalis et al., 1995).

Other lines of research also indicate that newborns are "tuned in" to the face as a social object. Andrew Meltzoff and Keith Moore (1983) found that within seventy-two hours of birth, babies not only look at faces but often mimic gestures such as moving the head, pursing the lips, or sticking out the tongue (see Figure 10.9). This rudimentary form of imitation occurs even when the model is a stranger (Meltzoff & Moore, 1992). In another study, newborns were videotaped as they watched an adult wear a happy, sad, or surprised expression. Observers who later saw only the tape were able to guess the adult's expression from changes in the baby's face (Field et al., 1982). What do these findings mean? It's not clear that newborns are capable of deliberate and coordinated imitation. But they do react automatically to certain facial cues, a reaction that has been observed not only in the United States but in India as well (Reissland, 1988). It's almost as if babies were born with a "social reflex," to the delight of parents all over the world.

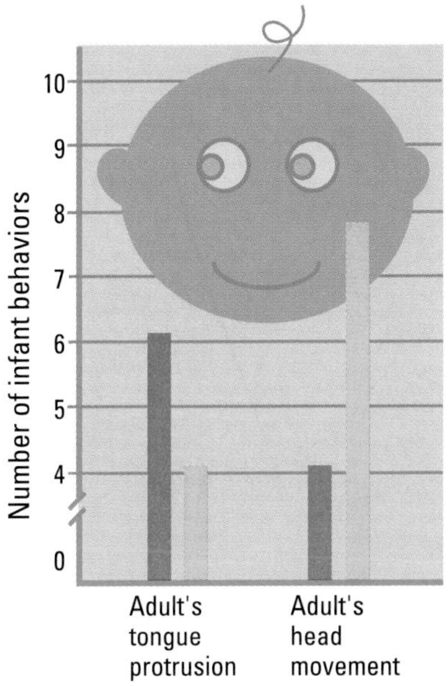

Figure 10.9 Newborn imitation An adult experimenter either stuck out his tongue or moved his head in front of newborn babies. Videotaped records showed that the infants were more likely to respond by imitating the same gesture (Meltzoff & Moore, 1989).

Hearing and Auditory Preferences Slam the nursery door while a newborn is asleep, and the baby will open its eyes wide and fling out its arms. Clearly, the newborn can hear. But what does it hear, and how well? As with vision, the human auditory system is not completely developed at birth. The baby's outer ear is very small, its eardrum does not vibrate effectively, and the auditory cortex is still immature. For the first week or so, the baby's ears are also clogged with amniotic fluid, which muffles sound. The result of all this is that the newborn baby is hard of hearing, compared to adults.

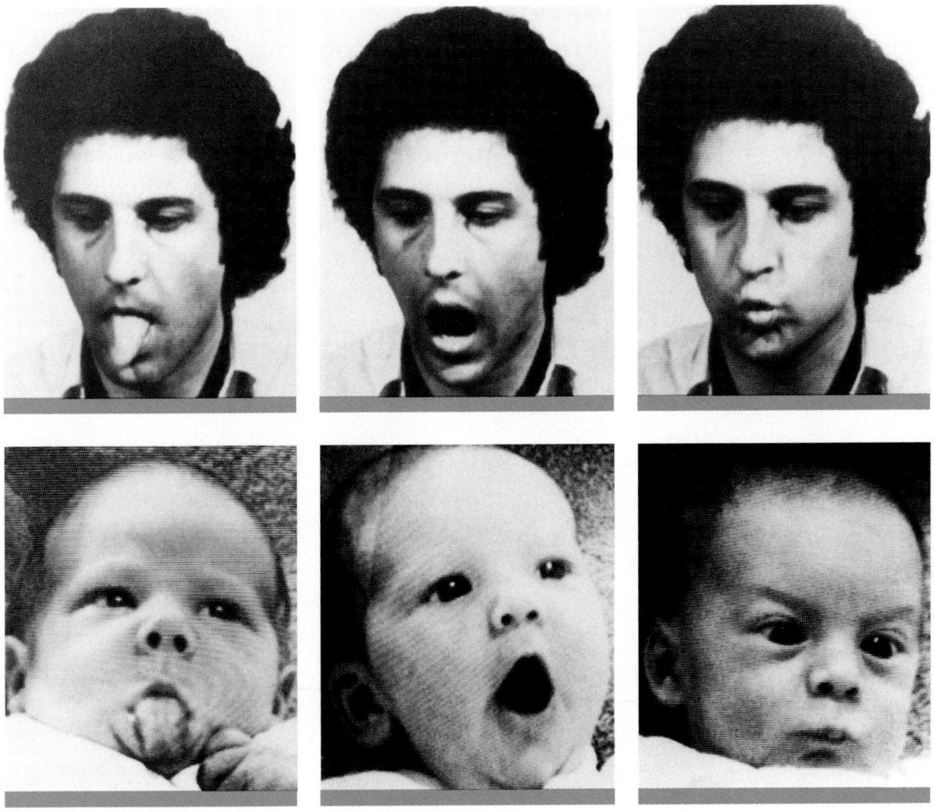

In his classic studies of infant imitation, Meltzoff found that 12- to 21-day-old infants imitated his facial expressions by sticking out their tongues, opening their mouths, and pursing their lips.

Though not in perfect form, the newborn reacts to life's sounds in consistent ways. If you stand on the baby's right or left side and shake a rattle, you'll notice that it slowly turns its head in your direction, as if trying to locate the source of the sound (see Chapter 3). Newborns have difficulty detecting low-pitch sounds, but they are particularly sensitive to high-pitch sounds, melodies, and the human voice (Aslin, 1989). They can tell the difference between tones that are one note apart on the musical scale, between the mother's voice and that of another woman, and between speech sounds that are as similar as *pa* and *ba*. As measured by changes in their sucking rate, newborn infants can distinguish among multisyllable words that vary in stress patterns or rhythm (Sansavini et al., 1997). And by twenty weeks old, they're more likely to turn their heads upon hearing the sound of their own names than to similar-sounding other names (Mandel et al., 1995).

In light of these findings, it's interesting to consider the way adults talk to babies. In cultures all over the world, men, women, and children use baby talk, or "motherese"—a form of speech that is slow, clear, simple, high in pitch, rhythmic, and songlike, just the kinds of sounds that will seize a newborn's attention (Fernald et al., 1989). How marvelously adaptive for the development of language! It's no wonder that infants prefer to hear baby talk over ordinary adult conversation (Fernald, 1985).

Taste and Smell Although nearsighted and somewhat hard of hearing, the newborn is well equipped for taste and smell. To illustrate, imagine the kind of face you'd make if a drop of sugar, lemon, or vinegar was put on your tongue. Regardless of age or culture, adults react to sweetness with a fleeting smile, to sour tastes with puckered lips, and to bitter tastes with a foul look of disgust. What about babies? To find out, researchers have tested newborns—many of whom were so young they had not yet been fed. Yet these babies made the same kinds of facial expressions as adults do—and in a more exaggerated manner (Rosenstein & Oster, 1988; Steiner, 1979). And when newborns—or even preterm infants—are fussy and crying, sugared water has a calming effect that plain water does not (Smith & Blass, 1996). Newborns are also sensitive to odors. When Steiner (1979) held sweet-smelling swabs under their noses, the babies smiled. Swabs of rotten egg made them

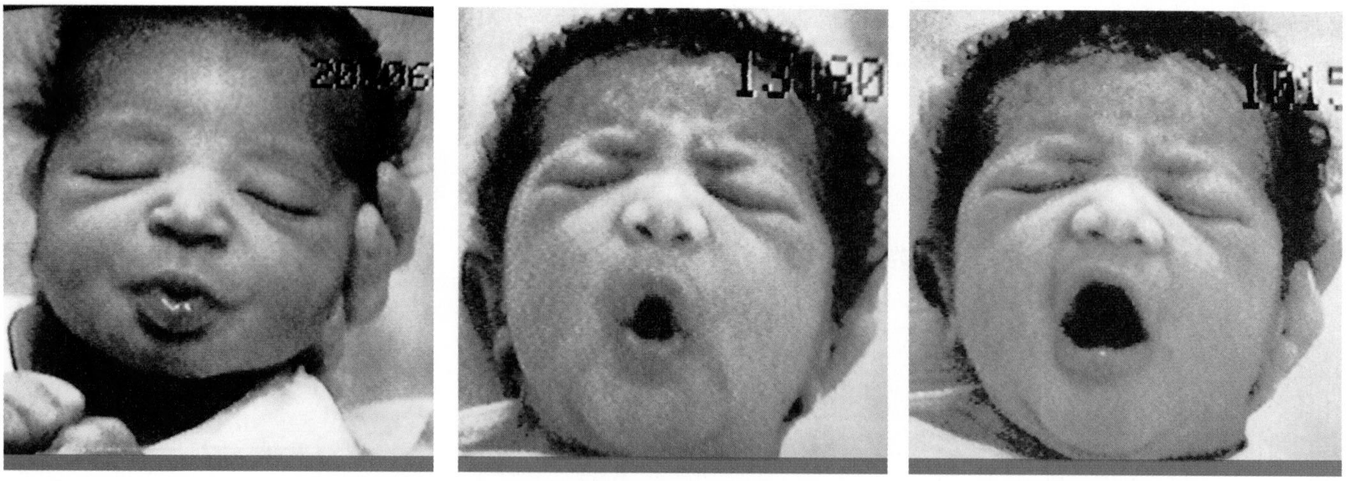

A newborn's sense of taste is evident from its behavior. As you can see, sweet, sour, and bitter tastes trigger very different facial expressions (Rosenstein & Oster, 1988).

grimace. The sense of smell is so well developed that at two weeks old, nursing infants are more attracted to the body odor of their own mother and other lactating females than to that of other women (Porter et al., 1992). No matter how tender the age, the nose knows.

The human newborn is not a miniature adult and is obviously too helpless to survive on its own. Thanks to recent research, however, we can now celebrate a newborn's impressive capacities. From the moment of birth, babies are equipped with many primitive but adaptive reflexes. They are also prepared to experience many forms of sensory stimulation, especially those provided by human contact—faces, voices, and mother's scent. And they are capable of rudimentary forms of learning and memory. For example, Carolyn Rovee-Collier (1988) hung a mobile over the crib of six-week-olds, attaching the mobile by a ribbon to one of their legs so they could move it. When these infants were brought back two weeks later, they remembered which leg to kick. Newborn capacities like these have existed for generations, but only now are we beginning to appreciate them.

The Infant and Growing Child

How do the brain and body develop in the first few years of life? What changes take place in the way children think, reason, and speak? Are child witnesses competent or too suggestible? Is an infant's first attachment to the mother "critical," and how is it affected by being in a day-care center? Finally, why are childhood friendships considered "developmental advantages"?

The newborn has come a long way—both in our minds and in its own short history of development. But there is so much more to come. First, there is an *infant*, from the Latin word meaning "without language." The infant grows into a walking and talking toddler, who then graduates on the first day of school to the category of *child*. Puberty spurs the *adolescent*, though what it means to be an *adult* is anybody's guess. Throughout the rest of this chapter, and in the next chapter, we look at biological, cognitive, and social aspects of development and consider the interplay among them.

Biological Development

During the first year or so, babies grow at a pace never to be equaled again. On average, babies double their birth weight in five months and triple it by their first birthday. They grow ten inches in height during the first year, and another four to six inches the year after. To the distress of parents without hand-me-downs, a baby's clothing size changes almost every month. Though it is not always accurate, there's a general rule of thumb you might find remarkable: By the second birthday, most babies have reached half of their adult height.

Physical Growth Matching the observable changes in body size, other aspects of growth also proceed at a fast pace. Cartilage turns to bone, muscle fibers thicken, and teeth break through the gums. Most impressive are the changes that occur in the brain and nervous system—and what these changes mean for cognitive and social development. At birth, an infant's brain weighs close to a pound and is completely equipped with all of the 100 billion neurons it will have in its lifetime. But the newborn's brain and nervous system are immature, and relatively few synaptic connections have been formed. The changes that then take place after birth are extraordinary. Starting in the first year, the neural axons grow longer, the dendrites increase in number, and a surplus of new synaptic connections are carved into the brain—trillions, more than can possibly be used (see Figure 10.10). Then over the next few years of childhood, the brain undergoes a pruning process in which often-used synaptic connections survive while unused connections are eliminated. The neurons also become more tightly wrapped in myelin sheath, the fatty substance that enhances the speed at which neural signals are transmitted. This process of myelination continues through infancy, childhood, and early adolescence.

The maturation of the brain is linked in intimate ways to other aspects of psychological development. For example, natural increases in the number of synaptic connections, or "pathways," in the brain are often accompanied by increases in cognitive ability (Fischer, 1987; Goldman-Rakic, 1987). Myelination shows similar patterns. At birth, the brainstem and spinal cord—which govern simple reflexes—are well myelinated and are in working order. The visual cortex is less well developed, as is the newborn's vision. Those parts of the cortex that control attention and information processing are not fully myelinated until the ages of four to seven years, which is when children become capable of reading and simple arithmetic (Parmelee & Sigman, 1983). In short, growth spurts in the brain correspond nicely to developments of the mind.

As we saw in Chapter 2, this correspondence is a two-way street: Just as the brain influences how people experience the world, it is also *affected* by that experience. As an example of how neural connections are sculpted by experience, studies have shown that rats flooded with visual stimulation formed more synaptic connections in the visual cortex, while those trained to run between pylons on runways formed new synaptic connections in the cerebellum, where balance and motor skills are coordinated. The developing brain is a dynamic and ever-changing structure—pro-

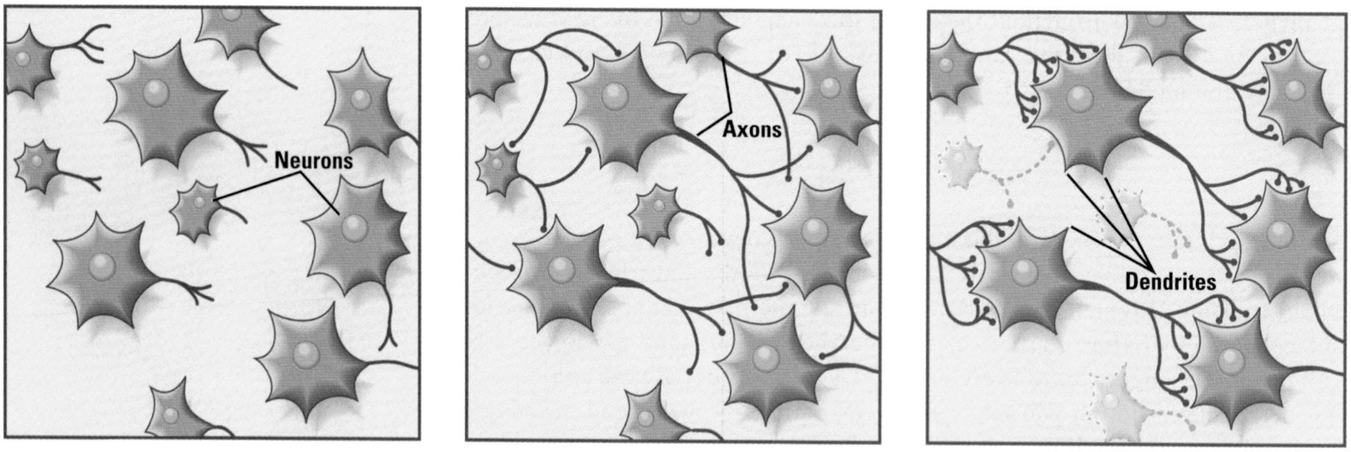

1 At birth, the infant's brain has a complete set of neurons but not very many synaptic connections

2 During the first year, the axons grow longer, the dentrites increase in number, and a surplus of new connections is formed.

3 Over the next few years, active connections are strengthened, while unused connections atrophy.

Figure 10.10 The developing brain At birth, the infant's brain has a complete set of neurons but relatively few synaptic connections (1). During the first year, the axons grow longer, the dendrites increase in number, and many new connections are formed (2). Over the next few years, the active circuits are strengthened, while those that are unused atrophy (3).

grammed only generally by genetics, but more specifically molded by life experience (Rosenzweig, 1996).

Motor Skills From infancy to childhood, physical growth—as measured by gains in height and weight—is the most predictable change that takes place. The second most predictable is the coordination of *motor skills*. As you can see in Figure 10.11, babies, on average, can lift their heads at 2 months, sit without support at 5.5 months, crawl at 10 months, and walk at 12 months. Children differ somewhat in their *rate* of motor development, but the *sequence* of events is usually the same: Lifting the head precedes sitting, which precedes crawling, and so on. More advanced activities such as running, jumping, climbing stairs, and throwing a ball develop later and are less predictable in their sequence. So are fine motor skills such as holding a pencil, tying a shoelace, and using a fork (Wade & Whiting, 1986).

It's important to realize that cultural factors also play a role. For example, infants in parts of Africa sit at an earlier age than their American peers because their parents use rolled-up blankets to prop them up into sitting positions in a hole in the ground. Yet these same precocious sitters are slower to crawl because their parents discourage it (Rogoff & Morelli, 1989). The physical environment also plays a role. An analysis of birth dates revealed that infants born in the summer and early fall began

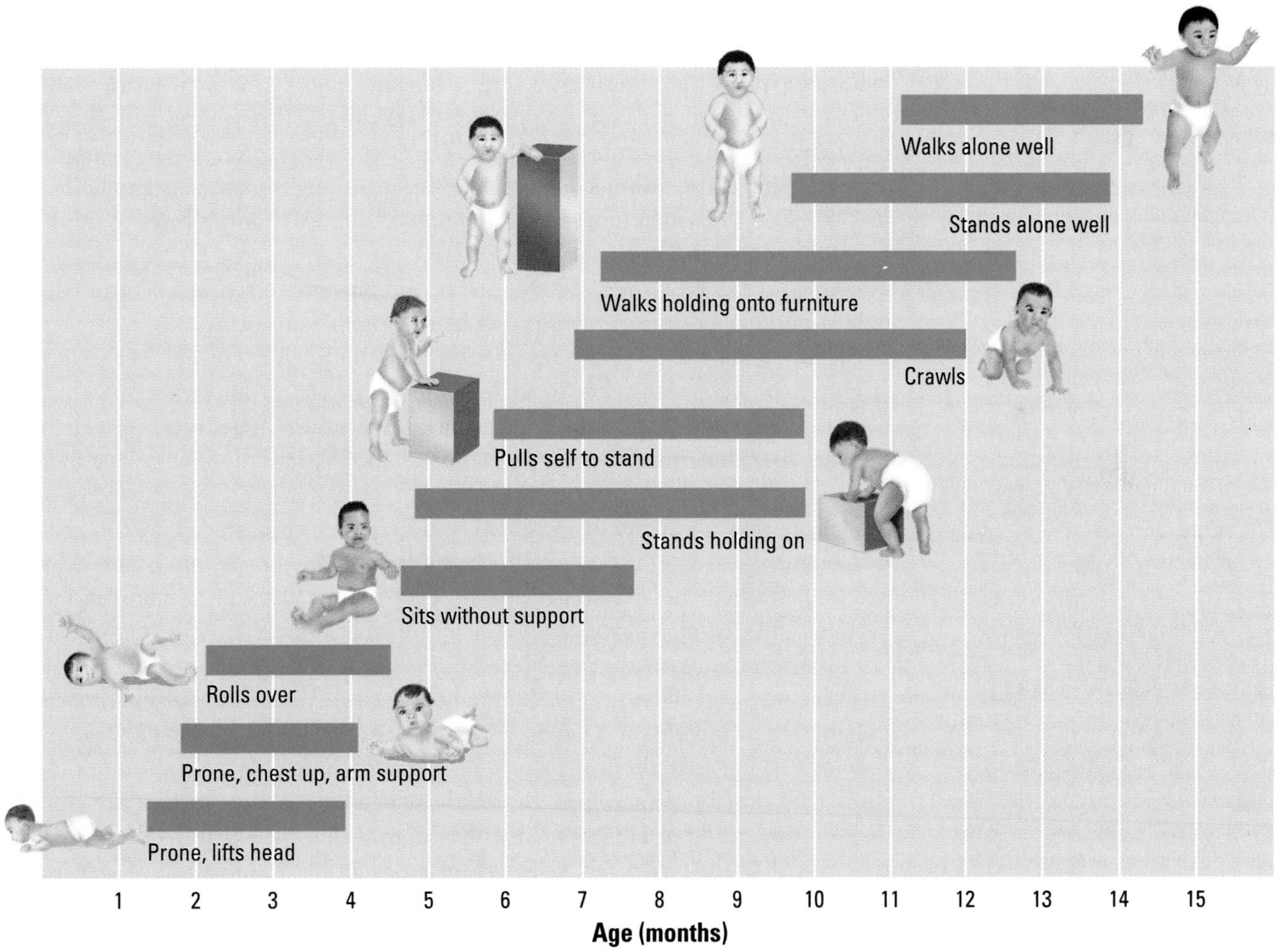

Figure 10.11 Milestones in motor development These bars show the average ages and variations for achievements ranging from lifting the head to walking alone (Frankenburg & Dodds, 1967).

to crawl three weeks later than did those from the same area who were born in the winter and spring. By the time summer and fall babies are ready to move about, the day is shorter and the temperature is colder (Benson, 1993).

Jean Piaget.

Cognitive Development

You don't have to be a psychologist to notice physical growth or the development of motor skills. The real challenge is to unravel the mystery of how children of different ages think—not just what they know but *how* they come to know it and the mistakes they make along the way. To understand this aspect of development, we turn to Jean Piaget (1896–1980), the most influential figure in the study of cognitive development.

Piaget's Theory Born in Switzerland, Piaget was a precocious boy interested in seashells, birds, and mechanics. He published his first article at the age of ten and was offered a curatorship at a natural-history museum in Geneva while he was in high school. At twenty-one, Piaget earned a Ph.D. in biology, then studied psychology in Paris and took a job administering intelligence tests to schoolchildren. As luck would have it, this experience proved to be a turning point—for Piaget and for psychology.

While testing, Piaget became intrigued by the mistakes that children made. Far from being random or idiosyncratic, he realized, these errors signaled that young children use a logic that is foreign to adults. To understand this logic, Piaget had children explain their answers, a simple but informative method. From these interviews, Piaget published a series of articles, and in 1921 he was named director of a child-development institute in Geneva. The seed was planted. In the years that followed, Piaget studied thousands of children, including his own. By the time he died in 1980, he had written more than forty books on how children come to think about people, nature, time, morality, and other aspects of the world (Piaget & Inhelder, 1969; Ginsberg & Opper, 1988). Today, anyone interested in cognitive development—parents, educators, or philosophers—begins with Piaget.

Piaget's theory rests on the assumption that children are curious, active, and constructive thinkers who want to understand the world around them. According to Piaget, infants and children form **schemas**, or mental representations of the world, in order to make sense of it. Through a process of **assimilation**, he said, children try to fit new information into their existing schemas. Through the process of **accommodation**, they modify existing schemas to fit new information. Viewed in this way, development is not a process by which children merely "copy and paste" what they are told. Rather, the creation of knowledge occurs "through a complex interplay between preexisting knowledge and new information gathered through interaction with the external world" (Siegler & Ellis, 1996, p. 212).

schemas In Piaget's theory, mental representations of the world that guide the processes of assimilation and accommodation.

assimilation In Piaget's theory, the process of incorporating and, if necessary, changing new information to fit existing cognitive structures.

accommodation In Piaget's theory, the process of modifying existing cognitive structures in response to new information.

In a study that illustrates nicely how children form and revise their conceptions in light of new information, Stella Vosniadou and William Brewer (1992) asked children of varying ages about the shape of the earth. Seeing that the ground they walk on is flat, preschoolers believe the earth as a whole is flat—either rectangular or disk-shaped. So what happens when they're told that the earth is spherical? Rather than just shed their incorrect schemas for an accurate representation, they incorporate the sphere into their beliefs that the earth is flat by constructing the synthetic models shown in Figure 10.12. Many first-graders adopt the "dual earth" notion that the earth is round but that humans live on a flat surface. By the third grade, many children see the world as a "flattened sphere" or as a "hollow sphere"—like a fishbowl with people living on the bottom. By fifth grade, most children have adopted the correct "sphere" model. Gradually then, through a dynamic interplay of assimilation and accommodation, children form new and accurate conceptions of, quite literally, the world.

Another assumption made by Piaget is that as children get older, they advance through a series of chronological *cognitive stages*, each distinguished by a specific kind of thinking. For Piaget, the child's cognitive development is like climbing a staircase, one step at a time. This view of development has two implications. First, even though some children advance more quickly than others, the sequence is universally the same: The first stage must precede the second, the second must precede the third, and so on. In this way, each stage holds both the fruits of the past and the seeds of the future. Second, even though the cognitive stages build upon one another, the increments are seen as qualitative and abrupt, not quantitative and gradual—in other words, like climbing stairs, not a ramp. As shown in Figure 10.13, Piaget described four stages in the development of the mind: (1) sensorimotor, (2) preoperational, (3) concrete operational, and (4) formal operational.

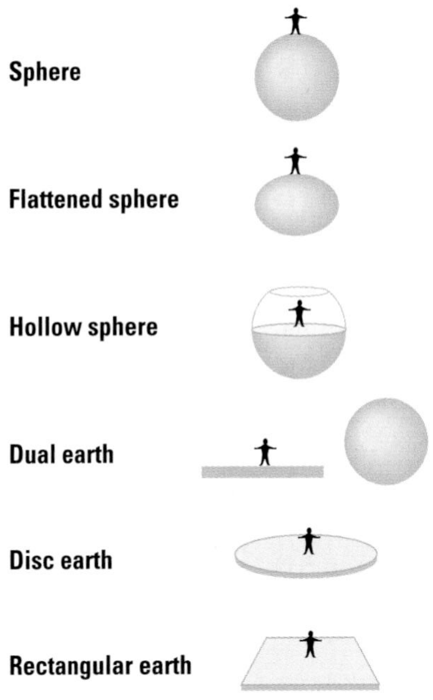

Figure 10.12 Changing schemas of the earth Compared to preschoolers, who think the world is flat, school-age children at first assimilate the spherical model into their schemas, then accommodate their schemas to form an accurate representation (Vosniadou & Brewer, 1992).

Sensorimotor Stage Beginning at birth and lasting about two years, infants come to know the world by touching, grasping, smelling, sucking, chewing, poking, prodding, banging, shaking, and manipulating objects. Piaget called this the **sensorimotor stage** of development. As far as infants are concerned, an object exists only for the moment and only insofar as it is in direct sensory contact. In fact, research shows that the way infants explore objects changes predictably with age. Beginning at one month old, they learn about the shape, texture, and substance of objects with the mouth (Gibson & Walker, 1984). At five months, they also acquire information with their hands (Streri & Pecheux, 1986) or by coordinating movement of the hands, eyes, and mouth together (Rochat, 1989). This sensorimotor mode can be seen in the way young babies try to stuff crayons, toys, and limbs into the mouth—

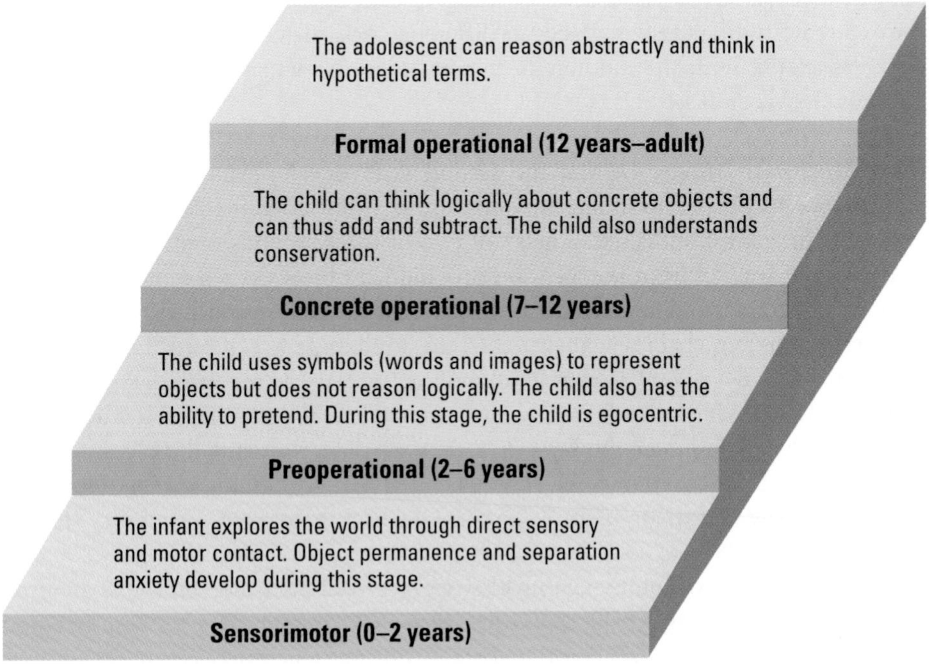

Figure 10.13 Piaget's stages of cognitive development Piaget portrayed development as a staircase in which the different steps, or stages, are distinguished by specific kinds of thinking.

sensorimotor stage Piaget's first stage of cognitive development, from birth to two years old, when infants come to know the world through their own actions.

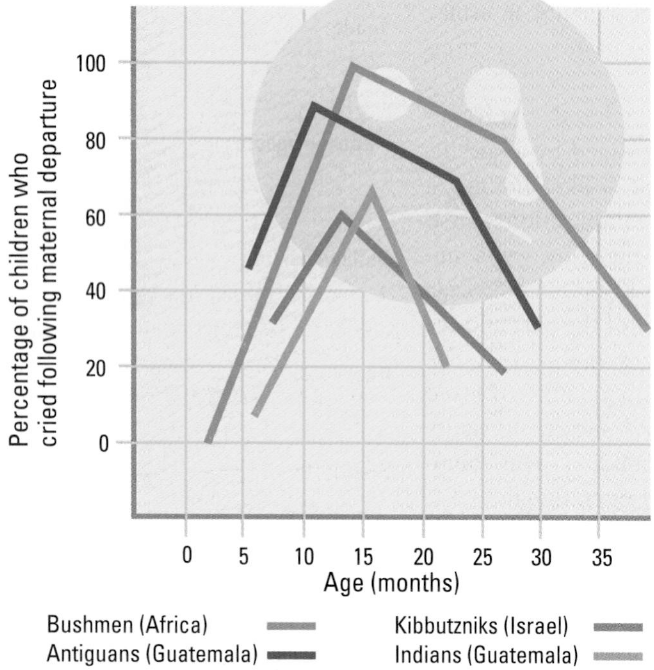

Figure 10.14 Separation anxiety Cross-cultural researchers have found that the rise and fall of separation anxiety follow a similar pattern among infants in different parts of the world (Kagan, 1976).

By uncovering the hidden toy, this baby is demonstrating object permanence.

object permanence Developing at six to eight months, an awareness that objects continue to exist after they disappear from view.

separation anxiety Among infants with object permanence, a fear reaction to the absence of their primary caretaker.

preoperational stage Piaget's second stage of cognitive development, when two- to six-year-olds become capable of reasoning in an intuitive, prelogical manner.

and in the way they pull, push, shake, squeeze, and bang everything they can get their fingers on.

According to Piaget, the crowning cognitive achievement of the sensorimotor stage is the development of **object permanence**, an awareness that objects continue to exist after they disappear from view. This may not seem to be much of an accomplishment, but Piaget (1952) noticed that whenever he covered a toy with his beret or a handkerchief, babies younger than eight months old did not protest, made no effort to retrieve it, and were unaware of its absence—even when the toy made noise. Quite literally, out of sight means out of mind. Given this lack of object permanence, it is no wonder that until babies approach their first birthday, they never seem to tire of playing peek-a-boo, a game in which each round is met with a fresh look of surprise.

Object permanence may be linked to important aspects of social development. It is probably not a coincidence that just as babies become capable of recalling objects that are out of view, they also begin to experience **separation anxiety**, a fear reaction to the absence of their primary caretaker. The baby who is not aware of its mother when she isn't perceptible will not seem distressed by her absence. However, the baby who has achieved object permanence is capable of missing its mother and cries frantically the moment she slips out of sight. As with other aspects of sensorimotor development, this pattern—of object permanence accompanied by several months of separation anxiety—can be seen in cultures all over the world (Kagan, 1976; Whiting & Edwards, 1988). Figure 10.14 provides a clear illustration of this point. Indeed, a recent longitudinal study of babies during the first year of life showed that although they matured at different rates, the cognitive gains they made were associated with the amount of distress they felt when separated from their mothers (Lewis et al., 1997).

Preoperational Stage During the second year, developments in memory lend permanence to people no longer in view, and peek-a-boo games give way to hide-and-seek. At eight months old, a delay of two or three seconds is enough for babies to become distracted from the location of a hidden object. At ten months, they can wait eight seconds, and at sixteen months, twenty to thirty seconds (Kail, 1990). At twenty months old, babies who watched an adult hide a Big Bird doll in a desk drawer or behind a pillow were able to find the toy even on the next day (DeLoache & Brown, 1983). The second year is also a time when children become more verbal and more abstract in their thinking. For the first time, words and images are used to symbolize objects. And one object may be used as a symbol for another—as when children pretend that their spoon is an airplane and their mouth a runway (Harris & Kavanaugh, 1993).

Despite enormous cognitive gains, the two-year-old does not think like an adult or even like a school-age child. According to Piaget, preschoolers between two and six years of age are in a **preoperational stage**, during which they reason in an intuitive, prelogical manner, unable to perform mental operations. There are two important features of preoperational thought. The first is that the child is **egocentric**, or self-centered—unable to adopt the perspective of another person. At this stage of development, children tend to assume that you can tell what they are thinking, that you know all the people in their lives, or that you can see a picture in a book they are reading. Play a hiding game with three-year-olds, and they will stand in full view and cover their eyes—assuming that if they cannot see, then they cannot be seen. Or eavesdrop on a conversation between four-year-olds and you will hear each of them jabbering away and taking turns—oblivious to what the other is saying. These "collective monologues" are also evidence of egocentrism.

A second limitation at this stage is that the preoperational child does not understand **conservation**, the idea that physical properties of an object stay the same despite superficial changes in appearance. To illustrate, take a tall, thin eight-ounce glass of lemonade and pour it into an eight-ounce cup that is shorter and wider. You and I know that the quantity of liquid stays the same regardless of changes in shape, but to the preschooler the tall, thin glass holds more to drink. As illustrated in Figure 10.15, there are other examples as well. Flatten a ball of clay and the preoperational child will think there is less. Roll the clay into a long thin snake, and the child will think there is more. Or if you use a handful of pennies, the child will think there are more if you spread them out than if you push them close together. What all these demonstrations show is that, until roughly the age of seven, children can't seem to *center* on two object features at a time (height and width, for example) or mentally reverse such operations as pouring, rolling, flattening, or spreading. Very simply, "What you see is what you get."

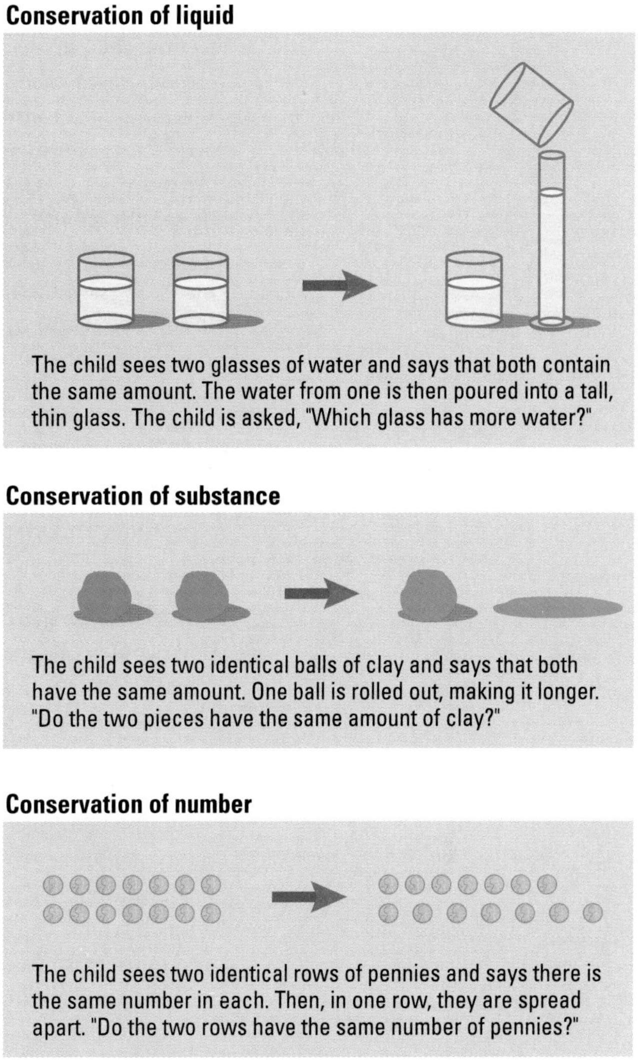

Figure 10.15 Tasks used to test conservation According to Piaget, the ability to conserve marks the transition from the preoperational to the concrete operational stages of cognitive development.

Egocentrism and failures at conservation both seem to have something in common: The preoperational child cannot think about objects or events in more than one way. Unable to see from another person's point of view or to take another perspective on the same object, toddlers have trouble distinguishing reality (what they know) from appearance (what they see). John Flavell and others (1986), for example, let nursery-school children feel a soft sponge that looked like a rock. When asked (1) what the object *really* is, and (2) what the object *looks like right now*, a majority of children gave the same response to both questions. Those who knew it was a sponge by feeling it also said it *looked* like a sponge, and those who said it looked like a rock also thought it *was* a rock. Many years ago, on Halloween, I discovered this confusion the hard way. In front of my four-year-old daughter, Briana, I put on a gorilla mask. She watched me put the mask on and knew it was me but then burst into tears, making me feel awful. It was as if appearance had become reality.

Concrete Operational Stage At about the age of seven, children advance to what Piaget called the **concrete operational stage**, during which they become

egocentric Self-centered, unable to adopt the perspective of another person.

conservation The concept that physical properties of an object remain the same despite superficial changes in appearance.

concrete operational stage Piaget's third stage of cognitive development, when six-year-olds become capable of logical reasoning.

capable of logical reasoning. As they enter school for the first time, children are able to take the perspective of another person and understand that various object properties can stay the same despite surface changes in appearance. They can now group similar objects into categories, order the objects according to size or number, and appreciate the logic that if A is greater than B, and B is greater than C, then A is greater than C. Capable of performing concrete operations, the first-grader can also be taught to add and subtract without counting (Resnick, 1989).

Piaget believed that conservation marks the beginning of a major advance in cognitive development, one that lasts to the age of eleven or twelve. However, even though concrete operational children appear to reason like adults do in response to specific problems, they do not think on an abstract level. The child may know that 2 is an even number and that 2 + 1 is an odd number, and they may well realize the same for 4 + 1, 6 + 1, and 100 + 1—but they will not necessarily put the pieces together to form the more general principle that any even number plus one yields an odd number. The ability to use methods of logic—inductive reasoning, deductive reasoning, and systematic hypothesis testing—is the hallmark of Piaget's next stage, the formal operational stage of cognitive development.

Formal Operational Stage What distinguishes Piaget's third and fourth levels of development is the ability to formulate solutions in advance and to reason on a logical, hypothetical level. To illustrate, imagine how you might approach the following test. You have four beakers, each containing a colorless chemical, and a dropper filled with potassium iodide. You are then told that when the potassium iodide is mixed with one or more of the four chemicals, it produces a bright yellow solution. Your task is to determine which chemicals to mix. Faced with this problem, the typical nine- or ten-year-old child will arbitrarily begin to mix chemicals, trying one combination after another until stumbling upon the solution. In contrast, the typical twelve- or thirteen-year-old will plan a systematic course of action, first adding potassium iodide to each beaker, then trying combinations of chemicals and keeping track of outcomes until the problem is solved (Inhelder & Piaget, 1958).

Unlike Piaget's first three stages, which appear roughly on schedule in different cultures, the **formal operational stage** does not characterize all non-Western adults. As we saw in Chapter 7, many Western adults are not necessarily formal operational in their problem solving, often falling back on rules of thumb known as heuristics. Piaget's point, however, is that adolescents and adults are cognitively *capable* of formal operations, whereas children are not.

Piaget's Legacy Piaget was an astute observer of children, and his writings single-handedly brought the study of cognitive development to life (Beilin, 1992; Brainerd, 1996; Flavell, 1996). Important practical lessons also stem from his theory—such as the idea that a given child may not be developmentally "ready" for reading, writing, arithmetic, taking turns, and other cognitive and social tasks. Today, many parents try to "jump-start" their children by enrolling them in academically rigorous preschools or by training them for athletics and other types of competition. Thanks to Piaget, however, many child-development experts are now quick to warn that children should not be pushed too early—before they have matured to the necessary stage of development (Elkind, 1989; Zigler, 1987).

Many of Piaget's writings have stirred both criticisms and vigorous defenses of his theory (Lourenco & Machado, 1996). Neo-Piagetian researchers are now revising and extending his work in important ways. One criticism is that Piaget's interview method was crude by today's standards. As a result, he underestimated young children's cognitive abilities and taxed their capacity to process task-relevant infor-

formal operational stage Piaget's fourth stage of cognitive development, when adolescents become capable of logic and abstract thought.

mation (Case, 1992). As illustrated in Figure 10.16, some studies have shown that babies even have an intuitive grasp of simple laws of physics. For example, they look longer at a ball that appears to roll through a solid object or at a ball that appears to stop in midair than at one that does *not* produce an unexpected physical outcome (Spelke et al., 1992; Baillargeon, 1994).

Other examples illustrate the point. Piaget thought that object permanence did not develop until eight months of age, when babies first try to retrieve toys that have been hidden from view. But what if a more sensitive measure were used? Renee Baillargeon (1986) recorded eye movements and found that six-month-olds reacted with surprise when a hidden object seemed to disappear. This suggests that an out-of-sight object is not out of mind at this age—or even at four months old (Baillargeon & De Vos, 1991). Similarly, Piaget thought that three- and four-year-olds are egocentric, unable to take the perspective of another person. Yet children at this age speak more simply to babies than to adults and show pictures to others with the front side facing the viewer (Gelman, 1979). Were Piaget's timetables wrong? Yes and no. Yes, it's clear that young children are often more precocious than Piaget had realized. But no, his developmental sequences—for example, the hypothesis that object permanence precedes conservation, which in turn precedes formal logic—have stood up well. Piaget may have underestimated the overall *rate* of development, but he was right about the *sequence* of achievements.

Figure 10.16 The infant's intuitive grasp of physics In this experiment, infants watched as an attractive box was pushed along a striped platform. In a physically possible version of the event, the box was pushed only to the edge. In an impossible version, it was pushed over most of the edge. Infants looked longer at the impossible event, suggesting that they have an intuitive grasp of gravity (Baillargeon, 1994).

A second question is often raised that goes right to the heart of Piaget's theory: Does cognitive development progress through a series of distinct stages, like a staircase, or is it more gradual, like a ramp? Or, as Robert Siegler (1996) has suggested, should cognitive development be depicted in waves, with the flow of new strategies overlapping with the ebb of old strategies? Robert Thatcher and others (1986) measured electrical brain activity in 577 humans ranging from two months old to young adulthood, and they spotted distinct growth spurts that corresponded roughly to the emergence of Piaget's stages. Yet Piaget's all-or-none view of development has been challenged inasmuch as children often master a concept in some tasks but not in others. Four-year-olds can order colors from light to dark, but they can't order sticks by length. Similarly, six-year-olds understand conservation in the pennies problem before they can solve the liquid or clay problems. These kinds of inconsistencies tell us that cognitive concepts don't burst into mind all at once but, instead, are used for one task at a time (Flavell, 1982). What, then, are we to conclude? Once again, Piaget was only partly correct. The pace of development is more rapid at some ages and in some cultures than others. But within these periods of rapid growth, it takes time for new skills to reach their full maturity.

Information-Processing Perspectives Today, many cognitive-development researchers examine age-related changes in the way that information is processed. From this perspective, cognitive development is characterized not by a transition from one qualitative stage of logic to another but by gradual increases both in the ability to attend selectively to one stimulus and in the ability to encode, store, and retrieve information from memory. These information-processing skills are acquired and refined throughout childhood. From this perspective, young children may fail a Piagetian task not because of how they think or the logic they use but because their attention wanders, they get distracted, and they forget elements of the problem (Kail & Bisanz, 1992; Siegler, 1996). Consider, for example, the finding that preoperational children cannot distinguish between appearance and reality. Catherine Rice and her colleagues (1997) presented three-year-olds with a sponge that looked like a rock. As in past studies, they could not separate the appearance from reality (if it looked like a rock, they thought it was a rock; if it felt like a sponge, they thought it looked like a sponge). But when a real rock and a normal-looking sponge were placed alongside the target object—which enabled the children to keep in mind both its apparent and its real identities—they were able to make the distinction and realize that the object was a sponge that looked like a rock.

One highly consistent change that takes place in childhood is in memory. On tests of short-term memory span, the average adult can recall about seven items of information (see Chapter 6). Among young children, this number increases steadily with age. Why? Some researchers have found that young children do not use the kinds of encoding, storage, and retrieval strategies that are common among adults. When you or I have to recall a phone number or grocery list, we try to repeat the items over and over. Not so among young children. In one experiment, children of varying ages were instructed to memorize objects presented in pictures, while a trained lip reader watched for signs of silent rehearsal. The result: The percentage of those who rehearsed increased from 10 percent among five-year-olds to 60 percent among seven-year-olds, to 85 percent among ten-year-olds (Flavell et al., 1966). Similar differences have been noted regarding the use of other memory aids (Kreutzer et al., 1975). Indeed, the memory abilities of young children are currently the subject of heated controversies in the courtroom (see pages 390–391).

The use of strategies may partly explain age differences in memory, but many researchers believe that the initial limitations and later increases in memory are also related to maturation of the brain and the efficiency with which information is processed. It turns out that there is a consistent age-related decline in performance *speed* at cognitive tasks. In a series of experiments, Robert Kail (1991) recorded the amount of time it took for seven- to twenty-one-year-old subjects to do various

Although Piaget estimated the ages at which certain cognitive skills develop, experience plays an important role. As with other children who work with clay or with liquid quantities, this young Indian potter is likely to understand the concept of conservation sooner than might be expected.

simple tasks. They were asked to name pictured objects, judge whether two letters flashed on a screen were the same, mentally rotate objects, move pegs from one side of a pegboard to the other, add two numbers, or press a button the moment they detected a target stimulus. The result: On all tasks, responses became quicker with age—and followed the same pattern of change. As depicted in Figure 10.17, information processing speeded up between the ages of seven and twelve, then leveled off. According to Kail, this general increase in speed stems from the biological maturation of the brain—specifically, perhaps, from the increased myelination of axons, which facilitates the transmission of neural impulses. This increase in speed may account for some of the stagelike performance increments typically found in cognitive-development research. It may also account for age differences in children's ability to read (Kail & Hall, 1994).

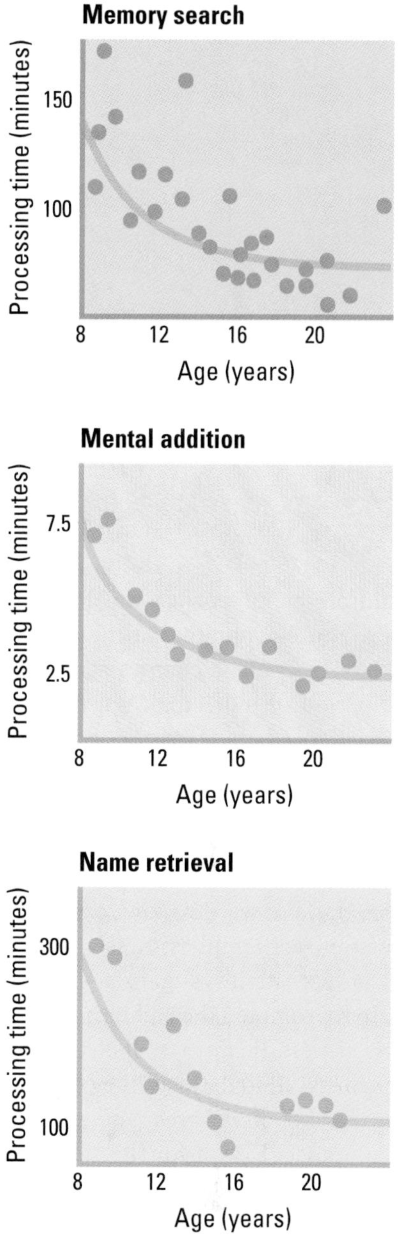

Figure 10.17 Speed of information processing In general, response times decline between the ages of seven and twelve, then level off. This same pattern appears in many tasks, including mental addition, memory search, and name retrieval (Kail, 1991).

Emergence of Language

Paralleling the changes that take place in the way children think is their development of language (see Table 10.2). Between the ages of one and six, children acquire a vocabulary consisting of an estimated 14,000 words, an average of 9 words per day. They also learn to combine words in ways that fit grammatical rules too complex for most of us to explain. What's amazing about these achievements is that boys and girls of all cultures absorb the words and grammar of language without formal instruction. It just happens. As in cognitive development, some children may speak sooner than others, but the sequence of achievements is the same for all (Brown, 1973; McNeil, 1970; Rice, 1989).

Developmental Sequence

Newborns communicate their needs by crying. In the second month, they also begin to use the tongue to make more articulated *cooing* sounds such as *oh* and *ah*. At about four months, babies begin playful **babbling**, vocalizing for the first time in ways that sound like human speech—*ah boo*, *da da*, and *ah gee*. As with crying and cooing, babbling is inborn. Regardless of whether the native language is English, French, Spanish, German, Hebrew, or Swahili, babies all over the world initially make the same sounds, including some they never hear at home (for example, the German *ch* and the rolled *r*). Even babies who are born deaf and cannot *hear* speech babble right on schedule.

Some time near the first birthday, give or take four months, babies utter their first real *words*. The sounds are brief and not clearly pronounced, but they are used to communicate meaning in the native tongue—for example, *ba* for *bottle*. For the next few months, babies speak one-word utterances, and the number of words in their vocabulary increases sharply (Woodward et al., 1994)—from 4 or 5 at twelve months to 30 at eighteen months to 250 at two years. These utterances are not random. Babies tend to name objects and actions that they desire (a bottle, favorite

Table 10.2 Early Milestones in the Emergence of Language

AGES	STAGES
1–2 months	Cooing (*oh, ah*)
4 months	Babbling (*ah boo*)
8–16 months	First words
24 months	2- and 3-word telegraphic speech
2–3 years	Multiword sentences
4 years	Adultlike, mostly grammatical speech

babbling Spontaneous vocalizations of basic speech sounds, which infants begin at about four months of age.

toys, "more"), especially those that involve motion (cars, a pet dog)—just as Piaget would expect of a sensorimotor child (Nelson, 1973).

At about two years of age, there is a vocabulary explosion, as children learn and accumulate hundreds of new words a year. At this stage, children will pick up a new word that they encounter in conversation—even when they hear it only once or twice. More important, they begin to form two- and three-word phrases. These early word combinations illustrate what is called **telegraphic speech** because—as in

telegraphic speech Early short form of speech in which the child omits unnecessary words—as telegrams once did ("More milk").

INTERSECTION

INFANCY AND CHILDHOOD AND LAW

The Child Witness: Competent to Testify?

On August 2, 1988, Margaret Kelly Michaels, a twenty-six-year-old preschool teacher, was found guilty of 115 counts of sex abuse committed at the Wee Care Nursery School in New Jersey. The charges against her were shocking. For a period of more than seven months, the jury was told, she danced nude in the classroom, forced children to drink her urine and eat her feces, stripped the children, licked peanut butter off their genitals, and raped them with knives, forks, spoons, and Lego blocks.

Were the children's stories accurate? On the one hand, there were striking consistencies in the testimonies of nineteen child witnesses. On the other hand, social workers and investigators who conducted the interviews often prompted the children with suggestive leading questions, told them that Michaels was a bad person, urged them to describe acts they had initially denied, offered bribes for disclosures, and pressured those who claimed ignorance. Except for this testimony, there was no physical evidence of abuse and no other witnesses—even though the acts were supposed to have occurred during school hours in an open classroom. Michaels was found guilty and sentenced to serve forty-seven years in prison. After serving five of those years, she was released when the state appeals court overturned the conviction on the ground that the children's testimony could not be trusted. "One day you're getting ready for work and making coffee, minding your business," said Michaels, "and the next minute you are an accused child molester."

Can suggestive interview procedures cause young children to confuse appearance and reality? With thousands of child-sex-abuse charges being filed in recent years against preschool teachers, babysitters, family members, and strangers, judges must struggle to decide: Are preschoolers competent to take the witness stand, or are they too suggestible, too prone to confuse reality and fantasy? To provide guidance to the courts, researchers have been studying children's eyewitness memory (Ceci & Bruck, 1995).

This research has evolved through stages. At first, simple laboratory experiments showed that preschoolers were more likely than older children and adults to incorporate misleading "trick" questions into their memories for simple stories (Ceci et al., 1987). Other studies showed that interviewers could get young children to change their memories, or at least their answers, simply by repeating a question over and over—a situation that implies that the answer already given is not good enough (Poole & White, 1991). But are young children suggestible about real-life, sometimes stressful, experiences? And what kinds of interview procedures are the most biasing?

In one study, Leichtman and Ceci (1995) told nursery-school children about a clumsy man named Sam

Margaret Kelly Michaels.

Stone who always broke things. A month later, the man visited the school, spent time in the classroom, and left without incident. The next day, the children were shown a ripped book and a soiled teddy bear and were asked what happened. Reasonably, no one said that they saw Stone cause the damage. But then, over the next ten weeks, they were asked suggestive questions ("I wonder if Sam Stone was wearing long pants or short pants when he ripped the book?"). The result: When a new, naive interviewer asked the children in the class to describe what happened, 72 percent of the three- and four-year-olds blamed Stone for the damage, and 45 percent said they saw him do it. One child "recalled" that Stone had taken a paintbrush and painted melted chocolate on the bear. Others "saw" him spill coffee, throw toys in the air, rip a book in anger, and soak the book in warm water until it fell apart.

Further research indicates that suggestibility effects are not limited to low-stress situations. Maggie Bruck and others (1995) interviewed five-year-old children who had visited their male pediatrician a year earlier for a physical examination and an immunization shot. Also during that visit, a female research assistant showed each child a poster, read a story, and gave out treats. Four interviews were conducted in a one-month period. During the first three sessions, half the children were falsely "reminded" about the day when the male doctor showed them the poster, read the story, and gave them treats while the female assistant gave them the examination, oral vaccine, and shot. During the fourth interview, when asked to recall what happened, those who were not misled were highly accurate in their recollections. But those given misinformation incorporated many false suggestions into their reports. Many even embellished the stories with nonsuggested new events—claiming, for example, that the female assistant had checked their ears and nose. In fact, the experimenters were able to manipulate children through false feedback into recalling that the immunization shots they received either hurt, causing them to cry, or did not hurt.

To summarize, recent research evidence makes it clear that repetition, misinformation, and leading questions can all bias a child's memory report—and that preschoolers are particularly vulnerable in this regard. At this point, the courts must seek to distinguish between true and false claims—and do so on a case-by-case basis. In addition, clear guidelines should be set for interviewing prospective child witnesses in an objective, nonbiasing manner.

telegrams, kept short for cost reasons—they include only nouns, verbs, and essential modifiers, yet make sense to the listener ("More juice" for "I want more juice," or "No sit chair" for "I don't want to sit in a chair"). It's interesting that these primitive forms of sentence contain the seeds of grammar—"more juice" rather than "juice more," for example. It's also interesting that the statements are often *overextensions*. For example, until different animals can be distinguished, the two-year-old who uses the word *doggie* to call the family pet will use the same word to refer to a cat, horse, or circus elephant. Language can tell us a lot about a child's developing knowledge of the world.

By the age of three, four, or five, a child's mind contains a small dictionary of words ready to be used correctly. Although new words are learned without explicit thought or instruction, an enriched linguistic environment can accelerate the process. For example, preschoolers who watched the educational TV show *Sesame Street* had larger vocabularies than those who did not (Rice et al., 1990). With increasing age, children construct longer and more complex sentences; learn to use plurals, pronouns, past tense, and other rules of grammar; and begin to appreciate puns and words with double meanings. At puberty, corresponding to the onset of Piaget's formal operational stage, children come to appreciate the use of abstract metaphors—"like two ships passing in the night."

Developmental Theories No one disputes the stages of language development in children or the sequence of those stages. But there are differences of opinion as to what it all means. Two issues in particular have been lively topics of controversy.

The first is our old friend the nature-nurture debate. In 1957, behaviorist B. F. Skinner wrote a book entitled *Verbal Behavior*, in which he argued that children learn to speak the way animals learn to run mazes. They associate objects and words, imitate adults, and repeat phrases that are met by social reinforcement. Through trial and error, for example, a baby of English-speaking parents learns to repeat the babbling sounds that excite mom and dad but not foreign sounds that leave them cold. In response to Skinner, linguist Noam Chomsky (1959, 1972) argued forcefully that the human brain is specially hard-wired for the acquisition of language. As we saw in Chapter 7, the evidence in for this biological position is impressive: Language grows at a rate that exceeds all other kinds of learning, two-year-olds construct telegraphic statements they couldn't possibly have heard from adults, and children learn to speak properly even though nobody really stops to correct their grammar.

To some extent, it is clear that human beings are genetically prepared for language the way that computers are prewired for programming (Pinker, 1994). The environment we live in may provide the software that determines *what* language we learn to speak, but biology provides the hardware that controls *when* and *how* we learn it. It's also clear that in the acquisition of language, there is a critical, or at least sensitive, period during the first few years of life when humans are most receptive to language learning (Lenneberg, 1967). Thus, when adolescents and adults learn a second language, they speak it with an accent. When children acquire the new language before puberty, however, they speak it without an accent. The same pattern is true in the acquisition of grammar. In a study of Asian immigrants to the United States, the younger they were as children when they moved, the higher was their score on a test of grammar (Johnson & Newport, 1989).

The second debate concerns a chicken-and-egg problem: What comes first, thought or language? Piaget (1976) believed that children must understand a concept before they can use words to describe it. Thus, babies cannot say, "All gone," or "Bye-bye," or use other words that refer to the disappearance of objects until they understand the concept of object permanence. However, other developmental psychologists believe that language shapes thought and that children develop concepts in order to understand the words they hear from others. Thus, the child who hears *dog* tries to understand the word by searching for objects that might fit (Bruner, 1983). It appears that both views are correct. That is, words and concepts emerge at roughly the same time—and the causal arrow points in both directions. Sometimes children use words to communicate what they already know, and sometimes they form concepts to fit the words they hear (Rice, 1989).

Soon after hatching, ducklings will follow the first moving object they see. In this photograph, the imprinted object was ethologist Konrad Lorenz.

Social Development

Born completely helpless, equipped with reflexes that orient toward people, responsive to human faces, voices, and odors, and prepared to mimic facial expressions on cue, the newborn is an inherently social animal. For eager parents, the baby's first smile is the warmest sign of all. It's funny sometimes how nature finds ways to lubricate a parent-newborn relationship. If you gently stroke or blow on a newborn's face, it reacts to this stimulation by contracting its muscles and pulling back its mouth into what looks like—you guessed it—a smile (Emde et al., 1976). In fact, babies don't crinkle up their eyes and flash real "social smiles" at people until they are at least six weeks old (Bower, 1982).

The Parent–Child Relationship Many developmental psychologists believe that a baby's first primary relationship to the mother or another caretaker sets the stage for social development. Clearly, it is critical in certain species of animals. Newly hatched ducks and geese, for example, will automatically follow their mother—an instinctive form of attachment called **imprinting**, which serves the purpose of keeping the young birds in proximity to their mother. Intrigued by how automatic the process is, Konrad Lorenz (1937) suspected that any moving, honking stimulus (whether it is the mother or not) will trigger this response. So he squatted, clucked, and moved about in front of birds hatched in an incubator, and it worked like a charm. One of Lorenz's favorite pictures shows him strolling through high grass trailed by a line of geese imprinted by his actions. In fact, geese will follow a wide variety of first-seen moving objects—decoys, rubber balls, wooden blocks, and even a striped metal pipe (Hess, 1959).

If baby birds are to follow the mother, they must be exposed to her within the first day or so, during a **critical period** for the development of imprinting. In humans, attachment is less automatic, the mother plays a more active role, and there is no "critical" period. Still, the infant does form a very deep and affectionate emotional bond called an **attachment**.

In his classic studies with rhesus monkeys, Harlow found that the babies clung to soft cloth "mothers"—and preferred this contact comfort to wire-mesh mothers that provided milk.

The First Attachment Beginning in the second half of the first year, accompanying the development of object permanence, infants all over the world form an intense, exclusive bond with their primary caretaker. This first relationship is highly charged with emotion and emerges with remarkable consistency from one culture to the next. Why? What motivates the infant? Years ago, psychologists assumed that infants would become attached to anyone who feeds them and satisfies their basic physiological needs. That assumption was then put to rest by a classic series of dramatic experiments by Harry Harlow (1958, 1971).

In the 1950s, Harlow was breeding rhesus monkeys to study learning. Infant monkeys were separated from their mothers, fed regularly, and housed in cages equipped with a blanket. At one point, Harlow noticed that the infants had become passionately attached to their blankets—as they would be to their mothers. It is interesting that, like Linus of the comic strip *Peanuts*, many normal children in the United States, Sweden, New Zealand, and elsewhere clutch security blankets (Passman, 1987). At any rate, this observation sparked in Harlow an interest in the possible origins of attachment: Are infants in general drawn to mother for the comfort of her warm and cuddly body or for the food and nourishment she provides? To answer this question, Harlow placed newborn monkeys into a cage that contained two substitute mothers—one was a wire-mesh cylinder with a wooden head; the other was covered with soft terrycloth. Both provided a bottle of milk with a nipple. It was no contest. The infant monkeys spent almost all of their time with the terrycloth doll. In fact, they continued clinging to the cloth substitute even when it did not contain a bottle for feeding. Given the choice, the infant monkeys preferred "contact comfort" over food. In later variations of this study, Harlow found that warmth and rocking motions further intensified the contact comfort provided by a cloth mother. It's clear that infants need more from parents than milk and a clean diaper.

Sadly, Harlow found that the infant monkeys raised with inanimate cloth substitutes grew into unhealthy adults, fearful in new settings, socially awkward, and sexually unable to function. But the discovery that contact comfort has therapeutic benefits for the isolated infant has proved useful. For example, consider the

imprinting Among newly hatched ducks and geese, an instinctive tendency to follow the mother.

critical period A period of time during which an organism must be exposed to a certain stimulus for proper development to occur.

attachment A deep emotional bond that an infant develops with its primary caretaker.

Premature babies will snuggle up to a "breathing" stuffed bear in their sleep. Shown here is the one-and-only original Teddy Bear, created in 1902 and named after President Theodore Roosevelt, who had refused to shoot a trapped bear.

predicament of a typical premature baby—kept in an incubator without physical contact and at risk for a whole host of problems later in life. Working in the maternity ward of a hospital, Saul Schanberg and Tiffany Field (1987) treated a group of premature babies with a forty-five-minute body massage for ten days, then compared their progress to others not receiving massage. The two groups drank the same amount of formula, but the massaged infants gained 47 percent more weight; were more alert, active, and coordinated; and left the hospital an average of six days earlier—for a savings of $3,000 per infant in expenses. More recent studies show that massage therapy has similarly beneficial effects on infants born to depressed mothers (Field et al., 1996). In another interesting intervention, Evelyn Thoman and others (1991) found that when the incubator was equipped with a soft blue teddy bear that gently "breathed" with the help of an air pump, premature babies snuggled up against the bear and slept more soundly in its presence. Additional research has shown that the breathing bear is a highly reinforcing source of stimulation (Thoman & Ingersoll, 1993).

Styles of Attachment Watch different parents and infants, and you'll notice that some attachments seem more intense than others. Is it possible to measure the intensity of this first relationship? How much of it depends on the parent and how much on the child? And does an infant's first attachment predict the quality of its social relationships later in life? Developmental psychologists are actively researching questions such as these about the attachment process (Main, 1996).

Drawing on evolutionary theory and on Harlow's studies with primates, psychiatrist John Bowlby (1969) theorized that infants are born with a repertoire of behaviors (such as sucking, gazing, clinging, and crying) that are designed to elicit nurturance from parents and lay a foundation for a strong relationship. Bowlby (1988) further argued that this attachment provides a secure base from which children can explore their surroundings and develop their cognitive and social skills. The impact of this first relationship, he said, influences future relationships and lasts a lifetime.

Is it possible to measure the quality of the infant-parent attachment? To study the process systematically, Mary Ainsworth and her colleagues (1978) created the **strange-situation test** in which the parent (usually the mother) brings the baby into an unfamiliar laboratory playroom and proceeds through a routine whereby the parent and a stranger come and go according to a set script. Based on how the infants react to the separations and reunions with the parent, they are classified as having either a secure or an insecure attachment. Infants with a **secure attachment** wander and explore the environment when the mother is present, react with distress when she leaves, and beam with sheer delight when she returns. These babies shower the returning parent with waves, smiles, laughter, hugs, and kisses. Infants having an **insecure attachment** are classified into two types. Some are anxious and *resistant*, clinging to the mother, crying when she leaves, and reacting with anger or indifference when she returns. These babies will often push the returning mother away, stiffen up, squirm, or even cry when picked up. Others are more detached and *avoidant*, not caring if the mother leaves and then ignoring her when she returns. Although a majority of babies worldwide are classified as having secure attachments, the percentage varies from culture to culture. In the United States, about two-thirds of infants tested in the strange situation are securely attached (Lamb et al., 1992; Van IJzendoorn & Kroonenberg, 1988)—and the classifications are generally the same whether the mother and child are tested in an unfamiliar setting or at home (Pederson & Moran, 1996).

strange-situation test A parent–infant "separation and reunion" procedure that is staged in a laboratory to test the security of a child's attachment.

secure attachment A parent–infant relationship in which the baby is secure when the parent is present, distressed by separation, and delighted by reunion.

insecure attachment A parent–infant relationship in which the baby clings to the parent, cries at separation, and reacts with anger or apathy to reunion.

It's hard to know for sure what causes a secure or insecure attachment. Clearly, parenting style is important. Mothers and fathers of securely attached babies are more sensitive to their needs, more affectionate, and more playful (Isabella & Belsky, 1991). The infant's temperament also plays a role, however, as securely attached babies are by nature less fussy and more easygoing than those who are not securely attached (Goldsmith & Lansky, 1987; Kagan et al., 1992). After several months, as you can imagine, the personalities of the parent and child become so tangled up that trying to separate the effects of one on the other is like trying to untie a twisted knot.

How important is this first relationship? Does a secure and trusting attachment with a mother or father provide a foundation for close friendships later in life? And what is the long-term fate of an insecurely attached infant? According to Bowlby, secure and insecure infants form "internal working models" of attachment figures—and these models influence their perceptions of others and their relationships later in life. Indeed, research shows that infants classified as securely attached at twelve-months-old are later more positive in their outlook toward others (Cassidy et al., 1996)—and are more popular, self-assured, and socially skilled in school (Ainsworth, 1989; Sroufe & Jacobvitz, 1989). Some researchers are further exploring the possibility that our attachments in infancy exert long-term effects on our romantic relationships as adults (Shaver & Clark, 1996). It's important, however, not to overstate this case by concluding that our future relationships are predetermined within the first year of life. The infant-to-child-to-adult correlation is far from perfect, and early attachments per se may not *cause* the differences that appear later in life. Responsive parents and easygoing infants may well continue in their positive ways long after the first-year attachment period has ended. These later interactions may prove to be just as important (Lamb, 1987).

The Day-Care Controversy If you've seen black-and-white reruns of *Leave It to Beaver*, *Father Knows Best*, or other TV shows produced in the 1950s, you are no doubt familiar with the image of the traditional, all-American family: a working father and a mother who stays home to take care of the house and kids. Today, the typical American child grows up in a vastly different environment consisting of either a single parent or two parents who both work outside the home. As a result, many infants and preschoolers in the United States spend much of their "attachment time" with babysitters, in day-care centers, or at home with other relatives. This scenario is not true of all societies. In China and Russia, mothers are encouraged to work full time while their children are cared for in state-supported institutions. And in Israel, mothers who live on rural collective settlements called *kibbutzim* work on the farm while child-care specialists raise the children in groups. The question is: Does nonmaternal child care for infants disrupt the security of attachment?

To begin with, what is the modern father's role as a second attachment figure? As a result of social changes that have taken place over the years, researchers just recently started to answer this question. The result: As a general rule, fathers spend less time with their infants than mothers do, and they tend to spend that time playing rather than feeding, bathing, dressing, or otherwise caring for the child. At home, infants seek contact with both parents equally and form attachments to both at about the same time. Yet in the strange-situation test, anxious infants prefer mothers to fathers (Cox et al., 1992; Parke, 1981; Lamb, 1986). This preference suggests that caring for the infant's needs is a key to attachment. Except for breast-feeding, fathers are as capable as mothers in this regard—and the more involved they are in the day-to-day routine, the stronger the attachment. Thus, it has been said that you can predict the closeness of the father-infant bond by counting how many diapers he changes in a week.

With increasing numbers of wives joining their husbands in the workplace, infants and preschoolers spend more of their time in day-care settings away from home. What is the impact of this experience? Should new parents—starting careers or struggling to make ends meet—be concerned about harmful long-term effects? As the research evidence mounts, professional opinion is divided. Some psychologists fear that full-time maternal employment may put infants at risk for insecure attachments and minor adjustment problems later in life (Belsky, 1988). Others are more optimistic about the impact of infant day care that is safe and stimulating and has a low adult-to-child ratio (Scarr, 1986).

After reviewing the research evidence, Alison Clarke-Stewart (1989) gave infant day care a cautious stamp of approval. Studies using the strange-situation test show that day-care infants whose mothers work full time are somewhat more likely than home-raised infants to be insecurely attached (36 percent to 29 percent). As young children, they are also somewhat more aggressive with peers and less obedient with parents. On the positive side, day-care infants are more outgoing and independent. Those placed in high-quality settings also go on to be more sociable and academically successful in elementary school (Field, 1991). Studies conducted in the United States, Norway, Sweden, New Zealand, and Great Britain further suggest that enriched infant day care can have positive effects on the growing child's cognitive development (Clark-Stewart et al., 1994; Broberg et al., 1997).

To summarize, there is no "bottom line." Day care and home care seem to foster somewhat different personal styles, though neither is necessarily better for healthy development. If an only parent has to work or if both parents work outside the home, day care is a viable option. What matters is not the *quantity* of time spent in one setting or the other but the *quality* of that time. Just as some parents are more attentive, loving, and stimulating than others, so too are some day-care centers. Those that are spacious, well equipped, and adequately staffed to provide individual attention and planned activities offer an excellent alternative to parents who work outside the home (Clarke-Stewart et al., 1994).

Beyond Attachment Attachment is just the first step in a long and complex relationship among mothers, fathers, sons, and daughters. Beginning at the age of two or three, children become more autonomous, independent, and even defiant. They stray from their parents, test the limits of authority, and spend increasing amounts of time playing with their brothers and sisters. Through TV and other cultural influences, boys and girls learn about sex roles and other stereotypes. The "terrible twos," toilet training, sibling rivalry, the first day of school, outside friendships, homework, the facts of life, and puberty are among the challenges that confront the growing child. Through it all, the parents—their behavior, attitudes, and discipline styles, whether they are happily married or divorced, whether they value obedience to authority or independence, whether they are strict or permissive, and so on—exert a profound influence on the child's social development (Bornstein, 1995).

Peer Relationships Developmental psychologists now realize that the mother-child attachment is only one factor in social development and that children also form key relationships with grandparents, siblings, teachers, classmates, and neighbors. The older the child is, the more important are *horizontal relationships*—friendships among peers, or equals (Hartup, 1989).

The growth of friendships may not progress through discrete stages, as in cognitive development, but certain patterns are evident. At one year old, infants show little interest in each other and come together only if drawn to the same person or toy. At first, these interactions breed friction, but with experience infants learn to take turns and minimize conflict. By the age of two, children prefer playing near each other rather than alone. By the age of four or five, they show clear preferences for some playmates over others. Although these relationships are quickly formed, quickly broken, and based on convenience, they mark the beginning of what can be called friendship (Berndt & Ladd, 1989; Collins & Gunnar, 1990).

It is interesting that almost all child relationships are between members of the same sex—not only in our culture but in others as well. Ask a three-year-old child to approach a peer, and he or she will stop farther away when that peer is of the opposite sex. Or watch children on a school playground, and you will see that four-year-olds spend three times as much time with playmates of the same sex than of the opposite sex (see Figure 10.18). By the age of six, this ratio is even higher, at 11 to 1 (Maccoby & Jacklin, 1987). From preschool to adolescence, only about 5 percent of all friendships are between boys and girls, and those that do exist often have sexual overtones (Thorne, 1986). Why is gender segregation so common? According to Eleanor Maccoby (1990), boys and girls prefer very different kinds of activities. Boys like competitive, rough-and-tumble play that takes up lots of space and involves large groups, while girls prefer to congregate at home with one or two close friends.

Just as attachments inside the home are important to healthy social development, so is the formation of friendships outside the home. To study this aspect of development, researchers ask schoolchildren to rate themselves and to nominate the

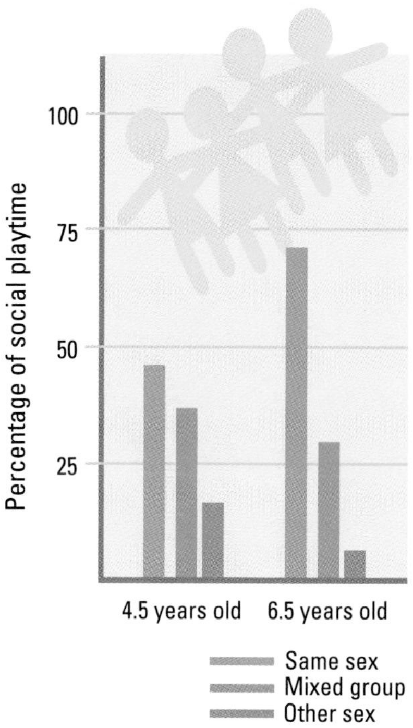

Figure 10.18 **Gender segregation at playtime** Observations of young children reveal that they are most likely to play in same-sex groups—a tendency that increases between the ages of four and six years (Maccoby & Jacklin, 1987).

Ethologists have observed that all young mammals (and some birds and reptiles) engage in social play. Such peer interactions may have evolved because they provide socialization and practice for adulthood. In predator species, the young often pounce, chomp, wrestle, and play-fight. Among prey species, including these macaque monkeys, the play tends to involve chasing and running.

classmates they like the most and the least. They may also get ratings from teachers and parents, observe behavior firsthand, and combine the results for each child. Using these methods, researchers have identified four types of school-age children—compared to those in the average majority—based on their "sociometric" status among peers. As described by Andrew Newcomb and his colleagues (1993), children can be classified as *popular* (sociable, skilled, and well liked), *rejected* (aggressive or withdrawn, lacking in social skills, and disliked), *controversial* (sociable but often aggressive, both liked and disliked), and *neglected* (less sociable and less aggressive than average, and seldom mentioned by peers).

As you might expect, popular children have the most friends at school (George & Hartmann, 1996) and derive the social and emotional benefits of these friendships (Newcomb & Bagwell, 1995). In contrast, children who are rejected by classmates are the ones who are the most "at risk." Longitudinal studies show that they are lonely and are more likely to drop out of school, have academic and drug problems, and have social-adjustment problems as adults (Parker & Asher, 1987; Asher & Coie, 1990). It's hard to know from these correlations if peer rejection is just part of a deeper problem or if it is the problem itself. And it's hard to know whether the emotional effects of peer rejection can be offset by family members, pets, or others. But it is clear that children's peer relations can be vital. Thus, Willard Hartup (1989) refers to friendships as "developmental advantages" (p. 125). He also notes, however, that more research is needed to determine whether these advantages depend on who the friends are, what they do together, and the nature and quality of the relationship (Hartup, 1996).

The Many Facets of Development

Thinking back over the material in this chapter, how are the biological, cognitive, and social aspects of development intertwined? In what ways are all influenced by both nature and nurture?

For the sake of convenience, developmental psychologists tend to separate the biological, cognitive, and social aspects of development. It's important to realize, however, that the way infants and children mature (the biological aspect), how they learn to think and speak (the cognitive aspect), and how they interact with others (the social aspect) are all intertwined. Thus, for example, only when the brain is sufficiently developed for infants to be capable of object permanence do they experience separation anxiety. A baby must have the capacity to be conscious of its mother and father when they are out of sight in order to be distressed by their absence (Kagan, 1984). Similarly, as suggested by Piaget, social relations inspire cognitive growth. By talking, sharing, playing, arguing, and watching one another, young children may learn from peer interactions to shed their egocentric ways and acquire logical skills such as conservation (Kerwin & Day, 1985). In short, biological, cognitive, and social development are intimately linked.

Now that we have zoomed in on the fine details of child development, let's step back and take a wide-angle look at the "big picture." As the material in this chapter clearly shows, both biological and environmental factors contribute to growth-related changes. Each of us is born with genetic predispositions, yet unique aspects of our experience can steer us in different directions. Nature and nurture are both vital in the development of the human infant and child.

Summary and Key Terms

Developmental psychology studies how people grow, mature, and change through the stages of the human life span.

Basic Developmental Questions

The Nature–Nurture Debate

Is behavior determined by a person's genetic blueprint or by environmental factors? This is the question posed by the **nature–nurture debate.** Recognizing that both factors are important, developmental psychologists try to measure their respective contributions. In the **twin-study method**, researchers compare the degree of similarity between identical and fraternal twins. **Adoption studies** compare identical twins raised in the same household to those raised apart.

Correlations from both twin and adoption studies can be used to calculate **heritability**, a statistic estimating the percentage of a trait's variability caused by genetic factors. Studies reveal strong genetic roots for many human traits, but this research also shows the importance of the environment. Children in a family are different in part because they experience nonshared environments. Complicating the nature–nurture debate is that the two factors are intertwined: Our genetic makeup can influence the environment we create and perceive.

Developmental-Research Strategies

There are two approaches to studying human development. In **cross-sectional studies**, people of different ages are examined at the same time and their responses compared. In **longitudinal studies**, the same subjects are retested at different times in their lives. Cross-sectional studies reveal differences between groups, but only longitudinal studies measure change as a function of age.

The Unborn Child

Genetic Building Blocks

A sperm cell and ovum unite to produce a single cell with forty-six rodlike **chromosomes**. The chromosomes are made up of **deoxyribonucleic acid (DNA)** molecules that contain many thousands of **genes**, the biochemical building blocks of an individual life.

Prenatal Development

In the germinal stage (the first two weeks after conception), the fertilized ovum, or **zygote**, divides into a cluster of cells that pass out of the Fallopian tube and attach to the uterine wall. At this point, the zygote becomes an **embryo**. During the embryonic stage (third to ninth weeks), body parts form and organs start to function. After the ninth week, the embryo becomes a **fetus**, which develops movement, circulation, and even the ability to recognize its mother's voice.

Teratogens are toxic substances that can harm the embryo or fetus. Babies of alcoholic mothers often show a pattern of birth defects known as **fetal alcohol syndrome (FAS)**. Even small doses of teratogens may be harmful. Smoking restricts the fetus's oxygen supply, and cocaine use by the mother correlates with social and cognitive difficulties for the infant and child.

The Birth Experience

The environment inside the womb, far from being tranquil, is full of sensory stimulation. At birth, however, newborns are bombarded by bright lights, noises, and a drop in temperature.

The Remarkable Newborn

To investigate how infants distinguish among stimuli, researchers often measure **habituation**, the tendency for attention to a novel stimulus to wane over time, and **recovery**, the tendency for a different stimulus to arouse new interest. These studies reveal that infants have remarkable abilities—even a rudimentary sense of arithmetic.

Reflexes

Babies are born with many adaptive reflexes, such as the **grasping reflex**, the **rooting reflex**, sucking, and swallowing.

Sensory Capacities

Though nearsighted, newborns can distinguish between light and dark, follow movements, notice facelike patterns, and mimic adult gestures. Though hard of hearing, they respond to the human voice, especially high pitches and melodic patterns. In taste and smell, newborns are very well developed.

The Infant and Growing Child

Biological Development

Babies grow rapidly in the first year. The brain and nervous system develop more synaptic connections and increased myelination. Motor skills also advance in a predictable sequence. Yet these biological aspects of development are influenced by environmental factors.

Cognitive Development

According to Piaget, infants and children form **schemas** in order to make sense of the world. Through **assimilation**, they try to fit new information into existing schemas. Through **accommodation**, they modify existing schemas to fit new information.

Piaget described four stages in cognitive development. In the **sensorimotor stage** (birth to two years), infants learn through sensory and motor contact. They develop **object permanence**, an awareness that objects continue to exist after they disappear from view, and **separation anxiety**, a fear reaction to the absence of a caretaker. In the **preoperational stage** (two to six years), children begin to reason in an intuitive, prelogical way. They are still **egocentric**, however, and they do not understand **conservation**—the concept that an object's physical properties stay the same despite superficial changes in appearance. The **concrete operational stage** (six to twelve years) brings logical reasoning but not abstract thought. Finally, at the **formal operational stage** (twelve years to adulthood), people learn to reason at an abstract level.

Piaget may have underestimated the rates of development, but he was right about the sequence. Likewise, he was only partly right about the sharp distinctions between stages. Many researchers study age-related changes in information processing. They have found that short-term memory and processing speed increase as children grow older.

Language development proceeds in a regular sequence: from cooing to **babbling**, single words, **telegraphic speech**, and full sentences. Evidence supports the view that humans are specially "wired" for language, that there is a critical period, and that words and concepts develop jointly, each influencing the other.

Social Development

Some animals exhibit **imprinting**, an instinctive tendency to follow the mother during a **critical period** just after birth. In humans, the process is less automatic, but infants form an **attachment**, a deep, affectionate emotional bond, with the primary caretaker. Studies with humans and monkeys show that "contact comfort" is an important source of attachment. The **strange-situation** test helps researchers distinguish between **secure attachment** and **insecure attachment**, a difference that results from both parenting style and the infant's own temperament. Although securely attached infants are later more independent and socially skilled, it isn't clear whether the early attachment causes these results.

Psychologists disagree about the effects of day care, but recent evidence shows that enriched, high-quality day care has more benefits than drawbacks.

Horizontal (peer) relationships—mostly between children of the same sex—become more important as the child grows older. Popular children enjoy the social and cognitive benefits of many friendships, while children rejected by their peers are most at risk for later adjustment problems.

The Many Facets of Development

Although psychologists differentiate among biological, cognitive, and social development, all three are closely linked—and all are affected by both nature and nurture.

In the Field Resources

Books

Kagan, J. (1994). *Galen's prophecy.* New York: Basic Books.

This book describes the exciting new research on inhibited and uninhibited infants—and how they are biologically predíposed to be shy or outgoing adults.

Maurer, D., & Maurer, C. (1988). *The world of the newborn.* New York: Basic Books.

What is life like in the womb, and shortly after birth? This beautifully written book describes in vivid detail how the world looks, sounds, smells, tastes, and feels to a newborn.

Films and Videos

Trading Places (1983, 106 min.)

This comedy plays with the nature–nurture question as two rich men arrange, to see what happens, for a stuffy young financial wizard and a black street hustler to trade places. (Dan Aykroyd, Eddie Murphy, Jamie Lee Curtis, Don Ameche, Ralph Bellamy.)

Internet

American Academy of Child and Adolescent Psychiatry (http://www.aacap.org/web/aacap/factsFam/)

AACAP offers "Facts for Families" about divorce, adoption, bedwetting, teen suicide, and other developmental issues.

Society for Research in Child Development (http://www.journals.uchicago.edu/SRCD/srcdhome.html)

This primary organization for child development researchers provides a list of publications and information on how to contact the society.

Youth and Children Resources Net (http://www.slip.net~scmetro/childco.htm)

Sponsored by the National Children's Coalition, this megasite offers news and newsgroups, resources, referrals, and national hotlines for and about children and teenagers.

Journals and Periodicals

Child Development
Developmental Psychology
Infant Behavior and Development
Journal of Experimental Child Psychology

11 *Adolescence and Adulthood*

The situation You know that people change as they get older, for better and for worse, and that development is a lifelong process. At the same time, you've heard it said that "age is a state of mind" and that "you're only as old as you feel." Hmm, you wonder. To what extent do people feel their chronological age? Do we tend to feel older than we are, or younger?

What's Your Prediction?

How old do people feel?

Imagine that you are a developmental psychologist. To answer this question, you need to ask people to tell you how old they feel. So you devise a questionnaire in which you ask respondents to write down their actual age and then to specify how old they feel, how old they look, how old they behave, and so on. You realize that you need to survey people of different ages, so you recruit high-school and college students, faculty members from your university, adults taking part in an educational workshop, and local senior citizen centers. You send out a total of 298 questionnaires, and 188 are completed and returned. Those who participate range in age from fourteen to eighty-three.

Make a prediction By averaging each respondent's answers to various "how old do you feel" questions, you can calculate his or her "subjective-age identity." So what do you think you'd find? How old do *you* feel? Look at Figure 11.1. The diagonal line that you see illustrates the pattern you would have if subjective ages were identical to chronological ages—in other words, if people felt exactly as young or old as they truly were. If you think that this is what happened, then all you have to do is trace over that existing line. Otherwise, use it as a guide and

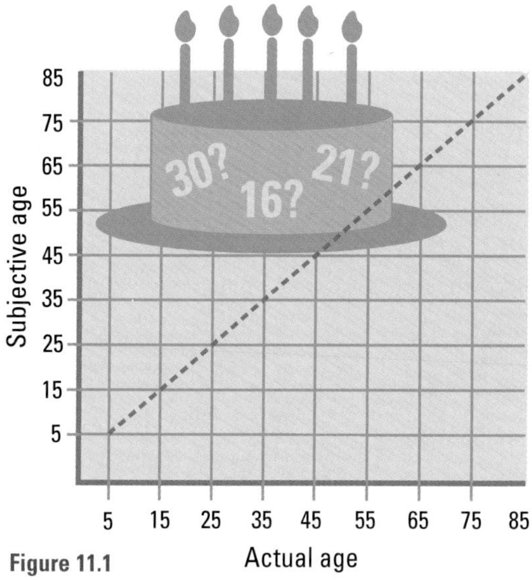

Figure 11.1

put an X at the age felt by the average 15-year-old, then do the same for those at the ages of 25, 35, 45, 55, 65, 75, and 85. If you think that people in a particular age group feel younger than they are, place the X below the existing line. If you think they feel older, put the X above the line. Connect the Xs and you'll have your predicted subjective-age line.

The results Based on research suggesting that life satisfaction has more to do with our subjective age than with our chronological age, Joann Montepare and Margie Lachman (1989) conducted the study just described. As you can see, the results are plotted alongside the comparison line in Figure 11.2. So how did you do? Look closely at the figure and you'll notice three interesting findings: (1) Teenagers in general feel older than they are; (2) adults feel younger; and (3) the tendency for adults to feel younger becomes more pronounced with advancing age.

What does it all mean? One of the most important and recurring questions in developmental psychology concerns the extent to which people change over the course of a lifetime, particularly during the adult years. We'll see in this chapter that development is a lifelong process in which we change—physically, cognitively, and socially—as we get older. We'll also see, however, that in other respects each of us is the same person today as we were five years ago and will remain that person five years from now. In this context, Montepare and Lachman's (1989) study shows, at least to some extent, that we age less in our minds than we do on the clock.

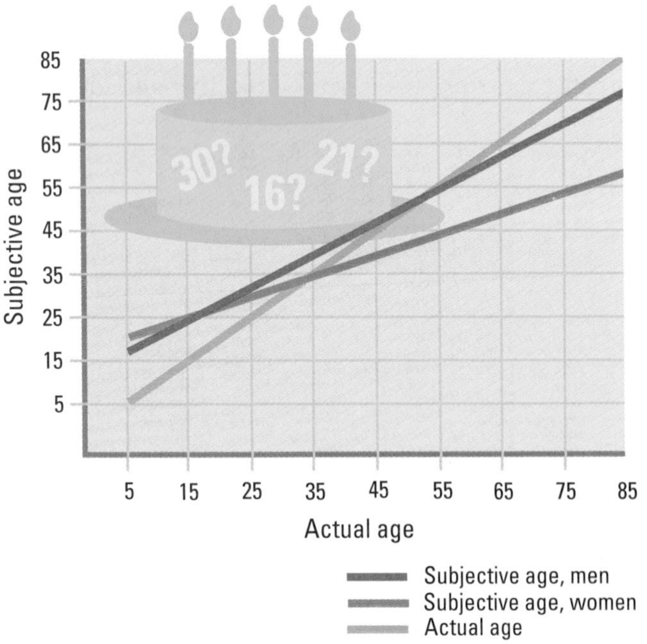

Figure 11.2

When it comes to understanding people, it often seems that poets, playwrights, philosophers, and artists are just a step ahead of the rest of us. In the seventh century BCE, the Greek poet Solon described nine stages in human development, beginning in the cradle and ending in the grave. Then, in roughly 500 BCE, the Chinese philosopher Confucius described six life phases spanning the ages of fifteen to seventy. Toward the end of the sixteenth century, William Shakespeare immortalized his vision of seven life stages. And in Sweden, an unnamed artist depicted the ages of man and woman in ten-decade pyramids that peak at the age of fifty. In some cultures, the human life span is pictured as a straight line. In others, it is thought of as a circle, spiral, square, or change of seasons (Kotre & Hall, 1990).

In light of all the wisdom inherited from past generations, it is ironic that researchers only recently began to appreciate the theme that is central to this chapter: Human development is a lifelong process. In Chapter 10, we examined the recurring controversy over the relative influences of nature and nurture. Over the years, developmental psychologists have also debated *stability* and *change,* a question concerning the extent to which humans change as they get older. Will an infant with a precocious smile turn into a sociable adult? Is the early-walking toddler a future athlete? Is the preschooler who clings to mom fated to become a dependent spouse later in life? And is the overanxious college student doomed to a life of anxiety? As in the nature–nurture debate, there are two contrasting, though not mutually exclusive, points of view.

For many years, it was assumed that our individual life scripts were written in infancy and childhood, waiting only to be acted out during our adult years. Freud felt that personality is largely formed by the sixth birthday, while Piaget claimed that the ultimate stage of cognitive development typically blossoms with puberty. These narrow views of the early years of life as critical may well describe changes in height, whereby early growth spurts are followed by a leveling off in adulthood. But such views do not yield an accurate picture when it comes to the full range of biological, cognitive, and social development. In this chapter, we will see that even though infancy and childhood are in some ways formative, each of us continues to change in important ways when we mature from adolescence to adulthood and old age. As our ancestors tried to tell us, development is a lifelong process.

Adolescence

Why is the timing of puberty important in the transition to adolescence? Do adolescents reach new cognitive milestones? What happens in parent–teenager relationships—and how do they change over time? Are peer influences good or bad? Why has adolescence been described as a period of "storm and stress"—and what's the evidence to support it?

Many cultures have initiation rites to celebrate the passage from childhood to adulthood. Among the African Thongas, when boys reach puberty they are beaten with clubs, shaved, stripped, exposed to cold, forced to eat unsavory foods, circumcised, and secluded for three months. Among certain Native American groups of North America, girls who menstruate for the first time are bathed, their bodies are painted red by older women, and they are isolated for four days. The ritual may vary, but most cultures have ways of marking adolescence. Confirmation, bar mitzvah, and the move into junior high school are some of the ways in which Westerners recognize this transitional time of life (Cohen, 1964).

Adolescence is to adulthood what infancy is to childhood—the dawn of a new era, like a second birth. Beginning with a biological event (puberty) and culminating in a social event (independence from parents), adolescence in the United States corresponds roughly to the teen years, thirteen to twenty. No longer a child but not yet an adult, the adolescent is in an important transitional phase of life—a time characterized by many biological, cognitive, and social changes (Graber et al., 1996).

It is interesting that the way psychologists have viewed adolescence has changed over the years. When Robert Enright and others (1987) analyzed articles on the topic that had been published during the past hundred years, they found that conceptions of adolescence have varied with changing political and economic conditions. During World Wars I and II, when young people were needed for factory

adolescence The period of life from puberty to adulthood, corresponding roughly to the ages of thirteen to twenty.

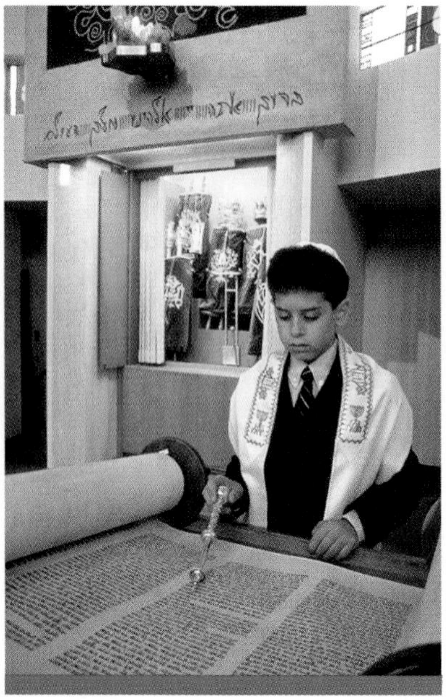

Many cultures celebrate the passage from childhood to adulthood. Dressed in buckskin and jewelry, an Apache girl is honored for her first menstrual period in an elaborate four-day ritual. At the age of thirteen, Jewish boys achieve their manhood in a religious ceremony known as a bar mitzvah.

work and military service, teenagers were described as competent and responsible, and adolescence as a life stage was thought to end by about age sixteen. Yet during the economically depressed 1890s and 1930s, when work was hard to find, teenagers were portrayed as incompetent and immature, and adolescence itself was thought to end at a later age. Perhaps political and economic conditions bias the way we view this phase of development—or perhaps these conditions actually affect the behaviors of adolescents. Either way, it's important to recognize that certain aspects of adolescence—and of other developmental periods as well—differ somewhat from one historical generation and culture to the next.

Biological Development

The biological motor of adolescence is **puberty,** the gradual onset of sexual maturation brought on by rising hormone levels—estrogen and progesterone in females, and testosterone in males. Plus or minus two years, girls reach puberty between the ages of eleven and thirteen, and boys between the ages of thirteen and fifteen. This sex difference can be seen in the rapid growth that propels children to almost their full adult height. Look at Figure 11.3, and you will see that the growth spurt begins a bit earlier for girls but lasts longer for boys, eventually leaving adult men an average of five inches taller than women.

For girls, puberty is marked by the first menstrual period, called **menarche.** Menarche is often a memorable event in a girl's life, one that she experiences with a mixture of pride, nervousness, and embarrassment (Greif & Ulman, 1982). Two factors influence a girl's reaction to her first period and to other physiological changes that signal her sexual maturity—budding breasts, pubic hair, and broadened hips. The first factor is *cultural practice.* For the Kurtatchi, who live on an island off the coast of New Guinea, menarche is a joyous village-wide event greeted

puberty The onset of adolescence, as evidenced by rapid growth, rising levels of sex hormones, and sexual maturity.

menarche A girl's first menstrual period.

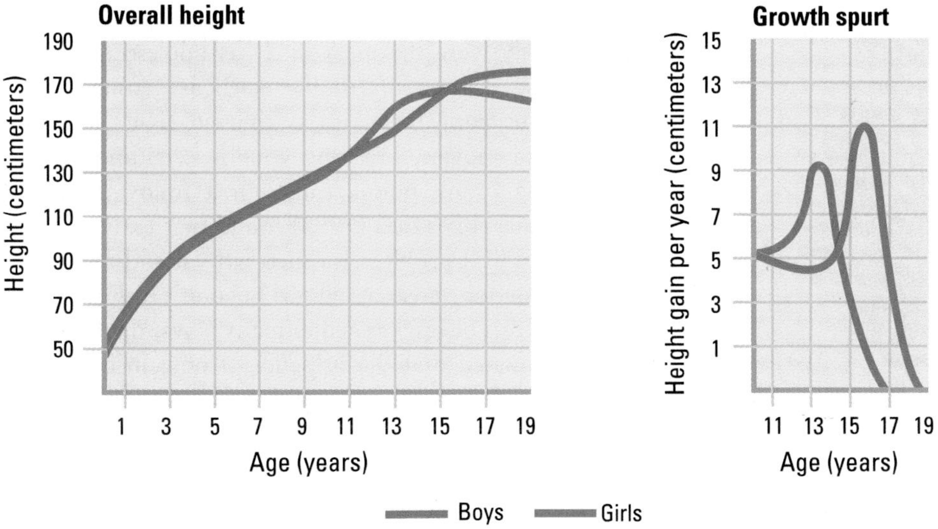

Figure 11.3 Adolescent growth spurts in height

by music, dance, food, and festivities. In many other cultures, however, menstruation—or "that time of the month"—is treated as too delicate a topic for conversation, and the menstruating woman is viewed warily by men. It's no wonder that many girls are secretive about their first period and tell only their mothers (Ruble & Brooks-Gunn, 1982).

The second factor that influences a girl's reaction to puberty is *timing*. In one study, Anne Petersen (1984) interviewed hundreds of adolescents and found that girls who mature earlier than most of their peers are usually less satisfied with their size, weight, and figure. A mature seventh- or eighth-grade girl may tower over her classmates and get teased about her appearance. Thus, as shown in Figure 11.4, girls who reach puberty early rather than "on time" or late are the most negative when asked to rate their own body image. They're also more likely to diet and develop eating disorders (Graber et al., 1994). The link to eating problems, however, is not that easy to interpret. Indicating that there's a complex interplay of factors at work, research shows that girls who reach puberty early are more likely to date and draw a watchful eye from parents—and that girls who have boyfriends and strained relations at home are also "at risk" for eating problems (Cauffman & Steinberg, 1996; Swarr & Richards, 1996).

Other researchers have found that early puberty presents additional adjustment problems. For example, girls who attain menarche early become more likely to spend time with older peers, have sex at an earlier age, get lower grades, and become involved in norm-breaking behaviors (Stattin & Magnusson, 1990). This timing effect is most true of those with a childhood history of behavior problems. In a longitudinal study conducted in New Zealand, Avshalom Caspi and Terrie Moffitt (1991) collected information from 348 girls nine, thirteen, and fifteen years old, their parents, and their teachers. They found that those

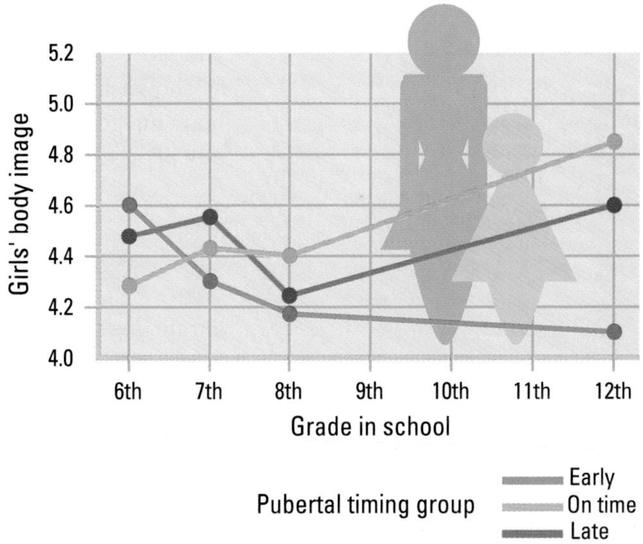

Figure 11.4 The timing of puberty and body images in girls On ratings of their own body image, early-maturing girls are more negative than others.

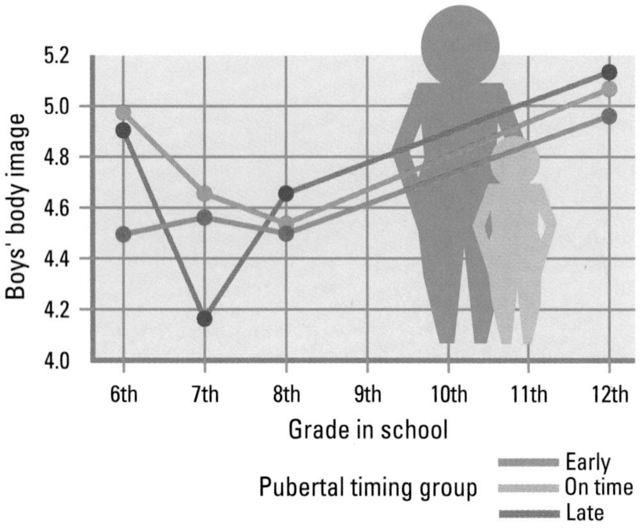

Figure 11.5 The timing of puberty and body images in boys On ratings of their own body image, late-maturing boys are the most negative, but they recover quickly.

who had difficulties before puberty *and* who reached puberty early were the most likely as adolescents to get into varying degrees of trouble (such as getting drunk, stealing items from classmates, getting into fights, sneaking into R-rated movies, breaking windows, cutting classes, and making prank phone calls). In a follow-up study, Caspi and his colleagues (1993) found that early maturation is more of a problem for girls who attend mixed-sex schools than for those at all-girl schools. Although this correlation can be interpreted in many ways, these investigators speculated that the presence of boys in mixed-sex schools provides "precocious" girls with additional opportunities for mischief.

It's interesting, by the way, that the timing of menarche is heavily influenced by environmental factors. In the 1800s, the average American girl didn't begin to menstruate until the age of seventeen. As a result of improved nutrition, the average girl now menstruates at a younger age, twelve or thirteen. There are also vast individual differences. Studies show that many models, gymnasts, and ballet dancers who exercise hard, diet, and lack body fat reach menarche relatively late in their teens (Brooks-Gunn & Warren, 1985). Recent studies also suggest that conflict in the family is associated with an earlier onset of menarche (Graber et al., 1995).

For boys, puberty is marked by the growth of the penis and testes, accompanied by facial hair, pubic hair, increased muscle mass, lowered voice, and broadened shoulders. Akin to menarche, the high point of male puberty is **spermarche,** the boy's first ejaculation, which usually occurs at about the age of fourteen (although it is not until a year later that the semen holds live sperm cells ready for reproduction). As with girls, some boys reach puberty before others. For boys, however, spermarche is a generally positive experience, and early maturation—which means being taller and stronger than peers—is a social asset (Gaddis & Brooks-Gunn, 1985; Stein & Reiser, 1994). Consistently, research has shown that early-maturing males excel in sports, are popular among peers, take leadership roles, and are more poised and self-confident than those who mature later (Jones, 1957; Petersen, 1988). Thus, as shown in Figure 11.5, boys who reach puberty early have a generally positive body image during these early years (Petersen, 1984). It's no wonder that the typical boy is on the lookout for whiskers, waiting for the chance to shave.

Cognitive Development

Paralleling the physical growth spurt brought on by puberty is what might be called a cognitive growth spurt. Adolescents who mature early get slightly higher scores on tests of intelligence than those who mature later (Newcombe & Baenninger, 1989). And you may recall Piaget's observation that adolescents are capable of logic, abstract thought, and hypothetical reasoning—hallmarks of the *formal operational* stage of cognitive development. This capacity for abstraction spurs teenagers to think critically, to challenge parents and society, and to contemplate possibilities. Eliot Turiel (1983) found that at the age of twelve or thirteen, adolescents begin to see various social conventions—for example, appropriate clothing, hairstyle, or the proper way to address a teacher—as arbitrary and unreasonable.

spermarche A boy's first ejaculation.

Despite the significant cognitive gains made at this stage, it's important to keep in mind that even as young adolescents start to flex their newly strengthened intellectual muscles, they are still somewhat *egocentric* in the way they think—and are highly self-conscious. Research shows that eighth- and ninth-graders always seem to think they are on "center stage," the focus of everyone's attention and unique among their peers (Elkind, 1967; Elkind & Bowen, 1979).

Moral Reasoning According to Piaget (1932), the adolescent's capacity for abstraction gives rise to a more mature form of **moral reasoning.** Piaget noticed that young children take rules literally, without regard for a person's intentions or motives or the circumstances. As far as the young child is concerned, the Little Leaguer who accidentally smacks a baseball into the windshield of a car is bad, and the parent who promises cookies only then to find the cupboard bare is a liar. Not until the age of ten or eleven do children think more flexibly about rules and evaluate others not just by what they do but *why* they do it. In this more advanced stage of reasoning, the Little Leaguer is not considered a bad person or the parent a liar for actions that produced negative outcomes they did not intend (Lickona, 1976; Strichartz & Burton, 1990).

Building on the idea that moral reasoning requires cognitive sophistication, Lawrence Kohlberg argued that adolescence is a particularly rich time of life for moral development (Kohlberg, 1981, 1984; Colby & Kohlberg, 1987). Kohlberg presented stories containing moral dilemmas to children, adolescents, and adults and asked them how these dilemmas should be resolved. To illustrate, consider the following classic story:

> In Europe, a woman was near death from cancer. One drug might save her, a form of radium that a druggist in the same town had recently discovered. The druggist was charging $2,000—10 times what the drug cost him to make. The sick woman's husband, Heinz, went to everyone he knew to borrow the money, but he could only get together about half of what it cost. He told the druggist that his wife was dying and asked him to sell it cheaper or let him pay later. But the druggist said, "No." The husband got desperate and broke into the man's store to steal the drug for his wife (Kohlberg, 1969, p. 379).

What do you think: Should Heinz have stolen the drug? Were his actions morally right or wrong, and why? Based on responses to stories like this one, Kohlberg proposed that people advance through three levels of moral thought, further divided into six stages. First, there is a *preconventional* level, in which moral dilemmas are resolved in ways that satisfy self-serving motives—so an act is moral if it enables a person to avoid punishment or obtain reward. Second is a *conventional* level, in which moral dilemmas are resolved in ways that reflect the laws of the land or norms set by parents and other sources of authority. Thus, an act is moral if it meets with social approval or maintains the social order. Third, adolescents and adults who attain Piaget's formal operational stage of cognitive development may also reach a *postconventional* level of moral thought, one based on abstract principles such as equality, justice, and the value of life. At this level, an act is moral if it affirms one's conscience—even if it violates the law. At each stage, there are possible reasons for and against stealing the drug (see Table 11.1).

Is this theory of moral development valid? Over the years, Kohlberg has drawn an enormous amount of attention, support, and criticism. To his credit, Kohlberg and others have found that as children and adolescents mature, they climb his moral

moral reasoning The way people think about and try to solve moral dilemmas.

Table 11.1 Kohlberg's Theory of Moral Development

Moral reasoning in response to the Heinz dilemma

Levels	*Stages*	*In favor of Heinz's stealing the drug*	*Against Heinz's stealing the drug*
I. Preconventional	Stage 1 *Punishment and obedience orientation:* Motivation to avoid punishment	"If you let your wife die, you will get in trouble."	"You shouldn't steal the drug because you'll be caught and sent to jail if you do."
	Stage 2 *Instrumental relativist orientation:* Motivation to obtain rewards	"It wouldn't bother you much to serve a little jail term, if you have your wife when you get out."	"He may not get much of a jail term if he steals the drug, but his wife will probably die before he gets out, so it won't do him much good."
II. Conventional	Stage 3 *Good boy–nice girl orientation:* Motivation to gain approval and to avoid disapproval	"No one will think you're bad if you steal the drug, but your family will think you're an inhuman husband if you don't."	"It isn't just the druggist who will think you're a criminal; everyone else will too."
	Stage 4 *Society-maintaining orientation:* Motivation to fulfill one's duty and to avoid feelings of guilt	"If you have any sense of honor, you won't let your wife die because you're afraid to do the only thing that will save her."	"You'll always feel guilty for your dishonesty and law-breaking."
III. Postconventional	Stage 5 *Social-contract orientation:*Motivation to follow rational, mutually agreed-upon principles and maintain the respect of others	"If you let your wife die, it would be out of fear, not out of reasoning it out."	"You would lose your standing and respect in the community and break the law."
	Stage 6 *Universal ethical principle orientation:* Motivation to uphold one's own ethical principles and avoid self-condemnation	"If you don't steal the drug, . . . you would have lived up to the outside rule of the law but you wouldn't have lived up to your own standards of conscience."	"If you stole the drug, . . .you'd condemn yourself because you wouldn't have lived up to your own conscience and standards of honesty."

Source: Adapted from L. Kohlberg (1969). Stage and sequence: the cognitive-developmental approach to socialization. In D.A. Goslin (Ed.), *Handbook of socialization theory and research.* Chicago: Rand McNally.

ladder in the predicted order, without skipping steps (Colby et al., 1983; Walker, 1989). Figure 11.6 shows that although most seven- to ten-year-olds are preconventional in their moral thinking, many thirteen- to sixteen-year-olds reason in conventional terms. Interestingly, researchers find that very few adolescents—or even mature adults, for that matter—resolve moral issues on a postconventional level.

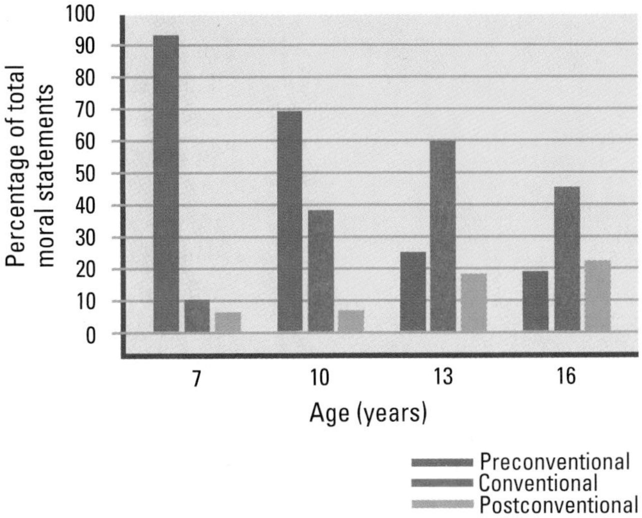

Figure 11.6 Levels of moral reasoning In response to standard moral dilemmas, most seven- to ten-year-olds are preconventional in their reasoning, while most thirteen- to sixteen-year-olds are conventional. Very few subjects resolved these dilemmas on a postconventional level (Colby et al., 1983).

Alternative Conceptions There are three major criticisms of Kohlberg's theory. The first is that his model is culturally biased. This is partly true. John Snarey (1985) reviewed forty-five studies conducted in twenty-eight countries and found that most children and adolescents—from Canada, Taiwan, Israel, Mexico, Turkey, and elsewhere—advanced at the same rate and in the same sequence through the first two levels. He also found, however, that only well-educated middle-class adults from complex urban societies consistently exhibited postconventional forms of morality based on abstract principles. When presented with Kohlberg's written dilemmas, many non-Westerners—including Tibetan Buddhist monks and respected village leaders from Kenya and Papua New Guinea—fail to reason at this third level. Why? In cultures that value friendship, belonging, and social responsibility more than rugged individualism, conventional moral reasoning is not only common but desirable. Thus, in a study that compared American and Indian children and adults, Joan Miller and David Bersoff (1992) found that in India, people operate by an alternative postconventional moral code in which obligation to a friend is more principled than obligation to justice.

A second criticism is that the model is gender biased. When Kohlberg first constructed his dilemmas, he tested only males and then used their responses as a moral yardstick. Yet according to Carol Gilligan (1982), women address moral issues "in a different voice." More concerned about compassion for others than about abstract rules, the female voice may be different, but it is not morally inferior. Gilligan's point has obvious intuitive appeal, but it lacks clear empirical support. On the one hand, public-opinion pollsters do find that women care more deeply than men about social issues and interpersonal relations. On the other hand, moral-development researchers find that women and men, on average, obtain very similar scores on Kohlberg's dilemmas (Rest, 1986; Walker, 1984). Also, in contrast to the assumption that people resolve moral dilemmas in set ways, as defined either by Kohlberg or by Gilligan, men and women are flexible in their reasoning. Studies by Dennis Krebs and his colleagues have shown that the kinds of moral judgments people make in real life depend on the situations they're in and the kinds of dilemmas they face (Krebs et al., 1991; Wark & Krebs, 1996).

Finally, many developmental psychologists have argued that Kohlberg's model is limited because morality consists of more than just an ability to think about hypothetical dilemmas in a manner that is cognitively sophisticated. Actions speak louder than words, say Kohlberg's critics. The real question is, does moral *reasoning* breed moral *conduct*? Are the postconventional thinkers kinder, more caring, or more virtuous in their daily affairs than those who are lower on the cognitive ladder? Do society's model citizens and philanthropists use higher levels of moral reasoning than drug pushers, racists, mobsters, and corrupt business executives? Available research offers two answers to these questions.

First, moral reasoning and behavior are very often related. Juvenile delinquents tend to score lower on Kohlberg's dilemmas than normal adolescents, and those with higher scores tend to behave in ways that are considered even more moral

(Blasi, 1980; Kurtines & Gewirtz, 1984). The second answer, however, is that it's entirely possible to live a moral life without "elitist" levels of cognitive reasoning. Think about Kohlberg's theory, then ask yourself: Are young children *a*moral, or less moral, than their cognitively superior parents? Children lack the cognitive equipment, but do they lack the emotional equipment underlying morality? According to Martin Hoffman (1984), morality in children is rooted in **empathy**—a capacity to experience joy for others who are happy and distress for those who are in pain. By this account, morality is present early in life. In the crib, infants often cry when they hear the sound of another baby crying. They feel no pain of their own, yet they are distressed, a possible sign of empathy. At less than two years old, babies have been observed giving food, toys, hugs, and kisses to others who show signs of distress—again, a possible sign of empathy (Zahn-Waxler et al., 1992). At the sight of a homeless person curled up on the floor of a bus station, even the preconventional young child reacts with sorrow and a desire to offer help (Damon, 1988; Eisenberg & Mussen, 1989).

As an alternative to Kohlberg's model of moral reasoning, Nancy Eisenberg (1992) argues that to predict changes in moral *behavior* it is better to examine how children and adolescents reason specifically about prosocial, helpful actions. So rather than present subjects of different ages with dilemmas that pit a rule against their own sense of right and wrong, Eisenberg presents situations in which the conflict is between one's own desires and the needs of another person. She then asks the subjects to choose a course of action and select among a set of reasons for engaging in that action. For example, subjects are asked to choose between getting an injured child's parents or going to a party, hoarding food after a flood or sharing with others, going to the beach or helping a friend study for a test, and so on.

Using a standard set of seven stories, and in longitudinal and cross-sectional studies, Eisenberg and others have found that prosocial reasoning follows a predictable developmental course. Preschool children are primarily hedonistic and self-centered in their responses; grade-school children are more other-oriented (but focused on what the person in need and others would think of them); and by late adolescence, there is an increase in feelings of guilt and sympathy, perspective-taking, and, ultimately, an inner sense of social responsibility. This pattern has been found in several countries—and there's a link between prosocial reasoning and helpfulness in actual behavior (Eisenberg et al., 1995; Carlo et al., 1996).

Moral Dilemmas in Law Each of us makes moral choices in our own lives and when called on to judge the actions of others, as when we sit on a jury. Juries have long been confronted with moral dilemmas like those constructed by Kohlberg. Before the Civil War, Northern juries regularly failed to convict people charged with aiding escaped slaves. During the turbulent Vietnam era, many juries refused to convict antiwar activists on political conspiracy charges. Today, cases involving battered women who retaliate against abusive husbands and crime victims who kill in self-defense present similar dilemmas. In cases like these, the jury has the power to vote its conscience—even if it means overruling or "nullifying" the law (Horowitz & Willging, 1991).

Particularly heart-wrenching are cases involving *euthanasia,* or assisted suicide—one of the most explosive moral and ethical issues of our time (Brigham & Pfeifer, 1996). Sometimes the issue involves physician-assisted suicide, as often practiced by Jack Kevorkian, a retired Michigan pathologist. As of the start of 1997, Kevorkian had presided over forty-six deaths. For three of these incidents, he was tried for murder—and in all three he was acquitted by a jury. Sometimes on trial are family members who are tried for what they say were acts of compassion on behalf of loved

empathy A feeling of joy for others who are happy and distress for those who are in pain.

ones who were suffering, terminally ill, and pleading for death. In some instances, juries have used a postconventional morality, voting for acquittal on the ground that compassion takes precedence over the letter of the law. Yet in other instances, juries have voted to convict. Illustrating the conventional form of moral reasoning, a juror in one such case said, "We had no choice. The law does not allow for sympathy" (Associated Press, 1985).

The conflict in these events is profound: The law strictly prohibits assisted suicide, yet many people who are terminally ill and in agony desperately want to die. Is it morally superior to condone assisted suicide? No, not necessarily. Kohlberg was always quick to note that moral development is measured not by *what* decision is made but by *how* that decision is reasoned. Indeed, any juror, judge, physician, or family member can decide against assisted suicide for reasons that are either conventional ("The law prohibits this act, so it's wrong") or postconventional ("A human life should never be sacrificed"). It's a sad and ironic postscript in this regard that Kohlberg himself—who had a chronic parasitic infection that caused him excruciating stomach pain—committed suicide in 1987, before his sixtieth birthday. He had discussed his predicament with a close friend and had concluded that someone with social responsibilities to others ought to go on. But overcome with pain and deeply depressed, he drowned himself in Boston Harbor (Hunt, 1993).

The actions of Jack Kevorkian embody a classic moral dilemma. Often referred to as "Dr. Death," Kevorkian has assisted in at least forty-six suicides involving terminally ill patients. He's been tried three times and acquitted each time by a jury. In recent polls, a fifth of all doctors said that they had actively helped end a patient's life (Van Biema, 1997).

Social Development

To many people, the word *teenager* is synonymous with torn jeans, loud music, wild hair, and long phone conversations. The teen years are a curious time of life. Absorbed in closer-than-ever friendships, newly aroused by sexual urges, needing to fit in and yet wanting to stand out, feeling caught between parents and peers, and anxious about the future, teens are fraught with mixed emotions. The highs are high, the lows are low, and the changes are frequent.

According to Erik Erikson (1963), all people pass through a series of life stages, each marked by a "crisis" that has to be resolved in order for healthy development to occur. During the transitional period of adolescence, the central task is to form an *identity,* or self-concept—hence, the term **identity crisis.** Some teenagers pass through this stage easily—clear about who they are, what values they hold, and what they want out of life. Others drift somewhat in confusion as they struggle to break from their parents, find the right friends, establish their sexual orientation, and set career goals for the future. For Erikson, this identity crisis is best described by a sign he once saw hanging in a cowboy bar: "I ain't what I ought to be, I ain't what I'm going to be, but I ain't what I was" (1959, p. 93).

In the United States and other countries with an ethnically diverse population, minority adolescents—caught between two cultures—must also establish an *ethnic identity.* Thus, African-, Hispanic-, and Asian-Americans may identify with the language and customs of their parent culture, their new national culture, or both. Jean Phinney (1990) notes that the process of ethnic identity formation typically begins in adolescence with a passive acceptance of the dominant culture, is then followed

identity crisis An adolescent's struggle to establish a personal identity, or self-concept.

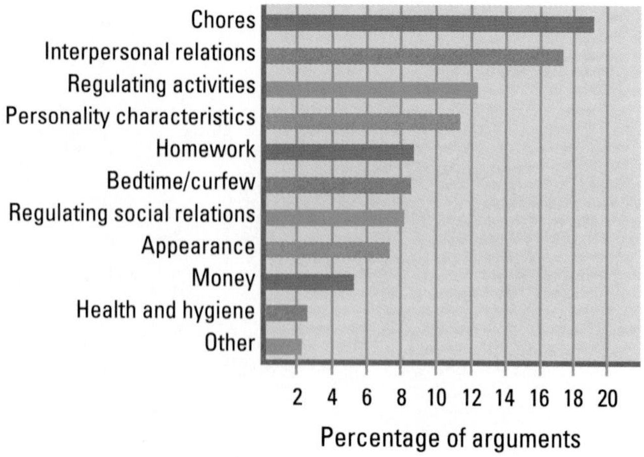

Figure 11.7 What do parents and teenagers fight about? Interviews with parents and adolescents of varying ages revealed that most arguments concern routine matters, not differences in deeply held values (Smetana, 1988).

in early adulthood by an awakening of interest in one's cultural roots, and culminates later in an ethnic identification. As you might expect, ethnic-group identity is stronger among immigrants who enter the host country as adults than it is among those who arrive at a younger, more formative age. This developmental process is described further in Chapter 14.

Research shows that adolescents experiment with different possible selves—the rebel, free spirit, workaholic, political activist, and so on—in search of their identity and that the process takes time (Waterman, 1982). First-year college students are thus less likely than seniors to say, "I know who I am and what I want out of life" (Constantinople, 1969). However long it takes, there are three aspects of social development that all adolescents must come to grips with: parent relationships, peer influences, and sexuality.

Parent Relationships For the mother or father of a cuddly newborn baby, it's hard to imagine that the intense emotional bond could ever be broken. To the parent of a teenager, it's no longer so hard to imagine. Whether the topic is a blaring stereo, school grades, money, or dirty laundry, it seems that parents and adolescents are often in a power struggle, involved in one squabble after another. As described by the mother of an eleven-year-old daughter, "It's like being bitten to death by ducks" (Steinberg, 1987, p. 36).

As children mature, what happens to their relationship with parents? Is conflict normal or easily avoided? Can the bond that once seemed so secure be shattered? And what effect does it all have on the family? By administering questionnaires, interviewing family members, and observing interactions in the laboratory and in the home, researchers are trying to answer these questions. What emerges from these studies is a portrait of parents and teenagers characterized by two changes. First, coinciding with the onset of puberty and physical maturation, there is a rise in tension between twelve- and thirteen-year-olds asserting their independence and parents, especially the mother. As shown in Figure 11.7, young adolescents and their parents argue about twice a week—but over routine household matters such as taking out the garbage, not about explosive issues such as sex, religion, or politics (Smetana, 1988). Despite vast cultural differences, similar interaction patterns have been observed among Chinese parents and adolescents in Hong Kong (Yau & Smetana, 1996).

A second change is that adolescents undergo a period marked by both *disengagement* and *transformation* in their relationships within the family. Reed Larson and his colleagues (1996) recently studied more than 200 Chicago-area boys and girls from fifth to eighth grades, then returned four years later when these same subjects were in the ninth to twelfth grades. For one week at a time, each subject carried an electronic pager and was signaled several times a day during normal waking hours. Whenever they were signaled, the subjects had to indicate where they were, who they were with, what they were doing, and how they felt. Together, the students provided a total of 16,477 reports. There were two key results. First, there was a steady decline in the sheer amount of waking time spent with family members—

> *"When I was a boy of 14, my father was so ignorant I could hardly stand to have the man around. But when I got to be 21, I was astonished at how much he had learnt in 7 years."*
>
> — MARK TWAIN

from 35 percent in the fifth grade to 14 percent in the twelfth grade. Interestingly, the students spent the same number of hours alone with mothers and fathers but "disengaged" from family group situations, siblings, and other relatives (see Figure 11.8). Second, there were marked changes in the way the students felt during family interactions. Specifically, they felt worse during the early-adolescent years of the seventh and eighth grades. But boys then became positively "transformed" in the family setting during the ninth and tenth grades, and girls followed suit in the eleventh and twelfth grades (see Figure 11.9).

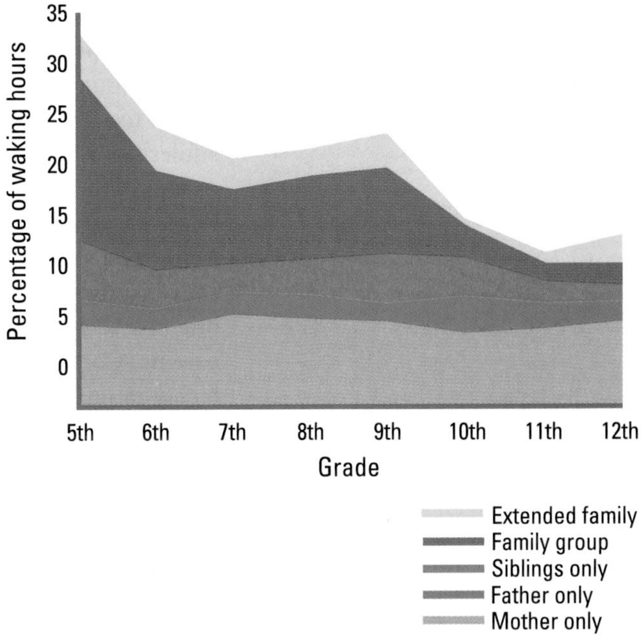

Figure 11.8 Patterns of adolescent "disengagement" from the family This study revealed that over the course of adolescent development, the amount of time spent with the family decreased by an average of 2.74 percent per year. As you can see, there was not a similar decline in time spent alone with parents (Larson et al., 1996).

It may seem as if parents and their young teenagers are at war or in a state of truce, like government and rebel forces, but most research indicates that the so-called generation gap has been blown out of proportion. To be sure, there are some minor skirmishes and some disengagement—all of which can be hard on parents while it lasts, increasing personal stress and straining marital relations (Silverberg & Steinberg, 1990). But typically there is peace, and seldom does the bickering leave a permanent scar on the parent–child relationship. In questionnaires and interviews, most adolescents say they admire their parents and accept their political and religious values (Adelson, 1986; Offer & Schonert-Reichl, 1992).

It's clear that the onset of puberty coincides with various changes and transformations. It's not clear, however, what to make of this correlation—so researchers, at least for now, can only speculate about possible interpretations (Holmbeck, 1996). Taking an evolutionary perspective, Laurence Steinberg (1989) argues that tensions within the family are triggered not by the adolescent's chronological age but by puberty. If it comes early, so does conflict. If puberty is late, the conflict is delayed. To clarify the complex link between the biology of adolescence and social relations at home, Steinberg notes that in many primate species living in the wild—gibbons and chimpanzees, for example—it's common for males and females at puberty to depart their group, search elsewhere for a mate, and reproduce outside the family. Even among humans, there is historical precedence for separating parents and their teenagers. Before many countries became industrialized, adolescents lived in a state of semiautonomy (living with parents but working to earn money), and in some cultures they were even subject to "extrusion" (sent to live in other households).

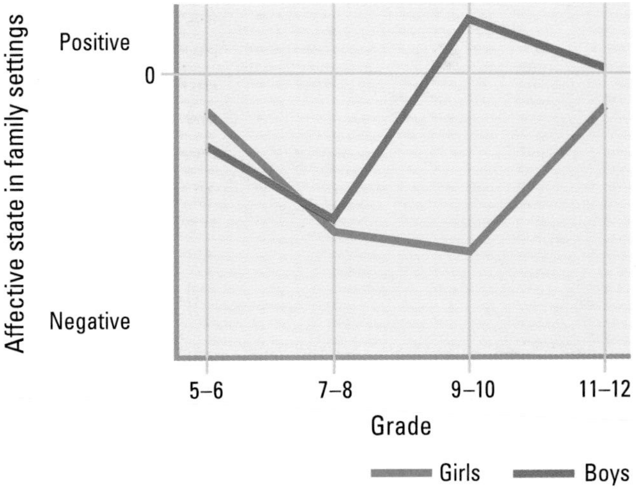

Figure 11.9 Patterns of adolescent "transformation" within the family Adolescents in the seventh and eighth grades felt worse while with the family, but affect was better among ninth- and tenth-grade boys and eleventh- and twelfth-grade girls (Larson et al., 1996).

According to Steinberg, the problem that exists today may stem from the fact that sexually mature offspring spend more time in the company of parents than ever before. A hundred years ago, adolescents left home at sixteen or seventeen, roughly the age at which they became mature. Now adolescents reach puberty at twelve or thirteen but live at home until the age of eighteen or older. So what does this tell us about parent-child relations? According to Steinberg (1987), everyone should feel reassured:

"Telling parents that fighting over taking out the garbage is related to the reproductive fitness of the species provides little solace—and doesn't help get the garbage out of the house, either. But parents need to recognize that quarreling with a teenager over mundane matters may be a normal part of family life during adolescence" (p. 39).

Peer Influences Another important aspect of adolescent social development is the heightened significance of peer groups and relations outside the home—long phone conversations, flirtation, and dating. For the first time, the child becomes primarily oriented to the world outside the home and may not even want to be seen with parents. Compared to early-childhood friendships, adolescent relationships can be highly intimate. It's not unusual for best friends to talk freely about their thoughts and feelings and to reveal some of their deepest, darkest secrets (Berndt, 1996).

Although most adolescents tend to retain the fundamental values of their parents, they look to peers for guidance on how to dress or wear their hair, what music to listen to, how to speak, and how to behave in ways that are acceptable. As social beings, we all exhibit a tendency to conform, at least to some extent. Is this tendency more pronounced in adolescence? Are junior- and senior-high-school students more vulnerable to peer pressure than adults? The answer is *yes,* especially during the early stages of adolescence. Thomas Berndt (1979) asked students in grades three, six, nine, and twelve how they would react if their friends tried to influence them to see a certain movie, go bowling, help a new kid on the block, or cheat on a test. The result: Conformity rose steadily with age, peaked in the ninth grade, then declined. The tendency to conform is much weaker for actions that are immoral or illegal, but younger adolescents are consistently the most likely followers, wanting desperately to fit in (Brown et al., 1986; Gavin & Furman, 1989).

Whether conforming to a new generation means eating live goldfish, dressing punk, shaving the head, or piercing an ear, conformity satisfies important needs in a teenager's life. It's important to realize that the socializing influence of peers—particularly close friends—can have both positive and negative effects on teenagers (Berndt, 1996). In a one-year longitudinal study, 1,000 ethnically diverse high-school students and their friends were asked about their school grades as well as their use of alcohol, marijuana, and other drugs. The result: Even after taking into account the fact that people are drawn to others who are similar, teenagers became even more like their friends over time. After a one-year period, those whose friends did well in school raised their own grades more than others who started with a similar academic record but whose friends did not do well in school. On the negative side, those whose friends were frequent drug users increased their own usage—again, compared to their peers who were similar at the start of the year but whose friends were less frequent users. Interestingly, students with warmer and more demanding parents were less vulnerable in this regard to the influence from friends (Mounts & Steinberg, 1995).

Sexuality Triggered by rising hormone levels and physical maturation, adolescent boys and girls are sexual beings, curious and easily aroused. The arousal of sexual impulses is a very natural part of adolescent development and the transition to adulthood. Whether teenagers *act* on these impulses, however, depends, in part, on social factors. As we saw in Chapter 8, national surveys of sexual practices—beginning with those conducted by Kinsey and his associates (1948, 1953)—have shown that there has been a constant 50–70 percent rate of sexual activity among boys but that the number of sexually active teenage girls climbed from a low of 10 percent in the 1940s to a high of more than 50 percent in the 1980s (Brooks-Gunn & Furstenberg, 1989). There are also marked cultural and ethnic differences. Teen rates of sexual activity are higher in western Europe but lower in Arab and Asian countries (Toufexis, 1993). And in the United States, the rates are higher among African Americans than among white Americans (Rodgers, 1996).

Although American teenagers are sexually more active today than at the time of Kinsey's survey, they are not always better informed about the health risks or more diligent in the use of contraceptives. In the United States, most pregnancies to girls under eighteen are unplanned and unwanted. All too often, they result in an abortion, a hasty and unhappy marriage, or an out-of-wedlock birth that forces the mother out of school and plunges her into poverty. With the spread of AIDS, unprotected sex can also prove fatal (Mann, 1992). Thankfully, after many years of skyrocketing teenage pregnancy rates, the numbers in the United States have recently started to decline (National Center for Health Statistics, 1996).

One reason for the unwanted pregnancies is that many teenagers in the United States do not use contraceptives the first time they have sex—and this pattern of neglect persists, particularly among those who are young, poor, and uneducated. The percentages vary from one sample to another, but they all reveal the same problem. In a questionnaire anonymously taken by 300 college students, for example, 63 percent of the women and 57 percent of the men admitted that neither they nor their partners used a contraceptive the first time they had sex (Darling et al., 1992). Why not? One reason is that they were often caught off guard, especially the first time. As one sixteen-year-old girl put it, "The first time, it was like totally out of the blue . . . I mean, you don't know it's coming, so how are you to be prepared?" (Stark, 1986, p. 28). A second reason why many teenagers do not plan for contraception is that they feel guilty about having sex. If one is ambivalent, it's easier to justify getting "swept off your feet" and "carried away" than it is to have premeditated sex (Byrne et al., 1993; Gerrard, 1987). A third reason is ignorance—and perhaps even the illusion of invulnerability ("It won't happen to me"). Many teenagers say they rely on withdrawal or the rhythm method as a means of birth control. Yet surveys consistently show that they know surprisingly little about reproductive physiology or about the safest time in the menstrual cycle (Morrison, 1985).

Perhaps improvements are needed in sex education. At home, too, many parents communicate uneasily about the birds and bees. And in school, most sex-education programs are brief and often are not focused on matters pertaining to contraception (Brooks-Gunn & Furstenberg, 1989). Adolescent sexuality is complex inasmuch as it is influenced by pubertal status, hormones, personality and risk-taking tendencies, identity seeking, peers, parents, the media, cultural institutions, and, of course, the desires of a prospective partner (Rodgers & Rowe, 1993). In short, there are no easy solutions to the kinds of problems that can arise. For male and female adolescents, however, it's clear that knowledge and protection are a necessary first step toward minimizing the possible negative consequences.

Adolescence and Mental Health

In 1904, G. Stanley Hall described adolescence as a time of "storm and stress," reflecting a widespread belief that teenagers suffer inner conflict and turmoil. Mood swings, identity crises, a rejection of traditional values, depression, drugs, unsafe sex, and suicide are among the stereotypic images of the adolescent overcome by raging hormones. Is there any truth to this image? Are teenagers really the hapless mental-health victims of one hormone attack after another?

Table 11.2 Common Concerns among the World's Teenagers

	Australia	Bangladesh	Hungary	Israel	Italy	Japan	Taiwan	Turkey	United States	West Germany	International Average
I feel so lonely	22	43	14	17	20	39	33	32	18	11	25
I frequently feel sad	27	36	24	28	25	55	26	34	25	17	29
My parents are ashamed of me	11	7	4	3	4	15	10	08	7	2	07

PERCENTAGE WHO AGREE

Source: Test items by D. Offer, E. Ostrov, & I. Howard (1981). *The adolescent: A psychological self-portrait.* New York: Basic Books.

No. Research shows that despite some of the transitional growing pains and mood swings of adolescence, severe emotional distress is neither inevitable nor widespread (Buchanan et al., 1992; Powers et al., 1989). Many years ago, cultural anthropologists Margaret Mead (1928) and Ruth Benedict (1959) described several nonindustrialized societies in which puberty passes uneventfully, without hoopla or turmoil. More recently, Daniel Offer and his colleagues (1981) distributed questionnaires to more than 20,000 junior- and senior-high-school students in different countries and found that most were happy and reasonably well adjusted. That's the good news. The bad news is that roughly 20 percent do develop serious emotional problems—which is high compared to younger children and roughly the same percentage as in adults. In a massive international survey, teenagers thirteen to nineteen years old agreed or disagreed with various statements from the Offer Self-Image Questionnaire. A sample of the results are shown in Table 11.2.

It's important to realize that many unhappy adolescents do grow up to become maladjusted later in life. For that reason, Offer (1987) urges parents and mental-health workers to abandon the old storm-and-stress view of youth and to understand that a teenager who cries for help may be in real trouble, not just "passing through a stage." In some cases, the tragic result is an attempted suicide (Lewinsohn et al., 1994).

Adulthood and Old Age

What is the human life span and how does it differ from the average life expectancy? What physical changes mark adult development? What about memory and intelligence—do people become more capable with age, or less? Is there a "typical" career path? What's the evidence for a midlife crisis and for despair in old age?

It's not altogether clear what separates adolescence from early adulthood. In most states, a person is legally old enough to drive a car at sixteen, to vote at eighteen, and to drink at twenty-one. The average American woman gets married at the age of twenty-three, the average man at twenty-five, and both are likely to become parents shortly thereafter. In educational terms, the average student in the United States graduates from high school at eighteen. Those who attend college graduate at twenty-two or older, depending on family and work obligations. Those who go on to professional or graduate school typically remain students for an additional three to six years after that.

"Some people mark off their life in years, others in events. I am one of the latter. . . . I did not become a young man at a particular year, like 13, but when a kid strolled into the store where I worked and called me 'mister.'"

— RICHARD COHEN

The starting point for adulthood may be debatable, but the endpoint is not. In all species of animals, there is a maximum **life span** that sets an upper limit on the oldest possible age of an organism under ideal conditions. Scientists have long held that just as a time clock has twenty-four hours in a day, our biological clocks contain a finite number of years in a life—about 120 among humans. Although this assumption still prevails, it is fast becoming a subject of controversy. In recent years, some biologists have managed to extend the life span of certain fruit flies, roundworms, and rodents through selective breeding, genetic manipulation, and alterations in diet (Fossell, 1996; Hayflick, 1996; Medina, 1996).

As verified by the Guinness Book of World Records, *Jeanne Calment of Arles, France, was the oldest living human ever recorded. Biologists see 120 as the upper limit of the human life span. But in February 1997, Calment celebrated her 122nd birthday. In August 1997, she died.*

In most species, the **life expectancy**—the actual number of years lived by an average member—is shorter than the maximum life span. On average, guinea pigs live to the tender age of 3; dogs, 10 to 15; chimpanzees, 15 to 20; elephants, 30 to 40; and eagles, 105 (Lansing, 1959). Among humans, the life expectancy is influenced not only by genetics but also by personality, nutrition, health practices, the environment, health care, and other factors. The average Roman in the year 1 CE lived to the age of 22. In the United States, the life expectancy rose from 36 in the nineteenth century to 47 in the year 1900, and to 76 in 1996. Women outlive men by an average of seven years.

Based on these trends, the U.S. Census Bureau projects that the average life expectancy will increase to 77 in the year 2000 and 78 in the year 2010. These numbers are somewhat deceptive, however, because some of the increase is due to a lowering of infancy and childhood mortality rates—not to the fact that adults in general are living longer than did their ancestors. Cultural variation is also common. According to the World Health Organization (1997), the average life expectancy is 40 in Sierra Leone, 53 in Bolivia, 58 in India, 69 in Mexico, and close to 80 in Japan. In the United States, there is also a racial gap, as white Americans live longer than African Americans—on average, 77 years compared to 70.

Biological Development

At birth, a human infant has billions of brain cells. From that point on, however, there is a steady process of attrition: Neurons die without replacement, and those that survive thin out. However, not all parts of the brain age at the same rate. In the brainstem, which controls many simple reflexes, there is little or no cell loss over time. Yet in the motor cortex and frontal lobes, which control motor and cognitive activity, thousands of neurons a day are lost, particularly after the age of fifty. By the time men and women are eighty, the brain weighs an average of 8 percent less than it did during the peak of adulthood. What's fascinating about this aspect of development is that the aging brain is simultaneously in a process of growth and decline. A newborn has a surplus of brain cells, so maturation involves the death of cells that are not used, coupled with the formation of new synaptic connections among those that remain. As we saw in Chapter 2, the human brain has great

life span The maximum possible age for members of a species.

life expectancy The number of years that an average member of a species is expected to live.

"When 1,200 Americans were asked when middle age begins, 41 percent said it's when you worry about health care, 42 percent said it was when the last child moves out, and 46 percent said it was when you no longer recognize the names of music groups on the radio."

— *NEWSWEEK* (1992)

plasticity, a capacity to change as a result of experience. In the brain of a mature adult, then, more can be accomplished with less (Creasey & Rapoport, 1985; Scheibel, 1995).

The Adult Years In addition to changes within the brain and nervous system, many other physical changes accompany development during the adult years (Whitbourne, 1996). Muscle strength, heart and lung capacity, speed of reflexes, and vision increase during the twenties, peak at about the age of thirty, then gradually start to decline. Also at that time, metabolism slows down, leading both men and women to lose their youthful physique and to gain weight. Does this mean that young adults who rely on physical skills are over the hill by the age of thirty? Absolutely not. It depends on one's diet, health, and exercise habits and on the physical demands of a particular activity.

Baseball statistician Bill James (1982) as well as Richard Schulz and his colleagues (1994) analyzed the full career records of major-league ballplayers and found that batters and pitchers peaked at the age of twenty-six. Football, basketball, and tennis players follow a similar age pattern. Yet world-class sprinters and swimmers peak in their teens and early twenties, while most professional bowlers and golfers reach the top of their game in their thirties. It all depends on whether a sport requires speed and agility, endurance, or power—which decline at different rates. Age sets limits on what the body can do, but adults who keep in shape can minimize the effects of aging and stretch performance beyond the average. As we will see in Chapter 18, regular exercise benefits both physical and mental health—and may even be associated on a short-term basis with improved functioning of the immune system (Simon, 1991; Solomon & Benton, 1994).

One inevitable biological event for women is **menopause,** the end of menstruation, which signals the end of fertility. At about the age of fifty, a woman's ovaries stop producing estrogen. The most common symptoms of this change are "hot flashes" (sudden feelings of warmth usually in the upper part of the body) and sometimes profuse sweating, dizziness, nausea, and headaches (Bates, 1981). Some women get moody, depressed, or anxious, but most are not terribly bothered by menopause—and most remain sexually active (Morokoff, 1988). In a survey of more than 8,000 middle-age women, 70 percent said they felt relieved, liberated, or unaffected by the change (McKinlay et al., 1987). Among those who do suffer, it's not clear whether the negative experience is linked to lowered estrogen levels or other aspects of aging, such as a fear of illness or the children leaving home. Consistently, large-scale studies have shattered the myth that menopause is a traumatic negative event in a woman's life (Matthews, 1992).

[Drawing by Cheney; © 1996 The New Yorker Magazine, Inc.]

"Happy fortieth. I'll take the muscle tone in your upper arms, the girlish timbre of your voice, your amazing tolerance for caffeine, and your ability to digest French fries. The rest of you can stay."

For men, there is no biological equivalent to menopause. Testosterone levels (which peak during adolescence) diminish only gradually, and even though the sperm count may drop, there is only a gradual loss of fertility. As with some women, some men pass through a difficult midlife period in which they question their marriage and career, worry about their health and sexual vigor, and feel frustrated about goals they did not achieve. For men and women alike, aging is not just a biological process but a psychological one as well.

menopause Among middle-age women, the end of menstruation and fertility.

Old Age As people enter their sixties and seventies, the cumulative effects of age begin to show, and the process seems to accelerate. Inside the body, brain cells die at a faster rate, the reflexes continue to slow, muscles continue to lose strength, the immune system begins to fail, bones become more brittle, joints stiffen, and there is a reduced sense of taste and smell. Resulting from a steady loss of visual acuity during adulthood, many older people are farsighted—and some have difficulty adapting to brightness or darkness. There are also noticeable auditory losses, as many older people report having trouble hearing high-pitched sounds, normal speech, and background noises. Perhaps most obvious are the effects of chronological age on appearance—including the wrinkles, stooped posture, thinned white hair, and shrinkage, as the average man loses about an inch in height, the average woman two inches. The physical changes and others are comprehensively reviewed in two recent books on the aging process (Birren & Schaie, 1995; Whitbourne, 1996).

When Ponce de León left Spain in 1513 and landed in what is now the state of Florida, he was looking for the legendary and mythical fountain of youth. Biologists say that it's impossible to reverse the body's aging process, but can it be slowed down? Can one's longevity be increased? According to current estimates, only one in a thousand readers of this textbook will live to celebrate a one hundredth birthday—and there's no secret formula for the rest of us. Osborn Segerberg (1982) interviewed 1,200 centenarians and found that many of them cited peculiar reasons for their longevity ("because I sleep with my head to the north," "because I don't believe in germs"). In fact, what you need is a mixture of healthy genes, a healthy lifestyle, and luck (Palmore, 1982).

It's often said that old age is a state of mind. But can a youthful mind produce a young body? Interested in this question, Ellen Langer (1989) and her associates designed a provocative experiment in which they tried to turn the clock back for men in their late seventies. Two groups of men were taken on a five-day country retreat. One group was encouraged to step back to the year 1959. They brought old photos and wrote autobiographical sketches in the present tense, but from the perspective of 1959. During their stay, these men listened to fifties-style music, saw old movies, talked about *The Honeymooners* and other classic TV shows, played *The Price Is Right* using 1950s prices, talked about old sports legends, read old issues of *Life,* and listened on an old radio to a speech by President Eisenhower. The second group of men enjoyed a similar retreat, except that they spent their time reminiscing about the year 1959 from the vantage point of the present. For these men, the experience meant current photos, recent magazines, and conversations that referred to 1959 in the past tense.

After five days, noticeable changes had taken place. When independent judges looked at photographs taken before and after the week, both groups of men looked younger. Even more striking, however, was that the men who mentally stepped back in time were in better physical condition than those who spent the same time reminiscing: They showed measurable increases in sitting height and joint flexibility, improved vision in one eye, and higher scores on a test of manual dexterity. These results led Langer (1989) to speculate that although aging is inevitable, perhaps the extent to which we show the symptoms of our age is not. For Ponce de León, a fountain of youth may have resided within the human mind.

In sports, as in other walks of life, career paths vary. In early 1997, at fourteen, American figure skater Tara Lipinski became the youngest U.S. champion. A few years ago, at the age of forty-five, George Foreman regained his long-lost title by becoming the oldest heavyweight champion in history.

Cognitive Development

The human body peaks at thirty, then gradually declines. But what about the trajectory of *cognitive* development through later adulthood and old age? Does a weakened body signal a feeble mind, or are the two paths separate? At what age do "growth" and "maturity" turn to "aging" when it comes to memory, intelligence, and the ability to be productive at one's work?

Memory and Forgetting Many people believe that as we age, we inevitably begin to forget names, faces, phone numbers, the car keys, and whatever else is personally important. According to this stereotype, men and women who are ready to retire are absentminded, if not senile. A deterioration of cognitive abilities is not, however, a necessary part of the aging process. Listen to the nostalgic remembrances of a parent or grandparent, and you will marvel at the ease with which he or she can vividly describe the details of an experience that took place a half-century ago. Research shows that certain experiences seem to leave an imprint on a person's memory, never to be erased. Sports, politics, wars, disasters, entertainment, and crime are topics that leave clear traces of newsprint on the mind (Howes & Katz, 1988). So are friends and acquaintances from earlier in life. Studies show that although elderly adults often cannot free-recall the names of high-school classmates, they have an uncanny ability to recognize names, recognize faces, and match them up (Bahrick et al., 1975).

When Ronald Reagan was president, comedians poked fun at his forgetfulness. But this issue lost its humor in November 1994 when Reagan announced that he has Alzheimer's disease. The former president was sober about his future. "As the disease progresses," he said, "the family often bears a heavy burden. I wish there was some way I could spare Nancy from this painful experience."

Clearly, there is much about our past that we tend not to forget, even as we get older. But study after study has shown that although the elderly are as capable as younger adults of recognizing stimuli they have seen before, there is a marked age-related decline in the ability to free-recall nonsense syllables, word lists, written prose, strings of numbers, names of people just introduced, map directions, geometric forms, faces, and other newly learned material (Light, 1991; Craik, 1992). The same results are found in *prospective* memory tasks, where the goal is to remember to do something in the future—like giving a message, removing food from the oven, or taking a medication. Although the research in this area is still in the early stages (Brandimonte et al., 1996), studies have revealed a consistent pattern. When subjects are asked, while working on a computer, to press a certain key every ten minutes, younger adults check the clock more frequently and outperform their elders at pressing the key on time. But when the task is to respond whenever a specific word is flashed on the screen, the age differences disappear. As with memory for past events, older people need more prompting, in the form of retrieval cues, to elevate their performance (Einstein et al., 1995).

There are two possible reasons for this age-related decline in memory. The first is strictly neurocognitive. Through a series of controlled experiments, Timothy Salthouse (1996) and others have discovered that as people get older, they process and react to information more slowly—and this loss of neural speed impairs performance on a whole range of cognitive tasks, including those used to test memory. The reason that slowness in the nervous system creates problems is that if it takes more time to process information—whether it's a list of names or grocery items—people will have less time to spend rehearsing the material or attending to items that appear later in the sequence, like getting "backed up" on an assembly line.

A second possible factor is that as people get older, they lose faith in their own cognitive abilities. Jane Berry and her colleagues (1989) administered a "memory self-efficacy" scale (a test that measures people's beliefs about their own retention skills) and found that sixty- to eighty-year-old adults were considerably less confident than eighteen- to thirty-year-olds (see Figure 11.10). As we saw, memory really does slip with age, but perhaps negative stereotypes and a lack of confidence can worsen the problem. The person who fears that he or she cannot remember directions, an appointment, or an old friend may not even try. Thus, when Becca Levy

(1996) boosted the confidence of older subjects by subliminally presenting them with words that depict old age in positive terms *(wise, learned, insightful),* their memory-test scores increased.

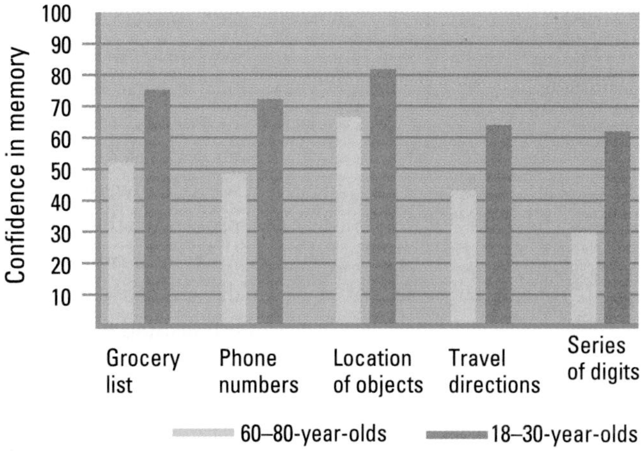

Figure 11.10 How good is your memory? Subjects were asked how confident they were (0–100) in their ability to perform various memory tasks. Consistently, elderly subjects were less confident than the younger subjects.

Alzheimer's Disease Although the brain and nervous system slow gradually as a natural part of aging, there are, sadly, many bright and sharp-witted adults who suffer from brain damage that causes dementia—a mental disorder characterized by severe cognitive impairments. Dementia can occur at any time during adulthood, but it is most likely to happen after age sixty-five and to strike about 10 percent of the elderly population. It is not part of the normal aging process but, rather, stems from damage to the brain caused by a stroke, a tumor, the long-term cumulative effects of alcohol, or certain kinds of diseases (Parks et al., 1993).

By far the most common cause of dementia is **Alzheimer's disease (AD)**, a progressive and irreversible brain disorder that afflicts mostly the elderly and kills brain cells at a terrifying pace. The statistics on AD are staggering. It is estimated that this disease claims as victims about 3 percent of adults aged sixty-five to seventy-four, 19 percent of those seventy-five to eighty-four, and 47 percent of those over eighty-five (Evans et al., 1989). At present, between 2 and 3 million Americans suffer from AD, which accounts for 40 to 50 percent of all nursing-home admissions. The estimated annual cost of AD in the United States is $80 billion (Zee, 1993).

Although the causes of cell death in AD are not fully known, researchers are in hot pursuit of clues (Parks et al., 1993; Terry et al., 1994). Many believe that AD results from a slow virus that invades the nervous system or from an accumulation of environmental toxins in the brain. Others find that AD destroys brain cells that produce acetylcholine, a neurotransmitter that plays an important role in memory. Still others find that one form of the disease is linked to genetic defects on the twenty-first, nineteenth, and fourteenth chromosomes. Whatever the causes, the effects of AD are devastating. It begins with lapses in memory and is soon followed by attention problems and an overall loss of cognitive functions. As the disease worsens over time, there are periods of disorientation, bursts of anger, depression, changes in mood and personality, and a steady deterioration of physical functions. Alzheimer's victims may lose track of a conversation, neglect to turn off a faucet or the stove, forget where they parked the car, or forget the name of a loved one. Compared to others of comparable age, Alzheimer's patients exhibit impairments in the simple classical conditioning of an eyeblink response (Solomon et al., 1995). To make matters worse, they often do not realize the extent of their problem (McGlynn & Kaszniak, 1991). In some cases, they lose the ability to recognize themselves in a mirror (Biringer et al., 1989). Typically, the onset of symptoms signals death within ten years.

There is no means of prevention and no cure for Alzheimer's disease. But there are adult day-care centers designed to help victims and provide relief and social support for the beleaguered families. For patients still in the early stages of AD, there are also memory-retraining programs to teach them how to use mnemonic devices and external memory aids. For more advanced AD patients, there are reality-orientation programs to help them stay aware of who and where they are (Heston & White, 1991).

Alzheimer's disease (AD) A progressive brain disorder that strikes older people, causing memory loss and other symptoms.

Intelligence Psychologists used to believe that intelligence—a concept, as we'll see in Chapter 12, that is not easily defined—peaks during the early twenties, declines gradually up to the age of fifty, then takes a dramatic downward turn from that point on. This view of development did not simply arise out of thin air, nor was it proposed by researchers extolling the power of youth. David Wechsler (1972), the psychologist who devised the most widely used adult intelligence test, was seventy-six years old when he wrote that "the decline of mental ability with age is part of the general process of the organism as a whole."

In light of numerous studies, we now know that old age does not necessarily mean diminished intelligence. The reason today's researchers are more optimistic about intellectual development later in life is that they realize that intelligence is not a single general trait. Rather, psychologists distinguish among different forms of intelligence—and although some forms decline with age, others do not. For example, Raymond Cattell (1963) and, later, John Horn (1982) distinguished between fluid and crystallized intelligence. **Fluid intelligence** is the ability to reason quickly and abstractly, solve problems of logic, detect letter or number sequences, or orient objects in two-dimensional space. In contrast, **crystallized intelligence** reflects more an accumulation of factual knowledge, skill, or expertise—as measured, for example, by the sheer size of one's vocabulary or the ability to add and subtract.

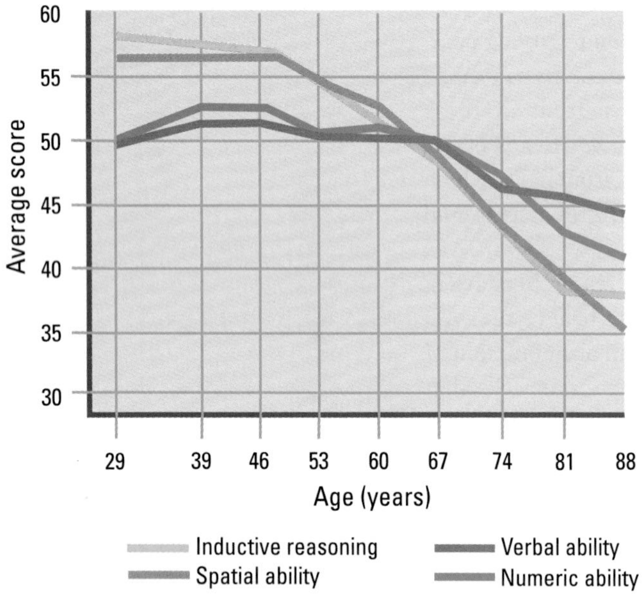

Figure 11.11 Age trends in measures of intelligence In this cross-sectional study, 1,628 adults took a battery of tests. Shown on the right are the results of four measures: two involving fluid intelligence (spatial ability and inductive reasoning) and two involving crystallized intelligence (verbal ability and numeric ability).

The distinction between fluid and crystallized intelligence is important because, when both are tested separately, two very different developmental patterns are found. In one large-scale study, for example, K. Warner Schaie and Sherry Willis (1993) tested more than 1,600 adults in age groups that ranged from twenty-nine to eighty-eight years old. As predicted, the fluid-intelligence test scores started to decline steadily through middle and late adulthood, but the measures of crystallized intelligence remained relatively stable—at least until subjects were in their seventies and eighties (see Figure 11.11). Additional research suggests that the developmental gains in crystallized intelligence come, in part, by reading books, newspapers, and magazines (Stanovich, West, & Harrison, 1995).

The fluid/crystallized distinction is related to two other developmental changes. First, as we saw, people lose mental *speed* as they get older. Whether a task involves recognizing pictures, folding paper, solving arithmetic problems or verbal analogies, dialing a telephone, proofreading, or assembling cubes, we get slower and slower over the life span (Cerella, 1985; Birren & Fisher, 1995; Salthouse, 1996)—and no one is immune, not even intellectually active but senior university professors (Shimamura et al., 1995). This helps to explain why age-related declines are greater on tests that are timed rather than untimed (Hertzog, 1989; Schaie, 1989) and on mental problems that are complex rather than simple (Salthouse, 1992). To illustrate the point, let's reconsider the Schaie and Willis (1993) study of adults twenty-nine to eighty-eight years old. In that study, three multiple-choice vocabulary tests were given to measure verbal ability, a form of crystallized intelligence: a standard untimed test, an untimed test consisting of difficult items, and a standard test that was timed. As shown in Figure 11.12, scores declined with age only in the speeded test. In the absence of time pres-

fluid intelligence A form of intelligence that involves the ability to reason logically and abstractly.

crystallized intelligence A form of intelligence that reflects the accumulation of verbal skills and factual knowledge.

sure, older subjects matched the performance of those literally half their age. It's worth noting, by the way, that older people can regain some of their diminished skills—even on measures of fluid intelligence—through cognitive training and practice (Willis, 1990; Schaie, 1996).

The second related change is that life experience, and hence age, is needed to cultivate *wisdom*—a form of intelligence that enables us to solve practical everyday problems (Baltes & Smith, 1990). Steven Cornelius and Avshalom Caspi (1987) asked adults ranging in age from twenty to seventy-eight to generate solutions to dilemmas that arise at home, at work, with friends and family, and so on (for example, "Your landlord refuses to make expensive repairs you want done. What should you do?"). The researchers measured problem-solving ability by having independent judges rate the quality of the solutions and found that these ratings increased steadily and consistently with the age of the subject. As Plato said, "The spiritual eyesight improves as the physical eyesight declines."

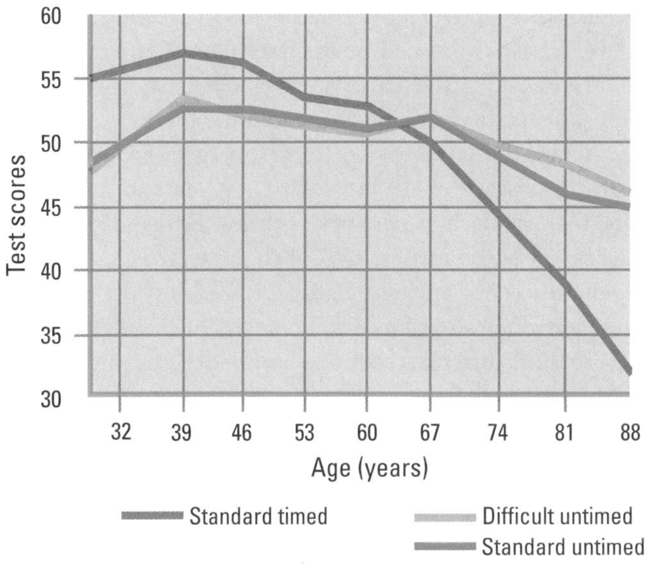

Figure 11.12 Timed vs. untimed vocabulary tests To measure verbal ability, Schaie and Willis (1993) administered (1) a standard untimed test, (2) a difficult untimed test, and (3) a standard timed test. As you can see, scores declined with age only in the timed test. In fact, performance on the two untimed tests peaked at the age of sixty-seven.

Social Development

Psychologists who study infants and young children can't help but be impressed by how accurately chronological age can be used to mark the milestones of social development. The first social smile is seen at six weeks and is predictably followed by attachment behaviors, separation anxiety, crawling, walking, first words, and so

I N T E R S E C T I O N

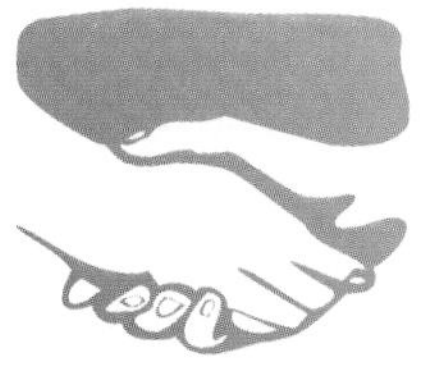

ADOLESCENCE AND ADULTHOOD AND BUSINESS

Career Trajectories

Look at some of history's prominent figures, and you'll see that they differ in terms of how productive they are—and when. Freud had 330 publications to his credit, Einstein had 248, and Darwin had 119. Thomas Edison held a record 1,093 U.S. patents, Picasso created 20,000 works of art, and Johann Sebastian Bach composed more than 1,000 pieces of music. Yet geneticist Gregor Mendel was famous on the basis of 7 scientific articles. With regard to timing, Mozart was only five years old when he wrote his first piece, and by fifteen he was an accomplished composer. Yet Italian composer Giuseppe Verdi was seventy-nine when he wrote the comic opera *Falstaff*, Benjamin Franklin invented bifocals at the age of seventy-eight and helped draft the U.S. Constitution at eighty-one, Marian Hart was eighty-four when she flew solo in a single-engine plane across the Atlantic, and Anna Mary "Grandma" Moses took up painting at seventy-eight and continued to the age of one hundred.

With such a diversity of careers, one wonders: Is there any regularity to career development? What normally happens to work productivity in adulthood? Sure, athletes peak when the body is in its prime. But what about people in careers that demand cognitive activity? Does productivity of output in these domains diminish with memory and mental speed or increase with knowledge and wisdom? Is there a typical trajectory?

While recognizing that individuals and their work situations differ in many ways, Dean Keith Simonton (1997) finds that career paths tend to follow a systematic pattern that is predictable by a person's career age. Over the years, Simonton and others have plotted the publication rates of various artists, psychologists, historians, philosophers, mathematicians, and other scholars. Across disciplines, the same basic pattern emerged: Productivity starts an upward climb in the first ten years of a career, which is usually in a person's twenties, peaks in the late thirties or early forties, and then undergoes a steady decline to retirement (see Figure 11.13). But just as athletes vary due to the physical demands of their sport, so too are there differences among careers. For example, the average mathematician (whose work requires fluid intelligence) peaks in the early thirties, whereas the average historian (whose scholarship benefits from a more accumulated crystallized intelligence) peaks later and stays productive well into the fifties and sixties. Individuals differ both in terms of how productive they are and whether they start their careers early or late, but the developmental trajectory is basically the same.

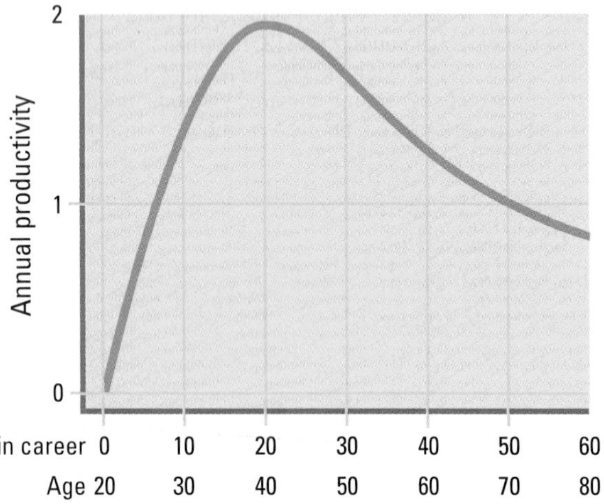

Figure 11.13 The "typical" career trajectory Although people differ in their overall potential and in whether they start their career early or late, this basic pattern is the same: growth in the first ten years, peaking during the next ten to twenty years, and a steady decline (Simonton, 1997).

Does this mean that performance on the job is doomed to suffer with age? On the one hand, research has shown that older adults are slower and less proficient at learning new job skills both in a laboratory setting and in the workplace (Kubeck et al., 1996; Salthouse et al., 1996). On the other hand, studies of government employees, military recruits, bank tellers, nurses, teachers, blue-collar workers, insurance agents, and others provide little evidence to suggest that actual performance on the job dwindles with age (Rhodes, 1983; Waldman & Avolio, 1986).

What accounts for the discrepancy? One explanation is that aging workers may learn how to compensate for their diminished physical abilities (Backman and Dixon, 1992; Morrow et al., 1994). To demonstrate this possibility, Timothy Salthouse (1984) tested the reaction time and skills of female typists ranging in age from nineteen to seventy-two years old. He found that the older, more experienced women were slower in their reaction times yet were able to type just as many words per minute. How? By scanning the text farther ahead. Indeed, when Salthouse limited the number of characters that could be viewed in advance, these veteran typists slowed down considerably. The same is true in complex games such as chess. Older players take longer to move and struggle more to remember board positions—but the moves they make are perfectly sound (Charness, 1985). As illustrated by the aging baseball pitcher who learns to compensate for his lost fastball by outsmarting the batter, experience and wisdom can be used to overcome the loss of youth.

---

on. Do adults similarly pass through an orderly succession of stages? Can chronological age be used to predict changes in self-concept, social relationships, or life satisfaction? Some say *yes,* others *no.*

Ages and Stages of Adulthood In contrast to the once-prevailing view that life patterns are set in early childhood, Erik Erikson (1963) proposed a life-span theory of development. According to Erikson, people mature through eight psychosocial stages, each marked by a crisis that has to be resolved. Stages 1 to 4 unfold in infancy and childhood; stage 5, in adolescence (the "identity crisis"); and stages 6 to 8, in the years of adulthood. In Erikson's view, those who emerge from adolescence with a sense of identity enter young adulthood, a time in which it's critical to fuse with someone else, to find *intimacy* through meaningful close friendships or marriage. The next stage is middle adulthood, a time when people feel the need to achieve *generativity,* by contributing to the welfare of a new generation—at work, at home, or in the community. Studies have shown that adults are more generative in their orientation than college students (McAdams & de St. Aubin, 1992). And among middle-age women, those who were the most generative were more politically active and cared more about others at work or their children at home (Peterson & Stewart, 1996). The final stage is late adulthood, a time in which it's important to gain *integrity,* a feeling that one's life has been worthwhile. Those who were fortunate enough to resolve their earlier crises enjoy a feeling of serenity and self-fulfillment. Those who are not so fortunate live their final years in regret and despair (see Table 11.3).

Building on Erikson's model, other theorists have tried to describe the stages of adulthood in finer detail, with a special emphasis on the middle years, the so-called prime of life (Gould, 1978; Vaillant, 1977). Perhaps the best known of these theories was proposed by Daniel Levinson. Based on extensive interviews with forty successful middle-age men and forty-five women, he proposed that just as there are four seasons in a year, there are four eras in a person's life: preadulthood, followed by early, middle, and late adulthood (Levinson et al., 1978; Levinson, 1996). According to this theory, our lives run in cycles that alternate from periods of stress and upheaval *between* eras to periods of relative calm *within* eras. Thus, each of us is likely to encounter rough times when we cross the transitional bridges to early adulthood (seventeen to twenty-two), middle adulthood (forty to forty-five), and late adulthood (sixty to sixty-five). The stages are shown in Figure 11.14.

During the transition to early adulthood, young adults shed their adolescence, build dreams, set goals for the future, and make choices that seem permanent—about a job, a spouse, a place to live. These choices are often reevaluated before people enter a busy but stable period of settling down. As men and women near forty, they reach a second turning point, during which they may question the paths

Table 11.3 Erikson's Eight Stages of Development

STAGES AND AGES	THE PRIMARY "CRISIS"
Infancy (0–1 year)	*Trust vs. mistrust*
Toddler (1–2 years)	*Autonomy vs. shame and doubt*
Preschool (3–5 years)	*Initiative vs. guilt*
Elementary school (6–12 years)	*Industry vs. inferiority*
Adolescence (13–19 years)	*Identity vs. role confusion* Adolescents struggle to break from parents and form an identity, or self-concept.
Young Adulthood (20–40 years)	*Intimacy vs. isolation* Having resolved the identity crisis, young adults seek intimacy in meaningful close relationships and marriage.
Middle Adulthood (40–65 years)	*Generativity vs. stagnation* Having achieved intimacy, middle-age adults seek to contribute to a new generation at work, at home, and in the community.
Late Adulthood (65 and over)	*Integrity vs. despair* Reflecting on life, older adults seek integrity, a sense that their lives were worthwhile.

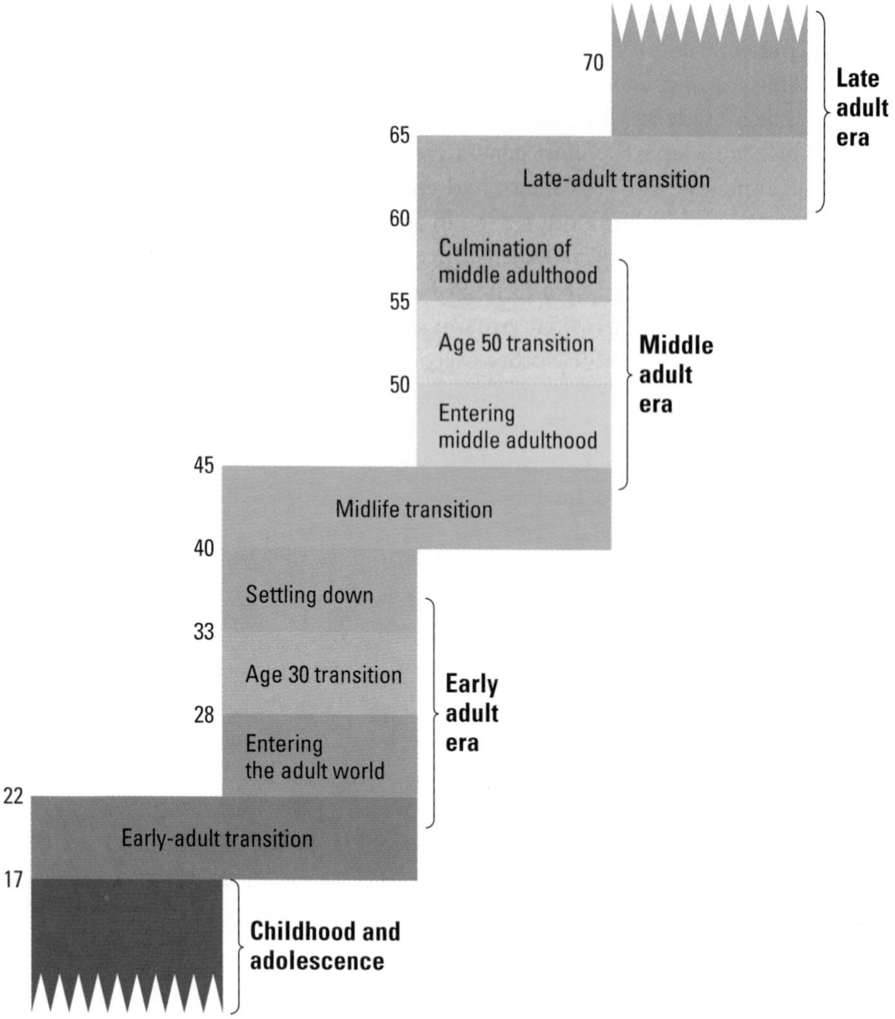

Figure 11.14 Levinson's "seasons" of the life cycle Levinson theorizes that there are four eras in a person's life (pre-, early, middle, and late adulthood) and that each is preceded by a potentially stressful period of transition.

[Drawing by Cline; © 1993 The New Yorker Magazine, Inc.]

"We're pushing forty. Shouldn't we have a house, or something?"

As Neugarten proposed, adults are guided in their development by culture- and generation-specific "social clocks."

they have taken and realize that the dreams of their youth are slipping away. Levinson described the early forties as a time when many men and women experience a midlife crisis. The final transition to late adulthood begins between sixty and sixty-five. Levinson only speculated about this era, but others have found that the period can prove gratifying to those who are healthy and active. Edwin Shneidman (1989) interviewed a group of male professionals in their seventies and found that they had a very positive outlook on life until their eighties. The same has been found in older women (Holahan, 1988). In the seasons of life, says Shneidman, the seventies are like "an Indian Summer."

Critical Events of Adulthood Erikson, Levinson, and other age-and-stage theorists believe that adults change in predictable ways and that these changes are linked to chronological age. But in light of the diversity of lifestyles across cultures and within a culture, which often lead people to take different developmental paths, others believe that the course of adult development is influenced by critical *events*—regardless of the age at which they occur. So what are these events? Ask people about turning points in their lives, and they inevitably mention starting school, graduation, their first job, getting married, having children, moving from one home to another, the death of a loved one, health changes, and world events (Ryff, 1989). As counselor Nancy Schlossberg put it, "Give me a roomful of 40-year-old women and you have told me nothing. What matters is what transitions she has experienced. Has she been 'dumped' by a husband, fired from her job, just had a breast removed, gone back to school, remarried, had her first book published? It is what has happened or not happened to her, and not how old she is that counts" (quoted in Rosenfeld & Stark, 1986, p. 69).

For certain milestones, timing can be critical. According to Bernice Neugarten (1979), people are sensitive to the ticking of a **social clock**—the set of culturally shared expectations, known to us all, concerning the best age for men and women to leave home, marry, start a career, have children, retire, and complete other life tasks. Social clocks differ from one culture to the next and from one generation to the next. In the 1950s, for example, most Americans believed that men and women should marry between the ages of nineteen and twenty-four and should start a career between twenty-four and twenty-six. Yet today, it's seen as more appropriate to attend college, then marry and settle down at a later age. In Neugarten's view, social clocks provide us with a developmental guideline, and people who are "out of sync" (for example, those who leave home too late or marry too young) will experience more stress than those who are "on time."

Not only are expected transitions important, but the fickle finger of fate can alter the course of development in profound and unanticipated ways. In a paper on the psychology of *chance encounters,* Albert Bandura (1982) noted that life paths are often turned by fortuitous events—as when a student is inspired to choose a career by a professor whose class happened to meet at a convenient hour or when a talented young athlete is permanently injured and sidelined by a hit-and-run driver. My own children delight in pointing out how they owe their lives to my graduate-school roommate: Had he not invited a crowd of his friends over one night, I would not have escaped the house, stumbled into a dance, and met their mother. These kinds of events cannot be anticipated, but autobiographers reflecting on the course of their own lives are often struck by the powerful influence of these chance encounters (Handel, 1987).

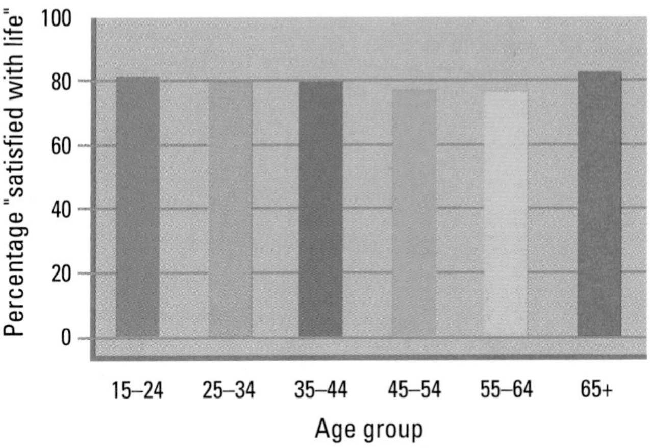

Figure 11.15 As shown, ratings of life satisfaction do not vary with age (Inglehart, 1990).

Life Satisfaction How happy are you today, compared to when you were fifteen? How satisfied with life do you expect to be in twenty-five years? And what about others: Do you think men and women in general are happier at twenty, forty-five, or seventy? As we saw earlier, adolescence is not inevitably filled with storm and stress. But consider other common assumptions: Are the twenties and thirties carefree and exciting? Do people in their forties suffer through a wrenching midlife crisis? Are the fifties calm and leisurely? Do the autumn years of retirement ring in sadness and depression? Recent studies cast new light on many of our beliefs.

Surveys of thousands of people around the world have shown that 75 to 80 percent say they are satisfied with life—and this percentage does not vary appreciably with age (Inglehart, 1990). As illustrated in Figure 11.15, this similarity across the life span is interesting, and perhaps a bit surprising, for two reasons. First, there's no evidence whatsoever for the turbulent midlife crisis popularized by Levinson, no

social clock A set of cultural expectations concerning the most appropriate ages for men and women to leave home, marry, start a career, have children, and retire.

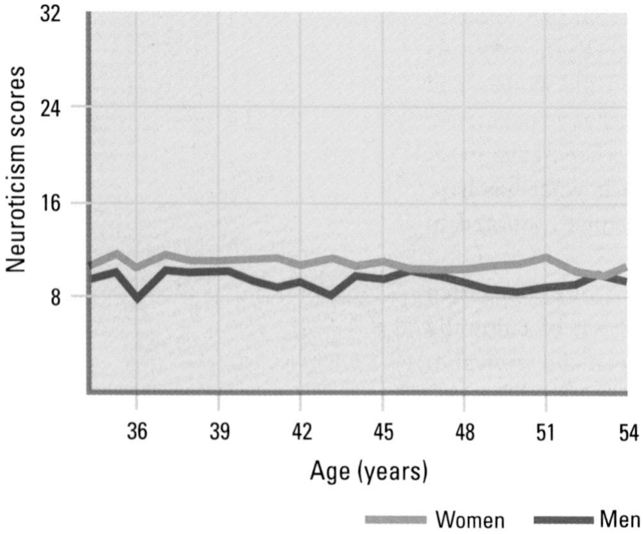

Figure 11.16 The myth of a "midlife crisis" Some 10,000 adults filled out a questionnaire that measured emotional instability. As shown, neither males nor females peaked during the supposedly turbulent forties (McCrae & Costa, 1990).

dip in satisfaction in middle age. In fact, the rates of divorce, marital discord, job change, admission for psychiatric care, and suicide do *not* increase among adults who are in their forties (Hunter & Sundel, 1989). To probe the matter further, Robert McCrae and Paul Costa (1990) administered to 350 men, thirty to sixty years old, a "Midlife Crisis Scale" that measured feelings of emptiness, inner turmoil, mortality, confusion, and unhappiness with job and family. Scores did not peak, or even show a blip, in the midlife forties. Next, they administered a questionnaire that measured anxiousness to 10,000 men and women, half of whom were between thirty-four and fifty-four years old. Again, as illustrated by the flat curve shown in Figure 11.16, there was no age at which men or women peaked in anxiousness—no sign of the so-called midlife crisis. Let's be clear about what these results mean. Clearly, we have ups and downs as we move through life. But the downs are not more likely to occur in our forties than in our twenties, thirties, fifties, or sixties.

The second "surprise" is that life satisfaction does not decline later in life, which is a blow to the stereotypic image of the elderly as sad, demoralized, and chronically worried. Although it's true that people have more medical problems as they age, older people are not as a group more prone to complain about their health, say they are distressed, or fall into a state of depression (Aldwin et al., 1989; Kessler et al., 1992; Newmann, 1989). In one cross-sectional study, for example, people ranging from twenty to ninety-eight years old were asked how often they suffered depressive symptoms such as crying spells, loneliness, loss of appetite, a lack of energy, and interpersonal problems. As shown in Figure 11.17, depression scores decreased from young adulthood to the middle and later years, and they did not rise again until the late seventies (Gatz & Hurwicz, 1990).

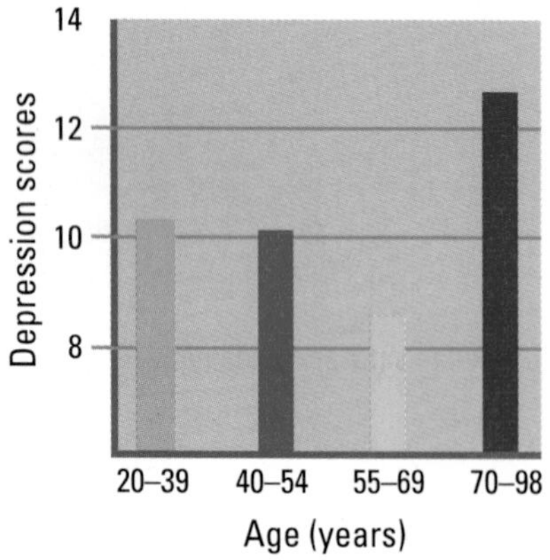

Figure 11.17 Are older people more depressed? People from twenty to ninety-eight years old indicated how often they had depressive symptoms. The scores decreased from young adulthood to the middle and later years, and they did not climb again until people approached eighty years old (Gatz & Hurwicz, 1990).

You might wonder why life satisfaction remains stable as we get older. Most psychologists agree that the recipe for subjective well-being contains two main ingredients: *love* and *work*. What's interesting is that these aspects of life are like some bottles of wine—they seem to get better with age. To be sure, every individual's life path is unique. Some people get married; others do not. Some are promoted at work; others get laid off. But there are general tendencies. At home, for example, marital satisfaction tends to decline when a young couple first has children (Belsky & Pensky, 1988) and continues to drop until the kids leave home, at which point husbands and wives report *increasing* levels of happiness (White & Edwards, 1990). Having children is an enriching experience, and parents initially are saddened by the departure of their last child—the so-called empty-nest syndrome. But raising a family is also a stressful experience that drains time, energy, and money from a marriage. So relationships are often strained when the nest is full and rejuvenated when it is empty. Job satisfaction also follows an upward pattern later in life—as people consistently report their highest levels of job satisfaction in late adulthood, before retirement (Rhodes, 1983; Warr, 1992). As people get older, they often advance to higher positions, get paid more money, and feel more committed to their work. In short, life satisfaction has more to do with the state of one's life at home and on the job than with chronological age.

Dying and Death

Humans are probably the only animals who know they are going to die or think about what it means. Many Westerners view death as a transition point in which the body ceases to exist but a soul lives on. Hindus and Buddhists believe in reincarnation. Still others view death as a final parting, period. The ways in which death is viewed, the intense emotions it elicits, how it is talked about, how dying people are treated, and how the dead are mourned all vary from one person, time, and culture to the next (Kearl, 1989).

Whatever their beliefs, people try to find ways to cope with the experience of dying and the terrifying prospect of their own demise. After interviewing hundreds of terminally ill patients, psychiatrist Elisabeth Kübler-Ross (1969) proposed that when people know they're dying, they pass through five stages in the coping process: (1) *denial* of their terminal condition ("It's not possible, it must be a mistake"); (2) *anger* and resentment, often directed at physicians and family members ("Why me? It isn't fair!"); (3) *bargaining* for more time ("God, let me live longer, and I'll be virtuous"); (4) *depression* accompanied by crying and refusal to see visitors ("Now I've lost everything I ever cared for"); and finally (5) *acceptance* of one's fate, often marked by a sense of peace and calm ("Oh well, what has to be, has to be").

Kübler-Ross's observations offer a glimpse at some of the ways in which people cope with dying. Not everyone passes in sequence through all the stages, however, and the experience can be quite different from one person to the next. Some patients struggle until the bitter end, while others accept their fate with quiet resignation (Kalish, 1981; Shneidman, 1984). For that reason, Kübler-Ross's stages should not be taken too literally. It may be reassuring for family members and friends to know that irrational denial and anger are common reactions, but it's also important to respect the uniqueness of the process. When a dying patient lashes out in anger or bursts into tears of depression, these feelings should be treated with sensitivity, not dismissed as signs of a person "just going through a stage."

The psychology of dying and death is fascinating but not well understood. We know that psychological factors such as a "will to live" can influence the timing of a person's death. For example, older people are more likely to die in the weeks that follow their birthday or another meaningful symbolic event than in the weeks that precede it (Phillips & Feldman, 1973; Phillips et al., 1992). It's not clearly understood how the will to live affects biological functions. We also know, as a result of recent interviews with 200 terminally ill patients, that about half occasionally wish for death, that about 10 percent seriously want to die, and that these desires are triggered most by depression, pain, and a lack of family support (Chochinov et al., 1995). Currently, three out of four Americans support a terminal patient's right to die. In addition, a growing number are preparing a living will, a legal document that asserts the right "to be allowed to die and not be kept alive by medications, artificial means, or heroic measures" (Shapiro, 1997; Van Biema, 1997). Finally, we know that at least some people who are pulled from the jaws of death and revived at the last moment report having extraordinary "near-death experiences" complete with soft music, visions of spirits separating from the body, traveling through a dark tunnel with a light at the end, meeting deceased friends and relatives, and so on. But we don't know if these reports are sheer fabrications or if they are the product of hallucinations induced by drugs, high fever, a gradual loss of oxygen, or a flood of endorphins washing over the brain (Siegel, 1980). For each of us, the mystery may be solved only by experience. Still, many psychologists feel that it's important to understand the process of dying in order to know "how death can serve life" (Feifel, 1990).

[Drawing by H. Martin; © 1991 The New Yorker Magazine, Inc.]

"Thornton, now that the children are grown and gone let's adopt a highway."

There is a widespread assumption that parents become lonely and despondent when the nest is empty, but there's no evidence to support this belief.

In Mali, in West Africa, the dead are buried in six-week-long communal funerals that are held only once every twelve years. In this ceremony, the bodies are tightly wrapped in cloths, hauled up a 300-foot cliff by rope, and put in burial caves that have been used for this purpose since the fifteenth century. The goal is to chase the collective spirits of the dead back to the afterworld.

Perspectives on the Life Cycle

Reflecting on this chapter, what are the positive ways to describe the aging process—and what are the negative? In what ways do people become very different with age, and in what ways do they stay basically the same?

This medieval painting by Hieronymus Bosch depicts a bright light-filled tunnel, a common vision in near-death experiences.

In this chapter, we have seen that biological, cognitive, and social development continues across the entire life span. Adolescence is not a mere extension of childhood but a time of rapid change—puberty, the capacity for sophisticated moral reasoning, identity formation, new relationships with parents, peer influences, and the onset of sexuality. Then come the various stages of adulthood and old age. Far from being one long and flat developmental plateau, these years are like a landscape filled with rolling hills, winding roads, peaks, and valleys. Physically, humans are in their prime at the age of thirty, then lose speed, power, sensory acuity, strength, and endurance. Cognitively, there are two courses of development. A small but steady decline occurs in mental speed, in the ability to recall new information, and in fluid intelligence. Yet autobiographical memories do not fade, and both crystallized intelligence and wisdom are relatively stable, if not incremental, with age. On the social front, the trajectories of development are more difficult to plot because they are influenced more by critical life events, social expectations, and chance encounters than by chronological age. The one pattern that remains clear is that life satisfaction peaks in late adulthood and doesn't diminish until we are very old, nearing death.

Buried underneath all the documented changes is an important detail—support for the expression that "the more things change, the more they stay the same." There is a recurring controversy in developmental psychology over the extent to which personal traits are stable or mutable over the course of life. It turns out that both conclusions are accurate. As we get older, biological, cognitive, and social changes will inevitably occur. We'll get slower, for example, and possibly wiser. Yet in other respects we are the same person today as we were ten years ago, and we will remain that person another ten years from now. Children who are well adjusted as adolescents are more likely than those with problems to be cheerful in adulthood (Block, 1981). Likewise, longitudinal studies have revealed that among those who are shy, smart, outgoing, anxious, calm, impulsive, conscientious, or open-minded, their relative standing on these attributes will also stay basically the same. In other words, individuals who are more withdrawn or outgoing than most of their peers at one point in their adulthood are likely to remain so when they are older.

> *"We do not count a man's years until he has nothing else to count."*
>
> — RALPH WALDO EMERSON

There's one last point worth making about continuity and its relationship to how old we feel. I know someone in his fifties but going on seventy, and someone else who is in his forties going on eighteen. It's often said that age is a state of mind. Indeed, there is some truth to this statement. Chronology may provide us with a rough measure of adult development, but as we saw in the study that opened this chapter, *subjective age*—that is, how old we feel—is, in some ways, as psychologically important as how old we really are.

Summary and Key Terms

For years, developmental psychologists have debated the question of stability versus change—whether characteristics evident early in life remain essentially the same as a person ages. It's true that early years are formative in some ways, but development is a lifelong process.

Adolescence

Adolescence is a transition from childhood to adulthood that corresponds roughly to ages thirteen to twenty in our society.

Biological Development

Adolescence begins with **puberty,** the onset of sexual maturation marked by rising levels of sex hormones and rapid growth. For girls, puberty brings **menarche,** the first menstrual period. Cultural practices and the timing of menarche influence a girl's reaction. Those who reach puberty early face embarrassment, adjustment problems, and a poor body image. For boys, puberty brings **spermarche,** the first ejaculation, as well as growth of the sexual organs and other physical changes. For boys, early maturation is a positive experience.

Cognitive Development

Adolescence is also a time of rapid cognitive growth. Entering what Piaget called the formal operational stage, teenagers begin to think critically and abstractly. In **moral reasoning,** they show more flexibility in interpreting rules than they did as children.

According to Kohlberg, moral reasoning develops in three stages: preconventional, conventional, and postconventional. But some critics see both cultural and gender bias in this theory, while others question how moral reasoning relates to behavior. Scores on Kohlberg's reasoning tasks correlate only modestly with prosocial behavior, and young children can act morally without the sophisticated reasoning. Children's morality is based on **empathy** for others. As illustrated by the recent controversy concerning euthanasia, or assisted suicide, people often confront moral dilemmas in legal contexts.

Social Development

An adolescent's struggle to establish a personal identity, or self-concept, is called an **identity crisis.** In an ethnically diverse society like the United States, finding one's personal identity can involve establishing an ethnic identity as well.

Young adolescents typically experience a rise in tension with parents characterized by bickering and disengagement from family activities. At the same time, peer relationships become more important. In early adolescence, peer pressure creates a tendency toward conformity, which can have both positive and negative effects. Sexuality is a natural part of adolescent development, but it can sometimes bring confusion and harmful consequences. American adolescents are sexually more active today than two generations ago, but they need greater knowledge of the risks and use of contraceptives.

Adolescence and Mental Health

Severe emotional distress is not more common among adolescents than among adults. Nevertheless, unhappy teenagers often become maladjusted adults, so parents should not dismiss mental-health struggles as just a passing stage.

Adulthood and Old Age

Biologists agree that each species has a maximum possible **life span,** which is greater than its average **life expectancy.** Among humans, the life expectancy varies across cultural and ethnic groups. In addition, women consistently outlive men.

Biological Development

The number of brain cells diminishes steadily after birth. Muscle strength and reflexes peak at about age thirty, then decline; also at that age, metabolism begins to slow, so that people tend to gain weight. For women, middle age brings **menopause,** the end of menstruation and fertility but without psychological effects. For men, there's only a gradual decline in fertility after adolescence, but no abrupt end.

When people are in their sixties and seventies, the aging process accelerates. The senses decline sharply, and the bones, joints, and immune system begin to deteriorate. Yet Langer's experiment suggests that a youthful state of mind can slow the rate at which people exhibit the symptoms of old age.

Cognitive Development

Aging need not mean cognitive decline. Autobiographical memories, for instance, survive into old age. Although experiments show an age-related decline in ability to free-recall new material, there is no comparable decline in recognition performance. The memory problems that do exist are largely due to a general slowing of neural processes. Older people also lack confidence needed for short-term memory tasks.

Dementia, a disorder resulting in severe cognitive damage, strikes 10 percent of the elderly population. The most common cause is **Alzheimer's disease (AD)**, which progressively destroys brain cells, causing memory loss and other symptoms.

Studies show that **fluid intelligence**, the ability to reason logically and abstractly, declines steadily in middle and late adulthood. However, **crystallized intelligence**, reflecting the accumulation of skills and factual knowledge, remains relatively stable over the life span. Similarly, mental speed decreases with age, but wisdom—the ability to solve practical problems—does not. Finally, although older workers find it harder to learn new skills, objective measures of job performance do not decline with age.

Social Development

Theorists such as Erikson and Levinson have described adulthood in terms of distinct stages. In this view, the stages are linked to chronological age, and the transitions produce stress. Other theorists believe that social development has less to do with age than with critical events such as marriage and having children. The **social clock** sets the expected times when major life events should occur. People are also influenced by fate in the form of chance encounters that change a person's life.

Despite prevailing stereotypes, recent research has found no evidence for a turbulent midlife crisis or demoralization of the elderly. Life satisfaction remains stable with age and depression rates decrease, at least until the very late years. The critical ingredients—love and work—both seem to improve with age.

Dying and Death

Kübler-Ross proposed five stages that people go through in coping with the knowledge of impending death: denial, anger, bargaining, depression, and acceptance. However, not everyone experiences these stages. Factors such as the will to live and near-death experiences remain a mystery.

Perspectives on the Life Cycle

Overall, research on human development suggests both stability and change. Biological, cognitive, and social changes do occur as people age. But on measures of many personal traits, people keep the same standing relative to their peers.

In the Field Resources

Books

Kotre, J., & Hall, E. (1990). *Seasons of life: Our dramatic journey from birth to death.* Boston: Little, Brown.

This nicely written book reports on psychological theories and studies on the topic of lifespan development—from the first day to the last.

Films and Videos

City Slickers (1991, 108 min)

This poignant comedy is about three male friends coming upon middle age who feel stuck in a rut. Searching for more, they vacation together at a ranch and gain fresh perspectives on their lives (Billy Crystal, Daniel Stern, Bruno Kirby, Jack Palance, Helen Slater, Patricia Wettig.)

The Breakfast Club (1985, 95 min.)

This film about five teenagers together for detention depicts the storm-and-stress of adolescence, identity formation, peer and parent relations, and sexual activity. (Emelio Estevez, Judd Nelson, Molly Ringwald, Anthony Michael Hall, Ally Sheedy.)

Internet

Adult Development & Aging—Division 20 (http://www.iog.wayne.edu/apadiv20.htm)

Provides information for professionals and others interested in adult development, a newsletter, student organization, and links to related sites on aging.

Alzheimer's Association (http://www.alz.org/)

Provides medical and research information, addresses for local chapters, a reading list, and caregiver resources.

Journals and Periodicals

Child Development
Developmental Psychology
Journal of Youth and Adolescence
Psychology and Aging

Telephone and Mail

Youth Crisis Hotline (1-800-448-4663)

12 *Intelligence*

INTELLIGENCE TESTS

The Stanford-Binet
The Wechsler Scales
Group Aptitude Tests
Are Intelligence Tests Accurate?
Are Intelligence Tests Biased?

THE NATURE OF INTELLIGENCE

General Intelligence
Gardner's "Frames of Mind"
Sternberg's Triarchic Theory

THE GREAT DEBATES

Nature and Nurture
Group Differences
Sex Differences

EDUCATION

Giftedness
Mental Retardation
The Self-fulfilling Prophecy

PERSPECTIVES ON INTELLIGENCE

The situation Just about everyone is curious about intelligence and the tests that are used to measure it. Most of the tests were created early in the twentieth century, and since then IQ scores have been used to determine academic potential in schools throughout the world. Hmm. The fact that people have been taking IQ tests for many years—and that you may have taken a test very similar to one taken by your parents and grandparents—raises a fascinating question: Have scores changed over time? Are people today more or less smart than a few years ago, or is human intelligence too stable a trait to change in so short a time?

What's Your Prediction?

Are people smarter today than in the past?

Being trained in psychology, you're accustomed to conducting experiments, often in the laboratory. To answer the question about IQ trends across generations, however, you'll need to use different methods. You'll need to gather old scores from IQ tests that were taken at different times by comparable groups of people. So you contact researchers all over the world and ask if they would send you test scores that have been compiled over the years. In particular, you want scores from tests that were never altered and were given to large groups of adults of different generations. You receive the data you need from a number of developed countries, including Australia, Austria, Belgium, Brazil, Canada, China, France, Germany, Great Britain, Israel, Japan, the Netherlands, New Zealand, Norway, Switzerland, and the United States. Now it's time to analyze the results.

Make a prediction As we'll see shortly, IQ tests are set so that the average score in the population is always 100. This means that if raw scores were to rise or fall over time, the scale would have to be readjusted like a thermostat in order to keep that average. The question is, what has happened to *raw scores* over the past seventy or so years? To make your prediction, look at Figure 12.1 and use the year 1920 as a starting point. Based on 1920 standards, which set the average IQ at 100, what do you think the raw, nonadjusted scores were in 1930, 1940, and other decades up to 1990? Has IQ steadily increased over time, decreased, fluctuated in response to historical events, or stayed essentially the same? Think carefully about the problem. Then, using

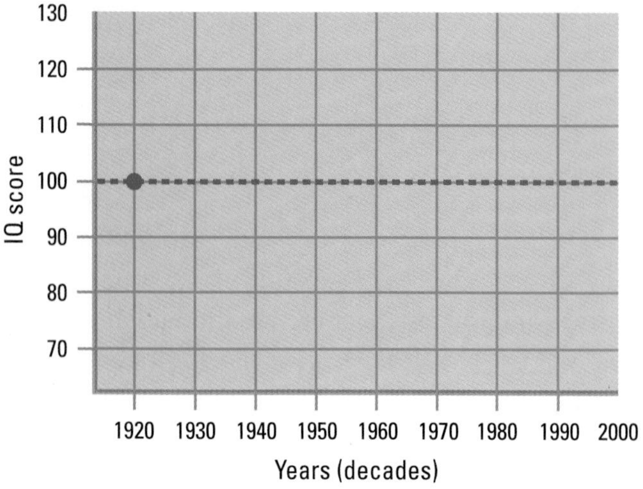

Figure 12. 1 Your predictions

Figure 12.1, plot your predicted trend for each decade before looking at the actual results.

The results When James Flynn (1987) first compiled the IQ scores in fourteen developed nations (he then added six more), the worldwide trend was unmistakable. Look at Figure 12.2 and you'll see that from one generation to the next, without exception, there have been steady and massive gains in IQ scores—so much so that today's average adult scores twenty-four points higher than in 1920. Named after its discoverer, this phenomenon is now known as the Flynn effect.

What does it all mean? For years, psychologists have hotly debated the nature of intelligence, the validity of standard IQ tests, and the extent to which being smart is the product of nature or nurture. Flynn's discovery that IQ scores have risen sharply over the years has provoked new discussion of these core issues. Is it possible that IQ has risen but that "intelligence" has not? What does the rise in IQ over such a short period of time imply about the genetic basis for intelligence? And what environmental factors could have caused the increase—could it be more time spent in school, parents with more education, better nutrition, or exposure to radio, TV, and computers? As we'll see in this chapter, the subject of intelligence is fascinating, complex, and frequently controversial.

Brace yourself, take a deep breath, and try to answer the following questions: How many miles apart are New York City and Los Angeles? In what ways are a lion and tiger alike? What does the word *disparate* mean? Why is copper used in electric wires? Now read the following series of numbers and, without taking a second look, try to repeat it backwards: *4 7 5 2 8 6*. If these questions seem familiar, it's because they are like those that are widely used to measure intelligence. The faster and more accurate you are, the higher your "IQ" will be. But what is an IQ, and what does the score mean? This chapter examines the controversial subject of human intelligence—what it is, how it's defined, how it's measured, the debates it has sparked, and the implications it has for educational policy. As we'll see, this facet of human development raises many profound, challenging questions (Neisser et al., 1996; Sternberg, 1994).

"Intelligence consists in recognizing opportunity."

— CHINESE PROVERB

Let's start with a definition: What really is intelligence? In 1921, fourteen prominent psychologists and educators were invited to answer this question, and they came up with fourteen different definitions, such as "the ability to carry on abstract thinking," "the capacity to learn or profit by experience," and "the capacity to acquire capacity" (Thorndike et al., 1921). How do these sound to you? When commuters, supermarket shoppers, and college students were handed a blank sheet of paper and asked to write down the characteristics of intelligence, they produced a long list of traits, including: reasons logically, makes sound decisions, sizes up situations well, speaks fluently, reads widely, is an expert on a particular subject, has many good ideas, accepts others for what they are, has an interest in world events, and thinks before speaking (Sternberg et al., 1981).

Clearly, the term **intelligence** means different things to different people. In fact, it's important to realize that your definition is influenced by the culture and generation in which you live. Many students I talk with are impressed by the combination of speed and general knowledge that enables contestants on TV game shows like *Jeopardy!* to win large sums of money. For some South Pacific islanders, however, intelligence is defined by one's ability to navigate the ocean from one island to the next. For the Kalahari Bushmen in Africa, it means having the skills needed for productive hunting and gathering. For gang members of an inner city, "street smarts" is what matters most. To accommodate the many ways in which people all over the world exhibit their intelligence, many psychologists prefer to define the concept in general terms, as *a capacity to learn from experience and adapt successfully to one's environment.*

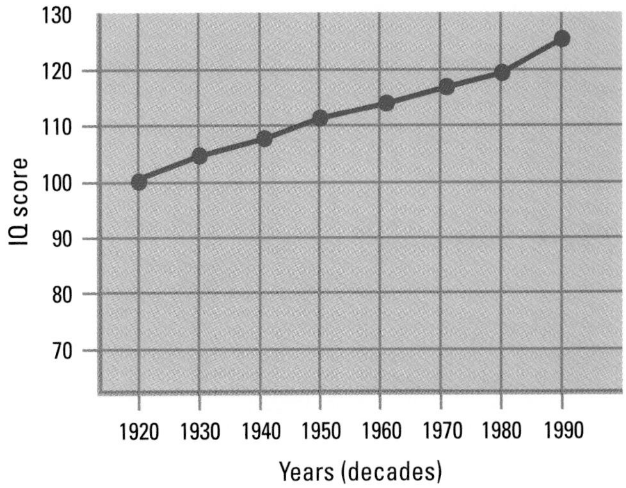

Figure 12. 2 The actual results

Intelligence Tests

What is intelligence, and why is it measured? What does *IQ* stand for, and how are IQ tests constructed? Are these tests accurate? Why do some people believe that the tests are biased?

The study of intelligence began with the instruments used to measure it. Like much of psychology, intelligence testing is long on tradition but short on history. About 4,000 years ago, the Chinese used civil-service exams to measure aptitude. But it was not until the end of the nineteenth century that modern forms of assessment were born. The first psychologist to devise such "mental tests" was Francis Galton (1883), Charles Darwin's cousin. Noticing that great achievements run in families like his own, Galton believed that intelligence was inherited. Like it or not, he said, all men and women are *not* created equal. Taking a page from Darwin's book on evolution, Galton went on to suggest that if intelligence could be objectively measured, then the normally slow processes of "natural selection" and "survival of the fittest" could be hastened through selective-breeding policies in which only the brightest of adults are encouraged to reproduce.

How did Galton measure intelligence? If you had visited the Chicago World's Fair in 1883 or London's International Health Exhibition in 1884, you could have been one of thousands to find out. For a small fee, a technician using Galton's state-of-the-art equipment would measure your muscular strength; the size of your head; your speed at reacting to signals; your ability to detect slight differences between two weights, lights, and tones; and other biologically rooted abilities. Afterward, you would receive an intelligence score printed on a card (Johnson et al., 1985). Galton's measures are intriguing, but by today's standards they are crude and without validity. Indeed, Galton noted that bright, accomplished adults did *not* get

intelligence The capacity to learn from experience and adapt successfully to one's environment.

*There are many conceptions of intelligence. One is to associate it with the kind of general knowledge that is needed to play—and win—*Jeopardy! *Intelligence can also be defined as the capacity to adapt to one's environment. Micronesians and other South Pacific islanders define intelligence in part by the ability to navigate long distances using information from ocean currents and the stars.*

higher-than-average test scores. What's worse, his elitist proposal for increasing the native intelligence of the human species through selective breeding laid the groundwork for what would become a bumpy road for the intelligence-testing movement that followed (Weinberg, 1989).

The Stanford-Binet

Across the English Channel, French psychologist Alfred Binet sought to measure intelligence for humane reasons: to enhance the education of children needing special assistance. In 1904, a few years after a law was passed requiring all French children to attend school, the Minister of Public Instruction hired Binet to develop an objective means of identifying children who would have difficulty with normal classwork. With the help of Theophile Simon, Binet (1905) developed a test that contained questions on problem solving, numbers, vocabulary, logical reasoning, general knowledge, and memory—the kinds of skills that are necessary in an academic setting. Binet and Simon wrote hundreds of questions, administered them to students in Paris, and recorded the average performance of children at different ages. Questions for the test were retained if answered correctly by an increasing number of children from one grade level to the next.

Once the test was complete, questions were arranged in order of increasing difficulty and administered by someone trained to score and interpret the results. Assuming that children develop in similar ways but at different rates, Binet and Simon used their test to determine a student's **mental age,** the average age of children who pass the same number of items. In other words, the average ten-year-old would have a mental age of ten. Those who are exceptionally bright would have a mental age that is higher (like an average older child), while those who are slow to develop would have one that is lower (like an average younger child). Practically speaking, mental age was a convenient way to score a child's intelligence because it suggested an appropriate grade placement in school.

mental age In an intelligence test, the average age of the children who achieve a certain level of performance.

After Binet died in 1911, the scale was translated into English and imported to the United States by Stanford University psychologist Lewis Terman (1916). The age norms in California were different from those in Paris, so Terman revised many of the questions, added items suitable for adults, published a set of American norms, and gave the test a new name, the **Stanford-Binet.** This test was then revised three more times (in 1937, 1960, and 1986). The most recent, the Stanford-Binet IV, contains fifteen subtests for use between the ages of two and twenty-three, takes about an hour to administer, and is still being used today. Ironically, Binet's work was barely known in France until the Stanford-Binet caught on in the United States. In 1971, sixty years after Binet's death, he and Simon were honored by a commemorative plaque installed at the school in Paris where it all began.

Back at Stanford, Terman was busy developing tests that could be administered in groups (including the popular *Stanford Achievement Test*), theorizing about the roots of intelligence (he favored nature over nurture as an explanation), and initiating a massive longitudinal study of gifted children (to be discussed later). Yet his most notable contribution was the concept of **IQ**, which stands for **intelligence quotient.** Basing his concept on an idea first offered by German psychologist William Stern, Terman proposed that performance on the Stanford-Binet be converted to a single score—a ratio derived by dividing mental age (MA) by the person's chronological age (CA), then multiplying the result by 100 to eliminate the decimal point. The concept is elegantly simple, yet powerful: $IQ = (MA / CA) \times 100$. Using this formula, you can see that people who are average (that is, those whose MA and CA are exactly the same) have an IQ of 100. A ten-year-old child with an MA of twelve has an IQ of 120, while a twelve-year-old with an MA of 10 has an IQ of 83.

Although IQ is a convenient way to represent a child's intelligence, it makes little sense for adults. The problem is that mental age does not continue to increase with chronological age but levels off as we get older. An average ten-year-old may be two MA years ahead of the average eight-year-old, but you can't really say the same for

Materials used in the Stanford-Binet.

Stanford-Binet An American version of Binet's intelligence test that yields an IQ score with an average of 100.

intelligence quotient (IQ) Originally defined as the ratio of mental age to chronological age, it now represents a person's performance relative to same-age peers.

someone who is twenty rather than eighteen or thirty rather than twenty-eight. When you consider specific examples, you can see that the results are ludicrous: If at eighteen you get the same score as the average thirty-six-year-old, your IQ would be 200; but if at thirty-six you had the same score as an average eighteen-year-old, your IQ would be 50. The solution was to drop Terman's quotient and assign IQ-like scores based instead on a person's performance *relative to the average of their same-age peers.*

In schools and other settings, the WISC is the most widely used individually administered IQ test for children.

The Wechsler Scales

Galton, Binet, and Terman all developed tests that reduced intelligence to a single score. But is that necessarily the most informative approach? David Wechsler (1939) didn't think so, so he constructed a test for adults that considers different aspects of intelligence. Wechsler's test has eleven subscales grouped within two major scales—one yielding a *verbal* score, and the other a nonverbal *performance* score useful for people who have language problems. He improved the test in 1955 and called it the **Wechsler Adult Intelligence Scale,** or **WAIS** (the test was revised again in 1981 and abbreviated WAIS-R). He also created similar tests for different age groups. For children six to sixteen years old, there is the *Wechsler Intelligence Scale for Children* (WISC III), and for preschoolers there is the *Wechsler Preschool and Primary Scale of Intelligence–Revised* (WPPSI–R).

Because the IQ scale was so deeply ingrained in public consciousness, Wechsler kept the same scoring system, setting the average at 100. Keep in mind, however, that if you took the WAIS, you would get three separate scores—one verbal, one performance, and the total (the most recent version of the Stanford-Binet also yields more than one score). To appreciate the kinds of skills measured on the test, try the questions in Figure 12.3. You'll notice that the verbal items call for comprehension, arithmetic, vocabulary, general information, analogies, and the ability to recall strings of digits. In contrast, the items in the nonverbal performance scale ask you to find missing picture parts, arrange cartoons in a logical sequence, reproduce block designs, assemble pieces of a jigsawlike puzzle, and copy symbols on paper. Today, Wechsler's scales are used more often in schools and clinics than any other individually administered tests (Lubin et al., 1984). Short forms are sometimes used as well, in which only certain subtests or certain items are sampled (Silverstein, 1990).

Group Aptitude Tests

The Stanford-Binet and the Wechsler scales are used to test one person at a time and take about an hour to administer. This procedure enables the examiner to interact with the test taker and observe whether he or she has trouble with instructions, loses attention, gets frustrated, or gives up too quickly. The disadvantage is that individualized tests are not practical for quick, large-scale assessment. During World War I, for example, the United States military needed an efficient way to screen recruits for service. With help from psychologists, two group tests were developed and administered to 1.7 million men—the Army Alpha Test, given in writing to those who could read English; and the Army Beta Test, given orally to those who could not (Lennon, 1985).

Wechsler Adult Intelligence Scale (WAIS) The most widely used IQ test for adults, it yields separate scores for verbal and performance subtests.

Today, group testing is a regular part of our lives. You are no doubt familiar with the Scholastic Assessment Test (SAT), a national rite of passage that many have

VERBAL SCALE

General Information
How many hours apart are Eastern Standard and Pacific time?

Similarities
In what way are boats and trains alike?

Arithmetic Reasoning
If eggs cost 96 cents a dozen, what does 1 egg cost?

Vocabulary
What does the word "procrastinate" mean?

Comprehension
Why do people buy automobile insurance?

Digit Span
Listen carefully to the following numbers. When I am through, I want you to repeat the numbers backwards: 4 8 7 5 2.

PERFORMANCE SCALE

Picture Completion
I'm going to show you a picture with an important part missing. Tell me what's missing:

Block Design
Using the sixteen blocks on the left, make the pattern shown on the right:

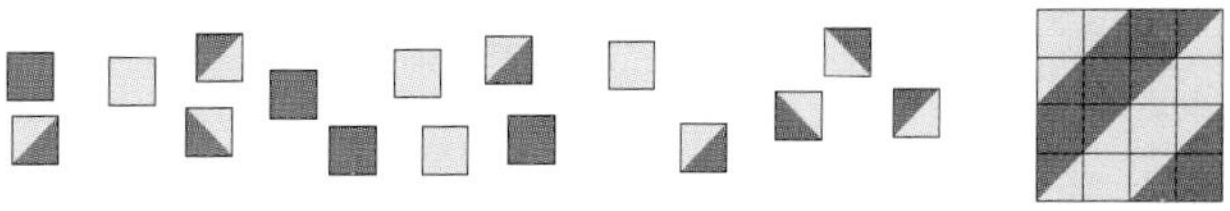

Object Assembly
If these pieces are put together correctly, they make something. Put them together as quickly as you can:

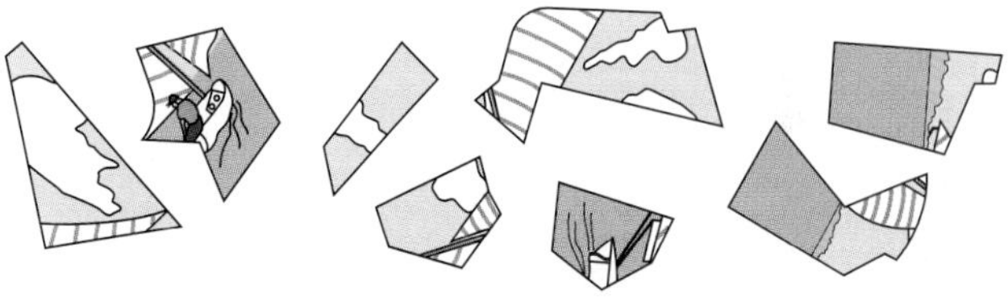

Picture Arrangement
The pictures tell a story. Put them in the right order to tell the story:

Coding
As quickly as you can, put the appropriate code symbols in the blank spaces:

Code

●	□	★	△	⫽
1	2	3	4	5

Test

3	5	2	4	1	2	4	3	5	2	1	4	3	5

Figure 12.3 Simulated items similar to those in the WAIS

learned to fear. The SAT is a grueling two-and-a-half-hour college entrance exam taken by more than a million college-bound seniors every year. The test, as introduced in 1926, was designed to measure both verbal and mathematical reasoning in a multiple-choice format. Now referred to as SAT-I, this test was revised in 1994 to include math questions that call for write-in answers (students can now use calculators), sentence-completion vocabulary items, and an increased emphasis on critical reading (see Figure 12.4). In addition, a number of SAT-II subject tests are available to assess knowledge of specific sciences, social studies, literature, and languages. The SATs are designed to supplement school grades as an objective predictor of academic performance. Instead of or in addition to the SAT, many students take the American College Test (ACT), a rival exam developed in 1939 that tests abilities in English, math, reading, and science reasoning. Comparable tests are also used to screen applicants for advanced education. If you choose to go on to graduate school, you'll have to take the Graduate Record Exam, or GRE. Similarly, for specialized professions, you would take the Medical College Admission Test (MCAT), the Law School Aptitude Test (LSAT), or the Graduate Management Admission Test (GMAT).

Underlying all these exams is the assumption that they measure academic *aptitude,* a potential for learning. Psychologists have hotly debated the extent to which this aptitude is influenced by innate potential as opposed to specific experiences at home and in school. For colleges and universities that use these tests for admissions purposes, the issue is irrelevant so long as the test scores can help to predict performance in college. But for students planning to take these exams, this issue has great practical relevance. Students want to know: Can you significantly boost your score by taking a six-week SAT-preparation course? Some ads have claimed that such courses can raise a student's total score by 100 points or more (DePalma, 1991).

Verbal

1. Choose the word or phrase that is most nearly *opposite* in meaning to the word in capital letters.

   WILT: (a) prevent (b) drain (c) expose (d) revive (e) stick

   [93 percent correctly answered d]

   GARNER: (a) disfigure (b) hedge (c) connect (d) forget (e) disperse

   (26 percent correctly answered e)

2. The question below consists of a related pair of words followed by five lettered pairs of words. Select the lettered pair that *best* expresses a relationship like that expressed in the original pair.

   SCOFF: DERISION (a) soothe : mollification (b) slander : repression (c) swear : precision (d) stimulate : appearance (e) startle : speediness

   [21 percent correctly answered a]

3. An accurate assessment of this shore community's _____ is complicated by the _____ migrations of part-time residents.

   (a) age...historical
   (b) revenue...negligible
   (c) geography...regional
   (d) population...seasonal
   (e) environment...predictable

   ANSWER: d

Mathematical

1. If $x^3 + y = x^3 + 5$, then $y =$
   (a) -5 (b) $-\sqrt[3]{5}$ (c) $\sqrt[3]{5}$ (d) 5 (e) 5^3

   [93 percent correctly answered d]

2. In the figure below, one side of the square is a diameter of the circle. If the area of the circle is *p* and the area of the square is *s*, which of the following must be true?

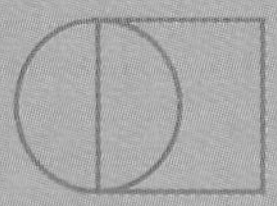

   I. $s > p$ II. $s \ngtr p$ III. $s < p$
   (a) None (b) I only (c) II only (d) III only (e) I and II

   [45 percent correctly answered b]

3. If the average of four numbers is 37 and the average of two of these numbers is 33, what is the average of the two other numbers?

   ANSWER: 41

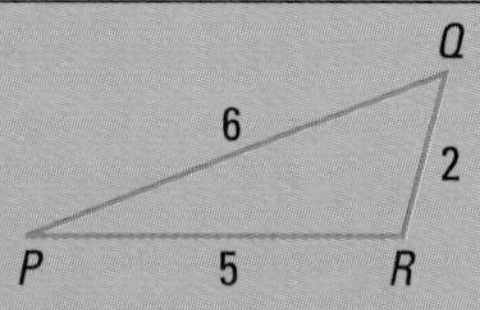

4. In Δ *PQR* above, point *S* (not shown) is on *QR* between *Q* and *R*. Grid in one possible value for the length of *PS*.

   ANSWER: 5.1

Figure 12.4 Sample items from the Scholastic Assessment Test (SAT)

According to the College Board, which administers the SAT, however, the test measures "developed abilities" acquired from an accumulation of life experiences both inside and outside the classroom (Donlon, 1984). Supporting this position is research showing that cramming for the SAT or taking a crash course can increase scores by an average of only 30 to 50 points on the 400–1600 scale. Claims of additional improvement are inflated by the fact that students who take SAT-preparation courses are generally motivated, more likely to practice on their own, and more likely to take the test a second time—which itself tends to raise scores (Kulik et al., 1984; Powers, 1993).

[Drawings by M. Twohy; ©1991 The New Yorker Magazine, Inc.]

"You're kidding! You count S.A.T.s?

Are Intelligence Tests Accurate?

Every year, millions of dollars are spent on intelligence testing. But what is the bottom line? Are the tests "accurate"? To answer this question fully, it's important to know that all psychological tests—including those designed to measure intelligence—must have three ingredients: standardization, reliability, and validity (Anastasi, 1988).

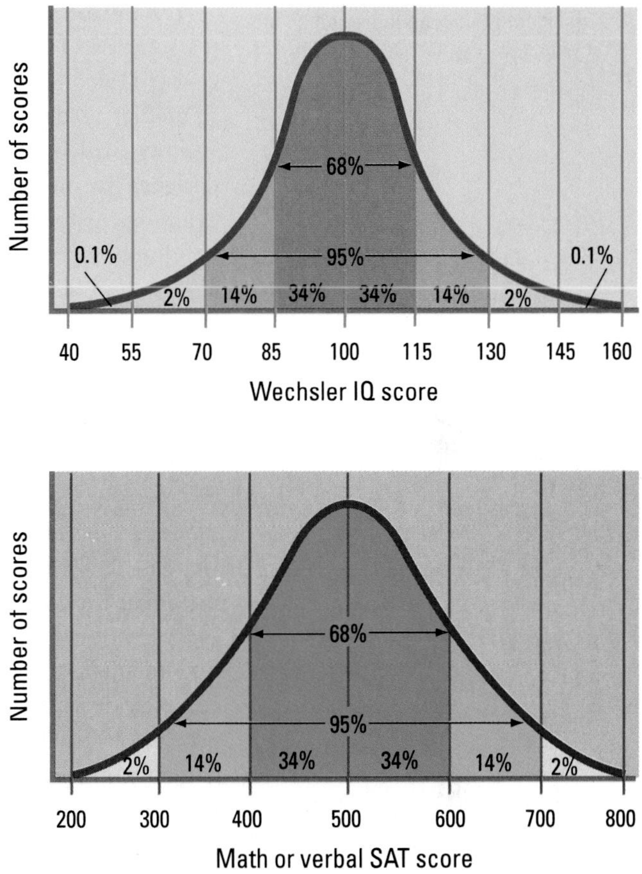

Figure 12.5 Distribution of scores on the WAIS and SAT

Standardization means that a test provides a standard of existing norms that can be used to interpret an individual's score. Suppose you took a 150-item SAT and then received a letter indicating that you had correctly answered 115 of the questions. How would you feel? Would you celebrate your success or lament your failure? As you can see, a raw score does not provide you with enough information. To interpret the number, you need to compare it to the performance of others. Standardization is achieved by administering a test to thousands of people similar to those for whom the test is designed. In the case of the Wechsler scales, the average was arbitrarily set at 100, with test scores distributed in a normal, bell-shape curve where roughly 68 percent of all scores fall between 85 and 115, 95 percent fall between 70 and 130, and 99 percent fall between 55 and 145. The SATs were first standardized in 1941, using a sample of more than 10,000 college-bound students. The verbal and math scores were each put on a scale ranging from 200 to 800, with their averages set at 500. In any case, regardless of whether a test's average is set at 100, 500, or 12 million, your *raw score*—the sheer number of correct answers—must be converted into a standardized *test score* that reflects the distance between your performance and the norm (see Figure 12.5).

The second ingredient is **reliability,** the consistency of a test's results. Two types of consistency are sought. One is **test-retest reliability,** the extent to which a test yields similar results on different occasions. Just as you would not trust a bathroom scale that shows moment-to-moment fluctuations in your weight, psychologists would not trust an IQ test that shows radical changes from one session to the next. Intelligence is thought to be a relatively stable trait, not one that varies much over a short period of time. To ensure that a scale has test-retest reliability, researchers test the same subjects on two occasions—say, a month or two apart—and calculate

standardization The procedure by which existing norms are used to interpret an individual's test score.

reliability The extent to which a test yields consistent results over time or using alternate forms.

test-retest reliability The degree to which a test yields consistent results when readministered at a later time.

"You can't build a hut, you don't know how to find edible roots and you know nothing about predicting the weather. In other words, you do *terribly* on our IQ test."

the correlation between their test and retest scores. The higher the correlation, the more reliable the scale.

The second kind of consistency is **split-half reliability,** the extent to which different forms of a test produce similar results. If you had two bathroom scales of the same brand and model, you would expect them to provide identical estimates of your weight. Likewise, alternate forms of an IQ test (often created by dividing it into odd and even items) should produce similar results. Using the test-retest and split-half methods, it's clear that the Stanford-Binet, WAIS, and SAT are reliable measures, all yielding correlations of about +.90. In fact, a study of 23,000 college seniors applying for graduate school showed a very high correlation of +.86 between their scores on the GRE (an exam much like the SAT) and their SAT performances four or more years earlier (Angoff, 1988).

The third essential ingredient is **validity,** a test's ability to measure or predict what it's supposed to. IQ tests may yield consistent scores, but do they indicate intelligence? Do college entrance exams measure aptitude? Better yet, are these tests able to predict academic success? Two kinds of validity are necessary. The first is **content validity,** which means that test items should adequately measure what they are designed to measure. Just as a science exam has science questions and a history exam has history questions, an IQ test should contain items that correspond to our definitions of intelligence. The second kind of validity is **criterion validity,** a test's ability to predict a concurrent or future outcome. For intelligence tests, the bottom line is the prediction of academic achievement.

Are IQ tests valid? It depends on what it is you're trying to predict. If the goal is to assess *academic performance,* then the tests pass with flying colors, particularly in the earlier school years. In elementary school, there is a high correlation among IQ, class grades, and achievement-test scores. There is a somewhat lower correlation between SAT scores and performance in college, but the combination of high-school grades and SAT scores is highly predictive of a student's grade-point average (Jensen, 1980; Linn, 1982). However, if the goal is to predict achievement in nonacademic walks of life, then IQ tests are more limited in their validity. Some psychologists believe that although these tests assess academic performance, they do not adequately measure the ability to adapt to life outside the classroom. The complex decisions made by successful corporate executives, the mental arithmetic used by hurried supermarket shoppers, and the handicapping strategies used by gamblers at a racetrack are all instances of practical, real-world intelligence unrelated to IQ (Sternberg et al., 1995).

Are Intelligence Tests Biased?

When Binet and Simon (1905) constructed their scale, they were trying to identify slow learners for placement in special classes. It soon became clear, however, that IQ tests can too easily be used as an instrument of prejudice and discrimination. One of the darkest episodes in psychology's history occurred just prior to World War I when immigrants from overseas arrived at Ellis Island, in the shadow of the Statue of Liberty. Just off the boat and exhausted from their long journey, the new arrivals were immediately tested—and in English, a language many of them could barely understand. Lo and behold, psychologist Henry Goddard (1917) concluded from the results that European Jews, Italians, Russians, and Hungarians were far less intelligent than the average American. Sadly, claims like this one fueled prejudice and contributed, at the time, to the passage of laws designed to restrict immigration.

Critics charge that intelligence tests are culturally biased, in that they favor some social groups over others. To the extent that a test calls for specific cultural knowl-

split-half reliability The degree to which alternate forms of a test yield consistent results.

validity The extent to which a test measures or predicts what it is designed to.

content validity The extent to which a test measures what it's supposed to measure.

criterion validity The extent to which a test can predict a concurrent or future outcome.

edge, it *is* biased. That's why Terman had to "Americanize" Binet's French test. But what about IQ testing in the United States, where Americans don't all share a common cultural heritage? Consider an issue that has deeply troubled many psychologists. Ever since intelligence tests were first administered, African Americans as a group have averaged 15 points lower than whites on IQ tests and 100 points lower on the SAT verbal and math tests (Jensen, 1994). Nobody disputes the fact that the difference exists. But disagreements arise as to what it means and what the social implications are.

Later, we'll see that there are many possible reasons for this difference. But for now, we'll examine one criticism in particular: that the question content within the tests favors the cultural and educational experiences of the white middle class (Garcia, 1981; Miller-Jones, 1989). If you take the Stanford-Binet or Wechsler test, for example, you may be asked: What is the color of rubies? What does C.O.D. mean? Who was Thomas Jefferson? To answer these questions, one needs to have knowledge of the dominant culture. It's also important to realize that a person's racial and ethnic background can also guide his or her perception of the testing situation, understanding of the task instructions, motivation to succeed, trust in the examiner, and other aspects of the experience (Helms, 1992). There are many subtle ways in which test scores can be influenced by a person's background—independent of his or her intelligence.

Advocates of IQ testing have replied to this criticism in two ways. The first is that group differences are found even on test items deemed "culture-fair" (see Figure 12.6)—namely, nonverbal items that do not require extensive knowledge of a particular culture, tasks such as reciting a series of letters or digits, classifying objects, forming a pattern with blocks, or putting together the pieces of a picture puzzle (Cattell, 1949; Raven et al., 1985). Second, intelligence and aptitude tests are statistically valid predictors of academic performance within a particular culture, the purpose for which they were designed—regardless of whether students are African American, white, Hispanic, or Asian (Kaplan, 1985).

Test bias has been debated not only in the laboratory but also in the courtroom (Elliott, 1987). In the 1979 case of *Larry P. v. Wilson Riles,* the parents of six African American students in San Francisco claimed that the school had harmed their children by placing them in "dead-end" classes for the educable mentally retarded (EMR), placements influenced by the results of IQ tests culturally biased against African Americans. To bolster their case, these parents pointed out that 27 percent of all EMR children in the state of California were African American, even though as a group they constituted only 10 percent of the school population. On the opposing side, the school board maintained that IQ tests were administered only to students who had already fallen behind and that the tests were valid—that is, they were predictive of the academic performance of African American children as well as whites. The trial lasted six months, generated 10,000 transcript pages, and included testimony from more than fifty witnesses, most of them psychologists. In the meantime, a nearly identical dispute reached center stage in the Chicago case of *P.A.S.E. v. Hannon* (1980). Once again, African American parents argued that IQ tests administered to their children were biased, local school officials defended the measures, and experts testified on both sides.

Mirroring the disagreements within psychology (Snyderman & Rothman, 1987), the judges in these two cases reached opposite decisions. In San Francisco, the judge concluded that IQ tests were culturally biased and banned their use in the California schools for placement purposes—ironically the very reason they were designed. Yet the Chicago judge concluded from the same evidence that intelligence tests are not discriminatory and that they offer a valid way to place children in

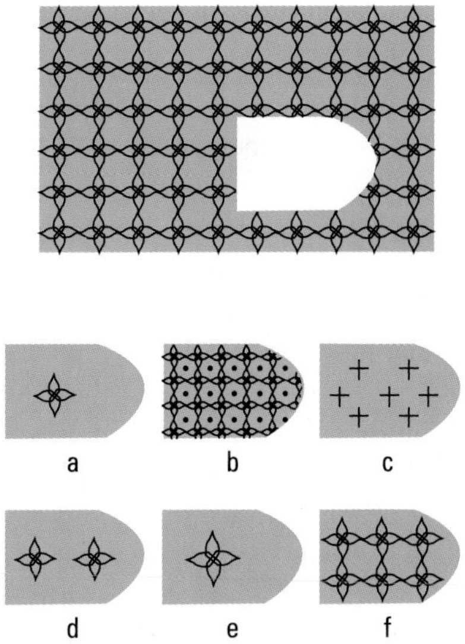

Figure 12.6 Sample item from Raven's "culture-fair" intelligence test In this test, the person is given a series of matrices and must complete each one by selecting the appropriate symbol from the accompanying choices.

appropriate classes. So are IQ tests culturally biased or not? To some extent, both sides are right. Disadvantaged minorities are handicapped on standardized measures, but they are also handicapped in the classroom. If IQ tests are culturally biased, it is precisely because they are meant to predict success in schools that are themselves part of the dominant culture. Thus, some experts have said that blaming IQ tests for reflecting society's problems is like killing the messenger who delivers the bad news. In this regard, there may also be some good news. In the most recent version of the Stanford-Binet, the race difference was 10 to 13 points, not 15, as in the past (Thorndike et al., 1986).

INTERSECTION

INTELLIGENCE AND EDUCATION

The Controversy Over Cultural Literacy

In December 1996, the schoolboard in Oakland, California, voted to recognize Black English, or "Ebonics" (derived from *ebony* and *phonics*), as a second language for African American students. The decision set off a storm of controversy, particularly within the African American community and was eventually withdrawn. In fact, however, this issue is part of an ongoing debate over the question of how important it is for people to learn the lessons of the predominant culture in a society. Some say it's wrong for intelligence tests to include items that are "biased"—specific to the culture in which they are used. Yet in a controversial bestseller entitled *Cultural Literacy: What Every American Needs to Know,* E. D. Hirsch, Jr. (1987), argued that "cultural literacy"—knowing basic facts in such topics as science, politics, literature, art, history, entertainment, history, sports, and geography—is a key to success.

According to Hirsch, every culture has a vocabulary of shared information. All Americans, for example, should know something about Shakespeare, Cinderella, the three branches of government, DNA, Superman, Martin Luther King, Jr.'s "I have a dream" speech, evolution, the location of the Rocky Mountains, the Bible, the founder of communism, the Dallas Cowboys, and so on. It's important to know these facts not just to play board games like Trivial Pursuit but also to thrive on a day-to-day basis. Cultural literacy is something we take for granted. But Americans who lack this vocabulary will have difficulty understanding what appears in daily newspapers, magazines, and popular books, all of which assume that readers know certain facts common within the culture.

Citing experiments showing that people read passages faster and with greater comprehension when they are familiar with the names, places, and contexts referred to in those passages, Hirsch argues that cultural literacy is "the oxygen of social intercourse" and that society's disadvantaged are doomed to failure without it. The solution, says Hirsch, is simple: Schools must impart cultural information to all students. Several years ago, the U.S. Department of Education concluded, in a report entitled *America's Challenge* (1990), that because American students are poorly informed about basic subjects, they are not adequately prepared for life in the twenty-first century. At the heart of this issue, however, are some controversial questions: Who's to say what core knowledge is essential? In a pluralistic nation such as ours, what people, places, and events belong in culture's dictionary? What are the "basics" that you would include? For ideas, consider some items presented in a paperback book entitled *Test Your Cultural Literacy* (Zahler & Zahler, 1993).

1. If you "bury the hatchet," you
   a. Ignore an insult.
   b. Spend too much money.
   c. Hide the evidence of a crime.
   d. Make peace.

2. The area that became Israel in 1948 was formerly known as
   a. Palestine. c. Syria.
   b. Jordan. d. Arabia.

3. How is AIDS transmitted?
   a. By contact between skin and skin.
   b. By exchange of body fluids.
   c. By bacterial infection.
   d. By an airborne virus.

4. An economic recession is a period of
   a. High spending.
   b. Low business activity.
   c. High prices.
   d. Increased production.

5. A silicon chip is part of a
   a. Floppy disk.
   b. Microcomputer.
   c. Cassette.
   d. Teleprinter.

6. What is the Koran?
   a. The ark in which the Jewish holy book is kept.
   b. The church built over Christ's tomb in Jerusalem.
   c. The name for Moses's Ten Commandments.
   d. The holy book of Islam.

7. In the case of *Brown v. Board of Education of Topeka,* the U.S. Supreme Court ruled that
   a. Public schools must be desegregated.
   b. Official school prayers were illegal.
   c. Children could not work in factories.
   d. Teenage girls could not get abortions.

8. Look at the map of Europe presented below. Which labeled section is Great Britain?
   a I.
   b. II.
   c. III.
   d. IV.

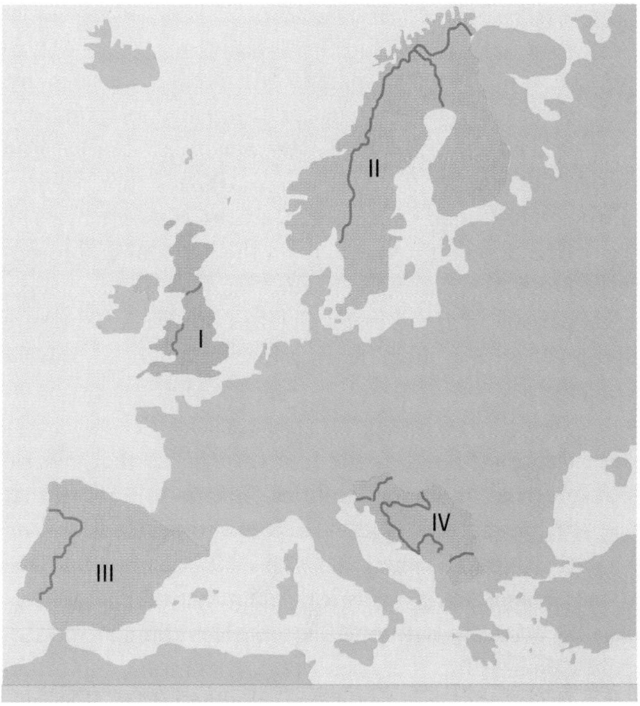

9. Who painted the portrait shown below?
   a. Rembrandt.
   b. Picasso.
   c. Leonardo da Vinci.
   d. Michelangelo.

10. What building is shown in the picture below?
    a. Mount Vernon.
    b. The White House.
    c. The Capitol.
    d. Monticello.

The correct answers are 1(d), 2(a), 3(b), 4(b), 5(b), 6(d), 7(a), 8(a), 9(c), and 10(c).

The Nature of Intelligence

Why do some psychologists believe that intelligence is a single general ability? Can a child's IQ be predicted in infancy? Can intelligence be "seen" in the brain? Why do some psychologists believe that there are multiple human intelligences? How do analytic, creative, and practical intelligences differ?

From the beginning, intelligence tests were constructed for strictly practical purposes—to identify slow learners in school, assign new military recruits, and select college applicants. Unfortunately, the initial emphasis on tests and measurements may have stunted the growth of theories concerning the very nature of intelligence—what it is, where it comes from, and how it is developed. As one psychologist put it, "Intelligence is whatever an intelligence test measures" (Boring, 1923).

One of the most unsatisfying aspects of IQ tests is that they reduce intelligence to a single uncomplicated number. But does that number tell a rich enough story about any person's intellect? For me, it certainly does not. I can write a decent sentence, I have more inventive research ideas than I can manage, I can hold my own in a game of Trivial Pursuit, and I can cut to the heart of a logical argument in a matter of seconds. But I can't for the life of me solve a Rubik's Cube, I have a lousy sense of direction, and it takes an embarrassing amount of time for me to assemble the pieces of a child's toy. It's amazing how a person can feel so smart and yet so dense all at once. The point is that you have to wonder whether a person's intelligence can really be summarized by a single IQ score or even by two scores, as in the WAIS and SAT.

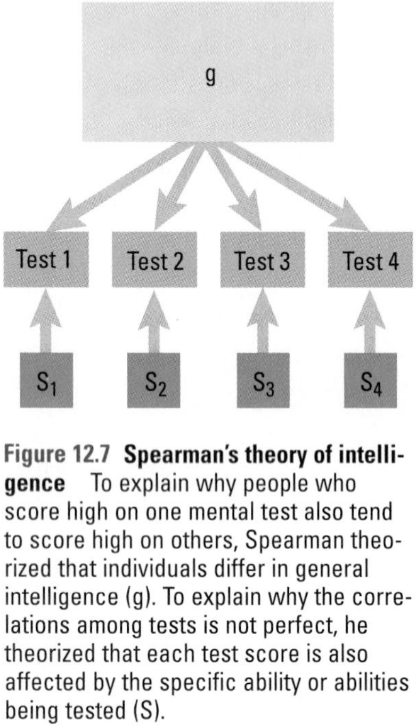

Figure 12.7 Spearman's theory of intelligence To explain why people who score high on one mental test also tend to score high on others, Spearman theorized that individuals differ in general intelligence (g). To explain why the correlations among tests is not perfect, he theorized that each test score is also affected by the specific ability or abilities being tested (S).

General Intelligence

Psychologists have long disagreed about whether there is one intelligence or many. Some theorists are "lumpers," who view different aspects of intelligence as part of a general underlying capacity. Others are "splitters," who divide intelligence into two or more specific abilities (Weinberg, 1989). Following in Binet's footsteps, all test developers make it a point to include many tasks and derive an IQ score by averaging a subject's performance on the different items. But is it then meaningful to calculate an average level of intelligence? Yes, according to the "lumpers"; some people are generally smarter and more capable than others, regardless of whether they are trying to program a computer, memorize a poem, learn a foreign language, solve a complex equation, or fix a car.

Factor Analysis Charles Spearman (1904) was the first to propose that **general intelligence** (abbreviated as g) underlies all mental abilities. Spearman noticed that people who excel at one task—say, verbal analogies—also tend to perform well on mazes, block designs, and other seemingly unrelated skills. To demonstrate the point, Spearman developed **factor analysis,** a statistical technique that is used to identify clusters of test items that correlate with one another. He administered different kinds of tests to subjects, calculated the between-item correlations, and found that although individuals may be more skilled in some areas than in others, the intellectual abilities are highly correlated. This pattern suggests that there is a general intelligence factor, g, that underlies our more specific abilities (see Figure 12.7). As far as Spearman was concerned—and many others as well—an individual's intelligence can, at least in a general way, be summarized by a single IQ score (Eysenck, 1982; Jensen, 1992; Carroll, 1993).

general intelligence (g) A broad intellectual-ability factor used to explain why performances on different intelligence-test items are often correlated.

factor analysis A statistical technique used to identify clusters of test items that correlate with one another.

Infant Measures and IQ One intriguing source of evidence for the concept of general intelligence comes from infancy-research laboratories. Until just a few years ago, psychologists had tried but failed to devise infant "intelligence tests" that could predict performance later in life. The age at which babies smile, turn the head toward a voice, inspect their fingers, track moving objects with their eyes, or start babbling, for example, are not related to measures of intelligence taken later in their early childhood (Bayley, 1949).

Thanks to the added sophistication that today's researchers bring to the study of infants, it's now possible to make modest predictions about intelligence from certain types of behavior. Specifically, recent longitudinal studies have shown that three- to six-month-old infants who are responsive to changes in a stimulus—as measured by their tendency to look more at stimuli that are new and different rather than old and familiar—score higher on standard IQ tests in early and middle childhood (Bornstein, 1989; Colombo, 1993; McCall & Carriger, 1995; Dougherty & Haith, 1997). These results—coupled with the fact that children's performance on preschool intelligence tests are even more predictive of IQ scores obtained in high school—suggest that a common ability may underlie the different measures of performance.

Neural Speed and Efficiency A second source of evidence is derived from research that equates general intelligence with mental speed and efficiency. Studies have shown that people with high IQs on standardized tests are quicker than average (in milliseconds) on a range of perceptual and cognitive tasks—such as inspecting stimuli, reacting to flashing lights, matching letters, solving certain types of problems, and retrieving general information from memory (Hunt, 1983; Vernon, 1987; Kranzler & Jensen, 1989; Deary & Stough, 1996).

These findings have led some researchers to claim that intelligent people are equipped with a nervous system that relays signals rapidly—thus enabling them to learn quickly and accumulate more knowledge. In fact, recent experiments have shown that neural transmission in certain parts of the brain is faster and more efficient in people with higher IQ scores. For example, Edward Reed and Arthur Jensen (1992) showed male college students black-and-white patterns while monitoring electrical activity in the visual pathway of their brains. In each subject, they recorded the average latency, or amount of time, it took for the brain to react once the stimulus was presented. Then they divided that figure by the length of the subject's head to get a more precise estimate of the speed at which neural impulses were conducted. The result: Those with quicker neural reactions also had higher scores on a written test of intelligence (see Figure 12.8).

Taking a somewhat different perspective, Richard Haier and others (1992) reasoned that intelligence could be defined by the efficient use of mental energy. Using PET scans to measure the rate at which the brain metabolizes glucose, they had subjects play Tetris, a computer game that requires moving and rotating variously shaped objects to create solid rows of blocks. They found that subjects with higher intelligence-test scores exhibited less energy use in the brain areas activated during this spatial task. They also found that subjects who were given daily practice with Tetris showed a decrease over time in glucose metabolism. Although more experimentation is needed, these initial findings suggest that people who are accomplished can work quickly and with less effort. As this evidence mounts, there is speculation that, in the future, it may be possible to devise neurological measures of intelligence (Matarazzo, 1992; Vernon, 1993).

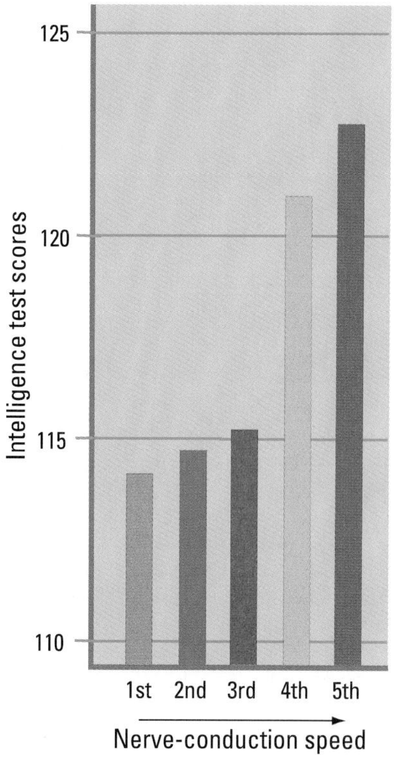

Figure 12.8 Neural speed and intelligence Reed and Jensen (1992) recorded the time it took for each subject's brain to react to visual stimuli, then ordered the subjects from the slowest (1) on this measure to the fastest (5). As you can see, the faster subjects also had higher scores on a written test of intelligence.

Multifactor Models Shortly after Spearman uncovered g, Louis Thurstone (1938) administered fifty-six different tests to college students, used factor analysis

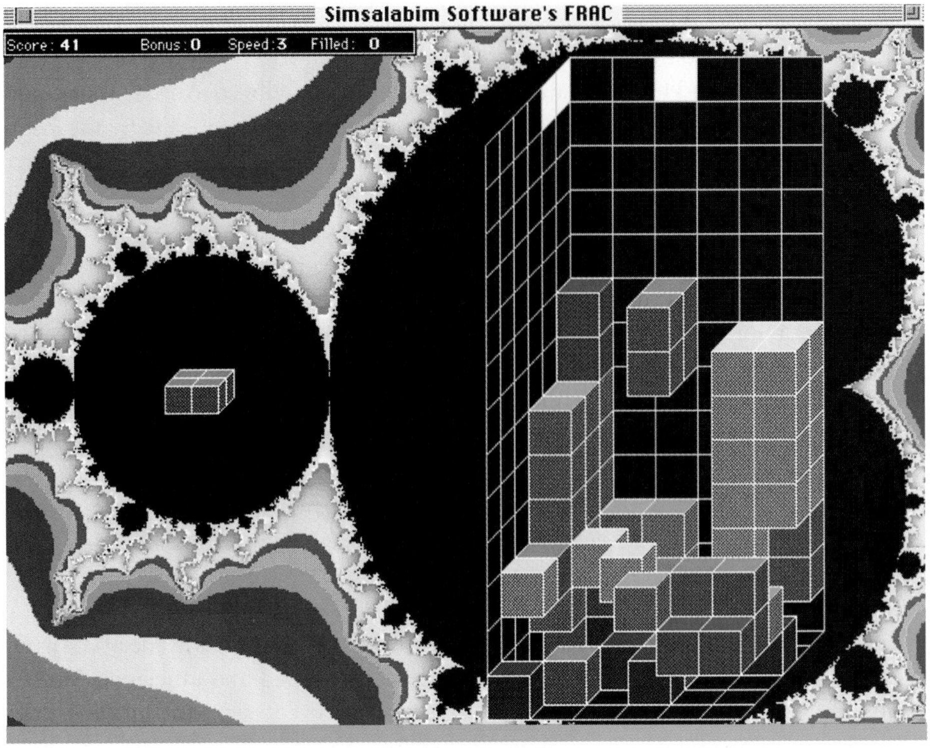

In computer games modeled after the original Tetris, players use spatial skills to rotate and orient different squared shapes to create a solid block.

to analyze the results, and concluded that human intelligence consists of seven factors, which he called primary mental abilities. For Thurstone, a person's intellectual profile cannot be captured by a single number. Other researchers agree with this emphasis on specific abilities but disagree on how many. John Horn and Raymond Cattell (1966) and Paul Kline (1991) said that there are two types of intelligence. J. P. Guilford (1967) believed that intelligence consists of 120 different factors—a number he later increased to 150 (Guilford, 1985).

At this point, research provides evidence for both a general intelligence and specific abilities. Scores on the eleven WAIS subscales are correlated (those who do well on one subscale also tend to do well on others)—evidence for a general intelligence. At the same time, it's not unusual for someone to score high on some of the subscales and low on others, as the correlations are far from perfect (usually in the .30 to .70 range)—evidence of separate mental abilities. So what does an IQ score tell us about the nature of intelligence? Were Albert Einstein, Jane Austen, and King Solomon similarly able individuals, or is that like comparing apples, oranges, and cherries? Many psychologists now believe that there's more to intelligence than IQ scores derived from paper-and-pencil tests. Two recent theories offer a broader view.

Gardner's "Frames of Mind"

multiple intelligences Gardner's theory that there are seven types of intelligence (linguistic, mathematical, spatial, musical, bodily-kinesthetic, interpersonal, intrapersonal).

In his 1983 book, *Frames of Mind,* Howard Gardner presents provocative evidence for the existence of **multiple intelligences,** each linked to a separate and independent system within the human brain. Gardner's main point is simple but revolutionary: The word *intelligence* is too narrowly used to describe cognitive abilities and does not adequately encompass the kinds of genius found in great musicians, poets, orators, dancers, athletes, and inspirational leaders all over the world. When basketball star Michael Jordan soars gracefully toward a hoop, evading blockers, and shooting with remarkable precision, isn't he exhibiting a form of intelligence? Can't the same be said about Stephen King, the horror novelist who makes readers tremble with his masterful use of language? And what about Martin Luther King, Jr., the civil-rights leader who stirred millions of Americans with his speeches and inspired massive social change?

Like a detective searching for fingerprints, smoking guns, and other clues, Gardner used converging lines of evidence to marshal support for his theory. He studied brain structures, diverse cultures, evolution, child development, and individuals with exceptional abilities—in other words, not just IQ tests. For example, the existence of **prodigies** (children who are normal in general but are highly precocious in a specific domain) and **idiot savants** (people who are mentally retarded yet are extraordinarily talented in some way) tells us that it's possible to have one kind of intelligence and lack another. Similarly, brain-damaged patients who lose certain abilities but retain others tell us that different intelligences can be traced to autonomous systems in the brain. In all, Gardner proposed that there are seven types of intelligence: linguistic, logical-mathematical, spatial, musical, bodily-kinesthetic, interpersonal, and intrapersonal. The first three fit easily within existing conceptions of intelligence. The last four represent a radical departure from tradition.

1. ***Linguistic intelligence*** is a verbal aptitude that is rooted in the auditory and speech centers of the brain and consists of the skills involved in speaking, listening, reading, and writing. Storytellers and poets who are sensitive to shades of meaning, syntax, sounds, inflections, and rhythm are linguistic geniuses. So are politicians, evangelists, and successful trial lawyers who know how to use language for persuasive purposes.
2. ***Logical-mathematical intelligence*** is the abstract reasoning skill necessary for solving puzzles and equations and programming computers. This form of intelligence blossoms early in childhood and is often displayed by "human calculators" who can perform rapid-fire mental arithmetic. In 1987, for example, an Indian woman named Shakuntala Devi stunned mathematicians by multiplying in her head two thirteen-digit numbers randomly dealt by a computer. It took her twenty-eight seconds to calculate the correct product: 18,947,668,177, 995,426,462,773,730 (*Guinness Book of World Records,* 1994).
3. ***Spatial intelligence*** is rooted in the right hemisphere of the brain and consists of the ability to visualize objects, find one's orientation in space, and navigate from one location to another (if you ever tried to find your way through a fun-house maze, you'll know the skill it takes). A Vietnamese refugee named Minh Thai was a spatial genius. He solved the Rubik's Cube, a highly complex three-dimensional puzzle, in twenty-three seconds—a world record. Great pilots, architects, mechanics, chess masters, and visual artists also exhibit spatial intelligence.
4. ***Musical intelligence*** is found in all cultures, has existed throughout history, flowers early in childhood, and involves an ability to appreciate the tonal qualities of sound, compose, and play an instrument. The concept of a "musical IQ" is supported by numerous case studies. The most prolific musical prodigy of all was Mozart, who learned to play a harpsichord at the age of three, composed at four, and performed in public at five. Then there's Noel Patterson, an autistic man with an IQ of 61 who can memorize melodies at the drop of a hat and play complex classical pieces by ear on the piano (Radford, 1990).

Tiger Woods was a prodigy in golf. At three years old (and with two years of experience), Woods scored a 48 in nine holes on a course in California. At fifteen, he was the youngest player ever to win a junior amateur title. At twenty he turned pro. At 21, he became the youngest golfer ever to win the coveted Masters Tournament—and broke the course record in doing so.

prodigy Someone who is highly precocious in a specific domain of endeavor.

idiot savant Someone who is mentally retarded but is extraordinarily talented in some ways.

According to Gardner, there are many types of intelligence. Working on metal sculpture, artist Richard Hunt uses spatial intelligence. Oprah Winfrey, who brilliantly combines linguistic and interpersonal intelligences, has been the most successful talk-show host for many years. Soaring toward the hoop, basketball legend Michael Jordan shows his extraordinary bodily-kinesthetic intelligence.

5. ***Bodily-kinesthetic intelligence*** is the ability to control the gross and fine movements of the body. This kind of ability is rooted in the motor cortex and probably evolved in humans for running, climbing, swimming, hunting, and fighting. This form of intelligence can be seen in the figure skater who varies the timing and speed of her jumps, flips, and spins with clocklike precision, and lands softly on the blade of her skate. It can also be seen in skilled dancers, athletes, and surgeons.
6. ***Interpersonal intelligence*** is the ability to understand other people—how they feel, what motivates them, what they like, and what they don't like. A person with these abilities can predict how others will act and, in turn, can interact smoothly. This form of intelligence can be found in successful politicians, salespersons, psychotherapists, and others with keen social skills. In *Leading Minds,* Gardner (1995) argued that great leaders have interpersonal intelligence.
7. ***Intrapersonal intelligence*** is the ability to have insight into one's own thoughts and feelings, to understand the causes and consequences of one's own actions, and, as a result, to make effective decisions. Self-insight is a highly adaptive form of intelligence.

Gardner's theory is controversial. Some psychologists agree that intelligence should be defined broadly enough to encompass musical genius, exquisite use of the body, and personal insight. Others feel that the theory stretches the concept too far. To his critics, Gardner says that there is nothing magical about the word *intelligence*—that to define it narrowly is to place cognitive and academic endeavors on a pedestal. The point is that all kinds of intelligence should be valued—on tests, in school, and in life. Whether you agree or not, Gardner has raised consciousness about what it means to have intelligence. Working in school systems, he also is exploring the implications of his theory for alternative, less standardized forms of education (Gardner, 1993). Still, further research is needed to evaluate his provocative ideas.

Sternberg's Triarchic Theory

"I knew exactly what our school psychologist looked like. Whenever she entered the classroom, I would panic: Her grand entry meant that we were about to take an IQ test, and the mere thought of it left me petrified. She was cold, impersonal, and as scary to me as the Wicked Witch of the West must have been to Dorothy. I really stunk on IQ tests" (quoted in Trotter, 1986, p. 56). Remarkably, this personal story is told by Robert Sternberg, now a psychology professor at Yale University and a leading expert on—you guessed it—intelligence.

Sternberg's initial poor performance piqued his curiosity about IQ tests. He overcame his test anxiety in the sixth grade, performed exceedingly well, and designed his own test of mental abilities as part of a science project. He then found a copy of the Stanford-Binet in a library book and administered the test to some of his classmates. The chief school psychologist found out and threatened to burn the book if Sternberg brought it back to class, so he didn't. After graduating from high school, however, Sternberg worked during summers as a research assistant at Educational Testing Service in New Jersey, home of the SAT. "Thus began my lifelong interest in intelligence. Call it the lure of the forbidden; or perhaps it was the experience of flunking those earlier tests. Whatever the impetus, my interest had been sparked, and it would continue throughout my life" (Sternberg, 1988).

In *The Triarchic Mind,* Sternberg proposed that there are three kinds of human intelligence: (1) analytic, (2) creative, and (3) practical. To bring this theory to life, Sternberg described three graduate students—Alice, Barbara, and Celia. *Alice* was smart by conventional criteria and was admitted to Yale as a top pick. She had an undergraduate grade-point average of 4.0, high scores on the GRE, and solid letters of recommendation. Yet Alice did *not* prove to be a strong graduate student. She did well enough on tests and was a sharp analytical thinker, but she lacked insight and could not generate creative research ideas. *Barbara* was different. Her GRE scores and grades were nothing to write home about, but her college professors raved about her insight and creativity. Barbara was not accepted into Yale, but Sternberg hired her as a research associate and found her exceptional: "Some of the most important work I've done was in collaboration with her," he said. *Celia* was the third student. Her grades, GRE scores, and letters were not the best, but they were good enough for admission. Celia lacked Alice's analytical ability and Barbara's creativity. Four years later, however, she was the most successful student on the job market. The reason: Celia had practical intelligence, or "street smarts." She did the kind of research that was in demand, sent her papers to the right journals, made the right contacts, and learned how to satisfy the requirements of her new profession. Like Barbara's creativity, hers was a form of intelligence that does not show up on IQ tests.

To summarize, Sternberg (1986, p. 62) has argued that there are different ways to be smart. "What you want to do is take the components (Alice's analytic intelligence), apply them to your experience (Barbara's creative intelligence), and use them to adapt to, select, and shape your environment (Celia's practical intelligence)." His **triarchic theory of intelligence** is depicted in Figure 12.9.

Analytic Intelligence

Alice's intelligence—what you might call school smarts—is characteristic of people who test well. Seeing intelligence in *analytic terms,* Sternberg and others have tried to understand how people answer the kinds of questions that regularly appear on traditional IQ tests—specifically, in terms of the mental steps or "components" they use to solve math problems, syllogisms, analogies, and so on.

What does it mean to process information intelligently? In our culture, as we have seen, it is common to equate intelligence with computerlike mental speed. Thus, smart people are often described as quick-witted and as fast learners. Indeed,

triarchic theory of intelligence Sternberg's theory that there are three kinds of intelligence: analytic, creative, and practical.

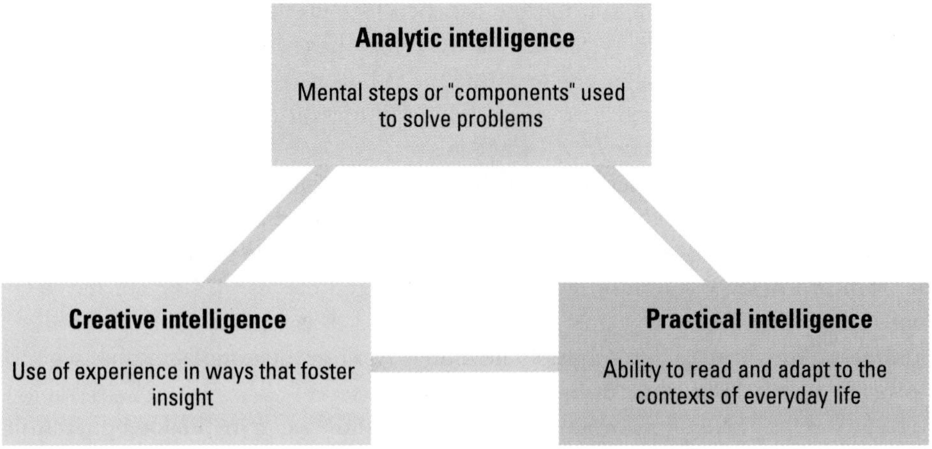

Figure 12.9 Sternberg's triarchic theory of intelligence

we saw earlier that people with high IQ scores respond quickly to various cognitive tasks. But Sternberg (1980) believes it's not that simple. He asked subjects to solve multiple-choice analogies such as "*Spouse* is to *husband* as *sibling* is to —— (father, brother, uncle, son)." To answer these kinds of questions, a problem solver must first *identify* the meaning of each term and then *compare* the terms to each other. In the sample problem, you have to recognize that *spouse* is a generic term for married person, that a *husband* is a male spouse, that *sibling* refers to persons born of the same parents, and so on. Next, you have to match what you know about these terms to each other. To separate the two components of this task, Sternberg put subjects through a timed two-step procedure. First, they read the question part of the analogy and pressed a button to signal when they were ready to move on. Next, they saw the multiple choices and pressed a button to select a response option. It turned out that subjects with higher IQ scores spent *more* time than others on the initial identification part of the task but were then quicker at making the necessary comparisons to find the answer. This study suggests that performance on complex thought tasks cannot be equated with sheer mental speed. People who excel on IQ tests seem to realize that the trick is to invest more time up front to comprehend the problem, then to pick up the pace (Galotti, 1989).

Creative Intelligence Barbara did not have classic academic school smarts, but she was gifted with a creative mind—the second facet of Sternberg's (1988) theory. According to the dictionary, **creativity** refers to "the mental processes that lead to solutions, conceptualizations, ideas, artistic forms, theories or products that are unique and novel" (Reber, 1985). To Sternberg, the key to creative intelligence is insight—an ability to know what information is relevant, find connections between old and new, combine facts that seem unrelated, and see the "big picture." It's certainly easy to come up with a list of creative geniuses who have used these skills in ways that have transformed our lives. Thomas Edison, who holds more than a thousand patented inventions, is an obvious choice. So are Rachel Carson (who pioneered the environmental movement in the United States), dancer-choreographer Martha Graham (who created a distinctive new style of modern dance), and Steve Jobs (the founder of Apple Computers, who first came up with the idea of making personal computers for the home).

creativity Intellectual and motivational processes that lead to novel solutions, ideas, artistic forms, or products.

Over the years, psychologists have tried to develop tests to measure our capacity for creative insight (Sternberg & Lubart, 1991). J. P. Guilford (1967) suggested that the critical factor is **divergent thinking,** the ability to think flexibly and to open the mind to a wide range of possible solutions. Several tests have been devised to measure divergent thinking. Guilford asked people to name as many uses as they could for common objects such as a brick. Skilled divergent thinkers came up with unconventional answers—use it to prop a door open, use it as a paper weight, break a window with it if you're locked out of the house, and so on. A second measure is the Symbolic Equivalents Test, in which people are asked to produce "symbolic equivalents" for various images. In response to the image of a candle burning low, for example, the divergent thinker is likely to imagine such analogous events as dying, a sunset, and water trickling down a drain (Barron, 1988). A third measure is the Remote Associates Test, in which people are shown three words and asked to come up with a fourth that links all the others. For example, the words *piano, record,* and *baseball,* are all linked to *player.* For *stool, powder,* and *ball,* the answer is *foot* (Mednick, 1962).

It's now clear that creativity requires more than just the divergent thought processes that promote insight. Creativity is also an attitude or an approach to a task. To be truly creative requires a personality that lends itself to being open-minded, adventurous, unconventional, and willing to take risks. It also requires a certain degree of inner drive, curiosity, interest, involvement, and passion—in other words, an intrinsically motivated state (see Chapter 8). In a series of studies, Teresa Amabile (1996) and others had subjects write poems, write stories, draw pictures, make paper collages, paint, and give creative solutions to business dilemmas. Consistently, they found that people are more creative when they feel interested and challenged by the work itself than when they feel pressured to make money, fulfill obligations, meet deadlines, win competitions, or impress others. In one study, Amabile had art experts rate the works of professional artists and found that their commissioned work (art they were contracted for) was judged as lower in quality than their noncommissioned work. To be most creative, it helps to be intrinsically motivated in relation to the task.

Psychologists are a long way from understanding creativity. It's clear that to compose music, design clothing, solve a difficult crime, or discover a chemical process, one needs the ability to process information and think in ways that spark flashes of insight. But it's also clear that creative achievements do not flow from great minds without lots of motivation, commitment, and hard work. Reflecting on his own prolific career, Thomas Edison thus concluded that "genius is one percent inspiration and ninety-nine percent perspiration."

Practical Intelligence According to Sternberg (1988), Celia epitomized the reason IQ tests are limited in their ability to predict success outside the classroom. Celia, you may recall, was the student who was the weakest on paper but then the most successful on the job market. The reason is that she had street smarts, or **practical intelligence**—the ability to size up new situations, figure out the unspoken "rules of the game," and do what is necessary to adapt to life's demands. Whether you are trying to start a career, buy a house, or make friends, says Sternberg, you need practical intelligence, not just IQ points.

More and more, psychologists are coming to appreciate how important practical intelligence is in nonacademic settings. What skills are involved? Nancy Cantor and John Kihlstrom (1987) said that what's critical is *social competence*—like Gardner's social or interpersonal intelligence, an ability to know the feelings, thoughts, and actions of other people. In a related vein, others believe that what's needed are *wisdom* and *common sense*—the kind of knowledge that grows with experience and

The U.S. Department of Education (1993) estimates that 90 million Americans lack competence at practical life tasks such as reading a bus schedule, computing the cost to carpet a room, writing a business letter, and balancing a checkbook.

divergent thinking The ability to think flexibly and entertain a wide range of possible solutions.

practical intelligence The ability to size up new situations and adapt to real-life demands.

New York City entrepreneur J.R. has practical intelligence, or street smarts. Each week he pays "scavengers" to collect bottles and cans. Then he carts thousands of them to a recycling center. For his efforts, J.R. averages $3,750 a week in profit.

enables us to make sound judgments (Staudinger & Baltes, 1994; Sternberg et al., 1995). Still others focus more narrowly on *emotional intelligence,* a sensitivity to how people are feeling coupled with an ability to motivate oneself and control one's own emotions—qualities that can be highly adaptive in social settings (Goleman, 1995; Mayer & Salovey, 1993).

In a book entitled *The Cloak of Competence,* Robert Edgarton (1967) related the story of a mentally retarded man who could not tell time and wore a broken watch. When he needed to know what time it was, he would approach a stranger and say, "Excuse me, I notice my watch isn't working. Could you tell me the correct time?" Using this ingenious strategy, which is an illustration of practical intelligence, the man overcame his handicap without embarrassment. In sharp contrast, I know a brilliant college professor with an intimidating intellect who eats the *New York Times* crossword puzzle for breakfast every morning. Yet he has no social skills, lacks what you might call common sense, and can't seem to teach, get papers published, run a committee meeting, or balance his checkbook. Clearly, this man lacks practical, down-to-earth street smarts. The moral of the story: Intelligence is not something you *have* but something you *use.*

The Great Debates

Why is debate about the nature and nurture of intelligence so politically loaded? What does the research tell us about the relative genetic and environmental influences? What do Head Start programs try to accomplish, and how successful are they? What group differences are found in test scores, and how might these differences be interpreted?

Intelligence testing is a "numbers game" with profound consequences for real people. IQ and aptitude scores help to determine which young children in need of parents are adopted quickly and which students are accepted into prestigious private schools. They determine whether a child is labeled as retarded or gifted, whether placed in the "bluebirds" or "cardinals" group at school. Later, these scores help to determine which students are admitted into elite colleges, are offered scholarships, and then have the best job prospects. As Richard Weinberg (1989) put it, "IQ tests play a pivotal role in allocating society's resources and opportunities" (p. 100). With the stakes so high, it's easy to see why those who study and measure intelligence find themselves in one emotional debate after another. In this section, we consider three heated issues: nature and nurture, racial and cultural differences, and sex differences.

Nature and Nurture

To what extent is intelligence determined by the forces of nature (genetics) and nurture (the environment)? How much does each factor contribute, and in what ways do they interact? This question looms over all others and is the most explosive. To see why this issue generates so much heat, let's step back in time and consider some of its social and political implications.

The Politics In the nineteenth century, Galton argued that intelligence was an inherited characteristic—and that only bright adults should be encouraged or even allowed to reproduce. Many years later, Henry Goddard (1917) tested new European immigrants to the United States, judged many as genetically inferior, and recommended that they be deported. In 1969, Arthur Jensen argued that IQ differences between black and white Americans were genetically rooted. Jensen was accused of being a racist and was jeered on campuses across the country. His writings influenced physicist William Shockley (the winner of a Nobel prize for inventing the transistor), who urged the U.S. government to start a voluntary sterilization program by offering to pay citizens with low IQ scores to undergo sterilization at a rate of $1,000 for each IQ point below 100. Along with some other Nobel prizewinners, Shockley deposited his sperm in a "sperm bank," to be used by women of superior intelligence.

In contrast, nurture advocates have attributed low IQ scores to nongenetic factors such as poverty, maternal drug use, poor nutrition, inadequate schooling, a lack of academic focus within the home, low expectations, and feelings of helplessness and despair. Focused on change, they have promoted social policies designed to enrich the educational experiences of disadvantaged children. In 1905, Binet wanted to identify slow learners so that they could receive special services (Binet & Simon, 1905). Sixty years later, in the United States, psychologists studying the effects of early experience on intelligence helped to inspire **Project Head Start,** a nationwide preschool program for children born of poor families. Similar intellectual-enrichment projects can now be found in other countries as well.

In light of the political implications, it is perhaps not surprising that the nature–nurture debate has been mired in scandal. When Jensen (1969) argued that racial differences were inherited and that educational-enrichment programs were doomed to fail, he based these conclusions heavily on the research of Cyril Burt, an eminent British psychologist who died in 1971. In a series of three studies published in 1943, 1955, and 1966, Burt had reported that the correlation in IQ scores was higher between identical twins reared apart than between fraternal twins reared together—convincing evidence for the role of genetics. When these data were closely inspected, however, they revealed a remarkable story. In *The Science and Politics of IQ,* Leon Kamin (1974) found that even though Burt kept adding new twins to his sample, the IQ correlations he reported never changed—a nearly impossible statistical outcome. Two years later, an article appeared in the *London Times* under the headline "Crucial Data Was Faked by Eminent Psychologist" (Gillie, 1976), followed by a rash of letters to the editor by other well-known researchers. Some claimed that Burt not only fudged his statistics but made up names for research assistants and subjects who did not exist (Hearnshaw, 1979). Others discredited Burt's results but concluded merely that he was careless (Fletcher, 1991; Joynson, 1989).

Whatever the truth may be, the Burt affair stands as a tall reminder that on politically tender topics, the conclusions that are drawn from research data should be made with caution—which brings us to *The Bell Curve* (1994), a highly controversial book by Richard Herrnstein, a psychologist who died just before the book was released, and Charles Murray, a political scientist. Based on their review of past research, these authors claimed that intelligence is a largely inherited trait, that it can be fully measured by standard IQ tests, and that IQ differences within society have created a castelike division between the highly intelligent "cognitive elite" and

Project Head Start A preschool intellectual-enrichment program for children born of poor families.

a lesser "cognitive underclass." Herrnstein and Murray argued that low IQ is the root cause of failure in school, poverty, welfare, crime, and other problems. They further argued that because IQ is so influenced by genetic factors, social programs designed to help the poor are doomed to fail. Although the book is not about race or ethnicity, the implication is that the existing IQ gap between African Americans and whites in the United States cannot be closed.

The Bell Curve aroused strong and instant public reaction. *Newsweek* called it "frightening stuff." *Time* described it as "845 pages of provocation with footnotes." Yet the *Wall Street Journal* decried those in the media who were engaged in "a frantic race to denounce and destroy Charles Murray." Among psychologists, some critics argued that Herrnstein and Murray overestimated the role of genetic factors. Others noted that correlations between IQ and social class cannot be taken to mean that IQ causes poverty. Some other third factor could give rise to both outcomes—or the causal arrow could point in the opposite direction. Thus, Stephen Ceci (1996) asks, "Is it better to be born rich or smart?" Finally, others challenged the pessimistic assumption that intelligence is a rigid trait that can be altered only minimally by environmental intervention. So, complex as it is, what is the scientific evidence?

The Science After many years of debate, most experts now agree that intelligence is influenced but not entirely determined by genetic factors. In support of this conclusion, Figure 12.10 summarizes the results of 111 studies of more than 100,000 twins and other relatives (Bouchard & McGue, 1981). You can see that genetically identical twins who grow up in the same home get highly similar scores on IQ tests—almost as if the same person had taken the test twice. But how much of this similarity is rooted in nature? To estimate the role of genetic factors, let's compare people who share a similar environment but differ in genetic relatedness. Three such

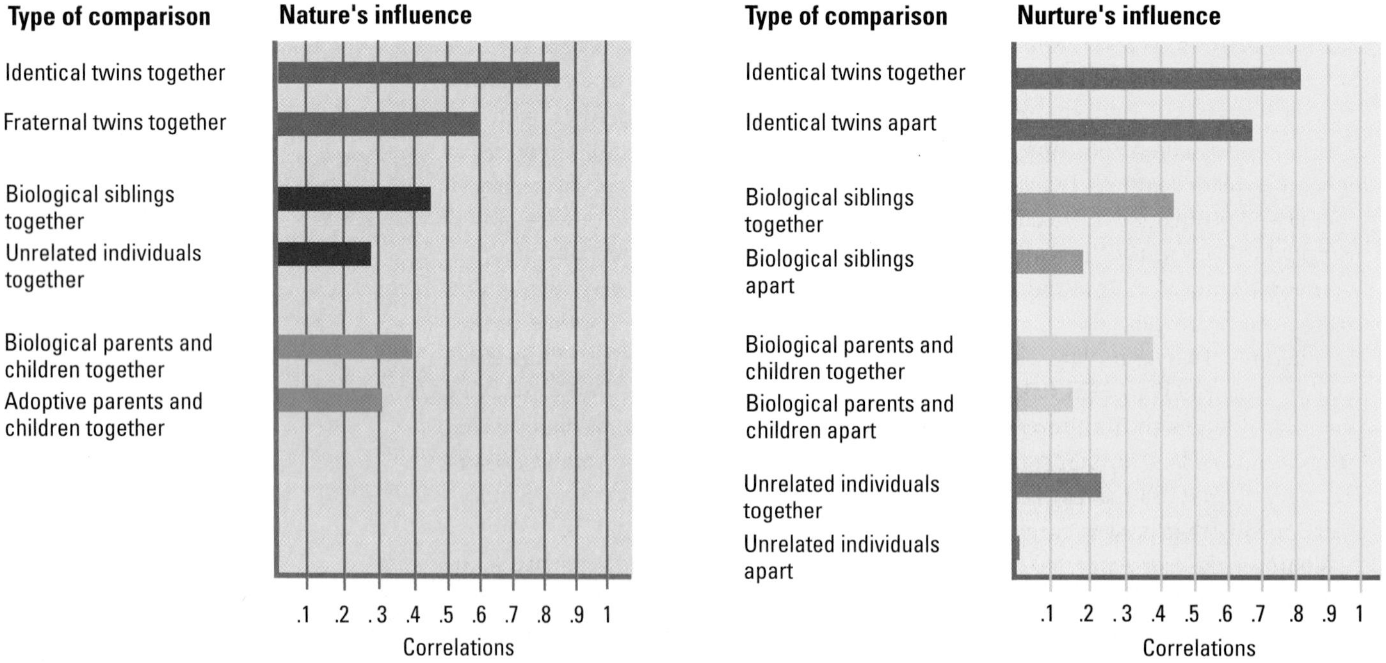

Figure 12.10 Nature's influence on IQ scores Studies reveal that the greater the genetic similarity between individuals, the more similar are their IQ scores (evidence for nature). These same studies reveal that individuals reared together have more similar IQ scores than those reared apart (evidence for nurture).

comparisons are worth noting: (1) Identical twins who are reared together (in fact, even those reared apart) are more similar than fraternal twins also reared together; (2) siblings who grow up together are more similar than unrelated individuals who grow up in the same home (even biological siblings reared apart show some degree of similarity); and (3) children are more similar to their biological parents than to adoptive parents. Additional research ties the genetic knot around IQ even tighter. Longitudinal studies show that the similarities do not diminish as blood relatives grow older—and that these similarities exist in verbal, mathematical, and spatial abilities; school grades; and vocational interests (McCartney et al., 1990; Plomin, 1988).

Nobody disputes the role of genetics, but it's clear that the same studies provide strong evidence for environmental influences. This pro-nurture conclusion is based on comparisons of people who have the same genetic relatedness but who live in different environments. As you can see in Figure 12.10, whenever they live together rather than apart there's more similarity between (1) identical twins, (2) siblings, (3) biological parents and children, and (4) unrelated individuals. In all instances, different environments reduce the impact of genetic relatedness. Based on all the results, it is safe to estimate that heredity accounts for about 50 percent of the population variation in intelligence, with environmental factors being responsible for the rest. Be clear about what this result means. It does not mean that 50 percent of your IQ is inherited—it means only that genetic factors are responsible for that portion of the differences among individuals in the population (Weinberg, 1989).

What environmental factors can influence intelligence? The possibilities are numerous: prenatal care, exposure to alcohol and other toxins, birth complications, malnutrition in the first few months of life, intellectual stimulation at home, stress, high-quality education, and so on (Bouchard & Segal, 1985). Just the sheer amount of time spent in school is important—which may account for why test scores drop during summer vacation and rise again during the school year (Ceci, 1991). One interesting variable is *family configuration*—the number and birth order of children in a home. According to Robert Zajonc (1976), a family's intellectual environment consists of the average absolute intelligence levels of all its members. Say, for example, that a family consisting of two adults with average IQs has an intellectual environment of 100. If the couple has a newborn baby (whose mental age is zero), the family average drops to 67 (200/3). If a second baby is born a year later, the average drops even lower, to 50. As children get older, their mental ages increase and raise the family's average. Consistent with this model, Zajonc and Mullally (1997) have found that IQ scores are slightly higher among first-borns and children from small families (because they spend much of their time in the company of adults) than among later-borns and those in large families (because they are surrounded by other children, unless their siblings are much older).

Head Start Programs Parents who provide an enriched and stimulating home—by hanging mobiles in the crib, reading bedtime stories, playing games, traveling, and so on—foster their child's intellectual growth. Children deprived of these learning experiences thus begin life at a tremendous disadvantage. It's like the old chicken-and-egg problem: Poverty lowers intelligence, and low intelligence leads people into poverty. Somehow, the vicious cycle must be broken.

In 1965, as part of President Johnson's War on Poverty, Project Head Start was launched with psychologist Edward Zigler as the program's first director. Head Start is a group of preschool programs for children born into low-income families. In some programs, teachers make house calls to train parents and engage the children in playing with building blocks, reading books, and other cognitive activities. In

Project Head Start is designed to enhance the intellectual development of children born into poverty.

other programs, children attend special preschools outside the home. Dedicated to helping those who are born into disadvantaged families—many of whom are minorities—Head Start serves hundreds of thousands of families across the country each year at a cost, as recently as 1990, of $2,803 per child (Zigler & Muenchow, 1992).

Skeptics wonder if it's worth the money, but research shows that the program has been reasonably successful. It cannot boost IQ scores into the gifted range, but in other ways, Head Start alumni surpass comparable others who don't take part. Entering school, they score about 10 points higher on IQ tests, are more confident, and are quicker to adjust to the demands of sitting in a classroom. Although the initial gain in IQ wears off over time, Head Start children in high-quality programs are later less likely to repeat grades or to be put into remedial classes—and are more likely to graduate from high school and hold after-school jobs (Woodhead, 1988; Lee et al., 1990). In addition, research shows that the younger children are when they get into Head Start, the better. In programs that target infants who are "at risk" due to low birth weight, low income, or low parental IQ, intelligence-test scores increase by as much as 9 points by the age of three (Brooks-Gunn et al., 1992; Ramey et al., 1992).

When it comes to academic success and failure, getting off on the right foot can make a difference. Reflecting on the program, Edward Zigler and Susan Muenchow (1992) note: "Head Start is the nation's most successful educational and social experiment. It was a pioneer in providing comprehensive services in a family-centered context, and it continues to offer the only real two-generational assault on poverty. Over 11 million children are better off today because of Head Start—in some cases, dramatically better off" (pp. 244–245).

Group Differences

One reason the nature–nurture debate is so filled with emotion is that certain racial and cultural groups score higher than others on measures of ability and achievement, and these differences ignite blunt claims concerning genetic superiority and inferiority. Let's start with an often-cited empirical fact: African Americans as a group have averaged 15 points lower than whites on IQ tests and 100 points lower on the SAT verbal and math tests (Jensen, 1994).

Why has this occurred? If heredity contributes to variations among individuals, doesn't it also account for differences found among groups? No, not necessarily. To be sure, a few psychologists have speculated that differing evolutionary pressures in Europe, Asia, and Africa have, over time, produced measurable differences among humans in brain size and intelligence (Rushton & Ankney, 1996). But as critics of *The Bell Curve* were correct to note, genetic variation among *individuals* within a group does not mean that differences among *groups* are genetically based. Compared to the average African American, white Americans grow up in more affluent homes and with better educational opportunities—differences that can account for the IQ gap (see Figure 12.11).

Two sets of research findings support this point. The first is from a study that asked: What would happen to the IQ scores of black children adopted into white middle-class homes? Sandra Scarr and Richard Weinberg (1976) studied 99 such cases in Minneapolis and found that the average IQ score was 110—well above the African American average and comparable to that of white children from similar families. When these adoptees were retested ten years later, similar results were found (Weinberg et al., 1992).

The second set of findings involves cross-cultural comparisons and historical trends. The cultural perspective reveals that the racial gap in IQ within the United States is not unique. Low scores are found in disadvantaged groups all over the world, including the Maoris of New Zealand, the "untouchables" in India, non-European Jews in Israel, and the Burakumin in Japan (Ogbu, 1978). From a historical perspective, it's clear that as a result of school desegregation and social programs such as Head Start, African Americans have had more educational doors opened in recent years than in the past. Paralleling these new opportunities, the racial gap in the Stanford-Binet has diminished somewhat (Thorndike et al., 1986)—and differences in reading and math achievement have substantially narrowed (Jones, 1984; Grissmer et al., 1994).

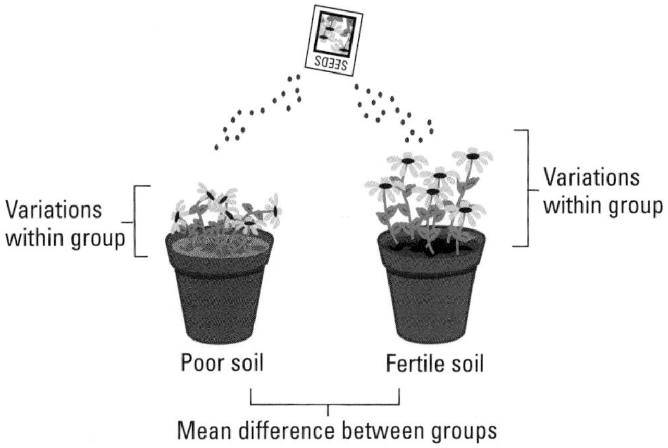

Figure 12.11 Explaining group differences To understand how genes can affect the variation among individuals but not account for differences among groups, imagine having an assortment of different seeds, with some more likely than others to grow into tall plants. Now take the mixture, randomly divide it into two groups, and plant one group in a pot of fertile soil and the other in a pot of barren soil. Among the seeds sown *within* a pot, the differences in growth may reflect genetic differences. Yet the average growth difference *between* the two pots will be largely due to their differing environments.

The recent achievements of Asian American immigrants are raising the nature–nurture questions once again. Compared to other groups, Asian American students get higher grades and SAT math scores, are more likely to attend and graduate from college, and are more likely to win National Merit Scholarships, Westinghouse Science Talent Searches, and Presidential Scholarships. It's no wonder that the news media refer to Japanese, Chinese, Korean, Vietnamese, Filipino, and Asian Indian students collectively as "The New Whiz Kids" (Sue & Okazaki, 1990). Are Asian Americans, in general, smarter than other groups? James Flynn (1991) analyzed more than a dozen IQ studies and found that despite the remarkable record of Asian Americans, their test scores were about average. Looking at IQ and employment statistics, Flynn went on to calculate that Chinese Americans as a group are as successful as white Americans with an average IQ of 120 would be—a pattern of "overachievement" that begs for an explanation.

Researchers are struggling to understand this phenomenon. Although some have suggested that the achievements of the Asian American community are influenced by genetic factors (Anderson, 1982), most attribute the success to cultural values that emphasize hard work, discipline, and respect for education. The support for this explanation is particularly strong when it comes to academic disparities in mathematics. In a series of studies, Harold Stevenson and others (1990, 1993) compared children in a wide range of schools in Taiwan, Japan, and the United States and found that by the fifth grade, Asian students were superior in number concepts, computation, word problems, and other aspects of math. However, the Asian students also found the schoolwork more difficult, were less confident of their own skills, and were less favorably evaluated by parents and teachers. Thus, American children and adults were more satisfied than Asians were despite lower levels of achievement (Crystal & Stevenson, 1991). Additional studies have shown that the Asian advantage in math continues into high school, where Taiwanese and Japanese students outperform Americans in algebra, geometry, trigonometry, and calculus (Chen & Stevenson, 1995). At this level, too, there are marked cultural differences

Lenny Ng is a son of Chinese immigrants. At ten, he scored 800 on the math SAT. At sixteen, he entered Harvard University. Julian Stanley, who founded the Study of Mathematically Precocious Youth at Johns Hopkins University, calls him "the most brilliant math prodigy I've ever met."

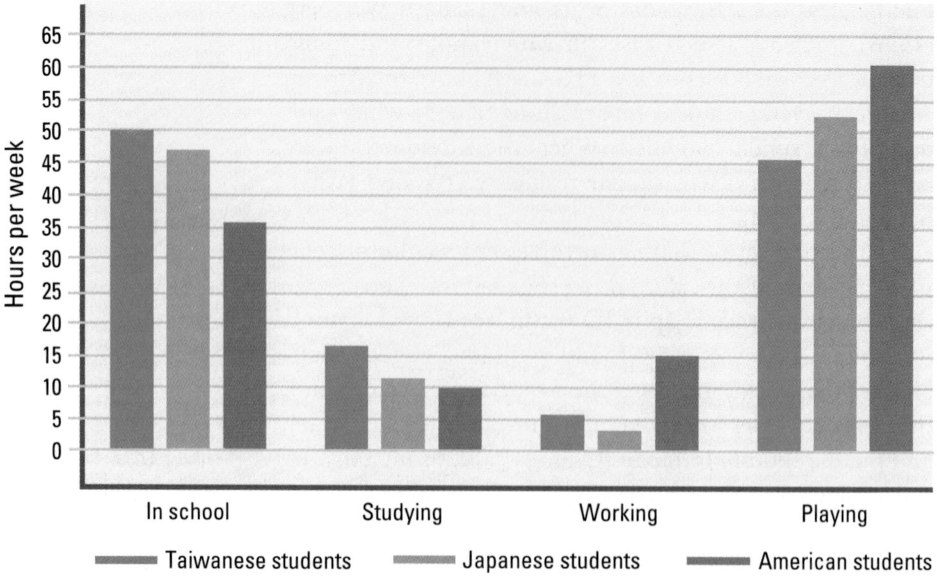

Figure 12.12 How American and Asian students spend their time Interviews with high-school students in Taiwan, Japan, and the United States revealed striking differences in the way they spend their time. Compared to those in the Asian populations, American students spent less time in school and less time studying but more time working and playing—which included extracurricular activities such as sports, time alone, time with friends, dating, and watching TV (Fuligni & Stevenson, 1995).

in the values placed on academics. When high-school students in the three countries were asked to account for their time, the differences were striking. As shown in Figure 12.12, students in Taiwan and Japan, relative to those in the United States, spend more time in school and more time studying, while the American students spend more time working, taking part in extracurricular activities, socializing with friends, and dating (Fuligni & Stevenson, 1995).

When you put the pieces together, it appears that Americans set lower standards and place a lower value on academic pursuits. Also consistent with this cultural explanation, Philip Ritter and Sanford Dornbusch (1989) surveyed thousands of high-school students in California and found that those of Asian descent were more likely than others to believe that success in life is linked to what they do in school. They also found that the longer an Asian family has lived in the United States, the lower is its level of achievement. Ironically, the cultural values that promote success for new Asian immigrants seem to erode as they become settled in their new homeland.

Sex Differences

When intelligence tests are constructed, a concerted effort is made to remove questions that prove more difficult for one sex than for the other—or at least to balance items favoring one sex with items favoring the other. The result is that total IQ scores are comparable for males and females. But what about specific abilities? Is there any truth to traditional gender stereotypes that depict math and spatial relations as masculine enterprises and language as the art of woman? Several years ago, Eleanor Maccoby and Carol Jacklin (1974) reviewed the research and found that it supported the stereotype. But because the issue has such profound implications for how parents treat their sons and daughters—and for how teachers treat male and female students—psychologists have been eager to understand the nature and extent of these differences. At this point, this is what we know.

- *Verbal abilities.* On verbal-aptitude tests, Janet Hyde and Marcia Linn (1988) analyzed data from millions of students tested between 1947 and 1980 and found that girls outscored boys but that the gender gap had narrowed. Still, on average, girls are better spellers. They also score slightly higher than boys on tests of reading comprehension, writing, and foreign languages (Hedges & Nowell, 1995; Stumpf & Stanley, 1996).
- *Mathematical abilities.* Girls are better at arithmetic in grade school, but males surpass females early in junior high school—a difference that continues to college and beyond and is found in other countries as well. On the math portion of the SAT, males have a 40–50-point edge, which is most evident among the highest-level math students (Benbow, 1988; Hyde et al., 1990). This difference may also underlie the fact that males score higher on high-school physics, chemistry, and computer-science achievement tests (Stumpf & Stanley, 1996).
- *Spatial abilities.* Consistently, males outperform females on spatial tasks such as mentally rotating objects to determine what they look like in another position and tracking moving objects in space (Linn & Petersen, 1985; Masters & Sanders, 1993). These skills are used in architecture, mechanical engineering, and certain other types of work. They may also account for the sex differences found in SAT math scores. In a recent study, male and female college students took the SAT and a mental-rotation task like the one depicted in Figure 12.13. As usual, male students outperformed females on the math portion of the SAT. But when the scores were statistically adjusted to account for differences in spatial ability, the gender gap in math disappeared. As shown in Figure 12.14, the male advantage in math is intimately tied to the difference in spatial skills (Casey et al., 1995).

So, why are there disparities in spatial relations? As you might expect, this question awakens the debate on the relative importance of nature and nurture. On the *biological* side, Camilla Benbow (1988) and others have speculated that sex differences in spatial abilities stem from the prenatal effects of sex hormones on the brain—that the male hormone testosterone slows the fetal development of the left hemisphere, thereby enhancing the growth of the right hemisphere, the side associated with spatial intelligence. Thus, highly talented math students are also more likely to be left-handed, nearsighted, and allergy sufferers—traits thought to be linked prenatally to high levels of testosterone exposure. More recently, David Geary (1996) speculated that the male spatial advantage evolved over time to support navigation, warfare, hunting, and other activities that require movement in three-dimensional space.

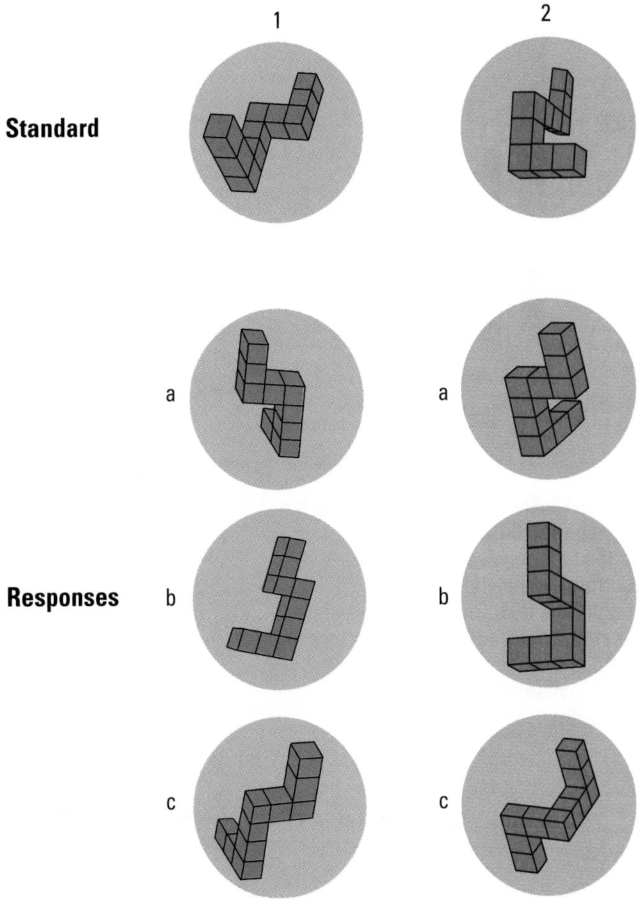

Figure 12.13 The mental rotation test of spatial ability For each standard shown on top, which of the three responses on the bottom shows a different view of the same object? The answers appear on page 467.

Studies show that experience with these games increases spatial test scores—for girls as well as boys.

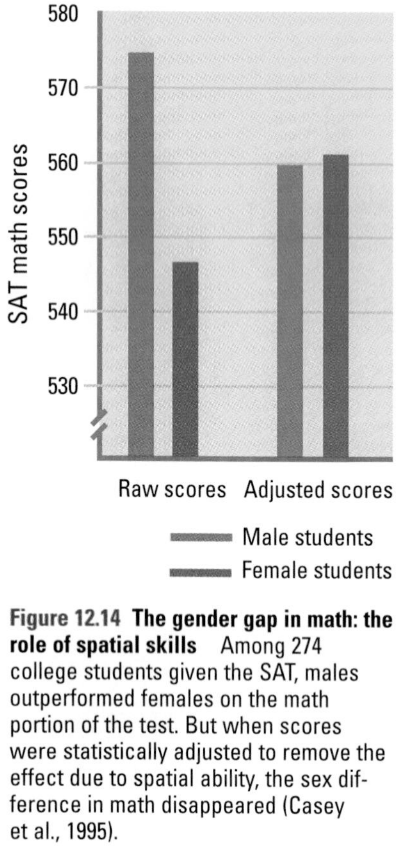

Figure 12.14 The gender gap in math: the role of spatial skills Among 274 college students given the SAT, males outperformed females on the math portion of the test. But when scores were statistically adjusted to remove the effect due to spatial ability, the sex difference in math disappeared (Casey et al., 1995).

On the *social* side, Jacquelynne Eccles (1985) and others attribute the gender gap to stereotypes of math as a masculine subject, less encouragement of girls by parents and teachers, and different experiences in childhood. For example, boys use spatial skills more often through contact sports, action-packed video games, construction sets, and "transformers" (plastic toys that can be "transformed" from one object to another). Consistent with this hypothesis, two studies have shown that playing action video games improves spatial-test performance—in girls as well as in boys (Okagaki & Frensch, 1994; Subrahmanyan & Greenfield, 1994).

Education

How are giftedness and mental retardation defined, and what education issues do they raise? What is the self-fulfilling prophecy, and how might the process influence the performance of students in the classroom?

Now that we have examined the major IQ tests, theories of intelligence, and the debates that have arisen, let's return to where it all started: the classroom. Ever since Binet's work in the schools of Paris, many psychologists have had uneasy feelings about the linkage between our conceptions of intelligence and education.

There are two principal questions. First, by focusing on the prediction of academic performance, have we accepted too narrow a conception of intelligence? There are many influential theorists who think so. Gardner (1983) complains that IQ tests completely ignore and devalue the musical, bodily-kinesthetic, and personal intelligences. Likewise, Sternberg (1988) says that these tests, like the school systems they service, do not recognize the potential for achievement inherent in people who have creative and practical intelligence. The second question concerns the impact of IQ testing on the quality of education. Once a child is identified as a fast, slow, or average learner, what next? Do those with unusually high or low IQ scores benefit from being identified as "special"? What are the educational implications? Because schools rely heavily on IQ tests to sort children into academic categories, it's important to raise these kinds of critical questions.

Answer to mental rotation test:
The correct answers are 1(a) and 2(b).

Giftedness

Popular stereotypes of gifted children include unflattering images of eccentric nerds and social misfits doomed to a life of failure—hence the expression "Early ripe, early rot." The story of William James Sidis, considered the world's greatest child prodigy, is a case in point. Sidis was born in 1898 in New York City, to Russian-immigrant parents. He was reading by the age of two, using a typewriter at three, and speaking Russian, French, German, and English at five. Sidis started school at the age of six and whizzed through seven grades in less than twelve months. That year, he devised a new table of logarithms and knew enough about human anatomy to pass a medical-school exam. At the age of eleven, Sidis was admitted into Harvard, where he astonished the Harvard Mathematical Club with a lecture on the fourth dimension. Despite this prodigious start, however, Sidis soon fizzled into obscurity. He dropped out of graduate school and spent most of his life in low-paying clerical jobs. When Sidis died at the age of forty-six, he was living in a rooming house alone, unemployed and penniless (Wallace, 1986).

Contrary to popular belief, this biographical pattern is atypical. In 1921, Lewis Terman (the Stanford psychologist who imported Binet's IQ scale) launched what was to become the most extensive longitudinal study of "genius" ever conducted. Terman studied 1,528 California schoolchildren, all with IQs over 135. He and subsequent researchers then followed the progress of their lives for years to come and found that as a group these men and women were healthy, well adjusted, happily married, and highly successful in school and in their careers. Many of the "Termites" went on to become eminent doctors, lawyers, authors, scientists, and professors. After retirement, many were happy and satisfied with their lives (Holahan & Sears, 1995). More contemporary longitudinal studies of gifted people are now underway, so more will be known in the years to come (Subotnik & Arnold, 1994).

It's impossible to know why William Sidis floundered while so many of Terman's subjects were successful. From an educational standpoint, however, it's important to know what it means to be "gifted" and how we can educate our bright and talented children. When Terman conducted his study, he selected subjects according to IQ tests. Today, giftedness is viewed in broader terms. For example, Joseph Renzulli (1986) proposed a three-ring conception of giftedness as a combination of above-average intelligence, task commitment, and creativity. Following in the footsteps of Gardner and Steinberg, others maintain that giftedness is not a general trait but, rather, one that is specific to a particular domain. Thus, many high-school students who get perfect scores on one academic subtest of the ACT do not fall within the gifted range on other subtests (Colangelo & Kerr, 1990). You can be a brilliant economist, physicist, writer, or computer programmer without being an intellectual jack-of-all-trades.

As a matter of policy, society has mixed feelings about how gifted children should be treated (Reis, 1989). On the one hand, we are troubled by a sense that it's unfair to provide special opportunities for an elite, chosen group of children, to the exclusion of others. On the other hand, we recognize that it's important to challenge bright minds and harvest their full potential in order to build a better future for everyone. An accelerated curriculum, special resource rooms, and after-school programs are some ways to enhance the educational experience. In 1971, for example, Julian Stanley of Johns Hopkins University pioneered what is now a nationwide talent search for gifted math students. By administering the math portion of the SAT to bright seventh-graders, Stanley and others identify as "mathematically precocious" those boys and girls with scores over 500 (a higher-than-average score for twelfth-graders, and the top percentage of seventh-graders). These students are offered advanced summer programs in math and science, accelerated college courses, and counseling for parents. It appears that participants enjoy the program and benefit from the experience, without showing signs of social or emotional stress (Stanley & Benbow, 1986; Richardson & Benbow, 1990).

Mental Retardation

At the opposite end of the continuum, children whose IQ scores are below 70 are evaluated to see if they are mentally retarded. **Mental retardation** is a term used to describe people with limited intellectual ability. It used to be the case that anyone who scored in the lowest 3–5 percent was identified as mentally retarded. Since test performance has little to do with the ability to function in nonacademic settings, however, the American Psychiatric Association (1994) raised its criteria. To be diagnosed as mentally retarded, a person must now have (1) an IQ score below 70, and (2) difficulty adapting to routine needs of life such as self-care and social interactions. Other causes of poor test performance—for example, physical illness or impaired vision or hearing—also have to be ruled out. Only about 1 percent of the population meets these criteria, with males outnumbering females (Landesman & Ramey, 1989).

There are four categories of mental retardation, varying in severity. As shown in Table 12.1, most retarded people are only mildly retarded. They have IQ scores in the 50–70 range and are sometimes referred to as "educable" because they are capable of achieving a sixth-grade level in reading and math. Usually, mildly retarded children live at home and attend public schools. Once diagnosed, they are given individualized education programs designed to meet their academic, social, and emotional needs, while keeping them as much as possible within the regular classroom (Schroeder et al., 1987). As Alfred Binet had hoped, these students can be taught at their own pace, enabling them to learn better and live more fulfilling lives. Unfortunately, the use of IQ tests for placement purposes can be risky—and may even backfire. The problem is this: Since the tests are not the perfect crystal ball, what happens to a child whose ability is underestimated? What happens if expectations are set too low?

The Self-fulfilling Prophecy

In 1948, sociologist Robert Merton told a story about Cartwright Millingville, president of the Last National Bank during the Depression. Although the bank was solvent, a rumor began to spread that it was floundering. Within hours, hundreds of depositors were lined up to withdraw their savings, until there was no money left. The rumor was false, but the bank eventually failed. Using stories such as this,

mental retardation A diagnostic category used for people with IQ scores below 70 who have difficulty adapting to the routine demands of life.

Table 12.1 Mental Retardation: Degrees of Severity

LEVEL	PERCENTAGE OF RETARDED PERSONS	TYPICAL IQ SCORES	ADAPTATION TO DEMANDS OF LIFE
Mild	85%	50–70	May learn academic skills up to a sixth-grade level. Adults may, with assistance, achieve self-supporting social and vocational skills.
Moderate	10%	35–49	May progress to a second-grade level. Adults may contribute to their own support by labor in sheltered workshops.
Severe	4%	20–34	May learn to talk and to perform simple work tasks under close supervision, but are generally unable to profit from vocational training.
Profound	1%	Below 20	Require constant aid and supervision.

Merton proposed that a person's expectation can actually lead to its own fulfillment—a phenomenon known as the **self-fulfilling prophecy.** As we'll see, there are three ways in which this can influence the educational process.

Teacher Expectancies Based on Merton's hypothesis, Robert Rosenthal and Lenore Jacobson (1968) wondered about the possible harmful effects of IQ testing. What happens to the educational experience of the child who receives a low score? Would it leave a permanent mark on his or her record, arouse negative expectations on the part of the teacher, and impair future performance? To examine the possible outcomes, Rosenthal and Jacobson told teachers in a San Francisco elementary school that certain pupils were on the verge of an intellectual growth spurt. The results of an IQ test were cited, but in fact the pupils were randomly selected. Rosenthal and Jacobson administered real tests eight months later and found that the so-called late bloomers (but not children assigned to a control group) had actually improved their scores by as much as thirty points and were evaluated more favorably by their classroom teachers.

When this study was published, it was greeted with chagrin. If high teacher expectations can increase student performance, can low expectations have the opposite effect? Could it be that children who get high scores are destined for success, while those who get low scores are doomed to failure, in part because educators hold different expectations of them? Many researchers were critical of the study and skeptical about the generality of the results. But the phenomenon is potentially too important to be swept under the proverbial rug. After reviewing other tests of the hypothesis, Rosenthal (1985) concluded that teacher expectations significantly predicted student performance 36 percent of the time.

How might teacher expectations be transformed into reality? There are two points of view. According to Rosenthal, the self-fulfilling prophecy can be viewed as a three-step process. First, the teacher forms an impression of the student early in the school year. This impression may be based on IQ-test scores or other information. Second, the teacher behaves in ways that are consistent with that first

self-fulfilling prophecy The idea that a person's expectation can lead to its own fulfillment (as in the effect of teacher expectations on student performance).

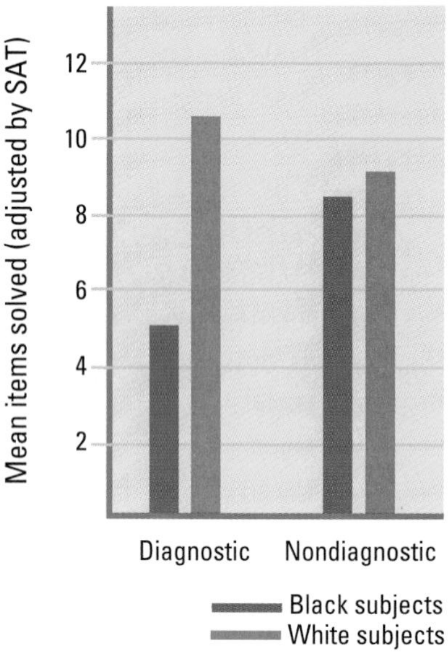

Figure 12.15 Stereotype vulnerability and test performance Steele and Aronson (1995) compared the performances (adjusted for their own ability) of African American and white students on a thirty-item verbal-reasoning test. When the significance of the test was underplayed, there were no differences (*right*). When the test was presented as diagnostic of verbal ability, the African American students performed worse (*left*). This result is consistent with the stereotype-vulnerability hypothesis.

impression. If the expectations are high rather than low, the teacher gives the student more praise, attention, and challenging homework. Third, the student unwittingly adjusts his or her own behavior according to the teacher's actions. If the signals are positive, the student may become energized. If negative, there may be a loss of interest and self-confidence. The cycle is thus complete and the expectations confirmed (Cooper & Good, 1983; Harris & Rosenthal, 1985).

Although the teacher-expectations effect can occur, Lee Jussim and his colleagues (1996) question whether teachers in real life are so prone in the first place to form erroneous impressions of their students. In many naturalistic studies, the expectations teachers have at the start of a school year are later confirmed by their students—a result that is consistent with the notion that the teachers had a hand in producing that outcome. But wait. That same result is also consistent with a more innocent possibility: Perhaps the expectations teachers form of their students are often *accurate.* There are times, Jussim admits, when teachers may stereotype a student and, without realizing it, behave in ways that create a self-fulfilling prophecy. But there may also be times when teachers can predict how their students will perform without necessarily influencing that performance.

Stereotype Vulnerability There's a second way in which expectations can set in motion a self-fulfilling prophecy. According to Claude Steele (1997), African Americans are painfully aware of the negative stereotypes people hold regarding their intelligence. As a result, academic test situations make African American students feel "vulnerable" to the stereotype and anxious about performance. Research on this hypothesis is still in the early stages, but so far the results suggest that this process may be at work.

Steele and Aronson (1995) administered a thirty-item verbal test to African American and white college students. Half the subjects were told that the items were merely a device that psychologists use to study the way people solve problems—a "nondiagnostic" instruction that was designed to underplay the testlike nature of the task. The other half were told that the items measured verbal-reasoning ability—a "diagnostic" instruction designed to make stereotype-vulnerable subjects anxious. As shown in Figure 12.15, African American and white subjects did not differ when given the low-key nondiagnostic instruction (their scores were statistically adjusted according to each subject's past verbal SAT in order to equalize initial differences in their actual abilities). In the diagnostic condition, however, the African American subjects exhibited a decrease in their own performance. With the task defined as an ability test, those feeling vulnerable to the stereotype, sadly, helped to confirm it. At this point, more research is needed to fully understand the process and all its ramifications.

Ability Grouping A third way in which IQ tests might actually influence (not just reflect) academic performance is by steering students onto a fast or slow track in the school curriculum. If you've read Aldous Huxley's *Brave New World,* you may recall the opening scene in the "Hatchery and Conditioning Centre," where human embryos only a few hours old are transformed into Alphas, Betas, Gammas, Deltas, or Epsilons and are programmed accordingly for a high-class or low-class future. In the foreword to this novel, Huxley (1932) expressed his personal fear that a "science of human differences" could be used to sort people early in life into fixed, immutable social ranks. This may sound like fanciful science fiction, but critics charge that intelligence tests are being used in the same manner to separate children according to their IQs (Tobias, 1989).

To cope with the tremendous diversity of children who attend public schools, educators try to group students who have similar academic abilities (Dornbusch et al., 1996). Teaching is easier when all students are on the same "wavelength." There are two ways to reduce student heterogeneity. One is *between-classroom grouping,* in which all the students in a grade are assigned to separate high-, average-, or low-level classes. A second way is *within-classroom grouping,* in which students mixed in the same classroom are put in separate instructional groups, usually for reading and math. What happens to students who are tracked at a young age, often based on a test score? What difference does it make to a child's education and self-esteem to belong to the fast "sharks" rather than the slow "goldfish"?

The main argument for between-classroom grouping is that by separating whole groups of children by ability, a teacher can prepare one curriculum to meet the needs of all students. The level and pace of instruction can be raised for those in the high class and lowered for those in the low class. Yet, as reasonable as this policy seems, this practice can have harmful effects on students who are dumped into slow classes because they don't test well. In elementary school, teachers in low-ability classes spend much of their time managing disruptive students, to the detriment of the others (Eder, 1981). In junior and senior high schools, high-track students read great literature, use computers, and learn critical thinking, expository writing, and other skills valuable for college. But in low-track classes, instructors are content to teach "functional literacy" (how to read signs, fill out forms, and so on), basic arithmetic, and rote memorization (Oakes, 1985). In short, a school's curriculum can be either enriched or watered down, depending on a student's placement—a placement that may constrain future performance. Ultimately, the rich get richer and the poor get poorer.

The alternative is within-classroom ability grouping, in which, as noted, mixed students from the same class are separated into groups assembled for math and reading. Most schools favor this approach, though the issue is complicated. After reviewing fourteen studies, Robert Slavin (1987) concluded that students who are in heterogeneous classes achieve more when they are grouped for instruction than when the class is taught as a whole and that between-class grouping is not similarly effective. So far, so good. But it's also important to consider the effects of such grouping on self-esteem. For many years, researchers were baffled by the fact that children in disadvantaged schools had higher academic self-esteem than those from more affluent schools. Apparently, children compare themselves to one another and feel smarter when they are surrounded by classmates who are relatively weak academically. In this respect, it's better to be a large fish in a small pond than a small fish in a large pond (Marsh & Parker, 1984). In terms of classroom composition, however, heterogeneity is like a two-edged sword: High-ability students gain confidence in the presence of weaker peers, but low-ability students lose confidence alongside their stronger peers. This result led David Reuman (1989) to conclude that "choosing within-classroom versus between-classroom grouping policies involves complicated tradeoffs" (p. 187).

Perspectives on Intelligence

Reflecting on the material in this chapter, how would you define intelligence? And what are the implications of the definition you choose?

For about a century now, psychologists have been trying to define, measure, understand, and enhance intelligence, an elusive concept. You can tell by the frequent use of the Stanford-Binet, Wechsler scales, SAT, and other instruments that ability testing is a booming enterprise. It's also one that should be viewed with a critical eye to safeguard against possible abuses. Intelligence is a many-splendored concept—more than just IQ, a magical number used to predict school performance. Intelligence shows up in one person's flair for writing, in a second person's ability to wheel-and-deal in business, and a third person's fluent mastery of five languages. It's the ability to process information with efficiency, generate creative ideas, and use one's skills to get ahead in life.

Underlying much of the tension that surrounds the study of intelligence is the nature–nurture debate. It is clear that both genetic and environmental factors contribute to an individual's intelligence. It's also clear that because racial and cultural groups have distinct life experiences, intellectual differences at the group level are hard to interpret. The same is true of the small differences that exist between men and women. Finally, it's important to consider the educational implications of using IQ tests for identification and placement purposes. On the one hand, objective measures of intelligence help us to predict academic potential and develop programs suitable for individual students. On the other hand, IQ tests can set in motion a self-fulfilling prophecy and steer students onto a fast or slow track in school. Either way, it's important to keep in mind that intelligence is not a tangible object but a word that describes the skills that enable you to make a better life for yourself and others.

Summary and Key Terms

Many psychologists define **intelligence** as a capacity to learn from experience and adapt successfully to one's environment.

Intelligence Tests

The Stanford-Binet

In the early 1900s, Binet and Simon developed a test to determine a student's **mental age**—the average age of children who achieve a given level of performance. Terman revised the test and renamed it the **Stanford-Binet.** He also scored the test by means of an **intelligence quotient (IQ):** mental age divided by chronological age and multiplied by 100. Today, an IQ represents a person's performance relative to the average of same-age peers.

The Wechsler Scales

To distinguish between different aspects of intelligence, the **Wechsler Adult Intelligence Scale (WAIS)** yields separate verbal and performance scores. There are also Wechsler scales for children.

Group Aptitude Tests

In contrast to the Stanford-Binet and Wechsler measures, which are individually administered, aptitude tests like the SAT and ACT are given in groups. Although these tests seek to distinguish aptitude from achievement, the two factors are difficult to separate.

Are Intelligence Tests Accurate?

To be accurate, a test must be standardized, reliable, and valid. **Standardization** means that the test provides a standard of norms that can be used to interpret a given score. **Reliability** means that the results are consistent. **Test-retest reliability** ensures that a test will yield similar results at different times; **split-half reliability** ensures that different forms of the test will produce similar results. **Validity** is the extent to which the test measures or predicts what it is supposed to. **Content validity** refers to whether test questions adequately measure the quality they were designed to measure (intelligence). **Criterion validity** concerns the test's ability to predict a concurrent or future outcome (academic achievement). These tests correlate highly with grades in school but are less predictive of adaptation to life outside.

Are Intelligence Tests Biased?

Some say that intelligence tests are culturally biased because scores are influenced by background factors such as the test taker's racial or ethnic group. Advocates of testing note that racial differences occur even on "culture-fair" items and that intelligence tests do predict academic performance.

The Nature of Intelligence

General Intelligence

Some psychologists believe in **general intelligence** (g), a broad factor underlying all mental abilities. By developing **factor analysis,** a statistical technique used to identify clusters of test items that correlate with one another, Spearman found that all intellectual abilities are linked to g. Recent studies show that childhood IQ scores are somewhat predictable from measures of infant responsiveness and that people with high IQ scores process information quickly and efficiently. Other researchers have divided intelligence into various components.

Gardner's "Frames of Mind"

Based in part on the existence of **prodigies** and **idiot savants,** Gardner proposed a theory of **multiple intelligences.** According to Gardner, different systems in the brain produce seven different types of intelligence: linguistic, logical-mathematical, spatial, musical, bodily-kinesthetic, interpersonal, and intrapersonal. The last four types stretch the concept of intelligence beyond traditional notions.

Sternberg's Triarchic Theory

According to Sternberg's **triarchic theory of intelligence,** there are three basic types of intelligence. Analytic intelligence is the kind of skill exhibited on traditional IQ tests and by school grades. It may relate to the sheer speed of neural transmission in the brain.

Creativity refers to the mental processes that lead to unique and novel solutions, ideas, artistic forms, or products. One key to creative insight is **divergent thinking,** the ability to think flexibly and entertain a wide range of possible solutions. Another key is intrinsic motivation, an inner drive and enthusiasm for a task.

Practical intelligence, the last of Sternberg's three types, is the ability to size up situations and adapt to real-life demands. This ability consists of social competence, wisdom, and emotional intelligence.

The Great Debates

Because test scores affect so many aspects of our lives, debates about intelligence testing have been heated.

Nature and Nurture

People have long disputed the extent to which intelligence is determined by nature (genetics) and by nurture (environment). Studies of twins and other family members show that heredity and environment each account for about half the population variation in intelligence. The recent publication of *The Bell Curve* brought this issue into the limelight.

The relationship between intelligence and poverty is a vicious cycle. Research indicates that programs such as **Project Head Start,** which intervenes early in a child's life to break the cycle, have a measurable impact on IQ and school success.

Group Differences

Are group differences in average IQ and SAT scores brought about by nature or by nurture? This issue is politically loaded. But research suggests that environmental factors can help to explain the relatively low scores by African Americans and the relatively high scores by Asian Americans.

Sex Differences

Whereas girls score somewhat higher on verbal tests, boys on average perform better in mathematical and visual-spatial tasks. Some researchers suggest the difference is biologically rooted, perhaps traceable to the prenatal effects of sex hormones. But others point to social explanations, such as gender differences in the spatial experiences of boys and girls.

Education

Giftedness

Contrary to stereotypes, gifted children as a group do well in later life. Today, many children identified as gifted are offered special programs. It appears that these students benefit from these programs.

Mental Retardation

For students with varying severity levels of **mental retardation,** individualized education programs can help meet special needs. On the other hand, test results may lead educators to underestimate a child's ability.

The Self-Fulfilling Prophecy

According to studies of the **self-fulfilling prophecy,** teacher expectations influence student performance. If teachers expect little of a child because of a low IQ score, that child will likely perform accordingly. The reason for this effect is not clear. Also, grouping or tracking, often based on intelligence tests, can harm students assigned to the slower groups. Within-classroom grouping seems less harmful in this respect than between-classroom grouping.

Perspectives on Intelligence

Intelligence is a complex concept and is expressed in many ways besides IQ. Because intelligence is influenced by both heredity and environment, group differences are hard to interpret. In education, intelligence testing can help identify students for special programs, but it can also limit the opportunities of those who don't score well.

In the Field Resources

Books

Gardner, H. (1983). *Frames of mind.* New York: Basic Books.

Gardner introduces his theory of multiple intelligences for the first time.

Sternberg, R.J. (1988). *The triarchic mind.* New York: Penguin Books.

Sternberg presents his tricomponent theory of intelligence.

Zigler, E., & Muenchow, S. (1992). *Head Start: The inside story of America's most successful educational experiment.* New York: Basic Books.

Coauthored by Head Start's first director, this book gives an inside look at the science and politics of Head Start—how it began, what it went through, and where it is today.

Films and Videos

I.Q. (1994, 106 min)

This is a cute love story about intelligence—and popular conceptions of it. With two men competing for one woman, this film depicts differences between analytical and practical intelligences (Tim Robbins, Meg Ryan, Walter Matthau.)

Rain Man (1988, 128 min.)

This film is about two brothers, one an autistic savant who has a mental calculator for numbers and an indelible memory for facts. He embodies the theory of multiple intelligences. (Dustin Hoffman, Tom Cruise, Valeria Golino.)

Internet

Educational Testing Service (http://www.ets.org/)

Has information about SATs, GREs, and other tests, practice questions, an on-line magazine, and links to education sites.

U.S. Department of Education (htp://www.ed.gov/)

Contains information about government education programs and services, studies, statistics, and press releases.

Journals and Periodicals

Journal of Educational Psychology
Child Development
Developmental Psychology
Intelligence

Telephone and Mail

U.S. Department of Education (1-800-USA-LEARN)

13 *Social Influences*

SOCIAL PERCEPTION

Making Attributions
Forming Impressions
Attraction

SOCIAL INFLUENCE

Conformity
Attitudes and Attitude Change
Group Processes

SOCIAL RELATIONS

Aggression
Altruism

The situation You see a newspaper ad for a psychology experiment that pays well, so you sign up. As you arrive at the laboratory, located at Yale University, you meet two men. One is the experimenter, a young man dressed in a white lab coat. The other is a pleasant middle-age man named Mr. Wallace. After introductions, the experimenter explains that you will be taking part in a study on the effects of punishment on learning. By a drawing of lots, it is determined that you'll serve as the "teacher" and Mr. Wallace as the "learner." So far, so good.

What's Your Prediction?

How far can people be pushed?

Before you know it, however, the situation takes on a more ominous tone. You find out that your job is to test the learner's memory and administer electric shocks of increasing intensity whenever he makes a mistake. You are taken to another room, where the experimenter straps Mr. Wallace into a chair, rolls up his sleeve, tapes electrodes onto his arm, and applies "electrode paste" to prevent blisters and burns. You overhear Mr. Wallace say that he has a heart problem and the experimenter reply that although the shocks are painful, they will not cause permanent damage. You then go back to the main room, where you're seated in front of a shock generator—a machine with thirty switches that range from 15 volts (labeled "slight shock") to 450 volts (labeled "XXX").

Your task is easy. First, you read a list of word-pairs to Mr. Wallace through a microphone. *Blue—phone. Girl—hat. Fish—spoon.* Then, you test his memory with a series of multiple-choice questions. The learner answers each question by pressing one of four switches that light up on the shock generator. If his answer is correct, you go to the next question. If it's incorrect, you announce the correct answer and shock him. As you press the shock switch, you can hear a buzzer go off in the learner's room. After each wrong answer, you're told, the shock intensity should be increased by 15 volts.

You don't realize it, but the experiment is rigged, and Mr. Wallace—who works for the experimenter—is not receiving any shocks. As the session proceeds, the learner makes more and more errors, leading you to work your way up the shock scale. As you reach 75 volts, you hear the learner grunt in pain. At 120 volts, he shouts. If you're still in it at 150 volts, he complains about his heart and cries out, "Experimenter! That's all. Get me out of here. I refuse to go on!" Screams of agony and protest follow. If you reach 300 volts, he absolutely refuses to go on. By the time you surpass 330 volts, the learner falls silent and is not heard from again. 360 volts. Zap. Not a peep. 420, 435, 450. Zap. Still no response. At some point, you turn to the experimenter. What should I do? Shouldn't we check on him? But in answer to your inquiries, the experimenter calmly repeats his commands: "Please continue." "The experiment requires that you continue." "You have no other choice, you *must* go on."

Make a prediction What do you do? Feeling caught between a rock and a hard place, do you follow your conscience or obey the experimenter? Do you stop at 45 volts? 150? 300? How would other subjects react? Would *anyone* in their right mind keep shocking the hapless Mr. Wallace all the way to 450 volts? Based on what you know about people, try to predict the point at which most subjects stopped and defied the experimenter. Make your prediction by circling a voltage level.

15	45	75	105	135	165	195	225
255	285	315	345	375	405	435	450

The results More than thirty years ago, social psychologist Stanley Milgram (1963) staged this situation to examine obedience to authority. When Milgram described the study to college students, adults, and a group of psychiatrists, they predicted that, on average, they would stop at 135 volts—and that almost *nobody* would go all the way. They were wrong. In Milgram's initial study, twenty-six out of forty men—that's 65 percent—delivered the ultimate punishment of 450 volts.

What does it all mean? Why did so many subjects obey the experimenter, even while thinking they were hurting a fellow human being? One possible explanation for these scary results is that Milgram's subjects—all of whom were male—were unusually cruel and sadistic. Who were these guys? Or maybe the result says something about men in general. What if the subjects were women instead? How far up the shock scale would they go? In a follow-up study, Milgram examined this question by putting forty women in the same situation. The result: 65 percent of the women tested administered 450 volts, identical to the number of men.

Hmm. Males and females, perhaps people in general, are willing if not eager to harm a fellow human being. As a sad commentary on human nature, perhaps Milgram's study says more about aggression than obedience. But how far would subjects go if *not* ordered to do so? What if the experimenter did not constantly prod the subjects to raise the voltage level? In this situation, Milgram found that only one subject out of forty (2.5 percent) pressed the last switch. Most stopped at 75 volts.

Milgram's subjects had acted out of obedience, not cruelty. In fact, most were visibly tormented by the experience. Many of those who administered 450 volts perspired, stuttered, trembled, bit their lips, and even burst into fits of nervous laughter. It was as if they wanted to stop but felt powerless to do so. What does it mean? When Nazis were tried for war crimes after World War II, their defense was: "I just followed orders." Intrigued by the power of authority implied by this statement, Milgram devised a laboratory situation to mimic the forces that operate in real-life crimes of obedience. As we'll see throughout this chapter, this classic research cries out the message of social psychology loud and clear: Other people can have a profound impact on our behavior.

Every now and then, an event comes along that seems to defy explanation. One such event took place in Los Angeles, in 1991. Police cars chased motorist Rodney King through the night, stopped his car, and cornered the unarmed black man on the street. A sergeant fired a 50,000-volt stun gun at King's chest, knocking him to the ground. Three other officers then clubbed him with their nightsticks, while eleven others looked on. King suffered a fractured skull, a crushed cheekbone, burn marks on the chest, a broken ankle, and internal injuries. To many, this horrifying incident was an act of racism, like an old-fashioned lynching. But then, on April 29, 1992, in the trial of four police officers charged with King's assault, a California jury returned verdicts of not guilty.

News of the jury's acquittals sparked a storm of anger in Los Angeles. At first, crowds gathered to protest the decision. But before long, mobs were rushing the streets, blocking traffic, setting buildings on fire, smashing windows, and looting stores. In a chilling incident that paralleled the King beating, members of a local gang pulled driver Reginald Denny from his truck, beat him senseless, and shot him in the leg. Thanks to four strangers who rushed Denny to the emergency room of a nearby hospital, he survived the attack. Still, others were killed and parts of the city were destroyed. One year later, the federal government retried the four officers for violating King's civil rights. Two of the officers were convicted by a second jury. The tension subsided.

This entire episode—the beating, the verdict, the riots, and the retrial—raises many questions. Was the King incident racially motivated? Why didn't the officers who saw the beating intervene to stop it? What persuaded the first jury to vote for acquittal and the second for conviction? What caused the mob violence that followed the first trial? And amid the chaos, what inspired four courageous citizens to rescue the fallen trucker? These questions—about social perceptions, conformity, persuasion, aggression, and altruism—are questions of **social psychology**, the study of how individuals think, feel, and behave in social situations.

social psychology The study of how individuals think, feel, and behave in social situations.

The videotaped beating of Rodney King (top left), *the riots that erupted after the police officers were acquitted* (top right), *and a group of residents working together on the cleanup after the riot* (bottom).

Social Perception

How do we come to know other people? What is the fundamental attribution error—and is it "fundamental"? Why are we so slow to revise our first impressions in light of new evidence? In liking, do birds of a feather flock together, or do opposites attract? And is physical beauty an objective characteristic or strictly in the eye of the beholder?

As social beings, humans are drawn to each other. We work together, play together, live together, and often make lifetime commitments to grow old together. In all our interactions, we engage in **social perception,** the process of coming to know and evaluate other persons. People are complex, not transparent, and it's not easy to form accurate impressions of them. So how do we do it? What kinds of evidence do we use? We cannot actually "see" inner dispositions or states of mind any more than a detective can see a crime that has already been committed. So, like the detective who tries to reconstruct events from physical traces, witnesses, and other clues, we observe the way people behave, try to explain that behavior, then put all the pieces together to form an impression.

Why were Israeli Prime Minister Netanyahu and Palestinian leader Yasser Arafat shaking hands? Did they really want to, or was the greeting compelled by the situation? In understanding people, we make attributions for their behavior. In this particular meeting, held in 1996, the rival leaders greeted each other—but at a distance. In the past, Netanyahu had said he would never shake Arafat's hand.

Making Attributions

Why did the police officers beat Rodney King senseless—were they angry or sadistic, or had King inflamed them? In trying to make sense of people from their actions, we need to understand what *causes* their behavior. What kinds of explanations do we come up with, and how do we go about making them? In *The Psychology of Interpersonal Relations,* Fritz Heider (1958) proposed that we are all "intuitive scientists" in the way we determine why people behave as they do. According to Heider, the explanations we come up with are called attributions, and the theory that describes the process is called **attribution theory.**

Attribution Theory Although there are numerous possible explanations for the events of human behavior, Heider found it useful to group our attributions into two major categories: personal and situational. The juries that tried the four police officers in the Rodney King case, for example, had to decide: Was the beating caused by characteristics of the officers (a *personal attribution*), or had King somehow provoked their actions (a *situational attribution*)? For the attribution theorist, the goal is not to determine the true causes of this event but, rather, to study our *perceptions* of the causes.

Following Heider, Harold Kelley (1967) theorized that people often make attributions on the basis of three types of information: consensus, distinctiveness, and consistency. To illustrate these concepts, imagine that you're standing on a street corner one hot, steamy evening, when all of a sudden a stranger bursts out of a cool, air-conditioned movie theater and blurts out, "Great movie!" Looking up, you don't recognize the film title, so you wonder what to make of this candid appraisal. Was the behavior (the rave review) caused by something about the person (the stranger), the stimulus (the film), or the specific circumstances (perhaps the comfortable theater)? Because you're possibly interested in spending an evening at the movies, how do you explain this incident?

Thinking like a scientist, you would probably seek *consensus information* to see how other persons react to the same stimulus. In other words, how do other moviegoers feel about this film? If others also rave about the film, the stranger's behavior is high in consensus and is thus attributed to the stimulus. If others are critical of the same film, the behavior is low in consensus and is attributed to the person.

social perception The processes by which we come to know and evaluate other persons.

attribution theory A set of theories that describe how people explain the causes of behavior.

"It's not you, Frank, it's me—I don't like you."

People make attributions all the time in an effort to make sense of their social world.

Still thinking like a scientist, you might want to have *distinctiveness information* to see how the same person reacts to different stimuli. In other words, how does this raving moviegoer react to other films? If this stranger is critical of many other films, then this rave review is highly distinctive and is attributed to the stimulus. If the stranger gushes about everything, then this review is low in distinctiveness and is attributed to the person, not to the film.

Finally, you might seek *consistency information* to see what happens to the behavior at another time when the person and the stimulus both remain the same. How does this moviegoer feel about this same film on other night? If the stranger raves about the film on video as well as in the theater, then the behavior is consistent. But if the stranger does not always enjoy the film, then the behavior is low in consistency. According to Kelley, behavior that is consistent is attributed to the stimulus when consensus and distinctiveness are also high, and to the person when they are low. Behaviors that are low in consistency are attributed to fleeting circumstances, such as the temperature of the movie theater (the theory and the predictions it makes are represented in Figure 13.1).

Kelley's attribution theory is logical, but does it describe the way that you and I analyze the behavior of others? To some extent, yes. Research shows that when people are asked to make attributions for someone's behavior, they often follow this logic and make attributions on the basis of consensus, distinctiveness, and consistency information (McArthur, 1972; Cheng & Novick, 1990; Fosterling, 1992). But as social perceivers, do we really analyze behavior in the way one might expect of a computer? Do we have the time, the desire, or the cognitive capacity for such mindful processes? Not always. With so much to explain and not enough time in a day, we often take mental shortcuts, cross our fingers, and get on with life (Fiske & Taylor, 1991). The problem is that with speed comes bias and perhaps even a loss of accuracy. We now examine two types of biases in attribution.

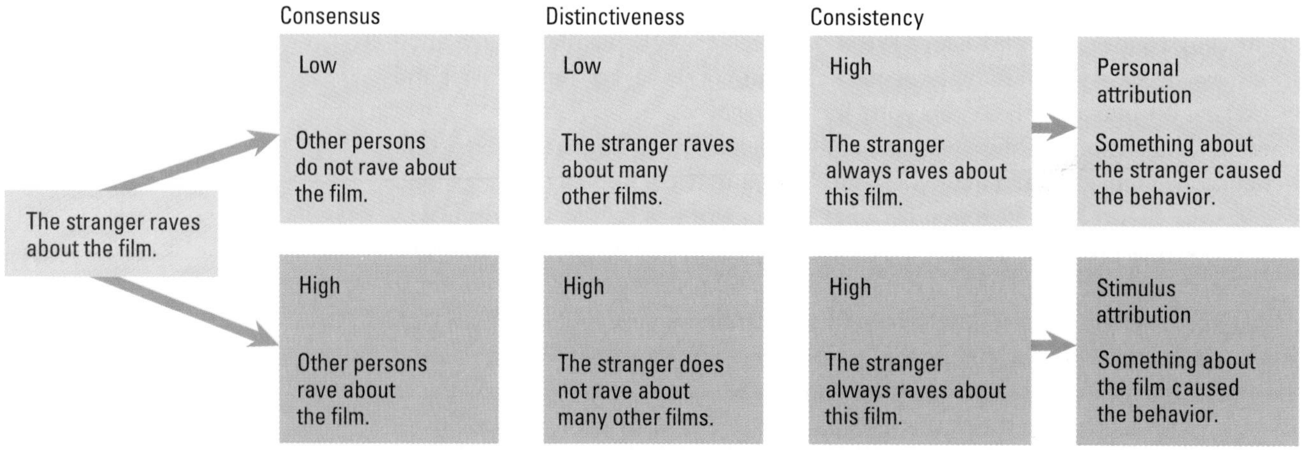

Figure 13.1 Kelley's attribution theory For behaviors that are consistent over time, attribution theory predicts that people make personal attributions under conditions of low consensus and distinctiveness (*top row*), and situational attributions under high consensus and distinctiveness (*bottom row*). Behaviors that are low in consistency (not shown) are attributed to passing circumstances.

The Fundamental Attribution Error By the time you complete this chapter, you will have learned the cardinal lesson of social psychology: People are influenced in profound ways by situations. This point seems obvious, right? So why, then, are parents often astonished to hear that their mischievous child, the family monster, is a perfect angel in school? And why are students often surprised to see that a favorite professor, an eloquent lecturer, can be awkward in informal conversation? These reactions are symptoms of a well-documented aspect of social perception. When people explain the behavior of others, they typically overestimate the role of personal factors and underestimate the role of the situation. This bias is so pervasive, and often so misleading, that it has been called the **fundamental attribution error** (Ross, 1977).

What are Michael Richards, Jason Alexander, Jerry Seinfeld, and Julia Louise-Dreyfus, really *like? As a consequence of the fundamental attribution error, TV viewers might assume that these actors are, in life, like Kramer, George, Jerry, and Elaine—the bizarre characters they play on* Seinfeld.

The fundamental attribution error was first discovered in a study by Edward Jones and Victor Harris (1967). In that study, subjects read a speech presumably written by a college student that was either for or against Fidel Castro, the communist leader of Cuba. Some subjects were told that the student had freely chosen his or her position; others were told that the student was assigned the position by an instructor. What was the student's true attitude? In response to this question, subjects sensibly judged the student's attitude from the speech when the position was freely chosen. So far, so good. But even when subjects knew that the student had no choice, they still inferred his or her attitude from the speech. Thus, the student who wrote for rather than against Castro was seen as more favorable toward the Cuban leader—whether that essay position was freely chosen or not. This finding has been repeated many times, typically with the same result: Except when subjects are highly motivated to make a careful judgment (Webster, 1993; Fein, 1996), they attribute the speaker's position to his or her attitude—regardless of the situation (Jones, 1990; Gilbert & Malone, 1995).

A fascinating study by Lee Ross and others (1977) exposes the fundamental attribution error in a familiar setting, the TV quiz show. By a flip of a coin, subjects were randomly assigned to play the role of either the questioner or the contestant in a quiz game, while spectators looked on. In front of the contestant and spectators, the experimenter instructed the questioner to write ten challenging questions from his or her own store of general knowledge. If you're a trivia buff, you can imagine how esoteric these questions might have been: Who was the first governor of Idaho? What team won the NHL Stanley Cup in 1968? It's no wonder that contestants correctly answered less than 40 percent of the questions asked. When the game was over, all participants rated the questioner's and contestant's general knowledge on a scale of 0 to 100.

Picture the events that transpired. The questioners appeared more knowledgeable than the contestants—after all, they knew all the answers. But a moment's reflection should remind us that the situation put the questioner at a huge advantage. So did subjects take the situation into account, or did they conclude that the questioners actually had more knowledge? As shown in Figure 13.2, the results were startling. Spectators rated the questioners as above average in their general knowledge and the contestants as below average. The contestants even rated themselves as inferior to their partners. Like the spectators, they too were fooled by the loaded situation.

fundamental attribution error A tendency to overestimate the impact of personal causes of behavior and to overlook the role of situations.

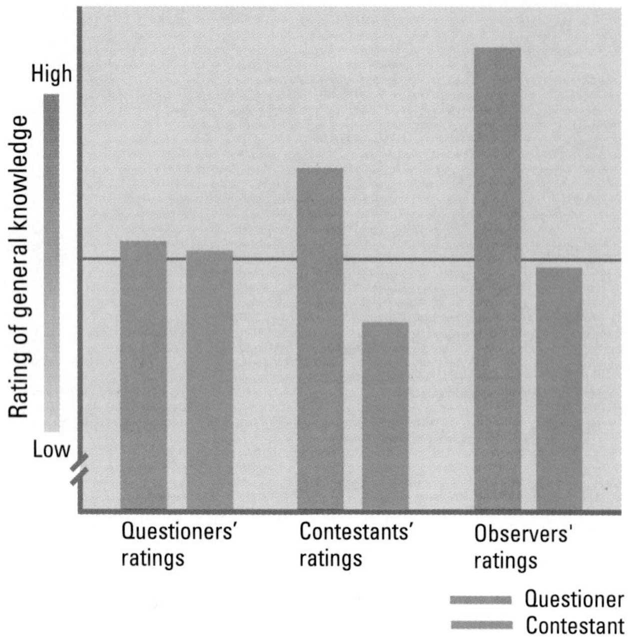

Figure 13.2 Fundamental attribution error in a TV quiz show The simulated quiz show put questioners at an advantage over contestants, yet observers still saw the questioners as more knowledgeable (*right*). Although questioners did not overrate their own general knowledge (*left*), contestants, like the observers, rated themselves as inferior (*middle*). These results illustrate the fundamental attribution error.

What's going on here? Why do social perceivers consistently make unwarranted attributions for behavior to persons and fail to appreciate the impact of situations? According to Daniel Gilbert and Patrick Malone (1995), the problem stems primarily from *how* attributions are made. Attribution theorists used to assume that people survey all the evidence and then decide on a personal or situational attribution. Instead, claims Gilbert, there is a two-step process: First, we identify the behavior and make a quick personal attribution; then, we correct or adjust that inference to account for situational influences. The first step is simple, natural, and automatic—like a reflex; the second one requires attention, thought, and effort.

Why is it so natural to attribute behavior to persons rather than to the situations they are in? Is this tendency universal, or is it limited to Western cultures in which individuals are seen as autonomous and responsible for their own actions? Indeed, many non-Western cultures take a more holistic view that focuses on the relationship between persons and their social roles. To see if these differing worldviews are related to attributions, Joan Miller (1984) asked people of varying ages from the United States and from India to describe what caused certain positive and negative behaviors they had observed in their lives. Among the youngest children, there were no cultural differences. With increasing age, however, the American subjects made more personal attributions, while the Indian subjects became more situational. These findings suggest that the fundamental attribution error may be unique to Western cultures (see Figure 13.3).

Self-Serving Attributions As logical as we try to be, our attributions are sometimes colored by an underlying need to maintain and enhance our self-esteem. Time and again, research has shown that when students receive their exam grades, those who do well take credit for the success; those who do poorly complain about the instructor and the questions. When professors have their articles accepted for publication, they assume it reflects on the high quality of their work; when articles are rejected, they blame the editor or the reviewers. In a whole range of situations, it seems that we are biased in the attributions we make for our own outcomes—taking quick credit for success but distancing ourselves from failure (Schlenker et al., 1990).

Other motives can also influence our attributions for the behavior of others. For example, William Klein and Ziva Kunda (1992) showed subjects the performance on a practice quiz of another subject, a male target, who was later expected to become either their partner or their opponent in a competition. In all cases, the target answered the practice questions correctly. The reason for his success? Hoping he was not too competent, subjects who thought that the target was to be their opponent perceived him as less able than those who thought he was their prospective partner. To justify their wishful thinking, the subjects reasoned that the task was easy and that luck was a contributing factor.

Forming Impressions

In the process of forming an impression of a person, making attributions is only the first step. A second step is to combine and integrate all the evidence into a coherent picture. Research shows that the impressions we form of people are generally based on a "weighting" and "averaging" of all the evidence (Anderson, 1981; Kashima & Kerekes, 1994). This same research also shows, however, that once we do form an impression of someone, we become less and less likely to revise our opinions in light of new, even contradictory evidence. As we'll see, first impressions are powerful.

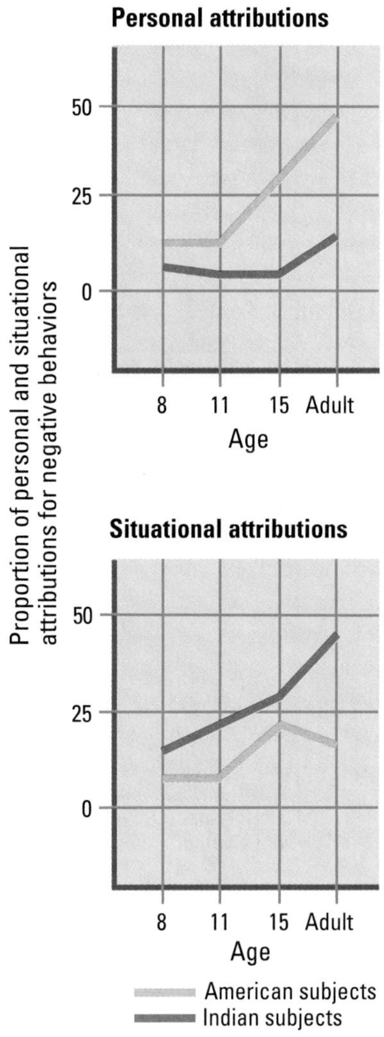

Figure 13.3 Fundamental attribution error: a Western bias? Subjects from the United States and India described the causes of various behaviors. Among young children, there were no cultural differences. With age, however, the Americans made more personal attributions and Indian subjects made more situational attributions.

Cognitive-Confirmation Biases It is often said that first impressions stick, and social psychologists are inclined to agree. In a classic demonstration of this phenomenon, Solomon Asch (1946) told a group of subjects that a person was "intelligent, industrious, impulsive, critical, stubborn, and envious." He then presented a second group with exactly the same list, but in reverse order. Logically, the two groups should have formed the same impression. Instead, however, subjects who heard the first list—in which the positive traits came first—were more favorable in their evaluations than those who heard the second list. The reason: People are influenced more by information they receive early in an interaction than by information that appears later—a finding known as the **primacy effect.**

The primacy effect occurs for two reasons. The first is that we become somewhat less attentive to later behavioral evidence once we have already formed an impression. Thus, when subjects in one study read a series of statements about someone, the amount of time they spent reading each statement declined steadily as they proceeded through the list (Belmore, 1987). Does this mean that we are doomed to a life of primacy? No, not necessarily. Tired, or unstimulated, one's attention may wane. Donna Webster and others (1996) found that college students "leaped to conclusions" about a person on the basis of preliminary information when they were mentally fatigued from having just taken a two-hour exam. But when they were alert and sufficiently motivated to keep from tuning out, this bias was diminished.

More unsettling is the second reason for primacy, known as the change-of-meaning hypothesis. Once people form an impression, they later interpret inconsistent information in light of that impression. Asch's research shows just how malleable the meaning of a trait can be. When people are told that a kind person is *calm,* they assume that he or she is gentle, peaceful, and serene. When a cruel person is said to be *calm,* however, the same word is interpreted to mean cool, shrewd, and calculating. There are many examples to illustrate the point. Based on your first impression, the word *proud* can mean self-respecting or conceited; *critical* can mean astute or picky; and *impulsive* can mean spontaneous or reckless (Hamilton & Zanna, 1974; Watkins & Peynircioglu, 1984).

> *"It is a capital mistake to theorize before you have all the evidence. It biases the judgment."*
>
> — ARTHUR CONAN DOYLE

A study by John Darley and Paget Gross (1983) illustrates this point in an important setting. In their study, subjects were asked to evaluate the academic potential of a fourth-grade girl named Hannah. Half of the subjects were led to believe that she was from an upper-middle-class home with educated, professional parents (high expectations). The other half were told that she lived in a run-down neighborhood and had poorly educated working parents (low expectations). As illustrated in Figure 13.4, subjects in the first group were somewhat more positive in their ratings of Hannah's ability than were those in the second group. Within each of these groups, however, half the subjects watched a videotape of Hannah taking a short achievement test. Her performance on the tape was not

primacy effect The tendency for impressions of others to be heavily influenced by information appearing early in an interaction.

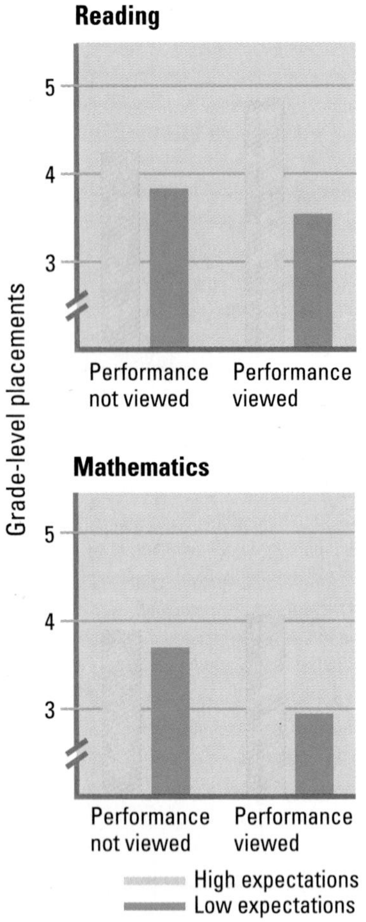

Figure 13.4 Mixed evidence: does it extinguish or fuel first impressions? Subjects rated the potential of a schoolgirl. Without seeing her test performance, those with high expectations rated her slightly higher than did those with low expectations. Among subjects who watched a tape of the girl taking a test, the expectations effect was even greater.

particularly high or low but was average—she correctly answered some hard questions but missed others that were easy. With all these subjects seeing the same objective-test performance, you would think that the difference between the high- and low-expectation groups would be completely wiped out. Yet among subjects who saw the tape, Hannah received even lower ability ratings from those with low expectations and even higher ratings from those with high expectations. Presenting a body of evidence did not extinguish the first-impression bias; it *fueled* it.

In events that are ambiguous enough to support contrasting interpretations, perceivers see what they expect to see. We are even biased in the way we interpret evidence that plainly disconfirms our opinions. Kari Edwards and Edward Smith (1996) presented both advocates and opponents of various issues—such as abortion, the death penalty, and affirmative action—with arguments that were compatible or incompatible with their own points of view. They found that subjects spent more time scrutinizing the incompatible arguments, saw more flaws in them, and rated them as weaker—particularly when they felt committed to their initial opinions. Additional studies have shown as well that people are quick to discredit evidence that contradicts the conclusions they want to reach (Ditto & Lopez, 1992; Kunda, 1990).

Behavioral-Confirmation Biases As social perceivers, we interpret new information in light of our existing beliefs and preferences. At times, we may even unwittingly *create* support for these beliefs and preferences. In Chapter 12, we saw that teachers who have positive or negative expectations of a student, perhaps based on an IQ score, alter their behavior toward that student, thus setting into motion a self-fulfilling prophecy (Rosenthal & Jacobson, 1968). The same process is at work in other settings as well. In a study of 34 corporate managers and 164 job applicants, Amanda Phillips and Robert Dipboye (1989) found that when the managers had positive expectations, they spent more interview time trying to impress rather than to evaluate the applicant and were more likely to make a favorable hiring decision. In another study involving actual job interviews, Thomas Dougherty and others (1994) found that interviewers with positive rather than negative expectations were warmer, more outgoing, and more cheerful in their demeanor. They also gave more information and spent more time selling the company.

How does this self-fulfilling prophecy work? How do social perceivers transform beliefs into reality? As shown by research on teacher expectations, the process involves a three-step chain of events (see Figure 13.5). First, a perceiver forms an opinion of a target person—based on the target's physical appearance, reputation, gender, race, or initial interactions. Second, the perceiver behaves in a manner that is consistent with that first impression. Third, the target unwittingly adjusts his or her behavior to the perceiver's actions (Darley & Fazio, 1980). By steering interactions with others along a path narrowed by our beliefs, we engage in a "behavioral-confirmation" bias that keeps us from judging others objectively. Thankfully, this bias is not inevitable. If we conceptualize the problem as a three-step process, it is possible to identify two links in the chain that can be broken to prevent a vicious cycle (Hilton & Darley, 1991; Snyder, 1993).

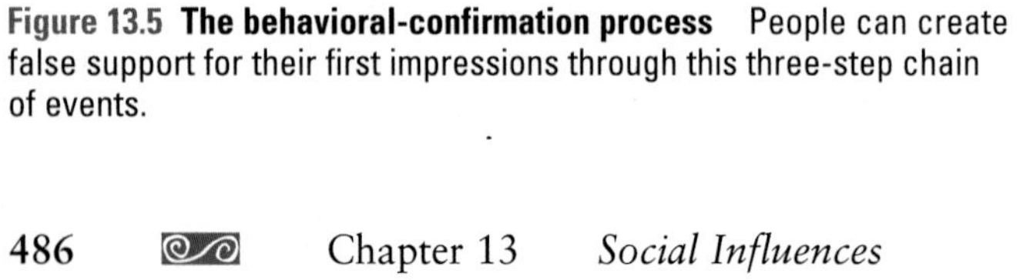

Figure 13.5 The behavioral-confirmation process People can create false support for their first impressions through this three-step chain of events.

First, there's the link between the perceiver's expectations and behavior toward the target. When perceivers are highly motivated to seek the truth (as when they evaluate the target as a possible teammate or opponent), when they can attend closely to the interaction, and when they are concerned about the way they are being judged by the target, they become more objective—and often do not confirm prior expectations (Neuberg, 1989; Copeland, 1994; Snyder & Haugen, 1994; Harris & Perkins, 1995). Next is the link between a perceiver's actions and a target's response. Often, the targets of our perceptions are not aware of the expectations that we have of them. But what if they were? How would you react, for example, if *you* knew that you were being cast in a particular light? When it happens to subjects in social-perception studies—especially when they think they are being misjudged—they often make it a point to behave in ways that contradict the perceiver's initial beliefs (Hilton & Darley, 1985; Swann & Ely, 1984). Clearly, the persons we perceive have their own prophecies to fulfill.

Thus far, we have discussed the way that people form and maintain their impressions of each other. It's important to recognize, however, that the process begins with a warm-blooded, motivated, emotional human being whose impressions are often positive or negative, not neutral. We now examine this evaluative aspect of social perception. First, we look at some of the factors that promote positive evaluations, or attraction. Later, in Chapter 14, we turn to the problem of prejudice, the dark side of social perception.

On MTV's Singled Out, *male and female contestants choose a date, without looking, from a group of fifty prospective dates. In the end, three finalists answer questions by the contestant. Consistent with the notion that people are drawn to others who are similar, finalists earn points for answers that match the contestant's. The person with the most points wins the date.*

Attraction

When you meet someone for the first time, what personal characteristics are you drawn to? Common sense is filled with contradiction: Does familiarity breed fondness or contempt? Do birds of a feather flock together, or do opposites attract? And is beauty the object of our desire, or do we think appearances are deceiving? Over the years, researchers have identified various determinants of attraction. Two of the most powerful are similarity and physical attractiveness.

Similarity and Liking Time and again, studies have revealed a general principle of attraction: The more exposure we have to a stimulus—whether it's a foreign word, a geometric form, a melody, or a face—the more we like it (Zajonc, 1968; Bornstein, 1989). In Chapter 4, we saw that this **mere-exposure effect** occurs even when the stimuli are presented subliminally, without the subject's awareness. Mere exposure can also influence our self-evaluations. Imagine, for example, that you had a photograph of yourself developed into two pictures—one that depicted your actual appearance, and the other a mirror-image copy. Which picture would you prefer? Which would a friend prefer? Theodore Mita and his colleagues (1977) tried this experiment with female college students and found that most preferred their own mirror images, while their friends liked the actual photos. In both cases, the preference was for the view of the face that was most familiar.

Although exposure tends to increase liking, interactions provide us with additional and relevant information about others. Imagine that you meet someone for the first time and strike up a conversation about politics, sports, restaurants, and your favorite band—only to realize that the two of you have a lot in common. Now

[Drawing by Weber; © 1996 The New Yorker Magazine, Inc.]

"The minute you walked into the room, I said to myself, 'Now, *he* looks interesting.'"

Research shows that people seek out others who are similar.

mere-exposure effect The attraction to a stimulus that results from increased exposure to it.

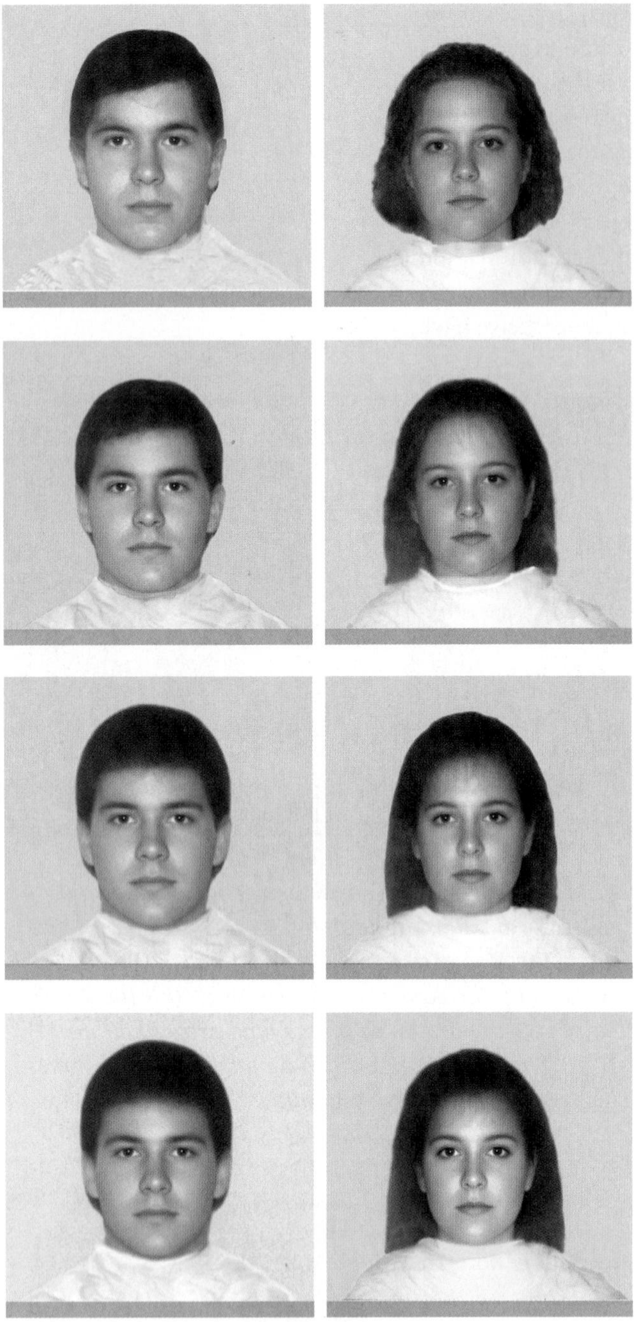

Figure 13.6 The beauty in "averaged" faces Using computer-generated composites like these, Langlois and Roggman (1990) found that images that combined the features of sixteen and thirty-two faces (rows 3 and 4) were seen as more attractive than composites derived from two and four faces (rows 1 and 2) or the individual faces on which they were based. When combined, "averaged" features produce attractive faces.

imagine the opposite experience, of meeting someone who is very different in his or her interests, values, and outlook on life. Which of these two strangers would you want to see again: the one who is similar or the one who is different?

As a general rule, people prefer to associate with others who are similar to themselves. According to Donn Byrne and his colleagues (1986), this effect on attraction consists of a two-step process: (1) We avoid others who are very different, then (2) among those who are left, we seek out those people who are the most similar to us. As a result, friends and couples are more likely than are randomly paired persons to share common attitudes and interests. They are also more likely to be similar in age, religion, race, level of education, height, intelligence, and economic status. The more similar two individuals are, the better are the chances that their relationship will last (Byrne, 1971).

Physical Attractiveness As we encounter and interact with people, our perceptions of them are influenced in subtle ways by their height, weight, skin color, hair color, and other aspects of outward appearance. Among Americans, blonds are considered fun-loving and sociable, and obese people are seen as weak-willed, lazy, and dependent. In the perception of men, height too is a factor—as suggested by the astonishing fact that between the years 1900 and 1996, the taller candidate for U.S. president won twenty-two out of twenty-four elections. Clearly, people see connections between outward appearance and personality (Alley, 1988; Bull & Rumsey, 1988; Herman et al., 1986).

The most influential aspect of appearance is physical attractiveness. As children, we were told that "beauty is only skin deep." Yet as adults, we prefer others who are good looking. Over the years, studies have shown that attractive people fare better in the way they are treated by teachers, job interviewers, judges, juries, and others (Hatfield & Sprecher, 1986). But wait. What is meant by the term *physical attractiveness?* Is beauty an objective and measurable quality, like height and weight? Or is beauty subjective, existing in the eye of the beholder?

Some psychologists believe that some faces are inherently more attractive than others. There are two sources of evidence for this "objective" view of beauty. First, when subjects rate faces on a 10-point scale, there is typically a high level of agreement over which are more or less attractive. In fact, people seem to prefer faces with eyes, noses, lips, and other features that are not too different from the average. Judith Langlois and Lori Roggman (1990) showed college students actual yearbook photos as well as computerized facial composites that "averaged" the features in these photos. Consistently, subjects preferred the averaged composites to the actual faces (see Figure 13.6). Other studies have since confirmed this effect (Langlois et al., 1994;

Rhodes & Tremewan, 1996). A second source of evidence is that babies who are too young to be aware of the cultural standards of beauty still prefer faces seen as attractive by adults. Judging from their eye movements, young infants spend more time gazing at attractive faces than at unattractive ones—regardless of whether the faces are young or old, male or female, or black or white (Langlois et al., 1991).

Other researchers argue that beauty is subjective and point to the influences of culture, time, and the circumstances of our perception. To enhance their appearance, people from different cultures use face painting, makeup, plastic surgery, scarring, hairstyling, the molding of bones, the filing of teeth, braces, and the piercing of body parts. What people find attractive in one part of the world may be repulsive in other parts of the world (Landau, 1989). Even within a culture, the standards change from one generation to the next. For example, Brett Silverstein and others (1986) examined the measurements of female models appearing in women's magazines between 1901 and 1981, and they found that "curvaceousness" (as measured by the bust-to-waist ratio) varied over time, with a boyish, slender look becoming most desirable in recent years. Finally, judgments of beauty can be inflated or deflated by various circumstances. For example, we evaluate others as more attractive after we have grown to like them (Gross & Crofton, 1977). On the other hand, subjects who viewed nude *Playboy* models later lowered their attractiveness ratings of average-looking women—the result of a contrast effect (Kenrick et al., 1989).

Consistent with the notion that beauty is in the eye of the beholder, people from different cultures enhance their appearance in different ways. Pictured here are a Mejecodoteri woman from Amazon Venezuela (top left), *a Maasi man from Kenya* (top right), *a woman from the state of Gujarat in India* (bottom left), *and a woman named Marilyn Monroe* (bottom right).

The bias for beauty seems so shallow, so superficial. Why are we drawn to people who are physically attractive? One notion is that it's rewarding to be in the company of others who are aesthetically appealing, or "easy on the eyes." In other words, we derive pleasure from beautiful men and women the same way we enjoy breathtaking scenery. Second, people associate beauty with other desirable qualities. Think about children's fairy tales, where Snow White and Cinderella are portrayed as beautiful *and* kind, and where the witch and stepsisters are depicted as ugly *and* cruel. Indeed, studies indicate that good-looking people are also assumed to be smart, successful, well adjusted, happy, confident, assertive, socially skilled, and popular (Dion et al., 1972; Eagly et al., 1991). It's true that good-looking people have more friends and a more active sex life. But beauty is *not* related to measures of intelligence, personality, adjustment, or self-esteem, where popular perceptions exaggerate the reality (Feingold, 1992).

So why does the physical-attractiveness stereotype endure? One possibility is that social perceivers may create support for their biased impressions. Think about the three-step model of the self-fulfilling prophecy described earlier. Mark Snyder and his colleagues (1977) demonstrated this phenomenon in a classic study of interpersonal

As in the story of Cinderella, the perceived link between beauty and goodness is evident even in classic children's fairy tales. (© *Disney Enterprises, Inc.*)

attraction. The subjects were unacquainted pairs of male and female college students. All subjects were given a background sketch of their partner, with men also receiving a photograph of an attractive or unattractive woman, supposedly their partner. At that point, the men rated their partners and then had a conversation over headphones. The result: Men who thought that their partner was physically attractive formed more positive impressions of her personality and were friendlier in their conversational behavior. And now for the clincher: The female subjects whose partners had seen the attractive photograph were later rated by listeners to the conversation as warmer, more confident, and more animated. Fulfilling their own prophecies, men who expected an attractive partner actually created one. This finding calls to mind the Greek myth of Pygmalion, who fell in love with the statue he had carved—and brought it to life.

Social Influence

What's the difference between public and private conformity? Just how far can people be pushed to obey the commands of an authority? What makes for a persuasive communication? Why is it that a change in behavior can elicit a change in attitude? When do groups arouse us, when do they relax us, and why do they sometimes make bad decisions?

Advertisers hire celebrities and supermodels to sell soft drinks, sneakers, and other products. Sports fans spread the "wave" and chant "de-fense" in a spectacular show of unison. Protestors, lost in a sea of anonymous faces, shed inhibitions and become transformed into a mob. Performers with stage fright tremble, turn pale, and freeze before appearing in front of an audience. These examples illustrate that people influence one another in various ways. As we'll see, the source of this influence may be a person or a group, the effect may be a change in behavior or attitude, and the change may be socially destructive (hurting others) or constructive (helping others).

Realizing the power of social influence, the photographer who took this picture anticipated that when one schoolgirl climbed the wall at the Tower of London, others would soon follow.

Conformity

As social animals, we are all vulnerable to subtle, reflexlike influences. We yawn when we see others yawning, and laugh when we hear others laughing. In one study, research confederates stopped on a busy street in New York City, looked up, and gawked at a window of a nearby building. A camera stationed behind the window showed that roughly 80 percent of passersby stopped and gazed up when they saw these confederates (Milgram et al., 1969).

SOCIAL INFLUENCES AND LAW

Social Perception in Jury Trials

It was called the trial of the century. When O. J. Simpson was tried for the murders of his former wife Nicole Brown and Ronald Goldman, the case involved celebrity, sports, sex, money, racial tension, and violence. As in a live theater, the trial was packed with drama. Outside the courthouse, TV cameras and microphones lined a parking-lot area that was called Camp OJ. Inside the courtroom, the jury struggled to decide whether Simpson stabbed his wife and her friend to death and, if so, whether the act was premeditated. The prosecution presented evidence in the form of pictures, witnesses, blood-soaked socks and a glove, shoeprints, and DNA tests. In turn, the defense argued that Simpson was at home at the time, that he was physically unable to overpower the two victims, and that the physical evidence could not be trusted. The trial lasted for nearly a year, and when it was over, the jury announced its controversial verdict: not guilty. For those who disagreed with it, Simpson was retried in a civil suit filed by the victims' families. In February 1997, that jury found Simpson liable for the murders and ordered him to pay the families more than $30 million.

Football Hall-of-Famer O. J. Simpson was charged with the murders of Nicole Brown Simpson and Ron Goldman. In 1996, he was quickly and unanimously acquitted by a criminal jury. Then in 1997, he was found liable for the murders and ordered to pay more than $30 million in damages by a unanimous civil jury. This case has raised many questions about the jury system.

Regardless of how one felt about the trials of O. J. Simpson, they illustrated the importance of social psychology at work in the legal system. Every day, ordinary people are brought together in a courtroom and empowered to make decisions of utmost importance. The trial consists of three stages. First, members of the community are summoned to court, sworn in, questioned, and selected. Next comes the presentation of testimony, arguments, and the judge's instructions. Third, jurors go off to deliberate as a group and strive to reach a common verdict. By law, juries are told to base their decisions only on evidence presented in court—not on extraneous factors. But is this ideal achieved? Over the years, social psychologists have examined some of the possible sources of bias.

Pretrial Publicity When cases are featured in the newspapers and on TV, does the pretrial publicity corrupt the jury? Public opinion surveys have shown that the more people know about a case, the more likely they are to presume the defendant guilty (Moran & Cutler, 1991). This result is not hard to explain. The information appearing in the news tends to come from the district attorney's office, so it typically reveals facts unfavorable to the defense. The real question is whether this exposure overwhelms the evidence—and the jury.

Norbert Kerr and his colleagues (1991) played a videotaped simulation of an armed-robbery trial to hundreds of subjects who took part in 108 mock juries. Before watching the tape, they were exposed to news clippings about the case. Some read material that was neutral, but others received information that implicated the defendant in another crime. As in court, mock jurors were told to base their decisions solely on the evidence. But the pretrial publicity had a marked effect. In groups exposed to the neutral story, 33 percent of the subjects voted guilty after the trial and deliberations. In groups exposed to an incriminating story, that figure increased to 48 percent. Why is pretrial publicity so harmful? Part of the problem is that it is revealed *before* the evidence—bringing primacy effects and first-impression biases into play. Indeed, additional studies have shown that jurors exposed to pretrial publicity later see the prosecutor's evidence as more incriminating (Otto et al., 1994). Clearly, justice demands that prospective jurors with knowledge about a case be excluded or that highly publicized cases be moved, if possible, to less informed communities.

Inadmissible Evidence In his opening statement, Simpson's defense lawyer Johnnie Cochran made reference to witnesses who would not later testify, eliciting objections from prosecuting attorneys. The trial judge sustained the objection and ordered the jury to disregard these references. Similar events from both sides occurred repeatedly. In each case, the jury was instructed to disregard the information.

Jurors often are exposed to extralegal information during a trial. By law, a judge may exclude from evidence any items that are inflammatory, are unreliable, or have been illegally obtained. If such information is disclosed at trial, the judge instructs jurors to disregard it. But can people really strike information from the mind the way a court reporter can strike it from the record? Can jurors resist the forbidden fruit of inadmissible testimony? Common sense suggests not, and so does the research.

In one study, Kassin and Sommers (1997) had mock jurors read a transcript of a double-murder trial based on evidence that was relatively weak, leading only 24 percent to vote guilty. Three other groups read the same case except that the state's evidence included a wiretapped phone conversation in which the defendant had confessed to a friend. In all cases, the defense lawyer objected to this disclosure. When the judge admitted the tape into evidence, the conviction rate rose considerably, to 79 percent. But when the judge excluded the tape and instructed jurors to disregard it, their reaction depended on the reason for the tape being excluded. When told to disregard the tape because it was barely audible and could not be trusted, subjects mentally erased the information, as they should, and delivered the same verdict as in the no-tape control group. But when told to disregard the item because it had been illegally obtained, 55 percent voted guilty. Despite the judge's warning, these subjects were unwilling to ignore testimony they found relevant merely on the basis of a legal "technicality."

Physical Appearances There is a third possible source of bias that is perhaps the most basic of all. As we saw, social perceivers are influenced by physical appearances. Does this bias extend into the courtroom, or is justice truly blind? Diane Berry and Leslie Zebrowitz (1988) speculated that adults with "baby-face" features (high eyebrows, large eyes, round cheeks, a large forehead, and a round chin) would be seen as naive and honest compared to "mature-face" adults—and that this perception would bias judgments in a legal proceeding. They showed mock jurors two versions of a trial. In one, the defendant was charged with negligence for forgetting to warn a customer about the hazard of a product he was selling. In the other version, the defendant was said to have deliberately misled a customer to make the sale. Interestingly, subjects were more likely to find the baby-face defendant negligent, a crime that "matched" his appearance. But they were less likely to judge him as guilty of the crime of deception. A similar pattern was uncovered in the decisions made by small-claims-court judges (Zebrowitz & McDonald, 1991). And other studies have shown that a defendant's physical attractiveness also plays a role: Among defendants whose appearances were rated from photographs, those seen as more attractive received lighter sentences and smaller fines from state judges (Stewart, 1980; Downs & Lyons, 1991).

The law states that verdicts should be based only on evidence presented in court. But jurors are ordinary people—which means that they are subject to the biases of social perception. Having identified some of the problems, researchers are now seeking ways to minimize these prejudicial effects.

Knowing that people are quick to imitate others, TV producers infuse situation comedies with canned laughter to make viewers think the shows are funny, political candidates trumpet inflated results from their own public-opinion polls to attract new voters, and bartenders stuff dollar bills into empty tip jars to draw more money from their customers. As they say, "Monkey see, monkey do."

Conformity, the tendency for people to bring their behavior in line with group norms, is a powerful fact of social life. Cast in a positive light, it promotes harmony, group solidarity, and peaceful coexistence—as when people assume their places in a waiting line. Cast in a negative light, conformity has harmful effects—as when people drink too heavily at parties or tell offensive ethnic jokes because others are

conformity A tendency to alter one's opinion or behavior in ways that are consistent with group norms.

doing the same. For the social psychologist, the goal is not to make moral judgments but, rather, to determine the factors that promote conformity and the reasons for it.

The Early Classics In 1936, Muzafer Sherif published a classic laboratory experiment on how norms develop in small groups. The subjects in his study, thinking they were in a visual-perception experiment, sat in a dark room, saw a beam of light, and then estimated the distance the light had moved. This procedure was repeated several times. Subjects didn't realize it, but the light never moved. The movement they thought they saw was merely an optical illusion. At first, subjects sat alone and reported their perceptions only to the experimenter (most estimates stabilized in the range of one to ten inches). Then, during the next few days, subjects returned to participate in three-person groups. Each time a beam of light was flashed, subjects stated their estimates one by one. As shown in Figure 13.7, initial estimates varied considerably, but the subjects eventually converged on a common perception, each group establishing its own set of norms.

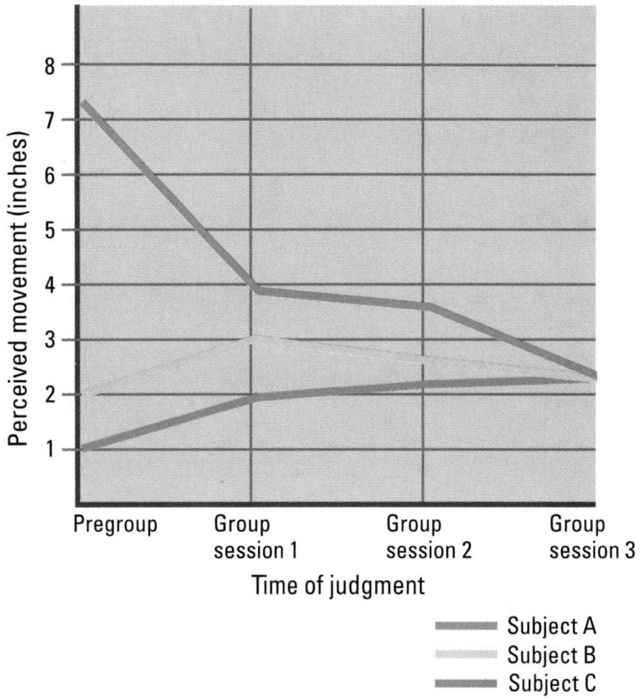

Figure 13.7 A classic case of suggestibility This group in Sherif's study illustrates how subjects' estimates of the apparent movement of light converged over time. Gradually, the group established its own set of norms.

Fifteen years after Sherif's experiment, Solomon Asch (1951) constructed a different situation. Imagine yourself as a subject in his study. You sign up for a psychology experiment, and when you arrive you find six other students waiting around a table. You take an empty seat, and the experimenter explains that he is measuring people's ability to make visual discriminations. As a warm-up, he asks you and the others to indicate which of three comparison lines is identical in length to a standard line (see Figure 13.8).

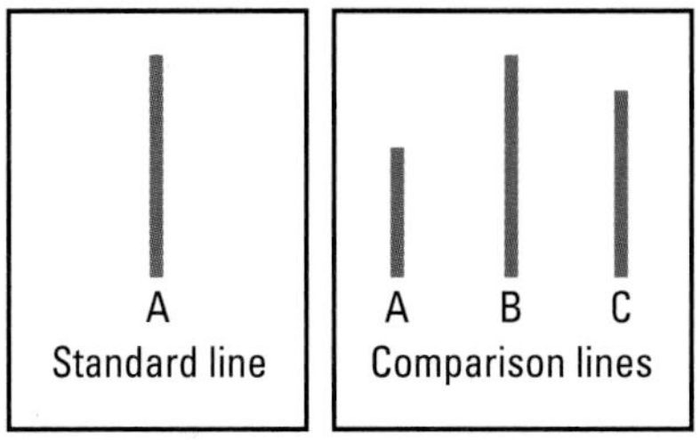

Figure 13.8 Line-judgment task in Asch's study Which comparison line—A, B, or C—is the same length as the standard line?

That seems easy enough. The experimenter then asks you all to take turns in order of your seating position. Starting on his left, the experimenter asks the first person for a judgment. Seeing that you are in the next-to-last position, you patiently await your turn. The opening moments pass uneventfully. The task is clear and everyone agrees on the answers. On the third set of lines, however, the first subject selects the wrong line. Huh? What happened? Did he suddenly lose his mind, his eyesight, or both? Before you know it, the next four subjects choose the same wrong line. Now it's your turn. Faced with what seems like an easy choice, you rub your eyes and take another look. What do you think? Better yet, what do you do? As you may have guessed by now, the other "subjects" were confederates trained to make incorrect judgments on certain trials. The right answers were clear. In a control group, where subjects made their judgments alone, performance was virtually errorless. Yet subjects in the experimental group went along with the incorrect majority 37 percent of the time. This result may seem surprising, but recent studies too have shown that people conform to the responses of others on a variety of cognitive tasks (Larsen, 1990; Schneider & Watkins, 1996).

Both Sherif and Asch found that people are influenced by the behavior of others. But there is an important difference in the types of conformity exhibited in these studies. Sherif's subjects were literally "in the dark"—uncertain of their own perceptions. Wanting to be correct, they looked to others for guidance and adopted the average of the group's estimates as their own. In Asch's study, however, the task was simple enough for subjects to see the lines with their own eyes. Most knew that the

After two uneventful rounds in Asch's line-judgment study the subject (number 6) faces a dilemma. Confederates 1 through 5 all gave the same wrong answer. Should he give his own or conform to theirs?

majority was wrong but went along to avoid becoming social outcasts. In short, there are two very different types of social influence: informational and normative (Deutsch & Gerard, 1955; Campbell & Fairey, 1989). **Informational influence** leads people to conform because they assume that the majority is correct. In the case of **normative influence,** people conform because they fear the social rejection that accompanies deviance. For good reason. Research shows that people who stray from the norm are disliked and often are ridiculed and laughed at (Levine, 1989)—especially in groups that need to reach a consensus (Kruglanski & Webster, 1991).

The distinction between the two types of social influence is important because they produce different types of conformity—private and public. Like beauty, conformity may be skin-deep or may penetrate beneath the surface. In *private conformity,* we change not only our behavior but our opinions as well. To conform at this level is to be genuinely persuaded that the majority is right. In contrast, *public conformity* refers to a temporary and superficial change in which we outwardly comply with the majority in our behavior but privately maintain our own beliefs.

In a study that demonstrates both processes, Robert S. Baron and his colleagues (1996) had subjects, in groups of three (the other two were confederates), act as eyewitnesses: First, they would see a picture of a person, then they would try to pick that person out of a lineup. In some groups, the task was difficult, like Sherif's, as they saw each picture only once, for half a second. For other subjects, the task was easier, like Asch's, in that they saw each picture twice for a total of ten seconds. How often did subjects conform when the confederates made the wrong identification? It depended on how motivated the subjects were. When the experimenter downplayed the task as only a "pilot study," the conformity rates were 35 percent when the task was difficult and 33 percent when it was easy. But when subjects were offered a financial incentive to do well, conformity went up to 51 percent when the task was difficult—and down to 16 percent when it was easy (see Figure 13.9). With pride and money on the line, the Sherif-like subjects conformed more, and the Asch-like subjects conformed less.

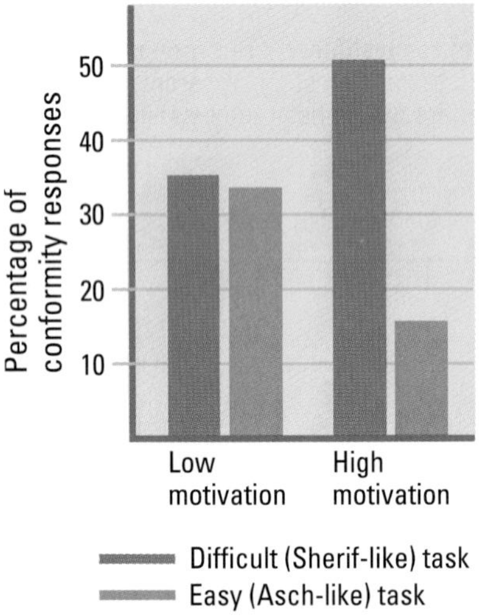

Figure 13.9 Private and public conformity Regardless of whether the task was difficult or easy, there were moderate levels of conformity when subjects had a low motivation (*left*). But when motivated (*right*), with pride and money on the line, subjects conformed more when the task was difficult, as in Sherif's study, and less when it was easy, as in Asch's study (Baron et al., 1996).

Majority Influence Realizing that people can be pressured by others is only the first step in understanding the process of social influence. The next step is to identify the situational factors that make us more or less likely to conform. One obvious factor is the size of a group. Common sense suggests that as a majority increases in size, so does its impact. Actually, it is not that simple. Asch (1956) varied the size of his groups—by using one, two, three, four, eight, or fifteen confederates—and found that conformity increased only up to a point. After four confederates, the amount of *additional* influence was negligible, subject to the law of diminishing returns (see Figure 13.10). Bibb Latané (1981) likens this impact on an individual to the way light bulbs illuminate a surface. Add a second bulb in a room, and the effect is dramatic. Add a tenth bulb, and its impact is barely noticed.

In Asch's initial study, subjects were pitted against a unanimous majority. But what if they had an ally, a partner in dissent? Put yourself in this situation: How do you think having an ally would affect *you?* Varying this aspect of his experiment, Asch found that the presence of just one confederate who gave the correct answer

informational influence Conformity motivated by the belief that others are correct.

normative influence Conformity motivated by a fear of social rejection.

reduced conformity by almost 80 percent. In fact, any dissenter—even one whose competence is called into question—can break the spell cast by a unanimous majority and reduce the pressure to conform (Allen & Levine, 1971).

Although the size of a majority and the presence of an ally influence the amount of pressure that is felt, people are most likely to conform when their attention is drawn to social norms (Cialdini et al., 1991). Of course, we must know what the norms are in a group in order to conform. This may sound like an obvious point, yet we often misperceive what is normative—as when others are afraid or embarrassed to publicly present their true views or behaviors. One common example concerns perceptions of alcohol usage. In university-wide surveys, Deborah Prentice and Dale Miller (1996) found that many students overestimated how comfortable their peers were with the drinking level on campus. They also found that the more positive students thought others were at the start of the school year, the more likely they were, eventually, to conform to this misperception in their own attitudes and behavior. The point is that we are influenced not by social norms per se but by our *perceptions* of those norms.

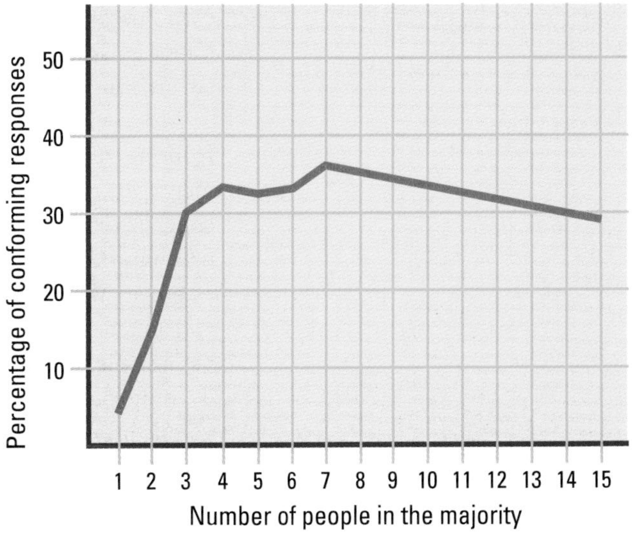

Figure 13.10 Group size and conformity By varying the number of confederates, Asch found that conformity increased with the size of the majority, but only up to a point. As you can see, fifteen had no more impact than did four.

Finally, cultural factors play a key role. In many Western cultures—most notably, the United States, Australia, Great Britain, Canada, and the Netherlands—autonomy and independence are highly valued. In contrast, many cultures of Asia, Africa, and Latin America place a value on social harmony and "fitting in" for the sake of the community. Among the Bantu of Zimbabwe, for example, an African people in which deviance is scorned, 51 percent of the subjects placed in an Asch-like study conformed to the majority's wrong answer—more than the number typically obtained in the West (Triandis, 1994; Bond & Smith, 1996).

Minority Influence It is not easy for individuals who express unpopular views to enlist support from others. Philosopher Bertrand Russell once said that "conventional people are roused to frenzy by departure from convention, largely because they regard such departure as criticism of themselves." Russell may have been right. People who challenge the status quo may be perceived as competent, but they are intensely disliked (Bassili & Provencal, 1988).

Maintaining independence in the face of social pressure to follow is difficult, but it is not impossible. In *The Dissenters,* anthropologist Langston Gwaltney (1986) interviewed "ordinary" nonconformists—an Irish man who befriended black people in a racist community, a New England grandmother who risked arrest to protest nuclear weapons, and a group of nuns who sued their church. Laboratory research also provides relevant evidence. Think about it. Asch's subjects conformed on 37 percent of the trials, but this means that they openly refused to acquiesce in the other 63 percent—a result that bears witness to the human spirit of independence (Friend et al., 1990).

How do nonconformists withstand the pressure to change? Better yet, how do they sometimes manage to sway the majority? According to Serge Moscovici (1985), majorities exert power by sheer numbers, but those in a minority derive their power by sticking to their positions in a persistent, unwavering, and self-confident manner. By holding firm, dissenters can get others to sit up, take notice, and rethink their

It may not be easy, but individuals sometimes resist the social pressure to conform.

own positions. Does it work? Yes. Dozens of studies have shown that dissenters who take a position and remain consistent over time are successful at producing minority influence (Wood et al., 1994).

Moscovici and his colleagues (1969) first observed this phenomenon by confronting real subjects with a *minority* of confederates who made incorrect judgments. In groups of six, subjects took part in what was believed to be a study of color perception. They viewed a series of blue slides and, for each, took turns naming the color. The task was simple—until two confederates described the slides as green. When these confederates were *consistent*—that is, when both made incorrect green judgments for all slides—one-third of all subjects incorrectly reported seeing at least one green slide. People can be influenced in important but subtle ways by minority opinion. Because of social pressures, we may be too intimidated to admit or even to recognize the influence. But it is there, and it is especially likely to materialize when subjects give their answers anonymously or in an indirect way (Clark & Maass, 1990; Moscovici & Personnaz, 1991).

Obedience to Authority Allen Funt, creator of the TV program *Candid Camera,* used to spend as much time observing people as most psychologists do. His conclusion: "The worst thing is how easily people can be led by any kind of authority figure, or even the most minimal signs of authority." Funt went on to describe the time he put up a road sign that read DELAWARE CLOSED TODAY. The reaction? "Motorists didn't question it. Instead they asked, 'Is Jersey open?'" (Zimbardo, 1985, p. 47).

Blind obedience may seem funny, but as the pages of history attest, the implications are sobering. In World War II, Nazi officials participated in the deaths of millions of Jewish men, women, and children. When they came to trial for these crimes, their defense was always the same: "I was just following orders." Was this episode a fluke? A historical aberration? In *Hitler's Willing Executioners,* historian Daniel Goldhagen (1996) argues on the basis of past records that many ordinary German people were willing, anti-Semitic participants in the Holocaust—not just following orders. On the other hand, human crimes of obedience are not unique to Nazi Germany and are committed all over the world, even today (Kelman & Hamilton, 1989). On one most extraordinary occasion, such obedience was carried to its limit: In 1978, 912 men and women of the People's Temple cult obeyed an order from the Reverend Jim Jones to kill themselves.

Taken to extreme, blind obedience can have tragic results. In World War II, Nazi officials killed millions of Jews in the Holocaust. Were these Germans willing participants, as suggested by Daniel Goldhagen in his 1996 book, Hitler's Willing Executioners, *or were they just following orders, as subjects did in Milgram's research?*

To study the power of authority, Stanley Milgram conducted the dramatic experiments described at the start of this chapter. In his 1974 book, *Obedience to Authority,* Milgram reported on the results of having put 1,000 subjects into a situation in which they were ordered by an experimenter to administer painful electric shocks to a confederate. Recall that subjects thought they were "teachers" in a study of the effects of punishment on learning and that each time the "learner" made a mistake, they were to deliver a shock of increasing intensity. The subjects could not actually see the learner, but they could hear grunts of pain, objections, loud screams, and eventual silence. Yet at each step, they were

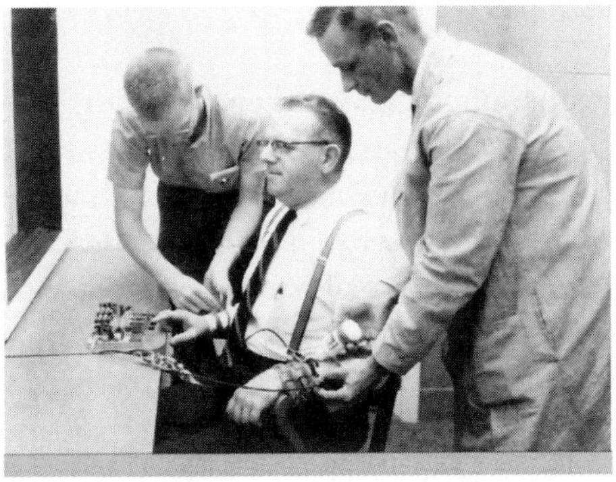

Milgram's subjects used the shock generator shown here to seemingly deliver up to 450 volts to a confederate who was strapped into his chair. (Copyright 1965 by Stanley Milgram. From the film Obedience, *distributed by Penn State Media Sales.)*

ordered to continue up the shock scale. Despite the pain subjects thought they were inflicting, and despite the guilt and anguish they were experiencing, 65 percent in Milgram's initial study delivered the ultimate punishment of 450 volts.

At first, these grim results led people to conclude that Milgram's subjects were heartless and cruel, not "normal" like you and me. On the contrary. Most subjects were tormented by the experience—and comparable levels of obedience were also then found among men, women, and college students all over the world (Miller, 1986; Blass, 1992), leading one author to ask, *Are We All Nazis?* (Askenasy, 1978). Indeed, high levels of obedience were found just a few years ago in studies much like Milgram's that were conducted in the Netherlands (Meeus & Raaijmakers, 1995).

The lesson of Milgram's research is clear. Although some people are more obedient than others, even decent human beings can be pushed to behave in ways that violate the conscience. Think about it. To me, the most striking aspect of Milgram's findings is that a psychology experimenter, unlike one's boss or military superior, cannot ultimately enforce any commands. Can you imagine the power that is wielded by real-life figures of authority? Not content merely to demonstrate obedience, Milgram altered aspects of his experimental situation in order to identify the factors that affect levels of obedience. Three types of factors were systematically varied:

- ***The authority.*** When Milgram moved his experiment from the prestigious campus of Yale University to a run-down city office building, arranged for the experimenter to issue his commands by telephone, or replaced the experimenter with an ordinary person, obedience levels dropped.
- ***The victim.*** In Milgram's main experiment, subjects were physically separated from the learner, so they could distance themselves emotionally from his pain and suffering. When the subject and learner were seated in the same room, however, especially when subjects had to touch the learner, levels of obedience declined.
- ***The situation.*** Two aspects of the experimental situation fueled the high levels of obedience: (1) The experimenter explicitly assumed responsibility for the victim's welfare, and (2) full obedience was reached gradually, each step requiring only 15 volts more than the last one. As Milgram (1965) said, people become "integrated in a situation that carries its own momentum. The subject's problem . . . is to become disengaged from a situation which is moving in an altogether ugly direction" (p. 73).

Attitudes and Attitude Change

People often change their behavior in response to social pressure from a group or figure of authority. These changes, however, are typically limited to one act in one situation at a fleeting moment in time. For the effects to endure, it is better to change attitudes, not just behavior. An **attitude** is a positive or negative reaction toward any person, object, or idea. People hold quite passionate attitudes about a whole range of issues—from abortion and political correctness to whether they prefer using a PC or a Mac. Thus, whether the goal is to win votes on election day, get consumers to buy a product, raise funds for a worthy cause, or combat sexual harassment in the military, attitude change is the key to a deeper, more lasting form of social influence (Eagly & Chaiken, 1993; Petty et al., 1997).

Persuasive Communications Persuasion, the process of changing attitudes, is a part of everyday life. The most common approach is to make a persuasive communication. Appeals made in person and through the mass media rely on the spoken word, the written word, and the picture that is worth a thousand words. What determines whether an appeal succeeds or fails? To understand why some approaches work and others do not, we need a road map of the persuasion process.

It's a familiar scene in American politics: Every four years, presidential candidates launch extensive campaigns for office. In a way, if you've seen one election, you've seen them all. The names and dates may change, but over and over again opposing candidates accuse each other of ducking the issues and turning the election into a popularity contest. Whether or not the accusations are true, they illustrate that politicians are keenly aware that votes can be won through two very different methods. They can stick to the issues, or they can base their appeal on other grounds.

To account for these varying approaches, Richard Petty and John Cacioppo (1986) proposed a two-track model of persuasion. When people have the ability and motivation to think critically about the contents of a message, they take the **central route to persuasion.** In these instances, people are influenced by the strength and quality of the arguments. When people do not have the ability or motivation to pay close attention to the issues, however, they take mental shortcuts along the **peripheral route to persuasion.** In this case, people may be influenced by a speaker's appearance, slogans, one-liners, emotions, audience reactions, and other superficial cues. This two-track model of persuasion—and others like it (Chaiken et al., 1989)—help to explain how voters, consumers, juries, and other targets of persuasion can seem so logical on some occasions, yet so illogical on others.

To understand the conditions that produce change on one route or the other, it's helpful to view persuasion as the outcome of three factors: a *source* (who), a *message* (says what, and how), and an *audience* (to whom). If a speaker is clear, if the message is relevant and important, if there is a bright and captive audience that cares deeply about the issues, then that audience will take the effortful central route. But if the source speaks too fast to comprehend, if the message is trivial, or if the audience is distracted, pressed for time, or uninterested, then the less strenuous peripheral route is taken. Particularly important is whether the target audience is personally involved in the issue under consideration. High involvement leads us to take the central route; low involvement, the peripheral route (Johnson & Eagly, 1989; Petty & Cacioppo, 1990). This model is illustrated in Figure 13.11.

The Source The communicator, or source of a message, is the first important consideration in changing attitudes. What makes some communicators more persuasive

attitude A positive or negative reaction to any person, object, or idea.

central route to persuasion A process in which people think carefully about a message and are influenced by its arguments.

peripheral route to persuasion A process in which people do not think carefully about a message and are influenced by superficial cues.

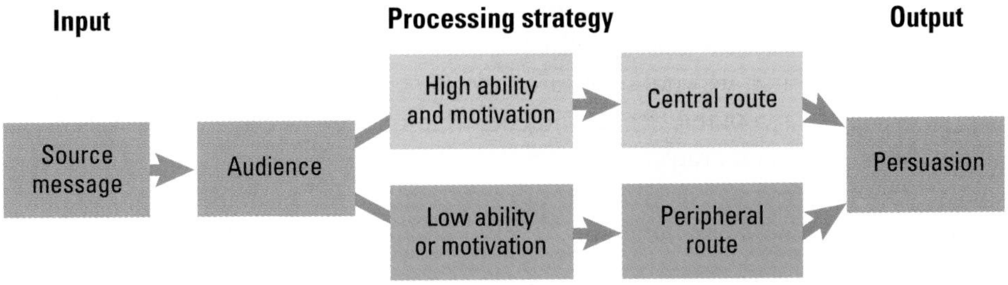

Figure 13.11 Two routes to persuasion Based on aspects of the source, message, and audience, people take either a "central" or a "peripheral" route to persuasion. On the central route, we are influenced by strong arguments and evidence. On the peripheral route, we are influenced more by superficial cues.

than others? There are two key characteristics: credibility and likability. To have credibility, a communicator must be perceived as both an *expert* and as one who can be *trusted* to tell the truth. Doctors, scientists, film critics, and other experts can have a disarming effect on us. To engender trust, however, they must also be seen as willing to state a position honestly and without compromise. If a source has been bought and paid for, has an ax to grind, or has something else to gain, then he or she will lose credibility. Using both expertise and trustworthiness to create high- and low-credibility sources, Shelly Chaiken and Durairaj Maheswaran (1994) thus found that subjects were more impressed by, and willing to purchase, a consumer product (a telephone answering machine) when they read a favorable review attributed to *Consumer Reports* rather than to a K-mart promotional pamphlet.

A second important characteristic is likability. As Dale Carnegie (1936) implied in the title of his classic, *How to Win Friends and Influence People,* being well liked and being persuasive go hand in hand. Thus, the speaker who is similar to us or is physically appealing has a unique advantage. In one study, Diane Mackie and others (1990) found that college students were more influenced by a speech on the SATs when the speaker was said to be from their own university than from another school. In another study, Chaiken (1979) had male and female assistants try to get students on campus to sign a petition and found that the more attractive the assistants were, the more signatures they were able to collect. It's no wonder that advertisers spend millions of dollars a year on celebrity endorsements from Cindy Crawford, Michael Jordan, Jerry Seinfeld, Tiger Woods, and other popular stars.

The Message Does the source hold the key to success? Are we so impressed by experts and so drawn to beautiful models that we uncritically embrace whatever they have to say? In light of what we know about the central and peripheral routes to persuasion, the answer is that it depends. When the target audience has a low level of involvement, superficial source characteristics make a difference. Under high involvement, however, a lack of substance cannot so easily be masked by style (Petty et al., 1997). So how can a message be constructed for maximum impact? Should it be crammed with facts or short and to the point? What about using one-sided versus two-sided arguments, and visual versus auditory media? Despite many years of research, there are no specific formulas—but there are answers. To illustrate, let us consider two strategic questions that confront all communicators.

Before making an appeal, the astute communicator knows that audience members are not blank slates but human beings endowed with preexisting attitudes and values. Knowing this, how discrepant a position should one advocate from that of an audience? Is it better to stake out an extreme position in the hope of stimulating the most change (as Newt Gingrich often does) or to preach moderation in order to avoid being rejected outright (as Bill Clinton tends to do)? There are two answers to this question. First, it's vital to ensure that one's arguments are based on premises that are at least acceptable to an audience (Holtgraves & Bailey, 1991). Second, communicators should argue for positions that are only moderately discrepant from that of the audience. Generally, the more discrepant the message, the greater the change. But there's a breaking point, beyond which too much discrepancy produces less change (Siero & Doosje, 1993).

A second common question concerns the arousal of emotion. Is it better to recite only facts and rational arguments or to stir up primitive emotions? This issue is often raised in discussions of the persuasive effects of fear, a common device. Magazine ads for condoms often use fear appeals—the most extreme being "I enjoy sex but I don't want to die for it" (Struckman-Johnson et al., 1990). Similarly blunt ads tell us that smoking "is a matter of life and breath" and that "this [a fried egg] is your brain on drugs." So does fear persuade? If so, is it better to arouse just a little nervousness or a full-blown anxiety attack? Over the years, researchers have measured the amount of attitude change produced by messages varying in fearfulness. Their results suggest that high-fear messages produce more change than low-fear messages—but only when they provide reassurance and instructions on how to avoid the threatened danger (Gleicher & Petty, 1992; Leventhal, 1970). Without guidance on how to cope, people panic and tune out. But when clear instructions are given, fear arousal is effective. Antismoking films thus work better when they show gory scenes of lung-cancer patients rather than charts filled with dry statistics. Similarly, driving-safety films have more impact when they show bloody human victims instead of controlled collisions involving crash dummies (Rogers, 1983).

It's interesting that just as fear sparks change, so does positive emotion. Food, drinks, a soft reclining chair, tender memories, pleasant music, and a breathtaking view can all lull us into a positive emotional state—ripe for persuasion. Why? One reason is that when people are in a good mood, they want to savor the moment, so they get mentally lazy and uncritically accepting of persuasive arguments (Isen, 1987). A second reason is that a good mood can be distracting, causing the mind to wander and making it more difficult to scrutinize a persuasive message (Mackie & Worth, 1989). Weakened in the motivation and the ability for critical thinking, people are easier to persuade when they're in a positive emotional state (Schwarz et al., 1991).

The Audience Source and message factors are important, but no persuasion strategy is complete without a consideration of the audience. Presentations that work on some people may fail with others. Are some individuals easier to persuade than others? No, not as a general rule. But people are responsive to different types of messages. For example, some people are more likely than others to take the central route to persuasion—and, therefore, to be focused on content. According to Cacioppo and Petty (1982), individuals differ in terms of how much they enjoy and engage in effortful cognitive activities or, as they call it, the *need for cognition*. Research shows that people with a high need for cognition are influenced by strong informational messages, while those who are low in the need for cognition are swayed more by a speaker's reputation, the applause of an audience, and other peripheral cues (Cacioppo et al., 1996).

According to Mark Snyder (1987), people who are highly concerned about their public image exhibit *self-monitoring:* a tendency to modify their behavior from one social situation to the next. As measured by the Self-Monitoring Scale, high self-monitors tend to say that "in different situations and with different people, I often act like different persons." As targets of influence, high self-monitors are thus drawn to messages that promise a desirable social image. In one study, subjects read information-oriented or image-oriented magazine advertisements. As predicted, high self-monitors were willing to pay more for products that were presented in image-oriented than in informational ads. To be persuasive, a message should meet the psychological needs of its audience (Snyder & DeBono, 1985).

Self-Persuasion Anyone who has ever acted on stage knows how easy it is to become so absorbed in a role that the experience seems real. Forced laughter can make an actor feel happy, and fake tears can turn to sadness. Even in real life, the effect can be dramatic. In 1974, Patty Hearst—a sheltered young college student from a wealthy family—was kidnapped by a revolutionary group. By the time she was arrested months later, she was carrying a gun and calling herself Tania. How could someone be so totally converted? In Hearst's own words, "I had thought I was humoring [my captors] by parroting their clichés and buzzwords without believing in them. . . . In trying to convince them I convinced myself."

The Patty Hearst case reveals the powerful effects of role playing. You don't have to be terrorized to be coaxed into doing something that contradicts your inner convictions. People often engage in attitude-discrepant behavior—as part of a job, for example, or to please others. This raises a profound question: What happens when people behave in ways that do not follow from their attitudes? We know that attitudes influence behavior. But can the causal arrow be reversed? That is, can a forced change in behavior spark a change in attitude?

Cognitive Dissonance Theory The answer to this question was provided by Leon Festinger's (1957) **cognitive dissonance** theory. According to Festinger, we hold many cognitions about ourselves and the world around us—and sometimes these cognitions clash. For example, you say you're on a diet, and yet you just dove headfirst into a chocolate mousse. Or you waited in line for hours to get into a concert, but then the band was disappointing. Or you baked under the hot summer sun, even though you knew of the health risks. In each case, there is inconsistency and conflict. You committed yourself to a course of action, but you realize that your behavior contradicts your attitude.

According to Festinger, these kinds of discrepancies often produce an unpleasant state of tension that he called cognitive dissonance. Attitude-discrepant behavior doesn't always arouse dissonance. If you broke a diet for a holiday dinner or if you thought that the mousse you ate was low in calories, you would be relatively free of tension. Attitude-discrepant behavior that is performed *freely* and with *knowledge* of the consequences, however, does arouse dissonance—and the motivation to reduce it. There are different ways to cope with this unpleasant state. Often the easiest is to change your attitude so that it becomes consistent with your behavior.

To understand dissonance theory, imagine for a moment that you are a subject in the classic study by Leon Festinger and J. Merrill Carlsmith (1959). The experimenter tells you that he is interested in various measures of performance. He hands you a wooden board containing forty-eight pegs in square holes and asks you to turn each peg to the left, then to the right, then back to the left, and again to the right. The routine seems endless. After thirty minutes, the experimenter comes to your rescue. Or does he? Just when you think things are looking up, he hands you another board, another assignment. For the next half-hour, you are to take twelve

cognitive dissonance An unpleasant psychological state often aroused when people behave in ways that are discrepant with their attitudes.

spools of thread off the board, put them back on, take them off, and so on. By now, you're just about ready to tear your hair out. As you think back over better times, even the first task begins to look good.

Finally, you've finished. After one of the longest hours of your life, the experimenter lets you in on a secret: There's more to this study than meets the eye. You were in the control group. To test the effects of motivation on performance, the experimenter will tell other subjects that the experiment is fun. You don't realize it, but you're being set up for a critical part of the study. Would you tell the next subject that the experiment is enjoyable? As you hem and haw, the experimenter offers to pay for your lie. Some subjects, like you, are offered a dollar; others, twenty dollars. Before you know it, you're in the waiting room trying to dupe an unsuspecting fellow student.

By means of this staged presentation, subjects were goaded into an attitude-discrepant behavior, an act that contradicted their private attitudes. They knew the experiment was dull, but they raved. Was cognitive dissonance aroused? It depended on how much subjects were paid. Suppose you were one of the lucky ones offered twenty dollars. Even by today's standards, that amount provides sufficient justification for telling a little white lie. Being well compensated, these subjects did not feel dissonance. But wait. Suppose you were offered only one dollar. Surely your integrity is worth more than that, don't you think? In this case, you do not have sufficient justification for going along. So you cope by changing your view of the task. If you can convince yourself that the experiment was interesting, then there is no conflict.

When the experiment was presumably over, subjects were asked to rate the pegboard tasks. Control-group subjects, who did not mislead a confederate, admitted the tasks were boring. So did those in the twenty-dollar condition, who had ample justification for what they did. Those paid only one dollar, however, rated the tasks as more enjoyable. After engaging in an attitude-discrepant behavior without sufficient justification, these subjects felt internally pressured to change their attitudes in order to reduce cognitive dissonance (see Figure 13.12).

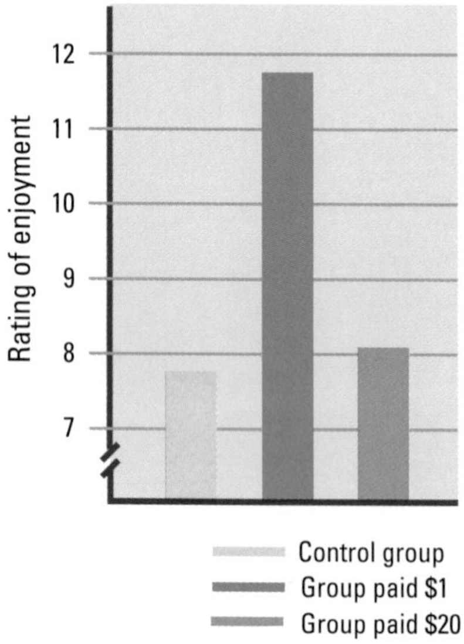

Figure 13.12 Festinger and Carlsmith's classic dissonance study How interesting is a boring task? Compared to subjects who did not have to lie and those paid $20 to do so, those paid only $1 later rated the task as more enjoyable. Having engaged in an attitude-discrepant behavior, these latter subjects reduced dissonance by changing their attitude.

Cognitive dissonance theory makes another interesting prediction: that people will change their attitudes to justify effort, money spent, time, or suffering. In the first test of this hypothesis, Eliot Aronson and Judson Mills (1959) invited female students to join a discussion group about sex. To get into the group, subjects were told they would have to pass an "embarrassment test." One set of subjects underwent a severe test (they had to recite obscene words and lurid passages), a second set took a mild test (they read a list of mildly sexual words), and a third set was admitted without an initiation. Subjects then listened in on a dreadfully boring discussion. How much fun was this discussion group? As predicted, those who had to endure a severe initiation liked the group more than the others did. There are some interesting implications. Research shows, for example, that the harder psychotherapy patients work at their treatment, the better they say they feel later (Axsom, 1989). Cognitive dissonance theory may also explain why college fraternities and sororities foster such lifelong loyalties or why 58 percent of Vietnam veterans, compared to 29 percent of others, say that "the U.S. was right to get involved in the Vietnam war" (Witteman, 1990). Perhaps even today, those who had risked their lives need to justify the nightmare they experienced.

Alternative Routes to Self-Persuasion Following Festinger, a generation of social psychologists has studied and refined the basic theory. Nobody disputes the fact that when people are coaxed into performing an attitude-discrepant behavior, they often go on to change their attitudes. In fact, people who have a high need for consistency are most likely to show the effect (Cialdini et al., 1995). But under what conditions, and why? According to Joel Cooper and Russell Fazio (1984), four conditions are necessary for change to occur: (1) The behavior has *negative consequences;* (2) the person feels *responsible* for these consequences; (3) the person becomes *physiologically aroused,* experiencing tension that needs to be reduced; and (4) the person *attributes* that arousal to his or her behavior.

The "why" question is still a matter of controversy. Some theorists argue that the attitude change is not fueled by a need to justify our actions but instead occurs as a rational process through which people draw conclusions about how they feel by observing their own behavior. In other words, subjects who lied about the boring task for a dollar reflected upon their actions and concluded that the task must have been interesting—or else why would they have said so (Bem, 1967)? Other theorists claim that the predominant motive is not to be consistent but to *appear* consistent, or favorable, to others. In this view, the subjects who lied simply did not want the experimenter to think they had sold out for a paltry sum of money (Tedeschi et al., 1971). Still others claim that the change in attitude is necessary for one's self-concept—that the subjects who lied had to view the task as fun in order to repair the damage done to their self-esteem (Steele, 1988; Thibodeau & Aronson, 1992).

Group Processes

When individuals assemble in groups, profound changes take place. The beating of Rodney King by four police officers was one example. So is the random violence and vandalism of street gangs, avid sports fans who scream at the top of their lungs in victory, high-powered business groups that make unusually risky decisions, and bloodthirsty lynch mobs seeking revenge. It's as if the group is casting a spell over the individual.

Social Facilitation First things first. How does the mere presence of others affect our behavior? Appropriately, this most basic question in social psychology was also the first to be tested. In 1898, Norman Triplett studied bicycle-racing records and discovered that cyclists were faster when they competed alongside others than when they pedaled alone against the clock. Intrigued by this finding, Triplett asked forty children simply to wind a fishing reel—sometimes alone, other times in pairs. Again, performance was faster among those who worked together than alone. Triplett's conclusion: The presence of others triggers "nervous energy," thereby enhancing performance.

Subsequently, many researchers confirmed that the presence of others speeds up performance on various cognitive and motor tasks (even ants excavate more and chickens eat more when they are in the company of other members of their species). At the same time, however, other researchers were observing performance declines. Why did the presence of others have such different effects on task performance? In 1965, Robert Zajonc solved the problem. He noted that (1) the presence of others increases arousal, and (2) arousal enhances the "dominant" response—that is, whatever response is most likely to occur. Zajonc reasoned that the dominant response is more likely to be the correct one when a task is easy (such as adding two numbers) but to be incorrect when the task is more difficult (such as solving a complex equation). The presence of other people should thus improve our performance on simple tasks but impair performance on tasks that are difficult. To demonstrate, Zajonc found that subjects who tried to memorize simple word associations (*mother-father*) performed better in the presence of others than alone, but

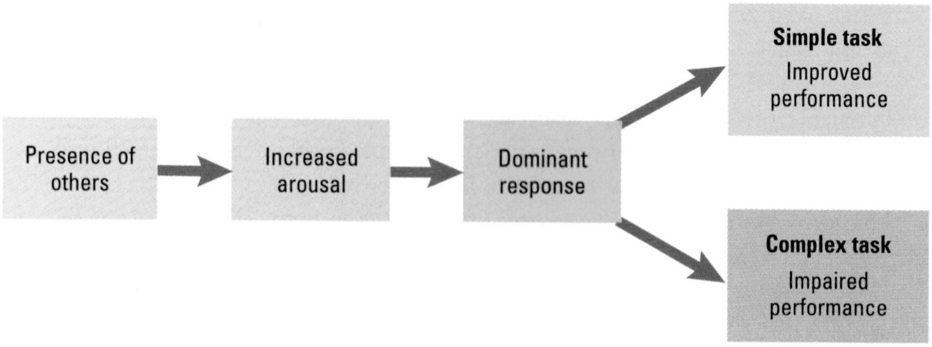

Figure 13.13 Social facilitation Zajonc theorized that the mere presence of others increases our arousal, which strengthens the "dominant" response. As a result, the presence of others improves performance on simple tasks but impairs performance on tasks that are complex.

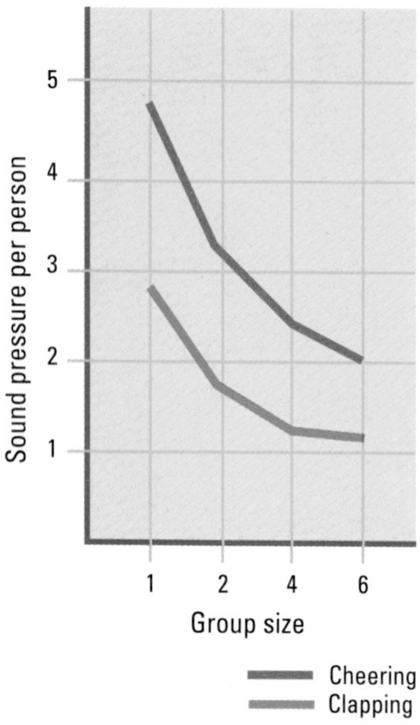

Figure 13.14 Social loafing Subjects were told to clap or cheer "as loud as you can"—either alone or in groups of two, four, or six. The more others there were, the less effort was exerted by each individual subject (Latané et al., 1979).

social facilitation The tendency for the presence of others to enhance performance on simple tasks and impair performance on complex tasks.

social loafing The tendency for people to exert less effort in group tasks for which individual contributions are pooled.

that those who tried to learn difficult associations (*mother-algebra*) did worse. This phenomenon is known as **social facilitation** (see Figure 13.13).

Is the mere presence of other actors or observers sufficient to produce social facilitation, as Zajonc suggested? Some social psychologists argue that we are aroused by others only when they are in a position to *evaluate* our performance. Others claim that we are aroused only when others drive us to *distraction*. Whatever the cause of the arousal, one fact is clear: In the company of other people, we perform better on tasks we're good at but worse on those we find difficult (Guerin, 1986).

Social Loafing

Social facilitation effects are found for *individual* tasks such as running a race, solving a problem, or memorizing a list. In these types of activities, one's own performance is easy to identify. But what about cooperative *joint* activities for which individual contributions are pooled? In a tug-of-war, say, does each person exert more effort when they compete as part of a team or alone?

To find out, Alan Ingham and his associates (1974) asked blindfolded subjects to pull on a rope "as hard as you can" and found that subjects pulled 18 percent harder when they knew they were alone than when they thought that three other subjects were pulling with them. Bibb Latané and others (1979) then asked subjects to clap or cheer "as loud as you can"—either alone or in groups of two, four, or six. The result: As individuals, subjects produced less noise when they thought they were part of a group than when they thought they were alone.

The Latané team (1979) coined the term **social loafing** to describe this group-produced reduction in individual effort. As illustrated in Figure 13.14, social loafing increases with group size: The more others there are, the less effort each subject exerts. In the clapping and cheering study, for example, two-person groups performed at only 71 percent of their individual capacity, four-person groups at 51 percent, and six-person groups at 40 percent.

Why do people slack off when others are there to pick up the slack? There are a few reasons. One is that people see their own contribution as unessential to the group's success. A second is that people are less concerned about being personally evaluated—in part because individual performance standards within a group are unclear. A third possibility is that people slack off in order to guard against looking like the "sucker" who works harder than everyone else. Putting the pieces together, researchers have concluded that social loafing occurs because individuals often do not see the connection between their own effort and the desired outcome (Karau & Williams, 1993; Sheppard, 1993).

Social loafing threatens work groups throughout Western society and, to a lesser extent, in Eastern cultures as well (Gabrenya et al., 1983). But it is not inevitable. Based on a meta-analysis of seventy-eight social-loafing studies, Steven Karau and Kipling Williams (1993) concluded that people are less likely to take a "free ride" when they think their individual performance can somehow be separated from the group's, when their own effort is needed for the group to succeed, when success will be amply rewarded, when the task is personally meaningful, or when the group consists of friends rather than strangers.

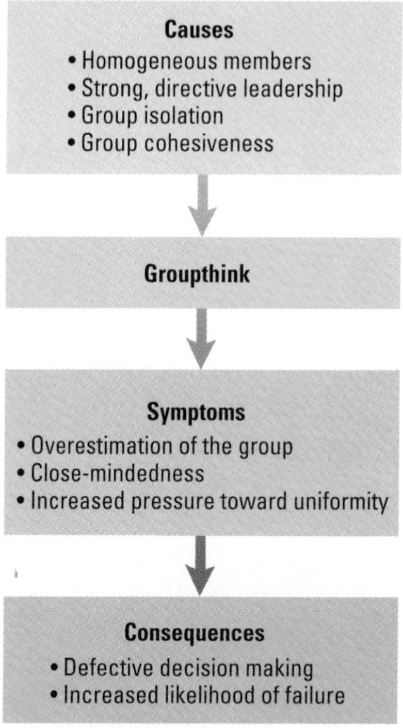

Figure 13.15 Groupthink

Groupthink In 1961, President Kennedy and his top advisers set into motion a half-baked plan to attack the Bay of Pigs in Cuba with 1,400 CIA-trained Cuban exiles. The invasion resulted in a quick and humiliating defeat, leaving Kennedy to wonder how such poor judgement could have come about. Curious for an answer, Irving Janis (1972, 1989) studied the decision-making procedures leading up to the Bay of Pigs fiasco, along with other miscalculations (such as the decision to escalate the Vietnam War, the Watergate coverup, and NASA's fatal decision to launch the *Challenger* space shuttle). What happened in the groups that made these blundering decisions? Was the process rational or irrational?

According to Janis, decision-making groups in politics, business, education, and other settings often fall prey to **groupthink**—a concurrence-seeking process in which the members convince themselves that their policies are correct. Insulated, tightly knit groups that value harmony and have a strong leader are most vulnerable to this conspiracy of silence. Groupthink seems to operate at two levels. In some cases, members suppress personal doubts on their own, often without realizing they are doing so; in other cases, they are openly and actively pressured into submission by a majority intolerant of dissent (McCauley, 1989). Some researchers disagree with Janis about the specific conditions that put decision-making groups "at risk" (Aldag & Fuller, 1993; Tetlock et al., 1992). In an interesting laboratory experiment, however, Marlene Turner and others (1992) assembled small problem-solving groups and found that when the groups were cohesive (the members wore name tags and thought about their similarities) and when they were under pressure (they feared the consequences of faulty decision making), they came up with lower-quality solutions.

[Drawing by Vietor; © 1987 The New Yorker Magazine, Inc.]

"This might not be ethical. Is that a problem for anybody?"

In insulated decision-making groups, members often fail to challenge existing policies.

The behavioral symptoms of groupthink are seen in three ways. First, the group tends to overestimate its own capacity. Group members harbor an illusion of invulnerability, an illusion of unanimity, and an exaggerated belief in the morality of their views. Second, group members become close-minded, rationalizing their own actions and stereotyping the targets of these actions. And third, there is great pressure toward uniformity. In the interests of group unity, members censor their thoughts and act as "mind guards" to prevent expressions of dissent. By inviting the pathological decision making outlined in Figure 13.15, groupthink raises the odds of miscalculation and failure.

Can groups inoculate themselves against this problem? After the Bay of Pigs fiasco, President Kennedy took active steps to make his decision-making process more constructive. Based on the safeguards Kennedy later adopted, Janis (1989) gave the following advice: (1) To avoid isolation, experts should be brought in and members should consult with impartial outsiders; (2) to reduce conformity pressures, the leader should not take a strong public stand early in the group discussion; and (3) to establish a norm of critical review, subgroups should separately discuss the same issue, a member should be assigned to play devil's advocate, and a "second-chance" meeting should be held to reconsider the preliminary decision.

groupthink A group decision-making style by which group members convince themselves that they are correct.

Social Relations

What kinds of aversive events predispose people to behave aggressively? Does alcohol spark or inhibit aggression? And what situational cues serve as "triggers?" In contrast, what is altruism—and why is it so difficult to define? Why do bystanders to an emergency often not intervene? And what situational factors influence helping behavior?

People relate to one another in different ways. Sometimes our interactions and the decisions we make are negative, hostile, and generally "antisocial." At other times, we are kind, helpful, charitable, and generally "prosocial" in our behavior. Let's examine these two contrasting tendencies and the situations that bring them out in us.

U.S. Marine paratroopers, after completing their training, receive their golden wings, with two pins on the back. In February 1997, it was revealed, as captured on videotape, that this achievement is marked by "blood pinning"—a barbaric hazing ritual in which veteran Marines punch, pound, and grind the pins into the chests of the new initiates, who scream and writhe in pain. As military leaders try to crack down on this "rite of passage," the tapes show that certain group situations can trigger unusually high levels of aggression.

aggression Behavior intended to inflict harm on another person.

Aggression

A nail-filled pipe bomb explodes at the Olympics in Atlanta. Six-year-old beauty-pageant star JonBenet Ramsey is found sexually abused and murdered in her basement in Boulder, Colorado. Ennis Cosby, son of Bill Cosby, is shot to death on a California freeway as he fixes a flat tire. A Palestinian visitor to the United States purchases an automatic weapon in Florida, flies to New York, and opens fire on a crowd of tourists in the Empire State Building. Boxer Mike Tyson deliberately bites the ear of Evander Holyfield during their championship bout in Las Vegas. The list of violent incidents seems endless.

In some ways, these acts of violence are so deviant that they shed little light on "normal" human nature. In other ways, however, they serve to remind us that **aggression**—behavior that is intended to inflict harm—is a common and contagious social disease. Every day, people all over the world are victims of wars between nations, conflicts between ethnic and religious groups, terrorist bombings, racism, street gangs, drug dealers, sexual assaults, domestic violence, police brutality, and suicide. Aggression is so prevalent that psychologists have desperately tried to pinpoint its origins. Some argue that aggression is programmed into human nature by instincts, genes, hormones, and other biological factors. Others emphasize the role of culture, social learning, and environmental stressors. As always, human behavior is not the product of either nature or nurture but is the interaction of both (Berkowitz, 1993).

Biological Roots On November 11, 1918, World War I ended. Shell-shocked, covered in mud, with lungs blasted by gas, millions of soldiers had died on the battlefields of Europe. What sinister forces of human nature could possibly explain the bloodshed? For Sigmund Freud (1920), who had earlier proposed that people were motivated by powerful life instincts, the war suggested that human beings are also driven by a self-destructive "death instinct." In the conflict between these opposing forces, said Freud, the death instinct is redirected—from oneself to others.

Based on his observations of animal behavior, Konrad Lorenz (1966) also viewed aggression as an inborn and adaptive instinct. According to Lorenz, successful aggressors gain access to food, water, and desirable mates. Thus, natural selection favors the evolution of an aggressive instinct. So are wars, crimes, and other acts of violence inevitable? Not necessarily. Both Freud and Lorenz argued that instinctual

INTERSECTION

SOCIAL INFLUENCES AND ENVIRONMENT

Population Density, Architecture, and Social Behavior

While social psychologists focus on the influences of others on our behavior, environmental psychologists study the impact of physical settings (Stokols, 1995). One of the most consistent findings in this area is that crowding often triggers antisocial behavior. From overpopulated cities to crowded neighborhoods, subway cars, dormitories, playgrounds, and prisons, this aspect of the physical environment affects the quality of our social lives.

Researchers have found it useful to distinguish between density and crowding. *Density* is an objective and quantifiable measure of the number of persons per unit space—as defined by square footage, number of housing units per acre, or number of rooms per building. In contrast, *crowding* is a psychological state that arises when one feels that there are too many people in a given space. This distinction helps to explain why high density can be experienced either as enjoyable (as in a basketball arena tightly packed with thousands of hometown fans) or as aversive (as in a jam-packed shopping mall during the week before Christmas). The feeling of being crowded is based not only on density but also on various personal, cultural, and architectural factors.

Many years ago, animal researchers found that high-density laboratory environments increased aggression among monkeys, rats, cats, hermit crabs, hogs, chickens, gerbils, fruit flies, and other species. For example, John Calhoun (1962) built different "rat universes," varied the population, and found that, despite an ample supply of food and water, the high-density conditions increased hyperactivity, aggression, cannibalism, withdrawal, and illness. Humans also show the effects of high-density living. In dormitories, college students who were assigned three to a room rather than two felt more crowded, disliked their roommates more, were less satisfied with the living conditions, felt a lack of control, and had lower grades (Baron et al., 1976; Gormley & Aiello, 1982). In off-campus housing, students living in crowded apartments were less likely to seek or to offer social support to housemates, or even to a stranger in need of support in an unrelated setting—a sign of social withdrawal (Evans & Lepore, 1993). And in prisons, as the number of inmates in a facility increases, so do rates of stress, violence, discipline problems, and deaths (Paulus, 1988).

High-density living may be overstimulating, arousing, and invasive of one's privacy and control, but the aversiveness of the experience is also influenced by architectural design. In an illustrative study, Andrew Baum and Stewart Valins (1979) found that first-year students living in corridor-style dorms—compared to those in dorms that were divided into suites—complained more about crowding and privacy, tried to avoid others both inside and outside the dorm, and had fewer friends among floormates. The two types of residences had the same amount of space per person, the same number of

Overcrowding can cause residents to lash out or withdraw. At the University of Cincinnati, Sander Hall—a twenty-six-story dorm that housed 1,300 students—was so beset by violence and vandalism that in 1991 the university literally blew the building up.

residents per floor, and comparable furnishings. Yet due to differences in spatial layout, the students living in the corridor-style dorms had to share more space (including bathrooms), found it harder to control their social contacts, and were under more stress.

Other aspects of architectural design and decor can also be used to offset the ill effects of density. For example, roommates feel less crowded in rooms where the floor space has been opened up with bunk beds. Rooms also feel larger when they are rectangular rather than square; when walls are straight-edged rather than curved; and when there are windows, sunlight, light-colored walls, and high ceilings (McAndrew, 1993). High-density homes are also more bearable if they have "architectural depth"—that is, when one has to pass through many spaces to get from one room to another. The more doors and walls that separate living areas, the easier it is for people to regulate social interactions. In a study of college students living in crowded off-campus housing, those who were in units with high levels of architectural depth were less psychologically distressed and less likely to show signs of social withdrawal (Evans et al., 1996). As environmental psychologists have noted, it is possible to design physical spaces in ways that buffer people against the adverse effects of high-density living.

aggressive impulses can be channeled into hunting, contact sports, intellectual debates, and other socially acceptable outlets.

Instinct theories—which are based on the assumption that aggression is unlearned and is characteristic of the whole species—have little influence today. One problem is that there are vast cultural differences that cannot be explained by instinct alone. The Arapesh of New Guinea live peacefully, for example, while the Yanomamo of the Amazon jungle are ferocious warriors. A second problem is that instinct-based explanations are logically circular: People are aggressive because of an instinct—which we know exists because people are aggressive.

Whether or not human aggression is fixed by instincts, it is subject to biological influences. Twin and adoption studies have suggested that genetic factors play a role—though it's not clear how large a role it is (DiLalla & Gottesman, 1991; Miles & Carey, 1997). There are, however, consistent sex differences: Compared to women, men report higher levels of physical aggression (Buss & Perry, 1992) and behave more aggressively in laboratory studies (Eagly & Steffen, 1986; Bettencourt & Miller, 1996; Knight et al., 1996). Indeed, in all countries in which criminal records are kept, more men than women commit violent crimes (Kenrick, 1987). Why? One possibility is that aggression is linked to the male sex hormone testosterone. In rats, mice, and other animals, testosterone injections increase levels of aggression, while castration—which lowers testosterone—has the opposite effect. In humans, correlational research shows that violent criminals have naturally higher levels of testosterone than those convicted of nonviolent crimes (Dabbs et al., 1987).

Finally, there is strong evidence to implicate alcohol in the commission of homicides, stabbings, child abuse, and other violent crimes. Laboratory experiments have shown that alcohol powerfully fuels aggression (Bushman, 1993)—particularly when subjects are frustrated (Ito et al., 1996). In one study, for example, subjects delivered more painful shocks, supposedly to another person, after drinking beverages spiked with 100-proof vodka or bourbon than after consuming nonalcoholic beverages (Taylor & Leonard, 1983). Why does alcohol bring this tendency out in us? According to Claude Steele and Robert Josephs (1990), people self-disclose more, take more risks, and behave more aggressively when they're drunk than sober. The reason, they say, is that alcohol leads us to lose touch with our values and become short-sighted about the consequences of our actions—thus evoking a state of "drunken excess."

Aversive Stimulation Aggression has biological roots, but it is also learned from experience and then is triggered by factors in the environment. What kinds of events unleash our aggressive impulses? And how can social influences be used to promote peace and nonviolence?

Put two rats in a cage together; subject them to painful shocks, loud noise, or intense heat; and a fight is likely to break out. Put people in unpleasant conditions—an overcrowded ghetto, a noisy construction site, a room filled with cigarette smoke, or the company of an obnoxious coworker—and they too become more likely to lash out. As a general rule, aversive stimulation sparks aggression (Berkowitz, 1983).

One type of aversive event that we all experience at times is frustration. In 1939, John Dollard and his associates proposed the hypothesis that frustration leads to aggression either against the source of frustration or against an innocent but vulnerable substitute, or scapegoat. Testing the implications of this **frustration-aggression hypothesis,** Carl Hovland and Robert Sears (1940) examined the link between economic hard times and racial violence. They analyzed the records from fourteen southern states during the years 1882–1930 and discovered a strong negative correlation between the value of cotton and lynchings: As the price of cotton fell, the number of lynchings increased. The same relationship has been verified in more recent analyses (Beck & Tolnay, 1990; Hepworth & West, 1988). Although this correlation cannot be interpreted in causal terms, experiments have confirmed that frustration sparks aggression in many contexts by arousing anger, fear, and other negative emotions (Berkowitz, 1989).

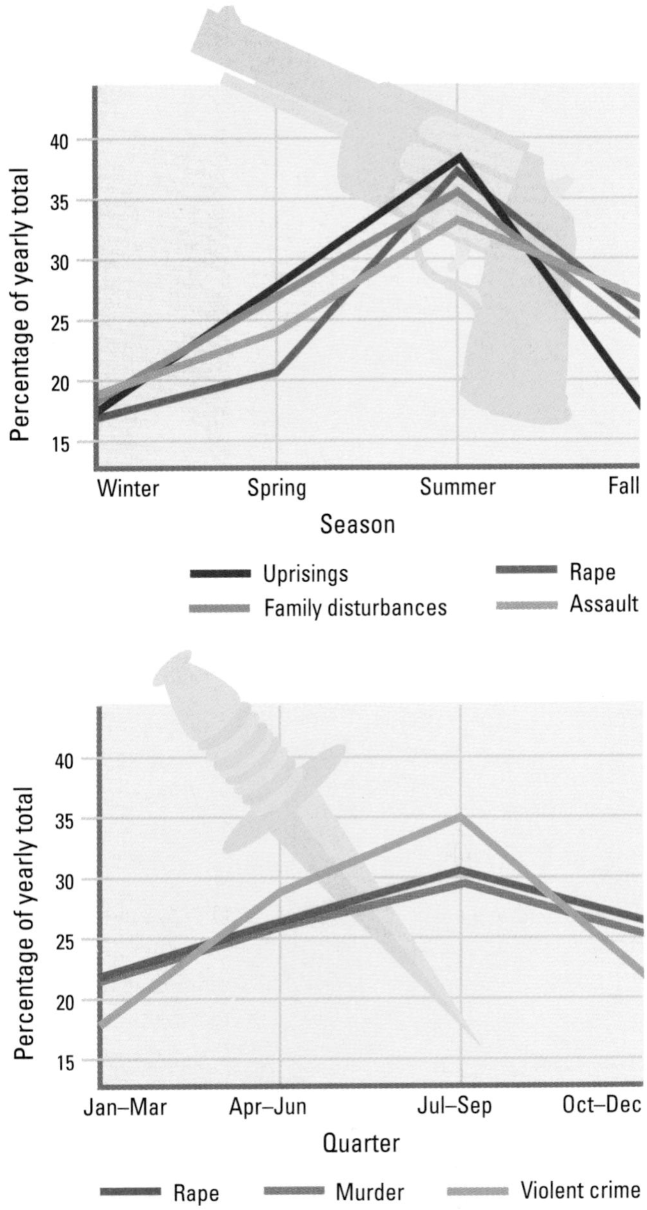

Figure 13.16 The link between heat and violence Worldwide weather records and crime statistics reveal that more violent crimes are committed during the summer than in the other seasons (Anderson, 1989).

The high temperatures of a "long, hot summer" also spark acts of violence. On the basis of worldwide weather records and crime statistics, correlational analyses reveal a strong link between heat and aggression. More violent crimes occur in the summer than in the winter, during hot years than in cooler years, and in hot cities than in cooler cities. As you can see in Figure 13.16, the numbers of political uprisings, riots, homicides, assaults, rapes, and reports of family violence all peak in the months of June, July, and August (Anderson, 1989). Indirect acts of aggression also increase in excessive heat. As temperatures rise above 90°F, laboratory subjects become more likely to interpret ambiguous events in hostile terms (Rule et al., 1987), drivers in cars without air-conditioning are more likely to honk their horns at other motorists (Kenrick & MacFarlane, 1984), and major-league baseball pitchers are more likely to hit batters with a pitch (Reifman et al., 1991). When people are "hot under the collar," tempers flare.

In this regard, cultural factors may also play a role—even within the same country. In a book entitled *Culture of Honor,* Richard Nisbett and Dov Cohen

frustration-aggression hypothesis The theory that frustration causes aggression.

Bringing the frustration-aggression hypothesis to life, baseball star Roberto Alomar spit into the face of umpire John Hirschbeck. Alomar, who is not normally quick-tempered, had just struck out on a close call at the plate during the final week of a tight pennant race.

(1996) analyzed crime statistics in the United States and found that rates of violence, over time, are consistently higher in the South than in all other regions. They speculate that this pattern reveals the workings of a culture whose men are highly protective of valued possessions, quick to defend against intruders, and anxious to project an image of strength. As a historical matter, they note that while northern towns were being settled mostly by farmers, the South was being settled by herders, whose "manly honor" is necessary to protect their flocks. Can this history be used to explain contemporary violence rates? Nisbett and Cohen examined public-opinion surveys and found that southern respondents were more likely to agree that "a man has the right to kill" in order to defend his family and house. They were also more likely to own guns, favor capital punishment, and retaliate for an insult in a laboratory experiment. At this point, you may be wondering, is it possible that violence in the South says more about climate, which is hot, than culture? Craig and Katherine Anderson (1996) used various statistical techniques to sort out these influences. They found that heat is associated with aggression regardless of regional factors and that the presumed effect of southern culture results primarily, though not entirely, from the generally high temperatures of the region.

Situational Cues Frustration, heat, and other aversive events predispose us to aggression by arousing negative affect. Once we are in this state of readiness, the presence of stimuli associated with aggression may then prompt us to act on this predisposition. Aversive events "load the gun," but situational cues get us to "pull the trigger." What situational cues have this effect?

Weapons The sights and sounds of violence are everywhere. In the United States, millions of adults own handguns. Daily TV news reports flood us with images of war, terrorism, and weapons of mass destruction. Does any of this matter? Yes. According to Leonard Berkowitz, the mere sight of an aggressive stimulus influences behavior. In a classic demonstration of this point, Berkowitz and Anthony LePage (1967) had male subjects administer electric shocks to a confederate who had insulted half the subjects right before the session. In one condition, only the shock-generating apparatus was present in the lab. In a second condition, a .38-caliber pistol and a 12-gauge shotgun were on the table near the shock button—supposedly left from a previous experiment. As measured by the number of shocks given, aggression was increased by the sight of the weapons. Subjects who were angered, and primed to aggress, retaliated more in the presence of the weapons than in their absence.

This provocative "weapons effect" has been replicated in some experiments but not in others. By statistically combining all the research, Michael Carlson and his colleagues (1990) concluded that the sight of weapons does increase aggression—except among subjects who figure out the true purpose of the experiment (when subjects realize that the guns are intended to heighten their aggression, they bend over backward to do the opposite). Do guns kill, or are people the problem? As Berkowitz likes to put it, "The finger pulls the trigger, but the trigger may also be pulling the finger."

Media Violence As if reality did not provide enough of a stimulus, the entertainment industry adds fuel to the fire. In an eighteen-hour sampling of television shows, *TV Guide* researchers taped the programs on ten major channels and counted a total of 1,846 acts of violence—including 175 killings, 389 assaults, 588 scenes depicting gunplay or menacing threats with a weapon, and 673 physical acts such as punching, pushing, and dragging. Among the culprits were news shows, movies, TV dramas, music videos, and toy commercials. The most violent programs of all: children's cartoons, in which heroes, villains, and Ninja Turtles fight an average of 26 battles an hour (Hickey, 1992).

Does exposure to TV violence promote aggression? Literally hundreds of studies have addressed this important question, often with alarming results. Correlational studies reveal that there is a link between the amount of TV violence watched by young boys and their subsequent level of aggression—a link commonly observed in the United States and Europe (Huesmann & Eron, 1986). In a longitudinal development study, for example, Leonard Eron (1987) found that a boy's exposure to TV violence at eight years old predicted criminal activity twenty-two years later. Critics are quick to point out that these correlations cannot be used to draw conclusions about cause and effect. After all, does exposure to TV violence cause aggression, or does being aggressive cause children to seek out violence on TV? Is it possible that poverty and other external conditions cause the tendency both to watch and to commit acts of aggression? (Freedman, 1988).

To pin down cause and effect, researchers observe subjects who are randomly assigned to watch violent or nonviolent events. Controlled laboratory studies of this sort show that exposure to aggressive models, either live or on film, has negative effects. In the first of these experiments, Albert Bandura and others (1961) found that preschool children were more likely to attack an inflated doll after watching an aggressive adult model than after watching a nonaggressive model. In a more recent study, Nicola

Playing violent video games, like watching violence on TV, may increase aggression in children.

Schutte and her associates (1988) found that children were more likely to hit another child after playing "Karetka," a violent video game, than after playing "Jungle Hunt," an exciting but nonviolent game. Among children and adolescents, exposure to aggressive models increases aggression—not just in laboratories but also in classrooms, playgrounds, and other settings (Wood et al., 1991).

Is there a solution? In 1994, the film *Natural Born Killers* was banned in Great Britain after copycat shooting sprees had occurred. In 1997, the American television industry instituted a new rating system for TV shows, modeled after the one used for movies, so that parents can regulate what their children watch. It remains to be seen whether this policy will help to curb violence. On the one hand, researchers have found that warning labels before TV shows heighten viewer interest and attraction to the "forbidden fruit" (Bushman & Stack, 1996). On the other hand, it's prudent to minimize children's exposure to violent models. At this point, only time will tell what the effect will be.

Deindividuation Earlier, we saw that the presence of others can arouse us (social facilitation) or relax us (social loafing), depending on the situation. At times, the influence of a group is even more profound and more troubling. Hidden in a faceless crowd, people tend to shed their normal inhibitions—sometimes resulting in violent acts of racism, looting, vandalism, sexual assaults, and riots. How can normal, law-abiding citizens turn into frenzied mobs that take the law into their own hands? The problem is that in large groups, people lose their sense of individuality, which results in a breakdown of their internal controls against deviant behavior. This depersonalized state of mind is called **deindividuation.**

Large groups promote deindividuation in two ways. First, people feel anonymous, if not "invisible," and less accountable for their actions. Anonymity has powerful effects. In one study, subjects who were dressed in white coats and Ku Klux Klan–style hoods, masking their bodies and faces, punished a confederate with longer electric shocks than did subjects who wore their regular clothing and name tags (Zimbardo, 1970). In a second study, Halloween trick-or-treaters who were invited to take one candy from a bowl were more likely to grab extras when they were nameless and in groups than when they appeared alone and were asked for their names (Diener et al., 1976).

A second aspect of deindividuation is a loss of self-consciousness. Have you ever been at a concert or a party with music blaring so loud that you could feel the room vibrate and your identity slipping away? When attention is diverted from the self by intense environmental stimulation, people momentarily lose track of their own values, morals, and internal standards of conduct—resulting in behavior that is impulsive, uninhibited, and often aggressive (Prentice-Dunn & Rogers, 1989). This effect may even grow with the size of the group. When Brian Mullen (1986) analyzed newspaper accounts of sixty lynchings that had occurred between 1899 and 1946, he discovered that the more people there were in the lynch mob, the more vicious were their actions.

Altruism

deindividuation A loss of individuality, often experienced in a group, that results in a breakdown of internal restraints against deviant behavior.

Everyone knows the horrid tales of obedience to authority in Nazi Germany. But, as depicted in the film *Schindler's List,* that same situation also exposed the brightest side of human nature—as Oskar Schindler and several other German citizens risked their lives to hide and protect Jewish friends and neighbors. Why did these heroes try to rescue those in need? And why did others not intervene?

Focusing on prosocial aspects of human interaction, many social psychologists study **altruism**, helping behavior that is motivated primarily by a desire to benefit a person other than oneself. When people are asked to list instances of helping in their own lives, they cite helping a classmate with homework, listening to a friend's problems, giving moral support, lending books or CDs, giving directions to someone who is lost, giving rides, and so on (McGuire, 1994). Everyday examples are not hard to find. Yet psychologists ask: Does altruism really exist, or is helping always selfishly motivated? And why do we sometimes fail to come to the aid of someone who needs it? These are just some of the puzzling questions asked about helping and the factors that influence it.

The Altruism Debate On the surface, altruism—as an act of self-sacrifice—seems personally maladaptive. The hero who risks life and limb to save a crime victim and the philanthropist who donates large sums of money come out losers in the exchange. Or do they? Evolutionary psychologists claim that in the fight for survival, helpfulness can perpetuate our own "selfish" genes (Dawkins, 1989). One way this may operate is that people of all cultures follow the norm of reciprocity—a moral code that directs us to help, not hurt, those who have helped us. Helping can thus be considered a long-term investment in the future. Evolutionary psychologists also point out that people are quick to help their own offspring, followed by other family members in proportion to their genetic relatedness and strangers who are similar to themselves. The result: self-sacrificing behavior that, paradoxically, promotes one's own genetic immortality (Rushton, 1989; Burnstein et al., 1994).

Binti Jua is a gorilla in the Brookfield Zoo, near Chicago. One day, a three-year-old boy fell eighteen feet into her area and was knocked unconscious. He was not a fellow ape. Yet with her baby clinging to her back, Binti scooped him up, cradled him, and took him to the door, where the keepers could reach him. She was a hero. But was her act one of "altruism"? Some say yes, *she was motivated by kindness and empathy. Others say she merely acted, as trained, to pick up and fetch objects that fall into her cage. This episode brings the altruism debate to life—even in the animal world.*

It is often said that helpfulness serves short-term personal interests as well. According to some theorists, people decide whether to intervene by weighing the costs (time, stress, the risk of injury) against the benefits (financial reward, praise, social approval, a feeling of satisfaction). This decision making may not be conscious, but if the anticipated benefits exceed the anticipated costs, we help; if not, we stay put. In other words, helping is motivated by self-serving goals (such as a desire for a "helper's high" or to avoid feeling guilty for not helping), not by altruism (Cialdini et al., 1973; Piliavin et al., 1981).

Are humans ever truly altruistic, or is our behavior always selfishly motivated? C. Daniel Batson (1991) argues that an act of assistance should be considered altruistic when the helper's main goal is to benefit someone in need—independent of the consequences for the helper. According to Batson's **empathy-altruism hypothesis**, diagrammed in Figure 13.17, people have two emotional reactions to someone in need: *personal distress* (guilt, anxiety, and discomfort) and *empathy* (sympathy and compassion for the other person). When the first reaction predominates, we help primarily to relieve our own discomfort—a self-centered, "egoistic" motivation. When the second reaction predominates, however, we help in order to alleviate the other's suffering—an altruistic motivation. In other words, says Batson, helping can satisfy both selfish and noble motives.

If Batson is correct, then empathy—a genuine, gut-level compassion for another person—is the engine that drives pure altruism. Can empathy inspire helping? How

altruism Helping behavior that is motivated primarily by a desire to benefit others, not oneself.

empathy-altruism hypothesis The proposition that an empathic response to a person in need produces altruistic helping.

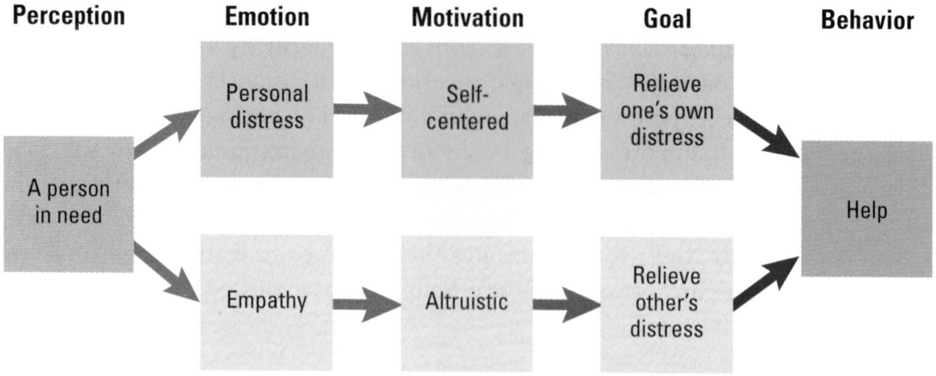

Figure 13.17 Two pathways to helping In response to someone needing help, people feel a combination of personal distress and empathy. Accordingly, there are two paths to helping: One is self-centered (aimed at the relief of one's own discomfort), and the other is altruistic (designed to alleviate the other's suffering).

can the two helping motives be distinguished? According to Batson, people who come face to face with a needy person—say, a beggar on the street or an accident victim—can relieve their *own* distress by offering help or by escaping the situation (out of sight, out of mind). For people with empathy for the victim, however, there is no mental escape. The *victim's* distress can be reduced only by helping.

To demonstrate, Batson and his coworkers (1981) devised a situation in which subjects watched a female accomplice, posing as another subject, receive electric shocks as part of an experiment. Over closed-circuit TV, they saw that she was upset and heard her say that she had suffered an electrical accident as a child. What next? Given a choice, would subjects leave the experiment, having already completed their part in it (escape), or would they volunteer to trade places with the accomplice (help)? As predicted by Batson, the choice subjects made depended on their feelings of empathy for the woman. Among those low in empathy (because her values were different from theirs), only 18 percent agreed to trade places. But among subjects who were high in empathy (because she shared similar values), 91 percent agreed to the trade. These latter subjects could have made themselves feel better by leaving, but instead they stayed to help the other person. Does this mean that pure altruism exists? Some say *yes* (Batson et al., 1989; Dovidio et al., 1990); others say *no* (Cialdini et al., 1987; Schaller & Cialdini, 1988).

Bystander Intervention This debate about human nature is fascinating, but what inspired social psychologists to study helping in the first place were hair-raising news stories about bystanders who fail to take action even when someone's life is in danger. The problem first made headlines in March 1964. Kitty Genovese was walking home from work in Queens, New York, at 3:20 in the morning. As she crossed the street from her car to her apartment, a man with a knife appeared. She ran, but he caught up and stabbed her. She cried frantically for help and screamed, "Oh my God, he stabbed me!...I'm dying, I'm dying!"—but to no avail. The man fled but then returned, raped her, and stabbed her eight more times, until she was dead. In the still of the night, the attack lasted for over half an hour. Thirty-eight neighbors heard the screams, turned lights on, and came to their windows. One couple even pulled chairs up to the window and turned out the light to see better. Yet nobody came down to help. Until it was over, nobody even called the police.

What happened? How could people have been so heartless and apathetic? How could they have remained passive while a neighbor was being murdered? Rather than blame the bystanders, Bibb Latané and John Darley (1970) focused on the social factors at work in this situation. In a series of important experiments, they staged emergencies, varied the conditions, and observed what happened. In one study, Darley and Latané (1968) took subjects to a cubicle and asked them to discuss the kinds of personal problems that college students face. For confidentiality purposes, they were told, subjects would communicate over an intercom system and the experimenter would not be listening. The subjects were also told to speak one at a time and to take turns. Some were assigned to two-person discussions, others to larger groups. Although the opening moments were uneventful, one subject (an accomplice) mentioned in passing that he had a seizure disorder that was sometimes triggered by pressure. Sure enough, when it came his turn to speak again, this subject struggled and pleaded for help:

> "I could really-er-use some help so if somebody would-er-give me a little h-help-uh-er-er-er c-could somebody-er-er-help-er-uh-uh-uh (choking sounds)...I'm gonna die-er-er-I'm...gonna die-er-help-er-er-seizure-er."

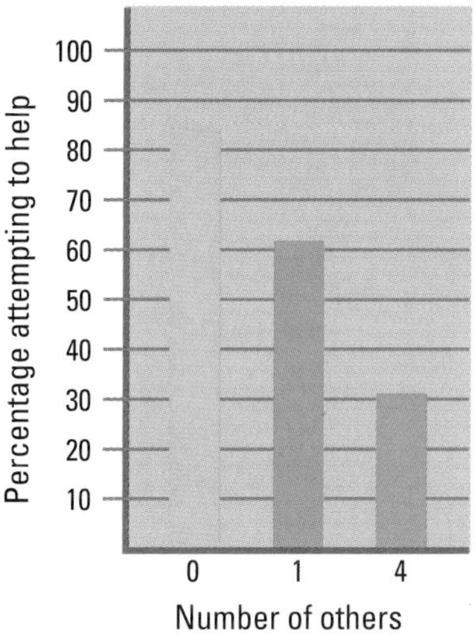

Figure 13.18 The bystander effect When subjects thought that they alone heard a seizure victim in need, the vast majority sought help. As the number of bystanders increased, however, they became less likely to intervene (Darley & Latané, 1968).

If you were in this situation, how would you react? Would you stop the experiment, dash out of your cubicle, and seek out the experimenter? As it turned out, the response was strongly influenced by the size of their group. Actually, all subjects participated alone, but they were led to believe that others were present and that there was a real crisis. Almost all subjects who thought they were in a two-person discussion left the room for help immediately. In the larger "groups," however, subjects were less likely to intervene and were slower to do so when they did. In fact, the larger the group was supposed to be, the less helping occurred (see Figure 13.18). This pattern of results was labeled the **bystander effect:** The more bystanders there are, the less likely a victim is to get help. In an emergency, the presence of others inhibits helping.

At first, this pioneering research seemed to defy all common sense. Isn't there safety in numbers? Don't we feel more secure rushing in to help when others are there for support? To fully understand what went wrong, Latané and Darley (1970) provided a careful, step-by-step analysis of the decision-making process in emergency situations. According to their scheme, bystanders help only when they *notice* the incident, *interpret* it as an emergency, *take responsibility* for helping, *decide* to intervene, and then *act* on that decision (see Figure 13.19).

This analysis of the intervention process sheds light on the bystander effect, as the presence of others can inhibit helping at each of the five steps. Consider, for example, the second requirement, that bystanders interpret an event as an emergency. Have you ever heard screaming from a nearby house and the sound of crashing objects, only to wonder if you were overhearing an assault or just a family quarrel? Cries of pain may sound like shrieks of laughter, and heart-attack victims may be mistaken for drunk. How do other bystanders influence our interpretation? Faced with a sudden, possibly dangerous event, everyone pretends to stay calm. As each person sees that others seem indifferent, they shrug it off. As a result, the event no longer feels like an emergency.

This process was observed in a study in which Latané and Darley (1970) had subjects fill out questionnaires alone or in groups of three. Shortly after the experimenter left, white smoke was pumped into the room through a vent. Alone, most subjects worried that there was a fire and quickly reported the smoke to the experimenter. Yet in the company of others, most subjects did not seek help. In some

bystander effect The finding that the presence of others inhibits helping in an emergency.

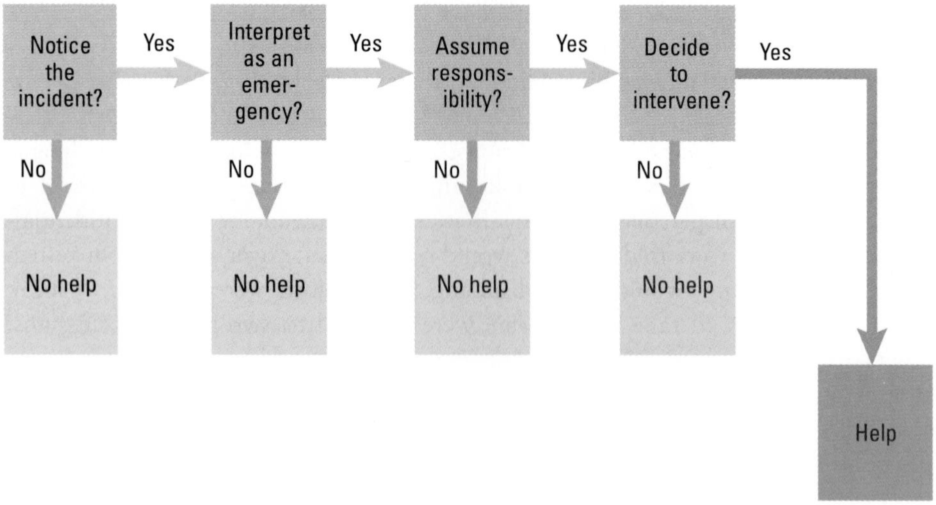

Figure 13.19 A model of bystander intervention This step-by-step analysis suggests several reasons for the fact that bystanders often do not help in emergencies.

groups, the smoke was so thick that subjects rubbed their eyes and waved the fumes away from their face as they worked on the questionnaires, but they did not call for help. Why not? In postexperiment interviews, they said they assumed the smoke was harmless steam, air-conditioning vapors, or even "truth gas"—but not a fire.

The presence of others also inhibits helping by causing a **diffusion of responsibility**, a belief that others will intervene. Thirty-eight people watched from their apartments and did nothing while Kitty Genovese was killed. Subjects in the group conditions of the seizure experiment also did not intervene. When subjects thought that they alone could hear the victim, making them solely responsible for his welfare, they took action. Many of those who thought that others were also present, however, behaved like the neighbors of Kitty Genovese: They stayed put because they assumed someone else was helping.

The bystander effect is powerful and scary. Over the years, researchers have observed behavior in different kinds of staged crises. Would subjects report a theft or a possible fire? Would they stop for a stranded motorist, help a woman who faints or sprains an ankle, or try to break up a fight? Would they rush to the aid of a seizure victim, a subway passenger who staggers and falls to the ground, or an experimenter who has an asthma attack? What are the odds that a person in need will actually receive help? Clearly, helping depends in complex ways on characteristics of the victim, the bystanders, and the situation (see Table 13.1). The fact remains, however, that a person is less likely to intervene in a group than when alone. Even more remarkable is that victims are more likely to get help from some*one* when their welfare rests on the shoulders of a single potential helper than when many others are present (Latané & Nida, 1981).

Social psychologists have studied a wide range of important behaviors—and in a wide range of important settings. From the studies of social perception, attraction, conformity, obedience, persuasion, group processes, aggression, and altruism, the research message is clear: We are influenced in profound ways by the words and actions of other people.

diffusion of responsibility In groups, a tendency for bystanders to assume that someone else will help.

Table 13.1 When Helping Is Most Likely to Occur

1. When the bystander is in a good mood
2. When the bystander feels guilty or needs a self-esteem boost
3. When the bystander observes someone else helping
4. When the bystander is not pressed for time
5. When the bystander is male and the victim female
6. When the victim makes a direct request for help
7. When the victim is physically attractive
8. When the victim appears to deserve help
9. When the victim is similar in some way to the bystander
10. In a small town or rural area, not a large city

Summary and Key Terms

Social psychology is the study of how individuals think, feel, and behave in social situations. The principle message is that people can influence each other's behavior in profound ways.

Social Perception

Social perception refers to the processes of coming to know and evaluate other people. To a large extent, the impressions we form of others are based on our observations of their behavior.

Making Attributions

People make attributions for other people's behavior. According to **attribution theory,** people analyze a person's behavior and its situational context in order to make a *personal attribution* or a *situational attribution.* According to Kelley, people use three types of information in making attributions: consensus (how other people react in the situation), distinctiveness (how the target person reacts in other situations), and consistency (how the target person reacts at different times).

Other studies point to attribution errors and biases. In explaining the behavior of others, we typically overestimate the role of personal factors, the **fundamental attribution error.** This tendency may be unique to cultures that value individualism. Attributions can also be biased by self-serving motivations, as people are more likely to make self-attributions for success than for failure.

Forming Impressions

In perceiving others, people are subject to a **primacy effect** by which first impressions weigh heavily and are highly resistant to change. Through various cognitive-confirmation biases, first impressions guide the way they interpret later contradictory evidence. Through behavioral-confirmation biases, we often alter our behavior and unwittingly shape others in ways that confirm our impressions.

Attraction

There are several factors that spark a positive impression, or attraction. The first is familiarity. Through the **mere-exposure effect,** exposure to a person increases liking. A second factor is physical attractiveness. People like others who are physically attractive and behave more warmly toward them. Third, people like others who are similar in attitudes and interests.

Social Influence

Conformity

Conformity is the tendency to change one's opinion or behavior in response to social norms. Classic studies by Sherif and Asch revealed two types of social influence. People demonstrating **informational influence** go along with the group and change their opinions because they believe the others are correct. **Normative influence** leads people to conform only in their public behavior because they fear social rejection.

Conformity increases with group size (up to a point) and with the salience of social norms. Conformity decreases when an ally is present. Cultural factors are also important, as more conformity is found in cultures that value social harmony. Nonconformists are often unpopular, but they can influence majorities by sticking to their positions with consistency and confidence.

History offers many examples of crimes committed in the name of obedience. Milgram's research showed that even decent people can violate the conscience on command. By varying characteristics of the authority, victim, and situation, he was able to determine what factors increase the likelihood of obedience.

Attitudes and Attitude Change

To have lasting effects, social influence must change not just behavior but **attitudes.** Attitude change, or persuasion, can occur in two ways. On the **central route to persuasion,** people think carefully about a message and are influenced by its arguments. On the **peripheral route to persuasion,** they rely on superficial cues. The central route requires the ability and motivation to process the communication carefully.

Persuasive communication is the outcome of three factors: source, message, and audience. Source credibility and likability increase persuasiveness. Messages are persuasive if the position taken is moderately discrepant and if it uses fear to motivate change or arouses positive emotions. Audience factors are also important, such as the need for cognition and self-monitoring.

Just as attitudes influence behavior, behavior can influence attitudes. Festinger argued that behaving in attitude-discrepant ways can create an unpleasant state of **cognitive dissonance.** This leads us to change our attitudes to match or justify our behavior. The evidence supports this basic effect and the conditions in which it occurs. Theorists continue to debate the reasons for it.

Group Processes

People behave differently in groups than when alone. Through **social facilitation,** the presence of others enhances performance on simple tasks but impairs performance on complex tasks. Zajonc explained that the mere presence of others increases arousal and triggers our dominant response. Others have proposed different interpretations. In joint activities, people often exert less effort than they would alone. This **social loafing** increases with group size because individuals do not see the link between their own effort and the desired group outcome.

Groupthink, a process in which members convince themselves that they are correct, is especially likely in groups that are isolated, cohesive, and homogeneous and have strong leadership. This process occurs because members feel invulnerable, become close-minded, and are pressured toward uniformity. Groupthink raises the odds of miscalculation and failure.

Social Relations

Aggression

Aggression is rooted in both human biology and social factors. Although instinct theories do not account for differences among cultures, there are biological influences, perhaps even a genetic component. Men are more aggressive than women, and aggression is also increased by alcohol.

In general, aversive stimulation sparks aggression. Studies of the **frustration-aggression hypothesis** show that frustration correlates with aggressive behavior. Intense summer heat is also linked to aggression. Once aversive stimulation arouses negative emotion, situational cues—such as the presence of weapons and exposure to violence—prompt us to turn the feeling into action. Aggression is also increased by **deindividuation,** a loss of individuality that people sometimes experience in large groups.

Altruism

Does **altruism**—that is, helping behavior primarily motivated by a desire to benefit others—really exist? Evolutionary psychologists theorize that by helping others we selfishly promote the long-term success of our own genes. Others say helping is motivated by short-term gains. According to Batson's **empathy-altruism hypothesis,** however, people react to someone else's need with both personal distress and empathy. When the latter reaction predominates, we have altruistic motivation.

Studies demonstrate a bystander effect in which the presence of others inhibits helping. The **bystander effect** can reduce our tendency to interpret an event as an emergency and create a **diffusion of responsibility,** a belief that others are providing the necessary help.

In the Field Resources

Books

Cialdini, R. B. (1993). *Influence: Science and practice* (3rd ed.). Glenview, IL: Scott, Foresman.

This captivating book describes six "weapons of influence" that are used by persuasive politicians, real estate agents, con artists, cult leaders, and others.

Milgram, S. (1974). *Obedience to authority.* New York: Harper & Row.

Milgram describes in vivid detail his classic series of experiments, what they tell us about human nature, and what ethical dilemmas he faced along the way.

Films and Videos

Schindler's List (1993, 184 min.)

With psychology's focus on the evils of the Holocaust, the story of Oskar Schindler, who risked his life to save Jews, illustrates altriusm—the bright side of human nature. (Liam Neeson, Ben Kingsley, Ralph Fiennes, Caroline Goodall, Johnathan Sagalle, Embeth Davidtz.)

Twelve Angry Men (1957, 95 min.)

This drama about a jury's deliberation beautifully depicts majority and minority influence, leadership, and deviance in small decision-making groups. (Henry Fonda, Lee J. Cobb, Ed Begley, E.G. Marshall, Jack Warden, Martin Balsam.)

Internet

The Institute for Social Research (http://www.isr.umich.edu/)

Presents the results of nationwide surveys of attitudes, lifestyles, and values, often reported in the media.

Journals and Periodicals

Journal of Applied Social Psychology
Journal of Experimental Social Psychology
Journal of Personality and Social Psychology
Journal of Social Issues
Personality and Social Psychology Bulletin

14 *Social and Cultural Groups*

What's Your Prediction?

Cultural influences on social interaction

The situation Having read some social psychology, you're interested in social interaction. Most of the studies you've read about took place in North America, and you're curious about the influences of culture both here and in other parts of the world. You already know that compared to most North Americans, people from Japan maintain a longer "polite" distance while interacting and that people from other countries, such as Venezuela, set a closer, more "intimate" distance. You assume that these different norms must cause occasional misunderstanding in cross-cultural interactions, and you want to explore this question.

You're at a large university and have access to students from different countries, all of whom speak English. What if students from Japan were to converse, in Japanese, as part of an American psychology experiment—would they adopt the usual polite distance or behave more like North Americans? What if they were to converse in English? Would that bring them even closer? Next, you wonder about students from Venezuela interacting in Spanish—would they "crowd" each other or increase the distance according to North American norms? Again, what if they were to converse in English?

To put these questions to the test, you recruit 105 male and female Japanese, Venezuelan, and American students for a study of conversations. You want to carefully control who they talk to, so you hire six confederates (two from each country) and arrange for all subjects to interact for five minutes with a same-sex partner from their own country. You also want to standardize the situation, so you train the confederates to behave in set ways and to discuss sports and hobbies. All the foreign students and confederates are bilingual, so you instruct half to speak in their native tongue and the other half in English. In each session, you then escort the subject and confederate into a room with a one-way mirror. The confederate sits first and you prompt the subject to pull up a chair. You then leave the room and videotape the conversation from behind the mirror. Later, you review the tape and measure to the nearest inch the distance of the subject's chair from the confederate's.

Make a prediction There are two questions being tested. First, will students from Japan, Venezuela, and the United States—talking to partners of the same sex and nationality—differ in the amount of distance they set? You might think that culturally ingrained interaction styles, like habits, are tough to break. On the other hand, you would not be surprised to find that people alter their behavior according to the situation they're in. Second, will students vary the distance according to the language they speak? Look at the table below and predict the number of inches from the confederate the subjects set themselves. Here are two items to help guide your predictions: (1) The range is 30 to 45 inches, and (2) on average, American subjects set a distance of 35 inches.

	SPEAKING NATIVE LANGUAGE		SPEAKING ENGLISH	
	Japanese	*Venezuelan*	*Japanese*	*Venezuelan*
Distance	_______	_______	_______	_______

The results The actual results are presented below. On the question of whether differences would be found among students speaking in their native tongue, the answer is *yes* (left). Compared to the American students, who were at 35 inches, the Japanese students sat farther and the Venezuelan students sat closer. On the question of what would happen when all subjects interacted in English, you can see that the differences between the Japanese and Venezuelan subjects vanished (right).

	SPEAKING NATIVE LANGUAGE		SPEAKING ENGLISH	
	Japanese	*Venezuelan*	*Japanese*	*Venezuelan*
Distance	40	32	39	40

What does it all mean? Like world travelers, psychologists have long known that just as people around the world speak different languages, they also differ in nonverbal aspects of communication—such as eye contact, the use of gestures, touching, and physical distance. In the study just described,

Nan Sussman and Howard Rosenfeld (1982) found that the interaction styles people exhibit in their own cultures can be observed in a controlled laboratory setting—a finding that reveals the subtle ways in which culture shapes our everyday behavior. They also found, however, that people alter their interaction styles, without being told to do so, in order to suit the situation they are in—a finding that is consistent with the message of social psychology. As we'll see in this chapter, both types of influences are important—not only in studies of different cultures but also in comparisons among ethnic groups and between men and women within a culture.

It's a sign of the times that Coca-Cola is being sold at Red Square in Moscow.

The first time I heard the song was at the 1964 World's Fair in Queens, New York. I was eleven years old at the time, and the exhibit was called "It's a Small World." After waiting in line, my family and I were seated in a "boat" that transported us from one large room of the exhibit to another and treated us to a fantasylike display that left a lasting imprint in my memory. There were hundreds of animated dolls colorfully dressed as children from all the continents of the world. As the dolls circled and moved about on mechanical platforms, you could hear children's voices singing in their native languages. The message of the exhibit: "There's so much that we share that it's time we're aware, it's a small world after all."

It's now thirty years later, and millions of people continue to tour this exhibit in the Disney parks of Florida, California, Paris, and Tokyo. And the message—that it's a small world—rings truer today than ever before. As many as a billion people have watched the Olympics on TV. Via satellite, the outbreak of war, floods, earthquakes, volcanic eruptions, royal weddings, and state funerals are broadcast live to all corners of the globe. People from different countries now communicate online and share information over the Internet. Thanks to various international trade agreements, you can wear Levi jeans, watch MTV, drink Coke, and eat McDonald's burgers in Moscow. And in the United States, you can drive a Japanese car, wear clothing made in Taiwan, and eat in restaurants that serve enchiladas, lasagna, wonton soup, pita bread, sushi, curried lamb, and other international delights.

As the people of the world come into greater contact with each other, one wonders: What challenges lie ahead as we approach the twenty-first century, when East meets West and North meets South in the global village? Does the "smallness" of the world homogenize different cultures and other groups, or does it sharpen our awareness of human diversity? What about migration patterns within countries? Consider the changes in the American landscape resulting from recent influxes of immigrants. Over the next few years, ethnic-minority groups will constitute a majority of the population in many cities in the United States. Will this increased heterogeneity breed tolerance of others who are different, or will it fuel prejudice and discrimination? And what about biological sex? With men and women often playing different roles at home and in the workplace, what questions are raised about the nature of men and women, their similarities and their differences?

[Published in *Hemisphere*; © Bob Schochet.]

"Very nice, but now can you take us to McDonald's?"

Immersed in our own way of life we sometimes fail to appreciate the richness and diversity of other cultures.

Over the years, social psychologists have found that people are deeply affected by the situations they are in. Milgram's obedience experiments illustrate this point in a dramatic way. In this regard, we'll see that social and cultural groups to which we belong—and, as a result, the ways in which we are similar to others and different—play a prominent role. The various issues addressed in this chapter converge on another important point: For people to get along, there needs to be mutual tolerance, understanding, and an appreciation of the diversity of human life. If I had to sum up all of psychology—and the theme of this chapter—in just one sentence, it would be this: Everyone is basically the same, yet no two people are alike.

The similarities among us are so self-evident that they are invisible, taken for granted. Regardless of whether you are male or female; regardless of whether the color of your skin is black, white, brown, yellow, or olive; and regardless of where in the world you live, you squint your eyes in bright sunlight, prefer sweet foods to bitter, get lightheaded when you drink too much alcohol, smile when you're happy, speak in "baby talk" to infants, have the capacity to hold seven or so items in short-term memory, forget events that took place when you were two years old, repeat behaviors that produce reinforcement, seek the company of others who are similar, respond to social pressure from peers, and react to trauma with anxiety or depression. Similarly, babies all over the world babble before uttering a word, fear strangers in the first year of life, think concretely before using abstract logic, and start yearning for sex during adolescence.

Despite the "universals" of human behavior, there are some differences—between cultures, between racial and ethnic groups within a culture, and between men and women. As we'll see, these differences are largely rooted in the various physical, economic, and social environments in which people live.

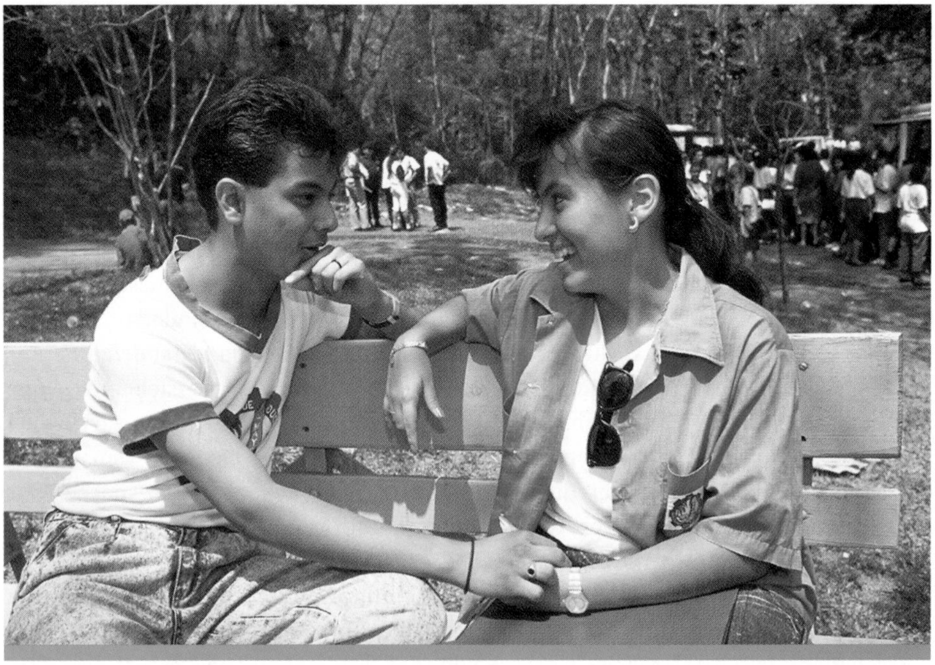

Despite cultural diversity, there are many similarities among the peoples of the world. Children crave the sweet taste of candy in Texas—and everywhere else. Teenagers flirt and think about sex in Honduras—and everywhere else.

Cross-Cultural Perspectives

What are individualism and collectivism, and how do cultures differ on this dimension? Is one orientation better, or more adaptive, than the other? Do cultures differ in the extent to which they breed conformity? Can culture influence the way people see themselves in relation to others?

For every two ticks of the second hand on your watch, 9 new babies are born and 3 people die. The net increase of 3 human lives per second means that the world's population grows by 10,600 per hour, 254,000 per day, 1.8 million per week, 7.7 million per month, and 93 million per year. According to the United Nations, there are almost 6 billion people in the world's total population, a number that is projected to reach 10 billion before the year 2050. Increasingly, then, people will need to live peacefully, and cooperatively.

Immersed in our own ways of life, it is all too easy to overlook an important fact: There is no dominant world culture. Look at Table 14.1, for example, and you'll see that of every 100 people in the 200 or so nations of the world, the U.S. Census Bureau estimates that 21 live in China, 16 live in India, and only 5 live in the United States. We humans are a heterogeneous lot. As a matter of *geography,* some of us live in large, heavily populated cities, while others live in small towns, affluent suburbs,

Table 14.1 Where in the World People Live

OF EVERY 100 PEOPLE	LIVE IN
21	China
16	India
5	United States
5	former Soviet Union
4	Indonesia
3	Brazil
2	Bangladesh
2	Japan
2	Mexico
2	Nigeria
2	Pakistan
1	Egypt
1	Ethiopia
1	France
1	Germany
1	Iran
1	Italy
1	Philippines
1	Thailand
1	Turkey
1	United Kingdom
1	Vietnam
25	All remaining countries

After China, India is the second most populous country in the world. This scene shows a Hindu woman at the holy river Ganges.

rural farming communities, hot and humid jungles, expansive deserts, high-altitude mountains, tropical islands, and icy arctic plains. Excluding the dialects, more than 6,000 different *languages* are spoken—including Chinese, English, Hindi, Spanish, Russian, Arabic, Malay, Bengali, Portuguese, French, German, and Japanese. There are also hundreds of *religions* that people identify with—the most popular being Christianity (32 percent), Islam (19 percent), Hinduism (14 percent), Buddhism (6 percent), Chinese folk religions (4 percent), New Asian religions (2 percent), various African ethnic-group religions (2 percent), and Judaism (0.4 percent). The remaining 20 percent of the world's population are atheists or simply are not affiliated with a religion.

In light of the many ways in which cultures differ, it can be difficult for cross-cultural psychologists to translate verbal research materials from one language into another. The goal is not to create literal translations but to create materials that are equivalent in their meaning. This process involves having one bilingual person translate an item—say, from English to Spanish—then having another bilingual person "back-translate" the item from Spanish into English. If there are discrepancies in meaning, the process is repeated until linguistic equivalence is achieved. Table 14.2 presents examples—from signs displayed around the world—of what can go wrong when simple sentences are poorly translated (Triandis, 1994).

Cultural Diversity: A Fact of Life

Linked together by space, language, religion, and historical bonds, each cultural group has its own ideology, folklore, music, political system, family structure, sexual mores, fashions, and foods. As world travelers come to learn, sometimes the hard way, there are also tremendous variations in local customs.

Visit an outdoor market in Iraq, and you should expect to barter or negotiate the price of everything you purchase. Plan a meeting with a native of Brazil, and don't

Table 14.2 Translation "Bloopers"

- "Drop your trousers here for best results" (a dry cleaner in Thailand).
- "You are invited to take advantage of the chambermaid" (a hotel in Japan).
- "Ladies are requested not to have children in the bar" (a cocktail lounge in Norway).
- "The manager has personally passed on the water served here" (a hotel in Mexico).
- "Take one of our horse-driven city tours—we guarantee no miscarriages" (a tourist agency in Czechoslovakia).
- "We take your bags and send them in all directions" (an airline in Denmark).

Source: H. C. Triandis (1994). *Culture and social behavior.* New York: McGraw-Hill.

be surprised if he or she is late. Nothing personal. In North America, it is common to sit casually opposite someone with your legs outstretched. Yet in Nepal, it's considered an insult to point the bottom of your feet at someone. In Turkey, heterosexual men can embrace, kiss on the cheek, and walk together hand in hand. Yet in North America, such public displays between men are considered unmanly. In Iran, Islamic women wear veils over the face; in many other countries, they paint their lips, shadow their eyes, and powder their faces with makeup. People in some parts of the world eat with forks and knives; others use chopsticks, bread, or their bare hands. Some people exchange greetings by shaking hands or waving; others lower the head and bow. As we saw at the start of this chapter, even the way we space ourselves while interacting is culturally determined. Americans, Germans, the British, and most northern Europeans maintain a polite distance between themselves and others—and feel "crowded" by the touchier, nose-to-nose style of the French, Greeks, Arabs, Mexicans, and people of Latin America. In the affairs of day-to-day living, each culture operates by its own implicit rules of conduct, or **social norms.** Social norms from one country to the next can be so different that people who travel for business or for pleasure should be mindful of local customs. As described in Roger Axtell's (1993) bestselling book, *Do's and Taboos around the World,* here are some helpful tips for the world traveler:

- *Greetings.* Waving and shaking hands may seem universal, but there are different rules for greeting. In Finland, you should give a firm handshake; in France, you should loosen the grip; in Zambia, you should use your left hand to support the right; and in Bolivia, you should extend your arm if your hand is dirty. In Japan, people bow; in Thailand, they put both hands together in a praying position on the chest; and in Fiji, they smile and raise their eyebrows. In Venezuela, Paraguay, and certain other parts of Latin America, it is common for people to hug, embrace, and kiss upon meeting. In most Arab countries, men greet one another by saying, "Salaam alaykum," then shaking hands and saying, "Kaif halak," and kissing each other on the cheek.

- *Nonverbal communication.* When you don't speak the native language, it's natural to use gestures. Watch out. In Bulgaria, nodding your head means "no" and shaking your head sideways means "yes." In Germany and Brazil, the American "okay" sign (forming a circle with your thumb and forefinger) is an obscene gesture. Personal space habits also vary across cultures. Japanese people prefer to keep a comfortable distance while interacting. But in Puerto Rico and much of Latin America, people stand very close—and backing off is

social norms Implicit rules of conduct according to which each culture operates.

considered an insult. Also beware of what you do with your eyes. In Latin America, locking eyes is a must, yet in Japan too much eye contact shows a lack of respect. If you're in the habit of stroking your cheek, you should know that in Italy, Greece, and Spain it means you find the person you're talking to attractive. And whatever you do, don't ever touch someone's head while in Buddhist countries, especially Thailand. The head is sacred.

- ***Table manners.*** So much human social activity revolves around eating that acceptance of local foods and table manners is important. First, be prepared for foods you may consider "exotic." For example, you may be served sheep's eyes in Saudi Arabia, raw fish in Japan, bear's paw soup in China...and lobster in the United States. Be mindful of strict religious prohibitions, and don't ask for beef in India or pork in Islamic countries. Table etiquette is also tricky. In Zambia, the guest should ask to be served, because it's impolite for the host to offer food first. In Saudi Arabia, you show your appreciation of a meal by stuffing yourself. As a dinner guest in Bolivia, you should clean your plate to prove you enjoyed the meal, but in India you should leave some food to signal to the host that you've had enough to eat. In parts of Pakistan, India, Malaysia, and Indonesia, you should never pass, accept, or touch food with your left hand.

- ***Gifts.*** Giving and accepting gifts are customary parts of social interaction. They also present an opportunity for misunderstanding. In Japan, gift giving is used to express friendship, gratitude, and respect. But beware: If you receive a gift, you should reciprocate—so don't get caught empty-handed. When you give a gift in Japan, however, make sure that it is not wrapped in white paper, because white is associated with death. In China, avoid using red ink because messages written in red imply the severing of a relationship. Of course, what you give is as important as how you present it. Never present a bottle of wine to a Muslim, because the Islamic faith prohibits alcohol. In Hong Kong, avoid clocks (which symbolize death) and sharp objects (which signify the breakup of a relationship). Flowers are nice, but in Guatemala white flowers are reserved for funerals, and in Chile yellow flowers signify contempt. If you visit someone in Greece, Morocco, and many Arab countries, be careful not to admire or praise any possession too much or your host will feel obligated to give it to you.

Just as cultures differ in their social norms, so too they differ in the extent to which people are expected to adhere to those norms. As an example, compare the United States and Japan. In the United States, parents teach their children to be self-reliant, independent, and assertive. In Japan, however, children are taught the values of conformity, loyalty, and harmony within the community. As we'll see, this comparison indicates that there are two very different cultural orientations toward persons and the groups to which they belong. One orientation centers on the individual, the other on the group.

Individualism and Collectivism: A Tale of Two Cultural Worldviews

In the movie *Mr. Baseball,* actor Tom Selleck plays an aging American baseball star who signs a contract with a team in Japan. Selleck plays a brash character who always swings for the home run, loafs at practice, defies his manager, argues with umpires, and throws his bat when frustrated—a personal style that offends the Japanese sense of decorum. At one point, Selleck's antics become so publicly humiliating to the team that he is suspended. American and Japanese values were caricatured somewhat in this

Table 14.3 Individualistic and Collectivist Orientations

1. If the group is slowing me down, it is better to leave it and work alone. (*I*)
2. I like my privacy. (*I*)
3. I can count on my relatives for help if I find myself in any kind of trouble. (*C*)
4. If you want something done right, you've got to do it yourself. (*I*)
5. It is reasonable for a son to continue his father's business. (*C*)
6. In the long run, the only person you can count on is yourself. (*I*)
7. I enjoy meeting and talking to my neighbors every day. (*C*)
8. I like to live close to my good friends. (*C*)
9. The bigger the family, the more family problems there are. (*I*)
10. There is everything to gain and nothing to lose for classmates to group themselves for study and discussion. (*C*)

Source: H. C. Triandis (1995). *Individualism and collectivism.* Boulder, CO: Westview Press.

film for the sake of art. But there is more than just a kernel of truth to the distinction. Baseball is popular in both countries and is played by the same set of rules. But while American players strive for personal glory as all-stars and national heroes, Japanese coaches caution their players that "lone wolves are the cancer of the team."

This comparison reveals just the tip of an iceberg. Over the years, social psychologists have observed that cultures differ in the extent to which they value **individualism** and the virtues of independence, autonomy, and self-reliance or **collectivism** and the virtues of interdependence, cooperation, and social harmony. Under the banner of individualism, personal goals take priority over group allegiances. In collectivist cultures, however, the person is, first and foremost, a loyal member of a family, team, company, church, state, and other groups (see Table 14.3). In what countries are these differing orientations most extreme? In a worldwide study of 116,000 employees of IBM, Geert Hofstede (1980) found that the most fiercely individualistic people were from the United States, Australia, Great Britain, Canada, and the Netherlands, in that order. The most collectivistic people were from Venezuela, Colombia, Pakistan, Peru, Taiwan, and China. So what is your cultural orientation? Read the statements in Table 14.3 and note whether you agree or disagree with them. People from collectivist cultures tend to agree with C statements; those from individualistic cultures tend to agree with the *I* statements.

Why are some cultures individualistic, and why are others collectivistic? Speculating on the origins of these orientations, Harry Triandis (1995) suggests that there are three key factors. The first is the *complexity* of a society. As people live in more complex industrialized societies—compared, for example, to a life of food gathering among desert nomads—there are more groups to identify with (family, hometown, alma mater, church, place of employment, political party, sports teams, social clubs, and so on), which means less loyalty to any one group and a greater focus on personal rather than collective goals. Second is the *affluence* of a society. As people prosper, they gain financial independence from one another, a condition that promotes social independence, mobility, and, again, a focus on personal rather than collective goals. The third factor is *heterogeneity*. Societies that are homogeneous or "tight" (where members share the same language, religion, and social customs) tend to be rigid and intolerant of those who veer from the norm. In contrast, societies that are culturally diverse or "loose" (where two or more cultures coexist) tend to be more permissive of dissent—thus allowing for greater individual expression.

individualism A cultural orientation in which personal goals and preferences take priority over group allegiances.

collectivism A cultural orientation in which cooperation and group harmony take priority over purely personal goals.

These photographs were taken of "average income" families posing in front of their homes and material possessions. Representing the individualistic orientation common in affluent societies is the Skeen family of Pearland, Texas (top). *From the collectivistic orientation found in more impoverished societies is the Natoma family of Kouakourou, Mali* (bottom).

It is interesting that individualistic values in the United States are even greater today than in the past. Consider this question: If you were a parent, what traits would you like your child to develop? When this question was asked of American mothers in 1924, many chose "strict obedience," "loyalty," and "good manners"—key characteristics of collectivism. But when American mothers were asked the same question fifty-four years later, in 1978, they cited "independence" and "tolerance of others"—important aspects of individualism. Due perhaps to the greater complexity, affluence, and diversity of Western life in general, similar trends were also found in Germany, Italy, and England (Remley, 1988)—and in laboratory experiments, where conformity rates are somewhat lower today than in the past (Bond & Smith, 1996). Even on the baseball diamonds of Japan—where ballplayers are expected to obey coaches and make personal sacrifices for the sake of the team, change is taking place (Whiting, 1989).

Conceptions of the Self Individualism and collectivism are so deeply ingrained in a culture that they mold our very self-conceptions and identities. According to Hazel Markus and Shinobu Kitayama (1991), people who grow up in individualistic countries see themselves as entities that are *independent*—distinct, autonomous, self-contained, and endowed with unique dispositions. By contrast, people from more collectivist countries hold *interdependent* views of the self as part of a larger social network that includes family, coworkers, friends, and others with whom they are socially connected. People with independent views say that "The only person you can count on is yourself" and "I enjoy being unique and different from others." In contrast, those with interdependent views are more likely to agree that "I'm partly to blame if one of my family members or coworkers fails" and "My happiness depends on the happiness of those around me" (Triandis, 1995; Singelis, 1994; Rhee et al., 1995). These contrasting orientations—one focused on the personal self, the other on the collective self—are depicted in Figure 14.1.

Research confirms that there is a close link between culture and conceptions of the self. David Trafimow and his colleagues (1991) had American and Chinese college students complete twenty sentences beginning with "I am . . ." As shown in Figure 14.2, the Americans were more likely to fill in the blank with personal trait descriptions ("I am shy"), whereas the Chinese were more likely to identify themselves by group affiliations ("I am a college student"). It's no wonder that in China, the family name comes *before* one's personal name. Similar differences have been found between Australian and Malaysian subjects (Bochner, 1994).

These differing conceptions of the self can influence the way people perceive themselves and others. Markus and Kitayama (1991) found two interesting differences between East and West. First, American college students see themselves as less similar to others than do Asian Indian students. This finding reinforces the idea that

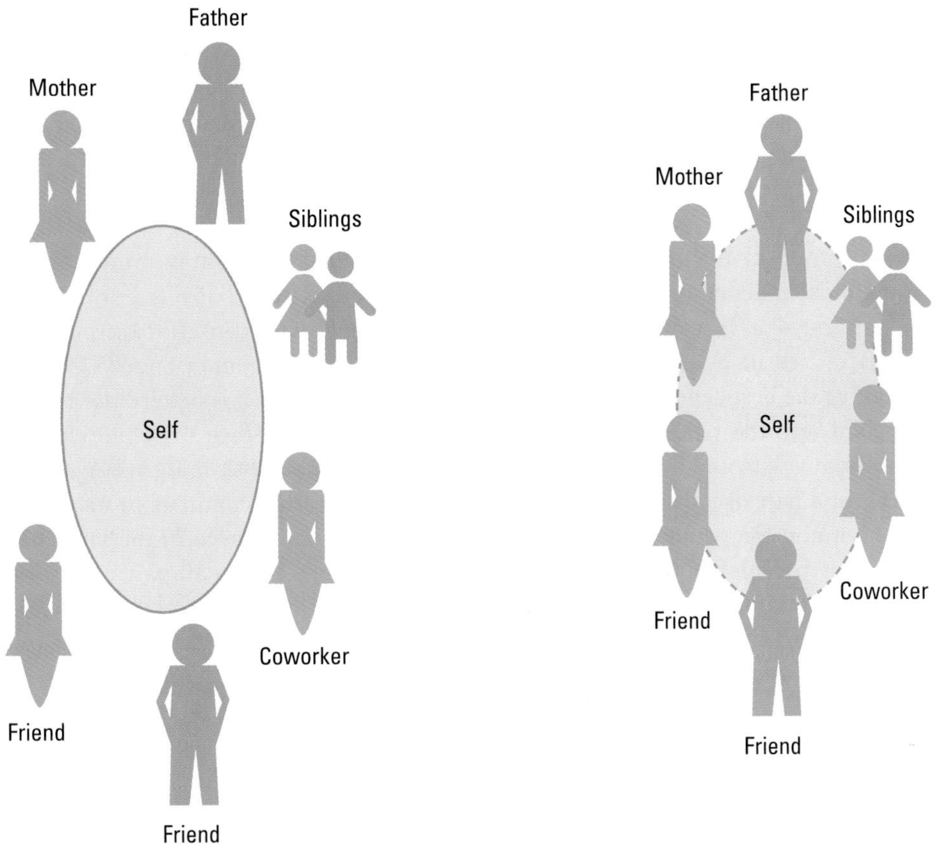

Figure 14.1 Self-conceptions Markus and Kitayama (1991) find that people from individualistic cultures see themselves as independent and distinct from others (left). In contrast, people in collectivist cultures see themselves as interdependent, as part of a larger social network (right).

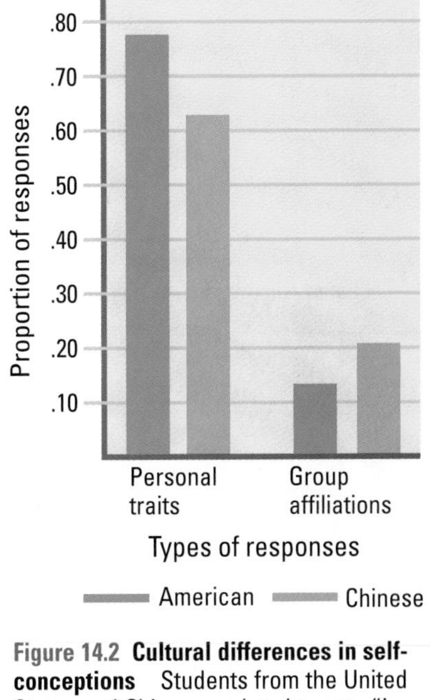

Figure 14.2 Cultural differences in self-conceptions Students from the United States and China completed twenty "I am ______" sentences. As shown, the Americans more often filled in the blank with personal qualities (*left*), while Chinese subjects were more likely to cite group affiliations (*right*).

people with independent conceptions of the self believe they are unique. Second, people in individualistic cultures strive for personal achievement, but those living in collectivist cultures derive more of their self-esteem through the status of a valued group. Thus, whereas North Americans overestimate their own contributions to a team effort, take credit for success, and blame others for failure, people from collectivist cultures underestimate their own role and present themselves in more modest, self-effacing terms in relation to others (Lee & Seligman, 1997). In a study that illustrates this point, Steven Heine and Darrin Lehman (1995) had students from Canada and Japan estimate the odds that certain positive and negative events would happen to them and to their peers. The result: Canadian students saw themselves, relative to their peers, as more likely to undergo the positive events and less likely to experience the negatives. But Japanese students rated themselves and peers as equally likely to experience the two types of events.

So are people from disparate cultures locked into thinking about the self in either personal or collective terms, or are both aspects of the self present in everyone, to be expressed according to the situation? Look again at the study depicted in Figure 14.2, where American students describe themselves more in terms of personal traits and where Chinese students cited more group affiliations. In a fascinating follow-up, Trafimow and his colleagues (1997) studied high-school and college students from Hong Kong, all of whom spoke English as a second language. One half of the subjects were given the "Who am I?" test in Chinese, and the other half took the

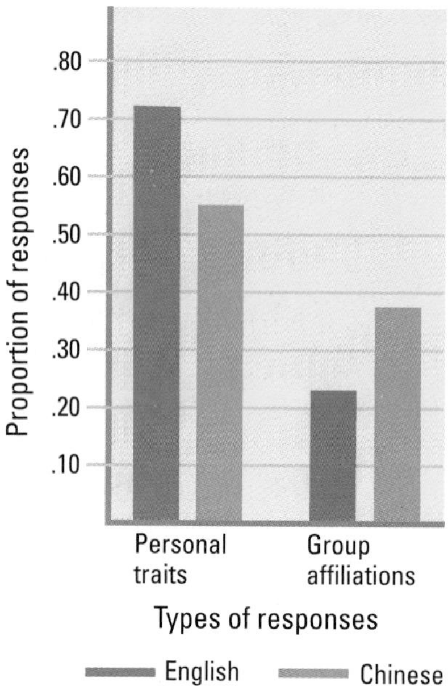

Figure 14.3 Can language bring out different aspects of the self? In this study, bilingual students from Hong Kong filled in the "I am _____" items in Chinese or in English. Suggesting that cultural orientation can bring out different aspects of the self, those who took the test in English focused more on personal traits (*left*), while those who took the test in Chinese were more focused on group affiliations (*right*).

test in English. Did this variation influence the results? Look at Figure 14.3, and you'll see that among these students from Hong Kong, those who described themselves in English focused more on personal traits, while those who took the test in Chinese focused more on group affiliations. It appears that all people have both personal and collective aspects of the self to draw on. The part that comes to mind depends on the situation.

Developmental Influences The culturally prescribed socialization practices that breed independence or interdependence begin soon after a baby is born. In the United States, a vast majority of middle-class parents who can afford it put their babies to bed in a separate room. Indeed, pediatrician Benjamin Spock (1945)—author of the best-selling child-care book ever—advised that it is better "not to take the child into the parents' bed for any reason" (p. 101). When my children were younger, my wife and I never thought twice about it. Separate sleeping arrangements were just a part of independence training. Yet in many other countries of the world, it is common for young children to sleep in the same room, even in the same bed, with their parents (Whiting & Edwards, 1988). Perhaps that is all part of *inter*dependence training. To many non-Americans, it is merciless to force helpless babies to lie alone in a dark room. Thus, when Mayan mothers from Guatemala were told of this practice, they reacted with shock, disapproval, and pity. As one disbelieving mother asked, "But there's someone else with them there, isn't there?" (Morelli et al., 1992).

Socialization fosters different cultural orientations in other ways, too. In individualistic cultures, parents are quick to wean infants from the breast and to toilet-train their toddlers out of diapers. Teenagers fight to separate from parents, and adults struggle to resolve the "identity crisis" that seems to plague us all. With all the focus on "me," the individual, it's no wonder that bookstore shelves are lined with paperbacks on how to "get in touch with your feelings," "speak your mind," "fulfill your potential," and become "self-actualized." In many ways, we take our cultural orientations for granted. In cultures that value freedom and individual rights, for example, we assume that people should marry for love and romance. Not so in all corners of the world. In parts of India, even today, families make arrangements for the future marriage of their children.

In 1994, Ichiro Suzuki, playing for the Orix Blue Wave, was the league's most valuable player. In sharp contrast to the suits uniformly worn by Japanese players off the field, Suzuki wears baggy jeans and a backward cap.

The Social Consequences Try as they do to be objective, cross-cultural researchers cannot help but make value judgments about the individualist and collectivist orientations. Is one orientation better, more adaptive, more productive, or more humane? There is no quick and simple answer. Predictably, individualists are less likely than collectivists to follow social norms. In Chapter 13, we saw that when American subjects were confronted with confederates who made incorrect perceptual judgments, they conformed to this incorrect majority 37 percent of the time (Asch, 1951). When similar tasks were given to subjects from collectivist cultures, conformity rates were even higher. Among the Bantu of Zimbabwe, where deviance is punished, 51 percent conformed. In fact, John Berry (1979) compared subjects from seventeen cultures and found that conformity rates ranged from a low of 18 percent among Inuit hunters of Baffin Island to a high of 60 percent among village-living Temne farmers of West Africa. More recent analyses have shown that conformity rates are generally higher in cultures that are collectivistic rather than individualistic in their orientation (Bond & Smith, 1996).

There is a drawback to individualism. If everyone focuses on personal goals, then the group as a whole suffers. The baseball player who worries more about his batting average than the team's winning percentage is a case in point (there's a scene in *Mr. Baseball* in which Tom Selleck defies his manager's call for a sacrifice bunt and strikes out swinging for a home run). We saw in Chapter 13 that people often exert less effort, or "loaf" on the job, when they work as part of a group than when they work alone (Latané et al., 1979). To many of us, it seems natural to slack off somewhat when others are there to pick up the slack. But social loafing is not equally strong all over the world. In fact, research shows that Chinese subjects in Taiwan work harder in a group than they do for themselves alone (Gabrenya et al., 1983). In collectivist cultures, what's good for the group is good for the self.

Exhibiting a collectivist orientation, 200 Amish men and women come together for a barn-raising. After an arsonist set fire to several barns in this Pennsylvania community, the men built new structures, while the women prepared lunch. This barn was rebuilt in ten hours.

Ironically, the benefit of collectivism may also be its main flaw. Intimately connected to groups, collectivists are loyal and team-spirited, willing to risk personal gain for the group's long-term well-being, and sometimes even willing to fight and die for their group. But how do collectivists behave toward members of other groups? Because they identify so strongly with their own, collectivists may be more likely to see their own norms as universal and exploit outsiders for competitive gain. In a study of interpersonal conflict, Kwok Leung (1988) found that Chinese subjects were less likely than Americans to pursue a conflict with a friend, but they were more likely to confront a stranger. As Triandis put it, "While collectivists are very nice to those who are members of their own groups, they can be very nasty, competitive, and uncooperative toward those who belong to other groups" (quoted in Goleman, 1990, p. 41). The result: The collective "we" may fuel intergroup tensions and promote ethnic, regional, national, and religious fighting against the collective "them."

Multicultural Perspectives

Is immigration a worldwide phenomenon or is it largely restricted to the United States? What is acculturation, and why is the process often stressful? What are the possible ways in which immigrants cope with the formation of an ethnic identity?

In June 1993, 300 Chinese men, women, and children left their families, crowded into a creaky, rusted freighter called the *Golden Venture,* traveled for four months over 17,000 miles, endured a ferocious Atlantic storm, and landed at 2 AM in Rockaway Beach, New York. The passengers clambered down the side of the vessel 200 yards from shore, and swam to the beach, where they were met by authorities. Most appeared dazed, disoriented, shivering cold, hungry, and in poor health. Why did these people pay thousands of dollars to illegal-alien smugglers and risk their lives on this dangerous and uncertain journey? Upset by the political and economic climate back home, they desperately wanted to start a new life.

[Drawing by B. Smaller; © 1996 The New Yorker Magazine, Inc.]

"I would share my cookies, but I'm afraid I'll set up a cycle of dependancy."

This "concern" is of an individualistic culture.

Ethnic Diversity: A Fact of Life

The names, dates, and places may change, but this script is replayed over and over again. In 1991, thousands of Albanians seeking political freedom stole into the night and sailed across the Adriatic Sea to Italy. Most but not all were sent back. In just

Seeking a new life, would-be immigrants from China wait off the coast of Mexico for entrance into the United States.

the past few years, thousands of Haitian refugees received political asylum in neighboring countries, Mexicans crossed the border into the United States, Afghans escaped war to Pakistan, Pakistanis moved to Great Britain, Turks sought employment in Germany, and Russian Jews moved from the former Soviet Union to Israel. Immigration is not the only source of ethnic diversity within a culture. In some cases, ethnic groups inhabit a country because they do not have their own homeland. Thus, many Sikhs live in India and Pakistan; Kurds inhabit Turkey and Iraq; Basques live in Spain; Tamils live in Sri Lanka; Palestinians are scattered throughout the Middle East; and Navajo, Sioux, and other Native Americans live within the United States (Demko, 1992).

In 1976, there were 67 Spanish-speaking radio stations in the United States. Now there are more than 300 (Market Segment Research, Inc.).

Like most countries, the United States has a culturally and ethnically mixed population—and is becoming even more so with time. According to the U.S. Bureau of the Census (1995), there are roughly 250 million U.S. citizens, 22 million of whom were born in another country. As categorized by the Census Bureau, 80 percent of the population are of European descent; 12 percent are of African descent; 9 percent are of Hispanic origin and trace their roots to Mexico, Puerto Rico, Central America, Cuba, and other Spanish-speaking countries; 3 percent are from Asia or the Pacific Islands; 1 percent are Native Americans, Eskimos, and Aleuts; and 4 percent are from other groups. These figures total more than 100 percent because some people identify with more than one ethnic category.

Growing racial and ethnic diversity within many countries around the world presents us all with new challenges and an uncertain future. How do the different groups within a culture coexist? Why, so often, is there animosity and conflict? More specifically, what are the causes and effects of discrimination, and how can this chronic social disease be treated? These and other questions have triggered, in recent years, an examination of multicultural research, the study of racial and ethnic groups within a culture.

Acculturation and Ethnic Identity

When people migrate from one country to another, they bring with them a cultural heritage and lifestyle that reach deep into the past. The result is that each racial or ethnic group is unique—similar to the dominant culture in some ways, different in others. For example, African American psychologist James Jones (1991) argues that compared to white American culture, African Americans tend to be more present-oriented, improvisational, expressive, spiritual, and emotional. Originating in Africa or among slaves of the American South, many black people have adopted a colorful and conspicuous behavior style—as seen in a certain slow, casual, rhythmic walk; in handshakes such as the "high five" and "thumb grasp"; and in sports, where athletes "spike" footballs into the end zone and "slam dunk" basketballs through the hoop (Majors, 1991).

Regardless of where racial or ethnic groups come from, how they get there, or why they leave their land of origin, all face the same core dilemma: whether to blend in and "assimilate" into the new culture or to retain a separate identity, language and all. There are two radically different historical perspectives on how this conflict between old and new should be managed. One is the romantic American ideal that all immigrant groups discard their heritage culture and blend into the American way of life. This assimilationist view is captured by the image of a *melting pot* in which different ethnic groups are mixed together to produce one harmonious mainstream culture. In the United States, this ideal is formalized in laws that require immigrants to renounce other citizenships, pass a test of American history, and take an oath of loyalty. The second approach encourages immigrants to retain their ancestral heritage, producing a culture that is ethnically diverse. In 1971, Canada adopted a policy of multiculturalism, in which the image of a melting pot was replaced by one of a colorful mosaic whereby each cultural group takes pride in its own unique

Ethnic diversity is a fact of life. In Dorchester, Massachusetts, these children represent twenty-four different nationalities.

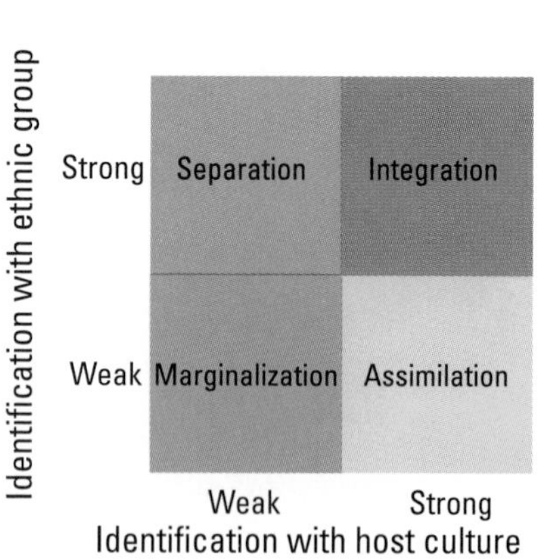

Figure 14.4 Acculturation strategies

identity and tolerates the differences among groups. Research shows, for example, that many recent Greek, Arab, and Italian immigrants to North America want their children to retain their own cultural identity (Moghaddam et al., 1993).

Torn between the need to fit in and a desire to retain their own heritage, ethnic-group members differ in the way they manage **acculturation**—the process by which persons are changed by their immersion in a new culture. John Berry and his colleagues (1989) noted that there are four types of coping strategies. At one extreme is *assimilation,* in which the person abandons the old for the new and completely embraces his or her host culture—its language, customs, identity, and ways of life. At the opposite extreme is *separation,* a pattern characterized by a desire to maintain one's ethnic traditions and not become part of the host culture. Native Americans who live on reservations and the Amish who live in Lancaster, Pennsylvania, are good examples. A third strategy is *integration,* a bicultural pattern in which the person tries to make the best of both worlds by retaining old traditions while, at the same time, adapting to the new way of life. The fourth strategy is *marginalization,* in which the person has no desire to maintain traditional ties or adopt the new host culture, perhaps due to prejudice and discrimination. These four types of acculturation strategies are summarized in Figure 14.4.

As a result of acculturation pressures, people who are caught between cultures come to identify with one or both of these cultures in the formation of an **ethnic identity.** Thus, French-speaking residents of Quebec may think of themselves as French, Canadian, French Canadian, or neither; Irish Americans may identify themselves as Irish, American, or Irish American. Jean Phinney (1990) notes that our ethnic identities are revealed in the way we label ourselves, our sense of belonging to a group, our pride in that group, and the extent to which we speak the language, study the history, follow the customs, and enjoy the food, music, dance, literature, holidays, and traditions. Phinney also notes that ethnic-identity formation typically begins in adolescence with a passive acceptance of the dominant culture, is followed in early adulthood by an awakening of interest in one's roots, and culminates later on in an ethnic identification. As you might expect, ethnic-group identification is stronger among immigrants who enter the host country as adults than it is among those who arrive at a younger, more formative age. Among people who adopt a new homeland—particularly among those who belong to a stigmatized minority group—ethnic identity is fundamental to their self-concept (Phinney, 1996).

Regardless of how immigrants, refugees, displaced natives, and other ethnic minorities adapt to their cultural environment, some individuals have a more difficult time than others in making the adjustment. The problem used to be called "culture shock." Now the term **acculturative stress** is used. Either way, studies show that entering a new culture may be accompanied by anxiety, depression, and other mental-health problems—and that these problems are linked to language barriers, a lack of familiarity with the host culture, a lack of education, rejection of one's group, prejudice, the absence of social-support services, and other factors (Berry et al., 1992). For example, Hispanic newcomers to the United States who were interviewed said they felt pressured to learn English, found it difficult to find suitable work, felt guilty about leaving their family and friends behind, did not make use of social services for fear of being deported, and felt that they were rejected because they were Latinos. Needless to say, these immigrants were under more stress at home and in the workplace than were Hispanics born in the United States (Cervantes et al., 1991).

Is there a healthy, optimum way for Hispanic Americans and others to cope with being strangers in a strange land, fish swimming outside of the mainstream? Con-

acculturation The process by which individuals are changed by their immersion in a new culture.

ethnic identity The part of a person's identity that is defined by an ethnic heritage, language, history, customs, and so on.

acculturative stress The stress and mental-health problems often found in immigrants trying to adjust to a new culture.

sider the acculturation strategies described earlier. Is it better to become "integrated" and bicultural, or should immigrants shed their native past in an effort to become fully "assimilated" into the host culture?

At this point, there is no clear answer. However, a study by Juan Sanchez and Diana Fernandez (1993) provides an important starting point. In Miami, these investigators administered questionnaires to 164 Hispanic college students who were born in Cuba, Puerto Rico, Latin America, Central America, or the United States. One questionnaire measured the extent to which subjects identified with their ethnic group ("I have a sense of belonging to Hispanic heritage"), a second measured the extent to which they identified with American culture ("I consider myself an American"), and the third assessed feelings of acculturative stress ("People look down on me if I practice customs of my culture," "It is difficult to show off my family"). As shown in Figure 14.5, students classified as integrated—that is, those who had a strong ethnic identification *and* embraced American culture—reported less acculturative stress than students who did not identify with one or both cultures. This correlation should be interpreted with caution. It may mean that identification with the host culture reduces stress—or that a lack of acculturative stress promotes identification. Either way, it's consistent with the increasingly popular notion that bicultural competence is psychologically adaptive, as it enables a person to alternate, without tension, between the two cultures (LaFromboise et al., 1993).

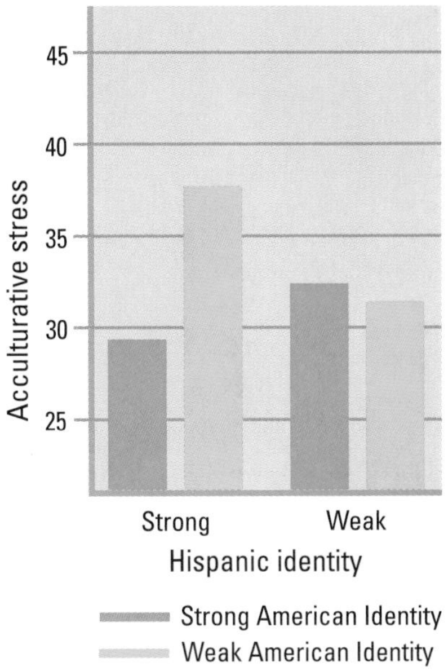

Figure 14.5 The link between cultural identity and acculturative stress In Miami, Hispanic American students answered questions about their Hispanic and American identities and acculturative stress. As shown, students who were "integrated" (*leftmost bar*) reported less stress than those who did not identify with one or both cultures.

At the same time, it's important to realize that not all immigrant groups face exactly the same challenges and that the integrated bicultural ideal is more or less difficult to achieve, depending on the fit between native and adopted homelands. In a book on Asian Americans, for example, Laura Uba (1994) notes that immigrants from Korea, China, Japan, and the Southeast Asian countries find that the values they learned at home clash in fundamental ways with those they encounter in the United States. Taught to be respectful, contained, and obedient, they feel pressured by teachers and peers to be more open, vocal, emotionally expressive, and assertive. Making the clash of cultures even more prominent is that many first-generation Asian American parents urge their children not to become too Americanized. In

Many cultural and ethnic groups in the United States retain the traditions of their homeland. Chinese Americans honor the Chinese New Year and Mexican Americans celebrate Cinco de Mayo.

The process of assimilation can cause old cultural traditions to become extinct—for better and for worse. This picture, taken in 1922, shows an Ainu woman. The Ainu people of Japan used to tattoo mustaches on their young daughters by rubbing soot into small knife cuts. The custom fell out of favor after the Ainu moved from the Kuril Islands to densely populated Hokkaido, where they became assimilated into Japanese society.

[Drawing by J. B. Handelsman; © 1995 The New Yorker Magazine, Inc.]

"That was a fine report, Barbara. But since the sexes speak different languages, I probably didn't understand a word of it."

discrimination Behavior directed against persons because of their affiliation with a social group.

doing so, they often prohibit dating and restrict other social activities. The result of these pressures is that "in the short run, biculturality can create cultural conflicts and stress for Asian American children who are trying to forge an identity" (Uba, 1994, pp. 126–127).

Immigrant groups from different parts of the world face unique challenges in the formation of an ethnic identity—and may need to cope in different ways. Of the many obstacles that confront ethnic minorities in any culture, the most vicious is **discrimination**—behavior directed against persons because of their affiliation with a social group. It is tempting to think of discrimination as a sin of the past. Unfortunately, recent incidents suggest that it still exists and that its victims are avoided, excluded, rejected, belittled, and attacked, often because of their skin color, language, ethnic and religious background, and customs. Discrimination has both cognitive and emotional roots. From a cognitive standpoint, it can often be traced to *stereotypes*—beliefs that associate whole groups of people with certain, sometimes unflattering, traits. Stereotypes have a depersonalizing effect on the way people perceive ethnic minorities. In addition, discrimination is often motivated by deep-seated *prejudice*—feelings of disdain toward others based on their membership in a particular group. As we'll see later in this chapter, stereotypes and prejudice are pervasive—and can be hurtful.

Gender: The Great Divide?

How are men and women similar? How are they different? Are the psychological differences between men and women primarily rooted in biological factors, or do they stem more from social experiences? What are some common gender stereotypes—and how accurate are they?

Do you sleep in the nude? Some 19 percent of men say *yes,* compared to only 6 percent of women. How much TV-watching time do you spend in charge of the remote control? Men estimate 55 percent, women 34 percent. How many articles of clothing do you buy in a year? Women estimate 52, men only 33. Are you afraid to walk at night within a mile of your home? Among women, 62 percent say *yes,* compared to 26 percent of men. Are you more likely to refuse sex than your partner is? To this question, 43 percent of women say *yes,* compared to only 22 percent of men. In search of a gender gap, pollsters have uncovered differences along every imaginable dimension—and then some (see Table 14.4).

As these examples illustrate, it is common for pollsters to find a "gender gap" in the ways that men and women describe their beliefs, attitudes, preferences, and behavior (Weiss, 1991). What do these results mean? Why are people so fascinated by even the silliest and most trivial of sex differences? And why, as Carol Jacklin (1989) put it, has the study of sex differences become a "national preoccupation"? Browse the shelves of any bookstore and you'll see one paperback title after another that addresses this intriguing topic. There are books for men and books for women, books that preach the masculine ideal and books that tell us how to be more feminine, books that portray men and women as similar and books that focus on the differences. In *You Just Don't Understand,* sociolinguist Deborah Tannen (1990) argues that women and men have different conversational styles, which often leads to misunderstanding. In *Brain Sex,* Ann Moir and David Jessel (1989) cite research

Table 14.4 Self-Reported Differences between Men and Women

ITEMS	MALES	FEMALES
% who consider themselves handsome or pretty	42	28
% who say they cry when they're blue	4	23
% married who think private time is important	32	46
% who look forward to hearing the telephone ring	20	37
% who consider themselves happy	90	90
% who believe in life elsewhere in the universe	41	32
% who frequently pray	26	39
% who feel guilty after eating candy	17	48
% who speak to their parents at least once a week	64	72
% who like to watch daytime soaps	7	33
% who think the U.S. president is underpaid	28	17
% who say they can be trusted	41	41
% who saw an X-rated movie last year	31	17

Source: D. E. Weiss (1991). *The great divide.* New York: Simon & Schuster.

evidence to conclude that men and women are different psychologically "because their brains are different" (p. 5).

On the topic of gender, as in the study of cultural and ethnic groups, we ask: In what ways are men and women different and in what ways are they alike? We have seen elsewhere in this book that there are sex differences in certain aspects of our cognitive, motivational, emotional, and interpersonal behavior—and that some of these differences are influenced by biological factors. In this chapter, we'll see that once a newborn baby is identified as male or female, powerful social forces as well come into play. In this section, we'll examine how our biological sex makes us members of a social group—and the implications of that identity for our behavior.

How Are Men and Women Different?

To children, the notion that there are innate differences between the sexes is immortalized in a poem: "What are little boys made of? Frogs and snails and puppy dogs' tails. . . . What are little girls made of? Sugar and spice and all that's nice." Ingredients aside, are males and females really that different?

Certain biological sex differences are a simple fact of life. At puberty, the onset of sexual maturation is brought on by rising hormone levels—estrogen and progesterone in females, testosterone in males. Girls reach puberty at about the age of eleven, boys at thirteen. On average, adult men are five inches taller than women and twenty to thirty pounds heavier, have 40 percent more muscle and 12 percent less fat, and sweat more. The average woman can arm-curl 52 percent as much weight as the average male and bench-press 37 percent as much. The average man has a million more red blood cells in each drop of blood, absorbs 30 percent less alcohol into his bloodstream (controlling for differences in body weight, this explains why men hold their liquor better than women), and has 10 percent more lung volume than women of the same size. Men are also more likely to be left-handed, snore in their sleep, become bald as they age, and have a deficiency in color

"Because my genetic programming *prevents* me from stopping to ask directions—*that's* why!"

Cartoonists often play up the popular notion that men and women have little in common.

vision. According to the National Center for Health Statistics (1996), the average American female, at birth, is expected to live for seventy-nine years, the average American male for seventy-two years.

Statistics such as these seem innocent enough—and are not a subject of debate. The biological approach becomes politically charged, however, when psychological differences between men and women are found and when these differences are attributed to sex hormones, brain anatomy, and other innate factors. The reason for the political heat is that our views on the nature of men and women will inform important policy questions such as whether military women should be allowed into combat, or whether men should be given equal consideration in child-custody suits. What reliable sex differences are there in human behavior, and why? Some scientists claim that men and women are so inherently different that to suggest otherwise is "to build a society based on a biological and scientific lie" (Moir & Jessel, 1989, p. 5). In *The Mismeasure of Woman,* psychologist Carol Tavris (1992) argues just as forcefully that "there is nothing *essential*—that is, universal and unvarying—in the natures of women and men" (Tavris, 1992, p. 21). Let's look at some of the evidence and consider the arguments on both sides.

One way in which men and women differ is in their sexual attitudes and behavior. As we saw in Chapter 8, surveys conducted worldwide show that, from adolescence through adulthood, men on average are more sexually permissive and adventurous than women. Indeed, men generally seem to view the world in more "sexualized" terms. In one study, for example, Antonia Abbey (1982) arranged for pairs of male and female college students to talk for five minutes, while other students observed these interactions. When she later questioned the actors and observers, Abbey found that the males were more sexually attracted to the females than vice versa—and that they rated the female actors as more promiscuous and seductive than the women had rated themselves. In another study, male subjects who read stories of various heterosexual dating scenarios were more likely than female subjects to assume that the women in these stories wanted to have sex (Muehlenhard, 1988). Other research confirms this point: Among men more than women, eye contact, a friendly remark, a brush against the arm, a compliment, and an innocent smile are often seen as sexual come-ons (Kowalski, 1993). These misperceptions occur not only in the laboratory but also between strangers, acquaintances, and casual friends who meet at parties, school, work, and other settings (Abbey, 1987; Saal et al., 1989).

Most men are also more physically aggressive than most women. Hunting, combat, rough-and-tumble play, and barroom brawls are all male-dominated activities. No matter when, where, or how you measure it, males on average exhibit more physical aggression than females. In Chapter 10, we saw that school-age boys are more likely than girls to play physical, competitive games (Maccoby, 1990). And in Chapter 13, we saw that men worldwide commit more violent crimes than do women (according to FBI statistics, 89 percent of all people arrested for murder, assault, and rape are male). In laboratory experiments in which subjects believe they are administering painful electric shocks to another person, men select higher voltage shocks (Eagly & Steffen, 1986; Bettencourt & Miller, 1996; Knight et al., 1996). And in public opinion polls, more men favor military solutions to world problems, the use of physical punishment to discipline children, and the death penalty (Weiss, 1991). Researchers may disagree about the size of the difference, but men are physically more aggressive than women.

Sex differences have also been found in cognitive abilities. In Chapter 12, we saw that although boys and girls are equally skilled at arithmetic in elementary school, male students begin to surpass females in mathematical problem solving in junior high school—and this difference persists into adulthood (in 1996, for example, male high-school students outscored their female peers by 35 points on the math portion of the SAT). Males also perform better on certain visual-spatial tasks (imagining how three-dimensional objects will appear when rotated, how flat objects appear when folded, or how solid objects appear when unfolded)—a difference that may account for part of the gender gap in math (Casey et al., 1995).

Paralleling the apparent male advantage in math and spatial relations, we saw that women typically perform better at grammar, spelling, reading comprehension, and certain verbal-fluency tasks. In elementary school, boys are four times more likely than girls to stutter and five to ten times more likely to have a reading disorder (Halpern, 1992). And in high school, girls score higher on tests of reading comprehension and foreign languages (Hedges & Nowell, 1995; Stumpf & Stanley, 1996). Finally, there are small but consistent sex differences in "social sensitivity." Specifically, women are better at using facial expressions, tones of voice, and other nonverbal cues to know how other people are feeling (J. A. Hall, 1984).

Why Are Men and Women Different?

Are male-female differences like the ones just described rooted in innate biological differences between the sexes? Or do these same disparities stem from the unequal social experiences that affect men and women? Let's examine these two perspectives.

Biological Perspectives Even before a baby is born, it has a full genetic heritage contained within its 23 pairs of chromosomes. The twenty-third pair controls one's sex. Everyone receives an X chromosome from the mother, but there's an equal chance that the father will donate an X or a short, stumpy Y chromosome to the pair. If the chromosome is an X, the offspring will be female (XX); if it is Y, the offspring will be male (XY).

Six or so weeks after conception, male and female embryos look very much the same and are similarly equipped. In those that are genetically female, ovaries are formed. In those that are genetically male, undescended testes secrete the male hormone *testosterone.* The presence of testosterone sparks the growth of the male sex organs, while its absence results in the development of female sex organs. In other words, having an XY or XX genetic endowment does not itself guarantee male or female development. If testosterone is not secreted in an XY embryo, the genetically male baby will be born with a girl's genitals. If testosterone is injected into an XX embryo, the genetic female will have the genitals of a normal male. During this stage of development, the fetal ovaries secrete very little estrogen and so play a minimal role in this process (Wilson et al., 1981; Breedlove, 1994).

Research suggests that certain differences between men and women may be linked to testosterone and estrogen (Gerall et al., 1992). These hormones are presumed to have two types of effects. First, in the prenatal life of an organism, they have long-term *organizational* effects on the developing nervous system—which may or may not account for the existence of certain differences between adult male and female brains (as we saw earlier in this book, experience can help mold the plastic brain). Then later in life, beginning at puberty, fluctuating levels of the sex hormones have short-term *activational* effects on behavior.

It is widely believed that testosterone fuels male sexual behavior. For that reason, castration (the surgical removal of the testes, which lowers testosterone production) has been used over the years to prepare harem guards, ensure celibacy, and rehabilitate sex offenders. Research shows that castration has the intended effect. Testosterone is not essential for sexual performance, but men with lowered levels often have less sexual interest and desire. There appears to be a similar link between ovarian hormones and sexuality in women. Estrogen is not necessary for performance, but sexual appetites fluctuate across the menstrual cycle (Carter, 1991).

There's also a strong connection between testosterone and aggression. If testosterone is injected into immature male mice, they attack other males; if they're castrated, aggression levels subside. Similarly, castration transforms a wild stallion into a gentler horse and an aggressive dog into a domesticated pet. In rats, monkeys, and other animal species, males become more aggressive at the onset of sexual maturation, when testosterone levels surge, and less aggressive as testosterone levels decline later in adulthood (this may explain why crime rates are consistently highest among male teenagers and young adults). James Dabbs and his coworkers (1987) measured testosterone in saliva samples taken from male prison inmates and found that those who had committed unprovoked violent crimes had the highest concentration levels. Dabbs and others (1990) then compared men of different occupations and found that football players had higher levels of testosterone than ministers did. These correlations do not prove that testosterone *causes* aggression in humans (competition can trigger the release of testosterone, so the link may be the other way around!). However, a good deal of animal research suggests that it does play a role (Archer, 1991; Collaer & Hines, 1995).

There is less evidence for the effects of testosterone on cognitive skills. According to Norman Geschwind and Peter Behan (1982), prenatal testosterone washes over the fetal brain. This slows the development of the left hemisphere, where language skills are housed, and it permits enhanced growth of the right hemisphere, which is associated with spatial skills. Consistent with this hypothesis that the male brain is right-dominated is the fact that more males than females are left-handed (as you may recall from Chapter 2, the right hemisphere controls the left half of the body and vice versa). This male right-dominance, speculated Geschwind and Behan, explains why most talented math students are male, why men perform better on visual-spatial tasks, and why women excel in various language-related tests. So is there a link between sex hormones and intellectual performance? It's too early to tell. There is some tantalizing evidence showing that on spatial tasks, males who reach puberty late due to unusually low testosterone levels perform worse than other males, while women with high testosterone levels outperform other women (Kimura & Hampson, 1994). In other studies, however, the results are small and not that consistent (Collaer & Hines, 1995).

Environmental Perspectives When a baby is born, the first question everyone asks is the same: "Is it a boy or a girl?" The newborn is then given a male or female name, dressed in blue or pink clothing, and showered with masculine or feminine gifts. Over the next few years, the typical boy receives toy trucks, baseball bats, building blocks, tools, guns, and chemistry sets, while his sister plays with dolls, stuffed animals, kitchen toys, sewing kits, and tea sets. In school, boys are guided into math and science, and girls are expected to seek out art, music, and literary activities. These distinctions persist in college, as male students are more likely to major in math, economics, and the hard sciences, while females predominate in education, arts, and the humanities. At work, men become doctors, builders, airline pilots, engineers, and bankers; women become secretaries, nurses, teachers, flight attendants, and bank tellers. The human male and female may love, work, play, and have families together, but in many ways, they are part of different social groups and live in different worlds.

"I think we've bent our genders about as far as they want to go."

Gender Roles The fact that males and females have different life experiences may explain the sex differences that are often observed. If you grew up in the United States, for example, you were probably taught to believe that it's more important for boys than for girls to learn to compete, fight, and defend themselves. Chances are, you also think it's more appropriate for the man to ask the woman for a date as well as to pay, drive, and initiate the good-night kiss.

Experience promotes sex differences through a process of social learning. Parents, teachers, and other socializing agents communicate **gender roles** to children at an early age, serve as same-sex role models, and use reward and punishment to shape up behaviors that are gender-appropriate. The models that surround children are powerful sources of influence. For example, Gary Levy (1989) found that girls with mothers who worked outside the home were more flexible in their perceptions of male and female sex roles than were those whose mothers worked in the home.

What transpires in the home is only part of what influences gender roles. Hugh Lytton and David Romney (1991) summarized the results of 172 studies and found that although parents tend to direct children to engage in sex-typed activities, in other ways they treat their sons and daughters in a similar manner. But the social learning of gender roles is supported by a host of other cultural institutions. Studies show that "Dick and Jane" readers, cartoons, TV shows, and magazines overportray male and female characters in traditional roles. Gone are the days when women were depicted only as homemakers who frantically shopped, cooked, and ironed everything in sight. Still, some sex stereotyping remains—for example, in TV commercials (Lovdal, 1989), children's books (Purcell & Stewart, 1990), and MTV music videos (Hansen, 1989). The result is that boys are taught to be masculine, while girls are taught to be feminine.

Experience shapes not only our behavior but also our beliefs. According to Sandra Bem (1981), experience leads people to form **gender schemas**—beliefs about men and women that influence the way we perceive ourselves and others. Research shows that children begin to identify themselves as boys or girls by the age of three—and then divide the world into masculine and feminine categories soon after that (Biernat, 1991; Martin et al., 1990). Even infants can tell the difference. In one study, nine-month-olds who were shown pictures of all-male or all-female faces spent less and less time looking—until a face of the opposite sex appeared. This result tells us what the infants themselves could not: That they can distinguish between men and women (Leinbach & Fagot, 1993).

In some cultures of the world, "sexist" traditions are quite strong. In Sudan, as currently ruled by Islamic fundamentalists, women must wear veils over the face and may not leave the country without permission from their fathers, husbands, or brothers. In Israel, where Jewish religious law prevails, a wife cannot get divorced without the consent of her husband—leaving thousands of women known as the Agunot ("the anchored") married against their will. In India, a Hindu system of dowries requires that the bride's family pay the groom cash and gifts equal to his social standing. As a result, girls are considered a burden on their parents. And in mainland China, where males are economically more valuable than females, and where the government controls the population growth by limiting each couple to one or two children, many female infants are aborted, abandoned, given up for adoption, or killed at birth (*Time,* 1990). Today, aided by ultrasound tests that reveal the sex of a fetus, parents are aborting increasing numbers of girls. Worldwide, 105 males are born for every 100 females. Yet in China, the sex ratio is 118 to 100 (see Figure 14.6).

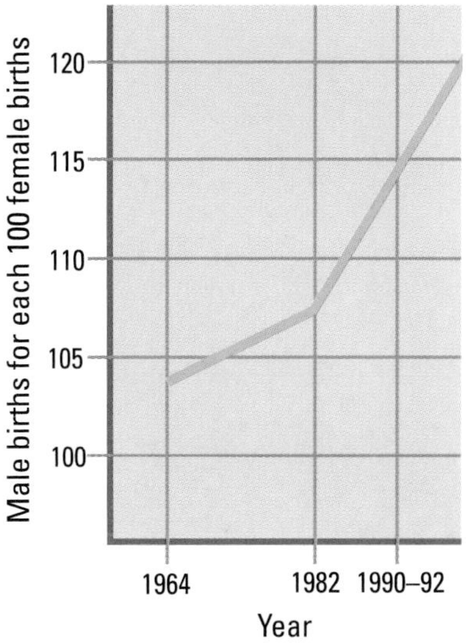

Figure 14.6 Sex ratios in China Birth statistics reveal that 118 boys are born for every 100 girls in China (by nature, this ratio is 105 to 100). Considered less valuable, female fetuses are being aborted in increasing numbers (Kristof, 1993).

gender roles Sex-typed behaviors promoted by social learning.

gender schemas Beliefs about men and women that influence the way we perceive ourselves and others.

Needless to say, prescribed sex roles vary widely from one culture to the next. Consider your reaction to statements such as "The first duty of a woman with young children is to home and family" and "When a man and woman live together, she should do the housework and he should do the heavier chores." People living in Nigeria, Pakistan, India, and Japan agree more with these statements than people from Germany, the Netherlands, Finland, or England—with Americans and Canadians falling between the two extremes (Williams & Best, 1990).

Even in places where gender gaps of the past have eroded, they have not completely disappeared. In the United States, 57 million women were employed in 1990—nearly double that of the 1960s. The number of women who now go on to become doctors, lawyers, accountants, and other professionals has risen sharply in recent years. And at home, more men today than in the past are cooking, cleaning, shopping, and changing diapers. Despite these changes, however, men and women continue to play different roles in the home. From interviews with working parents, sociologist Arlie Hochschild (1989) argued that wives more than husbands come home after work to a "second shift" of domestic and child-care duties. When the number of hours spent working outside and inside the home are combined, what emerges is a "leisure gap" that favors men.

Gender Stereotypes Cultures vary in their sex-role traditions, but stereotypes about men and women seem to be universal. If you had to describe the typical man and woman, what would you say? In a large-scale study, 2,800 college students from thirty countries were asked to check off adjectives from a list that are believed to describe men or women. Consistently, men were said to be adventurous, strong, dominant, assertive, task-oriented, aggressive, and independent. Just as consistently, women were said to be sensitive, gentle, dependent, emotional, sentimental, weak, submissive, and people-oriented (Williams & Best, 1982). These stereotypes are also evident in children's descriptions of others (Best & Williams, 1993).

Male and female stereotypes are so deeply ingrained in us that they influence our behavior literally from the moment a baby is born. In a fascinating study, first-time parents of fifteen girls and fifteen boys were interviewed within twenty-four hours of the birth. There were no actual differences between the male and female newborns in height, weight, or superficial physical appearance. Yet the parents of the girls rated their babies as softer, smaller, and more finely featured, while the fathers of boys described their sons as stronger, larger, more coordinated, and more alert (Rubin et al., 1974). When a similar study was conducted some twenty years later, the results were essentially the same (Karraker et al., 1995).

Gender stereotypes are so widespread that you may wonder if they are accurate and, if not, why they persist. Enlightened by years of research on sex differences, psychologists can now draw the following conclusion: Conventional wisdom contains a kernel of truth, but it may oversimplify and exaggerate that truth (Maccoby & Jacklin, 1974; Eagly & Wood, 1991; Feingold, 1994; Swim, 1994). Yes, most men are more competitive, aggressive, and assertive than most women. And yes, most women are more socially sensitive, nurturant, and cooperative than most men. But our stereotypes about these differences may be stronger and more numerous than the differences themselves.

A study by Carol Lynn Martin (1987) illustrates the point. She presented people with a list of thirty traits that were "masculine," "feminine," or neutral and asked them to circle those that were self-descriptive. A separate group of subjects received the same list and estimated, for each trait, the percentage of men and women in general for whom it was an accurate description. By comparing the percentage of male and female subjects who *actually* found the traits self-descriptive with the *estimated* percentages, Martin found that expectations outstripped reality. In actuality, the masculine traits were just slightly more self-descriptive of men and the feminine traits of women, but the estimated differences were more substantial. Like the cartoonist who draws caricatures, we seem to mentally stretch, expand, and enlarge the ways in which men and women differ.

Why, then, do exaggerated perceptions of difference endure? Alice Eagly's (1987) **social-roles theory** provides one possible explanation. According to Eagly, perceived sex differences are magnified by the unequal social roles occupied by men and women. The process involves three steps. First, through a combination of biological and social factors, a division of labor between the sexes has emerged over time—at home and in the work setting. Men are more likely to work in construction or business; women, to care for children and to take the lower-status jobs. Second, because people behave in ways that fit the roles they play, men are more likely than women to wield physical, social, and economic power. Third, these behavioral differences provide a continuing basis for sex stereotypes, leading us to perceive men as dominant "by nature" and women as domestic "by nature," when, in fact, the differences at least in part reflect the roles they play. In other words, says Eagly, our stereotypes are shaped by (and also confused with) the unequal distribution of men and women into different social roles (see Figure 14.7).

Social Roots of Sex Differences Clearly, the behavior of men and women all over the world is scripted by the gender roles they're expected to play. To what extent are the sex differences described earlier the product of socially constructed gender roles? Is it possible, for example, that the male strengths in mathematical problem solving and spatial skills are socially constructed? What about the interpersonal sensitivity of women?

Biologically oriented researchers offer convincing evidence that sex differences in mathematics have been so consistent over time and across cultures that they must be inborn. Socially oriented researchers, however, warn that these comparisons are misleading because boys and girls are not raised on a level playing field. For example, boys receive more support in math from parents and teachers (Chipman et al., 1985; Jacobs, 1991). Studying the development of math skills in children from hundreds of families, Jacquelynne Eccles and her colleagues (1990) found that parents who believe that girls are generally weak at math see their daughters as less competent, set lower expectations for them, and guide them in other directions. Sure enough, these girls lose interest and confidence and avoid future math-related pursuits. This may be why elementary-school girls—even though they do as well as or better than boys do in math—see themselves as less competent (Eccles et al., 1993). The single best predictor of math achievement-test scores is the number of math

Figure 14.7 A theory of gender stereotypes According to social-roles theory, stereotypes of men as dominant and women as nurturant or subordinate persist because of the different roles men and women play.

social-roles theory The theory that perceived sex differences are magnified by the different social roles occupied by men and women.

courses one has taken. But girls take fewer math courses than boys do (Yee & Eccles, 1988).

The strongest evidence for a cognitive gender gap is in performance on visual-spatial tasks. It may be possible, however, that at least part of the male advantage at these skills stems from differences in experience. Research shows that boys are permitted to stray farther from home than girls and engage in more "scouting" activities. Boys are more likely to own building blocks, erector sets, and other spatial-manipulation toys. They are also more likely to play billiards, basketball, and other sports that involve making judgments of moving objects. To some extent, the more spatial experience one has, the better is one's performance on visual-spatial tests. Thus, in one study, four-year-old boys *and girls* who were trained with wooden blocks, dominoes, Tinkertoys, and geometric shapes later scored higher on a spatial test than children who were not similarly trained (Baenninger & Newcombe, 1989). Similarly, studies have shown that playing action video games improves spatial-test performance in both boys and girls (Okagaki & Frensch, 1994; Subrahmanyan & Greenfield, 1994).

Turning from the cognitive to the social domain, studies reveal that women are more sensitive than men to how others are feeling—a skill often referred to as "female intuition." Some researchers speculate that this advantage is rooted in the left-dominant female brain (Moir & Jessel, 1989). Others argue that women acquire interpersonal sensitivity out of social necessity. According to Sara Snodgrass (1985), women are better than men at reading others for self-protective reasons—because they occupy subordinate roles in society. After all, isn't it more important for workers to know how the boss is feeling and for students to know how their professor is feeling than vice versa? To test this hypothesis, Snodgrass paired a man and a woman in each of several work teams and assigned one or the other to be the leader. In general, she found that the subordinate was more sensitive to the leader's nonverbal cues than the leader was to the subordinate's—regardless of gender. Snodgrass thus suggested that "women's intuition" be called "subordinate's intuition" to reflect the fact that low status, not sex, is what motivates our insight into others.

Putting Sex Differences in Perspective

"Not including purely physical differences, do you think men and women are basically similar or basically different?" When this question was asked in a 1993 Gallup poll, 56 percent of the men surveyed and 73 percent of the women chose the "different" option. But think about some of the well-established principles of psychology, and you may come to realize that men and women are similar in many ways that we take for granted. Differences make news; similarities do not.

Ponder the material presented elsewhere in this book and you'll see the point. Boys and girls alike crawl, walk, and smile at about the same age, and both become curious about sex in adolescence. Similarly, both men and women see better in daylight than in the dark, fall prey to optical illusions, and behave in ways that bring reward. Both men and women can hold about seven items in short-term memory, use shorthand cognitive heuristics in making judgments, and affiliate with others in times of stress. In their social behavior, both men and women are biased by their first impressions, are attracted to others who are similar, and are more likely to help others when they're alone than in a group of bystanders. The list of similarities that escape our daily notice is long and impressive. As human beings, men and women are more alike than different in many "invisible" ways.

SOCIAL AND CULTURAL GROUPS AND BUSINESS

Women in the Workplace

Ann Hopkins was hoping to become a partner in one of the largest accounting firms in the country. On paper, her record was impeccable. In just a few years, Hopkins had single-handedly brought in more than $25 million in contracts, the tops among her peers. Yet she was denied partnership while several less productive male candidates were promoted. Why? According to Hopkins, it was because she was a woman. As in most disputes, however, there were two sides to the story. The firm claimed Hopkins was overbearing, abrasive, and difficult to work with. One associate was said to have quit and sought employment elsewhere, presumably because he could not tolerate working with her.

Was Ann Hopkins rejected because of her personality, her gender, or a combination of the two? Hopkins took the case to court, where she testified that she was described by one partner as a "macho" woman who should attend "charm school." She was even advised to "wear makeup, have my hair styled, and wear jewelry."

Sex differences in occupations are sometimes so striking that we're quick to notice female construction workers and others who break the mold.

To make the case that these comments reveal sex discrimination, Hopkins called on social psychologist Susan Fiske to testify as an expert on stereotypes. Citing research on social perception, Fiske testified that Hopkins was seen as offensive only because her aggressive manner clashed with traditional conceptions of women and that in a predominantly male environment, everything she did was noticed, scrutinized, and blown out of proportion. Fiske concluded that Hopkins was a victim of sex discrimination, and the trial judge agreed. Then by a 6-to-3 vote, so did the U.S. Supreme Court (Fiske et al., 1991).

In recent years, women in the United States have made great strides in moving from the home to the workplace. Interestingly, however, gender gaps exist in the kinds of occupations that are filled by men and women. Think about it. How many female airline pilots have you met recently? What about male secretaries? Look at Table 14.5, and you'll see that even today, on the threshold of the twenty-first century, there are some striking sex differences in the workplace.

Differences also exist when it comes to positions of leadership. Look at the top of the list of America's Fortune 500 companies, and you will find that fewer than 10 percent of board-of-directors members are women. Despite the progress that has been made in entry- and middle-level positions, working women who seek positions of leadership are said to be blocked by a "glass ceiling"—a barrier so subtle that it's transparent yet so strong that it keeps them from climbing to the top of the corporate ladder (Morrison & Von Glinow, 1990).

In general, women are as qualified as men for positions of power. Research shows that male and female managers have similar aspirations, values, and skills (Dobbins & Platz, 1986; Howard & Bray, 1988). The main difference is that women are more open and democratic in their style—and are more likely to invite subordinates to participate in decision making (Eagly & Johnson, 1990). This result is consistent with Judy Rosener's (1990) conclusion, as reported in the *Harvard Business Review,* that today's leading women draw effectively on feminine qualities. It is also consistent with Sally Helgesen's (1990) observation that female managers interact more with subordinates, share power and information, and spin extensive networks, or "webs of inclusion"—a leadership style she calls the feminine advantage.

So why have so few women managed to reach the top? For women, the path to power—from their entry into the labor market, to recruitment in an organization, and up the promotion ladder—is something of an "obstacle course" (Ragins & Sundstrom, 1989). One reason is that many women are deeply conflicted about having to juggle a career and family responsibilities (Crosby, 1991). A second reason is that women tend to shy away from competitive, hierarchical positions that offer the potential for leadership in favor of jobs that involve helping other people (Pratto et al., 1997). A third reason is societal. Lingering stereotypes portray women as followers rather than leaders, and some people are uneasy about women in leadership roles. In one study, men and women who were seated at the head of the table in all-male or all-female groups were automatically tagged as leaders. In mixed-sex groups, however, this head-of-the-table bias applied only to men who sat in that position (Porter et al., 1985). In another study, subjects were observed from behind a one-way mirror as they took part in a discussion group with male and female confederates who were trained to behave similarly. Regardless of their sex, all confederates who played an assertive role were reasonably perceived as leaders. Yet subjects smiled and nodded less often, and frowned more often, in response to the female leaders than to the male leaders—a subtle but sure sign of disapproval (Butler & Geis, 1990). Combining the results of sixty-one studies, Eagly and her colleagues (1992) found that female leaders are devalued in comparison to equivalent males when they adopt a directive, task-oriented style of leadership or occupy traditionally "masculine" positions, as in business.

In 1997, Madeleine Albright broke through a glass ceiling by becoming the first woman ever to serve as U.S. Secretary of State. Soon after being sworn in, she visited China and the truce line in Korea.

Table 14.5 Sex Differences in Occupation

OCCUPATION	% MEN	% WOMEN
Airline pilot	96	4
Auto mechanic	99	1
Bartender	47	53
Child-care worker	3	97
Computer programmer	66	34
Dentist	90	10
Dental assistant	1	99
Grade-school teacher	14	86
College instructor	57	43
Lawyer, judge	77	23
Physician	78	22
Registered nurse	6	94
Telephone repairer	88	12
Telephone operator	13	87

Source: U.S. Bureau of the Census (1994).

Prejudice

How is prejudice a by-product of the way we think? Is stereotyping inevitable or can it be controlled? What motives seem to fuel prejudice all over the world? What are some of the social-psychological symptoms of racism in our society? In an ideal world, how can the problem be treated?

As people interact with others who are different in their culture, ethnic background, and gender, tolerance of diversity becomes a social necessity. Too often, however, people evaluate others negatively because they are members of a particular group. When that happens, we speak of **prejudice.**

Stories of prejudice today are not hard to find. In Germany, neo-Nazis terrorize Turkish immigrants. In the Middle East, Israelis and Palestinians fight what seems like an eternal battle. And in what used to be the Soviet Union, raging ethnic conflicts are almost too numerous to mention. The streets of America are also witness to bigotry. On the Long Island Railroad, a man expressed his "black rage" by shooting a carful of white commuters. On the campus of a large university, members of a fraternity painted their faces black and held a mock slave auction. In other incidents, swastikas were spray-painted on synagogue doors, and rocks and bottles were thrown at gay people in a parade.

Stories like these make the news on an all-too-regular basis, bringing to life an important point: People often dislike and resent others simply because they are different. Prejudice is one of the most tenacious social problems of modern times. Regardless of who the victims are, there are two roots to the problem: one cognitive, the other motivational.

The Cognitive Roots

To some extent, prejudice is a by-product of the beliefs we hold and the way we think. The beliefs are called stereotypes, and the cognitive processes that promote stereotyping are social categorization and the outgroup-homogeneity bias (Hilton & von Hippel, 1996).

How Stereotypes Are Formed

A **stereotype** is a belief that associates a whole group of people with certain traits. When you stop to think about it, the list of common stereotypes seems endless. Consider some examples: The Japanese are sneaky, athletes are brainless, Italians are emotional, Jews are materialistic, Californians are laid back, accountants are dull, college professors are absentminded, black people have rhythm, and used-car salespeople cannot be trusted as far as you can throw them. Now, how many of these images ring a bell? More important, how do they influence our evaluations of each other? There are many theories on how such stereotypes are born within the history of a culture. But social psychologists ask a different question: How do stereotypes operate in the minds of individuals, and how do they affect our judgments of others?

From a cognitive perspective, the formation of stereotypes involves two related processes. The first is that human beings naturally divide each other into groups based on sex, race, age, nationality, religion, and other attributes. This process is called **social categorization.** In some ways, social categorization is natural and adaptive. By grouping people the way we group foods, animals, furniture, and other objects, we make judgments quickly and easily and use past experience to guide interactions with people we've never met (Macrae et al., 1994). The problem is that categorization may lead us to magnify the differences *between* groups and overlook the differences among individuals *within* groups (Wilder, 1986; Stangor & Lange, 1994).

The second process that promotes stereotyping follows from the first. Although grouping people is like grouping objects, there is an important difference: In *social* categorization, we ourselves are members or nonmembers of the categories we employ. Groups that we identify with—our country, religion, political party, or even hometown sports team—are called *ingroups,* whereas groups other than our own are called *outgroups.* The tendency to make these distinctions has important psychological and social consequences.

prejudice Negative feelings toward others based solely on their membership in a certain group.

stereotype A belief that associates a group of people with certain traits.

social categorization The classification of persons into groups based on common attributes.

One consequence is that once we have carved the world up into "us" and "them," there is a pervasive tendency to assume that "they" are all alike—a phenomenon known as the **outgroup-homogeneity bias** (Linville & Jones, 1980). There are three types of research evidence for this bias. First, when people are asked to estimate how many group members share a certain stereotyped characteristic, percentage estimates are higher in ratings of outgroups than of ingroups. Second, when people are asked to estimate the range of differences within a population, that range is seen as narrower when the population being considered is an outgroup than an ingroup. Third, when people are asked to rate a group of individuals for how alike they are, outgroup members are seen as being more similar to each other than are ingroup members (Park & Judd, 1990; Ostrom & Sedikides, 1992).

Research shows that these effects are common—and there are many real life examples. Americans who arrive from Korea, China, Vietnam, Taiwan, and the Philippines see themselves as different from one another, but to the Western eye they are all Asian. Likewise, the people of Mexico, Puerto Rico, Central America, and Cuba distinguish among themselves, but others refer to them all as Hispanic. Business majors talk about "engineering types," engineers lump together "business types," conservatives see liberals as all the same, and while the natives of New York City proclaim their cultural and ethnic diversity, outsiders talk of the typical New Yorker. Apparently, when it comes to groups other than our own, particularly groups with which we are not familiar, "If you've seen one, you've seen them all."

Is Stereotyping Inevitable? As generalized beliefs, stereotypes offer us quick and convenient summaries of social groups. Yet as *over*generalized beliefs, they cause us to overlook the diversity within groups and form mistaken impressions of specific individuals. It's important to realize that our stereotypes may be positive or negative, accurate or inaccurate (Judd & Park, 1993; Lee et al., 1995). Unfortunately, many stereotypes cast groups in unfavorable light, sometimes with hurtful consequences. If we assume that these beliefs are born of the human tendency to categorize all objects, it's easy to justify the result as an innocent by-product of the way we think. But is this true? Is stereotyping inevitable? There are two points of view.

According to Anthony Greenwald and Mahzarin Banaji (1995), stereotypes are often activated without our awareness and operate at an unconscious or implicit level. It just happens. Various experiments illustrate the point. In one study, subjects worked on a computer while words such as *Harlem, slavery,* and *jazz* flashed across the screen so rapidly that they were not aware of the exposure. Yet moments later, in an unrelated task, they were more likely to see a fictional male target person as aggressive—consistent with the negative stereotype of African Americans (Devine, 1989). In a second study, subjects were instructed to complete word fragments such as *rice* and *polite.* When the items were presented on tape by an Asian woman, subjects who were also distracted by another task created words that are stereotypic of Asians, words such as *rice* and *polite* (Gilbert & Hixon, 1991). And in a third study, subjects worked at unscrambling sentences that depicted acts of aggression ("cuts off other drivers") or dependence ("won't go alone"). Later, ostensibly as part of a different experiment, subjects read about Donald or Donna, a male or female target person. Consistent with popular images of men and women, subjects exposed to the aggression phrases saw Donald as more aggressive, while those exposed to dependence phrases saw Donna as more dependent (Banaji et al., 1993). To some extent, it seems, the stereotypes we hold are "irrepressible" (Nelson et al., 1996).

outgroup-homogeneity bias The tendency to assume that "they" (members of groups other than our own) are all alike.

Clearly, stereotypes can be brought to mind without our awareness and can color our judgments of others. But this does not mean that each of us is inevitably trapped into evaluating people on the basis of social categories. Studies have shown that people are most likely to form an impression based on quick and simple stereotypes when they're busy or distracted (Gilbert & Hixon, 1991), pressed for time (Pratto & Bargh, 1991), mentally tired (Bodenhausen, 1990), and under the influence of alcohol (von Hippel et al., 1995). But these same studies, and others, have shown that people are less likely to use stereotypes when they are alert—and are motivated to form an accurate or nonstereotypic impression (Blair & Banaji, 1996). Thus, when subjects are trying to evaluate another subject whom they might need to complete a task or if they expect to compete against that person, then they manage to set aside their preexisting beliefs and make more individualized judgments (Fiske & Neuberg, 1990; Ruscher & Fiske, 1990).

Prejudice is one of the most tenacious social afflictions of our time. The problem, as shown by this young white supremacist, is that the hatred is passed from one generation to the next.

The Motivational Roots

From a cognitive perspective, stereotypes spring from the process of social categorization and the distinctions that are made between ingroups and outgroups. In other words, stereotypes are a by-product of the way people think. But is that all there is to it? If people could somehow be prevented from categorizing one another, would all the prejudice in the world be eliminated? Doubtful. The way we *think* about social groups is important, but there's another factor to consider: how we *feel* about the groups we encounter, and perhaps even our *need* to perceive them in a particular light.

Realistic Conflict Theory There are two major motivational theories of prejudice. The first is **realistic conflict theory,** which begins with a simple observation: Many intergroup conflicts in the world today stem from direct competition for valuable but limited resources (Levine & Campbell, 1972). As a matter of economics, one group may fare better than a neighboring group in a struggle for land, jobs, or power. The losers become frustrated, the winners feel threatened, and before long the conflict heats to a rapid boil. Chances are that a good deal of prejudice in the world is driven by the realities of competition (Taylor & Moghaddam, 1994).

Realistic conflict clearly accounts for part of the problem, as frustration evokes hostility, aggression, and the search for a scapegoat. From the years 1882 and 1930, for example, the number of black Americans lynched in the Deep South increased as cotton prices fell—a sign of economic frustration (Hovland & Sears, 1940; Beck & Tolnay, 1990). It has been suggested, for example, that the recent surge in racial tensions in the United States is linked to bitterness among some white Americans about affirmative-action policies that give preference to minorities (D'Souza, 1991).

The premise of realistic conflict theory seems compelling, but there's more to the story—much more. Research has shown that people are often prejudiced even when the quality of their lives is *not* directly threatened by the outgroup they despise—and that people are sensitive about the status of their ingroups relative to rival outgroups even when personal interests are not at stake. So is it possible that personal interests really *are* at stake, that our protectiveness of ingroups is nourished by a concern for the self? If so, might that explain why people all over the world seem to think that their own nation, culture, and religion are better and more deserving than others?

realistic conflict theory The theory that prejudice stems from intergroup competition for limited resources.

Social Identity Theory Questions about ingroups and outgroups were initially raised in a series of laboratory studies. In the first of these, Henri Tajfel and his

At the World Cup Soccer games of 1994, patriotic American fans basked in the glory of their team's success. Consistent with social identity theory, studies have shown that sports fans enjoy a temporary boost in self-esteem after "we win."

colleagues (1971) showed subjects a sequence of dotted slides and asked them to estimate the number of dots on each. The slides were flashed in rapid-fire succession, so the dots could not be counted. The experimenter then told subjects that some people are chronic "overestimators" and that others are "underestimators." As part of a second, separate task, subjects were then divided, supposedly for the sake of convenience, into groups of overestimators and underestimators (in fact, the assignments were random). Knowing who was in their group, subjects allocated points to each other for various tasks, points that reflected favorable judgments and could be cashed in for money.

This procedure was designed to create *minimal groups* of persons categorized by trivial similarities. The overestimators and underestimators were not bitter rivals, had no history of antagonism, and were not competing for a limited resource. Yet subjects allocated more points to members of their own group than to those of the outgroup. This pattern of discrimination, known as **ingroup favoritism,** is consistently observed. Even in groups that are constructed by the flip of a coin, subjects favor others with whom they are aligned (Messick & Mackie, 1989). They also make more favorable attributions for the successes of fellow ingroup members than of others (Weber, 1994).

Our preference for ingroups is so powerful that its effects can be measured by the language we use. According to Charles Perdue and others (1990), ingroup pronouns such as *we, us,* and *ours* trigger positive emotions, and outgroup pronouns such as *they, them,* and *theirs* elicit negative emotions. These investigators presented subjects with numerous pairs of letter strings on a computer—each pair containing both a pronoun and a nonsense syllable ("we-xeh," "they-yof"). Their task was to decide

ingroup favoritism The tendency to discriminate in favor of ingroups over outgroups.

as quickly as possible which letter string in each pair was a real word. They didn't realize it, but one nonsense syllable was always paired with ingroup pronouns, another with outgroup pronouns. Afterward, subjects were asked for their reactions to each of the nonsense syllables. The result: Those previously paired with ingroup words were seen as more pleasant than those paired with outgroup words. The ingroup-outgroup distinction has such emotional meaning for people that it can bias their views of an unfamiliar string of letters—or person.

To explain ingroup favoritism in the absence of realistic conflict, Tajfel (1982) and John Turner (1987) proposed **social identity theory.** According to this theory, each of us strives to enhance our self-esteem, which has two components: a *personal* identity and various collective or *social* identities that are based on the groups to which we belong. In other words, people can boost their self-esteem through their personal achievements or by affiliating with successful groups. What's nice about the need for social identity is that it leads us to derive pride from our connections with others. What's sad, however, is that often we feel the need to belittle "them" in order to feel secure about "us." Religious fervor, racial and ethnic conceit, and patriotism may all fulfill this darker side of our social identity. In this way, prejudice is nourished by a concern for oneself. The theory is summarized in Figure 14.8.

Social identity theory makes two predictions: (1) Threats to self-esteem should heighten the need to exhibit prejudice, and (2) expressions of prejudice should, in turn, restore one's self-esteem. Research generally supports these predictions (Hogg & Abrams, 1990; Turner et al., 1994)—particularly among people who are in a minority group as opposed to a large, overly inclusive majority (Brewer, 1991).

In a study that tested both components of social identity theory, Steven Fein and Steven Spencer (1997) gave subjects positive or negative feedback about their performance on a test of social and verbal skills—feedback that temporarily raised or lowered their self-esteem. These subjects then took part in what was supposed to be a second experiment in which they evaluated a job applicant. All subjects received a snapshot of a young woman, her resume, and a videotaped job interview. In half the cases, the woman was named Maria D'Agostino and was depicted as Catholic; in the other half, she was Julie Goldberg and was depicted as Jewish (on the campus where the study was conducted, students had a negative stereotype of the "Jewish American Princess" that was evoked by upper-middle-class Jewish women from New York). When this task was complete, subjects were retested for their self-esteem.

"It's not enough that we succeed. Cats must also fail."

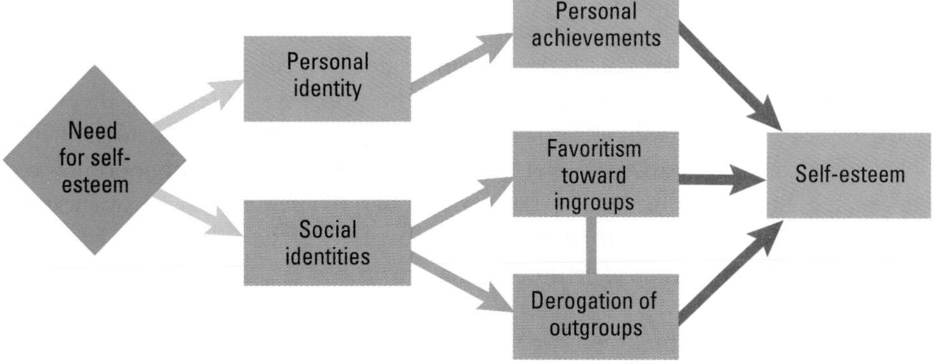

Figure 14.8 Social identity theory According to social identity theory, people strive to enhance self-esteem, which has two components: a personal identity and various social identities derived from the groups to which we belong. Thus, people can boost their self-image by viewing and treating ingroups more favorably than outgroups.

social identity theory The theory that people discriminate against outgroups in order to enhance their own self-esteem.

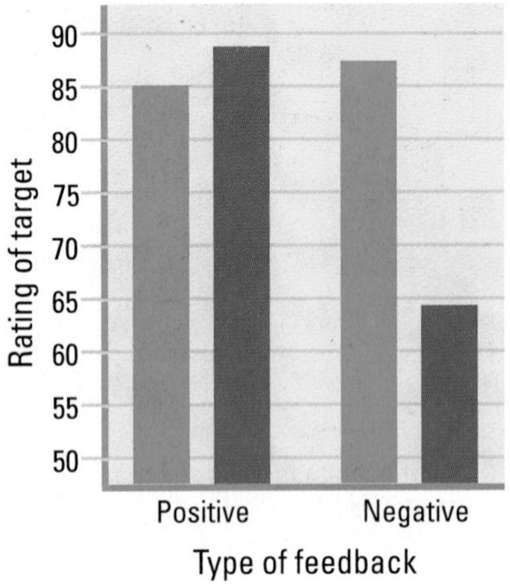

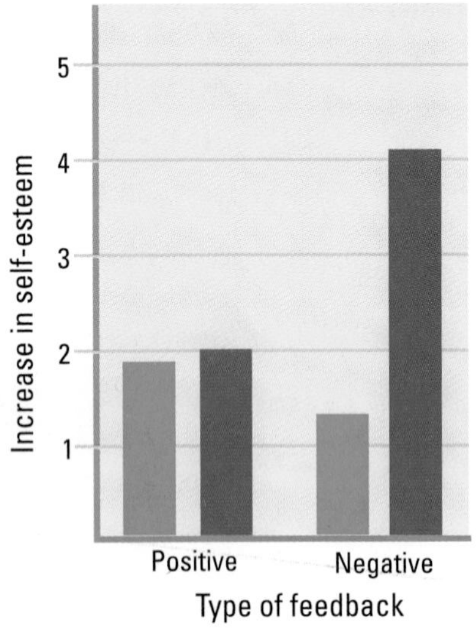

Figure 14.9 Derogation in the service of self-esteem Subjects received positive or negative feedback and then evaluated a female job applicant believed to be Italian or Jewish. There were two key results: (1) Subjects whose self-esteem had been lowered by negative feedback evaluated the woman less favorably when she was Jewish than Italian (*top*); and (2) negative-feedback subjects given the opportunity to belittle the Jewish woman showed a postexperiment increase in self-esteem (*bottom*) (Fein & Spencer, 1997).

As shown in Figure 14.9, there were two main results, both consistent with social identity theory. First, among subjects whose self-esteem had been lowered by negative feedback, Julie Goldberg was rated more negatively than Maria D'Agostino—even though their pictures and credentials were the same. Second, negative-feedback subjects given an opportunity to belittle the Jewish woman later exhibited a postexperiment increase in self-esteem. A blow to one's self-image evokes prejudice—and the expression of prejudice helps to restore that image. Other researchers as well have found support for this theory (Branscombe & Wann, 1994).

So far, we have seen that stereotypes are overgeneralized, easily activated images that lead us to overlook the diversity within social outgroups and to rush to judgment about specific individuals. We have also seen that prejudice can stem from competition for resources or the need to favor ingroups in the service of self-esteem. We now put these problems into concrete terms by focusing on racism, a common form of prejudice.

Racism in America

Slave trading. The Deep South. Abolitionists. The Civil War. Lynch mobs. Separate but equal. The Ku Klux Klan. Jackie Robinson. Sitting in the back of the bus. Martin Luther King, Jr. Civil rights. Malcolm X. School busing. *Roots.* Affirmative action. Rodney King. O. J. Simpson. Race relations in the United States have had a checkered, troubled, and emotional history—a history marked by both hatred and guilt, violent riots and peace marches, tolerance and intolerance, advances and setbacks. At the heart of it all, **racism:** a deep-seated form of prejudice that is based on the color of a person's skin. In the United States, this conflict is multidirectional, with all groups exhibiting prejudice in one form or another.

racism A deep-seated form of prejudice that is based on the color of a person's skin.

The Problem

I have been told, and I believe it, that because I am white I'll never really understand what it feels like to be a black person living in the United States. In a poignant, personal book titled *Race,* Studs Terkel (1992) interviewed ordinary Americans, black and white, about what he calls the American obsession. Terkel tells penetrating real-life stories that reveal the depth and scope of the problem.

In some cases, he observes overt, old-fashioned prejudice—for example, the new construction worker who complained bitterly about affirmative action because, as he put it, "they live like low lifes. Don't like to work. Let their homes run down." Yet in other cases, the prejudice is more subtle—as when Terkel's friend's wife, who is white and who sees herself as colorblind, drove through a black neighborhood in Chicago: "The people at the corners were all gesticulating at her. She was very frightened, turned up the windows, and drove determinedly. She discovered after several blocks, she was going the wrong way on a one-way street and they were trying to help her. Her assumption was they were blacks and were out to get her."

Another instance involved Terkel himself. He boarded a bus one morning and deposited his fare, only to have the driver, a young black man, say he was a dime short. Terkel was sure he had paid the right amount and was upset. But he fished into his pocket and dropped another dime into the box. "Oh, I understood the man," he thought. "I know the history of his people's bondage. It was his turn—a show of power, if only in a small way. If that's how it is, that's how it is. Oh, well." Then it happened. "As I was about to disembark, I saw a dime on the floor. My dime. I held it up to him. 'You were right.' He was too busy driving to respond. I waved: 'Take it easy.' 'You, too,' he replied. I've a hunch he'd been through something like this before" (p. 6).

This very subtle form of racism may seem invisible, but it can be humiliating to its victims. In *Color-Blind,* writer Ellis Cose (1997), who is African American, tells a story about how he was treated in a job interview some twenty years ago. He was an award-winning newspaper reporter at the time and was hoping to land a job with a national magazine. The editor he had met with was pleasant and gracious, but he said that the magazine did not have many black readers. "I don't know whether the editor had bothered to read my clippings, but then, the clips were somehow superfluous. . . . All the editor saw was a young black guy, and since *Esquire* was not in need of a young black guy, they were not in need of me . . . he had been so busy focusing on my race that he was incapable of seeing *me* or my work" (p. 150). Then a few years later, and in light of affirmative action, Cose was asked if he was interested in a position as a corporate director of equal opportunity. "I was stunned, for the question made no sense. I was an expert neither on personnel nor on equal employment law; I was, however, black, which seemed to be the most important qualification" (p. 156).

The Ku Klux Klan's burning cross is a powerful, spine-chilling symbol of racism.

The Symptoms Racism in the 1990s is a problem that poisons social relations between black and white people. Detecting racism is not as easy as it may seem. In 1933, Daniel Katz and Kenneth Braly found that many white college students believed that black Americans were lazy, happy-go-lucky, aggressive, and ignorant. Follow-up surveys taken in 1951, 1967, and 1982 showed that although these images have faded (Dovidio & Gaertner, 1986), negative stereotypes have not completely disappeared (Devine & Elliot, 1995).

Or have they? Research suggests that many people today are racially ambivalent. They want to see themselves as fair and are reluctant to express racist sentiments, but they still harbor feelings of anxiety and discomfort in the presence of people from other racial groups (Hass et al., 1992). So can public-opinion polls be trusted, or has racism simply gone underground? And what about the distrust of white people that many African Americans harbor? If people will not admit their biases to pollsters, or even to themselves, how can we know that this chronic social disease still exists? What are the symptoms? Better yet, what is the cure?

People may not openly express their prejudices, but racism can be subtle, distorting our perceptions and our behavior. In an old and classic demonstration of this point, Gordon Allport and Leo Postman (1947) showed white subjects a picture of a subway train filled with passengers. In the picture were a black man dressed in a suit and a white man holding a razor (see Figure 14.10). One subject viewed the scene briefly and described it to a second subject who had not seen it. The second subject communicated the description to a third subject and so on, through six rounds of communication. The result: The final subject's report often indicated that the black man, not the white man, was holding the razor. Some subjects even reported that he was waving the weapon in a threatening manner.

The way people interpret an event may also be influenced by race. In one study, white subjects watched on a TV monitor an interaction involving two men. A discussion

[Drawing by Cheney; © 1996 The New Yorker Magazine, Inc.]

Figure 14.10 How racist beliefs distort perceptions After looking at this drawing, one subject described it to a second, who described it to a third, and so on. After six rounds of communication, the final report often placed the razor blade held by the white man into the black man's hand (Allport & Postman, 1947).

developed into a heated argument, and one man seemed to shove the other. When the antagonist was white and the victim was black, only 17 percent of the subjects saw the shove as an act of violence. Most said it was just "horseplay." Yet when the antagonist was black and the victim white, the number of "violence" interpretations rose to 75 percent (Duncan, 1976). Similar results were found when the subjects were children (Lawrence, 1991; Sagar & Schofield, 1980).

Racist beliefs can also be detected without asking direct questions. Researchers have found that reaction time—the speed it takes to answer a question—can be used to uncover hidden prejudices. In one study, for example, white subjects read word pairs and pressed a button whenever they thought the words fit together. In each case, the word *blacks* or *whites* was paired with either a positive trait (*clean, smart,* etc.) or a negative trait (*stupid, lazy,* etc.). The results were revealing. Subjects did not openly associate *blacks* with negative terms or *whites* with positive terms. And they were equally quick to reject negative terms in both cases. However, subjects were quicker to respond to the positive words when they were paired with *whites* than with *blacks.* Since it takes less time to react to information that fits existing beliefs, this finding suggests that subjects were unconsciously predisposed to associate positive traits with *whites* more than with *blacks* (Dovidio et al., 1986; Gaertner & McLaughlin, 1983).

In Topeka, Kansas, in 1954, Linda Brown was forced to attended a segregated school after being denied admission to an all-white school. In Brown v. Board of Education, *the Supreme Court ruled that this separation of the public schools was unconstitutional.*

These results may seem subtle, but they suggest that racial prejudice may be so deeply ingrained in our culture that the negative images are as difficult to break as a bad habit (Devine, 1989). That's why Studs Terkel jumped to the conclusion that the black bus driver who said he was a dime short was being difficult when, in fact, the dime had fallen on the floor. The problem may be more common than we realize. When probed on the matter, many nonprejudiced white Americans admit that they are not always fair to blacks—an insight that causes them to feel embarrassed, guilty, and ashamed of themselves (Devine et al., 1991).

The Treatment In the United States, black and white people openly disagree about the extent to which racism still exists. Surveys show that most white Americans believe that racial discrimination is on the decline in housing, education, and employment, but most black Americans maintain that the problem still exists (Sigelman & Welch, 1991). There are also marked differences of opinion among highly paid athletes. Just a few years ago, *Sports Illustrated* surveyed 300 athletes who played in the NFL, in the NBA, and on Major League baseball teams. As shown in Figure 14.11, the results were striking: 63 percent of black respondents, compared to only 2 percent of their white teammates, believed that black people in their sport were victims of discrimination—in salaries, fan support, treatment by coaches, management opportunities, and commercial endorsements (Johnson, 1991).

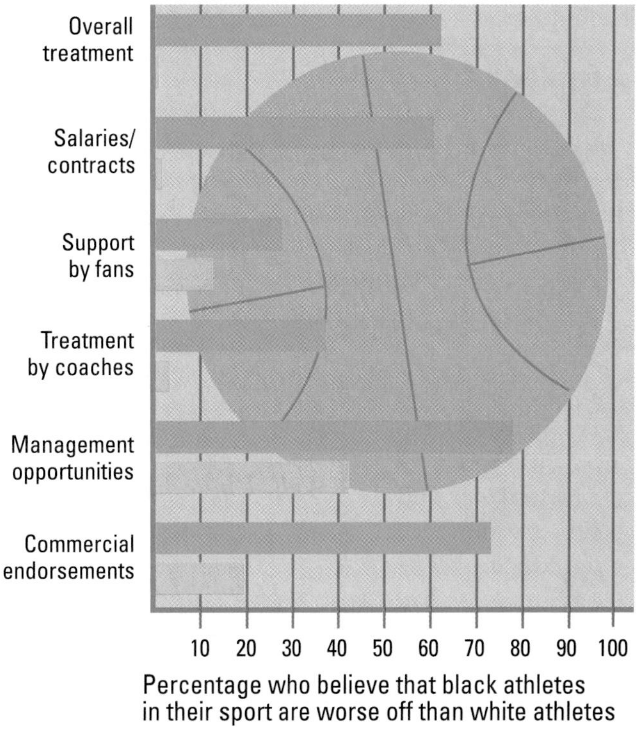

Figure 14.11 Perceptions of racial discrimination in sports *Sports Illustrated* surveyed 300 professional athletes and found that black and white athletes differed sharply in the belief that African Americans in their sport are subject to discrimination.

Racism is a social disease that gets transmitted from one generation to the next and afflicts millions of people from all groups. One wonders if it can be treated. Can people be joined cooperatively, perhaps, to foster a redrawing of the boundaries between "us" and "them"? In a laboratory study, Samuel Gaertner and others (1990) brought six subjects into the laboratory and divided them into two three-person groups. Each group took a name, wore color-coded ID tags, and worked on a decision-making task. Next, the groups were brought together and either listened to others discussing a problem (a neutral interaction) or joined forces to solve the problem themselves (a cooperative encounter). The strategy worked like a charm in two ways. First, despite initial allegiances, 58 percent of the subjects in the cooperative condition said they felt like one large group rather than two separate groups, an increase compared to only 28 percent in the neutral condition. Second, when subjects rated each other, those in the cooperative condition did not show the usual ingroup bias. Rather than derogate former outgroup members, they saw them as more likable, honest, and similar to the self. Thanks to cooperation, "they" became part of "us" (see Figure 14.12).

Is it possible to produce these kinds of effects on a large scale between racial or ethnic groups? Would it help to expose children to diversity at a young age? This large-scale "experiment" has been in progress, all across the country, in programs designed to desegregate the public schools.

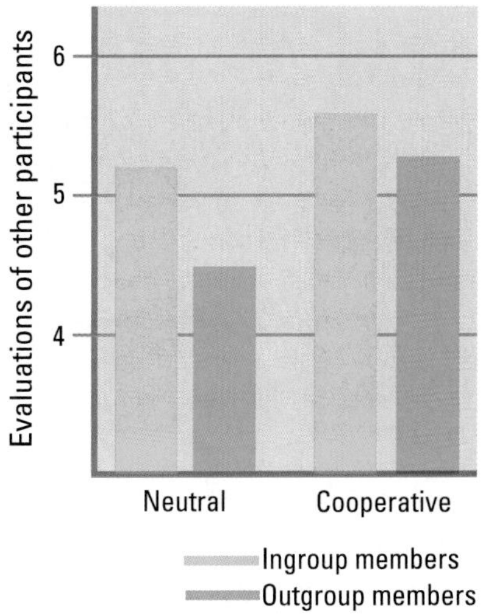

Figure 14.12 Using cooperation to make "them" part of "us" After working in separate three-person groups, six subjects were assembled for a neutral or cooperative interaction. After the neutral interaction, subjects later rated former ingroup members more favorably than former outgroup members (*left*). After the cooperative interaction, however, subjects did not exhibit this ingroup favoritism effect (*right*).

Problems and Prospects

Should the differences among diverse social and cultural groups be ignored or acknowledged?

When you stop to consider the ways in which all humans are similar, and share a common fate, the differences seem small and unimportant. Yet as we come into greater contact with people from other cultures, as our society becomes increasingly diverse, as gender-role boundaries continue to blur, and as tensions between black and white Americans stubbornly persist, it seems clear that we must recognize the differences among social groups if we are to understand, communicate, and be tolerant of one another.

SOCIAL AND CULTURAL GROUPS AND EDUCATION

Using Schools to Combat Racism

About forty-five years ago, the United States Supreme Court launched a bold and historic experiment in race relations. In the case of *Brown v. Board of Education of Topeka,* the Court ruled that racially separate schools were unequal, in violation of the Constitution. This opinion was informed by research suggesting that segregation had an adverse effect on the self-esteem and academic performance of black students and on prejudice itself (Allport et al., 1953).

> *See that man over there?*
>
> *Yes.*
>
> *Well, I hate him.*
>
> *But you don't know him.*
>
> *That's why I hate him.*
>
> — ALLPORT, 1954

Jackie Robinson and Branch Rickey discuss Robinson's contract with the Brooklyn Dodgers. This deal had great historical significance. The two men also went on to become good friends.

At the time, the Court's decision was controversial. Many Americans opposed school desegregation and argued that forcing interracial contact would only worsen matters. Others pinned their hopes on the **contact hypothesis,** which states that under certain conditions, direct contact between members of different groups will improve relations. For contact to have this effect, it was proposed, four conditions have to be met: (1) The two groups should be of equal status in the contact situation, (2) there should be personal interactions among individual members, (3) the groups should have a common goal that requires their cooperation—so that "them" can become part of "us," and (4) the contact should be supported by social norms, as set in part by people in authority.

Despite the Court's ruling, desegregation proceeded slowly. Many schools remained untouched until the 1970s. Then as the dust began to settle, research brought the sad news that there was little improvement in race relations (Stephan, 1986). Was the contact hypothesis wrong? It's hard to say. School desegregation had not produced desired changes, but the conditions necessary for effective intergroup contact had not been met. Nobody ever said that deeply rooted racism would be erased overnight just by throwing black and white people together. In fact, the four conditions necessary for contact to succeed did not exist in the schools.

First, the two groups did not come together on equal-status terms. When public schools were desegregated, the white children were from more affluent families and were better prepared than their black peers (Cohen, 1984). Second, personal interactions among black and white children were uncommon. Schools are not a melting pot, and desegregation does not ensure true integration. After the bus arrives, students gravitate toward members of their own race in the cafeteria and on the playground (Epstein, 1985; Schofield, 1982). Third, the typical classroom is filled with competition for a teacher's attention, grades, and so on—not the kinds of cooperative activities that bring people together to achieve a common goal. Fourth, school desegregation was not supported by social norms. Many principals, teachers, and state officials objected, and many parents boycotted busing—hardly an ingredient for success.

Although problems have plagued school-desegregation efforts, research shows that prejudice *can* be reduced in situations that satisfy the chief requirements of the contact hypothesis (Cook, 1985). Perhaps the most successful demonstration of this point took place on the baseball diamond. On April 15, 1947, Jackie Robinson played first base for the Brooklyn Dodgers—and became the first black man to break the color barrier in American sports. In a story told by Anthony Pratkanis and Marlene Turner (1994), Robinson's opportunity came through Dodger owner Branch Rickey, who felt that integrating baseball was both moral and good for the game. Rickey knew about the contact hypothesis and was assured by a social-scientist friend that a team can furnish the conditions for it to work: equal status among teammates, one-on-one interactions, dedication to a common goal, and a positive climate from the owner and coaching staff. The rest is history. Rickey signed Robinson and created the situation necessary for success. Baseball was integrated. In 1947, Jackie Robinson was named Rookie of the Year, and in 1962 he was elected into the Hall of Fame. At his induction ceremony, Robinson asked three people to stand beside him: his mother, his wife, and his friend Branch Rickey.

Can similar results be achieved in a school setting? Back in the classroom, Elliot Aronson and his colleagues (1978) developed a cooperative-learning method they called the "jigsaw classroom." In newly desegregated elementary schools in Texas and California, they assigned fifth-graders to small, racially and academically mixed groups. The material to be learned within each group was divided into subtopics, much the way a jigsaw puzzle is broken into pieces. Each student was responsible for learning one piece of the puzzle, after which all members took turns teaching their material to one another. Under this system, everyone—regardless of race, ability, or self-confidence—needs everyone else if the group as a whole is to succeed. The method produced impressive results. Compared to children in traditional classes, those in jigsaw classrooms grew to like one another more, were more tolerant, liked school more, and had higher self-esteem. On the academic front, test scores improved for minority students and remained the same for white students. As on interracial sports teams, the jigsaw classroom offers a promising way to create a truly integrated educational setting. It also provides a model of how to use personal contact to promote greater tolerance of diversity among children of all colors.

Currently, the policies spawned by Supreme Court's 1954 *Brown* decision are under attack. There is a growing sense among many white and African American urban leaders, and in the courts, that mandatory busing and forced integration are not a solution. There is also a growing sentiment in the African American community for "voluntary resegregation." And in California and other states where there are large Hispanic and Asian populations, true integration has become more complicated and more difficult to achieve. In a recent ruling, even the Supreme Court has changed its tune (*Missouri v. Jenkins,* 1996). At this point, it remains to be seen whether school districts will turn the clock back, redraw the color lines, and end school desegregation as we know it—and, if so, what the future effects will be on us all (Fineman, 1996; Kunen, 1996).

But what should be the goal? Should the differences among us be ignored or acknowledged? One view is that people should strive to become "blind" to culture, gender, and racial or ethnic heritage—categorizations that should have no bearing on the way we treat each other. In an ideal colorblind society, for example, healthy race relations demand that individuals be perceived, evaluated, and treated on a strictly personal basis. An alternative view is that people derive pride and a sense of belonging from their social connections and identities—and that while everyone should be treated equally and without discrimination, cultural, gender-based, and racial and ethnic diversity should be celebrated, not ignored. Clearly, there are similarities among us, and there are differences. The trick is not to focus exclusively on one or the other but to strike a balance.

contact hypothesis The proposition that in certain conditions, direct contact between members of rival groups will improve relations.

Summary and Key Terms

As the world becomes a global village, it's important to know the ways in which people from different cultural and ethnic groups are similar and different.

Cross-Cultural Perspectives

Cultural Diversity: A Fact of Life

People vary in their language, religion, geography, **social norms**—a culture's implicit rules of conduct—and in the degree to which they conform to these norms.

Individualism and Collectivism: A Tale of Two Cultural Worldviews

Cultures differ in their orientation toward **individualism** and **collectivism.** Individualistic cultures value independence and self-reliance, while collectivist cultures stress interdependence and cooperation. According to Triandis, societies that are complex, affluent, and heterogeneous are most likely to be individualistic.

Individualism and collectivism influence the extent to which we see the self as encompassing other people and groups with which we identify. In individualistic cultures, socialization practices are designed to foster independence; in collectivist cultures, the emphasis is on interdependence.

Each orientation has advantages and disadvantages. In collectivist societies, people are more likely to follow social norms, which promotes harmony and loyalty and discourage social loafing. But collectivism can also produce narrow-mindedness and a confrontational attitude toward outsiders.

Multicultural Perspectives

Ethnic Diversity: A Fact of Life

As ethnic diversity increases in the United States and elsewhere, more attention is being paid to **multiculturalism,** the study of diverse racial and ethnic groups within a culture.

Acculturation and Ethnic Identity

All ethnic groups face the dilemma of how to adapt to the larger society. Should they blend into a single "melting pot" or retain their heritage as part of a cultural "mosaic"? **Acculturation,** the process of change that occurs when people are immersed in a new culture, can occur in four ways: assimilation (abandoning the old culture for the new), separation (retaining the old and rejecting the new), integration (retaining the old *and* adapting to the new), or marginalization (identifying with neither culture).

Through acculturation, people establish an **ethnic identity,** which is revealed in language, customs, and a sense of belonging. But immigrants may also experience **acculturative stress,** resulting in various mental-health problems. The strategy of integration seems to correlate with less acculturative stress than the other three strategies, but different immigrant groups face different adjustment problems. A difficult obstacle for ethnic minorities is **discrimination,** behavior directed against people because of their affiliation with a social group. It stems from stereotypes and feelings of prejudice.

Gender: The Great Divide

Pollsters commonly find a "gender gap" between men and women, but is it real, and is its origin biological or environmental?

How Are Men and Women Different?

Certain biological sex differences are indisputable. Research has also established differences in the areas of sexuality, aggression, and cognitive skills. Men are more sexually permissive than women and see situations in more "sexualized" terms. They are also more physically aggressive than females. On average, males perform slightly better in mathematical problem solving and on some visual-spatial tasks. Females exhibit greater verbal fluency and social sensitivity.

Why Are Men and Women Different?

Some studies have linked sex differences in behavior to prenatal exposure to the sex hormones. Testosterone, the male sex hormone, has been associated with male sexual behavior and aggression. More research is needed to determine whether testosterone and estrogen, the female sex hormone, are similarly linked to performance on cognitive tasks.

Sex differences also result from contrasting life experiences. Through social learning, boys and girls come to understand **gender roles** they are expected to play. Experience also leads us to form **gender schemas,** beliefs about men and women that bias the way we perceive ourselves and others. In some cultures, sexist traditions are strong. Even in the United States, men and women occupy different roles in the workplace. Research suggests that gender stereotypes hold a kernel of truth but are exaggerated. According to **social-roles theory,** the sex differences we perceive are magnified by the different social roles occupied by men and women. In many ways we take for granted, men and women are more similar than different.

Prejudice

Prejudice refers to negative feelings toward others based solely on their membership in a certain group. Its roots can be both cognitive and motivational.

The Cognitive Roots

The cognitive roots of prejudice involve **stereotypes**—beliefs that associate a group of people with certain traits. Through a process of **social categorization,** we divide people into groups based on common attributes. We also distinguish ingroups (those we identify with) from outgroups (groups not our own). Although this process is natural and adaptive, the **outgroup-homogeneity bias** leads us to assume that members of outgroups are all alike.

Research suggests that stereotypes come to mind automatically and, at times, without conscious awareness. Studies also show that although stereotyping is cognitively inevitable, people are able to overcome the effects and judge others on a more individualized basis.

The Motivational Roots

Our motivations and emotions also play a role. The **realistic-conflict theory** holds that prejudice stems from intergroup competition for limited resources. But this explanation does not account for **ingroup favoritism** that appears even when resources aren't limited.

According to **social-identity theory,** the self contains not only a personal component but various social identities as well. Thus, people can boost their self-esteem by discriminating against outgroups. Research generally confirms that threats to self-esteem raise the need for prejudice and that expressions of prejudice in turn enhance self-esteem.

Racism in America

Racism, a deep-seated form of prejudice based on the color of a person's skin, is not as overt in the United States as it used to be, but studies find evidence of it in many settings. It influences our perceptions and our interpretations of events. As described by the **contact hypothesis,** the most effective way to combat prejudice is through personal, equal-status, cooperative contact between rival-group members in a situation in which the social norms for contact are favorable.

In the Field Resources

Books

Axtell, R. (1993). *Do's and taboos around the world* (3rd ed.). Wiley.

This entertaining bestseller describes cultural differences in customs and various norms for behavior. It is fun to read—and is sure to prove useful to the world traveler.

Moir, A., & Jessel, D. (1991). *Brain sex: The real difference between men and women.* New York: Dell.

This controversial bestseller presents the strong, though at times exaggerated, case that the male and female brains are different in ways that are psychologically meaningful.

Tavris, C. (1992). *The mismeasure of woman.* New York: Simon & Schuster.

This book critiques scientific evidence of sex differences and presents evidence for the proposition that men and women do not substantially differ in their psychological makeup.

Triandis, H. C. (1994). *Culture and social behavior.* New York: McGraw-Hill.

Written by a leading social psychologist, this book gives an up-to-date, authoritative look at cross-cultural research.

Films and Videos

Mr. Baseball (1992, 111 min.)

This comedy about an American ballplayer in Japan depicts the differences between individualist and collectivist cultures—and how they can clash. (Tom Selleck, Ken Takakura, Aya Takanshi, Dennis Haysbert, Tashi, Shioya, Kohsuke Toyohara.)

Tootsie (1982, 116 min.)

In this comedy, a struggling actor poses as a woman to land a role on TV. He comes to identify with women, leaving viewers thinking about sex differences and similarities. (Dustin Hoffman, Jessica Lange, Teri Garr, Dabney Coleman, Charles Durning, Bill Murray.)

Internet

International Association for Cross-Cultural Psychology (http://www.fit.edu/campuslife/clubs-org/iaccp/)

This organization lists books by its members, graduate programs in cross-cultural psychology, and Web resources.

U.S. Census Bureau (http://www.census.gov/)

Provides all sorts of interesting social and demographic information about the U.S. population (such as immigration statistics, languages spoken, and economic status).

Journals and Periodicals

Journal of Cross-Cultural Psychology
Journal of Personality and Social Psychology
Psychology of Women Quarterly
Sex Roles

15 *Personality*

The situation Based on research you've read, you know that an individual's personality consists of various, presumably enduring traits. You also know that many psychologists find it useful to describe personality by comparing people along five broad dimensions: (1) *neuroticism* (a proneness to anxiety and distress), (2) *extraversion* (a desire for social interaction, stimulation, and activity), (3) *openness* (a receptiveness to new experiences), (4) *agreeableness* (a selfless concern for others), and (5) *conscientiousness* (a tendency to be reliable, disciplined, and ambitious). Does one's relative standing on these traits stay basically the same over time, or does personality change with age, life experience, and other factors? If you're generally calm, outgoing, and open-minded now, will that be your profile later in life? What about the fact that a person's behavior differs, sometimes considerably, from one situation to another?

What's Your Prediction?

How stable is personality?

To determine the stability of personality, you decide to contact a large group of adults who completed a personality test six years earlier as part of another study. The test they filled out was designed to measure the top three of the five major traits (neuroticism, extraversion, openness). Overall, 635 people took the test—365 men and 270 women, ranging in age from twenty-five to ninety-one. In the original experiment, each person was given the test two times, with a six-month interval. Your goal now is to retest these same people on a newer version of the same scale. Most agree to take part in your study. But others, you come to learn, have died, moved, become disabled, or lost interest. In the end, you are able to recruit 398 of the original subjects. To each one, you mail the questionnaire, the instructions, and a stamped self-addressed envelope.

The questionnaire that you use is called the Neuroticism-Extraversion-Openness Personality Inventory, or NEO-PI. This test is the one most often used in research (Costa & McCrae, 1992). The NEO-PI contains 181 statements ("I am usually cheerful," "I really like most people I meet," "I have a very active imagination"). Next to each one, subjects rate on a 5-point scale how much they agree or disagree. The items measuring neuroticism, extraversion, and openness are dispersed throughout the test, but afterward you total the scores separately for each "subscale"—a procedure that yields three scores per subject. Once all tests are scored, the data are ready to be analyzed.

So what next? To determine the stability of the traits you measured, you need to take a longitudinal approach by comparing each subject's scores in the first and second tests. What is the *correlation* between the two sets of scores? If personality, like mood, were to fluctuate wildly from one moment to the next or if you were to pair the scores of one subject with those of another, randomly selected subject, the correlation would be 0 (remember, a correlation coefficient ranges from 0 to +1 or −1). At the other extreme, if personality were completely set in stone or if the same subjects were retested only six days, weeks, or months apart, the two sets of scores should be strongly and positively correlated, in the .90 range. The question is, How strongly correlated would the two sets of scores be after six *years?*

Make a prediction Six years ago, your 398 subjects took the test, which yielded three trait scores: one for neuroticism, another for extraversion, and a third for openness to experience. Now you have tested them again. How high do you think the correlations are between the two sets of scores? To give you a basis of comparison, the correlation coefficients that were found in earlier research when the test was readministered after only six months appear in the left-hand column of the table below. On a scale ranging from 0 (no correlation, no stability) to +1 (a perfect correlation, total stability), and using the six-month numbers as a guideline, predict the correlations that are found after six full years:

TRAIT	SIX MONTHS	SIX YEARS
Neuroticism	.87	______
Extraversion	.91	______
Openness	.86	______

The results The research just described is based on studies of adult personality that were conducted by Robert McCrae and Paul Costa (1990). So what did you predict? Does one's personality stay basically the same, or does it change over time? As shown below, the results revealed an extraordinary degree of stability—comparable, in fact, to that found after only six months.

TRAIT	SIX MONTHS	SIX YEARS
Neuroticism	.87	.83
Extraversion	.91	.82
Openness	.86	.83

What does it all mean? Think for a moment about your own personality—your basic feelings, attitudes, and ways of relating to others. Have you changed at all or stayed pretty much the same? When McCrae and Costa (1990) asked their subjects this question, 51 percent said they had stayed the same, 35 percent said they had changed a little, and 14 percent said they had changed a good deal. Were the self-perceptions of those who said they had changed accurate? Not according to the test scores. Costa and McCrae recalculated the test-retest correlations for only those subjects who said they had changed a lot—and the numbers were just as high.

As a general rule, personality is stable over time. Indeed, if it were not, you could not predict the kind of person you would be tomorrow, set a future career goal, or commit yourself to a marriage partner. This is not to say that we all stay the same as we get older. As we saw in Chapter 11, the aging process itself is accompanied by physical, sensory, and cognitive changes. As a result of life experiences, we may also change certain habits, attitudes, and behaviors. Even subtle shifts in personality are possible. When adults of different age groups are tested, for example, those who are older tend to score slightly lower on neuroticism, extraversion, and openness.

For clinical psychologists who work at helping people in distress, this research addresses a particularly critical question: Can people who suffer from anxiety, depression, or other types of mental disorders be helped? In Chapter 17, we'll see that they can. But as to the question of how much change is possible—and how difficult it is to facilitate that change—we'll see that the answer you come up with will depend, in part, on your theoretical orientation.

You might say that this woman "has personality." But then we all do. Individuals differ not in the amount of personality they have but in their distinctive patterns of thoughts, feelings, motives, and behaviors.

Browse through any bookstore and you will notice that the shelves are lined with pop-psych books that promise to reveal your true, hidden personality. All you have to do, they say, is analyze your diet (you are what you eat), color preferences (if you like red, you're said to be emotional), handwriting (short, clipped strokes mean that you're stingy), astrological signs (I've been told that I have a Taurus-like stubborn streak), facial characteristics (people with eyes set close together cannot be trusted), and body shape ("round" people are outgoing party animals).

Self-insight is not the only reason for all the interest in personality. Marketing experts categorize consumers so they can develop advertisements that appeal to certain segments of the market. Trial lawyers hire consultants to select jurors personally disposed to favor their client's case. Insurance companies generate profiles of high-risk clients prone to driving accidents. The FBI hires psychologists to probe the minds of terrorists and serial killers. Guidance counselors administer tests to tell whether someone is suited to working alone or with people. Even novelists use vivid personality sketches to develop their characters.

So what is **personality**? Although the word comes from the Latin *persona*, which means "mask," personality is more than just a face we wear in public. It's also what lies behind the mask—an enduring "inner core" that embodies an individual's distinct pattern of thoughts, feelings, motives, values, and behaviors. The study of personality seeks to describe individuals, the ways in which they are similar to one another, and the ways in which each is unique.

This chapter presents four major approaches to the study of personality: (1) psychoanalysis, (2) the cognitive social-learning approach, (3) the humanistic approach, and (4) the trait approach. Each perspective contains a set of theories that share certain assumptions about human nature—how personality forms and then develops;

personality An individual's distinct and relatively enduring pattern of thoughts, feelings, motives, and behaviors.

whether people are inherently good, bad, or neutral; the relative importance of biological and environmental factors; the role of unconscious determinants of behavior; and the question of stability and change. As we'll see, the scientific study of personality integrates theory, testing, and an interest in the clinical implications.

Psychoanalysis

What experiences inspired Freud to formulate psychoanalysis? What do dreams, jokes, and slips of the tongue have in common? Who were Jung and Adler, and how did these psychoanalytic theorists differ from Freud? What are projective tests—and how are they used? What is Freud's greatest legacy?

On the evening of May 6, 1856, at 6:30 PM, a baby boy was born in what is now the Czech Republic to Jakob and Amalie Freud. The boy arrived in a caul, a membrane that sometimes covers the infant's head at birth. Superstition had it that to be born in a caul is a good-luck omen—a sign that the baby will one day achieve fame and fortune. After one year of marriage, Jakob and Amalie had little money, but they were thrilled. They named the first of their six children Sigmund.

The boy grew up to be strong, healthy, and bright, at the top of his class in school. He enrolled at the University of Vienna at the age of seventeen, received a medical degree eight years later, and became a practicing neurologist. By his own admission, Freud was a driven young man, one who sorely wanted to make his mark on the world. In 1884, however, his desire for fame took a downward turn. He had heard about a "magic drug" with anesthetic powers, tried it, and enjoyed the uplifting effects it had on his mood and work. Thinking he was on the verge of a medical breakthrough, Freud prescribed the drug to a friend, who became hopelessly addicted and died of an overdose. The drug was cocaine. Having lost a friend, a patient, and a measure of respect in the medical community, Freud abandoned the drug and pursued other interests.

The Birth of Psychoanalysis

In 1885, Freud moved to Paris to study under Jean Charcot, an eminent French neurologist. Charcot was studying *hysteria,* a "conversion disorder" in which the patient experiences symptoms such as paralysis of the limbs, blindness, deafness, convulsions, and the like—without an organic basis (see Chapter 16). What's fascinating about hysteria is that the patient is not faking, yet there's nothing physically wrong. Charcot found that hysterical disorders often started with a traumatic event in the patient's childhood and that he could make the symptoms vanish by putting the patient under hypnosis. You can imagine how dazzled Freud was by the sight of "paralyzed" patients suddenly able to walk and of those who were "blind" suddenly able to see. Demonstrations like these filled Freud with a profound regard for the power of unconscious forces.

Back in Vienna, Freud became intrigued by the case of Anna O., a patient who suffered from hysterical paralysis of three limbs, impaired vision and speech, and a nervous cough. With the help of her physician, Josef Breuer, Anna was able to recall the events that precipitated her symptoms. As if a large block had been removed from her mind, Anna's symptoms slowly disappeared. Breuer had invented a *talking cure*. But something else happened that would also prove significant. After many sessions, Anna had become emotionally attached to Breuer. Freud was puzzled by the intensity of Anna's feelings, until one day when he had the same experience. Without provocation, a female patient lovingly threw her arms around Freud's neck. Freud had not sought the patient's affection, he said, and assumed he was not the real target of her passion. Without realizing it, he thought, this patient must have been transferring her feelings for someone else (maybe her father) onto him, a phenomenon Freud called *transference*.

Sigmund Freud and his daughter Anna—who went on to become a psychoanalyst in her own right.

Freud went into private practice but did not have much luck using hypnosis. He realized that not everyone could be hypnotized and that the so-called cures produced in hypnosis often did not last. To help patients recall and talk freely about their past, Freud came up with his first technique of psychotherapy, *free association*. The procedure is simple: The patient lies on a couch, relaxes, and says whatever comes to mind, no matter how trivial, embarrassing, or illogical it may seem. After many sessions, Freud noticed something curious. Although patients would produce streams of ideas leading to the unconscious, many seemed unable to talk or even think about painful and unpleasant memories. In fact, once on the brink of an important insight, they would often stop, go blank, lose their train of thought, or change the subject. Freud called this phenomenon resistance and concluded that it was part of an unconscious defensive process designed to keep unwanted thoughts under lock and key—and out of awareness.

Freud's Theory of Personality

Freud's clinical experiences laid a foundation for the theory he later developed. He was convinced that the traumas and conflicts of early childhood can have lasting effects, that we are ruled by unconscious forces, that what's unconscious can be brought out through free association, that we resist painful self-insights, and that we often transfer our feelings for one object onto another. Slowly but surely, the pieces were falling into place. In 1896, Freud used the term **psychoanalysis** for the first time. Then in 1900, he published *The Interpretation of Dreams,* the first of his twenty-four books and the one that marked the birth of what would become one of the broadest, most influential theories in modern history. The theory is summarized in Freud's (1940) last book, *An Outline of Psychoanalysis,* published one year after his death.

> *"Every man has reminiscences which he would not tell to everyone but only to his friends. He has other matters in mind which he would not reveal even to his friends, but only to himself, and that in secret. But there are other things which a man is afraid to tell even to himself, and every decent man has a number of such things stored away in his mind."*
>
> — FYODOR DOSTOYEVSKY

The Unconscious Underlying psychoanalysis is the assumption that personality is shaped largely by forces that act within a person's *unconscious*. To illustrate, Freud compared the human mind to an iceberg. Like the small tip of the iceberg that can be seen above the water, the conscious part consists of all that a person is aware of at a given moment. Below the surface is the vast region of the unconscious, which contains thoughts, feelings, and memories that are hidden from view. Part of this region lies just beneath the surface, in an area called the preconscious. Preconscious material is not threatening, just temporarily out of awareness and easy to bring to mind. The rest of the unconscious, however, is a deep, dark sea of secret urges, wishes, and drives. According to Freud, the mind keeps these unacceptable impulses out of awareness. Still, they rumble, make waves, and surface for air—in our dreams, our slips of the

psychoanalysis Freud's theory of personality and method of psychotherapy, both of which assume that our motives are largely unconscious.

tongue, the jokes we tell, the people we're attracted to, the anxieties we feel, and so on. In other words, only through psychoanalysis can we achieve meaningful insight into our personality.

What's in the unconscious? According to Freud, two major instincts motivate all of human behavior. The first is collectively referred to as the *life instincts*, which include the need for food, water, air, and sex. At the time of Freud's writing, the sex part raised eyebrows. Yet Freud felt it was critical because many of the childhood traumas that his patients told about were sexual in nature. Years later, after living through the stark destruction of World War I, Freud also proposed that there is a second, darker side of human nature—that buried within the unconscious is a *death instinct*, a need to reduce all tensions by returning to a calm lifeless state. Because these self-destructive impulses conflict with the more powerful life forces, reasoned Freud, they are turned away from the self and directed instead toward others. The fated result of the death instinct, then, is aggression—a problem that has plagued humans throughout history.

The Structure of Personality

Have you ever had a burning urge to kiss or embrace someone you're attracted to or to hit someone who has angered you, only to hear the haunting voice of your conscience? How do you resolve these dilemmas? Based on his clinical experiences, Freud believed that people are perpetually driven by inner conflicts (conscious vs. unconscious, free association vs. resistance, life vs. death)—and that compromise is a necessary solution. Freud thus divided the human personality into three interacting parts: the id, ego, and superego. These parts are not actual structures in the brain. Rather, they are concepts that Freud used to represent the different aspects of personality.

The **id** is the most primitive part of personality. Present at birth, it is a reservoir of instincts and biological drives that energize us. According to Freud, the id operates according to the **pleasure principle**, motivating us to seek immediate and total gratification of all desires. When a person is deprived of food, water, air, or sex, a state of tension builds until the need is satisfied. Thus, the id is a blind, pleasure-seeking part of us that aims for the reduction of all tension. If the impulsive, id-dominated infant could speak, it would scream: "I want it, and I want it *now*!"

The **superego** is a socially developed aspect of personality that motivates us to behave in ways that are moral, ideal, even perfect. Whereas the id pushes us to seek immediate gratification, the superego is a prude, a moralist, a part of us that shuns sex and other innate sources of pleasure. Where does the superego come from? According to Freud, children learn society's values from their parents. Through repeated experiences with reward for good behavior and punishment for bad, children eventually develop their own internal standards of what's right and wrong. There are two components to the superego. One is the *ego-ideal*, an image of the ideals we should strive for. The other is the *conscience*, a set of prohibitions that define how we should not behave. Once the superego is developed, people reward themselves internally for moral acts by feeling pride, and they punish themselves for immoral acts by suffering pangs of guilt.

The third aspect of personality is the **ego**, which mediates the conflict between the "wants" of the id and the "shoulds" of the superego. According to Freud, the ego is a pragmatic offshoot of the id, the part of personality that helps us achieve realistic forms of gratification. In contrast to the id (which strives for immediate gratification) and the superego (which seeks to inhibit the same impulses), the ego operates according to the **reality principle**—the goal being to reduce one's tensions, but only at the right time, in the right place, and in a socially appropriate manner. The ego is thus a

id In psychoanalysis, a primitive and unconscious part of personality that contains basic drives and operates according to the pleasure principle.

pleasure principle In psychoanalysis, the id's boundless drive for immediate gratification.

superego In psychoanalysis, the part of personality that consists of one's moral ideals and conscience.

ego In psychoanalysis, the part of personality that operates according to the reality principle and mediates the conflict between the id and superego.

reality principle In psychoanalysis, the ego's capacity to delay gratification.

master of compromise, the part of us that tries to satisfy our needs without offending our morals. The ego, said Freud, is the executive officer of the personality, the part that controls our behavior. Freud's model is illustrated in Figure 15.1.

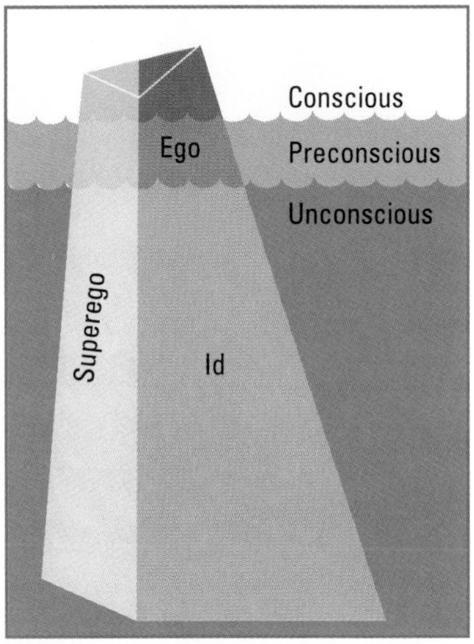

Figure 15.1 The structure of personality according to Freud

Psychosexual Development Over and over again, Freud the physician listened to patients tell wild tales about childhood traumas—tales involving sexual and aggressive encounters with mothers, fathers, neighbors, and dirty old uncles. Eventually, Freud came to believe that although some of the stories he heard were true, others were sheer fantasies, a product of overactive imaginations. From this experience, Freud drew two developmental conclusions: (1) that personality is shaped during the first few years of life, and (2) that the resolution of "psychosexual" conflicts is the key contributor. He went on to propose that children pass through an odyssey of **psychosexual stages** of development, with each stage defined by a different "erogenous zone," a part of the body that's most sensitive to erotic stimulation.

First comes the *oral stage*, which occurs in the first year of life, a time when the baby's mouth is the pleasure-seeking center of attention. Oral activity begins with the sucking of nipples, thumbs, and pacifiers, then moves on to biting, chewing, cooing, and other oral activities. In this stage, the infant is totally dependent on caretakers, feeding is a key activity, and weaning (the transition away from the breast or bottle) is a major source of conflict. Next comes the *anal stage*, which occurs during the second and third years of life, when the baby derives pleasure in the sensation of holding in and letting go of feces. There is a regular and enjoyable cycle of tension buildup and release. In this stage, however, toilet training brings the parent ("Wait!") and child ("I don't want to!") into sharp conflict. Between the ages of four and six, the child then enters the *phallic stage*, a time when pleasure is felt in the genital area. In this stage, children become fascinated with the body and can often be seen playing with their own sex organs in public, a habit that once again brings them into conflict with parents. To Freud, the single most dramatic conflict in psychosexual development takes place at this point.

There's a famous Greek tragedy in which the hero, an abandoned infant who goes on to become King Oedipus, returns as a young man to kill his father and marry his mother, both without realizing who they were. According to Freud, this legend exposes an unconscious human wish he called the **Oedipus complex**—a tendency for children to become sexually attracted to the parent of the opposite sex and to develop feelings of jealousy and rage toward the rival parent of the same sex. Freud's theory of male development is clear: The young boy wants his mother and hates his father for standing in the way. Because the father is bigger and more powerful, however, the boy develops *castration anxiety*, a fear that the father will retaliate by cutting off his son's prized genitals. For defensive reasons, the boy represses his sexual urge for the mother and tries to emulate the father, in a process known as **identification**. As a result, the boy becomes less anxious, derives partial satisfaction of his repressed wish for mom, and adopts his father's moral values. Freud admitted that his theory of female development is less clear. At some point, he says, the girl notices that her father has a penis but that she and her mother do not. Unconsciously, the girl blames and resents her mother for her deficiency, develops *penis envy*, and seeks to become daddy's little girl. Eventually, she realizes the futility of these feelings, represses her envy, and identifies with her mother. For both boys and girls, then, the identification part of the process is important: It means that the superego springs full blown from the Oedipus complex.

Once Oedipal conflicts are resolved, the child enters a long *latency period*, which lasts roughly between the ages of seven and twelve. In these middle years of

psychosexual stages Freud's stages of personality development during which pleasure is derived from different parts of the body (oral, anal, phallic, and genital).

Oedipus complex In psychoanalysis, a tendency for young children to become sexually attracted to the parent of the opposite sex and hostile toward the parent of the same sex.

identification In psychoanalysis, the process by which children internalize their parents' values and form a superego.

According to Freud, psychosexual development progresses through stages, each one of which is defined by a part of the body that is most sensitive. In the oral stage (top left), *everything is put into the mouth. During the anal stage* (top center), *toilet training brings the child and parents into conflict. The phallic stage* (top right) *centers around the Oedipus complex. Middle childhood is considered a calm latency period* (bottom left) *when sexual urges lie dormant. Beginning at puberty, the genital stage* (bottom right) *is marked by the emergence of adultlike sexual desires.*

childhood, sexual impulses lie dormant, as boys and girls concentrate on friends of the same sex and schoolwork. As parents come to appreciate, this is a time of calm between storms. Indeed, it precedes the fourth and final stage of psychosexual development—the *genital stage.* Starting at puberty, boys and girls emerge from their latency shells and feel the stirring of adultlike sexual urges for the first time. Once again, the ego must cope with an undeclared state of war between biological drives and social prohibitions.

According to Freud, one must pass successfully through all psychosexual stages in order to form a healthy personality and enjoy mature adult relationships. If children receive *too much* or *too little* gratification at an earlier stage, they will become stuck or "fixated" at that stage. **Fixation** is thus responsible for the development of the following personality types:

- *Oral.* If you were weaned too early or too late as an infant, you would become fixated at the oral stage and feel the need to smoke, drink, bite your nails, chew on pencils, or spend hours talking on the phone. You might also seek symbolic forms of oral gratification by becoming passive, dependent, and demanding—like a nursing infant.
- *Anal.* If, as a toddler, you were toilet-trained in a harsh and rigid manner, you would become anally fixated and react in one of two ways—either by becoming tight, stubborn, punctual, and overcontrolled (the holding-on, "anal-retentive" type) or by becoming rebellious, messy, and disorganized (the letting-go, "anal-expulsive" type).
- *Phallic.* If you masturbated freely during the preschool years or if all genital contact was prohibited, resulting in frustration, you would develop a phallic personality—one that is entirely self-centered, vain, arrogant, and in constant need of attention. The man who seems obsessed with building his muscles, wearing expensive clothing, and conquering women is a classic example.

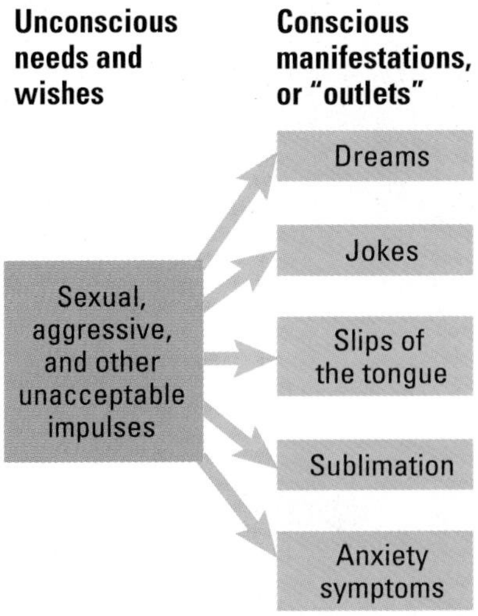

Figure 15.2 The dynamics of personality according to Freud In psychoanalysis, unconscious sexual and aggressive impulses find acceptable forms of expression.

The Dynamics of Personality

Influenced by the science of physics, Freud believed that the human mind has a constant, finite amount of "psychic energy," energy that cannot be created or destroyed but only transformed from one state to another. What this means for personality is that even though the id's instinctual impulses can be temporarily suppressed, its energy must find an outlet, a way to leak out. According to Freud, the ego searches for safe and normal outlets for these needs.

> *"Every impulse we strive to strangle broods in the mind, and poisons us."*
>
> — OSCAR WILDE

You may recall from Chapter 4 that in Freud's theory, the dreams you remember in the morning are a disguised, nonthreatening expression of your unconscious wishes. Pent-up energy is released while you're asleep, but in ways that are confusing, and therefore nonthreatening. The same is true of the so-called Freudian slips of the tongue and, as we'll see later, a defense mechanism known as sublimation. Even humor can serve as an outlet, as when people tell ethnic jokes to relieve hostile impulses and dirty jokes to ease their sexual tension. Disguised wish fulfillment—it's the compromise we strike with ourselves (see Figure 15.2).

To help minimize the anxiety that results from the clash between our wishes, morals, and reality, the ego uses powerful weapons: unconscious defense mechanisms that deny and distort our self-perceptions. Here are some common **defense mechanisms** described by Freud. See if you recognize any of them:

- **Repression** occurs when anxiety-provoking thoughts and memories are "forgotten" and pushed out of awareness. Freud believed that people repress unacceptable sexual and aggressive urges, traumas, and guilt feelings. In 1990, a woman jogging in Central Park, in New York, was raped, beaten, and left for dead by a gang of teenagers. She later testified that she could barely remember the attack—a possible sign of repression. According to Freud, this mechanism

fixation In psychoanalysis, a tendency to get "locked in" at early, immature stages of psychosexual development.

defense mechanisms Unconscious methods of minimizing anxiety by denying and distorting reality.

repression A defense mechanism in which personally threatening thoughts, memories, and impulses are banned from awareness.

of defense is a necessary prerequisite for all the others but is seldom an ultimate solution.

Denial is a primitive form of repression in which anxiety-filled external events not only are forgotten but also are barred from awareness in the first place (see no evil, hear no evil). Denial is common among terminally ill patients and in families that sometimes refuse to admit that a loved one is dying. It is also characteristic of smokers who refuse to recognize the health risks of their habit, husbands and wives who ignore signs of marital conflict, and politicians who manage to overlook corruption that takes place right under their noses.

Projection occurs when people attribute or "project" their own unacceptable impulses onto others. In Freud's view, a person who is sexually attracted to a friend's spouse, or to anyone else who is "off limits," might repress those feelings and consciously come to believe that the friend's spouse is attracted to him or her. In this way, "I lust for this person" is transformed into "This person lusts after me." Similarly, people who are prejudiced against certain racial or ethnic groups are quick to attribute their own hostile impulses to "them."

Reaction formation involves converting an unacceptable feeling into its opposite. Someone who brags may be masking feelings of inadequacy. Similarly, hatred can be transformed into love, and sadness into joy. Compared to "true" feelings, reaction formations often appear exaggerated. Examples include the mother who smothers with affection an unwanted child she secretly resents, the schoolboy who goes out of his way to taunt a girl he really likes, the antipornography crusader who deep down inside is aroused by sexually explicit material, and the vocal antigay activist who fights to cover up his own homosexual impulses.

Rationalization involves making excuses for one's failures and shortcomings. The fox in Aesop's fable who refused the grapes he could not reach "because they were sour" used rationalization. So do failing students who say they don't really care about grades, gamblers who justify their massive losses as entertainment costs, and scorned lovers who find fault with those who reject them.

Sublimation is the channeling of the id's repressed urges into socially acceptable substitute outlets. Freud saw this as the healthiest defense mechanism because it represents a genuine compromise among the id, ego, and superego. Thus, a person with pent-up hostile impulses may derive satisfaction by becoming a surgeon, football player, or critic. Similarly, a person may sublimate sexual needs by listening to others talk about sex or through music, art, dance, and other activities. Freud believed that civilization's greatest achievements spring from the wells of sexual and aggressive energy. He suggested, for example, that Leonardo da Vinci painted the famous *Mona Lisa* as a sublimation of his need for intimacy with a mother from whom he was separated at an early age. As for other men, the lyrics of an old song hint at how substitute gratification for repressed Oedipal urges can be achieved: "I want a girl just like the girl that married dear old dad!"

denial A primitive form of repression in which anxiety-filled external events are barred from awareness.

projection A defense mechanism in which people attribute or "project" their own unacceptable impulses onto others.

reaction formation A defense mechanism in which one converts an unacceptable feeling into its opposite.

rationalization A defense mechanism that involves making excuses for one's failures and shortcomings.

sublimation In psychoanalysis, the channeling of repressed sexual and aggressive urges into socially acceptable substitute outlets.

Freud's Legacy

Freud was born and raised in the prudish Victorian era, so his theory was met with a great deal of shock (Gay, 1988). Unconscious conflicts, dreams, jokes, and slips of the tongue that hold hidden meaning, erotic impulses churning in the innocent newborn baby, repression and other defense mechanisms that keep us from falling apart at the seams—it all seemed pretty wild. Still, Freud's legacy is remarkable. As we'll see, his ideas gave rise to other psychoanalytic theories and a whole class of personality tests. He also provided something for psychologists of other theoretical persuasions to shoot at—and build on.

Neo-Freudian Theorists Despite the controversy, Freud's emerging theory immediately attracted a group of followers, many of whom went on to propose competing theories. Make no mistake about it—these dissenters were psychoanalytically oriented. Following Freud, they assumed that unconscious factors play a critical role, that people need to resolve inner conflicts, and that personality is formed early in childhood. The main sticking point was—and, for many, still is—Freud's emphasis on s-e-x as a driving force.

Carl Jung was a favorite within Freud's inner circle, heir apparent to the throne of psychoanalysis. Jung (1928), however, complained that Freud viewed the brain "as an appendage to the genital glands," and he sought to change the theory in two ways. First, Jung maintained that the unconscious consists not only of repressed material from one's personal life but also of universal symbols and memories from our ancestral past—an inherited **collective unconscious**. That's why, said Jung, so many humans are born with an irrational fear of snakes; why we're drawn like magnets to fire, water, wind, and other natural elements; and why certain common themes appear in cultural myths and legends around the world. Jung's second shift in emphasis concerned the subject of personality development. He agreed that people strive for the satisfaction of biological drives. But he also felt that at the age of forty or so, we undergo a midlife transition, a time during which the youthful and vigorous pursuit of biological needs is replaced by deeper, more cerebral, even spiritual concerns. As far as Jung was concerned, personality development continues into adulthood.

Alfred Adler was another major theorist within Freud's inner circle. Like the others, Adler was trained in medicine. He broke with Freud, however, because he felt that personality was formed more from social conflicts than from sexual tension. According to Adler (1927), all humans feel small, helpless, and weak in the first few years of life, symptoms of what he termed an *inferiority complex*. As a result, we grow up trying unconsciously to compensate for these feelings and strive for superiority, while at the same time taking an interest in the welfare of others. Adler felt that Freud was so focused on the triangle of relationships among mother, father, and child that he neglected other family influences. Adler wrote, for example, about the impact of being first-, middle-, or later-born within the family, and he coined the term *sibling rivalry*.

Later generations of psychoanalytic theorists either viewed themselves as classical Freudians (Brenner, 1982) or extended the theory in two directions. One group followed in Adler's path by emphasizing that humans are inherently social animals. Erich Fromm (1941) maintained that as Western civilization abandoned the caste system, people felt freer and more independent but also more alone and isolated. Fromm argued that we unconsciously seek to "escape from freedom" by falling in love, getting married, having children, joining religious groups, and rallying behind powerful leaders. What distinguishes individuals from one another, he proposed, are the ways in which they resolve the conflict between freedom and unity. Karen Horney (1945) similarly claimed that all humans need love and security and become highly anxious when they feel isolated and alone. According to Horney, people have different ways of coping with this anxiety: Some are unconsciously driven to be

collective unconscious As proposed by Jung, a kind of memory bank that stores images and ideas that humans have accumulated over the course of evolution.

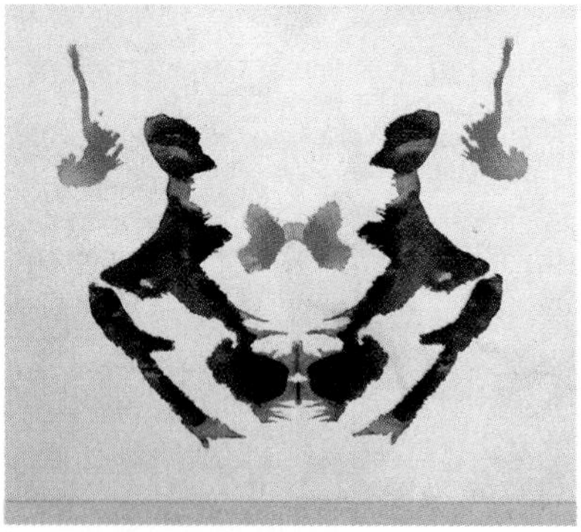

Figure 15.3 Sample Rorschach card According to psychoanalytically oriented psychologists, what you see in this inkblot—and how you see it—can be used to assess your personality.

loved, others to be feared, and still others to be admired. Again, the goal is to satisfy needs that are social, not biological.

A second group of psychoanalysts known as ego psychologists enlarged the role of the ego in personality. For Freud, the ego existed in order to accommodate the id and yet operate within the boundaries of reality, appease the superego, and ward off anxiety through the use of defense mechanisms. But according to daughter Anna Freud, Heinz Hartmann, David Rapaport, Erik Erikson, and other theorists, the ego is more than simply the id's brainy assistant. In their view, the ego is present at birth, is as basic as the id, and is the reason why people are often thoughtful as well as passionate. This ego helps to organize our thoughts, feelings, and memories, and it leads us to grow and pursue creative activities for the sake of enjoyment, not simply the reduction of tension (Westen, 1990). As ego psychologist Robert White (1975) put it, "Human beings have intrinsic urges which make them want to grow up."

Projective Personality Tests Psychoanalysis is founded on the assumption that the most meaningful parts of personality are locked away in an unconscious part of the mind. What this means is that one cannot truly get to know someone by asking direct questions. Searching for the key to this warehouse of personal secrets, Freud tried hypnosis, free association, and the interpretation of dreams—the "royal road to the unconscious." Is it possible to explore the mind without psychotherapy? Seeking a shortcut to the unconscious, psychoanalytic researchers and practitioners devised what's known as **projective tests**. A projective test asks people to respond to an ambiguous stimulus—a word out of context, an incomplete sentence, an inkblot, a fuzzy picture. The assumption is that if a stimulus has no inherent meaning and can accommodate a multitude of interpretations, then whatever people see must be a *projection* of their own needs, wishes, hopes, fears, and conflicts.

The most popular of the projective tests is the **Rorschach**, introduced in 1921 by Swiss psychiatrist Hermann Rorschach, which consists of a set of ten symmetrical inkblots—some in color, others in black and white. Look, for example, at the inkblot in Figure 15.3. What do you see? Is it a man with a beer belly wearing a bow tie? Two bats hanging from a wall? Two women bending over a pot? An upside-down frog? A bearskin rug? A butterfly? As you can imagine, stimuli like this can evoke wildly different interpretations. You may see crawling insects, animals, humans, sexual organs, or weapons or other inanimate objects. You may see a single large image, or you might dissect the inkblot into many smaller images. In fact, the examiner is interested not only in what you see but also in how you approach the task—whether you take two seconds per card or five minutes; whether you're sensitive to form or to color; and whether the images you report are common or uncommon. I'll never forget the time a graduate school friend of mine was learning to work with the Rorschach as part of her clinical training and used me as a guinea pig. Following a series of black-and-white inkblots, she turned over a bright, multi-colored design. "Wow, nice!" was my immediate reaction, at which point my friend raised an eyebrow and quickly jotted down some notes. Later, I was told that not everyone reacts as I did to the color—that my animated reaction meant I'm an emotional person.

projective tests Psychoanalytic personality tests that allow people to "project" unconscious needs, wishes, and conflicts onto ambiguous stimuli.

Rorschach A projective personality test in which people are asked to report what they see in a set of inkblots.

Over the years, many elaborate systems have been developed for scoring the Rorschach, which is still widely used in clinical practice. Critics say there are two problems. The first is that it lacks reliability, which means that two examiners often reach different conclusions from the same set of responses. The second problem is that the test lacks validity, which means that it does not discriminate among groups known to have different personalities (Hertz, 1986). In the most scathing critique,

Robyn Dawes (1994) called the Rorschach a "shoddy" instrument that "is not a valid test of anything" (p. 146).

Despite these criticisms, Rorschach users are now becoming more sophisticated. Based on past research, John Exner, Jr. (1993), developed a new, comprehensive, computerized scoring system. As a general rule, studies have shown that there are higher levels of reliability and validity than in the past (Parker et al., 1988)—but that these levels are still lower than is found in the kinds of "objective" tests to be described later (Acklin et al., 1992; Wood et al., 1996). As far as Rorschach users are concerned, however, skillful examiners can employ the test to understand how people think and to explore depths of personality that do not otherwise surface in questionnaires, interviews, or behavioral observations (Blatt, 1990; Exner, 1996; Weiner, 1997).

Figure 15.4 Sample TAT picture This ambiguous picture is used in the Thematic Apperception Test.

A second popular projective instrument is the **Thematic Apperception Test**, or **TAT**, introduced by Henry Murray. Murray (1938) had formulated a personality theory that distinguishes people by the kinds of psychological needs that motivate their behavior—such as the needs for power, achievement, nurturance, and affiliation. We saw in Chapter 8, in our discussion of achievement motivation, that to measure these needs, Murray (1943) developed a set of drawings of characters in ambiguous situations (plus one blank card, the ultimate projective test!) and asked subjects to tell a story about the "hero." Look, for example, at the picture presented in Figure 15.4. What do you think is going on? Who are the characters, and what's their relationship? What led up to this situation, and how will it all turn out? You can see that the possibilities are limitless—like a blank page awaiting your personal signature. The last time I showed this particular card to my students, I received a wide range of stories. Some said the woman in the shawl is the girl's mother, disappointed in her daughter's choice of a husband or career or in the fact that she's a lesbian. Others said that the girl is looking into the mirror, seeing herself as an old woman, alone and without a family. Still others said that the young woman is angry at her mother for driving her father out of the house.

The TAT is based on the assumption that people identify with the heroes and project their own needs into their responses. If someone tells one story after another about the loss of a loved one, resistance to authority, the struggle to achieve success, or fear of rejection, chances are that the particular theme is an important one for the person. As with the Rorschach, the TAT has been criticized for lacking reliability and validity (Anastasi, 1988). At the same time, certain TAT pictures have been reliably used to identify specific motives and predict behavior. As we saw in Chapter 8, for example, people whose TAT stories reveal a high rather than low *need for intimacy* think more about social relationships and spend more time talking, self-disclosing, smiling, and making eye contact when engaged in conversation (McAdams et al., 1984). In contrast, people whose stories reveal a high rather than low *need for achievement* set more realistic goals, persist more in the face of failure, are more likely to succeed at work, and derive more pride from their accomplishments (Atkinson, 1957; McClelland, 1985; Spangler, 1992). In many ways, the stories people tell when taking the TAT, and the themes they emphasize, are revealing of their personalities (Cramer, 1996).

Current Perspectives on Psychoanalysis

On November 29, 1993, *Time* magazine had a picture of Sigmund Freud on the cover, accompanied by three words: *"Is Freud Dead?"* It has now been more than a hundred years since Freud started putting together the pieces of psychoanalysis, a bold theory that would alter the course of psychology as a discipline. Needless to say, Freud and other psychoanalysts have

Thematic Apperception Test (TAT) A projective personality test in which people are asked to make up stories from a set of ambiguous pictures.

always attracted their share of critics, as new research developments within psychology lead us to modify or reject some propositions and to accept others.

There are three major criticisms of psychoanalysis. One is that as a theory of personality it paints too bleak a portrait of human nature. It was bad enough when Copernicus exposed the myth that earth is at the center of the universe and when Darwin said that humans were descended from apes. But when Freud claimed that we are driven, even as infants, by lustful, incestuous desires and antisocial aggressive impulses and that we are all at the mercy of unconscious forces beyond our control, he went too far. The theory was simply too pessimistic for many people to accept. Before World War II, for example, Albert Einstein wrote Freud and asked if he thought that war could be avoided. Freud wrote back a fourteen-page letter. The essence of his answer was *no*, war is inevitable.

The second criticism of psychoanalysis is that it does not meet acceptable standards of science. From the start, Freud based his whole theory on observations he made of his Vienna patients, hardly a representative group of human beings. He then proceeded to use the theory to explain family dynamics, mental illness, love and attraction, homosexuality, war, religion, suicide, crime and punishment, and the course of human history. Of course, after-the-fact explanations are easy, very much like betting on a horse after the race has been run. But can Freud's theory predict these kinds of events in advance?

The critics say *no*, which leads to the third major criticism of psychoanalysis: Carefully controlled research fails to support many of its propositions. One important example concerns the assumption that personality is completely formed in the first few years of life. In light of recent research, we now know that although early childhood experiences are formative and can have a lasting impact on us, development is, in many ways, a lifelong process (see Chapter 11). Freud's theory that childhood conflicts cause people to become fixated at certain psychosexual stages has also not stood the test of time. Research has shown that although oral, anal, and phallic personality types can be identified, they don't necessarily arise from difficulties experienced in weaning, toilet training, masturbation, or other psychosexual experiences. Even the Oedipus complex, the centerpiece of Freud's development theory, receives little support. Young boys and girls often do favor the opposite-sex parent and identify with the same-sex parent—but there's little hard evidence for castration anxiety, penis envy, or other sex-related motives (Fisher & Greenberg, 1977; Daly & Wilson, 1990).

So is Freud dead? The man is, but his influence clearly is not. In its classic form, psychoanalysis has some shortcomings and relatively few adherents. But many of its concepts have become so absorbed into mainstream psychology, not to mention popular culture, that it is very much alive—and continues to inspire new theories and research. As a physician, Freud almost single-handedly managed to convince the world that mental disorders are often psychological, not medical, in origin. As a personality theorist, he drew attention to the profound importance of the attachment bond between parents and the young child, the powerful unconscious filled with inner turmoil, and our arsenal of nonrational coping mechanisms. The theory may paint an unflattering portrait, psychoanalysts admit, but one must recognize the dark shadows of human nature in order to deal with them. Freud had the courage to expose this side of us and to penetrate beneath the surface of our behavior.

Perhaps the most enduring of Freud's ideas is his view of the mind as an iceberg. Today, virtually everyone agrees that the unconscious is vast and important—and that people have a limited awareness of why they think, feel, and behave as they do (Singer, 1990). Psychologists disagree, however, about the nature of the unconscious. Some maintain that it contains thoughts, wishes, impulses, memories, and other information that are actively blocked from awareness for self-protective reasons (Erdelyi, 1992; Bowers & Farvolden, 1996). Others maintain that the unconscious consists of innocent material that is not attended to, or else is forgotten, for strictly cognitive reasons (Greenwald, 1992; Kihlstrom et al., 1992). In a series of studies, Lloyd Silverman and his colleagues found that subjects are influenced by psychoanalytically charged messages flashed on a screen for four milliseconds—too quick to register in awareness. For example, after the Oedipal message "Mommy and I are one" is flashed, male subjects often report feeling happier and less anxious, even though they don't seem to know that a message was presented (Silverman & Weinberger, 1985). Researchers are now trying to determine just how reliable this result is and why it occurs (Balay & Shevrin, 1988; Hardaway, 1990).

A second enduring legacy of Freud's theory is his analysis of defense mechanisms. Based on the resistance shown by so many of his patients, Freud argued that people distort reality to ward off anxiety. Research shows that he was absolutely right. Some of us may be more defensive than others, but everyone harbors illusions about the self. We see ourselves in inflated terms, have an exaggerated sense of control over uncontrollable events, compare ourselves to others who are less fortunate, and think more optimistically than we should about our own future (Taylor & Brown, 1988)—and these illusions may help us cope with adversity (Taylor & Armor, 1996). Even young children exhibit the use of defense mechanisms (Cramer, 1990). Indeed, this part of Freud's theory can shed light on some of the most irrational, atrocious acts of humankind. For example, Robert Jay Lifton (1986) interviewed twenty-eight Nazi doctors who aided in the murder of millions of concentration-camp victims in World War II, and he found that these men psychologically covered their tracks through denial, rationalization, "psychic numbing," and other unconscious forms of self-deception.

If he were alive, Freud would have liked Lifton's analysis of the Nazi doctors. Freud himself had to escape Vienna when the Nazis stormed his hometown. He died in 1939, in London, at the age of eighty-three. Sixteen years later, a statue was unveiled in the courtyard of the University of Vienna, where he used to walk as a student. The inscription on the statue reads: "Sigmund Freud: who divined the famed riddle and was a man most mighty."

"And then I say to myself, 'If I really wanted to talk to her, why do I keep forgetting to dial 1 first?'"

Freud often interpreted forgetting as an unconscious but disguised form of wish fulfillment.

The Cognitive Social Learning Approach

What basic principles of learning laid the foundation for an alternative approach to personality? What is locus of control, and how do internals and externals differ? What is reciprocal determinism?

In contrast to psychoanalysis, **cognitive social learning theory** is an approach that views personality as the product of a continuous interaction between persons and their environments. This theory has its roots in the behavioral principles of classical and operant conditioning, social learning theory, and cognitive psychology. Let's trace the evolution of this important second approach.

cognitive social learning theory An approach to personality that focuses on social learning (modeling), acquired cognitive factors (expectancies, values), and the person-situation interaction.

Principles of Learning and Behavior

As psychoanalysis was emerging in Europe, a second movement was being conceived in animal laboratories in the United States and Russia. At the time, animal researchers were discovering some very powerful principles of learning and were spreading the new word of behaviorism—a scientific approach to psychology that focuses on environmental determinants of observable behavior. To the hard-core behaviorist, personality was a nonscientific figment of the Freudian imagination. After all, behaviorists had refused to muddy the scientific study of behavior by speculating about inner states of "mind." As we saw earlier in this book, the first spokesperson for this countermovement was John Watson, whose message was loud and clear:

> Give me a dozen healthy infants, well-formed, and my own specified world to bring them up in, and I'll guarantee to take any one at random and train him to become any type of specialist I might select—doctor, lawyer, artist, merchant-chief and, yes, even beggarman and thief, regardless of his talents, penchants, tendencies, abilities, vocations, and race of his ancestors (1925, p. 104).

At the same time that Freud was writing his classic book on dreams, animal researchers were discovering five simple but very powerful principles of learning: classical conditioning, operant conditioning, stimulus generalization, discrimination, and extinction (these are more fully described in Chapter 5).

The first, classical conditioning, was based on Ivan Pavlov's finding that the dogs in his laboratory would start to salivate before they were fed, in anticipation of the meal they were about to eat. By repeatedly sounding a buzzer before the presentation of food, Pavlov found that eventually the dogs would salivate as soon as the buzzer was sounded. Thus, the animals were trained to react to a neutral stimulus that was associated with food, which is an unconditioned stimulus that naturally elicits the reaction. The second major principle was operant conditioning, first shown by Edward Thorndike's discovery that organisms repeat behaviors that are rewarded. Working with cats and, later, with humans, Thorndike found that whatever solution succeeded for a subject on one puzzle was later tried on other puzzles as well. A few years later, B. F. Skinner tested the effects of reinforcement schedules on behavior by training rats to press bars and pigeons to peck at keys for food.

Both classical and operant conditioning researchers were making parallel discoveries not yet relevant to the study of personality. The first is stimulus generalization, the principle that once a response is learned in one situation, it may also be evoked in other, similar situations—as when Pavlov's dogs learned to salivate to tones that were similar but not identical to the conditioned stimulus. The second, opposite principle is discrimination: the learned tendency to distinguish between a conditioned stimulus and other stimuli—as when a child learns that having tantrums works on parents but not on teachers and friends. The third principle is extinction, the tendency for a conditioned response to diminish if not reinforced. Pavlov's dogs eventually stopped salivating to the buzzer if it was no longer followed by meat, and Skinner's animals stopped pressing bars when food pellets were no longer forthcoming.

These principles of learning and behavior were momentous discoveries in psychology, the new science of behavior. But what did drooling dogs, puzzled cats, and key-pecking pigeons have to do with personality? In a crude first attempt to answer this question, John Watson and his assistant Rosalie Rayner (1920) conducted a well-known but ethically questionable demonstration. As you may recall from Chapter 5, Watson and Rayner brought an eleven-month-old boy named Albert into contact with a harmless white rat, then repeatedly made a loud sound every time the boy reached for the animal. Soon poor Albert was terrified not only of the rat but also of rabbits, dogs, and a white furry coat. What was the point? Poking fun at

Freud and his followers, Watson declared that some day a psychoanalyst will meet a man named Albert with a fur-coat phobia, analyze his dreams, and conclude that his fear is related to a scolding he received from his white-haired mother. Such are the pitfalls of a nonscientific approach to personality, said Watson.

Picking up where Watson left off, B. F. Skinner emerged as behaviorism's most forceful and dedicated proponent. He coined the term "operant conditioning," studied different schedules of reinforcement, and wrote about how these principles could be used to socialize children, increase worker productivity, extinguish behavioral disorders, and build a better society. As far as Skinner was concerned, personality is nothing more than a collection of behavior patterns acquired, maintained, and—if necessary—modified by one's unique history of reinforcement.

Social-Learning Theory

Although Skinner offered a change of pace from psychoanalysis, many psychologists found his pointed focus on behavior too narrow and rejected his unwillingness to explore thoughts, feelings, motivations, and the richness and texture of the human personality. At the very least, it seemed that behaviorism had to be extended in two ways. Enter social-learning theory, an approach that examines the social and cognitive factors involved in learning and the development of personality. Leading the way were Albert Bandura, Julian Rotter, and Walter Mischel.

The first problem was to account for the fact that people often acquire new behavior patterns without having had personal experience with reward and punishment. According to Bandura (1977), people learn by observing and imitating others, a process called **modeling.** Children, for example, absorb what their parents say and how they act, pay close attention to TV characters and sports heroes, and emulate peers whom they admire. Research shows that modeling is a multistep process: We look, we learn, and we store in memory (learning). Then, if we are capable and motivated and if the time is right, we imitate (performance). Bandura thus reminded us that learning often takes place in a social context and that people can learn to become aggressive, helpful, fearful, moral, and so on by observing others (see Chapter 5).

The second important extension of behaviorism was to examine how our thoughts can influence the effects of reinforcement on behavior. Skinner had insisted that behavior is determined by actual reinforcement contingencies, but Julian Rotter (1954) argued that what really matters is how we perceive, interpret, and value the rewards in our lives. According to Rotter, human behavior in any given situation is determined by two broad factors: (1) our subjective *expectancy* that a specific act will be reinforced, and (2) the *value* of that reinforcement to us. If you expect that reading the rest of this textbook will help you learn psychology and earn a high grade for the course—and if these strike you as desirable outcomes—you'll probably read on. If you don't expect to learn from this book or if you don't really care, this may be the last paragraph you read. As far as personality is concerned, Rotter and his colleagues (1972) found that individuals differ both in the amount of control they expect to have over outcomes in their lives and in the kinds of outcomes they value.

Expanding on Rotter's model, Walter Mischel (1973, 1990) proposed a "cognitive" social-learning theory. According to Mischel, it is important to consider five "person variables" to understand how individuals interact with their environment. These person variables are (1) *competencies*—our mental and physical abilities, social skills, and creative talents, all of which influence what we strive for and what

modeling The social-learning process by which behavior is observed and imitated.

we can do; (2) *encoding strategies*—how we process information about other people and situations (for example, whether we tend to evaluate others in terms of their intelligence, friendliness, power, or physical appearance); (3) *expectancies*—our beliefs about the causes of success and failure and about other possible consequences of our actions (there are two types of expectancies: whether we can perform a particular behavior, and whether it will be reinforced); (4) *subjective values*—the kinds of outcomes we find more or less reinforcing (for example, whether we strive for love, security, excitement, respect, or dominance); and (5) *self-regulatory systems*—our ability to set goals, monitor and evaluate our progress, delay our short-term needs for gratification, and plan for the future. Self-regulation is an important and adaptive person variable. For example, Mischel and his colleagues (1989) have found that preschoolers who show they can defer their gratification in the laboratory—say, by waiting for a larger but delayed reward—grow up to become more competent, attentive, deliberate, and able to cope with real frustrations later in life.

Locus of Control

According to cognitive social learning theory, behavior is influenced not by actual reinforcements, as Skinner had maintained, but by our perceptions of control. Think about it. Is there a connection between how hard you study and the grades you receive, or does grading seem arbitrary? Does getting ahead require hard work and persistence, or is it simply a matter of being in the right place at the right time? Can individuals influence government policies, or are we at the mercy of powerful leaders? And what about the quality of your health, friendships, and financial well-being—are you in control?

According to Rotter (1966), individuals differ in their **locus of control**, defined as a generalized expectancy for the control of reinforcement. People who have an *internal* locus of control believe they are in charge of their own destiny. Those who have an *external* locus of control feel they are at the mercy of luck, fate, and powerful others. To assess these contrasting orientations, Rotter constructed a questionnaire known as the I-E Scale (see Table 15.1). Immediately, psychologists grasped the implications of having an internal or external locus of control. Over the years, more

locus of control A term referring to the expectancy that one's reinforcements are generally controlled by internal or external factors.

Table 15.1 Are You an Internal or an External?

1. a. No matter how hard you try, some people just don't like you.
   b. People who can't get others to like them don't understand how to get along with others.
2. a. One of the major reasons we have wars is because people don't take enough interest in politics.
   b. There will always be wars, no matter how hard people try to prevent them.
3. a. Sometimes I can't understand how teachers arrive at the grades they give.
   b. There is a direct connection between how hard I study and the grades I get.
4. a. The average citizen can have an influence in government decisions.
   b. This world is run by a few people in power, and there is not much the little guy can do about it.
5. a. Becoming a success is a matter of hard work; luck has little or nothing to do with it.
   b. Getting a good job depends mainly on being in the right place at the right time.
6. a. Most people don't realize the extent to which their lives are controlled by accidental happenings.
   b. There really is no such thing as "luck."

Source: J. B. Rotter (1966). Generalized expectancies for internal versus external control of reinforcement. *Psychological Monographs*, 80 (Whole No. 609).

than 2,000 studies using the I-E scale were published (Hunt, 1993). Studying people of different ages, cultures, and ethnic backgrounds, researchers found that internals, compared to externals, are more inquisitive, active, optimistic, hard-working, and persistent. They are also more likely to take preventive health measures, play an active role in social and political affairs, get high grades in school, and cope actively with stressful life events (Findley & Cooper, 1983; Lefcourt, 1982; Strickland, 1989; Rotter, 1990).

To see if you are an internal or an external, look at the six items from the I-E Scale in Table 15.1. For each item, circle the letter (a or b) of the statement you agree with more. Give yourself one point for each of the following answers: 1 (a), 2(b), 3(a), 4 (b), 5 (b), 6 (a). Next, add up your total number of points (from 0 to 6). The higher your score is, the more *external* is your generalized expectancy for control.

On one natural leg, this man competes in the long jump at the Paralympic Games. Such determination and persistence are hallmarks of an internal locus of control.

Although people differ in their locus of control, there are two important qualifications. The first is that it is entirely possible to have an internal orientation in some life situations but not in others. Look again at Table 15.1, and you'll see that the I-E Scale asks about control expectancies for a wide range of domains—including health, academics, friendships, career pursuits, and remote political and social events. The second is that individuals also differ in the extent to which they *want* control. Some of us care more deeply than others about making our own decisions or having an influence over others. People with a strong desire for control—regardless of whether they are internal or external in their expectancies—are more likely to become stressed and upset in situations that make them feel helpless (Burger, 1991).

Is an expectation for control adaptive? At first glance, it seems that an internal orientation is the key to health, success, and emotional well-being—and there is a great deal of research to support this point (Marshall, 1991). In a study of nursing-home patients, for example, 93 percent of those who by random assignment were given more control over minor daily affairs became happier, more active, and more alert when tested eighteen months later (Rodin, 1986). "No doubt about it," I tell my kids, "you need to believe in yourselves, take charge of your lives, open doors, and make things happen. As they say, the buck stops here" (point to yourself). But wait. Is an internal orientation *always* adaptive, or are there times when it's better to see life's reinforcements as beyond our command?

This is a tough question because there are two exceptions to the rule that it's better to be internal than external. First, an internal orientation can cause problems when we don't carefully distinguish between truly controllable and uncontrollable events. For example, people with an inflated sense of control are at risk to lose money gambling on games of pure chance (Langer, 1975). And victims of rape and other crimes often suffer greater distress when they blame themselves for having been careless or done something to provoke their attack (Janoff-Bulman, 1989; Frazier & Schauben, 1994). Second, an internal orientation can cause problems if it leads us to develop an overcontrolling, stress-inducing style of behavior—whether that means always having the last word in an argument, driving from the back seat of a car, or planning every detail of a leisurely vacation. Sometimes it is better to just let go (Wright et al., 1990). On this point, Japanese psychologist Hiroshi Azuma (1984) offers these Japanese proverbs: "Willow trees do not get broken by piled-up snow" and "The true tolerance is to tolerate the intolerable."

An internal orientation is adaptive—except in situations that are not truly controllable.

Self-Efficacy As noted, locus of control refers to the expectation that our behaviors can produce satisfying outcomes. But people also differ in the extent to which they think they can perform these reinforced behaviors in the first place. These concepts seem related, but in fact they refer to different beliefs, both of which are

"Amazing, three failed marriages, scores of disastrous relationships, many financial reversals, and countless physical ailments, but through it all I've always had good luck parking."

necessary for us to feel that we control the outcomes in our lives (Skinner, 1996). According to Bandura (1989), the latter expectations are based on feelings of competence, or **self-efficacy**. Although some people are generally more confident than others, Bandura believes that self-efficacy is a state of mind that varies from one specific task and situation to another. In other words, you may have a high self-efficacy about meeting new people but not about raising your grades. Or you may have a high self-efficacy about solving a math problem but not about writing a paper.

Bandura (1989) believes that with life full of "impediments, adversities, setbacks, frustrations, and inequities," a personal sense of self-efficacy is essential for success. How do we gain a belief in our own efficacy? Bandura cites four sources: (1) our own past experiences at successfully overcoming obstacles and failures; (2) our observations of similar others who overcome obstacles to succeed; (3) words of encouragement from family, friends, and others in our lives who urge us forward; and (4) feelings of relaxation and calm rather than tension during performance.

It's common for people to have feelings of self-efficacy in some life domains but not in others.

There are now numerous studies of self-efficacy, and this research indicates that the more of it you have at a particular task, the more likely you are to take on an activity, try hard, persist in the face of failure, and succeed. The implications for health are particularly striking. For example, people with a high self-efficacy on health-related matters are more likely, if they want, to stop smoking, abstain from alcohol, stay physically fit, and tolerate the pain of arthritis, migraine headaches, and childbirth (Maddux, 1991). People who have a high level of self-efficacy about their ability to cope with stress also exhibit an enhanced functioning of the immune system (Wiedenfeld et al., 1990).

Perspectives on Cognitive Social-learning Theory

Cognitive social-learning theorists believe that personality is rooted in the basic principles of learning. In contrast to psychoanalysis, this approach rests on the assumption that human behavior is derived more from external factors than by instincts and that personality is shaped by reinforcement, observation, and the development of learned abilities, expectancies, values, and information-processing strategies.

Although all learning-based theories of personality share this assumption, the more recent approach has come a long way from that taken by the hard-core behaviorists. In his facetious call for a dozen healthy infants, Watson claimed that he could mold people like clay through the use of reward and punishment. Years later, Skinner similarly argued that human behavior is shaped by external forces, by reinforcement contingencies beyond our awareness and control. Yet cognitive social-learning theorists maintain that personality emerges from an ongoing mutual interaction among persons, their actions, and their environments, a concept Bandura (1986) calls **reciprocal determinism.** The point is that environmental forces may help shape our personalities, but we can also choose and alter the situations we encounter and can interpret these situations in light of our own points of view. In Bandura's words, "Your behavior, internal personal factors, and environmental influences all operate interactively as determinants of each other" (p. 23). This concept is illustrated in Figure 15.5.

self-efficacy The belief that one is capable of performing the behaviors required to produce a desired outcome.

reciprocal determinism The view that personality emerges from a mutual interaction of individuals, their actions, and their environments.

To measure personality, cognitive social-learning theorists use fairly direct forms of assessment. One method is behavioral observation, in which subjects are observed either in real-life settings or in the laboratory. Another involves asking subjects to report on their own expectancies, values, and past behaviors using standardized interviews or questionnaires like the I-E Scale. Whatever the specific technique may be, information about an individual is measured in ways that are direct and to the point. No inkblots, no fuzzy pictures. To those in hot pursuit of the unconscious, the cognitive social-learning approach is doomed to shed light on only the tip of the iceberg. To others, this approach permits the study of personality in a more straightforward manner.

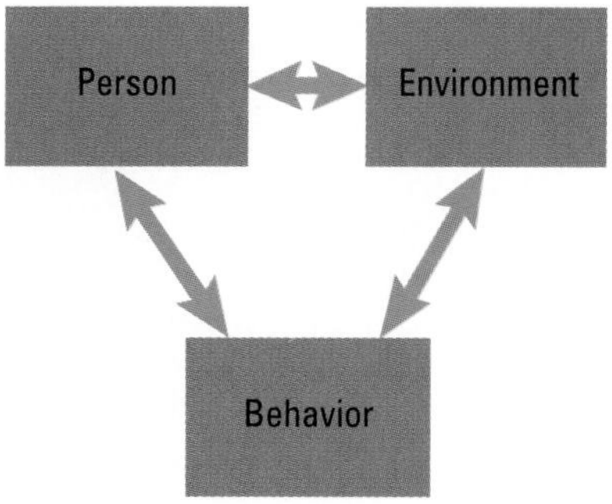

Figure 15.5 Reciprocal determinism

The Humanistic Approach

What are the tenets of a humanistic approach to personality? What clinical observations inspired Carl Rogers to theorize about the self? What are self-discrepancies, and what are their effects on our emotional well-being? What does it mean to be self-actualized—and what does it feel like?

Faced with a choice between psychoanalysis and behaviorism, many personality psychologists in the 1940s and 1950s had an uneasy feeling that something was missing, something vital about human nature. Freud had drawn attention to the darker forces of the unconscious, and Skinner was interested only in the effects of reinforcement on observable behavior. But what about the conscious mind, free will, subjective experiences, and the capacity for self-reflection? If we want to know about someone, can't we just ask? Are people really that mechanical? And isn't there a brighter side to human nature? In short, where's the *person* as we know it in personality? To fill the void, a "third force" was born—the **humanistic theory** of personality. Inspired by Carl Rogers and Abraham Maslow, a group of psychologists founded the Association of Humanistic Psychology and adopted four basic principles: (1) The experiencing person is of primary interest; (2) human choice, creativity, and self-actualization are the preferred topics of investigation; (3) meaningfulness must precede objectivity in the selection of research problems; and (4) ultimate value is placed on the dignity of the person.

Carl Rogers

Carl Rogers was the first self-proclaimed humanistic theorist. Born into a religious family in a Midwest farming town, Rogers attended a theological seminary for two years before deciding to become a clinical psychologist. He then received his degree in 1931, the same year that B. F. Skinner got his. Like Freud, Rogers spent his early years as a therapist treating emotionally troubled "clients." Yet unlike Freud, who was impressed by his patients' efforts to resist their own cures, Rogers was struck by how often his clients reflected on who they were ("I'd like to be more independent, but that just isn't me," "I just haven't been myself lately") and by their natural will to get better and reach their full potential. True, Rogers saw signs of temporary resistance and other ego defense mechanisms. But he was much more impressed by the self-concept—and by the underlying will to improve. If therapists provide warmth, a gentle, guiding hand, and a climate of uncritical acceptance, he said, clients will ultimately solve their own problems and find the road to health,

humanistic theory An approach to personality that focuses on the self, subjective experience, and the capacity for fulfillment.

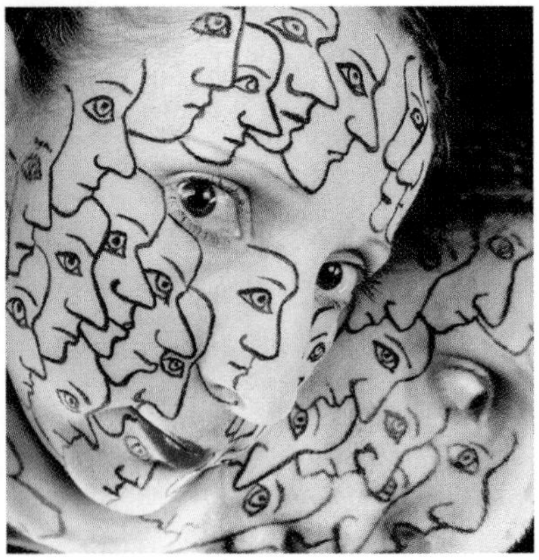

Manyness, *painted by Rimma Gerlovina and Valeriy Gerlovin, portrays the Rogerian notion that each person's sense of self is intimately linked to his or her interactions with significant others. (© Rimma Gerlovina and Valeriy Gerlovin,* Manyness, *1990, Ektacolor print, 39¼ × 39¼ inches.)*

happiness, and fulfillment. As far as Rogers was concerned, there is in each of us an inner wisdom.

Rogers's Theory The seeds of a new and different approach to personality were planted in fertile ground. From a humanist's standpoint, Rogers went on to develop client-centered therapy (1951) and a theory of personality, as described in his book *On Becoming a Person* (1961). According to Rogers, all living organisms are innately endowed with an actualizing tendency, a forward drive not only to survive but also to grow and reach their full genetic capacity. For thinking and feeling humans, there is also a natural need for self-actualization—a drive to behave in ways that are consistent with one's conscious identity, or self-concept. So far, so good. But problems arise because we are social animals, born helpless and dependent on others for approval, support, and love. In other words, there also develops within us a competing need, a need for positive regard. And therein lies the potential for conflict in the development of personality. Rogers, who was born and raised on a farm, saw many parallels among humans, plants, and other forms of life. He summarized his portrayal of the human drive for actualization in the following passage:

> During a vacation weekend some months ago I was standing on a headland overlooking one of the rugged coves which dot the coastline of Northern California. Several large rock outcroppings were at the mouth of the cove, and these received the full force of the great Pacific combers which, beating upon them, broke into mountains of spray before surging into the cliff-lined shore. As I watched the waves breaking over these large rocks in the distance, I noticed with surprise what appeared to be tiny palm trees on the rocks, no more than two or three feet high, taking the pounding of the breakers. Through my binoculars, I saw that these were some type of seaweed, with a slender "trunk" topped off with a head of leaves. As one examined a specimen in the interval between the waves it seemed clear that this fragile, erect, top-heavy plant would be utterly crushed and broken by the next breaker. When the wave crunched down upon it, the trunk bent almost flat, the leaves were whipped into a straight line by the torrent of the water, yet the moment the wave had passed, here was the plant again, erect, tough, resilient. It seemed incredible that it was able to take this incessant pounding hour after hour, day after night, week after week, perhaps for all I know, year after year, and all the time nourishing itself, extending its domain, reproducing itself; in short, maintaining and enhancing itself in this process which, in our shorthand, we call growth. Here in this palm-like seaweed was the tenacity of life, the forward thrust of life, the ability to push into an incredibly hostile environment and not only hold its own, but to adapt, develop, become itself. (1974, pp. 1–2)

Driven as humans are by the need for self-actualization *and* the need for positive regard, one of two general outcomes is possible. If you are fortunate enough to receive **unconditional positive regard** from parents and significant others—that is, if the important people in your life are loving and respectful despite your failures and setbacks, no ifs, ands, or buts—then life is rosy. Your need for positive regard is met, and you've got the green light to freely and openly pursue the all-important need for self-actualization. However, if you are subject to **conditional positive regard**—that is, if your parents, spouse, and close friends withdraw their love when your actions and life choices don't meet with their approval—then you get hung up trying to strike a balance between your true self and the kind of person others want you to

unconditional positive regard A situation in which the acceptance and love one receives from significant others is unqualified.

conditional positive regard A situation in which the acceptance and love one receives from significant others is contingent upon one's behavior.

become. The result is frustration, anxiety, and feelings of incongruence or "discrepancy" within the self. This theory is illustrated in Figure 15.6.

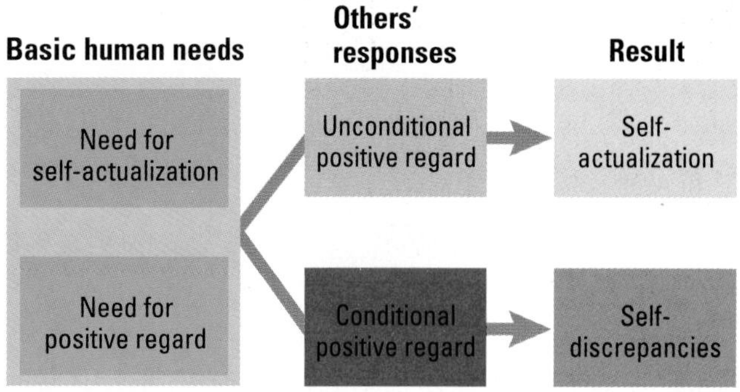

Figure 15.6 The personality theory of Carl Rogers According to Rogers, the needs for self-actualization and positive regard present a potential for conflict. Unconditional positive regard permits self-actualization, but conditional positive regard can result in self-discrepancies.

The Self-Concept From the start, Rogers sought empirical verification for his newly formulated theory. To evaluate the importance of the self-concept, he taped, transcribed, and analyzed many of his therapy sessions and found that, as treatment progressed, clients made more and more positive statements about themselves. Whatever self-discrepancies there were tended to diminish. More recent research confirms that people have clear, often complex beliefs about the self. According to Hazel Markus (1977), these beliefs are made up of a collection of **self-schemas**—specific beliefs about the self that influence how we interpret self-relevant information. It also appears that we think about—and are guided by—images of what we might become, would like to become, and are afraid of becoming in the future (Markus & Nurius, 1986; Ruvolo & Markus, 1992). Today, psychologists regard the self-concept as so central to personality that they have developed many different ways to measure it in young children, adolescents, and adults (Byrne, 1996).

Picking up where Rogers left off, E. Tory Higgins (1989) has confirmed the hypothesis that self-discrepancies breed emotional turmoil. According to his **self-discrepancy theory**, our self-esteem is defined by the match between how we see ourselves and how we want to see ourselves. To demonstrate, try the following exercise. On a blank sheet of paper, write down ten traits that describe the kind of person you think you *actually* are (smart? easygoing? sexy? excitable?). Next list ten traits that describe the kind of person you think you *ought* to be, characteristics that would enable you to meet your sense of duty, obligation, and responsibility. Then make a list of traits that describe an *ideal* of what you would like to be, an ideal that embodies your hopes, wishes, and dreams. If you follow these instructions, you should have three lists—your actual self, ought self, and ideal self.

Research shows that these trait lists can be used to predict your emotional well-being. The first list is your self-concept. The others represent your personal standards, or *self-guides*. To the extent that you fall short of meeting these standards, you will have a lowered self-esteem, negative emotions, and in extreme cases a psychological disorder. The specific consequence depends on which of the self-guides you don't achieve. If there's a discrepancy between your actual and ought selves, you'll feel guilty, ashamed, and resentful. You might even suffer from excessive fears and anxieties. If the discrepancy is between your actual and ideal selves, you'll feel disappointed, frustrated, sad, and unfulfilled. In extreme cases, you might become depressed. Based on a body of supportive research, these emotional and mental-health effects of self-discrepancies are summarized in Figure 15.7 (Scott & O'Hara, 1993; Strauman, 1989).

Carl Rogers believed that we form a self-concept from repeated interactions with the significant others in our lives. But are our self-discrepancies stable aspects of personality? Recently, Timothy Strauman (1996) examined this question. He tested college students twice, three years apart. In both sessions, he asked them to write down the kind of person they are, the kind of person they would like to be, and the kind of person they ought to be. The students exhibited some changes in terms of

self-schemas Specific beliefs about the self that influence how we interpret self-relevant information.

self-discrepancy theory The notion that discrepancies between one's self-concept and "ideal" and "ought" selves have negative emotional consequences.

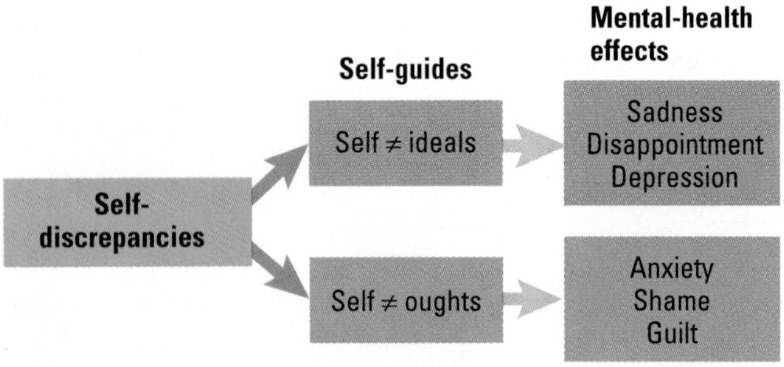

Figure 15.7 Self-discrepancy theory According to Higgins (1989), the emotional and mental-health consequences of self-discrepancy differ according to whether we fall short of our ideal or ought selves.

how they described themselves. But the amount of their self-discrepancies—between the actual self on the one hand and their ideal and ought selves on the other—stayed very much the same.

Abraham Maslow

Abraham Maslow was the second influential spokesperson for the humanistic approach to personality. Oddly enough, Maslow started out as a behaviorist conducting learning experiments with monkeys. Then came the birth of his first child. As most parents would agree, this was an eye-opening experience. Said Maslow, "I was stunned by the mystery and by the sense of not really being in control. I felt small and weak and feeble before all this. I'd say anyone who had a baby couldn't be a behaviorist." Over the years, Maslow (1954, 1968) went on to formulate a motivational theory of personality, focusing on how people strive to fulfill their utmost potential.

Maslow's Theory Have you ever met someone who seems to have it all—great looks, money, successful career, nice home, loving spouse, and wonderful children—and yet seems unsatisfied, searching for more? If so, then you'll appreciate the essence of Maslow's theory. As we saw in Chapter 8, Maslow (1954) theorized that all people are motivated to fulfill a hierarchy of needs, from the physiological needs basic to survival to the needs for safety and security, the needs for belongingness and love, and esteem-related needs for achievement, status, and recognition. In short, said Maslow, each of us strives in our own way to be biologically content, safe, loved, and respected. Only when these needs are met are we ready, willing, and able to strive for **self-actualization**—the distinctly human need to become everything one is capable of becoming.

Maslow's primary interest was in self-actualization, which he considered the ultimate state. Thus, he went out of his way to study happy, healthy, and productive individuals who embody the best that human nature has to offer. He interviewed a select group of acquaintances, and he used biographies to examine the lives of great historical figures such as Ludwig van Beethoven, Abraham Lincoln, Albert Einstein, and Eleanor Roosevelt. What did these self-actualized people have in common? Maslow (1968) saw self-actualization as a rare state of being in which a person is open to new experiences, spontaneous, playful, loving, realistic, accepting of others, creative, energetic, independent rather than conforming, and problem-focused rather than self-centered. If this set of traits sounds almost too good to be true, you're right. Maslow estimated that fewer than 1 percent of the world's adults are truly self-actualized. The rest of us are too busy trying to overcome obstacles in order to satisfy lower, more basic needs.

"No, I like my job. I like my apartment. I like my friends. I like our relationship. I'm just not sure I like what it all adds up to."

As Maslow had said, people who have all their basic needs fulfilled yearn for more—self-actualization.

self-actualization In humanistic personality theories, the need to fulfill one's unique potential.

The State of Self-Actualization Are you self-actualized? Based on Maslow's theory, Everett Shostrom (1965) developed the Personal Orientation Inventory, a

Table 15.2 Are You Self-Actualized?

1. I live in terms of my wants, likes, dislikes, and values.
2. I believe that man is essentially good and can be trusted.
3. I don't feel guilty when I'm selfish.
4. I believe it is important to accept others as they are.
5 I am not afraid of making mistakes.
6. I believe in saying what I feel in dealing with others.
7. I often make decisions spontaneously.
8. I welcome criticism as an opportunity for growth.
9. I enjoy detachment and privacy.
10. For me, work and play are the same.

Source: E. Shostrom (1965). An inventory for the measurement of self-actualization. *Educational and psychological measurement,* 24, 207–218

Self-actualization is a state of mind that we achieve on a temporary basis—during peak experiences.

lengthy questionnaire designed to assess various aspects of self-actualization—for example, the capacity for intimate contact, spontaneity, and self-acceptance (see Table 15.2). This scale was endorsed by Maslow and used in clinical settings. Research shows that people with high scores are psychologically healthier than those who receive low scores (Campbell et al., 1989; Knapp, 1976). A sample of ten statements from the Personal Orientation Inventory is given in Table 15.2. How many of the values thought to be associated with self-actualization do you possess?

If you're wondering what it feels like to be self-actualized, at least temporarily, try this: "Think about the most wonderful experiences of your life; happiest moments, ecstatic moments, moments of rapture, perhaps from being in love, or from listening to music or suddenly 'being hit' by a book or a painting, or from some great creative moment" (Maslow, 1968, p. 71). Maslow claimed that self-actualized individuals have more moments like these than other people do. Still, each of us enjoys an occasional **peak experience**, defined as a fleeting but intense moment of self-actualization in which we feel happy, absorbed, and capable of extraordinary performance. Music, sexual love, religion, nature, running, sports, creative pursuits, childbirth, and reminiscing are the most common situations people cite when asked about their peak experiences (Privette, 1983).

Based on Maslow's writings, Mihaly Csikszentmihalyi (1990) has studied a state of mind he calls flow, the "optimal experience." Under what conditions, Csikszentmihalyi asks, do we tend to become so fully immersed in an activity that we lose all track of time and all awareness of the self, forget our worries, and concentrate our energy on what we're doing, much to our benefit and enjoyment? I sometimes have this exquisite experience when I write, play baseball, or listen to music. Csikszentmihalyi interviewed athletes, dancers, artists, rock climbers, factory workers, chess masters, surgeons, sailors, elderly Korean women, Japanese motorcyclists, Navajo shepherds, and farmers in the Italian Alps, and he found that people from all parts of the world and from all walks of life describe a similar kind of experience—when what they're doing seems effortless and perfect, when they're so completely tuned in that nothing else seems to matter.

What precipitates flow? From his research, Csikszentmihalyi theorizes that the state arises when people engage in activities at which they are skilled—and at levels that are challenging in relation to their ability. As depicted in Figure 15.8, tasks that

peak experience A fleeting but intense moment of self-actualization in which people feel happy, absorbed, and extraordinarily capable.

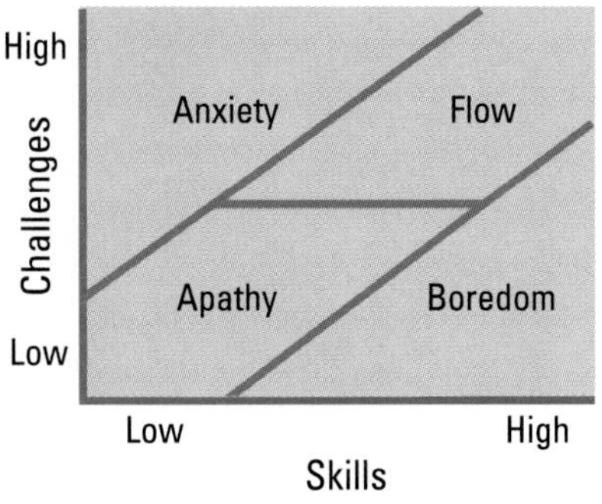

Figure 15.8 Flow, the optimal experience A state of "flow" arises when we engage in activities that we are skilled at and at levels that are challenging but not too difficult (Csikszentmihalyi, 1990).

are too easy result in boredom, while those that are too difficult cause anxiety. Also important is the capacity of these activities to present clear goals and immediate feedback. In some studies, for example, subjects carried portable beepers for a period of time and stopped to record on paper what they were doing, thinking, and feeling whenever the beeper went off. Supporting the flow model, subjects reported feeling more excited, more motivated, and more engaged at those times when they were involved in high-skill, high-challenge activities (Csikszentmihalyi & Csikszentmihalyi, 1988; Moneta & Csikszentmihalyi, 1996).

Other researchers have raised questions about the conditions that give rise to flow. In all sports, it seems, athletes who are hot and playing at the top of their game often talk about being "in the zone." In studies of amateur tennis players, basketball players, and golfers, Gary Stein and others (1995) found that although this state occurs in all sports ("My attention was focused entirely on what I was doing," "I felt in control of my game," "My performance felt effortless"), the conditions that produce it vary—depending on the competitive nature of the activity and the importance of winning.

Perspectives on the Humanistic Approach

When Carl Rogers (1974) looked back on his career and on his impact on psychology, counseling, and education, he concluded that "I expressed an idea whose time had come." The idea he referred to was that people are inherently good, that conscious mental experience is important, and that the self-concept lies at the heart of personality.

Humanistic psychologists have received praise for drawing our attention to this idea, for providing an alternative perspective on personality, and for stimulating interest among researchers in previously neglected topics related to the self. At the same time, they have been severely criticized for naively taking people's self-report statements at face value and for painting too rosy a picture of human nature while ignoring our demonstrated capacity for evil. Focused on the quest for self-actualization, humanistic psychologists have also been accused of inadvertently promoting the self-indulgent, "be true to yourself" approach to life that fosters the so-called me generation. Sure the self is important, say the critics, but where does the rest of the world fit in?

The Trait Approach

What are the main goals in a trait approach to personality? What are the "Big Five"? How are personality tests like the MMPI constructed, and what are their strengths and weaknesses? What evidence is there for the role of genetic factors in personality? What's an introvert, what's an extravert, and in what fundamental ways do they differ?

In 1919, a twenty-two-year-old psychology student from Indiana wrote a letter to Sigmund Freud to say he'd be traveling in Europe and would like to meet. Freud was the master, known worldwide, and the student wanted to feel his presence and maybe talk for a while. A meeting was arranged, so the student took a train to

Vienna, arrived on schedule, and entered the master's inner office. But Freud just sat there in silence, staring, waiting for his young, wide-eyed admirer to state his mission. Desperate to break the awkward stalemate, the student told about an incident he witnessed on the train that day involving a young boy who appeared to have a "dirt phobia." The boy complained that the seats were soiled and pleaded with his mother to keep dirty passengers from sitting nearby. The mother, it turned out, was a dominant, "well-starched" woman. Isn't that an interesting case? When the student finished telling his story, Freud paused, then leaned over and said in a soft voice, "And was that little boy you?"

Freud's young admirer was terribly embarrassed. Wishing he could disappear, he nervously changed the subject, babbled a bit, excused himself, and left. How could Freud have been so wrong? Was he so accustomed to analyzing the hidden motives of his anxious patients that he couldn't appreciate a man's simple curiosity? It turns out that the student was Gordon Allport, who went on to become one of the most important personality psychologists of all time. In an autobiography published the year he died, Allport (1967) said that this experience convinced him that before personality theorists search for deep, analytical explanations, they should start by trying to *describe* and *measure* the basic units of personality. In other words, first things first. This rule now guides what is known as the trait approach.

The Building Blocks of Personality

Working from the ground up, Allport and his colleague Henry Odbert (1936) combed through an unabridged English dictionary and came up with a list of 18,000 words that could be used to describe people. By eliminating synonyms, obscure words, and words referring to temporary states, they brought the list down to 4,500, then grouped words that were similar into about 200 clusters of related traits. For Allport, these **traits** were the building blocks of personality (though he was quick to point out that not all traits are relevant to all people, nor do they all have an influence on behavior).

To reduce Allport's list to a more manageable size and to construct a science of personality, Raymond Cattell (1965) used factor analysis, a statistical technique designed to identify clusters of items that correlate with one another. You may recall from Chapter 12 that this technique was used to distinguish among different aspects of intelligence. Cattell—who was a chemistry major in college—wanted to uncover the basic units of personality, much like chemistry's periodic table of elements. Are individuals who are passive also thoughtful, calm, and even-tempered? Do those who describe themselves as sociable also say they're easygoing, lively, and talkative? How many trait clusters are needed to fully describe personality? To answer these questions, Cattell collected people's ratings of themselves and others on various attributes, crunched the numbers through factor analysis, and found that personality consists of sixteen distinct units, which he called *source traits*. What distinguishes one individual from another, said Cattell, is that each of us has a unique combination of traits—high levels of some, and low levels of others—a pattern that is summarized by a personality "profile." To derive this profile, Cattell devised the Sixteen Personality Factors Questionnaire (16 PF), a 187-item scale that yields sixteen separate scores, one for each factor.

As factor analysis became more sophisticated, researchers began to notice that Cattell's model (and other existing models as well) could be simplified even further—and that five major factors often seemed to emerge from self-ratings, ratings of

trait A relatively stable predisposition to behave in a certain way.

others, and an assortment of personality questionnaires. This **five-factor model** has emerged consistently in studies of children, college students, and older adults; in men and women; in different languages; and in testing conducted in the United States, Canada, Finland, Germany, Japan, Poland, the Philippines, China, and other countries. As a result, these factors have been called the Big Five (Goldberg, 1993; Digman, 1990; McCrae & Costa, 1997; Paunonen et al., 1992; Wiggins, 1996).

Not everyone agrees with the five-factor model. Cattell still believes that five factors are too few. Hans Eysenck, whom we will meet shortly, thinks five is too many. Others see five as the right number but disagree about how the factors should be described. For the most part, however, evidence in support of the five-factor model is mounting. As represented in Table 15.3, most researchers are now convinced that the best way to describe personality and individual differences is to find where people stand on the following traits: (1) neuroticism (a proneness to anxiety and negative affect); (2) extraversion (a desire for social interaction, stimulation, and activity); (3) openness (a receptiveness to new experiences and ideas); (4) agreeableness (a selfless concern for others); and (5) conscientiousness (a tendency to be reliable, disciplined, and ambitious).

New tests have been developed to measure these five broad traits (Costa & McCrae, 1992)—and to use the scores to make predictions about behavior. In one study, for example, Winfred Arthur, Jr., and William Graziano (1996) tested large numbers of college students and recruits from a temporary-employment agency and found that subjects who scored low rather than high on the conscientiousness trait were more likely to have received a moving violation and more likely to have been involved in an automobile accident. As we'll see on pages 596–597, the Big Five have also been used to predict performance in the workplace.

Table 15.3 The "Big Five" Personality Factors

FACTOR	DESCRIPTION OF TRAITS
Neuroticism	Anxious vs. relaxed Insecure vs. secure Emotional vs. calm Self-pitying vs. content
Extraversion	Sociable vs. withdrawn Fun-loving vs. sober Friendly vs. aloof Adventurous vs. cautious
Openness	Original vs. conventional Imaginative vs. down-to-earth Broad interests vs. narrow interests Receptive vs. closed to new ideas
Agreeableness	Good-natured vs. irritable Soft-hearted vs. ruthless Courteous vs. rude Sympathetic vs. tough-minded
Conscientiousness	Well-organized vs. disorganized Dependable vs. undependable Hardworking vs. lazy Ambitious vs. easygoing

five-factor model A model of personality that consists of five basic traits: neuroticism, extraversion, openness, agreeableness, and conscientiousness.

Construction of Multitrait Inventories

As Allport had noted, the study of personality must begin not only with description but also with measurement. And so it did. One of the most important contributions of trait psychology is the construction of personality inventories, questionnaires designed to assess a whole multitude of traits (Wiggins & Pincus, 1992). Cattell's Sixteen Personality Factors Questionnaire is one such instrument. There are many others. The most widely used is the **Minnesota Multiphasic Personality Inventory,** or MMPI, a 550-item questionnaire originally developed in the 1940s to help in the diagnosis of psychological disorders (Hathaway & McKinley, 1983).

The MMPI is to personality measurement what the Stanford-Binet was to intelligence testing. Taking an empirical approach, Alfred Binet developed his test by generating a large number of problems, testing schoolchildren, and retaining those problems that were solved differently by fast and slow learners. The MMPI developers used a very similar strategy. They wrote hundreds of true-false statements, gave them to both normal adults and clinical patients with varying psychiatric diagnoses (depressed, paranoid, and so on), and then included in the final test only those items that were answered differently by the two groups—even if the content made little sense. The MMPI is filled with discriminating but odd items (for example, hysterical patients are more likely than others to answer *True* to "My fingers sometimes feel numb"). Indeed, satirist Art Buchwald once wrote a spoof of MMPI-like personality tests by creating his own items. Among them: "I think beavers work too hard," "Frantic screams make me nervous," and "My mother's uncle was a good man."

These MMPI scales have been used for more than fifty years. Many of the original items became dated, however, and the norms had been based on a predominantly white, rural, middle-class group of subjects. To bring the test up to date, new items were written and a more ethnically diverse cross-section of the United States was sampled. The result is a newer 567-item version known as MMPI-2 (Butcher et al., 1989; Butcher & Williams, 1992; Graham, 1990). As in the original test, MMPI-2 contains the ten *clinical scales* shown in Table 15.4. Eight of these are designed to distinguish between "normals" and diagnostic groups. Two others are used to measure the traits of masculinity-femininity and social introversion. It also contains fifteen *content scales* that measure work attitudes, family problems, and other characteristics. In addition, the MMPI and MMPI-2 contain a set of *validity scales* designed to expose test takers who are evasive, confused, lying to make a good impression, or defensive. Someone who answers *True* to many socially desirable but implausible statements such as "I never get angry" is assumed to be trying too hard to project a healthy image.

The MMPI-2 is easy to administer, and in contrast to the Rorschach and TAT, in which two examiners may reach different conclusions, the MMPI scoring is perfectly objective. Thus, a test taker's responses can be converted into a personality profile by computer. That's one reason why the test has been translated into more than 100 languages and is popular in both clinical and research settings. Test administrators must be cautious, however, about how to use the test and how to interpret the results. The test has good reliability and validity, but it is far from perfect (Helmes & Reddon, 1993). One needs to be particularly careful in interpreting the responses of test takers from subcultural groups that share different beliefs, values, ideals, and experiences. A pattern of responses may be normal in one culture and deviant in another.

Minnesota Multiphasic Personality Inventory (MMPI) A large-scale test designed to measure a multitude of psychological disorders and personality traits.

Table 15.4 Clinical and Validity Scales of the MMPI

CLINICAL SCALES	DESCRIPTIONS	SAMPLE ITEMS
1. Hypochondriasis	Excessive concern about self and physical health, fatigue, a pattern of complaining	"I have a great deal of stomach trouble."
2. Depression	Low morale, pessimistic about the future, passive, hopeless, unhappy, and sluggish	"I wish I could be as happy as others seem to be."
3. Hysteria	Use of physical symptoms to gain attention from others or avoid social responsibility	"I have had fainting spells."
4. Psychopathic deviation	Disregard for social rules and authority, impulsive, unreliable, self-centered, has shallow relationships	"In school I was sometimes sent to the principal for cutting up."
5. Masculinity/ Femininity	Identification with masculine and/or feminine sex roles	"I enjoy reading love stories."
6. Paranoia	Feelings of persecution and/or grandeur, suspiciousness, hypersensitivity, use of blame and projection	"I am sure I get a raw deal from life."
7. Psychasthenia	Anxiousness as exhibited in fears, self-doubt, worries, guilt, obsessions and compulsions	"I feel anxiety about something or someone almost all the time."
8. Schizophrenia	Feelings of social alienation, aloofness, confusion and disorientation, bizarre thoughts and sensations	"I often feel as if things were not real."
9. Mania	Hyperactivity, excitement, flakiness, elation, euphoria, and excessive optimism	"At times my thoughts race ahead faster than I could speak them."
10. Social introversion	Withdrawal from social contact, isolation, shyness, a reserved, inhibited, self-effacing style	"Whenever possible I avoid being in a crowd."
VALIDITY SCALES	**DESCRIPTIONS**	**SAMPLE ITEMS**
Cannot say	Evasiveness, as indicated by a high number of noncommittal, "Cannot say" responses	(None; this score consists of the number of "Cannot say" responses)
Lie scale	Tendency to present oneself favorably, not honestly, to fake a good impression	"I always tell the truth."
Infrequency scale	Tendency to "fake bad" by reporting unusual weaknesses and problems	"Everything tastes the same."
Correction	Subtle test-taking defensiveness, or lack of self-insight	"I have never felt better in my life than I do now."

Biological Roots of Personality

Many trait theories, even those that predate psychology's birth as a discipline, assume that there is a linkage between biological and personal dispositions. In the fifth century BCE, the Greek physician Hippocrates said that people could be classified into four temperament types, depending on which of their "humors," or body fluids, predominated: An excess of blood was associated with cheerfulness, black bile with sadness, yellow bile with anger, and phlegm with sluggishness. In the nineteenth century, German physician Franz Gall introduced phrenology, the pseudoscience that tried to link personality to brain structures that could be seen in the bumps on our head. Others used physiognomy, the idea that a person's character is revealed in the features of the face (for example, people with thin lips were said to be conscientious; those with thick lips, emotional).

Although these early theories were rejected, there is renewed interest in the connections between biology and personality. In 1954, William Sheldon studied thousands of adult men and concluded that there are three kinds of physique, each linked to a distinct type of personality. The *ectomorph,* said Sheldon, has a thin, frail body and a restrained, anxious, shy disposition. The *endomorph* has a soft, plump body and is relaxed, sociable, and easygoing. And the *mesomorph* has a strong, muscular build and is bold, assertive, and energetic. Sheldon reported high correlations between body types and personality, but his methods were flawed, and later research produced less impressive results.

Are there any biological underpinnings to personality? Yes, absolutely. Recall the nature–nurture debate and the twins study presented in Chapter 10. For a wide range of traits, studies have shown that (1) raised together, identical twins are more similar than fraternal twins, and (2) twins raised apart are as similar as those raised in the same home. Taken together, a growing body of research suggests that personality differences in the population are 40 to 50 percent genetically determined (Bouchard, 1994; Loehlin, 1992; Tellegen et al., 1988; DiLalla et al., 1996). As shown in Figure 15.9, this result is consistent with the results of a recent study in which the Big Five personality factors were measured in 123 pairs of identical twins and 127 pairs of fraternal twins (Lang et al., 1996).

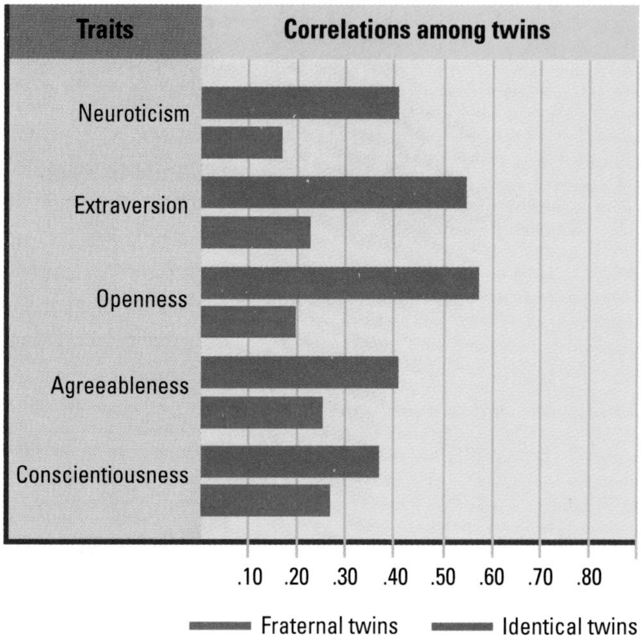

Figure 15.9 Genetic influences on personality Based on twin studies, these correlations provide estimates of the degrees to which various personality characteristics are inherited. Note that some traits have stronger genetic roots than others.

To the surprise of many psychologists, recent twin studies have revealed that there are also genetic links to characteristics that would seem to be determined entirely by personal experience. Specifically, identical twins are more similar than fraternal twins of the same sex in their attitudes toward sexuality, religion, and the death penalty (Tesser, 1993); in their vocational and personal interests (Lykken et al., 1993); and even in their risk of getting divorced (McGue & Lykken, 1992). Apparently, certain personality traits for which there is a genetic component predispose us to have certain types of experiences. It turns out, for example, that people who score high on measures of neuroticism, or anxiousness—for which there's a genetic basis—are more likely to get divorced than those who are low on this trait (Jockin et al., 1996).

Introversion and Extraversion

Psychologists may disagree over whether personality consists of 2, 5, 16, or 200 traits, but they all agree that the single most powerful dimension—one that can be seen in infants as well as adults, in cultures all over the world, and in questionnaires as well as behavior—is introversion–extraversion, one of the Big Five traits. The ancient Greeks and Romans noticed it, as have philosophers, physicians, and creative writers through the ages. Carl Jung wrote about individual differences on this dimension. So did Allport and Cattell. Even Pavlov said that some of the dogs in his classical-conditioning laboratory were more outgoing than others. But it was British psychologist Hans Eysenck who most clearly defined the trait, constructed a test to measure it, and proposed a provocative theory to explain its origin.

As described by Eysenck (1967), the typical **extravert** is someone who has many friends, likes parties, craves excitement, seeks adventure, takes chances, acts on the spur of the moment, and is uninhibited. In contrast, the typical **introvert** is low-keyed, has just a few close friends, shies away from stimulation, acts cautiously, and distrusts the impulse of the moment. Based on past writings, personal observations, and factor analyses of trait questionnaires, Eysenck developed a test that includes a measure of introversion and extraversion (see Table 15.5). Using this instrument, and others, researchers have found that extraverts are generally more talkative, prefer occupations that involve social contact, and take greater risks (Eysenck & Eysenck, 1985). The question is, What accounts for this broad and pervasive aspect of personality? To see whether you are an introvert or an extravert, go to Table 15.5 and answer the questions for yourself. If you said *yes* on most odd-numbered questions and *no* on the even-numbered ones in Table 15.5, you are relatively extraverted. If your answers are the other way around, then you're more of an introvert. Many people fall somewhere in the middle of the continuum.

[Drawing by Wilson; © 1995 The New Yorker Magazine, Inc.]

"But, in the end, you will become bored with that, too."

Extraverts have a constant appetite for stimulation and arousal—and may become easily bored.

Eysenck argues that individual differences are biologically rooted and that introverts have central nervous systems that are more sensitive to stimulation. According to Eysenck, people seek a moderate, comfortable level of CNS arousal. Introverts are easily overaroused, so they avoid intense sources of excitement. In contrast, extraverts are not so easily aroused, which leads them to approach high levels of excitement. Thus, it takes a more potent stimulus for the extravert to feel the "buzz." Research generally supports this hypothesis (Bullock & Gilliland, 1993;

Table 15.5 Are You an Introvert or an Extravert?

1. Are you usually carefree?
2. Do you generally prefer reading to meeting people?
3. Do you often long for excitement?
4. Are you mostly quiet when you're with others?
5. Do you often do things on the spur of the moment?
6. Are you slow and unhurried in the way you move?
7. Would you do almost anything for a dare?
8. Do you hate being in a crowd who plays jokes on one another?
9. Do you enjoy wild parties?
10. Do you like the kind of work you need to pay attention to?

Source: H. J. Eysenck & S. G. B. Eysenck (1964). *Manual of the Eysenck Personality Inventory.* London: University of London Press.

extravert A kind of person who seeks stimulation and is sociable and impulsive.

introvert A kind of person who avoids stimulation and is low-key and cautious.

Eysenck, 1990). For example, one study showed that when drops of natural lemon juice are placed on the tongue, most introverts salivate more than most extraverts (Deary et al., 1988). Others have shown that introverts are more easily aroused by caffeine and other stimulants—and are less easily relaxed by alcohol and other depressants (Stelmack, 1990). In short, says Eysenck, each of us is born with a nervous system that predisposes us to either love or hate large crowds, bright lights, blaring music, fast cars, roller coasters, suspenseful movies, spicy foods, and other, more social stimulants.

Fulfilling a promise he had made to himself after he had to bail out of a plane during World War II, former president George Bush landed his second parachute jump in 1997, at age seventy-two. This high-risk activity epitomizes the sensation-seeking component of extraversion.

As you can see, extraverts are not just more sociable and people-oriented than introverts. According to Marvin Zuckerman (1994), they are also more *sensation seeking*—a trait that leads people to drink, smoke, and use other drugs; seek out novel experiences; enjoy dangerous sports and other intense forms of stimulation; and gamble and take other risks for the thrill of it. As for the introvert, Elaine and Arthur Aron (1997) note that avoiding stimulating social situations is a smart and adaptive strategy for people sensitive to stimulation. In a series of studies, they found that subjects who described themselves as "highly sensitive" were more likely to report feeling overwhelmed by strong sensory input. Compared to others, they cry more easily, are more sensitive to daylight, are less tolerant of pain, are affected more by emotional films, and prefer country living to the city. Table 15.6 presents sample items from the tests that are used to measure both sensation-seeking and sensitivity.

Interestingly, the rudiments of introversion and extraversion can be seen in the predispositions of infants shortly after birth. Over the years, Jerome Kagan (1994) and his colleagues have studied children who are *inhibited* and *uninhibited* in temperament (most fall between these two extremes). At sixteen weeks old, inhibited infants—compared to those who are uninhibited—are more easily distressed and cry more in response to hanging mobiles, human speech, intense odors, and other types of stimulation. At two years of age, inhibited children are fearful, wary of strangers, and avoidant of novel situations, while their uninhibited peers are outgoing, adventurous, and quick to approach strangers and new situations. At five years old, socially inhibited children are shy and more easily aroused by mildly stressful tasks—as measured by increases in heart rate, dilation of the pupils, and a rise in

Table 15.6 What's Your Orientation to Stimulation?

SENSATION-SEEKING SCALE (Zuckerman, 1994)

1. I would like to try parachute jumping.
2. I like "wild" uninhibited parties.
3. I often like to get high.
4. I get bored seeing the same old faces.
5. I enjoy the company of people who are free and easy about sex.

HIGHLY SENSITIVE PERSON SCALE (Aron & Aron, 1997)

1. Do you startle easily?
2. Are you easily overwhelmed by strong sensory input?
3. Are you made uncomfortable by loud noises?
4. Do changes in your life shake you up?
5. Do you get rattled when you have a lot to do in a short amount of time?

norepinephrine. They often have more tension in the face muscles and are more likely to have higher-than-average levels of cortisol, a hormone associated with physiological arousal during stress.

Not all inhibited infants grow up to become inhibited adults. But two additional lines of research suggest that temperament is a biological predisposition. First, Stephen Suomi (1991) observed that infant rhesus monkeys also differ in their behavior at birth. Suomi calls the inhibited monkeys "uptight" and the uninhibited ones "laid back." He finds that the uptight monkeys, who are shy and anxious, also have the same physical attributes as Kagan's inhibited human infants. Second, Janet DiPietro and her colleagues (1996) monitored heart rate and motor activity in thirty-one human fetuses for twenty weeks prior to their birth. They found, through follow-up reports provided by the mothers, that the most active fetuses were later fussier, more difficult, and less adaptable as six-month-old babies. Apparently, certain aspects of an infant's temperament can be detected even before birth.

Perspectives: Do Traits Exist?

Intuitively, we are all trait psychologists. We use trait terms to describe ourselves and others, and we have preconceptions about how various characteristics relate to one another and to behavior. We assume that people who are unpredictable are also dangerous and that those who talk slowly are also slow-witted. We're surprised when a polite and unassuming coworker erupts in violence or when the sweet "girl next door" turns out to be the "other woman." Each of us tends to notice some traits more than others. One person may measure everyone by an intellectual yardstick, while others look for physical beauty, friendliness, a sense of humor, or a firm handshake. When I was younger, I used to think I could instantly tell all about people—

INTERSECTION

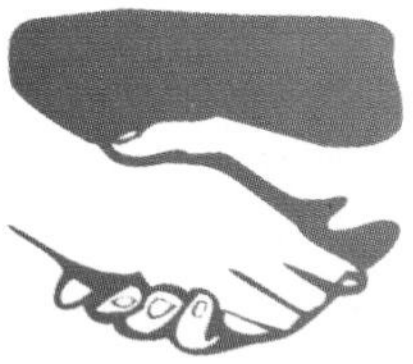

PERSONALITY AND BUSINESS

Using Personality Tests in Personnel Selection

On Christmas Eve 1996, Dan Reeves resigned as head coach of the New York Giants football team. At his press conference, Reeves criticized the organization's draft practices for relying too heavily on the psychological tests that prospective rookies must take. "So how valid is a two-hour test?" he asked. "When a psychologist has more to do with the draft than you do as a head coach, I have a problem with that" (Rhoden, 1996).

Anyone who has applied for a desirable job knows that you sometimes have to climb hurdles and jump through hoops to get hired. It's a familiar routine. You submit a resume and a list of references, fill out an application, and perhaps take the "hot seat" in a face-to-face interview. You may even be asked to bring in samples of your work or take a standardized test of intelligence, vocational interests, or personality. When it comes to personnel selection in business and industry, there are numerous methods—all designed to predict performance in the workplace (Landy et al., 1994; Borman et al., 1997).

The use of personality tests for employment purposes has been a source of controversy. Can scores on trait inventories be used to predict worker productivity, motivation, satisfaction, loyalty, or other aspects of job performance? For many years, the MMPI was used to assess a candidate's personality—even though it had been developed for the purpose of diagnosing mental disorders, and even though there was no clear link between MMPI test scores and work performance (Guion, 1965). Questions were also raised about whether it was ethical, or a violation of privacy, to require the testing of all prospective employees. People are free to refuse to take a test as part of an application process, but 52 percent of personnel managers surveyed said they automatically reject applicants who refuse to take a test (Blocklyn, 1988).

For predictive purposes, many organizations have sought more "scientific" methods of evaluation. It has been estimated, for example, that 3,000 firms in the United States and many more in Europe use "graphology," or handwriting analysis, to predict job-relevant traits such as honesty, sales ability, and leadership potential (Rafaeli & Klimoski, 1983). But controlled research does not support the claim that handwriting can be used in this way. In one study, professional graphologists were asked to predict various aspects of job performance by analyzing the handwriting contained in the autobiographical sketches of bank employees. From these same materials, the researchers themselves also made predictions. A comparison of predicted and actual employee performance revealed that the graphologists were no more effective than were the researchers. They were no more accurate than they would have been by flipping a coin (Ben-Shakhar et al., 1986).

Despite the initial problems and occasional misdirections, it now appears that certain personality tests can be used to predict a whole range of worker outcomes, including leadership potential, helpfulness, absenteeism, and theft (Goffin et al., 1996; Hogan et al., 1996). In particular, researchers have found that performance across different occupations can be significantly predicted by questionnaires that measure the Big Five personality factors. For example, extraverts are more likely than introverts to succeed as managers and salespersons, while workers in general benefit more from job training if they are high rather than low in their openness to new experiences. Recent reviews of this research have also revealed that, across the board, among skilled and unskilled workers alike, and in studies conducted in North America and Europe, conscientiousness—the trait of being dependable, responsible, organized, and persistent—is highly predictive of performance at work (Barrick & Mount, 1991; Tett et al., 1991; Salgado, 1997). Clearly, personality traits—not just measures of intelligence—are useful for predicting success and failure in the workplace (Goldberg, 1993; Hogan et al., 1996).

Dan Reeves the day he announced his resignation as head coach of the New York Giants. Reeves was critical of the organization for relying too heavily on "psychological tests" to make player selections.

One criticism of personality testing for employment purposes is that, as motivated test takers, job candidates can fake their responses in order to present themselves in a positive light. This is a serious possible drawback. Imagine having applied for a job you really wanted, and all that stands in your way are the results of a personality questionnaire. Isn't it possible that you would cover up your flaws, consciously or not, according to what you see as desirable? And wouldn't this render your test results invalid? The answer is *yes* to the first question, but *no* to the second. Industrial/organizational psychologists have found that people do bias their responses in a socially desirable direction—but that this does not diminish the value of the personality tests. Apparently, the ability to present oneself favorably is a sign of emotional stability and conscientiousness—traits that are predictive of success at work (Barrick & Mount, 1996; Ones et al., 1996).

whether they were relaxed or intense, competitive or cooperative, cautious or adventurous, and so on, by the way they played board games like Scrabble, Risk, and Monopoly.

Although it seems natural to think about people and their behavior in terms of traits, critics complain that the approach is limited. Psychoanalysts say it is superficial, cognitive social-learning theorists say it neglects situational factors, and humanists say it's cold and impersonal. By far the most serious attack, however, was Walter Mischel's (1968) startling claim that traits simply do not exist. After reviewing forty years of research, Mischel concluded that (1) personality test scores are not predictive of behavior, and (2) individuals do not act with traitlike consistency from one situation to the next. To illustrate, he cited a classic study by Hugh Hartshorne and Mark May (1928) in which they observed the moral conduct of thousands of children in school, at home, at parties, and so on. Seeking evidence for a trait of honesty, Hartshorne and May found that the children exhibited strikingly little cross-situational consistency in behavior. A child might pass up a chance to cheat in class or steal money from a dropped wallet but then be quick to cheat in an athletic event or lie to parents. Thus, said Mischel (1968), traits—as measured by personality tests—cannot reliably predict behavior.

Mischel's critique whipped up a tremendous controversy among personality psychologists wondering if traits were a mere figment of the imagination. After many years of debate and additional research, two main conclusions can be drawn. First, as noted by Seymour Epstein (1979), traits are highly informative—but only when they're used to predict an *aggregation* of behaviors. To measure personality, psychologists derive test scores by combining answers to several related questions. Similarly, says Epstein, behavior should be measured by combining several trait-related acts. Just as an IQ score is not expected to predict a grade in a particular class during a particular semester, your score on an introversion–extraversion scale cannot be expected to predict whether you will tell jokes at your next party. By the same token, just as an IQ score can predict grade point *averages,* a personality test can predict general behavior tendencies (Epstein & O'Brien, 1985; Moskowitz, 1982).

The second important conclusion is that behavior springs from complex *interactions* between persons and situations (Magnusson & Endler, 1977; Snyder & Ickes, 1985; Mischel & Shoda, 1995; Cervone, 1997). This interaction can take many forms. First, personality traits are expressed only in relevant situations. If you're the anxious type, you may break out in a cold sweat before a first date or public pres-entation but not when you're at home watching TV. Second, traits are expressed only in situations that do not constrain our behavior. Just about everyone is quiet and reserved in churches, libraries, and crowded elevators, but our unique personalities are free to emerge at home, at a party, or in the street. Third, people influence the situations they are in. The way we treat our friends, family, and others, for example, influences the treatment we receive in turn. Thus, child-development researchers who used to write about how parents shape their children now realize that children, even infants, shape their parents as well. Fourth, people choose settings that are compatible with their own personalities. Extraverts craving excitement are likely to visit amusement parks and casinos, but introverts seek out quiet restaurants, hiking trails, and other out-of-the-way places. Fifth, our personalities color the way we interpret and react to situations. Optimists see the proverbial glass as half-full, while pessimists see the same glass as half-empty. As Allport (1961) said, "The same fire that melts the butter hardens the egg" (p. 102).

Personality in Perspective

Reflecting on the material in this chapter, how are the four approaches to personality different—and how are they similar? How might an eclectic theorist combine the four approaches?

Now that you are familiar with the four major approaches to personality, you are in a position to evaluate each perspective for yourself. If you were to stop and think about your own life—say, to write your autobiography—which of the four approaches would best describe your personality and explain how you got that way?

To summarize, psychoanalysis emphasizes deep, unconscious conflicts, sex and aggression, defensive behavior, anxiety, and early childhood influences. Cognitive social-learning theory views personality as a socially acquired pattern of behavior, a learned response to how people perceive, interpret, and value the external reinforcements in their lives. Humanists believe that people are inherently good, that we have self-insight, and that personality springs from the desire and struggle to reach our full potential. The trait approach makes few value judgments about human nature, but it assumes that everyone can be compared on a standard set of dispositions that are consistent over time and, at least to some extent, genetically determined.

The four approaches also differ in their perspectives on change and in their approaches to the treatment of psychological disorders. Beginning with Freud, most psychoanalysts see the early years of childhood as formative, if not critical, to the development of personality—with relatively little room for change in adulthood. In fact, psychoanalytic therapists say that patients unconsciously resist the recovery process. The trait approach, with its emphasis on genetic determinants and the stability of core dispositions, also takes a relatively dim view of change. According to this view, people are biologically introverted or extraverted, and calm or anxious—thus leaving little room for variation. In contrast, the behavioral and cognitive social-learning theorists see people as flexible and influenced by environmental factors. According to this view, psychological disorders are learned—and can be unlearned just as well. The humanistic approach is equally clear in its view that people have not only the capacity but the will to change—and, specifically, to strive toward self-actualization.

It is important to realize that although we have discussed the four approaches as distinct, you don't necessarily have to choose a favorite or accept any one approach completely. Many personality psychologists are *eclectic,* which means that they accept bits and pieces of the different theories. Mix in some of Freud's unconscious, hold the sex, add a dash of reinforcement and a pinch of self-actualization, then administer a multitrait personality inventory, and you will have formed a new perspective from a blending of existing ingredients. It is also instructive to consider the possibility that each approach may better account for some aspects of personality than for others. Psychoanalysis may shed light on why we inexplicably feel troubled and anxious, cognitive social-learning theory may explain why having control is often so important to us, humanism may capture the experience of pursuing and catching lifelong dreams, and the trait approach may offer the best way to measure our unique predispositions. The human personality is so complex and multifaceted that all perspectives may be necessary.

Summary and Key Terms

The study of **personality**—an individual's distinct and relatively enduring pattern of thoughts, feelings, motives and behaviors—shows that personality characteristics are stable over time. There are four major approaches to personality.

Psychoanalysis

The Birth of Psychoanalysis

Just before the turn of the twentieth century, Freud used his clinical experience with hysteria to formulate **psychoanalysis.**

Freud's Theory of Personality

Psychoanalysis assumes that unconscious conflicts play a large part in shaping personality. Freud divided personality into three parts. The **id**—a primitive, unconscious reservoir of basic drives—operates according to the **pleasure principle.** The personality's moral part, the **superego,** consists of the ego-ideal and the conscience. The **ego** mediates between the id's "wants" and the superego's "shoulds" and follows a **reality principle** that allows for gratification of needs in a socially appropriate manner.

Freud believed that personality is shaped by conflicts that arise during the **psychosexual stages** of development. Young children pass through the oral, anal, and phallic stages. During the phallic stage (ages four to six), children experience the **Oedipus complex,** a tendency to become attracted to the parent of the opposite sex and hostile to the parent of the same sex. Children resolve this complex, however, and form an **identification** with the same-sex parent, internalizing the parent's values. At puberty, the genital stage begins. Too much or too little gratification in any of the first three stages can result in **fixation** at that stage and a distinct type of personality.

According to Freud, we feel anxiety when our impulses clash with morals, so the ego uses unconscious **defense mechanisms** that deny and distort reality. **Repression** helps us "forget" threatening thoughts, memories, and impulses by pushing them out of awareness. In **denial,** we bar anxiety-provoking thoughts from awareness in the first place. Through **projection,** we attribute our own unacceptable impulses to others. Through **reaction formation,** we convert an unacceptable feeling into its opposite. **Rationalization** involves making excuses for failures and shortcomings. And in **sublimation,** the healthiest defense mechanism, we channel repressed urges into socially acceptable substitute outlets.

Freud's Legacy

Freud's followers continued to focus on unconscious factors, inner conflicts, and early-childhood influences. Jung proposed that people are influenced by a **collective unconscious** consisting of memories from our ancestral past, and he argued that personality development continues into adulthood. Adler stressed social conflicts and developed the notions of sibling rivalry and the inferiority complex. More recent theorists have emphasized social needs or the role of the ego.

Psychoanalytic researchers also developed **projective tests** to reveal the unconscious through responses to ambiguous stimuli. The **Rorschach** uses inkblots. The **Thematic Apperception Test (TAT)** asks people to make up stories from a set of pictures.

Critics say that psychoanalysis takes too bleak a view of human nature and that its propositions are not supported by controlled research. Yet Freud's ideas, particularly those about the unconscious and defense mechanisms, have become an integral part of psychology.

The Cognitive Social-Learning Approach

Unlike psychoanalysis, **cognitive social-learning theory** sees personality as the result of a continuous interaction between persons and environments.

Principles of Learning and Behavior

Early behaviorists investigated classical conditioning, operant conditioning, and other key principles of learning. Watson and Skinner applied these principles to the study of personality.

Social Learning Theory

Social learning theory extended behaviorism to include social and cognitive factors. Through **modeling,** people can learn behavior by observing and imitating. Rotter and Mischel further showed that thoughts influence the link between reinforcement and behavior.

According to cognitive social learning theory, people differ in **locus of control**—expectations about the control of reinforcement. Internals, who believe they can control their own fate, tend to be healthier and more successful. People also differ in **self-efficacy,** the belief that they can perform the behaviors needed for a desired outcome. The more self-efficacy people have for a task, the more likely they are to succeed.

Perspectives on Cognitive Social-Learning Theory

Cognitive social-learning theory emphasizes **reciprocal determinism,** the notion that personality emerges from an ongoing interaction among individuals, their actions, and environments. Environmental forces shape our personalities, but we can choose, alter, and interpret the situations we encounter. To assess personality, cognitive social-learning theorists use direct methods such as behavioral observations and self-reports.

The Humanistic Approach

By the 1940s, some psychologists began to develop a **humanistic theory** of personality.

Carl Rogers

Impressed by his patients' self-insight and will to improve, Rogers theorized that we all have a natural need for self-actualization—that is, a drive to behave in ways consistent with our self-concepts. As social beings, however, we also have a competing need for positive regard. **Unconditional positive regard** from significant others frees us to pursue self-actualization. But if we receive **conditional positive regard,** we experience frustration, anxiety, and **self-discrepancies.**

Abraham Maslow

Maslow believed that people are motivated to fulfill a hierarchy of needs en route to **self-actualization,** the distinctly human need to become everything one is capable of becoming. Few people reach this state, though it is common to have momentary **peak experiences.**

Perspectives on the Humanistic Approach

Humanistic psychologists have been praised for focusing on the good in human beings, the self-concept, and conscious experience. They have been criticized for ignoring the darker side of human nature and relying too heavily on people's self-reports.

The Trait Approach

The Building Blocks of Personality

To study the basic units of personality, Allport compiled a list of 200 personality **traits.** With factor analysis, Cattell reduced these to 16 source traits. Now, researchers have condensed the list to a **five-factor model** consisting of 5 traits: neuroticism, extraversion, openness, agreeableness, and conscientiousness.

Construction of Multitrait Inventories

The trait approach gave rise to the construction of personality inventories such as the **Minnesota Multiphasic Personality Inventory (MMPI).**

Biological Roots of Personality

Different traits show different degrees of genetic linkage. According to recent estimates, many personality factors are 40 to 50 percent genetically determined in the population.

Introversion and Extraversion

One of the most powerful trait dimensions is introversion and extraversion. An **extravert** is sociable and impulsive and seeks stimulation. An **introvert** is low-keyed and cautious and avoids stimulation. Research suggests that extraverts are sensation seekers, while introverts are overly sensitive to stimulation. Recent studies reveal similar differences in temperament between inhibited and uninhibited infants and children.

Perspectives: Do Traits Exist?

Debates about trait theory lead to two major conclusions. First, traits can predict an aggregation of behaviors but not specific acts. Second, behavior springs from an interaction between traits and situations.

Personality in Perspective

Each of the approaches to personality has a different emphasis. To account for the full range of human experience, we may need to draw eclectically on all four theories.

In the Field Resources

Books

Csikszentmihalyi, M. (1990) *Flow: The psychology of optimal experience.* New York: Basic Books.

Written with a humanistic flair, this book is about being "in the zone"—strong, alert, highly focused, oblivious to outside distractions, and effortlessly in control.

Freud, S. (1917/1966). *Introductory lectures on psychoanalysis* (translated and edited by J. Strachey). New York: Norton.

In this popularly translated book, Freud talks about slips of the tongue, dreams, and psychological disorders.

Harary, K., & Donahue, E. (1994). *Who do you think you are? Explore your many-sided self with the Berkeley Personality Profile.* San Francisco: Harper.

This book, which is also available as a CD-ROM, enables the reader to assess and interpret his or her own personality with a test often used to measure the Big Five personality factors.

Internet

American Psychoanalytic Association (http://apsa.org/)

In this professional site, you can learn about psychoanalysis, search an extensive bibliography, and "find a psychoanalyst."

Association for Humanistic Psychology (http://ahpweb.bestware.net/)

This official AHP site contains a bibliography and links to other sites related to the humanistic perspective.

Sigmund Freud and the Freud Archives (http://plaza.interport.neg/nypsan/freudarc.html)

This collection of links related to Freud offers original writings, biographical material, photographs, and internet resources from libraries and museums.

Journals and Periodicals

Journal of Personality
Journal of Personality and Social Psychology
Journal of Personality Assessment
Journal of Research in Personality
Psychological Assessment

16 *Psychological Disorders*

PSYCHOLOGICAL DISORDERS: A GENERAL OUTLOOK
Defining Normal and Abnormal
Models of Abnormality
Diagnosis: A Necessary Step

ANXIETY DISORDERS
Generalized Anxiety Disorder
Panic Disorder
Phobic Disorder
Obsessive-compulsive Disorder

SOMATOFORM DISORDERS
Hypochondriasis
Conversion Disorder

DISSOCIATIVE DISORDERS
Amnesia and Fugue States
Dissociative Identity Disorder

MOOD DISORDERS
Major Depression
Theories of Depression
The Vicious Cycle of Depression
Suicide: The Ultimate "Solution"
Bipolar Disorder

SCHIZOPHRENIC DISORDERS
The Symptoms of Schizophrenia
Types of Schizophrenia
Theories of Schizophrenia

PERSONALITY DISORDERS
The Borderline Personality
The Antisocial Personality

WHAT NEXT?

The situation In clinical psychology, it's difficult but important to know the mental-health status of the nation and the kinds of problems most in need of attention. How common are different types of disorders? Are some segments of the population more "at risk" than others? And how can we make estimates that can be trusted?

Imagine that you have extensive experience at conducting personal interviews and that you get a call from the University of Michigan's National Research Center. Apparently, the center is planning a massive nationwide study to determine the prevalence in the United States of certain psychological disorders and wants to know if you can help conduct the interviews. You say *yes*, but first you need to attend a seven-day training program along with 157 other experienced interviewers recruited for the same study.

What's Your Prediction?

How common are psychological disorders?

Using a standard set of questions, interviewers in forty-eight states (excluding Hawaii and Alaska) get responses from a total of 8,098 men and women, fifteen to fifty-four years old—and carefully sampled to represent the national population. Some 75 percent are white, 12 percent black, 9 percent Hispanic, and 4 percent from other groups. With all respondents, your goal is to find out whether they have suffered from certain mental disorders during the course of their lives.

There are five types of disorders you ask about. One type is characterized by high and persistent levels of *anxiety*. Included in this category are people who are chronically anxious, who have panic attacks, who have intense fears of common objects and social situations, or who are afraid to leave the house. A second type are mood disorders, characterized primarily by *depression*. Included here are people who have suffered a bout of clinical depression or are chronically sad and "down in the dumps." The third type of disorder involves *substance abuse*. In this category are people who are addicted to alcohol or other drugs—or who abuse drugs in ways that cause physical, social, or legal harm. The fourth type is *schizophrenia*, a severe disorder marked by hallucinations, grossly distorted thoughts, bizarre behavior, and loss of contact with reality. Fifth is the *antisocial personality*, characterized by a blatant disregard for other people. Those diagnosed with this disorder repeatedly lie, steal, cheat, fight, assault others, and break the law—without feelings of remorse.

You interview people in your area from a list you're given. After you complete each interview, you send it to your regional supervisor, who checks to make sure that all the necessary questions were asked and answered. If responses are incomplete or unclear, the form is returned for you to go back and collect the missing information. If it is complete, the interview data are sent to the national office, where all the results are compiled and analyzed.

Make a prediction Think carefully about the five types of disorders described above. How prevalent are they? And are men and women equally "at risk"? For each disorder, use the table below to predict the percentages of men and women (from 0 to 100) who have ever suffered from it during the course of their lives.

	PERCENTAGE WHO HAVE EVER SUFFERED	
TYPES OF DISORDER	***Men***	***Women***
Anxiety	________%	________%
Depression	________%	________%
Substance abuse	________%	________%
Schizophrenia	________%	________%
Antisocial personality	________%	________%

The results When the responses were tallied, the results were consistent with previous research. Look at the table below, and you'll see, first, that the lifetime prevalence rate for both sexes combined is highest for substance abuse—followed, in order, by anxiety, depression, antisocial personality disorder, and schizophrenia. Second, notice that although men and women are equally vulnerable overall, they differ in the types of disorders they exhibit. Men are more likely to have substance abuse and antisocial personality problems, while women are more likely to suffer from anxiety and depression.

	PERCENTAGE WHO HAVE EVER SUFFERED	
TYPES OF DISORDER	***Men***	***Women***
Anxiety	19%	31%
Depression	15%	24%
Substance abuse	35%	18%
Schizophrenia	.6%	.8%
Antisocial personality	6%	1%

What does it all mean? In this study, Ronald Kessler and others (1994) conducted extensive interviews with a large national sample of respondents and provided much-needed information about the mental-health status of American men and women in the 1990s. For now, there are two aspects of these results that are worth noting. First, the numbers—which were somewhat higher than those found in an earlier national study (Robins & Regier, 1991)—represent *lifetime* prevalence rates. When Kessler et al. (1994) asked respondents about the past twelve months, the numbers were much lower. In other words, someone might experience anxiety or depression or might abuse drugs at one point in life but then recover.

A second important point is that the number of Americans likely to have a psychological problem is less than the sum for the different types of disorders. Add the percentages in the above table and it will appear that roughly three-quarters of all men and women will have a psychological disorder. Not so. As we'll see later in this chapter, people who have one problem often have others too—so that many of the respondents in this study were counted in more than one row. In fact, the lifetime rate for having at least one disorder was only 48 percent.

In this chapter, we'll discuss these disorders, and others that are less common, in greater detail. We will look not only at their incidence in the population but also at the possible causes, symptoms, and likely outcomes.

Have you ever lost a loved one to death, only to be stricken by grief, despair, and the numb feeling that life is not worth living? Have you ever been so nervous before making a speech or going on a date that your heart raced, your voice trembled, and your stomach tightened up? Have you ever been the victim of a car accident, then blocked out the whole experience? Have you ever jumped out of bed in the middle of the night, startled by a terrifying nightmare you couldn't seem to shake or by creaking noises you imagined to be the sound of an intruder? Have you ever been haunted by a tune you kept humming and couldn't get out of your mind, no matter how hard you tried? And have you ever heard the sound of laughter as you entered a room, only to wonder for a moment if everyone was looking and laughing at *you*?

Chances are that one or more of these descriptions will ring a familiar bell and provide you with a personal glimpse into the unhappy, disturbing, and sometimes scary world of psychological disorders. You don't have to be "crazy" to have these kinds of episodes. For some of us, they are rare and last for only brief periods of time. But for others, they are frequent, prolonged, and intense. Based on nationwide surveys, it is estimated that in any given one-year period, 28 percent of the adult population in the United States suffers from some form of psychological distress. In the course of a lifetime, one-third to one-half of all Americans will suffer from a problem serious enough to be diagnosed as a psychological disorder (Kessler et al., 1994; Regier et al., 1993).

These surveys, supplemented by clinical case studies, tell us that psychological disorders are often a temporary condition. No one is invulnerable in times of great stress, but most people are resilient in their capacity for recovery. For the clinical psychologist, the key point is that people experience changes in the status of their mental health, sometimes for the better, at other times for the worse. In this chapter, we examine the negative form of change—the causes and effects of psychological disorders.

Psychological Disorders: A General Outlook

In matters of mind and behavior, what separates normal from abnormal? What is the medical perspective on psychological disorders? What is the sociocultural perspective? What are pitfalls of diagnosis, and why is it necessary?

Before we discuss the wide array of mental-health problems that plague people all over the world, three general questions must be asked. First, when are thoughts, feelings, and behaviors defined as disordered? That is, when does a person cross the invisible line between health and illness, psychology and psycho*pathology*, normal and *ab*normal? Second, what biological and environmental factors put our psychological well-being at risk? Third, how can different problems be distinguished for the sake of understanding and treating those in need of assistance?

Defining Normal and Abnormal

"Oh, yeah? Well, I think *you're* the one with the biochemical imbalance."

In a recent journey through a subway station in New York City, I passed by a middle-age man in a neatly pressed blue suit who stood on a bench, waved his arms, and urged commuters to repent for their sins because the planet was due to explode. On the same bench, an older bearded man in a heavy wool coat lay all curled up, with his arms folded together, his eyes cast down to the ground, and a brown liquor bottle peaking out of his coat pocket. Once on the train, I sat next to a woman who was having an animated conversation with herself, and I watched a man who switched his seat several times during the ride. Crazy? For all I know, the other passengers—who slept, hid behind walls of newspapers, tuned into headphones, read books, and minded their own business—were wondering about me, the nosy guy who couldn't stop spying on everyone else.

People-watching experiences like this one demonstrate how tricky it can be to determine whether someone has a psychological disorder. Various criteria have been proposed over the years, and all have sparked controversy. A frequently cited definition is provided by the American Psychiatric Association (APA). According to the APA (1994), a pattern of behavior can be considered a **psychological disorder** if, and only if, it satisfies three conditions:

1. The person experiences significant pain or distress, an inability to work or play, an increased risk of death, or a loss of freedom in important areas of life.
2. The source of the problem resides within the person, due to biological factors, learned habits, or mental processes, and is not simply a normal response to specific life events such as the death of a loved one.
3. The problem is not a deliberate reaction to conditions such as poverty, prejudice, government policy, or other conflicts with society.

psychological disorder A condition in which a person's thoughts, feelings, or behavior is judged to be dysfunctional.

These criteria suggest some key points about a definition. One is that the term *abnormal* means more than just "different from the norm" in a statistical sense.

Nobel prizewinners and Olympic gold medalists are also atypical, but they're not clinically troubled. Also, what's normative in one cultural or ethnic group may be deviant in another. A second point is that normal and abnormal are merely locations along a continuum, not distinct conditions separated by a bright line. Think about it. At what point should nervousness be called "anxiety," or sadness "depression"? How much pain, distress, or impairment is too much? When is a person who is deeply but reasonably upset by a tragic life event in need of psychological assistance? And when it comes to people who are poverty-stricken or homeless, how can we tell that their actions are not a normal response to a hostile environment? These are difficult questions that can be addressed only on a case-by-case basis. A third point is that certain behavior patterns are considered abnormal not because they are disabling to the individual but because they threaten the safety and welfare of others. The model citizen who holds a prestigious, well-paying job but is abusive to his wife or children is an all-too-familiar example.

Finally, it's important to note that the criteria used to identify psychological disorders do not in themselves explain the source of those disorders or imply a certain form of treatment. As we will see, the unhealthy mind is sometimes the product of an unhealthy body and, thus, is treatable with drugs. Yet often the problem stems from deep-seated personal conflicts, bad habits, negative life experiences, daily stress, faulty processing of information, and sociocultural factors. Before describing the kinds of disorders from which so many of us suffer, let's examine these theoretical models.

"Enigma" controls his gag reflex and the muscles down to his stomach in order to swallow two feet of steel. What does this behavior reveal about him—is he normal or abnormal? What more information would you need to make such a judgment?

Models of Abnormality

When archaeologists unearth human bone fragments from thousands of years ago, they sometimes find a small hole that was drilled into the skull. The reason, some experts speculate, is that our prehistoric ancestors believed that mental disorders were caused by the intrusion of evil spirits into the body and that these spirits needed an opening to escape. In more recent times, these disorders were variously attributed to witchcraft, demonic possession, full moons, and other supernatural forces. Evil spirits were thus "driven out" through exorcism, torture, primitive forms of surgery, noise making, bloodletting, bitter potions, and starvation.

The Medical Perspective Today, there are more enlightened, naturalistic models of abnormality—medical, psychological, and sociocultural. Within the **medical model**, disordered thoughts, feelings, and behaviors are caused by physical disease. In 400 BCE, Greek physician Hippocrates, the founder of modern medicine, proposed that psychological disorders are caused by body-fluid imbalances. This perspective is an important one today, as researchers try to identify genetic links, damage to parts of the brain and nervous system, hormone imbalances, and neurotransmitter activity that is associated with various problems. The medical model is powerfully evoked by the language used to describe abnormality. Thus, we speak of *diagnosing* mental *illness* in *patients* so that *treatment, hospitalization*, and *therapy* will relieve the *symptoms* and produce a *cure*. In short, a strictly medical model holds that although mental disorders take on a psychological appearance, the underlying problems are physical in nature.

The medical approach is more humane than demonology, but it is not without critics. In *The Myth of Mental Illness*, psychiatrist Thomas Szasz (1961) argued that mental illness is a socially defined, relative concept used to cast aside people who

medical model The perspective that mental disorders are caused by biological conditions and can be treated through medical intervention.

are deviant ("If you talk to God, you are praying; if God talks to you, you have schizophrenia"). Szasz (1987) charged that psychologists, psychiatrists, and other mental-health experts are too quick to guard society's norms and values. What's worse, he claims, the label *sick* invites those with real problems to become passive—dependent upon doctors and drugs rather than relying upon their own inner strengths. These criticisms raise important and provocative questions, but they are misguided. Mental illness is *not* a myth, and it would be cruel to deny that many mental disorders have biological origins, consequences, and treatment possibilities.

The Psychological Perspective A second major approach to abnormal behavior is based on the **psychological model**, which holds that psychological disorders are caused and then maintained by a person's past and present life experiences. The list of negatively impactful events is a long one. Examples include prolonged illness, natural disasters, war, physical and sexual abuse, domestic violence, divorce, poverty, the death of a loved one, a lack of friendships, and persistent failure. This perspective was first born of Freud's interest in hysteria, a disorder in which the patient experiences bodily symptoms in the absence of physical damage. Freud and others believed that this disorder usually began with a traumatic event in childhood and that it could be treated successfully with *psycho*therapy, a form of "talking cure."

Today, there is not one psychological model of abnormality but many. Paralleling the major approaches to personality that were described in Chapter 15, three broad perspectives are worth keeping in mind. The first is psychoanalysis, which emphasizes the role of parental influences, unconscious conflicts, guilt, frustration, and an array of defense mechanisms used to ward off anxiety. According to this view, psychological disorders spring from inner conflicts so intense that they overwhelm our normal defenses. The second perspective is rooted in behaviorism and cognitive social-learning theories. In this view, abnormal behavior is a learned response to reward and punishment, further influenced by our perceptions, expectations, values, and role models. The third perspective is humanistic, which holds that mental disorders arise when we are blocked in our efforts to grow and achieve self-actualization. In this view, the self-concept is all-important.

The Sociocultural Perspective Whether one prefers to think in medical or psychological terms, it is important to realize that the sociocultural context in which we live affects the kinds of stresses we're exposed to, the kinds of disorders we're likely to have, and the treatment we're likely to receive. Particularly impressive evidence for this perspective comes from the fact that different types of disorders, or symptoms, appear in different cultures. A good example is provided by John Weisz and others (1993), who studied behavioral and emotional problems among teenagers in the United States and Thailand. Apparently, although problems are evident in both countries, they take very different forms. In the United States, troubled teens tend to act out by bullying others, getting into fights, or disobeying teachers. But in the Buddhist country of Thailand, where children are taught to inhibit expressions of negative emotion, troubled teenagers are more likely to sulk, refuse to talk, sleep too much, or become constipated.

Additional evidence of sociocultural influence comes from the fact that some disorders are found almost exclusively within specific groups. We saw in Chapter 8 that *anorexia nervosa* and *bulimia nervosa* (eating disorders that tend to affect adolescent girls and young women) strike primarily middle- and upper-class women of Westernized cultures—presumably because they feel most pressured to have a

psychological model The perspective that mental disorders are caused and maintained by one's life experiences.

slender appearance (Brumberg, 1988; Ruderman & Besbeas, 1992). Indeed, many women with eating disorders have negatively distorted images of their own bodies, often seeing themselves as overweight (Thompson, 1996). One particularly well-known **culture-bound syndrome** is *amok*, a brief period of brooding followed by a violent outburst, often resulting in murder. This disorder is frequently triggered by a perceived insult and is found only among men in Malaysia, Papua New Guinea, the Philippines, Polynesia, and Puerto Rico and among the Navajo. Another is *pibloktoq*, which is a brief period of extreme excitement, often followed by seizures and coma lasting up to twelve hours. During an attack of this condition, which is found only among arctic and subarctic Eskimo communities, the person may tear off his or her clothing, break furniture, shout obscenities, and eat feces—acts that are later reportedly forgotten (Simons & Hughes, 1993; American Psychiatric Association, 1994).

As you read this chapter, then, keep in mind that the kinds of experiences that trigger psychological disorders and the ways in which these disorders are expressed sometimes occur only in specific locations and sociocultural contexts.

Diagnosis: A Necessary Step

In science, as in other pursuits, it often helps to group people, objects, and situations that share similar properties. Biologists classify animals into species, archaeologists divide time into eras, and geographers split the earth into regions. Likewise, mental-health professionals find it enormously useful—for the sake of prediction, understanding, and treatment—to categorize mental disorders that involve similar patterns of behavior, or syndromes. This process of grouping and naming mental disorders is referred to as **diagnosis.**

The most widely used classification scheme in the United States is the American Psychiatric Association's *Diagnostic and Statistical Manual of Mental Disorders* (4th Edition), mercifully nicknamed **DSM-IV.** This manual provides a comprehensive list of more than 200 mental disorders grouped into seventeen broad categories. (Those discussed in this chapter are previewed in Table 16.1.) For each disorder, the prominent symptoms are described in concrete behavioral terms. Also presented are the prevalence rates for men and women, predisposing factors, the normal age of onset, and the expected outcome. Accompanying the manual are books with illustrative case studies and standardized interviews for use in making a diagnosis (Spitzer et al., 1994; Widiger et al., 1994). It is important to realize that DSM-IV, which was published in 1994, is only one link in an evolving chain of diagnostic schemes and was preceded by four earlier versions. DSM was first published in 1952, was substantially revised in 1968 (DSM-II), was substantially revised again in 1980 (DSM-III), and was updated in 1987 (DSM-III-R).

Over the years, critics of psychiatric diagnosis have voiced three concerns. The first was that the system lacked reliability. If two mental-health experts interview the same person, what are the chances that they will independently come up with the same diagnosis? Research on the earliest versions of DSM revealed low levels of reliability. However, more recent versions, including DSM-IV, base classifications on observable behavior and provide a checklist of specific, objective items to guide the diagnosis. As in medicine, the system is still not perfect, but reliability estimates are higher now than in the past (Matarazzo, 1983).

A second concern is that clinical judgments, like all other judgments that people make, may be biased by stereotypes about gender, race, age, socioeconomic status,

culture-bound syndromes Recurring patterns of maladaptive behavior that are limited to a specific cultural group or location.

diagnosis The process of identifying and grouping mental disorders with similar symptoms.

DSM-IV Nickname for the American Psychiatric Association's *Diagnostic and Statistical Manual of Mental Disorders* (4th Edition).

Table 16.1 DSM-IV Mental Disorders Described in this Chapter	
Anxiety disorders	Disorders in which intense anxiety is the main symptom. This category includes generalized anxiety and panic disorders, phobias, obsessive-compulsive disorder, and posttraumatic stress disorder.
Somatoform disorders	Disorders involving physical symptoms, such as paralysis or sensory loss, that are psychological in origin. This category includes hypochondriasis and conversion disorder (formerly known as hysteria).
Dissociative disorders	Disorders in which part of one's experience is detached from consciousness. This category includes amnesia, fugue states, and dissociative identity disorder (formerly known as multiple personality disorder).
Mood disorders	Disorders marked by severe mood disturbances, such as major depression, mania (elation), or an alternating pattern of both.
Schizophrenic disorders	A group of psychotic disorders characterized by a loss of contact with reality, hallucinations, delusions, disorganized thought and affect, and bizarre behavior.
Personality disorders	Long-term, inflexible, maladaptive patterns of behavior. This category includes the borderline and antisocial personality disorders.

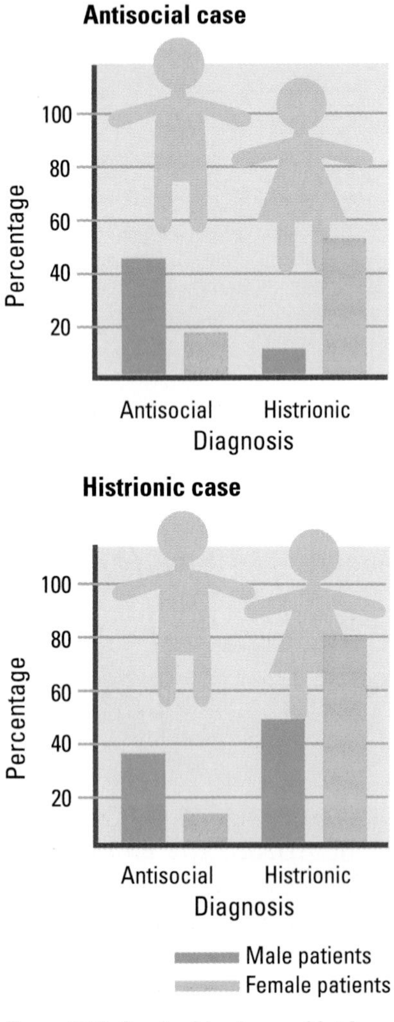

Figure 16.1 Gender bias in psychiatric diagnosis Clinical psychologists diagnosed a fictitious patient as "antisocial" when he was male and as "histrionic" when she was female—regardless of which disorder was described by the case history. This finding suggests that diagnosis can be biased by gender stereotypes.

ethnic background, and other social factors (Lopez, 1989). Gender provides a common example. In general, men and women suffer equally from mental disorders, but some specific problems are more common among men, others among women. Is it possible that these well-known differences influence a mental-health expert's judgment? We saw in Chapter 13 that people tend to see what they expect to see. Could the same be said of clinical diagnosis?

To examine this possibility, Maureen Ford and Thomas Widiger (1989) mailed a case history of a fictitious male or female adult to 354 clinical psychologists and asked them for a diagnosis. For some, the case depicted a classic "antisocial personality," a mostly male disorder characterized by self-centered behavior and a reckless disregard for rules. For other subjects, the case portrayed a "histrionic personality," a mostly female disorder characterized by excessive attention-seeking, emotionality, and flirtatiousness. As shown in Figure 16.1, the diagnoses that were made were clearly biased by gender. Regardless of which case history was read, the male patient was more likely to be labeled antisocial, and the female histrionic. Similar research suggests the possibility that African Americans are more often diagnosed—and misdiagnosed—as schizophrenic than are white patients with the same symptoms (Mukherjee et al., 1983).

A third concern is that diagnostic labels can adversely affect the way we perceive and treat those who suffer from mental disorders. In a provocative demonstration of how a label can take on a life of its own, psychologist David Rosenhan (1973) and seven colleagues visited twelve mental hospitals in five states, gave false names and occupations, and complained of hearing an unfamiliar disembodied voice say the words *thud*, *empty*, and *hollow*. On the basis of these reports, all the pseudopatients were diagnosed as schizophrenic and were admitted for treatment. From that point on, however, they answered all questions truthfully, behaved normally, followed instructions, and reported hearing no voices. Yet it took an average of nineteen days for Rosenhan and the others to get released (one was held for fifty-two days), and not a single psychiatrist, psychologist, social worker, or nurse uncovered the fraud (ironically, several real patients suspected that the researchers were journalists or investigators). Written case reports revealed that staff members sometimes interpreted normal behaviors in abnormal ways. Thus, when one pseudopatient paced the halls out of boredom, he was said to be "anxious." Another who was seen taking notes was said to be "paranoid." As with first impressions, a diagnostic label can be hard to remove. Indeed, we tend to see people through different eyes once they have been labeled mentally ill (Farina et al., 1992).

Thanks to the objective criteria provided in DSM-IV, and through the use of structured interviews and careful assessments of the patient's social and occupational functioning, diagnostic reliability has never been better. To some extent, the critics are correct in noting that clinical diagnosis is an imperfect human enterprise. As in medicine, mental-health professionals sometimes disagree on a patient, their judgments may subtly be influenced by stereotypes, and there is the ever-present danger that the labels will color the way people with disorders are perceived. Yet diagnosis is necessary. Just as physicians have to distinguish among heart disease, cancer, and pneumonia in order to prescribe the right treatment, psychologists and psychiatrists must distinguish among the different mental disorders. To ease the stigma associated with diagnostic categories, the American Psychiatric Association (1994) recommends that labels be applied to *behaviors*, not to *individuals*. It's better to say that a person has schizophrenia or an alcohol dependence than to call that person a schizophrenic or an alcoholic—terms that imply permanence.

In the remainder of this chapter, we consider some of the most common as well as some of the most bewildering disorders identified in DSM-IV. But first a word of caution: Watch out for "medical student's disease"—the tendency to see in yourself the disorders described in this chapter. If you are troubled or if you find it hard to function on a day-to-day basis, see someone about your problems. Otherwise, don't be alarmed. Bear in mind that normal and abnormal are points along a continuum and that everyone experiences some of the symptoms some of the time.

INTERSECTION

PSYCHOLOGICAL DISORDERS AND EDUCATION

Attention-Deficit Hyperactivity Disorder

This chapter is focused on adult psychological disorders. Among the diagnostic categories in DSM-IV, however, is one that pertains to problems that arise in infancy, childhood, or adolescence—often with adverse effects on academic achievement (Gaddes & Edgell, 1994; Barkley, 1997).

Almost every elementary-school classroom has at least one child, usually a boy, who is always on the go, lacks patience, and cannot sit still or sustain attention for an extended period of time. Among parents and teachers, children who fit this description are labeled hyperactive. Because these children also tend to be highly distractable and find it difficult to stay focused on a single task, they are diagnosed in DSM-IV as having *Attention-Deficit Hyperactivity Disorder*, or *ADHD*. The problem? As described by Sally Smith, founder of an elite private school for children with learning disabilities, "It's not that they are not paying attention. They are paying *too* much attention to *too* many things" (Hancock, 1996).

Research shows that the average two-year-old can attend to a constant stimulus for about seven minutes, that three-year-olds can do so for nine minutes, four-year-olds for thirteen minutes, and five-year-olds for fifteen minutes. The average first-grader can be expected to sit and work for up to an hour. Yet children with ADHD have three distinctive symptoms: they are *inattentive*,

In the classroom, children with ADHD have difficulty staying focused.

impulsive, and *hyperactive*. Thus, they are highly distractable, easily stimulated, quick to move from one task to another, and constantly on the lookout for new activities. In school, these children can't seem to stay in their seats, listen to the teacher, stand in line, or follow instructions. They constantly blurt out answers, wiggle their feet, climb on furniture, tap their pencils, lose things, and act as if being driven by a motor (Barkley, 1990).

ADHD affects an estimated 3 to 7 percent of all elementary schoolage children in North America and is more prevalent among boys than girls by about a 3 to 1 ratio. Among children diagnosed with ADHD, the problem persists into adolescence for 50 to 80 percent and into adulthood for 30 to 50 percent (Weiss & Hechtman, 1993). Many children with ADHD have behavioral and learning disabilities—and have trouble adjusting to structured settings such as a classroom. They tend to do poorly in school and have difficulty at reading, complex problem solving, and tasks that require fine motor coordination. The problems often continue into adolescence, resulting in low grades, and expulsion or early withdrawal from school (Klein & Mannuzza, 1991). As adults, they often have problems in marriage, social relationships, and employment (Barkley, 1997).

There are many theories about the causes of ADHD. According to one theory, children with ADHD exhibit extremely low levels of arousal in the central nervous system—and seek stimulation in order to raise that arousal level (Zentall & Zentall, 1983). In contrast, other researchers have examined differences in brain activity, diet, neurotransmitters, parenting styles, and social learning. Whatever its origins, most ADHD children can be successfully treated (though not cured) with *Ritalin*, a stimulant drug that increases arousal as well as the production of the neurotransmitters norepinephrine and dopamine. Nicknamed "Vitamin R," Ritalin is prescribed for about 600,000 children a year in the United States alone—the equivalent of 1 to 2 percent of the school-age population. Most ADHD children on Ritalin exhibit short-term increases in attention span, reductions in motor activity, and improvements in their classroom behavior and performance (Carlson & Bunner, 1993; Pelham et al., 1993).

It's important to be cautious in diagnosing ADHD—and not identify as disordered children who are merely active and rambunctious. It's also important, if Ritalin is prescribed, to combine its use with psychologically oriented therapies and classroom teaching strategies aimed at modifying the child's behavior and problem-solving skills. When she talks to children about Ritalin, teacher Sally Smith likes to hold up a ruler, point to the one-inch mark, and say, "This is how much Ritalin does for you. It makes you available to learn. You and your parents and teachers have to work on all the rest" (Hancock, 1996, p. 56). In this notable intersection of clinical psychology and education, it's clear that parents, teachers, psychologists, and physicians must collaborate in their efforts (Pelham, 1993).

Anxiety Disorders

What do cross-cultural studies tell us about the anxiety disorders? What is panic, and what are its biological and psychological origins? What's the difference between a simple and social phobia? And why do some people wash their hands hundreds of times a day?

Anyone who has faced military combat, the interview of a lifetime, a championship game, major surgery, or the menacing sound of a prowler in the house knows what anxiety feels like. On occasion, we all do. It's a nervous, jittery feeling of apprehension accompanied by a pounding heart, trembling hands, cold and sweaty palms, quivering voice, a dry mouth, dizziness, lightheadedness, a shortness of breath, an upset stomach, or diarrhea.

Generalized Anxiety Disorder

Anxiety is a normal response to threatening and stressful situations. As we saw earlier, however, about 25 percent of all Americans will at some time in life experience anxiety that is so intense, persistent, and disabling that it is considered to be a disorder (Kessler et al., 1994). Over the course of a lifetime, an estimated 5 percent of adults suffer what is known as **generalized anxiety disorder**—a persistent, gnawing undercurrent of "free-floating" (not linked to an identifiable source) anxiety (Wittchen et al., 1994). Feeling aroused and not knowing why, the person with a generalized anxiety disorder is highly sensitive to criticism, has difficulty making decisions, dwells on past mistakes, and worries constantly about money, work, family matters, and illness (Barlow, 1988). It is not clear, however, whether these are effects or causes of the disorder. Research suggests that people with generalized anxiety disorder are hypersensitive before they seek treatment—and remain so after the disorder is in remission (Eysenck, 1992).

Many people have anxiety attacks that are more focused. In particular, three such disorders are described in this section: panic, phobias, and obsessive-compulsive disorders. Before you read on, however, two points are worth noting. First, although the different anxiety disorders are in some ways distinct, most people who have one type are likely to exhibit the symptoms of at least one other type as well (Brown & Barlow, 1992; Sanderson et al., 1990). Second, although people all over the world suffer from intense anxiety, their specific symptoms are influenced by one's cultural upbringing (Good & Kleinman, 1985).

Consider the case of a twenty-five-year-old Chinese American patient. Shortly after having sex with a prostitute, he complained of a sudden burning pain in his penis, accompanied by a fear that his genitals were shrinking. He became terrified that his penis would retract into his abdomen, causing him to suffer and die. In a state of panic, he tried to masturbate in order to assure himself that all was well, but he could not achieve an erection. The young man became so desperate that he contemplated suicide. This case may sound unique, but it was not: The man was suffering from Koro (also called *suo-yang* in Chinese medical books), an anxiety disorder that has existed for hundreds of years in Southeast Asia. Typically found in young males, Koro is characterized by an acute panic attack lasting for days or weeks and by a fear that one's sexual organs will disappear into the body, causing death. A Koro epidemic swept through Singapore in 1967. Shortly after the Vietnam War, another thousand cases were reported in Thailand. Then in the 1980s, two waves of Koro spread through China. Many patients link the onset of this disorder to a sexual escapade, and treatment often consists of wearing a clamp that prevents retraction of the penis (Bernstein & Gaw, 1990).

Koro is only one example of an anxiety disorder that is restricted to a cultural group. There are others. In Mexico and certain Latin American cultures, people may be afflicted with *susto*—an intense fear reaction, insomnia, and irritability, believed to be brought on by the "evil eye" of voodoo or black magic. In Japan, there is *shinkeishitsu*—an emotional disorder in which people become so self-conscious and perfectionistic that they feel too inadequate to interact with others. And in China, there is *paleng*—a disorder in which sufferers wear several layers of clothing, even in the summer, because of a morbid fear that they will die from a loss of body heat.

generalized anxiety disorder A psychological disorder that is characterized by a constant state of anxiety not linked to an identifiable source.

The Scream *(Edward Munch, 1893)*

What do these cross-cultural comparisons tell us? At this point, two conclusions can be drawn. First, anxiety is universal and the *physiological* symptoms are the same from one culture to the next. Regardless of where one is born and raised, anxiety is a bodily reaction characterized by a shortness of breath, racing heart, trembling, and so on. Second, culture influences the *cognitive* component of anxiety. What symptoms people worry about, how they interpret those symptoms, and their beliefs about the causes of anxiety all depend on the values and ideologies to which they are exposed (Barlow, 1988; Good & Kleinman, 1985).

Panic Disorder

Norwegian artist Edward Munch (1863–1944) was a troubled man who knew all too well the meaning of the word *panic.* In 1893, Munch painted *The Scream,* a nightmarish portrait of a terrified person standing on a bridge under a blood-streaked sky, covering his or her ears and screaming in anguish as two ominous, shadowy people approach from behind. Said Munch, this image was inspired one day when "I was walking . . . and I felt a loud, unending scream piercing nature." Sometimes a picture really is worth a thousand words.

People who suffer from **panic disorder** experience frequent, sudden, intense rushes of anxiety, usually lasting for several minutes. The symptoms of a panic attack include chest pains and heart palpitations, hyperventilation, a shortness of breath, choking and smothering sensations, and fainting. These symptoms are often accompanied by feelings of unreality and detachment from one's body and by a fear of going crazy, losing control, or dying. Table 16.2 presents the percentages of panic-disordered patients who experience various symptoms. An attack is considered "panic" if it includes four or more of these symptoms (Barlow, 1988).

Research shows that panic strikes most often during the day but that it also frequently occurs between the hours of 1:30 and 3:30 AM, while people are asleep; that heart rates increase an average of thirty-nine beats per minute; and that the episodes last for approximately sixteen minutes, followed by exhaustion (Taylor et al., 1986).

Table 16.2 The Panic Button: Symptoms

SYMPTOMS	PERCENTAGES
Heart palpitations	87
Dizziness or faintness	87
Trembling or shaking	86
Fear of losing control	76
Shortness of breath	75
Hot flashes or chills	74
Excessive sweating	70
Numbness or tingling sensations	58
Depersonalization	57
Nausea or abdominal distress	56
Fear of dying	52
Choking sensation	50
Chest pains	38

Source: D. H. Barlow (1988). *Anxiety and its disorders.* New York, Guilford Press.

panic disorder A disorder characterized by sudden and intense rushes of anxiety without an apparent reason.

What's worse, those who get frequent panic attacks worry so much about embarrassing themselves in front of others (by falling, fainting, vomiting, gasping loudly for air, or losing bladder control) that they very often develop **agoraphobia**, a fear of being in public places that are hard to escape. People with agoraphobia are frequently prisoners in their own homes—afraid to stray into shopping malls, restaurants, sports arenas, theaters, airports, or train stations. The word itself comes from a Greek term meaning "fear of the marketplace."

Approximately one-third of all adults report that they have experienced panic during the past year (Norton et al., 1992). However, only 2 out of every 100—a majority of them women—suffer from panic disorder (Eaton et al., 1994; Kessler et al., 1994; Telch et al., 1989). What causes panic disorder? There are two major perspectives—one biological, the other psychological (McNally, 1994). Supporting a biological point of view, research shows that panic attacks tend to strike without warning or provocation and that the experience can be induced as well as treated with drugs (Barlow, 1988; Gorman et al., 1989). The psychological approach is supported by three kinds of evidence. First, many patients report that their first attack occurred shortly after an illness, miscarriage, or some other traumatic event (see Figure 16.2). Second, people with panic disorder are highly attuned to their bodily sensations and are prone to misinterpret the signals in ways that are "catastrophic." Feeling aroused, they are quick to fear that they are having a heart attack, stroke, or some other life-threatening ordeal—and this belief fuels the fire (Clark et al., 1997; Ehlers & Breuer, 1992; Schmidt & Trakowski, 1997). Among people prone to panic, for example, inhaling carbon dioxide sets off an otherwise adaptive "suffocation-alarm" (Klein, 1993). Third, psychological forms of therapy—such as relaxation training, breathing exercises, and various behavioral and cognitive techniques—can help alleviate panic attacks without the use of drugs (McNally, 1990; Michelson & Marchione, 1991; Rachman & Maser, 1988). To sum up: The human panic button can be activated by biological or psychological means.

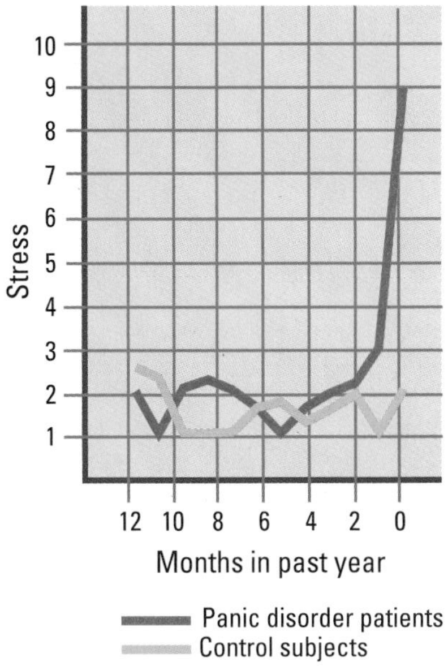

Figure 16.2 Stress and panic disorder Faravelli and Pallanti (1989) assessed the amount of stress felt by sixty-four panic-disorder patients and a group of "normal" controls. As shown, the patients had experienced a sharp increase in stress the month just prior to the onset of their symptoms.

Phobic Disorder

> *"A man who fears suffering is already suffering from what he fears."*
>
> — MICHEL DE MONTAIGNE

Every Sunday afternoon during football season, John Madden broadcasts a National Football League game on television. From one week to the next, regardless of whether the game is played in Philadelphia, Houston, Green Bay, or San Diego, Madden drives hundreds of miles in his own private bus. As inconvenient as this may seem, it is the only way Madden will travel. The reason? Despite his 260-pound, 6'4" frame and rough exterior, Madden is terrified of flying on airplanes.

Whereas panic strikes suddenly and without warning, phobias are focused and predictable. A **phobic disorder** is one in which a person reacts to an object or event with high levels of anxiety, knows that the reaction is irrational, and copes by avoidance. The word *phobia* comes from the name of the Greek god Phobos, who instilled fear in his enemies. The disorder itself is experienced by one out of eight Americans (Magee et al., 1996). There are two types of phobias. A **simple phobia** is an intense, irrational fear of a specific object or situation. The most common are a fear of heights, airplanes, closed spaces, blood, snakes, and spiders. But there are other, more idiosyncratic phobias as well. I once had a friend who would grip his car seat, stiffen up, and break into a cold sweat whenever we drove over a drawbridge with a metal-grating surface. Table 16.3 presents a partial list of simple phobias that have been identified and named over the years. Some names may sound familiar; others you may be able to figure out from the prefix (Maser, 1985).

agoraphobia An anxiety disorder in which the main symptom is an intense fear of public places.

phobic disorder An anxiety disorder characterized by an intense and irrational fear.

simple phobia An intense, irrational fear of a specific object or situation.

Table 16.3 Partial List of Simple Phobias

PHOBIA	FEARED OBJECT OR SITUATION
Acrophobia	Heights
Aerophobia	Flying
Agoraphobia	Public places
Aichmophobia	Sharp pointed objects
Aquaphobia	Water
Arachnaphobia	Spiders
Brontophobia	Thunderstorms
Claustrophobia	Closed spaces
Entomophobia	Insects
Hematophobia	Blood
Homilophobia	Sermons
Monophobia	Being alone
Mysophobia	Dirt and germs
Nycytophobia	Darkness
Ophidiophobia	Snakes
Parthenophobia	Virgins
Porphyrophobia	The color purple
Triskaidekaphobia	The number 13
Xenophobia	Strangers
Zoophobia	Animals

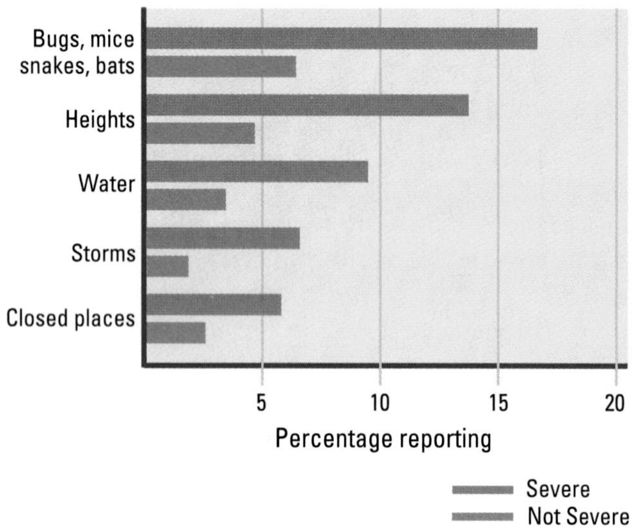

Figure 16.3 Frequency of the most prevalent simple phobias

A second type of phobic disorder is the **social phobia**, an exaggerated fear of situations that invite public scrutiny (Leary & Kowalski, 1995). Probably the most familiar example is public-speaking anxiety, or stage fright—a performer's worst nightmare. If you've ever had to make a public presentation, only to feel weak in the knees and hear your voice quiver, you will have endured at least a hint of this disorder. What is there to fear in public speaking? When people were asked this question, the most common responses were: shaking and showing other signs of anxiety, going blank, saying something foolish, and being unable to continue (Stein et al., 1996). For the social phobic, unbearable levels of self-consciousness are also evoked by other situations. Examples include eating at a public lunch counter, signing a check in front of a store clerk, and, for males, urinating in a crowded men's room. In private, these behaviors pose no problem. In the presence of others, however, they arouse so much fear that the situations are avoided at all costs. In extreme cases, the reaction becomes so debilitating that the person just stays at home (Turner & Beidel, 1989). The severe and less-severe frequencies of the most prevalent phobias are shown in Figure 16.3.

What causes phobic disorders? Many years ago, Freud argued that people with phobias are anxious about hidden impulses and cope by displacing their anxiety onto substitute objects that are less threatening and easier to avoid. To illustrate, he

social phobia An intense fear of situations that invite public scrutiny.

Certain phobic disorders occur with greater frequency than others. Some of the most common are ophidiophobia (a fear of snakes), acrophobia (a fear of heights), and claustrophobia (a fear of closed spaces).

wrote about the classic case of Little Hans, a five-year-old boy who would not leave home because he was terrified that he would be bitten by a horse. According to Freud (1909), Hans was in the midst of an Oedipal conflict and had converted an unconscious fear that his father would castrate him into a conscious fear of getting bitten by a horse. From a psychoanalytic perspective, then, the phobic object is merely a symbol for a deeper, more troubling problem.

In reaction to Freud's case study, behaviorist John Watson demonstrated with a baby named Little Albert that phobias can develop through conditioning (see Chapter 5). Since that time, researchers have found that phobias are learned by classical conditioning (Ost, 1992) and by the observation of someone else's fear reaction to an object. For example, Susan Mineka and Michael Cook (1993) found that when laboratory-raised rhesus monkeys saw wild monkeys of the same species react fearfully to the presence of a snake, they too became distressed and acquired an intense fear of snakes. To the behaviorist, then, phobias are derived from an experience or observation, then may spread through a process of stimulus generalization (thus, if a child is locked in a closet at a tender young age, he or she may acquire a specific fear of closets or a more general case of claustrophobia). In this view, the reason phobias last long after the precipitating experience is forgotten is that we avoid phobic objects, denying ourselves an opportunity to unlearn the fear.

A third view, also described in Chapter 5, is that humans are genetically programmed, or "prepared," to develop certain kinds of phobias. People all over the world fear darkness, heights, snakes, insects, and other harmless objects, some of which are never encountered. The reason, according to Seligman (1971), is that human beings are prepared by evolution to fear objects and situations that were harmful to our prehistoric ancestors.

Obsessive-Compulsive Disorder

Howard Hughes had it all. He was a billionaire, famous pilot, entrepreneur, and Hollywood producer. There was just one hitch: Hughes was tormented by an uncontrollable preoccupation with germs, eventually causing him to live the life of a hermit. He sealed all windows and doors with tape and spent many hours a day washing himself. His aides had to open doors with their feet to avoid contaminating doorknobs, wear white cotton gloves before serving his food, and deliver newspapers in stacks of three so he could slide the middle one out with a tissue. Toward the end of his life, Hughes became so overwhelmed by his own routines that he could not take care of himself. When he died, at the age of sixty-nine, his body was filthy and emaciated, his beard was scraggly, his teeth were rotted, and his fingernails were so long that they curled in on themselves—a sad and ironic ending for a man who had once said, "I want to live longer than my parents, so I avoid germs" (Fowler, 1986, p. 33).

Along with an estimated 4 million other Americans, Howard Hughes suffered from **obsessive-compulsive disorder (OCD)**—a crippling anxiety ailment characterized by constant *obsessions* (the intrusion into consciousness of persistent, often disturbing thoughts) and *compulsions* (behavior rituals performed in response to obsessions). OCD usually begins in late adolescence and early adulthood, affects men and women equally, and is found in India, England, Norway, Egypt, Nigeria, Japan, Hong Kong, and other countries around the world (Insel, 1984). People with OCD know that their habits are crazy, but they just can't stop themselves. Fearing shame and humiliation, many of them try to keep their actions a secret and wait years before seeking treatment.

What kinds of thoughts and behaviors haunt OCD patients? In a book entitled *The Boy Who Couldn't Stop Washing,* psychiatrist Judith Rapoport (1989) described one boy who washed his hands so much they became raw and bloodied from all the scrubbing; another boy who ran up and down a flight of stairs exactly sixty-three times every day; and a woman who was so determined to keep her eyebrows symmetrical that she plucked out each and every hair. Similarly, in *The Sky Is Falling,* Raeann Dumont (1996) described a woman who spent eight hours a day bathing; a man who couldn't leave a subway station without picking up all the litter; and a man whose apartment was stacked to the ceiling with dirty old clothes, dishes, newspapers, and other objects he had collected but could not bring himself to throw away. As bizarre as these stories sound, research shows that they accurately reflect the kinds of behaviors that plague OCD sufferers (Jenicke et al., 1986). The most common themes of this disorder, as reported in interviews with 100 OCD patients, are presented in Table 16.4. Most patients had multiple obsessions and compulsions (Jenicke et al., 1986).

Everyone has a few mild obsessions and compulsions. You may double- and triple-check your alarm clock at night, try to avoid stepping on sidewalk cracks, or feel a burning need to straighten out crooked wall hangings. Professional athletes

Table 16.4 Obsessive-Compulsive Disorder

THEMES OCD SUFFERERS OBSESS ABOUT	PERCENTAGE
Dirt, germs, contamination	55
Aggressive impulses	50
Need for symmetry	37
Bodily concerns	35
Forbidden sexual impulses	32
RITUALS OCD SUFFERERS PERFORM	**PERCENTAGE**
Checking	79
Washing	58
Counting	21

Source: M. A. Jenicke et al. (1986). *Obsessive-compulsive disorders: Theory and management.* Littleton, MA: PSG.

obsessive-compulsive disorder (OCD) An anxiety disorder defined by persistent thoughts (obsessions) and the need to perform repetitive acts (compulsions).

are especially known for their compulsive rituals. Many baseball players, for example, adjust their cap, tug at their shirt, bang their shoes, and run through a complicated sequence of superstitious gestures before every pitch. If these examples don't apply to you, try this: Do not imagine a white bear. Seriously, put this book down, and try not to think about white bears. See the problem? Daniel Wegner (1989) finds that when people actively try to suppress a particular thought, that thought intrudes into consciousness with remarkable frequency—like a newly developed obsession. What distinguishes these mild quirks from OCD is the intensity of the accompanying anxiety and the extent to which it interferes with one's life. Wegner and Zanakos (1994) devised a questionnaire they called the White Bear Suppression Inventory, and they found that individuals who agree with such statements as "I have thoughts I cannot stop" and "There are images that come to mind I cannot erase" are particularly prone to obsessional thinking.

There are many different theories about the causes of OCD. Psychoanalysts maintain that obsessive thoughts leak forbidden sexual and aggressive urges into consciousness, compelling the person to devise elaborate rituals as a countermeasure. In this view, compulsive washing symbolizes a person's need to cleanse the soul of dirty impulses. Behaviorally oriented theorists note that compulsions endure because they are reinforced by a reduction of the anxiety aroused by obsessive thoughts. Indeed, many compulsions can be extinguished in a few weeks by forcibly preventing the patient from responding to the obsession—for example, no washing allowed despite the buildup of anxiety (Foa et al., 1985).

Biological factors also play a role, as indicated by the fact that various antidepressant drugs help most sufferers of OCD to terminate their rituals (Rapoport, 1989). Also, PET scans of the brains of OCD patients have revealed abnormally high levels of activity in a group of nuclei that are involved in the control of habitual behaviors. In a PET study of eighteen OCD patients, Jeffrey Schwartz and others (1996) found that this area became less active after behavioral and cognitive therapy. For about ten weeks, patients were prevented from acting on their obsessions. Struck with the urge to wash for the umpteenth time of the day, for example, they were trained to label the urge a mere brain-triggered obsession and refocus their attention on a constructive activity such as gardening or golf. As Schwartz (1996) describes the process in his book *Brain Lock*, the refocusing procedure is designed to engage a new part of the brain, and this helps to "unlock" the area that had become stuck in its pattern. When it comes to OCD, it appears that the mind can change the brain.

Somatoform Disorders

What does it mean to be a hypochondriac? What is "glove anesthesia" and what is its psychological signficance?

Long before psychology became a discipline, physicians struggled with the problem of treating patients who complained of muscular aches and pains, upset stomachs, and other ailments for which an organic basis could not be found. According to DSM-IV, many of these patients suffer from a **somatoform disorder** (the word *somatoform* means "bodylike"), in which they experience bodily symptoms that are psychological rather than medical in origin. Somatoform disorders are not easy to diagnose. People who complain of an illness are not consciously faking

somatoform disorder A type of mental disorder in which a person experiences bodily symptoms that are psychological rather than medical in nature.

(a condition known as malingering), nor does their psychological distress cause physical damage (the way stress causes ulcers and migraine headaches, conditions that are "psychosomatic"). Illustrating that mind and body are hopelessly interlocked are two types of somatoform disorder: hypochondriasis and conversion disorder.

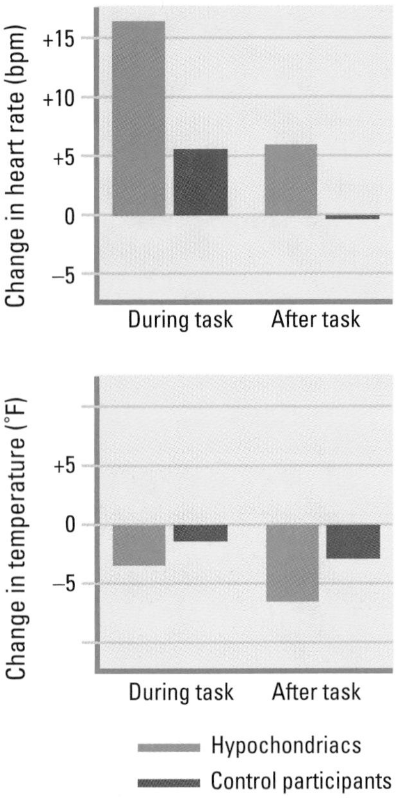

Figure 16.4 Sensitivity in people with hypochondriasis Hypochondriacal and control participants put their feet into ice-cold water for three minutes. Relative to their baseline levels, hypochondriacal participants had more elevated heart rates during the task—and later, in a posttask recovery period (*top*). They also had lowered hand temperatures during and after the task (*bottom*). These results suggest that hypochondriacs may be physiologically more reactive to stimulation than others (Gramling et al., 1996).

Hypochondriasis

While on his famed *Beagle* voyage around the world, Charles Darwin was constantly seasick. Then, beginning when his wife Emma became pregnant with their first of ten children and lasting for the rest of his life, he complained of nausea, numbness in the fingertips, indigestion, dizzy spells, chest pains, and other assorted ailments. Darwin was so pampered by his family that "the whole day was planned out to suit him, to be ready for reading aloud to him, to go on his walks with him, and to be constantly at hand to alleviate his daily discomforts" (Colp, 1977, p. 92).

If Darwin were alive today, he would be diagnosed as having **hypochondriasis,** a disorder involving a chronic and unwarranted preoccupation with one's own physical health. Hypochondriacs are highly sensitive to normal bodily sensations. Equipped with do-it-yourself medical books, thermometers, blood-pressure kits, and shelves lined with vitamins, they become alarmed the moment they sneeze, cough, feel warm, feel cool, get an itch, pull a muscle, or skip a heartbeat. Not wanting to hear words of reassurance, they tend to jump from one doctor to the next until they find one who takes their complaints seriously (Baur, 1988; Kellner, 1987). In general, hypochondriacs tend to set many health-related goals such as losing weight, relaxing, and managing stress (Lecci et al., 1996).

Some psychologists have speculated that hypochondriasis is a reaction to separation anxiety and the desire to stay helpless or that it is symptomatic of society's preoccupation with health. Others believe that it is caused by an oversensitive nervous system. Research shows that hypochondriacs not only are quicker to notice symptoms of illness but also are more distressed than others by loud noises, high and low temperatures, and hunger pains (Barsky et al., 1988). But are they more sensitive, prone to amplify bodily sensations? To test this hypothesis, Sandra Gramling and her colleagues (1996) used the MMPI to identify fifteen high-scoring hypochondriacal women and fifteen female controls. Each participant was asked to place her foot into a tub of ice water for three minutes—or until she could no longer tolerate it. Before, during, and afterward, heart rate and hand temperature were recorded. There were two telling results. First, the hypochondriacal women kept their feet in the tub for less time and rated the sensation as more unpleasant. In fact, only seven went the distance—compared to thirteen in the control group. Second, among those who did complete it, hypochondriacal participants had more elevated heart rates and lowered hand temperatures during the ice-water task—and afterward, during a posttask recovery period. People with hypochondriasis may be highly reactive to stimulation not just in their self-reports and behavior but also at a deeper physiological level (see Figure 16.4).

> *"Nothing is more fatal to Health, than the Over Care of it."*
>
> — BENJAMIN FRANKLIN

Whatever the causes of this somatoform disorder, two points are clear. First, hypochondriasis can easily become a lifelong pattern nourished by sympathy, attention, relief at work, excuse for failure, and other social rewards. Even Darwin realized before he died that "my head would have failed years ago had not my stomach saved me from a minute's over-work" (Colp, 1977, p. 70). Second, our sensitivity to bodily sensations falls on a continuum on which both extremes are maladaptive.

hypochondriasis A disorder characterized by an unwarranted preoccupation with one's physical health.

Just as the hypochondriac is too health-conscious, others are not attuned enough to the symptoms of illness, choosing instead to deny the body's warning signals, often to their own detriment (Strauss et al., 1990).

Conversion Disorder

A second somatoform disorder is **conversion disorder,** in which the person temporarily loses a bodily function without a physical cause. This problem is primarily found in young women, which is why Hippocrates in 400 bce called it *hysteria* (from the Greek word for "uterus")—and prescribed marriage as the cure. In the nineteenth century, Freud theorized that hysteria arose from traumas or deep-seated sexual conflicts and that the resulting anxiety was "converted" into physical ailments. The classic symptoms mimic neurological disorders such as paralysis, blindness, deafness, epilepsy, and anesthesia (a loss of feeling in a limb). This disorder was illustrated in a wave of cases in the 1970s, during a reign of terror in what used to be Cambodia. Shortly afterward, many women—who were tortured or, worse, saw their own children tortured and murdered—became psychologically blind. One woman, a refugee whose family had been killed and who had managed to escape to the United States, said, "I cried for four years. When I stopped crying, I was blind" (Rozee & Van Boemel, 1989).

How can one tell the difference between conversion disorder and actual nerve damage? It's not always easy. One clue is that the reported symptoms are sometimes not anatomically possible, as in the case of "glove anesthesia," shown in Figure 16.5. Another is that the symptoms may suddenly disappear—as when a "blind" patient manages to walk right through the doctor's office without bumping into furniture or a "paralyzed" patient walks in his or her sleep. How can a conversion disorder be distinguished from conscious faking? No diagnosis is foolproof, but there is one clue: Whereas people who fake ailments are always evasive and defensive about examination, true conversion patients tend to display *la belle indifference,* a nondefensive and curious lack of concern about their condition (Ford & Folks, 1985).

Sociocultural context seems to play an important role in the outbreak of somatoform disorders. Cases of hysterical paralysis, which Freud and his contemporaries reported at the turn of the century, are today rare. Perhaps it's because Western society is less sexually repressive than in Freud's era. Or perhaps we have become too sophisticated about psychological matters to believe that a person could be paralyzed for no apparent reason. Whatever the explanation, conversion-disorder cases are now few and far between. As a result, the subject has captured the imagination of many historians—including Mark Micale (1995), whose recent book, *Approaching Hysteria,* chronicles this curious "disease and its interpretations" from the ancient Greeks through the Middle Ages, nineteenth-century Europe, and today.

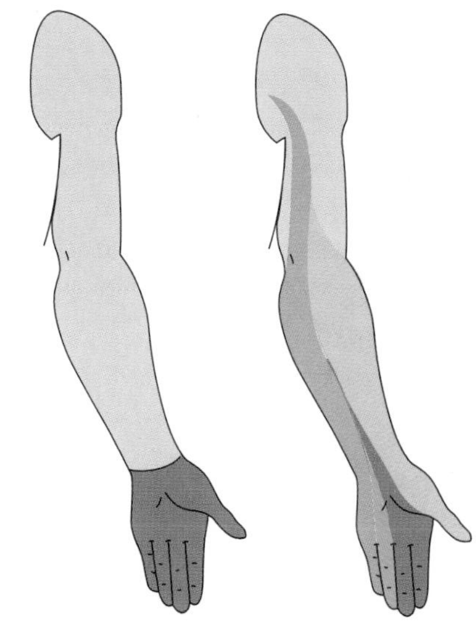

Figure 16.5 Glove anesthesia: a conversion disorder A person with "glove anesthesia" reports numbness in the hand from the wrist to the fingertips but continued sensation in other parts of the arm (*left*). This complaint can be diagnosed as a conversion disorder because it is anatomically impossible. If there is actual nerve damage, the sensory loss would extend to upper parts of the arm as well (*right*).

Dissociative Disorders

What is a dissociative disorder, and how does it differ from simple "tuning out"? What is dissociative identity disorder, how common is it, and why does it arouse so much skepticism?

Have you ever found yourself listening to someone talk, only to realize that you missed most of what was said? Were you ever in a place that was familiar but

conversion disorder A disorder in which a person temporarily loses a bodily function in the absence of a physical cause.

could not remember having been there before? And did you ever have trouble figuring out whether an experience that you had was real or just a dream? As with absentmindedness and other lapses of awareness, these phenomena are possible signs of dissociation—a process by which a portion of one's life becomes separated or detached from one's identity or conscious memory. Look at the experiences listed in Table 16.5, taken from the Dissociative Experiences Scale (Bernstein & Putnam, 1986). How many of these have you had, and how often? Some are common. In a survey of over a thousand adults in Canada, for example, 83 percent said they had occasionally "spaced out" on chunks of a conversation (Ross et al., 1990). In Japan, Belgium, the Netherlands, and the United States as well, studies have shown that people consistently report having such experiences (Ray, 1996; Ross, 1997).

In contrast to these normal episodes that we all experience, people diagnosed with a **dissociative disorder** have serious long-term memory gaps. In essence, these people have learned to cope with intense trauma and stress by mentally erasing unwanted parts of life from their memory. There are three types of dissociative disorders: amnesia, fugue state, and dissociative identity disorder (Michelson & Ray, 1996).

Amnesia and Fugue States

The most common dissociative disorder is **amnesia,** a partial or complete loss of memory. Amnesia can last for varying periods of time and can be caused by physical trauma such as head injury or alcohol intoxication. In a 1991 basketball game, for example, former Los Angeles Lakers star Magic Johnson fell on his back, hit his head on the hardwood floor, and was momentarily unable to recall the city he was in or the team he was playing against—a case of organic amnesia. Alternatively, the problem can sometimes be traced to a stressful event such as a car accident, a rape, or a physical beating. In these cases of dissociative amnesia, only self-relevant memories are blocked. Amnesia victims may forget who they are and where they live, but they remember clearly how to speak, read, drive a car, and recite information from general knowledge (Weingartner et al., 1983).

Dissociative **fugue states** (*fugue,* as in the word *fugitive,* means "flight") are more extensive than simple amnesia. In extreme cases, someone who slips into a fugue

Table 16.5 Types of Dissociative Experiences

1. Suddenly realizing, when you are listening to someone talk, that you did not hear part or all of what the person said.
2. Finding yourself in a place and having no idea how you got there.
3. Finding yourself dressed in clothes that you don't remember putting on.
4. Suddenly realizing, when you are driving a car, that you don't remember what has happened during all or part of the trip.
5. Losing the memories of important events in your life, such as your wedding or graduation.
6. Looking in a mirror and not recognizing yourself.
7. Feeling sometimes that other people, objects, and the world around you are not real.
8. Becoming so absorbed in a fantasy or daydream that it feels as though it was really happening to you.
9. Feeling sometimes as if you were looking at the world through a fog such that people and objects appear far away or unclear.
10. Feeling sometimes that your body does not seem to belong to you.

dissociative disorder A condition marked by a temporary disruption in one's memory, consciousness, or self-identity.

amnesia A dissociative disorder involving a partial or complete loss of memory.

fugue state A form of amnesia in which a person "forgets" his or her identity, wanders from home, and starts a new life.

state not only forgets his or her name but also wanders from home, takes on a new identity, remarries, gets a new job, and starts a new life. Then, just as suddenly, the person will "wake up"—disoriented and confused, oblivious to what has transpired, and eager to return home as if no time has passed. Fugue states may last for hours or for years. Sometimes, the victim's new life is more exciting and uninhibited than the old routine. At other times, it provides an escape from responsibility and danger. Fugue states are quite common, for example, among soldiers bound for combat. Either way, it is difficult—if not sometimes impossible—to tell whether a fugue victim has a genuine dissociative disorder or is faking (Schacter, 1986).

Chris Sizemore was the subject of The Three Faces of Eve, *a 1957 film about a woman with multiple personality disorder. Sizemore claims that she formed twenty-two different personalities to cope with "traumatic death experiences" she had at two years old.*

Dissociative Identity Disorder

The most dramatic instance of dissociation is **dissociative identity disorder (DID)**, an extremely rare condition in which a person displays two or more distinct identities (until DSM-IV was published in 1994, this condition was called *multiple personality disorder*). Sometimes, two opposing identities battle for control, as in the classic tale of Dr. Jekyll and Mr. Hyde. Sometimes, there are three personalities, as in *The Three Faces of Eve,* a film about a woman (played by actress Joanne Woodward) who alternated among Eve White, a timid housewife; Eve Black, a sexually promiscuous woman; and Jane, a balanced blend of the other two. In other cases, one dominant identity is accompanied by a host of subordinate personalities, as in the case of Sybil Dorsett, whose sixteen personalities were portrayed by actress Sally Field in the film *Sybil.*

Dissociative identity disorder is such a strange phenomenon that you might think it springs from the imaginative minds of playwrights and novelists. What are the facts and fictions about DID? According to DSM-IV, it is nine times more prevalent among women than men and is ordinarily preceded by a childhood history of repeated abuse. Summarizing five major studies of 843 DID patients, for example, Colin Ross and his colleagues (1990) found that more than 88 percent reported having been victims of sexual, physical, or emotional child abuse—a striking statistic that was confirmed in a later study conducted in the Netherlands (Boon & Draijer, 1993). This finding makes some sense. Children who are abused and are utterly defenseless learn early in life to cope by tuning out, divorcing a part of themselves from the pain and suffering, and constructing alternative persons within which to live (Ross, 1997).

In almost all cases, at least one personality is unable to recall what happens to the others (Putnam et al., 1986). In fact, the differences between personalities are at times extraordinary. Each may have its own voice, speech pattern, habits, memories, sexual orientation, clothing, and handwriting. Physical changes may also occur, as when two personalities within the same patient exhibit different brain-wave patterns, blood-pressure readings, eyeglass prescriptions, or reactions to medicine (Kluft, 1996). One man, for example, had a severe allergic skin reaction to orange juice when one personality was in control but not another (Braun, 1988). Based on interviews with 102 people with DID, which yielded the percentages associated with various symptoms. The most common symptoms of DID are presented in Table 16.6.

If you find the notion of multiple personalities hard to believe, you are not alone. Since the first case was reported, in 1817, fewer than 200 appeared in psychiatric journals up to the year 1970. Since that time, however, thousands of new cases have been reported. To be sure, DID can be found in most societies, but the frequency of the disorder and the form it takes vary greatly from one generation and culture to the next (Spanos, 1996). All this has skeptics wondering: Is the disorder really on the

dissociative identity disorder (DID) Formerly known as multiple personality disorder, it is a condition in which an individual develops two or more distinct identities.

Table 16.6 Symptoms of Dissociative Identity Disorder

SYMPTOMS	PERCENTAGES
Another person existing inside	90
Voices talking	87
Amnesia for childhood	83
Referring to self as "we" or "us"	74
Blank spells	68
Being told by others of unremembered events	63
Feelings of unreality	57
Strangers know the patient	44
Noticing that objects are missing	42
Coming out of a blank spell in a strange place	36
Objects are present that cannot be accounted for	31
Different handwriting styles	28

Source: C. A. Ross et al. (1990). Structured interview data on 102 cases of Multiple Personality Disorder from four centers. *American Journal of Psychiatry,* 147, p. 599.

rise? There are three possible explanations. One is that many patients are faking multiple personalities for personal gain, and therapists are simply unable to distinguish between true and false cases. A second is that therapists used to misdiagnose the problem and are now more sensitive to the symptoms. The third is that therapists now overdiagnose the disorder or, worse, are suggesting and reinforcing its presence in patients, thus producing a "psychiatric growth industry" (Weissberg, 1993).

If you've seen the 1996 movie thriller *Primal Fear*, you can appreciate the diagnostic dilemma. In that film, actor Richard Gere plays a lawyer who defends a man, played by Edward Norton, who murdered a priest. The defendant has enormous gaps in his memory and undergoes dramatic transformations in his demeanor, so Gere—and most viewers—come to believe that he has multiple personalities. Not until the film ends, however, and the defendant is found not guilty by reason of insanity, does he tell Gere that he had faked the disorder.

As bizarre as this situation may seem, it actually occurred several years ago in the case of Kenneth Bianchi, otherwise known as the Hillside Strangler. Based on convincing evidence, Bianchi was charged with brutally murdering ten California women. At first, he denied the charges. But then a psychologist hypnotized Bianchi and uncovered hidden personalities. During the hypnosis session, the psychologist said, "I've talked a bit to Ken, but I think perhaps there might be another part of Ken that I haven't talked to . . . Would you please come, Part, so I can talk to you too?" Lo and behold, a completely new personality named Steve Walker came out. Ranting and raving, using foul language, and smoking no-filter cigarettes, Steve confessed to the crimes and said he hated Ken because he was a "goodie two-shoes." According to Steve, Ken was innocent.

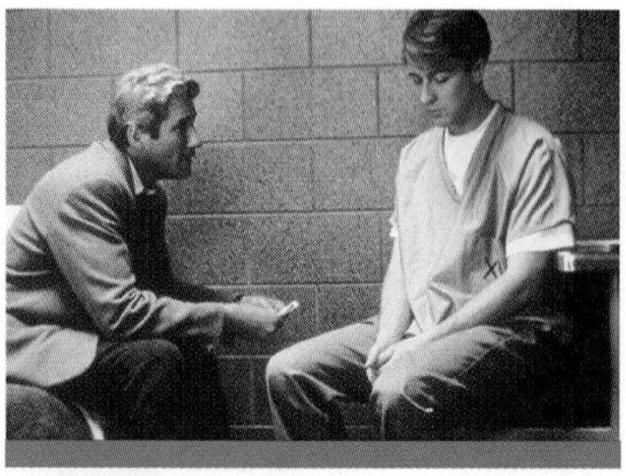

A scene from Primal Fear, *a film about a cold-blooded murderer who fakes a multiple personality to escape punishment for his crime.*

Was Steve a real personality, or was he born of convenience to help Ken escape punishment for his crimes? The dissociative disorders are a serious problem, one that inflicts profound suffering on those who have it. In this case, however, the local police were suspicious, so they hired psychiatrist Martin Orne to conduct further tests. At one point, Orne mentioned to Bianchi that real multiples usually have three or more personalities, not just two. The trap was set, and Ken fell in: The next time he was under hypnosis, Ken produced a third personality. Orne's trick—along with the discovery that Bianchi owned numerous books on psychology, hypnosis, and multiple personality—was convincing evidence. The jury that tried Bianchi found him guilty of murder (Orne et al., 1984; Schwarz, 1981).

Mood Disorders

Why is depression often called the "common cold" of mental disorders? What are the biological and psychological causes of depression? Do people who commit suicide leave clues of their intention? What is bipolar disorder, and why might it be linked to artistic creativity?

Personal experience tells us that mood can powerfully shade our view of ourselves, the world, and the future. On the roller coaster of life, the range of feelings is familiar to all of us: The exhilarating highs are on one end of the continuum, and the depths of despair are on the other. Land the job of your dreams, fall head over heels in love, or win a lottery, and you fly elatedly "on cloud 9." Lose a job or money, break up with a lover, struggle in school or at work, and you become sad, even depressed. These fluctuations are normal. Problems arise, however, when someone's mood state is so intense and so prolonged that it profoundly impairs the ability to function. There are two main types of **mood disorders:** major depression and bipolar disorder.

Major Depression

A chronic sufferer of depression, Winston Churchill referred to his condition as the "black dog" that followed him around. He was certainly not alone. The incidence of depression has increased dramatically in recent years (Klerman & Weissman, 1989). Currently, an estimated 12 percent of American males and 21 percent of females will suffer from major depression at some point in life (Kessler et al., 1994). The problem is so widespread that Churchill's black dog has been called the common cold of mental disorders.

> *"When you're depressed, you feel like you've got a thousand pounds on every limb of your body."*
>
> — ROD STEIGER

Depression is a mood disorder characterized by deep sadness and despair. Since these feelings are sometimes an appropriate and normal reaction to tragedy, someone is considered clinically depressed only if the episode arises without a discernible cause and lasts for two or more weeks. In addition to the effects on mood, symptoms include: (1) diminished pleasure or interest in food, sex, social banter, and other joys; (2) intense feelings of worthlessness, guilt, and self-blame; (3) restlessness and agitation, marked by difficulty sleeping, concentrating on work, and making decisions; (4) fatigue, slowness, and a lack of energy (in extreme cases, there is such a paralysis of the will that the person has to be pushed out of bed, washed, dressed, and fed by others); and (5) recurring thoughts of suicide and death. Indeed, up to 15 percent of people who are clinically depressed go on to kill themselves (American Psychiatric Association, 1994).

Consider some quick facts about depression. One is that about twice as many women as men seek treatment for depression—though the disparity is smaller in less-developed nations (Culbertson, 1997). This sex difference begins to appear in adolescence (Nolen-Hoeksema & Girgus, 1994). In part, it reflects the fact that

mood disorder A condition characterized by prolonged emotional extremes ranging from mania to depression.

depression A mood disorder characterized by sadness, despair, feelings of worthlessness, and low self-esteem.

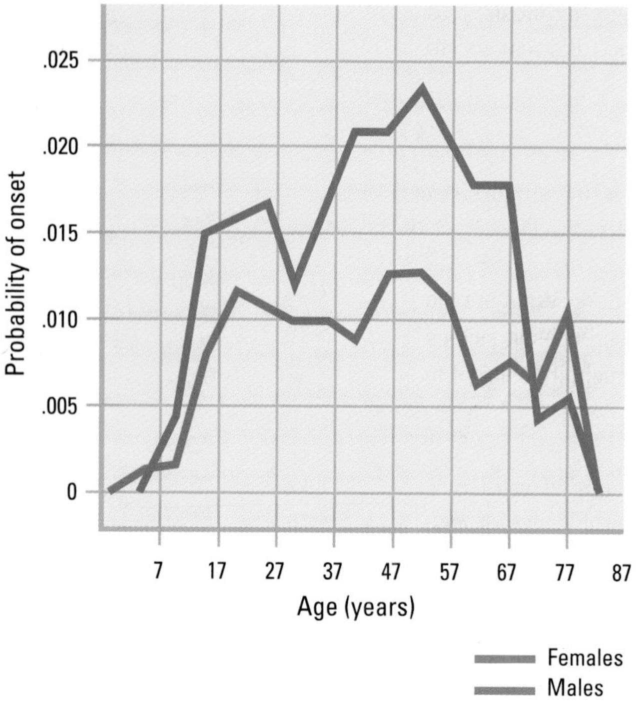

Figure 16.6 Depression: ages of first onset

women tend to confront their feelings, while men resort to alcohol, physical activity, and other means of distraction (Nolen-Hoeksema, 1990). Second, age is a relevant factor. As illustrated in Figure 16.6, depression is seldom identified for the first time in someone's life before adolescence, but then the age of first onset increases sharply, rises through adulthood, peaks at middle age, then declines (Lewinsohn et al., 1986). Third, people get depressed in all cultures of the world, though the specific form it takes may differ. For example, depressed people complain of headaches and "nerves" in Latino cultures, of "imbalance" in Chinese and Asian cultures, and of problems of the "heart" in Middle Eastern cultures (American Psychiatric Association, 1994). Fourth, the depression rate has been rising with each successive generation—a trend that has been found not only in the United States and Canada but also in France, Germany, Italy, Lebanon, New Zealand, Puerto Rico, and Taiwan (Cross-National Collaborative Group, 1992). Regardless of one's sex, age, culture, or generation, it's reassuring to know that depressive episodes often last only a few weeks. Sadly, however, 50 to 60 percent of those who suffer one major depression later have a recurrence that is longer-lasting and more severe (Maj et al., 1992; Winokur et al., 1993).

As we saw in Chapter 9, some people exhibit the symptoms of depression on a seasonal basis, after a succession of overcast days. This condition is known as *seasonal affective disorder (SAD),* and it strikes during the short, dark days of autumn and winter (Rosenthal, 1993). Every year, people with SAD who live in cold-winter regions of the world become listless, drowsy, and withdrawn. They sleep more, eat more, crave carbohydrates, gain weight, lose interest in sex, and falter at work and in social relationships. As described in Chapter 9, however, two hours a day of exposure to bright light is effective for many SAD sufferers.

Vincent van Gogh's Crows over the Wheatfield *is an intense and haunting portrayal of the French countryside under troubled skies. This may have been van Gogh's last painting before he committed suicide in 1890.*

Theories of Depression

As you might expect, psychologists have tried for many years to find a cure for this common cold of mental disorders. In order to treat and prevent depression, however, one must understand where it comes from and what factors serve to maintain it.

Biological Factors Ernest Hemingway killed himself with a shotgun. So did his father and brother. Then many years later, in June 1996, his granddaughter Margaux Hemingway committed suicide with a drug overdose. Clearly, say researchers, the depression that triggers suicide runs in families. But does this mean that depression is inherited, or is it the product of shared environments? Research shows that if one fraternal twin suffers a major depression, there is a 20 percent chance that at some point the other will too. Yet the rate for identical twins is closer to 50 percent—a comparison that reveals a genetic linkage (Tsuang & Faraone, 1990; Kendler et al., 1993; McGuffin, 1996). This finding suggests two compatible conclusions: (1) There is a genetic basis of depression, but (2) environmental factors also play a prominent role.

In all likelihood, genes influence mood disorders by acting on neurotransmitters, the biochemicals that relay impulses from one neuron to another. In the 1950s, doctors noticed that drugs used to treat blood pressure and tuberculosis often had dramatic side effects on a patient's mood—sometimes causing depression, at other times euphoria. Researchers then found that the same drugs also increase the supply of norepinephrine and serotonin, neurotransmitters that regulate moods and emotions. So what does it all mean? When the two strands of evidence were put together, it became apparent that depression is associated with lower-than-normal levels of these neurotransmitters—and that mania is caused by an overabundance. As we'll see in Chapter 17, the practical benefit of this discovery was the development of antidepressant drugs such as Prozac.

It is now clear that the link between biological states and mood is more complicated than was once believed. Antidepressants are effective for many people but not for everyone, and some drugs work without altering norepinephrine or serotonin levels (Depue & Iacono, 1989; McNeal & Cimbolic, 1986). Other biological factors may also play a role. For example, certain infectious diseases, neurological disorders, and vitamin deficiencies have mood-altering effects (Hollandsworth, 1990); many depressed people have higher-than-normal levels of cortisol, a stress hormone (Nemeroff, 1989); and people who suffer from the chronic pain of rheumatoid arthritis are also prone to become depressed (Brown, 1990). Researchers are currently trying to understand how and why these biological states are linked to depression, and whether they are causes or effects in the chain of events.

Psychological Factors In a 1917 paper entitled "Mourning and Melancholia," Sigmund Freud noted similarities between depression and the kind of grief that accompanies the death of a loved one. According to Freud, melancholia, like mourning, is a reaction to *loss*. The loss may involve the breakup of a relationship, financial decline, or failure to reach an important goal. Not everyone overreacts to these kinds of events. Among those who were abandoned or neglected as children, however, even a minor setback may cause them to retreat into a passive, dependent, childlike state. It can also awaken intense anger that is turned inward, or "internalized"—which is why people who are depressed often punish themselves with self-blame, feelings of worthlessness, and suicide.

Behaviorally oriented psychologists trace depression to our history of reinforcement and perception of control. According to Peter Lewinsohn (1974), people get depressed when they are unable to produce for themselves a high rate of positive reinforcement. Similarly, Martin Seligman (1975) has argued that depression is a form of **learned helplessness**, an expectation that one cannot control important life outcomes. In a series of experiments during the 1960s, Seligman found that dogs strapped into a harness and exposed to painful electric shocks soon became passive and gave up trying to escape—even in new situations where escape was possible. As applied to humans, this finding suggests that prolonged exposure to uncontrollable outcomes may similarly cause apathy, inactivity, a loss of motivation, and pessimism.

Realizing that perception is more important than reality, many psychologists now focus on social-cognitive aspects of depression. Several years ago, psychiatrist Aaron Beck (1967) noticed that his depressed patients viewed themselves, their world, and

learned helplessness A learned expectation that one cannot control important life outcomes, resulting in apathy and depression.

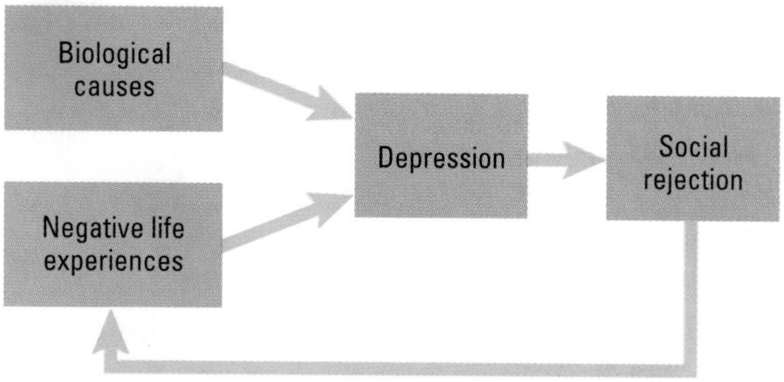

Figure 16.7 The vicious cycle of depression

the future through dark glasses. According to Beck, these patients distorted reality by focusing more attention on negative events than on positive ones—a pattern consistently found in research (Haaga et al., 1991). This bleak outlook is pervasive. Research shows that depressed people are not only down on themselves but also down on their parents and romantic partners (Gara et al., 1993).

Lynn Abramson, Gerald Metalsky, and Lauren Alloy (1989) further proposed that depression is a state of *hopelessness* brought on by the negative self-attributions that people make for failure. Specifically, some people have a **depressive explanatory style**, a tendency to attribute bad events to factors that are internal rather than external ("It's my fault"), stable rather than unstable ("It will not change"), and global rather than specific ("It affects other parts of my life"). Many studies now provide support for this proposition. Whether people are trying to explain social rejection, a sports defeat, low grades, or inability to solve an experimenter's puzzle, those who are depressed are more likely than others to blame factors that are within the self, are unlikely to change, and are broad enough to impair other aspects of life. The result is pessimism, hopelessness, and despair (Metalsky et al., 1993; Seligman, 1991).

Finally, humanistic theorists believe that people become depressed if they fail to achieve self-actualization. Consistent with this hypothesis, studies show that people feel unfulfilled and depressed when they perceive that there is a discrepancy between their actual and their ideal selves (Higgins, 1989)—particularly when the discrepancy is large and attention is focused on the self (Strauman, 1989; Pyszczynski & Greenberg, 1987). Within this framework, suicide is viewed as the last desperate attempt of an unfulfilled person to escape from the pain of self-awareness (Baumeister, 1990).

The Vicious Cycle of Depression

It's one of the sad ironies for men and women with depression: They desperately need social support and a shoulder to cry on, yet they behave in ways that drive away the most important people in their lives. The result is a vicious, self-perpetuating cycle: Depression elicits social rejection, which in turn worsens the depression (see Figure 16.7).

Do depressed people really elicit negative reactions and rejection? Are we all so cold-hearted that we turn our backs on those in need of emotional support? Sometimes, yes. When people are severely depressed, friends do try to cheer them up and offer a sympathetic ear, a shoulder to lean on, and advice. However, as psychotherapists are the first to admit, these efforts usually fail and the depression persists. The suffering person is filled with complaints, regrets, and expressions of self-pity, which makes social interaction unpleasant. What's worse, studies have shown that people who are depressed avoid eye contact, speak softly, are slow to respond, wear sad or blank facial expressions, and are negative in their demeanor—a pattern of behavior that is seen as rude, detached, and nonresponsive (Segrin & Abramson, 1994). The result is that people react to those who are depressed with mixed emotions—sorrow laced with irritation, anger, and a desire to avoid future contact (Coyne, 1976; Strack & Coyne, 1983; Gurtman, 1987; Sacco & Dunn, 1990). This vicious cycle may help to explain why strained friendships are common among people with depression (Coyne et al., 1987)—and why their social interactions, in general, are less intimate and rewarding (Nezlek et al., 1994).

depressive explanatory style The tendency for depressed people to attribute negative events to factors that are internal, stable, and global.

Suicide: The Ultimate "Solution"

"I don't believe it. I just saw him last week, and he looked fine." "I knew she was depressed, but I had no idea it was this bad. Why didn't she call me?" These statements are typical of how people react when someone they know commits suicide. Every year, about 31,000 Americans kill themselves—an average of one suicide every half-hour (Retterstol, 1993). And for every one person who actually commits suicide, there are ten to twenty others who try. To the average person, nothing about human behavior seems more puzzling or senseless. Yet to those who are depressed and in a state of mental pain and anguish, it often seems like the *only* solution (Maltsberger & Goldblatt, 1996; Shneidman, 1996).

> *"The thought of suicide is a great source of comfort; with it a calm passage is to be made across many a bad night."*
>
> — FRIEDRICH WILHELM NIETZSCHE

Who tries to commit suicide, and why? In the United States, statistics show that women are three times more likely to attempt suicide, but men are three to four times more likely to succeed. This difference reflects the fact that men often put a bullet to the head, while women are more likely to overdose on sleeping pills—a slower and less certain method. Either way, about 75 percent of suicides are committed by people who are depressed. In fact, the single best predictor of suicide potential is a sense of hopelessness. In one study, more than 2,000 psychiatric outpatients were tested and followed for up to seven years. Of the 17 who went on to commit suicide, 16 had initially gotten high scores on a "hopelessness scale" (Beck et al., 1990). In a survey of college students who had attempted suicide, the other factors most frequently cited were loneliness, depression, problems with lovers or parents, feelings of helplessness, grades, and money (Westefeld & Furr, 1987).

When do people who feel hopeless resort to suicide? Roy Baumeister (1990) theorized that the main purpose of suicide is to "escape from self." In his view, people think about suicide when they fail to achieve an important life goal, blame themselves for the failure, focus too much attention on the self, become sad and depressed, think in short-sighted terms as a way to escape mentally from the anguish, and, as a result, shed the inhibitions that normally prevent people from contemplating such drastic measures. In other words, suicide is a last resort, with the goal being "oblivion"—a complete loss of self-consciousness. Although it is impossible to test this theory directly, Baumeister presented an array of suicide research statistics compatible with his propositions. For example, consistent with the hypothesis that people who kill themselves are highly self-focused, he finds that compared to the farewell notes written by people who face death from illness, suicide notes contain more first-person pronouns (*I* and *me*).

These teenagers have all attempted suicide. Among the reasons most often cited in such cases are loneliness, depression, problems with boyfriends and girlfriends, grades, money, and feelings of helplessness.

Shocked friends and relatives always wonder: Should I have known? Could I have done something to prevent it? These are tough personal questions. Suicide is difficult to predict, and nobody should feel guilty about getting caught by surprise. But there are patterns to watch for (Shneidman, 1996). First, people who are depressed and who use drugs are particularly vulnerable—not while they are in the depths of despair, as you may think, but afterward, as they start to regain their energy and spirit. Second, about 90 percent of all suicides are preceded by remarks about one's death or departure—such as "Sometimes I wonder if life is worth living" or "You won't see me again" (note that only 2 or 3 percent of people who talk about suicide make the attempt, but of those who commit suicide, almost all had talked about it). Third, people preparing to kill themselves often leave telltale behavioral clues. They might start to put their papers in order, for example, pull back from prior commitments, take unusual risks, or give away prized possessions. Fourth, it helps to know that people who attempt suicide once are at a higher-than-average risk to do so again, even much later in life.

Is there a way to prevent suicide? If you are concerned about someone you know, Edwin Shneidman (1996) recommends that certain actions be taken. Stay close and communicate openly. If the person alludes to death, gives away valued possessions, or leaves other hints, it's best to inquire as to what's happening and, if necessary, ask directly, "Are you thinking about suicide?" Offer sympathy, suggest options, and most important of all—make sure the person gets professional help. In case of a crisis, call for help yourself.

Bipolar Disorder

In contrast to major depression, a *unipolar* disorder in which moods range from neutral to depressed, **bipolar disorder** produces wild fluctuations that range from *manic* (a euphoric, overactive state) to *depressed* (a state of hopelessness and apathy). In what used to be called "manic depression," bipolar-disorder patients alternate uncontrollably between the two extremes, in cycles that last from a few days to several months. One week, they are flying as high as a kite, bursting with energy and optimism. The next week, they have sunk to the depths of despair (see Figure 16.8).

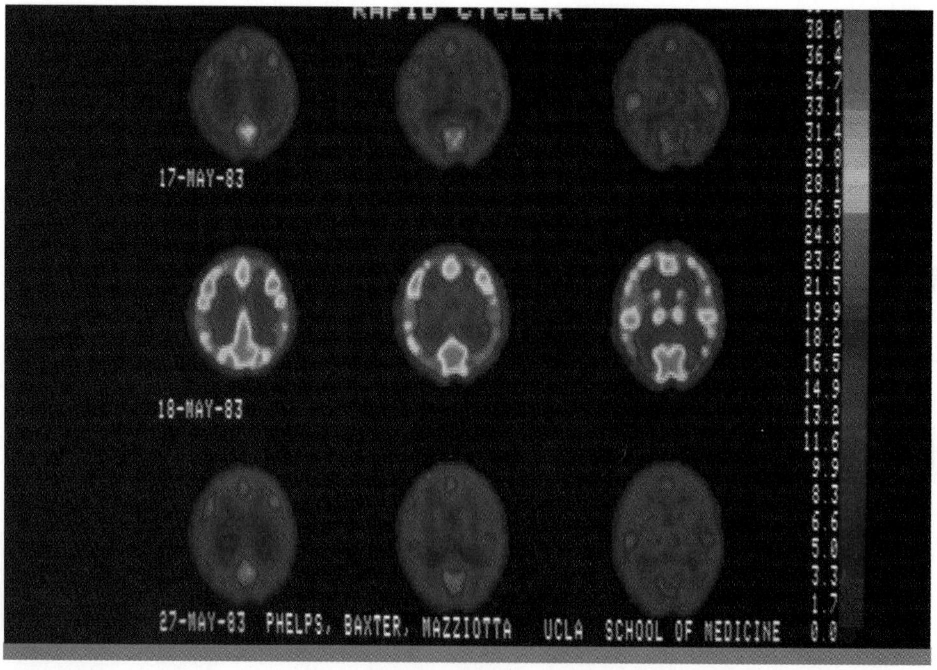

Figure 16.8 Brain activity in bipolar disorder The PET scans shown here were taken from the brain of a bipolar-disorder patient who alternated every 24–48 hours from depression (*top*) to mania (*middle*), and back to depression (*bottom*). Note that dark blues and greens mark low levels of activity; red, orange, and yellow mark higher levels of activity.

bipolar disorder A rare mood disorder characterized by wild fluctuations from mania (a euphoric, overactive state) to depression (a state of hopelessness and apathy).

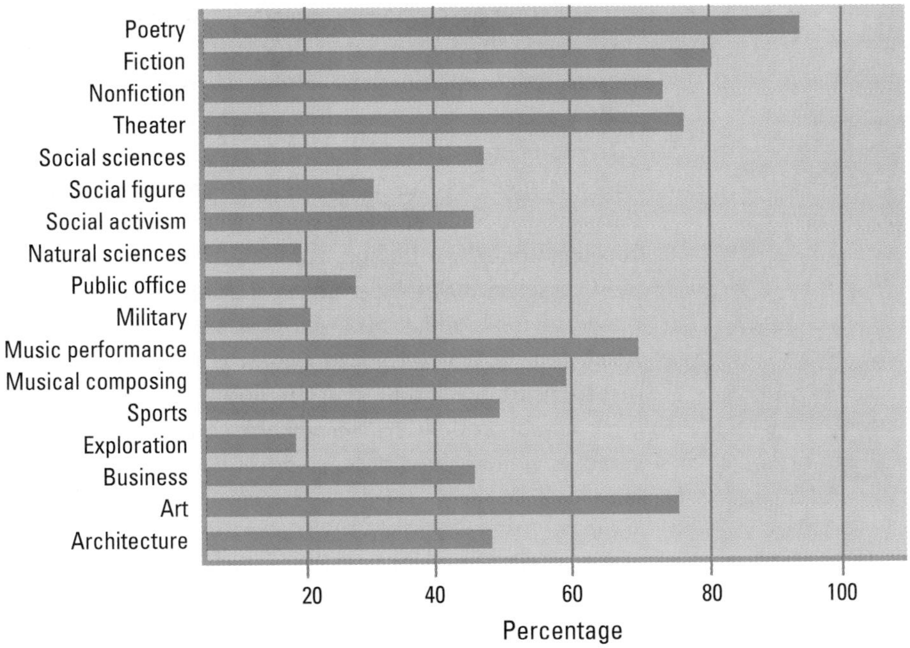

Figure 16.9 Is there a connection between creativity and mental illness? In a study of 1,005 successful twentieth-century people, Ludwig (1995) found that the lifetime rate of mental illness in general (not just bipolar disorder) was higher among those in the arts than in other professions. How can this phenomenon be explained?

What does the manic phase of this disorder feel like? What are the symptoms? In its early stages, mania is an exhilarating state of mind that many of us have enjoyed from time to time. The mildly manic person is boundless in energy, filled with self-esteem, and confident that no challenge is too daunting. With the mind racing at full speed, the manic person is entertaining, witty, imaginative, quick to see connections between ideas, and filled with ambitious and creative schemes.

More than 100 years ago, the German psychiatrist Emil Kraepelin (1883; reprinted 1923) observed that manic excitement "sets free powers that otherwise would be constrained by inhibition." The pages of history suggest he may have been right. In *Touched with Fire,* Kay Redfield Jamison (1993) notes that among the many creative geniuses who had bipolar disorder were composers Robert Schumann and George Frideric Handel, artist Vincent van Gogh, and writers Edgar Allan Poe, Ernest Hemingway, Eugene O'Neill, Sylvia Plath, F. Scott Fitzgerald, Mark Twain, Walt Whitman, Tennessee Williams, and Virginia Woolf. In *The Price of Greatness,* Arnold Ludwig (1995) reported on a biographical survey of more than 1,000 famous people of the twentieth century. He discovered that writers, poets, and artists were two to three times more likely to have bipolar disorder than successful professionals in business, science, sports, and public life. But he also found that they were more likely to suffer from alcoholism and other drug abuse, anxiety disorders, depression, and schizophrenic disorders (see Figure 16.9). As the philosopher Nietzsche once said, "One must harbor chaos within oneself to give birth to a dancing star."

Before jumping to the conclusion that bipolar disorder is worth having, you should know that there is a much darker side. As the disorder progresses, mania accelerates out of control, and "high" becomes "too high." The person becomes easily distracted, moves from one project to another, stays awake at night, and is extremely sensitive to stimulation. It has been said that to the manic person, a gentle breeze feels like a slap on the face and the dropping of a pin sounds like a clanging

"Those? Oh, just a few souvenirs from my bipolar-disorder days."

noise. People in an advanced state of mania also harbor delusions (false beliefs) of grandeur. They make promises they cannot keep, buy things they cannot afford, start new sexual relationships, and drag others into risky money-making schemes that are bound to fail. Socially, the charm and wit give way to behavior that embarrasses others. Fitting the stereotype of the "raving maniac," the person becomes loud, fast-talking, frenzied, and explosive. Even mild criticism may trigger anger and hostility. Finally, the manic phase is sometimes followed by major depression. Illustrating that what goes up must come down, bipolar-disorder sufferers either return to normal or hit the ground in a crash landing. A remarkable number of creative geniuses who reaped the benefits of their manic energy later killed themselves while depressed (Goodwin & Jamison, 1990; Ludwig, 1995).

Although bipolar disorder is a close relative of depression, the two are quite different. To begin with, bipolar disorder has a stronger genetic component. Thus, if one twin has it, the odds are about 72 percent that an identical twin will have it too, compared to only 13 or 14 percent for a fraternal twin of the same sex (Blehar et al., 1988; Tsuang & Faraone, 1990). Indeed, geneticists have linked bipolar disorder to a specific region of the eighteenth chromosome (MacKinnon et al., 1997). As we'll see in Chapter 17, bipolar disorder can be treated with the drug lithium.

"A monkey winked at me this morning."

Common in schizophrenia are delusions of reference, false beliefs that one is the recipient of others' actions.

schizophrenic disorders Disorders involving gross distortions of thoughts and perceptions and by loss of contact with reality.

Schizophrenic Disorders

What does the word *schizophrenia* mean? What are the five major symptoms of the schizophrenic disorders? What's the difference between a delusion and a hallucination? What evidence is there for the genetic and environmental roots of schizophrenia?

When you stop to think about "madness" or "insanity," what comes to mind? For many of us, the words alone evoke stereotyped images of people who stare blankly into space, talk gibberish to themselves, see imaginary pink animals, walk in circles, and erupt in fits of rage and violence. These images are not generally accurate, as we'll see, but they do come close to describing schizophrenia—the most dreaded of psychological disorders.

Schizophrenic disorders are marked by gross distortions of thought and perception and by a loss of contact with reality. In some cases, the disorder strikes suddenly between the ages of seventeen and twenty-five and is followed by a full recovery. In other cases, the disorder develops slowly, causes the person to deteriorate over a period of years and casts a life sentence on its victim—no parole, no time off for good behavior. Schizophrenia is found in all cultures of the world and affects men and women equally. It is estimated that slightly less than 1 percent of all Americans will exhibit a schizophrenic disorder within the course of a lifetime (Regier et al., 1988). The most likely age of first onset is eighteen to twenty-five for men, twenty-six to forty-five for women. This sex difference in age of onset shows up all over the world and has researchers puzzled (Gottesman, 1991; Straube & Oades, 1992).

The Symptoms of Schizophrenia

Translated from Greek, the word *schizophrenia* means "split brain." The so-called split is not between two or more inner selves, as in dissociative identity disorder, but rather between thoughts, beliefs, perceptions, emotions, motor behavior, and other brain functions. To people with schizophrenia, it's like being stuck in the "Twilight Zone" (Torrey, 1988).

There are five major symptoms that are found in people with a schizophrenic disorder. First and foremost, many of them exhibit *incoherent thinking*. The person may be mentally disorganized and confused, on a different wavelength than the rest of us. This problem is most evident in speech. Listen to people with this symptom talk, and you may well hear them create new words and drift illogically from one topic to another, making their statements sound like something of a "word salad." Often, for example, they will string together utterances that are only loosely associated. Eugen Bleuler (1911), the Swiss psychiatrist who gave schizophrenia its name, cited an example from one of his patients: "I wish you a happy, joyful, healthy, and fruitful year, and many good wine years to come as well as a healthy and good apple-year, and sauerkraut and cabbage and squash and seed year." In this sample of speech, the word fruitful set off a chain of food-related associations. The reason is that schizophrenic patients who exhibit disorganized thinking tend to have difficulty focusing attention on one stimulus and filtering out distractions (McGhie & Chapman, 1961; Freedman et al, 1987). In the autobiographies of fifty former patients, concentration problems were the most frequent thought-related complaint (Freedman, 1974).

In April 1997, Marshall Applewhite and thirty-eight followers of the Heaven's Gate cult committed mass suicide. Their actions were motivated by a socially constructed delusion—*that they would be taken from Earth to the Kingdom of Heaven by a spacecraft trailing the Hale-Bopp comet.*

A second symptom is the presence of **delusions,** or false beliefs. In schizophrenic minds all over the world, certain delusional themes appear with remarkable frequency. Among the most common are delusions of *influence*—the belief that one's thoughts are being broadcast in public, stolen from one's mind, or controlled by evil forces. Thus, one patient was convinced that his thoughts were publicized to others on a "mental ticker-tape," another spoke of having her thoughts "sucked out of my mind by a phrenological vacuum extractor," and a third believed "a radio was implanted in my skull." Also common are delusions of *grandeur* (that one is famous or powerful, capable of controlling weather, planets, and other people), delusions of *reference* (that one is the primary recipient of other peoples' actions), and delusions of *persecution* (that one is a target of secret plots by others).

A third symptom is the presence of **hallucinations,** sensory experiences that occur without actual stimulation. To hallucinate is to see, hear, smell, taste, or feel something that does not exist. The most common hallucinations are auditory. Many people with schizophrenia report that they "hear" the swishing or thumping sound of a heartbeat, musical choirs, or disembodied voices that comment on their lives, make accusations, and issue commands. "Son of Sam" David Berkowitz, who terrorized New York City in the 1970s by killing young women, claimed he was ordered to stalk and shoot his victims by the demonic voice of a barking dog. Sometimes, but less often, hallucinations occur in other sensory systems as well. People may "see" heavenly

delusions False beliefs that often accompany schizophrenia and other psychotic disorders.

hallucinations Sensory experiences that occur in the absence of actual stimulation.

visions, "smell" foul body odors, "taste" poison in their food, or "feel" a tingling, burning, or pricking sensation on their skin. Other perceptual distortions are also evident. According to numerous reports, lights seem brighter, colors more vibrant, and sounds more intense. And people's bodies often appear longer, shorter, smaller, rounder, or otherwise deformed—like viewing the world through a funhouse mirror.

The fourth symptom is a *disturbance of affect,* or emotional experience. Some schizophrenics have a flattened affect. They sit still for hours, wear a blank expression on the face, speak in a low and monotonic voice, avoid eye contact, and show little interest or concern in anything. As one psychiatrist described, "It is uncannily like interacting with a robot" (Torrey, 1988). Others express feelings that are highly animated and exaggerated or are inappropriate to the situation—crying to happy news, laughing at tragedy, or screaming in anger without external provocation.

The fifth symptom is *bizarre behavior.* Absorbed in an inner world of stimulation, perhaps confused by distorted perceptions of the outer world, people with schizophrenia often withdraw, go into social exile, and cease to function effectively at work. They may talk to themselves, repeat like parrots what others say, spend hours in statuelike poses, walk backward or in circles, take their clothes off in public, and so on. Remarkably, they also lack self-insight. People with schizophrenia often think that their word salads are coherent, their delusions and hallucinations real, and their emotions appropriate. As one former patient said, "I felt I was the only sane person in the world gone crazy" (see Table 16.7). Approximately 12 percent of people with schizophrenia commit suicide (Caldwell & Gottesman, 1990).

Table 16.7 Schizophrenia: A Personal Account

A little knowledge, people say, is a dangerous thing. My problems first started when I decided to go back to college at the age of 27. After taking a psychology course, I recognized signs of stress in myself and went for help. I was taking 16 credits, working full time in my business which was a day-care center, and taking care of my children in the absence of their father. He was working out of town and came home on weekends. During that school term, certain remarks made by my professors led me to the conclusion that they were working to rescue me from what they thought was an abusive marriage. And I, contrarily, was convinced that I wanted to stay married.

I felt particularly influenced by a foreign language instructor. I was convinced that this professor and I had a private means of communication and, because of this, interpreted what he said in class as personally relating to me. Sometimes the things I heard in class had no relation to the class purpose. One time, the professor asked the room at large, 'So your husband used to be a minister?' I had not divulged that information to him, but because I had recently told my baby-sitter that, I felt the incident was more than coincidence. I felt that there was a large network of people finding out about me, watching me on the street for some unknown reason. This feeling of lack of privacy soon grew into thinking my house was bugged, a fear I would have off and on for the next eight years. The bizarre and illogical things I heard people say were later dismissed as auditory hallucinations. They seemed very real to me, however.

On one occasion, I saw a personal experience of mine written on the blackboard in French and English. I did not recognize it as a hallucination at that time. This caused me considerable anguish, but I continued to act as normal as I could for fear that any bizarre behavior would cause me to lose my job. I did not talk about these things, so the only noticeable signs of my illness were that I became silent and withdrawn, not my usual ebullient and smiling self. I did not think I was sick, but that these things were being done to me. I was still able to function though I remember getting lunch ready very slowly as if working in molasses, each move an effort.

By Christmas, I heard an actor call me a liar over the TV, and I felt sure the media also knew about me. When I went to the store, I bought things that symbolically meant something else to me; each fruit, flavor, or color had a meaning that tied in with my delusion. For example, I would not buy Trix cereal, because it was associated with prostitution in my mind, but I bought a lot of Cheerios to make my day happier. The world of delusion soon became a world of imagined depravities that were a torment to my moralistic mind. I felt I was the only sane person in the world gone crazy (Anonymous, 1990, pp. 547–548).

Types of Schizophrenia

Even before Bleuler named the disorder, it was obvious that there are different kinds of schizophrenia, with each featuring different combinations of symptoms. In DSM-IV, five major types are distinguished (McGlashan & Fenton, 1991):

- *Disorganized.* A category used to describe those who exhibit illogical thinking, incoherent speech, a neglect of personal hygiene, exaggerated displays of emotion, and mannerisms that are silly and childish.
- *Catatonic.* A rare form of the disorder that features extremes in motor behavior ranging from motionless "stupors" to bursts of hyperactivity.
- *Paranoid.* A form in which the main symptom is being preoccupied with one or more delusions or hallucinations, often with extreme suspiciousness and hostility.
- *Undifferentiated.* A catch-all category for cases that exhibit a mixture of symptoms and do not clearly fit into another type.
- *Residual.* A diagnostic category that is used for people who had prior episodes of schizophrenia but are currently not experiencing the major symptoms.

The thoughts and emotions of people with schizophrenia can often be seen in their creative expressions. In the words of artist Sandra Milne, "This painting was done in response to my doctor's suggestion that I paint who I really was. Each person represents a side of me" (left). *Artist Maria Karasz says, "This is a picture of what happens when you have a nervous breakdown: the world explodes and the powers of cosmic destruction overwhelm your mind and soul with the screech of panic, fear of nonexistence, loud voices, bright lights, chaos, and confusion"* (right).

A catatonic stupor is an extreme form of withdrawal. While in this state, the person does not move or speak. In fact, an uncomfortable statuelike pose may be held for so long that the limbs become stiff and swollen.

In recent years, many clinical researchers have sought to determine which of the various symptoms of schizophrenia tend to appear together—in the same people, and at the same time. Although somewhat different classification schemes have been proposed, it is clear that there are at least two major types of symptoms (McGlashan & Fenton, 1992; Andreasen et al., 1995; Arndt et al., 1995). *Positive symptoms* consist of the cognitive, emotional, and behavioral *excesses*. Those that tend to appear together include delusions and hallucinations, which are exaggerations in beliefs and perceptions, as well as incoherent speech, inappropriate displays of emotion, and grossly bizarre behavior. In contrast are *negative symptoms* that are characterized by cognitive, emotional, and behavioral *deficits* such as apathy, blank looks, blunted affect, slowed movement and speech, and social withdrawal. Based on a study of 111 schizophrenic outpatients in an Iowa hospital, the estimated prevalence of both positive and negative symptoms is presented in Table 16.8. Note that delusions were the most common positive symptom and apathy the most common negative symptom.

Can people with schizophrenia be neatly classified into the two general types? No. On the one hand, research suggests that people with positive symptoms have a better predisorder state and a greater chance of recovery than those suffering from the negative symptoms. On the other hand, many patients exhibit both kinds of symptoms, so the two disorders often coexist (McGlashan & Fenton, 1992).

Theories of Schizophrenia

Can anyone stressed by adverse life circumstances "catch" a schizophrenic disorder, or are some of us more prone than others? Can the outbreak of schizophrenia in an adult be predicted in childhood? Indeed, are the causes biological, psychological, or a combination of both?

Biological Factors Family, twin, and adoption studies reveal a strong genetic basis for schizophrenic disorders (Holzman & Matthysse, 1990). You may recall that about 1 percent of the American population is diagnosed with schizophrenia at some point in life. However, the more closely related you are to someone with

Table 16.8 Positive and Negative Symptoms of Schizophrenia

POSITIVE SYMPTOMS	PERCENTAGE
Hallucinations	69
Delusions	84
Thought disorders	43
Bizarre behavior	26
NEGATIVE SYMPTOMS	**PERCENTAGE**
Apathy	90
Flattened affect	88
Social withdrawal	88
Inattention	66
Slowed or no speech	53

Source: N. C. Andreasen (1987). The diagnosis of schizophrenia. *Schizophrenia Bulletin,* 13, pp. 1–8.

schizophrenia, the greater the risk (see Figure 16.10). When one fraternal twin has it, the odds are 17 percent for the other. With an identical twin, however, the odds increase even further, to 48 percent—a number that remains high regardless of whether the twins are raised together or apart (Gottesman & Shields, 1982; Gottesman, 1991).

Searching for the biological origins of schizophrenia, many researchers find that a number of the positive symptoms are associated either with overactivity in the synapses where dopamine is the neurotransmitter or with an oversensitivity to dopamine. Three kinds of evidence support this linkage. First, antipsychotic drugs that block the activity of dopamine in the brain also lessen hallucinations, delusions, and other behavioral excesses. Second, amphetamines both increase dopamine activity and intensify these same symptoms (long-term usage or overdoses can even trigger schizophreniclike episodes in normal people). Third, autopsies on the brains of schizophrenic patients often reveal an excess of dopamine receptors (Wong et al., 1986; Seeman et al., 1993).

In contrast, the negative symptoms of schizophrenia are typically not affected by antipsychotic drugs or amphetamines. Instead, these symptoms—the flat affect, apathy, lack of speech, attention problems, immobility, and withdrawal—may be linked to structural defects in the brain. Brain scans of people with these symptoms thus reveal an enlargement of fluid-filled spaces called cerebral ventricles and a corresponding shrinkage of the cerebral cortex (Shelton & Weinberger, 1986; Raz & Raz, 1990).

Relationship	**Genetic relatedness**	**Risk**
Identical twins	100%	48%
Offspring of two schizophrenic parents	100%	46%
Fraternal twins	50%	17%
Offspring of one schizophrenic parent	50%	17%
Sibling	50%	9%
Nephew or niece	25%	4%
Spouse	0%	2%
Unrelated person	0%	1%

Figure 16.10 Genetic relationships and schizophrenia As shown, the lifetime risk of schizophrenia increases as a function of how genetically related a person is to someone else who is known to have schizophrenia (Gottesman, 1991, p. 96).

Psychological Factors Although there is a genetic basis for schizophrenia, 54 percent of those people born to two schizophrenic parents do *not* themselves develop the disorder. In other words, heredity may increase the risk, but it does not by itself predetermine one's fate. This notion has given rise to the **diathesis-stress model**, which states that people with a genetic or acquired vulnerability, or "diathesis," develop schizophrenia when exposed to high levels of stress (Meehl, 1962; Zubin & Spring, 1977; Fowles, 1992). What experiences act as triggering mechanisms?

To identify factors that predict the onset of schizophrenia, researchers in the United States, Canada, Israel, Finland, Denmark, and Sweden are conducting longitudinal studies in which high-risk children (those who have at least one schizophrenic parent) are followed closely as they grow older. The life experiences of the children who go on to develop schizophrenia are then compared to those who do not. So far, the results show that high-risk subjects who become schizophrenic were more likely to have had complications at birth and low birth weight. They were also more likely to have been separated from their mothers at an early age, to have fathers hospitalized for a mental disorder, to grow up in conflict-filled homes, to have a short attention span, and to have social problems in school (Asarnow, 1988). Can the future of a high-risk child be predicted? Perhaps. When psychology graduate students were shown old home movies of future schizophrenic patients and their healthy siblings—all of whom were normal while growing up—78 percent guessed

diathesis-stress model The theory that certain mental disorders (such as schizophrenia) develop when people with a genetic or acquired vulnerability are exposed to high levels of stress.

"Tell me, do you respond to treatment?"

People with a narcissistic-personality disorder are chronically vain, boastful, and pretentious.

correctly which of the children in the films went on to develop the disorder (Walker & Lewine, 1990).

As always, it is easier to identify factors that *predict* the onset of a disorder than to pinpoint its psychological *causes*. To see why, consider two classic findings that are interesting but hard to interpret. First, schizophrenia is most prevalent in the lowest socioeconomic classes of society. This pattern appears in studies all over the world and is sometimes taken to mean that poverty causes schizophrenia. Or is it the other way around? Perhaps schizophrenia—precisely because it is characterized by massive cognitive and social impairment—leads its sufferers to drop out of school, lose jobs, and drift downward into poverty. A second example is the well-publicized observation that parents of schizophrenics communicate to their offspring in ways that are inconsistent and confusing. This finding is often taken to suggest that faulty communication patterns at home can cause schizophrenia. Again, however, it is equally possible that the behavior of parents is not a cause but a *response* to the problem of communicating with preschizophrenic children. Which comes first, the chicken or the egg? Either way, it seems that biological and environmental forces combine to produce this very devastating disorder.

Personality Disorders

What are personality disorders, and what one distinguishing feature do they have in common? What does it mean to have a borderline personality? And why is there so much interest in antisocial personality disorder?

You have your own unique personality. So do I. We all do. You may be sloppy or meticulous, calm or emotional, self-centered or altruistic, cautious or impulsive, a loner or a social butterfly. However, if someone has a personality that is highly inflexible and maladaptive and that causes distress, the person is diagnosed as having a **personality disorder** (Livesley, 1995).

Among the disorders classified in DSM-IV, these are among the most controversial. People with personality disorders—an estimated 5 to 10 percent of the population—are not swamped with anxiety, depression, or confusion, nor have they lost touch with reality. In fact, they are not particularly motivated to change. The problem is that they are trapped by their own rigid ways in self-defeating patterns of behavior, patterns that begin to form in adolescence and then harden like plaster for the rest of life.

There are eleven personality disorders listed in DSM-IV—many of them quite colorful in their character. For example, there is the isolated and emotionally detached *schizoid personality*, the perfectionistic *obsessive-compulsive personality*, the highly sensitive and suspicious *paranoid personality*, the melodramatic and attention-seeking *histrionic personality*, the self-centered and ego-inflated *narcissistic personality*, and the *avoidant personality*, who so fears rejection that he or she does not start new relationships or make social commitments. Two others in particular have attracted widespread attention: (1) the borderline personality, which is quite common; and (2) the antisocial personality, which is socially destructive.

The Borderline Personality

personality disorders A group of disorders characterized by a personality that is highly inflexible and maladaptive.

Marilyn Monroe was famous for her beauty and her tremendous success in Hollywood. She was also known for being unpredictable, impulsive, insecure, impossible to live with, and yet desperately afraid to be alone. At the age of thirty-six, she shocked the world by killing herself with an overdose of sleeping pills. From what is known about her life, Marilyn Monroe did not have a serious anxiety, somatoform, conversion, or dissociative disorder, nor was she schizophrenic. At times, she was depressed. If she were alive today, however, she might well be diagnosed, along with 20 percent of all psychiatric patients and 3 to 5 percent of everyone else, as having a **borderline personality disorder** (Frances & Widiger, 1986).

Borderline personality disorder features a lack of identity and a pattern of instability in self-image, mood, and social relationships. People with this disorder (about two-thirds are women) are uncertain of who they are—in terms of their career goals, friends, values, and sometimes sexual orientation. They complain of feeling empty and bored, can't stand to be left alone, and are desperate for the company of others. Unhappily, people with a borderline personality cling to others with such fierce dependence that their relationships are stormy and do not last. They are impulsive—in the habit of running away, getting into fights, and jumping into bed with strangers. As a way to get attention, they are also notorious for committing acts of self-destruction. In a study of the lives of fifty-seven borderline patients, there were forty-two suicide threats, forty overdoses, thirty-eight cases of drug abuse, thirty-six acts of self-mutilation (slashing wrists, banging heads, burning skin with cigarettes, pulling out hair), thirty-six cases of sexual promiscuity, and fourteen car accidents caused by reckless driving (Gunderson, 1984).

The Antisocial Personality

The brutally cold, calculating, and callous individual is often depicted in books and in films such as *Silence of the Lambs* and *Copycat.* Unfortunately, the characters depicted in art come from real life. Every now and then, a crime story appears on the news that is so horrible it sends chills up my spine. Three high school students pour gasoline on their teacher and set her on fire. A man slashes the face of a model with a razor blade in exchange for $200. What kind of person is capable of these atrocities? Who are these monstrous creatures? In the nineteenth century, they were described as morally insane. More recently, they were called psychopaths, then sociopaths. Today, the term **antisocial personality disorder** is used to describe people who have "ice in their veins"—who behave in ways that are completely self-centered, irresponsible, and destructive, without regard for the welfare of others.

According to DSM-IV, the antisocial personality (ASP) is a disorder that applies to people who, as children, would cut school, run away from home, set fires, harm animals, steal, cheat, and get into fights—and who, as adults, drive recklessly, borrow money and do not return it, get into fights, behave irresponsibly as a spouse or parent, drink excessively, and engage in unlawful activities.

As you might expect, a person with ASP cannot hold a job or maintain a close relationship. But the most striking feature is that he (80 percent are men) lacks a conscience and feels no guilt, remorse, or empathy for his victims. He uses others for pleasure or profit then discards them. When intelligent, the person with ASP is not a common street criminal but a cool, manipulative, charming, and clever con artist who can seduce romantic companions with empty words of love, lie to business partners with a straight face, and sweet-talk his way out of trouble (Cleckley; 1976; Hare et al., 1991; Lykken, 1995). For the purpose of identifying individuals with ASP, Robert Hare (1993)—author of *Without Conscience*—created the *Psychopathy Checklist,* a widely used diagnostic and research tool. Some of the attributes to watch for that appear on this list are presented in Table 16.9.

borderline personality disorder A type of personality characterized by instability in one's self-image, mood, and social relationships and a lack of clear identity.

antisocial personality disorder A personality disorder involving a chronic pattern of self-centered, manipulative, and destructive behavior toward others.

Table 16.9 Some Attributes of the Antisocial Personality

- Is glib and charming
- Has a high need for stimulation
- Is a pathological liar
- Is cunning and manipulative
- Lacks remorse or guilt
- Has shallow affect
- Is callous and without empathy
- Has a parasitic lifestyle
- Has poor behavioral control
- Is sexually promiscuous
- Has no long-term goals
- Is irresponsible

Source: R. D. Hare (1993). *Without conscience: The disturbing world of the psychopaths among us.* New York: Pocket Books.

For many years, researchers have speculated about the causes of ASP. Some have tried to trace the disorder in childhood to broken homes, neglectful parents, and faulty role models that impede the formation of a superego and moral development. Others have measured brain-wave patterns and heart rates—and have found that people with antisocial personalities are less excitable than the average person and are not as easily startled. In fact, they remain physiologically calm in the face of electric shock, tense situations, and images of children screaming and crying—an attribute that makes them fearless (Blair et al., 1997; Patrick et al., 1993). Still others find that people diagnosed with ASP lack the ability to control their impulses—a problem that is worsened by their tendency to abuse alcohol and other disinhibiting drugs. Society can take some comfort in the fact that individuals with antisocial personalities who go on to become criminals tend to burn out and commit fewer crimes after age forty (Hare et al., 1988).

What Next?

In what way is the diagnosis of psychological disorders more complicated than it appears? What does "comorbidity" mean? And what does it mean to be legally insane?

Psychological disorders keep people from adapting in the most effective way to their environment. In this chapter, six types of disorders were described, each featuring different primary symptoms: intense anxiety, physical ailments and complaints, dissociation of the self from memory, extreme moods ranging from depression to euphoria, schizophrenic devastation of mental functions, and self-defeating patterns of behavior. Yet there are many more—such as disorders involving sex, sleep, impulse control, drug abuse, and development. Clearly, no aspect of our existence is immune to breakdown.

Now that you've seen the list of psychological disorders, you should note two ways in which the picture is more complicated than it appears. First, although each

PSYCHOLOGICAL DISORDERS AND LAW

The Insanity Defense

On July 22, 1991, Milwaukee police officers entered a one-bedroom apartment and encountered one of the most monstrous and disgusting crime scenes in American history. The stench was unbearable. There were photographs of dismembered bodies tacked on the walls; severed human heads, organs, and genitals in the refrigerator; and other body parts immersed in a vat of acid. The police soon arrested Jeffrey Dahmer, a thirty-one-year-old chocolate-factory worker, who went on to confess to a total of seventeen murders. In each case, he said, he would lure a young man to his apartment, drug, rape, and kill him; dismember the body; and store or eat the remains. Dahmer went to trial and entered a plea of insanity. After hearing two weeks of testimony, however, a Milwaukee jury voted by a 10-to-2 margin that he was sane. Dahmer was sentenced to life in prison, where he was later killed by inmates.

Was Jeffrey Dahmer really sane? How could a jury draw this conclusion about someone so calculating and so brutal? What does it mean to be sane, and when can a person be considered insane? To begin with, it's important to realize that *insanity* is a legal concept, not a psychological one. Insanity is not a diagnostic category and does not appear in DSM-IV. But it is an important concept in criminal law. Individuals who are charged with a crime can plead guilty or not guilty, or they can argue that they should not be held responsible in light of extraordinary circumstances. The law provides a variety of excusing conditions for this purpose. If a person commits a crime by accident, was coerced, or acted in self-defense, then he or she may argue for a verdict of not guilty. In a similar manner, the law permits an insanity defense, to protect from punishment those who cannot morally be faulted for their actions because they were mentally impaired while committing the crime (Hermann, 1983; Golding, 1992).

Over time, the courts have defined insanity in several different ways. In the nineteenth century, Great Britain and the United States adopted the rule that defendants were legally insane if, as a result of mental illness, they did not know what they were doing or that it was wrong. Critics argued that this definition too narrowly focused on a defendant's cognitive state and excluded those who knew what they were doing but could not control themselves. Some states thus added the "irresistible impulse" test by which defendants are considered insane if they lack the capacity to control their actions. Throughout the years, other definitions have been proposed. Today, the most common is one that combines three key elements. As defined by the Model Penal Code, defendants are not responsible for criminal conduct if (1) as a result of mental disorder, they cannot (2) appreciate the wrongfulness of their conduct or (3) conform to the law.

The insanity plea is a constant source of controversy. In 1843, a Scot named Daniel M'Naughten tried to assassinate British Prime Minister Robert Peel and mistakenly killed Peel's secretary. M'Naughten suffered from delusions of persecution and believed that Peel had plotted against him. He went to trial—but was found not guilty by reason of insanity. The public was outraged. In 1981, John Hinckley, Jr., shot and wounded President Reagan and was quickly apprehended. The shooting was witnessed by millions of TV viewers. Hinckley was tried in the District of Columbia, but this jury, too, returned a

Jeffrey Dahmer

verdict of not guilty by reason of insanity. Again, the public was outraged (Low et al., 1986).

Understandably, many people fear that the insanity defense opens up a loophole through which massive numbers of criminals can escape punishment for their crimes. But is that fear justified? Consider the following three questions: (1) What percentage of criminal defendants enter a plea of insanity? (2) Of those who do, what percentage succeed? (3) Of those who succeed, how many are set free?

Eric Silver and his colleagues (1994) compared public opinions on these questions to the actual figures gathered from forty-nine counties in eight different states and found that respondents, on average, clearly overestimated the overall impact of the insanity defense in criminal justice. Specifically, the public estimated that 37 percent of all criminal defendants raise the insanity defense, that 44 percent are acquitted, and that 26 percent of those acquitted are set free. In actuality, fewer than 1 percent of all defendants plead insanity, 26 percent are acquitted, and 15 percent of those acquitted are set free (the others are committed to a mental hospital). Put these numbers together, and you'll see that public opinion is highly distorted. For every 1,000 cases, people estimate that 163 defendants are acquitted by reason of insanity, and that 47 are set free. In actuality, 2 defendants in 1,000 are acquitted by reason of insanity, and only 3 in 10,000 are set free. In most cases, the person found to be insane spends as much time confined to a hospital as he or she would have spent in prison.

Despite the moral underpinnings of the insanity defense and the reassuring odds concerning the frequency of its usage, there are problems in its implementation. One is that many defendants who are evaluated for insanity engage in some form of malingering, or faking. To overcome this problem, psychologists have developed tests and interview methods to try to detect such faking (Rogers, 1988; Hall & Pritchard, 1996). A second problem is that judges often turn for expert opinion to clinical psychologists and psychiatrists who are trained to diagnose mental disorders—not to resolve disputes about criminal responsibility. Predictably, many insanity trials feature a battle of opposing experts who disagree in their assessments of the defendant (Dawes et al., 1989).

Is there a solution to the insanity dilemma? On the one hand, it seems inhumane to punish people who are not responsible for their actions. On the other hand, it seems repugnant to provide a loophole for violent criminals. In recent years, many courts have reformed their laws to discourage acquittals by reason of insanity. Although it remains to be seen what effect these changes will have on judges and juries, controversy will clearly continue to surround this awkward relationship between clinical psychology and the law.

disorder is presented separately in its own neat and tidy package, people diagnosed with one disorder often have symptoms of others as well—a common phenomenon known as **comorbidity** (Kendall & Clarkin, 1992; Kessler et al., 1994). People with phobias often suffer from obsessive-compulsive disorder, many of those with general-anxiety disorder are also depressed, those who are depressed often have sleep disorders, and people with schizophrenia often abuse drugs. In a similar vein, it's important to realize that psychological disorders do not exist in caricaturelike terms. Depression is considered a mood disorder, but it has cognitive symptoms; schizophrenia is considered a thought disorder, but it has a marked impact on emotion.

The second complication is that normal and abnormal are not distinct, well-defined categories but, rather, points on a continuum. Hence, people who are otherwise happy, healthy, and well adjusted may experience some of the symptoms of psychological disorders. On occasion, most of us have felt panic, phobic anxiety, mania, and depression. Most of us know what it's like to lose sleep when we're nervous or to worry excessively about our health when a contagious disease begins to spread. Most of us know what it's like to tune out for short periods of time and dissociate mentally from our surroundings. Sometimes we even catch brief, mild glimpses of schizophrenic symptoms. For example, the new parent who "hears" his or her newborn cry, only to see that the baby is fast asleep, is having an auditory hallucination. And the person who dines alone in a restaurant and self-consciously thinks everyone is watching is under some kind of delusion. In short, psychological

comorbidity The tendency for people diagnosed with one mental disorder to exhibit symptoms of other disorders as well.

order and disorder are not always black-and-white categories, but shades of gray. At times, diagnosis is a judgment call based on how intense, frequent, prolonged, and disabling the symptoms are.

Once psychological disorders are identified and diagnosed, and once we understand their causes, what next? At this point, we must return our attention to the underlying challenge of clinical psychology: the potential for positive *change*. As we saw in Chapter 15, personality remains relatively stable throughout adulthood. But what about the problems that afflict so many people? What about episodes of anxiety or depression? For those needing professional help, the answer is treatment—through drugs, counseling and psychotherapy, and other forms of intervention. Reflecting the hope and the reality that people can help other people change, the next chapter addresses these topics.

Summary and Key Terms

Psychological Disorders: A General Outlook

Because psychological disorders are widespread, it's important to define them, make distinctions among different types of problems, and know what factors put us at risk.

Defining Normal and Abnormal

The term **psychological disorder** has been defined in various ways. The APA definition stresses significant pain or dysfunctional behavior and an internal, involuntary source. Whatever definition is used, there is no strict line between normal and abnormal.

Models of Abnormality

The **medical model** attributes mental disorders to biological conditions. The **psychological model** locates the cause of disorder in past and present experiences. The sociocultural perspective stresses the importance of cultural context, as seen in **culture-bound syndromes,** recurring patterns of maladaptive behavior that are limited to a specific cultural group or location.

Diagnosis: A Necessary Step

Today, the process of **diagnosis**—the grouping and naming of mental disorders—is based on **DSM-IV.** Although diagnosis is more reliable than in the past, stereotypes can bias judgments, and diagnostic labels can then affect the way people are perceived and treated.

Anxiety Disorders

Anxiety is a nervous feeling of apprehension accompanied by physical symptoms, such as a pounding heart and trembling hands.

Generalized Anxiety Disorder

A constant state of anxiety not linked to an identifiable source is the mark of **generalized anxiety disorder.** Cross-cultural studies show that the physiological symptoms of anxiety are universal but that the cognitive component (the particular set of worries and interpretations) varies with the culture.

Panic Disorder

Panic disorder—characterized by frequent, sudden, intense rushes of anxiety for no apparent reason—is often accompanied by **agoraphobia,** a fear of public places. There is evidence for both biological and psychological causes.

Phobic Disorder

A **phobic disorder** is an intense and irrational fear. A **simple phobia** involves a fear of specific object, and a **social phobia** is a fear of a situation that invites public scrutiny. Freud attributed phobias to anxiety over hidden impulses; behaviorists stress conditioning and learning; others have linked common phobias to evolutionary programming or "preparedness."

Obsessive-Compulsive Disorder

In **obsessive-compulsive disorder (OCD),** the person is plagued by obsessions (persistent thoughts) and compulsions (the need to perform repetitive acts or rituals). Psychoanalysts, behaviorists, and biological psychologists have all offered explanations and possible therapies. For many people, OCD can be treated with antidepressants.

Somatoform Disorders

People with a **somatoform disorder** have bodily symptoms that are psychological rather than medical in origin.

Hypochondriasis

A disorder involving unwarranted preoccupation with one's physical health, **hypochondriasis** can become a lifelong pattern. People with this disorder may be acutely sensitive to stimulation.

Conversion Disorder

Conversion disorder is a temporary loss of a bodily function without a physical cause. It mainly affects young women but is far less common today than it was a hundred years ago—when it was called hysteria.

Dissociative Disorders

Many people have experiences in which they lose their memory for a portion of their lives or identity. A severe condition of this sort is known as a **dissociative disorder.**

Amnesia and Fugue States

Amnesia is a partial or complete loss of memory. Causes include physical trauma, alcohol, and stressful events. In the rarer forms known as **fugue states,** people forget their identity, wander away, and start a new life.

Dissociative Identity Disorder

In **dissociative identity disorder (DID),** which used to be called multiple personality disorder, the person develops two or more distinct personalities. Women exhibit this disorder more often than men and often have a history of abuse as children. Reported cases of DID are on the rise, a situation that has triggered controversy.

Mood Disorders

People normally have many fluctuations of mood. But prolonged emotional extremes that impair the ability to function are diagnosed as **mood disorders.**

Major Depression

Depression, a widespread mood disorder, brings feelings of deep sadness and despair without a discernible cause and lasts two weeks or more. Other symptoms include feelings of worthlessness, loss of sleep and appetite, hopelessness, and a lack of energy.

Theories of Depression

Twin studies show a genetic foundation for depression. Early research stressed the role of neurotransmitters, but now it appears that the connection between biology and mood is more complicated.

Psychological factors have also been noted. Freud considered depression a reaction to loss. Behaviorists link it to **learned helplessness,** an expectation that we cannot control important life outcomes. Social-cognitive theorists say that depressed people have a **depressive explanatory style,** a tendency to attribute negative events to factors that are internal, stable, global—and to assume that things will not change. Humanistic theories see depression as the result of the failure to reach self-actualization.

The Vicious Cycle of Depression

Depressed people often behave in ways that alienate others. Social rejection then intensifies the depression—a vicious cycle.

Suicide: The Ultimate "Solution"

Three-quarters of suicides are committed by depressed people. Baumeister sees suicide as an "escape from self" into oblivion. Clinically, scales of hopelessness are the best predictor. Among friends or relatives, signs of potential suicide include depression and drug use, remarks about death, and previous attempts.

Bipolar Disorder

People with **bipolar disorder** experience wild mood swings from depression at one extreme to mania (a euphoric, overactive state) at the other. Many famous artists had bipolar disorder, and their manic phases may have contributed to their brilliance. But mania may also spiral out of control, producing delusions and risky and embarrassing behavior. Though related to simple depression, bipolar disorder has a stronger genetic component.

Schizophrenic Disorders

Marked by gross distortions of thought and perception and a loss of contact with reality, **schizophrenic disorders** are equally common in women and men all over the world, though they tend to strike women at a later age.

The Symptoms of Schizophrenia

Schizophrenia's major symptoms are incoherent thinking, **delusions** (false beliefs), **hallucinations** (sensory experiences without actual stimulation), disturbance of affect (flattened, exaggerated, or inappropriate emotion), and bizarre behavior.

Types of Schizophrenia

DSM-IV lists five major types of schizophrenia: disorganized, catatonic, paranoid, undifferentiated, and residual. Researchers have found that two types of symptoms tend to appear together. Positive symptoms are behavioral excesses (such as delusions and hallucinations), and negative symptoms consist of behavioral deficits (such as flat affect and social withdrawal). Many patients exhibit symptoms of both kinds.

Theories of Schizophrenia

Twin, family, and adoption studies reveal a genetic basis for schizophrenia, linked to the neurotransmitter dopamine or to structural brain defects. But psychological factors also play a role. Some evidence supports the **diathesis-stress model,** which holds that people with genetic or acquired vulnerability develop schizophrenia when exposed to a high level of stress.

Personality Disorders

A person with a highly inflexible and maladaptive personality is said to have a **personality disorder.**

Borderline Personality

People with **borderline personality disorder** lack identity, cling to others, act impulsively, and are prone to self-destruction.

Antisocial Personality

Of those who have **antisocial personality disorder,** 80 percent are men. The condition produces a chronic pattern of self-centered, manipulative, and destructive behavior toward others. Its most notable feature is lack of conscience.

What Next?

Two facts make the picture of mental disorders more complicated than the categories suggest. First, people diagnosed with one disorder often show symptoms of other disorders as well—a phenomenon called **comorbidity.** Second, normality and abnormality are points on a continuum, with many points in between. After a mental disorder is diagnosed, the next step for the clinical psychologist is treatment—the topic of Chapter 17.

In the Field Resources

Books

Gottesman, I. I. (1991). *Schizophrenia genesis: The origins of madness.* New York: W. H. Freeman.

A leading researcher describes the genetic and environmental roots of this dreaded disorder—the course it takes, its toll on patients and their families, and treatment alternatives.

Jamison, K. R. (1995). *An unquiet mind.* New York: Vintage Books.

This bestseller is a personal and moving memoir of bipolar disorder from someone who has suffered from it. The author is a depression researcher whose work is cited in this text.

Marshall, J. R. (1994). *Social phobia: From shyness to stage fright.* New York: Basic Books.

Written by a psychiatrist, this book describes such social anxieties as fear of public speaking—and how they can be treated.

Films and Videos

Primal Fear (1996, 129 min.)

This gripping mystery portrays a murder defendant who exhibits multiple personalities. There are interesting scenes involving the defendant and psychiatrist. (Richard Gere, Laura Linney, John Mahoney, Frances McDormand, Edward Norton.)

Sybil (1977, 122 min.)

This TV drama tells the story of a woman diagnosed as having sixteen personalities—adopted as a response to childhood abuse. (Sally Field.)

Journals and Periodicals

American Journal of Psychiatry
Archives of General Psychiatry
Journal of Abnormal Psychology
Journal of Consulting and Clinical Psychology
Psychosomatic Medicine
Schizophrenia Bulletin

17 *Treatment*

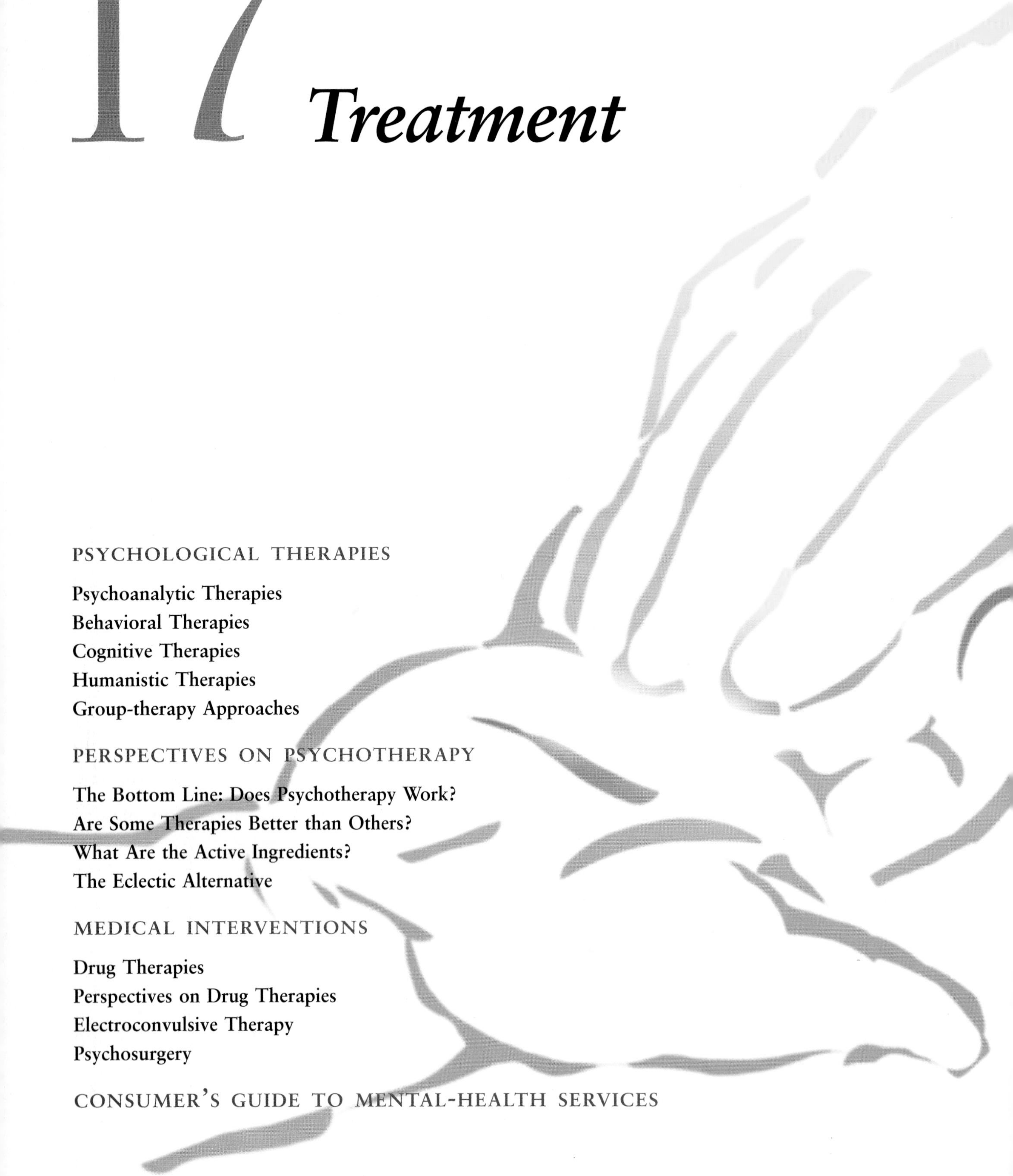

What's Your Prediction?

Consumer Reports *Evaluates psychological therapy*

The situation People who have personal problems—such as being anxious or depressed, drinking too much, having marital trouble, or feeling generally unhappy without knowing why—wonder where they can turn for help. Sometimes people turn to friends, relatives, clergy, or family doctors; at other times, they seek help from psychologists, psychiatrists, and other mental-health specialists. But do the specialists really help? Do psychotherapy and other forms of mental-health intervention produce the kind of improvement we all hope for?

In an effort to answer this question, *Consumer Reports (CR)* added a survey about psychotherapy to its annual questionnaire, in which readers are asked to rate laundry detergents, breakfast cereals, home appliances, automobiles, and other products and services. *CR* asked readers to fill out a special mental-health section "if at any time over the past three years you experienced stress or other emotional problems for which you sought help." The survey was mailed to 184,000 randomly selected subscribers; and 22,000 responded, a 13 percent response rate that is typical of *CR* surveys. Of those who did return it, 35 percent said they had a mental-health problem. Within this group, 40 percent sought some kind of professional help. Specifically, 2,900 readers sought help from a psychologist, psychiatrist, social worker, or marriage counselor; the others saw family doctors or self-help or support groups.

All respondents were asked to indicate the nature and severity of their distress and to provide background information about cost, insurance, the type of therapy they had, and other matters. Then they rated the extent to which their treatment helped with their specific problem (and, more generally, with their work and social lives and sense of personal fulfillment). They also indicated their overall level of satisfaction or dissatisfaction with the therapy.

Make a prediction On the question regarding improvement, respondents indicated whether the treatment made things a lot worse, somewhat worse, no different, somewhat better, or a lot better. How many reported *improvement*? Specifically, what percentage of the respondents do you think said that they were *somewhat better* or a *lot better* after treatment? Was it 10 percent? 25, 50, 90 percent? Next, consider the respondents' level of *satisfaction* with the therapy they received. What percentage do you think said they were *fairly* satisfied (very, or completely)? And what percentage were *highly* satisfied? Using the table below, make predictions for both sets of measures.

MEASURES	OVERALL RESPONSES
Improvement	_______ % Somewhat better
	_______ % A lot better
Satisfaction	_______ % Fairly satisfied
	_______ % Highly satisfied

The results In November 1995, *Consumer Reports* published the results of this survey (which is the largest ever conducted on the topic) and concluded that patients in general derive substantial benefit from psychotherapy. Just how substantial was the overall level of improvement? Combining all the respondents—regardless of the type of problem they had, the type of therapist they saw, or the amount of time they spent in treatment—the percentages of those who said they were a lot better—and satisfied—were striking. As you can see in the table below, a total of 86 percent felt they were improved after therapy and 89 percent were satisfied with the experience.

MEASURES	OVERALL RESPONSES
Improvement	44% Somewhat better
	42% A lot better
Satisfaction	27% Fairly satisfied
	62% Highly satisfied

What does it all mean? Over the years, the number of people seeking professional help for psychological problems has climbed. In light of soaring medical costs and health-insurance policy limits, those in need of help—the consumers of psychological treatments—need to know whether these treatments work. *Consumer Reports* has a reputation for being fair and objective in its evaluations. But are the survey results valid? Are *CR* subscribers representative of the population? Is it possible that people who were satisfied with their experience were more likely to take part in the survey than those not satisfied or that they would have felt better, eventually, without outside help? Is it possible that the self-reported improvements, which could not be verified, were exaggerated? Or is it possible that psychotherapy truly helps those in need?

When psychologist Martin Seligman (1995) presented the results to psychologists, he set off a wave of debate on bulletin boards on the Internet. In October 1996, the *American Psychologist* devoted an entire issue to commentary and debate about this study and what it meant. Some were critical of the study and its methods. Others, including Seligman, defended it and stood by the results. We'll revisit this controversy later in this chapter. We'll also see from other, more controlled, studies that psychological therapies (as well as medical interventions) *are* generally effective—that for people in distress, they offer hope, social support, and an opportunity to open up.

In *Love's Executioner and Other Tales of Psychotherapy*, Irvin Yalom (1989) tells the story of Betty, a twenty-seven-year-old female patient who was 5'2" and weighed 250 pounds. A few moments into the first meeting, Yalom asked his standard opening question, "So what ails?" Betty's reply: "Everything." She worked sixty hours a week, had no friends, cried every night, had frequent headaches, and spent weekends at home eating in front of the TV. According to Betty, she was too heavy for people to accept yet too depressed to lose weight. Had she sought professional help before? Yes, but without much success.

Throughout the first few weeks of therapy, Betty did not really open up. According to Yalom, she droned on about trivial work problems, giggled constantly, and put on silly accents—but she revealed nothing truly intimate about herself. To break the ice, Yalom confronted Betty with her avoidant tactics. Soon she began to open up (a frightening prospect, she said, "like jumping out of a plane without a parachute"). She became more engaged in the sessions and more interesting to talk to, but she was also more anxious. To speed up the process and provide a supportive social network, Yalom then put Betty into a therapy group, which worked wonders. She enrolled in a weight-reduction program, joined a bowling league, devoured her last honey-glazed doughnut, and went on a diet. As the months passed, Betty lost a great deal of weight. And with each new low, she would have flashbacks of emotionally charged events that had occurred when she was at that particular weight. At 150, for example, she recalled the death of her father. Swarms of painful memories poured out—her father's affectionate manner, his fight with cancer, how alone she felt when he died, and how afraid she was of dying the same way. There was one insight after another, until Betty became a happier, healthier, more confident woman. After fifteen months, the therapist and patient had their final session together. They reminisced about the past, looked forward to the future, embraced, and said good-bye.

As this story illustrates, the treatment of psychological distress is not only a science but also an art. Whereas some psychologists study the human mind and behavior in research, practicing clinical psychologists help people cope with real-life problems. Sometimes the goal is to treat the symptoms of a specific disorder or to help people cope with a stressful life event; at other times, it is to foster growth in those of us who are "normal" but not happy or content with the state of our lives. Whatever the problem, this chapter addresses three questions: (1) What treatments are available to people in need of psychological help? (2) Are the treatments effective? (3) And if so, why?

The methods for treating mental disorders are far from perfect, and are not always successful, but they've come a long way in a few short years (Gamwell &

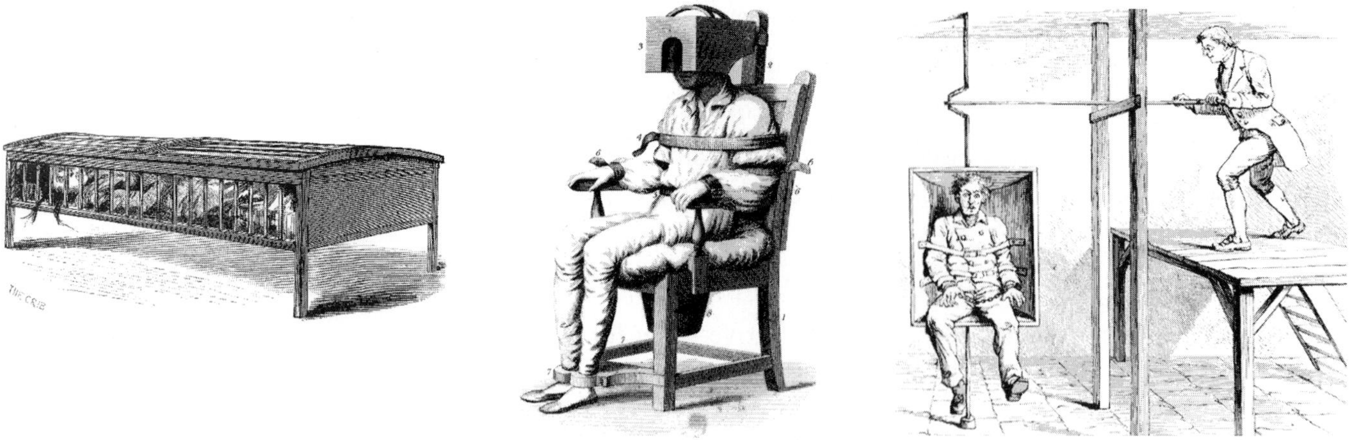

Figure 17.1 Old-fashioned "cures" for mental illness In the eighteenth century, many crude devices were used to treat mental illness. Among the more popular were the crib (used to restrain patients who would not stay in bed), the tranquilizing chair (used to calm those who were manic or violent), and the circulating swing (used to treat depression through high-speed rotation). Twentieth-century methods included cold packs, hot-steam showers, vibrating helmets, infrared-lightbulb cabinets, and electric "mummy bags."

Tomes, 1995; Stone, 1997). Our prehistoric ancestors believed that people with psychological disorders were inhabited by evil spirits—so they drilled holes in the skull large enough for these spirits to escape. In the seventeenth century, these same disorders were attributed to witchcraft and demonic possession and were "treated" with exorcism, noise making, bloodletting, beating, bitter potions, starvation, and torture. By the eighteenth century, people with mental disorders were considered ill but were hidden from public view—often chained to the walls of dark, dungeonlike hospitals called "asylums" (see Figure 17.1). Then during the nineteenth century, a spirit of humanitarian reform swept through many institutions in the United States and Europe. The inmates were unchained, housed in clean rooms with windows, and permitted to walk outside on hospital grounds.

At the turn of the twentieth century, major advances were made on two fronts. One was the finding that the symptoms of *hysteria* (such as paralysis of a limb or blindness) could be treated with hypnosis. The other was the discovery that a schizophrenia-like disorder called *general paresis*—which is marked by hallucinations, delusions, personality changes, and death—was caused by syphilis, a sexually transmitted genital infection. These developments now stand as symbols for the two predominant models of treatment: one psychological, the other medical. Today, as we'll see, these two models complement rather than compete with each other.

Psychological Therapies

What is psychoanalysis, and what is its goal for treatment? What principles underlie behavioral therapy, and what specific techniques are used? What are the main features of cognitive therapies? What is the humanistic approach? Why do therapists sometimes prefer to treat people in groups?

psychotherapy A term used to describe any treatment in which a trained professional uses psychological techniques to help someone in need of assistance.

The term **psychotherapy** is used to describe all forms of treatment in which a trained professional employs psychological techniques to help persons in need of assistance. Psychotherapy comes in many different forms. The trained professional may be a *clinical psychologist* (who attends graduate school, earns a Ph.D. in psychology, and conducts testing, diagnosis, treatment, and research), a *psychiatrist* (who attends medical school, receives an M.D., does a residency in psychiatry, and is the only mental-health professional who can prescribe drugs), a *counseling psychologist* (who receives a Ph.D. in counseling to help people with marital, family, and minor adjustment problems), or a *psychiatric social worker* (who earns a two-year master's degree in social work and has had special training in counseling). The person in need of assistance also varies from one case to another. He or she may suffer from one of the psychological disorders listed in DSM-IV or may simply feel inadequate, lonely, unimportant, or unloved and may just want more from life.

There is a vast array of techniques used in the practice of psychotherapy. Indeed, it has been estimated that there are more than 250 brands of psychotherapy to choose from (Herenk, 1980). A small number of therapists, who get too much attention from the media, use "faddish" techniques—for example, insulting patients to shake them up, having patients scream at the top of their lungs, or "regressing" them to infancy and into the womb. However, the vast majority of therapists are professionals who work with individuals, families, and groups and who are trained in one of the four major approaches: psychoanalytic, behavioral, cognitive, and humanistic. These approaches are described in the following pages.

Psychoanalytic Therapies

Imagine you are lying outstretched on a couch, with a soft pillow tucked underneath your head. You stare at the walls and ceiling, noticing subtle streaks of white paint, shadows, razor-thin cracks in the plaster, and dust on the drapes. You fixate on a small, neatly drilled hole in the wall from which a picture must have been hung. As your eyes examine every nook and cranny, however, your mind is elsewhere—in another time and place. You recall the tantrum you had on your first day of school, the fight your parents had after putting you to bed one night, the moment you were told that your favorite grandfather died, the peculiar dream you had the night before, or the way the family used to get together on Thanksgiving to eat, drink, and watch the parade on TV. As an image comes to mind, you talk about it and relive the emotions you felt. You laugh, you cry, you clench your teeth in anger as you become reabsorbed in the events of your own life. But you're not alone. Sitting behind you—listening to every word you say, commenting from time to time, and passing the Kleenex—is your "analyst."

Treated by Breuer in the 1880s, Anna O. played a pivotal role in the birth of psychoanalysis. Although her symptoms were only temporarily relieved under Breuer's care, she did eventually recover. Seventy years later, for the first time, her true identity was revealed. Her name was Bertha Pappenheim. When she died in 1936, she was a well-known defender of women's and children's rights.

Orthodox Psychoanalysis Ever since Josef Breuer and Sigmund Freud (1895) found that people often feel better after purging their minds of material buried in the unconscious, psychoanalysis has had a pervasive influence on the treatment of mental disorders. You may recall from Chapter 15 that Breuer treated a young female patient named Anna O., who suffered from hysterical blindness, paralysis of an arm, a nervous cough, and other symptoms of conversion disorder. This case was important in three ways. First, Breuer found that when Anna talked about herself, she sometimes stumbled upon memories that had been repressed for many years. Second, these insights often brought about a relief of her symptoms. Third, Anna became intensely attached to Breuer, eventually causing him, a married man, to terminate their sessions.

As a historical matter, questions have been raised concerning the actual nature and success of Breuer's treatment of Anna (Borch-Jacobsen, 1996). Nevertheless, Freud went on to use this case, and others like it, to develop psychoanalysis—the first

To encourage patients to relax, Freud had them recline on the couch in his study while he sat out of view. You can see this couch by visiting Freud's historic home in Vienna.

systematic method of "talking cure." Psychoanalysis is designed to achieve two goals: *catharsis*, a release of bottled-up psychic tension, and *insight*, or self-understanding. As we will see, these goals are achieved through the therapist's interpretation of three types of behavior: free association, resistance, and transference.

Free Association For Freud, the principal technique of psychoanalysis was born in 1892 with a patient named Elisabeth. At first, Freud had her lie down, close her eyes, think hard about a symptom, and try to recall the moment it started. Meanwhile, he asked pointed questions and pressed his hand against her forehead to help her concentrate. Then at one point, after many futile attempts, Elisabeth had an insight—but concerning a part of her life that was unrelated to the symptom she was trying to recall. Freud was taken by surprise. Why had she waited so long to reveal something so important? "I could have told you that the first time, but I didn't think that it was what you wanted," she said (quoted in Jones, 1953, p. 243). Humbled by this turn of events, Freud came up with a new set of rules. From now on, he said, follow your own train of thought. Elisabeth was agreeable but, in turn, asked Freud to stop asking so many irrelevant questions. This episode marked the first use of **free association**, the backbone of psychoanalysis. In free association, the patient lies back, relaxes, and talks about thoughts, wishes, memories, fantasies, physical sensations, dreams, and whatever else comes to mind—no matter how trivial, embarrassing, or crazy it may seem. No censorship. No interruption. In the meantime, the analyst listens attentively, trying to put together the pieces of an emerging puzzle.

Beginning with Freud's (1900) work on dreams, psychoanalysts have encouraged patients to free-associate about their dreams—the "royal road to the unconscious." As we saw in Chapter 4, this emphasis is based on the theory that pent-up psychic energy from repressed sexual and aggressive impulses is released when we're asleep, but in ways that are confusing and hard to interpret. According to Freud, the dreams you remember in the morning are well-disguised expressions of deep, hidden impulses. Thus, as patients describe the conscious *manifest content* of dreams, their analysts are busy trying to unmask the underlying *latent content*—what the dreams "really" mean.

Resistance Free association was only the beginning. Right from the start, Freud noticed something curious. His patients could talk for long periods of time and produce endless streams of ideas, but they often would not face unpleasant thoughts and memories. On the brink of an important but painful insight, patients would stop, go blank, lose their train of thought, change the subject, argue with the therapist, "forget" the next appointment, make jokes, call it quits, or seek another therapist. Freud called this pattern of avoidance **resistance** and concluded that it was part of an unconscious defensive process designed to keep threatening personal insights out of awareness.

In psychoanalysis, resistance is a double-edge sword. On the one hand, it slows down the course of therapy and may even bring it to a grinding halt. On the other hand, it signals that the patient is on the verge of exposing a psychic raw nerve and that therapy is moving in the right direction. Where there's smoke, there's fire;

free association A basic technique of psychoanalysis in which the patient says whatever comes to mind—freely and without censorship.

resistance In psychoanalysis, the tendency for patients to actively block or "resist" psychologically painful insights.

where there's resistance, there's emotional turmoil. The analyst's goal is to make the patient aware of the resistance by carefully interpreting what it means. "I notice you never want to talk about your mother" and "Why do you always make jokes when you discuss your illness?" are the kinds of interpretive statements analysts make in order to get at underlying problems and nudge patients toward difficult self-insights.

[Drawing by Henry Martin; © 1992 The New Yorker Magazine, Inc. All rights reserved.]

"Do you think your failure to bloom could be caused not just by improper location but also by a fear of having your blooms compared with those of other African violets?"

Transference Also critical to psychoanalysis is the therapist–patient relationship. Just as Anna O. became attached to Breuer, many of Freud's patients developed intense, unsolicited feelings toward him. Freud assumed that he was not the real target of these passions, so he speculated that people have an unconscious tendency to transfer feelings for parents, siblings, lovers, and other significant persons onto the therapist—a phenomenon he called **transference**. Sometimes the patient reacts with passionate love and affection (positive transference) but at other times with hatred, anger, and hostility (negative transference). Either way, the therapist is merely a convenient substitute for the person for whom these feelings are really meant. In fact, said Freud, therapists need to beware of their own tendency to "countertransfer" feelings they have for others onto their patients. In *Love's Executioner*, for example, Yalom (1989) freely admitted that when he started to treat Betty, the obese woman, he had to fight a lifelong aversion to people who are overweight—an aversion he traced to his own childhood.

> *"In a sonata all the themes that are going to appear are stated at the beginning. . . . One might think of one's first relationships as the themes of one's interpersonal life and all subsequent relationships as the development and recapitulation of those themes."*
>
> — MICHAEL KAHN

As with resistance, transference is a welcome disruption in psychoanalysis. It may slow down and complicate matters, but it also provides a window to the unconscious. When deeply rooted feelings are awakened in therapy, patients can more easily slip into the past and recall events from childhood. Again, the goal is for people to gain insight into their current relationships—to understand why they are attracted to certain kinds of people or why they shy away from commitments, need constant reassurance, or become fiercely possessive and jealous. To foster these kinds of transference-related insights, the psychoanalyst sits behind the patient, maintains a shadowy presence, and then interprets the transference reaction. Examples include: "You always seem to want my approval, the way you must have needed your mother's approval" and "You're angry because I won't tell you how to run your life, and you think I don't care. Is that why you're always upset with your boyfriend? He isn't bossy, so you think he doesn't care?"

Based on material provided by free association, resistance, and transference, psychoanalysts seek insight through a process of interpretation (see Table 17.1). One key factor in this endeavor is timing. Someone who is emotionally prepared to face painful ideas will feel relieved and enlightened by an interpretation. But for someone who is not, the technique will backfire, heightening anxiety and resistance. Psychoanalysis is thus a long, hard, and expensive process—typically requiring four or five fifty-minute sessions a week and lasting for some number of years. It's interesting that Freud's patients seldom stayed in psychoanalysis for more than a year. Since then, however, the process has become longer and more drawn out (it's been said that analysis used to last a year and marriage a lifetime but that now it's the opposite). If you ever saw the movie *Sleeper*, you'll recall that after having been frozen for 200 years, Woody Allen wakes up and says, in a semiserious tone, "If I had kept seeing my analyst, I'd almost be cured by now!"

Brief Psychoanalytic Therapies Inspired by neo-Freudian theorists such as Jung, Adler, Fromm, Horney, and Erikson (see Chapter 15) and by a practical need

transference In psychoanalysis, the tendency of patients to displace intense feelings for others onto the therapist.

Table 17.1 Psychoanalysis in Action

Taken from an actual therapy session, this dialogue illustrates one psychoanalyst's use of interpretation (Baker, 1985, pp. 41–42).

PATIENT:	You know, I really didn't want to come today. I just don't seem to have very much to talk about. (long silence) I'm just not really sure what to say; maybe you can suggest a topic.
THERAPIST:	You'd like for me to tell you what to talk about, to give you some structure?
PATIENT:	Sure, after all, that's what I'm paying you for. (pause) It seems that you just sit there all the time not saying anything. I'm not really sure this is helping very much.
THERAPIST:	Perhaps we should talk about your feeling that I'm not giving you what you want.
PATIENT:	It's not so much want, it's what I *need*. You always just sit there; you never give me advice; you never tell me what to do. I thought therapy would be different from this.
THERAPIST:	You expected more?
PATIENT:	I expected *something*. You know, it's a little irritating to pay out good money and feel like you're not getting your money's worth.
THERAPIST:	So it feels as if I'm cheating or depriving you in some way. Perhaps that is why you're feeling so angry today.
PATIENT:	I'm not feeling angry. (pause) Well . . . I guess I am a little. In fact, I really didn't even want to come.
THERAPIST:	Perhaps there's a relationship between those feelings . . . feeling angry and then wanting to withdraw.
PATIENT:	You know, I think I do that a lot. I feel uncomfortable being angry at you. It doesn't seem justified somehow and yet I do feel angry and feel like I just want to not come and not talk; or not pay my bill or do something to get even. I guess I do that a lot. I mean, when I get angry, I get quiet and I just don't talk.
THERAPIST:	Perhaps that is why you were so quiet at the beginning of the hour. It was a way of indirectly letting me know that you were angry, while at the same time protecting yourself and me from that anger and your fears of what it might do.
PATIENT:	I guess you are right. I am afraid of anger and I have a lot of difficulty letting people know directly when I feel they have done something bad or hurt me in some way. So I just . . . withdraw.

for shorter-term, less costly forms of treatment, most psychoanalytic therapists today use modified, nonorthodox techniques. They still share key aspects of Freud's approach—such as an appreciation for the importance of past experiences and unconscious processes. In general, however, these newer therapies are briefer, less intense, and more flexible. Sessions are usually scheduled once a week and for a limited period of time—usually just a few months rather than years. To accelerate the therapy process, many analysts now sit face-to-face with their patients and take a more active conversational role, often asking direct questions and prompting certain lines of inquiry. Unconscious resistance is still interpreted, and transference is still considered a useful vehicle for insight, but today's analyst tries to minimize these reactions or else to facilitate the process through role-playing exercises. There is also less time spent plunging into the past and more time spent addressing current life problems (Alexander & French, 1946; Luborsky, 1984; Crits-Christoph & Barber, 1991; Henry et al., 1994).

Controversies in Psychoanalysis Ever since Freud claimed that people are driven from birth by lustful desires and aggressive impulses and that they are at the mercy of unconscious forces beyond their control, psychoanalysis as a theory has been steeped in controversy. It is also controversial as a form of treatment. There are three main criticisms. The first, aimed at orthodox psychoanalysis, is that it takes too long and is too expensive, available only to those who are affluent. The second is that psychoanalytic interpretations can never be disproved. If a therapist interprets a patient's late arrival as a sign of resistance and the patient accepts this interpretation, it stands confirmed. If the patient emphatically denies the interpretation, the denial itself becomes proof of resistance, also "confirming" the initial interpretation ("heads I win, tails you lose"). A third criticism is that psychoanalysis is not truly therapeutic, that people are no better off after they come out than before they went in. We'll see later that this claim is unfair. Studies show that psychoanalytic therapy, like other types of psychotherapy, is generally effective. But must people dive head first into the past and open old wounds in order to solve current life problems? Many psychologists and psychiatrists do not think so. Psychoanalysis is thus on the decline, leaving many of its adherents in the United States wondering, "Is there a future for American psychoanalysis?" (Kirsner, 1990).

Despite the criticisms, psychoanalysis has left a permanent imprint on clinical theories, practice, and research (Nersessian & Kopff, 1996). Therapists from all orientations agree that resistance is a typical behavior among psychotherapy patients (Mahoney, 1991). Indeed, research shows that defensiveness and self-deception in general are normal, adaptive parts of human nature. Many practitioners also agree that transference and other aspects of the therapist–patient relationship are key to success (Horvath & Luborsky, 1993; Kahn, 1991). In addition, studies support Freud's claim that patients bring into therapy unique, consistent, and largely unconscious interaction styles from past relationships (Luborsky & Crits-Christoph, 1990). Even in laboratory studies, subjects have been shown to react to neutral strangers according to whether they resemble others from their own lives whom they liked or disliked (Andersen & Baum, 1994). Finally, many of us now take for granted the psychoanalytic assumptions that mental disorders are often rooted in childhood, that we often avoid thinking about deep-seated conflicts, and that insight has therapeutic value.

Behavioral Therapies

Psychoanalysis is an intensive form of therapy in which people are opened up, taken apart, and reassembled before they can be cured. In this approach, analysts have to get to the root of the "problem" in order to eliminate the "symptoms." Then along came Pavlov, Watson, Skinner, and other behaviorists. Armed with the principles of classical and operant conditioning, they argued that psychological disorders consist of maladaptive behaviors that are learned by reinforcement and can be unlearned in the same manner. Afraid to fly? Depressed? Think everyone is out to get you? Well, said the behaviorists, forget the past, ignore your dreams, keep unconscious urges in the closet, and stop waiting for pearls of wisdom to fall from the lips of your all-knowing analyst. Instead, tell me what it is you want to change about yourself. Then we'll make a list of concrete behavioral goals and try to achieve these goals as quickly as we can. Eliminate the symptom and you have solved the problem.

Whether one has a phobia, test anxiety, a sexual disorder, or an inability to stop smoking, it can often be treated by classical and operant conditioning and other

TREATMENT AND LAW

Repressed Memories on Trial

It is sometimes ironic how history repeats itself. It was the year 1900. While formulating his theory of psychoanalysis, Freud was listening to his patients recount horrifying tales of early childhood abuse. One after another, they told of incest and other traumas, often sexual in nature. But Freud soon came to believe that at least some of the stories he was being told were false, the figments of overactive imaginations. This development was a terrible blow, and Freud felt betrayed—until he concluded that his patients were not really lying. They truly believed that the incidents they talked about had happened.

Turning the clock forward, we find ourselves in the year 1990. In Redwood City, California, fifty-one-year-old George Franklin stood trial for the murder of an eight-year-old girl that had taken place more than twenty years earlier. For years, the crime was left unsolved. Then Eileen Franklin, the victim's friend—who was eight years old at the time of the girl's death—came forward to implicate the defendant, her father. According to Eileen, she had forgotten the incident and just recently had started to have flashbacks. She now remembers playing with her friend in the family van when the attack took place. She remembers seeing her father sexually assault the girl and raise his hands up, holding a rock. She remembers screams, a struggle, and the sight of her friend covered with blood, with a smashed silver ring on her finger. Based solely on her testimony, Franklin was convicted of first-degree murder and sentenced to prison. It was the first time that someone had been tried and convicted of murder on the basis of a newly recovered repressed memory.

In 1993, Steven Cook (left) filed a lawsuit against Cardinal Joseph Bernardin (right), in which he claimed that Bernardin had sexually molested him as a child. Months later, Cook dropped the charges and said that his "memories" (which had been "recovered" in hypnosis) were false. "My life will never be the same because of this," Bernardin said afterward. Cook died of AIDS in 1995, and Bernardin died of cancer in 1996.

The Franklin conviction was followed by a barrage of new charges. Alleged victims soon appeared in courtrooms and on daytime TV talk shows to tell horrifying tales of abuse, sometimes in the context of satanic-cult rituals. In many states, legal statutes of limitations that kept people from bringing cases forward after long periods of time were modified for those who recovered long-lost memories. As a result, thousands of men and women filed multimillion-dollar lawsuits against family members and others in their distant past, leaving the courts to decide how to treat this evidence. In one recent case, a federal court ruled to allow a sixty-eight-year-old woman to sue her cousin who, she alleged, sexually abused her when they were teenagers—a memory recovered fifty years later in therapy. Yet in another case, a federal court disallowed the testimony of a woman in her thirties who sued her aunt, uncle, and many others for repeatedly drugging her, raping her, and forcing her to drink blood from as early as the age of three—memories she recovered in hypnosis (Ewing, 1996).

These cases have now triggered a backlash against the use of repressed memories. Accused mothers, fathers, grandparents, and others sought each other out and formed the False Memory Syndrome Foundation, a nationwide support group. These people, too, had stories to tell about having their families and reputations torn apart by false accusations. Indeed, many repressed-memory accusers withdrew their claims—and some even joined their families in suing the therapists who brought the so-called memories out in the first place.

Childhood sex abuse is a crime that can have devastating and lasting consequences for mental health—and it may be far more common than was previously realized. Many psychotherapists point to cases in which patients had forgotten traumatic events until the memories sometimes surfaced years later, to be corroborated by independent evidence. But what should be done when there is no independent evidence? On one side of the debate are Ellen Bass and Laura Davis (1988), authors of *The Courage to Heal*, a book that is often described as the "bible" for the survivors of incest and childhood sex abuse. Though not trained in psychology, Bass and Davis provide readers with a list of symptoms to watch for, such as anxiety, depression, loss of appetite, intimacy problems, and dependence. And when a reader is in doubt? "If you are unable to remember any specific instances . . . but still have a feeling that something abusive happened to you, it probably did" (p. 21).

On the other side of the debate, Elizabeth Loftus (1993) warns that often a person's memories for remote-past events are not memories at all but images and ideas suggested by therapists eager to find the source of a patient's distress. Is it possible for one person to plant a false trauma memory into the mind of another? In *The Myth of Repressed Memory*, Loftus and Ketcham (1994) described some compelling demonstrations, including one in which a fourteen-year-old boy named Chris was told by his older brother Jim that he got lost in a mall when he was five years old and was found crying by a tall older man wearing a flannel shirt. The story was false. Yet a few days later, Chris "recalled" being scared, being asked by an older man if he was lost, and being scolded afterward by his mother. Two weeks later, he described even more fully what had happened: "I was with you guys for a second and I think I went over to look at the toy store . . . I thought I was never going to see my family again. I was really scared, you know. And then this old man, I think he was wearing blue flannel, came up to me . . . he was kind of old. He was kind of bald on top . . . he had like a ring of gray hair . . . and he had glasses."

As judges and juries struggle to sort facts from fictions, it is important to balance our concerns for both the victims of abuse and the victims of false accusations. Research suggests that people often avoid certain thoughts, and that events once forgotten can sometimes be recalled (Erdelyi, 1996). But can repressed-and-recovered memories of traumatic events be trusted? Within psychology, this controversy has become highly emotional—and divisive (Pezdek & Banks, 1996). Recently, the American Psychological Association assembled a task force to examine the issue, a mixed group composed of both researchers and therapists. The group could agree on little, except the following:

1. Sexual abuse is a pervasive problem.
2. Most people abused as children remember all or part of what happened.
3. It is possible to recall old memories that have been forgotten over time.
4. It is possible to construct false memories of events that did not occur.
5. There are gaps in our knowledge of the processes that lead to accurate versus inaccurate childhood memories.

Finally, let's return to the case of George Franklin. After Franklin spent five years in prison, his conviction was overturned by an appeals court on a matter of evidence. Franklin was freed and granted a new trial. It was revealed, however, that Eileen had recalled the event at a time when she was seeing a therapist and had undergone hypnosis, that the details she recounted had been published in the local newspaper, and that her reports had changed during the course of the investigation. To this day, there is no way to know whether her memory is true or false. In 1996, however, the prosecution—concerned about her credibility as a witness—chose not to retry Franklin. As the debate rages on, it is clear that these questions can be answered only on a case-by-case basis—and with the help of independent evidence.

well-established principles of learning. In a book on behavioral techniques, 158 specific procedures were described, including "anger-control therapy," "verbal-satiation therapy," and "implosion therapy" (Bellack & Hersen, 1985). Together, these various techniques are known as **behavioral therapy** (Bandura, 1969; Wolpe, 1982; Emmelkamp, 1994).

behavioral therapies Techniques used to modify disordered thoughts, feelings, and behaviors through the principles of learning.

Classical Conditioning Techniques As we saw in Chapter 5, *classical conditioning* is the Pavlovian process by which a once-neutral stimulus (a bell) comes to elicit an emotional or behavioral response (salivation) after being paired repeatedly with an unconditioned stimulus (food) that already has the power to elicit that reaction. In 1920, Watson and Rayner used this model to train a baby boy to react with fear to a white rat by pairing the rat with an aversive loud noise. If phobias and other disorders develop through classical conditioning, suggested Watson, then perhaps they can be erased in the same manner.

Flooding If Watson was right, it should be possible to treat certain disorders through *extinction*. After repeated presentations of a bell without food, Pavlov's dogs eventually stopped salivating in response to the sound. Similarly, people who confront a fearful situation without a negative consequence should see that the fear is unfounded. This idea gave rise to **flooding**—a technique in which a person is exposed to, or "flooded," with an anxiety-provoking stimulus until the anxiety is extinguished. Sometimes the person is guided to imagine the dreaded stimulus; at other times, the experience is firsthand. Someone with agoraphobia (a fear of being in public places), for example, might be taken by a reassuring therapist into a crowded shopping mall and kept there for hours until the fear subsides. This procedure is repeated several times until the anxiety is completely diminished. Flooding is generally effective, but success is not guaranteed. Some people can't bring themselves to confront their feared situation; others agree to but then panic, escape, and become even more anxious; still others complete the program but later experience a relapse (Barlow, 1988).

Systematic Desensitization Another powerful antidote for anxiety is *counterconditioning*—a procedure in which a person is trained to react to a feared stimulus with a positive response that is incompatible with anxiety. Mary Cover Jones (1924), a student of Watson's, sought to demonstrate that anxiety could be erased by associating a feared stimulus with a pleasurable experience. Jones treated a three-year-old boy named Peter, who had become intensely fearful of rabbits and other furry animals. One afternoon, Jones took Peter into a room with a caged rabbit, sat him at a table, and fed him milk and crackers. This routine was repeated several times, and each time the rabbit was moved closer as the boy devoured his snack. After a few weeks, Peter was holding the rabbit on his lap, stroking it with one hand, and eating with the other. Through the process of stimulus generalization, he shed his fear of other animals as well.

Thirty-four years after Jones reported on this case, Joseph Wolpe (1958) devised **systematic desensitization**, a technique that is now widely used in the treatment of phobias and other anxiety disorders. Based on the fact that a person cannot simultaneously feel anxious and relaxed, systematic desensitization is designed to condition people to respond to a feared stimulus with calm, not anxiety. There are three steps in this procedure: (1) relaxation training, (2) the construction of an anxiety hierarchy, and (3) gradual exposure. To see how systematic desensitization works, imagine that you are afraid to fly and that whenever you see an airplane on a runway, hear the thunderous noise of its engines, smell the fuel, or feel the vibrations, your heart races and you break into a cold sweat. You make an appointment with a behavior therapist, and before you know it you're ready to begin.

The first step is to learn how to relax in response to a cue from the therapist. This is accomplished through *relaxation training*—a procedure in which you are taught to concentrate on what it feels like to tighten and then relax various muscle groups throughout the body. Try it. Really. Sit back comfortably, loosen your clothing, take your shoes off, take a deep breath, and let your muscles get loose and heavy. Now wrinkle up your forehead, wrinkle it tighter, tighter again. Hold it for a few seconds. Now stop tensing, relax, and smooth it out. Picture your entire forehead and scalp

flooding A behavioral therapy technique in which the patient is saturated with a fear-provoking stimulus until the anxiety is extinguished.

systematic desensitization A behavioral therapy technique used to treat phobias and other anxiety disorders by pairing gradual exposure to an anxiety-provoking situation with relaxation.

becoming smoother. Now frown and crease your brows. Close your eyes, tighter and tighter. Feel the tension. Now relax, and let go. Keep your eyes closed gently, and notice the relaxation. Now clench your jaw and purse your lips, tighter and tighter. Press your tongue hard against the roof of your mouth, and feel the tension. All right, now relax. Relax your jaw, loosen your lips, let your mouth hang open, and let your tongue return to a comfortable position. Notice how relaxed you are all over. Let all your muscles go limp and feel the smoothness in your forehead, scalp, eyes, mouth, and lips. See how it feels to be relaxed.

The next step is to come up with an *anxiety hierarchy*, a graduated sequence of fear-provoking situations that you rate on a 100-point scale, ranging from mild to terrifying. In your case, the hierarchy might begin with "You see a newspaper ad for discount airfares" and progress to "You look out the window as the plane leaves the ground" (see Table 17.2).

Prepared with an ability to relax on cue and with a hierarchy of fear-provoking situations, you brace yourself for the third and final step. At this point, the therapist talks you into a state of relaxation and guides you through a gradual series of *exposures*. You're instructed to close your eyes and imagine the mildest fear-provoking situation in the hierarchy. If you keep your cool while visualizing this scene, you move on to the next item on the list. If you begin to get anxious, however, the therapist will instruct you to stop and relax. The scene is then revisited until it ceases to arouse anxiety. Lasting several sessions, this same routine is repeated for all items in the hierarchy until you are "cured" of the fear. This technique, in which the person mentally confronts the anxiety-provoking stimulus, is known as *imaginal exposure*. To ensure long-term success, however, many therapists prefer to use *in vivo exposure*—having the person confront the feared situations in real life. The ultimate test of whether you have conquered the fear of flying is in your ability to board an airplane, stay calm during the flight, and make the return trip later on.

In an intriguing new development, Barbara Rothbaum and others (1995) have been experimenting with exposure through the use of *virtual reality*. Imagine being

Table 17.2 A Sample Anxiety Hierarchy

The scenes in this hierarchy are typical of those used in the systematic desensitization of a fear of flying. The numbers to the left of each item represent one patient's subjective rating of how anxiety-provoking a situation is, on a scale from 0 to 100.

5	You see a newspaper ad for discount airfares.
10	You see a TV commercial for an airline.
20	A group of friends talks about arranging a trip that requires flying.
30	You visit a travel agent to make plane reservations.
35	The week before the trip, you get your plane tickets in the mail.
40	The night before the trip, you pull out your suitcase to pack.
55	You park your car near the departure terminal.
60	You check in, and the agent asks if you want a window or aisle seat.
65	The announcement is made that your flight is ready for passenger boarding.
70	You're in line, with ticket in hand, ready to board.
80	You're in your seat, and the flight attendant says, "Fasten your seatbelts for takeoff."
90	You feel the plane begin to roll down the runway.
95	You look out the window as the plane leaves the ground.

fearful of heights and peering down from the top edge of the Empire State Building. To achieve this sensation, the patient would wear a helmet with an electromagnetic sensor. The therapist would program the helmet with a computer-generated 3-D view of a virtual environment that changes with head and body movements. Thus, as part of systematic desensitization, patients can realistically experience what it feels like to stand on the roof of a virtual skyscraper, speak in front of a virtual audience, fly in a virtual airplane, or handle a virtual snake—all without leaving the therapist's office. Rothbaum and her colleagues tested this technique on college students fearful of heights and found that it was highly successful.

Systematic desensitization is a common and highly effective form of therapy and has been used to treat fears of dogs, snakes, blood, heights, open spaces, crowds, balloons, feathers, violins, dentists, tunnels, needles, and eating in public (Marks, 1987)—sometimes in a single session (Ost, 1989; Zinbarg et al., 1992). According to Wolpe (1982), systematic desensitization works via counterconditioning, by associating a new response (relaxation) to the feared stimulus. However, others find that exposure alone is all that's needed—with or without the relaxation (Rachman, 1990). Many home-bound agoraphobias, for example, benefit from an in vivo exposure treatment in which they are taken by their therapist, spouse, or a companion into crowded streets, shopping malls, and other progressively difficult situations (Foa & Kozak, 1986).

As shown in Figure 17.2, behavior therapists have used this technique with success to treat people with obsessive-compulsive disorder by exposing them to the situations that evoke obsessive thoughts but then preventing them from carrying out their compulsive rituals (Emmelkamp, 1982). This technique has also been used to help women with bulimia, an eating disorder that is characterized by cycles of binge eating and purging. Thus, the women are fed but prevented from vomiting (Wilson et al., 1986). In all cases, exposure-and-response-prevention causes an initial buildup of anxiety that eventually subsides, often with lasting success (Barlow & Lehman, 1996).

Sometimes it helps to watch the harmless exposure of others to an anxiety-provoking situation. In a study on the therapeutic effects of *modeling*, Albert Bandura and others (1969) had persons with snake phobias observe a filmed or live model handling snakes and found that these exposures—especially to a live model—increased the extent to which subjects were able to approach a snake without anxiety. In another study, medical patients who needed "hyperbaric oxygen therapy" (a stressful procedure in which they are locked for an hour in a narrow chamber containing pressurized oxygen) were more relaxed, completed more prescribed treatments, and required fewer days in the hospital when they first watched a filmed model coping with the same situation than when they did not (Allen et al., 1989). Even more effective is *participant modeling*, which combines passive exposure to a model with gradual practice (Ost et al., 1991).

Aversive Conditioning The aim of systematic desensitization is to get people to stay calm in safe situations. But when people are attracted to activities that are harmful—smoking, drinking, overeating, and other destructive habits—the opposite effect is sought. In these cases, behavioral therapists often use **aversion therapy**, a technique designed to elicit an aversive rather than pleasurable reaction to a harmful stimulus.

aversion therapy A behavioral therapy technique for classically conditioning people to react with aversion to alcohol and other harmful substances.

In the treatment of alcoholism, the goal of aversion therapy is to cause heavy drinkers to feel sick to the stomach at the sight, smell, and taste of liquor (see Figure 17.3 on page 662). There are a number of ways to achieve this objective. In one technique, the alcoholic drinker is given Antabuse (a drug that causes nausea when com-

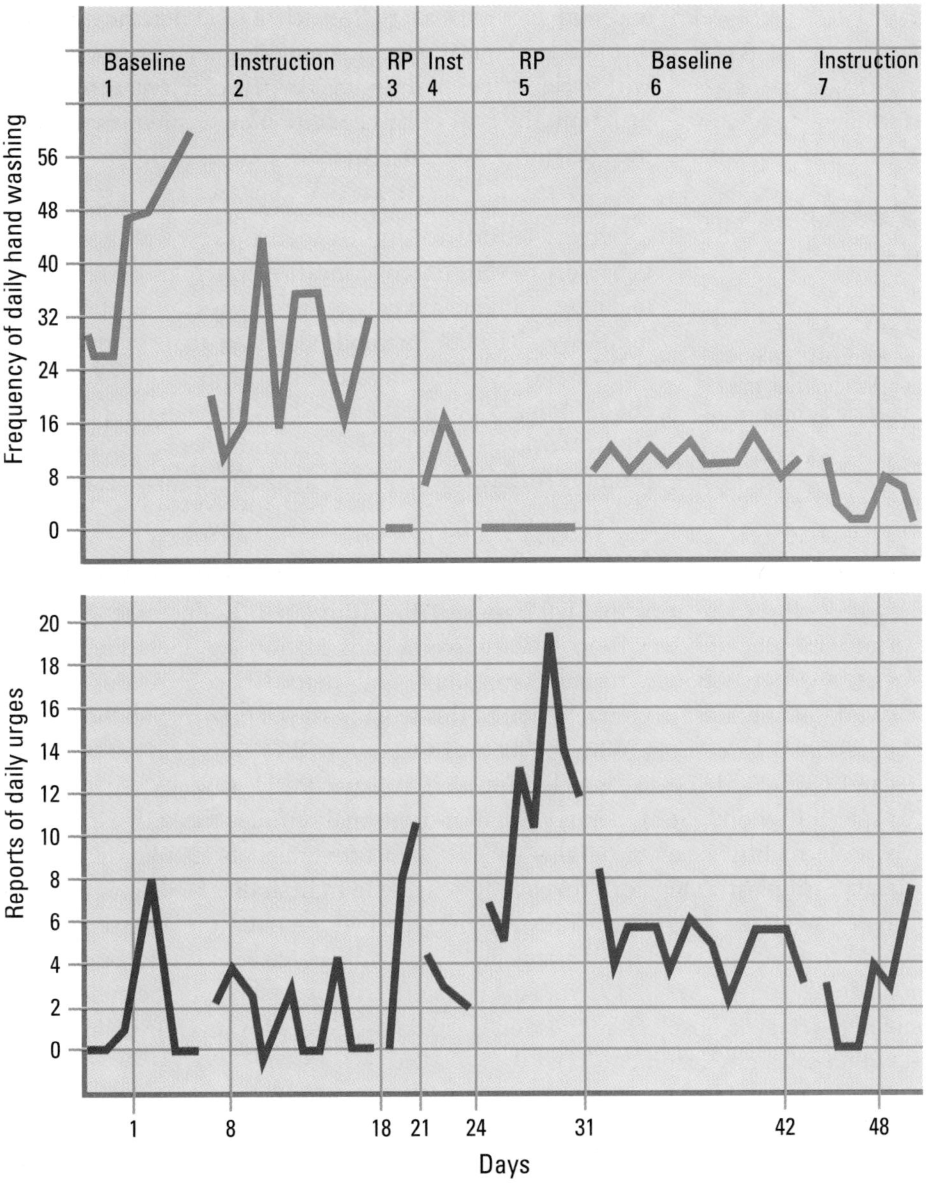

Figure 17.2 Therapeutic effects of exposure and response prevention A woman with a compulsive handwashing ritual was hospitalized and permitted for a week to wash as desired (baseline). During the next week, she was told to try to break the habit (instruction). This was followed by three days of denied access to running water (response prevention), another instruction, and more response prevention. This treatment was highly effective. After a few weeks, the woman was washing less often and getting fewer urges (Mills et al., 1973).

bined with certain other drugs, including alcohol) and then is taken to a darkened room (one designed to look much like a bar) and served beer, wine, gin, whiskey, or other favorite drinks. After a few minutes, the person vomits uncontrollably. This treatment has, in some cases, resulted in abstinence after five or six visits, followed by occasional booster sessions (Cannon et al., 1981). In a study of 685 hospitalized alcoholics treated with aversion therapy, 63 percent were still "dry" after one year, and 33 percent were still dry after three years (Wiens & Menustik, 1983).

By itself, aversion therapy is not a sufficient treatment for alcoholism. With people who are desperate and willing, however, this technique is sometimes used in conjunction with other forms of therapy (those being treated as such take an Antabuse pill every day, so if they drink they get sick). There are also nonchemical

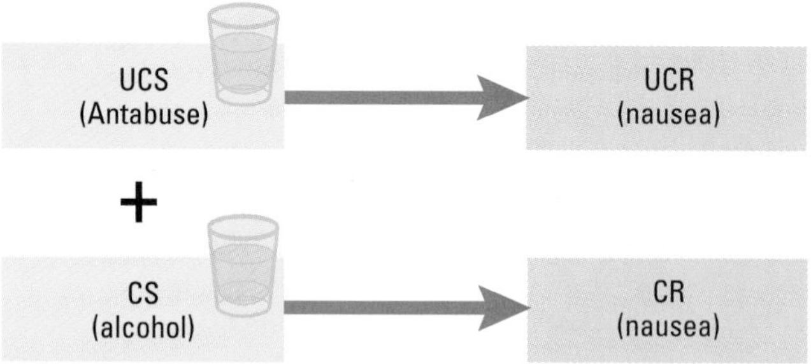

Figure 17.3 Aversion therapy to treat alcoholism In aversion therapy, the goal is eliminate the urge to drink by pairing alcohol with a chemical that causes nausea and vomiting. When used, this conditioning-based technique is typically accompanied by other forms of treatment.

aversion methods as well—such as having the problem drinker imagine unpleasant and disgusting scenes along with vivid images of drinking. As part of a larger treatment program, the goal of this conditioning technique is to suppress the urge to drink (Rimelle et al., 1995).

Operant-Conditioning Techniques While some behaviorists were discovering the principles of reinforcement by training animals to peck keys, press bars, and jump over barriers for food, water, or the termination of electric shock, others began using the methods of operant conditioning for clinical purposes. On the assumption that all the world's a Skinner box, reinforcement can be used to promote behaviors that are desirable and to extinguish those that are not.

Illustrating aversive conditioning, behavioral therapists use the "rapid-smoking technique" by forcing smokers who can't break the habit to puff continuously, every few seconds. For a period of time, this procedure is repeated over and over again until the urge to smoke is suppressed (Glasgow & Lichtenstein, 1987).

Reward and Punishment It is sometimes necessary to establish clear reinforcement programs to treat people who are severely disordered. In one case, a female patient with schizophrenia wore twenty-five pounds of clothing, including several dresses, sweaters, shawls, turbans, stockings, and coats. To control this bizarre behavior, the therapist in charge required this woman to weigh in at the door of the dining room before meals. Whether she was then allowed to enter and eat was contingent on a steadily decreasing clothing weight. After thirteen weeks, the problem was solved (Ayllon, 1963). Sometimes, in institutional settings, the staff establishes large-scale reinforcement programs called **token economies**. In a token economy, patients earn plastic chips or "tokens" for engaging in desirable behaviors (such as prompt attendance at group-therapy meetings). As with money, the tokens can then be used to purchase candy, TV privileges, weekend passes, books, and other commodities (Ayllon & Azrin, 1968). This is an effective way to shape behavior—not only in psychiatric hospitals but also in classrooms, homes for juvenile delinquents, and other settings (Kazdin, 1982).

Reward usually produces impressive changes, but punishment is sometimes necessary to eliminate dangerous or self-destructive behavior. In one study, punishment was used on nineteen autistic preschoolers who were uncommunicative and who injured themselves by pulling out hair, biting chunks of skin, and banging their heads against the wall. With help from their parents, these children were put into a two-year home-treatment program in which they were ignored, interrupted, or slapped on the thigh whenever they engaged in violent, self-abusive acts. By the first grade, nine of them were functioning normally in school—a remarkable accomplishment compared to those not treated with punishment and in light of previous failures with similar children (Lovaas, 1987).

token economy A large-scale behavior-change program in which the participants earn valuable tokens for engaging in desired target behaviors.

biofeedback An operant procedure in which people learn to control physiological responses with the help of "feedback" about their internal states.

Biofeedback Yoga specialist Swami Rama once astonished psychologists by proving in controlled laboratory tests that he could voluntarily slow down or speed up his pulse rate, stop his heart from pumping blood for seventeen seconds, raise or lower the temperature in his hand, and alter his brain-wave patterns. But is it possible? Can people control their physiological behavior? Yes, absolutely. In 1969, Neil Miller found that heart rates in animals could be conditioned to increase or decrease in response to rewarding, pleasurable brain stimulation.

As an outgrowth of this research, psychologists developed **biofeedback**, a procedure by which people learn to control their own autonomic processes by receiving continuous, moment-to-moment information, or feedback, in the form of visual or auditory displays. With the aid of electronic sensors attached to parts of the body and an instrument that records and amplifies the various signals, people can monitor and eventually regulate not only their heart rate but also their blood pressure, skin temperature, gastric acidity, hormone secretions, and muscle tension. Today, behavior therapists use biofeedback to treat hypertension, chronic back pain, ulcers, bedwetting, and other health problems (Hatch et al., 1987). In one series of studies, Edward Blanchard and others (1982) found that biofeedback can be used to help people with tension-related migraine headaches (see below). It's no wonder that biofeedback has been referred to as the "Yoga of the West" and as "electronic Zen" (Schwartz, 1995).

Social-Skills Training For people who are painfully shy, unresponsive, or socially awkward, there is **social-skills training**—lessons on how to speak clearly, make eye contact, maintain a comfortable amount of social distance, and respond appropriately to questions (Curran & Monti, 1982). In social-skills training, the therapist models the desired behaviors, the patient imitates and rehearses these behaviors in role-playing exercises, and the therapist responds with a combination of praise and constructive criticism. This reinforcement-based therapy produces impressive results. Studies show, for example, that it helps people with schizophrenia to interact with others more easily and to feel more comfortable in public situations (Benton & Schroeder, 1990).

One type of social-skills training that is currently popular is *assertiveness training* (Alberti & Emmons, 1986). Imagine that you are waiting in a long line for concert tickets and someone cuts in front of you. Or you are in a movie theater and the people behind you talk so loudly that you can't concentrate. Or a friend asks you for a lift to the airport, but you're too busy at the time. Or you take your car in for repairs, but when you pick it up you get a bill that is twice the estimated cost. How would you react in these situations? Would you speak up and assert yourself or hold your tongue and say nothing? For people who are passive and easily manipulated, assertiveness training—through the use of modeling and reinforcement—teaches people how to protect their own self-interests, resulting in treatment gains that may be enduring (Baggs & Spence, 1990).

social-skills training A form of behavioral therapy used to teach interpersonal skills through modeling, rehearsal, and reinforcement (e.g., assertiveness training).

INTERSECTION

TREATMENT AND HEALTH

Using Biofeedback to Treat Headaches

Have you ever had a pulsating headache so painful that you had to just lie down and close your eyes? If so, you're not alone. Surveys reveal that more than 90 percent of all adolescents and young adults have at least one such headache per year (Linet et al., 1989). In fact, in one survey 10 to 20 percent of respondents said *yes* to the question "Do you have a headache today?" (Rasmussen et al., 1991). For most people, headaches are infrequent, mild, and easily treatable with aspirin and rest in a dark, quiet room. But an estimated 11 million Americans suffer from headaches that are frequent, severe, and disabling (Stewart et al., 1992).

There are more than 100 different kinds of headaches. The two most common are migraines and tension types. *Migraine headaches* tend to strike several times a month, usually on one side of the head, and often around the eyes. They are accompanied by throbbing pain, nausea and vomiting, and a heightened sensitivity to noise, bright light, and physical exertion. In contrast, *tension headaches* are characterized by feelings of muscle tightness on both sides, often in the back of the neck or forehead. Studies show that headaches are more common among women than men (Stewart et al., 1992). They may be caused by such factors as high blood pressure, stress, too much or too little sleep, heat or cold, eyestrain, food allergies, alcohol, high altitude, and menstruation. Mild tension headaches can usually be treated with analgesics. For people who suffer from a chronic barrage of headaches, however, overuse of aspirin and other painkillers can trigger even more headaches and lose some of their impact over time (Hatch, 1993).

As an alternative, behaviorally oriented psychologists have successfully trained headache sufferers in the use of progressive muscle-relaxation techniques and biofeedback. In one series of studies, for example, Edward Blanchard and his colleagues showed that biofeedback can help people with tension-type headaches. In some cases, patients are provided with electromyographic (EMG) recordings of muscle tension in the face and scalp. For example, they may watch a light on an instrument panel that brightens as the muscles in the forehead, neck, or upper back tighten and dims as these muscles relax. Over time, this feedback enables the patient to control the EMG displays by learning to relax the right muscles (see Figure 17.4).

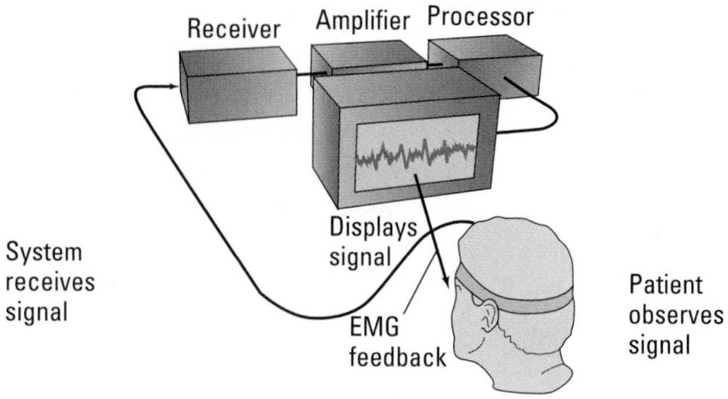

Figure 17.4 Biofeedback and the tension headache Using biofeedback, a headache sufferer learns to relax the forehead muscles by monitoring EMG recordings of tension in this region.

Another approach, which is typically used in the treatment of migraine headaches, is to provide patients with thermal biofeedback. In this procedure, sensors are attached to a finger and a beeping signal slows in rhythm as temperature rises. With experience, people learn to warm the finger, or even a hand or foot, thus bringing greater blood flow to that limb—and away from the head. Overall, biofeedback benefits more than 50 percent of tension-headache sufferers on a permanent, long-term basis (Blanchard, 1994). These results compare favorably with those produced by drug treatments—without the adverse side effects.

Cognitive Therapies

Behaviorists seek to modify maladaptive behavior through the use of classical and operant conditioning. But what matters most, stimulus–response connections and reinforcement per se, or the way we perceive these events? Reflecting psychology's interest in mental processes, many therapists use a more cognitive, rational approach. The result is **cognitive therapy**, a form of treatment designed to alter the maladaptive ways in which people interpret significant events in their lives (Hollon & Beck, 1994; J. Beck, 1995; Mahoney, 1995). To the cognitive therapist, "As you think, so shall you feel."

There are different brands of cognitive therapy and many techniques, but all have certain features in common. Based on the assumption that anxiety, depression, and other emotional disorders spring from the way we think, the goal is for people to open their minds, challenge their assumptions, and think about old problems in new ways. Cognitive therapy is short term, often limited to twenty sessions, and the therapist acts as a partner, friend, and teacher all rolled into one. Sessions are centered on concrete problems, and the therapist maintains a brisk, businesslike pace. Among the most prominent pioneers of this approach are Albert Ellis and Aaron Beck.

cognitive therapy A form of psychotherapy in which people are taught to think in more adaptive ways.

Rational-Emotive Therapy Though initially trained in psychoanalysis, Albert Ellis (1962) went on to develop **rational-emotive therapy**, or **RET**. According to Ellis, mental distress is caused not by upsetting events per se but by the rigid and maladaptive ways in which people construe these events. In other words, A (activating events) gives rise to B (beliefs), which in turn triggers C (emotional consequences). This A-B-C model is illustrated in Figure 17.5. The problem, said Ellis, is that too many of us hold beliefs that set us up for emotional turmoil. "I have to be liked by everyone," "I have to be perfect at whatever I do," and "Everyone gets what they deserve" are common beliefs that Ellis sees as irrational. The solution? Said Ellis, "My approach to psychotherapy is to zero in as quickly as possible on the client's basic philosophy of life; to get him to see exactly what this is and how it is inevitably self-defeating; and to persuade him to work his ass off, cognitively, emotively and behaviorally, to profoundly change it" (quoted in Warga, 1988, p. 57).

It's not easy to rid people of their lifelong assumptions or to get them to open their minds to new ways of thinking. To meet the task, RET therapists use blunt, confrontational techniques. "Why do you always have to make mountains out of tiny molehills?" "Where is it written that life is supposed to be fair?" "Who says you'll die if your marriage breaks up?" "What makes you think you'll be happier with more money?" are some of the argumentative questions typically asked. RET therapists also encourage their clients to step out of character, try new behaviors, and engage in "shame exercises." In one case, for example, Ellis instructed a shy young woman to sing at the top of her lungs in the subway, strike up conversations in the supermarket, flirt with men she liked, and even ask them for dates—so she could see that these actions did not bring life to a crashing end. Another part of RET is "psychoeducation," in which clients are lectured on the ABCs of emotional distress and given tapes of their own therapy sessions to review at home, along with booklets and audiotapes that teach the cognitive approach. Ellis himself made a series of self-help tapes, with straight-shooting titles such as "How to Stubbornly Refuse to Be Ashamed of Anything" (Bernard & DiGiuseppe, 1989).

Ellis's approach to psychotherapy may seem unconventional, but as a pioneer of the cognitive approach, he has made a substantial impact on the practice of psychotherapy. Although it's difficult to know precisely the extent to which patients benefit from RET (Haaga & Davison, 1993), studies designed to measure its effects on a patient's later adjustment and well-being have generally revealed positive results (Engels et al., 1993; Lyons & Woods, 1991). Reflecting immodestly on his own approach, Ellis (1996) recently said, "Most therapies help many clients to *feel better*. . . but only a few therapies help them *get better*" (p. 150).

Beck's Cognitive Therapy Like Ellis, Aaron Beck was trained in psychoanalysis, but he went on to devise a cognitive therapy when he noticed that his patients were

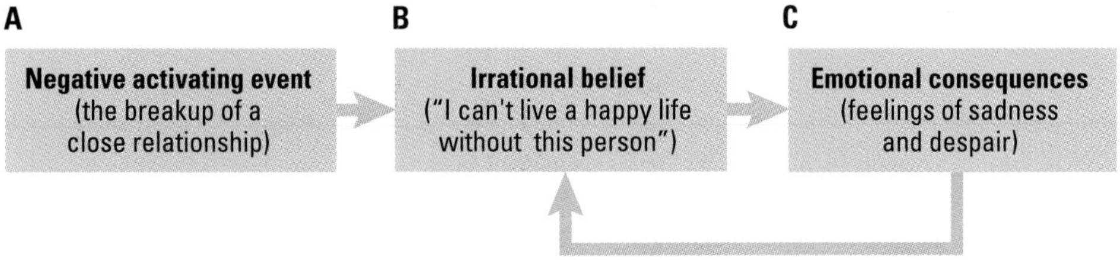

Figure 17.5 Ellis's A-B-C theory of emotional distress According to Ellis, emotional distress is caused by irrational thoughts and the assumptions people make. This distress, in turn, helps to sustain the irrational beliefs.

rational-emotive therapy (RET) A form of cognitive therapy in which people are confronted with their irrational, maladaptive beliefs.

filled with self-defeating beliefs (Beck, 1991). People who are depressed, for example, view themselves, their world, and the future through dark-colored glasses and make statements like "It's my fault," "I can't do anything right," "It's the story of my life," and "I'm a hopeless case" (Beck et al., 1979). People with anxiety disorders also think in ways that are maladaptive. They exaggerate the likelihood that they will fall victim to fatal accidents or diseases, and they engage in catastrophic thinking about their own bodies. When panic-disorder sufferers get aroused, for example, they often assume they're having a heart attack or a stroke—beliefs that further heighten their anxiety. Whether the problem is an eating disorder, a sexual disorder, an obsessive-compulsive disorder, drug abuse, or a fear of speaking in public, the problem contains an element of irrational thinking that can and should be changed (Beck, 1993).

All cognitive therapists share the same objectives, but they differ in style. Following Ellis, RET therapists forcefully confront clients with their irrational beliefs. In contrast, Beck—who has a soft, folksy manner—uses a gentler, more collaborative approach, helping people restructure the way they interpret events by means of a Socratic style of questioning. For a Beckian cognitive therapist, questions commonly asked include "What's the evidence for this idea?" "Are these facts, or your interpretation of the facts?" "Is there another way to look at the situation?" and "What's the worst that could happen?" (see Table 17.3).

There are many techniques that play an important role in Beck's cognitive therapy. One is to get clients to experience their distress in therapy. In one case, an eighteen-year-old woman who had frequent panic attacks was instructed to hyperventilate, which heightened her physiological arousal and triggered a state of panic. The therapist then helped her to interpret her bodily sensations in noncatastrophic terms. After four sessions, the woman's attacks subsided: "Every time my heart rate increased, I'd say, it's okay, it's no big deal" (Alford et al., 1990, p. 232). Keeping a diary is another important part of Beck's approach. Clients are encouraged to keep a daily log in which they describe the situation they were in, how they felt, what they were thinking, and how rational these thoughts were when they became upset. These assignments provide a basis for discussion and learning from one session to the next. Reading assignments, or bibliotherapy, are a third important technique. Clients are given books that explain the cognitive basis of psychological distress. Indeed, research shows that people benefit from reading cognitive-therapy self-help books that communicate the message "You feel the way you think" (Jamison & Scogin, 1995).

Cognitive therapy is popular among clinical psychologists. As noted, Ellis and Beck are the pioneers of the approach, but there are others as well. For example, Donald Meichenbaum (1985) uses stress-inoculation training, in which people are taught to make optimistic, positive self-statements—to insulate them from stress the way vaccines inoculate us against medical disease. Others within the cognitive tradition focus on problem-solving skills, feelings of self-efficacy, and behavioral self-control (Mahoney, 1995). Whatever the specific technique may be, cognitive therapy is now the most frequently taught orientation in American clinical-psychology graduate programs (Nevid et al., 1987) and is an effective form of treatment for a wide range of problems (Robins & Hayes, 1993).

Humanistic Therapies

When Carl Rogers was a young therapist, he noticed that his clients had a strong sense of self and an inner drive to grow, improve, and fulfill their potential. All the

Table 17.3 Beck's Cognitive Therapy in Action

The following dialogue between Beck and a client epitomizes his approach to therapy. When the client came in, he was upset over the poor job he did wallpapering a kitchen. Note how Beck gets the client to realize that he was exaggerating his negative appraisal (Beck et al., 1979, pp. 130–131).

THERAPIST:	Why didn't you rate wallpapering the kitchen as a mastery experience?
PATIENT:	Because the flowers didn't line up.
THERAPIST:	You did in fact complete the job?
PATIENT:	Yes.
THERAPIST:	Your kitchen?
PATIENT:	No, I helped a neighbor do his kitchen.
THERAPIST:	Did he do most of the work?
PATIENT:	No, I really did almost all of it. He hadn't wallpapered before.
THERAPIST:	Did anything else go wrong? Did you spill paste all over? Ruin the wallpaper? Leave a big mess?
PATIENT:	No, the only problem was that the flowers didn't line up.
THERAPIST:	Just how far off was this alignment of the flowers?
PATIENT:	(holding his fingers about an eighth of an inch apart) About this much.
THERAPIST:	On each strip of paper?
PATIENT:	No . . . on two or three pieces.
THERAPIST:	Out of how many?
PATIENT:	About twenty or twenty-five.
THERAPIST:	Did anyone else notice it?
PATIENT:	No, in fact my neighbor thought it was great.
THERAPIST:	Could you see the defect when you stood back and looked at the whole wall?
PATIENT:	Well, not really.

therapist has to do, he said, is provide warmth, a gentle, guiding hand, and a climate of uncritical acceptance, and clients will find the way to happiness and personal fulfillment. With this simple advice, the humanistic approach to psychotherapy was born. This approach (1) trusts a client's growth instincts; (2) focuses on feelings, not cognitions or behavior; (3) is oriented in the here-and-now, not in the distant past; and (4) makes the client responsible for change. Over the years, two types of humanistic therapy have had a marked impact on clinical practice: person-centered therapy and Gestalt therapy.

Person-Centered Therapy When 415 psychotherapists were asked to name the person who most influenced their work, Carl Rogers was cited more often than anyone else (Smith, 1982). The reason? In a profound way, Rogers redefined the role that a therapist should play: not detective, teacher, or adviser but a facilitator for the client. As Rogers put it, "Therapy is not a matter of doing something *to* the individual or inducing him to do something about himself. It is instead a matter of freeing him for normal growth and development" (1940, p. 7). Believing that people know what's right for themselves, Rogers let his clients call the shots. At various times, he referred to this approach as *nondirective, client-centered*, and *person-centered* (Farber et al., 1996).

Person-centered therapy is designed to provide a safe haven for people to clarify their feelings, their sense of who they are, and their hopes for what they would like to become, without fear of punishment or disapproval. To foster this process of self-exploration and discovery, person-centered therapists create a warm and caring relationship with the client. Specifically, they need to exhibit *empathy* (an ability to take the client's perspective in order to understand how he or she feels) and to offer *unconditional positive regard* (an unwavering respect for the client as a person—and these qualities have to be genuine, not put on) for people to open up and reveal themselves. Believing that counselors should not preach right or wrong, interpret problems, or give Dear Abby–like advice, person-centered therapists also use *reflection*, a nondirective, minimum-intervention technique in which the therapist actively listens to a client's statements, responding by paraphrasing what was said and seeking clarification. No interruption, no analysis, no evaluation. In this way, the therapist serves as a human mirror into which clients can see their feelings reflected clearly and without distortion. If psychotherapy were a dance, the person-centered client would lead, and the therapist would follow (see Table 17.4).

Underlying the Rogerian approach is the underlying belief that the client, not the therapist, is ultimately responsible for making positive changes. As such, one would expect that Rogers would play a less directive role than, say, cognitive therapists who seek to effect change through various interventions. Is there any evidence of this difference in therapist–client interactions? Interestingly, yes. Nathaniel Raskin (1996) examined published case transcripts and counted the number of lines spoken by therapists and their clients. He found that while cognitive therapists Ellis and Beck did 67 percent of the talking in their sessions, Rogers accounted for only 29 percent of the lines spoken in his sessions. His technique truly was "person-centered."

Gestalt Therapy

Have faith in human nature, encourage people to introspect, listen with a sympathetic ear, and guide with a gentle hand, and you are a humanistic psychologist in the mold of Carl Rogers. Focus on feelings that are unconscious, show an interest in dreams, and use techniques that are dramatic and confrontational, and you have **Gestalt therapy**, devised by humanistic psychologist Frederick (Fritz) Perls. Like Rogers, Gestalt therapists try to make people responsible for their own growth and development. In other ways, however, there is little resemblance. Forget about nondirective beating around the bush, Perls used to say. Instead, put clients on the "hot seat." When they speak in ways that are not brutally honest—by slipping into the past to avoid the present or by talking in general, abstract terms rather than in first-person—they should be challenged. "Do you really *need* to stay in this dysfunctional relationship, or do you *want* to?" "Do you *have* to work for seven days a week, or do you *choose* to?" "Is it that you *can't* say no, or that you *won't*?" "Why do you squirm in your seat, fold your arms, and cross your legs every time you say your sex life is fine?" "When you say it's hard for *people* to express anger, what you really mean is that *you* find it hard to show *your* anger. If that's what you mean, say so!" (Perls et al., 1951; Perls, 1969).

person-centered therapy A humanistic psychotherapy in which a warm and accepting environment is created to foster self-insight and acceptance.

Gestalt therapy A humanistic form of psychotherapy in which clients are aggressively prompted to express their feelings.

Group-Therapy Approaches

In the case study described at the start of this chapter, Yalom (1989) put Betty, his patient, into a therapy group. She felt isolated, craved companionship, and needed

Table 17.4 Person-Centered Therapy in Action

The following dialogue between Carl Rogers and a young man, who is upset over his relationship with his mother, illustrates the technique of reflection. Note how skillfully Rogers helped his client clarify his feelings toward his stepfather. Without prompting, he moved from a blunt statement of mutual hatred, to one of unilateral hatred, to an expression of respect (Raskin, 1985, pp. 167–168).

CLIENT:	You see I have a stepfather.
THERAPIST:	I see.
CLIENT:	Let's put it this way. My stepfather and I are not on the happiest terms in the world. And so, when he states some thing and, of course, she goes along, and I stand up and let her know that I don't like what he is telling me, well, she usually gives in to me.
THERAPIST:	I see.
CLIENT:	Sometimes, and sometimes it's just the opposite.
THERAPIST:	But part of what really makes for difficulty is the fact that you and your stepfather, as you say, are not . . . the relationship isn't completely rosy.
CLIENT:	Let's just put it this way, I hate him and he hates me. It's that way.
THERAPIST:	But you really hate him and you feel he really hates you.
CLIENT:	Well, I don't know if he hates me or not, but I know one thing, I don't like him whatsoever.
THERAPIST:	You can't speak for sure about his feelings because only he knows exactly what those are, but as far as you are concerned . . .
CLIENT:	. . . he knows how I feel about it.
THERAPIST:	You don't have any use for him.
CLIENT:	None whatsoever. And that's been for about eight years now.
THERAPIST:	So for about eight years you've lived with a person whom you have no respect for and really hate.
CLIENT:	Oh, I respect him.
THERAPIST:	Ah. Excuse me. I got that wrong.
CLIENT:	I have to respect him. I don't have to, but I do. But I don't love him, I hate him. I can't stand him.
THERAPIST:	There are certain things you respect him for, but that doesn't alter the fact that you definitely hate him and don't love him.
CLIENT:	That's the truth. I respect anybody who has bravery and courage, and he does.
THERAPIST:	. . . You do give him credit for the fact that he is brave, he has guts or something.
CLIENT:	Yeah. He shows that he can do a lot of things that, well, a lot of men can't.
THERAPIST:	M-hm, m-hm.
CLIENT:	And also he has asthma, and the doctor hasn't given him very long to live. And he, even though he knows he is going to die, he keeps working and he works at a killing pace, so I respect him for that, too.
THERAPIST:	M-hm. So I guess you're saying he really has . . .
CLIENT:	. . . what it takes.

Alcoholics Anonymous is a successful self-help group that ensures anonymity—which is why these members show only their backs to the camera. Meetings held in community settings usually begin with a reading of the AA Preamble: "Alcoholics Anonymous is a fellowship of men and women who share their experience, strength, and hope with each other that they may solve their common problem and help others to recover from alcoholism. The only requirement for membership is a desire to stop drinking. . . ."

a new perspective. Betty resisted the idea at first, but went along. It worked like a charm. At one point, a young man named Carlos revealed to the group that he was dying of cancer, the disease that had terrified Betty ever since it took the life of her father. At first, these encounters with Carlos made Betty acutely anxious. She became physically ill and obsessed with the fear that she too would get cancer, lose weight, and shrivel away. No wonder Betty was obese, they all thought—she was fighting the skin-and-bones image of her father before he died. Whether true or not, this insight was a key to Betty's problems. Soon she began to diet, with her therapy group acting as a supportive community, rooting her on with every pound she shed. One male member half-jokingly said he would take her to Hawaii for the weekend if she lost a hundred pounds. It was the first time a man had ever shown an interest in her.

As this story illustrates, **group therapy** provides a valuable alternative to individual psychotherapy. Typically, one or two therapists work with four to ten clients at a time, and often the clients have similar problems. The benefits are numerous, as groups furnish social support and encouragement, new outlooks on old problems, and interpersonal experience for those who are shy or socially awkward. The format and goals of a therapy group differ according to theoretical orientation.

In psychoanalytic groups, therapists interpret each member's interactions with the others in the same way that resistance and transference are interpreted in individual sessions. One psychoanalytic form of group therapy is *transactional analysis* (TA), in which the therapist analyzes the interactions between group members for clues concerning the individuals. In contrast, behavioral and cognitive groups seek to modify thoughts and behaviors, using members who have the same problem as both models and reinforcers. For example, social-skills training is often conducted in groups, as is systematic desensitization for people who have the same anxiety disorder (as when a group of people with agoraphobia are taken on a trip away from home). Among humanistic psychologists, groups are brought together to enhance personal development. One outgrowth of this approach is the *sensitivity-training* group, in which business executives, teachers, and others, in groups ranging in size from twelve to twenty persons, are taught to interact openly and with sensitivity. A close cousin of this is the encounter group, developed by Carl Rogers. In an *encounter group,* members express themselves with complete and brutal honesty—crying, yelling, laughing, and so on.

Encounter groups are not popular now, as they were in the 1960s and 1970s, but they gave rise to more specialized *self-help groups* in which people who share a common problem come together for mutual help and social support. The best known is Alcoholics Anonymous, or AA. AA was founded in 1935 and now has 2 million members worldwide. Many other groups are available—for people with AIDS, battered women, parents without partners, compulsive gamblers, teenage mothers, drug addicts, rape victims, weight watchers, smokers, newly arrived immigrants, families of cancer victims, and so on. The American Psychiatric Association (1989) estimates that in the United States alone, thousands of self-help groups service up to 15 million Americans. People helping one another is a promising

group therapy The simultaneous treatment of several clients in a group setting.

concept that no one should oppose. But are self-help groups effective? At present, these programs have not been systematically evaluated, so firm conclusions cannot be drawn (Christensen & Jacobson, 1994).

People often enter therapy as the result of problems that arise at home, so many psychologists prefer to treat families, not individuals. There is no single approach, but **family therapies** in general treat the family as an interdependent social "system" in which the whole is greater than the sum of its parts (Cox & Paley, 1997). The therapist observes family members together—how they relate, what roles they play, and what alliances they form. Indeed, researchers have tried to analyze these therapy interactions in systematic ways (Friedlander & Heatherington, 1989). Problems within the family vary—a boy acts out to get attention from two busy working parents; a husband and wife don't get along and use their daughter as a scapegoat; a child reaches adolescence, but the parents don't recognize her need for independence; a father drinks too much, but everyone denies it and says that "he's just under the weather." Whatever the problem, whole families are gathered in an effort to heal old wounds and prevent further conflict (Minuchin, 1974; Hazelrigg et al., 1987; Alexander et al., 1994).

Perspectives on Psychotherapy

How can the effectiveness of psychotherapy be measured? Does it work? Are some forms of therapy more effective than others? What do all therapies have in common? And what does it mean to be "eclectic" in approach?

> *"Two strangers meet by prearrangement; their purpose, to wrestle with life itself; their goal, to win from deadness more life for one of them; their risk, that one or both of them will find life filled with pain and anxiety for some period of time; their certainty, that if they persist in good faith with their struggle both will be changed in some measure."*
>
> — JAMES F. T. BUGENTAL

At the heart of psychotherapy is the assumption that people have a capacity for change. Thus, two questions loom over the entire enterprise: (1) Can humans help humans change? (2) Are some forms of helping better than others? (Mahoney, 1991). To those interested in the answers to these questions, Allen Bergin and Sol Garfield's (1994) *Handbook of Psychotherapy and Behavior Change* provides a comprehensive review of much of this research.

The Bottom Line: Does Psychotherapy Work?

Read case studies written by psychotherapists, and you'll have the impression that success is guaranteed. Ask people who have undergone psychotherapy, and three out of four will say they were "satisfied" or "very satisfied" with the outcome (Lebow, 1982). With such glowing reports, is there any reason for doubt?

Let's return to the *Consumer Reports* survey that opened this chapter. In that survey, 86 percent of those who saw a mental-health specialist reported feeling better after therapy and 89 percent were satisfied with the experience. In addition, psychiatrists, psychologists, and psychiatric social workers were all equally effective—more so than family doctors. On the basis of these findings, Seligman (1995) concluded that psychotherapy works. Yet many psychotherapy researchers were critical of the study, which was based solely on the self-reports of a nonrepresentative group of former clients (Jacobson & Christensen, 1996; Strupp, 1996). Steven Hollon (1996) said, "I am curious what the magazine would have found had it

family therapy Form of psychological treatment that treats the members of a family as an interactive system.

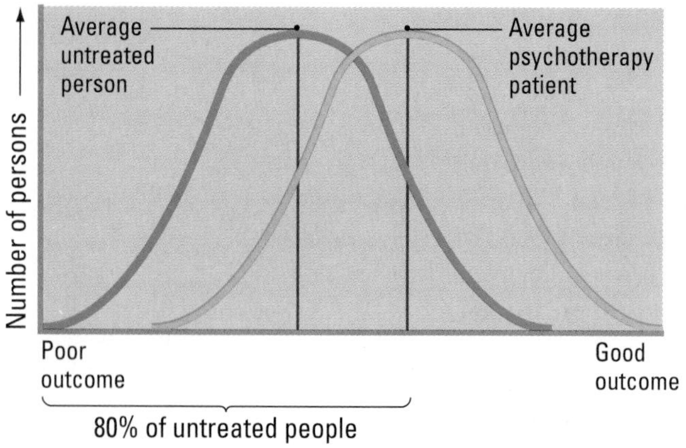

Figure 17.6 The benefits of psychotherapy Summarizing the results of 475 studies, Smith et al. (1980) found that the average psychotherapy client shows more improvement than 80 percent of the no-treatment controls.

surveyed the readers of supermarket tabloids regarding their experiences with psychics and faith healers. My suspicion is that people who make use of such 'professionals' are generally pleased with their services . . . I doubt that I would be prepared to believe that psychic healing works" (p. 1026). In response, Seligman (1996) noted that in a similar *CR* survey on lawyers, consumers were much more negative. "In fact, the devout reader of *CR* would do well to scan any of their articles on service professions; he or she will have a hard time finding any profession rated as highly as mental health professionals" (p. 1075).

As in the past, there are two reasons why researchers are cautious when it comes to using personal endorsements from clients—or therapists, for that matter—as a measure of the effectiveness of psychotherapy. First, both therapists and clients are motivated to believe that their efforts were successful. Therapists want to affirm their professional value and integrity, and clients need to justify their investment of time and money. Researchers thus seek independent and objective measures of improvement—for example, pre- to post-treatment changes in test scores, behavior, or third-party evaluations. The second problem is that some people get better on their own, without treatment. This improvement may occur as a result of support received from friends and family members or simply because "Time heals all wounds." (You know what they say about the common cold: "Take medicine and your stuffy nose will disappear in seven days; do nothing and it will last a whole week.") If psychotherapy is to be judged as effective, those who receive treatment should improve more than comparable others who do not. The question is whether they do.

In 1952, Hans Eysenck reviewed twenty-four psychotherapy studies and found that roughly two-thirds of all patients showed improvement. So far, so good. But there was a hitch: About two-thirds of people who were on waiting lists for therapy but were never actually treated also improved in the same period of time, on their own. Eysenck's blunt and pessimistic conclusion was that psychotherapy is worthless. His article stirred a major debate. Psychologists attacked the studies Eysenck had cited as well as his analysis of the results. It turned out, for example, that many of the control-group subjects were healthier initially than those who were treated, that some controls were taking drugs prescribed by physicians, and that they improved less than Eysenck believed (Bergin & Lambert, 1978).

Despite its shortcomings, Eysenck's article inspired an active, more sophisticated generation of clinical researchers determined to evaluate psychotherapy outcomes. By 1980, when Mary Lee Smith and others reviewed the available research, there were 475 published studies involving literally thousands of patients. Using meta-analysis to statistically combine the results of these studies, they found that psychotherapy was effective for a whole range of problems, including anxiety disorders, low self-esteem, social problems, and addiction. As shown in Figure 17.6, the average psychotherapy patient improved more than did 80 percent of the no-treatment controls. Smith and her colleagues (1980) concluded that "psychotherapy benefits people of all ages as reliably as schooling educates them, medicine cures them, or business turns a profit" (p. 183).

Although some psychologists still question the benefits of psychotherapy (Dawes, 1994), others have drawn similarly positive conclusions from the research evidence

(Shapiro & Shapiro, 1982; Lipsey & Wilson, 1993; Russell & Orlinsky, 1996, Shadish et al., 1997). Today, many clinical researchers are exploring the links between processes and outcomes. If a person started psychotherapy today, for example, how long would it take to feel better? Is there a timetable? Based on fifteen studies involving more than 2,400 clients, Kenneth Howard and others (1986) found that the percentage of people who improved increased with the number of therapy sessions *up to a point.* After six months, or twenty-six sessions, 70 percent of the outcomes were successful. From then on, however, the improvement rate leveled off and additional sessions contributed only little more to the final outcome (see Figure 17.7). In follow-up studies, Howard and his colleagues (1996) found that different aspects of a person's well-being change at different rates during the course of therapy. The improvement appears to occur in three stages. First, patients report that they "feel better," then they experience relief from the specific symptoms that drove them into therapy, and finally, they begin to function more effectively at work, at home, and in their social relationships.

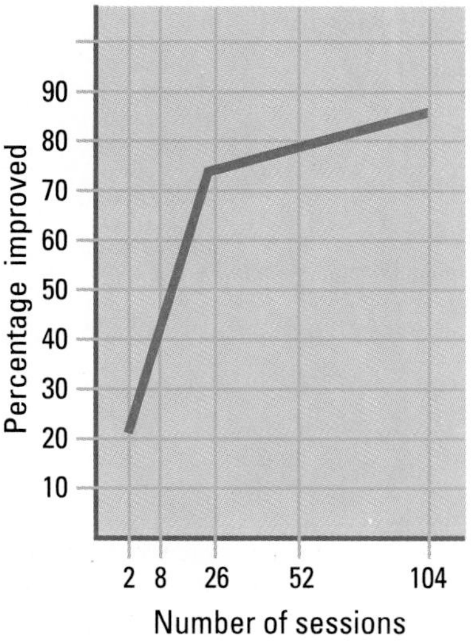

Figure 17.7 Improvement in psychotherapy: the more the better? A summary of fifteen studies indicates that there is continued improvement over twenty-six sessions but that the rate of improvement then levels off. At one session per week, six months seems to be an ideal amount of time.

Are Some Therapies Better than Others?

Some 80 percent of all therapy patients improve more than no-treatment controls; and 70 percent of those who improve do so within six months. These figures are interesting, you may think, but they are just averages, generalities. Don't some people derive more or less benefit than the average? Aren't some problems more amenable to change than others? And what about the differences among the psychoanalytic, behavioral, cognitive, and humanistic approaches? Interestingly, Smith and her colleagues (1980) did compare the different types of therapies, and they found a surprising result: All approaches were effective, and all were *equivalent*—that is, despite radical differences in techniques, no single approach was consistently superior to another. This conclusion, supported in other studies as well (Stiles et al., 1986; Seligman, 1995), has been called the "Dodo bird verdict" after the *Alice in Wonderland* character who declared, after a race, that "everyone has won, and all must have prizes."

The Dodo bird verdict poses a puzzling question: How can such different forms of treatment—ranging from a probing analysis of unconscious childhood conflicts, to a hard-nosed modification of behaviors or cognitions, to warm and nondirective reflection and acceptance—produce the same results? There are three good answers to this question. First, specific techniques are less critical to the final outcome than are personal characteristics of the client and therapist (Lambert & Bergin, 1994). Second, the different approaches may well be equivalent on average, but the value of any one technique depends on the problem to be solved. Behavioral forms of therapy are ideal for extinguishing phobias, compulsions, a fear of public speaking, and other specific anxiety-related ailments (Bowers & Clum, 1988). But it appears that cognitive therapy is more potent in the battle against depression (Dobson, 1989), and person-centered therapy is ideally suited to raising self-esteem (Smith et al., 1980). Perhaps with so many disorders listed in DSM-IV, psychotherapists should act as "matchmakers" and use different techniques with different clients. A third explanation is that all psychological therapies are more similar in important ways than one might think. In other words, despite the surface differences, all psychotherapies have a lot in common at a deeper level—and these common factors, not the specific techniques, provide the active ingredients necessary for change (Stiles et al., 1986; Strupp, 1989).

On the island of Bali, people with mental disorders are often seen as victims of witchcraft and are sent for treatment to a balian, *like the one shown here. Using massage, healing smoke, holy water, and other rituals, the* balian *would drive evil wind spirits from the patient's body. Like healers and shamans in other cultures,* balians *are often successful. Perhaps nonspecific factors that contribute to psychotherapy—such as hope and social support—are also at work in these rituals.*

What Are the Active Ingredients?

Regardless of differences in theoretical orientations and techniques, there are three common, "nonspecific" factors at work in all brands of psychotherapy.

A Supportive Relationship First, all therapists provide a *supportive relationship* characterized by warmth, trust, concern, encouragement, reassurance, acceptance, and a shoulder to cry on. Indeed, the better the working alliance is between a therapist and client, the more favorable the outcome—especially from the client's standpoint (Horvath & Symonds, 1991; Horvath & Luborsky, 1993). In one study, for example, schizophrenic patients who had a good rapport with their therapists were more likely than those who did not to remain in therapy, take their prescribed drugs, and improve in the end (Frank & Gunderson, 1991).

Why is this one-on-one human relationship so important? Hans Strupp (1996) believes that people find it immensely gratifying to be listened to with concern, empathy, and respect. "The simple and incontrovertible truth," he says, "is that if you are anxious or depressed, or if you are experiencing difficulties with significant people in your life, chances are that you feel better if you talk to someone you can trust" (p. 1017).

A Ray of Hope Second, all therapies offer a ray of *hope* to people who are typically unhappy, demoralized, and down on themselves. In all aspects of life, we are motivated by positive expectations, faith, and optimism (Seligman, 1991). The same is true in psychotherapy. It's even been suggested that high expectations are sufficient to produce change even when they are not justified (Prioleau et al., 1983). This suggestion is based on the **placebo effect**, a well-established medical phenomenon whereby patients will show more improvement when they are given an inactive drug, or placebo, than when they are not. Somehow, believing can help make it so—which is how faith healers, shamans, and witch doctors all over the world have been known to perform "miracle cures" with their rituals. So is that *all* there is to psychotherapy, just one big placebo effect? No, carefully controlled studies have shown that although people randomly assigned to receive a placebo therapy (bogus exercises, group discussions, self-help tapes, and sugar pills) improve more than those who do not, they typically do not improve as much as those who undergo actual psychotherapy (Barker et al., 1988). Hope may be necessary, but it's not sufficient.

An Opportunity to Open Up A third common ingredient is that all psychotherapies offer an ideal setting for *opening up*, a chance for people to confide in someone, spill their guts, and talk freely about their troubles—maybe for the first time ever. In a series of controlled studies on the healing power of opening up, James Pennebaker (1990) brought college students into a laboratory and asked them to write for twenty minutes about either past traumas or trivial events. He found that when people wrote about having been mistreated, the divorce of their parents, the death of a family pet, and other traumatic events, their systolic-blood-pressure levels rose during disclosure but then dipped below preexperiment levels. Afterward, they felt better, had a more positive outlook, and exhibited a decline in number of visits to the campus health center over the next six months. Other studies, too, have shown that keeping secrets is stressful—and that "letting it out" and "getting it off your chest" can have therapeutic effects on our mental and physical health (Pennebaker, 1997).

placebo effect The curative effect of an inactive treatment that results simply from the patient's belief in its therapeutic value.

Why does it help to open up? Why do *you* sometimes feel the need to talk out your problems? One possibility, recognized many years ago by Freud, is that the experience itself provides a much-needed *catharsis*, a discharge of psychic tension—like taking the lid off a boiling pot of water to slow the boiling. Another interpretation, favored by most psychotherapists, is that talking about a problem helps you to sort out your thoughts, understand it better, and gain *insight*, in cognitive terms. Whatever the reason, it's clear that psychotherapy provides an ideal setting for self-disclosure: The listener is patient, caring, and nonjudgmental—and what's said is kept in confidence. This last point is critical, because despite the potential for gain, opening up can also cause great distress when the people we choose to confide in react with rejection or unwanted advice, or—worse—disclose what was said to others (Kelly & McKillop, 1996).

Shortly after his only son, Ennis, was murdered, comedian Bill Cosby held an interview with newscaster and friend Dan Rather. Then he appeared on Dave Letterman's TV show and reminisced about his son. Deeply wounded by the tragedy, Cosby—who has a doctoral degree in education—may well have appreciated the therapeutic benefits of opening up.

The Eclectic Alternative

Psychoanalysis emerged from the medical model, behaviorists and humanists came forward in response to psychoanalysis, and cognitive therapies evolved from a desire to soften up hard-core behaviorism. Clearly, each approach staked out a position that seemed radically different from others. All that is changing now. Psychoanalytic therapists are playing a more active role than in the past to speed up the healing process. Behavioral and cognitive approaches have formed a hybrid known as cognitive-behavior therapy—and some of them now talk about unconscious processes and self-concepts. Person-centered therapists are more directive than they used to be, while many behaviorists are less directive.

As illustrated in Figure 17.8, national surveys show that more psychotherapists describe themselves as *eclectic*—which means that they borrow ideas and techniques from different approaches, as needed—rather than identify themselves with any single orientation (Smith, 1982; Beitman et al., 1989). More recent surveys suggest that this percentage has risen even higher over the past few years. Why is the trend toward an eclectic approach? And why are many psychotherapy researchers predicting more of the same in the years to come? The reasons are pragmatic. As health costs skyrocket and as people turn for insurance to managed-health-care programs, there is an increasing need for effective short-term therapies (Lazarus et al., 1992). Accordingly, specific treatment techniques should be chosen on a case-by-case basis, depending on the client, his or her problem, and the desired outcome (Norcross, 1991). In this vein, Arnold Lazarus (1996) describes the ideal clinician as an "authentic chameleon." Reflecting on his forty years of experience, Lazarus concludes that "a therapist must decide when and how to be directive, supportive, reflective, cold, warm, tepid, formal or informal. He/she must determine when and when not to be confrontational; when and whether to be earthy, chummy, or casual; when to self-disclose or remain enigmatic; when to be soft-nosed, gentle and tender, and when to come on like gangbusters" (pp. 143–144).

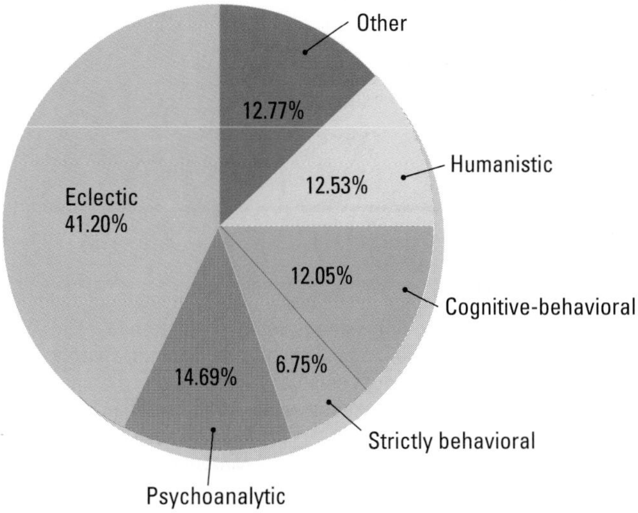

Figure 17.8 Orientations of psychotherapists Presented here are the results of a national survey in which 422 practicing clinical and counseling psychologists were asked to describe their theoretical orientations (Smith, 1982).

Medical Interventions

[© 1997 by Sidney Harris.]

"I utilize the best from Freud, the best from Jung and the best from my uncle Marty, a very smart fellow."

What are the main types of drugs used in the treatment of psychological disorders? What are the advantages of these drugs, and what are the drawbacks? What is electroconvulsive therapy, what is psychosurgery, and when, if ever, are these treatment methods used?

For people who suffer from severe anxiety, mood disorders, and schizophrenia, medical interventions may provide an alternative or supplement to psychotherapy. Based on established links among the brain, the mind, and behavior, there are three types of medical treatment available: drug therapy, electroshock therapy, and psychosurgery.

Drug Therapies

In 1952, French psychiatrists Jean Delay and Pierre Deniker eliminated the symptoms of a schizophrenic patient with a wonder drug called *chlorpromazine*. From then on, the use of drugs in the treatment of psychological disorders has risen in popularity. In the booming area of **psychopharmacology**, there is now a vast array of drugs available for therapeutic purposes (Schatzberg & Nemeroff, 1995). Most of them work by acting on neurotransmitters, the biochemicals that relay impulses between neurons. For the hundreds of thousands of people who used to languish in psychiatric wards and hospitals, these drugs opened doors to life in the community—for better and for worse (see Figure 17.9). Michael Gitlin's (1996) *The Psychotherapist's Guide to Psychopharmacology* describes these drugs in clear, nontechnical language—their trade names, purposes, dosage levels, effects on the brain and behavior, the benefits, potential side effects, and dangers. The main types are summarized in Table 17.5.

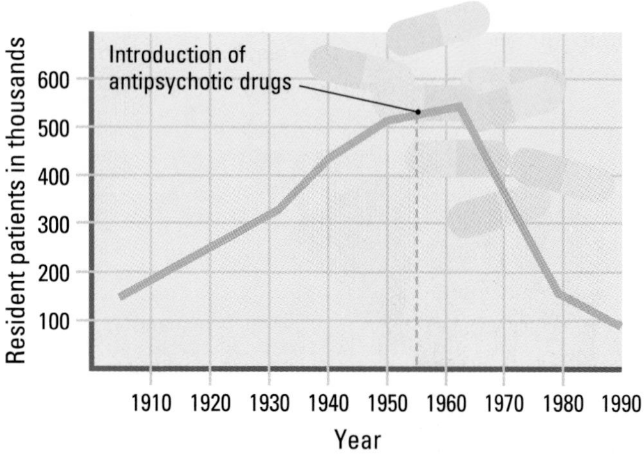

Figure 17.9 Antipsychotic drugs and hospitalization trends The inpatient population in U.S. mental hospitals has declined sharply since 1960, putting the treatment emphasis on outpatient community care. This trend resulted from the widespread use of antipsychotic drugs, which were introduced in the 1950s. Some benefited greatly from deinstitutionalization. Others—without families or a capacity to cope on their own—were left homeless.

Antianxiety Drugs Whether the cause is internal or external, and whether the condition is chronic or acute, there are many possible sources of anxiety and many people who at times suffer through it. Thus, it is no wonder there has always been a great demand for—and abuse of—**antianxiety drugs**, or tranquilizers. During the 1950s, many doctors prescribed *barbiturates* for anxious patients. Barbiturates combat anxiety by depressing central nervous system activity. They are effective but highly addictive. They help us to relax but also cause us to become clumsy and drowsy.

In the 1960s, a new class of tranquilizers was developed. Called *benzodiazepines*, they include chlordiazepoxide (Librium), diazepam (Valium), and alprazolam (Xanax). These drugs have the same desired calming effect and are less likely than barbiturates to cause drowsiness or addiction. Their impact is almost immediate, and they are most effective in treating generalized anxiety disorder, if taken regularly. Benzodiazepines are often prescribed by family doctors, not psychiatrists, for

psychopharmacology The study of the effects of drugs on psychological processes and disorders.

antianxiety drugs Tranquilizing medications used in the treatment of anxiety.

Table 17.5 Types of Drug Treatments

DRUG TYPE	TRADE NAME	BENEFICIAL EFFECTS
Antianxiety Drugs		
chlordiazepoxide	Librium	*Act as tranquilizers and, if taken regularly, can be used in the treatment of generalized anxiety disorder.*
diazepam	Valium	
alprazolam	Xanax	
buspirone	BuSpar	
Antidepressants		
imipramine	Tofranil	*Have mood-elevating effects and can relieve depression.*
fluoxetine	Prozac	
Mood Stabilizer		
lithium	Lithium Carbonate	*Calms mania and, if continuously taken, may reduce bipolar mood swings.*
Antipsychotic Drugs		
chlorpromazine	Thorazine	*Reduce hallucinations, delusions, and other positive symptoms of schizophrenia.*
clozapine	Clozaril	
risperidone	Risperdal	

people in the midst of a stressful time of life. These drugs are not as safe as once thought, however. They are dangerous when combined with alcohol, and they may produce temporary side effects such as slurred speech, dry mouth, lightheadedness, and diminished psychomotor control. When a regular user stops taking them, the result may be a two-week "rebound anxiety" more intense than ever (Julien, 1992). A drug called *buspirone*, which was first released in 1986, provides an alternative. It acts more slowly, usually taking a few days or weeks to have an effect, but it is also less likely to promote dependence or have unpleasant side effects (Lickey & Gordon, 1991).

Antidepressants In the 1950s, doctors noticed that drugs being used to treat high blood pressure and tuberculosis had dramatic side effects on mood—sometimes causing depression, other times euphoria. At about the same time, researchers found that these drugs also increased levels of the neurotransmitter norepinephrine, a chemical cousin of adrenaline found in a part of the brain that regulates mood and emotion. Together, these strands of evidence suggested that depression is associated with lower-than-needed norepinephrine levels. Later research also linked depression to serotonin. The practical result was the development of **antidepressants** such as *imipramine* (Tofranil)—drugs that tend to increase the supply of norepinephrine or serotonin and elevate mood. Studies have shown that the antidepressants are effective. They are not addictive and cause only minor side effects such as dry mouth, constipation, blurred vision, and fatigue.

Today, a new drug called *fluoxetine*—better known by its trade name, Prozac—is the most widely used antidepressant in the world (Cowley, 1994). By blocking the

antidepressants Drugs that relieve depression by increasing the supply of norepinephrine, serotonin, or dopamine.

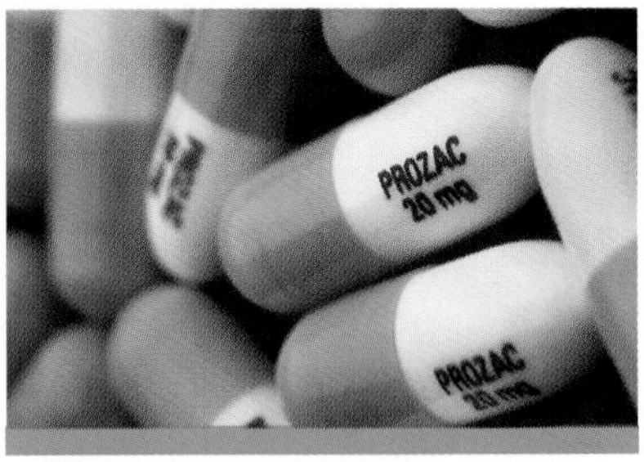

Encased in a small green-and-white capsule, Prozac is the most widely prescribed antidepressant in the world. There are 24 million users in 197 countries.

absorption and removal of serotonin from neural synapses, without affecting other neurotransmitters, Prozac is effective with relatively mild side effects (so are its younger cousins Luvox, Paxil, and Zoloft). Prozac has also been the subject of controversy. Many psychiatrists have observed that in some patients, Prozac does more than relieve depression. It also seems to transform their personality, making them happier, more self-confident and productive at work, and more engaged and relaxed in social situations. As a result, this "wonder drug" in a little green-and-white capsule is often prescribed for people who are not clinically depressed. This last development is unsettling and raises hard ethical questions concerning the proper use of psychoactive drugs (Kramer, 1993).

Mood Stabilizers For bipolar disorder—which is characterized by wild manic-depressive mood swings—different, mood-stabilizing drugs are used. The best known of these is **lithium**—an inexpensive mineral found in rocks, water, plants, and animals. Taken on a continuous basis, lithium can usually prevent moods from reeling out of control and is considered the most effective treatment in this regard (Schou, 1997). Common side effects include dry mouth, thirst, weight gain, excessive urination, fatigue, and tremors. Taken in dosages that are too high, lithium can prove dangerous, even life-threatening. For bipolar patients who do not respond to lithium or who cannot tolerate the side effects, other mood-stabilizing drugs can be used instead (Pope et al., 1991).

"Before Prozac, she loathed company."

Antipsychotic Drugs Not that long ago, people with schizophrenia who exhibited hallucinations, delusions, confused speech, exaggerated displays of emotion, paranoia, and bizarre behavior were dismissed as lost causes. All that changed in the 1950s, however, with the discovery of **antipsychotic drugs**, which reduce the intensity of these positive "uncontrollable" symptoms. As noted earlier, the first in this class of drugs was *chlorpromazine*, better known as Thorazine. By blocking the activity of dopamine, the neurotransmitter that has been linked to schizophrenia, antipsychotic drugs enable many people previously confined to hospital wards to live relatively normal lives.

Chlorpromazine has two drawbacks. The first is that it often does not relieve the negative symptoms of schizophrenia—symptoms such as flat affect, apathy, immobility, and social withdrawal, which may be linked to structural defects in the brain, not to dopamine (see Chapter 16). The second drawback is that very unpleasant side effects are common. In the worst of cases, these include Parkinson disease–like symptoms such as shaking and a loss of control over voluntary movements, stiff muscles, sluggishness, blunted affect, weight gain, and sexual impotence in men. These symptoms can sometimes be treated with other drugs. Still, psychiatrists and patients must weigh the benefits of relief from the symptoms of schizophrenia against the costs of drug-induced side effects (Gitlin, 1996).

Recent research suggests that *clozapine* (Clozaril), an antipsychotic medication first released in 1990, may be more effective than its predecessors. Clozapine operates through a different mechanism. Although it is effective at controlling hallucinations and other psychotic symptoms (even in some patients who do not respond to Thorazine), it does not have the undesirable side effects on motor functions. Yet for about 2 percent of those who take it, clozapine has a toxic effect on the white blood cells and increases the risk of a rare but fatal blood disorder. Released in 1994, an even newer drug, *risperidone* (Risperdal), seems to provide all the benefits of clozapine without the toxic effects. Gitlin (1996) thus projects that "in many ways, risperidone seems destined to become *the* first-line antipsychotic medication" (p. 394).

lithium A drug used to control mania and mood swings in people with bipolar disorder.

antipsychotic drugs Drugs that are used to control the positive symptoms of schizophrenia and other psychotic disorders.

Perspectives on Drug Therapies

"There's a place for drugs for some people, but they are overrated and overprescribed. In comparisons of psychotherapy and drugs, by and large drugs do not appear to be the superior treatment." "To say that psychiatric drugs are overrated is a stupid statement . . . For a wide range of psychiatric disorders, it's well documented that these drugs are the most effective treatments." The first of these remarks was made by psychologist Roger Greenberg, the second by psychiatrist Paul Bender (quoted in Goleman, 1989). Which of these statements is more true? Is psychological therapy preferable to drug therapy, or is it the other way around?

The debate over psychotherapy and drugs is as old as the split between psychology and medicine. But there is no winner, no right or wrong answer, no contest. In the spirit of taking an eclectic approach to the treatment of disorders, mental-health professionals are advised to make their judgments on an individual case basis and not exclude either approach as a matter of principle. Clearly, the drugs have helped hundreds of thousands of people once hidden away in psychiatric institutions, and they will continue to do so in years to come. And clearly, there are people with disorders who do not respond as well to psychological forms of treatment. There are reasons for caution, however. One is that some drugs produce side effects that are unpleasant and, at times, dangerous under high dosage levels. A second is that some drugs produce a physical or psychological dependence, leading patients to play a passive role in their own healing process. The person who gets into the habit of popping a Valium at the first sign of tension learns how to control the aversive symptoms of anxiety but not how to cope with the source of the problem.

In an effort to match treatments to specific disorders, many researchers are currently evaluating the relative effectiveness of psychological and drug therapies. So far neither approach has emerged as uniformly more effective. In one large-scale study, for example, the National Institute of Mental Health compared cognitive therapy, an interpersonal form of psychotherapy that focuses on social relations, an antidepressant, and a placebo control group in which the patients were given an inactive pill, attention, and encouragement. A total of 239 patients belonging to twenty-eight therapists in Oklahoma, Pennsylvania, and Washington, D.C., were randomly assigned to receive one form of treatment for a total of sixteen weeks. Among those in the placebo group, 29 percent were no longer depressed when the "treatment" was ended. In the other groups, that number was near 50 percent—and the psychological and drug therapies were equally effective (Elkin et al., 1989). Other research shows that the outcome changes over time—that for those who are depressed, cognitive therapy may be somewhat slower than antidepressants to take effect but is then more likely to last (Dobson, 1989; Hollon et al., 1991). With drugs that are used to combat depression and those used in the treatment of anxiety, patients are often kept for long periods of time on a "maintenance" dosage to lower the risk of a relapse (Thase & Kupfer, 1996; Lydiard et al., 1996).

Electroconvulsive Therapy

It used to be a terrifying experience, a Frankenstein-like nightmare come to life. The patient would be dragged kicking and screaming to a hospital table and strapped down by the arms and legs, only to watch as a white-coated physician leaned over to administer the pain. The patient would then be jolted by 100 volts of electricity to both sides of the skull, triggering seizures, unconsciousness, and muscle spasms

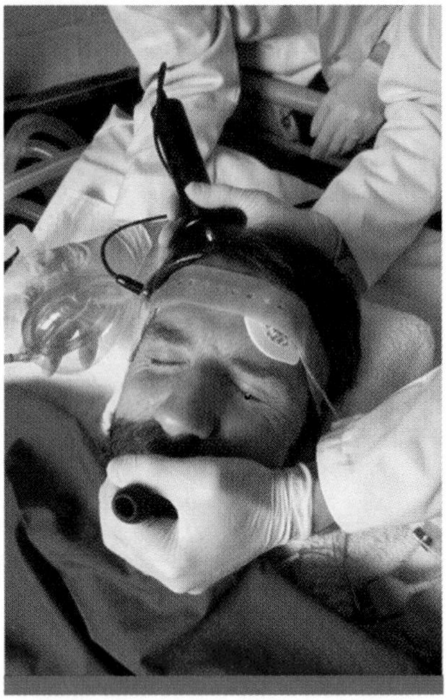

A person receiving electroconvulsive therapy. As shown, the shock is delivered to the right side of the head.

so violent that they sometimes resulted in broken bones. The shock also had a mind-scrambling effect, causing confusion and amnesia for chunks of time before and after the treatment.

Electroconvulsive therapy (ECT) has a curious history. In the nineteenth century, an "electric machine" was used to stimulate the nerves. But it was not until 1938 that an Italian doctor, Ugo Cerletti, introduced ECT—and the notion that mental illness could be cured by quite literally shocking the system. From the start, it was clear that ECT provided relief from depression. It was widely used in the 1950s and 1960s but soon fell out of favor as antidepressant drugs became available. Eventually, it made a quiet comeback when procedures were made safer and more humane. Today, consenting ECT patients are given a general anesthetic and a muscle relaxant to prevent injury from convulsions. They then receive briefer, milder shock to the right side of the head, which sets off a brain seizure that lasts for a minute or so. As in surgery, patients regain consciousness within minutes, unable to remember what happened. The entire process consists of ten or so sessions administered over a two-week period.

ECT is now a viable alternative for people who are deeply depressed, suicidal, and not responsive to psychological or drug therapies. It has also been used with some success to treat mania in people with bipolar disorder (Mukherjee et al., 1994) and some of the symptoms of schizophrenia (Fink & Sackeim, 1996). The convulsions triggered by electrical current to the brain provide quick, sometimes permanent relief. ECT is also safe, resulting in only 2 deaths per 100,000 treatments, a mortality rate lower than that for childbirth (Abrams, 1988; Endler & Persad, 1988). The reason ECT is effective, however—whether it works by stimulating inactive parts of the brain, inhibiting overactive parts, or triggering the release of scarce neurotransmitters—remains a mystery (Janicak et al., 1985; Sackeim, 1988). Brain scans of ECT patients show no signs of structural brain damage (Coffey et al., 1991; Devanand et al., 1994). As far as the side effects are concerned, however, they undergo a temporary state of confusion. When ECT patients regain consciousness, they often cannot recall events of the recent past and are disoriented about where they are and how they got there.

Psychosurgery

The most controversial of interventions is **psychosurgery,** the removal of portions of the brain for the purpose of treating psychological disorders. In 1935, Portuguese neurologist Egas Moniz performed the first *lobotomy,* a surgical procedure in which he cut the nerves that connect the frontal lobes to the rest of the brain, in order to tame patients who were agitated, manic, and violent. Moniz based this procedure on his belief that pathological mental activity occurred in the frontal lobes, which needed to be severed "to cut off the flow of morbid ideas." The operation was so highly regarded that in 1949 Moniz was awarded a Nobel prize in medicine. As reported in *The New York Times* (1949), "Hypochondriacs no longer thought they were going to die, would-be suicides found life acceptable, sufferers from persecution complex forgot the machinations of imaginary conspirators . . . Surgeons now think no more of operations on the brain than they do of removing an appendix."

Was the lobotomy all that it was cracked up to be? In a book entitled *Great and Desperate Cures,* Elliot Valenstein (1986) described how thousands of mentally ill patients around the world were mutilated on the operating table: "After drilling two or more holes in a patient's skull, a surgeon inserted into the brain any of various

electroconvulsive therapy (ECT) Electric-shock treatments that often relieve severe depression by triggering seizures in the brain.

psychosurgery The surgical removal of portions of the brain for the purpose of treating psychological disorders.

instruments—some resembling an apple corer, a butter spreader, or an ice pick—and, often without being able to see what he was cutting, destroyed parts of the brain" (p. 3). The results were often tragic. The lobotomy was supposed to relieve patients of crippling emotions, but it also profoundly altered their core personalities, creating people who were like robots: lethargic, flat, emotionless, unmotivated, and without aim or purpose. Talking about her lobotomized husband, one woman said, "His soul appears to be destroyed; he is not the man I once knew." Mercifully, this procedure was virtually extinguished when antipsychotic drugs came into use (Swayze, 1995).

Psychosurgery is more sophisticated today than in the past, enabling neurosurgeons to "damage the brain to save the mind" (Rodgers, 1992). Specific regions of the brain can now be destroyed with precision through ultrasonic irradiation or by sending electrical currents through fine wire electrodes. For people who are stricken with uncontrollable seizures, for example, the nerve fibers involved can be deactivated. Psychosurgery is also used sparingly, but with some success, on people incapacitated by chronic anxiety and depression or by severe obsessive-compulsive disorders that are not responsive to other forms of treatment (Baer et al., 1995). Still, there is debate over the science and ethics of psychosurgery, a treatment of last resort. After all, whether the outcome is positive or negative, the effect is irreversible.

Consumer's Guide to Mental-Health Services

What kinds of mental-health providers are available to consumers? For those in distress, how realistic are the possibilities for improvement?

Over the years, the number of Americans seeking professional help for psychological problems has climbed dramatically. The helpers are psychiatrists and clinical psychologists, psychiatric nurses and social workers, and marital and family counselors (see Figure 17.10). The kinds of help provided range from the most

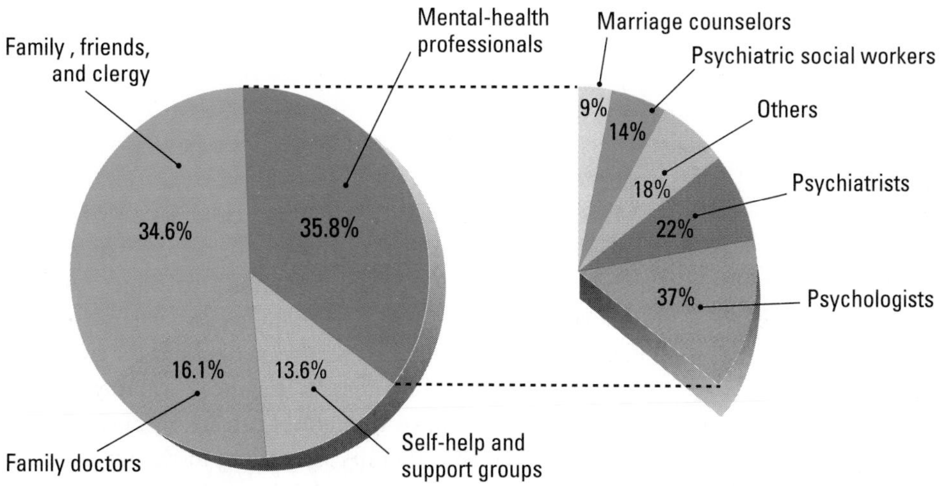

Figure 17.10 Where people turn for help The *Consumer Reports* study revealed that among respondents who had a psychological problem, many turned for help to friends, relatives, clergy, and family doctors. Among those who sought help within the mental-health profession, psychologists were seen more frequently than other types of specialists.

intensive one-on-one psychoanalysis to behavioral, cognitive, humanistic, and group therapies. In a small number of cases, obscure techniques are practiced, as in mandala therapy, electric-sleep therapy, alpha-wave therapy, deprivation therapy, and the Zaraleya Psychoenergetic Technique. And in a growing number of cases, people are turning to nonprofessionals, such as the many self-help and support groups that are widely available (Christensen & Jacobson, 1994).

Faced with an overwhelming array of treatment alternatives, people in the market for professional help have choices to make and problems to solve. One problem is that although someone must have a professional degree and supervised training to become licensed as a psychologist, anyone can hang up a shingle, offer a service, and call it therapy. From among those who are qualified, how do you select someone, and what kind of experience can you expect to have? Should you set your sights on psychotherapy or medical treatment? If you need help and don't know where to turn, it's probably best to start with personal recommendations from a close friend, relative, family doctor, or teacher. Or you might check with the college counseling service, which is free, or a community mental-health center. If you have health insurance that covers psychological services, find out if the policy covers what you want. If not, the hourly rates vary. Shop around and talk to two or three therapists until you are satisfied that you have found one you like, respect, and can work with. Talk openly about your goals and ask about fees, credentials, orientations, and values, to determine whether the two of you are on the same wavelength. Remember: The working relationship between therapist and client is an essential first step on the road to successful treatment.

All this brings us back to an important theme in the study of psychological disorders and treatment: the possibility of change. Under normal conditions, our personalities remain relatively stable throughout our adult lives. Individuals who are outgoing at one point in time are likely to remain that way later in life. But changes in behavior can be made—as when someone seeks to overcome shyness. When people suffer through a mental disorder, the need for change takes on an added dimension of importance. Some problems are relatively easy to overcome, others quite difficult. Through psychological and medical forms of therapy, however, the possibilities for improvement are real. Whether the specific goal is to overcome a fear, lower anxiety, lift depression, or clear the mind of illogical thoughts and perceptions, there is reason for hope, which is necessary for change.

Summary and Key Terms

Treatment raises the basic question of the possibilities and limits of human change. There are two primary models of treatment: psychological and medical.

Psychological Therapies

The term ***psychotherapy*** refers to all forms of treatment in which a trained professional uses psychological techniques to help people who are distressed. The four major approaches are psychoanalytic, behavioral, cognitive, and humanistic.

Psychoanalytic Therapies

Orthodox psychoanalysis aims for catharsis and insight. Its key technique, pioneered by Freud, is **free association,** in which patients say whatever comes to mind without censoring it. Often, the patient free associates about dreams while the therapist tries to get behind the manifest content to the latent content. **Resistance**—a patient's tendency to block painful thoughts—can be an obstacle but can also signal that therapy is heading in the right direction. The same is true of **transference,** whereby the patient displaces intense feelings for others onto the therapist. On the basis of these behaviors, the therapist offers interpretations to help the patient gain insight.

In briefer psychoanalytic therapies, the analyst plays a more active role, focuses less on the patient's past, and puts more emphasis on current life problems. The psychoanalytic approach has been criticized on various grounds. Yet despite the criticisms, it has left a strong mark on therapeutic practice.

Behavioral Therapies

Rather than search for deep problems, **behavioral therapies** use learning principles to modify the symptoms. Classical conditioning techniques include **flooding** the patient with an anxiety-provoking stimulus until the anxiety is extinguished. **Systematic desensitization,** a form of counterconditioning, pairs gradual exposure to an anxiety-provoking stimulus with relaxation training. **Aversion therapy** is designed to produce an aversive reaction to a harmful stimulus.

Other behavioral therapies use the principles of operant conditioning. **Token economies** reward patients for desirable behaviors; for dangerous behavior, punishment may be necessary. **Biofeedback**—learning to use feedback from the body to control physiological processes—is useful for health problems such as tension-related headaches. Assertiveness training and other types of **social skills training** use the techniques of modeling, rehearsal, and reinforcement.

Cognitive Therapies

Cognitive therapies focus on maladaptive perceptions and thoughts. Developed by Ellis, **rational-emotive therapy (RET)** bluntly confronts people with their irrational beliefs and provides "psychoeducation" on ways to change. Beck's cognitive therapy takes a more collaborative approach, giving clients homework assignments and role-playing exercises. These and other cognitive approaches are now the most common approaches to psychotherapy.

Humanistic Therapies

Acting as a facilitator, Rogers developed **person-centered therapy,** which creates a warm, caring environment to promote self-insight. Person-centered therapists offer empathy and unconditional positive regard. Through reflection, the therapist becomes an emotional mirror for the client. **Gestalt therapy,** developed by Perls, also makes clients responsible for their own change, but it focuses more on unconscious feelings and dreams, and it aggressively challenges clients to express their feelings.

Group-Therapy Approaches

An alternative to individual therapies, **group therapy** involves working with several clients simultaneously and together. In transactional analysis, a psychoanalytic therapist analyzes the interactions among group members. Behavioral and cognitive therapies can also take place in groups. Humanistic psychology has spawned sensitivity-training groups, encounter groups, and various self-help groups. In **family therapies,** the members of a family are treated together as an interdependent social system.

Perspectives on Psychotherapy

Is psychotherapy effective? Are some approaches better than others? What are the active ingredients of effective psychotherapy? These are among the important questions raised over the years.

The Bottom Line: Does Psychotherapy Work?

As the reaction to the recent *Consumer Reports* mental-health survey showed, psychologists have long argued about the effectiveness of psychotherapy. Meta-analysis has shown that psychotherapy patients experience more improvement, on average, than people who are not treated. After about six months of therapy, however, improvement rates appear to level off.

Are Some Therapies Better than Others?

Overall, the different forms of psychotherapy are about equally effective. Some work better on particular problems than others, but all share certain features in common that make them more similar in their effects than different.

What Are the Active Ingredients?

There are three common attributes of all therapies that constitute the active ingredients for a successful outcome: (1) a supportive relationship; (2) hope, which, as the **placebo effect** demonstrates, can itself produce improvement; and (3) an ideal setting in which the patient is able to open up and confide in another person.

The Eclectic Alternative

In need of speedy and effective forms of treatment, most therapists today use a pragmatic, eclectic strategy. Thus, they borrow ideas and techniques from the various approaches.

Medical Interventions

Medical interventions take three major forms: drug therapy; electroconvulsive, or shock, therapy; and psychosurgery.

Drug Therapies

Psychopharmacology is concerned with the effects of certain drugs on mental processes and disorders. **Antianxiety drugs** include buspirone and the widely used class of benzodiazepines. Research linking depression to neurotransmitters led to the development of **antidepressants,** such as the controversial new drug fluoxetine (Prozac). The mood stabilizer **lithium,** a mineral found in nature, can control mood swings in bipolar disorder. For schizophrenia and other psychotic disorders, **antipsychotic drugs** often reduce the positive symptoms, though often with side effects.

In the debate about the relative merits of psychoactive drugs and psychotherapy, there is no one answer. On the one hand, drugs have helped hundreds of thousands of patients; on the other, they can have unpleasant or dangerous side effects, and some produce physical or psychological dependence.

Electroconvulsive Therapy

Though once a nightmarelike experience, **electroconvulsive therapy (ECT)** now provides milder electric shock that can relieve severe depression by triggering seizures in the right side of the brain.

Psychosurgery

Psychosurgery, the most controversial medical intervention, involves removing portions of the brain to treat a psychological disorder. The technique of lobotomy, once popular, has fallen into disrepute. Today's psychosurgery is more sophisticated, targeting specific regions of the brain with ultrasonic irradiation or electrical currents. But safer methods are available, and the effects are irreversible.

Consumer's Guide to Mental Health Services

As more Americans look for help with psychological problems, a bewildering array of services have become available. Consumers should seek personal recommendations and talk frankly with prospective therapists. Psychological and medical therapies do offer hope, which is necessary for change.

In the Field Resources

Books

Dawes, R. M. (1994). *House of cards: Psychology and psychotherapy built on myth.* New York: Free Press.

Written by an eminent psychologist, this is a critical and controversial analysis of psychotherapy.

Engler, J., & Goleman, D. (1992). *The consumer's guide to psychotherapy.* New York: Simon & Schuster.

This 700-page handbook is designed to help people decide whether to seek therapy and then how to find and evaluate therapists.

Lickey, M. E., & Gordon, B. (1991). *Medicine and mental illness.* New York: W. H. Freeman.

Written for the student and interested layperson, this book provides an overview of drug therapies for psychological disorders.

Valenstein, E. S. (1986). *Great and desperate cures: The rise and decline of psychosurgery and other radical treatments for mental illness.* New York: Basic Books.

This book is a shocking exposé of psychosurgery as a form of treatment for psychological disorders—and the problems it has caused.

Films and Videos

One Flew Over the Cuckoo's Nest (1975, 129 min.)

In this drama, an inmate stirs trouble in a mental hospital. This film portrays the inhumane conditions that existed in some hospitals, ECT, and prefontal lobotomy. (Jack Nicholson, Louise Fletcher, William Redfield, Dean Brooks, Catman Crothers, Danny DeVito.)

Ordinary People (1980, 125 min.)

This drama depicts depression, suicide, and a family that is dysfunctional. Most impressive are seven psychotherapy scenes that show how therapy can work. (Donald Sutherland, Mary Tyler Moore, Judd Hirsch, Timothy Hutton.)

Internet

Mental Health Net (http://www.cmhc.com/)

A comprehensive on-line guide to mental health services, it has a "reading room" with ongoing opinion polls and discussion forums. It also has links to other mental health resources.

Self-help Resources Index (http://cmhc.com/selfhelp.htm)

Provides a "yellow pages" for mental health services and links to hundreds of self-help groups for such problems as druge abuse, depression, obesity, headaches, and stuttering.

Journals and Periodicals

American Journal of Psychiatry
Archives of General Psychiatry
Behavior Therapy
Journal of Abnormal Psychology
Journal of Consulting and Clinical Psychology
Psychotherapy

Telephone and Mail

American Self-help Clearinghouse (201-625-7101)
National Institutes of Mental Health (1-800-64-PANIC)

18 *Health and Well-being*

What's Your Prediction?

Does stress lower resistance?

The situation This time you really outdid yourself. You're one of 420 volunteers in a medical experiment for which you agreed to risk exposure to a common-cold virus. You'll be reimbursed for travel expenses, and for nine days you will receive free room and board in the clinic. So you pack your bags, check in, and sign an informed-consent statement.

The first two days are hectic. First you're given a complete medical examination, including a blood test. Then you fill out a stack of questionnaires. You answer questions about your mood, personality, health practices, and recent stressful experiences (such as a death in the family, pressures at work, or the breakup of a relationship). Then it happens. To simulate the person-to-person transmission of a virus, an attendant drops a clear liquid solution into your nose. If you're lucky, you were randomly assigned to the control group and receive only saline. If not, then you're in an experimental group and receive a low dose of a cold virus—just what you need. These exposures tend to produce illness at rates of 20 to 60 percent.

You are now quarantined in a large apartment for seven days—alone or with one or two roommates. Every day, you're examined by a nurse who takes your temperature, extracts a mucus sample, and looks for signs of a cold: sneezing, watery eyes, stuffy nose, hoarseness, sore throat, and cough (you don't know it, but the nurse also keeps track of the number of tissues you use). Basically, the researchers are interested in two results: (1) Are you infected (is there a virus in your system)? (2) Do you have a cold (as judged by the various symptoms)? What you don't realize is that the researchers are trying to see if there is a link between the recent stress in your life and your susceptibility to illness.

Make a prediction Based on the questionnaires initially filled out, you and others are classified as having a high or low level of stress in your life. Does this psychological factor make a person more or less vulnerable to viral infection? Among those who are infected, does recent life stress elevate the risk of catching a cold? All subjects were healthy at the start of the project—and not a single saline control subject developed a cold. Among those exposed to the virus, however, 82 percent became infected, and 46 percent caught a cold, symptoms and all. A virus is a virus, and there is no escape. But were the rates significantly different among the high- and low-stress groups? What do you think?

1. Were high-stress subjects more likely to become infected?	YES	NO
2. Were high-stress subjects more likely to catch a cold?	YES	NO

The results In 1985, the prestigious *New England Journal of Medicine* published a study that failed to find a significant link between psychological factors and medical outcomes. In an accompanying note, the journal's editor took the opportunity to scoff at the very notion that a person's mental state can affect his or her physical health. Six years later, Sheldon Cohen and others (1991) published the study just described in the same *New England Journal of Medicine*—an event that marked a "turning point in medical acceptance of a mind/body connection" (Kiecolt-Glaser & Glaser, 1993).

The results of this study were convincing. Life stress was not correlated with the rate of infection. Among those exposed to a virus, 85 percent of the high-stress subjects and 81 percent of the low-stress subjects became infected. Among those who were infected, however, high-stress subjects were more likely to catch a cold than were the low-stress subjects—53 percent compared to 40 percent. In fact, when subjects who had been housed with infected roommates were eliminated from the analysis (because of the risk that they had been reexposed), the high-stress subjects were still more likely to catch a cold than their low-stress counterparts—45 percent to 28 percent. Thus, once infected, people whose lives are filled with stress are particularly vulnerable to illness.

What does it all mean? This study reveals that there is a correlation between life stress and susceptibility to illness. Correlations do not prove causality, however, so one cannot conclude from this study alone that stress *per se* has this effect (it's theoretically possible, for example, that they are under stress because they are physically vulnerable). However, other researchers are finding that stress lowers resistance and compromises the immune system, the body's first line of defense against illness. Studies show that the activity of the immune system's white blood cells can be altered temporarily in subjects who are exposed to even a mildly stressful laboratory experience—such as a difficult mental task, a gruesome film, the recollection of bad memories, loud noise, or a bad social interaction (Kiecolt-Glaser et al., 1992).

This research has profound implications. Until recently, psychological and medical researchers alike believed that the human brain and immune system were separate and noninteracting. Not so. We now know that the organs of the immune system are richly endowed with nerve fibers, providing a direct pipeline to the brain—and that psychological factors, such as stress, can play an important role. The result is a new field that focuses on the seamless interplay of mental and physical health. This new field is called **psychoneuroimmunology (PNI)**: *psycho* for mind, *neuro* for the nervous system, and *immunology* for the immune system (Ader et al., 1991). Later in this chapter, we'll see that PNI is generating a great deal of excitement in all areas of psychology.

We've seen throughout this textbook that psychology is a remarkably diverse and eclectic discipline. Some psychologists define what they do as the study of the mind; others prefer to focus on behavior. Some are interested in the evolutionary and biological roots of human nature; others are interested more in cognitive and affective processes, growth and development, social and cultural factors, personality, or clinical disorders. Some of us build theories and conduct research to understand basic human processes; others want to apply what is known to improve health, education, law, life in the workplace, our interactions with the environment, and other aspects of the human condition. It has all become so diversified that Sigmund Koch (1993)—a prominent psychology historian—believes the discipline should be renamed the Psychological Studies.

Koch may have a point. A more important point, however, is that although psychology appears fragmented on the surface, many researchers in different areas of specialization unite in sharing a common objective: *to help improve upon our health and well-being and to enhance the quality of our lives.* In this chapter, we'll try to put psychology's puzzle pieces together. Beginning with the concept of the self and moving to the link between the mind and the body, we'll examine some of the new and exciting health-related questions that will be captivating researchers into the start of the twenty-first century.

Mind over Matter

In what ways has the study of psychology revealed the power of the human mind? What is the placebo effect, and what does it tell us?

Australian Aborigines believe that sorcerers have the power to cause death by pointing a bone at a person. The Kung of Africa believe that malaria can be caused by the death of a loved one. Many Western religious leaders maintain that faith heals all wounds. Shortly after the death of their wives, men die at a rate three times greater than others of the same age. In Fiji and other Pacific Islands, natives walk barefoot over beds of glowing hot coals without pain, burns, or blisters. Some doctors say they can prolong the lives of terminally ill patients through visualization (close your eyes, concentrate on the cancer in your body, and imagine that your disease-fighting white blood cells are gobbling up the cancer cells like Pac-Man).

psychoneuroimmunology (PNI) A new subfield of psychology that examines the interactions among psychological factors, the nervous system, and the immune system.

Walking barefoot on red-hot coals is an annual event at Mount Takao, Japan. This ritual may seem to demonstrate the power of mind over matter, but actually the wood coals are poor conductors of heat—and fire walkers often wet their feet before walking.

Still others advocate the power of positive thinking, laughter, confession, psychotherapy, prayer, meditation, yoga, jogging, subliminal self-help tapes, hypnosis, biofeedback, massage, acupuncture, social support, family pets, and screaming at the top of your lungs. Some of this advice is without merit. But as we'll see, a good deal of research supports the general point that we can improve our own health by learning to control not only our behavior but our minds as well.

In *The Healing Brain*, Robert Ornstein and David Sobel (1987) contend that "the brain minds the body," for the brain's primary function is not perception, consciousness, learning, thought, language, memory, motivation, or emotion—but health maintenance. According to Ornstein and Sobel, "The brain is the largest organ of secretion in the body, and the neuron, far from being like a chip within a computer, is a flesh-and-blood little gland, one that produces hundreds of chemicals. These chemicals do not, for the most part, serve thought or reason. They serve keeping the body out of trouble" (p. 11). Taking the argument one step further, Howard Friedman (1991), author of *The Self-Healing Personality*, notes that although he never saw a death certificate marked "death due to unhealthy personality," there is a link to chronic conditions such as headaches, ulcers, asthma, arthritis, and even cancer. And in *Mind-Body Deceptions*, Steven Dubrovsky (1997) argues that in "the psychosomatics of everyday life," the mind can often be used to heal the body. It all rings familiar the expression "Mind over matter."

The power we have to shape and alter our own experiences is a recurring theme in psychology. Elsewhere in this book, we saw that the perception of an object's size is determined not just by the size of its retinal image but also by the perceiver's knowledge of what the object is and its distance from the eye. We saw that accident victims who have an arm or leg amputated often feel pain in the missing limb even though no pain receptors are stimulated. And we saw that people often develop intense fears of harmless objects, construct memories of past events that did not occur, cure headaches with biofeedback, elevate their mood by smiling, and create self-fulfilling prophecies by behaving in ways that confirm their own beliefs.

One of the most profound illustrations of this theme is in the widely documented *placebo effect*—a psychological form of treatment routinely observed in medical circles. A placebo is any medical intervention (including inactive drugs, counseling, or surgery) designed to improve one's condition through the power of suggestion. In past years, sick people were forced to consume potions made of frog sperm, lizard tongues, crocodile dung, fly specks, unicorn horns, and ground snake. They were also subjected to shock treatments, bloodletting, forced vomiting, freezing, and blistering. It seems a miracle anyone survived. Yet accounts of early medical practices indicate that many people were "cured" by these peculiar remedies. Why? The patient's faith and hope are important parts of the healing process (White et al., 1985; Kirsch, 1990).

In a powerful demonstration of the placebo effect, Robert Sternbach (1964) gave to volunteer subjects a white sugar pill that contained no active ingredients. At first, subjects were told that the pill contained a drug that would stimulate a strong churning sensation in the stomach. The next time, they were told that it would reduce their stomach activity and make them feel full. On a third occasion, they were informed that the pill was only a placebo. The result: Subjects always swallowed the same tablet, yet they exhibited measurable changes in stomach activity consistent with their expectations. More recently, Montgomery and Kirsch (1996) recruited volunteers for an experiment on pain. The subjects put the index finger from each hand in a device onto which a metal bar was lowered, putting pressure on the finger. On one finger, but not the other, the experimenter applied a swab of brownish, medicinal-smelling "local anesthetic" to reduce pain. The solution was only a mixture of iodine, oil of thyme, and water—and it had no anesthetic properties. Yet subjects rated the pain to the placebo-treated finger as less intense and less unpleasant.

Over the years, placebos have been used to treat allergies, headaches, insomnia, constipation, skin rashes, upset stomachs, chronic pain, and other ailments. Indeed, in order to evaluate the effectiveness of any new drug or other form of treatment, researchers must demonstrate that the subjects who received that drug improved more than others who *believed* they had received it but did not. Only then can the actual effect of the treatment be separated from the placebo effect. Somehow, beliefs transform reality.

The placebo effect is not a magical occurrence or miracle, or even a purely mental phenomenon. And psychologists would not accept the claims made in the medical community solely on the basis of stories, anecdotes, and case studies. So how do placebos work? Is there a way to explain what Norman Cousins (1989) described as the biology of hope? Although the process is not well understood, research suggests that positive expectations—as communicated by a confident and enthusiastic expert—can trigger the release of endorphins, morphine-like substances that provide a temporary relief from pain (Levine et al., 1978). Others believe that by raising expectations, placebos relieve people of anxiety about being sick, thereby dampening the release of adrenaline and other stress hormones that lower the body's resistance (Taylor, 1986).

This chapter describes recent developments in the psychology of health and well-being on two fronts. First, we'll explore the topic of the self—the ways in which we think and feel about ourselves and the consequences of self-awareness for our mental and physical health. Next, we'll examine the topic of stress—what causes it, what effects it has on the body, and what coping mechanisms are most adaptive. As we'll see, people can use their minds to improve the quality of their lives.

The Self and Well-being

In what ways do people with high and low self-esteem differ? What role does self-awareness play? Is it more adaptive to harbor positive illusions or accurate perceptions of ourselves?

Have you ever been at a noisy gathering and yet managed to hear someone at the other end of the room mention your name? As noted in Chapter 4, this phenomenon is known as the cocktail party effect—the ability to pick a personally relevant stimulus out of a complex environment. This phenomenon shows that people are selective in their perceptions of the world. It also shows that the self is not just another stimulus—but an important object of our attention.

The Need for Self-esteem

You and I and just about everyone else are motivated by a need for **self-esteem**, and satisfying that need is critical to our entire outlook on life. People with high self-esteem tend to be happy, healthy, productive, and successful. They tend to persist longer at difficult tasks, sleep better at night, and have fewer ulcers. They are also more accepting of others and less likely to conform to peer pressure. In contrast, people with low self-esteem are more anxious, depressed, pessimistic about the future, and prone to failure (Brown, 1991).

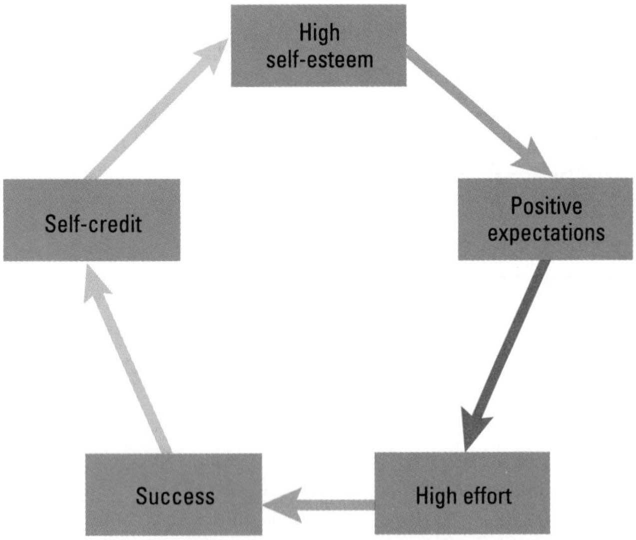

Figure 18.1 The self-esteem cycle High self-esteem is accompanied by positive expectations, which motivate behavior, improve performance, and reinforce the high self-esteem.

People with high self-esteem are confident and bring to new challenges a winning and motivating attitude. In contrast, people lacking in self-esteem also lack confidence, so they bring to new tasks a losing attitude that traps them in a vicious, self-defeating cycle (see Figure 18.1). Expecting to fail, they become anxious, exert less effort, and "tune out" on life's important challenges. Then when they do fail, people who are low in self-esteem blame themselves—which makes them feel worthless and even more incompetent (Brockner, 1983; Brown & Dutton, 1995). If that's not bad enough, people with low self-esteem may also be prone to illness. Research suggests that making people aware of their negative self-evaluations has adverse effects on the immune system, the body's capacity to ward off disease (Strauman et al., 1993).

One way to look at self-esteem is through the lens of self-discrepancy theory (Higgins, 1989). As we saw in Chapter 15, our self-esteem can be defined by the degree of match between how we see ourselves and how we want to see ourselves. In people who are high in self-esteem, the self-concept matches their personal standards. To the extent that we see ourselves as falling short of meeting these standards, our self-esteem is lowered and we feel sad or anxious or we experience other

self-esteem A positive or negative evaluation of the self.

negative emotions. It's clear that everyone must cope with some degree of self-discrepancy. After all, nobody is perfect. Yet we do not all suffer the consequences. The reason, according to Higgins, is that self-esteem depends on two factors. First is the amount of self-discrepancy we have (the more of it there is, the worse we feel). The second factor is the extent to which we focus on these self-discrepancies (the more focused we are, the greater is the harm). The question is, what makes us focus more or less on our personal shortcomings?

[Drawing by Twohy; © 1996 The New Yorker Magazine, Inc.]

The Self-awareness "Trap"

If you carefully review your daily routine—classes, work, leisure activities, social interactions, meals, and so on—you will probably be surprised at how little time you actually spend thinking about yourself. In a study that illustrates this point, more than 100 people, ranging in age from nineteen to sixty-three, were equipped for a week with electronic beepers that sounded on average every two hours between 7:30 AM and 10:30 PM. Each time the beepers went off, subjects interrupted whatever they were doing, wrote down what they were thinking at that moment, and filled out a questionnaire. Out of 4,700 observations, only 8 percent of all recorded thoughts were about the self. Even more interesting is that when subjects did think about themselves, they reported feeling relatively unhappy and wished they were doing something else (Csikszentmihalyi & Figurski, 1982).

This is an interesting correlation. Is it really unpleasant to think about ourselves? Is self-awareness a mental trap from which we need to escape? Perhaps. Many psychologists have found that self-focus brings out our personal shortcomings the way staring into a mirror draws our attention to every blemish on the face. According to **self-awareness theory**, certain situations predictably force us to turn inward and become the object of our own attention. When we talk about ourselves, glance in a mirror, stand before an audience or camera, watch ourselves on videotape, or behave in a conspicuous manner, we enter a state of heightened self-awareness that leads us to compare our behavior to some standard. This comparison often results in a negative discrepancy and a drop in self-esteem as we discover that we fall short of our ideals (Wicklund, 1975).

Just as certain situations trigger self-awareness, some people are generally more self-focused than others. As measured by the Self-consciousness Scale, research shows that individuals differ in the tendency to introspect on their inner thoughts and feelings and in their concern for how they appear to others (Fenigstein et al., 1975; Buss, 1980). A sample of items used to measure these traits is presented in Table 18.1. How many of these statements do you agree with?

Table 18.1 Sample Items to Measure Self-consciousness

- I'm always trying to figure myself out.
- I usually worry about making a good impression.
- One of the last things I do before leaving the house is look in the mirror.
- I'm alert to changes in my mood.
- I get embarrassed very easily.
- I have trouble working when someone is watching me.
- Large groups make me nervous.
- I'm constantly examining my motives.

self-awareness theory The theory that self-focused attention leads people to notice their shortcomings, thus motivating a change in behavior or an escape from self-awareness.

Looking into a mirror increases self-awareness—and often draws attention to our personal shortcomings.

Is self-consciousness an adaptive trait? In *Escaping the Self*, Roy Baumeister (1991) argued that contemporary Western culture places so much emphasis on selfhood and identity—as embodied in the so-called me generation—and that it is a constant burden to keep up. Just to maintain a positive image for ourselves and others, we read books on how to make a good impression, replace clothing when it is no longer fashionable, starve ourselves thin, spend countless dollars on cosmetic surgery, rationalize failure and rejection, and blush when we say something foolish in front of others. The more energy we invest in the self, the more we have to lose. Society is so enamored of, obsessed with, and addicted to the self, writes Baumeister, that "maintaining self-esteem can start to seem like a full-time job!" (p. 12).

If focusing on the self is a problem, what's the solution? Self-awareness theory suggests that there are two ways to cope with the discomfort: (1) behave in ways that might reduce one's self-discrepancies, or (2) withdraw from self-awareness. According to Charles Carver and Michael Scheier (1981), the solution chosen depends on whether you expect that you can successfully reduce the self-discrepancy—and whether you're satisfied with the progress you make once you try (Duval et al., 1992). If you are, you'll match your behavior to the standard; if not, you'll tune out, seek distractions, and turn attention away from the self. This process is depicted in Figure 18.2.

In general, research supports these predictions of self-awareness theory (Gibbons, 1990). When people are self-focused, they are more likely to behave in ways that are consistent with their values and socially accepted ideals. When the prospects for discrepancy reduction seem grim, however, they take the second route: escape from self-awareness. In one experiment, for example, subjects worked on a task in a room that did or did not have a full-length mirror facing them. Subjects who received negative feedback about their task performance were quicker to leave the room when it had a mirror to remind them of their failure than when it did not (Duval & Wicklund, 1972).

There are some disturbing health-related implications of escape as a coping strategy. One concerns the use of alcohol. According to Jay Hull, people often drown their sorrows in a bottle as a way to flee mentally from the negative effects of self-awareness. To demonstrate this process, Hull and Richard Young (1983) administered what was supposed to be an IQ test to male subjects, then gave them false feedback suggesting they had either succeeded or failed. Supposedly as part of a separate study, subjects were then asked to taste and rate different wines. They did not realize it, but the experimenters kept track of how much wine they drank during the fifteen-minute tasting period. As predicted, subjects who had high scores on the Self-consciousness Scale drank more after failure than after success, presum-

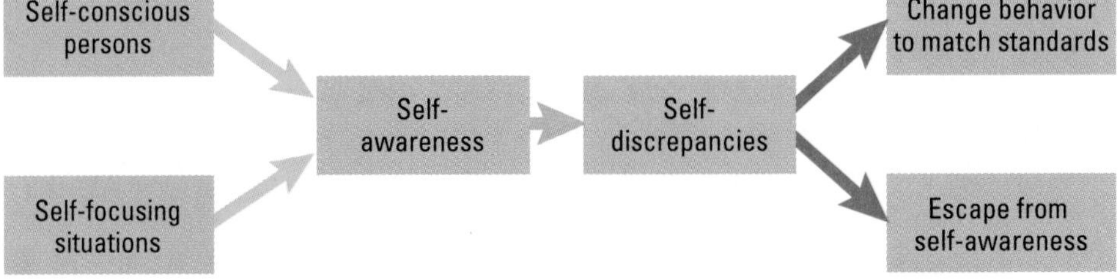

Figure 18.2 Self-awareness theory Focusing attention on the self makes us aware of our self-discrepancies. This awareness pressures us either to match our behavior to ideal standards or else to tune out.

ably to escape the negative implications for their self-esteem. Among subjects who were low in self-consciousness, there was no difference in alcohol consumption. Similar results were obtained in a study of men who had been hospitalized for alcoholism and then released. After three months, those who both were high in self-consciousness and were under stress were the most likely to relapse into heavy drinking (Hull et al., 1986).

According to Claude Steele and Robert Josephs (1990), alcoholic intoxication provides more than just a means of tuning out on the self. By causing people to lose touch with reality and shed their inhibitions, it also evokes a state of "drunken self-inflation." In one study, they had subjects rate their actual and ideal selves on thirty-five traits—some important to their self-esteem, others not important. After drinking either an 80-proof vodka cocktail or a harmless placebo, subjects rerated themselves on the same traits. As measured by the discrepancy between actual and ideal selves, subjects who had been drinking expressed inflated views of themselves on traits they considered important (Banaji & Steele, 1989).

[Drawing by Cline; © 1991 The New Yorker Magazine, Inc.]

"More wine! Less truth!"

People often drown their troubles in a bottle to escape the negative implications of self-awareness.

Positive Illusions

Self-awareness can force us to notice our shortcomings, so we turn away from unpleasant truths. We must be pretty good at it, because research consistently shows that most people think and speak highly of themselves. Time and again, subjects see positive traits as more self-descriptive than negative ones, they rate themselves more highly than they rate others, they rate themselves more highly than they are rated *by* others, they overestimate their contribution to team efforts, and they exaggerate their control over life events (Taylor, 1989). Illustrating the "mere ownership effect," people even judge the letters in their name more favorably than the other letters of the alphabet (Hoorens & Nuttin, 1993) and evaluate various consumer products that they own as better than comparable products they do not own (Beggan, 1992). It is not that we consciously flatter ourselves, either. The response is more like a mindless reflex. In fact, when subjects are busy or distracted as they make self-ratings, the judgments they come up with are quicker and even more favorable (Paulhus et al., 1989; Hixon & Swann, 1993).

Most people also exhibit "unrealistic optimism," a tendency to predict a uniquely bright and rosy future for themselves. As presented in Figure 18.3, college students asked to predict their own future compared to that of their classmates believed, on average, that they were more likely to graduate higher in their class, get a better job, earn a higher salary, have a happier marriage, and bear a gifted child. They also believed that they were less likely to get fired, get divorced, have a drinking problem, become depressed, become involved in a car accident, or suffer from a heart attack (Weinstein, 1980). Many other examples illustrate this point. In polls taken between 1952 and 1980, American voters—regardless of whether they had favored the ultimate winner or the loser—expected their favorite candidate to prevail by a 4-to-1 ratio (Granberg & Brent, 1983). Similarly, sports fans let their team preferences interfere with the bets they place, even when they're trying to be "objective" (Babad & Katz, 1991). In one study, students set their odds of getting divorced at only 20 percent, even though they knew that the divorce rate for new marriages is close to 50 percent (Kunda, 1987).

We can't all be better than average, nor can we all have a rosier future than everyone else. So how do we maintain such a generally positive outlook? How do we cope with our own faults, inadequacies, and an uncertain future? Simple. Using

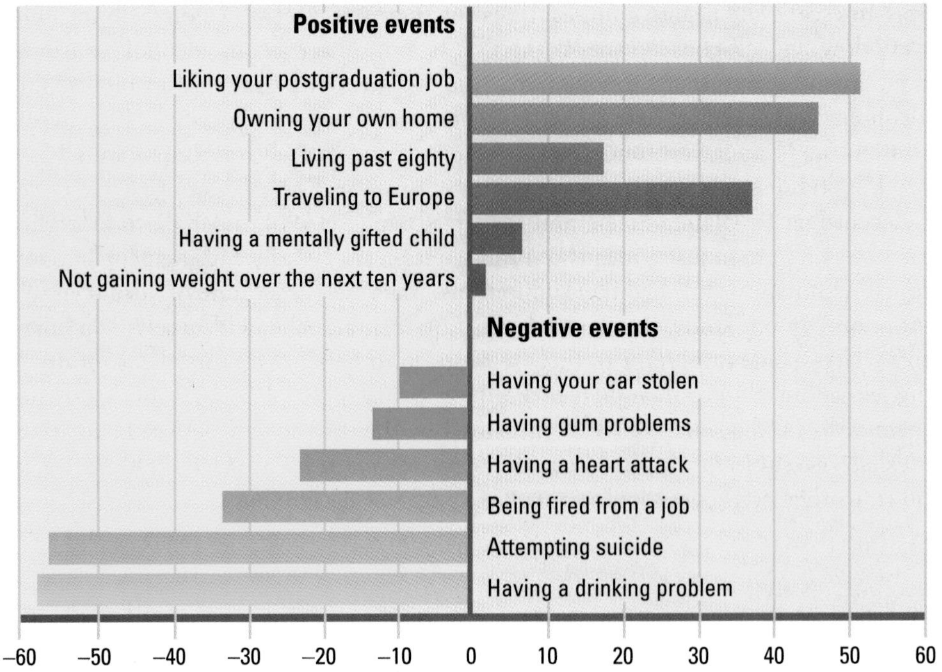

Figure 18.3 Unrealistic optimism When students were asked to predict their own future compared to that of their classmates of the same sex, they rated their own chances as above average for positive events and as below average for negative events.

cognitive strategies like the unconscious defense mechanisms described by Freud, we engage in **self-deception**—the processes by which we distort the information we have about ourselves (Lockard & Paulhus, 1988). Let's examine two such strategies: self-handicapping and downward comparisons.

Self-handicapping It is common for people who are failing or anticipating defeat to make excuses (Snyder et al., 1983). "I had a headache," "I don't test well," and "I was out partying all night" are among the many creative admissions we use to shield ourselves from what could be the most shattering implication of failure—a lack of ability. In what sounds like the ultimate paradox, there are times when we might even sabotage our own performance in order to preserve our self-esteem (Higgins et al., 1990).

As first described by Stephen Berglas and Edward Jones (1978), **self-handicapping** refers to actions people take to hinder their own performance in order to build an excuse for possible failure. To demonstrate, Berglas and Jones recruited college students for an experiment supposedly on the effects of drugs on intellectual performance. All subjects worked on a twenty-item analogies test and were told that they had done well, after which they expected to work on a second, similar test. For one group, the problems were relatively easy, leading subjects to expect more success; for a second group, the problems were insoluble, leading subjects to be confused about their initial performance and worried that they would fail. Before taking the second test, subjects were given a choice of two bogus drugs: Actavil, which was supposed to improve performance, or Pandocrin, which was supposed to impair it. Although no drugs were actually administered, most subjects who were confident about the upcoming test selected the Actavil; in contrast, male subjects (but not the

self-deception The processes by which people distort and hide unpleasant truths from themselves.

self-handicapping Behaviors designed to sabotage one's own performance and provide a subsequent excuse for failure.

females) who feared the outcome of the second test chose the Pandocrin. By handicapping themselves, these men set up a convenient excuse for failure.

Some people use self-handicapping as a defense more than others do—and there are different ways to do so. For example, men often handicap themselves by taking drugs or neglecting to practice, while women tend to cite stress and physical symptoms instead (Hirt et al., 1991). People also differ in the reasons they have for self-handicapping. Dianne Tice (1991) found that people who are low in self-esteem use self-handicapping to set up a defensive, face-saving excuse in case they fail, while those who are high in self-esteem use it as an opportunity to claim extra credit if they succeed. Other researchers have also found this difference in orientation (Rhodewalt et al., 1991; Wood et al., 1994). Whatever the goal, self-handicapping seems like an ingenious strategy: With the odds stacked against us, the self is both insulated from failure and enhanced by success. Of course, this strategy is not without considerable cost. Sure, it may ease the pressure to succeed, but sabotaging ourselves—by not preparing or practicing or by drinking too much, using drugs, or faking illness—also increases the risk of failure. Sometimes you just have to take chances in order to get ahead in life.

This college student sits drunk on a Texas beach during spring break. People may drink heavily to escape from past failure—and to set up a face-saving excuse for future failure.

Downward Comparisons A second way in which people maintain a positive glow is by making **downward social comparisons**. When victimized by tragic life events (perhaps a crime, accident, disease, or the death of a loved one), people like to *affiliate* with others in the same predicament who are adjusting well, role models who offer hope and guidance. But they prefer to *compare* themselves with others who are less successful, less happy, or less fortunate (Taylor & Lobel, 1989). When people who are low in self-esteem suffer a setback, downward comparisons have an uplifting effect on their mood and outlook for the future (Aspinwall & Taylor, 1993; Gibbons & McCoy, 1991).

Studies with cancer patients have shown that it helps to know that life could be worse. Many cancer patients contrast themselves to others who are *not* coping very well (Wood et al., 1985), and most believe that they're better off than their peers (Taylor et al., 1986). Interviews of women with breast-cancer tell the story. One woman who had only a lump removed wondered "how awful it must be for women who have had a full mastectomy." An older woman who had a mastectomy said: "The people I really feel sorry for are these young gals. To lose a breast when you're so young must be awful." Yet a young mastectomy patient derived comfort from the fact that "if I hadn't been married, this thing would have really gotten to me" (Taylor, 1989, p. 171). As these quotes poignantly illustrate, and as a great deal of research has shown, there's always someone else with whom we can favorably compare—and this downward comparison makes us feel better (VanderZee et al., 1996).

Are Positive Illusions Adaptive? Psychologists used to agree that an accurate perception of reality is vital to mental health. More and more, however, this view is being challenged by research on positive illusions. It is clear that many people delude themselves with overly high self-ratings and unrealistic optimism—and do so through the use of self-handicapping and downward comparisons. But are these illusions a sign of well-being or symptoms of disorder?

When Shelley Taylor and Jonathon Brown (1988) reviewed the relevant research, they noticed that people who are mildly depressed or low in self-esteem have less inflated and sometimes more realistic views of themselves than do others who are better adjusted. Their self-appraisals are more likely to match appraisals of them made by neutral others, they are less likely to exaggerate their control over

downward social comparison A way to boost self-esteem by comparing oneself to others who are less successful, less happy, or less fortunate.

uncontrollable events, they make more balanced predictions about the future, and they are more likely to compare themselves to similar others rather than to make downward comparisons. Based on these results, Taylor and Brown drew the provocative conclusion that when it comes to the self, positive illusions—not accurate perceptions of reality—promote health and well-being. In their words, "these illusions help make each individual's world a warmer and more active and beneficent place in which to live" (1988, p. 205). They may also help us cope with adversity (Taylor & Armor, 1996).

Baumeister and Steven Scher (1988) are not so sure that people are better off being eternal optimists than hard realists. Looking at a wide range of self-defeating behaviors, they conclude that positive illusions can give rise to chronic patterns of self-destruction—as when people escape from self-awareness through the use of alcohol and other drugs, self-handicap themselves into failure and underachievement, and deny health-related problems until it's too late for treatment. From an interpersonal point of view, C. Randall Colvin and his colleagues (1995) found that people who have inflated rather than realistic views of themselves were rated less favorably on certain dimensions by their own friends. In their studies, self-enhancing men were seen as assertive and ambitious, which are okay, but also as boastful, condescending, hostile, and less considerate of others. Self-enhancing women were seen as more hostile, more defensive and sensitive to criticism, more likely to overreact to minor setbacks, and less well liked by others.

Realism or illusion, which orientation is more adaptive? As psychologists debate the short-term and long-term consequences of positive illusions, it's clear that there is no simple answer (Colvin & Block, 1994; Taylor & Brown, 1994). For now, the picture that has emerged is this: People who harbor positive illusions about themselves are likely to enjoy the benefits and achievements of high self-esteem. But these same individuals may pay a price in other ways—as in their relations with others. Indeed, Baumeister and his colleagues (1996) have suggested that people who have high self-esteem are more likely to lash out angrily in response to negative feedback, rejection, and other threats to the ego. So what are we to conclude? Is it possible that positive illusions motivate us toward personal achievement but alienate us socially from others? Could it be that it's adaptive to see oneself in ways that are slightly inflated, but not too much? It will be interesting to see what researchers find in the years to come.

Stress and Health

What are the main sources of stress in our lives? What are the effects of stress on the body? What is the Type A personality, and why is it bad for your heart? How does the immune system work, and how is it affected by stress and other psychological states?

The reason psychologists are interested in mental health is obvious. But the field has also had a long-standing interest in physical health, a domain normally associated with medicine. Influenced by psychoanalysis, clinical psychologists used to study *psychosomatic* ailments such as asthma, ulcers, headaches, and constipation—conditions thought to result from unconscious conflicts. Working from a behavioral perspective, others later referred to these same ailments as *psychophysiological* disorders. Either way, it's clear that psychological states can influence physical well-being (Gatchel & Blanchard, 1993).

Over the past few years, increasing numbers of researchers have become interested in the emerging area of **health psychology**, the application of psychology to the promotion of physical health and the prevention and treatment of illness. You may wonder, what does psychology have to do with catching a cold, having a heart attack, or being afflicted by cancer? If you could turn the clock back a few years and ask your family doctor, his or her answer would be "very little." In the past, illness was considered a purely biological event. But this strict medical perspective has given way to a broader model that holds that health is a joint product of biological and psychological factors.

Part of the reason for this broadened view is that illness patterns over the years have changed in significant ways. Before the twentieth century, the principal causes of death were contagious diseases—polio, smallpox, tuberculosis, typhoid fever, malaria, influenza, pneumonia, and the like. In the United States, none of these infectious illnesses is currently a leading killer. Instead, Americans are most likely to die, in order of risk, from heart disease, cancer, strokes, and accidents (AIDS is eighth on the list)—problems that are often preventable through changes in mind and behavior (see Figure 18.4).

Although it's not possible to quantify the extent of the problem, psychological stress is known to be a potent killer. Regardless of who you are, when you were born, or where you live, you have no doubt experienced stress. Sitting in a rush-hour traffic jam, getting married or divorced, losing hours of work to a computer crash, getting into an argument with a close friend, worrying about an unwanted pregnancy or the health of your child, living in a noisy neighborhood, struggling to make financial ends meet, and caring for a loved one who is sick—these are the kinds of stresses and strains we all must learn to live with. Whether they are short-term or long-term, serious or mild, no one is immune and there is no escape. But there are ways to cope.

In this section, we examine three interrelated questions of relevance to your health and well-being: (1) What are some of the primary sources of stress? (2) What are the effects of stress on the body? (3) What are the most adaptive ways of coping with stress? Together, the answers to these questions provide a useful model of the stress-and-coping process (see Figure 18.5).

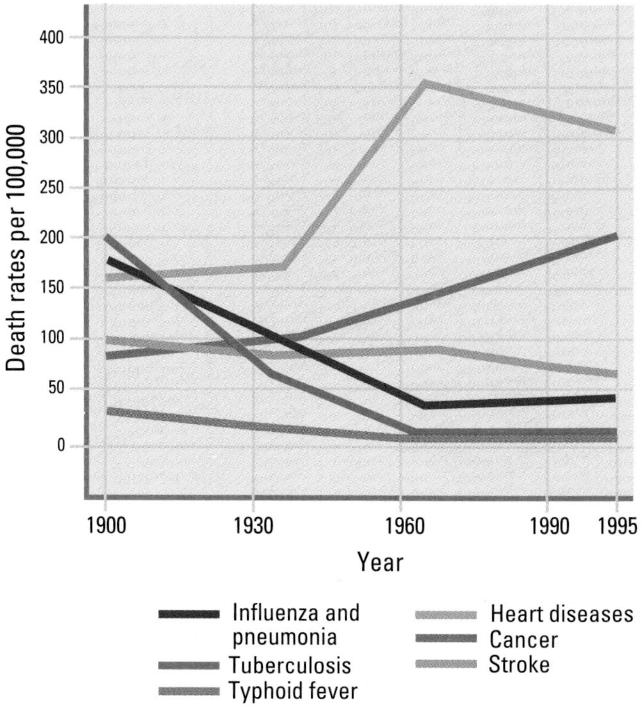

Figure 18.4 Leading causes of death, 1900–1995 As shown, heart disease, cancer, and strokes have replaced infectious diseases as the major causes of death in the United States.

The Sources of Stress

Stress is an unpleasant state of arousal that arises when we perceive that an event threatens our ability to cope effectively. There are many different sources of stress, or *stressors*. Try writing down the stressors in your own life, and you'll probably find that the items in your list can be divided into three major categories: catastrophes, major life events, and daily hassles.

Catastrophes It was the spring of 1997. As water levels rose, many North Dakota families removed whatever valuables they could from their homes. Many stayed to the bitter end, hoping that the river would not engulf their homes. The

health psychology The study of the links between psychological factors and physical health and illness.

stress An aversive state of arousal triggered by the perception that an event threatens our ability to cope effectively.

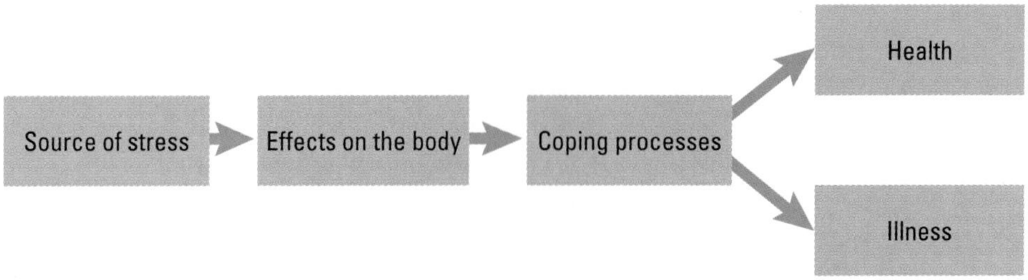

Figure 18.5 Stress and coping Advances in health psychology show that although stressful events have effects on the body, the way we cope with stress can promote health or illness.

flood dealt a devastating blow to many people. Other events that have similarly traumatic effects are car accidents, plane crashes, terrorist bombings, hurricanes, tornadoes, earthquakes, and violent crime.

Tornadoes have such devastating power that those who survive often exhibit posttraumatic stress disorder.

The harmful effects of catastrophic stressors on health are well documented. Paul and Gerald Adams (1984) examined the public records in Othello, Washington, before and after the 1980 eruption of the Mount Saint Helens volcano, which spewed thick layers of ash all over the community. They discovered that there were posteruption increases in calls made to a mental-health crisis line, police reports of domestic violence, referrals to the alcohol treatment center, and visits to the local hospital emergency room. Based on a review of fifty-two additional studies, Anthony Rubonis and Leonard Bickman (1991) concluded that high rates of psychological disorders are common after large-scale environmental disasters.

It has long been known that war in particular leaves deep and permanent psychological scars. Soldiers who experience combat see horrifying injuries, death, and destruction on a routine basis, leaving them with images and emotions that do not fade. In World War I, the problem was called shell shock. In World War II, it was called combat fatigue. It's now called **posttraumatic stress disorder (PTSD)** and is identified by such symptoms as recurring anxiety, sleeplessness, nightmares, vivid flashbacks, intrusive thoughts, attentional problems, and social withdrawal. To evaluate the extent of the problem, researchers at the Centers for Disease Control (1988) compared 7,000 Vietnam combat veterans with 7,000 noncombat veterans who served in the military at the same time, that is, more than twenty years before the study. They found that although the Vietnam War was a distant memory to most Americans, 15 percent of those who saw combat—twice as many as were in the comparison group—reported lingering symptoms of posttraumatic stress disorder. Those who had the most traumatic of experiences (crossing enemy lines, being ambushed or shot at, handling dead bodies) were five times more likely to suffer from nightmares, flashbacks, startle reactions, and other problems (Goldberg et al., 1990). Similar results have been found among older veterans of World War II and the Korean War (Fontana & Rosenheck, 1994; Spiro et al., 1994).

PTSD, a form of anxiety disorder, can be caused by traumas off the battlefield as well. Based on a nationwide survey of nearly 6,000 Americans, fifteen to fifty-four years old, Ronald Kessler and his colleagues (1995) estimated that 8 percent of the population (5 percent among men, 10 percent among women) have posttraumatic stress disorder in the course of a lifetime—and that the symptoms often persist for many years. Figure 18.6 indicates that different types of experiences produce these traumas (shown on the left are the percentages of men and women who had various experiences; shown on the right are the percentages of those for whom the experience was likely to have resulted in PTSD). In a study of Miami residents caught in a

posttraumatic stress disorder (PTSD) An anxiety disorder triggered by an extremely stressful event, such as combat.

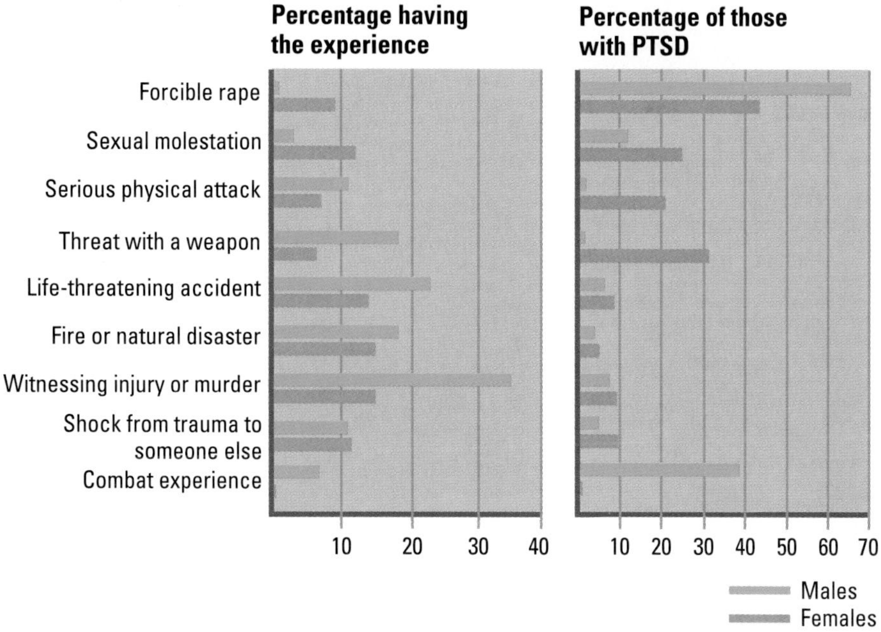

Figure 18.6 Lifetime rates of traumas and PTSD

major hurricane, Gail Ironson and others (1997) found that after a few months, one-third exhibited symptoms of PTSD—and that the more injury, property damage, and loss they suffered from the storm, the more severe their symptoms were.

It has long been recognized that combat leaves psychological scars and the symptoms of posttraumatic stress disorder.

Major Life Events Some people are lucky enough to avoid major catastrophes. But nobody can avoid stress. The reason, say some psychologists, is that change of any kind causes stress because it forces us to adapt to new circumstances. This hypothesis was first proposed by Thomas Holmes and Richard Rahe (1967), who interviewed hospital patients and found that their illnesses were often preceded by major changes in some aspect of their lives. Some of the changes were negative (being injured, divorced, or fired from a job), but others were positive (getting married, being promoted, or having a baby). To measure life stress, Holmes and Rahe thus devised the Social Readjustment Rating Scale (SRRS)—a checklist of forty-three major life changes, each assigned a numerical value based on the amount of readjustment it requires (see Table 18.2). The events listed, in order of stressfulness, can be used to estimate the amount of recent stress in your life (this scale does not include many events common among college students—such as changes in grades, graduation, and relationships with friends and lovers).

You may have seen the SRRS, or other questionnaires like it, in a book or magazine. The claim made is that the number of stress points or "life-change units" you accumulate in a recent period of time indicates the amount of stress you are under. I recall filling out such a questionnaire the year I finished graduate school. I received my Ph.D. One week later, my wife and I got married, moved 1,500 miles to a new state, rented a new apartment, and started new jobs. For the first and only time in her life, my wife developed an ulcer. Her doctor's first question: "Has anything changed in your life?"

The simple notion that change is inherently stressful has an intuitive ring about it. Indeed, research shows that people with high scores on the SRRS are more likely to come down with various physical illnesses (Dohrenwend & Dohrenwend, 1978;

Table 18.2 Sample Items from the Social Readjustment Rating Scale

LIFE EVENT	VALUE
1. Death of spouse	100
2. Divorce	73
3. Jail term or imprisonment	63
4. Death of a close family member	63
5. Major personal injury or illness	53
6. Marriage	50
7. Losing one's job	47
8. Pregnancy	40
9. Sexual difficulties	39
10. Addition of a new family member	39
11. Change in financial state	37
12. Death of a close friend	36
13. Change to a different line of work	36
14. Taking out a large mortgage	31
15. Change in status at work	29
16. Son or daughter leaving home	29
17. Outstanding personal achievement	28
18. Major change in work hours or conditions	20
19. Move to a new residence	20
20. Transfer to a new school	20
21. Taking out a loan (e.g., for a new car)	17
22. Change in sleeping habits	16
23. Change in eating habits	15
24. Vacation	13
25. Minor law violations (traffic tickets, etc.)	11

Source: T. H. Holmes & R. H. Rahe (1967). The social readjustment rating scale. *Journal of Psychosomatic Research*, 11, 213–218.

Maddi et al., 1987). But is change per se necessarily harmful? There are two problems with this notion. First, although there is a statistical link between negative events and illness, research does not similarly support the claim that positive "stressors"—taking a vacation, graduating, winning a lottery, starting a new career, or getting married—are similarly harmful (Stewart et al., 1986). Look carefully at the SRRS items in Table 18.2, and you'll see that most events on the list are negative. The second complicating factor is that the impact of any change depends on who the person is and how the change is interpreted. For example, moving to a new country is less stressful to immigrants who know their new language and culture (Berry et al., 1992), and having an abortion is less stressful to women who have the support of their family, partners, and friends (Major et al., 1990). The amount of change in a person's life may provide crude estimates of stress and future health, but the predictive equation is more complex.

Microstressors Think again about the sources of stress in your life, and catastrophes or exceptional events spring to mind. Researchers have found, however, that the most significant source of stress arises from the hassles that irritate us on a daily basis. Environmental factors such as population density, loud noise, extreme heat or cold, and cigarette smoke are all possible sources of stress. Car problems, waiting in lines, losing keys, arguments with friends, nosy neighbors, bad workdays, money troubles, and other "microstressors" also place a constant strain on us. Table 18.3 shows the events that most routinely stress children, college students, and adults (Kanner et al., 1981; Kanner et al., 1991; Kohn et al., 1990). Unfortunately, there is nothing "micro" about the impact of these stressors on our health and well-being. Studies show that the accumulation of daily hassles contributes more to illness than do major life events (DeLongis et al., 1982; Weinberger et al., 1987; Kohn et al., 1991).

There is one source of stress that plagues many people on a routine basis. At work, relentless job pressures can grind away at a person over time and cause *burnout*—a state of emotional exhaustion characterized by a feeling of distance from others and a diminished sense of personal accomplishment. Schoolteachers, doctors, nurses, police officers, social workers, and others in human-service professions are particularly at risk for burnout. Research shows that people who are burned out describe themselves as used up, drained, frustrated, hardened, apathetic, lacking in energy, and without motivation (Maslach, 1982; Cordes & Dougherty, 1993).

Table 18.3 Common Daily Hassles

CHILDREN AND EARLY ADOLESCENTS

- Having to clean up your room
- Being bored and having nothing to do
- Seeing that another kid can do something better
- Getting punished for doing something wrong
- Having to go to bed when you don't want to
- Being teased at school

COLLEGE STUDENTS

- Conflicts with a boyfriend or girlfriend
- Dissatisfaction with your athletic skills
- Having your trust betrayed by a friend
- Struggling to meet your own academic standards
- Not having enough leisure time
- Gossip concerning someone you care about
- Dissatisfaction with your physical appearance

MIDDLE-AGE ADULTS

- Concerns about weight
- Health of a family member
- Social obligations
- Inconsiderate smokers
- Concerns about money
- Misplacing or losing things
- Home maintenance
- Job security

Waiting helplessly in traffic is one of the most common microstressors in daily life.

Research also shows that people are most likely to experience burnout when there are not enough resources at work (such as support from supervisors, friendly relationships with coworkers, autonomy, and opportunities for advancement) to meet the demands of the job (Lee & Ashforth, 1996).

The Physiological Effects of Stress

The term *stress* was popularized by Hans Selye (1936, 1976), an endocrinologist. As a young medical student, Selye noticed that patients who were hospitalized for different illnesses often had similar symptoms, such as muscle weakness, a loss of weight and appetite, and a lack of ambition. Maybe these symptoms were part of a generalized response to an attack on the body, he thought. In the 1930s, Selye tested this hypothesis by exposing laboratory rats to various stressors, including heat, cold, heavy exercise, toxic substances, food deprivation, and electric shock. As anticipated, the different stressors all produced a similar physiological response: enlarged adrenal glands, shrunken lymph nodes, and bleeding stomach ulcers. Selye borrowed a term from engineering and called the reaction stress, a word that quickly became part of everyday language.

According to Selye, the body naturally responds to stress in a three-stage process he called the **general adaptation syndrome** (see Figure 18.7). Sparked by the recognition of a threat, any threat—predator, enemy soldier, speeding automobile, or virus—the body has an initial alarm reaction. To meet the challenge, adrenaline and other hormones are poured into the bloodstream, thus heightening physiological arousal. Heart rate, blood pressure, and breathing rates increase, while slower, long-term functions such as growth, digestion, and the operation of the immune system are inhibited. At this stage, the body mobilizes all its resources to ward off the threat. Next comes a resistance stage, during which the body remains aroused and on the alert. There is a continued release of stress hormones and local defenses are activated (if there is a virus, for example, immune-system antibodies are called into action). However, if the stress persists for a prolonged period of time (as in a failing marriage, high-pressure job, or poverty), the body will fall into an exhaustion stage. According to Selye, our antistress resources are limited. Eventually, resistance breaks down, putting us at risk for illness and even death.

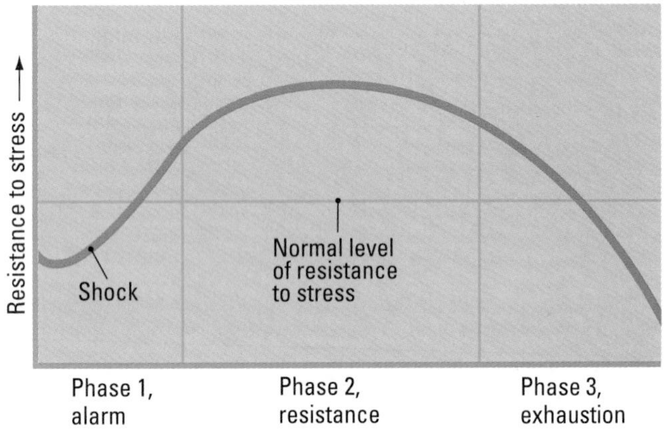

Figure 18.7 The general adaptation syndrome According to Selye, the human body responds to threat in three phases: alarm, resistance, and exhaustion.

Research has since revealed that different types of stressors elicit somewhat different bodily responses—and that exhaustion occurs not because the body's stress-fighting resources are limited but because the overuse of these resources causes other systems in the body to break down. Still, Selye's basic model makes an important point: Stress may be an adaptive, short-term reaction to threat, but over time it compromises our health and well-being. As we'll see in the coming pages, stress is linked to coronary heart disease and the workings of the immune system.

general adaptation syndrome A three-stage process (alarm, resistance, and exhaustion) by which the body responds to stress.

The stress response is found in all mammals. So why, asks neuroscientist Robert Sapolsky (1994), don't zebras get ulcers? Sapolsky notes that the physiological stress response is superbly designed through evolution to help animals mobilize to fight or escape in acute emergencies. For the zebra, this occurs when a hungry lion leaps out from a bush and sprints at top speed across the savanna. For humans, it occurs in combat or in competitive sports—and perhaps even on first dates and job interviews. But make a mental list of situations you find stressful, and you'll see that people become anxious over things that would make no sense to a zebra. "We humans live well enough and long enough, and are smart enough, to generate all sorts of stressful events purely in our heads," notes Sapolsky. "From the perspective of the evolution of the animal kingdom, psychological stress is a recent invention" (p. 5). The reason that stress causes ulcers and other illnesses, then, is that the response is designed for acute physical emergencies, yet we turn it on often and for prolonged periods of time as we worry about taxes, mortgages, family members, public speaking, career goals, and the inevitability of death.

Coronary Heart Disease Coronary heart disease (CHD) is a narrowing of the blood vessels that carry oxygen and nutrients to the heart muscle. It is currently the leading cause of death in the United States. An estimated 69 million Americans suffer from CHD. For many, the result is a heart attack, which occurs when the blood supply to the heart is blocked. This causes an uncomfortable feeling of pressure, fullness, squeezing, or pain in the center of the chest—and sometimes also sweating, dizziness, nausea, fainting, and a shortness of breath. Every year, 1.5 million Americans have heart attacks. One-third do not survive.

Several factors are known to increase the risk of CHD. The three most important are hypertension, or high blood pressure; cigarette smoking; and high cholesterol (others include a family history of CHD, obesity, and a lack of exercise). People with one of these three major risk factors are twice as likely to develop CHD, those with two risk factors are 3.5 times as likely, and those with all three are six times as likely. These statistics are compelling and should not be taken lightly. But combined, these factors account for fewer than half the known cases of CHD. What's missing from the equation is the fourth major risk factor: stress.

In 1956, cardiologists Meyer Friedman and Ray Rosenman were studying the relationship between cholesterol and coronary heart disease. After noticing that husbands were more likely than their wives to have CHD, they speculated that work-related stress might be the reason (at the time, most women did not work outside the home). To test this hypothesis, Friedman and Rosenman interviewed 3,000 healthy middle-age men. Those who seemed to be the most hard-driving, competitive, impatient, time-conscious, and quick to anger were classified as having a **Type A personality**. Roughly an equal number of those who were easygoing, relaxed, and laid back were classified as having a **Type B personality**. Interestingly, out of 258 men who eventually had heart attacks over the following nine years, 69 percent had been classified as Type As and only 31 percent were Type Bs (Rosenman et al., 1975).

The Type A personality of the so-called workaholic is made up of many traits, including competitive drive, a sense of time urgency, and a dangerous mix of anger, cynicism, and hostility (Friedman & Booth-Kewley, 1987; Matthews, 1988). In interviews and questionnaires, Type A people say they tend to walk fast and talk fast, work late hours, interrupt speakers in midsentence, get angry with people who are late, detest waiting in lines, race through yellow lights when they drive, lash out at others in frustration, strive to win at all costs, and save time by doing many things at once.

Type A personality A personality characterized by an impatient, hard-driving, and hostile pattern of behavior.

Type B personality A personality characterized by an easygoing, relaxed pattern of behavior.

Table 18.4 How "Hostile" Is Your Pattern of Behavior?
♦ When in the express checkout line at the supermarket, do you often count the items in the baskets of the people ahead of you to be sure they aren't over the limit?
♦ When an elevator doesn't come as quickly as it should, do your thoughts quickly focus on the inconsiderate behavior of the person on another floor who's holding it up?
♦ When someone criticizes you, do you quickly begin to feel annoyed?
♦ Do you frequently find yourself muttering at the television during a news broadcast?
♦ When you are held up in a slow line in traffic, do you quickly sense your heart pounding and your breath quickening?

Source: R. Williams (1993). Anger kills. New York: Times Books.

Over the years, researchers have found that not all the Type A personality traits are bad. Being time-pressured, competitive, and driven to achieve do not put us at risk. However, the one trait that is toxic and is related to an individual's proneness to CHD is *hostility*—as seen in people who are constantly angry, cynical, and mistrustful of others. People who are often in a negative emotional state are besieged by stress. But because the heart is just a dumb pump and the blood vessels merely hoses, "The cardiovascular stress-response basically consists of making them work harder for a while, and if you do that on a regular basis, they will wear out, just like any pump or hoses you could buy at Sears" (Sapolsky, 1994, p. 42). It's no wonder that, in the long run, a pattern of hostility and anger can be lethal (Siegman & Smith, 1994; Miller et al., 1996). Table 18.4 presents some questions that Redford Williams (1993) uses to help people assess their own level of hostility.

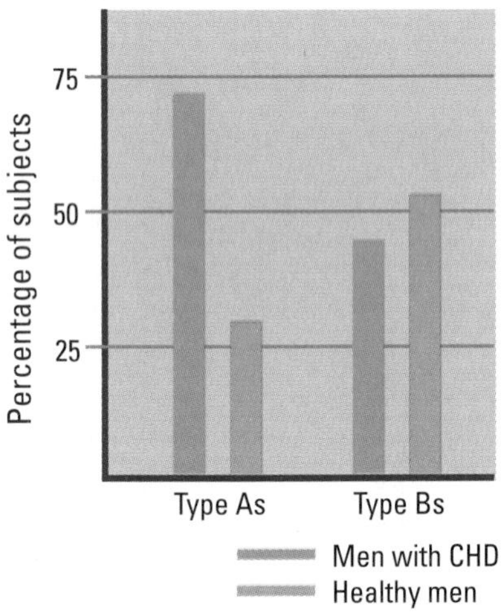

Figure 18.8 Personality and coronary heart disease Studies of middle-age men reveal that Type As are more likely than Type Bs to suffer from CHD (Miller et al., 1991).

The strength of the link between Type A behavior and coronary heart disease depends on how people are diagnosed. After Friedman and Rosenman's original study, many psychologists—in their haste to pursue this vital line of research—tried to identify Type A people using quick, easy-to-administer questionnaires instead of time-consuming interviews. The questionnaires, however, were not as predictive. Apparently, the Type A personality is more evident from a subject's interview *behavior* (whether he or she constantly checks the time, speaks quickly, and interrupts the interviewer) than from his or her *self-reports*. As shown in Figure 18.8, recent research confirms that when interviews are used to make the diagnosis, 70 percent of men who have CHD have a Type A personality—compared to only 46 percent of those who are healthy (Miller et al., 1991).

What explains the connection between Type A behavior and coronary heart disease? As shown in Figure 18.9, one explanation is that Type As are less health-

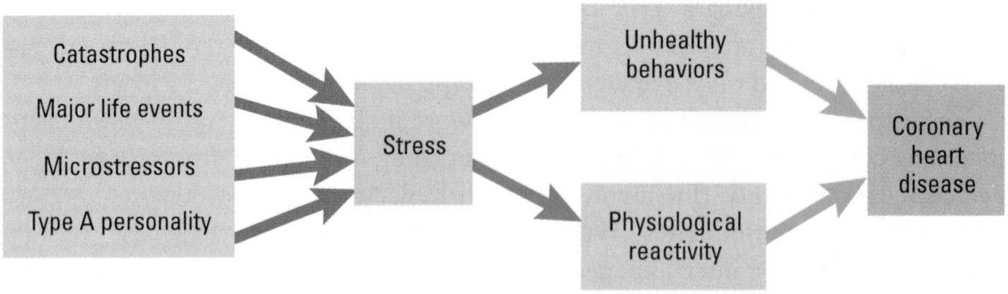

Figure 18.9 Pathways from stress to CHD Under stress, people (1) engage in less healthy behaviors (they smoke more, sleep less, and consume more caffeine and alcohol), and (2) are more physiologically reactive (they exhibit larger increases in pulse rate, blood pressure, and adrenaline level).

conscious than Type Bs. They tend to smoke more, consume more caffeine and alcohol, exercise less, sleep less, eat less healthy foods, and also be less likely to comply with health advice from doctors (Leiker & Hailey, 1988; Siegler, 1994). A second explanation is that Type A people are physiologically more reactive than Type Bs are. In tense social situations, they tend to react with greater increases in pulse rate, blood pressure, and adrenaline—a hormone that accelerates the build-up of fatty plaques on the artery walls, causing a hardening of the arteries (Krantz & Manuck, 1984; Harbin, 1989; Blascovich & Katkin, 1993; Suls & Wan, 1993).

INTERSECTION

HEALTH AND WELL-BEING AND ENVIRONMENT

Type A and B Cities: The Pace of Life and Death

In the 1950s, cardiologists Meyer Friedman and Ray Rosenman stumbled upon the idea that psychological stress may play a role in heart disease. They focused on *individuals* who differ in their Type A and B patterns of behavior. But is it also possible that the different orientations are triggered by the *environment* we live in?

Clearly, some places are more crowded, noisy, crime-ridden, drug-infested, and stressful than others. And clearly there are ways in which such unhealthy environments can "get under the skin" (Taylor et al., 1997). Are some places more than others likely to elicit Type A behavior? Anyone who has been to Wall Street and stood on the crowded floor of the New York Stock Exchange will vividly recall the frantic pace, the running, the noise, and the flashing stream of stock prices changing from one moment to the next. In contrast, anyone who has enjoyed an early morning stroll in a small rural town will recall an experience of calm and relaxation. It's hard to believe that these settings coexist on the same planet. This comparison does suggest, however, that just as we may be predisposed by our personalities to exhibit Type A or Type B behavior, environments can also lead us to behave in ways that pose more or less of a health risk.

Frantic, time-urgent, Type A behavior is a way of life on the floor of the New York Stock Exchange.

Do cities around the world, or even inside the borders of the United States, have different tempos? Do New Yorkers really live life in the fast lane? Are Californians as laid back as the popular image suggests? Indeed, can the pace of city life be measured, and, if so, how does it relate to the incidence of heart disease among inhabitants? Interested in these questions, Robert Levine (1990) examined thirty-six American cities of various sizes, nine from each of four regions (Northeast, Midwest, South, and West). Within each city, Levine determined the pace of life by collecting and then combining four measures: (1) the walking speed of downtown pedestrians on a clear summer weekday, (2) the amount of time it took bank tellers to fulfill a simple request for change, (3) the talking speed of postal clerks responding to a standardized question, and (4) the percentage of adults on the street wearing wristwatches. Levine also examined health statistics on the local death rates from heart disease (adjusted in each city for the average age of the population).

As you can see in Figure 18.10, the northeastern cities that were sampled had the fastest pace of life (the fastest cities, in order, were Boston, Buffalo, and New York), and the western cities on average had the slowest (the slowest cities, in order, were Los Angeles, Shreveport, Memphis, and San Diego). More important, the correlations showed that the quicker the pace, the higher was the incidence among inhabitants of death from heart disease. Think for a moment about this result. Why are

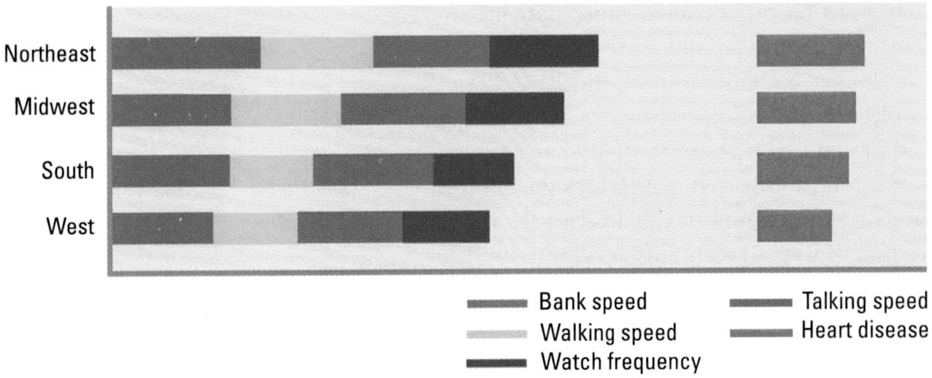

Figure 18.10 The pace of life in the different regions

has to acquire the classic Type A behavior pattern in order to cope with life in the Northeast). Another alternative is that people who are Type As seek out fast cities to live in, while those who are Type Bs migrate to slower-paced lifestyles. Still another interpretation is that the fast-paced cities tend to be found in colder climates, which means less active time outdoors or perhaps more cigarette smoking or other stress-reducing but harmful habits. Whatever the explanation, the link between the pace of city life and heart disease prompted Levine to suggest that the environment in which we live can be used to predict aspects of our health.

the residents of fast-paced environments more prone to heart disease? From the correlations alone, it is impossible to tell. One interpretation is that a city's pace causes inhabitants to develop the kinds of personality traits that are necessary for survival (in other words, maybe one

The Immune System

When it comes to the interaction between mind and body, the link between stress and the heart is just the tip of the iceberg. It now appears that stress also increases the risk of chronic back pain, diabetes, arthritis, appendicitis, upper respiratory infections, herpes, gum disease, the common cold, and some forms of cancer. How can stress have this wide range of disabling effects? Answer: By compromising the body's immune system—the first line of defense against illness (Glaser & Kiecolt-Glaser, 1994).

The **immune system** is a complex surveillance system that fights bacteria, viruses, parasites, fungi, and other "nonself" substances that invade the body. The system consists of more than a trillion specialized white blood cells called **lymphocytes** that originate in the bone marrow (*B cells*) and thymus (*T cells*), migrate to various organs, circulate through the bloodstream, and secrete chemical antibodies. These sharklike search-and-destroy cells protect us by patrolling the body twenty-four hours a day and attacking trespassers. Yet on occasion, they overreact and strike at benign material. This can result in "autoimmune" diseases such as multiple sclerosis, trigger allergic reactions to harmless pollen and ragweed, and cause the body to reject surgically transplanted organs. The immune system is also equipped with large scavenger cells known as *macrophages* ("big eaters") and *natural killer cells* (NK cells) that zero in on viruses and cancerous tumors. Serving as a sixth sense for foreign invaders, the immune system continually renews itself. During the few seconds it takes to read this sentence, your body will have produced 10 million new lymphocytes (see Figure 18.11).

immune system A biological surveillance system that detects and destroys "nonself" substances that invade the body.

lymphocytes Specialized white blood cells that secrete chemical antibodies and facilitate the immune response.

Many health psychologists—specializing in the new subfield of psychoneuroimmunology, or PNI—are now studying connections among the brain, behavior, and the immune system. Before we get into some of the fascinating results, let's pause for a moment and consider three of the methods that these researchers use to spy on the

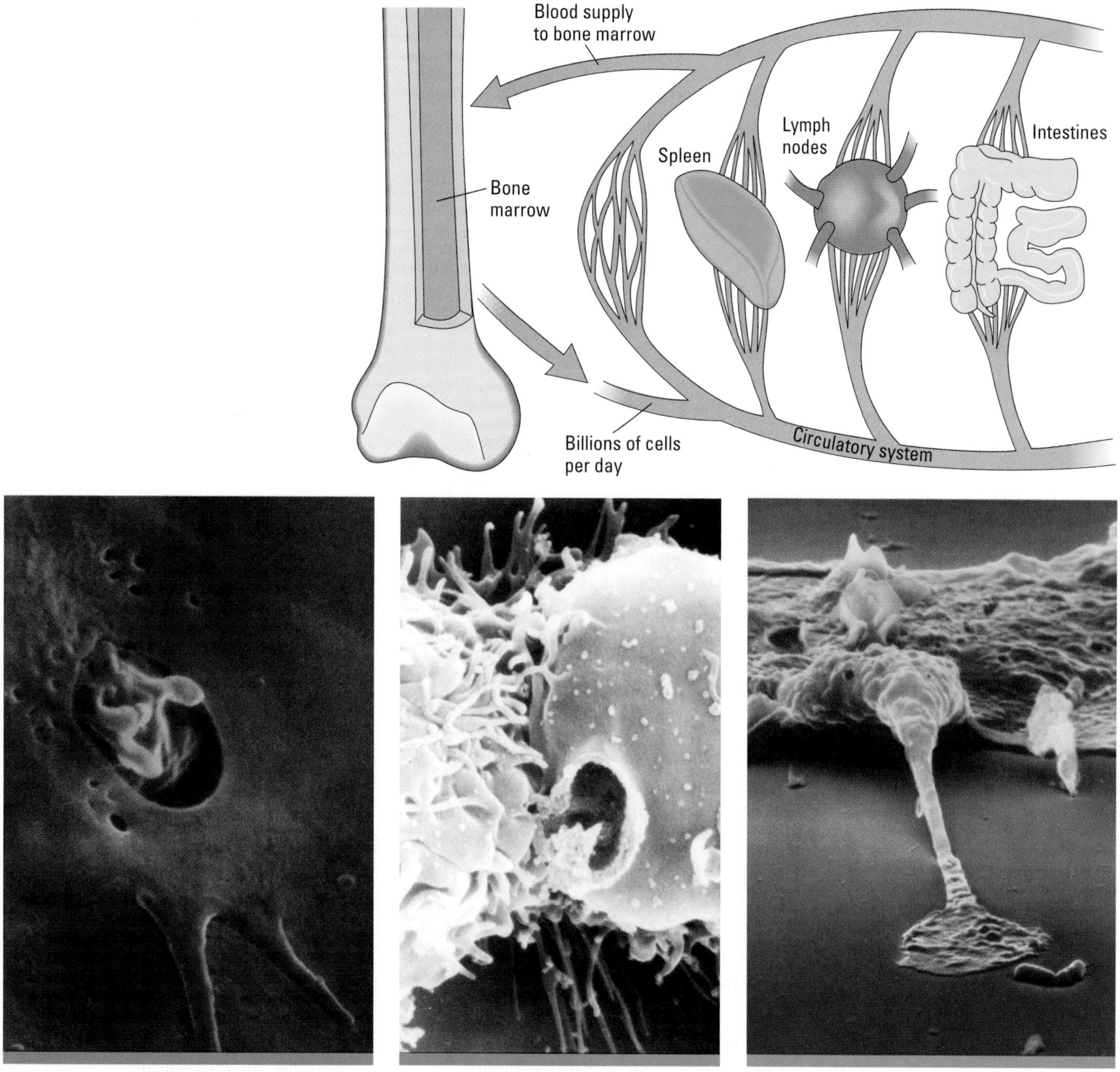

Figure 18.11 The immune system Originating in the bone marrow, lymphocytes move into certain organs and circulate continuously through the bloodstream. As pictured, a B cell migrates from the bone marrow to a blood vessel (left), a killer T cell locates and attacks a tumor cell (center), and a large macrophage prepares to trap and ingest a tiny bacterium (right).

operations of the immune system. One method is to take blood samples from animal or human subjects exposed to varying degrees of stress and simply count the numbers of lymphocytes and other white blood cells circulating in the bloodstream. A second is to extract blood, add cancerous tumor cells to the mix, and measure the extent to which the NK cells destroy the tumors. A third method is to "challenge" the living organism by injecting a foreign agent into the skin and measuring the amount of swelling that arises at the site of the injection. The more swelling there is, the more potent the immune reaction is assumed to be (Ader et al., 1991; Maier et al., 1994; Cohen & Herbert, 1996).

What Stress Does to the Immune System It's now clear that stress can affect the immune system, at least temporarily. The medical community used to reject the idea, but no longer. What changed? At first, animal experiments showed that rats exposed to noise, overcrowding, or inescapable shocks, and that primates separated from their social companions, exhibit a drop in immune-cell activity compared to nonexposed animals (Coe, 1993; Moynihan & Ader, 1996). A link was also observed in human subjects. Intrigued by the fact that people often become sick and die shortly after they are widowed, R. W. Barthrop and his colleagues (1977) took blood samples from twenty-six men and women whose spouses had just died. Compared to nonwidowed controls, these grief-stricken spouses exhibited a weakened immune response, as measured by T-cell activity. This was the first demonstration of its kind.

Additional studies soon revealed weakened immune responses in NASA astronauts after their reentry into the atmosphere and splashdown, in subjects deprived of sleep for a prolonged period of time, in students in the midst of final exams, in men and women recently divorced or separated, in people who are caring for a family member with Alzheimer's disease, in snake phobics exposed to a live snake, and in workers who had just lost their jobs (O'Leary, 1990). Even in the laboratory, subjects who are given complex arithmetic problems to solve or painful stimuli to tolerate exhibit changes in immune-cell activity—and these changes last for one or more hours after the stress has subsided (Cohen & Herbert, 1996).

In a particularly intriguing study, Arthur Stone and others (1994) paid forty-eight adult volunteers to take a harmless but novel protein pill every day for twelve weeks—a substance that would lead the immune system to respond by producing an antibody. Every day, the subjects completed a diary in which they reported on their moods and on experiences at work, at home, in financial matters, in leisure activities, and in relationships with their friends, spouses, and children. The subjects also gave daily saliva samples that were later used to measure the amount of the antibody that was produced. The results were striking, as are their implications: The more positive events subjects had in a given day, the more antibody was produced. The more negative the events, the less antibody was produced. In a direct way, daily experiences can strengthen or weaken our immune system's ability to protect us from illness.

We have seen that psychological states can "get into" the immune system. But how? To be sure, certain organs that play a key role in the immune system (the thymus, bone marrow, and lymph nodes) are richly endowed with nerve fibers, providing a direct pipeline to the brain. But what explains the link between stress and the activity of the lymphocytes? As illustrated in Figure 18.12, there are two possible ways this can happen. First, as described earlier, people who are stressed tend to smoke more, use more alcohol and drugs, sleep less, exercise less, and have poorer diets—behaviors that compromise the immune system. For example, one study showed that when healthy male adults were kept awake between 3:00 and 7:00 AM, natural-killer-cell activity diminished—and it returned to normal only after a full night of uninterrupted sleep (Irwin et al., 1994). Second, stress triggers the release of adrenaline and other stress hormones into the bloodstream—and these hormones suppress lymphocyte activity (Dhabhar & McEwen, 1995). The result is a temporary lowering of the body's resistance and increased susceptibility to illness (Cohen & Williamson, 1991).

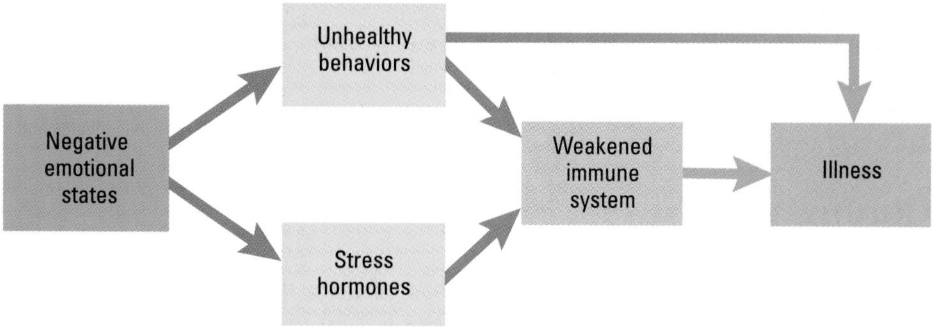

Figure 18.12 Pathways from stress to illness Negative emotional states may cause illness in two ways: (1) by promoting unhealthful behaviors (more alcohol, less sleep, and so on) and (2) by triggering the release of hormones that weaken the immune system by suppressing activity of the lymphocytes.

The Link between Stress and Illness At the start of this chapter, we saw that subjects who had reported high rather than low levels of everyday stress were more likely to catch a common cold after exposure to a cold virus (Cohen et al., 1991). This study is important because it demonstrated not only that stress can weaken the immune system but also that, as a result, it can leave us vulnerable to illness. Does stress have similar effects on more serious illnesses? Can it, for example, hasten the spread of cancer?

In an early test of this hypothesis, Madeline Visintainer and others (1982) implanted tumorous cancer cells into laboratory rats, some of whom were then repeatedly exposed to shocks they could not escape. After one month, 50 percent of the animals not shocked died of cancer. Yet relative to that baseline, the death rate climbed to 73 percent among those subjected to the inescapable shock. This study was among the first to show that psychological states—such as a feeling of helplessness—can influence the spread of cancer.

The growth of tumors in helpless white laboratory rats is interesting, but does the same principle apply to people? For obvious ethical reasons, researchers cannot fill human subjects with despair or inject lethal tumors into their bodies to test the cause-and-effect chain directly. But they can examine the medical records of people whose lives are struck by tragedy. Investigations of this sort have revealed that cancer appears more often than normal in people prone to being in a negative emotional state (Sklar & Anisman, 1981). In one large-scale study, investigators looked up 2,000 male workers of the Western Electric Company in Chicago whose personalities had been assessed in 1958. At the time, test scores indicated that some of the men were low in self-esteem, unhappy, and depressed. The result? Some twenty years later, these men were more likely than their coworkers to have died of cancer (Persky et al., 1987). Let's be clear about what these results mean. Nobody disputes the notion that cancer is caused by exposure to toxic substances and other biological factors. But individuals who are clinically depressed or under great stress have weakened immune systems—which, in some cases, may result in a higher death rate from cancer and other killer diseases (Herbert & Cohen, 1993; Andersen et al., 1994).

Toward the end of his life, Albert Schweitzer was asked for his opinion of traditional African medicine and the witch doctors who practice it. His reply: "The witch doctor succeeds for the same reason all the rest of us succeed. Each patient carries his own doctor inside him." More recently, Robert Ornstein and David Sobel (1987) referred to the human brain as an "internal pharmacy dispensing a stream

Following their nine days in orbit, these NASA astronauts pose soon after touching ground. Given what is known about the link between stress and immunity, their immune responses may have been in a weakened state when this picture was taken.

of powerful drugs" (p. 89). Whether it involves pharmacists or doctors, psychoneuroimmunology research suggests that the key is to find ways for each of us to tap our own inner resources.

Coping with Stress

Is it adaptive to block unwanted thoughts and emotions from awareness? Are relaxation and exercise truly healthful? What is the role played by feelings of control and optimism? Why is it said that friendships and other forms of social support are vital to our health and well-being?

Stress is inevitable. No one can prevent it. But we can try to minimize its harmful effects on our health. To understand how some people keep their composure while others crumble under the pressure, it is useful to examine the *coping* process and ask the question: What are some adaptive ways to cope with stress?

Coping Strategies

Leaving home. Taking exams. Breaking up with my college sweetheart. Working long nights on my thesis. Seeking employment in a competitive job market. Having children. Raising children. Facing academic pressures to publish or perish. Struggling to meet the deadline to complete this text. I could have coped with these sources of stress in any number of ways. In each case, I might have focused on solving the problem, talked to friends, invited distractions to pass the time, drunk myself silly, smiled and pretended that all was well—or I could have just freaked out.

Richard Lazarus and Susan Folkman (1984) distinguished two general types of coping strategies. The first is *problem-focused coping*, designed to reduce stress by overcoming the source of the problem. Difficulties in school? Study harder, hire a tutor, or reduce your workload. Marriage on the rocks? Talk it out or see a counselor. Problems at work? Consult with your boss or look for another job. The goal is to attack the source of your stress. A second approach is *emotion-focused coping,* in which one tries to manage the emotional turmoil, perhaps by learning to live with the problem rather than changing it. If you're struggling at school, at work, or in a relationship, you can keep a stiff upper lip and ignore the situation or make the best of it. According to Lazarus and Folkman, people take an active problem-focused approach when they think they can overcome the stressor, but they fall back on an emotion-focused approach when they see the problem as out of their control.

Thought Suppression One emotion-focused strategy people often use is to block stressful thoughts and feelings from awareness. I have used this strategy myself. As I recline in the dentist's chair with my mouth wide open and a bright light blinding my eyes, the sound of the drill and the grinding on my teeth send chills up my spine. To cope, I try to lock eyes with a gigantic toothbrush hanging on the wall or imagine that I'm lying on a warm, sunny beach. Ignore the noise and the pain, I say to myself. Think about something else.

This strategy, which is a form of *thought suppression*, can have a peculiar, paradoxical effect. Daniel Wegner (1994) conducted a series of experiments in which he had subjects say whatever came to mind into a microphone—and told half of them not to think about a white bear. As described in Chapter 4, Wegner found that subjects could not keep the image from popping to mind. What's more, he found that when subjects were permitted later to think about a white bear, those who had earlier tried to suppress the image were unusually preoccupied with it, providing evidence of a "rebound" effect. It is difficult to follow the command "Don't think about it"—and the harder you try, the less likely you are to succeed. The solution: focused self-distraction. In one study, Wegner told subjects to imagine a tiny red Volkswagen whenever the forbidden white bear intruded into consciousness, and the rebound effect vanished.

Try not to think of a white bear, and this image is likely to intrude upon consciousness with remarkable frequency.

What do white bears and red cars have to do with coping? Lots. When people try to force stressful thoughts or painful sensations out of awareness, they are doomed to fail. In fact, the problem may worsen. That's where focused self-distraction comes in. In a study of pain tolerance, Delia Cioffi and James Holloway (1993) had subjects put a hand into a bucket of ice-cold water and keep it there until they could no longer bear the pain. One group was instructed to avoid thinking about the sensation. A second group was told to form a mental picture of their room at home. Afterward, subjects who had coped through suppression were slower to recover from the pain than were those who used focused self-distraction. To manage stress—whether it's caused by physical pain, a strained romance, final exams, or problems at work—distraction ("think about lying on the beach") is a better coping strategy than mere suppression ("don't think about the dentist's drill").

It may be particularly maladaptive to keep secrets and hold in strong emotions. More than 100 years ago, Breuer and Freud (1895) theorized that emotional inhibition, or what they called strangulated affect, can cause mental illness. Current studies suggest it may be physically taxing as well. In the laboratory, James Gross and Robert Levenson (1997) showed female students funny, sad, and neutral films. Half the time, they instructed subjects to not let their feelings show. From a hidden camera, videotapes confirmed that when asked to conceal their feelings, subjects were less expressive. But physiological recordings revealed that as they watched the funny and sad films, subjects had a greater cardiovascular response when they tried to inhibit their feelings than when they did not. Physiologically, the effort to suppress the display of emotion backfired.

A recent study by Steve Cole and others (1996) pushes this point a suggestive but profound step further. These investigators identified eighty gay men in the Los Angeles area who were newly infected with the HIV virus but had no symptoms, administered various psychological tests, and monitored their progress every six months for nine years. They found that in men who were partly "in the closet"—compared to those who were completely open about their homosexuality—the infection spread more rapidly, causing them to die sooner. This correlation does not *prove* that "coming out" is healthier than "staying in," but it is consistent with other studies demonstrating the harmful effects of actively concealing one's thoughts and feelings.

Relaxation There are also ways to manage the physical symptoms of stress. One popular technique is *relaxation*. Years ago, cardiologist Herbert Benson (1975) recruited experienced meditators for a study and fitted them with various physiological measurement devices—including catheters in the veins and arteries. Subjects spent twenty minutes in a quiet resting state, then meditated, then returned to a normal state. There were no observable changes in their posture or level of physical activity. But the physiological results were striking. While meditating, subjects consumed 17 percent less oxygen—and also produced less carbon dioxide. Breathing

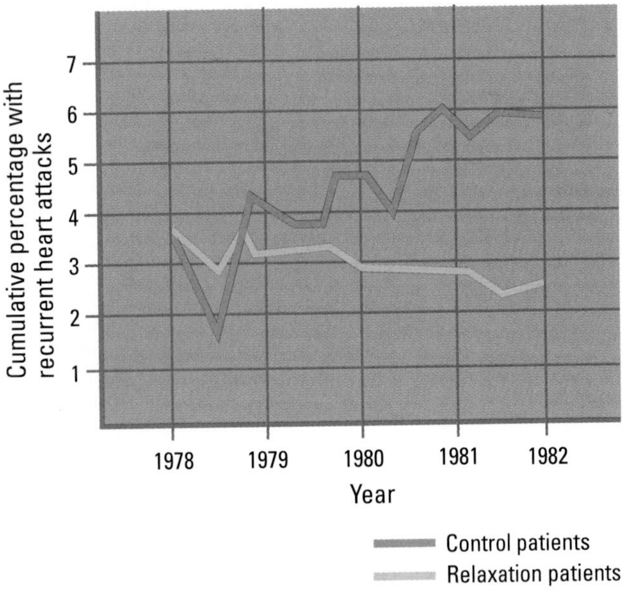

Figure 18.13 Relaxation and the heart After three years, heart-attack victims who were taught to relax their pace suffered fewer recurrences than did those who received only standard medical advice (Friedman & Ulmer, 1984).

slowed from fourteen or fifteen breaths per minute to ten or eleven breaths per minute. Blood tests showed there was a marked drop in the amount of lactate, a chemical typically associated with anxiety. Finally, brain-wave patterns were slower than those normally found in the waking state.

According to Benson, who went on to establish the Mind/Body Medical Institute at Harvard Medical School, anyone can be taught this "relaxation response." Try it. Sit quietly and comfortably, close your eyes, and relax all the muscles from your feet to your face. Then breathe deeply through the nose, and each time you exhale, silently utter some word (such as "one . . . one . . . one . . ."). As you proceed, let your mind drift freely. If anxiety-provoking thoughts pop into mind, refocus your attention on the word you are chanting and stay calm. Repeat this exercise once or twice a day, for ten to twenty minutes. Says Benson (1993), "By practicing two basic steps—the repetition of a sound, word, phrase, prayer, or muscular activity; and a passive return to the repetition whenever distracting thoughts recur—you can trigger a series of physiological changes that offer protection against stress" (p. 256).

Meditative relaxation can be powerfully effective. In one study, Friedman and Ulmer (1984) randomly assigned hundreds of heart attack patients to one of two treatment groups. In one group, they received standard medical advice on drugs, exercise, work, and diet. In the second group, they were also counseled on how to relax, slow down their pace, smile more, and take time to enjoy the moment. After three years, the relaxation patients had suffered only half as many repeat heart attacks as those in the control group (see Figure 18.13). In another study, Janice Kiecolt-Glaser and others (1985) found that relaxation can also fortify the immune system. Among a group of senior citizens, those who were trained in relaxation three times a week for one month felt better—and exhibited an increase in natural-killer-cell activity—compared to others in a no-treatment control group.

Aerobic Exercise A second way to manage stress is through *aerobic exercise*—sustained, vigorous physical activity designed to build heart and lung capacity and to enhance the body's use of oxygen. Walking, running, swimming, bicycling, cross-country skiing, and dancing are ideal forms of aerobic exercise. The health benefits seem clear. One large-scale study showed that men who burned at least 2,000 calories a week through exercise lived longer than those who were less active (Paffenbarger et al., 1986). Another study of both men and women showed that even a moderate amount of exercise is associated with increased longevity (Blair et al., 1989).

> *"Those who think they have not time for bodily exercise will sooner or later have to find time for illness."*
>
> — EDWARD STANLEY

Don't jump from these correlations to the causal conclusion that if you start running you'll live longer. It is possible, for example, that people who exercise regularly are also more health-conscious about eating, smoking, wearing seat belts, and other factors that contribute to longevity. Still, the effects of exercise on physical health are extensive. Research shows that exercise strengthens the heart, lowers blood pressure, aids in the metabolism of fats and carbohydrates, boosts self-esteem, elevates mood, and improves cognitive functioning (Simon, 1991). In a study involving mildly depressed female students, Lisa McCann and David Holmes (1984) randomly assigned some to take part in a ten-week aerobic-exercise program and others to a ten-week program of relaxation exercises. A third group received no treatment. Afterward, those who exercised were the most improved, scoring lowest on a measure of depression.

Physical fitness can also soften the toxic effects of stress on health. To demonstrate, Jonathon Brown (1991) brought college students into the laboratory, tested their aerobic fitness on an exercise bicycle, inquired about recent stressful events, and counted the number of illness visits they made to the university health center that year. The result: Life stress was linked to illness only among students who were out of shape. Those who were more physically fit absorbed more stress without an increase in illness (see Figure 18.14).

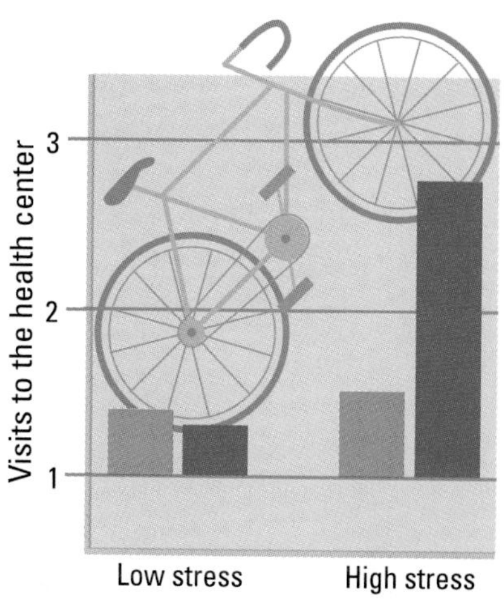

Figure 18.14 Fitness, stress, and health In a study of college students, life stress was associated with more visits to the health center among students low in aerobic fitness. Those who were high in fitness absorbed the stress with less illness (Brown, 1991).

The "Self-healing Personality"

For years, psychologists have speculated about very specific correlations between personality traits and illness. People who are anxious are doomed to get ulcers, we're told, just as angry types are prone to headaches, depressives are prone to cancer, weak and dependent types suffer from asthma, and workaholics die of heart attacks. In light of recent work on psychology and the immune system, others have considered the alternative possibility that there's a generic "disease-prone personality" consisting of a cluster of negative emotional states. According to this view, anger, anxiety, hostility, and depression all lead us to complain of bodily ailments (Watson & Pennebaker, 1989) and perhaps put us at risk for a whole range of illnesses (Friedman & Booth-Kewley, 1987). Whether the links are specific or general is a matter of dispute. However, most health researchers believe that certain traits are healthier and more adaptive than others (Adler & Matthews, 1994)—and that there is, in essence, a "self-healing personality" (Friedman, 1991).

Hardiness

Stress affects people differently, an observation that led Suzanne Kobasa (1979) to wonder why some of us are more resilient than others. Kobasa studied 200 business executives who were under stress. Many said they were frequently sick, affirming the link between stress and illness; others had managed to stay healthy. The two groups were similar in terms of age, education, job status, income, and ethnic and religious background. But from various tests, it was clear that they differed in their attitudes toward themselves, their jobs, and the people in their lives. Based on these differences, Kobasa identified a personality style she called **hardiness** and concluded that hardy people have three characteristics: (1) *commitment*, a sense of purpose with regard to work, family, and other domains; (2) *challenge*, an openness to new experiences and a desire to embrace change; and (3) *control*, the belief that one has the power to influence important future outcomes.

In general, research supports the point that hardiness acts as a buffer against stress (Funk, 1992)—and that control is the active ingredient. Studies have shown that the harmful effects of noise, crowding, heat, and other stressors are reduced when people think they can exert control over these aspects of their environment. Thus, rats exposed to electric shock are less likely to develop ulcers if they are trained to know they can avoid it; children awaiting a doctor's injection cope better when they're prepared with a pain-reducing cognitive strategy; nursing-home residents become healthier and more active when they're given more control over daily events; and patients with cancer, AIDS, and coronary heart disease are better adjusted, emotionally, when they think that they can influence the course of their illness (Rodin, 1986; Helgeson, 1992; Reed et al., 1993; Thompson et al., 1993).

hardiness A personality style that is characterized by commitment, challenge, and control and acts as a buffer against stress.

Optimism and Hope A second important trait in the self-healing personality is *optimism*, defined as a generalized tendency to expect positive outcomes. Are *you* an optimist or a pessimist? Do you look on the bright side and expect good things to happen, or do you tend to believe in Murphy's Law, that if something can go wrong, it will? By asking questions like these, Michael Scheier and Charles Carver (1985) categorized college students along this dimension and found that dispositional optimists reported fewer illness symptoms during the semester than did pessimists. Correlations between optimism and health are common. Other studies have shown that optimists are more likely to take a problem-focused approach to coping with stress; complete a rehabilitation program for alcoholics; make a quicker, fuller recovery from coronary-artery bypass surgery; and, among gay men concerned about AIDS, take a more active, less avoidant approach to the threat (Scheier & Carver, 1992).

"Cheerfulness is the very flower of health."

— JAPANESE PROVERB

In a book entitled *Learned Optimism*, Martin Seligman (1991) argues that optimism and pessimism are rooted in our "explanatory styles"—in the ways we explain good and bad events. Based on a large number of studies (Sweeney et al., 1986; Abramson et al., 1989), Seligman described the typical pessimist as someone who attributes failure to factors that are internal ("It was my fault"), permanent ("I'm all washed up"), and global ("I'm bad at everything")—and success to factors that are external ("I lucked out"), temporary ("The task was easy"), and specific ("It was my strength"). This explanatory style breeds despair and low self-esteem. In contrast, the typical optimist is someone who makes the opposite attributions. According to Seligman, optimists blame failure on factors that are external, temporary, and specific, while crediting success to factors that are internal, permanent, and global—an explanatory style that fosters hope, effort, and a high regard for oneself. Do *you* interpret events as an optimist or as a pessimist? Imagine the situations described in Table 18.5 and circle cause A or B—whichever you think is most likely. When you've finished, count the number of points you earned (in parentheses). A score of 0 indicates a high degree of pessimism; a score of 8 indicates a high degree of optimism (Seligman, 1991).

In the course of a lifetime, everyone has setbacks. Do optimists weather the storms better? Are they happier, healthier, and more successful? Do they have, in the words of Alan McGinnis (1987, p. 16), "the gift for turning stumbling blocks into stepping stones"? To find out, Christopher Peterson and others (1988) collected personal essays that were written in the 1940s by ninety-nine men who had just graduated from Harvard, and they analyzed these materials to determine what each subject's explanatory style was in his youth. Were these men optimists or pessimists? What eventually happened to them? Their health at age sixty was predictable from their explanatory styles thirty-five years earlier. Young optimists were healthier than young pessimists later in life. Why? A later study by Leslie Kamen-Siegel and colleagues (1991) provides a clue. These researchers measured explanatory style, took blood samples, and found that pessimists had a weaker immune response than optimists.

There's an old saying "While there's life, there's hope." It's possible that the opposite is also true: "While there's hope, there's life." In a remarkable illustration of this point, Susan Everson and others (1996) studied 2,428 middle-age men in Finland. Based on the extent to which they agreed with two simple statements ("I feel that it is impossible to reach the goals I would like to strive for" and "The future seems hopeless, and I can't believe that things are changing for the better"), the men were initially classified as having a high, medium, or low sense of hopelessness. When the investigators checked the death records roughly six years later, they found that the more hopeless the men were at the start, the more likely they were to have

Table 18.5 Explanatory-Styles Test

1. You forget your boyfriend's (girlfriend's) birthday:
   A. I'm not good at remembering birthdays. (0)
   B. I was preoccupied with other things. (1)
2. You stop a crime by calling the police:
   A. A strange noise caught my attention. (0)
   B. I was alert that day. (1)
3. You were extremely healthy all year:
   A. Few people around me were sick, so I wasn't exposed. (0)
   B. I made sure I ate well and got enough rest. (1)
4. You fail an important examination:
   A. I wasn't as smart as the others taking the exam. (0)
   B. I didn't prepare for it well. (1)
5. You ask someone to dance, and he (she) says no:
   A. I am not a good enough dancer. (0)
   B. He (she) doesn't like to dance. (1)
6. You gain weight over the holidays and you can't lose it:
   A. Diets don't work in the long run. (0)
   B. The diet I tried didn't work. (1)
7. You win the lottery:
   A. It was pure chance. (0)
   B. I picked the right numbers. (1)
8. You do extremely well in a job interview:
   A. I felt extremely confident during the interview. (0)
   B. I interview well. (1)

Source: M. E. P. Seligman (1991). Learned optimism. New York: Knopf.

died of various causes—even when the men were otherwise equated for their age and prior health status. Compared to those who were low in hopelessness, the highs were more than twice as likely to die from cancer and four times more likely to die of cardiovascular disease (see Figure 18.15).

As usual, we should be cautious in interpreting correlations—in this case, between optimism, pessimism, and longevity. Assuming that optimism is adaptive, however, and that it's better to be safe than sorry, Seligman (1991) believes that pessimists can be retrained—not through "mindless devices like whistling a happy tune" but by learning a new set of cognitive skills. According to Seligman, people can train themselves to make optimistic explanations by following three steps: (1) think about situations of adversity (losing in a sports competition, having a friend not return your calls); (2) consider the way you normally explain these events, and if it is pessimistic ("I always choke under pressure," "My friend does not really care about me"); then (3) dispute these explanations by looking closely at the facts ("My opponent played a great game," "My friend has been very busy"). Practice this exercise over and over again. You may find that changing a pessimistic outlook is like breaking a bad habit.

Social Support

We hear it all the time: No man (or woman) is an island, human beings are social animals, people need people, and to get by you need a little help from your friends. Is all this true? Do close family ties, lovers, buddies, community support groups, and

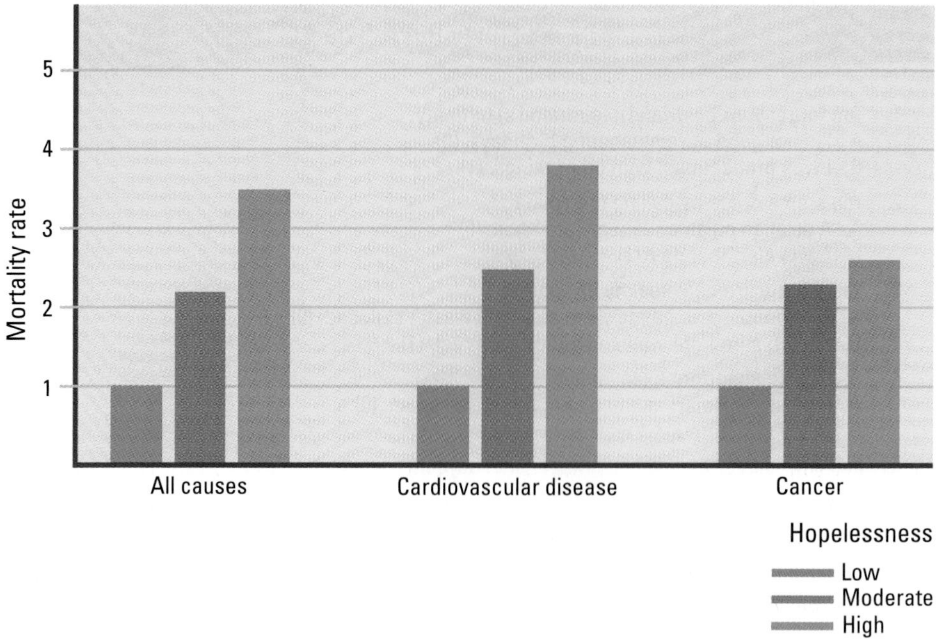

Figure 18.15 Hopelessness and the risk of death Among middle-age men in Finland, those who were initially high rather than low in hopelessness were more likely to die within six years—overall, from cancer, and from cardiovascular disease. On these same measures of mortality, those who were moderate in hopelessness fell between the two extremes.

relationships at work serve as a buffer against stress? The truth is: yes. An overwhelming amount of evidence now shows that **social support** has therapeutic effects on our psychological and physical health (Wills, 1990; Uchino et al., 1996).

Psychiatrist David Spiegel, of the Stanford University School of Medicine, came to appreciate the value of social connections several years ago when he organized support groups for women with advanced breast cancer. The groups met weekly in ninety-minute sessions to laugh, cry, share stories, and discuss ways of coping. Spiegel had fully expected the women to benefit, emotionally, from the experience. But he found something else he did not expect: These women lived an average of eighteen months longer than did similar others who did not attend these groups. According to Spiegel (1993), "The added survival time was longer than any medication or other known medical treatment could be expected to provide for women with breast cancer so far advanced" (pp. 331–332).

Similar discoveries were also made by other researchers. In one study, Lisa Berkman and Leonard Syme (1979) surveyed 7,000 residents of Alameda County, California, conducted a nine-year follow-up of mortality rates, and found that the more social contacts people had, the longer they lived. In fact, those who lived alone, had very few close friends or relatives, and did not participate in community groups died at a rate two to five times greater than those with more extensive social networks. This was true of both men and women, young and old, rich and poor, and people from all racial and ethnic backgrounds. James House and his colleagues (1988) then studied 2,754 adults interviewed during visits to their doctors. He found that the most socially active men were two to three times less likely to die within nine to twelve years than those of similar age who were more isolated. Socially active women were almost two times less likely to die. According to House, social isolation, statistically, is as predictive of early death as smoking or high cholesterol.

social support The healthful coping resources provided by friends and other people.

Research findings like these are now common. Married people are more likely than unmarried people to survive cancer for five years (Taylor, 1990), gay men infected with HIV are less likely to contemplate suicide if they have close ties than if they do not (Schneider et al., 1991), and people who have a heart attack are less likely to have a second one if they're living with someone than if they live alone (Case et al., 1992). Among students stressed by schoolwork and among the spouses of cancer patients, more social support is also associated with a stronger immune response (Baron et al., 1990; Jemmott & Magloire, 1988). Based on their review of eighty-one studies, Bert Uchino, John Cacioppo, and Janice Kiecolt-Glaser (1996) concluded that in times of stress, social support lowers blood pressure, lessens the secretion of stress hormones, and strengthens immune responses. There's no doubt about it: Being isolated from other people is hazardous to your health.

Human beings are inherently social creatures. Close and intimate relationships provide us with a buffer against stress and illness. *(Brancusi, Constantin (Rumanian, 1876–1957), "The Kiss," 1916. H: 23 inches, W: 13 inches, D: 10 inches. Limestone. Philadelphia Museum of Art: The Louise and Walter Arensberg Collection. Photo by Graydon Wood, 1994.)*

Our social connections can be therapeutic for many reasons. Friends encourage us to get out, exercise, eat regularly, or seek professional help. Emotionally, friends offer sympathy and reassurance in times of stress. Perhaps having a good friend around boosts our confidence, self-esteem, and sense of security. On an intellectual level, having someone to talk to provides a sounding board, new perspectives, and advice as we struggle for solutions to problems. Communicating helps us sort things out in our own minds (Clark, 1993).

It's important to talk about upsetting experiences. As we noted in Chapter 17, James Pennebaker (1990) conducted a number of studies in which he had college students talk to a hidden experimenter or into a tape recorder, or else simply write about a trauma they had experienced. While speaking, subjects were physiologically aroused and upset. Many tearfully recounted accidents, failures, instances of sex abuse, loneliness, rape, the divorce of their parents, shattered relationships, death, and their fears about the future. Soon, however, the subjects were feeling better than ever. Blood samples taken after the experiment revealed a heightened immune response relative to their baseline level, and in the ensuing months subjects who had "opened up" made 50 percent fewer visits to the campus health center. A comparison group of students who talked only about trivial matters did not similarly benefit from the experience.

The value of social support may be so basic that *any* bond formed with another living being—even the companionship of a pet—promotes health and survival (Beck & Katcher, 1983). In one study, heart-attack victims who owned pets were more likely to survive the year than those without pets (Friedmann et al., 1980). In a second study, elderly men and women made fewer visits to the doctor in times of stress if they had pet dogs than if they did not (Siegel, 1990). It may be that animals have a calming influence on us and provide a source of comfort. Karen Allen and others (1991) found that when female subjects (all of whom owned pet dogs) worked on a stressful laboratory task, those who had their pets with them became less physiologically aroused (as measured by changes in blood pressure, perspiration, and pulse rate) than those who were alone or had a human friend present. As companions, pets are wonderfully nonjudgmental.

Pets also provide us with companionship and "social" support.

Prospects for the Future

In what ways can we use our minds to protect our health? Why is it important not to overstate the role of psychological factors? When it comes to using psychology to promote health and well-being, what challenges lie ahead?

Psychologists from all areas of the discipline are seeking to better understand the factors that promote human health and well-being. With this goal in mind, they have made tremendous strides in recent years. We now know that self-awareness may lower rather than raise our self-esteem, that it may be healthy to harbor some positive illusions, that daily stress can kill us by overworking the heart and weakening the immune system, that it's unhealthy to suppress negative thoughts and emotions, and that certain coping strategies, a sense of control, hope, and social support can be used to restore the body's natural defenses. The mind is a powerful tool. The more we know about how to use it, the better off we'll be.

Psychology's latest discoveries are exciting, but it is also important to recognize the limitations. Recently established links among mind, behavior, and the immune system, for example, raise the hope that perhaps each of us has the power to slow the spread of cancer and other diseases. This is not an invitation to believe in miracles, however, nor does it mean that we should reject standard medical treatments and try instead to wish away our illnesses. If we smoke, if we're exposed to radiation, if we breathe polluted air or spend too much time baking in the hot sun, the risk of cancer will be increased—regardless of how relaxed, fit, determined, or upbeat we are and regardless of how many friends we have to support us. While appreciating the powers of the mind to influence the body, it's also important to guard against blaming the victims of terminal illness for their condition and making them feel guilty—as if dying were the ultimate failure. As Howard Friedman (1991) put it, "We must walk a fine line between blaming patients on the one hand and absolving them of any role in their health on the other" (p. 96).

Nowhere is this more true than with people who suffer from AIDS. Earlier, we noted that heart attacks, cancer, strokes, and accidents are now more common causes of death than infectious diseases. But AIDS, the first truly global epidemic, continues to spread at an alarming rate (see Figure 18.16). AIDS has been described as a recently exploded microbiological time bomb (Mann, 1992). In 1981, 5 homosexual men in North America were diagnosed with AIDS and were among 189 cases reported that year. By 1996, the number of AIDS cases in North America had skyrocketed to three-quarters of a million—and included heterosexual men, women, and children. And these figures were just the beginning. Worldwide, an estimated 22 million people are currently infected with HIV. The World Health Organization projects that by the year 2000, these numbers will climb even higher. From 1992 to 1996, the numbers stabilized in North America, Australia, and Western Europe, but there was an increase in live cases of 43 percent in Latin America, 37 percent in sub-Saharan Africa, 46 percent in North Africa and the Middle East, 238 percent in Eastern Europe and Central Asia, 261 percent in South and Southeast Asia, and 658 percent in East Asia and the Pacific (Purvis, 1997).

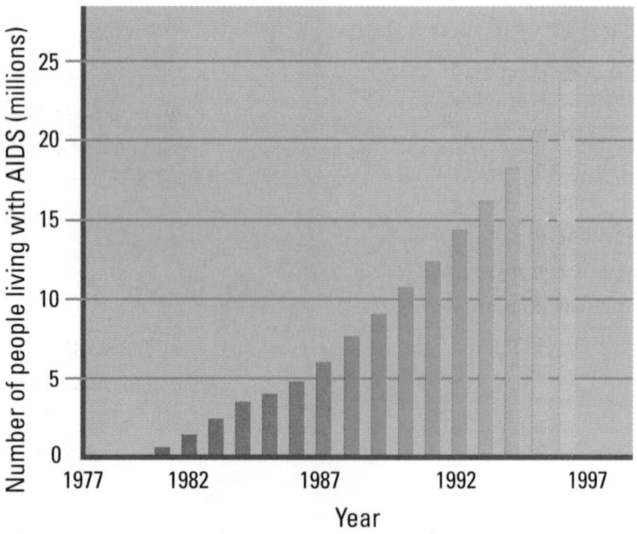

Figure 18.16 AIDS deaths Since the outbreak of AIDS in 1981, the number of cases worldwide has skyrocketed—and continues to do so. As shown, there are now more than 20 million people in the world living with AIDS.

The AIDS virus is transmitted from one person to another in infected blood, semen, vaginal secretions, and other body fluids. People who are HIV-positive may have no symptoms for several years and may not even realize they are infected. Eventually, however, the virus will ravage the immune system by destroying lymphocytes that help ward off disease. What's so scary about AIDS is that it is fatal, that it is increasing at a rate of one new case every few seconds, and that there is no vaccine or satisfactory treatment for it (Greene, 1993).

At present, the only way to control the spread of AIDS is to alter people's beliefs, motivations, and risk-taking behavior (Fisher & Fisher, 1992; Gerrard, Gibbons, & Bushman, 1996)—and that's where psychology comes in. When she was president of the Health Psychology Division of the American Psychological Association, Margaret Chesney (1993) noted that with the coming of the twenty-first century, psychologists need to design programs that will encourage voluntary AIDS testing, provide counseling to assist those who are positively identified, identify the nonbiological factors that influence the progression of AIDS in those who are infected, educate the public about the disease, and convince everyone—particularly adolescents—to limit their sexual activity or use condoms as a means of protection. As always, we can use our minds to help protect our lives.

Summary and Key Terms

Although psychology is a diverse field, all its branches share the objective of improving our health and well-being.

Mind over Matter

The mind's influence on the body, a frequent theme in psychology, can be seen in the placebo effect. Positive expectations increase the release of pain-relieving endorphins and suppress adrenaline and other stress hormones that reduce the body's resistance.

The Self and Well-being

As the "cocktail party effect" demonstrates, the self is an important object of our attention.

The Need for Self-Esteem

People strive to maintain a high level of **self-esteem.** Those with high self-esteem tend to be happy, healthy, and successful. Those with low self-esteem are more anxious, pessimistic, and prone to failure. According to self-discrepancy theory, self-esteem stems from a match between the way we see ourselves and the way we want to see ourselves. If our self-concept falls short of our standards, self-esteem declines. The more discrepancy there is and the more accessible it is to awareness, the more discomfort we feel.

The Self-Awareness "Trap"

According to **self-awareness theory,** certain situations raise our self-awareness and prompt us to compare our behavior to standards, often resulting in a loss of self-esteem. Individuals differ, however, in their tendencies toward self-consciousness. We can cope with self-awareness either by reducing self-discrepancies (trying to make our behavior match our standards) or by escaping from self-awareness. The escape strategy sometimes involves harmful actions such as getting intoxicated.

Positive Illusions

We also cope with inadequacies through **self-deception,** distorting and hiding unpleasant truths from ourselves. People tend to see themselves in favorable and inflated terms. Unrealistic optimism leads us to expect better outcomes for ourselves than for others. One way that people maintain positive illusions is by setting up advance excuses, or **self-handicapping,** to avoid the blame for failure. We also boost our spirits by making **downward social comparisons** with people who do not fare as well as we do.

Are positive illusions adaptive? Some research indicates that people with positive illusions have higher self-esteem, happiness, and health. On the other hand, certain kinds of self-deception can cause self-destructive behaviors, and recent studies suggest that people with inflated views of themselves are liked less by others.

Stress and Health

Researchers have taken a growing interest in **health psychology,** which applies psychology to the promotion of physical health and the prevention and treatment of illness. Among the influences on health, stress is especially important.

The Sources of Stress

Stress is an unpleasant state of arousal that occurs when we perceive that an event threatens our ability to cope. Catastrophes are one major type of stressor. **Posttraumatic**

stress disorder (PTSD) among combat veterans and other trauma victims produces long-lasting symptoms ranging from sleeplessness to social withdrawal.

According to one view, major life events—such as marriage, divorce, or promotion—cause stress. Research does show a link between negative life events and health problems, but no such connection for positive events. It's also important to recognize that people interpret events differently.

Daily hassles—microstressors—can have even more impact than major life events. Job pressures may cause burnout. Environmental factors such as crowding also play a role.

The Physiological Effects of Stress

Selye saw the body's response to stress as a **general adaptation syndrome** marked by the stages of alarm, resistance, and exhaustion. This model suggests that stress may be adaptive in the short term but a threat to health in the long term. According to Sapolsky, the problem for humans is that although the stress response is designed for occasional emergencies, psychological stress occurs often and for prolonged periods of time.

Other researchers have linked stress to coronary heart disease (CHD). People with a hostile **Type A personality** make up a greater percentage of those with CHD than people with a more relaxed **Type B personality.**

Stress also compromises the **immune system,** which relies on specialized white blood cells called **lymphocytes** and other types of cells to fight bacteria, viruses, and other invaders. Stress alters the activity of the various immune-system cells and can increase the likelihood of illness by weakening resistance. The new field of **psychoneuroimmunology** studies this interplay between the mind and the immune system.

Coping with Stress

Although we cannot prevent stress, we can minimize its effects on our health by means of active coping strategies.

Coping Strategies

Coping strategies can be divided broadly into problem-focused coping (overcoming the source of the problem) and emotion-focused coping (managing the emotional turmoil). Thought suppression, an emotion-focused strategy, doesn't usually work unless accompanied by focused self-distraction—deliberately thinking about something else. Relaxation techniques have been shown to boost the immune system. Aerobic exercise, which correlates with longevity and physical health, may also reduce the impact of stress.

The "Self-Healing Personality"

The personality style known as **hardiness,** which includes a strong sense of control, seems to act as a buffer against stress. Another important trait is optimism, which has been linked with health and a strong immune response. Optimism and pessimism are often related to explanatory style, and some researchers believe that people can train themselves to use optimistic explanations.

Social Support

Social support from friends and family members—or even pets—can reduce stress and promote health. Research shows that people with more social contacts survive illness better and live longer.

Prospects for the Future

Although psychology reveals strong connections between the mind and physical health, we should not assume that the mind can work miracles, nor should we blame people for their illnesses. Instead, psychology can be used to help us design public-health programs—an especially important endeavor during the current epidemic of AIDS.

In the Field Resources

Books

Friedman, H. S. (1991). *The self-healing personality: Why some people achieve health and others succumb to illness.* New York: Holt.

A health psychologist presents a research-based analysis of the factors that make some people healthier than others.

Goleman, D., & Gurin, J. (1993). *Mind/body medicine: How to use your mind for better health.* Yonkers, NY: Consumer Reports Books.

With contributions from leading researchers, this book has readable chapters on stress, relaxation, the immune system, and other mind-body issues in health and illness.

Sapolsky, R. M. (1994). *Why zebras don't get ulcers: A guide to stress, diseases, and coping.* New York: W. H. Freeman.

This engaging book details what stress does to the human body and the reason it breaks down our resistance to illness.

Taylor, S. E. (1989). *Positive illusions.* New York: Basic Books.

Drawing on various studies, Taylor makes the case that we are better off seeing ourselves through rose-colored glasses.

Internet

American Heart Association (http://www.amhrt.org/)

AHA offers news, risk-assessment tests, addresses for local offices, a heart and stroke guide, and other information.

American Cancer Society (http://www.acs.org/)

The ACS offers news releases, smoking and breast-cancer networks, publications, and addresses of local offices.

National Center for Health Statistics (http://www.cdc.gov/nchshome.htm)

Provides news, health statistics, answers to frequently asked questions, and links to other health sites.

The Society of Behavioral Medicine (http://psychweb.syr.edu/sbm/sisterorg.html)

Contains health resources, links to medical organizations, and links specific to various health problems.

World Health Organization (http://www.who.org/)

This WHO site provides updated health and disease statistics, links to other sites, and advice for international travelers.

Journals and Periodicals

Behavioral Medicine
Health Psychology
Journal of the American Medical Association
Journal of Social and Clinical Psychology
Psychosomatic Medicine

Telephone and Mail

Centers for Disease Control AIDS Information (1-800-342-2437)

Appendix
Statistics in Psychological Research

Everyday, we are besieged by claims backed by statistics. In our personal lives and in the news, we are presented with averages, percentages, probabilities, correlations, and margins of error. Whether we are reading *Consumer Reports, Sports Illustrated,* or the *New England Journal of Medicine,* an understanding of statistical concepts is vital to critical thinking.

Understanding and interpreting the results of psychological research also requires an understanding of the statistical methods that are used for describing and drawing conclusions from data. Chapter 1 introduced some terms and concepts associated with *descriptive statistics*—the numbers that psychologists use merely to describe and present their data—and with *inferential statistics*—the mathematical procedures used to draw conclusions from data and to make inferences about what they mean. Here, we present more details about these statistical analyses that will help you to evaluate research results.

Describing Data

Consider a hypothetical experiment on the effects of incentives on performance. The experimenter presents a list of problems to two groups of subjects. Each group must solve these problems within a fixed period of time, but for each correct answer, the low-incentive group is paid ten cents, while the high-incentive group gets one dollar. The hypothesis to be tested is the **null hypothesis,** the assertion that the independent variable manipulated by the experimenter will have no effect on the dependent variable. In this case, the null hypothesis holds that the size of the incentive (the independent variable) will not affect performance on the task (the dependent variable).

Assume that the experimenter has obtained a sample of subjects, assigned them randomly to the two incentive groups, and done everything possible to avoid the problems discussed in Chapter 1. The experiment has been run, and the researcher now has the data: a list of the number of correct answers given by each subject in each group. Now comes the first task of statistical analysis: describing the data in a way that is easy to understand.

The Frequency Histogram

The simplest way to describe the data is to draw up something like Table A.1—test scores obtained by thirteen subjects performing in a low-incentive condition and thirteen in a high-incentive condition—in which all the numbers are presented in a list. After glancing at the table, you might think that the high-incentive group seems to have done better than the low-incentive group, but the difference is not immediately obvious. A picture is worth a thousand words, so a more satisfactory way of presenting the same data is in a picturelike graphic known as a **frequency histogram** (see Figure A.1).

Construction of a histogram is simple. First, divide the scale for measuring the dependent variable (in this case, the number of correct solutions) into a number of categories, or "bins." The bins in our example are 1–2, 3–4, 5–6, 7–8, and 9–10. Next, sort the raw data into the appropriate bin. (For example, the score of a subject

null hypothesis The assertion that the independent variable will have no effect on the dependent variable.

frequency histogram A graphic presentation of data in which a set of bars is used to represent how frequently different values occur in a data set.

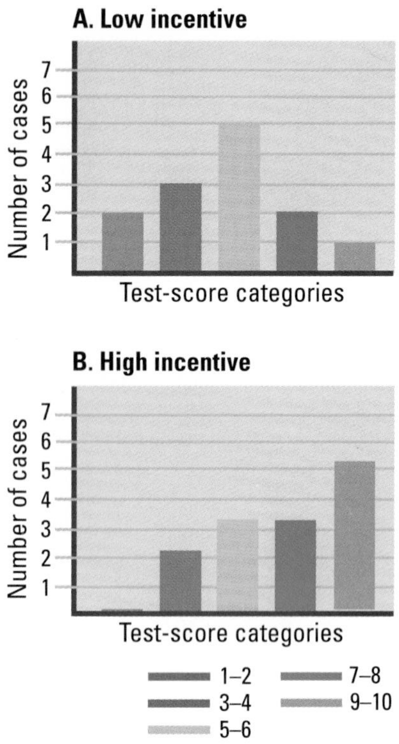

Figure A.1 Frequency histograms
The height of each bar of a histogram represents the number of scores falling within each range of score values. The pattern formed by these bars provides a visual image of how research results are distributed.

Table A.1 A Simple Data Set: Test Scores of Two Conditions

LOW INCENTIVE	HIGH INCENTIVE
4	6
6	4
2	10
7	10
6	7
8	10
3	6
5	7
2	5
3	9
5	9
9	3
5	8

who had 5 correct answers would go into the 5–6 bin, a score of 8 would go into the 7–8 bin, and so on.) Finally, for each bin, count the number of scores in that bin and draw a bar up to the height of that number on the vertical axis of a graph. The set of bars makes up the frequency histogram.

We are interested in comparing the scores of two groups, so two separate histograms are presented in Figure A.1: one for the high-incentive group, the other for the low-incentive group. Now the difference between groups that was difficult to see in Table A.1 becomes more clearly visible: More people in the high-incentive group obtained high scores than in the low-incentive group.

Histograms and other pictures are useful for visualizing and better understanding the "shape" of research data, but in order to analyze the results statistically, more is needed. For example, before we can tell whether two histograms are different statistically or just visually, the data that they represent must be summarized using descriptive statistics.

Descriptive Statistics

Descriptive statistics are used for basic purposes: (1) to measure the number of observations made; (2) to summarize the typical value of a set of data; (3) to summarize the spread, or variability, in a set of data; and (4) to express the correlation between two sets of data.

Sample Size

The easiest statistic to compute, abbreviated as N, simply describes the number of observations that make up a data set. In Table A.1, for example, $N = 13$ for each group, or 26 for the entire data set. Simple as it is, N plays a very important role in more sophisticated statistical analyses.

Measures of Central Tendency

Look at the histograms in Figure A.1, and you'll see that there is a difference in the pattern of scores between the two groups. But how much of a difference is it? What is the typical value, or the *central tendency,* that represents each group's performance? There are three measures of central tendency that capture this typical value: the mode, the median, and the mean. The *mode* is the value or score that occurs most often in the data set. The *median* is the middle score in the data set, the 50th percentile. If you list the scores in order from lowest to highest, half will fall above the median, half below it. The *mean* is the arithmetic average. To find the mean, add the values of all the scores and divide by the number of scores.

Measures of Variability

The variability, or dispersion, of scores in a set of data can be just as important as its central tendency. Are the scores clumped together or spread out? Basically, there are two ways to quantify the variability of scores. These measures are known as the range and the standard deviation.

The *range* is simply the difference between the highest and lowest values in a data set. For the results in Table A.1, the range for the low-incentive group is $9 - 2 = 7$; for the high-incentive group, the range is $10 - 3 = 7$.

The *standard deviation,* abbreviated as SD, measures the average difference between each score in a sample and the mean. To see how the standard deviation is derived, consider the data in Table A.2 and calculate, in order: (1) the mean of the set (in this example, $20/5 = 4$); (2) the difference, or *deviation* (D), of each score from that mean by subtracting the mean from each score (as in column 2 of Table A.2); and (3) the average of these deviations. Note that if you calculated the average

Table A.2 Calculating the Standard Deviation

RAW DATA	DIFFERENCE FROM MEAN = D	D^2
2	$2 - 4 = -2$	4
2	$2 - 4 = -2$	4
3	$3 - 4 = -1$	1
4	$4 - 4 = 0$	0
9	$9 - 4 = 5$	25
Mean = 20/5 = 4		$\Sigma D^2 = 34$

$$\text{Standard deviation} = \sqrt{\frac{\Sigma D^2}{N}} = \sqrt{\frac{34}{5}} = \sqrt{6.8} = 2.6$$

by finding the arithmetic mean, you would sum the deviations and find that the negative deviations exactly balance the positive ones, resulting in a mean difference of 0. Obviously, there is more than zero variation around the mean in the data set. So instead of using the arithmetic mean, we compute the standard deviation by squaring the deviations (which removes all negative values), summing these squared deviations, dividing by *N*, and then taking the square root of the result. These simple steps are outlined in more detail in Table A.2.

The Normal Distribution Now that we have described histograms and reviewed some descriptive statistics, we will reexamine how these methods of representing research data relate to some of the concepts discussed elsewhere in the book.

When psychology researchers collect multiple measurements and plot their data in histograms, the pattern that results often resembles that shown for the low-incentive group in Figure A.1. That is, the majority of scores tend to fall in the middle of the distribution, with fewer and fewer occurring as one moves toward the extremes. As more and more data are collected, and as smaller and smaller bins are used (perhaps containing only one value each), the histograms tend to smooth out, until they resemble the bell-shape curve known as the **normal distribution,** or *normal curve,* which is shown in Figure A.2a. When a distribution of scores follows a truly normal curve, its mean, median, and mode all have the same value. If the curve is normal, we can use its standard deviation to describe how any particular score stands in relation to the rest of the distribution.

Intelligence-test scores provide an example. As we saw in Chapter 12, IQ scores are distributed in a normal curve, with a mean, median, and mode of 100 and an SD of 15 (see Figure A.2b). In such a distribution, half of the population will have an IQ above 100, and half will be below 100. The shape of the true normal curve is such that 68 percent of the area under it lies within 1 standard deviation above and below the mean. In terms of IQ, this means that 68 percent of the population has an IQ somewhere between 85 (100 − 15) and 115 (100 + 15). Of the remaining 32 percent of the population, half falls more than 1 SD above the mean, and half falls more than 1 SD below the mean. Thus, 16 percent of the population has an IQ above 115, and 16 percent scores below 85.

The normal curve is also the basis for percentiles. A **percentile score** indicates the percentage of people or observations that fall below a given score in a normal distribution. In Figure A.2B, for example, the mean score (which is also the median)

normal distribution A symmetrical dispersion of scores in which the mean, median, and mode all have the same value.

percentile score The percentage of people or observations that fall below a given score in a normal distribution.

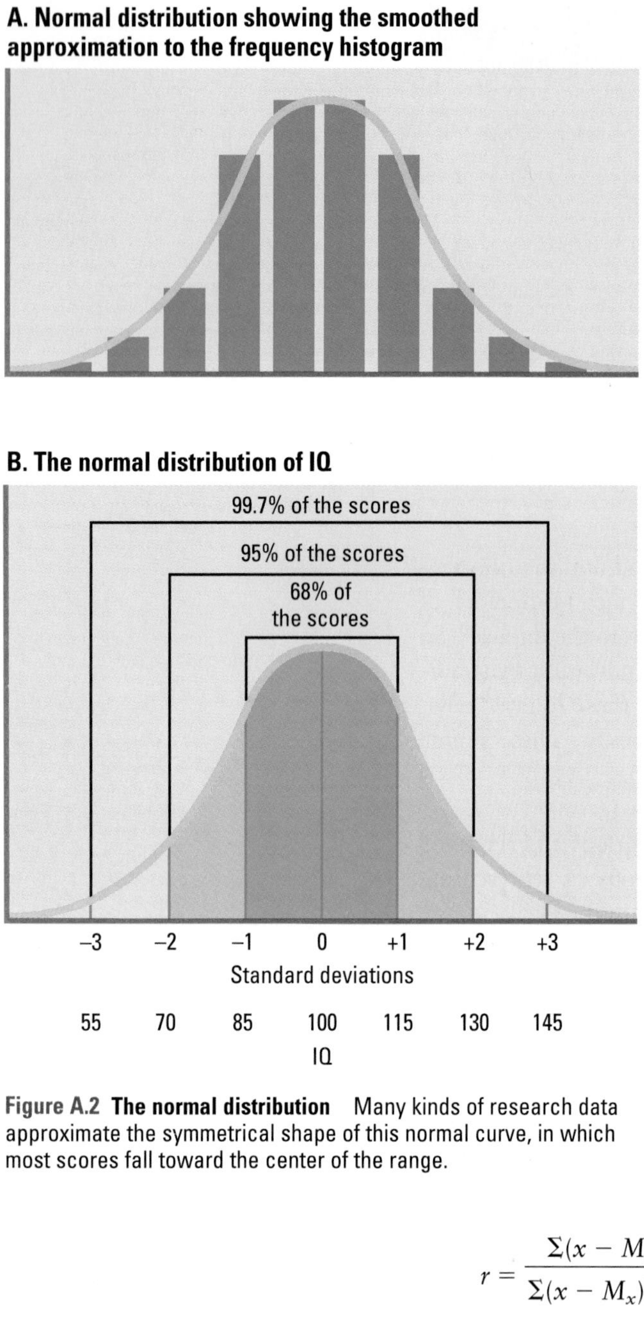

Figure A.2 The normal distribution Many kinds of research data approximate the symmetrical shape of this normal curve, in which most scores fall toward the center of the range.

lies at a point below which 50 percent of the scores fall. Thus, the mean of a normal distribution is at the 50th percentile. What does this mean for IQ? If you score 1 SD above the mean, your score is at a point above which only 16 percent of the population falls. This means that 84 percent of the population (100 percent − 16 percent) must be below that score; so this IQ score is at the 84th percentile. A score at 2 SDs above the mean is at the 97.5 percentile, because only 2.5 percent of the scores are above it in a normal distribution.

Scores may also be expressed in terms of their distance in standard deviations from the mean, producing what are called **standard scores.** A standard score of 1.5, for example, is 1.5 standard deviations from the mean.

Correlation Histograms, measures of central tendency, and measures of variability describe certain characteristics of one dependent variable at a time. However, psychologists are often concerned with describing the *relationship* between two variables. Measures of correlation are often used for this purpose. In Chapter 1, we discussed the meaning of a *correlation coefficient.* Here we describe how to calculate it.

Recall that correlations are based on the relationship between two sets of numbers associated with each subject or observation. The numbers may represent, say, a person's height and weight or the IQ of a parent and child. Table A.3 contains these kinds of data for four subjects from our incentives study who took the test twice. (As you may recall from Chapter 12, the correlation between their scores would be a measure of *test-retest reliability.*) The formula for computing the Pearson correlation, or r, is as follows:

$$r = \frac{\Sigma(x - M_x)(y - M_y)}{\Sigma(x - M_x)^2\Sigma(y - M_y)^2}$$

where:

x = each score on variable 1 (in this case, test 1)
y = each score on variable 2 (in this case, test 2)
M_x = the mean of the scores on variable 1
M_y = the mean of the scores on variable 2

The main function of the denominator in this formula is to ensure that the coefficient ranges from +1.00 to −1.00, no matter how large or small the values of the variables being correlated. The "action element" of this formula is the numerator. It is the result of multiplying the amounts by which each of two observations (x and y) differ from the means of their respective distributions (M_x and M_y). Notice that, if the two variables "go together" (so that, if one is large, the other is also large, and

standard score A value that indicates the distance, in standard deviations, between a given score and the mean of all the scores in a data set.

Table A.3 Calculating the Correlation Coefficient

SUBJECT	TEST 1	TEST 2	[STEP B] $(x - M_x)(y - M_y)$
A	1	3	$(1 - 3)(3 - 4) = (-2)(-1) = +2$
B	1	3	$(1 - 3)(3 - 4) = (-2)(-1) = +2$
C	4	5	$(4 - 3)(5 - 4) = (1)(1) = +1$
D	6	5	$(6 - 3)(5 - 4) = (3)(1) = +3$
[Step A]	$M_x = 3$	$M_y = 4$	$\Sigma(x - M_x)(y - M_y) = +8$
[Step C]	$\Sigma(x - M_x)^2 = 4 + 4 + 1 + 9 = 18$		
[Step D]	$\Sigma(y - M_y)^2 = 1 + 1 + 1 + 1 = 4$		

[Step E]

$$r = \frac{\Sigma(x - M_x)(y - M_y)}{\sqrt{\Sigma(x - M_x)^2 \Sigma(y - M_y)^2}} = \frac{8}{\sqrt{18 \times 4}} = \frac{8}{\sqrt{72}} = \frac{8}{8.48} = +.94$$

if one is small, the other is also small), then either both will tend to be above the mean of their distribution or both will tend to be below the mean of their distribution. When this is the case, $x - M_x$ and $y - M_y$ will both be positive, or they will both be negative. In either case, their product will always be positive, and the correlation coefficient will also be positive. If, on the other hand, the two variables go opposite to one another, such that, when one is large, the other is small, one of them is likely to be smaller than the mean of its distribution, so that either $x - M_x$ or $y - M_y$ will have a negative sign and the other a positive sign. Multiplying these differences together will always result in a product with a negative sign, and r will be negative as well.

Now compute the correlation coefficient for the data presented in Table A.3. The first step (Step A in the table) is to compute the mean (M) for each variable. M_x turns out to be 3, and M_y is 4. Next, calculate the numerator by finding the differences between each x and y value and its respective mean and then multiplying them (as in Step B of Table A.3). Notice, in this example, that the differences in each pair have like signs, so the correlation coefficient will be positive. The next step is to calculate the terms in the denominator; in this case, as shown in Steps C and D in Table A.3, they have values of 18 and 4. Finally, place all the terms in the formula and carry out the arithmetic (Step E). The result in this case is an r of + .94—which is a high and positive correlation, suggesting that performances on repeated tests are very closely related. A subject doing well the first time is very likely to do well again; a person doing poorly at first will probably do no better the second time.

Inferential Statistics

The descriptive statistics from the incentives experiment tell the experimenter that the performances of the high- and low-incentive groups differ. But there is some uncertainty. Is the difference large enough to be important? Does it represent a stable effect or a fluke? The researcher would like to have a *measure of confidence* that the difference between groups is genuine and reflects the impact of incentive on mental tasks in the real world, rather than the effect of the particular subjects used, the phase of the moon, or other random or uncontrolled factors. One way of determining confidence would be to run the experiment again with a new group of subjects. Confidence that incentives produced differences in performance would grow stronger if the same or a larger between-group difference occurs again. In reality, psychologists rarely repeat, or *replicate,* their experiments in exactly the same way three or four times. But *inferential statistics* provide a measure of how likely it was that results came about by chance. They put a precise mathematical value on the confidence or probability that rerunning the same experiment would yield similar (or even stronger) results.

Differences between Means: The *t* test One of the most important tools of inferential statistics is the ***t* test.** It allows the researcher to ask how likely it is that the difference between two means occurred by chance rather than as a function of the effect of the independent variable. When the *t* test or other inferential statistic says that the probability of chance effects is small enough (usually less than 5 percent), the results are said to be *statistically significant.* Conducting a *t* test of statistical significance requires the use of three descriptive statistics.

The first component of the *t* test is the size of the observed effect, the difference between the means. Recall that the mean is calculated by summing a group's scores and dividing by the number of scores. In the example shown in Table A.1, the mean of the high-incentive group is 94/13, or 7.23, and the mean of the low-incentive group is 65/13, or 5. Thus, the difference between the means for the high- and low-incentive groups is $7.23 - 5 = 2.23$.

Second, the standard deviation of scores in each group must be known. If the scores in a group are quite variable, the standard deviation will be large, indicating that chance may have played a large role in producing the results. The next replication of the study might generate a very different set of group scores. If the scores in a group are all very similar, however, the standard deviation will be small, which suggests that the same result would probably occur for that group if the study were repeated. Thus, the *difference* between groups is more likely to be significant when each group's standard deviation is small. If variability is high enough that the scores of two groups overlap (in Table A.1, for example, some people in the low-incentive group actually did better on the math test than some in the high-incentive group), the mean difference, though large, may not be statistically significant.

Third, we need to take the sample size, *N,* into account. The larger the number of subjects or observations, the more likely it is that a given difference between means is significant. This is so because, with larger samples, random factors within a group—the unusual performance of a few people who were sleepy or anxious or hostile, for example—are more likely to be canceled out by the majority, who better represent people in general. The same effect of sample size can be seen in flipping a coin. If you toss a quarter 5 times, you might not be too surprised if heads comes up 80 percent of the time. If you get 80 percent heads after 100 tosses, however, you might begin to suspect that this is probably not due to chance alone—that some other effect, perhaps bias in the coin, produced the results. For the same reason, a relatively small correlation coefficient—say, between diet and grades—might be statistically significant if it was based on 50,000 students. As the number of subjects increases, it becomes less likely that the correlation reflects the influence of a few oddball cases.

To summarize, as the differences between the means get larger, as *N* increases, and as standard deviations get smaller, *t* increases. This increase in *t* raises the researcher's confidence in the significance of the difference between means.

***t* test** A statistical test used to assess the likelihood that differences between two means occurred by chance.

Analysis of Variance Many psychology experiments are considerably more complex than simple comparisons between two groups. They often involve three or more experimental and control groups. Some experiments also include more than one independent variable. For example, suppose we had been interested not only in the effect of incentive size on performance but also in the effect of problem difficulty. We might then create six groups whose subjects would perform easy, moderate, or difficult problems with low or high incentives.

In an experiment like this, the results might be due to the incentive, the problem difficulty, or the combined effects (known as the *interaction*) of the two. Analyzing the size and source of these effects is typically accomplished through procedures known as *analysis of variance*. The details of analysis of variance are beyond the scope of this book. But for now, note that the statistical significance of each effect is influenced by differences between means, standard deviations, and sample sizes in much the same way as described for the *t* test.

For more detailed information about how analysis of variance and other inferential statistics are used to understand and interpret the results of psychological research, consider taking courses in research methods and statistics.

Summary and Key Terms

Psychological research generates data. Statistics are methods for describing and drawing conclusions from data.

Describing Data

Researchers often test the **null hypothesis,** which is the assertion that the independent variable will have no effect on the dependent variable.

The Frequency Histogram

Graphic representations such as **frequency histograms** provide visual descriptions of data, making them easier to understand.

Descriptive Statistics

Numbers that summarize the data are called descriptive statistics. The easiest statistic to compute is *N*, which gives the number of observations made. Measures of central tendency describe the typical value and include the mean, median, and mode. Variability is measured by the range and standard deviation.

Sets of data often follow a **normal distribution,** which means that most scores fall in the middle of the range, with fewer scores occurring as one moves toward the extremes. In a truly normal distribution, the mean, median, and mode are identical. In a normal distribution, a single observation can be described as a **percentile score,** which indicates the percentage of observations falling below it, and in terms of **standard scores,** which indicate its distance from the mean. Another type of descriptive statistic, a correlation coefficient, is used to measure the association between sets of scores.

Inferential Statistics

Researchers use inferential statistics to quantify the probability that conducting the same experiment again would yield similar results.

Differences between Means: The t test

One inferential statistic, the ***t* test,** assesses the likelihood that differences between two means occurred by chance or reflect the impact of an independent variable. Performing a *t* test requires using the difference between the means of two sets of data, the standard deviation of scores in each set, and the number of observations or subjects.

Analysis of Variance

When more than two groups are compared in an experiment, researchers typically rely on analysis of variance to interpret the results.

Glossary

absolute threshold The smallest amount of stimulation that can be detected.
accommodation In Piaget's theory, the process of modifying existing cognitive structures in response to new information.
accommodation The visual process by which lenses become rounded for viewing nearby objects and flatter for viewing remote objects.
acculturation The process by which individuals are changed by their immersion in a new culture.
acculturative stress The stress and mental-health problems often found in immigrants trying to adjust to a new culture.
acetylcholine (ACh) A neurotransmitter found throughout the nervous system that links the motor neurons and muscles.
achievement motivation A strong desire to accomplish difficult tasks, outperform others, and excel.
acquisition The formation of a learned response to a stimulus through the presentation of an unconditioned stimulus (classical conditioning) or reinforcement (operant conditioning).
action potential An electrical impulse that surges through an axon, caused by an influx of positive ions in the neuron.
activation-synthesis theory The theory that dreams result from the brain's attempt to make sense of random neural signals that fire during sleep.
adaptation-level theory The theory that people evaluate experiences in relation to current levels to which they have become accustomed.
adolescence The period of life from puberty to adulthood, corresponding roughly to the ages of thirteen to twenty.
adoption studies A method of testing nature and nurture by comparing twins and other siblings reared together with those separated by adoption.
afterimage A visual sensation that persists after prolonged exposure and removal of a stimulus.
aggression Behavior intended to inflict harm on another person.
agoraphobia An anxiety disorder in which the main symptom is an intense fear of public places.
algorithm A systematic problem-solving strategy that is guaranteed to produce a solution.
altruism Helping behavior that is motivated primarily by a desire to benefit others, not oneself.
Alzheimer's disease (AD) A progressive brain disorder that strikes older people, causing memory loss and other symptoms.
amnesia A dissociative disorder involving a partial or complete loss of memory.
amygdala A limbic structure that controls fear, anger, and aggression.
analogy A problem-solving heuristic that involves using an old solution as a model for a new, similar problem.
anchoring effect The tendency to use an initial value as an "anchor," or reference point, in making a new numerical estimate.
anorexia nervosa An eating disorder in which the person, usually an adolescent girl or young woman, limits her eating and becomes emaciated.
anterograde amnesia A memory disorder characterized by an inability to store new information in long-term memory.
antianxiety drugs Tranquilizing medications used in the treatment of anxiety.
antidepressants Drugs that relieve depression by increasing the supply of norepinephrine, serotonin, or dopamine.
antipsychotic drugs Drugs that are used to control the positive symptoms of schizophrenia and other psychotic disorders.
antisocial personality disorder A personality disorder involving a chronic pattern of self-centered, manipulative, and destructive behavior toward others.
aphasia The loss or impairment of language abilities following brain damage, often to the left hemisphere.
applied research Research that aims to solve practical human problems.
archival research A form of research that relies on existing records of past behavior.
arousal theory The notion that people are motivated to achieve and maintain an optimum level of bodily arousal.
assimilation In Piaget's theory, the process of incorporating and, if necessary, changing new information to fit existing cognitive structures.
association cortex Areas of the cortex that communicate with the sensory and motor areas and house the brain's higher mental processes.
attachment A deep emotional bond that an infant develops with its primary caretaker.
attention A state of awareness consisting of the sensations, thoughts, and feelings that one is focused on at a given moment.
attitude A positive or negative reaction to any person, object, or idea.
attribution theory A set of theories that describe how people explain the causes of behavior.
audition The sense of hearing.
auditory localization The ability to judge the direction a sound is coming from.
autobiographical memory The recollections people have of their own personal experiences and observations.
autonomic nervous system The branch of the peripheral nervous system that connects the CNS to the involuntary muscles, organs, and glands.
availability heuristic A tendency to estimate the likelihood of an event in terms of how easily instances of it can be recalled.
aversion therapy A behavioral therapy technique for classically conditioning people to react with aversion to alcohol, tobacco, and other harmful substances.
axon Extension of the cell body of a neuron that sends impulses to other neurons.

babbling Spontaneous vocalizations of basic speech sounds, which infants begin at about four months of age.
basic research "Pure science" research that tests theories and builds a foundation of knowledge.
behavioral genetics A subfield that examines the role of genetic factors on behavior.
behavioral neuroscience A subfield that studies the links among the brain, nervous system, and behavior.
behavioral observation A form of research that is based on the firsthand observation of a subject's behavior.

behavioral therapies Techniques used to modify disordered thoughts, feelings, and behaviors through the principles of learning.

behaviorism A school of thought that defines psychology as the scientific study of observable behavior.

belief perseverance The tendency to cling to beliefs even after they have been discredited.

binocular disparity A binocular cue for depth perception whereby the closer an object is to a perceiver, the more different the image is in each retina.

biofeedback An operant procedure in which people learn to control heart rate and other physiological responses with the help of "feedback" about their internal states.

biological rhythm Any periodic, more or less regular, fluctuation in a biological organism.

bipolar disorder A rare mood disorder characterized by wild fluctuations from mania (a euphoric, overactive state) to depression (a state of hopelessness and apathy).

blind spot A part of the retina through which the optic nerve passes. Lacking rods and cones, this spot is not responsive to light.

blindsight A condition caused by damage to the visual cortex in which a person encodes visual information without awareness.

borderline personality disorder A type of personality characterized by instability in one's self-image, mood, and social relationships and a lack of clear identity.

brainstem The inner core of the brain that connects to the spinal cord and contains the medulla, pons, and reticular formation.

Broca's area A region in the left hemisphere of the brain that directs the muscle movements in the production of speech.

bulimia nervosa An eating disorder found among young women that is marked by cycles of binge eating followed by purging.

bystander effect The finding that the presence of others inhibits helping in an emergency.

Cannon-Bard theory The theory that an emotion-eliciting stimulus simultaneously triggers physiological arousal and the experience of emotion.

case studies A type of research that involves making in-depth observations of individual persons.

CAT (computerized axial tomograph) scan A series of X rays taken from different angles and converted by computer into an image that depicts a horizontal slice of brain.

central nervous system (CNS) The network of nerves contained within the brain and spinal cord.

central route to persuasion A process in which people think carefully about a message and are influenced by its arguments.

cerebellum A primitive brainstem structure that controls balance and coordinates complex voluntary movements.

cerebral cortex The outermost covering of the brain, largely responsible for higher-order mental processes.

cerebral lateralization The tendency for each hemisphere of the brain to specialize in different functions.

childhood amnesia The inability of most people to recall events from before the age of three or four.

chromosomes Rodlike structures, found in all biological cells, that contain DNA molecules in the form of genes.

circadian rhythm A biological cycle, such as sleeping and waking, that occurs approximately every twenty-four hours.

classical conditioning A type of learning in which an organism comes to associate one stimulus with another (also called Pavlovian conditioning).

cocktail-party phenomenon The ability to attend selectively to one person's speech in the midst of competing conversations.

cognition A general term that refers to mental processes such as thinking, knowing, and remembering.

cognitive dissonance An unpleasant psychological state often aroused when people behave in ways that are discrepant with their attitudes.

cognitive neuroscience A subfield that studies the links among the brain, nervous system, and various mental activities.

cognitive social-learning theory An approach to personality that focuses on social learning (modeling), acquired cognitive factors (expectancies, values), and the person-situation interaction.

cognitive therapy A form of psychotherapy in which people are taught to think in more adaptive ways.

collective unconscious As proposed by Jung, a kind of memory bank that stores images and ideas that humans have accumulated over the course of evolution.

collectivism A cultural orientation in which cooperation and group harmony take priority over purely personal goals.

comorbidity The tendency for people diagnosed with one mental disorder to exhibit symptoms of other disorders as well.

concept A mental grouping of persons, ideas, events, or objects that share common properties.

concrete operational stage Piaget's third stage of cognitive development, when six-year-olds become capable of logical reasoning.

conditional positive regard A situation in which the acceptance and love one receives from significant others is contingent upon one's behavior.

conditioned response (CR) A learned response (salivation) to a classically conditioned stimulus (bell).

conditioned stimulus (CS) A neutral stimulus (bell) that comes to evoke a classically conditioned response (salivation).

conduction deafness Hearing loss caused by damage to the eardrum or bones in the middle ear.

cones Cone-shape photoreceptor cells in the retina that are sensitive to color.

confirmation bias The inclination to search only for evidence that will verify one's beliefs.

conformity A tendency to alter one's opinion or behavior in ways that are consistent with group norms.

consciousness An awareness of the sensations, thoughts, and feelings that one is attending to at a given moment.

conservation The concept that physical properties of an object remain the same despite superficial changes in appearance.

contact hypothesis The proposition that in certain conditions, direct contact between members of rival groups will improve relations.

content validity The extent to which a test measures what it's supposed to measure.

control group The condition of an experiment in which subjects are not exposed to the independent variable.

convergence A binocular cue for depth perception involving the turning inward of the eyes as an object gets closer.

conversion disorder A disorder in which a person temporarily loses a bodily function in the absence of a physical cause.

cornea The clear outer membrane that bends light so that it is sharply focused in the eye.

corpus callosum A bundle of nerve fibers that connects the left and right hemispheres.

correlation A statistical measure of the extent to which two variables are associated.

counterfactual thinking Imagining alternative scenarios and outcomes that might have happened but didn't.

creativity Intellectual and motivational processes that lead to novel solutions, ideas, artistic forms, or products.
criterion validity The extent to which a test can predict a concurrent or future outcome.
critical period A period of time during which an organism must be exposed to a certain stimulus for proper development to occur.
critical thinking The process of solving problems and making decisions through a careful evaluation of evidence.
cross-cultural research Studies designed to compare and contrast people of different cultures.
cross-sectional study A method of developmental research in which people of different ages are tested and compared.
crystallized intelligence A form of intelligence that reflects the accumulation of verbal skills and factual knowledge.
culture-bound syndrome Recurring patterns of maladaptive behavior that is limited to a specific cultural group or location.

dark adaptation A process of adjustment by which the eyes become more sensitive to light in a dark environment.
deception A research procedure used to mislead subjects about the true purposes of a study.
declarative memory Stored long-term knowledge of facts about ourselves and the world.
defense mechanisms Unconscious methods of minimizing anxiety by denying and distorting reality.
deindividuation A loss of individuality, often experienced in a group, that results in a breakdown of internal restraints against deviant behavior.
delusions False beliefs that often accompany schizophrenia and other psychotic disorders.
dendrites Extensions from the cell body of a neuron that receive incoming impulses.
denial A primitive form of repression in which anxiety-filled external events are barred from awareness.
deoxyribonucleic acid (DNA) The complex molecular structure of a chromosome that carries genetic information.
dependent variable A variable that is being measured in an experiment (the proposed effect).
depression A mood disorder characterized by sadness, despair, feelings of worthlessness, and low self-esteem.
depressive explanatory style The tendency for depressed people to attribute negative events to factors that are internal, stable, global.
depth perception The use of visual cues to estimate the depth and distance of objects.
developmental psychology The study of how people grow, mature, and change over the life span.
diagnosis The process of identifying and grouping mental disorders with similar symptoms.
diathesis-stress model The theory that certain mental disorders (such as schizophrenia) develop when people with a genetic or acquired vulnerability are exposed to high levels of stress.
diffusion of responsibility In groups, a tendency for bystanders to assume that someone else will help.
discrimination Behavior directed against persons because of their affiliation with a social group.
discrimination In classical and operant conditioning, the ability to distinguish between different stimuli.
discriminative stimulus A stimulus that signals the availability of reinforcement.
displacement The property of language that accounts for the capacity to communicate about matters that are not in the here-and-now.
display rules Social norms that regulate when, where, and how a person may express certain emotions.
dissociation A division of consciousness that permits one part of the mind to operate independent of another part.
dissociative disorder A condition marked by a temporary disruption in one's memory, consciousness, or self-identity.
dissociative identity disorder (DID) Formerly known as multiple personality disorder, it is a condition in which an individual develops two or more distinct identities.
divergent thinking The ability to think flexibly and entertain a wide range of possible solutions.
divided attention The ability to distribute one's attention and simultaneously engage in two or more activities.
dopamine A neurotransmitter that functions as an inhibitor and is involved in the control of voluntary movements.
downward social comparison A way to boost self-esteem by comparing oneself to others who are less successful, less happy, or less fortunate.
drive theory The notion that physiological needs arouse tension that motivates people to satisfy the need.
DSM-IV Nickname for the American Psychiatric Association's *Diagnostic and Statistical Manual of Mental Disorders* (4th Edition).
dualism The assumption that the body and mind are separate, though perhaps interacting, entities.

echoic memory A brief sensory memory for auditory input that lasts only two to three seconds.
ego In psychoanalysis, the part of personality that operates according to the reality principle and mediates the conflict between the id and superego.
egocentric Self-centered, unable to adopt the perspective of another person.
elaborative rehearsal A technique for transferring information into long-term memory by thinking about it in a deeper way.
electroconvulsive therapy (ECT) Electric-shock treatments that often relieve severe depression by triggering seizures in the brain.
electroencephalograph (EEG) An instrument used to measure electrical activity in the brain through electrodes placed on the scalp.
embryo The developing human organism, from two weeks to two months after conception.
emotion A feeling state characterized by physiological arousal, expressive behaviors, and a cognitive interpretation.
empathy A feeling of joy for others who are happy and distress for those who are in pain.
empathy-altruism hypothesis The proposition that an empathic response to a person in need produces altruistic helping.
encoding specificity The principle that any stimulus encoded along with an experience can later jog one's memory of that experience.
endocrine system A collection of ductless glands that regulate aspects of growth, reproduction, metabolism, and behavior by secreting hormones.
endorphin A morphinelike neurotransmitter that is produced in the brain and is linked to pain control and pleasure.
epidemiology The study of the distribution of illnesses in a population.
equity theory The notion that people want the ratio between input and outcome to be roughly the same for themselves as for others.
ethnic identity The part of a person's identity that is defined by an ethnic heritage, language, history, customs, and so on.

ethology The study of the behavior of animals in their natural habitat.

evolutionary psychology A subfield that uses the principles of evolution to understand human social behavior.

experiment A type of research in which the investigator varies some factors, keeps others constant, and measures the effects on randomly assigned subjects.

experimental group Any condition of an experiment in which subjects are exposed to an independent variable.

explicit memory The types of memory elicited through the conscious retrieval of recollections in response to direct questions.

extinction The elimination of a learned response by removal of the unconditioned stimulus (classical conditioning) or reinforcement (operant conditioning).

extrasensory perception (ESP) The alleged ability to perceive something without ordinary sensory information.

extravert A kind of person who seeks stimulation and is sociable and impulsive.

extrinsic motivation The desire to engage in an activity for money, recognition, or other tangible benefits.

facial electromyograph (EMG) An electronic instrument used by emotion researchers to record activity in the facial muscles.

facial-feedback hypothesis The hypothesis that changes in facial expression can produce corresponding changes in emotion.

factor analysis A statistical technique used to identify clusters of test items that correlate with one another.

family therapy Form of psychological treatment that treats the members of a family as an interactive system.

feature detectors Neurons in the visual cortex that respond to specific aspects of a visual stimulus (such as lines or angles).

fetal alcohol syndrome (FAS) A specific pattern of birth defects (stunted growth, facial deformity, and mental retardation) often found in the offspring of alcoholic mothers.

fetus The developing human organism, from nine weeks after conception to birth.

field research Research that is conducted in real-world locations.

five-factor model A model of personality that consists of five basic traits: neuroticism, extraversion, openness, agreeableness, and conscientiousness.

fixation In psychoanalysis, a tendency to get "locked in" at early, immature stages of psychosexual development.

fixed action pattern A species-specific behavior that is built into an animal's nervous system and triggered by a specific stimulus.

flashbulb memories Highly vivid and enduring memories, typically for events that are dramatic and emotional.

flooding A behavioral therapy technique in which the patient is saturated with a fear-provoking stimulus until the anxiety is extinguished.

fluid intelligence A form of intelligence that involves the ability to reason logically and abstractly.

forgetting curve A consistent pattern in which the rate of memory loss for input is steepest right after it is received and levels off over time.

formal operational stage Piaget's fourth stage of cognitive development, when adolescents become capable of logic and abstract thought.

fovea The center of the retina, where cones are clustered.

framing effect The biasing effects on decision making of the way in which a choice is worded, or "framed."

free association A basic technique of psychoanalysis in which the patient says whatever comes to mind—freely and without censorship.

free recall A type of explicit-memory task in which a person must reproduce information without the benefit of external cues (e.g., an essay exam).

frequency histogram A graphic presentation of data in which a set of bars is used to represent how frequently different values occur in a data set.

frustration-aggression hypothesis The theory that frustration causes aggression.

fugue state A form of amnesia in which a person "forgets" his or her identity, wanders from home, and starts a new life.

functional fixedness The tendency to think of objects only in terms of their usual functions, a limitation that disrupts problem solving.

fundamental attribution error A tendency to overestimate the impact of personal causes of behavior and to overlook the role of situations.

gate-control theory The theory that the spinal cord contains a neurological "gate" that blocks pain signals from the brain when flooded by competing signals.

gender roles Sex-typed behaviors promoted by social learning.

gender schemas Beliefs about men and women that influence the way we perceive ourselves and others.

general adaptation syndrome A three-stage process (alarm, resistance, and exhaustion) by which the body responds to stress.

general intelligence (g) A broad intellectual-ability factor used to explain why performances on different intelligence-test items are often correlated.

generalizability The extent to which a finding applies to a broad range of subject populations and circumstances.

generalized anxiety disorder A psychological disorder that is characterized by a constant state of anxiety not linked to an identifiable source.

generativity The property of language that accounts for the capacity to use a limited number of words to produce an infinite variety of expressions.

genes The biochemical units of heredity that govern the development of an individual life.

Gestalt psychology A school of thought rooted in the idea that the whole (perception) is greater than the sum of its parts (sensation).

Gestalt therapy A humanistic form of psychotherapy in which clients are aggressively prompted to express their feelings.

glial cells Nervous system cells, also called neuroglia, that provide structural support, insulation, and nutrients to the neurons.

grasping reflex In infants, an automatic tendency to grasp an object that stimulates the palm.

group therapy The simultaneous treatment of several clients in a group setting.

groupthink A group decision-making style by which group members convince themselves that they are correct.

gustatory system The structures responsible for the sense of taste.

habituation The tendency for attention to a stimulus to wane over time (often used to determine whether an infant has "learned" a stimulus); the tendency of an organism to become familiar with a stimulus as a result of repeated exposure.

hallucinations Sensory experiences that occur in the absence of actual stimulation.

hallucinogens Psychedelic drugs that distort perceptions and cause hallucinations (e.g., LSD, marijuana).

hardiness A personality style that is characterized by commitment, challenge, and control and acts as a buffer against stress.

Hawthorne effect The finding that workers who were put in a special experimental room became more productive regardless of what changes were made.

health psychology The study of the links between psychological factors and physical health and illness.

heritability A statistical estimate of the percentage of the variability of a trait within a group that is attributable to genetic factors.

heuristic A rule of thumb allowing one to make judgments that are quick but often in error.

hierarchy of needs Maslow's list of basic needs that have to be satisfied before people can become self-actualized.

hindsight bias The tendency to think after an event that we knew in advance what was going to happen.

hippocampus A limbic structure that plays a key role in the formation of new memories.

hormones Chemical messengers secreted from endocrine glands, into the bloodstream, to various organs throughout the body.

humanistic theory An approach to personality that focuses on the self, subjective experience, and the capacity for fulfillment.

hypermnesia A term referring to the unsubstantiated claim that hypnosis can be used to facilitate the retrieval of past memories.

hypnosis Attention-focusing procedures in which changes in a person's behavior or mental state are suggested.

hypnotic susceptibility The extent to which an individual is characteristically responsive to hypnosis.

hypochondriasis A disorder characterized by an unwarranted preoccupation with one's physical health.

hypothalamus A tiny limbic structure in the brain that helps regulate the autonomic nervous system, endocrine glands, emotions, and basic drives.

hypothesis A specific testable prediction, often derived from a theory.

iconic memory A fleeting sensory memory for visual images that lasts only a fraction of a second.

id In psychoanalysis, a primitive and unconscious part of personality that contains basic drives and operates according to the pleasure principle.

identification In psychoanalysis, the process by which children internalize their parents' values and form a superego.

identity crisis An adolescent's struggle to establish a personal identity, or self-concept.

idiot savant Someone who is mentally retarded but is extraordinarily talented in some way.

illusion of control The tendency for people to believe that they can control chance that mimic skill situations.

image A mental representation of visual information.

immune system A biological surveillance system that detects and destroys "nonself" substances that invade the body.

implicit memory A nonconscious recollection of a prior experience that is revealed indirectly by its effects on performance.

imprinting Among newly hatched ducks and geese, an instinctive tendency to follow the mother.

incentive theory The notion that people are motivated to behave in ways that produce a valued inducement.

independent variable Any variable that the researcher manipulates in an experiment (the proposed cause).

individualism A cultural orientation in which personal goals and preferences take priority over group allegiances.

information-processing model A model of memory in which information must pass through discrete stages via the processes of attention, encoding, storage, and retrieval.

informational influence Conformity motivated by the belief that others are correct.

informed consent The ethical requirement that prospective subjects receive enough information to permit them to decide freely whether or not to participate in a study.

ingroup favoritism The tendency to discriminate in favor of ingroups over outgroups.

insecure attachment A parent-infant relationship in which the baby clings to the parent, cries at separation, and reacts with anger or apathy to reunion.

insight A form of problem solving in which the solution seems to pop to mind all of a sudden.

insomnia An inability to fall asleep, stay asleep, or get the amount of sleep needed to function during the day.

instinct A fixed pattern of behavior that is unlearned, universal in a species, and "released" by specific stimuli.

intelligence The capacity to learn from experience and adapt successfully to one's environment.

intelligence quotient (IQ) Originally defined as the ratio of mental age to chronological age, it now represents a person's performance relative to same-age peers.

interneuron Central nervous system neurons that connect sensory inputs and motor outputs.

intrinsic motivation An inner drive that motivates people in the absence of external reward or punishment.

introspection Wundt's method of having trained observers report on their conscious, moment-to-moment reactions.

introvert A kind of person who avoids stimulation and is low-key and cautious.

iris The ring of muscle tissue that gives eyes their color and controls the size of the pupil.

James-Lange theory The theory that emotion stems from the physiological arousal that is triggered by an emotion-eliciting stimulus.

just-noticeable difference (JND) The smallest amount of change in a stimulus that can be detected.

kinesthetic system The structures distributed throughout the body that give us a sense of position and movement of body parts.

laboratory research Research conducted in an environment that can be regulated and in which subjects can be carefully observed.

latent content According to Freud, the unconscious, censored meaning of a dream.

latent learning Learning that occurs but is not exhibited in performance until there is an incentive to do so.

law of effect A law stating that responses followed by positive outcomes are repeated while those followed by negative outcomes are not.

learned helplessness A learned expectation that one cannot control important life outcomes, resulting in apathy and depression.

learning A relatively permanent change in knowledge or behavior that results from experience.

lens A transparent structure in the eye that focuses light on the retina.
life expectancy The number of years that an average member of a species is expected to live.
life span The maximum possible age for members of a species.
light adaptation The process of adjustment by which the eyes become less sensitive to light in a bright environment.
limbic system A set of loosely connected structures in the brain that help to regulate motivation, emotion, and memory.
linguistic relativity hypothesis The hypothesis that language determines, or at least influences, the way we think.
lithium A drug used to control mania and mood swings in people with bipolar disorder.
locus of control A term referring to the expectancy that one's reinforcements are generally controlled by internal or external factors.
long-term memory (LTM) A relatively permanent memory storage system that can hold vast amounts of information for many years.
longitudinal study A method of developmental research in which the same people are tested at different times to track changes related to age.
lucid dreaming A semiconscious dream state in which a sleeper is aware that he or she is dreaming.
lymphocytes Specialized white blood cells that secrete chemical antibodies and facilitate the immune response.

magnetic resonance imaging (MRI) A brain-scanning technique that uses magnetic fields and radio waves to produce clear, three-dimensional images.
maintenance rehearsal The use of sheer repetition to keep information in short-term memory.
manifest content According to Freud, the conscious dream content that is remembered in the morning.
means-end analysis A problem-solving heuristic that involves breaking down a larger problem into a series of subgoals.
medical model The perspective that mental disorders are caused by biological conditions and can be treated through medical intervention.
medulla A brainstem structure that controls vital involuntary functions.
memory The process by which information is retained for later use.
menarche A girl's first menstrual period.
menopause Among middle-age women, the end of menstruation and fertility.
mental age In an intelligence test, the average age of the children who achieve a certain level of performance.
mental models Intuitive theories about the way things work.
mental retardation A diagnostic category used for people with IQ scores below 70 who have difficulty adapting to the routine demands of life.
mental set The tendency to return to a problem-solving strategy that worked in the past.
mere exposure effect The attraction to a stimulus that results from increased exposure to it.
meta-analysis A set of statistical procedures used to review a body of evidence by combining the results of individual studies.
microsleep A brief episode of sleep that occurs in the midst of a wakeful activity.
Minnesota Multiphasic Personality Inventory (MMPI) A large-scale test designed to measure a multitude of psychological disorders and personality traits.
misattribution An explanation that shifts the perceived cause of arousal from the true source to another one.
misinformation effect The tendency to incorporate false postevent information into one's memory of the event itself.
mnemonics Memory aids designed to facilitate the recall of new information.
modeling The social-learning process by which behavior is observed and imitated.
monocular depth cues Distance cues, such as linear perspective, that enable us to perceive depth with one eye.
mood disorder A condition characterized by prolonged emotional extremes ranging from mania to depression.
moon illusion The tendency for people to see the moon as larger when it's low on the horizon than when it's overhead.
moral reasoning The way people think about and try to solve moral dilemmas.
morphemes In language, the smallest units that carry meaning (e.g., prefixes, root words, suffixes).
motivation An inner state that energizes people toward the fulfillment of a goal.
motor cortex The area of the cortex that sends impulses to voluntary muscles.
motor neurons Motion-producing neurons that transmit commands from the central nervous system to the muscles, glands, and organs.
Müller-Lyer illusion An illusion in which the perceived length of a line is altered by the position of other lines that enclose it.
multicultural research Studies of racial and ethnic minority groups within cultures.
multiple intelligences Gardner's theory that there are seven types of intelligence (linguistic, mathematical, spatial, musical, bodily-kinesthetic, interpersonal, intrapersonal).
myelin sheath A layer of fatty cells that is tightly wrapped around the axon to insulate it and speed the movement of electrical impulses.

narcolepsy A sleep disorder characterized by irresistible and sudden attacks of REM sleep during the day.
naturalistic observation The observation of behavior as it occurs naturally in real-world settings.
nature-nurture debate The debate over the extent to which human behavior is determined by genetics and the environment.
need for affiliation The desire to establish and maintain social contacts.
need for intimacy The desire for close relationships characterized by open and intimate communication.
need for power A strong desire to acquire prestige and influence over other people.
nerve deafness Hearing loss caused by damage to the structures of the inner ear.
neural graft A technique of transplanting healthy tissue from the nervous system of one animal into that of another.
neurons Nerve cells that serve as the building blocks of the nervous system.
neurotransmitters Chemical messengers in the nervous system that transmit information by crossing the synapse from one neuron to another.
normative influence Conformity motivated by a fear of social rejection.
normal distribution A symmetrical dispersion of scores in which the mean, median, and mode all have the same value.
NREM sleep The stages of sleep not accompanied by rapid eye movements.
null hypothesis The assertion that the independent variable will have no effect on the dependent variable.

obesity The state of having a surplus of body fat that causes a person to exceed his or her optimum weight by 20 percent.
object permanence Developing at six to eight months, an awareness that objects continue to exist after they disappear from view.
observational learning Learning that takes place when one observes and models the behavior of others.
obsessive-compulsive disorder (OCD) An anxiety disorder defined by persistent thoughts (obsessions) and the need to perform repetitive acts (compulsions).
Oedipus complex In psychoanalysis, a tendency for young children to become sexually attracted to the parent of the opposite sex and hostile toward the parent of the same sex.
olfactory system The structures responsible for the sense of smell.
operant conditioning The process by which organisms learn to behave in ways that produce reinforcement.
opiates A class of highly addictive drugs that depress neural activity and provide temporary relief from pain and anxiety (e.g., heroin, morphine).
opponent-process theory The theory that color vision is derived from three pairs of opposing receptors. The opponent colors are blue and yellow, red and green, and black and white.
optic nerve The pathway that carries visual information from the eyeball to the brain.
outgroup homogeneity bias The tendency to assume that "they" (members of groups other than our own) are all alike.

panic disorder A disorder characterized by sudden and intense rushes of anxiety, in the absence of any apparent reason.
parapsychology The study of ESP and other claims that cannot be explained by existing principles of science.
parasympathetic nervous system A branch of the autonomic nervous system that calms the body and conserves energy.
partial reinforcement effect The tendency for a schedule of partial reinforcement to strengthen later resistance to extinction.
peak experience A fleeting but intense moment of self-actualization in which people feel happy, absorbed, and extraordinarily capable.
percentile score The percentage of people or observations that fall below a given score in a normal distribution.
perception The processes by which people select, organize, and interpret sensations.
perceptual illusions Patterns of sensory input that give rise to misperceptions.
perceptual set The effects of prior experience and expectations on interpretations of sensory input.
peripheral nervous system (PNS) The network of nerves that radiate from the central nervous system to the rest of the body. The PNS comprises the somatic and autonomic nervous systems.
peripheral route to persuasion A process in which people do not think carefully about a message and are influenced by superficial cues.
person-centered therapy A humanistic psychotherapy in which a warm and accepting environment is created to foster self-insight and acceptance.
personality An individual's distinct and relatively enduring pattern of thoughts, feelings, motives, and behaviors.
personality disorders A group of disorders characterized by a personality that is highly inflexible and maladaptive.
PET (positron emission tomograph) scan A visual display of brain activity, as measured by the amount of glucose being used.
pheromones Chemicals secreted by animals that transmit signals to others, usually of the same species.
phobic disorder An anxiety disorder characterized by an intense and irrational fear.
phonemes The basic, distinct sounds of a spoken language.
phrenology The pseudoscientific theory that psychological characteristics are revealed by bumps on the skull.
physical dependence A physiological addiction in which a drug is needed to prevent symptoms of withdrawal.
pituitary gland A tiny gland in the brain that regulates growth and stimulates hormones in other endocrine glands at the command of the hypothalamus.
placebo effect The curative effect of an inactive treatment that results simply from the patient's belief in its therapeutic value.
plasticity A capacity to change as a result of experience.
pleasure principle In psychoanalysis, the id's boundless drive for immediate gratification.
polygraph An electronic device that records multiple channels of autonomic arousal and is often used as a lie-detector test.
pons A portion of the brainstem that plays a role in sleep and arousal.
Ponzo illusion An illusion in which the perceived length of a line is affected by linear perspective cues.
posthypnotic amnesia A reported tendency for hypnosis subjects to forget events that occurred during the induction.
posthypnotic suggestion A suggestion made to a subject in hypnosis to be carried out *after* the induction session is over.
posttraumatic stress disorder An anxiety disorder triggered by an extremely stressful event, such as combat.
practical intelligence The ability to size up new situations and to adapt to real-life demands.
prejudice Negative feelings toward others based solely on their membership in a certain group.
preoperational stage Piaget's second stage of cognitive development, when two- to six-year-olds become capable of reasoning in an intuitive, prelogical manner.
primacy effect The tendency for impressions of others to be heavily influenced by information appearing early in an interaction.
priming The tendency for a recently presented word or concept to facilitate, or "prime," responses in a subsequent situation.
proactive interference The tendency for previously learned material to disrupt the recall of new information.
procedural memory Stored long-term knowledge of learned habits and skills.
prodigy Someone who is highly precocious in a specific domain of endeavor.
Project Head Start A preschool intellectual-enrichment program for children born of poor families.
projection A defense mechanism in which people attribute or "project" their own unacceptable impulses onto others.
projective tests Psychoanalytic personality tests that allow people to "project" unconscious needs, wishes, and conflicts onto ambiguous stimuli.
prosopagnosia A condition stemming from damage to the temporal lobes that disrupts the ability to recognize familiar faces.
prototype A "typical" member of a category, one that has most of the defining features of that category.
psychoactive drug A chemical that alters perceptions, thoughts, moods, or behavior.
psychoanalysis Freud's theory of personality and method of psychotherapy, both of which assume that our motives are largely unconscious.

psychological dependence A condition in which drugs are needed to maintain a sense of well-being or relief from negative emotions.

psychological disorder A condition in which a person's thoughts, feelings, or behavior is judged to be dysfunctional.

psychological model The perspective that mental disorders are caused and maintained by one's life experiences.

psychology The scientific study of behavior and the mind.

psychoneuroimmunology (PNI) A new subfield of psychology that examines the interactions among psychological factors, the nervous system, and the immune system.

psychopharmacology The study of the effects of drugs on psychological processes and disorders.

psychophysics The study of the relationship between physical stimulation and subjective sensations.

psychosexual stages Freud's stages of personality development during which pleasure is derived from different parts of the body (oral, anal, phallic, and genital).

psychosurgery The surgical removal of portions of the brain for the purpose of treating psychological disorders.

psychotherapy A term used to describe any treatment in which a trained professional uses psychological techniques to help someone in need of assistance.

puberty The onset of adolescence, as evidenced by rapid growth, rising levels of sex hormones, and sexual maturity.

punishment In operant conditioning, any stimulus that decreases the likelihood of a prior response.

pupil The small round hole in the iris of the eye through which light passes.

REM sleep behavior disorder (RBD) A condition in which the skeletal muscles are not paralyzed during REM sleep, enabling a sleeper to act upon his or her nightmares, often violently.

replication The process of repeating a study to see if the results are reliable enough to be duplicated.

representativeness heuristic A tendency to estimate the likelihood of an event in terms of how typical it seems.

repression A defense mechanism in which personally threatening thoughts, memories, and impulses are banned from awareness.

resistance In psychoanalysis, the tendency for patients to actively block or "resist" psychologically painful insights.

reticular formation A group of nerve cells in the brainstem that help to control sleep, arousal, and attention.

retina The rear multilayer part of the eye where rods and cones convert light into neural impulses.

retroactive interference The tendency for new information to disrupt the memory of previously learned material.

retrograde amnesia A memory disorder characterized by an inability to retrieve long-term memories from the past.

reversible figure A drawing that one can perceive in different ways by reversing figure and ground.

rods Rod-shape photoreceptor cells in the retina that are highly sensitive to light.

rooting reflex In response to contact on the cheek, an infant's tendency to turn toward the stimulus and open its mouth.

Rorschach A projective personality test in which people are asked to report what they see in a set of inkblots.

racism A deep-seated form of prejudice that is based on the color of a person's skin.

random assignment The procedure of assigning subjects to conditions of an experiment in an arbitrary manner.

random sample A method of selection in which everyone in a population has an equal chance of being chosen.

rational-emotive therapy (RET) A form of cognitive therapy in which people are confronted with their irrational, maladaptive beliefs.

rationalization A defense mechanism that involves making excuses for one's failures and shortcomings.

reaction formation A defense mechanism in which one converts an unacceptable feeling into its opposite.

realistic conflict theory The theory that prejudice stems from intergroup competition for limited resources.

reality principle In psychoanalysis, the ego's capacity to delay gratification.

receptors Specialized neural cells that receive neurotransmitters.

reciprocal determinism The view that personality emerges from a mutual interaction of individuals, their actions, and their environments.

recognition A form of explicit-memory retrieval in which items are re-presented to a person who must determine if they were previously encountered.

recovery Following habituation to one stimulus, the tendency for a second stimulus to arouse new interest (often used to test whether infants can discriminate between stimuli).

reflex An inborn automatic response to a sensory stimulus.

reinforcement In operant conditioning, any stimulus that increases the likelihood of a prior response.

reliability The extent to which a test yields consistent results over time or using alternate forms.

REM sleep The rapid-eye-movement stage of sleep associated with dreaming.

scatterplot A graph in which paired scores (X, Y) for many subjects are plotted as single points to reveal the direction and strength of their correlation.

schemas Preconceptions about persons, objects, or events that bias the way that new information is interpreted and recalled. In Piaget's theory, mental representations of the world that guide the processes of assimilation and accommodation.

schizophrenic disorders Disorders involving gross distortions of thoughts and perceptions and by loss of contact with reality.

seasonal affective disorder (SAD) A form of depression that strikes during the late autumn and winter months.

secure attachment A parent-infant relationship in which the baby is secure when the parent is present, distressed by separation, and delighted by reunion.

sedatives A class of depressant drugs that slow down activity in the central nervous system (e.g., alcohol, barbiturates).

selective attention The ability to focus awareness on a single stimulus to the exclusion of other stimuli, as in the cocktail-party phenomenon.

self-actualization In humanistic personality theories, the need to fulfill one's unique potential.

self-awareness theory The theory that self-focused attention leads people to notice their shortcomings, thus motivating a change in behavior or an escape from self-awareness.

self-deception The processes by which people distort and hide unpleasant truths from themselves.

self-disclosure The sharing of intimate details about oneself with another person.

self-discrepancy theory The notion that discrepancies between one's self-concept and "ideal" and "ought" selves have negative emotional consequences.

self-efficacy The belief that one is capable of performing the behaviors required to produce a desired outcome.

self-esteem A positive or negative evaluation of the self.
self-fulfilling prophecy The idea that a person's expectation can lead to its own fulfillment (as in the effect of teacher expectations on student performance).
self-handicapping Behaviors designed to sabotage one's own performance and provide a subsequent excuse for failure.
self-report A method of observation that involves asking people to describe their own thoughts, feelings, or behavior.
self-schemas Specific beliefs about the self that influence how we interpret self-relevant information.
semantic network A complex web of semantic associations that link items in memory such that retrieving one item triggers the retrieval of others as well.
semanticity The property of language that accounts for the communication of meaning.
sensation The processes by which our sense organs receive information from the environment.
sensorimotor stage Piaget's first stage of cognitive development, from birth to two years old, when infants come to know the world through their own actions.
sensory adaptation A decline in sensitivity to a stimulus as a result of constant exposure.
sensory memory A memory storage system that records information from the senses for up to three seconds.
sensory neurons Neurons that send signals from the senses, skin, muscles, and internal organs to the central nervous system.
separation anxiety Among infants with object permanence, a fear reaction to the absence of their primary caretaker.
serial-position curve A U-shape pattern indicating the tendency to recall more items from the beginning and end of a list than from the middle.
set point A level of weight toward which a person's body gravitates.
sexual orientation A sexual preference for members of the same sex (homosexuality), opposite sex (heterosexuality), or both sexes (bisexuality).
sexual-response cycle The four physiological stages of sexual responding: excitement, plateau, orgasm, and resolution.
shape constancy The tendency to see an object as retaining its form despite changes in orientation.
shaping A procedure in which reinforcements are used to gradually guide an animal or person toward a specific behavior.
short-term memory (STM) A memory storage system that holds about seven items for up to twenty seconds before the material is transferred to long-term memory or is forgotten.
signal-detection theory The theory that detecting a stimulus is jointly determined by the signal and the subject's response criterion.
simple phobia An intense, irrational fear of a specific object or situation.
size constancy The tendency to view an object as constant in size despite changes in the size of the retinal image.
Skinner box An apparatus, invented by B. F. Skinner, used to study the effects of reinforcement on the behavior of laboratory animals.
sleep apnea A disorder in which a person repeatedly stops breathing during sleep and awakens gasping for air.
social categorization The classification of persons into groups based on common attributes.
social clock A set of cultural expectations concerning the most appropriate ages for men and women to leave home, marry, start a career, have children, and retire.
social facilitation The tendency for the presence of others to enhance performance on simple tasks and impair performance on complex tasks.
social loafing The tendency for people to exert less effort in group tasks for which individual contributions are pooled.
social norms Implicit rules of conduct according to which each culture operates.
social perception The processes by which we come to know and evaluate other persons.
social phobia An intense fear of situations that invite public scrutiny.
social psychology The study of how individuals think, feel, and behave in social situations.
social support The healthful coping resources provided by friends and other people.
social comparison theory The theory that people evaluate themselves by making comparisons with others.
social identity theory The theory that people discriminate against outgroups in order to enhance their own self-esteem.
social-roles theory The theory that perceived sex differences are magnified by the different social roles occupied by men and women.
social-skills training A form of behavioral therapy used to teach interpersonal skills through modeling, rehearsal, and reinforcement (e.g., assertiveness training).
soma The cell body of a neuron.
somatic nervous system The branch of the peripheral nervous system that transmits signals from the sensory organs to the CNS, and from the CNS to the skeletal muscles.
somatoform disorder A type of mental disorder in which a person experiences bodily symptoms that are psychological rather than medical in nature.
somatosensory cortex The area of the cortex that receives sensory information from the touch receptors in the skin.
spermarche A boy's first ejaculation.
split brain A surgically produced condition in which the corpus callosum is severed, thus cutting the link between the left and right hemispheres of the brain.
split-half reliability The degree to which alternate forms of a test yield consistent results.
spontaneous recovery The reemergence of an extinguished conditioned response after a rest period.
standard score A value that indicates the distance, in standard deviations, between a given score and the mean of all the scores in a data set.
standardization The procedure by which existing norms are used to interpret an individual's test score.
Stanford-Binet An American version of Binet's intelligence test that yields an IQ score with an average of 100.
statistics A branch of mathematics that is used for analyzing research data.
stereotype A belief that associates a group of people with certain traits.
stimulants A class of drugs that excite the central nervous system and energize behavior (e.g., amphetamines, cocaine).
stimulus generalization The tendency to respond to a stimulus that is similar to the conditioned stimulus.
strange-situation test A parent-infant "separation and reunion" procedure that is staged in a laboratory to test the security of a child's attachment.
stress An aversive state of arousal triggered by the perception that an event threatens our ability to cope effectively.
Stroop test A color-naming task that demonstrates the automatic nature of highly practiced activities such as reading.
sublimation In psychoanalysis, the channeling of repressed sexual and aggressive urges into socially acceptable substitute outlets.
subliminal message A stimulus that is presented below the threshold for awareness.

superego In psychoanalysis, the part of personality that consists of one's moral ideals and conscience.
survey A research method that involves interviewing or giving questionnaires to a large number of people.
syllogism A logical problem in which the goal is to determine the validity of a conclusion given two or more premises.
sympathetic nervous system A branch of the autonomic nervous system that controls the involuntary activities of various organs and mobilizes the body for fight or flight—that heightens arousal and energizes the body for action.
synapse The junction between the axon terminal of one neuron and the dendrites of another.
synesthesia A rare condition in which stimulation in one sensory modality triggers sensations in another sensory modality.
syntax Rules of grammar that govern the arrangement of words in a sentence.
systematic desensitization A behavioral therapy technique used to treat phobias and other anxiety disorders by pairing gradual exposure to an anxiety-provoking situation with relaxation.

***t* test** A statistical test used to assess the likelihood that differences between two means occurred by chance.
taste buds Nets of taste receptor cells.
telegraphic speech Early short form of speech in which the child omits unnecessary words—as telegrams once did ("More milk").
teratogens Toxic substances that can harm the embryo or fetus during prenatal development.
test-retest reliability The degree to which a test yields consistent results when readministered at a later time.
thalamus A limbic structure that relays neural messages between the senses and areas of the cerebral cortex.
Thematic Apperception Test (TAT) A projective personality test in which people are asked to make up stories from a set of ambiguous pictures.
theory An organized set of principles that describes, predicts, and explains some phenomenon.
threshold The level of stimulation needed to trigger a neural impulse.
token economy A large-scale behavior-change program in which the participants earn valuable tokens for engaging in desired target behaviors.
trait A relatively stable predisposition to behave in a certain way.
transduction The process by which physical energy is converted into sensory neural impulses.
transference In psychoanalysis, the tendency of patients to displace intense feelings for others onto the therapist.
trial and error A problem-solving strategy in which several solutions are attempted until one is found that works.
triarchic theory of intelligence Sternberg's theory that there are three kinds of intelligence: analytic, creative, and practical.
trichromatic theory A theory of color vision stating that the retina contains three types of color receptors—for red, blue, and green—and that these combine to produce all other colors.
twin-study method A method of testing nature and nurture by comparing pairs of identical and fraternal twins of the same sex.
two-factor theory of emotion The theory that emotion is based both on physiological arousal and on the cognitive interpretation of that arousal.
Type A personality A personality characterized by an impatient, hard-driving, and hostile pattern of behavior.
Type B personality A personality characterized by an easygoing, relaxed pattern of behavior.

unconditional positive regard A situation in which the accetance and love one receives from significant others is unqualified.
unconditioned response (UR) An unlearned response (salivation) to an unconditioned stimulus (food).
unconditioned stimulus (US) A stimulus (food) that triggers an unconditioned response (salivation).

validity The extent to which a test measures or predicts what it is designed to.
vestibular system The inner ear and brain structures that give us a sense of equilibrium.
visual cliff An apparatus used to test depth perception in infants and animals.
visual cortex Located in the back of the brain, it is the main information-processing center for visual information.

Weber's law The principle that the just-noticeable difference of a stimulus is a constant proportion despite variations in intensity.
Wechsler Adult Intelligence Scale (WAIS) The most widely used IQ test for adults, it yields separate scores for verbal and performance subtests.
Wernicke's area A region in the left hemisphere of the brain that is involved in the comprehension of language.
white noise A hissing sound that results from a combination of all frequencies of the sound spectrum.
working memory Term used to describe short-term memory as an active workspace where information is accessible for current use.

zygote A fertilized egg that undergoes a two-week period of rapid cell division and develops into an embryo.

References

Abbey, A. (1982). Sex differences in attributions for friendly behavior: Do males misperceive females' friendliness? *Journal of Personality and Social Psychology, 42,* 830–838.

Abbey, A. (1987). Misperceptions of friendly behavior as sexual interest: A survey of naturally occurring incidents. *Psychology of Women Quarterly, 11,* 173–194.

Abramov, I., & Gordon, J. (1994). Color appearance: On seeing red—or yellow, or green, or blue. *Annual Review of Psychology, 45,* 451–485.

Abrams, R. (1988). *Electroconvulsive therapy.* New York: Oxford University Press.

Abramson, L. Y., Metalsky, G., & Alloy, L. B. (1989). Hopelessness depression: A theory-based subtype. *Psychological Review, 96,* 358–372.

Ackerman, D. (1990). *A natural history of the senses.* New York: Random House.

Acklin, M., McDowell, C., II, & Orndoff, S. (1992). Statistical power and Rorschach: 1975–1991. *Journal of Personality Assessment, 59,* 366–379.

Adams, P. R., & Adams, G. R. (1984). Mount Saint Helens's ashfall: Evidence for a disaster stress reaction. *American Psychologist, 39,* 252–260.

Adams, R. J., & Maurer, D. (1984). Detection of contrast by the newborn and 2-month-old infant. *Infant Behavior and Development, 7,* 415–422.

Adelson, J. (1986). *Inventing adolescence: The political psychology of everyday schooling.* New Brunswick, NJ: Transaction.

Ader, R., & Cohen, N. (1985). CNS-immune system interactions: Conditioning phenomena. *Behavioral and Brain Sciences, 8,* 379–426.

Ader, R., & Cohen, N. (1993). Psychoneuroimmunology: Conditioning and stress. *Annual Review of Psychology, 44,* 53–85.

Ader, R., Felten, D. L., & Cohen, N. (Eds.). (1991). *Psychoneuroimmunology* (2nd ed.). San Diego: Academic Press.

Adler, A. (1927). *The practice and theory of individual psychology.* New York: Harcourt, Brace & World.

Adler, N., & Matthews, K. (1994). Health psychology: Why do some people get sick and some stay well? *Annual Review of Psychology, 45,* 229–259.

Ahrentzen, S., Joe, G. M., Skorpanich, M. A., & Evans, G. W. (1982). School environments and stress. In G. W. Evans (Ed.), *Environmental stress.* New York: Cambridge University Press.

Ainsworth, M. D. S. (1989). Attachments beyond infancy. *American Psychologist, 44,* 709–716.

Ainsworth, M. D. S., Blehar, M. C., Waters, E., & Wall, S. (1978). *Patterns of attachment: A psychological study of the Strange Situation.* Hillsdale, NJ: Erlbaum.

Ajzen, I. (1991). The theory of planned behavior. *Organizational Behavior and Human Decision Processes, 50,* 179–211.

Akerstedt, T. (1988). Sleepiness as a consequence of shift work. *Sleep, 11,* 17–34.

Akil, L. (1982). On the role of endorphins in pain modulation. In A. L. Beckman (Ed.), *The neural bases of behavior* (pp. 311–333). New York: Spectrum.

Alberti, R. E., & Emmons, M. L. (1986). *Your perfect right: A guide to assertive living* (5th ed.). San Luis Obispo, CA: Impact Publishers.

Aldag, R. J., & Fuller, S. R. (1993). Beyond fiasco: A reappraisal of the groupthink phenomenon and a new model of group decision processes. *Psychological Bulletin, 113,* 533–552.

Aldwin, C. M., Spiro, A., Bosse, R., & Levenson, M. R. (1989). Longitudinal findings from the normative aging study: 1. Does mental health change with age? *Psychology and Aging, 4,* 295–306.

Alessandri, D. M., Sullivan, R. W., Imaizumi, S., & Lewis, M. (1993). Learning and emotional responsivity in cocaine-exposed infants. *Developmental Psychology, 29,* 989–997.

Alexander, F., & French, T. M. (1946). *Psychoanalytic therapy: Principles and application.* New York: Ronald Press.

Alexander, J. F., Holtzworth-Munroe, A., & Jameson, P. (1994). The process and outcome of marital and family therapy: Research review and evaluation. In A. E. Bergin & S. L. Garfield (Eds.), *Handbook of psychotherapy and behavior change* (4th ed.). New York: Wiley.

Alford, B. A., Freeman, A., Beck, A. T., & Wright, F. D. (1990). Brief focused cognitive therapy of panic disorder. *Psychotherapy, 27,* 230–234.

Allen, J. B., Kenrick, D. T., Linder, D. E., & McCall, M. A. (1989). Arousal and attraction: A response-facilitation alternative to misattribution and negative-reinforcement models. *Journal of Personality and Social Psychology, 57,* 261–270.

Allen, K. D., Danforth, J. S., & Drabman, R. S. (1989). Videotaped modeling and film distraction for fear reduction in adults undergoing hyperbaric oxygen therapy. *Journal of Consulting and Clinical Psychology, 57,* 554–558.

Allen, K. M., Blascovich, J., Tomaka, J., & Kelsey, R. M. (1991). Presence of human friends and pet dogs as moderators of autonomic responses to stress in women. *Journal of Personality and Social Psychology, 61,* 582–589.

Allen, V. L., & Levine, J. M. (1971). Social support and conformity: The role of independent assessment of reality. *Journal of Experimental Social Psychology, 7,* 48–58.

Alley, T. R. (1988). *Social and applied aspects of perceiving faces.* Hillsdale, NJ: Erlbaum.

Alliger, G. M., Lilienfeld, S. O., & Mitchell, K. E. (1996). The susceptibility of overt and covert integrity tests to coaching and faking. *Psychological Science, 7,* 32–39.

Allison, T., & Cicchetti, D. V. (1976). Sleep in mammals: Ecological and constitutional correlates. *Science, 194,* 732–734.

Allport, F. H., et al. (1953). The effects of segregation and the consequences of desegregation: A social science statement. *Minneapolis Law Review, 37,* 429–440.

Allport, G. W. (1937). *Personality: A psychological interpretation.* New York: Holt, Rinehart & Winston.

Allport, G. W. (1961). *Pattern and growth in personality.* New York: Holt, Rinehart & Winston.

Allport, G. W. (1967). Gordon W. Allport. In E. G. Boring and G. Lindzey (Eds.), *A history of psychology in autobiography* (Vol. V). New York: Appleton-Century-Crofts.

Allport, G. W., & Odbert, H. S. (1936). Trait-names: A psycholexical study. *Psychological Monographs, 47* (Whole No. 1).

Allport, G. W., & Postman, L. J. (1947). *The psychology of rumor.* New York: Holt.

Altman, I., & Taylor, D. A. (1973). *Social penetration: the development of interpersonal relationships.* New York: Holt, Rinehart & Winston.

Alvarez-Borda, B., Ramirez-Amaya, V., Perez-Montfort, R., & Bermudez-Rattoni, F. (1995). Enhancement of antibody production by a learning paradigm. *Neurobiology of Learning and Memory, 64,* 103–105.

Amabile, T. M. (1996). *Creativity in context.* New York: Westview.

Ambady, N., & Rosenthal, R. (1992). Thin slices of expressive behavior as predictors of interpersonal consequences: A meta-analysis. *Psychological Bulletin, 111,* 256–274.

American Psychiatric Association (1989). *Treatments of psychiatric disorders.* Washington, DC: American Psychiatric Association.

American Psychiatric Association (1994). *Diagnostic and statistical manual of mental disorders* (4th ed.). Washington, DC: American Psychiatric Association.

American Psychological Association (1992). Ethical principles of psychologists and code of conduct. *American Psychologist, 47,* 1597–1611.

Amoore, J. E., Johnston, J. W., & Rubin, M. (1964). The stereochemical theory of odor. *Scientific American, 210,* 42–49.

Anand, B. K., & Brobeck, J. R. (1951). Localization of a "feeding center" in the hypothalamus of the rat. *Proceedings of the Society for Experimental Biology and Medicine, 77,* 323–324.

Anastasi, A. (1988). *Psychological testing* (6th ed.). New York: Macmillan.

Andersen, B. L., Kiecolt-Glaser, J. K., & Glaser, R. (1994). A biobehavioral model of cancer stress and disease course. *American Psychologist, 49,* 389–404.

Andersen, S. M., & Baum, A. (1994). Transference in interpersonal relations: Inferences and affect based on significant-other representations. *Journal of Personality, 62,* 459–497.

Anderson, A. (1982). The great Japanese IQ increase. *Nature, 297,* 180–181.

Anderson, C. A. (1989). Temperature and aggression: Ubiquitous effects of heat on occurrence of human violence. *Psychological Bulletin, 106,* 74–96.

Anderson, C. A., & Anderson, K. B. (1996). Violent crime rate studies in philosophical context: A destructive testing approach to heat and Southern culture of violence effects. *Journal of Personality and Social Psychology, 70,* 740–756.

Anderson, C. A., Lepper, M. R., & Ross, L. (1980). Perseverance of social theories: The role of explanation in the persistence of discredited information. *Journal of Personality and Social Psychology, 39,* 1037–1049.

Anderson, J. R. (1983). *The architecture of cognition.* Cambridge, MA: Harvard University Press.

Anderson, J. R. (1990). *Cognitive psychology and its implications* (3rd ed.). New York: W. H. Freeman.

Anderson, J. R., & Schooler, L. J. (1991). Reflections of the environment in memory. *Psychological Science, 2,* 396–408.

Anderson, M. J., Petros, T. V., Beckwith, B. E., Mitchell, W. W., & Fritz, S. (1991). Individual differences in the effect of time of day on long-term memory access. *American Journal of Psychology, 104,* 241–255.

Anderson, N. H. (1981). *Foundations of information integration theory.* New York: Academic Press.

Andreasen, N. C. (1987). The diagnosis of schizophrenia. *Schizophrenia Bulletin, 13,* 1–8.

Andreasen, N. C. (1988). Brain imaging: Applications in psychiatry. *Science, 239,* 1381–1388.

Andreasen, N. C., Arndt, S., Alliger, R., Miller, D., & Flaum, M. (1995). Symptoms of schizophrenia: Methods, meanings, and mechanisms. *Archives of General Psychiatry, 52,* 341–351.

Angoff, W. H. (1988). The nature-nurture debate, aptitudes, and group differences. *American Psychologist, 43,* 713–720.
Anisfeld, M. (1991). Neonatal imitation. *Developmental Review, 11,* 60–97.
Annett, J. (1985). *Left, right, hand and brain: The right shift theory.* London: Erlbaum.
Anonymous (1990). Behind the mask: A functional schizophrenic copes. *Schizophrenia Bulletin, 16,* 547–549.
Antrobus, J. (1991). Dreaming: Cognitive processes during cortical activation of high afferent thresholds. *Psychological Review, 98,* 96–121.
Archer, J. (1988). *The behavioural biology of aggression.* Cambridge: Cambridge University Press.
Archer, J. (1991). The influence of testosterone on human aggression. *British Journal of Psychology, 82,* 1–28.
Arndt, S., Andreasen, N. C., Flaum, M., Miller, D., & Nopoulos, P. (1995). A longitudinal study of symptom dimensions in schizophrenia. *Archives of General Psychiatry, 52,* 352–360.
Aron, A., Aron, E. N., & Smollan, D. (1992). Inclusion of other in the self scale and the structure of interpersonal closeness. *Journal of Personality and Social Psychology, 63,* 596–612.
Aron, E. N., & Aron, A. (1997). Sensory-processing sensitivity and its relation to introversion and emotionality. *Journal of Personality and Social Psychology, 73,* 345–368.
Aronoff, J., Woike, B. A., & Hyman, L. M. (1992). Which are the stimuli in facial displays of anger and happiness? Configurational bases of emotion recognition. *Journal of Personality and Social Psychology, 62,* 1050–1066.
Aronson, E., & Mills, J. (1959). The effect of severity of initiation on liking for a group. *Journal of Abnormal and Social Psychology, S9,* 177–181.
Aronson, E., Blaney, N., Stephan, C., Sikes, J., & Snapp, M. (1978). *The jigsaw classroom.* Beverly Hills, CA: Sage.
Arthur, W., Jr., & Graziano, W. G. (1996). The five-factor model, conscientiousness, and driving accident involvement. *Journal of Personality, 64,* 593–618.
Asarnow, J. R. (1988). Children at risk for schizophrenia: Converging lines of evidence. *Schizophrenia Bulletin, 14,* 613–631.
Asch, S. E. (1946). Forming impressions of personality. *Journal of Abnormal and Social Psychology, 41,* 258–290.
Asch, S. E. (1951). Effects of group pressure upon the modification and distortion of judgments. In H. Guetzkow (Ed.), *Groups, leadership, and men.* Pittsburgh, PA: Carnegie Press.
Asch, S. E. (1956). Studies of independence and conformity: A minority of one against a unanimous majority. *Psychological Monographs,* 70, 416.
Aschoff, J. (1981). *Handbook of behavioral neurobiology: Vol. 4. Biological rhythms.* New York: Plenum.
Aserinksy, E., & Kleitman, N. (1953). Regularly occurring periods of eye motility and concomitant phenomena during sleep. *Science, 118,* 273.
Ashcraft, M. H. (1989). *Human memory and cognition.* Glenview, IL: Scott, Foresman.
Aśhcraft, M. H. (1993). A personal case history of transient anemia. *Brain and Language, 44,* 47–57.
Asher, S. R., & Coie, J. D. (1990). *Peer rejection in childhood.* New York: Cambridge University Press.
Askenasy, H. (1978). *Are we all Nazis?* Secaucus, NJ: Lyle Stuart.
Aslin, R. N. (1989). Discrimination of frequency transitions by human infants. *Journal of the Acoustical Society of America, 86,* 582–590.
Aspinwall, L. G., & Taylor, S. E. (1993). The effects of social comparison direction, threat, and self-esteem on affect, self-evaluation, and expected success. *Journal of Personality and Social Psychology, 64,* 708–722.
Associated Press (1985, May 10). Man, 75, gets life for wife's death. *Kansas City Times,* p. A4.
Atkinson, J. W. (1957). Motivational determinants of risk-taking behavior. *Psychological Review, 64,* 359–372.
Atkinson, J. W. (1964). *An introduction to motivation.* New York: Van Nostrand.
Atkinson, J. W., & Litwin, G. H. (1960). Achievement motive and test anxiety conceived as motive to approach success and motive to avoid failure. *Journal of Abnormal and Social Psychology, 60,* 52–63.
Atkinson, R. C., & Shiffrin, R. M. (1968). Human memory: A proposed system and its control processes. In K. Spence & J. Spence (Eds.), *The psychology of learning and motivation: Advances in research and theory* (Vol. 2). New York: Academic Press.
Attie, I., & Brooks-Gunn, J. (1989). Development of eating problems in adolescent girls: A longitudinal study. *Developmental Psychology, 25,* 70–79.
Axelrod, S., & Apsche, J. (Eds.). (1983). *The effects of punishment on human behavior.* New York: Academic Press.
Axsom, D. (1989). Cognitive dissonance and behavior change in psychotherapy. *Journal of Experimental Social Psychology, 25,* 234–252.
Axtell, R. E. (1993). *Do's and taboos around the world* (3rd ed.). New York: Wiley.
Ayllon, T. (1963). Intensive treatment of psychotic behaviour by stimulus satiation and food reinforcement. *Behaviour Research and Therapy, 1,* 53–61.
Ayllon, T., & Azrin, N. H. (1968). *The token economy.* New York: Appleton-Century-Crofts.
Azar, B. (1996). Why is it that practice makes perfect? *APA Monitor,* January, p. 18.
Azuma, H. (1984). Secondary control as a heterogeneous category. *American Psychologist, 39,* 970–971.

Babad, E., & Katz, Y. (1991). Wishful thinking—against all odds. *Journal of Applied Social Psychology, 21,* 1921–1938.
Backlund, E. O., Grandburg, P. O., & Hamberger, B. (1985). Transplantation of adrenal medullary tissue to striatum in Parkinsonianism: First clinical trials. *Journal of Neurosurgery, 62,* 169–173.
Backman, L., and Dixon, R. A. (1992). Psychological compensation: A theoretical framework. *Psychological Bulletin, 112,* 259–283.
Baddeley, A. (1966). Short-term memory for word sequences as a function of acoustic, semantic, and formal similarity. *Quarterly Journal of Experimental Psychology, 18,* 362–365.
Baddeley, A. (1990). *Human memory: Theory and practice.* Boston: Allyn & Bacon.
Baddeley, A. (1992). Working memory. *Science, 255,* 556–559.
Baenninger, M., & Newcombe, N. (1989). The role of experience in spatial test performance: A meta-analysis. *Sex Roles, 20,* 327–344.
Baer, L., et al. (1995). Cingulotomy for intractable obsessive-compulsive disorder. *Archives of General Psychiatry,* 52, 384–392.
Baggs, K., & Spence, S. H. (1990). Effectiveness of booster sessions in the maintenance and enhancement of treatment gains following assertion training. *Journal of Consulting and Clinical Psychology, 58,* 845–854.
Bahill, A. T., & Karnavas, W. J. (1993). The perceptual illusion of baseball's rising fastball and breaking curveball. *Journal of Experimental Psychology: Human Perception and Performance, 19,* 3–14.
Bahrick, H. P. (1984). Semantic memory content in permastore: Fifty years of memory for Spanish learned in school. *Journal of Experimental Psychology: General, 113,* 1–35.
Bahrick, H. P., Bahrick, P. O., & Wittlinger, R. P. (1975). Fifty years of memory for names and faces: A cross-sectional approach. *Journal of Experimental Psychology: General, 104,* 54–75.
Bahrick, H. P., & Hall, L. K. (1991). Lifetime maintenance of high school mathematics content. *Journal of Experimental Psychology: General, 120,* 20–33.
Bahrick, H. P., Hall, L. K., & Berger, S. A. (1996). Accuracy and distortion in memory for high school grades. *Psychological Science, 7,* 265–271.
Bailey, J. M., & Pillard, R. C. (1991). A genetic study of male sexual orientation. *Archives of General Psychiatry, 48,* 1089–1096.
Bailey, J. M., Pillard, R. C., Neale, M. C., & Agyei, Y. (1993). Heritable factors influence sexual orientation in women. *Archives of General Psychiatry, 50,* 217–223.
Bailey, J. M., & Zucker, K. J. (1995). Childhood sex-typed behavior and sexual orientation: A conceptual analysis and quantitative review. *Developmental Psychology, 31,* 43–55.
Baillargeon, R. (1986). Representing the existence and the location of hidden objects: Object permanence in 6- and 8-month-old infants. *Cognition, 23,* 21–41.
Baillargeon, R. (1994). How do infants learn about the physical world? *Current Directions in Psychological Science, 5,* 133–140.
Baillargeon, R., & De Vos, J. (1991). Object permanence in young infants: Further evidence. Child *Development, 62,* 1227–1246.
Baker, E. L. (1985). Psychoanalysis and psychoanalytic therapy. In S. J. Lynn & J. P. Garske (Eds.), *Contemporary psychotherapies: Models and methods.* Columbus, OH: Merrill.
Balay, J., & Shevrin, H. (1988). The subliminal psychodynamic activation method: A critical review. *American Psychologist, 43,* 161–174.
Balch, W. R., & Lewis, B. S. (1996). Music-dependent memory: The roles of tempo change and mood mediation. *Journal of Experimental Psychology: Learning, Memory, and Cognition, 22,* 1354–1363.
Balota, D. A., & Paul, S. T. (1996). Summation of activation: Evidence from multiple primes that converge and diverge within semantic memory. *Journal of Experimental Psychology: Learning, Memory, and Cognition, 22,* 827–845.
Baltes, P. B., Cornelius, S. W., & Nesselroade, J. R. (1979). Cohort effects in developmental psychology. In J. R. Nesselroade & P. B. Baltes (Eds.), *Longitudinal research in the study of behavior and development* (pp. 61–87). New York: Academic Press.
Baltes, P. B., & Smith, J. (1990). Toward a psychology of wisdom and its ontogenesis. In R. J. Sternberg (Ed.), *Wisdom: Its nature, origins, and development* (pp. 87–120). New York: Cambridge University Press.
Banaji, M. R., & Steele, C. M. (1989). Alcohol and self-evaluation: Is a social cognition approach beneficial? *Social Cognition, 7,* 137–151.
Banaji, M. R., Hardin, C., & Rothman, A. J. (1993). Implicit stereotyping in person judgment. *Journal of Personality and Social Psychology, 65,* 272–281.
Bandura, A. (1969). *Principles of behavior modification.* New York: Holt, Rinehart & Winston.
Bandura, A. (1977). *Social learning theory.* Englewood Cliffs, NJ: Prentice-Hall.
Bandura, A. (1982). The psychology of chance encounters and life paths. *American Psychologist, 37,* 747–755.
Bandura, A. (1986). *Social foundations of thought and action: A social cognitive theory.* Englewood Cliffs, NJ: Prentice-Hall.
Bandura, A. (1989). Human agency in social cognitive theory. *American Psychologist, 44,* 1175–1184.

Bandura, A., Blanchard, E. B., & Ritter, B. (1969). Relative efficacy of desensitization and modeling approaches for inducing behavioral, affective, and attitudinal changes. *Journal of Personality and Social Psychology, 13,* 173–199.

Bandura, A., Ross, D., & Ross, S. A. (1961). Transmission of aggression through imitation of aggressive models. *Journal of Abnormal and Social Psychology,* 63, 575–582.

Banich, M. T. (1995). Interhemispheric processing: Theoretical considerations and empirical approaches. In R. J. Davidson & K. Hugdahl (Eds.), *Brain asymmetry* (pp. 427–450). Cambridge, MA: MIT Press.

Banks, M. S., & Salapatek, P. (1983). Infant visual perception. In M. M. Haith & J. J. Campos (Eds.), *Handbook of Child Psychology: Vol. 2. Infancy and Developmental Psychobiology* (4th ed., pp. 435–571). New York: Wiley.

Bar-Hillel, M. (1980). The base-rate fallacy in probability judgments. *Acta Psychologica, 44,* 211–213.

Barasch, M. (1993, August). The mind-body revolution. *Psychology Today,* pp. 58–63, 86, 90, 92.

Barbaro, N. M. (1988). Studies of PAG/PVG stimulation for pain relief in humans. *Progress in Brain Research, 77,* 165–173.

Barber, T. X. (1969). *Hypnosis: A scientific approach.* New York: Van Nostrand Reinhold.

Bargh, J. A., Chen, M., & Burrows, L. (1996). Automaticity of social behavior: Direct effects of trait construct and stereotype activation on action. *Journal of Personality and Social Psychology, 71,* 230–244.

Barker, S. L., Funk, S. C., & Houston, B. K. (1988). Psychological treatment versus nonspecific factors: A meta-analysis of conditions that engender comparable expectations for improvement. *Clinical Psychology Review, 8,* 579–594.

Barkley, R. A. (1990). *Attention-deficit hyperactivity disorder: A handbook for diagnosis and treatment.* New York: Guilford Press.

Barkley, R. A. (1997). Behavioral inhibition, sustained attention, and executive functions: Constructing a unifying theory of ADHD. *Psychological Bulletin, 121,* 65–94.

Barlow, D. H. (1988). *Anxiety and its disorders.* New York: Guilford Press.

Barlow, D. H., & Lehman, C. L. (1996). Advances in the psychosocial treatment of anxiety disorders: Implications for national health care. *Archives of General Psychiatry, 53,* 727–735.

Baron, R., Logan, H., Lilly, J., Inman, M., & Brennan, M. (1994). Negative emotion and message processing. *Journal of Experimental Social Psychology, 30,* 181–201.

Baron, R. M., Mandel, D. R., Adams, C. A., & Griffin, L. M. (1976). Effects of social density in university residential environments. *Journal of Personality and Social Psychology, 34,* 434–446.

Baron, R. S., Cutrona, C. E., Hicklin, D., Russell, D. W., & Lubaroff, D. M. (1990). Social support and immune function among spouses of cancer patients. *Journal of Personality and Social Psychology, 59,* 344–352.

Baron, R. S., Vandello, J. A., & Brunsman, B. (1996). The forgotten variable in conformity research: Impact of task importance on social influence. *Journal of Personality and Social Psychology, 71,* 915–927.

Baron-Cohen, S., Burt, L., Smith-Laittan, F., Harrison, J., & Bolton, P. (1996). Synaesthesia: Prevalence and familiality. *Perception, 25,* 1073–1079.

Baron-Cohen, S., Harrison, J. Goldstein, L. H., & Wyke, M. (1993). Coloured speech perception: Is synaesthesia what happens when modularity breaks down? *Perception, 22,* 419–426.

Barrick, M. R., & Mount, M. K. (1991). The big five personality dimensions and job performance: A meta-analysis. *Personnel Psychology, 44,* 1–26.

Barrick, M. R., & Mount, M. K. (1996). Effects of impression management and self-deception on the predictive validity of personality constructs. *Journal of Applied Psychology, 81,* 261–272.

Barron, F. (1988). Putting creativity to work. In R. Sternberg (Ed.), *The nature of creativity* (pp. 76–98). New York: Cambridge University Press.

Barsky, A. J., Goodson, J. D., Lane, R. S., & Cleary, P. D. (1988). The amplification of somatic symptoms. *Psychosomatic Medicine, 50,* 510–519.

Barthrop, R. W., Lazarus, L., Luckhurst, E., Kiloh, L. G., & Penny, R. (1977). Depressed lymphocyte function after bereavement. *Lancet, 1,* 834–839.

Bartlett, F. C. (1932). Remembering: *A study in experimental and social psychology.* Cambridge: Cambridge University Press.

Barton, J. (1994). Choosing to work at night: A moderating influence on individual tolerance to shift work. *Journal of Applied Psychology, 79,* 449–454.

Bartoushuk, L. M., & Beauchamp, G. K. (1994). Chemical senses. *Annual Review of Psychology, 45,* 419–449.

Baruss, I. (1987). Meta-analysis of definitions of consciousness. *Imagination, Cognition and Personality, 6,* 321–329.

Bashore, T. R., & Rapp, P. E. (1993). Are there alternatives to traditional polygraph procedures? *Psychological Bulletin, 113,* 3–22.

Bass, E., & Davis, L. (1988). *The courage to heal.* New York: Harper & Row.

Bassili, J. N., & Provencal, A. (1988). Perceiving minorities: A factor-analytic approach. *Personality and Social Psychology Bulletin, 14,* 5–15.

Bates, G. W. (1981). On the nature of the hot flash. *Clinical Obstetrics and Gynecology, 24,* 231.

Batson, C. D. (1991). *The altruism question: Toward a social-psychological answer.* Hillsdale, NJ: Erlbaum.

Batson, C. D., Batson, J. G., Griffitt, C. A., Barrientos, S., Brandt, J. R., Sprengelmeyer, P., & Bayly, M. J. (1989). Negative-state relief and the empathy-altruism hypothesis. *Journal of Personality and Social Psychology, 56,* 922–933.

Batson, C. D., Duncan, B. D., Ackerman, P., Buckley, T., & Birch, K. (1981). Is empathic emotion a source of altruistic motivation? *Journal of Personality and Social Psychology, 40,* 290–302.

Bauer, P. J. (1996). What do infants recall of their lives?: Memory for specific events by one- to two-year olds. *American Psychologist, 51,* 29–41.

Bauer, R. M., & Verfaellie, M. (1992). Memory dissociations: A cognitive psychophysiology perspective. In L. R. Squire & N. Butters (Eds.), *Neuropsychology of memory* (2nd ed., pp. 58–71). New York: Guilford Press.

Baum, A., & Valins, S. (1979). Architectural mediation of residential density and control: Crowding and the regulation of social contact. *Advances in Experimental Social Psychology, 12,* 131–175.

Baumeister, R. F. (1990). Suicide as escape from the self. *Psychological Review, 97,* 90–113.

Baumeister, R. F. (1991). *Escaping the self.* New York: Basic Books.

Baumeister, R. F., & Leary, M. R. (1996). The need to belong: Desire for interpersonal attachments as a fundamental human motivation. *Psychological Bulletin, 117,* 497–529.

Baumeister, R. F., & Scher, S. J. (1988). Self-defeating behavior patterns among normal individuals: Review and analysis of common self-destructive tendencies. *Psychological Bulletin, 104,* 3–22.

Baumeister, R. F., Smart, L., & Boden, J. M. (1996). Relation of threatened egotism to violence and aggression: The dark side of high self-esteem. *Psychological Review, 103,* 5–33.

Baur, S. (1988). *Hypochondria: Woeful imaginings.* Berkeley: University of California Press.

Bayley, N. (1949). Consistency and variability in the growth of intelligence from birth to eighteen years. *Journal of Genetic Psychology, 75,* 165–196.

Bayliss, G. C., Rolls, E. T., & Leonard, C. M. (1985). Selectivity between faces in the responses of a population of neurons in the cortex in the superior temporal sulcus of the monkey. *Brain Research, 342,* 91–102.

Bechara, A., Tranel, D., Damasio, R., Adolphs, C. R., & Damasio, A. (1995). Double dissociation of conditioning and declarative knowledge relative to the amygdala and hippocampus in humans. *Science, 269,* 1115–1118.

Beck, A. T. (1967). *Cognitive therapy and the emotional disorders.* New York: International Universities Press.

Beck, A. T. (1985). Cognitive therapy. In H. I. Kaplan & J. Sadock (Eds.), Comprehensive textbook of psychiatry (4th ed.). Baltimore: Williams & Wilkins.

Beck, A. T. (1991), Cognitive therapy: A 30-year retrospective. *American Psychologist, 46,* 368–375.

Beck, A. T. (1993). Cognitive therapy: Past, present, and future. *Journal of Consulting and Clinical Psychology, 61,* 194–198.

Beck, A. T., & Katcher, A. (1983). *Between pets and people: The importance of animal companionship.* New York: Putnam.

Beck, A. T., Brown, G., Berchick, R. J., Stewart, B. L., & Steer, R. A. (1990). Relationship between hopelessness and ultimate suicide: A replication with psychiatric outpatients. *American Journal of Psychiatry, 147,* 190–195.

Beck, A. T., Emery, G., & Greenberg, R. L. (1985). *Anxiety disorders and phobias: A cognitive perspective.* New York: Basic Books.

Beck, A. T., Rush, A. J., Shaw, B. F., & Emery, G. (1979). *Cognitive therapy of depression.* New York: Guilford Press.

Beck, E. M., & Tolnay, S. E. (1990). The killing fields of the Deep South: The market for cotton and the lynching of blacks, 1882–1930. *American Sociological Review, 55,* 526–539.

Beck, J. S. (1995). *Cognitive therapy: Basics and beyond.* New York: Guilford Press.

Becker, F. D. (1981). *Workspace.* New York: Praeger.

Begg, I., Anas, A., & Farinacci, S. (1992). Dissociation of processes in belief: Source recollection, statement familiarity, and the illusion of truth. *Journal of Experimental Psychology: General, 121,* 446–458.

Beggan, J. K. (1992). On the social nature of nonsocial perception: The mere ownership effect. *Journal of Personality and Social Psychology, 62,* 229–237.

Begley, S., & Ramo, J. C. (1993, November 1). Not just a pretty face. *Newsweek,* pp. 63–67.

Beilin, H. (1992). Piaget's enduring contribution to developmental psychology. *Developmental Psychology, 28,* 191–204.

Beitman, B. D., Goldfried, M. R., & Norcross, J. C. (1989). The movement toward integrating the psychotherapies: An overview. *American Journal of Psychiatry, 146,* 138–147.

Bell, A. P., Weinberg, M. S., & Hammersmith, S. K. (1981). *Sexual preference: Its development in men and women.* Bloomington: Indiana University Press.

Bellack, A. S., & Hersen, M. (Eds.). (1985). *Dictionary of behavior therapy techniques.* New York: Pergamon.

Belli, R. F., Lindsay, D. S., Gales, M. S., & McCarthy, T. T. (1994). Memory impairment and source misattribution in postevent misinformation experiments with short retention intervals. *Memory and Cognition,* 22, 40–54.

Belmore, S. M. (1987). Determinants of attention during impression formation. *Journal of Experimental Psychology: Learning, Memory, and Cognition, 13,* 480–489.

Belsky, J. (1988). The "effects" of infant daycare reconsidered. *Early Childhood Research Quarterly, 3,* 235–272.

Belsky, J., & Pensky, E. (1988). Marital changes across the transition to parenthood. *Marriage and Family Review, 12,* 133–156.
Bem, D. J. (1967). Self-perception: An alternative interpretation of cognitive dissonance phenomena. *Psychological Review, 74,* 183–200.
Bem, D. J. (1996). Exotic becomes erotic: A developmental theory of sexual orientation. *Psychological Review, 103,* 320–335.
Bem, D. J., & Honorton, C. (1994). Does Psi exist? Replicable evidence for an anomalous process of information transfer. *Psychological Bulletin, 115,* 4–18.
Bem, S. L. (1981). Gender schema theory: A cognitive account of sex typing. *Psychological Review, 88,* 354–364.
Ben-Shakhar, G., Bar-Hillel, M., Bilu, Y., Ben-Abba, E., & Flug, A. (1986). Can graphology predict occupational success? Two empirical studies and some methodological ruminations. *Journal of Applied Psychology, 71,* 645–653.
Benbow, C. P. (1988). Sex differences in mathematical reasoning ability in intellectually talented preadolescents: Their nature, effects, and possible causes. *Behavioral and Brain Sciences, 11,* 169–232.
Benca, R. M., Obermeyer, W. H., Thisted, R. A., & Gillin, J. C. (1992). Sleep and psychiatric disorders: A meta-analysis. *Archives of General Psychiatry, 49,* 651–658.
Benedict, R. (1959). *Patterns of culture.* Boston: Houghton Mifflin.
Benjamin, L. T., Jr. (1988). A history of teaching machines. *American Psychologist, 43,* 703–712.
Benjamin, L. T., Jr., Durkin, M., Link, M., Vestal, M., & Acord, J. (1992). Wundt's American doctoral students. *American Psychologist, 47,* 123–131.
Benson, H. (1975). *The relaxation response.* New York: Morrow.
Benson, H. (1993). The relaxation response. In D. Goleman & J. Gurin (Eds.), *Mind body medicine: How to use your mind for better health* (pp. 233–257). Yonkers, NY: Consumer Reports Books.
Benson, J. B. (1993). Season of birth and onset of locomotion: Theoretical and methodological implications. *Infant Behavior and Development, 16,* 69–81.
Benton, M. K., & Schroeder, H. E. (1990). Social skills training with schizophrenics: A meta-analytic evaluation. *Journal of Consulting and Clinical Psychology, 58,* 741–747.
Berg, J. H. (1987). Responsiveness and self-disclosure. In V. J. Derlega & J. H. Berg (Eds.), *Self-disclosure* (pp. 101–130). New York: Plenum.
Bergin, A. E., & Garfield, S. L. (Eds.). (1994). *Handbook of psychotherapy and behavior change* (4th ed.). New York: Wiley.
Bergin, A. E., & Lambert, M. J. (1978). The evaluation of therapeutic outcomes. In S. L. Garfield & A. E. Bergin (Eds.), *Handbook of psychotherapy and behavior change* (2nd ed., pp. 139–189). New York: Wiley.
Berglas, S., & Jones, E. E. (1978). Drug choice as a self-handicapping strategy in response to noncontingent success. *Journal of Personality and Social Psychology, 36,* 405–417.
Berkman, L., & Syme, S. L. (1979). Social networks, host resistance, and mortality: A nine-year follow-up study of Alameda County residents. *American Journal of Epidemiology, 109,* 186–204.
Berkowitz, L. (1983). Aversively stimulated aggression: Some parallels and differences in research with animals and humans. *American Psychologist, 38,* 1135–1144.
Berkowitz, L. (1989). Frustration-aggression hypothesis: Examination and reformulation. *Psychological Bulletin, 106,* 59–73.
Berkowitz, L. (1993). *Aggression: Its causes, consequences, and control.* New York: McGraw-Hill.
Berkowitz, L., & LePage, A. (1967). Weapons as aggression-eliciting stimuli. *Journal of Personality and Social Psychology, 7,* 202–207.
Berliner, D. C., & Calfee, R. C. (Eds.) (1996). *Handbook of educational psychology.* New York: Macmillan.
Bernard, M. E., & DiGiuseppe, R. (Eds.). (1989). *Inside rational-emotive therapy.* New York: Academic Press.
Berndt, T. (1996). Transitions in friendship and friends' influence. In J. A. Graber, J. Brooks-Gunn, & A. C. Petersen, (Eds.). *Transitions through adolescence: Interpersonal domains and context* (pp. 57–84). Mahwah, NJ: Erlbaum.
Berndt, T. J. (1979). Developmental changes in conformity to peers and parents. *Developmental Psychology, 15,* 606–616.
Berndt, T. J., & Ladd, G. W. (Eds.). (1989). *Peer relationships in child development.* New York: Wiley.
Burnstein, E., Crandall, C., & Kitayama, S. (1994). Some Neo-Darwinian decision rules for altruism: Weighing cues for inclusive fitness as a function of the biological importance of the decision. *Journal of Personality and Social Psychology, 67,* 773–789.
Bernstein, E. M., & Putnam, F. W. (1986). Development, reliability, and validity of a dissociation scale. *Journal of Nervous and Mental Disease, 174,* 727–735.
Bernstein, I. L., & Borson, S. (1986). Learned food aversion: A component of anorexia syndromes. *Psychological Review, 93,* 462–472.
Bernstein, R., & Gaw, A. (1990). Koro: Proposed classification for DSM-IV. *American Journal of Psychiatry, 147,* 1670–1674.
Berridge, A. P., & Valenstein, E. S. (1991). What psychological process mediates feeding evoked by electrical stimulation of the lateral hypothalamus? *Behavioral Neuroscience, 105,* 3–14.
Berridge, K. C., Venier, I. L., & Robinson, T. E. (1989). Taste reactivity analysis of 6-hydroxydopamine-induced aphagia: Implications for arousal and anhedonia hypotheses of dopamine function. *Behavioral Neuroscience, 103,* 3645.
Berry, D. S., & McArthur, L. Z. (1986). Perceiving character in faces: The impact of age-related craniofacial changes in social perception. *Psychological Bulletin, 100,* 3–18.
Berry, D. S., & McArthur, L. Z. (1988). What's in a face? Facial maturity and the attribution of legal responsibility. *Personality and Social Psychology Bulletin, 14,* 23–33.
Berry, J. M., West, R. L., & Dennehey, D. M. (1989). Reliability and validity of the memory self-efficacy questionnaire. *Developmental Psychology, 25,* 701–713.
Berry, J. W. (1979). A cultural ecology of social behavior. *Advances in Experimental Social Psychology, 12,* 177–206.
Berry, J. W., Kim, U., Power, S., Young, M., & Bujaki, M. (1989). Acculturation attitudes in plural societies. *Applied Psychology, 38,* 185–206.
Berry, J. W., Poortinga, Y. H., Segall, M. H., & Dasen, P. R. (1992). *Cross-cultural psychology: Research and applications.* New York: Cambridge University Press.
Berscheid, E. (1994). Interpersonal relationships. *Annual Review of Psychology, 45,* 79–129.
Berscheid, E., & Walster, E. (1974). A little bit about love. In T. Huston (Ed.), *Foundations of interpersonal attraction* (pp. 356–379). New York: Academic Press.
Berscheid, E., Snyder, M., & Omoto, A. M. (1989). The Relationship Closeness Inventory: Assessing the closeness of interpersonal relationships. *Journal of Personality and Social Psychology, 57,* 792–807.
Bersoff, D. E. (Ed.) (1995). *Ethical conflicts in psychology.* Washington, DC: American Psychological Association.
Best, D. L., & Williams, J. E. (1993). A cross-cultural viewpoint. In A. E. Beall & R. J. Sternberg (Eds.), *The psychology of gender* (pp. 215–248). New York: Guilford Press.
Bettencourt, B. A., & Miller, N. (1996). Gender differences in aggression as a function of provocation: A meta-analysis. *Psychological Bulletin, 119,* 422–447.
Beyer, S. (1990). Gender differences in the accuracy of self-evaluations of performance. *Journal of Personality and Social Psychology, 59,* 960–970.
Biederman, I. (1987). Recognition-by-components: A theory of human image understanding. *Psychological Review, 94,* 115–147.
Biernat, M. (1991). Gender stereotypes and the relationship between masculinity and femininity: A developmental analysis. *Journal of Personality and Social Psychology, 61,* 351–365.
Biner, P. M., Angle, S. T., Park, J. H., Mellinger, A. E., & Barber, B. C. (1995). Need state and the illusion of control. *Personality and Social Psychology Bulletin, 21,* 899–907.
Binet, A., & Simon, T. (1905). Methodes nouvelles pour le diagnostic du niveau intellectual des anormaux. *L'Annee Psychologique, 11,* 191–244.
Biringer, F., Anderson, J. R., & Strubel, D. (1989). Self-recognition in senile dementia. *Experimental Aging Research, 14,* 177–180.
Birren, J. E., & Fisher, L. M. (1995). Aging and speed of behavior: Possible consequences for psychological functioning. *Annual Review of Psychology, 46,* 329–353.
Birren, J. E., & Schaie, K. W. (Eds.) (1995). *Handbook of the psychology of aging* (4th ed.). San Diego: Academic Press.
Bjork, D. W. (1993). *B. F. Skinner: A life.* New York: Basic Books.
Bjork, E. L., & Bjork, R. A. (Eds.) (1996). *Memory.* San Diego: Academic Press.
Bjorklund, A. (1991). Neural transplantation—an experimental tool with clinical possibilities. *Trends in the Neurosciences, 14,* 319–322.
Blair, I. V., & Banaji, M. R. (1996). Automatic and controlled processes in stereotype priming. *Journal of Personality and Social Psychology, 70,* 1142–1163.
Blair, R. J. R., Jones, L., Clark, F., & Smith, M. (1997). The psychopathic individual: A lack of responsiveness to distress cues? *Psychophysiology, 34,* 192–198.
Blair, S. N., Kohl, H. W., Paffenbarger, R. S., Clark, D. G., Cooper, K. H., & Gibbons, L. W. (1989). Physical fitness and all-cause mortality: A prospective study of healthy men and women. *Journal of the American Medical Association, 262,* 2395–2401.
Blakeslee, S. (1993, June 1). Scanner pinpoints sites of thoughts as people see or speak. *The New York Times,* pp. C1, C3.
Blanchard, E. B. (1994). Behavioral medicine and health psychology. In A. E. Bergin & S. L. Garfield (Eds.), *Handbook of Psychotherapy and behavior change* (4th ed. pp. 701–733.) New York: Wiley.
Blanchard, E. B., et al. (1982). Biofeedback and relaxation training with three kinds of headache: Treatment effects and their prediction. *Journal of Consulting and Clinical Psychology, 50,* 562–575.
Blanchard, F. A., Lilly, T., & Vaughn, L. A. (1991). Reducing the expression of racial prejudice. *Psychological Science, 2,* 101–105.
Blaney, P. H. (1986). Affect and memory: A review. *Psychological Bulletin, 99,* 229–246.
Blascovich, J., & Katkin, E. S. (1993). *Cardiovascular reactivity to psychological stress and disease.* Washington, DC: American Psychological Association.
Blasi, A. (1980). Bridging moral cognition and moral action: A critical review of the literature. *Psychological Bulletin, 88,* 1–45.
Blass, T. (1992). The social psychology of Stanley Milgram. *Advances in Experimental Social Psychology, 25,* 227–329.
Blatt, S. J. (1990). The Rorschach: A test of perception or an evaluation of representation. *Journal of Personality Assessment, 55,* 394–416.
Blehar, M. C., & Rosenthal, N. E. (1989). Seasonal affective disorders and phototherapy: Report of a National Institute of Mental Health–sponsored workshop. *Archives of General Psychiatry, 46,* 469–474.

Blehar, M. C., Weissman, M. M., Gershon, E. S., Hirschfeld, R. M. A. (1988). Family and genetic studies of affective disorders. *Archives of General Psychiatry, 45,* 289–292.

Bleuler, E. (1911). *Dementia praecox oder gruppe der schizophrenien.* Leipzig, Germany: F. Deuticke.

Block, J. (1981). Some enduring and consequential structures of personality. In A. I. Rabin (Ed.), *Further explorations in personality.* New York: Wiley.

Block, J. R., & Yuker, H. E. (1989). *Can you believe your eyes?* New York: Gardner Press.

Blocklyn, P. L. (1988) Preemployment testing. *Personnel, 65,* 63–65.

Bloom, A. (1981). *The linguistic shaping of thought.* Hillsdale, NJ: Erlbaum.

Bloom, L. C., & Mudd, S. A. (1991). Depth of processing approach to face recognition: A test of two theories. *Journal of Experimental Psychology: Learning, Memory, and Cognition, 17,* 556–565.

Bochner, S. (1994). Cross-cultural differences in the self-concept: A test of Hofstede's individualism/collectivism distinction. *Journal of Cross Cultural Psychology, 25,* 273–283.

Bodenhausen, G. V. (1990). Stereotypes as judgmental heuristics: Evidence of circadian variations in discrimination. *Psychological Science, 1,* 319–322.

Boer, F., & Dunn, J. (Eds.). (1992). *Children's sibling relationships.* Hillsdale, NJ: Erlbaum.

Bogen, J. E. (1978). The callosal syndrome. In K. M. Heilman & E. Valenstein (Eds.), *Clinical Neuropsychology* (2nd ed., pp. 308–359). New York: Oxford University Press.

Boggiano, A. K., Harackiewicz, J. M., Bessette, M. M., & Main, D. S. (1985). Increasing children's interest through performance-contingent reward. *Social Cognition, 3,* 400–411.

Bolanowski, S. J., Jr., & Gescheider, G. A. (Eds.). (1991). *Ratio scaling of psychological magnitude: In honor of the memory of S. S. Stevens.* Hillsdale, NJ: Erlbaum.

Bolles, R. C. (1970). Species-specific defense reactions and avoidance learning. *Psychological Review, 77,* 32–48.

Bond, R., & Smith, P. B. (1996). Culture and conformity: A meta-analysis of studies using Asch's (1952b, 1956) line judgment task. *Psychological Bulletin, 119,* 111–137.

Boneau, C. A. (1990). Psychological literacy: A first approximation. *American Psychologist, 45,* 891–900.

Boneau, C. A. (1992). Observations on psychology's past and future. *American Psychologist, 47,* 1586–1596.

Booker, J. M., & Hellekson, C. J. (1992). Prevalence of seasonal affective disorder in Alaska. *American Journal of Psychiatry, 149,* 1176–1182.

Boon, S., & Draijer, N. (1993). Multiple personality disorder in the Netherlands: A clinical investigation of 71 patients. *American Journal of Psychiatry, 150,* 489–494.

Booth-Kewley, S., & Friedman, H. S. (1987). Psychological predictors of heart disease: A quantitative review. *Psychological Bulletin, 101,* 343–362.

Borbely, A. (1986). *The secrets of sleep.* New York: Basic Books.

Borch-Jacobsen, M. (1996). *Remembering Anna O.* London: Routledge.

Boring, E. G. (1923). Intelligence as the tests test it. *New Republic, 35,* 35–37.

Borman, W. C., Hanson, M. A., & Hedge, J. W. (1997). Personnel selection. *Annual Review of Psychology, 48,* 299–337.

Bornstein, M. H. (1989). Information processing (habituation) in infancy and stability in cognitive development. *Human Development, 32,* 129–136.

Bornstein, M. H. (Ed.) (1995). *Handbook of parenting (Volumes 1–4).* Mahwah, NJ: Erlbaum.

Bornstein, R. F. (1989). Exposure and affect: Overview and meta-analysis of research, 1968–1987. *Psychological Bulletin, 106,* 265–289.

Bornstein, R. F. (1992). Subliminal mere exposure effects. In R. F. Bornstein & T. S. Pittman (Eds.), *Perception without awareness: Cognitive, clinical, and social perspectives* (pp. 191–210). New York: Guilford Press.

Bornstein, R. F., & Pittman, T. S. (Eds.). (1992). *Perception without awareness: Cognitive, clinical, and social perspectives.* New York: Guilford Press.

Bornstein, R. F., Kale, A. R., & Cornell, K. R. (1990). Boredom as a limiting condition on the mere exposure effect. *Journal of Personality and Social Psychology, 58,* 791–800.

Bouchard, T. J., Jr. (1994). Genes, environment, and personality. *Science, 264,* 1700–1701.

Bouchard, T. J., Jr., Lykken, D. T., McGue, M., Segal, N. L., & Tellegen, A. (1990). Sources of human psychological differences: The Minnesota study of twins reared apart. *Science, 250,* 223–228.

Bouchard, T. J., Jr., & McGue, M. (1981). Familial studies of intelligence. *Science, 212,* 1055–1059.

Bouchard, T. J., Jr., & Segal, N. L. (1985). Environment and IQ. In B. B. Wolman (Ed.), *Handbook of intelligence: Theories, measurements, and applications* (pp. 391–464). New York: Wiley.

Bousfield, W. A. (1953). The occurrence of clustering in the recall of randomly arranged associates. *Journal of General Psychology, 49,* 229–240.

Bovbjerg, D. H., et al. (1990). Anticipatory immune suppression in women receiving cyclic chemotherapy for ovarian cancer. *Journal of Consulting and Clinical Psychology, 58,* 153–157.

Bovbjerg, D.H., et al. (1992). An experimental analysis of classically conditioned nausea during cancer chemotherapy. *Psychosomatic Medicine, 54,* 623–637.

Bower, G. H. (1970). Organizational factors in memory. *Cognitive Memory, 1,* 18–46.

Bower, G. H. (1981). Mood and memory. *American Psychologist, 36,* 129–148.

Bower, G. H., & Winzenz, D. (1970). Comparison of associative learning strategies. *Psychonomic Science, 20,* 119–120.

Bower, T. G. R. (1982). *Development in infancy* (2nd ed.). San Francisco: W. H. Freeman.

Bowers, K. S. (1992). Imagination and dissociation in hypnotic responding. *International Journal of Clinical and Experimental Hypnosis, 40,* 253–275.

Bowers, K. S., & Farvolden, P. (1996). Revisiting a century-old Freudian slip: From suggestion disavowed to the truth repressed. *Psychological Bulletin, 119,* 355–380.

Bowers, K. S., & Woody, E. Z. (1996). Hypnotic amnesia and the paradox of intentional forgetting. *Journal of Abnormal Psychology, 105,* 381–390.

Bowers, T. G., & Clum, G. A. (1988). Relative contribution of specific and non-specific treatment effects: Meta-analysis of placebo-controlled behavior therapy research. *Psychological Bulletin, 103,* 315–323.

Bowlby, J. (1969). *Attachment and loss: Volume 1. Attachment.* London: Hogarth.

Bowlby, J. (1988). *A secure base.* New York: Basic Books.

Boynton, R. M. (1988). Color vision. *Annual Review of Psychology, 39,* 69–100.

Bradshaw, J. L., & Nettleton, N. C. (1981). The nature of hemispheric specialization in man. *Behavioral and Brain Sciences, 4,* 51–91.

Brainerd, C. J. (1996). Piaget: A centennial celebration. *Psychological Science, 7,* 191–195.

Brandimonte, M., Einstein, G. O., & McDaniel, M. A. (Eds.). (1996). *Prospective memory: Theory and applications.* Mahwah, NJ: Erlbaum.

Branscombe, N. R., & Wann, D. L. (1994). Collective self-esteem consequences of outgroup derogation when a valued social identity is on trial. *European Journal of Social Psychology, 24,* 641–657.

Bransford, J. D., & Stein, B. S. (1984). *The ideal problem solver.* New York: W. H. Freeman.

Braun, B. G. (1988). *Treatment of multiple personality disorder.* Washington, DC: American Psychiatric Press.

Bray, G. A. (1986). Effects of obesity on health and happiness. In K. D. Brownell & J. P. Foreyt (Eds.), *Handbook of Eating Disorders.* New York: Basic Books.

Brean, H. (1958, March 31). What hidden sell is all about. *Life,* pp. 104–114.

Breedlove, S. M. (1994). Sexual differentiation of the human nervous system. *Annual Review of Psychology, 45,* 389–418.

Bregman, A. S. (1990). *Auditory scene analysis.* Cambridge MA: MIT Press.

Breland, K., & Breland, M. (1961). The misbehavior of organisms. *American Psychologist, 16,* 681–684.

Brenner, C. (1982). *The mind in conflict.* New York: International Universities Press.

Breuer, J., & Freud, S. (1895). Studies on hysteria. In J. Strachey, *The standard edition of the complete psychological works of Sigmund Freud.* London: Hogarth Press. (Reprinted in 1955.)

Brewer, M. B. (1991). The social self: On being the same and different at the same time. *Personality and Social Psychology Bulletin, 17,* 475–482.

Brewer, W. F., & Treyens, J. C. (1981). Role of schemata in memory for places. *Cognitive Psychology, 13,* 207–230.

Brickman, P., Coates, D., & Janoff-Bulman, R. J. (1978). Lottery winners and accident victims: Is happiness relative? *Journal of Personality and Social Psychology, 36,* 917–927.

Briere, J., & Lanktree, C. (1983). Sex role–related effects of sex bias in language. *Sex Roles, 9,* 625–632.

Brigham, J. C., & Malpass, R. S. (1985). The role of experience and contact in the recognition of faces of own- and other-race persons. *Journal of Social Issues, 41,* 139–155.

Brigham, J. C., & Pfeifer, J. E. (1996). Euthanasia: An introduction. *Journal of Social Issues, 52,* 1–11.

Broberg, A. G., Wessels, H., Lamb, M. E., & Hwang, C. P. (1997). Effects of day care on the development of cognitive abilities in 8-year-olds: A longitudinal study. *Developmental Psychology, 33,* 62–69.

Broca, P. (1861). Paul Broca on the speech centers (M. D. Boring, Trans.). In R. J. Herrnstein & E. G. Boring (Eds.), *A source book in the history of psychology.* Cambridge, MA: Harvard University Press. (Reprinted in 1965.)

Brockner, J. (1983). Low self-esteem and behavioral plasticity: Some implications. In L. Wheeler & P. Shaver (Eds.), *Review of personality and social psychology* (Vol. 4, pp. 237–271). Beverly Hills, CA: Sage.

Brody, L. R., & Hall, J. A. (1993). Gender and emotion. In M. Lewis & J. M. Haviland (Eds.), *Handbook of emotions* (pp. 447–460). New York: Guilford Press.

Bronfenbrenner, U., & Ceci, S. J. (1994). Nature-nurture reconceptualized in developmental perspective: A bioecological model. *Psychological Review, 101,* 568–586.

Brooks-Gunn, J., & Furstenberg, F. F., Jr. (1989). Adolescent sexual behavior. *American Psychologist, 44,* 249–257.

Brooks-Gunn, J., & Warren, M. P. (1985). The effects of delayed menarche in different contexts: Dance and nondance students. *Journal of Youth and Adolescence, 14,* 163–189.

Brooks-Gunn, J., Gross, R. T., Kraemer, H. C., Spiker, D., & Shapiro, S. (1992). Enhancing the cognitive outcomes of low birth weight, premature infants: For whom is the intervention most effective? *Pediatrics, 89,* 1209–1215.

Broughton, R. S. (1991). *Parapsychology: The controversial science.* New York: Ballantine Books.

Brown, A. S. (1991). A review of the tip-of-the-tongue experience. *Psychological Bulletin, 109,* 204–223.
Brown, A. S., & Murphy, D. R. (1989). Cryptomnesia: Delineating inadvertent plagiarism. *Journal of Experimental Psychology: Learning, Memory, and Cognition, 15,* 432–442.
Brown, A. S., & Nix, L. A. (1996). Turning lies into truths: Referential validation of falsehoods. *Journal of Experimental Psychology: Learning, Memory, and Cognition, 22,* 1088–1100.
Brown, B. B., Clasen, D. R., & Eicher, S. A. (1986). Perceptions of peer pressure, peer conformity dispositions, and self-reported behavior among adolescents. *Developmental Psychology, 22,* 521–530.
Brown, E. L., Deffenbacher, K. A., & Sturgill, W. (1977). Memory for faces and the circumstances of encounter. *Journal of Applied Psychology, 62,* 311–318.
Brown, G. K. (1990). A causal analysis of chronic pain and depression. *Journal of Abnormal Psychology, 99,* 127–137.
Brown, J. D. (1990). Evaluating one's abilities: Shortcuts and stumbling blocks on the road to self-knowledge. *Journal of Experimental Social Psychology, 26,* 149–167.
Brown, J. D. (1991). Staying fit and staying well: Physical fitness as a moderator of life stress. *Journal of Personality and Social Psychology, 60,* 555–561.
Brown, J. D., & Dutton, K. A. (1995). The thrill of victory, the complexity of defeat: Self-esteem and people's emotional reactions to success and failure. *Journal of Personality and Social Psychology, 68,* 712-722.
Brown, N. R., & Siegler, R. S. (1992). The role of availability in the estimation of national populations. *Memory and Cognition, 20,* 406–412.
Brown, R. (1973). *A first language: The early stages.* Cambridge, MA: Harvard University Press.
Brown, R., & Kulik, J. (1977). Flashbulb memories. *Cognition, 5,* 73–99.
Brown, R., & McNeill, D. (1966). The "tip of the tongue" phenomenon. *Journal of Verbal Learning and Verbal Behavior, 5,* 325–337.
Brown, T. A., & Barlow, D. H. (1992). Comorbidity among anxiety disorders: Implications for treatment and DSM-IV. *Journal of Consulting and Clinical Psychology, 60,* 835–844.
Brownell, K. D., & Fairburn, C. G. (Eds.). (1995). *Eating disorders and obesity: A comprehensive handbook.* New York: Guilford Press.
Brownell, K. D., & Wadden, T. A. (1992). Etiology and treatment of obesity: Understanding a serious, prevalent, and refractory disorder. *Journal of Consulting and Clinical Psychology, 60,* 505–517.
Bruck, M., Ceci, S. J., Francoeur, E., & Barr, R. (1995). "I hardly cried when I got my shot!" Influencing children's reports about a visit to their pediatrician. *Child Development, 66,* 193–208.
Brumberg, J. J. (1988). *Fasting girls: The emergence of anorexia nervosa as a modern disease.* Cambridge, MA: Harvard University Press.
Bruner, J. S. (1983). *Child's talk: Learning to use language.* New York: Norton.
Bruner, J. S., & Potter, M. C. (1964). Interference in visual recognition. *Science, 144,* 424–425.
Brunner, D. P., Kijk, D. J., Tobler, I., & Borbely, A. A. (1990). Effect of partial sleep stages and EEG power spectra: Evidence for non-REM and REM sleep homeostasis. *Electroencephalography and Clinical Neurophysiology, 75,* 492–499.
Bruyer, R. (1991). Covert face recognition in prosopagnosics: A review. *Brain and Cognition, 15,* 223–235.
Bryan, J. H., & Test, M. A. (1967). Models and helping: Naturalistic studies in aiding behavior. *Journal of Personality and Social Psychology, 6,* 400–407.
Buchanan, C. M., Eccles, J. S., & Becker, J. B. (1992). Are adolescents the victims of raging hormones? Evidence for activational effects of hormones on moods and behavior in adolescence. *Psychological Bulletin, 111,* 62–107.
Buck, L., & Axel, R. (1991). A novel multigene family may encode odorant receptors: A molecular basis for odor recognition. *Cell, 65,* 175–181.
Buckhout, R. (1974). Eyewitness testimony. *Scientific American, 231,* 23–31.
Buckley, J. T. (1996). Cold-nosed fleet puts heat on terrorism. *USA Today,* November 18, pp. 19A–20A.
Bull, R., & Rumsey, N. (1988). *The social psychology of facial appearance.* New York: Springer-Verlag.
Bullock, W. A., & Gilliland, K. (1993). Eysenck's arousal theory of introversion-extraversion: A converging measures investigation. *Journal of Personality and Social Psychology, 64,* 113–123.
Burger, J. M. (1991). Control. In V. Derlega, B. Winstead, & W. Jones (Eds.), *Personality* (pp. 287–312). Chicago: Nelson-Hall.
Burke, A., Heuer, F., & Reisberg, D. (1992). Remembering emotional events. *Memory and Cognition, 20,* 277–290.
Burton, H., & Sinclair, R. (1996). Somatosensory cortex and tactile perceptions. In L. Kruger (Ed.), *Pain and touch* (pp. 105–177). San Diego: Academic Press.
Bushman, B. J., & Cooper, H. M. (1990). Effects of alcohol on human aggression: An intergrative research review. *Psychological Bulletin, 107,* 341–354.
Bushman, B. J. (1993). Human aggression while under the influence of alcohol and other drugs: An integrative research review. *Current Directions in Psychological Science, 2,* 148–152.
Bushman, B. J., & Stack, A. D. (1996). Forbidden fruit versus tainted fruit: Effects of warning labels on attraction to television violence. *Journal of Experimental Psychology: Applied, 2,* 207–226.
Buske-Kirschbaum, A., Kirschbaum, C., Stierle, H., et al. (1994). Conditioned manipulation of natural killer (NK) cells in humans using a discriminative learning protocol. *Biological Psychology, 38,* 143–155.
Buske-Kirschbaum, A., Kirschbaum, C., Stierle, H., Lehnert, H., & Hellhammer, D. (1992). Conditioned increase in natural killer cell activity (NKCA) in humans. *Psychosomatic Medicine, 54,* 123–132.
Buss, A. H. (1980). *Self-consciousness and social anxiety.* San Francisco, CA: W. H. Freeman.
Buss, A. H., & Perry, M. (1992). The aggression questionnaire. *Journal of Personality and Social Psychology, 63,* 452–459.
Buss, D. M. (1988). The evolution of human intrasexual competition: Tactics of mate attraction. *Journal of Personality and Social Psychology, 54,* 616–628.
Buss, D. M. (1989). Sex differences in human mate preferences: Evolutionary hypotheses tested in 37 cultures. *Behavioral and Brain Sciences, 12,* 1–14.
Buss, D. M. (1994). *The evolution of desire.* New York: Basic Books.
Buss, D. M., & Shackelford, T. K. (1997). From vigilance to violence: Mate retention tactics in married couples. *Journal of Personality and Social Psychology,* in press.
Buss, D. M., Larsen, R. J., Westen, D., & Semmelroth, J. (1992). Sex differences in jealousy: Evolution, physiology, and psychology. *Psychological Science, 3,* 251–258.
Butcher, J. N., & Williams, C. L. (1992). *Essentials of MMPI-2 and MMPI-A interpretation.* Minneapolis: University of Minnesota Press.
Butcher, J. N., Dahlstrom, W. G., Graham, J. R., Tellegen, A., & Kaemmer, B. (1989). *MMPI-2: Minnesota Multiphasic Personality Inventory—2. Manual for administration and scoring.* Minneapolis: University of Minnesota Press.
Butler, D., & Geis, F. L. (1990). Nonverbal affect responses to male and female leaders: Implications for leadership evaluations. *Journal of Personality and Social Psychology, 58,* 48–59.
Buunk, B. P., Angleitner, A., Oubaid, V., & Buss, D. M. (1996). Sex differences in jealousy in evolutionary and cultural perspective: Tests from the Netherlands, Germany, and the United States. *Psychological Science, 7,* 359–363.
Buunk, B. P., & Hupka, R. B. (1987). Cross-cultural differences in the elicitation of sexual jealousy. *Journal of Sex Research, 23,* 12–22.
Byne, W., & Parsons, B. (1993). Human sexual orientation: The biological theories reappraised. *Archives of General Psychiatry, 50,* 228–239.
Byrne, B. M. (1996). *Measuring self-concept across the life span: Issues and instrumentation.* Washington, DC: American Psychological Association.
Byrne, D. (1971). *The attraction paradigm.* New York: Academic Press.
Byrne, D., Clore, G. L., & Smeaton, G. (1986). The attraction hypothesis: Do similar attitudes attract anything? *Journal of Personality and Social Psychology, 51,* 1167–1170.
Byrne, D., Kelley, K., & Fisher, W. A. (1993). Unwanted teenage pregnancies: Incidence, interpretation, and intervention. *Applied and Preventive Psychology, 2,* 101–113.

Cacioppo, J. T., & Petty, R. E. (1982). The need for cognition. *Journal of Personality and Social Psychology, 42,* 116–131.
Cacioppo, J. T., Marshall-Goodell, B. S., Tassinary, L. G., & Petty, R. E. (1992). Rudimentary determinants of attitudes: Classical conditioning is more effective when prior knowledge about the attitude stimulus is low than high. *Journal of Experimental Social Psychology, 28,* 207–233.
Cacioppo, J. T., Petty, R. E., Feinstein, J. A., Jarvis, W. B. G. (1996). Dispositional differences in cognitive motivation: The life and times of individuals varying in need for cognition. *Psychological Bulletin, 119,* 197–253.
Cairns, R. B., Gariepy, J. L., & Hood, K. E. (1990). Development, microevolution, and social behavior. *Psychological Review, 97,* 49–65.
Caldwell, C. B., & Gottesman, I. I. (1990). Schizophrenics kill themselves too: A review of risk factors for suicide. *Schizophrenia Bulletin, 16,* 571–589.
Calhoun, J. B. (1962). Population density and social pathology. *Scientific American, 206,* 139–148.
Camara, W. J., & Schneider, D. L. (1994). Integrity tests: Facts and unresolved issues. *American Psychologist, 49,* 112–119.
Cameron, J., & Pierce, W. D. (1994). Reinforcement, reward, and intrinsic motivation: A meta-analysis. *Review of Educational Research, 64,* 363–423.
Campbell, D. J., & Lee, C. (1988). Self-appraisal in performance evaluation: Development versus evaluation. *Academy Management Review, 13,* 302–313.
Campbell, J. D., & Fairey, P. J. (1989). Informational and normative routes to conformity. *Journal of Personality and Social Psychology, 57,* 457–468.
Campbell, J. M., Amerikaner, M., Swank, P., & Vincent, K. (1989). The relationship between the Hardiness Test and the Personal Orientation Inventory. *Journal of Research in Personality, 23,* 373–380.
Campos, J. J., Langer, A., & Krowtiz, A. (1970). Cardiac responses on the visual cliff in prelocomotor infants. *Science, 170,* 196–197.
Canfield, R. L., & Smith, E. G. (1996). Number-based expectations and sequential enumeration by 5-month-old infants. *Developmental Psychology, 32,* 269–279.
Cannon, D. S., Baker, T. B., & Wehl, C. K. (1981). Emetic and electric shock alcohol aversion therapy: Six- and twelve-month follow-up. *Journal of Consulting and Clinical Psychology, 49,* 360–368.
Cannon, W. B. (1927). The James-Lange theory of emotion: A critical examination and an alternative theory. *American Journal of Psychology, 39,* 106–124.

Cannon, W. B., & Washburn, A. L. (1912). An explanation of hunger. *American Journal of Physiology, 29,* 441–454.
Cantor, N., & Kihlstrom, J. F. (1987). *Personality and social intelligence.* Englewood Cliffs, NJ: Prentice-Hall.
Capaldi, E. D. (Ed.) (1996). *Why we eat what we eat: The psychology of eating.* Washington, DC: American Psychological Association.
Caplan, D. (1992). *Language: Structure, processing, and disorders.* Cambridge, MA: MIT Press.
Caramazza, A., & Hillis, A. E. (1991). Lexical organization of nouns and verbs in the brain. *Nature, 349,* 788–790.
Carlo, G., et al. (1996). A cross-national study on the relations among prosocial moral reasoning, gender role orientations, and prosocial behaviors. *Developmental Psychology, 32,* 231–240.
Carlson, C. L., & Bunner, M. R. (1993). Effects of methylphenidate on the academic performance of children with attention deficit hyperactivity disorder and learning disabilities. *School Psychology Review, 22,* 184–198.
Carlson, M., Marcus-Newhall, A., & Miller, N. (1990). Effects of situational aggressive cues: A quantitative review. *Journal of Personality and Social Psychology, 58,* 622–633.
Carmichael, L., Hogan, H. P., & Walter, A. (1932). An experimental study of the effect of language on the reproduction of visually perceived form. *Journal of Experimental Psychology, 15,* 73–86.
Carnegie, D. (1936). *How to win friends and influence people.* New York: Pocket Books. (Reprinted in 1972.)
Carroll, J. B. (1993). *Human cognitive abilities: A survey of factor-analytic studies.* Cambridge, England: University of Cambridge Press.
Carroll, J. M., & Russell, J. A. (1996). Do facial expressions signal specific emotions? Judging emotion from the face in context. *Journal of Personality and Social Psychology, 70,* 205–218.
Carskadon, M. A. (1993). Microsleep. In M. Carskadon (Ed.), *Encyclopedia of sleep and dreaming* (pp. 373–374). New York: Macmillan.
Carter, C. S. (1991). Hormonal influences on human sexual behavior. In J. B. Becker, S. M. Breedlove, & D. Crews (Eds.), *Behavioral endocrinology* (pp. 131–142). Cambridge, MA: MIT Press.
Cartwright, R. (1977, December). Happy endings for our dreams. *Psychology Today,* pp. 66–77.
Carver, C. S., & Scheier, M. F. (1981). *Attention and self-regulation: A control-theory approach to human behavior.* New York: Springer-Verlag.
Case, R. (1992). *The mind's staircase.* Hillsdale, NJ: Erlbaum.
Case, R. B., Moss, A. J., Case, N., McDermott, M., & Eberly, S. (1992). Living alone after myocardial infarction: Impact on prognosis. *Journal of the American Medical Association, 267,* 515–519.
Casey, M. B., Nuttall, R., Benbow, C. P., & Pezaris, E. (1995). The influence of spatial ability on gender differences in mathematics: College entrance test scores across diverse samples. *Developmental Psychology, 31,* 697–705.
Caspi, A., & Moffitt, T. E. (1991). Individual differences are accentuated during periods of social change: The sample case of girls at puberty. *Journal of Personality and Social Psychology, 61,* 157–168.
Caspi, A., Lynam, D., Moffitt, T. E., & Silva, P. A. (1993). Unraveling girls' delinquency: Biological, dispositional, and contextual contributions to adolescent misbehavior. *Developmental Psychology, 29,* 19–30.
Cassidy, J., Kirsh, S. J., Scolton, K. L., & Parke, R. D. (1996). Attachment and representations of peer relationships. *Developmental Psychology, 32,* 892–904.
Cattell, R. B. (1949). *The culture-free intelligence test.* Champaign, IL: Institute for Personality and Ability Testing.
Cattell, R. B. (1963). Theory of crystallized and fluid intelligence: A critical experiment. *Journal of Educational Psychology, 54,* 1–22.
Cattell, R. B. (1965). *The scientific analysis of personality.* Baltimore, MD: Penguin Books.
Cauffman, E., & Steinberg, L. (1996). Interactive effects of menarcheal status and dating on dieting and disordered eating among adolescent girls. *Developmental Psychology, 32,* 631–635.
Ceci, S. J. (1991). How much does schooling influence general intelligence and its cognitive components? A reassessment of the evidence. *Developmental Psychology, 27,* 703–722.
Ceci, S. J. (1996). *On intelligence: A bioecological treatise on intellectual development.* Cambridge, MA: Harvard University Press.
Ceci, S. J., & Bruck, M. (1995). *Jeopardy in the courtroom: A scientific analysis of children's testimony.* Washington, DC: American Psychological Association.
Ceci, S. J., Leichtman, M., & White, T. (in press). Interviewing preschoolers: Remembrances of things planted. In D. P. Peters (Ed.), *The child witness: Cognitive, social, and legal issues.* Netherlands: Kluwer.
Ceci, S. J., Ross, D. F., & Toglia, M. P. (1987). Suggestibility of children's memory: Psycholegal implications. *Journal of Experimental Psychology: General, 116,* 38–49.
Centers for Disease Control and Prevention (1993, July 19). *Newsweek,* p. 8.
Centers for Disease Control Vietnam Experience Study (1988). Health status of Vietnam veterans: I. Psychosocial characteristics. *Journal of the American Medical Association, 259,* 2701–2707.
Cerella, J. (1985). Information processing rates in the elderly. *Psychological Bulletin, 98,* 67–83.
Cernoch, J. M., & Porter, R. H. (1985). Recognition of maternal axillary odors by infants. *Child Development, 56,* 1593–1598.
Cervantes, R. C., Padilla, A. M., & de Snyder, N. S. (1991). The Hispanic Stress Inventory: A culturally relevant approach to psychosocial adjustment. *Psychological Assessment: A Journal of Consulting and Clinical Psychology, 3,* 438–447.
Cervone, D. (1997). Social-cognitive mechanisms and personality coherence: Self-knowledge, situational beliefs, and cross-situational coherence in perceived self-efficacy. *Psychological Science, 8,* 43–50.
Chaiken, S. (1979). Communicator physical attractiveness and persuasion. *Journal of Personality and Social Psychology, 37,* 1387–1397.
Chaiken, S., Liberman, A., & Eagly, A. (1989). Heuristic and systematic information processing within and beyond the persuasion context. In J. Uteman and J. A. Bargh (Eds.), *Unintended thought* (pp. 212–252). New York: Guilford Press.
Chaiken, S., & Maheswaran, D. (1994). Heuristic processing can bias systematic processing: Effects of source credibility, argument ambiguity, and task importance on attitude judgment. *Journal of Personality and Social Psychology, 66,* 460–473.
Chandler, C. C. (1991). How memory for an event is influenced by related events: Interference in modified recognition tests. *Journal of Experimental Psychology: Learning, Memory, and Cognition,* 17, 115–125.
Charness, N. (Ed.). (1985). *Aging and human performance.* Chicester, England: Wiley.
Chase, M. H., & Morales, F. R. (1983). Subthreshold excitatory activity and motorneuron discharge during REM periods of active sleep. *Science, 221,* 1195–1198.
Chase, W. G., & Simon, H. A. (1973). Perception in chess. *Cognitive Psychology, 4,* 55–81.
Cheek, J. M., & Briggs, S. R. (1990). Shyness as a personality trait. In W. R. Crozier (Ed.), *Shyness and embarrassment: Perspectives from social psychology* (pp. 315–337). New York: Cambridge University Press.
Chen, C., & Stevenson, H. W. (1995). Motivation and mathematics achievement: A comparative study of Asian-American, Caucasian-American, and East Asian high school students. *Child Development, 66,* 1215–1234.
Chen, C., Lee, S., & Stevenson, H. W. (1995). Response style and cross-cultural comparisons of rating scales among East Asian and North American students. *Psychological Science, 6,* 170–175.
Cheney, D. L., & Seyfarth, R. M. (1990). *How monkeys see the world.* Chicago: University of Chicago Press.
Cheney, D. L., & Seyfarth, R. M. (1992). Precis of *How monkeys see the world. Behavioral and Brain Sciences, 15,* 135–182.
Cheng, P. W., & Novick, L. R. (1990). A probabilistic contrast model of causal induction. *Journal of Personality and Social Psychology, 58,* 545–567.
Cheng, P. W., Holyoak, K. J., Nisbett, R. E., & Oliver, L. M. (1986). Pragmatic versus syntactic approaches to training deductive reasoning. *Cognitive Psychology, 18,* 293–328.
Cherry, E. C. (1953). Some experiments on the recognition of speech, with one and with two ears. *Journal of the Acoustical Society of America, 25,* 975–979.
Chesney, M. A. (1993). Health psychology in the 21st century: Acquired Immunodeficiency Syndrome as a harbinger of things to come. *Health Psychology, 12,* 259–268.
Chipman, S. F., Brush, L. R., & Wilson, D. M. (Eds.). (1985). *Women and mathematics.* Hillsdale, NJ: Erlbaum.
Chochinov, H. M., Wilson, K. G., Enns, M., Mowchun, N., Lander, S., Levitt, M., & Clinch, J. J. (1995). Desire for death in the terminally ill. *American Journal of Psychiatry, 152,* 1185–1191.
Chomsky, N. (1957). Syntactic structures. The Hague: Morton Publishers.
Chomsky, N. (1959). A review of B. F. Skinner's "Verbal Behavior." *Language, 35,* 26–58.
Chomsky, N. (1972). *Language and mind.* New York: Harcourt Brace Jovanovich.
Christensen, A., & Jacobson, N. S. (1994). Who (or what) can do psychotherapy: The status and challenge of nonprofessional therapies. *Psychological Science, 5,* 8–14.
Christianson, S. (1992). Emotional stress and eyewitness memory: A critical review. *Psychological Bulletin, 112,* 284–309.
Chumlea, W. C. (1982). Physical growth in adolescence. In B. Wolman (Ed.), *Handbook of developmental psychology.* Englewood Cliffs, NJ: Prentice-Hall.
Cialdini, R. B. (1988). *Influence: Science and practice* (2nd ed.). Glenview, IL: Scott, Foresman.
Cialdini, R. B., Darby, B. L., & Vincent, J. E. (1973). Transgressional altruism: A case for hedonism. *Journal of Personality and Social Psychology, 9,* 502–516.
Cialdini, R. B., Kallgren, C. A., & Reno, R. R. (1991). A focus theory of normative conduct: A theoretical refinement and reevaluation of the role of norms in human behavior. *Advances in Experimental Social Psychology, 24,* 201–234.
Cialdini, R. B., Schaller, M., Houlihan, D., Arps, K., Fultz, J., & Beaman, A. L. (1987). Empathy-based helping: Is it selflessly or selfishly motivated? *Journal of Personality and Social Psychology, 52,* 749–758.
Cialdini, R. B., Trost, M. R., & Newsom, J. T. (1995). Preference for consistency: The development of a valid measure and the discovery of surprising behavioral implications. *Journal of Personality and Social Psychology, 69,* 318–328.
Cioffi, D., & Holloway, J. (1993). Delayed costs of suppressed pain. *Journal of Personality and Social Psychology, 64,* 274–282.
Cipolli, C., Bolzani, R., Cornoldi, C., DeBeni, R., & Fagioli, I. (1993). Bizarreness effect in dream recall. *Sleep, 16,* 163–170.

Clark, D. M., Salkovskis, P. M., Ost, L. G., Breitholtz, E., Koehler, K. A., Westling, B. E., Jeavons, A., & Gelder, M. (1997). Misinterpretation of body sensations in panic disorder. *Journal of Consulting and Clinical Psychology, 65,* 203–213.
Clark, H. H. (1985). Language use and language users. In G. Lindzey & E. Aronson (Eds.), *Handbook of social psychology* (3rd ed., pp. 179–231). New York: Random House.
Clark, L. F. (1993). Stress and the cognitive-conversational benefits of social interaction. *Journal of Social and Clinical Psychology,* 12, 25–55.
Clark, R. D., & Maass, A. (1990). The effects of majority size on minority influence. *European Journal of Social Psychology, 20,* 99–117.
Clarke-Stewart, K. A. (1989). Infant day care: Maligned or malignant? *American Psychologist, 44,* 266–273.
Clarke-Stewart, K. A., Gruber, C. P., & Fitzgerald, L. M. (1994). *Children at home and in day care.* Mahwah, NJ: Erlbaum.
Cleckley, H. (1976). *The mask of sanity* (5th ed.). St. Louis: Mosby.
Coe, C. L. (1993). Psychosocial factors and immunity in nonhuman primates: A review. *Psychosomatic Medicine, 55,* 298–308. Coffey, C. E., et al. (1991). Brain anatomic effects of electroconvulsive therapy: A prospective magnetic resonance imaging study. *Archives of General Psychiatry, 48,* 1013–1021.
Coffey, C. E., et al. (1991). Brain anatomic effects of electroconvulsive therapy: A prospective magnetic resonance imaging study. *Archives of General Psychiatry, 48,* 1013–1021.
Cohen, E. G. (1984). The desegregated school: Problems in status power and interethnic climate. In N. Miller & M. B. Brewer (Eds.), *Groups in contact: The psychology of desegregation* (pp. 77–96). New York: Academic Press.
Cohen, G. (1989). *Memory in the real world.* Hillsdale, NJ: Erlbaum.
Cohen, J. D., & Schooler, J. W. (Eds.) (1997). *Scientific approaches to consciousness.* Hillsdale, NJ: Erlbaum.
Cohen, N. J., & Eichenhaum, H. (1993). *Memory, amnesia, and the hippocampal system.* Cambridge, MA: MIT Press.
Cohen, S., & Herbert, T. B. (1996). Health psychology: Psychological factors and physical disease from the perspective of human psychoneuroimmunology. *Annual Review of Psychology, 47,* 113–142.
Cohen, S., & Williamson, G. (1991). Stress and infectious disease in humans. *Psychological Bulletin, 109,* 5–24.
Cohen, S., Tyrrell, D. A. J., & Smith, A. P. (1991). Psychological stress and susceptibility to the common cold. *New England Journal of Medicine, 325,* 606–612.
Cohen, S., Tyrrell, D. A. J., & Smith, A. P. (1993). Negative life events, perceived stress, negative affect and susceptibility to the common cold. *Journal of Personality and Social Psychology, 64,* 131–140.
Cohen, W. (1997, January 27). Kid looks like the mailman? Genetic labs boom as the nation wonders who's daddy? *U.S. News & World Report,* p. 62.
Cohen, Y. (1964). *The transition from childhood to adolescence: Cross-cultural studies of initiation ceremonies, legal systems, and incest taboos.* Chicago: Aldine.
Coile, D. C., & Miller, N. E. (1984). How radical animal activists try to mislead humane people. *American Psychologist, 39,* 700–701.
Colangelo, N., & Kerr, B. A. (1990). Extreme academic talent: Profiles of perfect scorers. *Journal of Educational Psychology, 82,* 404–409.
Colby, A., & Kohlberg, L. (1987). *The measurement of moral judgment* (Vols. 1–2). New York: Cambridge University Press.
Colby, A., Kohlberg, L., Gibbs, J., & Lieberman, M. (1983). A longitudinal study of moral judgment. *Monographs of the Society for Research in Child Development, 48*(1–2, Serial No. 200).
Cole, S. W., Kemeny, M. E., Taylor, S. E., Visscher, B. R., & Fahey, J. L. (1996). Accelerated course of human immunodeficiency virus infection in gay men who conceal their homosexual identity. *Psychosomatic Medicine, 58,* 219–231.
Coleman, R. M. (1986). *Wide awake at 3:00 a.m.: By choice or by chance?* New York: W. H. Freeman.
Coles, R. (1997). *The moral intelligence of children.* New York: Random House.
Collaer, M. L., & Hines, M. (1995). Human behavioral sex differences: A role for gonadal hormones during early development? *Psychological Bulletin, 118,* 55–107.
Collins, A. M., & Loftus, E. F. (1975). A spreading-activation theory of semantic processing. *Psychological Review, 82,* 407–428.
Collins, N. L., & Miller, L. C. (1994). Self-disclosure and liking: A meta-analytic review. *Psychological Bulletin, 116,* 457–475.
Collins, W. A., & Gunnar, M. R. (1990). Social and personality development. *Annual Review of Psychology, 41,* 387–416.
Colombo, J. (1993). *Infant cognition: Predicting later intellectual functioning.* Thousand Oaks, CA: Sage.
Colp, R., Jr. (1977). *To be an invalid: The illness of Charles Darwin.* Chicago: University of Chicago Press.
Coltheart, M. (1980). Iconic memory and visual persistence. *Perception and Psychophysics, 27,* 183–228.
Colvin, C. R., & Block, J. (1994). Do positive illusions foster mental health? An examination of the Taylor and Brown formulation. *Psychological Bulletin, 116,* 3–20.
Colvin, C. R., Block, J., & Funder, D. C. (1995). Overly positive self-evaluations and personality: Negative implications for mental health. *Journal of Personality and Social Psychology, 68,* 1152–1162.
Condry, J., & Condry, S. (1976). Sex differences: A study of the eye of the beholder. *Child Development, 47,* 812–819.
Conel, J. L. (1939–1963). *The postnatal development of the human cerebral cortex* (Vols. I-VI). Cambridge, MA: Harvard University Press.
Conrad, R. (1964). Acoustic confusions in immediate memory. *British Journal of Psychology, 55,* 75–84.
Constantinople, A. (1969). An Eriksonian measure of personality development in college students. *Developmental Psychology, 1,* 357–372.
Consumer Reports (1995, November). Mental health: Does therapy help? pp. 734–739.
Conway, M. (1995). *Flashbulb memories.* Mahwah, NJ: Erlbaum.
Conway, M., Cohen, G., & Stanhope, N. (1991). On the very long-term retention of knowledge acquired through formal education: Twelve years of cognitive psychology. *Journal of Experimental Psychology: General, 120,* 395–409.
Conway, M., Collins, A. F., Gathercole, S. E., & Anderson, S. J. (1996). Recollections of true and false autobiographical memories. *Journal of Experimental Psychology: General, 125,* 69–95.
Cook, M., & Mineka, S. (1990). Selective association in the observational conditioning of fear in monkeys. *Behaviour Research and Therapy, 25,* 349–364.
Cook, S. W. (1985). Experimenting on social issues: The case of school desegregation. *American Psychologist, 40,* 452–460.
Cook, T. D., Cooper, H., Cordray, D. S., Hartmann, H., Hedges, L. V., Light, R. J., Louis, T. A., & Mosteller, F. (1992). *Meta-analysis for explanation: A casebook.* New York: Russell Sage Foundation.
Cooper, H., & Good, T. (1983). *Pygmalion grows up: Studies in the expectation communication process.* New York: Longman.
Cooper, J., & Fazio, R. H. (1984). A new look at dissonance theory. In L. Berkowitz (Ed.), *Advances in experimental social psychology* (Vol. 17, pp. 229–267). New York: Academic Press.
Cooper, M. L., Frone, M. R., Russell, M., & Mudar, P. (1995). Drinking to regulate positive and negative emotions: A motivational model of alcohol use. *Journal of Personality and Social Psychology, 69,* 990–1005.
Copeland, J. T. (1994). Prophecies of power: Motivational implications of social power for behavioral confirmation. *Journal of Personality and Social Psychology, 67,* 264–277.
Corballis, M. C. (1989). Laterality and human evolution. *Psychological Review, 96,* 492–505.
Cordes, C. L., & Dougherty, T. W. (1993). A review and integration of research on job burnout. *Academy of Management Review, 18,* 621–656.
Coren, S. (1993). *The left-hander syndrome.* New York: Vintage Books.
Coren, S. (1996). *Sleep thieves: An eye-opening exploration into science and mysteries of sleep.* New York: Free Press.
Coren, S., & Aks, D. J. (1990). Moon illusion in pictures: A multimechanism approach. *Journal of Experimental Psychology: Human Perception and Performance, 16,* 365–380.
Coren, S., & Halpern, D. F. (1991). Left-handedness: A marker for decreased survival fitness. *Psychological Bulletin, 109,* 90–106.
Corina, D. P., Vaid, J., & Belugi, U. (1992). The linguistic basis of left-hemisphere specialization. *Science, 255,* 1258–1260.
Cornelius, S. W., & Caspi, A. (1987). Everyday problem solving in adulthood and old age. *Psychology and Aging, 2,* 144–153.
Cose, E. (1996). *Color-Blind.* New York: HarperCollins.
Costa, P. T., Jr., & McCrae, R. M. (1992). *Revised NEO personality inventory: NEO PI and NEO Five Factor Inventory (NEO FFI Professional Manual).* Odessa, FL: Psychological Assessment Resources, Inc.
Costa, P. T., Jr., & Widiger, T. A. (Eds.) (1994). *Personality disorders and the five factor model of personality.* Washington, DC: American Psychological Association.
Cousins, N. (1989). *Head first: The biology of hope.* New York: Dutton.
Cowan, N. (1988). Evolving concepts of memory storage, selective attention, and their mutual constraints within the human information-processing system. *Psychological Bulletin, 104,* 163–191.
Cowan, N., Wood, N. L., & Borne, D. N. (1994). Reconfirmation of the short-term storage concept. *Psychological Science, 5,* 103–106.
Cowey, A., & Stoerig, P. (1991). The neurobiology of blindsight. *Trends in Neuroscience. 14,* 140–145.
Cowey, A., & Stoerig, P. (1992). Reflections on blindsight. In A. D. Milner & M. D. Rugg (Eds.), *The Neuropsychology of Consciousness.* London: Academic Press.
Cowley, G. (1994, February 7). The culture of Prozac. *Newsweek,* pp. 41–42.
Cox, M. J., & Paley, B. (1997). Families as systems. *Annual Review of Psychology, 48,* 243–267.
Cox, M. J., Owen, M. T., Henderson, V. K., & Margand, N. A. (1992). Prediction of infant-father and infant-mother attachment. *Developmental Psychology, 28,* 474–483.
Coyne, J. C. (1976). Depression and the responses of others. *Journal of Abnormal Psychology, 85,* 186–193.
Coyne, J. C., Kessler, R. C., Tal, M., Turnbull, J., Wortman, C., & Greden, J. (1987). Living with a depressed person: Burden and psychological distress. *Journal of Consulting and Clinical Psychology, 55,* 347–352.
Craik, F. I. M. (1992). In F. Craik & T. A. Salthouse (Eds.), *Handbook of aging and cognition.* Hillsdale, NJ: Erlbaum.
Craik, F. I. M., & Tulving, E. (1975). Depth of processing and the retention of words in episodic memory. *Journal of Experimental Psychology: General, 104,* 268–294.

Cramer, P. (1990). *The development of defense mechanisms: Theory, research, and assessment.* New York: Springer-Verlag.

Cramer, P. (1996). *Storytelling, narrative, and the Thematic Apperception Test.* New York: Guilford Press.

Crawford, H. J., Brown, A. M., & Moon, C. E. (1993). Sustained attentional and disattentional abilities: Differences between low and highly hypnotizable persons. *Journal of Abnormal Psychology, 102,* 534–543.

Crawford, H. J., Kitner-Triolo, M., Clarke, S. W., & Otesko, B. (1992). Transient positive and negative experiences accompanying stage hypnosis. *Journal of Abnormal Psychology, 101,* 663–667.

Creasey, H., & Rapoport, S. I. (1985). The aging human brain. *Annals of Neurology, 17,* 2–11.

Crits-Christoph, P., & Barber, J. (Eds.) (1991). *Handbook of short term dynamic psychotherapy.* New York: Basic Books.

Crocker, J., & Major, B. (1989). Social stigma and self-esteem: The self-protective properties of stigma. *Psychological Review, 96,* 608–630.

Crocker, J., Voelkl, K., Testa, M., & Major, B. (1991). Social stigma: The affective consequences of attributional ambiguity. *Journal of Personality and Social Psychology, 60,* 218–228.

Cropanzano, R. (Ed.) (1993). *Justice in the workplace: Approaching fairness in human resource management.* Mahwah, NJ: Erlbaum.

Crosby, F. J. (1991). *Juggling.* New York: Free Press.

Crosby, F., Bromley, S., & Saxe, L. (1980). Recent unobtrusive studies of black and white discrimination and prejudice: A literature review. *Psychological Bulletin, 87,* 546–563.

Cross-National Collaborative Group (1992). The changing rate of major depression. *Journal of the American Medical Association, 268,* 3008–3015.

Crowder, R. G. (1993). Short-term memory: Where do we stand? *Memory and Cognition, 21,* 142–145.

Crystal, D. S., & Stevenson, H. W. (1991). Mothers' perceptions of children's problems with mathematics: A cross-national comparison. *Journal of Educational Psychology, 83,* 372–376.

Csikszentmihalyi, M. (1990). *Flow: The psychology of optimal experience.* New York: Harper & Row.

Csikszentmihalyi, M., & Csikszentmihalyi, I. S. (Eds.) (1988). *Optimal experience: Psychological studies of flow in consciousness.* New York: Cambridge University Press.

Csikszentmihalyi, M., & Figurski, T. J. (1982). Self-awareness and aversive experience in everyday life. *Journal of Personality, 50,* 15–28.

Culbertson, F. M. (1997). Depression and gender: An international review. *American Psychologist, 52,* 25–31.

Curran, J. P., & Monti, P. M. (1982). *Social skills training: A practical handbook for assessment and treatment.* New York: Guilford Press.

Cutler, B. L., & Penrod, S. D. (1995). *Mistaken identification: The eyewitness, psychology, and the law.* New York: Cambridge University Press.

Czeisler, C. A., Johnson, M. P., Duffy, J. F., Brown, E. N., Ronda, J. M., & Kronauer, R. E. (1990). Exposure to bright light and darkness to treat physiologic maladaptation to night work. *New England Journal of Medicine, 322,* 1253–1259.

Czeisler, C. A., Kronauer, R. E., Allan, J. S., & Duffy, J. F. (1989). Bright light induction of strong (Type 0) resetting of the human circadian pacemaker. *Science, 244,* 1328–1333.

D'Souza, D. (1991). *Illiberal education: The politics of race and sex on campus.* New York: Free Press.

Dabbs, J. M., de La Rue, D., & Williams, P. M. (1990). Testosterone and occupational choice: Actors, ministers, and other men. *Journal of Personality and Social Psychology, 59,* 1261–1265.

Dabbs, J. M., Jr., Frady, R. L., Carr, T. S., & Besch, N. F. (1987). Saliva testosterone and criminal violence in young adult prison inmates. *Psychosomatic Medicine, 49,* 174–181.

Dallenbach, K. M. (1927). The temperature spots and end organs. *American Journal of Psychology, 54,* 431–433.

Dalton, P., & Wysocki, C. J. (1996). The nature and duration of adaptation following long-term odor exposure. *Perception and Psychophysics, 58,* 781–792.

Daly, M., & Wilson, M. (1990). Is parent-offspring conflict sex-linked? Freudian and Darwinian models. *Journal of Personality, 58,* 163–189.

Damon, W. (1988). *The moral child.* New York: Free Press.

Damos, D. (1992). *Multiple task performance.* London: Taylor Francis.

Darley, J. M., & Fazio, R. (1980). Expectancy confirmation processes arising in the social interaction sequence. *American Psychologist, 35,* 867–881.

Darley, J. M., & Gross, P. H. (1983). A hypothesis-confirming bias in labeling effects. *Journal of Personality and Social Psychology, 44,* 20–33.

Darley, J. M., & Latané, B. (1968). Bystander intervention in emergencies: Diffusion of responsibility. *Journal of Personality and Social Psychology, 8,* 377–383.

Darling, C. A., Davidson, J. K., & Passarello, L. C. (1992). The mystique of first intercourse among college youth: The role of partners, contraceptive practices, and psychological reactions. *Journal of Youth and Adolescence, 21,* 97–117.

Darwin, C. (1872). *The expression of the emotions in man and animals.* London: John Murray.

Darwin, C. (1859). *The origin of species.* New York: Washington Square Press. (Reprinted in 1963.)

Darwin, C. J., Turvey, M. T., & Crowder, R. G. (1972). An auditory analogue of the Sperling partial report procedure: Evidence for brief auditory storage. *Cognitive Psychology, 3,* 255–267.

Davey, G. C. L. (1995). Preparedness and phobias: Specific evolved associations or a generalized expectancy bias? *Behavioral and Brain Sciences, 18,* 289–325.

Davidson, R. J. (1993). The neuropsychology of emotion and affective style. In M. Lewis & J. M. Haviland (Eds.), *Handbook of emotions* (pp. 143–154). New York: Guilford Press.

Davidson, R. J., & Hugdahl, K. (Eds.) (1995). *Brain asymmetry.* Cambridge, MA: MIT Press.

Davidson, R. J., Ekman, P., Saron, C. D., Senulis, J. A., & Friesen, W. V. (1990). Approach-withdrawal and cerebral asymmetry: Emotional expression and brain physiology I. *Journal of Personality and Social Psychology, 58,* 330–341.

Davis, M. (1992). The role of the amygdala in fear and anxiety. *Annual Review of Neuroscience, 15,* 353–375.

Dawes, R. M. (1994). *House of cards: Psychology and psychotherapy built on myth.* New York: Free Press.

Dawes, R. M., Faust, D., & Meehl, P. E. (1989). Clinical versus actuarial judgment. *Science, 243,* 1668–1674.

Dawkins, R. (1989). *The selfish gene* (2nd ed.). Oxford: Oxford University Press.

Dawson, M. D., & Schell, A. M. (1982). Electrodermal responses to attended and nonattended significant stimuli during dichotic listening. *Journal of Experimental Psychology: Human Perception and Performance, 8,* 315–324.

Day, L. (1996). *Practical Intuition.* New York: Villard.

de Castro, J. M. (1994). Family and friends produce greater social facilitation of food intake than other companions. *Physiology and Behavior, 56,* 445–455.

de Castro, J. M., & Brewer, E. M. (1992). The amount eaten in meals by humans is a power function of the number of people present. *Physiology and Behavior, 51,* 121–125.

De Groot, A. D. (1965). *Thought and chance in chess.* The Hague: Moulton.

Deary, I. J., & Stough, C. (1996). Intelligence and inspection time: Achievements, prospects, and problems. *American Psychologist, 51,* 599–608.

Deary, I. J., Ramsay, H., Wilson, J. A., & Riad, M. (1988). Stimulated salivation: Correlations with personality and time of day effects. *Personality and Individual Differences, 9,* 903–909.

"Death Odds" (1990, September 24). *Newsweek,* p. 10.

DeCasper, A. J., & Fifer, W. P. (1980). Of human bonding: Newborns prefer their mothers' voices. *Science, 208,* 1174–1176.

DeCasper, A. J., & Sigafoos, A. D. (1983). The intrauterine heartbeat: A potent reinforcer for newborns. *Infant Behavior and Development, 6,* 19–25.

DeCasper, A. J., & Spence, M. J. (1986). Prenatal maternal speech influences newborns' perception of speech sounds. *Infant Behavior and Development, 9,* 133–150.

deCharms, R., & Moeller, G. H. (1962). Values expressed in American children's readers: 1800–1950. *Journal of Abnormal and Social Psychology, 64,* 136–142.

Deci, E. L. (1971). Effects of externally mediated rewards on intrinsic motivation. *Journal of Personality and Social Psychology, 18,* 105–115.

Deci, E. L., & Ryan, R. M. (1985). *Intrinsic motivation and self-determination in human behavior.* New York: Plenum.

Deci, E. L., Connell, J. P., & Ryan, R. M. (1989). Self-determination in a work organization. *Journal of Applied Psychology, 74,* 580–590.

DeLoache, J. S., & Brown, A. L. (1983). Very young children's memory for the location of objects in a large-scale environment. *Child Development, 54,* 888–897.

DeLongis, A., Coyne, J. C., Dakof, G., Folkman, S., & Lazarus, R. S. (1982). Relations of daily hassles, uplifts, and major life events to health status. *Health Psychology, 1,* 119–136.

Dement, W. C. (1992). *The sleepwatchers.* Stanford, CA: Stanford Alumni Association.

Dement, W. C., & Kleitman, N. (1957). The relation of eye movements during sleep to dream activity: An objective method for the study of dreaming. *Journal of Experimental Psychology, 53,* 339–346.

Demko, G. J. (1992). *Why in the world: Adventures in geography.* New York: Anchor Books.

Dempster, F. N. (1981). Memory span: Sources of individual and developmental differences. *Psychological Bulletin, 89,* 63–100.

Dempster, F. N. (1988). The spacing effect: A case study in the failure to apply the results of psychological research. *American Psychologist, 43,* 627–634.

DePalma, A. (1991, December 18). S.A.T. coaching raises scores, report says. *The New York Times,* p. C1.

Depue, R. A., & Iacono, W. G. (1989). Neurobehavioral aspects of affective disorders. *Annual Review of Psychology, 40,* 457–492.

Deregowski, J. B. (1989). Real space and represented space: Cross-cultural perspectives. *Brain and Behavioral Sciences, 12,* 51–119.

Derlega, V. J., Metts, S., Petronio, S., & Margulis, S. T. (1993). *Self-disclosure.* Newbury Park, CA: Sage.

Derlega, V. J., Winstead, B. A., Wong, P. T. P., & Hunter, S. (1985). Gender effects in an initial encounter: A case where men exceed women in disclosure. *Journal of Social and Personal Relations, 2,* 25–44.

Desimone, R. (1992). The physiology of memory: Recordings of things past. *Science, 258,* 245–246.
DeSteno, D. A., & Salovey, P. (1996). Evolutionary origins of sex differences in jealousy? Questioning the "fitness" model. *Psychological Science, 7,* 367–372.
Deutsch, M., & Gerard, H. B. (1955). A study of normative and informational social influences upon individual judgment. *Journal of Abnormal and Social Psychology, 51,* 629–636.
DeValois, R. L., & DeValois, K. K. (1975). Neural coding of color. In E. C. Carterette & M. P. Friedman (Eds.), *Handbook of perception: Vol. V. Seeing* (pp. 117–168). New York: Academic Press.
Devanand, D. P., Dwork, A. J., Hutchinson, M. S. E., Bolwig, T. G., & Sackeim, H. A. (1994). How does ECT alter brain structure? *American Journal of Psychiatry, 151,* 957–970.
Devine, P. G. (1989). Stereotypes and prejudice: Their automatic and controlled components. *Journal of Personality and Social Psychology, 56,* 5–18.
Devine, P. G., & Elliot, A. J. (1995). Are racial stereotypes really fading? The Princeton trilogy revisited. *Personality and Social Psychology Bulletin, 21,* 1139–1150.
Devine, P. G., Monteith, M. J., Zuwerink, J. R., & Elliot, A. J. (1991). Prejudice with and without compunction. *Journal of Personality and Social Psychology, 60,* 817–830.
Dewsbury, D. A. (1992). Comparative psychology and ethology: A reassessment. *American Psychologist, 47,* 208–215.
Dhabhar, F., & McEwen, B. (1995). *Journal of Immunology, 154,* 5511–5527.
Diamond, M. (1993). Homosexuality and bisexuality in different populations. *Archives of Sexual Behavior, 22,* 291–310.
Diener, E. (1984). Subjective well-being. *Psychological Bulletin, 95,* 542–575.
Diener, E., & Diener, C. (1996). Most people are happy. *Psychological Science, 7,* 181–185.
Diener, E., Diener, M., & Diener, C. (1995). Factors predicting the subjective well-being of nations. *Journal of Personality and Social Psychology, 69,* 851–864.
Diener, E., Emmons, R. A., Larsen, R. J., & Griffin, S. (1984). The Satisfaction with Life Scale. *Journal of Personality Assessment, 49,* 71–75.
Diener, E., Fraser, S. C., Beaman, A. L., & Kelem, R. T. (1976). Effects of deindividuation variables on stealing among Halloween trick-or-treaters. *Journal of Personality and Social Psychology, 33,* 178–183.
Diener, E., Horwitz, J., & Emmons, R. A. (1985). Happiness of the very wealthy. *Social Indicators Research, 16,* 263–274.
Digman, J. M. (1990). Personality structure: Emergence of the five factor model. *Annual Review of Psychology, 41,* 417–440.
DiLalla, D. L., Carey, G., Gottesman, I. I., & Bouchard, T. J. (1996). Heritability of MMPI personality indicators of psychopathology in twins reared apart. *Journal of Abnormal Psychology, 105,* 491–499.
DiLalla, L. F., & Gottesman, I. I. (1991). Biological and genetic contributions to violence—Widom's untold tale. *Psychological Bulletin, 109,* 125–129.
Dimberg, U. (1990). Facial electromyography and emotional reactions. *Psychophysiology, 27,* 481–494.
Dimberg, U., & Ohman, A. (1996). Behold the wrath: Psychophysiological responses to facial stimuli. *Motivation and Emotion, 20,* 149–181.
Dindia, K., & Allen, M. (1992). Sex differences in self-disclosure: A meta-analysis. *Psychological Bulletin, 112,* 106–124.
Dinges, D. F., Whitehouse, W. G., Orne, E. C., Powell, J. W., Orne, M. T., & Erdelyi, M. H. (1992). Evaluating hypnotic memory enhancement (hypermnesia and reminiscence) using multitrial forced recall. *Journal of Experimental Psychology: Learning, Memory, and Cognition, 18,* 1139–1147.
Dion, K. K., Berscheid, E., & Walster, E. (1972). What is beautiful is good. *Journal of Personality and Social Psychology, 24,* 285–290.
DiPietro, J. A., Hodgson, D. M., Costigan, K. A., Hilton, S. C., & Johnson, T. R. B. (1996). Fetal neurobehavioral development. *Child Development, 67,* 2553–2567.
DiPietro, J. A., Hodgson, D. M., Costigan, K. A., & Johnson, T. R. B. (1996). Fetal antecedents of infant temperament. *Child Development, 67,* 2568–2583.
Dittman, R. W., Kappes, M. E., & Kappes, M. H. (1992). Sexual behavior in adolescent and adult females with congenital adrenal hyperplasia. *Psychoneuroendocrinology, 17,* 153–170.
Ditto, P. H., & Lopez, D. F. (1992). Motivated skepticism: Use of differential decision criteria for preferred and nonpreferred conclusions. *Journal of Personality and Social Psychology, 63,* 568–584.
Dobbins, G. H., & Platz, S. J. (1986). Sex differences in leadership: How real are they? *Academy of Management Review, 11,* 118–127.
Doblin, R., & Kleiman, M. A. R. (1991). Medical use of marijuana. *Annals of Internal Medicine, 114,* 809–810.
Dobson, K. S. (1989). A meta-analysis of the efficacy of cognitive therapy for depression. *Journal of Consulting and Clinical Psychology, 57,* 414–419.
Dodson, C., & Reisberg, D. (1991). Indirect testing of eyewitness memory: The (non)effect of misinformation. *Bulletin of the Psychonomic Society, 29,* 333–336.
Dohrenwend, B. S., & Dohrenwend, B. P. (1978). Some issues in research on stressful life events. *Journal of Nervous and Mental Diseases, 166,* 7–15.
Dollard, J., Doob, L. W., Miller, N. E., Mowrer, O. H., & Sears, R. R. (1939). *Frustration and aggression.* New Haven, CT: Yale University Press.
Domjan, M., & Purdy, J. E. (1995). Animal research in psychology: More than meets the eye of the general psychology student. *American Psychologist, 50,* 496–503.
Donley, R. D., & Ashcraft, M. H. (1992). The methodology of testing naive beliefs in the physics classroom. *Memory and Cognition, 20,* 381–391.
Donlon, T. F. (Ed.) (1984). *The College Board technical handbook for the scholastic aptitude test and achievement tests.* New York: College Entrance Examination Board.
Donnelly, C., & McDaniel, M. (1993). Use of analogy in learning scientific concepts. *Journal of Experimental Psychology: Learning, Memory, and Cognition, 19,* 975–986.
Donnerstein, E., & Berkowitz, L. (1981). Victim reactions in aggressive erotic films as a factor in violence against women. *Journal of Personality and Social Psychology, 41,* 710–724.
Donnerstein, E., Linz, D., & Penrod, S. (1987). *The question of pornography.* New York: Free Press.
Dornbusch, S. M., Glasgow, K. L., & Lin, I. (1996). The social structure of schooling. *Annual Review of Psychology, 47,* 401–429.
Dostoevsky, F. (1960). *Notes from underground* (R. E. Matlaw, Trans.). New York: Dutton. (Original work published 1864.)
Doty, R. L., Applebaum, S., Zusho, H., & Settle, R. G. (1985). Sex differences in odor identification ability: A cross-cultural analysis. *Neuropsychologia, 23,* 667–672.
Dougherty, D. M., & Lewis, P. (1991). Stimulus generalization, discrimination, and peak shift in horses. *Journal of the Experimental Analysis of Behavior, 56,* 97–104.
Dougherty, T. M., & Haith, M. M. (1997). Infant expectations and reaction time as predictors of childhood speed of processing and IQ. *Developmental Psychology, 33,* 146–155.
Dougherty, T. W., Turban, D. B., & Callender, J. C. (1994). Confirming first impressions in the employment interview: A field study of interviewer behavior. *Journal of Applied Psychology, 79,* 659–665.
Dovidio, J. F., & Gaertner, S. L. (Eds.) (1986). *Prejudice, discrimination, and racism: Theory and research.* Orlando, FL: Academic Press.
Dovidio, J. F., Allen J. L., & Schroeder, D. A. (1990). Specificity of empathy-induced helping: Evidence for altruistic motivation. *Journal of Personality and Social Psychology, 59,* 249–260.
Downs, A. C., & Lyons, P. M. (1991). Natural observations of the links between attractiveness and initial legal judgments. *Personality and Social Psychology Bulletin, 17,* 541–547.
Driskell, J. E., Willis, R. P., & Copper, C. (1992). Effect of overlearning on retention. *Journal of Applied Psychology, 77,* 615–622.
Dubovsky, S. L. (1997). *Mind-body deceptions: The psychosomatics of everyday life.* New York: Norton.
Duclos, S. E., Laird, J. D., Schneider, E., Sexter, M., Stern, L., & Lighten, O. V. (1989). Emotion-specific effects of facial expressions and postures on emotional experience. *Journal of Personality and Social Psychology, 57,* 100–108.
Dudycha, G. J., & Dudycha, M. M. (1941). Childhood memories: A review of the literature. *Psychological Bulletin, 38,* 668–682.
Dumont, R. (1996). *The sky is falling: understanding and coping with phobias, panic, and obsessive-compulsive disorders.* New York: W. W. Norton.
Duncan, B. L. (1976). Differential social perception and attribution of intergroup violence: Testing the lower limits of stereotyping of blacks. *Journal of Personality and Social Psychology, 34,* 590–598.
Duncker, K. (1945). On problem-solving (L. S. Lees, Trans.). *Psychological Monographs, 58* (No. 270).
Dunn, D. S., & Wilson, T. D. (1990). When the stakes are high: A limit to the illusion-of-control effect. *Social Cognition, 8,* 305–323.
Dunn, J., & Plomin, R. (1990). Separate lives: *Why siblings are so different.* New York: Basic Books.
Dunn, J., Bretherton, I., & Munn, P. (1987). Conversations about feeling states between mothers and their young children. *Developmental Psychology, 23,* 132–139.
Dunning, D., Griffin, D. W., Milojkovic, J. D., & Ross, L. (1990). The overconfidence effect in social prediction. *Journal of Personality and Social Psychology, 58,* 568–581.
Dutton, D. G., & Aron, A. P. (1974). Some evidence for heightened sexual attraction under conditions of high anxiety. *Journal of Personality and Social Psychology, 23,* 510–517.
Duval, S., & Wicklund, R. A. (1972). *A theory of objective self-awareness.* New York: Academic Press.
Duval, S., Duval, V. H., & Mulilis, J. P. (1992). Effects of self-focus, discrepancy between self and standard, and outcome expectancy favorability on the tendency to match self to standard or to withdraw. *Journal of Personality and Social Psychology, 62,* 340–348.
Dywan, J., & Bowers, K. (1983). The use of hypnosis to enhance recall. *Science, 222,* 184–185.

Eagly, A. H., Ashmore, R. D., Makhijani, M. G., & Longo, L. C. (1991). What is beautiful is good, but . . . : A meta-analytic review of research on the physical attractiveness stereotype. *Psychology Bulletin, 110,* 107–128.
Eagly, A. H., & Johnson, B. T. (1990). Gender and leadership style: A meta-analysis. *Psychological Bulletin, 108,* 233–256.

Eagly, A. H. (1987). *Sex differences in social behavior: A social-role interpretation.* Hillsdale, NJ: Erlbaum.

Eagly, A. H., & Chaiken, S. (1993). *The psychology of attitudes.* Fort Worth, TX: Harcourt Brace Jovanovich.

Eagly, A. H., & Steffen, V. J. (1986). Gender and aggressive behavior: A meta-analytic review of the social psychology literature. *Psychological Bulletin, 100,* 309–330.

Eagly, A. H., & Wood, W. (1991). Explaining sex differences in social behavior: A meta-analytic perspective. *Personality and Social Psychology Bulletin, 17,* 306–315.

Eagly, A. H., Makhijani, M. G., & Klonsky, B. G. (1992). Gender and evaluation of leaders: A meta-analysis. *Psychological Bulletin, 111,* 3–22.

Eaton, W. W., et al. (1991). Panic and phobia. In L. N. Robins & D. A. Regier (Eds.), *Psychiatric disorders in America* (pp. 155–179). New York: Free Press.

Eaton, W. W., Kessler, R. C., Wittchen, H. U., & Magee, W. J. (1994). Panic and panic disorder in the United States. *American Journal of Psychiatry, 151,* 413–420.

Ebbinghaus, H. (1913). *Memory: A contribution to experimental psychology* (H. Roger & C. Bussenius, Trans.). New York: Teachers College Press. (Original work published 1885.)

Eccles, J. (1965). *The brain and unity of conscious experience: The 19th Arthur Stanley Eddington Memorial Lecture.* Cambridge: Cambridge University Press.

Eccles, J. P. (1985). Sex differences in achievement patterns. In T. B. Sonderegger (Ed.), *Nebraska symposium on motivation: Psychology and gender.* Lincoln: University of Nebraska Press.

Eccles, J. S., Jacobs, J. E., & Harold, R. D. (1990). Gender role stereotypes, expectancy effects, and parents' socialization of gender differences. *Journal of Social Issues, 46,* 183–201.

Eccles, J. S., Wigfield, A., Harold, R. D., & Blumenfeld, P. (1993). Age and gender differences in children's self- and task perceptions during elementary school. *Child Development, 64,* 830–847.

Eder, D. (1981). Ability grouping as a self-fulfilling prophecy: A microanalysis of teacher-student interaction. *Sociology of Education, 54,* 151–161.

Edgarton, R. (1967). *The cloak of competence.* Berkeley: University of California Press.

Edwards, B. (1979). *Drawing on the right side of the brain: A course in enhancing creativity and artistic confidence.* Los Angeles: Tarcher.

Edwards, K., & Smith, E. E. (1996). A disconfirmation bias in the evaluation of arguments. *Journal of Personality and Social Psychology, 71,* 5–24.

Efron, R. (1990). *The decline and fall of hemispheric specialization.* Hillsdale, NJ: Erlbaum.

Ehlers, A., & Breuer, P. (1992). Increased cardiac awareness in panic disorder. *Journal of Abnormal Psychology, 101,* 371–382.

Ehrlichman, H., & Eichenstein, R. (1992). Private wishes: Gender similarities and differences. *Sex Roles, 26,* 399–422.

Eibl-Eibesfeldt, I. (1989). *Human ethology.* New York: Aldine de Gruyter.

Eich, E. (1995). Mood as a mediator of place dependent memory. *Journal of Experimental Psychology: General, 124,* 293–308.

Eich, E., Macaulay, D., & Ryan, L. (1994). Mood dependent memory for events of the personal past. *Journal of Experimental Psychology: General, 123,* 201–215.

Einstein, G. O., McDaniel, M. A., & Lackey, S. (1989). Bizarre imagery, interference, and distinctiveness. *Journal of Experimental Psychology: Learning, Memory, and Cognition, 15,* 137–146.

Einstein, G. O., McDaniel, M. A., Richardson, S. L., Guynn, M. J., & Cunfer, A. (1995). Aging and prospective memory: Explaining the influences of self-initiated retrieval processes. *Journal of Experimental Psychology: Learning, Memory, and Cognition, 21,* 996–1007.

Eisenberg, N. (1992). *The caring child.* Cambridge, MA: Harvard University Press.

Eisenberg, N., & Mussen, P. H. (1989). *The roots of prosocial behavior in children.* New York: Cambridge University Press.

Eisenberg, N., Carlo, G., Murphy, B., & Van Court, P. (1995). Prosocial development in late adolescence: A longitudinal study. *Child Development, 66,* 1179–1197.

Eisenberger, R. (1992). Learned industriousness. *Psychological Review, 99,* 248–267.

Eisenberger, R., & Cameron, J. (1996). Detrimental effects of reward: Reality or myth? *American Psychologist, 51,* 1153–1166.

Ekman, P., & Davidson, R. J. (1993). Voluntary smiling changes regional brain activity. *Psychological Science, 4,* 342–345.

Ekman, P., & Friesen, W. V. (1974). Detecting deception from the body or face. *Journal of Personality and Social Psychology, 29,* 288–298.

Ekman, P., Davidson, R. J., & Friesen, W. V. (1990). The Duchenne smile: Emotional expression and brain physiology II. *Journal of Personality and Social Psychology, 58,* 342–353.

Ekman, P., Friesen, W. V., O'Sullivan, M., Chan, A., Diacoyanni-Tarlatzis, I., Heider, K., Krause, R., LeCompte, W. A., Pitcairn, T., Ricci-Bitti, P., Scherer, K., Tomita, M., & Tzavaras, A. (1987). Universals and cultural differences in the judgments of facial expressions of emotion. *Journal of Personality and Social Psychology, 53,* 712–717.

Ekman, P., Levenson, R. W., & Friesen, W. V. (1983). Autonomic nervous system activity distinguishes among emotions. *Science, 221,* 1208–1210.

Elbert, T., Pantev, C., Wienbruch, C., et al. (1995). Increased cortical representation of the fingers of the left hand in string players. *Science, 270,* 305–307.

Elkin, I., et al. (1989). National Institute of Mental Health treatment of depression collaborative research program. *Archives of General Psychiatry, 46,* 971–983.

Elkind, D. (1967). Egocentrism in adolescence. *Child Development, 38,* 1025–1034.

Elkind, D. (1989). *Miseducation: Preschoolers at risk.* New York: Knopf.

Elkind, D., & Bowen, R. (1979). Imaginary audience behavior in children and adolescents. *Developmental Psychology, 15,* 38–44.

Elliot, A. J., & Church, M. A. (1997). A hierarchical model of approach and avoidance achievement motivation. *Journal of Personality and Social Psychology, 72,* 218–232.

Elliott, R. (1987). *Litigating intelligence: IQ tests, special education, and social science in the courtroom.* Dover, MA: Auburn House.

Ellis, A. (1962). *Reason and emotion in psychotherapy.* New York: Lyle Stuart.

Ellis, A. (1989). Rational-emotive therapy. In R. J. Corcini & D. Wedding (Eds.), *Current psychotherapies* (4th ed.). Itasca, IL: Peacock.

Ellis, A. (1996). How I learned to help clients feel better *and* get better. *Psychotherapy, 33,* 149–151.

Ellis, A., & Hunt, R. R. (1989). *Fundamentals of human memory and cognition* (4th ed.). Dubuque, IA: William C. Brown.

Ellis, L., & Ames, M. A. (1987). Neurohormonal functioning and sexual orientation: A theory of homosexuality-heterosexuality. *Psychological Bulletin, 101,* 233–258.

Ellsworth, P. C. (1994). William James and emotion: Is a century of fame worth a century of misunderstanding? *Psychological Review, 101,* 222–229.

Emde, R. N., Gaensbauer, T. J., & Harmon, R. J. (1976). Emotional expression in infancy: A biobehavioral study. *Psychological Issues, 10*(Monograph 37).

Emmelkamp, P. M. G. (1982). *Phobic and obsessive-compulsive disorders: Theory, research, and practice.* New York: Plenum.

Emmelkamp, P. M. G. (1994). Behavior therapy with adults. In A. E. Bergin & S. L. Garfield (Eds.), *Handbook of psychotherapy and behavior change,* (4th ed.). New York: Wiley.

Endler, N. S., & Persad, E. (1988). *Electroconvulsive therapy: The myths and the realities.* Toronto: Hans Huber Publishers.

Engels, G. I., Garnefski, N., & Diekstra, R. (1993). Efficacy of rational-emotive therapy: A quantitative analysis. *Journal of Consulting and Clinical Psychology, 61,* 1083–1090.

Engen, T. (1982). *The perception of odors.* New York: Academic Press.

Engle, R. W., Cantor, J., & Carullo, J. J. (1992). Individual differences in working memory and comprehension: A test of four hypotheses. *Journal of Experimental Psychology: Learning, Memory, and Cognition, 18,* 972–992.

Enright, R. D., Levy, V. M., Harris, D., & Lapsley, D. K. (1987). *Journal of Youth and Adolescence, 16,* 541–559.

Epstein, J. L. (1985). After the bus arrives: Resegregation in desegregated schools. *Journal of Social Issues, 41,* 23–43.

Epstein, R., Kirshnit, C. E., Lanza, R. P., & Rubin, L. C. (1984). "Insight" in the pigeon: Antecedents and determinants of an intelligent performance. *Nature, 308,* 61–62.

Epstein, S. (1979). The stability of behavior: I. On predicting most of the people much of the time. *Journal of Personality and Social Psychology, 37,* 1097–1126.

Epstein, S., & O'Brien, E. J. (1985). The person-situation debate in historical and current perspective. *Psychological Bulletin, 98,* 513–537.

Erdelyi, M. H. (1985). *Psychoanalysis: Freud's cognitive psychology.* New York: W. H. Freeman.

Erdelyi, M. H. (1992). Psychodynamics and the unconscious. *American Psychologist, 47,* 784–787.

Erdelyi, M. H. (1996). *The recovery of unconscious memories: Hypermnesia and reminiscence.* Chicago: The University of Chicago Press.

Ericsson, K. A., & Chase, W. G. (1982). Exceptional memory. *American Scientist, 70,* 607–615.

Ericsson, K. A., Chase, W. G., & Faloon, S. (1980). Acquisition of a memory skill. *Science, 208,* 1181–1182.

Ericsson, K. A., Krampe, R. T., & Tesch-Romer, C. (1993). The role of deliberate practice in the acquisition of expert performance. *Psychological Review, 100,* 363–406.

Erikson, E. H. (1959). Identity and the life cycle. Psychological Issues (Monograph 1). New York: International Universities Press.

Erikson, E. H. (1963). *Childhood and society.* New York: Norton.

Eron, L. D. (1987). The development of aggressive behavior from the perspective of a developing behaviorism. *American Psychologist, 42,* 435–442.

Esteves, F., Dimberg, U., Parra, C., Ohman, A. (1994). Nonconscious associative learning: Pavlovian conditioning of skin conductance responses to masked fear-relevant facial stimuli. *Psychophysiology, 31,* 375–385.

Ether, J. T., Szuchman, L. T., & Rothberg, S. T. (1990). Everyday memory failure: Age differences in appraisal and attribution. *Psychology and Aging, 5,* 236–241.

Evans, D. A., et al. (1989). Prevalence of Alzheimer's disease in a community population of older persons: Higher than previously reported. *Journal of the American Medical Association, 262,* 2551–2556.

Evans, G. W., & Lepore, S. J. (1993). Household crowding and social support: A quasi-experimental analysis. *Journal of Personality and Social Psychology, 65,* 308–316.
Evans, G. W., Lepore, S. J., & Schroeder, A. (1996). The role of interior design elements in human responses to crowding. *Journal of Personality and Social Psychology, 70,* 41–46.
Everson, C. A. (1995). Functional consequences of sustained sleep deprivation in the rat. *Behavioural Brain Research, 69,* 43–54.
Everson, S. A., et al. (1996). Hopelessness and risk of mortality and incidence of myocardial infarction and cancer. *Psychosomatic Medicine, 58,* 103–121.
Ewing, C. P. (1996, July). Judicial notebook: Courts consider repressed memory. *APA Monitor,* p. 14.
Exner, J. E., Jr. (1993). *The Rorschach: A comprehensive system: Vol. 1. Basic foundations* (3rd ed.). New York: Wiley.
Exner, J. E., Jr. (1996). A comment on "The comprehensive system for the Rorschach: A critical examination." *Psychological Science, 7,* 11–13.
Eysenck, H. J. (1952). The effects of psychotherapy: An evaluation. *Journal of Consulting Psychology, 16,* 319–324.
Eysenck, H. J. (1967). *The biological basis of personality.* Springfield, IL: Thomas.
Eysenck, H. J. (1982). *A model for intelligence.* Berlin: Springer-Verlag.
Eysenck, H. J. (1990). Biological dimensions of personality. In L. A. Pervin (Ed.), *Handbook of personality theory and research* (pp. 244–276). New York: Guilford Press.
Eysenck, H. J., & Eysenck, M. W. (1985). *Personality and individual differences: A natural science approach.* New York: Plenum.
Eysenck, H. J., & Eysenck, S. G. B. (1964). *Manual of the Eysenck Personality Inventory.* London: University of London Press.
Eysenck, M. W. (1992). *Anxiety: The cognitive perspective.* Hillsdale, NJ: Erlbaum.

Fabes, R. A., & Martin, C. L. (1991). Gender and age stereotypes of emotionality. *Personality and Social Psychology Bulletin,* 17, 532–540.
Fantz, R. L. (1961). The origin of form perception. *Scientific American, 204,* 66–72.
Farah, M. J. (1989). The neural basis of mental imagery. *Trends in Neuroscience, 12,* 395–399.
Faravelli, C., & Pallanti, S. (1989). Recent life events and panic disorders. *American Journal of Psychiatry, 146,* 622–626.
Farber, B. A., Brink, D. C., & Raskin, P. M. (Eds.) (1996). *The psychotherapy of Carl Rogers: Cases and commentary.* New York: Guilford Press.
Farina, A., Fisher, J. D., & Fischer, E. H. (1992). Societal factors in the problems faced by deinstitutionalized psychiatric patients. In P. J. Fink & A. Tasman (Eds.), *Stigma and mental illness.* Washington, DC: American Psychiatric Press.
Farrell, P. A., Gates, W. K., Maksud, M. G., & Morgan, W. P. (1982). Increases in plasma beta-endorphin/beta-lipotropin immunoreactivity after treadmill running in humans. *Journal of Applied Psychology, 52,* 1245–1249.
Fay, R. E., Turner, C. F., Klassen, A. D., & Gagnon, J. H. (1989). Prevalence and patterns of same-gender sexual contact among men. *Science, 243,* 343–348.
Fechner, G. T. (1860). *Elements of psychophysics* (H. E. Alder, Trans.). New York: Holt, Rinehart & Winston. (Translated edition 1966.)
Fehr, B., & Russell, J. A. (1991). The concept of love: Viewed from a prototype perspective. *Journal of Personality and Social Psychology, 60,* 425–438.
Feifel, H. (1990). Psychology and death: Meaningful rediscovery. *American Psychologist, 45,* 537–543.
Fein, S. (1996). Effects of suspicion on attributional thinking and the correspondence bias. *Journal of Personality and Social Psychology, 70,* 1164–1184.
Fein, S., & Spencer, S. (1997). Prejudice as self–image maintenance: Affirming the self through negative evaluations of others. *Journal of Personality and Social Psychology, 73,* 31–44.
Fein, S., Hilton, J. L., & Miller, D. T. (1990). Suspicion of ulterior motivation and the correspondence bias. *Journal of Personality and Social Psychology, 58,* 753–764.
Feinberg, R. A. (1986). Credit cards as spending facilitating stimuli: A conditioning interpretation. *Journal of Consumer Research, 13,* 348–356.
Feingold, A. (1992). Good-looking people are not what we think. *Psychological Bulletin, 111,* 304–341.
Feingold, A. (1994). Gender differences in personality: A meta-analysis. *Psychological Bulletin, 116,* 429–456.
Fenigstein, A., Scheier, M. F., & Buss, A. H. (1975). Public and private self-consciousness: Assessment and theory. *Journal of Consulting and Clinical Psychology, 43,* 522–527.
Fennell, M. J. (1989). Depression. In K. Hawton, P. Salkovskis, J. Kirk, & D. Clark (Eds.), *Cognitive behaviour therapy for psychiatric problems* (pp. 167–234). New York: Oxford Medical Publications.
Fernald, A. (1985). Four-month-old infants prefer to listen to motherese. *Infant Behavior and Development, 8,* 181–195.
Fernald, A., Taeschner, T., Dunn, J., Papousek, M., Boysson-Bardies, B. D., & Fukui, I. (1989). A cross-linguistic study of prosodic modifications in mothers' and fathers' speech to preverbal infants. *Journal of Child Language, 16,* 477–501.
Fernandez, E., & Turk, D. C. (1992). Sensory and affective components of pain: Separation and synthesis. *Psychological Bulletin, 112,* 205–217.
Ferster, C. B., & Skinner, B. F. (1957). *Schedules of reinforcement.* New York: Appleton-Century-Crofts.
Festinger, L. (1957). *A theory of cognitive dissonance.* Stanford, CA: Stanford University Press.
Festinger, L., & Carlsmith, J. M. (1959). Cognitive consequences of forced compliance. *Journal of Abnormal and Social Psychology, 58,* 203–210.
Field, T. (1991). Quality infant day-care and grade school behavior and performance. *Child Development, 62,* 863–870.
Field, T., Cohen, D., Garcia, R., & Greenberg, R. (1984). Mother-stranger face discrimination by the newborn. *Infant Behavior and Development, 7,* 19–25.
Field, T., Grizzle, N., Scafidi, F., Abrams, S., Richardson, S., Kuhn, C., & Schanberg, S. (1996). Massage therapy for infants of depressed mothers. *Infant Behavior and Development, 19,* 107–112.
Field, T., Woodson, R., Greenberg, R., & Cohen, D. (1982). Discrimination and imitation of facial expressions by neonates. *Science, 218,* 179–181.
Fifer, W. P., & Moon, C. M. (1995). The effects of fetal experience with sound. In J. Lecanuet, W. P. Fifer, N. A. Krasnegor, & W. P. Smotherman (Eds.), *Fetal development: A psychobiological perspective* (pp. 351–366). Mahwah, NJ: Erlbaum.
Findley, M. J., & Cooper, H. M. (1983). Locus of control and academic achievement: A literature review. *Journal of Personality and Social Psychology, 44,* 419–427.
Fineman, H. (1996, April 29). Redrawing the color lines. *Newsweek,* pp. 34–36.
Fink, M., & Sackeim, H. A. (1996). Convulsive therapy in schizophrenia? *Schizophrenia Bulletin, 22,* 27–40.
Firestein, S., & Werblin, F. (1989). Odor-induced membrane currents in vertebrate-olfactory receptor neurons. *Science, 244,* 79–82.
Fischer, K. W. (1987). Relations between brain and cognitive development. *Child Development, 58,* 623–632.
Fischhoff, B. (1975). Hindsight/foresight: The effect of outcome knowledge on judgment under uncertainty. *Journal of Experimental Psychology: Human Perception and Performance, 1,* 288–299.
Fischhoff, B., Slovic, P., & Lichtenstein, S. (1977). Knowing with certainty: The appropriateness of extreme confidence. *Journal of Experimental Psychology: Human Perception and Performance, 3,* 552–564.
Fishbein, M. (1980). A theory of reasoned action: Some applications and implications. In H. E. Howe & M. M. Page (Eds.), *Nebraska Symposium on Motivation* (Vol. 27, pp. 65–116). Lincoln: University of Nebraska Press.
Fisher, G. H. (1968). Ambiguity of form: Old and new. *Perception and Psychophysics, 4,* 189–192.
Fisher, J. D., & Fisher, W. A. (1992). Changing AIDS-risk behavior. *Psychological Bulletin, 111,* 455–474.
Fisher, S., & Greenberg, R. P. (1977). *The scientific credibility of Freud's theories and therapy.* New York: Columbia University Press.
Fiske, D. W., & Maddi, S. R. (1961). *The functions of varied experience.* Homewood, IL: Dorsey.
Fiske, S. T., & Neuberg, S. L. (1990). A continuum of impression formation from category-based to individuating processes: Influences of information and motivation on attention and interpretation. *Advances in Experimental Social Psychology, 23,* 1–74.
Fiske, S. T., & Taylor, S. E. (1991). *Social cognition.* New York: McGraw-Hill.
Fiske, S. T., Bersoff, D. N., Borgida, E., Deaux, K., & Heilman, M. E. (1991). Social science research on trial: Use of sex stereotyping research in *Price Waterhouse v. Hopkins. American Psychologist, 46,* 1049–1060.
Fitzgerald, J. M. (1988). Vivid memories and the reminiscence phenomenon: The role of self-narrative. *Human Development, 31,* 261–273.
Flavell, J. H. (1982). Structures, stages, and sequences in cognitive development. In W. A. Collins (Ed.), *The concept of development: The Minnesota symposia on child psychology* (Vol. 15). Hillsdale, NJ: Erlbaum.
Flavell, J. H. (1996). Piaget's legacy. *Psychological Science, 7,* 200–203.
Flavell, J. H., Beach, D. R., & Chinsky, J. M. (1966). Spontaneous verbal rehearsal in a memory task as a function of age. *Child Development, 37,* 283–299.
Flavell, J. H., Green, F. L., & Flavell, E. R. (1986). Development of knowledge about the appearance-reality distinction. *Monographs of the Society for Research in Child Development, 51* (1, Serial No. 212).
Flavell, J. H., Miller, P. H., & Miller, S. A. (1993). *Cognitive development* (3rd ed.). Englewood Cliffs, NJ: Prentice-Hall.
Fleming, I. A., Baum, A., & Weiss, L. (1987). Social density and perceived control as mediators of crowding stress in high-density residential neighborhoods. *Journal of Personality and Social Psychology, 52,* 899–906.
Fletcher, R. (1991). *Science, ideology, and the media: The Cyril Burt scandal.* New Brunswick, NJ: Transaction.
Flor, H., et al. (1995). Phantom-limb pain as a perceptual correlate of cortical reorganization following arm amputation. *Nature, 375,* 482–484.
Flynn, J. R. (1991). *Asian-Americans: Achievement beyond IQ.* Hillsdale, NJ: Erlbaum.
Flynn, J. R. (1987). Massive IQ gains in 14 nations: What IQ tests really measure. *Psychology Bulletin, 101,* 171–191.
Foa, E. B., & Kozak, M. J. (1986). Emotional processing of fear: Exposure to corrective information. *Psychological Bulletin, 99,* 20–35.
Foa, E. B., Steketee, G., & Grayson, J. B. (1985). Imaginal and in vivo exposure: A comparison with obsessive-compulsive checkers. *Behavior Therapy, 16,* 292–302.

Fontana, A., & Rosenheck, R. (1994). Traumatic war stressors and psychiatric symptoms among World War II, Korean, and Vietnam War veterans. *Psychology and Aging, 9,* 27–33.

Ford, C. V., & Folks, D. G. (1985). Conversion disorders: An overview. *Psychosomatics, 26,* 371–374, 380–383.

Ford, M. R., & Widiger, T. A. (1989). Sex bias in the diagnosis of histrionic and antisocial personality disorders. *Journal of Consulting and Clinical Psychology, 57,* 301–305.

Fossel, M. (1996). *Reversing human aging.* New York: Morrow.

Fosterling, F. (1992). The Kelley model as an analysis of variance analogy: How far can it be taken? *Journal of Experimental Social Psychology, 28,* 475–490.

Foulke, E. (1991). Braille. In M. A. Heller & W. Schiff (Eds.), *The psychology of touch* (pp. 219–233). Hillsdale, NJ: Erlbaum.

Fouts, R. S., Fouts, D. H., & Van Cantfort, T. E. (1989). The infant Loulis learns signs from cross-fostered chimpanzees. In R. A. Gardner, B. T. Gardner, & T. E. Van Cantfort (Eds.), *Teaching sign language to chimpanzees* (pp. 280–292). Albany: State University of New York Press.

Fowler, M. J., Sullivan, M. J., & Ekstrand, B. R. (1973). Sleep and memory. *Science, 179,* 302–304.

Fowler, R. D. (1986, May). Howard Hughes: A psychological autopsy. *Psychology Today,* pp. 22–33.

Fowles, D. C. (1992). Schizophrenia: Diathesis-stress revisited. *Annual Review of psychology, 43,* 303–336.

Fox, N. A. (1991). If it's not left, it's right: Electroencephalograph asymmetry and the development of emotion. *American Psychologist, 46,* 863–872.

Fox, N. A., Coplan, R. J., Rubin, K. H., Porges, S. W., Calkins, S. D., Long, J. M., Marshall, T. R., & Stewart, S. (1995). Frontal activation asymmetry and social competence at four years of age. *Child Development, 66,* 1770–1784.

Frances, A. J., & Widiger, T. (1986). The classification of personality disorders: An overview of problems and solutions. *Annual Review of Psychiatry, 5,* 240–257.

Frank, A. F., & Gunderson, J. G. (1991). The role of the therapist alliance in the treatment of schizophrenia: Relationship to course and outcome. *Archives of General Psychiatry, 47,* 228–236.

Frank, M. G., Ekman, P., & Friesen, W. V. (1993). Behavioral markers and recognizability of the smile of enjoyment. *Journal of Personality and Social Psychology, 64,* 83–93.

Frankenburg, W., Dodds, J., Archer, P., Shapiro, H., & Bresnick, B. (1992). The Denver II: A major revision and restandardization of the Denver Developmental Screening Test. *Pediatrics, 89,* 91–97.

Frazier, P., & Schauben, L. (1994). Causal attributions and recovery from rape and other stressful events. *Journal of Social and Clinical Psychology, 13,* 1–14.

Freedman, B. J. (1974). The perceptual experience of perpetual and cognitive disturbances in schizophrenia: A review of autobiographical accounts. *Archives of General Psychiatry, 30,* 333–340.

Freedman, J. L. (1988). Television violence and aggression: What the evidence shows. *Applied Social Psychology Annual, 8,* 144–162.

Freedman, J. L., Cunningham, J. A., & Krismer, K. (1992). Inferred values and the reverse-incentive effect in induced compliance. *Journal of Personality and Social Psychology, 62,* 357–368.

Freedman, R., et al. (1987). Neurobiological studies of sensory gating in schizophrenia. *Schizophrenia Bulletin, 13,* 669–678.

Freud, S. (1900). *The interpretation of dreams.* In Vols. 4 and 5 of the Standard edition. London: Hogarth.

Freud, S. (1909). Analysis of a phobia in a five-year-old boy. In *Collected works of Sigmund Freud* (Vol. 10). London: Hogarth. (Reprinted in 1956.)

Freud, S. (1920). *Beyond the pleasure principle: A study of the death instinct in human aggression* (J. Strachey, Trans.). New York: Bantam Books. (Reprinted in 1959.)

Freud, S. (1917). Mourning and melancholia. In J. Riviere (Trans.), *Collected papers* (Vol. 4). London: Hogarth Press. (Reprinted in 1924.)

Freud, S. (1940). *An outline of psychoanalysis.* In Vol. 23 of the *Standard edition.* London: Hogarth.

Freud, S. (1905). Fragments of an analysis of a case of hysteria. *Collected papers* (Vol. 3). New York: Basic Books. (Reprinted in 1959.)

Fridlund, A. J. (1994). *Human facial expression: An evolutionary view.* San Diego: Academic Press.

Friedlander, M. L., & Heatherington, L. (1989). Analyzing relational control in family therapy interviews. *Journal of Counseling Psychology, 36,* 139–148.

Friedman, H. S. (1991). *The self-healing personality.* New York: Henry Holt.

Friedman, H. S., & Booth-Kewley, S. (1987). The "disease-prone personality": A meta-analytic view of the construct. *American Psychologist, 42,* 539–555.

Friedman, M., & Rosenman, R. F. (1974). *Type A behavior and your heart.* New York: Knopf.

Friedman, M., & Ulmer, D. (1984). *Treating Type A behavior—and your heart.* New York: Knopf.

Friedman, W. J. (1993). Memory for the time of past events. *Psychological Bulletin, 113,* 44–66.

Friedmann, E., Katcher, A. H., Lynch, J. J., & Thomas, S. A. (1980). Animal companions and one-year survival of patients after discharge from a coronary care unit. *Public Health Reports, 95,* 307–312.

Friend, R., Rafferty, Y., & Bramel, D. (1990). A puzzling misinterpretation of the Asch "conformity" study. *European Journal of Social Psychology, 20,* 29–44.

Frijda, N. H. (1986). *The emotions.* New York: Cambridge University Press.

Fromm, E. (1941). *Escape from freedom.* New York: Farrar & Rinehart.

Fromm, E., & Nash, M. (1992). *Contemporary hypnosis research.* New York: Guilford Press.

Fuligni, A. J., & Stevenson, H. W. (1995). Time use and mathematics achievement among American, Chinese, and Japanese high school students. *Child Development, 66,* 830–842.

Funk, S. C. (1992). Hardiness: A review of theory and research. *Health Psychology, 11,* 335–345.

Fuster, J. M. (1989). *The prefrontal cortex: Anatomy, physiology, and neuropsychology of the frontal lobe.* New York: Raven Press.

Fuster, J. M. (1995). *Memory in the cerebral cortex.* Cambridge, MA: MIT Press.

Gabrenya, W. K., Jr., Latané, B., & Wang, Y. E. (1983). Social loafing in cross-cultural perspective: Chinese in Taiwan. *Journal of Cross-Cultural Psychology, 14,* 368–384.

Gabrieli, J. D., Desmond, J. E., Demb, J. B., Wagner, A. D., Stone, M. V., Vaidya, C. J., & Glover, G. H. (1996). Functional magnetic resonance imaging of semantic memory processes in the frontal lobes. *Psychological Science, 7,* 278–283.

Gackenbach, J., & Bosveld, J. (1989). *Control your dreams.* New York: Harper & Row.

Gaddes, W. H., & Edgell, D. (1994). *Learning disabilities and brain function: A neuropsychological approach* (3rd ed.). New York: Springer-Verlag.

Gaddis, A., & Brooks-Gunn, J. (1985). The male experience of pubertal change. *Journal of Youth and Adolescence, 14,* 61–69.

Gaertner, S. L., & McLaughlin, J. P. (1983). Racial stereotypes: Associations and ascriptions of positive and negative characteristics. *Social Psychology Quarterly, 46,* 23–30.

Gaertner, S. L., Mann, J. A., Dovidio, J. F., Murrell, A. J., & Pomare, M. (1990). How does cooperation reduce intergroup bias? *Journal of Personality and Social Psychology, 59,* 692–704.

Gage, F. H. (1993). Fetal implants put to the test. *Nature, 361,* 405–406.

Galanter, E. (1962). Contemporary psychophysics. In R. Brown, E. Galanter, H. Hess, & G. Mandler (Eds.), *New directions in psychology.* New York: Holt, Rinehart & Winston.

Gallant, J. L., Braun, J., & Van Essen, D. C. (1993). Selectivity for polar, hyperbolic, and Cartesian gratings in macaque visual cortex. *Science, 259,* 100–103.

Galotti, K. M. (1989). Approaches to studying formal and everyday reasoning. *Psychological Bulletin, 105,* 331–351.

Galton, F. (1883). *Inquiries into human faculty and its development.* London: Dent.

Gamwell, L., & Tomes, N. (1995). *Madness in America: Cultural and medical perceptions of mental illness before 1914.* Ithaca, NY: Cornell University Press.

Gara, M. A., Woolfolk, R. L., Cohen, B. D., Goldston, R. B., Allen, L. A., & Novalany, J. (1993). Perception of self and other in major depression. *Journal of Abnormal Psychology, 102,* 93–100

Garcia, J. (1981). The logic and limits of mental aptitude testing. *American Psychologist, 36,* 1172–1180.

Garcia, J., & Koelling, R. A. (1966). The relation of cue to consequence in avoidance learning. *Psychonomic Science, 4,* 123–124.

Gardner, H. (1983). Frames of mind: *The theory of multiple intelligences.* New York: Basic Books.

Gardner, H. (1993). *Multiple intelligences: The theory in practice.* New York: Basic Books.

Gardner, H. (1995). *Leading minds: An anatomy of leadership.* New York: Basic Books.

Gardner, R. A., & Gardner, B. I. (1969). Teaching sign language to a chimpanzee. *Science, 165,* 664–672.

Gardner, R. A., & Gardner, B. T. (1978). Comparative psychology and language acquisition. *Annuals of the New York Academy of Science, 309,* 37–76.

Garner, D. M., & Wooley, S. C. (1991). Confronting the failure of behavioral and dietary treatments for obesity. *Clinical Psychology Review, 11,* 729–780.

Garry, M., Manning, C. G., Loftus, E. F., & Sherman, S. J. (1997). Imagination inflation: Imagining a childhood event inflates confidence that it occurred. *Psychonomic Bulletin and Review,* in press.

Gatchel, R. J., & Blanchard, E. B. (Eds.). (1993). *Psychophysiological disorders.* Washington, DC: American Psychological Association.

Gatz, M., & Hurwicz, M. L. (1990). Are old people more depressed? Cross-sectional data on Center for Epidemiological Studies depression scale factors. *Psychology and Aging, 5,* 284–290.

Gavin, L., & Furman, W. (1989). Age differences in adolescents' perceptions of their peer groups. *Developmental Psychology, 25,* 827–834.

Gawin, F. H. (1991). Cocaine addiction: Psychology and neurophysiology. *Science, 251,* 1580–1586.

Gay, P. (1988). Freud: A life for our time. New York: Norton.

Gazzaniga, M. S. (1967). The split brain in man. *Scientific American,* 24–29.

Gazzaniga, M. S. (1970). *The bisected brain.* New York: Appleton-Century-Crofts.

Gazzaniga, M. S. (1985). *The social brain.* New York: Basic Books.

Gazzaniga, M. S. (1992). *Nature's mind: The roots of thinking, emotions, sexuality, language, and intelligence.* New York: Basic Books.

Gazzaniga, M. S., & LeDoux, J. E. (1978). *The integrated mind.* New York: Plenum.

Geary, D. C. (1996). Sexual selection and sex differences in mathematical abilities. *Behavioral and Brain Sciences, 19,* 229–284.

Geldard, F. A. (1972). *The human senses* (2nd ed.). New York: Wiley.

Gelman, R. (1979). Preschool thought. *American Psychologist, 34,* 900–905.

Gentner, D., & Stevens, A. L. (Eds.). (1983). *Mental models.* Hillsdale, NJ: Erlbaum.

George, J. T., & Hopkins, B. L. (1989). Multiple effects of performance-contigent pay for waitpersons. *Journal of Applied Behavior Analysis, 22,* 131–141.

George, T. P., & Hartmann, D. P. (1996). Friendship networks of unpopular, average, and popular children. *Child Development, 67,* 2301–2316.

Gerall, A. A., Moltz, H., & Ward, I. L. (Eds.). (1992). *Handbook of behavioral neurobiology: Vol. 11. Sexual differentiation.* New York: Plenum.

Gerrard, M. (1987). Sex, sex guilt, and contraceptive use revisited: The 1980s. *Journal of Personality and Social Psychology, 52,* 975–980.

Gerrard, M., Gibbons, F. X., & Bushman, B. J. (1996). Relation between perceived vulnerability in HIV and precautionary sexual behavior. *Psychological Bulletin, 119,* 390–409.

Gescheider, G. A. (1985). *Psychophysics: Method, theory, and application* (2nd ed.). Hillsdale, NJ: Erlbaum.

Geschwind, N. (1979). Specializations of the human brain. *Scientific American, 241,* 180–199.

Geschwind, N., & Behan, P. (1982). Left-handedness: Association with immune disease, migraine, and left-handed learning disorder. *Proceedings of the National Academy of Sciences, 79,* 5097–5100.

Gesell, A. L. (1940). *The first five years of life: A guide to the study of the preschool child.* New York: Harper.

Gevins, A., et al. (1996). High resolution evoked potential imaging of the cortical dynamics of human working memory. *Electroencephalography and Clinical Neurophysiology, 98,* 327–348.

Gibbons, F. X. (1990). Self-attention and behavior: A review and theoretical update. In M. P. Zanna (Ed.), *Advances in experimental social psychology,* (Vol. 23, pp. 249–303). New York: Academic Press.

Gibbons, F. X., & McCoy, S. B. (1991). Self-esteem, similarity, and reactions to active versus passive downward comparison. *Journal of Personality and Social Psychology, 60,* 414–424.

Gibson, E., & Walk, R. D. (1960). The visual cliff. *Scientific American, 202,* 80–92.

Gibson, E. J., & Walker, A. S. (1984). Development of knowledge of visual-tactual affordances of substance. *Child Development, 55,* 453–461.

Gibson, H. B. (1991). Can hypnosis compel people to commit harmful, immoral and criminal acts? A review of the literature. *Contemporary Hypnosis, 8,* 129–140.

Gibson, J. J. (1962). Observations on active touch. *Psychological Review, 69,* 477–491.

Gibson, J. J. (1979). *The ecological approach to visual perception.* Boston: Houghton Mifflin.

Gick, M. L., & Holyoak, K. J. (1980). Analogical problem solving. *Cognitive Psychology, 12,* 306–355.

Gilbert, A. N., & Wysocki, C. J. (1987, October). The smell survey results. *National Geographic,* pp. 514–525.

Gilbert, D. T., & Hixon, J. G. (1991). The trouble of thinking: Activation and application of stereotypic beliefs. *Journal of Personality and Social Psychology, 60, 509–517.*

Gilbert, D. T., & Malone, P. S. (1995). The correspondence bias. *Psychological Bulletin, 117,* 21–38.

Gillie, O. (1976, October 24). Crucial data was faked by eminent psychologist. *London Sunday Times.*

Gilligan, C. (1982). *In a different voice: Psychological theory and women's development.* Cambridge, MA: Harvard University Press.

Gilovich, T. (1983). Biased evaluation and persistence in gambling. *Journal of Personality and Social Psychology, 40,* 797–808.

Gilovich, T. (1991). *How we know what isn't so: The fallibility of human reason in everyday life.* New York: Free Press.

Ginsburg, H., & Opper, S. (1988). *Piaget's theory of intellectual development* (3rd ed.). Englewood Cliffs, NJ: Prentice-Hall.

Ginty, D. D., et al. (1993). Regulation of CREB phosphorylation in the suprachiasmatic nucleus by light and a circadian clock. *Science, 260,* 238–241.

Gitlin, M. J. (1996). *The psychotherapist's guide to psychopharmacology* (2nd ed.). New York: Free Press.

Glanzer, M., & Cunitz, A. (1966). Two storage mechanisms in free recall. *Journal of Verbal Learning and Verbal Behavior, 5,* 351–360.

Glaser, R. (1990). The reemergence of learning theory within instructional research. *American Psychologist, 45,* 29–39.

Glaser, R., & Kiecolt-Glaser, J. K. (Eds.) (1994). *Handbook of stress and immunity.* San Diego: Academic Press.

Glasgow, R. E., & Lichtenstein, E. (1987). Long-term effects of behavioral smoking cessation interventions. *Behavior Therapy, 18,* 297–324.

Glass, A. L., & Holyoak, K. J. (1986). *Cognition* (2nd ed.). New York: Random House.

Glass, D. C. (1977). *Behavior patterns, stress, and coronary disease.* Hillsdale, NJ: Erlbaum.

Glass, J. D., & Johnson, R. T. (1996). Human immunodeficiency virus and the brain. *Annual Review of Neuroscience, 19,* 1–26.

Gleicher, F., & Petty, R. E. (1992). Expectations of reassurance influence the nature of fear-stimulated attitude change. *Journal of Experimental Social Psychology, 28,* 86–100.

Glenn, N. D. (1990). Quantitative research on marital quality in the 1980s: A critical review. *Journal of Marriage and the Family, 52,* 818–831.

Gobet, F., & Simon, H. A. (1996). Recall of random and distorted chess positions: Implications for the theory of expertise. *Memory and Cognition, 24,* 493–503.

Goddard, H. H. (1917). Mental tests and the immigrant. *The Journal of Delinquency, 2,* 243–277.

Godden, D. R., & Baddeley, A. D. (1975). Context-dependent memory in two natural environments: On land and underwater. *British Journal of Psychology, 66,* 325–332.

Goebel, B. L., & Brown, D. (1981). Age differences in motivation related to Maslow's need hierarchy. *Developmental Psychology, 17,* 809–815.

Goethals, G. R., & Reckman, R. F. (1973). The perception of consistency in attitudes. *Journal of Experimental Social Psychology, 9,* 491–501.

Goffin, R. D., Rothstein, M. G., & Johnston, N. G. (1996). Personality testing and the assessment center: Incremental validity for managerial selection. *Journal of Applied Psychology, 81,* 746–756.

Golay, M., & Rollyson, C. (1996). *Where America stands 1996.* New York: Wiley.

Gold, P. E. (1992). Modulation of memory processing: Enhancement of memory in rodents and humans. In L. Squire & N. Butters (Eds.), *Neuropsychology of memory* (2nd ed., pp. 402–414). New York: Guilford Press.

Gold, P. E. (1993). *Cognitive enhancers in animals and humans: From hormones to brains.* Paper presented at the annual meeting of the American Psychological Society. Chicago, IL.

Goldberg, L. R. (1990). An alternative "description of personality": The big-five factor structure. *Journal of Personality and Social Psychology, 59,* 1216–1229.

Goldberg, L. R. (1993). The structure of phenotypic personality. *American Psychologist, 48,* 26–34.

Goldberg, L. R., Grenier, J. R., Guion, R., Sechrest, L. B., & Wing, H. (1991). *Questionnaires used in the prediction of trustworthiness in pre-employment selection decisions: An A.P.A. Task Force Report.* Washington, DC: American Psychological Association.

Goldhagen, D. J. (1996). *Hitler's willing executioners: Ordinary Germans and the Holocaust.* New York: Knopf.

Golding, S. L. (1992). The adjudication of criminal responsibility: A review of theory and research. In D. Kagehiro & W. Laufer (Eds.), *Handbook of psychology and law.* New York: Springer-Verlag.

Goldman-Rakic, P. S. (1987). Development of cortical circuitry and cognitive function. *Child Development, 58,* 601–622.

Goldsmith, H. H., & Lansky, J. A. (1987). Maternal and infant temperamental predictors of attachment: A meta-analytic review. *Journal of Consulting and Clinical Psychology, 55,* 805–816

Goldstein, A. G., Chance, J. E., & Schneller, G. R. (1989). Frequency of eyewitness identification in criminal cases: A survey of prosecutors. *Bulletin of the Psychonomic Society, 27,* 71–74.

Goldstein, S. R., & Young, C. A. (1996). "Evolutionary" stable strategy of handedness in major league baseball. *Journal of Comparative Psychology, 110,* 164–169.

Goleman, D. (1989, October 17). Critics challenge reliance on drugs in psychiatry. *The New York Times,* p. C1.

Goleman, D. (1990, December 25). The group and the self: New focus on a cultural rift. *The New York Times,* pp. 37, 41.

Goleman, D. (1995). *Emotional intelligence.* New York: Bantam.

Golomb, J., de Leon, M. J., Kluger, A., George, A. E., Tarshish, C., & Ferris, S. H. (1993). Hippocampal atrophy in normal aging: An association with recent memory impairment. *Archives of Neurology, 50,* 967–973.

Good, B. J., & Kleinman, A. M. (1985). Culture and anxiety: Cross-cultural evidence for the patterning of anxiety disorders. In A. H. Tuma & J. D. Maser (Eds.), *Anxiety and the anxiety disorders.* Hillsdale, NJ: Erlbaum.

Good, K., & Chanoff, D. (1991). *Into the heart.* New York: Simon & Schuster.

Goodall, J. (1986). *The chimpanzees of Gombe: Patterns of behavior.* Cambridge, MA: Harvard University Press.

Goodman, G. S., Aman, C., & Hirschman, J. (1987). Child sexual and physical abuse. In S. Ceci, M. Toglia, & D. Ross (Eds.), *Children's eyewitness testimony* (pp. 1–23). New York: Springer-Verlag.

Goodwin, F. K., & Jamison, K. R. (1990). *Manic depressive illness.* New York: Oxford University Press.

Gordon, S. (1986, October). What kids need to know. *Psychology Today,* pp. 22–26.

Gorman, J. M., Liebowitz, M. R., Fyer, A. J., & Stein, J. (1989). A neuroanatomical hypothesis for panic disorder. *American Journal of Psychiatry, 146,* 148–161.

Gormley, F. F., & Aiello, J. R. (1982). Social density, interpersonal relationships, and residential crowding stress. *Journal of Applied Social Psychology, 12,* 22–36.

Gortmaker, S. L., Must, A., Perrin, J. M., Sobol, A. M., & Dietz, W. H. (1993). Social and economic consequences of overweight in adolescence and young adulthood. *New England Journal of Medicine, 329,* 1008–1012.

Gosselin, P., Kirouac, G., & Dore, F. Y. (1995). Components and recognition of facial expression in the communication of emotion by actors. *Journal of Personality and Social Psychology, 68,* 83–96.

Gottesman, I. I. (1991). *Schizophrenia genesis: The origins of madness.* San Francisco: W. H. Freeman.
Gottesman, I. I., & Shields, J. (1982). *Schizophrenia: The epigenetic puzzle.* New York: Cambridge University Press.
Gould, J. L., & Marler, P. (1987). Learning by instinct. *Scientific American, 256* (1), 74–75.
Gould, R. L. (1978). *Transformations: Growth and change in adult life.* New York: Simon & Schuster.
Graber, J. A., Brooks-Gunn, J., & Petersen, A. C. (Eds.) (1996). *Transitions through adolescence: Interpersonal domains and context.* Mahwah, NJ: Erlbaum.
Graber, J. A., Brooks-Gunn, J., & Warren, M. P. (1995). The antecedents of menarcheal age: Heredity, family environment, and stressful life events. *Child Development, 66,* 346–359.
Graber, J. A., Brooks-Gunn, J., Paikoff, R. L., & Warren, M. P. (1994). Prediction of eating problems: An 8-year study of adolescent girls. *Developmental Psychology, 30,* 823–834.
Graffin, N. F., Ray, W. J., & Lundy, R. (1995). EEG concomitants of hypnosis and hypnotic susceptibility. *Journal of Abnormal Psychology, 104,* 123–131.
Graham, J. R. (1990). *MMPI-2: Assessing personality and psychopathology.* New York: Oxford University Press.
Granberg, D., & Brent, E. (1983). When prophecy bends: The preference-expectation link in U.S. presidential elections. *Journal of Personality and Social Psychology, 45,* 477–491.
Gramling, S. E., Clawson, E. P., & McDonald, M. K. (1996). Perceptual and cognitive abnormality model of hypochondriasis: Amplification and physiological reactivity in women. *Psychosomatic Medicine, 58,* 423–431.
Green, D. M., & Swets, J. A. (1966). *Signal detection theory and psychophysics.* New York: Wiley.
Greenberg, J. (1982). Approaching equity and avoiding inequity in groups and organizations. In J. Greenberg & R. L. Cohen (Eds.), *Equity and justice in social behavior* (pp. 389–435). New York: Academic Press.
Greenberg, J. (1988). Equity and workplace status: A field experiment. *Journal of Applied Psychology, 73,* 606–613.
Greenberg, J. (1993). Stealing in the name of justice: Informational and interpersonal moderators of theft reactions to underpayment equity. *Organizational Behavior and Human Decision Processes, 54,* 81–103.
Greene, W. C. (1993, September). AIDS and the immune system. *Scientific American,* pp. 99–105.
Greenough, W. T., Black, J. E., & Wallace, C. S. (1987). Experience and brain development. *Child Development, 58,* 539–559.
Greenough, W. T., Withers, G. S., & Wallace, C. S. (1990). Morphological changes in the nervous system arising from behavioral experience: What is the evidence they are involved in learning and memory? In L. R. Squire & E. Lindenlaub (Eds.), *The biology of memory* (pp. 159–185). Stuttgart: Schattauer.
Greenspan, J. D., & Bolanowski, S. J. (1996). The psychophysics of tactile perception and its peripheral physiological basis. In L. Kruger (Ed.), *Pain and touch* (pp. 25–103). San Diego: Academic Press.
Greenwald, A. G. (1980). The totalitarian ego: Fabrication and revision of personal history. *American Psychologist, 35,* 603–618.
Greenwald, A. G. (1992). New Look 3: Unconscious cognition reclaimed. *American Psychologist, 47,* 766–779.
Greenwald, A. G., & Banaji, M. R. (1989). The self as a memory system: Powerful but ordinary. *Journal of Personality and Social Psychology, 57,* 41–54.
Greenwald, A. G., & Banaji, M. R. (1995). Implicit social cognition: Attitudes, self-esteem, and stereotypes. *Psychological Review, 102,* 4–27.
Greenwald, A. G., Spangenberg, E. R., Pratkanis, A. R., & Eskenazi, J. (1991). Double-blind tests of subliminal self-help audiotapes. *Psychological Science, 2,* 119–122.
Gregory, R. L. (1990). *Eye and brain: The psychology of seeing* (4th ed.). Princeton, NJ: Princeton University Press.
Greif, E. B., & Ulman, K. J. (1982). The psychological impact of menarche on early adolescent females: A review of the literature. *Child Development, 53,* 1413–1430.
Griffin, D. R. (1992). *Animal minds.* Chicago: University of Chicago Press.
Griggs, R. A., & Cox, J. R. (1982). The elusive thematic-materials effect in Wason's selection task. *British Journal of Psychology, 73,* 407–420.
Grilo, C. M., & Pogue-Geile, M. (1991). The nature of environmental influences in weight and obesity: A behavior genetic analysis. *Psychological Bulletin, 110,* 520–537.
Grissmer, D. W., Kirby, S. N., Berends, M., & Williamson, S. (1994). *Student achievement and the changing American family.* Santa Monica, CA: RAND Corporation.
Gross, A. E., & Crofton, C. (1977). What is good is beautiful. *Sociometry, 40,* 85–90.
Gross, C. G., Rocha-Miranda, E. C., & Bender, D. B. (1972). Visual properties of neurons in the inferotemporal cortex of the macaque. *Journal of Neurophysiology, 35,* 96–111.
Gross, J. J., & Levenson, R. W. (1997). Hiding feelings: The acute effects of inhibiting negative and positive emotion. *Journal of Abnormal Psychology, 106,* 95–103.
Grossman, M., & Wood, W. (1993). Sex differences in intensity of emotional experience: A social role interpretation. *Journal of Personality and Social Psychology, 65,* 1010–1022.
Grunwald, L., & Goldberg, J. (1993, July). The amazing minds of infants. *Life,* pp. 46–56.
Guerin, B. (1986). Mere presence effects in humans: A review. *Journal of Experimental Social Psychology, 22,* 38–77.
Guilford, J. P. (1967). *The nature of human intelligence.* New York: McGraw-Hill.
Guilford, J. P. (1985). The structure-of-intellect model. In B. B. Wolman (Ed.), *Handbook of intelligence: Theories, measurements, and applications* (pp. 225–266). New York: Wiley.
Guilleminault, C., & Roth, T. (1993). Hypersomnia. In M. A. Carskadon (Ed.), *Encyclopedia of Sleep and Dreaming* (pp. 287–288). New York: Macmillan.
Guinness Book of World Records. (1994). New York: Bantam Books.
Guion, R. M. (1965). *Personnel testing.* New York: McGraw-Hill.
Gump, P. V. (1987). School and classroom environments. In D. Stokols & I. Altman (Eds.), *Handbook of Environmental Psychology* (Vol. 1). New York: Wiley.
Gunderson, J. G. (1984). *Borderline personality disorder.* Washington, DC: American Psychiatric Press.
Gurtman, M. B. (1987). Depressive affect and disclosures as factors in interpersonal rejection. *Cognitive Therapy and Research, 11,* 87–100.
Guthrie, J. P., Ash, R. A., & Bendapudi, V. (1995). Additional validity evidence for measures of morningness. *Journal of Applied Psychology, 80,* 186–190.
Guttman, N., & Kalish, H. (1956). Discriminability and stimulus generalization. *Journal of Experimental Psychology, 51,* 79–88.
Gwaltney, L. (1986). *The dissenters.* New York: Random House.

Haaga, D., & Davison, G. C. (1993). An appraisal of rational-emotive therapy. *Journal of Consulting and Clinical Psychology, 61,* 215–220.
Haaga, D. A., Dyck, M. J., & Ernst, D. (1991). Empirical status of cognitive theory of depression. *Psychological Bulletin, 110,* 215–236.
Haddock, G., Zanna, M. P., & Esses, V. M. (1993). Assessing the structure of prejudicial attitudes: The case of attitudes toward homosexuals. *Journal of Personality and Social Psychology, 65,* 1105–1118.
Haier, R. J., Siegel, B., Tang, C., Abel, L., & Buchsbaum, M. S. (1992). Intelligence and changes in regional cerebral glucose metabolic rate following learning. *Intelligence, 16,* 415–426.
Hailman, J. P. (1969). How an instinct is learned. *Scientific American, 221,* 98–106.
Haist, F., Shimamura, A. P., & Squire, L. R. (1992). On the relationship between recall and recognition memory. *Journal of Experimental Psychology: Learning, Memory, and Cognition, 18,* 691–702.
Haith, M. (1980). *Rules that babies look by.* Hillsdale, NJ: Erlbaum.
Hall, C. S., & Van de Castle, R. (1966). *The content analysis of dreams.* New York: Appleton-Century-Crofts.
Hall, G. S. (1904). *Adolescence.* New York: Appleton-Century-Crofts.
Hall, J. A. (1984). *Nonverbal sex differences: Communication accuracy and expressive style.* Baltimore: Johns Hopkins University Press.
Hall, J. A., & Veccia, E. M. (1990). More "touching" observations: New insights on men, women, and interpersonal touch. *Journal of Personality and Social Psychology, 59,* 1155–1162.
Hall, H. V., & Pritchard, D. A. (1996). *Detecting malingering and deception: Forensic distortion analysis (FDA).* Delray Beach, FL: St. Lucie Press.
Halpern, A. R. (1986). Memory for tune titles after organized or unorganized presentation. *American Journal of Psychology, 99,* 57–70.
Halpern, A. R., & Deveraux, S. D. (1989). Lucky numbers: Choice strategies in the Pennsylvania Number game. *Bulletin of the Psychonomic Society, 27,* 167–170.
Halpern, D. F. (1992). *Sex differences in cognitive abilities.* Hillsdale, NJ: Erlbaum.
Halpern, D. F., & Coren, S. (1993). Left-handedness and life span: A reply to Harris. *Psychological Bulletin, 114,* 235–241.
Hamilton, D. L., & Zanna, M. P. (1974). Context effects in impression formation: Changes in connotative meaning. *Journal of Personality and Social Psychology, 29,* 649–654.
Hamilton, M. C. (1988). Using masculine generics: Does generic "he" increase male bias in the user's imagery? *Sex Roles, 19,* 785–799.
Hampton, R. R., & Shettleworth, S. J. (1996). Hippocampus and memory in a food-storing and in a nonstoring bird species. *Behavioral Neuroscience, 110,* 946–964.
Hancock, L. (1996, March 18). Mother's little helper. *Newsweek,* pp. 51–56.
Handel, A. (1987). Personal theories about the life-span development of one's self in autobiographical self-presentations of adults. *Human Development, 30,* 83–98.
Hanna, E., & Meltzoff, A. N. (1993). Peer imitation by toddlers in laboratory, home, and day-care contexts: Implications for social learning and memory. *Developmental Psychology, 29,* 701–710.
Hansen, C. H. (1989). Priming sex-role stereotypic event schemas with rock music videos: Effects on impression favorability, trait inferences, and recall of a subsequent male-female interaction. *Basic and Applied Social Psychology, 10,* 371–391.
Hansen, C. H., & Hansen, R. D. (1988). Finding the face in the crowd: An anger superiority effect. *Journal of Personality and Social Psychology, 54,* 917–924.
Harbin, T. J. (1989). The relationship between the Type A behavior pattern and physiological responsivity: Quantitative review. *Psychophysiology, 26,* 110–119.

Hardaway, R. A. (1990). Subliminally activated symbolic fantasies: Facts and artifacts. *Psychological Bulletin, 107,* 177–195.
Hardin, C., & Banaji, M. R. (1993). The influence of language on thought. *Social Cognition, 11,* 277–308.
Hare, R. D. (1993). *Without conscience: The disturbing world of the psychopaths among us.* New York: Pocket Books.
Hare, R. D., Hart, S. D., & Harpur, T. (1991). Psychopathy and the DSM-IV criteria for antisocial personality disorder. *Journal of Abnormal Psychology, 100,* 391–398.
Hare, R. D., McPherson, L. M., & Forth, A. E. (1988). Male psychopaths and their criminal careers. *Journal of Consulting and Clinical Psychology, 56,* 710–714.
Hargadon, R., Bowers, K. S., & Woody, E. Z. (1995). Does counterpain imagery mediate hypnotic responding? *Journal of Abnormal Psychology, 104,* 508–516.
Harkins, D. A., & Uzgiris, I. C. (1991). Hand-use matching between mothers and infants during the first year. *Infant Behavior and Development, 14,* 289–298.
Harlow, H. F. (1958). The nature of love. *American Psychologist, 13,* 673–685.
Harlow, H. F. (1971). *Learning to love.* San Francisco: Albion.
Harlow, J. M. (1868). Recovery from the passage of an iron bar through the head. *Massachusetts Medical Society Publication, 2,* 327–347.
Harris, B. (1979). Whatever happened to Little Albert? *American Psychologist, 34,* 151–160.
Harris, C. R., & Christenfeld, N. (1996). Gender, jealousy, and reason. *Psychological Science, 7,* 364–366.
Harris, J. R. (1995). Where is the child's environment? A group socialization theory of development. *Psychological Review, 102,* 458–489.
Harris, L. J. (1988). Right-brain training: Some reflections on the application of research on cerebral hemispheric specialization to education. In D. L. Molfese & S. J. Segalowitz (Eds.), *Brain lateralization in children,* pp. 207–235. New York: Guilford Press.
Harris, L. J. (1993). Do left-handers die sooner than right-handers? Commentary on Coren and Halpern's (1991) "Left-handedness: A marker for decreased survival fitness." *Psychological Bulletin, 114,* 203–234.
Harris, M. J., & Perkins, R. (1995). Effects of distraction on interpersonal expectancy effects: A social interaction test of the cognitive busyness hypothesis. *Social Cognition, 13,* 163–182.
Harris, M. J., & Rosenthal, R. (1985). Mediation of interpersonal expectancy effects. *Psychological Bulletin, 97,* 363–386.
Harris, P. L., & Kavanaugh, R. D. (1993). Young children's understanding of pretense. *Monographs of the Society for Research in Child Development, 58* (1, Serial No. 231).
Harris, R. J., & Monaco, G. E. (1978). Psychology of pragmatic implication: Information processing between the lines. *Journal of Experimental Psychology: General, 107,* 1–22.
Harrison, A. A., & Saeed, L. (1977). Let's make a deal: An analysis of revelations and stipulations in lonely hearts advertisements. *Journal of Personality and Social Psychology, 35,* 257–264.
Hartshorne, H., & May, M. (1928). *Studies in deceit.* New York: Macmillan.
Hartup, W. W. (1989). Social relationships and their developmental significance. *American Psychologist, 44,* 120–126.
Hartup, W. W. (1996). The company they keep: Friendships and their developmental significance. *Child Development, 67,* 1–13.
Hasher, L., & Zacks, R. T. (1984). Automatic processing of fundamental information: The case of frequency. *American Psychologist, 39,* 1372–1388.
Hass, R. G., Katz, I., Rizzo, N., Bailey, J., & Moore, L. (1992). When racial ambivalence evokes negative affect, using a disguised measure of mood. *Personality and Social Psychology Bulletin, 18,* 786–797.
Hassett, J. (1978). *A primer of psychophysiology.* San Francisco: W. H. Freeman.
Hatch, J. P. (1993). Headache. In R. J. Gatchel & E. B. Blanchard (Eds.), *Psychophysiological disorders* (pp. 111–150). Washington, DC: American Psychological Association.
Hatch, J. P., Fisher, J. G., & Rugh, J. D. (1987). *Biofeedback: Studies in clinical efficacy.* New York: Plenum.
Hatfield, E. (1988). Passionate and compassionate love. In R. J. Sternberg & M. L. Barnes (Eds.), *The psychology of love.* New Haven, CT: Yale University Press.
Hatfield, E., & Sprecher, S. (1986). *Mirror, mirror . . . The importance of looks in everyday life.* Albany, NY: State University of New York Press.
Hathaway, S. R., & McKinley, J. C. (1983). *Minnesota Multiphasic Personality Inventory: Manual for administration and scoring.* New York: Psychological Corporation.
Hawkins, S. A., & Hastie, R. (1990). Hindsight: Biased judgments of past events after the outcomes are known. *Psychological Bulletin, 107,* 311–327.
Hayes, C. (1951). *The ape in our house.* New York: Harper.
Hayflick, L. (1996). *How and why we age.* New York: Ballantine.
Hazelrigg, M. D., Cooper, H. M., & Borduin, C. (1987). Evaluating the effectiveness of family therapies: An integrative review and analysis. *Psychological Bulletin, 101,* 428–442.
He, L. F. (1987). Involvement of endogenous opioid peptides in acupuncture analgesia. *Pain, 31,* 99–121.
Hearnshaw, L. S. (1979). *Cyril Burt: Psychologist.* Ithaca, NY: Cornell University Press.
Heatherton, T. F., & Weinberger, J. L. (Eds.). (1994). *Can personality change?* Washington, DC: American Psychological Association.
Hecht, H., & Proffitt, D. R. (1995). The price of expertise: Effects of experience on the water-level task. *Psychological Science, 6,* 90–95.
Hedges, L. B., & Nowell, A. (1995). Sex differences in mental test scores, variability, and numbers of high-scoring individuals. *Science, 269,* 41–45.
Heider, F. (1958). *The psychology of interpersonal relations.* New York: Wiley.
Heinberg, L. J., & Thompson, J. K. (1995). Body image and televised images of thinness and attractiveness: A controlled laboratory investigation. *Journal of Social and Clinical Psychology, 14,* 325–338.
Heine, S. J., & Lehman, D. R. (1995). Cultural variation in unrealistic optimism: Does the West feel more invulnerable than the East? *Journal of Personality and Social Psychology, 68,* 595–607.
Helgesen, S. (1990). *The female advantage: Women's ways of leadership.* New York: Doubleday Currency.
Helgeson, V. S. (1992). Moderators of the relation between perceived control and adjustment to chronic illness. *Journal of Personality and Social Psychology, 63,* 652-666.
Heller, M. A., & Schiff, W. (Eds.). (1991). *The psychology of touch: Theory and application.* Hillsdale, NJ: Erlbaum.
Hellige, J. B. (1990). Hemispheric asymmetry. *Annual Review of Psychology, 41,* 55–80.
Helmes, E., & Reddon, J. R. (1993). A perspective on developments in assessing psychopathology: A critical review of the MMPI–2. *Psychological Bulletin, 113,* 453–471.
Helmholtz, H. von. (1852). On the theory of compound colours. *Philosophical Magazine, 4,* 519–534.
Helms, J. E. (1992). Why is there no study of cultural equivalence in standardized cognitive ability testing? *American Psychologist, 47,* 1083–1101.
Hendrick, S. S. (1981). Self-disclosure and marital satisfaction. *Journal of Personality and Social Psychology, 40,* 1150–1159.
Heneman, H. G., & Schwab, D. P. (1985). Pay satisfaction: Its multidimensional nature and measurement. *International Journal of Psychology, 20,* 129–141.
Henley, N. M. (1977). *Body politics: Power, sex, and nonverbal communication.* Englewood Cliffs, NJ: Prentice-Hall.
Henry, K. R. (1984). Cochlear damage resulting from exposure to four different octave bands of noise at three different ages. *Behavioral Neuroscience, 1,* 107–117.
Henry, W. A. (1994, June 27). Pride and prejudice. *Time,* pp. 54–59.
Henry, W. P., Strupp, H. H., Schacht, T. E., & Gaston, L. (1994). Psychodynamic approaches. In A. E. Bergin & S. L. Garfield (Eds.), *Handbook of psychotherapy and behavior change* (4th ed.) (pp. 467–508). New York: Wiley.
Hensel, H. (1981). *Thermoreception and temperature regulation.* London: Academic Press.
Henslin, J. M. (1967). Craps and magic. *American Journal of Sociology, 73,* 316–330.
Hepper, P. G., Shahidullah, S., & White, R. (1990). Origins of fetal handedness. *Nature, 347,* 431.
Hepworth, J. T., & West, S. G. (1988). Lynchings and the economy: A time-series reanalysis of Hovland and Sears (1940). *Journal of Personality and Social Psychology, 55,* 239–247.
Herbert, T. B., & Cohen, S. (1993). Depression and immunity: A meta-analytic review. *Psychological Bulletin, 113,* 472–486.
Herek, G. M. (1988). Heterosexuals' attitudes toward lesbians and gay men: Correlates and gender differences. *Journal of Sex Research, 25,* 451–477.
Herenk, R. (Ed.). (1980). *The psychotherapy handbook: The A to Z guide to more than 250 therapies in use today.* New York: New American Library.
Hering, E. (1878). *Outlines of a theory of the light sense* (L. Hurvich & D. Jameson, Trans.). Cambridge, MA: Harvard University Press.
Herman, C. P., Zanna, M. P., & Higgins, E. T. (1986). *Physical appearance, stigma, and social behavior: The Ontario Symposium* (Vol. 3). Hillsdale, NJ: Erlbaum.
Herman, L. M., Kuczaj, S. A., & Holder, M. D. (1993). Responses to anomalous gestural sequences by a language-trained dolphin: Evidence for processing of semantic relations and syntactic information. *Journal of Experimental Psychology: General, 122,* 184–194.
Hermann, D. H. J. (1983). *The insanity defense: Philosophical, historical, and legal perspectives.* Springfield, IL: C. C. Thomas.
Herrnstein, R. J., & Murray, C. (1994). *The bell curve: Intelligence and class structure in American life.* New York: Free Press.
Hershenson, M. (Ed.). (1989). *The moon illusion.* Hillsdale, NJ: Erlbaum.
Hertz, M. R. (1986). Rorschach bound: A 50-year memoir. *Journal of Personality Assessment, 50,* 396–416.
Hertzog, C. (1989). Influences of cognitive slowing on age differences in intelligence. *Developmental Psychology, 25,* 636–651.
Hess, E. H. (1959). Imprinting. *Science, 130,* 133–144.
Heston, L. L., & White, J. A. (1991). *The vanishing mind: A practical guide to Alzheimer's disease and other dementias.* New York: W. H. Freeman.
Hetherington, A. W., & Ranson, S. W. (1942). The spontaneous activity and food intake of rats with hypothalamic lesions. *American Journal of Physiology, 136,* 609–617.
Hetherington, E. M., Reiss, D., & Plomin, R. (Eds.). (1994). *Separate social worlds of siblings: The impact of nonshared environment on development.* Hillsdale, NJ: Erlbaum.
Heyes, C. M., & Galef, B. G., Jr. (1996). *Social learning in animals: The roots of culture.* New York: Academic Press.

Heyser, C. J., Spear, N. E., & Spear, L. P. (1993). Effects of prenatal exposure to cocaine on conditional discrimination learning in adult rats. *Behavioral Neuroscience, 106,* 837–845.
Hickey, N. (1992, August 22). How much violence? *TV Guide,* pp. 10–11.
Higgins, E. T. (1989). Self-discrepancy theory: What patterns of self-beliefs cause people to suffer? In L. Berkowitz (Ed.), *Advances in experimental social psychology* (Vol. 22, pp. 93–136). New York: Academic Press.
Higgins, E. T., Bond, R. N., Klein, R., & Strauman, T. (1986). Self-discrepancies and emotional vulnerability: How magnitude, accessibility, and type of discrepancy influence affect. *Journal of Personality and Social Psychology, 51,* 5–15.
Higgins, R. L., Snyder, C. R., & Berglas, S. (1990). *Self-handicapping: The paradox that isn't.* New York: Plenum.
Hilgard, E. R. (1982). Hypnotic susceptibility and implications for measurement. *International Journal of Clinical and Experimental Hypnosis, 30,* 394–403.
Hilgard, E. R. (1986). *Divided consciousness: Multiple controls in human thought and action.* New York: Wiley-Interscience.
Hilgard, E. R. (1987). *Psychology in America: A historical survey.* San Diego: Harcourt Brace Jovanovich.
Hilgard, E. R. (1992). Divided consciousness and dissociation. *Consciousness and Cognition, 1,* 16–31.
Hilgard, E. R., Morgan, A. H., & MacDonald, H. (1975). Pain and dissociation in the cold pressor test: A study of "hidden reports" through automatic key-pressing and automatic talking. *Journal of Abnormal Psychology, 84,* 280–289.
Hilgard, J. R. (1979). *Personality and hypnosis: A study of imaginative involvement.* Chicago: University of Chicago Press.
Hill, C. A. (1987). Affiliation motivation: People who need people...but in different ways. *Journal of Personality and Social Psychology, 52,* 1008–1018.
Hill, R. M., Hegemeir, S., & Tennyson, L. M. (1989). The fetal alcohol syndrome: A multihandicapped child. *Neuro-Toxicology, 10,* 585–596.
Hilton, D. (1995). The social context of reasoning: Conversational inference and rational judgment. *Psychological Bulletin, 118,* 248–271.
Hilton, J. L., & Darley, J. M. (1985). Constructing other persons: A limit on the effect. *Journal of Experimental Social Psychology, 21,* 1–18.
Hilton, J. L., & von Hippel, W. (1996). Stereotypes. *Annual Review of Psychology, 47,* 237–271.
Hilts, P. J. (1995). *Memory's ghost: The strange tale of Mr. M and the nature of memory.* New York: Simon & Schuster.
Hirsch, E. D., Jr. (1987). *Cultural literacy: What every American needs to know.* Boston: Houghton Mifflin.
Hirsh, I. J., & Watson, C. S. (1996). Auditory psychophysics and perception. *Annual Review of Psychology, 47,* 461–484.
Hirt, E. R., Deppe, R. K., & Gordon, L. J. (1991). Self-reported versus behavioral self-handicapping: Empirical evidence for a theoretical distinction. *Journal of Personality and Social Psychology, 61,* 981–991.
Hixon, J. G., & Swann, W. B., Jr. (1993). When does introspection bear fruit? Self-reflection, self-insight, and interpersonal choices. *Journal of Personality and Social Psychology, 64,* 35–43.
Hobbes, T. (1919). *Leviathan.* London: J. M. Dent. (Original work published 1651.)
Hobden, K., & Pliner, P. (1995). Effects of a model on food neophobia in humans. *Appetite, 25,* 101–113.
Hobson, J. A. (1988). *The dreaming brain.* New York: Basic Books.
Hobson, J. A. (1989). *Sleep.* New York: Scientific American.
Hobson, J. A., & McCarley, R. W. (1977). The brain as a dream state generator: An activational-synthesis hypothesis of the dream process. *American Journal of Psychiatry, 134,* 1335–1348.
Hochberg, J. E. (1978). *Perception* (2nd ed). Englewood Cliffs, NJ: Prentice-Hall.
Hochschild, A. R. (1989). *The second shift: Working parents and the revolution at home.* New York: Viking.
Hofmann, A. (1980). *LSD: My problem child.* New York: McGraw-Hill.
Hoffer, B. J., & Olson, L. (1991). Ethical issues in brain cell transplantation. *Trends in the Neurosciences, 14,* 384–388.
Hoffman, C., Lau, I., & Johnson, D. R. (1986). The linguistic relativity of person cognition: An English-Chinese comparison. *Journal of Personality and Social Psychology, 51,* 1097–1105.
Hoffman, E. (1989). *Lost in translation: A life in a new language.* New York: Dutton.
Hoffman, L. W. (1989). Effects of maternal employment in the two-parent family. *American Psychologist, 44,* 283–292.
Hoffman, M. L. (1984). Empathy, its limitations, and its role in a comprehensive moral theory. In J. Gewirtz & W. Kurtines (Eds.), *Morality, moral development, and moral behavior* (pp. 283–302). New York: Wiley.
Hoffner, C., & Badzinski, D. M. (1989). Children's integration of facial and situational cues to emotion. *Child Development, 60,* 411–422.
Hoffstein, V., Mateika, S., & Anderson, D. (1994). Snoring: Is it in the ear of the beholder? *Sleep, 17,* 522–526.
Hofstede, G. (1980). *Culture's consequences.* Beverly Hills, CA: Sage.
Hogan, R., Hogan, J., & Roberts, B. W. (1996). Personality measurement and employment decisions: Questions and answers. *American Psychologist, 51,* 469–477.
Hogg, M. A., & Abrams, D. (1990). Social motivation, self-esteem and social identity. In D. Abrams & M. Hogg (Eds.), *Social identity theory: Constructive and critical advances* (pp. 28–47). New York: Springer-Verlag.
Holahan, C. K. (1988). Relation of life goals at age 70 to activity participation and health and psychological well-being among Terman's gifted men and women. *Psychology and Aging, 3,* 286–291.
Holahan, C. K., & Sears, R. R. (1995). *The gifted group in later maturity.* Palo Alto, CA: Stanford University Press.
Holden, C. (1980, November). Twins reunited. *Science, 80,* 55–59.
Holding, D. H. (1989). *Human skills* (2nd ed.). New York: Wiley.
Hollandsworth, J. G., Jr. (1990). *The physiology of psychological disorders.* New York: Plenum.
Hollins, M., Faldowski, R., Rao, S., & Young, F. (1993). Perceptual dimensions of tactile surface texture: A multidimensional scaling analysis. *Perception and Psychophysics, 54,* 697–705.
Hollon, S. D. (1996). The efficacy and effectiveness of psychotherapy relative to medications. *American Psychologist, 51,* 1025–1030.
Hollon, S. D., & Beck, A. T. (1994). Cognitive and cognitive-behavioral therapies. In A. E. Bergin & S. L. Garfield (Eds.), *Handbook of Psychotherapy and Behavior Change* (4th ed., pp. 428–466). New York: Wiley.
Hollon, S. D., Shelton, R. C., & Loosen, P. T. (1991). Cognitive therapy and pharmacotherapy for depression. *Journal of Consulting and Clinical Psychology, 59,* 88–99.
Holmbeck, G. (1996). A model of family relational transformations during the transition to adolescence: Parent-adolescent conflict and adaptation. In J. A. Graber, J. Brooks-Gunn, & A. C. Petersen, (Eds.). *Transitions through adolescence: Interpersonal domains and context* (pp. 167–199). Mahwah, NJ: Erlbaum.
Holmes, T. H., & Rahe, R. H. (1967). The Social Readjustment Rating Scale. *Journal of Psychosomatic Research, 11,* 213–218.
Holtgraves, T., & Bailey, C. (1991). Premise acceptability and message effectiveness. *Basic and Applied Social Psychology, 12,* 157–176.
Holtgraves, T., & Skeel, J. (1992). Cognitive biases in playing the lottery: Estimating the odds and choosing the numbers. *Journal of Applied Social Psychology, 22,* 934–952.
Holton, S. D., Shelton, R. C., & Loosen, P. T. (1991). Cognitive therapy and pharmacotherapy for depression. *Journal of Consulting and Clinical Psychology, 59,* 88–99.
Holyoak, K. J., & Spellman, B. A. (1993). Thinking. *Annual Review of Psychology, 44,* 265–315.
Holyoak, K. J., & Thagard, P. (1997). The analogical mind. *American Psychologist, 52,* 35–44.
Holzman, P. S., & Matthysse, S. (1990). The genetics of schizophrenia: A review. *Psychological Science, 1,* 279–286.
Honts, C. R., Raskin, D. C., and Kircher, J. C. (1994). Mental and physical countermeasures reduce the accuracy of polygraph tests. *Journal of Applied Psychology, 79,* 252–259.
Hooper, J., & Teresi, D. (1986). *The 3-pound universe—the brain.* New York: Laurel.
Hoorens, V., & Nuttin, J. M. (1993). Overvaluation of own attributes: Mere ownership or subjective frequency? *Social Cognition, 11,* 177–200.
Hopkins, W. D. (1996). Chimpanzee handedness revisited: 55 years since Finch (1941). *Psychonomic Bulletin and Review, 3,* 449–457.
Hoptman, M. J., & Davidson, R. J. (1994). How and why do the two cerebral hemispheres interact? *Psychological Bulletin, 116,* 195–219.
Horn, J. C. (1987). Bigger pay for better work. *Psychology Today, 21*(1), 54–57.
Horn, J. L. (1982). The aging of human abilities. In B. B. Wolman (Ed.), *Handbook of developmental psychology* (pp. 847–870). Englewood Cliffs, NJ: Prentice-Hall.
Horn, J. L., & Cattell, R. C. (1966). Refinement and test of the theory of fluid and crystallized general intelligences. *Journal of Educational Psychology, 57,* 253–270.
Horne, J. A. (1988). *Why we sleep: The functions of sleep in humans and other animals.* Oxford, England: Oxford University Press.
Horne, J. A., & Reyner, L. A. (1996). Counteracting driver sleepiness: Effects of napping, caffeine, and placebo. *Psychophysiology, 33,* 306–309.
Horner, K. L., Rushton, J. P., & Vernon, P. A. (1986). Relation between aging and research productivity of academic psychologists. *Psychology and Aging, 1,* 319–324.
Horney, K. (1945). *Our inner conflicts.* New York: Norton.
Horowitz, I. A., & Willging, T. E. (1991). Changing views of jury power: The nullification debate, 1787–1988. *Law and Human Behavior, 15,* 165–182.
Horvath, A. O., & Luborsky, L. (1993). The role of the therapeutic alliance in psychotherapy. *Journal of Consulting and Clinical Psychology, 61,* 561–573.
Horvath, A. O., & Symonds, B. D. (1991). Relation between working alliance and outcome in psychotherapy: A meta-analysis. *Journal of Counseling Psychology, 38,* 139–149.
Horvath, F. (1984). Detecting deception in eyewitness cases: Problems and prospects in use of the polygraph. In G. Wells & E. Loftus (Eds.), *Eyewitness testimony: Psychological perspectives* (pp. 214–255). New York: Cambridge University Press.
Hothersall, D. (1990). *History of psychology* (2nd ed.). New York: McGraw-Hill.
House, J. S., Landis, K. R., & Umberson, D. (1988). Social relationships and health. *Science, 241,* 540–545.
Hovland, C. I., & Sears, R. R. (1940). Minor studies in aggression: VI. Correlation of lynchings with economic indices. *Journal of Psychology, 9,* 301–310.
Howard, A., & Bray, D. W. (1988). *Managerial lives in transition.* New York: Guilford Press.

Howard, I. P. (1986). The perception of posture, self-motion, and the visual vertical. In K. R. Boff, L. Kaufman, & J. P. Thomas (Eds.), *Handbook of perception and human performance* (Vol. 1). New York: Wiley.

Howard, K. I., Cornille, T. A., Lyons, J. S., Vessey, J. T., Lueger, R. J., & Saunders, S. M. (1996). Patterns of mental health service utilization. *Archives of General Psychiatry, 53,* 696–703.

Howard, K. I., Kopta, S. M., Krause, M. S., & Orlinsky, D. E. (1986). The dose-effect relationship in psychotherapy. *American Psychologist, 41,* 159–164.

Howard, K. I., Moras, K., Brill, P. L., Martinovich, Z., & Lutz, W. (1996). Evaluation of psychotherapy: Efficacy, effectiveness, and patient progress. *American Psychologist, 51,* 1059–1064.

Howe, M. L., & Courage, M. L. (1993). On resolving the enigma of infantile amnesia. *Psychological Bulletin, 113,* 305–326.

Howes, J. L., & Katz, A. N. (1988). Assessing remote memory with an improved public events questionnaire. *Psychology and Aging, 3,* 142–150.

Hubel, D. H. (1979). The brain. *Scientific American.*

Hubel, D. H. (1988). *Eye, brain, and vision.* New York: Scientific American Library.

Hubel, D. H., & Wiesel, T. N. (1962). Receptive fields, binocular interaction and functional architecture in the cat's visual cortex. *Journal of Physiology, 160,* 106–154.

Hubel, D. H., & Wiesel, T. N. (1979). Brain mechanisms of vision. *Scientific American, 241,* 150–162.

Hudson, W. (1960). Pictorial depth perception in sub-cultural groups in Africa. *Journal of Social Psychology, 52,* 183–208.

Hudspeth, A. J. (1985). The cellular basis of hearing: The biophysics of hair cells. *Science, 230,* 745–752.

Huesmann, L. R., & Eron, L. D. (Eds.). (1986). Television and the aggressive child: *A cross-national comparison.* Hillsdale, NJ: Erlbaum.

Hugdahl, K., Satz, P., Mitrushina, M., & Miller, E. N. (1993). Left-handedness and old age: Do left-handers die earlier? *Neuropsychologia, 31,* 325–333.

Hughes, J., Smith, T. W., Kosterlitz, A. W., Fothergill, L. A., Morgan, B. A., & Morris, H. R. (1975). Identification of two related pentapeptides from the brain with potent opiate against activity. *Nature, 258,* 577–579.

Hull, C. L. (1943). *Principles of behavior.* New York: Appleton-Century-Crofts.

Hull, J. G., & Young, R. D. (1983). Self-consciousness, self-esteem, and success-failure as determinants of alcohol consumption in male social drinkers. *Journal of Personality and Social Psychology, 44,* 1097–1109.

Hull, J. G., Young, R. D., & Jouriles, E. (1986). Applications of the self-awareness model of alcohol consumption: Predicting patterns of use and abuse. *Journal of Personality and Social Psychology, 51,* 790–796.

Humphries, S. A., Johnson, M. H., & Long, N. R. (1996). An investigation of the gate control theory of pain using the experimental pain stimulus of potassium iontophoresis. *Perception and Psychophysics, 58,* 693–703.

Hunt, E. (1983). On the nature of intelligence. *Science, 219,* 141–146.

Hunt, E., & Agnoli, F. (1991). The Whorfian hypothesis: A cognitive psychology perspective. *Psychological Review, 9,* 377–389.

Hunt, M. (1993). *The story of psychology.* New York: Doubleday.

Hunter, S., & Sundel, M. (Eds.). (1989). *Midlife myths: Issues, findings, and practice implications.* Newbury Park, CA: Sage.

Hur, Y. M., & Bouchard, T. J., Jr. (1995). Genetic influences on perceptions of childhood family environment: A reared apart twin study. *Child Development, 66,* 330–345.

Hurt, H. T., Scott, M. D., & McCroskey, J. C. (1978). *Communication in the classroom.* Reading, MA: Addison-Wesley.

Huxley, A. (1932). *Brave new world.* London: Chatto & Windus.

Hyde, J. S., & Linn, M. C. (1988). Gender differences in verbal ability: A meta-analysis. *Psychological Bulletin, 104,* 53–69.

Hyde, J. S., Fennema, E., & Lamon, S. (1990). Gender differences in mathematics performance: A meta-analysis. *Psychological Bulletin, 107,* 139–155.

Hyman, I., Husband, T., & Billings, F. (1995). False memories of childhood experiences. *Applied Cognitive Psychology, 9,* 181–198.

Hyman, R. (1989). *The elusive quarry: A scientific appraisal of psychical research.* Buffalo, NY: Prometheus Books.

Hyman, R. (1994). Anomaly or artifact? Comments on Bem and Honorton. *Psychological Bulletin, 115,* 19–24.

Iaccino, J. F. (1993). *Left brain-right brain differences: Inquiries, evidence, and new approaches.* Hillsdale, NJ: Erlbaum.

Ingham, A. G., Levinger, G., Graves, J., & Peckham, V. (1974). The Ringelmann effect: Studies of group size and group performance. *Journal of Experimental Social Psychology, 10,* 371–384.

Inglehart, R. (1990). *Culture shift in advanced industrial society.* Princeton, NJ: Princeton University Press.

Ingram, R. E. (1990). Self-focused attention in clinical disorders: Review and a conceptual model. *Psychological Bulletin, 107,* 156–176.

Inhelder, B., & Piaget, J. (1958). *The growth of logical thinking from childhood to adolescence.* New York: Basic Books.

Insel, T. R. (Ed.). (1984). *New findings in obsessive-compulsive disorder.* Washington, DC: American Psychiatric Press.

Intons-Peterson, M. (1993). Imaginal priming. *Journal of Experimental Psychology: Learning, Memory, and Cognition, 19,* 223–235.

Intraub, H., Bender, R. S., & Mangels, J. A. (1992). Looking at pictures but remembering scenes. *Journal of Experimental Psychology: Learning, Memory, and Cognition, 18,* 180–191.

Ironson, G., et al. (1997). Posttraumatic stress symptoms, intrusive thoughts, loss, and immune function after Hurricane Andrew. *Psychosomatic Medicine, 59,* 128–141.

Irwin, M., Mascovich, S., Gillin, J. C., Willoughby, R., Pike, J., & Smith, T. L. (1994). Partial sleep deprivation reduces natural killer cell activity in humans. *Psychosomatic Medicine, 56,* 493–498.

Isaacson, W. (1997, January 13). In search of the real Bill Gates. *Time,* pp. 45–57.

Isabella, R. A., & Belsky, J. (1991). Interactional synchrony and the origins of infant-mother attachment: A replication study. *Child Development, 62,* 373–384.

Isen, A. M. (1987). Positive affect, cognitive processes, and social behavior. In L. Berkowitz (Ed.), *Advances in experimental social psychology* (Vol. 20, pp. 203–253). New York: Academic Press.

Isha, A., & Sagi, D. (1995). Common mechanisms of imagery and perception. *Science, 268,* 1772–1774.

Ito, T. A., Miller, N., & Pollock, V. E. (1996). Alcohol and aggression: A meta-analysis on the moderating effects of inhibitory cues, triggering events, and self-focused attention. *Psychological Bulletin, 120,* 60–82.

Izard, C. E. (1990). Facial expressions and the regulation of emotions. *Journal of Personality and Social Psychology, 58,* 487–498.

Izard, C. E. (1993). Four systems for emotion activation: Cognitive and noncognitive processes. *Psychological Review, 100,* 68–90.

Izard, C. E., Fatauzzo, C. A., Castle, J. M., Haynes, O. M., Rayias, M. F., & Putnam, P. H. (1995). The ontogeny and significance of infants' facial expressions in the first 9 months of life. *Developmental Psychology, 31,* 997–1013.

Izard, C. E., Huebner, R., Risser, D., McGinnes, G., & Dougherty, L. (1980). The young infant's ability to produce discrete emotion expressions. *Developmental Psychology, 16,* 132–140.

Jacklin, C. N. (1989). Female and male: Issues of gender. *American Psychologist, 44,* 127–133.

Jackson, H. J. (1958). In J. Taylor (Ed.), *Selected writings of John Hughlings Jackson.* New York: Basic Books.

Jacobs, G. H. (1993). The distribution and nature of colour vision among the mammals. *Biological Review, 68,* 413–471.

Jacobs, J. E. (1991). Influence of gender stereotypes on parent and child mathematics attitudes. *Journal of Educational Psychology, 83,* 518–527.

Jacobson, J. L., & Jacobson, S. W. (1996). Methodological considerations in behavioral toxicology in infants and children. *Developmental Psychology, 32,* 390–403.

Jacobson, N. S., & Christensen, A. (1996). Studying the effectiveness of psychotherapy: How well can clinical trials do the job? *American Psychologist, 51,* 1031–1039.

Jacobson, N. S., & Hollon, S. D. (1996). Cognitive-behavior therapy versus pharmacotherapy: Now that the jury's returned its verdict, it's time to present the rest of the evidence. *Journal of Consulting and Clinical Psychology, 64,* 74–80.

Jacobson, S. W., Jacobson, J. L., Sokol, R. J., Martier, S. S., & Ager, J. W. (1993). Prenatal alcohol exposure and infant information processing ability. *Child Development, 64,* 1706–1721.

Jacoby, L. L., Kelley, C. M., Brown, J., & Jasechko, J. (1989). Becoming famous overnight: Limits on the ability to avoid unconscious influences of the past. *Journal of Personality and Social Psychology, 56,* 326–338.

Jacoby, L. L., Lindsay, D. S., & Toth, J. P. (1992). Unconscious influences revealed: Attention, awareness, and control. *American Psychologist, 47,* 802–809.

Jacoby, L. L., Toth, J. P., & Yonelinas, A. P. (1993). Separating conscious and unconscious influences on memory: Measuring recollection. *Journal of Experimental Psychology: General, 122,* 139–154.

Jacowitz, K. E., & Kahneman, D. (1995). Measures of anchoring in estimation tasks. *Personality and Social Psychology Bulletin, 21,* 1161–1166.

James, B. (1982). *The Bill James Baseball Abstract.* New York: Ballantine.

James, W. (1884). What is an emotion? *Mind, 9,* 188–205.

James, W. (1890). *Principles of psychology* (Vols. 1–2). New York: Holt.

Jamison, C., & Scogin, F. (1995). The outcome of cognitive bibliotherapy with adults. *Journal of Consulting and Clinical Psychology, 63,* 644–650.

Jamison, K. R. (1993). *Touched with fire: Manic-depressive illness and the artistic temperament.* New York: Free Press.

Janicak, P. G., Davis, J. M., Gibbons, R. D., Ericksen, S., Chang, S., & Gallagher, P. (1985). Efficacy of ECT: A meta-analysis. *American Journal of Psychiatry, 142,* 297–302.

Janis, I. L. (1972). *Groupthink.* Boston: Houghton Mifflin.

Janis, I. L. (1989). *Crucial decisions: Leadership in policy-making and crisis management.* New York: Free Press.

Janiszewski, C., & Warlop, L. (1993). The influence of classical conditioning procedures on subsequent attention to the conditioned brand. *Journal of Consumer Research, 20,* 171–189.

Janoff-Bulman, R. (1989). The benefits of illusions, the threat of disillusionment, and the limitations of inaccuracy. *Journal of Social and Clinical Psychology, 8,* 158–175.

Jansari, A., & Parkin, A. J. (1996). Things that go bump in your life: Explaining the reminiscence bump in autobiographical memory. *Psychology and Aging, 11,* 85–91.

Jaroff, L. (1993, November). Lies of the mind. *Time,* pp. 52–59.

Jemmott, J. B., III, & Magloire, K. (1988). Academic stress, social support, and secretary immunoglobin. *Journal of Personality and Social Psychology, 55,* 803–810.

Jenicke, M. A., Baer, L., & Minichiello, W. E. (1986). Obsessive-compulsive disorders: *Theory and management.* Littleton, MA: PSG.

Jenkins, J. G., & Dallenbach, K. M. (1924). Oblivescence during sleep and waking. *American Journal of Psychology, 35,* 605–612.

Jenkins, S. R. (1994). Need for power and women's careers over 14 years: Structural power, job satisfaction, and motive change. *Journal of Personality and Social Psychology, 66,* 155–165.

Jennings (Walstedt), J., Geis, F. L., & Brown, V. (1980). Influence of television commercials on women's self-confidence and independent judgment. *Journal of Personality and Social Psychology, 38,* 203–210.

Jensen, A. R. (1969). How much can we boost IQ and scholastic achievement? *Harvard Educational Review, 39,* 1–123.

Jensen, A. R. (1980). *Bias in mental testing.* New York: Free Press.

Jensen, A. R. (1992). Understanding *g* in terms of information processing. *Educational Psychology Review, 4,* 271–308.

Jessell, T. M., & Kelly, D. D. (1991). Pain and analgesia. In E. R. Kandel, J. H. Schwartz, & T. M. Jessell (Eds.), *Principles of neural science* (3rd ed., pp. 385–399). New York: Elsevier.

Jockin, V., McGue, M., & Lykken, D. T. (1996). Personality and divorce: A genetic analysis. *Journal of Personality and Social Psychology, 71,* 288–299.

John, E. R., Prichep, L. S., Fridman, J., & Easton, P. (1988). Neurometrics: Assisted differential diagnosis of brain dysfunction. *Science, 239,* 162–169.

John, O. P. (1990). The "Big Five" factor taxonomy: Dimensions of personality in the natural language and in questionnaires. In L. A. Pervin (Ed.), *Handbook of personality theory and research* (pp. 66–100). New York: Guilford Press.

Johnson, B. T., & Eagly, A. H. (1989). Effects of involvement on persuasion: A meta-analysis. *Psychological Bulletin, 106,* 290–314.

Johnson, D. (1990). Animal rights and human lives: Time for scientists to right the balance. *Psychological Science, 1,* 213–214.

Johnson, G. (1995, June 6). Chimp talk debate: Is it really language? *The New York Times,* p. C1.

Johnson, J. E., Christie, J. F., & Yawkey, T. D. (1987). *Play and early childhood development.* Glenview, IL: Scott, Foresman.

Johnson, J. S., & Newport, E. L. (1989). Critical period effects in second language learning: The influence of maturational state on the acquisition of English as a second language. *Cognitive Psychology, 21,* 60–99.

Johnson, K. M., Gutkin, T. B., & Plake, B. S. (1991). Use of modeling to enhance children's interrogative strategies. *Journal of School Psychology, 29,* 81–88.

Johnson, M. H., Dziurawiec, S., Ellis, H. D., & Morton, J. (1991). Newborns' preferential tracking of faces and its subsequent decline. *Cognition, 40,* 1–19.

Johnson, M. K., Hashtroudi, S., & Lindsay, D. S. (1993). Source monitoring. *Psychological Bulletin, 114,* 3–28.

Johnson, R. C., McClearn, G. E., Yuen, S., Nagoshi, C. T., Ahern, F. M., & Cole, R. E. (1985). Galton's data a century later. *American Psychologist, 40,* 875–892.

Johnson, W. O. (1991). How far have we come? *Sports Illustrated, 75*(6), 39–47.

Johnson-Laird, P. N. (1983). *Mental models.* Cambridge, MA: Harvard University Press.

Jones, E. (1953). *The life and work of Sigmund Freud.* New York: Basic Books.

Jones, E. E. (1990). *Interpersonal perception.* New York: W. H. Freeman.

Jones, E. E., & Harris, V. A. (1967). The attribution of attitudes. *Journal of Experimental Social Psychology, 3,* 1–24.

Jones, E. E., & Pulos, S. M. (1993). Comparing the process in psychodynamic and cognitive-behavioral therapies. *Journal of Consulting and Clinical Psychology, 61,* 306–316.

Jones, J. L. (Ed.) (1991). *Black psychology* (3rd ed.). Berkeley, CA: Cobb & Henry.

Jones, K. L., Smith, D. W., Ulleland, C. N., & Streissguth, A. P. (1973). Patterns of malformation in the offspring of chronic alcoholic mothers. *Lancet, 1,* 1267–1271.

Jones, L. V. (1984). White-black achievement differences: The narrowing gap. *American Psychologist, 39,* 1207–1213.

Jones, M. C. (1924). A laboratory study of fear: The case of Peter. *Journal of Genetic Psychology, 31,* 308–315.

Jones, M. C. (1957). The late careers of boys who were early- or late-maturers. *Child Development, 28,* 115–128.

Josephs, R. A., Markus, H. R., & Tafarodi, R. W. (1992). Gender and self- esteem. *Journal of Personality and Social Psychology, 63,* 391–402.

Jourard, S. M. (1971). *Self-disclosure: An experimental analysis of the transparent self.* New York: Wiley.

Joynson, R. B. (1989). *The Burt affair.* London: Routledge.

Judd, C. M., & Park, B. (1993). Definition and assessment of accuracy in social stereotypes. *Psychological Review, 100,* 109–128.

Judge, T. A., & Welbourne, T. M. (1994). A confirmatory investigation of the dimensionality of the pay satisfaction questionnaire. *Journal of Applied Psychology, 79,* 461–466.

Julien, R. M. (1992). *A primer of drug action* (6th ed.). New York: W. H. Freeman.

Jung, C. G. (1928). *Contributions to analytical psychology.* New York: Harcourt Brace.

Jussim, L., Eccles, J., & Madon, S. (1996). Social perception, social stereotypes, and teacher expectations: The quest for the powerful self-fulfilling prophecy. *Advances in Experimental Social Psychology, 28,* 281–387.

Just, M. A., & Carpenter, P. A. (1992). A capacity theory of comprehension: Individual differences in working memory. *Psychological Review, 99,* 122–149.

Kagan, J. (1976). Emergent themes in human development. *American Scientist, 64,* 186–196.

Kagan, J. (1984). *The nature of the child.* New York: Basic Books.

Kagan, J. (1994). *Galen's prophecy: Temperament in human nature.* New York: Basic Books.

Kagan, J., Reznick, J. S., & Snidman, N. (1990). Biological bases of childhood shyness. *Science, 240,* 167–171.

Kagan, J., Snidman, N., & Arcus, D. M. (1992). Initial reactions to unfamiliarity. *Current Directions in Psychological Science, 1,* 171–174.

Kahn, M. (1991). *Between therapist and client: The new relationship.* New York: W. H. Freeman.

Kahneman, D., & Miller, D. T. (1986). Norm theory: Comparing reality to its alternatives. *Psychological Review, 93,* 136–153.

Kahneman, D., & Tversky, A. (1972). Subjective probability: A judgement of representativeness. *Cognitive Psychology, 3,* 430–454.

Kahneman, D., & Tversky, A. (1973). On the psychology of prediction. *Psychological Review, 80,* 237–251.

Kahneman, D., & Tversky, A. (1984). Choices, values, and frames. *American Psychologist, 39,* 341–350.

Kahneman, D., & Tversky, A. (1996). On the reality of cognitive illusions. *Psychological Review, 103,* 582–591.

Kahneman, D., Slovic, P., & Tversky, A. (Eds.). (1982). *Judgement under uncertainty: Heuristics and biases.* New York: Cambridge University Press.

Kail, R. (1990). *The development of memory in children* (3rd ed.). New York: W. H. Freeman.

Kail, R. (1991). Developmental changes in speed of processing during childhood and adolescence. *Psychological Bulletin, 109,* 490–501.

Kail, R., & Bisanz, J. (1992). The information-processing perspective on cognitive development in childhood and adolescence. In R. J. Sternberg & C. A. Berg (Eds.), *Intellectual development.* New York: Cambridge University Press.

Kail, R., & Hall, L. K. (1994). Processing speed, naming speed, and reading. *Developmental Psychology, 30,* 949–954.

Kalin, N. H., Shelton, S. E., Davidson, R. J., & Lynn, D. E. (1996). A new method for aversive Pavlovian conditioning of heart rate in rhesus monkeys. *Physiology and Behavior, 60,* 1043–1046.

Kalish, R. A. (1981). *Death, grief, and caring relationships.* Monterey, CA: Wadsworth.

Kamen-Siegel, L., Rodin, J., Seligman, M. E. P., & Dwyer, J. (1991). Explanatory style and cell-mediated immunity in elderly men and women. *Health Psychology, 10,* 229–235.

Kamin, L. J. (1974). *The science and politics of IQ.* New York: Wiley.

Kandel, E. R. (1979). Small systems of neurons. *Scientific American, 241,* 66–87.

Kane, J. M., Honigfeld, G., Singer, J., Meltzer, H., & The Clozaril Collaborative Study Group (1988). Clozapine for the treatment-resistant schizophrenic. *Archives of General Psychiatry, 45,* 789–796.

Kanner, A. D., Coyne, J. C., Schaefer, C., & Lazarus, R. S. (1981). Comparison of two modes of stress measurement: Daily hassles and uplifts versus major life events. *Journal of Behavioral Medicine, 4,* 1–39.

Kanner, A. D., Feldman, S. S., Weinberger, D. A., & Ford, M. F. (1991). Uplifts, hassles, and adaptational outcomes in early adolescents. In A. Monat & R. S. Lazarus (Eds.), *Stress and coping: An anthology* (pp. 158–181). New York: Columbia University Press.

Kaplan, C. A., & Simon, H. A. (1990). In search of insight. *Cognitive Psychology, 22,* 374–419.

Kaplan, R. M. (1985). The controversy related to the use of psychological tests. In B. B. Wolman (Ed.), *Handbook of intelligence: Theories, measurements, and applications* (pp. 465–504). New York: Wiley.

Karau, S. J., & Williams, K. D. (1993). Social loafing: A meta-analytic review and theoretical integration. *Journal of Personality and Social Psychology, 65,* 681–706.

Karni, A., & Ungerleider, L. (1996). Comorbidity and treatment implications. *Journal of Consulting and Clinical Psychology, 60,* 833–834.

Karraker, K. H., Vogel, D. A., & Lake, M. (1995). Parents' gender-stereotyped perceptions of newborns: The eye of the beholder revisited. *Sex Roles, 33,* 687–701.

Kashima, Y., & Kerekes, A. R. Z. (1994). A distributed memory model of averaging phenomena in person impression formation. *Journal of Experimental Social Psychology, 30,* 407–455.

Kasper, S., & Rosenthal, N. E. (1989). Anxiety and depression in seasonal affective disorders. In P. Kendall & D. Watson (Eds.), *Anxiety and depression: Distinct and overlapping features* (pp. 341–375). San Diego: Academic Press.

Kassin, S. M. (1997). The psychology of confession evidence. *American Psychologist, 52,* 221–233.

Kassin, S. M., & Sommers, S. R. (1997). Inadmissible testimony, instructions to disregard, and the jury: Substantive versus procedural considerations. *Personality and Social Psychology Bulletin, 23,* 1046–1054.

Kassin, S. M., & Wrightsman, L. S. (1988). *The American jury on trial: Psychological perspectives.* Washington, DC: Hemisphere.
Kassin, S. M., Ellsworth, P. C., & Smith, V. L. (1989). The general acceptance of psychological research on eyewitness testimony. *American Psychologist, 44,* 1089–1098.
Katz, D., & Braly, K. (1933). Racial stereotypes of 100 college students. *Journal of Abnormal and Social Psychology, 28,* 280–290.
Kaufman, L., & Rock, I. (1962). The moon illusion. (Vol I). *Science, 136,* 953–961.
Kazdin, A. E. (1982). The token economy: A decade later. *Journal of Applied Behavior Analysis, 15,* 431–445.
Kearl, M. C. (1989). *A sociology of death and dying.* New York: Oxford University Press.
Kecklund, G., & Akerstedt, T. (1993). Sleepiness in long distance truck driving: An ambulatory EEG study of night driving. *Ergonomics, 36,* 1007–1017.
Keesey, R. E. (1995). A set-point model of weight regulation. In K. D. Brownell & C. G. Fairburn (Eds.), *Eating disorders and obesity* (pp. 46–50). New York: Guilford Press.
Keith, J. R., & McVety, K. M. (1988). Latent place learning in a novel environment and the influences of prior training in rats. *Psychobiology, 16,* 146–151.
Kelley, H. H. (1967). Attribution theory in social psychology. In D. Levine (Ed.), *Nebraska Symposium on Motivation* (Vol. 15, pp. 192–241). Lincoln, NE: University of Nebraska Press.
Kellman, P. J., & Spelke, E. S. (1983). Perception of partly occluded objects in infancy. *Cognitive psychology, 15,* 483–524.
Kellner, R. (1987). Hypochondriasis and somatization. *Journal of the American Medical Association, 258,* 2718–2722.
Kellogg, W. N., & Kellogg, L. A. (1933). *The ape and the child.* New York: McGraw-Hill.
Kelly, A. E., & McKillop, K. J. (1996). Consequences of revealing personal secrets. *Psychological Bulletin, 120,* 450–465.
Kelly, D. D. (1991). Disorders of sleep and consciousness. In E. R. Kandel, J. H. Schwartz & T. M. Jessell (Eds.), Principles of Neural Science (3rd. ed., pp. 805–819). New York: Elsevier.
Kelman, H. C., & Hamilton, V. L. (1989). *Crimes of obedience: Toward a social psychology of authority and responsibility.* New Haven, CT: Yale University Press.
Kendall, P. C., & Clarkin, J. F. (1992). Introduction to special section: Comorbidity and treatment implications. *Journal of Consulting and Clinical Psychology, 60,* 833–834.
Kendler, H. H. (1993). Psychology and the ethics of social policy. *American Psychologist, 48,* 1046–1053.
Kendler, K. S., MacLean, C., Neale, M., Kessler, R., Heath, A., & Eaves, L. (1991). The genetic epidemiology of bulimia nervosa. *American Journal of Psychiatry, 148,* 1627–1637.
Kendler, K. S., Neale, M. C., Kessler, R. C., Heath, A. C., & Eaves, L. J. (1993). The lifetime history of major depression in women. Reliability of diagnosis and heritability. *Archives of General Psychiatry, 50,* 863–870.
Kenrick, D. T. (1987). Gender, genes, and the social environment. *Review of Personality and Social Psychology, 8,* 14–43.
Kenrick, D. T. (1994). Evolutionary social psychology: From sexual selection to social cognition. *Advances in Experimental Social Psychology, 26,* 75–121.
Kenrick, D. T., & Keefe, R. C. (1992). Age preferences in mates reflect sex differences in human reproductive strategies. *Behavioral and Brain Sciences, 15,* 75–91.
Kenrick, D. T., & MacFarlane, S. W. (1984). Ambient temperature and horn-honking: A field study of the heat/aggression relationship. *Environment and Behavior, 18,* 179–191.
Kenrick, D. T., Gutierres, S. E., & Goldberg, L. L. (1989). Influence of popular erotica on judgments of strangers and mates. *Journal of Experimental Social Psychology, 25,* 159–167.
Kerkhof, G. A. (1985). Inter-individual differences in the human circadian system: A review. *Biological Psychology, 20,* 83–112.
Kerr, N. L., Kramer, G. P., Carroll, J. S., & Alfini, J. J. (1991). On the effectiveness of voir dire in criminal cases with prejudicial pretrial publicity: An empirical study. *The American University Law Review, 40,* 665–701.
Kerwin, M. L. E., & Day, J. D. (1985). Peer influences on cognitive development. In J. Pryor & J. Day (Eds.), *The development of social cognition* (pp. 211–228). New York: Springer-Verlag.
Kessler, R. C., Foster, C., Webster, P. S., & House, J. S. (1992). The relationship between age and depressive symptoms in two national surveys. *Psychology and Aging, 7,* 117–126.
Kessler, R. C., McGonagle, K. A., Zhao, S., Nelson, C. B., Hughes, M., Eshleman, S., Wittchen, H. U., & Kendler, K. S. (1994). Lifetime and 12-month prevalence of DSM–III-R psychiatric disorders in the United States. *Archives of General Psychiatry, 51,* 8–19.
Kessler, R. C., Sonnega, A., Bromet, E., Hughes, M., & Nelson, C. B. (1995). Post-traumatic stress disorder in the National Comorbidity Survey. *Archives of General Psychiatry, 52,* 1048–1060.
Key, W. B. (1973). *Subliminal seduction.* Englewood Cliffs, NJ: Signet.
Key, W. B. (1989). *The age of manipulation.* New York: Holt.
Kiecolt-Glaser, J. K., & Glaser, R. (1992). Psychoneuroimmunology: Can psychological interventions modulate immunity? *Journal of Consulting and Clinical Psychology, 60,* 569–575.
Kiecolt-Glaser, J. K., & Glaser, R. (1993). Mind and immunity. In D. Goleman & J. Gurin (Eds.), *Mind body medicine* (pp. 39–61). Yonkers, NY: Consumer Reports Books.
Kiecolt-Glaser, J. K., Cacioppo, J. T., Malarkey, W. B., & Glaser, R. (1992). Acute psychological stressors and short-term immune changes: What, why, for whom, and to what extent? *Psychosomatic Medicine, 54,* 680–685.
Kiecolt-Glaser, J. K., Glaser, R., et al. (1985). Psychosocial enhancement of immunocompetence in a geriatric population. *Health Psychology, 4,* 25–41.
Kiewra, K. A., et al. (1991). Note-taking functions and techniques. *Journal of Educational Psychology, 83,* 240–245.
Kihlstrom, J. F. (1985). Hypnosis. *Annual Review of Psychology, 36,* 385–418.
Kihlstrom, J. F., Barnhardt, T. M., & Tataryn, D. J. (1987). The psychological unconscious: Found, lost, and regained. *American Psychologist, 47,* 788–791.
Kihlstrom, J. F., Schacter, D. L., Cork, R. C., Hurt, C. A., & Behr, S. E. (1990). Implicit and explicit memory following surgical anesthesia. *Psychological Science, 1,* 303–306.
Kimball, M. M. (1989). A new perspective on women's math achievement. *Psychological Bulletin, 105,* 198–214.
Kimble, D. P. (1990). Functional effects of neural grafting in the mammalian central nervous system. *Psychological Bulletin, 108,* 462–479.
Kimble, D. P. (1992). *Biological Psychology* (2nd ed.). Fort Worth, TX: Harcourt Brace Jovanovich.
Kimmel, A. J. (1991). Predictable biases in the ethical decision-making of American psychologists. *American Psychologist, 46,* 786–788.
Kimura, D., & Hampson, E. (1994). Cognitive pattern in men and women is influenced by fluctuations in sex hormones. *Current Directions in Psychological Science, 3,* 57–61.
Kinnunen, T., Zamanksi, H. S., and Block, M. L. (1994). Is the hypnotized subject lying? *Journal of Abnormal Psychology, 103,* 184–191.
Kinsey, A. C., Pomeroy, W. B., & Martin, C. E. (1948). *Sexual behavior in the human male.* Philadelphia: W. B. Saunders.
Kinsey, A. C., Pomeroy, W. B., Martin, C. E., & Gebhard, P. H. (1953). *Sexual behavior in the human female.* Philadelphia: W. B. Saunders.
Kirsch, I. (1990). *Changing expectations: A Key to effective psychotherapy.* Pacific Grove, CA: Brooks/Cole.
Kirsch, I., & Lynn, S. J. (1995). Altered state of hypnosis: Changes in theoretical landscape. *American Psychologist, 50,* 846–858.
Kirsch, I., Montgomery, G., & Sapirstein, G. (1995). Hypnosis as an adjunct cognitive-behavioral psychotherapy: A meta-analysis. *Journal of Consulting and Clinical Psychology, 63,* 214–220.
Kirsch, I., Silva, C. E., Carone, J. E., Johnston, J. D., & Simon, B. (1989). The surreptitious observation design: An experimental paradigm for distinguishing artifact from essence in hypnosis. *Journal of Abnormal Psychology, 98,* 132–136.
Kirsch, I., Silva, C. E., Comey, G., & Reed, S. (1995). A spectral analysis of cognitive and personality variables in hypnosis: Empirical disconfirmation of the two-factor model of hypnotic responding. *Journal of Personality and Social Psychology, 69,* 167–175.
Kirsner, D. (1990). Is there a future for American psychoanalysis? *Psychoanalytic Review, 77,* 175–200.
Kitayama, S., and Markus, H. R. (Eds.). (1994). Emotion and culture: *Empirical studies of mutual influence.* Washington, DC: American Psychological Association.
Klatsky, R. A., & Lederman, S. J. (1992). Stages of manual exploration in haptic object identification. *Perception and Psychophysics, 52,* 661–670.
Klein, D. F. (1993). False suffocation alarms, spontaneous panics, and related conditions: An integrative hypothesis. *Archives of General Psychiatry, 50,* 306–317.
Klein, R., & Mannuzza, S. (1991). Long-term outcome of hyperactive children: A review. *Journal of the American Academy of Child and Adolescent Psychiatry, 30,* 383–387.
Klein, W. M., & Kunda, Z. (1992). Motivated person perception: Constructing justifications for desired beliefs. *Journal of Experimental Social Psychology, 28,* 135–168.
Kleiner, K. A. (1987). Amplitude and phase spectra as indices of infants' pattern preferences. *Infant Behavior and Development, 10,* 49–59.
Kleinke, C. L. (1986). Gaze and eye contact: A research review. *Psychological Bulletin, 100,* 78–100.
Kleinmuntz, B., & Szucko, J. J. (1984). Lie detection in ancient and modern times. *American Psychologist, 39,* 766–776.
Kleitman, N. (1963). *Sleep and wakefulness.* Chicago: University of Chicago Press.
Klerman, G. L., & Weissman, M. M. (1989). Increasing rates of depression. *Journal of the American Medical Association, 261,* 2229–2235.
Kline, P. (1991). *Intelligence: The psychometric view.* New York: Routledge, Chapman & Hall.
Klivington, K. A. (Ed.). (1989). *The science of mind.* Cambridge, MA; MIT Press.
Kluegel, J. R. (1990). Trends in whites' explanations of the black-white gap in socioeconomic status, 1977–1989. *American Sociological Review, 55,* 512–525.
Kluft, R. P. (1996). Dissociative identity disorder. In L. K. Michelson & W. J. Ray (Eds.), *Handbook of dissociation: Theoretical, empirical, and clinical perspectives* (pp. 337–366). New York: Plenum.
Knapp, R. R. (1976). *Handbook for the Personal Orientation Inventory.* San Diego: Edits Publishers.

Knight, G. P., Fabes, R. A., & Higgins, D. A. (1996). Concerns about drawing causal inferences from meta-analyses: An example in the study of gender differences in aggression. *Psychological Bulletin, 119,* 410–421.

Kobasa, S. C. (1979). Stressful life events, personality, and health: An inquiry into hardiness. *Journal of Personality and Social Psychology, 37,* 1–11.

Koch, S. (1993). "Psychology" or "the psychological studies"? *American Psychologist, 48,* 902–904.

Koffka, K. (1935). *Principles of gestalt psychology.* New York: Harcourt, Brace & World.

Kohlberg, L. (1969). Stage and sequence: The cognitive-developmental approach to socialization. In D. A. Goslin (Ed.), *Handbook of socialization theory and research.* Chicago: Rand McNally.

Kohlberg, L. (1981). *Essays on moral development: Vol. 1. The philosophy of moral development.* New York: Harper & Row.

Kohlberg, L. (1984). *Essays on moral development: Vol. 2. The psychology of moral development.* New York: Harper & Row.

Kohler, W. (1925). *The mentality of apes.* London: Pelican.

Kohler, W. (1947). *Gestalt psychology.* New York: Liveright.

Kohn, A. (1993). *Punished by rewards.* Boston: Houghton Mifflin.

Kohn, P. M., Lafreniere, K., & Gurevich, M. (1990). The inventory of college students' recent life experiences: A decontaminated hassles scale for a special population. *Journal of Behavioral Medicine, 13,* 619–630.

Kohn, P. M., Lafreniere, K., & Gurevich, M. (1991). Hassles, health, and personality. *Journal of Personality and Social Psychology, 61,* 478–482.

Kolb, B., & Whishaw, I. Q. (1990). *Fundamentals of human neuropsychology* (3rd ed.). New York: W. H. Freeman.

Konishi, M. (1993). Listening with two ears. *Scientific American, 268,* 66–73.

Koriat, A., & Goldsmith, M. (1996). Memory metaphors and the real-life/laboratory controversy: Correspondence versus storehouse conceptions of memory. *Behavioral and Brain Sciences, 19,* 167–228.

Korn, J. H., Davis, R., & Davis, S. F. (1991). Historians' and chairpersons' judgments of eminence among psychologists. *American Psychologist, 46,* 789–792.

Kosonen, P., & Winne, P. (1995). Effects of teaching statistical laws of reasoning about everyday problems. *Journal of Educational Psychology, 87,* 33–46.

Kosslyn, S. M. (1980). *Image and mind.* Cambridge, MA: Harvard University Press.

Kosslyn, S. M. (1994). *Image and brain: The resolution of the imagery debate.* Cambridge, MA: MIT Press.

Kotovsky, K., Hayes, J. R., & Simon, H. A. (1985). Why are some problems hard? Evidence from Tower of Hanoi. *Cognitive Psychology, 17,* 248–294.

Kotre, J. (1995). *White gloves: How we create ourselves through memory.* New York: Free Press.

Kotre, J., & Hall, E. (1990). *Seasons of life.* Boston: Little, Brown.

Kovecses, Z. (1990). *Emotion concepts.* New York: Springer-Verlag.

Kowalski, R. M. (1993). Inferring sexual interest from behavioral cues: Effects of gender and sexually relevant attitudes. *Sex Roles, 29,* 13–36.

Kraepelin, E. (1883). *Textbook of psychiatry.* New York: Macmillan. (Reprinted in 1923).

Kramer, P. D. (1993). *Listening to Prozac.* New York: Viking.

Krantz, D. S., & Manuck, S. B. (1984). Acute psychophysiologic reactivity and risk of cardiovascular disease: A review and methodological critique. *Psychological Bulletin, 96,* 435–464.

Kranzler, J. H., & Jensen, A. R. (1989). Inspection time and intelligence: A meta-analysis. *Intelligence, 13,* 329–347.

Krasne, F. B., & Glanzman, D. L. (1995). What we can learn from invertebrate learning. *Annual Review of Psychology, 46,* 585–624.

Krebs, D. L., Denton, K. L., Vermeulen, S. C., Carpendale, J. I., & Bush, A. (1991). Structural flexibility in moral judgment. *Journal of Personality and Social Psychology, 61,* 1012–1023.

Kreitler, S., Weissler, K., Krietler, H., & Brunner, D. (1991). The relation of smoking to psychological and physiological risk factors for coronary heart disease. *Personality and Individual Differences, 12,* 487–495.

Kreutzer, M. A., Leonard, C., & Flavell, J. H. (1975). An interview study of children's knowledge about memory. *Monographs of the Society for Research in Child Development, 40*(1, Serial No. 159), 1–58.

Kristof, N. D. (1993, July 21). Peasants of China discover new way to weed out girls. *The New York Times,* pp. A1, A6.

Kruger, L. (Ed.) (1996). *Pain and touch.* San Diego: Academic Press.

Kruglanski, A. W., & Webster, D. M. (1991). Group members' reactions to opinion deviates and conformists at varying degrees of proximity to decision deadline and of environmental noise. *Journal of Personality and Social Psychology, 61,* 212–225.

Krumhansil, C. L. (1991). Music psychology: Tonal structures in perception and memory. *Annual Review of Psychology, 42,* 277–303.

Kryter, K. D. (1994). *The handbook of hearing and the effects of noise.* San Diego: Academic Press.

Kubeck, J. E., Delp, N. D., Haslett, T. K., & McDaniel, M. A. (1996). Does job-related training performance decline with age? *Psychology and Aging, 11,* 92–107.

Kübler-Ross, E. (1969). *On death and dying.* New York: Macmillan.

Küebli, J., & Fivush, R. (1992). Gender differences in parent-child conversations about past emotions. *Sex Roles, 27,* 683–698.

Kuffler, S. W. (1953). Discharge patterns and functional organization of mammalian retina. *Journal of Neurophysiology, 16,* 37–68.

Kuhn, D. (1991). *The skills of argument.* Cambridge, England: Cambridge University Press.

Kulik, J. A., Bangert-Drowns, R. L., & Kulik, C. (1984). Effectiveness of coaching for aptitude tests. *Psychological Bulletin, 95,* 179–188.

Kulik, J. A., Mahler, H. I. M. (1989). Stress and affiliation in a hospital setting: Preoperative roommate preferences. *Personality and Social Psychology Bulletin, 15,* 183–193.

Kulik, J. A., Mahler, H. I. M., & Earnest, A. (1994). Social comparison and affiliation under threat: Going beyond the affiliate-choice paradigm. *Journal of Personality and Social Psychology, 66,* 301–309.

Kulik, J. A., Mahler, H. I. M., & Moore, P. J. (1996). Social comparison and affiliation under threat: Effects of recovery from major surgery. *Journal of Personality and Social Psychology, 71,* 967–979.

Kumon-Nakamura, S., Glucksberg, S., & Brown, M. (1995). How about another piece of pie: The allusional pretense theory of discourse. *Journal of Experimental Psychology: General, 124,* 3–21.

Kunda, Z. (1987). Motivated inference: Self-serving generation and evaluation of causal theories. *Journal of Personality and Social Psychology, 53,* 636–647.

Kunda, Z. (1990). Motivated reasoning. *Psychological Bulletin, 108,* 480–498.

Kunen, J. S. (1996, April 29). The end of integration. *Time,* pp. 39–45.

Kuntz-Wilson, W., & Zaionc, R. B. (1980). Affective discrimination of stimuli that cannot be recognized. *Science, 207,* 557–558.

Kurdek, L. A. (1991). Sexuality in homosexual and heterosexual couples. In K. McKinney & S. Sprecher (Eds.), *Sexuality in close relationships* (pp. 177–191). Hillsdale, NJ: Erlbaum.

Kurtines, W. M., & Gewirtz, J. L. (Eds.). (1984). *Morality, moral behavior, and moral development.* New York: Wiley.

LaBerge, S. P. (1992). *Physiological studies of lucid dreaming.* Hillsdale, NJ: Erlbaum.

LaFrance, M., & Banaji, M. (1992). Toward a reconsideration of the gender-emotion relationship. *Review of Personality and Social Psychology, 14,* 178–201.

LaFromboise, T., Coleman, H., & Gerton, J. (1993). Psychological impact of biculturalism: Evidence and theory. *Psychological Bulletin, 114,* 395–412.

Laird, J. D. (1974). Self-attribution of emotion: The effects of expressive behavior on the quality of emotional experience. *Journal of Personality and Social Psychology, 33,* 475–486.

Lamb, M. (1986). *The father's role: Applied perspectives.* New York: Wiley.

Lamb, M. (1987). Predictive implications of individual differences in attachment. *Journal of Consulting and Clinical Psychology, 55,* 817–824.

Lamb, M., Sternberg, K. J., & Prodromidis, M. (1992). Nonmaternal care and the security of the infant-mother attachment: A reanalysis of the data. *Infant Behavior and Development, 15,* 71–83.

Lambert, M. J., & Bergin, A. E. (1994). The effectiveness of psychotherapy. In A. Bergin & S. Garfield (Eds.), *Handbook of psychotherapy and behavior change* (4th ed., pp. 143–189). New York: Wiley.

Land, M. F., & Fernald, R. D. (1992). The evolution of eyes. *Annual Review of Neuroscience, 15,* 1–29.

Landau, T. (1989). *About faces: The evolution of the human face.* New York: Anchor Books.

Landesman, S., & Ramey, C. (1989). Developmental psychology and mental retardation: Integrating scientific principles with treatment practices. *American Psychologist, 44,* 409–415.

Landy, F. J., Shankster, L. J., & Kohler, S. S. (1994). Personnel selection and placement. *Annual Review of Psychology, 45,* 261–296.

Lang, K. L., Livesley, W. J., & Vernon, P. A. (1996). Heritability of the Big Five personality dimensions and their facets: A twin study. *Journal of Personality, 64,* 577–591.

Lang, P. J. (1995). The emotion probe: Studies of motivation and attention. *American Psychologist, 50,* 372–385.

Langer, E. J. (1975). The illusion of control. *Journal of Personality and Social Psychology, 32,* 311–328.

Langer, E. J. (1989). *Mindfulness.* Reading, MA: Addison-Wesley.

Langevin, B., Sukkar, F., Leger, P., Guez, A., & Robert, D. (1992). Sleep apnea syndromes (SAS) of specific etiology: Review and incidence from a sleep laboratory. *Sleep, 15,* S25–S32.

Langley, G. (Ed.). (1989). *Animal experimentation: The consensus changes.* New York: Chapman & Hall.

Langlois, J. H., & Roggman, L. A. (1990). Attractive faces are only average. *Psychological Science, 1,* 115–121.

Langlois, J. H., Ritter, J. M., Roggman, L. A., & Vaughn, L. S. (1991). Facial diversity and infant preferences for attractive faces. *Developmental Psychology, 27,* 79–84.

Langlois, J. H., Roggman, L. A., & Musselman, L. (1994). What is average and what is not average about attractive faces? *Psychological Science, 5,* 214–220.

Lansing, A. K. (1959). *General biology of senescence.* In J. E. Birren (Ed.), Handbook of aging and the individual. Chicago: University of Chicago Press.

LaPiere, R. T. (1934). Attitudes vs. action. *Social Forces, 13,* 230–237.

Larry P. v. *Wilson Riles,* 495 F. Supp. 926 (N. D. Cal. 1979).

Larsen, K. S. (1990). The Asch conformity experiment: Replication and transhistorical comparisons. Journal of *Social Behavior and Personality, 5,* 163–168.

Larsen, R. J., & Diener, E. (1992). Promises and problems with the circumplex model of emotion. *Review of Personality and Social Psychology, 13,* 25–59.

Larsen, R. J., & Kasimatis, M. (1990). Individual differences in entrainment of mood to the weekly calendar. *Journal of Personality and Social Psychology, 58,* 164–171.

Larson, R. W., Richards, M. H., Moneta, G., Holmbeck, G., & Duckett, E. (1996). Changes in adolescents' daily interactions with their families from ages 10 to 18: Disengagement and transformation. *Developmental Psychology, 32,* 744–754.

Lashley, K. S. (1950). In search of the engram. In *Society for Experimental Biology, Symposium 4,* 454–482.

Latané, B. (1981). The psychology of social impact. *American Psychologist, 36,* 343–356.

Latané, B., & Darley, J. M. (1970). *The unresponsive bystander: Why doesn't he help?* New York: Appleton-Century-Crofts.

Latané, B., & Nida, S. (1981). Ten years of research on group size and helping. *Psychological Bulletin, 89,* 308–324.

Latané, B., & Werner, C. (1978). Regulation of social contact in laboratory rats: Time, not distance. *Journal of Personality and Social Psychology, 36,* 1128–1137.

Latané, B., Williams, K., & Harkins, S. (1979). Many hands make light the work: The causes and consequences of social loafing. *Journal of Personality and Social Psychology, 37,* 822–832.

Lattal, K. A. (1992). B. F. Skinner and psychology: Introduction to the special issue. *American Psychologist, 47,* 1269–1272.

Laumann, E. O., Gagnon, J. H., Michael, R. T., & Michaels, S. (1994). *The social organization of sexuality.* Chicago: University of Chicago Press.

Lawrence, V. W. (1991). Effect of socially ambiguous information on white and black children's behavioral and trait perceptions. *Merrill-Palmer Quarterly, 37,* 619–630.

Lazarus, A. A. (1996). Some reflections after 40 years of trying to be an effective psychotherapist. *Psychotherapy, 33,* 142–145.

Lazarus, A. A., Beutler, L. E., & Norcross, J. C. (1992). The future of technical eclecticism. *Psychotherapy, 29,* 11–20.

Lazarus, R. S. (1984). On the primacy of cognition. *American Psychologist, 39,* 124–129.

Lazarus, R. S. (1991). Cognition and motivation in emotion. *American Psychologist, 46,* 352–367.

Lazarus, R. S. (1993). From psychological stress to the emotions: A history of changing outlooks. *Annual Review of Psychology, 44,* 1–21.

Lazarus, R. S., & Folkman, S. (1984). *Stress, appraisal, and coping.* New York: Springer.

Lazarus, R. S., & Lazarus, B. N. (1994). *Passion and reason: Making sense of our emotions.* New York: Oxford University Press.

Leahey, T. H. (1992). The mythical revolutions of American psychology. *American Psychologist, 47,* 308–318.

Leary, D. E. (1992). William James and the art of human understanding. *American Psychologist, 47,* 152–160.

Leary, M. R., & Kowalski, R. M. (1995). *Social anxiety.* New York: Guilford Press.

Lebow, J. (1982). Consumer satisfaction with mental health treatment. *Psychological Bulletin, 91,* 244–259.

Lecanuet, J., Fifer, W. P., Krasnegor, N. A., & Smotherman, W. P. (Eds.) (1995). *Fetal development: A psychobiological perspective.* Mahwah, NJ: Erlbaum.

Leccese, A. P. (1991). *Drugs and society.* Englewood Cliffs, NJ: Prentice-Hall.

Lecci, L., Karoly, P., Ruehlman, L. S., & Lanyon, R. I. (1996). Goal-relevant dimensions of hypochondriacal tendencies and their relation to symptom manifestation and psychological distress. *Journal of Abnormal Psychology, 105,* 42–52.

LeDoux, J. E. (1993). Emotional networks in the brain. In M. Lewis, & J. M. Haviland (Eds.), *Handbook of emotions* (pp. 109–118). New York: Guilford Press.

LeDoux, J. E. (1996). *The emotional brain: The mysterious underpinnings of emotional life.* New York: Simon & Schuster.

LeDoux, J. E., Wilson, D. H., & Gazzaniga, M. S. (1977). A divided mind: Observation on the conscious properties of the separated hemispheres. *Annals of Neurology, 2,* 417–421.

Lee, R. T., Ashforth, B. E. (1996). A meta-analytic examination of the correlates of the three dimensions of job burnout. *Journal of Applied Psychology, 81,* 123–133.

Lee, V. E., Brooks-Gunn, J., Schnur, E., & Liaw, F. R. (1990). Are Head Start effects sustained? A longitudinal follow-up of comparison of disadvantaged children attending Head Start, no preschool, and other preschool programs. *Child Development, 61,* 495–507.

Lee, Y. T., & Seligman, M. E. P. (1997). Are Americans more optimistic than the Chinese? *Personality and Social Psychology Bulletin, 23,* 32–40.

Lee, Y. T., Jussim, L. J., & McCauley, C. R. (1995). *Stereotype accuracy: Toward appreciating group differences.* Washington, DC: American Psychological Association.

Lefcourt, H. M. (1982). *Locus of control: Current trends in theory and research.* Hillsdale, NJ: Erlbaum.

Lefebvre, P. P., Malgrange, B., Staecker, H., Moonen, G., & Van De Water, T. R. (1993). Retinoic acid stimulates regeneration of mammalian hair cells. *Science, 260,* 692–695.

Leger, D. (1994). The cost of sleep-related accidents: A report for the National Commission on Sleep Disorders Research. *Sleep, 17,* 84–93.

Lehman, D. R., & Nisbett, R. E. (1990). A longitudinal study of the effects of undergraduate training on reasoning. *Developmental Psychology, 26,* 952–960.

Lehman, H. C. (1953). *Age and achievement.* Princeton, NJ: Princeton University Press.

Leibowitz, H. W., Brislin, R., Perlmutter, L., & Hennessy, R. (1969). Ponzo perspective illusion as a manifestation of space perception. *Science, 166,* 1174–1176.

Leichtman, M. D., & Ceci, S. J. (1995). The effects of stereotypes and suggestions on preschoolers' reports. *Developmental Psychology, 31,* 568–578.

Leigh, B. C., & Stacy, A. W. (1993). Alcohol outcome expectancies: Scale construction and predictive utility in higher-order confirmatory models. *Psychological Assessment, 5,* 216–229.

Leigh, B. C., Temple, M. T., & Trocki, K. F. (1993). The sexual behavior of U.S. adults: Results from a national survey. *American Journal of Public Health, 83,* 1400–1408.

Leiker, M., & Hailey, B. J. (1988). A link between hostility and disease: Poor health habits? *Behavioral Medicine, 3,* 129–133.

Leinbach, M. D., & Fagot, B. I. (1993). Categorical habituation to male and female faces: Gender schematic processes in infancy. *Infant Behavior and Development, 16,* 317–332.

Leitenberg, H., & Henning, K. (1995). Sexual fantasy. *Psychological Bulletin, 117,* 469–496.

Lenneberg, E. H. (1967). *Biological foundations of language.* New York: Wiley.

Lennon, R. T. (1985). Group tests of intelligence. In B. Wolman (Ed.), *Handbook of intelligence: Theories, measurement, and applications* (pp. 825–845). New York: Wiley.

Leon, M. (1992). The neurobiology of filial learning. *Annual Review of Psychology, 43,* 377–398.

Lepper, M. R., & Cordova, D. I. (1992). A desire to be taught: Instructional consequences of intrinsic motivation. *Motivation and Emotion, 16,* 187–208.

Lepper, M. R., & Greene, D. (Eds.). (1978). *The hidden costs of reward.* Hillsdale, NJ: Erlbaum.

Lepper, M. R., Greene, D., & Nisbett, R. E. (1973). Undermining children's intrinsic interest with extrinsic reward: A test of the "overjustification" hypothesis. *Journal of Personality and Social Psychology, 28,* 129–137.

Leung, K. (1988). Some determinants of conflict avoidance. *Journal of Cross-Cultural Psychology, 19,* 125–136.

LeVay, S. (1991). A difference in hypothalamic structure between heterosexual and homosexual men. *Science, 253,* 1034–1037.

LeVay, S. (1993). *The sexual brain.* Cambridge, MA: MIT Press.

LeVay, S., & Mamer, D. H. (1994). Evidence for a biological influence in male homosexuality. *Scientific American, 270*(5), 44–49.

Levenson, R. W. (1992). Autonomic nervous system differences among emotions. *Psychological Science, 3,* 23–27.

Levenson, R. W., Ekman, P., Heider, K., & Friesen, W. V. (1992). Emotion and autonomic nervous system activity in the Minangkabau of West Sumatra. *Journal of Personality and Social Psychology, 62,* 972–988.

Leventhal, H. (1970). Findings and theory in the study of fear communications. In L. Berkowitz (Ed.), *Advances in experimental social psychology* (Vol. 5). New York: Academic Press.

Levin, I. P., & Gaeth, J. (1988). How consumers are affected by the framing of attribute information before and after consuming the product. *Journal of Consumer Research, 15,* 374–378.

Levin, I. P., Schnittjer, S. K., & Thee, S. L. (1988). Information framing effects in social and personal decisions. *Journal of Experimental Social Psychology, 24,* 520–529.

Levine, J. D., Gordon, N. C., & Fields, H. L. (1978). The mechanism of placebo analgesia. *Lancet, 2,* 654–657.

Levine, J. M. (1989). Reaction to opinion deviance in small groups. In P. B. Paulus (Ed.), *Psychology of group influence* (2nd ed., pp. 187–231). Hillsdale, NJ: Erlbaum.

Levine, R. A., & Campbell, D. T. (1972). *Ethnocentrism: Theories of conflict, ethnic attitudes, and group behavior.* New York: Wiley.

Levine, R. V. (1990). The pace of life. *American Scientist, 78,* 450–459.

Levinson, D. J. (1996). *The seasons of a woman's life.* New York: Knopf.

Levinson, D. J., Darrow, C. N., Klein, E. B., Levinson, M. H., McKee, B. (1978). *The seasons of a man's life.* New York: Knopf.

Levy, B. (1996). Improving memory in old age through implicit self-stereotyping. *Journal of Personality and Social Psychology, 71,* 1092–1107.

Levy, G. D. (1989). Relations among aspects of children's social environments, gender schematization, gender role knowledge, and flexibility. *Sex Roles, 21,* 803–823.

Levy, J., Trevarthen, C., & Sperry, R. W. (1972). Perception of bilateral chimeric figures following hemispheric disconnection. *Brain, 95,* 61–78.

Lewinsohn, P. M. (1974). A behavioral approach to depression. In R. Friedman & M. Katz (Eds.), *The psychology of depression: Contemporary theory and research.* Washington, DC: Winston-Wiley.

Lewinsohn, P. M., & Rosenbaum, M. (1987). Recall of parental behavior by acute depressives, remitted depressives, and nondepressives. *Journal of Personality and Social Psychology, 52,* 611–619.

Lewinsohn, P. M., Duncan, E. M., Stanton, A. K., & Hautzinger, M. (1986). Age at first onset for nonbipolar depression. *Journal of Abnormal Psychology, 95,* 378–383.

Lewinsohn, P. M., Rohde, P., & Seeley, J. R. (1994). Psychosocial risk factors for future adolescent suicide attempts. *Journal of Consulting and Clinical Psychology, 62,* 297–305.

Lewis, M. D., Koroshegyi, C., Douglas, L., & Kampe, K. (1997). Age-specific associations between emotional responses to separation and cognitive performance in infancy. *Developmental Psychology, 33,* 32–42.

Lewis, M., & Bendersky, M. (Eds.) (1995). *Mothers, babies, and cocaine: The role of toxins in development.* Mahwah, NJ: Erlbaum.

Lewis, P., & Boylan, P. (1979). Fetal breathing: A review. *American Journal of Obstetrics and Gynecology, 134,* 587–598.

Lewontin, R. (1970). Race and intelligence. *Bulletin of the Atomic Scientists, 26,* 2–8.

Lichtman, S. W., et al. (1992). Discrepancy between self-reported and actual caloric intake and exercise in obese subjects. *New England Journal of Medicine, 327,* 1893–1898.

Lickey, M. E., & Gordon, B. (1991). *Medicine and mental illness.* New York: W. H. Freeman.

Lickona, T. (1976). *Research on Piaget's theory of moral development.* In T. Lickona (Ed.), Moral development and behavior. New York: Holt, Rinehart & Winston.

Lieberman, P. (1984). *The biology and evolution of language.* Cambridge, MA: Harvard University Press.

Lifton, R. J. (1986). *The Nazi doctors.* New York: Basic Books.

Light, L. L. (1991). Memory and aging: Four hypotheses in search of data. *Annual Review of Psychology, 42,* 333–376.

Linden, E. (1993, March 22). Can animals think? *Time,* pp. 52–61.

Lindsay, P. H., & Norman, D. A. (1977). *Human information processing.* New York: Academic Press.

Lindsay, R. C. L., Wells, G. L., & O'Conner, F. J. (1989). Mock-juror belief of accurate and inaccurate eyewitnesses: A replication and extension. *Law and Human Behavior, 13,* 333–339.

Lindsley, O. (1992). Precision teaching: Discoveries and effects. *Journal of Applied Behavior Analysis, 25,* 51–57.

Lindvall, O., et al. (1992). Transplantation of fetal dopamine neurons in Parkinson's disease: One year clinical and neurophysiological observations in two patients with putiminal implants. *Annals of Neurology, 31,* 155–165.

Linet, M. G., Stewart, W. F., Celentano, D. D., Ziegler, D., & Sprecher, M. (1989). An epidemiologic study of headache among adolescents and young adults. *Journal of the American Medical Association, 261,* 2211–2216.

Linn, M. C., & Petersen, A. (1985). Emergence and characterization of sex differences in spatial ability: A meta-analysis. *Child Development, 56,* 1479–1498.

Linn, R. L. (1982). Ability testing: Individual differences, prediction, and differential prediction. In A. K. Wigdor & W. R. Garner (Eds.), *Ability testing: Uses, consequences, and controversies* (Part II). Washington, DC: National Academy Press.

Linton, M. (1982). Transformations of memory in everyday life. In U. Neisser (Ed.), *Memory observed: Remembering in natural contexts* (pp. 77–91). San Francisco: W. H. Freeman.

Linville, P. W., & Jones, E. E. (1980). Polarized appraisals of out-group members. *Journal of Personality and Social Psychology, 38,* 689–703.

Linville, P. W., Fischer, G. W., & Fischhoff, B. (1992). Perceived risk and decision-making involving AIDS. In J. B. Pryor & G. D. Reeder (Eds.), *The social psychology of HIV infection.* Hillsdale, NJ: Erlbaum.

Linz, D., Donnerstein, E., & Penrod, S. (1988). Effects of long-term exposure to violent and sexually degrading depictions of women. *Journal of Personality and Social Psychology, 55,* 758–768.

Lipsey, M. W., & Wilson, D. B. (1993). The efficacy of psychological, educational, and behavioral treatment: Confirmation from metaanalysis. *American Psychologist, 48,* 1181–1209.

Lipsitt, L. (1971, December). Babies: They're a lot smarter than they look. *Psychology Today,* p. 23.

Liu, S. S. (1971). Differential conditioning and stimulus generalization of the rabbit's nictitating membrane response. *Journal of Comparative and Physiological Psychology, 77,* 136–142.

Livesley, W. J. (Ed.) (1995). *The DSM-IV personality disorders.* New York: Guilford Press.

Livingstone, M., & Hubel, D. (1988). Segregation of form, color, movement, and depth: Anatomy, physiology, and perception. *Science, 240,* 740–749.

Lockard, J. S., & Paulhus, D. L. (1988). *Self-deception: An adaptive mechanism?* Upper Saddle River, NJ: Prentice Hall.

Locke, E. A., & Latham, G. P. (1990). *A theory of goal-setting and task performance.* Englewood Cliffs, NJ: Prentice Hall.

Loehlin, J. C. (1992). *Genes and environment in personality development.* Newbury Park, CA: Sage Publications.

Loehlin, J. C., Willerman, L., & Horn, J. M. (1987). Personality resemblance in adoptive families: A 10-year follow-up. *Journal of Personality and Social Psychology, 53,* 961–969.

Loehlin, J. C., Willerman, L., & Horn, J. M. (1988). Human behavior genetics. *Annual Review of Psychology, 38,* 101–133.

Loftus, E. F. (1979). *Eyewitness testimony.* Cambridge, MA: Harvard University Press.

Loftus, E. F. (1993a). The reality of repressed memories. *American Psychologist, 48,* 518–537.

Loftus, E. F. (1993b). Desperately seeking memories of the first few years of childhood: The reality of early memories. *Journal of Experimental Psychology: General, 122,* 274–277.

Loftus, E. F., & Ketcham, K. (1991). *Witness for the defense: The accused, the eyewitness, and the expert who puts memory on trial.* New York: St. Martin's Press.

Loftus, E. F., & Ketcham, K. (1994). *The myth of repressed memory: False memories and allegations of sexual abuse.* New York: St. Martin's Press.

Loftus, E. F., & Klinger, M. R. (1992). Is the unconscious smart or dumb? *American Psychologist, 47,* 761–765.

Loftus, E. F., & Loftus, G. R. (1980). On the permanence of stored information in the human brain. *American Psychologist, 35,* 409–420.

Loftus, E. F., & Palmer, J. C. (1974). Reconstruction of automobile destruction: An example of the interaction between language and memory. *Journal of Verbal Learning and Verbal Behavior, 13,* 585–589.

Loftus, E. F., Donders, K., Hoffman, H. G., & Schooler, J. W. (1989). Creating new memories that are quickly accessed and confidently held. *Memory and Cognition, 17,* 607–616.

Loftus, E. F., Loftus, G. R., & Messo, J. (1987). Some facts about "weapon focus." *Law and Human Behavior, 11,* 55–62.

Loftus, E. F., Miller, D. G., & Burns, H. J. (1978). Semantic integration of verbal information into visual memory. *Journal of Experimental Psychology: Human Learning and Memory, 4,* 19–31.

Loftus, G. R., Duncan, J., & Gehrig, P. (1992). On the time course of perceptual information that results from a brief visual presentation. *Journal of Experimental Psychology: Human Perception and Performance, 18,* 530–549.

Logan, G. (1992). Attention and preattention in theories of automaticity. *American Journal of Psychology, 105,* 317–340.

Logothetis, N. K., & Schall, J. D. (1989). Neuronal correlates of subjective visual perception. *Science, 245,* 761–763.

Logue, A. W. (1991). *The psychology of eating and drinking: An introduction.* New York: W. H. Freeman.

Lopez, S. R. (1989). Patient variable biases in clinical judgment: Conceptual overview and methodological considerations. *Psychological Bulletin, 106,* 184–203.

Lorenz, K. (1937). Imprinting. *The Auk, 54,* 245–273.

Lorenz, K. (1966). *On aggression.* New York: Harcourt, Brace & World.

Lourenco, O., & Machado, A. (1996). In defense of Piaget's theory: A reply to 10 common criticisms. *Psychological Review, 103,* 143–164.

Lovaas, O. I. (1987). Behavioral treatment and normal educational and intellectual functioning in young autistic children. *Journal of Consulting and Clinical Psychology, 55,* 3–9.

Lovdal, L. T. (1989). Sex role messages in television commercials: An update. *Sex Roles, 21,* 715–724.

Low, P. W., Jeffries, J. C., & Bonnie, R. J. (1986). *The trial of John Hinckley, Jr.: A case study in the insanity defense.* Mineola, NY: Foundation Press.

Lu, Z.-L., Williamson, S. J., & Kaufman, L. (1992). Behavioral lifetime of human auditory sensory memory predicted by physiological measures. *Science, 258,* 1668–1670.

Lubin, B., Larson, R. M., & Matarazzo, J. D. (1984). Patterns of psychological test usage in the United States: 1935–1982. *American Psychologist, 39,* 451–454.

Luborsky, L. (1984). *Principles of psychoanalytic psychotherapy.* New York: Basic Books.

Luborsky, L., & Crits-Christoph, P. (1990). *Understanding transference: The CCRT method.* New York: Basic Books.

Lubow, R. E., & Fein, O. (1996). Pupillary size in response to a visual guilty knowledge test: New technique for the detection of deception. *Journal of Experimental Psychology: Applied, 2,* 164–177.

Lucy, J. A. (1992). *Language diversity and thought: A reformulation of the linguistic relativity hypothesis.* New York: Cambridge University Press.

Ludwig, A. M. (1995). *The price of greatness: Resolving the creativity and madness controversy.* New York: Guilford Press.

Luria, A. R. (1968). *The mind of a mnemonist.* New York: Basic Books.

Luthans, F., Paul, R., & Baker, D. (1981). An experimental analysis of the impact of contingent reinforcement on salespersons' performance behavior. *Journal of Applied Psychology, 66,* 314–323.

Lutz, W. (1989). *Doublespeak.* New York: Harper Perennial.

Lydiard, R. B., Brawman-Mintzer, O., & Ballenger, J. C. (1996). Recent developments in the psychopharmacology of anxiety disorders. *Journal of Consulting and Clinical Psychology, 64,* 660–668.

Lykken, D. T. (1981). *A tremor in the blood: Uses and abuses of the lie detector.* New York: McGraw-Hill.

Lykken, D. T. (1995). *The antisocial personalities.* Mahwah, NJ: Erlbaum.

Lykken, D. T., Bouchard, T. J., Jr., McGue, M., & Tellegen, A. (1993). Heritability of interests: A twin study. *Journal of Applied Psychology, 78,* 649–661.

Lykken, D. T., & Tellegen, A. (1996). Happiness is a stochastic phenomenon. *Psychological Science, 7,* 186–189.

Lynch, G., & Baudry, M. (1984). The biochemistry of memory: A new and specific hypothesis. *Science, 224,* 1057–1064.

Lynn, S. J., Rhue, J. W., & Weekes, J. R. (1990). Hypnotic involuntariness: A social cognitive analysis. *Psychological Review, 97,* 169–184.

Lyons, L. C., & Woods, P. J. (1991). The efficacy of rational-emotive therapy: A quantitative review of outcome research. *Clinical Psychology Review, 11,* 357–369.

Lytton, H., Romney, D. M. (1991). Parents' differential socialization of boys and girls: A meta-analysis. *Psychological Bulletin, 109,* 267–296.

Maccoby, E. E. (1990). Gender and relationships: A developmental account. *American Psychologist, 45,* 513–520.

Maccoby, E. E., & Jacklin, C. N. (1974). *The psychology of sex differences.* Palo Alto, CA: Stanford University Press.

Maccoby, E. E., & Jacklin, C. N. (1987). Gender segregation in childhood. In H. W. Reese (Ed.), *Advances in child development and behavior* (Vol. 20, pp. 239–287).

MacCoun, R. J. (1993). Drugs and the law: A psychological analysis of drug prohibition. *Psychological Bulletin, 113,* 497–512.

Mackayey, W. R., Malley, J. E., & Stewart, A. J. (1991). Remembering autobiographically consequential experiences: Content analysis of psychologists' accounts of their lives. *Psychology and Aging, 6,* 50–59.

Mackie, D. M., & Worth, L. T. (1989). Processing deficits and the mediation of positive affect in persuasion. *Journal of Personality and Social Psychology, 57,* 27–40.

Mackie, D. M., Worth, L. T., & Asuncion, A. G. (1990). Processing of persuasive in-group messages. *Journal of Personality and Social Psychology, 58,* 812–822.

MacKinnon, D. F., Jamison, K. R., & DePaulo, J. R. (1997). Genetics of manic depressive illness. *Annual Review of Psychology, 20,* 355–373.

MacLeod, C. M. (1991). Half a century of research on the Stroop effect: An integrative review. *Psychological Bulletin, 109,* 163–203.

MacLeod-Morgan, C., & Lack, L. (1982). Hemispheric specificity: A physiological concomitant of hypnotizability. *Psychophysiology, 19,* 687–690.

Macmillan, M. B. (1986). A wonderful journey through skull and brains: The travels of Mr. Gage's tamping iron. *Brain and Cognition, 5,* 67–104.

MacQueen, G., Marshall, J., Perdue, M., Siegal, S., & Bienenstock, J. (1989). Pavlovian conditioning of rat mast cells to secrete rat mast cell protease 11. *Science, 234,* 83–85.

Macrae, C. N., Milne, A. B., & Bodenhausen, G. V. (1994). Stereotypes as energy-saving devices: A peek inside the cognitive toolbox. *Journal of Personality and Social Psychology, 66,* 37–47.

Maddi, S. R., Bartone, P. T., & Puccetti, M. C. (1987). Stressful events are indeed a factor in physical illness: Reply to Schroeder and Costa (1984). *Journal of Personality and Social Psychology, 52,* 833–843.

Maddux, J. E. (1991). Self-efficacy. In C. R. Snyder & D. R. Forsyth (Eds.), *Handbook of social and clinical psychology: The health perspective* (pp. 57–78). New York: Pergamon Press.

Madigan, S., & O'Hara, R. (1992). Short-term memory at the turn of the century: Mary Whiten Calkins's memory research. *American Psychologist, 47,* 170–174.

Madrazo, I., Drucker-Colin, R., Diaz, V., Martinez-Mata, J., Torres, C., & Becerril, J. J. (1987). Open microsurgical autograft of adrenal medulla to the right caudate nucleus in two patients with intractable Parkinson's disease. *New England Journal of Medicine, 316,* 831–834.

Magee, W. J., Eaton, W. W., Wittchen, H. U., McGonagle, K. A., & Kessler, R. C. (1996). Agoraphobia, simple phobia, and social phobia in the National Comorbidity Survey. *Archives of General Psychiatry, 53,* 159–168.

Magnusson, D., & Endler, N. S. (Eds.) (1977). *Personality at the crossroads: Current issues in interactional psychology.* Hillsdale, NJ: Erlbaum.

Mahoney, M. J. (1991). *Human change processes.* New York: Basic Books.

Mahoney, M. J. (Ed.) (1995). *Cognitive and constructive psychotherapies: Theory, research, and practice.* New York: Springer.

Mahowald, M. W., & Schenck, C. H. (1989). Narcolepsy. In G. Adelman (Ed.), *Neuroscience year: Supplement 1 to the Encyclopedia of Neuroscience.* Boston: Birkhauser.

Maier, S. F., Watkins, L. R., & Fleshner, M. (1994). Psychoneuroimmunology: The interface between behavior, the brain, and immunity. *American Psychologist, 49,* 1004–1017.

Main, M. (1996). Introduction to the special section on attachment and psychopathology: 2. Overview of the field of attachment. *Journal of Consulting and Clinical Psychology, 64,* 237–243.

Maj, M., Veltro, F., Pirozzi, R., Lobrace, S., & Magliano, L. (1992). Pattern of recurrence of illness after recovery from an episode of major depression: A prospective study. *Journal of Personality and Social Psychology, 62,* 795–800.

Major, B., Cozzarelli, C., Sciacchitano, A. M., Cooper, M. L., Testa, M., & Mueller, P. M. (1990). Perceived social support, self-efficacy, and adjustment to abortion. *Journal of Personality and Social Psychology, 59,* 452–463.

Major, B., McFartin, D. B., & Gagnon, D. (1984). Overworked and underpaid: On the nature of gender differences in personal entitlement. *Journal of Personality and Social Psychology, 47,* 1399–1412.

Major, B., Schmidlin, A. M., & Williams, L. (1990). Gender patterns in social touch: The impact of setting and age. *Journal of Personality and Social Psychology, 58,* 634–643.

Majors, R. (1991). *Nonverbal behaviors and communication styles among African Americans.* In R. Jones (Ed.), *Black psychology* (pp. 269–294). Berkeley, CA: Cobb & Henry.

Malamuth, N. M., & Check, J. V. P. (1981). The effects of mass media exposure on acceptance of violence against women: A field experiment. *Journal of Research in Personality, 15,* 436–446.

Malpass, R. S., & Devine, P. G. (1981). Eyewitness identification: Lineup instructions and the absence of the offender. *Journal of Applied Psychology, 66,* 482–489.

Maltsberger, J. T., & Goldblatt, M. J. (Eds.) (1996). *Essential papers on suicide.* New York: New York University Press.

Mandel, D. R., Jusczyk, P. W., & Pisoni, D. B. (1995). Infants' recognition of the sound patterns of their own names. *Psychological Science, 6,* 314–317.

Mandler, G. (1980). Recognizing: The judgment of previous occurrence. *Psychological Review, 87,* 252–271.

Mann, J. M. (1992). AIDS—the second decade: A global perspective. *Journal of Infectious Diseases, 165,* 245–250.

Marcel, A. J. (1983). Conscious and unconscious perception: Experiments on visual masking and word recognition. *Cognitive Psychology, 15,* 197–237.

Mark, V. H., & Ervin, F. R. (1970). *Violence and the brain.* New York: Harper & Row.

Marks, D. F. (1986). Investigating the paranormal. *Nature, 320,* 119–124.

Marks, G. A., Shaffrey, J. P., Oksenberg, A., Speciale, S. G., & Roffwarg, H. P. (1995). A functional role for the REM sleep in brain maturation. *Behavioural Brain Research, 69,* 1–11.

Marks, I. M. (1987). *Fears, phobias, and rituals: Panic, anxiety, and their disorders.* New York: Oxford University Press.

Markus, H. (1977). Self-schemata and processing information about the self. *Journal of Personality and Social Psychology, 35,* 63–78.

Markus, H., & Kitayama, S. (1991). Culture and the self: Implications for cognition, emotion, and motivation. *Psychological Review, 98,* 224–253.

Markus, H., & Nurius, P. (1986). *Possible selves.* American Psychologist, 41, 954–969.

Marsh, H. W., & Parker, J. W. (1984). Determinants of student self-concept: Is it better to be a relatively large fish in a small pond even if you don't learn to swim as well? *Journal of Personality and Social Psychology, 47,* 213–231.

Marsh, R. L., & Bower, G. H. (1993). Eliciting cryptomnesia: Unconscious plagiarism in a puzzle task. *Journal of Experimental Psychology: Learning, Memory, and Cognition, 19,* 673–688.

Marsh, R. L., & Landau, J. D. (1995). Item availability in cryptomnesia: Assessing its role in two paradigms of unconscious plagiarism. *Journal of Experimental Psychology: Learning, Memory, and Cognition, 21,* 1568–1582.

Marshall, D. A., & Moulton, D. G. (1981). Olfactory sensitivity to xionone in humans and dogs. *Chemical Senses, 6,* 53–61.

Marshall, G. N. (1991). A multidimensional analysis of internal health locus of control belief: Separating the wheat from the chaff? *Journal of Personality and Social Psychology, 61,* 483–491.

Martin, C. L. (1987). A ratio measure of sex stereotyping. *Journal of Personality and Social Psychology, 52,* 489–499.

Martin, C. L., Wood, C. H., & Little, J. K. (1990). The development of gender stereotype components. *Child Development, 61,* 1891–1904.

Martin, G., & Pear, J. (1992). *Behavior modification: What it is and how to do it* (4th ed.). Englewood Cliffs, NJ: Prentice-Hall.

Martin, J. H. (1991). Coding and processing of sensory information. In E. R. Kandel, J. H. Schwartz, & T. M. Jessell (Eds.), *Principles of neural science* (3rd ed., pp. 329–340). New York: Elsevier.

Martin, J. H., Brost, J. C. M., & Hilal, S. (1991). Imaging the living brain. In E. R. Kandel, J. H. Schwartz, & T. M. Jessell (Eds.), *Principles of neural science* (3rd ed., pp. 309–324). New York: Elsevier.

Martin, L. (1986). "Eskimo words for snow": A case study in the genesis and decay of an anthropological example. *American Anthropologist, 88,* 418–423.

Maser, J. D. (1985). List of phobias. In A. H. Tuma & J. D. Maser (Eds.), *Anxiety and the anxiety disorders.* Hillsdale, NJ: Erlbaum.

Maslach, C. (1982). *Burnout: The cost of caring.* Englewood Cliffs, NJ: Prentice-Hall.

Maslow, A. (1954). *Motivation and personality.* New York: Harper.

Maslow, A. (1968). *Toward a psychology of being.* New York: Van Nostrand.

Masters, M. S., & Sanders, B. (1993). Is the gender difference in mental rotation disappearing? *Behavior Genetics, 23,* 337–341.

Masters, W. H., & Johnson, V. E. (1966). *Human sexual response.* Boston: Little, Brown.

Matarazzo, J. D. (1983). The reliability of psychiatric and psychological diagnosis. *Clinical Psychology Review, 3,* 103–145.

Matarazzo, J. D. (1992). Psychological testing and assessment in the 21st century. *American Psychologist, 47,* 1007–1018.

Matsumoto, D., & Ekman, P. (1989). Japanese-American cultural differences in intensity ratings of facial expressions of emotion. *Motivation and Emotion, 13,* 143–157.

Matsumoto, D., Kudoh, T., Scherer, K., & Wallbott, H. (1988). Antecedents and reactions to emotions in the United States and Japan. *Journal of Cross-Cultural Psychology, 19,* 267–286.

Matthews, K. A. (1988). CHD and Type A behavior: Update on and alternative to the Booth-Kewley and Friedman quantitative review. *Psychological Bulletin, 104,* 373–380.

Matthews, K. A. (1992). Myths and realities of the menopause. *Psychosomatic Medicine, 54,* 1–9.

Maurer, D., & Maurer, C. (1988). *The world of the newborn.* New York: Basic Books.

Mauro, R., Sato, K., & Tucker, J. (1992). The role of appraisal in human emotions: A cross-cultural study. *Journal of Personality and Social Psychology, 62,* 301–317.
Mayer, J. D., & Salovey, P. (1993). The intelligence of emotional intelligence. *Intelligence, 17,* 433–442.
Mazur, A., Booth, A., & Dabbs, J. M., Jr. (1992). Testosterone and chess competition. *Social Psychology Quarterly, 55,* 70–77.
McAdams, D. P. (1989). *Intimacy: The need to be close.* New York: Doubleday.
McAdams, D. P., & Constantian, C. A. (1983). Intimacy and affiliation motives in daily living: An experience sampling analysis. *Journal of Personality and Social Psychology, 45,* 851–861.
McAdams, D. P., & de St. Aubin, E. (1992). A theory of generativity and its assessment through self-report, behavioral acts, and narrative themes in autobiography. *Journal of Personality and Social Psychology, 62,* 1003–1015.
McAdams, D. P., Jackson, R. J., & Kirshnit, C. (1984). Looking, laughing, and smiling in dyads as a function of intimacy motivation and reciprocity. *Journal of Personality, 52,* 261–273.
McAndrew, F. T. (1993). *Environmental psychology.* Pacific Grove, CA: Brooks/Cole.
McArthur, L. A. (1972). The how and what of why: Some determinants and consequences of causal attribution. *Journal of Personality and Social Psychology, 22,* 171–193.
McCall, M., & Belmont, H. J. (1996). Credit card insignia and restaurant tipping: Evidence for an associative link. *Journal of Applied Psychology, 81,* 609–613.
McCall, R. B., & Carriger, M. S. (1995). A meta-analysis of infant habituation and recognition memory performance as predictors of later IQ. *Child Development, 64,* 57–79.
McCann, I. L., & Holmes, D. S. (1984). Influence of aerobic exercise on depression. *Journal of Personality and Social Psychology, 46,* 1142–1147.
McCartney, K., Harris, M. J., & Bernieri, F. (1990). Growing up and growing apart: A developmental meta-analysis of twin studies. *Psychological Bulletin, 107,* 226–237.
McCaul, K. D., & Malott, J. (1984). Distraction and coping with pain. *Psychological Bulletin, 95,* 516–533.
McCauley, C. (1989). The nature of social influence in groupthink: Compliance and internalization. *Journal of Personality and Social Psychology, 57,* 250–260.
McClelland, D. C. (1985). *Human motivation.* Glenview, IL: Scott, Foresman.
McClelland, D. C., Atkinson, J. W., Clark, R. A., & Lowell, E. (1953). *The achievement motive.* New York: Appleton-Century-Crofts.
McClelland, D. C., & Koestner, R. (1992). The achievement motive. In C. P. Smith, J. W. Atkinson, D. C. McClelland, & J. Veroff (Eds.), *Motivation and personality: Handbook of thematic content analysis* (pp. 143–152). New York: Cambridge University Press.
McClelland, D. C., Koestner, R., & Weinberger, J. (1989). How do self-attributed and implicit motives differ? *Psychological Review, 96,* 690–702.
McClelland, J. L., McNaughton, B. L., & O'Reilly, R. C. (1995). Why there are complementary learning systems in the hippocampus and neocortex: Insights from the successes and failures of connectionist models of learning and memory. *Psychological Review, 102,* 419–457.
McCloskey, M., & Kuhl, D. (1983). Naive physics: The curvilinear impetus principle and its role in interactions with moving objects. *Journal of Experimental Psychology: Learning, Memory, and Cognition, 9,* 146–156.
McCloskey, M., & Zaragoza, M. (1985). Misleading postevent information and memory for events: Arguments and evidence against memory impairment hypotheses. *Journal of Experimental Psychology, 114,* 3–18.
McCloskey, M., Washburn, A., & Felch, L. (1983). Intuitive physics: The straight-down belief and its origin. *Journal of Experimental Psychology: Learning, Memory, and Cognition, 9,* 636–649.
McCloskey, M., Wible, C. G., & Cohen, N. J. (1988). Is there a special flashbulb-memory mechanism? *Journal of Experimental Psychology: General, 117,* 171–181.
McConkey, K. M., & Sheehan, P. W. (1995). *Hypnosis, memory, and behavior in criminal investigation.* New York: Guilford Press.
McConnell, A. R., & Fazio, R. H. (1996). Women and men as people: Effects of gender-marked language. *Personality and Social Psychology Bulletin, 22,* 1004–1013.
McCormick, D. A., & Thompson, R. F. (1984). Cerebellum: Essential involvement in the classically conditioned eyelid response. *Science, 223,* 296–299.
McCrae, R. R., & Costa, P. T., Jr. (1990). *Personality in adulthood.* New York: Guilford Press.
McCrae, R. R., & Costa, P. T., Jr. (1997). Personality trait structure as a human universal. *American Psychologist, 52,* 509–516.
McDaniel, M. A., Einstein, G. O., DeLosh, E. L., May, C. P., & Brady, P. (1995). The bizarreness effect: It's not surprising, it's complex. *Journal of Experimental Psychology: Learning, Memory, and Cognition, 21,* 422–435.
McGaugh, J. L. (1990). Significance and remembrance: The role of neuromodulatory systems. *Psychological Science, 1,* 15–25.
McGhie, A., & Chapman, J. (1961). Disorders of attention and perception in early schizophrenia. *British Journal of Medical Psychology, 34,* 102–116.
McGinnis, A. L. (1987). *The power of optimism.* San Francisco: Harper & Row.
McGlashan, T. H., & Fenton, W. S. (1991). Classical subtypes for schizophrenia: Literature review for DSM-IV. *Schizophrenia Bulletin, 17,* 609–623.
McGlashan, T. H., & Fenton, W. S. (1992). The positive-negative distinction in schizophrenia: Review of natural history validators. *Archives of General Psychiatry, 49,* 63–72.
McGlone, J. (1980). Sex differences in human brain asymmetry: A critical survey. *The Behavioral and Brain Sciences, 3,* 215–263.
McGlynn, S. M., & Kaszniak, A. W. (1991). When metacognition fails: Impaired awareness of deficit in Alzheimer's disease. *Journal of Cognitive Neuroscience, 3,* 183–189.
McGue, M., & Lykken, D. T. (1992). Genetic influence on risk of divorce. *Psychological Science, 3,* 368–373.
McGue, M., Bacon, S., & Lykken, D. T. (1993). Personality stability and change in early adulthood: A behavioral genetic analysis. *Developmental Psychology, 29,* 96–109.
McGuffin, P., Katz, R., Watkins, S., & Rutherford, J. (1996). A hospital-based twin register of the heritability of DSM-IV unipolar depression. *Archives of General Psychiatry, 53,* 129–136.
McGuire, A. M. (1994). Helping behaviors in the natural environment: Dimensions and correlates of helping. *Personality and Social Psychology Bulletin, 20,* 45–56.
McIntosh, D. N. (1996). Facial feedback hypothesis: Evidence, implications, and directions. *Motivation and Emotion, 20,* 121–147.
McKim, W. A. (1991). *Drugs and behavior.* Engelwood Cliffs, NJ: Prentice-Hall.
McKinlay, J. B., McKinlay, S. M., & Brambilla, D. J. (1987). Health status and utilization behavior associated with menopause. *American Journal of Epidemiology, 125,* 110–121.
McKinlay, J. B., McKinlay, S. M., & Brambilla, D. J. (1987). The relative contributions of endocrine changes and social circumstances to depression in middle-aged women. Journal of *Health and Social Behavior, 28,* 345–363.
McNally, R. J. (1987). Preparedness and phobias: A review. *Psychological Bulletin, 101,* 283–303.
McNally, R. J. (1990). Psychological approaches to panic disorder: A review. *Psychological Bulletin, 108,* 403–419.
McNally, R. J. (1994). *Panic disorder: A critical analysis.* New York: Guilford Press.
McNamara, T. P. (1992). Priming and the constraints it places on theories of memory and retrieval. *Psychological Review, 99,* 650–662.
McNamara, T. P. (1994). Theories of priming: II. Types of primes. *Journal of Experimental Psychology: Learning, Memory, and Cognition, 20,* 507–520.
McNeal, E. T., & Cimbolic, P. (1986). Antidepressants and biochemical theories of depression. *Psychological Bulletin, 99,* 361–374.
McNeill, D. (1970). *The acquisition of language: The study of developmental psycholinguistics.* New York: Harper & Row.
McReynolds, P. (1996). Lightner Witmer: A centennial tribute. *American Psychologist, 51,* 237–240.
McWhorter, K. T. (1988). *Study and thinking skills in college.* Glenview, IL: Scott, Foresman.
Mead, M. (1928). *Coming of age in Samoa.* New York: Morrow.
Medina, J. J. (1996). *The clock of ages: Why we age—how we age—winding back the clock.* New York: Cambridge University Press.
Mednick, S. A. (1962). The associative basis of the creative process. *Psychological Review, 69,* 220–232.
Medvec, V. H., & Savitsky, K. (1997). When doing better means feeling worse: The effects of categorical cutoff points on counterfactual thinking and satisfaction. *Journal of Personality and Social Psychology, 72,* 1284–1296.
Medvec, V. H., Madey, S. F., & Gilovich, T. (1995). When less is more: Counterfactual thinking and satisfaction among Olympic medalists. *Journal of Personality and Social Psychology, 69,* 603–610.
Meehl, P. E. (1962). Schizotaxia, schizotypy, schizophrenia. *American Psychologist, 17,* 827–838.
Meeus, W. H. J., & Raaijmakers, Q. A. W. (1995). Obedience in modern society: The Utrecht studies. *Journal of Social Issues, 51,* 155–175.
Meichenbaum, D. (1985). *Stress inoculation training.* New York: Pergamon.
Meizack, R., & Wall, P. (1965). Pain mechanisms: A new theory. *Science, 150,* 971–979.
Meltzoff, A. N., & Moore, M. K. (1983). Imitation of facial and manual gestures by human neonates. *Child Development, 54,* 702–709.
Meltzoff, A. N., & Moore, M. K. (1989). Imitation in newborn infants: Exploring the range of gestures imitated and the underlying mechanisms. *Developmental Psychology, 25,* 954–962.
Meltzoff, A. N., & Moore, M. K. (1992). Early imitation within a functional framework: The importance of person identity, movement, and development. *Infant Behavior and Development, 15,* 479–505.
Melzack, R., & Wall, P. (1965). Pain mechanisms: A new theory. *Science,* 150, 971–979.
Melzack, R., & Wall, P. (1982). *The challenge of pain.* New York: Penguin Books.
Merikle, P., & Skanes, H. E. (1992). Subliminal self-help audiotapes: A search for placebo effects. *Journal of Applied Psychology, 77,* 772–776.
Merikle, P. M., & Reingold, E. M. (1992). Measuring unconscious perceptual processes. In R. F. Bornstein & T. S. Pittman (Eds.), *Perception without awareness.* New York: Guilford Press.
Mesquita, B., & Frijda, N. H. (1992). Cultural variations in emotions: A review. *Psychological Bulletin, 112,* 179–204.
Messick, D. M., & Mackie, D. M. (1989). Intergroup relations. *Annual Review of Psychology, 40,* 51–81.

Metalsky, G. I., Joiner, T. E., Hardin, T. S., & Abramson, L. Y. (1993). Depressive reactions to failure in a naturalistic setting: A test of the hopelessness and self-esteem theories of depression. *Journal of Abnormal Psychology, 102,* 101–109.
Metcalfe, J., & Weibe, D. (1987). Intuition in insight and non-insight problem solving. *Memory and Cognition, 15,* 238–246.
Metcalfe, J., Funnell, M., & Gazzaniga, M. S. (1995). Right-hemisphere memory superiority: Studies of a split-brain patient. *Psychological Science, 6,* 157–164.
Meyer, D. E., & Schvaneveldt, R. W. (1971). Facilitation in recognizing pairs of words: Evidence of a dependence between retrieval operations. *Journal of Experimental Psychology, 90,* 227–234.
Meyer, G. E., & Hilterbrand, K. (1984). Does it pay to be "Bashful"? The seven dwarfs and long-term memory. *American Journal of Psychology, 97,* 47–55.
Micale, M. S. (1995). *Approaching hysteria: Disease and its interpretations.* Princeton, NJ: Princeton University Press.
Michelson, L. K., & Marchione, K. (1991). Behavioral, cognitive, and pharmacological treatments of panic disorder with agoraphobia: Critique and synthesis. *Journal of Consulting and Clinical Psychology, 59,* 100–114.
Michelson, L. K., & Ray, W. J. (Eds.) (1996). *Handbook of dissociation: Theoretical, empirical, and clinical perspectives.* New York: Plenum.
Middlebrooks, J. C., & Green, D. M. (1991). Sound localization by human listeners. *Annual Review of Psychology, 42,* 135–159.
Miles, D. R., & Carey, G. (1997). Genetic and environmental architecture of human aggression. *Journal of Personality and Social Psychology, 72,* 207–217.
Milgram, S. (1963). Behavioral study of obedience. *Journal of Abnormal and Social Psychology, 67,* 371–378.
Milgram, S. (1965). Some conditions of obedience and disobedience to authority. *Human Relations, 18,* 57–76.
Milgram, S. (1974). *Obedience to authority: An experimental view.* New York: Harper & Row.
Milgram, S., Bickman, L., & Berkowitz, L. (1969). Note on the drawing power of crowds of different size. *Journal of Personality and Social Psychology, 13,* 79–82.
Miller, A. G. (1986). *The obedience experiments: A case study of controversy in social science.* New York: Praeger.
Miller, G. (1991). *The science of words.* New York: Freeman.
Miller, G. A. (1956). The magical number seven plus or minus two: Some limits on our capacity for processing information. *Psychological Review, 63,* 81–97.
Miller, I. J., & Reedy, F. E. (1990). Variations in human taste bud density and taste intensity perception. *Physiology and Behavior, 47,* 1213–1219.
Miller, J. G. (1984). Culture and the development of everyday social explanation. *Journal of Personality and Social Psychology, 46,* 961–978.
Miller, J. G., & Bersoff, D. M. (1992). Culture and moral judgment: How are conflicts between justice and interpersonal responsibilities resolved? *Journal of Personality and Social Psychology, 62,* 541–554.
Miller, M. E., & Bowers, K. S. (1993). Hypnotic analgesia: Dissociated experience or dissociated control? *Journal of Abnormal Psychology, 102,* 29–38.
Miller, N. E. (1969). Learning of visceral and glandular responses. *Science, 163,* 434–445.
Miller, N. E. (1985). The value of behavioral research on animals. *American Psychologist, 40,* 423–440.
Miller, N. S., & Gold, M. S. (1994). LSD and Ecstasy: Pharmacology, phenomenology, and treatment. *Psychiatric Annals, 24,* 131–133.
Miller, R. R., Barnet, R. C., & Grahame, N. J. (1995). Assessment of the Rescorla-Wagner model. *Psychological Bulletin, 117,* 363–386.
Miller, T. Q., Smith, T. W., Turner, C. W., Guijarro, M. L., & Hallet, A. J. (1996). A meta-analytic review of research on hostility and physical health. *Psychological Bulletin, 119,* 322–348.
Miller, T. Q., Turner, C. W., Tindale, R. S., Posavac, E. J., & Dugon, B. L. (1991). Reasons for the trend toward null findings in research on Type A behavior. *Psychological Bulletin, 110,* 469–485.
Miller-Jones, D. (1989). Culture and testing. *American Psychologist, 44,* 360–366.
Mills, H. L., Agras, W. S., Barlow, D. H., & Mills, J. R. (1973). Compulsive rituals treated by response prevention. *Archives of General Psychiatry, 28,* 524–529.
Milner, B., Corkin, S., & Teuber, H. L. (1968). Further analysis of the hippocampal amnesic syndrome: 14-year follow-up study of H. M. *Neuropsychologica, 6,* 215–234.
Mineka, S., & Cook, M. (1993). Mechanisms involved in the observational conditioning of fear. *Journal of Experimental Psychology: General, 122,* 23–38.
Minuchin, S. (1974). *Families and family therapy.* Cambridge, MA: Harvard University Press.
Mischel, W. (1968). *Personality and assessment.* New York: Wiley.
Mischel, W. (1973). Toward a cognitive social-learning reconceptualization of personality. *Psychological Review, 80,* 252–283.
Mischel, W. (1990). Personality dispositions revisited and revised: A view after three decades. In L. A. Pervin (Ed.), *Handbook of personality theory and research* (pp. 111–134). New York: Guilford Press.
Mischel, W., & Shoda, Y. (1995). A cognitive-affective system theory of personality: Reconceptualizing situations, dispositions, dynamics, and invariance in personality structure. *Psychological Review, 102,* 246–268.
Mischel, W., Shoda, Y., & Rodriguez, M. L. (1989). Delay of gratification in children. *Science, 244,* 933–938.
Mita, T. H., Dermer, M., & Knight, J. (1977). Reversed facial images and the mere-exposure hypothesis. *Journal of Personality and Social Psychology, 35,* 597–601.
Mitchell, P. (1976). Act of love: *The killing of George Zygmanik.* New York: Knopf.
Mitchell, T. R. (1974). Expectancy models of job satisfaction, occupational preference, and effort: A theoretical, methodological, and empirical appraisal. *Psychological Bulletin, 81,* 1096–1112.
Mitler, M. M., Aldrich, M. S., Koob, G. F., & Zarcone, V. I. (1994). Narcolepsy and its treatment with stimulants. *Sleep, 17,* 352–371.
Mitler, M. M., Carskadon, M. A., Czeisler, C. A., Dement, W. C., Dinges, D. F., & Graeber, R. C. (1988). Catastrophes, sleep, and public policy: A consensus report. *Sleep, 11,* 100–109.
Moghaddam, F. M., Taylor, D. M., & Wright, S. C. (1993). *Social psychology in cross-cultural perspective.* New York: W. H. Freeman.
Moir, A., & Jessel, D. (1989). *Brain sex: The real difference between men and women.* New York: Dell.
Moneta, G. B., & Csikszentmihalyi, M. (1996). The effect of perceived challenges and skills on the quality of subjective experience. *Journal of Personality, 64,* 275–310.
Mongeluzi, D. L., Rosellini, R. A., Caldarone, B. J., Stock, H. S., & Abrahamson, G. C. (1996). Pavlovian aversive conditioning using carbon dioxide as the unconditioned stimulus. *Journal of Experimental Psychology: Animal Behavior Processes, 22,* 244–257.
Monk, T. H. (1987). Coping with the stress of jet-lag. *Work & Stress, 1,* 163–166.
Monk, T. H. (1988). Coping with the stress of shift work. *Work & Stress, 2,* 169–172.
Montepare, J. M., & Lachman, M. E. (1989). "You're only as old as you feel": Self perceptions of age, fears of aging, and life satisfaction from adolescence to old age. *Psychology and Aging, 4,* 73–78.
Montepare, J. M., & McArthur, L. Z. (1988). Impressions of people created by age-related qualities of their gait. *Journal of Personality and Social Psychology, 55,* 547–556.
Montgomery, G., & Kirsch, I. (1996). Mechanisms of placebo pain reduction: An empirical investigation. *Psychological Science, 7,* 174–176.
Moore, B. C. J. (Ed.) (1995). *Hearing.* San Diego: Academic Press.
Moore, T. E. (1982). Subliminal advertising: What you see is what you get. *Journal of Marketing, 46,* 38–47.
Moran, G., & Cutler, B. L. (1991). The prejudicial impact of pretrial publicity. *Journal of Applied Social Psychology, 21,* 345–367.
Morawetz, D. (1989). Behavioral self-help treatment for insomnia: A controlled evaluation. *Behavior Therapy, 20,* 365–379.
Moray, N. (1959). Attention in dichotic listening: Affective cues and the influence of instructions. *Quarterly Journal of Experimental Psychology, 11,* 56–60.
Morelli, G. A., Rogoff, B., Oppenheim, D., & Goldsmith, D. (1992). Cultural variation in infants' sleeping arrangements: Questions of independence. *Developmental Psychology, 28,* 604–613.
Mori, D., Chaiken, S., & Pliner, P. (1987). Eating lightly and the self-presentation of femininity. *Journal of Personality and Social Psychology, 53,* 693–702.
Morin, C. M., Culbert, J. P., & Schwartz, S. M. (1994). Non-pharmacological interventions for insomnia: A meta-analysis of treatment efficacy. *American Journal of Psychiatry, 151,* 1172–1180.
Morokoff, P. J. (1988). Sexuality in perimenopausal and postmenopausal women. *Psychology of Women Quarterly, 12,* 489–511.
Morris, M. W., & Nisbett, R. E. (1993). Tools of the trade: Deductive schemas taught in psychology and philosophy. In R. E. Nisbett (Ed.), *Rules for reasoning* (pp. 228–256). Hillsdale, NJ: Erlbaum.
Morrison, A. M., & Von Glinow, M. A. (1990). Women and minorities in management. *American Psychologist, 45,* 200–208.
Morrison, D. C. (1988). Marine mammals join the navy. *Science, 242,* 1503–1504.
Morrison, D. M. (1985). Adolescent contraceptive behavior: A review. *Psychological Bulletin, 98,* 538–568.
Morrow, D., Leirer, V., Altieri, P., and Fitzsimmons, C. (1994). When expertise reduces age differences in performance. *Psychology and Aging, 9,* 134–148.
Morton, J., & Johnson, M. H. (1991). CONSPEC and CONLERN: A two-process theory of infant face recognition. *Psychological Review, 98,* 164–181.
Moscovici, S. (1985). Social influence and conformity. In G. Lindzey & E. Aronson (Eds.), *The handbook of social psychology* (3rd ed., pp. 347–412). New York: Random House.
Moscovici, S., & Personnaz, B. (1991). Studies in social influence: VI. Is Lenin orange or red? Imagery and social influence. *European Journal of Social Psychology, 21,* 101–118.
Moscovici, S., Lage, E., & Naffrechoux, M. (1969). Influence of a consistent minority on the responses of a majority in a color perception task. *Sociometry, 32,* 365–380.
Moskowitz, D. S. (1982). Coherence and cross-situational generality in personality: A new analysis of old problems. *Journal of Personality and Social Psychology, 43,* 754–768.
Moulton, J., Robinson, G. M., & Elias, C. (1978). Sex bias in language use: "Neutral pronouns that aren't." *American Psychologist, 33,* 1032–1036.
Mounts, N. S., & Steinberg, L. (1995). An ecological analysis of peer influence on adolescent grade point average and drug use. *Developmental Psychology, 31,* 915–922.
Moynihan J. A., & Ader, R. (1996). Psychoneuroimmunology: Animal models of disease. *Psychosomatic Medicine, 58,* 546–558.

Mozell, M. M., Smith, B., Smith, P., Sullivan, R., & Swender, P. (1969). Nasal chemoreception in flavor identification. *Archives of Otolaryngology, 90,* 367–373.

Muehlenhard, C. L. (1988). Misinterpreted dating behaviors and the risk of date rape. *Journal of Social and Clinical Psychology, 6,* 20–37.

Mukherjee, S., Sackheim, H. A., & Schnur, D. B. (1994). Electroconvulsive therapy of acute manic episodes: A review of 50 years' experience. *American Journal of Psychiatry, 151,* 169–176.

Mukherjee, S., Shukla, S., Woodle, J., Rosen, A. M., & Olarte, S. (1983). Misdiagnosis of schizophrenia in bipolar patients: A multiethnic comparison. *American Journal of Psychiatry, 140,* 1571–1574.

Mulder, H. E., Van Olphen, A. F., Bosman, A., & Smoorenburg, G. F. (1992). Phoneme recognition by deaf individuals using the multichannel nucleus cochlear implant. *Acta Otolaryngology, 112,* 946–955.

Mullen, B. (1986). Atrocity as a function of lynch mob composition: A self-attention perspective. *Personality and Social Psychology Bulletin, 12,* 187–197.

Mullington, J., & Broughton, R. (1993). Scheduled naps in the management of daytime sleepiness in narcolepsy-cataplexy. *Sleep, 16,* 444–456.

Murray, B. (1996). Psychology remains top college major. *APA Monitor,* February, pp. 1, 42.

Murray, H. A. (1938). *Explorations in personality.* New York: Oxford University Press.

Murray, H. A. (1943). *Thematic Apperception Test: Pictures and manual.* Cambridge, MA: Harvard University Press.

Murray, S. L., Holmes, J. G., & Griffin, D. W. (1996). The benefits of positive illusions: Idealization and the construction of satisfaction in close relationships. *Journal of Personality and Social Psychology, 70,* 79–98.

Murtagh, D. R. R., & Greenwood, K. M. (1995). Identifying effective psychological treatments for insomnia: A meta-analysis. *Journal of Consulting and Clinical Psychology, 63,* 79–89.

Mustillo, P. (1985). Binocular mechanisms mediating crossed and uncrossed stereopsis. *Psychological Bulletin, 97,* 187–201.

Mydans, S. (1990, January). For jurors, facts could not be sifted from fantasies. *The New York Times,* p. A18.

Myers, D. G. (1993). *The pursuit of happiness.* New York: Avon.

Myers, D. G., & Diener, E. (1995). Who is happy? *Psychological Science, 6,* 10–19.

Nadon, R., Hoyt, I. P., Register, P. A., & Kihlstrom, J. F. (1991). Absorption and hypnotizability: Context effects reexamined. *Journal of Personality and Social Psychology, 60,* 144–153.

Nathans, J. (1989). The genes for color vision. *Scientific American, 260,* 42–49.

Nathans, J., Piantanida, T. P., Eddy, R. L., Shows, T. B., & Hogness, D. S. (1986). Molecular genetics of inherited variation in human color vision. *Science, 232,* 203–210.

National Center for Health Statistics (1996). Teenage birth rates down in a majority of states. Hyattsville, MD: Public Health Service.

National Law Journal (1990, September 10). Rock group not liable for deaths, p. 33.

Nebes, R. D. (1990). The commissurotomized brain: Introduction. In R. D. Nebes & S. Corkin (Eds.), *Handbook of neuropsychology* (Vol. 4). Amsterdam, Netherlands: Elsevier.

Neiberg, P., Marks, J. S., McLaren, N. M., & Remongton, P. (1985). The fetal tobacco syndrome. *Journal of the American Medical Association, 253,* 2998–2999.

Neill, S. R. (1982). Preschool design and child behavior. *Journal of Child Psychology and Psychiatry, 23,* 309–318.

Neisser, U. (1967). *Cognitive psychology.* New York: Appleton-Century-Crofts.

Neisser, U. (1981). John Dean's memory: A case study. *Cognition, 9,* 1–22.

Neisser, U., & Becklen, R. (1975). Selective looking: Attending to visually specified events. *Cognitive Psychology, 7,* 480–494.

Neisser, U., et al. (1996). Intelligence: Knowns and unknowns. *American Psychologist, 51,* 77–101.

Nelson, C. A. (1995). The ontogeny of human memory: A cognitive neuroscience perspective. *Developmental Psychology, 31,* 723–738.

Nelson, K. (1973). Structure and strategy in learning to talk. *Monographs of the Society for Research in Child Development, 38*(Whole No. 149).

Nelson, T. E., Acker, M., & Manis, M. (1996). Irrepressible stereotypes. *Journal of Experimental Social Psychology, 32,* 13–38.

Nemeroff, C. B. (1989). Clinical significance of psychoneuroendocrinology in psychiatry: Focus on the thyroid and adrenal. *Journal of Clinical Psychiatry, 50,* 13–20.

Nersessian, E., & Kopff, R. G., Jr. (Eds.) (1996). *Textbook of psychoanalysis.* Washington, DC: American Psychiatric Press.

Neuberg, S. L. (1989). The goal of forming accurate impressions during social interactions: Attenuating the impact of negative expectancies. *Journal of Personality and Social Psychology, 56,* 374–386.

Neugarten, B. L. (1979). Time, age, and the life cycle. *American Journal of Psychiatry, 136,* 887–894.

Nevid, J. S., Lavi, B., & Primavera, L. H. (1987). Principal components analysis of therapeutic orientations of doctoral programs in clinical psychology. *Journal of Clinical Psychology, 43,* 723–729.

Nevin, J. A. (1988). Behavioral momentum and the partial reinforcement effect. *Psychological Bulletin, 103,* 44–56.

Newcomb, A. F., & Bagwell, C. L. (1995). Children's friendship relations: A meta-analytic review. *Psychological Bulletin, 117,* 306–347.

Newcomb, A. F., Bukowski, W. M., & Pattee, L. (1993). Children's peer relations: A meta-analytic review of popular, rejected, neglected, controversial, and average sociometric status. *Psychological Bulletin, 113,* 99–128.

Newcombe, F., & Ratcliff, G. (1990). Disorders of visuospatial analysis. In H. Goodglass & A. R. Damasio (Eds.), *Handbook of Neuropsychology* (Vol. 2). Amsterdam, Netherlands: Elsevier.

Newcombe, N., & Fox, N. A. (1994). Infantile amnesia: Through a glass darkly. Child Development, 65, 31–40.

Newcombe, N. S., & Baenninger, M. (1989). Biological change and cognitive ability in adolescence. In G. Adams, R. Montemayor, & T. Gullotta (Eds.), *Biology of adolescent behavior and development* (pp. 168–191). Newbury Park, CA: Sage.

Newell, A., & Simon, H. (1972). *Human problem solving.* Englewood Cliffs, NJ: Prentice-Hall.

Newell, A., Shaw, J. G., & Simon, H. A. (1958). Elements of a theory of human problem solving. Psychological Review, 65, 151–166.

Newmann, J. P. (1989). Aging and depression. *Psychology and Aging, 4,* 150–165.

Nezlek, J. B., Imbrie, M., & Shean, G. D. (1994). Depression and everyday social interaction. *Journal of Personality and Social Psychology, 67,* 1101–1111.

Ng, S. H. (1990). Androcentric coding of *man* and *his* in memory by language users. *Journal of Experimental Social Psychology, 26,* 455–464.

Nicholls, J. G., Martin, A. R., & Wallace, B. G. (1992). *From neuron to brain.* Sunderland, MA: Sinauer.

Nickerson, R. S., & Adams, M. J. (1979). Long-term memory for a common object. *Cognitive Psychology, 11,* 287–307.

Nielson, S. L., & Sarason, I. G. (1981). Emotion, personality, and selective attention. *Journal of Personality and Social Psychology, 41,* 945–960.

Nijhawan, R. (1991). Three-dimensional Müller-Lyer illusion. *Perception and Psychophysics, 49,* 333–341.

Nimmons, D. (1994, March). Sex and the brain. *Discover,* pp. 64–71.

Nisbett, R. E., & Cohen, D. (1996). *Culture of honor: The psychology of violence in the South.* New York: Westview.

Nisbett, R. E., Fong, G. T., Lehman, D. R., & Cheng, P. W. (1987). Teaching reasoning. *Science, 238,* 625–631.

Nisbett, R. E., & Wilson, T. D. (1977). Telling more than we can know: Verbal reports on mental processes. *Psychological Review, 84,* 231–259.

Noble, J., & McConkey, K. M. (1995). Hypnotic sex change: Creating and challenging a delusion in the laboratory. *Journal of Abnormal Psychology, 104,* 69–74.

Nolen-Hoeksema, S. (1990). *Sex differences in depression.* Palo Alto, CA: Stanford University Press.

Nolen-Hoeksema, S., & Girgus, J. S. (1994). The emergence of gender differences in depression during adolescence. *Psychological Bulletin, 115,* 424–443.

Nolen-Hoeksema, S., Morrow, J., & Fredrickson, N. (1993). Response styles and the duration of episodes of depressed mood. *Journal of Abnormal Psychology, 102,* 20–28.

Norcross, J. C. (1991). Prescriptive matching in psychotherapy: An introduction. *Psychotherapy, 28,* 439–443.

Norton, G. R., Cox, B., & Malan, J. (1992). Nonclinical panickers: A critical review. *Clinical Psychology Review, 12,* 121–139.

Norton, K. I., Olds, T. S., Olive, S., & Dank, S. (1996). Ken and Barbie at life size. *Sex Roles, 34,* 287–294.

O'Connor, S. C., Rosenblood, L. K. (1996). Affiliation motivation in everyday experience: A theoretical comparison. *Journal of Personality and Social Psychology, 70,* 513–522.

O'Leary, A. (1990). Stress, emotion, and human immune function. *Psychological Bulletin, 108,* 363–382.

Oakes, J. (1985). *Keeping track: How schools structure inequality.* New Haven, CT: Yale University Press.

Oakman, J. M., & Woody, E. Z. (1996). A taxometric analysis of hypnotic susceptibility. *Journal of Personality and Social Psychology, 71,* 980–991.

Offer, D. (1987). In defense of adolescents. *Journal of the American Medical Association, 257,* 3407–3408.

Offer, D., Ostrov, E., & Howard, I. (1981). *The adolescent: A psychological self-portrait.* New York: Basic Books.

Offer, D., & Schonert-Reichl, K. A. (1992). Debunking the myths of adolescence: Findings from recent research. *Journal of the American Academy of Child and Adolescent Psychiatry, 31,* 1003–1013.

Ogbu, J. U. (1978). *Minority education and caste: The American system in cross-cultural perspective.* New York: Academic Press.

Ogilvy, D. (1985). Ogilvy on advertising. New York: Vintage Books. Ohman, A. (1986). Face the beast and fear the face: Animal and social fears as prototypes for evolutionary analyses of emotion. *Psychophysiology, 23,* 123–145.

Ohman, A. (1986). Face the beast and fear the face: Animal and social fears as prototypes for evolutionary analyses of emotion. *Psychophysiology, 23,* 123–145.

Okagaki, L., and Frensch, P. A. (1994). Effects of video game playing on measures of spatial performance: Gender effects in late adolescence. *Journal of Applied Developmental Psychology, 15,* 33–58.

Olds, J., & Milner, P. M. (1954). Positive reinforcement produced by electrical stimulation of septal area and other regions of the rat brain. *Journal of Comparative and Physiological Psychology, 47,* 419–427.

Oliver, M. B., & Hyde, J. S. (1993). Gender differences in sexuality: A meta-analysis. *Psychological Bulletin, 114,* 29–51.
Olness, K. (1993). Hypnosis: The power of attention. In D. Goleman & J. Gurin (Eds.), *Mind body medicine* (pp. 277–290). Yonkers, New York: Consumer Reports Books.
Olson, J. M. (1988). Misattribution, preparatory information, and speech anxiety. *Journal of Personality and Social Psychology, 54,* 758–767.
Olzak, S., & Nagel, J. (1986). *Competitive ethnic relations.* New York: Academic Press.
Ones, D. S., Viswesvaran, C., & Reiss, A. D. (1996). Role of social desirability in personality testing for personnel selection: The red herring. *Journal of Applied Psychology, 81,* 660–679.
Ones, D. S., Viswesvaran, C., & Schmidt, F. L. (1993). Comprehensive meta-analysis of integrity test validities: Findings and implications for personnel selection and theories of job performance. *Journal of Applied Psychology, 78,* 679–703.
Oren, D. (1995). *How to beat jet lag.* New York: Henry Holt.
Orne, M. T., & Evans, F. J. (1965). Social control in the psychological experiment: Antisocial behavior and hypnosis. *Journal of Personality and Social Psychology, 1,* 189–200.
Orne, M. T., Dinges, D. F., & Orne, E. C. (1984). The differential diagnosis of multiple personality in the forensic court. *International Journal of Clinical and Experimental Hypnosis, 32,* 118–169.
Ornstein, R. E. (1972). *The psychology of consciousness.* San Francisco: W. H. Freeman.
Ornstein, R. E. (1978). The split and whole brain. *Human Nature, 1,* 76–83.
Ornstein, R., & Sobel, D. (1987). *The healing brain.* New York: Simon & Schuster.
Ost, L.-G. (1989). One-session treatment for specific phobias. *Behavioral Research and Therapy, 27,* 1–7.
Ost, L.-G. (1992). Blood and injection phobia: Background and cognitive, physiological, and behavioral variables. *Journal of Abnormal Psychology, 101,* 68–74.
Ost, L.-G., Salkovskis, P. M., & Helistrom, K. (1991). One-session therapist-directed exposure vs. self-exposure in the treatment of spider phobia. *Behavior Therapy, 22,* 407–422.
Ostrom, T. M., & Sedikides, C. (1992). Out-group homogeneity effects in natural and minimal groups. *Psychological Bulletin, 112,* 536–552.
Ottati, V. C., Riggle, E. J., Wyer, R. S., Schwarz, N., & Kuklinski, J. (1989). Cognitive and affective bases of opinion survey responses. *Journal of Personality and Social Psychology, 57,* 404–415.
Otto, A. L., Penrod, S. D., & Dexter, H. R. (1994). The biasing impact of pretrial publicity on juror judgments. *Law and Human Behavior, 18,* 453–469.
Overman, W. H., Bachevalier, J., Schuhmann, E., & Ryan, P. (1996). Cognitive gender differences in very young children parallel biologically based cognitive gender differences in monkeys. *Behavioral Neuroscience, 110,* 673–684.

P.A.S.E. v. *Hannon,* 506 F. Supp. 931 (N. D. Ill. 1980).
Packard, V. (1957). *The hidden persuaders.* New York: Pocket Books.
Paffenbarger, R. S., Jr., Hyde, R. T., Wing, A. L., & Hsieh, C. (1986). Physical activity, all-cause mortality, and longevity of college alumni. *New England Journal of Medicine, 314,* 605–613.
Paivio, A. (1969). Mental imagery in associative learning and memory. *Psychological Review, 76,* 241–263.
Paivio, A. (1986). *Mental representations: A dual coding approach.* New York: Oxford University Press.
Palfai, T., & Jankiewicz, H. (1991). *Drugs and human behavior.* Dubuque, IA: William C. Brown.
Palmore, E. B. (1982). Predictors of the longevity difference: A 25-year follow-up. *The Gerontologist, 22,* 513–518.
Panskepp, J. (1986). The anatomy of emotions. In R. Plutchik & H. Kellerman (Eds.), *Emotion: Theory, research, and experience—Biological foundations of emotion* (Vol. 3, pp. 91–124). San Diego: Academic Press.
Panskepp, J. (1992). A critical role for "affective neuroscience" in resolving what is basic about basic emotions. *Psychological Review, 99,* 554–560.
Parducci, A. (1995). *Happiness, pleasure, and judgment: The contextual theory and its applications.* Mahwah, NJ: Erlbaum.
Park, B., & Judd, C. M. (1990). Measures and models of perceived group variability. *Journal of Personality and Social Psychology, 59,* 173–191.
Parke, R. D. (1981). *Fathers.* Cambridge, MA: Harvard University Press.
Parker, J. G., & Asher, S. R. (1987). Peer relations and later adjustment: Are low-accepted children "at risk"? *Psychological Bulletin, 102,* 357–389.
Parker, K., Hanson, R., & Hinsley, J. (1988). MMPI, Rorschach, and WAIS: A meta-analytic comparison of reliability, stability, and validity. *Psychological Bulletin, 103,* 367–373.
Parker, L. E., & Lepper, M. R. (1992). Effects of fantasy contexts on children's learning and motivation: Making learning more fun. *Journal of Personality and Social Psychology, 62,* 625–633.
Parks, R. W., Zee, R. F., & Wilson, R. S. (Eds.) (1993). *Neuropsychology of Alzheimer's disease and other dementias.* New York: Oxford University Press.
Parmelee, A. H., Jr., & Sigman, M. D. (1983). Perinatal brain development and behavior. In P. H. Mussen (Ed.), *Handbook of child psychology: Vol. 2. Infancy and developmental psychobiology.* New York: Wiley.
Pascalis, O., de Schonen, S., Morton, J., DeRuelle, C., & Fabre-Grenet, M. (1995). Mother's face recognition by neonates: A replication and an extension. *Infant Behavior and Development, 18,* 79–85.
Pascual-Leone, A., Camarota, A., Wassermann, E. M., et al. (1993). Modulation of motor cortical outputs to the reading hand of braille readers. *Annals of Neurology, 34,* 33–37.
Passman, R. H. (1987). Attachments to inanimate objects: Are children who have security blankets insecure? *Journal of Consulting and Clinical Psychology, 55,* 825–830.
Patrick, C. J., & Iacono, W. G. (1991). Validity of the control question polygraph test: The problem of sampling bias. *Journal of Applied Psychology, 76,* 229–238.
Patrick, C. J., Bradley, M. M., & Lang, P. J. (1993). Emotion in the criminal psychopath: Startle reflex modulation. *Journal of Abnormal Psychology, 102,* 82–92.
Patterson, F., & Linden, E. (1981). *The education of Koko.* New York: Holt, Rinehart & Winston.
Patterson, M. L. (1983). *Nonverbal behavior: A functional perspective.* New York: Springer-Verlag.
Paulesu, E., Harrison, J., Baron-Cohen, S., et al. (1995). The physiology of coloured hearing: A PET activation study of colour-word synesthesia. *Brain, 118,* 661–676.
Paulhus, D., Graf, P., & Van Selst, M. (1989). Attentional load increases the positivity of self-presentation. *Social Cognition, 7,* 389–400.
Paulos, J. A. (1988). *Innumeracy: Mathematical illiteracy and its consequences.* New York: Hill and Wang.
Paulus, P. B. (1988). *Prison crowding: A psychological perspective.* New York: Springer-Verlag.
Paunonen, S. V., Jackson, D. N., Trzebinski, J., & Fosterling, F. (1992). Personality structure across cultures: A multi-method evaluation. *Journal of Personality and Social Psychology, 62,* 447–456.
Pavlov, I. (1927). *Conditioned reflexes.* Oxford, England: Oxford University Press.
Pavot, W., & Diener, E. (1993). Review of the Satisfaction with Life Scale. *Psychological Assessment, 5,* 164–172.
Payne, J. W., Bettman, J. R., & Johnson, E. J. (1992). Behavioral decision research: A constructive processing approach. *Annual Review of Psychology, 43,* 87–131.
Pearce, J. M. (1987). A model for stimulus generalization in Pavlovian conditioning. *Psychological Review, 94,* 61–73.
Pederson, D. R., & Moran, G. (1996). Expressions of the attachment relationship outside the strange situation. *Child Development, 67,* 915–927.
Pelham, W. E. (1993). Pharmacotherapy for children with attention deficit hyperactivity disorder. *School Psychology Review, 22,* 199–227.
Pelham, W. E., Carlson, C. L., Sams, S. E., Vallano, G., et al. (1993). Separate and combined effects of methylphenidate and behavior modification on boys with attention deficit hyperactivity disorder in the classroom. *Journal of Consulting and Clinical Psychology, 61,* 506–515.
Penfield, W., & Perot, P. (1963). The brain's record of auditory and visual experience. *Brain, 86,* 595–696.
Penfield, W., & Roberts, L. (1959). *Speech and brain mechanisms.* Princeton, NJ: Princeton University Press.
Pennebaker, J. W. (1990). *Opening up: The healing power of confiding in others.* New York: Morrow.
Pennebaker, J. W. (1997). Writing about emotional experiences as a therapeutic process. *Psychological Science, 8,* 162–166.
Pepperberg, I. M. (1991). A communicative approach to animal cognition: A study of the conceptual abilities of an African grey parrot. In C. A. Ristau (Ed.), *Cognitive ethology: The minds of other animals* (pp. 153–186). Hillsdale, NJ: Erlbaum.
Pepperberg, I. M. (1994). Numerical competence in an African gray parrot. *Journal of Comparative Psychology, 108,* 36–44.
Pepperberg, I. M., & McLaughlin, M. A. (1996). Effect of avian-human joint attention on allospecific vocal learning by grey parrots *(Psittacus erithacus). Journal of Comparative Psychology, 110,* 286–297.
Perdue, C. W., Dovidio, J. F., Gurtman, M. B., & Tyler, R. B. (1990). Us and them: Social categorization and the process of intergroup bias. *Journal of Personality and Social Psychology, 59,* 475–486.
Perlow, M. J., Freed, W. J., Hoffer, B. J., Seiger, A., Olson, L., & Wyatt, R. J. (1979). Brain grafts reduce motor abnormalities produced by destruction of nigrostriatal dopamine system. *Science, 204,* 643–646.
Perls, F. S. (1969). *Gestalt therapy verbatim.* Lafayette, CA: Real People Press.
Perls, F. S., Heffertine, R. F., & Goodman, P. (1951). *Gestalt therapy.* New York: Julian Press.
Persky, V. W., Kempthorne-Rawson, J., & Shekelle, R. B. (1987). Personality and risk of cancer: 20-year follow-up of the Western Electric Study. *Psychosomatic Medicine, 49,* 435–449.
Pert, C. B., & Snyder, S. H. (1973). Opiate receptor: Demonstration in nervous tissue. *Science, 179,* 1011–1014.
Petersen, A. C. (1984). The early adolescence study: An overview. *Journal of Early Adolescence, 4,* 103–106.
Petersen, A. C. (1985). Pubertal development as a cause of disturbance: Myths, realities, and unanswered questions. *Genetic, Social, and General Psychology Monographs, 111,* 205–232.
Petersen, A. C. (1988). Adolescent development. *Annual Review of Psychology, 39,* 583–607.

Peterson, B. E., & Stewart, A. J. (1996). Antecedents and contexts of generativity motivation at midlife. *Psychology and Aging, 11,* 21–33.

Peterson, C., Seligman, M. E. P., & Vaillant, G. E. (1988). Pessimistic explanatory style is a risk factor for physical illness: A thirty-five-year longitudinal study. *Journal of Personality and Social Psychology, 55,* 23–27.

Peterson, D., & Goodall, J. (1993). *Visions of Caliban.* Boston: Houghton Mifflin.

Peterson, L. R., & Peterson, M. J. (1959). Short-term retention of individual verbal items. *Journal of Experimental Psychology, 58,* 193–198.

Peterson, S. E., & Fiez, J. A. (1993). The processing of single words studied with positron emission tomography. *Annual Review of Neuroscience, 16,* 509–530.

Peterson, S. E., Fox, P. T., Mintun, M. A., Posner, J. I., & Raichle, M. E. (1989). Studies of the processing of single words using averaged positron emission tomographic measurements of cerebral blood flow change. *Journal of Cognitive Neuroscience, 1,* 153–170.

Petty, M. M., Singleton, B., & Connell, D. W. (1992). An experimental evaluation of an organizational incentive plan in the electric utility industry. *Journal of Applied Psychology, 77,* 427–436.

Petty, R. E., & Cacioppo, J. T. (1986). *Communication and persuasion: Central and peripheral routes to attitude change.* New York: Springer-Verlag.

Petty, R. E., & Cacioppo, J. T. (1990). Involvement and persuasion: Tradition versus integration. *Psychological Bulletin, 107,* 367–374.

Petty, R. E., Wegener, D. T., & Fabrigar, L. R. (1997). Attitudes and attitude change. *Annual Review of Psychology, 48,* 609–647.

Pezdek, K., & Banks, W. P. (Eds.) (1996). *The recovered memory/false memory debate.* San Diego: Academic Press.

Pezdek, K., Whetstone, T., Reynolds, K., Askari, N., & Dougherty, T. (1989). Memory for real-world scenes: The role of consistency with schema expectation. *Journal of Experimental Psychology: Learning, Memory, and Cognition, 15,* 587–595.

Phares, E. J. (1976). *Locus of control in personality.* Morristown, NJ: General Learning Press.

Phelps, M. E., & Mazziotta, J. C. (1985). Positron-emission tomography: Human brain function and biochemistry. *Science, 228,* 799–809.

Phillips, A. P., & Dipboye, R. L. (1989). Correlational tests of predictions from a process model of the interview. *Journal of Applied Psychology, 74,* 41–52.

Phillips, D. P., & Feldman, K. A. (1973). A dip in deaths before ceremonial occasions: Some new relationships between social integration and mortality. *American Sociological Review, 38,* 678–696.

Phillips, D. P., Van Voorhees, C. A., & Ruth, T. E. (1992). The birth day: Lifeline or deadline? *Psychosomatic Medicine, 54,* 532–542.

Phillips, R. B., Sharma, R., Premachandra, B. R., Vaughn, A. J., & Reyes-Lee, M. (1996). Intrauterine exposure to cocaine: Effect on neurobehavior of neonates. *Infant Behavior and Development, 19,* 71–81.

Phinney, J. S. (1990). Ethnic identity in adolescents and adults: Review of research. *Psychological Bulletin, 108,* 499–514.

Phinney, J. S. (1996). When we talk about American ethnic groups, what do we mean? *American Psychologist, 51,* 918–927.

Piaget, J. (1932). *The moral judgment of the child.* New York: Harcourt, Brace & World.

Piaget, J. (1936). *The origins of intelligence in children.* New York: International University Press. (Reprinted in 1952.)

Piaget, J. (1932). *The moral judgment of the child.* New York: Free Press. (Reprinted in 1965.)

Piaget, J. (1976). *The grasp of consciousness: Action and concept in the young child.* Cambridge, MA: Harvard University Press.

Piaget, J., & Inhelder, B. (1969). *The psychology of the child.* New York: Basic Books.

Piccione, C., Hilgard, E. R., & Zimbardo, P. G. (1989). On the degree of stability of measured hypnotizability over a 25-year period. *Journal of Personality and Social Psychology, 56,* 289–295.

Piliavin, J. A., Dovidio, J. F., Gaertner, S. S., & Clark, R. D., III (1981). *Emergency intervention.* New York: Academic Press.

Pillemer, D. B., Picariello, M. L., & Pruett, J. C. (1994). Very long-term memories of a salient preschool event. Applied *Cognitive Psychology, 8,* 95–106.

Pillemer, D. B., Picariello, M. L., Law, A. B., & Reichman, J. S. (1996). Memories of college: The importance of educational episodes. In D. C. Rubin (Ed.), *Remembering our past: Studies in autobiographical memory* (pp. 318–337). New York: Cambridge University Press.

Pinker, S. (1994). *The language instinct: How the mind creates language.* New York: HarperCollins.

Pliner, P., & Chaiken, S. (1990). Eating, social motives, and self-presentation in men and women. *Journal of Experimental Social Psychology,* 26, 240–254.

Pliner, P., Pelchat, M., & Grabski, M. (1993). Reduction of neophobia in humans by exposure to novel foods. *Appetite, 20,* 111–123.

Plomin, R. (1988). The nature and nurture of cognitive abilities. In R. J. Sternberg (Ed.), *Advances in the psychology of human intelligence* (Vol. 4, pp. 1–33). Hillsdale, NJ: Erlbaum.

Plomin, R. (1989). Environment and genes: Determinants of behavior. *American Psychologist, 44,* 105–111.

Plomin, R., & McClearn, G. E. (Eds.). (1993). *Nature, nurture, and psychology.* Washington, DC: American Psychological Association.

Plomin, R., et al. (1993). Genetic change and continuity from fourteen to twenty months: The MacArthur longitudinal twin study. *Child Development, 64,* 1354–1376.

Plomin, R., Reiss, D., Hetherington, E. M., & Howe, G. W. (1994). Nature and nurture: Genetic contributions to measures of the family environment. *Developmental Psychology, 30,* 32–43.

Plous, S. (1991). An attitude survey of animal rights activists. *Psychological Science, 2,* 194–196.

Plous, S. (1996). Attitudes toward the use of animals in psychological research and education: Results from a national survey of psychology majors. *Psychological Science, 7,* 352–358.

Plutchik, R. (1980). *Emotion: A psychoevolutionary synthesis.* New York: Harper & Row.

Poincuré, H. (1929). *The foundations of science.* New York: Science House.

Poizner, H., Klima, E. S., & Bellugi, U. (1990). *What the hands reveal about the brain.* Cambridge, MA: MIT Press.

Poling, A., Schlinger, H. D., Jr., Starin, S., & Blakely, E. (1990). *Psychology: A behavioral overview.* New York: Plenum.

Poole, D. A., & White, L. T. (1991). Effects of question repetition on the eyewitness testimony of children and adults. *Developmental Psychology, 27,* 975–986.

Poole, G. D., & Craig, K. D. (1992). Judgments of genuine, suppressed, and faked facial expressions of pain. *Journal of Personality and Social Psychology, 63,* 797–805.

Pope, H. G., Jr., McElroy, S. L., Keck, P. E., Jr., & Hudson, J. I. (1991). Valproate in the treatment of acute mania. *Archives of General Psychiatry, 48,* 62–68.

Pope, K. S., & Vetter, V. A. (1992). Ethical dilemmas encountered by members of the American Psychological Association: A national survey. *American Psychologist, 47,* 397–411.

Popkin, J. (1994, March 14). Tricks of the trade. *U.S. News & World Report,* pp. 48–52.

Porac, C., & Coren, S. (1981). *Lateral preferences and human behavior.* New York: Springer-Verlag.

Porte, H. S., & Hobson, J. A. (1996). Physical motion in dreams: One measure of three theories. *Journal of Abnormal Psychology, 105,* 329–335.

Porter, D., & Neuringer, A. (1984). Music discrimination by pigeons. *Journal of Experimental Psychology: Animal Behavior Processes, 10,* 138–148.

Porter, N., Geis, F. L., Cooper, E., & Newman, E. (1985). Androgyny and leadership in mixed-sex groups. *Journal of Personality and Social Psychology, 49,* 808–823.

Porter, R. H., Makin, J. W., Davis, L. B., & Christensen, K. M. (1992). Breast-fed infants respond to olfactory cues from their own mother and unfamiliar lactating females. *Infant Behavior and Development, 15,* 85–93.

Posner, M. I., & Raichle, M. E. (1994). *Images of mind.* New York: Scientific American Library.

Poulson, C. L., et al. (1991). Generalized vocal imitation in infants. *Journal of Experimental Child Psychology, 51,* 267–279.

Powers, D. E. (1993). Coaching for the SAT: A summary of the summaries and an update. *Educational Measurement Issues and Practice, 12,* 24–30.

Powers, L. I., Hauser, S. T., & Kilner, L. A. (1989). Adolescent mental health. *American Psychologist, 44,* 200–208.

Pratkanis, A. R. (1992). The cargo-cult science of subliminal persuasion. *Skeptical Inquirer, 16,* 260–272.

Pratkanis, A. R., & Aronson, E. (1992). *Age of propaganda: The everyday use and abuse of persuasion.* San Francisco: W. H. Freeman.

Pratkanis, A. R., & Turner, M. E. (1994). Nine principles of successful affirmative action: Mr. Branch Rickey, Mr. Jackie Robinson, and the integration of baseball. *Nine: A Journal of Baseball History and Social Policy Perspectives, 3,* 36–65.

Pratkanis, A. R., Eskenazi, J., & Greenwald, A. G. (1994). What you expect is what you believe (but not necessarily what you get): A test of the effectiveness of subliminal self-help audiotapes. *Basic and Applied Social Psychology, 15,* 251–276.

Pratto, F., & Bargh, J. A. (1991). Stereotyping based on apparently individuating information: Trait and global components of sex stereotypes under attention overload. *Journal of Experimental Social Psychology, 27,* 26–47.

Pratto, F., Stallworth, L. M., Sidanius, J., & Siers, B. (1997). The gender gap in occupational role attainment: A social dominance approach. *Journal of Personality and Social Psychology, 72,* 37–53.

Premack, A., & Premack, D. (1983). *The mind of an ape.* New York: Norton.

Premack, D. (1971). Language in chimpanzee? *Science, 172,* 808–822.

Prentice, D. A., & Miller, D. T. (1996). Pluralistic ignorance and the perpetuation of social norms by unwitting actors. *Advances in Experimental Social Psychology, 28,* 161–209.

Prentice-Dunn, S., & Rogers, R. W. (1989). Deindividuation and the self-regulation of behavior. In P. B. Paulus (Ed.), *Psychology of group influence* (2nd ed.). Hillsdale, NJ: Erlbaum.

Previde, E. P., & Poli, M. D. (1996). Social learning in the golden hamster *(Mesocricetus auratus). Journal of Comparative Psychology, 110,* 203–208.

Prioleau, L., Murdock, M., & Brody, N. (1983). An analysis of psychotherapy versus placebo studies. *Behavioral and Brain Sciences, 6,* 275–310.

Pritchard, R. D., Jones, S. D., Roth, P. L., Stuebing, K. K., & Ekeberg, S. E. (1988). Effects of group feedback, goal setting, and incentives on organizational productivity. *Journal of Applied Psychology, 73,* 337–358.

Privette, G. (1983). Peak experience, peak performance, and flow: A comparative analysis of positive human experiences. *Journal of Personality and Social Psychology, 45,* 1361–1368.

Pullum, G. K. (1991). *The great Eskimo vocabulary hoax and other irreverent essays on the study of language.* Chicago: University of Chicago Press.
Purcell, P., & Stewart, L. (1990). Dick and Jane in 1989. *Sex Roles, 22,* 177–185.
Purvis, A. (1997, January 6). The global epidemic. *Time,* pp. 76–78.
Putnam, F. W., Guroff, J. J., Silberman, E. K., Barban, L., & Post, R. M. (1986). The clinical phenomenology of multiple personality disorder: 100 recent cases. *Journal of Clinical Psychiatry, 47,* 285–293.
Pyszczynski, T., & Greenberg, J. (1987). Self-regulatory preservation and the depressive self-focusing style: A self-awareness theory of reactive depression. *Psychological Bulletin, 201,* 122–138.

Quinn, P. C., Burke, S., & Rush, A. (1993). Part-whole perception in early infancy: Evidence for perceptual grouping produced by lightness similarity. *Infant Behavior and Development, 16,* 19–42.

Rachman, S. J. (1990). *Fear and courage* (2nd ed.). San Francisco: W. H. Freeman.
Rachman, S., & Maser, J. D. (Eds.) (1988). *Panic: Psychological perspectives.* Hillsdale, NJ: Erlbaum.
Radford, J. (1990). *Child prodigies and exceptional early achievers.* New York: Free Press.
Rafaeli, A., & Klimoski, R. J. (1983). Predicting sales success through handwriting analysis: An evaluation of the effects of training and handwriting sample context. *Journal of Applied Psychology, 68,* 212–217.
Ragins, B. R., & Sundstrom, E. (1989). Gender and power in organizations: A longitudinal perspective. *Psychological Bulletin, 105,* 51–88.
Raichle, M. E. (1994). Images of the mind: Studies with modern imaging techniques. *Annual Review of Psychology, 45,* 333–356.
Rajaram, S., & Roediger, H. L., III. (1993). Direct comparisons of four implicit memory tests. *Journal of Experimental Psychology: Learning, Memory, and Cognition, 19,* 765–776.
Rajecki, D. W., Bledsoe, S. B., & Rasmussen, J. L. (1991). Successful personal ads: Gender differences and similarities in offers, stipulations, and outcomes. *Basic and Applied Social Psychology, 12,* 457–469.
Raloff, J. (1982). Noise can be hazardous to your health. *Science News, 121,* 377–381.
Ralph, M. R., Foster, R. G., Davis, F. C., & Menaker, M. (1990). Transplanted suprachiasmatic nucleus determines circadian period. *Science, 247,* 975–978.
Ramey, C. T., Bryant, D. M., Wasik, B. H., Sparling, J. J., Fendt, K. H., & LaVange, L. M. (1992). Infant health and development program for low weight, premature infants: Program elements, family participation, and child intelligence. *Pediatrics, 89,* 454–465.
Randi, J. (1980). *Flim-Flam: The truth about unicorns, para-psychology, and other delusions.* New York: Lippincott & Crowell.
Rapoport, J. L. (1989). *The boy who couldn't stop washing: The experience and treatment of obsessive-compulsive disorder.* New York: Plume.
Raskin, D. C. (1986). The polygraph in 1986: Scientific, professional, and legal issues surrounding application and acceptance of polygraph evidence. *Utah Law Review,* 29–74.
Raskin, N. J. (1985). Client-centered therapy. In S. Lynn & J. Garske (Eds.), *Contemporary psychotherapies: Models and methods* (pp. 155–190). Columbus, OH: Charles E. Merrill.
Raskin, N. J. (1996). The case of Loretta: A psychiatric inpatient. In B. A. Farber, D. C. Brink, & P. M. Raskin (Eds.). *The psychotherapy of Carl Rogers: Cases and commentary* (pp. 44–56). New York: Guilford Press.
Rasmussen, B. K., Jensen, R., Schroll, M., & Olesen, J. (1991). Epidemiology of headache in a general population—a prevalence study. *Journal of Clinical Epidemiology, 44,* 1147–1157.
Raven, J. C., Court, J. H., & Raven, J. (1985). *A manual for Raven's progressive matrices and vocabulary scales.* London: H. K. Lewis.
Ray, W. J. (1996). Dissociation in normal populations. In L. K. Michelson & W. J. Ray (Eds.), *Handbook of dissociation: Theoretical, empirical, and clinical perspectives* (pp. 51–68). New York: Plenum.
Raz, S., & Raz, N. (1990). Structural brain abnormalities in the major psychoses: A quantitative review of the evidence from computerized imaging. *Psychological Bulletin, 108,* 93–108.
Read, J. D. (1996). From a passing thought to a false memory in 2 minutes: Confusing real and illusory events. *Psychonomic Bulletin & Review, 3,* 105–111.
Reber, A. S. (1985). *The Penguin dictionary of psychology.* New York: Viking.
Reber, A. S. (1993). *Implicit learning and tacit knowledge: An essay on the cognitive unconscious.* New York: Oxford University Press.
Rechtschaffen, A., & Bergmann, B. M. (1995). Sleep deprivation in the rat by the disk-over-water method. *Behavioural Brain Research, 69,* 55–63.
Redelmeier, D. A., & Tibshirani, R. J. (1997). Association between cellular-telephone calls and motor vehicle collisions. *New England Journal of Medicine, 336,* 453–458.
Reed, C. F., & Krupinski, E. A. (1992). The target in the celestial (moon) illusion. *Journal of Experimental Psychology: Human Perception and Performance, 18,* 247–256.
Reed, G. M., Taylor, S. E., & Kemeny, M. E. (1993). Perceived control and psychological adjustment in gay men with AIDS. *Journal of Applied Social Psychology, 23,* 791–824.
Reed, P., & Richards, A. (1996). The von Restorff effect in rats *(Rattus norvegicus). Journal of Comparative Psychology, 110,* 193–198.
Reed, S. B., Kirsch, I., Wickless, C., Moffitt, K. H., & Taren, P. (1996). Reporting biases in hypnosis: Suggestion or compliance? *Journal of Abnormal Psychology, 105,* 142–145.
Reed, T. E., & Jensen, A. R. (1992). Conduction velocity in a brain nerve pathway of normal adults correlates with intelligence level. *Intelligence, 16,* 259–272.
Regan, P. C., & Berscheid, E. (1997). Gender differences in characteristics desired in a potential sexual and marriage partner. *Journal of Psychology & Human Sexuality, 9,* 25–37.
Regier, D. A., Narrow, W., Rae, D., Manderschied, R., Locke, B., & Goodwin, F. (1993). The de facto U. S. mental and addictive disorders service system: Epidemiologic catchment area prospective 1-year prevalence rates of disorders and services. *Archives of General Psychiatry, 50,* 85–94.
Reifman, A. S., Larrick, R. P., & Fein, S. (1991). Temper and temperature on the diamond: The heat-aggression relationship in major league baseball. *Personality and Social Psychology Bulletin, 17,* 580–585.
Reis, S. M. (1989). Reflections on policy affecting the education of gifted and talented students: Past and future perspectives. *American Psychologist, 44,* 399–408.
Reisberg, D. (1997). *Cognition: Exploring the science of the mind.* New York: Norton.
Reisenzein, R. (1983). The Schachter theory of emotion: Two decades later. *Psychological Bulletin, 94,* 239–264.
Reisenzein, R. (1994). Pleasure-arousal theory and the intensity of emotions. *Journal of Personality and Social Psychology, 67,* 525–539.
Reiser, M. (1980). *Handbook of investigative hypnosis.* Los Angeles: LEHI.
Reiser, M., & Nielson, M. (1980). Investigative hypnosis: A developing specialty. *American Journal of Clinical Hypnosis, 23,* 75–83.
Reissland, N. (1988). Neonatal imitation in the first hour of life: Observations in rural Nepal. *Developmental Psychology, 24,* 464–469.
Remley, A. (1988, October). The great parental value shift: From obedience to independence. *Psychology Today,* pp. 56–59.
Renault, E. M., Signoret, J. L., Debruille, B., Breton, F., & Bolgert, F. (1989). Brain potentials reveal covert facial recognition in prosopagnosia. *Neuropsychologia, 27,* 905–912.
Renzulli, J. S. (1986). The three-ring conception of giftedness: A developmental model for creative productivity. In R. J. Sternberg & J. E. Davidson (Eds.), *Conceptions of giftedness* (pp. 53–92). New York: Cambridge University Press.
Rescorla, R. A. (1968). Probability of shock in the presence and absence of CS in fear conditioning. *Journal of Comparative and Physiological Psychology, 66,* 1–5.
Rescorla, R. A. (1980). *Pavlovian second-order conditioning.* Hillsdale, NJ: Erlbaum.
Rescorla, R. A. (1987). A Pavlovian analysis of goal-directed behavior. *American Psychologist, 42,* 119–129.
Rescorla, R. A. (1988). Pavlovian conditioning: It's not what you think it is. *American Psychologist, 43,* 151–160.
Resnick, L. R. (1989). Developing mathematical knowledge. *American Psychologist, 44,* 162–169.
Resnick, S. M. (1992). Positron emission tomography in psychiatric illness. *Current Directions in Psychological Science, 1,* 92–98.
Rest, J. R. (1986). *Moral development: Advances in research and theory.* New York: Praeger.
Restak, R. M. (1988). *The mind.* New York: Bantam.
Retterstol, N. (1993). *Suicide: A European perspective.* New York: Cambridge University Press.
Reuman, D. A. (1989). How social comparison mediates the relation between ability-grouping practices and students' achievement expectancies in mathematics. *Journal of Educational Psychology, 81,* 178–189.
Rhee, E., Uleman, J. S., Lee, H. K., & Roman, R. J. (1995). Spontaneous self-descriptions and ethnic identities in individualistic and collectivistic cultures. *Journal of Personality and Social Psychology, 69,* 142–152.
Rhoden, W. C. (1996, December 24). A two-hour psychological test turns into Giants' lightning rod. *The New York Times,* pp. B1, B10.
Rhodes, G., & Tremewan, T. (1996). Averageness, exaggeration, and facial attractiveness. *Psychological Science, 7,* 105–110.
Rhodes, S. R. (1983). Age-related differences in work attitudes and behavior: A review and conceptual analysis. *Psychological Bulletin, 93,* 328–367.
Rhodewalt, F., Morf, C., Hazlett, S., & Fairfield, M. (1991). Self-handicapping: The role of discounting and augmentation in the preservation of self-esteem. *Journal of Personality and Social Psychology, 61,* 122–131.
Rhue, J. W., Lynn, S. J., & Kirsch, I. (Eds.) (1993). *Handbook of clinical hypnosis.* Washington, DC: American Psychological Association.
Rice, C., Koinis, D., Sullivan, K., Tager-Flusberg, H., & Winner, H. (1997). When 3-year-olds pass the appearance-reality test. *Developmental Psychology, 33,* 54–61.
Rice, M. L. (1989). Children's language acquisition. *American Psychologist, 44,* 149–156.

Rice, M. L., Huston, A. C., Truglio, R., & Wright, J. (1990). Words from "Sesame Street": Learning vocabulary while viewing. *Developmental Psychology, 26,* 421–428.

Richardson, J. T. E., & Zucco, G. M. (1989). Cognition and olfaction: A review. *Psychological Bulletin, 105,* 352–360.

Richardson, T. M., & Benbow, C. P. (1990). Long-term effects of acceleration on the social-emotional adjustment of mathematically precocious youths. *Journal of Educational Psychology, 82,* 464–470.

Riefer, D. M., & Rouder, J. N. (1992). A multinomial modeling analysis of the mnemonic benefits of bizarre imagery. *Memory and Cognition, 20,* 601–611.

Rilling, M. (1996). The mystery of vanished citations: James McConnell's forgotten 1960s quest for planarian learning, a biochemical engram, and celebrity. *American Psychologist, 51,* 589–598.

Rimmele, C. T., Howard, M. O., & Hilfrink, M. L. (1995). Aversion therapies. In R. K. Hester & W. R. Miller (Eds.). *Handbook of alcoholism treatment approaches: Effective alternatives* (2nd ed.) (pp. 134–147). Boston: Allyn & Bacon.

Rips, L. J. (1975). Inductive judgments about natural categories. *Journal of Verbal Learning and Verbal Behavior, 14,* 665–681.

Ristau, C. A. (Ed.) (1991). *Cognitive ethology: The minds of other animals.* Hillsdale, NJ: Erlbaum.

Ritter, P. L., & Dornbusch, S. M. (1989, March). *Ethnic variation in family influences on academic achievement.* Paper presented at the American Educational Research Association Meeting, San Francisco.

Robins, C. J., & Hayes, A. M. (1993). An appraisal of cognitive therapy. *Journal of Consulting and Clinical Psychology, 61,* 205–214.

Robins, L. N., & Regier, D. A. (Eds.) (1991). *Psychiatric disorders in America: The epidemiologic catchment area study.* New York: Free Press.

Robinson, I., Ziss, K., Ganza, B., Katz, S., & Robinson, E. (1991). Twenty years of the sexual revolution, 1965–1985: An update. *Journal of Marriage and the Family, 53,* 216–220.

Robinson, J. L., Kagan, J., Reznick, J. S., & Corley, R. (1992). The heritability of inhibited and uninhibited behavior: A twin study. *Developmental Psychology, 28,* 1030–1037.

Rochat, P. (1989). Object manipulation and exploration in 2- to 5-month-old infants. *Developmental Psychology, 25,* 871–884.

Rock, I. (1997). *Indirect perception.* Cambridge, MA: MIT Press.

Rock, I., & Palmer, S. (1990). The legacy of Gestalt psychology. *Scientific American,* 84–90.

Rodgers, J. E. (1992). *Psychosurgery: Damaging the brain to save the mind.* New York: HarperCollins.

Rodgers, J. L. (1996). Sexual transitions in adolescence. In J. A. Graber, J. Brooks-Gunn, & A. C. Petersen, (Eds.), *Transitions through adolescence: Interpersonal domains and context* (pp. 85–110). Mahwah, NJ: Erlbaum.

Rodgers, J. L., & Rowe, D. C. (1993). Social contagion and adolescent sexual behavior: A developmental EMOSA model. *Psychological Review, 100,* 479–510.

Rodin, J. (1986). Aging and health: Effects of the sense of control. *Science, 233,* 1271–1276.

Roediger, H. L., III. (1990). Implicit memory: Retention without remembering. *American Psychologist, 45,* 1043–1056.

Roediger, H. L., III. & McDermott, K. B. (1995). Creating false memories: Remembering words not presented in lists. *Journal of Experimental Psychology: Learning, Memory, and Cognition, 21,* 803–814.

Roese, N. J., & Olson, J. M. (Eds.) (1995). *What might have been: The social psychology of counterfactual thinking.* Mahwah, NJ: Erlbaum.

Roethlisberger, F. J., & Dickson, W. J. (1939). *Management and the worker.* Cambridge, MA: Harvard University Press.

Roffwarg, H. P., Muzio, J. N., & Dement, W. C. (1966). Ontogenetic development of the human sleep-dream cycle. *Science, 152,* 604–619.

Rogers, C. R. (1951). *Client-centered therapy.* Boston: Houghton Mifflin.

Rogers, C. R. (1961). *On becoming a person.* Boston: Houghton Mifflin.

Rogers, C. R. (1963). Actualizing tendency in relation to "motives" and to consciousness. In M. Jones (Ed.), *Nebraska symposium on motivation.* Lincoln: University of Nebraska Press.

Rogers, C. R. (1970). *Carl Rogers on encounter groups.* New York: Harper & Row.

Rogers, C. R. (1974). In retrospect: Forty-six years. *American Psychologist, 29,* 115–123.

Rogers, P. (1993, February 15). How many gays are there? *Newsweek,* p. 46.

Rogers, R. (1988). *Clinical assessment of malingering and deception.* New York: Guilford Press.

Rogers, R. W. (1983). Cognitive and psychological processes in fear appeals and attitude change: A revised theory of protection motivation. In J. Cacioppo & R. Petty (Eds.), *Social psychophysiology: A sourcebook* (pp. 153–176). New York: Guilford Press.

Rogers, T. B., Kuiper, N. A., & Kirker, W. S. (1977). Self-reference and the encoding of personal information. *Journal of Personality and Social Psychology, 35,* 677–688.

Rogoff, B., & Morelli, G. (1989). Perspectives on children's development from cultural psychology. *American Psychologist, 44,* 343–348.

Romney, A. K., Brewer, D. D., & Batchelder, W. H. (1993). Predicting clustering from semantic structure. *Psychological Science, 4,* 28–34.

Roper Reports (1989, May).

Rorschach, H. (1921). *Psychodiagnostik.* Bern, Switzerland: Bircher.

Rosch, E. (1973). On the internal structure of perceptual and semantic categories. In T. E. Moore (Ed.). *Cognitive development and the acquisition of language.* New York: Academic Press.

Rosch, E. (1975). Cognitive representations of semantic categories. *Journal of Experimental Psychology: General, 104,* 192–223.

Roseman, I. J., Spindel, M. S., & Jose, P. E. (1990). Appraisals of emotion-eliciting events: Testing a theory of discrete emotions. *Journal of Personality and Social Psychology, 59,* 899–915.

Rosen, R. C., & Ashton, A. K. (1993). Psychosexual drugs: Empirical status of the "new aphrodisiacs." *Archives of Sexual Behavior, 22,* 521–543.

Rosener, J. B. (1990). Ways women lead. *Harvard Business Review, 68,* 119–125.

Rosenfeld, A., & Stark, E. (1986, May). The prime of our lives. *Psychology Today,* pp. 62–72.

Rosenfeld, J. P. (1995). Alternative views of Bashore and Rapp's alternatives to traditional polygraphy: A critique. *Psychological Bulletin, 117,* 159–166.

Rosenfield, P., Lambert, N. M., & Black, A. (1985). Desk arrangement effects on pupil classroom behavior. *Journal of Educational Psychology, 77,* 101–108.

Rosenhan, D. L. (1973). On being sane in insane places. *Science, 179,* 250–258.

Rosenman, R. H., Brand, R. J., Jenkins, C. D., Friedman, M., Strau, R., & Wurm, M. (1975). Coronary heart disease in the Western Collaborative Group Study: Final follow-up experience of $8\frac{1}{2}$ years. *Journal of the American Medical Association, 233,* 872–877.

Rosenstein, D., & Oster, H. (1988). Differential facial responses to four basic tastes in newborns. *Child Development, 59,* 1555–1568.

Rosenthal, N. E. (1993). *Winter blues: Seasonal affective disorder, what it is and how to overcome it.* New York: Guilford Press.

Rosenthal, R. (1985). From unconscious experimenter bias to teacher expectancy effects. In J. B. Dusek, V. C. Hall, & W. J. Meyer (Eds.), *Teacher expectancies.* Hillsdale, NJ: Erlbaum.

Rosenthal, R. (1991). *Meta-analytic procedures for social research* (2nd ed.). Newbury Park, CA: Sage.

Rosenthal, R., & Jacobson, L. (1968). *Pygmalion in the classroom: Teacher expectation and pupils' intellectual development.* New York: Holt, Rinehart & Winston.

Rosenzweig, M. R. (1984). Experience, memory, and the brain. *American Psychologist, 39,* 365–376.

Rosenzweig, M. R. (1996). Aspects of the search for neural mechanisms of memory. *Annual Review of Psychology, 47,* 1–32.

Rosnow, R. L., Rotheram-Borus, M. J., Ceci, S. J., Blanck, P. D., & Koocher, G. P. (1993). The institutional review board as a mirror of scientific and ethical standards. *American Psychologist, 48,* 821–826.

Ross, C. A. (1994). *The Osiris complex: Case studies in multiple personality disorder.* Toronto: University of Toronto Press.

Ross, C. A. (1997). *Dissociative identity disorder.* New York: Wiley.

Ross, C. A., Joshi, S., & Currie, R. (1990). Dissociative experiences in the general population. *American Journal of Psychiatry, 147,* 1547–1552.

Ross, C. A., Miller, S. D., Reagor, P., Bjornson, L., Fraser, G. A., & Anderson, G. (1990). Structured interview data on 102 cases of multiple personality disorder from four centers. *American Journal of Psychiatry, 147,* 596–601.

Ross, D. F., Read, J. D., & Toglia, M. P. (Eds.) (1994). *Adult eyewitness testimony: Current trends and developments.* New York: Cambridge University Press.

Ross, L. (1977). The intuitive psychologist and his shortcomings: Distortions in the attribution process. In L. Berkowitz (Ed.), *Advances in experimental social psychology* (Vol. 10). New York: Academic Press.

Ross, L., Amabile, T. M., & Steinmetz, J. L. (1977). Social roles, social control, and biases in social-perception processes. *Journal of Personality and Social Psychology, 35,* 485–494.

Ross, M. (1989). The relation of implicit theories to the construction of personal histories. *Psychological Review, 96,* 341–357.

Ross, M., & Sicoly, F. (1979). Egocentric biases in availability and attribution. *Journal of Personality and Social Psychology, 37,* 322–336.

Ross, R. T., & LoLordo, V. M. (1987). Evaluation of the relation between Pavlovian occasion-setting and instrumental discriminative stimuli. *Journal of Experimental Psychology: Animal Behavior Processes, 13,* 3–16.

Roth, T., Roehrs, T., & Zorick, F. (1987). Sleep disorders. In G. Adelman (Ed.), *Encyclopedia of neuroscience.* Boston: Birkhauser.

Rothbaum, B. O., Hodges, L. F., Kooper, R., Opdyke, D., Williford, J. S., & North, M. (1995). Effectiveness of computer-generated (virtual reality) graded exposure in the treatment of acrophobia. *American Journal of Psychiatry, 152,* 626–628.

Rotter, J. B. (1954). *Social learning and clinical psychology.* Englewood Cliffs, NJ: Prentice-Hall.

Rotter, J. B. (1966). Generalized expectancies for internal versus external control of reinforcement. *Psychological Monographs, 80* (Whole No. 609).

Rotter, J. B. (1990). Internal versus external control of reinforcement: A case history of a variable. *American Psychologist, 45,* 489–493.

Rotter, J. B., Chance, J. E., & Phares, E. J. (Eds.) (1972). *Applications of a social learning theory of personality.* New York: Holt, Rinehart & Winston.

Rousseau, D. L. (1992). Case studies in pathological science. *American Scientist, 80,* 54–63.

Rovee-Collier, C. (1988). The joy of kicking: Memories, motives, and mobiles. In P. Solomon, G. Goethals, C. Kelley, & B. Stephens (Eds.), *Memory; Interdisciplinary approaches*. New York: Springer-Verlag.

Rovee-Collier, C., Hankins, E., & Bhatt, R. (1992). Textons, visual pop-out effects, and object recognition in infancy. *Journal of Experimental Psychology: General, 121,* 435–445.

Rowe, D. C. (1994). *The limits of family influence: Genes, experience, and behavior.* New York: Guilford Press

Rozee, P. D., & Van Boemel, G. V. (1989). The psychological effects of war trauma and abuse on older Cambodian refugee women. *Women and Therapy, 8,* 23–50.

Rozin, E. (1983). *Ethnic cuisine: The flavor-principle cookbook.* Brattleboro, VT: Stephen Greene Press.

Rozin, P., & Fallon, A. E. (1987). A perspective on disgust. *Psychological Review, 94,* 23–41.

Rubin, D. C. (Ed.) (1996). *Remembering our past: Studies in autobiographical memory.* New York: Cambridge University Press.

Rubin, D. C., & Kozin, M. (1986). Vivid memories. *Cognition, 16,* 81–95.

Rubin, D. C., & Wenzel, A. E. (1996). One hundred years of forgetting: A quantitative description of retention. *Psychological Review, 103,* 734–760.

Rubin, J. Z., Provenzano, F. J., & Luria, Z. (1974). The eye of the beholder: Parents' views on sex of newborns. *American Journal of Orthopsychiatry, 44,* 512–519.

Ruble, D. N., & Brooks-Gunn, J. (1982). The experience of menarche. *Child Development, 53,* 1557–1566.

Rubonis, A. V., & Bickman, L. (1991). Psychological impairment in the wake of disaster: The disaster-psychopathology relationship. *Psychological Bulletin, 109,* 384–399.

Ruderman, A. J., & Besbeas, M. (1992). Psychological characteristics of dieters and bulimics. *Journal of Abnormal Psychology, 101,* 383–390.

Rule, B. G., Taylor, B. R., & Dobbs, A. R. (1987). Priming effects of heat on aggressive thoughts. *Social Cognition, 5,* 131–143.

Rumbaugh, D. M. (1977). *Language learning by a chimpanzee: The Lana project.* New York: Academic Press.

Rumelhart, D. E., & McClelland, J. L. (1986). On learning the past tenses of English verbs. In J. L. McClelland & D. E. Rumelhart (Eds.), *Parallel distributed processing: Explorations in the microstructure of cognition: Vol 2. Psychological and biological models* (pp. 216–271). Cambridge, MA: MIT Press.

Rumelhart, D. E., McClelland, J. L., & the PDP Research Group (1986). *Parallel distributed processing: Vol. 1. Foundations.* Cambridge, MA: MIT Press.

Ruscher, J. B., & Fiske, S. T. (1990). Interpersonal competition can cause individuating processes. *Journal of Personality and Social Psychology, 58,* 832–843.

Rushton, J. P. (1989). Genetic similarity, human altruism, and group selection. *Behavioral and Brain Sciences, 12,* 503–559.

Rushton, J. P., & Ankney, C. D. (1996). Brain size and cognitive ability: Correlations with age, sex, social class, and race. *Psychonomic Bulletin & Review, 3,* 21–36.

Russell, J. A. (1980). A circumplex model of affect. *Journal of Personality and Social Psychology, 39,* 1161–1178.

Russell, J. A. (1991). Culture and the categorization of emotions. *Psychological Bulletin, 110,* 426–450.

Russell, J. A. (1994). Is there universal recognition of emotion from facial expression? A review of cross-cultural studies. *Psychological Bulletin, 115,* 102–141.

Russell, J. A. (1995). Facial expressions of emotion: What lies beyond minimal universality? *Psychological Bulletin, 118,* 379–391.

Russell, M. J. (1976). Human olfactory communication. *Nature (London), 260,* 520–522.

Russell, R. L., & Orlinsky, D. E. (1996). Psychotherapy research in historical perspective: Implications for mental health care policy. *Archives of General Psychiatry, 53,* 708–715.

Russon, A. E., Bard, K. A., & Parker, S. T. (Eds.) (1996). *Reaching into thought: The minds of the great apes.* New York: Cambridge University Press.

Ruvolo, A., & Markus, H. (1992). Possible selves and performance: The power of self-relevant imagery. *Social Cognition, 9,* 95–124.

Ryckman, R. M., Robbins, M. A., Kazcor, L. M., & Gold, J. A. (1989). Male and female raters' stereotyping of male and female physiques. *Personality and Social Psychology Bulletin, 15,* 244–251.

Ryff, C. D. (1989). In the eye of the beholder: Views of psychological well-being among middle-aged and older adults. *Psychology and Aging, 4,* 195–210.

Saal, F. E., Johnson, C. B., & Weber, N. (1989). Friendly or sexy? Friendly or sex? It may depend on whom you ask. *Psychology of Women Quarterly, 13,* 263–276.

Sacco, W. P., & Dunn, V. K. (1990). Effect of actor depression on observer attributions: Existence and impact of negative attributions toward the depressed. *Journal of Personality and Social Psychology, 59,* 517–524.

Sachs, J. (1967). Recognition memory for syntactic and semantic aspects of connected discourse. *Perception and Psychophysics, 2,* 437–442.

Sack, R. L., Lewy, A. J., White, D. M., Singer, C. M., Fireman, M. J., & Vandiver, R. (1990). Morning vs. evening light treatment for winter depression: Evidence that the therapeutic effects of light are mediated by circadian phase shift. *Archives of General Psychiatry, 47,* 343–351.

Sackeim, H. A. (1988). Mechanisms of action of electroconvulsive therapy. In A. J. Francis & R. E. Hales (Eds.), *Review of Psychiatry* (Vol. 7). Washington, DC: American Psychiatric Press.

Sacks, O. (1983). *Awakenings.* New York: Dutton.

Sacks, O. (1985). *The man who mistook his wife for a hat and other clinical tales.* New York: Summit Books.

Sacks, O. (1995). *An anthropologist on Mars: Seven paradoxical tales.* New York: Knopf.

Sagar, H. A., & Schofield, J. W. (1980). Racial and behavioral cues in black and white children's perceptions of ambiguously aggressive acts. *Journal of Personality and Social Psychology, 39,* 590–598.

Salgado, J. F. (1997). The five factor model of personality and job performance in the European community. *Journal of Applied Psychology, 82,* 30–43.

Salovey, P. (Ed.) (1991). *The psychology of jealousy and envy.* New York: Guilford Press.

Salthouse, T. A. (1984). Effects of age and skill in typing. *Journal of Experimental Psychology: General, 113,* 345–371.

Salthouse, T. A. (1992). Why do adult age differences increase with task complexity? *Developmental Psychology, 28,* 905–918.

Salthouse, T. A. (1996). The processing-speed theory of adult age differences in cognition. *Psychological Review, 103,* 403–428.

Salthouse, T. A., Hambrick, D. Z., Lukas, K. E., & Dell, T. C. (1996). Determinants of adult age differences on synthetic work performance. *Journal of Experimental Psychology: Applied, 2,* 305–329.

Sams, M., Hari, R., Rif, J., & Knuutila, J. (1993). The human auditory memory trace persists about 10 sec: Neuromagnetic evidence. *Journal of Cognitive Neuroscience, 5,* 363–370.

Sanchez, J. I., & Fernandez, D. M. (1993). Acculturative stress among Hispanics: A bidimensional model of ethnic identification. *Journal of Applied Social Psychology, 23,* 654–668.

Sanderson, D. W. (1993). *Smileys.* Sebastopol, CA: O'Reilly.

Sanderson, W. C., DiNardo, P. A., Rapee, R. M., & Barlow, D. H. (1990). Syndrome comorbidity in patients diagnosed with a DSMIII-R anxiety disorder. *Journal of Abnormal Psychology, 99,* 308–312.

Sansavini, A., Bertoncini, J., & Giovanelli, G. (1997). Newborns discriminate the rhythm of multisyllabic stressed words. *Developmental Psychology, 33,* 3–11.

Sapir, E. (1941). *Language, culture, and personality: Essays in honor of Edward Sapir* (L. Sapir, Ed.). Menasha, WI: Sapir Memorial Publication Fund.

Sapolsky, R. M. (1994). *Why zebras don't get ulcers: A guide to stress, diseases, and coping.* New York: W. H. Freeman.

Sarbin, T. R. (1992). Accounting for "dissociative" actions without invoking mentalistic constructs. *Consciousness and Cognition, 1,* 54–58.

Sarter, M., Bernston, G. G., & Cacioppo, J. T. (1996). Brain imaging and cognitive neuroscience: Toward strong inference in attributing function to structure. *American Psychologist, 51,* 13–21.

Sary, G., Vogels, R., & Orban, G. A. (1993). Cue-invariant shape selectivity of macaque inferior temporal neurons. *Science, 260,* 995–997.

Savage-Rumbaugh, S. (1990). Language acquisition in a nonhuman species: Implications for the innateness debate. *Developmental Psychobiology, 23,* 599–620.

Savage-Rumbaugh, S., Murphy, J., Sevcik, R. A., Brakke, K. E., Williams, S. L., & Rumbaugh, D. M. (1993). Language comprehension in ape and child. *Monographs of the Society for Research in Child Development, 58* (3–4, Serial No. 233).

Saxe, L., Dougherty, D., & Cross, T. (1985). The validity of polygraph testing: Scientific analysis and public controversy. *American Psychologist, 38,* 355–366.

Scarr, S. (1986). *Mother care/other care.* New York: Basic Books.

Scarr, S., & McCartney, K. (1983). How people make their own environments: A theory of genotype → environment effects. *Child Development, 54,* 424–435.

Scarr, S., & Weinberg, R. A. (1976). I.Q. test performance of black children adopted by white families. *American Psychologist, 31,* 726–739.

Scarr, S., & Weinberg, R. A. (1983). The Minnesota adoption studies: Genetic differences and malleability. *Child Development, 54,* 260–267.

Schab, F. R. (1990). Odors and the remembrance of things past. *Journal of Experimental Psychology: Learning, Memory, and Cognition, 16,* 648–655.

Schab, F. R., & Crowder, R. G. (Eds.) (1995). *Memory for odors.* Mahwah, NJ: Erlbaum.

Schachter, S. (1959). *The psychology of affiliation.* Palo Alto, CA: Stanford University Press.

Schachter, S. (1964). The interaction of cognitive and physiological determinants of emotional state. In L. Berkowitz (Ed.), *Advances in experimental social psychology* (Vol. 1, pp. 49–80). New York: Academic Press.

Schachter, S., & Gross, L. (1968). Manipulated time and eating behavior. *Journal of Personality and Social Psychology, 10,* 98–106.

Schachter, S., & Singer, J. E. (1962). Cognitive, social, and physiological determinants of emotional state. *Psychological Review, 69,* 379–399.

Schacter, D. L. (1986). Amnesia and crime: How much do we really know? *American Psychologist, 41,* 286–295.

Schacter, D. L. (1987). Implicit memory: History and current status. *Journal of Experimental Psychology: Learning, Memory, and Cognition, 13,* 501–518.

Schacter, D. L. (1992). Understanding implicit memory: A cognitive neuroscience approach. *American Psychologist, 47,* 559–569.
Schacter, D. L. (1996). *Searching for memory.* New York: Basic Books.
Schacter, D. L., Reiman, E., Curran, T., Yun, L. S., Bandy, D., McDermott, K. B., & Roediger, H. L. (1996). Neuroanatomical correlates of veridical and illusory recognition memory: Evidence from positron emission tomography. *Neuron, 17,* 267–274.
Schaie, K. W. (1989). Perceptual speed in adulthood: Cross-sectional and longitudinal studies. *Psychology and Aging, 4,* 443–453.
Schaie, K. W. (1996). *Intellectual development in adulthood: The Seattle Longitudinal Study.* New York: Cambridge University Press.
Schaie, K. W. (Ed.) (1983). *Longitudinal studies of adult psychological development.* New York: Guilford Press.
Schaie, K. W., & Willis, S. L. (1993). Age difference patterns of psychometric intelligence in adulthood: Generalizability within and across ability domains. *Psychology and Aging, 8,* 44–55.
Schaller, M., & Cialdini, R. B. (1988). The economics of empathic helping: Support for a mood management motive. *Journal of Experimental Social Psychology, 24,* 163–181.
Schanberg, S. M., & Field, T. M. (1987). Sensory deprivation stress and supplemental stimulation in the rat pup and preterm human neonate. *Child Development, 58,* 1431–1447.
Schatzberg, A. F., & Nemeroff, C. B. (Eds.) (1995). *The American Psychiatric Press textbook of psychopharmacology.* Washington, DC: American Psychiatric Press.
Scheflin, A. W., & Shapiro, J. L. (1989). *Trance on trial.* New York: Guilford Press.
Scheibel, A. B. (1995). Structural and functional changes in the aging brain. In J. E. Birren & K. W. Schaie (Eds.), *Handbook of the psychology of aging,* 4th ed. (pp. 78–128). San Diego: Academic Press.
Scheier, M. F., & Carver, C. S. (1985). Optimism, coping, and health: Assessment and implications of generalized outcome expectancies. *Health Psychology, 4,* 219–247.
Scheier, M. F., & Carver, C. S. (1992). Effects of optimism on psychological and physical well-being: Theoretical overview and empirical update. *Cognitive Therapy and Research, 16,* 201–228.
Schenck, C. H. (1993). REM sleep behavior disorder. In M. A. Carskadon (Ed.), *Encyclopedia of Sleep and Dreaming* (pp. 499–505). New York: Macmillan.
Scherer, K. R., & Wallbott, H. G. (1994). Evidence for universality and cultural variation of differential emotion response patterning. *Journal of Personality and Social Psychology, 66,* 310–328.
Schiff, W. (1980). *Perception: An applied approach.* Boston: Houghton Mifflin.
Schiller, F. (1992). *Paul Broca.* New York: Oxford University Press.
Schlenker, B. R., Weigold, M. F., & Hallam, J. R. (1990). Self-serving attributions in social context: Effects of self-esteem and social pressure. *Journal of Personality and Social Psychology, 58,* 855–863.
Schmidt, F. L. (1992). What do data really mean? Research findings, meta-analysis, and cumulative knowledge in psychology. *American Psychologist, 47,* 1173–1181.
Schmidt, N. B., & Trakowski, J. H. (1997). Body vigilance in panic disorder: Evaluating attention to bodily perturbations. *Journal of Consulting and Clinical Psychology, 65,* 214–220.
Schmidt, S. R. (1991). Can we have a distinctive theory of memory? *Memory and Cognition, 19,* 523–542.
Schnapf, J. L., Kraft, T. W., & Baylor, D. A. (1987). Spectral sensitivity of human cone photoreceptors. *Nature, 325,* 439–441.
Schneider, D. J., & Shiffrin, R. M. (1977). Controlled and automatic human information processing: I. Detection, search, and attention. *Psychological Review, 84,* 1–66.
Schneider, D. M., & Watkins, M. J. (1996). Response conformity in recognition testing. *Psychonomic Bulletin & Review, 3,* 481–485.
Schneider, S. G., Taylor, S. E., Hammen, C., Kemeny, M. E., & Dudley, J. (1991). Factors influencing suicide intent in gay and bisexual suicide ideators: Differing models for men with and without human immunodeficiency virus. *Journal of Personality and Social Psychology, 61,* 776–788.
Schofield, J. W. (1982). *Black and white in school: Trust, tension, or tolerance?* New York: Praeger.
Schooler, J. W., & Engstler-Schooler, T. Y. (1990). Verbal overshadowing of visual memories: Some things are better left unsaid. *Cognitive Psychology, 17,* 36–71.
Schooler, J. W., Ohlsson, S., & Brooks, K. (1993). Thoughts beyond words: When language overshadows insight. *Journal of Experimental Psychology: General, 122,* 166–183.
Schou, M. (1997). Forty years of lithium treatment. *Archives of General Psychiatry, 54,* 9–13.
Schroeder, S. R., Schroeder, C. S., & Landesman, S. (1987). Psychological services in educational settings to persons with mental retardation. *American Psychologist, 42,* 805–807.
Schulz, R., Musa, D., Staszewski, J., & Siegler, R. S. (1994). The relationship between age and major league baseball performance: Implications for development. *Psychology and Aging, 9,* 274–286.
Schutte, N. S., Malouff, J. M., Post-Gorden, J. C., & Rodasta, A. L. (1988). Effects of playing videogames on children's aggressive and other behaviors. *Journal of Applied Social Psychology, 18,* 454–460.
Schwartz, A., & Schwartz, R. M. (1993). *Depression—Theories and treatments: Psychological, biological, and social perspectives.* New York: Columbia University Press.
Schwartz, B., & Reisberg, D. (1991). *Learning and memory.* New York: Norton.
Schwartz, J. M. (1996). *Brain lock.* New York: HarperCollins.
Schwartz, J. M., Stoessel, P. W., Baxter, L. R., Martin, K. M., & Phelps, M. E. (1996). Systematic changes in cerebral glucose metabolic rate after successful behavior modification treatment of obsessive-compulsive disorder. *Archives of General Psychiatry, 53,* 109–113.
Schwartz, M. S., et al. (1995). *Biofeedback: A practitioner's guide* (2nd ed.). New York: Guilford Press.
Schwartz, P. J., Brown, C., Wehr, T. A., & Rosenthal, N. E. (1996). Winter seasonal affective disorder: A follow-up study of the first 59 patients of the National Institute of Mental Health seasonal studies program. *American Journal of Psychiatry, 153,* 1028–1036.
Schwarz, J. R. (1981). *The Hillside strangler: A murderer's mind.* New York: New American Library.
Schwarz, N., Bless, H., & Bohner, G. (1991). Mood and persuasion: Affective states influence the processing of persuasive communications, *Advances in Experimental Social Psychology, 24,* 161–199.
Scott, L., & O'Hara, M. W. (1993). Self-discrepancies in clinically anxious and depressed university students. *Journal of Abnormal Psychology, 102,* 282–287.
Scoville, W. B., & Milner, B. (1957). Loss of recent memory after bilateral hippocampal lesions. *Journal of Neurology, Neurosurgery, and Psychiatry, 20,* 11–21.
Searle, J. R. (1992). *The rediscovery of the mind.* Cambridge, MA: MIT Press.
Sebel, P. S., Bonke, B., Winograd, E. (1993). *Memory and awareness in anesthesia.* Englewood Cliffs, NJ: Prentice Hall.
Sedikides, C., & Ostrom, T. M. (Eds.) (1993). Perceptions of group variability. *Social Cognition, 11* (1).
Seeman, P., Guan, H-C., & Van Tol, H. H. M. (1993). Dopamine D4 receptors elevated in schizophrenia. *Nature, 365,* 441–445.
Segall, M. H., Campbell, D. T., & Herskovitz, M. J. (1966). *The influence of culture on visual perception.* Indianapolis, IN: Bobbs-Merrill.
Segerberg, O. (1982). *Living to be 100: 1200 who did and how they did it.* New York: Scribner.
Segrin, C., & Abramson, L. Y. (1994). Negative reactions to depressive behaviors: A communications theories analysis. *Journal of Abnormal Psychology, 103,* 655–668.
Seligman, M. E. P. (1971). Phobias and preparedness. *Behavior Therapy, 2,* 307–320.
Seligman, M. E. P. (1975). *Helplessness: On depression, development, and death.* San Francisco: W. H. Freeman.
Seligman, M. E. P. (1991). *Learned optimism.* New York: Knopf.
Seligman, M. E. P. (1995). The effectiveness of psychotherapy: The *Consumer Reports* Study. *American Psychologist, 50,* 965–974.
Seligman, M. E. P. (1996). Science as an ally of practice. *American Psychologist, 51,* 1072–1079.
Selye, H. (1936). A syndrome produced by diverse nocuous agents. *Nature, 138,* 32.
Selye, H. (1976). *The stress of life.* New York: McGraw-Hill.
Semb, G. B., Ellis, J. A., & Araujo, J. (1993). Long-term memory for knowledge learned in school. *Journal of Educational Psychology, 85,* 305–316.
Sepple, C. P., & Read, N. W. (1989). Gastrointestinal correlates of the development of hunger in man. *Appetite, 13,* 183–191.
Sergent, J. (1983). The role of the input in visual hemispheric asymmetries. *Psychological Bulletin, 93,* 481–512.
Sergent, J. (1990). Furtive incursions into bicameral minds. *Brain, 113,* 537–568.
Shadish, W. R., et al. (1997). Evidence that therapy works in clinically representative conditions. *Journal of Consulting and Clinical Psychology, 65,* 355–365.
Shah, P., & Miyake, A. (1996). The separability of working memory resources for spatial thinking and language processing: An individual differences approach. *Journal of Experimental Psychology: General, 125,* 4–27.
Shapiro, D., & Shapiro, D. (1982). Meta-analysis of comparative therapy outcome studies: A replication and refinement. *Psychological Bulletin, 92,* 581–604.
Shapiro, J. P. (1997, January 13). Euthanasia's home. *U.S. News & World Report,* pp. 22–27.
Shapley, R. (1990). Visual sensitivity and parallel retinocortical channels. *Annual Review of Psychology, 41,* 635–658.
Shaver, P. R., & Clark, C. L. (1996). Forms of adult romantic attachment and their cognitive and emotional underpinnings. In G. G. Noam & K. W. Fischer (Eds.), *Development and vulnerability in close relationships* (pp. 29–58). Mahwah, NJ: Erlbaum.
Shearn, D., Bergman, E., Hill, D., Abel, A., & Hinds, L. (1990). Facial coloration and temperature responses in blushing. *Psychophysiology, 27,* 687–693.
Sheehan, P. W., Statham, D., & Jamieson, G. A. (1991). Pseudomemory effects and their relationship to level of susceptibility to hypnosis and state instruction. *Journal of Personality and Social Psychology, 60,* 130–137.
Sheldon, W. H. (1954). *Atlas of man: A guide for somatotyping the adult male of all ages.* New York: Harper & Row.
Shelton, R. C., & Weinberger, D. R. (1986). X-ray computerized tomography studies in schizophrenia: Review and synthesis. In H. A. Nasrallah & D. R. Weinberger (Eds.), *The neurology of schizophrenia.* Amsterdam, Netherlands: Elsevier.

Shepard, R. N. (1990). *Mind sights.* New York: W. H. Freeman.
Shepard, R. N., & Cooper, L. A. (1982). *Mental images and their transformations.* Cambridge, MA: MIT Press.
Shepard, R. N., & Metzler, J. (1971). Mental rotation of three-dimensional objects. *Science, 171,* 701–703.
Sheppard, J. A. (1993). Productivity loss in performance groups: A motivation analysis. *Psychological Bulletin, 113,* 67–81.
Shepperd, J. A. (1993). Student derogation of the Scholastic Aptitude Test: Biases in perceptions and presentations of college board scores. *Basic and Applied Social Psychology, 14,* 455–473.
Sherif, M. (1936). *The psychology of social norms.* New York: Harper.
Sherrod, D. (1989). The influence of gender on same-sex friendships. In C. Hendrick (Ed.), *Review of Personality and Social Psychology* (Vol. 10, pp. 164–186). Newbury Park, CA: Sage.
Sherry, D. F. (1992). Memory, the hippocampus, and natural selection: Studies of food-storing birds. In L. Squire & N. Butters (Eds.), *Neuropsychology of Memory* (2nd ed., pp. 521–532). New York: Guilford Press.
Shiffrin, R. M. (1993). Short-term memory: A brief commentary. *Memory and Cognition, 21,* 193–197.
Shimamura, A. P. (1986). Priming effects in amnesia: Evidence for a dissociable memory function. *Quarterly Journal of Experimental Psychology, 38A,* 619–644.
Shimamura, A. P., Berry, J. M., Mangels, J. A., Rusting, C. L., & Jurica, P. J. (1995). Memory and cognitive abilities in university professors: Evidence for successful aging. *Psychological Science, 6,* 271–277.
Shneidman, E. (1989). The Indian summer of life: A preliminary study of septuagenarians. *American Psychologist, 44,* 684–694.
Shneidman, E. (Ed.) (1984). *Death: Current perspectives.* Palo Alto, CA: Mayfield.
Shneidman, E. S. (1996). *The suicidal mind.* New York: Oxford University Press.
Shostrom, E. (1965). An inventory for the measurement of self-actualization. *Educational and Psychological Measurement, 24,* 207–218.
Shuell, T. J. (1996). Teaching and learning in a classroom context. In D. C. Berliner & R. C. Calfee (Eds.), *Handbook of educational psychology* (pp. 726–764). New York: Macmillan.
Shulgin, A. T. (1986). The background and chemistry of MDMA. *Journal of Psychoactive Drugs, 18,* 291–303.
Shurin, M. R., Kusnecov, A. W., Riechman, S. E. & Rabin, B. (1995). The effect of a conditioned aversive stimulus on the immune response in three strains of rat. *Psychoneuroendocrinology, 20,* 837–849.
Sidey, H. (1993, August 9). The flood: A broken heartland. *Time,* p. 28.
Siegel, J. M. (1990). Stressful life events and use of physician services among the elderly. *Journal of Personality and Social Psychology, 58,* 1081–1086.
Siegel, J. M., et al. (1991). Neuronal activity in narcolepsy: Identification of cataplexy-related cells in the medial medulla. *Science, 252,* 1315–1318.
Siegel, R. K. (1980). The psychology of life after death. *American Psychologist, 35,* 911–931.
Siegel, R. K. (1989). *Intoxication: Life in pursuit of artificial paradise.* New York: Dutton.
Siegler, I. C. (1994). Hostility and risk: Demographic and lifestyle variables. In A. W. Siegman & T. W. Smith (Eds.), *Anger, hostility, and the heart* (pp. 199–214). Mahwah, NJ: Erlbaum.
Siegler, R. S. (1996). *Emerging minds: The process of change in children's thinking.* New York: Oxford University Press.
Siegler, R. S., & Ellis, S. (1996). Piaget on childhood. *Psychological Science, 7,* 211–215.
Siegman, A., & Boyle, S. (1993). Voices of fear and anxiety and sadness and depression: The effects of speech rate and loudness on fear and anxiety and sadness and depression. *Journal of Abnormal Psychology, 102,* 430–437.
Siegman, A. W. & Smith, T. W. (Eds.) (1994). *Anger, hostility, and the heart.* Mahwah, NJ: Erlbaum.
Siero, F. W., & Doosje, B. J. (1993). Attitude change following persuasive communication: Integrating social judgment theory and the Elaboration Likelihood Model. *European Journal of Social Psychology, 23,* 541–554.
Sigelman, L., & Welch, S. (1991). *Black Americans' views of racial inequality: The dream deferred.* New York: Cambridge University Press.
Silbersweig, D. A., Stern, E., Cahill, C., et al. (1995). A functional neuroanatomy of hallucinations in schizophrenia. *Nature, 378,* 176–179.
Silveira, J. (1971). *Incubation: The effect of interruption timing and length on problem solution and quality of problem processing.* Unpublished doctoral dissertation. University of Oregon, Eugene.
Silver, E., Cirincione, C., & Steadman, H. J. (1994). Demythologizing inaccurate perceptions of the insanity defense. *Law and Human Behavior, 18,* 63–70.
Silverberg, S. B., & Steinberg, L. (1990). Psychological well-being of parents with early adolescent children. *Developmental Psychology, 26,* 658–666.
Silverman, K., Evans, S. M., Strain, E. C., & Griffiths, R. R. (1992). Withdrawal syndrome after the double-blind cessation of caffeine consumption. *New England Journal of Medicine, 327,* 1109–1114.
Silverman, L., & Weinberger, J. (1985). Mommy and I are one: Implications for psychotherapy. *American Psychologist, 40,* 1296–1308.
Silverstein, A. B. (1990). Short forms of individual intelligence tests. *Psychological Assessment: A Journal of Consulting and Clinical Psychology, 2,* 3–11.
Silverstein, B., Perdue, L., & Kelly, E. (1986). The role of the mass media in promoting a thin standard of bodily attractiveness for women. *Sex Roles, 14,* 519–532.
Simmons, J. V. (1981). *Project sea hunt: A report on prototype development and tests.* Technical Report 746, Naval Ocean Systems Center, San Diego.
Simon, H. A. (1975). The functional equivalence of problem solving skills. *Cognitive Psychology, 7,* 268–288.
Simon, H. A. (1989). The scientist as a problem solver. In D. Kiahr and K. Kotovsky (Eds.), *Complex information processing: The impact of Herbert Simon.* Hillsdale, NJ: Erlbaum.
Simon, H. B. (1991). Exercise and human immune function. In R. Ader, D. E. Felton, & N. Cohen (Eds.), *Psychoneuroimmunology* (2nd ed.), pp. 869–895. New York: Academic Press.
Simon, S. A., & Roper, S. D. (1993). *Mechanisms of taste transduction.* Boca Raton, FL: CRC Press.
Simons, R. C., & Hughes, C. C . (1993). Culture-bound syndromes. In A. C. Gaw (Ed.), *Culture, ethnicity, and mental illness* (pp. 75–99). Washington, DC: American Psychological Association.
Simonton, D. K. (1997). Creative productivity: A predictive and explanatory model of career trajectories and landmarks. *Psychological Review, 104,* 66–89.
Simpson, G. B. (1989). Varieties of ambiguity: What are we seeking? In D. S. Gorfein (Ed.), *Resolving semantic ambiguity.* New York: Springer-Verlag.
Simpson, J. A. (1987). The dissolution of romantic relationships: Factors involved in relationship stability and emotional distress. *Journal of Personality and Social Psychology, 53,* 683–692.
Simpson, J. A., & Kenrick, D. T. (Ed.) (1997). *Evolutionary social psychology.* Mahwah, NJ: Erlbaum.
Sinden, J. D., Hodges, H., & Gray, J. A. (1995). Neural transplantation and recovery of cognitive function. *Behavioral and Brain Sciences, 18,* 10–35.
Singelis, T. M. (1994). The measurement of independent and interdependent self-construals. *Personality and Social Psychology Bulletin, 20,* 580–591.
Singer, J. L. (Ed.) (1990). *Repression and dissociation: Implications for personality theory, psychopathology, and health.* Chicago: University of Chicago Press.
Skinner, B. F. (1938). *The behavior of organisms.* New York: Appleton-Century-Crofts.
Skinner, B. F. (1948). "Superstition" in the pigeon. *Journal of Experimental Psychology, 38,* 168–172.
Skinner, B. F. (1948). *Walden two.* New York: Macmillan.
Skinner, B. F. (1956). A case history in scientific method. *American Psychologist, 11,* 221–233.
Skinner, B. F. (1957). *Verbal behavior.* New York: Appleton-Century-Crofts.
Skinner, B. F. (1971). *Beyond freedom and dignity.* New York: Knopf.
Skinner, B. F. (1988). *The school of the future.* Paper presented at the annual meeting of the American Psychological Association, Atlanta, GA.
Skinner, B. F. (1990). Can psychology be a science of mind? *American Psychologist, 45,* 1206–1210.
Skinner, E. A. (1996). A guide to constructs of control. *Journal of Personality and Social Psychology, 71,* 549–570.
Sklar, L. S., & Anisman, H. (1981). Stress and cancer. *Psychological Bulletin, 89,* 369–406.
Sladek, J. R., & Shoulson, I. (1988). Neural transplantation: A call for patience rather than patients. *Science, 240,* 1386–1388.
Slater, A., Mattock, A., & Brown, E. (1990). Size constancy at birth: Newborn infants' responses to retinal and real size. *Journal of Experimental Child Psychology, 49,* 314–322.
Slavin, R. E. (1987). Ability grouping and student achievement in elementary schools: A best-evidence synthesis. *Review of Educational Research, 57,* 293–336.
Slobin, D. I. (1966). Grammatical transformations and sentence comprehension in childhood and adulthood. *Journal of Verbal Learning and Verbal Behavior, 5,* 219–227.
Slovic, P., Fischoff, B., & Lichtenstein, S. (1982). Facts versus fears: Understanding perceived risk. In D. Kahneman, P. Slovic, & A. Tversky (Eds.), *Judgment under uncertainty: Heuristics and biases* (pp. 463–489). New York: Cambridge University Press.
Smetana, J. G. (1988). Concepts of self and social convention: Adolescents' and parents' reasoning about hypothetical and actual family conflicts. In M. R. Gunnar & W. A. Collins (Eds.), *Development during the transition to adolescence: Minnesota symposia on child psychology* (Vol. 21, pp. 79–122). Hillsdale, NJ: Erlbaum.
Smith, B. A., & Blass, E. M. (1996). Taste-mediated calming in premature, preterm, and full-term human infants. *Developmental Psychology, 32,* 1084–1089.
Smith, C. A., & Ellsworth, P. C. (1985). Patterns of cognitive appraisal in emotion. *Journal of Personality and Social Psychology, 48,* 813–838.
Smith, C. A., Haynes, K. N., Lazarus, R. S., & Pope, L. K. (1993). In search of the "hot" cognitions: Attributions, appraisals, and their relation to emotion. *Journal of Personality and Social Psychology, 65,* 916–929.
Smith, C. S., Reilly, C., & Midkiff, K. (1989). Evaluation of three circadian rhythm questionnaires with suggestions for an improved measure of morningness. *Journal of Applied Psychology, 74,* 728–738.
Smith, D. (1982). Trends in counseling and psychotherapy. *American Psychologist, 37,* 802–809.
Smith, E. E., Shoben, E. J., & Ripps, L. J. (1974). Structure and processes in semantic memory: A featural model for semantic decisions. *Psychological Review, 81,* 214–241.

Smith, M. C. (1983). Hypnotic memory enhancement of witnesses: Does it work? *Psychological Bulletin, 94,* 387–407.

Smith, M. L., Glass, G. V., & Miller, T. I. (1980). *The benefits of psychotherapy.* Baltimore: Johns Hopkins University Press.

Smith, R. F., Mattran, K. M., Kurkjian, M. F., & Kurtz, S. L. (1989). Alterations in offspring behavior induced by chronic prenatal cocaine dosing. *Neurotoxicology and Teratology, 11,* 35–38.

Smith, R. W., & Kounios, J. (1996). Sudden insight: All-or-none processing revealed by speed-accuracy decomposition. *Journal of Experimental Psychology: Learning, Memory, and Cognition, 22,* 1443–1462.

Smith, V. L. (1991). Prototypes in the courtroom: Lay representations of legal concepts. *Journal of Personality and Social Psychology, 61,* 857–872.

Smotherman, W. P., & Robinson, S. R. (1996). The development of behavior before birth. *Developmental Psychology, 32,* 425–434.

Snarey, J. R. (1985). Cross-cultural universality of social-moral development: A critical review of Kohlbergian research. *Psychological Bulletin, 97,* 202–233.

Sno, H. N., & Linszen, D. H. (1990). The déjà vu experience: Remembrance of things past? *American Journal of Psychiatry, 147,* 1587–1595.

Snodgrass, S. E. (1985). Women's intuition: The effect of subordinate roles on interpersonal sensitivity. *Journal of Personality and Social Psychology, 49,* 146–155.

Snyder, C. R., Higgins, R. L., & Stucky, R. J. (1983). *Excuses: Masquerades in search of grace.* New York: Wiley.

Snyder, M. (1987). *Public appearances/private realities: The psychology of self-monitoring.* New York: W. H. Freeman.

Snyder, M. (1993). Motivational foundations of behavioral confirmation. *Advances in Experimental Social Psychology, 25,* 67–114.

Snyder, M., & DeBono, K. (1985). Appeals to image and claims about quality: Understanding the psychology of advertising. *Journal of Personality and Social Psychology, 49,* 586–597.

Snyder, M., & Haugen, J. A. (1994). Why does behavioral confirmation occur? A functional perspective on the role of the perceiver. *Journal of Experimental Social Psychology, 30,* 218–246.

Snyder, M., & Ickes, W. (1985). Personality and social behavior. In G. Lindzey & E. Aronson (Eds.), *Handbook of social psychology* (3rd ed., Vol. II, pp. 883–948). Reading, MA: Addison-Wesley.

Snyder, M., Tanke, E. D., & Berscheid, E. (1977). Social perception and interpersonal behavior: On the self-fulfilling nature of social stereotypes. *Journal of Personality and Social Psychology, 35,* 656–666.

Snyder, S. H. (1992). Nitric oxide: First in a new class of neurotransmitters? *Science, 257,* 494–496.

Snyder, S. H. (1996). *Drugs and the brain* (2nd ed.). New York: Scientific American Library.

Snyderman, M., & Rothman, S. (1987). Survey of expert opinion on intelligence and aptitude testing. *American Psychologist, 42,* 137–144.

Sokolov, E. M. (1963). Higher nervous functions: The orienting reflex. *Annual Review of Physiology, 25,* 545–580.

Solomon, G. F., & Benton, D. (1994). Psychoneuroimmunologic aspects of aging. In R. Glaser & J. Kiecolt-Glaser (Eds.), *Handbook of stress and immunity* (pp. 341–364). San Diego: Academic Press.

Solomon, P. R., Brett, M., Groccia-Ellison, M., Oyler, C., Tomasi, M., & Pendlebury, W. W. (1995). Classical conditioning in patients with Alzheimer's disease: A multi-day study. *Psychology and Aging, 10,* 248–254.

Solomon, R. L. (1980). The opponent-process theory of motivation. *American Psychologist, 35,* 691–712.

Sommer, R. (1967). Classroom ecology. *Journal of Applied Behavioral Science, 3,* 489–503.

Spangler, W. D. (1992). Validity of questionnaire and TAT measures of need for achievement: Two meta-analyses. *Psychological Bulletin, 112,* 140–154.

Spangler, W. D., & House, R. J. (1991). Presidential effectiveness and the leadership motive profile. *Journal of Personality and Social Psychology, 60,* 439–455.

Spanos, N. P. (1986). Hypnotic behavior: A social-psychological interpretation of amnesia, analgesia, and "trance-logic." *Behavioral and Brain Sciences, 9,* 449–467.

Spanos, N. P. (1996). *Multiple identities and false memories: A sociocognitive perspective.* Washington, DC: American Psychological Association.

Spanos, N. P., & Katsanis, J. (1989). Effects of instructional set of nonvolition during hypnotic and nonhypnotic analgesia. *Journal of Personality and Social Psychology, 56,* 182–188.

Spanos, N. P., Burgess, C. A., Roncon, V., Wallace-Capretta, S., & Cross, P. (1993). Surreptitiously observed hypnotic responding in simulators and in skill-trained and untrained high hypnotizables. *Journal of Personality and Social Psychology, 65,* 391–398.

Spanos, N. P., Stenstrom, R. J., & Johnson, J. C. (1988). Hypnosis, placebo, and suggestion in the treatment of warts. *Psychosomatic Medicine, 50,* 245–260.

Spear, N. E., Spear, L. P., & Woodruff, M. L. (Eds.) (1995). *Neurobehavioral plasticity: Learning, development, and response to brain insults.* Mahwah, NJ: Erlbaum.

Spearman, C. (1904). General intelligence objectively determined and measured. *American Journal of Psychology, 15,* 201–293.

Spelke, E. S., Breinlinger, K., Macomber, J., & Jacobson, K. (1992). Origins of knowledge. *Psychological Review, 99,* 605–632.

Sperling, G. (1960). The information available in brief visual presentations. *Psychological Monographs, 74*(Whole No. 11), 1–29.

Sperry, R. W. (1966). Brain bisection and consciousness. In J. Eccles (Ed.), *Brain and conscious experience.* New York: Springer-Verlag.

Sperry, R. W. (1968). Hemisphere deconnection and unity in conscious awareness. *American Psychologist, 23,* 723–733.

Sperry, R. W. (1982). Some effects of disconnecting the cerebral hemispheres. *Science, 217,* 1223–1226, 1250.

Sperry, R. W. (1993). The impact and promise of the cognitive revolution. *American Psychologist, 48,* 878–885.

Spiegel, D. (1993). Social support: How friends, family, and groups can help. In D. Goleman & J. Gurin (Eds.), *Mind body medicine: How to use your mind for better health* (pp. 331–350). Yonkers, NY: Consumer Reports Books.

Spiro, A., III., Schnurr, P. P., & Aldwin, C. M. (1994). Combat-related posttraumatic stress disorder symptoms in older men. *Psychology and Aging, 9,* 17–26.

Spitzer, R. L., Gibbon, M., Skodol, A. E., Williams, J. B., & First, M. B. (Eds.) (1994). *DSM-IV casebook.* Washington, DC: American Psychiatric Press.

Spock, B. J. (1945). *The common sense book of child and baby care.* New York: Duell, Sloan, & Pearce.

Springer, S. P., & Deutsch, G. (1989). *Left brain, right brain* (3rd ed.). New York: W. H. Freeman.

Squire, L. R. (1992). Memory and the hippocampus: A synthesis from findings with rats, monkeys, and humans. *Psychological Review, 99,* 195–231.

Squire, L. R., & Butters, N. (Eds.) (1992). *Neuropsychology of memory* (2nd ed.). New York: Guilford Press.

Squire, L. R., & Zola-Morgan, S. (1991). The medial temporal lobe memory system. *Science, 253,* 1380–1386.

Sroufe, L. A., & Jacobvitz, D. (1989). Diverging pathways, developmental transformations, multiple etiologies, and the problem of continuity in development. *Human Development, 32,* 196–203.

Staats, A. W., & Staats, C. K. (1958). Attitudes established by classical conditioning. *Journal of Abnormal and Social Psychology, 57,* 37–40.

Stangor, C., & Lange, J. E. (1994). Mental representations of social groups: Advances in understanding stereotypes and stereotyping. *Advances in Experimental Social Psychology, 26,* 357–416.

Stangor, C., Sullivan, L. A., & Ford, T. E. (1991). Affective and cognitive determinants of prejudice. *Social Cognition, 9,* 359–380.

Stanley, J. C., & Benbow, C. P. (1986). Youths who reason exceptionally well mathematically. In R. J. Sternberg & J. E. Davidson (Eds.), *Conceptions of giftedness* (pp. 361–387). New York: Cambridge University Press.

Stanovich, K. E., West, R. F., & Harrison, M. R. (1995). Knowledge growth and maintenance across the life span: The role of print exposure. *Developmental Psychology, 31,* 811–826.

Stapp, J., Tucker, A. M., & VandenBos, G. R. (1983). Census of psychological personnel. *American Psychologist, 40,* 1317–1351.

Stark, E. (1984, October). To sleep, perchance to dream. *Psychology Today,* p. 16.

Stark, E. (1986, October). Young, innocent, and pregnant. *Psychology Today,* pp. 28–35.

Staszewski, J. J. (1988). Skilled memory and expert mental calculation. In M. T. H. Chi, R. Blaser, & M. J. Farr (Eds.), *The nature of expertise* (pp. 71–128). Hillsdale, NJ: Erlbaum.

Stattin, H., & Magnusson, D. (1990). *Pubertal maturation in female development.* Hillsdale, NJ: Erlbaum.

Staudinger, U. M., & Baltes, P. B. (1994). Psychology of wisdom. In R. J. Sternberg (Ed.), *The encyclopedia of intelligence* (pp. 1143–1152). New York: Macmillan.

Steblay, N. M. (1992). A meta-analytic review of the weapon-focus effect. *Law and Human Behavior, 16,* 413–424.

Steele, C. M. (1988). The psychology of self-affirmation: Sustaining the integrity of the self. *Advances in Experimental Social Psychology, 21,* 261–302.

Steele, C. M. (1997). A threat in the air: How stereotypes shape the intellectual identities and performance of women and African Americans. *American Psychologist,* in press.

Steele, C. M., & Aronson, J. (1995). Stereotype threat and the intellectual test performance of African Americans. *Journal of Personality and Social Psychology, 69,* 797–811.

Steele, C. M., & Josephs, R. A. (1990). Alcohol myopia: Its prized and dangerous effects. *American Psychologist, 45,* 921–933.

Steele, S. (1990). *The content of our character.* New York: St. Martin's Press.

Stein, B. E., & Meredith, M. A. (1993). *The merging of the senses.* Cambridge, MA: MIT Press.

Stein, D. G., & Glasier, M. M. (1995). Some practical and theoretical issues concerning fetal brain tissue grafts as therapy for brain dysfunctions. *Behavioral and Brain Sciences, 18,* 36–45.

Stein, G. L., Kimiecik, J. C., Daniels, J., & Jackson, S. A. (1995). Psychological antecedents of flow in recreational sport. *Personality and Social Psychology Bulletin, 21,* 125–135.

Stein, J. H., & Reiser, L. W. (1994). A study of white middle-class adolescent boys' responses to "semenarche" (the first ejaculation). *Journal of Youth and Adolescence, 23,* 373–384.

Stein, M. B., Walker, J. R., & Forde, D. R. (1996). Public-speaking fears in a community sample. *Archives of General Psychiatry, 53,* 169–174.

Steinberg, L. (1987, September). Bound to bicker. *Psychology Today,* pp. 36–39.
Steinberg, L. (1989). Pubertal maturation and parent-adolescent distance: An evolutionary perspective. In G. Adams, R. Montemayor, & T. Gullotta (Eds.), *Biology of adolescent behavior and development.* Newbury Park, CA: Sage.
Steiner, J. (1979). Human facial expressions in response to taste and smell stimulation. In H. Reese & L. P. Lipsitt (Eds.), *Advances in child development and behavior* (Vol. 13, pp. 257–295). New York: Academic Press.
Stellar, E. (1954). The physiology of motivation. *Psychological Review, 61,* 5–22.
Stelmack, R. M. (1990). Biological bases of extraversion: Psychophysiological evidence. *Journal of Personality, 58,* 293–311.
Stephan, W. G. (1986). The effects of school desegregation: An evaluation 30 years after *Brown.* In M. J. Saks & L. Saxe (Eds.), *Advances in applied social psychology* (Vol. 3, pp. 181–206). Hillsdale, NJ: Erlbaum.
Stepper, S., & Strack, F. (1993). Proprioceptive determinants of emotional and nonemotional feelings. *Journal of Personality and Social Psychology, 64,* 211–220.
Sternbach, R. A. (1964). The effects of instructional sets of autonomic responsivity. *Psychophysiology, 1,* 67–72.
Sternberg, R. J. (1980). Sketch of a componential subtheory of human intelligence. *Behavioral and Brain Sciences, 3,* 573–584.
Sternberg, R. J. (1985). *Beyond IQ.* Cambridge, MA: Cambridge University Press.
Sternberg, R. J. (1988). *The triarchic mind: A new theory of human intelligence.* New York: Viking.
Sternberg, R. J. (Ed.) (1988). *The nature of creativity: Contemporary psychological perspectives.* New York: Cambridge University Press.
Sternberg, R. J. (Ed.) (1990). *Wisdom: Its nature, origins, and development.* New York: Cambridge University Press.
Sternberg, R. J. (Ed.) (1994). *The encyclopedia of intelligence.* New York: Macmillan.
Sternberg, R. J., & Davidson, J. E. (Eds.) (1995). *The nature of insight.* Cambridge, MA: MIT Press.
Sternberg, R. J., & Lubart, T. I. (1991). An investment theory of creativity and its development. *Human development, 34,* 1–31.
Sternberg, R. J., & Okagaki, L. (1989). Continuity and discontinuity in intellectual development are not a matter of "either-or." *Human Development, 32,* 158–166.
Sternberg, R. J., Conway, B. E., Ketron, J. L., & Bernstein, M. (1981). People's conceptions of intelligence. *Journal of Personality and Social Psychology, 41,* 37–55.
Sternberg, R. J., Wagner, R. K., Williams, W. M., & Horvath, J. A. (1995). Testing common sense. *American Psychologist, 50,* 912–927.
Stevens, J. C., Foulke, E., & Patterson, M. Q. (1996). Tactile acuity, aging, and braille reading in long-term blindness. *Journal of Experimental Psychology: Applied, 2,* 91–106.
Stevenson, H. W., Chen, C., & Lee, S. Y. (1993). Mathematics achievement in Chinese, Japanese, and American children: Ten years later. *Science, 259,* 53–58.
Stevenson, H. W., Lee, S., Chen, C., Stigler, J., Fan, L., & Ge, F. (1990). Mathematics achievement of children in China and the United States. *Child Development, 61,* 1053–1066.
Stewart, A. J., Sokol, M., Healy, J. M., & Chester, N. L. (1986). Longitudinal studies of psychological consequences of life changes in children and adults. *Journal of Personality and Social Psychology, 50,* 143–151.
Stewart, J. E., II. (1980). Defendant's attractiveness as a factor in the outcome of criminal trials: An observational study. *Journal of Applied Social Psychology, 10,* 348–361.
Stewart, W. F., Lipton, R. B., Celentano, D. D., & Reed, M. L. (1992). Prevalence of migraine headache in the United States: Relation to age, income, race, and other sociodemographic factors. *Journal of the American Medical Association, 267,* 84–89.
Stigler, J., Shweder, R. A., & Herdt, G. (Eds.) (1990). *Cultural psychology: Essays on comparative human development.* New York: Cambridge University Press.
Stiles, W. B., Shapiro, D. A., & Elliott, R. (1986). Are all psychotherapies equivalent? *American Psychologist, 41,* 165–180.
Stipek, D. J. (1996). Motivation and instruction. In D. C. Berliner & R. C. Calfee (Eds.), *Handbook of Educational Psychology* (pp. 85–113). New York: Macmillan.
Stobin, D. I. (1966). Grammatical transformations and sentence comprehension in childhood and adulthood. *Journal of Verbal Learning and Verbal Behavior, 5,* 219–227.
Stokols, D. (1995). The paradox of environmental psychology, *American Psychology, 50,* 821–837.
Stone, A. A., Neale, J. M., Cox, D. S., Napoli, A., Valdimarsdottir, H., & Kennedy-Moore, E. (1994). Daily events are associated with a secretory immune response to an oral antigen in men. *Health Psychology, 13,* 440–446.
Stone, M. H. (1997). *Healing the mind: A history of psychiatry from antiquity to present.* New York: Norton.
Strack, F., Argyle, M., & Schwarz, N. (Eds.) (1991). *Subjective well-being.* London: Pergamon.
Strack, S., & Coyne, J. C. (1983). Social confirmation of dysphoria: Shared and private reactions to depression. *Journal of Personality and Social Psychology, 44,* 798–806.
Straube, E. R., & Oades, R. D. (1992). *Schizophrenia: Empirical research and findings.* San Diego: Academic Press.
Strauman, T. J. (1989). Self-discrepancies in clinical depression and social phobia: Cognitive structures that underly emotional disorders? *Journal of Abnormal Psychology, 98,* 5–14.
Strauman, T. J. (1996). Stability within the self: A longitudinal study of the structural implications of self-discrepancy theory. *Journal of Personality and Social Psychology, 71,* 1142–1153.
Strauman, T. J., Lemieux, A. M., & Coe, C. L. (1993). Self-discrepancy and natural killer cell activity: Immunological consequences of negative self-evaluation. *Journal of Personality and Social Psychology, 64,* 1042–1052.
Strauss, D. H., Spitzer, R. L., Muskin, P. R. (1990). Maladaptive denial of physical illness: A proposal for DSM-IV. *American Journal of Psychiatry, 147,* 1168–1172.
Streissguth, A. P., Barr, H. M., Bookstein, F. L., & Sampson, P. D. (1993). *The enduring effects of prenatal alcohol exposure on child development: Birth through 7 years.* Ann Arbor: University of Michigan Press.
Streissguth, A. P., Barr, H. M., Sampson, P. D., Darby, B. L., & Martin, C. (1989). IQ at age 4 in relation to maternal alcohol use and smoking during pregnancy. *Developmental Psychology, 25,* 3–11.
Streri, A., & Pecheux, M. G. (1986). Tactual habituation and discrimination of form in infancy: A comparison with vision. *Child Development, 57,* 100–104.
Strichartz, A. F., & Burton, R. V. (1990). Lies and truth: A study of the development of the concept. *Child Development, 61,* 211–220.
Stricker, E. (1990). *Handbook of behavioral neurobiology: Volume 10: Neurobiology of food and water intake.* New York: Plenum.
Strickland, B. R. (1989). Internal-external control expectancies: From contingency to creativity. *American Psychologist, 44,* 1–12.
Stroop, J. R. (1935). Studies of interference in serial verbal reactions. *Journal of Experimental Psychology, 18,* 643–662.
Strube, M. J., & Werner, C. (1985). Relinquishment of control and the Type A behavior pattern. *Journal of Personality and Social Psychology, 48,* 688–701.
Struckman-Johnson, C. J., Gilliland, R. G., Struckman-Johnson, D. L., & North, T. C. (1990). The effects of fear of AIDS and gender on responses to fear-arousing condom advertisements. *Journal of Applied Social Psychology, 20,* 1396–1410.
Strupp, H. H. (1989). Psychotherapy: Can the practitioner learn from the researcher? *American Psychologist, 44,* 717–724.
Strupp, H. H. (1996). The tripartite model and the *Consumer Reports* study. *American Psychologist, 51,* 1017–1024.
Stumpf, H., & Stanley, J. C. (1996). Gender-related differences on the college board's advanced placement and achievement tests, 1982–1992. *Journal of Educational Psychology, 88,* 353–364.
Stunkard, A. J., Harris, J. R., Pedersen, N. L., & McClearn, G. E. (1990). The body-mass index of twins who have been reared apart. *New England Journal of Medicine, 332,* 1483–1487.
Subotnik, R. F., & Arnold, K. D. (Eds.) (1994). *Beyond Terman: Contemporary longitudinal studies of giftedness and talent.* Norwood, NJ: Ablex.
Subrahmanyan, K., and Greenfield, P. M. (1994). Effects of video game practice on spatial skills in girls and boys. *Journal of Applied Developmental Psychology, 15,* 13–32.
Sue, S., & Okazaki, S. (1990). Asian-American educational achievements: A phenomenon in search of an explanation. *American Psychologist, 45,* 913–920.
Suh, E., Diener, E., & Fujita, F. (1996). Events and subjective well-being: Only recent events matter. *Journal of Personality and Social Psychology, 70,* 1091–1102.
Sullivan, C. E., Issa, F. G., Berthon-Jones, M., & Eves, L. (1981). Reversal of obstructive sleep apnea by continuous positive airway pressure applied through the nares. *Lancet,* 862–865.
Sullivan, R. M., Taborsky-Barbar, S., Mendoza, R., Itino, A., Leon, M., et al. (1991). Olfactory classical conditioning in neonates. *Pediatrics, 87,* 511–518.
Suls, J., & Wan, C. K. (1993). The relationship between trait hostility and cardiovascular reactivity: A quantitative review and analysis. *Psychophysiology, 30,* 615–636.
Sundstrom, E. (1986). *Work places.* New York: Cambridge University Press.
Suomi, S. J. (1991). Uptight and laid-back monkeys: Individual differences in the response to social challenges. In S. Branch, W. Hall, & J. E. Dooling (Eds.), *Plasticity of development.* Cambridge, MA: MIT Press.
Sussman, N., & Rosenfeld, H. (1982). Influence of culture, language, and sex on interpersonal distance. *Journal of Personality and Social Psychology, 42,* 66–74.
Suzuki, K. (1991). Moon illusion simulated in complete darkness: Planetarium experiment reexamined. *Perception and Psychophysics, 49,* 349–354.
Swann, W. B., Jr., & Ely, R. J. (1984). A battle of wills: Self-verification versus behavioral confirmation. *Journal of Personality and Social Psychology, 46,* 1287–1302.
Swanson, H. L. (1996). Individual and age-related differences in children's working memory. *Memory and Cognition, 24,* 70–82.
Swarr, A. E., & Richards, M. H. (1996). Longitudinal effects of adolescent girls' pubertal development, perceptions of pubertal timing, and parental relations on eating problems. *Developmental Psychology, 32,* 636–646.
Swayze, V. W. (1995). Frontal leukotomy and related psychosurgical procedures in the era before antipsychotics (1935–1954): A historical overview. *American Journal of Psychiatry, 152,* 505–515.

Sweeney, P. D., Anderson, K., & Bailey, S. (1986). Attributional style in depression: A meta-analytic review. *Journal of Personality and Social Psychology, 50,* 974–991.
Swets, J. A. (1996). *Signal detection theory and ROC analysis in psychology and diagnostics.* Mahwah, NJ: Erlbaum.
Swets, J. A., & Bjork, R. A. (1990). Enhancing human performance: An evaluation of "new age" techniques considered by the U.S. Army. *Psychological Science, 1,* 85–96.
Swim, J. K. (1994). Perceived versus meta-analytic effect sizes: An assessment of the accuracy of gender stereotypes. *Journal of Personality and Social Psychology, 66,* 21–36.
Swim, J. K., Borgida, E., Maruyama, G., & Myers, D. G. (1989). Joan McKay versus John McKay: Do gender stereotypes bias evaluations? *Psychological Bulletin, 105,* 409–429.
Switzer, J. Y. (1990). The impact of generic word choices: An empirical investigation of age- and sex-related differences. *Sex Roles, 22,* 69–82.
Szasz, T. (1961). *The myth of mental illness.* New York: Harper & Row.
Szasz, T. (1987). *Insanity: The idea and its consequences.* New York: Wiley.
Szymczyk, J. (1995, August 14). Animals, vegetables, and minerals. *Newsweek,* p. 10.

Tajfel, H. (Ed.) (1982). *Social identity and intergroup relations.* London: Cambridge University Press.
Tajfel, H., Billig, M. G., Bundy, R. P., & Flament, C. (1971). Social categorization and intergroup behavior. *European Journal of Social Psychology, 1,* 149–178.
Takeuchi, A. H., & Hulse, S. H. (1993). Absolute pitch. *Psychological Bulletin, 113,* 345–361.
Tang, S., & Hall, V. C. (1995). The overjustification effect: A meta-analysis. *Applied Cognitive Psychology, 9,* 365–404.
Tangney, J. P., Miller, R. S., Flicker, L., & Barlow, D. H. (1996). Are shame, guilt, and embarrassment distinct emotions? *Journal of Personality and Social Psychology, 70,* 1256–1269.
Tannen, D. (1990). *You just don't understand: Women and men in conversation.* New York: Morrow.
Tartter, V. C. (1986). *Language processes.* New York: Holt, Rinehart & Winston.
Tassinary, L. G., & Cacioppo, J. T. (1992). Unobservable facial actions and emotion. *Psychological Science, 3,* 28–33.
Tavris, C. (1992). *The mismeasure of woman.* New York: Simon & Schuster.
Taylor, C. B., Sheikh, J., Agras, W. S., Roth, W. T., Margraf, J., Ehlers, A., Maddock, R., & Gossard, D. (1986). Self-report of panic attacks: Agreement with heart rate changes. *American Journal of Psychiatry, 143,* 478–482.
Taylor, D. M., & Moghaddam, F. M. (1994). *Theories of intergroup relations* (2nd ed.). Westport, CT: Praeger.
Taylor, S. E. (1986). *Health psychology.* New York: Random House.
Taylor, S. E. (1989). *Positive illusions: Creative self-deception and the healthy mind.* New York: Basic Books.
Taylor, S. E. (1990). Health psychology: The science and the field. *American Psychologist, 45,* 40–50.
Taylor, S. E., & Armor, D. A . (1996). Positive illusions and coping with adversity. *Journal of Personality, 64,* 873–898.
Taylor, S. E., & Brown, J. D. (1988). Illusion and well-being: A social psychological perspective on mental health. *Psychological Bulletin, 103,* 193–210.
Taylor, S. E., & Brown, J. D. (1994). Positive illusions and well-being revisited: Separating fact from fiction. *Psychological Bulletin, 116,* 21–27.
Taylor, S. E., & Lobel, M. (1989). Social comparison activity under threat: Downward evaluation and upward contacts. *Psychological Review, 96,* 569–575.
Taylor, S. E., Falke, R. L., Shoptaw, S. J., & Lichtman, R. R. (1986). Social support, social groups, and the cancer patient. *Journal of Consulting and Clinical Psychology, 54,* 608–615.
Taylor, S. E., Repetti, R. L., & Seeman, T. (1997). Health psychology: What is an unhealthy environment and how does it get under the skin? *Annual Review of Psychology, 48,* 411–447.
Taylor, S. P., & Leonard, K. E. (1983). Alcohol and human physical aggression. In R. G. Geen & E. I. Donnerstein (Eds.), *Aggression; Theoretical and empirical reviews* (Vol. 2, pp. 77–101). New York: Academic Press.
Teas, D. C. (1989). Auditory physiology: Present trends. *Annual Review of Psychology, 40,* 405–429.
Tedeschi, J. T., Schlenker, B. R., & Bonoma, T. V. (1971). Cognitive dissonance: Private ratiocination or public spectacle? *American Psychologist,* 26, 685–695.
Teitelbaum, P., & Epstein, A. N. (1962). The lateral hypothalamic syndrome: Recovery of feeding and drinking after lateral hypothalamic lesions. *Psychological Review, 69,* 74–90.
Telch, M. J., Lucas, J. A., & Nelson, P. (1989). Nonclinical panic in college students: An investigation of prevalence and symptomatology. *Journal of Abnormal Psychology, 98,* 300–306.
Tellegen, A., Lykken, D. T., Bouchard, T. J., Jr., Wilcox, K. J., & Rich, S. (1988). Personality similarity in twins reared apart and together. *Journal of Personality and Social Psychology, 54,* 1031–1039.
Terkel, S. (1972). *Working.* New York. Pantheon.
Terkel, S. (1992). *Race: How blacks and whites think and feel about the American obsession.* New York: New Press.
Terman, L. M. (1916). *The measurement of intelligence.* Boston: Houghton Mifflin.
Terman, M., Terman, J., Quitkin, F., McGrath, P., Stewart, J., & Rafferty, B. (1989). Light therapy for seasonal affective disorder: A review of efficacy. *Neuropsychopharmacology, 2,* 1–22.
Terrace, H. S. (1985). In the beginning was the "name." *American Psychologist, 40,* 1011–1028.
Terrace, H. S. (1986). *Nim: A chimpanzee who learned sign language.* New York: Columbia University Press.
Terrace, H. S., Petitto, L. A., Sanders, R. J., & Bever, T. G. (1979). Can an ape create a sentence? *Science, 206,* 891–902.
Terry, R. D., Katzman, R., & Bick, K. L. (Eds.) (1994). *Alzheimer's disease.* New York: Raven Press.
Tesser, A. (1993). The importance of heritability in psychological research: The case of attitudes. *Psychological Review, 100,* 129–142.
Tetlock, P. E., Peterson, R. S., McGuire, C., Chang, S., & Feld, P. (1992). Assessing political group dynamics: A test of the groupthink model. *Journal of Personality and Social Psychology, 63,* 403–425.
Tett, R. P., Jackson, D. N., & Rothstein, M. (1991). Personality measures as predictors of job performance: A meta-analytic review. *Personnel Psychology, 44,* 703–742.
Thach, W. T., Goodkin, H. P., & Keating, J. G. (1992). The cerebellum and the adaptive coordination of movement. *Annual Review of Neuroscience, 15,* 403–442.
Thal, L. J. (1992). Cholinomimetic therapy in Alzheimer's disease. In L. Squire & N. Butters (Eds.), *Neuropsychology of memory* (2nd ed., pp. 277–284). New York: Guilford Press.
Thapar, A., & Greene, R. L. (1993). Evidence against a short-term store account of long-term recency effects. *Memory and Cognition, 21,* 329–337.
Thase, M. E., & Kupfer, D. J. (1996). Recent developments in the pharmacotherapy of mood disorders. *Journal of Consulting and Clinical Psychology, 64,* 646–659.
Thatcher, R. W., Walker, R. A., & Giudice, S. (1986). Human cerebral hemispheres develop at different rates and different ages. *Science, 236,* 1110–1113.
Thessing, V. C., Anch, A. M., Muelbach, M. J., Schweitzer, P. K., & Walsh, J. K. (1994). Two- and 4-hour bright-light exposure differentially affect sleepiness and performance the subsequent night. *Sleep, 17,* 140–145.
Thibodeau, R., & Aronson, E. (1992). Taking a closer look: Reasserting the role of the self-concept in dissonance theory. *Personality and Social Psychology Bulletin, 18,* 591–602.
Thoman, E. B., & Ingersoll, E. W. (1993). Learning in premature infants. *Developmental Psychology, 29,* 692–700.
Thoman, E. B., Ingersoll, E. W., & Acebo, C. (1991). Premature infants seek rhythmic stimulation, and the experience facilitates neurobehavioral development. *Journal of Developmental and Behavioral Pediatrics, 12,* 11–18.
Thompson, J. G. (1988). *The psychobiology of emotions.* New York: Plenum.
Thompson, J. K. (Ed.) (1996). *Body image, eating disorders, and obesity.* Washington, DC: American Psychological Association.
Thompson, J. K., & Gray, J. J. (1995). Development and validation of a new body image assessment scale. *Journal of Personality Assessment, 64,* 258–269.
Thompson, S. C., Sobolew-Shubin, A., Galbraith, M., Schwankovsky, L., & Cruzen, D. (1993). Maintaining perceptions of control: Finding perceived control in low-control circumstances. *Journal of Personality and Social Psychology, 64,* 293–304.
Thorndike, E. L. (1898). Animal intelligence: An experimental study of the associative processes in animals. *Psychological Monographs, 2* (Whole No. 8).
Thorndike, E. L. (1911). *Animal intelligence: Experimental studies.* New York: Macmillan.
Thorndike, E. L., et al. (1921). Intelligence and its measurement: A symposium. *Journal of Educational Psychology, 12,* 123–247.
Thorndike, R. L., Hagen, E. P., & Sattler, J. M. (1986). *Technical manual for the Stanford-Binet Intelligence Scale: Fourth edition.* Chicago: Riverside.
Thorne, B. (1986). Girls and boys together . . . but mostly apart: Gender arrangements in elementary schools. In W. W. Hartup & Z. Rubin (Eds.), *Relationships and development* (pp. 167–184). Hillsdale, NJ: Erlbaum.
Thurstone, L. L. (1938). *Primary mental abilities.* Chicago: University of Chicago Press.
Tice, D. M. (1991). Esteem protection or enhancement? Self-handicapping motives and attributions differ by trait self-esteem. *Journal of Personality and Social Psychology, 60,* 711–725.
Timberlake, W. (1993). Animal behavior: A continuing synthesis. *Annual Review of Psychology, 44,* 675–708.
Time (1990). Women: The road ahead. (Special Issue)
Time (1994, June 27), p. 26.
Tinbergen, N. (1951). *The study of instinct.* New York: Oxford University Press.
Tobias, S. (1989, September). Tracked to fail. *Psychology Today,* 54–60.
Tolman, E. C. (1948). Cognitive maps in rats and men. *Psychological Review, 55,* 189–208.
Tolman, E. C., & Honzik, C. H. (1930). Introduction and removal of reward and maze performance in rats. *University of California Publications in Psychology, 4,* 257–275.
Tomarken, A. J., Davidson, R. J., Wheeler, R. E., & Doss, R. C. (1992). Individual differences in anterior brain asymmetry and fundamental dimensions of emotion. *Journal of Personality and Social Psychology, 62,* 676–687.

Top, T. J. (1991). Sex bias in the evaluation of performance in the scientific, artistic, and literary professions: A review. *Sex Roles, 24,* 73–106.
Torrey, E. F. (1988). *Surviving schizophrenia: A family manual.* New York: Harper & Row.
Totterdell, P., Spelten, E., Smith, L., Barton, J., & Folkard, S. (1995). Recovery from work shifts: How long does it take? *Journal of Applied Psychology, 80,* 43–57.
Toufexis, A. (1989, June 12). Our violent kids. *Time,* pp. 52–58.
Toufexis, A. (1991, August 15). Now hear this—if you can. *Time,* pp. 33–34.
Toufexis, A. (1993, May 24). Sex has many accents. *Time,* p. 66.
Tourangeau, R., Rasinski, K. A., & D'Andrade, R. (1991). Attitude structure and belief accessibility. *Journal of Experimental Social Psychology, 27,* 48–75.
Townsend, B., Cotter, N., Van Compernolled, J., & White, R. L. (1987). Pitch perception of cochlear implant subjects. *Journal of the Acoustical Society of America, 82,* 106–114.
Trafimow, D., Silverman, E. S., Fan, R. M. T., & Law, J. S. F. (1997). The effects of language and priming on the relative accessibility of the private self and collective self. *Journal of Cross-Cultural Psychology, 28,* 107–123.
Trafimow, D., Triandis, H. C., & Goto, S. G. (1991). Some tests of the distinction between the private and collective self. *Journal of Personality and Social Psychology, 60,* 649–655.
Tranel, D., & Damasio, A. R. (1985). Knowledge without awareness: An autonomic index of facial recognition by prosopagnosics. *Science, 228,* 1453–1454.
Travis, J. (1994). Glia: The brain's other cells. *Science, 266,* 970–972.
Treisman, A., Viera, A., & Hayes, A. (1992). Automaticity and preattentive processes. *American Journal of Psychology, 105,* 341–362.
Triandis, H. C. (1994). *Culture and social behavior.* New York: McGraw-Hill.
Triandis, H. C. (1995). *Individualism and collectivism.* Boulder, CO: Westview Press.
Triplett, N. (1898). The dynamogenic factors in pacemaking and competition. *American Journal of Psychology, 9,* 507–533.
Trope, Y. (1986). Identification and inferential processes in dispositional attribution. *Psychological Review, 93,* 239–257.
Trotter, R. J. (1986, August). Three heads are better than one. *Psychology Today,* pp. 56–62.
Tsuang, M. T., & Faraone, S. V. (1990). *The genetics of mood disorders.* Baltimore, MD: Johns Hopkins University Press.
Tulving, E. (1985). How many memory systems are there? *American Psychologist, 40,* 385–398.
Tulving, E., & Schacter, D. L. (1990). Priming and human memory systems. *Science, 247,* 301–306.
Turiel, E. (1983). *The development of social knowledge: Morality and convention.* New York: Cambridge University Press.
Turkkan, J. S. (1989). Classical conditioning: The new hegemony. *Behavioral and Brain Sciences, 12,* 121–179.
Turnbull, C. M. (1961). *The forest people: A study of the Pygmies of the Congo.* New York: Clarion.
Turner, J. C. (1987). *Rediscovering the social group: A self-categorization theory.* Oxford, England: Basil Blackwell.
Turner, J. C., Oakes, P. J., Haslam, S. A., & McGarty, C. (1994). Self and collective: Cognition and social context. *Personality and Social Psychology Bulletin, 20,* 454–463.
Turner, M. E., Pratkanis, A. R., Probasco, P., & Leve, C. (1992). Threat, cohesion, and group effectiveness: Testing a social identity maintenance perspective on groupthink. *Journal of Personality and Social Psychology, 63,* 781–796.
Turner, S. M., & Beidel, D. C. (1989). Social phobia: Clinical syndrome, diagnosis, and comorbidity. *Clinical Psychology Review, 9,* 3–18.
Tversky, A., & Kahneman, D. (1971). Belief in the law of small numbers. *Psychological Bulletin, 76,* 105–110.
Tversky, A., & Kahneman, D. (1973). Availability: A heuristic for judging frequency and probability. *Cognitive Psychology, 5,* 207–232.
Tversky, A., & Kahneman, D. (1981). The framing of decisions and the psychology of choice. *Science, 211,* 453–458.
Tversky, B., & Tuchin, M. (1989). A reconciliation of the evidence on eyewitness testimony: Comments on McCloskey and Zaragoza. *Journal of Experimental Psychology, 118,* 86–91.
Tyler, R. S., Lowder, M. W., Parkinson, A. J. (1995). Performance of adult Ineraid and Nucleus cochlear implant patients after 3.5 years of use. *Audiology, 34,* 135–144.
Tyron, R. C. (1940). Genetic differences in maze learning in rats. *Yearbook of the National Society for Studies in Education, 39,* 111–119.

U.S. Department of Education (1990). *America's challenge: Accelerating academic achievement* (1990). Princeton, NJ: Educational Testing Service.
U.S. Department of Education (1993). *Adult literacy in America* (1993). Princeton, NJ: Educational Testing Service.
U.S. Bureau of the Census (1991). *World Population Profile.*
Uba, L. (1994). *Asian Americans: Personality patterns, identity, and mental health.* New York: Guilford Press.
Uchino, B. N., Cacioppo, J. T., & Kiecolt-Glaser, J. K. (1996). The relationship between social support and physiological processes: A review with emphasis on underlying mechanisms and implications for health. *Psychological Bulletin, 119,* 488–531.
Ucros, C. G. (1989). Mood state-dependent memory: A meta-analysis. *Cognition and Emotion, 3,* 139–167.
Underwood, B. J. (1957). Interference and forgetting. *Psychological Review, 64,* 49–60.
Usher, J. A., & Neisser, U. (1993). Childhood amnesia and the beginnings of memory for four early life events. *Journal of Experimental Psychology: General, 122,* 155–165.

Vaillant, G. E. (1977). *Adaptation to life.* Boston: Little, Brown.
Valenstein, E. S. (1986). *Great and desperate cures: The rise and decline of psychosurgery and other radical treatments for mental illness.* New York: Basic Books.
Valenza, E., Simion, F., Cassia, V. M., & Umilta, C. (1996). Face preference at birth. *Journal of Experimental Psychology: Human Perception and Performance, 22,* 892–903.
Vallone, R. P., Griffin, D. W., Lin, S., & Ross, L. (1990). Overconfident prediction of future actions and outcomes by self and others. *Journal of Personality and Social Psychology, 58,* 582–592.
Van Biema, D. (1997, January 13). Is there a right to die? *Time,* pp. 60–61.
Van de Castle, R. L. (1994). *Our dreaming mind.* New York: Ballantine Books.
Van Giffen, K., & Haith, M. M. (1984). Infant visual response to gestalt geometric forms. *Infant Behavior and Development, 7,* 335–346.
Van IJzendoorn, M. H., & Kroonenberg, P. M. (1988). Cross-cultural patterns of attachment: A meta-analysis of the Strange Situation. *Child Development, 59,* 147–156.
VanderZee, K. I., Buunk, B. P., DeRuiter, J. H., Tempelaar, R., VanSonderen, E., & Sanderman, R. (1996). Social comparison and the subjective well-being of cancer patients. *Basic and Applied Social Psychology, 18,* 453–468.
Vauclair, J. (1996). *Animal cognition: An introduction to modern comparative psychology.* Cambridge, MA: Harvard University Press.
Vauclair, J., Fagot, J., & Hopkins, W. D. (1993). Rotation of mental images in baboons when the visual input is directed to the left cerebral hemisphere. *Psychological Science, 4,* 99–103.
Veenhoven, R. (1993). *Happiness in nations.* Rotterdam, Netherlands: Risbo.
Verma, A., Hirsch, D. J., Glatt, C. E., Ronnett, G. V., & Snyder, S. H. (1993). Carbon monoxide: A putative neural messenger. *Science, 259,* 381–384.
Vernon, P. A. (1987). *Speed of information-processing and intelligence.* Norwood, NJ: Ablex.
Vernon, P. A. (Ed.) (1993). *Biological approaches to the study of human intelligence.* Norwood, NJ: Ablex.
Vimal, R. L. P., Pokorny, J., & Smith, V. C. (1987). Appearance of steadily viewed lights. *Vision Research, 27,* 1309–1318.
Visintainer, M., Volpicelli, J., & Seligman, M. (1982). Tumor rejection in rats after inescapable or escapable shock. *Science, 216,* 437–439.
Vogel, D. A., Lake, M. A., Evans, S., & Karraker, K. H. (1991). Children's and adults' sex-stereotyped perceptions of infants. *Sex Roles, 24,* 605–616.
von Frisch, K. (1974). Decoding the language of the bee. *Science, 185,* 663–668.
von Hippel, W., Sekaquaptewa, D., & Vargas, P. (1995). On the role of encoding processes in stereotype maintenance. *Advances in Experimental Social Psychology, 27,* 177–254.
Vosniadou, S., & Brewer, W. F. (1992). Mental models of the earth: A study of conceptual change in childhood. *Cognitive Psychology, 24,* 535–585.
Vroom, V. H. (1964). *Work and motivation.* New York: Wiley.

Wade, M. G., & Whiting, H. T. A. (Eds.) (1986). *Motor development in children: Aspects of coordination and control.* Dordrecht, Netherlands: Martinus Nijhoff.
Wade, N. (1990). *Visual allusions: Pictures of Perception.* Hillsdale, NJ: Erlbaum.
Wagenaar, W. A. (1988). *Paradoxes of gambling behavior.* Hillsdale, NJ: Erlbaum.
Wagner, H. L., MacDonald, C. J., & Manstead, A. S. R. (1986). Communication of individual emotions by spontaneous facial expressions. *Journal of Personality and Social Psychology, 50,* 737–743.
Wagstaff, G. F. (1981). *Hypnosis, compliance, and belief.* New York: St. Martin's Press.
Wald, G. (1964). The receptors of human color vision. *Science, 145,* 1007–1017.
Waldman, D. A., & Avolio, B. J. (1986). A meta-analysis of age differences in job performance. *Journal of Applied Psychology, 71,* 33–38.
Walk, R. D. (1981). *Perceptual development.* Monterey, CA: Brooks/Cole.
Walker, E., & Lewine, R. J. (1990). Prediction of adult-onset schizophrenia from childhood home movies of the patients. *American Journal of Psychiatry, 147,* 1052–1056.
Walker, L. J. (1984). Sex differences in the development of moral reasoning: A critical review. *Child Development, 55,* 677–691.
Walker, L. J. (1989). A longitudinal study of moral reasoning. *Child Development, 60,* 157–166.
Wallace, A. (1986). *The prodigy: A biography of William James Sidis, the world's greatest child prodigy.* London: Macmillan.
Wallace, W. P. (1965). Review of the historical, empirical, and theoretical status of the von Restorff phenomenon. *Psychological Bulletin, 63,* 410–424.

Wallis, C. (1995, March 6). How to live to be 120. *Time,* p. 85.
Walton, G. E., Bower, N. J. A., & Bower, T. G. R. (1992). Recognition of familiar faces by newborns. *Infant Behavior and Development, 15,* 265–269.
Warchol, M. E., Lambert, P. R., Goldstein, B. J., Forge, A., & Corwin, J. T. (1993). Regenerative proliferation in inner ear sensory epithelia from adult guinea pigs and humans. *Science, 259,* 1619–1622.
Warga, C. (1988, September). Profile: Albert Ellis. *Psychology Today,* pp. 55–58.
Wark, G. R., & Krebs, D. L. (1996). Gender and dilemma differences in real-life moral judgment. *Developmental Psychology, 32,* 220–230.
Warr, P. (1992). Age and occupational well-being. *Psychology and Aging, 7,* 37–45.
Warrington, E. K., & Weiskrantz, L. (1970). Amnesic syndrome: Consolidation or retrieval? *Nature, 228,* 629–630.
Wason, P. C. (1960). On the failure to eliminate hypotheses in a conceptual task. *Quarterly Journal of Experimental Psychology, 12,* 129–140.
Wasserman, E. A. (1993). Comparative cognition: Beginning the second century of the study of animal intelligence. *Psychological Bulletin, 113,* 211–228.
Waterman, A. S. (1982). Identity development from adolescence to adulthood: An extension of theory and a review of research. *Developmental Psychology, 18,* 341–358.
Watkins, L. R., & Mayer, D. J. (1982). Organization of endogenous opiate and nonopiate pain control systems. *Science, 216,* 1185–1192.
Watkins, M. J., & Peynircioglu, Z. F. (1984). Determining perceived meaning during impression formation: Another look at the meaning change hypothesis. *Journal of Personality and Social Psychology, 46,* 1005–1016.
Watson, D., & Pennebaker, J. W. (1989). Health complaints, stress, and distress: Exploring the central role of negative affectivity. *Psychological Review, 96,* 234–254.
Watson, D. L., & Tharp, R. G. (1989). *Self-directed behavior: Self-modification for personal adjustment.* Pacific Grove, CA: Brooks/Cole.
Watson, J. B. (1913). Psychology as the behaviorist views it. *Psychological Review, 20,* 158–177.
Watson, J. B. (1925). *Behaviorism.* New York: Norton.
Watson, J. B. (1927). The myth of the unconscious. *Harper's, 155,* 502–508.
Watson, J. B., & Rayner, R. (1920). Conditioned emotional reactions. *Journal of Experimental Psychology, 3,* 1–14.
Watson, R. I., & Evans, R. B. (1991). *The great psychologists: A history of psychological thought.* New York: HarperCollins.
Weaver, C. A., III. (1993). Do you need a "flash" to form a flashbulb memory? *Journal of Experimental Psychology: General, 122,* 39–46.
Webb, W. B. (1992). *Sleep the gentle tyrant* (2nd ed.). Bolton, MA: Anker.
Weber, E. H. (1834). *De pulen, resorptione, auditu et tactu: Annotationes anatomicae et physiologicae.* Leipzig, Germany: Kohler.
Weber, J. G. (1994). The nature of ethnocentric attribution bias: Ingroup protection or enhancement? *Journal of Experimental Social Psychology, 30,* 482–504.
Webster, D. M. (1993). Motivated augmentation and reduction of the overattribution bias. *Journal of Personality and Social Psychology, 65,* 261–271.
Webster, D. M., Richter, L., & Kruglanski, A. W. (1996). On leaping to conclusions when feeling tired: Mental fatigue effects on impressional primacy. *Journal of Experimental Social Psychology, 32,* 181–195.
Wechsler, D. (1939). *The measurement of adult intelligence.* Baltimore: Williams & Wilkins.
Wechsler, D. (1972). "Hold" and "don't hold" test. In S. M. Chown (Ed.), *Human aging.* New York: Penguin.
Wechsler, D. (1981). *Manual for the Wechsler Adult Intelligence Scale—Revised.* New York: Psychological Corporation.
Wegner, D. M. (1989). *White bears and other unwanted thoughts: Suppression, obsession, and the psychology of mental control.* New York: Viking.
Wegner, D. M. (1994). Ironic processes of mental control. *Psychological Review, 101,* 34–52.
Wegner, D. M., & Zanakos, S. (1994). Chronic thought suppression. *Journal of Personality,* 62, 615–640.
Weil, A. T. (1974, July). Parapsychology: Andrew Weil's search for the true Geller: Part II. The letdown. *Psychology Today,* pp. 74–78, 82.
Weil, A., & Rosen, W. (1993). *From chocolate to morphine: Everyday mind-altering drugs.* Boston: Houghton Mifflin.
Weinberg, R. A. (1989). Intelligence and IQ: Landmark issues and great debates. *American Psychologist,* 44, 98–104.
Weinberg, R. A., Scarr, S., & Waldman, I. D. (1992). The Minnesota transracial adoption study: The follow-up of IQ test performance at adolescence. *Intelligence, 16,* 117–135.
Weinberger, H., Hiner, S. L., & Tierney, W. M. (1987). In support of hassles as a measure of stress in predicting health outcomes. *Journal of Behavioral Medicine, 10,* 481–500.
Weiner, B. (1985). An attributional theory of achievement motivation and emotion. *Psychological Review, 92,* 548–573.
Weiner, B. (1989). *Human motivation.* Mahwah, NJ: Erlbaum.
Weiner, I. B. (1997). Current status of the Rorschach inkblot method. *Journal of Personality Assessment, 68,* 5–19.
Weingardt, K. R., Loftus, E. F., & Lindsay, D. S. (1995). Misinformation revisited: New evidence on the suggestibility of memory. *Memory and Cognition, 23,* 72–82.
Weingartner, H., Grafman, J., Boutelle, W., Kaye, W., & Martin, P. R. (1983). Forms of memory failure. *Science, 221,* 380–382.
Weinstein, N. D. (1980). Unrealistic optimism about future life events. *Journal of Personality and Social Psychology,* 39, 806–820.
Weinstein, S. (1968). Intensive and extensive aspects of tactile sensitivity as a function of body part, sex, and laterality. In D. R. Kenshalo (Ed.), *The skin senses* (pp. 195–218). Springfield, IL: Thomas.
Weisberg, R. W. (1986). *Creativity: Genius and other myths.* New York: W. H. Freeman.
Weisberg, R. W. (1992). Metacognition and insight during problem solving: Comment on Metcalfe. *Journal of Experimental Psychology: Learning, Memory, and Cognition, 18,* 426–431.
Weiskrantz, L. (1995). Blindsight: Not an island unto itself. *Current Directions in Psychological Science, 4,* 146–151.
Weiss, D. E. (1991). *The great divide.* New York: Simon & Schuster.
Weiss, G., & Hechtman, L. (1993). *Hyperactive children grown up.* New York: Guilford Press.
Weissberg, M. (1993). Multiple personality disorder and iatrogenesis: The cautionary tale of Anna O. *International Journal of Clinical and Experimental Hypnosis, 41,* 15–34.
Weisz, J. R., Suwanlert, S., Chaiyasit, W., Weiss, B., Achenbach, T. M., & Eastman, K. L. (1993). Behavioral and emotional problems among Thai and American adolescents: Parent reports for ages 12–16. *Journal of Abnormal Psychology, 102,* 395–403.
Wells, G. L. (1993). What do we know about eyewitness identification? *American Psychologist, 48,* 553–571.
Wells, G. L., Lindsay, R. C. L., & Ferguson, T. J. (1979). Accuracy, confidence, and juror perceptions in eyewitness identification. *Journal of Applied Psychology,* 64, 440–448.
Wells, G. L., & Murray, D. M. (1984). Eyewitness confidence. In G. Wells & E.Loftus (Eds.), *Eyewitness testimony: Psychological perspectives* (pp. 155–170). New York: Cambridge University Press.
Wenk, G. L. (1989). An hypothesis on the role of glucose in the mechanism of action of cognitive enhancers. *Psychopharmacology, 99,* 431–438.
Wernicke, C. (1874). *Das aphasische symptomenkomplex.* Breslau, Poland: Cohn und Weigart.
West, P. D. B., & Evans, E. F. (1990). Early detection of hearing damage in young listeners resulting from exposure to amplified music. *British Journal of Audiology, 24,* 89–103.
Westefeld, J. S., & Furr, S. R. (1987). Suicide and depression among college students. *Professional Psychology: Research and Practice, 18,* 119–123.
Westen, D. (1990). Psychoanalytic approaches to personality. In L. A. Pervin (Ed.), *Handbook of personality theory and research.* New York: Guilford Press.
Wheeler, L., & Miyake, K. (1992). Social comparison in everyday life. *Journal of Personality and Social Psychology, 62,* 760–773.
Wheeler, M. A. (1995). Improvement in recall over time without repeated testing: Spontaneous recovery revisited. *Journal of Experimental Psychology: Learning, Memory, and Cognition, 21,* 173–184.
Whitbourne, S. K. (1996). *The aging individual: Physical and psychological perspectives.* New York: Springer.
White, G. L., & Mullen, P. E. (1990). *Jealousy: Theory, research, and clinical strategies.* New York: Guilford Press.
White, G. L., Fishbein, S., & Rutstein, J. (1981). Passionate love and misattribution of arousal. *Journal of Personality and Social Psychology, 41,* 52–62.
White, L., & Edwards, J. N. (1990). Emptying the nest and parental well-being: An analysis of national panel data. *American Sociological Review, 55,* 235–242.
White, L., Tursky, B., & Schwartz, G. E. (1985). *Placebo: Theory, research, and mechanisms.* New York: Guilford Press.
White, N. M., & Milner, P. M. (1992). The psychobiology of reinforcers. *Annual Review of Psychology, 43,* 443–471.
White, R. W. (1975). *Lives in progress* (3rd ed.). New York: Holt, Rinehart & Winston.
Whiting, R. (1989). *You gotta have wa.* New York: Macmillan.
Whiting, B. B., & Edwards, C. P. (1988). *Children of different worlds.* Cambridge, MA: Harvard University Press.
Whitney, P. (1986). Processing category terms in context: Instantiations as inferences. *Memory and Cognition, 14,* 39–48.
Whorf, B. L. (1956). Science and linguistics. In J. B. Carroll (Ed.), *Language, thought, and reality: Selected writings of Benjamin Lee Whorf* (pp. 207–219). Cambridge, MA: MIT Press.
Wicklund, R. A. (1975). Objective self-awareness. In L. Berkowitz (Ed.), *Advances in experimental social psychology* (Vol 8, pp. 233–275). New York: Academic Press.
Widiger, T. A., Frances, A. J., Pincus, H. A., First, M. B., Ross, R., & Davis, W. (Eds.) (1994). *DSM-IV Sourcebook.* Washington, DC: American Psychiatric Press.
Wiedenfeld, S. A., O'Leary, A., Bandura, A., Brown, S., Levine, S., & Raska, K. (1990). Impact of perceived self-efficacy in coping with stressors on coping with the immune system. *Journal of Personality and Social Psychology, 59,* 1082–1094.
Wiens, A. N., & Menustik, C. E. (1983). Treatment outcome and patient characteristics in an aversion therapy program for alcoholism. *American Psychologist, 38,* 1089–1096.
Wierzbicka, A. (1985). Different cultures, different languages, different speech acts. *Journal of Pragmatics, 9,* 145–178.

Wiggins, J. S. (Ed.) (1996). *The five-factor model of personality: Theoretical perspectives.* New York: Guilford Press.
Wiggins, J. S., & Pincus, A. L. (1992). Personality: Structure and assessment. *Annual Review of Psychology, 43,* 473–504.
Wilder, D. A. (1986). Social categorization: Implications for creation and reduction of intergroup bias. In L. Berkowitz (Ed.), *Advances in experimental social psychology* (Vol. 19, pp. 291–355). New York: Academic Press.
Wilder, D. A., & Shapiro, P. (1991). Facilitation of outgroup stereotypes by enhanced ingroup identity. *Journal of Experimental Social Psychology, 27,* 431–452.
Williams, G. C., Grow, V. M., Freedman, Z. R., & Ryan, R. M. (1996). Motivational predictors of weight loss and weight-loss maintenance. *Journal of Personality and Social Psychology, 70,* 115–176.
Williams, J. E., & Best, D. L. (1982). *Measuring sex stereotypes: A thirty-nation study.* Beverly Hills, CA: Sage.
Williams, J. E., & Best, D. L. (1990). *Sex and psyche: Gender and self viewed cross-culturally.* Newbury Park, CA: Sage.
Williams, J. M. G., Mathews, A., & MacLeod, C. (1996). The emotional Stroop task and psychopathology. *Psychological Bulletin, 120,* 3–24.
Williams, R. (1993). *Anger kills.* New York: Times Books.
Willis, S. L. (1990). Introduction to the special section on cognitive training in later adulthood. *Developmental Psychology, 26,* 875–878.
Wills, T. A. (Ed.) (1990). Social support in social and clinical psychology. *Journal of Social and Clinical Psychology, 9.* (Special Issue)
Wilson, G. T., Rossiter, E., Kleinfield, E. I., & Lindholm, L. (1986). Cognitive-behavioral treatment of bulimia nervosa: A controlled evaluation. *Behavior Research and Therapy, 24,* 277–288.
Wilson, J. D., George, F. W., & Griffin, J. E. (1981). The hormonal control of sexual development. *Science, 211,* 1278–1284.
Wilson, T. D., Houston, C. E., Brekke, N., & Etling, K. M. (1996). A new look at anchoring effects: Basic anchoring and its antecedents. *Journal of Experimental Psychology: General, 125,* 387–402.
Windschitl, P. D. (1996). Memory for faces: Evidence of retrieval-based impairment. *Journal of Experimental Psychology: Learning, Memory, and Cognition, 22,* 1101–1122.
Winger, G., Hofmann, F. G., & Woods, J. H. (1992). *A handbook on drug and alcohol abuse* (3rd. ed.). New York: Oxford University Press.
Winn, P. (1995). The lateral hypothalamus and motivated behavior: An old syndrome reassessed and a new perspective gained. *Psychological Science, 4,* 182–187.
Winograd, E., & Neisser, U. (Eds.) (1992). *Affect and accuracy in recall: Studies of 'flashbulb' memories.* New York: Cambridge University Press.
Winokur, G., Coryell, W., Keller, M., Endicott, J., & Akiskall, H. S. (1993). A prospective follow-up of patients with bipolar and primary unipolar affective disorder. *Archives of General Psychiatry, 50,* 457–465.
Winter, D. G. (1973). *The power motive.* New York: Free Press.
Winter, D. G. (1993). Power, affiliation, and war: Three tests of a motivational model. *Journal of Personality and Social Psychology, 65,* 532–545.
Wise, R. A. (1996). Addictive drugs and brain stimulation reward. *Annual Review of Neuroscience, 19,* 319–340.
Wise, R. A., & Rompre, P. P. (1989). Brain dopamine and reward. *Annual Review of Psychology, 40,* 191–225.
Wittchen, H. U., Zhao, S., Kessler, R. C., & Eaton, W. W. (1994). DSM–III-R generalized anxiety disorder in the National Comorbidity Survey. *Archives of General Psychiatry, 51,* 355–364.
Witteman, P. A. (1990, April 30). Vietnam: 15 years later. *Time,* pp. 19–21.
Wittig, R. (1993). Continuous positive airway pressure. In M. A. Carskadon (Ed.), *Encyclopedia of Sleep and Dreaming* (pp. 139–141). New York: Macmillan.
Wolpe, J. (1958). *Psychotherapy by reciprocal inhibition.* Palo Alto, CA: Stanford University Press.
Wolpe, J. (1982). *The practice of behavior therapy* (3rd ed.). New York: Pergamon.
Wong, D. F., et al. (1986). Positron emission tomography reveals elevated D–2 dopamine receptors in drug-naive schizophrenics. *Science, 234,* 1558–1563.
Wood, J. M., Nezworski, M. T., & Stejskal, W. J. (1996). The comprehensive system for the Rorschach: A critical examination. Psychological *Science, 7,* 3–10.
Wood, J. V., Giordano-Beech, M., Taylor, K. L., Michela, J. L., & Gaus, V. (1994). Strategies for social comparison among people with low self-esteem: Self-protection and self-enhancement. *Journal of Personality and Social Psychology, 67,* 713–731.
Wood, J. V., Taylor, S. E., & Lichtman, R. R. (1985). Social comparison in adjustment to breast cancer. *Journal of Personality and Social Psychology, 49,* 1169–1183.
Wood, N. L., & Cowan, N. (1995). The cocktail party phenomenon revisited: Attention and memory in the classic selective learning procedure of Cherry (1953). *Journal of Experimental Psychology: General, 124,* 243–262.
Wood, W., Lundgren, S., Ouellette, J. A., Busceme, S., & Blackstone, T. (1994). Minority influence: A meta-analytic review of social influence processes. *Psychological Bulletin, 115,* 323–345.
Wood, W., Wong, F. Y., & Chachere, J. G. (1991). Effects of media violence on viewers' aggression in unconstrained social interaction. *Psychological Bulletin, 109,* 371–383.
Woodhead, M. (1988). When psychology informs public policy: The case of early childhood intervention. *American Psychologist, 43,* 443–454.
Woodward, A. L., Markman, E. M., & Fitzsimmons, C. M. (1994). Rapid word-learning in 13- and 18-month-olds. *Developmental Psychology, 30,* 553–566.
Wright, J. W. (Ed.) (1993). *The Universal Almanac.* Kansas City, MO: Andrews & McMeel.
Wright, L., von Bussman, K., Friedman, A., Khoury, M., & Owens, F. (1990). Exaggerated social control and its relationship to the Type A behavior pattern. *Journal of Research in Personality, 24,* 258–269.
Wynn, K. (1992). Addition and subtraction by human infants. *Nature, 358,* 749–750.
Wynn, K. (1996). Infants' individuation and enumeration of actions. *Psychological Science, 7,* 164–169.
Wyrwicka, W., & Dobrzecka, C. (1960). Relationship between feeding and satiation centers of the hypothalamus, *Science, 132,* 805–806.

Yalom, I. D. (1989). *Love's executioner and other tales of psychotherapy.* New York: HarperCollins.
Yam, P. (1995). James Randi: A skeptically inquiring mind. *Scientific American, 273,* 34–35.
Yau, J., & Smetana, J. G. (1996). Adolescent-parent conflict among Chinese adolescents in Hong Kong. *Child Development, 67,* 1262–1275.
Yee, D. K., & Eccles, J. S. (1988). Parent perceptions and attributions for children's math achievement. *Sex Roles, 19,* 317–333.
Young, A. W., & De Haan, E. H. F. (1992). Face recognition and awareness after brain injury. In A. D. Milner & M. D. Rugg (Eds.), *The neuropsychology of consciousness.* London: Academic Press.
Young, K. T. (1990). American conceptions of infant development from 1955 to 1984: What the experts are telling parents. *Child Development, 61,* 17–28.
Young, T. (1802). On the theory of light and colors. *Philosophical Transactions of the Royal Society of London, 92,* 12–48.
Yuille, J. C., & Tollestrup, P. A. (1990). Some effects of alcohol on eye witness memory. *Journal of Applied Psychology, 75,* 268–273.

Zahler, D., & Zahler, K. A. (1993). *Test your cultural literacy* (2nd ed.). New York: ARCO.
Zahn-Waxler, C., Radke-Yarrow, M., Wagner, E., & Chapman, M. (1992). Development of concern for others. *Developmental Psychology, 28,* 126–136.
Zajonc, R. B. (1965). Social facilitation. *Science, 149,* 269–274.
Zajonc, R. B. (1968). Attitudinal effects of mere exposure. *Journal of Personality and Social Psychology Monograph,* 9 (2, part 2), 1–27.
Zajonc, R. B. (1976). Family configuration and intelligence. *Science, 192,* 227–236.
Zajonc, R. B. (1984). On the primacy of affect. *American Psychologist, 39,* 117–123.
Zajonc, R. B. (1986). The decline and rise of Scholastic Aptitude Scores: A prediction derived from the confluence model. *American Psychologist, 41,* 862–867.
Zajonc, R. B. (1993). Brain temperature and subjective emotional experience. In M. Lewis & J. M. Haviland (Eds.), *Handbook of emotions* (pp. 209–220). New York: Guilford Press.
Zajonc, R. B., & Mullally, P. R. (1997). Birth order: Reconciling conflicting effects. *American Psychologist, 52,* 685–699.
Zajonc, R. B., Murphy, S. T., & Inglehart, M. (1989). Feeling and facial efference: Implications of the vascular theory of emotion. *Psychological Review, 96,* 395–416.
Zebrowitz, L. A., & McDonald, S. M. (1991). The impact of litigants' babyfacedness and attractiveness on adjudications in small claims courts. *Law and Human Behavior,* 603–624.
Zechmeister, E. B., & Johnson, J. E. (1992). Critical thinking: A functional approach. Belmont, CA: Wadsworth.
Zee, R. F. (1993). Neuropsychological functioning in Alzheimer's disease. In R. W. Parks, R. F. Zee, & R. S. Wilson (Eds.), *Neuropsychology of Alzheimer's Disease and other dementias* (pp. 3–80). New York: Oxford University Press.
Zeki, S. (1992). The visual image in mind and brain. *Scientific American, 267,* 68–76.
Zentall, S. S., & Zentall, T. R. (1983). Optimal stimulation: A model of disordered activity and performance in normal and deviant children. *Psychological Bulletin, 94,* 446–471.
Zentall, T. R., Sutton, J. E., & Sherburne, L. M. (1996). True imitative learning in pigeons. *Psychological Science, 7,* 343–346.
Zigler, E. (1987). Formal schooling for 4-year-olds? No. *American Psychologist, 42,* 254–260.
Zigler, E., & Muenchow, S. (1992). *Head Start: The inside story of America's most successful educational experiment.* New York: Basic Books.
Zillman, D. (1983). Transfer of excitation in emotional behavior. In J. Cacioppo and R. Petty (Eds.), *Social psychophysiology: A sourcebook* (pp. 215–240). New York: Guilford Press.
Zillman, D., & Bryant, J. (Eds.) (1989). *Pornography: Research advances and policy considerations.* Hillsdale, NJ: Erlbaum.
Zimbardo, P. G. (1970). The human choice: Individuation, reason, and order versus deindividuation, impulse, and chaos. In W. J. Arnold & D. Levine

(Eds.), *Nebraska Symposium on Motivation: 1969* (Vol. 17, pp. 237–307). Lincoln: University of Nebraska Press.

Zimbardo, P. G. (1985, June). Laugh where we must, be candid where we can. *Psychology Today,* pp. 43–47.

Zimmerberg, B., and Gray, M. S. (1992). The effects of cocaine on maternal behaviors in the rat. *Physiology and Behavior, 52,* 379–384.

Zinbarg, R. E., Barlow, D. H., Brown, T. A., & Hertz, R. M. (1992). Cognitive-behavioral approaches to the nature and treatment of anxiety disorders. *Annual Review of Psychology, 43,* 235–267.

Zola-Morgan, S. (1995). Localization of brain function: The legacy of Franz Gall (1758–1828). *Annual Review of Neuroscience, 18,* 359–383.

Zubin, J., & Spring, B. (1977). Vulnerability—A new view of schizophrenia. *Journal of Abnormal Psychology, 86,* 103–126.

Zuckerman, M. (1979). *Sensation seeking: Beyond the optimal level of arousal.* Hillsdale, NJ: Erlbaum.

Zuckerman, M. (1990). The psychophysiology of sensation seeking. *Journal of Personality, 58,* 313–345.

Zuckerman, M. (1994). *Behavioral expressions and biosocial bases of sensation seeking.* New York: Cambridge University Press.

Credits

PHOTO CREDITS

Chapter 1 **Page 6:** Corbis-Bettman *(top);* **p. 6:** Brown Brothers *(bottom);* **p. 7:** Stock Montage, Inc./Historical Pictures Collection; **p. 11:** Annie GriffithsBelt *(left);* **p. 11:** Dan McCoy/Rainbow *(right);* **p. 15:** Yoav Levy/Phototake NYC *(top);* **p. 15:** Richard Lord/The Image Works *(bottom);* **p. 17:** Joe McNally/Sygma; **p. 19:** UPI/Corbis-Bettmann; **p. 20:** P. Breese/Gamma-Liaison, Inc.; **p. 27:** Brad Bower/Mercury Pictures *(left);* **p. 27:** Paul S. Conklin *(right).*

Chapter 2 **Page 39:** From Damasio, H., Grabowski, T., Frank, R., Galaburda, AM, Damasio, AR, "The Return of Phineas Gage: Clues about the brain from the skull of a famous patient." *Science, 264,* 1102-1105, 1994. Department of Neurology and Image Analysis Facility, University of Iowa *(top);* **p. 39:** Martin Rotker/Phototake NYC *(bottom);* **p. 44:** CNRI/Science Photo Library/Photo Researchers, Inc.; **p. 44:** Howard Sochurek/Howard Sochurek, Inc.; **p. 45:** CNRI/Science Photo Library/Photo Researchers, Inc.; **p. 49:** Ken Whitmore/Tony Stone Images; **p. 51:** Drs. John Mazziota and Michael E. Phelps/UCLA School of Medicine; **p. 52:** Dan McCoy/Rainbow *(top);* **p. 52:** SAM Technology, Inc. *(bottom);* **p. 63:** Oxford University Press, England; **p. 64:** Oxford University Press, England; **p. 66:** Marcus E. Raichle, M.D. Courtesy Dr. M.E. Raichle, Washington University School of Medicine, research based upon "Nature," vol. 331, pg. 585-589, 1988; **p. 70:** Joe Puglies/AP/Wide World Photos; **p. 71:** Bob Strong/SIPA Press.

Chapter 3 **Page 82:** Bob Krist/Tony Stone Images; **p. 86:** Omikron/Photo Researchers, Inc.; **p. 90:** Fritz Goro/Life Magazine, Time Warner, Inc.; **p. 91:** Hart-Davis/Science Photo Library Photo Researchers, Inc. Ishihara, "Test for Color Deficiency." Courtesy Kanehara Shuppan Co., Ltd. Offered exclusively in the USA by Graham-Field, Inc., Hauppauge, New York; **p. 94:** Lennart Nilsson/Bonnier Alba AB, BEHOLD MAN, p. 206-207; **p. 95:** James M. Kubus/James M. Kubus Photography; **p. 98:** Billy Hustace/Tony Stone Images *(top);* **p. 98:** Institut Pasteur/CNRI/Phototake NYC (bottom); **p. 100:** Omikron/Photo Researchers, Inc.; **p. 101:** Terry Vine/Tony Stone Images; **p. 103:** Colorsport/SIPA Press; **p. 104:** Daemmrich/Stock Boston; **p. 106:** American Psychological Association; **p. 107:** American Psychological Association; **p. 108:** Art Wolfe/Tony Stone Images; **p. 109:** David Austen/Tony Stone Images *(top);* **p. 109:** Chantra Pramkaew *(bottom left);* **p. 109:** Copyright 1998 C. Herscovici, Brussels/Artists Rights Society (ARS), New York. Magritte, René (Belgian, 1898-1967), "La conditione humaine," 1933, canvas/oil on canvas, 1.000 × .810 × .016 (39-3/8 × 31-7/8 × 5/8). Copyright 1997 Board of Trustees, National Gallery of Art, Washington, Gift of the Collectors Committee, 1933 *(bottom right);* **p. 110:** David Wells/The Image Works; **p. 110:** David Wells/The Image Works; **p. 111:** James King-Holmes/W Industries/Science Photo Library/Photo Researchers, Inc.; **p. 112:** Topham/The Image Works *(top);* **p. 112:** Werner Krutein/Photovault/ Gamma-Liaison, Inc. *(bottom);* **p. 113:** M. Granitsas/The Image Works *(top);* **p. 113:** M. Everton/The Image Works *(bottom);* **p. 116:** Petyer Pearson/Tony Stone Images; **p. 117:** Michael Dwyer/Stock Boston; **p. 118:** David Olsen/Tony Stone Images *(left);* **p. 118:** Michael J. Howell/Stock Boston *(right);* **p. 120:** Dick Ruhl; **p. 121:** Dick Ruhl.

Chapter 4 **Page 131:** Sam Sargent/Gamma-Liaison, Inc.; **p. 132:** Paul S. Conklin; **p. 137:** Tom Ives/Sygma *(right);* **p. 137:** A. Galvano/Gamma-Liaison, Inc. *(left);* **p. 140:** Arnulf Husmo/Tony Stone Images; **p. 141:** Will & Deni McIntyre/Science Source/Photo Researchers, Inc.; **p. 147:** J.A. Hobson, Harvard Medical School/Photo Researchers, Inc. *(left);* **p. 147:** The Lucidity Institute *(right);* **p. 151:** Dr. Carlos H. Schenck; **p. 152:** Brian Phillips/The Image Works; **p. 159:** Corbis-Bettmann; **p. 160:** Dan McCoy/Rainbow *(left);* **p. 160:** Tony Savino/The Image Works *(right);* **p. 160:** Cary Wolinsky/Tony Stone Images *(bottom).*

Chapter 5 **Page 172:** Treat Davidson/National Audubon Society/Photo Researchers, Inc. *(top);* **p. 172:** Wolfgang Kaehler/Gamma-Liaison, Inc. *(bottom);* **p. 175:** The Granger Collection; **p. 183:** J.-L. Atlan/Sygma; **p. 187:** Yoav Levy/Phototake NYC; **p. 189:** Jan Kopec/Tony Stone Images *(left);* **p. 189:** Ellen Shub *(right);* **p. 193:** Agence France Presse/Corbis-Bettmann; **p. 194:** Culver Pictures, Inc.; **p. 195:** Jon Riley/Tony Stone Images *(left);* **p. 195:** Rob Nelson/Black Star *(right);* **p. 196:** Charles Gupton/Stock Boston; **p. 201:** Everett Collection.

Chapter 6 **Page 209:** Corbis-Bettmann; **p. 211:** "Color of Memory," watercolor, collage by Richard E. Schaffer. Photo courtesy of Daniel L. Schacter Collection; **p. 213:** Dave Cannon/Tony Stone Images; **p. 216:** Enrico Ferorelli; **p. 224:** Lori Adamski Peek/Tony Stone Images *(left);* **p. 224:** Kathleen Campbell/Gamma-Liaison, Inc. *(right);* **p. 227:** Gregory K. Scott/Photo Researchers, Inc.; **p. 229:** © Disney Enterprises, Inc.; **p. 230:** Christopher Morris/Black Star *(top);* **p. 230:** R. Maiman/Sygma *(bottom);* **p. 243:** Prof. William F. Brewer; **p. 244:** Loftus EF, Miller DG, Burns HJ (1978). Semantic integration of verbal information into a visual memory. *Journal of Experimental Psychology;* Human Learning and Memory, 4, 19-31; **p. 247:** Eric Reiman, University of Arizona/ Science Photo Laboratory/Photo Researchers, Inc.; **p. 250:** NASA Headquarters.

Chapter 7 **Page 258:** Frank Siteman/Stock Boston *(top left);* **p. 258:** M. Antman/The Image Works *(top right);* **p. 258:** Dan McCoy/Rainbow *(bottom);* **p. 262:** I. Uimonen/Sygma; **p. 271:** John Chiasson/Gamma-Liaison, Inc.; **p. 273:** AP/Wide World Photos; **p. 276:** Kenneth H. Thomas/Photo Researchers, Inc. *(left);* **p. 276:** Gary Brettnacher/Tony Stone Images *(right);* **p. 277:** Owen Franken/Stock Boston; **p. 280:** Michael Goldman/Time Life Syndication; **p. 281:** Michael Nichols/ Magnum Photos, Inc.; **p. 285:** James Balog/Tony Stone Images *(top);* **p. 285:** Ben Blankenburg/Stock Boston *(bottom).*

Chapter 8 **Page 295:** Sam Sargent/Gamma-Liaison, Inc. *(top);* **p. 295:** William R. Sallaz/Duomo Photography *(bottom);* **p. 297:** Iwago Photographic *(top);* **p. 297:** Addison Geary/Stock Boston *(bottom);* **p. 300:** Richard Howard/Richard Howard Photography; **p. 304:** Gilles Mingasson/Gamma-Liaison, Inc. *(left);* **p. 305:** Joel Sartore/National Geographic Society *(right);* **p. 306:** Identigene; **p. 309:** B. Daemmrich/The Image Works; **p. 314:** Fred Prouser/SIPA Press; **p. 315:** Irvington Publishers.

Chapter 9 **Page 329:** Joe McNally/Sygma; **p. 330:** Chad Slattery/Tony Stone Images; **p. 335:** Jim McHugh/Outline Press Syndicate, Inc. *(top);* **p. 335:** Paul Ekman, Ph.D./Consulting Psychologists Press, Inc. *(bottom);* **p. 336:** Courtesy Dr. Carroll Izard; **p. 337:** Matthew Stockman/All-Sport Photography U.S.A., Inc.; **p. 346:** Mark Lennihan/AP/Wide World Photos *(left);* **p. 346:** Markel/Gamma-Liaison, Inc. *(right);* **p. 349:** Mark Downey/Lucid Images; **p. 351:** Bryan and Cherry Alexander.

Chapter 10 **Page 364:** Michael Nichols/Magnum Photos, Inc.; **p. 366:** Reuters/Jeff Mitchell/Archive Photos; **p. 369:** Photo Lennart Nilsson/ Bonnier Alba AB, A CHILD IS BORN, Dell Publishing Company; **p. 371:** Professor Anthony J. DeCasper; **p. 373:** J. Pavlovsky/Sygma; **p. 374:** Joe McNally/Sygma; **p. 375:** Joe McNally/Sygma; **p. 377:** From: A.N. Meltzoff & M.K. Moore (1977). "Imitation of facial and manual gestures by human neonates." *Science, 198,* 75-78; **p. 378:** Rosenstein, D.S., and Oster, H. (1988), "Differential Facial Responses to Four Basic Tastes in Newborns." CHILD DEVELOPMENT, 59, 1555-1568; **p. 382:** American Psychological Association; **p. 384:** Goodman/ Monkmeyer Press; **p. 388:** Mandal Ranjir/Photo Researchers, Inc.; **p. 390:** Mike Derer/AP/Wide World Photos; **p. 392:** Nina Leen/Time Life Syndication; **p. 393:** Martin Rogers/Stock Boston; **p. 394:** Smithsonian Institution; **p. 397:** Mitsuaki Iwago/Minden Pictures.

Chapter 11 **Page 406:** Miro Vintoniv/Stock Boston *(left);* **p. 406:** Stephen Trimble *(right);* **p. 413:** John C. Hillery/Reuters/Corbis-Bettmann; **p. 419:** Figaro Magazine/Gamma-Liaison, Inc.; **p. 421:** Stu Forster/Allsport Photography (USA), Inc. *(top);* **p. 421:** Lennox McLendon/AP/Wide World Photos *(bottom);* **p. 423:** Steve Grayson/ Reuters/Archive Photos; **p. 431:** Carol Beckwith/Angela Fisher/Robert Estall Photo Agency; **p. 432:** Bosch, Hieronymus. Diptych: Paradise and Ascension into the Empyrean. Palazzo Ducale, Venice, Italy. Cameraphoto/Art Resource, NY.

Chapter 12 **Page 439:** Photofest *(left);* **p. 439:** Rick Smolan/Stock Boston *(right);* **p. 441:** Riverside Publishing; **p. 442:** Bob Daemmrich/The Image

Works; **p. 449:** Leonardo da Vinci (1452-1519) La Gioconda (Mona Lisa), Oil on wood (1503 and 1506). 77 × 53 cm. Louvre, Paris. Erich Lessing/Art Resource, NY *(top)*; **p. 449:** Sandra Baker/Gamma-Liaison, Inc. *(bottom)*; **p. 452:** Max Tegmark Courtesy of Simsalabim Software; **p. 453:** David Strick/Outline Press Syndicate Inc. *(top)*; **p. 453:** Michael Cohen/Sygma *(bottom)*; **p. 454:** Michael Mauney/Tony Stone Images *(left)*; **p. 454:** Harpo/Kingworld/Photofest *(middle)*; **p. 454:** Andy Hayt/Time Inc. Magazines, Sports Illustrated *(right)*; **p. 458:** Ralph Ginzburg; **p. 462:** Jacques Chenet/Woodfin Camp & Associates; **p. 463:** Patrick Harbron/ Outline Press Syndicate Inc.; **p. 466:** Arthur Tilley/Tony Stone Images.

Chapter 13 **Page 480:** Rob Crandall/Stock Boston *(left)*; **p. 480:** Scott Weersing/The Enterprise/Gamma-Liaison, Inc. *(right)*; **p. 480:** Allan Tannenbaum/Sygma *(below)*; **p. 481:** Adel Hana/AP/Wide World Photos; **p. 483:** Photofest; **p. 487:** Everett Collection; **p. 488:** Dr. Judith Langlois; **p. 489:** Gerard Pile/Tony Stone Images *(top left)*; **p. 489:** Art Wolfe/Tony Stone Images *(top right)*; **p. 489:** Anthony Cassidy/Tony Stone Images *(bottom left)*; **p. 489:** Sunset Boulevard/Sygma *(bottom right)*; **p. 490:** © Disney Enterprises, Inc. *(top)*; **p. 490:** Bob Krist *(bottom)*; **p. 491:** E. Agostini/Gamma-Liaison, Inc.; **p. 494:** Photo by William Vandivert and *Scientific American*. From "Opinions and Social Pressure" by Solomon E. Asch, November 1955. Copyright 1995 by Scientific American, Inc.; **p. 496:** AP/Wide World Photos; **p. 497:** Copyright 1965 by Stanley Milgram. From the film OBEDIENCE, distributed by Penn State Media Sales; **p. 506:** CNN/AP/Wide World Photos; **p. 507:** David Baxter/University of Cincinnati; **p. 510:** Reuters/Mike Blake/Archive Photos; **p. 511:** Acclaim Entertainment Inc.; **p. 513:** Robert Allison/ Contact Press Images.

Chapter 14 **Page 523:** Georges de Keerle/Sygma; **p. 524:** L. Kolvoord/ The Image Works *(left)*; **p. 524:** Bob Daemmrich/Bob Daemmrich Photography *(right)*; **p. 526:** Mark Downey/Lucid Images; **p. 530:** Peter Menzel/Material World; **p. 532:** Toshihiro Kitagawa/AFL-CIO; **p. 533:** John Launis/Black Star; **p. 534:** John Gibbins/SABA Press Photos, Inc.; **p. 535:** Boston Globe; **p. 538:** National Geographic Society *(top)*; **p. 537:** Paul S. Conklin *(bottom left)*; **p. 537:** Bob Daemmrich/Bob Daemmrich Photography *(bottom right)*; **p. 547:** Zigy Kaluzny/Tony Stone Images; **p. 548:** Reuters/Choo Yon-Kong/Archive Photos; **p. 551:** Rob Nelson/ Black Star; **p. 552:** Lois Bernstein/AP/Wide World Photos; **p. 555:** Owen Franken/Sygma; **p. 556:** Carol Iwasaki/Time Life Syndication; **p. 558:** AP/Wide World Photos.

Chapter 15 **Page 565:** Ann Purcell/Photo Researchers, Inc.; **p. 567:** Photo by Max Halberstatt, Mary Evans Picture Library. Freud copyrights courtesy of W. E. Freud; **p. 570:** Elizabeth Crews Photography *(top left)*; **p. 570:** Margaret Miller/Photo Researchers, Inc.*(top middle)*; **p. 570:** Louie Psihoyos/Matrix International *(top right)*; **p. 570:** Mark Downey/Lucid Images *(bottom left)*; **p. 570:** Richard Hutchings/Photo Researchers, Inc. *(bottom right)*; **p. 574:** Yoav Levy/Phototake NYC; **p. 575:** Harvard University Press; **p. 581:** B. Daemmrich/The Image Works *(top)*; **p. 581:** Kevin Horan/Tony Stone Images *(bottom)*; **p. 584:** © Rimma Gerlovina and Valeriy Gerlovin, *Manyness*, 1990, Ektacolor print, 39 1/4 × 39 1/4 inches; **p. 587:** Bruce McClelland/AP/Wide World Photos; **p. 595:** Mike Nelson/Agence France Presse/Corbis-Bettman; **p. 595:** Reuters/Mike Nelson/Archive Photos; **p. 597:** Dith Pran/New York Times Pictures.

Chapter 16 **Page 607:** Joe McNally/Matrix International; **p. 612:** Jose Azel/Aurora & Quanta Productions; **p. 614:** Edvard Munch, "The Scream," Oslo, National Gallery. Scala/Art Resource, NY; **p. 617:** Rod Planck/Tony Stone Images *(top left)*; **p. 617:** Mark Downey/Lucid Images *(top right)*; **p. 617:** Bobbie Kingsley/Photo Researchers, Inc. *(bottom)*; **p. 623:** David Longstreath/AP/Wide World Photos; **p. 624:** Gregory Hoblit/Sygma; **p. 626:** Gogh, Vincent van. "Wheatfield with Crows," 1890. Van Gogh Museum, Amsterdam, The Netherlands. Art Resource, NY; **p. 629:** Rob Nelson/Black Star; **p. 630:** Drs. Lewis Baxter and Michael Phelps, UCLA School of Medicine; **p. 633:** Internet/AP/ Wide World Photos; **p. 635:** Sandra Milne *(left)*; **p. 635:** Marisa Karasz *(right)*; **p. 636:** Grunnitus/Monkmeyer Press; **p. 641:** Mark Elias/AP/ Wide World Photos.

Chapter 17 **Page 650:** Stock Montage Inc./Historical Pictures Collection *(left)*; **p. 650:** Engraving from Rush, B., Observations on the tranquilizer. Phila. Med. Mus. n.s.: plate opps. p. 169, 1810. Courtesy National Library of Medicine *(middle)*; **p. 650:** Culver Pictures, Inc. *(right)*; **p. 651:** Mary Evans/Sigmund Freud copyrights. Mary Evans Picture Library; **p. 652:** Sygma; **p. 656:** AP/Wide World Photos *(left)*; **p. 656:** James Schnepf/Gamma-Liason, Inc. *(right)*; **p. 662:** John Chiasson/Gamma-Liaison, Inc.; **p. 670:** Hank Morgan/Science Source/Photo Researchers, Inc.; **p. 674:** Dashow/Anthro-Photo; **p. 675:** Elena Seibert/Outline Press Syndicate, Inc.; **p. 678:** Paul S. Howell/Gamma-Liaison, Inc.; **p. 680:** W W & D McIntyre/Photo Researchers, Inc.

Chapter 18 **Page 690:** FujiFotos/The Image Works; **p. 694:** Robert Brenner/PhotoEdit; **p. 697:** Bob Daemmrich/Bob Daemmrich Photography; **p. 700:** Sheila Beougher/Gamma-Liaison, Inc.; **p. 701:** David Leeson/The Image Works; **p. 704:** Krees Van den Berg/Photo Researchers, Inc.; **p. 707:** Owen Franken/Stock Boston; **p. 709:** Robert Becker, Ph. D./Custom Medical Stock Photo *(left)*; **p. 709:** Dr. Gilla Kaplan/The Rockefeller University *(middle)*; **p. 709:** Copyright Boehringer Ingelheim International GmbH, THE INCREDIBLE MACHINE, **p. 709:** Photo by Lennart Nilsson/Bonnier Alba AB *(right)*; **p. 711:** NASA; **p. 713:** Tom Walker/Stock Boston; **p. 719:** Brancusi, Constantin (Rumanian, 1876-1957), "The Kiss," 1916. H: 23 inches, W: 13 inches, D: 10 inches. Limestone. Philadelphia Museum of Art: The Louise and Walter Arensberg Collection. Photo by Graydon Wood, 1994 *(top)*; **p. 719:** Eastcott/The Image Works *(bottom)*.

TEXT CREDITS

The publishers acknowledge the copyright owners for permission to reprint the following copyrighted materials.

Pages 64-65, *extract:* Sergent, J. (1990). Furtive incursions into bicameral minds. *Brain, 113,* 537-568. Copyright © 1990 by *Brain.* Reprinted with permission of the publishers and the author's estate.

Page 218, *Figure 6.8:* Baddeley, A., & Hitch, G.J. (1974). Working memory. In G.H. Bower (Ed.), *The psychology of learning and motivation,* Vol. VIII, (pp. 47-90). New York: Academic Press.

Page 220, *Figure 6.10:* Crowder, R.G. (1993). Where do we stand? *Memory and Cognition, 21,* 142-145, Reprinted by permission of Psychonomic Society.

Page 236, *Table 6.3:* Baddeley, A. (1990). *Human memory: Theory and practice.* Copyright © 1990 by Allyn and Bacon. Reprinted/adapted by permission.

Page 249, *Figure 6.25:* Pillemer, D.B., Picariello, M.L., Law, A.B., & Reichman, J.S. (1996). Memories of college: The importance of educational episodes. In D.C. Rubin (Ed.), *Remembering our past: Studies in autobiographical memory.* New York: Cambridge University Press. Reprinted with permission.

Page 260, *Figure 7.4:* Vauclair, J., Fagot, J., & Hopkins, W.D. (1993). Rotation of mental images in baboons when visual input is directed to the left cerebral hemisphere. *Psychological Science, 4,* 100. Reprinted with permission of Cambridge University Press.

Page 283, *Table 7.3:* Savage-Rumbaugh, et al. (1993). Language comprehension in ape and child. *Monographs of the Society for Research in Child Development, 58,* (3-4): 111-210. Copyright © 1993 by Society for Research in Child Development. Reprinted with permission of the publishers.

Page 301, *Figure 8.4:* Adapted from Stunkard, A.J., Harris, J.R., Pedersen, N.L. & McClearn, G.E. (1990). The body-mass index of twins who have been reared apart. *New England Journal of Medicine, 322* (21), 1483-1487.

Page 303, *Figure 8.5:* Thompson, J.K., & Gray, J.J. (1995). Development and validation of a new body image assessment scale. *Journal of Personality Assessment, 46,* 258-269. Reprinted with permission.

Page 306, *Figure 8.6:* Kenrick, D.T., & Keefe, R.C. (1992). Age preferences in mates reflect sex differences in human reproductive strategies. *Behavioral and Brain Sciences, 15,* 81.
Page 310, *Figure 8.8:* Bailey, J.M., Pillard, R.C., Neale, M.C., & Agyei, Y. (1993). Heritable factors influence sexual orientation in women. *Archives of General Psychiatry, 50,* 217. Reprinted with permission of the American Medical Association.

Page 311, *Figure 8.9:* Bem, D.J. (1996). Exotic becomes erotic: A developmental theory of sexual orientation. *Psychological Review, 103,* 320-335. Copyright © 1996 by the American Psychological Asssociation. Reprinted with permission.

Page 319, *Figure 8.13:* Deci, E.L. (1971). Effects of externally mediated rewards on intrinsic motivation. *Journal of Personality and Social Psychology, 18,* 105-115. Copyright © 1971 by the American Psychological Association. Reprinted with permission.

Page 334, *Figure 9.7:* Reprinted with permission from Fridlund, A.J. (1994). *Human facial expression: An evolutionary view.* San Diego: Academic Press.

Page 344, *Figure 9.12:* LeDoux, J. E. (1994). Emotion, memory and the brain. *Scientific American,* June 1994. Illustration on p. 56 by Roberto Osi. Reprinted with permission of the artist.

Page 347, *Figure 9.14:* Lang, P.J. (1995). The emotion probe: Studies of motivation and attention. *American Psychologist, 50,* 372-385. Copyright © 1995 by the American Psychological Association. Reprinted with permission.

Page 387, *Figure 10.16:* Baillargeon, R. (1994). How do infants learn about the physical world? *Current Directions in Psychological Science, 5,* 133-140. Reprinted with permission of Cambridge University Press.

Page 407, *Figure 11.4:* Graber, J.A., Brooks-Gunn, J., & Petersen, A.C. (1996). *Transitions through adolescence: Interpersonal domains and context* (p. 43). Mahwah, NJ: Lawrence Erlbaum Associates. Reprinted with permission.

Page 408, *Figure 11.5:* Graber, J. A., Brooks-Gunn, J., & Petersen, A.C. (1996). *Transitions through adolescence: Interpersonal domains and context* (p. 44). Mahwah, NJ: Lawrence Erlbaum Associates. Reprinted with permission.

Page 410: *Table 11.1:* Kohlberg, L. (1969). Stage and sequence: The cognitive-development approach to socialization. In D. Goslin (Ed.) *Handbook of socialization theory and research.* Chicago: Rand McNally. Copyright © 1997 by David Goslin. Reprinted with the permission of the publishers.

Page 426, *Figure 11.13:* Simonton, D.K. (1997). Creative productivity: A predictive and explanatory model of career trajectories and landmarks. *Psychological Review, 4,* 86. Reprinted with permission of Academic Press.

Page 429, *Figure 11.15:* Myers, D.G., & Diener, E. (1995). Who is happy? *Psychological Science, 6,* 11. Reprinted with permission of Cambridge University Press.

Pages 448-449, *boxed material:* Zahler, D., & Zahler, K.A. (1993). *Test your cultural literacy* (2nd ed.). Copyright © 1988, 1993 by Diane Zahler and Kathy A. Zahler. Reprinted with permission of Macmillan General Reference USA, a Simon & Schuster Macmillan Company.

Page 451, *Figure 12.8:* Reed, T.E., & Jensen, A.R. (1992). Conduxtion celocity in a brain nerve pathway of normal adults correlates with intelligence. *Intelligence, 16,* 266, fig 12.8. Reprinted with permission of Ablex Publishing Corp.

Page 464, *Figure 12.12:* Adapted from Fuligni, A.J., & Stevenson, H.W. (1995). Time use and mathematics achievement among American, Chinese, and Japanese high school students. *Child Development, 66,* 830-842. © Society for Research in Child Development, Inc.

Page 470, *Figure 12.15:* Steele, C.M., & Aronson, J. (1995). Stereotype threat and the intellectual test performance of African Americans. *Journal of Personality and Social Psychology, 69,* 802. Copyright © 1995 by the American Psychological Association. Reprinted with permission.

Page 527, *Table 14.2:* Triandis, H.C. (1994). *The adolescent: A psychological self-portrait.* Copyright © 1994 by McGraw-Hill. Reprinted with the permission of the publishers.

Page 529, *Table 14.3:* Triandis, H.C. (1995). *Individualism and collectivism.* Copyright © 1995 by Westview Press. Reprinted with the permission of the publishers.

Page 531, *Figure 14.2:* Trafimow, D., Triandis, H.C., & Goto, S.G. (1991). Some tests of the distinction between the private and collective self. *Journal of Personality and Social Psychology, 60,* 649-655. Copyright © 1991 by the American Psychological Association. Reprinted with permission.
Page 532, *Figure 14.3:* Trafimow, D., Silverman, E.S., Fan, R.M.T., & Law, J.S.F. (1997). The effects of language and priming on the relative accessibility of the private self and collective self. *Journal of Cross-Cultural Psychology, 28,* 107-123. Copyright © 1997 by Sage Periodicals Press. Reprinted by permission of Sage Publications, Inc.

Page 554, *Figure 14.9:* Fein, S., & Spencer, S. (1997). Prejudice as self-image maintenance: Affirming the self through negative evaluations of others. *Journal of Personality and Social Psychology, 73,* 31-44. Copyright © 1997 by the American Psychological Association. Reprinted with permission.

Page 557, *Figure 14.12:* Gaertner, S.L., Mann, J.A., Dovidio, J.F., Murrell, A.J., & Pomare, M. (1990). How does cooperation reduce intergroup bias? *Journal of Personality and Social Psychology, 59,* 692-704. Copyright © 1990 by the American Psychological Association. Reprinted with permission.

Page 584, *extract:* Rogers, C.R. (1961) On becoming a person. Excerpted from *On becoming a person.* Copyright © 1961 by Carl R. Rogers. Reprinted by permission of Houghton Mifflin Company. All rights reserved.

Page 593, *Figure 15.9:* After Lang, K.L., Livesley, W.J., & Vernon, P.A. (1996). Heritability of the Big Five personality dimensions and their facets: A twin study. *Journal of Personality, 64,* (3), 577-591.

Page 595, *Table 15.6:* Zuckerman, M. (1994). *Behavioral expressions and biosocial bases of sensation seeking.* Copyright © 1994 by Cambridge University Press. Reprinted with permission of the publishers.

Page 595, *Table 15.6:* Aron, E.N. & Aron, A. (1997). Sensory-processing sensitivity and its relation to introversion and emotionality. *Journal of Personality and Social Psychology, 73:* 352. Reprinted with the permission of the publishers.

Page 616, *Figure 16.3:* Robins, Lee N. & Regier, Darrel A. (1991) *Psychiatric disorders in America: The epidemiologic catchment area study.* Copyright © 1991 by Lee N. Robins and Darrel A. Regier. Reprinted with permission of The Free Press, a division of Simon & Schuster.

Page 620, *Figure 16.4:* Gramling, S.E., Clawson, E.P., McDonaled, M.K. (1996). Perceptual and cognitive abnormality of hypochodriasis: Amplification and physiological reactivity in women. *Psychosomatic Medicine, 58,* 428. Copyright © 1996 William & Wilkins.

Page 634, *Table 16.7:* Anonymous (1990). Behind the mask: A functional schizophrenic copes. *Schizophrenia Bulletin, 16,* 547-549. Reprinted with permission of the publishers.

Page 640, *Table 16.9:* Hare, R.D. (1993). *Without conscience: The disturbing world of the psychopaths among us.* Copyright © 1993 by Robert Hare. Reprinted with the permission of Pocket Books, a division of Simon & Schuster.

Page 654, *Table 17.1:* Baker, E.L. (1985). Psychoanalysis and psychoanalytic therapy. In S.J. Lynn & J.P. Garske (Eds.), *Contemporary psychotherapies: Models and methods.* Copyright © 1985 by Charles E. Merrill. Reprinted with permission of the publishers.

Page 667, *Table 17.3:* Beck, A.T., et al. (1979). *Cognitive theory of depression.* Copyright © by Guilford Publications, Inc. Reprinted with permission of the publishers.

Page 669, *Table 17.4:* Raskin, N.J. (1985). Client-centered therapy. In S.J. Lynn & J.P. Garske (Eds.), *Contemporary psychotherapies: Models and methods.* Copyright © 1985 by Charles E. Merrill. Reprinted with the permission of the publishers.

Page 704, *Figure 18.7:* Kessler, R.C., Sonnega, A., Bromet, E., Hughes, M., & Nelson, C.B. (1995). Posttraumatic stress disorder in the National Comorbidity Survey. *Archives of General Psychiatry, 52,* 1052. Reprinted with permission of the American Medical Association.

Page 706, *Table 18.4:* Williams, R. (1993). *Anger kills.* Copyright © 1993 by Times Books. Reprinted with the permission of the publishers.

Page 717, *Table 18.5:* Seligman, M.E.P. (1991). *Learned optimism.* Copyright © 1991 by Knopf. Reprinted with the permission of the publishers.

Author Index

Subject Index

create™

Course Business Statistics

Course Number **BADM 220**

Hudson Valley Community College

Business

create™

http://create.mcgraw-hill.com

ISBN-10: 1308158750 ISBN-13: 9781308158754

Contents

Online Supplements

Credits

Online Supplements

Statistical Techniques in

BUSINESS & ECONOMICS

The McGraw-Hill/Irwin Series in Operations and Decision Sciences

SUPPLY CHAIN MANAGEMENT

Benton
Purchasing and Supply Chain Management
Third Edition

Bowersox, Closs, Cooper, and Bowersox
Supply Chain Logistics Management
Fourth Edition

Burt, Petcavage, and Pinkerton
Supply Management
Eighth Edition

Johnson, Leenders, and Flynn
Purchasing and Supply Management
Fourteenth Edition

Simchi-Levi, Kaminsky, and Simchi-Levi
Designing and Managing the Supply Chain: Concepts, Strategies, Case Studies
Third Edition

PROJECT MANAGEMENT

Brown and Hyer
Managing Projects: A Team-Based Approach
First Edition

Larson and Gray
Project Management: The Managerial Process
Fifth Edition

SERVICE OPERATIONS MANAGEMENT

Fitzsimmons and Fitzsimmons
Service Management: Operations, Strategy, Information Technology
Eighth Edition

MANAGEMENT SCIENCE

Hillier and Hillier
Introduction to Management Science: A Modeling and Case Studies Approach with Spreadsheets
Fifth Edition

Stevenson and Ozgur
Introduction to Management Science with Spreadsheets
First Edition

MANUFACTURING CONTROL SYSTEMS

Jacobs, Berry, Whybark, and Vollmann
Manufacturing Planning & Control for Supply Chain Management
Sixth Edition

BUSINESS RESEARCH METHODS

Cooper and Schindler
Business Research Methods
Twelfth Edition

BUSINESS FORECASTING

Wilson, Keating, and John Galt Solutions, Inc.
Business Forecasting
Sixth Edition

LINEAR STATISTICS AND REGRESSION

Kutner, Nachtsheim, and Neter
Applied Linear Regression Models
Fourth Edition

BUSINESS SYSTEMS DYNAMICS

Sterman
Business Dynamics: Systems Thinking and Modeling for a Complex World
First Edition

OPERATIONS MANAGEMENT

Cachon and Terwiesch
Matching Supply with Demand: An Introduction to Operations Management
Third Edition

Finch
Interactive Models for Operations and Supply Chain Management
First Edition

Jacobs and Chase
Operations and Supply Chain Management
Fourteenth Edition

Jacobs and Chase
Operations and Supply Chain Management: The Core
Third Edition

Jacobs and Whybark
Why ERP? A Primer on SAP Implementation
First Edition

Schroeder, Goldstein, and Rungtusanatham
Operations Management in the Supply Chain: Decisions and Cases
Sixth Edition

Stevenson
Operations Management
Eleventh Edition

Swink, Melnyk, Cooper, and Hartley
Managing Operations across the Supply Chain
Second Edition

PRODUCT DESIGN

Ulrich and Eppinger
Product Design and Development
Fifth Edition

BUSINESS MATH

Slater and Wittry
Math for Business and Finance: An Algebraic Approach
First Edition

Slater and Wittry
Practical Business Math Procedures
Eleventh Edition

Slater and Wittry
Practical Business Math Procedures, Brief Edition
Eleventh Edition

BUSINESS STATISTICS

Bowerman, O'Connell, and Murphree
Business Statistics in Practice
Seventh Edition

Bowerman, O'Connell, Murphree, and Orris
Essentials of Business Statistics
Fourth Edition

Doane and Seward
Applied Statistics in Business and Economics
Fourth Edition

Lind, Marchal, and Wathen
Basic Statistics for Business and Economics
Eighth Edition

Lind, Marchal, and Wathen
Statistical Techniques in Business and Economics
Sixteenth Edition

Jaggia and Kelly
Business Statistics: Communicating with Numbers
First Edition

Jaggia and Kelly
Essentials of Business Statistics: Communicating with Numbers
First Edition

Statistical Techniques in

BUSINESS & ECONOMICS

SIXTEENTH EDITION

DOUGLAS A. LIND
Coastal Carolina University and The University of Toledo

WILLIAM G. MARCHAL
The University of Toledo

SAMUEL A. WATHEN
Coastal Carolina University

Mc Graw Hill Education

STATISTICAL TECHNIQUES IN BUSINESS & ECONOMICS, SIXTEENTH EDITION
Published by McGraw-Hill Education, 2 Penn Plaza, New York, NY 10121.

This book is printed on acid-free paper.

1 2 3 4 5 6 7 8 9 0 DOW/DOW 1 0 9 8 7 6 5 4

ISBN 978-0-07-802052-0
MHID 0-07-802052-2

Senior Vice President, Products & Markets: *Kurt L. Strand*
Vice President, Content Production & Technology Services: *Kimberly Meriwether David*
Managing Director: *Douglas Reiner*
Senior Brand Manager: *Thomas Hayward*
Executive Director of Development: *Ann Torbert*
Development Editor: *Kaylee Putbrese*
Director of Digital Content: *Doug Ruby*
Digital Development Editor: *Meg B. Maloney*
Senior Marketing Manager: *Heather A. Kazakoff*
Content Project Manager: *Diane L. Nowaczyk*
Content Project Manager: *Brian Nacik*
Senior Buyer: *Carol A. Bielski*
Design: *Jana Singer*
Cover Image: *Adrianna Williams/The Image Bank/Getty Images*
Lead Content Licensing Specialist: *Keri Johnson*
Typeface: *9.5/11 Helvetica Neue 55*
Compositor: *Aptara®, Inc.*
Printer: *R. R. Donnelley*

All credits appearing on page or at the end of the book are considered to be an extension of the copyright page.

Library of Congress Cataloging-in-Publication Data

Lind, Douglas A.
Statistical techniques in business & economics / Douglas A. Lind, Coastal Carolina University and The University of Toledo, William G. Marchal, The University of Toledo, Samuel A. Wathen, Coastal Carolina University. — Sixteenth edition.
pages cm. — (The McGraw-Hill/Irwin series in operations and decision sciences)
Includes index.
ISBN 978-0-07-802052-0 (alk. paper) — ISBN 0-07-802052-2 (alk. paper)
1. Social sciences—Statistical methods. 2. Economics—Statistical methods. 3. Commercial statistics. I. Marchal, William G. II. Wathen, Samuel Adam. III. Title. IV. Title: Statistical techniques in business and economics.
HA29.M268 2015
519.5—dc23

2013035290

www.mhhe.com

DEDICATION

To Jane, my wife and best friend, and our sons, their wives, and our grandchildren: Mike and Sue (Steve and Courtney), Steve and Kathryn (Kennedy, Jake, and Brady), and Mark and Sarah (Jared, Drew, and Nate).

Douglas A. Lind

To my newest grandchildren (George Orn Marchal, Liam Brophy Horowitz, and Eloise Larae Marchal Murray), newest son-in-law (James Miller Nicholson), and newest wife (Andrea).

William G. Marchal

To my wonderful family: Isaac, Hannah, and Barb.

Samuel A. Wathen

A NOTE FROM THE AUTHORS

Over the years, we have received many compliments on this text and understand that it's a favorite among students. We accept that as the highest compliment and continue to work very hard to maintain that status.

The objective of *Statistical Techniques in Business and Economics* is to provide students majoring in management, marketing, finance, accounting, economics, and other fields of business administration with an introductory survey of the many applications of descriptive and inferential statistics. We focus on business applications, but we also use many exercises and examples that relate to the current world of the college student. A previous course in statistics is not necessary, and the mathematical requirement is first-year algebra.

In this text, we show beginning students every step needed to be successful in a basic statistics course. This step-by-step approach enhances performance, accelerates preparedness, and significantly improves motivation. Understanding the concepts, seeing and doing plenty of examples and exercises, and comprehending the application of statistical methods in business and economics are the focus of this book.

The first edition of this text was published in 1967. At that time, locating relevant business data was difficult. That has changed! Today, locating data is not a problem. The number of items you purchase at the grocery store is automatically recorded at the checkout counter. Phone companies track the time of our calls, the length of calls, and the identity of the person called. Credit card companies maintain information on the number, time and date, and amount of our purchases. Medical devices automatically monitor our heart rate, blood pressure, and temperature from remote locations. A large amount of business information is recorded and reported almost instantly. CNN, USA Today, and MSNBC, for example, all have websites that track stock prices with a delay of less than 20 minutes.

Today, skills are needed to deal with a large volume of numerical information. First, we need to be critical consumers of information presented by others. Second, we need to be able to reduce large amounts of information into a concise and meaningful form to enable us to make effective interpretations, judgments, and decisions. All students have calculators and most have either personal computers or access to personal computers in a campus lab. Statistical software, such as Microsoft Excel and Minitab, is available on these computers. The commands necessary to achieve the software results are available in Appendix C at the end of the book. We use screen captures within the chapters, so the student becomes familiar with the nature of the software output.

Because of the availability of computers and software, it is no longer necessary to dwell on calculations. We have replaced many of the calculation examples with interpretative ones, to assist the student in understanding and interpreting the statistical results. In addition, we now place more emphasis on the conceptual nature of the statistical topics. While making these changes, we still continue to present, as best we can, the key concepts, along with supporting interesting and relevant examples.

WHAT'S NEW IN THIS SIXTEENTH EDITION?

We have made changes to this edition that we think you and your students will find useful and timely.

- We reorganized the chapters so that each section corresponds to a learning objective. The learning objectives have been revised.
- We expanded the hypothesis testing procedure in Chapter 10 to six steps, emphasizing the interpretation of test results.

- We have revised example/solution sections in various chapters:
  - Chapter 5 now includes a new example/solution used to demonstrate contingency tables and tree diagrams. Also the example/solution demonstrating the combination formula has been revised.
  - Chapter 6 includes a revised example/solution demonstrating the binomial distribution.
  - Chapter 15 includes a new example/solution demonstrating contingency table analysis.
- We have revised the simple regression example in Chapter 13 and increased the number of observations to better illustrate the principles of simple linear regression.
- We have reordered the nonparametric chapters to follow the traditional statistics chapters.
- We moved the sections on one- and two-sample tests of proportions, placing all analysis of nominal data in one chapter: Nonparametric Methods: Nominal Level Hypothesis Tests.
- We combined the answers to the Self-Review Exercises into a new appendix.
- We combined the Software Commands into a new appendix.
- We combined the Glossaries in the section reviews into a single Glossary that follows the appendices at the end of the text.
- We improved graphics throughout the text.

HOW ARE CHAPTERS ORGANIZED TO ENGAGE STUDENTS AND PROMOTE LEARNING?

Chapter Learning Objectives

Each chapter begins with a set of learning objectives designed to provide focus for the chapter and motivate student learning. These objectives, located in the margins next to the topic, indicate what the student should be able to do after completing each section in the chapter.

MERRILL LYNCH recently completed a study of online investment portfolios for a sample of clients. For the 70 participants in the study, organize these data into a frequency distribution. (See Exercise 43 and LO2-3.)	**LEARNING OBJECTIVES** *When you have completed this chapter, you will be able to:* **LO2-1** Summarize qualitative variables with frequency and relative frequency tables. **LO2-2** Display a frequency table using a bar or pie chart. **LO2-3** Summarize quantitative variables with frequency and relative frequency distributions. **LO2-4** Display a frequency distribution using a histogram or frequency polygon.

Chapter Opening Exercise

A representative exercise opens the chapter and shows how the chapter content can be applied to a real-world situation.

Introduction to the Topic

Each chapter starts with a review of the important concepts of the previous chapter and provides a link to the material in the current chapter. This step-by-step approach increases comprehension by providing continuity across the concepts.

> INTRODUCTION
>
> Chapter 2 began our study of descriptive statistics. To summarize raw data into a meaningful form, we organized qualitative data into a frequency table and portrayed the results in a bar chart. In a similar fashion, we organized quantitative data into a frequency distribution and portrayed the results in a histogram. We also looked at other graphical techniques such as pie charts to portray qualitative data and frequency polygons to portray quantitative data.
>
> This chapter is concerned with two numerical ways of describing quantitative variables, namely, **measures of location** and **measures of dispersion.** Measures of location are often referred to as averages. The purpose of a measure of location is to pinpoint the center of a distribution of data. An

Example/Solution

After important concepts are introduced, a solved example is given. This example provides a how-to illustration and shows a relevant business application that helps students answer the question, "What will I use this for?"

> **EXAMPLE**
>
> The service departments at Tionesta Ford Lincoln Mercury and Sheffield Motors Inc., two of the four Applewood Auto Group dealerships, were both open 24 days last month. Listed below is the number of vehicles serviced last month at the two dealerships. Construct dot plots and report summary statistics to compare the two dealerships.

Tionesta Ford Lincoln Mercury

Monday	Tuesday	Wednesday	Thursday	Friday	Saturday
23	33	27	28	39	26
30	32	28	33	35	32
29	25	36	31	32	27
35	32	35	37	36	30

Self-Reviews

Self-Reviews are interspersed throughout each chapter and closely patterned after the preceding examples. They help students monitor their progress and provide immediate reinforcement for that particular technique.

> SELF-REVIEW 4-2
>
> The Quality Control department of Plainsville Peanut Company is responsible for checking the weight of the 8-ounce jar of peanut butter. The weights of a sample of nine jars produced last hour are:

7.69	7.72	7.8	7.86	7.90	7.94	7.97	8.06	8.09

> (a) What is the median weight?
> (b) Determine the weights corresponding to the first and third quartiles.

Statistics in Action

Statistics in Action articles are scattered throughout the text, usually about two per chapter. They provide unique and interesting applications and historical insights in the field of statistics.

STATISTICS IN ACTION

If you wish to get some attention at the next gathering you attend, announce that you believe that at least two people present were born on the same date—that is, the same day of the year but not necessarily the same year. If there are 30 people in the room,

Definitions

Definitions of new terms or terms unique to the study of statistics are set apart from the text and highlighted for easy reference and review. They also appear in the Glossary at the end of the book.

JOINT PROBABILITY A probability that measures the likelihood two or more events will happen concurrently.

Formulas

Formulas that are used for the first time are boxed and numbered for reference. In addition, a formula card is bound into the back of the text that lists all the key formulas.

SPECIAL RULE OF MULTIPLICATION $P(A \text{ and } B) = P(A)P(B)$ **[5–5]**

Exercises

Exercises are included after sections within the chapter and at the end of the chapter. Section exercises cover the material studied in the section.

EXERCISES

33. $P(A_1) = .60$, $P(A_2) = .40$, $P(B_1 | A_1) = .05$, and $P(B_1 | A_2) = .10$. Use Bayes' theorem to determine $P(A_1 | B_1)$.

34. $P(A_1) = .20$, $P(A_2) = .40$, $P(A_3) = .40$, $P(B_1 | A_1) = .25$, $P(B_1 | A_2) = .05$, and $P(B_1 | A_3) = .10$. Use Bayes' theorem to determine $P(A_3 | B_1)$.

35. The Ludlow Wildcats baseball team, a minor league team in the Cleveland Indians organization, plays 70% of their games at night and 30% during the day. The team wins 50% of their night games and 90% of their day games. According to today's newspaper, they won yesterday. What is the probability the game was played at night?

36. Dr. Stallter has been teaching basic statistics for many years. She knows that 80% of the students will complete the assigned problems. She has also determined that among those who do their assignments, 90% will pass the course. Among those students who do not do

Computer Output

The text includes many software examples, using Excel, MegaStat®, and Minitab.

APPLEWOOD AUTO GROUP

	A	B	C	D	E	F	G	H
1	Age	Profit	Location	Vehicle-Type	Previous		*Profit*	
2	21	$1,387	Tionesta	Sedan	0			
3	23	$1,754	Sheffield	SUV	1		Mean	1843.17
4	24	$1,817	Sheffield	Hybrid	1		Standard Error	47.97
5	25	$1,040	Sheffield	Compact	0		Median	1882.50
6	26	$1,273	Kane	Sedan	1		Mode	1915.00
7	27	$1,529	Sheffield	Sedan	1		Standard Deviation	643.63
8	27	$3,082	Kane	Truck	0		Sample Variance	414256.61
9	28	$1,951	Kane	SUV	1		Kurtosis	-0.22
10	28	$2,692	Tionesta	Compact	0		Skewness	-0.24
11	29	$1,342	Kane	Sedan	2		Range	2998
12	29	$1,206	Sheffield	Sedan	0		Minimum	294
13	30	$443	Kane	Sedan	3		Maximum	3292
14	30	$1,621	Sheffield	Truck	1		Sum	331770
15	30	$754	Olean	Sedan	2		Count	180

HOW DOES THIS TEXT REINFORCE STUDENT LEARNING?

BY CHAPTER

Chapter Summary

Each chapter contains a brief summary of the chapter material, including the vocabulary and the critical formulas.

CHAPTER SUMMARY

I. A random variable is a numerical value determined by the outcome of an experiment.
II. A probability distribution is a listing of all possible outcomes of an experiment and the probability associated with each outcome.
A. A discrete probability distribution can assume only certain values. The main features are:
1. The sum of the probabilities is 1.00.
2. The probability of a particular outcome is between 0.00 and 1.00.
3. The outcomes are mutually exclusive.
B. A continuous distribution can assume an infinite number of values within a specific range.
III. The mean and variance of a probability distribution are computed as follows.
A. The mean is equal to:

$$\mu = \Sigma[xP(x)] \qquad [6\text{–}1]$$

B. The variance is equal to:

$$\sigma^2 = \Sigma[(x - \mu)^2P(x)] \qquad [6\text{–}2]$$

Pronunciation Key

This tool lists the mathematical symbol, its meaning, and how to pronounce it. We believe this will help the student retain the meaning of the symbol and generally enhance course communications.

PRONUNCIATION KEY

SYMBOL	MEANING	PRONUNCIATION
$P(A)$	Probability of *A*	*P* of *A*
$P(\sim A)$	Probability of not *A*	*P* of not *A*
$P(A \text{ and } B)$	Probability of *A* and *B*	*P* of *A* and *B*
$P(A \text{ or } B)$	Probability of *A* or *B*	*P* of *A* or *B*
$P(A\|B)$	Probability of *A* given *B* has happened	*P* of *A* given *B*
$_nP_r$	Permutation of *n* items selected *r* at a time	*Pnr*
$_nC_r$	Combination of *n* items selected *r* at a time	*Cnr*

Chapter Exercises

Generally, the end-of-chapter exercises are the most challenging and integrate the chapter concepts. The answers and worked-out solutions for all odd-numbered exercises are in Appendix D at the end of the text. Many exercises are noted with a data file icon in the margin. For these exercises, there are data files in Excel format located on the text's website, www.mhhe.com/lind16e. These files help students use statistical software to solve the exercises.

CHAPTER EXERCISES

41. The amount of cola in a 12-ounce can is uniformly distributed between 11.96 ounces and 12.05 ounces.
a. What is the mean amount per can?
b. What is the standard deviation amount per can?
c. What is the probability of selecting a can of cola and finding it has less than 12 ounces?
d. What is the probability of selecting a can of cola and finding it has more than 11.98 ounces?
e. What is the probability of selecting a can of cola and finding it has more than 11.00 ounces?

42. A tube of Listerine Tartar Control toothpaste contains 4.2 ounces. As people use the toothpaste, the amount remaining in any tube is random. Assume the amount of toothpaste remaining in the tube follows a uniform distribution. From this information, we can determine the following information about the amount remaining in a toothpaste tube without invading anyone's privacy.
a. How much toothpaste would you expect to be remaining in the tube?
b. What is the standard deviation of the amount remaining in the tube?
c. What is the likelihood there is less than 3.0 ounces remaining in the tube?
d. What is the probability there is more than 1.5 ounces remaining in the tube?

43. Many retail stores offer their own credit cards. At the time of the credit application, the customer is given a 10% discount on the purchase. The time required for the credit application process follows a uniform distribution with the times ranging from 4 minutes to 10 minutes.
a. What is the mean time for the application process?
b. What is the standard deviation of the process time?
c. What is the likelihood a particular application will take less than 6 minutes?

Data Set Exercises

The last several exercises at the end of each chapter are based on three large data sets. These data sets are printed in Appendix A in the text and are also on the text's website. These data sets present the students with real-world and more complex applications.

DATA SET EXERCISES

(The data for these exercises are available at the text website: www.mhhe.com/lind16e.)

74. Refer to the Real Estate data, which report information on homes sold in the Goodyear, Arizona, area during the last year.
a. The mean selling price (in $ thousands) of the homes was computed earlier to be $221.10, with a standard deviation of $47.11. Use the normal distribution to estimate the percentage of homes selling for more than $280.0. Compare this to the actual results. Does the normal distribution yield a good approximation of the actual results?
b. The mean distance from the center of the city is 14.629 miles, with a standard deviation of 4.874 miles. Use the normal distribution to estimate the number of homes 18 or more miles but less than 22 miles from the center of the city. Compare this to the actual results. Does the normal distribution yield a good approximation of the actual results?

Software Commands

Software examples using Excel, MegaStat®, and Minitab are included throughout the text. The explanations of the computer input commands are placed at the end of the text in Appendix C.

CHAPTER 5

5–1. The Excel Commands to determine the number of permutations shown on page 164 are:
a. Click on the **Formulas** tab in the top menu, then, on the far left, select **Insert Function *fx*.**
b. In the **Insert Function** box, select **Statistical** as the category, then scroll down to **PERMUT** in the **Select a function list.** Click **OK.**
c. In the **PERM** box after **Number,** enter *8* and in the **Number_chosen** box enter *3*. The correct answer of *336* appears twice in the box.

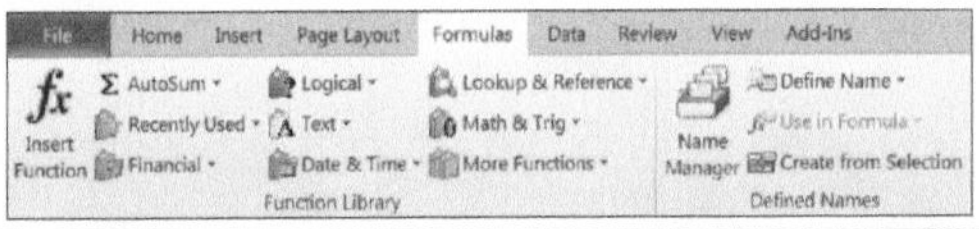

Answers to Self-Review

The worked-out solutions to the Self-Reviews are provided at the end of the text in Appendix E.

16–7 a.

		Rank			
x	*y*	*x*	*y*	*d*	d^2
805	23	5.5	1	4.5	20.25
777	62	3.0	9	−6.0	36.00
820	60	8.5	8	0.5	0.25
682	40	1.0	4	−3.0	9.00
777	70	3.0	10	−7.0	49.00
810	28	7.0	2	5.0	25.00
805	30	5.5	3	2.5	6.25
840	42	10.0	5	5.0	25.00
777	55	3.0	7	−4.0	16.00
820	51	8.5	6	2.5	6.25
				0	193.00

BY SECTION

Section Reviews

After selected groups of chapters (1–4, 5–7, 8 and 9, 10–12, 13 and 14, 15 and 16, and 17 and 18), a Section Review is included. Much like a review before an exam, these include a brief **overview** of the chapters and **problems for review.**

A REVIEW OF CHAPTERS 1–4

This section is a review of the major concepts and terms introduced in Chapters 1–4. Chapter 1 began by describing the meaning and purpose of statistics. Next we described the different types of variables and the four levels of measurement. Chapter 2 was concerned with describing a set of observations by organizing it into a frequency distribution and then portraying the frequency distribution as a histogram or a frequency polygon. Chapter 3 began by describing measures of location, such as the mean, weighted mean, median, geometric mean, and mode. This chapter also included measures of dispersion, or spread. Discussed in this section were the range, variance, and standard deviation. Chapter 4 included several graphing techniques such as dot plots, box plots, and scatter diagrams. We also discussed the coefficient of skewness, which reports the lack of symmetry in a set of data.

Cases

The review also includes continuing cases and several small cases that let students make decisions using tools and techniques from a variety of chapters.

CASES

A. Century National Bank

The following case will appear in subsequent review sections. Assume that you work in the Planning Department of the Century National Bank and report to Ms. Lamberg. You will need to do some data analysis and prepare a short written report. Remember, Mr. Selig is the president of the bank, so you will want to ensure that your report is complete and accurate. A copy of the data appears in Appendix A.6.

Century National Bank has offices in several cities in the Midwest and the southeastern part of the United States. Mr. Dan Selig, president and CEO, would like to know the characteristics of his checking account customers. What is the balance of a typical customer?

How many other bank services do the checking account customers use? Do the customers use the ATM service and, if so, how often? What about debit cards? Who uses them, and how often are they used?

balances for the four branches. Is there a difference among the branches? Be sure to explain the difference between the mean and the median in your report.

3. Determine the range and the standard deviation of the checking account balances. What do the first and third quartiles show? Determine the coefficient of skewness and indicate what it shows. Because Mr. Selig does not deal with statistics daily, include a brief description and interpretation of the standard deviation and other measures.

B. Wildcat Plumbing Supply Inc.: Do We Have Gender Differences?

Wildcat Plumbing Supply has served the plumbing needs of Southwest Arizona for more than 40 years. The company was founded by Mr. Terrence St. Julian and is run today by

Practice Test

The Practice Test is intended to give students an idea of content that might appear on a test and how the test might be structured. The Practice Test includes both objective questions and problems covering the material studied in the section.

PRACTICE TEST

There is a practice test at the end of each review section. The tests are in two parts. The first part contains several objective questions, usually in a fill-in-the-blank format. The second part is problems. In most cases, it should take 30 to 45 minutes to complete the test. The problems require a calculator. Check the answers in the Answer Section in the back of the book.

Part 1—Objective

1. The science of collecting, organizing, presenting, analyzing, and interpreting data to assist in making effective decisions is called ________. 1. ________
2. Methods of organizing, summarizing, and presenting data in an informative way are called ________. 2. ________
3. The entire set of individuals or objects of interest or the measurements obtained from all individuals or objects of interest are called the ________. 3. ________
4. List the two types of variables. 4. ________

WHAT TECHNOLOGY CONNECTS STUDENTS TO BUSINESS STATISTICS?

MCGRAW-HILL *CONNECT®* *BUSINESS STATISTICS*

Less Managing. More Teaching. Greater Learning.

McGraw-Hill *Connect® Business Statistics* is an online assignment and assessment solution that connects students with the tools and resources they'll need to achieve success. McGraw-Hill *Connect® Business Statistics* helps prepare students for their future by enabling faster learning, more efficient studying, and higher retention of knowledge.

McGraw-Hill *Connect® Business Statistics* Features

Connect® Business Statistics offers a number of powerful tools and features to make managing assignments easier, so faculty can spend more time teaching. With *Connect Business Statistics,* students can engage with their coursework anytime and anywhere, making the learning process more accessible and efficient. *Connect® Business Statistics* offers you the features described below.

Simple Assignment Management

With *Connect® Business Statistics,* creating assignments is easier than ever, so you can spend more time teaching and less time managing. The assignment management function enables you to

- Create and deliver assignments easily with selectable end-of-chapter questions and test bank items.
- Streamline lesson planning, student progress reporting, and assignment grading to make classroom management more efficient than ever.
- Go paperless with the eBook and online submission and grading of student assignments.

Smart Grading

When it comes to studying, time is precious. *Connect® Business Statistics* helps students learn more efficiently by providing feedback and practice material when they need it, where they need it. When it comes to teaching, your time is also precious. The grading function enables you to

- Have assignments scored automatically, giving students immediate feedback on their work and side-by-side comparisons with correct answers.
- Access and review each response; manually change grades or leave comments for students to review.
- Reinforce classroom concepts with practice tests and instant quizzes.

Instructor Library

The *Connect® Business Statistics* Instructor Library is your repository for additional resources to improve student engagement in and out of class. You can select and use any asset that enhances your lecture.

Student Study Center

The *Connect® Business Statistics* Student Study Center is the place for students to access additional resources. The Student Study Center

- Offers students quick access to lectures, practice materials, eBooks, and more.
- Provides instant practice material and study questions, easily accessible on the go.

LearnSmart

Students want to make the best use of their study time. The LearnSmart adaptive self-study technology within *Connect® Business Statistics* provides students with a seamless combination of practice, assessment, and remediation for every concept in the textbook. LearnSmart's intelligent software adapts to every student response and automatically delivers concepts that advance the student's understanding while reducing time devoted to the concepts already mastered. The result for every student is the fastest path to mastery of the chapter concepts. LearnSmart

- Applies an intelligent concept engine to identify the relationships between concepts and to serve new concepts to each student only when he or she is ready.
- Adapts automatically to each student, so students spend less time on the topics they understand and practice more those they have yet to master.
- Provides continual reinforcement and remediation, but gives only as much guidance as students need.
- Integrates diagnostics as part of the learning experience.
- Enables you to assess which concepts students have efficiently learned on their own, thus freeing class time for more applications and discussion.

LearnSmart Achieve

LearnSmart Achieve is a revolutionary new learning system that combines a continually adaptive learning experience with necessary course resources to focus students on mastering concepts they don't already know. The program adjusts to each student individually as he or she progresses, creating just-in-time learning experiences by presenting interactive content that is tailored to each student's needs. A convenient time-management feature and reports for instructors also ensure students stay on track.

Student Progress Tracking

Connect® Business Statistics keeps instructors informed about how each student, section, and class is performing, allowing for more productive use of lecture and office hours. The progress-tracking function enables you to

- View scored work immediately and track individual or group performance with assignment and grade reports.
- Access an instant view of student or class performance relative to learning objectives.
- Collect data and generate reports required by many accreditation organizations, such as AACSB and AICPA.

McGraw-Hill *Connect® Plus Business Statistics*

McGraw-Hill reinvents the textbook learning experience for the modern student with *Connect® Plus Busin*
Statistics. A seamless integration of an eBook and *Connect® Business Statistics, Connect® Plus Business S*
tics provides all of the *Connect Business Statistics* features plus the following:

- An integrated eBook, allowing for anytime, anywhere access to the textbook.
- Dynamic links between the problems or questions you assign to your students and the location i
  where that problem or question is covered.
- A powerful search function to pinpoint and connect key concepts in a snap.

In short, *Connect® Business Statistics* offers you and your students powerful tools and featur
your time and energies, enabling you to focus on course content, teaching, and student learnin
ness Statistics also offers a wealth of content resources for both instructors and students. Th
thoroughly tested system supports you in preparing students for the world that awaits.

For more information about *Connect,* go to www.mcgrawhillconnect.com, or contact your local McGraw-Hill sales representative.

COURSESMART

CourseSmart is a new way to find and buy eTextbooks. At CourseSmart you can save up to 50% of the cost of your print textbook, reduce your impact on the environment, and gain access to powerful web tools for learning. Try a free chapter to see if it's right for you. Visit www.CourseSmart.com and search by title, author, or ISBN.

TEGRITY CAMPUS: LECTURES 24/7

Tegrity Campus is a service that makes class time available 24/7 by automatically capturing every lecture in a searchable format for students to review when they study and complete assignments. With a simple one-click start-and-stop process, you capture all computer screens and corresponding audio. Students can replay any part of any class with easy-to-use browser-based viewing on a PC or Mac.

Educators know that the more students can see, hear, and experience class resources, the better they learn. In fact, studies prove it. With Tegrity Campus, students quickly recall key moments by using Tegrity Campus's unique search feature. This search helps students efficiently find what they need, when they need it, across an entire semester of class recordings. Help turn all your students' study time into learning moments immediately supported by your lecture.

To learn more about Tegrity watch a two-minute Flash demo at http://tegritycampus.mhhe.com.

ASSURANCE OF LEARNING READY

Many educational institutions today are focused on the notion of *assurance of learning*, an important element of some accreditation standards. *Statistical Techniques in Business & Economics* is designed specifically to support your assurance of learning initiatives with a simple, yet powerful solution.

Each test bank question for *Statistical Techniques in Business & Economics* maps to a specific chapter learning objective listed in the text. You can use our test bank software, EZ Test and EZ Test Online, or *Connect® Business Statistics* to easily query for learning objectives that directly relate to the learning objectives for your course. You can then use the reporting features of EZ Test to aggregate student results in similar fashion, making the collection and presentation of assurance of learning data simple and easy.

MCGRAW-HILL CUSTOMER CARE CONTACT INFORMATION

At McGraw-Hill, we understand that getting the most from new technology can be challenging. That's why our services don't stop after you purchase our products. You can e-mail our product specialists 24 hours a day to get product-training online. Or you can search our knowledge bank of frequently asked questions on our support website. For customer support, call **800-331-5094,** e-mail hmsupport@mcgraw-hill.com, or visit www.mhhe.com/support. One of our technical support analysts will be able to assist you in a timely fashion.

WHAT SOFTWARE IS AVAILABLE WITH THIS TEXT?

MEGASTAT® FOR MICROSOFT EXCEL®

MegaStat® by J. B. Orris of Butler University is a full-featured Excel statistical analysis add-in that is available on the MegaStat website at www.mhhe.com/megastat (for purchase). MegaStat works with recent versions of Microsoft Excel® (Windows and Mac OS X). See the website for details on supported versions.

Once installed, MegaStat will always be available on the Excel add-ins ribbon with no expiration date or data limitations. MegaStat performs statistical analyses within an Excel workbook. When a MegaStat menu item is selected, a dialog box pops up for data selection and options. Since MegaStat is an easy-to-use extension of Excel, students can focus on learning statistics without being distracted by the software. Ease-of-use features include Auto Expand for quick data selection and Auto Label detect.

MegaStat does most calculations found in introductory statistics textbooks, such as descriptive statistics, frequency distributions, and probability calculations as well as hypothesis testing, ANOVA chi-square, and regression (simple and multiple). MegaStat output is carefully formatted and appended to an output worksheet.

Video tutorials are included that provide a walkthrough using MegaStat for typical business statistics topics. A context-sensitive help system is built into MegaStat and a User's Guide is included in PDF format.

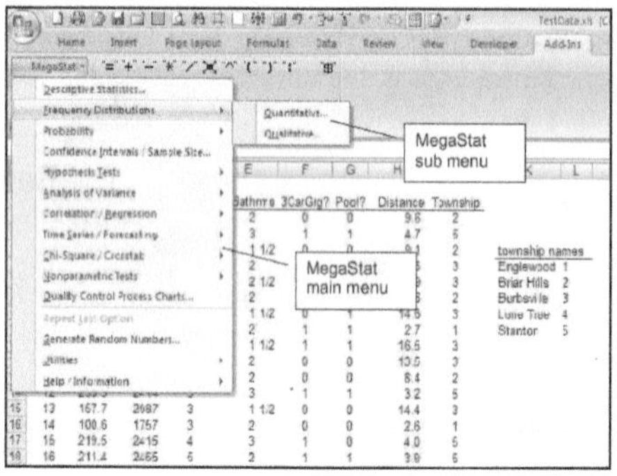

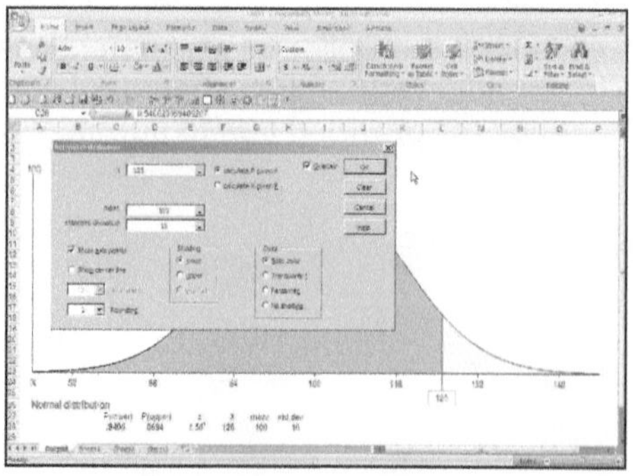

MINITAB®/SPSS®/JMP®

Minitab® Student Version 14, SPSS® Student Version 18.0, and JMP® Student Edition Version 8 are software tools that are available to help students solve the business statistics exercises in the text. Each can be packaged with any McGraw-Hill business statistics text.

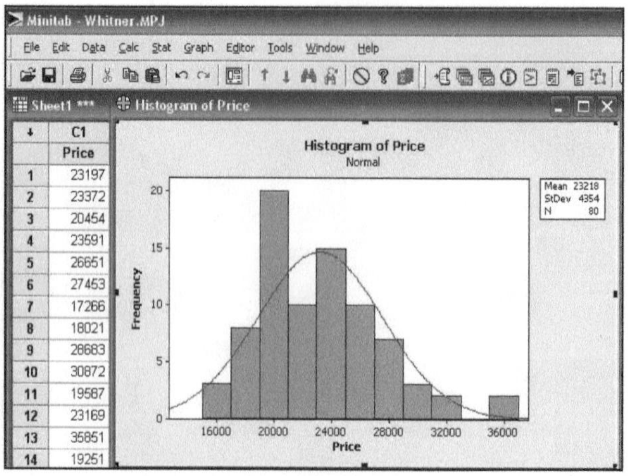

ONLINE LEARNING CENTER:
www.mhhe.com/lind16e

The Online Learning Center (OLC) provides the instructor with a complete Instructor's Manual in Word format, the complete Test Bank in both Word files and computerized EZ Test format, Instructor PowerPoint slides, text art files, an introduction to ALEKS®, an introduction to McGraw-Hill Connect Business Statistics™, and more.

EZ TEST

All test bank questions are available in an EZ Test electronic format. Included are a number of multiple-choice, true/false, and short-answer questions and problems. The answers to all questions are given, along with a rating of the level of difficulty, chapter goal the question tests, Bloom's taxonomy question type, and the AACSB knowledge category.

WebCT/Blackboard/eCollege

All of the material in the Online Learning Center is also available in portable WebCT, Blackboard, or eCollege content "cartridges" provided free to adopters of this text.

WebCT

Do More The **Best** of **Both Worlds**

eCollege

WHAT RESOURCES ARE AVAILABLE FOR STUDENTS?

ALEKS®

ALEKS is an assessment and learning program that provides individualized instruction in Business Statistics, Business Math, and Accounting. Available online, ALEKS interacts with students much like a skilled human tutor, with the ability to assess precisely a student's knowledge and provide instruction on the exact topics the student is most ready to learn. By providing topics to meet individual students' needs, allowing students to move between explanation and practice, correcting and analyzing errors, and defining terms, ALEKS helps students to master course content quickly and easily.

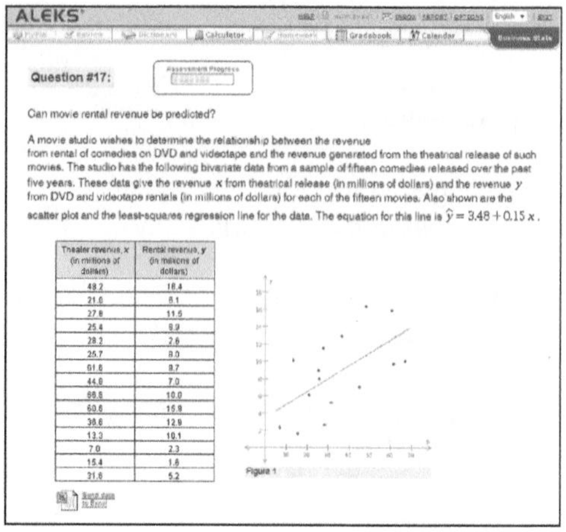

ALEKS also includes a new instructor module with powerful, assignment-driven features and extensive content flexibility. ALEKS simplifies course management and allows instructors to spend less time with administrative tasks and more time directing student learning. To learn more about ALEKS, visit www.aleks.com.

ONLINE LEARNING CENTER: www.mhhe.com/lind16e

The Online Learning Center (OLC) provides students with the following content:

- Quizzes
- PowerPoints
- Data sets/files
- Appendixes
- Chapter 20

BUSINESS STATISTICS CENTER (BSC): www.mhhe.com/bstat

The BSC contains links to statistical publications and resources, software downloads, learning aids, statistical websites and databases, and McGraw-Hill product websites and online courses.

BSC BUSINESS STATISTICS CENTER

ACKNOWLEDGMENTS

This edition of *Statistical Techniques in Business and Economics* is the product of many people: students, colleagues, reviewers, and the staff at McGraw-Hill/Irwin. We thank them all. We wish to express our sincere gratitude to the survey and focus group participants, and the reviewers:

Reviewers

Sung K. Ahn
Washington State University–Pullman

Vaughn S. Armstrong
Utah Valley University

Scott Bailey
Troy University

Douglas Barrett
University of North Alabama

Arnab Bisi
Purdue University

Pamela A. Boger
Ohio University–Athens

Emma Bojinova
Canisius College

Ann Brandwein
Baruch College

Giorgio Canarella
California State University–Los Angeles

Lee Cannell
El Paso Community College

James Carden
University of Mississippi

Mary Coe
St. Mary College of California

Anne Davey
Northeastern State University

Neil Desnoyers
Drexel University

Nirmal Devi
Embry Riddle Aeronautical University

David Doorn
University of Minnesota–Duluth

Ronald Elkins
Central Washington University

Vickie Fry
Westmoreland County Community College

Xiaoning Gilliam
Texas Tech University

Mark Gius
Quinnipiac University

Clifford B. Hawley
West Virginia University

Peter M. Hutchinson
Saint Vincent College

Lloyd R. Jaisingh
Morehead State University

Ken Kelley
University of Notre Dame

Mark Kesh
University of Texas

Melody Kiang
California State University–Long Beach

Morris Knapp
Miami Dade College

David G. Leupp
University of Colorado–Colorado State

Teresa Ling
Seattle University

Cecilia Maldonado
Georgia Southwestern State University

John D. McGinnis
Pennsylvania State–Altoona

Mary Ruth J. McRae
Appalachian State University

Jackie Miller
The Ohio State University

Carolyn Monroe
Baylor University

Valerie Muehsam
Sam Houston State University

Tariq Mughal
University of Utah

Elizabeth J. T. Murff
Eastern Washington University

Quinton Nottingham
Virginia Polytechnic Institute and State University

René Ordonez
Southern Oregon University

Ed Pappanastos
Troy University

Michelle Ray Parsons
Aims Community College

Robert Patterson
Penn State University

Joseph Petry
University of Illinois at Urbana-Champaign

Germain N. Pichop
Oklahoma City Community College

Tammy Prater
Alabama State University

Michael Racer
University of Memphis

Darrell Radson
Drexel University

Steven Ramsier
Florida State University

Emily N. Roberts
University of Colorado–Denver

Christopher W. Rogers
Miami Dade College

Stephen Hays Russell
Weber State University

Martin Sabo
Community College of Denver

Farhad Saboori
Albright College

Amar Sahay
Salt Lake Community College and University of Utah

Abdus Samad
Utah Valley University

Nina Sarkar
Queensborough Community College

Roberta Schini
West Chester University of Pennsylvania

Robert Smidt
California Polytechnic State University

Gary Smith
Florida State University

Stanley D. Stephenson
Texas State University–San Marcos
Debra Stiver
University of Nevada–Reno
Bedassa Tadesse
University of Minnesota–Duluth
Stephen Trouard
Mississippi College
Elzbieta Trybus
California State University–Northridge
Daniel Tschopp
Daemen College
Sue Umashankar
University of Arizona
Bulent Uyar
University of Northern Iowa
Jesus M. Valencia
Slippery Rock University
Joseph Van Matre
University of Alabama at Birmingham
Raja Vatti
St. John's University
Holly Verhasselt
University of Houston–Victoria
Angie Waits
Gadsden State Community College
Bin Wang
St. Edwards University
Kathleen Whitcomb
University of South Carolina
Blake Whitten
University of Iowa
Oliver Yu
San Jose State University
Zhiwei Zhu
University of Louisiana

Survey and Focus Group Participants

Nawar Al-Shara
American University
Charles H. Apigian
Middle Tennessee State University
Nagraj Balakrishnan
Clemson University
Philip Boudreaux
University of Louisiana at Lafayette
Nancy Brooks
University of Vermont
Qidong Cao
Winthrop University
Margaret M. Capen
East Carolina University
Robert Carver
Stonehill College
Jan E. Christopher
Delaware State University
James Cochran
Louisiana Tech University
Farideh Dehkordi-Vakil
Western Illinois University
Brant Deppa
Winona State University
Bernard Dickman
Hofstra University
Casey DiRienzo
Elon University
Erick M. Elder
University of Arkansas at Little Rock
Nicholas R. Farnum
California State University–Fullerton
K. Renee Fister
Murray State University
Gary Franko
Siena College
Maurice Gilbert
Troy State University
Deborah J. Gougeon
University of Scranton
Christine Guenther
Pacific University
Charles F. Harrington
University of Southern Indiana
Craig Heinicke
Baldwin-Wallace College
George Hilton
Pacific Union College
Cindy L. Hinz
St. Bonaventure University
Johnny C. Ho
Columbus State University
Shaomin Huang
Lewis-Clark State College
J. Morgan Jones
University of North Carolina at Chapel Hill
Michael Kazlow
Pace University
John Lawrence
California State University–Fullerton
Sheila M. Lawrence
Rutgers, The State University of New Jersey
Jae Lee
State University of New York at New Paltz
Rosa Lemel
Kean University
Robert Lemke
Lake Forest College
Francis P. Mathur
California State Polytechnic University, Pomona
Ralph D. May
Southwestern Oklahoma State University
Richard N. McGrath
Bowling Green State University
Larry T. McRae
Appalachian State University
Dragan Miljkovic
Southwest Missouri State University
John M. Miller
Sam Houston State University
Cameron Montgomery
Delta State University
Broderick Oluyede
Georgia Southern University
Andrew Paizis
Queens College
Andrew L. H. Parkes
University of Northern Iowa
Paul Paschke
Oregon State University
Srikant Raghavan
Lawrence Technological University
Surekha K. B. Rao
Indiana University Northwest

Timothy J. Schibik
University of Southern Indiana
Carlton Scott
University of California, Irvine
Samuel L. Seaman
Baylor University
Scott J. Seipel
Middle Tennessee State University
Sankara N. Sethuraman
Augusta State University
Daniel G. Shimshak
University of Massachusetts, Boston
Robert K. Smidt
California Polytechnic State University
William Stein
Texas A&M University
Robert E. Stevens
University of Louisiana at Monroe
Debra Stiver
University of Nevada–Reno
Ron Stunda
Birmingham-Southern College
Edward Sullivan
Lebanon Valley College
Dharma Thiruvaiyaru
Augusta State University
Daniel Tschopp
Daemen College
Bulent Uyar
University of Northern Iowa
Lee J. Van Scyoc
University of Wisconsin–Oshkosh
Stuart H. Warnock
Tarleton State University
Mark H. Witkowski
University of Texas at San Antonio
William F. Younkin
University of Miami
Shuo Zhang
State University of New York, Fredonia
Zhiwei Zhu
University of Louisiana at Lafayette

Their suggestions and thorough reviews of the previous edition and the manuscript of this edition make this a better text.

Special thanks go to a number of people. Professor Malcolm Gold, Avila University, reviewed the page proofs and the solutions manual, checking text and exercises for accuracy. Professor Jose Lopez-Calleja, Miami Dade College–Kendall, prepared the test bank. Professor Vickie Fry, Westmoreland County Community College, accuracy checked the *Connect* exercises.

We also wish to thank the staff at McGraw-Hill. This includes Thomas Hayward, Senior Brand Manager; Kaylee Putbrese, Development Editor; Diane Nowaczyk, Content Project Manager; and others we do not know personally, but who have made valuable contributions.

ENHANCEMENTS TO STATISTICAL TECHNIQUES IN BUSINESS & ECONOMICS, 16E

MAJOR CHANGES MADE TO INDIVIDUAL CHAPTERS:

CHAPTER 1 What Is Statistics?

- New photo and chapter opening exercise on the Nook Color sold by Barnes & Noble.
- New introduction with new graphic showing the increasing amount of information collected and processed with new technologies.
- New ordinal scale example based on rankings of states based on business climate.
- The chapter includes several new examples.
- Chapter is more focused on the revised learning objectives and improving the chapter's flow.
- Revised exercise 17 is based on economic data.

CHAPTER 2 Describing Data: Frequency Tables, Frequency Distributions, and Graphic Presentation

- Revised Self-Review 2–3 to include data.
- Updated the company list in revised exercise 38.
- New or revised exercises 45, 47, and 48.

CHAPTER 3 Describing Data: Numerical Measures

- Reorganized chapter based on revised learning objectives.
- Replaced the mean deviation with more emphasis on the variance and standard deviation.
- Updated statistics in action.

CHAPTER 4 Describing Data: Displaying and Exploring Data

- Updated exercise 22 with 2012 New York Yankee player salaries.

CHAPTER 5 A Survey of Probability Concepts

- New explanation of odds compared to probabilities.
- New exercise 21.
- New example/solution for demonstrating contingency tables and tree diagrams.
- New contingency table exercise 31.
- Revised example/solution demonstrating the combination formula.

CHAPTER 6 Discrete Probability Distributions

- Revised the section on the binomial distribution.
- Revised example/solution demonstrating the binomial distribution.
- Revised Self-Review 6–4 applying the binomial distribution.
- New exercise 10 using the number of "underwater" loans.
- New exercise using a raffle at a local golf club to demonstrate probability and expected returns.

CHAPTER 7 Continuous Probability Distributions

- Updated Statistics in Action.
- Revised Self-Review 7–2 based on daily personal water consumption.
- Revised explanation of the Empirical Rule as it relates to the normal distribution.

CHAPTER 8 Sampling Methods and the Central Limit Theorem

- New example of simple random sampling and the application of the table of random numbers.
- The discussions of systematic random, stratified random, and cluster sampling have been revised.
- Revised exercise 44 based on the price of a gallon of milk.

CHAPTER 9 Estimation and Confidence Intervals

- New Statistics in Action describing EPA fuel economy.
- New separate section on point estimates.
- Integration and application of the central limit theorem.
- A revised simulation demonstrating the interpretation of confidence level.
- New presentation on using the t table to find z values.
- A revised discussion of determining the confidence interval for the population mean.
- Expanded section on calculating sample size.
- New exercise 12 (milk consumption).

CHAPTER 10 One-Sample Tests of Hypothesis

- New example/solution involving airport parking.
- Revised software solution and explanation of p-values.
- New exercises 17 (daily water consumption) and 19 (number of text messages by teenagers).
- Conducting a test of hypothesis about a population proportion is moved to Chapter 15.
- New example introducing the concept of hypothesis testing.
- Sixth step added to the hypothesis testing procedure emphasizing the interpretation of the hypothesis test results.

CHAPTER 11 Two-Sample Tests of Hypothesis

- New introduction to the chapter.
- Section of two-sample tests about proportions moved to Chapter 15.

- Changed subscripts in example/solution for easier understanding.
- Updated exercise with 2012 New York Yankee player salaries.

CHAPTER 12 Analysis of Variance

- New introduction to the chapter.
- New exercise 24 using the speed of browsers to search the Internet.
- Revised exercise 33 comparing learning in traditional versus online courses.
- New section on Comparing Two Population Variances.
- New example illustrating the comparison of variances.
- Revised section on two-way ANOVA with interaction with new examples and revised example/solution.
- Revised the names of the airlines in the one-way ANOVA example.
- Changed the subscripts in example/solution for easier understanding.
- New exercise 30 (flight times between Los Angeles and San Francisco).

CHAPTER 13 Correlation and Linear Regression

- Rewrote the introduction section to the chapter.
- The data used as the basis for the North American Copier Sales example/solution used throughout the chapter has been changed and expanded to 15 observations to more clearly demonstrate the chapter's learning objectives.
- Revised section on transforming data using the economic relationship between price and sales.
- New exercises 35 (transforming data), 36 (Masters prizes and scores), 43 (2012 NFL points scored versus points allowed), 44 (store size and sales), and 61 (airline distance and fare).

CHAPTER 14 Multiple Regression Analysis

- Rewrote the section on evaluating the multiple regression equation.
- More emphasis on the regression ANOVA table.
- Enhanced the discussion of the *p*-value in decision making.
- More emphasis on calculating the variance inflation factor to evaluate multicollinearity.

CHAPTER 15 Nonparametric Methods: Nominal Level Hypothesis Tests

- Moved and renamed chapter.
- Moved one-sample and two-sample tests of proportions from Chapters 10 and 11 to Chapter 15.
- New example introducing goodness-of-fit tests.
- Removed the graphical methods to evaluate normality.
- Revised section on contingency table analysis with a new example/solution.
- Revised Data Set exercises.

CHAPTER 16 Nonparametric Methods: Analysis of Ordinal Data

- Moved and renamed chapter.
- New example/solution and self-review demonstrating a hypothesis test about the median.
- New example/solution demonstrating the rank-order correlation.

CHAPTER 17 Index Numbers

- Moved chapter to follow nonparametric statistics.
- Updated dates, illustrations, and examples.
- Revised example/solution demonstrating the use of the Production Price Index to deflate sales dollars.
- Revised example/solution demonstrating the comparison of the Dow Jones Industrial Average and the Nasdaq using indexing.
- New self-review about using indexes to compare two different measures over time.
- Revised Data Set Exercise.

CHAPTER 18 Time Series and Forecasting

- Moved chapter to follow nonparametric statistics and index numbers.
- Updated dates, illustrations, and examples.
- Revised section on the components of a time series.
- Revised graphics for better illustration.

CHAPTER 19 Statistical Process Control and Quality Management

- Updated 2012 Malcolm Baldrige National Quality Award winners.

BRIEF CONTENTS

CONTENTS

What Is Statistics?

1

BARNES & NOBLE recently began selling an electronic book reader called the Nook Color. With this device, you can download from a selection of over two million e-books, newspapers, and magazines. It displays downloaded materials in full color. Assume you know the number of Nook Color units sold each day for the last month at the Barnes & Noble store at the Market Commons Mall in Riverside, California. Describe a condition in which this information could be considered a sample. Illustrate a second situation in which the same data would be regarded as a population. (See Exercise 11 and LO1-3.)

LEARNING OBJECTIVES

When you have completed this chapter, you will be able to:

LO1-1 Explain why knowledge of statistics is important.

LO1-2 Define statistics and provide an example of how statistics is applied.

LO1-3 Differentiate between descriptive and inferential statistics.

LO1-4 Classify variables as qualitative or quantitative, and discrete or continuous.

LO1-5 Distinguish between nominal, ordinal, interval, and ratio levels of measurement.

LO1-6 List the values associated with the practice of statistics.

INTRODUCTION

Suppose you work for a large company and your supervisor asks you to decide if a new version of a smartphone should be produced and sold. You start by thinking about the product's innovations and new features. Then, you stop and realize the weight of the decision. The product will need to make a profit so the pricing and the costs of production and distribution are all very important. The decision to introduce the product is based on many alternatives. So how will you know? Where do you start?

Without a long experience in the industry, beginning to develop an intelligence that will make you an expert is essential. You select three other people to work with and meet with them. The conversation focuses on what you need to know and what information and data you need. In your meeting, many questions are asked. How many competitors are already in the market? How are smartphones priced? What design features do competitors' products have? What features does the market require? What do customers want in a smartphone? What do customers like about the existing products? The answers will be based on business intelligence consisting of data and information collected through customer surveys, engineering analysis, and market research. In the end, your presentation to support your decision regarding the introduction of a new smartphone is based on the statistics that you use to summarize and organize your data, the statistics that you use to compare the new product to existing products, and the statistics to estimate future sales, costs, and revenues. The statistics will be the focus of the conversation that you will have with your supervisor about this very important decision.

As a decision maker, you will need to acquire and analyze data to support your decisions. The purpose of this text is to develop your knowledge of basic statistical techniques and methods and how to apply them to develop the business and personal intelligence that will help you make decisions.

LO1-1
Explain why knowledge of statistics is important.

WHY STUDY STATISTICS?

If you look through your university catalogue, you will find that statistics is required for many college programs. As you investigate a future career in accounting, economics, human resources, finance, or other business area, you will also discover that statistics is required as part of these college programs. So why is an education in statistics a requirement in so many disciplines?

A major driver of the requirement for statistics knowledge is the technologies available for capturing data. Examples include the technology that Google uses to track how Internet users access websites. As people use Google to search the Internet, Google records every search and then uses these data to sort and prioritize the results for future Internet searches. One recent estimate indicates that Google processes 20,000 terabytes of information per day. Big-box retailers like Target, Walmart, Kroger, and others scan every purchase and use the data to manage the distribution of products, to make decisions about marketing and sales, and to track daily and even hourly sales. Police departments collect and use data to provide city residents with maps that communicate information about crimes committed and their location. Every organization is collecting and using data to develop knowledge and intelligence that will help people make informed decisions, and to track the implementation of their decisions. The graphic to the left shows the amount of data generated every minute (www.domo.com). A good working knowledge of statistics is useful for summarizing and organizing data to provide information that is useful and supportive of decision making. Statistics is used to make valid comparisons and to predict the outcomes of decisions.

In summary, there are at least three reasons for studying statistics: (1) data are collected everywhere and require statistical knowledge to

make the information useful, (2) statistical techniques are used to make professional and personal decisions, and (3) no matter what your career, you will need a knowledge of statistics to understand the world and to be conversant in your career. An understanding of statistics and statistical method will help you make more effective personal and professional decisions.

LO1-2
Define statistics and provide an example of how statistics is applied.

WHAT IS MEANT BY STATISTICS?

This question can be rephrased in two, subtly different ways: what are statistics and what is statistics? To answer the first question, a statistic is a number used to communicate a piece of information. Examples of **statistics** are:

- The inflation rate is 2%.
- Your grade point average is 3.5.
- The price of a new Tesla premium electric sedan is $85,400.

Each of these statistics is a numerical fact and communicates a very limited piece of information that is not very useful by itself. However, if we recognize that each of these statistics is part of a larger discussion, then the question "what **is** statistics" is applicable. Statistics is the set of knowledge and skills used to organize, summarize, and analyze data. The results of statistical analysis will start interesting conversations in the search for knowledge and intelligence that will help us make decisions. For example:

- The inflation rate for the calendar year was 2%. By applying statistics we could compare this year's inflation rate to the past observations of inflation. Is it higher, lower, or about the same? Is there a trend of increasing or decreasing inflation? Is there a relationship between interest rates and government bonds?
- Your grade point average (GPA) is 3.5. By collecting data and applying statistics, you can determine the required GPA to be admitted to the Master of Business Administration program at the University of Chicago, Harvard, or the University of Michigan. You can determine the likelihood that you would be admitted to a particular program. You may be interested in interviewing for a management position with Procter & Gamble. What GPA does Procter & Gamble require for college graduates with a bachelor's degree? Is there a range of acceptable GPAs?
- You are budgeting for a new car. You would like to own an electric car with a small carbon footprint. The price for the Tesla premium electric sedan is $85,400. By collecting additional data and applying statistics, you can analyze the alternatives. For example, another choice is a hybrid car that runs on both gas and electricity such as a Toyota Prius. It can be purchased for about $27,000. Another hybrid, the Chevrolet Volt, costs about $32,000. What are the differences in the cars' specifications? What additional information can be collected and summarized so that you can make a good purchase decision?

Another example of using statistics to provide information to evaluate decisions is the distribution and market share of Frito-Lay products. Data are collected on each of the Frito-Lay product lines. These data include the market share and the pounds of product sold. Statistics is used to present this information in a bar chart in Chart 1–1. It clearly shows Frito-Lay's dominance in the potato, corn, and tortilla chip markets. It also shows the absolute measure of pounds of each product line consumed in the United States.

These examples show that statistics is more than the presentation of numerical information. Statistics is about collecting and processing information to create a conversation, to stimulate additional questions, and to provide a basis for making decisions. Specifically, we define statistics as:

STATISTICS The science of collecting, organizing, presenting, analyzing, and interpreting data to assist in making more effective decisions.

STATISTICS IN ACTION

We call your attention to a feature of our textbook—*Statistics in Action*. Read each one carefully to get an appreciation of the wide application of statistics in management, economics, nursing, law enforcement, sports, and other disciplines.

- In 2013, *Forbes* published a list of the richest Americans. William Gates, founder of Microsoft Corporation, is the richest. His net worth is estimated at $66.0 billion. (www.forbes.com)
- In 2013, the four largest privately owned American companies, ranked by revenue, were Cargill, Koch Industries, Mars, and Bechtel. (www.forbes.com)
- In the United States, a typical high school graduate earns $652 per week, a typical college graduate with a bachelor's degree earns $1,066 per week, and a typical college graduate with a master's degree earns $1,300 per week. (www.bls.gov/emp/ep_chart_001.htm)

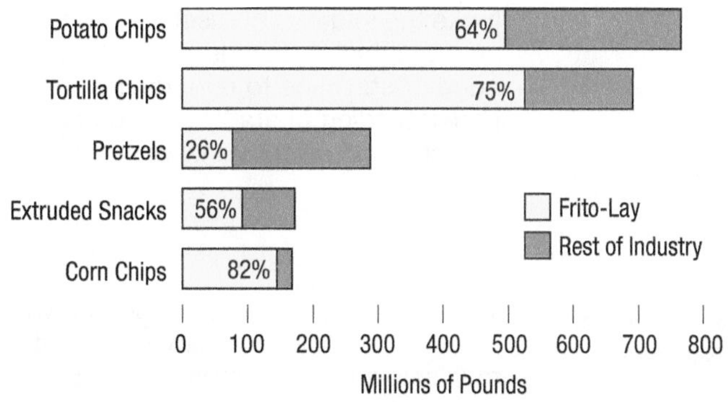

CHART 1–1 Frito-Lay Volume and Share of Major Snack Chip Categories in U.S. Supermarkets

In this book, you will learn the basic techniques and applications of statistics that you can use to support your decisions, both personal and professional. To start, we will differentiate between descriptive and inferential statistics.

LO1-3
Differentiate between descriptive and inferential statistics.

TYPES OF STATISTICS

When we use statistics to generate information for decision making from data, we use either descriptive statistics or inferential statistics. Their application depends on the questions asked and the type of data available.

Descriptive Statistics

Masses of unorganized data—such as the census of population, the weekly earnings of thousands of computer programmers, and the individual responses of 2,000 registered voters regarding their choice for president of the United States—are of little value as is. However, descriptive statistics can be used to organize data into a meaningful form. We define **descriptive statistics** as:

DESCRIPTIVE STATISTICS Methods of organizing, summarizing, and presenting data in an informative way.

The following are examples that apply descriptive statistics to summarize a large amount of data and provide information that is easy to understand.

- There are a total of 46,837 miles of interstate highways in the United States. The interstate system represents only 1% of the nation's total roads but carries more than 20% of the traffic. The longest is I-90, which stretches from Boston to Seattle, a distance of 3,099 miles. The shortest is I-878 in New York City, which is 0.70 mile in length. Alaska does not have any interstate highways, Texas has the most interstate miles at 3,232, and New York has the most interstate routes with 28.
- The average person spent $103.00 on traditional Valentine's Day merchandise in 2013. This is an increase of $0.50 from 2012. As in previous years, men spent nearly twice the amount women spent on the holiday. The average man spent $135.35 to impress the people in his life while women only spent $72.28. Family pets also feel the love; the average person spent $3.27 on his or her furry friends, up from $2.17 last year.

Statistical methods and techniques to generate descriptive statistics are presented in Chapters 2 and 4. These include organizing and summarizing data with frequency distributions and presenting frequency distributions with charts and graphs.

In addition, statistical measures to summarize the characteristics of a distribution are discussed in Chapter 3.

Inferential Statistics

Sometimes we must make decisions based on a limited set of data. For example, we would like to know the operating characteristics, such as fuel efficiency measured by miles per gallon, of sport utility vehicles (SUVs) currently in use. If we spent a lot of time, money, and effort, all the owners of SUVs could be surveyed. In this case, our goal would be to survey the **population** of SUV owners.

POPULATION The entire set of individuals or objects of interest or the measurements obtained from all individuals or objects of interest.

However, based on inferential statistics, we can survey a limited number of SUV owners and collect a **sample** from the population.

SAMPLE A portion, or part, of the population of interest.

Samples are often used to obtain reliable estimates of population parameters. (Sampling is discussed in Chapter 8). In the process, we make trade-offs between the time, money, and effort to collect the data and the error of estimating a population parameter. The process of sampling SUVs is illustrated in the following graphic. In this example, we would like to know the mean or average SUV fuel efficiency. To estimate the mean of the population, six SUVs are sampled and the mean of their MPG is calculated.

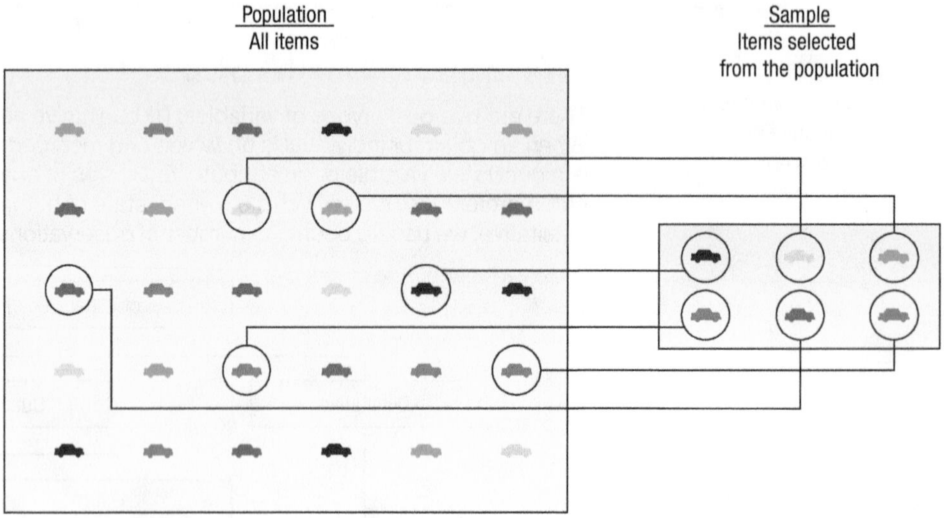

So, the sample of six SUVs represents evidence from the population that we use to reach an inference or conclusion about the average MPG for all SUVs. The process of sampling from a population with the objective of estimating properties of a population is called **inferential statistics.**

INFERENTIAL STATISTICS The methods used to estimate a property of a population on the basis of a sample.

Inferential statistics is widely applied to learn something about a population in business, agriculture, politics, and government, as shown in the following examples:

- Television networks constantly monitor the popularity of their programs by hiring Nielsen and other organizations to sample the preferences of TV viewers. For example, 10.5% of a sample of households with TVs watched *The Big Bang Theory* during the week of February 25, 2012 (www.nielsen.com). These program ratings are used to make decisions about advertising rates and whether to continue or cancel a program.
- In 2012, a sample of 40 U.S. Internal Revenue Service volunteer program sites was selected and the volunteer tax preparers were tested with three standard tax returns. The sample indicated that tax returns were completed with a 49% accuracy rate. In this example, the statistics are used to make decisions about how to improve the accuracy rate by correcting the most common errors and improving the training of volunteers. (www.treasury.gov/tigta/auditreports/2012reports/201240088fr.pdf)

A feature of our text is self-review problems. There are a number of them interspersed throughout each chapter. The first self-review follows. Each self-review tests your comprehension of preceding material. The answer and method of solution are given in Appendix E. You can find the answer to the following self-review in 1–1 in Appendix E. We recommend that you solve each one and then check your answer.

SELF-REVIEW 1–1

The answers are in Appendix E.

The Atlanta-based advertising firm Brandon and Associates asked a sample of 1,960 consumers to try a newly developed chicken dinner by Boston Market. Of the 1,960 sampled, 1,176 said they would purchase the dinner if it is marketed.

(a) What could Brandon and Associates report to Boston Market regarding acceptance of the chicken dinner in the population?

(b) Is this an example of descriptive statistics or inferential statistics? Explain.

LO1-4
Classify variables as qualitative or quantitative, and discrete or continuous.

TYPES OF VARIABLES

There are two basic types of variables: (1) qualitative and (2) quantitative (see Chart 1–2). When an object or individual is observed and recorded as a nonnumeric characteristic, it is a qualitative variable or an attribute. Examples of qualitative variables are gender, beverage preference, type of vehicle owned, state of birth, and eye color. When a variable is qualitative, we usually count the number of observations for each category and determine

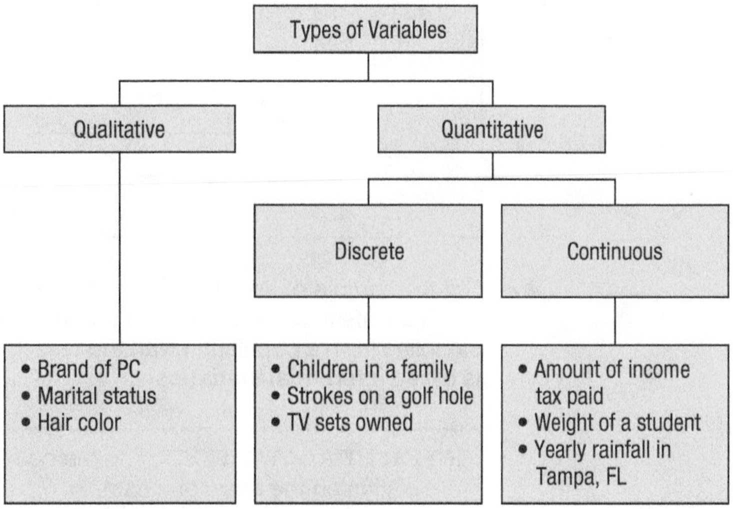

CHART 1–2 Summary of the Types of Variables

what percent are in each category. For example, if we observe the variable eye color, what percent of the population has blue eyes and what percent has brown eyes? If the variable is type of vehicle, what percent of the total number of cars sold last month were SUVs? Qualitative variables are often summarized in charts and bar graphs (Chapter 2).

When a variable can be reported numerically, the variable is called a quantitative variable. Examples of quantitative variables are the balance in your checking account, the ages of company presidents, the life of a car battery (such as 42 months), and the number of people employed by a company.

Quantitative variables are either discrete or continuous. Discrete variables can assume only certain values, and there are "gaps" between the values. Examples of discrete variables are the number of bedrooms in a house (1, 2, 3, 4, etc.), the number of cars arriving at Exit 25 on I-4 in Florida near Walt Disney World in an hour (326, 421, etc.), and the number of students in each section of a statistics course (25 in section A, 42 in section B, and 18 in section C). We count, for example, the number of cars arriving at Exit 25 on I-4, and we count the number of statistics students in each section. Notice that a home can have 3 or 4 bedrooms, but it cannot have 3.56 bedrooms. Thus, there is a "gap" between possible values. Typically, discrete variables are counted.

Observations of a continuous variable can assume any value within a specific range. Examples of continuous variables are the air pressure in a tire and the weight of a shipment of tomatoes. Other examples are the ounces of raisins in a box of raisin bran cereal and the duration of flights from Orlando to San Diego. Grade point average (GPA) is a continuous variable. We could report the GPA of a particular student as 3.2576952. The usual practice is to round to 3 places—3.258. Typically, continuous variables result from measuring.

LO1-5
Distinguish between nominal, ordinal, interval, and ratio levels of measurement.

LEVELS OF MEASUREMENT

Data can be classified according to levels of measurement. The level of measurement determines how data should be summarized and presented. It will also indicate the type of statistical analysis that can be performed. Here are two examples of the relationship between measurement and how we apply statistics. There are six colors of candies in a bag of M&Ms. Suppose we assign brown a value of 1, yellow 2, blue 3, orange 4, green 5, and red 6. What kind of variable is the color of an M&M? It is a qualitative variable. Suppose someone summarizes M&M color by adding the assigned color values, divides the sum by the number of M&Ms, and reports that the mean color is 3.56. How do we interpret this statistic? You are correct in concluding that it has no meaning as a measure of M&M color. As a qualitative variable, we can only report the count and percentage of each color in a bag of M&Ms. As a second example, in a high school track meet there are eight competitors in the 400-meter run. We report the order of finish and that the mean finish is 4.5. What does the mean finish tell us? Nothing! In both of these instances, we have not used the appropriate statistics for the level of measurement.

There are four levels of measurement: nominal, ordinal, interval, and ratio. The lowest, or the most primitive, measurement is the nominal level. The highest is the ratio level of measurement.

Nominal-Level Data

For the **nominal level of measurement,** observations of a qualitative variable are measured and recorded as labels or names. The labels or names can only be classified and counted. There is no particular order to the labels.

NOMINAL LEVEL OF MEASUREMENT Data recorded at the nominal level of measurement is represented as labels or names. They have no order. They can only be classified and counted.

STATISTICS IN ACTION

Where did statistics get its start? In 1662 John Graunt published an article called "Natural and Political Observations Made upon Bills of Mortality." The author's "observations" were the result of a study and analysis of a weekly church publication called "Bill of Mortality," which listed births, christenings, and deaths and their causes. Graunt realized that the Bills of Mortality represented only a fraction of all births and deaths in London. However, he used the data to reach broad conclusions about the impact of disease, such as the plague, on the general population. His logic is an example of statistical inference. His analysis and interpretation of the data are thought to mark the start of statistics.

The classification of the six colors of M&M milk chocolate candies is an example of the nominal level of measurement. We simply classify the candies by color. There is no natural order. That is, we could report the brown candies first, the orange first, or any of the other colors first. Recording the variable gender is another example of the nominal level of measurement. Suppose we count the number of students entering a football game with a student ID and report how many are men and how many are women. We could report either the men or the women first. For the data measured at the nominal level, we are limited to counting the number in each category of the variable. Often, we convert these counts to percentages. For example, a study of the color of M&M candies reports the following results (www.sensationalcolor.com/color-trends/most-popular-colors-177/mam-colors.html):

Color	Percent in a bag
Blue	24%
Green	20
Orange	16
Yellow	14
Red	13
Brown	13

To process the data for a variable measured at the nominal level, we often numerically code the labels or names. For example, if we are interested in measuring the home state for students at East Carolina University, we would assign a student's home state of Alabama a code of 1, Alaska a code of 2, Arizona a 3, and so on. Using this procedure with an alphabetical listing of states, Wisconsin is coded 49 and Wyoming 50. Realize that the number assigned to each state is still a label or name. The reason we assign numerical codes is to facilitate counting the number of students from each state with statistical software. Note that assigning numbers to the states does not give us license to manipulate the codes as numerical information. Specifically, in this example, 1 + 2 = 3 corresponds to Alabama + Alaska = Arizona. Clearly, the nominal level of measurement does not permit any mathematical operation that has any valid interpretation.

Ordinal-Level Data

The next higher level of measurement is the **ordinal level.** For this level of measurement a qualitative variable or attribute is either ranked or rated on a relative scale.

ORDINAL LEVEL OF MEASUREMENT Data recorded at the ordinal level of measurement is based on a relative ranking or rating of items based on a defined attribute or qualitative variable. Variables based on this level of measurement are only ranked or counted.

Best Business Climate
1. Texas
2. Utah
3. Virginia
4. Florida
5. Louisiana
6. Indiana
7. South Carolina
8. Tennessee
9. Georgia
10. Nebraska

For example, many businesses make decisions about where to locate their facilities; in other words, where is the best place for their business? Business Facilities (www.businessfacilities.com) publishes a list of the top 10 states for the "best business climate." The 2012 rankings are shown to the left. They are based on the evaluation of 20 different factors, including the cost of labor, business tax climate, quality of life, transportation infrastructure, educated workforce, and economic growth potential to rank states based on the attribute "best business climate."

This is an example of an ordinal scale because the states are ranked in order of best to worst business climate. That is, we know the relative order of the states

based on the attribute. For example, in 2012 Texas had the best business climate. Louisiana was fifth, and that was better than South Carolina but not as good as Virginia. Notice that we cannot say that Texas's business climate is five times better than Louisiana's business climate because the magnitude of the differences between the states is not known.

Another example of the ordinal level measure is based on a scale that measures an attribute. This type of scale is used when students rate instructors on a variety of attributes. One attribute may be: "Overall, how do you rate the quality of instruction in this class?" A student's response is recorded on a relative scale of inferior, poor, good, excellent, and superior. An important characteristic of using a relative measurement scale is that we cannot distinguish the magnitude of the differences between groups. We do not know if the difference between "Superior" and "Good" is the same as the difference between "Poor" and "Inferior."

Table 1–1 lists the frequencies of student ratings of instructional quality for Professor James Brunner in an Introduction to Finance course. The data are summarized based on the order of the scale used to rate the instructor. That is, they are summarized by the number of students who indicated a rating of superior (6), good (28), and so on. We can also convert the frequencies to percentages. About 37.8% of the students rated the instructor as good.

TABLE 1–1 Rating of a Finance Professor

Rating	Frequency
Superior	6
Good	28
Average	25
Poor	12
Inferior	3

Interval-Level Data

The **interval level of measurement** is the next highest level. It includes all the characteristics of the ordinal level, but, in addition, the difference or interval between values is meaningful.

INTERVAL LEVEL OF MEASUREMENT For data recorded at the interval level of measurement, the interval or the distance between values is meaningful. The interval level of measurement is based on a scale with a known unit of measurement.

The Fahrenheit temperature scale is an example of the interval level of measurement. Suppose the high temperatures on three consecutive winter days in Boston are 28, 31, and 20 degrees Fahrenheit. These temperatures can be easily ranked, but we can also determine the interval or distance between temperatures. This is possible because 1 degree Fahrenheit represents a constant unit of measurement. That is, the distance between 10 and 15 degrees Fahrenheit is 5 degrees, and is the same as the 5-degree distance between 50 and 55 degrees Fahrenheit. It is also important to note that 0 is just a point on the scale. It does not represent the absence of the condition. The measurement of zero degrees Fahrenheit does not represent the absence of heat or cold. But by our own measurement scale, it is cold! A major limitation of a variable measured at the interval level is that we cannot make statements similar to 20 degrees Fahrenheit is twice as warm as 10 degrees Fahrenheit.

Another example of the interval scale of measurement is women's dress sizes. Listed below is information on several dimensions of a standard U.S. woman's dress.

Size	Bust (in)	Waist (in)	Hips (in)
8	32	24	35
10	34	26	37
12	36	28	39
14	38	30	41
16	40	32	43
18	42	34	45
20	44	36	47
22	46	38	49
24	48	40	51
26	50	42	53
28	52	44	55

Why is the "size" scale an interval measurement? Observe that as the size changes by two units (say from size 10 to size 12 or from size 24 to size 26), each of the measurements increases by 2 inches. To put it another way, the intervals are the same.

There is no natural zero point for dress size. A "size 0" dress does not have "zero" material. Instead, it would have a 24-inch bust, 16-inch waist, and 27-inch hips. Moreover, the ratios are not reasonable. If you divide a size 28 by a size 14, you do not get the same answer as dividing a size 20 by a size 10. Neither ratio is equal to two, as the "size" number would suggest. In short, if the distances between the numbers make sense, but the ratios do not, then you have an interval scale of measurement.

Ratio-Level Data

Almost all quantitative variables are recorded on the **ratio level of measurement.** The ratio level is the "highest" level of measurement. It has all the characteristics of the interval level, but, in addition, the 0 point and the ratio between two numbers are both meaningful.

RATIO LEVEL OF MEASUREMENT Data recorded at the ratio level of measurement are based on a scale with a known unit of measurement and a meaningful interpretation of zero on the scale.

Examples of the ratio scale of measurement include wages, units of production, weight, changes in stock prices, distance between branch offices, and height. Money is also a good illustration. If you have zero dollars, then you have no money, and a wage of $50 per hour is two times the wage of $25 per hour. Weight is also measured at the ratio level of measurement. If a scale is correctly calibrated, then it will read 0 when nothing is on the scale. Further, something that weighs 1 pound is half as heavy as something that weighs 2 pounds.

Table 1–2 illustrates the ratio scale of measurement for the variable, annual income for four father-and-son combinations. Observe that the senior Lahey earns twice as much as his son. In the Rho family, the son makes twice as much as the father.

TABLE 1–2 Father–Son Income Combinations

Name	Father	Son
Lahey	$80,000	$ 40,000
Nale	90,000	30,000
Rho	60,000	120,000
Steele	75,000	130,000

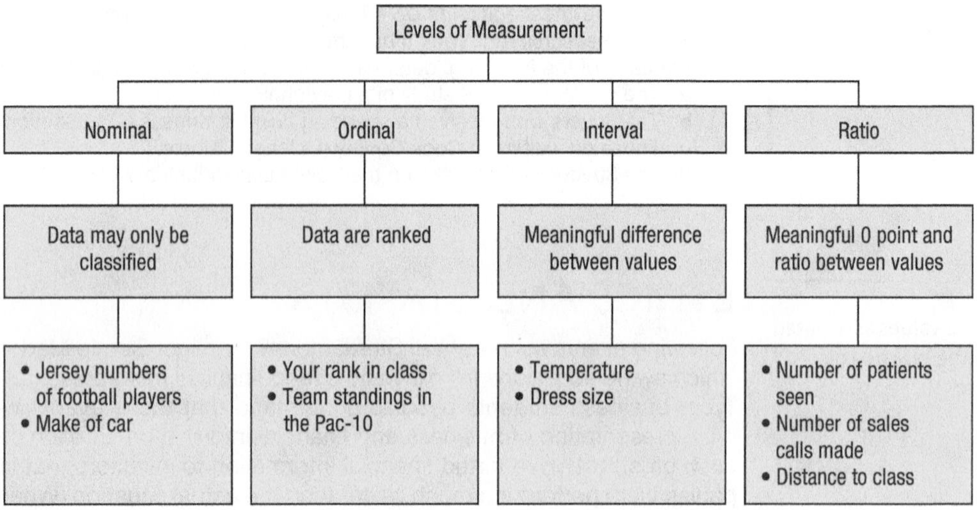

CHART 1–3 Summary and Examples of the Characteristics for Levels of Measurement

Chart 1–3 summarizes the major characteristics of the various levels of measurement. The level of measurement will determine the type of statistical methods that can be used to analyze a variable. Statistical methods to analyze variables measured on a nominal level are discussed in Chapter 15; methods for ordinal-level variables are discussed in Chapter 16. Statistical methods to analyze variables measured on an interval or ratio level are presented in Chapters 9 through 14.

SELF-REVIEW 1–2

What is the level of measurement reflected by the following data?

(a) The age of each person in a sample of 50 adults who listen to one of the 1,230 talk radio stations in the United States is

35	29	41	34	44	46	42	42	37	47
30	36	41	39	44	39	43	43	44	40
47	37	41	27	33	33	39	38	43	22
44	39	35	35	41	42	37	42	38	43
35	37	38	43	40	48	42	31	51	34

(b) In a survey of 200 luxury-car owners, 100 were from California, 50 from New York, 30 from Illinois, and 20 from Ohio.

EXERCISES

The answers to the odd-numbered exercises are in Appendix D.

1. What is the level of measurement for each of the following variables?
   a. Student IQ ratings.
   b. Distance students travel to class.
   c. The jersey numbers of a sorority soccer team.
   d. A student's state of birth.
   e. A student's academic class—that is, freshman, sophomore, junior, or senior.
   f. Number of hours students study per week.

2. The *San Francisco Chronicle* is a large newspaper published daily. What is the level of measurement for each of the following variables?
   a. The number of papers sold each Sunday during 2014.
   b. The departments, such as editorial, advertising, sports, etc.
   c. The number of papers sold by county.
   d. The number of years with the paper for each employee.

3. Look in the latest edition of *USA Today* or your local newspaper and find examples of each level of measurement. Write a brief memo summarizing your findings.
4. For each of the following, determine whether the group is a sample or a population.
   a. The participants in a study of a new cholesterol drug.
   b. The drivers who received a speeding ticket in Kansas City last month.
   c. Those on welfare in Cook County (Chicago), Illinois.
   d. The 30 stocks that make up the Dow Jones Industrial Average.

LO1-6
List the values associated with the practice of statistics.

ETHICS AND STATISTICS

Following events such as Wall Street money manager Bernie Madoff's Ponzi scheme, which swindled billions from investors, and financial misrepresentations by Enron and Tyco, business students need to understand that these events were based on the misrepresentation of business and financial information. In each case, people within each organization reported financial information to investors that indicated the companies were performing much better than the actual situation. When the true financial information was reported, the companies were worth much less than advertised. The result was many investors lost all or nearly all of the money that they had invested.

The article "Statistics and Ethics: Some Advice for Young Statisticians," in *The American Statistician* 57, no. 1 (2003), offers guidance. The authors advise us to practice statistics with integrity and honesty, and urge us to "do the right thing" when collecting, organizing, summarizing, analyzing, and interpreting numerical information. The real contribution of statistics to society is a moral one. Financial analysts need to provide information that truly reflects a company's performance so as not to mislead individual investors. Information regarding product defects that may be harmful to people must be analyzed and reported with integrity and honesty. The authors of *The American Statistician* article further indicate that when we practice statistics, we need to maintain "an independent and principled point-of-view" when analyzing and reporting findings and results.

As you progress through this text, we will highlight ethical issues in the collection, analysis, presentation, and interpretation of statistical information. We also hope that, as you learn about using statistics, you will become a more informed consumer of information. For example, you will question a report based on data that do not fairly represent the population, a report that does not include all relevant statistics, one that includes an incorrect choice of statistical measures, or a presentation that introduces bias in a deliberate attempt to mislead or misrepresent.

COMPUTER SOFTWARE APPLICATIONS

Using statistics to process and analyze data requires computer software. Throughout our text, we show the application of Microsoft Excel and, occasionally, Minitab. University and college computers usually have Microsoft Excel. Your computer may already be packaged with Microsoft Excel. If not, the Microsoft Office package with Excel is often sold at a reduced academic price through your university or college. In this text, we use Excel for the majority of the applications. We also use an Excel add-in called MegaStat. If your instructor requires this package, it is available at www.mhhe.com/megastat. This add-in gives Excel the capability to produce additional statistical reports. Occasionally, we use Minitab to illustrate an application. See www.minitab.com for further information. Minitab also offers discounted academic pricing. If you are using an Apple Mac computer with Excel, you should download the free, trial version of Stat Plus at www.analystsoft.com. It is a statistical software package that will integrate with Excel for Mac computers.

The following example shows the application of Excel to perform a statistical analysis. In Chapters 2, 3, and 4, we illustrate software methods for summarizing and

describing data. An example used in these chapters refers to the Applewood Auto Group data set. These data and other data sets and files are available on the text's student website, www.mhhe.com/lind16e. The Applewood data set has several variables that were measured for 180 vehicles sold by the Applewood Auto Group. The following shows Excel's calculation of several statistics for the variable profit. The Excel output reveals, among other things, that there were 180 vehicles sold, the mean (average) profit per vehicle was $1,843.17, and the amount of profit ranged from $294 to $3,292. Throughout the text, the illustrations of Excel are supported by instructions so that you can learn how to apply Excel to do statistical analysis. The instructions are presented in Appendix C of this text.

APPLEWOOD AUTO GROUP.xlsx

	A	B	C	D	E	F	G	H
1	Age	Profit	Location	Vehicle-Type	Previous		*Profit*	
2	33	$1,889	Olean	SUV	1			
3	47	$1,461	Kane	Sedan	0		Mean	1843.17
4	44	$1,532	Tionesta	SUV	3		Standard Error	47.97
5	53	$1,220	Olean	Sedan	0		Median	1882.50
6	51	$1,674	Sheffield	Sedan	1		Mode	1915.00
7	41	$2,389	Kane	Truck	1		Standard Deviation	643.63
8	58	$2,058	Kane	SUV	1		Sample Variance	414256.61
9	35	$1,919	Tionesta	SUV	1		Kurtosis	-0.22
10	45	$1,266	Olean	Sedan	0		Skewness	-0.24
11	54	$2,991	Tionesta	Sedan	0		Range	2998
12	56	$2,695	Kane	Sedan	2		Minimum	294
13	41	$2,165	Tionesta	SUV	0		Maximum	3292
14	38	$1,766	Sheffield	SUV	0		Sum	331770
15	48	$1,952	Tionesta	Compact	1		Count	180

At the option of your instructor, and depending on the software system available, we urge you to apply a computer package to the exercises in the **Data Set Exercises** section in each chapter. It will relieve you of the tedious calculations and allow you to concentrate on the statistical analysis.

CHAPTER SUMMARY

I. Statistics is the science of collecting, organizing, presenting, analyzing, and interpreting data to assist in making more effective decisions.

II. There are two types of statistics.
- **A.** Descriptive statistics are procedures used to organize and summarize data.
- **B.** Inferential statistics involve taking a sample from a population and making estimates about a population based on the sample results.
  - **1.** A population is an entire set of individuals or objects of interest or the measurements obtained from all individuals or objects of interest.
  - **2.** A sample is a part of the population.

III. There are two types of variables.
- **A.** A qualitative variable is nonnumeric.
  - **1.** Usually we are interested in the number or percent of the observations in each category.
  - **2.** Qualitative data are usually summarized in graphs and bar charts.
- **B.** There are two types of quantitative variables and they are usually reported numerically.
  - **1.** Discrete variables can assume only certain values, and there are usually gaps between values.
  - **2.** A continuous variable can assume any value within a specified range.

IV. There are four levels of measurement.
  A. With the nominal level, the data are sorted into categories with no particular order to the categories.
  B. The ordinal level of measurement presumes that one classification is ranked higher than another.
  C. The interval level of measurement has the ranking characteristic of the ordinal level of measurement plus the characteristic that the distance between values is a constant size.
  D. The ratio level of measurement has all the characteristics of the interval level, plus there is a 0 point and the ratio of two values is meaningful.

CHAPTER EXERCISES

5. Explain the difference between qualitative and quantitative variables. Give an example of qualitative and quantitative variables.

6. Explain the difference between a sample and a population.

7. Explain the difference between a discrete and a continuous variable. Give an example of each not included in the text.

8. For the following situations, would you collect information using a sample or a population? Why?
  a. Statistics 201 is a course taught at a university. Professor Rauch has taught nearly 1,500 students in the course over the past 5 years. You would like to know the average grade for the course.
  b. As part of a research project, you need to report the average profit as a percentage of revenue for the #1-ranked corporation in the Fortune 500 for each of the last 10 years.
  c. You are looking forward to graduation and your first job as a salesperson for one of five large pharmaceutical corporations. Planning for your interviews, you will need to know about each company's mission, profitability, products, and markets.
  d. You are shopping for a new MP3 music player such as the Apple iPod. The manufacturers advertise the number of music tracks that can be stored in the memory. Usually, the advertisers assume relatively short, popular songs to estimate the number of tracks that can be stored. You, however, like Broadway musical tunes and they are much longer. You would like to estimate how many Broadway tunes will fit on your MP3 player.

9. Exits along interstate highways were formerly numbered successively from the western or southern border of a state. However, the Department of Transportation has recently changed most of them to agree with the numbers on the mile markers along the highway.
  a. What level of measurement were data on the consecutive exit numbers?
  b. What level of measurement are data on the milepost numbers?
  c. Discuss the advantages of the newer system.

10. A poll solicits a large number of college undergraduates for information on the following variables: the name of their cell phone provider (AT&T, Verizon, and so on), the numbers of minutes used last month (200, 400, for example), and their satisfaction with the service (Terrible, Adequate, Excellent, and so forth). What is the level of measurement for each of these three variables?

11. Barnes & Noble recently began selling an electronic book reader called the Nook Color. With this device, you can download over two million e-books and newpapers and magazines. It displays downloaded materials in full color. Assume you know the number of Nook Color units sold each day for the last month at the Barnes & Noble store at the Market Commons Mall in Riverside, California. Describe a condition in which this information could be considered a sample. Illustrate a second situation in which the same data would be regarded as a population.

12. Utilize the concepts of sample and population to describe how a presidential election is unlike an "exit" poll of the electorate.

13. Place these variables in the following classification tables. For each table, summarize your observations and evaluate if the results are generally true. For example, salary is reported as a continuous quantitative variable. It is also a continuous ratio-scaled variable.
  a. Salary
  b. Gender
  c. Sales volume of MP3 players
  d. Soft drink preference
  e. Temperature
  f. SAT scores
  g. Student rank in class

h. Rating of a finance professor
i. Number of home computers

	Discrete Variable	Continuous Variable
Qualitative		
Quantitative		a. Salary

	Discrete	Continuous
Nominal		
Ordinal		
Interval		
Ratio		a. Salary

14. Using data from such publications as the *Statistical Abstract of the United States, The World Almanac, Forbes,* or your local newspaper, give examples of the nominal, ordinal, interval, and ratio levels of measurement.

15. The Struthers Wells Corporation employs more than 10,000 white-collar workers in its sales offices and manufacturing facilities in the United States, Europe, and Asia. A sample of 300 U.S. workers revealed 120 would accept a transfer to a location outside the United States. On the basis of these findings, write a brief memo to Ms. Wanda Carter, Vice President of Human Services, regarding all white-collar workers in the firm and their willingness to relocate.

16. AVX Stereo Equipment, Inc., recently began a "no-hassles" return policy. A sample of 500 customers who recently returned items showed 400 thought the policy was fair, 32 thought it took too long to complete the transaction, and the rest had no opinion. On the basis of this information, make an inference about customer reaction to the new policy.

17. *The Wall Street Journal's* website, www.wsj.com, reported the number of cars and light-duty trucks sold by the eight largest automakers in the first 2 months of 2013. Compare the 2013 data to the first 2 months of 2009 as reported below.

	Year-to-Date Sales	
Manufacturer	**Through February 2013**	**Through February 2009**
General Motors Corp.	419,013	252,701
Ford Motor Company	361,713	185,825
Toyota Motor Sales USA Inc.	324,102	226,870
Chrysler LLC	256,746	146,207
American Honda Motor Co. Inc.	201,613	142,606
Nissan North America Inc.	180,555	108,133
Hyundai Motor America	96,024	55,133
Mazda Motor of America Inc.	46,255	31,821

a. Compare the total sales for the eight automakers. Has there been an increase or a decrease in sales for 2013 compared to the same period in 2009?
b. The total number of cars and light-duty trucks sold in 2013 was 2.234 million while 1.346 million were sold in 2009. Compute the market share for each of the companies. Has there been a change in the market share for any of the companies?
c. Compute the percentage change in sales for each of the eight companies. Which companies had a significant change in sales?

18. The following chart depicts the average amounts spent by consumers on holiday gifts.

Holiday Spending	Amount
Family	$451.34
Friends	$ 85.60
Co-workers	$ 22.40
Others	$ 44.52

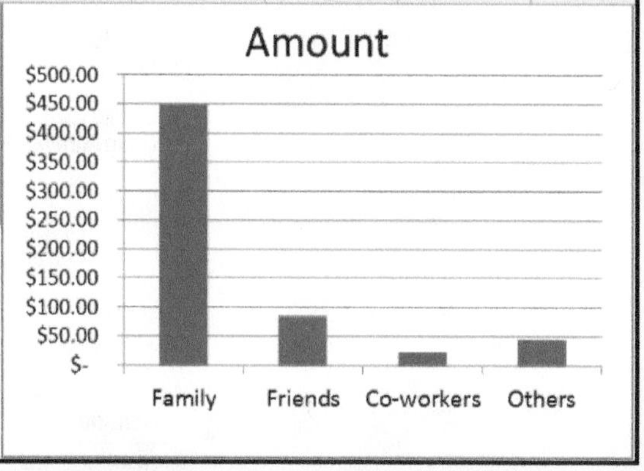

Write a brief report summarizing the amounts spent during the holidays. Be sure to include the total amount spent and the percent spent by each group.

19. The following chart depicts the earnings in billions of dollars for ExxonMobil for the period 2003 until 2012. Write a brief report discussing the earnings at ExxonMobil during the period. Was one year higher than the others? Did the earnings increase, decrease, or stay the same over the period?

Year	Earnings ($ billions)
2003	14.5
2004	16.7
2005	24.3
2006	26.2
2007	26.5
2008	45.2
2009	19.3
2010	30.5
2011	41.1
2012	44.9

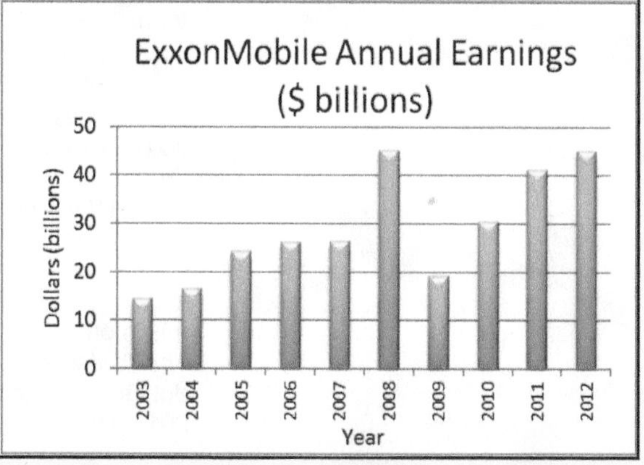

DATA SET EXERCISES

(The data for these exercises are available at the text website www.mhhe.com/lind16e.)

20. Refer to the Real Estate data, which report information on homes sold in the Goodyear, Arizona, area last year. Consider the following variables: selling price, number of bedrooms, township, and distance from the center of the city.
a. Which of the variables are qualitative and which are quantitative?
b. Determine the level of measurement for each of the variables.

21. Refer to the Baseball 2012 data, which report information on the 30 Major League Baseball teams for the 2012 season. Consider the following variables: number of wins, payroll, season attendance, whether the team is in the American or National League, and the number of home runs hit.
a. Which of these variables are quantitative and which are qualitative?
b. Determine the level of measurement for each of the variables.

22. Refer to the Buena School District bus data, which report information on the school district's bus fleet.
a. Which of the variables are qualitative and which are quantitative?
b. Determine the level of measurement for each variable.

Describing Data:

FREQUENCY TABLES, FREQUENCY DISTRIBUTIONS, AND GRAPHIC PRESENTATION

2

MERRILL LYNCH recently completed a study of online investment portfolios for a sample of clients. For the 70 participants in the study, organize these data into a frequency distribution. (See Exercise 43 and LO2-3.)

LEARNING OBJECTIVES

When you have completed this chapter, you will be able to:

LO2-1 Summarize qualitative variables with frequency and relative frequency tables.

LO2-2 Display a frequency table using a bar or pie chart.

LO2-3 Summarize quantitative variables with frequency and relative frequency distributions.

LO2-4 Display a frequency distribution using a histogram or frequency polygon.

INTRODUCTION

The highly competitive automobile retailing industry in the United States has changed dramatically in recent years. These changes spurred events such as the

- bankruptcies of General Motors and Chrysler in 2009.
- elimination of well-known brands like Pontiac and Saturn.
- closing of over 1,500 local dealerships.
- collapse of consumer credit availability.
- consolidation of dealership groups.

Traditionally, a local family owned and operated the community dealership, which might have included one or two manufacturers or brands, like Pontiac and GMC Trucks or Chrysler and the popular Jeep line. Recently, however, skillfully managed and well-financed companies have been acquiring local dealerships throughout the country. As these groups acquire the local dealerships, they often bring standardized selling practices, common software and hardware technology platforms, and management reporting techniques. The goal of these new organizations is to provide an improved buying experience for the consumer, while increasing profitability. Megadealerships often employ over 10,000 people, generate several billion dollars in annual sales, own more than 50 franchises, and are traded on the New York Stock Exchange or NASDAQ. Today, the largest megadealership is AutoNation (ticker symbol AN). Others include Penske Auto Group (PAG and second largest), Asbury Automotive Group (ABG), and Hendrick Auto Group (which is privately held).

The Applewood Auto Group is an ownership group that includes four dealerships. The group sells a wide range of vehicles, including the inexpensive but popular Korean brands Kia and Hyundai, BMW and Volvo sedans and luxury SUVs, and a full line of Ford and Chevrolet cars and trucks.

Ms. Kathryn Ball is a member of the senior management team at Applewood Auto Group, which has its corporate offices adjacent to Kane Motors. She is responsible for tracking and analyzing vehicle sales and the profitability of those vehicles. Kathryn would like to summarize the profit earned on the vehicles sold with tables, charts, and graphs that she would review monthly. She wants to know the profit per vehicle sold, as well as the lowest and highest amount of profit. She is also interested in describing the demographics of the buyers. What are their ages? How many vehicles have they previously purchased from one of the Applewood dealerships? What type of vehicle did they purchase?

The Applewood Auto Group operates four dealerships:

- ***Tionesta Ford Lincoln Mercury*** sells the Ford, Lincoln, and Mercury cars and trucks.
- ***Olean Automotive Inc.*** has the Nissan franchise as well as the General Motors brands of Chevrolet, Cadillac, and GMC Trucks.
- ***Sheffield Motors Inc.*** sells Buick, GMC trucks, Hyundai, and Kia.
- ***Kane Motors*** offers the Chrysler, Dodge, and Jeep line as well as BMW and Volvo.

APPLEWOOD AUTO GROUP

	A	B	C	D	E
1	Age	Profit	Location	Vehicle-Type	Previous
2	21	$1,387	Tionesta	Sedan	0
3	23	$1,754	Sheffield	SUV	1
4	24	$1,817	Sheffield	Hybrid	1
5	25	$1,040	Sheffield	Compact	0
6	26	$1,273	Kane	Sedan	1
7	27	$1,529	Sheffield	Sedan	1
8	27	$3,082	Kane	Truck	0
9	28	$1,951	Kane	SUV	1
10	28	$2,692	Tionesta	Compact	0
11	29	$1,206	Sheffield	Sedan	0
12	29	$1,342	Kane	Sedan	2
13	30	$443	Kane	Sedan	3
14	30	$754	Olean	Sedan	2
15	30	$1,621	Sheffield	Truck	1

Every month, Ms. Ball collects data from each of the four dealerships and enters them into an Excel spreadsheet. Last month the Applewood Auto Group sold 180 vehicles at the four dealerships. A copy of the first few observations appears to the left. The variables collected include:

- ***Age***—the age of the buyer at the time of the purchase.

- ***Profit***—the amount earned by the dealership on the sale of each vehicle.
- ***Location***—the dealership where the vehicle was purchased.
- ***Vehicle type***—SUV, sedan, compact, hybrid, or truck.
- ***Previous***—the number of vehicles previously purchased at any of the four Applewood dealerships by the consumer.

The entire data set is available at the McGraw-Hill website (www.mhhe.com/lind16e) and in Appendix A.4 at the end of the text.

LO2-1
Summarize qualitative variables with frequency and relative frequency tables.

CONSTRUCTING FREQUENCY TABLES

Recall from Chapter 1 that techniques used to describe a set of data are called descriptive statistics. Descriptive statistics organize data to show the general pattern of the data, to identify where values tend to concentrate, and to expose extreme or unusual data values. The first technique we discuss is a **frequency table.**

FREQUENCY TABLE A grouping of qualitative data into mutually exclusive and collectively exhaustive classes showing the number of observations in each class.

In Chapter 1, we distinguished between qualitative and quantitative variables. To review, a qualitative variable is nonnumeric, that is, it can only be classified into distinct categories. Examples of qualitative data include political affiliation (Republican, Democrat, Independent), state of birth (Alabama, . . . , Wyoming), and method of payment for a purchase at Barnes & Noble (cash, check, debit, or credit). On the other hand, quantitative variables are numerical in nature. Examples of quantitative data relating to college students include the price of their textbooks, their age, and the number of credit hours they are registered for this semester.

In the Applewood Auto Group data set, there are five variables for each vehicle sale: age of the buyer, amount of profit, dealer that made the sale, type of vehicle sold, and number of previous purchases by the buyer. The dealer and the type of vehicle are *qualitative* variables. The amount of profit, the age of the buyer, and the number of previous purchases are *quantitative* variables.

Suppose Ms. Ball wanted to summarize last month's sales by location. To summarize this qualitative data, we classify the vehicles sold last month according to their location: Tionesta, Olean, Sheffield, or Kane. We use location to develop a frequency table with four mutually exclusive (distinctive) classes. This means that a particular vehicle cannot belong to more than one class. Each vehicle is uniquely classified into one of the four mutually exclusive locations. In addition, the frequency table must be collectively exhaustive. This means that every vehicle is accounted for in the table. This frequency table is shown in Table 2–1. The number of observations, representing the sales at each location, is called the class frequency. So the class frequency for vehicles sold at the Kane location is 52.

TABLE 2–1 Frequency Table for Vehicles Sold Last Month at Applewood Auto Group by Location

Location	Number of Cars
Kane	52
Olean	40
Sheffield	45
Tionesta	43
Total	180

Relative Class Frequencies

You can convert class frequencies to relative class frequencies to show the fraction of the total number of observations in each class. A relative frequency captures the relationship between a class total and the total number of observations. In the vehicle sales example, we may want to know the percentage of total cars sold at each of the four locations. To convert a frequency distribution to a relative frequency distribution, each of the class frequencies is divided by the total number of observations. For example, the fraction of vehicles sold last month at the Kane location is 0.289, found by 52 divided by 180. The relative frequency for each location is shown in Table 2–2.

TABLE 2–2 Relative Frequency Table of Vehicles Sold by Type Last Month at Applewood Auto Group

Location	Number of Cars	Relative Frequency	Found by
Kane	52	.289	52/180
Olean	40	.222	40/180
Sheffield	45	.250	45/180
Tionesta	43	.239	43/180
Total	180	1.000	

LO2-2
Display a frequency table using a bar or pie chart.

GRAPHIC PRESENTATION OF QUALITATIVE DATA

The most common graphic form to present a qualitative variable is a **bar chart.** In most cases, the horizontal axis shows the variable of interest. The vertical axis shows the frequency or fraction of each of the possible outcomes. A distinguishing feature of a bar chart is there is distance or a gap between the bars. That is, because the variable of interest is qualitative, the bars are not adjacent to each other. Thus, a bar chart graphically describes a frequency table using a series of uniformly wide rectangles, where the height of each rectangle is the class frequency.

BAR CHART A graph that shows qualitative classes on the horizontal axis and the class frequencies on the vertical axis. The class frequencies are proportional to the heights of the bars.

We use the Applewood Auto Group data as an example (Chart 2–1). The variable of interest is the location where the vehicle was sold and the number of vehicles sold at each location is the class frequency. We label the horizontal axis with the four locations and scale the vertical axis with the number sold. The height of the bars, or rectangles, corresponds to the number of vehicles at each location. There were 52 vehicles sold last month at the Kane location, so the height of the Kane bar is 52; the height of the bar for the Olean location is 40. The variable location is of nominal scale, so the order of the locations on the horizontal axis does not matter. Listing this variable alphabetically, as shown in Chart 2–1, or in order of decreasing frequencies is also appropriate.

Another useful type of chart for depicting qualitative information is a **pie chart.**

PIE CHART A chart that shows the proportion or percentage that each class represents of the total number of frequencies.

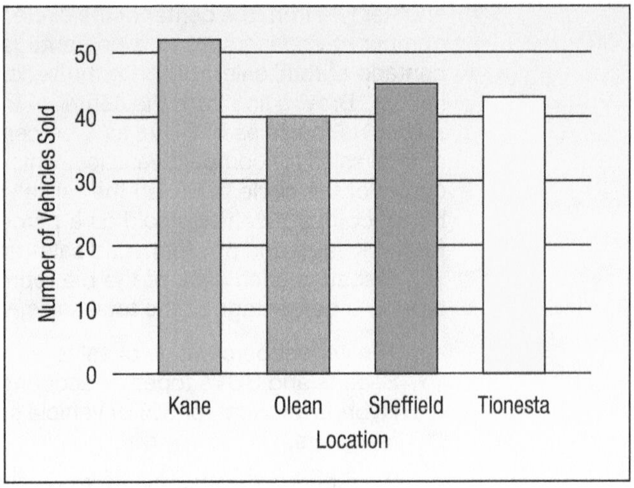

CHART 2–1 Number of Vehicles Sold by Location

We explain the details of constructing a pie chart using the information in Table 2–3, which shows the frequency and percent of cars sold by the Applewood Auto Group for each vehicle type.

TABLE 2–3 Vehicle Sales by Type at Applewood Auto Group

Vehicle Type	Number Sold	Percent Sold
Sedan	72	40
SUV	54	30
Compact	27	15
Truck	18	10
Hybrid	9	5
Total	180	100

The first step to develop a pie chart is to mark the percentages 0, 5, 10, 15, and so on evenly around the circumference of a circle (see Chart 2–2). To plot the 40% of total sales represented by sedans, draw a line from the center of the circle to 0 and

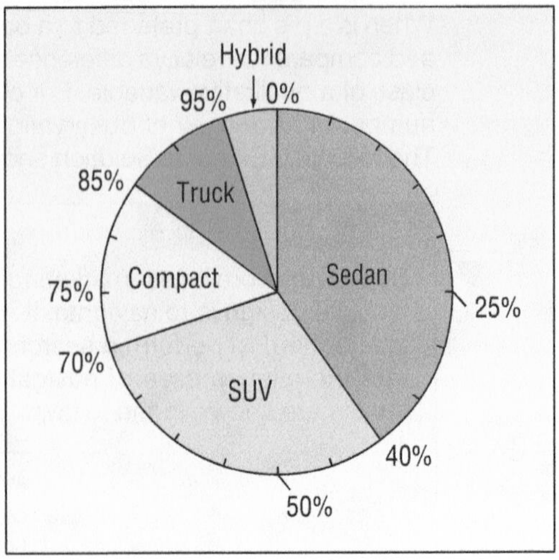

CHART 2–2 Pie Chart of Vehicles by Type

another line from the center of the circle to 40%. The area in this "slice" represents the number of sedans sold as a percentage of the total sales. Next, add the SUV's percentage of total sales, 30%, to the sedan's percentage of total sales, 40%. The result is 70%. Draw a line from the center of the circle to 70%, so the area between 40 and 70 shows the sales of SUVs as a percentage of total sales. Continuing, add the 15% of total sales for compact vehicles, which gives us a total of 85%. Draw a line from the center of the circle to 85, so the "slice" between 70% and 85% represents the number of compact vehicles sold as a percentage of the total sales. The remaining 10% for truck sales and 5% for hybrid sales are added to the chart using the same method.

Because each slice of the pie represents the relative frequency of each vehicle type as a percentage of the total sales, we can easily compare them:

- The largest percentage of sales is for sedans.
- Sedans and SUVs together account for 70% of vehicle sales.
- Hybrids account for 5% of vehicle sales, in spite of being on the market for only a few years.

We can use Excel software to quickly count the number of cars for each vehicle type and create the frequency table, bar chart, and pie chart below. The Excel tool is called a Pivot Table. The instructions to produce these descriptive statistics and charts are given in Appendix C.

APPLEWOOD AUTO GROUP

Row Labels	Count of Vehicle-Type
Sedan	72
SUV	54
Compact	27
Truck	18
Hybrid	9
Grand Total	**180**

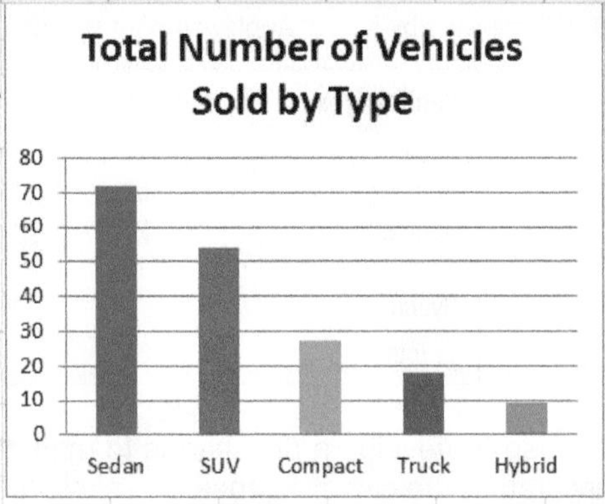

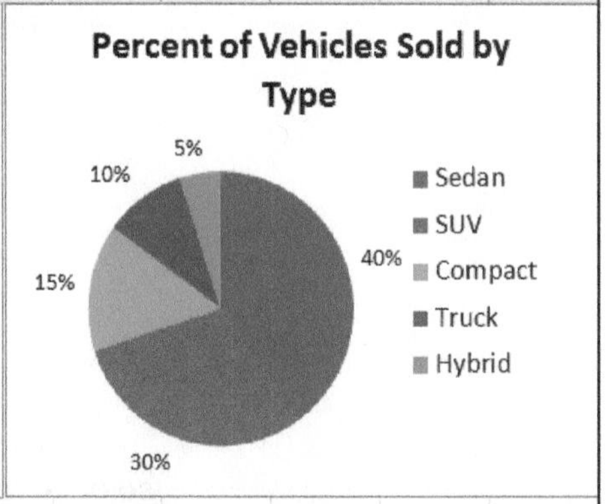

Pie and bar charts both serve to illustrate frequency and relative frequency tables. When is a pie chart preferred to a bar chart? In most cases, pie charts are used to show and compare the relative differences in the percentage of observations for each value or class of a qualitative variable. Bar charts are preferred when the goal is to compare the number or frequency of observations for each value or class of a qualitative variable. The following Example/Solution shows another application of bar and pie charts.

EXAMPLE

SkiLodges.com is test marketing its new website and is interested in how easy its website design is to navigate. It randomly selected 200 regular Internet users and asked them to perform a search task on the website. Each person was asked to rate the relative ease of navigation as poor, good, excellent, or awesome. The results are shown in the following table:

Awesome	102
Excellent	58
Good	30
Poor	10

1. What type of measurement scale is used for ease of navigation?
2. Draw a bar chart for the survey results.
3. Draw a pie chart for the survey results.

SOLUTION

The data are measured on an ordinal scale. That is, the scale is ranked in relative ease when moving from "poor" to "awesome." Also, the interval between each rating is unknown so it is impossible, for example, to conclude that a rating of good is twice the value of a poor rating.

We can use a bar chart to graph the data. The vertical scale shows the relative frequency and the horizontal scale shows the values of the ease-of-navigation variable.

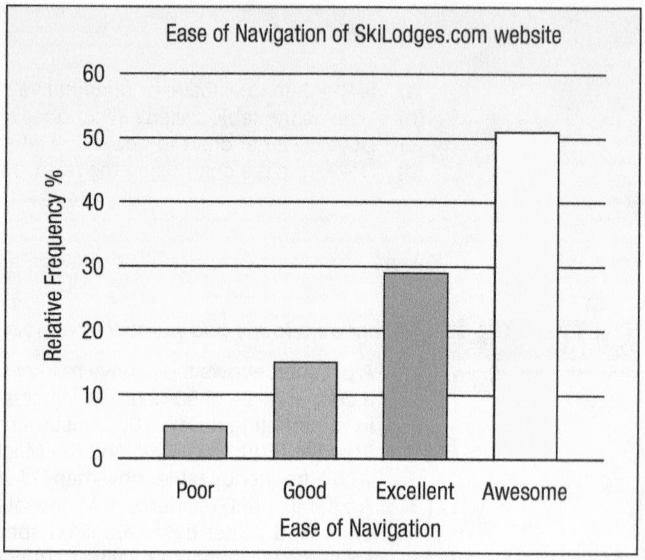

A pie chart can also be used to graph these data. The pie chart emphasizes that more than half of the respondents rate the relative ease of using the website awesome.

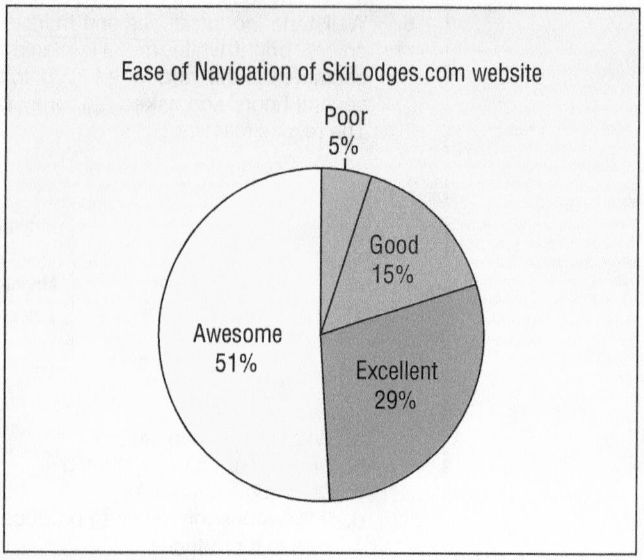

SELF-REVIEW 2–1

The answers are in Appendix E.

DeCenzo Specialty Food and Beverage Company has been serving a cola drink with an additional flavoring, Cola-Plus, that is very popular among its customers. The company is interested in customer preferences for Cola-Plus versus Coca-Cola, Pepsi, and a lemon-lime beverage. They ask 100 randomly sampled customers to take a taste test and select the beverage they prefer most. The results are shown in the following table:

Beverage	Number
Cola-Plus	40
Coca-Cola	25
Pepsi	20
Lemon-Lime	15
Total	100

(a) Is the data qualitative or quantitative? Why?
(b) What is the table called? What does it show?
(c) Develop a bar chart to depict the information.
(d) Develop a pie chart using the relative frequencies.

EXERCISES

The answers to the odd-numbered exercises are at the end of the book in Appendix D.

1. A pie chart shows the relative market share of cola products. The "slice" for Pepsi-Cola has a central angle of 90 degrees. What is its market share?
2. In a marketing study, 100 consumers were asked to select the best digital music player from the iPod, the iRiver, and the Magic Star MP3. To summarize the consumer responses with a frequency table, how many classes would the frequency table have?
3. A total of 1,000 residents in Minnesota were asked which season they preferred. One hundred liked winter best, 300 liked spring, 400 liked summer, and 200 liked fall. Develop a frequency table and a relative frequency table to summarize this information.
4. Two thousand frequent business travelers are asked which midwestern city they prefer: Indianapolis, Saint Louis, Chicago, or Milwaukee. One hundred liked Indianapolis best, 450 liked Saint Louis, 1,300 liked Chicago, and the remainder preferred Milwaukee. Develop a frequency table and a relative frequency table to summarize this information.
5. Wellstone Inc. produces and markets replacement covers for cell phones in five different colors: bright white, metallic black, magnetic lime, tangerine orange, and fusion red. To estimate the demand for each color, the company set up a kiosk in the Mall of America for several hours and asked randomly selected people which cover color was their favorite. The results follow:

Bright white	130
Metallic black	104
Magnetic lime	325
Tangerine orange	455
Fusion red	286

   a. What is the table called?
   b. Draw a bar chart for the table.
   c. Draw a pie chart.
   d. If Wellstone Inc. plans to produce 1 million cell phone covers, how many of each color should it produce?

6. A small business consultant is investigating the performance of several companies. The fourth-quarter sales for last year (in thousands of dollars) for the selected companies were:

Company	Fourth-Quarter Sales ($ thousands)
Hoden Building Products	$ 1,645.2
J & R Printing Inc.	4,757.0
Long Bay Concrete Construction	8,913.0
Mancell Electric and Plumbing	627.1
Maxwell Heating and Air Conditioning	24,612.0
Mizelle Roofing & Sheet Metals	191.9

The consultant wants to include a chart in his report comparing the sales of the six companies. Use a bar chart to compare the fourth-quarter sales of these corporations and write a brief report summarizing the bar chart.

LO2-3
Summarize quantitative variables with frequency and relative frequency distributions.

CONSTRUCTING FREQUENCY DISTRIBUTIONS

In Chapter 1 and earlier in this chapter, we distinguished between qualitative and quantitative data. In the previous section, using the Applewood Automotive Group data, we summarized two qualitative variables: the location of the sale and the type of vehicle sold. We created frequency and relative frequency tables and depicted the results in bar and pie charts.

The Applewood Auto Group data also includes several quantitative variables: the age of the buyer, the profit earned on the sale of the vehicle, and the number of previous purchases. Suppose Ms. Ball wants to summarize last month's sales by profit earned. We can describe profit using a **frequency distribution.**

FREQUENCY DISTRIBUTION A grouping of quantitative data into mutually exclusive and collectively exhaustive classes showing the number of observations in each class.

How do we develop a frequency distribution? The following example shows the steps to construct a frequency distribution. Remember, our goal is to construct tables, charts, and graphs that will quickly reveal the concentration, extreme values, and shape of the data.

EXAMPLE

We return to the situation where Ms. Kathryn Ball of the Applewood Auto Group wants to summarize the quantitative variable profit with a frequency distribution and display the distribution with charts and graphs. With this information, Ms. Ball can easily answer the following questions: What is the typical profit on each sale? What is the largest or maximum profit on any sale? What is the smallest or minimum profit on any sale? Around what value do the profits tend to cluster?

SOLUTION

To begin, we need the profits for each of the 180 vehicle sales, which are listed in Table 2–4. This information is called raw or ungrouped data because it is simply a listing of the individual, observed profits. It is possible to search the list and find the smallest or minimum profit ($294) and the largest or maximum profit ($3,292),

STATISTICS IN ACTION

In 1788, James Madison, John Jay, and Alexander Hamilton anonymously published a series of essays entitled *The Federalist*. These Federalist papers were an attempt to convince the people of New York that they should ratify the Constitution. In the course of history, the authorship of most of these papers became known, but 12 remained contested. Through the use of statistical analysis, and particularly the study of the frequency of the use of various words, we can now conclude that James Madison is the likely author of the 12 papers. In fact, the statistical evidence that Madison is the author is overwhelming.

but that is about all. It is difficult to determine a typical profit or to visualize where the profits tend to cluster. The raw data are more easily interpreted if we summarize the data with a frequency distribution as follows.

TABLE 2–4 Profit on Vehicles Sold Last Month by the Applewood Auto Group

Maximum

$1,387	$2,148	$2,201	$ 963	$ 820	$2,230	$3,043	$2,584	$2,370
1,754	2,207	996	1,298	1,266	2,341	1,059	2,666	2,637
1,817	2,252	2,813	1,410	1,741	3,292	1,674	2,991	1,426
1,040	1,428	323	1,553	1,772	1,108	1,807	934	2,944
1,273	1,889	352	1,648	1,932	1,295	2,056	2,063	2,147
1,529	1,166	482	2,071	2,350	1,344	2,236	2,083	1,973
3,082	1,320	1,144	2,116	2,422	1,906	2,928	2,856	2,502
1,951	2,265	1,485	1,500	2,446	1,952	1,269	2,989	783
2,692	1,323	1,509	1,549	369	2,070	1,717	910	1,538
1,206	1,760	1,638	2,348	978	2,454	1,797	1,536	2,339
1,342	1,919	1,961	2,498	1,238	1,606	1,955	1,957	2,700
443	2,357	2,127	294	1,818	1,680	2,199	2,240	2,222
754	2,866	2,430	1,115	1,824	1,827	2,482	2,695	2,597
1,621	732	1,704	1,124	1,907	1,915	2,701	1,325	2,742
870	1,464	1,876	1,532	1,938	2,084	3,210	2,250	1,837
1,174	1,626	2,010	1,688	1,940	2,639	377	2,279	2,842
1,412	1,762	2,165	1,822	2,197	842	1,220	2,626	2,434
1,809	1,915	2,231	1,897	2,646	1,963	1,401	1,501	1,640
2,415	2,119	2,389	2,445	1,461	2,059	2,175	1,752	1,821
1,546	1,766	335	2,886	1,731	2,338	1,118	2,058	2,487

Minimum

Step 1: **Decide on the number of classes.** A useful recipe to determine the number of classes (k) is the "2 to the k rule." This guide suggests you select the smallest number (k) for the number of classes such that 2^k (in words, 2 raised to the power of k) is greater than the number of observations (n). In the Applewood Auto Group example, there were 180 vehicles sold. So $n = 180$. If we try $k = 7$, which means we would use 7 classes, $2^7 = 128$, which is less than 180. Hence, 7 is too few classes. If we let $k = 8$, then $2^8 = 256$, which is greater than 180. So the recommended number of classes is 8.

Step 2: **Determine the class interval.** Generally, the **class interval** is the same for all classes. The classes all taken together must cover at least the distance from the minimum value in the data up to the maximum value. Expressing these words in a formula:

$$i \geq \frac{\text{Maximum value} - \text{Minimum value}}{k}$$

where i is the class interval, and k is the number of classes.

For the Applewood Auto Group, the minimum value is $294 and the maximum value is $3,292. If we need 8 classes, the interval should be:

$$i \geq \frac{\text{Maximum value} - \text{Minimum value}}{k} = \frac{\$3{,}292 - \$294}{8} = \$374.75$$

In practice, this interval size is usually rounded up to some convenient number, such as a multiple of 10 or 100. The value of $400 is a reasonable choice.

Step 3: Set the individual class limits. State clear class limits so you can put each observation into only one category. This means you must avoid overlapping or unclear class limits. For example, classes such as "$1,300–$1,400" and "$1,400–$1,500" should not be used because it is not clear whether the value $1,400 is in the first or second class. In this text, we will generally use the format $1,300 **up to** $1,400 and $1,400 **up to** $1,500 and so on. With this format, it is clear that $1,399 goes into the first class and $1,400 in the second.

Because we always round the class interval up to get a convenient class size, we cover a larger than necessary range. For example, using 8 classes with an interval of $400 in the Applewood Auto Group example results in a range of 8($400) = $3,200. The actual range is $2,998, found by ($3,292 − $294). Comparing that value to $3,200, we have an excess of $202. Because we need to cover only the range (*Maximum* − *Minimum*), it is natural to put approximately equal amounts of the excess in each of the two tails. Of course, we should also select convenient class limits. A guideline is to make the lower limit of the first class a multiple of the class interval. Sometimes this is not possible, but the lower limit should at least be rounded. So here are the classes we could use for these data.

Classes
$ 200 up to $ 600
600 up to 1,000
1,000 up to 1,400
1,400 up to 1,800
1,800 up to 2,200
2,200 up to 2,600
2,600 up to 3,000
3,000 up to 3,400

Step 4: Tally the vehicle profit into the classes. To begin, the profit from the sale of the first vehicle in Table 2–4 is $1,387. It is tallied in the $1,000 up to $1,400 class. The second profit in the first row of Table 2–4 is $2,148. It is tallied in the $1,800 up to $2,200 class. The other profits are tallied in a similar manner. When all the profits are tallied, the table would appear as:

Profit	Frequency
$ 200 up to $ 600	𝍸 III
600 up to 1,000	𝍸 𝍸 I
1,000 up to 1,400	𝍸 𝍸 𝍸 𝍸 III
1,400 up to 1,800	𝍸 𝍸 𝍸 𝍸 𝍸 𝍸 𝍸 III
1,800 up to 2,200	𝍸 𝍸 𝍸 𝍸 𝍸 𝍸 𝍸 𝍸 𝍸
2,200 up to 2,600	𝍸 𝍸 𝍸 𝍸 𝍸 II
2,600 up to 3,000	𝍸 𝍸 𝍸 IIII
3,000 up to 3,400	IIII

Step 5: Count the number of items in each class. The number of observations in each class is called the **class frequency.** In the $200 up to $600 class there are 8 observations, and in the $600 up to $1,000 class there are 11 observations. Therefore, the class frequency in

the first class is 8 and the class frequency in the second class is 11. There are a total of 180 observations in the entire set of data. So the sum of all the frequencies should be equal to 180.

TABLE 2–5 Frequency Distribution of Profit for Vehicles Sold Last Month at Applewood Auto Group

Profit	Frequency
$ 200 up to $ 600	8
600 up to 1,000	11
1,000 up to 1,400	23
1,400 up to 1,800	38
1,800 up to 2,200	45
2,200 up to 2,600	32
2,600 up to 3,000	19
3,000 up to 3,400	4
Total	180

Now that we have organized the data into a frequency distribution (see Table 2–5), we can summarize the profits of the vehicles for the Applewood Auto Group. Observe the following:

1. The profits from vehicle sales range between $200 and $3,400.
2. The vehicle profits are classified using a class interval of $400. The class interval is determined by subtracting consecutive lower or upper class limits. For example, the lower limit of the first class is $200, and the lower limit of the second class is $600. The difference is the class interval of $400.
3. The profits are concentrated between $1,000 and $3,000. The profit on 157 vehicles, or 87%, was within this range.
4. For each class, we can determine the typical profit or **class midpoint.** It is halfway between the lower or upper limits of two consecutive classes. It is computed by adding the lower or upper limits of consecutive classes and dividing by 2. Referring to Table 2–5, the lower class limit of the first class is $200, and the next class limit is $600. The class midpoint is $400, found by ($600 + $200)/2. The midpoint best represents, or is typical of, the profits of the vehicles in that class. Applewood sold 8 vehicles with a typical profit of $400.
5. The largest concentration, or highest frequency, of vehicles sold is in the $1,800 up to $2,200 class. There are 45 vehicles in this class. The class midpoint is $2,000. So we say that the typical profit in the class with the highest frequency is $2,000.

By presenting this information to Ms. Ball, we give her a clear picture of the distribution of the vehicle profits for last month.

We admit that arranging the information on profits into a frequency distribution does result in the loss of some detailed information. That is, by organizing the data into a frequency distribution, we cannot pinpoint the exact profit on any vehicle, such as $1,387, $2,148, or $2,201. Further, we cannot tell that the actual minimum profit for any vehicle sold is $294 or that the maximum profit was $3,292. However, the lower limit of the first class and the upper limit of the last class convey essentially the same meaning. Likely, Ms. Ball will make the same judgment if she knows the smallest profit is about $200 that she will if she knows the exact profit is $292. The advantages of summarizing the 180 profits into a more understandable and organized form more than offset this disadvantage.

When we summarize raw data with frequency distributions, equal class intervals are preferred. However, in certain situations unequal class intervals may be necessary to avoid a large number of classes with very small frequencies. Such is the case in Table 2–6. The U.S. Internal Revenue Service uses unequal-sized class intervals for adjusted gross income on individual tax returns to summarize the number of individual tax returns. If we use our method to find equal class intervals, the 2^k rule results in 25 classes, and a class interval of \$400,000, assuming \$0 and \$10,000,000 as the minimum and maximum values for adjusted gross income. Using equal class intervals, the first 13 classes in Table 2–6 would be combined into one class of about 99.9% of all tax returns and 24 classes for the 0.1% of the returns with an adjusted gross income above \$400,000. Using equal class intervals does not provide a good understanding of the raw data. In this case, good judgment in the use of unequal class intervals, as demonstrated in Table 2–6, is required to show the distribution of the number of tax returns filed, especially for incomes under \$500,000.

TABLE 2–6 Adjusted Gross Income for Individuals Filing Income Tax Returns

Adjusted Gross Income	Number of Returns (in thousands)
No adjusted gross income	178.2
\$ 1 up to 5,000	1,204.6
5,000 up to 10,000	2,595.5
10,000 up to 15,000	3,142.0
15,000 up to 20,000	3,191.7
20,000 up to 25,000	2,501.4
25,000 up to 30,000	1,901.6
30,000 up to 40,000	2,502.3
40,000 up to 50,000	1,426.8
50,000 up to 75,000	1,476.3
75,000 up to 100,000	338.8
100,000 up to 200,000	223.3
200,000 up to 500,000	55.2
500,000 up to 1,000,000	12.0
1,000,000 up to 2,000,000	5.1
2,000,000 up to 10,000,000	3.4
10,000,000 or more	0.6

SELF-REVIEW 2–2

The commissions earned for the first quarter of last year by the 11 members of the sales staff at Master Chemical Company are:

\$1,650 \$1,475 \$1,510 \$1,670 \$1,595 \$1,760 \$1,540 \$1,495 \$1,590 \$1,625 \$1,510

(a) What are the values such as \$1,650 and \$1,475 called?
(b) Using \$1,400 up to \$1,500 as the first class, \$1,500 up to \$1,600 as the second class, and so forth, organize the quarterly commissions into a frequency distribution.
(c) What are the numbers in the right column of your frequency distribution called?
(d) Describe the distribution of quarterly commissions, based on the frequency distribution. What is the largest concentration of commissions earned? What is the smallest, and the largest? What is the typical amount earned?

Relative Frequency Distribution

It may be desirable, as we did earlier with qualitative data, to convert class frequencies to relative class frequencies to show the proportion of the total number of observations in each class. In our vehicle profits, we may want to know what percentage of the vehicle profits are in the \$1,000 up to \$1,400 class. In another study, we may want to know what percentage of the employees used 5 up to 10 personal leave days last year. To convert a frequency distribution to a *relative* frequency distribution, each of the class frequencies is divided by the total number of observations. From the distribution of vehicle profits, Table 2–5, the relative frequency for the \$1,000 up to \$1,400 class is 0.128, found by dividing 23 by 180. That is, profit on 12.8% of the vehicles sold is between \$1,000 and \$1,400. The relative frequencies for the remaining classes are shown in Table 2–7.

TABLE 2–7 Relative Frequency Distribution of Profit for Vehicles Sold Last Month at Applewood Auto Group

Profit	Frequency	Relative Frequency	Found by
\$ 200 up to \$ 600	8	.044	8/180
600 up to 1,000	11	.061	11/180
1,000 up to 1,400	23	.128	23/180
1,400 up to 1,800	38	.211	38/180
1,800 up to 2,200	45	.250	45/180
2,200 up to 2,600	32	.178	32/180
2,600 up to 3,000	19	.106	19/180
3,000 up to 3,400	4	.022	4/180
Total	180	1.000	

As we mentioned in Chapter 1, there are many software packages that perform statistical calculations. Throughout this text, we will show the output from Microsoft Excel, MegaStat (a Microsoft Excel add-in), and Minitab (a statistical software package).

APPLEWOOD AUTO GROUP

	A	B	C
1	Profit Class	Frequency	Relative Frequency
2	200-600	8	4.44%
3	600-1000	11	6.11%
4	1000-1400	23	12.78%
5	1400-1800	38	21.11%
6	1800-2200	45	25.00%
7	2200-2600	32	17.78%
8	2600-3000	19	10.56%
9	3000-3400	4	2.22%
10	Grand Total	180	100.00%

On page 22 of this chapter, we used the Pivot Table tool in Excel to create a frequency table. We use the same Excel tool to create frequency and relative frequency distributions for the profit variable in the Applewood Auto Group data. The necessary steps for the table to the left are given in the Software Commands section in Appendix C.

SELF-REVIEW 2–3

Barry Bonds of the San Francisco Giants established a new single-season Major League Baseball home run record by hitting 73 home runs during the 2001 season. Listed below is the sorted distance of each of the 73 home runs.

320	320	347	350	360	360	360	361	365	370
370	375	375	375	375	380	380	380	380	380
380	390	390	391	394	396	400	400	400	400
405	410	410	410	410	410	410	410	410	410
410	410	411	415	415	416	417	417	420	420
420	420	420	420	420	420	429	430	430	430
430	430	435	435	436	440	440	440	440	440
450	480	488							

(a) For this data, show that seven classes would be used to create a frequency distribution using the 2^k rule.
(b) Show that a class interval of 30 would summarize the data in seven classes.
(c) Construct frequency and relative frequency distributions for the data with seven classes and a class interval of 30. Start the first class with a lower limit of 300.
(d) How many home runs traveled a distance of 360 up to 390 feet?
(e) What percentage of the home runs traveled a distance of 360 up to 390 feet?
(f) What percentage of the home runs traveled a distance of 390 feet or more?

EXERCISES

This icon indicates that the data are available at the text website: www.mhhe.com/lind16e. You will be able to download the data directly into Excel or Minitab from this site.

7. A set of data consists of 38 observations. How many classes would you recommend for the frequency distribution?
8. A set of data consists of 45 observations between $0 and $29. What size would you recommend for the class interval?
9. A set of data consists of 230 observations between $235 and $567. What class interval would you recommend?
10. A set of data contains 53 observations. The minimum value is 42 and the maximum value is 129. The data are to be organized into a frequency distribution.
    a. How many classes would you suggest?
    b. What would you suggest as the lower limit of the first class?
11. Wachesaw Manufacturing Inc. produced the following number of units in the last 16 days.

For **DATA FILE**, please visit www.mhhe.com/lind16e

27	27	27	28	27	25	25	28
26	28	26	28	31	30	26	26

The information is to be organized into a frequency distribution.
    a. How many classes would you recommend?
    b. What class interval would you suggest?
    c. What lower limit would you recommend for the first class?
    d. Organize the information into a frequency distribution and determine the relative frequency distribution.
    e. Comment on the shape of the distribution.
12. The Quick Change Oil Company has a number of outlets in the metropolitan Seattle area. The daily number of oil changes at the Oak Street outlet in the past 20 days are:

For **DATA FILE**, please visit www.mhhe.com/lind16e

65	98	55	62	79	59	51	90	72	56
70	62	66	80	94	79	63	73	71	85

The data are to be organized into a frequency distribution.
    a. How many classes would you recommend?
    b. What class interval would you suggest?
    c. What lower limit would you recommend for the first class?
    d. Organize the number of oil changes into a frequency distribution.
    e. Comment on the shape of the frequency distribution. Also determine the relative frequency distribution.
13. The manager of the BiLo Supermarket in Mt. Pleasant, Rhode Island, gathered the following information on the number of times a customer visits the store during a month. The responses of 51 customers were:

For **DATA FILE**, please visit www.mhhe.com/lind16e

5	3	3	1	4	4	5	6	4	2	6	6	6	7	1
1	14	1	2	4	4	4	5	6	3	5	3	4	5	6
8	4	7	6	5	9	11	3	12	4	7	6	5	15	1
1	10	8	9	2	12									

    a. Starting with 0 as the lower limit of the first class and using a class interval of 3, organize the data into a frequency distribution.
    b. Describe the distribution. Where do the data tend to cluster?
    c. Convert the distribution to a relative frequency distribution.

For **DATA FILE**, please visit www.mhhe.com/lind16e

14. The food services division of Cedar River Amusement Park Inc. is studying the amount that families who visit the amusement park spend per day on food and drink. A sample of 40 families who visited the park yesterday revealed they spent the following amounts:

$77	$18	$63	$84	$38	$54	$50	$59	$54	$56	$36	$26	$50	$34	$44
41	58	58	53	51	62	43	52	53	63	62	62	65	61	52
60	60	45	66	83	71	63	58	61	71					

a. Organize the data into a frequency distribution, using seven classes and 15 as the lower limit of the first class. What class interval did you select?
b. Where do the data tend to cluster?
c. Describe the distribution.
d. Determine the relative frequency distribution.

LO2-4
Display a frequency distribution using a histogram or frequency polygon.

GRAPHIC PRESENTATION OF A FREQUENCY DISTRIBUTION

Sales managers, stock analysts, hospital administrators, and other busy executives often need a quick picture of the distributions of sales, stock prices, or hospital costs. These distributions can often be depicted by the use of charts and graphs. Three charts that will help portray a frequency distribution graphically are the histogram, the frequency polygon, and the cumulative frequency polygon.

Histogram

A **histogram** for a frequency distribution based on quantitative data is similar to the bar chart showing the distribution of qualitative data. The classes are marked on the horizontal axis and the class frequencies on the vertical axis. The class frequencies are represented by the heights of the bars. However, there is one important difference based on the nature of the data. Quantitative data are usually measured using scales that are continuous, not discrete. Therefore, the horizontal axis represents all possible values, and the bars are drawn adjacent to each other to show the continuous nature of the data.

HISTOGRAM A graph in which the classes are marked on the horizontal axis and the class frequencies on the vertical axis. The class frequencies are represented by the heights of the bars, and the bars are drawn adjacent to each other.

EXAMPLE

Below is the frequency distribution of the profits on vehicle sales last month at the Applewood Auto Group.

Profit	Frequency
$ 200 up to $ 600	8
600 up to 1,000	11
1,000 up to 1,400	23
1,400 up to 1,800	38
1,800 up to 2,200	45
2,200 up to 2,600	32
2,600 up to 3,000	19
3,000 up to 3,400	4
Total	180

STATISTICS IN ACTION

Florence Nightingale is known as the founder of the nursing profession. However, she also saved many lives by using statistical analysis. When she encountered an unsanitary condition or an undersupplied hospital, she improved the conditions and then used statistical data to document the improvement. Thus, she was able to convince others of the need for medical reform, particularly in the area of sanitation. She developed original graphs to demonstrate that, during the Crimean War, more soldiers died from unsanitary conditions than were killed in combat.

Construct a histogram. What observations can you reach based on the information presented in the histogram?

SOLUTION

The class frequencies are scaled along the vertical axis (*Y*-axis) and either the class limits or the class midpoints along the horizontal axis. To illustrate the construction of the histogram, the first three classes are shown in Chart 2–3.

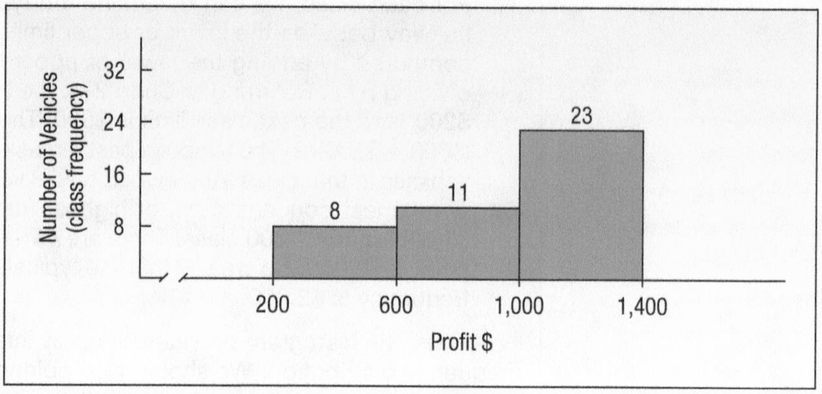

CHART 2–3 Construction of a Histogram

From Chart 2–3 we note the profit on eight vehicles was $200 up to $600. Therefore, the height of the column for that class is 8. There are 11 vehicle sales where the profit was $600 up to $1,000. So, logically, the height of that column is 11. The height of the bar represents the number of observations in the class.

This procedure is continued for all classes. The complete histogram is shown in Chart 2–4. Note that there is no space between the bars. This is a feature of the histogram. Why is this so? Because the variable plotted on the horizontal axis is a continuous variable. In a bar chart, the scale of measurement is often nominal and the vertical bars are separated. This is an important distinction between the histogram and the bar chart.

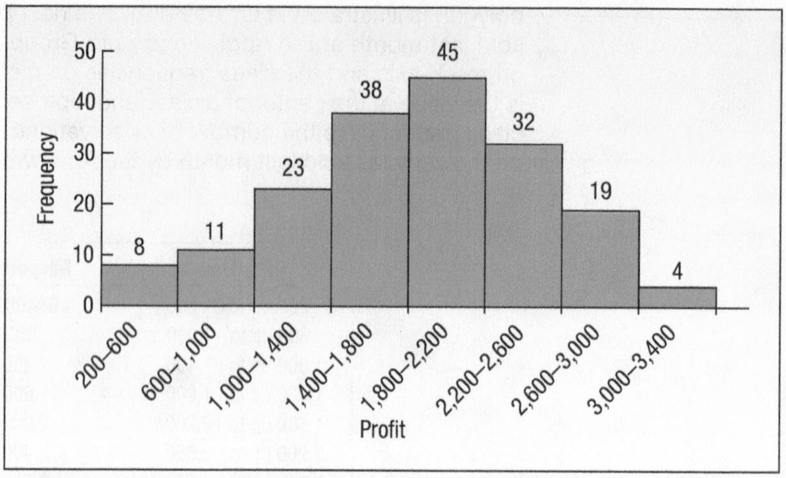

CHART 2–4 Histogram of the Profit on 180 Vehicles Sold at the Applewood Auto Group

We can make the following statements using Chart 2–4. They are the same as the observations based on Table 2–5 on page 28.

1. The profits from vehicle sales range between $200 and $3,400.
2. The vehicle profits are classified using a class interval of $400. The class interval is determined by subtracting consecutive lower or upper class limits. For example, the lower limit of the first class is $200, and the lower limit of the second class is $600. The difference is the class interval or $400.
3. The profits are concentrated between $1,000 and $3,000. The profit on 157 vehicles, or 87%, was within this range.
4. For each class, we can determine the typical profit or class midpoint. It is halfway between the lower or upper limits of two consecutive classes. It is computed by adding the lower or upper limits of consecutive classes and dividing by 2. Referring to Chart 2–4, the lower class limit of the first class is $200, and the next class limit is $600. The class midpoint is $400, found by ($600 + $200)/2. The midpoint best represents, or is typical of, the profits of the vehicles in that class. Applewood sold 8 vehicles with a typical profit of $400.
5. The largest concentration, or highest frequency of vehicles sold, is in the $1,800 up to $2,200 class. There are 45 vehicles in this class. The class midpoint is $2,000. So we say that the typical profit in the class with the highest frequency is $2,000.

Thus, the histogram provides an easily interpreted visual representation of a frequency distribution. We should also point out that we would have made the same observations and the shape of the histogram would have been the same had we used a relative frequency distribution instead of the actual frequencies. That is, if we had used the relative frequencies of Table 2–7, we would have had a histogram of the same shape as Chart 2–4. The only difference is that the vertical axis would have been reported in percentage of vehicles instead of the number of vehicles. The Excel commands to create Chart 2–4 are given in Appendix C.

Frequency Polygon

A **frequency polygon** also shows the shape of a distribution and is similar to a histogram. It consists of line segments connecting the points formed by the intersections of the class midpoints and the class frequencies. The construction of a frequency polygon is illustrated in Chart 2–5 on the next page. We use the profits from the cars sold last month at the Applewood Auto Group. The midpoint of each class is scaled on the *X*-axis and the class frequencies on the *Y*-axis. Recall that the class midpoint is the value at the center of a class and represents the typical values in that class. The class frequency is the number of observations in a particular class. The profit earned on the vehicles sold last month by the Applewood Auto Group is repeated below.

Profit	Midpoint	Frequency
$ 200 up to $ 600	$ 400	8
600 up to 1,000	800	11
1,000 up to 1,400	1,200	23
1,400 up to 1,800	1,600	38
1,800 up to 2,200	2,000	45
2,200 up to 2,600	2,400	32
2,600 up to 3,000	2,800	19
3,000 up to 3,400	3,200	4
Total		180

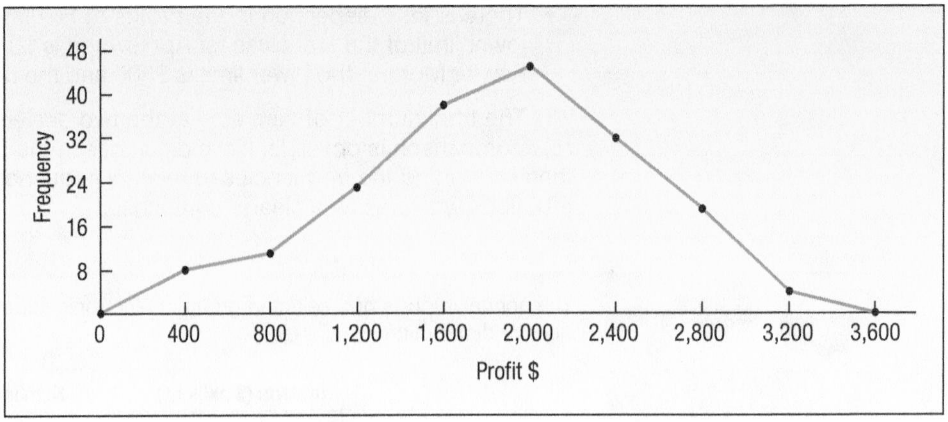

CHART 2–5 Frequency Polygon of Profit on 180 Vehicles Sold at Applewood Auto Group

As noted previously, the $200 up to $600 class is represented by the midpoint $400. To construct a frequency polygon, move horizontally on the graph to the midpoint, $400, and then vertically to 8, the class frequency, and place a dot. The x and the y values of this point are called the *coordinates.* The coordinates of the next point are $x = 800$ and $y = 11$. The process is continued for all classes. Then the points are connected in order. That is, the point representing the lowest class is joined to the one representing the second class and so on. Note in Chart 2–5 that, to complete the frequency polygon, midpoints of $0 and $3,600 are added to the X-axis to "anchor" the polygon at zero frequencies. These two values, $0 and $3,600, were derived by subtracting the class interval of $400 from the lowest midpoint ($400) and by adding $400 to the highest midpoint ($3,200) in the frequency distribution.

Both the histogram and the frequency polygon allow us to get a quick picture of the main characteristics of the data (highs, lows, points of concentration, etc.). Although the two representations are similar in purpose, the histogram has the advantage of depicting each class as a rectangle, with the height of the rectangular bar representing the number in each class. The frequency polygon, in turn, has an advantage over the histogram. It allows us to compare directly two or more frequency distributions. Suppose Ms. Ball wants to compare the profit per vehicle sold at Applewood Auto Group with a similar auto group, Fowler Auto in Grayling, Michigan. To do this, two frequency polygons are constructed, one on top of the other, as in Chart 2–6. Two things are clear from the chart:

- The typical vehicle profit is larger at Fowler Motors—about $2,000 for Applewood and about $2,400 for Fowler.

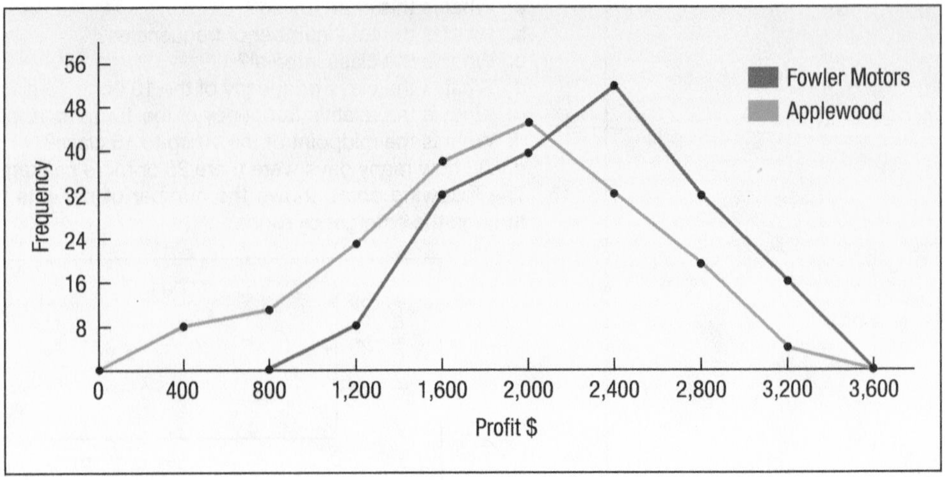

CHART 2–6 Distribution of Profit at Applewood Auto Group and Fowler Motors

- There is less dispersion in the profits at Fowler Motors than at Applewood. The lower limit of the first class for Applewood is $0 and the upper limit is $3,600. For Fowler Motors, the lower limit is $800 and the upper limit is the same: $3,600.

The total number of cars sold at the two dealerships is about the same, so a direct comparison is possible. If the difference in the total number of cars sold is large, then converting the frequencies to relative frequencies and then plotting the two distributions would allow a clearer comparison.

SELF-REVIEW 2–4

The annual imports of a selected group of electronic suppliers are shown in the following frequency distribution.

Imports ($ millions)	Number of Suppliers
2 up to 5	6
5 up to 8	13
8 up to 11	20
11 up to 14	10
14 up to 17	1

(a) Portray the imports as a histogram.
(b) Portray the imports as a relative frequency polygon.
(c) Summarize the important facets of the distribution (such as classes with the highest and lowest frequencies).

EXERCISES

15. Molly's Candle Shop has several retail stores in the coastal areas of North and South Carolina. Many of Molly's customers ask her to ship their purchases. The following chart shows the number of packages shipped per day for the last 100 days.

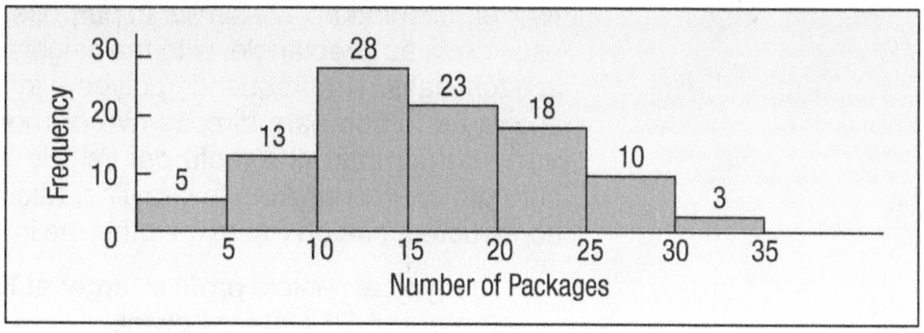

a. What is this chart called?
b. What is the total number of frequencies?
c. What is the class interval?
d. What is the class frequency of the 10 up to 15 class?
e. What is the relative frequency of the 10 up to 15 class?
f. What is the midpoint of the 10 up to 15 class?
g. On how many days were there 25 or more packages shipped?

16. The following chart shows the number of patients admitted daily to Memorial Hospital through the emergency room.

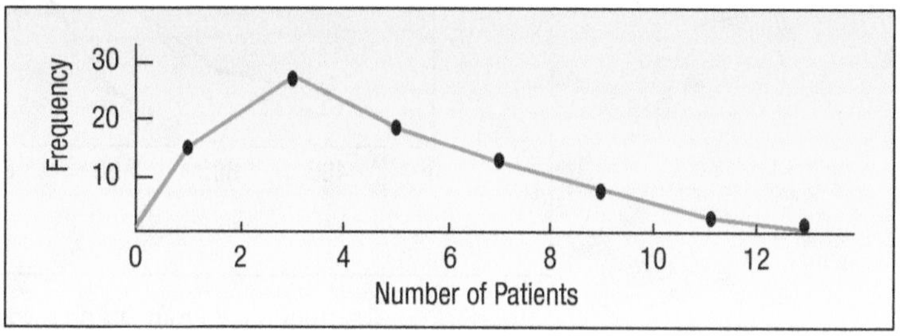

a. What is the midpoint of the 2 up to 4 class?
b. How many days were 2 up to 4 patients admitted?
c. What is the class interval?
d. What is this chart called?

17. The following frequency distribution reports the number of frequent flier miles, reported in thousands, for employees of Brumley Statistical Consulting Inc. during the most recent quarter.

Frequent Flier Miles (000)	Number of Employees
0 up to 3	5
3 up to 6	12
6 up to 9	23
9 up to 12	8
12 up to 15	2
Total	50

a. How many employees were studied?
b. What is the midpoint of the first class?
c. Construct a histogram.
d. A frequency polygon is to be drawn. What are the coordinates of the plot for the first class?
e. Construct a frequency polygon.
f. Interpret the frequent flier miles accumulated using the two charts.

18. Ecommerce.com, a large Internet retailer, is studying the lead time (elapsed time between when an order is placed and when it is filled) for a sample of recent orders. The lead times are reported in days.

Lead Time (days)	Frequency
0 up to 5	6
5 up to 10	7
10 up to 15	12
15 up to 20	8
20 up to 25	7
Total	40

a. How many orders were studied?
b. What is the midpoint of the first class?
c. What are the coordinates of the first class for a frequency polygon?
d. Draw a histogram.
e. Draw a frequency polygon.
f. Interpret the lead times using the two charts.

Cumulative Frequency Distributions

Consider once again the distribution of the profits on vehicles sold by the Applewood Auto Group. Suppose we were interested in the number of vehicles that sold for a profit of less than $1,400 or the profit earned on the lowest-selling 40% of the vehicles. These values can be approximated by developing a **cumulative frequency distribution** and portraying it graphically in a **cumulative frequency polygon.**

EXAMPLE

The frequency distribution of the profits earned at Applewood Auto Group is repeated from Table 2–5.

Profit	Frequency
\$ 200 up to \$ 600	8
600 up to 1,000	11
1,000 up to 1,400	23
1,400 up to 1,800	38
1,800 up to 2,200	45
2,200 up to 2,600	32
2,600 up to 3,000	19
3,000 up to 3,400	4
Total	180

Construct a cumulative frequency polygon to answer the following two questions. Seventy-five percent of the vehicles sold earned a profit of less than what amount? Sixty of the vehicles earned a profit of less than what amount?

SOLUTION

As the names imply, a cumulative frequency distribution and a cumulative frequency polygon require *cumulative frequencies.* To construct a cumulative frequency distribution, refer to the preceding table and note that there were eight vehicles in which the profit earned was less than \$600. Those 8 vehicles, plus the 11 in the next higher class, for a total of 19, earned a profit of less than \$1,000. The cumulative frequency for the next higher class is 42, found by 8 + 11 + 23. This process is continued for all the classes. All the vehicles earned a profit of less than \$3,400. (See Table 2–8.)

TABLE 2–8 Cumulative Frequency Distribution for Profit on Vehicles Sold Last Month at Applewood Auto Group

Profit	Cumulative Frequency	Found by
Less than \$ 600	8	8
Less than 1,000	19	8 + 11
Less than 1,400	42	8 + 11 + 23
Less than 1,800	80	8 + 11 + 23 + 38
Less than 2,200	125	8 + 11 + 23 + 38 + 45
Less than 2,600	157	8 + 11 + 23 + 38 + 45 + 32
Less than 3,000	176	8 + 11 + 23 + 38 + 45 + 32 + 19
Less than 3,400	180	8 + 11 + 23 + 38 + 45 + 32 + 19 + 4

To plot a cumulative frequency distribution, scale the upper limit of each class along the *X*-axis and the corresponding cumulative frequencies along the *Y*-axis. To provide additional information, you can label the vertical axis on the left in units and the vertical axis on the right in percent. In the Applewood Auto Group,

the vertical axis on the left is labeled from 0 to 180 and on the right from 0 to 100%. The value of 50% corresponds to 90 vehicles.

To begin, the first plot is at $x = 200$ and $y = 0$. None of the vehicles sold for a profit of less than $200. The profit on 8 vehicles was less than $600, so the next plot is at $x = 600$ and $y = 8$. Continuing, the next plot is $x = 1{,}000$ and $y = 19$. There were 19 vehicles that sold for a profit of less than $1,000. The rest of the points are plotted and then the dots connected to form Chart 2–7.

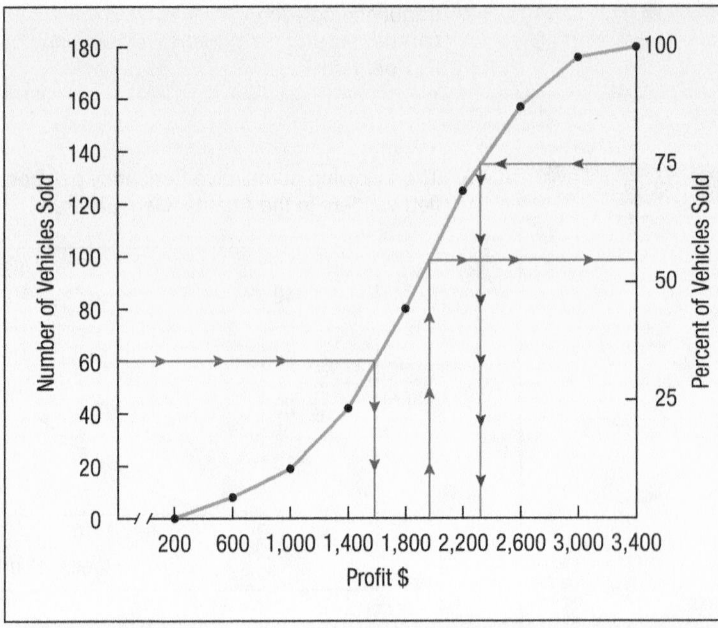

CHART 2–7 Cumulative Frequency Polygon for Profit on Vehicles Sold Last Month at Applewood Auto Group

Using Chart 2–7 to find the amount of profit on 75% of the cars sold, draw a horizontal line from the 75% mark on the right-hand vertical axis over to the polygon, then drop down to the *X*-axis and read the amount of profit. The value on the *X*-axis is about $2,300, so we estimate that 75% of the vehicles sold earned a profit of $2,300 or less for the Applewood group.

To find the highest profit earned on 60 of the 180 vehicles, we use Chart 2–7 to locate the value of 60 on the left-hand vertical axis. Next, we draw a horizontal line from the value of 60 to the polygon and then drop down to the *X*-axis and read the profit. It is about $1,600, so we estimate that 60 of the vehicles sold for a profit of less than $1,600. We can also make estimates of the percentage of vehicles that sold for less than a particular amount. To explain, suppose we want to estimate the percentage of vehicles that sold for a profit of less than $2,000. We begin by locating the value of $2,000 on the *X*-axis, move vertically to the polygon, and then horizontally to the vertical axis on the right. The value is about 56%, so we conclude 56% of the vehicles sold for a profit of less than $2,000.

SELF-REVIEW 2–5

A sample of the hourly wages of 15 employees at Home Depot in Brunswick, Georgia, was organized into the following table.

Hourly Wages	Number of Employees
$ 8 up to $10	3
10 up to 12	7
12 up to 14	4
14 up to 16	1

(a) What is the table called?
(b) Develop a cumulative frequency distribution and portray the distribution in a cumulative frequency polygon.
(c) On the basis of the cumulative frequency polygon, how many employees earn less than $11 per hour?

EXERCISES

19. The following cumulative frequency polygon shows the hourly wages of a sample of certified welders in the Atlanta, Georgia, area.

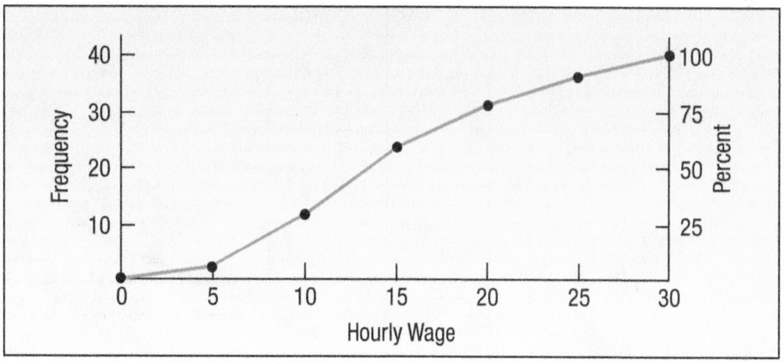

a. How many welders were studied?
b. What is the class interval?
c. About how many welders earn less than $10.00 per hour?
d. About 75% of the welders make less than what amount?
e. Ten of the welders studied made less than what amount?
f. What percent of the welders make less than $20.00 per hour?

20. The following cumulative frequency polygon shows the selling price ($000) of houses sold in the Billings, Montana, area.

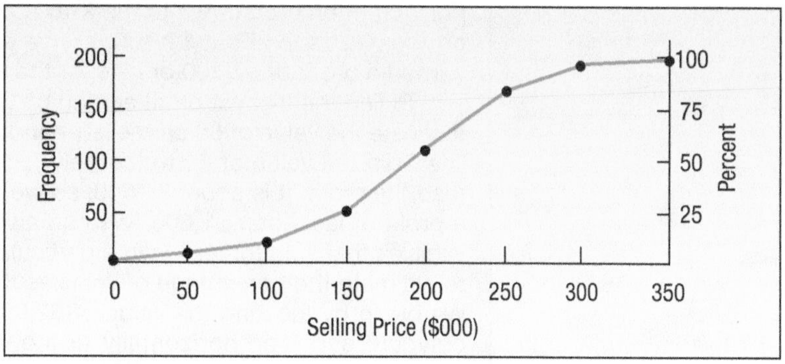

a. How many homes were studied?
b. What is the class interval?

c. One hundred homes sold for less than what amount?
d. About 75% of the homes sold for less than what amount?
e. Estimate the number of homes in the $150,000 up to $200,000 class.
f. About how many homes sold for less than $225,000?

21. The frequency distribution representing the number of frequent flier miles accumulated by employees at Brumley Statistical Consulting Inc. is repeated from Exercise 17.

Frequent Flier Miles (000)	Frequency
0 up to 3	5
3 up to 6	12
6 up to 9	23
9 up to 12	8
12 up to 15	2
Total	50

a. How many employees accumulated less than 3,000 miles?
b. Convert the frequency distribution to a cumulative frequency distribution.
c. Portray the cumulative distribution in the form of a cumulative frequency polygon.
d. Based on the cumulative frequency polygon, about 75% of the employees accumulated how many miles or less?

22. The frequency distribution of order lead time at Ecommerce.com from Exercise 18 is repeated below.

Lead Time (days)	Frequency
0 up to 5	6
5 up to 10	7
10 up to 15	12
15 up to 20	8
20 up to 25	7
Total	40

a. How many orders were filled in less than 10 days? In less than 15 days?
b. Convert the frequency distribution to a cumulative frequency distribution.
c. Develop a cumulative frequency polygon.
d. About 60% of the orders were filled in less than how many days?

CHAPTER SUMMARY

I. A frequency table is a grouping of qualitative data into mutually exclusive and collectively exhaustive classes showing the number of observations in each class.
II. A relative frequency table shows the fraction of the number of frequencies in each class.
III. A bar chart is a graphic representation of a frequency table.
IV. A pie chart shows the proportion each distinct class represents of the total number of observations.
V. A frequency distribution is a grouping of data into mutually exclusive and collectively exhaustive classes showing the number of observations in each class.
  A. The steps in constructing a frequency distribution are
    1. Decide on the number of classes.
    2. Determine the class interval.
    3. Set the individual class limits.
    4. Tally the raw data into classes.
    5. Count the number of tallies in each class.
  B. The class frequency is the number of observations in each class.
  C. The class interval is the difference between the limits of two consecutive classes.
  D. The class midpoint is halfway between the limits of consecutive classes.

VI. A relative frequency distribution shows the percent of observations in each class.

VII. There are three methods for graphically portraying a frequency distribution.

A. A histogram portrays the number of frequencies in each class in the form of a rectangle.

B. A frequency polygon consists of line segments connecting the points formed by the intersection of the class midpoint and the class frequency.

C. A cumulative frequency distribution shows the number or percent of observations less than a given value.

CHAPTER EXERCISES

23. Describe the similarities and differences of qualitative and quantitative variables. Be sure to include the following:

a. What level of measurement is required for each variable type?

b. Can both types be used to describe both samples and populations?

24. Describe the similarities and differences between a frequency table and a frequency distribution. Be sure to include which requires qualitative data and which requires quantitative data.

25. Alexandra Damonte will be building a new resort in Myrtle Beach, South Carolina. She must decide how to design the resort based on the type of activities that the resort will offer to its customers. A recent poll of 300 potential customers showed the following results about customers' preferences for planned resort activities:

Like planned activities	63
Do not like planned activities	135
Not sure	78
No answer	24

a. What is the table called?

b. Draw a bar chart to portray the survey results.

c. Draw a pie chart for the survey results.

d. If you are preparing to present the results to Ms. Damonte as part of a report, which graph would you prefer to show? Why?

For **DATA FILE**, please visit www.mhhe.com/lind16e

26. Speedy Swift is a package delivery service that serves the greater Atlanta, Georgia, metropolitan area. To maintain customer loyalty, one of Speedy Swift's performance objectives is on-time delivery. To monitor its performance, each delivery is measured on the following scale: early (package delivered before the promised time), on-time (package delivered within 5 minutes of the promised time), late (package delivered more than 5 minutes past the promised time), lost (package never delivered). Speedy Swift's objective is to deliver 99% of all packages either early or on-time. Another objective is to never lose a package.

Speedy collected the following data for last month's performance:

On-time	On-time	Early	Late	On-time	On-time	On-time	On-time	Late	On-time
Early	On-time	On-time	Early	On-time	On-time	On-time	On-time	On-time	On-time
Early	On-time	Early	On-time	On-time	On-time	Early	On-time	On-time	On-time
Early	On-time	On-time	Late	Early	Early	On-time	On-time	On-time	Early
On-time	Late	Late	On-time	On-time	On-time	On-time	On-time	On-time	On-time
On-time	Late	Early	On-time	Early	On-time	Lost	On-time	On-time	On-time
Early	Early	On-time	On-time	Late	Early	Lost	On-time	On-time	On-time
On-time	On-time	Early	On-time	Early	On-time	Early	On-time	Late	On-time
On-time	Early	On-time	On-time	On-time	Late	On-time	Early	On-time	On-time
On-time	On-time	On-time	On-time	On-time	Early	Early	On-time	On-time	On-time

a. What scale is used to measure delivery performance? What kind of variable is delivery performance?

b. Construct a frequency table for delivery performance for last month.

c. Construct a relative frequency table for delivery performance last month.
d. Construct a bar chart of the frequency table for delivery performance for last month.
e. Construct a pie chart of on-time delivery performance for last month.
f. Analyze the data summaries and write an evaluation of last month's delivery performance as it relates to Speedy Swift's performance objectives. Write a general recommendation for further analysis.

27. A data set consists of 83 observations. How many classes would you recommend for a frequency distribution?

28. A data set consists of 145 observations that range from 56 to 490. What size class interval would you recommend?

29. The following is the number of minutes to commute from home to work for a group of 25 automobile executives.

For **DATA FILE**, please visit www.mhhe.com/lind16e

28	25	48	37	41	19	32	26	16	23	23	29	36
31	26	21	32	25	31	43	35	42	38	33	28	

a. How many classes would you recommend?
b. What class interval would you suggest?
c. What would you recommend as the lower limit of the first class?
d. Organize the data into a frequency distribution.
e. Comment on the shape of the frequency distribution.

30. The following data give the weekly amounts spent on groceries for a sample of 45 households.

For **DATA FILE**, please visit www.mhhe.com/lind16e

$271	$363	$159	$ 76	$227	$337	$295	$319	$250
279	205	279	266	199	177	162	232	303
192	181	321	309	246	278	50	41	335
116	100	151	240	474	297	170	188	320
429	294	570	342	279	235	434	123	325

a. How many classes would you recommend?
b. What class interval would you suggest?
c. What would you recommend as the lower limit of the first class?
d. Organize the data into a frequency distribution.

31. A social scientist is studying the use of iPods by college students. A sample of 45 students revealed they played the following number of songs yesterday.

For **DATA FILE**, please visit www.mhhe.com/lind16e

4	6	8	7	9	6	3	7	7	6	7	1	4	7	7
4	6	4	10	2	4	6	3	4	6	8	4	3	3	6
8	8	4	6	4	6	5	5	9	6	8	8	6	5	10

Organize the above information into a frequency distribution.
a. How many classes would you suggest?
b. What is the most suitable class interval?
c. What is the lower limit of the initial class?
d. Create the frequency distribution.
e. Describe the profile of the distribution.

32. David Wise handles his own investment portfolio, and has done so for many years. Listed below is the holding time (recorded to the nearest whole year) between purchase and sale for his collection of 36 stocks.

For **DATA FILE**, please visit www.mhhe.com/lind16e

8	8	6	11	11	9	8	5	11	4	8	5	14	7	12	8	6	11	9	7
9	15	8	8	12	5	9	8	5	9	10	11	3	9	8	6				

a. How many classes would you propose?
b. What class interval would you suggest?
c. What quantity would you use for the lower limit of the initial class?
d. Using your responses to parts (a), (b), and (c), create a frequency distribution.
e. Identify the appearance of the frequency distribution.

For **DATA FILE**, please visit www.mhhe.com/lind16e

33. You are exploring the music in your iTunes library. The total play counts over the past year for the 27 songs on your "smart playlist" are shown below. Make a frequency distribution of the counts and describe its shape. It is often claimed that a small fraction of a person's songs will account for most of their total plays. Does this seem to be the case here?

128	56	54	91	190	23	160	298	445	50
578	494	37	677	18	74	70	868	108	71
466	23	84	38	26	814	17			

For **DATA FILE**, please visit www.mhhe.com/lind16e

34. The monthly issues of the *Journal of Finance* are available on the Internet. The table below shows the number of times an issue was downloaded over the last 33 months. Suppose that you wish to summarize the number of downloads with a frequency distribution.

312	2,753	2,595	6,057	7,624	6,624	6,362	6,575	7,760	7,085	7,272
5,967	5,256	6,160	6,238	6,709	7,193	5,631	6,490	6,682	7,829	7,091
6,871	6,230	7,253	5,507	5,676	6,974	6,915	4,999	5,689	6,143	7,086

a. How many classes would you propose?
b. What class interval would you suggest?
c. What quantity would you use for the lower limit of the initial class?
d. Using your responses to parts (a), (b), and (c), create a frequency distribution.
e. Identify the appearance of the frequency distribution.

35. The following histogram shows the scores on the first exam for a statistics class.

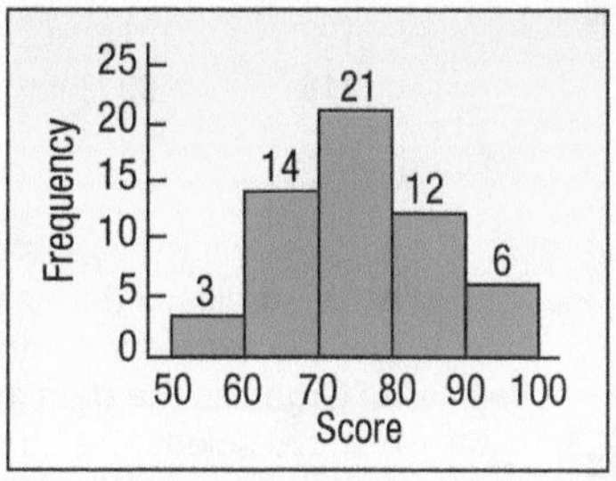

a. How many students took the exam?
b. What is the class interval?
c. What is the class midpoint for the first class?
d. How many students earned a score of less than 70?

36. The following chart summarizes the selling price of homes sold last month in the Sarasota, Florida, area.

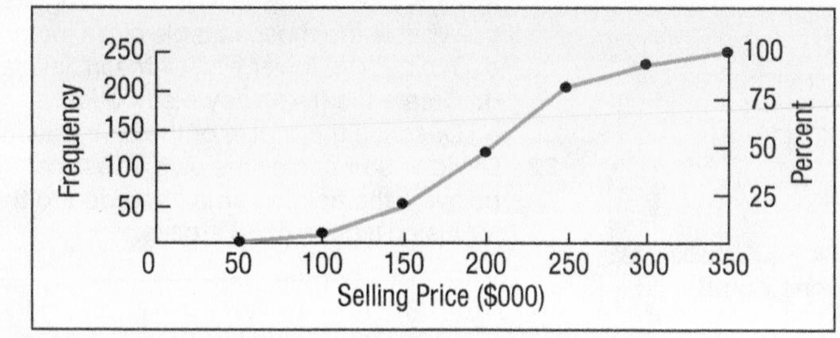

a. What is the chart called?
b. How many homes were sold during the last month?
c. What is the class interval?
d. About 75% of the houses sold for less than what amount?
e. One hundred seventy-five of the homes sold for less than what amount?

For **DATA FILE**, please visit www.mhhe.com/lind16e

37. A chain of sport shops catering to beginning skiers, headquartered in Aspen, Colorado, plans to conduct a study of how much a beginning skier spends on his or her initial purchase of equipment and supplies. Based on these figures, it wants to explore the possibility of offering combinations, such as a pair of boots and a pair of skis, to induce customers to buy more. A sample of 44 cash register receipts revealed these initial purchases:

$140	$ 82	$265	$168	$ 90	$114	$172	$230	$142
86	125	235	212	171	149	156	162	118
139	149	132	105	162	126	216	195	127
161	135	172	220	229	129	87	128	126
175	127	149	126	121	118	172	126	

a. Arrive at a suggested class interval.
b. Organize the data into a frequency distribution using a lower limit of $70.
c. Interpret your findings.

For **DATA FILE**, please visit www.mhhe.com/lind16e

38. The numbers of outstanding shares for 24 publicly traded companies are listed in the following table.

Company	Number of Outstanding Shares (millions)	Company	Number of Outstanding Shares (millions)
Southwest Airlines	738	Costco	436
FIRSTENERGY	418	Home Depot	1,495
Harley Davidson	226	DTE Energy	172
Entergy	178	Dow Chemical	1,199
Chevron	1,957	Eastman Kodak	272
Pacific Gas and Electric	430	American Electric Power	485
DuPont	932	ITT Corporation	93
Westinghouse Solar	22	Ameren	243
Northeast Utilities	314	Virginia Electric and Power	575
Facebook	1,067	Public Service Electric & Gas	506
Google, Inc.	64	Consumers Energy	265
Apple	941	Starbucks	744

a. Using the number of outstanding shares, summarize the companies with a frequency distribution.
b. Display the frequency distribution with a frequency polygon.
c. Create a cumulative frequency distribution of the companies.
d. Display the cumulative frequency distribution with a cumulative frequency polygon.
e. Based on the cumulative frequency distribution, 75% of the companies have less than "what number" of outstanding shares?
f. Write a brief analysis of this group of companies based on your statistical summaries of "number of outstanding shares."

39. A recent survey showed that the typical American car owner spends $2,950 per year on operating expenses. Below is a breakdown of the various expenditure items. Draw an appropriate chart to portray the data and summarize your findings in a brief report.

Expenditure Item	Amount
Fuel	$ 603
Interest on car loan	279
Repairs	930
Insurance and license	646
Depreciation	492
Total	$2,950

For **DATA FILE**, please visit www.mhhe.com/lind16e

40. Midland National Bank selected a sample of 40 student checking accounts. Below are their end-of-the-month balances.

$404	$ 74	$234	$149	$279	$215	$123	$ 55	$ 43	$321
87	234	68	489	57	185	141	758	72	863
703	125	350	440	37	252	27	521	302	127
968	712	503	489	327	608	358	425	303	203

a. Tally the data into a frequency distribution using $100 as a class interval and $0 as the starting point.
b. Draw a cumulative frequency polygon.
c. The bank considers any student with an ending balance of $400 or more a "preferred customer." Estimate the percentage of preferred customers.
d. The bank is also considering a service charge to the lowest 10% of the ending balances. What would you recommend as the cutoff point between those who have to pay a service charge and those who do not?

41. Residents of the state of South Carolina earned a total of $69.5 billion in adjusted gross income. Seventy-three percent of the total was in wages and salaries; 11% in dividends, interest, and capital gains; 8% in IRAs and taxable pensions; 3% in business income pensions; 2% in Social Security; and the remaining 3% from other sources. Develop a pie chart depicting the breakdown of adjusted gross income. Write a paragraph summarizing the information.

For **DATA FILE**, please visit www.mhhe.com/lind16e

42. A recent study of home technologies reported the number of hours of personal computer usage per week for a sample of 60 persons. Excluded from the study were people who worked out of their home and used the computer as a part of their work.

9.3	5.3	6.3	8.8	6.5	0.6	5.2	6.6	9.3	4.3
6.3	2.1	2.7	0.4	3.7	3.3	1.1	2.7	6.7	6.5
4.3	9.7	7.7	5.2	1.7	8.5	4.2	5.5	5.1	5.6
5.4	4.8	2.1	10.1	1.3	5.6	2.4	2.4	4.7	1.7
2.0	6.7	1.1	6.7	2.2	2.6	9.8	6.4	4.9	5.2
4.5	9.3	7.9	4.6	4.3	4.5	9.2	8.5	6.0	8.1

a. Organize the data into a frequency distribution. How many classes would you suggest? What value would you suggest for a class interval?
b. Draw a histogram. Interpret your result.

For **DATA FILE**, please visit www.mhhe.com/lind16e

43. Merrill Lynch recently completed a study regarding the size of online investment portfolios (stocks, bonds, mutual funds, and certificates of deposit) for a sample of clients in the 40 up to 50 years old age group. Listed following is the value of all the investments in thousands of dollars for the 70 participants in the study.

$669.9	$ 7.5	$ 77.2	$ 7.5	$125.7	$516.9	$ 219.9	$645.2
301.9	235.4	716.4	145.3	26.6	187.2	315.5	89.2
136.4	616.9	440.6	408.2	34.4	296.1	185.4	526.3
380.7	3.3	363.2	51.9	52.2	107.5	82.9	63.0
228.6	308.7	126.7	430.3	82.0	227.0	321.1	403.4
39.5	124.3	118.1	23.9	352.8	156.7	276.3	23.5
31.3	301.2	35.7	154.9	174.3	100.6	236.7	171.9
221.1	43.4	212.3	243.3	315.4	5.9	1,002.2	171.7
295.7	437.0	87.8	302.1	268.1	899.5		

a. Organize the data into a frequency distribution. How many classes would you suggest? What value would you suggest for a class interval?
b. Draw a histogram. Interpret your result.

44. A total of 5.9% of the prime-time viewing audience watched shows on ABC, 7.6% watched shows on CBS, 5.5% on Fox, 6.0% on NBC, 2.0% on Warner Brothers, and 2.2% on UPN. A total of 70.8% of the audience watched shows on other cable networks, such as CNN and ESPN. You can find the latest information on TV viewing from the following website: http://www.zap2it.com/tv/ratings/. Develop a pie chart or a bar chart to depict this information. Write a paragraph summarizing your findings.

45. Refer to the following chart:

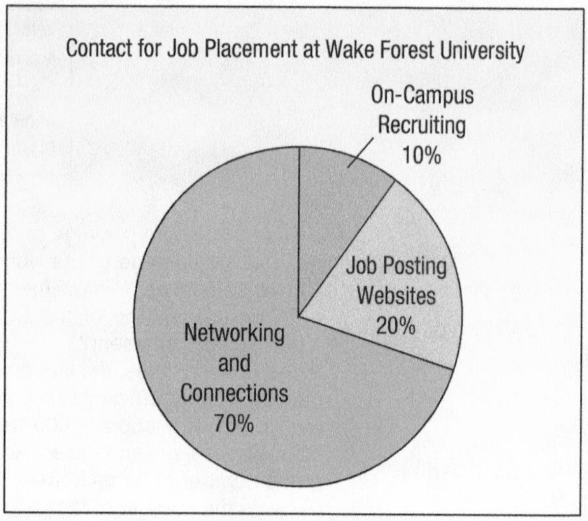

a. What is the name given to this type of chart?

b. Suppose that 1,000 graduates will start a new job shortly after graduation. Estimate the number of graduates whose first contact for employment occurred through networking and other connections.

c. Would it be reasonable to conclude that about 90% of job placements were made through networking, connections, and job posting websites? Cite evidence.

46. The following chart depicts the annual revenues, by type of tax, for the state of Georgia. The chart was developed using Kids Zone, an NCES project. Their website is nces.ed.gov/nceskids/createagraph/.

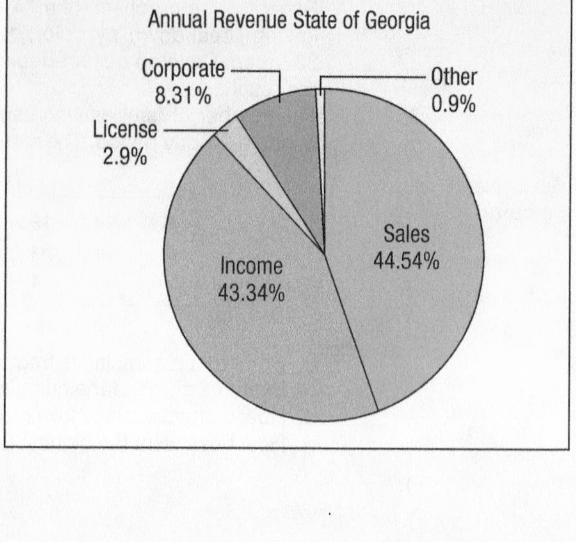

a. What percentage of the state revenue is accounted for by sales tax and individual income tax?
b. Which category will generate more revenue: corporate taxes or license fees?
c. The total annual revenue for the state of Georgia is $6.3 billion. Estimate the amount of revenue in billions of dollars for sales taxes and for individual taxes.

47. In 2011, the United States exported a total of $281 billion worth of products to Canada. The five largest categories were:

Product	Amount
Vehicles	$46.9
Machinery	44.2
Electrical machinery	27.1
Mineral fuel and oil	18.4
Plastic	12.6

a. Use a software package to develop a bar chart.
b. What percentage of the United States' total exports to Canada is represented by the two categories "Mineral fuel and oil" and "Vehicles"?
c. What percentage of the top five exported products do "Mineral fuel and oil" and "Vehicles" represent?

For **DATA FILE**, please visit www.mhhe.com/lind16e

48. In the United States, the industrial revolution of the early 20th century changed farming by making it more efficient. For example, in 1910 U.S. farms used 24.2 million horses and mules and only about 1,000 tractors. By 1960, 4.6 million tractors were used and only 3.2 million horses and mules. An outcome of making farming more efficient is the reduction of the number of farms from over 6 million in 1920 to about 2.2 million farms today. Listed below is the number of farms, in thousands, for each of the 50 states. Summarize the data and write a paragraph that describes your findings.

49	1	16	49	82	36	5	2	48	47
8	26	76	62	92	66	86	30	8	13
8	55	81	42	108	29	47	3	4	10
21	36	52	32	75	87	39	63	1	27
32	78	248	17	7	47	40	23	78	11

49. One of the most popular candies in the United States is M&M's, which are produced by the Mars Company. In the beginning M&M's were all brown; more recently they were produced in red, green, blue, orange, brown, and yellow. You can read about the history of the product, find ideas for baking, purchase the candies in the colors of your school or favorite team, and learn the percent of each color in the standard bags at www.m-ms.com. Recently, the purchase of a 14-ounce bag of M&M's Plain had 444 candies with the following breakdown by color: 130 brown, 98 yellow, 96 red, 35 orange, 52 blue, and 33 green. Develop a chart depicting this information and write a paragraph summarizing the results.

For **DATA FILE**, please visit www.mhhe.com/lind16e

50. The number of families who used the Minneapolis YWCA day care service was recorded during a 30-day period. The results are as follows:

31	49	19	62	24	45	23	51	55	60
40	35	54	26	57	37	43	65	18	41
50	56	4	54	39	52	35	51	63	42

a. Construct a cumulative frequency distribution.
b. Sketch a graph of the cumulative frequency polygon.
c. How many days saw fewer than 30 families utilize the day care center?
d. How busy were the highest 80% of the days?

DATA SET EXERCISES

(The data for these exercises are available at the text website: www.mhhe.com/lind16e.)

51. Refer to the Real Estate data, which reports information on homes sold in the Goodyear, Arizona, area during the last year. Select an appropriate class interval and organize the selling prices into a frequency distribution. Write a brief report summarizing your findings. Be sure to answer the following questions in your report.
   a. Around what values do the data tend to cluster?
   b. Based on the frequency distribution, what is the typical selling price in the first class? What is the typical selling price in the last class?
   c. Draw a cumulative frequency distribution. How many homes sold for less than \$200,000? Estimate the percent of the homes that sold for more than \$220,000. What percent of the homes sold for less than \$125,000?
   d. Refer to the variable regarding the townships. Draw a bar chart showing the number of homes sold in each township. Are there any differences or is the number of homes sold about the same in each township?

52. Refer to the Baseball 2012 data that report information on the 30 Major League Baseball teams for the 2012 season. Create a frequency distribution for the the team payroll variable and answer the following questions.
   a. What is the typical payroll for a team? What is the range of the payrolls?
   b. Comment on the shape of the distribution. Does it appear that any of the teams have a payroll that is out of line with the others?
   c. Draw a cumulative frequency distribution. Thirty percent of the teams have a payroll of less than what amount? About how many teams have total payroll of less than \$100,000,000?

53. Refer to the Buena School District bus data. Select the variable referring to the number of miles traveled last month, and then organize these data into a frequency distribution.
   a. What is a typical amount of miles traveled? What is the range?
   b. Comment on the shape of the distribution. Are there any outliers in terms of miles driven?
   c. Draw a cumulative frequency distribution. Forty percent of the buses were driven fewer than how many miles? How many buses were driven less than 850 miles?
   d. Refer to the variables regarding the bus type and the number of seats in each bus. Draw a pie chart of each variable and comment on your findings.

3 Describing Data:

NUMERICAL MEASURES

THE KENTUCKY DERBY is held the first Saturday in May at Churchill Downs in Louisville, Kentucky. The race track is one and one-quarter miles. The table in Exercise 82 shows the winners since 1990, their margin of victory, the winning time, and the payoff on a $2 bet. Determine the mean and median for the variables winning time and payoff on a $2 bet. (See Exercise 82 and LO3-1.)

LEARNING OBJECTIVES

When you have completed this chapter, you will be able to:

LO3-1 Compute and interpret the mean, the median, and the mode.

LO3-2 Compute a weighted mean.

LO3-3 Compute and interpret the geometric mean.

LO3-4 Compute and interpret the range, variance, and standard deviation.

LO3-5 Explain and apply Chebyshev's theorem and the Empirical Rule.

LO3-6 Compute the mean and standard deviation of grouped data.

INTRODUCTION

Chapter 2 began our study of descriptive statistics. To summarize raw data into a meaningful form, we organized qualitative data into a frequency table and portrayed the results in a bar chart. In a similar fashion, we organized quantitative data into a frequency distribution and portrayed the results in a histogram. We also looked at other graphical techniques such as pie charts to portray qualitative data and frequency polygons to portray quantitative data.

This chapter is concerned with two numerical ways of describing quantitative variables, namely, **measures of location** and **measures of dispersion.** Measures of location are often referred to as averages. The purpose of a measure of location is to pinpoint the center of a distribution of data. An average is a measure of location that shows the central value of the data. Averages appear daily on TV, on various websites, in the newspaper, and in other journals. Here are some examples:

- The average U.S. home changes ownership every 11.8 years.
- An American receives an average of 568 pieces of mail per year.
- The average American home has more TV sets than people. There are 2.73 TV sets and 2.55 people in the typical home.
- The average American couple spends $20,398 for their wedding, while their budget is 50% less. This does not include the cost of a honeymoon or engagement ring.
- The average price of a theater ticket in the United States is $7.50, according to the National Association of Theatre Owners.

If we consider only measures of location in a set of data, or if we compare several sets of data using central values, we may draw an erroneous conclusion. In addition to measures of location, we should consider the **dispersion**—often called the *variation* or the *spread*—in the data. As an illustration, suppose the average annual income of executives for Internet-related companies is $80,000, and the average income for executives in pharmaceutical firms is also $80,000. If we looked only at the average incomes, we might wrongly conclude that the distributions of the two salaries are the same. However, we need to examine the dispersion or spread of the distributions of salary. A look at the salary ranges indicates that this conclusion of equal distributions is not correct. The salaries for the executives in the Internet firms range from $70,000 to $90,000, but salaries for the marketing executives in pharmaceuticals range from $40,000 to $120,000. Thus, we conclude that although the average salaries are the same for the two industries, there is much more spread or dispersion in salaries for the pharmaceutical executives. To describe the dispersion, we will consider the range, the variance, and the standard deviation.

STATISTICS IN ACTION

Did you ever meet the "average" American man? Well, his name is Robert (that is the nominal level of measurement) and he is 31 years old (that is the ratio level), is 69.5 inches tall (again the ratio level of measurement), weighs 172 pounds, wears a size 9½ shoe, has a 34-inch waist, and wears a size 40 suit. In addition, the average man eats 4 pounds of potato chips, watches 1,456 hours of TV, and eats 26 pounds of bananas each year, and also sleeps 7.7 hours per night.

The average American woman is 5′ 4″ tall and weighs 140 pounds, while the average American model is 5′ 11″ tall and weighs 117 pounds. On any given day, almost half of the women in the United States are on a diet. Idolized in the 1950s, Marilyn Monroe would be considered overweight by today's standards. She fluctuated between a size 14 and a size 18 dress, and was a healthy and attractive woman.

MEASURES OF LOCATION

LO3-1
Compute and interpret the mean, the median, and the mode.

We begin by discussing measures of location. There is not just one measure of location; in fact, there are many. We will consider five: the arithmetic mean, the median, the mode, the weighted mean, and the geometric mean. The arithmetic mean is the most widely used and widely reported measure of location. We study the mean as both a population parameter and a sample statistic.

The Population Mean

Many studies involve all the values in a population. For example, there are 12 sales associates employed at the Reynolds Road Carpet Outlet. The mean amount of commission they earned last month was $1,345. This is a population value because we considered the commission of *all* the sales associates. Other examples of a population mean would be:

- The mean closing price for Johnson & Johnson stock for the last 5 days is $64.75.
- The mean number of hours of overtime worked last week by the six welders in the welding department of Butts Welding Inc. is 6.45 hours.
- Caryn Tirsch began a website last month devoted to organic gardening. The mean number of hits on her site for the 31 days in July was 84.36.

For raw data—that is, data that have not been grouped in a frequency distribution—the population mean is the sum of all the values in the population divided by the number of values in the population. To find the population mean, we use the following formula.

$$\text{Population mean} = \frac{\text{Sum of all the values in the population}}{\text{Number of values in the population}}$$

Instead of writing out in words the full directions for computing the population mean (or any other measure), it is more convenient to use the shorthand symbols of mathematics. The mean of the population using mathematical symbols is:

POPULATION MEAN $$\mu = \frac{\Sigma x}{N} \qquad \textbf{[3–1]}$$

where:

μ represents the population mean. It is the Greek lowercase letter "mu."
N is the number of values in the population.
x represents any particular value.
Σ is the Greek capital letter "sigma" and indicates the operation of adding.
Σx is the sum of the x values in the population.

Any measurable characteristic of a population is called a **parameter.** The mean of a population is an example of a parameter.

PARAMETER A characteristic of a population.

EXAMPLE

There are 42 exits on I-75 through the state of Kentucky. Listed below are the distances between exits (in miles).

11	4	10	4	9	3	8	10	3	14	1	10	3	5
2	2	5	6	1	2	2	3	7	1	3	7	8	10
1	4	7	5	2	2	5	1	1	3	3	1	2	1

Why is this information a population? What is the mean number of miles between exits?

SOLUTION

This is a population because we are considering all the exits on I-75 in Kentucky. We add the distances between each of the 42 exits. The total distance is 192 miles. To find the arithmetic mean, we divide this total by 42. So the arithmetic mean is 4.57 miles, found by 192/42. From formula (3–1):

$$\mu = \frac{\Sigma x}{N} = \frac{11 + 4 + 10 + \cdots + 1}{42} = \frac{192}{42} = 4.57$$

How do we interpret the value of 4.57? It is the typical number of miles between exits. Because we considered all the exits on I-75 in Kentucky, this value is a population parameter.

The Sample Mean

As explained in Chapter 1, we often select a sample from the population to estimate a specific characteristic of the population. Smucker's quality assurance department needs to be assured that the amount of orange marmalade in the jar labeled as containing 12 ounces actually contains that amount. It would be very expensive and time-consuming to check the weight of each jar. Therefore, a sample of 20 jars is selected, the mean of the sample is determined, and that value is used to estimate the amount in each jar.

For raw data—that is, ungrouped data—*the mean is the sum of all the sampled values divided by the total number of sampled values.* To find the mean for a sample:

$$\text{Sample mean} = \frac{\text{Sum of all the values in the sample}}{\text{Number of values in the sample}}$$

The mean of a sample and the mean of a population are computed in the same way, but the shorthand notation used is different. The formula for the mean of a *sample* is:

SAMPLE MEAN $$\bar{x} = \frac{\Sigma x}{n}$$ **[3–2]**

where:

$\bar{x}$ represents the sample mean. It is read "x bar."
n is the number of values in the sample.
x represents any particular value.
Σ is the Greek capital letter "sigma" and indicates the operation of adding.
Σx is the sum of the x values in the sample.

The mean of a sample, or any other measure based on sample data, is called a **statistic.** If the mean weight of a sample of 10 jars of Smucker's orange marmalade is 11.5 ounces, this is an example of a statistic.

STATISTIC A characteristic of a sample.

EXAMPLE

Verizon is studying the number of minutes used by clients in a particular cell phone rate plan. A random sample of 12 clients showed the following number of minutes used last month.

90	77	94	89	119	112
91	110	92	100	113	83

What is the arithmetic mean number of minutes used?

SOLUTION

Using formula (3–2), the sample mean is:

$$\text{Sample mean} = \frac{\text{Sum of all values in the sample}}{\text{Number of values in the sample}}$$

$$\bar{x} = \frac{\Sigma x}{n} = \frac{90 + 77 + \cdots + 83}{12} = \frac{1{,}170}{12} = 97.5$$

The arithmetic mean number of minutes used last month by the sample of cell phone users is 97.5 minutes.

Properties of the Arithmetic Mean

The arithmetic mean is a widely used measure of location. It has several important properties:

1. **To compute a mean, the data must be measured at the interval or ratio level.** Recall from Chapter 1 that ratio-level data include such data as ages, incomes, and weights, with the distance between numbers being constant.
2. **All the values are included in computing the mean.**
3. **The mean is unique.** That is, there is only one mean in a set of data. Later in the chapter, we will discover a measure of location that might appear twice, or more than twice, in a set of data.
4. **The sum of the deviations of each value from the mean is zero.** Expressed symbolically:

$$\Sigma(x - \bar{x}) = 0$$

As an example, the mean of 3, 8, and 4 is 5. Then:

$$\begin{aligned}\Sigma(x - \bar{x}) &= (3 - 5) + (8 - 5) + (4 - 5)\\ &= -2 + 3 - 1\\ &= 0\end{aligned}$$

Thus, we can consider the mean as a balance point for a set of data. To illustrate, we have a long board with the numbers 1, 2, 3, . . . , 9 evenly spaced on it. Suppose three bars of equal weight were placed on the board at numbers 3, 4, and 8, and the balance point was set at 5, the mean of the three numbers. We would find that the

board is balanced perfectly! The deviations below the mean (−3) are equal to the deviations above the mean (+3). Shown schematically:

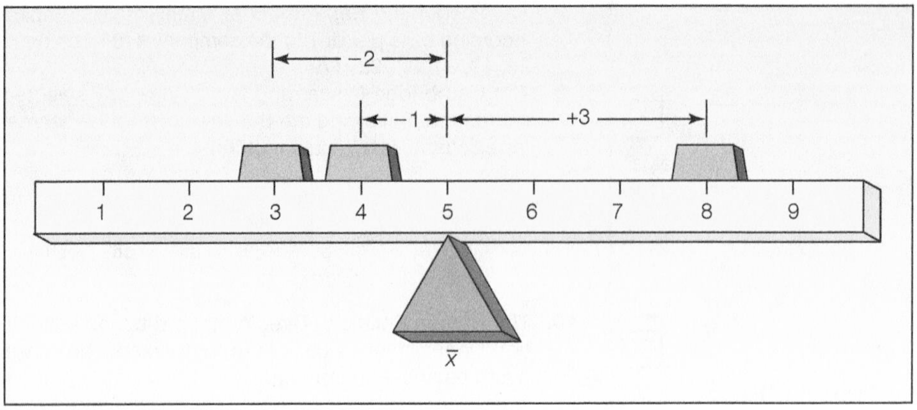

The mean does have a weakness. Recall that the mean uses the value of every item in a sample, or population, in its computation. If one or two of these values are either extremely large or extremely small compared to the majority of data, the mean might not be an appropriate average to represent the data. For example, suppose the annual incomes of a sample of financial planners at Merrill Lynch are \$62,900, \$61,600, \$62,500, \$60,800, and \$1,200,000. The mean income is \$289,560. Obviously, it is not representative of this group because all but one financial planner has an income in the \$60,000 to \$63,000 range. One income (\$1.2 million) is unduly affecting the mean.

SELF-REVIEW 3-1

1. The annual incomes of a sample of middle-management employees at Westinghouse are \$62,900, \$69,100, \$58,300, and \$76,800.
   (a) Give the formula for the sample mean.
   (b) Find the sample mean.
   (c) Is the mean you computed in (b) a statistic or a parameter? Why?
   (d) What is your best estimate of the population mean?
2. All the students in advanced Computer Science 411 are a population. Their course grades are 92, 96, 61, 86, 79, and 84.
   (a) Give the formula for the population mean.
   (b) Compute the mean course grade.
   (c) Is the mean you computed in (b) a statistic or a parameter? Why?

EXERCISES

The answers to the odd-numbered exercises are in Appendix D.

1. Compute the mean of the following population values: 6, 3, 5, 7, 6.
2. Compute the mean of the following population values: 7, 5, 7, 3, 7, 4.
3. **a.** Compute the mean of the following sample values: 5, 9, 4, 10.
b. Show that $\Sigma(x - \bar{x}) = 0$.
4. **a.** Compute the mean of the following sample values: 1.3, 7.0, 3.6, 4.1, 5.0.
b. Show that $\Sigma(x - \bar{x}) = 0$.
5. Compute the mean of the following sample values: 16.25, 12.91, 14.58.
6. Suppose you go to the grocery store and spend \$61.85 for the purchase of 14 items. What is the mean price per item?

For Exercises 7–10, (a) compute the arithmetic mean and (b) indicate whether it is a statistic or a parameter.

7. There are 10 salespeople employed by Midtown Ford. The number of new cars sold last month by the respective salespeople were 15, 23, 4, 19, 18, 10, 10, 8, 28, 19.

8. The accounting department at a mail-order company counted the following numbers of incoming calls per day to the company's toll-free number during the first 7 days in May: 14, 24, 19, 31, 36, 26, 17.

For **DATA FILE**, please visit www.mhhe.com/lind16e

9. The Cambridge Power and Light Company selected a random sample of 20 residential customers. Following are the amounts, to the nearest dollar, the customers were charged for electrical service last month:

54	48	58	50	25	47	75	46	60	70
67	68	39	35	56	66	33	62	65	67

For **DATA FILE**, please visit www.mhhe.com/lind16e

10. The Human Relations Director at Ford began a study of the overtime hours in the Inspection Department. A sample of 15 workers showed they worked the following number of overtime hours last month.

13	13	12	15	7	15	5	12
6	7	12	10	9	13	12	

11. AAA Heating and Air Conditioning completed 30 jobs last month with a mean revenue of $5,430 per job. The president wants to know the total revenue for the month. Based on the limited information, can you compute the total revenue? What is it?

12. A large pharmaceutical company hires business administration graduates to sell its products. The company is growing rapidly and dedicates only 1 day of sales training for new salespeople. The company's goal for new salespeople is $10,000 per month. The goal is based on the current mean sales for the entire company, which is $10,000 per month. After reviewing the retention rates of new employees, the company finds that only 1 in 10 new employees stays longer than 3 months. Comment on using the current mean sales per month as a sales goal for new employees. Why do new employees leave the company?

The Median

We have stressed that, for data containing one or two very large or very small values, the arithmetic mean may not be representative. The center for such data can be better described by a measure of location called the **median.**

To illustrate the need for a measure of location other than the arithmetic mean, suppose you are seeking to buy a condominium in Palm Aire. Your real estate agent says that the typical price of the units currently available is $110,000. Would you still want to look? If you had budgeted your maximum purchase price at $75,000, you might think they are out of your price range. However, checking the prices of the individual units might change your mind. They are $60,000, $65,000, $70,000, and $80,000, and a superdeluxe penthouse costs $275,000. The arithmetic mean price is $110,000, as the real estate agent reported, but one price ($275,000) is pulling the arithmetic mean upward, causing it to be an unrepresentative average. It does seem that a price around $70,000 is a more typical or representative average, and it is. In cases such as this, the median provides a more valid measure of location.

MEDIAN The midpoint of the values after they have been ordered from the minimum to the maximum values.

The median price of the units available is \$70,000. To determine this, we order the prices from the minimum value (\$60,000) to the maximum value (\$275,000) and select the middle value (\$70,000). For the median, the data must be at least an ordinal level of measurement.

Prices Ordered from Minimum to Maximum		Prices Ordered from Maximum to Minimum
\$ 60,000		\$275,000
65,000		80,000
70,000	← Median →	70,000
80,000		65,000
275,000		60,000

Note that there is the same number of prices below the median of \$70,000 as above it. The median is, therefore, unaffected by extremely low or high prices. Had the highest price been \$90,000, or \$300,000, or even \$1 million, the median price would still be \$70,000. Likewise, had the lowest price been \$20,000 or \$50,000, the median price would still be \$70,000.

In the previous illustration, there are an *odd* number of observations (five). How is the median determined for an *even* number of observations? As before, the observations are ordered. Then by convention to obtain a unique value we calculate the mean of the two middle observations. So for an even number of observations, the median may not be one of the given values.

EXAMPLE

Facebook is a popular social networking website. Users can add friends and send them messages, and update their personal profiles to notify friends about themselves and their activities. A sample of 10 adults revealed they spent the following number of hours last month using Facebook.

3	5	7	5	9	1	3	9	17	10

Find the median number of hours.

SOLUTION

Note that the number of adults sampled is even (10). The first step, as before, is to order the hours using Facebook from the minimum value to the maximum value. Then identify the two middle times. The arithmetic mean of the two middle observations gives us the median hours. Arranging the values from minimum to maximum:

1	3	3	5	5	7	9	9	10	17

The median is found by averaging the two middle values. The middle values are 5 hours and 7 hours, and the mean of these two values is 6. We conclude that the typical adult Facebook user spends 6 hours per month at the website. Notice that the median is not one of the values. Also, half of the times are below the median and half are above it.

The major properties of the median are:

1. **It is not affected by extremely large or small values.** Therefore, the median is a valuable measure of location when such values do occur.
2. **It can be computed for ordinal-level data or higher.** Recall from Chapter 1 that ordinal-level data can be ranked from low to high.

The Mode

The **mode** is another measure of location.

MODE The value of the observation that appears most frequently.

The mode is especially useful in summarizing nominal-level data. As an example of its use for nominal-level data, a company has developed five bath oils. The bar chart in Chart 3–1 shows the results of a marketing survey designed to find which bath oil consumers prefer. The largest number of respondents favored Lamoure, as evidenced by the highest bar. Thus, Lamoure is the mode.

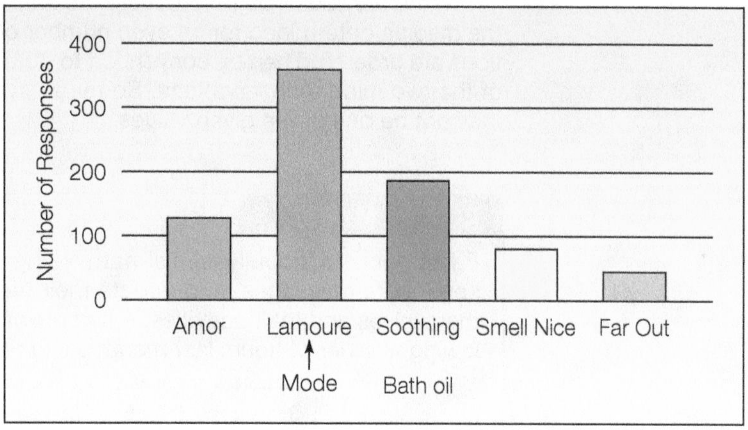

CHART 3–1 Number of Respondents Favoring Various Bath Oils

EXAMPLE

Recall the data regarding the distance in miles between exits on I-75 in Kentucky. The information is repeated below.

11	4	10	4	9	3	8	10	3	14	1	10	3	5
2	2	5	6	1	2	2	3	7	1	3	7	8	10
1	4	7	5	2	2	5	1	1	3	3	1	2	1

What is the modal distance?

SOLUTION

The first step is to organize the distances into a frequency table. This will help us determine the distance that occurs most frequently.

Distance in Miles between Exits	Frequency
1	8
2	7
3	7
4	3
5	4
6	1
7	3
8	2
9	1
10	4
11	1
14	1
Total	42

The distance that occurs most often is 1 mile. This happens eight times—that is, there are eight exits that are 1 mile apart. So the modal distance between exits is 1 mile.

Which of the three measures of location (mean, median, or mode) best represents the central location of these data? Is the mode the best measure of location to represent the Kentucky data? No. The mode assumes only the nominal scale of measurement and the variable miles is measured using the ratio scale. We calculated the mean to be 4.57 miles. See page 53. Is the mean the best measure of location to represent these data? Probably not. There are several cases in which the distance between exits is large. These values are affecting the mean, making it too large and not representative of the distances between exits. What about the median? The median distance is 3 miles. That is, half of the distances between exits are 3 miles or less. In this case, the median of 3 miles between exits is probably a more representative measure of the distance between exits.

In summary, we can determine the mode for all levels of data—nominal, ordinal, interval, and ratio. The mode also has the advantage of not being affected by extremely high or low values.

The mode does have disadvantages, however, that cause it to be used less frequently than the mean or median. For many sets of data, there is no mode because no value appears more than once. For example, there is no mode for this set of price data because every value occurs once: $19, $21, $23, $20, and $18. Conversely, for some data sets there is more than one mode. Suppose the ages of the individuals in a stock investment club are 22, 26, 27, 27, 31, 35, and 35. Both the ages 27 and 35 are modes. Thus, this grouping of ages is referred to as *bimodal* (having two modes). One would question the use of two modes to represent the location of this set of age data.

SELF-REVIEW 3–2

1. A sample of single persons in Towson, Texas, receiving Social Security payments revealed these monthly benefits: $852, $598, $580, $1,374, $960, $878, and $1,130.
   (a) What is the median monthly benefit?
   (b) How many observations are below the median? Above it?
2. The number of work stoppages in the automobile industry for selected months are 6, 0, 10, 14, 8, and 0.
   (a) What is the median number of stoppages?
   (b) How many observations are below the median? Above it?
   (c) What is the modal number of work stoppages?

EXERCISES

13. What would you report as the modal value for a set of observations if there were a total of:
    a. 10 observations and no two values were the same?
    b. 6 observations and they were all the same?
    c. 6 observations and the values were 1, 2, 3, 3, 4, and 4?

For Exercises 14–16, determine the (a) mean, (b) median, and (c) mode.

14. The following is the number of oil changes for the last 7 days at the Jiffy Lube located at the corner of Elm Street and Pennsylvania Avenue.

41	15	39	54	31	15	33

15. The following is the percent change in net income from last year to this year for a sample of 12 construction companies in Denver.

5	1	−10	−6	5	12	7	8	6	5	−1	11

16. The following are the ages of the 10 people in the video arcade at the Southwyck Shopping Mall at 10 a.m.

12	8	17	6	11	14	8	17	10	8

For **DATA FILE**, please visit www.mhhe.com/lind16e

17. Several indicators of long-term economic growth in the United States and their annual percent change are listed below.

Economic Indicator	Percent Change	Economic Indicator	Percent Change
Inflation	4.5%	Real GNP	2.9%
Exports	4.7	Investment (residential)	3.6
Imports	2.3	Investment (nonresidential)	2.1
Real disposable income	2.9	Productivity (total)	1.4
Consumption	2.7	Productivity (manufacturing)	5.2

    a. What is the median percent change?
    b. What is the modal percent change?

For **DATA FILE**, please visit www.mhhe.com/lind16e

18. Sally Reynolds sells real estate along the coastal area of Northern California. Below are her total annual commissions between 2002 and 2012. Find the mean, median, and mode of the commissions she earned for the 11 years.

Year	Amount (thousands)
2002	$237.51
2003	233.80
2004	206.97
2005	248.14
2006	164.69
2007	292.16
2008	269.11
2009	225.57
2010	255.33
2011	202.67
2012	206.53

For **DATA FILE**, please visit www.mhhe.com/lind16e

19. The accounting firm of Rowatti and Koppel specializes in income tax returns for self-employed professionals, such as physicians, dentists, architects, and lawyers. The firm employs 11 accountants who prepare the returns. For last year, the number of returns prepared by each accountant was:

58	75	31	58	46	65	60	71	45	58	80

Find the mean, median, and mode for the number of returns prepared by each accountant. If you could report only one, which measure of location would you recommend reporting?

For **DATA FILE**, please visit www.mhhe.com/lind16e

20. The demand for the video games provided by Mid-Tech Video Games Inc. has exploded in the last several years. Hence, the owner needs to hire several new technical people to keep up with the demand. Mid-Tech gives each applicant a special test that Dr. McGraw, the designer of the test, believes is closely related to the ability to create video games. For the general population, the mean on this test is 100. Below are the scores on this test for the applicants.

95	105	120	81	90	115	99	100	130	10

The president is interested in the overall quality of the job applicants based on this test. Compute the mean and the median scores for the 10 applicants. What would you report to the president? Does it seem that the applicants are better than the general population?

The Relative Positions of the Mean, Median, and Mode

Refer to the histogram in Chart 3–2. It is a symmetric distribution, which is also mound-shaped. This distribution *has the same shape on either side of the center*. If the histogram were folded in half, the two halves would be identical. For any symmetric distribution, the mode, median, and mean are located at the center and are always equal. They are all equal to 30 years in Chart 3–2. We should point out that there are symmetric distributions that are not mound-shaped.

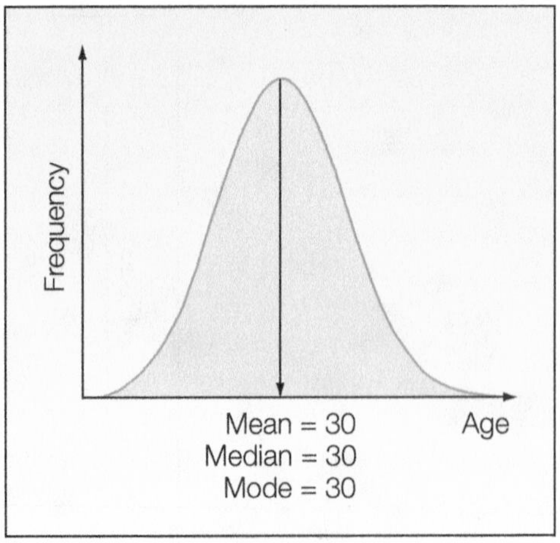

CHART 3–2 A Symmetric Distribution

The number of years corresponding to the highest point of the curve is the *mode* (30 years). Because the distribution is symmetrical, the *median* corresponds to the point where the distribution is cut in half (30 years). Also, because the arithmetic mean is the balance point of a distribution (as shown on page 55), and the distribution is symmetric, the arithmetic mean is 30. Logically, any of the three measures would be appropriate to represent the distribution's center.

If a distribution is nonsymmetrical, or **skewed,** the relationship among the three measures changes. In a **positively skewed distribution,** such as the distribution of weekly income in Chart 3–3, the arithmetic mean is the largest of the three measures. Why? Because the mean is influenced more than the median or mode by a few extremely high values. The median is generally the next largest measure in a positively skewed frequency distribution. The mode is the smallest of the three measures.

If the distribution is highly skewed, the mean would not be a good measure to use. The median and mode would be more representative.

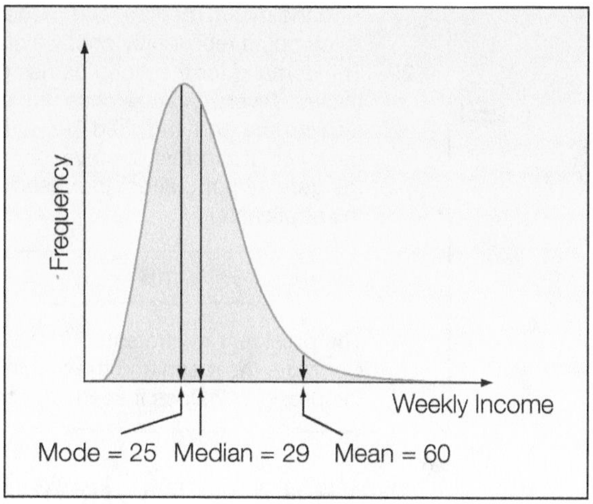

CHART 3–3 A Positively Skewed Distribution

Conversely, if a distribution is **negatively skewed,** such as the distribution of tensile strength in Chart 3–4, the mean is the lowest of the three measures. The mean is, of course, influenced by a few extremely low observations. The median is greater than the arithmetic mean, and the modal value is the largest of the three measures. Again, if the distribution is highly skewed, the mean should not be used to represent the data.

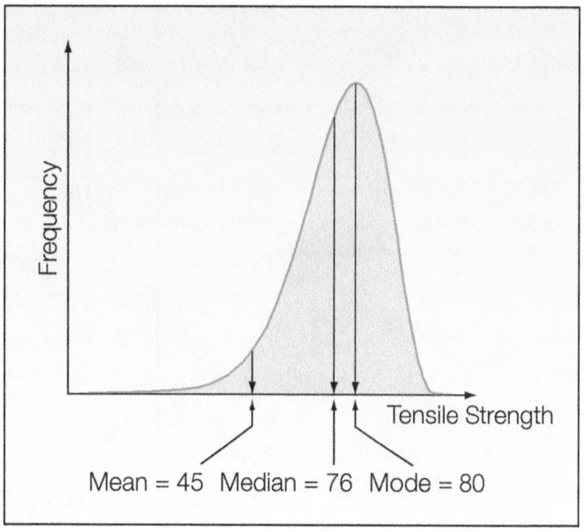

CHART 3–4 A Negatively Skewed Distribution

SELF-REVIEW 3–3

The weekly sales from a sample of Hi-Tec electronic supply stores were organized into a frequency distribution. The mean of weekly sales was computed to be \$105,900, the median \$105,000, and the mode \$104,500.

(a) Sketch the sales in the form of a smoothed frequency polygon. Note the location of the mean, median, and mode on the X-axis.

(b) Is the distribution symmetrical, positively skewed, or negatively skewed? Explain.

EXERCISES

21. The unemployment rate in the state of Alaska by month is given in the table below:

Jan	Feb	Mar	Apr	May	Jun	Jul	Aug	Sep	Oct	Nov	Dec
8.7	8.8	8.7	7.8	7.3	7.8	6.6	6.5	6.5	6.8	7.3	7.6

For **DATA FILE**, please visit www.mhhe.com/lind16e

For **DATA FILE**, please visit www.mhhe.com/lind16e

a. What is the arithmetic mean of the Alaska unemployment rates?
b. Find the median and the mode for the unemployment rates.
c. Compute the arithmetic mean and median for just the winter (Dec–Mar) months. Is it much different?

22. Big Orange Trucking is designing an information system for use in "in-cab" communications. It must summarize data from eight sites throughout a region to describe typical conditions. Compute an appropriate measure of central location for the variables wind direction, temperature, and pavement.

City	Wind Direction	Temperature	Pavement
Anniston, AL	West	89	Dry
Atlanta, GA	Northwest	86	Wet
Augusta, GA	Southwest	92	Wet
Birmingham, AL	South	91	Dry
Jackson, MS	Southwest	92	Dry
Meridian, MS	South	92	Trace
Monroe, LA	Southwest	93	Wet
Tuscaloosa, AL	Southwest	93	Trace

Software Solution

We can use a statistical software package to find many measures of location.

EXAMPLE

Table 2–4 on page 26 shows the profit on the sales of 180 vehicles at Applewood Auto Group. Determine the mean and the median selling price.

SOLUTION

The mean, median, and modal amounts of profit are reported in the following output (highlighted in the screen shot). (Reminder: The instructions to create the output appear in the **Software Commands** in Appendix C.) There are 180 vehicles in the study, so using a calculator would be tedious and prone to error.

APPLEWOOD AUTO GROUP

	A	B	C	D	E	F	G	H
1	Age	Profit	Location	Vehicle-Type	Previous		*Profit*	
2	21	$1,387	Tionesta	Sedan	0			
3	23	$1,754	Sheffield	SUV	1		Mean	1843.17
4	24	$1,817	Sheffield	Hybrid	1		Standard Error	47.97
5	25	$1,040	Sheffield	Compact	0		Median	1882.50
6	26	$1,273	Kane	Sedan	1		Mode	1915.00
7	27	$1,529	Sheffield	Sedan	1		Standard Deviation	643.63
8	27	$3,082	Kane	Truck	0		Sample Variance	414256.61
9	28	$1,951	Kane	SUV	1		Kurtosis	-0.22
10	28	$2,692	Tionesta	Compact	0		Skewness	-0.24
11	29	$1,342	Kane	Sedan	2		Range	2998
12	29	$1,206	Sheffield	Sedan	0		Minimum	294
13	30	$443	Kane	Sedan	3		Maximum	3292
14	30	$1,621	Sheffield	Truck	1		Sum	331770
15	30	$754	Olean	Sedan	2		Count	180

The mean profit is $1,843.17 and the median is $1,882.50. These two values are less than $40 apart, so either value is reasonable. We can also see from the Excel output that there were 180 vehicles sold and their total profit was $331,770.00. We will describe the meaning of standard error, standard deviation, and other measures reported on the output later in this chapter and in later chapters.

What can we conclude? The typical profit on a vehicle is about $1,850. Management at Applewood might use this value for revenue projections. For example, if the dealership could increase the number sold in a month from 180 to 200, this would result in an additional estimated $37,000 of revenue, found by 20($1,850).

LO3-2
Compute a weighted mean.

THE WEIGHTED MEAN

The weighted mean is a convenient way to compute the arithmetic mean when there are several observations of the same value. To explain, suppose the nearby Wendy's Restaurant sold medium, large, and Biggie-sized soft drinks for $.90, $1.25, and $1.50, respectively. Of the last 10 drinks sold, 3 were medium, 4 were large, and 3 were Biggie-sized. To find the mean price of the last 10 drinks sold, we could use formula (3–2).

$$\overline{x} = \frac{\$.90 + \$.90 + \$.90 + \$1.25 + \$1.25 + \$1.25 + \$1.25 + \$1.50 + \$1.50 + \$1.50}{10}$$

$$\overline{x} = \frac{\$12.20}{10} = \$1.22$$

The mean selling price of the last 10 drinks is $1.22.

An easier way to find the mean selling price is to determine the weighted mean. That is, we multiply each observation by the number of times it happens. We will refer to the weighted mean as $\overline{x}_w$. This is read "x bar sub w."

$$\overline{x}_w = \frac{3(\$0.90) + 4(\$1.25) + 3(\$1.50)}{10} = \frac{\$12.20}{10} = \$1.22$$

In this case, the weights are frequency counts. However, any measure of importance could be used as a weight. In general, the weighted mean of a set of numbers designated $x_1, x_2, x_3, \ldots, x_n$ with the corresponding weights $w_1, w_2, w_3, \ldots, w_n$ is computed by:

WEIGHTED MEAN

$$\overline{x}_w = \frac{w_1x_1 + w_2x_2 + w_3x_3 + \cdots + w_nx_n}{w_1 + w_2 + w_3 + \cdots + w_n} \qquad [3\text{–}3]$$

This may be shortened to:

$$\overline{x}_w = \frac{\Sigma(wx)}{\Sigma w}$$

Note that the denominator of a weighted mean is always the sum of the weights.

EXAMPLE

The Carter Construction Company pays its hourly employees $16.50, $19.00, or $25.00 per hour. There are 26 hourly employees, 14 of whom are paid at the $16.50 rate, 10 at the $19.00 rate, and 2 at the $25.00 rate. What is the mean hourly rate paid the 26 employees?

SOLUTION

To find the mean hourly rate, we multiply each of the hourly rates by the number of employees earning that rate. From formula (3–3), the mean hourly rate is

$$\bar{x}_w = \frac{14(\$16.50) + 10(\$19.00) + 2(\$25.00)}{14 + 10 + 2} = \frac{\$471.00}{26} = \$18.1154$$

The weighted mean hourly wage is rounded to $18.12.

SELF-REVIEW 3–4

Springers sold 95 Antonelli men's suits for the regular price of $400. For the spring sale, the suits were reduced to $200 and 126 were sold. At the final clearance, the price was reduced to $100 and the remaining 79 suits were sold.

(a) What was the weighted mean price of an Antonelli suit?

(b) Springers paid $200 a suit for the 300 suits. Comment on the store's profit per suit if a salesperson receives a $25 commission for each one sold.

EXERCISES

23. In June, an investor purchased 300 shares of Oracle (an information technology company) stock at $20 per share. In August, she purchased an additional 400 shares at $25 per share. In November, she purchased an additional 400 shares, but the stock declined to $23 per share. What is the weighted mean price per share?

24. The Bookstall Inc. is a specialty bookstore concentrating on used books sold via the Internet. Paperbacks are $1.00 each, and hardcover books are $3.50. Of the 50 books sold last Tuesday morning, 40 were paperback and the rest were hardcover. What was the weighted mean price of a book?

25. The Loris Healthcare System employs 200 persons on the nursing staff. Fifty are nurse's aides, 50 are practical nurses, and 100 are registered nurses. Nurse's aides receive $8 an hour, practical nurses $15 an hour, and registered nurses $24 an hour. What is the weighted mean hourly wage?

26. Andrews and Associates specialize in corporate law. They charge $100 an hour for researching a case, $75 an hour for consultations, and $200 an hour for writing a brief. Last week one of the associates spent 10 hours consulting with her client, 10 hours researching the case, and 20 hours writing the brief. What was the weighted mean hourly charge for her legal services?

LO3-3
Compute and interpret the geometric mean.

THE GEOMETRIC MEAN

The geometric mean is useful in finding the average change of percentages, ratios, indexes, or growth rates over time. It has a wide application in business and economics because we are often interested in finding the percentage changes in sales, salaries, or economic figures, such as the gross domestic product, which compound or build on each other. The geometric mean of a set of n positive numbers is defined as the nth root of the product of n values. The formula for the geometric mean is written:

GEOMETRIC MEAN $$GM = \sqrt[n]{(x_1)(x_2)\cdots(x_n)} \qquad [3\text{–}4]$$

The geometric mean will always be less than or equal to (never more than) the arithmetic mean. Also, all the data values must be positive.

As an example of the geometric mean, suppose you receive a 5% increase in salary this year and a 15% increase next year. The average annual percent increase is

9.886, not 10.0. Why is this so? We begin by calculating the geometric mean. Recall, for example, that a 5% increase in salary is 105%. We will write it as 1.05.

$$GM = \sqrt{(1.05)(1.15)} = 1.09886$$

This can be verified by assuming that your monthly earning was \$3,000 to start and you received two increases of 5% and 15%.

Raise 1 =	\$3,000(.05) =	\$150.00
Raise 2 =	\$3,150(.15) =	472.50
Total		\$622.50

Your total salary increase is \$622.50. This is equivalent to:

\$3,000.00(.09886) =	\$296.58
\$3,296.58(.09886) =	325.90
	\$622.48 is about \$622.50

The following example shows the geometric mean of several percentages.

EXAMPLE

The return on investment earned by Atkins Construction Company for four successive years was 30%, 20%, −40%, and 200%. What is the geometric mean rate of return on investment?

SOLUTION

The number 1.3 represents the 30% return on investment, which is the "original" investment of 1.0 plus the "return" of 0.3. The number 0.6 represents the loss of 40%, which is the original investment of 1.0 less the loss of 0.4. This calculation assumes the total return each period is reinvested or becomes the base for the next period. In other words, the base for the second period is 1.3 and the base for the third period is (1.3)(1.2) and so forth.

Then the geometric mean rate of return is 29.4%, found by

$$GM = \sqrt[n]{(x_1)(x_2)\cdots(x_n)} = \sqrt[4]{(1.3)(1.2)(0.6)(3.0)} = \sqrt[4]{2.808} = 1.294$$

The geometric mean is the fourth root of 2.808. So, the average rate of return (compound annual growth rate) is 29.4%.

Notice also that if you compute the arithmetic mean [(30 + 20 − 40 + 200)/4 = 52.5], you would have a much larger number, which would overstate the true rate of return!

A second application of the geometric mean is to find an average percentage change over a period of time. For example, if you earned \$45,000 in 2000 and \$100,000 in 2012, what is your annual rate of increase over the period? It is 6.88%. The rate of increase is determined from the following formula.

RATE OF INCREASE OVER TIME

$$GM = \sqrt[n]{\frac{\text{Value at end of period}}{\text{Value at start of period}}} - 1 \qquad \textbf{[3–5]}$$

In the above box, n is the number of periods. An example will show the details of finding the average annual percent increase.

EXAMPLE

During the decade of the 1990s, and into the 2000s, Las Vegas, Nevada, was the fastest-growing city in the United States. The population increased from 258,295 in 1990 to 584,539 in 2011. This is an increase of 326,244 people, or a 126.3% increase over the period. The population has more than doubled. What is the average *annual* percent increase?

SOLUTION

There are 21 years between 1990 and 2011, so $n = 21$. Then formula (3–5) for the geometric mean as applied to this problem is:

$$GM = \sqrt[21]{\frac{\text{Value at end of period}}{\text{Value at start of period}}} - 1.0 = \sqrt[21]{\frac{584{,}539}{258{,}295}} - 1.0 = 1.0397 - 1.0 = .0397$$

To summarize, the steps to compute the geometric mean are:

1. Divide the value at the end of the period by the value at the beginning of the period.
2. Find the *n*th root of the ratio, where *n* is the number of periods.
3. Subtract one.

The value of .0397 indicates that the average annual growth over the period was 3.97%. To put it another way, the population of Las Vegas increased at a rate of 3.97% per year from 1990 to 2011.

SELF-REVIEW 3–5

1. The percent increase in sales for the last 4 years at Combs Cosmetics were 4.91, 5.75, 8.12, and 21.60.
   (a) Find the geometric mean percent increase.
   (b) Find the arithmetic mean percent increase.
   (c) Is the arithmetic mean equal to or greater than the geometric mean?
2. Production of Cablos trucks increased from 23,000 units in 1993 to 120,520 in 2013. Find the geometric mean annual percent increase.

EXERCISES

27. Compute the geometric mean of the following percent increases: 8, 12, 14, 26, and 5.

28. Compute the geometric mean of the following percent increases: 2, 8, 6, 4, 10, 6, 8, and 4.

29. Listed below is the percent increase in sales for the MG Corporation over the last 5 years. Determine the geometric mean percent increase in sales over the period.

9.4	13.8	11.7	11.9	14.7

30. In 1996, a total of 14,968,000 taxpayers in the United States filed their individual tax returns electronically. By the year 2010, the number increased to 99,000,000. What is the geometric mean annual increase for the period?

31. The Consumer Price Index is reported monthly by the U.S. Bureau of Labor Statistics. It reports the change in prices for a market basket of goods from one period to another. The index for 2000 was 172.2. By 2012, it increased to 229.6. What was the geometric mean annual increase for the period?

32. JetBlue Airways is an American low-cost airline headquartered in New York City. Its main base is John F. Kennedy International Airport. JetBlue's revenue in 2002 was $635.2 million. By 2012, revenue had increased to $3,788.0 million. What was the geometric mean annual increase for the period?

33. In 1985, there were 340,213 cell phone subscribers in the United States. By 2012, the number of cell phone subscribers increased to 327,577,529. What is the geometric mean annual increase for the period?

34. The information below shows the cost for a year of college in public and private colleges in 2002–03 and 2012–13. What is the geometric mean annual increase for the period for the two types of colleges? Compare the rates of increase.

Type of College	2002–03	2012–13
Public	$ 4,960	$ 8,655
Private	18,056	29,056

LO3-4
Compute and interpret the range, variance, and standard deviation.

WHY STUDY DISPERSION?

A measure of location, such as the mean, median, or mode, only describes the center of the data. It is valuable from that standpoint, but it does not tell us anything about the spread of the data. For example, if your nature guide told you that the river ahead averaged 3 feet in depth, would you want to wade across on foot without additional information? Probably not. You would want to know something about the variation in the depth. Is the maximum depth of the river 3.25 feet and the minimum 2.75 feet? If that is the case, you would probably agree to cross. What if you learned the river depth ranged from 0.50 foot to 5.5 feet? Your decision would probably be not to cross. Before making a decision about crossing the river, you want information on both the typical depth and the dispersion in the depth of the river.

A small value for a measure of dispersion indicates that the data are clustered closely, say, around the arithmetic mean. The mean is therefore considered representative of the data. Conversely, a large measure of dispersion indicates that the mean is not reliable. Refer to Chart 3–5. The 100 employees of Hammond Iron Works Inc., a steel fabricating company, are organized into a histogram based on the number of years of employment with the company. The mean is 4.9 years, but the spread of the data is from 6 months to 16.8 years. The mean of 4.9 years is not very representative of all the employees.

STATISTICS IN ACTION

The U.S. Postal Service has tried to become more "user friendly" in the last several years. A recent survey showed that customers were interested in more *consistency* in the time it takes to make a delivery. Under the old conditions, a local letter might take only one day to deliver, or it might take several. "Just tell me how many days ahead I need to mail the birthday card to Mom so it gets there on her birthday, not early, not late," was a common complaint. The level of consistency is measured by the standard deviation of the delivery times.

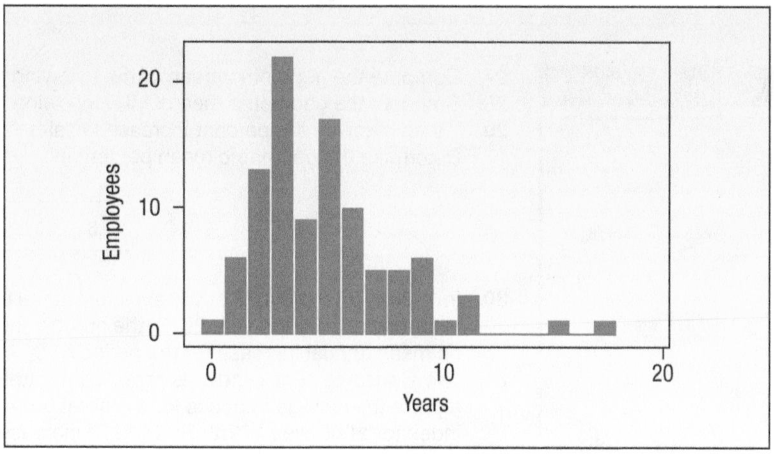

CHART 3–5 Histogram of Years of Employment at Hammond Iron Works Inc.

A second reason for studying the dispersion in a set of data is to compare the spread in two or more distributions. Suppose, for example, that the new Vision Quest LCD computer monitor is assembled in Baton Rouge and also in Tucson. The arithmetic mean hourly output in both the Baton Rouge plant and the Tucson plant is 50.

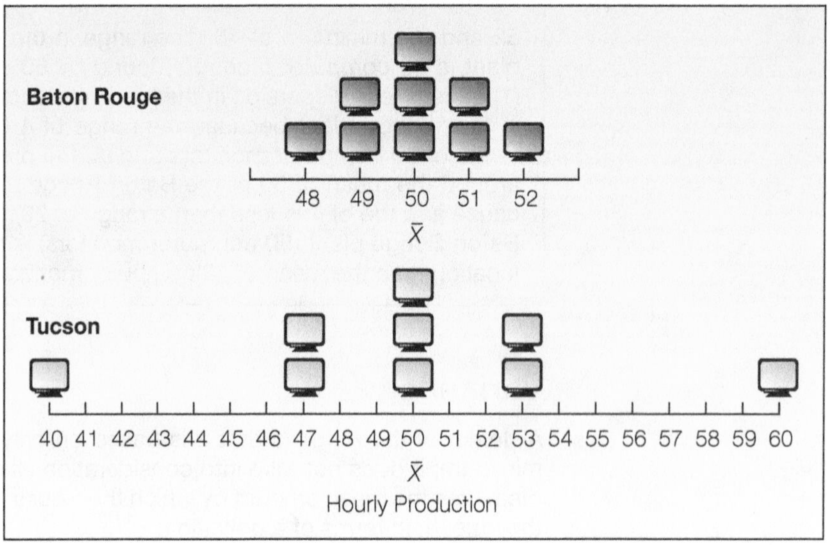

CHART 3–6 Hourly Production of Computer Monitors at the Baton Rouge and Tucson Plants

Based on the two means, you might conclude that the distributions of the hourly outputs are identical. Production records for 9 hours at the two plants, however, reveal that this conclusion is not correct (see Chart 3–6). Baton Rouge production varies from 48 to 52 assemblies per hour. Production at the Tucson plant is more erratic, ranging from 40 to 60 per hour. Therefore, the hourly output for Baton Rouge is clustered near the mean of 50; the hourly output for Tucson is more dispersed.

We will consider several measures of dispersion. The range is based on the maximum and minimum values in the data set; that is, only two values are considered. The variance and the standard deviation use all the values in a data set and are based on deviations from the arithmetic mean.

Range

The simplest measure of dispersion is the **range.** It is the difference between the maximum and minimum values in a data set. In the form of an equation:

RANGE	Range = Maximum value − Minimum value	**[3–6]**

The range is widely used in statistical process control (SPC) applications because it is very easy to calculate and understand.

EXAMPLE

Refer to Chart 3–6 above. Find the range in the number of computer monitors produced per hour for the Baton Rouge and the Tucson plants. Interpret the two ranges.

SOLUTION

The range of the hourly production of computer monitors at the Baton Rouge plant is 4, found by the difference between the maximum hourly production of

52 and the minimum of 48. The range in the hourly production for the Tucson plant is 20 computer monitors, found by 60 − 40. We therefore conclude that (1) there is less dispersion in the hourly production in the Baton Rouge plant than in the Tucson plant because the range of 4 computer monitors is less than a range of 20 computer monitors and (2) the production is clustered more closely around the mean of 50 at the Baton Rouge plant than at the Tucson plant (because a range of 4 is less than a range of 20). Thus, the mean production in the Baton Rouge plant (50 computer monitors) is a more representative measure of location than the mean of 50 computer monitors for the Tucson plant.

Variance

A defect of the range is that it is based on only two values, the maximum and the minimum; it does not take into consideration all of the values. The **variance** does. It measures the mean amount by which the values in a population, or sample, vary from their mean. In terms of a definition:

VARIANCE The arithmetic mean of the squared deviations from the mean.

The following example illustrates how the variance is used to measure dispersion.

EXAMPLE

The chart below shows the number of cappuccinos sold at the Starbucks in the Orange County airport and the Ontario, California, airport between 4 and 5 p.m. for a sample of 5 days last month.

California Airports	
Orange County	Ontario
20	20
40	45
50	50
60	55
80	80

Determine the mean, median, range, and variance for each location. Comment on the similarities and differences in these measures.

SOLUTION

The mean, median, and range for each of the airport locations are reported below as part of an Excel spreadsheet.

	A	B	C
1		California Airports	
2		Orange County	Ontario
3		20	20
4		40	45
5		50	50
6		60	55
7		80	80
8			
9	Mean	50	50
10	Median	50	50
11	Range	60	60

Notice that all three of the measures are exactly the same. Does this indicate that there is no difference in the two sets of data? We get a clearer picture if we calculate the variance. First, for Orange County:

F	G	H
Calculation of Variance for Orange County		
Number Sold	Each Value - Mean	Squared Deviation
20	20 - 50 = -30	900
40	40 - 50 = -10	100
50	50 - 50 = 0	0
60	60 - 50 = 10	100
80	80 - 50 = 30	900
	Total	2000

$$\text{Variance} = \frac{\Sigma(x-\mu)^2}{N} = \frac{(-30^2) + (-10^2) + 0^2 + 10^2 + 30^2}{5} = \frac{2{,}000}{5} = 400$$

The variance is 400. That is, the average squared deviation from the mean is 400.

The following shows the detail of determining the variance for the number of cappuccinos sold at the Ontario Airport.

Calculation of Variance for Ontario		
Number Sold	Each Value - Mean	Squared Deviation
20	20 - 50 = -30	900
45	45 - 50 = -5	25
50	50 - 50 = 0	0
55	55 - 50 = 5	25
80	80 - 50 = 30	900
	Total	1850

$$\text{Variance} = \frac{\Sigma(x-\mu)^2}{N} = \frac{(-30^2) + (-5^2) + 0^2 + 5^2 + 30^2}{5} = \frac{1{,}850}{5} = 370$$

So the mean, median, and range of the cappuccinos sold are the same at the two airports, but the variances are different. The variance at Orange County is 400, but it is 370 at Ontario.

Let's interpret and compare the results of our measures for the two Starbucks airport locations. The mean and median of the two locations are exactly the same,

50 cappuccinos sold. These measures of location suggest the two distributions are the same. The range for both locations is also the same, 60. However, recall that the range provides limited information about the dispersion because it is based on only two of the observations.

The variances are not the same for the two airports. The variance is based on the differences between each observation and the arithmetic mean. It shows the closeness or clustering of the data relative to the mean or center of the distribution. Compare the variance for Orange County of 400 to the variance for Ontario of 370. Based on the variance, we conclude that the dispersion for the sales distribution of the Ontario Starbucks is more concentrated—that is, nearer the mean of 50—than for the Orange County location.

The variance has an important advantage over the range. It uses all the values in the computation. Recall that the range uses only the highest and the lowest values.

SELF-REVIEW 3–6

The weights of containers being shipped to Ireland are (in thousands of pounds):

95	103	105	110	104	105	112	90

(a) What is the range of the weights?
(b) Compute the arithmetic mean weight.
(c) Compute the variance of the weights.

EXERCISES

For Exercises 35–38, calculate the (a) range, (b) arithmetic mean, (c) variance, and (d) interpret the statistics.

35. There were five customer service representatives on duty at the Electronic Super Store during last weekend's sale. The numbers of HDTVs these representatives sold are 5, 8, 4, 10, and 3.

36. The Department of Statistics at Western State University offers eight sections of basic statistics. Following are the numbers of students enrolled in these sections: 34, 46, 52, 29, 41, 38, 36, and 28.

37. Dave's Automatic Door installs automatic garage door openers. The following list indicates the number of minutes needed to install 10 door openers: 28, 32, 24, 46, 44, 40, 54, 38, 32, and 42.

38. All eight companies in the aerospace industry were surveyed as to their return on investment last year. The results are (in percent) 10.6, 12.6, 14.8, 18.2, 12.0, 14.8, 12.2, and 15.6.

For **DATA FILE**, please visit www.mhhe.com/lind16e

39. Ten young adults living in California rated the taste of a newly developed sushi pizza topped with tuna, rice, and kelp on a scale of 1 to 50, with 1 indicating they did not like the taste and 50 that they did. The ratings were:

34	39	40	46	33	31	34	14	15	45

In a parallel study, 10 young adults in Iowa rated the taste of the same pizza. The ratings were:

28	25	35	16	25	29	24	26	17	20

As a market researcher, compare the potential markets for sushi pizza.

For **DATA FILE**, please visit www.mhhe.com/lind16e

40. The personnel files of all eight employees at the Pawnee location of Acme Carpet Cleaners Inc. revealed that during the last 6-month period they lost the following number of days due to illness:

2	0	6	3	10	4	1	2

All eight employees during the same period at the Chickpee location of Acme Carpets revealed they lost the following number of days due to illness:

2	0	1	0	5	0	1	0

As the director of human relations, compare the two locations. What would you recommend?

Population Variance

In the previous example, we developed the concept of variance as a measure of dispersion. Similar to the mean, we can calculate the variance of a population or the variance of a sample. The formula to compute the population variance is:

POPULATION VARIANCE $$\sigma^2 = \frac{\Sigma(x - \mu)^2}{N}$$ **[3–7]**

where:

σ^2 is the population variance (σ is the lowercase Greek letter sigma). It is read as "sigma squared."
x is the value of a particular observation in the population.
μ is the arithmetic mean of the population.
N is the number of observations in the population.

The process for computing the variance is implied by the formula.

1. Begin by finding the mean.
2. Find the difference between each observation and the mean, and square that difference.
3. Sum all the squared differences.
4. Divide the sum of the squared differences by the number of items in the population.

So the population variance is the mean of the squared difference between each value and the mean. For populations whose values are near the mean, the variance will be small. For populations whose values are dispersed from the mean, the population variance will be large.

The variance overcomes the weakness of the range by using all the values in the population, whereas the range uses only the maximum and minimum values. We overcome the issue where $\Sigma(x - \mu) = 0$ by squaring the differences. Squaring the differences will always result in nonnegative values. The following is a another example that illustrates the calculation and interpretation of the variance.

EXAMPLE

The number of traffic citations issued last year by month in Beaufort County, South Carolina, is reported below.

Citations by Month

January	February	March	April	May	June	July	August	September	October	November	December
19	17	22	18	28	34	45	39	38	44	34	10

Determine the population variance.

SOLUTION

Because we are studying all the citations for a year, the data comprise a population. To determine the population variance, we use formula (3–7). The table below details the calculations.

Month	Citations (x)	$x - \mu$	$(x - \mu)^2$
January	19	−10	100
February	17	−12	144
March	22	−7	49
April	18	−11	121
May	28	−1	1
June	34	5	25
July	45	16	256
August	39	10	100
September	38	9	81
October	44	15	225
November	34	5	25
December	10	−19	361
Total	348	0	1,488

1. We begin by determining the arithmetic mean of the population. The total number of citations issued for the year is 348, so the mean number issued per month is 29.

$$\mu = \frac{\Sigma x}{N} = \frac{19 + 17 + \cdots + 10}{12} = \frac{348}{12} = 29$$

2. Next we find the difference between each observation and the mean. This is shown in the third column of the table. Recall that earlier in the chapter (page 54) we indicated that the sum of the differences between each value and the mean is 0. In this example, the sum of the differences between the mean and the number of citations each month is 0.
3. The next step is to square the difference for each month. That is shown in the fourth column of the table. All the squared differences will be positive. Note that squaring a negative value, or multiplying a negative value by itself, always results in a positive value.
4. The squared differences are totaled. The total of the fourth column is 1,488. That is the term $\Sigma(x - \mu)^2$.
5. Finally, we divide the squared differences by N, the number of observations in the population.

$$\sigma^2 = \frac{\Sigma(x - \mu)^2}{N} = \frac{1{,}488}{12} = 124$$

So, the population variance for the number of citations is 124.

Like the range, the variance can be used to compare the dispersion in two or more sets of observations. For example, the variance for the number of citations issued in Beaufort County was just computed to be 124. If the variance in the number of citations issued in Marlboro County, South Carolina, is 342.9, we conclude that (1) there is less dispersion in the distribution of the number of citations issued in Beaufort County than in Marlboro County (because 124 is less than 342.9) and (2) the number of citations in Beaufort County is more closely clustered around the mean of 29 than for the number of citations issued in Marlboro County. Thus the mean number of citations issued in Beaufort County is a more representative measure of location than the mean number of citations in Marlboro County.

Population Standard Deviation

When we compute the variance, it is important to understand the unit of measure and what happens when the differences in the numerator are squared. That is, in the previous example, the number of monthly citations is the variable. When we calculate the variance, the unit of measure for the variance is citations squared. Using "squared citations" as a unit of measure is cumbersome.

There is a way out of this difficulty. By taking the square root of the population variance, we can transform it to the same unit of measurement used for the original data. The square root of 124 citations squared is 11.14 citations. The units are now simply citations. The square root of the population variance is the **population standard deviation.**

POPULATION STANDARD DEVIATION

$$\sigma = \sqrt{\frac{\Sigma(x - \mu)^2}{N}} \qquad [3\text{–}8]$$

SELF-REVIEW 3–7

The Philadelphia office of Price Waterhouse Coopers LLP hired five accounting trainees this year. Their monthly starting salaries were $3,536; $3,173; $3,448; $3,121; and $3,622.

(a) Compute the population mean.
(b) Compute the population variance.
(c) Compute the population standard deviation.
(d) The Pittsburgh office hired six trainees. Their mean monthly salary was $3,550, and the standard deviation was $250. Compare the two groups.

EXERCISES

41. Consider these five values a population: 8, 3, 7, 3, and 4.
  a. Determine the mean of the population.
  b. Determine the variance.

42. Consider these six values a population: 13, 3, 8, 10, 8, and 6.
  a. Determine the mean of the population.
  b. Determine the variance.

43. The annual report of Dennis Industries cited these primary earnings per common share for the past 5 years: $2.68, $1.03, $2.26, $4.30, and $3.58. If we assume these are population values, what is:
  a. The arithmetic mean primary earnings per share of common stock?
  b. The variance?

44. Referring to Exercise 43, the annual report of Dennis Industries also gave these returns on stockholder equity for the same 5-year period (in percent): 13.2, 5.0, 10.2, 17.5, and 12.9.
  a. What is the arithmetic mean return?
  b. What is the variance?

45. Plywood Inc. reported these returns on stockholder equity for the past 5 years: 4.3, 4.9, 7.2, 6.7, and 11.6. Consider these as population values.
  a. Compute the range, the arithmetic mean, the variance, and the standard deviation.
  b. Compare the return on stockholder equity for Plywood Inc. with that for Dennis Industries cited in Exercise 44.

46. The annual incomes of the five vice presidents of TMV Industries are $125,000; $128,000; $122,000; $133,000; and $140,000. Consider this a population.
  a. What is the range?
  b. What is the arithmetic mean income?
  c. What is the population variance? The standard deviation?
  d. The annual incomes of officers of another firm similar to TMV Industries were also studied. The mean was $129,000 and the standard deviation $8,612. Compare the means and dispersions in the two firms.

Sample Variance and Standard Deviation

The formula for the population mean is $\mu = \Sigma x/N$. We just changed the symbols for the sample mean; that is, $\bar{x} = \Sigma x/n$. Unfortunately, the conversion from the population variance to the sample variance is not as direct. It requires a change in the denominator. Instead of substituting n (number in the sample) for N (number in the population), the denominator is $n - 1$. Thus the formula for the **sample variance** is:

SAMPLE VARIANCE $$s^2 = \frac{\Sigma(x - \bar{x})^2}{n - 1}$$ **[3–9]**

where:

- s^2 is the sample variance.
- x is the value of each observation in the sample.
- $\bar{x}$ is the mean of the sample.
- n is the number of observations in the sample.

Why is this change made in the denominator? Although the use of n is logical since $\bar{x}$ is used to estimate μ, it tends to underestimate the population variance, σ^2. The use of $(n - 1)$ in the denominator provides the appropriate correction for this tendency. Because the primary use of sample statistics like s^2 is to estimate population parameters like σ^2, $(n - 1)$ is preferred to n in defining the sample variance. We will also use this convention when computing the sample standard deviation.

EXAMPLE

The hourly wages for a sample of part-time employees at Home Depot are \$12, \$20, \$16, \$18, and \$19. What is the sample variance?

SOLUTION

The sample variance is computed by using formula (3–9).

$$\bar{x} = \frac{\Sigma x}{n} = \frac{\$85}{5} = \$17$$

Hourly Wage (x)	$x - \bar{x}$	$(x - \bar{x})^2$
\$12	−\$5	25
20	3	9
16	−1	1
18	1	1
19	2	4
\$85	0	40

$$s^2 = \frac{\Sigma(x - \bar{x})^2}{n - 1} = \frac{40}{5 - 1}$$

$$= 10 \text{ in dollars squared}$$

The sample standard deviation is used as an estimator of the population standard deviation. As noted previously, the population standard deviation is the square root of the population variance. Likewise, the *sample standard deviation is the square root of the sample variance*. The sample standard deviation is determined by:

SAMPLE STANDARD DEVIATION

$$s = \sqrt{\frac{\Sigma(x - \bar{x})^2}{n - 1}} \qquad [3\text{–}10]$$

EXAMPLE

The sample variance in the previous example involving hourly wages was computed to be 10. What is the sample standard deviation?

SOLUTION

The sample standard deviation is \$3.16, found by $\sqrt{10}$. Note again that the sample variance is in terms of dollars squared, but taking the square root of 10 gives us \$3.16, which is in the same units (dollars) as the original data.

Software Solution

On page 63, we used Excel to determine the mean, median, and mode of profit for the Applewood Auto Group data. You will also note that it lists the sample variance and sample standard deviation. Excel, like most other statistical software, assumes the data are from a sample.

APPLEWOOD AUTO GROUP

	A	B	C	D	E	F	G	H
1	Age	Profit	Location	Vehicle-Type	Previous		Profit	
2	21	$1,387	Tionesta	Sedan	0			
3	23	$1,754	Sheffield	SUV	1		Mean	1843.17
4	24	$1,817	Sheffield	Hybrid	1		Standard Error	47.97
5	25	$1,040	Sheffield	Compact	0		Median	1882.50
6	26	$1,273	Kane	Sedan	1		Mode	1915.00
7	27	$1,529	Sheffield	Sedan	1		Standard Deviation	643.63
8	27	$3,082	Kane	Truck	0		Sample Variance	414256.61
9	28	$1,951	Kane	SUV	1		Kurtosis	-0.22
10	28	$2,692	Tionesta	Compact	0		Skewness	-0.24
11	29	$1,342	Kane	Sedan	2		Range	2998
12	29	$1,206	Sheffield	Sedan	0		Minimum	294
13	30	$443	Kane	Sedan	3		Maximum	3292
14	30	$1,621	Sheffield	Truck	1		Sum	331770
15	30	$754	Olean	Sedan	2		Count	180

SELF-REVIEW 3–8

The years of service for a sample of seven employees at a State Farm Insurance claims office in Cleveland, Ohio, are 4, 2, 5, 4, 5, 2, and 6. What is the sample variance? Compute the sample standard deviation.

EXERCISES

For Exercises 47–52, do the following:

a. Compute the sample variance.
b. Determine the sample standard deviation.

47. Consider these values a sample: 7, 2, 6, 2, and 3.
48. The following five values are a sample: 11, 6, 10, 6, and 7.
49. Dave's Automatic Door, referred to in Exercise 37, installs automatic garage door openers. Based on a sample, following are the times, in minutes, required to install 10 door openers: 28, 32, 24, 46, 44, 40, 54, 38, 32, and 42.
50. The sample of eight companies in the aerospace industry, referred to in Exercise 38, was surveyed as to their return on investment last year. The results are 10.6, 12.6, 14.8, 18.2, 12.0, 14.8, 12.2, and 15.6.
51. The Houston, Texas, Motel Owner Association conducted a survey regarding weekday motel rates in the area. Listed below is the room rate for business-class guests for a sample of 10 motels.

For **DATA FILE**, please visit www.mhhe.com/lind16e

$101	$97	$103	$110	$78	$87	$101	$80	$106	$88

52. A consumer watchdog organization is concerned about credit card debt. A survey of 10 young adults with credit card debt of more than $2,000 showed they paid an average of just over $100 per month against their balances. Listed below are the amounts each young adult paid last month.

For **DATA FILE**, please visit www.mhhe.com/lind16e

$110	$126	$103	$93	$99	$113	$87	$101	$109	$100

LO3-5
Explain and apply Chebyshev's theorem and the Empirical Rule.

INTERPRETATION AND USES OF THE STANDARD DEVIATION

The standard deviation is commonly used as a measure to compare the spread in two or more sets of observations. For example, the standard deviation of the biweekly amounts invested in the Dupree Paint Company profit-sharing plan is computed to be $7.51. Suppose these employees are located in Georgia. If the standard deviation for a group of employees in Texas is $10.47, and the means are about the same, it indicates that the amounts invested by the Georgia employees are not dispersed as much as those in Texas (because $7.51 < $10.47). Since the amounts invested by the Georgia employees are clustered more closely about the mean, the mean for the Georgia employees is a more reliable measure than the mean for the Texas group.

STATISTICS IN ACTION

Most colleges report the "average class size." This information can be misleading because average class size can be found in several ways. If we find the number of students *in each class* at a particular university, the result is the mean number of students per class. If we compile a list of the class sizes for each student and find the mean class size, we might find the mean to be quite different. One school found the mean number of students in each of its 747 classes to be 40. But when it found the mean from a list of the class sizes of each

(continued)

Chebyshev's Theorem

We have stressed that a small standard deviation for a set of values indicates that these values are located close to the mean. Conversely, a large standard deviation reveals that the observations are widely scattered about the mean. The Russian mathematician P. L. Chebyshev (1821–1894) developed a theorem that allows us to determine the minimum proportion of the values that lie within a specified number of standard deviations of the mean. For example, according to **Chebyshev's theorem,** at least three out of every four, or 75%, of the values must lie between the mean plus two standard deviations and the mean minus two standard deviations. This relationship applies regardless of the shape of the distribution. Further, at least eight of nine values, or 88.9%, will lie between plus three standard deviations and minus three standard deviations of the mean. At least 24 of 25 values, or 96%, will lie between plus and minus five standard deviations of the mean.

Chebyshev's theorem states:

CHEBYSHEV'S THEOREM For any set of observations (sample or population), the proportion of the values that lie within k standard deviations of the mean is at least $1 - 1/k^2$, where k is any value greater than 1.

EXAMPLE

The arithmetic mean biweekly amount contributed by the Dupree Paint employees to the company's profit-sharing plan is \$51.54, and the standard deviation is \$7.51. At least what percent of the contributions lie within plus 3.5 standard deviations and minus 3.5 standard deviations of the mean?

SOLUTION

About 92%, found by

$$1 - \frac{1}{k^2} = 1 - \frac{1}{(3.5)^2} = 1 - \frac{1}{12.25} = 0.92$$

(continued from p. 78)

student, it was 147. Why the disparity? Because there are few students in the small classes and a larger number of students in the larger classes, which has the effect of increasing the mean class size when it is calculated this way. A school could reduce this mean class size for each student by reducing the number of students in each class. That is, cut out the large freshman lecture classes.

The Empirical Rule

Chebyshev's theorem applies to any set of values; that is, the distribution of values can have any shape. However, for a symmetrical, bell-shaped distribution such as the one in Chart 3–7, we can be more precise in explaining the dispersion about the mean. These relationships involving the standard deviation and the mean are described by the **Empirical Rule,** sometimes called the **Normal Rule.**

EMPIRICAL RULE For a symmetrical, bell-shaped frequency distribution, approximately 68% of the observations will lie within plus and minus one standard deviation of the mean; about 95% of the observations will lie within plus and minus two standard deviations of the mean; and practically all (99.7%) will lie within plus and minus three standard deviations of the mean.

These relationships are portrayed graphically in Chart 3–7 for a bell-shaped distribution with a mean of 100 and a standard deviation of 10.

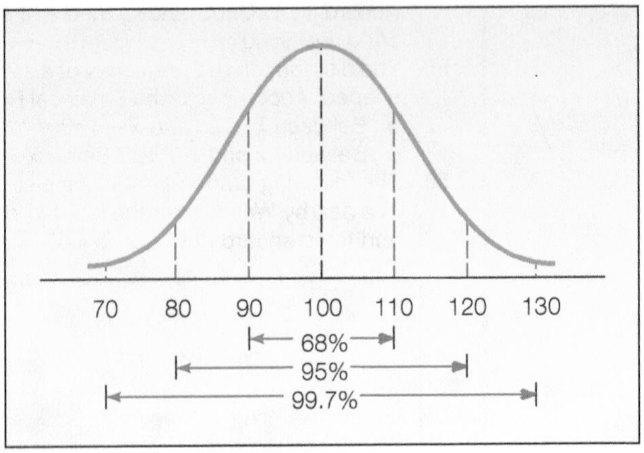

CHART 3–7 A Symmetrical, Bell-Shaped Curve Showing the Relationships between the Standard Deviation and the Percentage of Observations

Applying the Empirical Rule, if a distribution is symmetrical and bell-shaped, practically all of the observations lie between the mean plus and minus three standard deviations. Thus, if $\bar{x} = 100$ and $s = 10$, practically all the observations lie between $100 + 3(10)$ and $100 - 3(10)$, or 70 and 130. The estimated range is therefore 60, found by $130 - 70$.

Conversely, if we know that the range is 60 and the distribution is bell-shaped, we can approximate the standard deviation by dividing the range by 6. For this illustration: range ÷ 6 = 60 ÷ 6 = 10, the standard deviation.

EXAMPLE

A sample of the rental rates at University Park Apartments approximates a symmetrical, bell-shaped distribution. The sample mean is \$500; the standard deviation is \$20. Using the Empirical Rule, answer these questions:

1. About 68% of the monthly rentals are between what two amounts?
2. About 95% of the monthly rentals are between what two amounts?
3. Almost all of the monthly rentals are between what two amounts?

SOLUTION

1. About 68% are between \$480 and \$520, found by $\bar{x} \pm 1s = \$500 \pm 1(\$20)$.
2. About 95% are between \$460 and \$540, found by $\bar{x} \pm 2s = \$500 \pm 2(\$20)$.
3. Almost all (99.7%) are between \$440 and \$560, found by $\bar{x} \pm 3s = \$500 \pm 3(\$20)$.

SELF-REVIEW 3–9

The Pitney Pipe Company is one of several domestic manufacturers of PVC pipe. The quality control department sampled 600 10-foot lengths. At a point 1 foot from the end of the pipe, they measured the outside diameter. The mean was 14.0 inches and the standard deviation 0.1 inch.

(a) If the shape of the distribution is not known, at least what percent of the observations will be between 13.85 inches and 14.15 inches?

(b) If we assume that the distribution of diameters is symmetrical and bell-shaped, about 95% of the observations will be between what two values?

EXERCISES

53. According to Chebyshev's theorem, at least what percent of any set of observations will be within 1.8 standard deviations of the mean?

54. The mean income of a group of sample observations is \$500; the standard deviation is \$40. According to Chebyshev's theorem, at least what percent of the incomes will lie between \$400 and \$600?

55. The distribution of the weights of a sample of 1,400 cargo containers is symmetric and bell-shaped. According to the Empirical Rule, what percent of the weights will lie:

a. Between $\bar{x} - 2s$ and $\bar{x} + 2s$?

b. Between $\bar{x}$ and $\bar{x} + 2s$? Below $\bar{x} - 2s$?

56. The following graph portrays the distribution of the number of Biggie-sized soft drinks sold at a nearby Wendy's for the last 141 days. The mean number of drinks sold per day is 91.9 and the standard deviation is 4.67.

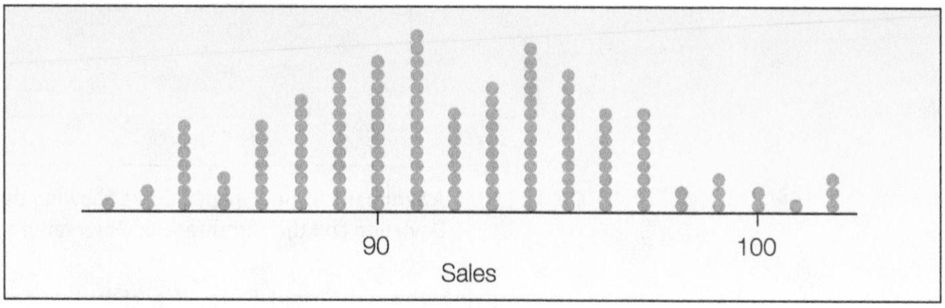

If we use the Empirical Rule, sales will be between what two values on 68% of the days? Sales will be between what two values on 95% of the days?

LO3-6
Compute the mean and standard deviation of grouped data.

THE MEAN AND STANDARD DEVIATION OF GROUPED DATA

In most instances, measures of location, such as the mean, and measures of dispersion, such as the standard deviation, are determined by using the individual values. Statistical software packages make it easy to calculate these values, even for large data sets. However, sometimes we are given only the frequency distribution and wish to estimate the mean or standard deviation. In the following discussion, we show how we can estimate the mean and standard deviation from data organized into a frequency distribution. We should stress that a mean or a standard deviation from grouped data is an *estimate* of the corresponding actual values.

STATISTICS IN ACTION

Buster Posey of the San Francisco Giants had the highest batting average, at .336, during the 2012 Major League Baseball season. Tony Gwynn hit .394 in the strike-shortened season of 1994, and Ted Williams hit .406 in 1941. No one has hit over .400 since 1941. The mean batting average has remained constant at about .260 for more than 100 years, but the standard deviation declined from .049 to .031. This indicates less dispersion in the batting averages today and helps explain the lack of any .400 hitters in recent times.

Arithmetic Mean of Grouped Data

To approximate the arithmetic mean of data organized into a frequency distribution, we begin by assuming the observations in each class are represented by the *midpoint* of the class. The mean of a sample of data organized in a frequency distribution is computed by:

ARITHMETIC MEAN OF GROUPED DATA

$$\bar{x} = \frac{\Sigma fM}{n} \qquad [3\text{–}11]$$

where:

- $\bar{x}$ is the designation for the sample mean.
- M is the midpoint of each class.
- f is the frequency in each class.
- fM is the frequency in each class times the midpoint of the class.
- ΣfM is the sum of these products.
- n is the total number of frequencies.

EXAMPLE

The computations for the arithmetic mean of data grouped into a frequency distribution will be shown based on the Applewood Auto Group profit data. Recall in Chapter 2, in Table 2–7 on page 30, we constructed a frequency distribution for the vehicle profit. The information is repeated below. Determine the arithmetic mean profit per vehicle.

Profit	Frequency
$ 200 up to $ 600	8
600 up to 1,000	11
1,000 up to 1,400	23
1,400 up to 1,800	38
1,800 up to 2,200	45
2,200 up to 2,600	32
2,600 up to 3,000	19
3,000 up to 3,400	4
Total	180

SOLUTION

The mean vehicle selling price can be estimated from data grouped into a frequency distribution. To find the estimated mean, assume the midpoint of each class is representative of the data values in that class. Recall that the midpoint of a class is halfway between the lower class limits of two consecutive classes. To

find the midpoint of a particular class, we add the lower limits of two consecutive classes and divide by 2. Hence, the midpoint of the first class is \$400, found by (\$200 + \$600)/2. We assume the value of \$400 is representative of the eight values in that class. To put it another way, we assume the sum of the eight values in this class is \$3,200, found by 8(\$400). We continue the process of multiplying the class midpoint by the class frequency for each class and then sum these products. The results are summarized in Table 3–1.

TABLE 3–1 Profit on 180 Vehicles Sold Last Month at Applewood Auto Group

Profit	Frequency (f)	Midpoint (M)	fM
\$ 200 up to \$ 600	8	\$ 400	\$ 3,200
600 up to 1,000	11	800	8,800
1,000 up to 1,400	23	1,200	27,600
1,400 up to 1,800	38	1,600	60,800
1,800 up to 2,200	45	2,000	90,000
2,200 up to 2,600	32	2,400	76,800
2,600 up to 3,000	19	2,800	53,200
3,000 up to 3,400	4	3,200	12,800
Total	180		\$333,200

Solving for the arithmetic mean using formula (3–11), we get:

$$\bar{x} = \frac{\Sigma fM}{n} = \frac{\$333{,}200}{180} = \$1{,}851.11$$

We conclude that the mean profit per vehicle is about \$1,851.

Standard Deviation of Grouped Data

To calculate the standard deviation of data grouped into a frequency distribution, we need to adjust formula (3–10) slightly. We weight each of the squared differences by the number of frequencies in each class. The formula is:

STANDARD DEVIATION, GROUPED DATA

$$s = \sqrt{\frac{\Sigma f(M - \bar{x})^2}{n - 1}} \qquad [3\text{–}12]$$

where:

- s is the symbol for the sample standard deviation.
- M is the midpoint of the class.
- f is the class frequency.
- n is the number of observations in the sample.
- $\bar{x}$ is the designation for the sample mean.

EXAMPLE

Refer to the frequency distribution for the Applewood Auto Group profit data reported in Table 3–1. Compute the standard deviation of the vehicle selling prices.

SOLUTION

Following the same practice used earlier for computing the mean of data grouped into a frequency distribution, f is the class frequency, M the class midpoint, and n the number of observations.

Profit	Frequency (f)	Midpoint (M)	fM	$(M - \bar{x})$	$(M - \bar{x})^2$	$f(M - \bar{x})^2$
$ 200 up to $ 600	8	400	3,200	−1,451	2,105,401	16,843,208
600 up to 1,000	11	800	8,800	−1,051	1,104,601	12,150,611
1,000 up to 1,400	23	1,200	27,600	−651	423,801	9,747,423
1,400 up to 1,800	38	1,600	60,800	−251	63,001	2,394,038
1,800 up to 2,200	45	2,000	90,000	149	22,201	999,045
2,200 up to 2,600	32	2,400	76,800	549	301,401	9,644,832
2,600 up to 3,000	19	2,800	53,200	949	900,601	17,111,419
3,000 up to 3,400	4	3,200	12,800	1,349	1,819,801	7,279,204
Total	180		333,200			76,169,780

To find the standard deviation:

Step 1: Subtract the mean from the class midpoint. That is, find $(M - \bar{x})$ = ($400 − $1,851 = −$1,451) for the first class, for the second class ($800 − $1,851 = −$1,051), and so on.

Step 2: Square the difference between the class midpoint and the mean. For the first class, it would be $(\$400 - \$1{,}851)^2 = 2{,}105{,}401$, for the second class $(\$800 - \$1{,}851)^2 = 1{,}104{,}601$, and so on.

Step 3: Multiply the squared difference between the class midpoint and the mean by the class frequency. For the first class, the value is $8(\$400 - \$1{,}851)^2 = 16{,}843{,}208$; for the second, $11(\$800 - \$1{,}851)^2 = 12{,}150{,}611$, and so on.

Step 4: Sum the $f(M - \bar{x})^2$. The total is 76,169,920. To find the standard deviation, we insert these values in formula (3–12).

$$s = \sqrt{\frac{\Sigma f(M - \bar{x})^2}{n - 1}} = \sqrt{\frac{76{,}169{,}780}{180 - 1 -}} = 652.33$$

The mean and the standard deviation calculated from the data grouped into a frequency distribution are usually close to the values calculated from raw data. The grouped data result in some loss of information. For the vehicle profit example, the mean profit reported in the Excel output on page 63 is $1,843.17 and the standard deviation is $643.63. The respective values estimated from data grouped into a frequency distribution are $1,851.11 and $652.33. The difference in the means is $7.94, or about 0.4%. The standard deviations differ by $8.70, or 1.4%. Based on the percentage difference, the estimates are very close to the actual values.

SELF-REVIEW 3–10

The net incomes of a sample of large importers of antiques were organized into the following table:

Net Income ($ millions)	Number of Importers
2 up to 6	1
6 up to 10	4
10 up to 14	10
14 up to 18	3
18 up to 22	2

(a) What is the table called?
(b) Based on the distribution, what is the estimate of the arithmetic mean net income?
(c) Based on the distribution, what is the estimate of the standard deviation?

EXERCISES

57. When we compute the mean of a frequency distribution, why do we refer to this as an *estimated* mean?

58. Estimate the mean and the standard deviation of the following frequency distribution.

Class	Frequency
0 up to 5	2
5 up to 10	7
10 up to 15	12
15 up to 20	6
20 up to 25	3

59. Estimate the mean and the standard deviation of the following frequency distribution.

Class	Frequency
20 up to 30	7
30 up to 40	12
40 up to 50	21
50 up to 60	18
60 up to 70	12

60. SCCoast, an Internet provider in the Southeast, developed the following frequency distribution on the age of Internet users. Estimate the mean and the standard deviation.

Age (years)	Frequency
10 up to 20	3
20 up to 30	7
30 up to 40	18
40 up to 50	20
50 up to 60	12

61. The IRS was interested in the number of individual tax forms prepared by small accounting firms. The IRS randomly sampled 50 public accounting firms with 10 or fewer employees in the Dallas–Fort Worth area. The following frequency table reports the results of the study. Estimate the mean and the standard deviation.

Number of Clients	Frequency
20 up to 30	1
30 up to 40	15
40 up to 50	22
50 up to 60	8
60 up to 70	4

62. Advertising expenses are a significant component of the cost of goods sold. Listed below is a frequency distribution showing the advertising expenditures for 60 manufacturing companies located in the Southwest. Estimate the mean and the standard deviation of advertising expenses.

Advertising Expenditure ($ millions)	Number of Companies
25 up to 35	5
35 up to 45	10
45 up to 55	21
55 up to 65	16
65 up to 75	8
Total	60

ETHICS AND REPORTING RESULTS

In Chapter 1, we discussed the ethical and unbiased reporting of statistical results. While you are learning about how to organize, summarize, and interpret data using statistics, it is also important to understand statistics so that you can be an intelligent consumer of information.

In this chapter, we learned how to compute numerical descriptive statistics. Specifically, we showed how to compute and interpret measures of location for a data set: the mean, median, and mode. We also discussed the advantages and disadvantages for each statistic. For example, if a real estate developer tells a client that the average home in a particular subdivision sold for $150,000, we assume that $150,000 is a representative selling price for all the homes. But suppose that the client also asks what the median sales price is, and the median is $60,000. Why was the developer only reporting the mean price? This information is extremely important to a person's decision making when buying a home. Knowing the advantages and disadvantages of the mean, median, and mode is important as we report statistics and as we use statistical information to make decisions.

We also learned how to compute measures of dispersion: range, variance, and standard deviation. Each of these statistics also has advantages and disadvantages. Remember that the range provides information about the overall spread of a distribution. However, it does not provide any information about how the data are clustered or concentrated around the center of the distribution. As we learn more about statistics, we need to remember that when we use statistics we must maintain an independent and principled point of view. Any statistical report requires objective and honest communication of the results.

CHAPTER SUMMARY

I. A measure of location is a value used to describe the center of a set of data.

A. The arithmetic mean is the most widely reported measure of location.

1. It is calculated by adding the values of the observations and dividing by the total number of observations.

a. The formula for a population mean of ungrouped or raw data is

$$\mu = \frac{\Sigma x}{N} \qquad \textbf{[3–1]}$$

b. The formula for the mean of a sample is

$$\bar{x} = \frac{\Sigma x}{n} \qquad \textbf{[3–2]}$$

c. The formula for the sample mean of data in a frequency distribution is

$$\bar{x} = \frac{\Sigma fM}{n} \quad \textbf{[3–11]}$$

2. The major characteristics of the arithmetic mean are:
a. At least the interval scale of measurement is required.
b. All the data values are used in the calculation.
c. A set of data has only one mean. That is, it is unique.
d. The sum of the deviations from the mean equals 0.

B. The median is the value in the middle of a set of ordered data.
1. To find the median, sort the observations from minimum to maximum and identify the middle value.
2. The major characteristics of the median are:
a. At least the ordinal scale of measurement is required.
b. It is not influenced by extreme values.
c. Fifty percent of the observations are larger than the median.
d. It is unique to a set of data.

C. The mode is the value that occurs most often in a set of data.
1. The mode can be found for nominal-level data.
2. A set of data can have more than one mode.

D. The weighted mean is found by multiplying each observation by its corresponding weight.
1. The formula for determining the weighted mean is

$$\bar{x}_w = \frac{w_1x_1 + w_2x_2 + w_3x_3 + \cdots + w_nx_n}{w_1 + w_2 + w_3 + \cdots + w_n} \quad \textbf{[3–3]}$$

E. The geometric mean is the nth root of the product of n positive values.
1. The formula for the geometric mean is

$$GM = \sqrt[n]{(x_1)(x_2)(x_3)\cdots(x_n)} \quad \textbf{[3–4]}$$

2. The geometric mean is also used to find the rate of change from one period to another.

$$GM = \sqrt[n]{\frac{\text{Value at end of period}}{\text{Value at beginning of period}}} - 1 \quad \textbf{[3–5]}$$

3. The geometric mean is always equal to or less than the arithmetic mean.

II. The dispersion is the variation or spread in a set of data.

A. The range is the difference between the maximum and minimum values in a set of data.
1. The formula for the range is

$$\text{Range} = \text{Maximum value} - \text{Minimum value} \quad \textbf{[3–6]}$$

2. The major characteristics of the range are:
a. Only two values are used in its calculation.
b. It is influenced by extreme values.
c. It is easy to compute and to understand.

B. The variance is the mean of the squared deviations from the arithmetic mean.
1. The formula for the population variance is

$$\sigma^2 = \frac{\Sigma(x - \mu)^2}{N} \quad \textbf{[3–7]}$$

2. The formula for the sample variance is

$$s^2 = \frac{\Sigma(x - \bar{x})^2}{n - 1} \quad \textbf{[3–9]}$$

3. The major characteristics of the variance are:
a. All observations are used in the calculation.
b. The units are somewhat difficult to work with; they are the original units squared.

C. The standard deviation is the square root of the variance.
1. The major characteristics of the standard deviation are:
a. It is in the same units as the original data.
b. It is the square root of the average squared distance from the mean.
c. It cannot be negative.
d. It is the most widely reported measure of dispersion.

2. The formula for the sample standard deviation is

$$s = \sqrt{\frac{\Sigma(x - \bar{x})^2}{n - 1}} \qquad \textbf{[3–10]}$$

3. The formula for the standard deviation of grouped data is

$$s = \sqrt{\frac{\Sigma f(M - \bar{x})^2}{n - 1}} \qquad \textbf{[3–12]}$$

III. We use the standard deviation to describe a frequency distribution by applying Chebyshev's theorem or the Empirical Rule.

A. Chebyshev's theorem states that regardless of the shape of the distribution, at least $1 - 1/k^2$ of the observations will be within k standard deviations of the mean, where k is greater than 1.

B. The Empirical Rule states that for a bell-shaped distribution about 68% of the values will be within one standard deviation of the mean, 95% within two, and virtually all within three.

PRONUNCIATION KEY

SYMBOL	MEANING	PRONUNCIATION
μ	Population mean	*mu*
Σ	Operation of adding	*sigma*
Σx	Adding a group of values	*sigma x*
$\bar{x}$	Sample mean	*x bar*
$\bar{x}_w$	Weighted mean	*x bar sub w*
GM	Geometric mean	*G M*
ΣfM	Adding the product of the frequencies and the class midpoints	*sigma f M*
σ^2	Population variance	*sigma squared*
σ	Population standard deviation	*sigma*

CHAPTER EXERCISES

63. The accounting firm of Crawford and Associates has five senior partners. Yesterday the senior partners saw six, four, three, seven, and five clients, respectively.

a. Compute the mean and median number of clients seen by the partners.

b. Is the mean a sample mean or a population mean?

c. Verify that $\Sigma(x - \mu) = 0$.

64. Owens Orchards sells apples in a large bag by weight. A sample of seven bags contained the following numbers of apples: 23, 19, 26, 17, 21, 24, 22.

a. Compute the mean and median number of apples in a bag.

b. Verify that $\Sigma(x - \bar{x}) = 0$.

For **DATA FILE**, please visit www.mhhe.com/lind16e

65. A sample of households that subscribe to United Bell Phone Company for landline phone service revealed the following number of calls received per household last week. Determine the mean and the median number of calls received.

52	43	30	38	30	42	12	46	39	37
34	46	32	18	41	5				

For **DATA FILE**, please visit www.mhhe.com/lind16e

66. The Citizens Banking Company is studying the number of times the ATM located in a Loblaws Supermarket at the foot of Market Street is used per day. Following are the number of times the machine was used daily over each of the last 30 days. Determine the mean number of times the machine was used per day.

83	64	84	76	84	54	75	59	70	61
63	80	84	73	68	52	65	90	52	77
95	36	78	61	59	84	95	47	87	60

For **DATA FILE**, please visit www.mhhe.com/lind16e

67. A recent study of the laundry habits of Americans included the time in minutes of the wash cycle. A sample of 40 observations follows. Determine the mean and the median of a typical wash cycle.

35	37	28	37	33	38	37	32	28	29
39	33	32	37	33	35	36	44	36	34
40	38	46	39	37	39	34	39	31	33
37	35	39	38	37	32	43	31	31	35

For **DATA FILE**, please visit www.mhhe.com/lind16e

68. Trudy Green works for the True-Green Lawn Company. Her job is to solicit lawn-care business via the telephone. Listed below is the number of appointments she made in each of the last 25 hours of calling. What is the arithmetic mean number of appointments she made per hour? What is the median number of appointments per hour? Write a brief report summarizing the findings.

9	5	2	6	5	6	4	4	7	2	3	6	3
4	4	7	8	4	4	5	5	4	8	3	3	

69. The Split-A-Rail Fence Company sells three types of fence to homeowners in suburban Seattle, Washington. Grade A costs $5.00 per running foot to install, Grade B costs $6.50 per running foot, and Grade C, the premium quality, costs $8.00 per running foot. Yesterday, Split-A-Rail installed 270 feet of Grade A, 300 feet of Grade B, and 100 feet of Grade C. What was the mean cost per foot of fence installed?

70. Rolland Poust is a sophomore in the College of Business at Scandia Tech. Last semester he took courses in statistics and accounting, 3 hours each, and earned an A in both. He earned a B in a 5-hour history course and a B in a 2-hour history of jazz course. In addition, he took a 1-hour course dealing with the rules of basketball so he could get his license to officiate high school basketball games. He got an A in this course. What was his GPA for the semester? Assume that he receives 4 points for an A, 3 for a B, and so on. What measure of location did you just calculate?

71. The table below shows the percent of the labor force that is unemployed and the size of the labor force for three counties in northwest Ohio. Jon Elsas is the Regional Director of Economic Development. He must present a report to several companies that are considering locating in northwest Ohio. What would be an appropriate unemployment rate to show for the entire region?

County	Percent Unemployed	Size of Workforce
Wood	4.5	15,300
Ottawa	3.0	10,400
Lucas	10.2	150,600

For **DATA FILE**, please visit www.mhhe.com/lind16e

72. The American Diabetes Association recommends a blood glucose reading of less than 130 for those with Type 2 diabetes. Blood glucose measures the amount of sugar in the blood. Below are the readings for February for a person recently diagnosed with Type 2 diabetes.

112	122	116	103	112	96	115	98	106	111
106	124	116	127	116	108	112	112	121	115
124	116	107	118	123	109	109	106		

a. What is the arithmetic mean glucose reading?
b. What is the median glucose reading?
c. What is the modal glucose reading?

73. The metropolitan area of Los Angeles–Long Beach, California, showed the largest increase in the number of jobs between 1989 and 2010. The number of jobs increased from 5,164,900 to 6,286,800. What was the geometric mean expected yearly rate of increase?

74. A recent article suggested that, if you earn $25,000 a year today and the inflation rate continues at 3% per year, you'll need to make $33,598 in 10 years to have the same buying power. You would need to make $44,771 if the inflation rate jumped to 6%. Confirm that these statements are accurate by finding the geometric mean rate of increase.

75. The ages of a sample of Canadian tourists flying from Toronto to Hong Kong were 32, 21, 60, 47, 54, 17, 72, 55, 33, and 41.

a. Compute the range.
b. Compute the standard deviation.

76. The weights (in pounds) of a sample of five boxes being sent by UPS are 12, 6, 7, 3, and 10.

a. Compute the range.
b. Compute the standard deviation.

77. The enrollments of the 13 public universities in the state of Ohio are listed below.

For **DATA FILE**, please visit www.mhhe.com/lind16e

College	Enrollment
University of Akron	26,666
Bowling Green State University	17,298
Central State University	2,152
University of Cincinnati	33,347
Cleveland State University	17,529
Kent State University	27,706
Miami University	16,924
Ohio State University	56,387
Ohio University	25,223
Shawnee State University	4,630
University of Toledo	21,500
Wright State University	16,762
Youngstown State University	13,813

a. Is this a sample or a population?
b. What is the mean enrollment?
c. What is the median enrollment?
d. What is the range of the enrollments?
e. Compute the standard deviation.

78. Health issues are a concern of managers, especially as they evaluate the cost of medical insurance. A recent survey of 150 executives at Elvers Industries, a large insurance and financial firm located in the Southwest, reported the number of pounds by which the executives were overweight. Compute the mean and the standard deviation.

Pounds Overweight	Frequency
0 up to 6	14
6 up to 12	42
12 up to 18	58
18 up to 24	28
24 up to 30	8

79. The Apollo space program lasted from 1967 until 1972 and included 13 missions. The missions lasted from as little as 7 hours to as long as 301 hours. The duration of each flight is listed below.

For **DATA FILE**, please visit www.mhhe.com/lind16e

9	195	241	301	216	260	7	244	192	147
10	295	142							

a. Explain why the flight times are a population.
b. Find the mean and median of the flight times.
c. Find the range and the standard deviation of the flight times.

INTRODUCTION

Chapter 2 began our study of descriptive statistics. In order to transform raw or ungrouped data into a meaningful form, we organize the data into a frequency distribution. We present the frequency distribution in graphic form as a histogram or a frequency polygon. This allows us to visualize where the data tend to cluster, the largest and the smallest values, and the general shape of the data.

In Chapter 3, we first computed several measures of location, such as the mean, median, and mode. These measures of location allow us to report a typical value in the set of observations. We also computed several measures of dispersion, such as the range, variance, and standard deviation. These measures of dispersion allow us to describe the variation or the spread in a set of observations.

We continue our study of descriptive statistics in this chapter. We study (1) dot plots, (2) stem-and-leaf displays, (3) percentiles, and (4) box plots. These charts and statistics give us additional insight into where the values are concentrated as well as the general shape of the data. Then we consider bivariate data. In bivariate data, we observe two variables for each individual or observation. Examples include the number of hours a student studied and the points earned on an examination; whether a sampled product is acceptable or not and the shift on which it is manufactured; and the amount of electricity used in a month by a homeowner and the mean daily high temperature in the region for the month.

LO4-1
Construct and interpret a dot plot.

DOT PLOTS

Recall for the Applewood Auto Group data, we summarized the profit earned on the 180 vehicles sold into eight classes. When we organized the data into the eight classes, we lost the exact value of the observations. A **dot plot,** on the other hand, groups the data as little as possible, and we do not lose the identity of an individual observation. To develop a dot plot, we display a dot for each observation along a horizontal number line indicating the possible values of the data. If there are identical observations or the observations are too close to be shown individually, the dots are "piled" on top of each other. This allows us to see the shape of the distribution, the value about which the data tend to cluster, and the largest and smallest observations. Dot plots are most useful for smaller data sets, whereas histograms tend to be most useful for large data sets. An example will show how to construct and interpret dot plots.

EXAMPLE

The service departments at Tionesta Ford Lincoln Mercury and Sheffield Motors Inc., two of the four Applewood Auto Group dealerships, were both open 24 days last month. Listed below is the number of vehicles serviced last month at the two dealerships. Construct dot plots and report summary statistics to compare the two dealerships.

Tionesta Ford Lincoln Mercury					
Monday	**Tuesday**	**Wednesday**	**Thursday**	**Friday**	**Saturday**
23	33	27	28	39	26
30	32	28	33	35	32
29	25	36	31	32	27
35	32	35	37	36	30

Sheffield Motors Inc.					
Monday	Tuesday	Wednesday	Thursday	Friday	Saturday
31	35	44	36	34	37
30	37	43	31	40	31
32	44	36	34	43	36
26	38	37	30	42	33

SOLUTION

The Minitab system provides a dot plot and outputs the mean, median, maximum, and minimum values, and the standard deviation for the number of cars serviced at each dealership over the last 24 working days.

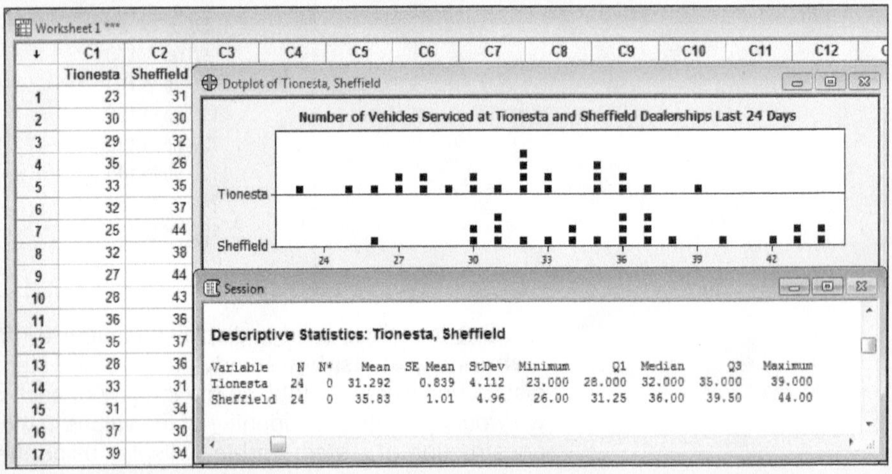

The dot plots, shown in the center of the output, graphically illustrate the distributions for each dealership. The plots show the difference in the location and dispersion of the observations. By looking at the dot plots, we can see that the number of vehicles serviced at the Sheffield dealership is more widely dispersed and has a larger mean than at the Tionesta dealership. Several other features of the number of vehicles serviced are:

- Tionesta serviced the fewest cars in any day, 23.
- Sheffield serviced 26 cars during their slowest day, which is 4 cars less than the next lowest day.
- Tionesta serviced exactly 32 cars on four different days.
- The numbers of cars serviced cluster around 36 for Sheffield and 32 for Tionesta.

From the descriptive statistics, we see Sheffield serviced a mean of 35.83 vehicles per day. Tionesta serviced a mean of 31.292 vehicles per day during the same period. So Sheffield typically services 4.54 more vehicles per day. There is also more dispersion, or variation, in the daily number of vehicles serviced at Sheffield than at Tionesta. How do we know this? The standard deviation is larger at Sheffield (4.96 vehicles per day) than at Tionesta (4.112 cars per day).

LO4-2
Construct and describe a stem-and-leaf display.

STEM-AND-LEAF DISPLAYS

In Chapter 2, we showed how to organize data into a frequency distribution so we could summarize the raw data into a meaningful form. The major advantage to organizing the data into a frequency distribution is we get a quick visual picture of the shape of the distribution without doing any further calculation. To put it another way, we can see where the data are concentrated and also determine whether there are any extremely large or small values. There are two disadvantages, however, to organizing the data into a frequency distribution: (1) we lose the exact identity of each value and (2) we are not sure how the values within each class are distributed. To explain, the following frequency distribution shows the number of advertising spots purchased by the 45 members of the Greater Buffalo Automobile Dealers Association in 2010. We observe that 7 of the 45 dealers purchased at least 90 but less than 100 spots. However, are the spots purchased within this class clustered about 90, spread evenly throughout the class, or clustered near 99? We cannot tell.

Number of Spots Purchased	Frequency
80 up to 90	2
90 up to 100	7
100 up to 110	6
110 up to 120	9
120 up to 130	8
130 up to 140	7
140 up to 150	3
150 up to 160	3
Total	45

One technique used to display quantitative information in a condensed form is the **stem-and-leaf display.** An advantage of the stem-and-leaf display over a frequency distribution is we do not lose the identity of each observation. In the above example, we would not know the identity of the values in the 90 up to 100 class. To illustrate the construction of a stem-and-leaf display using the number of advertising spots purchased, suppose the seven observations in the 90 up to 100 class are 96, 94, 93, 94, 95, 96, and 97. The **stem** value is the leading digit or digits, in this case 9. The **leaves** are the trailing digits. The stem is placed to the left of a vertical line and the leaf values to the right.

The values in the 90 up to 100 class would appear as follows:

```
9 | 6 4 3 4 5 6 7
```

It is also customary to sort the values within each stem from smallest to largest. Thus, the second row of the stem-and-leaf display would appear as follows:

```
9 | 3 4 4 5 6 6 7
```

With the stem-and-leaf display, we can quickly observe that two dealers purchased 94 spots and the number of spots purchased ranged from 93 to 97. A stem-and-leaf display is similar to a frequency distribution with more information, that is, the identity of the observations is preserved.

STEM-AND-LEAF DISPLAY A statistical technique to present a set of data. Each numerical value is divided into two parts. The leading digit(s) becomes the stem and the trailing digit the leaf. The stems are located along the vertical axis, and the leaf values are stacked against each other along the horizontal axis.

The following example explains the details of developing a stem-and-leaf display.

EXAMPLE

Listed in Table 4–1 is the number of 30-second radio advertising spots purchased by each of the 45 members of the Greater Buffalo Automobile Dealers Association last year. Organize the data into a stem-and-leaf display. Around what values do the number of advertising spots tend to cluster? What is the fewest number of spots purchased by a dealer? The largest number purchased?

TABLE 4–1 Number of Advertising Spots Purchased by Members of the Greater Buffalo Automobile Dealers Association

96	93	88	117	127	95	113	96	108	94	148	156
139	142	94	107	125	155	155	103	112	127	117	120
112	135	132	111	125	104	106	139	134	119	97	89
118	136	125	143	120	103	113	124	138			

SOLUTION

From the data in Table 4–1, we note that the smallest number of spots purchased is 88. So we will make the first stem value 8. The largest number is 156, so we will have the stem values begin at 8 and continue to 15. The first number in Table 4–1 is 96, which has a stem value of 9 and a leaf value of 6. Moving across the top row, the second value is 93 and the third is 88. After the first 3 data values are considered, your chart is as follows.

Stem	Leaf
8	8
9	6 3
10	
11	
12	
13	
14	
15	

Organizing all the data, the stem-and-leaf chart looks as follows.

Stem	Leaf
8	8 9
9	6 3 5 6 4 4 7
10	8 7 3 4 6 3
11	7 3 2 7 2 1 9 8 3
12	7 5 7 0 5 5 0 4
13	9 5 2 9 4 6 8
14	8 2 3
15	6 5 5

The usual procedure is to sort the leaf values from the smallest to largest. The last line, the row referring to the values in the 150s, would appear as:

15	5	5	6

The final table would appear as follows, where we have sorted all of the leaf values.

Stem	Leaf
8	8 9
9	3 4 4 5 6 6 7
10	3 3 4 6 7 8
11	1 2 2 3 3 7 7 8 9
12	0 0 4 5 5 5 7 7
13	2 4 5 6 8 9 9
14	2 3 8
15	5 5 6

You can draw several conclusions from the stem-and-leaf display. First, the minimum number of spots purchased is 88 and the maximum is 156. Two dealers purchased less than 90 spots, and three purchased 150 or more. You can observe, for example, that the three dealers who purchased more than 150 spots actually purchased 155, 155, and 156 spots. The concentration of the number of spots is between 110 and 130. There were nine dealers who purchased between 110 and 119 spots and eight who purchased between 120 and 129 spots. We can also tell that within the 120 to 129 group the actual number of spots purchased was spread evenly throughout. That is, two dealers purchased 120 spots, one dealer purchased 124 spots, three dealers purchased 125 spots, and two purchased 127 spots.

We can also generate this information on the Minitab software system. We have named the variable *Spots.* The Minitab output is below. You can find the Minitab commands that will produce this output in Appendix C.

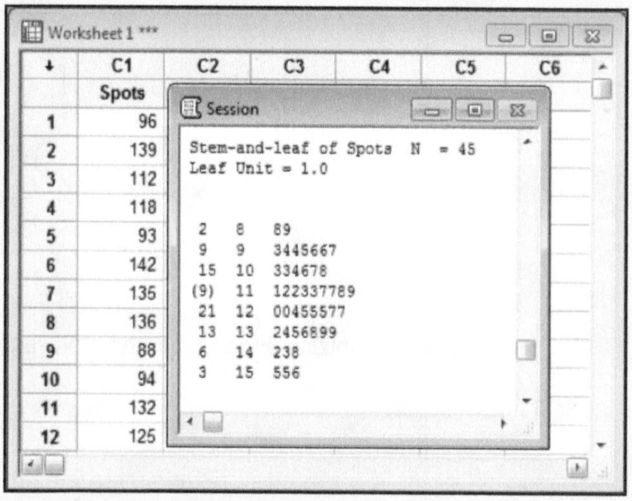

The Minitab solution provides some additional information regarding cumulative totals. In the column to the left of the stem values are numbers such as 2, 9, 15, and so on. The number 9 indicates there are 9 observations that have occurred before the value of 100. The number 15 indicates that 15 observations have occurred prior to 110. About halfway down the column the number 9 appears in parentheses. The parentheses indicate that the middle value or median appears in that row and there are nine values in this group. In this case, we describe the middle value as the value below which half of the observations occur. There are a total of 45 observations, so the middle value, if the data were arranged from smallest to largest, would be the 23rd observation; its value is 118. After the median, the values begin to decline. These values represent the "more than" cumulative totals. There are 21 observations of 120 or more, 13 of 130 or more, and so on.

Which is the better choice, a dot plot or a stem-and-leaf chart? This is really a matter of personal choice and convenience. For presenting data, especially with a large number of observations, you will find dot plots are more frequently used. You will see dot plots in analytical literature, marketing reports, and occasionally in annual reports. If you are doing a quick analysis for yourself, stem-and-leaf tallies are handy and easy, particularly on a smaller set of data.

SELF-REVIEW 4–1

1. The number of employees at each of the 142 Home Depot stores in the Southeast region is shown in the following dot plot.

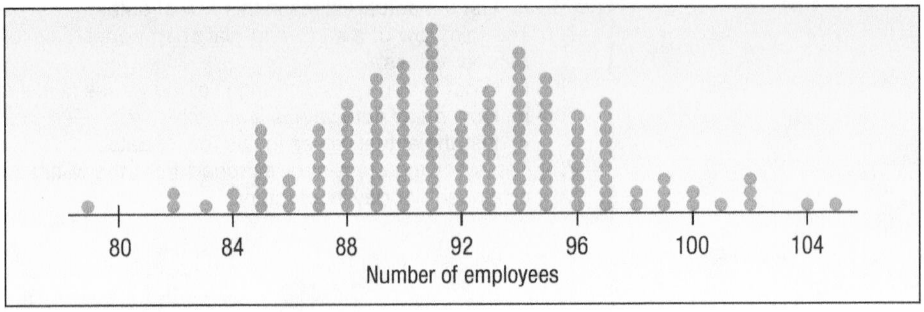

   (a) What are the maximum and minimum numbers of employees per store?
   (b) How many stores employ 91 people?
   (c) Around what values does the number of employees per store tend to cluster?
2. The rate of return for 21 stocks is:

8.3	9.6	9.5	9.1	8.8	11.2	7.7	10.1	9.9	10.8	
10.2	8.0	8.4	8.1	11.6	9.6	8.8	8.0	10.4	9.8	9.2

Organize this information into a stem-and-leaf display.
   (a) How many rates are less than 9.0?
   (b) List the rates in the 10.0 up to 11.0 category.
   (c) What is the median?
   (d) What are the maximum and the minimum rates of return?

EXERCISES

1. Describe the differences between a histogram and a dot plot. When might a dot plot be better than a histogram?
2. Describe the differences between a histogram and a stem-and-leaf display.
3. Consider the following chart.

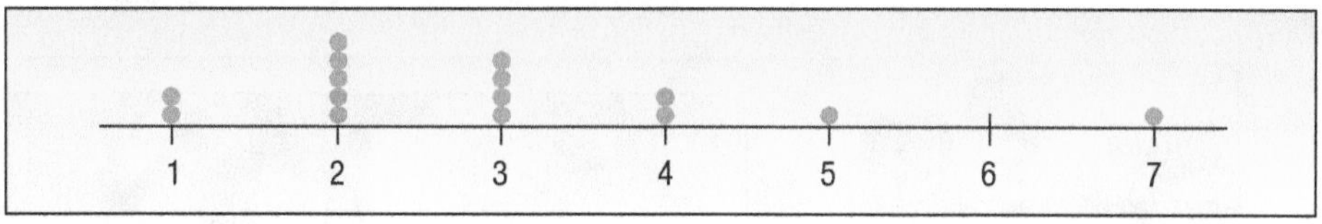

a. What is this chart called?
b. How many observations are in the study?
c. What are the maximum and the minimum values?
d. Around what values do the observations tend to cluster?

4. The following chart reports the number of cell phones sold at Radio Shack for the last 26 days.

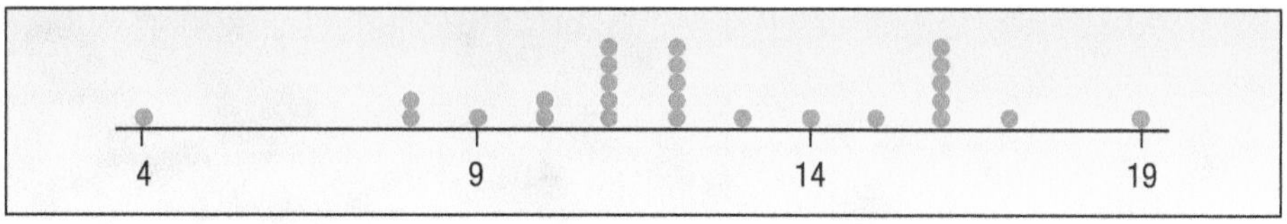

a. What are the maximum and the minimum numbers of cell phones sold in a day?
b. What is a typical number of cell phones sold?

5. The first row of a stem-and-leaf chart appears as follows: 62 | 1 3 3 7 9. Assume whole number values.
a. What is the "possible range" of the values in this row?
b. How many data values are in this row?
c. List the actual values in this row of data.
6. The third row of a stem-and-leaf chart appears as follows: 21 | 0 1 3 5 7 9. Assume whole number values.
a. What is the "possible range" of the values in this row?
b. How many data values are in this row?
c. List the actual values in this row of data.
7. The following stem-and-leaf chart from the Minitab software shows the number of units produced per day in a factory.

1	3	8
1	4	
2	5	6
9	6	0133559
(7)	7	0236778
9	8	59
7	9	00156
2	10	36

a. How many days were studied?
b. How many observations are in the first class?
c. What are the minimum value and the maximum value?

d. List the actual values in the fourth row.
e. List the actual values in the second row.
f. How many values are less than 70?
g. How many values are 80 or more?
h. What is the median?
i. How many values are between 60 and 89, inclusive?

8. The following stem-and-leaf chart reports the number of movies rented per day at Video Connection on the corner of Fourth and Main Streets.

3	12	689
6	13	123
10	14	6889
13	15	589
15	16	35
20	17	24568
23	18	268
(5)	19	13456
22	20	034679
16	21	2239
12	22	789
9	23	00179
4	24	8
3	25	13
1	26	
1	27	0

a. How many days were studied?
b. How many observations are in the last class?
c. What are the maximum and the minimum values in the entire set of data?
d. List the actual values in the fourth row.
e. List the actual values in the next to the last row.
f. On how many days were less than 160 movies rented?
g. On how many days were 220 or more movies rented?
h. What is the middle value?
i. On how many days were between 170 and 210 movies rented?

For **DATA FILE**, please visit www.mhhe.com/lind16e

9. A survey of the number of phone calls made by a sample of 16 Verizon subscribers last week revealed the following information. Develop a stem-and-leaf chart. How many calls did a typical subscriber make? What were the maximum and the minimum number of calls made?

52	43	30	38	30	42	12	46	39
37	34	46	32	18	41	5		

For **DATA FILE**, please visit www.mhhe.com/lind16e

10. Aloha Banking Co. is studying ATM use in suburban Honolulu. A sample of 30 ATMs showed they were used the following number of times yesterday. Develop a stem-and-leaf chart. Summarize the number of times each ATM was used. What were the typical, minimum, and maximum number of times each ATM was used?

83	64	84	76	84	54	75	59	70	61
63	80	84	73	68	52	65	90	52	77
95	36	78	61	59	84	95	47	87	60

LO4-3
Identify and compute measures of position.

MEASURES OF POSITION

The standard deviation is the most widely used measure of dispersion. However, there are other ways of describing the variation or spread in a set of data. One method is to determine the *location* of values that divide a set of observations into equal parts. These measures include **quartiles, deciles,** and **percentiles.**

Quartiles divide a set of observations into four equal parts. To explain further, think of any set of values arranged from the minimum to the maximum. In Chapter 3, we called the middle value of a set of data arranged from the minimum to the maximum the median. That is, 50% of the observations are larger than the median and 50% are smaller. The median is a measure of location because it pinpoints the center of the data. In a similar fashion, **quartiles** divide a set of observations into four equal parts. The first quartile, usually labeled Q_1, is the value below which 25% of the observations occur, and the third quartile, usually labeled Q_3, is the value below which 75% of the observations occur.

Similarly, **deciles** divide a set of observations into 10 equal parts and **percentiles** into 100 equal parts. So if you found that your GPA was in the 8th decile at your university, you could conclude that 80% of the students had a GPA lower than yours and 20% had a higher GPA. If your GPA was in the 92nd percentile, then 92% of students had a GPA less than your GPA and only 8% of students had a GPA greater than your GPA. Percentile scores are frequently used to report results on such national standardized tests as the SAT, ACT, GMAT (used to judge entry into many master of business administration programs), and LSAT (used to judge entry into law school).

Quartiles, Deciles, and Percentiles

To formalize the computational procedure, let L_p refer to the location of a desired percentile. So if we want to find the 92nd percentile we would use L_{92}, and if we wanted the median, the 50th percentile, then L_{50}. For a number of observations, n, the location of the *Pth* percentile, can be found using the formula:

LOCATION OF A PERCENTILE $$L_p = (n + 1)\frac{P}{100}$$ **[4–1]**

An example will help to explain further.

EXAMPLE

Listed below are the commissions earned last month by a sample of 15 brokers at Morgan Stanley Smith Barney's Oakland, California, office. Morgan Stanley Smith Barney is an investment company with offices located throughout the United States.

\$2,038	\$1,758	\$1,721	\$1,637	\$2,097	\$2,047	\$2,205	\$1,787	\$2,287
1,940	2,311	2,054	2,406	1,471	1,460			

Locate the median, the first quartile, and the third quartile for the commissions earned.

SOLUTION

The first step is to sort the data from the smallest commission to the largest.

$1,460	$1,471	$1,637	$1,721	$1,758	$1,787	$1,940	$2,038
2,047	2,054	2,097	2,205	2,287	2,311	2,406	

The median value is the observation in the center and is the same as the 50th percentile, so P equals 50. So the median or L_{50} is located at $(n + 1)(50/100)$, where n is the number of observations. In this case, that is position number 8, found by $(15 + 1)(50/100)$. The eighth-largest commission is $2,038. So we conclude this is the median and that half the brokers earned commissions more than $2,038 and half earned less than $2,038. The result using formula (4–1) to find the median is the same as the method presented in Chapter 3.

Recall the definition of a quartile. Quartiles divide a set of observations into four equal parts. Hence 25% of the observations will be less than the first quartile. Seventy-five percent of the observations will be less than the third quartile. To locate the first quartile, we use formula (4–1), where $n = 15$ and $P = 25$:

$$L_{25} = (n + 1)\frac{P}{100} = (15 + 1)\frac{25}{100} = 4$$

and to locate the third quartile, $n = 15$ and $P = 75$:

$$L_{75} = (n + 1)\frac{P}{100} = (15 + 1)\frac{75}{100} = 12$$

Therefore, the first and third quartile values are located at positions 4 and 12, respectively. The fourth value in the ordered array is $1,721 and the twelfth is $2,205. These are the first and third quartiles.

In the above example, the location formula yielded a whole number. That is, we wanted to find the first quartile and there were 15 observations, so the location formula indicated we should find the fourth ordered value. What if there were 20 observations in the sample, that is $n = 20$, and we wanted to locate the first quartile? From the location formula (4–1):

$$L_{25} = (n + 1)\frac{P}{100} = (20 + 1)\frac{25}{100} = 5.25$$

We would locate the fifth value in the ordered array and then move .25 of the distance between the fifth and sixth values and report that as the first quartile. Like the median, the quartile does not need to be one of the actual values in the data set.

To explain further, suppose a data set contained the six values 91, 75, 61, 101, 43, and 104. We want to locate the first quartile. We order the values from the minimum to the maximum: 43, 61, 75, 91, 101, and 104. The first quartile is located at

$$L_{25} = (n + 1)\frac{P}{100} = (6 + 1)\frac{25}{100} = 1.75$$

The position formula tells us that the first quartile is located between the first and the second values and it is .75 of the distance between the first and the second values.

STATISTICS IN ACTION

John W. Tukey (1915–2000) received a PhD in mathematics from Princeton in 1939. However, when he joined the Fire Control Research Office during World War II, his interest in abstract mathematics shifted to applied statistics. He developed effective numerical and graphical methods for studying patterns in data. Among the graphics he developed are the stem-and-leaf diagram and the box-and-whisker plot or box plot. From 1960 to 1980, Tukey headed the statistical division of NBC's election night vote projection team. He became renowned in 1960 for preventing an early call of victory for Richard Nixon in the presidential election won by John F. Kennedy.

The first value is 43 and the second is 61. So the distance between these two values is 18. To locate the first quartile, we need to move .75 of the distance between the first and second values, so .75(18) = 13.5. To complete the procedure, we add 13.5 to the first value, 43, and report that the first quartile is 56.5.

We can extend the idea to include both deciles and percentiles. To locate the 23rd percentile in a sample of 80 observations, we would look for the 18.63 position.

$$L_{23} = (n + 1)\frac{P}{100} = (80 + 1)\frac{23}{100} = 18.63$$

To find the value corresponding to the 23rd percentile, we would locate the 18th value and the 19th value and determine the distance between the two values. Next, we would multiply this difference by 0.63 and add the result to the smaller value. The result would be the 23rd percentile.

Statistical software is very helpful when describing and summarizing data. Excel, Minitab, and MegaStat, a statistical analysis Excel add-in, all provide summary statistics that include quartiles. For example, Minitab's summary of the Smith Barney commission data, shown below, includes the first and third quartiles, and other statistics. Based on the reported quartiles, 25% of the commissions earned were less than $1,721 and 75% were less than $2,205. These are the same values we calculated using formula (4–1).

Sheet1 ***

↓	C1
	Commissions
1	1460
2	1471
3	1637
4	1721

Session

Descriptive Statistics: Commissions

Variable	N	N*	Mean	SE Mean	StDev	Minimum	Q1	Median	Q3	Maximum
Commissions	15	0	1947.9	77.1	298.8	1460.0	1721.0	2038.0	2205.0	2406.0

SmithBarney.xlsx

	A	B	C	D
1	Commissions			
2	1460			
3	1471		Equation 4-1	
4	1637		Quartile 1	1721
5	1721			
6	1758		Quartile 3	2205
7	1787			
8	1940		Excel Method	
9	2038		Quartile 1	1739.5
10	2047			
11	2054		Quartile 3	2151
12	2097			
13	2205			
14	2287			
15	2311			
16	2406			

There are ways other than formula (4–1) to locate quartile values. For example, another method uses $0.25n + 0.75$ to locate the position of the first quartile and $0.75n + 0.25$ to locate the position of the third quartile. We will call this the *Excel Method.* In the Smith Barney data, this method would place the first quartile at position 4.5 (.25 × 15 + .75) and the third quartile at position 11.5 (.75 × 15 + .25). The first quartile would be interpolated as 0.5, or one-half the difference between the fourth- and the fifth-ranked values. Based on this method, the first quartile is $1739.5, found by ($1,721 + 0.5[$1,758 − $1,721]). The third quartile, at position 11.5, would be $2,151, or one-half the distance between the eleventh- and the twelfth-ranked values, found by ($2,097 + 0.5[$2,205 − $2,097]). Excel, as shown in the Smith Barney and Applewood examples, can compute quartiles using either of the two methods. **Please note the text uses formula (4–1) to calculate quartiles.**

Is the difference between the two methods important? No. Usually it is just a nuisance. In general, both methods calculate values that will support the statement that approximately 25% of the values are less than the value of the first quartile, and approximately 75% of the data values are less than the value of the third quartile. When the sample is large, the difference in the results from the two methods is small. For example, in the Applewood Auto Group data there are 180 vehicles. The

APPLEWOOD AUTO GROUP.xlsx

	A	B	C	D	E
1	**Age**	**Profit**			
2	44	$294			
3	40	$323		Equation 4-1	
4	42	$335		1st Quartile	1415.5
5	40	$352			
6	46	$369		3rd Quartile	2275.5
7	53	$377			
8	**30**	**$443**			
9	40	$482		Excel Method	
10	37	$732		1st Quartile	1422.5
11	**30**	**$754**			
12	62	$783		3rd Quartile	2268.5

quartiles computed using both methods are shown to the left. Based on the variable profit, 45 of the 180 values (25%) are less than both values of the first quartile, and 135 of the 180 values (75%) are less than both values of the third quartile.

When using Excel, be careful to understand the method used to calculate quartiles. In Excel 2007, quartiles are calculated using the *Excel Method.* Excel 2010 provides both methods to calculate quartiles. The Excel 2010 commands to compute the quartiles are shown in Appendix C.

SELF-REVIEW 4–2

The Quality Control department of Plainsville Peanut Company is responsible for checking the weight of the 8-ounce jar of peanut butter. The weights of a sample of nine jars produced last hour are:

7.69	7.72	7.8	7.86	7.90	7.94	7.97	8.06	8.09

(a) What is the median weight?
(b) Determine the weights corresponding to the first and third quartiles.

EXERCISES

For **DATA FILE**, please visit www.mhhe.com/lind16e

For **DATA FILE**, please visit www.mhhe.com/lind16e

For **DATA FILE**, please visit www.mhhe.com/lind16e

11. Determine the median and the first and third quartiles in the following data.

46	47	49	49	51	53	54	54	55	55	59

12. Determine the median and the first and third quartiles in the following data.

5.24	6.02	6.67	7.30	7.59	7.99	8.03	8.35	8.81	9.45
9.61	10.37	10.39	11.86	12.22	12.71	13.07	13.59	13.89	15.42

13. The Thomas Supply Company Inc. is a distributor of gas-powered generators. As with any business, the length of time customers take to pay their invoices is important. Listed below, arranged from smallest to largest, is the time, in days, for a sample of The Thomas Supply Company Inc. invoices.

13	13	13	20	26	27	31	34	34	34	35	35	36	37	38
41	41	41	45	47	47	47	50	51	53	54	56	62	67	82

a. Determine the first and third quartiles.
b. Determine the second decile and the eighth decile.
c. Determine the 67th percentile.

For **DATA FILE**, please visit www.mhhe.com/lind16e

14. Kevin Horn is the national sales manager for National Textbooks Inc. He has a sales staff of 40 who visit college professors all over the United States. Each Saturday morning he requires his sales staff to send him a report. This report includes, among other things, the number of professors visited during the previous week. Listed below, ordered from smallest to largest, are the number of visits last week.

38	40	41	45	48	48	50	50	51	51	52	52	53	54	55	55	55	56	56	57
59	59	59	62	62	62	63	64	65	66	66	67	67	69	69	71	77	78	79	79

a. Determine the median number of calls.
b. Determine the first and third quartiles.
c. Determine the first decile and the ninth decile.
d. Determine the 33rd percentile.

LO4-4 Construct and analyze a box plot.

BOX PLOTS

A **box plot** is a graphical display, based on quartiles, that helps us picture a set of data. To construct a box plot, we need only five statistics: the minimum value, Q_1 (the first quartile), the median, Q_3 (the third quartile), and the maximum value. An example will help to explain.

EXAMPLE

Alexander's Pizza offers free delivery of its pizza within 15 miles. Alex, the owner, wants some information on the time it takes for delivery. How long does a typical delivery take? Within what range of times will most deliveries be completed? For a sample of 20 deliveries, he determined the following information:

$$\text{Minimum value} = 13 \text{ minutes}$$
$$Q_1 = 15 \text{ minutes}$$
$$\text{Median} = 18 \text{ minutes}$$
$$Q_3 = 22 \text{ minutes}$$
$$\text{Maximum value} = 30 \text{ minutes}$$

Develop a box plot for the delivery times. What conclusions can you make about the delivery times?

SOLUTION

The first step in drawing a box plot is to create an appropriate scale along the horizontal axis. Next, we draw a box that starts at Q_1 (15 minutes) and ends at Q_3 (22 minutes). Inside the box we place a vertical line to represent the median (18 minutes). Finally, we extend horizontal lines from the box out to the minimum value (13 minutes) and the maximum value (30 minutes). These horizontal lines outside of the box are sometimes called "whiskers" because they look a bit like a cat's whiskers.

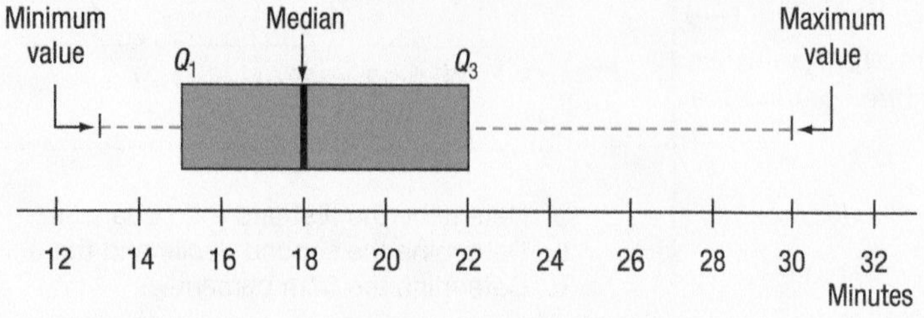

The box plot also shows the interquartile range of delivery times between Q1 and Q3. The **interquartile range** is 7 minutes and indicates that 50% of the deliveries are between 15 and 22 minutes.

The box plot also reveals that the distribution of delivery times is positively skewed. In Chapter 3, we defined skewness as the lack of symmetry in a set of data. How do we know this distribution is positively skewed? In this case, there are actually two pieces of information that suggest this. First, the dashed line to the right of the box from 22 minutes (Q_3) to the maximum time of 30 minutes is longer than the dashed line from the left of 15 minutes (Q_1) to the minimum value of 13 minutes. To put it another way, the 25% of the data larger than the third quartile is more spread out than the 25% less than the first quartile. A second indication of positive skewness is that the median is not in the center of the box. The distance from the first quartile to the median is smaller than the distance from the median to the third quartile. We know that the number of delivery times between 15 minutes and 18 minutes is the same as the number of delivery times between 18 minutes and 22 minutes.

EXAMPLE

Refer to the Applewood Auto Group data. Develop a box plot for the variable age of the buyer. What can we conclude about the distribution of the age of the buyer?

SOLUTION

Minitab was used to develop the following chart and summary statistics.

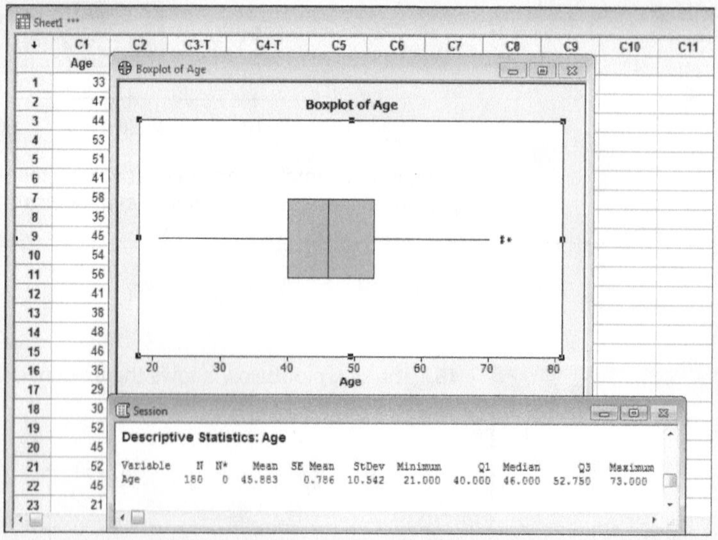

The median age of the purchaser is 46 years, 25% of the purchasers are less than 40 years of age, and 25% are more than 52.75 years of age. Based on the summary information and the box plot, we conclude:

- Fifty percent of the purchasers are between the ages of 40 and 52.75 years.
- The distribution of ages is symmetric. There are two reasons for this conclusion. The length of the whisker above 52.75 years (Q_3) is about the same

length as the whisker below 40 years (Q_1). Also, the area in the box between 40 years and the median of 46 years is about the same as the area between the median and 52.75.

There are three asterisks (*) above 70 years. What do they indicate? In a box plot, an asterisk identifies an **outlier.** An outlier is a value that is inconsistent with the rest of the data. It is defined as a value that is more than 1.5 times the interquartile range smaller than Q_1 or larger than Q_3. In this example, an outlier would be a value larger than 71.875 years, found by:

$$\textit{Outlier} > Q_3 + 1.5(Q_3 - Q_1) = 52.75 + 1.5(52.75 - 40) = 71.875$$

An outlier would also be a value less than 20.875 years.

$$\textit{Outlier} < Q_1 - 1.5(Q_3 - Q_1) = 40 - 1.5(52.75 - 40) = 20.875$$

From the box plot, we conclude there are three purchasers 72 years of age or older and none less than 21 years of age. Technical note: In some cases, a single asterisk may represent more than one observation because of the limitations of the software and space available. It is a good idea to check the actual data. In this instance, there are three purchasers 72 years old or older; two are 72 and one is 73.

SELF-REVIEW 4–3

The following box plot shows the assets in millions of dollars for credit unions in Seattle, Washington.

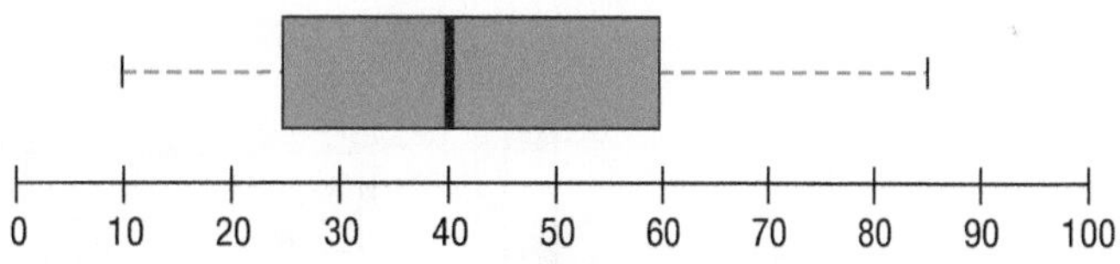

What are the smallest and largest values, the first and third quartiles, and the median? Would you agree that the distribution is symmetrical? Are there any outliers?

EXERCISES

15. The box plot below shows the amount spent for books and supplies per year by students at four-year public colleges.

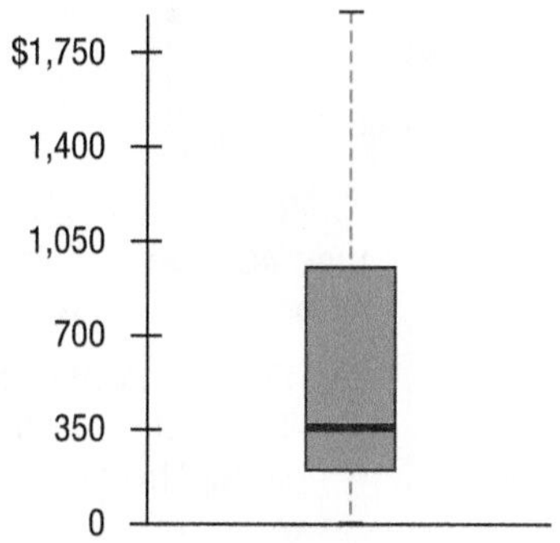

a. Estimate the median amount spent.
b. Estimate the first and third quartiles for the amount spent.
c. Estimate the interquartile range for the amount spent.
d. Beyond what point is a value considered an outlier?
e. Identify any outliers and estimate their value.
f. Is the distribution symmetrical or positively or negatively skewed?

16. The box plot shows the undergraduate in-state charge per credit hour at four-year public colleges.

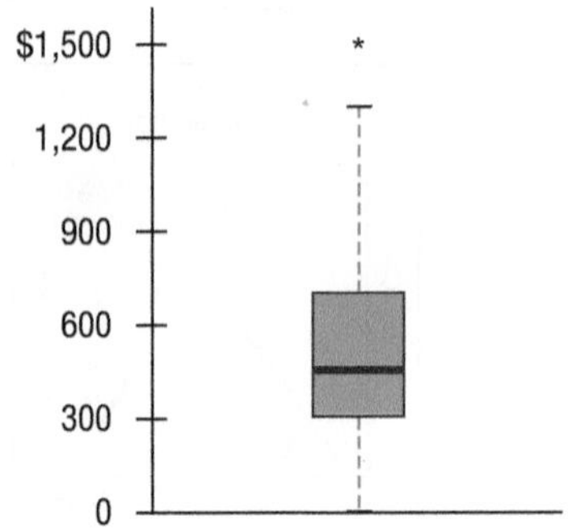

a. Estimate the median.
b. Estimate the first and third quartiles.
c. Determine the interquartile range.
d. Beyond what point is a value considered an outlier?
e. Identify any outliers and estimate their value.
f. Is the distribution symmetrical or positively or negatively skewed?

17. In a study of the gasoline mileage of model year 2013 automobiles, the mean miles per gallon was 27.5 and the median was 26.8. The smallest value in the study was 12.70 miles per gallon, and the largest was 50.20. The first and third quartiles were 17.95 and 35.45 miles per gallon, respectively. Develop a box plot and comment on the distribution. Is it a symmetric distribution?

For **DATA FILE**, please visit www.mhhe.com/lind16e

18. A sample of 28 time shares in the Orlando, Florida, area revealed the following daily charges for a one-bedroom suite. For convenience, the data are ordered from smallest to largest. Construct a box plot to represent the data. Comment on the distribution. Be sure to identify the first and third quartiles and the median.

$116	$121	$157	$192	$207	$209	$209
229	232	236	236	239	243	246
260	264	276	281	283	289	296
307	309	312	317	324	341	353

LO4-5
Compute and interpret the coefficient of skewness.

SKEWNESS

In Chapter 3, we described measures of central location for a set of observations by reporting the mean, median, and mode. We also described measures that show the amount of spread or variation in a set of data, such as the range and the standard deviation.

Another characteristic of a set of data is the shape. There are four shapes commonly observed: symmetric, positively skewed, negatively skewed, and bimodal. In a **symmetric** set of observations the mean and median are equal and the data values are evenly spread around these values. The data values below the mean and median are a mirror image of those above. A set of values is **skewed to the right** or **positively skewed** if there is a single peak, but the values extend much farther to the right of the peak than to the left of the peak. In this case, the mean is larger than the median. In a **negatively skewed** distribution there is a single peak, but the observations extend

farther to the left, in the negative direction, than to the right. In a negatively skewed distribution, the mean is smaller than the median. Positively skewed distributions are more common. Salaries often follow this pattern. Think of the salaries of those employed in a small company of about 100 people. The president and a few top executives would have very large salaries relative to the other workers and hence the distribution of salaries would exhibit positive skewness. A **bimodal distribution** will have two or more peaks. This is often the case when the values are from two or more populations. This information is summarized in Chart 4-1.

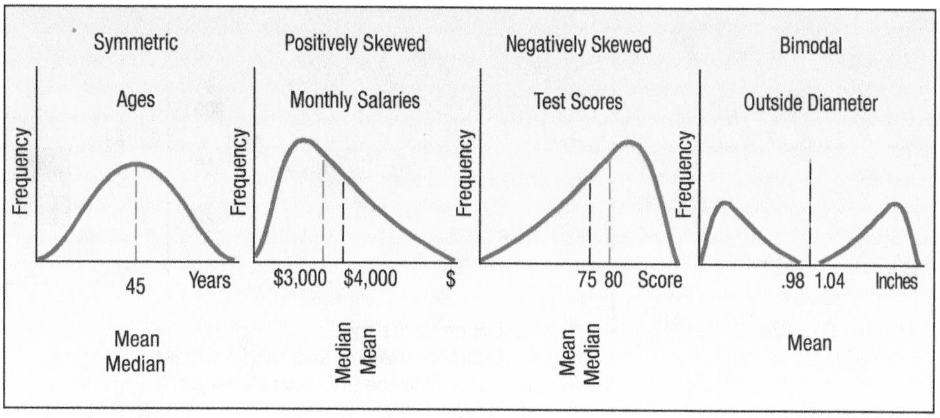

CHART 4-1 Shapes of Frequency Polygons

There are several formulas in the statistical literature used to calculate skewness. The simplest, developed by Professor Karl Pearson (1857–1936), is based on the difference between the mean and the median.

STATISTICS IN ACTION

The late Stephen Jay Gould (1941–2002) was a professor of zoology and professor of geology at Harvard University. In 1982, he was diagnosed with cancer and had an expected survival time of 8 months. However, never to be discouraged, his research showed that the distribution of survival time is dramatically skewed to the right and showed that not only do 50% of similar cancer patients survive more than 8 months, but that the survival time could be years rather than months! In fact, Dr. Gould lived another 20 years. Based on his experience, he wrote a widely published essay titled "The Median Is Not the Message."

PEARSON'S COEFFICIENT OF SKEWNESS

$$sk = \frac{3(\bar{x} - \text{Median})}{s} \qquad [4\text{–}2]$$

Using this relationship, the coefficient of skewness can range from −3 up to 3. A value near −3, such as −2.57, indicates considerable negative skewness. A value such as 1.63 indicates moderate positive skewness. A value of 0, which will occur when the mean and median are equal, indicates the distribution is symmetrical and there is no skewness present.

In this text, we present output from Minitab and Excel. Both of these software packages compute a value for the coefficient of skewness based on the cubed deviations from the mean. The formula is:

SOFTWARE COEFFICIENT OF SKEWNESS

$$sk = \frac{n}{(n-1)(n-2)}\left[\sum\left(\frac{x-\bar{x}}{s}\right)^3\right] \qquad [4\text{–}3]$$

Formula (4–3) offers an insight into skewness. The right-hand side of the formula is the difference between each value and the mean, divided by the standard deviation. That is the portion $(x - \bar{x})/s$ of the formula. This idea is called **standardizing.** We will discuss the idea of standardizing a value in more detail in Chapter 7 when we describe the normal probability distribution. At this point, observe that the result is to report the difference between each value and the mean in units of the standard deviation. If this difference is positive, the particular value is larger than the mean; if the

value is negative, the standardized quantity is smaller than the mean. When we cube these values, we retain the information on the direction of the difference. Recall that in the formula for the standard deviation [see formula (3–10)] we squared the difference between each value and the mean, so that the result was all nonnegative values.

If the set of data values under consideration is symmetric, when we cube the standardized values and sum over all the values, the result would be near zero. If there are several large values, clearly separate from the others, the sum of the cubed differences would be a large positive value. If there are several small values clearly separate from the others, the sum of the cubed differences will be negative.

An example will illustrate the idea of skewness.

EXAMPLE

Following are the earnings per share for a sample of 15 software companies for the year 2013. The earnings per share are arranged from smallest to largest.

\$0.09	\$0.13	\$0.41	\$0.51	\$ 1.12	\$ 1.20	\$ 1.49	\$3.18
3.50	6.36	7.83	8.92	10.13	12.99	16.40	

Compute the mean, median, and standard deviation. Find the coefficient of skewness using Pearson's estimate and the software methods. What is your conclusion regarding the shape of the distribution?

SOLUTION

These are sample data, so we use formula (3–2) to determine the mean

$$\bar{x} = \frac{\Sigma x}{n} = \frac{\$74.26}{15} = \$4.95$$

The median is the middle value in a set of data, arranged from smallest to largest. In this case, the middle value is \$3.18, so the median earnings per share is \$3.18.

We use formula (3–10) on page 77 to determine the sample standard deviation.

$$s = \sqrt{\frac{\Sigma(x - \bar{x})^2}{n - 1}} = \sqrt{\frac{(\$0.09 - \$4.95)^2 + \cdots + (\$16.40 - \$4.95)^2}{15 - 1}} = \$5.22$$

Pearson's coefficient of skewness is 1.017, found by

$$sk = \frac{3(\bar{x} - \text{Median})}{s} = \frac{3(\$4.95 - \$3.18)}{\$5.22} = 1.017$$

This indicates there is moderate positive skewness in the earnings per share data.

We obtain a similar, but not exactly the same, value from the software method. The details of the calculations are shown in Table 4–2. To begin, we find the difference between each earnings per share value and the mean and divide this result by the standard deviation. We have referred to this as standardizing. Next, we cube, that is, raise to the third power, the result of the first step. Finally, we sum the cubed values. The details for the first company, that is, the company with an earnings per share of \$0.09, are:

$$\left(\frac{x - \bar{x}}{s}\right)^3 = \left(\frac{0.09 - 4.95}{5.22}\right)^3 = (-0.9310)^3 = -0.8070$$

TABLE 4–2 Calculation of the Coefficient of Skewness

Earnings per Share	$\dfrac{(x - \bar{x})}{s}$	$\left(\dfrac{x - \bar{x}}{s}\right)^3$
0.09	−0.9310	−0.8070
0.13	−0.9234	−0.7873
0.41	−0.8697	−0.6579
0.51	−0.8506	−0.6154
1.12	−0.7337	−0.3950
1.20	−0.7184	−0.3708
1.49	−0.6628	−0.2912
3.18	−0.3391	−0.0390
3.50	−0.2778	−0.0214
6.36	0.2701	0.0197
7.83	0.5517	0.1679
8.92	0.7605	0.4399
10.13	0.9923	0.9772
12.99	1.5402	3.6539
16.40	2.1935	10.5537
		11.8274

When we sum the 15 cubed values, the result is 11.8274. That is, the term $\Sigma[(x - \bar{x})/s]^3 = 11.8274$. To find the coefficient of skewness, we use formula (4–3), with $n = 15$.

$$sk = \frac{n}{(n-1)(n-2)}\sum\left(\frac{x-\bar{x}}{s}\right)^3 = \frac{15}{(15-1)(15-2)}(11.8274) = 0.975$$

We conclude that the earnings per share values are somewhat positively skewed. The following Minitab summary reports the descriptive measures, such as the mean, median, and standard deviation of the earnings per share data. Also included are the coefficient of skewness and a histogram with a bell-shaped curve superimposed.

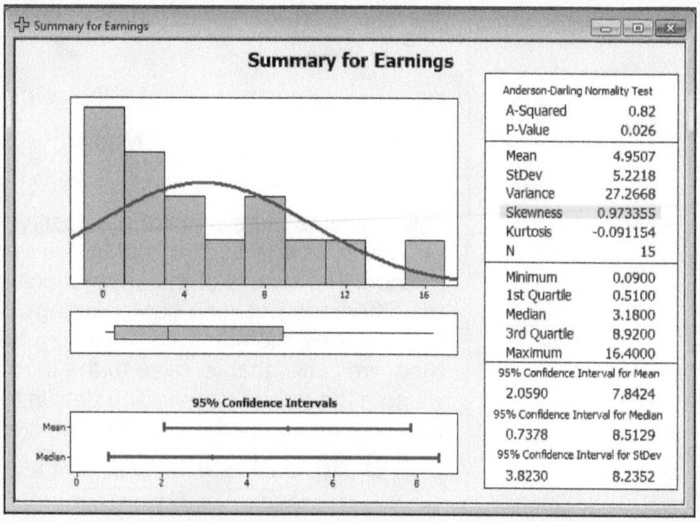

SELF-REVIEW 4–4

A sample of five data entry clerks employed in the Horry County Tax Office revised the following number of tax records last hour: 73, 98, 60, 92, and 84.

(a) Find the mean, median, and the standard deviation.
(b) Compute the coefficient of skewness using Pearson's method.
(c) Calculate the coefficient of skewness using the software method.
(d) What is your conclusion regarding the skewness of the data?

EXERCISES

For Exercises 19–22:

a. Determine the mean, median, and the standard deviation.
b. Determine the coefficient of skewness using Pearson's method.
c. Determine the coefficient of skewness using the software method.

For **DATA FILE**, please visit www.mhhe.com/lind16e

19. The following values are the starting salaries, in $000, for a sample of five accounting graduates who accepted positions in public accounting last year.

36.0	26.0	33.0	28.0	31.0

For **DATA FILE**, please visit www.mhhe.com/lind16e

20. Listed below are the salaries, in $000, for a sample of 15 chief financial officers in the electronics industry.

$516.0	$548.0	$566.0	$534.0	$586.0	$529.0
546.0	523.0	538.0	523.0	551.0	552.0
486.0	558.0	574.0			

For **DATA FILE**, please visit www.mhhe.com/lind16e

21. Listed below are the commissions earned ($000) last year by the 15 sales representatives at Furniture Patch Inc.

$ 3.9	$ 5.7	$ 7.3	$10.6	$13.0	$13.6	$15.1	$15.8	$17.1
17.4	17.6	22.3	38.6	43.2	87.7			

For **DATA FILE**, please visit www.mhhe.com/lind16e

22. Listed below are the salaries for the 2012 New York Yankees Major League Baseball team.

Player	Salary	Player	Salary
Alex Rodriguez	$30,000,000	Boone Logan	$1,875,000
Mark Teixeira	23,125,000	Joba Chamberlain	1,675,000
CC Sabathia	23,000,000	David Robertson	1,600,000
Derek Jeter	15,729,364	Raul Ibanez	1,100,000
Mariano Rivera	14,940,025	Eric Chavez	900,000
Robinson Cano	14,000,000	Michael Pineda	528,475
Rafael Soriano	11,000,000	Ivan Nova	527,200
Nick Swisher	10,250,000	Clay Rapada	525,000
Curtis Granderson	10,000,000	Eduardo Nunez	523,800
Hiroki Kuroda	10,000,000	Cory Wade	508,925
Russell Martin	7,500,000	David Aardsma	500,000
Freddy Garcia	4,000,000	Chris Stewart	482,500
Pedro Feliciano	3,750,000	Austin Romine	482,000
Phil Hughes	3,200,000	Cesar Cabral	480,000
Brett Gardner	2,800,000	Brad Meyers	480,000
Andruw Jones	2,000,000		

LO4-6
Create and interpret a scatter diagram.

DESCRIBING THE RELATIONSHIP BETWEEN TWO VARIABLES

In Chapter 2 and the first section of this chapter, we presented graphical techniques to summarize the distribution of a single variable. We used a histogram in Chapter 2 to summarize the profit on vehicles sold by the Applewood Auto Group. Earlier in this chapter, we used dot plots and stem-and-leaf displays to visually summarize a set of data. Because we are studying a single variable, we refer to this as **univariate** data.

There are situations where we wish to study and visually portray the relationship between two variables. When we study the relationship between two variables, we refer to the data as **bivariate.** Data analysts frequently wish to understand the relationship between two variables. Here are some examples:

- Tybo and Associates is a law firm that advertises extensively on local TV. The partners are considering increasing their advertising budget. Before doing so, they would like to know the relationship between the amount spent per month on advertising and the total amount of billings for that month. To put it another way, will increasing the amount spent on advertising result in an increase in billings?
- Coastal Realty is studying the selling prices of homes. What variables seem to be related to the selling price of homes? For example, do larger homes sell for more than smaller ones? Probably. So Coastal might study the relationship between the area in square feet and the selling price.
- Dr. Stephen Givens is an expert in human development. He is studying the relationship between the height of fathers and the height of their sons. That is, do tall fathers tend to have tall children? Would you expect Dwight Howard, the 6′ 11″, 265-pound professional basketball player, to have relatively tall sons?

One graphical technique we use to show the relationship between variables is called a **scatter diagram.**

To draw a scatter diagram, we need two variables. We scale one variable along the horizontal axis (*X*-axis) of a graph and the other variable along the vertical axis (*Y*-axis). Usually one variable depends to some degree on the other. In the third example above, the height of the son *depends* on the height of the father. So we scale the height of the father on the horizontal axis and that of the son on the vertical axis.

We can use statistical software, such as Excel, to perform the plotting function for us. *Caution:* You should always be careful of the scale. By changing the scale of either the vertical or the horizontal axis, you can affect the apparent visual strength of the relationship.

Following are three scatter diagrams (Chart 4–2). The one on the left shows a rather strong positive relationship between the age in years and the maintenance cost last year for a sample of 10 buses owned by the city of Cleveland, Ohio. Note that as the age of the bus increases, the yearly maintenance cost also increases. The example in the center, for a sample of 20 vehicles, shows a rather strong indirect relationship between the odometer reading and the auction price. That is, as the number of miles driven increases, the auction price decreases. The example on the right depicts the relationship between the height and yearly salary for a sample of 15 shift supervisors. This graph indicates there is little relationship between their height and yearly salary.

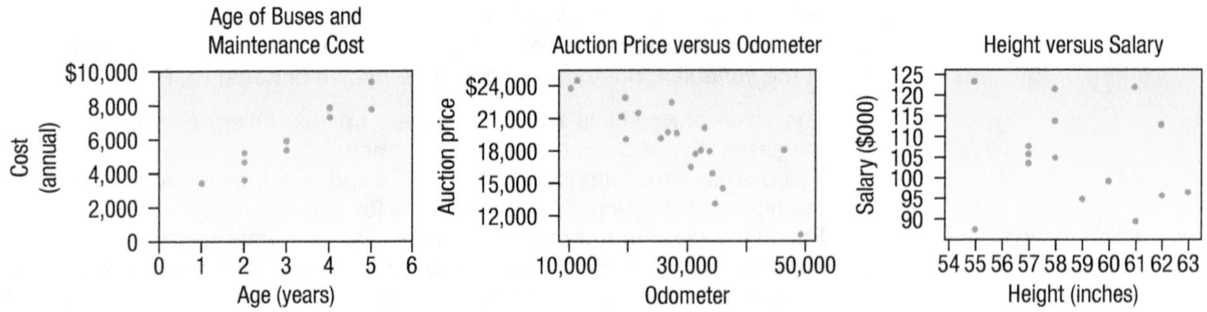

CHART 4–2 Three Examples of Scatter Diagrams.

EXAMPLE

In the introduction to Chapter 2, we presented data from the Applewood Auto Group. We gathered information concerning several variables, including the profit earned from the sale of 180 vehicles sold last month. In addition to the amount of profit on each sale, one of the other variables is the age of the purchaser. Is there a relationship between the profit earned on a vehicle sale and the age of the purchaser? Would it be reasonable to conclude that more profit is made on vehicles purchased by older buyers?

SOLUTION

We can investigate the relationship between vehicle profit and the age of the buyer with a scatter diagram. We scale age on the horizontal, or *X*-axis, and the profit on the vertical, or *Y*-axis. We assume profit depends on the age of the purchaser. As people age, they earn more income and purchase more expensive cars which, in turn, produce higher profits. We use Excel to develop the scatter diagram. The Excel commands are in Appendix C.

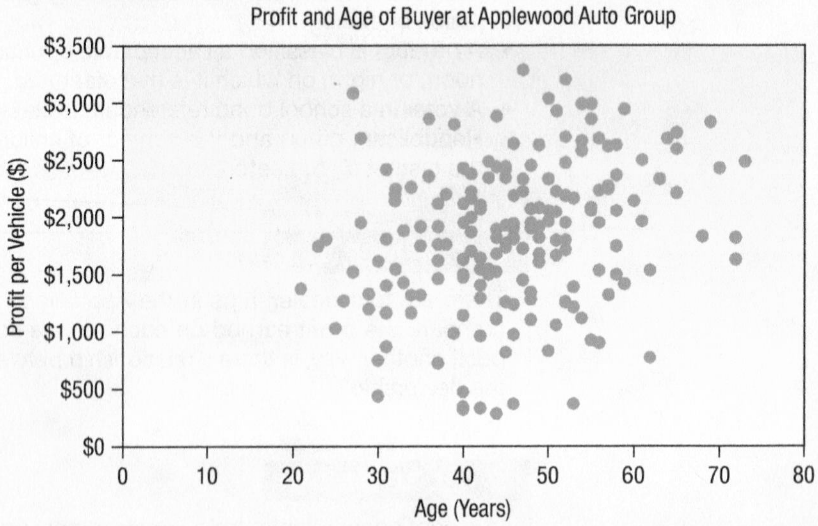

The scatter diagram shows a rather weak positive relationship between the two variables. It does not appear there is much relationship between the vehicle profit and the age of the buyer. In Chapter 13, we will study the relationship between variables more extensively, even calculating several numerical measures to express the relationship between variables.

In the preceding example, there is a weak positive, or direct, relationship between the variables. There are, however, many instances where there is a relationship between the variables, but that relationship is inverse or negative. For example:

- The value of a vehicle and the number of miles driven. As the number of miles increases, the value of the vehicle decreases.
- The premium for auto insurance and the age of the driver. Auto rates tend to be the highest for younger drivers and less for older drivers.
- For many law enforcement personnel, as the number of years on the job increases, the number of traffic citations decreases. This may be because personnel become more liberal in their interpretations or they may be in supervisor positions and not in a position to issue as many citations. But in any event, as age increases, the number of citations decreases.

LO4-7
Develop and explain a contingency table.

CONTINGENCY TABLES

A scatter diagram requires that both of the variables be at least interval scale. In the Applewood Auto Group example, both age and vehicle profit are ratio scale variables. Height is also ratio scale as used in the discussion of the relationship between the height of fathers and the height of their sons. What if we wish to study the relationship between two variables when one or both are nominal or ordinal scale? In this case, we tally the results in a **contingency table.**

CONTINGENCY TABLE A table used to classify observations according to two identifiable characteristics.

A contingency table is a cross-tabulation that simultaneously summarizes two variables of interest. For example:

- Students at a university are classified by gender and class (freshman, sophomore, junior, or senior).
- A product is classified as acceptable or unacceptable and by the shift (day, afternoon, or night) on which it is manufactured.
- A voter in a school bond referendum is classified as to party affiliation (Democrat, Republican, other) and the number of children that voter has attending school in the district (0, 1, 2, etc.).

EXAMPLE

There are four dealerships in the Applewood Auto Group. Suppose we want to compare the profit earned on each vehicle sold by the particular dealership. To put it another way, is there a relationship between the amount of profit earned and the dealership?

SOLUTION

In a contingency table, both variables only need to be nominal or ordinal. In this example, the variable dealership is a nominal variable and the variable profit is a ratio variable. To convert profit to an ordinal variable, we classify the variable profit into two categories, those cases where the profit earned is more than the median and those cases where it is less. On page 63 we calculated the median profit for all sales last month at Applewood Auto Group to be $1,882.50.

Contingency Table Showing the Relationship between Profit and Dealership

Above/Below Median Profit	Kane	Olean	Sheffield	Tionesta	Total
Above	25	20	19	26	90
Below	27	20	26	17	90
Total	52	40	45	43	180

By organizing the information into a contingency table, we can compare the profit at the four dealerships. We observe the following:

- From the Total column on the right, 90 of the 180 cars sold had a profit above the median and half below. From the definition of the median, this is expected.
- For the Kane dealership, 25 out of the 52, or 48%, of the cars sold were sold for a profit more than the median.
- The percentage of profits above the median for the other dealerships are 50% for Olean, 42% for Sheffield, and 60% for Tionesta.

We will return to the study of contingency tables in Chapter 5 during the study of probability and in Chapter 15 during the study of nonparametric methods of analysis.

SELF-REVIEW 4–5

The rock group Blue String Beans is touring the United States. The following chart shows the relationship between concert seating capacity and revenue in $000 for a sample of concerts.

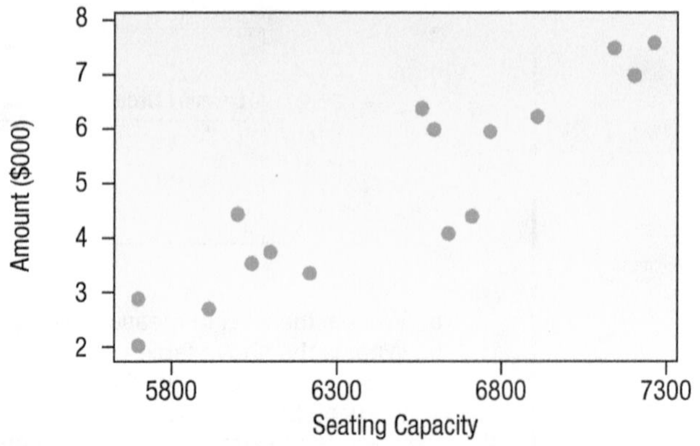

(a) What is the diagram called?
(b) How many concerts were studied?
(c) Estimate the revenue for the concert with the largest seating capacity.
(d) How would you characterize the relationship between revenue and seating capacity? Is it strong or weak, direct or inverse?

EXERCISES

For **DATA FILE**, please visit www.mhhe.com/lind16e

23. Develop a scatter diagram for the following sample data. How would you describe the relationship between the values?

x-Value	*y*-Value	*x*-Value	*y*-Value
10	6	11	6
8	2	10	5
9	6	7	2
11	5	7	3
13	7	11	7

24. Silver Springs Moving and Storage Inc. is studying the relationship between the number of rooms in a move and the number of labor hours required for the move. As part of the analysis, the CFO of Silver Springs developed the following scatter diagram.

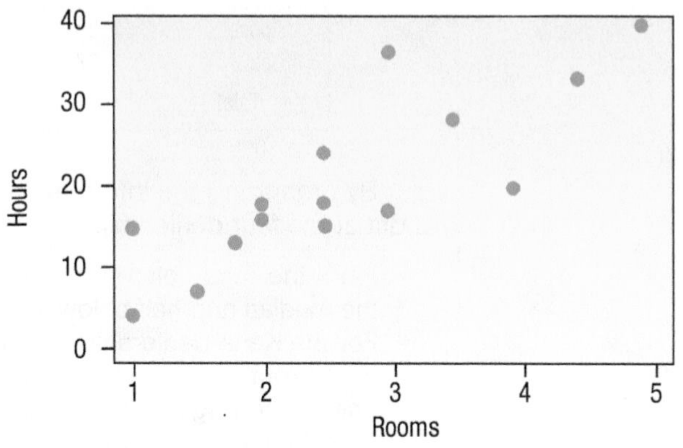

a. How many moves are in the sample?
b. Does it appear that more labor hours are required as the number of rooms increases, or do labor hours decrease as the number of rooms increases?

25. The Director of Planning for Devine Dining Inc. wishes to study the relationship between the gender of a guest and whether the guest orders dessert. To investigate the relationship, the manager collected the following information on 200 recent customers.

	Gender		
Dessert Ordered	**Male**	**Female**	**Total**
Yes	32	15	47
No	68	85	153
Total	100	100	200

a. What is the level of measurement of the two variables?
b. What is the above table called?
c. Does the evidence in the table suggest men are more likely to order dessert than women? Explain why.

26. Ski Resorts of Vermont Inc. is considering a merger with Gulf Shores Beach Resorts Inc. of Alabama. The board of directors surveyed 50 stockholders concerning their position on the merger. The results are reported below.

	Opinion			
Number of Shares Held	**Favor**	**Oppose**	**Undecided**	**Total**
Under 200	8	6	2	16
200 up to 1,000	6	8	1	15
Over 1,000	6	12	1	19
Total	20	26	4	50

a. What level of measurement is used in this table?
b. What is this table called?
c. What group seems most strongly opposed to the merger?

CHAPTER SUMMARY

I. A dot plot shows the range of values on the horizontal axis and the number of observations for each value on the vertical axis.
  A. Dot plots report the details of each observation.
  B. They are useful for comparing two or more data sets.
II. A stem-and-leaf display is an alternative to a histogram.
  A. The leading digit is the stem and the trailing digit the leaf.
  B. The advantages of a stem-and-leaf display over a histogram include:
    1. The identity of each observation is not lost.
    2. The digits themselves give a picture of the distribution.
    3. The cumulative frequencies are also shown.
III. Measures of location also describe the shape of a set of observations.
  A. Quartiles divide a set of observations into four equal parts.
    1. Twenty-five percent of the observations are less than the first quartile, 50% are less than the second quartile, and 75% are less than the third quartile.
    2. The interquartile range is the difference between the third quartile and the first quartile.
  B. Deciles divide a set of observations into 10 equal parts and percentiles into 100 equal parts.
IV. A box plot is a graphic display of a set of data.
  A. A box is drawn enclosing the regions between the first quartile and the third quartile.
    1. A line is drawn inside the box at the median value.
    2. Dotted line segments are drawn from the third quartile to the largest value to show the highest 25% of the values and from the first quartile to the smallest value to show the lowest 25% of the values.
  B. A box plot is based on five statistics: the maximum and minimum values, the first and third quartiles, and the median.
V. The coefficient of skewness is a measure of the symmetry of a distribution.
  A. There are two formulas for the coefficient of skewness.
    1. The formula developed by Pearson is:

$$sk = \frac{3(\bar{x} - \text{Median})}{s} \qquad \textbf{[4–2]}$$

    2. The coefficient of skewness computed by statistical software is:

$$sk = \frac{n}{(n-1)(n-2)}\left[\sum\left(\frac{x-\bar{x}}{s}\right)^3\right] \qquad \textbf{[4–3]}$$

VI. A scatter diagram is a graphic tool to portray the relationship between two variables.
  A. Both variables are measured with interval or ratio scales.
  B. If the scatter of points moves from the lower left to the upper right, the variables under consideration are directly or positively related.
  C. If the scatter of points moves from the upper left to the lower right, the variables are inversely or negatively related.
VII. A contingency table is used to classify nominal-scale observations according to two characteristics.

PRONUNCIATION KEY

SYMBOL	MEANING	PRONUNCIATION
L_p	Location of percentile	*L* sub *p*
Q_1	First quartile	*Q* sub 1
Q_3	Third quartile	*Q* sub 3

CHAPTER EXERCISES

27. A sample of students attending Southeast Florida University is asked the number of social activities in which they participated last week. The chart below was prepared from the sample data.

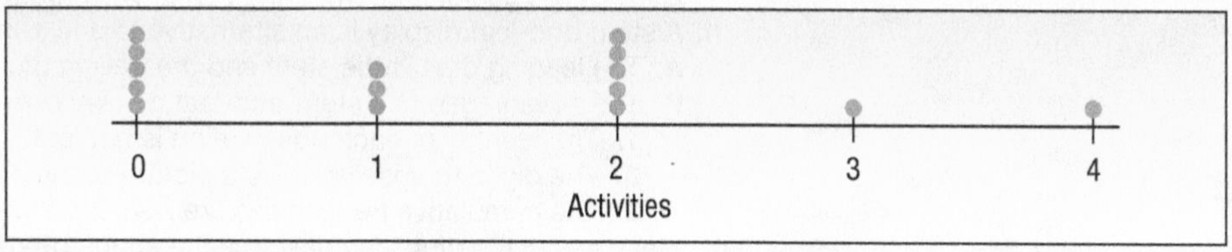

a. What is the name given to this chart?
b. How many students were in the study?
c. How many students reported attending no social activities?

28. Doctor's Care is a walk-in clinic, with locations in Georgetown, Moncks Corner, and Aynor, at which patients may receive treatment for minor injuries, colds, and flu, as well as physical examinations. The following charts report the number of patients treated in each of the three locations last month.

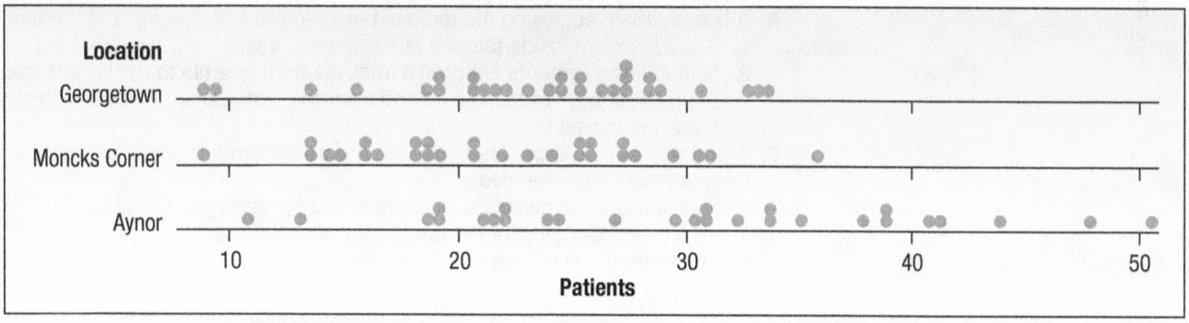

Describe the number of patients served at the three locations each day. What are the maximum and minimum numbers of patients served at each of the locations?

For **DATA FILE**, please visit www.mhhe.com/lind16e

29. The screen size for 23 LCD televisions is given below. Make a stem-and-leaf display of this variable.

46	52	46	40	42	46	40	37	46	40	52	32	37	32	52
40	32	52	40	52	46	46	52							

For **DATA FILE**, please visit www.mhhe.com/lind16e

30. The top 25 companies (by market capitalization) operating in the Washington, DC, area along with the year they were founded and the number of employees are given below. Make a stem-and-leaf display of each of these variables and write a short description of your findings.

Company Name	Year Founded	Employees
AES Corp.	1981	30,000
American Capital Strategies Ltd.	1986	484
AvalonBay Communities Inc.	1978	1,767
Capital One Financial Corp.	1995	31,800
Constellation Energy Group Inc.	1816	9,736
Coventry Health Care Inc.	1986	10,250
Danaher Corp.	1984	45,000
Dominion Resources Inc.	1909	17,500
Fannie Mae	1938	6,450
Freddie Mac	1970	5,533

(*continued*)

Company Name	Year Founded	Employees
Gannett Co.	1906	49,675
General Dynamics Corp.	1952	81,000
Genworth Financial Inc.	2004	7,200
Harman International Industries Inc.	1980	11,246
Host Hotels & Resorts Inc.	1927	229
Legg Mason Inc.	1899	3,800
Lockheed Martin Corp.	1995	140,000
Marriott International Inc.	1927	151,000
MedImmune Inc.	1988	2,516
NII Holdings Inc.	1996	7,748
Norfolk Southern Corp.	1982	30,594
Pepco Holdings Inc.	1896	5,057
Sallie Mae	1972	11,456
Sprint Nextel Corp.	1899	64,000
T. Rowe Price Group Inc.	1937	4,605
The Washington Post Co.	1877	17,100

For **DATA FILE**, please visit www.mhhe.com/lind16e

31. In recent years, due to low interest rates, many homeowners refinanced their home mortgages. Linda Lahey is a mortgage officer at Down River Federal Savings and Loan. Below is the amount refinanced for 20 loans she processed last week. The data are reported in thousands of dollars and arranged from smallest to largest.

59.2	59.5	61.6	65.5	66.6	72.9	74.8	77.3	79.2
83.7	85.6	85.8	86.6	87.0	87.1	90.2	93.3	98.6
100.2	100.7							

a. Find the median, first quartile, and third quartile.
b. Find the 26th and 83rd percentiles.
c. Draw a box plot of the data.

For **DATA FILE**, please visit www.mhhe.com/lind16e

32. A study is made by the recording industry in the United States of the number of music CDs owned by 25 senior citizens and 30 young adults. The information is reported below.

Seniors									
28	35	41	48	52	81	97	98	98	99
118	132	133	140	145	147	153	158	162	174
177	180	180	187	188					

Young Adults									
81	107	113	147	147	175	183	192	202	209
233	251	254	266	283	284	284	316	372	401
417	423	490	500	507	518	550	557	590	594

a. Find the median and the first and third quartiles for the number of CDs owned by senior citizens. Develop a box plot for the information.
b. Find the median and the first and third quartiles for the number of CDs owned by young adults. Develop a box plot for the information.
c. Compare the number of CDs owned by the two groups.

For **DATA FILE**, please visit www.mhhe.com/lind16e

33. The corporate headquarters of *Bank.com,* a new Internet company that performs all banking transactions via the Internet, is located in downtown Philadelphia. The director of human resources is making a study of the time it takes employees to get to work. The city is planning to offer incentives to each downtown employer if they will encourage their

employees to use public transportation. Below is a listing of the time to get to work this morning according to whether the employee used public transportation or drove a car.

Public Transportation									
23	25	25	30	31	31	32	33	35	36
37	42								

Private									
32	32	33	34	37	37	38	38	38	39
40	44								

a. Find the median and the first and third quartiles for the time it took employees using public transportation. Develop a box plot for the information.

b. Find the median and the first and third quartiles for the time it took employees who drove their own vehicle. Develop a box plot for the information.

c. Compare the times of the two groups.

34. The following box plot shows the number of daily newspapers published in each state and the District of Columbia. Write a brief report summarizing the number published. Be sure to include information on the values of the first and third quartiles, the median, and whether there is any skewness. If there are any outliers, estimate their value.

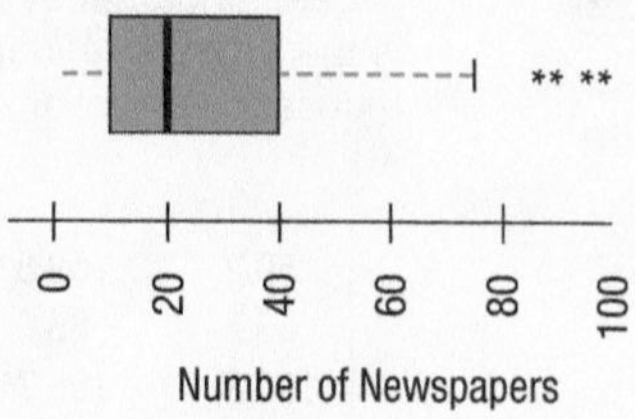

35. Walter Gogel Company is an industrial supplier of fasteners, tools, and springs. The amounts of its invoices vary widely, from less than $20.00 to more than $400.00. During the month of January the company sent out 80 invoices. Here is a box plot of these invoices. Write a brief report summarizing the invoice amounts. Be sure to include information on the values of the first and third quartiles, the median, and whether there is any skewness. If there are any outliers, approximate the value of these invoices.

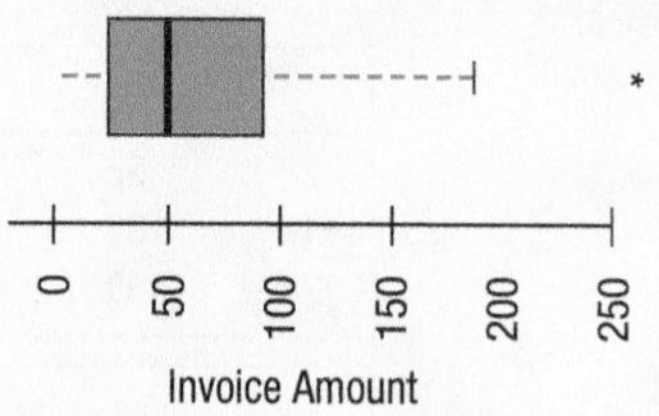

For **DATA FILE**, please visit www.mhhe.com/lind16e

36. The American Society of PeriAnesthesia Nurses (ASPAN; www.aspan.org) is a national organization serving nurses practicing in ambulatory surgery, preanesthesia, and postanesthesia care. The organization consists of the 40 components listed below.

State/Region	Membership	State/Region	Membership
Alabama	95	Illinois	562
Arizona	399	Indiana	270
Maryland, Delaware, DC	531	Iowa	117
Connecticut	239	Kentucky	197
Florida	631	Louisiana	258
Georgia	384	Michigan	411
Hawaii	73	Massachusetts	480

(continued)

State/Region	Membership	State/Region	Membership
Maine	97	California	1,165
Minnesota, Dakotas	289	New Mexico	79
Missouri, Kansas	282	Pennsylvania	575
Mississippi	90	Rhode Island	53
Nebraska	115	Colorado	409
North Carolina	542	South Carolina	237
Nevada	106	Texas	1,026
New Jersey, Bermuda	517	Tennessee	167
Alaska, Idaho, Montana, Oregon, Washington	708	Utah	67
New York	891	Virginia	414
Ohio	708	Vermont, New Hampshire	144
Oklahoma	171	Wisconsin	311
Arkansas	68	West Virginia	62

Use statistical software to answer the following questions.

a. Find the mean, median, and standard deviation of the number of members per component.

b. Find the coefficient of skewness, using the software. What do you conclude about the shape of the distribution of component size?

c. Compute the first and third quartiles using formula (4–1).

d. Develop a box plot. Are there any outliers? Which components are outliers? What are the limits for outliers?

For **DATA FILE**, please visit www.mhhe.com/lind16e

37. McGivern Jewelers is located in the Levis Square Mall just south of Toledo, Ohio. Recently it ran an advertisement in the local newspaper reporting the shape, size, price, and cut grade for 33 of its diamonds currently in stock. The information is reported below.

Shape	Size (carats)	Price	Cut Grade	Shape	Size (carats)	Price	Cut Grade
Princess	5.03	$44,312	Ideal cut	Round	0.77	$2,828	Ultra ideal cut
Round	2.35	20,413	Premium cut	Oval	0.76	3,808	Premium cut
Round	2.03	13,080	Ideal cut	Princess	0.71	2,327	Premium cut
Round	1.56	13,925	Ideal cut	Marquise	0.71	2,732	Good cut
Round	1.21	7,382	Ultra ideal cut	Round	0.70	1,915	Premium cut
Round	1.21	5,154	Average cut	Round	0.66	1,885	Premium cut
Round	1.19	5,339	Premium cut	Round	0.62	1,397	Good cut
Emerald	1.16	5,161	Ideal cut	Round	0.52	2,555	Premium cut
Round	1.08	8,775	Ultra ideal cut	Princess	0.51	1,337	Ideal cut
Round	1.02	4,282	Premium cut	Round	0.51	1,558	Premium cut
Round	1.02	6,943	Ideal cut	Round	0.45	1,191	Premium cut
Marquise	1.01	7,038	Good cut	Princess	0.44	1,319	Average cut
Princess	1.00	4,868	Premium cut	Marquise	0.44	1,319	Premium cut
Round	0.91	5,106	Premium cut	Round	0.40	1,133	Premium cut
Round	0.90	3,921	Good cut	Round	0.35	1,354	Good cut
Round	0.90	3,733	Premium cut	Round	0.32	896	Premium cut
Round	0.84	2,621	Premium cut				

a. Develop a box plot of the variable price and comment on the result. Are there any outliers? What is the median price? What are the values of the first and the third quartiles?

b. Develop a box plot of the variable size and comment on the result. Are there any outliers? What is the median price? What are the values of the first and the third quartiles?

c. Develop a scatter diagram between the variables price and size. Be sure to put price on the vertical axis and size on the horizontal axis. Does there seem to be an association between the two variables? Is the association direct or indirect? Does any point seem to be different from the others?

d. Develop a contingency table for the variables shape and cut grade. What is the most common cut grade? What is the most common shape? What is the most common combination of cut grade and shape?

For **DATA FILE**, please visit www.mhhe.com/lind16e

38. Listed below is the amount of commissions earned last month for the eight members of the sales staff at Best Electronics. Calculate the coefficient of skewness using both methods. *Hint:* Use of a spreadsheet will expedite the calculations.

980.9	1,036.5	1,099.5	1,153.9	1,409.0	1,456.4	1,718.4	1,721.2

For **DATA FILE**, please visit www.mhhe.com/lind16e

39. Listed below is the number of car thefts in a large city over the last week. Calculate the coefficient of skewness using both methods. *Hint:* Use of a spreadsheet will expedite the calculations.

3	12	13	7	8	3	8

40. The manager of Information Services at Wilkin Investigations, a private investigation firm, is studying the relationship between the age (in months) of a combination printer, copier, and fax machine and its monthly maintenance cost. For a sample of 15 machines, the manager developed the following chart. What can the manager conclude about the relationship between the variables?

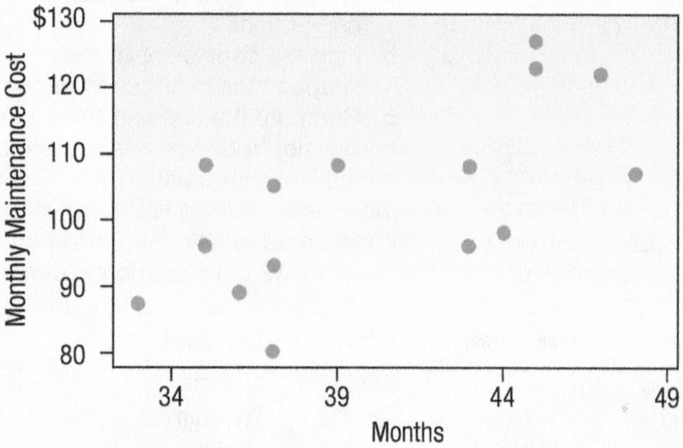

For **DATA FILE**, please visit www.mhhe.com/lind16e

41. An auto insurance company reported the following information regarding the age of a driver and the number of accidents reported last year. Develop a scatter diagram for the data and write a brief summary.

Age	Accidents	Age	Accidents
16	4	23	0
24	2	27	1
18	5	32	1
17	4	22	3

42. Wendy's offers eight different condiments (mustard, catsup, onion, mayonnaise, pickle, lettuce, tomato, and relish) on hamburgers. A store manager collected the following information on the number of condiments ordered and the age group of the customer. What can you conclude regarding the information? Who tends to order the most or least number of condiments?

	Age			
Number of Condiments	Under 18	18 up to 40	40 up to 60	60 or older
0	12	18	24	52
1	21	76	50	30
2	39	52	40	12
3 or more	71	87	47	28

43. Here is a table showing the number of employed and unemployed workers 20 years or older by gender in the United States.

	Number of Workers (000)	
Gender	**Employed**	**Unemployed**
Men	70,415	4,209
Women	61,402	3,314

a. How many workers were studied?
b. What percent of the workers were unemployed?
c. Compare the percent unemployed for the men and the women.

DATA SET EXERCISES

(The data for these exercises is available at the text website: www.mhhe.com/lind16e.)

44. Refer to the Real Estate data, which reports information on homes sold in the Goodyear, Arizona, area during the last year. Prepare a report on the selling prices of the homes. Be sure to answer the following questions in your report.
a. Develop a box plot. Estimate the first and the third quartiles. Are there any outliers?
b. Develop a scatter diagram with price on the vertical axis and the size of the home on the horizontal. Does there seem to be a relationship between these variables? Is the relationship direct or inverse?
c. Develop a scatter diagram with price on the vertical axis and distance from the center of the city on the horizontal axis. Does there seem to be a relationship between these variables? Is the relationship direct or inverse?

45. Refer to the Baseball 2012 data that report information on the 30 Major League Baseball teams for the 2012 season.
a. In the data set, the variable, built, is the year that a stadium was constructed. Using this variable, create a new variable, age, by subtracting the value of the variable, built, from the current year for each team. Develop a box plot with the new variable, age. Are there any outliers? If so, which of the stadiums are outliers?
b. Using the variable, payroll, create a box plot. Are there any outliers? Compute the quartiles using formula (4–1). How does the New York Yankees' payroll compare to other team payrolls? Write a brief summary of your analysis.
c. Draw a scatter diagram with the variable, wins, on the vertical axis and payroll on the horizontal axis. What are your conclusions?
d. Using the variable, wins, draw a dot plot. What can you conclude from this plot?

46. Refer to the Buena School District bus data.
a. Refer to the maintenance cost variable. Develop a box plot. What are the first and third quartiles? Are there any outliers?
b. Determine the median maintenance cost. Based on the median, develop a contingency table with bus manufacturer as one variable and whether the maintenance cost was above or below the median as the other variable. What are your conclusions?

A REVIEW OF CHAPTERS 1–4

This section is a review of the major concepts and terms introduced in Chapters 1–4. Chapter 1 began by describing the meaning and purpose of statistics. Next we described the different types of variables and the four levels of measurement. Chapter 2 was concerned with describing a set of observations by organizing it into a frequency distribution and then portraying the frequency distribution as a histogram or a frequency polygon. Chapter 3 began by describing measures of location, such as the mean, weighted mean, median, geometric mean, and mode. This chapter also included measures of dispersion, or spread. Discussed in this section were the range, variance, and standard deviation. Chapter 4 included several graphing techniques such as dot plots, box plots, and scatter diagrams. We also discussed the coefficient of skewness, which reports the lack of symmetry in a set of data.

Throughout this section we stressed the importance of statistical software, such as Excel and Minitab. Many computer outputs in these chapters demonstrated how quickly and effectively a large data set can be organized into a frequency distribution, several of the measures of location or measures of variation calculated, and the information presented in graphical form.

PROBLEMS

For **DATA FILE**, please visit www.mhhe.com/lind16e

1. A sample of 50 funds deposited in First Federal Savings Bank's MCA (miniature checking account) revealed the following amounts.

$124	$ 14	$150	$289	$ 52	$156	$203	$ 82	$ 27	$248
39	52	103	58	136	249	110	298	251	157
186	107	142	185	75	202	119	219	156	78
116	152	206	117	52	299	58	153	219	148
145	187	165	147	158	146	185	186	149	140

Use a statistical software package such as Excel or Minitab to help answer the following questions.

a. Determine the mean, median, and standard deviation.
b. Determine the first and third quartiles.
c. Develop a box plot. Are there any outliers? Do the amounts follow a symmetric distribution or are they skewed? Justify your answer.
d. Organize the distribution of funds into a frequency distribution.
e. Write a brief summary of the results in parts a to d.

For **DATA FILE**, please visit www.mhhe.com/lind16e

2. Listed below are the 44 U.S. presidents and their age as they began their terms in office.

Number	Name	Age	Number	Name	Age
1	Washington	57	23	B. Harrison	55
2	J. Adams	61	24	Cleveland	55
3	Jefferson	57	25	McKinley	54
4	Madison	57	26	T. Roosevelt	42
5	Monroe	58	27	Taft	51
6	J. Q. Adams	57	28	Wilson	56
7	Jackson	61	29	Harding	55
8	Van Buren	54	30	Coolidge	51
9	W. H. Harrison	68	31	Hoover	54
10	Tyler	51	32	F. D. Roosevelt	51
11	Polk	49	33	Truman	60
12	Taylor	64	34	Eisenhower	62
13	Fillmore	50	35	Kennedy	43
14	Pierce	48	36	L. B. Johnson	55
15	Buchanan	65	37	Nixon	56
16	Lincoln	52	38	Ford	61
17	A. Johnson	56	39	Carter	52
18	Grant	46	40	Reagan	69
19	Hayes	54	41	G. H. W. Bush	64
20	Garfield	49	42	Clinton	46
21	Arthur	50	43	G. W. Bush	54
22	Cleveland	47	44	Obama	47

Use a statistical software package such as Excel or Minitab to help answer the following questions.

a. Determine the mean, median, and standard deviation.
b. Determine the first and third quartiles.

c. Develop a box plot. Are there any outliers? Do the amounts follow a symmetric distribution or are they skewed? Justify your answer.
d. Organize the distribution of ages into a frequency distribution.
e. Write a brief summary of the results in parts a to d.

3. Listed below is the per capita income for the 50 states and the District of Columbia.

For **DATA FILE**, please visit www.mhhe.com/lind16e

State	Amount	State	Amount
Alabama	$30,894	Montana	$30,790
Alaska	38,138	Nebraska	34,440
Arizona	31,936	Nevada	38,994
Arkansas	28,473	New Hampshire	39,753
California	39,626	New Jersey	46,763
Colorado	39,491	New Mexico	29,929
Connecticut	50,762	New York	44,027
Delaware	39,131	North Carolina	32,247
DC	57,746	North Dakota	32,763
Florida	36,720	Ohio	33,320
Georgia	32,095	Oklahoma	32,391
Hawaii	37,023	Oregon	33,299
Idaho	29,920	Pennsylvania	36,825
Illinois	38,409	Rhode Island	37,523
Indiana	32,288	South Carolina	29,767
Iowa	33,038	South Dakota	32,030
Kansas	34,799	Tennessee	32,172
Kentucky	29,729	Texas	35,166
Louisiana	31,821	Utah	29,406
Maine	32,095	Vermont	34,871
Maryland	43,788	Virginia	39,540
Massachusetts	46,299	Washington	38,212
Michigan	33,788	West Virginia	28,206
Minnesota	38,859	Wisconsin	34,405
Mississippi	27,028	Wyoming	40,655
Missouri	32,789		

Use a statistical software package such as Excel or Minitab to help answer the following questions.
a. Determine the mean, median, and standard deviation.
b. Determine the first and third quartiles.
c. Develop a box plot. Are there any outliers? Do the amounts follow a symmetric distribution or are they skewed? Justify your answer.
d. Organize the distribution of funds into a frequency distribution.
e. Write a brief summary of the results in parts a to d.

4. A sample of 12 homes sold last week in St. Paul, Minnesota, revealed the following information. Draw a scatter diagram. Can we conclude that, as the size of the home (reported below in thousands of square feet) increases, the selling price (reported in $ thousands) also increases?

Home Size (thousands of square feet)	Selling Price ($ thousands)	Home Size (thousands of square feet)	Selling Price ($ thousands)
1.4	100	1.3	110
1.3	110	0.8	85
1.2	105	1.2	105
1.1	120	0.9	75
1.4	80	1.1	70
1.0	105	1.1	95

5. Refer to the following diagram.

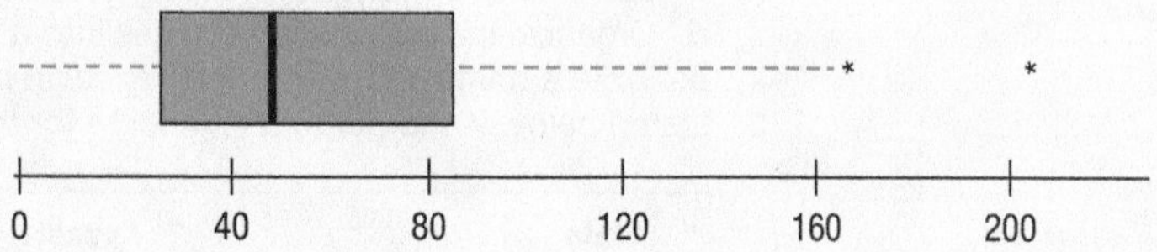

a. What is the graph called?
b. What are the median, and first and third quartile values?
c. Is the distribution positively skewed? Tell how you know.
d. Are there any outliers? If yes, estimate these values.
e. Can you determine the number of observations in the study?

CASES

A. Century National Bank

The following case will appear in subsequent review sections. Assume that you work in the Planning Department of the Century National Bank and report to Ms. Lamberg. You will need to do some data analysis and prepare a short written report. Remember, Mr. Selig is the president of the bank, so you will want to ensure that your report is complete and accurate. A copy of the data appears in Appendix A.6.

Century National Bank has offices in several cities in the Midwest and the southeastern part of the United States. Mr. Dan Selig, president and CEO, would like to know the characteristics of his checking account customers. What is the balance of a typical customer?

How many other bank services do the checking account customers use? Do the customers use the ATM service and, if so, how often? What about debit cards? Who uses them, and how often are they used?

To better understand the customers, Mr. Selig asked Ms. Wendy Lamberg, director of planning, to select a sample of customers and prepare a report. To begin, she has appointed a team from her staff. You are the head of the team and responsible for preparing the report. You select a random sample of 60 customers. In addition to the balance in each account at the end of last month, you determine (1) the number of ATM (automatic teller machine) transactions in the last month; (2) the number of other bank services (a savings account, a certificate of deposit, etc.) the customer uses; (3) whether the customer has a debit card (this is a bank service in which charges are made directly to the customer's account); and (4) whether or not interest is paid on the checking account. The sample includes customers from the branches in Cincinnati, Ohio; Atlanta, Georgia; Louisville, Kentucky; and Erie, Pennsylvania.

1. Develop a graph or table that portrays the checking balances. What is the balance of a typical customer? Do many customers have more than $2,000 in their accounts? Does it appear that there is a difference in the distribution of the accounts among the four branches? Around what value do the account balances tend to cluster?
2. Determine the mean and median of the checking account balances. Compare the mean and the median balances for the four branches. Is there a difference among the branches? Be sure to explain the difference between the mean and the median in your report.
3. Determine the range and the standard deviation of the checking account balances. What do the first and third quartiles show? Determine the coefficient of skewness and indicate what it shows. Because Mr. Selig does not deal with statistics daily, include a brief description and interpretation of the standard deviation and other measures.

B. Wildcat Plumbing Supply Inc.: Do We Have Gender Differences?

Wildcat Plumbing Supply has served the plumbing needs of Southwest Arizona for more than 40 years. The company was founded by Mr. Terrence St. Julian and is run today by his son Cory. The company has grown from a handful of employees to more than 500 today. Cory is concerned about several positions within the company where he has men and women doing essentially the same job but at different pay. To investigate, he collected the information below. Suppose you are a student intern in the Accounting Department and have been given the task to write a report summarizing the situation.

Yearly Salary ($000)	Women	Men
Less than 30	2	0
30 up to 40	3	1
40 up to 50	17	4
50 up to 60	17	24
60 up to 70	8	21
70 up to 80	3	7
80 or more	0	3

To kick off the project, Mr. Cory St. Julian held a meeting with his staff and you were invited. At this meeting, it was suggested that you calculate several measures of location, create charts or draw graphs such as a cumulative

frequency distribution, and determine the quartiles for both men and women. Develop the charts and write the report summarizing the yearly salaries of employees at Wildcat Plumbing Supply. Does it appear that there are pay differences based on gender?

C. Kimble Products: Is There a Difference In the Commissions?

At the January national sales meeting, the CEO of Kimble Products was questioned extensively regarding the company policy for paying commissions to its sales representatives. The company sells sporting goods to two major markets. There are 40 sales representatives who call directly on large-volume customers, such as the athletic departments at major colleges and universities and professional sports franchises. There are 30 sales representatives who represent the company to retail stores located in shopping malls and large discounters such as Kmart and Target.

Upon his return to corporate headquarters, the CEO asked the sales manager for a report comparing the commissions earned last year by the two parts of the sales team. The information is reported below. Write a brief report. Would you conclude that there is a difference? Be sure to include information in the report on both the central tendency and dispersion of the two groups.

Commissions Earned by Sales Representatives Calling on Athletic Departments ($)

354	87	1,676	1,187	69	3,202	680	39	1,683	1,106
883	3,140	299	2,197	175	159	1,105	434	615	149
1,168	278	579	7	357	252	1,602	2,321	4	392
416	427	1,738	526	13	1,604	249	557	635	527

Commissions Earned by Sales Representatives Calling on Large Retailers ($)

1,116	681	1,294	12	754	1,206	1,448	870	944	1,255
1,213	1,291	719	934	1,313	1,083	899	850	886	1,556
886	1,315	1,858	1,262	1,338	1,066	807	1,244	758	918

PRACTICE TEST

There is a practice test at the end of each review section. The tests are in two parts. The first part contains several objective questions, usually in a fill-in-the-blank format. The second part is problems. In most cases, it should take 30 to 45 minutes to complete the test. The problems require a calculator. Check the answers in the Answer Section in the back of the book.

Part 1—Objective

1. The science of collecting, organizing, presenting, analyzing, and interpreting data to assist in making effective decisions is called ________. 1. ________
2. Methods of organizing, summarizing, and presenting data in an informative way are called ________. 2. ________
3. The entire set of individuals or objects of interest or the measurements obtained from all individuals or objects of interest are called the ________. 3. ________
4. List the two types of variables. 4. ________ ________
5. The number of bedrooms in a house is an example of a ________. (discrete variable, continuous variable, qualitative variable—pick one) 5. ________
6. The jersey numbers of Major League Baseball players are an example of what level of measurement? 6. ________
7. The classification of students by eye color is an example of what level of measurement? 7. ________
8. The sum of the differences between each value and the mean is always equal to what value? 8. ________
9. A set of data contained 70 observations. How many classes would the 2^k method suggest to construct a frequency distribution? 9. ________
10. What percent of the values in a data set are always larger than the median? 10. ________
11. The square of the standard deviation is the ________. 11. ________
12. The standard deviation assumes a negative value when ________. (all the values are negative, at least half the values are negative, or never—pick one.) 12. ________
13. Which of the following is least affected by an outlier? (mean, median, or range—pick one) 13. ________

Part 2—Problems

1. The Russell 2000 index of stock prices increased by the following amounts over the last 3 years.

18%	4%	2%

What is the geometric mean increase for the 3 years? ________

2. The information below refers to the selling prices ($000) of homes sold in Warren, Pennsylvania, during 2014.

Selling Price ($000)	Frequency
120.0 up to 150.0	4
150.0 up to 180.0	18
180.0 up to 210.0	30
210.0 up to 240.0	20
240.0 up to 270.0	17
270.0 up to 300.0	10
300.0 up to 330.0	6

a. What is the class interval? ________
b. How many homes were sold in 2014? ________
c. How many homes sold for less than $210,000? ________
d. What is the relative frequency of the 210 up to 240 class? ________
e. What is the midpoint of the 150 up to 180 class? ________
f. The selling prices range between what two amounts? ________

3. A sample of eight college students revealed they owned the following number of CDs.

52	76	64	79	80	74	66	69

a. What is the mean number of CDs owned? ________
b. What is the median number of CDs owned? ________
c. What is the 40th percentile? ________
d. What is the range of the number of CDs owned? ________
e. What is the standard deviation of the number of CDs owned? ________

4. An investor purchased 200 shares of the Blair Company for $36 each in July of 2012, 300 shares at $40 each in September 2013, and 500 shares at $50 each in January 2014. What is the investor's weighted mean price per share? ________

5. During the 2014 Super Bowl, 30 million pounds of snack food were eaten. The chart below depicts this information.

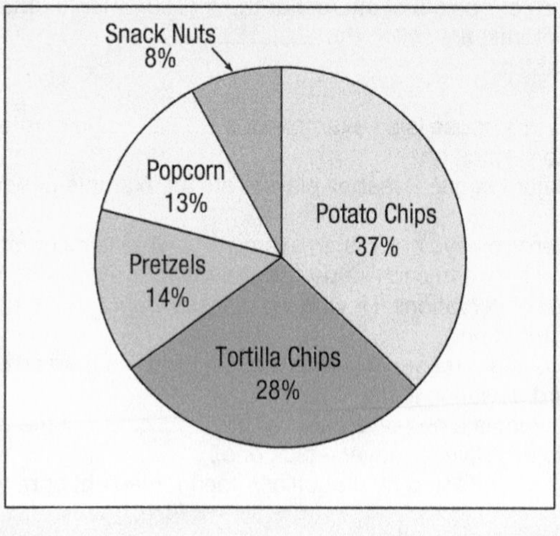

a. What is the name given to this graph? ________
b. Estimate, in millions of pounds, the amount of potato chips eaten during the game. ________
c. Estimate the relationship of potato chips to popcorn. (twice as much, half as much, three times, none of these—pick one) ________
d. What percent of the total do potato chips and tortilla chips comprise? ________

A Survey of Probability Concepts

5

RECENT SURVEYS **indicate 60% of tourists to China visited the Forbidden City, the Temple of Heaven, the Great Wall, and other historical sites in or near Beijing. Forty percent visited Xi'an and its magnificent terra-cotta soldiers, horses, and chariots, which lay buried for over 2,000 years. Thirty percent of the tourists went to both Beijing and Xi'an. What is the probability that a tourist visited at least one of these places? (See Exercise 76 and LO5-3.)**

LEARNING OBJECTIVES

When you have completed this chapter, you will be able to:

LO5-1 Define the terms *probability, experiment, event,* and *outcome.*

LO5-2 Assign probabilities using a classical, empirical, or subjective approach.

LO5-3 Calculate probabilities using the rules of addition.

LO5-4 Calculate probabilities using the rules of multiplication.

LO5-5 Compute probabilities using a contingency table.

LO5-6 Calculate probabilities using Bayes' theorem.

LO5-7 Determine the number of outcomes using principles of counting.

INTRODUCTION

The emphasis in Chapters 2, 3, and 4 is on descriptive statistics. In Chapter 2, we organize the profits on 180 vehicles sold by the Applewood Auto Group into a frequency distribution. This frequency distribution shows the smallest and the largest profits and where the largest concentration of data occurs. In Chapter 3, we use numerical measures of location and dispersion to locate a typical profit on vehicle sales and to examine the variation in the profit of a sale. We describe the variation in the profits with such measures of dispersion as the range and the standard deviation. In Chapter 4, we develop charts and graphs, such as a scatter diagram or a dot plot, to further describe the data graphically.

Descriptive statistics is concerned with summarizing data collected from past events. We now turn to the second facet of statistics, namely, *computing the chance that something will occur in the future*. This facet of statistics is called **statistical inference** or **inferential statistics.**

Seldom does a decision maker have complete information to make a decision. For example:

- Toys and Things, a toy and puzzle manufacturer, recently developed a new game based on sports trivia. It wants to know whether sports buffs will purchase the game. "Slam Dunk" and "Home Run" are two of the names under consideration. To investigate, the president of Toys and Things decided to hire a market research firm. The firm selected a sample of 800 consumers from the population and asked each respondent for a reaction to the new game and its proposed titles. Using the sample results, the company can estimate the proportion of the population that will purchase the game.
- The quality assurance department of a U.S. Steel mill must assure management that the quarter-inch wire being produced has an acceptable tensile strength. Clearly, not all the wire produced can be tested for tensile strength because testing requires the wire to bestretched until it breaks—thus destroying it. So a random sample of 10 pieces is selected and tested. Based on the test results, all the wire produced is deemed to be either acceptable or unacceptable.
- Other questions involving uncertainty are: Should the daytime drama *Days of Our Lives* be discontinued immediately? Will a newly developed mint-flavored cereal be profitable if marketed? Will Charles Linden be elected to county auditor in Batavia County?

Statistical inference deals with conclusions about a population based on a sample taken from that population. (The populations for the preceding illustrations are all consumers who like sports trivia games, all the quarter-inch steel wire produced, all television viewers who watch soaps, all who purchase breakfast cereal, and so on.)

Because there is uncertainty in decision making, it is important that all the known risks involved be scientifically evaluated. Helpful in this evaluation is *probability theory,* which has often been referred to as the science of uncertainty. The use of probability theory allows the decision maker with only limited information to analyze

the risks and minimize the gamble inherent, for example, in marketing a new product or accepting an incoming shipment possibly containing defective parts.

Because probability concepts are so important in the field of statistical inference (to be discussed starting with Chapter 8), this chapter introduces the basic language of probability, including such terms as *experiment, event, subjective probability,* and *addition* and *multiplication rules*.

LO5-1

Define the terms *probability, experiment, event,* and *outcome.*

WHAT IS A PROBABILITY?

No doubt you are familiar with terms such as *probability, chance,* and *likelihood*. They are often used interchangeably. The weather forecaster announces that there is a 70% chance of rain for Super Bowl Sunday. Based on a survey of consumers who tested a newly developed toothpaste with a banana flavor, the probability is .03 that, if marketed, it will be a financial success. (This means that the chance of the banana-flavor toothpaste being accepted by the public is rather remote.) What is a probability? In general, it is a numerical value that describes the chance that something will happen.

PROBABILITY A value between zero and one, inclusive, describing the relative possibility (chance or likelihood) an event will occur.

A probability is frequently expressed as a decimal, such as .70, .27, or .50. However, it may be given as a fraction such as 7/10, 27/100, or 1/2. It can assume any number from 0 to 1, inclusive. If a company has only five sales regions, and each region's name or number is written on a slip of paper and the slips put in a hat, the probability of selecting one of the five regions is 1. The probability of selecting from the hat a slip of paper that reads "Pittsburgh Steelers" is 0. Thus, the probability of 1 represents something that is certain to happen, and the probability of 0 represents something that cannot happen.

The closer a probability is to 0, the more improbable it is the event will happen. The closer the probability is to 1, the more sure we are it will happen. The relationship is shown in the following diagram along with a few of our personal beliefs. You might, however, select a different probability for Slo Poke's chances to win the Kentucky Derby or for an increase in federal taxes.

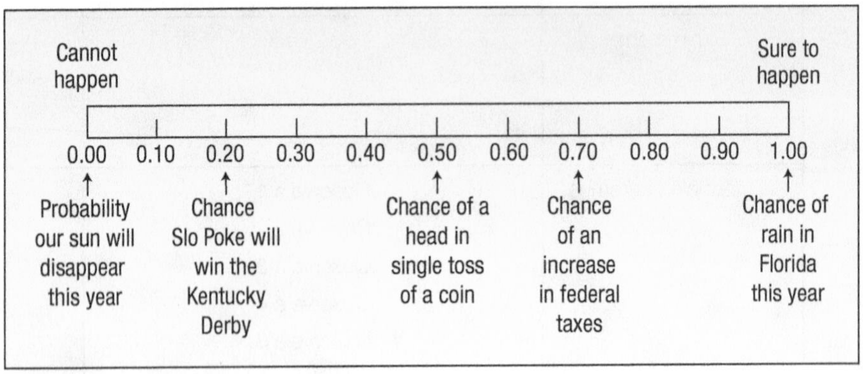

Sometimes, the likelihood of an event is expressed using the term *odds*. To explain, someone says the odds are "five to two" that an event will occur. This means that in a total of seven trials (5 + 2), the event will occur five times and not occur two times. Using odds, we can compute the probability that the event occurs as 5/(5 + 2) or 5/7. So, if the odds in favor of an event are x to y, the probability of the event is $x/(x + y)$.

Three key words are used in the study of probability: **experiment, outcome,** and **event.** These terms are used in our everyday language, but in statistics they have specific meanings.

EXPERIMENT A process that leads to the occurrence of one and only one of several possible results.

This definition is more general than the one used in the physical sciences, where we picture someone manipulating test tubes or microscopes. In reference to probability, an experiment has two or more possible results, and it is uncertain which will occur.

OUTCOME A particular result of an experiment.

For example, the tossing of a coin is an experiment. You are unsure of the outcome. When a coin is tossed, one particular outcome is a "head." The alternative outcome is a "tail." Similarly, asking 500 college students if they would travel more than 100 miles to attend a Mumford and Sons concert is an experiment. In this experiment, one possible outcome is that 273 students indicate they would travel more than 100 miles to attend the concert. Another outcome is that 317 students would attend the concert. Still another outcome is that 423 students indicate they would attend the concert. When one or more of the experiment's outcomes are observed, we call this an event.

EVENT A collection of one or more outcomes of an experiment.

Examples to clarify the definitions of the terms *experiment, outcome,* and *event* are presented in the following figure.

In the die-rolling experiment, there are six possible outcomes, but there are many possible events. When counting the number of members of the board of directors for Fortune 500 companies over 60 years of age, the number of possible outcomes can be anywhere from zero to the total number of members. There are an even larger number of possible events in this experiment.

Experiment	Roll a die	Count the number of members of the board of directors for Fortune 500 companies who are over 60 years of age
All possible outcomes	Observe a 1 Observe a 2 Observe a 3 Observe a 4 Observe a 5 Observe a 6	None is over 60 One is over 60 Two are over 60 ... 29 are over 60 ... ... 48 are over 60 ...
Some possible events	Observe an even number Observe a number greater than 4 Observe a number 3 or less	More than 13 are over 60 Fewer than 20 are over 60

SELF-REVIEW 5–1

Video Games Inc. recently developed a new video game. Its playability is to be tested by 80 veteran game players.

(a) What is the experiment?
(b) What is one possible outcome?
(c) Suppose 65 players tried the new game and said they liked it. Is 65 a probability?
(d) The probability that the new game will be a success is computed to be −1.0. Comment.
(e) Specify one possible event.

LO5-2
Assign probabilities using a classical, empirical, or subjective approach.

APPROACHES TO ASSIGNING PROBABILITIES

In this section, we describe three ways to assign a probability to an event: classical, empirical, and subjective. The classical and empirical methods are objective and are based on information and data. The subjective method is based on a person's belief or estimate of an event's likelihood.

Classical Probability

Classical probability is based on the assumption that the outcomes of an experiment are *equally likely*. Using the classical viewpoint, the probability of an event happening is computed by dividing the number of favorable outcomes by the number of possible outcomes:

CLASSICAL PROBABILITY

$$\text{Probability of an event} = \frac{\text{Number of favorable outcomes}}{\text{Total number of possible outcomes}} \qquad [5\text{–}1]$$

EXAMPLE

Consider an experiment of rolling a six-sided die. What is the probability of the event "an even number of spots appear face up"?

SOLUTION

The possible outcomes are:

a one-spot	a four-spot
a two-spot	a five-spot
a three-spot	a six-spot

There are three "favorable" outcomes (a two, a four, and a six) in the collection of six equally likely possible outcomes. Therefore:

$$\text{Probability of an even number} = \frac{3}{6} \begin{matrix} \leftarrow \\ \leftarrow \end{matrix} \boxed{\frac{\text{Number of favorable outcomes}}{\text{Total number of possible outcomes}}}$$

$$= .5$$

The mutually exclusive concept appeared earlier in our study of frequency distributions in Chapter 2. Recall that we create classes so that a particular value is included in only

one of the classes and there is no overlap between classes. Thus, only one of several events can occur at a particular time.

MUTUALLY EXCLUSIVE The occurrence of one event means that none of the other events can occur at the same time.

The variable "gender" presents mutually exclusive outcomes, male and female. An employee selected at random is either male or female but cannot be both. A manufactured part is acceptable or unacceptable. The part cannot be both acceptable and unacceptable at the same time. In a sample of manufactured parts, the event of selecting an unacceptable part and the event of selecting an acceptable part are mutually exclusive.

If an experiment has a set of events that includes every possible outcome, such as the events "an even number" and "an odd number" in the die-tossing experiment, then the set of events is **collectively exhaustive.** For the die-tossing experiment, every outcome will be either even or odd. So the set is collectively exhaustive.

COLLECTIVELY EXHAUSTIVE At least one of the events must occur when an experiment is conducted.

If the set of events is collectively exhaustive and the events are mutually exclusive, the sum of the probabilities is 1. Historically, the classical approach to probability was developed and applied in the 17th and 18th centuries to games of chance, such as cards and dice. It is unnecessary to do an experiment to determine the probability of an event occurring using the classical approach because the total number of outcomes is known before the experiment. The flip of a coin has two possible outcomes; the roll of a die has six possible outcomes. We can logically arrive at the probability of getting a tail on the toss of one coin or three heads on the toss of three coins.

The classical approach to probability can also be applied to lotteries. In South Carolina, one of the games of the Education Lottery is "Pick 3." A person buys a lottery ticket and selects three numbers between 0 and 9. Once per week, the three numbers are randomly selected from a machine that tumbles three containers each with balls numbered 0 through 9. One way to win is to match the numbers and the order of the numbers. Given that 1,000 possible outcomes exist (000 through 999), the probability of winning with any three-digit number is 0.001, or 1 in 1,000.

Empirical Probability

Empirical or **relative frequency** is the second type of objective probability. It is based on the number of times an event occurs as a proportion of a known number of trials.

EMPIRICAL PROBABILITY The probability of an event happening is the fraction of the time similar events happened in the past.

The formula to determine an empirical probability is:

$$\text{Empirical probability} = \frac{\text{Number of times the event occurs}}{\text{Total number of observations}}$$

The empirical approach to probability is based on what is called the law of large numbers. The key to establishing probabilities empirically is that more observations will provide a more accurate estimate of the probability.

LAW OF LARGE NUMBERS Over a large number of trials, the empirical probability of an event will approach its true probability.

To explain the law of large numbers, suppose we toss a fair coin. The result of each toss is either a head or a tail. With just one toss of the coin the empirical probability for heads is either zero or one. If we toss the coin a great number of times, the probability of the outcome of heads will approach .5. The following table reports the results of seven different experiments of flipping a fair coin 1, 10, 50, 100, 500, 1,000, and 10,000 times and then computing the relative frequency of heads. Note as we increase the number of trials, the empirical probability of a head appearing approaches .5, which is its value based on the classical approach to probability.

Number of Trials	Number of Heads	Relative Frequency of Heads
1	0	.00
10	3	.30
50	26	.52
100	52	.52
500	236	.472
1,000	494	.494
10,000	5,027	.5027

What have we demonstrated? Based on the classical definition of probability, the likelihood of obtaining a head in a single toss of a fair coin is .5. Based on the empirical or relative frequency approach to probability, the probability of the event happening approaches the same value based on the classical definition of probability.

This reasoning allows us to use the empirical or relative frequency approach to finding a probability. Here are some examples.

- Last semester, 80 students registered for Business Statistics 101 at Scandia University. Twelve students earned an A. Based on this information and the empirical approach to assigning a probability, we estimate the likelihood a student will earn an A is .15.
- Kobe Bryant of the Los Angeles Lakers made 381 out of 451 free throw attempts during the 2011–12 NBA season. Based on the empirical rule of probability, the likelihood of him making his next free throw attempt is .845.

Life insurance companies rely on past data to determine the acceptability of an applicant as well as the premium to be charged. Mortality tables list the likelihood a person of a particular age will die within the upcoming year. For example, the likelihood a 20-year-old female will die within the next year is .00105.

The empirical concept is illustrated with the following example.

EXAMPLE

On February 1, 2003, the Space Shuttle *Columbia* exploded. This was the second disaster in 113 space missions for NASA. On the basis of this information, what is the probability that a future mission is successfully completed?

SOLUTION

We use letters or numbers to simplify the equations. P stands for probability and A represents the event of a successful mission. In this case, $P(A)$ stands for the probability a future mission is successfully completed.

$$\text{Probability of a successful flight} = \frac{\text{Number of successful flights}}{\text{Total number of flights}}$$

$$P(A) = \frac{111}{113} = .98$$

We can use this as an estimate of probability. In other words, based on past experience, the probability is .98 that a future space shuttle mission will be safely completed.

The following Venn diagram shows two events that are not mutually exclusive. The two events overlap to illustrate the joint event that some people have visited both attractions.

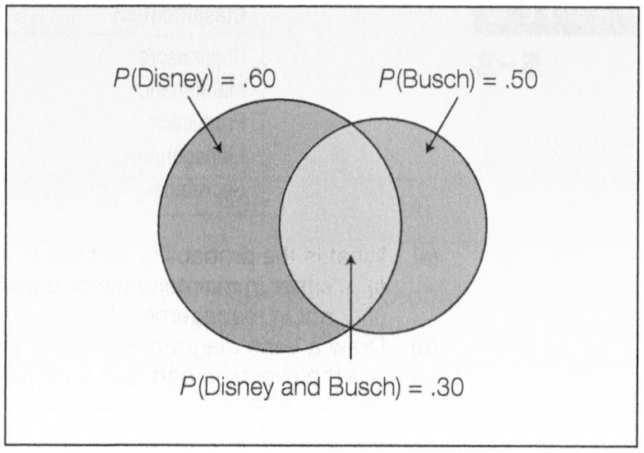

JOINT PROBABILITY A probability that measures the likelihood two or more events will happen concurrently.

So the general rule of addition, which is used to compute the probability of two events that are not mutually exclusive, is:

GENERAL RULE OF ADDITION $P(A \text{ or } B) = P(A) + P(B) - P(A \text{ and } B)$ **[5–4]**

For the expression $P(A \text{ or } B)$, the word *or* suggests that A may occur or B may occur. This also includes the possibility that A and B may occur. This use of *or* is sometimes called an **inclusive.** You could also write $P(A \text{ or } B \text{ or both})$ to emphasize that the union of the events includes the intersection of A and B.

If we compare the general and special rules of addition, the important difference is determining if the events are mutually exclusive. If the events *are* mutually exclusive, then the joint probability $P(A \text{ and } B)$ is 0 and we could use the special rule of addition. Otherwise, we must account for the joint probability and use the general rule of addition.

EXAMPLE

What is the probability that a card chosen at random from a standard deck of cards will be either a king or a heart?

SOLUTION

We may be inclined to add the probability of a king and the probability of a heart. But this creates a problem. If we do that, the king of hearts is counted with the kings and also with the hearts. So, if we simply add the probability of a king (there are 4 in a deck of 52 cards) to the probability of a heart (there are 13 in a deck of 52 cards) and report that 17 out of 52 cards meet the requirement, we have counted the king of hearts twice. We need to subtract 1 card from the 17 so the king of hearts is counted only once. Thus, there are 16 cards that are either hearts or kings. So the probability is 16/52 = .3077.

Card	Probability	Explanation
King	$P(A) = 4/52$	4 kings in a deck of 52 cards
Heart	$P(B) = 13/52$	13 hearts in a deck of 52 cards
King of Hearts	$P(A \text{ and } B) = 1/52$	1 king of hearts in a deck of 52 cards

From formula (5–4):

$$P(A \text{ or } B) = P(A) + P(B) - P(A \text{ and } B)$$
$$= 4/52 + 13/52 - 1/52$$
$$= 16/52, \text{ or } .3077$$

A Venn diagram portrays these outcomes, which are not mutually exclusive.

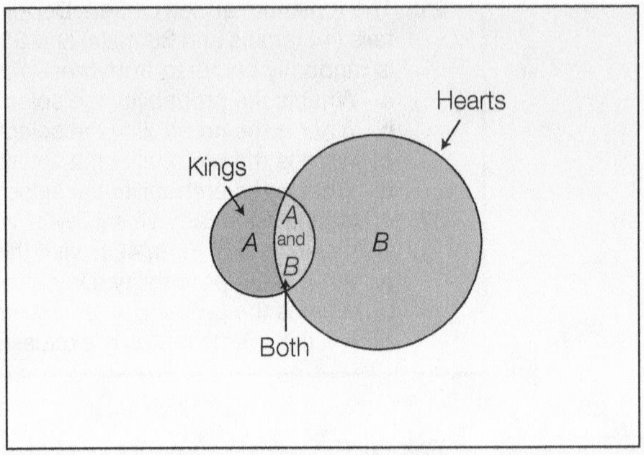

SELF-REVIEW 5–4

Routine physical examinations are conducted annually as part of a health service program for General Concrete Inc. employees. It was discovered that 8% of the employees need corrective shoes, 15% need major dental work, and 3% need both corrective shoes and major dental work.
(a) What is the probability that an employee selected at random will need either corrective shoes or major dental work?
(b) Show this situation in the form of a Venn diagram.

EXERCISES

For **DATA FILE**, please visit www.mhhe.com/lind16e

11. The events *A* and *B* are mutually exclusive. Suppose $P(A) = .30$ and $P(B) = .20$. What is the probability of either *A* or *B* occurring? What is the probability that neither *A* nor *B* will happen?
12. The events *X* and *Y* are mutually exclusive. Suppose $P(X) = .05$ and $P(Y) = .02$. What is the probability of either *X* or *Y* occurring? What is the probability that neither *X* nor *Y* will happen?
13. A study of 200 advertising firms revealed their income after taxes:

Income after Taxes	Number of Firms
Under $1 million	102
$1 million to $20 million	61
$20 million or more	37

a. What is the probability an advertising firm selected at random has under $1 million in income after taxes?
b. What is the probability an advertising firm selected at random has either an income between $1 million and $20 million, or an income of $20 million or more? What rule of probability was applied?

14. The chair of the board of directors says, "There is a 50% chance this company will earn a profit, a 30% chance it will break even, and a 20% chance it will lose money next quarter."
a. Use an addition rule to find the probability the company will not lose money next quarter.
b. Use the complement rule to find the probability it will not lose money next quarter.

15. Suppose the probability you will get an A in this class is .25 and the probability you will get a B is .50. What is the probability your grade will be above a C?
16. Two coins are tossed. If *A* is the event "two heads" and *B* is the event "two tails," are *A* and *B* mutually exclusive? Are they complements?

17. The probabilities of the events *A* and *B* are .20 and .30, respectively. The probability that both *A* and *B* occur is .15. What is the probability of either *A* or *B* occurring?
18. Let $P(X) = .55$ and $P(Y) = .35$. Assume the probability that they both occur is .20. What is the probability of either *X* or *Y* occurring?
19. Suppose the two events *A* and *B* are mutually exclusive. What is the probability of their joint occurrence?
20. A student is taking two courses, history and math. The probability the student will pass the history course is .60, and the probability of passing the math course is .70. The probability of passing both is .50. What is the probability of passing at least one?
21. The aquarium at Sea Critters Depot contains 140 fish. Eighty of these fish are green swordtails (44 female and 36 male) and 60 are orange swordtails (36 female and 24 males.). A fish is randomly captured from the aquarium:
    a. What is the probability the selected fish is a green swordtail?
    b. What is the probability the selected fish is male?
    c. What is the probability the selected fish is a male green swordtail?
    d. What is the probability the selected fish is either a male or a green swordtail?
22. A National Park Service survey of visitors to the Rocky Mountain region revealed that 50% visit Yellowstone Park, 40% visit the Tetons, and 35% visit both.
    a. What is the probability a vacationer will visit at least one of these attractions?
    b. What is the probability .35 called?
    c. Are the events mutually exclusive? Explain.

LO5-4
Calculate probabilities using the rules of multiplication.

RULES OF MULTIPLICATION TO CALCULATE PROBABILITY

In this section, we discuss the rules for computing the likelihood that two events both happen, or their joint probability. For example, 16% of the 2012 tax returns were prepared by H&R Block and 75% of those returns showed a refund. What is the likelihood a person's tax form was prepared by H&R Block and the person received a refund? Venn diagrams illustrate this as the intersection of two events. To find the likelihood of two events happening, we use the rules of multiplication. There are two rules of multiplication: the special rule and the general rule.

Special Rule of Multiplication

The special rule of multiplication requires that two events *A* and *B* are independent. Two events are independent if the occurrence of one event does not alter the probability of the occurrence of the other event.

INDEPENDENCE The occurrence of one event has no effect on the probability of the occurrence of another event.

One way to think about independence is to assume that events *A* and *B* occur at different times. For example, when event *B* occurs after event *A* occurs, does *A* have any effect on the likelihood that event *B* occurs? If the answer is no, then *A* and *B* are independent events. To illustrate independence, suppose two coins are tossed. The outcome of a coin toss (head or tail) is unaffected by the outcome of any other prior coin toss (head or tail).

For two independent events *A* and *B*, the probability that *A* and *B* will both occur is found by multiplying the two probabilities. This is the **special rule of multiplication** and is written symbolically as:

SPECIAL RULE OF MULTIPLICATION $P(A \text{ and } B) = P(A)P(B)$ **[5–5]**

For three independent events, A, B, and C, the special rule of multiplication used to determine the probability that all three events will occur is:

$$P(A \text{ and } B \text{ and } C) = P(A)P(B)P(C)$$

EXAMPLE

A survey by the American Automobile Association (AAA) revealed 60% of its members made airline reservations last year. Two members are selected at random. What is the probability both made airline reservations last year?

SOLUTION

The probability the first member made an airline reservation last year is .60, written $P(R_1) = .60$, where R_1 refers to the fact that the first member made a reservation. The probability that the second member selected made a reservation is also .60, so $P(R_2) = .60$. Because the number of AAA members is very large, you may assume that R_1 and R_2 are independent. Consequently, using formula (5–5), the probability they both make a reservation is .36, found by:

$$P(R_1 \text{ and } R_2) = P(R_1)P(R_2) = (.60)(.60) = .36$$

All possible outcomes can be shown as follows. R means a reservation is made, and $\sim R$ means no reservation is made.

With the probabilities and the complement rule, we can compute the joint probability of each outcome. For example, the probability that neither member makes a reservation is .16. Further, the probability of the first or the second member (special addition rule) making a reservation is .48 (.24 + .24). You can also observe that the outcomes are mutually exclusive and collectively exhaustive. Therefore, the probabilities sum to 1.00.

Outcomes	Joint Probability	
R_1 R_2	(.60)(.60) =	.36
R_1 $\sim R_2$	(.60)(.40) =	.24
$\sim R_1$ R_2	(.40)(.60) =	.24
$\sim R_1$ $\sim R_2$	(.40)(.40) =	.16
Total		1.00

SELF-REVIEW 5–5

From experience, Teton Tire knows the probability is .95 that a particular XB-70 tire will last 60,000 miles before it becomes bald or fails. An adjustment is made on any tire that does not last 60,000 miles. You purchase four XB-70s. What is the probability all four tires will last at least 60,000 miles?

General Rule of Multiplication

If two events are not independent, they are referred to as **dependent.** To illustrate dependency, suppose there are 10 cans of soda in a cooler; 7 are regular and 3 are diet. A can is selected from the cooler. The probability of selecting a can of diet soda is 3/10, and the probability of selecting a can of regular soda is 7/10. Then a second can is selected from the cooler, without returning the first. The probability the second

is diet depends on whether the first one selected was diet or not. The probability that the second is diet is:

2/9, if the first can is diet. (Only two cans of diet soda remain in the cooler.)
3/9, if the first can selected is regular. (All three diet sodas are still in the cooler.)

The fraction 2/9 (or 3/9) is called a **conditional probability** because its value is conditional on (dependent on) whether a diet or regular soda was the first selection from the cooler.

CONDITIONAL PROBABILITY The probability of a particular event occurring, given that another event has occurred.

In the general rule of multiplication, the conditional probability is required to compute the joint probability of two events that are not independent. For two events, *A* and *B*, that are not independent, the conditional probability is represented as $P(B|A)$, and expressed as the probability of *B* given *A*. Or the probability of *B* is conditional on the occurrence and effect of event *A*. Symbolically, the general rule of multiplication for two events that are not independent is:

GENERAL RULE OF MULTIPLICATION $P(A \text{ and } B) = P(A)P(B|A)$ **[5–6]**

EXAMPLE

A golfer has 12 golf shirts in his closet. Suppose 9 of these shirts are white and the others blue. He gets dressed in the dark, so he just grabs a shirt and puts it on. He plays golf two days in a row and does not launder and return the used shirts to the closet. What is the likelihood both shirts selected are white?

SOLUTION

The event that the first shirt selected is white is W_1. The probability is $P(W_1) = 9/12$ because 9 of the 12 shirts are white. The event that the second shirt selected is also white is identified as W_2. The conditional probability that the second shirt selected is white, given that the first shirt selected is also white, is $P(W_2|W_1) = 8/11$. Why is this so? Because after the first shirt is selected, there are only 11 shirts remaining in the closet and 8 of these are white. To determine the probability of 2 white shirts being selected, we use formula (5–6).

$$P(W_1 \text{ and } W_2) = P(W_1)P(W_2|W_1) = \left(\frac{9}{12}\right)\left(\frac{8}{11}\right) = .55$$

So the likelihood of selecting two shirts and finding them both to be white is .55.

We can extend the general rule of multiplication to more than two events. For three events *A*, *B*, and *C*, the formula is:

$$P(A \text{ and } B \text{ and } C) = P(A)P(B|A)P(C|A \text{ and } B)$$

In the case of the golf shirt example, the probability of selecting three white shirts without replacement is:

$$P(W_1 \text{ and } W_2 \text{ and } W_3) = P(W_1)P(W_2|W_1)P(W_3|W_1 \text{ and } W_2) = \left(\frac{9}{12}\right)\left(\frac{8}{11}\right)\left(\frac{7}{10}\right) = .38$$

So the likelihood of selecting three shirts without replacement and all being white is .38.

SELF-REVIEW 5–6

The board of directors of Tarbell Industries consists of eight men and four women. A four-member search committee is to be chosen at random to conduct a nationwide search for a new company president.

(a) What is the probability all four members of the search committee will be women?
(b) What is the probability all four members will be men?
(c) Does the sum of the probabilities for the events described in parts (a) and (b) equal 1? Explain.

LO5-5
Compute probabilities using a contingency table.

CONTINGENCY TABLES

Often we tally the results of a survey in a two-way table and use the results of this tally to determine various probabilities. We described this idea beginning on page 116 in Chapter 4. To review, we refer to a two-way table as a contingency table.

CONTINGENCY TABLE A table used to classify sample observations according to two or more identifiable categories or classes.

STATISTICS IN ACTION

In 2000 George W. Bush won the U.S. presidency by the slimmest of margins. Many election stories resulted, some involving voting irregularities, others raising interesting election questions. In a local Michigan election, there was a tie between two candidates for an elected position. To break the tie, the candidates drew a slip of paper from a box that contained two slips of paper, one marked "Winner" and the other unmarked. To determine which candidate drew first, election officials flipped a coin. The winner of the coin flip also drew the winning slip of paper. But was the coin flip really necessary? No, because the two events are independent. Winning the coin flip did not alter the probability of either candidate drawing the winning slip of paper.

A contingency table is a cross-tabulation that simultaneously summarizes two variables of interest and their relationship. The level of measurement can be nominal. Below are several examples.

- One hundred fifty adults were asked their gender and the number of Facebook accounts they used. The following table summarizes the results.

	Gender		
Facebook Accounts	**Men**	**Women**	**Total**
0	20	40	60
1	40	30	70
2 or more	10	10	20
Total	70	80	150

- The American Coffee Producers Association reports the following information on age and the amount of coffee consumed in a month.

	Coffee Consumption			
Age (Years)	**Low**	**Moderate**	**High**	**Total**
Under 30	36	32	24	92
30 up to 40	18	30	27	75
40 up to 50	10	24	20	54
50 and over	26	24	29	79
Total	90	110	100	300

According to this table, each of the 300 respondents is classified according to two criteria: (1) age and (2) the amount of coffee consumed.

The following example shows how the rules of addition and multiplication are used when we employ contingency tables.

EXAMPLE

Last month, the National Association of Theater Managers conducted a survey of 500 randomly selected adults. The survey asked respondents their age and the number of times they saw a movie in a theater. The results are summarized in Table 5–1.

TABLE 5–1 Number of Movies Attended per Month by Age

		Age			
Movies per Month		**Less than 30** B_1	**30 up to 60** B_2	**60 or Older** B_3	**Total**
0	A_1	15	50	10	75
1 or 2	A_2	25	100	75	200
3, 4, or 5	A_3	55	60	60	175
6 or more	A_4	5	15	30	50
Total		100	225	175	500

The association is interested in understanding the probabilities that an adult will see a movie in a theater, especially for adults 60 and older. This information is useful for making decisions regarding discounts on tickets and concessions for seniors. Determine the probability of:

1. Selecting an adult who attended 6 or more movies per month.
2. Selecting an adult who attended 2 or fewer movies per month.
3. Selecting an adult who attended 6 or more movies per month **or** is 60 years of age or older.
4. Selecting an adult who attended 6 or more movies per month **given** the person is 60 years of age or older.
5. Selecting an adult who attended 6 or more movies per month **and** is 60 years of age or older.

and we will determine the

6. Independence of the number of movies per month attended and the age of the adult.

SOLUTION

Table 5–1 is called a contingency table. In a contingency table, an individual or an object is classified according to two criteria. In this example, a sampled adult is classified by age and by the number of movies attended per month. The rules of addition [formulas (5–2) and (5–4)] and the rules of multiplication [formulas (5–5) and (5–6)] allow us to answer the various probability questions based on the contingency table.

1. To find the probability that a randomly selected adult attended 6 or more movies per month, focus on the row labeled “6 or more” (also labeled A_4) in Table 5–1. The table shows that 50 of the total of 500 adults are in this class. Using the empirical approach, the probability is computed:

$$P(\text{6 or more}) = P(A_4) = \frac{50}{500} = .10$$

This probability indicates 10% of the 500 adults attend 6 or more movies per month.

2. To determine the probability of randomly selecting an adult who went to 2 or fewer movies per month, two outcomes must be combined: attending 0 movies per month and attending 1 or 2 movies per month. These two outcomes are mutually exclusive. That is, a person can only be classified as attending 0 movies per month, or 1 or 2 movies per month, not both. Because the two outcomes are mutually exclusive, we use the special rule of addition [formula (5–2)] by adding the probabilities of attending no movies and attending 1 or 2 movies:

$$P[(\text{attending } 0) \text{ or } (\text{attending 1 or 2})] = P(A_1) + P(A_2) = \left(\frac{75}{500} + \frac{200}{500}\right) = .55$$

So 55% of the adults in the sample attended 2 or fewer movies a month.

3. To determine the probability of randomly selecting an adult who went to "6 or more" movies per month or whose age is "60 or older," we again use the rules of addition. However, in this case the outcomes are **not** mutually exclusive. Why is this? Because a person can attend more than 6 movies per month, be 60 or older, or be both. So the two groups are not mutually exclusive because it is possible that a person would be counted in both groups. To determine this probability, the general rule of addition [formula (5–4)] is used.

$$P[(6 \text{ or more}) \text{ or } (60 \text{ or older})] = P(A_4) + P(B_3) - P(A_4 \text{ and } B_3)$$
$$= \left(\frac{50}{500} + \frac{175}{500} - \frac{30}{500}\right) = .39$$

So 39% of the adults are either 60 or older, attend 6 or more movies per month, or both.

4. To determine the probability of selecting a person who attends 6 or more movies per month given that the person is 60 or older, focus only on the column labeled B_3 in Table 5–1. That is, we are only interested in the 175 adults who are 60 or older. Of these 175 adults, 30 attended 6 or more movies. Using the general rule of multiplication [formula (5–6)]:

$$P[(6 \text{ or more}) \text{ given } (60 \text{ or older})] = P(A_4|B_3) = \frac{30}{175} = .17$$

Of the 500 adults, 17% of adults who are 60 or older attend 6 or more movies per month. This is called a conditional probability because the probability is based on the "condition" of being the age of 60 or older. Recall that in part (1), 10% of all adults attend 6 or more movies per month; here we see that 17% of adults who are 60 or older attend movies. This is valuable information for theater managers regarding the characteristics of their customers.

5. The probability a person attended 6 or more movies and is 60 or older is based on two conditions and they must both happen. That is, the two outcomes "6 or more movies" (A_4) and "60 or older" (B_3) must occur jointly. To find this joint probability we use the special rule of multiplication [formula (5–6)].

$$P[(6 \text{ or more}) \text{ and } (60 \text{ or older})] = P(A_4 \text{ and } B_3) = P(A_4)\, P(B_3|A_4)$$

To compute the joint probability, first compute the simple probability of the first outcome, A_4, randomly selecting a person who attends 6 or more movies. To find the probability, refer to row A_4 in Table 5–1. There are 50 of 500 adults that attended 6 or more movies. So $P(A_4) = 50/500$.

Next, compute the conditional probability $P(B_3|A_4)$. This is the probability of selecting an adult who is 60 or older given that the person attended 6 or more movies. The conditional probability is:

$$P[(60 \text{ or older}) \text{ given } (60 \text{ or more})] = P(B_3|A_4) = 30/50$$

Using these two probabilities, the joint probability that an adult attends 6 or more movies and is 60 or older is:

$$P[(6 \text{ or more}) \text{ and } (60 \text{ or older})] = P(A_4 \text{ and } B_3) = P(A_4)\, P(B_3|A_4)$$
$$= (50/500)(30/50) = .06$$

Based on the sample information from Table 5–1, the probability that an adult is both over 60 and attended 6 or more movies is 6%. It is important to know that the 6% is relative to all 500 adults.

Is there another way to determine this joint probability without using the special rule of multiplication formula? Yes. Look directly at the cell where row A_4, attends 6 or more movies, and column B_3, 60 or older, intersect. There are 30 adults in this cell that meet both criteria, so $P(A_4 \text{ and } B_3) = 30/500 = .06$. This is the same as computed with the formula.

6. Are the events independent? We can answer this question with the help of the results in part 4. In part 4 we found the probability of selecting an adult who was 60 or older given that the adult attended 6 or more movies was .17. If age is not a factor in movie attendance then we would expect the probability of a person who is 30 or less that attended 6 or more movies to also be 17%. That is, the two conditional probabilities would be the same. The probability that an adult attends 6 or more movies per month given the adult is less than 30 years old is:

$$P[(6 \text{ or more}) \text{ given } (\text{less than } 30)] = \frac{5}{100} = .05$$

Because these two probabilities are not the same, the number of movies attended and age are not independent. To put it another way, for the 500 adults, age is related to the number of movies attended. In Chapter 15, we investigate this concept of independence in greater detail.

SELF-REVIEW 5–7

Refer to Table 5–1 on page 150 to find the following probabilities.
(a) What is the probability of selecting an adult that is 30 up to 60 years old?
(b) What is the probability of selecting an adult who is under 60 years of age?
(c) What is the probability of selecting an adult who is less than 30 years old or attended no movies?
(d) What is the probability of selecting an adult who is less than 30 years old and went to no movies?

Tree Diagrams

A **tree diagram** is a visual that is helpful in organizing and calculating probabilities for problems similar to the previous example/solution. This type of problem involves several stages and each stage is illustrated with a branch of the tree. The branches of a tree diagram are labeled with probabilities. We will use the information in Table 5–1 to show the construction of a tree diagram.

1. We begin the construction by drawing a box with the variable, age, on the left to represent the root of the tree (see Chart 5–2).

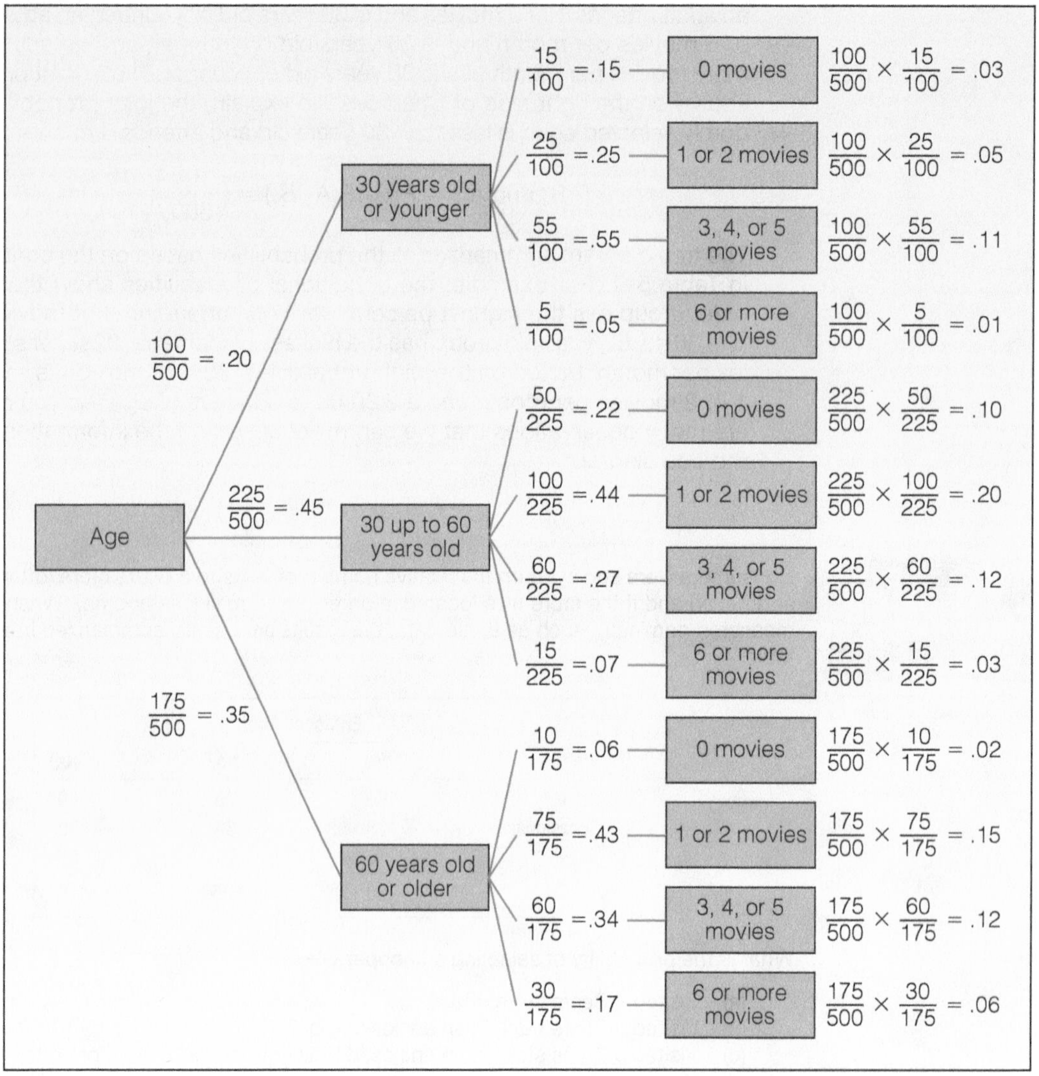

CHART 5–2 Tree Diagram Showing Age and Number of Movies Attended

2. There are three main branches going out from the root. The upper branch represents the outcome that an adult is less than 30 years old. The branch is labeled with the probability, $P(B_1) = 100/500$. The next branch represents the outcome that adults are 30 up to 60 years old. This branch is labeled with the probability $P(B_2) = 225/500$. The remaining branch is labeled $P(B_3) = 175/500$.
3. Four branches "grow" out of each of the four main branches. These branches represent the four categories of movies attended per month—0; 1 or 2; 3, 4, or 5; and 6 or more. The upper branches of the tree represent the conditional probabilities that an adult did not attend any movies given they are less than 30 years old. These are written $P(A_1|B_1)$, $P(A_2|B_1)$, $P(A_3|B_1)$, and $P(A_4|B_1)$ where A_1 refers to attending no movies; A_2 attending 1 or 2 movies per month; A_3 attending 3, 4, or 5 movies per month; and A_4 attending 6 or more movies per month. For the upper branch of the tree, these probabilities are 15/100, 25/100, 55/100, and 5/100. We write the conditional probabilities in a similar fashion on the other branches.
4. Finally we determine the various joint probabilities. For the top branches, the events are an adult attends no movies per month and is 30 years old or younger;

an adult attends 1 or 2 movies and is 30 years old or younger; an adult attends 3, 4, or 5 movies per month and is 30 years old or younger; and an adult attends 6 or more movies per month and is 30 years old or younger. These joint probabilities are shown on the right side of Chart 5–2. To explain, the joint probability that a randomly selected adult is less than 30 years old and attends 0 movies per month is:

$$P(B_1 \text{ and } A_1) = P(B_1)P(A_1|B_1) = \left(\frac{100}{500}\right)\left(\frac{15}{100}\right) = .03$$

The tree diagram summarizes all the probabilities based on the contingency table in Table 5–1. For example, the conditional probabilities show that the 60-and-older group has the highest percentage, 17%, attending 6 or movies per month. The 30-to-60-year-old group has the highest percentage, 22%, of seeing no movies per month. Based on the joint probabilities, 20% of the adults sampled attend 1 or 2 movies per month and are 30 up to 60 years of age. As you can see, there are many observations that we can make based on the information presented in the tree diagram.

SELF-REVIEW 5–8

Consumers were surveyed on the relative number of visits to a Sears store (often, occasional, and never) and if the store was located in an enclosed mall (yes and no). When variables are measured nominally, such as these data, the results are usually summarized in a contingency table.

	Enclosed Mall		
Visits	**Yes**	**No**	**Total**
Often	60	20	80
Occasional	25	35	60
Never	5	50	55
	90	105	195

What is the probability of selecting a shopper who:

(a) Visited a Sears store often?
(b) Visited a Sears store in an enclosed mall?
(c) Visited a Sears store in an enclosed mall or visited a Sears store often?
(d) Visited a Sears store often, given that the shopper went to a Sears store in an enclosed mall?

In addition:

(e) Are the number of visits and the enclosed mall variables independent?
(f) What is the probability of selecting a shopper who visited a Sears store often and it was in an enclosed mall?
(g) Draw a tree diagram and determine the various joint probabilities.

EXERCISES

23. Suppose $P(A) = .40$ and $P(B|A) = .30$. What is the joint probability of A and B?
24. Suppose $P(X_1) = .75$ and $P(Y_2|X_1) = .40$. What is the joint probability of X_1 and Y_2?
25. A local bank reports that 80% of its customers maintain a checking account, 60% have a savings account, and 50% have both. If a customer is chosen at random, what is the probability the customer has either a checking or a savings account? What is the probability the customer does not have either a checking or a savings account?
26. All Seasons Plumbing has two service trucks that frequently need repair. If the probability the first truck is available is .75, the probability the second truck is available is .50, and the probability that both trucks are available is .30, what is the probability neither truck is available?

For **DATA FILE**, please visit www.mhhe.com/lind16e

27. Refer to the following table.

Second Event	First Event A_1	A_2	A_3	Total
B_1	2	1	3	6
B_2	1	2	1	4
Total	3	3	4	10

a. Determine $P(A_1)$.
b. Determine $P(B_1 | A_2)$.
c. Determine $P(B_2 \text{ and } A_3)$.

28. Three defective electric toothbrushes were accidentally shipped to a drugstore by Cleanbrush Products along with 17 nondefective ones.
a. What is the probability the first two electric toothbrushes sold will be returned to the drugstore because they are defective?
b. What is the probability the first two electric toothbrushes sold will not be defective?

For **DATA FILE**, please visit www.mhhe.com/lind16e

29. Each salesperson at Puchett, Sheets, and Hogan Insurance Agency is rated either below average, average, or above average with respect to sales ability. Each salesperson is also rated with respect to his or her potential for advancement—either fair, good, or excellent. These traits for the 500 salespeople were cross-classified into the following table.

Sales Ability	Potential for Advancement Fair	Good	Excellent
Below average	16	12	22
Average	45	60	45
Above average	93	72	135

a. What is this table called?
b. What is the probability a salesperson selected at random will have above average sales ability and excellent potential for advancement?
c. Construct a tree diagram showing all the probabilities, conditional probabilities, and joint probabilities.

30. An investor owns three common stocks. Each stock, independent of the others, has equally likely chances of (1) increasing in value, (2) decreasing in value, or (3) remaining the same value. List the possible outcomes of this experiment. Estimate the probability at least two of the stocks increase in value.

31. A survey of 545 college students asked: What is your favorite winter sport? And, what type of college do you attend? The results are summarized below:

College Type	Favorite Winter Sport Snowboarding	Skiing	Ice Skating	Total
Junior College	68	41	46	155
Four-Year College	84	56	70	210
Graduate School	59	74	47	180
Total	211	171	163	545

Using these 545 students as the sample, a student from this study is randomly selected.
a. What is the probability of selecting a student whose favorite sport is skiing?
b. What is the probability of selecting a junior-college student?
c. If the student selected is a four-year-college student, what is the probability that the student prefers ice skating?
d. If the student selected prefers snowboarding, what is the probability that the student is in junior college?
e. If a graduate student is selected, what is the probability that the student prefers skiing or ice skating?

32. If you ask three strangers about their birthdays, what is the probability (a) All were born on Wednesday? (b) All were born on different days of the week? (c) None was born on Saturday?

LO5-6
Calculate probabilities using Bayes' theorem.

BAYES' THEOREM

In the 18th century, Reverend Thomas Bayes, an English Presbyterian minister, pondered this question: Does God really exist? Being interested in mathematics, he attempted to develop a formula to arrive at the probability God does exist based on evidence available to him on earth. Later Pierre-Simon Laplace refined Bayes' work and gave it the name "Bayes' theorem." In a workable form, **Bayes' theorem** is:

BAYES' THEOREM
$$P(A_i|B) = \frac{P(A_i)P(B|A_i)}{P(A_1)P(B|A_1) + P(A_2)P(B|A_2)} \quad \textbf{[5–7]}$$

Assume in formula (5–7) that the events A_1 and A_2 are mutually exclusive and collectively exhaustive, and A_i refers to either event A_1 or A_2. Hence A_1 and A_2 are in this case complements. The meaning of the symbols used is illustrated by the following example.

Suppose 5% of the population of Umen, a fictional Third World country, have a disease that is peculiar to that country. We will let A_1 refer to the event "has the disease" and A_2 refer to the event "does not have the disease." Thus, we know that if we select a person from Umen at random, the probability the individual chosen has the disease is .05, or $P(A_1) = .05$. This probability, $P(A_1) = P(\text{has the disease}) = .05$, is called the **prior probability.** It is given this name because the probability is assigned before any empirical data are obtained.

PRIOR PROBABILITY The initial probability based on the present level of information.

The prior probability a person is not afflicted with the disease is therefore .95, or $P(A_2) = .95$, found by $1 - .05$.

There is a diagnostic technique to detect the disease, but it is not very accurate. Let B denote the event "test shows the disease is present." Assume that historical evidence shows that if a person actually has the disease, the probability that the test will indicate the presence of the disease is .90. Using the conditional probability definitions developed earlier in this chapter, this statement is written as:

$$P(B|A_1) = .90$$

Assume the probability is .15 that for a person who actually does not have the disease the test will indicate the disease is present.

$$P(B|A_2) = .15$$

Let's randomly select a person from Umen and perform the test. The test results indicate the disease is present. What is the probability the person actually has the disease? In symbolic form, we want to know $P(A_1|B)$, which is interpreted as: $P(\text{has the disease}\,|\,\text{the test results are positive})$. The probability $P(A_1|B)$ is called a **posterior probability.**

POSTERIOR PROBABILITY A revised probability based on additional information.

With the help of Bayes' theorem, formula (5–7), we can determine the posterior probability.

$$P(A_1|B) = \frac{P(A_1)P(B|A_1)}{P(A_1)P(B|A_1) + P(A_2)P(B|A_2)}$$
$$= \frac{(.05)(.90)}{(.05)(.90) + (.95)(.15)} = \frac{.0450}{.1875} = .24$$

STATISTICS IN ACTION

A recent study by the National Collegiate Athletic Association (NCAA) reported that of 150,000 senior boys playing on their high school basketball team, 64 would make a professional team. To put it another way, the odds of a high school senior basketball player making a professional team are 1 in 2,344. From the same study:

1. The odds of a high school senior basketball player playing some college basketball are about 1 in 40.
2. The odds of a high school senior playing college basketball as a senior in college are about 1 in 60.
3. If you play basketball as a senior in college, the odds of making a professional team are about 1 in 37.5.

So the probability that a person has the disease, given that he or she tested positive, is .24. How is the result interpreted? If a person is selected at random from the population, the probability that he or she has the disease is .05. If the person is tested and the test result is positive, the probability that the person actually has the disease is increased about fivefold, from .05 to .24.

In the preceding problem, we had only two mutually exclusive and collectively exhaustive events, A_1 and A_2. If there are n such events, $A_1, A_2, \cdots, A_n$, Bayes' theorem, formula (5–7), becomes

$$P(A_i|B) = \frac{P(A_i)P(B|A_i)}{P(A_1)P(B|A_1) + P(A_2)P(B|A_2) + \cdots + P(A_n)P(B|A_n)}$$

With the preceding notation, the calculations for the Umen problem are summarized in the following table.

Event, A_i	Prior Probability, $P(A_i)$	Conditional Probability, $P(B \mid A_i)$	Joint Probability, $P(A_i \text{ and } B)$	Posterior Probability, $P(A_i \mid B)$
Disease, A_1	.05	.90	.0450	.0450/.1875 = .24
No disease, A_2	.95	.15	.1425	.1425/.1875 = .76
			$P(B)$ = .1875	1.00

Another illustration of Bayes' theorem follows.

E X A M P L E

A manufacturer of cell phones purchases a particular microchip, called the LS-24, from three suppliers: Hall Electronics, Schuller Sales, and Crawford Components. Thirty percent of the LS-24 chips are purchased from Hall Electronics, 20% from Schuller Sales, and the remaining 50% from Crawford Components. The manufacturer has extensive histories on the three suppliers and knows that 3% of the LS-24 chips from Hall Electronics are defective, 5% of chips from Schuller Sales are defective, and 4% of the chips purchased from Crawford Components are defective.

When the LS-24 chips arrive from the three suppliers, they are placed directly in a bin and not inspected or otherwise identified by supplier. A worker selects a chip for installation and finds it defective. What is the probability that it was manufactured by Schuller Sales?

S O L U T I O N

As a first step, let's summarize some of the information given in the problem statement.

- There are three mutually exclusive and collectively exhaustive events, that is, three suppliers.

A_1 The LS-24 was purchased from Hall Electronics.
A_2 The LS-24 was purchased from Schuller Sales.
A_3 The LS-24 was purchased from Crawford Components.

- The prior probabilities are:

  $P(A_1) = .30$ The probability the LS-24 was manufactured by Hall Electronics.
  $P(A_2) = .20$ The probability the LS-24 was manufactured by Schuller Sales.
  $P(A_3) = .50$ The probability the LS-24 was manufactured by Crawford Components.

- The additional information can be either:

  B_1 The LS-24 is defective, or
  B_2 The LS-24 is not defective.

- The following conditional probabilities are given.

  $P(B_1|A_1) = .03$ The probability that an LS-24 chip produced by Hall Electronics is defective.
  $P(B_1|A_2) = .05$ The probability that an LS-24 chip produced by Schuller Sales is defective.
  $P(B_1|A_3) = .04$ The probability that an LS-24 chip produced by Crawford Components is defective.

- A chip is selected from the bin. Because the chips are not identified by supplier, we are not certain which supplier manufactured the chip. We want to determine the probability that the defective chip was purchased from Schuller Sales. The probability is written $P(A_2|B_1)$.

Look at Schuller's quality record. It is the worst of the three suppliers. Now that we have found a defective LS-24 chip, we suspect that $P(A_2|B_1)$ is greater than $P(A_2)$. That is, we expect the revised probability to be greater than .20. But how much greater? Bayes' theorem can give us the answer. As a first step, consider the tree diagram in Chart 5–3.

The events are dependent, so the prior probability in the first branch is multiplied by the conditional probability in the second branch to obtain the joint probability. The joint probability is reported in the last column of Chart 5–3. To

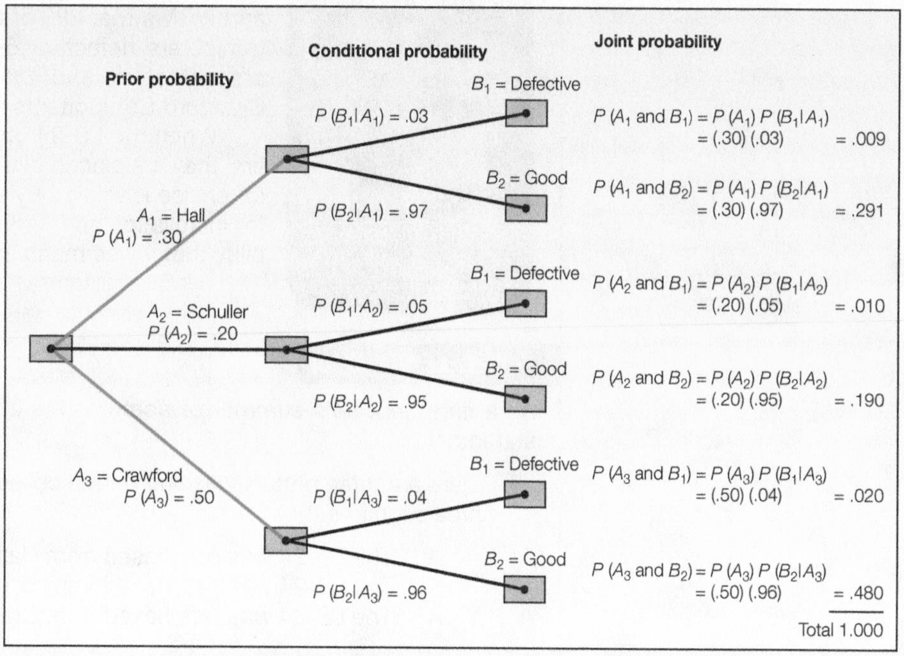

CHART 5–3 Tree Diagram of the Cell Phone Manufacturing Problem

construct the tree diagram of Chart 5–3, we used a time sequence that moved from the supplier to the determination of whether the chip was defective.

What we need to do is reverse the time process. That is, instead of moving from left to right in Chart 5–3, we need to move from right to left. We have a defective chip, and we want to determine the likelihood that it was purchased from Schuller Sales. How is that accomplished? We first look at the joint probabilities as relative frequencies out of 1,000 cases. For example, the likelihood of a defective LS-24 chip that was produced by Hall Electronics is .009. So of 1,000 cases, we would expect to find 9 defective chips produced by Hall Electronics. We observe that in 39 of 1,000 cases the LS-24 chip selected for assembly will be defective, found by 9 + 10 + 20. Of these 39 defective chips, 10 were produced by Schuller Sales. Thus, the probability that the defective LS-24 chip was purchased from Schuller Sales is 10/39 = .2564. We have now determined the revised probability of $P(A_2|B_1)$. Before we found the defective chip, the likelihood that it was purchased from Schuller Sales was .20. This likelihood has been increased to .2564.

This information is summarized in the following table.

Event, A_i	Prior Probability, $P(A_i)$	Conditional Probability, $P(B_1|A_i)$	Joint Probability, $P(A_i \text{ and } B_1)$	Posterior Probability, $P(A_i|B_1)$
Hall	.30	.03	.009	.009/.039 = .2308
Schuller	.20	.05	.010	.010/.039 = .2564
Crawford	.50	.04	.020	.020/.039 = .5128
			$P(B_1)$ = .039	1.0000

The probability the defective LS-24 chip came from Schuller Sales can be formally found by using Bayes' theorem. We compute $P(A_2|B_1)$, where A_2 refers to Schuller Sales and B_1 to the fact that the selected LS-24 chip was defective.

$$P(A_2|B_1) = \frac{P(A_2)P(B_1|A_2)}{P(A_1)P(B_1|A_1) + P(A_2)P(B_1|A_2) + P(A_3)(B_1|A_3)}$$

$$= \frac{(.20)(.05)}{(.30)(.03) + (.20)(.05) + (.50)(.04)} = \frac{.010}{.039} = .2564$$

This is the same result obtained from Chart 5–3 and from the conditional probability table.

SELF-REVIEW 5–9

Refer to the preceding example and solution.

(a) Design a formula to find the probability the part selected came from Crawford Components, given that it was a good chip.

(b) Compute the probability using Bayes' theorem.

EXERCISES

33. $P(A_1) = .60$, $P(A_2) = .40$, $P(B_1|A_1) = .05$, and $P(B_1|A_2) = .10$. Use Bayes' theorem to determine $P(A_1|B_1)$.

34. $P(A_1) = .20$, $P(A_2) = .40$, $P(A_3) = .40$, $P(B_1|A_1) = .25$, $P(B_1|A_2) = .05$, and $P(B_1|A_3) = .10$. Use Bayes' theorem to determine $P(A_3|B_1)$.

35. The Ludlow Wildcats baseball team, a minor league team in the Cleveland Indians organization, plays 70% of their games at night and 30% during the day. The team wins 50% of their night games and 90% of their day games. According to today's newspaper, they won yesterday. What is the probability the game was played at night?

36. Dr. Stallter has been teaching basic statistics for many years. She knows that 80% of the students will complete the assigned problems. She has also determined that among those who do their assignments, 90% will pass the course. Among those students who do not do

their homework, 60% will pass. Mike Fishbaugh took statistics last semester from Dr. Staller and received a passing grade. What is the probability that he completed the assignments?

37. The credit department of Lion's Department Store in Anaheim, California, reported that 30% of their sales are cash, 30% are paid with a credit card, and 40% with a debit card. Twenty percent of the cash purchases, 90% of the credit card purchases, and 60% of the debit card purchases are for more than $50. Ms. Tina Stevens just purchased a new dress that cost $120. What is the probability that she paid cash?

38. One-fourth of the residents of the Burning Ridge Estates leave their garage doors open when they are away from home. The local chief of police estimates that 5% of the garages with open doors will have something stolen, but only 1% of those closed will have something stolen. If a garage is robbed, what is the probability the doors were left open?

LO5-7

Determine the number of outcomes using principles of counting.

PRINCIPLES OF COUNTING

If the number of possible outcomes in an experiment is small, it is relatively easy to count them. There are six possible outcomes, for example, resulting from the roll of a die, namely:

If, however, there are a large number of possible outcomes, such as the number of heads and tails for an experiment with 10 tosses, it would be tedious to count all the possibilities. They could have all heads, one head and nine tails, two heads and eight tails, and so on. To facilitate counting, we describe three formulas: the **multiplication formula** (not to be confused with the multiplication *rule* described earlier in the chapter), the **permutation formula,** and the **combination formula.**

The Multiplication Formula

We begin with the multiplication formula.

MULTIPLICATION FORMULA If there are m ways of doing one thing and n ways of doing another thing, there are $m \times n$ ways of doing both.

In terms of a formula:

MULTIPLICATION FORMULA Total number of arrangements = $(m)(n)$ **[5–8]**

This can be extended to more than two events. For three events m, n, and o:

$$\text{Total number of arrangements} = (m)(n)(o)$$

EXAMPLE

An automobile dealer wants to advertise that for $29,999 you can buy a convertible, a two-door sedan, or a four-door model with your choice of either wire wheel covers or solid wheel covers. Based on the number of models and wheel covers, how many different vehicles can the dealer offer?

SOLUTION

Of course, the dealer could determine the total number of different cars by picturing and counting them. There are six.

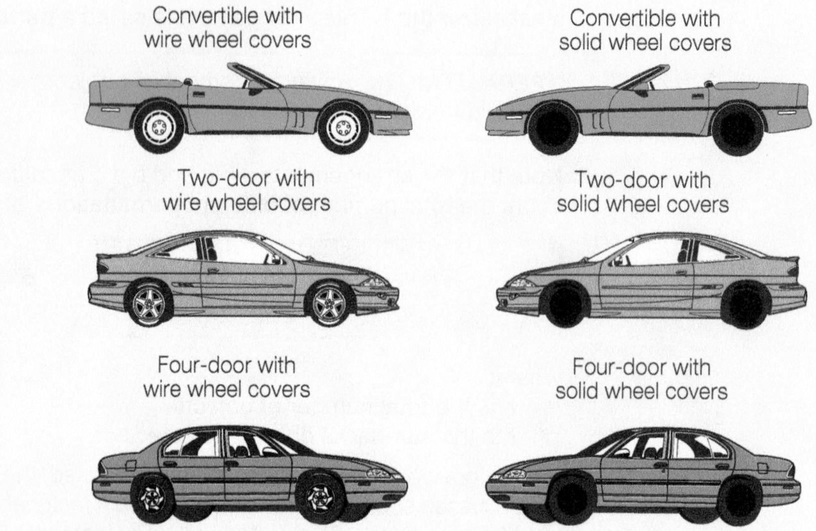

We can employ the multiplication formula as a check (where m is the number of models and n the wheel cover type). From formula (5–8):

$$\text{Total possible arrangements} = (m)(n) = (3)(2) = 6$$

It was not difficult to count all the possible model and wheel cover combinations in this example. Suppose, however, that the dealer decided to offer eight models and six types of wheel covers. It would be tedious to picture and count all the possible alternatives. Instead, the multiplication formula can be used. In this case, there are $(m)(n) = (8)(6) = 48$ possible arrangements.

Note in the preceding applications of the multiplication formula that there were *two or more groupings from which you made selections*. The automobile dealer, for example, offered a choice of models and a choice of wheel covers. If a home builder offered you four different exterior styles of a home to choose from and three interior floor plans, the multiplication formula would be used to find how many different arrangements were possible. There are 12 possibilities.

SELF-REVIEW 5–10

1. The Women's Shopping Network on cable TV offers sweaters and slacks for women. The sweaters and slacks are offered in coordinating colors. If sweaters are available in five colors and the slacks are available in four colors, how many different outfits can be advertised?
2. Pioneer manufactures three models of stereo receivers, two MP3 docking stations, four speakers, and three CD carousels. When the four types of components are sold together, they form a "system." How many different systems can the electronics firm offer?

The Permutation Formula

The multiplication formula is applied to find the number of possible arrangements for two or more groups. In contrast, we use the **permutation formula** to find the number of possible arrangements when there is a single group of objects. Illustrations of this type of problem are:

- Three electronic parts, a transistor, an LED, and a synthesizer, are assembled into a plug-in unit for a television. The parts can be assembled in any order. How many different ways can the three parts be assembled?
- A machine operator must make four safety checks before starting his machine. It does not matter in which order the checks are made. In how many different ways can the operator make the checks?

One order for the first illustration might be the transistor first, the LED second, and the synthesizer third. This arrangement is called a **permutation.**

> **PERMUTATION** Any arrangement of r objects selected from a single group of n possible objects.

Note that the arrangements *a b c* and *b a c* are different permutations. The formula to count the total number of different permutations is:

> **PERMUTATION FORMULA** $${}_nP_r = \frac{n!}{(n-r)!} \qquad \textbf{[5–9]}$$

where:

n is the total number of objects.
r is the number of objects selected.

Before we solve the two problems illustrated, the permutations and combinations (to be discussed shortly) use a notation called *n factorial*. It is written $n!$ and means the product of $n(n-1)(n-2)(n-3)\cdots(1)$. For instance, $5! = 5 \cdot 4 \cdot 3 \cdot 2 \cdot 1 = 120$.

Many of your calculators have a button with $x!$ that will perform this calculation for you. It will save you a great deal of time. For example the Texas Instrument TI-36X calculator has the following key: $x!$

It is the "third function," so check your users' manual or the Internet for instructions.

The factorial notation can also be canceled when the same number appears in both the numerator and the denominator, as shown below.

$$\frac{6!3!}{4!} = \frac{6 \cdot 5 \cdot \cancel{4} \cdot \cancel{3} \cdot \cancel{2} \cdot \cancel{1}(3 \cdot 2 \cdot 1)}{\cancel{4} \cdot \cancel{3} \cdot \cancel{2} \cdot \cancel{1}} = 180$$

By definition, zero factorial, written 0!, is 1. That is, $0! = 1$.

EXAMPLE

Referring to the group of three electronic parts that are to be assembled in any order, in how many different ways can they be assembled?

SOLUTION

There are three electronic parts to be assembled, so $n = 3$. Because all three are to be inserted in the plug-in unit, $r = 3$. Solving using formula (5–9) gives:

$${}_nP_r = \frac{n!}{(n-r)!} = \frac{3!}{(3-3)!} = \frac{3!}{0!} = \frac{3!}{1} = 6$$

We can check the number of permutations arrived at by using the permutation formula. We determine how many "spaces" have to be filled and the possibilities for each "space." In the problem involving three electronic parts, there are three locations in the plug-in unit for the three parts. There are three possibilities for the first place, two for the second (one has been used up), and one for the third, as follows:

$$(3)(2)(1) = 6 \text{ permutations}$$

The six ways in which the three electronic parts, lettered *A*, *B*, *C*, can be arranged are:

ABC	*BAC*	*CAB*	*ACB*	*BCA*	*CBA*

In the previous example, we selected and arranged all the objects, that is $n = r$. In many cases, only some objects are selected and arranged from the n possible objects. We explain the details of this application in the following example.

EXAMPLE

Betts Machine Shop Inc. has eight screw machines but only three spaces available in the production area for the machines. In how many different ways can the eight machines be arranged in the three spaces available?

SOLUTION

There are eight possibilities for the first available space in the production area, seven for the second space (one has been used up), and six for the third space. Thus:

$$(8)(7)(6) = 336,$$

that is, there are a total of 336 different possible arrangements. This could also be found by using formula (5–9). If $n = 8$ machines and $r = 3$ spaces available, the formula leads to

$$_nP_r = \frac{n!}{(n-r)!} = \frac{8!}{(8-3)!} = \frac{8!}{5!} = \frac{(8)(7)(6)\cancel{5!}}{\cancel{5!}} = 336$$

The Combination Formula

If the order of the selected objects is *not* important, any selection is called a **combination.** Logically, the number of combinations is always less than the number of permutations. The formula to count the number of r object combinations from a set of n objects is:

COMBINATION FORMULA $$_nC_r = \frac{n!}{r!(n-r)!} \quad \textbf{[5–10]}$$

For example, if executives Able, Baker, and Chauncy are to be chosen as a committee to negotiate a merger, there is only one possible combination of these three; the committee of Able, Baker, and Chauncy is the same as the committee of Baker, Chauncy, and Able. Using the combination formula:

$$_nC_r = \frac{n!}{r!(n-r)!} = \frac{3 \cdot 2 \cdot 1}{3 \cdot 2 \cdot 1(1)} = 1$$

EXAMPLE

The Grand 16 movie theater uses teams of three employees to work the concession stand each evening. There are seven employees available to work each evening. How many different teams can be scheduled to staff the concession stand?

SOLUTION

According to formula (5–10), there are 35 combinations, found by

$$_7C_3 = \frac{n!}{r!(n-r)!} = \frac{7!}{3!(7-3)!} = \frac{7!}{3!4!} = 35$$

The seven employees taken three at a time would create the possibility of 35 different teams.

When the number of permutations or combinations is large, the calculations are tedious. Computer software and handheld calculators have "functions" to compute these numbers. The Excel output for the location of the eight screw machines in the production area of Betts Machine Shop Inc. is shown below. There are a total of 336 arrangements.

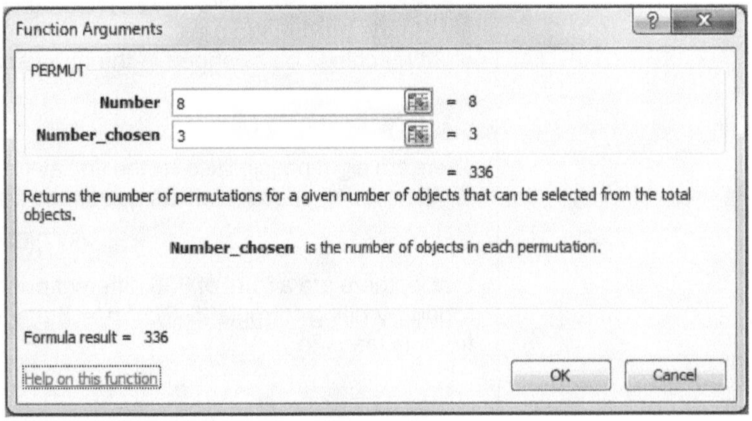

Below is the output for the number of teams at the Grand 16 movie theater. Three employees are chosen from seven possible employees.

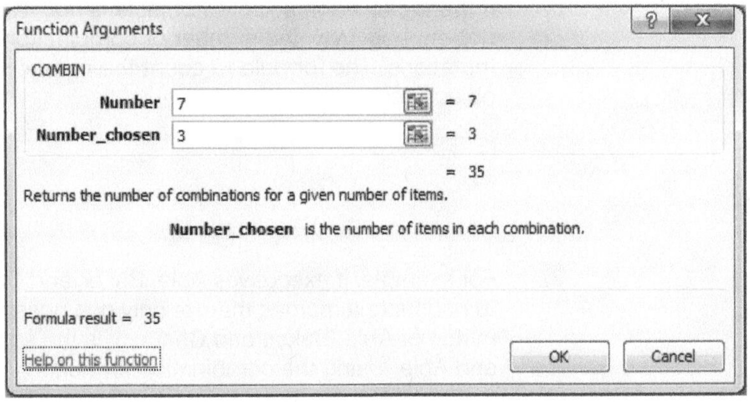

SELF-REVIEW 5–11

1. A musician wants to write a score based on only five chords: B-flat, C, D, E, and G. However, only three chords out of the five will be used in succession, such as C, B-flat, and E. Repetitions, such as B-flat, B-flat, and E, will not be permitted.
   (a) How many permutations of the five chords, taken three at a time, are possible?
   (b) Using formula (5–9), how many permutations are possible?
2. The 10 numbers 0 through 9 are to be used in code groups of four to identify an item of clothing. Code 1083 might identify a blue blouse, size medium; the code group 2031 might identify a pair of pants, size 18; and so on. Repetitions of numbers are not permitted. That is, the same number cannot be used twice (or more) in a total sequence. For example, 2256, 2562, or 5559 would not be permitted. How many different code groups can be designed?
3. In the preceding example/solution involving the Grand 16 movie theater, there were 35 possible teams of three taken from seven employees.
   (a) Use formula (5–10) to show this is true.
   (b) The manager of the theater wants to plan for staffing the concession stand with teams of five employees on the weekends to serve the larger crowds. From the seven employees, how many teams of five employees are possible?

4. In a lottery game, three numbers are randomly selected from a tumbler of balls numbered 1 through 50.
   (a) How many permutations are possible?
   (b) How many combinations are possible?

EXERCISES

39. Solve the following:
a. 40!/35!
b. ${}_7P_4$
c. ${}_5C_2$

40. Solve the following:
a. 20!/17!
b. ${}_9P_3$
c. ${}_7C_2$

41. A pollster randomly selected 4 of 10 available people. How many different groups of 4 are possible?

42. A telephone number consists of seven digits, the first three representing the exchange. How many different telephone numbers are possible within the 537 exchange?

43. An overnight express company must include five cities on its route. How many different routes are possible, assuming that it does not matter in which order the cities are included in the routing?

44. A representative of the Environmental Protection Agency (EPA) wants to select samples from 10 landfills. The director has 15 landfills from which she can collect samples. How many different samples are possible?

45. A national pollster has developed 15 questions designed to rate the performance of the president of the United States. The pollster will select 10 of these questions. How many different arrangements are there for the order of the 10 selected questions?

46. A company is creating three new divisions and seven managers are eligible to be appointed head of a division. How many different ways could the three new heads be appointed? Hint: Assume the division assignment makes a difference.

CHAPTER SUMMARY

I. A probability is a value between 0 and 1 inclusive that represents the likelihood a particular event will happen.
  A. An experiment is the observation of some activity or the act of taking some measurement.
  B. An outcome is a particular result of an experiment.
  C. An event is the collection of one or more outcomes of an experiment.

II. There are three definitions of probability.
  A. The classical definition applies when there are n equally likely outcomes to an experiment.
  B. The empirical definition occurs when the number of times an event happens is divided by the number of observations.
  C. A subjective probability is based on whatever information is available.

III. Two events are mutually exclusive if by virtue of one event happening the other cannot happen.

IV. Events are independent if the occurrence of one event does not affect the occurrence of another event.

V. The rules of addition refer to the probability that any of two or more events can occur.
  A. The special rule of addition is used when events are mutually exclusive.

$$P(A \text{ or } B) = P(A) + P(B) \qquad \textbf{[5–2]}$$

  B. The general rule of addition is used when the events are not mutually exclusive.

$$P(A \text{ or } B) = P(A) + P(B) - P(A \text{ and } B) \qquad \textbf{[5–4]}$$

STATISTICS IN ACTION

Government statistics show there are about 1.7 automobile-caused fatalities for every 100,000,000 vehicle-miles. If you drive 1 mile to the store to buy your lottery ticket and then return home, you have driven 2 miles. Thus the probability that you will join this statistical group on your next 2-mile round trip is $2 \times 1.7/100{,}000{,}000 = 0.000000034$. This can also be stated as "One in 29,411,765." Thus, if you drive to the store to buy your Powerball ticket, your chance of being killed (or killing someone else) is more than 4 times greater than the chance that you will win the Powerball Jackpot, one chance in 120,526,770. **http://www.durangobill.com/Powerball Odds.html**

C. The complement rule is used to determine the probability of an event happening by subtracting the probability of the event not happening from 1.

$$P(A) = 1 - P(\sim A) \qquad \textbf{[5–3]}$$

VI. The rules of multiplication are applied when two or more events occur simultaneously.

A. The special rule of multiplication refers to events that are independent.

$$P(A \text{ and } B) = P(A)P(B) \qquad \textbf{[5–5]}$$

B. The general rule of multiplication refers to events that are not independent.

$$P(A \text{ and } B) = P(A)P(B|A) \qquad \textbf{[5–6]}$$

C. A joint probability is the likelihood that two or more events will happen at the same time.

D. A conditional probability is the likelihood that an event will happen, given that another event has already happened.

E. Bayes' theorem is a method of revising a probability, given that additional information is obtained. For two mutually exclusive and collectively exhaustive events:

$$P(A_1|B) = \frac{P(A_1)P(B|A_1)}{P(A_1)P(B|A_1) + P(A_2)P(B|A_2)} \qquad \textbf{[5–7]}$$

VII. There are three counting rules that are useful in determining the number of outcomes in an experiment.

A. The multiplication rule states that if there are m ways one event can happen and n ways another event can happen, then there are mn ways the two events can happen.

$$\text{Number of arrangements} = (m)(n) \qquad \textbf{[5–8]}$$

B. A permutation is an arrangement in which the order of the objects selected from a specific pool of objects is important.

$$_nP_r = \frac{n!}{(n - r)!} \qquad \textbf{[5–9]}$$

C. A combination is an arrangement where the order of the objects selected from a specific pool of objects is not important.

$$_nC_r = \frac{n!}{r!(n - r)!} \qquad \textbf{[5–10]}$$

PRONUNCIATION KEY

SYMBOL	MEANING	PRONUNCIATION
$P(A)$	Probability of *A*	*P* of *A*
$P(\sim A)$	Probability of not *A*	*P* of not *A*
$P(A \text{ and } B)$	Probability of *A* and *B*	*P* of *A* and *B*
$P(A \text{ or } B)$	Probability of *A* or *B*	*P* of *A* or *B*
$P(A\|B)$	Probability of *A* given *B* has happened	*P* of *A* given *B*
$_nP_r$	Permutation of *n* items selected *r* at a time	*Pnr*
$_nC_r$	Combination of *n* items selected *r* at a time	*Cnr*

CHAPTER EXERCISES

47. The marketing research department at Pepsico plans to survey teenagers about a newly developed soft drink. Each will be asked to compare it with his or her favorite soft drink.

a. What is the experiment?

b. What is one possible event?

48. The number of times a particular event occurred in the past is divided by the number of occurrences. What is this approach to probability called?

49. The probability that the cause and the cure for all cancers will be discovered before the year 2020 is .20. What viewpoint of probability does this statement illustrate?

For **DATA FILE**, please visit www.mhhe.com/lind16e

50. Berdine's Chicken Factory has several stores in the Hilton Head, South Carolina, area. When interviewing applicants for server positions, the owner would like to include information on the amount of tip a server can expect to earn per check (or bill). A study of 500 recent checks indicated the server earned the following amounts in tips per 8-hour shift.

Amount of Tip	Number
\$0 up to \$ 20	200
20 up to 50	100
50 up to 100	75
100 up to 200	75
200 or more	50
Total	500

a. What is the probability of a tip of \$200 or more?
b. Are the categories "\$0 up to \$20," "\$20 up to \$50," and so on considered mutually exclusive?
c. If the probabilities associated with each outcome were totaled, what would that total be?
d. What is the probability of a tip of up to \$50?
e. What is the probability of a tip of less than \$200?

51. Winning all three "Triple Crown" races is considered the greatest feat of a pedigree racehorse. After a successful Kentucky Derby, Corn on the Cob is a heavy favorite at 2 to 1 odds to win the Preakness Stakes.
a. If he is a 2 to 1 favorite to win the Belmont Stakes as well, what is his probability of winning the Triple Crown?
b. What do his chances for the Preakness Stakes have to be in order for him to be "even money" to earn the Triple Crown?

52. The first card selected from a standard 52-card deck is a king.
a. If it is returned to the deck, what is the probability that a king will be drawn on the second selection?
b. If the king is not replaced, what is the probability that a king will be drawn on the second selection?
c. What is the probability that a king will be selected on the first draw from the deck and another king on the second draw (assuming that the first king was not replaced)?

53. Armco, a manufacturer of traffic light systems, found that under accelerated-life tests, 95% of the newly developed systems lasted 3 years before failing to change signals properly.
a. If a city purchased four of these systems, what is the probability all four systems would operate properly for at least 3 years?
b. Which rule of probability does this illustrate?
c. Using letters to represent the four systems, write an equation to show how you arrived at the answer to part (a).

54. Refer to the following picture.

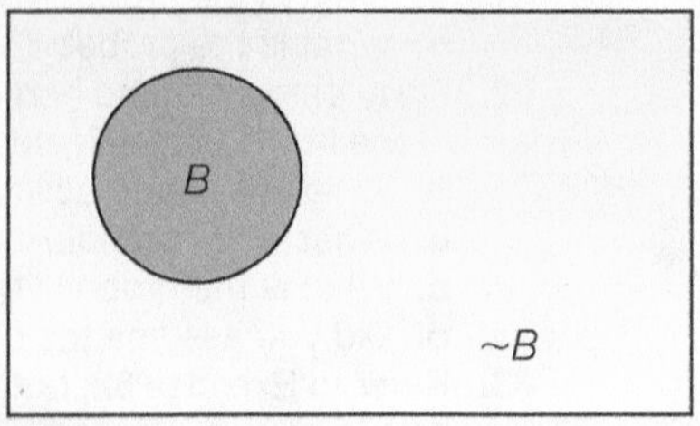

a. What is the picture called?
b. What rule of probability is illustrated?
c. B represents the event of choosing a family that receives welfare payments. What does $P(B) + P(\sim B)$ equal?

55. In a management trainee program at Claremont Enterprises, 80% of the trainees are female and 20% male. Ninety percent of the females attended college, and 78% of the males attended college.
   a. A management trainee is selected at random. What is the probability that the person selected is a female who did not attend college?
   b. Are gender and attending college independent? Why?
   c. Construct a tree diagram showing all the probabilities, conditional probabilities, and joint probabilities.
   d. Do the joint probabilities total 1.00? Why?

56. Assume the likelihood that any flight on Delta Airlines arrives within 15 minutes of the scheduled time is .90. We randomly selected a Delta flight on four different days.
   a. What is the likelihood all four of the selected flights arrived within 15 minutes of the scheduled time?
   b. What is the likelihood that none of the selected flights arrived within 15 minutes of the scheduled time?
   c. What is the likelihood at least one of the selected flights did not arrive within 15 minutes of the scheduled time?

57. There are 100 employees at Kiddie Carts International. Fifty-seven of the employees are hourly workers, 40 are supervisors, 2 are secretaries, and the remaining employee is the president. Suppose an employee is selected:
   a. What is the probability the selected employee is an hourly worker?
   b. What is the probability the selected employee is either an hourly worker or a supervisor?
   c. Refer to part (b). Are these events mutually exclusive?
   d. What is the probability the selected employee is neither an hourly worker nor a supervisor?

58. Buster Posey of the San Francisco Giants had the highest batting average in the 2012 Major League Baseball season. His average was .336. So assume the probability of getting a hit is .336 for each time he batted. In a particular game, assume he batted three times.
   a. This is an example of what type of probability?
   b. What is the probability of getting three hits in a particular game?
   c. What is the probability of not getting any hits in a game?
   d. What is the probability of getting at least one hit?

59. Four women's college basketball teams are participating in a single-elimination holiday basketball tournament. If one team is favored in its semifinal match by odds of 2 to 1 and another squad is favored in its contest by odds of 3 to 1, what is the probability that:
   a. Both favored teams win their games?
   b. Neither favored team wins its game?
   c. At least one of the favored teams wins its game?

60. There are three clues labeled "daily double" on the game show *Jeopardy.* If three equally matched contenders play, what is the probability that:
   a. A single contestant finds all three "daily doubles"?
   b. The returning champion gets all three of the "daily doubles"?
   c. Each of the players selects precisely one of the "daily doubles"?

61. Brooks Insurance Inc. wishes to offer life insurance to men age 60 via the Internet. Mortality tables indicate the likelihood of a 60-year-old man surviving another year is .98. If the policy is offered to five men age 60:
   a. What is the probability all five men survive the year?
   b. What is the probability at least one does not survive?

62. Forty percent of the homes constructed in the Quail Creek area include a security system. Three homes are selected at random:
   a. What is the probability all three of the selected homes have a security system?
   b. What is the probability none of the three selected homes has a security system?
   c. What is the probability at least one of the selected homes has a security system?
   d. Did you assume the events to be dependent or independent?

63. Refer to Exercise 62, but assume there are 10 homes in the Quail Creek area and 4 of them have a security system. Three homes are selected at random:
   a. What is the probability all three of the selected homes have a security system?
   b. What is the probability none of the three selected homes has a security system?
   c. What is the probability at least one of the selected homes has a security system?
   d. Did you assume the events to be dependent or independent?

64. There are 20 families living in the Willbrook Farms Development. Of these families, 10 prepared their own federal income taxes for last year, 7 had their taxes prepared by a local professional, and the remaining 3 by H&R Block.
a. What is the probability of selecting a family that prepared their own taxes?
b. What is the probability of selecting two families, both of which prepared their own taxes?
c. What is the probability of selecting three families, all of which prepared their own taxes?
d. What is the probability of selecting two families, neither of which had their taxes prepared by H&R Block?

65. The board of directors of Saner Automatic Door Company consists of 12 members, 3 of whom are women. A new policy and procedures manual is to be written for the company. A committee of three is randomly selected from the board to do the writing.
a. What is the probability that all members of the committee are men?
b. What is the probability that at least one member of the committee is a woman?

66. A recent survey reported in *BloombergBusinessweek* dealt with the salaries of CEOs at large corporations and whether company shareholders made money or lost money.

For **DATA FILE**, please visit www.mhhe.com/lind16e

	CEO Paid More Than $1 Million	CEO Paid Less Than $1 Million	Total
Shareholders made money	2	11	13
Shareholders lost money	4	3	7
Total	6	14	20

If a company is randomly selected from the list of 20 studied, what is the probability:
a. The CEO made more than $1 million?
b. The CEO made more than $1 million or the shareholders lost money?
c. The CEO made more than $1 million given the shareholders lost money?
d. Of selecting two CEOs and finding they both made more than $1 million?

67. Althoff and Roll, an investment firm in Augusta, Georgia, advertises extensively in the *Augusta Morning Gazette,* the newspaper serving the region. The *Gazette* marketing staff estimates that 60% of Althoff and Roll's potential market read the newspaper. It is further estimated that 85% of those who read the *Gazette* remember the Althoff and Roll advertisement.
a. What percent of the investment firm's potential market sees and remembers the advertisement?
b. What percent of the investment firm's potential market sees, but does not remember, the advertisement?

68. An Internet company located in Southern California has season tickets to the Los Angeles Lakers basketball games. The company president always invites one of the four vice presidents to attend games with him, and claims he selects the person to attend at random. One of the four vice presidents has not been invited to attend any of the last five Lakers home games. What is the likelihood this could be due to chance?

69. A computer-supply retailer purchased a batch of 1,000 CD-R disks and attempted to format them for a particular application. There were 857 perfect CDs, 112 CDs were usable but had bad sectors, and the remainder could not be used at all.
a. What is the probability a randomly chosen CD is not perfect?
b. If the disk is not perfect, what is the probability it cannot be used at all?

70. An investor purchased 100 shares of Fifth Third Bank stock and 100 shares of Santee Electric Cooperative stock. The probability the bank stock will appreciate over a year is .70. The probability the electric utility will increase over the same period is .60. Assume the two events are independent.
a. What is the probability both stocks appreciate during the period?
b. What is the probability the bank stock appreciates but the utility does not?
c. What is the probability at least one of the stocks appreciates?

71. Flashner Marketing Research Inc. specializes in providing assessments of the prospects for women's apparel shops in shopping malls. Al Flashner, president, reports that he assesses the prospects as good, fair, or poor. Records from previous assessments show that 60% of the time the prospects were rated as good, 30% of the time fair, and 10% of the time poor. Of those rated good, 80% made a profit the first year; of those rated fair, 60% made a profit the first year; and of those rated poor, 20% made a profit the first year. Connie's Apparel was one of Flashner's clients. Connie's Apparel made a profit last year. What is the probability that it was given an original rating of poor?

72. Two boxes of men's Old Navy shirts were received from the factory. Box 1 contained 25 mesh polo shirts and 15 Super-T shirts. Box 2 contained 30 mesh polo shirts and 10 Super-T shirts. One of the boxes was selected at random, and a shirt was chosen at random from that box to be inspected. The shirt was a mesh polo shirt. Given this information, what is the probability that the mesh polo shirt came from box 1?

73. With each purchase of a large pizza at Tony's Pizza, the customer receives a coupon that can be scratched to see if a prize will be awarded. The probability of winning a free soft drink is 0.10, and the probability of winning a free large pizza is 0.02. You plan to eat lunch tomorrow at Tony's. What is the probability:

a. That you will win either a large pizza or a soft drink?
b. That you will not win a prize?
c. That you will not win a prize on three consecutive visits to Tony's?
d. That you will win at least one prize on one of your next three visits to Tony's?

74. For the daily lottery game in Illinois, participants select three numbers between 0 and 9. A number cannot be selected more than once, so a winning ticket could be, say, 307 but not 337. Purchasing one ticket allows you to select one set of numbers. The winning numbers are announced on TV each night.

a. How many different outcomes (three-digit numbers) are possible?
b. If you purchase a ticket for the game tonight, what is the likelihood you will win?
c. Suppose you purchase three tickets for tonight's drawing and select a different number for each ticket. What is the probability that you will not win with any of the tickets?

75. Several years ago, Wendy's Hamburgers advertised that there are 256 different ways to order your hamburger. You may choose to have, or omit, any combination of the following on your hamburger: mustard, ketchup, onion, pickle, tomato, relish, mayonnaise, and lettuce. Is the advertisement correct? Show how you arrive at your answer.

76. Recent surveys indicate 60% of tourists to China visited the Forbidden City, the Temple of Heaven, the Great Wall, and other historical sites in or near Beijing. Forty percent visited Xi'an with its magnificent terra-cotta soldiers, horses, and chariots, which lay buried for over 2,000 years. Thirty percent of the tourists went to both Beijing and Xi'an. What is the probability that a tourist visited at least one of these places?

77. A new chewing gum has been developed that is helpful to those who want to stop smoking. If 60% of those people chewing the gum are successful in stopping smoking, what is the probability that in a group of four smokers using the gum at least one quits smoking?

78. Reynolds Construction Company has agreed not to erect all "look-alike" homes in a new subdivision. Five exterior designs are offered to potential home buyers. The builder has standardized three interior plans that can be incorporated in any of the five exteriors. How many different ways can the exterior and interior plans be offered to potential home buyers?

79. A new sports car model has defective brakes 15% of the time and a defective steering mechanism 5% of the time. Let's assume (and hope) that these problems occur independently. If one or the other of these problems is present, the car is called a "lemon." If both of these problems are present, the car is a "hazard." Your instructor purchased one of these cars yesterday. What is the probability it is:

a. A lemon?
b. A hazard?

80. The state of Maryland has license plates with three numbers followed by three letters. How many different license plates are possible?

81. There are four people being considered for the position of chief executive officer of Dalton Enterprises. Three of the applicants are over 60 years of age. Two are female, of which only one is over 60.

a. What is the probability that a candidate is over 60 and female?
b. Given that the candidate is male, what is the probability he is less than 60?
c. Given that the person is over 60, what is the probability the person is female?

82. Tim Bleckie is the owner of Bleckie Investment and Real Estate Company. The company recently purchased four tracts of land in Holly Farms Estates and six tracts in Newburg Woods. The tracts are all equally desirable and sell for about the same amount.

a. What is the probability that the next two tracts sold will be in Newburg Woods?
b. What is the probability that of the next four sold at least one will be in Holly Farms?
c. Are these events independent or dependent?

83. A computer password consists of four characters. The characters can be one of the 26 letters of the alphabet. Each character may be used more than once. How many different passwords are possible?

84. A case of 24 cans contains 1 can that is contaminated. Three cans are to be chosen randomly for testing.
 a. How many different combinations of three cans could be selected?
 b. What is the probability that the contaminated can is selected for testing?

85. A puzzle in the newspaper presents a matching problem. The names of 10 U.S. presidents are listed in one column, and their vice presidents are listed in random order in the second column. The puzzle asks the reader to match each president with his vice president. If you make the matches randomly, how many matches are possible? What is the probability all 10 of your matches are correct?

86. Two components, *A* and *B*, operate in series. Being in series means that for the system to operate, both components *A* and *B* must work. Assume the two components are independent. What is the probability the system works under these conditions? The probability *A* works is .90 and the probability *B* functions is also .90.

87. Horwege Electronics Inc. purchases TV picture tubes from four different suppliers. Tyson Wholesale supplies 20% of the tubes, Fuji Importers 30%, Kirkpatricks 25%, and Parts Inc. 25%. Tyson Wholesale tends to have the best quality, as only 3% of its tubes arrive defective. Fuji Importers' tubes are 4% defective, Kirkpatricks' 7%, and Parts Inc.'s are 6.5% defective.
 a. What is the overall percent defective?
 b. A defective picture tube was discovered in the latest shipment. What is the probability that it came from Tyson Wholesale?

88. ABC Auto Insurance classifies drivers as good, medium, or poor risks. Drivers who apply to them for insurance fall into these three groups in the proportions 30%, 50%, and 20%, respectively. The probability a "good" driver will have an accident is .01, the probability a "medium" risk driver will have an accident is .03, and the probability a "poor" driver will have an accident is .10. The company sells Mr. Brophy an insurance policy and he has an accident. What is the probability Mr. Brophy is:
 a. A "good" driver?
 b. A "medium" risk driver?
 c. A "poor" driver?

89. You take a trip by air that involves three independent flights. If there is an 80% chance each specific leg of the trip is on time, what is the probability all three flights arrive on time?

90. The probability a D-Link network server is down is .05. If you have three independent servers, what is the probability that at least one of them is operational?

91. Twenty-two percent of all liquid crystal displays (LCDs) are manufactured by Samsung. What is the probability that in a collection of three independent LCD purchases, at least one is a Samsung?

DATA SET EXERCISES

(The data for these exercises are available at the text website: www.mhhe.com/lind16e.)

92. Refer to the Real Estate data, which report information on homes sold in the Goodyear, Arizona, area during the last year.
 a. Sort the data into a table that shows the number of homes that have a pool versus the number that don't have a pool in each of the five townships. If a home is selected at random, compute the following probabilities.
  1. The home is in Township 1 or has a pool.
  2. Given that it is in Township 3, that it has a pool.
  3. The home has a pool and is in Township 3.
 b. Sort the data into a table that shows the number of homes that have a garage attached versus those that don't in each of the five townships. If a home is selected at random, compute the following probabilities:
  1. The home has a garage attached.
  2. The home does not have a garage attached, given that it is in Township 5.
  3. The home has a garage attached and is in Township 3.
  4. The home does not have a garage attached or is in Township 2.

93. Refer to the Baseball 2012 data, which reports information on the 30 Major League Baseball teams for the 2012 season. Set up three variables:
 - Divide the teams into two groups, those that had a winning season and those that did not. That is, create a variable to count the teams that won 81 games or more, and those that won 80 or less.

- Create a new variable for attendance, using three categories: attendance less than 2.0 million, attendance of 2.0 million up to 3.0 million, and attendance of 3.0 million or more.
- Create a variable that shows the teams that play in a stadium less than 15 years old versus one that is 15 years old or more.

Answer the following questions.

a. Create a table that shows the number of teams with a winning season versus those with a losing season by the three categories of attendance. If a team is selected at random, compute the following probabilities:
   1. The team had a winning season.
   2. The team had a winning season or attendance of more than 3.0 million.
   3. The team had a winning season given attendance was more than 3.0 million.
   4. The team has a winning season and attracted fewer than 2.0 million fans.

b. Create a table that shows the number of teams with a winning season versus those that play in new or old stadiums. If a team is selected at random, compute the following probabilities:
   1. Selecting a team with a winning season.
   2. The likelihood of selecting a team with a winning record and playing in a new stadium.
   3. The team had a winning record or played in a new stadium.

94. Refer to the data on the school buses in the Buena School District. Set up a variable that divides the age of the buses into three groups: new (less than 5 years old), medium (5 but less than 10 years), and old (10 or more years). The median maintenance cost is $456. Based on this value, create a variable for those less than or equal to the median (low maintenance) and those more than the median (high maintenance). Finally, develop a table to show the relationship between maintenance cost and age of the bus.

a. What percentage of the buses are new?
b. What percentage of the new buses have low maintenance?
c. What percentage of the old buses have high maintenance?
d. Does maintenance cost seem to be related to the age of the bus? Hint: Compare the maintenance cost of the old buses with the cost of the new buses? Would you conclude maintenance cost is independent of the age?

Discrete Probability Distributions

6

RECENT STATISTICS SUGGEST that 15% of those who visit a retail site on the Web make a purchase. A retailer wished to verify this claim. To do so, she selected a sample of 16 "hits" to her site and found that 4 had actually made a purchase. What is the likelihood of exactly four purchases? How many purchases should she expect? What is the likelihood that four or more "hits" result in a purchase? (See Exercise 49 and LO6-4.)

LEARNING OBJECTIVES

When you have completed this chapter, you will be able to:

LO6-1 Identify the characteristics of a probability distribution.

LO6-2 Distinguish between discrete and continuous random variables.

LO6-3 Compute the mean, variance, and standard deviation of a discrete probability distribution.

LO6-4 Explain the assumptions of the binomial distribution and apply it to calculate probabilities.

LO6-5 Explain the assumptions of the hypergeometric distribution and apply it to calculate probabilities.

LO6-6 Explain the assumptions of the Poisson distribution and apply it to calculate probabilities.

INTRODUCTION

Chapters 2 through 4 are devoted to descriptive statistics. We describe raw data by organizing the data into a frequency distribution and portraying the distribution in tables, graphs, and charts. Also, we compute a measure of location—such as the arithmetic mean, median, or mode—to locate a typical value near the center of the distribution. The range and the standard deviation are used to describe the spread in the data. These chapters focus on describing *something that has already happened.*

Starting with Chapter 5, the emphasis changes—we begin examining *something that could happen.* We note that this facet of statistics is called *statistical inference.* The objective is to make inferences (statements) about a population based on a number of observations, called a sample, selected from the population. In Chapter 5, we state that a probability is a value between 0 and 1 inclusive, and we examine how probabilities can be combined using rules of addition and multiplication.

This chapter begins the study of **probability distributions.** A probability distribution gives the entire range of values that can occur based on an experiment. A probability distribution is similar to a relative frequency distribution. However, instead of describing the past, it describes a likely future event. For example, a drug manufacturer may claim a treatment will cause weight loss for 80% of the population. A consumer protection agency may test the treatment on a sample of six people. If the manufacturer's claim is true, it is *almost impossible* to have an outcome where no one in the sample loses weight and it is *most likely* that five out of the six do lose weight.

In this chapter, we discuss the mean, variance, and standard deviation of a probability distribution. We also discuss three frequently occurring probability distributions: the binomial, hypergeometric, and Poisson.

LO6-1
Identify the characteristics of a probability distribution.

WHAT IS A PROBABILITY DISTRIBUTION?

A probability distribution shows the possible outcomes of an experiment and the probability of each of these outcomes.

PROBABILITY DISTRIBUTION A listing of all the outcomes of an experiment and the probability associated with each outcome.

Below are the major characteristics of a probability distribution.

CHARACTERISTICS OF A PROBABILITY DISTRIBUTION

1. The probability of a particular outcome is between 0 and 1 inclusive.
2. The outcomes are mutually exclusive.
3. The list of outcomes is exhaustive. So the sum of the probabilities of the outcomes is equal to 1.

How can we generate a probability distribution? The following example will explain.

EXAMPLE

Suppose we are interested in the number of heads showing face up on three tosses of a coin. This is the experiment. The possible results are zero heads, one head, two heads, and three heads. What is the probability distribution for the number of heads?

SOLUTION

There are eight possible outcomes. A tail might appear face up on the first toss, another tail on the second toss, and another tail on the third toss of the coin. Or we might get a tail, tail, and head, in that order. We use the multiplication formula for counting outcomes (5–8). There are (2)(2)(2) or 8 possible results. These results are shown on the next page.

Possible Result	Coin Toss First	Second	Third	Number of Heads
1	T	T	T	0
2	T	T	H	1
3	T	H	T	1
4	T	H	H	2
5	H	T	T	1
6	H	T	H	2
7	H	H	T	2
8	H	H	H	3

Note that the outcome "zero heads" occurred only once, "one head" occurred three times, "two heads" occurred three times, and the outcome "three heads" occurred only once. That is, "zero heads" happened one out of eight times. Thus, the probability of zero heads is one-eighth, the probability of one head is three-eighths, and so on. The probability distribution is shown in Table 6–1. Because one of these outcomes must happen, the total of the probabilities of all possible events is 1.000. This is always true. The same information is shown in Chart 6–1.

TABLE 6–1 Probability Distribution for the Events of Zero, One, Two, and Three Heads Showing Face Up on Three Tosses of a Coin

Number of Heads, x	Probability of Outcome, $P(x)$
0	$\frac{1}{8} = .125$
1	$\frac{3}{8} = .375$
2	$\frac{3}{8} = .375$
3	$\frac{1}{8} = .125$
Total	$\frac{8}{8} = 1.000$

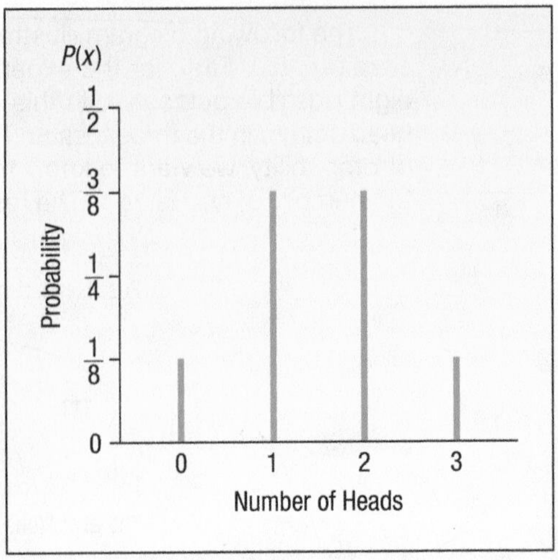

CHART 6–1 Graphical Presentation of the Number of Heads Resulting from Three Tosses of a Coin and the Corresponding Probability

Refer to the coin-tossing example in Table 6–1. We write the probability of x as $P(x)$. So the probability of zero heads is P(0 heads) = .125, and the probability of one head is P(1 head) = .375, and so forth. The sum of these mutually exclusive probabilities is 1; that is, from Table 6–1, .125 + .375 + .375 + .125 = 1.00.

SELF-REVIEW 6–1

The possible outcomes of an experiment involving the roll of a six-sided die are a one-spot, a two-spot, a three-spot, a four-spot, a five-spot, and a six-spot.
(a) Develop a probability distribution for the number of possible spots.
(b) Portray the probability distribution graphically.
(c) What is the sum of the probabilities?

LO6-2
Distinguish between discrete and continuous random variables.

RANDOM VARIABLES

In any experiment of chance, the outcomes occur randomly. So it is often called a *random variable.* For example, rolling a single die is an experiment: Any one of six possible outcomes can occur. Some experiments result in outcomes that are quantitative (such as dollars, weight, or number of children), and others result in qualitative outcomes (such as color or religious preference). Each value of the random variable is associated with a probability to indicate the chance of a particular outcome. A few examples will further illustrate what is meant by a **random variable.**

- If we count the number of employees absent from the day shift on Monday, the number might be 0, 1, 2, 3, . . . The number absent is the random variable.
- If we weigh four steel bars, the weights might be 2,492 pounds, 2,497 pounds, 2,506 pounds, and so on. The weight is the random variable.
- Other random variables might be the number of defective lightbulbs produced in an hour at the Cleveland Company Inc., the grade level (9, 10, 11, or 12) of the members of the St. James High School girls' basketball team, the number of runners in the 2013 New York City Marathon, and the daily number of drivers charged with driving under the influence of alcohol in Brazoria County, Texas, last month.

RANDOM VARIABLE A quantity resulting from an experiment that, by chance, can assume different values.

The following diagram illustrates the terms *experiment, outcome, event,* and *random variable.* First, for the experiment where a coin is tossed three times, there are eight possible outcomes. In this experiment, we are interested in the event that one head occurs in the three tosses. The random variable is the number of heads. In terms of probability, we want to know the probability of the event that the random variable, the number of heads, is 1. The result is P(1 head in 3 tosses) = .375.

Possible *outcomes* for three coin tosses

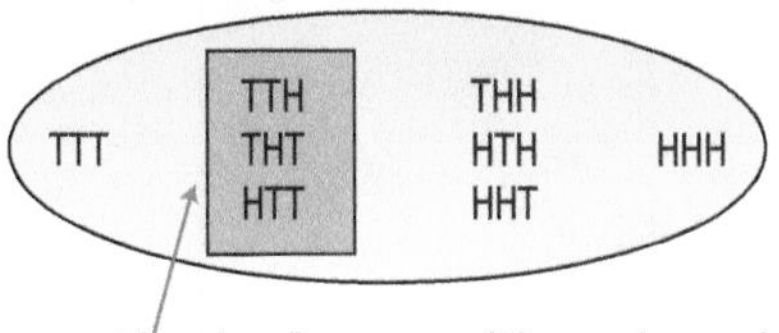

The *event* {one head} occurs and the *random variable* $x = 1$.

A random variable may be either *discrete* or *continuous.*

Discrete Random Variable

A discrete random variable can assume only a certain number of separated values. For example, the Bank of the Carolinas counts the number of credit cards carried for a group of customers. The data are summarized with the following frequency table.

Number of Credit Cards	Percent
0	3%
1	10%
2	18%
3	21%
4 or more	48%
Total	100%

In this frequency table, the number of cards carried is the discrete random variable.

DISCRETE RANDOM VARIABLE A random variable that can assume only certain clearly separated values.

A discrete random variable can, in some cases, assume fractional or decimal values. These values must be separated—that is, have distance between them. As an example, the scores awarded by judges for technical competence and artistic form in figure skating are decimal values, such as 7.2, 8.9, and 9.7. Such values are discrete because there is distance between scores of, say, 8.3 and 8.4. A score cannot be 8.34 or 8.347, for example.

Continuous Random Variable

On the other hand, a random variable can be continuous. If we measure something such as the width of a room, the height of a person, or the pressure in an automobile tire, the variable is a *continuous random variable.* It can assume one of an infinitely large number of values, within certain limitations. As examples:

- The times of commercial flights between Atlanta and Los Angeles are 4.67 hours, 5.13 hours, and so on. The random variable is the time in hours.
- Tire pressure, measured in pounds per square inch (psi), for a new Chevy Trailblazer might be 32.78 psi, 31.62 psi, 33.07 psi, and so on. In other words, any values between 28 and 35 could reasonably occur. The random variable is the tire pressure.

As with discrete random variables, the likelihood of a continuous random variable can be summarized with a **probability distribution.** So what is the difference between a probability distribution and a random variable? A random variable reports the particular outcome of an experiment. A probability distribution reports all the possible outcomes as well as the corresponding probability.

The tools used, as well as the probability interpretations, are different for discrete and continuous probability distributions. This chapter is limited to the discussion and interpretation of discrete distributions. In the next chapter, we discuss continuous distributions. How do you tell the difference between the two types of distributions? Usually a discrete distribution is the result of counting something, such as:

- The number of heads appearing when a coin is tossed 3 times.
- The number of students earning an A in this class.
- The number of production employees absent from the second shift today.
- The number of 30-second commercials on NBC from 8 to 11 p.m. tonight.

Continuous distributions are usually the result of some type of measurement, such as:

- The length of each song on the latest Linkin Park CD.
- The weight of each student in this class.
- The temperature outside as you are reading this book.
- The age in years of each of the 161,000 Ford Motor Company employees.

LO6-3
Compute the mean, variance, and standard deviation of a probability distribution.

THE MEAN, VARIANCE, AND STANDARD DEVIATION OF A DISCRETE PROBABILITY DISTRIBUTION

In Chapter 3, we discussed measures of location and variation for a frequency distribution. The mean reports the central location of the data, and the variance describes the spread in the data. In a similar fashion, a probability distribution is summarized by its mean and variance. We identify the mean of a probability distribution by the lowercase Greek letter mu (μ) and the standard deviation by the lowercase Greek letter sigma (σ).

Mean

The mean is a typical value used to represent the central location of a probability distribution. It also is the long-run average value of the random variable. The mean of a probability distribution is also referred to as its **expected value.** It is a weighted average where the possible values of a random variable are weighted by their corresponding probabilities of occurrence.

The mean of a discrete probability distribution is computed by the formula:

MEAN OF A PROBABILITY DISTRIBUTION $$\mu = \Sigma[xP(x)] \quad \textbf{[6–1]}$$

where $P(x)$ is the probability of a particular value x. In other words, multiply each x value by its probability of occurrence, and then add these products.

Variance and Standard Deviation

The mean is a typical value used to summarize a discrete probability distribution. However, it does not describe the amount of spread (variation) in a distribution. The variance does this. The formula for the variance of a probability distribution is:

VARIANCE OF A PROBABILITY DISTRIBUTION $$\sigma^2 = \Sigma[(x - \mu)^2 P(x)] \quad \textbf{[6–2]}$$

The computational steps are:

1. Subtract the mean from each value of the random variable, and square this difference.
2. Multiply each squared difference by its probability.
3. Sum the resulting products to arrive at the variance.

The standard deviation, σ, is found by taking the positive square root of σ^2; that is, $\sigma = \sqrt{\sigma^2}$.

An example will help explain the details of the calculation and interpretation of the mean and standard deviation of a probability distribution.

EXAMPLE

John Ragsdale sells new cars for Pelican Ford. John usually sells the largest number of cars on Saturday. He has developed the following probability distribution for the number of cars he expects to sell on a particular Saturday.

Number of Cars Sold, x	Probability, $P(x)$
0	.1
1	.2
2	.3
3	.3
4	.1
Total	1.0

1. What type of distribution is this?
2. On a typical Saturday, how many cars does John expect to sell?
3. What is the variance of the distribution?

SOLUTION

1. This is a discrete probability distribution for the random variable called "number of cars sold." Note that John expects to sell only within a certain range of cars; he does not expect to sell 5 cars or 50 cars. Further, he cannot sell half a car. He can sell only 0, 1, 2, 3, or 4 cars. Also, the outcomes are mutually exclusive—he cannot sell a total of both 3 and 4 cars on the same Saturday. The sum of the possible outcomes total 1. Hence, these circumstance qualify as a probability distribution.
2. The mean number of cars sold is computed by weighting the number of cars sold by the probability of selling that number and adding or summing the products, using formula (6–1):

$$\begin{aligned}\mu &= \Sigma[xP(x)]\\ &= 0(.1) + 1(.2) + 2(.3) + 3(.3) + 4(.1)\\ &= 2.1\end{aligned}$$

These calculations are summarized in the following table.

Number of Cars Sold, x	Probability, $P(x)$	$x \cdot P(x)$
0	.1	0.0
1	.2	0.2
2	.3	0.6
3	.3	0.9
4	.1	0.4
Total	1.0	$\mu = 2.1$

How do we interpret a mean of 2.1? This value indicates that, over a large number of Saturdays, John Ragsdale expects to sell a mean of 2.1 cars a day. Of course, it is not possible for him to sell *exactly* 2.1 cars on any

particular Saturday. However, the expected value can be used to predict the arithmetic mean number of cars sold on Saturdays in the long run. For example, if John works 50 Saturdays during a year, he can expect to sell (50) (2.1) or 105 cars just on Saturdays. Thus, the mean is sometimes called the expected value.

3. The following table illustrates the steps to calculate the variance using formula (6–2). The first two columns repeat the probability distribution. In column three, the mean is subtracted from each value of the random variable. In column four, the differences from column three are squared. In the fifth column, each squared difference in column four is multiplied by the corresponding probability. The variance is the sum of the values in column five.

Number of Cars Sold, x	Probability, $P(x)$	$(x - \mu)$	$(x - \mu)^2$	$(x - \mu)^2 P(x)$
0	.1	0 − 2.1	4.41	0.441
1	.2	1 − 2.1	1.21	0.242
2	.3	2 − 2.1	0.01	0.003
3	.3	3 − 2.1	0.81	0.243
4	.1	4 − 2.1	3.61	0.361
				$\sigma^2 = 1.290$

Recall that the standard deviation, σ, is the positive square root of the variance. In this example, $\sqrt{\sigma^2} = \sqrt{1.290} = 1.136$ cars. How do we apply a standard deviation of 1.136 cars? If salesperson Rita Kirsch also sold a mean of 2.1 cars on Saturdays, and the standard deviation in her sales was 1.91 cars, we would conclude that there is more variability in the Saturday sales of Ms. Kirsch than in those of Mr. Ragsdale (because 1.91 > 1.136).

SELF-REVIEW 6–2

The Pizza Palace offers three sizes of cola. The smallest size sells for \$0.80, the medium for \$0.90, and the large for \$1.20. Thirty percent of the drinks sold are small, 50% are medium, and 20% are large. Create a probability distribution for the random variable price and answer the following questions.

(a) Is this a discrete probability distribution? Indicate why or why not.
(b) Compute the mean amount charged for a cola.
(c) What is the variance in the amount charged for a cola? The standard deviation?

EXERCISES

For **DATA FILE**, please visit www.mhhe.com/lind16e

1. Compute the mean and variance of the following discrete probability distribution.

x	$P(x)$
0	.2
1	.4
2	.3
3	.1

For **DATA FILE**, please visit www.mhhe.com/lind16e

2. Compute the mean and variance of the following discrete probability distribution.

x	$P(x)$
2	.5
8	.3
10	.2

3. Compute the mean and variance of the following probability distribution.

x	$P(x)$
5	.1
10	.3
15	.2
20	.4

4. Which of these variables are discrete and which are continuous random variables?
a. The number of new accounts established by a salesperson in a year.
b. The time between customer arrivals to a bank ATM.
c. The number of customers in Big Nick's barber shop.
d. The amount of fuel in your car's gas tank.
e. The number of minorities on a jury.
f. The outside temperature today.

For **DATA FILE**, please visit www.mhhe.com/lind16e

5. The information below is the number of daily emergency service calls made by the volunteer ambulance service of Walterboro, South Carolina, for the last 50 days. To explain, there were 22 days on which there were two emergency calls, and 9 days on which there were three emergency calls.

Number of Calls	Frequency
0	8
1	10
2	22
3	9
4	1
Total	50

a. Convert this information on the number of calls to a probability distribution.
b. Is this an example of a discrete or continuous probability distribution?
c. What is the mean number of emergency calls per day?
d. What is the standard deviation of the number of calls made daily?

For **DATA FILE**, please visit www.mhhe.com/lind16e

6. The director of admissions at Kinzua University in Nova Scotia estimated the distribution of student admissions for the fall semester on the basis of past experience. What is the expected number of admissions for the fall semester? Compute the variance and the standard deviation of the number of admissions.

Admissions	Probability
1,000	.6
1,200	.3
1,500	.1

For **DATA FILE**, please visit www.mhhe.com/lind16e

7. Belk Department Store is having a special sale this weekend. Customers charging purchases of more than \$50 to their Belk credit card will be given a special Belk Lottery card. The customer will scratch off the card, which will indicate the amount to be taken off the total amount of the purchase. Listed below are the amount of the prize and the percent of the time that amount will be deducted from the total amount of the purchase.

Prize Amount	Probability
\$ 10	.50
25	.40
50	.08
100	.02

a. What is the mean amount deducted from the total purchase amount?
b. What is the standard deviation of the amount deducted from the total purchase?

For **DATA FILE**, please visit www.mhhe.com/lind16e

8. The Downtown Parking Authority of Tampa, Florida, reported the following information for a sample of 250 customers on the number of hours cars are parked and the amount they are charged.

Number of Hours	Frequency	Amount Charged
1	20	$ 3.00
2	38	6.00
3	53	9.00
4	45	12.00
5	40	14.00
6	13	16.00
7	5	18.00
8	36	20.00
	250	

a. Convert the information on the number of hours parked to a probability distribution. Is this a discrete or a continuous probability distribution?
b. Find the mean and the standard deviation of the number of hours parked. How would you answer the question: How long is a typical customer parked?
c. Find the mean and the standard deviation of the amount charged.

LO6-4
Explain the assumptions of the binomial distribution and apply it to calculate probabilities.

BINOMIAL PROBABILITY DISTRIBUTION

The **binomial probability distribution** is a widely occurring discrete probability distribution. To describe experimental outcomes with a binomial distribution, there are four requirements. The first requirement is there are only two possible outcomes on a particular experimental trial. For example, on a test, a true/false question is either true or false. In a resort, a housekeeping supervisor reviews an employee's work and evaluates it as acceptable or unacceptable. A key characteristic of the two outcomes is that they must be mutually exclusive. This means that the answer to a true/false question must be either true or false but cannot be both true and false at the same time. Another example is the outcome of a sales call. Either a customer purchases or does not purchase the product, but the sale cannot result in both outcomes. Frequently, we refer to the two possible outcomes of a binomial experiment as a "success" and a "failure." However, this distinction does not imply that one outcome is good and the other is bad, only that there are two mutually exclusive outcomes.

The second binomial requirement is that the random variable is the number of successes for a fixed and known number of trials. For example, we flip a coin five times and count the number of times a head appears in the five flips, we randomly select 10 employees and count the number who are older than 50 years of age, or we randomly select 20 boxes of Kellogg's Raisin Bran and count the number that weigh more than the amount indicated on the package. In each example, we count the number of successes from the fixed number of trials.

A third requirement is that we know the probability of a success and it is the same for each trial. Three examples are:

- For a test with 10 true/false questions, we know there are 10 trials and the probability of correctly guessing the answer for any of the 10 trials is 0.5. Or, for a test with 20 multiple-choice questions with four options and only one correct answer, we know that there are 20 trials and the probability of randomly guessing the correct answer for each of the 20 trials is 0.25.

- Bones Albaugh is a Division I college basketball player who makes 70% of his foul shots. If he has five opportunities in tonight's game, the likelihood he will be successful on each of the five attempts is 0.70.
- In a recent poll, 18% of adults indicated a Snickers bar was their favorite candy bar. We select a sample of 15 adults and ask each for his or her favorite candy bar. The likelihood a Snickers bar is the answer for each adult is 0.18.

The final requirement of a binomial probability distribution is that each trial is *independent* of any other trial. Independent means there is no pattern to the trials. The outcome of a particular trial does not affect the outcome of any other trial. Two examples are:

- A young family has two children, both boys. The probability of a third birth being a boy is still .50. That is, the gender of the third child is independent of the gender of the other two.
- Suppose 20% of the patients served in the emergency room at Waccamaw Hospital do not have insurance. If the second patient served on the afternoon shift today did not have insurance, that does not affect the probability the third, the tenth, or any of the other patients will or will not have insurance.

BINOMIAL PROBABILITY EXPERIMENT

1. An outcome on each trial of an experiment is classified into one of two mutually exclusive categories—a success or a failure.
2. The random variable is the number of successes in a fixed number of trials.
3. The probability of success is the same for each trial.
4. The trials are independent, meaning that the outcome of one trial does not affect the outcome of any other trial.

How Is a Binomial Probability Computed?

To construct a particular binomial probability, we use (1) the number of trials and (2) the probability of success on each trial. For example, if the Hannah Landscaping Company plants 10 Norfolk pine trees today knowing that 90% of these trees survive, we can compute the binomial probability that exactly 8 trees survive. In this case the number of trials is the 10 trees, the probability of success is .90, and the number of successes is eight. In fact, we can compute a binomial probability for any number of successes from 0 to 10 surviving trees.

A binomial probability is computed by the formula:

BINOMIAL PROBABILITY FORMULA $$P(x) = {}_nC_x \pi^x (1 - \pi)^{n-x} \quad \textbf{[6–3]}$$

where:

C denotes a combination.
n is the number of trials.
x is the random variable defined as the number of successes.
π is the probability of a success on each trial.

We use the Greek letter π (pi) to denote a binomial population parameter. Do not confuse it with the mathematical constant 3.1416.

EXAMPLE

There are five flights daily from Pittsburgh via US Airways into the Bradford Regional Airport in Bradford, Pennsylvania. Suppose the probability that any flight arrives late is .20. What is the probability that none of the flights are late today? What is the probability that exactly one of the flights is late today?

SOLUTION

We can use formula (6–3). The probability that a particular flight is late is .20, so let $\pi = .20$. There are five flights, so $n = 5$, and X, the random variable, refers to the number of successes. In this case, a "success" is a flight that arrives late. Because there are no late arrivals, $x = 0$.

$$P(0) = {}_nC_x(\pi)^x(1 - \pi)^{n-x}$$
$$= {}_5C_0(.20)^0(1 - .20)^{5-0} = (1)(1)(.3277) = .3277$$

The probability that exactly one of the five flights will arrive late today is .4096, found by

$$P(1) = {}_nC_x(\pi)^x(1 - \pi)^{n-x}$$
$$= {}_5C_1(.20)^1(1 - .20)^{5-1} = (5)(.20)(.4096) = .4096$$

The entire binomial probability distribution with $\pi = .20$ and $n = 5$ is shown in the following bar chart. We observe that the probability of exactly three late flights is .0512 and from the bar chart that the distribution of the number of late arrivals is positively skewed.

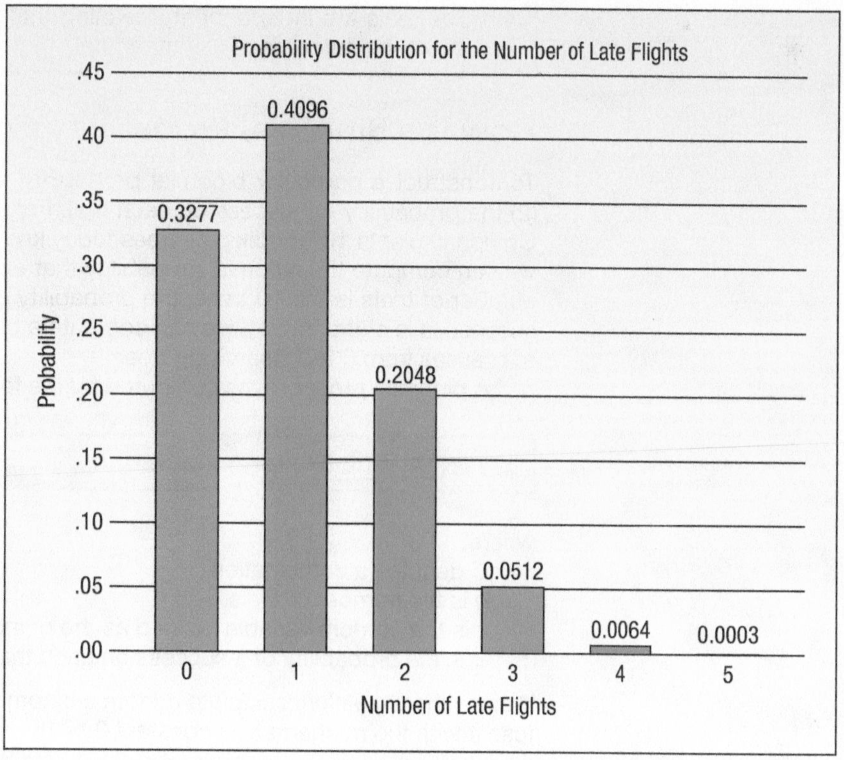

The mean (μ) and the variance (σ^2) of a binomial distribution are computed in a "shortcut" fashion by:

MEAN OF A BINOMIAL DISTRIBUTION	$\mu = n\pi$	**[6–4]**

VARIANCE OF A BINOMIAL DISTRIBUTION	$\sigma^2 = n\pi(1 - \pi)$	**[6–5]**

For the example regarding the number of late flights, recall that $\pi = .20$ and $n = 5$. Hence:

$$\mu = n\pi = (5)(.20) = 1.0$$

$$\sigma^2 = n\pi(1 - \pi) = 5(.20)(1 - .20) = .80$$

The mean of 1.0 and the variance of .80 can be verified from formulas (6–1) and (6–2). The probability distribution from the bar chart on the previous page and the details of the calculations are shown below.

Number of Late Flights, x	$P(x)$	$xP(x)$	$x - \mu$	$(x - \mu)^2$	$(x - \mu)^2P(x)$
0	0.3277	0.0000	−1	1	0.3277
1	0.4096	0.4096	0	0	0
2	0.2048	0.4096	1	1	0.2048
3	0.0512	0.1536	2	4	0.2048
4	0.0064	0.0256	3	9	0.0576
5	0.0003	0.0015	4	16	0.0048
		$\mu = 1.0000$			$\sigma^2 = 0.7997$

Binomial Probability Tables

Formula (6–3) can be used to build a binomial probability distribution for any value of n and π. However, for a larger n, the calculations take more time. For convenience, the tables in Appendix B.1 show the result of using the formula for various values of n and π. Table 6–2 shows part of Appendix B.1 for $n = 6$ and various values of π.

TABLE 6–2 Binomial Probabilities for $n = 6$ and Selected Values of π

	$n = 6$ Probability										
$x\backslash\pi$	**.05**	.1	.2	.3	.4	.5	.6	.7	.8	.9	.95
0	**.735**	.531	.262	.118	.047	.016	.004	.001	.000	.000	.000
1	**.232**	.354	.393	.303	.187	.094	.037	.010	.002	.000	.000
2	**.031**	.098	.246	.324	.311	.234	.138	.060	.015	.001	.000
3	**.002**	.015	.082	.185	.276	.313	.276	.185	.082	.015	.002
4	**.000**	.001	.015	.060	.138	.234	.311	.324	.246	.098	.031
5	**.000**	.000	.002	.010	.037	.094	.187	.303	.393	.354	.232
6	**.000**	.000	.000	.001	.004	.016	.047	.118	.262	.531	.735

EXAMPLE

In the Southwest, 5% of all cell phone calls are dropped. What is the probability that out of six randomly selected calls, none was dropped? Exactly one? Exactly two? Exactly three? Exactly four? Exactly five? Exactly six out of six?

SOLUTION

The binomial conditions are met: (a) there are only two possible outcomes (a particular call is either dropped or not dropped), (b) there are a fixed number of trials (6), (c) there is a constant probability of success (.05), and (d) the trials are independent.

Refer to Table 6–2 on the previous page for the probability of exactly zero dropped calls. Go down the left margin to an x of 0. Now move horizontally to the column headed by a π of .05 to find the probability. It is .735. The values in Table 6–2 are rounded to three decimal places.

The probability of exactly one dropped call in a sample of six calls is .232. The complete binomial probability distribution for $n = 6$ and $\pi = .05$ is:

Number of Dropped Calls, x	Probability of Occurrence, $P(x)$	Number of Dropped Calls, x	Probability of Occurrence, $P(x)$
0	.735	4	.000
1	.232	5	.000
2	.031	6	.000
3	.002		

Of course, there is a slight chance of getting exactly five dropped calls out of six random selections. It is .00000178, found by inserting the appropriate values in the binomial formula:

$$P(5) = {}_6C_5(.05)^5(.95)^1 = (6)(.05)^5(.95) = .00000178$$

For six out of the six, the exact probability is .000000016. Thus, the probability is very small that five or six calls will be dropped in six trials.

We can compute the mean or expected value of the distribution of the number defective:

$$\mu = n\pi = (6)(.05) = 0.30$$

$$\sigma^2 = n\pi(1 - \pi) = 6(.05)(.95) = 0.285$$

SELF-REVIEW 6–3

Ninety-five percent of the employees at the J. M. Smucker Company plant on Laskey Road have their bimonthly wages sent directly to their bank by electronic funds transfer. This is also called direct deposit. Suppose we select a random sample of seven employees.
(a) Does this situation fit the assumptions of the binomial distribution?
(b) What is the probability that all seven employees use direct deposit?
(c) Use formula (6–3) to determine the exact probability that four of the seven sampled employees use direct deposit.
(d) Use Excel to verify your answers to parts (b) and (c).

Appendix B.1 is limited. It gives probabilities for n values from 1 to 15 and π values of .05, .10, . . . , .90, and .95. A software program can generate the probabilities for a specified number of successes, given n and π. The Excel output on the next page shows the probability when $n = 40$ and $\pi = .09$. Note that the number of successes stops at 15 because the probabilities for 16 to 40 are very close to 0. The instructions are detailed in the Software Commands in Appendix C.

	A	B
1	Success	Probability
2	0	0.0230
3	1	0.0910
4	2	0.1754
5	3	0.2198
6	4	0.2011
7	5	0.1432
8	6	0.0826
9	7	0.0397
10	8	0.0162
11	9	0.0057
12	10	0.0017
13	11	0.0005
14	12	0.0001
15	13	0.0000
16	14	0.0000
17	15	0.0000

Several additional points should be made regarding the binomial probability distribution.

1. If n remains the same but π increases from .05 to .95, the shape of the distribution changes. Look at Table 6–3 and Chart 6–2. The distribution for a π of .05 is positively skewed. As π approaches .50, the distribution becomes symmetrical. As π goes beyond .50 and moves toward .95, the probability distribution becomes negatively skewed. Table 6–3 highlights probabilities for $n = 10$ and a π of .05, .10, .20, .50, and .70. The graphs of these probability distributions are shown in Chart 6–2.

TABLE 6–3 Probability of 0, 1, 2, . . . Successes for a π of .05, .10, .20, .50, and .70, and an n of 10

$x \backslash \pi$	.05	.1	.2	.3	.4	.5	.6	.7	.8	.9	.95
0	.599	.349	.107	.028	.006	.001	.000	.000	.000	.000	.000
1	.315	.387	.268	.121	.040	.010	.002	.000	.000	.000	.000
2	.075	.194	.302	.233	.121	.044	.011	.001	.000	.000	.000
3	.010	.057	.201	.267	.215	.117	.042	.009	.001	.000	.000
4	.001	.011	.088	.200	.251	.205	.111	.037	.006	.000	.000
5	.000	.001	.026	.103	.201	.246	.201	.103	.026	.001	.000
6	.000	.000	.006	.037	.111	.205	.251	.200	.088	.011	.001
7	.000	.000	.001	.009	.042	.117	.215	.267	.201	.057	.010
8	.000	.000	.000	.001	.011	.044	.121	.233	.302	.194	.075
9	.000	.000	.000	.000	.002	.010	.040	.121	.268	.387	.315
10	.000	.000	.000	.000	.000	.001	.006	.028	.107	.349	.599

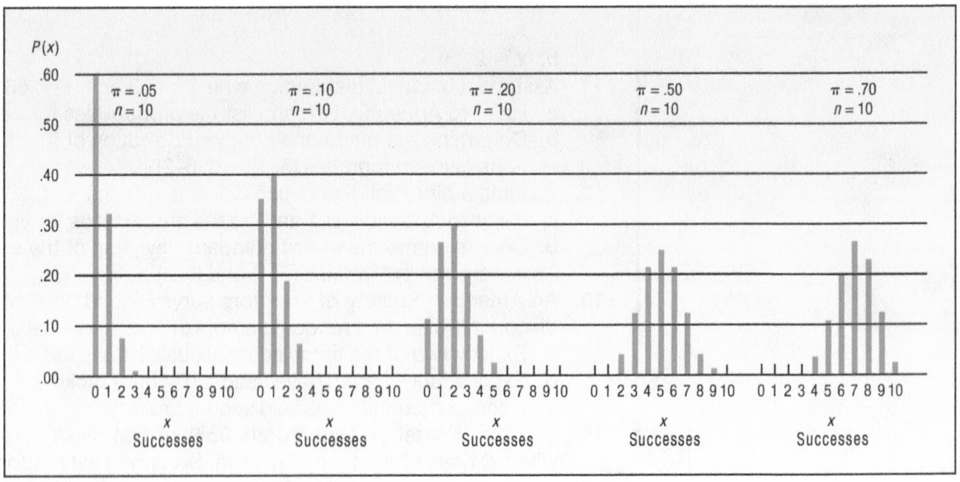

CHART 6–2 Graphing the Binomial Probability Distribution for a π of .05, .10, .20, .50, and .70, and an n of 10

2. If π, the probability of success, remains the same but n becomes larger, the shape of the binomial distribution becomes more symmetrical. Chart 6–3 shows a situation where π remains constant at .10 but n increases from 7 to 40.

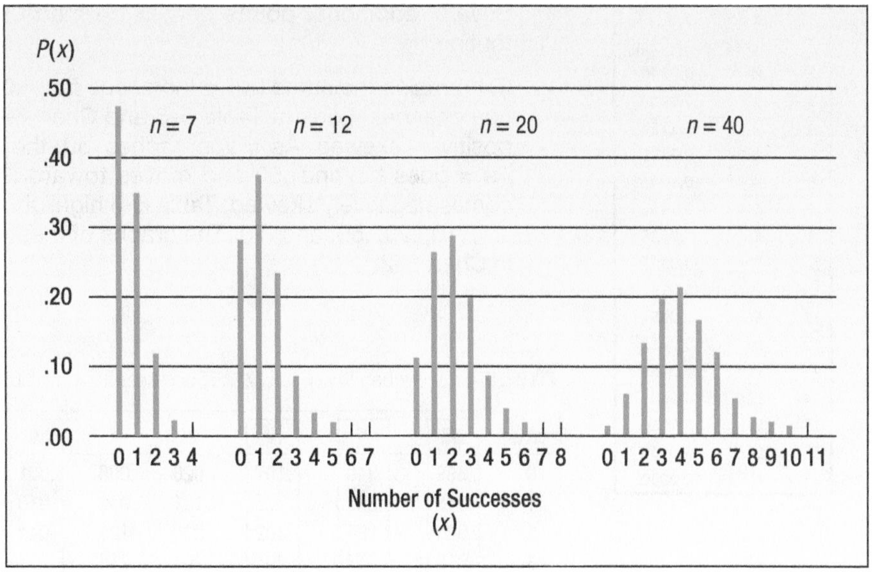

CHART 6–3 Chart Representing the Binomial Probability Distribution for a π of .10 and an n of 7, 12, 20, and 40

EXERCISES

9. In a binomial situation, $n = 4$ and $\pi = .25$. Determine the probabilities of the following events using the binomial formula.
   a. $x = 2$
   b. $x = 3$
10. In a binomial situation, $n = 5$ and $\pi = .40$. Determine the probabilities of the following events using the binomial formula.
    a. $x = 1$
    b. $x = 2$
11. Assume a binomial distribution where $n = 3$ and $\pi = .60$.
    a. Refer to Appendix B.1, and list the probabilities for values of x from 0 to 3.
    b. Determine the mean and standard deviation of the distribution from the general definitions given in formulas (6–1) and (6–2).
12. Assume a binomial distribution where $n = 5$ and $\pi = .30$.
    a. Refer to Appendix B.1 and list the probabilities for values of x from 0 to 5.
    b. Determine the mean and standard deviation of the distribution from the general definitions given in formulas (6–1) and (6–2).
13. An American Society of Investors survey found 30% of individual investors have used a discount broker. In a random sample of nine individuals, what is the probability:
    a. Exactly two of the sampled individuals have used a discount broker?
    b. Exactly four of them have used a discount broker?
    c. None of them has used a discount broker?
14. The U.S. Postal Service reports 95% of first-class mail within the same city is delivered within 2 days of the time of mailing. Six letters are randomly sent to different locations.
    a. What is the probability that all six arrive within 2 days?
    b. What is the probability that exactly five arrive within 2 days?
    c. Find the mean number of letters that will arrive within 2 days.
    d. Compute the variance and standard deviation of the number that will arrive within 2 days.

For **DATA FILE**, please visit www.mhhe.com/lind16e

15. Industry standards suggest that 10% of new vehicles require warranty service within the first year. Jones Nissan in Sumter, South Carolina, sold 12 Nissans yesterday.
    a. What is the probability that none of these vehicles requires warranty service?
    b. What is the probability exactly one of these vehicles requires warranty service?
    c. Determine the probability that exactly two of these vehicles require warranty service.
    d. Compute the mean and standard deviation of this probability distribution.

For **DATA FILE**, please visit www.mhhe.com/lind16e

For **DATA FILE**, please visit www.mhhe.com/lind16e

For **DATA FILE**, please visit www.mhhe.com/lind16e

For **DATA FILE**, please visit www.mhhe.com/lind16e

16. A telemarketer makes six phone calls per hour and is able to make a sale on 30% of these contacts. During the next 2 hours, find:
   a. The probability of making exactly four sales.
   b. The probability of making no sales.
   c. The probability of making exactly two sales.
   d. The mean number of sales in the 2-hour period.

17. A recent survey by the American Accounting Association revealed 23% of students graduating with a major in accounting select public accounting. Suppose we select a sample of 15 recent graduates.
   a. What is the probability two select public accounting?
   b. What is the probability five select public accounting?
   c. How many graduates would you expect to select public accounting?

18. It is reported that 16% of American households use a cell phone exclusively for their telephone service. In a sample of eight households,
   a. Find the probability that no household uses a cell phone as their exclusive telephone service.
   b. Find the probability that exactly 5 households exclusively use a cell phone for telephone service.
   c. Find the mean number of households exclusively using cell phones.

Cumulative Binomial Probability Distributions

We may wish to know the probability of correctly guessing the answers to 6 *or more* true/false questions out of 10. Or we may be interested in the probability of *selecting less than two* defectives at random from production during the previous hour. In these cases, we need cumulative frequency distributions similar to the ones developed in Chapter 2. See page 37. The following example will illustrate.

EXAMPLE

A study by the Illinois Department of Transportation concluded that 76.2% of front seat occupants used seat belts. That is, both occupants of the front seat were using their seat belts. Suppose we decide to compare that information with current usage. We select a sample of 12 vehicles.

1. What is the probability the front seat occupants in exactly 7 of the 12 vehicles selected are wearing seat belts?
2. What is the probability the front seat occupants in at least 7 of the 12 vehicles are wearing seat belts?

SOLUTION

This situation meets the binomial requirements.

- In a particular vehicle, both the front seat occupants are either wearing seat belts or they are not. There are only two possible outcomes.
- There are a fixed number of trials, 12 in this case, because 12 vehicles are checked.
- The probability of a "success" (occupants wearing seat belts) is the same from one vehicle to the next: 76.2%.
- The trials are independent. If the fourth vehicle selected in the sample has all the occupants wearing their seat belts, this does not have any effect on the results for the fifth or tenth vehicle.

To find the likelihood the occupants of *exactly* 7 of the sampled vehicles are wearing seat belts, we use formula (6–3). In this case, $n = 12$ and $\pi = .762$.

$$P(x = 7) = {}_{12}C_7(.762)^7(1 - .762)^{12-7} = 792(.149171)(.000764) = .0902$$

So we conclude the likelihood that the occupants of exactly 7 of the 12 sampled vehicles will be wearing their seat belts is about 9%. We often use, as we did in

this equation, a bar "|" to mean "given that." So in this equation we want to know the probability that x is equal to 7 "given that the number of trials is 12 and the probability of a success is .762."

To find the probability that the occupants in seven or more of the vehicles will be wearing seat belts, we use formula (6–3) from this chapter as well as the special rule of addition from the previous chapter. See formula (5–2) on page 140.

Because the events are mutually exclusive (meaning that a particular sample of 12 vehicles cannot have both a *total* of 7 and a *total* of 8 vehicles where the occupants are wearing seat belts), we find the probability of 7 vehicles where the occupants are wearing seat belts, the probability of 8, and so on up to the probability that occupants of all 12 sample vehicles are wearing seat belts. The probability of each of these outcomes is then totaled.

$$P(x \geq 7) = P(x = 7) + P(x = 8) + P(x = 9) + P(x = 10) + P(x = 11) + P(x = 12)$$

$$= .0902 + .1805 + .2569 + .2467 + .1436 + .0383$$

$$= .9562$$

So the probability of selecting 12 cars and finding that the occupants of 7 or more vehicles were wearing seat belts is .9562. This information is shown on the following Excel spreadsheet. There is a slight difference in the software answer due to rounding. The Excel commands are similar to those detailed in the Software Commands in Appendix C.

Cumulative Binomial.xlsx

	A	B	C	D
1	Success	Probability		
2	0	0.0000		
3	1	0.0000		
4	2	0.0000		
5	3	0.0002		
6	4	0.0017		
7	5	0.0088		
8	6	0.0329		
9	7	0.0902		
10	8	0.1805		
11	9	0.2569		
12	10	0.2467		
13	11	0.1436		
14	12	0.0383		
15		0.9563		

Sum of Probabilities for 7 or more successes

SELF-REVIEW 6–4

A recent study revealed that 40% of women in the San Diego metropolitan area who work full time also volunteer in the community. Suppose we randomly select eight women in the San Diego area.

(a) What are the values for n and π?
(b) What is the probability exactly three of the women volunteer in the community?
(c) What is the probability at least one of the women volunteers in the community?

EXERCISES

19. In a binomial distribution, $n = 8$ and $\pi = .30$. Find the probabilities of the following events.
- **a.** $x = 2$.
- **b.** $x \leq 2$ (the probability that x is equal to or less than 2).
- **c.** $x \geq 3$ (the probability that x is equal to or greater than 3).

20. In a binomial distribution, $n = 12$ and $\pi = .60$. Find the following probabilities.
- **a.** $x = 5$.
- **b.** $x \leq 5$.
- **c.** $x \geq 6$.

For **DATA FILE**, please visit www.mhhe.com/lind16e

21. In a recent study, 90% of the homes in the United States were found to have large-screen TVs. In a sample of nine homes, what is the probability that:
   a. All nine have large-screen TVs?
   b. Less than five have large-screen TVs?
   c. More than five have large-screen TVs?
   d. At least seven homes have large-screen TVs?

For **DATA FILE**, please visit www.mhhe.com/lind16e

22. A manufacturer of window frames knows from long experience that 5% of the production will have some type of minor defect that will require an adjustment. What is the probability that in a sample of 20 window frames:
   a. None will need adjustment?
   b. At least one will need adjustment?
   c. More than two will need adjustment?

For **DATA FILE**, please visit www.mhhe.com/lind16e

23. The speed with which utility companies can resolve problems is very important. GTC, the Georgetown Telephone Company, reports it can resolve customer problems the same day they are reported in 70% of the cases. Suppose the 15 cases reported today are representative of all complaints.
   a. How many of the problems would you expect to be resolved today? What is the standard deviation?
   b. What is the probability 10 of the problems can be resolved today?
   c. What is the probability 10 or 11 of the problems can be resolved today?
   d. What is the probability more than 10 of the problems can be resolved today?

For **DATA FILE**, please visit www.mhhe.com/lind16e

24. It is asserted that 80% of the cars approaching an individual toll booth in New Jersey are equipped with an E-ZPass transponder. Find the probability that in a sample of six cars:
   a. All six will have the transponder.
   b. At least three will have the transponder.
   c. None will have a transponder.

LO6-5
Explain the assumptions of the hypergeometric distribution and apply it to calculate probabilities.

HYPERGEOMETRIC PROBABILITY DISTRIBUTION

For the binomial distribution to be applied, the probability of a success must stay the same for each trial. For example, the probability of guessing the correct answer to a true/false question is .50. This probability remains the same for each question on an examination. Likewise, suppose that 40% of the registered voters in a precinct are Republicans. If 27 registered voters are selected at random, the probability of choosing a Republican on the first selection is .40. The chance of choosing a Republican on the next selection is also .40, assuming that the sampling is done *with replacement,* meaning that the person selected is put back in the population before the next person is selected.

Most sampling, however, is done *without replacement.* Thus, if the population is small, the probability of a success will change for each observation. For example, if the population consists of 20 items, the probability of selecting a particular item from that population is 1/20. If the sampling is done without replacement, after the first selection there are only 19 items remaining; the probability of selecting a particular item on the second selection is only 1/19. For the third selection, the probability is 1/18, and so on. This assumes that the population is **finite**—that is, the number in the population is known and relatively small in number. Examples of a finite population are 2,842 Republicans in the precinct, 9,241 applications for medical school, and the 18 2014 Dakota 4x4 Crew Cabs at Helfman Dodge Chrysler Jeep in Houston, TX.

Recall that one of the criteria for the binomial distribution is that the probability of success remains the same from trial to trial. Because the probability of success does not remain the same from trial to trial when sampling is from a relatively small population without replacement, the binomial distribution should not be used. Instead, the **hypergeometric distribution** is applied. Therefore, (1) if a sample is selected from a finite population without replacement and (2) if the size of the sample n is more than

5% of the size of the population N, then the hypergeometric distribution is used to determine the probability of a specified number of successes or failures. It is especially appropriate when the size of the population is small.

The formula for the hypergeometric distribution is:

HYPERGEOMETRIC DISTRIBUTION $$P(x) = \frac{({}_{S}C_{x})({}_{N-S}C_{n-x})}{{}_{N}C_{n}}$$ **[6–6]**

where:

N is the size of the population.
S is the number of successes in the population.
x is the number of successes in the sample. It may be 0, 1, 2, 3, ...
n is the size of the sample or the number of trials.
C is the symbol for a combination.

In summary, a hypergeometric probability distribution has these characteristics:

HYPERGEOMETRIC PROBABILITY EXPERIMENT

1. An outcome on each trial of an experiment is classified into one of two mutually exclusive categories—a success or a failure.
2. The random variable is the number of successes in a fixed number of trials.
3. The trials are *not independent.*
4. We assume that we sample from a finite population without replacement and $n/N > 0.05$. So, the probability of a success *changes* for each trial.

The following example illustrates the details of determining a probability using the hypergeometric distribution.

EXAMPLE

PlayTime Toys Inc. employs 50 people in the Assembly Department. Forty of the employees belong to a union and 10 do not. Five employees are selected at random to form a committee to meet with management regarding shift starting times. What is the probability that four of the five selected for the committee belong to a union?

SOLUTION

The population in this case is the 50 Assembly Department employees. An employee can be selected for the committee only once. Hence, the sampling is done without replacement. Thus, the probability of selecting a union employee, for example, changes from one trial to the next. The hypergeometric distribution is appropriate for determining the probability. In this problem,

N is 50, the number of employees.
S is 40, the number of union employees.
x is 4, the number of union employees selected.
n is 5, the number of employees selected.

We wish to find the probability 4 of the 5 committee members belong to a union. Inserting these values into formula (6–6):

$$P(4) = \frac{({}_{40}C_4)({}_{50-40}C_{5-4})}{{}_{50}C_5} = \frac{(91{,}390)(10)}{2{,}118{,}760} = .431$$

Thus, the probability of selecting 5 assembly workers at random from the 50 workers and finding 4 of the 5 are union members is .431.

Table 6–4 shows the hypergeometric probabilities of finding 0, 1, 2, 3, 4, and 5 union members on the committee.

TABLE 6–4 Hypergeometric Probabilities ($n = 5, N = 50$, and $S = 40$) for the Number of Union Members on the Committee

Union Members	Probability
0	.000
1	.004
2	.044
3	.210
4	.431
5	.311
	1.000

In order for you to compare the two probability distributions, Table 6–5 shows the hypergeometric and binomial probabilities for the PlayTime Toys Inc. example. Because 40 of the 50 Assembly Department employees belong to the union, we let $\pi = .80$ for the binomial distribution. The binomial probabilities for Table 6–5 come from the binomial distribution with $n = 5$ and $\pi = .80$.

TABLE 6–5 Hypergeometric and Binomial Probabilities for PlayTime Toys Inc. Assembly Department

Number of Union Members on Committee	Hypergeometric Probability, $P(x)$	Binomial Probability ($n = 5$ and $\pi = .80$)
0	.000	.000
1	.004	.006
2	.044	.051
3	.210	.205
4	.431	.410
5	.311	.328
	1.000	1.000

When the binomial requirement of a constant probability of success cannot be met, the hypergeometric distribution should be used. However, as Table 6–5 shows, under certain conditions the results of the binomial distribution can be used to approximate the hypergeometric. This leads to a rule of thumb:

If selected items are not returned to the population, the binomial distribution can be used to closely approximate the hypergeometric distribution when $n < .05N$. In words, the binomial will suffice if the sample is less than 5% of the population.

	A	B
1	Union Members	Probability
2	0	0.000
3	1	0.004
4	2	0.044
5	3	0.210
6	4	0.431
7	5	0.311

A hypergeometric distribution can be created using Excel. See the output on the left. The necessary steps are given in Appendix C in the back of the text.

SELF-REVIEW 6–5

Horwege Discount Brokers plans to hire five new financial analysts this year. There is a pool of 12 approved applicants, and George Horwege, the owner, decides to randomly select those who will be hired. There are eight men and four women among the approved applicants. What is the probability that three of the five hired are men?

EXERCISES

25. A CD contains 10 songs; 6 are classical and 4 are rock and roll. In a sample of three songs, what is the probability that exactly two are classical? Assume the samples are drawn without replacement.
26. A population consists of 15 items, 10 of which are acceptable. In a sample of four items, what is the probability that exactly three are acceptable? Assume the samples are drawn without replacement.
27. The Riverton Branch of the National Bank of Wyoming has 10 real estate loans over $1,000,000. Of these 10 loans, 3 are "underwater." A loan is underwater if the amount of the loan is greater than the value of the property. The chief loan officer decided to randomly select two of these loans to determine if they met all banking standards. What is the probability that neither of the selected loans is underwater?
28. The Computer Systems Department has eight faculty, six of whom are tenured. Dr. Vonder, the chairman, wants to establish a committee of three department faculty members to review the curriculum. If she selects the committee at random:
    a. What is the probability all members of the committee are tenured?
    b. What is the probability that at least one member is not tenured? (Hint: For this question, use the complement rule.)
29. Keith's Florists has 15 delivery trucks, used mainly to deliver flowers and flower arrangements in the Greenville, South Carolina, area. Of these 15 trucks, 6 have brake problems. A sample of five trucks is randomly selected. What is the probability that two of those tested have defective brakes?
30. The game called Lotto sponsored by the Louisiana Lottery Commission pays its largest prize when a contestant matches all 6 of the 40 possible numbers. Assume there are 40 ping-pong balls each with a single number between 1 and 40. Any number appears only once, and the winning balls are selected without replacement.
    a. The commission reports that the probability of matching all the numbers are 1 in 3,838,380. What is this in terms of probability?
    b. Use the hypergeometric formula to find this probability.

    The lottery commission also pays if a contestant matches four or five of the six winning numbers. Hint: Divide the 40 numbers into two groups, winning numbers and nonwinning numbers.

    c. Find the probability, again using the hypergeometric formula, for matching 4 of the 6 winning numbers.
    d. Find the probability of matching 5 of the 6 winning numbers.

LO6-6
Explain the assumptions of the Poisson distribution and apply it to calculate probabilities.

POISSON PROBABILITY DISTRIBUTION

The **Poisson probability distribution** describes the number of times some event occurs during a specified interval. The interval may be time, distance, area, or volume.

The distribution is based on two assumptions. The first assumption is that the probability is proportional to the length of the interval. The second assumption is that the intervals are independent. To put it another way, the longer the interval, the larger the probability, and the number of occurrences in one interval does not affect the other intervals. This distribution is also a limiting form of the binomial distribution when the probability of a success is very small and n is large. It is often referred to as the "law of improbable events," meaning that the probability, π, of a particular event's happening is quite small. The Poisson distribution is a discrete probability distribution because it is formed by counting.

The Poisson probability distribution has these characteristics:

POISSON PROBABILITY EXPERIMENT

1. The random variable is the number of times some event occurs during a defined interval.
2. The probability of the event is proportional to the size of the interval.
3. The intervals do not overlap and are independent.

This probability distribution has many applications. It is used as a model to describe the distribution of errors in data entry, the number of scratches and other imperfections in newly painted car panels, the number of defective parts in outgoing shipments, the number of customers waiting to be served at a restaurant or waiting to get into an attraction at Disney World, and the number of accidents on I–75 during a three-month period.

The Poisson distribution is described mathematically by the formula:

POISSON DISTRIBUTION $$P(x) = \frac{\mu^x e^{-\mu}}{x!} \qquad \textbf{[6–7]}$$

where:

μ (mu) is the mean number of occurrences (successes) in a particular interval.
e is the constant 2.71828 (base of the Napierian logarithmic system).
x is the number of occurrences (successes).
$P(x)$ is the probability for a specified value of x.

The mean number of successes, μ, is found by $n\pi$, where n is the total number of trials and π the probability of success.

MEAN OF A POISSON DISTRIBUTION $$\mu = n\pi \qquad \textbf{[6–8]}$$

The variance of the Poisson is equal to its mean. If, for example, the probability that a check cashed by a bank will bounce is .0003, and 10,000 checks are cashed, the mean and the variance for the number of bad checks is 3.0, found by $\mu = n\pi = 10{,}000(.0003) = 3.0$.

Recall that for a binomial distribution there are a fixed number of trials. For example, for a four-question multiple-choice test there can only be zero, one, two, three, or four successes (correct answers). The random variable, x, for a Poisson distribution, however, can assume an *infinite number of values*—that is, 0, 1, 2, 3, 4, 5, . . . However, *the probabilities become very small after the first few occurrences* (successes).

To illustrate the Poisson probability computation, assume baggage is rarely lost by Northeast Airlines. Most flights do not experience any mishandled bags; some have one bag lost; a few have two bags lost; rarely a flight will have three lost bags; and so on. Suppose a random sample of 1,000 flights shows a total of 300 bags were lost. Thus, the arithmetic mean number of lost bags per flight is 0.3, found by 300/1,000. If the number of lost bags per flight follows a Poisson distribution with $\mu = 0.3$, we can compute the various probabilities using formula (6–7):

$$P(x) = \frac{\mu^x e^{-\mu}}{x!}$$

For example, the probability of not losing any bags is:

$$P(0) = \frac{(0.3)^0(e^{-0.3})}{0!} = 0.7408$$

STATISTICS IN ACTION

Near the end of World War II, the Germans developed rocket bombs, which were fired at the city of London. The Allied military command didn't know whether these bombs were fired at random or whether they had an aiming device. To investigate, the city of London was divided into 586 square regions. The distribution of hits in each square was recorded as follows:

Hits	0	1	2	3	4	5
Regions	229	221	93	35	7	1

To interpret, the above chart indicates that 229 regions were not hit with one of the bombs. Seven regions were hit four times. Using the Poisson distribution, with a mean of 0.93 hits per region, the expected number of hits is as follows:

Hits	0	1	2	3	4	5 or more
Regions	231.2	215.0	100.0	31.0	7.2	1.6

Because the actual number of hits was close to the expected number of hits, the military command concluded that the bombs were falling at random. The Germans had not developed a bomb with an aiming device.

In other words, 74% of the flights will have no lost baggage. The probability of exactly one lost bag is:

$$P(1) = \frac{(0.3)^1(e^{-0.3})}{1!} = 0.2222$$

Thus, we would expect to find exactly one lost bag on 22% of the flights.

Poisson probabilities can also be found in the table in Appendix B.2.

EXAMPLE

Recall from the previous illustration that the number of lost bags follows a Poisson distribution with a mean of 0.3. Use Appendix B.2 to find the probability that no bags will be lost on a particular flight. What is the probability exactly one bag will be lost on a particular flight? When should the supervisor become suspicious that a flight is having too many lost bags?

SOLUTION

Part of Appendix B.2 is repeated as Table 6–6. To find the probability of no lost bags, locate the column headed "0.3" and read down that column to the row labeled "0." The probability is .7408. That is the probability of no lost bags. The probability of one lost bag is .2222, which is in the next row of the table, in the same column. The probability of two lost bags is .0333, in the row below; for three lost bags, it is .0033; and for four lost bags, it is .0003. Thus, a supervisor should not be surprised to find one lost bag but should expect to see more than one lost bag infrequently.

TABLE 6–6 Poisson Table for Various Values of μ (from Appendix B.2)

	μ								
x	**0.1**	**0.2**	**0.3**	**0.4**	**0.5**	**0.6**	**0.7**	**0.8**	**0.9**
0	0.9048	0.8187	0.7408	0.6703	0.6065	0.5488	0.4966	0.4493	0.4066
1	0.0905	0.1637	0.2222	0.2681	0.3033	0.3293	0.3476	0.3595	0.3659
2	0.0045	0.0164	0.0333	0.0536	0.0758	0.0988	0.1217	0.1438	0.1647
3	0.0002	0.0011	0.0033	0.0072	0.0126	0.0198	0.0284	0.0383	0.0494
4	0.0000	0.0001	0.0003	0.0007	0.0016	0.0030	0.0050	0.0077	0.0111
5	0.0000	0.0000	0.0000	0.0001	0.0002	0.0004	0.0007	0.0012	0.0020
6	0.0000	0.0000	0.0000	0.0000	0.0000	0.0000	0.0001	0.0002	0.0003
7	0.0000	0.0000	0.0000	0.0000	0.0000	0.0000	0.0000	0.0000	0.0000

These probabilities can also be found using Excel. The commands to compute Poisson probabilities are in Appendix C.

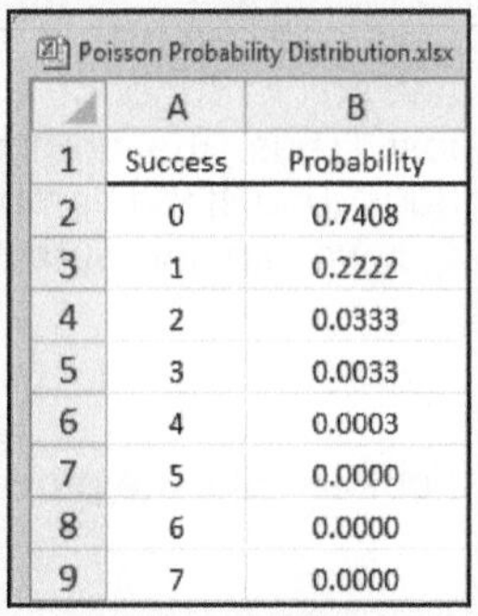
Poisson Probability Distribution.xlsx

	A	B
1	Success	Probability
2	0	0.7408
3	1	0.2222
4	2	0.0333
5	3	0.0033
6	4	0.0003
7	5	0.0000
8	6	0.0000
9	7	0.0000

Earlier in this section, we mentioned that the Poisson probability distribution is a limiting form of the binomial. That is, we could estimate a binomial probability using the Poisson.

The Poisson probability distribution is characterized by the number of times an event happens during some interval or continuum. Examples include:

- The number of misspelled words per page in a newspaper.
- The number of calls per hour received by Dyson Vacuum Cleaner Company.
- The number of vehicles sold per day at Hyatt Buick GMC in Durham, North Carolina.
- The number of goals scored in a college soccer game.

In each of these examples, there is some type of continuum—misspelled words per page, calls per hour, vehicles per day, or goals per game.

In the previous example, we investigated the number of bags lost per flight, so the continuum was a "flight." We knew the mean number of bags of luggage lost per flight, but we did not know the number of passengers or the probability of a bag being lost. We suspected the number of passengers was fairly large and the probability of a passenger losing his or her bag of luggage was small. In the following example, we use the Poisson distribution to estimate a binomial probability when *n*, the number of trials, is large and π, the probability of a success, small.

EXAMPLE

Coastal Insurance Company underwrites insurance for beachfront properties along the Virginia, North and South Carolina, and Georgia coasts. It uses the estimate that the probability of a named Category III hurricane (sustained winds of more than 110 miles per hour) or higher striking a particular region of the coast (for example, St. Simons Island, Georgia) in any one year is .05. If a homeowner takes a 30-year mortgage on a recently purchased property in St. Simons, what is the likelihood that the owner will experience at least one hurricane during the mortgage period?

SOLUTION

To use the Poisson probability distribution, we begin by determining the mean or expected number of storms meeting the criterion hitting St. Simons during the 30-year period. That is:

$$\mu = n\pi = 30(.05) = 1.5$$

where:

n is the number of years, 30 in this case.
π is the probability a hurricane meeting the strength criteria comes ashore.
μ is the mean or expected number of storms in a 30-year period.

To find the probability of at least one storm hitting St. Simons Island, Georgia, we first find the probability of no storms hitting the coast and subtract that value from 1.

$$P(x \geq 1) = 1 - P(x = 0) = 1 - \frac{\mu^0 e^{-1.5}}{0!} = 1 - .2231 = .7769$$

We conclude that the likelihood a hurricane meeting the strength criteria will strike the beachfront property at St. Simons during the 30-year period when the mortgage is in effect is .7769. To put it another way, the probability St. Simons will be hit by a Category III or higher hurricane during the 30-year period is a little more than 75%.

We should emphasize that the continuum, as previously described, still exists. That is, there are expected to be 1.5 storms hitting the coast per 30-year period. The continuum is the 30-year period.

In the preceding case, we are actually using the Poisson distribution as an estimate of the binomial. Note that we've met the binomial conditions outlined on page 183.

- There are only two possible outcomes: a hurricane hits the St. Simons area or it does not.
- There are a fixed number of trials, in this case 30 years.
- There is a constant probability of success; that is, the probability of a hurricane hitting the area is .05 each year.
- The years are independent. That means if a named storm strikes in the fifth year, that has no effect on any other year.

To find the probability of at least one storm striking the area in a 30-year period using the binomial distribution:

$$P(x \geq 1) = 1 - P(x = 0) = 1 - [{}_{30}C_0(.05)^0(.95)^{30}] = 1 - [(1)(1)(.2146)] = .7854$$

The probability of at least one hurricane hitting the St. Simons area during the 30-year period using the binomial distribution is .7854.

Which answer is correct? Why should we look at the problem both ways? The binomial is the more "technically correct" solution. The Poisson can be thought of as an approximation for the binomial, when n, the number of trials is large, and π, the probability of a success, is small. We look at the problem using both distributions to emphasize the convergence of the two discrete distributions. In some instances, using the Poisson may be the quicker solution, and as you see there is little practical difference in the answers. In fact, as n gets larger and π smaller, the difference between the two distributions gets smaller.

The Poisson probability distribution is always positively skewed and the random variable has no specific upper limit. The Poisson distribution for the lost bags example/solution where $\mu = 0.3$, is highly skewed. As μ becomes larger, the Poisson distribution becomes more symmetrical. For example, Chart 6–4 shows the distributions of

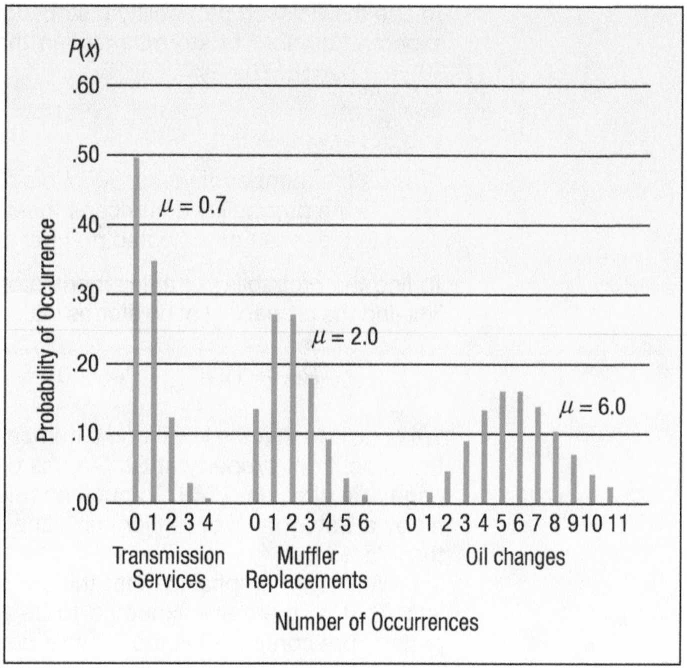

CHART 6–4 Poisson Probability Distributions for Means of 0.7, 2.0, and 6.0

the number of transmission services, muffler replacements, and oil changes per day at Avellino's Auto Shop. They follow Poisson distributions with means of 0.7, 2.0, and 6.0, respectively.

In summary, the Poisson distribution is a family of discrete distributions. All that is needed to construct a Poisson probability distribution is the mean number of defects, errors, and so on—designated as μ.

SELF-REVIEW 6–6

From actuary tables, Washington Insurance Company determined the likelihood that a man age 25 will die within the next year is .0002. If Washington Insurance sells 4,000 policies to 25-year-old men this year, what is the probability they will pay on exactly one policy?

EXERCISES

31. In a Poisson distribution $\mu = 0.4$.
- **a.** What is the probability that $x = 0$?
- **b.** What is the probability that $x > 0$?

32. In a Poisson distribution $\mu = 4$.
- **a.** What is the probability that $x = 2$?
- **b.** What is the probability that $x \leq 2$?
- **c.** What is the probability that $x > 2$?

33. Ms. Bergen is a loan officer at Coast Bank and Trust. From her years of experience, she estimates that the probability is .025 that an applicant will not be able to repay his or her installment loan. Last month she made 40 loans.
- **a.** What is the probability that three loans will be defaulted?
- **b.** What is the probability that at least three loans will be defaulted?

34. Automobiles arrive at the Elkhart exit of the Indiana Toll Road at the rate of two per minute. The distribution of arrivals approximates a Poisson distribution.
- **a.** What is the probability that no automobiles arrive in a particular minute?
- **b.** What is the probability that at least one automobile arrives during a particular minute?

35. It is estimated that 0.5% of the callers to the Customer Service department of Dell Inc. will receive a busy signal. What is the probability that of today's 1,200 callers at least 5 received a busy signal?

36. In the past, schools in Los Angeles County have closed an average of 3 days each year for weather emergencies. What is the probability that schools in Los Angeles County will close for 4 days next year?

CHAPTER SUMMARY

I. A random variable is a numerical value determined by the outcome of an experiment.

II. A probability distribution is a listing of all possible outcomes of an experiment and the probability associated with each outcome.
- **A.** A discrete probability distribution can assume only certain values. The main features are:
  1. The sum of the probabilities is 1.00.
  2. The probability of a particular outcome is between 0.00 and 1.00.
  3. The outcomes are mutually exclusive.
- **B.** A continuous distribution can assume an infinite number of values within a specific range.

III. The mean and variance of a probability distribution are computed as follows.
- **A.** The mean is equal to:

$$\mu = \Sigma[xP(x)] \qquad \textbf{[6–1]}$$

- **B.** The variance is equal to:

$$\sigma^2 = \Sigma[(x - \mu)^2 P(x)] \qquad \textbf{[6–2]}$$

IV. The binomial distribution has the following characteristics.

A. Each outcome is classified into one of two mutually exclusive categories.

B. The distribution results from a count of the number of successes in a fixed number of trials.

C. The probability of a success remains the same from trial to trial.

D. Each trial is independent.

E. A binomial probability is determined as follows:

$$P(x) = {}_nC_x \pi^x(1 - \pi)^{n-x} \qquad \textbf{[6–3]}$$

F. The mean is computed as:

$$\mu = n\pi \qquad \textbf{[6–4]}$$

G. The variance is

$$\sigma^2 = n\pi(1 - \pi) \qquad \textbf{[6–5]}$$

V. The hypergeometric distribution has the following characteristics.

A. There are only two possible outcomes.

B. The probability of a success is not the same on each trial.

C. The distribution results from a count of the number of successes in a fixed number of trials.

D. It is used when sampling without replacement from a finite population.

E. A hypergeometric probability is computed from the following equation:

$$P(x) = \frac{({}_SC_x)({}_{N-S}C_{n-x})}{({}_NC_n)} \qquad \textbf{[6–6]}$$

VI. The Poisson distribution has the following characteristics.

A. It describes the number of times some event occurs during a specified interval.

B. The probability of a "success" is proportional to the length of the interval.

C. Nonoverlapping intervals are independent.

D. It is a limiting form of the binomial distribution when n is large and π is small.

E. A Poisson probability is determined from the following equation:

$$P(x) = \frac{\mu^x e^{-\mu}}{x!} \qquad \textbf{[6–7]}$$

F. The mean and the variance are:

$$\mu = n\pi \qquad \textbf{[6–8]}$$

$$\sigma^2 = n\pi$$

CHAPTER EXERCISES

37. What is the difference between a random variable and a probability distribution?

38. For each of the following indicate whether the random variable is discrete or continuous.

a. The length of time to get a haircut.

b. The number of cars a jogger passes each morning while running.

c. The number of hits for a team in a high school girls' softball game.

d. The number of patients treated at the South Strand Medical Center between 6 and 10 p.m. each night.

e. The distance your car traveled on the last fill-up.

f. The number of customers at the Oak Street Wendy's who used the drive-through facility.

g. The distance between Gainesville, Florida, and all Florida cities with a population of at least 50,000.

For **DATA FILE**, please visit www.mhhe.com/lind16e

39. An investment will be worth \$1,000, \$2,000, or \$5,000 at the end of the year. The probabilities of these values are .25, .60, and .15, respectively. Determine the mean and variance of the worth of the investment.

40. The following notice appeared in the golf shop at a Myrtle Beach, South Carolina, golf course.

> **Blackmoor Golf Club Members**
>
> The golf shop is holding a raffle to win a
> TaylorMade R9 10.5° Regular Flex Driver ($300 value).
> Tickets are $5.00 each.
> Only 80 tickets will be sold.
> Please see the golf shop to get your tickets!

John Underpar buys a ticket.

a. What are Mr. Underpar's possible monetary outcomes?
b. What are the probabilities of the possible outcomes?
c. Summarize Mr. Underpar's "experiment" as a probability distribution.
d. What is the mean or expected value of the probability distribution? Explain your result.
e. If all 80 tickets are sold, what is the expected return to the Club?

For **DATA FILE**, please visit www.mhhe.com/lind16e

41. Croissant Bakery Inc. offers special decorated cakes for birthdays, weddings, and other occasions. It also has regular cakes available in its bakery. The following table gives the total number of cakes sold per day and the corresponding probability. Compute the mean, variance, and standard deviation of the number of cakes sold per day.

Number of Cakes Sold in a Day	Probability
12	.25
13	.40
14	.25
15	.10

For **DATA FILE**, please visit www.mhhe.com/lind16e

42. The payouts for the Powerball lottery and their corresponding odds and probabilities of occurrence are shown below. The price of a ticket is $1.00. Find the mean and standard deviation of the payout. Hint: Don't forget to include the cost of the ticket and its corresponding probability.

Divisions	Payout	Odds	Probability
Five plus Powerball	$50,000,000	146,107,962	0.000000006844
Match 5	200,000	3,563,609	0.000000280614
Four plus Powerball	10,000	584,432	0.000001711060
Match 4	100	14,255	0.000070145903
Three plus Powerball	100	11,927	0.000083836351
Match 3	7	291	0.003424657534
Two plus Powerball	7	745	0.001340482574
One plus Powerball	4	127	0.007812500000
Zero plus Powerball	3	69	0.014285714286

43. In a recent survey, 35% indicated chocolate was their favorite flavor of ice cream. Suppose we select a sample of 10 people and ask them to name their favorite flavor of ice cream.

a. How many of those in the sample would you expect to name chocolate?
b. What is the probability exactly four of those in the sample name chocolate?
c. What is the probability four or more name chocolate?

For **DATA FILE**, please visit www.mhhe.com/lind16e

44. Thirty percent of the population in a southwestern community are Spanish-speaking Americans. A Spanish-speaking person is accused of killing a non-Spanish-speaking American and goes to trial. Of the first 12 potential jurors, only 2 are Spanish-speaking Americans, and 10 are not. The defendant's lawyer challenges the jury selection, claiming bias against her client. The government lawyer disagrees, saying that the probability of this particular jury composition is common. Compute the probability and discuss the assumptions.

45. An auditor for Health Maintenance Services of Georgia reports 40% of policyholders 55 years or older submit a claim during the year. Fifteen policyholders are randomly selected for company records.

a. How many of the policyholders would you expect to have filed a claim within the last year?
b. What is the probability that 10 of the selected policyholders submitted a claim last year?
c. What is the probability that 10 or more of the selected policyholders submitted a claim last year?
d. What is the probability that more than 10 of the selected policyholders submitted a claim last year?

46. Tire and Auto Supply is considering a 2-for-1 stock split. Before the transaction is finalized, at least two-thirds of the 1,200 company stockholders must approve the proposal. To evaluate the likelihood the proposal will be approved, the CFO selected a sample of 18 stockholders. He contacted each and found 14 approved of the proposed split. What is the likelihood of this event, assuming two-thirds of the stockholders approve?

47. A federal study reported that 7.5% of the U.S. workforce has a drug problem. A drug enforcement official for the state of Indiana wished to investigate this statement. In her sample of 20 employed workers:

a. How many would you expect to have a drug problem? What is the standard deviation?
b. What is the likelihood that *none* of the workers sampled has a drug problem?
c. What is the likelihood *at least one* has a drug problem?

48. The Bank of Hawaii reports that 7% of its credit card holders will default at some time in their life. The Hilo branch just mailed out 12 new cards today.

a. How many of these new cardholders would you expect to default? What is the standard deviation?
b. What is the likelihood that *none* of the cardholders will default?
c. What is the likelihood *at least one* will default?

49. Recent statistics suggest that 15% of those who visit a retail site on the World Wide Web make a purchase. A retailer wished to verify this claim. To do so, she selected a sample of 16 "hits" to her site and found that 4 had actually made a purchase.

a. What is the likelihood of exactly four purchases?
b. How many purchases should she expect?
c. What is the likelihood that four or more "hits" result in a purchase?

50. In Chapter 19, we discuss *acceptance sampling.* Acceptance sampling is a statistical method used to monitor the quality of purchased parts and components. To ensure the quality of incoming parts, a purchaser or manufacturer normally samples 20 parts and allows one defect.

a. What is the likelihood of accepting a lot that is 1% defective?
b. If the quality of the incoming lot was actually 2%, what is the likelihood of accepting it?
c. If the quality of the incoming lot was actually 5%, what is the likelihood of accepting it?

51. Unilever Inc. recently developed a new body wash with a scent of ginger. Their research indicates that 30% of men like the new scent. To further investigate, Unilever's marketing research group randomly selected 15 men and asked them if they liked the scent. What is the probability that six or more men like the ginger scent in the body wash?

52. Dr. Richmond, a psychologist, is studying the daytime television viewing habits of college students. She believes 45% of college students watch soap operas during the afternoon. To further investigate, she selects a sample of 10.

a. Develop a probability distribution for the number of students in the sample who watch soap operas.
b. Find the mean and the standard deviation of this distribution.
c. What is the probability of finding exactly four students who watch soap operas?
d. What is the probability less than half of the students selected watch soap operas?

For **DATA FILE**, please visit www.mhhe.com/lind16e

53. A recent study conducted by Penn, Shone, and Borland, on behalf of LastMinute.com, revealed that 52% of business travelers plan their trips less than two weeks before departure. The study is to be replicated in the tri-state area with a sample of 12 frequent business travelers.

a. Develop a probability distribution for the number of travelers who plan their trips within two weeks of departure.

b. Find the mean and the standard deviation of this distribution.

c. What is the probability exactly 5 of the 12 selected business travelers plan their trips within two weeks of departure?

d. What is the probability 5 or fewer of the 12 selected business travelers plan their trips within two weeks of departure?

54. The Internal Revenue Service is studying the category of charitable contributions. A sample of 25 returns is selected from young couples between the ages of 20 and 35 who had an adjusted gross income of more than $100,000. Of these 25 returns, five had charitable contributions of more than $1,000. Four of these returns are selected for a comprehensive audit.

a. Explain why the hypergeometric distribution is appropriate.

b. What is the probability exactly one of the four audited had a charitable deduction of more than $1,000?

c. What is the probability at least one of the audited returns had a charitable contribution of more than $1,000?

55. The law firm of Hagel and Hagel is located in downtown Cincinnati. There are 10 partners in the firm; 7 live in Ohio and 3 in northern Kentucky. Ms. Wendy Hagel, the managing partner, wants to appoint a committee of 3 partners to look into moving the firm to northern Kentucky. If the committee is selected at random from the 10 partners, what is the probability that:

a. One member of the committee lives in northern Kentucky and the others live in Ohio?

b. At least one member of the committee lives in northern Kentucky?

56. Topten is a leading source on energy-efficient products. Their list of the top seven vehicles in terms of fuel efficiency for 2014 includes three Hondas.

a. Determine the probability distribution for the number of Hondas in a sample of two cars chosen from the top seven.

b. What is the likelihood that in the sample of two at least one Honda is included?

57. The position of chief of police in the city of Corry, Pennsylvania, is vacant. A search committee of Corry residents is charged with the responsibility of recommending a new chief to the city council. There are 12 applicants, 4 of whom are either female or members of a minority. The search committee decides to interview all 12 of the applicants. To begin, they randomly select four applicants to be interviewed on the first day, and none of the four is female or a member of a minority. The local newspaper, the *Corry Press*, suggests discrimination in an editorial. What is the likelihood of this occurrence?

For **DATA FILE**, please visit www.mhhe.com/lind16e

58. Listed below is the population by state for the 15 states with the largest population. Also included is whether that state's border touches the Gulf of Mexico, the Atlantic Ocean, or the Pacific Ocean (coastline).

Rank	State	Population	Coastline
1	California	36,553,215	Yes
2	Texas	23,904,380	Yes
3	New York	19,297,729	Yes
4	Florida	18,251,243	Yes
5	Illinois	12,852,548	No
6	Pennsylvania	12,432,792	No
7	Ohio	11,466,917	No
8	Michigan	10,071,822	No
9	Georgia	9,544,750	Yes
10	North Carolina	9,061,032	Yes
11	New Jersey	8,685,920	Yes
12	Virginia	7,712,091	Yes
13	Washington	6,468,424	Yes
14	Massachusetts	6,449,755	Yes
15	Indiana	6,345,289	No

Note that 5 of the 15 states do not have any coastline. Suppose three states are selected at random. What is the probability that:

a. None of the states selected has any coastline?

b. Exactly one of the selected states has a coastline?

c. At least one of the selected states has a coastline?

59. The sales of Lexus automobiles in the Detroit area follow a Poisson distribution with a mean of 3 per day.

a. What is the probability that no Lexus is sold on a particular day?

b. What is the probability that for 5 consecutive days at least one Lexus is sold?

60. Suppose 1.5% of the antennas on new Nokia cell phones are defective. For a random sample of 200 antennas, find the probability that:

a. None of the antennas is defective.

b. Three or more of the antennas are defective.

61. A study of the checkout lines at the Safeway Supermarket in the South Strand area revealed that between 4 and 7 p.m. on weekdays there is an average of four customers waiting in line. What is the probability that you visit Safeway today during this period and find:

a. No customers are waiting?

b. Four customers are waiting?

c. Four or fewer are waiting?

d. Four or more are waiting?

62. An internal study by the Technology Services department at Lahey Electronics revealed company employees receive an average of two non-work-related e-mails per hour. Assume the arrival of these e-mails is approximated by the Poisson distribution.

a. What is the probability Linda Lahey, company president, received exactly one non-work-related e-mail between 4 p.m. and 5 p.m. yesterday?

b. What is the probability she received five or more non-work-related e-mails during the same period?

c. What is the probability she did not receive any non-work-related e-mails during the period?

63. Recent crime reports indicate that 3.1 motor vehicle thefts occur each minute in the United States. Assume that the distribution of thefts per minute can be approximated by the Poisson probability distribution.

a. Calculate the probability exactly *four* thefts occur in a minute.

b. What is the probability there are *no* thefts in a minute?

c. What is the probability there is *at least one* theft in a minute?

64. Recent difficult economic times have caused an increase in the foreclosure rate of home mortgages. Statistics from the Penn Bank and Trust Company show their monthly foreclosure rate is now 1 loan out of every 136 loans. Last month the bank approved 300 loans.

a. How many foreclosures would you expect the bank to have last month?

b. What is the probability of exactly two foreclosures?

c. What is the probability of at least one foreclosure?

65. The National Aeronautics and Space Administration (NASA) has experienced two disasters. The *Challenger* exploded over the Atlantic Ocean in 1986, and the *Columbia* disintegrated on reentry over East Texas in 2003. Based on the first 113 missions, and assuming failures occur at the same rate, consider the next 23 missions. What is the probability of exactly two failures? What is the probability of no failures?

66. According to the "January theory," if the stock market is up for the month of January, it will be up for the year. If it is down in January, it will be down for the year. According to an article in *The Wall Street Journal,* this theory held for 29 out of the last 34 years. Suppose there is no truth to this theory; that is, the probability it is either up or down is .50. What is the probability this could occur by chance? You will probably need a software package such as Excel or Minitab.

67. During the second round of the 1989 U.S. Open golf tournament, four golfers scored a hole in one on the sixth hole. The odds of a professional golfer making a hole in one are estimated to be 3,708 to 1, so the probability is 1/3,709. There were 155 golfers participating in the second round that day. Estimate the probability that four golfers would score a hole in one on the sixth hole.

68. Suppose the National Hurricane Center forecasts that hurricanes will hit the strike area with a .95 probability.

a. What probability distribution does this follow?

b. If there are 10 hurricanes this season, what is the probability that all reach the strike area?

c. What is the probability at least one of 10 hurricanes reaches land outside the strike area?

69. A recent CBS News survey reported that 67% of adults felt the U.S. Treasury should continue making pennies.

Suppose we select a sample of 15 adults.

a. How many of the 15 would we expect to indicate that the Treasury should continue making pennies? What is the standard deviation?

b. What is the likelihood that exactly eight adults would indicate the Treasury should continue making pennies?

c. What is the likelihood at least eight adults would indicate the Treasury should continue making pennies?

DATA SET EXERCISES

(The data for these exercises are available at the text website: www.mhhe.com/lind16e.)

70. Refer to the Real Estate data, which report information on homes sold in the Goodyear, Arizona, area last year.

a. Create a probability distribution for the number of bedrooms. Compute the mean and the standard deviation of this distribution.

b. Create a probability distribution for the number of bathrooms. Compute the mean and the standard deviation of this distribution.

71. Refer to the Baseball 2012 data. Compute the mean number of home runs per game. To do this, first find the mean number of home runs per team for 2012. Next, divide this value by 162 (a season comprises 162 games). Then multiply by 2 because there are two teams in each game. Use the Poisson distribution to estimate the number of home runs that will be hit in a game. Find the probability that:

a. There are no home runs in a game.

b. There are two home runs in a game.

c. There are at least four home runs in a game.

7 Continuous Probability Distributions

CRUISE SHIPS of the Royal Viking line report that 80% of their rooms are occupied during September. For a cruise ship having 800 rooms, what is the probability that 665 or more are occupied in September? (See Exercise 60 and LO7-4.)

LEARNING OBJECTIVES

When you have completed this chapter, you will be able to:

LO7-1 Describe the uniform probability distribution and use it to calculate probabilities.

LO7-2 Describe the characteristics of a normal probability distribution.

LO7-3 Describe the standard normal probability distribution and use it to calculate probabilities.

LO7-4 Approximate the binomial probability distribution using the standard normal probability distribution to calculate probabilities.

LO7-5 Describe the exponential probability distribution and use it to calculate probabilities.

INTRODUCTION

Chapter 6 began our study of probability distributions. We consider three *discrete* probability distributions: binomial, hypergeometric, and Poisson. These distributions are based on discrete random variables, which can assume only clearly separated values. For example, we select for study 10 small businesses that began operations during the year 2010. The number still operating in 2013 can be 0, 1, 2, . . . , 10. There cannot be 3.7, 12, or −7 still operating in 2013. In this example, only certain outcomes are possible and these outcomes are represented by clearly separated values. In addition, the result is usually found by counting the number of successes. We count the number of the businesses in the study that are still in operation in 2013.

We continue our study of probability distributions by examining *continuous* probability distributions. A continuous probability distribution usually results from measuring something, such as the distance from the dormitory to the classroom, the weight of an individual, or the amount of bonus earned by CEOs. As an example, at Dave's Inlet Fish Shack flounder is the featured, fresh-fish menu item. The distribution of the amount of flounder sold per day has a mean of 10.0 pounds per day and a standard deviation of 3.0 pounds per day. This distribution is continuous because Dave, the owner, "measures" the amount of flounder sold each day. It is important to realize that a continuous random variable has an infinite number of values within a particular range. So, for a continuous random variable, probability is for a range of values. The probability for a specific value of a continuous random variable is 0.

This chapter shows how to use three continuous probability distributions: the uniform probability distribution, the normal probability distribution, and the exponential probability distribution.

LO7-1
Describe the uniform probability distribution and use it to calculate probabilities.

THE FAMILY OF UNIFORM PROBABILITY DISTRIBUTIONS

The uniform probability distribution is the simplest distribution for a continuous random variable. This distribution is rectangular in shape and is completely defined by its minimum and maximum values. Here are some examples that follow a uniform distribution.

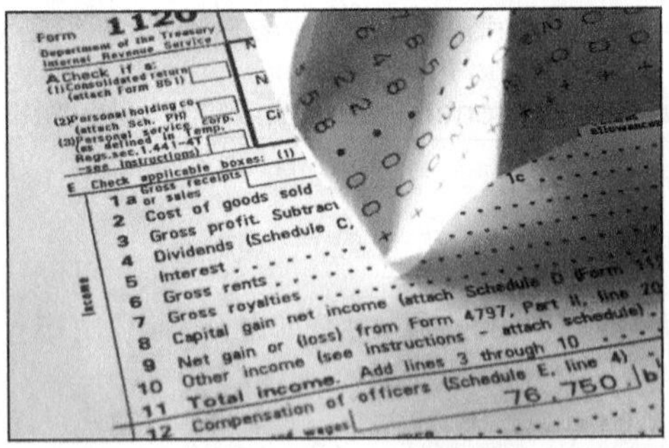

- The sales of gasoline at the Kwik Fill in Medina, New York, follow a uniform distribution that varies between 2,000 and 5,000 gallons per day. The random variable is the number of gallons sold per day and is continuous within the interval between 2,000 gallons and 5,000 gallons.
- Volunteers at the Grand Strand Public Library prepare federal income tax forms. The time to prepare form 1040-EZ follows a uniform distribution over the interval between 10 minutes and 30 minutes. The random variable is the number of minutes to complete the form, and it can assume any value between 10 and 30.

A uniform distribution is shown in Chart 7–1. The distribution's shape is rectangular and has a minimum value of *a* and a maximum of *b*. Also notice in Chart 7–1 the height of the distribution is constant or uniform for all values between *a* and *b*.

The mean of a uniform distribution is located in the middle of the interval between the minimum and maximum values. It is computed as:

MEAN OF THE UNIFORM DISTRIBUTION $$\mu = \frac{a + b}{2}$$ **[7–1]**

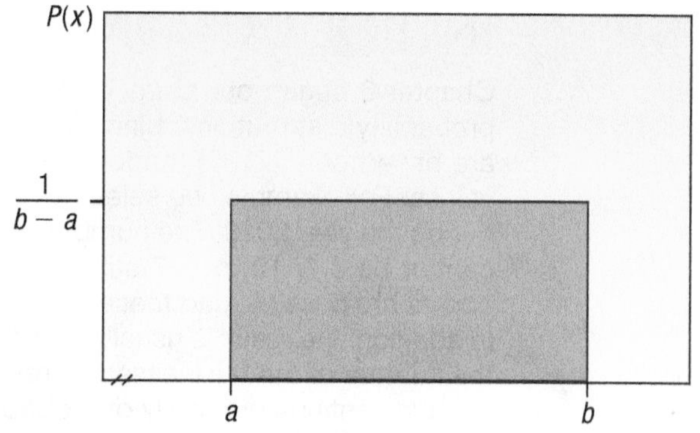

CHART 7–1 A Continuous Uniform Distribution

The standard deviation describes the dispersion of a distribution. In the uniform distribution, the standard deviation is also related to the interval between the maximum and minimum values.

STANDARD DEVIATION OF THE UNIFORM DISTRIBUTION $$\sigma = \sqrt{\frac{(b-a)^2}{12}}$$ **[7–2]**

The equation for the uniform probability distribution is:

UNIFORM DISTRIBUTION $$P(x) = \frac{1}{b-a} \text{ if } a \le x \le b \text{ and 0 elsewhere}$$ **[7–3]**

As we described in Chapter 6, probability distributions are useful for making probability statements concerning the values of a random variable. For distributions describing a continuous random variable, areas within the distribution represent probabilities. In the uniform distribution, its rectangular shape allows us to apply the area formula for a rectangle. Recall that we find the area of a rectangle by multiplying its length by its height. For the uniform distribution, the height of the rectangle is $P(x)$, which is $1/(b - a)$. The length or base of the distribution is $b - a$. So if we multiply the height of the distribution by its entire range to find the area, the result is always 1.00. To put it another way, the total area within a continuous probability distribution is equal to 1.00. In general

$$\text{Area} = (\text{height})(\text{base}) = \frac{1}{(b-a)}(b-a) = 1.00$$

So if a uniform distribution ranges from 10 to 15, the height is 0.20, found by $1/(15 - 10)$. The base is 5, found by $15 - 10$. The total area is:

$$\text{Area} = (\text{height})(\text{base}) = \frac{1}{(15-10)}(15-10) = 1.00$$

An example will illustrate the features of a uniform distribution and how we calculate probabilities using it.

EXAMPLE

Southwest Arizona State University provides bus service to students while they are on campus. A bus arrives at the North Main Street and College Drive stop every 30 minutes between 6 a.m. and 11 p.m. during weekdays. Students arrive

at the bus stop at random times. The time that a student waits is uniformly distributed from 0 to 30 minutes.

1. Draw a graph of this distribution.
2. Show that the area of this uniform distribution is 1.00.
3. How long will a student "typically" have to wait for a bus? In other words, what is the mean waiting time? What is the standard deviation of the waiting times?
4. What is the probability a student will wait more than 25 minutes?
5. What is the probability a student will wait between 10 and 20 minutes?

SOLUTION

In this case, the random variable is the length of time a student must wait. Time is measured on a continuous scale, and the wait times may range from 0 minutes up to 30 minutes.

1. The graph of the uniform distribution is shown in Chart 7–2. The horizontal line is drawn at a height of .0333, found by 1/(30 − 0). The range of this distribution is 30 minutes.

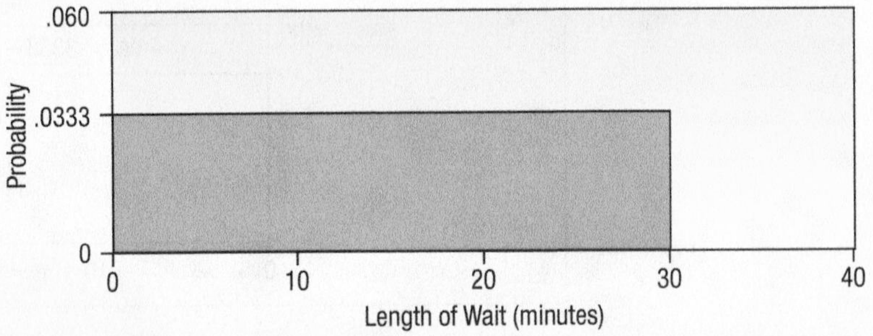

CHART 7–2 Uniform Probability Distribution of Student Waiting Times

2. The times students must wait for the bus are uniform over the interval from 0 minutes to 30 minutes, so in this case *a* is 0 and *b* is 30.

$$\text{Area} = (\text{height})(\text{base}) = \frac{1}{(30-0)}(30-0) = 1.00$$

3. To find the mean, we use formula (7–1).

$$\mu = \frac{a+b}{2} = \frac{0+30}{2} = 15$$

The mean of the distribution is 15 minutes, so the typical wait time for bus service is 15 minutes.

To find the standard deviation of the wait times, we use formula (7–2).

$$\sigma = \sqrt{\frac{(b-a)^2}{12}} = \sqrt{\frac{(30-0)^2}{12}} = 8.66$$

The standard deviation of the distribution is 8.66 minutes. This measures the variation in the student wait times.

4. The area within the distribution for the interval 25 to 30 represents this particular probability. From the area formula:

$$P(25 < \text{wait time} < 30) = (\text{height})(\text{base}) = \frac{1}{(30-0)}(5) = .1667$$

So the probability a student waits between 25 and 30 minutes is .1667. This conclusion is illustrated by the following graph.

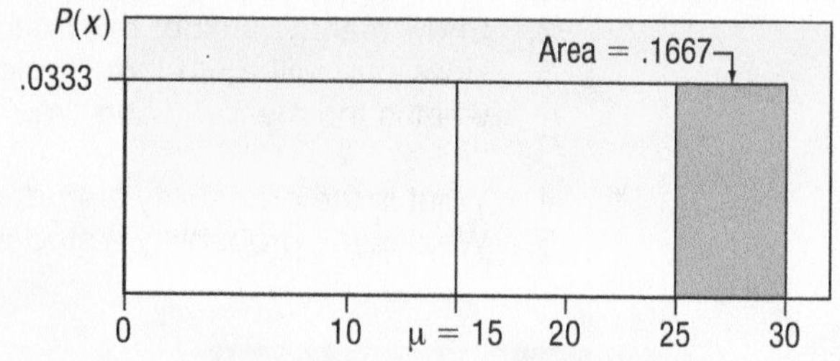

5. The area within the distribution for the interval 10 to 20 represents the probability.

$$P(10 < \text{wait time} < 20) = (\text{height})(\text{base}) = \frac{1}{(30-0)}(10) = .3333$$

We can illustrate this probability as follows.

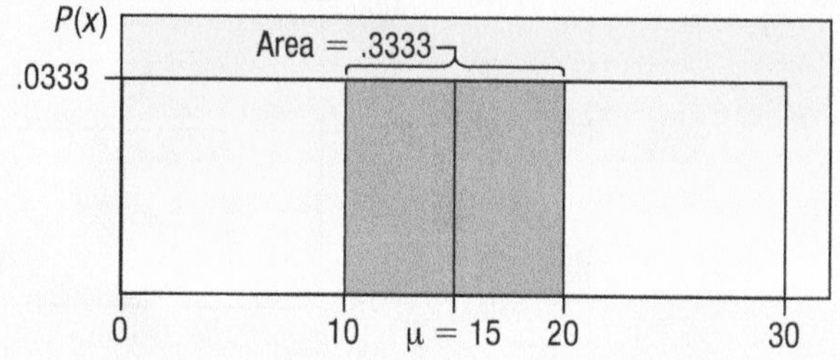

SELF-REVIEW 7–1

Australian sheepdogs have a relatively short life. The length of their life follows a uniform distribution between 8 and 14 years.
(a) Draw this uniform distribution. What are the height and base values?
(b) Show the total area under the curve is 1.00.
(c) Calculate the mean and the standard deviation of this distribution.
(d) What is the probability a particular dog lives between 10 and 14 years?
(e) What is the probability a dog will live less than 9 years?

EXERCISES

1. A uniform distribution is defined over the interval from 6 to 10.
   a. What are the values for *a* and *b*?
   b. What is the mean of this uniform distribution?
   c. What is the standard deviation?
   d. Show that the total area is 1.00.
   e. Find the probability of a value more than 7.
   f. Find the probability of a value between 7 and 9.
2. A uniform distribution is defined over the interval from 2 to 5.
   a. What are the values for *a* and *b*?
   b. What is the mean of this uniform distribution?
   c. What is the standard deviation?

d. Show that the total area is 1.00.
e. Find the probability of a value more than 2.6.
f. Find the probability of a value between 2.9 and 3.7.

3. The closing price of Schnur Sporting Goods Inc. common stock is uniformly distributed between $20 and $30 per share. What is the probability that the stock price will be:
a. More than $27?
b. Less than or equal to $24?

4. According to the Insurance Institute of America, a family of four spends between $400 and $3,800 per year on all types of insurance. Suppose the money spent is uniformly distributed between these amounts.
a. What is the mean amount spent on insurance?
b. What is the standard deviation of the amount spent?
c. If we select a family at random, what is the probability they spend less than $2,000 per year on insurance per year?
d. What is the probability a family spends more than $3,000 per year?

5. The April rainfall in Flagstaff, Arizona, follows a uniform distribution between 0.5 and 3.00 inches.
a. What are the values for *a* and *b*?
b. What is the mean amount of rainfall for the month? What is the standard deviation?
c. What is the probability of less than an inch of rain for the month?
d. What is the probability of *exactly* 1.00 inch of rain?
e. What is the probability of more than 1.50 inches of rain for the month?

6. Customers experiencing technical difficulty with their Internet cable hookup may call an 800 number for technical support. It takes the technician between 30 seconds and 10 minutes to resolve the problem. The distribution of this support time follows the uniform distribution.
a. What are the values for *a* and *b* in minutes?
b. What is the mean time to resolve the problem? What is the standard deviation of the time?
c. What percent of the problems take more than 5 minutes to resolve?
d. Suppose we wish to find the middle 50% of the problem-solving times. What are the end points of these two times?

LO7-2
Describe the characteristics of a normal probability distribution.

THE FAMILY OF NORMAL PROBABILITY DISTRIBUTIONS

Next we consider the normal probability distribution. Unlike the uniform distribution [see formula (7–3)] the normal probability distribution has a very complex formula.

NORMAL PROBABILITY DISTRIBUTION $$P(x) = \frac{1}{\sigma\sqrt{2\pi}} e^{-\left[\frac{(x-\mu)^2}{2\sigma^2}\right]} \quad \textbf{[7–4]}$$

However, do not be bothered by how complex this formula looks. You are already familiar with many of the values. The symbols μ and σ refer to the mean and the standard deviation, as usual. The Greek symbol π is a constant and its value is approximately 22/7 or 3.1416. The letter *e* is also a constant. It is the base of the natural log system and is approximately equal to 2.718. *x* is the value of a continuous random variable. So a normal distribution is based on—that is, it is defined by—its mean and standard deviation.

You will not need to make calculations using formula (7–4). Instead you will use a table, given in Appendix B.3, to find various probabilities. These probabilities can also be calculated using Excel functions as well as other statistical software.

The normal probability distribution has the following characteristics:

- It is **bell-shaped** and has a single peak at the center of the distribution. The arithmetic mean, median, and mode are equal and located in the center of the distribution. The total area under the curve is 1.00. Half the area under the normal curve is to the right of this center point and the other half, to the left of it.
- It is **symmetrical** about the mean. If we cut the normal curve vertically at the center value, the two halves will be mirror images.
- It falls off smoothly in either direction from the central value. That is, the distribution is **asymptotic:** The curve gets closer and closer to the *X*-axis but never actually touches it. To put it another way, the tails of the curve extend indefinitely in both directions.
- The location of a normal distribution is determined by the mean, μ. The dispersion or spread of the distribution is determined by the standard deviation, σ.

These characteristics are shown graphically in Chart 7–3.

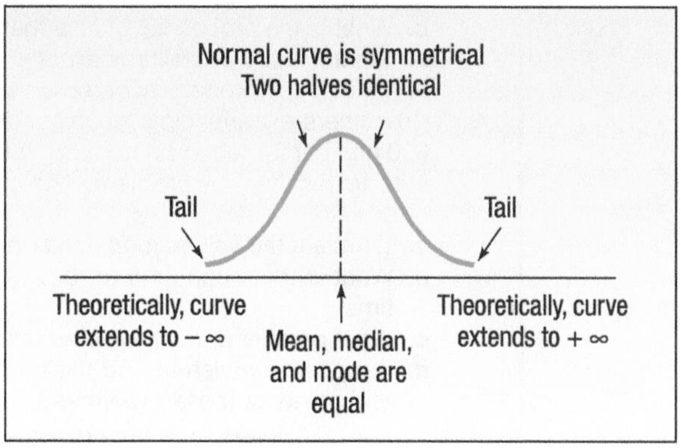

CHART 7–3 Characteristics of a Normal Distribution

There is not just one normal probability distribution, but rather a "family" of them. For example, in Chart 7–4 the probability distributions of length of employee service in three different plants are compared. In the Camden plant, the mean is 20 years and the standard deviation is 3.1 years. There is another normal probability distribution for the length of service in the Dunkirk plant, where $\mu = 20$ years and $\sigma = 3.9$ years. In the Elmira plant, $\mu = 20$ years and $\sigma = 5.0$ years. Note that the means are the same but the standard deviations are different. As the standard deviation gets smaller, the distribution becomes more narrow and "peaked."

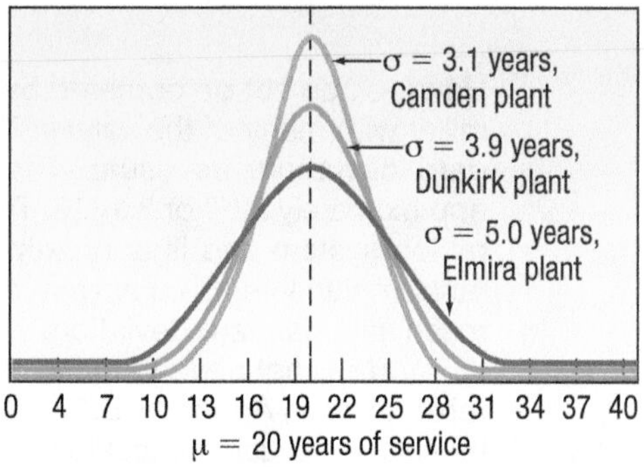

CHART 7–4 Normal Probability Distributions with Equal Means but Different Standard Deviations

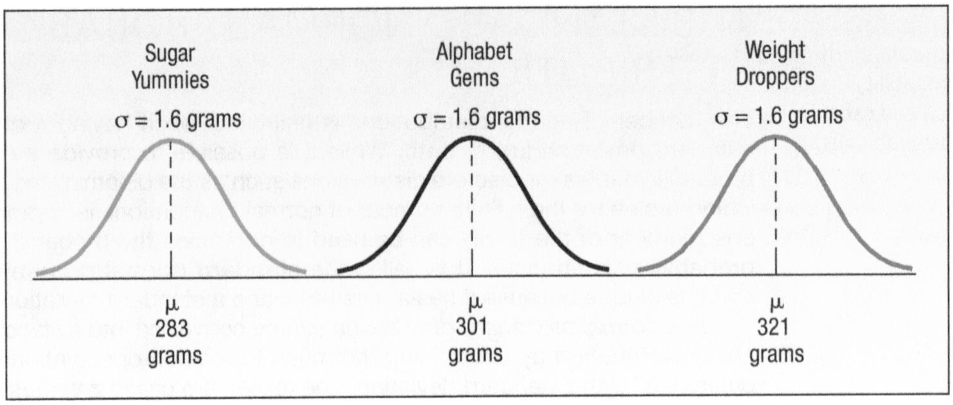

CHART 7–5 Normal Probability Distributions Having Different Means but Equal Standard Deviations

Chart 7–5 shows the distribution of box weights of three different cereals. The weights follow a normal distribution with different means but identical standard deviations.

Finally, Chart 7–6 shows three normal distributions having different means and standard deviations. They show the distribution of tensile strengths, measured in pounds per square inch (psi), for three types of cables.

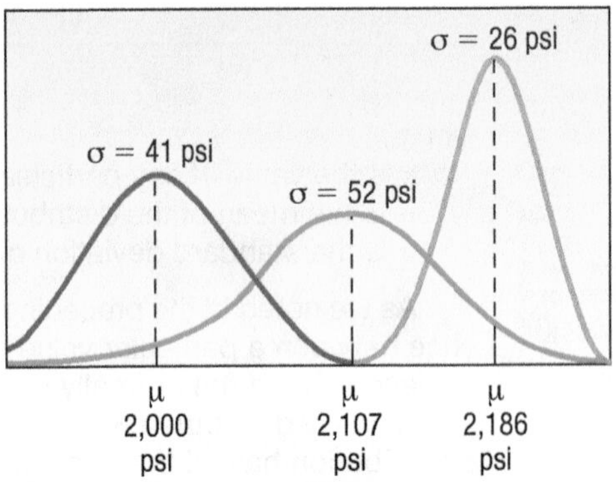

CHART 7–6 Normal Probability Distributions with Different Means and Standard Deviations

In Chapter 6, recall that discrete probability distributions show the specific likelihood a discrete value will occur. For example, on page 184, the binomial distribution is used to calculate the probability that none of the five flights arriving at the Bradford Pennsylvania Regional Airport would be late.

With a continuous probability distribution, areas below the curve define probabilities. The total area under the normal curve is 1.0. This accounts for all possible outcomes. Because a normal probability distribution is symmetric, the area under the curve to the left of the mean is 0.5, and the area under the curve to the right of the mean is 0.5. Apply this to the distribution of Sugar Yummies in Chart 7–5. It is normally distributed with a mean of 283 grams. Therefore, the probability of filling a box with more than 283 grams is 0.5 and the probability of filling a box with less than 283 grams is 0.5. We can also determine the probability that a box weighs between 280 and 286 grams. However, to determine this probability we need to know about the standard normal probability distribution.

LO7-3
Describe the standard normal probability distribution and use it to calculate probabilities.

THE STANDARD NORMAL PROBABILITY DISTRIBUTION

The number of normal distributions is unlimited, each having a different mean (μ), standard deviation (σ), or both. While it is possible to provide a limited number of probability tables for discrete distributions such as the binomial and the Poisson, providing tables for the infinite number of normal distributions is impractial. Fortunately, one member of the family can be used to determine the probabilities for all normal probability distributions. It is called the **standard normal probability distribution,** and it is unique because it has a mean of 0 and a standard deviation of 1.

Any *normal probability distribution* can be converted into a *standard normal probability distribution* by subtracting the mean from each observation and dividing this difference by the standard deviation. The results are called ***z* values** or ***z* scores.**

> ***z* VALUE** The signed distance between a selected value, designated *x*, and the mean, μ, divided by the standard deviation, σ.

So, a *z* value is the distance from the mean, measured in units of the standard deviation. The formula for this conversion is:

STANDARD NORMAL VALUE

$$z = \frac{x - \mu}{\sigma} \quad [7\text{–}5]$$

where:

x is the value of any particular observation or measurement.
μ is the mean of the distribution.
σ is the standard deviation of the distribution.

STATISTICS IN ACTION

An individual's skills depend on a combination of many hereditary and environmental factors, each having about the same amount of weight or influence on the skills. Thus, much like a binomial distribution with a large number of trials, many skills and attributes follow the normal distribution. For example, the SAT Reasoning Test is the most widely used standardized test for college admissions in the United States. Scores are based on a normal distribution with a mean of 1,500 and a standard deviation of 300.

As we noted in the preceding definition, a *z* value expresses the distance or difference between a particular value of *x* and the arithmetic mean in units of the standard deviation. Once the normally distributed observations are standardized, the *z* values are normally distributed with a mean of 0 and a standard deviation of 1. Therefore, the *z* distribution has all the characteristics of any normal probability distribution. These characteristics are listed on page 212. The table in Appendix B.3 (also on the inside back cover) lists the probabilities for the standard normal probability distribution. A small portion of this table follows.

TABLE 7–1 Areas under the Normal Curve

z	0.00	0.01	0.02	0.03	0.04	0.05	...
1.3	0.4032	0.4049	0.4066	0.4082	0.4099	0.4115	
1.4	0.4192	0.4207	0.4222	0.4236	0.4251	0.4265	
1.5	0.4332	0.4345	0.4357	0.4370	0.4382	0.4394	
1.6	0.4452	0.4463	0.4474	0.4484	0.4495	0.4505	
1.7	0.4554	0.4564	0.4573	0.4582	0.4591	0.4599	
1.8	0.4641	0.4649	0.4656	0.4664	0.4671	0.4678	
1.9	0.4713	0.4719	0.4726	0.4732	0.4738	0.4744	
⋮							

Applications of the Standard Normal Distribution

The standard normal distribution is very useful for determining probabilities for any normally distributed random variable. The basic procedure is to find the z value for a particular value of the random variable based on the mean and standard deviation of its distribution. Then, using the z value, we can use the standard normal distribution to find various probabilities. The following example/solution describes the details of the application.

EXAMPLE

The weekly incomes of shift foremen in the glass industry follow the normal probability distribution with a mean of \$1,000 and a standard deviation of \$100. What is the z value for the income, let's call it x, of a foreman who earns \$1,100 per week? For a foreman who earns \$900 per week?

SOLUTION

Using formula (7–5), the z values corresponding to the two x values (\$1,100 and \$900) are:

For $x = \$1{,}100$:

$$z = \frac{x - \mu}{\sigma} = \frac{\$1{,}100 - \$1{,}000}{\$100} = 1.00$$

For $x = \$900$:

$$z = \frac{x - \mu}{\sigma} = \frac{\$900 - \$1{,}000}{\$100} = -1.00$$

The z of 1.00 indicates that a weekly income of \$1,100 is one standard deviation above the mean, and a z of -1.00 shows that a \$900 income is one standard deviation below the mean. Note that both incomes (\$1,100 and \$900) are the same distance (\$100) from the mean.

SELF-REVIEW 7–2

A recent national survey concluded that the typical person consumes 48 ounces of water per day. Assume daily water consumption follows a normal probability distribution with a standard deviation of 12.8 ounces.

(a) What is the z value for a person who consumes 64 ounces of water per day? Based on this z value, how does this person compare to the national average?
(b) What is the z value for a person who consumes 32 ounces of water per day? Based on this z value, how does this person compare to the national average?

The Empirical Rule

The Empirical Rule is introduced in Chapter 3 on page 79. It states that if a random variable is normally distributed, then:

1. Approximately 68% of the observations will lie within plus and minus one standard deviation of the mean.
2. About 95% of the observations will lie within plus and minus two standard deviations of the mean.
3. Practically all, or 99.7% of the observations, will lie within plus and minus three standard deviations of the mean.

Now, knowing how to apply the standard normal probability distribution, we can verify the Empirical Rule. For example, one standard deviation from the mean is the same as a z value of 1.00. When we refer to the standard normal probability table, a z value of 1.00 corresponds to a probability of 0.3413. So what percent of the observations will lie within plus and minus one standard deviation of the mean? We multiply (2)(0.3413), which equals 0.6826, or approximately 68% of the observations are within plus and minus one standard deviation of the mean.

The Empirical Rule is summarized in the following graph.

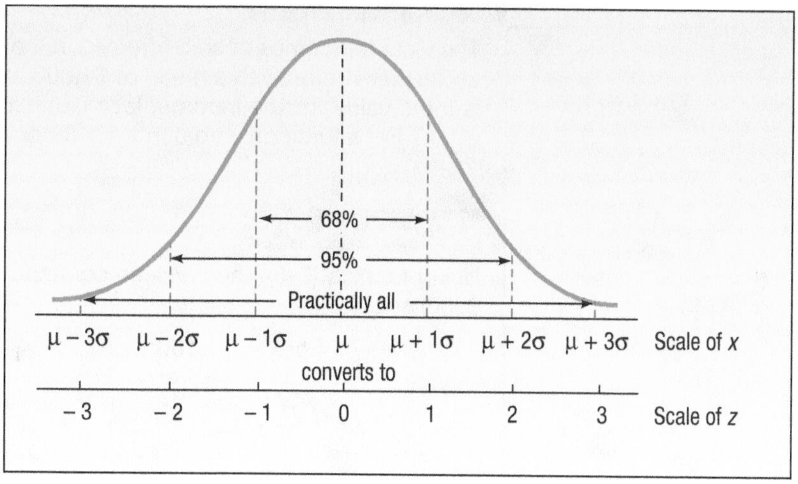

Transforming measurements to standard normal deviates changes the scale. The conversions are also shown in the graph. For example, $\mu + 1\sigma$ is converted to a z value of 1.00. Likewise, $\mu - 2\sigma$ is transformed to a z value of -2.00. Note that the center of the z distribution is zero, indicating no deviation from the mean, μ.

EXAMPLE

As part of its quality assurance program, the Autolite Battery Company conducts tests on battery life. For a particular D-cell alkaline battery, the mean life is 19 hours. The useful life of the battery follows a normal distribution with a standard deviation of 1.2 hours. Answer the following questions.

1. About 68% of the batteries failed between what two values?
2. About 95% of the batteries failed between what two values?
3. Virtually all of the batteries failed between what two values?

SOLUTION

We can use the Empirical Rule to answer these questions.

1. About 68% of the batteries will fail between 17.8 and 20.2 hours, found by $19.0 \pm 1(1.2)$ hours.
2. About 95% of the batteries will fail between 16.6 and 21.4 hours, found by $19.0 \pm 2(1.2)$ hours.
3. Practically all failed between 15.4 and 22.6 hours, found by $19.0 \pm 3(1.2)$ hours.

This information is summarized on the following chart.

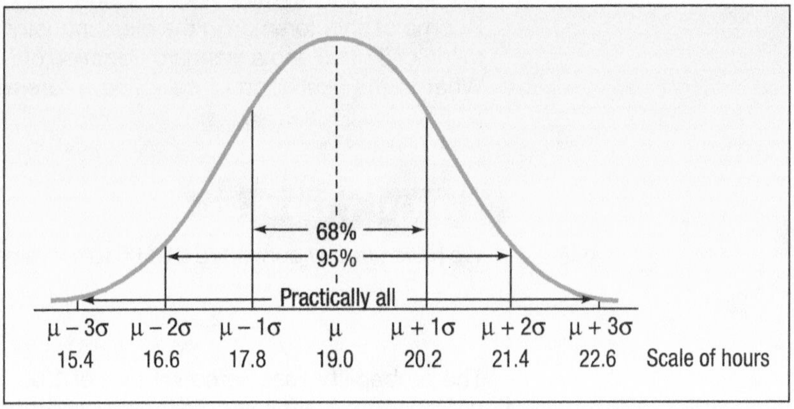

SELF-REVIEW 7–3

The distribution of the annual incomes of a group of middle-management employees at Compton Plastics approximates a normal distribution with a mean of $47,200 and a standard deviation of $800.

(a) About 68% of the incomes lie between what two amounts?
(b) About 95% of the incomes lie between what two amounts?
(c) Virtually all of the incomes lie between what two amounts?
(d) What are the median and the modal incomes?
(e) Is the distribution of incomes symmetrical?

EXERCISES

7. Explain what is meant by this statement: "There is not just one normal probability distribution but a 'family' of them."

8. List the major characteristics of a normal probability distribution.

9. The mean of a normal probability distribution is 500; the standard deviation is 10.
   a. About 68% of the observations lie between what two values?
   b. About 95% of the observations lie between what two values?
   c. Practically all of the observations lie between what two values?

10. The mean of a normal probability distribution is 60; the standard deviation is 5.
   a. About what percent of the observations lie between 55 and 65?
   b. About what percent of the observations lie between 50 and 70?
   c. About what percent of the observations lie between 45 and 75?

11. The Kamp family has twins, Rob and Rachel. Both Rob and Rachel graduated from college 2 years ago, and each is now earning $50,000 per year. Rachel works in the retail industry, where the mean salary for executives with less than 5 years' experience is $35,000 with a standard deviation of $8,000. Rob is an engineer. The mean salary for engineers with less than 5 years' experience is $60,000 with a standard deviation of $5,000. Compute the z values for both Rob and Rachel and comment on your findings.

12. A recent article in the *Cincinnati Enquirer* reported that the mean labor cost to repair a heat pump is $90 with a standard deviation of $22. Monte's Plumbing and Heating Service completed repairs on two heat pumps this morning. The labor cost for the first was $75 and it was $100 for the second. Assume the distribution of labor costs follows the normal probability distribution. Compute z values for each and comment on your findings.

Finding Areas under the Normal Curve

The next application of the standard normal distribution involves finding the area in a normal distribution between the mean and a selected value, which we identify as x. The following example/solution will illustrate the details.

EXAMPLE

In the example/solution first described on page 215, we reported that the weekly income of shift foreman in the glass industry followed the normal distribution with a mean of \$1,000 and a standard deviation of \$100. That is, $\mu = \$1{,}000$ and $\sigma = \$100$. What is the likelihood of selecting a foreman whose weekly income is between \$1,000 and \$1,100?

SOLUTION

We have already converted \$1,100 to a *z* value of 1.00 using formula (7–5). To repeat:

$$z = \frac{X - \mu}{\sigma} = \frac{\$1{,}100 - \$1{,}000}{\$100} = 1.00$$

The probability associated with a *z* of 1.00 is available in Appendix B.3. A portion of Appendix B.3 follows. To locate the probability, go down the left column to 1.0, and then move horizontally to the column headed .00. The value is .3413.

z	0.00	0.01	0.02
⋮	⋮	⋮	⋮
0.7	.2580	.2611	.2642
0.8	.2881	.2910	.2939
0.9	.3159	.3186	.3212
1.0	.3413	.3438	.3461
1.1	.3643	.3665	.3686
⋮	⋮	⋮	⋮

The area under the normal curve between \$1,000 and \$1,100 is .3413. We could also say 34.13% of the shift foremen in the glass industry earn between \$1,000 and \$1,100 weekly, or the likelihood of selecting a foreman and finding his or her income is between \$1,000 and \$1,100 is .3413.

This information is summarized in the following diagram.

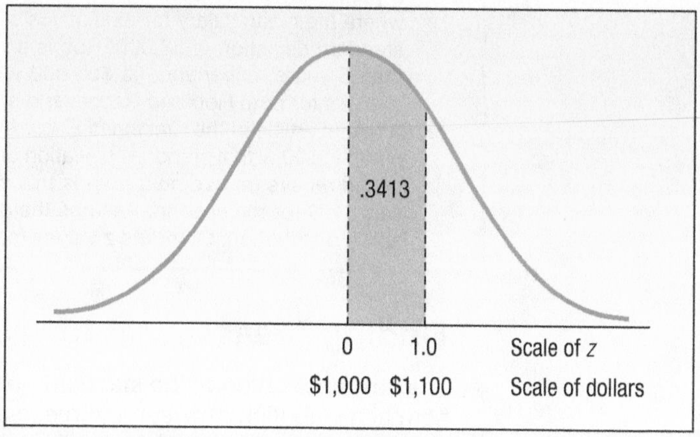

STATISTICS IN ACTION

Many processes, such as filling soda bottles and canning fruit, are normally distributed. Manufacturers must guard against both over- and underfilling. If they put too much in the can or bottle, they are giving away their product. If they put too little in, the customer may feel cheated and the government may question the label description. "Control charts," with limits drawn three standard deviations above and below the mean, are routinely used to monitor this type of production process.

In the example/solution just completed, we are interested in the probability between the mean and a given value. Let's change the question. Instead of wanting to know the probability of selecting at random a foreman who earned between $1,000 and $1,100, suppose we wanted the probability of selecting a foreman who earned less than $1,100. In probability notation, we write this statement as *P*(weekly income < $1,100). The method of solution is the same. We find the probability of selecting a foreman who earns between $1,000, the mean, and $1,100. This probability is .3413. Next, recall that half the area, or probability, is above the mean and half is below. So the probability of selecting a foreman earning less than $1,000 is .5000. Finally, we add the two probabilities, so .3413 + .5000 = .8413. About 84% of the foremen in the glass industry earn less than $1,100 per week. See the following diagram.

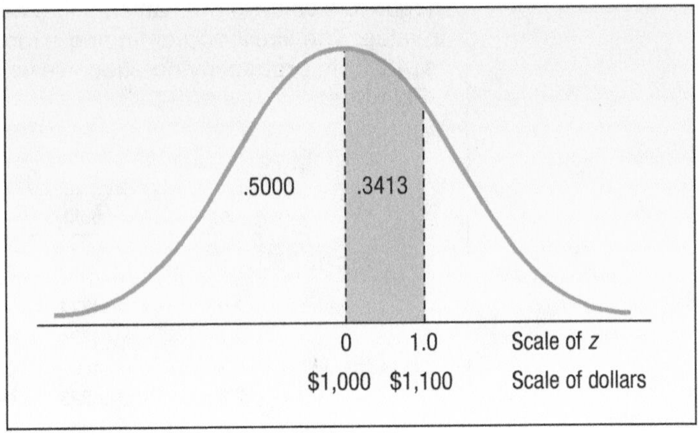

Excel will calculate this probability. The necessary commands are in the **Software Commands** in Appendix C. The answer is .8413, the same as we calculated.

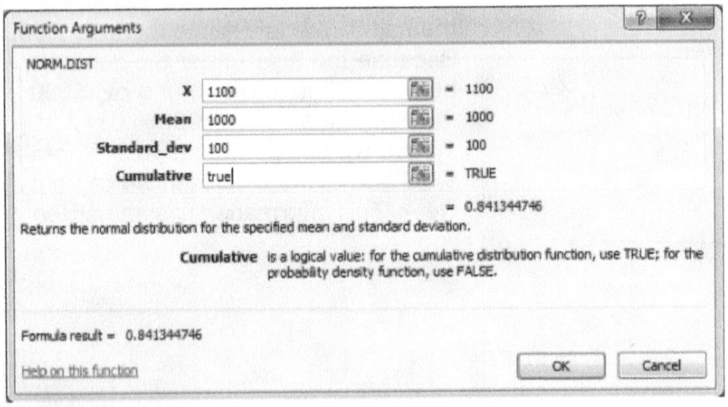

EXAMPLE

Refer to the example/solution first discussed on page 215 regarding the weekly income of shift foremen in the glass industry. The distribution of weekly incomes follows the normal probability distribution, with a mean of $1,000 and a standard deviation of $100. What is the probability of selecting a shift foreman in the glass industry whose income is:

1. Between $790 and $1,000?
2. Less than $790?

SOLUTION

We begin by finding the z value corresponding to a weekly income of \$790. From formula (7–5):

$$z = \frac{X - \mu}{s} = \frac{\$790 - \$1{,}000}{\$100} = -2.10$$

See Appendix B.3. Move down the left margin to the row 2.1 and across that row to the column headed 0.00. The value is .4821. So the area under the standard normal curve corresponding to a z value of 2.10 is .4821. However, because the normal distribution is symmetric, the area between 0 and a negative z value is the same as that between 0 and the corresponding positive z value. The likelihood of finding a foreman earning between \$790 and \$1,000 is .4821. In probability notation, we write $P(\$790 < \text{weekly income} < \$1{,}000) = .4821$.

z	0.00	0.01	0.02
⋮	⋮	⋮	⋮
2.0	.4772	.4778	.4783
2.1	.4821	.4826	.4830
2.2	.4861	.4864	.4868
2.3	.4893	.4896	.4898
⋮	⋮	⋮	⋮

The mean divides the normal curve into two identical halves. The area under the half to the left of the mean is .5000, and the area to the right is also .5000. Because the area under the curve between \$790 and \$1,000 is .4821, the area below \$790 is .0179, found by .5000 − .4821. In probability notation, we write $P(\text{weekly income} < \$790) = .0179$.

So we conclude that 48.21% of the foremen have weekly incomes between \$790 and \$1,000. Further, we can anticipate that 1.79% earn less than \$790 per week. This information is summarized in the following diagram.

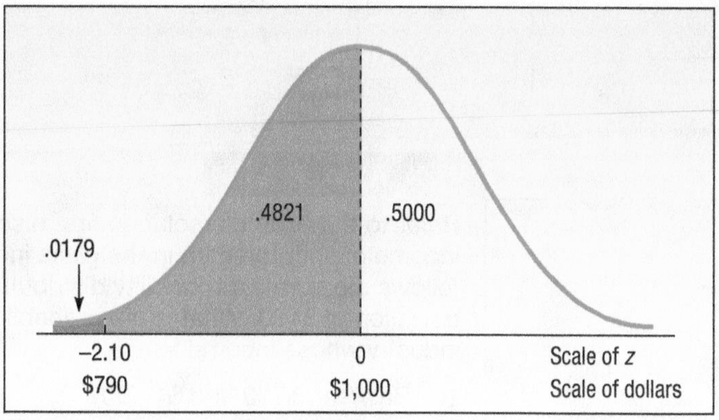

SELF-REVIEW 7–4

The temperature of coffee sold at the Coffee Bean Cafe follows the normal probability distribution, with a mean of 150 degrees. The standard deviation of this distribution is 5 degrees.
(a) What is the probability that the coffee temperature is between 150 degrees and 154 degrees?
(b) What is the probability that the coffee temperature is more than 164 degrees?

EXERCISES

13. A normal population has a mean of 20.0 and a standard deviation of 4.0.
  a. Compute the *z* value associated with 25.0.
  b. What proportion of the population is between 20.0 and 25.0?
  c. What proportion of the population is less than 18.0?

14. A normal population has a mean of 12.2 and a standard deviation of 2.5.
  a. Compute the *z* value associated with 14.3.
  b. What proportion of the population is between 12.2 and 14.3?
  c. What proportion of the population is less than 10.0?

15. A recent study of the hourly wages of maintenance crew members for major airlines showed that the mean hourly salary was $20.50, with a standard deviation of $3.50. Assume the distribution of hourly wages follows the normal probability distribution. If we select a crew member at random, what is the probability the crew member earns:
  a. Between $20.50 and $24.00 per hour?
  b. More than $24.00 per hour?
  c. Less than $19.00 per hour?

16. The mean of a normal probability distribution is 400 pounds. The standard deviation is 10 pounds.
  a. What is the area between 415 pounds and the mean of 400 pounds?
  b. What is the area between the mean and 395 pounds?
  c. What is the probability of selecting a value at random and discovering that it has a value of less than 395 pounds?

Another application of the normal distribution involves combining two areas, or probabilities. One of the areas is to the right of the mean and the other to the left.

EXAMPLE

Continuing the example/solution first discussed on page 215 using the weekly income of shift foremen in the glass industry, weekly income follows the normal probability distribution, with a mean of $1,000 and a standard deviation of $100. What is the area under this normal curve between $840 and $1,200?

SOLUTION

The problem can be divided into two parts. For the area between $840 and the mean of $1,000:

$$z = \frac{\$840 - \$1,000}{\$100} = \frac{-\$160}{\$100} = -1.60$$

For the area between the mean of $1,000 and $1,200:

$$z = \frac{\$1,200 - \$1,000}{\$100} = \frac{\$200}{\$100} = 2.00$$

The area under the curve for a z of -1.60 is .4452 (from Appendix B.3). The area under the curve for a z of 2.00 is .4772. Adding the two areas: $.4452 + .4772 = .9224$. Thus, the probability of selecting an income between \$840 and \$1,200 is .9224. In probability notation, we write $P(\$840 < \text{weekly income} < \$1{,}200) = .4452 + .4772 = .9224$. To summarize, 92.24% of the foremen have weekly incomes between \$840 and \$1,200. This is shown in a diagram:

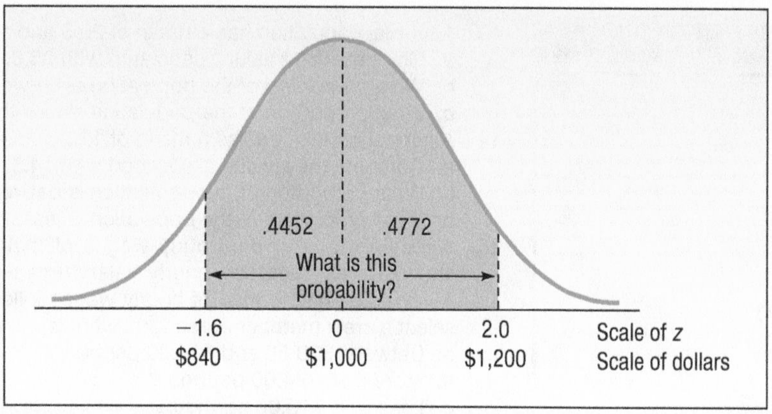

Another application of the normal distribution involves determining the area between values on the *same* side of the mean.

EXAMPLE

Returning to the weekly income distribution of shift foremen in the glass industry ($\mu = \$1{,}000$, $\sigma = \$100$), what is the area under the normal curve between \$1,150 and \$1,250?

SOLUTION

The situation is again separated into two parts, and formula (7–5) is used. First, we find the z value associated with a weekly salary of \$1,250:

$$z = \frac{\$1{,}250 - \$1{,}000}{\$100} = 2.50$$

Next we find the z value for a weekly salary of \$1,150:

$$z = \frac{\$1{,}150 - \$1{,}000}{\$100} = 1.50$$

From Appendix B.3, the area associated with a z value of 2.50 is .4938. So the probability of a weekly salary between \$1,000 and \$1,250 is .4938. Similarly, the area associated with a z value of 1.50 is .4332, so the probability of a weekly salary between \$1,000 and \$1,150 is .4332. The probability of a weekly salary between \$1,150 and \$1,250 is found by subtracting the area associated with a z value of 1.50 (.4332) from that associated with a z of 2.50 (.4938). Thus, the probability of a weekly salary between \$1,150 and \$1,250 is .0606. In probability notation, we write $P(\$1{,}150 < \text{weekly income} < \$1{,}250) = .4938 - .4332 = .0606$.

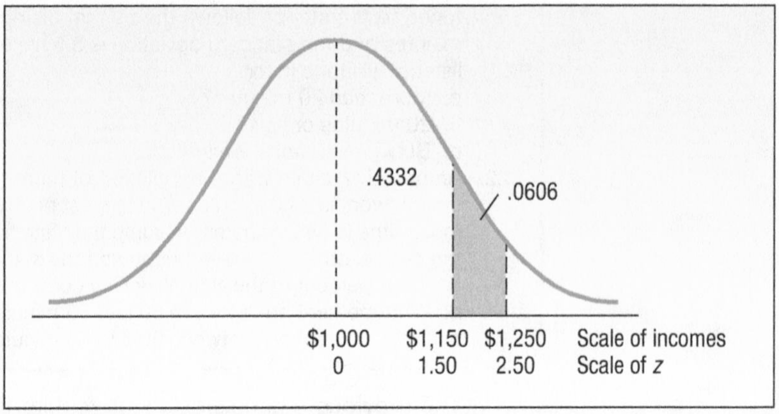

To summarize, there are four situations for finding the area under the standard normal probability distribution.

1. To find the area between 0 and z or ($-z$), look up the probability directly in the table.
2. To find the area beyond z or ($-z$), locate the probability of z in the table and subtract that probability from .5000.
3. To find the area between two points on different sides of the mean, determine the z values and add the corresponding probabilities.
4. To find the area between two points on the same side of the mean, determine the z values and subtract the smaller probability from the larger.

SELF-REVIEW 7–5

Refer to Self-Review 7–4. The temperature of coffee sold at the Coffee Bean Cafe follows the normal probability distribution with a mean of 150 degrees. The standard deviation of this distribution is 5 degrees.
(a) What is the probability the coffee temperature is between 146 degrees and 156 degrees?
(b) What is the probability the coffee temperature is more than 156 but less than 162 degrees?

EXERCISES

17. A normal distribution has a mean of 50 and a standard deviation of 4.
 a. Compute the probability of a value between 44.0 and 55.0.
 b. Compute the probability of a value greater than 55.0.
 c. Compute the probability of a value between 52.0 and 55.0.

18. A normal population has a mean of 80.0 and a standard deviation of 14.0.
 a. Compute the probability of a value between 75.0 and 90.0.
 b. Compute the probability of a value of 75.0 or less.
 c. Compute the probability of a value between 55.0 and 70.0.

19. According to the Internal Revenue Service, the mean tax refund for the year 2013 was $3,000. Assume the standard deviation is $450 and that the amounts refunded follow a normal probability distribution.
 a. What percent of the refunds are more than $3,100?
 b. What percent of the refunds are more than $3,100 but less than $3,500?
 c. What percent of the refunds are more than $2,250 but less than $3,500?

20. The distribution of the number of viewers for the *American Idol* television show follows a normal distribution with a mean of 29 million and a standard deviation of 5 million. What is the probability next week's show will:
 a. Have between 30 and 34 million viewers?
 b. Have at least 23 million viewers?
 c. Exceed 40 million viewers?

21. WNAE, an all-news AM station, finds that the distribution of the lengths of time listeners are tuned to the station follows the normal distribution. The mean of the distribution is 15.0 minutes and the standard deviation is 3.5 minutes. What is the probability that a particular listener will tune in for:
    a. More than 20 minutes?
    b. 20 minutes or less?
    c. Between 10 and 12 minutes?
22. Among U.S. cities with a population of more than 250,000, the mean one-way commute time to work is 24.3 minutes. The longest one-way travel time is in New York City, where the mean time is 38.3 minutes. Assume the distribution of travel times in New York City follows the normal probability distribution and the standard deviation is 7.5 minutes.
    a. What percent of the New York City commutes are for less than 30 minutes?
    b. What percent are between 30 and 35 minutes?
    c. What percent are between 30 and 40 minutes?

The previous example/solutions require finding the percent of the observations located between two observations or the percent of the observations above, or below, a particular observation x. A further application of the normal distribution involves finding the value of the observation x when the percent above or below the observation is given.

EXAMPLE

Layton Tire and Rubber Company wishes to set a minimum mileage guarantee on its new MX100 tire. Tests reveal the mean mileage is 67,900 with a standard deviation of 2,050 miles and that the distribution of miles follows the normal probability distribution. Layton wants to set the minimum guaranteed mileage so that no more than 4% of the tires will have to be replaced. What minimum guaranteed mileage should Layton announce?

SOLUTION

The facets of this case are shown in the following diagram, where x represents the minimum guaranteed mileage.

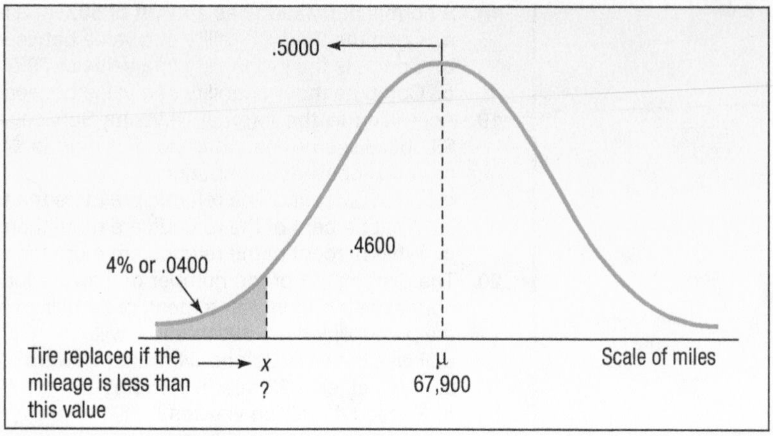

Inserting these values in formula (7–5) for z gives:

$$z = \frac{x - \mu}{\sigma} = \frac{x - 67{,}900}{2{,}050}$$

There are two unknowns in this equation, z and x. To find x, we first find z, and then solve for x. Recall from the characteristics of a normal curve that the area to the left of μ is .5000. The area between μ and x is .4600, found by .5000 − .0400. Now refer to Appendix B.3. Search the body of the table for the area closest to .4600. The closest area is .4599. Move to the margins from this value and read the z value of 1.75. Because the value is to the left of the mean, it is actually −1.75. These steps are illustrated in Table 7–2.

TABLE 7–2 Selected Areas under the Normal Curve

z ...	.03	.04	.05	.06
⋮	⋮	⋮	⋮	⋮
1.5	.4370	.4382	.4394	.4406
1.6	.4484	.4495	.4505	.4515
1.7	.4582	.4591	.4599	.4608
1.8	.4664	.4671	.4678	.4686

Knowing that the distance between μ and x is -1.75σ or $z = -1.75$, we can now solve for x (the minimum guaranteed mileage):

$$z = \frac{x - 67{,}900}{2{,}050}$$

$$-1.75 = \frac{x - 67{,}900}{2{,}050}$$

$$-1.75(2{,}050) = x - 67{,}900$$

$$x = 67{,}900 - 1.75(2{,}050) = 64{,}312$$

So Layton can advertise that it will replace for free any tire that wears out before it reaches 64,312 miles, and the company will know that only 4% of the tires will be replaced under this plan.

Excel will also find the mileage value. See the following output. The necessary commands are given in the **Software Commands** in Appendix C.

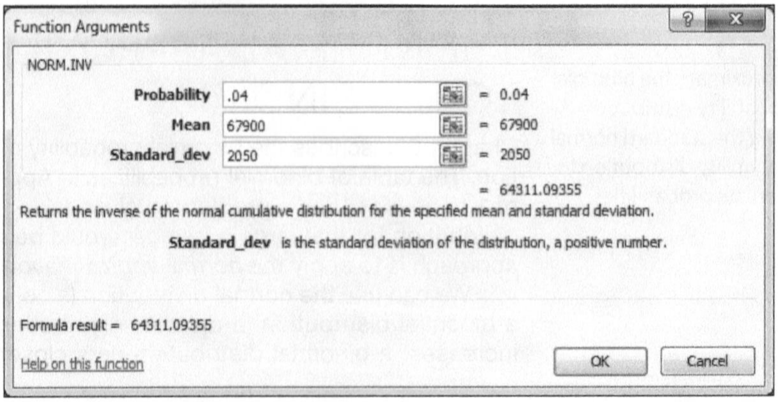

SELF-REVIEW 7–6

An analysis of the final test scores for Introduction to Business reveals the scores follow the normal probability distribution. The mean of the distribution is 75 and the standard deviation is 8. The professor wants to award an A to students whose score is in the highest 10%. What is the dividing point for those students who earn an A and those earning a B?

EXERCISES

23. A normal distribution has a mean of 50 and a standard deviation of 4. Determine the value below which 95% of the observations will occur.

24. A normal distribution has a mean of 80 and a standard deviation of 14. Determine the value above which 80% of the values will occur.

25. Assume that the hourly cost to operate a commercial airplane follows the normal distribution with a mean of $2,100 per hour and a standard deviation of $250. What is the operating cost for the lowest 3% of the airplanes?

26. The SAT Reasoning Test is perhaps the most widely used standardized test for college admissions in the United States. Scores are based on a normal distribution with a mean of 1500 and a standard deviation of 300. Clinton College would like to offer an honors scholarship to students who score in the top 10% of this test. What is the minimum score that qualifies for the scholarship?

27. According to media research, the typical American listened to 195 hours of music in the last year. This is down from 290 hours 4 years earlier. Dick Trythall is a big country and western music fan. He listens to music while working around the house, reading, and riding in his truck. Assume the number of hours spent listening to music follows a normal probability distribution with a standard deviation of 8.5 hours.

a. If Dick is in the top 1% in terms of listening time, how many hours did he listen last year?

b. Assume that the distribution of times 4 years earlier also follows the normal probability distribution with a standard deviation of 8.5 hours. How many hours did the 1% who listen to the *least* music actually listen?

28. For the most recent year available, the mean annual cost to attend a private university in the United States was $26,889. Assume the distribution of annual costs follows the normal probability distribution and the standard deviation is $4,500. Ninety-five percent of all students at private universities pay less than what amount?

29. In economic theory, a "hurdle rate" is the minimum return that a person requires before he or she will make an investment. A research report says that annual returns from a specific class of common equities are distributed according to a normal distribution with a mean of 12% and a standard deviation of 18%. A stock screener would like to identify a hurdle rate such that only 1 in 20 equities is above that value. Where should the hurdle rate be set?

30. The manufacturer of a laser printer reports the mean number of pages a cartridge will print before it needs replacing is 12,200. The distribution of pages printed per cartridge closely follows the normal probability distribution and the standard deviation is 820 pages. The manufacturer wants to provide guidelines to potential customers as to how long they can expect a cartridge to last. How many pages should the manufacturer advertise for each cartridge if it wants to be correct 99% of the time?

LO7-4
Approximate the binomial probability distribution using the standard normal probability distribution to calculate probabilities.

THE NORMAL APPROXIMATION TO THE BINOMIAL

Chapter 6 describes the binomial probability distribution, which is a discrete distribution. The table of binomial probabilities in Appendix B.1 goes successively from an n of 1 to an n of 15. If a problem involved taking a sample of 60, generating a binomial distribution for that large a number would be very time-consuming. A more efficient approach is to apply the *normal approximation to the binomial*.

We can use the normal distribution (a continuous distribution) as a substitute for a binomial distribution (a discrete distribution) for large values of n because, as n increases, a binomial distribution gets closer and closer to a normal distribution.

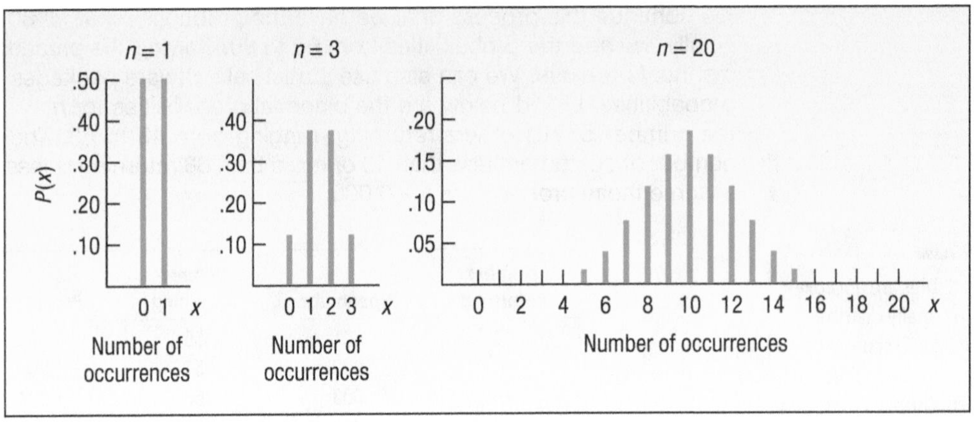

CHART 7–7 Binomial Distributions for an n of 1, 3, and 20, Where $\pi = .50$

Chart 7–7 depicts the change in the shape of a binomial distribution with $\pi = .50$ from an n of 1, to an n of 3, to an n of 20. Notice how the case where $n = 20$ approximates the shape of the normal distribution. That is, compare the case where $n = 20$ to the normal curve in Chart 7–3 on page 212.

When can we use the normal approximation to the binomial? The normal probability distribution is a good approximation to the binomial probability distribution when $n\pi$ and $n(1 - \pi)$ are both at least 5. However, before we apply the normal approximation, we must make sure that our distribution of interest is in fact a binomial distribution. Recall from Chapter 6 that four criteria must be met:

1. There are only two mutually exclusive outcomes to an experiment: a "success" and a "failure."
2. The distribution results from counting the number of successes in a fixed number of trials.
3. The probability of a success, π, remains the same from trial to trial.
4. Each trial is independent.

Continuity Correction Factor

To show the application of the normal approximation to the binomial and the need for a correction factor, suppose the management of the Santoni Pizza Restaurant found that 70% of its new customers return for another meal. For a week in which 80 new (first-time) customers dined at Santoni's, what is the probability that 60 or more will return for another meal?

Notice the binomial conditions are met: (1) There are only two possible outcomes—a customer either returns for another meal or does not return. (2) We can count the number of successes, meaning, for example, that 57 of the 80 customers return. (3) The trials are independent, meaning that if the 34th person returns for a second meal, that does not affect whether the 58th person returns. (4) The probability of a customer returning remains at .70 for all 80 customers.

Therefore, we could use the binomial formula (6–3) described on page 183.

$$P(x) = {}_nC_x\,(\pi)^x\,(1 - \pi)^{n-x}$$

To find the probability 60 or more customers return for another pizza, we need to first find the probability exactly 60 customers return. That is:

$$P(x = 60) = {}_{80}C_{60}\,(.70)^{60}\,(1 - .70)^{20} = .063$$

Next we find the probability that exactly 61 customers return. It is:

$$P(x = 61) = {}_{80}C_{61}\,(.70)^{61}\,(1 - .70)^{19} = .048$$

We continue this process until we have the probability that all 80 customers return. Finally, we add the probabilities from 60 to 80. Solving the preceding problem in this manner is tedious. We can also use statistical software packages to find the various probabilities. Listed below are the binomial probabilities for $n = 80$, $\pi = .70$, and x, the number of customers returning, ranging from 43 to 68. The probability of any number of customers less than 43 or more than 68 returning is less than .001. We can assume these probabilities are 0.000.

Number Returning	Probability	Number Returning	Probability
43	.001	56	.097
44	.002	57	.095
45	.003	58	.088
46	.006	59	.077
47	.009	60	.063
48	.015	61	.048
49	.023	62	.034
50	.033	63	.023
51	.045	64	.014
52	.059	65	.008
53	.072	66	.004
54	.084	67	.002
55	.093	68	.001

We can find the probability of 60 or more returning by summing .063 + .048 + · · · + .001, which is .197. However, a look at the plot below shows the similarity of this distribution to a normal distribution. All we need do is "smooth out" the discrete probabilities into a continuous distribution. Furthermore, working with a normal distribution will involve far fewer calculations than working with the binomial.

The trick is to let the discrete probability for 56 customers be represented by an area under the continuous curve between 55.5 and 56.5. Then let the probability for 57 customers be represented by an area between 56.5 and 57.5, and so on. This is just the opposite of rounding off the numbers to a whole number.

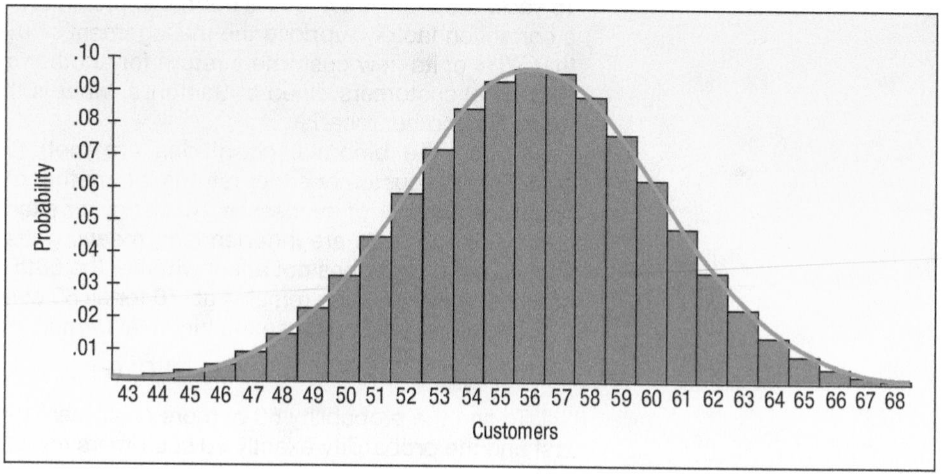

Because we use the normal distribution to determine the binomial probability of 60 or more successes, we must subtract, in this case, .5 from 60. The value .5 is called the **continuity correction factor.** This small adjustment is made because a continuous

STATISTICS IN ACTION

Many variables are approximately, normally distributed, such as IQ scores, life expectancies, and adult height. This implies that nearly all observations occur within 3 standard deviations of the mean. On the other hand, observations that occur beyond 3 standard deviations from the mean are extremely rare. For example, the mean adult male height is 68.2 inches (about 5 feet 8 inches) with a standard deviation of 2.74. This means that almost all males are between 60.0 inches (5 feet) and 76.4 inches (6 feet 4 inches). LeBron James, a professional basketball player with the Miami Heat, is 80 inches, or 6 feet 8 inches, which is clearly beyond 3 standard deviations from the mean. The height of a standard doorway is 6 feet 8 inches, and should be high enough for almost all adult males, except for a rare person like LeBron James.

As another example, the driver's seat in most vehicles is set to comfortably fit a person who is at least 159 cm (62.5 inches) tall. The distribution of heights of adult women is approximately a normal distribution with a mean of 161.5 cm and a standard deviation of 6.3 cm. Thus about 35% of adult women will not fit comfortably in the driver's seat.

distribution (the normal distribution) is being used to approximate a discrete distribution (the binomial distribution). Subtracting, $60 - .5 = 59.5$.

CONTINUITY CORRECTION FACTOR The value .5 subtracted or added, depending on the question, to a selected value when a discrete probability distribution is approximated by a continuous probability distribution.

How to Apply the Correction Factor

Only four cases may arise. These cases are:

1. For the probability *at least* x occur, use the area *above* $(x - .5)$.
2. For the probability that *more than* x occur, use the area *above* $(x + .5)$.
3. For the probability that x *or fewer* occur, use the area *below* $(x + .5)$.
4. For the probability that *fewer than* x occur, use the area *below* $(x - .5)$.

To use the normal distribution to approximate the probability that 60 or more first-time Santoni customers out of 80 will return, follow the procedure shown below.

Step 1: Find the z value corresponding to an x of 59.5 using formula (7–5), and formulas (6–4) and (6–5) for the mean and the variance of a binomial distribution:

$$\mu = n\pi = 80(.70) = 56$$

$$\sigma^2 = n\pi(1 - \pi) = 80(.70)(1 - .70) = 16.8$$

$$\sigma = \sqrt{16.8} = 4.10$$

$$z = \frac{x - \mu}{\sigma} = \frac{59.5 - 56}{4.10} = 0.85$$

Step 2: Determine the area under the normal curve between a μ of 56 and an x of 59.5. From step 1, we know that the z value corresponding to 59.5 is 0.85. So we go to Appendix B.3 and read down the left margin to 0.8, and then we go horizontally to the area under the column headed by .05. That area is .3023.

Step 3: Calculate the area beyond 59.5 by subtracting .3023 from .5000 ($.5000 - .3023 = .1977$). Thus, .1977 is the probability that 60 or more first-time Santoni customers out of 80 will return for another meal. In probability notation, $P(\text{customers} > 59.5) = .5000 - .3023 = .1977$. The facets of this problem are shown graphically:

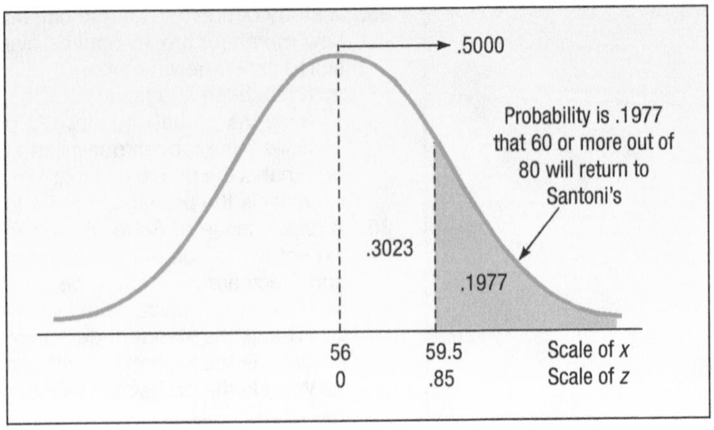

No doubt you will agree that using the normal approximation to the binomial is a more efficient method of estimating the probability of 60 or more first-time customers returning. The result compares favorably with that computed on page 228, using the binomial distribution. The probability using the binomial distribution is .197, whereas the probability using the normal approximation is .1977.

SELF-REVIEW 7–7

A study by Great Southern Home Insurance revealed that none of the stolen goods were recovered by the homeowners in 80% of reported thefts.

(a) During a period in which 200 thefts occurred, what is the probability that no stolen goods were recovered in 170 or more of the robberies?

(b) During a period in which 200 thefts occurred, what is the probability that no stolen goods were recovered in 150 or more robberies?

EXERCISES

31. Assume a binomial probability distribution with $n = 50$ and $\pi = .25$. Compute the following:
- **a.** The mean and standard deviation of the random variable.
- **b.** The probability that x is 15 or more.
- **c.** The probability that x is 10 or less.

32. Assume a binomial probability distribution with $n = 40$ and $\pi = .55$. Compute the following:
- **a.** The mean and standard deviation of the random variable.
- **b.** The probability that x is 25 or greater.
- **c.** The probability that x is 15 or less.
- **d.** The probability that x is between 15 and 25, inclusive.

33. Dottie's Tax Service specializes in federal tax returns for professional clients, such as physicians, dentists, accountants, and lawyers. A recent audit by the IRS of the returns she prepared indicated that an error was made on 7% of the returns she prepared last year. Assuming this rate continues into this year and she prepares 80 returns, what is the probability that she makes errors on:
- **a.** More than six returns?
- **b.** At least six returns?
- **c.** Exactly six returns?

34. Shorty's Muffler advertises it can install a new muffler in 30 minutes or less. However, the work standards department at corporate headquarters recently conducted a study and found that 20% of the mufflers were not installed in 30 minutes or less. The Maumee branch installed 50 mufflers last month. If the corporate report is correct:
- **a.** How many of the installations at the Maumee branch would you expect to take more than 30 minutes?
- **b.** What is the likelihood that fewer than eight installations took more than 30 minutes?
- **c.** What is the likelihood that eight or fewer installations took more than 30 minutes?
- **d.** What is the likelihood that exactly 8 of the 50 installations took more than 30 minutes?

35. A study conducted by the nationally known Taurus Health Club revealed that 30% of its new members are 15 pounds overweight. A membership drive in a metropolitan area resulted in 500 new members.
- **a.** It has been suggested that the normal approximation to the binomial be used to determine the probability that 175 or more of the new members are 15 pounds overweight. Does this problem qualify as a binomial problem? Explain.
- **b.** What is the probability that 175 or more of the new members are 15 pounds overweight?
- **c.** What is the probability that 140 or more new members are 15 pounds overweight?

36. A recent issue of *Bride Magazine* suggested that couples planning their wedding should expect two-thirds of those who are sent an invitation to respond that they will attend. Rich and Stacy are planning to be married later this year. They plan to send 197 invitations.
- **a.** How many guests would you expect to accept the invitation?
- **b.** What is the standard deviation?
- **c.** What is the probability 140 or more will accept the invitation?
- **d.** What is the probability exactly 140 will accept the invitation?

LO7-5

Describe the exponential probability distribution and use it to calculate probabilities.

THE FAMILY OF EXPONENTIAL DISTRIBUTIONS

So far in this chapter, we have considered two continuous probability distributions, the uniform and the normal. The next continuous distribution we consider is the exponential distribution. This continuous probability distribution usually describes times between events in a sequence. The actions occur independently at a constant rate per unit of time or length. Because time is never negative, an exponential random variable is always positive. The exponential distribution usually describes situations such as:

- The service time for customers at the information desk of the Dallas Public Library.
- The time between "hits" on a website.
- The lifetime of an electrical component.
- The time until the next phone call arrives in a customer service center.

The exponential probability distribution is positively skewed. That differs from the uniform and normal distributions, which were both symmetric. Moreover, the distribution is described by only one parameter, which we will identify as λ (pronounced "lambda"). λ is often referred to as the "rate" parameter. The following chart shows the change in the shape of the exponential distribution as we vary the value of λ from 1/3 to 1 to 2. Observe that as we decrease λ, the shape of the distribution changes to become "less skewed."

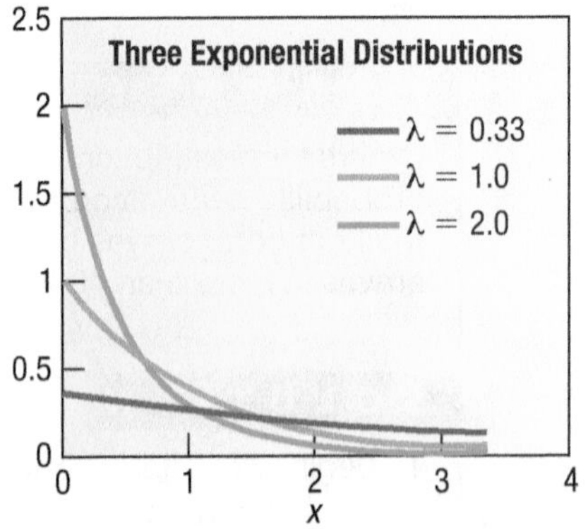

Another feature of the exponential distribution is its close relationship to the Poisson distribution. The Poisson is a discrete probability distribution and also has a single parameter, μ. We described the Poisson distribution starting on page 194 in Chapter 6. It too is a positively skewed distribution. To explain the relationship between the Poisson and the exponential distributions, suppose the rate customers arrive at a family restaurant during the dinner hour is six per hour. We use the Poisson distribution to find the probability in any particular dinner hour that two customers arrive, or that seven arrive, and so on. So we have a Poisson distribution with a mean of 6. But suppose instead of studying the number of customers *arriving in an hour,* we wished to study the time *between their arrivals*. The time between arrivals is a continuous distribution because time is measured as a continuous random variable. If customers arrive at a rate of six per hour, then logically the typical or mean time between arrivals is 1/6 of an hour, or 10 minutes. We need to be careful here to be consistent with our units, so let's stay with 1/6 of an hour. So in general, if we know customers arrive at a certain rate per hour, which we call μ, then we can expect the mean time between arrivals to be $1/\mu$. The rate parameter λ is equal to $1/\mu$. So in our restaurant arrival example, $\lambda = 1/6$.

The graph of the exponential distribution starts at the value of λ when the random variable's (x) value is 0. The distribution declines steadily as we move to the right with increasing values of x. Formula (7–6) describes the exponential probability distribution with λ as rate parameter. As we described with the Poisson distribution on page 194, e is a mathematical constant equal to 2.71828. It is the basis of the Napierian logarithmic system. It is a pleasant surprise that both the mean and the standard deviation of the exponential probability distribution are equal to $1/\lambda$.

EXPONENTIAL DISTRIBUTION $P(x) = \lambda e^{-\lambda x}$ **[7–6]**

With continuous distributions, we do not address the probability that a distinct value will occur. Instead, areas or regions below the graph of the probability distribution between two specified values give the probability the random variable is in that interval. A table, such as Appendix B.3 for the normal distribution, is not necessary for the exponential distribution. The area under the exponential density function is found by a formula and the necessary calculations can be accomplished with a handheld calculator that has an e^x key. Most statistical software packages will also calculate exponential probabilities by inputting the rate parameter, λ, only. The probability of obtaining an arrival value less than a particular value of x is:

FINDING A PROBABILITY USING THE EXPONENTIAL DISTRIBUTION $P(\text{Arrival time} < x) = 1 - e^{-\lambda x}$ **[7–7]**

EXAMPLE

Orders for prescriptions arrive at a pharmacy website according to an exponential probability distribution at a mean of one every 20 seconds. Find the probability the next order arrives in less than 5 seconds. Find the probability the next order arrives in more than 40 seconds.

SOLUTION

To begin, we determine the rate parameter λ, which in this case is 1/20. To find the probability, we insert 1/20 for λ and 5 for x in formula (7–7).

$$P(\text{Arrival time} < 5) = 1 - e^{-\frac{1}{20}(5)} = 1 - e^{-0.25} = 1 - .7788 = .2212$$

So we conclude there is a 22% chance the next order will arrive in less than 5 seconds. The region is identified as the rust-colored area under the curve.

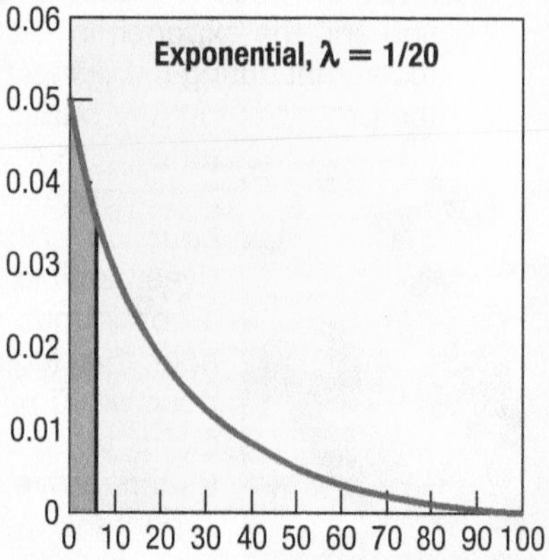

The preceding computations addressed the area in the left-tail area of the exponential distribution with $\lambda = 1/20$ and the area between 0 and 5—that is, the area that is below 5 seconds. What if you are interested in the right-tail area? It is found using the complement rule. See formula (5–3) on page 142 in Chapter 5. To put it another way, to find the probability the next order will arrive in more than 40 seconds, we find the probability the order arrives in less than 40 seconds and subtract the result from 1.00. We show this in two steps.

1. Find the probability an order is received *in less than* 40 seconds.

$$P(\text{Arrival} < 40) = 1 - e^{-\frac{1}{20}(40)} = 1 - .1353 = .8647$$

2. Find the probability an order is received *in more than* 40 seconds.

$$P(\text{Arrival} > 40) = 1 - P(\text{Arrival} < 40) = 1 - .8647 = .1353$$

We conclude that the likelihood that it will be 40 seconds or more before the next order is received at the pharmacy is 13.5%.

In the preceding example/solution, when we apply the exponential probability distribution to compute the probability that the arrival time is greater than 40 seconds, you probably observed that there is some redundancy. In general, if we wish to find the likelihood of a time greater than some value x, such as 40, the complement rule is applied as follows:

$$P(\text{Arrival} > x) = 1 - P(\text{Arrival} < x) = 1 - (1 - e^{-\lambda x}) = e^{-\lambda x}$$

In other words, when we subtract formula (7–7) from 1 to find the area in the right tail, the result is $e^{-\lambda x}$. Thus, the probability that more than 40 seconds go by before the next order arrives is computed without the aid of the complement rule as follows:

$$P(\text{Arrival} > 40) = e^{-\frac{1}{20}(40)} = .1353$$

The result is shown in the following graph.

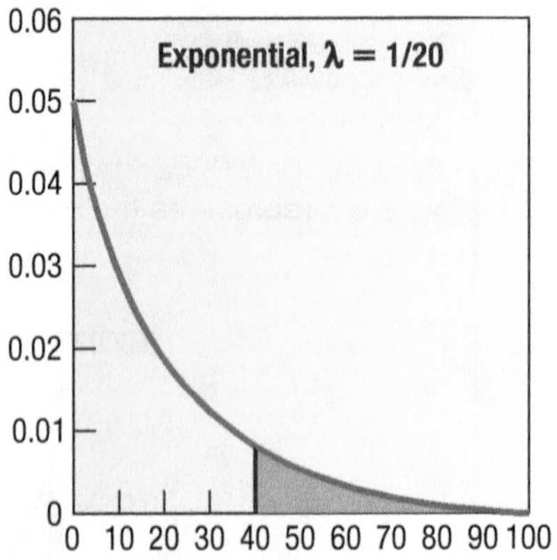

What if you wish to determine the probability that it will take more than 5 seconds but less than 40 seconds for the next order to arrive? Use formula (7–7) with an x value of 40 and then subtract the value of formula (7–7) when x is 5.

In symbols, you can write this as:

$$P(5 \le x \le 40) = P(\text{Arrival} \le 40) - P(\text{Arrival} \le 5)$$

$$= (1 - e^{-\frac{1}{20}(40)}) - (1 - e^{-\frac{1}{20}(5)}) = .8647 - .2212 = .6435$$

We conclude that 64% of the time, the time between orders will be between 5 seconds and 40 seconds.

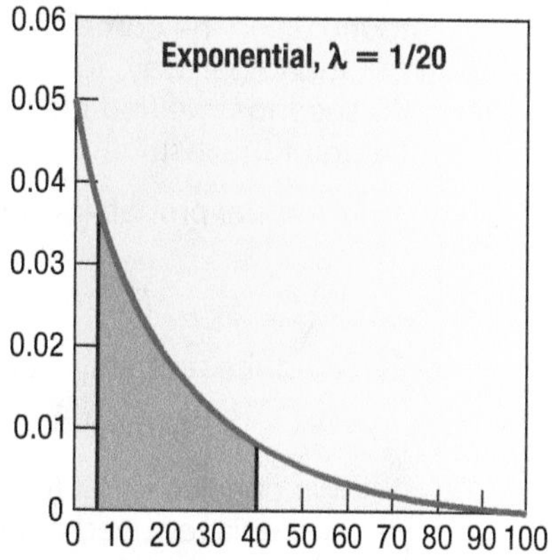

Previous examples require finding the percentage of the observations located between two values or the percentage of the observations above or below a particular value, x. We can also use formula (7–7) in "reverse" to find the value of the observation x when the percentage above or below the observation is given. The following example/solution illustrates this situation.

EXAMPLE

Compton Computers wishes to set a minimum lifetime guarantee on its new power supply unit. Quality testing shows the time to failure follows an exponential distribution with a mean of 4,000 hours. Compton wants a warranty period such that only 5% of the power supply units fail during that period. What value should they set for the warranty period?

SOLUTION

Note that 4,000 hours is a mean and not a rate. Therefore, we must compute λ as 1/4,000, or 0.00025 failure per hour. A diagram of the situation is shown below, where x represents the minimum guaranteed lifetime.

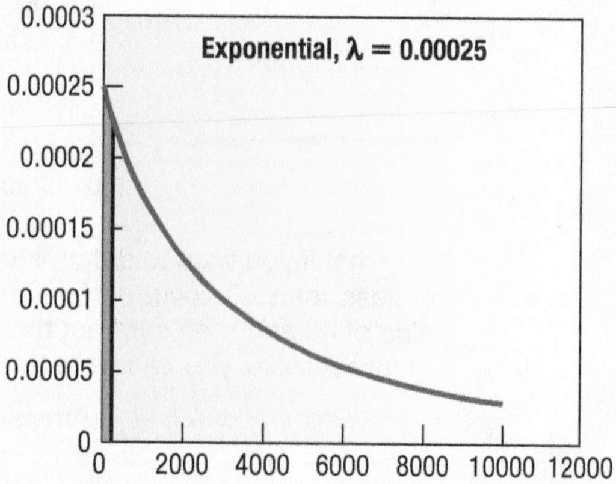

We use formula (7–7) and essentially work backward for the solution. In this case, the rate parameter is 4,000 hours and we want the area, as shown in the diagram, to be .05.

$$P(\text{Arrival time} < x) = 1 - e^{(-\lambda x)}$$

$$.05 = 1 - e^{-\frac{1}{4{,}000}(x)}$$

Next, we solve this equation for x. So, we subtract 1 from both sides of the equation and multiply by -1 to simplify the signs. The result is:

$$.95 = e^{-\frac{1}{4{,}000}(x)}$$

Next, we take the natural log of both sides and solve for x:

$$\ln(.95) = -\frac{1}{4{,}000}x$$

$$-(.051293294) = -\frac{1}{4{,}000}x$$

$$x = 205.17$$

In this case, $x = 205.17$. Hence, Compton can set the warranty period at 205 hours and expect about 5% of the power supply units to be returned.

SELF-REVIEW 7–8

The time between ambulance arrivals at the Methodist Hospital emergency room follows an exponential distribution with a mean of 10 minutes.

(a) What is the likelihood the next ambulance will arrive in 15 minutes or less?
(b) What is the likelihood the next ambulance will arrive in more than 25 minutes?
(c) What is the likelihood the next ambulance will arrive in more than 15 minutes but less than 25?
(d) Find the 80th percentile for the time between ambulance arrivals. (This means only 20% of the runs are longer than this time.)

EXERCISES

37. Waiting times to receive food after placing an order at the local Subway sandwich shop follow an exponential distribution with a mean of 60 seconds. Calculate the probability a customer waits:
- **a.** Less than 30 seconds.
- **b.** More than 120 seconds.
- **c.** Between 45 and 75 seconds.
- **d.** Fifty percent of the patrons wait less than how many seconds? What is the median?

38. The lifetime of plasma and LCD TV sets follows an exponential distribution with a mean of 100,000 hours. Compute the probability a television set:
- **a.** Fails in less than 10,000 hours.
- **b.** Lasts more than 120,000 hours.
- **c.** Fails between 60,000 and 100,000 hours of use.
- **d.** Find the 90th percentile. So 10% of the TV sets last more than what length of time?

39. The Bureau of Labor Statistics' *American Time Use Survey* showed that the amount of time spent using a computer for leisure varied greatly by age. Individuals age 75 and over averaged 0.3 hour (18 minutes) per day using a computer for leisure. Individuals ages 15 to 19 spend 1.0 hour per day using a computer for leisure. If these times follow an exponential distribution, find the proportion of each group that spends:
- **a.** Less than 15 minutes per day using a computer for leisure.
- **b.** More than 2 hours.
- **c.** Between 30 minutes and 90 minutes using a computer for leisure.
- **d.** Find the 20th percentile. Eighty percent spend more than what amount of time?

40. The cost per item at a supermarket follows an exponential distribution. There are many inexpensive items and a few relatively expensive ones. The mean cost per item is \$3.50. What is the percentage of items that cost:
a. Less than \$1?
b. More than \$4?
c. Between \$2 and \$3?
d. Find the 40th percentile. Sixty percent of the supermarket items cost more than what amount?

CHAPTER SUMMARY

I. The uniform distribution is a continuous probability distribution with the following characteristics.
A. It is rectangular in shape.
B. The mean and the median are equal.
C. It is completely described by its minimum value a and its maximum value b.
D. It is described by the following equation for the region from a to b:

$$P(x) = \frac{1}{b - a} \quad \textbf{[7–3]}$$

E. The mean and standard deviation of a uniform distribution are computed as follows:

$$\mu = \frac{(a + b)}{2} \quad \textbf{[7–1]}$$

$$\sigma = \sqrt{\frac{(b - a)^2}{12}} \quad \textbf{[7–2]}$$

II. The normal probability distribution is a continuous distribution with the following characteristics.
A. It is bell-shaped and has a single peak at the center of the distribution.
B. The distribution is symmetric.
C. It is asymptotic, meaning the curve approaches but never touches the X-axis.
D. It is completely described by its mean and standard deviation.
E. There is a family of normal probability distributions.
1. Another normal probability distribution is created when either the mean or the standard deviation changes.
2. The normal probability distribution is described by the following formula:

$$P(x) = \frac{1}{\sigma\sqrt{2\pi}} e^{-\left[\frac{(x - \mu)^2}{2\sigma^2}\right]} \quad \textbf{[7–4]}$$

III. The standard normal probability distribution is a particular normal distribution.
A. It has a mean of 0 and a standard deviation of 1.
B. Any normal probability distribution can be converted to the standard normal probability distribution by the following formula.

$$z = \frac{X - \mu}{\sigma} \quad \textbf{[7–5]}$$

C. By standardizing a normal probability distribution, we can report the distance of a value from the mean in units of the standard deviation.

IV. The normal probability distribution can approximate a binomial distribution under certain conditions.
A. $n\pi$ and $n(1 - \pi)$ must both be at least 5.
1. n is the number of observations.
2. π is the probability of a success.
B. The four conditions for a binomial probability distribution are:
1. There are only two possible outcomes.
2. π remains the same from trial to trial.

3. The trials are independent.
4. The distribution results from a count of the number of successes in a fixed number of trials.

C. The mean and variance of a binomial distribution are computed as follows:

$$\mu = n\pi$$

$$\sigma^2 = n\pi(1 - \pi)$$

D. The continuity correction factor of .5 is used to extend the continuous value of x one-half unit in either direction. This correction compensates for approximating a discrete distribution by a continuous distribution.

V. The exponential probability distribution describes times between events in a sequence.

A. The actions occur independently at a constant rate per unit of time or length.

B. The probability density is given by the formula:

$$P(x) = \lambda e^{-\lambda x} \quad \textbf{[7–6]}$$

C. It is nonnegative, is positively skewed, declines steadily to the right, and is asymptotic.

D. The area under the curve is given by the formula

$$P(\text{Arrival time} < x) = 1 - e^{-\lambda x} \quad \textbf{[7–7]}$$

E. Both the mean and standard deviation are $1/\lambda$.

CHAPTER EXERCISES

41. The amount of cola in a 12-ounce can is uniformly distributed between 11.96 ounces and 12.05 ounces.

a. What is the mean amount per can?
b. What is the standard deviation amount per can?
c. What is the probability of selecting a can of cola and finding it has less than 12 ounces?
d. What is the probability of selecting a can of cola and finding it has more than 11.98 ounces?
e. What is the probability of selecting a can of cola and finding it has more than 11.00 ounces?

42. A tube of Listerine Tartar Control toothpaste contains 4.2 ounces. As people use the toothpaste, the amount remaining in any tube is random. Assume the amount of toothpaste remaining in the tube follows a uniform distribution. From this information, we can determine the following information about the amount remaining in a toothpaste tube without invading anyone's privacy.

a. How much toothpaste would you expect to be remaining in the tube?
b. What is the standard deviation of the amount remaining in the tube?
c. What is the likelihood there is less than 3.0 ounces remaining in the tube?
d. What is the probability there is more than 1.5 ounces remaining in the tube?

43. Many retail stores offer their own credit cards. At the time of the credit application, the customer is given a 10% discount on the purchase. The time required for the credit application process follows a uniform distribution with the times ranging from 4 minutes to 10 minutes.

a. What is the mean time for the application process?
b. What is the standard deviation of the process time?
c. What is the likelihood a particular application will take less than 6 minutes?
d. What is the likelihood an application will take more than 5 minutes?

44. The time patrons at the Grande Dunes Hotel in the Bahamas spend waiting for an elevator follows a uniform distribution between 0 and 3.5 minutes.

a. Show that the area under the curve is 1.00.
b. How long does the typical patron wait for elevator service?
c. What is the standard deviation of the waiting time?
d. What percent of the patrons wait for less than a minute?
e. What percent of the patrons wait more than 2 minutes?

45. The net sales and the number of employees for aluminum fabricators with similar characteristics are organized into frequency distributions. Both are normally distributed. For the net sales, the mean is \$180 million and the standard deviation is \$25 million. For the number of employees, the mean is 1,500 and the standard deviation is 120. Clarion Fabricators had sales of \$170 million and 1,850 employees.
a. Convert Clarion's sales and number of employees to *z* values.
b. Locate the two *z* values.
c. Compare Clarion's sales and number of employees with those of the other fabricators.

46. The accounting department at Weston Materials Inc., a national manufacturer of unattached garages, reports that it takes two construction workers a mean of 32 hours and a standard deviation of 2 hours to erect the Red Barn model. Assume the assembly times follow the normal distribution.
a. Determine the *z* values for 29 and 34 hours. What percent of the garages take between 32 hours and 34 hours to erect?
b. What percent of the garages take between 29 hours and 34 hours to erect?
c. What percent of the garages take 28.7 hours or less to erect?
d. Of the garages, 5% take how many hours or more to erect?

47. A recent report indicated a typical family of four spends \$490 per month on food. Assume the distribution of food expenditures for a family of four follows the normal distribution, with a standard deviation of \$90 per month.
a. What percent of the families spend more than \$30 but less than \$490 per month on food?
b. What percent of the families spend less than \$430 per month on food?
c. What percent spend between \$430 and \$600 per month on food?
d. What percent spend between \$500 and \$600 per month on food?

48. A study of long-distance phone calls made from General Electric Corporate Headquarters in Fairfield, Connecticut, revealed the length of the calls, in minutes, follows the normal probability distribution. The mean length of time per call was 4.2 minutes and the standard deviation was 0.60 minute.
a. What fraction of the calls lasts between 4.2 and 5 minutes?
b. What fraction of the calls lasts more than 5 minutes?
c. What fraction of the calls lasts between 5 and 6 minutes?
d. What fraction of the calls lasts between 4 and 6 minutes?
e. As part of her report to the president, the director of communications would like to report the length of the longest (in duration) 4% of the calls. What is this time?

49. Shaver Manufacturing Inc. offers dental insurance to its employees. A recent study by the human resource director shows the annual cost per employee per year followed the normal probability distribution, with a mean of \$1,280 and a standard deviation of \$420 per year.
a. What fraction of the employees costs more than \$1,500 per year for dental expenses?
b. What fraction of the employees costs between \$1,500 and \$2,000 per year?
c. Estimate the percent that did not have any dental expense.
d. What was the cost for the 10% of employees who incurred the highest dental expense?

50. The annual commissions earned by sales representatives of Machine Products Inc., a manufacturer of light machinery, follow the normal probability distribution. The mean yearly amount earned is \$40,000 and the standard deviation is \$5,000.
a. What percent of the sales representatives earn more than \$42,000 per year?
b. What percent of the sales representatives earn between \$32,000 and \$42,000?
c. What percent of the sales representatives earn between \$32,000 and \$35,000?
d. The sales manager wants to award the sales representatives who earn the largest commissions a bonus of \$1,000. He can award a bonus to 20% of the representatives. What is the cutoff point between those who earn a bonus and those who do not?

51. According to the South Dakota Department of Health, the number of hours of TV viewing per week is higher among adult women than adult men. A recent study showed women spent an average of 34 hours per week watching TV, and men, 29 hours per week. Assume that the distribution of hours watched follows the normal distribution for both groups, and that the standard deviation among the women is 4.5 hours and is 5.1 hours for the men.
a. What percent of the women watch TV less than 40 hours per week?
b. What percent of the men watch TV more than 25 hours per week?
c. How many hours of TV do the 1% of women who watch the most TV per week watch? Find the comparable value for the men.

52. According to a government study among adults in the 25- to 34-year age group, the mean amount spent per year on reading and entertainment is $1,994. Assume that the distribution of the amounts spent follows the normal distribution with a standard deviation of $450.
   a. What percent of the adults spend more than $2,500 per year on reading and entertainment?
   b. What percent spend between $2,500 and $3,000 per year on reading and entertainment?
   c. What percent spend less than $1,000 per year on reading and entertainment?

53. Management at Gordon Electronics is considering adopting a bonus system to increase production. One suggestion is to pay a bonus on the highest 5% of production based on past experience. Past records indicate weekly production follows the normal distribution. The mean of this distribution is 4,000 units per week and the standard deviation is 60 units per week. If the bonus is paid on the upper 5% of production, the bonus will be paid on how many units or more?

54. Fast Service Truck Lines uses the Ford Super Duty F-750 exclusively. Management made a study of the maintenance costs and determined the number of miles traveled during the year followed the normal distribution. The mean of the distribution was 60,000 miles and the standard deviation 2,000 miles.
   a. What percent of the Ford Super Duty F-750s logged 65,200 miles or more?
   b. What percent of the trucks logged more than 57,060 but less than 58,280 miles?
   c. What percent of the Fords traveled 62,000 miles or less during the year?
   d. Is it reasonable to conclude that any of the trucks were driven more than 70,000 miles? Explain.

55. Best Electronics Inc. offers a "no hassle" returns policy. The number of items returned per day follows the normal distribution. The mean number of customer returns is 10.3 per day and the standard deviation is 2.25 per day.
   a. In what percent of the days are there eight or fewer customers returning items?
   b. In what percent of the days are between 12 and 14 customers returning items?
   c. Is there any chance of a day with no returns?

56. A recent news report indicated that 20% of all employees steal from their company each year. If a company employs 50 people, what is the probability that:
   a. Fewer than five employees steal?
   b. More than five employees steal?
   c. Exactly five employees steal?
   d. More than 5 but fewer than 15 employees steal?

57. The *Orange County Register,* as part of its Sunday health supplement, reported that 64% of American men over the age of 18 consider nutrition a top priority in their lives. Suppose we select a sample of 60 men. What is the likelihood that:
   a. 32 or more consider nutrition important?
   b. 44 or more consider nutrition important?
   c. More than 32 but fewer than 43 consider nutrition important?
   d. Exactly 44 consider diet important?

58. It is estimated that 10% of those taking the quantitative methods portion of the CPA examination fail that section. Sixty students are taking the exam this Saturday.
   a. How many would you expect to fail? What is the standard deviation?
   b. What is the probability that exactly two students will fail?
   c. What is the probability at least two students will fail?

59. The Georgetown, South Carolina, Traffic Division reported 40% of high-speed chases involving automobiles result in a minor or major accident. During a month in which 50 high-speed chases occur, what is the probability that 25 or more will result in a minor or major accident?

60. Cruise ships of the Royal Viking line report that 80% of their rooms are occupied during September. For a cruise ship having 800 rooms, what is the probability that 665 or more are occupied in September?

61. The goal at U.S. airports handling international flights is to clear these flights within 45 minutes. Let's interpret this to mean that 95% of the flights are cleared in 45 minutes, so 5% of the flights take longer to clear. Let's also assume that the distribution is approximately normal.
   a. If the standard deviation of the time to clear an international flight is 5 minutes, what is the mean time to clear a flight?
   b. Suppose the standard deviation is 10 minutes, not the 5 minutes suggested in part (a). What is the new mean?
   c. A customer has 30 minutes from the time her flight lands to catch her limousine. Assuming a standard deviation of 10 minutes, what is the likelihood that she will be cleared in time?

62. The funds dispensed at the ATM machine located near the checkout line at the Kroger's in Union, Kentucky, follows a normal probability distribution with a mean of \$4,200 per day and a standard deviation of \$720 per day. The machine is programmed to notify the nearby bank if the amount dispensed is very low (less than \$2,500) or very high (more than \$6,000).

a. What percent of the days will the bank be notified because the amount dispensed is very low?

b. What percent of the time will the bank be notified because the amount dispensed is high?

c. What percent of the time will the bank not be notified regarding the amount of funds dispersed?

63. The weights of canned hams processed at Henline Ham Company follow the normal distribution, with a mean of 9.20 pounds and a standard deviation of 0.25 pound. The label weight is given as 9.00 pounds.

a. What proportion of the hams actually weigh less than the amount claimed on the label?

b. The owner, Glen Henline, is considering two proposals to reduce the proportion of hams below label weight. He can increase the mean weight to 9.25 and leave the standard deviation the same, or he can leave the mean weight at 9.20 and reduce the standard deviation from 0.25 pound to 0.15. Which change would you recommend?

64. The *Cincinnati Enquirer,* in its Sunday business supplement, reported that full-time employees in the region work an average of 43.9 hours per week. The article further indicated that about one-third of those employed full time work less than 40 hours per week.

a. Given this information and assuming that number of hours worked follows the normal distribution, what is the standard deviation of the number of hours worked?

b. The article also indicated that 20% of those working full time work more than 49 hours per week. Determine the standard deviation with this information. Are the two estimates of the standard deviation similar? What would you conclude?

65. Most four-year automobile leases allow up to 60,000 miles. If the lessee goes beyond this amount, a penalty of 20 cents per mile is added to the lease cost. Suppose the distribution of miles driven on four-year leases follows the normal distribution. The mean is 52,000 miles and the standard deviation is 5,000 miles.

a. What percent of the leases will yield a penalty because of excess mileage?

b. If the automobile company wanted to change the terms of the lease so that 25% of the leases went over the limit, where should the new upper limit be set?

c. One definition of a low-mileage car is one that is 4 years old and has been driven less than 45,000 miles. What percent of the cars returned are considered low-mileage?

66. The price of shares of Bank of Florida at the end of trading each day for the last year followed the normal distribution. Assume there were 240 trading days in the year. The mean price was \$42.00 per share and the standard deviation was \$2.25 per share.

a. What percent of the days was the price over \$45.00? How many days would you estimate?

b. What percent of the days was the price between \$38.00 and \$40.00?

c. What was the stock's price on the *highest* 15% of days?

67. The annual sales of romance novels follow the normal distribution. However, the mean and the standard deviation are unknown. Forty percent of the time sales are more than 470,000, and 10% of the time sales are more than 500,000. What are the mean and the standard deviation?

68. In establishing warranties on HDTVs, the manufacturer wants to set the limits so that few will need repair at the manufacturer's expense. On the other hand, the warranty period must be long enough to make the purchase attractive to the buyer. For a new HDTV, the mean number of months until repairs are needed is 36.84 with a standard deviation of 3.34 months. Where should the warranty limits be set so that only 10% of the HDTVs need repairs at the manufacturer's expense?

69. DeKorte Tele-Marketing Inc. is considering purchasing a machine that randomly selects and automatically dials telephone numbers. DeKorte Tele-Marketing makes most of its calls during the evening, so calls to business phones are wasted. The manufacturer of the machine claims that its programming reduces the calling to business phones to 15% of all calls. To test this claim, the director of purchasing at DeKorte programmed the machine to select a sample of 150 phone numbers. What is the likelihood that more than 30 of the phone numbers selected are those of businesses, assuming the manufacturer's claim is correct?

70. A carbon monoxide detector in the Wheelock household activates once every 200 days on average. Assume this activation follows the exponential distribution. What is the probability that:

a. There will be an alarm within the next 60 days?
b. At least 400 days will pass before the next alarm?
c. It will be between 150 and 250 days until the next warning?
d. Find the median time until the next activation.

71. "Boot time" (the time between the appearance of the Bios screen to the first file that is loaded in Windows) on Eric Mouser's personal computer follows an exponential distribution with a mean of 27 seconds. What is the probability his "boot" will require:

a. Less than 15 seconds?
b. More than 60 seconds?
c. Between 30 and 45 seconds?
d. What is the point below which only 10% of the boots occur?

72. The time between visits to a U.S. emergency room for a member of the general population follows an exponential distribution with a mean of 2.5 years. What proportion of the population:

a. Will visit an emergency room within the next 6 months?
b. Will not visit the ER over the next 6 years?
c. Will visit an ER next year, but not this year?
d. Find the first and third quartiles of this distribution.

73. The times between failures on a personal computer follow an exponential distribution with a mean of 300,000 hours. What is the probability of:

a. A failure in less than 100,000 hours?
b. No failure in the next 500,000 hours?
c. The next failure occurring between 200,000 and 350,000 hours?
d. What are the mean and standard deviation of the time between failures?

DATA SET EXERCISES

(The data for these exercises are available at the text website: **www.mhhe.com/lind16e**.)

74. Refer to the Real Estate data, which report information on homes sold in the Goodyear, Arizona, area during the last year.

a. The mean selling price (in $ thousands) of the homes was computed earlier to be $221.10, with a standard deviation of $47.11. Use the normal distribution to estimate the percentage of homes selling for more than $280.0. Compare this to the actual results. Does the normal distribution yield a good approximation of the actual results?
b. The mean distance from the center of the city is 14.629 miles, with a standard deviation of 4.874 miles. Use the normal distribution to estimate the number of homes 18 or more miles but less than 22 miles from the center of the city. Compare this to the actual results. Does the normal distribution yield a good approximation of the actual results?

75. Refer to the Baseball 2012 data, which report information on the 30 Major League Baseball teams for the 2012 season.

a. The mean attendance per team for the season was 2.495 million, with a standard deviation of 0.6421 million. Use the normal distribution to estimate the number of teams with attendance of more than 3.5 million. Compare that estimate with the actual number. Comment on the accuracy of your estimate.
b. The mean team salary was $98.023 million, with a standard deviation of $36.832 million. Use the normal distribution to estimate the number of teams with a team salary of more than $50 million. Compare that estimate with the actual number. Comment on the accuracy of the estimate.

76. Refer to the Buena School District bus data.

a. Refer to the maintenance cost variable. The mean maintenance cost for last year is $450.29, with a standard deviation of $53.69. Estimate the number of buses with a cost of more than $500. Compare that with the actual number.
b. Refer to the variable on the number of miles driven. The mean is 830.11 and the standard deviation is 42.19 miles. Estimate the number of buses traveling more than 900 miles. Compare that number with the actual value.

A REVIEW OF CHAPTERS 5–7

The chapters in this section consider methods of dealing with uncertainty. In Chapter 5, we describe the concept of probability. A *probability* is a value between 0 and 1 that expresses the likelihood a particular event will occur. We also looked at methods to calculate probabilities using rules of addition and multiplication; presented principles of counting, including permutations and combinations; and described situations for using Bayes' theorem.

Chapter 6 describes *discrete* probability distributions. Discrete probability distributions list all possible outcomes of an experiment and the probability associated with each outcome. We describe three discrete probability distributions: the *binomial distribution,* the *hypergeometric distribution,* and the *Poisson distribution.* The requirements for the binomial distribution are there are only two possible outcomes for each trial, there is a constant probability of success, there are a fixed number of trials, and the trials are independent. The binomial distribution lists the probabilities for the number of successes in a fixed number of trials. The hypergeometric distribution is similar to the binomial, but the probability of success is not constant, so the trials are not independent. The Poisson distribution is characterized by a small probability of success in a large number of trials. It has the following characteristics: the random variable is the number of times some event occurs in a fixed interval, the probability of a success is proportional to the size of the interval, and the intervals are independent and do not overlap.

Chapter 7 describes three continuous probability distributions: the *uniform distribution,* the *normal distribution,* and the *exponential distribution.* The uniform probability distribution is rectangular in shape and is defined by minimum and maximum values. The mean and the median of a uniform probability distribution are equal, and it does not have a mode.

A normal probability distribution is the most widely used and widely reported distribution. Its major characteristics are that it is bell-shaped and symmetrical, completely described by its mean and standard deviation, and asymptotic, that is, it falls smoothly in each direction from its peak but never touches the horizontal axis. There is a family of normal probability distributions—each with its own mean and standard deviation. There are an unlimited number of normal probability distributions.

To find the probabilities for any normal probability distribution, we convert a normal distribution to a *standard normal probability distribution* by computing *z* values. A *z* value is the distance between *x* and the mean in units of the standard deviation. The standard normal probability distribution has a mean of 0 and a standard deviation of 1. It is useful because the probability for any event from a normal probability distribution can be computed using standard normal probability tables (see Appendix B.3).

The exponential probability distribution describes the time between events in a sequence. These events occur independently at a constant rate per unit of time or length. The exponential probability distribution is positively skewed, with λ as the "rate" parameter. The mean and standard deviation are equal and are the reciprocal of λ.

PROBLEMS

1. Proactine, a new medicine for acne, is claimed by the manufacturer to be 80% effective. It is applied to the affected area of a sample of 15 people. What is the probability that:
   a. All 15 will show significant improvement?
   b. Fewer than 9 of 15 will show significant improvement?
   c. 12 or more people will show significant improvement?
2. Customers at the Bank of Commerce of Idaho Falls, Idaho, default at a rate of .005 on small home-improvement loans. The bank has approved 400 small home-improvement loans. Assuming the Poisson probability distribution applies to this problem:
   a. What is the probability that no homeowners out of the 400 will default?
   b. How many of the 400 are expected not to default?
   c. What is the probability that three or more homeowners will default on their small home-improvement loans?
3. A study of the attendance at the University of Alabama's basketball games revealed that the distribution of attendance is normally distributed with a mean of 10,000 and a standard deviation of 2,000.
   a. What is the probability a particular game has an attendance of 13,500 or more?
   b. What percent of the games have an attendance between 8,000 and 11,500?
   c. Ten percent of the games have an attendance of how many or less?
4. Daniel-James Insurance Company will insure an offshore Mobil Oil production platform against weather losses for one year. The president of Daniel-James estimates the following losses for that platform (in millions of dollars) with the accompanying probabilities:

Amount of Loss ($ millions)	Probability of Loss
0	.98
40	.016
300	.004

a. What is the expected amount Daniel-James will have to pay to Mobil in claims?
b. What is the likelihood that Daniel-James will actually lose less than the expected amount?
c. Given that Daniel-James suffers a loss, what is the likelihood that it is for $300 million?
d. Daniel-James has set the annual premium at $2.0 million. Does that seem like a fair premium? Will it cover its risk?

5. The distribution of the number of school-age children per family in the Whitehall Estates area of Grand Junction, Colorado, is:

Number of children	0	1	2	3	4
Percent of families	40	30	15	10	5

a. Determine the mean and standard deviation of the number of school-age children per family in Whitehall Estates.
b. A new school is planned in Whitehall Estates. An estimate of the number of school-age children is needed. There are 500 family units. How many children would you estimate?
c. Some additional information is needed about only the families having children. Convert the preceding distribution to one for families with children. What is the mean number of children among families that have children?

6. The following table shows a breakdown of the 113th U.S. Congress by party affiliation.

	Party		
	Democrats	**Republicans**	**Total**
House	234	201	435
Senate	46	54	100
Total	280	255	535

a. A member of Congress is selected at random. What is the probability of selecting a Republican?
b. Given that the person selected is a member of the House of Representatives, what is the probability he or she is a Republican?
c. What is the probability of selecting a member of the House of Representatives or a Democrat?

CASES

A. Century National Bank

Refer to the Century National Bank data. Is it reasonable that the distribution of checking account balances approximates a normal probability distribution? Determine the mean and the standard deviation for the sample of 60 customers. Compare the actual distribution with the theoretical distribution. Cite some specific examples and comment on your findings.

Divide the account balances into three groups, of about 20 each, with the smallest third of the balances in the first group, the middle third in the second group, and those with the largest balances in the third group. Next, develop a table that shows the number in each of the categories of the account balances by branch. Does it appear that account balances are related to the branch? Cite some examples and comment on your findings.

B. Elections Auditor

An item such as an increase in taxes, recall of elected officials, or an expansion of public services can be placed on the ballot if a required number of valid signatures are collected on the petition. Unfortunately, many people will sign the petition even though they are not registered to vote in that particular district, or they will sign the petition more than once.

Sara Ferguson, the elections auditor in Venango County, must certify the validity of these signatures after the petition is officially presented. Not surprisingly, her staff is overloaded, so she is considering using statistical methods to validate the pages of 200 signatures, instead of validating each individual signature. At a recent professional meeting, she found that, in some communities in the state, election officials were checking only five signatures on each page and rejecting the entire page if two or more signatures were invalid. Some people are concerned that five may not be enough to make a good decision. They suggest that you should check 10 signatures and reject the page if 3 or more are invalid.

In order to investigate these methods, Sara asks her staff to pull the results from the last election and sample

30 pages. It happens that the staff selected 14 pages from the Avondale district, 9 pages from the Midway district, and 7 pages from the Kingston district. Each page had 200 signatures, and the data below show the number of invalid signatures on each.

Use the data to evaluate Sara's two proposals. Calculate the probability of rejecting a page under each of the approaches. Would you get about the same results by examining every single signature? Offer a plan of your own, and discuss how it might be better or worse than the two plans proposed by Sara.

Avondale	Midway	Kingston
9	19	38
14	22	39
11	23	41
8	14	39
14	22	41
6	17	39
10	15	39
13	20	
8	18	
8		
9		
12		
7		
13		

C. Geoff "Applies" His Education

Geoff Brown is the manager for a small telemarketing firm and is evaluating the sales rate of experienced workers in order to set minimum standards for new hires. During the past few weeks, he has recorded the number of successful calls per hour for the staff. These data appear next along with some summary statistics he worked out with a statistical software package. Geoff has been a student at the local community college and has heard of many different kinds of probability distributions (binomial, normal, hypergeometric, Poisson, etc.). Could you give Geoff some advice on which distribution to use to fit these data as well as possible and how to decide when a probationary employee should be accepted as having reached full production status? This is important because it means a pay raise for the employee, and there have been some probationary employees in the past who have quit because of discouragement that they would never meet the standard.

Successful sales calls per hour during the week of August 14:

4	2	3	1	4	5	5	2	3	2	2	4	5	2	5	3	3	0
1	3	2	8	4	5	2	2	4	1	5	5	4	5	1	2	4	

Descriptive statistics:

N	MEAN	MEDIAN	TRMEAN	STDEV	SEMEAN
35	3.229	3.000	3.194	1.682	0.284
MIN	MAX	Q1	Q3		
0.0	8.000	2.000	5.000		

Which distribution do you think Geoff should use for his analysis?

D. CNP Bank Card

Before banks issue a credit card, they usually rate or score the customer in terms of his or her projected probability of being a profitable customer. A typical scoring table appears below.

Age	**Under 25** (12 pts.)	**25–29** (5 pts.)	**30–34** (0 pts.)	**35+** (18 pts.)
Time at same address	**<1 yr.** (9 pts.)	**1–2 yrs.** (0 pts.)	**3–4 yrs.** (13 pts.)	**5+ yrs.** (20 pts.)
Auto age	**None** (18 pts.)	**0–1yr.** (12 pts.)	**2–4 yrs.** (13 pts.)	**5+ yrs.** (3 pts.)
Monthly car payment	**None** (15 pts.)	**\$1–\$99** (6 pts.)	**\$100–\$299** (4 pts.)	**\$300+** (0 pts.)
Housing cost	**\$1–\$199** (0 pts.)	**\$200–\$399** (10 pts.)	**Owns** (12 pts.)	**Lives with relatives** (24 pts.)
Checking/ savings accounts	**Both** (15 pts.)	**Checking only** (3 pts.)	**Savings only** (2 pts.)	**Neither** (0 pts.)

The score is the sum of the points on the six items. For example, Sushi Brown is under 25 years old (12 pts.), has lived at the same address for 2 years (0 pts.), owns a 4-year-old car (13 pts.), with car payments of \$75 (6 pts.), housing cost of \$200 (10 pts.), and a checking account (3 pts.). She would score 44.

A second chart is then used to convert scores into the probability of being a profitable customer. A sample chart of this type appears below.

Score	30	40	50	60	70	80	90
Probability	.70	.78	.85	.90	.94	.95	.96

Sushi's score of 44 would translate into a probability of being profitable of approximately .81. In other words, 81% of customers like Sushi will make money for the bank card operations.

Here are the interview results for three potential customers.

Name	David Born	Edward Brendan	Ann McLaughlin
Age	42	23	33
Time at same address	9	2	5
Auto age	2	3	7
Monthly car payment	\$140	\$99	\$175
Housing cost	\$300	\$200	Owns clear
Checking/savings accounts	Both	Checking only	Neither

1. Score each of these customers and estimate their probability of being profitable.
2. What is the probability that all three are profitable?
3. What is the probability that none of them are profitable?
4. Find the entire probability distribution for the number of profitable customers among this group of three.
5. Write a brief summary of your findings.

PRACTICE TEST

Part 1—Objective

1. Under what conditions will a probability be greater than 1 or 100%? 1. ________
2. An ________ is the observation of some activity or the act of taking some type of measurement. 2. ________
3. An ________ is the collection of one or more outcomes to an experiment. 3. ________
4. A ________ probability is the likelihood that two or more events will happen at the same time. 4. ________
5. In a (5a) ________, the order in which the events are counted is important, but in a (5b) ________, it is not important. 5. a. ________ 5. b. ________
6. In a discrete probability distribution, the sum of the possible outcomes is equal to ________. 6. ________
7. Which of the following is *NOT* a requirement of the binomial distribution? (constant probability of success, three or more outcomes, the result of counts) 7. ________
8. How many normal distributions are there? (1, 10, 30, 1,000, or infinite—pick one) 8. ________
9. How many standard normal distributions are there? (1, 10, 30, 1,000, or infinite—pick one) 9. ________
10. What is the probability of finding a z value between 0 and -0.76? 10. ________
11. What is the probability of finding a z value greater than 1.67? 11. ________
12. Two events are ________ if the occurrence of one event does not affect the occurrence of another event. 12. ________
13. Two events are ________ if by virtue of one event happening the other cannot happen. 13. ________
14. Which of the following is not true regarding the normal probability distribution? (asymptotic, family of distributions, only two outcomes, 50% of the observations greater than the mean) 14. ________
15. Which of the following statements best describes the shape of a normal probability distribution? (bell-shaped, uniform, V-shaped, no constant shape) 15. ________

Part 2—Problems

1. Fred Friendly, CPA, has 20 tax returns to prepare before the April 15th deadline. It is late at night so he decides to do two more before going home. In his stack of accounts, 12 are personal, 5 are businesses, and 3 are for charitable organizations. If he selects the two returns at random, what is the probability:
   a. Both are businesses?
   b. At least one is a business?
2. The IRS reports that 15% of returns where the adjusted gross income is more than $1,000,000 will be subject to a computer audit. For the year 2013, Fred Friendly, CPA, completed 16 returns where the adjusted gross income was more than $1,000,000.
   a. What is the probability exactly one of these returns will be audited?
   b. What is the probability at least one will be audited?
3. Fred works in a tax office with five other CPAs. There are five parking spots beside the office. In how many different ways can the cars belonging to the CPAs be arranged in the five spots? Assume they all drive to work.
4. Fred decided to study the number of exemptions claimed on personal tax returns he prepared in 2012. The data are summarized in the following table.

Exemptions	Percent
1	20
2	50
3	20
4	10

   a. What is the mean number of exemptions per return?
   b. What is the variance of the number of exemptions per return?

5. In a memo to all those involved in tax preparation, the IRS indicated that the mean amount of refund was $1,600 with a standard deviation of $850. Assume the distribution of the amounts returned follows the normal distribution.
   a. What percent of the refunds were between $1,600 and $2,000?
   b. What percent of the refunds were between $900 and $2,000?
   c. According to the above information, what percent of the refunds were less than $0; that is, the taxpayer owed the IRS.
6. For the year 2013, Fred Friendly completed a total of 80 returns. He developed the following table summarizing the relationship between number of dependents and whether or not the client received a refund.

	Dependents			
Refund	**1**	**2**	**3 or more**	**Total**
Yes	20	20	10	50
No	10	20	0	30
Total	30	40	10	80

   a. What is the name given to this table?
   b. What is the probability of selecting a client who received a refund?
   c. What is the probability of selecting a client who received a refund or had one dependent?
   d. Given that the client received a refund, what is the probability he or she had one dependent?
   e. What is the probability of selecting a client who did *not* receive a refund and had one dependent?
7. The IRS offers taxpayers the choice of allowing the IRS to compute the amount of their tax refund. During the busy filing season, the number of returns received at the Springfield Service Center that request this service follows a Poisson distribution with a mean of three per day. What is the probability that on a particular day:
   a. There are no requests?
   b. Exactly three requests appear?
   c. Five or more requests take place?
   d. There are no requests on two consecutive days?

Sampling Methods and the Central Limit Theorem

8

THE NIKE annual report says that the average American buys 6.5 pairs of sports shoes per year. Suppose the population standard deviation is 2.1 and that a sample of 81 customers will be examined next year. What is the standard error of the mean in this experiment? (See Exercise 45 and LO8-4.)

LEARNING OBJECTIVES

When you have completed this chapter, you will be able to:

LO8-1 Explain why populations are sampled and describe four methods to sample a population.

LO8-2 Define sampling error.

LO8-3 Demonstrate the construction of a sampling distribution of the sample mean.

LO8-4 Recite the central limit theorem and define the mean and standard error of the sampling distribution of the sample mean.

LO8-5 Apply the central limit theorem to calculate probabilities.

STATISTICS IN ACTION

With the significant role played by inferential statistics in all branches of science, the availability of large sources of random numbers has become a necessity. The first book of random numbers, containing 41,600 random digits generated by L. Tippett, was published in 1927. In 1938, R. A. Fisher and F. Yates published 15,000 random digits generated using two decks of cards. In 1955, RAND Corporation published a million random digits, generated by the random frequency pulses of an electronic roulette wheel. By 1970, applications of sampling required billions of random numbers. Methods have since been developed for generating, using a computer, digits that are "almost" random and hence are called *pseudo-random*. The question of whether a computer program can be used to generate numbers that are truly random remains a debatable issue.

LO8-1
Explain why populations are sampled and describe four methods to sample a population.

INTRODUCTION

Chapters 2 through 4 emphasize techniques to describe data. To illustrate these techniques, we organize the profits for the sale of 180 vehicles by the four dealers included in the Applewood Auto Group into a frequency distribution and compute various measures of location and dispersion. Such measures as the mean and the standard deviation describe the typical profit and the spread in the profits. In these chapters, the emphasis is on describing the condition of the data. That is, we describe something that has already happened.

In Chapter 5, we begin to lay the foundation for statistical inference with the study of probability. Recall that in statistical inference our goal is to determine something about a *population* based only on the *sample*. The population is the entire group of individuals or objects under consideration, and the sample is a part or subset of that population. Chapter 6 extends the probability concepts by describing three discrete probability distributions: the binomial, the hypergeometric, and the Poisson. Chapter 7 describes three continuous probability distributions: the uniform, normal, and exponential. Probability distributions encompass all possible outcomes of an experiment and the probability associated with each outcome. We use probability distributions to evaluate the likelihood something occurs in the future.

This chapter begins our study of sampling. Sampling is a process of selecting items from a population so we can use this information to make judgments or inferences about the population. We begin this chapter by discussing methods of selecting a sample from a population. Next, we construct a distribution of the sample mean to understand how the sample means tend to cluster around the population mean. Finally, we show that for any population the shape of this sampling distribution tends to follow the normal probability distribution.

SAMPLING METHODS

In Chapter 1, we said the purpose of inferential statistics is to find something about a population based on a sample. A sample is a portion or part of the population of interest. In many cases, sampling is more feasible than studying the entire population. In this section, we discuss the major reasons for sampling, and then several methods for selecting a sample.

Reasons to Sample

When studying characteristics of a population, there are many practical reasons why we prefer to select portions or samples of a population to observe and measure. Here are some of the reasons for sampling:

1. **To contact the whole population would be time-consuming.** A candidate for a national office may wish to determine her chances for election. A sample poll using the regular staff and field interviews of a professional polling firm would take only 1 or 2 days. Using the same staff and interviewers and working 7 days a week, it would take nearly 200 years to contact all the voting population! Even if a large staff of interviewers could be assembled, the benefit of contacting all of the voters would probably not be worth the time.
2. **The cost of studying all the items in a population may be prohibitive.** Public opinion polls and consumer testing organizations, such as Harris International, CBS News Polls, and Zogby International, usually contact fewer than 2,000 of the nearly 60 million families in the United States. One consumer panel–type organization charges $40,000 to mail samples and tabulate responses to test a product (such as breakfast cereal, cat food, or perfume). The same product test using all 60 million families would be too expensive to be worthwhile.
3. **The physical impossibility of checking all items in the population.** Some populations are infinite. It would be impossible to check all the water in Lake Erie for bacterial levels, so we select samples at various locations. The populations of

fish, birds, snakes, deer, and the like are large and are constantly moving, being born, and dying. Instead of even attempting to count all the ducks in Canada or all the fish in Lake Pontchartrain, we make estimates using various techniques—such as counting all the ducks on a pond selected at random, tracking fish catches, or netting fish at predetermined places in the lake.

4. **The destructive nature of some tests.** If the wine tasters at the Sutter Home Winery in California drank all the wine to evaluate the vintage, they would consume the entire crop, and none would be available for sale. In the area of industrial production, steel plates, wires, and similar products must have a certain minimum tensile strength. To ensure that the product meets the minimum standard, the Quality Assurance Department selects a sample from the current production. Each piece is stretched until it breaks and the breaking point (usually measured in pounds per square inch) recorded. Obviously, if all the wire or all the plates were tested for tensile strength, none would be available for sale or use. For the same reason, only a few seeds are tested for germination by Burpee Seeds Inc. prior to the planting season.
5. **The sample results are adequate.** Even if funds were available, it is doubtful the additional accuracy of a 100% sample—that is, studying the entire population—is essential in most problems. For example, the federal government uses a sample of grocery stores scattered throughout the United States to determine the monthly index of food prices. The prices of bread, beans, milk, and other major food items are included in the index. It is unlikely that the inclusion of all grocery stores in the United States would significantly affect the index because the prices of milk, bread, and other major foods usually do not vary by more than a few cents from one chain store to another.

Simple Random Sampling

The most widely used type of sampling is a **simple random sample.**

> **SIMPLE RANDOM SAMPLE** A sample selected so that each item or person in the population has the same chance of being included.

To illustrate the selection process for a simple random sample, suppose the population of interest is the 750 Major League Baseball players on the active rosters of the 30 teams at the end of the 2012 season. The president of the players' union wishes to form a committee of 10 players to study the issue of concussions. One way of ensuring that every player in the population has the same chance of being chosen to serve on the Concussion Committee is to write each name of the 750 players on a slip of paper and place all the slips of paper in a box. After the slips of paper have been thoroughly mixed, the first selection is made by drawing a slip of paper from the box identifying the first player. The slip of paper is not returned to the box. (Note that the probability of each selection does increase because the slip is not replaced. However, the differences are very small. The probability of each selection is about 0.0013, rounded to four decimal places). This process is repeated nine more times to form the committee.

Of course, the process of writing all the players' names on a slip of paper is very time-consuming. A more convenient method of selecting a random sample is to use a **table of random numbers** such as the one in Appendix B.4. In this case the union president would prepare a list of all 750 players and number each of the players from 1 to 750 with a computer application. Using a table of random numbers, we would randomly pick a starting place in the table, and then select 10 three-digit numbers between 001 and 750. A computer can also be used to generate random numbers. These numbers would correspond with the 10 players in the list that will be asked to participate on the committee. As the name simple random sampling implies, the probability of selecting any number between 001 and 750 is the same. Thus, the

probability of selecting the player assigned the number 131 is the same as the probability of selecting player 722 or player 382. Using random numbers to select players for the committee removes any bias from the selection process.

The following example shows how to select random numbers using a portion of a random number table illustrated below. First, we choose a starting point in the table. One way of selecting the starting point is to close your eyes and point at a number in the table. Any starting point will do. Another way is to randomly pick a column and row. Suppose the time is 3:04. Using the hour, three o'clock, pick the third column and then, using the minutes, four, move down to the fourth row of numbers. The number is 03759. Because there are only 750 players, we will use the first three digits of a five-digit random number. Thus, 037 is the number of the first player to be a member of the sample. To continue selecting players, we could move in any direction. Suppose we move right. The first three digits of the number to the right of 03759 are 447. Player number 447 is the second player selected to be on the committee. The next three-digit number to the right is 961. You skip 961 as well as the next number 784 because there are only 750 players. The third player selected is number 189. We continue this process until we have 10 players.

50525	57454	28455	68226	34656	38884	39018
72507	53380	53827	42486	54465	71819	91199
34986	74297	00144	38676	89967	98869	39744
68851	27305	03759	44723	96108	78489	18910
06738	62879	03910	17350	49169	03850	18910
11448	10734	05837	24397	10420	16712	94496
		Starting point	Second player			Third player

STATISTICS IN ACTION

Is discrimination taking a bite out of your paycheck? Before you answer, consider a recent article in *Personnel Journal.* These findings indicate that attractive men and women earn about 5% more than average lookers, who in turn earn about 5% more than their plain counterparts. This is true for both men and women. It is also true for a wide range of occupations, from construction work to auto repair to telemarketing, occupations for which it would seem that looks would not matter.

Statistical packages such as Minitab and spreadsheet packages such as Excel have software that will select a simple random sample. The following example/solution uses Excel to select a random sample from a list of the data.

EXAMPLE

Jane and Joe Miley operate the Foxtrot Inn, a bed and breakfast in Tryon, North Carolina. There are eight rooms available for rent at this B&B. Listed below is the number of these eight rooms rented each day during June 2013. Use Excel to select a sample of five nights during the month of June.

June	Rentals	June	Rentals	June	Rentals
1	0	11	3	21	3
2	2	12	4	22	2
3	3	13	4	23	3
4	2	14	4	24	6
5	3	15	7	25	0
6	4	16	0	26	4
7	2	17	5	27	1
8	3	18	3	28	1
9	4	19	6	29	3
10	7	20	2	30	3

SOLUTION

Excel will select the random sample and report the results. On the first sampled date, four of the eight rooms were rented. On the second sampled date in June, seven of the eight rooms were rented. The information is reported in column D of the Excel spreadsheet. The Excel steps are listed in the **Software Commands** in

Appendix C. The Excel system performs the sampling *with* replacement. This means it is possible for the same day to appear more than once in a sample.

	A	B	C	D
1	Day of June	Rentals		Sample
2	1	0		4
3	2	2		7
4	3	3		4
5	4	2		3
6	5	3		1
7	6	4		
8	7	2		
9	8	3		
10	9	4		
11	10	7		
12	11	3		
13	12	4		
14	13	4		
15	14	4		

SELF-REVIEW 8–1

The following class roster lists the students enrolling in an introductory course in business statistics. Three students are to be randomly selected and asked various questions regarding course content and method of instruction.

(a) The numbers 00 through 45 are handwritten on slips of paper and placed in a bowl. The three numbers selected are 31, 7, and 25. Which students would be included in the sample?

(b) Now use the table of random digits, Appendix B.4, to select your own sample.

(c) What would you do if you encountered the number 59 in the table of random digits?

CSPM 264 01 BUSINESS & ECONOMIC STAT
8:00 AM 9:40 AM MW ST 118 LIND D

RANDOM NUMBER	NAME	CLASS RANK	RANDOM NUMBER	NAME	CLASS RANK
00	ANDERSON, RAYMOND	SO	23	MEDLEY, CHERYL ANN	SO
01	ANGER, CHERYL RENEE	SO	24	MITCHELL, GREG R	FR
02	BALL, CLAIRE JEANETTE	FR	25	MOLTER, KRISTI MARIE	SO
03	BERRY, CHRISTOPHER G	FR	26	MULCAHY, STEPHEN ROBERT	SO
04	BOBAK, JAMES PATRICK	SO	27	NICHOLAS, ROBERT CHARLES	JR
05	BRIGHT, M. STARR	JR	28	NICKENS, VIRGINIA	SO
06	CHONTOS, PAUL JOSEPH	SO	29	PENNYWITT, SEAN PATRICK	SO
07	DETLEY, BRIAN HANS	JR	30	POTEAU, KRIS E	JR
08	DUDAS, VIOLA	SO	31	PRICE, MARY LYNETTE	SO
09	DULBS, RICHARD ZALFA	JR	32	RISTAS, JAMES	SR
10	EDINGER, SUSAN KEE	SR	33	SAGER, ANNE MARIE	SO
11	FINK, FRANK JAMES	SR	34	SMILLIE, HEATHER MICHELLE	SO
12	FRANCIS, JAMES P	JR	35	SNYDER, LEISHA KAY	SR
13	GAGHEN, PAMELA LYNN	JR	36	STAHL, MARIA TASHERY	SO
14	GOULD, ROBYN KAY	SO	37	ST. JOHN, AMY J	SO
15	GROSENBACHER, SCOTT ALAN	SO	38	STURDEVANT, RICHARD K	SO
16	HEETFIELD, DIANE MARIE	SO	39	SWETYE, LYNN MICHELE	SO
17	KABAT, JAMES DAVID	JR	40	WALASINSKI, MICHAEL	SO
18	KEMP, LISA ADRIANE	FR	41	WALKER, DIANE ELAINE	SO
19	KILLION, MICHELLE A	SO	42	WARNOCK, JENNIFER MARY	SO
20	KOPERSKI, MARY ELLEN	SO	43	WILLIAMS, WENDY A	SO
21	KOPP, BRIDGETTE ANN	SO	44	YAP, HOCK BAN	SO
22	LEHMANN, KRISTINA MARIE	JR	45	YODER, ARLAN JAY	JR

STATISTICS IN ACTION

Random and unbiased sampling methods are extremely important to make valid statistical inferences. In 1936, a straw vote to predict the outcome of the presidential race between Franklin Roosevelt and Alfred Landon was done. Ten million ballots in the form of returnable postcards were sent to addresses taken from telephone directories and automobile registrations. A high proportion of the ballots were returned, with 59% in favor of Landon and 41% favoring Roosevelt. On Election Day, Roosevelt won with 61% of the vote. Landon had 39%. In the mid-1930s people who had telephones and drove automobiles clearly did not represent American voters!

Systematic Random Sampling

The simple random sampling procedure is awkward in some research situations. For example, Stood's Grocery Market needs to sample their customers to study the length of time customers spend in the store. Simple random sampling is not an effective method. Practically, we do not have a list of customers, so assigning random numbers to customers is impossible. Instead, we can use **systematic random sampling** to select a representative sample. Using this method for Stood's Grocery Market, we decide to select 100 customers over 4 days, Monday through Thursday. We will select 25 customers a day and begin the sampling at different times each day: 8 a.m., 11 a.m., 4 p.m., and 7 p.m. We write the 4 times and 4 days on slips of paper and put them in two hats—one hat for the days and the other hat for the times. We select one slip from each hat. This ensures that the time of day is randomly assigned for each day. Suppose we selected 4 p.m. for the starting time on Monday. Next we select a random number between 1 and 10; it is 6. Our selection process begins on Monday at 4 p.m. by selecting the sixth customer to enter the store. Then, we select every 10th (16th, 26th, 36th) customer until we reach the goal of 25 customers. For each of these sampled customers, we measure the length of time the customer spends in the store.

> **SYSTEMATIC RANDOM SAMPLE** A random starting point is selected, and then every *k*th member of the population is selected.

Simple random sampling is used in the selection of the days, the times, and the starting point. But the systematic procedure is used to select the actual customer.

Before using systematic random sampling, we should carefully observe the physical order of the population. When the physical order is related to the population characteristic, then systematic random sampling should not be used because the sample could be biased. For example, if we wanted to audit the invoices in a file drawer that were ordered in increasing dollar amounts, systematic random sampling would not guarantee an unbiased random sample. Other sampling methods should be used.

Stratified Random Sampling

When a population can be clearly divided into groups based on some characteristic, we may use **stratified random sampling.** It guarantees each group is represented in the sample. The groups are called **strata.** For example, college students can be grouped as full time or part time; as male or female; or as freshman, sophomore, junior, or senior. Usually the strata are formed based on members' shared attributes or characteristics. A random sample from each stratum is taken in a number proportional to the stratum's size when compared to the population. Once the strata are defined, we apply simple random sampling within each group or stratum to collect the sample.

> **STRATIFIED RANDOM SAMPLE** A population is divided into subgroups, called strata, and a sample is randomly selected from each stratum.

For instance, we might study the advertising expenditures for the 352 largest companies in the United States. The objective of the study is to determine whether firms with high returns on equity (a measure of profitability) spend more on advertising than firms with low returns on equity. To make sure the sample is a fair representation of the 352 companies, the companies are grouped on percent return on equity. Table 8–1 shows the strata and the relative frequencies. If simple random sampling is used, observe that firms in the 3rd and 4th strata have a high chance of selection (probability of 0.87) while firms in the other strata have a small chance of selection (probability of 0.13). We might not select any firms in stratum 1 or 5 *simply by chance*. However, stratified random sampling will guarantee that at least one firm in each of strata 1 and 5 is represented in the sample.

TABLE 8–1 Number Selected for a Proportional Stratified Random Sample

Stratum	Profitability (return on equity)	Number of Firms	Relative Frequency	Number Sampled
1	30% and over	8	0.02	1*
2	20 up to 30%	35	0.10	5*
3	10 up to 20%	189	0.54	27
4	0 up to 10%	115	0.33	16
5	Deficit	5	0.01	1
Total		352	1.00	50

*0.02 of 50 = 1, 0.10 of 50 = 5, etc.

Let's say that 50 firms are selected for intensive study. Then based on probability, 1 firm, or (0.02)(50), should be randomly selected from stratum 1. We would randomly select 5, or (0.10)(50), firms from stratum 2. In this case, the number of firms sampled from each stratum is proportional to the stratum's relative frequency in the population. Stratified sampling has the advantage, in some cases, of more accurately reflecting the characteristics of the population than does simple random or systematic random sampling.

Cluster Sampling

Another common type of sampling is **cluster sampling.** It is often employed to reduce the cost of sampling a population scattered over a large geographic area.

CLUSTER SAMPLING A population is divided into clusters using naturally occurring geographic or other boundaries. Then, clusters are randomly selected and a sample is collected by randomly selecting from each cluster.

Suppose you want to determine the views of residents in the greater Chicago, Illinois, metropolitan area about state and federal environmental protection policies. Selecting a random sample of residents in this region and personally contacting each one would be time-consuming and very expensive. Instead, you could employ cluster sampling by subdividing the region into small units, perhaps by counties. These are often called *primary units.*

There are 12 counties in the greater Chicago metropolitan area. Suppose you randomly select 3 counties. The 3 chosen are La Porte, Cook, and Kenosha (see Chart 8–1 below). Next, you select a random sample of the residents in each of these counties and interview them. This is also referred to as sampling through an *intermediate unit.* In this case, the intermediate unit is the county. (Note that this is a combination of cluster sampling and simple random sampling.)

The discussion of sampling methods in the preceding sections did not include all the sampling methods available to a researcher. Should you become involved in a

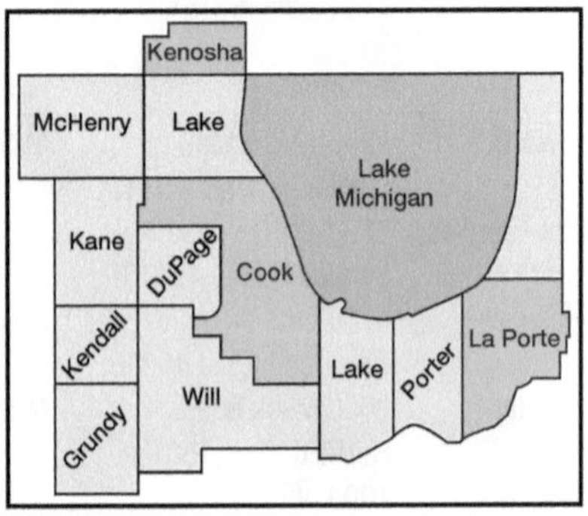

CHART 8–1 The counties of the greater Chicago, Illinois, metropolitan area.

major research project in marketing, finance, accounting, or other areas, you would need to consult books devoted solely to sample theory and sample design.

SELF-REVIEW 8–2

Refer to Self-Review 8–1 and the class roster on page 251. Suppose a systematic random sample will select every ninth student enrolled in the class. Initially, the fourth student on the list was selected at random. That student is numbered 03. Remembering that the random numbers start with 00, which students will be chosen to be members of the sample?

EXERCISES

1. The following is a list of 24 Marco's Pizza stores in Lucas County. The stores are identified by numbering them 00 through 23. Also noted is whether the store is corporate-owned (C) or manager-owned (M). A sample of four locations is to be selected and inspected for customer convenience, safety, cleanliness, and other features.

ID No.	Address	Type	ID No.	Address	Type
00	2607 Starr Av	C	12	2040 Ottawa River Rd	C
01	309 W Alexis Rd	C	13	2116 N Reynolds Rd	C
02	2652 W Central Av	C	14	3678 Rugby Dr	C
03	630 Dixie Hwy	M	15	1419 South Av	C
04	3510 Dorr St	C	16	1234 W Sylvania Av	C
05	5055 Glendale Av	C	17	4624 Woodville Rd	M
06	3382 Lagrange St	M	18	5155 S Main	M
07	2525 W Laskey Rd	C	19	106 E Airport Hwy	C
08	303 Louisiana Av	C	20	6725 W Central	M
09	149 Main St	C	21	4252 Monroe	C
10	835 S McCord Rd	M	22	2036 Woodville Rd	C
11	3501 Monroe St	M	23	1316 Michigan Av	M

a. The random numbers selected are 08, 18, 11, 54, 02, 41, and 54. Which stores are selected?
b. Use the table of random numbers to select your own sample of locations.
c. A sample is to consist of every seventh location. The number 03 is the starting point. Which locations will be included in the sample?
d. Suppose a sample is to consist of three locations, of which two are corporate-owned and one is manager-owned. Select a sample accordingly.

2. The following is a list of 29 hospitals in the Cincinnati (Ohio) and Northern Kentucky region. The hospitals are identified by numbering them 00 through 28. Also included is whether the hospital is a general medical/surgical hospital (M/S) or a specialty hospital (S). We are interested in estimating the average number of full- and part-time nurses employed in the area hospitals.
a. A sample of five hospitals is to be randomly selected. The random numbers are 09, 16, 00, 49, 54, 12, and 04. Which hospitals are included in the sample?
b. Use a table of random numbers to develop your own sample of five hospitals.

ID Number	Name	Address	Type	ID Number	Name	Address	Type
00	Bethesda North	10500 Montgomery Cincinnati, Ohio 45242	M/S	05	Middletown Regional	105 McKnight Drive Middletown, Ohio 45044	M/S
01	Ft. Hamilton–Hughes	630 Eaton Avenue Hamilton, Ohio 45013	M/S	06	Clermont Mercy Hospital	3000 Hospital Drive Batavia, Ohio 45103	M/S
02	Jewish Hospital– Kenwood	4700 East Galbraith Rd. Cincinnati, Ohio 45236	M/S	07	Mercy Hospital– Anderson	7500 State Road Cincinnati, Ohio 45255	M/S
03	Mercy Hospital– Fairfield	3000 Mack Road Fairfield, Ohio 45014	M/S	08	Bethesda Oak Hospital	619 Oak Street Cincinnati, Ohio 45206	M/S
04	Mercy Hospital– Hamilton	100 Riverfront Plaza Hamilton, Ohio 45011	M/S	09	Children's Hospital Medical Center	3333 Burnet Avenue Cincinnati, Ohio 45229	M/S

ID Number	Name	Address	Type
10	Christ Hospital	2139 Auburn Avenue Cincinnati, Ohio 45219	M/S
11	Deaconess Hospital	311 Straight Street Cincinnati, Ohio 45219	M/S
12	Good Samaritan Hospital	375 Dixmyth Avenue Cincinnati, Ohio 45220	M/S
13	Jewish Hospital	3200 Burnet Avenue Cincinnati, Ohio 45229	M/S
14	University Hospital	234 Goodman Street Cincinnati, Ohio 45267	M/S
15	Providence Hospital	2446 Kipling Avenue Cincinnati, Ohio 45239	M/S
16	St. Francis–St. George Hospital	3131 Queen City Avenue Cincinnati, Ohio 45238	M/S
17	St. Elizabeth Medical Center, North Unit	401 E. 20th Street Covington, Kentucky 41014	M/S
18	St. Elizabeth Medical Center, South Unit	One Medical Village Edgewood, Kentucky 41017	M/S
19	St. Luke's Hospital West	7380 Turfway Drive Florence, Kentucky 41075	M/S
20	St. Luke's Hospital East	85 North Grand Avenue Ft. Thomas, Kentucky 41042	M/S
21	Care Unit Hospital	3156 Glenmore Avenue Cincinnati, Ohio 45211	S
22	Emerson Behavioral Science	2446 Kipling Avenue Cincinnati, Ohio 45239	S
23	Pauline Warfield Lewis Center for Psychiatric Treat.	1101 Summit Road Cincinnati, Ohio 45237	S
24	Children's Psychiatric No. Kentucky	502 Farrell Drive Covington, Kentucky 41011	S
25	Drake Center Rehab—Long Term	151 W. Galbraith Road Cincinnati, Ohio 45216	S
26	No. Kentucky Rehab Hospital—Short Term	201 Medical Village Edgewood, Kentucky	S
27	Shriners Burns Institute	3229 Burnet Avenue Cincinnati, Ohio 45229	S
28	VA Medical Center	3200 Vine Cincinnati, Ohio 45220	S

c. A sample is to consist of every fifth location. We select 02 as the starting point. Which hospitals will be included in the sample?

d. A sample is to consist of four medical and surgical hospitals and one specialty hospital. Select an appropriate sample.

3. Listed below are the 35 members of the Metro Toledo Automobile Dealers Association. We would like to estimate the mean revenue from dealer service departments. The members are identified by numbering them 00 through 34.

ID Number	Dealer
00	Dave White Acura
01	Autofair Nissan
02	Autofair Toyota-Suzuki
03	George Ball's Buick GMC Truck
04	Yark Automotive Group
05	Bob Schmidt Chevrolet
06	Bowling Green Lincoln Mercury Jeep Eagle
07	Brondes Ford
08	Brown Honda
09	Brown Mazda
10	Charlie's Dodge
11	Thayer Chevrolet/Toyota
12	Spurgeon Chevrolet Motor Sales, Inc.
13	Dunn Chevrolet
14	Don Scott Chevrolet
15	Dave White Chevrolet Co.
16	Dick Wilson Infinity
17	Doyle Buick
18	Franklin Park Lincoln Mercury
19	Genoa Motors
20	Great Lakes Ford Nissan
21	Grogan Towne Chrysler
22	Hatfield Motor Sales
23	Kistler Ford, Inc.
24	Lexus of Toledo
25	Mathews Ford Oregon, Inc.
26	Northtowne Chevrolet
27	Quality Ford Sales, Inc.
28	Rouen Chrysler Jeep Eagle
29	Saturn of Toledo
30	Ed Schmidt Jeep Eagle
31	Southside Lincoln Mercury
32	Valiton Chrysler
33	Vin Divers
34	Whitman Ford

a. We want to select a random sample of five dealers. The random numbers are 05, 20, 59, 21, 31, 28, 49, 38, 66, 08, 29, and 02. Which dealers would be included in the sample?

b. Use the table of random numbers to select your own sample of five dealers.

c. A sample is to consist of every seventh dealer. The number 04 is selected as the starting point. Which dealers are included in the sample?

4. Listed next are the 27 Nationwide Insurance agents in the Toledo, Ohio, metropolitan area. The agents are identified by numbering them 00 through 26. We would like to estimate the mean number of years employed with Nationwide.

ID Number	Agent	ID Number	Agent	ID Number	Agent
00	**Bly Scott** 3332 W Laskey Rd	10	**Heini Bernie** 7110 W Centra	19	**Riker Craig** 2621 N Reynolds Rd
01	**Coyle Mike** 5432 W Central Av	11	**Hinckley Dave** 14 N Holland Sylvania Rd	20	**Schwab Dave** 572 W Dussel Dr
02	**Denker Brett** 7445 Airport Hwy	12	**Joehlin Bob** 3358 Navarre Av	21	**Seibert John H** 201 S Main
03	**Denker Rollie** 7445 Airport Hwy	13	**Keisser David** 3030 W Sylvania Av	22	**Smithers Bob** 229 Superior St
04	**Farley Ron** 1837 W Alexis Rd	14	**Keisser Keith** 5902 Sylvania Av	23	**Smithers Jerry** 229 Superior St
05	**George Mark** 7247 W Central Av	15	**Lawrence Grant** 342 W Dussel Dr	24	**Wright Steve** 105 S Third St
06	**Gibellato Carlo** 6616 Monroe St	16	**Miller Ken** 2427 Woodville Rd	25	**Wood Tom** 112 Louisiana Av
07	**Glemser Cathy** 5602 Woodville Rd	17	**O'Donnell Jim** 7247 W Central Av	26	**Yoder Scott** 6 Willoughby Av
08	**Green Mike** 4149 Holland Sylvania Rd	18	**Priest Harvey** 5113 N Summit St		
09	**Harris Ev** 2026 Albon Rd				

a. We want to select a random sample of four agents. The random numbers are 02, 59, 51, 25, 14, 29, 77, 69, and 18. Which dealers would be included in the sample?

b. Use the table of random numbers to select your own sample of four agents.

c. A sample is to consist of every seventh dealer. The number 04 is selected as the starting point. Which agents will be included in the sample?

LO8-2
Define sampling error.

SAMPLING "ERROR"

In the previous section, we discussed sampling methods that are used to select a sample that is an unbiased representation of the population. In each method, the selection of every possible sample of a specified size from a population has a known chance or probability. This is another way to describe an unbiased sampling method.

Samples are used to estimate population characteristics. For example, the mean of a sample is used to estimate the population mean. However, since the sample is a part or portion of the population, it is unlikely that the sample mean would be *exactly equal* to the population mean. Similarly, it is unlikely that the sample standard deviation would be *exactly equal* to the population standard deviation. We can therefore expect a difference between a *sample statistic* and its corresponding *population parameter*. This difference is called **sampling error.**

SAMPLING ERROR The difference between a sample statistic and its corresponding population parameter.

The following example/solution clarifies the idea of sampling error.

EXAMPLE

Refer to the example/solution on page 250, where we studied the number of rooms rented at the Foxtrot Inn bed and breakfast in Tryon, North Carolina. The population is the number of rooms rented each of the 30 days in June 2013. Find the mean of the population. Use Excel or other statistical software to select three random samples of 5 days. Calculate the mean of each sample and compare it to the population mean. What is the sampling error in each case?

SOLUTION

During the month, there were a total of 94 rentals. So the mean number of units rented per night is 3.13. This is the population mean. Hence we designate this value with the Greek letter μ.

$$\mu = \frac{\Sigma x}{N} = \frac{0 + 2 + 3 + \cdots + 3}{30} = \frac{94}{30} = 3.13$$

The first random sample of five nights resulted in the following number of rooms rented: 4, 7, 4, 3, and 1. The mean of this sample of 5 nights is 3.80 rooms, which we designate as $\bar{x}_1$. The bar over the x reminds us that it is a sample mean and the subscript 1 indicates it is the mean of the first sample.

$$\bar{x}_1 = \frac{\Sigma x}{n} = \frac{4 + 7 + 4 + 3 + 1}{5} = \frac{19}{5} = 3.80$$

The sampling error for the first sample is the difference between the population mean (3.13) and the first sample mean (3.80). Hence, the sampling error is $(\bar{x}_1 - \mu) = 3.80 - 3.13 = 0.67$. The second random sample of 5 days from the population of all 30 days in June revealed the following number of rooms rented: 3, 3, 2, 3, and 6. The mean of these five values is 3.40, found by

$$\bar{x}_2 = \frac{\Sigma x}{n} = \frac{3 + 3 + 2 + 3 + 6}{5} = 3.40$$

The sampling error is $(\bar{x}_2 - \mu) = 3.4 - 3.13 = 0.27$. In the third random sample, the mean was 1.80 and the sampling error was -1.33.

Each of these differences, 0.67, 0.27, and -1.33, is the sampling error made in estimating the population mean. Sometimes these errors are positive values, indicating that the sample mean overestimated the population mean; other times they are negative values, indicating the sample mean was less than the population mean.

	A	B	C	D	E	F	G
1	Day of June	Rentals			Sample 1	Sample 2	Sample 3
2	1	0			4	3	0
3	2	2			7	3	0
4	3	3			4	2	3
5	4	2			3	3	3
6	5	3			1	6	3
7	6	4		Totals	19	17	9
8	7	2		Sample means	3.80	3.40	1.80
9	8	3					
10	9	4					
11	10	7					
12	11	3					
13	12	4					
14	13	4					
15	14	4					

In this case, where we have a population of 30 values and samples of 5 values, there is a very large number of possible samples—142,506 to be exact! To find this value, use the combination formula (5–10) on page 163. Each of the 142,506 different samples has the same chance of being selected. Each sample may have a different sample mean and therefore a different sampling error. The value of the sampling error is based on the particular one of the 142,506 different possible samples selected. Therefore, the sampling errors are random and occur by chance. If you were to determine the sum of these sampling errors over a large number of samples, the result would be very close to zero. This is true because the sample mean is an *unbiased estimator* of the population mean.

LO8-3
Demonstrate the construction of a sampling distribution of the sample mean.

SAMPLING DISTRIBUTION OF THE SAMPLE MEAN

In the previous section, we defined sampling error and presented the results when we compared a sample statistic, such as the sample mean, to the population mean. To put it another way, when we use the sample mean to estimate the population mean, how can we determine how accurate the estimate is? How does:

- A quality-assurance supervisor decide if a machine is filling 20-ounce bottles with 20 ounces of cola based only on a sample of 10 filled bottles?
- CNN/*USA Today* or ABC News/*Washington Post* make accurate statements about the average years of education for voters in a presidential race based on a sample of 1,200 registered voters out of a voting population of nearly 90 million?

To answer these questions, we first develop a *sampling distribution of the sample mean*.

The sample means in the previous example/solution varied from one sample to the next. The mean of the first sample of 5 days was 3.80 rooms, and the second sample mean was 3.40 rooms. The population mean was 3.13 rooms. If we organized the means of all possible samples of 5 days into a probability distribution, the result is called the **sampling distribution of the sample mean.**

SAMPLING DISTRIBUTION OF THE SAMPLE MEAN A probability distribution of all possible sample means of a given sample size.

The following example/solution illustrates the construction of a sampling distribution of the sample mean. We have intentionally used a small population to highlight the relationship between the population mean and the various sample means.

EXAMPLE

Tartus Industries has seven production employees (considered the population). The hourly earnings of each employee are given in Table 8–2.

TABLE 8–2 Hourly Earnings of the Production Employees of Tartus Industries

Employee	Hourly Earnings	Employee	Hourly Earnings
Joe	$7	Jan	$7
Sam	7	Art	8
Sue	8	Ted	9
Bob	8		

1. What is the population mean?
2. What is the sampling distribution of the sample mean for samples of size 2?
3. What is the mean of the sampling distribution?
4. What observations can be made about the population and the sampling distribution?

SOLUTION

Here are the solutions to the questions.

1. The population is small so it is easy to calculate the population mean. It is $7.71, found by:

$$\mu = \frac{\Sigma x}{N} = \frac{\$7 + \$7 + \$8 + \$8 + \$7 + \$8 + \$9}{7} = \$7.71$$

We identify the population mean with the Greek letter μ. Recall from earlier chapters, Greek letters are used to represent population parameters.

2. To arrive at the sampling distribution of the sample mean, we need to select all possible samples of 2 without replacement from the population, then compute the mean of each sample. There are 21 possible samples, found by using formula (5–10) on page 163.

$$_NC_n = \frac{N!}{n!(N-n)!} = \frac{7!}{2!(7-2)!} = 21$$

where $N = 7$ is the number of items in the population and $n = 2$ is the number of items in the sample.

TABLE 8–3 Sample Means for All Possible Samples of 2 Employees

Sample	Employees	Hourly Earnings	Sum	Mean	Sample	Employees	Hourly Earnings	Sum	Mean
1	Joe, Sam	$7, $7	$14	$7.00	12	Sue, Bob	$8, $8	$16	$8.00
2	Joe, Sue	7, 8	15	7.50	13	Sue, Jan	8, 7	15	7.50
3	Joe, Bob	7, 8	15	7.50	14	Sue, Art	8, 8	16	8.00
4	Joe, Jan	7, 7	14	7.00	15	Sue, Ted	8, 9	17	8.50
5	Joe, Art	7, 8	15	7.50	16	Bob, Jan	8, 7	15	7.50
6	Joe, Ted	7, 9	16	8.00	17	Bob, Art	8, 8	16	8.00
7	Sam, Sue	7, 8	15	7.50	18	Bob, Ted	8, 9	17	8.50
8	Sam, Bob	7, 8	15	7.50	19	Jan, Art	7, 8	15	7.50
9	Sam, Jan	7, 7	14	7.00	20	Jan, Ted	7, 9	16	8.00
10	Sam, Art	7, 8	15	7.50	21	Art, Ted	8, 9	17	8.50
11	Sam, Ted	7, 9	16	8.00					

The 21 sample means from all possible samples of 2 that can be drawn from the population of 7 employees are shown in Table 8–3. These 21 sample means are used to construct a probability distribution. This is called the sampling distribution of the sample mean, and it is summarized in Table 8–4.

TABLE 8–4 Sampling Distribution of the Sample Mean for $n = 2$

Sample Mean	Number of Means	Probability
$7.00	3	.1429
7.50	9	.4285
8.00	6	.2857
8.50	3	.1429
	21	1.0000

3. Using the data in Table 8–3, the mean of the sampling distribution of the sample mean is obtained by summing the various sample means and dividing the sum by the number of samples. The mean of all the sample means is usually written $\mu_{\bar{x}}$. The μ reminds us that it is a population value because we have considered all possible samples of two employees from the population of seven employees. The subscript $\bar{x}$ indicates that it is the sampling distribution of the sample mean.

$$\mu_{\bar{x}} = \frac{\text{Sum of all sample means}}{\text{Total number of samples}} = \frac{\$7.00 + \$7.50 + \$7.50 + \cdots + \$8.00 + \$8.50}{21}$$

$$= \frac{\$162}{21} = \$7.71$$

4. Refer to Chart 8–2. It shows the population distribution based on the data in Table 8–2 and the distribution of the sample mean based on the data in Table 8–4. These observations can be made:
   a. The mean of the distribution of the sample mean ($7.71) is equal to the mean of the population: $\mu = \mu_{\bar{X}}$.
   b. The spread in the distribution of the sample mean is less than the spread in the population values. The sample means range from $7.00 to $8.50, while the population values vary from $7.00 up to $9.00. If we continue to increase the sample size, the spread of the distribution of the sample mean becomes smaller.
   c. The shape of the sampling distribution of the sample mean and the shape of the frequency distribution of the population values are different. The distribution of the sample mean tends to be more bell-shaped and to approximate the normal probability distribution.

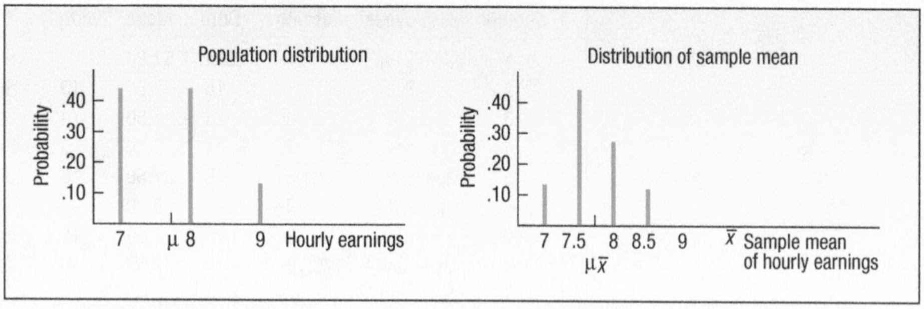

CHART 8–2 Distributions of Population Values and Sample Mean

In summary, we took all possible random samples from a population and for each sample calculated a sample statistic (the mean amount earned). This example illustrates important relationships between the population distribution and the sampling distribution of the sample mean:

1. The mean of the sample means is exactly equal to the population mean.
2. The dispersion of the sampling distribution of the sample mean is narrower than the population distribution.
3. The sampling distribution of the sample mean tends to become bell-shaped and to approximate the normal probability distribution.

Given a bell-shaped or normal probability distribution, we will be able to apply concepts from Chapter 7 to determine the probability of selecting a sample with a specified sample mean. In the next section, we will show the importance of sample size as it relates to the sampling distribution of the sample mean.

SELF-REVIEW 8–3

The years of service of the five executives employed by Standard Chemicals are:

Name	Years
Mr. Snow	20
Ms. Tolson	22
Mr. Kraft	26
Ms. Irwin	24
Mr. Jones	28

(a) Using the combination formula, how many samples of size 2 are possible?
(b) List all possible samples of two executives from the population and compute their means.
(c) Organize the means into a sampling distribution.
(d) Compare the population mean and the mean of the sample means.
(e) Compare the dispersion in the population with that in the distribution of the sample mean.
(f) A chart portraying the population values follows. Is the distribution of population values normally distributed (bell-shaped)?

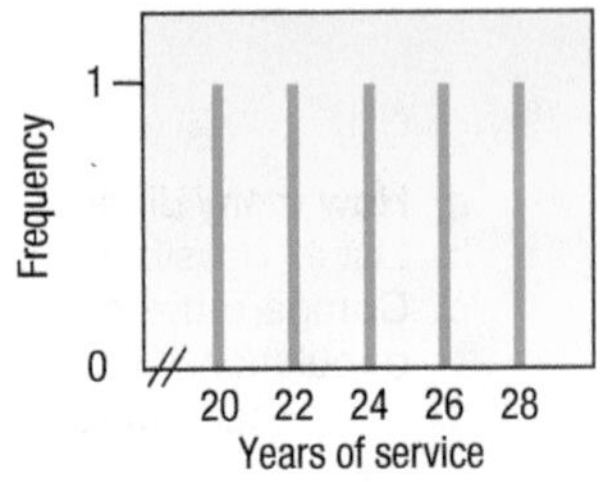

(g) Is the distribution of the sample mean computed in part (c) starting to show some tendency toward being bell-shaped?

EXERCISES

5. A population consists of the following four values: 12, 12, 14, and 16.
   a. List all samples of size 2, and compute the mean of each sample.
   b. Compute the mean of the distribution of the sample mean and the population mean. Compare the two values.
   c. Compare the dispersion in the population with that of the sample mean.

6. A population consists of the following five values: 2, 2, 4, 4, and 8.
   a. List all samples of size 2, and compute the mean of each sample.
   b. Compute the mean of the distribution of sample means and the population mean. Compare the two values.
   c. Compare the dispersion in the population with that of the sample means.

7. A population consists of the following five values: 12, 12, 14, 15, and 20.
   a. List all samples of size 3, and compute the mean of each sample.
   b. Compute the mean of the distribution of sample means and the population mean. Compare the two values.
   c. Compare the dispersion in the population with that of the sample means.

8. A population consists of the following five values: 0, 0, 1, 3, 6.
   a. List all samples of size 3, and compute the mean of each sample.
   b. Compute the mean of the distribution of sample means and the population mean. Compare the two values.
   c. Compare the dispersion in the population with that of the sample means.

9. In the law firm Tybo and Associates, there are six partners. Listed next is the number of cases each partner actually tried in court last month.

Partner	Number of Cases
Ruud	3
Wu	6
Sass	3
Flores	3
Wilhelms	0
Schueller	1

   a. How many different samples of size 3 are possible?
   b. List all possible samples of size 3, and compute the mean number of cases in each sample.
   c. Compare the mean of the distribution of sample means to the population mean.
   d. On a chart similar to Chart 8–2, compare the dispersion in the population with that of the sample means.

10. There are five sales associates at Mid-Motors Ford. The five associates and the number of cars they sold last week are:

Sales Associate	Cars Sold
Peter Hankish	8
Connie Stallter	6
Juan Lopez	4
Ted Barnes	10
Peggy Chu	6

a. How many different samples of size 2 are possible?
b. List all possible samples of size 2, and compute the mean of each sample.
c. Compare the mean of the sampling distribution of the sample mean with that of the population.
d. On a chart similar to Chart 8–2, compare the dispersion in sample means with that of the population.

LO8-4
Recite the central limit theorem and define the mean and standard error of the sampling distribution of the sample mean.

THE CENTRAL LIMIT THEOREM

In this section, we examine the **central limit theorem.** Its application to the sampling distribution of the sample mean, introduced in the previous section, allows us to use the normal probability distribution to create confidence intervals for the population mean (described in Chapter 9) and perform tests of hypothesis (described in Chapter 10). The central limit theorem states that, for large random samples, the shape of the sampling distribution of the sample mean is close to the normal probability distribution. The approximation is more accurate for large samples than for small samples. This is one of the most useful conclusions in statistics. We can reason about the distribution of the sample mean with absolutely no information about the shape of the population distribution from which the sample is taken. In other words, the central limit theorem is true for all distributions.

A formal statement of the central limit theorem follows.

CENTRAL LIMIT THEOREM If all samples of a particular size are selected from any population, the sampling distribution of the sample mean is approximately a normal distribution. This approximation improves with larger samples.

If the population follows a normal probability distribution, then for any sample size the sampling distribution of the sample mean will also be normal. If the population distribution is symmetrical (but not normal), you will see the normal shape of the distribution of the sample mean emerge with samples as small as 10. On the other hand, if you start with a distribution that is skewed or has thick tails, it may require samples of 30 or more to observe the normality feature. This concept is summarized in Chart 8–3 for various population shapes. Observe the convergence to a normal distribution regardless of the shape of the population distribution.

The idea that the distribution of the sample means from a population that is not normal will converge to normality is illustrated in Charts 8–4, 8–5, and 8–6. We will discuss this example in more detail shortly, but Chart 8–4 is a graph of a discrete probability distribution that is positively skewed. There are many possible samples of 5 that might be selected from this population. Suppose we randomly select 25 samples of size 5 from the population portrayed in Chart 8–4 and compute the mean of each sample. These results are shown in Chart 8–5. Notice that the shape of the distribution of sample means has changed from the shape of the original population even though we selected only 25 of the many possible samples. To put it another way, we selected 25 random samples of 5 each from a population that is positively skewed and found the distribution of sample means has changed from the shape of the population. As we take larger samples, that is, $n = 20$ instead of $n = 5$, we will find the distribution of the

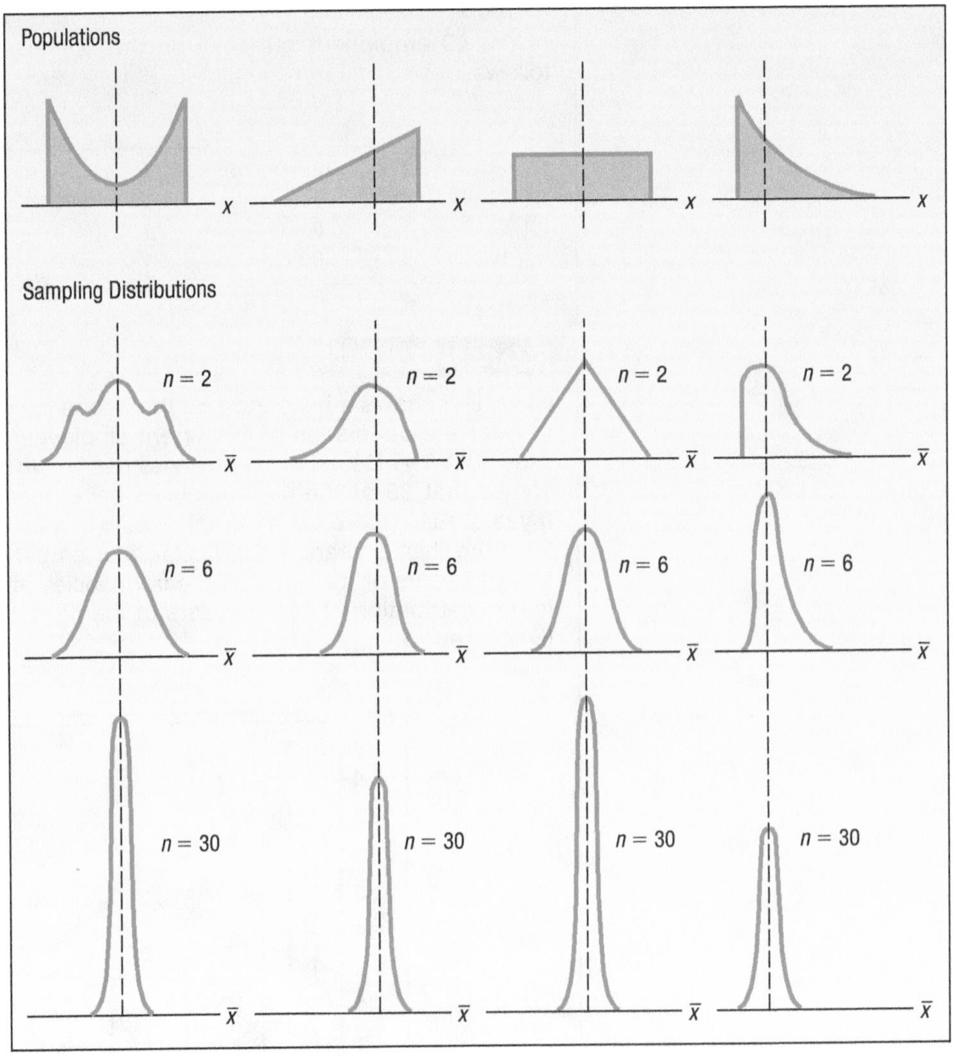

CHART 8–3 Results of the Central Limit Theorem for Several Populations

sample mean will approach the normal distribution. Chart 8–6 shows the results of 25 random samples of 20 observations each from the same population. Observe the clear trend toward the normal probability distribution. This is the point of the central limit theorem. The following example/solution will underscore this condition.

EXAMPLE

Ed Spence began his sprocket business 20 years ago. The business has grown over the years and now employs 40 people. Spence Sprockets Inc. faces some major decisions regarding health care for these employees. Before making a final decision on what health care plan to purchase, Ed decides to form a committee of five representative employees. The committee will be asked to study the health care issue carefully and make a recommendation as to what plan best fits the employees' needs. Ed feels the views of newer employees toward health care may differ from those of more experienced employees. If Ed randomly selects this committee, what can he expect in terms of the mean years with Spence Sprockets for those on the committee? How does the shape of the distribution of years of service of all employees (the population) compare with the shape of the sampling distribution of the mean? The years of service (rounded to the nearest year)

of the 40 employees currently on the Spence Sprockets Inc. payroll are as follows.

11	4	18	2	1	2	0	2	2	4
3	4	1	2	2	3	3	19	8	3
7	1	0	2	7	0	4	5	1	14
16	8	9	1	1	2	5	10	2	3

SOLUTION

Chart 8–4 shows a histogram for the frequency distribution of the years of service for the population of 40 current employees. This distribution is positively skewed. Why? Because the business has grown in recent years, the distribution shows that 29 of the 40 employees have been with the company less than 6 years. Also, there are 11 employees who have worked at Spence Sprockets for more than 6 years. In particular, four employees have been with the company 12 years or more (count the frequencies above 12). So there is a long tail in the distribution of service years to the right, that is, the distribution is positively skewed.

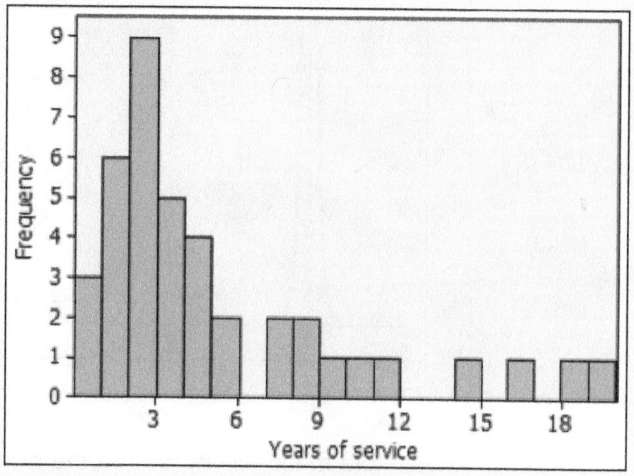

CHART 8–4 Years of Service for Spence Sprockets Inc. Employees

Let's consider the first of Ed Spence's problems. He would like to form a committee of five employees to look into the health care question and suggest what type of health care coverage would be most appropriate for the majority of workers. How should he select the committee? If he selects the committee randomly, what might he expect in terms of mean years of service for those on the committee?

To begin, Ed writes the years of service for each of the 40 employees on pieces of paper and puts them into an old baseball hat. Next, he shuffles the pieces of paper and randomly selects five slips of paper. The years of service for these five employees are 1, 9, 0, 19, and 14 years. Thus, the mean years of service for these five sampled employees is 8.60 years. How does that compare with the population mean? At this point, Ed does not know the population mean, but the number of employees in the population is only 40, so he decides to calculate

the mean years of service for *all* his employees. It is 4.8 years, found by adding the years of service for *all* the employees and dividing the total by 40.

$$\mu = \frac{11 + 4 + 18 + \cdots + 2 + 3}{40} = 4.80$$

The difference between a sample mean ($\bar{x}$) and the population mean (μ) is called **sampling error**. In other words, the difference of 3.80 years between the sample mean of 8.60 and the population mean of 4.80 is the sampling error. It is due to chance. Thus, if Ed selected these five employees to constitute the committee, their mean years of service would be larger than the population mean.

What would happen if Ed put the five pieces of paper back into the baseball hat and selected another sample? Would you expect the mean of this second sample to be exactly the same as the previous one? Suppose he selects another sample of five employees and finds the years of service in this sample to be 7, 4, 4, 1, and 3. This sample mean is 3.80 years. The result of selecting 25 samples of five employees and computing the mean for each sample is shown in Table 8–5 and Chart 8–5. There are actually 658,008 possible samples of 5 from the population of 40 employees, found by the combination formula (5–9) for 40 things taken 5 at a time. Notice the difference in the shape of the population and the distribution of these sample means. The population of the years of service for employees (Chart 8–4) is positively skewed, but the

TABLE 8–5 Twenty-Five Random Samples of Five Employees

	Sample Data						
Sample	**Obs 1**	**Obs 2**	**Obs 3**	**Obs 4**	**Obs 5**	**Sum**	**Mean**
A	1	9	0	19	14	43	8.6
B	7	4	4	1	3	19	3.8
C	8	19	8	2	1	38	7.6
D	4	18	2	0	11	35	7.0
E	4	2	4	7	18	35	7.0
F	1	2	0	3	2	8	1.6
G	2	3	2	0	2	9	1.8
H	11	2	9	2	4	28	5.6
I	9	0	4	2	7	22	4.4
J	1	1	1	11	1	15	3.0
K	2	0	0	10	2	14	2.8
L	0	2	3	2	16	23	4.6
M	2	3	1	1	1	8	1.6
N	3	7	3	4	3	20	4.0
O	1	2	3	1	4	11	2.2
P	19	0	1	3	8	31	6.2
Q	5	1	7	14	9	36	7.2
R	5	4	2	3	4	18	3.6
S	14	5	2	2	5	28	5.6
T	2	1	1	4	7	15	3.0
U	3	7	1	2	1	14	2.8
V	0	1	5	1	2	9	1.8
W	0	3	19	4	2	28	5.6
X	4	2	3	4	0	13	2.6
Y	1	1	2	3	2	9	1.8

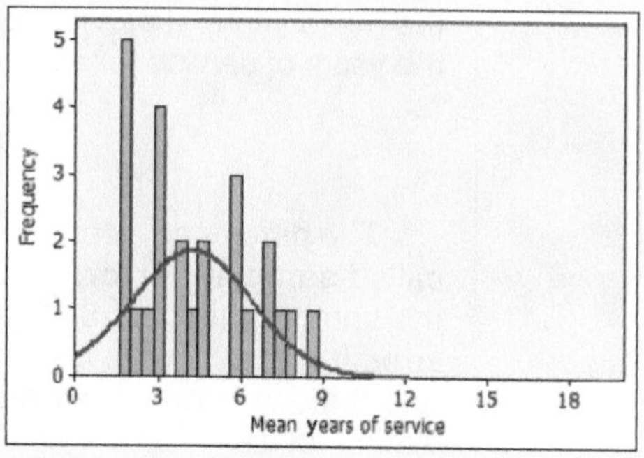

CHART 8–5 Histogram of Mean Years of Service for 25 Samples of Five Employees

distribution of these 25 sample means does not reflect the same positive skew. There is also a difference in the range of the sample means versus the range of the population. The population ranged from 0 to 19 years, whereas the sample means range from 1.6 to 8.6 years.

Now let's change the example by increasing the size of each sample from 5 employees to 20. Table 8–6 reports the result of selecting 25 samples of 20 employees each and computing their sample means. These sample means are

TABLE 8–6 Twenty-Five Random Samples of 20 Employees

	Sample Data							
Sample	Obs 1	Obs 2	Obs 3	–	Obs 19	Obs 20	Sum	Mean
A	3	8	3	–	4	16	79	3.95
B	2	3	8	–	3	1	65	3.25
C	14	5	0	–	19	8	119	5.95
D	9	2	1	–	1	3	87	4.35
E	18	1	2	–	3	14	107	5.35
F	10	4	4	–	2	1	80	4.00
G	5	7	11	–	2	4	131	6.55
H	3	0	2	–	16	5	85	4.25
I	0	0	18	–	2	3	80	4.00
J	2	7	2	–	3	2	81	4.05
K	7	4	5	–	1	2	84	4.20
L	0	3	10	–	0	4	81	4.05
M	4	1	2	–	1	2	88	4.40
N	3	16	1	–	11	1	95	4.75
O	2	19	2	–	2	2	102	5.10
P	2	18	16	–	4	3	100	5.00
Q	3	2	3	–	3	1	102	5.10
R	2	3	1	–	0	2	73	3.65
S	2	14	19	–	0	7	142	7.10
T	0	1	3	–	2	0	61	3.05
U	1	0	1	–	9	3	65	3.25
V	1	9	4	–	2	11	137	6.85
W	8	1	9	–	8	7	107	5.35
X	4	2	0	–	2	5	86	4.30
Y	1	2	1	–	1	18	101	5.05

shown graphically in Chart 8–6. Compare the shape of this distribution to the population (Chart 8–4) and to the distribution of sample means where the sample is $n = 5$ (Chart 8–5). You should observe two important features:

1. The shape of the distribution of the sample mean is different from that of the population. In Chart 8–4, the distribution of all employees is positively skewed. However, as we select random samples from this population, the shape of the distribution of the sample mean changes. As we increase the size of the sample, the distribution of the sample mean approaches the normal probability distribution. This illustrates the central limit theorem.
2. There is less dispersion in the sampling distribution of the sample mean than in the population distribution. In the population, the years of service ranged from 0 to 19 years. When we selected samples of 5, the sample means ranged from 1.6 to 8.6 years, and when we selected samples of 20, the means ranged from 3.05 to 7.10 years.

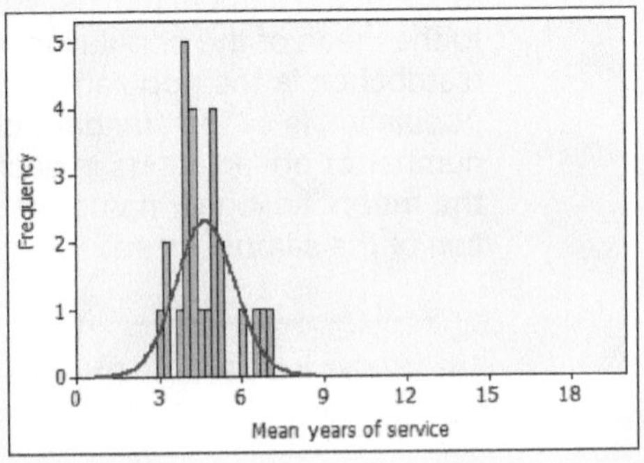

CHART 8–6 Histogram of Mean Years of Service for 25 Samples of 20 Employees

We can also compare the mean of the sample means to the population mean. The mean of the 25 samples of 20 employees reported in Table 8–6 is 4.676 years.

$$\mu_{\bar{X}} = \frac{3.95 + 3.25 + \cdots + 4.30 + 5.05}{25} = 4.676$$

We use the symbol $\mu_{\bar{X}}$ to identify the mean of the distribution of the sample mean. The subscript reminds us that the distribution is of the sample mean. It is read "mu sub x bar." We observe that the mean of the sample means, 4.676 years, is very close to the population mean of 4.80.

What should we conclude from this example? The central limit theorem indicates that, regardless of the shape of the population distribution, the sampling distribution of the sample mean will move toward the normal probability distribution. The larger the number of observations in each sample, the stronger the convergence. The Spence Sprockets Inc. example shows how the central limit theorem works. We began with a positively skewed population (Chart 8–4). Next, we selected 25 random samples of 5 observations, computed the mean of each sample, and finally organized these 25 sample means into a histogram (Chart 8–5). We observe a change in the shape of the sampling distribution of the sample mean from that of the population. The movement is from a positively skewed distribution to a distribution that has the shape of the normal probability distribution.

To further illustrate the effects of the central limit theorem, we increased the number of observations in each sample from 5 to 20. We selected 25 samples of 20 observations each and calculated the mean of each sample. Finally, we organized these

sample means into a histogram (Chart 8–6). The shape of the histogram in Chart 8–6 is clearly moving toward the normal probability distribution.

If you go back to Chapter 6 where several binomial distributions with a "success" proportion of .10 are shown in Chart 6–3 on page 188, you can see yet another demonstration of the central limit theorem. Observe as n increases from 7 through 12 and 20 up to 40 that the profile of the probability distributions moves closer and closer to a normal probability distribution. Chart 8–6 on page 267 also shows the convergence to normality as n increases. This again reinforces the fact that, as more observations are sampled from any population distribution, the shape of the sampling distribution of the sample mean will get closer and closer to a normal distribution.

The central limit theorem itself (reread the definition on page 262) does not say anything about the dispersion of the sampling distribution of the sample mean or about the comparison of the mean of the sampling distribution of the sample mean to the mean of the population. However, in our Spence Sprockets example, we did observe that there was less dispersion in the distribution of the sample mean than in the population distribution by noting the difference in the range in the population and the range of the sample means. We observe that the mean of the sample means is close to the mean of the population. It can be demonstrated that the mean of the sampling distribution is the population mean (i.e., $\mu_{\bar{x}} = \mu$), and if the standard deviation in the population is σ, the standard deviation of the sample means is $\sigma/\sqrt{n}$, where n is the number of observations in each sample. We refer to $\sigma/\sqrt{n}$ as the **standard error of the mean.** Its longer name is actually the *standard deviation of the sampling distribution of the sample mean*.

STANDARD ERROR OF THE MEAN $$\sigma_{\bar{x}} = \frac{\sigma}{\sqrt{n}} \qquad [8\text{–}1]$$

In this section, we also came to other important conclusions.

1. The mean of the distribution of sample means will be *exactly* equal to the population mean if we are able to select all possible samples of the same size from a given population. That is:

$$\mu = \mu_{\bar{x}}$$

   Even if we do not select all samples, we can expect the mean of the distribution of sample means to be close to the population mean.
2. There will be less dispersion in the sampling distribution of the sample mean than in the population. If the standard deviation of the population is σ, the standard deviation of the distribution of sample means is $\sigma/\sqrt{n}$. Note that when we increase the size of the sample, the standard error of the mean decreases.

SELF-REVIEW 8–4

Refer to the Spence Sprockets Inc. data on page 264. Select 10 random samples of five employees each. Use the methods described earlier in the chapter and the Table of Random Numbers (Appendix B.4) to find the employees to include in the sample. Compute the mean of each sample and plot the sample means on a chart similar to Chart 8–4. What is the mean of your 10 sample means?

EXERCISES

11. Appendix B.4 is a table of random numbers that are uniformly distributed. Hence, each digit from 0 to 9 has the same likelihood of occurrence.
   a. Draw a graph showing the population distribution of random numbers. What is the population mean?
   b. Following are the first 10 rows of five digits from the table of random numbers in Appendix B.4. Assume that these are 10 random samples of five values each. Determine

the mean of each sample and plot the means on a chart similar to Chart 8–4. Compare the mean of the sampling distribution of the sample mean with the population mean.

0	2	7	1	1
9	4	8	7	3
5	4	9	2	1
7	7	6	4	0
6	1	5	4	5
1	7	1	4	7
1	3	7	4	8
8	7	4	5	5
0	8	9	9	9
7	8	8	0	4

For **DATA FILE**, please visit www.mhhe.com/lind16e

12. Scrapper Elevator Company has 20 sales representatives who sell its product throughout the United States and Canada. The number of units sold last month by each representative is listed below. Assume these sales figures to be the population values.

2	3	2	3	3	4	2	4	3	2	2	7	3	4	5	3	3	3	3	5

a. Draw a graph showing the population distribution.
b. Compute the mean of the population.
c. Select five random samples of 5 each. Compute the mean of each sample. Use the methods described in this chapter and Appendix B.4 to determine the items to be included in the sample.
d. Compare the mean of the sampling distribution of the sample mean to the population mean. Would you expect the two values to be about the same?
e. Draw a histogram of the sample means. Do you notice a difference in the shape of the distribution of sample means compared to the shape of the population distribution?

13. Consider all of the coins (pennies, nickels, quarters, etc.) in your pocket or purse as a population. Make a frequency table beginning with the current year and counting backward to record the ages (in years) of the coins. For example, if the current year is 2013, then a coin with 2011 stamped on it is 2 years old.
a. Draw a histogram or other graph showing the population distribution.
b. Randomly select five coins and record the mean age of the sampled coins. Repeat this sampling process 20 times. Now draw a histogram or other graph showing the distribution of the sample means.
c. Compare the shapes of the two histograms.

14. Consider the digits in the phone numbers on a randomly selected page of your local phone book a population. Make a frequency table of the final digit of 30 randomly selected phone numbers. For example, if a phone number is 555-9704, record a 4.
a. Draw a histogram or other graph of this population distribution. Using the uniform distribution, compute the population mean and the population standard deviation.
b. Also record the sample mean of the final four digits (9704 would lead to a mean of 5). Now draw a histogram or other graph showing the distribution of the sample means.
c. Compare the shapes of the two histograms.

LO8-5
Apply the central limit theorem to calculate probabilities.

USING THE SAMPLING DISTRIBUTION OF THE SAMPLE MEAN

The previous discussion is important because most business decisions are made on the basis of sample information. Here are some examples.

1. Arm & Hammer Company wants to ensure that its laundry detergent actually contains 100 fluid ounces, as indicated on the label. Historical summaries from

the filling process indicate the mean amount per container is 100 fluid ounces and the standard deviation is 2 fluid ounces. The quality technician in her 10 a.m. check of 40 containers finds the mean amount per container is 99.8 fluid ounces. Should the technician shut down the filling operation?

2. A. C. Nielsen Company provides information to organizations advertising on television. Prior research indicates that adult Americans watch an average of 6.0 hours per day of television. The standard deviation is 1.5 hours. For a sample of 50 adults in the greater Boston area, would it be reasonable that we could randomly select a sample and find that they watch an average of 6.5 hours or more of television per day?
3. Haughton Elevator Company wishes to develop specifications for the number of people who can ride in a new oversized elevator. Suppose the mean weight for an adult is 160 pounds and the standard deviation is 15 pounds. However, the distribution of weights does not follow the normal probability distribution. It is positively skewed. What is the likelihood that for a sample of 30 adults their mean weight is 170 pounds or more?

We can answer the questions in each of these situations using the ideas discussed in the previous section. In each case, we have a population with information about its mean and standard deviation. Using this information and sample size, we can determine the distribution of sample means and compute the probability that a sample mean will fall within a certain range. The sampling distribution will be normally distributed under two conditions:

1. When the samples are taken from populations known to follow the normal distribution. In this case, the size of the sample is not a factor.
2. When the shape of the population distribution is not known or the shape is known to be nonnormal, sample size is important. In general, the sampling distribution will be normally distributed as the sample size approaches infinity. In practice, a sampling distribution will be close to a normal distribution with samples of at least 30 observations.

We use formula (7–5) from the previous chapter to convert any normal distribution to the standard normal distribution. Using formula (7–5) to compute z values, we can use the standard normal table, Appendix B.3, to find the probability that an observation is within a specific range. The formula for finding a z value is:

$$z = \frac{x - \mu}{\sigma}$$

In this formula, x is the value of the random variable, μ is the population mean, and σ is the population standard deviation.

However, most business decisions refer to a sample—not just one observation. So we are interested in the distribution of $\overline{X}$, the sample mean, instead of X, the value of one observation. That is the first change we make in formula (7–5). The second is that we use the standard error of the mean of n observations instead of the population standard deviation. That is, we use $\sigma/\sqrt{n}$ in the denominator rather than σ. Therefore, to find the likelihood of a sample mean within a specified range, we first use the following formula to find the corresponding z value. Then we use Appendix B.3 or statistical software to determine the probability.

FINDING THE z VALUE OF $\overline{x}$ WHEN THE POPULATION STANDARD DEVIATION IS KNOWN

$$z = \frac{\overline{x} - \mu}{\sigma/\sqrt{n}} \qquad \textbf{[8–2]}$$

The following example/solution will show the application.

EXAMPLE

The Quality Assurance Department for Cola, Inc. maintains records regarding the amount of cola in its jumbo bottle. The actual amount of cola in each bottle is critical but varies a small amount from one bottle to the next. Cola, Inc. does not wish to underfill the bottles because it will have a problem with truth in labeling. On the other hand, it cannot overfill each bottle because it would be giving cola away, hence reducing its profits. Records maintained by the Quality Assurance Department indicate that the amount of cola follows the normal probability distribution. The mean amount per bottle is 31.2 ounces and the population standard deviation is 0.4 ounce. At 8 a.m. today the quality technician randomly selected 16 bottles from the filling line. The mean amount of cola contained in the bottles is 31.38 ounces. Is this an unlikely result? Is it likely the process is putting too much soda in the bottles? To put it another way, is the sampling error of 0.18 ounce unusual?

SOLUTION

We use the results of the previous section to find the likelihood that we could select a sample of 16 (n) bottles from a normal population with a mean of 31.2 (μ) ounces and a population standard deviation of 0.4 (σ) ounce and find the sample mean to be 31.38 ($\bar{x}$) or more. We use formula (8–2) to find the value of z.

$$z = \frac{\bar{x} - \mu}{\sigma/\sqrt{n}} = \frac{31.38 - 31.20}{0.4/\sqrt{16}} = 1.80$$

The numerator of this equation, $\bar{x} - \mu = 31.38 - 31.20 = .18$, is the sampling error. The denominator, $\sigma/\sqrt{n} = 0.4/\sqrt{16} = 0.1$, is the standard error of the sampling distribution of the sample mean. So the z values express the sampling error in standard units—in other words, the standard error.

Next, we compute the likelihood of a z value greater than 1.80. In Appendix B.3, locate the probability corresponding to a z value of 1.80. It is .4641. The likelihood of a z value greater than 1.80 is .0359, found by .5000 − .4641.

What do we conclude? It is unlikely, less than a 4% chance, we could select a sample of 16 observations from a normal population with a mean of 31.2 ounces and a population standard deviation of 0.4 ounce and find the sample mean equal to or greater than 31.38 ounces. We conclude the process is putting too much cola in the bottles. The quality technician should see the production supervisor about reducing the amount of soda in each bottle. This information is summarized in Chart 8–7.

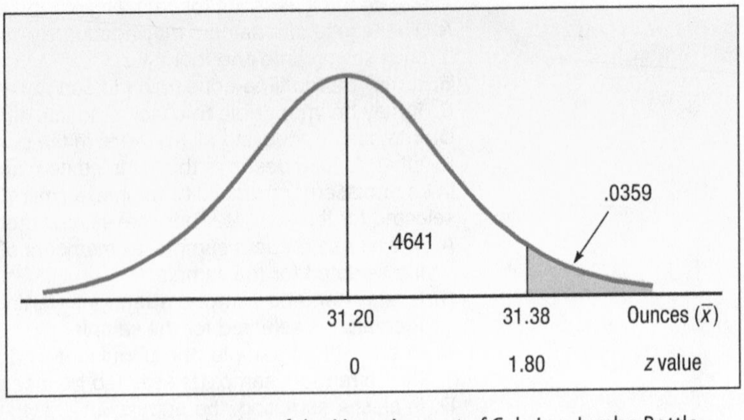

CHART 8–7 Sampling Distribution of the Mean Amount of Cola in a Jumbo Bottle

SELF-REVIEW 8–5

Refer to the Cola, Inc. information. Suppose the quality technician selected a sample of 16 jumbo bottles that averaged 31.08 ounces. What can you conclude about the filling process?

EXERCISES

15. A normal population has a mean of 60 and a standard deviation of 12. You select a random sample of 9. Compute the probability the sample mean is:
   a. Greater than 63.
   b. Less than 56.
   c. Between 56 and 63.

16. A normal population has a mean of 75 and a standard deviation of 5. You select a sample of 40. Compute the probability the sample mean is:
   a. Less than 74.
   b. Between 74 and 76.
   c. Between 76 and 77.
   d. Greater than 77.

17. In a certain section of Southern California, the distribution of monthly rent for a one-bedroom apartment has a mean of $2,200 and a standard deviation of $250. The distribution of the monthly rent does not follow the normal distribution. In fact, it is positively skewed. What is the probability of selecting a sample of 50 one-bedroom apartments and finding the mean to be at least $1,950 per month?

18. According to an IRS study, it takes a mean of 330 minutes for taxpayers to prepare, copy, and electronically file a 1040 tax form. This distribution of times follows the normal distribution and the standard deviation is 80 minutes. A consumer watchdog agency selects a random sample of 40 taxpayers.
   a. What is the standard error of the mean in this example?
   b. What is the likelihood the sample mean is greater than 320 minutes?
   c. What is the likelihood the sample mean is between 320 and 350 minutes?
   d. What is the likelihood the sample mean is greater than 350 minutes?

CHAPTER SUMMARY

I. There are many reasons for sampling a population.
   A. The results of a sample may adequately estimate the value of the population parameter, thus saving time and money.
   B. It may be too time-consuming to contact all members of the population.
   C. It may be impossible to check or locate all the members of the population.
   D. The cost of studying all the items in the population may be prohibitive.
   E. Often testing destroys the sampled item and it cannot be returned to the population.

II. In an unbiased or probability sample, all members of the population have a chance of being selected for the sample. There are several probability sampling methods.
   A. In a simple random sample, all members of the population have the same chance of being selected for the sample.
   B. In a systematic sample, a random starting point is selected, and then every *k*th item thereafter is selected for the sample.
   C. In a stratified sample, the population is divided into several groups, called strata, and then a random sample is selected from each stratum.
   D. In cluster sampling, the population is divided into primary units, then samples are drawn from the primary units.

III. The sampling error is the difference between a population parameter and a sample statistic.

IV. The sampling distribution of the sample mean is a probability distribution of all possible sample means of the same sample size.

A. For a given sample size, the mean of all possible sample means selected from a population is equal to the population mean.

B. There is less variation in the distribution of the sample mean than in the population distribution.

C. The standard error of the mean measures the variation in the sampling distribution of the sample mean. The standard error is found by:

$$\sigma_{\bar{X}} = \frac{\sigma}{\sqrt{n}} \quad \textbf{[8–1]}$$

D. If the population follows a normal distribution, the sampling distribution of the sample mean will also follow the normal distribution for samples of any size. If the population is not normally distributed, the sampling distribution of the sample mean will approach a normal distribution when the sample size is at least 30. Assume the population standard deviation is known. To determine the probability that a sample mean falls in a particular region, use the following formula.

$$z = \frac{\bar{x} - \mu}{\sigma/\sqrt{n}} \quad \textbf{[8–2]}$$

PRONUNCIATION KEY

SYMBOL	MEANING	PRONUNCIATION
$\mu_{\bar{X}}$	Mean of the sampling distribution of the sample mean	*mu sub x bar*
$\sigma_{\bar{X}}$	Population standard error of the sample mean	*sigma sub x bar*

CHAPTER EXERCISES

19. The 25 retail stores located in the North Towne Square Mall numbered 00 through 24 are:

00	Elder-Beerman	09	Lion Store	18	County Seat
01	Sears	10	Bootleggers	19	Kid Mart
02	Deb Shop	11	Formal Man	20	Lerner
03	Frederick's of Hollywood	12	Leather Ltd.	21	Coach House Gifts
04	Petries	13	B Dalton Bookseller	22	Spencer Gifts
05	Easy Dreams	14	Pat's Hallmark	23	CPI Photo Finish
06	Summit Stationers	15	Things Remembered	24	Regis Hairstylists
07	E. B. Brown Opticians	16	Pearle Vision Express		
08	Kay-Bee Toy & Hobby	17	Dollar Tree		

a. If the following random numbers are selected, which retail stores should be contacted for a survey? 11, 65, 86, 62, 06, 10, 12, 77, and 04

b. Select a random sample of four retail stores. Use Appendix B.4.

c. A systematic sampling procedure is to be used. The first store is to be contacted and then every third store. Which stores will be contacted?

20. The Medical Assurance Company is investigating the cost of a routine office visit to family-practice physicians in the Rochester, New York, area. The following is a list of 39 family-practice physicians in the region. Physicians are to be randomly selected and contacted regarding their charges. The 39 physicians have been coded from 00 to 38. Also noted is whether they are in practice by themselves (S), have a partner (P), or are in a group practice (G).

Number	Physician	Type of Practice	Number	Physician	Type of Practice
00	R. E. Scherbarth, M.D.	S	20	Gregory Yost, M.D.	P
01	Crystal R. Goveia, M.D.	P	21	J. Christian Zona, M.D.	P
02	Mark D. Hillard, M.D.	P	22	Larry Johnson, M.D.	P
03	Jeanine S. Huttner, M.D.	P	23	Sanford Kimmel, M.D.	P
04	Francis Aona, M.D.	P	24	Harry Mayhew, M.D.	S
05	Janet Arrowsmith, M.D.	P	25	Leroy Rodgers, M.D.	S
06	David DeFrance, M.D.	S	26	Thomas Tafelski, M.D.	S
07	Judith Furlong, M.D.	S	27	Mark Zilkoski, M.D.	G
08	Leslie Jackson, M.D.	G	28	Ken Bertka, M.D.	G
09	Paul Langenkamp, M.D.	S	29	Mark DeMichiei, M.D.	G
10	Philip Lepkowski, M.D.	S	30	John Eggert, M.D.	P
11	Wendy Martin, M.D.	S	31	Jeanne Fiorito, M.D.	P
12	Denny Mauricio, M.D.	P	32	Michael Fitzpatrick, M.D.	P
13	Hasmukh Parmar, M.D.	P	33	Charles Holt, D.O.	P
14	Ricardo Pena, M.D.	P	34	Richard Koby, M.D.	P
15	David Reames, M.D.	P	35	John Meier, M.D.	P
16	Ronald Reynolds, M.D.	G	36	Douglas Smucker, M.D.	S
17	Mark Steinmetz, M.D.	G	37	David Weldy, M.D.	P
18	Geza Torok, M.D.	S	38	Cheryl Zaborowski, M.D.	P
19	Mark Young, M.D.	P			

a. The random numbers obtained from Appendix B.4 are 31, 94, 43, 36, 03, 24, 17, and 09. Which physicians should be contacted?
b. Select a random sample of four physicians using the random numbers of Appendix B.4.
c. A sample is to consist of every fifth physician. The number 04 is selected as the starting point. Which physicians will be contacted?
d. A sample is to consist of two physicians in solo practice (S), two in partnership (P), and one in group practice (G). Select a sample accordingly. Explain your procedure.

21. A population consists of the following three values: 1, 2, and 3.
a. Sampling with replacement, list all possible samples of size 2 and compute the mean of every sample.
b. Find the means of the distribution of the sample mean and the population mean. Compare the two values.
c. Compare the dispersion of the population with that of the sample mean.
d. Describe the shapes of the two distributions.

22. In the Department of Education at UR University, student records suggest that the population of students spends an average of 5.5 hours per week playing organized sports. The population's standard deviation is 2.2 hours per week. Based on a sample of 121 students, Healthy Lifestyles Incorporated (HLI) would like to apply the central limit theorem to make various estimates.
a. Compute the standard error of the sample mean.
b. What is the chance HLI will find a sample mean between 5 and 6 hours?
c. Calculate the probability that the sample mean will be between 5.3 and 5.7 hours.
d. How strange would it be to obtain a sample mean greater than 6.5 hours?

23. The manufacturer of eComputers, an economy-priced computer, recently completed the design for a new laptop model. eComputer's top management would like some assistance in pricing the new laptop. Two market research firms were contacted and asked to prepare a pricing strategy. Marketing-Gets-Results tested the new eComputers laptop with 50 randomly selected consumers who indicated they plan to purchase a laptop within the next year. The second marketing research firm, called Marketing-Reaps-Profits, test-marketed the new eComputers laptop with 200 current laptop owners. Which of the marketing research companies' test results will be more useful? Discuss why.

24. Answer the following questions in one or two well-constructed sentences.
a. What happens to the standard error of the mean if the sample size is increased?
b. What happens to the distribution of the sample means if the sample size is increased?

c. When using the distribution of sample means to estimate the population mean, what is the benefit of using larger sample sizes?

25. There are 25 motels in Goshen, Indiana. The number of rooms in each motel follows:

90	72	75	60	75	72	84	72	88	74	105	115	68	74	80	64	104	82	48	58	60	80	48	58	100

a. Using a table of random numbers (Appendix B.4), select a random sample of five motels from this population.
b. Obtain a systematic sample by selecting a random starting point among the first five motels and then select every fifth motel.
c. Suppose the last five motels are "cut-rate" motels. Describe how you would select a random sample of three regular motels and two cut-rate motels.

26. As a part of their customer-service program, United Airlines randomly selected 10 passengers from today's 9 a.m. Chicago–Tampa flight. Each sampled passenger is to be interviewed in depth regarding airport facilities, service, and so on. To identify the sample, each passenger was given a number on boarding the aircraft. The numbers started with 001 and ended with 250.
a. Select 10 usable numbers at random using Appendix B.4.
b. The sample of 10 could have been chosen using a systematic sample. Choose the first number using Appendix B.4, and then list the numbers to be interviewed.
c. Evaluate the two methods by giving the advantages and possible disadvantages.
d. In what other way could a random sample be selected from the 250 passengers?

27. Suppose your statistics instructor gave six examinations during the semester. You received the following grades (percent correct): 79, 64, 84, 82, 92, and 77. Instead of averaging the six scores, the instructor indicated he would randomly select two grades and compute the final percent correct based on the two percents.
a. How many different samples of two test grades are possible?
b. List all possible samples of size 2 and compute the mean of each.
c. Compute the mean of the sample means and compare it to the population mean.
d. If you were a student, would you like this arrangement? Would the result be different from dropping the lowest score? Write a brief report.

28. At the downtown office of First National Bank, there are five tellers. Last week, the tellers made the following number of errors each: 2, 3, 5, 3, and 5.
a. How many different samples of two tellers are possible?
b. List all possible samples of size 2 and compute the mean of each.
c. Compute the mean of the sample means and compare it to the population mean.

29. The Quality Control Department employs five technicians during the day shift. Listed below is the number of times each technician instructed the production foreman to shut down the manufacturing process last week.

Technician	Shutdowns	Technician	Shutdowns
Taylor	4	Rousche	3
Hurley	3	Huang	2
Gupta	5		

a. How many different samples of two technicians are possible from this population?
b. List all possible samples of two observations each and compute the mean of each sample.
c. Compare the mean of the sample means with the population mean.
d. Compare the shape of the population distribution with the shape of the distribution of the sample means.

30. The Appliance Center has six sales representatives at its North Jacksonville outlet. Listed below is the number of refrigerators sold by each last month.

Sales Representative	Number Sold	Sales Representative	Number Sold
Zina Craft	54	Jan Niles	48
Woon Junge	50	Molly Camp	50
Ernie DeBrul	52	Rachel Myak	52

a. How many samples of size 2 are possible?
b. Select all possible samples of size 2 and compute the mean number sold.
c. Organize the sample means into a frequency distribution.
d. What is the mean of the population? What is the mean of the sample means?
e. What is the shape of the population distribution?
f. What is the shape of the distribution of the sample mean?

31. Power +, Inc. produces AA batteries used in remote-controlled toy cars. The mean life of these batteries follows the normal probability distribution with a mean of 35.0 hours and a standard deviation of 5.5 hours. As a part of its quality assurance program, Power +, Inc. tests samples of 25 batteries.
a. What can you say about the shape of the distribution of the sample mean?
b. What is the standard error of the distribution of the sample mean?
c. What proportion of the samples will have a mean useful life of more than 36 hours?
d. What proportion of the sample will have a mean useful life greater than 34.5 hours?
e. What proportion of the sample will have a mean useful life between 34.5 and 36.0 hours?

32. CRA CDs Inc. wants the mean lengths of the "cuts" on a CD to be 135 seconds (2 minutes and 15 seconds). This will allow the disk jockeys to have plenty of time for commercials within each 10-minute segment. Assume the distribution of the length of the cuts follows the normal distribution with a population standard deviation of 8 seconds. Suppose we select a sample of 16 cuts from various CDs sold by CRA CDs Inc.
a. What can we say about the shape of the distribution of the sample mean?
b. What is the standard error of the mean?
c. What percent of the sample means will be greater than 140 seconds?
d. What percent of the sample means will be greater than 128 seconds?
e. What percent of the sample means will be greater than 128 but less than 140 seconds?

33. Recent studies indicate that the typical 50-year-old woman spends $350 per year for personal-care products. The distribution of the amounts spent follows a normal distribution with a standard deviation of $45 per year. We select a random sample of 40 women. The mean amount spent for those sampled is $335. What is the likelihood of finding a sample mean this large or larger from the specified population?

34. Information from the American Institute of Insurance indicates the mean amount of life insurance per household in the United States is $110,000. This distribution follows the normal distribution with a standard deviation of $40,000.
a. If we select a random sample of 50 households, what is the standard error of the mean?
b. What is the expected shape of the distribution of the sample mean?
c. What is the likelihood of selecting a sample with a mean of at least $112,000?
d. What is the likelihood of selecting a sample with a mean of more than $100,000?
e. Find the likelihood of selecting a sample with a mean of more than $100,000 but less than $112,000.

35. The mean age at which men in the United States marry for the first time follows the normal distribution with a mean of 24.8 years. The standard deviation of the distribution is 2.5 years. For a random sample of 60 men, what is the likelihood that the age at which they were married for the first time is less than 25.1 years?

36. A recent study by the Greater Los Angeles Taxi Drivers Association showed that the mean fare charged for service from Hermosa Beach to Los Angeles International Airport is $21 and the standard deviation is $3.50. We select a sample of 15 fares.
a. What is the likelihood that the sample mean is between $20 and $23?
b. What must you assume to make the above calculation?

37. Crossett Trucking Company claims that the mean weight of its delivery trucks when they are fully loaded is 6,000 pounds and the standard deviation is 150 pounds. Assume that the population follows the normal distribution. Forty trucks are randomly selected and weighed. Within what limits will 95% of the sample means occur?

38. The mean amount purchased by a typical customer at Churchill's Grocery Store is $23.50, with a standard deviation of $5.00. Assume the distribution of amounts purchased follows the normal distribution. For a sample of 50 customers, answer the following questions.
a. What is the likelihood the sample mean is at least $25.00?
b. What is the likelihood the sample mean is greater than $22.50 but less than $25.00?
c. Within what limits will 90% of the sample means occur?

39. The mean performance score on a physical fitness test for Division I student-athletes is 947 with a standard deviation of 205. If you select a random sample of 60 of these students, what is the probability the mean is below 900?

40. Suppose we roll a fair die two times.

a. How many different samples are there?

b. List each of the possible samples and compute the mean.

c. On a chart similar to Chart 8–2, compare the distribution of sample means with the distribution of the population.

d. Compute the mean and the standard deviation of each distribution and compare them.

41. Following is a list of the 50 states with the numbers 0 through 49 assigned to them.

For **DATA FILE**, please visit www.mhhe.com/lind16e

Number	State	Number	State
0	Alabama	25	Montana
1	Alaska	26	Nebraska
2	Arizona	27	Nevada
3	Arkansas	28	New Hampshire
4	California	29	New Jersey
5	Colorado	30	New Mexico
6	Connecticut	31	New York
7	Delaware	32	North Carolina
8	Florida	33	North Dakota
9	Georgia	34	Ohio
10	Hawaii	35	Oklahoma
11	Idaho	36	Oregon
12	Illinois	37	Pennsylvania
13	Indiana	38	Rhode Island
14	Iowa	39	South Carolina
15	Kansas	40	South Dakota
16	Kentucky	41	Tennessee
17	Louisiana	42	Texas
18	Maine	43	Utah
19	Maryland	44	Vermont
20	Massachusetts	45	Virginia
21	Michigan	46	Washington
22	Minnesota	47	West Virginia
23	Mississippi	48	Wisconsin
24	Missouri	49	Wyoming

a. You wish to select a sample of eight from this list. The selected random numbers are 45, 15, 81, 09, 39, 43, 90, 26, 06, 45, 01, and 42. Which states are included in the sample?

b. You wish to use a systematic sample of every sixth item and the digit 02 is chosen as the starting point. Which states are included?

42. Human Resource Consulting (HRC) surveyed a random sample of 60 Twin Cities construction companies to find information on the costs of their health care plans. One of the items being tracked is the annual deductible that employees must pay. The Minnesota Department of Labor reports that historically the mean deductible amount per employee is $502 with a standard deviation of $100.

a. Compute the standard error of the sample mean for HRC.

b. What is the chance HRC finds a sample mean between $477 and $527?

c. Calculate the likelihood that the sample mean is between $492 and $512.

d. What is the probability the sample mean is greater than $550?

43. Over the past decade, the mean number of hacking attacks experienced by members of the Information Systems Security Association is 510 per year with a standard deviation of 14.28 attacks. The number of attacks per year is normally distributed. Suppose nothing in this environment changes.

a. What is the likelihood this group will suffer an average of more than 600 attacks in the next 10 years?

b. Compute the probability the mean number of attacks over the next 10 years is between 500 and 600.

c. What is the possibility they will experience an average of less than 500 attacks over the next 10 years?

STATISTICS IN ACTION

On all new cars, a fuel economy estimate is prominently displayed on the window sticker as required by the Environmental Protection Agency (EPA). Often, fuel economy is a factor in a consumer's choice of a new car because of fuel costs or environmental concerns. The fuel estimates for a 2010 BMW 328i Sedan (6-cylinder, automatic) are 18 miles per gallon (mpg) in the city and 28 on the highway. The EPA recognizes that actual fuel economy may differ from the estimates by noting, "No test can simulate all possible combinations of conditions and climate, driver behavior, and car care habits. Actual mileage depends on how, when, and where the vehicle is driven. The EPA has found that the mpg obtained by most drivers will be within a few mpg of the estimates." In fact, the window sticker also includes an interval estimate for fuel economy: 14 to 22 mpg in the city and 23 to 33 mpg on the highway.

INTRODUCTION

The previous chapter began our discussion of statistical inference. We introduced both the reasons for, and the methods of, sampling. The reasons for sampling were:

- Contacting the entire population is too time-consuming.
- Studying all the items in the population is often too expensive.
- The sample results are usually adequate.
- Certain tests are destructive.
- Checking all the items is physically impossible.

There are several methods of sampling. Simple random sampling is the most widely used method. With this type of sampling, each member of the population has the same chance of being selected to be a part of the sample. Other methods of sampling include systematic sampling, stratified sampling, and cluster sampling.

Chapter 8 assumes information about the population, such as the mean, the standard deviation, or the shape of the population, is known. In most business situations, such information is not available. In fact, the purpose of sampling may be to estimate some of these values. For example, you select a sample from a population and use the mean of the sample to estimate the mean of the population.

This chapter considers several important aspects of sampling. We begin by studying **point estimates.** A point estimate is a single value (point) derived from a sample and used to estimate a population value. For example, suppose we select a sample of 50 junior executives and ask how many hours they worked last week. Compute the mean of this sample of 50 and use the value of the sample mean as a point estimate of the unknown population mean. However, a point estimate is a single value. A more informative approach is to present a range of values where we expect the population parameter to occur. Such a range of values is called a **confidence interval.**

Frequently in business we need to determine the size of a sample. How many voters should a polling organization contact to forecast the election outcome? How many products do we need to examine to ensure our quality level? This chapter also develops a strategy for determining the appropriate number of observations in the sample.

POINT ESTIMATE FOR A POPULATION MEAN

LO9-1 Compute and interpret a point estimate of a population mean.

A point estimate is a single statistic used to estimate a population parameter. Suppose Best Buy Inc. wants to estimate the mean age of people who purchase LCD HDTV televisions. They select a random sample of 50 recent purchases, determine the age of each buyer, and compute the mean age of the buyers in the sample. The mean of this sample is a point estimate of the population mean.

POINT ESTIMATE The statistic, computed from sample information, that estimates a population parameter.

The following examples illustrate point estimates of population means.

1. Tourism is a major source of income for many Caribbean countries, such as Barbados. Suppose the Bureau of Tourism for Barbados wants an estimate of the mean amount spent by tourists visiting the country. It would not be feasible to contact each tourist. Therefore, 500 tourists are randomly selected as they depart the country and asked in detail about their spending while visiting Barbados. The mean amount spent by the sample of 500 tourists is an estimate of the unknown population parameter. That is, we let the sample mean serve as a point estimate of the population mean.

2. Litchfield Home Builders Inc. builds homes in the southeastern region of the United States. One of the major concerns of new buyers is the date when the home will be completed. Recently, Litchfield has been telling customers, "Your home will be completed 45 working days from the date we begin installing drywall." The customer relations department at Litchfield wishes to compare this pledge with recent experience. A sample of 50 homes completed this year revealed that the point estimate of the population mean is 46.7 working days from the start of drywall to the completion of the home. Is it reasonable to conclude that the population mean is still 45 days and that the difference between the sample mean (46.7 days) and the proposed population mean (45 days) is sampling error? In other words, is the sample mean significantly different from the population mean?

3. Recent medical studies indicate that exercise is an important part of a person's overall health. The director of human resources at OCF, a large glass manufacturer, wants an estimate of the number of hours per week employees spend exercising. A sample of 70 employees reveals the mean number of hours of exercise last week is 3.3. This value is a point estimate of the unknown population mean.

The sample mean, $\bar{x}$, is not the only point estimate of a population parameter. For example, p, a sample proportion, is a point estimate of π, the population proportion; and s, the sample standard deviation, is a point estimate of σ, the population standard deviation.

LO9-2
Compute and interpret a confidence interval for a population mean.

CONFIDENCE INTERVALS FOR A POPULATION MEAN

A point estimate, however, tells only part of the story. While we expect the point estimate to be close to the population parameter, we would like to measure how close it really is. A confidence interval serves this purpose. For example, we estimate the mean yearly income for construction workers in the New York–New Jersey area is \$85,000. The range of this estimate might be from \$81,000 to \$89,000. We can describe how confident we are that the population parameter is in the interval. We might say, for instance, that we are 90% confident that the mean yearly income of construction workers in the New York–New Jersey area is between \$81,000 and \$89,000.

CONFIDENCE INTERVAL A range of values constructed from sample data so that the population parameter is likely to occur within that range at a specified probability. The specified probability is called the *level of confidence*.

To compute a confidence interval for a population mean, we will consider two situations:

- We use sample data to estimate μ with $\bar{x}$, and the population standard deviation (σ) is known.
- We use sample data to estimate μ with $\bar{x}$, and the population standard deviation is unknown. In this case, we substitute the sample standard deviation (s) for the population standard deviation (σ).

There are important distinctions in the assumptions between these two situations. We first consider the case where σ is known.

Population Standard Deviation, Known σ

A confidence interval is computed using two statistics: the sample mean, $\bar{x}$, and the standard deviation. From previous chapters, you know that the standard deviation is an important statistic because it measures the dispersion, or variation, of a population or sample distribution. In computing a confidence interval, the standard deviation is used to compute the limits of the confidence interval.

To demonstrate the idea of a confidence interval, we start with one simplifying assumption. That assumption is that we know the value of the population standard deviation, σ. Typically, we know the population standard deviation in situations where we have a long history of collected data. Examples are data from monitoring processes that fill soda bottles or cereal boxes, and the results of the SAT Reasoning Test (for college admission). Knowing σ allows us to simplify the development of a confidence interval because we can use the standard normal distribution from Chapter 8.

Recall that the sampling distribution of the sample mean is the distribution of all sample means, $\bar{x}$, of sample size n from a population. The population standard deviation, σ, is known. From this information, and the central limit theorem, we know that the sampling distribution follows the normal probability distribution with a mean of μ and a standard deviation $\sigma/\sqrt{n}$. Also recall that this value is called the standard error.

The results of the central limit theorem allow us to make the following general confidence interval statements using z-statistics:

1. Ninety-five percent of all confidence intervals computed from random samples selected from a population will contain the population mean. These intervals are computed using a z-statistic equal to 1.96.
2. Ninety percent of all confidence intervals computed from random samples selected from a population will contain the population mean. These confidence intervals are computed using a z-statistic equal to 1.65.

These confidence interval statements provide examples of *levels of confidence* and are called a **95% confidence interval** and a **90% confidence interval.** The *95%* and *90%* are the levels of confidence and refer to the percentage of similarly constructed intervals that would include the parameter being estimated—in this case, μ, the population mean.

How are the values of 1.96 and 1.65 obtained? First, let's look for the z value for a 95% confidence interval. The following diagram and Table 9–1 will help explain. Table 9–1 is a reproduction of Appendix B.3, the standard normal table. However, many rows and columns have been eliminated to allow us to better focus on particular rows and columns.

1. First, we divide the confidence level in half, so .9500/2 = .4750.
2. Next, we find the value .4750 in the body of Table 9–1. Note that .4750 is located in the table at the intersection of a row and a column.
3. Locate the corresponding row value in the left margin, which is 1.9, and the column value in the top margin, which is .06. Adding the row and column values gives us a z value of 1.96.
4. Thus, the probability of finding a z value between 0 and 1.96 is .4750.
5. Likewise, because the normal distribution is symmetric, the probability of finding a z value between -1.96 and 0 is also .4750.
6. When we add these two probabilities, the probability that a z value is between -1.96 and 1.96 is .9500.

For the 90% level of confidence, we follow the same steps. First, one-half of the desired confidence interval is .4500. A search of Table 9–1 does not reveal this exact value. However, it is between two values, .4495 and .4505. As in step three,

we locate each value in the table. The first, .4495, corresponds to a z value of 1.64 and the second, .4505, corresponds to a z value of 1.65. To be conservative, we will select the larger of the two z values, 1.65, and the exact level of confidence is 90.1%, or 2(0.4505). Next, the probability of finding a z value between −1.65 and 0 is .4505, and the probability that a z value is between −1.65 and 1.65 is .9010.

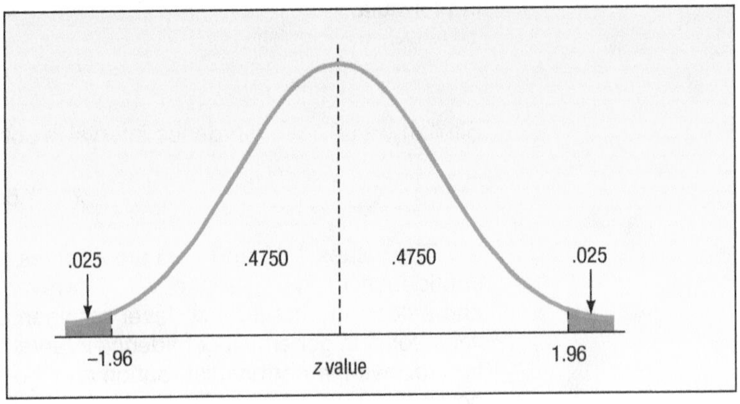

TABLE 9–1 The Standard Normal Table for Selected Values

z	0.00	0.01	0.02	0.03	0.04	0.05	0.06	0.07
⋮	⋮	⋮	⋮	⋮	⋮	⋮	⋮	⋮
1.5	0.4332	0.4345	0.4357	0.4370	0.4382	0.4394	0.4406	0.4418
1.6	0.4452	0.4463	0.4474	0.4484	0.4495	0.4505	0.4515	0.4525
1.7	0.4554	0.4564	0.4573	0.4582	0.4591	0.4599	0.4608	0.4616
1.8	0.4641	0.4649	0.4656	0.4664	0.4671	0.4678	0.4686	0.4693
1.9	0.4713	0.4719	0.4726	0.4732	0.4738	0.4744	0.4750	0.4756
2.0	0.4772	0.4778	0.4783	0.4788	0.4793	0.4798	0.4803	0.4808
2.1	0.4821	0.4826	0.4830	0.4834	0.4838	0.4842	0.4846	0.4850
2.2	0.4861	0.4864	0.4868	0.4871	0.4875	0.4878	0.4881	0.4884

How do we determine a 95% confidence interval? The width of the interval is determined by two factors: (1) the level of confidence, as described in the previous section, and (2) the size of the standard error of the mean. To find the standard error of the mean, recall from the previous chapter [see formula (8–1) on page 268] that the standard error of the mean reports the variation in the distribution of sample means. It is really the standard deviation of the distribution of sample means. The formula is repeated below:

$$\sigma_{\bar{x}} = \frac{\sigma}{\sqrt{n}}$$

where:

- $\sigma_{\bar{x}}$ is the symbol for the standard error of the mean. We use a Greek letter because it is a population value, and the subscript $\bar{x}$ reminds us that it refers to a sampling distribution of the sample means.
- σ is the population standard deviation.
- n is the number of observations in the sample.

The size of the standard error is affected by two values. The first is the standard deviation of the population. The larger the population standard deviation, σ, the larger $\sigma/\sqrt{n}$. If the population is homogeneous, resulting in a small population standard deviation, the standard error will also be small. However, the standard error is also affected by the number of observations in the sample. A large number of observations in the sample will result in a small standard error of estimate, indicating that there is less variability in the sample means.

We can summarize the calculation for a 95% confidence interval using the following formula:

$$\bar{x} \pm 1.96 \frac{\sigma}{\sqrt{n}}$$

Similarly, a 90.1% confidence interval is computed as follows:

$$\bar{x} \pm 1.65 \frac{\sigma}{\sqrt{n}}$$

The values 1.96 and 1.65 are z values corresponding to the 95% and the 90.1% confidence intervals, respectively. However, we are not restricted to these values. We can select any confidence level between 0 and 100% and find the corresponding value for z. In general, a confidence interval for the population mean when the population follows the normal distribution and the population standard deviation is known is computed by:

CONFIDENCE INTERVAL FOR A POPULATION MEAN WITH σ KNOWN

$$\bar{x} \pm z \frac{\sigma}{\sqrt{n}} \quad \textbf{[9–1]}$$

To explain these ideas, consider the following example. Del Monte Foods distributes diced peaches in 4.5-ounce plastic cups. To ensure that each cup contains at least the required amount, Del Monte sets the filling operation to dispense 4.51 ounces of peaches and gel in each cup. Of course, not every cup will contain exactly 4.51 ounces of peaches and gel. Some cups will have more and others less. From historical data, Del Monte knows that 0.04 ounce is the standard deviation of the filling process and that the amount, in ounces, follows the normal probability distribution. The quality control technician selects a sample of 64 cups at the start of each shift, measures the amount in each cup, computes the mean fill amount, and then develops a 95% confidence interval for the population mean. Using the confidence interval, is the process filling the cups to the desired amount? This morning's sample of 64 cups had a sample mean of 4.507 ounces. Based on this information, the 95% confidence interval is:

$$\bar{x} \pm 1.96 \frac{\sigma}{\sqrt{n}} = 4.507 \pm 1.96 \frac{0.04}{\sqrt{64}} = 4.507 \pm 0.0098$$

The 95% confidence interval estimates that the population mean is between 4.4972 ounces and 4.5168 ounces of peaches and gel. Recall that the process is set to fill each cup with 4.51 ounces. Because the desired fill amount of 4.51 ounces is in this interval, we conclude that the filling process is achieving the desired results. In other words, it is reasonable to conclude that the sample mean of 4.507 could have come from a population distribution with a mean of 4.51 ounces.

In this example, we observe that the population mean of 4.51 ounces is in the confidence interval. But this is not always the case. If we selected 100 samples of

64 cups from the population, calculated the sample mean, and developed a confidence interval based on each sample, we would expect to find the population mean in about 95 of the 100 intervals. Or, in contrast, about five of the intervals would not contain the population mean. From Chapter 8, this is called sampling error. The following example details repeated sampling from a population.

EXAMPLE

The American Management Association is studying the income of store managers in the retail industry. A random sample of 49 managers reveals a sample mean of $45,420. The standard deviation of this population is $2,050. The association would like answers to the following questions:

1. What is the population mean?
2. What is a reasonable range of values for the population mean?
3. How do we interpret these results?

SOLUTION

Generally, distributions of salary and income are positively skewed because a few individuals earn considerably more than others, thus skewing the distribution in the positive direction. Fortunately, the central limit theorem states that the sampling distribution of the mean becomes a normal distribution as sample size increases. In this instance, a sample of 49 store managers is large enough that we can assume that the sampling distribution will follow the normal distribution. Now to answer the questions posed in the example.

1. **What is the population mean?** In this case, we do not know. We do know the sample mean is $45,420. Hence, our best estimate of the unknown population value is the corresponding sample statistic. Thus, the sample mean of $45,420 is a *point estimate* of the unknown population mean.
2. **What is a reasonable range of values for the population mean?** The association decides to use the 95% level of confidence. To determine the corresponding confidence interval, we use formula (9–1):

$$\bar{x} \pm z\frac{\sigma}{\sqrt{n}} = \$45{,}420 \pm 1.96\frac{\$2{,}050}{\sqrt{49}} = \$45{,}420 \pm \$574$$

   The confidence interval limits are $44,846 and $45,994. The degree or level of confidence is 95% and the confidence interval is from $44,846 to $45,994. The ±$574 is called the margin of error.
3. **How do we interpret these results?** Suppose we select many samples of 49 store managers, perhaps several hundred. For each sample, we compute the mean and then construct a 95% confidence interval, such as we did in the previous section. We could expect about 95% of these confidence intervals to contain the *population* mean. About 5% of the intervals would not contain the population mean annual income, which is μ. However, a particular confidence interval either contains the population parameter or it does not. The following diagram shows the results of selecting samples from the population of store managers in the retail industry, computing the mean of each, and then, using formula (9–1), determining a 95% confidence interval for the population mean. Note that not all intervals include the population mean. Both the endpoints of the fifth sample are less than the population mean. We attribute this to sampling error, and it is the risk we assume when we select the level of confidence.

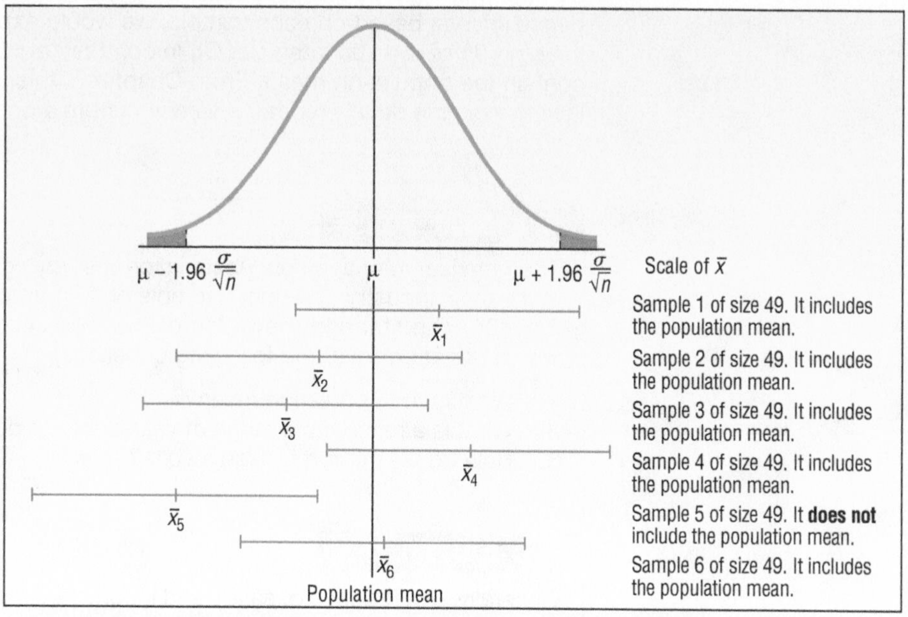

A Computer Simulation

With the aid of a computer, we can easily create random samples of a desired sample size, *n,* from a population. For each sample of *n* observations with corresponding numerical values, we can calculate the sample mean. With the sample mean, population standard deviation, and confidence level, we can determine the confidence interval for each sample. Then, using all samples and the confidence intervals, we can find the frequency that the population mean is included in the confidence intervals. The following example does just that.

EXAMPLE

From many years in the automobile leasing business, Town Bank knows that the mean distance driven on an automobile with a four-year lease is 50,000 miles and the standard deviation is 5,000 miles. These are population values. Suppose Town Bank would like to experiment with the idea of sampling to estimate the population mean of 50,000 miles. Town Bank decides to choose a sample size of 30 observations and a 95% confidence interval to estimate the population mean. Based on the experiment, we want to find the proportion of 95% confidence intervals that include the population mean of 50,000. We expect about 95%, or 57 of the 60 intervals, will include the population mean. To make the calculations easier to understand, we'll conduct the study in thousands of miles, instead of miles.

SOLUTION

Using statistical software, 60 random samples with a sample size of 30 are generated and the sample means for each sample computed. Then, using the *n* of 30 and a standard error of 0.913 ($\sigma/\sqrt{n} = 5/\sqrt{30}$), a 95% confidence interval is computed for each sample. The results of the experiment are shown next.

	Sample Observations													Sample	95% Confidence Limits	
Sample	1	2	3	4	5	–	–	–	26	27	28	29	30	Mean	Lower Limit	Upper Limit
1	56	47	47	48	58	–	–	–	55	62	48	61	57	51.6	49.811	53.389
2	55	51	52	40	53	–	–	–	47	54	55	55	45	50.77	48.981	52.559
3	42	46	48	46	41	–	–	–	50	52	50	47	45	48.63	46.841	50.419
4	52	49	55	47	49	–	–	–	46	56	49	43	50	49.9	48.111	51.689
5	48	50	53	48	45	–	–	–	46	51	61	49	47	49.03	47.241	50.819
6	**49**	**44**	**47**	**46**	**48**	–	–	–	**51**	**44**	**51**	**52**	**43**	**47.73**	45.941	49.519
7	50	53	39	50	46	–	–	–	55	47	43	50	57	50.2	48.411	51.989
8	47	51	49	58	44	–	–	–	49	57	54	48	48	51.17	49.381	52.959
9	51	44	47	56	45	–	–	–	45	51	49	49	52	50.33	48.541	52.119
10	45	44	52	52	56	–	–	–	52	51	52	50	48	50	48.211	51.789
11	43	52	54	46	54	–	–	–	43	46	49	52	52	51.2	49.411	52.989
12	57	53	48	42	55	–	–	–	49	44	46	46	48	49.8	48.011	51.589
13	53	39	47	51	53	–	–	–	42	44	44	55	58	49.6	47.811	51.389
14	56	55	45	43	57	–	–	–	48	51	52	55	47	49.03	47.241	50.819
15	49	50	39	45	44	–	–	–	49	43	44	51	51	49.37	47.581	51.159
16	46	44	55	53	55	–	–	–	44	53	53	43	44	50.13	48.341	51.919
17	**64**	**52**	**55**	**55**	**43**	–	–	–	**58**	**46**	**52**	**58**	**55**	**52.47**	50.681	54.259
18	57	51	60	40	53	–	–	–	50	51	53	46	52	50.1	48.311	51.889
19	50	49	51	57	45	–	–	–	53	52	40	45	52	49.6	47.811	51.389
20	45	46	53	57	49	–	–	–	49	43	43	53	48	49.47	47.681	51.259
21	52	45	51	52	45	–	–	–	43	49	49	58	53	50.43	48.641	52.219
22	**48**	**48**	**52**	**49**	**40**	–	–	–	**50**	**47**	**54**	**51**	**45**	**47.53**	45.741	49.319
23	48	50	50	53	44	–	–	–	48	57	52	44	39	49.1	47.311	50.889
24	51	51	40	54	52	–	–	–	54	45	50	57	48	50.13	48.341	51.919
25	48	63	41	52	41	–	–	–	48	50	48	44	53	49.33	47.541	51.119
26	47	45	48	59	49	–	–	–	44	47	49	55	42	49.63	47.841	51.419
27	52	45	60	51	52	–	–	–	52	50	54	46	52	49.4	47.611	51.189
28	46	48	46	57	51	–	–	–	51	50	51	41	52	49.33	47.541	51.119
29	46	48	45	42	48	–	–	–	49	43	59	46	50	48.27	46.481	50.059
30	55	48	47	48	48	–	–	–	47	59	54	51	42	50.53	48.741	52.319
31	58	49	56	46	46	–	–	–	44	51	47	51	46	50.77	48.981	52.559
32	53	54	52	58	55	–	–	–	53	52	45	44	51	50	48.211	51.789
33	50	57	56	51	51	–	–	–	58	47	50	56	46	49.7	47.911	51.489
34	61	48	49	53	54	–	–	–	46	46	56	45	54	50.03	48.241	51.819
35	43	42	43	46	49	–	–	–	49	49	56	51	45	49.43	47.641	51.219
36	39	48	48	51	44	–	–	–	54	52	47	50	52	50.07	48.281	51.859
37	48	43	57	42	54	–	–	–	52	50	59	50	52	50.17	48.381	51.959
38	55	43	49	57	45	–	–	–	41	51	51	52	52	49.5	47.711	51.289
39	47	49	58	54	54	–	–	–	50	56	51	56	58	50.37	48.581	52.159
40	47	56	41	50	54	–	–	–	46	56	61	61	45	51.6	49.811	53.389
41	48	47	42	47	62	–	–	–	44	47	49	55	43	49.43	47.641	51.219
42	**46**	**49**	**43**	**36**	**52**	–	–	–	**45**	**51**	**46**	**51**	**43**	**47.67**	45.881	49.459
43	44	48	49	48	51	–	–	–	47	52	51	48	49	49.63	47.841	51.419
44	45	52	54	54	49	–	–	–	49	45	53	50	52	49.07	47.281	50.859
45	54	46	54	45	48	–	–	–	55	38	56	50	62	49.53	47.741	51.319
46	48	50	49	52	51	–	–	–	53	57	58	46	50	49.9	48.111	51.689
47	54	55	46	55	50	–	–	–	56	54	50	55	51	50.5	48.711	52.289
48	45	47	47	63	44	–	–	–	45	53	42	53	50	50.1	48.311	51.889
49	47	47	48	54	56	–	–	–	50	48	54	49	51	49.93	48.141	51.719
50	45	61	51	45	54	–	–	–	55	52	47	45	53	51.03	49.241	52.819
51	49	62	43	49	48	–	–	–	49	58	42	58	52	51.07	49.281	52.859
52	54	52	62	43	54	–	–	–	51	57	49	58	55	50.17	48.381	51.959

(continued)

53	46	50	59	56	46	–	–	–	50	51	52	54	53	50.47	48.681	52.259
54	52	50	48	48	58	–	–	–	58	52	43	61	54	51.77	49.981	53.559
55	45	44	46	56	46	–	–	–	43	45	63	48	56	49.37	47.581	51.159
56	60	50	56	51	43	–	–	–	45	43	49	59	54	50.37	48.581	52.159
57	59	56	43	47	52	–	–	–	49	54	50	50	57	49.53	47.741	51.319
58	52	55	48	51	40	–	–	–	53	51	51	52	47	49.77	47.981	51.559
59	53	50	44	53	52	–	–	–	47	50	55	46	51	50.07	48.281	51.859
60	55	54	50	52	43	–	–	–	57	50	48	47	53	52.07	50.281	53.859

To explain, in the first row, the computer software computed 30 random observations based on a distribution with a mean of 50 and a standard deviation of 5. To conserve space, only observations 1 through 5 and 26 through 30 are listed. The first sample's mean is computed and listed as 51.6. In the next columns, the upper and lower limits of the 95% confidence interval for the first sample are shown. The confidence interval calculation for the first sample follows:

$$\bar{x} \pm 1.96\frac{\sigma}{\sqrt{n}} = 51.6 \pm 1.96\frac{5}{\sqrt{30}} = 51.6 \pm 1.789$$

This calculation is repeated for all the other samples. The results of the experiment show that 56, or 93.33%, of the sixty 95% confidence intervals include the population mean of 50. Four, or 6.67%, do not include the population mean. The 6.67% is close to the estimate that 5% of the intervals will not include the population mean. The particular intervals are samples 6, 17, 22, and 42. They are highlighted in yellow. This is another example of sampling error, or the possibility that a particular random sample may not be a good representation of the population and that the confidence interval based on the sample does not include the value of the population parameter.

SELF-REVIEW 9–1

The Bun-and-Run is a franchise fast-food restaurant located in the Northeast specializing in half-pound hamburgers, fish sandwiches, and chicken sandwiches. Soft drinks and French fries are also available. The Planning Department of Bun-and-Run Inc. reports that the distribution of daily sales for restaurants follows the normal distribution and that the population standard deviation is $3,000. A sample of 40 showed the mean daily sales to be $20,000.

(a) What is the population mean?
(b) What is the best estimate of the population mean? What is this value called?
(c) Develop a 95% confidence interval for the population mean.
(d) Interpret the confidence interval.

EXERCISES

1. A sample of 49 observations is taken from a normal population with a standard deviation of 10. The sample mean is 55. Determine the 99% confidence interval for the population mean.
2. A sample of 81 observations is taken from a normal population with a standard deviation of 5. The sample mean is 40. Determine the 95% confidence interval for the population mean.
3. A sample of 250 observations is selected from a normal population for which the population standard deviation is known to be 25. The sample mean is 20.
   - **a.** Determine the standard error of the mean.
   - **b.** Explain why we can use formula (9–1) to determine the 95% confidence interval.
   - **c.** Determine the 95% confidence interval for the population mean.
4. Suppose you know σ and you want an 85% confidence level. What value would you use as z in formula (9–1)?

5. A research firm conducted a survey to determine the mean amount steady smokers spend on cigarettes during a week. They found the distribution of amounts spent per week followed the normal distribution with a population standard deviation of \$5. A sample of 49 steady smokers revealed that $\bar{x}$ = \$20.
   a. What is the point estimate of the population mean? Explain what it indicates.
   b. Using the 95% level of confidence, determine the confidence interval for μ. Explain what it indicates.
6. Refer to the previous exercise. Suppose that 64 smokers (instead of 49) were sampled. Assume the sample mean remained the same.
   a. What is the 95% confidence interval estimate of μ?
   b. Explain why this confidence interval is narrower than the one determined in the previous exercise.
7. Bob Nale is the owner of Nale's Quick Fill. Bob would like to estimate the mean number of gallons of gasoline sold to his customers. Assume the number of gallons sold follows the normal distribution with a population standard deviation of 2.30 gallons. From his records, he selects a random sample of 60 sales and finds the mean number of gallons sold is 8.60.
   a. What is the point estimate of the population mean?
   b. Develop a 99% confidence interval for the population mean.
   c. Interpret the meaning of part (b).
8. Dr. Patton is a professor of English. Recently she counted the number of misspelled words in a group of student essays. She noted the distribution of misspelled words per essay followed the normal distribution with a population standard deviation of 2.44 words per essay. For her 10 a.m. section of 40 students, the mean number of misspelled words was 6.05. Construct a 95% confidence interval for the mean number of misspelled words in the population of student essays.

Population Standard Deviation, σ Unknown

In the previous section, we assumed the population standard deviation was known. In the case involving Del Monte 4.5-ounce cups of peaches, there would likely be a long history of measurements in the filling process. Therefore, it is reasonable to assume the standard deviation of the population is available. However, in most sampling situations the population standard deviation (σ) is not known. Here are some examples where we wish to estimate the population means and it is unlikely we would know the population standard deviations. Suppose each of these studies involves students at West Virginia University.

- The Dean of the Business College wants to estimate the mean number of hours full-time students work at paying jobs each week. He selects a sample of 30 students, contacts each student, and asks them how many hours they worked last week. From the sample information, he can calculate the sample mean, but it is not likely he would know or be able to find the *population* standard deviation (σ) required in formula (9–1). He could calculate the standard deviation of the sample and use that as an estimate, but he would not likely know the population standard deviation.
- The Dean of Students wants to estimate the distance the typical commuter student travels to class. She selects a sample of 40 commuter students, contacts each, and determines the one-way distance from each student's home to the center of campus. From the sample data, she calculates the mean travel distance, that is, $\bar{x}$. It is unlikely the standard deviation of the population would be known or available, again making formula (9–1) unusable.
- The Director of Student Loans wants to estimate the mean amount owed on student loans at the time of his/her graduation. The director selects a sample of 20 graduating students and contacts each to find the information. From the sample information, the director can estimate the mean amount. However, to develop a confidence interval using formula (9–1), the population standard deviation is necessary. It is not likely this information is available.

STATISTICS IN ACTION

William Gosset was born in England in 1876 and died there in 1937. He worked for many years at Arthur Guinness, Sons and Company. In fact, in his later years he was in charge of the Guinness Brewery in London. Guinness preferred its employees to use pen names when publishing papers, so in 1908, when Gosset wrote "The Probable Error of a Mean," he used the name "Student." In this paper, he first described the properties of the *t* distribution.

Fortunately we can use the sample standard deviation to estimate the population standard deviation. That is, we use *s*, the sample standard deviation, to estimate σ, the population standard deviation. But in doing so, we cannot use formula (9–1). Because we do not know σ, we cannot use the *z* distribution. However, there is a remedy. We use the sample standard deviation and replace the *z* distribution with the *t* distribution.

The *t* distribution is a continuous probability distribution, with many similar characteristics to the *z* distribution. William Gosset, an English brewmaster, was the first to study the *t* distribution.

He was particularly concerned with the exact behavior of the distribution of the following statistic:

$$t = \frac{\overline{x} - \mu}{s/\sqrt{n}}$$

where *s* is an estimate of σ. He was especially worried about the discrepancy between *s* and σ when *s* was calculated from a very small sample. The *t* distribution and the standard normal distribution are shown graphically in Chart 9–1. Note particularly that the *t* distribution is flatter, more spread out, than the standard normal distribution. This is because the standard deviation of the *t* distribution is larger than that of the standard normal distribution.

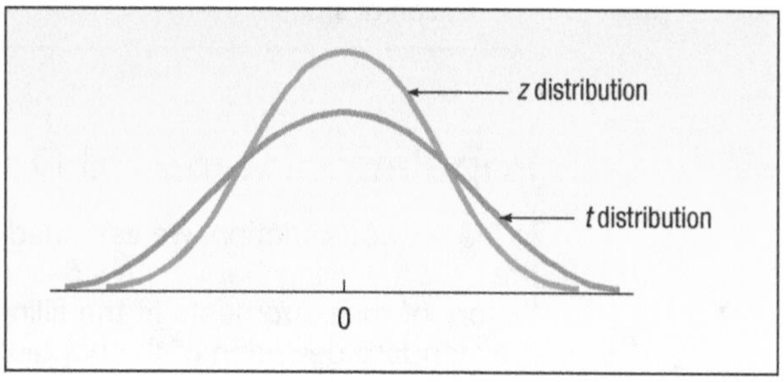

CHART 9–1 The Standard Normal Distribution and Student's *t* Distribution

The following characteristics of the *t* distribution are based on the assumption that the population of interest is normal, or nearly normal.

- It is, like the *z* distribution, a continuous distribution.
- It is, like the *z* distribution, bell-shaped and symmetrical.
- There is not one *t* distribution, but rather a family of *t* distributions. All *t* distributions have a mean of 0, but their standard deviations differ according to the sample size, *n*. There is a *t* distribution for a sample size of 20, another for a sample size of 22, and so on. The standard deviation for a *t* distribution with 5 observations is larger than for a *t* distribution with 20 observations.
- The *t* distribution is more spread out and flatter at the center than the standard normal distribution (see Chart 9–1). As the sample size increases, however, the *t* distribution approaches the standard normal distribution because the errors in using *s* to estimate σ decrease with larger samples.

Because Student's *t* distribution has a greater spread than the *z* distribution, the value of *t* for a given level of confidence is larger in magnitude than the corresponding *z* value. Chart 9–2 shows the values of *z* for a 95% level of confidence and of *t* for the same level of confidence when the sample size is $n = 5$. How we obtained the actual value of *t* will be explained shortly. For now, observe that for the same level of confidence the *t* distribution is flatter or more spread out than the standard normal distribution.

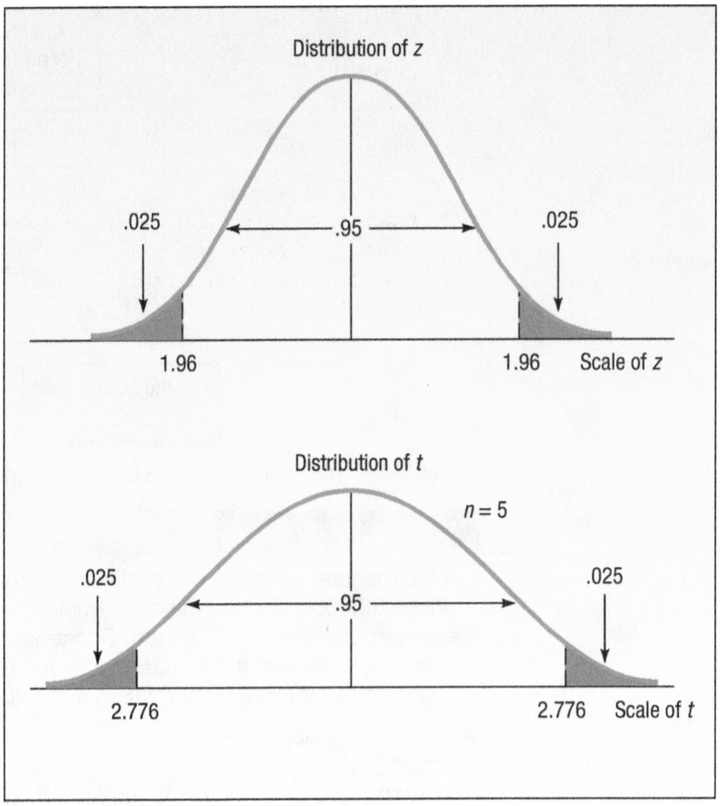

CHART 9–2 Values of z and t for the 95% Level of Confidence

To develop a confidence interval for the population mean using the t distribution, we adjust formula (9–1) as follows.

CONFIDENCE INTERVAL FOR THE POPULATION MEAN, σ UNKNOWN

$$\bar{x} \pm t\frac{s}{\sqrt{n}} \quad [9\text{–}2]$$

To determine a confidence interval for the population mean with an unknown standard deviation, we:

1. Assume the sampled population is either normal or approximately normal. This assumption may be questionable for small sample sizes, and becomes more valid with larger sample sizes.
2. Estimate the population standard deviation (σ) with the sample standard deviation (s).
3. Use the t distribution rather than the z distribution.

We should be clear at this point. We base the decision on whether to use the t or the z on whether or not we know σ, the population standard deviation. If we know the population standard deviation, then we use z. If we do not know the population standard deviation, then we must use t. Chart 9–3 summarizes the decision-making process.

The following example will illustrate a confidence interval for a population mean when the population standard deviation is unknown and how to find the appropriate value of t in a table.

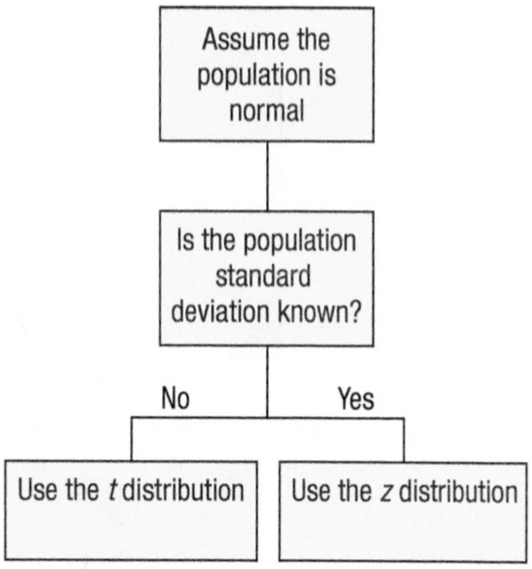

CHART 9–3 Determining When to Use the *z* Distribution or the *t* Distribution

EXAMPLE

A tire manufacturer wishes to investigate the tread life of its tires. A sample of 10 tires driven 50,000 miles revealed a sample mean of 0.32 inch of tread remaining with a standard deviation of 0.09 inch. Construct a 95% confidence interval for the population mean. Would it be reasonable for the manufacturer to conclude that after 50,000 miles the population mean amount of tread remaining is 0.30 inch?

SOLUTION

To begin, we assume the population distribution is normal. In this case, we don't have a lot of evidence, but the assumption is probably reasonable. We know the sample standard deviation is .09 inch. We use formula (9–2):

$$\bar{x} \pm t\frac{s}{\sqrt{n}}$$

From the information given, $\bar{x} = 0.32$, $s = 0.09$, and $n = 10$. To find the value of t, we use Appendix B.5, a portion of which is reproduced in Table 9–2. Appendix B.5

TABLE 9–2 A Portion of the *t* Distribution

	Confidence Intervals				
	80%	90%	95%	98%	99%
	Level of Significance for One-Tailed Test				
df	0.10	0.05	0.025	0.010	0.005
	Level of Significance for Two-Tailed Test				
	0.20	0.10	0.05	0.02	0.01
1	3.078	6.314	12.706	31.821	63.657
2	1.886	2.920	4.303	6.965	9.925
3	1.638	2.353	3.182	4.541	5.841
4	1.533	2.132	2.776	3.747	4.604
5	1.476	2.015	2.571	3.365	4.032
6	1.440	1.943	2.447	3.143	3.707
7	1.415	1.895	2.365	2.998	3.499
8	1.397	1.860	2.306	2.896	3.355
9	1.383	1.833	2.262	2.821	3.250
10	1.372	1.812	2.228	2.764	3.169

is also reproduced on the inside back cover of the text. The first step for locating t is to move across the columns identified for "Confidence Intervals" to the level of confidence requested. In this case, we want the 95% level of confidence, so we move to the column headed "95%." The column on the left margin is identified as "*df.*" This refers to the number of degrees of freedom. The number of degrees of freedom is the number of observations in the sample minus the number of samples, written $n - 1$. In this case, it is $10 - 1 = 9$. Why did we decide there were 9 degrees of freedom? When sample statistics are being used, it is necessary to determine the number of values that are *free to vary.*

To illustrate the meaning of degrees of freedom: Assume that the mean of four numbers is known to be 5. The four numbers are 7, 4, 1, and 8. The deviations of these numbers from the mean must total 0. The deviations of +2, −1, −4, and +3 do total 0. If the deviations of +2, −1, and −4 are known, then the value of +3 is fixed (restricted) in order to satisfy the condition that the sum of the deviations must equal 0. Thus, 1 degree of freedom is lost in a sampling problem involving the standard deviation of the sample because one number (the arithmetic mean) is known. For a 95% level of confidence and 9 degrees of freedom, we select the row with 9 degrees of freedom. The value of t is 2.262.

To determine the confidence interval, we substitute the values in formula (9–2).

$$\bar{x} \pm t\frac{s}{\sqrt{n}} = 0.32 \pm 2.262\frac{0.09}{\sqrt{10}} = 0.32 \pm .064$$

The endpoints of the confidence interval are 0.256 and 0.384. How do we interpret this result? If we repeated this study 200 times, calculating the 95% confidence interval with each sample's mean and the standard deviation, we expect 190 of the intervals would include the population mean. Ten of the intervals would not include the population mean. This is the effect of sampling error. A further interpretation is to conclude that the population mean is in this interval. The manufacturer can be reasonably sure (95% confident) that the mean remaining tread depth is between 0.256 and 0.384 inch. Because the value of 0.30 is in this interval, it is possible that the mean of the population is 0.30.

Here is another example to clarify the use of confidence intervals. Suppose an article in your local newspaper reported that the mean time to sell a residential property in the area is 60 days. You select a random sample of 20 homes sold in the last year and find the mean selling time is 65 days. Based on the sample data, you develop a 95% confidence interval for the population mean. You find that the endpoints of the confidence interval are 62 days and 68 days. How do you interpret this result? You can be reasonably confident the population mean is within this range. The value proposed for the population mean, that is, 60 days, is not included in the interval. It is not likely that the population mean is 60 days. The evidence indicates the statement by the local newspaper may not be correct. To put it another way, it seems unreasonable to obtain the sample you did from a population that had a mean selling time of 60 days.

The following example will show additional details for determining and interpreting a confidence interval. We used Minitab to perform the calculations.

EXAMPLE

The manager of the Inlet Square Mall, near Ft. Myers, Florida, wants to estimate the mean amount spent per shopping visit by customers. A sample of 20 customers reveals the following amounts spent.

$48.16	$42.22	$46.82	$51.45	$23.78	$41.86	$54.86
37.92	52.64	48.59	50.82	46.94	61.83	61.69
49.17	61.46	51.35	52.68	58.84	43.88	

What is the best estimate of the population mean? Determine a 95% confidence interval. Interpret the result. Would it be reasonable to conclude that the population mean is \$50? What about \$60?

SOLUTION

The mall manager assumes that the population of the amounts spent follows the normal distribution. This is a reasonable assumption in this case. Additionally, the

confidence interval technique is quite powerful and tends to commit any errors on the conservative side if the population is not normal. We should not make the normality assumption when the population is severely skewed or when the distribution has "thick tails." In Chapter 16, we present methods for handling this issue if we cannot make the normality assumption. In this case, the normality assumption is reasonable.

The population standard deviation is not known. Hence, it is appropriate to use the *t* distribution and formula (9–2) to find the confidence interval. We use the Minitab system to find the mean and standard deviation of this sample. The results are shown below.

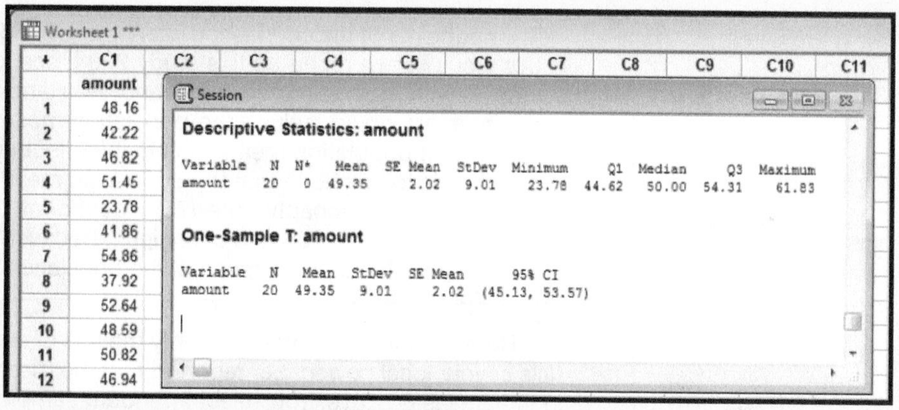

Worksheet 1 ***

↓	C1
	amount
1	48.16
2	42.22
3	46.82
4	51.45
5	23.78
6	41.86
7	54.86
8	37.92
9	52.64
10	48.59
11	50.82
12	46.94

Session

Descriptive Statistics: amount

Variable	N	N*	Mean	SE Mean	StDev	Minimum	Q1	Median	Q3	Maximum
amount	20	0	49.35	2.02	9.01	23.78	44.62	50.00	54.31	61.83

One-Sample T: amount

Variable	N	Mean	StDev	SE Mean	95% CI
amount	20	49.35	9.01	2.02	(45.13, 53.57)

The mall manager does not know the population mean. The sample mean is the best estimate of that value. From the pictured Minitab output, the mean is \$49.35, which is the best estimate, the *point estimate,* of the unknown population mean.

We use formula (9–2) to find the confidence interval. The value of *t* is available from Appendix B.5. There are $n - 1 = 20 - 1 = 19$ degrees of freedom. We move across the row with 19 degrees of freedom to the column for the 95% confidence level. The value at this intersection is 2.093. We substitute these values into formula (9–2) to find the confidence interval.

$$\bar{x} \pm t\frac{s}{\sqrt{n}} = \$49.35 \pm 2.093\frac{\$9.01}{\sqrt{20}} = \$49.35 \pm \$4.22$$

The endpoints of the confidence interval are \$45.13 and \$53.57. It is reasonable to conclude that the population mean is in that interval.

The manager of Inlet Square wondered whether the population mean could have been \$50 or \$60. The value of \$50 is within the confidence interval. It is reasonable that the population mean could be \$50. The value of \$60 is not in the confidence interval. Hence, we conclude that the population mean is unlikely to be \$60.

The calculations to construct a confidence interval are also available in Excel. The output follows. Note that the sample mean ($49.35) and the sample standard deviation ($9.01) are the same as those in the Minitab calculations. In the Excel output, the last line also includes the margin of error, which is the amount that is added and subtracted from the sample mean to form the endpoints of the confidence interval. This value is found from

$$t\frac{s}{\sqrt{n}} = 2.093\frac{\$9.01}{\sqrt{20}} = \$4.22$$

shopping

	A	B	C	D	E
1	Amount		Amount		
2	48.16				
3	42.22		Mean	49.35	
4	46.82		Standard Error	2.02	
5	51.45		Median	50.00	
6	23.78		Mode	#N/A	
7	41.86		Standard Deviation	9.01	
8	54.86		Sample Variance	81.22	
9	37.92		Kurtosis	2.26	
10	52.64		Skewness	-1.00	
11	48.59		Range	38.05	
12	50.82		Minimum	23.78	
13	46.94		Maximum	61.83	
14	61.83		Sum	986.96	
15	61.69		Count	20.00	
16	49.17		Confidence Level(95.0%)	4.22	
17	61.46				
18	51.35				
19	52.68				
20	58.84				
21	43.88				

Before doing the confidence interval exercises, we would like to point out a useful characteristic of the *t* distribution that will allow us to use the *t* table to quickly find both *z* and *t* values. Earlier in this section, on page 290, we detailed the characteristics of the *t* distribution. The last point indicated that as we increase the sample size the *t* distribution approaches the *z* distribution. In fact, when we reach an infinitely large sample, the *t* distribution is exactly equal to the *z* distribution.

To explain, Table 9–3 is a portion of Appendix B.5, with the degrees of freedom between 4 and 99 omitted. To find the appropriate *z* value for a 95% confidence interval, we begin by going to the confidence interval section and selecting the column headed "95%." Move down that column to the last row, which is labeled "∞," or infinite degrees of freedom. The value reported is 1.960, the same value that we found using the standard normal distribution in Appendix B.3. This confirms the convergence of the *t* distribution to the *z* distribution.

What does this mean for us? Instead of searching in the body of the *z* table, we can go to the last row of the *t* table and find the appropriate value to build a confidence interval. An additional benefit is that the values have three decimal places. So, using this table for a 90% confidence interval, go down the column headed "90%" and see the value 1.645, which is a more precise *z* value that can be used for the 90%

confidence level. Other z values for 98% and 99% confidence intervals are also available with three decimals. Note that we will use the t table, which is summarized in Table 9–3, to find the z values with three decimals for all following exercises and problems.

TABLE 9–3 Student's t Distribution

df (degrees of freedom)	Confidence Interval					
	80%	90%	95%	98%	99%	99.9%
	Level of Significance for One-Tailed Test, α					
	0.1	0.05	0.02	0.01	0.001	0.0005
	Level of Significance for Two-Tailed Test, α					
	0.2	0.1	0.05	0.02	0.01	0.001
1	3.078	6.314	12.706	31.821	63.657	636.619
2	1.886	2.920	4.303	6.965	9.925	31.599
3	1.638	2.353	3.182	4.541	5.841	12.924
⋮	⋮	⋮	⋮	⋮	⋮	⋮
100	1.290	1.660	1.984	2.364	2.626	3.390
120	1.289	1.658	1.980	2.358	2.617	3.373
140	1.288	1.656	1.977	2.353	2.611	3.361
160	1.287	1.654	1.975	2.350	2.607	3.352
180	1.286	1.653	1.973	2.347	2.603	3.345
200	1.286	1.653	1.972	2.345	2.601	3.340
∞	1.282	1.645	1.960	2.326	2.576	3.291

SELF-REVIEW 9–2

Dottie Kleman is the "Cookie Lady." She bakes and sells cookies at locations in the Philadelphia area. Ms. Kleman is concerned about absenteeism among her workers. The information below reports the number of days absent for a sample of 10 workers during the last two-week pay period.

4	1	2	2	1	2	2	1	0	3

(a) Determine the mean and the standard deviation of the sample.
(b) What is the population mean? What is the best estimate of that value?
(c) Develop a 95% confidence interval for the population mean. Assume that the population distribution is normal.
(d) Explain why the t distribution is used as a part of the confidence interval.
(e) Is it reasonable to conclude that the typical worker does not miss any days during a pay period?

EXERCISES

9. Use Appendix B.5 to locate the value of t under the following conditions.
 a. The sample size is 12 and the level of confidence is 95%.
 b. The sample size is 20 and the level of confidence is 90%.
 c. The sample size is 8 and the level of confidence is 99%.

10. Use Appendix B.5 to locate the value of t under the following conditions.
 a. The sample size is 15 and the level of confidence is 95%.
 b. The sample size is 24 and the level of confidence is 98%.
 c. The sample size is 12 and the level of confidence is 90%.

11. The owner of Britten's Egg Farm wants to estimate the mean number of eggs produced per chicken. A sample of 20 chickens shows they produced an average of 20 eggs per month with a standard deviation of 2 eggs per month.
 a. What is the value of the population mean? What is the best estimate of this value?
 b. Explain why we need to use the t distribution. What assumption do you need to make?

c. For a 95% confidence interval, what is the value of *t*?
d. Develop the 95% confidence interval for the population mean.
e. Would it be reasonable to conclude that the population mean is 21 eggs? What about 25 eggs?

12. The U.S. Dairy Industry wants to estimate the mean yearly milk consumption. A sample of 16 people reveals the mean yearly consumption to be 60 gallons with a standard deviation of 20 gallons. Assume the population distribution is normal.
a. What is the value of the population mean? What is the best estimate of this value?
b. Explain why we need to use the *t* distribution. What assumption do you need to make?
c. For a 90% confidence interval, what is the value of *t*?
d. Develop the 90% confidence interval for the population mean.
e. Would it be reasonable to conclude that the population mean is 63 gallons?

For **DATA FILE**, please visit www.mhhe.com/lind16e

13. Merrill Lynch Securities and Health Care Retirement Inc. are two large employers in downtown Toledo, Ohio. They are considering jointly offering child care for their employees. As a part of the feasibility study, they wish to estimate the mean weekly child-care cost of their employees. A sample of 10 employees who use child care reveals the following amounts spent last week.

$107	$92	$97	$95	$105	$101	$91	$99	$95	$104

Develop a 90% confidence interval for the population mean. Interpret the result.

For **DATA FILE**, please visit www.mhhe.com/lind16e

14. The Greater Pittsburgh Area Chamber of Commerce wants to estimate the mean time workers who are employed in the downtown area spend getting to work. A sample of 15 workers reveals the following number of minutes spent traveling.

29	38	38	33	38	21	45	34
40	37	37	42	30	29	35	

Develop a 98% confidence interval for the population mean. Interpret the result.

LO9-3
Compute and interpret a confidence interval for a population proportion.

A CONFIDENCE INTERVAL FOR A POPULATION PROPORTION

The material presented so far in this chapter uses the ratio scale of measurement. That is, we use such variables as incomes, weights, distances, and ages. We now want to consider situations such as the following:

- The career services director at Southern Technical Institute reports that 80% of its graduates enter the job market in a position related to their field of study.
- A company representative claims that 45% of Burger King sales are made at the drive-through window.
- A survey of homes in the Chicago area indicated that 85% of the new construction had central air conditioning.
- A recent survey of married men between the ages of 35 and 50 found that 63% felt that both partners should earn a living.

These examples illustrate the nominal scale of measurement when the outcome is limited to

two values. In these cases, an observation is classified into one of two mutually exclusive groups. For example, a graduate of Southern Tech either entered the job market in a position related to his or her field of study or not. A particular Burger King customer either made a purchase at the drive-through window or did not make a purchase at the drive-through window. We can talk about the groups in terms of proportions.

> **PROPORTION** The fraction, ratio, or percent indicating the part of the sample or the population having a particular trait of interest.

As an example of a proportion, a recent survey indicated that 92 out of 100 people surveyed favored the continued use of daylight savings time in the summer. The sample proportion is 92/100, or .92, or 92%. If we let p represent the sample proportion, x the number of "successes," and n the number of items sampled, we can determine a sample proportion as follows.

SAMPLE PROPORTION

$$p = \frac{x}{n} \qquad [9\text{–}3]$$

The population proportion is identified by π. Therefore, π refers to the percent of successes in the population. Recall from Chapter 6 that π is the proportion of "successes" in a binomial distribution. This continues our practice of using Greek letters to identify population parameters and Roman letters to identify sample statistics.

To develop a confidence interval for a proportion, we need to meet the following assumptions.

1. The binomial conditions, discussed in Chapter 6, have been met. Briefly, these conditions are:
   a. The sample data are the number of successes in n trials.
   b. There are only two possible outcomes. (We usually label one of the outcomes a "success" and the other a "failure.")
   c. The probability of a success remains the same from one trial to the next.
   d. The trials are independent. This means the outcome on one trial does not affect the outcome on another.
2. The values $n\pi$ and $n(1 - \pi)$ should both be greater than or equal to 5. This condition allows us to invoke the central limit theorem and employ the standard normal distribution, that is, z, to complete a confidence interval.

Developing a point estimate for a population proportion and a confidence interval for a population proportion is similar to doing so for a mean. To illustrate, John Gail is running for Congress from the third district of Nebraska. From a random sample of 100 voters in the district, 60 indicate they plan to vote for him in the upcoming election. The sample proportion is .60, but the population proportion is unknown. That is, we do not know what proportion of voters in the *population* will vote for Mr. Gail. The sample value, .60, is the best estimate we have of the unknown population parameter. So we let p, which is .60, be an estimate of π, which is not known.

To develop a confidence interval for a population proportion, we use:

CONFIDENCE INTERVAL FOR A POPULATION PROPORTION

$$p \pm z\sqrt{\frac{p(1-p)}{n}} \qquad [9\text{–}4]$$

An example will help to explain the details of determining a confidence interval and interpreting the result.

STATISTICS IN ACTION

Many survey results reported in newspapers, in news magazines, and on TV use confidence intervals. For example, a recent survey of 800 TV viewers in Toledo, Ohio, found 44% watched the evening news on the local CBS affiliate. The article went on to indicate the margin of error was 3.4%. The margin of error is actually the amount that is added and subtracted from the point estimate to find the endpoints of a confidence interval. From formula (9–4) and the 95% level of confidence:

$$z\sqrt{\frac{p(1-p)}{n}} = 1.96\sqrt{\frac{.44(1-.44)}{800}} = 0.034$$

EXAMPLE

The union representing the Bottle Blowers of America (BBA) is considering a proposal to merge with the Teamsters Union. According to BBA union bylaws, at least three-fourths of the union membership must approve any merger. A random sample of 2,000 current BBA members reveals 1,600 plan to vote for the merger proposal. What is the estimate of the population proportion? Develop a 95% confidence interval for the population proportion. Basing your decision on this sample information, can you conclude that the necessary proportion of BBA members favor the merger? Why?

SOLUTION

First, calculate the sample proportion from formula (9–3). It is .80, found by

$$p = \frac{x}{n} = \frac{1,600}{2,000} = .80$$

Thus, we estimate that 80% of the population favor the merger proposal. We determine the 95% confidence interval using formula (9–4). The z value corresponding to the 95% level of confidence is 1.96.

$$p \pm z\sqrt{\frac{p(1-p)}{n}} = .80 \pm 1.96\sqrt{\frac{.80(1-.80)}{2,000}} = .80 \pm .018$$

The endpoints of the confidence interval are .782 and .818. The lower endpoint is greater than .75. Hence, we conclude that the merger proposal will likely pass because the interval estimate includes values greater than 75% of the union membership.

To review the interpretation of the confidence interval: If the poll was conducted 100 times with 100 different samples, we expect the confidence intervals constructed from 95 of the samples would contain the true population proportion. In addition, the interpretation of a confidence interval can be very useful in decision making and play a very important role especially on election night. For example, Cliff Obermeyer is running for Congress from the 6th District of New Jersey. Suppose 500 voters are contacted upon leaving the polls and 275 indicate they voted for Mr. Obermeyer. We will assume that the exit poll of 500 voters is a random sample of those voting in the 6th District. That means that 55% of those in the sample voted for Mr. Obermeyer. Based on formula (9–3):

$$p = \frac{x}{n} = \frac{275}{500} = .55$$

Now, to be assured of election, he must earn *more than* 50% of the votes in the population of those voting. At this point, we know a point estimate, which is .55, of the population of voters that will vote for him. But we do not know the percent in the population that will ultimately vote for the candidate. So the question is: Could we take a sample of 500 voters from a population where 50% or less of the voters support Mr. Obermeyer and find that 55% of the sample support him? To put it another way, could the sampling error, which is $p - \pi = .55 - .50 = .05$ be due to chance, or is the population of voters who support Mr. Obermeyer greater than .50? If we develop a confidence interval for the sample proportion and find that the lower endpoint is greater than .50, then we conclude that the proportion of voters supporting Mr. Obermeyer is greater than .50. What does that mean? Well, it means he should be elected! What if .50 is in the interval? Then we conclude that he is not assured of

a majority and we cannot conclude he will be elected. In this case, using the 95% significance level and formula (9–4):

$$p \pm z\sqrt{\frac{p(1-p)}{n}} = .55 \pm 1.96\sqrt{\frac{.55(1-.55)}{500}} = .55 \pm .044$$

So the endpoints of the confidence interval are .55 − .044 = .506 and .55 + .044 = .594. The value of .50 is not in this interval. So we conclude that probably *more than 50%* of the voters support Mr. Obermeyer and that is enough to get him elected.

Is this procedure ever used? Yes! It is exactly the procedure used by television networks, news magazines, and polling organizations on election night.

SELF-REVIEW 9–3

A market survey was conducted to estimate the proportion of homemakers who would recognize the brand name of a cleanser based on the shape and the color of the container. Of the 1,400 homemakers sampled, 420 were able to identify the brand by name.
(a) Estimate the value of the population proportion.
(b) Develop a 99% confidence interval for the population proportion.
(c) Interpret your findings.

EXERCISES

15. The owner of the West End Kwick Fill Gas Station wishes to determine the proportion of customers who use a credit card or debit card to pay at the pump. He surveys 100 customers and finds that 80 paid at the pump.
a. Estimate the value of the population proportion.
b. Develop a 95% confidence interval for the population proportion.
c. Interpret your findings.

16. Ms. Maria Wilson is considering running for mayor of the town of Bear Gulch, Montana. Before completing the petitions, she decides to conduct a survey of voters in Bear Gulch. A sample of 400 voters reveals that 300 would support her in the November election.
a. Estimate the value of the population proportion.
b. Develop a 99% confidence interval for the population proportion.
c. Interpret your findings.

17. The Fox TV network is considering replacing one of its prime-time crime investigation shows with a new family-oriented comedy show. Before a final decision is made, network executives commission a sample of 400 viewers. After viewing the comedy, 250 indicated they would watch the new show and suggested it replace the crime investigation show.
a. Estimate the value of the population proportion.
b. Develop a 99% confidence interval for the population proportion.
c. Interpret your findings.

18. Schadek Silkscreen Printing Inc. purchases plastic cups on which to print logos for sporting events, proms, birthdays, and other special occasions. Zack Schadek, the owner, received a large shipment this morning. To ensure the quality of the shipment, he selected a random sample of 300 cups. He found 15 to be defective.
a. What is the estimated proportion defective in the population?
b. Develop a 95% confidence interval for the proportion defective.
c. Zack has an agreement with his supplier that he is to return lots that are 10% or more defective. Should he return this lot? Explain your decision.

LO9-4
Calculate the required sample size to estimate a population proportion or population mean.

CHOOSING AN APPROPRIATE SAMPLE SIZE

When working with confidence intervals, one important variable is sample size. However, in practice, sample size is not a variable. It is a decision we make so that our estimate of a population parameter is a good one. Our decision is based on three variables:

1. The margin of error the researcher will tolerate.
2. The level of confidence desired, for example, 95%.
3. The variation or dispersion of the population being studied.

The first variable is the *margin of error.* It is designated as E and is the amount that is added and subtracted to the sample mean (or sample proportion) to determine the endpoints of the confidence interval. For example, in a study of wages, we may decide that we want to estimate the mean wage of the population with a margin of error of plus or minus \$1,000. Or, in an opinion poll, we may decide that we want to estimate the population proportion with a margin of error of plus or minus 3.5%. The margin of error is the amount of error we are willing to tolerate in estimating a population parameter. You may wonder why we do not choose small margins of error. There is a trade-off between the margin of error and sample size. A small margin of error will require a larger sample and more money and time to collect the sample. A larger margin of error will permit a smaller sample and result in a wider confidence interval.

The second choice is the *level of confidence.* In working with confidence intervals, we logically choose relatively high levels of confidence such as 95% and 99%. To compute the sample size, we need the z-statistic that corresponds to the chosen level of confidence. The 95% level of confidence corresponds to a z value of 1.96, and a 90% level of confidence corresponds to a z value of 1.645 (using the t table). Notice that larger sample sizes (and more time and money to collect the sample) correspond with higher levels of confidence. Also, notice that we use a z-statistic.

The third choice to determine the sample size is the *population standard deviation.* If the population is widely dispersed, a large sample is required. On the other hand, if the population is concentrated (homogeneous), the required sample size will be smaller. Often, we do not know the population standard deviation. Here are three suggestions for finding a value for the population standard deviation.

1. **Conduct a pilot study.** This is the most common method. Suppose we want an estimate of the number of hours per week worked by students enrolled in the College of Business at the University of Texas. To test the validity of our questionnaire, we use it on a small sample of students. From this small sample, we compute the standard deviation of the number of hours worked and use this value as the population standard deviation.
2. **Use a comparable study.** Use this approach when there is an estimate of the standard deviation from another study. Suppose we want to estimate the number of hours worked per week by refuse workers. Information from certain state or federal agencies that regularly study the workforce may provide a reliable value to use for the population standard deviation.
3. **Use a range-based approach.** To use this approach, we need to know or have an estimate of the largest and smallest values in the population. Recall from Chapter 3, the Empirical Rule states that virtually all the observations could be expected to be within plus or minus 3 standard deviations of the mean, assuming that the distribution follows the normal distribution. Thus, the distance between the largest and the smallest values is 6 standard deviations. We can estimate the standard deviation as one-sixth of the range. For example, the director of operations at University Bank wants to estimate the number of checks written per month by college students. She believes that the distribution of the number of checks written follows the normal distribution. The minimum and maximum numbers written per month are 2 and 50, so the range is 48, found by $(50 - 2)$. Then eight checks per month, 48/6, would be the value we would use for the population standard deviation.

Sample Size to Estimate a Population Mean

To estimate a population mean, we can express the interaction among these three factors and the sample size in the following formula. Notice that this formula is the margin of error used to calculate the endpoints of confidence intervals to estimate a population mean!

$$E = z\frac{\sigma}{\sqrt{n}}$$

Solving this equation for n yields the following result.

SAMPLE SIZE FOR ESTIMATING THE POPULATION MEAN	$n = \left(\frac{z\sigma}{E}\right)^2$	[9–5]

where:

n is the size of the sample.
z is the standard normal value corresponding to the desired level of confidence.
σ is the population standard deviation.
E is the maximum allowable error.

The result of this calculation is not always a whole number. When the outcome is not a whole number, the usual practice is to round up *any* fractional result to the next whole number. For example, 201.21 would be rounded up to 202.

EXAMPLE

A student in public administration wants to estimate the mean monthly earnings of city council members in large cities. The error in estimating the mean is to be less than $100 with a 95% level of confidence. The student found a report by the Department of Labor that reported a standard deviation of $1,000. What is the required sample size?

SOLUTION

The maximum allowable error, E, is $100. The value of z for a 95% level of confidence is 1.96, and the value of the standard deviation is $1,000. Substituting these values into formula (9–5) gives the required sample size as:

$$n = \left(\frac{z\sigma}{E}\right)^2 = \left(\frac{(1.96)(\$1{,}000)}{\$100}\right)^2 = (19.6)^2 = 384.16$$

The computed value of 384.16 is rounded up to 385. A sample of 385 is required to meet the specifications. If the student wants to increase the level of confidence, for example to 99%, this will require a larger sample. Using the t table, the z value for a 99% level of confidence is 2.576.

$$n = \left(\frac{z\sigma}{E}\right)^2 = \left(\frac{(2.576)(\$1{,}000)}{\$100}\right)^2 = (25.76)^2 = 663.58$$

We recommend a sample of 664. Observe how much the change in the confidence level changed the size of the sample. An increase from the 95% to the 99% level of confidence resulted in an increase of 279 observations, or 72% [(664/385) × 100]. This would greatly increase the cost of the study, in terms of both time and money. Hence, the level of confidence should be considered carefully.

Sample Size to Estimate a Population Proportion

To determine the sample size for a proportion, the same three variables need to be specified:

1. The margin of error.
2. The desired level of confidence.
3. The variation or dispersion of the population being studied.

For the binomial distribution, the margin of error is:

$$E = z\sqrt{\frac{\pi(1 - \pi)}{n}}$$

Solving this equation for n yields the following equation

SAMPLE SIZE FOR THE POPULATION PROPORTION

$$n = \pi(1 - \pi)\left(\frac{z}{E}\right)^2 \qquad \textbf{[9–6]}$$

where:

n is the size of the sample.
z is the standard normal value corresponding to the desired level of confidence.
π is the population proportion.
E is the maximum allowable error.

The choices for the z-statistic and the margin of error, E, are the same as the choices for estimating the population mean. However, the population variance of the binomial distribution is represented by $\pi(1 - \pi)$. To find a value of the population proportion, we would find a comparable study or conduct a pilot study. If a reliable value cannot be found, then a value of .50 should be used for π. Note that $\pi(1 - \pi)$ has the largest value using 0.50 and, therefore, without a good estimate of the population proportion, overstates the sample size. This difference will not hurt the estimate of the population proportion.

EXAMPLE

The study in the previous example also estimates the proportion of cities that have private refuse collectors. The student wants the margin of error to be within .10 of the population proportion, the desired level of confidence is 90%, and no estimate is available for the population proportion. What is the required sample size?

SOLUTION

The estimate of the population proportion is to be within .10, so $E = .10$. The desired level of confidence is .90, which corresponds to a z value of 1.645, using the t table. Because no estimate of the population proportion is available, we use .50. The suggested number of observations is

$$n = (.5)(1 - .5)\left(\frac{1.645}{.10}\right)^2 = 67.65$$

The student needs a random sample of 68 cities.

SELF-REVIEW 9–4

The registrar wants to estimate the arithmetic mean grade point average (GPA) of all graduating seniors during the past 10 years. GPAs range between 2.0 and 4.0. The mean GPA is to be estimated within plus or minus .05 of the population mean. Based on prior experience, the population standard deviation is 0.279. Use the 99% level of confidence. Will you assist the college registrar in determining how many transcripts to study?

EXERCISES

19. A population is estimated to have a standard deviation of 10. We want to estimate the population mean within 2, with a 95% level of confidence. How large a sample is required?

20. We want to estimate the population mean within 5, with a 99% level of confidence. The population standard deviation is estimated to be 15. How large a sample is required?

21. The estimate of the population proportion is to be within plus or minus .05, with a 95% level of confidence. The best estimate of the population proportion is .15. How large a sample is required?

22. The estimate of the population proportion is to be within plus or minus .10, with a 99% level of confidence. The best estimate of the population proportion is .45. How large a sample is required?

23. A survey is being planned to determine the mean amount of time corporation executives watch television. A pilot survey indicated that the mean time per week is 12 hours, with a standard deviation of 3 hours. It is desired to estimate the mean viewing time within one-quarter hour. The 95% level of confidence is to be used. How many executives should be surveyed?

24. A processor of carrots cuts the green top off each carrot, washes the carrots, and inserts six to a package. Twenty packages are inserted in a box for shipment. To test the weight of the boxes, a few were checked. The mean weight was 20.4 pounds; the standard deviation, 0.5 pound. How many boxes must the processor sample to be 95% confident that the sample mean does not differ from the population mean by more than 0.2 pound?

25. Suppose the U.S. president wants an estimate of the proportion of the population who support his current policy toward revisions in the health care system. The president wants the estimate to be within .04 of the true proportion. Assume a 95% level of confidence. The president's political advisors estimated the proportion supporting the current policy to be .60.
   a. How large of a sample is required?
   b. How large of a sample would be necessary if no estimate were available for the proportion supporting current policy?

26. Past surveys reveal that 30% of tourists going to Las Vegas to gamble spend more than $1,000. The Visitor's Bureau of Las Vegas wants to update this percentage.
   a. The new study is to use the 90% confidence level. The estimate is to be within 1% of the population proportion. What is the necessary sample size?
   b. The Bureau feels the sample size determined above is too large. What can be done to reduce the sample? Based on your suggestion, recalculate the sample size.

LO9-5
Adjust a confidence interval for finite populations.

FINITE-POPULATION CORRECTION FACTOR

The populations we have sampled so far have been very large or infinite. What if the sampled population is not very large? We need to make some adjustments in the way we compute the standard error of the sample means and the standard error of the sample proportions.

A population that has a fixed upper bound is *finite.* For example, there are 12,179 students enrolled at Eastern Illinois University, there are 40 employees at Spence Sprockets, Chrysler assembled 917 Jeep Wranglers at the Alexis Avenue plant yesterday, or there were 65 surgical patients at St. Rose Memorial Hospital in Sarasota yesterday. A finite population can be rather small; it could be all the students registered for this class. It can also be very large, such as all senior citizens living in Florida.

For a finite population, where the total number of objects or individuals is N and the number of objects or individuals in the sample is n, we need to adjust the standard errors in the confidence interval formulas. To put it another way, to find the confidence interval for the mean, we adjust the standard error of the mean in formulas (9–1) and (9–2). If we are determining the confidence interval for a proportion, then we need to adjust the standard error of the proportion in formula (9–4).

This adjustment is called the **finite-population correction factor.** It is often shortened to *FPC* and is:

$$FPC = \sqrt{\frac{N - n}{N - 1}}$$

Why is it necessary to apply a factor, and what is its effect? Logically, if the sample is a substantial percentage of the population, the estimate is more precise. Note the effect of the term $(N - n)/(N - 1)$. Suppose the population is 1,000 and the sample is 100. Then this ratio is $(1{,}000 - 100)/(1{,}000 - 1)$, or 900/999. Taking the square root gives the correction factor, .9492. Multiplying this correction factor by the standard error *reduces* the standard error by about 5% $(1 - .9492 = .0508)$. This reduction in the size of the standard error yields a smaller range of values in estimating the population mean or the population proportion. If the sample is 200, the correction factor is .8949, meaning that the standard error has been reduced by more than 10%. Table 9–4 shows the effects of various sample sizes.

TABLE 9–4 Finite-Population Correction Factor for Selected Samples When the Population Is 1,000

Sample Size	Fraction of Population	Correction Factor
10	.010	.9955
25	.025	.9879
50	.050	.9752
100	.100	.9492
200	.200	.8949
500	.500	.7075

So if we wished to develop a confidence interval for the mean from a finite population and the population standard deviation was unknown, we would adjust formula (9–2) as follows:

$$\bar{x} \pm t\frac{s}{\sqrt{n}}\left(\sqrt{\frac{N-n}{N-1}}\right)$$

We would make a similar adjustment to formula (9–4) in the case of a proportion.

The following example summarizes the steps to find a confidence interval for the mean.

EXAMPLE

There are 250 families residing in Scandia, Pennsylvania. A random sample of 40 of these families revealed the mean annual church contribution was $450 and the standard deviation of this was $75.

1. What is the population mean? What is the best estimate of the population mean?
2. Develop a 90% confidence interval for the population mean. What are the endpoints of the confidence interval?
3. Using the confidence interval, explain why the population mean could be $445. Could the population mean be $425? Why?

SOLUTION

First, note the population is finite. That is, there is a limit to the number of people residing in Scandia, in this case 250.

1. We do not know the population mean. This is the value we wish to estimate. The best estimate we have of the population mean is the sample mean, which is $450.

2. The formula to find the confidence interval for a population mean follows.

$$\bar{x} \pm t\frac{s}{\sqrt{n}}\left(\sqrt{\frac{N-n}{N-1}}\right)$$

In this case, we know $\bar{x} = 450$, $s = 75$, $N = 250$, and $n = 40$. We do not know the population standard deviation, so we use the t distribution. To find the appropriate value of t, we use Appendix B.5, and move across the top row to the column headed 90%. The degrees of freedom are $df = n - 1 = 40 - 1 = 39$, so we move to the cell where the df row of 39 intersects with the column headed 90%. The value is 1.685. Inserting these values in the formula:

$$\bar{x} \pm t\frac{s}{\sqrt{n}}\left(\sqrt{\frac{N-n}{N-1}}\right)$$

$$= \$450 \pm 1.685\frac{\$75}{\sqrt{40}}\left(\sqrt{\frac{250-40}{250-1}}\right) = \$450 \pm \$19.98\sqrt{.8434} = \$450 \pm \$18.35$$

The endpoints of the confidence interval are \$431.65 and \$468.35.

3. It is likely that the population mean is more than \$431.65 but less than \$468.35. To put it another way, could the population mean be \$445? Yes, but it is not likely that it is \$425. Why is this so? Because the value \$445 is within the confidence interval and \$425 is not within the confidence interval.

SELF-REVIEW 9–5

The same study of church contributions in Scandia revealed that 15 of the 40 families sampled attend church regularly. Construct the 95% confidence interval for the proportion of families attending church regularly.

EXERCISES

27. Thirty-six items are randomly selected from a population of 300 items. The sample mean is 35 and the sample standard deviation 5. Develop a 95% confidence interval for the population mean.

28. Forty-nine items are randomly selected from a population of 500 items. The sample mean is 40 and the sample standard deviation 9. Develop a 99% confidence interval for the population mean.

29. The attendance at the Savannah Colts minor league baseball game last night was 400. A random sample of 50 of those in attendance revealed that the mean number of soft drinks consumed per person was 1.86, with a standard deviation of 0.50. Develop a 99% confidence interval for the mean number of soft drinks consumed per person.

30. There are 300 welders employed at Maine Shipyards Corporation. A sample of 30 welders revealed that 18 graduated from a registered welding course. Construct the 95% confidence interval for the proportion of all welders who graduated from a registered welding course.

CHAPTER SUMMARY

I. A point estimate is a single value (statistic) used to estimate a population value (parameter).

II. A confidence interval is a range of values within which the population parameter is expected to occur.

   A. The factors that determine the width of a confidence interval for a mean are:

      1. The number of observations in the sample, *n*.

      2. The variability in the population, usually estimated by the sample standard deviation, *s*.

      3. The level of confidence.

         a. To determine the confidence limits when the population standard deviation is known, we use the *z* distribution. The formula is

$$\bar{X} \pm z\frac{\sigma}{\sqrt{n}} \qquad \textbf{[9–1]}$$

         b. To determine the confidence limits when the population standard deviation is unknown, we use the *t* distribution. The formula is

$$\bar{X} \pm t\frac{s}{\sqrt{n}} \qquad \textbf{[9–2]}$$

III. The major characteristics of the *t* distribution are:

   A. It is a continuous distribution.

   B. It is mound-shaped and symmetrical.

   C. It is flatter, or more spread out, than the standard normal distribution.

   D. There is a family of *t* distributions, depending on the number of degrees of freedom.

IV. A proportion is a ratio, fraction, or percent that indicates the part of the sample or population that has a particular characteristic.

   A. A sample proportion is found by *x*, the number of successes, divided by *n*, the number of observations.

   B. We construct a confidence interval for a sample proportion from the following formula.

$$p \pm z\sqrt{\frac{p(1-p)}{n}} \qquad \textbf{[9–4]}$$

V. We can determine an appropriate sample size for estimating both means and proportions.

   A. There are three factors that determine the sample size when we wish to estimate the mean.

      1. The margin of error, *E*.

      2. The desired level of confidence.

      3. The variation in the population.

      4. The formula to determine the sample size for the mean is

$$n = \left(\frac{z\sigma}{E}\right)^2 \qquad \textbf{[9–5]}$$

   B. There are three factors that determine the sample size when we wish to estimate a proportion.

      1. The margin of error, *E*.

      2. The desired level of confidence.

      3. A value for π to calculate the variation in the population.

      4. The formula to determine the sample size for a proportion is

$$n = \pi(1-\pi)\left(\frac{z}{E}\right)^2 \qquad \textbf{[9–6]}$$

VI. For a finite population, the standard error is adjusted by the factor $\sqrt{\frac{N-n}{N-1}}$.

CHAPTER EXERCISES

31. A random sample of 85 group leaders, supervisors, and similar personnel at General Motors revealed that, on average, they spent 6.5 years in a particular job before being promoted. The standard deviation of the sample was 1.7 years. Construct a 95% confidence interval.

32. A state meat inspector in Iowa has been given the assignment of estimating the mean net weight of packages of ground chuck labeled "3 pounds." Of course, he realizes that the weights cannot be precisely 3 pounds. A sample of 36 packages reveals the mean weight to be 3.01 pounds, with a standard deviation of 0.03 pound.

a. What is the estimated population mean?

b. Determine a 95% confidence interval for the population mean.

33. As part of their business promotional package, the Milwaukee Chamber of Commerce would like an estimate of the mean cost per month to lease a one-bedroom apartment. A random sample of 40 apartments currently available for lease showed the mean cost per month was $323. The standard deviation of the sample was $25.

a. Develop a 98% confidence interval for the population mean.

b. Would it be reasonable to conclude that the population mean is $350 per month?

34. A recent survey of 50 executives who were laid off during a recent recession revealed it took a mean of 26 weeks for them to find another position. The standard deviation of the sample was 6.2 weeks. Construct a 95% confidence interval for the population mean. Is it reasonable that the population mean is 28 weeks? Justify your answer.

35. Marty Rowatti recently assumed the position of director of the YMCA of South Jersey. He would like some current data on how long current members of the YMCA have been members. To investigate, suppose he selects a random sample of 40 current members. The mean length of membership of those included in the sample is 8.32 years and the standard deviation is 3.07 years.

a. What is the mean of the population?

b. Develop a 90% confidence interval for the population mean.

c. The previous director, in the summary report she prepared as she retired, indicated the mean length of membership was now "almost 10 years." Does the sample information substantiate this claim? Cite evidence.

36. The American Restaurant Association collected information on the number of meals eaten outside the home per week by young married couples. A survey of 60 couples showed the sample mean number of meals eaten outside the home was 2.76 meals per week, with a standard deviation of 0.75 meal per week. Construct a 99% confidence interval for the population mean.

37. The National Collegiate Athletic Association (NCAA) reported that the mean number of hours spent per week on coaching and recruiting by college football assistant coaches during the season was 70. A random sample of 50 assistant coaches showed the sample mean to be 68.6 hours, with a standard deviation of 8.2 hours.

a. Using the sample data, construct a 99% confidence interval for the population mean.

b. Does the 99% confidence interval include the value suggested by the NCAA? Interpret this result.

c. Suppose you decided to switch from a 99% to a 95% confidence interval. Without performing any calculations, will the interval increase, decrease, or stay the same? Which of the values in the formula will change?

38. The Human Relations Department of Electronics Inc. would like to include a dental plan as part of the benefits package. The question is: How much does a typical employee and his or her family spend per year on dental expenses? A sample of 45 employees reveals the mean amount spent last year was $1,820, with a standard deviation of $660.

a. Construct a 95% confidence interval for the population mean.

b. The information from part (a) was given to the president of Electronics Inc. He indicated he could afford $1,700 of dental expenses per employee. Is it possible that the population mean could be $1,700? Justify your answer.

39. A student conducted a study and reported that the 95% confidence interval for the mean ranged from 46 to 54. He was sure that the mean of the sample was 50, that the standard deviation of the sample was 16, and that the sample size was at least 30, but could not remember the exact number. Can you help him out?

40. A recent study by the American Automobile Dealers Association revealed the mean amount of profit per car sold for a sample of 20 dealers was $290, with a standard deviation of $125. Develop a 95% confidence interval for the population mean.

41. A study of 25 graduates of four-year colleges by the American Banker's Association revealed the mean amount owed by a student in student loans was $14,381. The standard deviation of the sample was $1,892. Construct a 90% confidence interval for the population mean. Is it reasonable to conclude that the mean of the population is actually $15,000? Tell why or why not.
42. An important factor in selling a residential property is the number of people who look through the home. A sample of 15 homes recently sold in the Buffalo, New York, area revealed the mean number looking through each home was 24 and the standard deviation of the sample was 5 people. Develop a 98% confidence interval for the population mean.
43. Warren County Telephone Company claims in its annual report that "the typical customer spends $60 per month on local and long-distance service." A sample of 12 subscribers revealed the following amounts spent last month.

For **DATA FILE**, please visit www.mhhe.com/lind16e

$64	$66	$64	$66	$59	$62	$67	$61	$64	$58	$54	$66

   a. What is the point estimate of the population mean?
   b. Develop a 90% confidence interval for the population mean.
   c. Is the company's claim that the "typical customer" spends $60 per month reasonable? Justify your answer.
44. The manufacturer of a new line of ink-jet printers would like to include as part of its advertising the number of pages a user can expect from a print cartridge. A sample of 10 cartridges revealed the following number of pages printed.

For **DATA FILE**, please visit www.mhhe.com/lind16e

2,698	2,028	2,474	2,395	2,372	2,475	1,927	3,006	2,334	2,379

   a. What is the point estimate of the population mean?
   b. Develop a 95% confidence interval for the population mean.
45. Dr. Susan Benner is an industrial psychologist. She is currently studying stress among executives of Internet companies. She has developed a questionnaire that she believes measures stress. A score above 80 indicates stress at a dangerous level. A random sample of 15 executives revealed the following stress level scores.

For **DATA FILE**, please visit www.mhhe.com/lind16e

94	78	83	90	78	99	97	90	97	90	93	94	100	75	84

   a. Find the mean stress level for this sample. What is the point estimate of the population mean?
   b. Construct a 95% confidence level for the population mean.
   c. According to Dr. Benner's test, is it reasonable to conclude that the mean stress level of Internet executives is 80? Explain.
46. As a condition of employment, Fashion Industries applicants must pass a drug test. Of the last 220 applicants, 14 failed the test. Develop a 99% confidence interval for the proportion of applicants who fail the test. Would it be reasonable to conclude that 10% of the applicants fail the test? Explain.
47. Fashion Industries randomly tests its employees throughout the year. Last year in the 400 random tests conducted, 14 employees failed the test. Develop a 99% confidence interval for the proportion of applicants that fail the test. Would it be reasonable to conclude that 5% of the employees cannot pass the random drug test? Explain.
48. During a national debate on changes to health care, a cable news service performs an opinion poll of 500 small-business owners. It shows that 65% of small-business owners do not approve of the changes. Develop a 95% confidence interval for the proportion opposing health care changes. Comment on the result.
49. There are 20,000 eligible voters in York County, South Carolina. A random sample of 500 York County voters revealed 350 plan to vote to return Louella Miller to the state senate. Construct a 99% confidence interval for the proportion of voters in the county who plan to vote for Ms. Miller. From this sample information, is it reasonable to conclude that Ms. Miller will receive a majority of the votes?
50. In a poll to estimate presidential popularity, each person in a random sample of 1,000 voters was asked to agree with one of the following statements:
   1. The president is doing a good job.
   2. The president is doing a poor job.
   3. I have no opinion.

A total of 560 respondents selected the first statement, indicating they thought the president was doing a good job.

a. Construct a 95% confidence interval for the proportion of respondents who feel the president is doing a good job.

b. Based on your interval in part (a), is it reasonable to conclude that a majority of the population believes the president is doing a good job?

51. Police Chief Edward Wilkin of River City reports 500 traffic citations were issued last month. A sample of 35 of these citations showed the mean amount of the fine was $54, with a standard deviation of $4.50. Construct a 95% confidence interval for the mean amount of a citation in River City.

52. The First National Bank of Wilson has 650 checking account customers. A recent sample of 50 of these customers showed 26 have a Visa card with the bank. Construct the 99% confidence interval for the proportion of checking account customers who have a Visa card with the bank.

53. It is estimated that 60% of U.S. households subscribe to cable TV. You would like to verify this statement for your class in mass communications. If you want your estimate to be within 5 percentage points, with a 95% level of confidence, how large of a sample is required?

54. You need to estimate the mean number of travel days per year for outside salespeople. The mean of a small pilot study was 150 days, with a standard deviation of 14 days. If you must estimate the population mean within 2 days, how many outside salespeople should you sample? Use the 90% confidence level.

55. You are to conduct a sample survey to determine the mean family income in a rural area of central Florida. The question is, how many families should be sampled? In a pilot sample of 10 families, the standard deviation of the sample was $500. The sponsor of the survey wants you to use the 95% confidence level. The estimate is to be within $100. How many families should be interviewed?

56. *Families USA,* a monthly magazine that discusses issues related to health and health costs, surveyed 20 of its subscribers. It found that the annual health insurance premiums for a family with coverage through an employer averaged $10,979. The standard deviation of the sample was $1,000.

a. Based on this sample information, develop a 90% confidence interval for the population mean yearly premium.

b. How large a sample is needed to find the population mean within $250 at 99% confidence?

57. Passenger comfort is influenced by the amount of pressurization in an airline cabin. Higher pressurization permits a closer-to-normal environment and a more relaxed flight. A study by an airline user group recorded the corresponding air pressure on 30 randomly chosen flights. The study revealed a mean equivalent pressure of 8,000 feet with a standard deviation of 300 feet.

a. Develop a 99% confidence interval for the population mean equivalent pressure.

b. How large a sample is needed to find the population mean within 25 feet at 95% confidence?

58. A random sample of 25 people employed by the Florida state authority established they earned an average wage (including benefits) of $65.00 per hour. The sample standard deviation was $6.25 per hour.

a. What is the population mean? What is the best estimate of the population mean?

b. Develop a 99% confidence interval for the population mean wage (including benefits) for these employees.

c. How large a sample is needed to assess the population mean with an allowable error of $1.00 at 95% confidence?

59. A film alliance used a random sample of 50 U.S. citizens to estimate that the typical American spent 78 hours watching videos and DVDs last year. The standard deviation of this sample was 9 hours.

a. Develop a 95% confidence interval for the population mean number of hours spent watching videos and DVDs last year.

b. How large a sample should be used to be 90% confident the sample mean is within 1.0 hour of the population mean?

60. Dylan Jones kept careful records of the fuel efficiency of his new car. After the first nine times he filled up the tank, he found the mean was 23.4 miles per gallon (mpg) with a sample standard deviation of 0.9 mpg.

a. Compute the 95% confidence interval for his mpg.

b. How many times should he fill his gas tank to obtain a margin of error below 0.1 mpg?

61. A survey of 36 randomly selected "iPhone" owners showed that the purchase price has a mean of \$416 with a sample standard deviation of \$180.
  a. Compute the standard error of the sample mean.
  b. Compute the 95% confidence interval for the mean.
  c. How large a sample is needed to estimate the population mean within \$10?

62. You plan to conduct a survey to find what proportion of the workforce has two or more jobs. You decide on the 95% confidence level and state that the estimated proportion must be within 2% of the population proportion. A pilot survey reveals that 5 of the 50 sampled hold two or more jobs. How many in the workforce should be interviewed to meet your requirements?

63. The proportion of public accountants who have changed companies within the last 3 years is to be estimated within 3%. The 95% level of confidence is to be used. A study conducted several years ago revealed that the percent of public accountants changing companies within 3 years was 21.
  a. To update this study, the files of how many public accountants should be studied?
  b. How many public accountants should be contacted if no previous estimates of the population proportion are available?

64. As part of an annual review of its accounts, a discount brokerage selects a random sample of 36 customers. Their accounts are reviewed for total account valuation, which showed a mean of \$32,000, with a sample standard deviation of \$8,200. What is a 90% confidence interval for the mean account valuation of the population of customers?

65. The National Weight Control Registry tries to mine secrets of success from people who have lost at least 30 pounds and kept it off for at least a year. It reports that out of 2,700 registrants, 459 were on low-carbohydrate diets (less than 90 grams a day).
  a. Develop a 95% confidence interval for this fraction.
  b. Is it possible that the population percentage is 18%?
  c. How large a sample is needed to estimate the proportion within 0.5%?

66. Near the time of an election, a cable news service performs an opinion poll of 1,000 probable voters. It shows that the Republican contender has an advantage of 52% to 48%.
  a. Develop a 95% confidence interval for the proportion favoring the Republican candidate.
  b. Estimate the probability that the Democratic candidate is actually leading.
  c. Repeat the above analysis based on a sample of 3,000 probable voters.

67. A sample of 352 subscribers to *Wired* magazine shows the mean time spent using the Internet is 13.4 hours per week, with a sample standard deviation of 6.8 hours. Find the 95% confidence interval for the mean time *Wired* subscribers spend on the Internet.

68. The Tennessee Tourism Institute (TTI) plans to sample information center visitors entering the state to learn the fraction of visitors who plan to camp in the state. Current estimates are that 35% of visitors are campers. How large a sample would you take to estimate at a 95% confidence level the population proportion with an allowable error of 2%?

DATA SET EXERCISES

(The data for these exercises are available at the text website: **www.mhhe.com/lind16e**.)

69. Refer to the Real Estate data, which report information on homes sold in the Goodyear, Arizona, area during the last year.
  a. Develop a 95% confidence interval for the mean selling price of the homes.
  b. Develop a 95% confidence interval for the mean distance the home is from the center of the city.
  c. Develop a 95% confidence interval for the proportion of homes with an attached garage.
  d. To report your findings, write a business style memo to Gary Loftus, the president of the Goodyear Chamber of Commerce.

70. Refer to the Baseball 2012 data, which report information on the 30 Major League Baseball teams for the 2012 season. Assume the 2012 data represents a sample.
  a. Develop a 95% confidence interval for the mean number of home runs per team.
  b. Develop a 95% confidence interval for the mean number of errors committed by each team.
  c. Develop a 95% confidence interval for the mean number of stolen bases for each team.

71. Refer to the Buena School District bus data.
  a. Develop a 95% confidence interval for the mean bus maintenance.
  b. Develop a 95% confidence interval for the mean bus miles.
  c. Write a business memo to the state transportation official to report your results.

A REVIEW OF CHAPTERS 8–9

We began Chapter 8 by describing the reasons sampling is necessary. We sample because it is often impossible to study every item, or individual, in some populations. It would be too expensive and time-consuming, for example, to contact and record the annual incomes of all U.S. bank officers. Also, sampling often destroys the product. A drug manufacturer cannot test the properties of each vitamin tablet manufactured because there would be none left to sell. To estimate a population parameter, therefore, we select a sample from the population. A sample is a part of the population. Care must be taken to ensure that every member of our population has a chance of being selected; otherwise, the conclusions might be biased. A number of probability-type sampling methods can be used, including *simple random, systematic, stratified,* and *cluster sampling.*

Regardless of the sampling method selected, a sample statistic is seldom equal to the corresponding population parameter. For example, the mean of a sample is seldom exactly the same as the mean of the population. The difference between this sample statistic and the population parameter is the *sampling error.*

In Chapter 8, we demonstrated that, if we select all possible samples of a specified size from a population and calculate the mean of these samples, the result will be exactly equal to the population mean. We also showed that the dispersion in the distribution of the sample means is equal to the population standard deviation divided by the square root of the sample size. This result is called the standard error of the mean. There is less dispersion in the distribution of the sample means than in the population. In addition, as we increase the number of observations in each sample, we decrease the variation in the sampling distribution.

The central limit theorem is the foundation of statistical inference. It states that, if the population from which we select the samples follows the normal probability distribution, the distribution of the sample means will also follow the normal distribution. If the population is not normal, it will approach the normal probability distribution as we increase the size of the sample.

Our focus in Chapter 9 was point estimates and interval estimates. A point estimate is a single value used to estimate a population parameter. An interval estimate is a range of values within which we expect the population parameter to occur. For example, based on a sample, we estimate that the mean annual income of all professional house painters in Atlanta, Georgia (the population), is $45,300. That estimate is called a *point estimate.* If we state that the population mean is probably in the interval between $45,200 and $45,400, that estimate is called an *interval estimate.* The two endpoints ($45,200 and $45,400) are the *confidence limits* for the population mean. We also described procedures for establishing a confidence interval for a population mean when the population standard deviation is not known and for a population proportion. In this chapter, we also provided a method to determine the necessary sample size based on the dispersion in the population, the level of confidence desired, and the desired precision of the estimate or margin of error.

PROBLEMS

1. A recent study indicated that women took an average of 8.6 weeks of unpaid leave from their jobs after the birth of a child. Assume that this distribution follows the normal probability distribution with a standard deviation of 2.0 weeks. We select a sample of 35 women who recently returned to work after the birth of a child. What is the likelihood that the mean of this sample is at least 8.8 weeks?
2. The manager of Tee Shirt Emporium reports that the mean number of shirts sold per week is 1,210, with a standard deviation of 325. The distribution of sales follows the normal distribution. What is the likelihood of selecting a sample of 25 weeks and finding the sample mean to be 1,100 or less?
3. The owner of the Gulf Stream Café wished to estimate the mean number of lunch customers per day. A sample of 40 days revealed a mean of 160 per day, with a standard deviation of 20 per day. Develop a 98% confidence interval for the mean number of customers per day.
4. The manager of the local Hamburger Express wishes to estimate the mean time customers spend at the drive-through window. A sample of 20 customers experienced a mean waiting time of 2.65 minutes, with a standard deviation of 0.45 minute. Develop a 90% confidence interval for the mean waiting time.
5. Defiance Tool and Die has 293 sales offices throughout the world. The VP of Sales is studying the usage of its copy machines. A random sample of six of the sales offices revealed the following number of copies made in each selected office last week.

826	931	1,126	918	1,011	1,101

Develop a 95% confidence interval for the mean number of copies per week.

6. John Kleman is the host of KXYZ Radio 55 AM drive-time news in Denver. During his morning program, John asks listeners to call in and discuss current local and national news. This morning, John was concerned with the number of hours children under 12 years of age watch TV per day. The last five callers reported that their children watched the following number of hours of TV last night.

3.0	3.5	4.0	4.5	3.0

Would it be reasonable to develop a confidence interval from these data to show the mean number of hours of TV watched? If yes, construct an appropriate confidence interval and interpret the result. If no, why would a confidence interval not be appropriate?
7. Historically, Widgets Manufacturing Inc. produces 250 widgets per day. Recently the new owner bought a new machine to produce more widgets per day. A sample of 16 days' production revealed a mean of 240 units with a standard deviation of 35. Construct a confidence interval for the mean number of widgets produced per day. Does it seem reasonable to conclude that the mean daily widget production has changed? Justify your conclusion.
8. A manufacturer of cell phone batteries wants to estimate the useful life of its battery (in thousands of hours). The estimate is to be within 0.10 (100 hours). Assume a 95% level of confidence and that the standard deviation of the useful life of the battery is 0.90 (900 hours). Determine the required sample size.
9. The manager of a home improvement store wishes to estimate the mean amount of money spent in the store. The estimate is to be within $4.00 with a 95% level of confidence. The manager does not know the standard deviation of the amounts spent. However, he does estimate that the range is from $5.00 up to $155.00. How large of a sample is needed?
10. In a sample of 200 residents of Georgetown County, 120 reported they believed the county real estate taxes were too high. Develop a 95% confidence interval for the proportion of residents who believe the tax rate is too high. Does it seem reasonable to conclude that 50% of the voters believe that taxes are too high?
11. In recent times, the percent of buyers purchasing a new vehicle via the Internet has been large enough that local automobile dealers are concerned about its impact on their business. The information needed is an estimate of the proportion of purchases via the Internet. How large of a sample of purchasers is necessary for the estimate to be within 2 percentage points with a 98% level of confidence? Current thinking is that about 8% of the vehicles are purchased via the Internet.
12. Historically, the proportion of adults over the age of 24 who smoke has been .30. In recent years, much information has been published and aired on radio and TV that smoking is not good for one's health. A sample of 500 adults revealed only 25% of those sampled smoked. Develop a 98% confidence interval for the proportion of adults who currently smoke. Does it seem reasonable to conclude that the proportion of adults who smoke has changed?
13. The auditor of the state of Ohio needs an estimate of the proportion of residents who regularly play the state lottery. Historically, about 40% regularly play, but the auditor would like some current information. How large a sample is necessary for the estimate to be within 3 percentage points, with a 98% level of confidence?

CASE

Century National Bank

Refer to the description of Century National Bank at the end of the Review of Chapters 1–4 on page 125. When Mr. Selig took over as president of Century several years ago, the use of debit cards was just beginning. He would like an update on the use of these cards. Develop a 95% confidence interval for the proportion of customers using these cards. On the basis of the confidence interval, is it reasonable to conclude that more than half of the customers use a debit card? Write a brief report interpreting the results.

PRACTICE TEST

Part 1—Objective

1. If each item in the population has the same chance of being selected, this is called a ________. 1. ____________
2. The difference between the population mean and the sample mean is called the ________. 2. ____________

3. The ________ is the standard deviation of the distribution of sample means. 3. ____________
4. If the sample size is increased, the variance of the sample means will ________. (become smaller, become larger, not change) 4. ____________
5. A single value used to estimate a population parameter is called a ________. 5. ____________
6. A range of values within which the population parameter is expected to occur is called a ________. 6. ____________
7. Which of the following does *not* affect the width of a confidence interval? (sample size, variation in the population, level of confidence, size of population) 7. ____________
8. The fraction of a population that has a particular characteristic is called a ________. 8. ____________
9. Which of the following is not a characteristic of the *t* distribution? (positively skewed, continuous, mean of zero, based on degrees of freedom) 9. ____________
10. To determine the required sample size of a proportion when no estimate of the population proportion is available, what value is used? 10. ____________

Part 2—Problems

1. Americans spend an average (mean) of 12.2 minutes (per day) in the shower. The distribution of times follows the normal distribution with a population standard deviation of 2.3 minutes. What is the likelihood that the mean time per day for a sample of 12 Americans was 11 minutes or less?
2. A recent study of 26 Conway, South Carolina, residents revealed they had lived at their current address an average of 9.3 years. The standard deviation of the sample was 2 years.
   a. What is the population mean?
   b. What is the best estimate of the population mean?
   c. What is the standard error of estimate?
   d. Develop a 90% confidence interval for the population mean.
3. A recent federal report indicated that 27% of children ages 2 to 5 ate a vegetable at least five times a week. How large a sample is needed to estimate the true population proportion within 2% with a 98% level of confidence? Be sure to use the information contained in the federal report.
4. The Philadelphia Area Transit Authority wishes to estimate the proportion of central city workers that use public transportation to get to work. A sample of 100 workers revealed that 64 used public transportation. Develop a 95% confidence interval for the population proportion.

One-Sample Tests of Hypothesis

10

DOLE PINEAPPLE INC. is concerned that the 16-ounce can of sliced pineapple is being overfilled. Assume the standard deviation of the process is .03 ounce. The quality control department took a random sample of 50 cans and found that the arithmetic mean weight was 16.05 ounces. At the 5% level of significance, can we conclude that the mean weight is greater than 16 ounces? Determine the *p*-value. (See Exercise 26 and LO10-5.)

LEARNING OBJECTIVES

When you have completed this chapter, you will be able to:

LO10-1 Define a hypothesis.

LO10-2 Explain the process of testing a hypothesis.

LO10-3 Apply the six-step procedure for testing a hypothesis.

LO10-4 Distinguish between a one-tailed and a two-tailed test of hypothesis.

LO10-5 Conduct a test of a hypothesis about a population mean.

LO10-6 Compute and interpret a *p*-value.

LO10-7 Use a *t* statistic to test a hypothesis.

LO10-8 Compute the probability of a Type II error.

STATISTICS IN ACTION

LASIK is a 15-minute surgical procedure that uses a laser to reshape an eye's cornea with the goal of improving eyesight. Research shows that about 5% of all surgeries involve complications such as glare, corneal haze, overcorrection or undercorrection of vision, and loss of vision. In a statistical sense, the research tests a null hypothesis that the surgery will not improve eyesight with the alternative hypothesis that the surgery will improve eyesight. The sample data of LASIK surgery shows that 5% of all cases result in complications. The 5% represents a Type I error rate. When a person decides to have the surgery, he or she expects to reject the null hypothesis. In 5% of future cases, this expectation will not be met. (Source: *American Academy of Ophthalmology Journal,* Vol. 16, no. 43.)

INTRODUCTION

Chapter 8 began our study of statistical inference. We described how we could select a random sample to estimate the value of a population parameter. For example, we selected a sample of five employees at Spence Sprockets, found the number of years of service for each sampled employee, computed the mean years of service, and used the sample mean to estimate the mean years of service for all employees. In other words, we estimated a population parameter from a sample statistic.

Chapter 9 continued the study of statistical inference by developing a confidence interval. A confidence interval is a range of values within which we expect the population parameter to occur. In this chapter, rather than develop a range of values within which we expect the population parameter to occur, we develop a procedure to test the validity of a statement about a population parameter. Some examples of statements we might want to test are:

- The mean speed of automobiles passing milepost 150 on the West Virginia Turnpike is 68 miles per hour.
- The mean number of miles driven by those leasing a Chevy TrailBlazer for 3 years is 32,000 miles.
- The mean time an American family lives in a particular single-family dwelling is 11.8 years.
- The mean starting salary for a 2013 graduate from a four-year business program is $51,541. This is an increase of 2.2% from 2011.
- According to the Kelley Blue Book (www.kbb.com), a 2013 Ford Edge averages 19 miles per gallon in the city.
- The mean cost to remodel a home office is $10,500.

This chapter and several of the following chapters cover statistical hypothesis testing. We begin by defining what we mean by a statistical hypothesis and statistical hypothesis testing. Next, we outline the steps in statistical hypothesis testing. Then we conduct tests of hypothesis for means. In the last section of the chapter, we describe possible errors due to sampling in hypothesis testing.

LO10-1
Define a hypothesis.

WHAT IS A HYPOTHESIS?

A hypothesis is a statement about a population. Data are then collected to check the reasonableness of the statement. To begin, we need to define the word *hypothesis.* In the U.S. legal system, a person is presumed innocent until proven guilty. A jury hypothesizes that a person charged with a crime is innocent and then reviews the evidence to assess if there is enough evidence to claim that the person is not innocent or guilty as charged. In a similar sense, a patient goes to a physician and reports various symptoms. On the basis of the symptoms, the physician will order certain diagnostic tests, then, according to the symptoms and the test results, determine the treatment to be followed.

In statistical analysis, we make a claim—that is, state a hypothesis—collect data, and then use the data to test the claim. We define a statistical hypothesis as follows.

HYPOTHESIS A statement about a population parameter subject to verification.

In most cases, the population is so large that it is not feasible to study all the items, objects, or persons in the population. For example, it would not be possible to contact every systems analyst in the United States to find his or her monthly income. Likewise, the quality assurance department at Cooper Tire cannot check each tire produced to determine whether it will last more than 60,000 miles.

As noted in Chapter 8, an alternative to measuring or interviewing the entire population is to take a sample from the population. We can, therefore, test a statement to determine whether the sample does or does not support the statement concerning the population.

LO10-2
Explain the process of testing a hypothesis.

WHAT IS HYPOTHESIS TESTING?

The terms *hypothesis testing* and *testing a hypothesis* are used interchangeably. Hypothesis testing starts with a statement, or assumption, about a population parameter—such as the population mean. This statement is referred to as a hypothesis. A hypothesis might be that the mean monthly commission of sales associates in retail electronics stores, such as h. h. gregg, is \$2,000. We cannot contact all h. h. gregg sales associates to determine that the mean is \$2,000. The cost of locating and interviewing every h. h. gregg electronics sales associate in the United States would be exorbitant. To test the validity of the hypothesis ($\mu = \$2{,}000$), we must select a sample from the population of all h. h. gregg electronics sales associates, calculate sample statistics, and based on certain decision rules reject or fail to reject the hypothesis. A sample mean of \$1,000 per month is much less than \$2,000 per month and we would most likely reject the hypothesis. However, suppose the sample mean is \$1,995. Can we attribute the \$5 difference between \$1,995 and \$2,000 to sampling error? Or is this difference of \$5 statistically significant?

> **HYPOTHESIS TESTING** A procedure based on sample evidence and probability theory to determine whether the hypothesis is a reasonable statement.

LO10-3
Apply the six-step procedure for testing a hypothesis.

SIX-STEP PROCEDURE FOR TESTING A HYPOTHESIS

There is a six-step procedure that systematizes hypothesis testing; when we get to step 5, we are ready to reject or not reject the hypothesis. However, hypothesis testing as used by statisticians does not provide proof that something is true, in the manner in which a mathematician "proves" a statement. It does provide a kind of "proof beyond a reasonable doubt," in the manner of the court system. Hence, there are specific rules of evidence, or procedures, that are followed. The steps are shown in the following diagram. We will discuss in detail each of the steps.

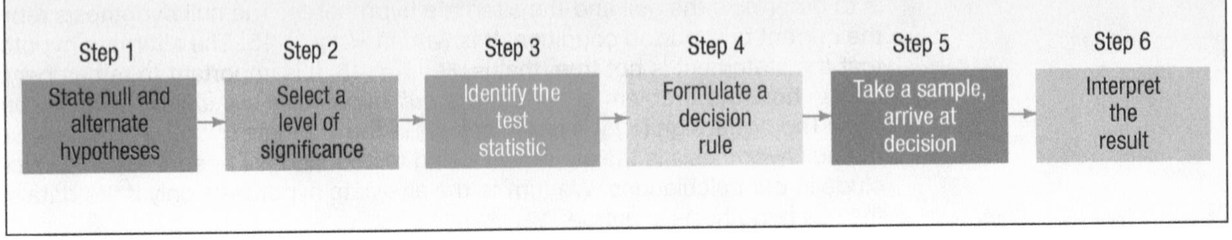

Step 1: State the Null Hypothesis (H_0) and the Alternate Hypothesis (H_1)

The first step is to state the hypothesis being tested. It is called the **null hypothesis,** designated H_0, and read "*H sub zero.*" The capital letter *H* stands for hypothesis, and the subscript zero implies "no difference." There is usually a "not" or a "no" term in the null hypothesis, meaning that there is "no change." For example, the null hypothesis is that the mean number of miles driven on the steel-belted tire is not different from 60,000. The null hypothesis would be written H_0: $\mu = 60{,}000$. Generally speaking, the null hypothesis is developed for the purpose of testing. We either reject or fail to reject the null hypothesis. The null hypothesis is a statement that is not rejected unless our sample data provide convincing evidence that it is false.

We should emphasize that, if the null hypothesis is not rejected on the basis of the sample data, we cannot say that the null hypothesis is true. To put it another way, failing to reject the null hypothesis does not prove that H_0 is true; it means we have *failed to disprove* H_0. To prove without any doubt the null hypothesis is true, the population parameter would have to be known. To actually determine it, we would have to test, survey, or count every item in the population. This is usually not feasible. The alternative is to take a sample from the population.

It should also be noted that we often begin the null hypothesis by stating, "There is no *significant* difference between . . ." or "The mean impact strength of the glass is not *significantly* different from. . . ." When we select a sample from a population, the sample statistic is usually numerically different from the hypothesized population parameter. As an illustration, suppose the hypothesized impact strength of a glass plate is 70 psi, and the mean impact strength of a sample of 12 glass plates is 69.5 psi. We must make a decision about the difference of 0.5 psi. Is it a true difference, that is, a significant difference, or is the difference between the sample statistic (69.5) and the hypothesized population parameter (70.0) due to chance (sampling)? To answer this question, we conduct a test of significance, commonly referred to as a test of hypothesis. To define what is meant by a null hypothesis:

> **NULL HYPOTHESIS** A statement about the value of a population parameter developed for the purpose of testing numerical evidence.

The **alternate hypothesis** describes what you will conclude if you reject the null hypothesis. It is written H_1 and is read "*H sub one.*" It is also referred to as the research hypothesis. The alternate hypothesis is accepted if the sample data provide us with enough statistical evidence that the null hypothesis is false.

> **ALTERNATE HYPOTHESIS** A statement that is accepted if the sample data provide sufficient evidence that the null hypothesis is false.

The following example will help clarify what is meant by the null hypothesis and the alternate hypothesis. A recent article indicated the mean age of U.S. commercial aircraft is 15 years. To conduct a statistical test regarding this statement, the first step is to determine the null and the alternate hypotheses. The null hypothesis represents the current or reported condition. It is written H_0: $\mu = 15$. The alternate hypothesis is that the statement is not true, that is, H_1: $\mu \neq 15$. It is important to remember that no matter how the problem is stated, *the null hypothesis will always contain the equal sign.* The equal sign (=) will never appear in the alternate hypothesis. Why? Because the null hypothesis is the statement being tested, and we need a specific value to include in our calculations. We turn to the alternate hypothesis only if the data suggest the null hypothesis is untrue.

Step 2: Select a Level of Significance

After setting up the null hypothesis and alternate hypothesis, the next step is to state the level of significance.

LEVEL OF SIGNIFICANCE The probability of rejecting the null hypothesis when it is true.

The level of significance is designated α, the Greek letter alpha. It is also sometimes called the level of risk. This may be a more appropriate term because it is the risk you take of rejecting the null hypothesis when it is really true.

There is no one level of significance that is applied to all tests. A decision is made to use the .05 level (often stated as the 5% level), the .01 level, the .10 level, or any other level between 0 and 1. Traditionally, the .05 level is selected for consumer research projects, .01 for quality assurance, and .10 for political polling. You, the researcher, must decide on the level of significance *before* formulating a decision rule and collecting sample data.

To illustrate how it is possible to reject a true hypothesis, suppose a firm manufacturing personal computers uses a large number of printed circuit boards. Suppliers bid on the boards, and the one with the lowest bid is awarded a sizable contract. Suppose the contract specifies that the computer manufacturer's quality-assurance department will sample all incoming shipments of circuit boards. If more than 6% of the boards sampled are substandard, the shipment will be rejected. The null hypothesis is that the incoming shipment of boards contains 6% or less substandard boards. The alternate hypothesis is that more than 6% of the boards are defective.

A shipment of 4,000 circuit boards was received from Allied Electronics, and the quality assurance department selected a random sample of 50 circuit boards for testing. Of the 50 circuit boards sampled, 4 boards, or 8%, were substandard. The shipment was rejected because it exceeded the maximum of 6% substandard printed circuit boards. If the shipment was actually substandard, then the decision to return the boards to the supplier was correct. However, suppose the 4 substandard printed circuit boards selected in the sample of 50 were the only substandard boards in the shipment of 4,000 boards. Then only $\frac{1}{10}$ of 1% were defective ($4/4,000 = .001$). In that case, less than 6% of the entire shipment was substandard and rejecting the shipment was an error. In terms of hypothesis testing, we rejected the null hypothesis when we should have failed to reject the null hypothesis. By rejecting a true null hypothesis, we committed a Type I error. The probability of committing a Type I error is α.

TYPE I ERROR Rejecting the null hypothesis, H_0, when it is true.

The probability of committing another type of error, called a Type II error, is designated by the Greek letter beta (β).

TYPE II ERROR Not rejecting the null hypothesis when it is false.

The firm manufacturing personal computers would commit a Type II error if, unknown to the manufacturer, an incoming shipment of printed circuit boards from Allied Electronics contained 15% substandard boards, yet the shipment was

accepted. How could this happen? Suppose 2 of the 50 boards in the sample (4%) tested were substandard, and 48 of the 50 were good boards. According to the stated procedure, because the sample contained less than 6% substandard boards, the shipment was accepted. It could be that *by chance* the 48 good boards selected in the sample were the only acceptable ones in the entire shipment consisting of thousands of boards!

In retrospect, the researcher cannot study every item or individual in the population. Thus, there is a possibility of two types of error—a Type I error, wherein the null hypothesis is rejected when it should not be rejected, and a Type II error, wherein the null hypothesis is not rejected when it should have been rejected.

We often refer to the probability of these two possible errors as *alpha*, α, and *beta*, β. Alpha (α) is the probability of making a Type I error, and beta (β) is the probability of making a Type II error. The following table summarizes the decisions the researcher could make and the possible consequences.

Null Hypothesis	Researcher: Does Not Reject H_0	Researcher: Rejects H_0
H_0 is true	Correct decision	Type I error
H_0 is false	Type II error	Correct decision

Step 3: Select the Test Statistic

There are many test statistics. In this chapter, we use both z and t as the test statistics. In later chapters, we will use such test statistics as F and χ^2, called chi-square.

TEST STATISTIC A value, determined from sample information, used to determine whether to reject the null hypothesis.

In hypothesis testing for the mean (μ) when σ is known, the test statistic z is computed by:

TESTING A MEAN, σ KNOWN

$$z = \frac{\bar{x} - \mu}{\sigma/\sqrt{n}} \qquad [10\text{–}1]$$

The z value is based on the sampling distribution of $\bar{x}$, which follows the normal distribution with a mean ($\mu_{\bar{x}}$) equal to μ and a standard deviation $\sigma_{\bar{x}}$, which is equal to $\sigma/\sqrt{n}$. We can thus determine whether the difference between $\bar{x}$ and μ is statistically significant by finding the number of standard deviations $\bar{x}$ is from μ, using formula (10–1).

Step 4: Formulate the Decision Rule

A decision rule is a statement of the specific conditions under which the null hypothesis is rejected and the conditions under which it is not rejected. The region or area of rejection defines the location of all those values that are so large or so small that the probability of their occurrence under a true null hypothesis is rather remote.

Chart 10–1 portrays the rejection region for a test of significance that will be conducted later in the chapter.

STATISTICS IN ACTION

During World War II, allied military planners needed estimates of the number of German tanks. The information provided by traditional spying methods was not reliable, but statistical methods proved to be valuable. For example, espionage and reconnaissance led analysts to estimate that 1,550 tanks were produced during June 1941. However, using the serial numbers of captured tanks and statistical analysis, military planners estimated that only 244 tanks were produced. The actual number produced, as determined from German production records, was 271. The estimate using statistical analysis turned out to be much more accurate. A similar type of analysis was used to estimate the number of Iraqi tanks destroyed during Desert Storm.

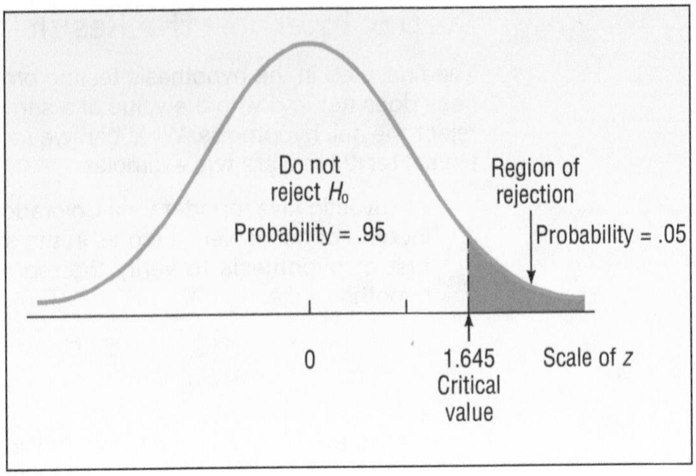

CHART 10–1 Sampling Distribution of the Statistic *z*, a Right-Tailed Test, .05 Level of Significance

Note in the chart that:

- The area where the null hypothesis is not rejected is to the left of 1.645. We will explain how to get the 1.645 value shortly.
- The area of rejection is to the right of 1.645.
- A one-tailed test is being applied. (This will also be explained later.)
- The .05 level of significance was chosen.
- The sampling distribution of the statistic z follows the normal probability distribution.
- The value 1.645 separates the regions where the null hypothesis is rejected and where it is not rejected.
- The value 1.645 is the **critical value.**

CRITICAL VALUE The dividing point between the region where the null hypothesis is rejected and the region where it is not rejected.

Step 5: Make a Decision

The fifth step in hypothesis testing is to compute the value of the test statistic, compare its value to the critical value, and make a decision to reject or not to reject the null hypothesis. Referring to Chart 10–1, if, based on sample information, z is computed to be 2.34, the null hypothesis is rejected at the .05 level of significance. The decision to reject H_0 was made because 2.34 lies in the region of rejection, that is, beyond 1.645. We reject the null hypothesis, reasoning that it is highly improbable that a computed z value this large is due to sampling error (chance).

Had the computed value been 1.645 or less, say 0.71, the null hypothesis is not rejected. It is reasoned that such a small computed value could be attributed to chance, that is, sampling error. As we have emphasized, only one of two decisions is possible in hypothesis testing—either reject or do not reject the null hypothesis.

However, because the decision is based on a sample, it is always possible to make either of two decision errors. It is possible to make a Type I error when the null hypothesis is rejected when it should not be rejected. Or it is also possible to make a Type II error when the null hypothesis is not rejected and it should have been rejected. Fortunately, we can decide on the probability of making a Type I error, α (alpha), and we can compute the probabilities associated with a Type II error, β (beta).

Step 6: Interpret the Result

The final step in the hypothesis testing procedure is to interpret the results. The process does not end with the value of a sample statistic or the decision to reject or not reject the null hypothesis. What can we say or report based on the results of the statistical test? Here are two examples:

- An investigative reporter for a Colorado newspaper reports that the mean monthly income of convenience stores in the state is \$130,000. You decide to conduct a test of hypothesis to verify the report. The null hypothesis and the alternate hypothesis are:

$$H_0: \mu = \$130{,}000$$
$$H_1: \mu \neq \$130{,}000$$

  A sample of convenience stores provides a sample mean and standard deviation, and you compute a z statistic. The results of the hypothesis test result in a decision to not reject the null hypothesis. How do you interpret the result? Be cautious with your interpretation because by not rejecting the null hypothesis, you did not prove the null hypothesis to be true. Based on the sample data, the difference between the sample mean and hypothesized population mean was not large enough to reject the null hypothesis.
- In a recent speech to students, the dean of the College of Business reported that the mean credit card debt for college students is \$3,000. You decide to conduct a test of hypothesis to investigate the statement's truth. The null hypothesis and the alternate hypothesis are:

$$H_0: \mu = \$3{,}000$$
$$H_1: \mu \neq \$3{,}000$$

  A sample of college students provides a sample mean and standard deviation, and you compute a z statistic. The results of the hypothesis test result in a decision to reject the null hypothesis. How do you interpret the result? The evidence does not support the dean's statement. You have disproved the null hypothesis with a stated probability of a Type I error, α. Based on the sample data, the mean amount of student credit card debt is different from \$3,000.

SUMMARY OF THE STEPS IN HYPOTHESIS TESTING

1. Establish the null hypothesis (H_0) and the alternate hypothesis (H_1).
2. Select the level of significance, that is, α.
3. Select an appropriate test statistic.
4. Formulate a decision rule based on steps 1, 2, and 3 above.
5. Make a decision regarding the null hypothesis based on the sample information.
6. Interpret the results of the test.

Before actually conducting a test of hypothesis, we describe the difference between a one-tailed test of significance and a two-tailed test.

LO10-4
Distinguish between a one-tailed and a two-tailed test of hypothesis.

ONE-TAILED AND TWO-TAILED TESTS OF SIGNIFICANCE

Refer to Chart 10–1. It shows a one-tailed test. It is called a one-tailed test because the rejection region is only in one tail of the curve. In this case, it is in the right, or upper, tail of the curve. To illustrate, suppose that the packaging department at General Foods

Corporation is concerned that some boxes of Grape Nuts are significantly overweight. The cereal is packaged in 453-gram boxes, so the null hypothesis is H_0: $\mu \leq 453$. This is read, "the population mean (μ) is equal to or less than 453." The alternate hypothesis is, therefore, H_1: $\mu > 453$. This is read, "μ is greater than 453." Note that the inequality sign in the alternate hypothesis (>) points to the region of rejection in the upper tail. (See Chart 10–1.) Also observe that the null hypothesis includes the equal sign. That is, H_0: $\mu \leq 453$. The equality condition always appears in H_0, never in H_1.

Chart 10–2 portrays a situation where the rejection region is in the left (lower) tail of the standard normal distribution. As an illustration, consider the problem of automobile manufacturers, large automobile leasing companies, and other organizations that purchase large quantities of tires. They want the tires to average, say, 60,000 miles of wear under normal usage. They will, therefore, reject a shipment of tires if tests reveal that the mean life of the tires is significantly below 60,000 miles. They gladly accept a shipment if the mean life is greater than 60,000 miles! They are not concerned with this possibility, however. They are concerned only if they have sample evidence to conclude that the tires will average less than 60,000 miles of useful life. Thus, the test is set up to satisfy the concern of the automobile manufacturers that *the mean life of the tires is not less than 60,000 miles.* This statement appears in the null hypothesis. The null and alternate hypotheses in this case are written H_0: $\mu \geq 60{,}000$ and H_1: $\mu < 60{,}000$.

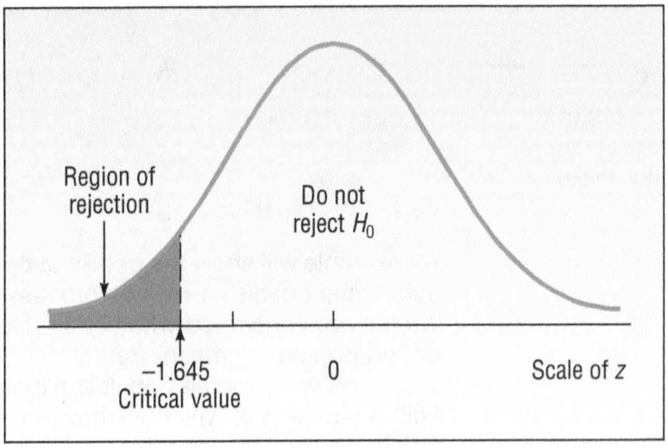

CHART 10–2 Sampling Distribution for the Statistic *z*, Left-Tailed Test, .05 Level of Significance

One way to determine the location of the rejection region is to look at the direction in which the inequality sign in the alternate hypothesis is pointing (either < or >). In the tire wear problem, it is pointing to the left, and the rejection region is therefore in the left tail.

In summary, a test is *one-tailed* when the alternate hypothesis, H_1, states a direction, such as:

H_0: The mean income of female stockbrokers is *less than or equal to* \$65,000 per year.
H_1: The mean income of female stockbrokers is *greater than* \$65,000 per year.

If no direction is specified in the alternate hypothesis, we use a *two-tailed* test. Changing the previous problem to illustrate, we can say:

H_0: The mean income of female stockbrokers is \$65,000 per year.
H_1: The mean income of female stockbrokers is *not equal to* \$65,000 per year.

If the null hypothesis is rejected and H_1 accepted in the two-tailed case, the mean income could be significantly greater than \$65,000 per year or it could be significantly less than \$65,000 per year. To accommodate these two possibilities, the 5% area of

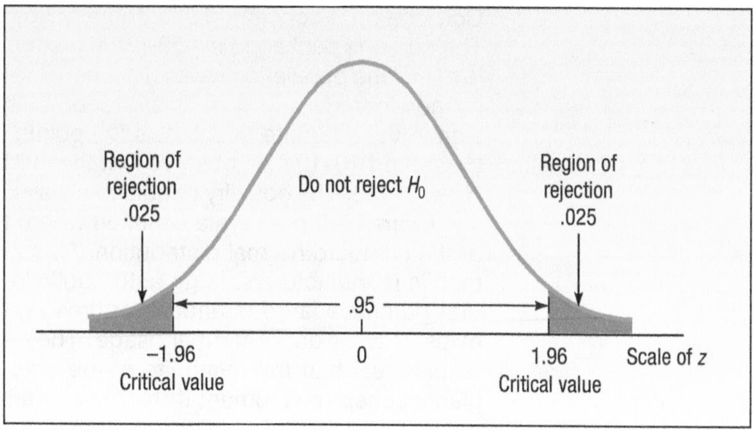

CHART 10–3 Regions of Nonrejection and Rejection for a Two-Tailed Test, .05 Level of Significance

rejection is divided equally into the two tails of the sampling distribution (2.5% each). Chart 10–3 shows the two areas and the critical values. Note that the total area in the normal distribution is 1.0000, found by .9500 + .0250 + .0250.

LO10-5
Conduct a test of a hypothesis about a population mean.

TESTING FOR A POPULATION MEAN: KNOWN POPULATION STANDARD DEVIATION

A Two-Tailed Test

An example will show the details of the six-step hypothesis testing procedure and the subsequent decision-making process. We also wish to use a two-tailed test. That is, we are *not* concerned whether the sample results are larger or smaller than the proposed population mean. Rather, we are interested in whether it is *different from* the proposed value for the population mean. We begin, as we did in the previous chapter, with a situation in which we have historical information about the population and in fact know its standard deviation.

EXAMPLE

Jamestown Steel Company manufactures and assembles desks and other office equipment at several plants in western New York State. The weekly production of the Model A325 desk at the Fredonia Plant follows a normal probability distribution with a mean of 200 and a standard deviation of 16. Recently, because of market expansion, new production methods have been introduced and new employees hired. The vice president of manufacturing would like to investigate whether there has been a *change* in the weekly production of the Model A325 desk. Is the mean number of desks produced at the Fredonia Plant *different from* 200 at the .01 significance level?

SOLUTION

In this example, we know two important pieces of information: (1) the population of weekly production follows the normal distribution and (2) the standard deviation of this normal distribution is 16 desks per week. So it is appropriate to use the *z* statistic. We use the statistical hypothesis testing procedure to investigate whether the production rate has changed from 200 per week.

Step 1: State the null hypothesis and the alternate hypothesis. The null hypothesis is "The population mean is 200." The alternate hypothesis is "The mean is different from 200" or "The mean is not 200." These two hypotheses are written:

$$H_0: \mu = 200$$
$$H_1: \mu \neq 200$$

This is a *two-tailed test* because the alternate hypothesis does not state a direction. In other words, it does not state whether the mean production is greater than 200 or less than 200. The vice president wants only to find out whether the production rate is different from 200.

Before moving to Step 2, we wish to emphasize two points.

- The null hypothesis has the equal sign. Why? Because the value we are testing is always in the null hypothesis. Logically, the alternate hypothesis never contains the equal sign.
- Both the null hypothesis and the alternate hypothesis contain Greek letters—in this case μ, which is the symbol for the population mean. Tests of hypothesis **always** refer to population parameters, never to sample statistics. To put it another way, you will never see the symbol $\bar{x}$ as part of the null hypothesis or the alternate hypothesis.

Step 2: Select the level of significance. In the example description, the significance level selected is .01. This is α, the probability of committing a Type I error, and it is the probability of rejecting a true null hypothesis.

Step 3: Select the test statistic. The test statistic is *z* when the population standard deviation is known. Transforming the production data to standard units (*z* values) permits their use not only in this problem but also in other hypothesis-testing problems. Formula (10–1) for *z* is repeated next with the various letters identified.

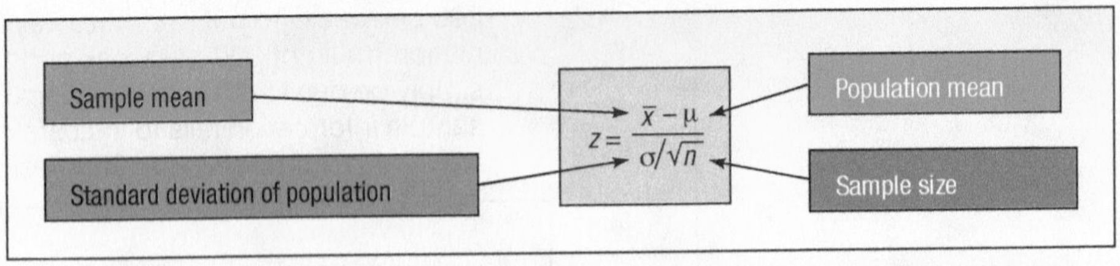

Step 4: Formulate the decision rule. We formulate the decision rule by first determining the critical values of *z*. Because this is a two-tailed test, half of .01, or .005, is placed in each tail. The area where H_0 is not rejected, located between the two tails, is therefore .99. Using the Student's *t* Distribution table in Appendix B.5, move to the top margin called "Level of Significance for Two-Tailed Tests, α," select the column with $\alpha = .01$, and move to the last row, which is labeled ∞,

or infinite degrees of freedom. The z value in this cell is 2.576. For your convenience, Appendix B.5, Student's t Distribution, is repeated in the inside back cover. All the facets of this problem are shown in the diagram in Chart 10–4.

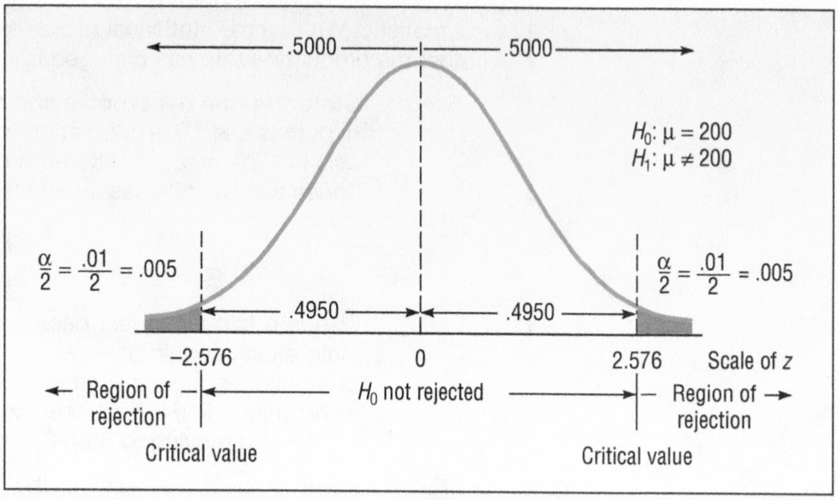

CHART 10–4 Decision Rule for the .01 Significance Level

The decision rule is: if the computed value of z is not between −2.576 and 2.576, reject the null hypothesis. If z falls between −2.576 and 2.576, do not reject the null hypothesis.

Step 5: Make a decision. Take a sample from the population (weekly production), compute z, apply the decision rule, and arrive at a decision to reject H_0 or not to reject H_0. The mean number of desks produced last year (50 weeks because the plant was shut down 2 weeks for vacation) is 203.5. The standard deviation of the population is 16 desks per week. Computing the z value from formula (10–1):

$$z = \frac{\bar{x} - \mu}{\sigma/\sqrt{n}} = \frac{203.5 - 200}{16/\sqrt{50}} = 1.547$$

Because 1.547 does not fall in the rejection region, we decide not to reject H_0.

Step 6: Interpret the result. We did not reject the null hypothesis, so we have failed to show that the population mean has changed from 200 per week. To put it another way, the difference between the population mean of 200 per week and the sample mean of 203.5 could simply be due to chance. What should we tell the vice president? The sample information fails to indicate that the new production methods resulted in a change in the 200-desks-per-week production rate.

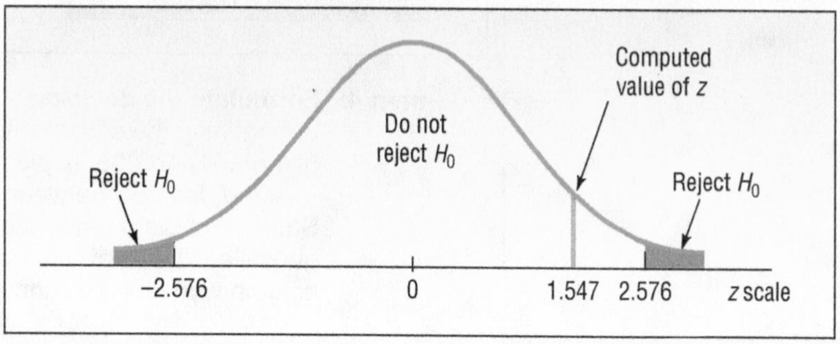

Did we prove that the assembly rate is still 200 per week? Not really. What we did, technically, was *fail to disprove the null hypothesis.* Failing to disprove the hypothesis that the population mean is 200 is not the same thing as proving it to be true. As we suggested in the chapter introduction, the conclusion is analogous to the American judicial system. To explain, suppose a person is accused of a crime but is acquitted by a jury. If a person is acquitted of a crime, the conclusion is that there was not enough evidence to prove the person guilty. The trial did not prove that the individual was innocent, only that there was not enough evidence to prove the defendant guilty. That is what we do in statistical hypothesis testing when we do not reject the null hypothesis. The correct interpretation is that we have failed to disprove the null hypothesis.

We selected the significance level, .01 in this case, before setting up the decision rule and sampling the population. This is the appropriate strategy. The significance level should be set by the investigator, but it should be determined *before* gathering the sample evidence and not changed based on the sample evidence.

How does the hypothesis testing procedure just described compare with that of confidence intervals discussed in the previous chapter? When we conducted the test of hypothesis regarding the production of desks, we changed the units from desks per week to a z value. Then we compared the computed value of the test statistic (1.547) to that of the critical values (-2.576 and 2.576). Because the computed value was in the region where the null hypothesis was not rejected, we concluded that the population mean could be 200. To use the confidence interval approach, on the other hand, we would develop a confidence interval, based on formula (9–1). See page 284. The interval would be from 197.671 to 209.329, found by $203.5 \pm 2.576(16/\sqrt{50})$. Note that the proposed population value, 200, is within this interval. Hence, we would conclude that the population mean could reasonably be 200.

In general, H_0 is rejected if the confidence interval does not include the hypothesized value. If the confidence interval includes the hypothesized value, then H_0 is not rejected. So the "do not reject region" for a test of hypothesis is equivalent to the proposed population value occurring in the confidence interval.

SELF-REVIEW 10–1

Heinz, a manufacturer of ketchup, uses a particular machine to dispense 16 ounces of its ketchup into containers. From many years of experience with the particular dispensing machine, Heinz knows the amount of product in each container follows a normal distribution with a mean of 16 ounces and a standard deviation of 0.15 ounce. A sample of 50 containers filled last hour revealed the mean amount per container was 16.017 ounces. Does this evidence suggest that the mean amount dispensed is different from 16 ounces? Use the .05 significance level.

(a) State the null hypothesis and the alternate hypothesis.
(b) What is the probability of a Type I error?
(c) Give the formula for the test statistic.
(d) State the decision rule.
(e) Determine the value of the test statistic.
(f) What is your decision regarding the null hypothesis?
(g) Interpret, in a single sentence, the result of the statistical test.

A One-Tailed Test

In the previous example/solution, we emphasized that we were concerned only with reporting to the vice president whether there had been a change in the mean number

of desks assembled at the Fredonia Plant. We were not concerned with whether the change was an increase or a decrease in the production.

To illustrate a one-tailed test, let's change the problem. Suppose the vice president wants to know whether there has been an *increase* in the number of units assembled. Can we conclude, because of the improved production methods, that the mean number of desks assembled in the last 50 weeks was more than 200? Look at the difference in the way the problem is formulated. In the first case, we wanted to know whether there was a *difference* in the mean number assembled, but now we want to know whether there has been an *increase*. Because we are investigating different questions, we will set our hypotheses differently. The biggest difference occurs in the alternate hypothesis. Before, we stated the alternate hypothesis as "different from"; now we want to state it as "greater than." In symbols:

A two-tailed test:	A one-tailed test:
H_0: $\mu = 200$	H_0: $\mu \leq 200$
H_1: $\mu \neq 200$	H_1: $\mu > 200$

The critical values for a one-tailed test are different from a two-tailed test at the same significance level. In the previous example/solution, we split the significance level in half and put half in the lower tail and half in the upper tail. In a one-tailed test, we put all the rejection region in one tail. See Chart 10–5.

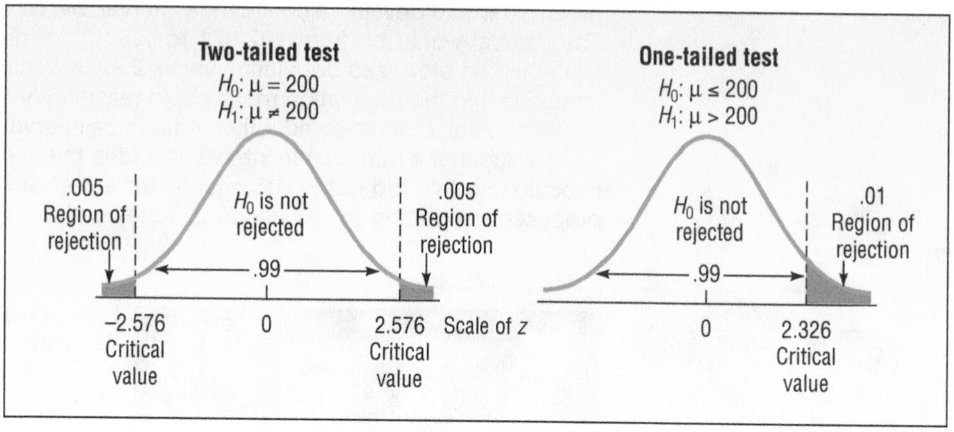

CHART 10–5 Rejection Regions for Two-Tailed and One-Tailed Tests, $\alpha = .01$

For the one-tailed test, the critical value of *z* is 2.326. Using the Student's *t* Distribution table in Appendix B.5 or inside the back cover, move to the top heading called "Level of Significance for One-Tailed Tests, α," select the column with $\alpha = .01$, and move to the last row, which is labeled ∞, or infinite degrees of freedom. The *z* value in this cell is 2.326.

LO10-6
Compute and interpret a *p*-value.

p-VALUE IN HYPOTHESIS TESTING

In testing a hypothesis, we compare the test statistic to a critical value. A decision is made to either reject the null hypothesis or not to reject it. So, for example, if the critical value is 1.96 and the computed value of the test statistic is 2.19, the decision is to reject the null hypothesis.

In recent years, spurred by the availability of computer software, additional information is often reported on the strength of the rejection. That is, how confident are we in rejecting the null hypothesis? This approach reports the probability (assuming that the null hypothesis is true) of getting a value of the test statistic at least as extreme as

the value actually obtained. This process compares the probability, called the **p-value,** with the significance level. If the *p*-value is smaller than the significance level, H_0 is rejected. If it is larger than the significance level, H_0 is not rejected.

> **p-VALUE** The probability of observing a sample value as extreme as, or more extreme than, the value observed, given that the null hypothesis is true.

STATISTICS IN ACTION

There is a difference between *statistically significant* and *practically significant.* To explain, suppose we develop a new diet pill and test it on 100,000 people. We conclude that the typical person taking the pill for 2 years lost 1 pound. Do you think many people would be interested in taking the pill to lose 1 pound? The results of using the new pill were statistically significant but not practically significant.

Determining the *p*-value not only results in a decision regarding H_0, but it gives us additional insight into the strength of the decision. A very small *p*-value, such as .0001, indicates that there is little likelihood the H_0 is true. On the other hand, a *p*-value of .2033 means that H_0 is not rejected, and there is little likelihood that it is false.

How do we find the *p*-value? To calculate *p*-values, we will need to use the *z* table (Appendix B.3 or inside the back cover), and, to use this table, we will round *z* test statistics to two decimals. To illustrate how to compute a *p*-value, we will use the example in which we tested the null hypothesis that the mean number of desks produced per week at Fredonia was 200. We did not reject the null hypothesis because the *z* value of 1.547 fell in the region between −2.576 and 2.576. We agreed not to reject the null hypothesis if the computed value of *z* fell in this region. Rounding 1.547 to 1.55 and using the *z* table, the probability of finding a *z* value of 1.55 or more is .0606, found by .5000 − .4394. To put it another way, the probability of obtaining an $\bar{X}$ greater than 203.5 if $\mu = 200$ is .0606. To compute the *p*-value, we need to be concerned with the region less than −1.55 as well as the values greater than 1.55 (because the rejection region is in both tails). The two-tailed *p*-value is .1212, found by 2(.0606). The *p*-value of .1212 is greater than the significance level of .01 decided upon initially, so H_0 is not rejected. The details are shown in the following graph. Notice for the two-tailed hypothesis test, the *p*-value is represented by areas in both tails of the distribution. Then the *p*-value can easily be compared with the significance level. The same decision rule is used as in the one-sided test.

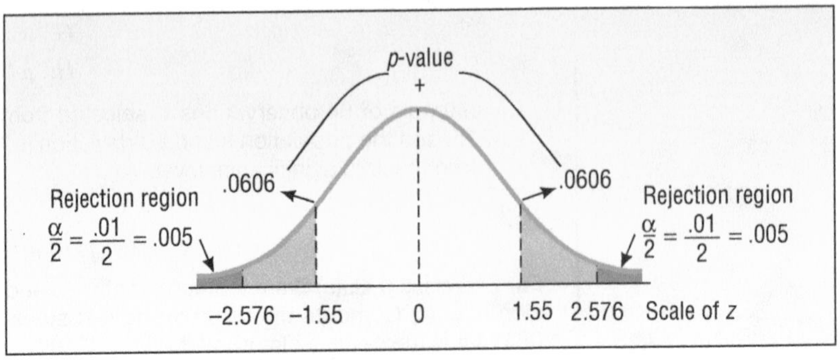

A *p*-value is a way to express the likelihood that H_0 is false. But how do we interpret a *p*-value? We have already said that if the *p*-value is less than the significance level, then we reject H_0; if it is greater than the significance level, then we do not reject H_0. Also, if the *p*-value is very large, then it is likely that H_0 is true. If the *p*-value is small, then it is likely that H_0 is not true. The following box will help to interpret *p*-values.

> **INTERPRETING THE WEIGHT OF EVIDENCE AGAINST H_0** If the *p*-value is less than
> (a) .10, we have *some* evidence that H_0 is not true.
> (b) .05, we have *strong* evidence that H_0 is not true.
> (c) .01, we have *very strong* evidence that H_0 is not true.
> (d) .001, we have *extremely strong* evidence that H_0 is not true.

SELF-REVIEW 10–2

Refer to Self-Review 10–1.

(a) Suppose the next to the last sentence is changed to read: Does this evidence suggest that the mean amount dispensed is *more than* 16 ounces? State the null hypothesis and the alternate hypothesis under these conditions.
(b) What is the decision rule under the new conditions stated in part (a)?
(c) A second sample of 50 filled containers revealed the mean to be 16.040 ounces. What is the value of the test statistic for this sample?
(d) What is your decision regarding the null hypothesis?
(e) Interpret, in a single sentence, the result of the statistical test.
(f) What is the *p*-value? What is your decision regarding the null hypothesis based on the *p*-value? Is this the same conclusion reached in part (d)?

EXERCISES

For Exercises 1–4, answer the questions: (a) Is this a one- or two-tailed test? (b) What is the decision rule? (c) What is the value of the test statistic? (d) What is your decision regarding H_0? (e) What is the *p*-value? Interpret it.

1. A sample of 36 observations is selected from a normal population. The sample mean is 49, and the population standard deviation is 5. Conduct the following test of hypothesis using the .05 significance level.

$$H_0: \mu = 50$$
$$H_1: \mu \neq 50$$

2. A sample of 36 observations is selected from a normal population. The sample mean is 12, and the population standard deviation is 3. Conduct the following test of hypothesis using the .01 significance level.

$$H_0: \mu \leq 10$$
$$H_1: \mu > 10$$

3. A sample of 36 observations is selected from a normal population. The sample mean is 21, and the population standard deviation is 5. Conduct the following test of hypothesis using the .05 significance level.

$$H_0: \mu \leq 20$$
$$H_1: \mu > 20$$

4. A sample of 64 observations is selected from a normal population. The sample mean is 215, and the population standard deviation is 15. Conduct the following test of hypothesis using the .025 significance level.

$$H_0: \mu \geq 220$$
$$H_1: \mu < 220$$

For Exercises 5–8: (a) State the null hypothesis and the alternate hypothesis. (b) State the decision rule. (c) Compute the value of the test statistic. (d) What is your decision regarding H_0? (e) What is the *p*-value? Interpret it.

5. The manufacturer of the X-15 steel-belted radial truck tire claims that the mean mileage the tire can be driven before the tread wears out is 60,000 miles. Assume the mileage wear follows the normal distribution and the standard deviation of the distribution is 5,000 miles. Crosset Truck Company bought 48 tires and found that the mean mileage for its trucks is 59,500 miles. Is Crosset's experience different from that claimed by the manufacturer at the .05 significance level?
6. The waiting time for customers at MacBurger Restaurants follows a normal distribution with a population standard deviation of 1 minute. At the Warren Road MacBurger, the quality-assurance department sampled 50 customers and found that the mean waiting time was 2.75 minutes. At the .05 significance level, can we conclude that the mean waiting time is less than 3 minutes?
7. A recent national survey found that high school students watched an average (mean) of 6.8 DVDs per month with a population standard deviation of 1.8. The distribution of DVDs watched per month follows the normal distribution. A random sample of 36 college students revealed that the mean number of DVDs watched last month was 6.2. At the .05 significance level, can we conclude that college students watch fewer DVDs a month than high school students?

8. At the time she was hired as a server at the Grumney Family Restaurant, Beth Brigden was told, "You can average \$80 a day in tips." Assume the population of daily tips is normally distributed with a standard deviation of \$9.95. Over the first 35 days she was employed at the restaurant, the mean daily amount of her tips was \$84.85. At the .01 significance level, can Ms. Brigden conclude that her daily tips average more than \$80?

LO10-7

Use a *t* statistic to test a hypothesis.

TESTING FOR A POPULATION MEAN: POPULATION STANDARD DEVIATION UNKNOWN

In the preceding example, we knew σ, the population standard deviation, and that the population followed the normal distribution. In most cases, however, the population standard deviation is unknown. Thus, σ must be based on prior studies or estimated by the sample standard deviation, *s*. The population standard deviation in the following example is not known, so the sample standard deviation is used to estimate σ.

To find the value of the test statistic, we use the *t* distribution and revise formula (10–1) as follows:

TESTING A MEAN, σ UNKNOWN

$$t = \frac{\bar{x} - \mu}{s/\sqrt{n}} \qquad \textbf{[10–2]}$$

with $n - 1$ degrees of freedom, where:

$\bar{x}$ is the sample mean.
μ is the hypothesized population mean.
s is the sample standard deviation.
n is the number of observations in the sample.

We encountered this same situation when constructing confidence intervals in the previous chapter. See pages 289–296 in Chapter 9. We summarized this problem in Chart 9–3 on page 292. Under these conditions, the correct statistical procedure is to replace the standard normal distribution with the *t* distribution. To review, the major characteristics of the *t* distribution are:

- It is a continuous distribution.
- It is bell-shaped and symmetrical.
- There is a family of *t* distributions. Each time the degrees of freedom change, a new distribution is created.
- As the number of degrees of freedom increases, the shape of the *t* distribution approaches that of the standard normal distribution.
- The *t* distribution is flatter, or more spread out, than the standard normal distribution.

The following example/solution shows the details.

EXAMPLE

The McFarland Insurance Company Claims Department reports the mean cost to process a claim is \$60. An industry comparison showed this amount to be larger than most other insurance companies, so the company instituted cost-cutting measures. To evaluate the effect of the cost-cutting measures, the supervisor of the Claims Department selected a random sample of 26 claims processed last

month and recorded the cost to process each claim. The sample information is reported below.

$45	$49	$62	$40	$43	$61
48	53	67	63	78	64
48	54	51	56	63	69
58	51	58	59	56	57
38	76				

At the .01 significance level, is it reasonable to conclude that the mean cost to process a claim is now less than $60?

SOLUTION

We will use the six-step hypothesis testing procedure.

Step 1: State the null hypothesis and the alternate hypothesis. The null hypothesis is that the population mean is at least $60. The alternate hypothesis is that the population mean is less than $60. We can express the null and alternate hypotheses as follows:

$$H_0: \mu \geq \$60$$
$$H_1: \mu < \$60$$

The test is *one*-tailed because we want to determine whether there has been a *reduction* in the cost. The inequality in the alternate hypothesis points to the region of rejection in the left tail of the distribution.

Step 2: Select the level of significance. We decided on the .01 significance level.

Step 3: Select the test statistic. The test statistic in this situation is the t distribution. Why? First, it is reasonable to conclude that the distribution of the cost per claim follows the normal distribution. We can confirm this from the histogram in the center of the following Minitab output. Observe the normal distribution superimposed on the frequency distribution.

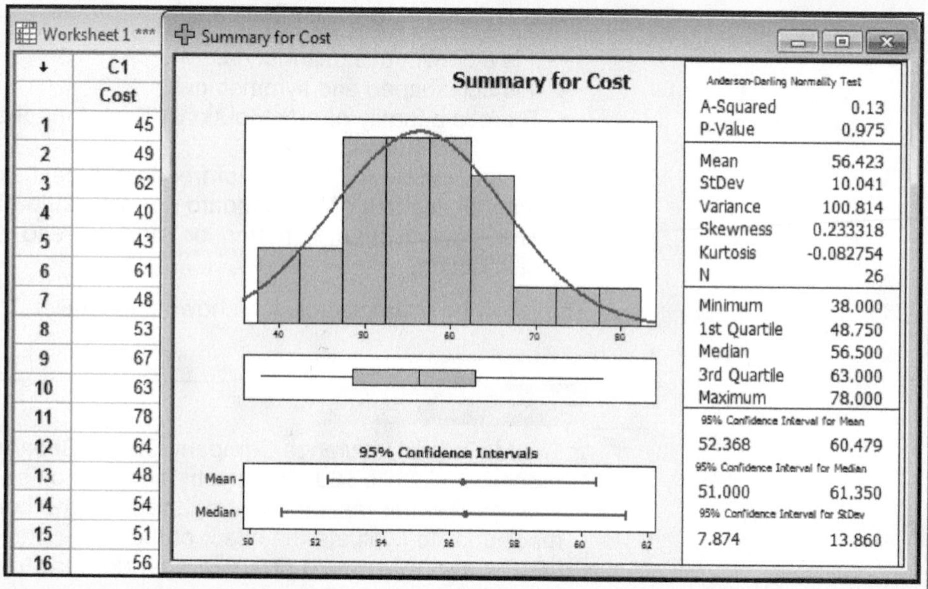

We do not know the standard deviation of the population. So we substitute the sample standard deviation. The value of the test statistic is computed by formula (10–2):

$$t = \frac{\bar{x} - \mu}{s/\sqrt{n}}$$

Step 4: Formulate the decision rule. The critical values of t are given in Appendix B.5, a portion of which is shown in Table 10–1. Appendix B.5 is also repeated in the back inside cover of the text. The far left column of the table is labeled "*df*" for degrees of freedom. The number of degrees of freedom is the total number of observations in the sample minus the number of populations sampled, written $n - 1$. In this case, the number of observations in the sample is 26, and we sampled 1 population, so there are $26 - 1 = 25$ degrees of freedom. To find the critical value, first locate the row with the appropriate degrees of freedom. This row is shaded in Table 10–1. Next, determine whether the test is one-tailed or two-tailed. In this case, we have a one-tailed test, so find the portion of the table that is labeled "one-tailed." Locate the column with the selected significance level. In this example, the significance level is .01. Move down the column labeled "0.01" until it intersects the row with 25 degrees of freedom. The value is 2.485. Because this is a one-sided test and the rejection region is in the left tail, the critical value is negative. The decision rule is to reject H_0 if the value of t is less than -2.485.

TABLE 10–1 A Portion of the *t* Distribution Table

	Confidence Intervals					
	80%	90%	95%	98%	99%	99.9%
	Level of Significance for One-Tailed Test, α					
df	0.10	0.05	0.025	0.01	0.005	0.0005
	Level of Significance for Two-Tailed Test, α					
	0.20	0.10	0.05	0.02	0.01	0.001
⋮	⋮	⋮	⋮	⋮	⋮	⋮
21	1.323	1.721	2.080	2.518	2.831	3.819
22	1.321	1.717	2.074	2.508	2.819	3.792
23	1.319	1.714	2.069	2.500	2.807	3.768
24	1.318	1.711	2.064	2.492	2.797	3.745
25	1.316	1.708	2.060	2.485	2.787	3.725
26	1.315	1.706	2.056	2.479	2.779	3.707
27	1.314	1.703	2.052	2.473	2.771	3.690
28	1.313	1.701	2.048	2.467	2.763	3.674
29	1.311	1.699	2.045	2.462	2.756	3.659
30	1.310	1.697	2.042	2.457	2.750	3.646

Step 5: Make a decision. From the Minitab output, to the right of the histogram, the mean cost per claim for the sample of 26 observations is \$56.42. The standard deviation of this sample is \$10.04. We insert these values in formula (10–2) and compute the value of t:

$$t = \frac{\bar{x} - \mu}{s/\sqrt{n}} = \frac{\$56.42 - \$60}{\$10.04/\sqrt{26}} = -1.818$$

Because -1.818 lies in the region to the right of the critical value of -2.485 (see Chart 10–6), the null hypothesis is not rejected at the .01 significance level.

Step 6: Interpret the result. We have not disproved the null hypothesis. The sample of claims could have been selected from a population with a mean cost of \$60 per claim. To put it another way, the difference of \$3.58 (\$56.42 − \$60.00) between the sample mean and the population mean could be due to sampling error. The test results do not allow the claims department manager to conclude that the cost-cutting measures have been effective.

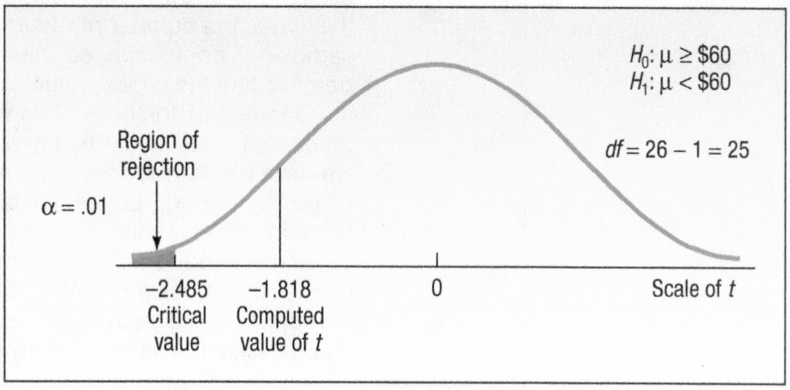

CHART 10–6 Rejection Region, *t* Distribution, .01 Significance Level

In the previous example, the mean and the standard deviation were computed using Minitab. The following example/solution shows the details when the sample mean and sample standard deviation are calculated from sample data.

EXAMPLE

The Myrtle Beach International Airport's short-term parking lot is close to the terminal, so someone meeting an incoming passenger has only a short walk to the baggage claim area, a good place to meet. To decide if the short-term lot has enough parking places, the manager of airport parking needs to know if the mean time in the lot is more than 40 minutes. A sample of 12 recent customers showed they were in the lot the following lengths of time, in minutes.

55	49	53	47	39	27	64	48	48	53	37	56

At the .05 significance level, is it reasonable to conclude that the mean time in the lot is more than 40 minutes?

SOLUTION

We begin by stating the null hypothesis and the alternate hypothesis. In this case, the question is whether the population mean could be more than 40 minutes. So this is a one-tailed test. We state the two hypotheses as follows:

$$H_0: \mu \leq 40$$

$$H_1: \mu > 40$$

There are 11 degrees of freedom, found by $n - 1 = 12 - 1 = 11$. The critical t value is 1.796, found by referring to Appendix B.5 for a one-tailed test, using $\alpha = .05$ with 11 degrees of freedom. The decision rule is: Reject the null hypothesis if the computed t is greater than 1.796. This information is summarized in Chart 10–7.

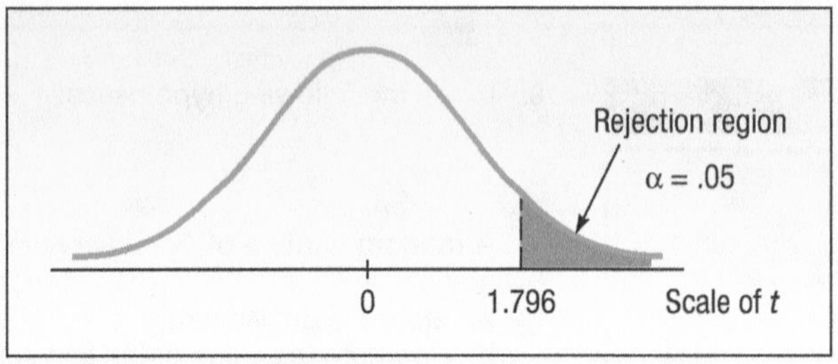

CHART 10–7 Rejection Region, One-Tailed Test, Student's t Distribution, $\alpha = .05$

We calculate the sample mean using formula (3–2) and the sample standard deviation using formula (3–8). The sample mean is 48 hours, and the sample standard deviation is 9.835 hours. The details of the calculations are shown in Table 10–2.

TABLE 10–2 Calculations of Sample Mean and Standard Deviation Parking Times

Customer	x, Minutes	$(x - \bar{x})^2$
1	55	49
2	49	1
3	53	25
4	47	1
5	39	81
6	27	441
7	64	256
8	48	0
9	48	0
10	53	25
11	37	121
12	56	64
Total	576	1064

$$\bar{x} = \frac{\Sigma x}{n} = \frac{576}{12} = 48$$

$$s = \sqrt{\frac{\Sigma(x - \bar{x})^2}{n - 1}} = \sqrt{\frac{1064}{12 - 1}} = 9.835$$

Now we are ready to compute the value of t, using formula (10–2).

$$t = \frac{\bar{x} - \mu}{s/\sqrt{n}} = \frac{48 - 40}{9.835/\sqrt{12}} = 2.818$$

The null hypothesis that the population mean is less than or equal to 40 minutes is rejected because the computed t value of 2.818 lies in the area to the right of 1.796. We conclude that the time customers spend in the lot is more than 40 minutes. This result indicates that the airport may need to add more parking places.

SELF-REVIEW 10–3

The mean life of a battery used in a digital clock is 305 days. The lives of the batteries follow the normal distribution. The battery was recently modified to last longer. A sample of 20 of the modified batteries had a mean life of 311 days with a standard deviation of 12 days. Did the modification increase the mean life of the battery?

(a) State the null hypothesis and the alternate hypothesis.
(b) Show the decision rule graphically. Use the .05 significance level.
(c) Compute the value of *t*. What is your decision regarding the null hypothesis? Briefly summarize your results.

EXERCISES

9. Given the following hypotheses:

$$H_0: \mu \leq 10$$
$$H_1: \mu > 10$$

A random sample of 10 observations is selected from a normal population. The sample mean was 12 and the sample standard deviation 3. Using the .05 significance level:

a. State the decision rule.
b. Compute the value of the test statistic.
c. What is your decision regarding the null hypothesis?

10. Given the following hypotheses:

$$H_0: \mu = 400$$
$$H_1: \mu \neq 400$$

A random sample of 12 observations is selected from a normal population. The sample mean was 407 and the sample standard deviation 6. Using the .01 significance level:

a. State the decision rule.
b. Compute the value of the test statistic.
c. What is your decision regarding the null hypothesis?

11. The Rocky Mountain district sales manager of Rath Publishing Inc., a college textbook publishing company, claims that the sales representatives make an average of 40 sales calls per week on professors. Several reps say that this estimate is too low. To investigate, a random sample of 28 sales representatives reveals that the mean number of calls made last week was 42. The standard deviation of the sample is 2.1 calls. Using the .05 significance level, can we conclude that the mean number of calls per salesperson per week is more than 40?

12. The management of White Industries is considering a new method of assembling its golf cart. The present method requires 42.3 minutes, on the average, to assemble a cart. The mean assembly time for a random sample of 24 carts, using the new method, was 40.6 minutes, and the standard deviation of the sample was 2.7 minutes. Using the .10 level of significance, can we conclude that the assembly time using the new method is faster?

13. The mean income per person in the United States is $40,000, and the distribution of incomes follows a normal distribution. A random sample of 10 residents of Wilmington, Delaware, had a mean of $50,000 with a standard deviation of $10,000. At the .05 level of significance, is that enough evidence to conclude that residents of Wilmington, Delaware, have more income than the national average?

For **DATA FILE**, please visit www.mhhe.com/lind16e

14. Most air travelers now use e-tickets. Electronic ticketing allows passengers to not worry about a paper ticket, and it costs the airline companies less to handle than paper ticketing. However, in recent times the airlines have received complaints from passengers regarding their e-tickets, particularly when connecting flights and a change of airlines were involved. To investigate the problem, an independent watchdog agency contacted a random sample of 20 airports and collected information on the number of complaints the airport had with e-tickets for the month of March. The information is reported below.

14	14	16	12	12	14	13	16	15	14
12	15	15	14	13	13	12	13	10	13

At the .05 significance level, can the watchdog agency conclude the mean number of complaints per airport is less than 15 per month?

a. What assumption is necessary before conducting a test of hypothesis?
b. Plot the number of complaints per airport in a frequency distribution or a dot plot. Is it reasonable to conclude that the population follows a normal distribution?
c. Conduct a test of hypothesis and interpret the results.

A Software Solution

The Minitab statistical software system, used in earlier chapters and the previous section, provides an efficient method for conducting a one-sample test of hypothesis for a population mean. The steps to generate the following output are shown in Appendix C.

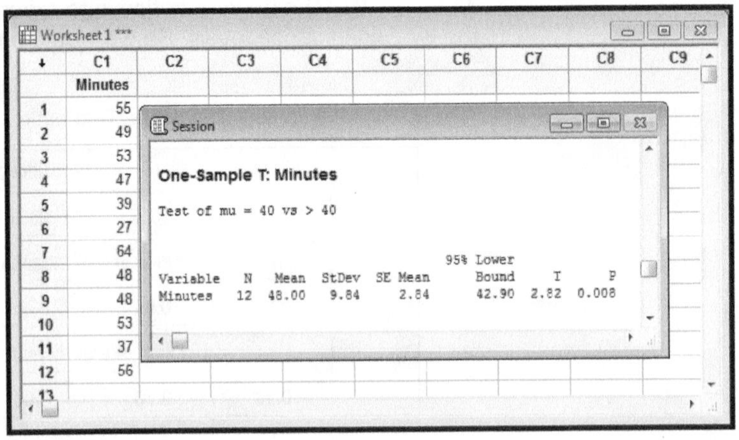

An additional feature of most statistical software packages is to report the *p*-value, which gives additional information on the null hypothesis. The *p*-value is the probability of a *t* value as extreme or more extreme than the computed *t* value, given that the null hypothesis is true. Using the Minitab analysis from the previous Parking Lot example, the *p*-value of .008 is the likelihood of a *t* value of 2.82 or larger, given a population mean of 40. Thus, comparing the *p*-value to the significance level tells us whether the null hypothesis was close to being rejected, barely rejected, and so on.

To explain further, refer to the diagram below. The *p*-value of .008 is the brown shaded area and the significance level is the total amber and brown shaded area. Because the *p*-value of .008 is less than the significance level of .05, the null hypothesis is rejected. Had the *p*-value been larger than the significance level—say, .06, .19, or .57—the null hypothesis would not be rejected.

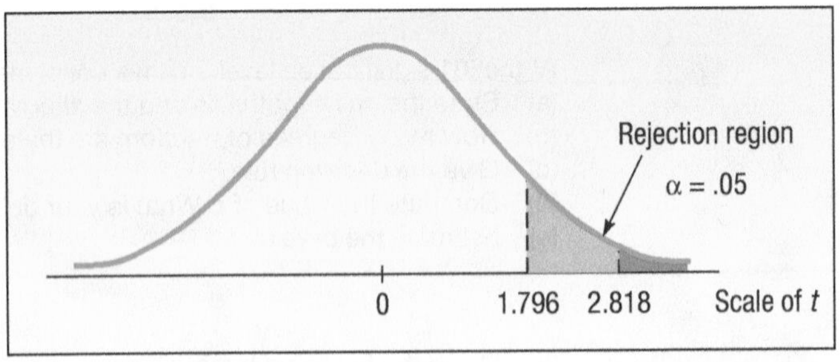

In the preceding example, the alternate hypothesis was one-sided, and the upper (right) tail of the *t* distribution contained the rejection region. The *p*-value is the area to the right of 2.818 for a *t* distribution with 11 degrees of freedom.

What if we were conducting a two-sided test, so that the rejection region is in both the upper and the lower tails? That is, in the Parking Lot example, if H_1 were stated as $\mu \neq 40$, we would have reported the *p*-value as the area to the right of 2.818 plus the value to the left of −2.818. Both of these values are .008, so the *p*-value is $.008 + .008 = .016$.

How can we estimate a *p*-value without a computer? To illustrate, recall that, in the example/solution regarding the length of time at the Parking Lot, we rejected the

null hypothesis that $\mu \leq 40$ and accepted the alternate hypothesis that $\mu > 40$. The significance level was .05, so logically the *p*-value is less than .05. To estimate the *p*-value more accurately, go to Appendix B.5 and find the row with 11 degrees of freedom. The computed *t* value of 2.818 is between 2.718 and 3.106. (A portion of Appendix B.5 is reproduced as Table 10–3.) The one-tailed significance level corresponding to 2.718 is .01, and for 3.106 it is .005. Therefore, the *p*-value is between .005 and .01. The usual practice is to report that the *p*-value is less than the larger of the two significance levels. So we would report "the *p*-value is less than .01."

TABLE 10–3 A Portion of Student's *t* Distribution

	Confidence Intervals					
	80%	90%	95%	98%	99%	99.9%
	Level of Significance for One-Tailed Test, α					
df	0.10	0.05	.0025	0.01	0.005	0.0005
	Level of Significance for Two-Tailed Test, α					
	0.20	0.10	0.05	0.02	0.01	0.001
⋮	⋮	⋮	⋮	⋮	⋮	⋮
9	1.383	1.833	2.262	2.821	3.250	4.781
10	1.372	1.812	2.228	2.764	3.169	4.587
11	1.363	1.796	2.201	2.718	3.106	4.437
12	1.356	1.782	2.179	2.681	3.055	4.318
13	1.350	1.771	2.160	2.650	3.012	4.221
14	1.345	1.761	2.145	2.624	2.977	4.140
15	1.341	1.753	2.131	2.602	2.947	4.073

SELF-REVIEW 10–4

A machine is set to fill a small bottle with 9.0 grams of medicine. A sample of eight bottles revealed the following amounts (grams) in each bottle.

9.2	8.7	8.9	8.6	8.8	8.5	8.7	9.0

At the .01 significance level, can we conclude that the mean weight is less than 9.0 grams?
(a) State the null hypothesis and the alternate hypothesis.
(b) How many degrees of freedom are there?
(c) Give the decision rule.
(d) Compute the value of *t*. What is your decision regarding the null hypothesis?
(e) Estimate the *p*-value.

EXERCISES

15. Given the following hypotheses:

$$H_0: \mu \geq 20$$
$$H_1: \mu < 20$$

A random sample of five resulted in the following values: 18, 15, 12, 19, and 21. Assume a normal population. Using the .01 significance level, can we conclude the population mean is less than 20?

a. State the decision rule.
b. Compute the value of the test statistic.
c. What is your decision regarding the null hypothesis?
d. Estimate the *p*-value.

16. Given the following hypotheses:

$$H_0: \mu = 100$$
$$H_1: \mu \neq 100$$

A random sample of six resulted in the following values: 118, 105, 112, 119, 105, and 111. Assume a normal population. Using the .05 significance level, can we conclude the mean is different from 100?

a. State the decision rule.
b. Compute the value of the test statistic.
c. What is your decision regarding the null hypothesis?
d. Estimate the *p*-value.

For **DATA FILE**, please visit www.mhhe.com/lind16e

17. The amount of water consumed each day by a healthy adult follows a normal distribution with a mean of 1.4 liters. A health campaign promotes the consumption of at least 2.0 liters per day. A sample of 10 adults after the campaign shows the following consumption in liters:

1.5	1.6	1.5	1.4	1.9	1.4	1.3	1.9	1.8	1.7

At the .01 significance level, can we conclude that water consumption has increased? Calculate and interpret the *p*-value.

For **DATA FILE**, please visit www.mhhe.com/lind16e

18. The liquid chlorine added to swimming pools to combat algae has a relatively short shelf life before it loses its effectiveness. Records indicate that the mean shelf life of a 5-gallon jug of chlorine is 2,160 hours (90 days). As an experiment, Holdlonger was added to the chlorine to find whether it would increase the shelf life. A sample of nine jugs of chlorine had these shelf lives (in hours):

2,159	2,170	2,180	2,179	2,160	2,167	2,171	2,181	2,185

At the .025 level, has Holdlonger increased the shelf life of the chlorine? Estimate the *p*-value.

For **DATA FILE**, please visit www.mhhe.com/lind16e

19. A Washington, D.C., "think tank" announces the typical teenager sent 50 text messages per day in 2013. To update that estimate, you phone a sample of 12 teenagers and ask them how many text messages they sent the previous day. Their responses were:

51	175	47	49	44	54	145	203	21	59	42	100

At the .05 level, can you conclude that the mean number is greater than 50? Estimate the *p*-value and describe what it tells you.

For **DATA FILE**, please visit www.mhhe.com/lind16e

20. Hugger Polls contends that an agent conducts a mean of 53 in-depth home surveys every week. A streamlined survey form has been introduced, and Hugger wants to evaluate its effectiveness. The number of in-depth surveys conducted during a week by a random sample of 15 agents are:

53	57	50	55	58	54	60	52	59	62	60	60	51	59	56

At the .05 level of significance, can we conclude that the mean number of interviews conducted by the agents is more than 53 per week? Estimate the *p*-value.

LO10-8
Compute the probability of a Type II error.

TYPE II ERROR

Recall that the level of significance, identified by the symbol α, is the probability that the null hypothesis is rejected when it is true. This is called a Type I error. The most common levels of significance are .05 and .01 and are set by the researcher at the outset of the test.

In a hypothesis-testing situation there is also the possibility that a null hypothesis is not rejected when it is actually false. That is, we accept a false null hypothesis. This is called a Type II error. The probability of a Type II error is identified by the Greek letter beta (β). The following example illustrates the details of determining the value of β.

EXAMPLE

Western Wire Products purchases steel bars to make cotter pins. Past experience indicates that the mean tensile strength of all incoming shipments is 10,000 psi and that the standard deviation, σ, is 400 psi.

To make a decision about incoming shipments of steel bars, Western Wire Products set up a rule for the quality-control inspector to follow: "Take a sample of 100 steel bars. At the .05 significance level, if the sample mean ($\bar{x}$) strength falls between 9,922 psi and 10,078 psi, accept the lot. Otherwise, the lot is to be rejected." Refer to Chart 10–8, Region A. It shows the region where each lot is rejected and where it is not rejected. The mean of this distribution is designated μ_0. The tails of the curve represent the probability of making a Type I error, that is, rejecting the incoming lot of steel bars when in fact it is a good lot, with a mean of 10,000 psi.

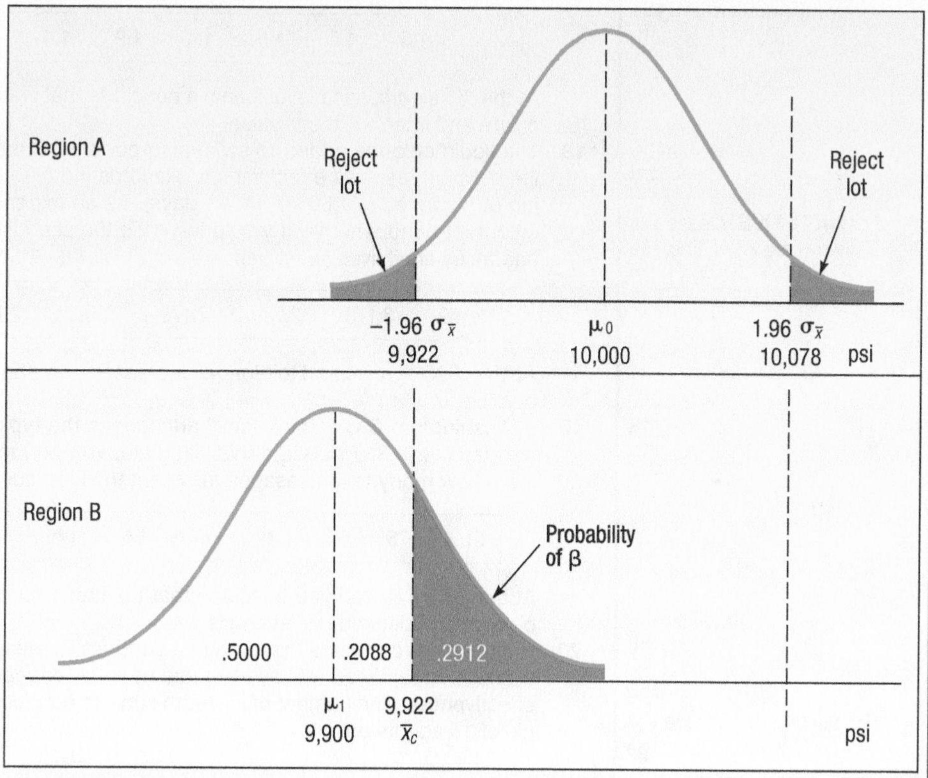

CHART 10–8 Charts Showing Type I and Type II Errors

Suppose the unknown population mean of an incoming lot, designated μ_1, is really 9,900 psi. What is the probability that the quality-control inspector will fail to reject the shipment (a Type II error)?

SOLUTION

The probability of committing a Type II error, as represented by the shaded area in Chart 10–8, Region B, is computed by determining the area under the normal curve that lies above 9,922 pounds. The calculation of the areas under the normal curve was discussed in Chapter 7. Reviewing briefly, it is necessary first to determine the probability of the sample mean falling between 9,900 and 9,922. Then this probability is subtracted from .5000 (which represents all the area beyond the mean of 9,900) to arrive at the probability of making a Type II error.

The number of standard units (z value) between the mean of the incoming lot (9,900), designated by μ_1, and $\bar{X}_c$, representing the critical value for 9,922, is computed by:

TYPE II ERROR

$$z = \frac{\bar{X}_c - \mu_1}{\sigma/\sqrt{n}} \quad \textbf{[10–3]}$$

With $n = 100$ and $\sigma = 400$, the value of z is 0.55:

$$z = \frac{\bar{X}_c - \mu_1}{\sigma/\sqrt{n}} = \frac{9{,}922 - 9{,}900}{400/\sqrt{100}} = \frac{22}{40} = 0.55$$

The area under the curve between 9,900 and 9,922 (a z value of 0.55) is .2088. The area under the curve beyond 9,922 pounds is .5000 − .2088, or .2912; this is the probability of making a Type II error—that is, accepting an incoming lot of steel bars when the population mean is 9,900 psi.

Another illustration, in Chart 10–9, Region C, depicts the probability of accepting a lot when the population mean is 10,120. To find the probability:

$$z = \frac{\bar{X}_c - \mu_1}{\sigma/\sqrt{n}} = \frac{10{,}078 - 10{,}120}{400/\sqrt{100}} = -1.05$$

The probability that z is less than −1.05 is .1469, found by .5000 − .3531. Therefore, β, or the probability of a Type II error, is .1469. Caution: If the difference between μ_0 and μ_1 is relatively small, the probability of a Type II error may occur in both tails. This eventuality is not considered here.

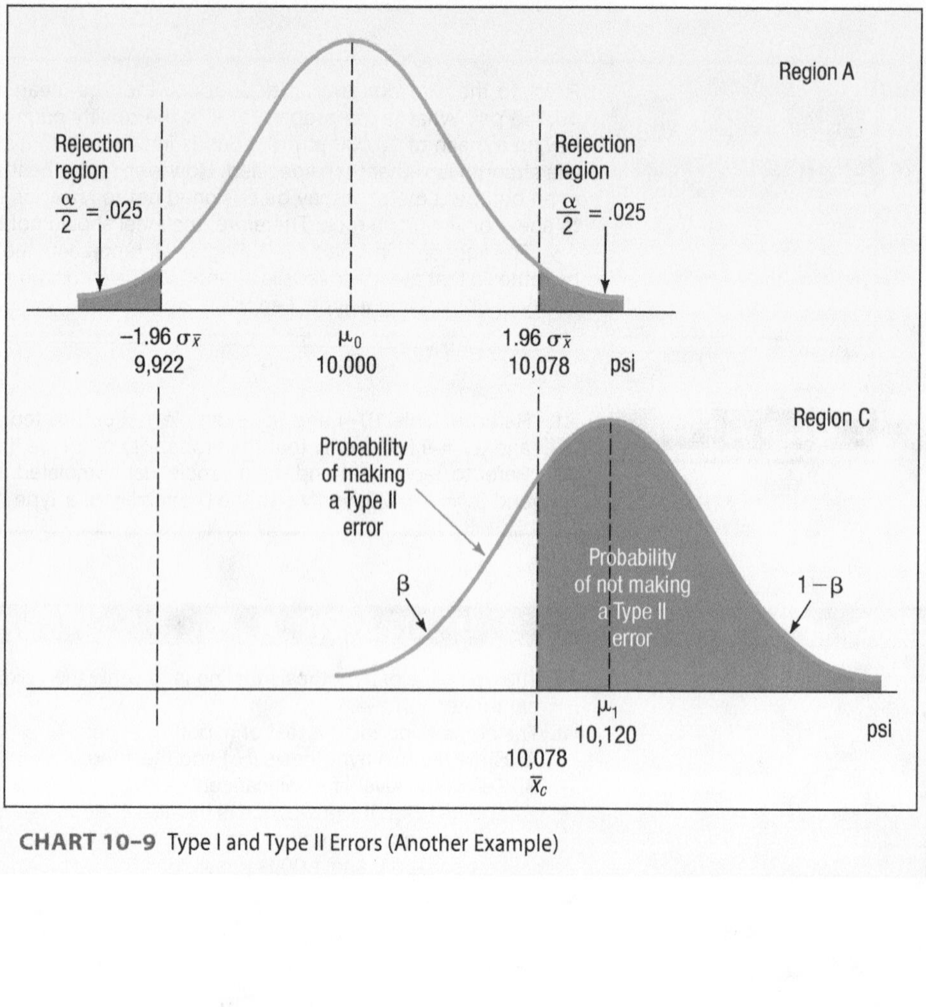

CHART 10–9 Type I and Type II Errors (Another Example)

Using the methods illustrated by Charts 10–8 Region B and 10-9 Region C, the probability of accepting a hypothesis as true when it is actually false can be determined for any value of μ_1.

Type II error probabilities are shown in the center column of Table 10–4 for selected values of μ_1, given in the left column. The right column gives the probability of not making a Type II error, which is also known as the power of a test.

TABLE 10–4 Probabilities of a Type II Error for $\mu_0 = 10{,}000$ Pounds and Selected Alternative Means, .05 Level of Significance

Selected Alternative Mean (μ_1)	Probability of Type II Error (β)	Probability of Not Making a Type II Error ($1 - \beta$)
9,820	.0054	.9946
9,880	.1469	.8531
9,900	.2912	.7088
9,940	.6736	.3264
10,000	—*	—
10,060	.6736	.3264
10,100	.2912	.7088
10,120	.1469	.8531
10,180	.0054	.9946

*It is not possible to make a Type II error when $\mu_1 = \mu_0$.

SELF-REVIEW 10–5

Refer to the previous example. Suppose the true mean of an incoming lot of steel bars is 10,180 psi. What is the probability that the quality control inspector will accept the bars as having a mean of 10,000 psi? (It sounds implausible that steel bars will be rejected if the tensile strength is higher than specified. However, it may be that the cotter pin has a dual function in an outboard motor. It may be designed not to shear off if the motor hits a small object, but to shear off if it hits a rock. Therefore, the steel should not be *too* strong.)

The light area in Chart 10–9, Region C, represents the probability of falsely accepting the hypothesis that the mean tensile strength of the incoming steel is 10,000 psi. What is the probability of committing a Type II error?

EXERCISES

21. Refer to Table 10–4 and the example just completed. With $n = 100$, $\sigma = 400$, $\bar{x}_c = 9{,}922$, and $\mu_1 = 9{,}880$, verify that the probability of a Type II error is .1469.

22. Refer to Table 10–4 and the example just completed. With $n = 100$, $\sigma = 400$, $\bar{x}_c = 10{,}078$, and $\mu_1 = 10{,}100$, verify that the probability of a Type II error is .2912.

CHAPTER SUMMARY

I. The objective of hypothesis testing is to verify the validity of a statement about a population parameter.

II. The steps to conduct a test of hypothesis are:

A. State the null hypothesis (H_0) and the alternate hypothesis (H_1).

B. Select the level of significance.

1. The level of significance is the likelihood of rejecting a true null hypothesis.

2. The most frequently used significance levels are .01, .05, and .10, but any value between 0 and 1.00 is possible.

C. Select the test statistic.
  1. A test statistic is a value calculated from sample information used to determine whether to reject the null hypothesis.
  2. Two test statistics were considered in this chapter.
    a. The standard normal distribution (the *z* distribution) is used when the population follows the normal distribution and the population standard deviation is known.
    b. The *t* distribution is used when the population follows the normal distribution and the population standard deviation is unknown.

D. State the decision rule.
  1. The decision rule indicates the condition or conditions when the null hypothesis is rejected.
  2. In a two-tailed test, the rejection region is evenly split between the upper and lower tails.
  3. In a one-tailed test, all of the rejection region is in either the upper or the lower tail.

E. Select a sample, compute the value of the test statistic, and make a decision regarding the null hypothesis.

F. Interpret the results of your decision.

III. A *p*-value is the probability that the value of the test statistic is as extreme as the value computed, when the null hypothesis is true.

IV. When testing a hypothesis about a population mean:
  A. If the population standard deviation, σ, is known, the test statistic is the standard normal distribution and is determined from:

$$z = \frac{\bar{x} - \mu}{\sigma/\sqrt{n}} \qquad \textbf{[10–1]}$$

  B. If the population standard deviation is not known, *s* is substituted for σ. The test statistic is the *t* distribution, and its value is determined from:

$$t = \frac{\bar{x} - \mu}{s/\sqrt{n}} \qquad \textbf{[10–2]}$$

  The major characteristics of the *t* distribution are:
  1. It is a continuous distribution.
  2. It is mound-shaped and symmetrical.
  3. It is flatter, or more spread out, than the standard normal distribution.
  4. There is a family of *t* distributions, depending on the number of degrees of freedom.

V. There are two types of errors that can occur in a test of hypothesis.
  A. A Type I error occurs when a true null hypothesis is rejected.
    1. The probability of making a Type I error is equal to the level of significance.
    2. This probability is designated by the Greek letter α.
  B. A Type II error occurs when a false null hypothesis is not rejected.
    1. The probability of making a Type II error is designated by the Greek letter β.
    2. The likelihood of a Type II error is found by

$$z = \frac{\bar{x}_c - \mu_1}{\sigma/\sqrt{n}} \qquad \textbf{[10–3]}$$

PRONUNCIATION KEY

SYMBOL	MEANING	PRONUNCIATION
H_0	Null hypothesis	*H sub zero*
H_1	Alternate hypothesis	*H sub one*
$\alpha/2$	Two-tailed significance level	*Alpha over 2*
$\bar{x}_c$	Limit of the sample mean	*x bar sub c*
μ_0	Assumed population mean	*mu sub zero*

CHAPTER EXERCISES

23. According to the local union president, the mean gross income of plumbers in the Salt Lake City area follows the normal probability distribution with a mean of \$45,000 and a standard deviation of \$3,000. A recent investigative reporter for KYAK TV found, for a sample of 120 plumbers, the mean gross income was \$45,500. At the .10 significance level, is it reasonable to conclude that the mean income is not equal to \$45,000? Determine the *p*-value.

For **DATA FILE**, please visit www.mhhe.com/lind16e

24. Rutter Nursery Company packages its pine bark mulch in 50-pound bags. From a long history, the production department reports that the distribution of the bag weights follows the normal distribution and the standard deviation of this process is 3 pounds per bag. At the end of each day, Jeff Rutter, the production manager, weighs 10 bags and computes the mean weight of the sample. Below are the weights of 10 bags from today's production.

45.6	47.7	47.6	46.3	46.2	47.4	49.2	55.8	47.5	48.5

   a. Can Mr. Rutter conclude that the mean weight of the bags is less than 50 pounds? Use the .01 significance level.
   b. In a brief report, tell why Mr. Rutter can use the *z* distribution as the test statistic.
   c. Compute the *p*-value.

25. A new weight-watching company, Weight Reducers International, advertises that those who join will lose, on the average, 10 pounds the first two weeks with a standard deviation of 2.8 pounds. A random sample of 50 people who joined the new weight reduction program revealed the mean loss to be 9 pounds. At the .05 level of significance, can we conclude that those joining Weight Reducers on average will lose less than 10 pounds? Determine the *p*-value.
26. Dole Pineapple Inc. is concerned that the 16-ounce can of sliced pineapple is being overfilled. Assume the standard deviation of the process is .03 ounce. The quality-control department took a random sample of 50 cans and found that the arithmetic mean weight was 16.05 ounces. At the 5% level of significance, can we conclude that the mean weight is greater than 16 ounces? Determine the *p*-value.
27. According to a recent survey, Americans get a mean of 7 hours of sleep per night. A random sample of 50 students at West Virginia University revealed the mean length of time slept last night was 6 hours and 48 minutes (6.8 hours). The standard deviation of the sample was 0.9 hour. At the 5% level of significance, is it reasonable to conclude that students at West Virginia sleep less than the typical American? Compute the *p*-value.
28. A statewide real estate sales agency, Farm Associates, specializes in selling farm property in the state of Nebraska. Its records indicate that the mean selling time of farm property is 90 days. Because of recent drought conditions, the agency believes that the mean selling time is now greater than 90 days. A statewide survey of 100 farms sold recently revealed that the mean selling time was 94 days, with a standard deviation of 22 days. At the .10 significance level, has there been an increase in selling time?
29. According to the Census Bureau, 3.13 people reside in the typical American household. A sample of 25 households in Arizona retirement communities showed the mean number of residents per household was 2.86 residents. The standard deviation of this sample was 1.20 residents. At the .05 significance level, is it reasonable to conclude the mean number of residents in the retirement community household is less than 3.13 persons?
30. A recent article in *Vitality* magazine reported that the mean amount of leisure time per week for American men is 40.0 hours. You believe this figure is too large and decide to conduct your own test. In a random sample of 60 men, you find that the mean is 37.8 hours of leisure per week and that the standard deviation of the sample is 12.2 hours. Can you conclude that the information in the article is untrue? Use the .05 significance level. Determine the *p*-value and explain its meaning.

For **DATA FILE**, please visit www.mhhe.com/lind16e

31. According to a study by the Federal Reserve Board, the rate charged on credit card debt is more than 14%. Listed below is the interest rate charged on a sample of 10 credit cards.

14.6	16.7	17.4	17.0	17.8	15.4	13.1	15.8	14.3	14.5

   Is it reasonable to conclude the mean rate charged is greater than 14%? Use the .01 significance level.

For **DATA FILE**, please visit www.mhhe.com/lind16e

32. A recent article in *The Wall Street Journal* reported that the home equity loan rate is now less than 6%. A sample of eight small banks in the Midwest revealed the following home equity loan rates (in percent):

4.8	5.3	6.5	4.8	6.1	5.8	6.2	5.6

At the .01 significance level, can we conclude that the home equity loan rate for small banks is less than 6%? Estimate the *p*-value.

For **DATA FILE**, please visit www.mhhe.com/lind16e

33. A recent study revealed the typical American coffee drinker consumes an average of 3.1 cups per day. A sample of 12 senior citizens revealed they consumed the following amounts of coffee, reported in cups, yesterday.

3.1	3.3	3.5	2.6	2.6	4.3	4.4	3.8	3.1	4.1	3.1	3.2

At the .05 significance level, do these sample data suggest there is a difference between the national average and the sample mean from senior citizens?

For **DATA FILE**, please visit www.mhhe.com/lind16e

34. The postanesthesia care area (recovery room) at St. Luke's Hospital in Maumee, Ohio, was recently enlarged. The hope was that with the enlargement the mean number of patients per day would be more than 25. A random sample of 15 days revealed the following numbers of patients.

25	27	25	26	25	28	28	27	24	26	25	29	25	27	24

At the .01 significance level, can we conclude that the mean number of patients per day is more than 25? Estimate the *p*-value and interpret it.

For **DATA FILE**, please visit www.mhhe.com/lind16e

35. www.golfsmith.com receives an average of 6.5 returns per day from online shoppers. For a sample of 12 days, it received the following numbers of returns.

0	4	3	4	9	4	5	9	1	6	7	10

At the .01 significance level, can we conclude the mean number of returns is less than 6.5?

For **DATA FILE**, please visit www.mhhe.com/lind16e

36. During recent seasons, Major League Baseball has been criticized for the length of the games. A report indicated that the average game lasts 3 hours and 30 minutes. A sample of 17 games revealed the following times to completion. (Note that the minutes have been changed to fractions of hours, so that a game that lasted 2 hours and 24 minutes is reported at 2.40 hours.)

2.98	2.40	2.70	2.25	3.23	3.17	2.93	3.18	2.80
2.38	3.75	3.20	3.27	2.52	2.58	4.45	2.45	

Can we conclude that the mean time for a game is less than 3.50 hours? Use the .05 significance level.

For **DATA FILE**, please visit www.mhhe.com/lind16e

37. Watch Corporation of Switzerland claims that its watches on average will neither gain nor lose time during a week. A sample of 18 watches provided the following gains (+) or losses (−) in seconds per week.

−0.38	−0.20	−0.38	−0.32	+0.32	−0.23	+0.30	+0.25	−0.10
−0.37	−0.61	−0.48	−0.47	−0.64	−0.04	−0.20	−0.68	+0.05

Is it reasonable to conclude that the mean gain or loss in time for the watches is 0? Use the .05 significance level. Estimate the *p*-value.

For **DATA FILE**, please visit www.mhhe.com/lind16e

38. Listed below is the rate of return for one year (reported in percent) for a sample of 12 mutual funds that are classified as taxable money market funds.

4.63	4.15	4.76	4.70	4.65	4.52	4.70	5.06	4.42	4.51	4.24	4.52

Using the .05 significance level, is it reasonable to conclude that the mean rate of return is more than 4.50%?

For **DATA FILE**, please visit www.mhhe.com/lind16e

39. Many grocery stores and large retailers such as Walmart and Kmart have installed self-checkout systems so shoppers can scan their own items and cash out themselves. How do customers like this service and how often do they use it? Listed below is the number of customers using the service for a sample of 15 days at a Walmart location.

120	108	120	114	118	91	118	92	104	104
112	97	118	108	117					

Is it reasonable to conclude that the mean number of customers using the self-checkout system is more than 100 per day? Use the .05 significance level.

For **DATA FILE**, please visit www.mhhe.com/lind16e

40. For a recent year, the mean fare to fly from Charlotte, North Carolina, to Chicago, Illinois, on a discount ticket was \$267. A random sample of 13 round-trip discount fares on this route last month gives:

\$321	\$286	\$290	\$330	\$310	\$250	\$270	\$280	\$299	\$265	\$291	\$275	\$281

At the .01 significance level, can we conclude that the mean fare has increased? What is the *p*-value?

41. The publisher of *Celebrity Living* claims that the mean sales for personality magazines that feature people such as Angelina Jolie or Paris Hilton are 1.5 million copies per week. A sample of 10 comparable titles shows a mean weekly sales last week of 1.3 million copies with a standard deviation of 0.9 million copies. Do these data contradict the publisher's claim? Use the 0.01 significance level.

42. A United Nations report shows the mean family income for Mexican migrants to the United States is \$27,000 per year. A FLOC (Farm Labor Organizing Committee) evaluation of 25 Mexican family units reveals a mean to be \$30,000 with a sample standard deviation of \$10,000. Does this information disagree with the United Nations report? Apply the 0.01 significance level.

43. The cost of weddings in the United States has skyrocketed in recent years. As a result, many couples are opting to have their weddings in the Caribbean. A Caribbean vacation resort recently advertised in *Bride Magazine* that the cost of a Caribbean wedding was less than \$10,000. Listed below is a total cost in \$000 for a sample of 8 Caribbean weddings.

9.7	9.4	11.7	9.0	9.1	10.5	9.1	9.8

At the .05 significance level, is it reasonable to conclude the mean wedding cost is less than \$10,000 as advertised?

44. The American Water Works Association reports that the per capita water use in a single-family home is 69 gallons per day. Legacy Ranch is a relatively new housing development. The builders installed more efficient water fixtures, such as low-flush toilets, and subsequently conducted a survey of the residences. Thirty-six owners responded, and the sample mean water use per day was 64 gallons with a standard deviation of 8.8 gallons per day. At the .10 level of significance, is that enough evidence to conclude that residents of Legacy Ranch use less water on average?

45. A cola-dispensing machine is set to dispense 9.00 ounces of cola per cup, with a standard deviation of 1.00 ounce. The manufacturer of the machine would like to set the control limit in such a way that, for samples of 36, 5% of the sample means will be greater than the upper control limit, and 5% of the sample means will be less than the lower control limit.

a. At what value should the control limit be set?

b. If the population mean shifts to 8.6, what is the probability of detecting the change?

c. If the population mean shifts to 9.6, what is the probability of detecting the change?

46. The owners of the Westfield Mall wished to study customer shopping habits. From earlier studies, the owners were under the impression that a typical shopper spends 0.75 hour at the mall, with a standard deviation of 0.10 hour. Recently the mall owners added some specialty restaurants designed to keep shoppers in the mall longer. The consulting firm, Brunner and Swanson Marketing Enterprises, was hired to evaluate the effects of the

restaurants. A sample of 45 shoppers by Brunner and Swanson revealed that the mean time spent in the mall had increased to 0.80 hour.

a. Develop a test of hypothesis to determine if the mean time spent in the mall changed. Use the .10 significance level.

b. Suppose the mean shopping time actually increased from 0.75 hour to 0.79 hours. What is the probability of making a Type II error?

c. When Brunner and Swanson reported the information in part (b) to the mall owners, the owners believed that the probability of making a Type II error was too high. How could this probability be reduced?

47. The following null and alternate hypotheses are given.

$$H_0: \mu \leq 50$$
$$H_1: \mu > 50$$

Suppose the population standard deviation is 10. The probability of a Type I error is set at .01 and the probability of a Type II error at .30. Assume that the population mean shifts from 50 to 55. How large a sample is necessary to meet these requirements?

48. An insurance company, based on past experience, estimates the mean damage for a natural disaster in its area is $5,000. After introducing several plans to prevent loss, it randomly samples 200 policyholders and finds the mean amount per claim was $4,800 with a standard deviation of $1,300. Does it appear the prevention plans were effective in reducing the mean amount of a claim? Use the .05 significance level.

49. A national grocer's magazine reports the typical shopper spends 8 minutes in line waiting to check out. A sample of 24 shoppers at the local Farmer Jack's showed a mean of 7.5 minutes with a standard deviation of 3.2 minutes. Is the waiting time at the local Farmer Jack's less than that reported in the national magazine? Use the .05 significance level.

DATA SET EXERCISES

(The data for these exercises are available at the text website: www.mhhe.com/lind16e.)

50. Refer to the Real Estate data, which report information on the homes sold in Goodyear, Arizona, last year.

a. A recent article in the *Arizona Republic* indicated that the mean selling price of the homes in the area is more than $220,000. Can we conclude that the mean selling price in the Goodyear, AZ, area is more than $220,000? Use the .01 significance level. What is the *p*-value?

b. The same article reported the mean size was more than 2,100 square feet. Can we conclude that the mean size of homes sold in the Goodyear, AZ, area is more than 2,100 square feet? Use the .01 significance level. What is the *p*-value?

51. Refer to the Baseball 2012 data, which report information on the 30 Major League Baseball teams for the 2012 season.

a. Conduct a test of hypothesis to determine whether the mean salary of the teams was different from $80.0 million. Use the .05 significance level.

b. Using a 5% significance level, conduct a test of hypothesis to determine whether the mean attendance was more than 2,000,000 per team.

52. Refer to the Buena School District bus data.

a. Select the variable for the number of miles traveled last month. Conduct a test of hypothesis to determine whether the mean number of miles traveled is equal to 840. Use the .01 significance level. Find the *p*-value and explain what it means.

b. Using the maintenance cost variable, conduct a test of hypothesis to determine whether the mean maintenance cost is less than $500 at the .05 significance level. Determine the *p*-value and interpret the result.

11 Two-Sample Tests of Hypothesis

GIBBS BABY FOOD COMPANY wishes to compare the weight gain of infants using its brand versus its competitor's. A sample of 40 babies using the Gibbs products revealed a mean weight gain of 7.6 pounds in the first three months after birth. For the Gibbs brand, the population standard deviation of the sample is 2.3 pounds. A sample of 55 babies using the competitor's brand revealed a mean increase in weight of 8.1 pounds. The population standard deviation is 2.9 pounds. At the .05 significance level, can we conclude that babies using the Gibbs brand gained less weight? (See Exercise 3 and LO11-1.)

LEARNING OBJECTIVES

When you have completed this chapter, you will be able to:

LO11-1 Test a hypothesis that two independent population means are equal, assuming that the population standard deviations are known and equal.

LO11-2 Test a hypothesis that two independent population means are equal, with unknown population standard deviations.

LO11-3 Test a hypothesis about the mean population difference between paired or dependent observations.

LO11-4 Explain the difference between dependent and independent samples.

INTRODUCTION

Chapter 10 began our study of hypothesis testing. We described the nature of hypothesis testing and conducted tests of a hypothesis in which we compared the results of a single sample to a population value. That is, we selected a single random sample from a population and conducted a test of whether the proposed population value was reasonable. Recall in Chapter 10 that we selected a sample of the number of desks assembled per week at Jamestown Steel Company to determine whether there was a change in the production rate. Similarly, we sampled the cost to process insurance claims to determine if cost-cutting measures resulted in a mean less than the current $60 per claim. In both cases, we compared the results of a *single* sample statistic to a population parameter.

In this chapter, we expand the idea of hypothesis testing to two populations. That is, we select random samples from two different populations to determine whether the population means are equal. Some questions we might want to test are:

1. Is there a difference in the mean value of residential real estate sold by male agents and female agents in south Florida?
2. At Grabit Software, Inc., do customer service employees receive more calls for assistance during the morning or afternoon?
3. In the fast-food industry, is there a difference in the mean number of days absent between young workers (under 21 years of age) and older workers (more than 60 years of age)?
4. Is there an increase in the production rate if music is piped into the production area?

We begin this chapter with the case in which we select random samples from two independent populations and wish to investigate whether these populations have the same mean.

STATISTICS IN ACTION

The U.S. presidential election of 2000 turned out to be one of the closest in history. The news media were unable to project a winner, and the final decision, including recounts and court decisions, took more than five weeks. This was not the only election in which there was controversy. Shortly before the 1936 presidential election, *The New York Times* carried the headline: "*Digest* Poll Gives Landon 32 States: Landon Leads 4–3." However, Alfred Landon of Kansas was not elected president. In fact, Roosevelt won by more than 11 million votes and received 523 Electoral College votes. How could the headline have been so wrong?

(continued on p. 350)

TWO-SAMPLE TESTS OF HYPOTHESIS: INDEPENDENT SAMPLES

LO11-1
Test a hypothesis that two independent population means are equal, assuming that the population standard deviations are known and equal.

A city planner in Florida wishes to know whether there is a difference in the mean hourly wage rate of plumbers and electricians in central Florida. A financial accountant wishes to know whether the mean rate of return for high-yield mutual funds is different from the mean rate of return on global mutual funds. In each of these cases, there are two independent populations. In the first case, the plumbers represent one population and the electricians, the other. In the second case, high-yield mutual funds are one population and global mutual funds, the other.

In each of these cases, to investigate the question, we would select a random sample from each population and compute the mean of the two samples. If the two population means are the same, that is, the mean hourly rate is the same for the plumbers and the electricians, we would expect the *difference* between the two sample means to be zero. But what if our sample results yield a difference other than zero? Is that difference due to chance or is it because there is a real difference in the hourly earnings? A two-sample test of means will help to answer this question.

We do need to return to the results of Chapter 8. Recall that we showed that a distribution of sample means would tend to approximate the normal distribution. We need to again assume that a distribution of sample means will follow the normal

(continued from p. 349)

The *Literary Digest* collected a sample of voters from lists of telephone numbers, automobile registrations, and *Digest* readers. In 1936 not many people could afford a telephone or an automobile. In addition, those who read the *Digest* tended to be wealthier and vote Republican. Thus, the population that was sampled did not represent the population of voters. A second problem was with the nonresponses. More than 10 million people were sent surveys, and more than 2.3 million responded. However, no attempt was made to see whether those responding represented a cross-section of all the voters.

With modern computers and survey methods, samples are carefully selected and checked to ensure they are representative. What happened to the *Literary Digest*? It went out of business shortly after the 1936 election.

distribution. It can be shown mathematically that the distribution of the differences between sample means for two normal distributions is also normal.

We can illustrate this theory in terms of the city planner in Tampa, Florida. To begin, let's assume some information that is not usually available. Suppose that the population of plumbers has a mean of \$30.00 per hour and a standard deviation of \$5.00 per hour. The population of electricians has a mean of \$29.00 and a standard deviation of \$4.50. Now, from this information it is clear that the two population means are not the same. The plumbers actually earn \$1.00 per hour more than the electricians. But we cannot expect to uncover this difference each time we sample the two populations.

Suppose we select a random sample of 40 plumbers and a random sample of 35 electricians and compute the mean of each sample. Then, we determine the difference between the sample means. It is this difference between the sample means that holds our interest. If the populations have the same mean, then we would expect the difference between the two sample means to be zero. If there is a difference between the population means, then we expect to find a difference between the sample means.

To understand the theory, we need to take several pairs of samples, compute the mean of each, determine the difference between the sample means, and study the distribution of the differences in the sample means. Because of our study of the distribution of sample means in Chapter 8, we know that the distribution of the sample means follows the normal distribution. If the two distributions of sample means follow the normal distribution, then we can reason that the distribution of their differences will also follow the normal distribution. This is the first hurdle.

The second hurdle refers to the mean of this distribution of differences. If we find the mean of this distribution is zero, that implies that there is no difference in the two populations. On the other hand, if the mean of the distribution of differences is equal to some value other than zero, either positive or negative, then we conclude that the two populations do not have the same mean.

To report some concrete results, let's return to the city planner in Tampa, Florida. Table 11–1 shows the result of selecting 20 different samples of 40 plumbers and

TABLE 11–1 The Mean Hourly Earnings of 20 Random Samples of Plumbers and Electricians and the Differences between the Means

Sample	Plumbers	Electricians	Difference
1	\$29.80	\$28.76	\$1.04
2	30.32	29.40	0.92
3	30.57	29.94	0.63
4	30.04	28.93	1.11
5	30.09	29.78	0.31
6	30.02	28.66	1.36
7	29.60	29.13	0.47
8	29.63	29.42	0.21
9	30.17	29.29	0.88
10	30.81	29.75	1.06
11	30.09	28.05	2.04
12	29.35	29.07	0.28
13	29.42	28.79	0.63
14	29.78	29.54	0.24
15	29.60	29.60	0.00
16	30.60	30.19	0.41
17	30.79	28.65	2.14
18	29.14	29.95	−0.81
19	29.91	28.75	1.16
20	28.74	29.21	−0.47

35 electricians, computing the mean of each sample, and finding the difference between the two sample means. In the first case, the sample of 40 plumbers has a mean of $29.80, and for the 35 electricians the mean is $28.76. The difference between the sample means is $1.04. This process was repeated 19 more times. Observe that in 17 of the 20 cases, the differences are positive because the mean of the plumbers is larger than the mean of the electricians. In two cases, the differences are negative because the mean of the electricians is larger than the mean of the plumbers. In one case, the means are equal.

Our final hurdle is that we need to know something about the *variability* of the distribution of differences. To put it another way, what is the standard deviation of this distribution of differences? Statistical theory shows that when we have independent populations, as in this case, the distribution of the differences has a variance (standard deviation squared) equal to the sum of the two individual variances. This means that we can add the variances of the two sampling distributions. To put it another way, the variance of the difference in sample means ($\bar{x}_1 - \bar{x}_2$) is equal to the sum of the variance for the plumbers and the variance for the electricians.

VARIANCE OF THE DISTRIBUTION OF DIFFERENCES IN MEANS

$$\sigma^2_{\bar{x}_1-\bar{x}_2} = \frac{\sigma_1^2}{n_1} + \frac{\sigma_2^2}{n_2} \quad [11\text{–}1]$$

The term $\sigma^2_{\bar{x}_1-\bar{x}_2}$ looks complex but need not be difficult to interpret. The σ^2 portion reminds us that it is a variance, and the subscript $\bar{x}_1 - \bar{x}_2$ that it is a distribution of differences in the sample means.

We can put this equation in a more usable form by taking the square root, so that we have the standard deviation of the distribution or "standard error" of the differences. Finally, we standardize the distribution of the differences. The result is the following equation.

TWO-SAMPLE TEST OF MEANS—KNOWN σ

$$z = \frac{\bar{x}_1 - \bar{x}_2}{\sqrt{\frac{\sigma_1^2}{n_1} + \frac{\sigma_2^2}{n_2}}} \quad [11\text{–}2]$$

Before we present an example, let's review the assumptions necessary for using formula (11–2).

- The two populations follow normal distributions.
- The two samples are unrelated, that is, independent.
- The standard deviations for both populations are known.

The following example shows the details of the test of hypothesis for two population means.

EXAMPLE

Customers at the FoodTown Supermarket have a choice when paying for their groceries. They may check out and pay using the standard cashier-assisted checkout, or they may use the new Fast Lane procedure. In the standard

procedure, a FoodTown employee scans each item and puts it on a short conveyor, where another employee puts it in a bag and then into the grocery cart. In the Fast Lane procedure, the customer scans each item, bags it, and places the bags in the cart him- or herself. The Fast Lane procedure is designed to reduce the time a customer spends in the checkout line.

The Fast Lane facility was recently installed at the Byrne Road FoodTown location. The store manager would like to know if the mean checkout time using the standard checkout method is longer than using the Fast Lane. She gathered the following sample information. The time is measured from when the customer enters the line until all his or her bags are in the cart. Hence the time includes both waiting in line and checking out. What is the *p*-value?

Customer Type	Sample Mean	Population Standard Deviation	Sample Size
Standard	5.50 minutes	0.40 minute	50
Fast Lane	5.30 minutes	0.30 minute	100

SOLUTION

We use the six-step hypothesis-testing procedure to investigate the question.

Step 1: State the null hypothesis and the alternate hypothesis. The null hypothesis is that the mean standard checkout time is less than or equal to the mean Fast Lane checkout time. In other words, the difference of 0.20 minute between the mean checkout time for the standard method and the mean checkout time for Fast Lane is due to chance. The alternate hypothesis is that the mean checkout time is larger for those using the standard method. We will let μ_S refer to the mean checkout time for the population of standard customers and μ_F the mean checkout time for the Fast Lane customers. The null and alternative hypotheses are:

$$H_0: \mu_S \leq \mu_F$$
$$H_1: \mu_S > \mu_F$$

Step 2: Select the level of significance. The significance level is the probability that we reject the null hypothesis when it is actually true. This likelihood is determined prior to selecting the sample or performing any calculations. The .05 and .01 significance levels are the most common, but other values, such as .02 and .10, are also used. In theory, we may select any value between 0 and 1 for the significance level. In this case, we selected the .01 significance level.

Step 3: Determine the test statistic. In Chapter 10, we used the standard normal distribution (that is, *z*) and *t* as test statistics. In this case, we use the *z* distribution as the test statistic because we assume the

STATISTICS IN ACTION

Do you live to work or work to live? A recent poll of 802 working Americans revealed that, among those who considered their work as a career, the mean number of hours worked per day was 8.7. Among those who considered their work as a job, the mean number of hours worked per day was 7.6.

two population distributions are both normal and the standard deviations of both populations are known.

Step 4: Formulate a decision rule. The decision rule is based on the null and the alternate hypotheses (i.e., one-tailed or two-tailed test), the level of significance, and the test statistic used. We selected the .01 significance level and the z distribution as the test statistic, and we wish to determine whether the mean checkout time is longer using the standard method. We set the alternate hypothesis to indicate that the mean checkout time is longer for those using the standard method than the Fast Lane method. Hence, the rejection region is in the upper tail of the standard normal distribution (a one-tailed test). To find the critical value, go to Student's t distribution (Appendix B.5). In the table headings, find the row labeled **"Level of Significance for One-Tailed Test"** and select the column for an alpha of .01. Go to the bottom row with infinite degrees of freedom. The z critical value is 2.326. So the decision rule is to reject the null hypothesis if the value of the test statistic exceeds 2.326. Chart 11–1 depicts the decision rule.

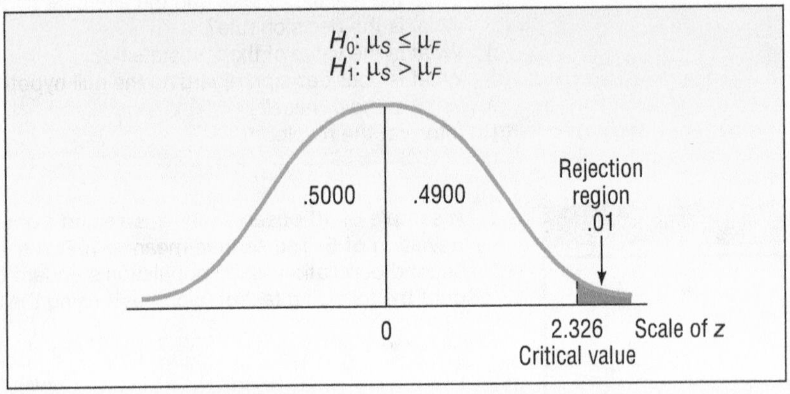

CHART 11–1 Decision Rule for One-Tailed Test at .01 Significance Level

Step 5: Make the decision regarding H_0. We use formula (11–2) to compute the value of the test statistic.

$$z = \frac{\bar{x}_S - \bar{x}_F}{\sqrt{\dfrac{\sigma_S^2}{n_S} + \dfrac{\sigma_F^2}{n_F}}} = \frac{5.5 - 5.3}{\sqrt{\dfrac{0.40^2}{50} + \dfrac{0.30^2}{100}}} = \frac{0.2}{0.064031} = 3.123$$

The computed value of 3.123 is larger than the critical value of 2.326. Our decision is to reject the null hypothesis and accept the alternate hypothesis.

Step 6: Interpret the result. The difference of .20 minute between the mean checkout times is too large to have occurred by chance. We conclude the Fast Lane method is faster.

What is the p-value for the test statistic? Recall that the p-value is the probability of finding a value of the test statistic this extreme when the null hypothesis is true. To calculate the p-value, we need the probability of a z value larger than 3.123. From Appendix B.3, we cannot find the probability associated with 3.123. The largest value available is 3.09. The area corresponding to 3.09 is .4990. In this case, we can report that the p-value is less than .0010, found by .5000 − .4990. We conclude that there is very little likelihood that the null hypothesis is true!

In summary, the criteria for using formula (11–2) are:

1. *The samples are from independent populations*. This means the checkout time for the Fast Lane customers is unrelated to the checkout time for the other customers. For example, Mr. Smith's checkout time does not affect any other customer's checkout time.
2. *Both populations follow the normal distribution.* In the FoodTown example, the population of times in both the standard checkout line and the Fast Lane follow normal distributions.
3. *Both population standard deviations are known*. In the FoodTown example, the population standard deviation of the Fast Lane times was 0.30 minute. The population standard deviation of the standard checkout times was 0.40 minute.

SELF-REVIEW 11–1

Tom Sevits is the owner of the Appliance Patch. Recently Tom observed a difference in the dollar value of sales between the men and women he employs as sales associates. A sample of 40 days revealed the men sold a mean of $1,400 worth of appliances per day. For a sample of 50 days, the women sold a mean of $1,500 worth of appliances per day. Assume the population standard deviation for men is $200 and for women $250. At the .05 significance level, can Mr. Sevits conclude that the mean amount sold per day is larger for the women?

(a) State the null hypothesis and the alternate hypothesis.
(b) What is the decision rule?
(c) What is the value of the test statistic?
(d) What is your decision regarding the null hypothesis?
(e) What is the *p*-value?
(f) Interpret the result.

EXERCISES

1. A sample of 40 observations is selected from one population with a population standard deviation of 5. The sample mean is 102. A sample of 50 observations is selected from a second population with a population standard deviation of 6. The sample mean is 99. Conduct the following test of hypothesis using the .04 significance level.

$$H_0: \mu_1 = \mu_2$$
$$H_1: \mu_1 \neq \mu_2$$

a. Is this a one-tailed or a two-tailed test?
b. State the decision rule.
c. Compute the value of the test statistic.
d. What is your decision regarding H_0?
e. What is the *p*-value?

2. A sample of 65 observations is selected from one population with a population standard deviation of 0.75. The sample mean is 2.67. A sample of 50 observations is selected from a second population with a population standard deviation of 0.66. The sample mean is 2.59. Conduct the following test of hypothesis using the .08 significance level.

$$H_0: \mu_1 \leq \mu_2$$
$$H_1: \mu_1 > \mu_2$$

a. Is this a one-tailed or a two-tailed test?
b. State the decision rule.
c. Compute the value of the test statistic.
d. What is your decision regarding H_0?
e. What is the *p*-value?

Note: Use the six-step hypothesis-testing procedure to solve the following exercises.

3. Gibbs Baby Food Company wishes to compare the weight gain of infants using its brand versus its competitor's. A sample of 40 babies using the Gibbs products revealed a mean weight gain of 7.6 pounds in the first three months after birth. For the Gibbs brand, the population standard deviation of the sample is 2.3 pounds. A sample of 55 babies using the competitor's brand revealed a mean increase in weight of 8.1 pounds. The population standard deviation is 2.9 pounds. At the .05 significance level, can we conclude that babies using the Gibbs brand gained less weight? Compute the *p*-value and interpret it.

4. As part of a study of corporate employees, the director of human resources for PNC Inc. wants to compare the distance traveled to work by employees at its office in downtown Cincinnati with the distance for those in downtown Pittsburgh. A sample of 35 Cincinnati employees showed they travel a mean of 370 miles per month. A sample of 40 Pittsburgh employees showed they travel a mean of 380 miles per month. The population standard deviations for the Cincinnati and Pittsburgh employees are 30 and 26 miles, respectively. At the .05 significance level, is there a difference in the mean number of miles traveled per month between Cincinnati and Pittsburgh employees?

5. Women's height is a suspected factor for difficult deliveries, that is, shorter women are more likely to have Caesarean sections. A medical researcher found in a sample of 45 women who had a normal delivery that their mean height was 61.4 inches. A second sample of 39 women who had a Caesarean section had a mean height of 60.6 inches. Assume that the population of heights of normal deliveries has a population standard deviation of 1.2 inches. Also assume that the heights of the population of women who had Caesarean section births has a standard deviation of 1.1 inches. Are those who had a Caesarean section shorter? Use the .05 significance level. Find the *p*-value and explain what it means.

6. Mary Jo Fitzpatrick is the vice president for Nursing Services at St. Luke's Memorial Hospital. Recently she noticed in the job postings for nurses that those that are unionized seem to offer higher wages. She decided to investigate and gathered the following information.

Group	Mean Wage	Population Standard Deviation	Sample Size
Union	$20.75	$2.25	40
Nonunion	$19.80	$1.90	45

Would it be reasonable for her to conclude that union nurses earn more? Use the .02 significance level. What is the *p*-value?

LO11-2
Test a hypothesis that two independent population means are equal, with unknown population standard deviations.

COMPARING POPULATION MEANS WITH UNKNOWN POPULATION STANDARD DEVIATIONS

In the previous section, we used the standard normal distribution and z as the test statistic to test a hypothesis that two population means from independent populations were equal. The hypothesis tests presumed that the populations were normally distributed and that we knew the population standard deviations. However, in most cases, we do not know the population standard deviations. We can overcome this problem, as we did in the one-sample case in the previous chapter, by substituting the sample standard deviation (s) for the population standard deviation (σ). See formula (10–2) on page 331.

Two-Sample Pooled Test

In this section, we describe another method for comparing the sample means of two independent populations to determine if the sampled populations could reasonably have the same mean. The method described does *not* require that we know the standard deviations of the populations. This gives us a great deal more flexibility when investigating the difference in sample means. There are two major differences in this test and the previous test described in this chapter.

1. We assume the sampled populations have equal but unknown standard deviations. Because of this assumption, we combine or "pool" the sample standard deviations.
2. We use the t distribution as the test statistic.

The formula for computing the value of the test statistic t is similar to formula (11–2), but an additional calculation is necessary. The two sample standard deviations are pooled to form a single estimate of the unknown population standard deviation. In essence, we compute a weighted mean of the two sample standard deviations and use this value as an estimate of the unknown population standard deviation. The weights are the degrees of freedom that each sample provides. Why do we need to pool the sample standard deviations? Because we assume that the two populations have equal standard deviations, the best estimate we can make of that value is to combine or pool all the sample information we have about the value of the population standard deviation.

The following formula is used to pool the sample standard deviations. Notice that two factors are involved: the number of observations in each sample and the sample standard deviations themselves.

POOLED VARIANCE

$$s_p^2 = \frac{(n_1 - 1)s_1^2 + (n_2 - 1)s_2^2}{n_1 + n_2 - 2} \qquad \textbf{[11–3]}$$

where:

s_1^2 is the variance (standard deviation squared) of the first sample.
s_2^2 is the variance of the second sample.

The value of t is computed from the following equation.

TWO-SAMPLE TEST OF MEANS—UNKNOWN σ'S

$$t = \frac{\bar{x}_1 - \bar{x}_2}{\sqrt{s_p^2\left(\frac{1}{n_1} + \frac{1}{n_2}\right)}} \qquad \textbf{[11–4]}$$

where:

$\bar{x}_1$ is the mean of the first sample.
$\bar{x}_2$ is the mean of the second sample.
n_1 is the number of observations in the first sample.
n_2 is the number of observations in the second sample.
s_p^2 is the pooled estimate of the population variance.

The number of degrees of freedom in the test is the total number of items sampled minus the total number of samples. Because there are two samples, there are $n_1 + n_2 - 2$ degrees of freedom.

To summarize, there are three requirements or assumptions for the test.

1. The sampled populations are approximately normally distributed.
2. The sampled populations are independent.
3. The standard deviations of the two populations are equal.

The following example/solution explains the details of the test.

EXAMPLE

Owens Lawn Care Inc. manufactures and assembles lawnmowers that are shipped to dealers throughout the United States and Canada. Two different procedures have been proposed for mounting the engine on the frame of the lawnmower. The question is: Is there a difference in the mean time to mount the engines on the frames of the lawnmowers? The first procedure was developed by longtime Owens employee Herb Welles (designated as procedure W), and the other procedure was

developed by Owens Vice President of Engineering William Atkins (designated as procedure A). To evaluate the two methods, we conduct a time and motion study. A sample of five employees is timed using the Welles method and six using the Atkins method. The results, in minutes, are shown below. Is there a difference in the mean mounting times? Use the .10 significance level.

Welles (minutes)	Atkins (minutes)
2	3
4	7
9	5
3	8
2	4
	3

SOLUTION

Following the six steps to test a hypothesis, the null hypothesis states that there is no difference in mean mounting times between the two procedures. The alternate hypothesis indicates that there is a difference.

$$H_0: \mu_W = \mu_A$$
$$H_1: \mu_W \neq \mu_A$$

The required assumptions are:

- The observations in the Welles sample are *independent* of the observations in the Atkins sample.
- The two populations follow the normal distribution.
- The two populations have equal standard deviations.

Is there a difference between the mean assembly times using the Welles and the Atkins methods? The degrees of freedom are equal to the total number of items sampled minus the number of samples. In this case, that is $n_W + n_A - 2$. Five assemblers used the Welles method and six the Atkins method. Thus, there are 9 degrees of freedom, found by $5 + 6 - 2$. The critical values of t, from Appendix B.5 for $df = 9$, a two-tailed test, and the .10 significance level, are -1.833 and 1.833. The decision rule is portrayed graphically in Chart 11–2. We do not reject the null hypothesis if the computed value of t falls between -1.833 and 1.833.

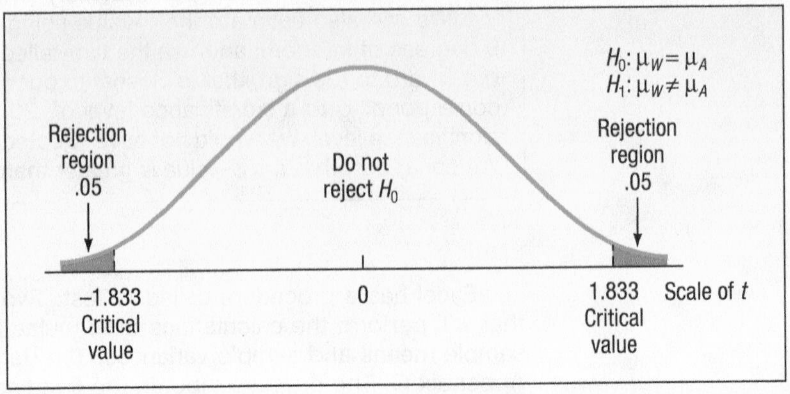

CHART 11–2 Regions of Rejection, Two-Tailed Test, $df = 9$, and .10 Significance Level

We use three steps to compute the value of t.

Step 1: Calculate the sample standard deviations. To compute the sample standard deviations, we use formula (3–11) from page 81. See the details below.

Welles Method		Atkins Method	
x_W	$(x_W - \bar{x}_W)^2$	x_A	$(x_A - \bar{x}_A)^2$
2	$(2-4)^2 = 4$	3	$(3-5)^2 = 4$
4	$(4-4)^2 = 0$	7	$(7-5)^2 = 4$
9	$(9-4)^2 = 25$	5	$(5-5)^2 = 0$
3	$(3-4)^2 = 1$	8	$(8-5)^2 = 9$
2	$(2-4)^2 = 4$	4	$(4-5)^2 = 1$
20	34	3	$(3-5)^2 = 4$
		30	22

$$\bar{x}_W = \frac{\Sigma x_W}{n_W} = \frac{20}{5} = 4 \qquad \bar{x}_A = \frac{\Sigma x_A}{n_A} = \frac{30}{6} = 5$$

$$s_W = \sqrt{\frac{\Sigma(x_W - \bar{x}_W)^2}{n_W - 1}} = \sqrt{\frac{34}{5-1}} = 2.9155 \qquad s_A = \sqrt{\frac{\Sigma(x_A - \bar{x}_A)^2}{n_A - 1}} = \sqrt{\frac{22}{6-1}} = 2.0976$$

Step 2: Pool the sample variances. We use formula (11–3) to pool the sample variances (standard deviations squared).

$$s_p^2 = \frac{(n_W - 1)s_W^2 + (n_A - 1)s_A^2}{n_W + n_A - 2} = \frac{(5-1)(2.9155)^2 + (6-1)(2.0976)^2}{5+6-2} = 6.2222$$

Step 3: Determine the value of t. The mean mounting time for the Welles method is 4.00 minutes, found by $\bar{x}_W = 20/5$. The mean mounting time for the Atkins method is 5.00 minutes, found by $\bar{x}_A = 30/6$. We use formula (11–4) to calculate the value of t.

$$t = \frac{\bar{x}_W - \bar{x}_A}{\sqrt{s_p^2\left(\frac{1}{n_W} + \frac{1}{n_A}\right)}} = \frac{4.00 - 5.00}{\sqrt{6.2222\left(\frac{1}{5} + \frac{1}{6}\right)}} = -0.662$$

The decision is not to reject the null hypothesis because −0.662 falls in the region between −1.833 and 1.833. Our conclusion is that the sample data failed to show a difference between the mean assembly times of the two methods.

We can also estimate the p-value using Appendix B.5. Locate the row with 9 degrees of freedom, and use the two-tailed test column. Find the t value, without regard to the sign, that is closest to our computed value of 0.662. It is 1.383, corresponding to a significance level of .20. Thus, even had we used the 20% significance level, we would not have rejected the null hypothesis of equal means. We can report that the p-value is greater than .20.

Excel has a procedure called "t-Test: Two Sample Assuming Equal Variances" that will perform the calculations of formulas (11–3) and (11–4) as well as find the sample means and sample variances. The details of the procedure are provided in Appendix C. The data are input in the first two columns of the Excel spreadsheet. They are labeled "Welles" and "Atkins." The output follows. The value of t, called the "t Stat," is −0.662, and the two-tailed p-value is .525. As we would expect, the

p-value is larger than the significance level of .10. The conclusion is not to reject the null hypothesis.

welles and atkins.xlsx

	A	B	C	D	E	F
1	Welles	Atkins		t-Test: Two-Sample Assuming Equal Variances		
2	2	3				
3	4	7			*Welles*	*Atkins*
4	9	5		Mean	4.000	5.000
5	3	8		Variance	8.500	4.400
6	2	4		Observations	5.000	6.000
7		3		Pooled Variance	6.222	
8				Hypothesized Mean Difference	0.000	
9				df	9.000	
10				t Stat	-0.662	
11				P(T<=t) one-tail	0.262	
12				t Critical one-tail	1.833	
13				P(T<=t) two-tail	0.525	
14				t Critical two-tail	2.262	

SELF-REVIEW 11–2

The production manager at Bellevue Steel, a manufacturer of wheelchairs, wants to compare the number of defective wheelchairs produced on the day shift with the number on the afternoon shift. A sample of the production from 6 day shifts and 8 afternoon shifts revealed the following number of defects.

Day	5	8	7	6	9	7		
Afternoon	8	10	7	11	9	12	14	9

At the .05 significance level, is there a difference in the mean number of defects per shift?

(a) State the null hypothesis and the alternate hypothesis.
(b) What is the decision rule?
(c) What is the value of the test statistic?
(d) What is your decision regarding the null hypothesis?
(e) What is the p-value?
(f) Interpret the result.
(g) What are the assumptions necessary for this test?

EXERCISES

For Exercises 7 and 8: (a) state the decision rule, (b) compute the pooled estimate of the population variance, (c) compute the test statistic, (d) state your decision about the null hypothesis, and (e) estimate the p-value.

7. The null and alternate hypotheses are:

$$H_0: \mu_1 = \mu_2$$
$$H_1: \mu_1 \neq \mu_2$$

A random sample of 10 observations from one population revealed a sample mean of 23 and a sample standard deviation of 4. A random sample of 8 observations from another population revealed a sample mean of 26 and a sample standard deviation of 5. At the .05 significance level, is there a difference between the population means?

8. The null and alternate hypotheses are:

$$H_0: \mu_1 = \mu_2$$
$$H_1: \mu_1 \neq \mu_2$$

A random sample of 15 observations from the first population revealed a sample mean of 350 and a sample standard deviation of 12. A random sample of 17 observations from the second population revealed a sample mean of 342 and a sample standard deviation of 15. At the .10 significance level, is there a difference in the population means?

Note: Use the six-step hypothesis testing procedure for the following exercises.

9. Listed below are the 25 players on the opening-day roster of the 2013 New York Yankees Major League Baseball team, their salaries, and fielding positions.

Player	Salary (US$)	Position
CC Sabathia	24,285,714	Pitcher
Hiroki Kuroda	15,000,000	Pitcher
Andy Pettitte	12,000,000	Pitcher
Mariano Rivera	10,000,000	Pitcher
Phil Hughes	7,150,000	Pitcher
Boone Logan	3,150,000	Pitcher
David Robertson	3,100,000	Pitcher
Joba Chamberlain	1,875,000	Pitcher
Shawn Kelley	935,000	Pitcher
Ivan Nova	575,600	Pitcher
David Phelps	512,425	Pitcher
Adam Warren	490,525	Pitcher
Lyle Overbay	850,000	First Base
Robinson Cano	15,000,000	Second Base
Kevin Youkilis	12,000,000	Third Base
Francisco Cervelli	515,350	Catcher
Chris Stewart	515,100	Catcher
Brett Gardner	2,850,000	Center Field
Travis Hafner	2,000,000	Designated Hitter
Vernon Wells	24,642,857	Left Field
Ben Francisco	1,200,000	Left Field
Ichiro Suzuki	6,500,000	Right Field
Brennan Boesch	1,500,000	Right Field
Jayson Nix	900,000	Shortstop
Eduardo Nunez	533,300	Shortstop

Sort the players into two groups, pitchers (P) and nonpitchers (position players). Assume equal population standard deviations for the position players and the pitchers. Test the hypothesis that mean salaries of pitchers and nonpitchers are equal using the .01 significance level.

10. A recent study compared the time spent together by single- and dual-earner couples. According to the records kept by the wives during the study, the mean amount of time spent together watching television among the single-earner couples was 61 minutes per day, with a standard deviation of 15.5 minutes. For the dual-earner couples, the mean number of minutes spent watching television was 48.4 minutes, with a standard deviation of 18.1 minutes. At the .01 significance level, can we conclude that the single-earner couples on average spend more time watching television together? There were 15 single-earner and 12 dual-earner couples studied.

For **DATA FILE**, please visit www.mhhe.com/lind16e

11. Ms. Lisa Monnin is the budget director for Nexus Media Inc. She would like to compare the daily travel expenses for the sales staff and the audit staff. She collected the following sample information.

Sales ($)	131	135	146	165	136	142	
Audit ($)	130	102	129	143	149	120	139

At the .10 significance level, can she conclude that the mean daily expenses are greater for the sales staff than the audit staff? What is the p-value?

For **DATA FILE**, please visit www.mhhe.com/lind16e

12. The Tampa Bay (Florida) Area Chamber of Commerce wanted to know whether the mean weekly salary of nurses was larger than that of school teachers. To investigate, they

collected the following information on the amounts earned last week by a sample of school teachers and nurses.

School Teachers ($)	845	826	827	875	784	809	802	820	829	830	842	832
Nurses ($)	841	890	821	771	850	859	825	829				

Is it reasonable to conclude that the mean weekly salary of nurses is higher? Use the .01 significance level. What is the *p*-value?

Unequal Population Standard Deviations

In the previous sections, it was necessary to assume that the populations had equal standard deviations. To put it another way, we did not know the population standard deviations, but we assumed they were equal. In many cases, this is a reasonable assumption, but what if it is not? In the next chapter, we present a formal method for testing this equal variance assumption. In Chapter 16 we describe a test of hypothesis that does not require either the equal variance or the normality assumption.

If it is not reasonable to assume the population standard deviations are equal, then we use a statistic very much like formula (11–2). The sample standard deviations, s_1 and s_2, are used in place of the respective population standard deviations. In addition, the degrees of freedom are adjusted downward by a rather complex approximation formula. The effect is to reduce the number of degrees of freedom in the test, which will require a larger value of the test statistic to reject the null hypothesis.

The formula for the *t* statistic is:

TEST STATISTIC FOR NO DIFFERENCE IN MEANS, UNEQUAL VARIANCES

$$t = \frac{\bar{x}_1 - \bar{x}_2}{\sqrt{\dfrac{s_1^2}{n_1} + \dfrac{s_2^2}{n_2}}} \qquad \textbf{[11–5]}$$

The degrees of freedom statistic is found by:

DEGREES OF FREEDOM FOR UNEQUAL VARIANCE TEST

$$df = \frac{[(s_1^2/n_1) + (s_2^2/n_2)]^2}{\dfrac{(s_1^2/n_1)^2}{n_1 - 1} + \dfrac{(s_2^2/n_2)^2}{n_2 - 1}} \qquad \textbf{[11–6]}$$

where n_1 and n_2 are the respective sample sizes and s_1 and s_2 are the respective sample standard deviations. If necessary, this fraction is rounded down to an integer value. An example will explain the details.

EXAMPLE

Personnel in a consumer testing laboratory are evaluating the absorbency of paper towels. They wish to compare a set of store brand towels to a similar group of name brand ones. For each brand they dip a ply of the paper into a tub of fluid, allow the paper to drain back into the vat for 2 minutes, and then evaluate the amount of liquid the paper has taken up from the vat. A random sample of nine store brand paper towels absorbed the following amounts of liquid in milliliters.

8	8	3	1	9	7	5	5	12

An independent random sample of 12 name brand towels absorbed the following amounts of liquid in milliliters:

12	11	10	6	8	9	9	10	11	9	8	10

Use the .10 significance level and test if there is a difference in the mean amount of liquid absorbed by the two types of paper towels.

SOLUTION

To begin, let's assume that the amounts of liquid absorbed follow the normal probability distribution for both the store brand and the name brand towels. We do not know either of the population standard deviations, so we are going to use the *t* distribution as the test statistic. The assumption of equal population standard deviations does not appear reasonable. The amount of absorption in the store brand ranges from 1 ml to 12 ml. For the name brand, the amount of absorption ranges from 6 ml to 12 ml. That is, there is considerably more variation in the amount of absorption in the store brand than in the name brand. We observe the difference in the variation in the following dot plot provided by Minitab. The software commands to create a Minitab dot plot are given on page 746.

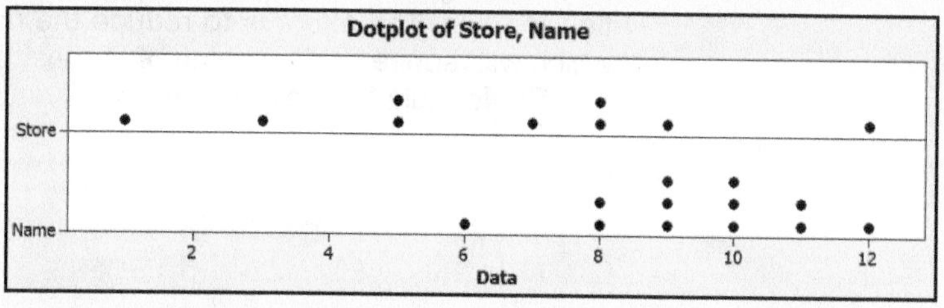

So we decide to use the *t* distribution and assume that the population standard deviations are not the same.

In the six-step hypothesis testing procedure, the first step is to state the null hypothesis and the alternate hypothesis. The null hypothesis is that there is no difference in the mean amount of liquid absorbed between the two types of paper towels. The alternate hypothesis is that there is a difference.

$$H_0: \mu_1 = \mu_2$$
$$H_0: \mu_1 \neq \mu_2$$

The significance level is .10 and the test statistic follows the *t* distribution. Because we do not wish to assume equal population standard deviations, we adjust the degrees of freedom using formula (11–6). To do so, we need to find the sample standard deviations. We can use the Minitab system to quickly find these results. The respective sample sizes are $n_1 = 9$ and $n_2 = 12$ and the respective standard deviations are 3.321 ml and 1.621 ml.

Variable	*n*	Mean	Standard Deviation
Store	9	6.444	3.321
Name	12	9.417	1.621

Inserting this information into formula (11–6):

$$df = \frac{[(s_1^2/n_1) + (s_2^2/n_2)]^2}{\dfrac{(s_1^2/n_1)^2}{n_1 - 1} + \dfrac{(s_2^2/n_2)^2}{n_2 - 1}} = \frac{[(3.321^2/9) + (1.621^2/12)]^2}{\dfrac{(3.321^2/9)^2}{9 - 1} + \dfrac{(1.621^2/12)^2}{12 - 1}} = \frac{1.4444^2}{.1877 + .0044} = 10.86$$

The usual practice is to round down to the integer, so we use 10 degrees of freedom. From Appendix B.5 with 10 degrees of freedom, a two-tailed test, and the .10 significance level, the critical t values are -1.812 and 1.812. Our decision rule is to reject the null hypothesis if the computed value of t is less than -1.812 or greater than 1.812.

To find the value of the test statistic, we use formula (11–5). Recall that the mean amount of absorption for the store paper towels is 6.444 ml and 9.417 ml for the brand.

$$t = \frac{\bar{x}_1 - \bar{x}_2}{\sqrt{\dfrac{s_1^2}{n_1} + \dfrac{s_2^2}{n_2}}} = \frac{6.444 - 9.417}{\sqrt{\dfrac{3.321^2}{9} + \dfrac{1.621^2}{12}}} = -2.474$$

The computed value of t is less than the lower critical value, so our decision is to reject the null hypothesis. We conclude that the mean absorption rate for the two towels is not the same. The Minitab output for this example follows.

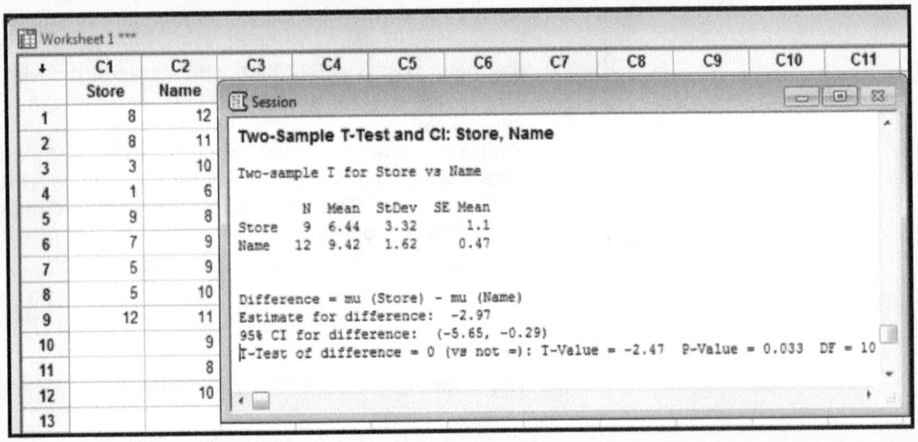

SELF-REVIEW 11–3

It is often useful for companies to know who their customers are and how they became customers. A credit card company is interested in whether the owner of the card applied for the card on his or her own or was contacted by a telemarketer. The company obtained the following sample information regarding end-of-the-month balances for the two groups.

Source	Mean	Standard Deviation	Sample Size
Applied	$1,568	$356	10
Contacted	1,967	857	8

Is it reasonable to conclude the mean balance is larger for the credit card holders that were contacted by telemarketers than for those who applied on their own for the card? Assume the population standard deviations are not the same. Use the .05 significance level.

(a) State the null hypothesis and the alternate hypothesis.
(b) How many degrees of freedom are there?
(c) What is the decision rule?
(d) What is the value of the test statistic?
(e) What is your decision regarding the null hypothesis?
(f) Interpret the result.

EXERCISES

For exercises 13 and 14, assume the sample populations do not have equal standard deviations and use the .05 significance level: (a) determine the number of degrees of freedom, (b) state the decision rule, (c) compute the value of the test statistic, and (d) state your decision about the null hypothesis.

13. The null and alternate hypotheses are:

$$H_0: \mu_1 = \mu_2$$
$$H_1: \mu_1 \neq \mu_2$$

A random sample of 15 items from the first population showed a mean of 50 and a standard deviation of 5. A sample of 12 items for the second population showed a mean of 46 and a standard deviation of 15.

14. The null and alternate hypotheses are:

$$H_0: \mu_1 \leq \mu_2$$
$$H_1: \mu_1 > \mu_2$$

A random sample of 20 items from the first population showed a mean of 100 and a standard deviation of 15. A sample of 16 items for the second population showed a mean of 94 and a standard deviation of 8. Use the .05 significant level.

15. A recent survey compared the costs of adoption through public and private agencies. For a sample of 16 adoptions through a public agency, the mean cost was $21,045, with a standard deviation of $835. For a sample of 18 adoptions through a private agency, the mean cost was $22,840, with a standard deviation of $1,545. Can we conclude the mean cost is larger for adopting children through a private agency? Use the .05 significance level.

For **DATA FILE**, please visit www.mhhe.com/lind16e

16. Suppose you are an expert on the fashion industry and wish to gather information to compare the amount earned per month by models featuring Liz Claiborne attire with those of Calvin Klein. The following is the amount ($000) earned per month by a sample of 15 Claiborne models:

$5.0	$4.5	$3.4	$3.4	$6.0	$3.3	$4.5	$4.6	$3.5	$5.2
4.8	4.4	4.6	3.6	5.0					

The following is the amount ($000) earned by a sample of 12 Klein models.

$3.1	$3.7	$3.6	$4.0	$3.8	$3.8	$5.9	$4.9	$3.6	$3.6
2.3	4.0								

Is it reasonable to conclude that Claiborne models earn more? Use the .05 significance level and assume the population standard deviations are not the same.

LO11-3
Test a hypothesis about the mean population difference between paired or dependent observations.

TWO-SAMPLE TESTS OF HYPOTHESIS: DEPENDENT SAMPLES

In the example/solution beginning on page 356, we tested the difference between the means from two independent populations. We compared the mean time required to mount an engine using the Welles method to the time to mount the engine using the Atkins method. The samples were *independent,* meaning that the sample of assembly times using the Welles method was in no way related to the sample of assembly times using the Atkins method.

There are situations, however, in which the samples are not independent. To put it another way, the samples are *dependent* or *related*. As an example, Nickel Savings and Loan employs two firms, Schadek Appraisals and Bowyer Real Estate, to appraise the value of the real estate properties on which it makes loans. It is important that these two firms be similar in their appraisal values. To review the consistency of the two appraisal firms, Nickel Savings randomly selects 10 homes and has both Schadek Appraisals and Bowyer Real Estate appraise the values of the selected homes. For each home, there will

be a pair of appraisal values. That is, for each home there will be an appraised value from both Schadek Appraisals and Bowyer Real Estate. The appraised values depend on, or are related to, the home selected. This is also referred to as a **paired sample.**

For hypothesis testing, we are interested in the distribution of the *differences* in the appraised value of each home. Hence, there is only one sample. To put it more formally, we are investigating whether the mean of the distribution of differences in the appraised values is 0. The sample is made up of the *differences* between the appraised values determined by Schadek Appraisals and the values from Bowyer Real Estate. If the two appraisal firms are reporting similar estimates, then sometimes Schadek Appraisals will be the higher value and sometimes Bowyer Real Estate will have the higher value. However, the mean of the distribution of differences will be 0. On the other hand, if one of the firms consistently reports the larger appraisal values, then the mean of the distribution of the differences will not be 0.

We will use the symbol μ_d to indicate the population mean of the distribution of differences. We assume the distribution of the population of differences is approximately normally distributed. The test statistic follows the t distribution and we calculate its value from the following formula:

PAIRED *t* TEST
$$t = \frac{\bar{d}}{s_d/\sqrt{n}} \quad \textbf{[11–7]}$$

There are $n - 1$ degrees of freedom and

$\bar{d}$ is the mean of the difference between the paired or related observations.
s_d is the standard deviation of the differences between the paired or related observations.
n is the number of paired observations.

The standard deviation of the differences is computed by the familiar formula for the standard deviation [see formula (3–11)], except d is substituted for x. The formula is:

$$s_d = \sqrt{\frac{\Sigma(d - \bar{d})^2}{n - 1}}$$

The following example illustrates this test.

EXAMPLE

Recall that Nickel Savings and Loan wishes to compare the two companies it uses to appraise the value of residential homes. Nickel Savings selected a sample of 10 residential properties and scheduled both firms for an appraisal. The results, reported in $000, are:

Home	Schadek	Bowyer
1	235	228
2	210	205
3	231	219
4	242	240
5	205	198
6	230	223
7	231	227
8	210	215
9	225	222
10	249	245

At the .05 significance level, can we conclude there is a difference between the firms' mean appraised home values?

SOLUTION

The first step is to state the null and the alternate hypotheses. In this case, a two-tailed alternative is appropriate because we are interested in determining whether there is a *difference* in the firms' appraised values. We are not interested in showing whether one particular firm appraises property at a higher value than the other. The question is whether the sample differences in the appraised values could have come from a population with a mean of 0. If the population mean of the differences is 0, then we conclude that there is no difference between the two firms' appraised values. The null and alternate hypotheses are:

$$H_0: \mu_d = 0$$
$$H_1: \mu_d \neq 0$$

There are 10 homes appraised by both firms, so $n = 10$, and $df = n - 1 = 10 - 1 = 9$. We have a two-tailed test, and the significance level is .05. To determine the critical value, go to Appendix B.5 and move across the row with 9 degrees of freedom to the column for a two-tailed test and the .05 significance level. The value at the intersection is 2.262. This value appears in the box in Table 11–2 on the next page. The decision rule is to reject the null hypothesis if the computed value of t is less than −2.262 or greater than 2.262. Here are the computational details.

Home	Schadek	Bowyer	Difference, d	$(d - \bar{d})$	$(d - \bar{d})^2$
1	235	228	7	2.4	5.76
2	210	205	5	0.4	0.16
3	231	219	12	7.4	54.76
4	242	240	2	−2.6	6.76
5	205	198	7	2.4	5.76
6	230	223	7	2.4	5.76
7	231	227	4	−0.6	0.36
8	210	215	−5	−9.6	92.16
9	225	222	3	−1.6	2.56
10	249	245	4	−0.6	0.36
			46	0	174.40

$$\bar{d} = \frac{\Sigma d}{n} = \frac{46}{10} = 4.60$$

$$s_d = \sqrt{\frac{\Sigma(d - \bar{d})^2}{n - 1}} = \sqrt{\frac{174.4}{10 - 1}} = 4.402$$

Using formula (11–7), the value of the test statistic is 3.305, found by

$$t = \frac{\bar{d}}{s_d/\sqrt{n}} = \frac{4.6}{4.402/\sqrt{10}} = \frac{4.6}{1.3920} = 3.305$$

Because the computed t falls in the rejection region, the null hypothesis is rejected. The population distribution of differences does not have a mean of 0. We conclude that there is a difference between the firms' mean appraised home values. The largest difference of $12,000 is for Home 3. Perhaps that would be an appropriate place to begin a more detailed review.

To find the *p*-value, we use Appendix B.5 and the section for a two-tailed test. Move along the row with 9 degrees of freedom and find the values of *t* that are closest to our calculated value. For a .01 significance level, the value of *t* is 3.250. The computed value is larger than this value, but smaller than the value of 4.781 corresponding to the .001 significance level. Hence, the *p*-value is less than .01. This information is highlighted in Table 11–2.

TABLE 11–2 A Portion of the *t* Distribution from Appendix B.5

	Confidence Intervals					
	80%	90%	95%	98%	99%	
	Level of Significance for One-Tailed Test					
df	0.10	0.05	0.025	0.01	0.005	
	Level of Significance for Two-Tailed Test					
	0.20	0.10	0.05	0.02	0.01	0.001
1	3.078	6.314	12.706	31.821	63.657	636.619
2	1.886	2.920	4.303	6.965	9.925	31.599
3	1.638	2.353	3.182	4.541	5.841	12.924
[illegible]	[illegible]	2.132	2.776	3.747	4.604	8.610
[illegible]	[illegible]	2.015	2.571	3.365	4.032	6.869
6	1.440	1.943	2.447	3.143	3.707	5.959
7	1.415	895	2.365	2.998	3.499	5.408
8	1.397	1.860	2.306	2.896	3.355	5.041
9	1.383	1.833	2.262	2.821	3.250	4.781
10	1.372	1.812	2.228	2.764	3.169	4.587

p-value between 0.01 and 0.001

Critical *t*-statistic for 0.05

Excel has a procedure called "t-Test: Paired Two-Sample for Means" that will perform the calculations of formula (11–7). The output from this procedure is given below.

The computed value of *t* is 3.305, and the two-tailed *p*-value is .009. Because the *p*-value is less than .05, we reject the hypothesis that the mean of the distribution of the differences between the appraised values is zero. In fact, this *p*-value is between .01 and .001. There is a small likelihood that the null hypothesis is true.

paired t test

	A	B	C	D	E	F	G
1	Home	Schadek	Bowyer		t-Test: Paired Two-Sample for Means		
2	1	235	228				
3	2	210	205			*Schadek*	*Bowyer*
4	3	231	219		Mean	226.800	222.200
5	4	242	240		Variance	208.844	204.178
6	5	205	198		Observations	10.000	10.000
7	6	230	223		Pearson Correlation	0.953	
8	7	231	227		Hypothesized Mean Difference	0.000	
9	8	210	215		df	9.000	
10	9	225	222		t Stat	3.305	
11	10	249	245		P(T<=t) one-tail	0.005	
12					t Critical one-tail	1.833	
13					P(T<=t) two-tail	0.009	
14					t Critical two-tail	2.262	
15							

LO11-4
Explain the difference between dependent and independent samples.

COMPARING DEPENDENT AND INDEPENDENT SAMPLES

Beginning students are often confused by the difference between tests for independent samples [formula (11–4)] and tests for dependent samples [formula (11–7)]. How do we tell the difference between dependent and independent samples? There are two types of dependent samples: (1) those characterized by a measurement, an intervention of some type, and then another measurement; and (2) a matching or pairing of the observations. To explain further:

1. The first type of dependent sample is characterized by a measurement followed by an intervention of some kind and then another measurement. This could be called a "before" and "after" study. Two examples will help to clarify. Suppose we want to show that, by placing speakers in the production area and playing soothing music, we are able to increase production. We begin by selecting a sample of workers and measuring their output under the current conditions. The speakers are then installed in the production area, and we again measure the output of the same workers. There are two measurements, before placing the speakers in the production area and after. The intervention is placing speakers in the production area.

   A second example involves an educational firm that offers courses designed to increase test scores and reading ability. Suppose the firm wants to offer a course that will help high school juniors increase their SAT scores. To begin, each student takes the SAT in the junior year in high school. During the summer between the junior and senior year, they participate in the course that gives them tips on taking tests. Finally, during the fall of their senior year in high school, they retake the SAT. Again, the procedure is characterized by a measurement (taking the SAT as a junior), an intervention (the summer workshops), and another measurement (taking the SAT during their senior year).
2. The second type of dependent sample is characterized by matching or pairing observations. The previous example/solution regarding Nickel Savings illustrates dependent samples. A property is selected and both firms appraise the same property. As a second example, suppose an industrial psychologist wishes to study the intellectual similarities of newly married couples. She selects a sample of newlyweds. Next, she administers a standard intelligence test to both the man and woman to determine the difference in the scores. Notice the matching that occurred: comparing the scores that are paired or matched by marriage.

Why do we prefer dependent samples to independent samples? By using dependent samples, we are able to reduce the variation in the sampling distribution. To illustrate, we will use the Nickel Savings and Loan example/solution just completed. Suppose we assume that we have two independent samples of real estate property for appraisal and conduct the following test of hypothesis, using formula (11–4). The null and alternate hypotheses are:

$$H_0\colon \mu_1 = \mu_2$$
$$H_1\colon \mu_1 \neq \mu_2$$

There are now two independent samples of 10 each. So the number of degrees of freedom is $10 + 10 - 2 = 18$. From Appendix B.5, for the .05 significance level, H_0 is rejected if t is less than -2.101 or greater than 2.101.

We use Excel to find the means and standard deviations of the two independent samples as shown on page 745 in the Chapter 3 section of Appendix C. The Excel instructions to find the pooled variance and the value of the "t Stat" are on page 750 in Appendix C. These values are highlighted in yellow.

Independent t test.xlsx

	A	B	C	D	E	F	G
1	Home	Schadek	Bowyer		t-Test: Two-Sample Assuming Equal Variances		
2	1	235	228				
3	2	210	205			*Schadek*	*Bowyer*
4	3	231	219		Mean	226.800	222.200
5	4	242	240		Variance	208.844	204.178
6	5	205	198		Observations	10.000	10.000
7	6	230	223		Pooled Variance	206.511	
8	7	231	227		Hypothesized Mean Difference	0.000	
9	8	210	215		df	18.000	
10	9	225	222		t Stat	0.716	
11	10	249	245		P(T<=t) one-tail	0.242	
12					t Critical one-tail	1.734	
13	Mean =	226.80	222.20		P(T<=t) two-tail	0.483	
14	S =	14.45	14.29		t Critical two-tail	2.101	

The mean of the appraised value of the 10 properties by Schadek is \$226,800, and the standard deviation is \$14,500. For Bowyer Real Estate, the mean appraised value is \$222,200, and the standard deviation is \$14,290. To make the calculations easier, we use \$000 instead of \$. The value of the pooled estimate of the variance from formula (11–3) is

$$s_p^2 = \frac{(n_1 - 1)s_1^2 + (n_2 - 1)s_2^2}{n_1 + n_2 - 2} = \frac{(10 - 1)(14.45^2) + (10 - 1)(14.29)^2}{10 + 10 - 2} = 206.50$$

From formula (11–4), t is 0.716.

$$t = \frac{\bar{x}_1 - \bar{x}_2}{\sqrt{s_p^2\left(\frac{1}{n_1} + \frac{1}{n_2}\right)}} = \frac{226.8 - 222.2}{\sqrt{206.50\left(\frac{1}{10} + \frac{1}{10}\right)}} = \frac{4.6}{6.4265} = 0.716$$

The computed t (0.716) is less than 2.101, so the null hypothesis is not rejected. We cannot show that there is a difference in the mean appraisal value. That is not the same conclusion that we got before! Why does this happen? The numerator is the same in the paired observations test (4.6). However, the denominator is smaller. In the paired test, the denominator is 1.3920 (see the calculations on page 366). In the case of the independent samples, the denominator is 6.4265. There is more variation or uncertainty. This accounts for the difference in the t values and the difference in the statistical decisions. The denominator measures the standard error of the statistic. When the samples are *not* paired, two kinds of variation are present: differences between the two appraisal firms and the difference in the value of the real estate. Properties numbered 4 and 10 have relatively high values, whereas number 5 is relatively low. These data show how different the values of the property are, but we are really interested in the difference between the two appraisal firms.

In sum, when we can pair or match observations that measure differences for a common variable, a hypothesis test based on dependent samples is more sensitive to detecting a significant difference than a hypothesis test based on independent samples. In the case of comparing the property valuations by Schadek Appraisals and Bowyer Real Estate, the hypothesis test based on dependent samples eliminates the variation between the values of the properties and focuses only on the comparisons in the two appraisals for each property. There is a bit of bad news here. In the dependent samples test, the degrees of freedom are half of what they are if the samples are not paired. For the real estate example, the degrees of freedom drop from 18 to 9 when the observations are paired. However, in most cases, this is a small price to pay for a better test.

SELF-REVIEW 11–4

Advertisements by Sylph Fitness Center claim that completing its course will result in losing weight. A random sample of eight recent participants showed the following weights before and after completing the course. At the .01 significance level, can we conclude the students lost weight?

Name	Before	After
Hunter	155	154
Cashman	228	207
Mervine	141	147
Massa	162	157
Creola	211	196
Peterson	164	150
Redding	184	170
Poust	172	165

(a) State the null hypothesis and the alternate hypothesis.
(b) What is the critical value of t?
(c) What is the computed value of t?
(d) Interpret the result. What is the p-value?
(e) What assumption needs to be made about the distribution of the differences?

EXERCISES

17. The null and alternate hypotheses are:

$$H_0: \mu_d \leq 0$$
$$H_1: \mu_d > 0$$

The following sample information shows the number of defective units produced on the day shift and the afternoon shift for a sample of four days last month.

	Day			
	1	2	3	4
Day shift	10	12	15	19
Afternoon shift	8	9	12	15

At the .05 significance level, can we conclude there are more defects produced on the day shift?

18. The null and alternate hypotheses are:

$$H_0: \mu_d = 0$$
$$H_1: \mu_d \neq 0$$

The following paired observations show the number of traffic citations given for speeding by Officer Dhondt and Officer Meredith of the South Carolina Highway Patrol for the last five months.

	Number of Citations Issued				
	May	June	July	August	September
Officer Dhondt	30	22	25	19	26
Officer Meredith	26	19	20	15	19

At the .05 significance level, is there a difference in the mean number of citations given by the two officers?

Note: Use the six-step hypothesis testing procedure to solve the following exercises.

For **DATA FILE**, please visit www.mhhe.com/lind16e

19. The management of Discount Furniture, a chain of discount furniture stores in the Northeast, designed an incentive plan for salespeople. To evaluate this innovative plan, 12 salespeople

were selected at random, and their weekly incomes before and after the plan were recorded.

Salesperson	Before	After
Sid Mahone	$320	$340
Carol Quick	290	285
Tom Jackson	421	475
Andy Jones	510	510
Jean Sloan	210	210
Jack Walker	402	500
Peg Mancuso	625	631
Anita Loma	560	560
John Cuso	360	365
Carl Utz	431	431
A. S. Kushner	506	525
Fern Lawton	505	619

Was there a significant increase in the typical salesperson's weekly income due to the innovative incentive plan? Use the .05 significance level. Estimate the p-value, and interpret it.

20. The federal government recently granted funds for a special program designed to reduce crime in high-crime areas. A study of the results of the program in eight high-crime areas of Miami, Florida, yielded the following results.

	Number of Crimes by Area							
	A	B	C	D	E	F	G	H
Before	14	7	4	5	17	12	8	9
After	2	7	3	6	8	13	3	5

Has there been a decrease in the number of crimes since the inauguration of the program? Use the .01 significance level. Estimate the p-value.

CHAPTER SUMMARY

I. In comparing two population means, we wish to know whether they could be equal.

A. We are investigating whether the distribution of the difference between the means could have a mean of 0.

B. The test statistic follows the standard normal distribution if the population standard deviations are known.

1. The two populations follow normal distributions.
2. The samples are from independent populations.
3. The formula to compute the value of z is

$$z = \frac{\bar{x}_1 - \bar{x}_2}{\sqrt{\frac{\sigma_1^2}{n_1} + \frac{\sigma_2^2}{n_2}}} \qquad \textbf{[11–2]}$$

II. The test statistic to compare two means is the t distribution if the population standard deviations are not known.

A. Both populations are approximately normally distributed.

B. The populations must have equal standard deviations.

C. The samples are independent.

D. Finding the value of t requires two steps.

1. The first step is to pool the standard deviations according to the following formula:

$$s_p^2 = \frac{(n_1 - 1)s_1^2 + (n_2 - 1)s_2^2}{n_1 + n_2 - 2} \qquad \textbf{[11–3]}$$

2. The value of t is computed from the following formula:

$$t = \frac{\bar{x}_1 - \bar{x}_2}{\sqrt{s_p^2\left(\frac{1}{n_1} + \frac{1}{n_2}\right)}} \quad \textbf{[11–4]}$$

3. The degrees of freedom for the test are $n_1 + n_2 - 2$.

III. If we cannot assume the population standard deviations are equal, we adjust the degrees of freedom and the formula for finding t.

A. We determine the degrees of freedom based on the following formula.

$$df = \frac{[(s_1^2/n_1) + (s_2^2/n_2)]^2}{\frac{(s_1^2/n_1)^2}{n_1 - 1} + \frac{(s_2^2/n_2)^2}{n_2 - 1}} \quad \textbf{[11–6]}$$

B. The value of the test statistic is computed from the following formula.

$$t = \frac{\bar{x}_1 - \bar{x}_2}{\sqrt{\frac{s_1^2}{n_1} + \frac{s_2^2}{n_2}}} \quad \textbf{[11–5]}$$

IV. For dependent samples, we assume the distribution of the paired differences between the populations has a mean of 0.

A. We first compute the mean and the standard deviation of the sample differences.

B. The value of the test statistic is computed from the following formula:

$$t = \frac{\bar{d}}{s_d/\sqrt{n}} \quad \textbf{[11–7]}$$

PRONUNCIATION KEY

SYMBOL	MEANING	PRONUNCIATION
s_p^2	Pooled sample variance	*s sub p squared*
$\bar{x}_1$	Mean of the first sample	*x bar sub 1*
$\bar{x}_2$	Mean of the second sample	*x bar sub 2*
$\bar{d}$	Mean of the difference between dependent observations	*d bar*
s_d	Standard deviation of the difference between dependent observations	*s sub d*

CHAPTER EXERCISES

21. A recent study focused on the number of times men and women who live alone buy take-out dinner in a month. Assume that the distributions follow the normal probability distribution and the population standard deviations are equal. The information is summarized below.

Statistic	Men	Women
Sample mean	24.51	22.69
Sample standard deviation	4.48	3.86
Sample size	35	40

At the .01 significance level, is there a difference in the mean number of times men and women order take-out dinners in a month? What is the p-value?

22. Clark Heter is an industrial engineer at Lyons Products. He would like to determine whether there are more units produced on the night shift than on the day shift. Assume the population standard deviation for the number of units produced on the day shift is 21 and is 28 on the night shift. A sample of 54 day-shift workers showed that the mean number of units produced was 345. A sample of 60 night-shift workers showed that the mean number of units produced was 351. At the .05 significance level, is the number of units produced on the night shift larger?

23. Fry Brothers Heating and Air Conditioning Inc. employs Larry Clark and George Murnen to make service calls to repair furnaces and air-conditioning units in homes. Tom Fry, the owner, would like to know whether there is a difference in the mean number of service calls they make per day. Assume the population standard deviation for Larry Clark is 1.05 calls per day and 1.23 calls per day for George Murnen. A random sample of 40 days last year showed that Larry Clark made an average of 4.77 calls per day. For a sample of 50 days George Murnen made an average of 5.02 calls per day. At the .05 significance level, is there a difference in the mean number of calls per day between the two employees? What is the *p*-value?

24. A coffee manufacturer is interested in whether the mean daily consumption of regular-coffee drinkers is less than that of decaffeinated-coffee drinkers. Assume the population standard deviation for those drinking regular coffee is 1.20 cups per day and 1.36 cups per day for those drinking decaffeinated coffee. A random sample of 50 regular-coffee drinkers showed a mean of 4.35 cups per day. A sample of 40 decaffeinated-coffee drinkers showed a mean of 5.84 cups per day. Use the .01 significance level. Compute the *p*-value.

25. A cell phone company offers two plans to its subscribers. At the time new subscribers sign up, they are asked to provide some demographic information. The mean yearly income for a sample of 40 subscribers to Plan A is $57,000 with a standard deviation of $9,200. For a sample of 30 subscribers to Plan B, the mean income is $61,000 with a standard deviation of $7,100. At the .05 significance level, is it reasonable to conclude the mean income of those selecting Plan B is larger? What is the *p*-value?

26. A computer manufacturer offers a help line that purchasers can call for help 24 hours a day, 7 days a week. Clearing these calls for help in a timely fashion is important to the company's image. After telling the caller that resolution of the problem is important, the caller is asked whether the issue is software or hardware related. The mean time it takes a technician to resolve a software issue is 18 minutes with a standard deviation of 4.2 minutes. This information was obtained from a sample of 35 monitored calls. For a study of 45 hardware issues, the mean time for the technician to resolve the problem was 15.5 minutes with a standard deviation of 3.9 minutes. This information was also obtained from monitored calls. At the .05 significance level, does it take longer to resolve software issues? What is the *p*-value?

27. One of the music industry's most pressing questions is: Can paid download stores contend nose-to-nose with free peer-to-peer download services? Data gathered over the last 12 months show Apple's iTunes was used by an average of 1.65 million households with a sample standard deviation of 0.56 million family units. Over the same 12 months WinMX (a no-cost P2P download service) was used by an average of 2.2 million families with a sample standard deviation of 0.30 million. Assume the population standard deviations are not the same. Using a significance level of .05, test the hypothesis of no difference in the mean number of households picking either variety of service to download songs.

28. Businesses, particularly those in the food preparation industry such as General Mills, Kellogg, and Betty Crocker, regularly use coupons as a brand allegiance builder to stimulate their retailing. There is uneasiness that the users of paper coupons are different from the users of e-coupons (coupons disseminated by means of the Internet). One survey recorded the age of each person who redeemed a coupon along with the type (either electronic or paper). The sample of 35 e-coupon users had a mean age of 33.6 years with a standard deviation of 10.9, while a similar sample of 25 traditional paper-coupon clippers had a mean age of 39.5 with a standard deviation of 4.8. Assume the population standard deviations are not the same. Using a significance level of .01, test the hypothesis of no difference in the mean ages of the two groups of coupon clients.

29. The owner of Bun 'N' Run Hamburgers wishes to compare the sales per day at two locations. The mean number sold for 10 randomly selected days at the Northside site was 83.55, and the standard deviation was 10.50. For a random sample of 12 days at the Southside location, the mean number sold was 78.80 and the standard deviation was 14.25. At the .05 significance level, is there a difference in the mean number of hamburgers sold at the two locations? What is the *p*-value?

For **DATA FILE**, please visit www.mhhe.com/lind16e

30. The Engineering Department at Sims Software Inc. recently developed two chemical solutions designed to increase the usable life of computer disks. A sample of disks treated with the first solution lasted 86, 78, 66, 83, 84, 81, 84, 109, 65, and 102 hours. Those treated with the second solution lasted 91, 71, 75, 76, 87, 79, 73, 76, 79, 78, 87, 90, 76, and 72 hours. Assume the population standard deviations are not the same. At the .10 significance level, can we conclude that there is a difference in the length of time the two types of treatment lasted?

For **DATA FILE**, please visit www.mhhe.com/lind16e

31. The Willow Run Outlet Mall has two Haggar Outlet Stores, one located on Peach Street and the other on Plum Street. The two stores are laid out differently, but both store managers claim their layout maximizes the amounts customers will purchase on impulse. A sample of 10 customers at the Peach Street store revealed they spent the following amounts more than planned: \$17.58, \$19.73, \$12.61, \$17.79, \$16.22, \$15.82, \$15.40, \$15.86, \$11.82, and \$15.85. A sample of 14 customers at the Plum Street store revealed they spent the following amounts more than they planned: \$18.19, \$20.22, \$17.38, \$17.96, \$23.92, \$15.87, \$16.47, \$15.96, \$16.79, \$16.74, \$21.40, \$20.57, \$19.79, and \$14.83. At the .01 significance level, is there a difference in the mean amounts purchased on impulse at the two stores?

For **DATA FILE**, please visit www.mhhe.com/lind16e

32. Grand Strand Family Medical Center treats minor medical emergencies for visitors to the Myrtle Beach area. There are two facilities, one in the Little River Area and the other in Murrells Inlet. The Quality Assurance Department wishes to compare the mean waiting time for patients at the two locations. Samples of the waiting times for each location, reported in minutes, follow:

Location	Waiting Time											
Little River	31.73	28.77	29.53	22.08	29.47	18.60	32.94	25.18	29.82	26.49		
Murrells Inlet	22.93	23.92	26.92	27.20	26.44	25.62	30.61	29.44	23.09	23.10	26.69	22.31

Assume the population standard deviations are not the same. At the .05 significance level, is there a difference in the mean waiting time?

For **DATA FILE**, please visit www.mhhe.com/lind16e

33. Commercial Bank and Trust Company is studying the use of its automatic teller machines (ATMs). Of particular interest is whether young adults (under 25 years) use the machines more than senior citizens. To investigate further, samples of customers under 25 years of age and customers over 60 years of age were selected. The number of ATM transactions last month was determined for each selected individual, and the results are shown below. At the .01 significance level, can bank management conclude that younger customers use the ATMs more?

Under 25	10	10	11	15	7	11	10	9			
Over 60	4	8	7	7	4	5	1	7	4	10	5

For **DATA FILE**, please visit www.mhhe.com/lind16e

34. Two boats, the *Prada* (Italy) and the *Oracle* (U.S.A.), are competing for a spot in the upcoming *America's Cup* race. They race over a part of the course several times. Below are a sample of times in minutes for each boat. Assume the population standard deviations are not the same. At the .05 significance level, can we conclude that there is a difference in their mean times?

Boat	Time (minutes)											
Prada (Italy)	12.9	12.5	11.0	13.3	11.2	11.4	11.6	12.3	14.2	11.3		
Oracle (U.S.A.)	14.1	14.1	14.2	17.4	15.8	16.7	16.1	13.3	13.4	13.6	10.8	19.0

For **DATA FILE**, please visit www.mhhe.com/lind16e

35. The manufacturer of an MP3 player wanted to know whether a 10% reduction in price is enough to increase the sales of its product. To investigate, the owner randomly selected eight outlets and sold the MP3 player at the reduced price. At seven randomly selected outlets, the MP3 player was sold at the regular price. Reported below is the number of units sold last month at the regular and reduced prices at the randomly selected outlets. At the .01 significance level, can the manufacturer conclude that the price reduction resulted in an increase in sales?

Regular price	138	121	88	115	141	125	96	
Reduced price	128	134	152	135	114	106	112	120

For **DATA FILE**, please visit www.mhhe.com/lind16e

36. A number of minor automobile accidents occur at various high-risk intersections in Teton County despite traffic lights. The Traffic Department claims that a modification in the type of light will reduce these accidents. The county commissioners have agreed to a proposed experiment. Eight intersections were chosen at random, and the lights at those intersections were modified. The numbers of minor accidents during a six-month period before and after the modifications were:

	Number of Accidents							
	A	**B**	**C**	**D**	**E**	**F**	**G**	**H**
Before modification	5	7	6	4	8	9	8	10
After modification	3	7	7	0	4	6	8	2

At the .01 significance level, is it reasonable to conclude that the modification reduced the number of traffic accidents?

For **DATA FILE**, please visit www.mhhe.com/lind16e

37. Lester Hollar is vice president for human resources for a large manufacturing company. In recent years, he has noticed an increase in absenteeism that he thinks is related to the general health of the employees. Four years ago, in an attempt to improve the situation, he began a fitness program in which employees exercise during their lunch hour. To evaluate the program, he selected a random sample of eight participants and found the number of days each was absent in the six months before the exercise program began and in the six months following the exercise program. Below are the results. At the .05 significance level, can he conclude that the number of absences has declined? Estimate the *p*-value.

Employee	Before	After
1	6	5
2	6	2
3	7	1
4	7	3
5	4	3
6	3	6
7	5	3
8	6	7

For **DATA FILE**, please visit www.mhhe.com/lind16e

38. The president of the American Insurance Institute wants to compare the yearly costs of auto insurance offered by two leading companies. He selects a sample of 15 families, some with only a single insured driver, others with several teenage drivers, and pays each family a stipend to contact the two companies and ask for a price quote. To make the data comparable, certain features, such as the deductible amount and limits of liability, are standardized. The data for the sample of families and their two insurance quotes are reported below. At the .10 significance level, can we conclude that there is a difference in the amounts quoted?

Family	Midstates Car Insurance	Gecko Mutual Insurance
Becker	$2,090	$1,610
Berry	1,683	1,247
Cobb	1,402	2,327
Debuck	1,830	1,367
DuBrul	930	1,461
Eckroate	697	1,789
German	1,741	1,621
Glasson	1,129	1,914
King	1,018	1,956
Kucic	1,881	1,772
Meredith	1,571	1,375
Obeid	874	1,527
Price	1,579	1,767
Phillips	1,577	1,636
Tresize	860	1,188

39. Fairfield Homes is developing two parcels near Pigeon Fork, Tennessee. In order to test different advertising approaches, it uses different media to reach potential buyers. The mean annual family income for 15 people making inquiries at the first development is $150,000, with a standard deviation of $40,000. A corresponding sample of 25 people at the second development had a mean of $180,000, with a standard deviation of $30,000. Assume the population standard deviations are the same. At the .05 significance level, can Fairfield conclude that the population means are different?

40. A candy company taste-tested two chocolate bars, one with almonds and one without almonds. A panel of testers rated the bars on a scale of 0 to 5, with 5 indicating the highest taste rating. If the bar had almonds, the rating was assigned a code of 1; if the bar did not have almonds, the rating was assigned a code of 0. Assume the population standard deviations are equal. At the .05 significance level, do the ratings show a difference between chocolate bars with or without almonds?

Rating	With/Without	Rating	With/Without
3	1	1	1
1	1	4	0
0	0	4	0
2	1	2	1
3	1	3	0
1	1	4	0

For **DATA FILE**, please visit www.mhhe.com/lind16e

41. An investigation of the effectiveness of an antibacterial soap in reducing operating room contamination resulted in the accompanying table. The new soap was tested in a sample of eight operating rooms in the greater Seattle area during the last year. The following table reports the contamination levels before and after the use of the soap for each operating room.

	Operating Room							
	A	B	C	D	E	F	G	H
Before	6.6	6.5	9.0	10.3	11.2	8.1	6.3	11.6
After	6.8	2.4	7.4	8.5	8.1	6.1	3.4	2.0

At the .05 significance level, can we conclude the contamination measurements are lower after use of the new soap?

For **DATA FILE**, please visit www.mhhe.com/lind16e

42. The following data on annual rates of return were collected from five randomly selected stocks listed on the New York Stock Exchange ("the big board") and five randomly selected stocks listed on NASDAQ. Assume the population standard deviations are the same. At the .10 significance level, can we conclude that the annual rates of return are higher on the big board?

NYSE	NASDAQ
17.16	15.80
17.08	16.28
15.51	16.21
8.43	17.97
25.15	7.77

For **DATA FILE**, please visit www.mhhe.com/lind16e

43. The city of Laguna Beach operates two public parking lots. The Ocean Drive parking lot can accommodate up to 125 cars and the Rio Rancho parking lot can accommodate up to 130 cars. City planners are considering increasing the size of the lots and changing the fee structure. To begin, the Planning Office would like some information on the number of cars in the lots at various times of the day. A junior planner officer is assigned the task of visiting the two lots at random times of the day and evening and counting the number of cars in the lots. The study lasted over a period of one month. Below is the number of cars in the lots for 25 visits of the Ocean Drive lot and 28 visits of the Rio Rancho lot. Assume the population standard deviations are equal.

Ocean Drive												
89	115	93	79	113	77	51	75	118	105	106	91	54
63	121	53	81	115	67	53	69	95	121	88	64	
Rio Rancho												
128	110	81	126	82	114	93	40	94	45	84	71	74
92	66	69	100	114	113	107	62	77	80	107	90	129
105	124											

Is it reasonable to conclude that there is a difference in the mean number of cars in the two lots? Use the .05 significance level.

For **DATA FILE**, please visit www.mhhe.com/lind16e

44. The amount of income spent on housing is an important component of the cost of living. The total costs of housing for homeowners might include mortgage payments, property taxes, and utility costs (water, heat, electricity). An economist selected a sample of

20 homeowners in New England and then calculated these total housing costs as a percent of monthly income, 5 years ago and now. The information is reported below. Is it reasonable to conclude the percent is less now than 5 years ago?

Homeowner	Five Years Ago	Now	Homeowner	Five Years Ago	Now
1	17%	10%	11	35%	32%
2	20	39	12	16	32
3	29	37	13	23	21
4	43	27	14	33	12
5	36	12	15	44	40
6	43	41	16	44	42
7	45	24	17	28	22
8	19	26	18	29	19
9	49	28	19	39	35
10	49	26	20	22	12

For **DATA FILE**, please visit www.mhhe.com/lind16e

45. The CVS Pharmacy located on US 17 in Murrells Inlet has been one of the busiest pharmaceutical retail stores in South Carolina for many years. To try and capture more business in the area, CVS top management opened another store about 6 miles west on SC 707. After a few months, CVS management decided to compare the business volume at the two stores. One way to measure business volume is to count the number of cars in the store parking lots on random days and times. The results of the survey from the last 3 months of the year are reported below. To explain, the first observation was on October 2 at 20:52 military time (8:52 p.m.). At that time there were four cars in the US 17 lot and nine cars in the SC 707 lot. At the .05 significance level, is it reasonable to conclude that, based on vehicle counts, the US 17 store has more business volume than the SC 707 store?

		Vehicle Count	
Date	Time	US 17	SC 707
Oct 2	20:52	4	9
Oct 11	19:30	5	7
Oct 15	22:08	9	12
Oct 19	11:42	4	5
Oct 25	15:32	10	8
Oct 26	11:02	9	15
Nov 3	11:22	13	7
Nov 5	19:09	20	3
Nov 8	15:10	15	14
Nov 9	13:18	15	11
Nov 15	22:38	13	11
Nov 17	18:46	16	12
Nov 21	15:44	17	8
Nov 22	15:34	15	3
Nov 27	21:42	20	6
Nov 29	9:57	17	13
Nov 30	17:58	5	9
Dec 3	19:54	7	13
Dec 15	18:20	11	6
Dec 16	18:25	14	15
Dec 17	11:08	8	8
Dec 22	21:20	10	3
Dec 24	15:21	4	6
Dec 25	20:21	7	9
Dec 30	14:25	19	4

46. A goal of financial literacy for children is to learn how to manage money wisely. One question is: How much money do children have to manage? A recent study by Schnur Educational Research Associates randomly sampled 15 children between 8 and 10 years old and 18 children between 11 and 14 years old and recorded their monthly allowance. Is it reasonable to conclude that the mean allowance received by children between 11 and 14 years is more than the allowance received by children between 8 and 10 years? Use the .01 significance level. What is the *p*-value?

8–10 Years	11–14 Years	8–10 Years	11–14 Years
6	19	6	11
13	14	5	8
10	12	7	14
6	8	9	9
14	9	14	20
6	11	12	19
7	9		11
7	8		12
10	8		20

DATA SET EXERCISES

(The data for these exercises are available at the text website: www.mhhe.com/lind16e.)

47. Refer to the Real Estate data, which report information on the homes sold in Goodyear, Arizona, last year.
   a. At the .05 significance level, can we conclude that there is a difference in the mean selling price of homes with a pool and homes without a pool?
   b. At the .05 significance level, can we conclude that there is a difference in the mean selling price of homes with an attached garage and homes without an attached garage?
   c. At the .05 significance level, can we conclude that there is a difference in the mean selling price of homes in Township 1 and Township 2?

48. Refer to the Baseball 2012 data, which report information on the 30 Major League Baseball teams for the 2012 season.
   a. At the .05 significance level, can we conclude that there is a difference in the mean salary of teams in the American League versus teams in the National League?
   b. At the .05 significance level, can we conclude that there is a difference in the mean home attendance of teams in the American League versus teams in the National League?
   c. Compute the mean and the standard deviation of the number of wins for the 10 teams with the highest salaries. Do the same for the 10 teams with the lowest salaries. At the .05 significance level, is there a difference in the mean number of wins for the two groups?

49. Refer to the Buena School District bus data. Is there a difference in the mean maintenance cost for the diesel versus the gasoline buses? Use the .05 significance level.

Analysis of Variance

12

A SOFTWARE DESIGN COMPANY is creating a new, faster search engine. The search engine is clearly faster, but initial tests indicate there is more variation in the time to perform a search. A sample of 16 different searches showed that the standard deviation of the search time was 22 hundredths of a second for the new search engine and 12 hundredths of a second for the current search engine. At the .05 significance level, can we conclude that there is more variation in the search time of the new search engine? (See Exercise 24 and LO12-1.)

LEARNING OBJECTIVES

When you have completed this chapter, you will be able to:

LO12-1 Apply the *F* distribution to test a hypothesis that two population variances are equal.

LO12-2 Use ANOVA to test a hypothesis that three or more population means are equal.

LO12-3 Use confidence intervals to test and interpret differences between pairs of population means.

LO12-4 Use a blocking variable in a two-way ANOVA to test a hypothesis that three or more population means are equal.

LO12-5 Perform a two-way ANOVA with interaction and describe the results.

INTRODUCTION

In this chapter, we continue our discussion of hypothesis testing. Recall that in Chapters 10 and 11 we examined the general theory of hypothesis testing. We described the case where a sample was selected from the population. We used the z distribution (the standard normal distribution) or the t distribution to determine whether it was reasonable to conclude that the population mean was equal to a specified value. We tested whether two population means are the same. In this chapter, we expand our idea of hypothesis tests. We describe a test for variances and then a test that simultaneously compares several means to determine if they came from equal populations.

LO12-1
Apply the *F* distribution to test a hypothesis that two population variances are equal.

COMPARING TWO POPULATION VARIANCES

In Chapter 11, we tested hypotheses about equal population means. The tests differed based on our assumptions regarding whether the population standard deviations or variances were equal or unequal. In this chapter, the assumption about equal population variances is also important. In this section, we present a way to statistically test this assumption. The test is based on the *F* distribution.

The *F* Distribution

The probability distribution used in this chapter is the *F* distribution. It was named to honor Sir Ronald Fisher, one of the founders of modern-day statistics. The test statistic for several situations follows this probability distribution. It is used to test whether two samples are from populations having equal variances, and it is also applied when we want to compare several population means simultaneously. The simultaneous comparison of several population means is called **analysis of variance (ANOVA).** In both of these situations, the populations must follow a normal distribution, and the data must be at least interval-scale.

What are the characteristics of the *F* distribution?

1. **There is a family of *F* distributions.** A particular member of the family is determined by two parameters: the degrees of freedom in the numerator and the degrees of freedom in the denominator. The shape of the distribution is illustrated by the following graph. There is one *F* distribution for the combination of 29 degrees of freedom in the numerator (*df*) and 28 degrees of freedom in the denominator. There is another *F* distribution for 19 degrees of freedom in the numerator and 6 degrees of freedom in the denominator. The final distribution shown has 6 degrees of freedom in the numerator and 6 degrees of freedom in the denominator. We will describe the concept of degrees of freedom later in the chapter. Note that the shapes of the distributions change as the degrees of freedom change.

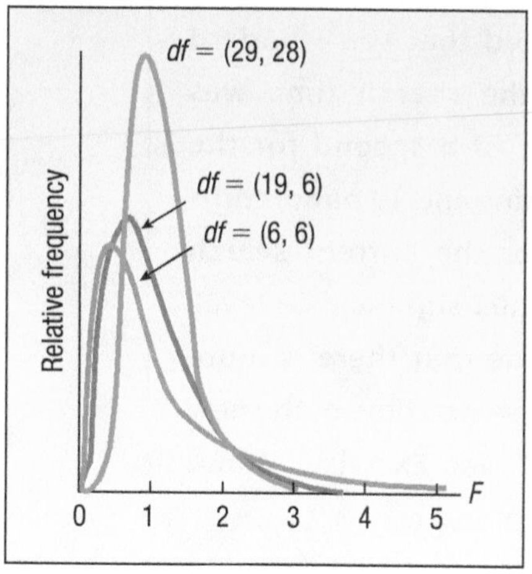

2. **The *F* distribution is continuous.** This means that it can assume an infinite number of values between zero and positive infinity.
3. **The *F* distribution cannot be negative.** The smallest value *F* can assume is 0.
4. **It is positively skewed.** The long tail of the distribution is to the right-hand side. As the number of degrees of freedom increases in both the numerator and denominator, the distribution approaches a normal distribution.
5. **It is asymptotic.** As the values of *F* increase, the distribution approaches the horizontal axis but never touches it. This is similar to the behavior of the normal probability distribution, described in Chapter 7.

Testing a Hypothesis of Equal Population Variances

The first application of the *F* distribution that we describe occurs when we test the hypothesis that the variance of one normal population equals the variance of another normal population. The following examples will show the use of the test:

- A health services corporation manages two hospitals in Knoxville, Tennessee: St. Mary's North and St. Mary's South. In each hospital, the mean waiting time in the Emergency Department is 42 minutes. The hospital administrator believes that the St. Mary's North Emergency Department has more variation in waiting time than St. Mary's South.

- The mean rate of return on two types of common stock may be the same, but there may be more variation in the rate of return in one than the other. A sample of 10 technology and 10 utility stocks shows the same mean rate of return, but there is likely more variation in the technology stocks.
- A study by the marketing department for a large newspaper found that men and women spent about the same amount of time per day surfing the Net. However, the same report indicated there was nearly twice as much variation in time spent per day among the men than the women.

The *F* distribution is also used to test assumptions for some statistical tests. Recall that in the previous chapter we used the *t* test to investigate whether the means of two independent populations differed. To employ that test, we sometimes assume that the variances of two normal populations are the same. See this list of assumptions on page 356. The *F* distribution is used to test the assumption that the variances of two normal populations are equal.

Regardless of whether we want to determine whether one population has more variation than another population or validate an assumption for a statistical test, we first state the null hypothesis. The null hypothesis is that the variance of one normal population, σ_1^2, equals the variance of another normal population, σ_2^2. The alternate hypothesis could be that the variances differ. In this instance, the null hypothesis and the alternate hypothesis are:

$$H_0: \sigma_1^2 = \sigma_2^2$$
$$H_1: \sigma_1^2 \neq \sigma_2^2$$

To conduct the test, we select a random sample of n_1 observations from one population and a random sample of n_2 observations from the second population. The test statistic is defined as follows.

TEST STATISTIC FOR COMPARING TWO VARIANCES

$$F = \frac{s_1^2}{s_2^2} \quad [12\text{–}1]$$

The terms s_1^2 and s_2^2 are the respective sample variances. If the null hypothesis is true, the test statistic follows the F distribution with $n_1 - 1$ and $n_2 - 1$ degrees of freedom. To reduce the size of the table of critical values, the *larger* sample variance is placed in the numerator; hence, the tabled F ratio is always larger than 1.00. Thus, the right-tail critical value is the only one required. The critical value of F for a two-tailed test is found by dividing the significance level in half ($\alpha/2$) and then referring to the appropriate degrees of freedom in Appendix B.6. An example will illustrate.

EXAMPLE

Lammers Limos offers limousine service from Government Center in downtown Toledo, Ohio, to Metro Airport in Detroit. Sean Lammers, president of the company, is considering two routes. One is via U.S. 25 and the other via I-75. He wants to study the time it takes to drive to the airport using each route and then compare the results. He collected the following sample data, which is reported in minutes. Using the .10 significance level, is there a difference in the variation in the driving times for the two routes?

U.S. Route 25	Interstate 75
52	59
67	60
56	61
45	51
70	56
54	63
64	57
	65

SOLUTION

The mean driving times along the two routes are nearly the same. The mean time is 58.29 minutes for the U.S. 25 route and 59.0 minutes along the I-75 route. However, in evaluating travel times, Mr. Lammers is also concerned about the variation in the travel times. The first step is to compute the two sample variances. We'll use formula (3–11) to compute the sample standard deviations. To obtain the sample variances, we square the standard deviations.

U.S. Route 25

$$\bar{x} = \frac{\Sigma x}{n} = \frac{408}{7} = 58.29 \qquad s = \sqrt{\frac{\Sigma(x - \bar{x})^2}{n - 1}} = \sqrt{\frac{485.43}{7 - 1}} = 8.9947$$

Interstate 75

$$\bar{x} = \frac{\Sigma x}{n} = \frac{472}{8} = 59.00 \qquad s = \sqrt{\frac{\Sigma(x - \bar{x})^2}{n - 1}} = \sqrt{\frac{134}{8 - 1}} = 4.3753$$

There is more variation, as measured by the standard deviation, in the U.S. 25 route than in the I-75 route. This is consistent with his knowledge of the two routes; the U.S. 25 route contains more stoplights, whereas I-75 is a limited-access interstate highway. However, the I-75 route is several miles longer. It is important that the service offered be both timely and consistent, so he decides to conduct a statistical test to determine whether there really is a difference in the variation of the two routes.

We use the six-step hypothesis test procedure.

Step 1: We begin by stating the null hypothesis and the alternate hypothesis. The test is two-tailed because we are looking for a difference in the variation of the two routes. We are *not* trying to show that one route has more variation than the other. For this example/solution, the subscript 1 indicates information for U.S. 25; the subscript 2 indicates information for I-75.

$$H_0: \sigma_1^2 = \sigma_2^2$$
$$H_1: \sigma_1^2 \neq \sigma_2^2$$

Step 2: We selected the .10 significance level.

Step 3: The appropriate test statistic follows the *F* distribution.

Step 4: The critical value is obtained from Appendix B.6, a portion of which is reproduced as Table 12–1. Because we are conducting a two-tailed test, the tabled significance level is .05, found by $\alpha/2 = .10/2 = .05$. There are $n_1 - 1 = 7 - 1 = 6$ degrees of freedom in the numerator and $n_2 - 1 = 8 - 1 = 7$ degrees of freedom in the denominator. To find the critical value, move horizontally across the top portion of the *F* table (Table 12–1 or Appendix B.6) for the .05 significance level to 6 degrees of freedom in the numerator. Then move down that column to the critical value opposite 7 degrees of freedom in the denominator. The critical value is 3.87. Thus, the decision rule is: Reject the null hypothesis if the ratio of the sample variances exceeds 3.87.

TABLE 12–1 Critical Values of the *F* Distribution, $\alpha = .05$

Degrees of Freedom for Denominator	Degrees of Freedom for Numerator 5	6	7	8
1	230	234	237	239
2	19.3	19.3	19.4	19.4
3	9.01	8.94	8.89	8.85
4	6.26	6.16	6.09	6.04
5	5.05	4.95	4.88	4.82
6	4.39	4.28	4.21	4.15
7	3.97	3.87	3.79	3.73
8	3.69	3.58	3.50	3.44
9	3.48	3.37	3.29	3.23
10	3.33	3.22	3.14	3.07

Step 5: Next we compute the ratio of the two sample variances, determine the value of the test statistic, and make a decision regarding the null hypothesis. Note that formula (12–1) refers to the sample *variances*,

but we calculated the sample *standard deviations*. We need to square the standard deviations to determine the variances.

$$F = \frac{s_1^2}{s_2^2} = \frac{(8.9947)^2}{(4.3753)^2} = 4.23$$

The decision is to reject the null hypothesis because the computed F value (4.23) is larger than the critical value (3.87).

Step 6: We conclude there is a difference in the variation in the time to travel the two routes. Mr. Lammers will want to consider this in his scheduling.

The usual practice is to determine the F ratio by putting the larger of the two sample variances in the numerator. This will force the F ratio to be at least 1.00. This allows us to always use the right tail of the F distribution, thus avoiding the need for more extensive F tables.

A logical question arises: Is it possible to conduct one-tailed tests? For example, suppose in the previous example we suspected that the variance of the times using the U.S. 25 route, σ_1^2, is larger than the variance of the times along the I-75 route, σ_2^2. We would state the null and the alternate hypothesis as

$$H_0: \sigma_1^2 \le \sigma_2^2$$
$$H_1: \sigma_1^2 > \sigma_2^2$$

The test statistic is computed as s_1^2/s_2^2. Notice that we labeled the population with the suspected large variance as population 1. So s_1^2 appears in the numerator. The F ratio will be larger than 1.00, so we can use the upper tail of the F distribution. Under these conditions, it is not necessary to divide the significance level in half. Because Appendix B.6 gives us only the .05 and .01 significance levels, we are restricted to these levels for one-tailed tests and .10 and .02 for two-tailed tests unless we consult a more complete table or use statistical software to compute the F statistic.

The Excel software has a procedure to perform a test of variances. Below is the output. The computed value of F is the same as that determined by using formula (12–1).

Variance Test

	A	B	C	D	E	F	G
1	U.S. 25	Interstate 75		F-Test Two-Sample for Variances			
2	52	59			*U.S. 25*	*Interstate 75*	
3	67	60		Mean	58.29	59.00	
4	56	61		Variance	80.90	19.14	
5	45	51		Observations	7.00	8.00	
6	70	56		df	6.00	7.00	
7	54	63		F	4.23		
8	64	57		P(F<=f) one-tail	0.04		
9		65		F Critical one-tail	3.87		
10							

SELF-REVIEW 12–1

Steele Electric Products Inc. assembles electrical components for cell phones. For the last 10 days, Mark Nagy has averaged 9 rejects, with a standard deviation of 2 rejects per day. Debbie Richmond averaged 8.5 rejects, with a standard deviation of 1.5 rejects, over the same period. At the .05 significance level, can we conclude that there is more variation in the number of rejects per day attributed to Mark?

EXERCISES

1. What is the critical F value for a sample of six observations in the numerator and four in the denominator? Use a two-tailed test and the .10 significance level.
2. What is the critical F value for a sample of four observations in the numerator and seven in the denominator? Use a one-tailed test and the .01 significance level.
3. The following hypotheses are given.

$$H_0: \sigma_1^2 = \sigma_2^2$$
$$H_1: \sigma_1^2 \neq \sigma_2^2$$

A random sample of eight observations from the first population resulted in a standard deviation of 10. A random sample of six observations from the second population resulted in a standard deviation of 7. At the .02 significance level, is there a difference in the variation of the two populations?
4. The following hypotheses are given.

$$H_0: \sigma_1^2 \leq \sigma_2^2$$
$$H_1: \sigma_1^2 > \sigma_2^2$$

A random sample of five observations from the first population resulted in a standard deviation of 12. A random sample of seven observations from the second population showed a standard deviation of 7. At the .01 significance level, is there more variation in the first population?
5. Arbitron Media Research Inc. conducted a study of the iPod listening habits of men and women. One facet of the study involved the mean listening time. It was discovered that the mean listening time for men was 35 minutes per day. The standard deviation of the sample of the 10 men studied was 10 minutes per day. The mean listening time for the 12 women studied was also 35 minutes, but the standard deviation of the sample was 12 minutes. At the .10 significance level, can we conclude that there is a difference in the variation in the listening times for men and women?
6. A stockbroker at Critical Securities reported that the mean rate of return on a sample of 10 oil stocks was 12.6% with a standard deviation of 3.9%. The mean rate of return on a sample of 8 utility stocks was 10.9% with a standard deviation of 3.5%. At the .05 significance level, can we conclude that there is more variation in the oil stocks?

LO12-2
Use ANOVA to test a hypothesis that three or more population means are equal.

ANOVA: ANALYSIS OF VARIANCE

The F distribution is used to perform a wide variety of hypothesis tests. For example, when the equality of more than two population means is tested, the Analysis of Variance (ANOVA) technique is used and the F statistic is used as the test statistic.

ANOVA Assumptions

The ANOVA to test the equality of more than two population means requires that three assumptions are true:

1. The populations follow the normal distribution.
2. The populations have equal standard deviations (σ).
3. The populations are independent.

When these conditions are met, F is used as the distribution of the test statistic.

Why do we need to study ANOVA? Why can't we just use the test of differences in population means discussed in the previous chapter? We could compare the population means two at a time. The major reason is the unsatisfactory buildup of Type I error. To explain further, suppose we have four different methods (A, B, C, and D) of training new recruits to be firefighters. We randomly assign each of the 40 recruits in this year's class to one of the four methods. At the end of the training program, we administer to the four groups a common test to measure understanding of firefighting techniques. The question is: Is there a difference in the mean test scores among the four groups? An answer to this question will allow us to compare the four training methods.

Using the t distribution to compare the four population means, we would have to conduct six different t tests. That is, we would need to compare the mean scores for the

four methods as follows: A versus B, A versus C, A versus D, B versus C, B versus D, and C versus D. For each *t* test, suppose we choose an $\alpha = .05$. Therefore, the probability of a Type I error, rejecting the null when it is true, is .05. The complement is the probability of .95 that we do not reject the null when it is true. Because we conduct six separate (independent) tests, the probability that all six tests result in correct decisions is:

$$P(All\ correct) = (.95)(.95)(.95)(.95)(.95)(.95) = .735$$

To find the probability of at least one error due to sampling, we subtract this result from 1. Thus, the probability of at least one incorrect decision due to sampling is $1 - .735 = .265$. To summarize, if we conduct six independent tests using the *t* distribution, the likelihood of rejecting a true null hypothesis because of sampling error is an unsatisfactory .265. The ANOVA technique allows us to compare population means simultaneously at a selected significance level. It avoids the buildup of Type I error associated with testing many hypotheses.

ANOVA was first developed for applications in agriculture, and many of the terms related to that context remain. In particular, the term *treatment* is used to identify the different populations being examined. For example, treatment refers to how a plot of ground was treated with a particular type of fertilizer. The following illustration will clarify the term *treatment* and demonstrate an application of ANOVA.

EXAMPLE

Joyce Kuhlman manages a regional financial center. She wishes to compare the productivity, as measured by the number of customers served, among three employees. Four days are randomly selected and the number of customers served by each employee is recorded. The results are:

Wolfe	White	Korosa
55	66	47
54	76	51
59	67	46
56	71	48

SOLUTION

Is there a difference in the mean number of customers served? Chart 12–1 illustrates how the populations would appear if there were a difference in the treatment means. Note that the populations follow the normal distribution and the variation in each population is the same. However, the means are *not* the same.

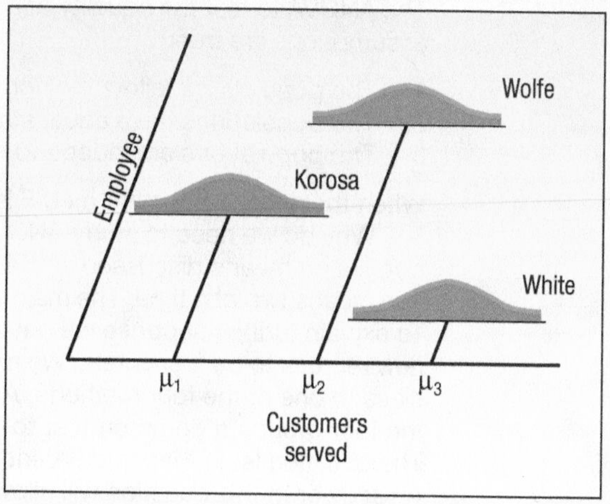

CHART 12–1 Case Where Treatment Means Are Different

Suppose the populations are the same. That is, there is no difference in the (treatment) means. This is shown in Chart 12–2. This would indicate that the population means are the same. Note again that the populations follow the normal distribution and the variation in each of the populations is the same.

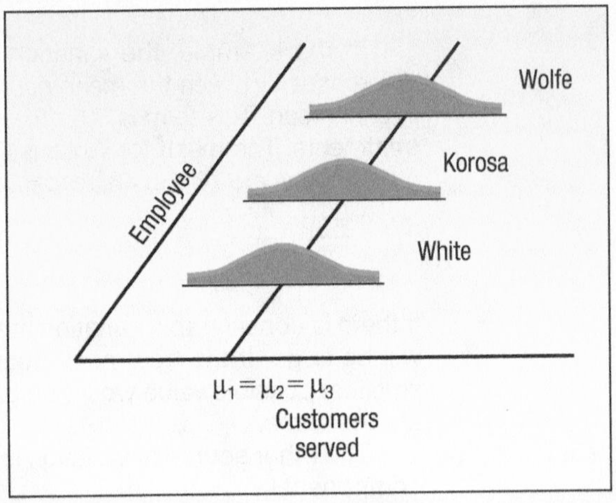

CHART 12–2 Case Where Treatment Means Are the Same

The ANOVA Test

How does the ANOVA test work? Recall that we want to determine whether the various sample means came from a single population or populations with different means. We actually compare these sample means through their variances. To explain, on page 385 we listed the assumptions required for ANOVA. One of those assumptions was that the standard deviations of the various normal populations had to be the same. We take advantage of this requirement in the ANOVA test. The underlying strategy is to estimate the population variance (standard deviation squared) two ways and then find the ratio of these two estimates. If this ratio is about 1, then logically the two estimates are the same, and we conclude that the population means are the same. If the ratio is quite different from 1, then we conclude that the population means are not the same. The *F* distribution serves as a referee by indicating when the ratio of the sample variances is too much greater than 1 to have occurred by chance.

Refer to the example/solution in the previous section. The manager wants to determine whether there is a difference in the mean number of customers served. To begin, find the overall mean of the 12 observations. It is 58, found by $(55 + 54 + \cdots + 48)/12$. Next, for each of the 12 observations find the difference between the particular value and the overall mean. Each of these differences is squared and these squares summed. This term is called the **total variation.**

TOTAL VARIATION The sum of the squared differences between each observation and the overall mean.

In our example, the total variation is 1,082, found by $(55 - 58)^2 + (54 - 58)^2 + \cdots + (48 - 58)^2$.

Next, break this total variation into two components: that which is due to the **treatments** and that which is **random.** To find these two components, determine

the mean of each of the treatments. The first source of variation is due to the treatments.

TREATMENT VARIATION The sum of the squared differences between each treatment mean and the grand or overall mean.

In the example, the variation due to the treatments is the sum of the squared differences between the mean number of customers served by each employee and the overall mean. This term is 992. To calculate it, we first find the mean of each of the three treatments. The mean for Wolfe is 56 customers, found by $(55 + 54 + 59 + 56)/4$. The other means are 70 and 48, respectively. The sum of the squares due to the treatments is:

$$(56 - 58)^2 + (56 - 58)^2 + \cdots + (48 - 58)^2 = 4(56 - 58)^2 + 4(70 - 58)^2 + 4(48 - 58)^2$$
$$= 992$$

If there is considerable variation among the treatment means, it is logical that this term will be large. If the treatment means are similar, this term will be a small value. The smallest possible value would be zero. This would occur when all the treatment means are the same.

The other source of variation is referred to as the **random** component, or the error component.

RANDOM VARIATION The sum of the squared differences between each observation and its treatment mean.

In the example, this term is the sum of the squared differences between each value and the mean for that particular employee. The error variation is 90.

$$(55 - 56)^2 + (54 - 56)^2 + \cdots + (48 - 48)^2 = 90$$

We determine the test statistic, which is the ratio of the two estimates of the population variance, from the following equation.

$$F = \frac{\text{Estimate of the population variance based on the differences among the sample means}}{\text{Estimate of the population variance based on the variation within the sample}}$$

Our first estimate of the population variance is based on the treatments, that is, the difference *between* the means. It is 992/2. Why did we divide by 2? Recall from Chapter 3, to find a sample variance [see formula (3–11)], we divide by the number of observations minus one. In this case, there are three treatments, so we divide by 2. Our first estimate of the population variance is 992/2.

The variance estimate *within* the treatments is the random variation divided by the total number of observations less the number of treatments—that is, $90/(12 - 3)$. Hence, our second estimate of the population variance is 90/9. This is actually a generalization of formula (11–5), where we pooled the sample variances from two populations.

The last step is to take the ratio of these two estimates.

$$F = \frac{992/2}{90/9} = 49.6$$

Because this ratio is quite different from 1, we can conclude that the treatment means are not the same. There is a difference in the mean number of customers served by the three employees.

Here's another example, which deals with samples of different sizes.

EXAMPLE

Recently airlines cut services, such as meals and snacks during flights, and started charging for checked luggage. A group of four carriers hired Brunner Marketing Research Inc. to survey passengers regarding their level of satisfaction with a recent flight. The survey included questions on ticketing, boarding, in-flight service, baggage handling, pilot communication, and so forth. Twenty-five questions offered a range of possible answers: excellent, good, fair, or poor. A response of excellent was given a score of 4, good a 3, fair a 2, and poor a 1. These responses were then totaled, so the total score was an indication of the satisfaction with the flight. The greater the score, the higher the level of satisfaction with the service. The highest possible score was 100.

Brunner randomly selected and surveyed passengers from the four airlines. Below is the sample information. Is there a difference in the mean satisfaction level among the four airlines? Use the .01 significance level.

Northern	WTA	Pocono	Branson
94	75	70	68
90	68	73	70
85	77	76	72
80	83	78	65
	88	80	74
		68	65
		65	

SOLUTION

We will use the six-step hypothesis-testing procedure.

Step 1: State the null hypothesis and the alternate hypothesis. The null hypothesis is that the mean scores are the same for the four airlines.

$$H_0: \mu_N = \mu_W = \mu_P = \mu_B$$

The alternate hypothesis is that the mean scores are not all the same for the four airlines.

H_1: The mean scores are not all equal.

We can also think of the alternate hypothesis as "at least two mean scores are not equal."

If the null hypothesis is not rejected, we conclude that there is no difference in the mean scores for the four airlines. If H_0 is rejected, we conclude that there is a difference in at least one pair of mean scores, but at this point we do not know which pair or how many pairs differ.

Step 2: Select the level of significance. We selected the .01 significance level.

Step 3: Determine the test statistic. The test statistic follows the *F* distribution.

Step 4: Formulate the decision rule. To determine the decision rule, we need the critical value. The critical value for the *F* statistic is found in Appendix B.6. The critical values for the .05 significance level are found on the first page and the .01 significance level on the second page. To use this table, we need to know the degrees of freedom in the numerator and the denominator. The degrees of freedom in the

numerator equal the number of treatments, designated as *k,* minus 1. The degrees of freedom in the denominator are the total number of observations, *n,* minus the number of treatments. For this problem, there are four treatments and a total of 22 observations.

$$\text{Degrees of freedom in the numerator} = k - 1 = 4 - 1 = 3$$

$$\text{Degrees of freedom in the denominator} = n - k = 22 - 4 = 18$$

Refer to Appendix B.6 and the .01 significance level. Move horizontally across the top of the page to 3 degrees of freedom in the numerator. Then move down that column to the row with 18 degrees of freedom. The value at this intersection is 5.09. So the decision rule is to reject H_0 if the computed value of F exceeds 5.09.

Step 5: Select the sample, perform the calculations, and make a decision. It is convenient to summarize the calculations of the F statistic in an **ANOVA table.** The format for an ANOVA table is as follows. Statistical software packages also use this format.

ANOVA Table

Source of Variation	Sum of Squares	Degrees of Freedom	Mean Square	F
Treatments	SST	$k - 1$	$SST/(k - 1) = MST$	MST/MSE
Error	SSE	$n - k$	$SSE/(n - k) = MSE$	
Total	SS total	$n - 1$		

There are three values, or sum of squares, used to compute the test statistic F. You can determine these values by obtaining SS total and SSE, then finding SST by subtraction. The SS total term is the total variation, SST is the variation due to the treatments, and SSE is the variation within the treatments or the random error.

We usually start the process by finding SS total. This is the sum of the squared differences between each observation and the overall mean. The formula for finding SS total is:

$$\text{SS total} = \Sigma(x - \bar{x}_G)^2 \qquad \textbf{[12–2]}$$

where:

x is each sample observation.
$\bar{x}_G$ is the overall or grand mean.

Next determine SSE or the sum of the squared errors. This is the sum of the squared differences between each observation and its respective treatment mean. The formula for finding SSE is:

$$\text{SSE} = \Sigma(x - \bar{x}_c)^2 \qquad \textbf{[12–3]}$$

where:

$\bar{x}_c$ is the sample mean for treatment c.

The SSE is calculated:

$$\text{SSE} = \Sigma(x - \bar{x}_N)^2 + \Sigma(x - \bar{x}_W)^2 + \Sigma(x - \bar{x}_P)^2 + \Sigma(x - \bar{x}_B)^2$$

The detailed calculations of SS total and SSE for this example follow. To determine the values of SS total and SSE we start by calculating the overall or grand mean. There are 22 observations and the total is 1,664, so the grand mean is 75.64.

$$\bar{x}_G = \frac{1{,}664}{22} = 75.64$$

	Northern	WTA	Pocono	Branson	Total
	94	75	70	68	
	90	68	73	70	
	85	77	76	72	
	80	83	78	65	
		88	80	74	
			68	65	
			65		
Column total	349	391	510	414	1,664
n	4	5	7	6	22
Mean	87.25	78.20	72.86	69.00	75.64

Grand Mean

Next we find the deviation of each observation from the grand mean, square those deviations, and sum this result for all 22 observations. For example, the first sampled passenger had a score of 94 and the overall or grand mean is 75.64. So $(x - \bar{x}_G) = 94 - 75.64 = 18.36$. For the last passenger, $(x - \bar{x}_G) = 65 - 75.64 = -10.64$. The calculations for all other passengers follow.

Northern	WTA	Pocono	Branson
18.36	−0.64	−5.64	−7.64
14.36	−7.64	−2.64	−5.64
9.36	1.36	0.36	−3.64
4.36	7.36	2.36	−10.64
	12.36	4.36	−1.64
		−7.64	−10.64
		−10.64	

Then square each of these differences and sum all the values. Thus, for the first passenger:

$$(x - \bar{x}_G)^2 = (94 - 75.64)^2 = (18.36)^2 = 337.09$$

Finally, sum all the squared differences as formula (12–2) direct
Our SS total value is 1,485.10.

	Northern	WTA	Pocono	Branson	Total
	337.09	0.41	31.81	58.37	
	206.21	58.37	6.97	31.81	
	87.61	1.85	0.13	13.25	
	19.01	54.17	5.57	113.21	
		152.77	19.01	2.69	
			58.37	113.21	
			113.21		
Total	649.92	267.57	235.07	332.54	1,485.10

SS Total

To compute the term SSE, find the deviation between each observation and its treatment mean. In the example, the mean of the first treatment (that is, the passengers on Northern Airlines) is 87.25, found by $\bar{x}_N = 349/4$. The subscript N refers to Northern Airlines.

STATISTICS IN ACTION

Have you ever waited in line for a telephone and it seemed like the person using the phone talked on and on? There is evidence that people actually talk longer on public telephones when someone is waiting. In a recent survey, researchers measured the length of time that 56 shoppers in a mall spent on the phone (1) when they were alone, (2) when a person was using the adjacent phone, and (3) when a person was using an adjacent phone and someone was waiting to use the phone. The study, using the one-way ANOVA technique, showed that the mean time using the telephone was significantly less when the person was alone.

The first passenger rated Northern a 94, so $(x - \bar{x}_N) = (94 - 87.25) = 6.75$. The first passenger in the WTA group responded with a total score of 75, so $(x - \bar{x}_W) = (75 - 78.20) = -3.2$. The detail for all the passengers follows.

Northern	WTA	Pocono	Branson
6.75	−3.2	−2.86	−1
2.75	−10.2	0.14	1
−2.25	−1.2	3.14	3
−7.25	4.8	5.14	−4
	9.8	7.14	5
		−4.86	−4
		−7.86	

Each of these values is squared and then summed for all 22 observations. The four column totals can also be summed to find SSE. The values are shown in the following table.

	Northern	WTA	Pocono	Branson	Total
	45.5625	10.24	8.18	1	
	7.5625	104.04	0.02	1	
	5.0625	1.44	9.86	9	
	52.5625	23.04	26.42	16	
		96.04	50.98	25	
			23.62	16	SSE
			61.78		
Total	110.7500	234.80	180.86	68	594.41

So the SSE value is 594.41. That is, $\Sigma(x - \bar{x}_c)^2 = 594.41$.

Finally, we determine SST, the sum of the squares due to the treatments, by subtraction.

$$\text{SST} = \text{SS total} - \text{SSE} \qquad \textbf{[12–4]}$$

For this example:

$$\text{SST} = \text{SS total} - \text{SSE} = 1{,}485.10 - 594.41 = 890.69.$$

To find the computed value of *F*, work your way across the ANOVA table. The degrees of freedom for the numerator and the denominator are the same as in step 4 on page 389 when we were finding the critical value of *F*. The term **mean square** is another expression for an estimate of the variance. The mean square for treatments is SST divided by its degrees of freedom. The result is the **mean square for treatments** and is written MST. Compute the **mean square error** in a similar fashion. To be precise, divide SSE by its degrees of freedom. To complete the process and find *F*, divide MST by MSE.

Insert the particular values of *F* into an ANOVA table and compute the value of *F* as follows.

Source of Variation	Sum of Squares	Degrees of Freedom	Mean Square	*F*
Treatments	890.69	3	296.90	8.99
Error	594.41	18	33.02	
Total	1,485.10	21		

The computed value of F is 8.99, which is greater than the critical value of 5.09, so the null hypothesis is rejected.

Step 6: Interpret the result. We conclude the population means are not all equal. At this point, the results of the ANOVA only show that at least one pair of mean satisfaction scores are not the same among the four airlines. We cannot statistically show which airlines differ in satisfaction or which airlines have the highest or lowest satisfaction scores. The techniques for determining how the airlines differ are presented in the next section.

The calculations in the previous example/solution are tedious if the number of observations in each treatment is large. Many software packages will perform the calculations and output the results. In the following illustration, Excel is used to calculate the descriptive statistics and ANOVA for the previous example/solution involving airlines and passenger ratings. There are some slight differences between the software output and the previous calculations. These differences are due to rounding.

Airline Anova

Northern	WTA	Pocono	Branson
94	75	70	68
90	68	73	70
85	77	76	72
80	83	78	65
	88	80	74
		68	65
		65	

Anova: Single Factor

SUMMARY

Groups	Count	Sum	Average	Variance
Northern	4	349	87.250	36.917
WTA	5	391	78.200	58.700
Pocono	7	510	72.857	30.143
Branson	6	414	69.000	13.600

ANOVA

Source of Variation	SS	df	MS	F	P-value	F crit
Between Groups	890.684	3	296.895	8.99	0.0007	3.160
Within Groups	594.407	18	33.023			
Total	1485.091	21				

Notice Excel uses the term "Between Groups" for treatments and "Within Groups" for error. However, they have the same meanings. The p-value is .0007. This is the probability of finding a value of the test statistic this large or larger when the null hypothesis is true. To put it another way, it is the likelihood of calculating an F value larger than 8.99 with 3 degrees of freedom in the numerator and 18 degrees of freedom in the denominator. So when we reject the null hypothesis in this instance, there is a very small likelihood of committing a Type I error!

SELF-REVIEW 12–2

Citrus Clean is a new all-purpose cleaner being test-marketed by placing displays in three different locations within various supermarkets. The number of 12-ounce bottles sold from each location within the supermarket is reported below.

Near bread	18	14	19	17
Near beer	12	18	10	16
Other cleaners	26	28	30	32

At the .05 significance level, is there a difference in the mean number of bottles sold at the three locations?

(a) State the null hypothesis and the alternate hypothesis.
(b) What is the decision rule?
(c) Compute the values of SS total, SST, and SSE.
(d) Develop an ANOVA table.
(e) What is your decision regarding the null hypothesis?

For **DATA FILE**, please visit www.mhhe.com/lind16e

18. There are three hospitals in the Tulsa, Oklahoma, area. The following data show the number of outpatient surgeries performed on Monday, Tuesday, Wednesday, Thursday, and Friday at each hospital last week. At the .05 significance level, can we conclude there is a difference in the mean number of surgeries performed by hospital or by day of the week?

	Number of Surgeries Performed		
Day	**St. Luke's**	**St. Vincent**	**Mercy**
Monday	14	18	24
Tuesday	20	24	14
Wednesday	16	22	14
Thursday	18	20	22
Friday	20	28	24

LO12-5 Perform a two-way ANOVA with interaction and describe the results.

TWO-WAY ANOVA WITH INTERACTION

In the previous section, we studied the separate or independent effects of two variables, or factors, on a response variable, travel time. In the example/solution, the two factors were the bus routes and the drivers and the response was travel time. The analysis shows two significant results. First, the mean travel times between routes, averaged over all drivers, are different. Second, the mean travel times between the five drivers, averaged over all the routes, are different. What could explain these differences? The differences between routes may simply be related to differences in the distance of the routes. We really didn't study the distance of the various routes. Perhaps the differences are explained by how fast, on average, the drivers drive regardless of the route.

There is another effect that may influence travel time that we have not considered. This is called the **interaction effect** between route and driver on travel time. That is, differences in travel time may depend on both the driver and the route. For example, it is possible that one of the drivers is especially good driving one of the routes. Perhaps one driver knows how to effectively time the traffic lights or how to avoid heavily congested intersections for one or more of the routes. In this case, differences in mean travel time may depend on the combined effect of driver and route. The results of the interaction of driver and route can provide interesting information.

INTERACTION The effect of one factor on a response variable differs depending on the value of another factor.

Interaction Plots

An everyday illustration of interaction is the effect of diet and exercise on body weight. It is generally agreed that body weight (the response variable) can be affected by two factors, diet and exercise. However, research shows there is also a combined or *interaction* effect of diet and exercise on weight loss. That is, the amount of weight loss will be different and depend on diet AND whether people exercise.

The following graph, or interaction plot, illustrates the interaction of diet and exercise. First, for people who do not exercise, the mean weight losses for Diet 1 and Diet 2 are plotted. These are connected with the blue line. Clearly, there is a difference in weight loss for the two diets. Second, for people who did exercise, the mean weight losses for Diet 1 and Diet 2 are plotted. These are connected with the green line. Again, there is a clear difference in weight loss between Diet 1 and Diet 2 for people who exercise. The plot also shows an interaction effect between diet and exercise on weight

loss. Notice the two lines are not parallel to each other. For Diet 1, the mean weight loss is more when people also exercise. For Diet 2, the mean weight loss is also more when people also exercise, but the weight loss is much greater than for Diet 1. So, what is the effect of diet and exercise on weight loss? It depends on the combined, or interaction, effects of diet and exercise.

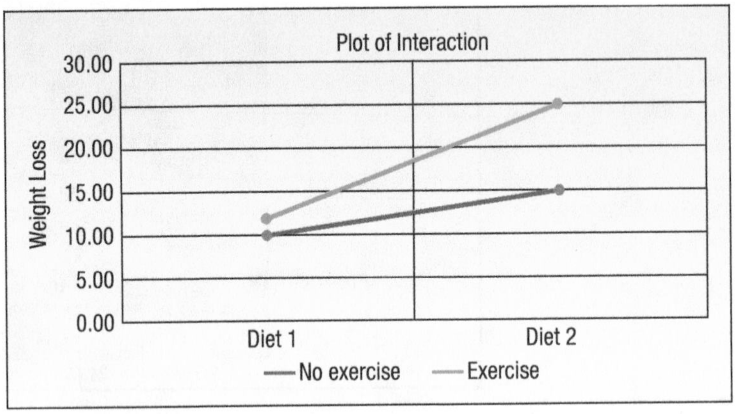

How would the interaction plot look if there were no interaction? The following graph shows an analysis of diet and exercise with no interaction.

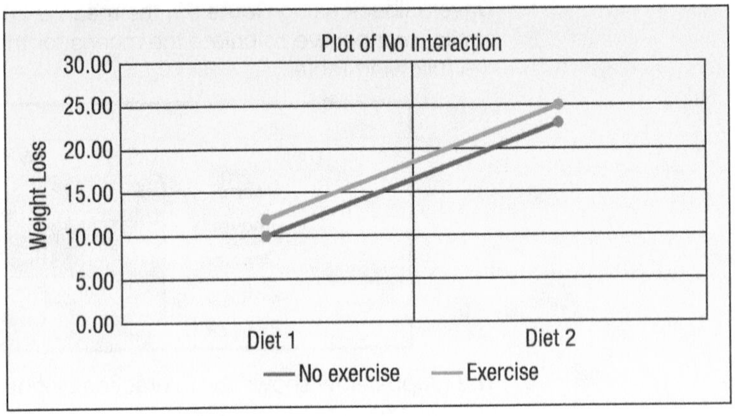

In this case the lines are parallel. Comparing the means, the effect of exercise on weight loss for Diet 1 and Diet 2 is the same. The estimated weight loss is about two pounds. In addition, the effect of diet is the same whether people exercise or not. It is about 13 pounds.

Testing for Interaction

To test for an interaction effect, we use a two-way ANOVA with interaction. To illustrate, we return to the previous WARTA example/solution. Restating the issue facing WARTA management: They want to expand bus service from downtown Warren to Starbrick. So far they have concluded, based on statistical analysis, that there is a difference in the mean travel time along the four proposed routes and a difference in the mean travel times of the five drivers. But it is possible that the combination, or the interaction between routes and drivers, has a significant effect on mean travel time.

In this analysis, we call the two variables, route and driver, **factors.** We refer to the variable, travel time, as the **response** variable. To test for interaction, the sample data must be replicated for each route. In this case, each driver drives each route three times so there are three observed times for each route/driver combination. This information is summarized in the following Excel spreadsheet.

	Routes				
	US 6	West End	Hickory St	Route 59	Means for Drivers
Deans	18	17	21	22	
	15	14	20	19	
	21	20	22	25	19.50
Snaverly	16	23	23	22	
	19	19	24	20	
	13	25	22	24	20.83
Ormson	21	21	26	22	
	19	23	24	24	
	14	25	28	20	22.25
Zollaco	23	22	29	25	
	21	24	30	20	
	25	20	28	26	24.42
Filbeck	25	24	28	28	
	24	25	29	30	Grand Mean
	26	23	27	26	26.25
Means for Routes	20.00	21.67	25.40	23.53	22.65

To evaluate interaction effects, a useful first step is to plot the means for each driver/route combination. For the driver/route combination Driver Deans using Route 6, the mean is 18 minutes, found by (18 + 15 + 21)/3. For the driver/route combination Driver Filbeck using Route 59, the mean is 28 minutes, found by (28 + 30 + 26)/3. In a similar manner we calculate the means for the other cells and summarize the results in the following table.

	Routes			
Drivers	US 6	West End	Hickory St	Route 59
Deans	18	17	21	22
Snaverly	16	22.33	23	22
Ormson	18	23	26	22
Zollaco	23	22	29	23.67
Filbeck	25	24	28	28

The graph below shows the interaction plot using the information in the above table. The vertical axis is the travel time in minutes. The four routes are labeled on the horizontal axis and each line plots the mean travel times for each driver for all four routes. For example, the green line reports average travel times for Deans for each of the four routes.

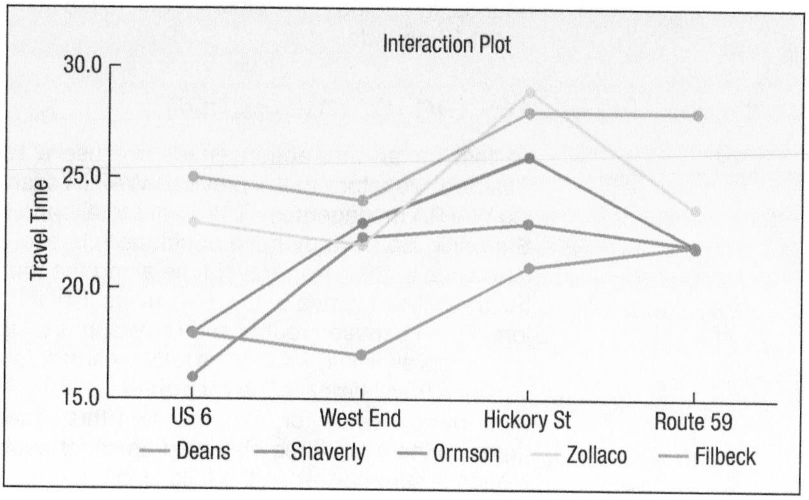

From the graph, what observations can be made about the interaction of driver and route on travel time? Most importantly, the lines are not parallel. Because the five lines are clearly not parallel, there is an interaction effect of driver and route on travel time; that is, travel time depends on the combined effect of driver and route.

Note the differences in travel times. For the U.S. 6 route, Snaverly has the lowest or fastest mean travel time. Deans has the lowest mean travel time for the West End and Hickory Street routes. Zollaco has the slowest average time for the Hickory Street route. There are many other observations that lead to the general observation that travel time is related to the combined effects of driver AND route. The critical question is whether the observed interactions are significant or the differences are due to chance.

Hypothesis Tests for Interaction

The next step is to conduct statistical tests to further investigate the possible interaction effects. In summary, our study of travel times has several questions:

- Is there an interaction between routes and drivers on mean travel times?
- Are the mean travel times for drivers the same?
- Are the mean travel times for the routes the same?

Of the three questions, we are most interested in the test for interactions.

We formalize these ideas into three sets of hypotheses:

1. H_0: There is no interaction between drivers and routes.
   H_1: There is interaction between drivers and routes.
2. H_0: The driver means are the same.
   H_1: The driver means are *not* the same.
3. H_0: The route means are the same.
   H_1: The route means are *not* the same.

We test each of these hypotheses as we did in the previous section using the F distribution. The tests are summarized with the following ANOVA table. It is similar to the two-way ANOVA in the previous section with the addition of the Interaction source of variation. In addition, we refer to the driver effect as **Factor A** and the route effect as **Factor B.** Each of these hypotheses is tested using the familiar F statistic.

Source of Variation	Sum of Squares	*df*	Mean Square	*F*
Factor A (driver)	SSA	$k - 1$	MSA = SSA/$(k - 1)$	MSA/MSE
Factor B (route)	SSB	$b - 1$	MSB = SSA/$(b - 1)$	MSB/MSE
Interaction	SSI	$(k - 1)(b - 1)$	MSI = SSI/$[(k - 1)(b - 1)]$	MSI/MSE
Error	SSE	$n - kb$	MSE = SSE/$(n - kb)$	
Total		$n - 1$		

To test the hypotheses for a two-way ANOVA with interaction, we use the ANOVA: Two-Factor with Replication in the Data Analysis add-in for Excel. The details of using Excel are summarized in Appendix C. The following ANOVA table shows the results of the analysis. We use the p-values to test each hypothesis. Using the .05 significance level, the null hypotheses are rejected if the computed p-value is less than .05.

ANOVA						
Source of Variation	*SS*	*df*	*MS*	*F*	*P-value*	*F crit*
Drivers	353.5667	4	88.39167	17.21916	0.0000	2.605975
Routes	244.9833	3	81.66111	15.90801	0.0000	2.838745
Interaction	125.7667	12	10.48056	2.041667	0.0456	2.003459
Error	205.3333	40	5.133333			
Total	929.65	59				

Reviewing the results of the ANOVA, the *p*-value for the interaction effect of .0456 is less than our significance level of. 05, so our decision is to reject the null hypothesis of no interaction and conclude that the combination of route and driver has a significant effect on the response variable, travel time.

A significant interaction effect provides important information about the combined effects of the variables. If interaction is present, then a test of differences in the factor means using a one-way ANOVA for each level of the other factor is the next step. This analysis requires some time and work to complete, but the results are usually enlightening.

We will continue the analysis by conducting a one-way ANOVA for each route by testing the hypothesis H_0: Driver travel times are equal. The results follow.

US 6; H_0: Driver times are equal						
Source of Variation	*SS*	*df*	*MS*	*F*	*P-value*	*F crit*
Between Groups	174	4	43.5	6.04167	0.010	3.478
Within Groups	72	10	7.2			
Total	246	14				

West End; H_0: Driver times are equal						
Source of Variation	*SS*	*df*	*MS*	*F*	*P-value*	*F crit*
Between Groups	88.6667	4	22.1667	4.05488	0.033	3.478
Within Groups	54.6667	10	5.46667			
Total	143.333	14				

Hickory; H_0: Driver times are equal						
Source of Variation	*SS*	*df*	*MS*	*F*	*P-value*	*F crit*
Between Groups	135.6	4	33.9	21.1875	0.000	3.478
Within Groups	16	10	1.6			
Total	151.6	14				

Route 59; H_0: Driver times are equal						
Source of Variation	*SS*	*df*	*MS*	*F*	*P-value*	*F crit*
Between Groups	81.0667	4	20.2667	3.23404	0.060	3.478
Within Groups	62.6667	10	6.26667			
Total	143.733	14				

The results of the one-way ANOVA show there are significant differences in the mean travel times among the drivers for every route, except Route 59 with a *p*-value of 0.06. A review of the interaction plot may reveal some of the differences. For example, for the West End route, the graph suggests that Deans has the best mean travel time. Further statistical analysis would test pairs of mean travel times to determine the significant differences between driver travel times for each route that has a significant *p*-value.

SELF-REVIEW 12–5

See the following ANOVA table.

ANOVA					
Source of Variation	**SS**	***df***	**MS**	***F***	***p*-value**
Factor A	6.41	3	2.137	3.46	0.0322
Factor B	5.01	2	2.507	4.06	0.0304
Interaction	33.15	6	5.525	8.94	0.0000
Error	14.83	24	0.618		
Total	59.41	35			

Use the .05 significance level to answer the following questions.

(a) How many levels does Factor A have? Is there a significant difference among the Factor A means? How do you know?

(b) How many levels does Factor B have? Is there a significant difference among the Factor B means? How do you know?

(c) How many observations are there in each cell? Is there a significant interaction between Factor A and Factor B on the response variable? How do you know?

EXERCISES

For **DATA FILE**, please visit www.mhhe.com/lind16e

19. Consider the following sample data for a two-factor ANOVA analysis. There are two levels (heavy and light) of factor A (weight), and three levels (small, medium, and large) of factor B (size). For each combination of size and weight, there are three observations.

		Size		
		Small	**Medium**	**Large**
		23	20	11
	Heavy	21	32	20
		25	26	20
Weight				
		13	20	11
	Light	32	17	23
		17	15	8

Compute an ANOVA with statistical software, and use the .05 significance level to answer the following questions.

a. Is there a difference in the Size means?

b. Is there a difference in the Weight means?

c. Is there a significant interaction between Weight and Size?

20. Consider the following partially completed two-way ANOVA table. Suppose there are four levels of Factor A and three levels of Factor B. The number of replications per cell is 5. Complete the table and test to determine if there is a significant difference in Factor A means, Factor B means, or the interaction means. Use the .05 significance level. (Hint: estimate the values from the *F* table.)

ANOVA				
Source	**SS**	***df***	**MS**	***F***
Factor A	75			
Factor B	25			
Interaction	300			
Error	600			
Total	1000			

For **DATA FILE**, please visit www.mhhe.com/lind16e

21. The distributor of the *Wapakoneta Daily News,* a regional newspaper serving western Ohio, is considering three types of dispensing machines or "racks." Management wants to know if the different machines affect sales. These racks are designated as J-1000, D-320, and UV-57. Management also wants to know if the placement of the racks either inside or outside supermarkets affects sales. Each of six similar stores was randomly assigned a machine and location combination. The data below are the number of papers sold over four days.

Position/Machine	J-1000	D-320	UV-57
Inside	33, 40, 30, 31	29, 28, 33, 33	47, 39, 39, 45
Outside	43, 36, 41, 40	48, 45, 40, 44	37, 32, 36, 35

a. Draw the interaction graph. Based on your observations, is there an interaction effect? Based on the graph, describe the interaction effect of machine and position.
b. Compute an ANOVA with statistical software, and use the 0.05 level to test for position, machine, and interaction effects on sales. Report the statistical results.
c. Compare the inside and outside mean sales for each machine using statistical techniques. What do you conclude?

For **DATA FILE**, please visit www.mhhe.com/lind16e

22. A large company is organized into three functional areas: manufacturing, marketing, and research and development. The employees claim that the company pays women less than men for similar jobs. The company randomly selected four males and four females in each area and recorded their weekly salaries in dollars.

Area/Gender	Female	Male
Manufacturing	1016, 1007, 875, 968	978, 1056, 982, 748
Marketing	1045, 895, 848, 904	1154, 1091, 878, 876
Research and Development	770, 733, 844, 771	926, 1055, 1066, 1088

a. Draw the interaction graph. Based on your observations, is there an interaction effect? Based on the graph, describe the interaction effect of gender and area on salary.
b. Compute an ANOVA with statistical software, and use the 0.05 level to test for gender, area, and interaction effects on salary. Report the statistical results.
c. Compare the male and female mean sales for each area using statistical techniques. What do you recommend to the distributor?

CHAPTER SUMMARY

I. The characteristics of the *F* distribution are:
   A. It is continuous.
   B. Its values cannot be negative.
   C. It is positively skewed.
   D. There is a family of *F* distributions. Each time the degrees of freedom in either the numerator or the denominator change, a new distribution is created.

II. The *F* distribution is used to test whether two population variances are the same.
   A. The sampled populations must follow the normal distribution.
   B. The larger of the two sample variances is placed in the numerator, forcing the ratio to be at least 1.00.
   C. The value of *F* is computed using the following equation:

$$F = \frac{s_1^2}{s_2^2} \quad [12\text{–}1]$$

III. A one-way ANOVA is used to compare several treatment means.
   A. A treatment is a source of variation.
   B. The assumptions underlying ANOVA are:
      1. The samples are from populations that follow the normal distribution.
      2. The populations have equal standard deviations.
      3. The populations are independent.

C. The information for finding the value of F is summarized in an ANOVA table.

1. The formula for SS total, the sum of squares total, is:

$$\text{SS total} = \Sigma(x - \bar{x}_G)^2 \qquad \textbf{[12–2]}$$

2. The formula for SSE, the sum of squares error, is:

$$\text{SSE} = \Sigma(x - \bar{x}_c)^2 \qquad \textbf{[12–3]}$$

3. The formula for the SST, the sum of squares treatment, is found by subtraction.

$$\text{SST} = \text{SS total} - \text{SSE} \qquad \textbf{[12–4]}$$

4. This information is summarized in the following ANOVA table and the value of F is determined.

Source of Variation	Sum of Squares	Degrees of Freedom	Mean Square	F
Treatments	SST	$k - 1$	$\text{SST}/(k - 1) = \text{MST}$	MST/MSE
Error	SSE	$n - k$	$\text{SSE}/(n - k) = \text{MSE}$	
Total	SS total	$n - 1$		

IV. If a null hypothesis of equal treatment means is rejected, we can identify the pairs of means that differ from the following confidence interval.

$$(\bar{x}_1 - \bar{x}_2) \pm t\sqrt{\text{MSE}\left(\frac{1}{n_1} + \frac{1}{n_2}\right)} \qquad \textbf{[12–5]}$$

V. In a two-way ANOVA, we consider a second treatment variable.

A. The second treatment variable is called the blocking variable.

B. It is determined using the following equation:

$$\text{SSB} = k\Sigma(\bar{x}_b - \bar{x}_G)^2 \qquad \textbf{[12–6]}$$

C. The SSE term, or sum of squares error, is found from the following equation.

$$\text{SSE} = \text{SS total} - \text{SST} - \text{SSB} \qquad \textbf{[12–7]}$$

D. The F statistics for the treatment variable and the blocking variable are determined in the following table.

Source of Variation	Sum of Squares	Degrees of Freedom	Mean Square	F
Treatments	SST	$k - 1$	$\text{SST}/(k - 1) = \text{MST}$	MST/MSE
Blocks	SSB	$b - 1$	$\text{SSB}/(b - 1) = \text{MSB}$	MSB/MSE
Error	SSE	$(k - 1)(b - 1)$	$\text{SSE}/[(k - 1)(b - 1)] = \text{MSE}$	
Total	SS total	$n - 1$		

VI. In a two-way ANOVA with repeated observations, we consider two treatment variables and the possible interaction between the variables. The complete ANOVA table including interactions is:

Source	Sum of Squares	*df*	Mean Square	F
Factor A	SSA	$k - 1$	$\text{SSA}/(k - 1) = \text{MSA}$	MSA/MSE
Factor B	SSB	$b - 1$	$\text{SSB}/(b - 1) = \text{MSB}$	MSB/MSE
Interaction	SSI	$(k - 1)(b - 1)$	$\text{SSI}/[(k - 1)(b - 1)] = \text{MSI}$	MSI/MSE
Error	SSE	$n - kb$	$\text{SSE}/(n - kb) = \text{MSE}$	
Total	SS total	$n - 1$		

PRONUNCIATION KEY

SYMBOL	MEANING	PRONUNCIATION
SS total	Sum of squares total	*S S total*
SST	Sum of squares treatment	*S S T*
SSE	Sum of squares error	*S S E*
MSE	Mean square error	*M S E*
SSB	Block sum of squares	*S S B*
SSI	Sum of squares interaction	*S S I*

CHAPTER EXERCISES

23. A real estate agent in the coastal area of Georgia wants to compare the variation in the selling price of homes on the oceanfront with those one to three blocks from the ocean. A sample of 21 oceanfront homes sold within the last year revealed the standard deviation of the selling prices was $45,600. A sample of 18 homes, also sold within the last year, that were one to three blocks from the ocean revealed that the standard deviation was $21,330. At the .01 significance level, can we conclude that there is more variation in the selling prices of the oceanfront homes?

24. A software design company is creating a new, faster search engine. The search engine is clearly faster, but initial tests indicate there is more variation in the time to perform a search. A sample of 16 different searches showed that the standard deviation of the search time was 22 hundredths of a second for the new search engine and 12 hundredths of a second for the current search engine. At the .05 significance level, can we conclude that there is more variation in the search time of the new search engine?

For **DATA FILE**, please visit www.mhhe.com/lind16e

25. There are two Chevrolet dealers in Jamestown, New York. The mean monthly sales at Sharkey Chevy and Dave White Chevrolet are about the same. However, Tom Sharkey, the owner of Sharkey Chevy, believes his sales are more consistent. Below are the numbers of new cars sold at Sharkey in the last 7 months and for the last 8 months at Dave White. Do you agree with Mr. Sharkey? Use the .01 significance level.

Sharkey	98	78	54	57	68	64	70	
Dave White	75	81	81	30	82	46	58	101

26. Random samples of five were selected from each of three populations. The sum of squares total was 100. The sum of squares due to the treatments was 40.
a. Set up the null hypothesis and the alternate hypothesis.
b. What is the decision rule? Use the .05 significance level.
c. Complete the ANOVA table. What is the value of F?
d. What is your decision regarding the null hypothesis?

27. In an ANOVA table, MSE was equal to 10. Random samples of six were selected from each of four populations, where the sum of squares total was 250.
a. Set up the null hypothesis and the alternate hypothesis.
b. What is the decision rule? Use the .05 significance level.
c. Complete the ANOVA table. What is the value of F?
d. What is your decision regarding the null hypothesis?

28. The following is a partial ANOVA table.

Source	Sum of Squares	*df*	Mean Square	*F*
Treatment		2		
Error			20	
Total	500	11		

Complete the table and answer the following questions. Use the .05 significance level.

a. How many treatments are there?
b. What is the total sample size?
c. What is the critical value of *F*?
d. Write out the null and alternate hypotheses.
e. What is your conclusion regarding the null hypothesis?

For **DATA FILE**, please visit www.mhhe.com/lind16e

29. A consumer organization wants to know whether there is a difference in the price of a particular toy at three different types of stores. The price of the toy was checked in a sample of five discount stores, five variety stores, and five department stores. The results are shown below. Use the .05 significance level.

Discount	Variety	Department
$12	$15	$19
13	17	17
14	14	16
12	18	20
15	17	19

For **DATA FILE**, please visit www.mhhe.com/lind16e

30. Jacob Lee is a frequent traveler between Los Angeles and San Francisco. For the past month, he wrote down the flight times on three different airlines. The results are:

Goust	Jet Red	Cloudtran
51	50	52
51	53	55
52	52	60
42	62	64
51	53	61
57	49	49
47	50	49
47	49	
50	58	
60	54	
54	51	
49	49	
48	49	
48	50	

a. Use the .05 significance level and the six-step hypothesis-testing process to check if there is a difference in the mean flight times among the three airlines.
b. Develop a 95% confidence interval for the difference in the means between Goust and Cloudtran.

For **DATA FILE**, please visit www.mhhe.com/lind16e

31. The City of Maumee comprises four districts. Chief of Police Andy North wants to determine whether there is a difference in the mean number of crimes committed among the four districts. He examined the records from six randomly selected days and recorded the number of crimes. At the .05 significance level, can Chief North conclude that there is a difference in the mean number of crimes among the four districts?

Number of Crimes			
Rec Center	**Key Street**	**Monclova**	**Whitehouse**
13	21	12	16
15	13	14	17
14	18	15	18
15	19	13	15
14	18	12	20
15	19	15	18

For **DATA FILE**, please visit www.mhhe.com/lind16e

32. A study of the effect of television commercials on 12-year-old children measured their attention span, in seconds. The commercials were for clothes, food, and toys. At the .05 significance level, is there a difference in the mean attention span of the children for the various commercials? Are there significant differences between pairs of means? Would you recommend dropping one of the three commercial types?

Clothes	Food	Toys
26	45	60
21	48	51
43	43	43
35	53	54
28	47	63
31	42	53
17	34	48
31	43	58
20	57	47
	47	51
	44	51
	54	

For **DATA FILE**, please visit www.mhhe.com/lind16e

33. When only two treatments are involved, ANOVA and the Student's t test (Chapter 11) result in the same conclusions. Also, $t^2 = F$. As an example, 14 randomly selected Introduction to History students were divided into two groups, one consisting of 6 students and the other of 8. One group took the course in the normal lecture format. The other group of 8 students took the course via the Internet. At the end of the course, each group was given a 50-item test. The following is a list of the number correct for each of the two groups.

Traditional Lecture	Internet
19	32
17	28
23	31
22	26
17	23
16	24
	27
	25

a. Using analysis of variance techniques, test H_0 that the two mean test scores are equal; $\alpha = .05$.
b. Using the t test from Chapter 11, compute t.
c. Interpret the results.

34. There are four auto body shops in Bangor, Maine, and all claim to promptly serve customers. To check if there is any difference in service, customers are randomly selected from each repair shop and their waiting times in days are recorded. The output from a statistical software package is:

Summary				
Groups	**Count**	**Sum**	**Average**	**Variance**
Body Shop A	3	15.4	5.133333	0.323333
Body Shop B	4	32	8	1.433333
Body Shop C	5	25.2	5.04	0.748
Body Shop D	4	25.9	6.475	0.595833

ANOVA					
Source of Variation	**SS**	***df***	**MS**	***F***	***p*-value**
Between Groups	23.37321	3	7.791069	9.612506	0.001632
Within Groups	9.726167	12	0.810514		
Total	33.09938	15			

Is there evidence to suggest a difference in the mean waiting times at the four body shops? Use the .05 significance level.

35. The fuel efficiencies for a sample of 27 compact, midsize, and large cars are entered into a statistical software package. Analysis of variance is used to investigate if there is a difference in the mean mileage of the three cars. What do you conclude? Use the .01 significance level.

Summary				
Groups	**Count**	**Sum**	**Average**	**Variance**
Compact	12	268.3	22.35833	9.388106
Midsize	9	172.4	19.15556	7.315278
Large	6	100.5	16.75	7.303

Additional results are shown below.

ANOVA					
Source of Variation	**SS**	***df***	**MS**	***F***	***p*-value**
Between Groups	136.4803	2	68.24014	8.258752	0.001866
Within Groups	198.3064	24	8.262766		
Total	334.7867	26			

36. Three assembly lines are used to produce a certain component for an airliner. To examine the production rate, a random sample of six hourly periods is chosen for each assembly line and the number of components produced during these periods for each line is recorded. The output from a statistical software package is:

Summary				
Groups	**Count**	**Sum**	**Average**	**Variance**
Line A	6	250	41.66667	0.266667
Line B	6	260	43.33333	0.666667
Line C	6	249	41.5	0.7

ANOVA					
Source of Variation	**SS**	***df***	**MS**	***F***	***p*-value**
Between Groups	12.33333	2	6.166667	11.32653	0.001005
Within Groups	8.166667	15	0.544444		
Total	20.5	17			

a. Use a .01 level of significance to test if there is a difference in the mean production of the three assembly lines.
b. Develop a 99% confidence interval for the difference in the means between Line B and Line C.

37. The postal service sorts mail as Priority Mail Express, Priority Mail, First-Class Mail, or Standard Mail. Over a period of 3 weeks, 18 of each type were mailed from the Network Distribution Center in Altanta, Georgia, to Des Moines, Iowa. The total delivery time in days was recorded. Minitab was used to perform the ANOVA. The results follow:

```
Source   DF      SS      MS      F      P
Factor    3  30.298  10.099  11.90  0.000
Error    68  57.705   0.849
Total    71  88.003

S = 0.9212    R-Sq = 34.43%    R-Sq(adj) = 31.54%

Level                    N    Mean   StDev
Priority Mail Express   18  1.0694  0.7652
Priority Mail           18  1.7210  1.0829
First-Class Mail        18  2.5211  0.9097
Standard Mail           18  2.6840  0.8991

Priority Mail Express subtracted from:

                   Lower  Center   Upper
Priority Mail     0.0389  0.6516  1.2644
First-Class Mail  0.8390  1.4517  2.0645
Standard Mail     1.0018  1.6146  2.2273

                  ------+---------+---------+---------+---
Priority Mail                     (------*-----)
First-Class Mail                          (------*-----)
Standard Mail                               (-----*-----)
                  ------+---------+---------+---------+---
                      -1.0       0.0       1.0       2.0

Priority Mail subtracted from:

                   Lower  Center   Upper
First-Class Mail  0.1874  0.8001  1.4128
Standard Mail     0.3502  0.9629  1.5757

                  ------+---------+---------+---------+---
First-Class Mail                    (-----*-----)
Standard Mail                         (-----*-----)
                  ------+---------+---------+---------+---
                      -1.0       0.0       1.0       2.0

First-Class Mail subtracted from:

                 Lower  Center   Upper
Standard Mail  -0.4499  0.1628  0.7756

               ------+---------+---------+---------+---
Standard Mail              (-----*-----)
               ------+---------+---------+---------+---
                   -1.0       0.0       1.0       2.0
```

Using the ANOVA results, compare the average delivery times of the four different types of mail.

38. For your e-mail, you use a filter to block spam from your inbox. The number of items blocked by day of week is recorded and Minitab is used to perform the analysis that follows. Here are the results:

```
Source  DF      SS     MS     F      P
Factor   6  1242.5  207.1  6.66  0.000
Error   48  1493.1   31.1
Total   54  2735.7

S = 5.577   R-Sq = 45.42%   R-Sq(adj) = 38.60%


Level       N    Mean  StDev
Monday     10  71.926  5.435
Tuesday     9  64.329  6.890
Wednesday   7  73.322  2.936
Thursday    8  60.539  4.268
Friday      8  73.709  5.369
Saturday    5  64.436  6.729
Sunday      8  68.810  6.384

Monday subtracted from:
                Lower   Center   Upper  ---------+---------+---------+---------+
Tuesday       -12.749   -7.597  -2.444        (----*-----)
Wednesday      -4.130    1.396   6.922                 (----*-----)
Thursday      -16.706  -11.387  -6.068    (-----*----)
Friday         -3.536    1.783   7.103                (-----*----)
Saturday      -13.632   -7.490  -1.348       (------*-----)
Sunday         -8.436   -3.117   2.203             (----*----)
                                        ---------+---------+---------+---------+
                                              -10         0        10        20

Tuesday subtracted from:
               Lower  Center   Upper    ---------+---------+---------+---------+
Wednesday      3.341   8.993  14.644                          (-----*-----)
Thursday      -9.239  -3.790   1.659              (----*-----)
Friday         3.931   9.380  14.829                           (----*-----)
Saturday      -6.148   0.107   6.362                 (-----*-----)
Sunday        -0.969   4.480   9.929                      (----*-----)
                                        ---------+---------+---------+---------+
                                              -10         0        10        20

Wednesday subtracted from:
               Lower   Center   Upper   ---------+---------+---------+---------+
Thursday     -18.587  -12.783  -6.979   (-----*-----)
Friday        -5.416    0.388   6.191                 (----*-----)
Saturday     -15.452   -8.886  -2.319       (-----*------)
Sunday       -10.316   -4.512   1.291            (----*-----)
                                        ---------+---------+---------+---------+
                                              -10         0        10        20

Thursday subtracted from:
              Lower  Center   Upper     ---------+---------+---------+---------+
Friday        7.563  13.170  18.777                                (----*-----)
Saturday     -2.496   3.897  10.290                      (-----*-----)
Sunday        2.663   8.270  13.877                           (----*-----)
                                        ---------+---------+---------+---------+
                                              -10         0        10        20

Friday subtracted from:
               Lower  Center   Upper    ---------+---------+---------+---------+
Saturday     -15.666  -9.273  -2.880       (------*-----)
Sunday       -10.507  -4.900   0.707            (-----*-----)
                                        ---------+---------+---------+---------+
                                              -10         0        10        20

Saturday subtracted from:
              Lower  Center   Upper     ---------+---------+---------+---------+
Sunday       -2.020   4.373  10.766                      (-----*------)
                                        ---------+---------+---------+---------+
                                              -10         0        10
```

Using the ANOVA results, compare the average number of items blocked for each day of the week.

For **DATA FILE**, please visit www.mhhe.com/lind16e

39. Shank's Inc., a nationwide advertising firm, wants to know whether the size of an advertisement and the color of the advertisement make a difference in the response of magazine readers. A random sample of readers is shown ads of four different colors and three different sizes. Each reader is asked to give the particular combination of size and color a rating between 1 and 10. Assume that the ratings follow the normal distribution. The rating for each combination is shown in the following table (for example, the rating for a small red ad is 2).

	Color of Ad			
Size of Ad	**Red**	**Blue**	**Orange**	**Green**
Small	2	3	3	8
Medium	3	5	6	7
Large	6	7	8	8

Is there a difference in the effectiveness of an advertisement by color and by size? Use the .05 level of significance.

For **DATA FILE**, please visit www.mhhe.com/lind16e

40. There are four McBurger restaurants in the Columbus, Georgia, area. The numbers of burgers sold at the respective restaurants for each of the last 6 weeks are shown below. At the .05 significance level, is there a difference in the mean number sold among the four restaurants when the factor of week is considered?

	Restaurant			
Week	**Metro**	**Interstate**	**University**	**River**
1	124	160	320	190
2	234	220	340	230
3	430	290	290	240
4	105	245	310	170
5	240	205	280	180
6	310	260	270	205

a. Is there a difference in the treatment means?
b. Is there a difference in the block means?

For **DATA FILE**, please visit www.mhhe.com/lind16e

41. The city of Tucson, Arizona, employs people to assess the value of homes for the purpose of establishing real estate tax. The city manager sends each assessor to the same five homes and then compares the results. The information is given below, in thousands of dollars. Can we conclude that there is a difference in the assessors? Use the .05 significance level.

	Assessor			
Home	**Zawodny**	**Norman**	**Cingle**	**Holiday**
A	$53.0	$55.0	$49.0	$45.0
B	50.0	51.0	52.0	53.0
C	48.0	52.0	47.0	53.0
D	70.0	68.0	65.0	64.0
E	84.0	89.0	92.0	86.0

a. Is there a difference in the treatment means?
b. Is there a difference in the block means?

For **DATA FILE**, please visit www.mhhe.com/lind16e

42. Martin Motors has in stock three cars of the same make and model. The Sales Manager would like to compare the gas consumption of the three cars (labeled car A, car B, and car C) using four different types of gasoline. For each trial, a gallon of gasoline was added to an empty tank, and the car was driven until it ran out of gas. The following table shows the number of miles driven in each trial.

	Distance (miles)		
Types of Gasoline	**Car A**	**Car B**	**Car C**
Regular	22.4	20.8	21.5
Super regular	17.0	19.4	20.7
Unleaded	19.2	20.2	21.2
Premium unleaded	20.3	18.6	20.4

Using the .05 level of significance:

a. Is there a difference among types of gasoline?

b. Is there a difference in the cars?

43. A research firm wants to compare the miles per gallon of unleaded regular, mid-grade, and super premium gasolines. Because of differences in the performance of different automobiles, seven different automobiles were selected and treated as blocks. Therefore, each brand of gasoline was tested with each type of automobile. The results of the trials, in miles per gallon, are shown in the following table. At the .05 significance level, is there a difference in the gasolines or automobiles?

For **DATA FILE**, please visit www.mhhe.com/lind16e

Automobile	Regular	Mid-grade	Super Premium
1	21	23	26
2	23	22	25
3	24	25	27
4	24	24	26
5	26	26	30
6	26	24	27
7	28	27	32

44. Three supermarket chains in the Denver area each claims to have the lowest overall prices. As part of an investigative study on supermarket advertising, the *Denver Daily News* conducted a study. First, a random sample of nine grocery items was selected. Next, the price of each selected item was checked at each of the three chains on the same day. At the .05 significance level, is there a difference in the mean prices at the supermarkets or for the items?

For **DATA FILE**, please visit www.mhhe.com/lind16e

Item	Super$	Ralph's	Lowblaws
1	$1.12	$1.02	$1.07
2	1.14	1.10	1.21
3	1.72	1.97	2.08
4	2.22	2.09	2.32
5	2.40	2.10	2.30
6	4.04	4.32	4.15
7	5.05	4.95	5.05
8	4.68	4.13	4.67
9	5.52	5.46	5.86

45. Listed below are the weights (in grams) of a sample of M&M's Plain candies, classified according to color. Use a statistical software system to determine whether there is a difference in the mean weights of candies of different colors. Use the .05 significance level.

For **DATA FILE**, please visit www.mhhe.com/lind16e

Red	Orange	Yellow	Brown	Tan	Green
0.946	0.902	0.929	0.896	0.845	0.935
1.107	0.943	0.960	0.888	0.909	0.903
0.913	0.916	0.938	0.906	0.873	0.865
0.904	0.910	0.933	0.941	0.902	0.822
0.926	0.903	0.932	0.838	0.956	0.871
0.926	0.901	0.899	0.892	0.959	0.905
1.006	0.919	0.907	0.905	0.916	0.905
0.914	0.901	0.906	0.824	0.822	0.852
0.922	0.930	0.930	0.908		0.965
1.052	0.883	0.952	0.833		0.898
0.903		0.939			
0.895		0.940			
		0.882			
		0.906			

46. There are four radio stations in Midland. The stations have different formats (hard rock, classical, country/western, and easy listening), but each is concerned with the number of minutes of music played per hour. From a sample of 10 randomly selected hours from each

station, the sum of squared differences between each observation and the mean for its respective radio station, $\Sigma(x - \bar{x}_C)^2$, are:

Hard rock station:	126.29	Country/western station:	166.79
Classical station:	233.34	Easy listening station:	77.57

The total sum of squares for the data is: SS total = 1,099.61.

a. Determine SSE.
b. Determine SST.
c. Complete an ANOVA table.
d. At the .05 significance level, is there a difference in the treatment means?
e. If the mean for the hard rock station is 51.32 and the mean for the country/western station is 50.85, determine if there is a difference using the .05 significance level.

For **DATA FILE**, please visit www.mhhe.com/lind16e

47. The American Accounting Association recently conducted a study to compare the weekly wages of men and women employed in either the public or private sector of accounting. Random samples of five men and five women were selected in each group.

	Sector	
Gender	**Public**	**Private**
Men	$ 978	$1,335
	1,035	1,167
	964	1,236
	996	1,317
	1,117	1,192
Women	$ 863	$1,079
	975	1,160
	999	1,063
	1,019	1,110
	1,037	1,093

a. Draw an interaction plot of men and women means by sector.
b. Compute an ANOVA with statistical software and, using the .05 significance level, test the interaction effect of gender and sector on wages.
c. Based on your results in part (b), conduct the appropriate tests of hypotheses for differences in factor means.
d. Interpret the results in a brief report.

For **DATA FILE**, please visit www.mhhe.com/lind16e

48. Robert Altoff is vice president for engineering for a manufacturer of household washing machines. As part of new product development, he wishes to determine the optimal length of time for the washing cycle. A part of the development is to study the relationship between the detergent used (four brands) and the length of the washing cycle (18, 20, 22, or 24 minutes). In order to run the experiment, 32 standard household laundry loads (having equal amounts of dirt and the same total weights) are randomly assigned to the 16 detergent-washing cycle combinations. The results (in pounds of dirt removed) are shown below.

	Cycle Time (min)			
Detergent Brand	**18**	**20**	**22**	**24**
A	0.13	0.12	0.19	0.15
	0.11	0.11	0.17	0.18
B	0.14	0.15	0.18	0.20
	0.10	0.14	0.17	0.18
C	0.16	0.15	0.18	0.19
	0.17	0.14	0.19	0.21
D	0.09	0.12	0.16	0.15
	0.13	0.13	0.16	0.17

a. Draw an interaction plot of the detergent means by cycle time.
b. Compute the ANOVA with statistical software and, using the .05 significance level, test the interaction effect of brand and cycle time on "dirt removed."
c. Based on your results in part (b), conduct the appropriate tests of hypotheses for differences in factor means.
d. Interpret the results in a brief report.

DATA SET EXERCISES

(The data for these exercises are available at the text website: www.mhhe.com/lind16e.)

49. Refer to the Real Estate data, which report information on the homes sold in the Goodyear, Arizona, area last year.
   a. At the .02 significance level, is there a difference in the variability of the selling prices of the homes that have a pool versus those that do not have a pool?
   b. At the .02 significance level, is there a difference in the variability of the selling prices of the homes with an attached garage versus those that do not have an attached garage?
   c. At the .05 significance level, is there a difference in the mean selling price of the homes among the five townships?
50. Refer to the Baseball 2012 data, which report information on the 30 Major League Baseball teams for the 2012 season.
   a. At the .10 significance level, is there a difference in the variation in team salary among the American and National League teams?
   b. Create a variable that classifies a team's total attendance into three groups: less than 2.0 (million), 2.0 up to 3.0, and 3.0 or more. At the .05 significance level, is there a difference in the mean number of games won among the three groups?
   c. Using the same attendance variable developed in part (b), is there a difference in the mean number of home runs hit per team? Use the .05 significance level.
   d. Using the same attendance variable developed in part (b), is there a difference in the mean salary of the three groups? Use the .05 significance level.
51. Refer to the Buena School District bus data.
   a. Conduct a test of hypothesis to reveal whether the mean maintenance cost is equal for each of the bus manufacturers. Use the .01 significance level.
   b. Conduct a test of hypothesis to determine whether the mean miles traveled is equal for each bus manufacturer. Use the .05 significance level.
   c. Develop a 95% confidence interval for the disparity in the average maintenance cost between buses made by Bluebird and Thompson.

A REVIEW OF CHAPTERS 10–12

This section is a review of the major concepts and terms introduced in Chapters 10, 11, and 12. Chapter 10 began our study of hypothesis testing. A hypothesis is a statement about the value of a population parameter. In statistical hypothesis testing, we begin by making a statement about the value of the population parameter in the null hypothesis. We establish the null hypothesis for the purpose of testing. When we complete the testing, our decision is either to reject or to fail to reject the null hypothesis. If we reject the null hypothesis, we conclude that the alternate hypothesis is true. The alternate hypothesis is "accepted" only if we show that the null hypothesis is false. We also refer to the alternate hypothesis as the research hypothesis. Most of the time we want to prove the alternate hypothesis.

In Chapter 10, we selected random samples from a single population and tested whether it was reasonable that the population parameter under study equaled a particular value. For example, we wish to investigate whether the mean tenure of those holding the position of CEO in large firms is 12 years. We select a sample of CEOs, compute the sample mean, and compare the mean of the sample to the population. The single population under consideration is the length of tenure of CEOs of large firms. We described methods for conducting the test when the population standard deviation was available and when it was not available.

In Chapter 11, we extended the idea of hypothesis testing to whether two independent random samples came from populations having the same or equal population means. For example, St. Mathews Hospital operates an urgent care facility on both the north and south sides of Knoxville, Tennessee. The research question is: Is the mean waiting time for patients visiting the two facilities the same? To investigate, we select a random sample from each of the facilities and compute the sample means. We test the null hypothesis that the mean waiting time is the same at the two facilities. The alternate hypothesis is that the mean waiting time is not the same for the two facilities. If the population standard deviations are known, we use the *z* distribution as the test statistic. If the population standard deviations are not known, the test statistic follows the *t* distribution.

Our discussion in Chapter 11 also concerned dependent samples. The test statistic is the *t* distribution and we assume that the distribution of differences follows the normal distribution. One typical paired sample problem calls for recording an individual's blood pressure before administering medication and then again afterward in order to evaluate the effectiveness of the medication. We also considered the case of testing two population proportions. For example, the production manager wished to compare the proportion of defects on the day shift with that of the second shift.

Chapter 11 dealt with the difference between two population means. Chapter 12 presented tests for variances and a procedure called the *analysis of variance,* or *ANOVA*. ANOVA is used to simultaneously determine whether several independent normal populations have the same mean. This is accomplished by comparing the variances of the random samples selected from these populations. We apply the usual hypothesis-testing procedure, but we use the *F* distribution as the test statistic. Often the calculations are tedious, so a software package is recommended.

As an example of analysis of variance, a test could be conducted to resolve whether there is any difference in effectiveness among five fertilizers on the weight of popcorn ears. This type of analysis is referred to as *one-factor ANOVA* because we are able to draw conclusions about only one factor, called a *treatment*. If we want to draw conclusions about the simultaneous effects of more than one factor or variable, we use the *two-factor ANOVA* technique. Both the one-factor and two-factor tests use the *F distribution* as the distribution of the test statistic. The *F* distribution is also the distribution of the test statistic used to find whether one normal population has more variation than another.

An additional feature of the two-factor ANOVA is the possibility that interactions may exist between the factors. There is an *interaction* if the response to one of the factors depends on the level of the other factor. Fortunately, the ANOVA is easily extended to include a test for interactions.

PROBLEMS

For problems 1–6, state: (a) the null and the alternate hypotheses, (b) the decision rule, and (c) the decision regarding the null hypothesis, (d) then interpret the result.

1. A machine is set to produce tennis balls so the mean bounce is 36 inches when the ball is dropped from a platform of a certain height. The production supervisor suspects that the mean bounce has changed and is less than 36 inches. As an experiment, a sample of 12 balls was dropped from the platform and the mean height of the bounce was 35.5 inches, with a standard deviation of 0.9 inch. At the .05 significance level, can the supervisor conclude that the mean bounce height is less than 36 inches?

For **DATA FILE**, please visit www.mhhe.com/lind16e

2. It was hypothesized that road construction workers do not engage in productive work 20 minutes on the average out of every hour. Some claimed the nonproductive time is greater than 20 minutes. An actual study was conducted at a construction site, using a stopwatch and other ways of checking the work habits. A random check of workers revealed the following unproductive times, in minutes, during a one-hour period (exclusive of regularly scheduled breaks):

10	25	17	20	28	30	18	23	18

Using the .05 significance level, is it reasonable to conclude the mean unproductive time is greater than 20 minutes?

3. A test is to be conducted involving the mean holding power of two glues designed for plastic. First, a small plastic hook was coated at one end with Epox glue and fastened to a sheet of plastic. After it dried, weight was added to the hook until it separated from the sheet of plastic. The weight was then recorded. This was repeated until 12 hooks were tested. The same procedure was followed for Holdtite glue, but only 10 hooks were used. The sample results, in pounds, were:

	Epox	Holdtite
Sample mean	250	252
Sample standard deviation	5	8
Sample size	12	10

At the .01 significance level, is there a difference between the mean holding power of Epox and that of Holdtite?

For **DATA FILE**, please visit www.mhhe.com/lind16e

4. Pittsburgh Paints wishes to test an additive formulated to increase the life of paints used in the hot and arid conditions of the Southwest. The top half of a piece of wood was painted using the regular paint. The bottom half was painted with the paint including the additive. The same procedure was followed for a total of 10 pieces. Then each piece was subjected to brilliant light. The data, the number of hours each piece lasted before it faded beyond a certain point, follow:

	Number of Hours by Sample									
	A	B	C	D	E	F	G	H	I	J
Without additive	325	313	320	340	318	312	319	330	333	319
With additive	323	313	326	343	310	320	313	340	330	315

Using the .05 significance level, determine whether the additive is effective in prolonging the life of the paint.

5. A Buffalo, New York, cola distributor is featuring a super-special sale on 12-packs. She wonders where in the grocery store to place the cola for maximum attention. Should it be near the front door of the grocery stores, in the cola section, at the checkout registers, or near the milk and other dairy products? Four stores with similar total sales cooperated in an experiment. In one store, the 12-packs were stacked near the front door, in another they were placed near the checkout registers, and so on. Sales were checked at specified times in each store for exactly four minutes. The results were:

Cola at the Door	In Soft Drink Section	Near Registers	Dairy Section
$6	$ 5	$ 7	$10
8	10	10	9
3	12	9	6
7	4	4	11
	9	5	
		7	

The Buffalo distributor wants to find out whether there is a difference in the mean sales for cola stacked at the four locations in the store. Use the .05 significance level.

For **DATA FILE**, please visit www.mhhe.com/lind16e

6. Williams Corporation is investigating the effects of educational background on employee performance. A potential relevant variable in this case is the self-rated social status of the employee. The company has recorded the annual sales volumes (in $000) achieved by sales employees in each of the categories below. Perform a complete two-way analysis of variance (including the possibility of interactions) on the data and describe what your results suggest.

	School Type		
Self-Rated Social Status	**Ivy League**	**State-supported**	**Small Private**
Low	62, 61	68, 64	70, 70
Medium	68, 64	74, 68	62, 65
High	70, 71	57, 60	57, 56

7. A school supervisor is reviewing initial wages of former students (in $000). Samples were taken over 3 years for four different majors (accounting, administration, finance, and marketing). For each combination of major and year, three former students were sampled.

Major/Year	2010	2011	2012
Accounting	75.4, 69.8, 62.3	73.9, 78.8, 62.0	64.2, 80.8, 68.2
Administration	61.5, 59.9, 62.1	63.9, 57.6, 66.5	74.2, 67.5, 58.1
Finance	63.6, 70.2, 72.2	69.2, 72.5, 67.2	74.7, 66.4, 77.9
Marketing	71.3, 69.2, 66.4	74.0, 67.6, 61.7	60.0, 61.3, 62.5

a. Here is an interaction plot of the information. What does it reveal?

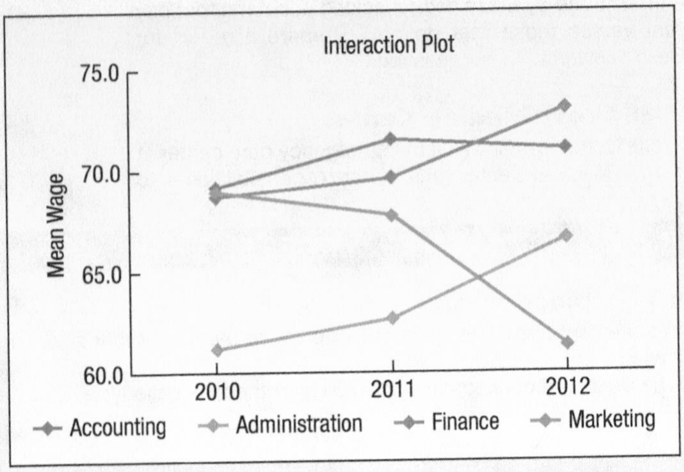

b. Write out all of the pairs of null and alternative hypotheses you would apply for a two-way ANOVA.

c. Here is the statistical software output. Use the 0.05 level to check for interactions.

Source	DF	SS	MS	F	P
Major	3	329.20	109.732	3.39	0.034
Year	2	7.32	3.659	0.11	0.894
Interaction	6	183.57	30.595	0.94	0.482
Error	24	777.29	32.387		
Total	35	1297.37			

d. If proper, test the other hypotheses at the .05 significance level. If it is not appropriate, describe why you should not do the tests.

CASES

A. Century National Bank

Refer to the description of Century National Bank at the end of the Review of Chapters 1–4 on page 128.

With many other options available, customers no longer let their money sit in a checking account. For many years the mean checking balance has been $1,600. Do the sample data indicate that the mean account balance has declined from this value?

Recent years have also seen an increase in the use of ATM machines. When Mr. Selig took over the bank, the mean number of transactions per month per customer was 8; now he believes it has increased to more than 10. In fact, the advertising agency that prepares TV commercials for Century would like to use this on the new commercial being designed. Is there sufficient evidence to conclude that the mean number of transactions per customer is more than 10 per month? Could the advertising agency say the mean is more than 9 per month?

The bank has branch offices in four different cities: Cincinnati, Ohio; Atlanta, Georgia; Louisville, Kentucky; and Erie, Pennsylvania. Mr. Selig would like to know whether there is a difference in the mean checking account balances among the four branches. If there are differences, between which branches do these differences occur?

Mr. Selig is also interested in the bank's ATMs. Is there a difference in ATM use among the branches? Also, do customers who have debit cards tend to use ATMs differently from those who do not have debit cards? Is there a difference in ATM use by those with checking accounts that pay interest versus those that do not? Prepare a report for Mr. Selig answering these questions.

B. Bell Grove Medical Center

Ms. Gene Dempsey manages the emergency care center at Bell Grove Medical Center. One of her responsibilities is to have enough nurses so that incoming patients needing service can be handled promptly. It is stressful for patients to wait a long time for emergency care even when their care needs are not life threatening. Ms. Dempsey gathered the following information regarding the number of patients over the last several weeks. The center is not open on weekends. Does it appear that there are any differences in the number of patients served by the day of the week? If there are differences, which days seem to be the busiest? Write a brief report summarizing your findings.

Date	Day	Patients
9-29-06	Monday	38
9-30-06	Tuesday	28
10-1-06	Wednesday	28
10-2-06	Thursday	30
10-3-06	Friday	35
10-6-06	Monday	35
10-7-06	Tuesday	25
10-8-06	Wednesday	22
10-9-06	Thursday	21
10-10-06	Friday	32
10-13-06	Monday	37
10-14-06	Tuesday	29
10-15-06	Wednesday	27
10-16-06	Thursday	28
10-17-06	Friday	35
10-20-06	Monday	37
10-21-06	Tuesday	26
10-22-06	Wednesday	28
10-23-06	Thursday	23
10-24-06	Friday	33

PRACTICE TEST

Part 1—Objective

1. A statement about the value of a population parameter that always includes the equal sign is called the ________. 1. ________
2. The likelihood of rejecting a true null hypothesis is called the ________. 2. ________

3. Assuming the null hypothesis is true, the likelihood of finding a value of the test statistic at least as extreme as the one found in the sample is called the ________. 3. ________
4. When conducting a test of hypothesis about a single population mean, the z distribution is used as the test statistic only when the ________ is known. 4. ________
5. In a two-sample test of hypothesis for means, if the population standard deviations are not known, *what must we assume about the shape of the populations?* 5. ________
6. A value calculated from sample information used to determine whether to reject the null hypothesis is called the ________. 6. ________
7. In a two-tailed test, the rejection region is ________. (all in the upper tail, all in the lower tail, split evenly between the two tails, none of these—pick one) 7. ________
8. Which of the following is not a characteristic of the F distribution? (continuous, positively skewed, range from $-\infty$ to ∞, family of distributions) 8. ________
9. To perform a one-way ANOVA, the treatments must be ________. (independent, mutually exclusive, continuous) 9. ________
10. In a one-way ANOVA, there are four treatments and six observations in each treatment. What are the degrees of freedom for the F distribution? 10. ________

Part 2—Problems

For problems 1 and 2, state the null and alternate hypotheses and the decision rule, make a decision regarding the null hypothesis, and interpret the result.

1. The Park Manager at Fort Fisher State Park in North Carolina believes the typical summer visitor spends more than 90 minutes in the park. A sample of 18 visitors during the months of June, July, and August revealed the mean time in the park for visitors was 96 minutes, with a standard deviation of 12 minutes. At the .01 significance level, is it reasonable to conclude the mean time in the park is greater than 90 minutes?
2. Is there a difference in the mean miles traveled per week by each of two taxicab companies operating in the Grand Strand area? The *Sun News*, the local paper, is investigating and obtained the following sample information. At the .05 significance level, is it reasonable to conclude there is a difference in the mean miles traveled? Assume equal population variances.

Variable	Yellow Cab	Horse and Buggy Cab Company
Mean miles	837	797
Standard deviation	30	40
Sample size	14	12

3. The results of a one-way ANOVA are reported below. Use the .05 significance level.

ANOVA

Source of Variation	SS	*df*	MS	*F*
Between groups	6.892202	2	3.446101	4.960047
Within groups	12.50589	18	0.694772	
Total	19.3981	20		

Answer the following questions.

a. How many treatments are in the study?
b. What is the total sample size?
c. What is the critical value of F?
d. Write out the null hypothesis and the alternate hypothesis.
e. What is your decision regarding the null hypothesis?
f. Can we conclude the treatment means differ?

13 Correlation and Linear Regression

AN AIR TRAVEL SERVICE samples domestic airline flights to explore the relationship between airfare and distance. The service would like to know if there is a correlation between airfare and flight distance. If there is a correlation, what percentage of the variation in airfare is accounted for by distance? How much does each additional mile add to the fare? (See Exercise 61 and LO13-2, LO13-3, and LO13-5.)

LEARNING OBJECTIVES

When you have completed this chapter, you will be able to:

LO13-1 Explain the purpose of correlation analysis.

LO13-2 Calculate a correlation coefficient to test and interpret the relationship between two variables.

LO13-3 Apply regression analysis to estimate the linear relationship between two variables.

LO13-4 Evaluate the significance of the slope of the regression equation.

LO13-5 Evaluate a regression equation's ability to predict using the standard estimate of the error and the coefficient of determination.

LO13-6 Calculate and interpret confidence and prediction intervals.

LO13-7 Use a log function to transform a nonlinear relationship.

INTRODUCTION

STATISTICS IN ACTION

The space shuttle *Challenger* exploded on January 28, 1986. An investigation of the cause examined four contractors: Rockwell International for the shuttle and engines, Lockheed Martin for ground support, Martin Marietta for the external fuel tanks, and Morton Thiokol for the solid fuel booster rockets. After several months, the investigation blamed the explosion on defective O-rings produced by Morton Thiokol. A study of the contractor's stock prices showed an interesting happenstance. On the day of the *Challenger* explosion, Morton Thiokol stock was down 11.86% and the stock of the other three lost only 2 to 3%. Can we conclude that financial markets predicted the outcome of the investigation?

Chapters 2 through 4 presented *descriptive statistics.* We organized raw data into a frequency distribution and computed several measures of location and measures of dispersion to describe the major characteristics of the distribution. In Chapters 5 through 7, we described probability, and from probability statements, we created probability distributions. In Chapter 8, we began the study of *statistical inference,* where we collected a sample to estimate a population parameter such as the population mean or population proportion. In addition, we used the sample data to test a hypothesis about a population mean or a population proportion, the difference between two population means, or the equality of several population means. Each of these tests involved just *one* interval- or ratio-level variable, such as the profit made on a car sale, the income of bank presidents, or the number of patients admitted each month to a particular hospital.

In this chapter, we shift the emphasis to the study of relationships between two interval- or ratio-level variables. In all business fields, identifying and studying relationships between variables can provide information on ways to increase profits, methods to decrease costs, or variables to predict demand. In marketing products, many firms use price reductions through coupons and discount pricing to increase sales. In this example, we are interested in the relationship between two variables: price reductions and sales. To collect the data, a company can test-market a variety of price reduction methods and observe sales. We hope to confirm a relationship that decreasing price leads to increased sales. In economics, you will find many relationships between two variables that are the basis of economics, such as price and demand.

As another familiar example, recall in Chapter 4 we used the Applewood Auto Group data to show the relationship between two variables with a scatter diagram. We plotted the profit for each vehicle sold on the vertical axis and the age of the buyer on the horizontal axis. See the statistical software output on page 95. In that graph, we observed that as the age of the buyer increased, the profit for each vehicle also increased.

Other examples of relationships between two variables are:

- Does the amount Healthtex spends per month on training its sales force affect its monthly sales?
- Is the number of square feet in a home related to the cost to heat the home in January?
- In a study of fuel efficiency, is there a relationship between miles per gallon and the weight of a car?
- Does the number of hours that students study for an exam influence the exam score?

In this chapter, we carry this idea further. That is, we develop numerical measures to express the relationship between two variables. Is the relationship strong or weak? Is it direct or inverse? In addition, we develop an equation to express the relationship between variables. This will allow us to estimate one variable on the basis of another.

To begin our study of relationships between two variables, we examine the meaning and purpose of **correlation analysis.** We continue by developing an equation that will allow us to estimate the value of one variable based on the value of another. This is called **regression analysis.** We will also evaluate the ability of the equation to accurately make estimations.

WHAT IS CORRELATION ANALYSIS?

LO13-1

Explain the purpose of correlation analysis.

When we study the relationship between two interval- or ratio-scale variables, we often start with a scatter diagram. This procedure provides a visual representation of the relationship between the variables. The next step is usually to calculate the correlation

TABLE 13–1 Number of Sales Calls and Copiers Sold for 15 Salespeople

Sales Representative	Sales Calls	Copiers Sold
Brian Virost	96	41
Carlos Ramirez	40	41
Carol Saia	104	51
Greg Fish	128	60
Jeff Hall	164	61
Mark Reynolds	76	29
Meryl Rumsey	72	39
Mike Kiel	80	50
Ray Snarsky	36	28
Rich Niles	84	43
Ron Broderick	180	70
Sal Spina	132	56
Soni Jones	120	45
Susan Welch	44	31
Tom Keller	84	30

coefficient. It provides a quantitative measure of the strength of the relationship between two variables. As an example, the sales manager of North American Copier Sales, which has a large sales force throughout the United States and Canada, wants to determine whether there is a relationship between the number of sales calls made in a month and the number of copiers sold that month. The manager selects a random sample of 15 representatives and determines, for each representative, the number of sales calls made and the number of copiers sold. This information is reported in Table 13–1.

By reviewing the data, we observe that there does seem to be some relationship between the number of sales calls and the number of units sold. That is, the salespeople who made the most sales calls sold the most units. However, the relationship is not "perfect" or exact. For example, Soni Jones made fewer sales calls than Jeff Hall, but she sold more units.

In addition to the graphical techniques in Chapter 4, we will develop numerical measures to precisely describe the relationship between the two variables, sales calls and copiers sold. This group of statistical techniques is called **correlation analysis.**

CORRELATION ANALYSIS A group of techniques to measure the relationship between two variables.

The basic idea of correlation analysis is to report the relationship between two variables. The usual first step is to plot the data in a **scatter diagram.** An example will show how a scatter diagram is used.

EXAMPLE

North American Copier Sales sells copiers to businesses of all sizes throughout the United States and Canada. Ms. Marcy Bancer was recently promoted to the position of national sales manager. At the upcoming sales meeting, the sales representatives from all over the country will be in attendance. She would like to impress upon them the importance of making that extra sales call each day. She decides to gather some information on the relationship between the number of sales calls and the number of copiers sold. She selects a random sample of 15 sales representatives and determines the number of sales calls they made last month and the number of copiers they sold. The sample information is reported in

Table 13–1. What observations can you make about the relationship between the number of sales calls and the number of copiers sold? Develop a scatter diagram to display the information.

SOLUTION

Based on the information in Table 13–1, Ms. Bancer suspects there is a relationship between the number of sales calls made in a month and the number of copiers sold. Ron Broderick sold the most copiers last month and made 180 sales calls. On the other hand, Ray Snarsky, Carlos Ramirez, and Susan Welch made the fewest calls: 36, 40, and 44. They also had the lowest number of copiers sold among the sampled representatives.

The implication is that the number of copiers sold is related to the number of sales calls made. As the number of sales calls increases, it appears the number of copiers sold also increases. We refer to number of sales calls as the **independent variable** and number of copiers sold as the **dependent variable.**

The independent variable provides the basis for estimating or predicting the dependent variable. For example, we would like to predict the expected number of copiers sold if a salesperson makes 100 sales calls. In the randomly selected sample data, the independent variable—sales calls—is a random number.

The dependent variable is the variable that is being predicted or estimated. It can also be described as the result or outcome for a particular value of the independent variable. The dependent variable is random. That is, for a given value of the independent variable, there are many possible outcomes for the dependent variable.

It is common practice to scale the dependent variable (copiers sold) on the vertical or Y-axis and the independent variable (number of sales calls) on the horizontal or X-axis. To develop the scatter diagram of the North American Copier Sales information, we begin with the first sales representative, Brian Virost. Brian made 96 sales calls last month and sold 41 copiers, so $x = 96$ and $y = 41$. To plot this point, move along the horizontal axis to $x = 96$, then go vertically to $y = 41$ and place a dot at the intersection. This process is continued until all the paired data are plotted, as shown in Chart 13–1.

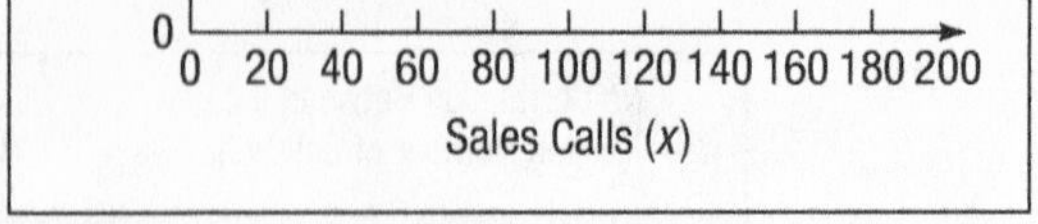

CHART 13–1 Scatter Diagram Showing Sales Calls and Copiers Sold

The scatter diagram shows graphically that the sales representatives who make more calls tend to sell more copiers. It is reasonable for Ms. Bancer, the national sales manager, to tell her salespeople that the more sales calls they make, the more copiers they can expect to sell. Note that, while there appears to be a positive relationship between the two variables, all the points do not fall on a line. In the following section, you will measure the strength and direction of this relationship between two variables by determining the correlation coefficient.

LO13-2
Calculate a correlation coefficient to test and interpret the relationship between two variables.

THE CORRELATION COEFFICIENT

Originated by Karl Pearson about 1900, the **correlation coefficient** describes the strength of the relationship between two sets of interval-scaled or ratio-scaled variables. Designated *r*, it is often referred to as *Pearson's r* and as the *Pearson product-moment correlation coefficient*. It can assume any value from −1.00 to +1.00 inclusive. A correlation coefficient of −1.00 or +1.00 indicates *perfect correlation*. For example, a correlation coefficient for the preceding example computed to be +1.00 would indicate that the number of sales calls and the number of copiers sold are perfectly related in a positive linear sense. A computed value of −1.00 would reveal that sales calls and the number of copiers sold are perfectly related in an inverse linear sense. How the scatter diagram would appear if the relationship between the two variables were linear and perfect is shown in Chart 13–2.

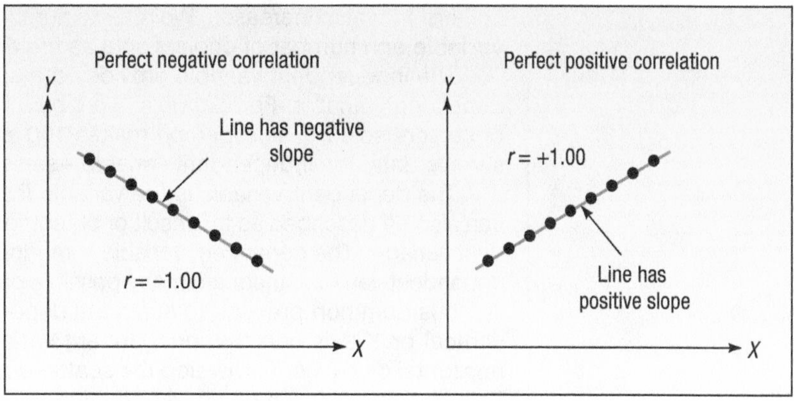

CHART 13–2 Scatter Diagrams Showing Perfect Negative Correlation and Perfect Positive Correlation

If there is absolutely no relationship between the two sets of variables, Pearson's *r* is zero. A correlation coefficient *r* close to 0 (say, .08) shows that the linear relationship is quite weak. The same conclusion is drawn if $r = -.08$. Coefficients of −.91 and +.91 have equal strength; both indicate very strong correlation between the two variables. Thus, *the strength of the correlation does not depend on the direction (either − or +).*

Scatter diagrams for $r = 0$, a weak *r* (say, −.23), and a strong *r* (say, +.87) are shown in Chart 13–3. Note that, if the correlation is weak, there is considerable scatter about a line drawn through the center of the data. For the scatter diagram representing a strong relationship, there is very little scatter about the line. This indicates, in the example shown on the chart, that hours studied is a good predictor of exam score.

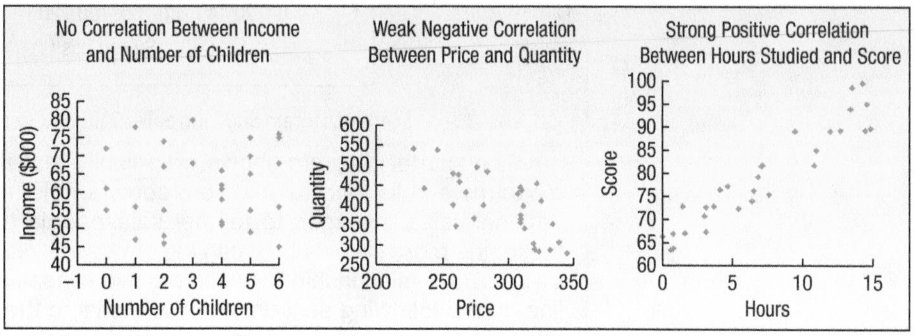

CHART 13–3 Scatter Diagrams Depicting Zero, Weak, and Strong Correlation

The following drawing summarizes the strength and direction of the correlation coefficient.

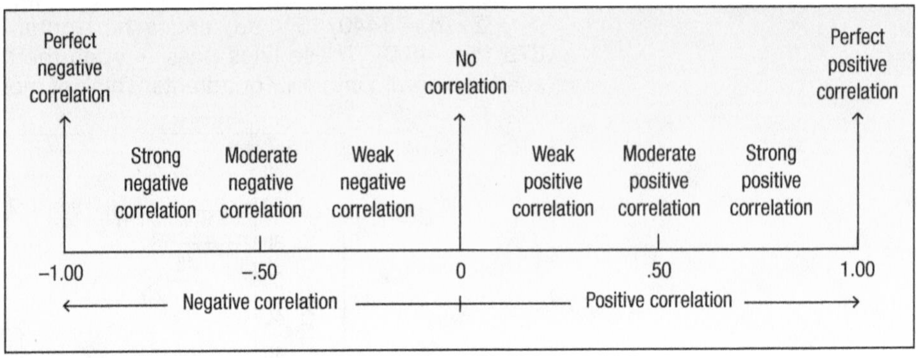

CORRELATION COEFFICIENT A measure of the strength of the linear relationship between two variables.

The characteristics of the correlation coefficient are summarized below.

CHARACTERISTICS OF THE CORRELATION COEFFICIENT

1. The sample correlation coefficient is identified by the lowercase letter r.
2. It shows the direction and strength of the linear relationship between two interval- or ratio-scale variables.
3. It ranges from -1 up to and including $+1$.
4. A value near 0 indicates there is little linear relationship between the variables.
5. A value near 1 indicates a direct or positive linear relationship between the variables.
6. A value near -1 indicates an inverse or negative linear relationship between the variables.

How is the value of the correlation coefficient determined? We will use the North American Copier Sales in Table 13–1 as an example. It is replicated in Table 13–2 for

TABLE 13–2 Number of Sales Calls and Copiers Sold for 15 Salespeople

Sales Representative	Sales Calls	Copiers Sold
Brian Virost	96	41
Carlos Ramirez	40	41
Carol Saia	104	51
Greg Fish	128	60
Jeff Hall	164	61
Mark Reynolds	76	29
Meryl Rumsey	72	39
Mike Kiel	80	50
Ray Snarsky	36	28
Rich Niles	84	43
Ron Broderick	180	70
Sal Spina	132	56
Soni Jones	120	45
Susan Welch	44	31
Tom Keller	84	30
Total	1440	675

your convenience. We begin with a scatter diagram, similar to Chart 13–2. Draw a vertical line through the data values at the mean of the x-values and a horizontal line at the mean of the y-values. In Chart 13–4, we've added a vertical line at 96 calls ($\bar{x} = \Sigma x/n = 1440/15 = 96$) and a horizontal line at 45.0 copiers ($\bar{y} = \Sigma y/n = 675/15 = 45.0$). These lines pass through the "center" of the data and divide the scatter diagram into four quadrants. Think of moving the origin from (0, 0) to (96, 45).

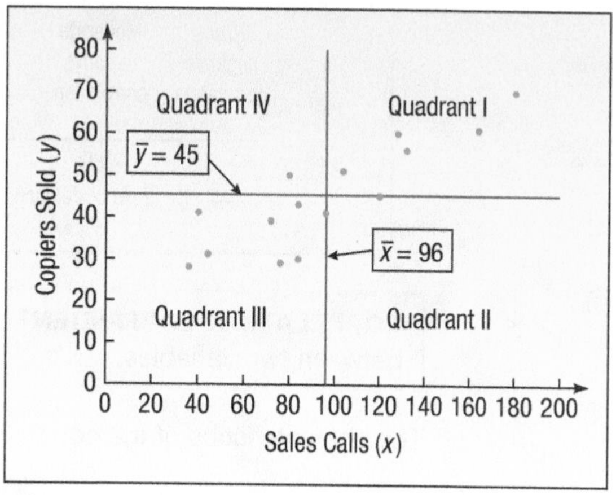

CHART 13–4 Computation of the Correlation Coefficient

Two variables are positively related when the number of copiers sold is above the mean and the number of sales calls is also above the mean. These points appear in the upper-right quadrant (labeled Quadrant I) of Chart 13–4. Similarly, when the number of copiers sold is less than the mean, so is the number of sales calls. These points fall in the lower-left quadrant of Chart 13–4 (labeled Quadrant III). For example, the third person on the list in Table 13–2, Carol Saia, made 104 sales calls and sold 51 copiers. These values are above their respective means, so this point is located in Quadrant I, which is in the upper-right quadrant. She made 8 more calls than the mean number of sales calls and sold 6 more than the mean number sold. Tom Keller, the last name on the list in Table 13–2, made 84 sales calls and sold 30 copiers. Both of these values are less than their respective means, hence this point is in the lower-left quadrant. Tom made 12 fewer sales calls and sold 15 fewer copiers than the respective means. The deviations from the mean number of sales calls and the mean number of copiers sold are summarized in Table 13–3 for the 15 sales representatives. The sum of the products of the deviations from the respective means is 6672. That is, the term $\Sigma(x - \bar{x})(y - \bar{y}) = 6672$.

In both the upper-right and the lower-left quadrants, the product of $(x - \bar{x})(y - \bar{y})$ is positive because both of the factors have the same sign. In our example, this happens for all sales representatives except Mike Kiel. Mike made 80 sales calls (which is less than the mean) but sold 50 machines (which is more than the mean). We can therefore expect the correlation coefficient to have a positive value.

If the two variables are inversely related, one variable will be above the mean and the other below the mean. Most of the points in this case occur in the upper-left and lower-right quadrants, that is, Quadrants II and IV. Now $(x - \bar{x})$ and $(y - \bar{y})$ will have opposite signs, so their product is negative. The resulting correlation coefficient is negative.

What happens if there is no linear relationship between the two variables? The points in the scatter diagram will appear in all four quadrants. The negative products of $(x - \bar{x})(y - \bar{y})$ offset the positive products, so the sum is near zero. This leads to a correlation coefficient near zero. So, the term $\Sigma(x - \bar{x})(y - \bar{y})$ drives the strength as well as the sign of the relationship between the two variables.

TABLE 13–3 Deviations from the Mean and Their Products

Sales Representative	Sales Calls (x)	Copiers Sold (y)	$x - \bar{x}$	$y - \bar{y}$	$(x - \bar{x})(y - \bar{y})$
Brian Virost	96	41	0	−4	0
Carlos Ramirez	40	41	−56	−4	224
Carol Saia	104	51	8	6	48
Greg Fish	128	60	32	15	480
Jeff Hall	164	61	68	16	1,088
Mark Reynolds	76	29	−20	−16	320
Meryl Rumsey	72	39	−24	−6	144
Mike Kiel	80	50	−16	5	−80
Ray Snarsky	36	28	−60	−17	1,020
Rich Niles	84	43	−12	−2	24
Ron Broderick	180	70	84	25	2,100
Sal Spina	132	56	36	11	396
Soni Jones	120	45	24	0	0
Susan Welch	44	31	−52	−14	728
Tom Keller	84	30	−12	−15	180
Totals	1440	675	0	0	6,672

The correlation coefficient is also unaffected by the units of the two variables. For example, if we had used hundreds of copiers sold instead of the number sold, the correlation coefficient would be the same. The correlation coefficient is independent of the scale used if we divide the term $\Sigma(x - \bar{x})(y - \bar{y})$ by the sample standard deviations. It is also made independent of the sample size and bounded by the values +1.00 and −1.00 if we divide by $(n - 1)$.

This reasoning leads to the following formula:

CORRELATION COEFFICIENT

$$r = \frac{\Sigma(x - \bar{x})(y - \bar{y})}{(n - 1)s_x s_y} \qquad [13\text{–}1]$$

To compute the correlation coefficient, we use the standard deviations of the sample of 15 sales calls and 15 copiers sold. We could use formula (3–12) to calculate the sample standard deviations or we could use a software package. For the specific Excel and Minitab commands, see the **Software Commands** in Appendix C. The following is the Excel output. The standard deviation of the number of sales calls is 42.76 and of the number of copiers sold 12.89.

	A	B	C	D	E	F	G	H
1		Sales Representative	Sales Calls (x)	Copiers Sold (y)			Sales Calls (x)	Copiers Sold (y)
2		Brian Virost	96	41		Mean	96.00	45.00
3		Carlos Ramirez	40	41		Standard Error	11.04	3.33
4		Carol Saia	104	51		Median	84.00	43.00
5		Greg Fish	128	60		Mode	84.00	41.00
6		Jeff Hall	164	61		Standard Deviation	42.76	12.89
7		Mark Reynolds	76	29		Sample Variance	1828.57	166.14
8		Meryl Rumsey	72	39		Kurtosis	-0.32	-0.73
9		Mike Kiel	80	50		Skewness	0.46	0.36
10		Ray Snarsky	36	28		Range	144.00	42.00
11		Rich Niles	84	43		Minimum	36.00	28.00
12		Ron Broderick	180	70		Maximum	180.00	70.00
13		Sal Spina	132	56		Sum	1440.00	675.00
14		Soni Jones	120	45		Count	15.00	15.00
15		Susan Welch	44	31				
16		Tom Keller	84	30				
17		Total	1440	675				

We now insert these values into formula (13–1) to determine the correlation coefficient:

$$r = \frac{\Sigma(x - \bar{x})(y - \bar{y})}{(n - 1)s_x s_y} = \frac{6672}{(15 - 1)(42.76)(12.89)} = 0.865$$

How do we interpret a correlation of 0.865? First, it is positive, so we conclude there is a direct relationship between the number of sales calls and the number of copiers sold. This confirms our reasoning based on the scatter diagram, Chart 13–4. The value of 0.865 is fairly close to 1.00, so we conclude that the association is strong.

We must be careful with the interpretation. The correlation of 0.865 indicates a strong positive linear association between the variables. Ms. Bancer would be correct to encourage the sales personnel to make that extra sales call because the number of sales calls made is related to the number of copiers sold. However, does this mean that more sales calls *cause* more sales? No, we have not demonstrated cause and effect here, only that the two variables—sales calls and copiers sold—are related.

If there is a strong relationship (say, .97) between two variables, we are tempted to assume that an increase or decrease in one variable *causes* a change in the other variable. For example, historically, the consumption of Georgia peanuts and the consumption of aspirin have a strong correlation. However, this does not indicate that an increase in the consumption of peanuts *caused* the consumption of aspirin to increase. Likewise, the incomes of professors and the number of inmates in mental institutions have increased proportionately. Further, as the population of donkeys has decreased, there has been an increase in the number of doctoral degrees granted. Relationships such as these are called **spurious correlations.** What we can conclude when we find two variables with a strong correlation is that there is a relationship or association between the two variables, not that a change in one causes a change in the other.

EXAMPLE

The Applewood Auto Group's marketing department believes younger buyers purchase vehicles on which lower profits are earned and the older buyers purchase vehicles on which higher profits are earned. They would like to use this information as part of an upcoming advertising campaign to try to attract older buyers, for whom the profits tend to be higher. Develop a scatter diagram depicting the relationship between vehicle profits and age of the buyer. Use statistical software to determine the correlation coefficient. Would this be a useful advertising feature?

SOLUTION

Using the Applewood Auto Group example, the first step is to graph the data using a scatter plot. It is shown in Chart 13–5.

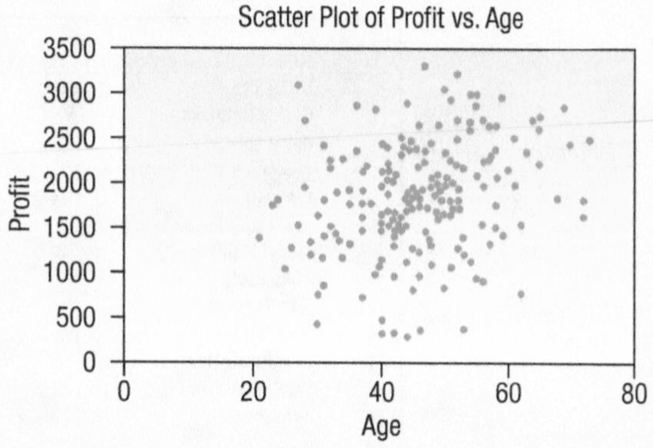

CHART 13–5 Scatter Diagram of Profit versus Age for the Applewood Auto Group Data

The scatter diagram suggests that a positive relationship does exist between age and profit; however, that relationship does not appear strong.

The next step is to calculate the correlation coefficient to evaluate the relative strength of the relationship. Statistical software provides an easy way to calculate the value of the correlation coefficient. The Excel output follows.

	Age	*Profit*
Age	1	
Profit	0.262	1

For these data, $r = 0.262$. To evaluate the relationship between a buyer's age and the profit on a car sale:

1. The relationship is positive or direct. Why? Because the sign of the correlation coefficient is positive. This confirms that as the age of the buyer increases, the profit on a car sale also increases.
2. The relationship between the two variables is weak. For a positive relationship, values of the correlation coefficient close to one indicate stronger relationships. In this case, $r = 0.262$. It is closer to zero, and we would observe that the relationship is not very strong.

It is not recommended that Applewood use this information as part of an advertising campaign to attract older, more profitable buyers.

SELF-REVIEW 13–1

Haverty's Furniture is a family business that has been selling to retail customers in the Chicago area for many years. The company advertises extensively on radio, TV, and the Internet, emphasizing low prices and easy credit terms. The owner would like to review the relationship between sales and the amount spent on advertising. Below is information on sales and advertising expense for the last four months.

Month	Advertising Expense ($ million)	Sales Revenue ($ million)
July	2	7
August	1	3
September	3	8
October	4	10

(a) The owner wants to forecast sales on the basis of advertising expense. Which variable is the dependent variable? Which variable is the independent variable?
(b) Draw a scatter diagram.
(c) Determine the correlation coefficient.
(d) Interpret the strength of the correlation coefficient.

EXERCISES

1. The following sample observations were randomly selected.

x	4	5	3	6	10
y	4	6	5	7	7

Determine the correlation coefficient and interpret the relationship between x and y.

For **DATA FILE**, please visit www.mhhe.com/lind16e

2. The following sample observations were randomly selected.

x	5	3	6	3	4	4	6	8
y	13	15	7	12	13	11	9	5

Determine the correlation coefficient and interpret the relationship between *x* and *y*.

For **DATA FILE**, please visit www.mhhe.com/lind16e

3. Bi-lo Appliance Super-Store has outlets in several large metropolitan areas in New England. The general sales manager aired a commercial for a digital camera on selected local TV stations prior to a sale starting on Saturday and ending Sunday. She obtained the information for Saturday–Sunday digital camera sales at the various outlets and paired it with the number of times the advertisement was shown on the local TV stations. The purpose is to find whether there is any relationship between the number of times the advertisement was aired and digital camera sales. The pairings are:

Location of TV Station	Number of Airings	Saturday–Sunday Sales ($ thousands)
Providence	4	15
Springfield	2	8
New Haven	5	21
Boston	6	24
Hartford	3	17

   a. What is the dependent variable?
   b. Draw a scatter diagram.
   c. Determine the correlation coefficient.
   d. Interpret these statistical measures.

For **DATA FILE**, please visit www.mhhe.com/lind16e

4. The production department of Celltronics International wants to explore the relationship between the number of employees who assemble a subassembly and the number produced. As an experiment, two employees were assigned to assemble the subassemblies. They produced 15 during a one-hour period. Then four employees assembled them. They produced 25 during a one-hour period. The complete set of paired observations follows.

Number of Assemblers	One-Hour Production (units)
2	15
4	25
1	10
5	40
3	30

   The dependent variable is production; that is, it is assumed that different levels of production result from a different number of employees.
   a. Draw a scatter diagram.
   b. Based on the scatter diagram, does there appear to be any relationship between the number of assemblers and production? Explain.
   c. Compute the correlation coefficient.

For **DATA FILE**, please visit www.mhhe.com/lind16e

5. The city council of Pine Bluffs is considering increasing the number of police in an effort to reduce crime. Before making a final decision, the council asked the chief of police to survey other cities of similar size to determine the relationship between the number of police and the number of crimes reported. The chief gathered the following sample information.

City	Police	Number of Crimes	City	Police	Number of Crimes
Oxford	15	17	Holgate	17	7
Starksville	17	13	Carey	12	21
Danville	25	5	Whistler	11	19
Athens	27	7	Woodville	22	6

a. Which variable is the dependent variable and which is the independent variable? Hint: Which of the following makes better sense: Cities with more police have fewer crimes, or cities with fewer crimes have more police? Explain your choice.
b. Draw a scatter diagram.
c. Determine the correlation coefficient.
d. Interpret the correlation coefficient. Does it surprise you that the correlation coefficient is negative?

For **DATA FILE**, please visit www.mhhe.com/lind16e

6. The owner of Maumee Ford-Mercury-Volvo wants to study the relationship between the age of a car and its selling price. Listed below is a random sample of 12 used cars sold at the dealership during the last year.

Car	Age (years)	Selling Price ($000)	Car	Age (years)	Selling Price ($000)
1	9	8.1	7	8	7.6
2	7	6.0	8	11	8.0
3	11	3.6	9	10	8.0
4	12	4.0	10	12	6.0
5	8	5.0	11	6	8.6
6	7	10.0	12	6	8.0

a. Draw a scatter diagram.
b. Determine the correlation coefficient.
c. Interpret the correlation coefficient. Does it surprise you that the correlation coefficient is negative?

Testing the Significance of the Correlation Coefficient

Recall that the sales manager of North American Copier Sales found the correlation between the number of sales calls and the number of copiers sold was 0.865. This indicated a strong positive association between the two variables. However, only 15 salespeople were sampled. Could it be that the correlation in the population is actually 0? This would mean the correlation of 0.865 was due to chance. The population in this example is all the salespeople employed by the firm.

Resolving this dilemma requires a test to answer the obvious question: Could there be zero correlation in the population from which the sample was selected? To put it another way, did the computed r come from a population of paired observations with zero correlation? To continue our convention of allowing Greek letters to represent a population parameter, we will let ρ represent the correlation in the population. It is pronounced "rho."

We will continue with the illustration involving sales calls and copiers sold. We employ the same hypothesis testing steps described in Chapter 10. The null hypothesis and the alternate hypothesis are:

H_0: $\rho = 0$ (The correlation in the population is zero.)
H_1: $\rho \neq 0$ (The correlation in the population is different from zero.)

From the way H_1 is stated, we know that the test is two-tailed.

The formula for t is:

t TEST FOR THE CORRELATION COEFFICIENT

$$t = \frac{r\sqrt{n-2}}{\sqrt{1-r^2}} \quad \text{with } n-2 \text{ degrees of freedom} \qquad \textbf{[13–2]}$$

Using the .05 level of significance, the decision rule states that if the computed t falls in the area between plus 2.160 and minus 2.160, the null hypothesis is not rejected. To locate the critical value of 2.160, refer to Appendix B.5 for $df = n - 2 = 15 - 2 = 13$. See Chart 13–6.

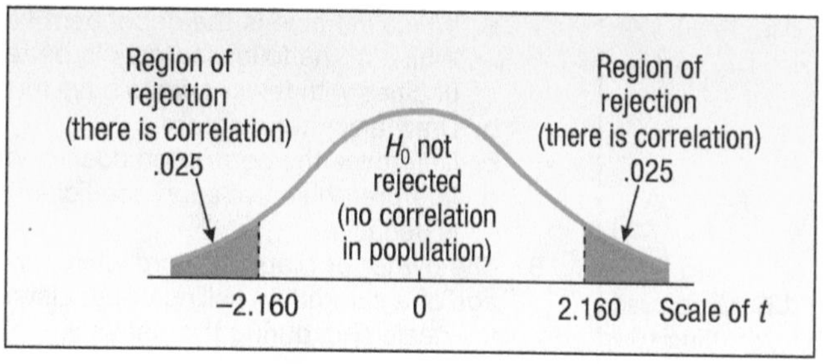

CHART 13–6 Decision Rule for Test of Hypothesis at .05 Significance Level and 13 *df*

Applying formula (13–2) to the example regarding the number of sales calls and units sold:

$$t = \frac{r\sqrt{n-2}}{\sqrt{1-r^2}} = \frac{.865\sqrt{15-2}}{\sqrt{1-.865^2}} = 6.216$$

The computed t is in the rejection region. Thus, H_0 is rejected at the .05 significance level. Hence we conclude the correlation in the population is not zero. This indicates to the sales manager that there is correlation with respect to the number of sales calls made and the number of copiers sold in the population of salespeople.

We can also interpret the test of hypothesis in terms of p-values. A p-value is the likelihood of finding a value of the test statistic more extreme than the one computed, when H_0 is true. To determine the p-value, go to the t distribution in Appendix B.5 and find the row for 13 degrees of freedom. The value of the test statistic is 6.216, so in the row for 13 degrees of freedom and a two-tailed test, find the value closest to 6.216. For a two-tailed test at the 0.001 significance level, the critical value is 4.221. Because 6.216 is greater than 4.221, we conclude that the p-value is less than 0.001.

Both Minitab and Excel will report the correlation between two variables. In addition to the correlation, Minitab reports the p-value for the test of hypothesis that the correlation in the population between the two variables is 0. The Minitab output follows.

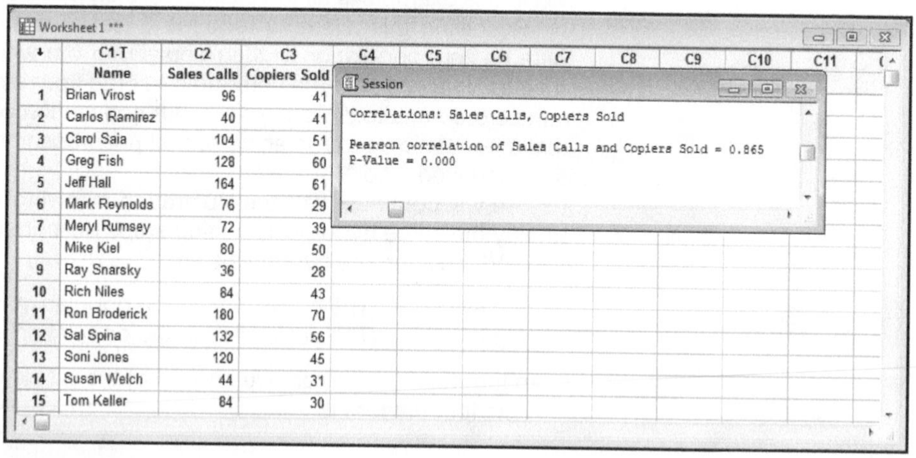

	C1-T Name	C2 Sales Calls	C3 Copiers Sold
1	Brian Virost	96	41
2	Carlos Ramirez	40	41
3	Carol Saia	104	51
4	Greg Fish	128	60
5	Jeff Hall	164	61
6	Mark Reynolds	76	29
7	Meryl Rumsey	72	39
8	Mike Kiel	80	50
9	Ray Snarsky	36	28
10	Rich Niles	84	43
11	Ron Broderick	180	70
12	Sal Spina	132	56
13	Soni Jones	120	45
14	Susan Welch	44	31
15	Tom Keller	84	30

EXAMPLE

In the example on page 435, we found that the correlation coefficient between the profit on the sale of a vehicle by the Applewood Auto Group and the age of the person that purchased the vehicle was 0.262. Because the sign of the correlation coefficient was positive, we concluded there was a direct relationship between the two variables. However, because the amount of correlation was low—that is, near

zero—we concluded that an advertising campaign directed toward the older buyers, where there is a large profit, was not warranted. We can test our conclusion by conducting a hypothesis test that the correlation coefficient is greater than zero using the .05 significance level.

SOLUTION

To test the hypothesis, we need to clarify the sample and population issues. Let's assume that the data collected on the 180 vehicles sold by the Applewood Group is a sample from the population of *all* vehicles sold over many years by the Applewood Auto Group. The Greek letter ρ is the correlation coefficient in the population and r the correlation coefficient in the sample.

Our next step is to set up the null hypothesis and the alternate hypothesis. We test the null hypothesis that the correlation coefficient is equal to or less than zero. The alternate hypothesis is that there is positive correlation between the two variables.

H_0: $\rho \leq 0$ (The correlation in the population is negative or equal to zero.)
H_1: $\rho > 0$ (The correlation in the population is positive.)

This is a one-tailed test because we are interested in confirming a positive association between the variables. The test statistic follows the t distribution with $n - 2$ degrees of freedom, so the degrees of freedom are $180 - 2 = 178$. However, the value for 178 degrees of freedom is not in Appendix B.5. The closest value is 180, so we will use that value. Our decision rule is to reject the null hypothesis if the computed value of the test statistic is greater than 1.653.

We use formula (13–2) to find the value of the test statistic.

$$t = \frac{r\sqrt{n-2}}{\sqrt{1-r^2}} = \frac{0.262\sqrt{180-2}}{\sqrt{1-0.262^2}} = 3.622$$

Comparing the value of our test statistic of 3.622 to the critical value of 1.653, we reject the null hypothesis. We conclude that the sample correlation coefficient of 0.262 is too large to have come from a population with no correlation. To put our results another way, there is a positive correlation between profits and age in the population.

This result is confusing and seems contradictory. On one hand, we observed that the correlation coefficient did not indicate a very strong relationship and that the Applewood Auto Group marketing department should not use this information for its promotion and advertising decisions. On the other hand, the hypothesis test indicated that the correlation coefficient is not equal to zero and that a positive relationship between age and profit exists. How can this be? We must be very careful about the application of the hypothesis test results. The hypothesis test shows a statistically significant result. However, this result does not necessarily support a practical decision to start a new marketing and promotion campaign to older purchasers. In fact, the relatively low correlation coefficient is an indication that the outcome of a new marketing and promotion campaign to older potential purchasers is, at best, uncertain.

SELF-REVIEW 13–2

A sample of 25 mayoral campaigns in medium-sized cities with populations between 50,000 and 250,000 showed that the correlation between the percent of the vote received and the amount spent on the campaign by the candidate was .43. At the .05 significance level, is there a positive association between the variables?

EXERCISES

7. The following hypotheses are given.

$$H_0: \rho \leq 0$$
$$H_1: \rho > 0$$

A random sample of 12 paired observations indicated a correlation of .32. Can we conclude that the correlation in the population is greater than zero? Use the .05 significance level.

8. The following hypotheses are given.

$$H_0: \rho \geq 0$$
$$H_1: \rho < 0$$

A random sample of 15 paired observations has a correlation of −.46. Can we conclude that the correlation in the population is less than zero? Use the .05 significance level.

9. Pennsylvania Refining Company is studying the relationship between the pump price of gasoline and the number of gallons sold. For a sample of 20 stations last Tuesday, the correlation was .78. At the .01 significance level, is the correlation in the population greater than zero?

10. A study of 20 worldwide financial institutions showed the correlation between their assets and pretax profit to be .86. At the .05 significance level, can we conclude that there is positive correlation in the population?

11. The Airline Passenger Association studied the relationship between the number of passengers on a particular flight and the cost of the flight. It seems logical that more passengers on the flight will result in more weight and more luggage, which in turn will result in higher fuel costs. For a sample of 15 flights, the correlation between the number of passengers and total fuel cost was .667. Is it reasonable to conclude that there is positive association in the population between the two variables? Use the .01 significance level.

For **DATA FILE**, please visit www.mhhe.com/lind16e

12. The Student Government Association at Middle Carolina University wanted to demonstrate the relationship between the number of beers a student drinks and his or her blood alcohol content (BAC). A random sample of 18 students participated in a study in which each participating student was randomly assigned a number of 12-ounce cans of beer to drink. Thirty minutes after they consumed their assigned number of beers, a member of the local sheriff's office measured their blood alcohol content. The sample information is reported below.

Student	Beers	BAC	Student	Beers	BAC
1	6	0.10	10	3	0.07
2	7	0.09	11	3	0.05
3	7	0.09	12	7	0.08
4	4	0.10	13	1	0.04
5	5	0.10	14	4	0.07
6	3	0.07	15	2	0.06
7	3	0.10	16	7	0.12
8	6	0.12	17	2	0.05
9	6	0.09	18	1	0.02

Use a statistical software package to answer the following questions.

a. Develop a scatter diagram for the number of beers consumed and BAC. Comment on the relationship. Does it appear to be strong or weak? Does it appear to be positive or inverse?
b. Determine the correlation coefficient.
c. At the .01 significance level, is it reasonable to conclude that there is a positive relationship in the population between the number of beers consumed and the BAC? What is the *p*-value?

LO13-3 Apply regression analysis to estimate the linear relationship between two variables.

REGRESSION ANALYSIS

In the previous sections of this chapter, we evaluated the direction and the significance of the linear relationship between two variables by finding the correlation coefficient. Regression analysis is another method to examine a linear relationship between two variables. This analysis uses the basic concepts of correlation but provides much more

information by expressing the linear relationship between two variables in the form of an equation. Using this equation, we will be able to estimate the value of the dependent variable *Y* based on a selected value of the independent variable *X*. The technique used to develop the equation and provide the estimates is called **regression analysis.**

In Table 13–1, we reported the number of sales calls and the number of units sold for a sample of 15 sales representatives employed by North American Copier Sales. Chart 13–1 portrayed this information in a scatter diagram. Recall that we tested the significance of the correlation coefficient ($r = 0.865$) and concluded that a significant relationship exists between the two variables. Now we want to develop a linear equation that expresses the relationship between the number of sales calls, the independent variable, and the number of units sold, the dependent variable. The equation for the line used to estimate *Y* on the basis of *X* is referred to as the **regression equation.**

REGRESSION EQUATION An equation that expresses the linear relationship between two variables.

Least Squares Principle

In regression analysis, our objective is to use the data to position a line that best represents the relationship between the two variables. Our first approach is to use a scatter diagram to visually position the line.

The scatter diagram in Chart 13–1 is reproduced in Chart 13–7, with a line drawn with a ruler through the dots to illustrate that a line would probably fit the data. However, the line drawn using a straight edge has one disadvantage: Its position is based in part on the judgment of the person drawing the line. The hand-drawn lines in Chart 13–8 represent the judgments of four people. All the lines except line *A* seem to be reasonable. That is, each line is centered among the graphed data. However, each would result in a different estimate of units sold for a particular number of sales calls.

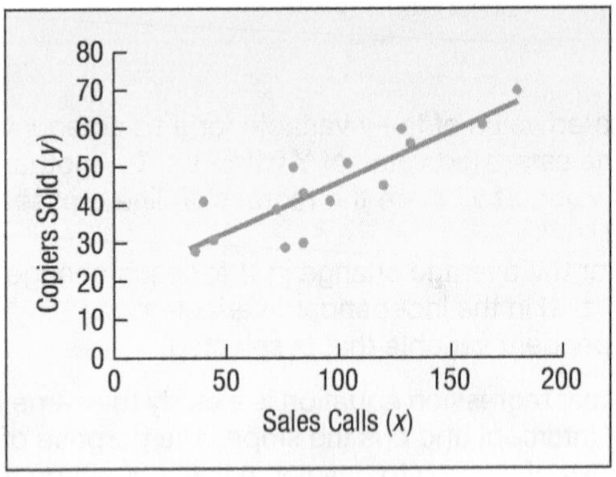

CHART 13–7 Sales Calls and Copiers Sold for 15 Sales Representatives

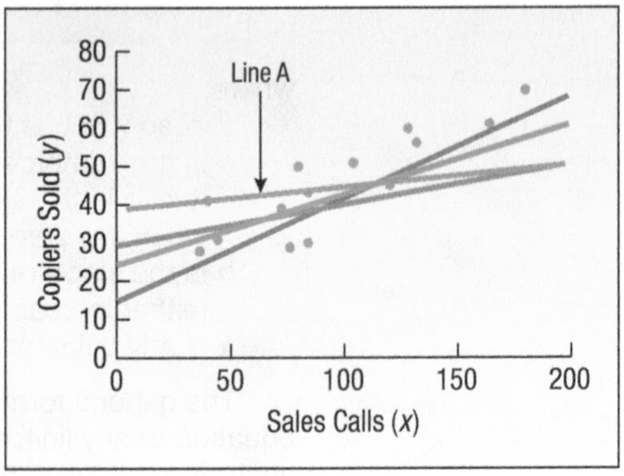

CHART 13–8 Four Lines Superimposed on the Scatter Diagram

We would prefer a method that results in a single, best regression line. This method is called the least squares principle. It gives what is commonly referred to as the "best-fitting" line.

LEAST SQUARES PRINCIPLE A mathematical procedure that uses the data to position a line with the objective of minimizing the sum of the squares of the vertical distances between the actual *y* values and the predicted values of *y*.

To illustrate this concept, the same data are plotted in the three charts that follow. The dots are the actual values of *y*, and the asterisks are the predicted values of *y* for a given value of *x*. The regression line in Chart 13–9 was determined using the least squares method. It is the best-fitting line because the sum of the squares of the vertical deviations about it is at a minimum. The first plot ($x = 3, y = 8$) deviates by 2 from the line, found by $10 - 8$. The deviation squared is 4. The squared deviation for the plot $x = 4, y = 18$ is 16. The squared deviation for the plot $x = 5, y = 16$ is 4. The sum of the squared deviations is 24, found by $4 + 16 + 4$.

Assume that the lines in Charts 13–10 and 13–11 were drawn with a straight edge. The sum of the squared vertical deviations in Chart 13–10 is 44. For Chart 13–11, it is 132. Both sums are greater than the sum for the line in Chart 13–9, found by using the least squares method.

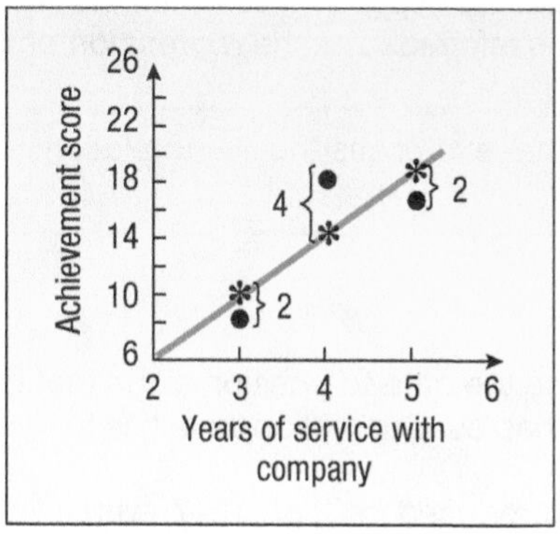

CHART 13–9 The Least Squares Line

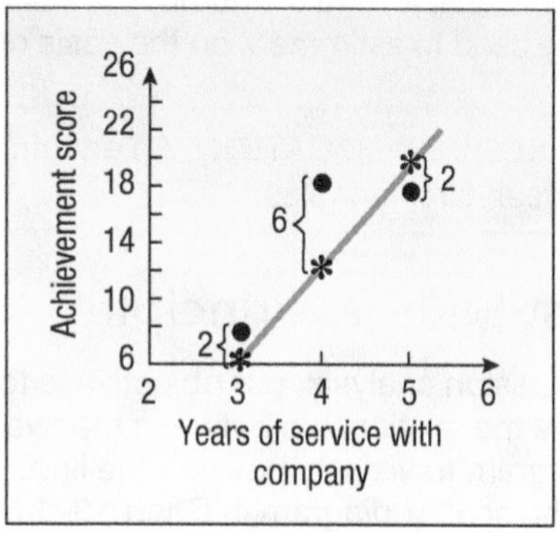

CHART 13–10 Line Drawn with a Straight Edge

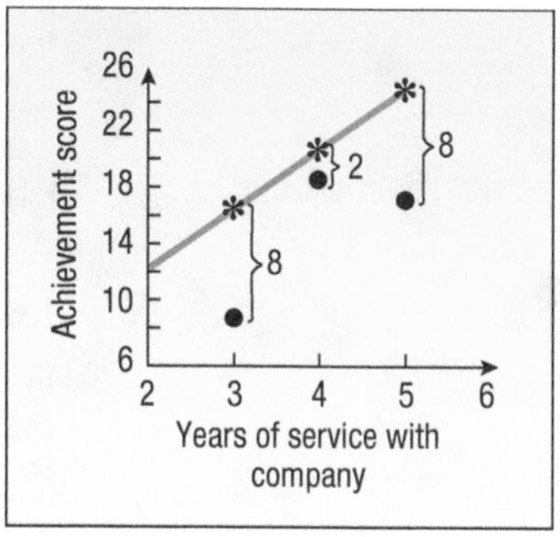

CHART 13–11 Different Line Drawn with a Straight Edge

The equation of a line has the form

GENERAL FORM OF LINEAR REGRESSION EQUATION	$\hat{y} = a + bx$	**[13–3]**

where:

$\hat{y}$, read *y* hat, is the estimated value of the *y* variable for a selected *x* value.

a is the *y*-intercept. It is the estimated value of *Y* when $x = 0$. Another way to put it is: *a* is the estimated value of *y* where the regression line crosses the *Y*-axis when *x* is zero.

b is the slope of the line, or the average change in $\hat{y}$ for each change of one unit (either increase or decrease) in the independent variable *x*.

x is any value of the independent variable that is selected.

The general form of the linear regression equation is exactly the same form as the equation of any line. *a* is the *Y* intercept and *b* is the slope. The purpose of regression analysis is to calculate the values of *a* and *b* to develop a linear equation that best fits the data.

The formulas for *a* and *b* are:

SLOPE OF THE REGRESSION LINE	$b = r\left(\frac{s_y}{s_x}\right)$	**[13–4]**

where:

r is the correlation coefficient.

s_y is the standard deviation of *y* (the dependent variable).

s_x is the standard deviation of *x* (the independent variable).

Y-INTERCEPT $a = \bar{y} - b\bar{x}$ **[13–5]**

where:

$\bar{y}$ is the mean of y (the dependent variable).
$\bar{x}$ is the mean of x (the independent variable).

EXAMPLE

Recall the example involving North American Copier Sales. The sales manager gathered information on the number of sales calls made and the number of copiers sold for a random sample of 15 sales representatives. As a part of her presentation at the upcoming sales meeting, Ms. Bancer, the sales manager, would like to offer specific information about the relationship between the number of sales calls and the number of copiers sold. Use the least squares method to determine a linear equation to express the relationship between the two variables. What is the expected number of copiers sold by a representative who made 100 calls?

SOLUTION

The first step in determining the regression equation is to find the slope of the least squares regression line. That is, we need the value of b. On page 434, we determined the correlation coefficient r (0.865). In the Excel output on page 433, we determined the standard deviation of the independent variable x (42.76) and the standard deviation of the dependent variable y (12.89). The values are inserted in formula (13–4).

$$b = r\left(\frac{s_y}{s_x}\right) = .865\left(\frac{12.89}{42.76}\right) = 0.2608$$

Next, we need to find the value of a. To do this, we use the value for b that we just calculated as well as the means for the number of sales calls and the number of copiers sold. These means are also available in the Excel worksheet on page 433. From formula (13–5):

$$a = \bar{y} - b\bar{x} = 45 - .2608(96) = 19.9632$$

Thus, the regression equation is $\hat{y} = 19.9632 + 0.2608x$. So if a salesperson makes 100 calls, he or she can expect to sell 46.0432 copiers, found by $\hat{y} = 19.9632 + 0.2608x = 19.9632 + 0.2608(100)$. The b value of .2608 indicates that for each additional sales call, the sales representative can expect to increase the number of copiers sold by about 0.2608. To put it another way, 20 additional sales calls in a month will result in about five more copiers being sold, found by $0.2608(20) = 5.216$.

The a value of 19.9632 is the point where the equation crosses the Y-axis. A literal translation is that if no sales calls are made, that is $x = 0$, 19.9632 copiers will be sold. Note that $x = 0$ is outside the range of values included in the sample and, therefore, should not be used to estimate the number of copiers sold. The sales calls ranged from 36 to 180, so estimates should be limited to that range.

Drawing the Regression Line

The least squares equation $\hat{y} = 19.9632 + 0.2608x$ can be drawn on the scatter diagram. The fifth sales representative in the sample is Jeff Hall. He made 164 calls. His estimated number of copiers sold is $\hat{y} = 19.9632 + 0.2608(164) = 62.7344$.The plot $x = 164$ and $\hat{y} = 62.7344$ is located by moving to 164 on the X-axis and then going

STATISTICS IN ACTION

In finance, investors are interested in the trade-off between returns and risk. One technique to quantify risk is a regression analysis of a company's stock price (dependent variable) and an average measure of the stock market (independent variable). Often the Standard and Poor's (S&P) 500 Index is used to estimate the market. The regression coefficient, called beta in finance, shows the change in a company's stock price for a one-unit change in the S&P Index. For example, if a stock has a beta of 1.5, then when the S&P index increases by 1%, the stock price will increase by 1.5%. The opposite is also true. If the S&P decreases by 1%, the stock price will decrease by 1.5%. If the beta is 1.0, then a 1% change in the index should show a 1% change in a stock price. If the beta is less than 1.0, then a 1% change in the index shows less than a 1% change in the stock price.

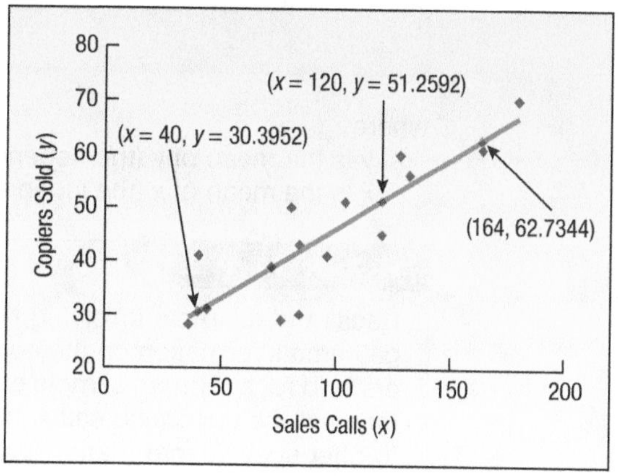

CHART 13–12 The Line of Regression Drawn on the Scatter Diagram

vertically to 62.7344. The other points on the regression equation can be determined by substituting a particular value of x into the regression equation and calculating $\hat{y}$. All the points are connected to give the line. See Chart 13–12.

Sales Representative	Sales Calls (x)	Copiers Sold (y)	Estimated Sales ($\hat{y}$)
Brian Virost	96	41	45.0000
Carlos Ramirez	40	41	30.3952
Carol Saia	104	51	47.0864
Greg Fish	128	60	53.3456
Jeff Hall	164	61	62.7344
Mark Reynolds	76	29	39.7840
Meryl Rumsey	72	39	38.7408
Mike Kiel	80	50	40.8272
Ray Snarsky	36	28	29.3520
Rich Niles	84	43	41.8704
Ron Broderick	180	70	66.9072
Sal Spina	132	56	54.3888
Soni Jones	120	45	51.2592
Susan Welch	44	31	31.4384
Tom Keller	84	30	41.8704

The least squares regression line has some interesting and unique features. First, it will always pass through the point $(\bar{x}, \bar{y})$. To show this is true, we can use the mean number of sales calls to predict the number of copiers sold. In this example, the mean number of sales calls is 96, found by $\bar{x} = 1440/15$. The mean number of copiers sold is 45.0, found by $\bar{y} = 675/15$. If we let $x = 96$ and then use the regression equation to find the estimated value for $\hat{y}$, the result is:

$$\hat{y} = 19.9632 + 0.2608(96) = 45$$

The estimated number of copiers sold is exactly equal to the mean number of copiers sold. This simple example shows the regression line will pass through the point represented by the two means. In this case, the regression equation will pass through the point $x = 96$ and $y = 45$.

Second, as we discussed earlier in this section, there is no other line through the data where the sum of the squared deviations is smaller. To put it another way, the term $\Sigma(y - \hat{y})^2$ is smaller for the least squares regression equation than for any other equation. We use the Excel system to demonstrate this result in the following printout.

	A	B	C	D	E	F	G	H	I	J
1	Sales Rep	Sales Calls (x)	Copiers Sold (y)	Estimated Sales $\hat{y}$	$(y-\hat{y})$	$(y-\hat{y})^2$	y*	(y - y*)^2	y**	(y - y**)^2
2	Brian Virost	96	41	45.0000	-4.0000	16.0000	44.4000	11.5600	41.6000	0.3600
3	Carlos Ramirez	40	41	30.3952	10.6048	112.4618	29.0000	144.0000	29.0000	144.0000
4	Carol Saia	104	51	47.0864	3.9136	15.3163	46.6000	19.3600	43.4000	57.7600
5	Greg Fish	128	60	53.3456	6.6544	44.2810	53.2000	46.2400	48.8000	125.4400
6	Jeff Hall	164	61	62.7344	-1.7344	3.0081	63.1000	4.4100	56.9000	16.8100
7	Mark Reynolds	76	29	39.7840	-10.7840	116.2947	38.9000	98.0100	37.1000	65.6100
8	Meryl Rumsey	72	39	38.7408	0.2592	0.0672	37.8000	1.4400	36.2000	7.8400
9	Mike Kiel	80	50	40.8272	9.1728	84.1403	40.0000	100.0000	38.0000	144.0000
10	Ray Snarsky	36	28	29.3520	-1.3520	1.8279	27.9000	0.0100	28.1000	0.0100
11	Rich Niles	84	43	41.8704	1.1296	1.2760	41.1000	3.6100	38.9000	16.8100
12	Ron Broderick	180	70	66.9072	3.0928	9.5654	67.5000	6.2500	60.5000	90.2500
13	Sal Spina	132	56	54.3888	1.6112	2.5960	54.3000	2.8900	49.7000	39.6900
14	Soni Jones	120	45	51.2592	-6.2592	39.1776	51.0000	36.0000	47.0000	4.0000
15	Susan Welch	44	31	31.4384	-0.4384	0.1922	30.1000	0.8100	29.9000	1.2100
16	Tom Keller	84	30	41.8704	-11.8704	140.9064	41.1000	123.2100	38.9000	79.2100
17	Total				0.0000	587.1108		597.8000		793.0000

In Columns A, B, and C in the Excel spreadsheet above, we duplicated the sample information on sales and copiers sold from Table 13–1. In column D, we provide the estimated sales values, the $\hat{y}$ values, as calculated above.

In column E, we calculate the **residuals,** or the error values. This is the difference between the actual values and the predicted values. That is, column E is $(y - \hat{y})$. For Soni Jones,

$$\hat{y} = 19.9632 + 0.2608(120) = 51.2592$$

Her actual value is 45. So the residual, or error of estimate, is

$$(y - \hat{y}) = (45 - 51.2592) = -6.2592$$

This value reflects the amount the predicted value of sales is "off" from the actual sales value.

Next, in Column F, we square the residuals for each of the sales representatives and total the result. The total is 587.111.

$$\Sigma(y - \hat{y})^2 = 16.0000 + 112.4618 + \cdots + 140.9064 = 587.1108$$

This is the sum of the squared differences or the least squares value. There is no other line through these 15 data points where the sum of the squared differences is smaller.

We can demonstrate the least squares criterion by choosing two arbitrary equations that are close to the least squares equation and determining the sum of the squared differences for these equations. In column G, we use the equation $y^* = 18 + 0.275x$ to find the predicted value. Notice this equation is very similar to the least squares equation. In Column H, we determine the residuals and square these residuals. For the first sales representative, Brian Virost,

$$y^* = 18 + 0.275(96) = 44.4$$

$$(y - y^*)^2 = (41 - 44.4)^2 = 11.56$$

This procedure is continued for the other 14 sales representatives and the squared residuals totaled. The result is 597.8. This is a larger value (597.8 is more than 587.1108) than the residuals for the least squares line.

In columns I and J on the output, we repeat the above process for yet another equation $y^{**} = 20 + 0.225x$. Again, this equation is similar to the least squares equation. The details for Brian Virost are:

$$y^{**} = 20 + 0.225x = 20 + 0.225(96) = 41.6$$

$$(y - y^{**})^2 = (41 - 41.6)^2 = 0.36$$

This procedure is continued for the other 14 sales representatives and the residuals totaled. The result is 793, which is also larger than the least squares values.

What have we shown with the example? The sum of the squared residuals $[\Sigma(y - \hat{y})^2]$ for the least squares equation is smaller than for other selected lines. The

bottom line is you will not be able to find a line passing through these data points where the sum of the squared residuals is smaller.

SELF-REVIEW 13–3

Refer to Self-Review 13–1, where the owner of Haverty's Furniture Company was studying the relationship between sales and the amount spent on advertising. The advertising expense and sales revenue, both in millions of dollars, for the last 4 months are repeated below.

Month	Advertising Expense ($ million)	Sales Revenue ($ million)
July	2	7
August	1	3
September	3	8
October	4	10

(a) Determine the regression equation.
(b) Interpret the values of *a* and *b*.
(c) Estimate sales when $3 million is spent on advertising.

EXERCISES

For **DATA FILE**, please visit www.mhhe.com/lind16e

13. The following sample observations were randomly selected.

x:	4	5	3	6	10
y:	4	6	5	7	7

a. Determine the regression equation.
b. Determine the value of $\hat{y}$ when *x* is 7.

For **DATA FILE**, please visit www.mhhe.com/lind16e

14. The following sample observations were randomly selected.

x:	5	3	6	3	4	4	6	8
y:	13	15	7	12	13	11	9	5

a. Determine the regression equation.
b. Determine the value of $\hat{y}$ when *x* is 7.

For **DATA FILE**, please visit www.mhhe.com/lind16e

15. Bradford Electric Illuminating Company is studying the relationship between kilowatt-hours (thousands) used and the number of rooms in a private single-family residence. A random sample of 10 homes yielded the following.

Number of Rooms	Kilowatt-Hours (thousands)	Number of Rooms	Kilowatt-Hours (thousands)
12	9	8	6
9	7	10	8
14	10	10	10
6	5	5	4
10	8	7	7

a. Determine the regression equation.
b. Determine the number of kilowatt-hours, in thousands, for a six-room house.

For **DATA FILE**, please visit www.mhhe.com/lind16e

16. Mr. James McWhinney, president of Daniel-James Financial Services, believes there is a relationship between the number of client contacts and the dollar amount of sales. To document this assertion, Mr. McWhinney gathered the following sample information. The *x* column indicates the number of client contacts last month and the *y* column shows the value of sales ($ thousands) last month for each client sampled.

Number of Contacts, x	Sales ($ thousands), y	Number of Contacts, x	Sales ($ thousands), y
14	24	23	30
12	14	48	90
20	28	50	85
16	30	55	120
46	80	50	110

a. Determine the regression equation.
b. Determine the estimated sales if 40 contacts are made.

For **DATA FILE**, please visit www.mhhe.com/lind16e

17. A recent article in *Bloomberg Businessweek* listed the "Best Small Companies." We are interested in the current results of the companies' sales and earnings. A random sample of 12 companies was selected and the sales and earnings, in millions of dollars, are reported below.

Company	Sales ($ millions)	Earnings ($ millions)	Company	Sales ($ millions)	Earnings ($ millions)
Papa John's International	$89.2	$4.9	Checkmate Electronics	$17.5	$ 2.6
Applied Innovation	18.6	4.4	Royal Grip	11.9	1.7
Integracare	18.2	1.3	M-Wave	19.6	3.5
Wall Data	71.7	8.0	Serving-N-Slide	51.2	8.2
Davidson & Associates	58.6	6.6	Daig	28.6	6.0
Chico's FAS	46.8	4.1	Cobra Golf	69.2	12.8

Let sales be the independent variable and earnings be the dependent variable.
a. Draw a scatter diagram.
b. Compute the correlation coefficient.
c. Determine the regression equation.
d. For a small company with $50.0 million in sales, estimate the earnings.

For **DATA FILE**, please visit www.mhhe.com/lind16e

18. We are studying mutual bond funds for the purpose of investing in several funds. For this particular study, we want to focus on the assets of a fund and its five-year performance. The question is: Can the five-year rate of return be estimated based on the assets of the fund? Nine mutual funds were selected at random, and their assets and rates of return are shown below.

Fund	Assets ($ millions)	Return (%)	Fund	Assets ($ millions)	Return (%)
AARP High Quality Bond	$622.2	10.8	MFS Bond A	$494.5	11.6
Babson Bond L	160.4	11.3	Nichols Income	158.3	9.5
Compass Capital Fixed Income	275.7	11.4	T. Rowe Price Short-term	681.0	8.2
Galaxy Bond Retail	433.2	9.1	Thompson Income B	241.3	6.8
Keystone Custodian B-1	437.9	9.2			

a. Draw a scatter diagram.
b. Compute the correlation coefficient.
c. Write a brief report of your findings for parts (a) and (b).
d. Determine the regression equation. Use assets as the independent variable.
e. For a fund with $400.0 million in sales, determine the five-year rate of return (in percent).

19. Refer to Exercise 5. Assume the dependent variable is number of crimes.
a. Determine the regression equation.
b. Estimate the number of crimes for a city with 20 police officers.
c. Interpret the regression equation.

20. Refer to Exercise 6.
a. Determine the regression equation.
b. Estimate the selling price of a 10-year-old car.
c. Interpret the regression equation.

LO13-4
Evaluate the significance of the slope of the regression equation.

TESTING THE SIGNIFICANCE OF THE SLOPE

In the prior section, we showed how to find the equation of the regression line that best fits the data. The method for finding the equation is based on the *least squares principle.* The purpose of the regression equation is to quantify a linear relationship between two variables.

The next step is to analyze the regression equation by conducting a test of hypothesis to see if the slope of the regression line is different from zero. Why is this important? If we can show that the slope of the line in the population is different from zero, then we can conclude that using the regression equation adds to our ability to predict or forecast the dependent variable based on the independent variable. If we cannot demonstrate that this slope is different from zero, then we conclude there is no merit to using the independent variable as a predictor. To put it another way, if we cannot show the slope of the line is different from zero, we might as well use the mean of the dependent variable as a predictor, rather than use the regression equation.

Following from the hypothesis-testing procedure in Chapter 10, the null and alternative hypotheses are:

$$H_0: \beta = 0$$
$$H_1: \beta \neq 0$$

We use β (the Greek letter beta) to represent the population slope for the regression equation. This is consistent with our policy to identify population parameters by Greek letters. We assumed the information regarding North American Copier Sales, Table 13–2, is a sample. Be careful here. Remember, this is a single sample, but when we selected a particular salesperson we identified two pieces of information: how many customers they called on and how many copiers they sold. It is still a single sample, however.

We identified the slope value as b. So our computed slope b is based on a sample and is an estimate of the population's slope, identified as β. The null hypothesis is that the slope of the regression equation in the population is zero. If this is the case, the regression line is horizontal and there is no relationship between the independent variable, X, and the dependent variable, Y. In other words, the value of the dependent variable is the same for any value of the independent variable and does not offer us any help in estimating the value of the dependent variable.

What if the null hypothesis is rejected? If the null hypothesis is rejected and the alternate hypothesis accepted, this indicates that the slope of the regression line for the population is not equal to zero. That is, knowing the value of the independent variable allows us to make a better estimate of the dependent variable. To put it another way, a significant relationship exists between the two variables.

Before we test the hypothesis, we use statistical software to determine the needed regression statistics. We continue to use the North American Copier Sales data from Table 13–2 and use Excel to perform the necessary calculations. The following spreadsheet shows three tables to the right of the sample data.

	A	B	C	D	E	F	G	H	I	J
1	Sales Representative	Sales calls (x)	Copiers Sold (y)		SUMMARY OUTPUT					
2	Brian Virost	96	41							
3	Carlos Ramirez	40	41		*Regression Statistics*					
4	Carol Saia	104	51		Multiple R	0.865				
5	Greg Fish	128	60		R Square	0.748				
6	Jeff Hall	164	61		Adjusted R Square	0.728				
7	Mark Reynolds	76	29		Standard Error	6.720				
8	Meryl Rumsey	72	39		Observations	15				
9	Mike Kiel	80	50							
10	Ray Snarsky	36	28		ANOVA					
11	Rich Niles	84	43			*df*	*SS*	*MS*	*F*	*Significance F*
12	Ron Broderick	180	70		Regression	1	1738.89	1738.89	38.5031	3.19277E-05
13	Sal Spina	132	56		Residual	13	587.11	45.1623		
14	Sani Jones	120	45		Total	14	2326			
15	Susan Welch	44	31							
16	Tom Keller	84	30			*Coefficients*	*Standard Error*	*t Stat*	*P-value*	
17					Intercept	19.9800	4.389675533	4.55159	0.00054	
18					Sales calls (x)	0.2606	0.042001817	6.20509	3.2E-05	

1. Starting on the top are the *Regression Statistics.* We will use this information later in the chapter, but notice that the "Multiple R" value is familiar. It is .865, which is the correlation coefficient we calculated using formula (13–1).
2. Next is an ANOVA table. This is a useful table for summarizing regression information. We will refer to it later in this chapter and use it extensively in the next chapter when we study multiple regression.
3. At the bottom, highlighted in blue, is the information needed to conduct our test of hypothesis regarding the slope of the line. It includes the value of the slope, which is 0.2606, and the intercept, which is 19.98. (Note that these values for the slope and the intercept are slightly different from those computed on page 443. These small differences are due to rounding.) In the column to the right of the regression coefficient is a column labeled "Standard Error." This is a value similar to the standard error of the mean. Recall that the standard error of the mean reports the variation in the sample means. In a similar fashion, these standard errors report the possible variation in slope and intercept values. The standard error of the slope coefficient is 0.0420.

To test the null hypothesis, we use the t-distribution with $(n - 2)$ and the following formula.

TEST FOR THE SLOPE

$$t = \frac{b - 0}{s_b} \quad \text{with } n - 2 \text{ degrees of freedom} \qquad \textbf{[13–6]}$$

where:

b is the estimate of the regression line's slope calculated from the sample information.

s_b is the standard error of the slope estimate, also determined from sample information.

Our first step is to set the null and the alternative hypotheses. They are:

$$H_0: \beta \leq 0$$
$$H_1: \beta > 0$$

Notice that we have a one-tailed test. If we do not reject the null hypothesis, we conclude that the slope of the regression line in the population could be zero. This means the independent variable is of no value in improving our estimate of the dependent variable. In our case, this means that knowing the number of sales calls made by a representative does not help us predict the sales.

If we reject the null hypothesis and accept the alternative, we conclude the slope of the line is greater than zero. Hence, the independent variable is an aid in predicting the dependent variable. Thus, if we know the number of sales calls made by a representative, this will help us forecast that representative's sales. We also know, because we have demonstrated that the slope of the line is greater than zero—that is, positive—that more sales calls will result in the sale of more copiers.

The t-distribution is the test statistic; there are 13 degrees of freedom, found by $n - 2 = 15 - 2$. We use the .05 significance level. From Appendix B.5, the critical value is 1.771. Our decision rule is to reject the null hypothesis if the value computed from formula (13–6) is greater than 1.771. We apply formula (13–6) to find t.

$$t = \frac{b - 0}{s_b} = \frac{0.2606 - 0}{0.042} = 6.205$$

The computed value of 6.205 exceeds our critical value of 1.771, so we reject the null hypothesis and accept the alternative hypothesis. We conclude that the slope of the line is greater than zero. The independent variable, number of sales calls, is useful in estimating copier sales.

The table also provides us information on the *p*-value of this test. This cell is highlighted in purple. So we could select a significance level, say .05, and compare that value with the *p*-value. In this case, the calculated *p*-value in the table is reported in exponential notation and is equal to 0.0000319, so our decision is to reject the null hypothesis. An important caution is that the *p*-values reported in the statistical software are usually for a two-*tailed test.*

Before moving on, here is an interesting note. Observe that on page 439, when we conducted a test of hypothesis regarding the correlation coefficient for these same data using formula (13–2), we obtained the same value of the *t*-statistic, $t = 6.205$. Actually, when comparing the results of simple linear regression and correlation analysis, the two tests are equivalent and will always yield exactly the same values of *t* and the same *p*-values.

SELF-REVIEW 13–4

Refer to Self-Review 13–1, where the owner of Haverty's Furniture Company studied the relationship between the amount spent on advertising in a month and sales revenue for that month. The amount of sales is the dependent variable and advertising expense, the independent variable. The regression equation in that study was $\hat{y} = 1.5 + 2.2x$ for a sample of 5 months. Conduct a test of hypothesis to show there is a positive relationship between advertising and sales. From statistical software, the standard error of the regression coefficient is 0.42. Use the .05 significance level.

EXERCISES

21. Refer to Exercise 5. The regression equation is $\hat{y} = 29.29 - 0.96x$, the sample size is 8, and the standard error of the slope is 0.22. Use the .05 significance level. Can we conclude that the slope of the regression line is less than zero?

22. Refer to Exercise 6. The regression equation is $\hat{y} = 11.18 - 0.49x$, the sample size is 12, and the standard error of the slope is 0.23. Use the .05 significance level. Can we conclude that the slope of the regression line is less than zero?

23. Refer to Exercise 17. The regression equation is $\hat{y} = 1.85 + .08x$, the sample size is 12, and the standard error of the slope is 0.03. Use the .05 significance level. Can we conclude that the slope of the regression line is *different from zero*?

24. Refer to Exercise 18. The regression equation is $\hat{y} = 9.9198 - 0.00039x$, the sample size is 9, and the standard error of the slope is 0.0032. Use the .05 significance level. Can we conclude that the slope of the regression line is less than zero?

LO13-5
Evaluate a regression equation's ability to predict using the standard estimate of the error and the coefficient of determination.

EVALUATING A REGRESSION EQUATION'S ABILITY TO PREDICT

The Standard Error of Estimate

The results of the regression analysis for North American Copier Sales show a significant relationship between number of sales calls and the number of sales made. By substituting the names of the variables into the equation, it can be written as:

$$\text{Number of copiers sold} = 19.9632 + 0.2608\ (\text{Number of sales calls})$$

The equation can be used to estimate the number of copiers sold for any given "number of sales calls" within the range of the data. For example, if the number of sales calls is 84, then we can predict the number of copiers sold. It is 41.8704, found by 19.9632 + 0.2608(84). However, the data show two sales representatives with 84 sales calls and 30 and 43 copiers sold. So, is the regression equation a good predictor of "Number of copiers sold"?

Perfect prediction, which is finding the exact outcome, is practically impossible in almost all disciplines including economics and business. For example:

- A large electronics firm, with production facilities throughout the United States, has a stock option plan for employees. Suppose there is a relationship between the number of years employed and the number of shares owned. This relationship is likely because, as number of years of service increases, the number of shares an employee earns also increases. If we observe all employees with 20 years of service, they would most likely own different numbers of shares.
- A real estate developer in the southwest United States studied the relationship between the income of buyers and the size, in square feet, of the home they purchased. The developer's analysis shows that as the income of a purchaser increases, the size of the home purchased will also increase. However, all buyers with an income of $70,000 will not purchase a home of exactly the same size.

What is needed, then, is a measure that describes how precise the prediction of Y is based on X or, conversely, how inaccurate the estimate might be. This measure is called the **standard error of estimate.** The standard error of estimate is symbolized by $s_{y \cdot x}$. The subscript, $y \cdot x$, is interpreted as the standard error of y for a given value of x. It is the same concept as the standard deviation discussed in Chapter 3. The standard deviation measures the dispersion around the mean. The standard error of estimate measures the dispersion about the regression line for a given value of x.

STANDARD ERROR OF ESTIMATE A measure of the dispersion, or scatter, of the observed values around the line of regression for a given value of x.

The standard error of estimate is found using formula (13–7).

STANDARD ERROR OF ESTIMATE

$$s_{y \cdot x} = \sqrt{\frac{\Sigma(y - \hat{y})^2}{n - 2}} \quad [13\text{–}7]$$

The calculation of the standard error of estimate requires the sum of the squared differences between each observed value of y and the predicted value of y, which is identified as $\hat{y}$ in the numerator. This calculation is illustrated in the spreadsheet on page 445. See cell G13 in the spreadsheet. It is a very important value. It is the numerator in the calculation of the standard error of estimate.

$$s_{y \cdot x} = \sqrt{\frac{\Sigma(y - \hat{y})^2}{n - 2}} = \sqrt{\frac{587.11}{15 - 2}} = 6.720$$

The standard error of estimate can be calculated using statistical software such as Excel. It is included in Excel's regression analysis and highlighted in yellow on page 448. Its value is 6.720.

If the standard error of estimate is small, this indicates that the data are relatively close to the regression line and the regression equation can be used to predict y with little error. If the standard error of estimate is large, this indicates that the data are widely scattered around the regression line and the regression equation will not provide a precise estimate of y.

The Coefficient of Determination

Using the standard error of estimate provides a relative measure of a regression equation's ability to predict. We will use it to provide more specific information about a

prediction in the next section. In this section, another statistic is explained that will provide a more interpretable measure of a regression equation's ability to predict. It is called the coefficient of determination, or R-square.

> **COEFFICIENT OF DETERMINATION** The proportion of the total variation in the dependent variable Y that is explained, or accounted for, by the variation in the independent variable X.

The coefficient of determination is easy to compute. It is the correlation coefficient squared. Therefore, the term R-square is also used. With the North American Copier Sales data, the correlation coefficient for the relationship between the number of copiers sold and the number of sales calls is 0.865. If we compute $(0.865)^2$, the coefficient of determination is 0.748. See the blue (Multiple R) and green (R-square) highlighted cells in the spreadsheet on page 448. To better interpret the coefficient of determination, convert it to a percentage. Hence, we say that 74.8% of the variation in the number of copiers sold is explained, or accounted for, by the variation in the number of sales calls.

How well can the regression equation predict number of copiers sold with number of sales calls made? If it were possible to make perfect predictions, the coefficient of determination would be 100%. That would mean that the independent variable, number of sales calls, explains or accounts for all the variation in the number of copiers sold. A coefficient of determination of 100% is associated with a correlation coefficient of $+1.0$ or -1.0. Refer to Chart 13–2, which shows that a perfect prediction is associated with a perfect linear relationship where all the data points form a perfect line in a scatter diagram. Our analysis shows that only 74.8% of the variation in copiers sold is explained by the number of sales calls. Clearly, these data do not form a perfect line. Instead, the data are scattered around the best-fitting, least squares regression line, and there will be error in the predictions. In the next section, the standard error of estimate is used to provide more specific information regarding the error associated with using the regression equation to make predictions.

SELF-REVIEW 13–5

Refer to Self-Review 13–1, where the owner of Haverty's Furniture Company studied the relationship between the amount spent on advertising in a month and sales revenue for that month. The amount of sales is the dependent variable and advertising expense is the independent variable.

(a) Determine the standard error of estimate.
(b) Determine the coefficient of determination.
(c) Interpret the coefficient of determination.

EXERCISES

(You may wish to use a software package such as Excel, Minitab, or Megastat to assist in your calculations.)

25. Refer to Exercise 5. Determine the standard error of estimate and the coefficient of determination. Interpret the coefficient of determination.

26. Refer to Exercise 6. Determine the standard error of estimate and the coefficient of determination. Interpret the coefficient of determination.

27. Refer to Exercise 15. Determine the standard error of estimate and the coefficient of determination. Interpret the coefficient of determination.

28. Refer to Exercise 16. Determine the standard error of estimate and the coefficient of determination. Interpret the coefficient of determination.

Relationships among the Correlation Coefficient, the Coefficient of Determination, and the Standard Error of Estimate

On page 451, we described the standard error of estimate. Recall that it measures how close the actual values are to the regression line. When the standard error is small, it indicates that the two variables are closely related. In the calculation of the standard error, the key term is

$$\Sigma(y - \hat{y})^2$$

If the value of this term is small, then the standard error will also be small.

The correlation coefficient measures the strength of the linear association between two variables. When the points on the scatter diagram appear close to the line, we note that the correlation coefficient tends to be large. Therefore, the correlation coefficient and the standard error of the estimate are inversely related. As the strength of a linear relationship between two variables increases, the correlation coefficient increases and the standard error of the estimate decreases.

We also noted that the square of the correlation coefficient is the coefficient of determination. The coefficient of determination measures the percentage of the variation in *Y* that is explained by the variation in *X*.

A convenient vehicle for showing the relationship among these three measures is an ANOVA table. See the highlighted portion of the spreadsheet below. This table is similar to the analysis of variance table developed in Chapter 12. In that chapter, the total variation was divided into two components: variation due to the *treatments* and that due to *random error.* The concept is similar in regression analysis. The total variation is divided into two components: (1) variation explained by the *regression* (explained by the independent variable) and (2) the *error,* or *residual.* This is the unexplained variation. These three sources of variance (total, regression, and residual) are identified in the first column of the spreadsheet ANOVA table. The column headed "*df*" refers to the degrees of freedom associated with each category. The total number of degrees of freedom is $n - 1$. The number of degrees of freedom in the regression is 1 because there is only one independent variable. The number of degrees of freedom associated with the error term is $n - 2$. The term SS located in the middle of the ANOVA table refers to the sum of squares. You should note that the total degrees of freedom are equal to the sum of the regression and residual (error) degrees of freedom, and the total sum of squares is equal to the sum of the regression and residual (error) sum of squares. This is true for any ANOVA table.

	A	B	C
1	Sales Representive	Sales Calls (x)	Copiers Sold (y)
2	Brian Virost	96	41
3	Carlos Ramirez	40	41
4	Carol Saia	104	51
5	Greg Fish	128	60
6	Jeff Hall	164	61
7	Mark Reynolds	76	29
8	Meryl Rumsey	72	39
9	Mike Kiel	80	50
10	Ray Snarsky	36	28
11	Rich Niles	84	43
12	Ron Broderick	180	70
13	Sal Spina	132	56
14	Sani Jones	120	45
15	Susan Welch	44	31
16	Tom Keller	84	30
17			
18			

SUMMARY OUTPUT

Regression Statistics	
Multiple R	0.865
R Square	0.748
Adjusted R Square	0.728
Standard Error	6.720
Observations	15

ANOVA

	df	SS	MS	F	Significance F
Regression	1	1738.89	1738.89	38.50312548	3.19277E-05
Residual	13	587.11	45.162308		
Total	14	2326			

	Coefficients	*Standard Error*	*t Stat*	*P-value*
Intercept	19.9800	4.389675533	4.5515893	0.000543565
Sales Calls (X)	0.2606	0.042001817	6.2050887	3.19277E-05

The ANOVA sum of squares are:

$$\text{Regression Sum of Squares} = \text{SSR} = \Sigma(\hat{y} - \bar{y})^2 = 1738.89$$

$$\text{Residual or Error Sum of Squares} = \text{SSE} = \Sigma(y - \hat{y})^2 = 587.11$$

$$\text{Total Sum of Squares} = \text{SS Total} = \Sigma(y - \bar{y})^2 = 2326.0$$

Recall that the coefficient of determination is defined as the percentage of the total variation (SS Total) explained by the regression equation (SSR). Using the ANOVA table, the reported value of R-square can be validated.

COEFFICIENT OF DETERMINATION $$r^2 = \frac{\text{SSR}}{\text{SS Total}} = 1 - \frac{\text{SSE}}{\text{SS Total}} \quad \textbf{[13–8]}$$

Using the values from the ANOVA table, the coefficient of determination is 1738.89/2326.0 = 0.748. Therefore, the more variation of the dependent variable (SS Total) explained by the independent variable (SSR), the higher the coefficient of determination.

We can also express the coefficient of determination in terms of the error or residual variation:

$$r^2 = 1 - \frac{\text{SSE}}{\text{SS Total}} = 1 - \frac{587.11}{2326.0} = 1 - 0.252 = 0.748$$

As illustrated in formula 13–8, the coefficient of determination and the residual or error sum of squares are inversely related. The higher the unexplained or error variation as a percentage of the total variation, the lower is the coefficient of determination. In this case, 25.2% of the total variation in the dependent variable is error or residual variation.

The final observation that relates the correlation coefficient, the coefficient of determination, and the standard error of estimate is to show the relationship between the standard error of estimate and SSE. By substituting [SSE Residual or Error Sum of Squares = SSE = $\Sigma(y - \hat{y})^2$] into the formula for the standard error of estimate, we find:

STANDARD ERROR OF ESTIMATE $$s_{y \cdot x} = \sqrt{\frac{\text{SSE}}{n - 2}} \quad \textbf{[13–9]}$$

In sum, regression analysis provides two statistics to evaluate the predictive ability of a regression equation: the standard error of the estimate and the coefficient of determination. When reporting the results of a regression analysis, the findings must be clearly explained, especially when using the results to make predictions of the dependent variable. The report must always include a statement regarding the coefficient of determination so that the relative precision of the prediction is known to the reader of the report. Objective reporting of statistical analysis is required so that the readers can make their own decisions.

EXERCISES

29. Given the following ANOVA table:

Source	*DF*	SS	MS	*F*
Regression	1	1000.0	1000.0	26.00
Error	13	500.0	38.46	
Total	14	1500.0		

a. Determine the coefficient of determination.

b. Assuming a direct relationship between the variables, what is the correlation coefficient?

c. Determine the standard error of estimate.

30. On the first statistics exam, the coefficient of determination between the hours studied and the grade earned was 80%. The standard error of estimate was 10. There were 20 students in the class. Develop an ANOVA table for the regression analysis of hours studied as a predictor of the grade earned on the first statistics exam.

LO13-6

Calculate and interpret confidence and prediction intervals.

STATISTICS IN ACTION

Studies indicate that for both men and women, those who are considered good looking earn higher wages than those who are not. In addition, for men there is a correlation between height and salary. For each additional inch of height, a man can expect to earn an additional $250 per year. So a man 6′6″ tall receives a $3,000 "stature" bonus over his 5′6″ counterpart. Being overweight or underweight is also related to earnings, particularly among women. A study of young women showed the heaviest 10% earned about 6% less than their lighter counterparts.

INTERVAL ESTIMATES OF PREDICTION

The standard error of estimate and the coefficient of determination are two statistics that provide an overall evaluation of the ability of a regression equation to predict a dependent variable. Another way to report the ability of a regression equation to predict is specific to a stated value of the independent variable. For example, we can predict the number of copiers sold (y) for a selected value of number of sales calls made (x). In fact, we can calculate a confidence interval for the predicted value of the dependent variable for a selected value of the independent variable.

Assumptions Underlying Linear Regression

Before we present the confidence intervals, the assumptions for properly applying linear regression should be reviewed. Chart 13–13 illustrates these assumptions.

1. For each value of x, there are corresponding y values. These y values follow the normal distribution.
2. The means of these normal distributions lie on the regression line.
3. The standard deviations of these normal distributions are all the same. The best estimate we have of this common standard deviation is the standard error of estimate ($s_{y \cdot x}$).
4. The y values are statistically independent. This means that in selecting a sample, a particular x does not depend on any other value of x. This assumption is particularly important when data are collected over a period of time. In such situations, the errors for a particular time period are often correlated with those of other time periods.

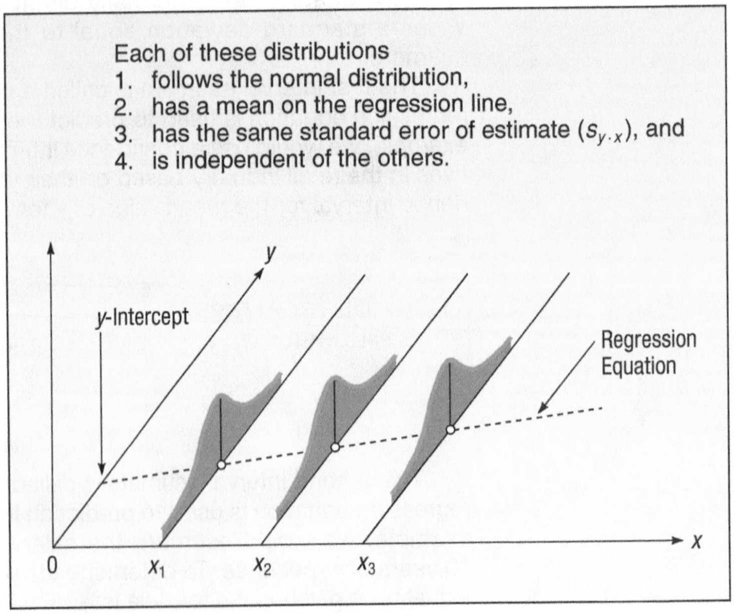

CHART 13–13 Regression Assumptions Shown Graphically

Recall from Chapter 7 that if the values follow a normal distribution, then the mean plus or minus one standard deviation will encompass 68% of the observations, the mean plus or minus two standard deviations will encompass 95% of the observations,

and the mean plus or minus three standard deviations will encompass virtually all of the observations. The same relationship exists between the predicted values $\hat{y}$ and the standard error of estimate ($s_{y \cdot x}$).

1. $\hat{y} \pm s_{y \cdot x}$ will include the middle 68% of the observations.
2. $\hat{y} \pm 2s_{y \cdot x}$ will include the middle 95% of the observations.
3. $\hat{y} \pm 3s_{y \cdot x}$ will include virtually all the observations.

We can now relate these assumptions to North American Copier Sales, where we studied the relationship between the number of sales calls and the number of copiers sold. If we drew a parallel line 6.72 units above the regression line and another 6.72 units below the regression line, about 68% of the points would fall between the two lines. Similarly, a line 13.44[$2s_{y \cdot x} = 2(6.72)$] units above the regression line and another 13.44 units below the regression line should include about 95% of the data values.

As a rough check, refer to column E in the Excel spreadsheet on page 445. Four of the 15 deviations exceed one standard error of estimate. That is, the deviations of Carlos Ramirez, Mark Reynolds, Mike Keil, and Tom Keller all exceed 6.72 (one standard error). All values are less than 13.44 units away from the regression line. In short, 11 of the 15 deviations are within one standard error and all are within two standard errors. That is a fairly good result for a relatively small sample.

Constructing Confidence and Prediction Intervals

When using a regression equation, two different predictions can be made for a selected value of the independent variable. The differences are subtle but very important and are related to the assumptions stated in the last section. Recall that for any selected value of the independent variable (X), the dependent variable (Y) is a random variable that is normally distributed with a mean $\hat{Y}$. Each distribution of Y has a standard deviation equal to the regression analysis's standard error of estimate.

The first interval estimate is called a **confidence interval.** This is used when the regression equation is used to predict the mean value of Y for a given value of x. For example, we would use a confidence interval to estimate the mean salary of all executives in the retail industry based on their years of experience. To determine the confidence interval for the mean value of y for a given x, the formula is:

CONFIDENCE INTERVAL FOR THE MEAN OF *Y*, GIVEN *X*

$$\hat{y} \pm t s_{y \cdot x}\sqrt{\frac{1}{n} + \frac{(x - \bar{x})^2}{\Sigma(x - \bar{x})^2}} \qquad \textbf{[13–10]}$$

The second interval estimate is called a prediction interval. This is used when the regression equation is used to predict an individual y ($n = 1$) for a given value of x. For example, we would estimate the salary of a particular retail executive who has 20 years of experience. To determine the prediction interval for an estimate of an individual for a given x, the formula is:

PREDICTION INTERVAL FOR *Y*, GIVEN *X*

$$\hat{y} \pm t s_{y \cdot x}\sqrt{1 + \frac{1}{n} + \frac{(x - \bar{x})^2}{\Sigma(x - \bar{x})^2}} \qquad \textbf{[13–11]}$$

EXAMPLE

We return to the North American Copier Sales illustration. Determine a 95% confidence interval for all sales representatives who make 50 calls, and determine a prediction interval for Sheila Baker, a West Coast sales representative who made 50 calls.

SOLUTION

We use formula (13–10) to determine a confidence level. Table 13–4 includes the necessary totals and a repeat of the information of Table 13–2 on page 431.

TABLE 13–4 Determining Confidence and Prediction Intervals

Sales Representative	Sales Calls (x)	Copiers Sold (y)	$(x - \bar{x})$	$(x - \bar{x})^2$
Brian Virost	96	41	0	0
Carlos Ramirez	40	41	−56	3,136
Carol Saia	104	51	8	64
Greg Fish	128	60	32	1,024
Jeff Hall	164	61	68	4,624
Mark Reynolds	76	29	−20	400
Meryl Rumsey	72	39	−24	576
Mike Kiel	80	50	−16	256
Ray Snarsky	36	28	−60	3,600
Rich Niles	84	43	−12	144
Ron Broderick	180	70	84	7,056
Sal Spina	132	56	36	1,296
Sani Jones	120	45	24	576
Susan Welch	44	31	−52	2,704
Tom Keller	84	30	−12	144
Total	1440	675	0	25,600

The first step is to determine the number of copiers we expect a sales representative to sell if he or she makes 50 calls. It is 33.0032, found by

$$\hat{y} = 19.9632 + 0.2608x = 19.9632 + 0.2608(50) = 33.0032$$

To find the t value, we need to first know the number of degrees of freedom. In this case, the degrees of freedom are $n - 2 = 15 - 2 = 13$. We set the confidence level at 95%. To find the value of t, move down the left-hand column of Appendix B.5 to 13 degrees of freedom, then move across to the column with the 95% level of confidence. The value of t is 2.160.

In the previous section, we calculated the standard error of estimate to be 6.720. We let $x = 50$, and from Table 13–4, the mean number of sales calls is 96.0 (1440/15) and $\Sigma(x - \bar{x})^2 = 25{,}600$. Inserting these values in formula (13–10), we can determine the confidence interval.

$$\text{Confidence Interval} = \hat{y} \pm ts_{y \cdot x}\sqrt{\frac{1}{n} + \frac{(x - \bar{x})^2}{\Sigma(x - \bar{x})^2}}$$

$$= 33.0032 \pm 2.160(6.720)\sqrt{\frac{1}{15} + \frac{(50 - 96)^2}{25{,}600}}$$

$$= 33.0032 \pm 5.6090$$

Thus, the 95% confidence interval for all sales representatives who make 50 calls is from 27.3942 up to 38.6122. To interpret, let's round the values. If a sales representative makes 50 calls, he or she can expect to sell 33 copiers. It is likely the sales will range from 27.4 to 38.6 copiers.

Suppose we want to estimate the number of copiers sold by Sheila Baker, who made 50 sales calls. The 95% prediction interval is determined as follows:

$$\text{Prediction Interval} = \hat{y} \pm ts_{y\cdot x}\sqrt{1 + \frac{1}{n} + \frac{(x - \bar{x})^2}{\Sigma(x - \bar{x})^2}}$$

$$= 33.0032 \pm 2.160(6.720)\sqrt{1 + \frac{1}{15} + \frac{(50 - 96)^2}{25{,}600}}$$

$$= 33.0032 \pm 15.5612$$

Thus, the interval is from 17.442 up to 48.5644 copiers. We conclude that the number of office machines sold will be between about 17.4 and 48.6 for a particular sales representative, such as Sheila Baker, who makes 50 calls. This interval is quite large. It is much larger than the confidence interval for all sales representatives who made 50 calls. It is logical, however, that there should be more variation in the sales estimate for an individual than for a group.

The following Minitab graph shows the relationship between the least squares regression line (in the center), the confidence interval (shown in crimson), and the prediction interval (shown in green). The bands for the prediction interval are always further from the regression line than those for the confidence interval. Also, as the values of x move away from the mean number of calls (96) in either direction, the confidence interval and prediction interval bands widen. This is caused by the numerator of the right-hand term under the radical in formulas (13–10) and (13–11). That is, as the term increases, the widths of the confidence interval and the prediction interval also increase. To put it another way, there is less precision in our estimates as we move away, in either direction, from the mean of the independent variable.

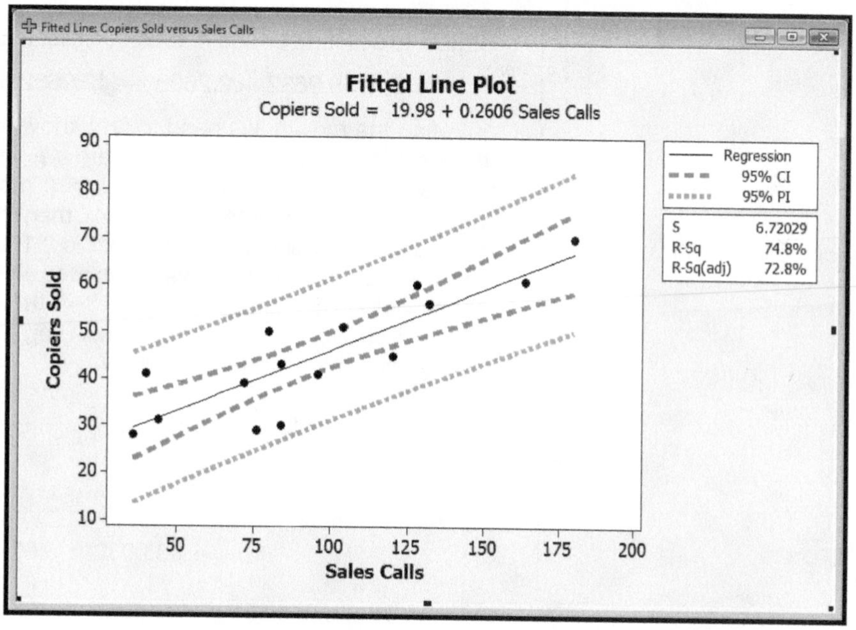

We wish to emphasize again the distinction between a confidence interval and a prediction interval. A confidence interval refers to the mean of all cases for a given value of x and is computed by formula (13–10). A prediction interval refers to a particular, single case for a given value of x and is computed using formula (13–11). The prediction interval will always be wider because of the extra 1 under the radical in the second equation.

SELF-REVIEW 13–6

Refer to the sample data in Self-Review 13–1, where the owner of Haverty's Furniture was studying the relationship between sales and the amount spent on advertising. The advertising expense and sales revenue, both in millions of dollars, for the last 4 months are repeated below.

Month	Advertising Expense ($ million)	Sales Revenue ($ million)
July	2	7
August	1	3
September	3	8
October	4	10

The regression equation was computed to be $\hat{y} = 1.5 + 2.2x$, and the standard error 0.9487. Both variables are reported in millions of dollars. Determine the 90% confidence interval for the typical month in which \$3 million was spent on advertising.

EXERCISES

31. Refer to Exercise 13.
   a. Determine the .95 confidence interval for the mean predicted when $x = 7$.
   b. Determine the .95 prediction interval for an individual predicted when $x = 7$.

32. Refer to Exercise 14.
   a. Determine the .95 confidence interval for the mean predicted when $x = 7$.
   b. Determine the .95 prediction interval for an individual predicted when $x = 7$.

33. Refer to Exercise 15.
   a. Determine the .95 confidence interval, in thousands of kilowatt-hours, for the mean of all six-room homes.
   b. Determine the .95 prediction interval, in thousands of kilowatt-hours, for a particular six-room home.

34. Refer to Exercise 16.
   a. Determine the .95 confidence interval, in thousands of dollars, for the mean of all sales personnel who make 40 contacts.
   b. Determine the .95 prediction interval, in thousands of dollars, for a particular salesperson who makes 40 contacts.

LO13-7
Use a log function to transform a nonlinear relationship.

TRANSFORMING DATA

Regression analysis describes the relationship between two variables. A requirement is that this relationship be linear. The same is true of the correlation coefficient. It measures the strength of a linear relationship between two variables. But what if the relationship is not linear? The remedy is to rescale one or both of the variables so the new relationship is linear. For example, instead of using the actual values of the dependent variable, y, we would create a new dependent variable by computing the log to the base 10 of y, Log(y). This calculation is called a transformation. Other common

transformations include taking the square root, taking the reciprocal, or squaring one or both of the variables.

Thus, two variables could be closely related, but their relationship is not linear. Be cautious when you are interpreting the correlation coefficient or a regression equation. These statistics may indicate there is no linear relationship, but there could be a relationship of some other nonlinear or curvilinear form. The following example explains the details.

EXAMPLE

GroceryLand Supermarkets is a regional grocery chain with over 300 stores located in the midwestern United States. The corporate director of marketing for GroceryLand wishes to study the effect of price on the weekly sales of two-liter bottles of their private-brand diet cola. The objectives of the study are:

1. To determine whether there is a relationship between selling price and weekly sales. Is this relationship direct or indirect? Is it strong or weak?
2. To determine the effect of price increases or decreases on sales. Can we effectively forecast sales based on the price?

SOLUTION

To begin the project, the marketing director meets with the vice president of sales and other company staff members. They decide that it would be reasonable to price the two-liter bottle of their private-brand diet cola from $0.50 up to $2.00. To collect the data needed to analyze the relationship between price and sales, the marketing director selects a random sample of 20 stores and then randomly assigns a selling price for the two-liter bottle of diet cola between $0.50 and $2.00 to each selected store. The director contacts each of the 20 store managers included in the study to tell them the selling price and ask them to report the sales for the product at the end of the week. The results are reported below. For example, store number 17 sold 181 two-liter bottles of diet cola at $0.50 each.

GroceryLand Sales and Price Data

Store Number	Price	Sales
17	0.50	181
121	1.35	33
227	0.79	91
135	1.71	13
6	1.38	34
282	1.22	47
172	1.03	73
296	1.84	11
143	1.73	15
66	1.62	20

GroceryLand Sales and Price Data

Store Number	Price	Sales
30	0.76	91
127	1.79	13
266	1.57	22
117	1.27	34
132	0.96	74
120	0.52	164
272	0.64	129
120	1.05	55
194	0.72	107
105	0.75	119

To examine the relationship between Price and Sales, we use regression analysis setting *Price* as the independent variable and *Sales* as the dependent

variable. The analysis will provide important information about the relationship between the variables. The analysis is summarized in the following Minitab output.

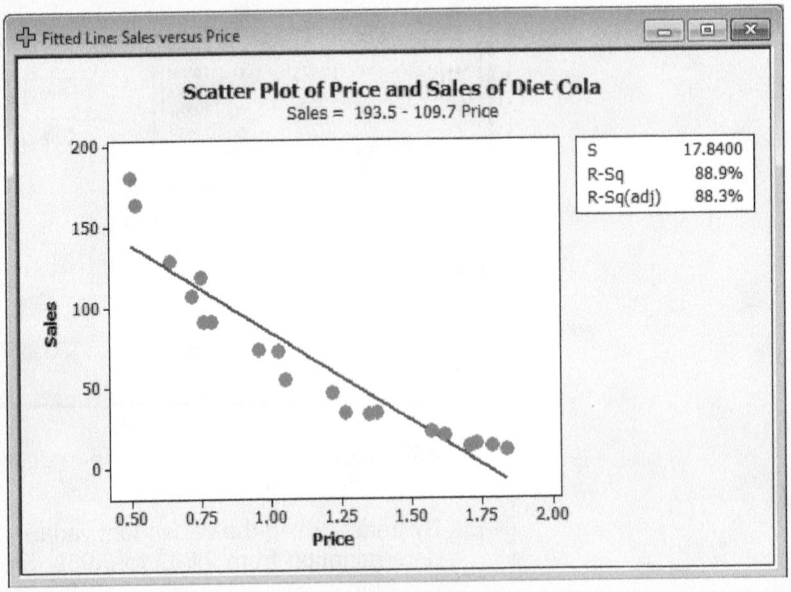

From the output, we can make these conclusions:

1. The relationship between the two variables is inverse or indirect. As the *Price* of the cola increases, the *Sales* of the product decreases. Given basic economic theory of price and demand, this is expected.
2. There is a strong relationship between the two variables. The coefficient of determination is 88.9%. So 88.9% of the variation in *Sales* is accounted for by the variation in *Price*. From the coefficient of determination, we can compute the correlation coefficient as the square root of the coefficient of determination. The correlation coefficient is the square root of 0.889, or 0.943. The sign of the correlation coefficient is negative because sales are inversely related to price. Therefore, the correlation coefficient is −0.943.
3. Before continuing our summary of conclusions, we should look carefully at the scatter diagram and the plot of the regression line. The assumption of a linear relationship is tenuous. If the relationship is linear, the data points should be distributed both above and below the line over the entire range of the independent variable. However, for the highest and lowest prices, the data points are above the regression line. For the selling prices in the middle, most of the data points are below the regression line. So the linear regression equation does not effectively describe the relationship between *Price* and *Sales.* A transformation of the data is needed to create a linear relationship.

By transforming one of the variables, we may be able to change the nonlinear relationship between the variables to a linear relationship. Of the possible choices, the director of marketing decides to transform the dependent variable, *Sales,* by taking the logarithm to the base 10 of each *Sales* value. Note the new variable, *Log-Sales,* in the following analysis. Now, the regression

analysis uses *Log-Sales* as the dependent variable and *Price* as the independent variable. This analysis is reported below.

Groceryland.MTW ***

↓	C1 Store Number	C2 Price	C3 Sales	C4 Log-Sales
1	17	0.50	181	2.25768
2	121	1.35	33	1.51851
3	227	0.79	91	1.95904
4	135	1.71	13	1.11394
5	6	1.38	34	1.53148
6	282	1.22	47	1.67210
7	172	1.03	73	1.86332
8	296	1.84	11	1.04139
9	143	1.73	15	1.17609
10	66	1.62	20	1.30103
11	30	0.76	91	1.95904
12	127	1.79	13	1.11394
13	266	1.57	22	1.34242
14	117	1.27	34	1.53148
15	132	0.96	74	1.86923
16	120	0.52	164	2.21484
17	272	0.64	129	2.11059
18	120	1.05	55	1.74036
19	194	0.72	107	2.02938
20	105	0.75	119	2.07555

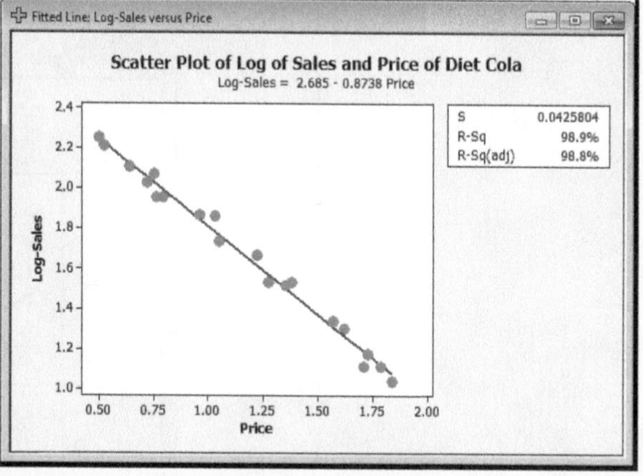

What can we conclude from the regression analysis using the transformation of the dependent variable *Sales?*

1. By transforming the dependent variable, *Sales,* we increase the coefficient of determination from 0.889 to 0.989. So *Price* now explains nearly all of the variation in *Log-Sales.*
2. Compare this result with the scatter diagram before we transformed the dependent variable. The transformed data seem to fit the linear relationship requirement much better. Observe that the data points are both above and below the regression line over the range of *Price.*
3. The regression equation is $\hat{y} = 2.685 - 0.8738x$. The sign of the slope value is negative, confirming the inverse association between the variables. We can use the new equation to estimate sales and study the effect of changes in price. For example, if we decided to sell the two-liter bottle of diet cola for \$1.25, the predicted *Log-Sales* is:

$$\hat{y} = 2.685 - 0.8738x = 2.685 - 0.8738(1.25) = 1.593$$

Remember that the regression equation now predicts the log, base10, of *Sales.* Therefore, we must undo the transformation by taking the antilog of 1.593, which is $10^{1.593}$, or 39.174. So, if we price the two-liter diet cola product at \$1.25, the predicted weekly sales are 39 bottles. If we increase the price to \$2.00, the regression equation would predict a value of .9374. Taking the antilog, $10^{.9374}$, the predicted sales decrease to 8.658, or, rounding, 9 two-liter bottles per week. Clearly, as price increases, sales decrease. This relationship will be very helpful to GroceryLand when making pricing decisions for this product.

EXERCISES

35. Given the following sample of five observations, develop a scatter diagram, using *x* as the independent variable and *y* as the dependent variable, and compute the correlation coefficient. Does the relationship between the variables appear to be linear? Try squaring the *x* variable and then develop a scatter diagram and determine the correlation coefficient. Summarize your analysis.

x	−8	−16	12	2	18
y	58	247	153	3	341

For **DATA FILE**, please visit www.mhhe.com/lind16e

36. Every April, The Masters—one of the most prestigious golf tournaments on the PGA golf tour—is played in Augusta, Georgia. In 2013, 60 players received prize money. The 2013 winner, Adam Scott of Australia, earned a prize of $1,440,000. Miguel Cabrera finished in second place, earning $864,000. Jason Day finished in third place, earning $544,000. The data are briefly summarized below. Each player has three corresponding variables: finishing position or rank, score, and prize (in dollars). The complete file is in the data sets available on the text website, www.mhhe.com/lind16e, labeled as Ex13-36. We want to study the relationship between score and prize.

Position	Player	Score	Prize
1	Scott	279	$1,440,000
2	Cabrera	279	$864,000
3	Day	281	$544,000
Tied 4	Woods	283	$352,000
Tied 4	Leishman	283	$352,000
.	.	.	.
.	.	.	.
Tied 54	Bradley	297	$18,320
Tied 54	Lyle	297	$18,320
Tied 54	Mickelson	297	$18,320
Tied 54	Piercy	297	$18,320
58	Na	301	$17,920
59	Peterson	302	$17,760
60	Pettersson	304	$17,600

a. Using *Score* as the independent variable and *Prize* as the dependent variable, develop a scatter diagram. Does the relationship appear to be linear? Does it seem reasonable that as *Score* increases the *Prize* decreases?
b. What percentage of the variation in the dependent variable, *Prize,* is accounted for by the independent variable, *Score*?
c. Calculate a new variable, *Log-Prize*, computing the log to the base 10 of *Prize*. Draw a scatter diagram with *Log-Prize* as the dependent variable and *Score* as the independent variable.
d. Develop a regression equation and compute the coefficient of determination using *Log-Prize* as the dependent variable.
e. Compare the coefficient of determination in parts (b) and (d). What do you conclude?
f. Write out the regression equation developed in part (d). If a player shot a total of 280 for the four rounds, how much would you expect that player to earn?

CHAPTER SUMMARY

I. A scatter diagram is a graphic tool to portray the relationship between two variables.
- **A.** The dependent variable is scaled on the *Y*-axis and is the variable being estimated.
- **B.** The independent variable is scaled on the *X*-axis and is the variable used as the predictor.

II. The correlation coefficient measures the strength of the linear association between two variables.
- **A.** Both variables must be at least the interval scale of measurement.
- **B.** The correlation coefficient can range from −1.00 to 1.00.
- **C.** If the correlation between the two variables is 0, there is no association between them.
- **D.** A value of 1.00 indicates perfect positive correlation, and a value of −1.00 indicates perfect negative correlation.

E. A positive sign means there is a direct relationship between the variables, and a negative sign means there is an inverse relationship.
F. It is designated by the letter r and found by the following equation:

$$r = \frac{\Sigma(x - \bar{x})(y - \bar{y})}{(n - 1)s_x s_y} \quad \textbf{[13–1]}$$

G. To test a hypothesis that a population correlation is different from 0, we use the following statistic:

$$t = \frac{r\sqrt{n - 2}}{\sqrt{1 - r^2}} \quad \text{with } n - 2 \text{ degrees of freedom} \quad \textbf{[13–2]}$$

III. In regression analysis, we estimate one variable based on another variable.
A. The variable being estimated is the dependent variable.
B. The variable used to make the estimate or predict the value is the independent variable.
1. The relationship between the variables is linear.
2. Both the independent and the dependent variables must be interval or ratio scale.
3. The least squares criterion is used to determine the regression equation.
IV. The least squares regression line is of the form $\hat{y} = a + bx$.
A. $\hat{y}$ is the estimated value of y for a selected value of x.
B. a is the constant or intercept.
1. It is the value of $\hat{y}$ when $x = 0$.
2. a is computed using the following equation.

$$a = \bar{y} - b\bar{x} \quad \textbf{[13–5]}$$

C. b is the slope of the fitted line.
1. It shows the amount of change in $\hat{y}$ for a change of one unit in x.
2. A positive value for b indicates a direct relationship between the two variables. A negative value indicates an inverse relationship.
3. The sign of b and the sign of r, the correlation coefficient, are always the same.
4. b is computed using the following equation.

$$b = r\left(\frac{s_y}{s_x}\right) \quad \textbf{[13–4]}$$

D. x is the value of the independent variable.
V. For a regression equation, the slope is tested for significance.
A. We test the hypothesis that the slope of the line in the population is 0.
1. If we do not reject the null hypothesis, we conclude there is no relationship between the two variables.
2. The test is equivalent to the test for the correlation coefficient.
B. When testing the null hypothesis about the slope, the test statistic is with $n - 2$ degrees of freedom:

$$t = \frac{b - 0}{s_b} \quad \textbf{[13–6]}$$

VI. The standard error of estimate measures the variation around the regression line.
A. It is in the same units as the dependent variable.
B. It is based on squared deviations from the regression line.
C. Small values indicate that the points cluster closely about the regression line.
D. It is computed using the following formula.

$$s_{y \cdot x} = \sqrt{\frac{\Sigma(y - \hat{y})^2}{n - 2}} \quad \textbf{[13–7]}$$

VII. The coefficient of determination is the proportion of the variation of a dependent variable explained by the independent variable.
A. It ranges from 0 to 1.0.
B. It is the square of the correlation coefficient.
C. It is found from the following formula.

$$r^2 = \frac{\text{SSR}}{\text{SS Total}} = 1 - \frac{\text{SSE}}{\text{SS Total}} \quad \textbf{[13–8]}$$

VIII. Inference about linear regression is based on the following assumptions.

A. For a given value of x, the values of Y are normally distributed about the line of regression.

B. The standard deviation of each of the normal distributions is the same for all values of x and is estimated by the standard error of estimate.

C. The deviations from the regression line are independent, with no pattern to the size or direction.

IX. There are two types of interval estimates.

A. In a confidence interval, the mean value of y is estimated for a given value of x.

1. It is computed from the following formula.

$$\hat{y} \pm ts_{y \cdot x}\sqrt{\frac{1}{n} + \frac{(x - \bar{x})^2}{\Sigma(x - \bar{x})^2}} \quad \textbf{[13–10]}$$

2. The width of the interval is affected by the level of confidence, the size of the standard error of estimate, and the size of the sample, as well as the value of the independent variable.

B. In a prediction interval, the individual value of y is estimated for a given value of x.

1. It is computed from the following formula.

$$\hat{y} \pm ts_{y \cdot x}\sqrt{1 + \frac{1}{n} + \frac{(x - \bar{x})^2}{\Sigma(x - \bar{x})^2}} \quad \textbf{[13–11]}$$

2. The difference between formulas (13–10) and (13–11) is the 1 under the radical.

a. The prediction interval will be wider than the confidence interval.

b. The prediction interval is also based on the level of confidence, the size of the standard error of estimate, the size of the sample, and the value of the independent variable.

PRONUNCIATION KEY

SYMBOL	MEANING	PRONUNCIATION
Σxy	Sum of the products of x and y	*Sum x y*
ρ	Correlation coefficient in the population	*Rho*
$\hat{y}$	Estimated value of Y	*y hat*
$s_{y \cdot x}$	Standard error of estimate	*s sub y dot x*
r^2	Coefficient of determination	*r square*

CHAPTER EXERCISES

37. A regional commuter airline selected a random sample of 25 flights and found that the correlation between the number of passengers and the total weight, in pounds, of luggage stored in the luggage compartment is 0.94. Using the .05 significance level, can we conclude that there is a positive association between the two variables?

38. A sociologist claims that the success of students in college (measured by their GPA) is related to their family's income. For a sample of 20 students, the correlation coefficient is 0.40. Using the 0.01 significance level, can we conclude that there is a positive correlation between the variables?

39. An Environmental Protection Agency study of 12 automobiles revealed a correlation of 0.47 between engine size and emissions. At the .01 significance level, can we conclude that there is a positive association between these variables? What is the *p*-value? Interpret.

For **DATA FILE**, please visit www.mhhe.com/lind16e

40. A suburban hotel derives its revenue from its hotel and restaurant operations. The owners are interested in the relationship between the number of rooms occupied on a nightly basis and the revenue per day in the restaurant. Below is a sample of 25 days (Monday through Thursday) from last year showing the restaurant income and number of rooms occupied.

Day	Revenue	Occupied	Day	Revenue	Occupied
1	$1,452	23	14	$1,425	27
2	1,361	47	15	1,445	34
3	1,426	21	16	1,439	15
4	1,470	39	17	1,348	19
5	1,456	37	18	1,450	38
6	1,430	29	19	1,431	44
7	1,354	23	20	1,446	47
8	1,442	44	21	1,485	43
9	1,394	45	22	1,405	38
10	1,459	16	23	1,461	51
11	1,399	30	24	1,490	61
12	1,458	42	25	1,426	39
13	1,537	54			

Use a statistical software package to answer the following questions.

a. Does the revenue seem to increase as the number of occupied rooms increases? Draw a scatter diagram to support your conclusion.

b. Determine the correlation coefficient between the two variables. Interpret the value.

c. Is it reasonable to conclude that there is a positive relationship between revenue and occupied rooms? Use the .10 significance level.

d. What percent of the variation in revenue in the restaurant is accounted for by the number of rooms occupied?

For **DATA FILE**, please visit www.mhhe.com/lind16e

41. The table below shows the number of cars (in millions) sold in the United States for various years and the percent of those cars manufactured by GM.

Year	Cars Sold (millions)	Percent GM	Year	Cars Sold (millions)	Percent GM
1950	6.0	50.2	1985	15.4	40.1
1955	7.8	50.4	1990	13.5	36.0
1960	7.3	44.0	1995	15.5	31.7
1965	10.3	49.9	2000	17.4	28.6
1970	10.1	39.5	2005	16.9	26.9
1975	10.8	43.1	2010	11.6	19.1
1980	11.5	44.0			

Use a statistical software package to answer the following questions.

a. Is the number of cars sold directly or indirectly related to GM's percentage of the market? Draw a scatter diagram to show your conclusion.

b. Determine the correlation coefficient between the two variables. Interpret the value.

c. Is it reasonable to conclude that there is a negative association between the two variables? Use the .01 significance level.

d. How much of the variation in GM's market share is accounted for by the variation in cars sold?

42. For a sample of 32 large U.S. cities, the correlation between the mean number of square feet per office worker and the mean monthly rental rate in the central business district is −.363. At the .05 significance level, can we conclude that there is a negative association between the two variables?

43. For each of the 32 National Football League teams, the numbers of points scored and allowed during the 2012 season are shown below.

Team	Conference	Points Scored	Points Allowed	Team	Conference	Points Scored	Points Allowed
Chicago Bears	NFC	375	277	Cincinnati Bengals	AFC	391	320
Green Bay Packers	NFC	433	336	Baltimore Ravens	AFC	398	344
Minnesota Vikings	NFC	379	348	Pittsburgh Steelers	AFC	336	314
Detroit Lions	NFC	372	437	Cleveland Browns	AFC	302	368
Seattle Seahawks	NFC	412	245	New England Patriots	AFC	557	331
San Francisco 49ers	NFC	397	273	Miami Dolphins	AFC	288	317
St. Louis Rams	NFC	299	348	Buffalo Bills	AFC	344	435
Arizona Cardinals	NFC	250	357	New York Jets	AFC	281	375
Atlanta Falcons	NFC	419	299	Denver Broncos	AFC	481	289
New Orleans Saints	NFC	461	454	San Diego Chargers	AFC	350	350
Tampa Bay Buccaneers	NFC	389	394	Oakland Raiders	AFC	290	443
Carolina Panthers	NFC	357	363	Kansas City Chiefs	AFC	211	425
New York Giants	NFC	429	344	Houston Texans	AFC	416	331
Washington Redskins	NFC	436	388	Indianapolis Colts	AFC	357	387
Dallas Cowboys	NFC	376	400	Tennessee Titans	AFC	330	471
Philadelphia Eagles	NFC	280	444	Jacksonville Jaguars	AFC	255	444

Assuming these are sample data, answer the following questions. You may use statistical software to assist you.

a. What is the correlation coefficient between these variables? Are you surprised the association is negative? Interpret your results.
b. Find the coefficient of determination. What does it say about the relationship?
c. At the .05 significance level, can you conclude there is a negative association between "points scored" and "points allowed"?
d. At the .05 significance level, can you conclude there is a negative association between "points scored" and "points allowed" for each conference?

For **DATA FILE**, please visit www.mhhe.com/lind16e

44. The Cotton Mill is an upscale chain of women's clothing stores, located primarily in the southwest United States. Due to recent success, The Cotton Mill's top management is planning to expand by locating new stores in other regions of the country. The director of planning has been asked to study the relationship between yearly sales and the store size. As part of the study, the director selects a sample of 25 stores and determines the size of the store in square feet and the sales for last year. The sample data follow. The use of statistical software is suggested.

Store Size (thousands of square feet)	Sales (millions $)	Store Size (thousands of square feet)	Sales (millions $)
3.7	9.18	0.4	0.55
2.0	4.58	4.2	7.56
5.0	8.22	3.1	2.23
0.7	1.45	2.6	4.49
2.6	6.51	5.2	9.90
2.9	2.82	3.3	8.93
5.2	10.45	3.2	7.60
5.9	9.94	4.9	3.71
3.0	4.43	5.5	5.47
2.4	4.75	2.9	8.22
2.4	7.30	2.2	7.17
0.5	3.33	2.3	4.35
5.0	6.76		

a. Draw a scatter diagram. Use store size as the independent variable. Does there appear to be a relationship between the two variables. Is it positive or negative?
b. Determine the correlation coefficient and the coefficient of determination. Is the relationship strong or weak? Why?
c. At the .05 significance level, can we conclude there is a significant positive correlation?

45. The manufacturer of Cardio Glide exercise equipment wants to study the relationship between the number of months since the glide was purchased and the time, in hours, the equipment was used last week.

For **DATA FILE**, please visit www.mhhe.com/lind16e

Person	Months Owned	Hours Exercised	Person	Months Owned	Hours Exercised
Rupple	12	4	Massa	2	8
Hall	2	10	Sass	8	3
Bennett	6	8	Karl	4	8
Longnecker	9	5	Malrooney	10	2
Phillips	7	5	Veights	5	5

a. Plot the information on a scatter diagram. Let hours of exercise be the dependent variable. Comment on the graph.
b. Determine the correlation coefficient. Interpret.
c. At the .01 significance level, can we conclude that there is a negative association between the variables?

46. The following regression equation was computed from a sample of 20 observations:

$$\hat{y} = 15 - 5x$$

SSE was found to be 100 and SS total, 400.
a. Determine the standard error of estimate.
b. Determine the coefficient of determination.
c. Determine the correlation coefficient. (Caution: Watch the sign!)

47. City planners believe that larger cities are populated by older residents. To investigate the relationship, data on population and median age in 10 large cities were collected.

For **DATA FILE**, please visit www.mhhe.com/lind16e

City	Population (in millions)	Median Age
Chicago, IL	2.833	31.5
Dallas, TX	1.233	30.5
Houston, TX	2.144	30.9
Los Angeles, CA	3.849	31.6
New York, NY	8.214	34.2
Philadelphia, PA	1.448	34.2
Phoenix, AZ	1.513	30.7
San Antonio, TX	1.297	31.7
San Diego, CA	1.257	32.5
San Jose, CA	0.930	32.6

a. Plot these data on a scatter diagram with median age as the dependent variable.
b. Find the correlation coefficient.
c. A regression analysis was performed and the resulting regression equation is Median Age = 31.4 + 0.272 Population. Interpret the meaning of the slope.
d. Estimate the median age for a city of 2.5 million people.
e. Here is a portion of the regression software output. What does it tell you?

```
Predictor        Coef    SE Coef        T        P
Constant      31.3672     0.6158    50.94    0.000
Population     0.2722     0.1901     1.43    0.190
```

f. Using the .10 significance level, test the significance of the slope. Interpret the result. Is there a significant relationship between the two variables?

48. Emily Smith decides to buy a fuel-efficient used car. Here are several vehicles she is considering, with the estimated cost to purchase and the age of the vehicle.

For **DATA FILE**, please visit www.mhhe.com/lind16e

Vehicle	Estimated Cost	Age
Honda Insight	$5,555	8
Toyota Prius	$17,888	3
Toyota Prius	$9,963	6
Toyota Echo	$6,793	5
Honda Civic Hybrid	$10,774	5
Honda Civic Hybrid	$16,310	2
Chevrolet Prizm	$2,475	8
Mazda Protege	$2,808	10
Toyota Corolla	$7,073	9
Acura Integra	$8,978	8
Scion xB	$11,213	2
Scion xA	$9,463	3
Mazda3	$15,055	2
Mini Cooper	$20,705	2

a. Plot these data on a scatter diagram with estimated cost as the dependent variable.
b. Find the correlation coefficient.
c. A regression analysis was performed and the resulting regression equation is Estimated Cost = 18358 − 1534 Age. Interpret the meaning of the slope.
d. Estimate the cost of a five-year-old car.
e. Here is a portion of the regression software output. What does it tell you?

```
Predictor        Coef     SE Coef        T        P
Constant        18358        1817    10.10    0.000
Age           -1533.6       306.3    -5.01    0.000
```

f. Using the .10 significance level, test the significance of the slope. Interpret the result. Is there a significant relationship between the two variables?

49. The National Highway Association is studying the relationship between the number of bidders on a highway project and the winning (lowest) bid for the project. Of particular interest is whether the number of bidders increases or decreases the amount of the winning bid.

For **DATA FILE**, please visit www.mhhe.com/lind16e

Project	Number of Bidders, x	Winning Bid ($ millions), y	Project	Number of Bidders, x	Winning Bid ($ millions), y
1	9	5.1	9	6	10.3
2	9	8.0	10	6	8.0
3	3	9.7	11	4	8.8
4	10	7.8	12	7	9.4
5	5	7.7	13	7	8.6
6	10	5.5	14	7	8.1
7	7	8.3	15	6	7.8
8	11	5.5			

a. Determine the regression equation. Interpret the equation. Do more bidders tend to increase or decrease the amount of the winning bid?
b. Estimate the amount of the winning bid if there were seven bidders.
c. A new entrance is to be constructed on the Ohio Turnpike. There are seven bidders on the project. Develop a 95% prediction interval for the winning bid.
d. Determine the coefficient of determination. Interpret its value.

For **DATA FILE**, please visit www.mhhe.com/lind16e

50. Mr. William Profit is studying companies going public for the first time. He is particularly interested in the relationship between the size of the offering and the price per share. A sample of 15 companies that recently went public revealed the following information.

Company	Size ($ millions), x	Price per Share, y	Company	Size ($ millions), x	Price per Share, y
1	9.0	10.8	9	160.7	11.3
2	94.4	11.3	10	96.5	10.6
3	27.3	11.2	11	83.0	10.5
4	179.2	11.1	12	23.5	10.3
5	71.9	11.1	13	58.7	10.7
6	97.9	11.2	14	93.8	11.0
7	93.5	11.0	15	34.4	10.8
8	70.0	10.7			

a. Determine the regression equation.
b. Conduct a test to determine whether the slope of the regression line is positive.
c. Determine the coefficient of determination. Do you think Mr. Profit should be satisfied with using the size of the offering as the independent variable?

For **DATA FILE**, please visit www.mhhe.com/lind16e

51. Bardi Trucking Co., located in Cleveland, Ohio, makes deliveries in the Great Lakes region, the Southeast, and the Northeast. Jim Bardi, the president, is studying the relationship between the distance a shipment must travel and the length of time, in days, it takes the shipment to arrive at its destination. To investigate, Mr. Bardi selected a random sample of 20 shipments made last month. Shipping distance is the independent variable and shipping time is the dependent variable. The results are as follows:

Shipment	Distance (miles)	Shipping Time (days)	Shipment	Distance (miles)	Shipping Time (days)
1	656	5	11	862	7
2	853	14	12	679	5
3	646	6	13	835	13
4	783	11	14	607	3
5	610	8	15	665	8
6	841	10	16	647	7
7	785	9	17	685	10
8	639	9	18	720	8
9	762	10	19	652	6
10	762	9	20	828	10

a. Draw a scatter diagram. Based on these data, does it appear that there is a relationship between how many miles a shipment has to go and the time it takes to arrive at its destination?
b. Determine the correlation coefficient. Can we conclude that there is a positive correlation between distance and time? Use the .05 significance level.
c. Determine and interpret the coefficient of determination.
d. Determine the standard error of estimate.
e. Would you recommend using the regression equation to predict shipping time? Why or why not.

For **DATA FILE**, please visit www.mhhe.com/lind16e

52. Super Markets Inc. is considering expanding into the Scottsdale, Arizona, area. You, as director of planning, must present an analysis of the proposed expansion to the operating committee of the board of directors. As a part of your proposal, you need to include information on the amount people in the region spend per month for grocery items. You would also like to include information on the relationship between the amount spent for grocery items and income. Your assistant gathered the following sample information.

Household	Amount Spent	Monthly Income
1	$ 555	$4,388
2	489	4,558
⋮	⋮	⋮
39	1,206	9,862
40	1,145	9,883

a. Let the amount spent be the dependent variable and monthly income the independent variable. Create a scatter diagram, using a software package.
b. Determine the regression equation. Interpret the slope value.
c. Determine the correlation coefficient. Can you conclude that it is greater than 0?

53. Below is information on the price per share and the dividend for a sample of 30 companies.

For **DATA FILE**, please visit www.mhhe.com/lind16e

Company	Price per Share	Dividend
1	$20.00	$ 3.14
2	22.01	3.36
⋮	⋮	⋮
29	77.91	17.65
30	80.00	17.36

a. Calculate the regression equation using selling price based on the annual dividend.
b. Test the significance of the slope.
c. Determine the coefficient of determination. Interpret its value.
d. Determine the correlation coefficient. Can you conclude that it is greater than 0 using the .05 significance level?

54. A highway employee performed a regression analysis of the relationship between the number of construction work-zone fatalities and the number of unemployed people in a state. The regression equation is Fatalities = 12.7 + 0.000114 (Unemp). Some additional output is:

Predictor	Coef	SE Coef	T	P
Constant	12.726	8.115	1.57	0.134
Unemp	0.00011386	0.00002896	3.93	0.001

Analysis of Variance

Source	DF	SS	MS	F	P
Regression	1	10354	10354	15.46	0.001
Residual Error	18	12054	670		
Total	19	22408			

a. How many states were in the sample?
b. Determine the standard error of estimate.
c. Determine the coefficient of determination.
d. Determine the correlation coefficient.
e. At the .05 significance level, does the evidence suggest there is a positive association between fatalities and the number unemployed?

55. A regression analysis relating the current market value in dollars to the size in square feet of homes in Greene County, Tennessee, follows. The regression equation is: Value = −37,186 + 65.0 Size.

Predictor	Coef	SE Coef	T	P
Constant	−37186	4629	−8.03	0.000
Size	64.993	3.047	21.33	0.000

Analysis of Variance

Source	DF	SS	MS	F	P
Regression	1	13548662082	13548662082	454.98	0.000
Residual Error	33	982687392	29778406		
Total	34	14531349474			

a. How many homes were in the sample?
b. Compute the standard error of estimate.
c. Compute the coefficient of determination.
d. Compute the correlation coefficient.
e. At the .05 significance level, does the evidence suggest a positive association between the market value of homes and the size of the home in square feet?

56. The following table shows the mean annual percent return on capital (profitability) and the mean annual percentage sales growth for eight aerospace and defense companies.

For **DATA FILE**, please visit www.mhhe.com/lind16e

Company	Profitability	Growth
Alliant Techsystems	23.1	8.0
Boeing	13.2	15.6
General Dynamics	24.2	31.2
Honeywell	11.1	2.5
L-3 Communications	10.1	35.4
Northrop Grumman	10.8	6.0
Rockwell Collins	27.3	8.7
United Technologies	20.1	3.2

a. Compute the correlation coefficient. Conduct a test of hypothesis to determine if it is reasonable to conclude that the population correlation is greater than zero. Use the .05 significance level.
b. Develop the regression equation for profitability based on growth. Can we conclude that the slope of the regression line is negative?
c. Use a software package to determine the residual for each observation. Which company has the largest residual?

57. The following data show the retail price for 12 randomly selected laptop computers along with their corresponding processor speeds in gigahertz.

For **DATA FILE**, please visit www.mhhe.com/lind16e

Computers	Speed	Price	Computers	Speed	Price
1	2.0	$2,017	7	2.0	$2,197
2	1.6	922	8	1.6	1,387
3	1.6	1,064	9	2.0	2,114
4	1.8	1,942	10	1.6	2,002
5	2.0	2,137	11	1.0	937
6	1.2	1,012	12	1.4	869

a. Develop a linear equation that can be used to describe how the price depends on the processor speed.
b. Based on your regression equation, is there one machine that seems particularly over- or underpriced?
c. Compute the correlation coefficient between the two variables. At the .05 significance level, conduct a test of hypothesis to determine if the population correlation is greater than zero.

58. A consumer buying cooperative tested the effective heating area of 20 different electric space heaters with different wattages. Here are the results.

For **DATA FILE**, please visit www.mhhe.com/lind16e

Heater	Wattage	Area	Heater	Wattage	Area
1	1,500	205	11	1,250	116
2	750	70	12	500	72
3	1,500	199	13	500	82
4	1,250	151	14	1,500	206
5	1,250	181	15	2,000	245
6	1,250	217	16	1,500	219
7	1,000	94	17	750	63
8	2,000	298	18	1,500	200
9	1,000	135	19	1,250	151
10	1,500	211	20	500	44

a. Compute the correlation between the wattage and heating area. Is there a direct or an indirect relationship?
b. Conduct a test of hypothesis to determine if it is reasonable that the coefficient is greater than zero. Use the .05 significance level.
c. Develop the regression equation for effective heating based on wattage.
d. Which heater looks like the "best buy" based on the size of the residual?

59. A dog trainer is exploring the relationship between the size of the dog (weight in pounds) and its daily food consumption (measured in standard cups). Below is the result of a sample of 18 observations.

For **DATA FILE**, please visit www.mhhe.com/lind16e

Dog	Weight	Consumption	Dog	Weight	Consumption
1	41	3	10	91	5
2	148	8	11	109	6
3	79	5	12	207	10
4	41	4	13	49	3
5	85	5	14	113	6
6	111	6	15	84	5
7	37	3	16	95	5
8	111	6	17	57	4
9	41	3	18	168	9

a. Compute the correlation coefficient. Is it reasonable to conclude that the correlation in the population is greater than zero? Use the .05 significance level.
b. Develop the regression equation for cups based on the dog's weight. How much does each additional cup change the estimated weight of the dog?
c. Is one of the dogs a big undereater or overeater?

60. Waterbury Insurance Company wants to study the relationship between the amount of fire damage and the distance between the burning house and the nearest fire station. This information will be used in setting rates for insurance coverage. For a sample of 30 claims for the last year, the director of the actuarial department determined the distance from the fire station (x) and the amount of fire damage, in thousands of dollars (y). The MegaStat output is reported below.

ANOVA table

Source	SS	df	MS	F
Regression	1,864.5782	1	1,864.5782	38.83
Residual	1,344.4934	28	48.0176	
Total	3,209.0716	29		

Regression output

Variables	Coefficients	Std. Error	t(df = 28)
Intercept	12.3601	3.2915	3.755
Distance–X	4.7956	0.7696	6.231

Answer the following questions.
a. Write out the regression equation. Is there a direct or indirect relationship between the distance from the fire station and the amount of fire damage?
b. How much damage would you estimate for a fire 5 miles from the nearest fire station?
c. Determine and interpret the coefficient of determination.
d. Determine the correlation coefficient. Interpret its value. How did you determine the sign of the correlation coefficient?
e. Conduct a test of hypothesis to determine if there is a significant relationship between the distance from the fire station and the amount of damage. Use the .01 significance level and a two-tailed test.

For **DATA FILE**, please visit www.mhhe.com/lind16e

61. An air travel service samples domestic airline flights to explore the relationship between airfare and distance. The service would like to know if there is a correlation between airfare and flight distance. If there is a correlation, what percentage of the variation in airfare is accounted for by distance? How much does each additional mile add to the fare? The data follow.

Origin	Destination	Distance	Fare
Detroit, MI	Myrtle Beach, SC	636	$109
Baltimore, MD	Sacramento, CA	2,395	252
Las Vegas, NV	Philadelphia, PA	2,176	221
Sacramento, CA	Seattle, WA	605	151
Atlanta, GA	Orlando, FL	403	138
Boston, MA	Miami, FL	1,258	209
Chicago, IL	Covington, KY	264	254
Columbus, OH	Minneapolis, MN	627	259
Fort Lauderdale, FL	Los Angeles, CA	2,342	215
Chicago, IL	Indianapolis, IN	177	128
Philadelphia, PA	San Francisco, CA	2,521	348
Houston, TX	Raleigh/Durham, NC	1,050	224
Houston, TX	Midland/Odessa, TX	441	175
Cleveland, OH	Dallas/Ft.Worth, TX	1,021	256
Baltimore, MD	Columbus, OH	336	121
Boston, MA	Covington, KY	752	252
Kansas City, MO	San Diego, CA	1,333	206
Milwaukee, WI	Phoenix, AZ	1,460	167
Portland, OR	Washington, DC	2,350	308
Phoenix, AZ	San Jose, CA	621	152
Baltimore, MD	St. Louis, MO	737	175
Houston, TX	Orlando, FL	853	191
Houston, TX	Seattle, WA	1,894	231
Burbank, CA	New York, NY	2,465	251
Atlanta, GA	San Diego, CA	1,891	291
Minneapolis, MN	New York, NY	1,028	260
Atlanta, GA	West Palm Beach, FL	545	123
Kansas City, MO	Seattle, WA	1,489	211
Baltimore, MD	Portland, ME	452	139
New Orleans, LA	Washington, DC	969	243

a. Draw a scatter diagram with *Distance* as the independent variable and *Fare* as the dependent variable. Is the relationship direct or indirect?

b. Compute the correlation coefficient. At the .05 significance level, is it reasonable to conclude that the correlation coefficient is greater than zero?

c. What percentage of the variation in *Fare* is accounted for by *Distance* of a flight?

d. Determine the regression equation. How much does each additional mile add to the fare? Estimate the fare for a 1,500-mile flight.

e. A traveler is planning to fly from Atlanta to London Heathrow. The distance is 4,218 miles. She wants to use the regression equation to estimate the fare. Explain why it would not be a good idea to estimate the fare for this international flight with the regression equation.

DATA SET EXERCISES

(The data for these exercises are available at the text website: www.mhhe.com/lind16e.)

62. Refer to the Real Estate data, which reports information on homes sold in Goodyear, Arizona, last year.

a. Let selling price be the dependent variable and size of the home the independent variable. Determine the regression equation. Estimate the selling price for a home with an

area of 2,200 square feet. Determine the 95% confidence interval and the 95% prediction interval for the selling price of a home with 2,200 square feet.

b. Let selling price be the dependent variable and distance from the center of the city the independent variable. Determine the regression equation. Estimate the selling price of a home 20 miles from the center of the city. Determine the 95% confidence interval and the 95% prediction interval for homes 20 miles from the center of the city.

c. Can you conclude that the independent variables "distance from the center of the city" and "selling price" are negatively correlated and that the area of the home and the selling price are positively correlated? Use the .05 significance level. Report the *p*-value of the test. Summarize your results in a brief report.

63. Refer to the Baseball 2012 data, which reports information on the 2012 Major League Baseball season. Let attendance be the dependent variable and total team salary, in millions of dollars, be the independent variable. Determine the regression equation and answer the following questions.

a. Draw a scatter diagram. From the diagram, does there seem to be a direct relationship between the two variables?

b. What is the expected attendance for a team with a salary of $80.0 million?

c. If the owners pay an additional $30 million, how many more people could they expect to attend?

d. At the .05 significance level, can we conclude that the slope of the regression line is positive? Conduct the appropriate test of hypothesis.

e. What percentage of the variation in attendance is accounted for by salary?

f. Determine the correlation between attendance and team batting average and between attendance and team ERA. Which is stronger? Conduct an appropriate test of hypothesis for each set of variables.

64. Refer to the Buena School bus data. Develop a regression equation that expresses the relationship between age of the bus and maintenance. The age of the bus is the independent variable.

a. Draw a scatter diagram. What does this diagram suggest as to the relationship between the two variables? Is it direct or indirect? Does it appear to be strong or weak?

b. Develop a regression equation. How much does an additional year add to the maintenance cost. What is the estimated maintenance cost for a 10-year-old bus?

c. Conduct a test of hypothesis to determine whether the slope of the regression line is greater than zero. Use the .05 significance level. Interpret your findings from parts (a), (b), and (c) in a brief report.

14 Multiple Regression Analysis

THE MORTGAGE DEPARTMENT of the Bank of New England is studying data from recent loans. Of particular interest is how such factors as the value of the home being purchased, education level of the head of the household, age of the head of the household, current monthly mortgage payment, and gender of the head of the household relate to the family income. Are the proposed variables effective predictors of the dependent variable family income? (See the example/solution on page 508, LO14-1.)

LEARNING OBJECTIVES

When you have completed this chapter, you will be able to:

LO14-1 Use multiple regression analysis to describe and interpret a relationship between several independent variables and a dependent variable.

LO14-2 Evaluate how well a multiple regression equation fits the data.

LO14-3 Test hypotheses about the relationships inferred by a multiple regression model.

LO14-4 Evaluate the assumptions of multiple regression.

LO14-5 Use and interpret a qualitative, dummy variable in multiple regression.

LO14-6 Include and interpret an interaction effect in multiple regression analysis.

LO14-7 Apply stepwise regression to develop a multiple regression model.

LO14-8 Apply multiple regression techniques to develop a linear model.

INTRODUCTION

In Chapter 13, we described the relationship between a pair of interval- or ratio-scaled variables. We began the chapter by studying the correlation coefficient, which measures the strength of the relationship. A coefficient near plus or minus 1.00 (−.88 or .78, for example) indicates a very strong linear relationship, whereas a value near 0 (−.12 or .18, for example) indicates that the relationship is weak. Next we developed a procedure to determine a linear equation to express the relationship between the two variables. We referred to this as a *regression line.* This line describes the relationship between the variables. It also describes the overall pattern of a dependent variable (y) to a single independent or explanatory variable (x).

In multiple linear correlation and regression, we use additional independent variables (denoted $x_1, x_2, \ldots$, and so on) that help us better explain or predict the dependent variable (y). Almost all of the ideas we saw in simple linear correlation and regression extend to this more general situation. However, the additional independent variables do lead to some new considerations. Multiple regression analysis can be used either as a descriptive or as an inferential technique.

LO14-1
Use multiple regression analysis to describe and interpret a relationship between several independent variables and a dependent variable.

MULTIPLE REGRESSION ANALYSIS

The general descriptive form of a multiple linear equation is shown in formula (14–1). We use k to represent the number of independent variables. So k can be any positive integer.

GENERAL MULTIPLE REGRESSION EQUATION

$$\hat{y} = a + b_1x_1 + b_2x_2 + b_3x_3 + \cdots + b_kx_k \quad [14\text{–}1]$$

where:

a is the intercept, the value of $\hat{y}$ when all the X's are zero.

b_j is the amount by which $\hat{y}$ changes when that particular x_j increases by one unit, with the values of all other independent variables held constant. The subscript j is simply a label that helps to identify each independent variable; it is not used in any calculations. Usually the subscript is an integer value between 1 and k, which is the number of independent variables. However, the subscript can also be a short or abbreviated label. For example, age could be used as a subscript.

In Chapter 13, the regression analysis described and tested the relationship between a dependent variable, $\hat{y}$, and a single independent variable, x. The relationship between $\hat{y}$ and x was graphically portrayed by a line. When there are two independent variables, the regression equation is

$$\hat{y} = a + b_1x_1 + b_2x_2$$

Because there are two independent variables, this relationship is graphically portrayed as a plane and is shown in Chart 14–1. The chart shows the residuals as the difference between the actual y and the fitted $\hat{y}$ on the plane. If a multiple regression analysis includes more than two independent variables, we cannot use a graph to illustrate the analysis since graphs are limited to three dimensions.

To illustrate the interpretation of the intercept and the two regression coefficients, suppose the selling price of a home is directly related to the number of rooms and *inversely* related to its age. We let x_1 refer to the number of rooms, x_2 to the age of the home in years, and y to the selling price of the home in thousands of dollars ($000).

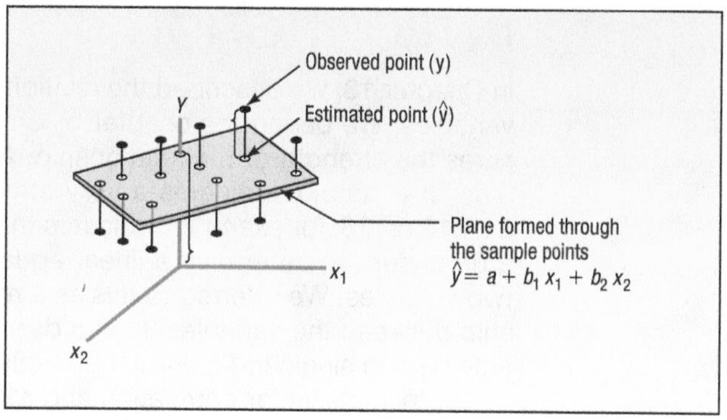

CHART 14–1 Regression Plane with 10 Sample Points

Suppose the regression equation, calculated using statistical software, is:

$$\hat{y} = 21.2 + 18.7x_1 - 0.25x_2$$

The intercept value of 21.2 indicates the regression equation (plane) intersects the *y*-axis at 21.2. This happens when both the number of rooms and the age of the home are zero. We could say that $21,200 is the average value of a property without a house.

The first regression coefficient, 18.7, indicates that for each increase of one room in the size of a home, the selling price will increase by $18.7 thousand ($18,700), regardless of the age of the home. The second regression coefficient, −0.25, indicates that for each increase of one year in age, the selling price will *decrease* by $.25 thousand ($250), regardless of the number of rooms. As an example, a seven-room home that is 30 years old is expected to sell for $144,600.

$$\hat{y} = 21.2 + 18.7x_1 - 0.25x_2 = 21.2 + 18.7(7) - 0.25(30) = 144.6$$

The values for the coefficients in the multiple linear equation are found by using the method of least squares. Recall from the previous chapter that the least squares method makes the sum of the squared differences between the fitted and actual values of *y* as small as possible, that is, the term $\Sigma(y - \hat{y})^2$ is minimized. The calculations are very tedious, so they are usually performed by a statistical software package.

In the following example, we show a multiple regression analysis using three independent variables employing Excel that produces a standard set of statistics and reports. Statistical software such as Minitab, Megastat, and others provide advanced regression analysis techniques.

EXAMPLE

Salsberry Realty sells homes along the East Coast of the United States. One of the questions most frequently asked by prospective buyers is: If we purchase this home, how much can we expect to pay to heat it during the winter? The research department at Salsberry has been asked to develop some guidelines regarding heating costs for single-family homes. Three variables are thought to relate to the heating costs: (1) the mean daily outside temperature, (2) the number of inches of insulation in the attic, and (3) the age in years of the furnace. To investigate, Salsberry's research department selected a random sample of 20 recently sold homes. It determined the cost to heat each home last January, as well as the January outside temperature in the region, the number of inches of insulation in the attic, and the age of the furnace. The sample information is reported in Table 14–1.

STATISTICS IN ACTION

Many studies indicate a woman will earn about 70% of what a man would for the same work. Researchers at the University of Michigan Institute for Social Research found that about one-third of the difference can be explained by such social factors as differences in education, seniority, and work interruptions. The remaining two-thirds is not explained by these social factors.

TABLE 14–1 Factors in January Heating Cost for a Sample of 20 Homes

Home	Heating Cost ($)	Mean Outside Temperature (°F)	Attic Insulation (inches)	Age of Furnace (years)
1	$250	35	3	6
2	360	29	4	10
3	165	36	7	3
4	43	60	6	9
5	92	65	5	6
6	200	30	5	5
7	355	10	6	7
8	290	7	10	10
9	230	21	9	11
10	120	55	2	5
11	73	54	12	4
12	205	48	5	1
13	400	20	5	15
14	320	39	4	7
15	72	60	8	6
16	272	20	5	8
17	94	58	7	3
18	190	40	8	11
19	235	27	9	8
20	139	30	7	5

The data in Table 14–1 are available in Excel worksheet format at the textbook website, www.mhhe.com/lind16e. The basic instructions for using Excel for these data are in the Software Commands in Appendix C.

Determine the multiple regression equation. Which variables are the independent variables? Which variable is the dependent variable? Discuss the regression coefficients. What does it indicate if some coefficients are positive and some coefficients are negative? What is the intercept value? What is the estimated heating cost for a home if the mean outside temperature is 30 degrees, there are 5 inches of insulation in the attic, and the furnace is 10 years old?

SOLUTION

We begin the analysis by defining the dependent and independent variables. The dependent variable is the January heating cost. It is represented by y. There are three independent variables:

- The mean outside temperature in January, represented by x_1.
- The number of inches of insulation in the attic, represented by x_2.
- The age in years of the furnace, represented by x_3.

Given these definitions, the general form of the multiple regression equation follows. The value $\hat{y}$ is used to estimate the value of y.

$$\hat{y} = a + b_1x_1 + b_2x_2 + b_3x_3$$

Now that we have defined the regression equation, we are ready to use Excel to compute all the statistics needed for the analysis. The output from Excel is shown on the following page.

To use the regression equation to predict the January heating cost, we need to know the values of the regression coefficients, b_j. These are highlighted in the

software reports. The software uses the variable names or labels associated with each independent variable. The regression equation intercept, *a*, is labeled "intercept" in the Excel output.

	A	B	C	D
1	Cost	Temp	Insul	Age
2	250	35	3	6
3	360	29	4	10
4	165	36	7	3
5	43	60	6	9
6	92	65	5	6
7	200	30	5	5
8	355	10	6	7
9	290	7	10	10
10	230	21	9	11
11	120	55	2	5
12	73	54	12	4
13	205	48	5	1
14	400	20	5	15
15	320	39	4	7
16	72	60	8	6
17	272	20	5	8
18	94	58	7	3
19	190	40	8	11
20	235	27	9	8
21	139	30	7	5

SUMMARY OUTPUT

Regression Statistics	
Multiple R	0.897
R Square	0.804
Adjusted R Square	0.767
Standard Error	51.049
Observations	20

ANOVA

	df	*SS*	*MS*	*F*	*Significance F*
Regression	3	171220.473	57073.491	21.901	0.000
Residual	16	41695.277	2605.955		
Total	19	212915.750			

	Coefficients	*Standard Error*	*t Stat*	*P-value*
Intercept	427.194	59.601	7.168	0.000
Temp	-4.583	0.772	-5.934	0.000
Insul	-14.831	4.754	-3.119	0.007
Age	6.101	4.012	1.521	0.148

In this case, the estimated regression equation is:

$$\hat{y} = 427.194 - 4.583x_1 - 14.831x_2 + 6.101x_3$$

We can now estimate or predict the January heating cost for a home if we know the mean outside temperature, the inches of insulation, and the age of the furnace. For an example home, the mean outside temperature for the month is 30 degrees (x_1), there are 5 inches of insulation in the attic (x_2), and the furnace is 10 years old (x_3). By substituting the values for the independent variables:

$$\hat{y} = 427.194 - 4.583(30) - 14.831(5) + 6.101(10) = 276.56$$

The estimated January heating cost is $276.56.

The regression coefficients, and their algebraic signs, also provide information about their individual relationships with the January heating cost. The regression coefficient for mean outside temperature is −4.583. The coefficient is negative and shows an inverse relationship between heating cost and temperature. This is not surprising. As the outside temperature increases, the cost to heat the home decreases. The numeric value of the regression coefficient provides more information. If we increase temperature by 1 degree and hold the other two independent variables constant, we can estimate a decrease of $4.583 in monthly heating cost. So if the mean temperature in Boston is 25 degrees and it is 35 degrees in Philadelphia, all other things being the same (insulation and age of furnace), we expect the heating cost would be $45.83 less in Philadelphia.

The attic insulation variable also shows an inverse relationship: the more insulation in the attic, the less the cost to heat the home. So the negative sign for this coefficient is logical. For each additional inch of insulation, we expect the cost to heat the home to decline $14.83 per month, holding the outside temperature and the age of the furnace constant.

The age of the furnace variable shows a direct relationship. With an older furnace, the cost to heat the home increases. Specifically, for each additional year older the furnace is, we expect the cost to increase $6.10 per month.

SELF-REVIEW 14–1

There are many restaurants in northeastern South Carolina. They serve beach vacationers in the summer, golfers in the fall and spring, and snowbirds in the winter. Bill and Joyce Tuneall manage several restaurants in the North Jersey area and are considering moving to Myrtle Beach, SC, to open a new restaurant. Before making a final decision, they wish to investigate existing restaurants and what variables seem to be related to profitability. They gather sample information where profit (reported in $000) is the dependent variable and the independent variables are:

x_1 the number of parking spaces near the restaurant.
x_2 the number of hours the restaurant is open per week.
x_3 the distance from the SkyWheel, a landmark in Myrtle Beach.
x_4 the number of servers employed.
x_5 the number of years the current owner operated the restaurant.

The following is part of the output obtained using statistical software.

Predictor	Coefficient	SE Coefficient	t
Constant	2.50	1.50	1.667
x_1	3.00	1.50	2.000
x_2	4.00	3.00	1.333
x_3	-3.00	0.20	-15.000
x_4	0.20	0.05	4.000
x_5	1.00	1.50	0.667

(a) What is the amount of profit for a restaurant with 40 parking spaces that is open 72 hours per week, is 10 miles from the SkyWheel, has 20 servers, and has been operated by the current owner for 5 years?
(b) Interpret the values of b_2 and b_3 in the multiple regression equation.

EXERCISES

1. The director of marketing at Reeves Wholesale Products is studying monthly sales. Three independent variables were selected as estimators of sales: regional population, per capita income, and regional unemployment rate. The regression equation was computed to be (in dollars):

$$\hat{y} = 64{,}100 + 0.394x_1 + 9.6x_2 - 11{,}600x_3$$

   a. What is the full name of the equation?
   b. Interpret the number 64,100.
   c. What are the estimated monthly sales for a particular region with a population of 796,000, per capita income of $6,940, and an unemployment rate of 6.0%?

2. Thompson Photo Works purchased several new, highly sophisticated processing machines. The production department needed some guidance with respect to qualifications needed by an operator. Is age a factor? Is the length of service as an operator (in years) important? In order to explore further the factors needed to estimate performance on the new processing machines, four variables were listed:

   x_1 = Length of time an employee was in the industry
   x_2 = Mechanical aptitude test score
   x_3 = Prior on-the-job rating
   x_4 = Age

   Performance on the new machine is designated *y*.

   Thirty employees were selected at random. Data were collected for each, and their performances on the new machines were recorded. A few results are:

Name	Performance on New Machine, y	Length of Time in Industry, x_1	Mechanical Aptitude Score, x_2	Prior on-the-Job Performance, x_3	Age, x_4
Mike Miraglia	112	12	312	121	52
Sue Trythall	113	2	380	123	27

The equation is:

$$\hat{y} = 11.6 + 0.4x_1 + 0.286x_2 + 0.112x_3 + 0.002x_4$$

a. What is this equation called?
b. How many dependent variables are there? Independent variables?
c. What is the number 0.286 called?
d. As age increases by one year, how much does estimated performance on the new machine increase?
e. Carl Knox applied for a job at Photo Works. He has been in the business for 6 years and scored 280 on the mechanical aptitude test. Carl's prior on-the-job performance rating is 97, and he is 35 years old. Estimate Carl's performance on the new machine.

3. A consulting group was hired by the Human Resources Department at General Mills, Inc. to survey company employees regarding their degree of satisfaction with their quality of life. A special index, called the index of satisfaction, was used to measure satisfaction. Six factors were studied, namely, age at the time of first marriage (x_1), annual income (x_2), number of children living (x_3), value of all assets (x_4), status of health in the form of an index (x_5), and the average number of social activities per week—such as bowling and dancing (x_6). Suppose the multiple regression equation is:

$$\hat{y} = 16.24 + 0.017x_1 + 0.0028x_2 + 42x_3 + 0.0012x_4 + 0.19x_5 + 26.8x_6$$

a. What is the estimated index of satisfaction for a person who first married at 18, has an annual income of $26,500, has three children living, has assets of $156,000, has an index of health status of 141, and has 2.5 social activities a week on the average?
b. Which would add more to satisfaction, an additional income of $10,000 a year or two more social activities a week?

4. Cellulon, a manufacturer of home insulation, wants to develop guidelines for builders and consumers on how the thickness of the insulation in the attic of a home and the outdoor temperature affect natural gas consumption. In the laboratory, it varied the insulation thickness and temperature. A few of the findings are:

Monthly Natural Gas Consumption (cubic feet), y	Thickness of Insulation (inches), x_1	Outdoor Temperature (°F), x_2
30.3	6	40
26.9	12	40
22.1	8	49

On the basis of the sample results, the regression equation is:

$$\hat{y} = 62.65 - 1.86x_1 - 0.52x_2$$

a. How much natural gas can homeowners expect to use per month if they install 6 inches of insulation and the outdoor temperature is 40 degrees F?
b. What effect would installing 7 inches of insulation instead of 6 have on the monthly natural gas consumption (assuming the outdoor temperature remains at 40 degrees F)?
c. Why are the regression coefficients b_1 and b_2 negative? Is this logical?

LO14-2
Evaluate how well a multiple regression equation fits the data.

EVALUATING A MULTIPLE REGRESSION EQUATION

Many statistics and statistical methods are used to evaluate the relationship between a dependent variable and more than one independent variable. Our first step was to write the relationship in terms of a multiple regression equation. The next step follows on the concepts presented in Chapter 13 by using the information in an ANOVA table to evaluate how well the equation fits the data.

The ANOVA Table

As in Chapter 13, the statistical analysis of a multiple regression equation is summarized in an ANOVA table. To review, the total variation of the dependent variable, y, is divided into two components: (1) *regression,* or the variation of y explained by all the independent variables, and (2) *the error or residual,* or unexplained variation of y. These two categories are identified in the first column of an ANOVA table below. The column headed "*df*" refers to the degrees of freedom associated with each category. The total number of degrees of freedom is $n - 1$. The number of degrees of freedom in the regression is equal to the number of independent variables in the multiple regression equation. We call the regression degrees of freedom k. The number of degrees of freedom associated with the error term is equal to the total degrees of freedom minus the regression degrees of freedom. In multiple regression, the degrees of freedom are $n - (k + 1)$.

Source	***df***	**SS**	**MS**	***F***
Regression	k	SSR	MSR = SSR/k	MSR/MSE
Residual or error	$n - (k + 1)$	SSE	MSE = SSE/$[n - (k + 1)]$	
Total	$n - 1$	SS total		

The term "SS" located in the middle of the ANOVA table refers to the sum of squares. Notice that there is a sum of squares for each source of variation. The sum of squares column shows the amount of variation attributable to each source. The total variation of the dependent variable, y, is summarized in SS total. You should note that this is simply the numerator of the usual formula to calculate any variation—in other words, the sum of the squared deviations from the mean. It is computed as:

$$\text{Total Sum of Squares} = \text{SS total} = \Sigma(y - \bar{y})^2$$

As we have seen, the total sum of squares is the sum of the regression and residual sum of squares. The regression sum of squares is the sum of the squared differences between the estimated or predicted values, $\hat{y}$, and the overall mean of y. The regression sum of squares is found by:

$$\text{Regression Sum of Squares} = \text{SSR} = \Sigma(\hat{y} - \bar{y})^2$$

The residual sum of squares is the sum of the squared differences between the observed values of the dependent variable, y, and their corresponding estimated or predicted values, $\hat{y}$. Notice that this difference is the error of estimating or predicting the dependent variable with the multiple regression equation. It is calculated as:

$$\text{Residual or Error Sum of Squares} = \text{SSE} = \Sigma(y - \hat{y})^2$$

We will use the ANOVA table information from the previous example to evaluate the regression equation to estimate January heating costs.

	A	B	C	D
1	Cost	Temp	Insul	Age
2	250	35	3	6
3	360	29	4	10
4	165	36	7	3
5	43	60	6	9
6	92	65	5	6
7	200	30	5	5
8	355	10	6	7
9	290	7	10	10
10	230	21	9	11
11	120	55	2	5
12	73	54	12	4
13	205	48	5	1
14	400	20	5	15
15	320	39	4	7
16	72	60	8	6
17	272	20	5	8
18	94	58	7	3
19	190	40	8	11
20	235	27	9	8

SUMMARY OUTPUT

Regression Statistics	
Multiple R	0.897
R Square	0.804
Adjusted R Square	0.767
Standard Error	51.049
Observations	20

ANOVA

	df	*SS*	*MS*	*F*	*Significance F*
Regression	3	171220.473	57073.491	21.901	0.000
Residual	16	41695.277	2605.955		
Total	19	212915.750			

	Coefficients	*Standard Error*	*t Stat*	*P-value*
Intercept	427.194	59.601	7.168	0.000
Temp	-4.583	0.772	-5.934	0.000
Insul	-14.831	4.754	-3.119	0.007
Age	6.101	4.012	1.521	0.148

Multiple Standard Error of Estimate

We begin with the **multiple standard error of estimate.** Recall that the standard error of estimate is comparable to the standard deviation. To explain the details of the standard error of estimate, refer to the first sampled home in row 2 in the Excel spreadsheet on the previous page. The actual heating cost for the first observation, y, is \$250; the outside temperature, x_1, is 35 degrees; the depth of insulation, x_2, is 3 inches; and the age of the furnace, x_3, is 6 years. Using the regression equation developed in the previous section, the estimated heating cost for this home is:

$$\begin{aligned}\hat{y} &= 427.194 - 4.583x_1 - 14.831x_2 + 6.101x_3\\ &= 427.194 - 4.583(35) - 14.831(3) + 6.101(6)\\ &= 258.90\end{aligned}$$

So we would estimate that a home with a mean January outside temperature of 35 degrees, 3 inches of insulation, and a 6-year-old furnace would cost \$258.90 to heat. The actual heating cost was \$250, so the residual—which is the difference between the actual value and the estimated value—is $y - \hat{y} = 250 - 258.90 = -8.90$. This difference of \$8.90 is the random or unexplained error for the first home sampled. Our next step is to square this difference—that is, find $(y - \hat{y})^2 = (250 - 258.90)^2 = (-8.90)^2 = 79.21$.

If we repeat this calculation for the other 19 observations and sum all 20 squared differences, the total will be the residual or error sum of squares from the ANOVA table. Using this information, we can calculate the multiple standard error of the estimate as:

MULTIPLE STANDARD ERROR OF ESTIMATE

$$s_{Y.123...k} = \sqrt{\frac{\Sigma(y - \hat{y})^2}{n - (k + 1)}} = \sqrt{\frac{SSE}{n - (k + 1)}} \qquad [14\text{–}2]$$

where:

y is the actual observation.
$\hat{y}$ is the estimated value computed from the regression equation.
n is the number of observations in the sample.
k is the number of independent variables.
SSE is the Residual Sum of Squares from an ANOVA table.

There is more information in the ANOVA table that can be used to compute the multiple standard error of estimate. The column headed "MS" reports the mean squares for the regression and residual variation. These values are calculated as the sum of squares divided by the corresponding degrees of freedom. The multiple standard error of estimate is equal to the square root of the residual MS, which is also called the mean square error or the MSE.

$$s_{Y.123...K} = \sqrt{MSE} = \sqrt{2605.995} = \$51.05$$

How do we interpret the standard error of estimate of 51.05? It is the typical "error" when we use this equation to predict the cost. First, the units are the same as the dependent variable, so the standard error is in dollars, \$51.05. Second, we expect the residuals to be approximately normally distributed, so about 68% of the residuals will be within ±\$51.05 and about 95% within ±2(51.05), or ±\$102.10. As before with similar measures of dispersion, such as the standard error of estimate in Chapter 13, a smaller multiple standard error indicates a better or more effective predictive equation.

Coefficient of Multiple Determination

Next, let's look at the coefficient of multiple determination. Recall from the previous chapter the coefficient of determination is defined as the percent of variation in the

dependent variable explained, or accounted for, by the independent variable. In the multiple regression case, we extend this definition as follows.

COEFFICIENT OF MULTIPLE DETERMINATION The percent of variation in the dependent variable, y, explained by the set of independent variables, x_1, x_2, x_3, . . . x_k.

The characteristics of the coefficient of multiple determination are:

1. **It is symbolized by a capital *R* squared.** In other words, it is written as R^2 because it behaves like the square of a correlation coefficient.
2. **It can range from 0 to 1.** A value near 0 indicates little association between the set of independent variables and the dependent variable. A value near 1 means a strong association.
3. **It cannot assume negative values.** Any number that is squared or raised to the second power cannot be negative.
4. **It is easy to interpret.** Because R^2 is a value between 0 and 1, it is easy to interpret, compare, and understand.

We can calculate the coefficient of determination from the information found in the ANOVA table. We look in the sum of squares column, which is labeled SS in the Excel output, and use the regression sum of squares, SSR, then divide by the total sum of squares, SS total.

COEFFICIENT OF MULTIPLE DETERMINATION

$$R^2 = \frac{\text{SSR}}{\text{SS total}} \quad [14\text{–}3]$$

We can use the regression and the total sum of squares from the ANOVA table highlighted in the Excel output on page 483 and compute the coefficient of determination.

$$R^2 = \frac{\text{SSR}}{\text{SS total}} = \frac{171{,}220.473}{212{,}915.750} = .804$$

How do we interpret this value? We conclude that the independent variables (outside temperature, amount of insulation, and age of furnace) explain, or account for, 80.4% of the variation in heating cost. To put it another way, 19.6% of the variation is due to other sources, such as random error or variables not included in the analysis. Using the ANOVA table, 19.6% is the error sum of squares divided by the total sum of squares. Knowing that the SSR + SSE = SS total, the following relationship is true.

$$1 - R^2 = 1 - \frac{\text{SSR}}{\text{SS total}} = \frac{\text{SSE}}{\text{SS total}} = \frac{41{,}695.277}{212{,}915.750} = .196$$

Adjusted Coefficient of Determination

The coefficient of determination tends to increase as more independent variables are added to the multiple regression model. Each new independent variable causes the predictions to be more accurate. That, in turn, makes SSE smaller and SSR larger. Hence, R^2 increases only because the total number of independent variables increases and not because the added independent variable is a good predictor of the dependent variable. In fact, if the number of variables, k, and the sample size, n, are equal, the coefficient of determination is 1.0. In practice, this situation is rare and would also be ethically questionable. To balance the effect that the number of independent variables has on the coefficient of multiple determination, statistical software packages use an *adjusted* coefficient of multiple determination.

ADJUSTED COEFFICIENT OF DETERMINATION

$$R^2_{adj} = 1 - \frac{\dfrac{SSE}{n-(k+1)}}{\dfrac{SS\,total}{n-1}} \qquad [14\text{–}4]$$

The error and total sum of squares are divided by their degrees of freedom. Notice especially the degrees of freedom for the error sum of squares include *k*, the number of independent variables. For the cost of heating example, the adjusted coefficient of determination is:

$$R^2_{adj} = 1 - \frac{\dfrac{41{,}695.277}{20-(3+1)}}{\dfrac{212{,}915.750}{20-1}} = 1 - \frac{2{,}605.955}{11{,}206.092} = 1 - .233 = .767$$

If we compare the R^2 (0.80) to the adjusted R^2 (0.767), the difference in this case is small.

SELF-REVIEW 14–2

Refer to Self-Review 14–1 on the subject of restaurants in Myrtle Beach. The ANOVA portion of the regression output is presented below.

Analysis of Variance

Source	DF	SS	MS
Regression	5	100	20
Residual Error	20	40	2
Total	25	140	

(a) How large was the sample?
(b) How many independent variables are there?
(c) How many dependent variables are there?
(d) Compute the standard error of estimate. About 95% of the residuals will be between what two values?
(e) Determine the coefficient of multiple determination. Interpret this value.
(f) Find the coefficient of multiple determination, adjusted for the degrees of freedom.

EXERCISES

5. Consider the ANOVA table that follows.

Analysis of Variance

Source	DF	SS	MS	F	P
Regression	2	77.907	38.954	4.14	0.021
Residual Error	62	583.693	9.414		
Total	64	661.600			

a. Determine the standard error of estimate. About 95% of the residuals will be between what two values?
b. Determine the coefficient of multiple determination. Interpret this value.
c. Determine the coefficient of multiple determination, adjusted for the degrees of freedom.

6. Consider the ANOVA table that follows.

Analysis of Variance

Source	DF	SS	MS	F
Regression	5	3710.00	742.00	12.89
Residual Error	46	2647.38	57.55	
Total	51	6357.38		

a. Determine the standard error of estimate. About 95% of the residuals will be between what two values?
b. Determine the coefficient of multiple determination. Interpret this value.
c. Determine the coefficient of multiple determination, adjusted for the degrees of freedom.

LO14-3
Test hypotheses about the relationships inferred by a multiple regression model.

INFERENCES IN MULTIPLE LINEAR REGRESSION

Thus far, multiple regression analysis has been viewed only as a way to describe the relationship between a dependent variable and several independent variables. However, the least squares method also has the ability to draw inferences or generalizations about the relationship for an entire population. Recall that when you create confidence intervals or perform hypothesis tests as a part of inferential statistics, you view the data as a random sample taken from some population.

In the multiple regression setting, we assume there is an unknown population regression equation that relates the dependent variable to the k independent variables. This is sometimes called a **model** of the relationship. In symbols we write:

$$Y = \alpha + \beta_1 X_1 + \beta_2 X_2 + \cdots + \beta_k X_k$$

This equation is analogous to formula (14–1) except the coefficients are now reported as Greek letters. We use the Greek letters to denote *population parameters*. Then under a certain set of assumptions, which will be discussed shortly, the computed values of a and b_j are sample statistics. These sample statistics are point estimates of the corresponding population parameters α and β_j. For example, the sample regression coefficient b_2 is a point estimate of the population parameter β_2. The sampling distribution of these point estimates follows the normal probability distribution. These sampling distributions are each centered at their respective parameter values. To put it another way, the means of the sampling distributions are equal to the parameter values to be estimated. Thus, by using the properties of the sampling distributions of these statistics, inferences about the population parameters are possible.

Global Test: Testing the Multiple Regression Model

We can test the ability of the independent variables $X_1, X_2, \ldots, X_k$ to explain the behavior of the dependent variable Y. To put this in question form: Can the dependent variable be estimated without relying on the independent variables? The test used is referred to as the **global test.** Basically, it investigates whether it is possible all the independent variables have zero regression coefficients.

To relate this question to the heating cost example, we will test whether the independent variables (amount of insulation in the attic, mean daily outside temperature, and age of furnace) effectively estimate home heating costs. In testing a hypothesis, we first state the null hypothesis and the alternate hypothesis. In the heating cost example, there are three independent variables. Recall that b_1, b_2, and b_3 are sample regression coefficients. The corresponding coefficients in the population are given the symbols β_1, β_2, and β_3. We now test whether the regression coefficients in the population are all zero. The null hypothesis is:

$$H_0: \beta_1 = \beta_2 = \beta_3 = 0$$

The alternate hypothesis is:

$$H_1: \text{Not all the } \beta_i\text{'s are } 0.$$

If the null hypothesis is true, it implies the regression coefficients are all zero and, logically, are of no value in estimating the dependent variable (heating cost). Should that be the case, we would have to search for some other independent variables—or take a different approach—to predict home heating costs.

To test the null hypothesis that the multiple regression coefficients are all zero, we employ the F distribution introduced in Chapter 12. We will use the .05 level of significance. Recall these characteristics of the F distribution:

1. **There is a family of *F* distributions.** Each time the degrees of freedom in either the numerator or the denominator change, a new F distribution is created.

2. **The *F* distribution cannot be negative.** The smallest possible value is 0.
3. **It is a continuous distribution.** The distribution can assume an infinite number of values between 0 and positive infinity.
4. **It is positively skewed.** The long tail of the distribution is to the right-hand side. As the number of degrees of freedom increases in both the numerator and the denominator, the distribution approaches the normal probability distribution. That is, the distribution will move toward a symmetric distribution.
5. **It is asymptotic.** As the values of *X* increase, the *F* curve will approach the horizontal axis, but will never touch it.

The *F*-statistic to test the global hypothesis follows. As in Chapter 12, it is the ratio of two variances. In this case, the numerator is the regression sum of squares divided by its degrees of freedom, *k*. The denominator is the residual sum of squares divided by its degrees of freedom, $n - (k + 1)$. The formula follows.

GLOBAL TEST

$$F = \frac{SSR/k}{SSE/[n - (k + 1)]} \qquad [14\text{–}5]$$

Using the values from the ANOVA table on page 480, the *F*-statistic is

$$F = \frac{SSR/k}{SSE/[n - (k + 1)]} = \frac{171{,}220.473/3}{41{,}695.277/[20 - (3 + 1)]} = 21.90$$

Remember that the *F*-statistic tests the basic null hypothesis that two variances or, in this case, two mean squares are equal. In our global multiple regression hypothesis test, we will reject the null hypothesis, H_0, that all regression coefficients are zero when the regression mean square is larger in comparison to the residual mean square. If this is true, the *F*-statistic will be relatively large and in the far right tail of the *F* distribution, and the *p*-value will be small, that is, less than our choice of significance level of 0.05. Thus, we will reject the null hypothesis.

As with other hypothesis-testing methods, the decision rule can be based on either of two methods: (1) comparing the test statistic to a critical value or (2) calculating a *p*-value based on the test statistic and comparing the *p*-value to the significance level. The critical value method using the *F*-statistic requires three pieces of information: (1) the numerator degrees of freedom, (2) the denominator degrees of freedom, and (3) the significance level. The degrees of freedom for the numerator and the denominator are reported in the Excel ANOVA table that follows. The ANOVA output is highlighted in light green. The top number in the column marked "*df*" is 3, indicating there are 3 degrees of freedom in the numerator. This value corresponds to the number of independent variables. The middle number in the "*df*" column (16) indicates that there are 16 degrees of freedom in the denominator. The number 16 is found by $n - (k - 1) = 20 - (3 - 1) = 16$.

	A	B	C	D	G	H	I	J	K	L	M
1	Cost	Temp	Insul	Age		SUMMARY OUTPUT					
2	250	35	3	6							
3	360	29	4	10		*Regression Statistics*					
4	165	36	7	3		Multiple R	0.897				
5	43	60	6	9		R Square	0.804				
6	92	65	5	6		Adjusted R Square	0.767				
7	200	30	5	5		Standard Error	51.049				
8	355	10	6	7		Observations	20				
9	290	7	10	10							
10	230	21	9	11		ANOVA					
11	120	55	2	5			*df*	*SS*	*MS*	*F*	*Significance F*
12	73	54	12	4		Regression	3	171220.473	57073.491	21.901	0.000
13	205	48	5	1		Residual	16	41695.277	2605.955		
14	400	20	5	15		Total	19	212915.750			
15	320	39	4	7							
16	72	60	8	6			*Coefficients*	*Standard Error*	*t Stat*	*P-value*	
17	272	20	5	8		Intercept	427.194	59.601	7.168	0.000	
18	94	58	7	3		Temp	-4.583	0.772	-5.934	0.000	
19	190	40	8	11		Insul	-14.831	4.754	-3.119	0.007	
20	235	27	9	8		Age	6.101	4.012	1.521	0.148	

The critical value of F is found in Appendix B.6. Using the table for the .05 significance level, move horizontally to 3 degrees of freedom in the numerator, then down to 16 degrees of freedom in the denominator, and read the critical value. It is 3.24. The region where H_0 is not rejected and the region where H_0 is rejected are shown in the following diagram.

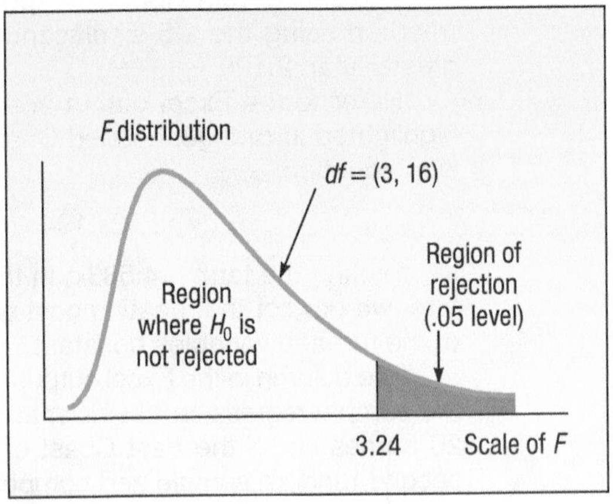

Continuing with the global test, the decision rule is: Do not reject the null hypothesis, H_0, that all the regression coefficients are 0 if the computed value of F is less than or equal to 3.24. If the computed F is greater than 3.24, reject H_0 and accept the alternate hypothesis, H_1.

The computed value of F is 21.90, which is in the rejection region. The null hypothesis that all the multiple regression coefficients are zero is therefore rejected. This means that at least one of the independent variables has the ability to explain the variation in the dependent variable (heating cost). We expected this decision. Logically, the outside temperature, the amount of insulation, or the age of the furnace has a great bearing on heating costs. The global test assures us that they do.

Testing the null hypothesis can also be based on a p-value, which is reported in the statistical software output for all hypothesis tests. In the case of the F-statistic, the p-value is defined as the probability of observing an F-value as large or larger than the F test statistic, assuming the null hypothesis is true. If the p-value is less than our selected significance level, then we decide to reject the null hypothesis. The ANOVA shows the F-statistic's p-value is equal to 0.000. It is clearly less than our significance level of 0.05. Therefore, we decide to reject the global null hypothesis and conclude that at least one of the regression coefficients is not equal to zero.

Evaluating Individual Regression Coefficients

So far we have shown that at least one, but not necessarily all, of the regression coefficients is not equal to zero and thus useful for predictions. The next step is to test the independent variables *individually* to determine which regression coefficients may be 0 and which are not.

Why is it important to know if any of the β_i's equal 0? If a β could equal 0, it implies that this particular independent variable is of no value in explaining any variation in the dependent value. If there are coefficients for which H_0 cannot be rejected, we may want to eliminate them from the regression equation.

Our strategy is to use three sets of hypotheses: one for temperature, one for insulation, and one for age of the furnace.

For temperature:	For insulation:	For furnace age:
H_0: $\beta_1 = 0$	H_0: $\beta_2 = 0$	H_0: $\beta_3 = 0$
H_1: $\beta_1 \neq 0$	H_1: $\beta_2 \neq 0$	H_1: $\beta_3 \neq 0$

We will test the hypotheses at the .05 level. Note that these are two-tailed tests.

The test statistic follows Student's t distribution with $n - (k + 1)$ degrees of freedom. The number of sample observations is n. There are 20 homes in the study, so $n = 20$. The number of independent variables is k, which is 3. Thus, there are $n - (k + 1) = 20 - (3 + 1) = 16$ degrees of freedom.

The critical value for t is in Appendix B.5. For a two-tailed test with 16 degrees of freedom using the .05 significance level, H_0 is rejected if t is less than -2.120 or greater than 2.120.

Refer to the Excel output in the previous section. (See page 488.) The column highlighted in orange, headed Coefficients, shows the values for the multiple regression equation:

$$\hat{y} = 427.194 - 4.583x_1 - 14.831x_2 + 6.101x_3$$

Interpreting the term $-4.583x_1$ in the equation: For each degree increase in temperature, we predict that heating cost will decrease \$4.58, holding the insulation and age of the furnace variables constant.

The column in the Excel output labeled "Standard Error" shows the standard error of the sample regression coefficients. Recall that Salsberry Realty selected a sample of 20 homes along the East Coast of the United States. If Salsberry Realty selected a second random sample and computed the regression coefficients for that sample, the values would not be exactly the same. If the sampling process was repeated many times, we could construct a sampling distribution for each of these regression coefficients. The column labeled "Standard Error" estimates the variability for each of these regression coefficients. The sampling distributions of the coefficients follow the t distribution with $n - (k + 1)$ degrees of freedom. Hence, we are able to test the independent variables individually to determine whether the regression coefficients differ from zero. The formula is:

TESTING INDIVIDUAL REGRESSION COEFFICIENTS

$$t = \frac{b_i - 0}{s_{b_i}} \quad [14\text{–}6]$$

The b_i refers to any one of the regression coefficients, and s_{b_i} refers to the standard deviation of that distribution of the regression coefficient. We include 0 in the equation because the null hypothesis is $\beta_i = 0$.

To illustrate this formula, refer to the test of the regression coefficient for the independent variable temperature. From the output on page 488, the regression coefficient for temperature is -4.583. The standard deviation of the sampling distribution of the regression coefficient for the independent variable temperature is 0.772. Inserting these values in formula (14–6):

$$t = \frac{b_1 - 0}{s_{b_1}} = \frac{-4.583 - 0}{0.772} = -5.937$$

The computed value of t is -5.937 for temperature (the small difference between the computed value and that shown on the Excel output is due to rounding) and -3.119 for insulation. Both of these t-values are in the rejection region to the left of -2.120. Thus, we conclude that the regression coefficients for the temperature and insulation variables are *not* zero. The computed t for the age of the furnace is 1.521, so we conclude that the coefficient could equal 0. The independent variable age of the furnace is not a significant predictor of heating cost. The results of these hypothesis tests indicate that the analysis should focus on temperature and insulation as predictors of heating cost.

We can also use p-values to test the individual regression coefficients. Again, these are commonly reported in statistical software output. The computed value of t for temperature on the Excel output is -5.934 and has a p-value of 0.000. Because the p-value is less than 0.05, the regression coefficient for the independent variable temperature is not equal to zero and should be included in the equation to

predict heating costs. For insulation, the value of t is -3.119 and has a p-value of 0.007. As with temperature, the p-value is less than 0.05, so we conclude that the insulation regression coefficient is not equal to zero and should be included in the equation to predict heating cost. In contrast to temperature and insulation, the p-value to test the "age of the furnace" regression coefficient is 0.148. It is clearly greater than 0.05, so we conclude that the "age of furnace" regression coefficient could equal 0. Further, as an independent variable it is not a significant predictor of heating cost. Thus, age of furnace should not be included in the equation to predict heating costs.

At this point, we need to develop a strategy for deleting independent variables. In the Salsberry Realty case, there were three independent variables. For the age of the furnace variable, we failed to reject the null hypothesis that the regression coefficient was zero. It is clear that we should drop that variable and rerun the regression equation. Below is the Excel output where heating cost is the dependent variable and outside temperature and amount of insulation are the independent variables.

	A	B	C	D
1	Cost	Temp	Insul	Age
2	250	35	3	6
3	360	29	4	10
4	165	36	7	3
5	43	60	6	9
6	92	65	5	6
7	200	30	5	5
8	355	10	6	7
9	290	7	10	10
10	230	21	9	11
11	120	55	2	5
12	73	54	12	4
13	205	48	5	1
14	400	20	5	15
15	320	39	4	7
16	72	60	8	6
17	272	20	5	8
18	94	58	7	3
19	190	40	8	11
20	235	27	9	8

SUMMARY OUTPUT

Regression Statistics	
Multiple R	0.881
R Square	0.776
Adjusted R Square	0.749
Standard Error	52.982
Observations	20

ANOVA

	df	*SS*	*MS*	*F*	*Significance F*
Regression	2	165194.521	82597.261	29.424	0.000
Residual	17	47721.229	2807.131		
Total	19	212915.750			

	Coefficients	*Standard Error*	*t Stat*	*P-value*
Intercept	490.286	44.410	11.040	0.000
Temp	-5.150	0.702	-7.337	0.000
Insul	-14.718	4.934	-2.983	0.008

Summarizing the results from this new output:

1. The new regression equation is:

$$\hat{y} = 490.286 - 5.150x_1 - 14.718x_2$$

   Notice that the regression coefficients for outside temperature (x_1) and amount of insulation (x_2) are similar to but not exactly the same as when we included the independent variable age of the furnace. Compare the above equation to that in the Excel output on page 488. Both of the regression coefficients are negative as in the earlier equation.

2. The details of the global test are as follows:

$$H_0: \beta_1 = \beta_2 = 0$$
$$H_1: \text{Not all of the } \beta_i\text{'s} = 0$$

   The F distribution is the test statistic and there are $k = 2$ degrees of freedom in the numerator and $n - (k + 1) = 20 - (2 + 1) = 17$ degrees of freedom in the denominator. Using the .05 significance level and Appendix B.6, the decision rule is to reject H_0 if F is greater than 3.59. We compute the value of F as follows:

$$F = \frac{\text{SSR}/k}{\text{SSE}/[n - (k + 1)]} = \frac{165{,}194.521/2}{47{,}721.229/[20 - (2 + 1)]} = 29.424$$

   Because the computed value of F (29.424) is greater than the critical value (3.59), the null hypothesis is rejected and the alternate accepted. We conclude that at least one of the regression coefficients is different from 0.

Using the p-value, the F test statistic (29.424) has a p-value (0.000), which is clearly less than 0.05. Therefore, we reject the null hypothesis and accept the alternate. We conclude that at least one of the regression coefficients is different from 0.

3. The next step is to conduct a test of the regression coefficients individually. We want to determine if one or both of the regression coefficients are different from 0. The null and alternate hypotheses for each of the independent variables are:

Outside Temperature	Insulation
$H_0: \beta_1 = 0$	$H_0: \beta_2 = 0$
$H_1: \beta_1 \neq 0$	$H_1: \beta_2 \neq 0$

The test statistic is the t distribution with $n - (k + 1) = 20 - (2 + 1) = 17$ degrees of freedom. Using the .05 significance level and Appendix B.5, the decision rule is to reject H_0 if the computed value of t is less than -2.110 or greater than 2.110.

Outside Temperature

$$t = \frac{b_1 - 0}{s_{b_1}} = \frac{-5.150 - 0}{0.702} = -7.337$$

Insulation

$$t = \frac{b_2 - 0}{s_{b_2}} = \frac{-14.718 - 0}{4.934} = -2.983$$

In both tests, we reject H_0 and accept H_1. We conclude that each of the regression coefficients is different from 0. Both outside temperature and amount of insulation are useful variables in explaining the variation in heating costs.

Using p-values, the p-value for the temperature t-statistic is 0.000 and the p-value for the insulation t-statistic is 0.008. Both p-values are less than 0.05, so in both tests we reject the null hypothesis and conclude that each of the regression coefficients is different from 0. Both outside temperature and amount of insulation are useful variables in explaining the variation in heating costs.

In the heating cost example, it was clear which independent variable to delete. However, in some instances which variable to delete may not be as clear-cut. To explain, suppose we develop a multiple regression equation based on five independent variables. We conduct the global test and find that some of the regression coefficients are different from zero. Next, we test the regression coefficients individually and find that three are significant and two are not. The preferred procedure is to drop the single independent variable with the *smallest absolute* t *value* or *largest* p*-value* and rerun the regression equation with the four remaining variables, then, on the new regression equation with four independent variables, conduct the individual tests. If there are still regression coefficients that are not significant, again drop the variable with the smallest absolute t value or the largest, nonsignificant p-value. To describe the process in another way, we should delete only one variable at a time. Each time we delete a variable, we need to rerun the regression equation and check the remaining variables.

This process of selecting variables to include in a regression model can be automated, using Excel, Minitab, MegaStat, or other statistical software. Most of the software systems include methods to sequentially remove and/or add independent variables and at the same time provide estimates of the percentage of variation explained (the R-square term). Two of the common methods are **stepwise regression** and **best subset regression.** It may take a long time, but in the extreme we could compute every regression between the dependent variable and any possible subset of the independent variables.

Unfortunately, on occasion, the software may work "too hard" to find an equation that fits all the quirks of your particular data set. The suggested equation may not represent the relationship in the population. Judgment is needed to choose among the equations presented. Consider whether the results are logical. They should have a simple interpretation and be consistent with your knowledge of the application under study.

SELF-REVIEW 14–3

The regression output about eating places in Myrtle Beach is repeated below (see earlier self-reviews).

Predictor	Coefficient	SE Coefficient	t	p-value
Constant	2.50	1.50	1.667	0.111
x_1	3.00	1.50	2.000	0.056
x_2	4.00	3.00	1.333	0.194
x_3	-3.00	0.20	-15.000	0.000
x_4	0.20	0.05	4.000	0.000
x_5	1.00	1.50	0.667	0.511

Analysis of Variance

Source	DF	SS	MS	F	p-value
Regression	5	100	20	10	0.000
Residual Error	20	40	2		
Total	25	140			

(a) Perform a global test of hypothesis to check if any of the regression coefficients are different from 0. What do you decide? Use the .05 significance level.
(b) Do an individual test of each independent variable. Which variables would you consider eliminating? Use the .05 significance level.
(c) Outline a plan for possibly removing independent variables.

EXERCISES

7. Given the following regression output,

Predictor	Coefficient	SE Coefficient	t	p-value
Constant	84.998	1.863	45.62	0.000
x_1	2.391	1.200	1.99	0.051
x_2	-0.409	0.172	-2.38	0.021

Analysis of Variance

Source	DF	SS	MS	F	p-value
Regression	2	77.907	38.954	4.138	0.021
Residual Error	62	583.693	9.414		
Total	64	661.600			

answer the following questions:

a. Write the regression equation.
b. If x_1 is 4 and x_2 is 11, what is the expected or predicted value of the dependent variable?
c. How large is the sample? How many independent variables are there?
d. Conduct a global test of hypothesis to see if any of the set of regression coefficients could be different from 0. Use the .05 significance level. What is your conclusion?
e. Conduct a test of hypothesis for each independent variable. Use the .05 significance level. Which variable would you consider eliminating?
f. Outline a strategy for deleting independent variables in this case.

8. The following regression output was obtained from a study of architectural firms. The dependent variable is the total amount of fees in millions of dollars.

Predictor	Coefficient	SE Coefficient	t	p-value
Constant	7.987	2.967	2.690	0.010
x_1	0.122	0.031	3.920	0.000
x_2	-1.220	0.053	-2.270	0.028
x_3	-0.063	0.039	-1.610	0.114
x_4	0.523	0.142	3.690	0.001
x_5	-0.065	0.040	-1.620	0.112

Analysis of Variance

Source	DF	SS	MS	F	p-value
Regression	5	371000	742	12.89	0.000
Residual Error	46	2647.38	57.55		
Total	51	6357.38			

x_1 is the number of architects employed by the company.
x_2 is the number of engineers employed by the company.
x_3 is the number of years involved with health care projects.
x_4 is the number of states in which the firm operates.
x_5 is the percent of the firm's work that is health care–related.

a. Write out the regression equation.
b. How large is the sample? How many independent variables are there?
c. Conduct a global test of hypothesis to see if any of the set of regression coefficients could be different from 0. Use the .05 significance level. What is your conclusion?
d. Conduct a test of hypothesis for each independent variable. Use the .05 significance level. Which variable would you consider eliminating first?
e. Outline a strategy for deleting independent variables in this case.

LO14-4
Evaluate the assumptions of multiple regression.

EVALUATING THE ASSUMPTIONS OF MULTIPLE REGRESSION

In the previous section, we described the methods to statistically evaluate the multiple regression equation. The results of the test let us know if at least one of the coefficients was not equal to zero and we described a procedure of evaluating each regression coefficient. We also discussed the decision-making process for including and excluding independent variables in the multiple regression equation.

It is important to know that the validity of the statistical global and individual tests rely on several assumptions. So if the assumptions are not true, the results might be biased or misleading. However, strict adherence to the following assumptions is not always possible. Fortunately, the statistical techniques discussed in this chapter work well even when one or more of the assumptions are violated. Even if the values in the multiple regression equation are "off" slightly, our estimates using a multiple regression equation will be closer than any that could be made otherwise. Usually the statistical procedures are robust enough to overcome violations of some assumptions.

In Chapter 13, we listed the necessary assumptions for regression when we considered only a single independent variable. (See page 455.) The assumptions for multiple regression are similar.

1. **There is a linear relationship.** That is, there is a straight-line relationship between the dependent variable and the set of independent variables.
2. **The variation in the residuals is the same for both large and small values of $\hat{y}$.** To put it another way, $(y - \hat{y})$ is unrelated to whether $\hat{y}$ is large or small.
3. **The residuals follow the normal probability distribution.** Recall the residual is the difference between the actual value of y and the estimated value $\hat{y}$. So the term $(y - \hat{y})$ is computed for every observation in the data set. These residuals should approximately follow a normal probability distribution. In addition, the mean of the residuals is 0.
4. **The independent variables should not be correlated.** That is, we would like to select a set of independent variables that are not themselves correlated.
5. **The residuals are independent.** This means that successive observations of the dependent variable are not correlated. This assumption is often violated when time is involved with the sampled observations.

In this section, we present a brief discussion of each of these assumptions. In addition, we provide methods to validate these assumptions and indicate the consequences if these assumptions cannot be met. For those interested in additional discussion, Kutner, Nachtscheim, Neter, and Li, *Applied Linear Statistical Models,* 5th ed. (McGraw-Hill: 2005), is an excellent reference.

Linear Relationship

Let's begin with the linearity assumption. The idea is that the relationship between the set of independent variables and the dependent variable is linear. If we are considering two independent variables, we can visualize this assumption. The two independent variables and the dependent variable would form a three-dimensional space. The regression equation would then form a plane as shown on page 478. We can evaluate this assumption with scatter diagrams and residual plots.

Using Scatter Diagrams The evaluation of a multiple regression equation should always include a scatter diagram that plots the dependent variable against each independent variable. These graphs help us to visualize the relationships and provide some initial information about the direction (positive or negative), linearity, and strength of the relationship. For example, the scatter diagrams for the home heating

example follow. The plots suggest a fairly strong negative, linear relationship between heating cost and temperature, and a negative relationship between heating cost and insulation.

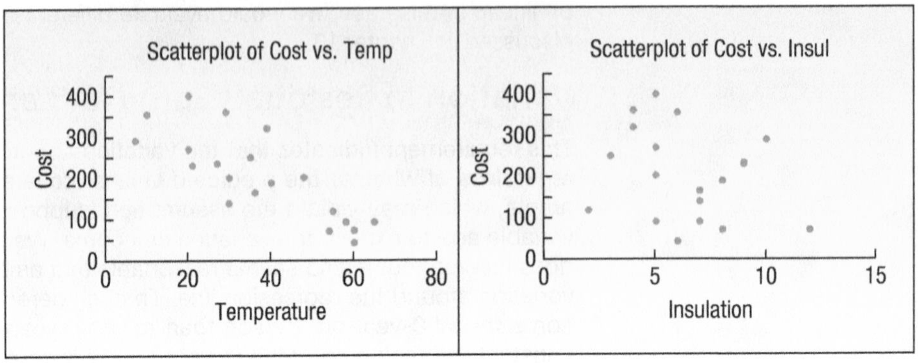

Using Residual Plots Recall that a residual ($y - \hat{y}$) can be computed using the multiple regression equation for each observation in a data set. In Chapter 13, we discussed the idea that the best regression line passed through the center of the data in a scatter plot. In this case, you would find a good number of the observations above the regression line (these residuals would have a positive sign) and a good number of the observations below the line (these residuals would have a negative sign). Further, the observations would be scattered above and below the line over the entire range of the independent variable.

The same concept is true for multiple regression, but we cannot graphically portray the multiple regression. However, plots of the residuals can help us evaluate the linearity of the multiple regression equation. To investigate, the residuals are plotted on the vertical axis against the predictor variable, $\hat{y}$. The graph on the left below shows the residual plots for the home heating cost example. Notice the following:

- The residuals are plotted on the vertical axis and are centered around zero. There are both positive and negative residuals.
- The residual plots show a random distribution of positive and negative values across the entire range of the variable plotted on the horizontal axis.
- The points are scattered and there is no obvious pattern, so there is no reason to doubt the linearity assumption.

This plot supports the assumption of linearity.

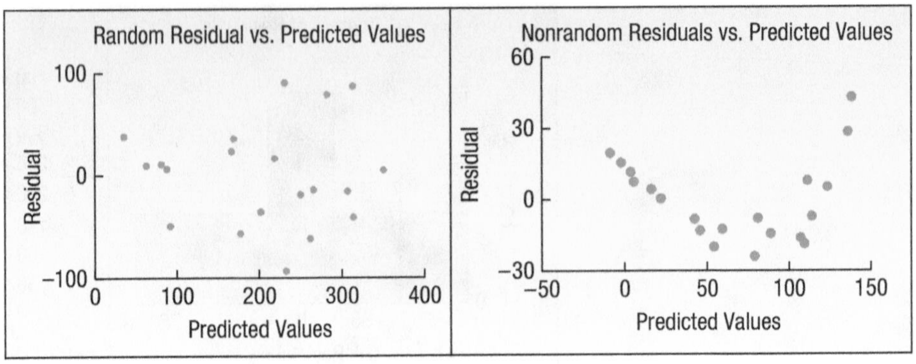

If there is a pattern to the points in the scatter plot, further investigation is necessary. For example, the graph at the bottom of the previous page shows nonrandom residuals. See that the residual plot does *not* show a random distribution of positive and negative values across the entire range of the variable plotted on the horizontal axis. In fact, the graph shows a curvature to the residual plots. This indicates the relationship may not be linear. In this case, we would evaluate different transformations of the equation as discussed in Chapter 13.

Variation in Residuals Same for Large and Small $\hat{y}$ Values

This requirement indicates that the variation about the predicted values is constant, regardless of whether the predicted values are large or small. To cite a specific example, which may violate the assumption, suppose we use the single independent variable age to explain the variation in income. We suspect that as age increases so does income, but it also seems reasonable that as age increases there may be more variation around the regression line. That is, there will likely be more variation in income for a 50-year-old person than for a 35-year-old person. The requirement for constant variation around the regression line is called **homoscedasticity.**

HOMOSCEDASTICITY The variation around the regression equation is the same for all of the values of the independent variables.

To check for homoscedasticity, the residuals are plotted against the fitted values of y. This is the same graph that we used to evaluate the assumption of linearity. (See page 495.) Based on the scatter diagram in that software output, it is reasonable to conclude that this assumption has not been violated.

Distribution of Residuals

To be sure that the inferences we make in the global and individual hypothesis tests are valid, we evaluate the distribution of residuals. Ideally, the residuals should follow a normal probability distribution.

To evaluate this assumption, we can organize the residuals into a frequency distribution. The Histogram of Residuals graph is shown on the left for the home heating cost example. Although it is difficult to show that the residuals follow a normal distribution with only 20 observations, it does appear the normality assumption is reasonable.

Excel offers another graph that helps to evaluate the assumption of normally distributed residuals. It is a called a Normal Probability Plot and is shown to the right of the histogram. The normal probability plot supports the assumption of normally distributed residuals if the plotted points are fairly close to a straight line drawn from the lower left to the upper right of the graph. This plot supports the assumption of normally distributed residuals.

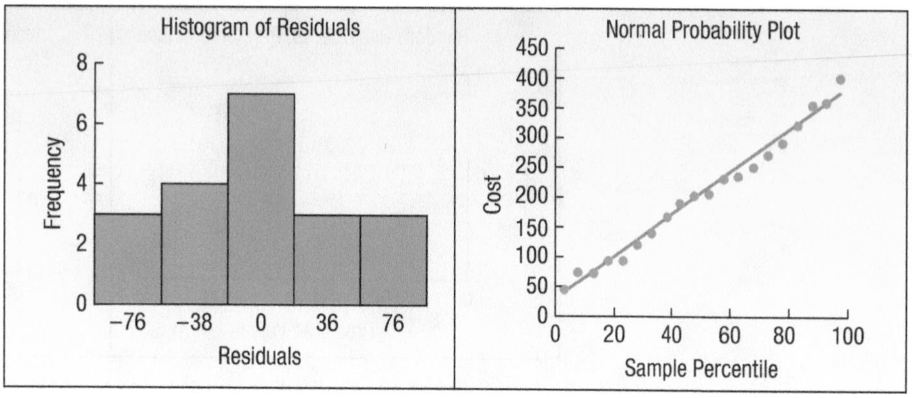

In this case, both graphs support the assumption that the residuals follow the normal probability distribution. Therefore, the inferences that we made based on the global and individual hypothesis tests are supported with the results of this evaluation.

Multicollinearity

Multicollinearity exists when independent variables are correlated. Correlated independent variables make it difficult to make inferences about the individual regression coefficients and their individual effects on the dependent variable. In practice, it is nearly impossible to select variables that are completely unrelated. To put it another way, it is nearly impossible to create a set of independent variables that are not correlated to some degree. However, a general understanding of the issue of multicollinearity is important.

First, multicollinearity does not affect a multiple regression equation's ability to predict the dependent variable. However, when we are interested in evaluating the relationship between each independent variable and the dependent variable, multicollinearity may show unexpected results.

For example, if we use two highly multicollinear variables, high school GPA and high school class rank, to predict the GPA of incoming college freshmen (dependent variable), we would expect that both independent variables would be positively related to the dependent variable. However, because the independent variables are highly correlated, one of the independent variables may have an unexpected and inexplicable negative sign. In essence, these two independent variables are redundant in that they explain the same variation in the dependent variable.

A second reason to avoid correlated independent variables is they may lead to erroneous results in the hypothesis tests for the individual independent variables. This is due to the instability of the standard error of estimate. Several clues that indicate problems with multicollinearity include the following:

1. An independent variable known to be an important predictor ends up having a regression coefficient that is not significant.
2. A regression coefficient that should have a positive sign turns out to be negative, or vice versa.
3. When an independent variable is added or removed, there is a drastic change in the values of the remaining regression coefficients.

In our evaluation of a multiple regression equation, an approach to reducing the effects of multicollinearity is to carefully select the independent variables that are included in the regression equation. A general rule is if the correlation between two independent variables is between −0.70 and 0.70, there likely is not a problem using both of the independent variables. A more precise test is to use the **variance inflation factor.** It is usually written *VIF*. The value of *VIF* is found as follows:

VARIANCE INFLATION FACTOR $$VIF = \frac{1}{1 - R_j^2} \qquad \textbf{[14–7]}$$

The term R_j^2 refers to the coefficient of determination, where the selected *independent variable* is used as a dependent variable and the remaining independent variables are used as independent variables. A *VIF* greater than 10 is considered unsatisfactory, indicating that the independent variable should be removed from the analysis. The following example will explain the details of finding the *VIF*.

EXAMPLE

Refer to the data in Table 14–1, which relate the heating cost to the independent variables outside temperature, amount of insulation, and age of furnace. Develop a correlation matrix for all the independent variables. Does it appear there is a problem with multicollinearity? Find and interpret the variance inflation factor for each of the independent variables.

SOLUTION

We begin by finding the correlation matrix for the dependent variable and the three independent variables. A correlation matrix shows the correlation between all pairs of the variables. A portion of that output follows:

	Cost	*Temp*	*Insul*	*Age*
Cost	1.000			
Temp	–0.812	1.000		
Insul	–0.257	–0.103	1.000	
Age	0.537	–0.486	0.064	1.000

The highlighted area indicates the correlation among the independent variables. Because all of the correlations are between −.70 and .70, we do not suspect problems with multicollinearity. The largest correlation among the independent variables is −0.486 between age and temperature.

To confirm this conclusion, we compute the *VIF* for each of the three independent variables. We will consider the independent variable temperature first. We use Excel to find the multiple coefficient of determination with temperature as the *dependent variable* and amount of insulation and age of the furnace as independent variables. The relevant Excel output follows.

SUMMARY OUTPUT

Regression Statistics	
Multiple R	0.491
R Square	0.241
Adjusted R Square	0.152
Standard Error	16.031
Observations	20

ANOVA

	df	*SS*	*MS*	*F*	*Significance F*
Regression	2	1390.291	695.145	2.705	0.096
Residual	17	4368.909	256.995		
Total	19	5759.200			

The coefficient of determination is .241, so inserting this value into the *VIF* formula:

$$VIF = \frac{1}{1 - R_1^2} = \frac{1}{1 - .241} = 1.32$$

The *VIF* value of 1.32 is less than the upper limit of 10. This indicates that the independent variable temperature is not strongly correlated with the other independent variables.

Again, to find the *VIF* for insulation we would develop a regression equation with insulation as the *dependent variable* and temperature and age of furnace as independent variables. For this equation, the R^2 is .011 and, using formula (14–7), the *VIF* for insulation would be 1.011. To find the *VIF* for age, we would develop a regression equation with age as the dependent variable and temperature and insulation as the independent variables. For this equation, the R^2 is .236 and, using formula (14–7), the *VIF* for age would be 1.310. All the *VIF* values are less than 10. Hence, we conclude there is not a problem with multicollinearity in this example.

Independent Observations

The fifth assumption about regression and correlation analysis is that successive residuals should be independent. This means that there is not a pattern to the residuals, the residuals are not highly correlated, and there are not long runs of positive or negative residuals. When successive residuals are correlated, we refer to this condition as **autocorrelation.**

Autocorrelation frequently occurs when the data are collected over a period of time. For example, we wish to predict yearly sales of Ages Software Inc. based on the time and the amount spent on advertising. The dependent variable is yearly sales and the independent variables are time and amount spent on advertising. It is likely that for a period of time the actual points will be above the regression plane (remember there are two independent variables) and then for a period of time the points will be below the regression plane. The graph below shows the residuals plotted on the vertical axis and the fitted values $\hat{y}$ on the horizontal axis. Note the run of residuals above the mean of the residuals, followed by a run below the mean. A scatter plot such as this would indicate possible autocorrelation.

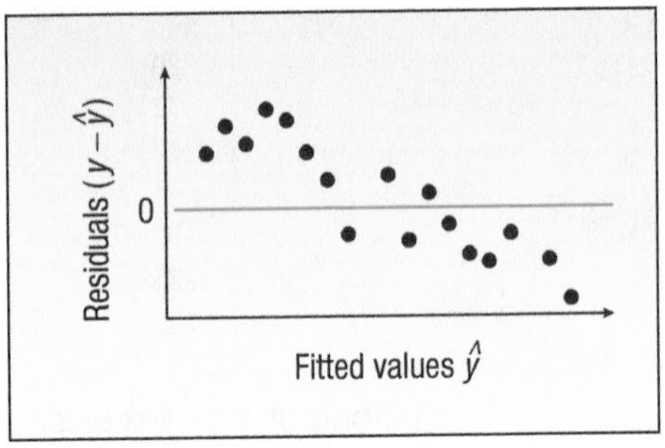

There is a test for autocorrelation, called the Durbin-Watson. It is discussed in Chapter 18.

LO14-5
Use and interpret a qualitative, dummy variable in multiple regression.

QUALITATIVE INDEPENDENT VARIABLES

In the previous example/solution regarding heating cost, the two independent variables outside temperature and insulation were quantitative; that is, numerical in nature. Frequently we wish to use nominal-scale variables—such as gender, whether the home has a swimming pool, or whether the sports team was the home or the visiting team—in our analysis. These are called **qualitative variables** because they describe a particular quality, such as male or female. To use a qualitative variable in regression analysis, we use a scheme of **dummy variables** in which one of the two possible conditions is coded 0 and the other 1.

DUMMY VARIABLE A variable in which there are only two possible outcomes. For analysis, one of the outcomes is coded a 1 and the other a 0.

STATISTICS IN ACTION

In recent years, multiple regression has been used in a variety of legal proceedings. It is particularly useful in cases alleging discrimination by gender or race. As an example, suppose that a woman alleges that Company X's wage rates are unfair to women. To support the claim, the plaintiff produces data showing that, on the average, women earn less than men. In response, Company X argues that its wage rates are based on experience, training, and skill and that its female employees, on the average, are younger and less experienced than the male employees. In fact, the company might further argue that the current situation is actually due to its recent successful efforts to hire more women.

For example, we are interested in estimating an executive's salary on the basis of years of job experience and whether he or she graduated from college. "Graduation from college" can take on only one of two conditions: yes or no. Thus, it is considered a qualitative variable.

Suppose in the Salsberry Realty example that the independent variable "garage" is added. For those homes without an attached garage, 0 is used; for homes with an attached garage, a 1 is used. We will refer to the "garage" variable as x_4. The data from Table 14–2 are entered into the Excel system. Recall that the variable "age of the furnace" is not included in the analysis because we determined that it was not significantly related to heating cost.

TABLE 14–2 Home Heating Costs, Temperature, Insulation, and Presence of a Garage for a Sample of 20 Homes

Cost, y	Temperature, x_1	Insulation, x_2	Garage, x_4
$250	35	3	0
360	29	4	1
165	36	7	0
43	60	6	0
92	65	5	0
200	30	5	0
355	10	6	1
290	7	10	1
230	21	9	0
120	55	2	0
73	54	12	0
205	48	5	1
400	20	5	1
320	39	4	1
72	60	8	0
272	20	5	1
94	58	7	0
190	40	8	1
235	27	9	0
139	30	7	0

The output from Excel is:

	A	B	C	D
1	Cost	Temp	Insul	Garage
2	250	35	3	0
3	360	29	4	1
4	165	36	7	0
5	43	60	6	0
6	92	65	5	0
7	200	30	5	0
8	355	10	6	1
9	290	7	10	1
10	230	21	9	0
11	120	55	2	0
12	73	54	12	0
13	205	48	5	1
14	400	20	5	1
15	320	39	4	1
16	72	60	8	0
17	272	20	5	1
18	94	58	7	0
19	190	40	8	1
20	235	27	9	0

SUMMARY OUTPUT

Regression Statistics	
Multiple R	0.933
R Square	0.870
Adjusted R Square	0.845
Standard Error	41.618
Observations	20

ANOVA

	df	*SS*	*MS*	*F*	*Significance F*
Regression	3	185202.269	61734.090	35.641	0.000
Residual	16	27713.481	1732.093		
Total	19	212915.750			

	Coefficients	*Standard Error*	*t Stat*	*P-value*
Intercept	393.666	45.001	8.748	0.000
Temp	-3.963	0.653	-6.072	0.000
Insul	-11.334	4.002	-2.832	0.012
Garage	77.432	22.783	3.399	0.004

What is the effect of the garage variable? Should it be included in the analysis? To show the effect of the variable, suppose we have two houses exactly alike

next to each other in Buffalo, New York; one has an attached garage and the other does not. Both homes have 3 inches of insulation, and the mean January temperature in Buffalo is 20 degrees. For the house without an attached garage, a 0 is substituted for x_4 in the regression equation. The estimated heating cost is \$280.404, found by:

$$\hat{y} = 393.666 - 3.963x_1 - 11.334x_2 + 77.432x_4$$
$$= 393.666 - 3.963(20) - 11.334(3) + 77.432(0) = 280.404$$

For the house with an attached garage, a 1 is substituted for x_4 in the regression equation. The estimated heating cost is \$357.836, found by:

$$\hat{y} = 393.666 - 3.963x_1 - 11.334x_2 + 77.432x_4$$
$$= 393.666 - 3.963(20) - 11.334(3) + 77.432(1) = 357.836$$

The difference between the estimated heating costs is \$77.432 (\$357.836 − \$280.404). Hence, we can expect the cost to heat a house with an attached garage to be \$77.432 more than the cost for an equivalent house without a garage.

We have shown the difference between the two types of homes to be \$77.432, but is the difference significant? We conduct the following test of hypothesis.

$$H_0: \beta_4 = 0$$
$$H_1: \beta_4 \neq 0$$

The information necessary to answer this question is in the output at the bottom of the previous page. The regression coefficient for the independent variable garage is \$77.432, and the standard deviation of the sampling distribution is 22.783. We identify this as the fourth independent variable, so we use a subscript of 4. (Remember we dropped age of the furnace, the third independent variable.) Finally, we insert these values in formula (14–6).

$$t = \frac{b_4 - 0}{s_{b_4}} = \frac{77.432 - 0}{22.783} = 3.399$$

There are three independent variables in the analysis, so there are $n - (k + 1) = 20 - (3 + 1) = 16$ degrees of freedom. The critical value from Appendix B.5 is 2.120. The decision rule, using a two-tailed test and the .05 significance level, is to reject H_0 if the computed t is to the left of -2.120 or to the right of 2.120. Because the computed value of 3.399 is to the right of 2.120, the null hypothesis is rejected. We conclude that the regression coefficient is not zero. The independent variable garage should be included in the analysis.

Using the p-value approach, the computed t value of 3.399 has a p-value of 0.004. This value is less than the .05 significance level. Therefore, we reject the null hypothesis. We conclude that the regression coefficient is not zero and the independent variable garage should be included in the analysis.

Is it possible to use a qualitative variable with more than two possible outcomes? Yes, but the coding scheme becomes more complex and will require a series of dummy variables. To explain, suppose a company is studying its sales as they relate to advertising expense by quarter for the last 5 years. Let sales be the dependent variable and advertising expense be the first independent variable, x_1. To include the qualitative information regarding the quarter, we use three additional independent variables. For the variable x_2, the five observations referring to the first quarter of each of the 5 years are coded 1 and the other quarters 0. Similarly, for x_3 the five observations referring to the second quarter are coded 1 and the other quarters 0. For x_4, the five observations referring to the third quarter are coded 1 and the other quarters 0. An observation that does not refer to any of the first three quarters must refer to the fourth quarter, so a distinct independent variable referring to this quarter is not necessary.

SELF-REVIEW 14–4

A study by the American Realtors Association investigated the relationship between the commissions earned by sales associates last year and the number of months since the associates earned their real estate licenses. Also of interest in the study is the gender of the sales associate. Below is a portion of the regression output. The dependent variable is commissions, which is reported in \$000, and the independent variables are months since the license was earned and gender (female = 1 and male = 0).

Regression Analysis

Regression Statistics	
Multiple R	0.801
R Square	0.642
Adjusted R Square	0.600
Standard Error	3.219
Observations	20

ANOVA

	df	*SS*	*MS*	*F*	*p-value*
Regression	2	315.9291	157.9645	15.2468	0.0002
Residual	17	176.1284	10.36049		
Total	19	492.0575			

	Coefficients	*Standard Error*	*t Stat*	*p-value*
Intercept	15.7625	3.0782	5.121	.0001
Months	0.4415	0.0839	5.262	.0001
Gender	3.8598	1.4724	2.621	.0179

(a) Write out the regression equation. How much commission would you expect a female agent to make who earned her license 30 months ago?
(b) Do the female agents on the average make more or less than the male agents? How much more?
(c) Conduct a test of hypothesis to determine if the independent variable gender should be included in the analysis. Use the .05 significance level. What is your conclusion?

LO14-6
Include and interpret an interaction effect in a multiple regression analysis.

REGRESSION MODELS WITH INTERACTION

In Chapter 12, we discussed interaction among independent variables. To explain, suppose we are studying weight loss and assume, as the current literature suggests, that diet and exercise are related. So the dependent variable is amount of change in weight and the independent variables are diet (yes or no) and exercise (none, moderate, significant). We are interested in whether there is interaction among the independent variables. That is, if those studied maintain their diet and exercise significantly, will that increase the mean amount of weight lost? Is total weight loss more than the sum of the loss due to the diet effect and the loss due to the exercise effect?

We can expand on this idea. Instead of having two nominal-scale variables, diet and exercise, we can examine the effect (interaction) of several ratio-scale variables. For example, suppose we want to study the effect of room temperature (68, 72, 76, or 80 degrees Fahrenheit) and noise level (60, 70, or 80 decibels) on the number of units produced. To put it another way, does the combination of noise level in the room and the temperature of the room have an effect on the productivity of the workers? Would the workers in a quiet, cool room produce more units than those in a hot, noisy room?

In regression analysis, interaction is examined as a separate independent variable. An interaction prediction variable can be developed by multiplying the data values in one independent variable by the values in another independent variable, thereby creating a new independent variable. A two-variable model that includes an interaction term is:

$$Y = \alpha + \beta_1 X_1 + \beta_2 X_2 + \beta_3 X_1 X_2$$

The term X_1X_2 is the *interaction term.* We create this variable by multiplying the values of X_1 and X_2 to create the third independent variable. We then develop a regression equation using the three independent variables and test the significance of the third independent variable using the individual test for independent variables, described earlier in the chapter. An example will illustrate the details.

EXAMPLE

Refer to the heating cost example and the data in Table 14–1. Is there an interaction between the outside temperature and the amount of insulation? If both variables are increased, is the effect on heating cost greater than the sum of savings from warmer temperature and the savings from increased insulation separately?

SOLUTION

The information from Table 14–1 for the independent variables temperature and insulation is repeated below. We create the interaction variable by multiplying the temperature variable by the insulation. For the first sampled home, the value temperature is 35 degrees and insulation is 3 inches so the value of the interaction variable is 35 × 3 = 105. The values of the other interaction products are found in a similar fashion.

	A	B	C	D
1	Cost	Temp	Insul	Temp X Insul
2	250	35	3	105
3	360	29	4	116
4	165	36	7	252
5	43	60	6	360
6	92	65	5	325
7	200	30	5	150
8	355	10	6	60
9	290	7	10	70
10	230	21	9	189
11	120	55	2	110
12	73	54	12	648
13	205	48	5	240
14	400	20	5	100
15	320	39	4	156
16	72	60	8	480
17	272	20	5	100
18	94	58	7	406
19	190	40	8	320
20	235	27	9	243
21	139	30	7	210

SUMMARY OUTPUT

Regression Statistics	
Multiple R	0.893
R Square	0.798
Adjusted R Square	0.760
Standard Error	51.846
Observations	20

ANOVA

	df	*SS*	*MS*	*F*	*Significance F*
Regression	3	169908.452	56636.151	21.070	0.000
Residual	16	43007.298	2687.956		
Total	19	212915.750			

	Coefficients	*Standard Error*	*t Stat*	*P-value*
Intercept	598.070	92.265	6.482	0.000
Temp	-7.811	2.124	-3.678	0.002
Insul	-30.161	12.621	-2.390	0.030
Temp X Insul	0.385	0.291	1.324	0.204

We find the multiple regression using temperature, insulation, and the interaction of temperature and insulation as independent variables. The regression equation is reported below.

$$\hat{y} = 598.070 - 7.811x_1 - 30.161x_2 + 0.385x_1x_2$$

The question we wish to answer is whether the interaction variable is significant. We will use the .05 significance level. In terms of a hypothesis:

$$H_0: \beta_3 = 0$$

$$H_1: \beta_3 \neq 0$$

There are $n - (k + 1) = 20 - (3 + 1) = 16$ degrees of freedom. Using the .05 significance level and a two-tailed test, the critical values of t are -2.120 and 2.120. We reject the null hypothesis if t is less than -2.120 or t is greater than 2.120. From the output, $b_3 = 0.385$ and $s_{b_3} = 0.291$. To find the value of t, we use formula (14–6).

$$t = \frac{b_3 - 0}{s_{b_3}} = \frac{0.385 - 0}{0.291} = 1.324$$

Because the computed value of 1.324 is less than the critical value of 2.120, we do not reject the null hypothesis. In addition, the p-value of .204 exceeds .05. We conclude that there is not a significant interaction between temperature and insulation.

There are other situations that can occur when studying interaction among independent variables.

1. It is possible to have a three-way interaction among the independent variables. In our heating example, we might have considered the three-way interaction between temperature, insulation, and age of the furnace.
2. It is possible to have an interaction where one of the independent variables is nominal scale. In our heating cost example, we could have studied the interaction between temperature and garage.

Studying all possible interactions can become very complex. However, careful consideration to possible interactions among independent variables can often provide useful insight into the regression models.

LO14-7
Apply stepwise regression to develop a multiple regression model.

STEPWISE REGRESSION

In our heating cost example (see sample information in Table 14–1), we considered three independent variables: the mean outside temperature, the amount of insulation in the home, and the age of the furnace. To obtain the equation, we first ran a global or "all at once" test to determine if any of the regression coefficients were significant. When we found at least one to be significant, we tested the regression coefficients individually to determine which were important. We kept the independent variables that had significant regression coefficients and left the others out. By retaining the independent variables with significant coefficients, we found the regression equation that used the fewest independent variables. This made the regression equation easier to interpret. Then we considered the qualitative variable, garage, and found that it was significantly related to heating cost. The variable, garage, was added to the equation.

We are now going to describe a technique called **stepwise regression.** This technique is more efficient for building an equation that only includes independent variables with significant regression coefficients.

> **STEPWISE REGRESSION** A step-by-step method to determine a regression equation that begins with a single independent variable and adds or deletes independent variables one by one. Only independent variables with nonzero regression coefficients are included in the regression equation.

In the stepwise method, we develop a sequence of equations. The first equation contains only one independent variable. However, this independent variable is the one from the set of proposed independent variables that explains the most variation in the dependent variable. Stated differently, if we compute all the simple correlations between each independent variable and the dependent variable, the stepwise method first selects the independent variable with the strongest correlation with the dependent variable.

Next, the stepwise method looks at the remaining independent variables and then selects the one that will explain the largest percentage of the variation yet unexplained. We continue this process until all the independent variables with significant regression coefficients are included in the regression equation. The advantages to the stepwise method are:

1. Only independent variables with significant regression coefficients are entered into the equation.
2. The steps involved in building the regression equation are clear.
3. It is efficient in finding the regression equation with only significant regression coefficients.
4. The changes in the multiple standard error of estimate and the coefficient of determination are shown.

The stepwise Minitab output for the heating cost problem follows. Note that the final equation, which is reported in the column labeled 3, includes the independent variables temperature, garage, and insulation. These are the same independent variables that were included in our equation using the global test and the test for individual independent variables. (See page 500.) The independent variable age, for age of the furnace, is not included because it is not a significant predictor of cost.

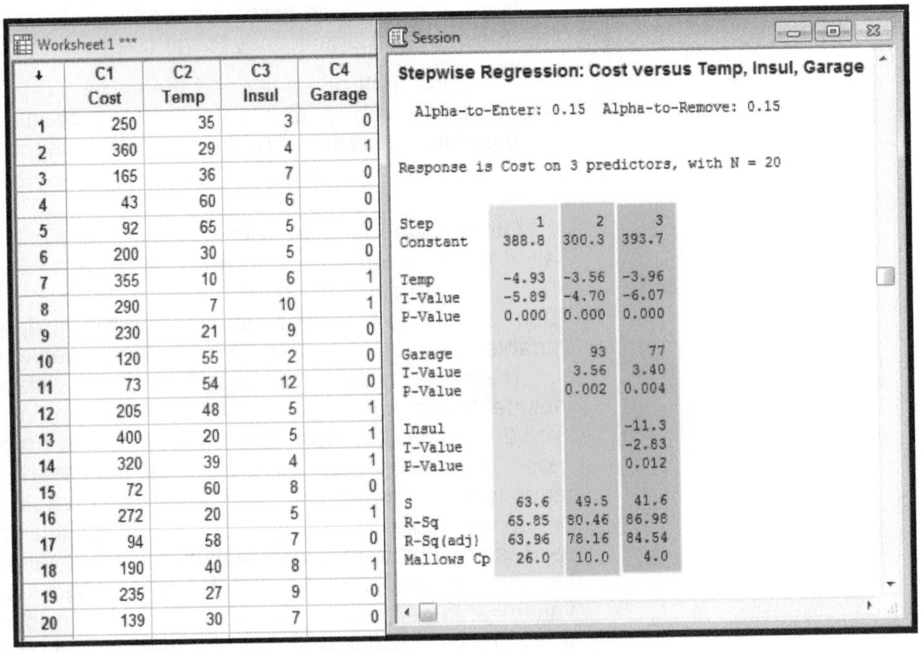
Worksheet 1 ***

↓	C1 Cost	C2 Temp	C3 Insul	C4 Garage
1	250	35	3	0
2	360	29	4	1
3	165	36	7	0
4	43	60	6	0
5	92	65	5	0
6	200	30	5	0
7	355	10	6	1
8	290	7	10	1
9	230	21	9	0
10	120	55	2	0
11	73	54	12	0
12	205	48	5	1
13	400	20	5	1
14	320	39	4	1
15	72	60	8	0
16	272	20	5	1
17	94	58	7	0
18	190	40	8	1
19	235	27	9	0
20	139	30	7	0

Session

Stepwise Regression: Cost versus Temp, Insul, Garage

```
Alpha-to-Enter: 0.15  Alpha-to-Remove: 0.15

Response is Cost on 3 predictors, with N = 20

Step              1       2       3
Constant      388.8   300.3   393.7

Temp          -4.93   -3.56   -3.96
T-Value       -5.89   -4.70   -6.07
P-Value       0.000   0.000   0.000

Garage                   93      77
T-Value                3.56    3.40
P-Value               0.002   0.004

Insul                          -11.3
T-Value                        -2.83
P-Value                        0.012

S              63.6    49.5    41.6
R-Sq          65.85   80.46   86.98
R-Sq(adj)     63.96   78.16   84.54
Mallows Cp     26.0    10.0     4.0
```

Reviewing the steps and interpreting output:

1. The stepwise procedure selects the independent variable temperature first. This variable explains more of the variation in heating cost than any of the other three proposed independent variables. Temperature explains 65.85% of the variation in heating cost. The regression equation is:

   $$\hat{y} = 388.8 - 4.93x_1$$

   There is an inverse relationship between heating cost and temperature. For each degree the temperature increases, heating cost is reduced by $4.93.
2. The next independent variable to enter the regression equation is garage. When this variable is added to the regression equation, the coefficient of determination is increased from 65.85% to 80.46%. That is, by adding garage as an independent variable, we increase the coefficient of determination by 14.61 percentage points. The regression equation after step 2 is:

   $$\hat{y} = 300.3 - 3.56x_1 + 93.0x_2$$

   Usually the regression coefficients will change from one step to the next. In this case, the coefficient for temperature retained its negative sign, but it changed from −4.93 to −3.56. This change is reflective of the added influence of the independent variable garage. Why did the stepwise method select the independent variable garage instead of either insulation or age? The increase in R^2, the coefficient of determination, is larger if garage is included rather than either of the other two variables.
3. At this point, there are two unused variables remaining, insulation and age. Notice on the third step the procedure selects insulation and then stops. This indicates

the variable insulation explains more of the remaining variation in heating cost than the age variable does. After the third step, the regression equation is:

$$\hat{y} = 393.7 - 3.96x_1 + 77.0x_2 - 11.3x_3$$

At this point, 86.98% of the variation in heating cost is explained by the three independent variables temperature, garage, and insulation. This is the same R^2 value and regression equation we found on page 500 except for rounding differences.

4. Here, the stepwise procedure stops. This means the independent variable age does not add significantly to the coefficient of determination.

The stepwise method developed the same regression equation, selected the same independent variables, and found the same coefficient of determination as the global and individual tests described earlier in the chapter. The advantage to the stepwise method is that it is more direct than using a combination of the global and individual procedures.

Other methods of variable selection are available. The stepwise method is also called the **forward selection method** because we begin with no independent variables and add one independent variable to the regression equation at each iteration. There is also the **backward elimination method,** which begins with the entire set of variables and eliminates one independent variable at each iteration.

The methods described so far look at one variable at a time and decide whether to include or eliminate that variable. Another approach is the **best-subset regression.** With this method, we look at the best model using one independent variable, the best model using two independent variables, the best model with three, and so on. The criterion is to find the model with the largest R^2 value, regardless of the number of independent variables. Also, each independent variable does not necessarily have a nonzero regression coefficient. Since each independent variable could either be included or not included, there are $2^k - 1$ possible models, where k refers to the number of independent variables. In our heating cost example, we considered four independent variables so there are 15 possible regression models, found by $2^4 - 1 = 16 - 1 = 15$. We would examine all regression models using one independent variable, all combinations using two variables, all combinations using three independent variables, and the possibility of using all four independent variables. The advantages to the best-subset method is it may examine combinations of independent variables not considered in the stepwise method. The process is available in Minitab and MegaStat.

EXERCISES

For **DATA FILE**, please visit www.mhhe.com/lind16e

9. The production manager of High Point Sofa and Chair, a large furniture manufacturer located in North Carolina, is studying the job performance ratings of a sample of 15 electrical repairmen employed by the company. An aptitude test is required by the human resources department to become an electrical repairman. The production manager was able to get the score for each repairman in the sample. In addition, he determined which of the repairmen were union members (code = 1) and which were not (code = 0). The sample information is reported below.

Worker	Job Performance Score	Aptitude Test Score	Union Membership
Abbott	58	5	0
Anderson	53	4	0
Bender	33	10	0
Bush	97	10	0
Center	36	2	0
Coombs	83	7	0
Eckstine	67	6	0
Gloss	84	9	0
Herd	98	9	1

(continued)

Worker	Job Performance Score	Aptitude Test Score	Union Membership
Householder	45	2	1
Iori	97	8	1
Lindstrom	90	6	1
Mason	96	7	1
Pierse	66	3	1
Rohde	82	6	1

a. Use a statistical software package to develop a multiple regression equation using the job performance score as the dependent variable and aptitude test score and union membership as independent variables.
b. Comment on the regression equation. Be sure to include the coefficient of determination and the effect of union membership. Are these two variables effective in explaining the variation in job performance?
c. Conduct a test of hypothesis to determine if union membership should be included as an independent variable.
d. Repeat the analysis considering possible interaction terms.

For **DATA FILE**, please visit www.mhhe.com/lind16e

10. Cincinnati Paint Company sells quality brands of paints through hardware stores throughout the United States. The company maintains a large sales force whose job it is to call on existing customers as well as look for new business. The national sales manager is investigating the relationship between the number of sales calls made and the miles driven by the sales representative. Also, do the sales representatives who drive the most miles and make the most calls necessarily earn the most in sales commissions? To investigate, the vice president of sales selected a sample of 25 sales representatives and determined:

- The amount earned in commissions last month (y)
- The number of miles driven last month (x_1)
- The number of sales calls made last month (x_2)

The information is reported below.

Commissions ($000)	Calls	Driven
22	139	2,371
13	132	2,226
33	144	2,731
⋮	⋮	⋮
25	127	2,671
43	154	2,988
34	147	2,829

Develop a regression equation including an interaction term. Is there a significant interaction between the number of sales calls and the miles driven?

For **DATA FILE**, please visit www.mhhe.com/lind16e

11. An art collector is studying the relationship between the selling price of a painting and two independent variables. The two independent variables are the number of bidders at the particular auction and the age of the painting, in years. A sample of 25 paintings revealed the following sample information.

Painting	Auction Price	Bidders	Age
1	3,470	10	67
2	3,500	8	56
3	3,700	7	73
⋮	⋮	⋮	⋮
23	4,660	5	94
24	4,710	3	88
25	4,880	1	84

a. Develop a multiple regression equation using the independent variables number of bidders and age of painting to estimate the dependent variable auction price. Discuss the equation. Does it surprise you that there is an inverse relationship between the number of bidders and the price of the painting?
b. Create an interaction variable and include it in the regression equation. Explain the meaning of the interaction. Is this variable significant?
c. Use the stepwise method and the independent variables for the number of bidders, the age of the painting, and the interaction between the number of bidders and the age of the painting. Which variables would you select?

For **DATA FILE**, please visit www.mhhe.com/lind16e

12. A real estate developer wishes to study the relationship between the size of home a client will purchase (in square feet) and other variables. Possible independent variables include the family income, family size, whether there is a senior adult parent living with the family (1 for yes, 0 for no), and the total years of education beyond high school for the husband and wife. The sample information is reported below.

Family	Square Feet	Income (000s)	Family Size	Senior Parent	Education
1	2,240	60.8	2	0	4
2	2,380	68.4	2	1	6
3	3,640	104.5	3	0	7
4	3,360	89.3	4	1	0
5	3,080	72.2	4	0	2
6	2,940	114	3	1	10
7	4,480	125.4	6	0	6
8	2,520	83.6	3	0	8
9	4,200	133	5	0	2
10	2,800	95	3	0	6

Develop an appropriate multiple regression equation. Which independent variables would you include in the final regression equation? Use the stepwise method.

LO14-8
Apply multiple regression techniques to develop a linear model.

REVIEW OF MULTIPLE REGRESSION

We described many topics involving multiple regression in this chapter. In this section of the chapter, we focus on a single example with a solution that reviews the procedure and guides your application of multiple regression analysis.

EXAMPLE

The Bank of New England is a large financial institution serving the New England states as well as New York and New Jersey. The mortgage department of the Bank of New England is studying data from recent loans. Of particular interest is how such factors as the value of the home being purchased ($000), education level of the head of the household (number of years, beginning with first grade), age of the head of the household, current monthly mortgage payment (in dollars), and gender of the head of the household (male = 1, female = 0) relate to the family income. The mortgage department would like to know whether these variables are effective predictors of family income.

SOLUTION

Consider a random sample of 25 loan applications submitted to the Bank of New England last month. A portion of the sample information is shown in Table 14–3. The entire data set is available at the website (www.mhhe.com/lind16e) and is identified as Bank of New England.

TABLE 14–3 Information on Sample of 25 Loans by the Bank of New England

Loan	Income ($000)	Value ($000)	Education	Age	Mortgage	Gender
1	100.7	190	14	53	230	1
2	99.0	121	15	49	370	1
3	102.0	161	14	44	397	1
⋮	⋮	⋮	⋮	⋮	⋮	⋮
23	102.3	163	14	46	142	1
24	100.2	150	15	50	343	0
25	96.3	139	14	45	373	0

We begin by calculating the correlation matrix shown below. It shows the relationship between each of the independent variables and the dependent variable. It helps to identify the independent variables that are more closely related to the dependent variable (family income). The correlation matrix also reveals the independent variables that are highly correlated and possibly redundant.

	Income	Value	Education	Age	Mortgage	Gender
Income	1					
Value	0.720	1				
Education	0.188	−0.144	1			
Age	0.243	0.220	0.621	1		
Mortgage	0.116	0.358	−0.210	−0.038	1	
Gender	0.486	0.184	0.062	0.156	−0.129	1

What can we learn from this correlation matrix?

1. The first column shows the correlations between each of the independent variables and the dependent variable family income. Observe that each of the independent variables is positively correlated with family income. The value of the home has the strongest correlation with family income. The level of education of the person applying for the loan and the current mortgage payment have a weak correlation with family income. These two variables are candidates to be dropped from the regression equation.
2. All possible correlations among the independent variables are identified with the green background. Our standard is to look for correlations that exceed an absolute value of .700. None of the independent variables are strongly correlated with each other. This indicates that multicollinearity is not likely.

Next, we compute the multiple regression equation using all the independent variables. The software output follows.

	A	B	C	D	E	F
1	SUMMARY OUTPUT					
2						
3	*Regression Statistics*					
4	Multiple R	0.866				
5	R Square	0.750				
6	Adjusted R Square	0.684				
7	Standard Error	1.478				
8	Observations	25				
9						
10	ANOVA					
11		*df*	*SS*	*MS*	*F*	*P-value*
12	Regression	5	124.322	24.864	11.385	0.000
13	Residual	19	41.494	2.184		
14	Total	24	165.815			
15						
16		*Coefficients*	*Standard Error*	*t Stat*	*P-value*	
17	Intercept	70.606	7.464	9.459	0.000	
18	Value ($000)	0.072	0.012	5.769	0.000	
19	Education	1.624	0.603	2.693	0.014	
20	Age	-0.122	0.078	-1.566	0.134	
21	Mortgage	-0.001	0.003	-0.319	0.753	
22	Gender	1.807	0.623	2.901	0.009	

The coefficients of determination, that is, both R^2 and adjusted R^2, are reported at the top of the summary output and highlighted in yellow. The R^2 value is 75.0%, so the five independent variables account for three-quarters of the variation in family income. The adjusted R^2 measures the strength of the relationship between the set of independent variables and family income and also accounts for the number of variables in the regression equation. The adjusted R^2 indicates that the five variables account for 68.4% of the variance of family income. Both of these suggest that the proposed independent variables are useful in predicting family income.

The output also includes the regression equation.

$$\hat{y} = 70.606 + 0.072(Value) + 1.624(Education) - 0.122(Age) - 0.001(Mortgage) + 1.807(Gender)$$

Be careful in this interpretation. Both income and the value of the home are in thousands of dollars. Here is a summary:

1. An increase of $1,000 in the value of the home suggests an increase of $72 in family income. An increase of 1 year of education increases income by $1,624, another year older reduces income by $122, and an increase of $1,000 in the mortgage reduces income by $1.
2. If a male is head of the household, the value of family income will increase by $1,807. Remember that "female" was coded 0 and "male" was coded 1, so a male head of household is positively related to home value.
3. The age of the head of household and monthly mortgage payment are inversely related to family income. This is true because the sign of the regression coefficient is negative.

Next we conduct the global hypothesis test. Here we check to see if any of the regression coefficients are different from 0. We use the .05 significance level.

$$H_0: \beta_1 = \beta_2 = \beta_3 = \beta_4 = \beta_5 = 0$$
$$H_1: \text{Not all the } \beta\text{s are 0.}$$

The *p*-value from the table (cell F12) is 0.000. Because the *p*-value is less than the significance level, we reject the null hypothesis and conclude that at least one of the regression coefficients is not equal to zero.

Next we evaluate the individual regression coefficients. The *p*-values to test each regression coefficient are reported in cells E18 through E22 in the software output on the previous page. The null hypothesis and the alternate hypothesis are:

$$H_0: \beta_i = 0$$
$$H_1: \beta_i \neq 0$$

The subscript *i* represents any particular independent variable. Again using .05 significance levels, the *p*-values for the regression coefficients for home value, years of education, and gender are all less than .05. We conclude that these regression coefficients are not equal to zero and are significant predictors of family income. The *p*-value for age and mortgage amount are greater than the significance level of .05, so we do not reject the null hypotheses for these variables. The regression coefficients are not different from zero and are not related to family income.

Based on the results of testing each of the regression coefficients, we conclude that the variables age and mortgage amount are not effective predictors of family income. Thus, they should be removed from the multiple regression equation. Remember that we must remove one independent variable at a time and redo the analysis to evaluate the overall effect of removing the variable. Our strategy is to remove the variable with the smallest *t*-statistic or the largest *p*-value. This variable is mortgage amount. The result of the regression analysis without the mortgage variable follows.

	A	B	C	D	E	F
1	SUMMARY OUTPUT					
2						
3	*Regression Statistics*					
4	Multiple R	0.865				
5	R Square	0.748				
6	Adjusted R Square	0.698				
7	Standard Error	1.444				
8	Observations	25				
9						
10	ANOVA					
11		*df*	*SS*	*MS*	*F*	*P-value*
12	Regression	4	124.099	31.025	14.874	0.000
13	Residual	20	41.716	2.086		
14	Total	24	165.815			
15						
16		*Coefficients*	*Standard Error*	*t Stat*	*P-value*	
17	Intercept	70.159	7.165	9.791	0.000	
18	Value ($000)	0.070	0.011	6.173	0.000	
19	Education	1.647	0.585	2.813	0.011	
20	Age	-0.122	0.076	-1.602	0.125	
21	Gender	1.846	0.596	3.096	0.006	

Observe that the R^2 and adjusted R^2 change very little without the mortgage variable. Also observe that the *p*-value associated with age is greater than the .05

significance level. So next we remove the age variable and redo the analysis. The regression output with the variables age and mortgage amount removed follows.

	A	B	C	D	E	F
1	SUMMARY OUTPUT					
2						
3	*Regression Statistics*					
4	Multiple R	0.846				
5	R Square	0.716				
6	Adjusted R Square	0.676				
7	Standard Error	1.497				
8	Observations	25				
9						
10	ANOVA					
11		*df*	*SS*	*MS*	*F*	*P-value*
12	Regression	3	118.743	39.581	17.658	0.000
13	Residual	21	47.072	2.242		
14	Total	24	165.815			
15						
16		*Coefficients*	*Standard Error*	*t Stat*	*P-value*	
17	Intercept	74.527	6.870	10.849	0.000	
18	Value ($000)	0.063	0.011	5.803	0.000	
19	Education	1.016	0.449	2.262	0.034	
20	Gender	1.770	0.616	2.872	0.009	

From this output, we conclude:

1. The R^2 and adjusted R^2 values have declined but only slightly. Using all five independent variables, the R^2 value was .750. With the two nonsignificant variables removed, the R^2 and adjusted R^2 values are .716 and .676, respectively. We prefer the equation with the fewer number of independent variables. It is easier to interpret.
2. In ANOVA, we observe that the *p*-value is less than .05. Hence, at least one of the regression coefficients is not equal to zero.
3. Reviewing the significance of the individual coefficients, the *p*-values associated with each of the remaining independent variables are less than .05. We conclude that all the regression coefficients are different from zero. Each independent variable is a useful predictor of family income.

Our final step is to examine the regression assumptions, listed on page 494, with our regression model. The first assumption is that there is a linear relationship between each independent variable and the dependent variable. It is not necessary to review the dummy variable Gender because there are only two possible outcomes. Below are the scatter plots of family income versus home value and family income versus years of education.

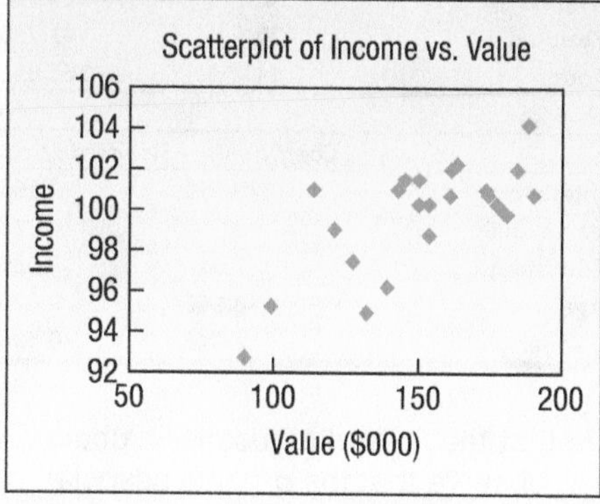

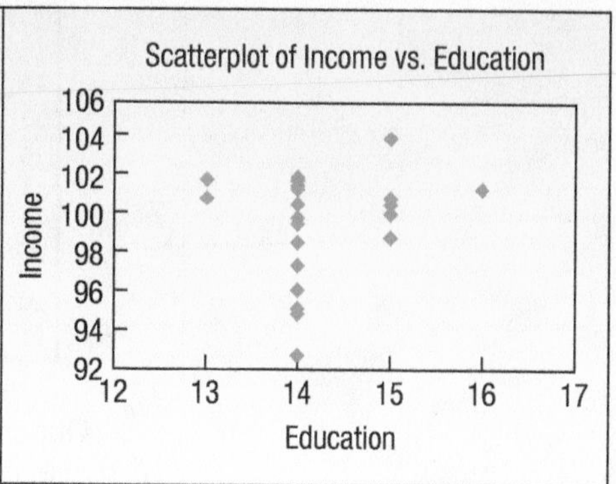

The scatter plot of income versus home value shows a general increasing trend. As the home value increases, so does family income. The points appear to be linear. That is, there is no observable nonlinear pattern in the data. The scatter plot on the right, of income versus years of education, shows that the data are measured to the nearest year. The measurement is to the nearest year and is a discrete variable. Given the measurement method, it is difficult to determine if the relationship is linear or not.

A plot of the residuals is also useful to evaluate the overall assumption of linearity. Recall that a residual is $(y - \hat{y})$, the difference between the actual value of the dependent variable (y) and the predicted value of the dependent variable ($\hat{y}$). Assuming a linear relationship, the distribution of the residuals should show about an equal proportion of negative residuals (points above the line) and positive residuals (points below the line) centered on zero. There should be no observable pattern to the plots. The graph follows.

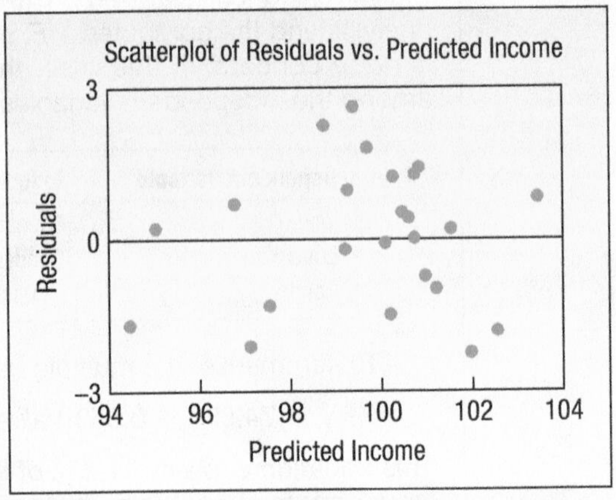

There is no discernable pattern to the plot, so we conclude that the linearity assumption is reasonable.

If the linearity assumption is valid, then the distribution of residuals should follow the normal probability distribution with a mean of zero. To evaluate this assumption, we will use a histogram and a normal probability plot.

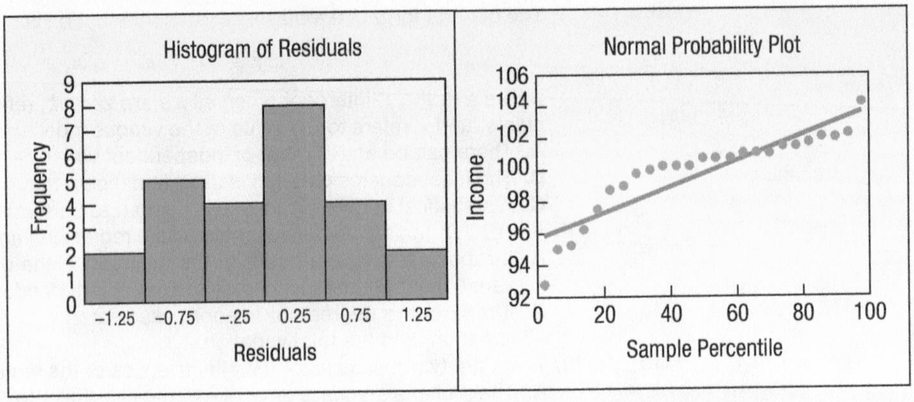

In general, the histogram on the left shows the major characteristics of a normal distribution, that is, a majority of observations in the middle and centered on the mean of zero, with lower frequencies in the tails of the distribution. The normal probability plot on the right is based on a cumulative normal probability distribution. The line shows the standardized cumulative normal distribution. The green

dots show the cumulative distribution of the residuals. To confirm the normal distribution of the residuals, the green dots should be close to the line. This is true for most of the plot. However, we would note that there are departures and even perhaps a nonlinear pattern in the residuals in the lower part of the graph. As before, we are looking for serious departures from linearity and these are not indicated in these graphs.

The final assumption refers to multicollinearity. This means that the independent variables should not be highly correlated. We suggested a rule of thumb that multicollinearity would be a concern if the correlations among independent variables were close to 0.7 or −0.7. There are no violations of this guideline.

There is a statistic that is used to more precisely evaluate multicollinearity, the variance inflation factor (*VIF*). To calculate the *VIF*s, we need to do a regression analysis for each independent variable as a function of the other independent variables. From each of these regression analyses, we need the R^2 to compute the *VIF* using formula (14–7). The following table shows the R^2 for each regression analysis and the computed *VIF*. If the *VIF*s are less than 10, then multicollinearity is not a concern. In this case, the *VIF*s are all less than 10, so multicollinearity among the independent variables is not a concern.

Dependent Variable	Independent Variables	*R*-square	*VIF*
Value	Education and Gender	0.058	1.062
Education	Gender and Value	0.029	1.030
Gender	Value and Education	0.042	1.044

To summarize, the multiple regression equation is

$$\hat{y} = 74.527 + 0.063(Value) + 1.016(Education) + 1.770(Gender)$$

This equation explains 71.6% of the variation in family income. There are no major departures from the multiple regression assumptions of linearity, normally distributed residuals, and multicollinearity.

CHAPTER SUMMARY

I. The general form of a multiple regression equation is:

$$\hat{y} = a + b_1x_1 + b_2x_2 + \cdots + b_kx_k \qquad \textbf{[14–1]}$$

where a is the Y-intercept when all x's are zero, b_j refers to the sample regression coefficients, and x_j refers to the value of the various independent variables.

A. There can be any number of independent variables.

B. The least squares criterion is used to develop the regression equation.

C. A statistical software package is needed to perform the calculations.

II. An ANOVA table summarizes the multiple regression analysis.

A. It reports the total amount of the variation in the dependent variable and divides this variation into that explained by the set of independent variables and that not explained.

B. It reports the degrees of freedom associated with the independent variables, the error variation, and the total variation.

III. There are two measures of the effectiveness of the regression equation.

A. The multiple standard error of estimate is similar to the standard deviation.

1. It is measured in the same units as the dependent variable.

2. It is based on squared deviations from the regression equation.

3. It ranges from 0 to plus infinity.

4. It is calculated from the following equation.

$$s_{Y.123...k} = \sqrt{\frac{\Sigma(y - \hat{y})^2}{n - (k + 1)}} \qquad \textbf{[14–2]}$$

B. The coefficient of multiple determination reports the percent of the variation in the dependent variable explained by the variation in the set of independent variables.

1. It may range from 0 to 1.

2. It is also based on squared deviations from the regression equation.

3. It is found by the following equation.

$$R^2 = \frac{\text{SSR}}{\text{SS total}} \quad \textbf{[14–3]}$$

4. When the number of independent variables is large, we adjust the coefficient of determination for the degrees of freedom as follows.

$$R^2_{\text{adj}} = 1 - \frac{\dfrac{\text{SSE}}{n - (k + 1)}}{\dfrac{\text{SS total}}{n - 1}} \quad \textbf{[14–4]}$$

IV. A global test is used to investigate whether any of the independent variables have a regression coefficient that differs significantly from zero.

A. The null hypothesis is: All the regression coefficients are zero.

B. The alternate hypothesis is: At least one regression coefficient is not zero.

C. The test statistic is the F distribution with k (the number of independent variables) degrees of freedom in the numerator and $n - (k + 1)$ degrees of freedom in the denominator, where n is the sample size.

D. The formula to calculate the value of the test statistic for the global test is:

$$F = \frac{\text{SSR}/k}{\text{SSE}/[n - (k + 1)]} \quad \textbf{[14–5]}$$

V. The test for individual variables determines which independent variables have regression coefficients that differ significantly from zero.

A. The variables that have zero regression coefficients are usually dropped from the analysis.

B. The test statistic is the t distribution with $n - (k + 1)$ degrees of freedom.

C. The formula to calculate the value of the test statistic for the individual test is:

$$t = \frac{b_i - 0}{s_{b_i}} \quad \textbf{[14–6]}$$

VI. There are five assumptions to use multiple regression analysis.

A. The relationship between the dependent variable and the set of independent variables must be linear.

1. To verify this assumption, develop a scatter diagram and plot the residuals on the vertical axis and the fitted values on the horizontal axis.

2. If the plots appear random, we conclude the relationship is linear.

B. The variation is the same for both large and small values of $\hat{y}$.

1. Homoscedasticity means the variation is the same for all fitted values of the dependent variable.

2. This condition is checked by developing a scatter diagram with the residuals on the vertical axis and the fitted values on the horizontal axis.

3. If there is no pattern to the plots—that is, they appear random—the residuals meet the homoscedasticity requirement.

C. The residuals follow the normal probability distribution.

1. This condition is checked by developing a histogram of the residuals or a normal probability plot.

2. The mean of the distribution of the residuals is 0.

D. The independent variables are not correlated.

1. A correlation matrix will show all possible correlations among independent variables. Signs of trouble are correlations larger than 0.70 or less than −0.70.

2. Signs of correlated independent variables include when an important predictor variable is found insignificant, when an obvious reversal occurs in signs in one or more of

the independent variables, or when a variable is removed from the solution, there is a large change in the regression coefficients.

3. The variance inflation factor is used to identify correlated independent variables.

$$VIF = \frac{1}{1 - R_j^2} \quad \text{[14–7]}$$

E. Each residual is independent of other residuals.

1. Autocorrelation occurs when successive residuals are correlated.
2. When autocorrelation exists, the value of the standard error will be biased and will return poor results for tests of hypothesis regarding the regression coefficients.

VII. Several techniques help build a regression model.

A. A dummy or qualitative independent variable can assume one of two possible outcomes.

1. A value of 1 is assigned to one outcome and 0 to the other.
2. Use formula (14–6) to determine if the dummy variable should remain in the equation.

B. Interaction is the case in which one independent variable (such as x_2) affects the relationship with another independent variable (x_1) and the dependent variable (y).

C. Stepwise regression is a step-by-step process to find the regression equation.

1. Only independent variables with nonzero regression coefficients enter the equation.
2. Independent variables are added one at a time to the regression equation.

PRONUNCIATION KEY

SYMBOL	MEANING	PRONUNCIATION
b_1	Regression coefficient for the first independent variable	*b sub 1*
b_k	Regression coefficient for any independent variable	*b sub k*
$s_{Y.123...k}$	Multiple standard error of estimate	*s sub Y dot 1, 2, 3 . . . k*

CHAPTER EXERCISES

13. A multiple regression equation yields the following partial results.

Source	Sum of Squares	*df*
Regression	750	4
Error	500	35

a. What is the total sample size?
b. How many independent variables are being considered?
c. Compute the coefficient of determination.
d. Compute the standard error of estimate.
e. Test the hypothesis that none of the regression coefficients is equal to zero. Let $\alpha = .05$.

14. In a multiple regression equation, two independent variables are considered, and the sample size is 25. The regression coefficients and the standard errors are as follows.

$$b_1 = 2.676 \qquad s_{b_1} = 0.56$$
$$b_2 = -0.880 \qquad s_{b_2} = 0.71$$

Conduct a test of hypothesis to determine whether either independent variable has a coefficient equal to zero. Would you consider deleting either variable from the regression equation? Use the .05 significance level.

15. The following output was obtained.

Analysis of Variance			
Source	DF	SS	MS
Regression	5	100	20
Residual Error	20	40	2
Total	25	140	

Predictor	Coefficient	SE Coefficient	t
Constant	3.00	1.50	2.00
x_1	4.00	3.00	1.33
x_2	3.00	0.20	15.00
x_3	0.20	0.05	4.00
x_4	-2.50	1.00	-2.50
x_5	3.00	4.00	0.75

a. What is the sample size?
b. Compute the value of R^2.
c. Compute the multiple standard error of estimate.
d. Conduct a global test of hypothesis to determine whether any of the regression coefficients are significant. Use the .05 significance level.
e. Test the regression coefficients individually. Would you consider omitting any variable(s)? If so, which one(s)? Use the .05 significance level.

16. In a multiple regression equation, $k = 5$ and $n = 20$, the MSE value is 5.10, and SS total is 519.68. At the .05 significance level, can we conclude that any of the regression coefficients are not equal to 0?

17. The district manager of Jasons, a large discount electronics chain, is investigating why certain stores in her region are performing better than others. She believes that three factors are related to total sales: the number of competitors in the region, the population in the surrounding area, and the amount spent on advertising. From her district, consisting of several hundred stores, she selects a random sample of 30 stores. For each store, she gathered the following information.

y = total sales last year (in \$ thousands)
x_1 = number of competitors in the region
x_2 = population of the region (in millions)
x_3 = advertising expense (in \$ thousands)

The sample data were run on Minitab, with the following results.

Analysis of Variance			
Source	DF	SS	MS
Regression	3	3050	1016.67
Residual Error	26	2200	84.62
Total	29	5250	

Predictor	Coefficient	SE Coefficient	t
Constant	14.00	7.00	2.00
x_1	-1.00	0.70	-1.43
x_2	30.00	5.20	5.77
x_3	0.20	0.08	2.50

a. What are the estimated sales for the Bryne store, which has four competitors, a regional population of 0.4 (400,000), and an advertising expense of 30 ($30,000)?
b. Compute the R^2 value.
c. Compute the multiple standard error of estimate.
d. Conduct a global test of hypothesis to determine whether any of the regression coefficients are not equal to zero. Use the .05 level of significance.
e. Conduct tests of hypothesis to determine which of the independent variables have significant regression coefficients. Which variables would you consider eliminating? Use the .05 significance level.

18. Suppose that the sales manager of a large automotive parts distributor wants to estimate as early as April the total annual sales of a region. On the basis of regional sales, the total sales for the company can also be estimated. If, based on past experience, it is found that the April estimates of annual sales are reasonably accurate, then in future years the April forecast could be used to revise production schedules and maintain the correct inventory at the retail outlets.

Several factors appear to be related to sales, including the number of retail outlets in the region stocking the company's parts, the number of automobiles in the region registered as of April 1, and the total personal income for the first quarter of the year. Five independent variables were finally selected as being the most important (according to the sales manager). Then the data were gathered for a recent year. The total annual sales for that year for each region were also recorded. Note in the following table that for region 1 there were 1,739 retail outlets stocking the company's automotive parts, there were 9,270,000 registered automobiles in the region as of April 1, and so on. The sales for that year were $37,702,000.

Annual Sales ($ millions), y	Number of Retail Outlets, x_1	Number of Automobiles Registered (millions), x_2	Personal Income ($ billions), x_3	Average Age of Automobiles (years), x_4	Number of Supervisors, x_5
37.702	1,739	9.27	85.4	3.5	9.0
24.196	1,221	5.86	60.7	5.0	5.0
32.055	1,846	8.81	68.1	4.4	7.0
3.611	120	3.81	20.2	4.0	5.0
17.625	1,096	10.31	33.8	3.5	7.0
45.919	2,290	11.62	95.1	4.1	13.0
29.600	1,687	8.96	69.3	4.1	15.0
8.114	241	6.28	16.3	5.9	11.0
20.116	649	7.77	34.9	5.5	16.0
12.994	1,427	10.92	15.1	4.1	10.0

a. Consider the following correlation matrix. Which single variable has the strongest correlation with the dependent variable? The correlations between the independent variables outlets and income and between cars and outlets are fairly strong. Could this be a problem? What is this condition called?

	sales	outlets	cars	income	age
outlets	0.899				
cars	0.605	0.775			
income	0.964	0.825	0.409		
age	−0.323	−0.489	−0.447	−0.349	
bosses	0.286	0.183	0.395	0.155	0.291

b. The output for all five variables is shown below. What percent of the variation is explained by the regression equation?

```
The regression equation is
Sales = −19.7 − 0.00063 outlets + 1.74 cars + 0.410 income
        + 2.04 age − 0.034 bosses

    Predictor        Coef       SE Coef        T        P
    Constant      −19.672         5.422    −3.63    0.022
    outlets     −0.000629      0.002638    −0.24    0.823
    cars           1.7399        0.5530     3.15    0.035
    income        0.40994       0.04385     9.35    0.001
    age            2.0357        0.8779     2.32    0.081
    bosses        −0.0344        0.1880    −0.18    0.864

Analysis of Variance
    SOURCE          DF       SS       MS        F        P
    Regression       5  1593.81   318.76   140.36    0.000
    Residual Error   4     9.08     2.27
    Total            9  1602.89
```

c. Conduct a global test of hypothesis to determine whether any of the regression coefficients are not zero. Use the .05 significance level.

d. Conduct a test of hypothesis on each of the independent variables. Would you consider eliminating "outlets" and "bosses"? Use the .05 significance level.

e. The regression has been rerun below with "outlets" and "bosses" eliminated. Compute the coefficient of determination. How much has R^2 changed from the previous analysis?

```
The regression equation is
Sales = −18.9 + 1.61 cars + 0.400 income + 1.96 age

           Predictor          Coef       SE Coef          T          P
           Constant        −18.924         3.636      −5.20      0.002
           cars             1.6129        0.1979       8.15      0.000
           income          0.40031       0.01569      25.52      0.000
           age              1.9637        0.5846       3.36      0.015

Analysis of Variance
           SOURCE              DF         SS         MS          F          P
           Regression           3    1593.66     531.22     345.25      0.000
           Residual Error       6       9.23       1.54
           Total                9    1602.89
```

f. Following is a histogram of the residuals. Does the normality assumption appear reasonable?

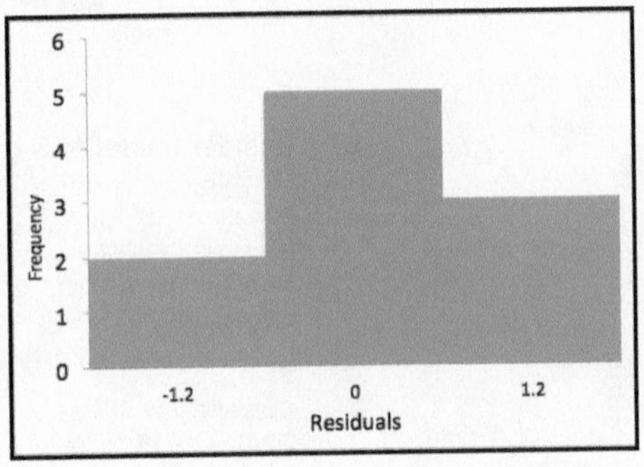

g. Following is a plot of the fitted values of y (i.e., $\hat{y}$) and the residuals. Do you see any violations of the assumptions?

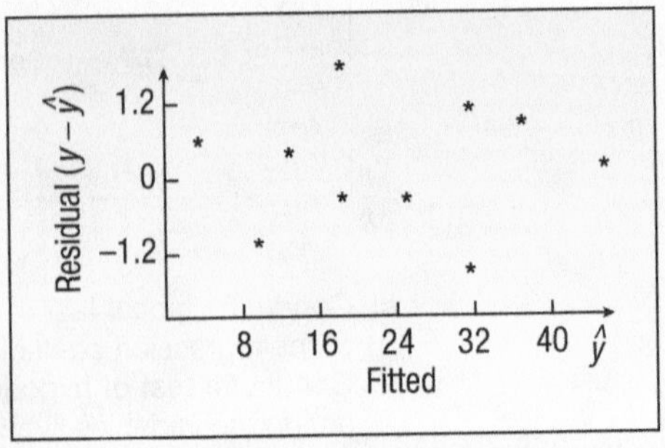

19. The administrator of a new paralegal program at Seagate Technical College wants to estimate the grade point average in the new program. He thought that high school GPA, the

verbal score on the Scholastic Aptitude Test (SAT), and the mathematics score on the SAT would be good predictors of paralegal GPA. The data on nine students are:

Student	High School GPA	SAT Verbal	SAT Math	Paralegal GPA
1	3.25	480	410	3.21
2	1.80	290	270	1.68
3	2.89	420	410	3.58
4	3.81	500	600	3.92
5	3.13	500	490	3.00
6	2.81	430	460	2.82
7	2.20	320	490	1.65
8	2.14	530	480	2.30
9	2.63	469	440	2.33

a. Consider the following correlation matrix. Which variable has the strongest correlation with the dependent variable? Some of the correlations among the independent variables are strong. Does this appear to be a problem?

	legal	gpa	verbal
gpa	0.911		
verbal	0.616	0.609	
math	0.487	0.636	0.599

b. Consider the following output. Compute the coefficient of multiple determination.

```
The regression equation is
Legal = -0.411 + 1.20 GPA + 0.00163 Verbal - 0.00194 Math

Predictor          Coef        SE Coef          T          P
Constant        -0.4111         0.7823      -0.53      0.622
GPA              1.2014         0.2955       4.07      0.010
Verbal         0.001629       0.002147       0.76      0.482
Math          -0.001939       0.002074      -0.94      0.393

Analysis of Variance
SOURCE            DF          SS          MS          F          P
Regression         3      4.3595      1.4532      10.33      0.014
Residual Error     5      0.7036      0.1407
Total              8      5.0631

SOURCE     DF     Seq SS
GPA         1     4.2061
Verbal      1     0.0303
Math        1     0.1231
```

c. Conduct a global test of hypothesis from the preceding output. Does it appear that any of the regression coefficients are not equal to zero?

d. Conduct a test of hypothesis on each independent variable. Would you consider eliminating the variables "verbal" and "math"? Let $\alpha = .05$.

e. The analysis has been rerun without "verbal" and "math." See the following output. Compute the coefficient of determination. How much has R^2 changed from the previous analysis?

```
The regression equation is
Legal = −0.454 + 1.16 GPA

Predictor          Coef      SE Coef         T         P
Constant        −0.4542       0.5542     −0.82     0.439
GPA              1.1589       0.1977      5.86     0.001

Analysis of Variance
SOURCE              DF         SS         MS         F         P
Regression           1     4.2061     4.2061     34.35     0.001
Residual Error       7     0.8570     0.1224
Total                8     5.0631
```

f. Following is a histogram of the residuals. Does the normality assumption for the residuals seem reasonable?

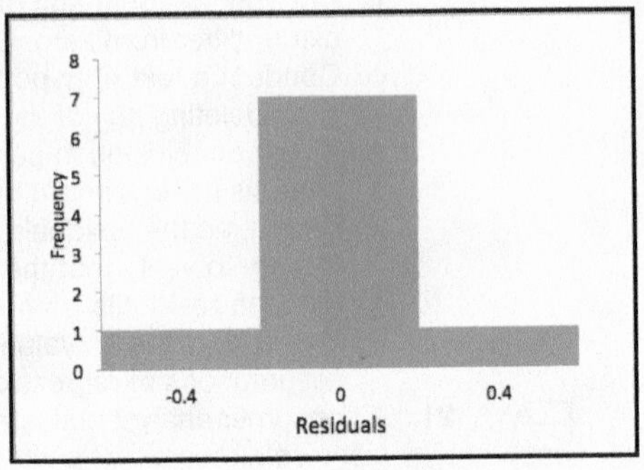

g. Following is a plot of the residuals and the $\hat{y}$ values. Do you see any violation of the assumptions?

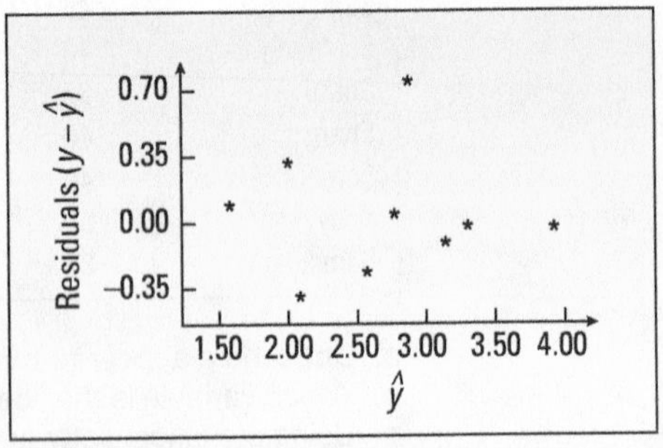

For **DATA FILE**, please visit www.mhhe.com/lind16e

20. Mike Wilde is president of the teachers' union for Otsego School District. In preparing for upcoming negotiations, he would like to investigate the salary structure of classroom teachers in the district. He believes there are three factors that affect a teacher's salary: years of experience, a rating of teaching effectiveness given by the principal, and whether the teacher has a master's degree. A random sample of 20 teachers resulted in the following data.

Salary ($ thousands), y	Years of Experience, x_1	Principal's Rating, x_2	Master's Degree,* x_3
31.1	8	35	0
33.6	5	43	0
29.3	2	51	1
⋮	⋮	⋮	⋮
30.7	4	62	0
32.8	2	80	1
42.8	8	72	0

*1 = yes, 0 = no.

a. Develop a correlation matrix. Which independent variable has the strongest correlation with the dependent variable? Does it appear there will be any problems with multicollinearity?
b. Determine the regression equation. What salary would you estimate for a teacher with 5 years' experience, a rating by the principal of 60, and no master's degree?
c. Conduct a global test of hypothesis to determine whether any of the regression coefficients differ from zero. Use the .05 significance level.
d. Conduct a test of hypothesis for the individual regression coefficients. Would you consider deleting any of the independent variables? Use the .05 significance level.
e. If your conclusion in part (d) was to delete one or more independent variables, run the analysis again without those variables.
f. Determine the residuals for the equation of part (e). Use a stem-and-leaf chart or a histogram to verify that the distribution of the residuals is approximately normal.
g. Plot the residuals computed in part (f) in a scatter diagram with the residuals on the Y-axis and the $\hat{y}$ values on the X-axis. Does the plot reveal any violations of the assumptions of regression?

For **DATA FILE**, please visit www.mhhe.com/lind16e

21. A consumer analyst collected the following data on the screen sizes of popular LCD televisions sold recently at a large retailer:

Manufacturer	Screen	Price	Manufacturer	Screen	Price
Sharp	46	$1473.00	Sharp	37	$1314.50
Samsung	52	2300.00	Sharp	32	853.50
Samsung	46	1790.00	Sharp	52	2778.00
Sony	40	1250.00	Samsung	40	1749.50
Sharp	42	1546.50	Sharp	32	1035.00
Samsung	46	1922.50	Samsung	52	2950.00
Samsung	40	1372.00	Sony	40	1908.50
Sharp	37	1149.50	Sony	52	3103.00
Sharp	46	2000.00	Sony	46	2606.00
Sony	40	1444.50	Sony	46	2861.00
Sony	52	2615.00	Sony	52	3434.00
Samsung	32	747.50			

a. Does there appear to be a linear relationship between the screen size and the price?
b. Which variable is the "dependent" variable?
c. Using statistical software, determine the regression equation. Interpret the value of the slope in the regression equation.
d. Include the manufacturer in a multiple linear regression analysis using a "dummy" variable. Does it appear that some manufacturers can command a premium price? *Hint:* You will need to use a set of indicator variables.
e. Test each of the individual coefficients to see if they are significant.
f. Make a plot of the residuals and comment on whether they appear to follow a normal distribution.
g. Plot the residuals versus the fitted values. Do they seem to have the same amount of variation?

For **DATA FILE**, please visit www.mhhe.com/lind16e

22. A regional planner is studying the demographics in a region of a particular state. She has gathered the following data on nine counties.

County	Median Income	Median Age	Coastal
A	$48,157	57.7	1
B	48,568	60.7	1
C	46,816	47.9	1
D	34,876	38.4	0
E	35,478	42.8	0
F	34,465	35.4	0
G	35,026	39.5	0
H	38,599	65.6	0
J	33,315	27.0	0

a. Is there a linear relationship between the median income and median age?
b. Which variable is the "dependent" variable?
c. Use statistical software to determine the regression equation. Interpret the value of the slope in a simple regression equation.
d. Include the aspect that the county is "coastal" or not in a multiple linear regression analysis using a "dummy" variable. Does it appear to be a significant influence on incomes?
e. Test each of the individual coefficients to see if they are significant.
f. Make a plot of the residuals and comment on whether they appear to follow a normal distribution.
g. Plot the residuals versus the fitted values. Do they seem to have the same amount of variation?

For **DATA FILE**, please visit www.mhhe.com/lind16e

23. Great Plains Roofing and Siding Company Inc. sells roofing and siding products to home repair retailers, such as Lowe's and Home Depot, and commercial contractors. The owner is interested in studying the effects of several variables on the value of shingles sold ($000). The marketing manager is arguing that the company should spend more money on advertising, while a market researcher suggests it should focus more on making its brand and product more distinct from its competitors.

The company has divided the United States into 26 marketing districts. In each district, it collected information on the following variables: volume of sales (in thousands of dollars), advertising dollars (in thousands), number of active accounts, number of competing brands, and a rating of district potential.

Sales (000s)	Advertising Dollars (000s)	Number of Accounts	Number of Competitors	Market Potential
79.3	5.5	31	10	8
200.1	2.5	55	8	6
163.2	8.0	67	12	9
200.1	3.0	50	7	16
146.0	3.0	38	8	15
177.7	2.9	71	12	17
⋮	⋮	⋮	⋮	⋮
93.5	4.2	26	8	3
259.0	4.5	75	8	19
331.2	5.6	71	4	9

Conduct a multiple regression analysis to find the best predictors of sales.
a. Draw a scatter diagram comparing sales volume with each of the independent variables. Comment on the results.
b. Develop a correlation matrix. Do you see any problems? Does it appear there are any redundant independent variables?
c. Develop a regression equation. Conduct the global test. Can we conclude that some of the independent variables are useful in explaining the variation in the dependent variable?

d. Conduct a test of each of the independent variables. Are there any that should be dropped?

e. Refine the regression equation so the remaining variables are all significant.

f. Develop a histogram of the residuals and a normal probability plot. Are there any problems?

g. Determine the variance inflation factor for each of the independent variables. Are there any problems?

For **DATA FILE**, please visit www.mhhe.com/lind16e

24. The *Times-Observer* is a daily newspaper in Metro City. Like many city newspapers, the *Times-Observer* is suffering through difficult financial times. The circulation manager is studying other newspapers in similar cities in the United States and Canada. She is particularly interested in what variables relate to the number of subscriptions to the newspaper. She is able to obtain the following sample information on 25 newspapers in similar cities. The following notation is used:

Sub = Number of subscriptions (in thousands)
Popul = The metropolitan population (in thousands)
Adv = The advertising budget of the newspaper (in $ hundreds)
Income = The median family income in the metropolitan area (in $ thousands)

Paper	Sub	Popul	Adv	Income
1	37.95	588.9	13.2	35.1
2	37.66	585.3	13.2	34.7
3	37.55	566.3	19.8	34.8
⋮	⋮	⋮	⋮	⋮
23	38.83	629.6	22.0	35.3
24	38.33	680.0	24.2	34.7
25	40.24	651.2	33.0	35.8

a. Determine the regression equation.

b. Conduct a global test of hypothesis to determine whether any of the regression coefficients are not equal to zero.

c. Conduct a test for the individual coefficients. Would you consider deleting any coefficients?

d. Determine the residuals and plot them against the fitted values. Do you see any problems?

e. Develop a histogram of the residuals. Do you see any problems with the normality assumption?

For **DATA FILE**, please visit www.mhhe.com/lind16e

25. Fred G. Hire is the manager of human resources at Crescent Tool and Die Inc. As part of his yearly report to the CEO, he is required to present an analysis of the salaried employees. Because there are over 1,000 employees, he does not have the staff to gather information on each salaried employee, so he selects a random sample of 30. For each employee, he records monthly salary; service at Crescent, in months; gender (1 = male, 0 = female); and whether the employee has a technical or clerical job. Those working technical jobs are coded 1, and those who are clerical 0.

Sampled Employee	Monthly Salary	Length of Service	Age	Gender	Job
1	$1,769	93	42	1	0
2	1,740	104	33	1	0
3	1,941	104	42	1	1
⋮	⋮	⋮	⋮	⋮	⋮
28	1,791	131	56	0	1
29	2,001	95	30	1	1
30	1,874	98	47	1	0

a. Determine the regression equation, using salary as the dependent variable and the other four variables as independent variables.

b. What is the value of R^2? Comment on this value.

c. Conduct a global test of hypothesis to determine whether any of the independent variables are different from 0.
d. Conduct an individual test to determine whether any of the independent variables can be dropped.
e. Rerun the regression equation, using only the independent variables that are significant. How much more does a man earn per month than a woman? Does it make a difference whether the employee has a technical or a clerical job?

For **DATA FILE**, please visit www.mhhe.com/lind16e

26. Many regions along the coast in North and South Carolina and Georgia have experienced rapid population growth over the last 10 years. It is expected that the growth will continue over the next 10 years. This has motivated many of the large grocery store chains to build new stores in the region. The Kelley's Super Grocery Stores Inc. chain is no exception. The director of planning for Kelley's Super Grocery Stores wants to study adding more stores in this region. He believes there are two main factors that indicate the amount families spend on groceries. The first is their income and the other is the number of people in the family. The director gathered the following sample information.

Family	Food	Income	Size
1	$5.04	$ 73.98	4
2	4.08	54.90	2
3	5.76	94.14	4
⋮	⋮	⋮	⋮
23	4.56	38.16	3
24	5.40	43.74	7
25	4.80	48.42	5

Food and income are reported in thousands of dollars per year, and the variable size refers to the number of people in the household.
a. Develop a correlation matrix. Do you see any problems with multicollinearity?
b. Determine the regression equation. Discuss the regression equation. How much does an additional family member add to the amount spent on food?
c. What is the value of R^2? Can we conclude that this value is greater than 0?
d. Would you consider deleting either of the independent variables?
e. Plot the residuals in a histogram. Is there any problem with the normality assumption?
f. Plot the fitted values against the residuals. Does this plot indicate any problems with homoscedasticity?

For **DATA FILE**, please visit www.mhhe.com/lind16e

27. An investment advisor is studying the relationship between a common stock's price to earnings (P/E) ratio and factors that she thinks would influence it. She has the following data on the earnings per share (EPS) and the dividend percentage (Yield) for a sample of 20 stocks.

Stock	P/E	EPS	Yield
1	20.79	$2.46	1.42
2	3.03	2.69	4.05
3	44.46	−0.28	4.16
⋮	⋮	⋮	⋮
18	30.21	1.71	3.07
19	32.88	0.35	2.21
20	15.19	5.02	3.50

a. Develop a multiple linear regression with P/E as the dependent variable.
b. Are either of the two independent variables an effective predictor of P/E?
c. Interpret the regression coefficients.
d. Do any of these stocks look particularly undervalued?
e. Plot the residuals and check the normality assumption. Plot the fitted values against the residuals.
f. Does there appear to be any problems with homoscedasticity?
g. Develop a correlation matrix. Do any of the correlations indicate multicollinearity?

For **DATA FILE**, please visit www.mhhe.com/lind16e

28. The Conch Café, located in Gulf Shores, Alabama, features casual lunches with a great view of the Gulf of Mexico. To accommodate the increase in business during the summer vacation season, Fuzzy Conch, the owner, hires a large number of servers as seasonal help. When he interviews a prospective server, he would like to provide data on the amount a server can earn in tips. He believes that the amount of the bill and the number of diners are both related to the amount of the tip. He gathered the following sample information.

Customer	Amount of Tip	Amount of Bill	Number of Diners
1	$7.00	$48.97	5
2	4.50	28.23	4
3	1.00	10.65	1
⋮	⋮	⋮	⋮
28	2.50	26.25	2
29	9.25	56.81	5
30	8.25	50.65	5

a. Develop a multiple regression equation with the amount of tips as the dependent variable and the amount of the bill and the number of diners as independent variables. Write out the regression equation. How much does another diner add to the amount of the tips?
b. Conduct a global test of hypothesis to determine if at least one of the independent variables is significant. What is your conclusion?
c. Conduct an individual test on each of the variables. Should one or the other be deleted?
d. Use the equation developed in part (c) to determine the coefficient of determination. Interpret the value.
e. Plot the residuals. Is it reasonable to assume they follow the normal distribution?
f. Plot the residuals against the fitted values. Is it reasonable to conclude they are random?

For **DATA FILE**, please visit www.mhhe.com/lind16e

29. The president of Blitz Sales Enterprises sells kitchen products through television commercials, often called infomercials. He gathered data from the last 15 weeks of sales to determine the relationship between sales and the number of infomercials.

Infomercials	Sales ($000s)	Infomercials	Sales ($000s)
20	3.2	22	2.5
15	2.6	15	2.4
25	3.4	25	3.0
10	1.8	16	2.7
18	2.2	12	2.0
18	2.4	20	2.6
15	2.4	25	2.8
12	1.5		

a. Determine the regression equation. Are the sales predictable from the number of commercials?
b. Determine the residuals and plot a histogram. Does the normality assumption seem reasonable?

For **DATA FILE**, please visit www.mhhe.com/lind16e

30. The director of special events for Sun City believed that the amount of money spent on fireworks displays on the 4th of July was predictive of attendance at the Fall Festival held in October. She gathered the following data to test her suspicion.

4th of July ($000)	Fall Festival (000)	4th of July ($000)	Fall Festival (000)
10.6	8.8	9.0	9.5
8.5	6.4	10.0	9.8
12.5	10.8	7.5	6.6
9.0	10.2	10.0	10.1
5.5	6.0	6.0	6.1
12.0	11.1	12.0	11.3
8.0	7.5	10.5	8.8
7.5	8.4		

Determine the regression equation. Is the amount spent on fireworks related to attendance at the Fall Festival? Evaluate regression assumptions by examining the residuals.

For **DATA FILE**, please visit www.mhhe.com/lind16e

31. You are a new hire at Laurel Woods Real Estate, which specializes in selling foreclosed homes via public auction. Your boss has asked you to use the following data (mortgage balance, monthly payments, payments made before default, and final auction price) on a random sample of recent sales in order to estimate what the actual auction price will be.

Loan	Monthly Payments	Payments Made	Auction Price
$ 85,600	$ 985.87	1	$16,900
115,300	902.56	33	75,800
103,100	736.28	6	43,900
⋮	⋮	⋮	⋮
119,400	1,021.23	58	69,000
90,600	836.46	3	35,600
104,500	1,056.37	22	63,000

a. Carry out a global test of hypothesis to verify if any of the regression coefficients are different from zero.
b. Do an individual test of the independent variables. Would you remove any of the variables?
c. If it seems one or more of the independent variables is not needed, remove it and work out the revised regression equation.

32. Think about the figures from the previous exercise. Add a new variable that describes the potential interaction between the loan amount and the number of payments made. Then do a test of hypothesis to check if the interaction is significant.

DATA SET EXERCISES

(The data for these exercises are available at the text website: www.mhhe.com/lind16e.)

33. Refer to the Real Estate data, which report information on homes sold in Goodyear, Arizona. Use the selling price of the home as the dependent variable and determine the regression equation with number of bedrooms, size of the house, center of the city, and number of bathrooms as independent variables.
a. Use a statistical software package to determine the multiple regression equation. Discuss each of the variables. For example, are you surprised that the regression coefficient for distance from the center of the city is negative? How much does a garage or a swimming pool add to the selling price of a home?
b. Determine the value of the Intercept.
c. Develop a correlation matrix. Which independent variables have strong or weak correlations with the dependent variable? Do you see any problems with multicollinearity?
d. Conduct the global test on the set of independent variables. Interpret.
e. Conduct a test of hypothesis on each of the independent variables. Would you consider deleting any of the variables? If so, which ones?

f. Rerun the analysis until only significant regression coefficients remain in the analysis. Identify these variables.
g. Develop a histogram or a stem-and-leaf display of the residuals from the final regression equation developed in part (f). Is it reasonable to conclude that the normality assumption has been met?
h. Plot the residuals against the fitted values from the final regression equation developed in part (f). Plot the residuals on the vertical axis and the fitted values on the horizontal axis.

34. Refer to the Baseball 2012 data, which report information on the 30 Major League Baseball teams for the 2012 season. Let the number of games won be the dependent variable and the following variables be independent variables: team batting average, number of stolen bases, number of errors committed, team ERA, number of home runs, and whether the team plays in the American or the National League.
a. Use a statistical software package to determine the multiple regression equation. Discuss each of the variables. For example, are you surprised that the regression coefficient for ERA is negative? Is the number of wins affected by whether the team plays in the National or the American League?
b. Find the coefficient of determination for this set of independent variables.
c. Develop a correlation matrix. Which independent variables have strong or weak correlations with the dependent variable? Do you see any problems with multicollinearity?
d. Conduct a global test on the set of independent variables. Interpret.
e. Conduct a test of hypothesis on each of the independent variables. Would you consider deleting any of the variables? If so, which ones?
f. Rerun the analysis until only significant regression coefficients remain in the analysis. Identify these variables.
g. Develop a histogram or a stem-and-leaf display of the residuals from the final regression equation developed in part (f). Is it reasonable to conclude that the normality assumption has been met?
h. Plot the residuals against the fitted values from the final regression equation developed in part (f). Plot the residuals on the vertical axis and the fitted values on the horizontal axis.

35. Refer to the Buena School District bus data. First, add a variable to change the type of bus (diesel or gasoline) to a qualitative variable. If the bus type is diesel, then set the qualitative variable to 0. If the bus type is gasoline, then set the qualitative variable to 1. Develop a regression equation using statistical software with maintenance as the dependent variable and age, miles, and bus type as the independent variables.
a. Write out the multiple regression equation analysis. Discuss each of the variables.
b. Determine the value of R^2. Interpret.
c. Develop a correlation matrix. Which independent variables have strong or weak correlations with the dependent variable? Do you see any problems with multicollinearity?
d. Conduct the global test on the set of independent variables. Interpret.
e. Conduct a test of hypothesis on each of the independent variables. Would you consider deleting any of the variables? If so, which ones?
f. Rerun the analysis until only significant regression coefficients remain in the analysis. Identify these variables.
g. Develop a histogram or a stem-and-leaf display of the residuals from the final regression equation developed in part (f). Is it reasonable to conclude that the normality assumption has been met?
h. Plot the residuals against the fitted values from the final regression equation developed in part (f) against the fitted values of Y. Plot the residuals on the vertical axis and the fitted values on the horizontal axis.

A REVIEW OF CHAPTERS 13–14

This section is a review of the major concepts and terms introduced in Chapters 13 and 14. Chapter 13 noted that the strength of the relationship between the independent variable and the dependent variable can be measured by the *correlation coefficient.* The correlation coefficient is designated by the letter r. It can assume any value between −1.00 and +1.00 inclusive. Coefficients of −1.00 and +1.00 indicate a perfect relationship, and 0 indicates no relationship. A value near 0, such

as −.14 or .14, indicates a weak relationship. A value near −1 or +1, such as −.90 or +.90, indicates a strong relationship. Squaring *r* gives the *coefficient of determination,* also called R^2. It indicates the proportion of the total variation in the dependent variable explained by the independent variable.

Likewise, the strength of the relationship between several independent variables and a dependent variable is measured by the *coefficient of multiple determination,* R^2. It measures the proportion of the variation in *y* explained by two or more independent variables.

The linear relationship in the simple case involving one independent variable and one dependent variable is described by the equation $\hat{y} = a + bx$. For *k* independent variables, $x_1, x_2, \ldots x_k$, the same multiple regression equation is

$$\hat{y} = a + b_1x_1 + b_2x_2 + \cdots + b_kx_k$$

Solving for $b_1, b_2, \ldots, b_k$ would involve tedious calculations. Fortunately, this type of problem can be quickly solved using one of the many statistical software packages and spreadsheet packages. Various measures, such as the coefficient of determination, the multiple standard error of estimate, the results of the global test, and the test of the individual variables, are reported in the output of most statistical software programs.

PROBLEMS

1. The accounting department at Box and Go Apparel wishes to estimate the net profit for each of the chain's many stores on the basis of the number of employees in the store, overhead costs, average markup, and theft loss. A few statistics from the stores are:

Store	Net Profit ($ thousands)	Number of Employees	Overhead Cost ($ thousands)	Average Markup (percent)	Theft Loss ($ thousands)
1	$846	143	$79	69%	$52
2	513	110	64	50	45

   a. The dependent variable is ________.
   b. The general equation for this problem is ________.
   c. The multiple regression equation was computed to be $\hat{y} = 67 + 8x_1 - 10x_2 + 0.004x_3 - 3x_4$. What are the predicted sales for a store with 112 employees, an overhead cost of $65,000, a markup rate of 50%, and a loss from theft of $50,000?
   d. Suppose R^2 was computed to be .86. Explain.
   e. Suppose that the multiple standard error of estimate was 3 (in $ thousands). Explain what this means in this problem.

2. Quick-print firms in a large downtown business area spend most of their advertising dollars on displays on bus benches. A research project involves predicting monthly sales based on the annual amount spent on placing ads on bus benches. A sample of quick-print firms revealed these advertising expenses and sales:

Firm	Annual Bus Bench Advertising ($ thousands)	Monthly Sales ($ thousands)
A	2	10
B	4	40
C	5	30
D	7	50
E	3	20

   a. Draw a scatter diagram.
   b. Determine the correlation coefficient.
   c. What is the coefficient of determination?

d. Compute the regression equation.
e. Estimate the monthly sales of a quick-print firm that spends $4,500 on bus bench advertisements.
f. Summarize your findings.

3. The following ANOVA output is given.

Analysis of Variance			
Source	DF	SS	MS
Regression	4	1050.8	262.70
Residual Error	20	83.8	4.19
Total	24	1134.6	
Predictor	Coefficient	SE Coefficient	t
Constant	70.06	2.13	32.89
x_1	0.42	0.17	2.47
x_2	0.27	0.21	1.29
x_3	0.75	0.30	2.50
x_4	0.42	0.07	6.00

a. Compute the coefficient of determination.
b. Compute the multiple standard error of estimate.
c. Conduct a test of hypothesis to determine whether any of the regression coefficients are different from zero.
d. Conduct a test of hypothesis on the individual regression coefficients. Can any of the variables be deleted?

CASES

A. The Century National Bank

Refer to the Century National Bank data. Using checking account balance as the dependent variable and using as independent variables the number of ATM transactions, the number of other services used, whether the individual has a debit card, and whether interest is paid on the particular account, write a report indicating which of the variables seem related to the account balance and how well they explain the variation in account balances. Should all of the independent variables proposed be used in the analysis or can some be dropped?

B. Terry and Associates: The Time to Deliver Medical Kits

Terry and Associates is a specialized medical testing center in Denver, Colorado. One of the firm's major sources of revenue is a kit used to test for elevated amounts of lead in the blood. Workers in auto body shops, those in the lawn care industry, and commercial house painters are exposed to large amounts of lead and thus must be randomly tested. It is expensive to conduct the test, so the kits are delivered on demand to a variety of locations throughout the Denver area.

Kathleen Terry, the owner, is concerned about setting appropriate costs for each delivery. To investigate, Ms. Terry gathered information on a random sample of 50 recent deliveries. Factors thought to be related to the cost of delivering a kit were:

Prep The time in minutes between when the customized order is phoned into the company and when it is ready for delivery.
Delivery The actual travel time in minutes from Terry's plant to the customer.
Mileage The distance in miles from Terry's plant to the customer.

Sample Number	Cost	Prep	Delivery	Mileage	Sample Number	Cost	Prep	Delivery	Mileage
1	$32.60	10	51	20	6	$22.63	9	20	11
2	23.37	11	33	12	7	22.63	9	39	11
3	31.49	6	47	19	8	21.53	10	23	10
4	19.31	9	18	8	9	21.16	13	20	8
5	28.35	8	88	17	10	21.53	10	32	10

Sample Number	Cost	Prep	Delivery	Mileage	Sample Number	Cost	Prep	Delivery	Mileage
11	$28.17	5	35	16	31	$24.29	7	35	13
12	20.42	7	23	9	32	19.56	2	12	6
13	21.53	9	21	10	33	22.63	8	30	11
14	27.55	7	37	16	34	21.16	5	13	8
15	23.37	9	25	12	35	21.16	11	20	8
16	17.10	15	15	6	36	19.68	5	19	8
17	27.06	13	34	15	37	18.76	5	14	7
18	15.99	8	13	4	38	17.96	5	11	4
19	17.96	12	12	4	39	23.37	10	25	12
20	25.22	6	41	14	40	25.22	6	32	14
21	24.29	3	28	13	41	27.06	8	44	16
22	22.76	4	26	10	42	21.96	9	28	9
23	28.17	9	54	16	43	22.63	8	31	11
24	19.68	7	18	8	44	19.68	7	19	8
25	25.15	6	50	13	45	22.76	8	28	10
26	20.36	9	19	7	46	21.96	13	18	9
27	21.16	3	19	8	47	25.95	10	32	14
28	25.95	10	45	14	48	26.14	8	44	15
29	18.76	12	12	5	49	24.29	8	34	13
30	18.76	8	16	5	50	24.35	3	33	12

1. Develop a multiple linear regression equation that describes the relationship between the cost of delivery and the other variables. Do these three variables explain a reasonable amount of the variation in the dependent variable? Estimate the delivery cost for a kit that takes 10 minutes for preparation, takes 30 minutes to deliver, and must cover a distance of 14 miles.
2. Test to determine that at least one regression coefficient differs from zero. Also test to see whether any of the variables can be dropped from the analysis. If some of the variables can be dropped, rerun the regression equation until only significant variables are included.
3. Write a brief report interpreting the final regression equation.

PRACTICE TEST

Part 1—Objective

1. In a scatter diagram, the dependent variable is always scaled on which axis? 1. ____________
2. What level of measurement is required to compute the correlation coefficient? 2. ____________
3. If there is no correlation between two variables, what is the value of the correlation coefficient? 3. ____________
4. Which of the following values indicates the strongest correlation between two variables? (.65, −.77, 0, −.12) 4. ____________
5. Under what conditions will the coefficient of determination assume a value greater than 1? 5. ____________

Given the following regression equation, $\hat{Y} = 7 - .5X$, and that the coefficient of determination is .81, answer questions 6, 7, and 8.

6. At what point does the regression equation cross the *Y*-axis? 6. ____________
7. An increase of 1 unit in the independent variable will result in what amount of an increase or decrease in the dependent variable? 7. ____________
8. What is the correlation coefficient? (Be careful of the sign.) 8. ____________
9. If all the data points in a scatter diagram were on the regression line, what would be the value of the standard error of estimate? 9. ____________
10. In a multiple regression equation, what is the maximum number of independent variables allowed? (2, 10, 30, unlimited) 10. ____________
11. In multiple regression analysis, we assume what type of relationship between the dependent variable and the set of independent variables? (linear, multiple, curved, none of these) 11. ____________
12. The difference between Y and $\hat{Y}$ is called a ________. 12. ____________

13. For a particular dummy variable, such as gender, how many different outcomes are possible? **13.** ________
14. What is the term given to a table that shows all possible correlation coefficients between the dependent variable and all the independent variables and among all the independent variables? **14.** ________
15. If there is a linear relationship between the dependent variable and the set of independent variables, a graph of the residuals will show what type of distribution? **15.** ________

Part 2—Problems

1. Given the following software output:

Regression Analysis

ANOVA Table

Source	SS	*df*	MS	*F*	*p*-value
Regression	129.7275	1	129.7275	14.50	.0007
Residual	250.4391	28	8.9443		
Total	380.1667	29			

Regression Output

Variables	Coefficients	Standard Error	t ($df = 28$)
Intercept	90.6190	1.5322	59.141
Slope	−0.9401	0.2468	−3.808

a. What is the sample size?
b. Write out the regression equation. Interpret the slope and intercept values.
c. If the value of the independent variable is 10, what is the value of the dependent variable?
d. Calculate the coefficient of determination. Interpret this value.
e. Calculate the correlation coefficient. Conduct a test of hypothesis to determine if there is a significant negative association between the variables.

2. Given the following software output.

Regression Analysis

ANOVA Table

Source	SS	*df*	MS	*F*	*p-value*
Regression	227.0928	4	56.7732	9.27	0.000
Residual	153.0739	25	6.1230		
Total	380.1667	29			

Regression Output

Variables	Coefficients	Standard Error	t ($df = 25$)	*p*-value
Intercept	68.3366	8.9752	7.614	0.000
X_1	0.8595	0.3087	2.784	0.010
X_2	−0.3380	0.8381	−0.403	0.690
X_3	−0.8179	0.2749	−2.975	0.006
X_4	−0.5824	0.2541	−2.292	0.030

a. How large is the sample size?
b. How many independent variables are in the study?
c. Determine the coefficient of determination.
d. Conduct a global test of hypothesis. Can you conclude at least one of the independent variables does not equal zero? Use the .01 significance level.
e. Conduct an individual test of hypothesis on each of the independent variables. Would you consider dropping any of the independent variables? If so, which variable or variables would you drop? Use the .01 significance level.

Nonparametric Methods:

NOMINAL LEVEL HYPOTHESIS TESTS

15

FOR MANY YEARS, TV executives used the guideline that 30% of the audience were watching each of the traditional big three prime-time networks and 10% were watching cable stations on a weekday night. A random sample of 500 viewers in the Tampa–St. Petersburg, Florida, area last Monday night showed that 165 homes were tuned in to the ABC affiliate, 140 to the CBS affiliate, 125 to the NBC affiliate, and the remainder were viewing a cable station. At the .05 significance level, can we conclude that the guideline is still reasonable? (See Exercise 24 and LO15-3.)

LEARNING OBJECTIVES

When you have completed this chapter, you will be able to:

LO15-1 Test a hypothesis about a population proportion.

LO15-2 Test a hypothesis about two population proportions.

LO15-3 Test a hypothesis comparing an observed set of frequencies to an expected frequency distribution.

LO15-4 Explain the limitations of using the chi-square statistic in goodness-of-fit tests.

LO15-5 Test a hypothesis that an observed frequency distribution is normally distributed.

LO15-6 Perform a chi-square test for independence on a contingency table.

INTRODUCTION

In Chapters 9 through 12 we describe tests of hypothesis for data of interval or ratio scale. Examples of interval and ratio scale data include the scores on the first statistics examination in your class, the incomes of corporate executive officers in technology companies, or years of employment of production workers at the BMW plant in Greer, South Carolina.

We conducted hypothesis tests about a single population mean (Chapter 10), about two population means (Chapter 11), and about three or more population means (Chapter 12). For these tests we use interval or ratio data and assume the populations follow the normal probability distribution. However, there are hypothesis tests that do not require any assumption regarding the shape of the population. Hence, the assumption of a normal population is not necessary. These tests are referred to as non-parametric hypothesis tests.

In this chapter, we begin with tests of hypothesis for nominal scale data. Recall that nominal scale data are simply classified into mutually exclusive categories. In the first two sections of this chapter we describe tests of proportions. In these tests individuals or objects are classified into one of two mutually exclusive groups. Examples include gender (male or female), quality (acceptable or unacceptable), diabetes (yes or no), and airline flight arrivals (on time or late).

We also expand the nominal scale tests to include situations where data are classified into several mutually exclusive categories. The scale of measurement is still nominal, but there are several categories. Examples include the colors of M&M Plain Candies (red, green, blue, yellow, orange, and brown), brand of peanut butter purchased (Peter Pan, Jif, Skippy, and others), or days of the workweek (Monday, Tuesday, Wednesday, Thursday, and Friday). We introduce the chi-square distribution as a new test statistic. It is most often used when there are more than two nominal scale categories.

LO15-1
Test a hypothesis about a population proportion.

TEST A HYPOTHESIS OF A POPULATION PROPORTION

Beginning on page 297 in Chapter 9, we discussed confidence intervals for proportions. We can also conduct a test of hypothesis for a proportion. Recall that a proportion is the ratio of the number of successes to the number of observations. We let X refer to the number of successes and n the number of observations, so the proportion of successes in a fixed number of trials is X/n. Thus, the formula for computing a sample proportion, p, is $p = X/n$. Consider the following potential hypothesis-testing situations.

- Historically, General Motors reports that 70% of leased vehicles are returned with less than 36,000 miles. A recent sample of 200 vehicles returned at the end of their lease showed 158 had less than 36,000 miles. Has the proportion increased?
- The American Association of Retired Persons (AARP) reports that 60% of retired people under the age of 65 would return to work on a full-time basis if a suitable job were available. A sample of 500 retirees under 65 revealed 315 would return to work. Can we conclude that more than 60% would return to work?
- Able Moving and Storage Inc. advises its clients for long-distance residential moves that their household goods will be delivered in 3 to 5 days from the time they are picked up. Able's records show it is successful 90% of the time with this claim. A recent audit revealed it was successful 190 times out of 200. Can the company conclude its success rate has increased?

Some assumptions must be made and conditions met before testing a population proportion. To test a hypothesis about a population proportion, a random sample is

chosen from the population. It is assumed that the binomial assumptions discussed in Chapter 6 are met: (1) the sample data collected are the result of counts; (2) the outcome of an experiment is classified into one of two mutually exclusive categories—a "success" or a "failure"; (3) the probability of a success is the same for each trial; and (4) the trials are independent, meaning the outcome of one trial does not affect the outcome of any other trial. This test is appropriate when both $n\pi$ and $n(1 - \pi)$ are at least 5. n is the sample size, and π is the population proportion. It takes advantage of the fact that a binomial distribution can be approximated by the normal distribution.

EXAMPLE

A Republican governor of a western state is thinking about running for reelection. Historically, to be reelected, a Republican candidate needs to earn at least 80% of the vote in the northern section of the state. The governor hires a polling organization to survey the voters in the northern section of the state and determine what percent would vote for him. The polling organization will survey 2,000 voters. Use a statistical hypothesis-testing procedure to assess the governor's chances of reelection.

SOLUTION

This situation regarding the governor's reelection meets the binomial conditions.

- There are only two possible outcomes. That is, a sampled voter will either vote or not vote for the governor.
- The probability of a success is the same for each trial. In this case, the likelihood a particular sampled voter will support reelection is .80.
- The trials are independent. This means, for example, the likelihood the 23rd voter sampled will support reelection is not affected by what the 24th or 52nd voter does.
- The sample data are the result of counts. We are going to count the number of voters who support reelection in the sample of 2,000.

We can use a normal approximation to the binomial distribution if both $n\pi$ and $n(1 - \pi)$ exceed 5. In this case, $n = 2{,}000$ and $\pi = 0.80$. (π is the proportion of the vote in the northern part of the state, or 80%, needed to be elected.) Thus, $n\pi = 2{,}000(.80) = 1{,}600$ and $n(1 - \pi) = 2{,}000(1 - .80) = 400$. Both 1,600 and 400 are clearly greater than 5.

Step 1: State the null hypothesis and the alternate hypothesis. The null hypothesis, H_0, is that the population proportion π is .80 or larger. The alternate hypothesis, H_1, is that the proportion is less than .80. From a practical standpoint, the incumbent governor is concerned only when the proportion is less than .80. If it is equal to or greater than .80, he will have no problem; that is, the sample data would indicate he will probably be reelected. These hypotheses are written symbolically as:

$$H_0: \pi \geq .80$$
$$H_1: \pi < .80$$

H_1 states a direction. Thus, as noted previously, the test is one-tailed with the inequality sign pointing to the tail of the distribution containing the region of rejection.

Step 2: Select the level of significance. The level of significance is .05. This is the likelihood that a true hypothesis will be rejected.

Step 3: Select the test statistic. z is the appropriate statistic, found by:

TEST OF HYPOTHESIS, ONE PROPORTION

$$z = \frac{p - \pi}{\sqrt{\frac{\pi(1 - \pi)}{n}}} \quad \textbf{[15–1]}$$

where:

π is the population proportion.
p is the sample proportion.
n is the sample size.

Step 4: Formulate the decision rule. The critical value or values of z form the dividing point or points between the regions where H_0 is rejected and where it is not rejected. Because the alternate hypothesis states a direction, this is a one-tailed test. The sign of the inequality points to the left, so only the left side of the curve is used. (See Chart 15–1.) The significance level is .05. This probability is in the left tail and determines the region of rejection. The area between zero and the critical value is .4500, found by .5000 − .0500. Referring to Appendix B.3, go to the column indicating a .05 significance level for a one-tailed test, find the row with infinite degrees of freedom, and read the z value of 1.645. The decision rule is, therefore: Reject the null hypothesis and accept the alternate hypothesis if the computed value of z falls to the left of −1.645; otherwise do not reject H_0.

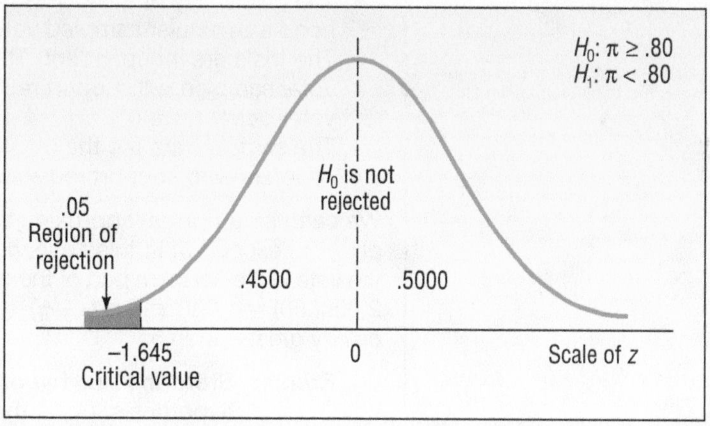

CHART 15–1 Rejection Region for the .05 Level of Significance, One-Tailed Test

Step 5: Make a decision. Select a sample and make a decision about H_0. A sample survey of 2,000 potential voters in the northern part of the state revealed that 1,550 planned to vote for the incumbent governor. Is the sample proportion of .775 (found by 1,550/2,000) close enough to .80 to conclude that the difference is due to sampling error? In this case:

p is .775, the proportion in the sample who plan to vote for the governor.
n is 2,000, the number of voters surveyed.
π is .80, the hypothesized population proportion.
z is a normally distributed test statistic when the hypothesis is true and the other assumptions are true.

Using formula (15–1) and computing z gives

$$z = \frac{p - \pi}{\sqrt{\frac{\pi(1-\pi)}{n}}} = \frac{\frac{1,550}{2,000} - .80}{\sqrt{\frac{.80(1-.80)}{2,000}}} = \frac{.775 - .80}{\sqrt{.00008}} = -2.80$$

The computed value of z (−2.80) is less than the critical value, so the null hypothesis is rejected at the .05 level. The difference of 2.5 percentage points between the sample percent (77.5%) and the hypothesized population percent in the northern part of the state necessary to carry the state (80%) is statistically significant. From Appendix B.3, the probability of a z value between zero and −2.80 is .4974. So the p-value is .0026, found by .5000 − .4974. Because the p-value is less than the significance level, the null hypothesis is rejected.

Step 6: Interpret the result. The governor can conclude that he does not have the necessary support in the northern section of the state to win reelection. To put it another way, the evidence at this point does not support the claim that the incumbent governor will return to the governor's mansion for another 4 years.

SELF-REVIEW 15–1

A recent insurance industry report indicated that 40% of those persons involved in minor traffic accidents this year have been involved in at least one other traffic accident in the last 5 years. An advisory group decided to investigate this claim, believing it was too large. A sample of 200 traffic accidents this year showed 74 persons were also involved in another accident within the last 5 years. Use the .01 significance level.

(a) Can we use z as the test statistic? Tell why or why not.
(b) State the null hypothesis and the alternate hypothesis.
(c) Show the decision rule graphically.
(d) Compute the value of z and state your decision regarding the null hypothesis.
(e) Determine and interpret the p-value.

EXERCISES

1. The following hypotheses are given.

$$H_0: \pi \leq .70$$
$$H_1: \pi > .70$$

A sample of 100 observations revealed that $p = .75$. At the .05 significance level, can the null hypothesis be rejected?

a. State the decision rule.
b. Compute the value of the test statistic.
c. What is your decision regarding the null hypothesis?

2. The following hypotheses are given.

$$H_0: \pi = .40$$
$$H_1: \pi \neq .40$$

A sample of 120 observations revealed that $p = .30$. At the .05 significance level, can the null hypothesis be rejected?

a. State the decision rule.
b. Compute the value of the test statistic.
c. What is your decision regarding the null hypothesis?

Note: It is recommended that you use the six-step hypothesis-testing procedure in solving the following problems.

3. The National Safety Council reported that 52% of American turnpike drivers are men. A sample of 300 cars traveling southbound on the New Jersey Turnpike yesterday revealed that 170 were driven by men. At the .01 significance level, can we conclude that a larger proportion of men were driving on the New Jersey Turnpike than the national statistics indicate?
4. A recent article reported that a job awaits only one in three new college graduates. The major reasons given were an overabundance of college graduates and a weak economy. A survey of 200 recent graduates from your school revealed that 80 students had jobs. At the .01 significance level, can we conclude that a larger proportion of students at your school have jobs?
5. Chicken Delight claims that 90% of its orders are delivered within 10 minutes of the time the order is placed. A sample of 100 orders revealed that 82 were delivered within the promised time. At the .10 significance level, can we conclude that less than 90% of the orders are delivered in less than 10 minutes?
6. Research at the University of Toledo indicates that 50% of students change their major area of study after their first year in a program. A random sample of 100 students in the College of Business revealed that 48 had changed their major area of study after their first year of the program. Has there been a significant decrease in the proportion of students who change their major after the first year in this program? Test at the .05 level of significance.

LO15-2
Test a hypothesis about two population proportions.

TWO-SAMPLE TESTS ABOUT PROPORTIONS

In the previous section, we considered a test of a single population proportion. However, we are often interested also in whether two sample proportions come from populations that are equal. Here are several examples.

- The vice president of human resources wishes to know whether there is a difference in the proportion of hourly employees who miss more than 5 days of work per year at the Atlanta and the Houston plants.
- General Motors is considering a new design for the Chevy Malibu. The design is shown to a group of potential buyers under 30 years of age and another group over 60 years of age. General Motors wishes to know whether there is a difference in the proportion of the two groups who like the new design.
- A consultant to the airline industry is investigating the fear of flying among adults. Specifically, the company wishes to know whether there is a difference in the proportion of men versus women who are fearful of flying.

In the above cases, each sampled item or individual can be classified as a "success" or a "failure." That is, in the Chevy Malibu example, each potential buyer is classified as "liking the new design" or "not liking the new design." We then compare the proportion in the under-30 group with the proportion in the over-60 group who indicated they liked the new design. Can we conclude that the differences are due to chance? In this study, there is no measurement obtained, only classifying the individuals or objects.

To conduct the test, we assume each sample is large enough that the normal distribution will serve as a good approximation of the binomial distribution. The test statistic follows the standard normal distribution. We compute the value of z from the following formula:

TWO-SAMPLE TEST OF PROPORTIONS

$$z = \frac{p_1 - p_2}{\sqrt{\dfrac{p_c(1 - p_c)}{n_1} + \dfrac{p_c(1 - p_c)}{n_2}}} \qquad [15\text{–}2]$$

where:

n_1 is the number of observations in the first sample.
n_2 is the number of observations in the second sample.
p_1 is the proportion in the first sample possessing the trait.
p_2 is the proportion in the second sample possessing the trait.
p_c is the pooled proportion possessing the trait in the combined samples. It is called the pooled estimate of the population proportion and is computed from the following formula.

POOLED PROPORTION

$$p_c = \frac{x_1 + x_2}{n_1 + n_2} \quad \textbf{[15–3]}$$

where:

x_1 is the number possessing the trait in the first sample.
x_2 is the number possessing the trait in the second sample.

The following example will illustrate the two-sample test of proportions.

EXAMPLE

Manelli Perfume Company recently developed a new fragrance that it plans to market under the name Heavenly. A number of market studies indicate that Heavenly has very good market potential. The sales department at Manelli is particularly interested in whether there is a difference in the proportions of young and older women who would purchase Heavenly if it were marketed. There are two independent populations, a population consisting of the young women and a population consisting of the older women. Each sampled woman will be asked to smell Heavenly and indicate whether she likes the fragrance well enough to purchase a bottle.

SOLUTION

We will use the usual six-step hypothesis-testing procedure.

Step 1: State H_0 and H_1. In this case, the null hypothesis is: "There is no difference in the proportion of young women and older women who prefer Heavenly." We designate π_1 as the proportion of young women who would purchase Heavenly and π_2 as the proportion of older women who would purchase it. The alternate hypothesis is that the two proportions are not equal.

$$H_0: \pi_1 = \pi_2$$
$$H_1: \pi_1 \neq \pi_2$$

Step 2: Select the level of significance. We choose the .05 significance level in this example.

Step 3: Determine the test statistic. The test statistic follows the standard normal distribution. The value of the test statistic can be computed from formula (15–2).

Step 4: Formulate the decision rule. Recall that the alternate hypothesis from **Step 1** does not state a direction, so this is a two-tailed test. To find the critical value, go to Student's *t* distribution (Appendix B.5). In the table headings, find the row labeled **"Level of Significance for Two-Tailed Test"** and select the column for an alpha of .05. Go to the bottom row with infinite degrees of freedom. The *z* critical value is 1.960, so the critical values are −1.960 and 1.960. As before, if the computed test statistic is less than −1.960 or greater than 1.960, the null hypothesis is rejected. This information is summarized in Chart 15–2.

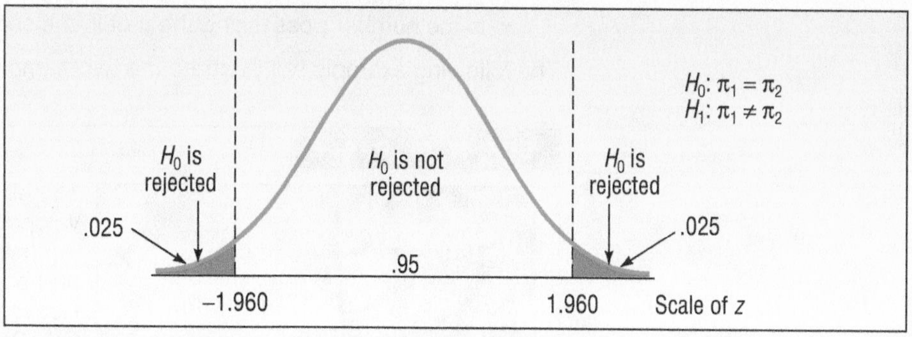

CHART 15–2 Decision Rules for Heavenly Fragrance Test, .05 Significance Level

Step 5: Select a sample and make a decision. A random sample of 100 young women revealed 19 liked the Heavenly fragrance well enough to purchase it. Similarly, a sample of 200 older women revealed 62 liked the fragrance well enough to make a purchase. We let p_1 refer to the young women and p_2 to the older women.

$$p_1 = \frac{x_1}{n_1} = \frac{19}{100} = .19 \qquad p_2 = \frac{x_2}{n_2} = \frac{62}{200} = .31$$

The research question is whether the difference of .12 in the two sample proportions is due to chance or whether there is a difference in the proportion of young and older women who like the Heavenly fragrance.

Next, we combine or pool the sample proportions. We use formula (15–3).

$$p_c = \frac{x_1 + x_2}{n_1 + n_2} = \frac{19 + 62}{100 + 200} = \frac{81}{300} = 0.27$$

Note that the pooled proportion is closer to .31 than to .19 because more older women than young women were sampled.

We use formula (15–2) to find the value of the test statistic.

$$z = \frac{p_1 - p_2}{\sqrt{\dfrac{p_c(1 - p_c)}{n_1} + \dfrac{p_c(1 - p_c)}{n_2}}} = \frac{.19 - .31}{\sqrt{\dfrac{.27(1 - .27)}{100} + \dfrac{.27(1 - .27)}{200}}} = -2.207$$

The computed value of −2.207 is in the area of rejection; that is, it is to the left of −1.960. Therefore, the null hypothesis is rejected at the .05 significance level. To put it another way, we reject the null hypothesis that the proportion of young women who would purchase Heavenly is equal to the proportion of older women who would purchase Heavenly.

To find the *p*-value, we need to round the *z* test statistic from −2.207 to −2.21 so that we can use the table Areas under the Normal Curve in Appendix B.3. In the table, find the likelihood, or probability, of a *z* value less than −2.21 or greater than 2.21. The probability corresponding to 2.21 is .4864, so the likelihood of finding the value of the test statistic to be less than −2.21 or greater than 2.21 is:

$$p\text{-value} = 2(.5000 - .4864) = 2(.0136) = .0272$$

The *p*-value of .0272 is less than the significance level of .05, so our decision is to reject the null hypothesis.

Step 6: Interpret the result. The results of the hypothesis test indicate younger and older women purchase Heavenly at different rates or proportions.

The MegaStat add-in for Excel has a procedure to determine the value of the test statistic and compute the *p*-value. Notice that the MegaStat output includes the two sample proportions, the value of *z*, and the *p*-value. The difference in the *p*-value is rounding. The results follow.

Hypothesis test for two independent proportions

p1	*p2*	p_c	
0.19	0.31	0.27	p (as decimal)
19/100	62/200	81/300	p (as fraction)
19.	62.	81.	X
100	200	300	n
		-0.12	difference
		0.	hypothesized difference
		0.0544	std. error
		-2.21	z
		.0273	p-value (two-tailed)

SELF-REVIEW 15–2

Of 150 adults who tried a new peach-flavored Peppermint Pattie, 87 rated it excellent. Of 200 children sampled, 123 rated it excellent. Using the .10 level of significance, can we conclude that there is a significant difference in the proportion of adults and the proportion of children who rate the new flavor excellent?

(a) State the null hypothesis and the alternate hypothesis.
(b) What is the probability of a Type I error?
(c) Is this a one-tailed or a two-tailed test?
(d) What is the decision rule?
(e) What is the value of the test statistic?
(f) What is your decision regarding the null hypothesis?
(g) What is the *p*-value? Explain what it means in terms of this problem.

EXERCISES

7. The null and alternate hypotheses are:

$$H_0: \pi_1 \leq \pi_2$$
$$H_1: \pi_1 > \pi_2$$

A sample of 100 observations from the first population indicated that X_1 is 70. A sample of 150 observations from the second population revealed X_2 to be 90. Use the .05 significance level to test the hypothesis.
   a. State the decision rule.
   b. Compute the pooled proportion.
   c. Compute the value of the test statistic.
   d. What is your decision regarding the null hypothesis?

8. The null and alternate hypotheses are:

$$H_0: \pi_1 = \pi_2$$
$$H_1: \pi_1 \neq \pi_2$$

A sample of 200 observations from the first population indicated that x_1 is 170. A sample of 150 observations from the second population revealed x_2 to be 110. Use the .05 significance level to test the hypothesis.
   a. State the decision rule.
   b. Compute the pooled proportion.
   c. Compute the value of the test statistic.
   d. What is your decision regarding the null hypothesis?

Note: Use the six-step hypothesis-testing procedure in solving the following exercises.

9. The Damon family owns a large grape vineyard in western New York along Lake Erie. The grapevines must be sprayed at the beginning of the growing season to protect against various insects and diseases. Two new insecticides have just been marketed: Pernod 5 and Action. To test their effectiveness, three long rows were selected and sprayed with Pernod 5, and three others were sprayed with Action. When the grapes ripened, 400 of the vines treated with Pernod 5 were checked for infestation. Likewise, a sample of 400 vines sprayed with Action were checked. The results are:

Insecticide	Number of Vines Checked (sample size)	Number of Infested Vines
Pernod 5	400	24
Action	400	40

At the .05 significance level, can we conclude that there is a difference in the proportion of vines infested using Pernod 5 as opposed to Action?

10. GfK Custom Research North America conducted identical surveys 5 years apart. One question asked of women was "Are most men basically kind, gentle, and thoughtful?" The earlier survey revealed that, of the 3,000 women surveyed, 2,010 said that they were. The later revealed 1,530 of the 3,000 women surveyed thought that men were kind, gentle, and thoughtful. At the .05 level, can we conclude that women think men are less kind, gentle, and thoughtful in the later survey compared with the earlier one?

11. A nationwide sample of influential Republicans and Democrats was asked as a part of a comprehensive survey whether they favored lowering environmental standards so that high-sulfur coal could be burned in coal-fired power plants. The results were:

	Republicans	Democrats
Number sampled	1,000	800
Number in favor	200	168

At the .02 level of significance, can we conclude that there is a larger proportion of Democrats in favor of lowering the standards? Determine the p-value.

12. The research department at the home office of New Hampshire Insurance conducts ongoing research on the causes of automobile accidents, the characteristics of the drivers, and so on. A random sample of 400 policies written on single persons revealed 120 had at

least one accident in the previous three-year period. Similarly, a sample of 600 policies written on married persons revealed that 150 had been in at least one accident. At the .05 significance level, is there a significant difference in the proportions of single and married persons having an accident during a three-year period? Determine the *p*-value.

LO15-3
Test a hypothesis comparing an observed set of frequencies to an expected frequency distribution.

GOODNESS-OF-FIT TESTS: COMPARING OBSERVED AND EXPECTED FREQUENCY DISTRIBUTIONS

Next, we compare two distributions of nominal scale data that are summarized by several categories. For example, a life insurance company classified its policies into four categories: whole life, level term, decreasing term, and others. The table below shows the historical relative frequency distribution of the policy types.

Policy Type	Percent
Whole life	40
Level term	25
Decreasing term	15
Other	20

The insurance company wishes to compare this distribution with the distribution of policy types purchased by a sample of 2,000 young married adults. In situations where the data are nominally scaled and we wish to compare two distributions, we call this a goodness-of-fit test. A goodness-of-fit test is one of the most commonly used statistical tests. It is particularly useful because it requires only the nominal level of measurement. So we can conduct a test of hypothesis on data that have been classified into categories or groups.

Hypothesis Test of Equal Expected Frequencies

Our first illustration of a goodness-of-fit test involves the case when the expected frequencies are equal. As the full name implies, the purpose of the goodness-of-fit test is to compare an observed frequency distribution to an expected frequency distribution. An example will describe the hypothesis-testing situation.

EXAMPLE

Bubba's Fish and Pasta is a chain of restaurants located along the Gulf Coast of Florida. Bubba, the owner, is considering adding steak to his menu. Before doing so, he decides to hire Magnolia Research, LLC, to conduct a survey of adults as to their favorite meal when eating out. Magnolia selected a sample 120 adults and asked each to indicate his or her favorite meal when dining out. The results are reported below.

TABLE 15–1 Favorite Entrée as Selected by a Sample of 120 Adults

Favorite Entrée	Frequency
Chicken	32
Fish	24
Meat	35
Pasta	29
Total	120

Is it reasonable to conclude there is no preference among the four entrées?

SOLUTION

If there is no difference in the popularity of the four entrées, we would expect the observed frequencies to be equal—or nearly equal. To put it another way, we would expect as many adults to indicate they preferred chicken as fish. Thus, any discrepancy in the observed and expected frequencies is attributed to sampling error or chance.

What is the level of measurement in this problem? Notice that when a person is selected, we can only classify the selected adult as to the entrée preferred. We do not get a reading or a measurement of any kind. The "measurement" or "classification" is based on the selected entrée. In addition, there is no natural order to the favorite entrée. No one entrée is assumed better than another. Therefore, the nominal scale is appropriate.

If the entrées are equally popular, we would expect 30 adults to select each meal. Why is this so? If there are 120 adults in the sample and four categories, we expect that one-fourth of those surveyed would select each entrée. So 30, found by 120/4, is the expected frequency for each category or cell, assuming there is no preference for any of the entrées. This information is summarized in Table 15–2. An examination of the data indicates meat is the entrée selected most frequently (35 out of 120) and fish is selected least frequently (24 out of 120). Is the difference in the number of times each entrée is selected due to chance, or should we conclude that the entrées are not equally preferred?

TABLE 15–2 Observed and Expected Frequencies for Survey of 120 Adults

Favorite Meal	Observed Frequency, f_o	Expected Frequency, f_e
Chicken	32	30
Fish	24	30
Meat	35	30
Pasta	29	30
Total	120	120

To investigate the issue, we use the six-step hypothesis-testing procedure.

Step 1: State the null hypothesis and the alternate hypothesis. The null hypothesis, H_0, is that there is no difference between the set of observed frequencies and the set of expected frequencies. In other words, any difference between the two sets of frequencies is attributed to sampling error. The alternate hypothesis, H_1, is that there is a difference between the observed and expected sets of frequencies. If the null hypothesis is rejected and the alternate hypothesis is

accepted, we conclude the preferences are not equally distributed among the four categories (cells).

H_0: There is no difference in the proportion of adults selecting each entrée.
H_1: There is a difference in the proportion of adults selecting each entrée.

Step 2: Select the level of significance. We selected the .05 significance level. The probability is .05 that a true null hypothesis is rejected.

Step 3: Select the test statistic. The test statistic follows the chi-square distribution, designated by χ^2.

CHI-SQUARE TEST STATISTIC

$$\chi^2 = \Sigma\left[\frac{(f_o - f_e)^2}{f_e}\right] \quad \textbf{[15–4]}$$

with $k - 1$ degrees of freedom, where:
k is the number of categories.
f_o is an observed frequency in a particular category.
f_e is an expected frequency in a particular category.

We will examine the characteristics of the chi-square distribution in more detail shortly.

Step 4: Formulate the decision rule. Recall that the decision rule in hypothesis testing is the value that separates the region where we do not reject H_0 from the region where H_0 is rejected. This number is called the *critical value.* As we will soon see, the chi-square distribution is really a family of distributions. Each distribution has a slightly different shape, depending on the number of degrees of freedom. The number of degrees of freedom is $k - 1$, where k is the number of categories. In this particular problem, there are four categories, the four meal entrées. Because there are four categories, there are $k - 1 = 4 - 1 = 3$ degrees of freedom. As noted, a category is called a *cell,* and there are four cells. The critical value for 3 degrees of freedom and the .05 level of significance is found in Appendix B.7. A portion of that table is shown in Table 15–3. The critical value is 7.815, found by locating 3 degrees of freedom in the left margin and then moving horizontally (to the right) and reading the critical value in the .05 column.

TABLE 15–3 A Portion of the Chi-Square Table

Degrees of Freedom	Right-Tail Area			
df	.10	.05	.02	.01
1	2.706	3.841	5.412	6.635
2	4.605	5.991	7.824	9.210
3	6.251	7.815	9.837	11.345
4	7.779	9.488	11.668	13.277
5	9.236	11.070	13.388	15.086

The decision rule is to reject the null hypothesis if the computed value of chi-square is greater than 7.815. If it is less than or equal to 7.815, we fail to reject the null hypothesis. Chart 15–3 shows the decision rule.

STATISTICS IN ACTION

For many years, researchers and statisticians believed that all variables were normally distributed. In fact, it was generally assumed to be a universal law. However, Karl Pearson observed that experimental data were not always normally distributed but there was no way to prove his observations were correct. To solve this problem, Pearson discovered the chi-square statistic that basically compares an observed frequency distribution with an assumed normal distribution. His discovery proved that all variables were not normally distributed.

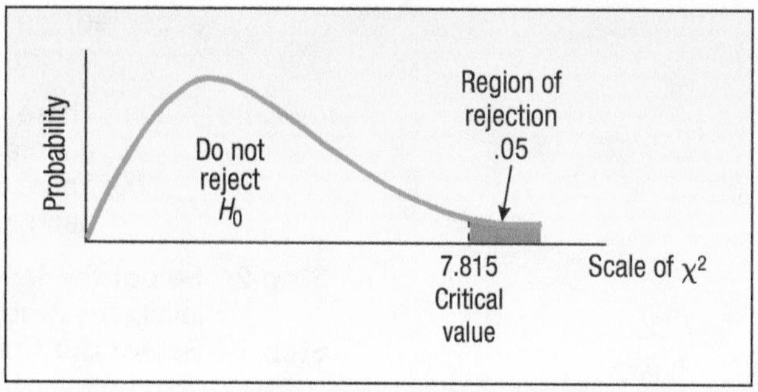

CHART 15–3 Chi-Square Probability Distribution for 3 Degrees of Freedom, Showing the Region of Rejection, .05 Level of Significance

The decision rule indicates that if there are large differences between the observed and expected frequencies, resulting in a computed χ^2 of more than 7.815, the null hypothesis should be rejected. However, if the differences between f_o and f_e are small, the computed χ^2 value will be 7.815 or less, and the null hypothesis should not be rejected. The reasoning is that such small differences between the observed and expected frequencies are probably due to chance. Remember, the 120 observations are a sample of the population.

Step 5: Compute the value of chi-square and make a decision. Of the 120 adults in the sample, 32 indicated their favorite entrée was chicken. The counts were reported in Table 15–1. The calculations for chi-square follow. (Note again that the expected frequencies are the same for each cell.)

Column D: Determine the differences between each f_o and f_e. That is, $f_o - f_e$. The sum of these differences is zero.
Column E: Square the difference between each observed and expected frequency, that is, $(f_o - f_e)^2$.
Column F: Divide the result for each observation by the expected frequency, that is, $(f_o - f_e)^2/f_e$. Finally, sum these values. The result is the value of χ^2, which is 2.20.

	A	B	C	D	E	F	G
1	Favorite Entrée	f_o	f_e	$(f_o - f_e)$	$(f_o - f_e)^2$	$(f_o - f_e)^2/f_e$	
2	Chicken	32	30	2	4	0.133	
3	Fish	24	30	-6	36	1.200	
4	Meat	35	30	5	25	0.833	χ^2 Value
5	Pasta	29	30	-1	1	0.033	
6	Total	120	120			2.200	

The computed χ^2 of 2.20 is not in the rejection region. It is less than the critical value of 7.815. The decision, therefore, is to not reject the null hypothesis.

Step 6: Interpret the results. We conclude that the differences between the observed and the expected frequencies could be due to chance. The data do not suggest that the preferences among the four entrées are different.

We can use Megastat to compute the goodness-of-fit test as follows. The steps are shown in the **Software Commands** in Appendix C. The computed value of

chi-square is 2.20, the same value obtained in our earlier calculations. Also note the *p*-value is .5319, much larger than .05.

Goodness-of-Fit Test

observed	expected	O − E	(O − E)²/E	% of chisq
32	30.000	2.000	0.133	6.06
24	30.000	−6.000	1.200	54.55
35	30.000	5.000	0.833	37.88
29	30.000	−1.000	0.033	1.52
120	120.000	0.000	2.200	100.00

2.20	chi-square
3	df
.5319	p-value

The distribution of the chi-square statistic has the following characteristics.

1. **Chi-square values are never negative.** This is because the difference between f_o and f_e is squared, that is, $(f_o - f_e)^2$.
2. **There is a family of chi-square distributions.** There is a chi-square distribution for 1 degree of freedom, another for 2 degrees of freedom, another for 3 degrees of freedom, and so on. In this type of problem, the number of degrees of freedom is determined by $k - 1$, where k is the number of categories. Therefore, the shape of the chi-square distribution does *not* depend on the size of the sample, but on the number of categories used. For example, if 200 employees of an airline were classified into one of three categories—flight personnel, ground support, and administrative personnel—there would be $k - 1 = 3 - 1 = 2$ degrees of freedom.
3. **The chi-square distribution is positively skewed.** However, as the number of degrees of freedom increases, the distribution begins to approximate the normal probability distribution. Chart 15–4 shows the distributions for selected degrees of freedom. Notice that for 10 degrees of freedom the curve is approaching a normal distribution.

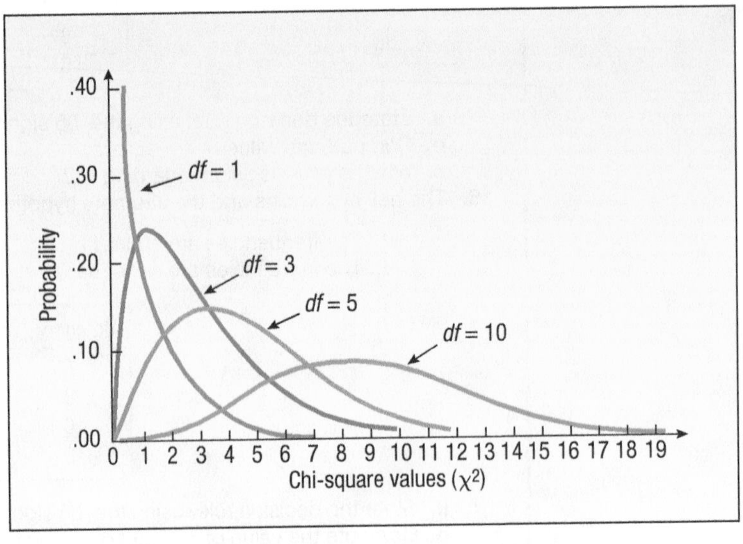

CHART 15–4 Chi-Square Distributions for Selected Degrees of Freedom

SELF-REVIEW 15–3

The human resources director at Georgetown Paper Inc. is concerned about absenteeism among hourly workers. She decides to sample the company records to determine whether absenteeism is distributed evenly throughout the six-day workweek. The hypotheses are:

H_0: Absenteeism is evenly distributed throughout the workweek.
H_1: Absenteeism is *not* evenly distributed throughout the workweek.

The sample results are:

	Number Absent		Number Absent
Monday	12	Thursday	10
Tuesday	9	Friday	9
Wednesday	11	Saturday	9

(a) What are the numbers 12, 9, 11, 10, 9, and 9 called?
(b) How many categories (cells) are there?
(c) What is the *expected* frequency for each day?
(d) How many degrees of freedom are there?
(e) What is the chi-square critical value at the 1% significance level?
(f) Compute the χ^2 test statistic.
(g) What is the decision regarding the null hypothesis?
(h) Specifically, what does this indicate to the human resources director?

EXERCISES

13. In a particular chi-square goodness-of-fit test, there are four categories and 200 observations. Use the .05 significance level.
a. How many degrees of freedom are there?
b. What is the critical value of chi-square?

14. In a particular chi-square goodness-of-fit test, there are six categories and 500 observations. Use the .01 significance level.
a. How many degrees of freedom are there?
b. What is the critical value of chi-square?

15. The null hypothesis and the alternate hypothesis are:

H_0: The frequencies are equal.
H_1: The frequencies are not equal.

Category	f_o
A	10
B	20
C	30

a. State the decision rule, using the .05 significance level.
b. Compute the value of chi-square.
c. What is your decision regarding H_0?

16. The null hypothesis and the alternate hypothesis are:

H_0: The frequencies are equal.
H_1: The frequencies are not equal.

Category	f_o
A	10
B	20
C	30
D	20

a. State the decision rule, using the .05 significance level.
b. Compute the value of chi-square.
c. What is your decision regarding H_0?

17. A six-sided die is rolled 30 times and the numbers 1 through 6 appear as shown in the following frequency distribution. At the .10 significance level, can we conclude that the die is fair?

Outcome	Frequency	Outcome	Frequency
1	3	4	3
2	6	5	9
3	2	6	7

18. Classic Golf Inc. manages five courses in the Jacksonville, Florida, area. The director of golf wishes to study the number of rounds of golf played per weekday at the five courses. He gathered the following sample information. At the .05 significance level, is there a difference in the number of rounds played by day of the week?

Day	Rounds
Monday	124
Tuesday	74
Wednesday	104
Thursday	98
Friday	120

For **DATA FILE**, please visit www.mhhe.com/lind16e

19. A group of department store buyers viewed a new line of dresses and gave their opinions of them. The results were:

Opinion	Number of Buyers	Opinion	Number of Buyers
Outstanding	47	Good	39
Excellent	45	Fair	35
Very good	40	Undesirable	34

Because the largest number (47) indicated the new line is outstanding, the head designer thinks that this is a mandate to go into mass production of the dresses. The head sweeper (who somehow became involved in this) believes that there is not a clear mandate and claims that the opinions are evenly distributed among the six categories. He further states that the slight differences among the various counts are probably due to chance. Test the null hypothesis that there is no significant difference among the opinions of the buyers. Test at the .01 level of risk. Follow a formal approach; that is, state the null hypothesis, the alternate hypothesis, and so on.

For **DATA FILE**, please visit www.mhhe.com/lind16e

20. The safety director of a large steel mill took samples at random from company records of minor work-related accidents and classified them according to the time the accident took place.

Time	Number of Accidents	Time	Number of Accidents
8 up to 9 a.m.	6	1 up to 2 p.m.	7
9 up to 10 a.m.	6	2 up to 3 p.m.	8
10 up to 11 a.m.	20	3 up to 4 p.m.	19
11 up to 12 p.m.	8	4 up to 5 p.m.	6

Using the goodness-of-fit test and the .01 level of significance, determine whether the accidents are evenly distributed throughout the day. Write a brief explanation of your conclusion.

Hypothesis Test of Unequal Expected Frequencies

The expected frequencies (f_e) in the previous example/solution involving preferred entrées were all equal. According to the null hypothesis, it was expected that of the

120 adults in the study, an equal number would select each of the four entrées. So we expect 30 to select chicken, 30 to select fish, and so on. The chi-square test can also be used if the expected frequencies are not equal.

The following example illustrates the case of unequal frequencies and also gives a practical use of the chi-square goodness-of-fit test—namely, to find whether a local experience differs from the national experience.

EXAMPLE

The American Hospital Administrators Association (AHAA) reports the following information concerning the number of times senior citizens are admitted to a hospital during a one-year period. Forty percent are not admitted; 30% are admitted once; 20% are admitted twice, and the remaining 10% are admitted three or more times.

A survey of 150 residents of Bartow Estates, a community devoted to active seniors located in central Florida, revealed 55 residents were not admitted during the last year, 50 were admitted to a hospital once, 32 were admitted twice, and the rest of those in the survey were admitted three or more times. Can we conclude the survey at Bartow Estates is consistent with the information reported by the AHAA? Use the .05 significance level.

SOLUTION

We begin by organizing the above information into Table 15–4. Clearly, we cannot compare percentages given in the study by AHAA to the frequencies reported for the Bartow Estates. However, these percentages can be converted to expected frequencies, f_e. According to AHAA, 40% of the Bartow residents in the survey did not require hospitalization. Thus, if there is no difference between the national experience and those of Bartow Estates, then 40% of the 150 seniors surveyed (60 residents) would not have been hospitalized. Further, 30% of those surveyed were admitted once (45 residents), and so on. The observed frequencies for Bartow residents and the expected frequencies based on the percents in the national study are given in Table 15–4.

TABLE 15–4 Summary of Study by AHAA and a Survey of Bartow Estates

Number of Times Admitted	AHAA Percent of Total	Number of Bartow Residents (f_o)	Expected Number of Bartow Residents (f_e)
0	40	55	60
1	30	50	45
2	20	32	30
3 or more	10	13	15
Total	100	150	

The null hypothesis and the alternate hypothesis are:

H_0: There is no difference between local and national experience for hospital admissions.

H_1: There is a difference between local and national experience for hospital admissions.

To find the decision rule, we use Appendix B.7 and the .05 significance level. There are four admitting categories, so the degrees of freedom are $df = 4 - 1 = 3$.

STATISTICS IN ACTION

Many state governments operate lotteries to help fund education. In many lotteries, numbered balls are mixed and selected by a machine. In a Select Three game, numbered balls are selected randomly from three groups of balls numbered zero through nine. Randomness would predict that the frequency of each number is equal. How would you test if the machine ensured a random selection process? A chi-square, goodness-of-fit test could be used to investigate this question.

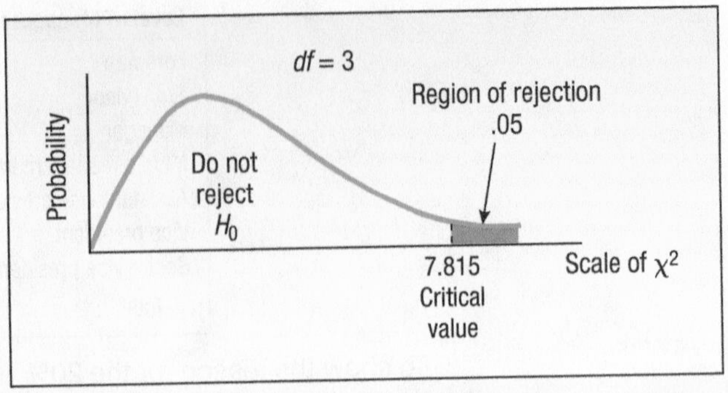

CHART 15–5 Decision Criteria for the Bartow Estates Research Study

The critical value is 7.815. Therefore, the decision rule is to reject the null hypothesis if $\chi^2 > 7.815$. The decision rule is portrayed in Chart 15–5.

Now to compute the chi-square test statistic:

Number of Times Admitted	f_o	f_e	$(f_o - f_e)$	$(f_o - f_e)^2$	$(f_o - f_e)^2/f_e$
0	55	60	−5	25	0.4167
1	50	45	5	25	0.5556
2	32	30	2	4	0.1333
3 or more	13	15	−2	4	0.2667
Total	150				1.3723 (χ^2 value)

The computed value of χ^2 (1.3723) lies to the left of 7.815. Thus, we cannot reject the null hypothesis. We conclude that the survey results do not provide evidence of a difference between the local and national experience for hospital admissions.

LO15-4
Explain the limitations of using the chi-square statistic in goodness-of-fit tests.

LIMITATIONS OF CHI-SQUARE

If there is an unusually small expected frequency in a cell, chi-square (if applied) might result in an erroneous conclusion. This can happen because f_e appears in the denominator, and dividing by a very small number makes the quotient quite large! Two generally accepted policies regarding small cell frequencies are:

1. If there are only two cells, the *expected* frequency in each cell should be at least 5. The computation of chi-square would be permissible in the following problem, involving a minimum f_e of 6.

Individual	f_o	f_e
Literate	641	642
Illiterate	7	6

2. For more than two cells, chi-square should *not* be used if more than 20% of the f_e cells have expected frequencies less than 5. According to this policy, it would not be appropriate to use the goodness-of-fit test on the following data. Three of the seven cells, or 43%, have expected frequencies (f_e) of less than 5.

Level of Management	f_o	f_e
Foreman	30	32
Supervisor	110	113
Manager	86	87
Middle management	23	24
Assistant vice president	5	2
Vice president	5	4
Senior vice president	4	1
Total	263	263

To show the reason for the 20% policy, we conducted the goodness-of-fit test on the above data on the levels of management. The MegaStat output follows.

Goodness of Fit Test

observed	expected	O - E	$(O - E)^2 / E$	% of chisq
30	32.000	-2.000	0.125	0.89
110	113.000	-3.000	0.080	0.57
86	87.000	-1.000	0.011	0.08
23	24.000	-1.000	0.042	0.30
5	2.000	3.000	4.500	32.12
5	4.000	1.000	0.250	1.78
4	1.000	3.000	9.000	64.25
263	263.000	0.000	14.008	100.00

14.01 chi-square
6 df
.0295 p-value

For this test at the .05 significance level, H_0 is rejected if the computed value of chi-square is greater than 12.592. The computed value is 14.008, so we reject the null hypothesis that the observed frequencies represent a random sample from the population of the expected values. Examine the MegaStat output. More than 98% of the computed chi-square value is accounted for by the three vice president categories [(4.500 + .250 + 9.000)/14.008 = 0.9815]. Logically, too much weight is being given to these categories.

The issue can be resolved by combining categories if it is logical to do so. In the above example, we combine the three vice president categories, which satisfies the 20% policy.

Level of Management	f_o	f_e
Foreman	30	32
Supervisor	110	113
Manager	86	87
Middle management	23	24
Vice president	14	7
Total	263	263

The computed value of chi-square with the revised categories is 7.258. See the following MegaStat output. This value is less than the critical value of 9.488 for the .05 significance level. The null hypothesis is, therefore, not rejected at the .05 significance level. This indicates there is not a significant difference between the observed distribution and the expected distribution.

Goodness-of-Fit Test

Observed	Expected	O - E	(O - E)² / E	% of chisq
30	32.000	-2.000	0.125	1.72
110	113.000	-3.000	0.080	1.10
86	87.000	-1.000	0.011	0.16
23	24.000	-1.000	0.042	0.57
14	7.000	7.000	7.000	96.45
263	263.000	0.000	7.258	100.00

7.26 chi-square
4 df
.1229 p-value

SELF-REVIEW 15–4

The American Accounting Association classifies accounts receivable as "current," "late," and "not collectible." Industry figures show that 60% of accounts receivable are current, 30% are late, and 10% are not collectible. Massa and Barr, a law firm in Greenville, Ohio, has 500 accounts receivable: 320 are current, 120 are late, and 60 are not collectible. Are these numbers in agreement with the industry distribution? Use the .05 significance level.

EXERCISES

21. The following hypotheses are given:

H_0: Forty percent of the observations are in category A, 40% are in B, and 20% are in C.
H_1: The distribution of the observations is not as described in H_0.

We took a sample of 60, with the results below.

Category	f_o
A	30
B	20
C	10

a. State the decision rule using the .01 significance level.
b. Compute the value of chi-square.
c. What is your decision regarding H_0?

22. The chief of security for Mall of the Dakotas was directed to study the problem of missing goods. He selected a sample of 100 boxes that had been tampered with and ascertained that, for 60 of the boxes, the missing pants, shoes, and so on were attributed to shoplifting. For 30 other boxes, employees had stolen the goods, and for the remaining 10 boxes he blamed poor inventory control. In his report to the mall management, can he say that shoplifting is *twice* as likely to be the cause of the loss as compared with either employee theft or poor inventory control and that employee theft and poor inventory control are equally likely? Use the .02 significance level.

23. The bank credit card department of Carolina Bank knows from experience that 5% of its card holders have had some high school, 15% have completed high school, 25% have had some college, and 55% have completed college. Of the 500 card holders whose cards

have been called in for failure to pay their charges this month, 50 had some high school, 100 had completed high school, 190 had some college, and 160 had completed college. Can we conclude that the distribution of card holders who do not pay their charges is different from all others? Use the .01 significance level.

24. For many years, TV executives used the guideline that 30% of the audience were watching each of the traditional big three prime-time networks and 10% were watching cable stations on a weekday night. A random sample of 500 viewers in the Tampa–St. Petersburg, Florida, area last Monday night showed that 165 homes were tuned in to the ABC affiliate, 140 to the CBS affiliate, and 125 to the NBC affiliate, with the remainder viewing a cable station. At the .05 significance level, can we conclude that the guideline is still reasonable?

LO15-5
Test a hypothesis that an observed frequency distribution is normally distributed.

TESTING THE HYPOTHESIS THAT A DISTRIBUTION IS NORMAL

We use a goodness-of-fit test to compare an observed frequency distribution to an expected frequency distribution. In the example/solution regarding Bubba's Fish and Pasta (page 543), the observed frequencies are the count of each entrée selected for a sample of 120 adults. We determine the expected frequencies by assuming there is no preference for any of the four entrées, so we expect that one-fourth of the sample, or 30 adults, selects each entrée. In this section, we want to test a hypothesis that a distribution is normal by using the goodness-of-fit test to compare an observed frequency distribution to an expected frequency distribution that is normal. Why is this test important? In Chapter 11, when we tested for differences in two population means, we assumed the two populations followed the normal distribution. We made the same assumption in Chapter 12 when we tested if several population means were equal. In Chapter 13 on page 455 we assume the distribution of the residuals in a least squares regression analysis follow the normal probability distribution.

The following example/solution provides the details of a goodness-of-fit test to investigate the reasonableness of the normality assumption.

EXAMPLE

On page 28 in Chapter 2 we use a frequency distribution to organize the profits from the Applewood Auto Group's sale of 180 vehicles. The frequency distribution is repeated in Table 15–5.

TABLE 15–5 Frequency Distribution of Profits for Vehicles Sold Last Month by Applewood Auto Group

Profit	Frequency
$ 200 up to $ 600	8
600 up to 1,000	11
1,000 up to 1,400	23
1,400 up to 1,800	38
1,800 up to 2,200	45
2,200 up to 2,600	32
2,600 up to 3,000	19
3,000 up to 3,400	4
Total	180

Using statistical software, on page 63 in Chapter 3 we determined that the mean profit on a vehicle for the Applewood Auto Group was \$1,843.17 and that the standard deviation was \$643.63. Is it reasonable to conclude that the profit data is a sample obtained from a normal population? To put it another way, do the profit data follow a normal population? We use the .05 significance level.

SOLUTION

To test for a normal distribution, we need to find the expected frequencies for each class in the distribution, assuming that the expected distribution follows a normal probability distribution. We start with the normal distribution by calculating probabilities for each class. Then we use these probabilities to compute the expected frequencies for each class.

To begin, we need to find the area, or probability, for each of the eight classes in Table 15–5, assuming a normal population with a mean of \$1,843.17 and a standard deviation of \$643.63. To find this probability, we adapt formula (7–1) from Chapter 7 replacing μ with $\bar{x}$ and σ with s. So we use the following formula to determine the various values of z.

$$z = \frac{x - \bar{x}}{s}$$

In this case, z is the value of the standard normal statistic; $\bar{x}$, \$1,843.17, is the sample mean; and s, \$643.63, is the sample standard deviation. To illustrate, we select class \$200 up to \$600 from Table 15–5. We want to determine the expected frequency in this class, assuming the distribution of profits follows a normal distribution. First, we find the z value corresponding to \$200.

$$z = \frac{x - \bar{x}}{s} = \frac{\$200 - \$1{,}843.17}{\$643.63} = -2.55$$

This indicates that the lower limit of this class is 2.55 standard deviations below the mean. From Appendix B.3, the probability of finding a z value less than -2.55 is $.5000 - .4946 = .0054$.

For the upper limit of the \$200 up to \$600 class:

$$z = \frac{x - \bar{x}}{s} = \frac{\$600 - \$1{,}843.17}{\$643.63} = -1.93$$

The area to the left of \$600 is the probability of a z value less than -1.93. To find this value, we again use Appendix B.3 and reason that $.5000 - .4732 = .0268$.

Finally, to find the area between \$200 and \$600:

$$P(\$200 < x < \$600) = P(-2.55 < z < -1.93) = .0268 - .0054 = .0214$$

That is, about 2.14% of the vehicles sold will result in a profit of between \$200 and \$600.

There is a chance that the profit earned is less than \$200. To find this probability:

$$P(x < \$200) = P(z < -2.55) = .5000 - .4946 = .0054$$

We enter these two probabilities in the second and third rows of column 3 in Table 15–6.

TABLE 15–6 Profits at Applewood Auto Group, *z* Values, Areas under the Normal Distribution, and Expected Frequencies

Profit	*z* Values	Area	Found by	Expected Frequency
Under $200	Under −2.55	.0054	0.5000 − 0.4946	0.97
$ 200 up to $ 600	−2.55 up to −1.93	.0214	0.4946 − 0.4732	3.85
600 up to 1,000	−1.93 up to −1.31	.0683	0.4732 − 0.4049	12.29
1,000 up to 1,400	−1.31 up to −0.69	.1500	0.4049 − 0.2549	27.00
1,400 up to 1,800	−0.69 up to −0.07	.2270	0.2549 − 0.0279	40.86
1,800 up to 2,200	−0.07 up to 0.55	.2367	0.0279 + 0.2088	42.61
2,200 up to 2,600	0.55 up to 1.18	.1722	0.3810 − 0.2088	31.00
2,600 up to 3,000	1.18 up to 1.80	.0831	0.4641 − 0.3810	14.96
3,000 up to 3,400	1.80 up to 2.42	.0281	0.4922 − 0.4641	5.06
3,400 or more	2.42 or more	.0078	0.5000 − 0.4922	1.40
Total		1.0000		180.00

Logically, if we sold 180 vehicles, we would expect to earn a profit of between $200 and $600 on 3.852 vehicles, found by .0214(180). We would expect to sell 0.972 vehicle with a profit of less than $200, found by 180(.0054). We continue this process for the remaining classes. This information is summarized in Table 15–7. Don't be concerned that we are reporting fractional vehicles.

TABLE 15–7 Computations of the Chi-Square Statistic

Profit	f_o	f_e	$(f_o - f_e)$	$(f_o - f_e)^2$	$(f_o - f_e)^2/f_e$
Under $600	8	4.82	3.18	10.1124	2.098
$ 600 up to $1,000	11	12.29	−1.29	1.6641	.135
1,000 up to 1,400	23	27.00	−4.00	16.0000	.593
1,400 up to 1,800	38	40.86	−2.86	8.1796	.200
1,800 up to 2,200	45	42.61	2.39	5.7121	.134
2,200 up to 2,600	32	31.00	1.00	1.0000	.032
2,600 up to 3,000	19	14.96	4.04	16.3216	1.091
3,000 and over	4	6.46	−2.46	6.0516	.937
Total	180	180.00	0		5.220

Before continuing, we should emphasize one of the limitations of tests using chi-square as the test statistic. The second limitation on page 551 indicates that if more than 20% of the cells have *expected frequencies* of less than 5, some of the categories should be combined. In Table 15–6, there are three classes in which the expected frequencies are less than 5. Hence, we combine the "Under $200" class with the "$200 up to $600" class and the "$3,400 or more" class with the "$3,000 up to $3,400" class. So the expected frequency in the "Under $600" class is now 4.82, found by 0.97 plus 3.85. We do the same for the "$3,000 and over" class: 5.06 + 1.40 = 6.46. The results are shown in Table 15–7. The computed value of chi-square is 5.220.

Now let's put this information into the formal hypothesis-testing format. The null and alternate hypotheses are:

H_0: The population of profits follows the normal distribution.
H_1: The population of profits does not follow the normal distribution.

To determine the critical value of chi-square, we need to know the degrees of freedom. In this case, there are 8 categories, or classes, so the degrees of freedom are $k - 1 = 8 - 1 = 7$. In addition, the values \$1,843.17, the mean profit, and \$643.63, the standard deviation of the Applewood Auto Group profits, were computed from a sample. When we estimate population parameters from sample data, we lose a degree of freedom for each estimate. So we lose two more degrees of freedom for estimating the population mean and the population standard deviation. Thus, the number of degrees of freedom in this problem is 5, found by $k - 2 - 1 = 8 - 2 - 1 = 5$.

From Appendix B.7, using the .05 significance level, the critical value of chi-square is 11.070. Our decision rule is to reject the null hypothesis if the computed value of chi-square is more than 11.070.

Now, to compute the value of chi-square, we use formula (15–4):

$$\chi^2 = \sum \frac{(f_o - f_e)^2}{f_e} = \frac{(8 - 4.82)^2}{4.82} + \cdots + \frac{(4 - 6.46)^2}{6.46} = 5.220$$

The values for each class are shown in the right-hand column of Table 15–7, as well as the column total, which is 5.220. Because the computed value of 5.220 is less than the critical value, we do not reject the null hypothesis. We conclude the evidence does not suggest the distribution of profits is other than normal.

To expand on the calculation of the number of degrees of freedom, if we know the mean and the standard deviation of a population and wish to find whether some sample data conform to a normal, the degrees of freedom are $k - 1$. On the other hand, suppose we have sample data grouped into a frequency distribution, but we do not know the value of the population mean and the population standard deviation. In this case, the degrees of freedom are $k - 2 - 1$. In general, when we use sample statistics to estimate population parameters, we lose a degree of freedom for each parameter we estimate. This is parallel to the situation on page 488 of Chapter 14, the chapter on multiple regression, where we lost a degree of freedom in the denominator of the F statistic for each independent variable considered.

EXERCISES

For **DATA FILE**, please visit www.mhhe.com/lind16e

25. The IRS is interested in the number of individual tax forms prepared by small accounting firms. The IRS randomly sampled 50 public accounting firms with 10 or fewer employees in the Dallas–Fort Worth area. The following frequency table reports the results of the study. Assume the sample mean is 44.8 clients and the sample standard deviation is 9.37 clients. Is it reasonable to conclude that the sample data are from a population that follows a normal probability distribution? Use the .05 significance level.

Number of Clients	Frequency
20 up to 30	1
30 up to 40	15
40 up to 50	22
50 up to 60	8
60 up to 70	4

For **DATA FILE**, please visit www.mhhe.com/lind16e

26. Advertising expenses are a significant component of the cost of goods sold. Listed below is a frequency distribution showing the advertising expenditures for 60 manufacturing companies located in the Southwest. The mean expense is \$52.0 million and the standard

deviation is $11.32 million. Is it reasonable to conclude the sample data are from a population that follows a normal probability distribution? Use the .05 significance level.

Advertising Expense ($ Million)	Number of Companies
25 up to 35	5
35 up to 45	10
45 up to 55	21
55 up to 65	16
65 up to 75	8
Total	60

LO15-6
Perform a chi-square test for independence on a contingency table.

CONTINGENCY TABLE ANALYSIS

In Chapter 4, we discussed bivariate data, where we studied the relationship between two variables. We described a contingency table, which simultaneously summarizes two nominal-scale variables of interest. For example, a sample of students enrolled in the School of Business is classified by gender (male or female) and major (accounting, management, finance, marketing, or quantitative methods). This classification is based on the nominal scale because there is no natural order to the classifications.

We discussed contingency tables in Chapter 5. On page 150, we illustrated the relationship between the number of movies attended per month and the age of the attendee. We can use the chi-square distribution to test whether two nominal-scaled variables are related or not. To put it another way, is one variable *independent* of the other?

Here are some examples where we are interested in testing whether two nominal-scaled variables are related.

- Ford Motor Company operates an assembly plant in Dearborn, Michigan. The plant operates three shifts per day, 5 days a week. The quality control manager wishes to compare the quality level on the three shifts. Vehicles are classified by quality level (acceptable, unacceptable) and shift (day, afternoon, night). Is there a difference in the quality level on the three shifts? That is, is the quality of the product related to the shift when it was manufactured? Or is the quality of the product independent of the shift on which it was manufactured?
- A sample of 100 drivers who were stopped for speeding violations was classified by gender and whether or not they were wearing a seat belt. For this sample, is wearing a seatbelt related to gender?
- Does a male released from federal prison make a different adjustment to civilian life if he returns to his hometown or if he goes elsewhere to live? The two variables are adjustment to civilian life and place of residence. Note that both variables are measured on the nominal scale.

The following example/solution provides the details of the analysis and possible conclusions.

EXAMPLE

Rainbow Chemical, Inc. employs hourly and salaried employees. The vice president of human resources surveyed a random sample of 380 employees about his/her satisfaction level with the current health care benefits program. The employees were then classified according to the pay type, i.e., salary or hourly. The results are shown in Table 15–8.

TABLE 15–8 Health Care Satisfaction Level for Rainbow Chemical Employees

Pay Type	Satisfied	Neutral	Dissatisfied	Total
Salary	30	17	8	55
Hourly	140	127	58	325
Total	170	144	66	380

At the .05 significance level, is it reasonable to conclude that pay type and level of satisfaction with the health care benefits are related?

SOLUTION

The first step is to state the null hypothesis and the alternate hypothesis.

H_0: There is no relationship between level of satisfaction and pay type.
H_1: There is a relationship between level of satisfaction and pay type.

The significance level, as requested by the HR vice president, is .05. The level of measurement for pay type is the nominal scale. The satisfaction level with health benefits is actually the ordinal scale, but we use it as a nominal-scale variable. Each sampled employee is classified by two criteria: the level of satisfaction with benefits and pay type. The information is tabulated into Table 15–8, which is called a contingency table.

We use the chi-square distribution as the test statistic. To determine the critical value of chi-square, we need to know the degrees of freedom (*df*) calculated as:

$$df = (\text{Number of rows} - 1)(\text{Number of columns} - 1) = (r - 1)(c - 1)$$

In this example/solution there are 2 rows and 3 columns, so there are 2 degrees of freedom.

$$df = (r - 1)(c - 1) = (2 - 1)(3 - 1) = 2$$

To find the critical value for 2 degrees of freedom and the .05 level, refer to Appendix B.7. Move down the degrees of freedom column in the left margin to the row with 2 degrees of freedom. Move across this row to the column headed .05. At the intersection, the chi-square critical value is 5.991. The decision rule is to reject the null hypothesis if the computed value of χ^2 is greater than 5.991. See Chart 15–6.

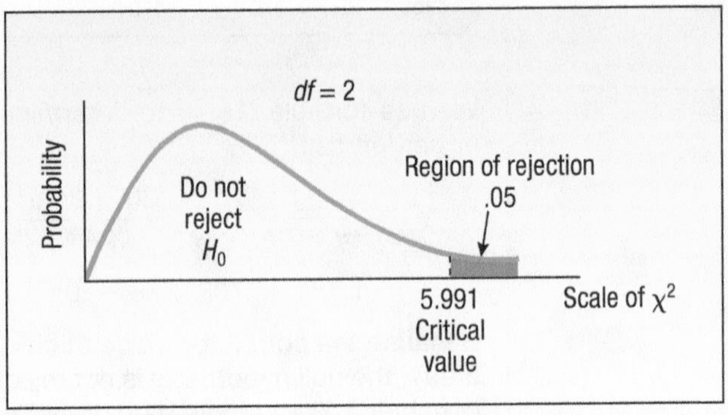

CHART 15–6 Chi-Square Distribution for 2 Degree of Freedom

Next we compute the chi-square value χ^2, using formula (15–4). The observed frequencies, f_o, are shown in Table 15–9. How are the corresponding expected frequencies, f_e, determined? To begin, notice from Table 15–8 that 55 of the 380 Rainbow Chemical employees sampled are salaried. So the fraction of salaried employees in the sample is 55/380 = .14474. *If there is no relationship* between pay type and level of satisfaction with the health care benefits program, we would expect about the same fraction of the employees who are satisfied with the health care to be salaried. There are 170 employees who are satisfied with the health care program, so the expected number of satisfied employees who are salaried is 24.61, found by (.14474)(170). Thus, the expected frequency for the upper-left cell is 24.61. Likewise, if there were no relationship between satisfaction level and pay type, we would expect .14474 of the 144 employees, or 20.84, who were neutral about the health care program to be salaried. We continue this process, filling in the remaining cells. It is not necessary to calculate each of these cell values; some may be determined by subtraction.

The expected frequency for any cell is determined by:

EXPECTED FREQUENCY $$f_e = \frac{(\text{Row total})(\text{Column total})}{(\text{Grand total})} \quad \textbf{[15–5]}$$

From this formula, the expected frequency for the upper-left cell in Table 15–8 is:

$$f_e = \frac{(\text{Row total})(\text{Column total})}{(\text{Grand total})} = \frac{(55)(170)}{380} = 24.61$$

The observed frequencies, f_o, and the expected frequencies, f_e, for all of the cells in the contingency table are listed in Table 15–9. Note there are slight differences due to rounding.

TABLE 15–9 Observed and Expected Frequencies

	Satisfaction Level with Health Care						
	Satisfied		Neutral		Dissatisfied		
Pay Type	f_o	f_e	f_o	f_e	f_o	f_e	**Total**
Salary	30	24.61	17	20.84	8	9.55	55
Hourly	140	145.39	127	123.16	58	56.45	325
Total	170	170.00	144	144.00	66	66.00	380

We use formula (15–4) to determine the value of chi-square. Starting with the upper-left cell:

$$\chi^2 = \sum\frac{(f_o - f_e)^2}{f_e} = \frac{(30 - 24.61)^2}{24.61} + \frac{(17 - 20.84)^2}{20.84} + \cdots + \frac{(58 - 56.45)^2}{56.45}$$
$$= 1.181 + .708 + \cdots + .043 = 2.506$$

Because the computed value of chi-square (2.506) lies in the region to the left of 5.991, the null hypothesis is not rejected at the .05 significance level. What do we conclude? The sample data do not provide evidence that pay type and satisfaction level with health care benefits are related.

The following output is from the Megastat Excel add-in.

Chi-square Contingency Table Test for Independence

Pay Type		Satisfaction Level with Health Care			
		Satisfied	Neutral	Dissatisfied	Total
Salary	Observed	**30**	**17**	**8**	55
	Expected	24.61	20.84	9.55	55.00
Hourly	Observed	**140**	**127**	**58**	325
	Expected	145.39	123.16	56.45	325.00
Total	Observed	170	144	66	380
	Expected	170.00	144.00	66.00	380.00
		2.506 chi-square 2 df 0.286 *p*-value			

Observe that the value of chi-square is the same as that computed earlier, 2.506. In addition, the *p*-value, .286, is reported. So the probability of finding a value of the test statistic as large or larger, assuming the null hypothesis is true, is .286. The *p*-value also results in the same decision: do not reject the null hypothesis.

SELF-REVIEW 15–5

A social scientist sampled 140 people and classified them according to income level and whether or not they played a state lottery in the last month. The sample information is reported below. Is it reasonable to conclude that playing the lottery is related to income level? Use the .05 significance level.

	Income			
	Low	Middle	High	Total
Played	46	28	21	95
Did not play	14	12	19	45
Total	60	40	40	140

(a) What is this table called?
(b) State the null hypothesis and the alternate hypothesis.
(c) What is the decision rule?
(d) Determine the value of chi-square.
(e) Make a decision on the null hypothesis. Interpret the result.

EXERCISES

For **DATA FILE**, please visit www.mhhe.com/lind16e

27. The director of advertising for the *Carolina Sun Times,* the largest newspaper in the Carolinas, is studying the relationship between the type of community in which a subscriber resides and the section of the newspaper he or she reads first. For a sample of readers, she collected the sample information in the following table.

	National News	Sports	Comics
City	170	124	90
Suburb	120	112	100
Rural	130	90	88

At the .05 significance level, can we conclude there is a relationship between the type of community where the person resides and the section of the paper read first?

For **DATA FILE**, please visit www.mhhe.com/lind16e

28. Four brands of lightbulbs are being considered for use in the final assembly area of the Ford F-150 truck plant in Dearborn, Michigan. The director of purchasing asked for samples of 100 from each manufacturer. The numbers of acceptable and unacceptable bulbs from each manufacturer are shown below. At the .05 significance level, is there a difference in the quality of the bulbs?

	Manufacturer			
	A	B	C	D
Unacceptable	12	8	5	11
Acceptable	88	92	95	89
Total	100	100	100	100

For **DATA FILE**, please visit www.mhhe.com/lind16e

29. The quality control department at Food Town Inc., a grocery chain in upstate New York, conducts a monthly check on the comparison of scanned prices to posted prices. The chart below summarizes the results of a sample of 500 items last month. Company management would like to know whether there is any relationship between error rates on regularly priced items and specially priced items. Use the .01 significance level.

	Regular Price	Advertised Special Price
Undercharge	20	10
Overcharge	15	30
Correct price	200	225

30. The use of cellular phones in automobiles has increased dramatically in the last few years. Of concern to traffic experts, as well as manufacturers of cellular phones, is the effect on accident rates. Is someone who is using a cellular phone more likely to be involved in a traffic accident? What is your conclusion from the following sample information? Use the .05 significance level.

	Had Accident in the Last Year	Did Not Have an Accident in the Last Year
Uses a cell phone	25	300
Does not use a cell phone	50	400

CHAPTER SUMMARY

I. This chapter considered tests of hypothesis for nominal level data.

II. When we sample from a single population and the variable of interest has only two possible outcomes, we call this a test of proportion.

A. The binomial conditions must be met.

B. Both $n\pi$ and $n(1-\pi)$ must be at least 5.

C. The test statistic is

$$z = \frac{p - \pi}{\sqrt{\dfrac{\pi(1-\pi)}{n}}} \qquad [15\text{–}1]$$

III. We can also test whether two samples came from populations with an equal proportion of successes.

A. The two sample proportions are pooled using the following formula:

$$p_c = \frac{x_1 + x_2}{n_1 + n_2} \qquad [15\text{–}3]$$

B. We compute the value of the test statistic from the following formula:

$$z = \frac{p_1 - p_2}{\sqrt{\frac{p_c(1 - p_c)}{n_1} + \frac{p_c(1 - p_c)}{n_2}}} \quad \textbf{[15–2]}$$

IV. The characteristics of the chi-square distribution are:
- **A.** The value of chi-square is never negative.
- **B.** The chi-square distribution is positively skewed.
- **C.** There is a family of chi-square distributions.
  1. Each time the degrees of freedom change, a new distribution is formed.
  2. As the degrees of freedom increase, the distribution approaches a normal distribution.

V. A goodness-of-fit test will show whether an observed set of frequencies could have come from a hypothesized population distribution.
- **A.** The degrees of freedom are $k - 1$, where k is the number of categories.
- **B.** The formula for computing the value of chi-square is

$$\chi^2 = \sum \frac{(f_o - f_e)^2}{f_e} \quad \textbf{[15–4]}$$

VI. A goodness-of-fit test can also be used to determine whether a sample of observations is from a normal population.
- **A.** First, find the mean and standard deviation of the sample data.
- **B.** Group the data into a frequency distribution.
- **C.** Convert the class limits to z values and find the standard normal probability distribution for each class.
- **D.** For each class, find the expected normally distributed frequency by multiplying the standard normal probability distribution by the class frequency.
- **E.** Calculate the chi-square goodness-of-fit statistic based on the observed and expected class frequencies.
- **F.** Find the expected frequency in each cell by determining the product of the probability of finding a value in each cell by the total number of observations.
- **G.** If we use the information on the sample mean and the sample standard deviation from the sample data, the degrees of freedom are $k - 3$.

VII. A contingency table is used to test whether two traits or characteristics are related.
- **A.** Each observation is classified according to two traits.
- **B.** The expected frequency is determined as follows:

$$f_e = \frac{\text{(Row total)(Column total)}}{\text{Grand total}} \quad \textbf{[15–5]}$$

- **C.** The degrees of freedom are found by:

$$df = (\text{Rows} - 1)(\text{Columns} - 1)$$

- **D.** The usual hypothesis testing procedure is used.

PRONUNCIATION KEY

SYMBOL	MEANING	PRONUNCIATION
p_c	Pooled proportion	*p sub c*
χ^2	Probability distribution	*ki square*
f_o	Observed frequency	*f sub oh*
f_e	Expected frequency	*f sub e*

CHAPTER EXERCISES

31. A coin toss is used to decide which team gets the ball first in most sports. It involves little effort and is believed to give each side the same chance. In 47 Super Bowl games, the National Football Conference has won the coin flip 31 times. Meanwhile, the American

Football Conference has won only 16 times. Use the six-step hypothesis-testing procedure at the .01 significance level to test whether these data suggest a fair coin flip.

a. Why can you employ Z as the test statistic?
b. State the null and alternate hypotheses.
c. Make a diagram of the decision rule.
d. Evaluate the test statistic and make the decision.
e. What is the p-value and what does that imply?

32. According to a study by the American Pet Food Dealers Association, 63% of U.S. households own pets. A report is being prepared for an editorial in the *San Francisco Chronicle.* As a part of the editorial, a random sample of 300 households showed 210 own pets. Do these data disagree with the Pet Food Dealers Association's data? Use a .05 level of significance.

33. Tina Dennis is the comptroller for Meek Industries. She believes that the current cash-flow problem at Meek is due to the slow collection of accounts receivable. She believes that more than 60% of the accounts are in arrears more than 3 months. A random sample of 200 accounts showed that 140 were more than 3 months old. At the .01 significance level, can she conclude that more than 60% of the accounts are in arrears for more than three months?

34. The policy of the Suburban Transit Authority is to add a bus route if more than 55% of the potential commuters indicate they would use the particular route. A sample of 70 commuters revealed that 42 would use a proposed route from Bowman Park to the downtown area. Does the Bowman-to-downtown route meet the STA criterion? Use the .05 significance level.

35. Past experience at the Crowder Travel Agency indicated that 44% of those persons who wanted the agency to plan a vacation for them wanted to go to Europe. During the most recent season, a sampling of 1,000 persons was selected at random from the files. It was found that 480 persons wanted to go to Europe on vacation. Has there been a significant shift upward in the percentage of persons who want to go to Europe? Test at the .05 significance level.

36. Research in the gaming industry showed that 10% of all slot machines in the United States stop working each year. Short's Game Arcade has 60 slot machines and only 3 failed last year. At the .05 significance level, test whether these data contradict the research report.

a. Why can you employ z as the test statistic?
b. State the null and alternate hypotheses.
c. Evaluate the test statistic and make the decision.
d. What is the p-value and what does that imply?

37. An urban planner claims that, nationally, 20% of all families renting condominiums move during a given year. A random sample of 200 families renting condominiums in the Dallas Metroplex revealed that 56 moved during the past year. At the .01 significance level, does this evidence suggest that a larger proportion of condominium owners moved in the Dallas area? Determine the p-value.

38. After a losing season, there is a great uproar to fire the head football coach. In a random sample of 200 college alumni, 80 favor keeping the coach. Test at the .05 level of significance whether the proportion of alumni who support the coach is less than 50%.

39. During the 1990s, the fatality rate for lung cancer was 80 per 100,000 people. After the turn of the century and the establishment of newer treatments and adjustment in public health advertising, a random sample of 10,000 people exhibits only six deaths due to lung cancer. Test at the .05 significance level whether that data are proof of a reduced fatality rate for lung cancer.

40. Each month the National Association of Purchasing Managers surveys purchasing managers and publishes the NAPM index. One of the questions asked on the survey is: Do you think the economy is contracting? Last month, of the 300 responding managers, 160 answered yes to the question. This month, 170 of the 290 managers indicated they felt the economy was contracting. At the .05 significance level, can we conclude that a larger proportion of the purchasing managers believe the economy is contracting this month?

41. As part of a recent survey among dual-wage-earner couples, an industrial psychologist found that 990 men out of the 1,500 surveyed believed the division of household duties was fair. A sample of 1,600 women found 970 believed the division of household duties was fair. At the .01 significance level, is it reasonable to conclude that the proportion of men who believe the division of household duties is fair is larger? What is the p-value?

42. There are two major cell phone providers in the Colorado Springs, Colorado, area, one called HTC and the other, Mountain Communications. We want to investigate whether there is a difference in the proportion of times a customer is able to successfully access the Internet. During a one-week period, 500 calls were placed at random times throughout the day and night to HTC; 450 of the calls were successful. A similar one-week study with Mountain Communications showed that 352 of 400 calls were successful. At the .01 significance level, is there a difference in the percent of time that cell phone connections are successful?
43. The Consumer Confidence Survey is a monthly review that measures consumer confidence in the U.S. economy. It is based on a typical sample of 5,000 U.S. households. Last month 9.1% of consumers said conditions were "good." In the prior month, only 8.5% said they were "good." Use the six-step hypothesis-testing method at the .05 level of significance to see whether you can determine if there is an increase in the share asserting conditions are "good." Find the *p*-value and explain what it means.
44. A study was conducted to determine if there was a difference in the humor content in British and American trade magazine advertisements. In an independent random sample of 270 American trade magazine advertisements, 56 were humorous. An independent random sample of 203 British trade magazines contained 52 humorous ads. Do these data provide evidence at the .05 significance level that there is a difference in the proportion of humorous ads in British versus American trade magazines?
45. The AP-Petside.com poll contacted 300 married women and 200 married men. All owned pets. One hundred of the women and 36 of the men replied that their pets are better listeners than their spouses. At the .05 significance level, is there a difference between the responses of women and men?
46. The National Basketball Association had 39 African-American top executives (presidents or vice presidents) among its 388 senior managers. Meanwhile, Major League Baseball had only 11 African Americans among its 307 top administrators. Test at the .05 significance level if this reveals the NBA has significantly more African-American participation in higher levels of management.
47. Vehicles heading west on Front Street may turn right, turn left, or go straight ahead at Elm Street. The city traffic engineer believes that half of the vehicles will continue straight through the intersection. Of the remaining half, equal proportions will turn right and left. Two hundred vehicles were observed, with the following results. Can we conclude that the traffic engineer is correct? Use the .10 significance level.

	Straight	Right Turn	Left Turn
Frequency	112	48	40

48. The publisher of a sports magazine plans to offer new subscribers one of three gifts: a sweatshirt with the logo of their favorite team, a coffee cup with the logo of their favorite team, or a pair of earrings also with the logo of their favorite team. In a sample of 500 new subscribers, the number selecting each gift is reported below. At the .05 significance level, is there a preference for the gifts or should we conclude that the gifts are equally well liked?

Gift	Frequency
Sweatshirt	183
Coffee cup	175
Earrings	142

49. In a particular metro area, there are three commercial television stations, each with its own news program from 6:00 to 6:30 p.m. According to a report in this morning's local newspaper, a random sample of 150 viewers last night revealed 53 watched the news on WNAE (channel 5), 64 watched on WRRN (channel 11), and 33 on WSPD (channel 13). At the .05 significance level, is there a difference in the proportion of viewers watching the three channels?

For **DATA FILE**, please visit www.mhhe.com/lind16e

50. There are four entrances to the Government Center Building in downtown Philadelphia. The building maintenance supervisor would like to know if the entrances are equally utilized. To

investigate, 400 people were observed entering the building. The number using each entrance is reported below. At the .01 significance level, is there a difference in the use of the four entrances?

Entrance	Frequency
Main Street	140
Broad Street	120
Cherry Street	90
Walnut Street	50
Total	400

For **DATA FILE**, please visit www.mhhe.com/lind16e

51. The owner of a mail-order catalog would like to compare her sales with the geographic distribution of the population. According to the U.S. Bureau of the Census, 21% of the population lives in the Northeast, 24% in the Midwest, 35% in the South, and 20% in the West. Listed below is a breakdown of a sample of 400 orders randomly selected from those shipped last month. At the .01 significance level, does the distribution of the orders reflect the population?

Region	Frequency
Northeast	68
Midwest	104
South	155
West	73
Total	400

For **DATA FILE**, please visit www.mhhe.com/lind16e

52. Banner Mattress and Furniture Company wishes to study the number of credit applications received per day for the last 300 days. The sample information is reported below.

Number of Credit Applications	Frequency (Number of Days)
0	50
1	77
2	81
3	48
4	31
5 or more	13

To interpret, there were 50 days on which no credit applications were received, 77 days on which only one application was received, and so on. Would it be reasonable to conclude that the population distribution is Poisson with a mean of 2.0? Use the .05 significance level. (*Hint:* To find the expected frequencies use the Poisson distribution with a mean of 2.0. Find the probability of exactly one success given a Poisson distribution with a mean of 2.0. Multiply this probability by 300 to find the expected frequency for the number of days in which there was exactly one application. Determine the expected frequency for the other days in a similar manner.)

For **DATA FILE**, please visit www.mhhe.com/lind16e

53. Each of the digits in a raffle is thought to have the same chance of occurrence. The table shows the frequency of each digit for consecutive drawings in a California lottery. Perform the chi-square test to see if you reject the hypothesis at the .05 significance level that the digits are from a uniform population.

Digit	Frequency	Digit	Frequency
0	44	5	24
1	32	6	31
2	23	7	27
3	27	8	28
4	23	9	21

For **DATA FILE**, please visit www.mhhe.com/lind16e

54. John Isaac Inc., a designer and installer of industrial signs, employs 60 people. The company recorded the type of the most recent visit to a doctor by each employee. A national assessment conducted in 2014 found that 53% of all physician visits were to primary care physicians, 19% to medical specialists, 17% to surgical specialists, and 11% to emergency departments. Test at the .01 significance level if Isaac employees differ significantly from the survey distribution. Here are their results:

Visit Type	Number of Visits
Primary care	29
Medical specialist	11
Surgical specialist	16
Emergency	4

For **DATA FILE**, please visit www.mhhe.com/lind16e

55. The Eckel Manufacturing Company believes that their hourly wages follow a normal probability distribution. To confirm this, 270 employees were sampled, organized into the following frequency distribution. Use the methods on pages 82–83 of Chapter 3 to find the mean and standard deviation of these data grouped into a frequency distribution. At the .10 significance level, is it reasonable to conclude that the distribution of hourly wages follows a normal distribution?

Hourly Wage	Frequency
$5.50 up to $ 6.50	20
6.50 up to 7.50	24
7.50 up to 8.50	130
8.50 up to 9.50	68
9.50 up to 10.50	28
Total	270

For **DATA FILE**, please visit www.mhhe.com/lind16e

56. The National Cable and Telecommunications Association recently reported that the mean number of HDTVs per household in the United States is 2.30 with a standard deviation of 1.474 sets. A sample of 100 homes in Boise, Idaho, revealed the following sample information.

Number of HDTVs	Number of Households
0	7
1	27
2	28
3	18
4	10
5 or more	10
Total	100

At the .05 significance level, is it reasonable to conclude that the number of HDTVs per household follows a normal distribution? (*Hint:* Use limits such as 0.5 up to 1.5, 1.5 up to 2.5, and so on.)

For **DATA FILE**, please visit www.mhhe.com/lind16e

57. A survey investigated the public's attitude toward the federal deficit. Each sampled citizen was classified as to whether he or she felt the government should reduce the deficit or increase the deficit, or if the individual had no opinion. The sample results of the study by gender are reported below.

Gender	Reduce the Deficit	Increase the Deficit	No Opinion
Female	244	194	68
Male	305	114	25

At the .05 significance level, is it reasonable to conclude that gender is independent of a person's position on the deficit?

58. A study regarding the relationship between age and the amount of pressure sales personnel feel in relation to their jobs revealed the following sample information. At the .01 significance level, is there a relationship between job pressure and age?

	Degree of Job Pressure		
Age (years)	**Low**	**Medium**	**High**
Less than 25	20	18	22
25 up to 40	50	46	44
40 up to 60	58	63	59
60 and older	34	43	43

For **DATA FILE**, please visit www.mhhe.com/lind16e

59. The claims department at Wise Insurance Company believes that younger drivers have more accidents and, therefore, should be charged higher insurance rates. Investigating a sample of 1,200 Wise policyholders revealed the following breakdown on whether a claim had been filed in the last 3 years and the age of the policyholder. Is it reasonable to conclude that there is a relationship between the age of the policyholder and whether or not the person filed a claim? Use the .05 significance level.

Age Group	No Claim	Claim
16 up to 25	170	74
25 up to 40	240	58
40 up to 55	400	44
55 or older	190	24
Total	1,000	200

For **DATA FILE**, please visit www.mhhe.com/lind16e

60. A sample of employees at a large chemical plant was asked to indicate a preference for one of three pension plans. The results are given in the following table. Does it seem that there is a relationship between the pension plan selected and the job classification of the employees? Use the .01 significance level.

	Pension Plan		
Job Class	**Plan A**	**Plan B**	**Plan C**
Supervisor	10	13	29
Clerical	19	80	19
Labor	81	57	22

For **DATA FILE**, please visit www.mhhe.com/lind16e

61. Did you ever purchase a bag of M&M's candies and wonder about the distribution of colors? You can go to the website www.baking.m-ms.com and click the United States on the map, then click **About M&M's,** then **Products** and **Peanut,** and find the percentage breakdown according to the manufacturer, as well as a brief history of the product. Did you know in the beginning they were all brown? For peanut M&M's, 12% are brown, 15% yellow, 12% red, 23% blue, 23% orange, and 15% green. A 6-oz. bag purchased at the Book Store at Coastal Carolina University had 14 brown, 13 yellow, 14 red, 12 blue, 7 orange, and 12 green. Is it reasonable to conclude that the actual distribution agrees with the

expected distribution? Use the .05 significance level. Conduct your own trial. Be sure to share with your instructor.

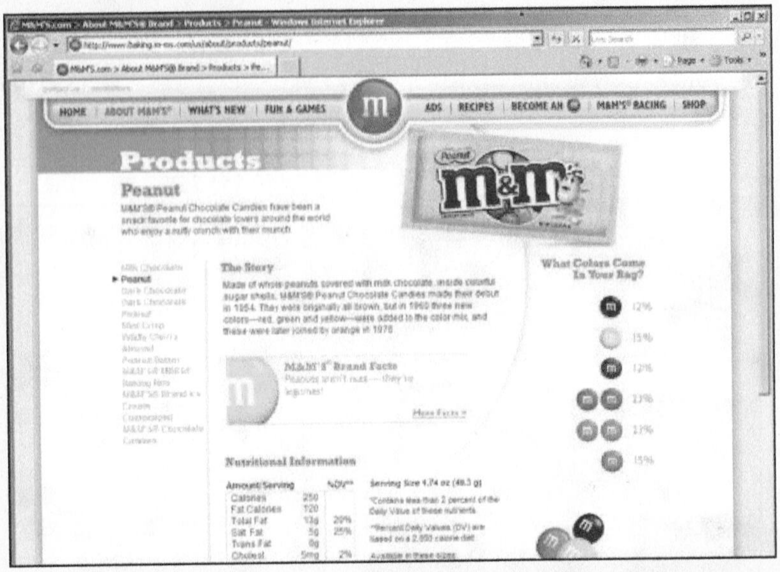

DATA SET EXERCISES

(The data for these exercises are available at the text website: www.mhhe.com/lind16e.)

62. Refer to the Real Estate data, which report information on homes sold in Goodyear, Arizona, and the surrounding area last year.

a. Determine the proportion of homes that have an attached garage. At the .05 significance level, can we conclude that more than 60% of the homes sold in the Goodyear, Arizona, area had an attached garage? What is the *p*-value?

b. Determine the proportion of homes that have a pool. At the .05 significance level, can we conclude that more than 60% of the homes sold in the Goodyear, Arizona, area had a pool? What is the *p*-value?

c. Develop a contingency table that shows whether a home has a pool and the township in which the house is located. Is there an association between the variables pool and township? Use the .05 significance level.

d. Develop a contingency table that shows whether a home has an attached garage and the township in which the home is located. Is there an association between the variables attached garage and township? Use the .05 significance level.

63. Refer to the Baseball 2012 data, which report information on the 30 Major League Baseball teams for the 2012 season. Set up a variable that divides the teams into two groups, those that had a winning season and those that did not. There are 162 games in the season, so define a winning season as having won 81 or more games. Next, find the median team salary and divide the teams into two salary groups. Let the 15 teams with the largest salaries be in one group and the 15 teams with the smallest salaries be in the other. At the .05 significance level, is there a relationship between salaries and winning?

64. Refer to the Buena School District bus data.

a. Suppose we consider a bus "old" if it has been in service more than 8 years. At the .01 significance level, can we conclude that less than 40% of the district's buses are old? Report the *p*-value.

b. Find the median maintenance cost and the median age of the buses. Organize the data into a two-by-two contingency table, with buses above and below the median of each variable. Determine whether the age of the bus is related to the amount of the maintenance cost. Use the .05 significance level.

c. Is there a relationship between the maintenance cost and the manufacturer of the bus? Use the breakdown in part (b) for the buses above and below the median maintenance cost and the bus manufacturers to create a contingency table. Use the .05 significance level.

16 Nonparametric Methods:

ANALYSIS OF ORDINAL DATA

ASSEMBLY WORKERS AT Coastal Computers Inc. assemble one or two subassemblies and insert them in a frame. Executives at CC think that the employees would have more pride in their work if they assembled all components and tested the completed computer. A sample of 25 employees is selected to test the idea. Twenty liked assembling the entire unit and testing it. At the .05 level, can we conclude the employees preferred assembling the entire unit? (See Exercise 8 and LO16-1.)

LEARNING OBJECTIVES

When you have completed this chapter, you will be able to:

LO16-1 Use the sign test to compare two dependent populations.

LO16-2 Test a hypothesis about a median using the sign test.

LO16-3 Test a hypothesis of dependent populations using the Wilcoxon signed-rank test.

LO16-4 Test a hypothesis of independent populations using the Wilcoxon rank-sum test.

LO16-5 Test a hypothesis of several independent populations using the Kruskal-Wallis test.

LO16-6 Test and interpret a nonparametric hypothesis test of correlation.

INTRODUCTION

In Chapter 15, we introduced tests of hypothesis for *nominal-scale* variables. Recall from Chapter 1 that the nominal level of measurement implies the data can only be classified into categories, and there is no particular order to the categories. The purpose of these tests is to determine whether an observed set of frequencies, f_o, is significantly different from a corresponding set of expected frequencies, f_e. Likewise, if you are interested in the relationship between two characteristics—such as gender and his or her music preference—you would tally the data into a contingency table and use the chi-square distribution as the test statistic. For both these types of problems, no assumptions need to be made about the shape of the population. We do not have to assume, for example, that the population of interest follows the normal distribution, as we did with the tests of hypotheses in Chapters 10 through 12.

This chapter continues our discussion of hypothesis tests designed especially for nonparametric data. For these tests, we do not need to assume anything about the shape of the population distribution. Sometimes, we use the term *distribution-free tests*. These tests do require that the responses can be ranked or ordered. So the responses must be measured with an ordinal, interval, or ratio scale. An example of an ordinal scale is executive title. Corporate executives can be ranked as assistant vice president, vice president, senior vice president, and president. A vice president is ranked higher than an assistant vice president, a senior vice president is ranked higher than a vice president, and so on.

In this chapter, we consider five distribution-free tests and the Spearman coefficient of rank correlation. The tests are the sign test, the median test, the Wilcoxon signed-rank test, the Wilcoxon rank-sum test, and the Kruskal-Wallis analysis of variance by ranks.

LO16-1
Use the sign test to compare two dependent populations.

THE SIGN TEST

The **sign test** is based on the sign of a difference between two related observations. We usually designate a plus sign for a positive difference and a minus sign for a negative difference. For example, a dietitian wishes to see if a person's cholesterol level will decrease if the diet is supplemented by a certain mineral. She selects a sample of 20 production workers over the age of 40 and measures the workers' cholesterol level. After the 20 subjects take the mineral for six weeks, they are tested again. If the cholesterol level has dropped, a plus sign is recorded. If it has increased, a negative sign is recorded. If there is no change, a zero is recorded (and that person is dropped from the study). For a sign test, we are not concerned with the magnitude of the difference, only the direction of the difference.

The sign test has many applications. One is for "before/ after" experiments. To illustrate, an evaluation is to be made on a new tune-up program for automobiles. We record the number of miles traveled per gallon of gasoline before the tune-up and again after the tune-up. If the tune-up is not effective—that is, it had no effect on performance—then about half of the automobiles tested would show an increase in miles per gallon and the other half a decrease. A "+" sign is assigned to an increase, a "−" sign to a decrease.

A product-preference experiment illustrates another use of the sign test. Taster's Choice markets two kinds of coffee: decaffeinated and regular. Its market research department wants to determine whether coffee drinkers prefer decaffeinated or regular coffee. Coffee drinkers are given two small, unmarked cups of coffee, and each is asked his or her preference. Preference for decaffeinated could be coded "+" and preference for regular "−."

In a sense, the data are ordinal level because the coffee drinkers give their preferred coffee the higher rank; they rank the other kind below it. Here again, if the population of consumers do not have a preference, we would expect half of the sample of coffee drinkers to prefer decaffeinated and the other half regular coffee.

We can best show the application of the sign test by an example. We will use a "before/after" experiment.

EXAMPLE

The director of information systems at Samuelson Chemicals recommended that an in-plant training program be instituted for certain managers. The objective is to improve the computer knowledge base in the Payroll, Accounting, and Production Planning Departments.

A sample of 15 managers is randomly selected from the three departments. Each manager is rated on his or her computer knowledge by a panel of experts. They were rated as being either outstanding, excellent, good, fair, or poor. (See Table 16–1.) After the three-month training program, the same panel of experts rated each manager's computer knowledge again. The two ratings (before and after) are shown along with the sign of the difference. A "+" sign indicates improvement, and a "−" sign indicates that the manager's competence using databases had declined after the training program.

TABLE 16–1 Competence Before and After the Training Program

	Name	Before	After	Sign of Difference
	T. J. Bowers	Good	Outstanding	+
	Sue Jenkins	Fair	Excellent	+
	James Brown	Excellent	Good	−
	Tad Jackson	Poor	Good	+
Dropped from analysis	~~Andy Love~~	~~Excellent~~	~~Excellent~~	~~0~~
	Sarah Truett	Good	Outstanding	+
	Antonia Aillo	Poor	Fair	+
	Jean Unger	Excellent	Outstanding	+
	Coy Farmer	Good	Poor	−
	Troy Archer	Poor	Good	+
	V. A. Jones	Good	Outstanding	+
	Juan Guillen	Fair	Excellent	+
	Candy Fry	Good	Fair	−
	Arthur Seiple	Good	Outstanding	+
	Sandy Gumpp	Poor	Good	+

We are interested in whether the in-plant training program increased the managers' computer knowledge. That is, are the managers more knowledgeable after the training program than before?

SOLUTION

We will use the six-step hypothesis-testing procedure.

Step 1: State the null hypothesis and the alternate hypothesis.

$H_0: \pi \leq .50$ There has been no change in the computer knowledge base of the managers as a result of the training program.

$H_1: \pi > .50$ There has been an increase in the computer knowledge base of the managers as a result of the training program.

STATISTICS IN ACTION

A recent study of undergraduate students at the University of Michigan revealed the students with the worst attendance records also tended to earn the lowest grades. Does that surprise you? Students who were absent less than 10% of the time tended to earn a B or better. The same study also found that students who sat in the front of the class earned higher grades than those who sat in the back.

The symbol π refers to the proportion in the population with a particular characteristic. If we *do not reject* the null hypothesis, it will indicate the training program has produced no change in the knowledge base, or that knowledge actually decreased. If we *reject* the null hypothesis, it will indicate that the knowledge of the managers has increased as a result of the training program.

The test statistic follows the binomial probability distribution. It is appropriate because the sign test meets all the binomial assumptions, namely:

1. There are only two outcomes: a "success" and a "failure." A manager either increased his or her knowledge (a success) or did not.
2. For each trial, the probability of success is assumed to be .50. Thus, the probability of a success is the same for all trials (managers in this case).
3. The total number of trials is fixed (15 in this experiment).
4. Each trial is independent. This means, for example, that Arthur Seiple's performance in the three-month course is unrelated to Sandy Gumpp's performance.

Step 2: Select a level of significance. We chose the .10 level.

Step 3: Decide on the test statistic. It is the *number of plus signs* resulting from the experiment.

Step 4: Formulate a decision rule. Fifteen managers were enrolled in the training course, but Andy Love showed no increase or decrease in computer knowledge. (See Table 16–1.) He was, therefore, eliminated from the study because he could not be assigned to either group, so $n = 14$. From the binomial probability distribution table in Appendix B.1, for an n of 14 and a probability of .50, we copied the binomial probability distribution in Table 16–2. The number of successes is in column 1, the probabilities of success in column 2, and the cumulative probabilities in column 3. To arrive at the cumulative probabilities, we *add* the probabilities of success in column 2 from the bottom. For illustration, to get the cumulative probability of 11 or more successes, we add $.000 + .001 + .006 + .022 = .029$.

This is a one-tailed test because the alternate hypothesis gives a direction. The inequality (>) points to the right. Thus, the region of rejection is in the upper tail. If the inequality sign pointed toward the left tail (<), the region of rejection would be in the lower tail. If that were the case, we would add the probabilities in column 2 *down* to get the cumulative probabilities in column 3.

Recall that we selected the .10 level of significance. To arrive at the decision rule for this problem, we go to the cumulative probabilities in Table 16–2, column 3. We read up from the bottom until we come to the *cumulative probability nearest to but not exceeding the level of significance* (.10). That cumulative probability is .090. The number of successes (plus signs) corresponding to .090 in column 1 is 10. Therefore, the decision rule is: If the number of pluses in the sample is 10 or more, the null hypothesis is rejected and the alternate hypothesis accepted.

To repeat: We add the probabilities up from the bottom because the direction of the inequality (>) is toward the right, indicating that the region of rejection is in the upper tail. If the number of plus signs in the sample is 10 or more, we reject the null hypothesis; otherwise, we do not reject H_0. The region of rejection is portrayed in Chart 16–1.

TABLE 16–2 Binomial Probability Distribution for $n = 14, \pi = .50$

Number of Successes	Probability of Success		Cumulative Probability
0	0.000	↑	1.000
1	0.001		0.999
2	0.006		0.998
3	0.022		0.992
4	0.061		0.970
5	0.122		0.909
6	0.183		0.787
7	0.209	**Add up**	0.604
8	0.183	↑	0.395
9	0.122		0.212
10	0.061		0.090 ← .000 + .001 + .006 + .022 + .061
11	0.022		0.029
12	0.006		0.007
13	0.001		0.001
14	0.000		0.000

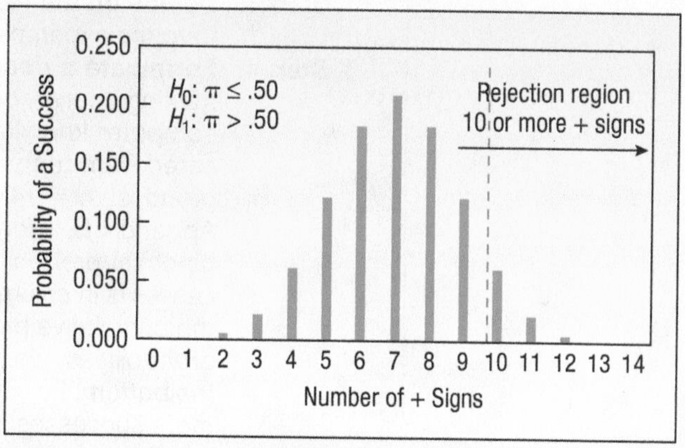

CHART 16–1 Binomial Distribution, $n = 14, \pi = .50$

What procedure is followed for a two-tailed test? We combine (add) the probabilities of success in the two tails until we come as close to the desired level of significance (α) as possible without exceeding it. In this example, α is .10. The probability of 3 or fewer successes is .029, found by .000 + .001 + .006 + .022. The probability of 11 or more successes is also .029. Adding the two probabilities gives .058. This is the closest we can come to .10 without exceeding it. Had we included the probabilities of 4 and 10 successes, the total would be .180, which exceeds .10. Hence, the decision rule for a two-tailed test would be to reject the null hypothesis if there are 3 or fewer plus signs, or 11 or more plus signs.

Step 5: Make a decision regarding the null hypothesis. Eleven out of the 14 managers in the training course increased their computer knowledge. The number 11 is in the rejection region, which starts at 10, so H_0 is rejected.

Step 6: Interpret the results. We conclude that the three-month training course was effective. It increased the computer knowledge of the managers.

If the alternate hypothesis does not give a direction—for example, H_0: $\pi = .50$ and H_1: $\pi \neq .50$—the test of hypothesis is *two-tailed*. In such cases, there are two rejection regions—one in the lower tail and one in the upper tail. If $\alpha = .10$ and the test is two-tailed, the area in each tail is .05 ($\alpha/2 = .10/2 = .05$). Self-Review 16–1 illustrates this.

SELF-REVIEW 16–1

Recall the Taster's Choice example described on page 571, involving a consumer test to determine the preference for decaffeinated versus regular coffee. Use the .10 significance level. The null and alternate hypotheses are:

$$H_0: \pi = .50 \qquad n = 12$$
$$H_1: \pi \neq .50$$

(a) Is this a one-tailed or a two-tailed test of hypothesis?
(b) Show the decision rule in a chart.
(c) Letting consumer preference for decaffeinated coffee be a "+" and preference for regular coffee a "−," it was found that two customers preferred decaffeinated. What is your decision? Explain.

EXERCISES

1. The following hypothesis-testing situation is given: H_0: $\pi \leq .50$ and H_1: $\pi > .50$. The significance level is .10, and the sample size is 12.
   a. What is the decision rule?
   b. There were nine successes. What is your decision regarding the null hypothesis? Explain.
2. The following hypothesis-testing situation is given: H_0: $\pi = .50$ and H_1: $\pi \neq .50$. The significance level is .05, and the sample size is 9.
   a. What is the decision rule?
   b. There were five successes. What is your decision regarding the null hypothesis?
3. Calorie Watchers has low-calorie breakfasts, lunches, and dinners. If you join the club, you receive two packaged meals a day. Calorie Watchers claims that you can eat anything you want for the third meal and still lose at least 5 pounds the first month. Members of the club are weighed before commencing the program and again at the end of the first month. The experiences of a random sample of 11 enrollees are:

Name	Weight Change	Name	Weight Change
Foster	Lost	Hercher	Lost
Taoka	Lost	Camder	Lost
Lange	Gained	Hinckle	Lost
Rousos	Lost	Hinkley	Lost
Stephens	No change	Justin	Lost
Cantrell	Lost		

   We are interested in whether there has been a weight loss as a result of the Calorie Watchers program.
   a. State H_0 and H_1.
   b. Using the .05 level of significance, what is the decision rule?
   c. What is your conclusion about the Calorie Watchers program?
4. Many new stockbrokers resist giving presentations to bankers and certain other groups. Sensing this lack of self-confidence, management arranged to have a confidence-building seminar for a sample of new stockbrokers and enlisted Career Boosters for a three-week

course. Before the first session, Career Boosters measured the level of confidence of each participant. It was measured again after the three-week seminar. The before and after levels of self-confidence for the 14 in the course are shown below. Self-confidence was classified as being either negative, low, high, or very high.

Stockbroker	Before Seminar	After Seminar	Stockbroker	Before Seminar	After Seminar
J. M. Martin	Negative	Low	F. M. Orphey	Low	Very high
T. D. Jagger	Negative	Negative	C. C. Ford	Low	High
A. D. Hammer	Low	High	A. R. Utz	Negative	Low
T. A. Jones Jr.	Very high	Low	M. R. Murphy	Low	High
B. G. Dingh	Low	High	P. A. Lopez	Negative	Low
D. A. Skeen	Low	High	B. K. Pierre	Low	High
C. B. Simmer	Negative	High	N. S. Walker	Low	Very high

The purpose of this study is to find whether Career Boosters was effective in raising the self-confidence of the new stockbrokers. That is, was the level of self-confidence higher after the seminar than before it? Use the .05 significance level.

a. State the null and alternate hypotheses.

b. Using the .05 level of significance, state the decision rule—either in words or in chart form.

c. Draw conclusions about the seminar offered by Career Boosters.

Using the Normal Approximation to the Binomial

If the number of observations in the sample is larger than 10, the normal distribution can be used to approximate the binomial. In Chapter 6 on page 185, we computed the mean of the binomial distribution from $\mu = n\pi$ and the standard deviation from $\sigma = \sqrt{n\pi(1-\pi)}$. In this case, $\pi = .50$, so the equations reduce to $\mu = .50n$ and $\sigma = .50\sqrt{n}$, respectively.

The test statistic z is

SIGN TEST, $n > 10$

$$z = \frac{(x \pm .50) - \mu}{\sigma} \quad [16\text{–}1]$$

If the number of pluses or minuses is *more than n/2*, we use the following form as the test statistic:

SIGN TEST, $n > 10$, + SIGNS MORE THAN $n/2$

$$z = \frac{(x - .50) - \mu}{\sigma} = \frac{(x - .50) - .50n}{.50\sqrt{n}} \quad [16\text{–}2]$$

If the number of pluses or minuses is *less than n/2*, the test statistic z is

SIGN TEST, $n > 10$, + SIGNS LESS THAN $n/2$

$$z = \frac{(x + .50) - \mu}{\sigma} = \frac{(x + .50) - .50n}{.50\sqrt{n}} \quad [16\text{–}3]$$

In the preceding formulas, x is the number of plus (or minus) signs. The value $+.50$ or $-.50$ is the *continuity correction factor,* discussed in Chapter 7 on page 227. Briefly, it is applied when a continuous distribution such as the normal distribution (which we are using) is used to approximate a discrete distribution (the binomial).

The following example illustrates the details of the sign test when n is greater than 10.

EXAMPLE

The market research department of Cola, Inc. has the assignment of testing a new soft drink. There are two versions of the drink under consideration. One version is sweet and the other bitter. The market research department selects a random sample of 64 consumers. Each consumer will taste both the sweet cola (labeled A) and the bitter one (labeled B) and indicate a preference. Conduct a test of hypothesis to determine if there is a difference in the preference for the sweet and bitter tastes. Use the .05 significance level.

SOLUTION

Step 1: State the null and alternate hypotheses.

H_0: $\pi = .50$ There is no preference.
H_1: $\pi \neq .50$ There is a preference.

Step 2: Select a level of significance. It is .05, which is stated in the problem.

Step 3: Select the test statistic. It is z, given in formula (16–1).

$$z = \frac{(x \pm .50) - \mu}{\sigma}$$

where $\mu = .50n$ and $\sigma = .50\sqrt{n}$.

Step 4: Formulate the decision rule. Using Appendix B.5, *Student's t Distribution,* with infinite degrees of freedom, for a two-tailed test (because H_1 states that $\pi \neq .50$) and the .05 significance level, the critical values are +1.960 and −1.960. Therefore, do not reject H_0 if the computed z value is between +1.960 and −1.960. Otherwise, reject H_0 and accept H_1.

Step 5: Compute *z*, compare the computed value with the critical value, and make a decision regarding H_0. Preference for cola A was given a "+" sign and preference for B a "−" sign. Out of the 64 in the sample, 42 preferred the sweet taste, which is cola A. Therefore, there are 42 pluses. Since 42 is *more than* $n/2 = 64/2 = 32$, we use formula (16–2) for z:

$$z = \frac{(x - .50) - .50n}{.50\sqrt{n}} = \frac{(42 - .50) - .50(64)}{.50\sqrt{64}} = 2.38$$

The computed z of 2.38 is beyond the critical value of 1.96. Therefore, the null hypothesis of no difference is rejected at the .05 significance level.

Step 6: Interpret the results. There is evidence of a difference in consumer preference. That is, we conclude consumers prefer one cola over another.

The p-value is the probability of finding a z value larger than 2.38 or smaller than −2.38. To compute the p-value, we first use Appendix B.3, *Areas under the Normal Curve,* and find the probability that a z value greater than 2.38 is .5000 − .4913 = .0087. For a two-tailed test, this probability is multiplied by two; the p-value is .0174. So the probability of obtaining a sample statistic this extreme when the null hypothesis is true is less than 2%.

SELF-REVIEW 16–2

The human resources department at Ford Motor Company began a pilot health education program at the beginning of the year. The study director randomly selected 100 employees to participate in the program. In the first week of January, the blood pressure of each employee was recorded. To evaluate the effectiveness of the program, the blood pressure of the same 100 employees was recorded in July. Eighty employees showed a reduction in blood pressure. Can we conclude that the program was effective in reducing blood pressure?

(a) State the null hypothesis and the alternate hypothesis.
(b) What is the decision rule for a significance level of .05?
(c) Compute the value of the test statistic.
(d) What is your decision regarding the null hypothesis?
(e) Interpret your decision.

EXERCISES

5. A sample of 45 overweight men participated in an exercise program. At the conclusion of the program, 32 had lost weight. At the .05 significance level, can we conclude the program is effective?
  a. State the null hypothesis and the alternate hypothesis.
  b. State the decision rule.
  c. Compute the value of the test statistic.
  d. What is your decision regarding the null hypothesis?

6. A sample of 60 college students was given a special training program designed to improve their time management skills. One month after completing the course, the students were contacted and asked whether the skills learned in the program were effective. A total of 42 responded yes. At the .05 significance level, can we conclude the program is effective?
  a. State the null hypothesis and the alternate hypothesis.
  b. State the decision rule.
  c. Compute the value of the test statistic.
  d. What is your decision regarding the null hypothesis?

7. Pierre's Restaurant announced that on Thursday night the menu would consist of unusual gourmet items, such as squid, rabbit, snails from Scotland, and dandelion greens. As part of a larger survey, a sample of 81 regular customers was asked whether they preferred the regular menu or the gourmet menu. Forty-three preferred the gourmet menu. At the .02 level, can we conclude the customers preferred the gourmet menu?

8. Assembly workers at Coastal Computers Inc. assemble just one or two subassemblies and insert them in a frame. The executives at CC think that the employees would have more pride in their work if they assembled all of the subassemblies and tested the complete computer. A sample of 25 employees was selected to experiment with the idea. After a training program, each was asked his or her preference. Twenty liked assembling the entire unit and testing it. At the .05 level, can we conclude the employees preferred assembling the entire unit? Explain the steps you used to arrive at your decision.

LO16-2
Test a hypothesis about a median using the sign test.

TESTING A HYPOTHESIS ABOUT A MEDIAN

Most of the tests of hypothesis we have conducted so far involved the population mean or a proportion. The sign test is one of the few tests that can be used to test the value of a median. Recall from Chapter 3 that the median is the value above which half of the observations lie and below which the other half lie. For hourly wages of $7, $9, $11, and $18, the median is $10. Half of the wages are above $10 an hour and the other half below $10.

To conduct a test of hypothesis, a value above the median is assigned a plus sign, and a value below the median is assigned a minus sign. If a value is the same as the median, it is dropped from further analysis.

EXAMPLE

The U.S. Bureau of Labor Statistics reported in 2012 that the median amount spent eating out by American families is $2,505 annually. The food editor of the *Portland (Oregon) Tribune* wishes to know if the citizens of Portland differ from

this national value in the last year in terms of eating out. She selected a random sample of 102 couples and found 60 spent more than \$2,505 last year eating out, 40 spent less than \$2,505, and surprisingly 2 spent exactly \$2,505. At the .10 significance level, is it reasonable to conclude that the median amount spent this year in Portland, Oregon, is not equal to \$2,505?

SOLUTION

If the population median is \$2,505, then we expect about half of the sampled couples spent more than \$2,505 last year and about half less than \$2,505. After discarding the two couples that spent exactly \$2,505, we would expect 50 to be above the median and 50 to be below the median. Is the difference between the 60 couples that spent more than \$2,505 and the number expected to spend more than \$2,505 attributable to chance? Is the median some value other than \$2,505? The statistical test for the median will help answer this question.

The null and the alternate hypotheses are:

$$H_0\text{: Median} = \$2{,}505$$
$$H_1\text{: Median} \neq \$2{,}505$$

This is a two-tailed test because the alternate hypothesis does not indicate a direction. That is, we are not interested in whether the median is less than or greater than \$2,505, only that it is different from \$2,505. The test statistic meets the binomial assumptions. That is:

1. An observation is either larger or smaller than the proposed median, so there are only two possible outcomes.
2. The probability of a success remains constant at .50. That is, $\pi = .50$.
3. The couples selected as part of the sample represent independent trials.
4. We count the number of successes in a fixed number of trials. In this case, we consider 100 couples and count the number who spend more than \$2,505 annually on eating out.

The usable sample size is 100 and π is .50, so $n\pi = 100(.50) = 50$ and $n(1 - \pi) = 100(1 - .50) = 50$, which are both larger than 5, so we use the normal distribution to approximate the binomial. That is, we actually use the standard normal distribution as the test statistic. The significance level is .10, so $\alpha/2 = .10/2 = .05$, which is the area in each tail of a normal distribution. From Appendix B.5, in the row with infinite degrees of freedom, the critical values are −1.645 and 1.645. The decision rule is to reject the null hypothesis if z is less than −1.645 or greater than 1.645.

We use formula (16–2) for z because 60 is greater than $n/2$ or $(100/2 = 50)$.

$$z = \frac{(x - .5) - .5n}{.50\sqrt{n}} = \frac{(60 - .5) - 50(100)}{.50\sqrt{100}} = 1.90$$

The null hypothesis is rejected because the computed value of 1.90 is greater than the critical value of 1.645. The sample evidence indicates that the median amount spent annually is *not* \$2,505. The food editor in Portland should conclude that there is a difference in the median amount spent annually last year in Portland as compared with that reported by the U.S. Bureau of Labor Statistics in 2012. The p-value is .0574, found by 2(.5000 − .4713). The p-value is smaller than the significance level of .10 for this test. So based on the p-value and a significance level of .10, we also reject the null hypothesis and conclude that Portland couples spend an amount that is different from the national median value.

SELF-REVIEW 16–3

After reading the results of the Portland, Oregon, study, the food editor of the *Tampa Times* decided to conduct a similar study. The Tampa food editor decides to alter the study slightly by investigating whether families in her region spend *more than* a median amount of $2,505. A sample of 64 Tampa couples revealed 42 spent more than $2,505 per year eating out. Use the .05 significance level.

EXERCISES

9. The median salary for a chiropractor in the United States is $81,500 per year, according to the U.S. Department of Labor. A group of recent graduates believe this amount is too low. In a random sample of 205 chiropractors who recently graduated, 170 began with a salary of more than $81,500 and five earned a salary of exactly $81,500.
  a. State the null and alternate hypotheses.
  b. State the decision rule. Use the .05 significance level.
  c. Do the necessary computations and interpret the results.

10. Central Airlines claims that the median price of a round-trip ticket from Chicago to Jackson Hole, Wyoming, is $503. This claim is being challenged by the Association of Travel Agents, who believe the median price is less than $503. A random sample of 400 round-trip tickets from Chicago to Jackson Hole revealed 160 tickets were below $503. None of the tickets was exactly $503. Let $\alpha = .05$.
  a. State the null and alternate hypotheses.
  b. What is your decision regarding H_0? Interpret.

LO16-3
Test a hypothesis of dependent populations using the Wilcoxon signed-rank test.

WILCOXON SIGNED-RANK TEST FOR DEPENDENT POPULATIONS

The paired *t* test (page 364), described in Chapter 11, has two requirements. First, the samples must be dependent. Recall that dependent samples are characterized by a measurement, some type of intervention, and then another measurement. For example, a large company began a "wellness" program at the start of the year. Twenty workers were enrolled in the weight reduction portion of the program. To begin, all participants were weighed. Next they dieted, did the exercise, and so forth in an attempt to lose weight. At the end of the program, which lasted 6 months, all participants were weighed again. The difference in their weight between the start and the end of the program is the variable of interest. Note that there is a measurement, an intervention, and then another measurement.

The second requirement for the paired *t* test is that the distribution of the differences follow the normal probability distribution. In the company wellness example, this would require that the differences in the weights of the population of participants follow the normal probability distribution. In that case, this assumption is reasonable. However, there are instances when we want to study the differences between dependent observations where we cannot assume that the distribution of the differences approximates a normal distribution. Frequently, we encounter a problem with the normality assumption when the level of measurement in the samples is ordinal, rather than interval or ratio. For example, suppose there are 10 surgical patients on 3 East today. The nursing supervisor asks Nurse Benner and Nurse Jurris to rate each of the 10 patients on a scale of 1 to 10, according to the difficulty of patient care. The distribution of the differences in the ratings probably would not approximate the normal distribution, and, therefore, the paired *t* test would not be appropriate.

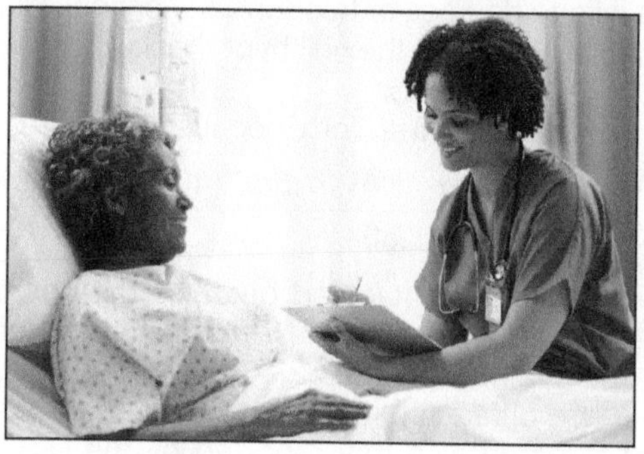

In 1945, Frank Wilcoxon developed a nonparametric test, based on the differences in dependent samples, where the normality assumption is not required. This test is called the **Wilcoxon signed-rank test.** The following example details its application.

EXAMPLE

Fricker's is a family restaurant chain located primarily in the southeastern part of the United States. It offers a full dinner menu, but its specialty is chicken. Recently, Bernie Frick, the owner and founder, developed a new spicy flavor for the batter in which the chicken is cooked. Before replacing the current flavor, he wants to be sure that patrons will like the spicy flavor better.

To begin his taste test, Bernie selects a random sample of 15 customers. Each sampled customer is given a small piece of the current chicken and asked to rate its overall taste on a scale of 1 to 20. A value near 20 indicates the participant liked the flavor, whereas a score near 0 indicates they did not like the flavor. Next, the same 15 participants are given a sample of the new chicken with the spicier flavor and again asked to rate its taste on a scale of 1 to 20. The results are reported below. Is it reasonable to conclude that the spicy flavor is preferred? Use the .05 significance level.

Participant	Score Spicy Flavor	Score Current Flavor
Arquette	14	12
Jones	8	16
Fish	6	2
Wagner	18	4
Badenhop	20	12
Hall	16	16
Fowler	14	5
Virost	6	16
Garcia	19	10
Sundar	18	10
Miller	16	13
Peterson	18	2
Boggart	4	13
Hein	7	14
Whitten	16	4

SOLUTION

Each participant is asked to rate both flavors of chicken. So the scores are dependent or related and, for each participant, we compute the difference between the ratings for the spicy flavor and the current flavor. The resulting value shows the amount the participants favor one flavor over the other. If we choose to subtract the current flavor score from the spicy flavor score, a positive result is the "amount" the participant favors the spicy flavor. Negative difference scores indicate the participant favored the current flavor. Because of the subjective nature of the scores, we are not confident that the distribution of the differences follows the normal distribution. We decide to use the nonparametric Wilcoxon signed-rank test.

As usual, we will use the six-step hypothesis-testing procedure. The null hypothesis is that there is no difference in the rating of the chicken flavors by the

participants. The alternate hypothesis is that the ratings are higher for the spicy flavor. More formally:

H_0: There is no difference in the ratings of the two flavors.
H_1: The spicy ratings are higher.

This is a one-tailed test. Why? Because Bernie Frick, the owner of Fricker's, will want to change his chicken flavor only if the sample participants show that the population of customers like the new flavor better. The significance level is .05, as stated on the previous page.

The steps to conduct the Wilcoxon signed-rank test are as follows.

1. Compute the difference between the spicy flavor score and the current flavor score for each participant. For example, Arquette's spicy flavor score was 14 and current flavor score was 12, so the amount of the difference is 2. For Jones, the difference is −8, found by 8 − 16, and for Fish it is 4, found by 6 − 2. The differences for all participants are shown in column D of Table 16–3.

TABLE 16–3 Flavor Rating for Current and Spicy Flavors

A	B	C	D	E	F	G	H	I
Participant	Score Spicy Flavor	Score Current Flavor	Difference in Score	Absolute Difference	Rank	Signed Rank R^+	R^-	
Arquette	14	12	2	2	1	1		
Jones	8	16	−8	8	6		6	
Fish	6	2	4	4	3	3		
Wagner	18	4	14	14	13	13		
Badenhop	20	12	8	8	6	6		
Hall	16	16	0	*	*			
Fowler	14	5	9	9	9	9		
Virost	6	16	−10	10	11		11	
Garcia	19	10	9	9	9	9		
Sundar	18	10	8	8	6	6		
Miller	16	13	3	3	2	2		
Peterson	18	2	16	16	14	14		
Boggart	4	13	−9	9	9		9	Smaller rank sum
Hein	7	14	−7	7	4		4	
Whitten	16	4	12	12	12	12		
					Sums	75	30	

2. Only the positive and negative differences are considered further. That is, if the difference in flavor scores is 0, that participant is dropped from further analysis and the number in the sample reduced. From Table 16–3, Hall, the sixth participant, scored both the spicy and the current flavor a 16. Hence, Hall is dropped from the study and the usable sample size reduced from 15 to 14.
3. Determine the absolute differences for the values computed in column D. Recall that in an absolute difference we ignore the sign of the difference and focus on the magnitude of the differences in scores. The absolute differences are shown in column E.

4. Next, rank the absolute differences from smallest to largest. Arquette, the first participant, scored the spicy chicken a 14 and the current a 12. The difference of 2 in the two taste scores is the smallest absolute difference, so it is given a ranking of 1. The next largest difference is 3, given by Miller, so it is given a rank of 2. The other differences are ranked in a similar manner. There are three participants who rated the difference in the flavor as 8. That is, Jones, Badenhop, and Sundar each had a difference of 8 between their rating of the spicy flavor and the current flavor. To resolve this issue, we average the ranks involved and report the average rank for each. This situation involves the ranks 5, 6, and 7, so all three participants are assigned the rank of 6. The same situation occurs for those participants with a difference of 9. The ranks involved are 8, 9, and 10, so those participants are assigned a rank of 9.
5. Each assigned rank in column F is then given the same sign as the original difference, and the results are reported in column G or H. For example, the second participant has a difference score of −8 and a rank of 6. So the value of 6 is recorded for Jones in the R^- section of column H.
6. Finally, the R^+ and R^- columns are totaled. The sum of the positive ranks is 75 and the sum of the negative ranks is 30. The smaller of the two rank sums is used as the test statistic and referred to as T.

The critical values for the Wilcoxon signed-rank test are located in Appendix B.8. A portion of that table is shown below. The α row is used for one-tailed tests and the 2α row for two-tailed tests. In this case, we want to show that customers like the spicy taste better, which is a one-tailed test, so we select the α row. We chose the .05 significance level, so move to the right to the column headed .05. Go down that column to the row where n is 14. (Recall that one person in the study rated the chicken flavors the same and was dropped from the study, making the usable sample size 14.) The value at the intersection is 25, so the critical value is 25. The decision rule is to reject the null hypothesis if the *smaller* of the rank sums is 25 or less. The value obtained from Appendix B.8 is the *largest value in the rejection region*. To put it another way, our decision rule is to reject H_0 if the smaller of the two rank sums is 25 or less. In this case, the smaller rank sum is 30, so the decision is not to reject the null hypothesis. We cannot conclude there is a difference in the flavor ratings between the current and the spicy. The study has failed to show that customers prefer the new flavor. Mr. Frick should stay with the current flavor of chicken.

n	2α .15 α .075	.10 .05	.05 .025	.04 .02	.03 .015	.02 .01	.01 .005
4	0						
5	1	0					
6	2	2	0	0			
7	4	3	2	1	0	0	
8	7	5	3	3	2	1	0
9	9	8	5	5	4	3	1
10	12	10	8	7	6	5	3
11	16	13	10	9	8	7	5
12	19	17	13	12	11	9	7
13	24	21	17	16	14	12	9
14	28	25	21	19	18	15	12
15	33	30	25	23	21	19	15

SELF-REVIEW 16–4

The assembly area of Gotrac Products was recently redesigned. Installing a new lighting system and purchasing new workbenches were two features of the redesign. The production supervisor would like to know if the changes resulted in an improvement in worker productivity. To investigate, she selected a sample of 11 workers and determined the production rate before and after the changes. The sample information is reported below.

Operator	Production Before	Production After	Operator	Production Before	Production After
S. M.	17	18	U. Z.	10	22
D. J.	21	23	Y. U.	20	19
M. D.	25	22	U. T.	17	20
B. B.	15	25	Y. H.	24	30
M. F.	10	28	Y. Y.	23	26
A. A.	16	16			

(a) How many usable pairs are there? That is, what is n?
(b) Use the Wilcoxon signed-rank test to determine whether the new procedures actually increased production. Use the .05 level and a one-tailed test.
(c) What assumption are you making about the distribution of the differences in production before and after redesign?

EXERCISES

11. An industrial psychologist selected a random sample of seven young urban professional couples who own their homes. The size of their home (square feet) is compared with that of their parents. At the .05 significance level, can we conclude that the professional couples live in larger homes than their parents?

Couple Name	Professional	Parent	Couple Name	Professional	Parent
Gordon	1,725	1,175	Kuhlman	1,290	1,360
Sharkey	1,310	1,120	Welch	1,880	1,750
Uselding	1,670	1,420	Anderson	1,530	1,440
Bell	1,520	1,640			

12. Toyota USA is studying the effect of regular versus high-octane gasoline on the fuel economy of its new high-performance, 3.5-liter, V6 engine. Ten executives are selected and asked to maintain records on the number of miles traveled per gallon of gas. The results are:

	Miles per Gallon			Miles per Gallon	
Executive	Regular	High-Octane	Executive	Regular	High-Octane
Bowers	25	28	Rau	38	40
Demars	33	31	Greolke	29	29
Grasser	31	35	Burns	42	37
DeToto	45	44	Snow	41	44
Kleg	42	47	Lawless	30	44

At the .05 significance level, is there a difference in the number of miles traveled per gallon between regular and high-octane gasoline?

13. A new assembly-line procedure to increase production has been suggested by Mr. Mump. To test whether the new procedure is superior to the old procedure, a random sample of 15 assembly-line workers was selected. The number of units produced in an hour under the old procedure was determined, then the new Mump procedure was

introduced. After an appropriate break-in period, their production was measured again. The results were:

	Production			Production	
Employee	Old System	Mump Method	Employee	Old System	Mump Method
A	60	64	I	87	84
B	40	52	J	80	80
C	59	58	K	56	57
D	30	37	L	21	21
E	70	71	M	99	108
F	78	83	N	50	56
G	43	46	0	56	62
H	40	52			

At the .05 significance level, can we conclude the production is greater using the Mump method?

a. State the null and alternate hypotheses.
b. State the decision rule.
c. Arrive at a decision regarding the null hypothesis.

14. It has been suggested that daily production of a subassembly would be increased if better lighting were installed and background music and free coffee and doughnuts were provided during the day. Management agreed to try the scheme for a limited time. A listing of the number of subassemblies produced per week before and after the new work environment for each employee follows.

Employee	Past Production Record	Production after Installing Lighting, Music, etc.	Employee	Past Production Record	Production after Installing Lighting, Music, etc.
JD	23	33	WWJ	21	25
SB	26	26	OP	25	22
MD	24	30	CD	21	23
RCF	17	25	PA	16	17
MF	20	19	RRT	20	15
UHH	24	22	AT	17	9
IB	30	29	QQ	23	30

Using the Wilcoxon signed-rank test, determine whether the suggested changes are worthwhile.

a. State the null hypothesis.
b. You decide on the alternate hypothesis.
c. You decide on the level of significance.
d. State the decision rule.
e. Compute T and arrive at a decision.
f. What did you assume about the distribution of the differences?

LO16-4
Test a hypothesis of independent populations using the Wilcoxon rank-sum test.

WILCOXON RANK-SUM TEST FOR INDEPENDENT POPULATIONS

One test specifically designed to determine whether two *independent* samples came from equivalent populations is the **Wilcoxon rank-sum test.** This test is an alternative to the two-sample t test described on page 355 in Chapter 11. Recall that the t test requires that the two populations follow the normal distribution and have equal population variances. These conditions are not required for the Wilcoxon rank-sum test.

The Wilcoxon rank-sum test is based on the sum of ranks. The data are ranked as if the observations were part of a single sample. If the null hypothesis is true, then the ranks will be about evenly distributed between the two samples, and the sum of the ranks for the two samples will be about the same. That is, the low, medium, and high ranks should be about equally divided between the two samples. If the alternate hypothesis is true, one of the samples will have more of the lower ranks and, thus, a smaller rank sum. The other sample will have more of the higher ranks and, therefore, a larger rank sum. If each of the samples contains *at least eight observations,* the standard normal distribution is used as the test statistic. We use the following formula to find the value of the test statistic.

WILCOXON RANK-SUM TEST

$$z = \frac{W - \dfrac{n_1(n_1 + n_2 + 1)}{2}}{\sqrt{\dfrac{n_1 n_2(n_1 + n_2 + 1)}{12}}} \qquad [16\text{–}4]$$

where:

n_1 is the number of observations from the first population.
n_2 is the number of observations from the second population.
W is the sum of the ranks from the first population.

EXAMPLE

Dan Thompson, the president of CEO Airlines, recently noted an increase in the number of no-shows for flights out of Atlanta. He is particularly interested in determining whether there are more no-shows for flights that originate from Atlanta compared with flights leaving Chicago. A sample of nine flights from Atlanta and eight from Chicago are reported in Table 16–4. At the .05 significance level, can we conclude that there are more no-shows for the flights originating in Atlanta?

TABLE 16–4 Number of No-Shows for Scheduled Flights

Atlanta	Chicago
11	13
15	14
10	10
18	8
11	16
20	9
24	17
22	21
25	

SOLUTION

If the populations of no-shows follow the normal probability distribution and have equal variances, the two-sample *t* test, discussed on page 356 in Chapter 11, is appropriate. In this case, Mr. Thompson believes these two conditions cannot be met. Therefore, a nonparametric test, the Wilcoxon rank-sum test, is appropriate.

If the number of no-shows is the same for Atlanta and Chicago, then we expect the sum of the ranks for the two distributions to be about the same. Or to put

it another way, the average rank of the two groups will be about the same. If the number of no-shows is not the same, we expect the average of the ranks to be quite different.

Mr. Thompson believes there are more no-shows for Atlanta flights. Thus, a one-tailed test is appropriate. The null and alternate hypotheses are:

H_0: The number of no-shows for Atlanta is the same or less than the number of no-shows for Chicago.
H_1: The number of no-shows for Atlanta is more than the number of no-shows for Chicago.

The test statistic follows the standard normal distribution. At the .05 significance level, we find from the last row in Appendix B.5 the critical value of z is 1.645. The null hypothesis is rejected if the computed value of z is greater than 1.645.

The alternate hypothesis is that there are more no-shows in Atlanta, which means that distribution is located to the right of the Chicago distribution. The details of rank assignment are shown in Table 16–5. We rank the observations from *both* samples as if they were a single group. The Chicago flight with only 8 no-shows had the fewest, so it is assigned a rank of 1. The Chicago flight with 9 no-shows is ranked 2, and so on. The Atlanta flight with 25 no-shows is the highest, so it is assigned the largest rank, 17. There are also two instances of tied ranks. There are Atlanta and Chicago flights that each have 10 no-shows. There are also two Atlanta flights with 11 no-shows. How do we handle these ties? The solution is to average the ranks involved and assign the average rank to both flights. In the case involving 10 no-shows, the ranks involved are 3 and 4. The mean of these ranks is 3.5, so a rank of 3.5 is assigned to both the Atlanta and the Chicago flights with 10 no-shows.

TABLE 16–5 Ranked Number of No-Shows

Atlanta		Chicago	
No-Shows	**Rank**	**No-Shows**	**Rank**
11	5.5	13	7
15	9	14	8
10	3.5	10	3.5
18	12	8	1
11	5.5	16	10
20	13	9	2
24	16	17	11
22	15	21	14
25	17		
	96.5		56.5

Atlanta rank sum

The sum of the ranks for the Atlanta flights is 96.5. This is the value of W in formula (16–4). From Table 16–5, there are nine flights originating in Atlanta and eight in Chicago, so $n_1 = 9$ and $n_2 = 8$. Computing z from formula (16–4) gives:

$$z = \frac{W - \dfrac{n_1(n_1 + n_2 + 1)}{2}}{\sqrt{\dfrac{n_1 n_2(n_1 + n_2 + 1)}{12}}} = \frac{96.5 - \dfrac{9(9 + 8 + 1)}{2}}{\sqrt{\dfrac{9(8)(9 + 8 + 1)}{12}}} = 1.49$$

Because the computed z value (1.49) is less than 1.645, the null hypothesis is not rejected. The evidence does not show a difference in the distributions of the number of no-shows. That is, it appears that the number of no-shows is the same in Atlanta as in Chicago. The p-value of .0681, found by determining the area to the right of 1.49 (.5000 − .4319), indicates the same result.

MegaStat software can produce the same results. The MegaStat p-value is .0679, which is close to the value we calculated. The difference is due to rounding in the statistical software and a correction for ties.

Wilcoxon - Mann/Whitney Test

n	sum of ranks	
9	96.5	Atlanta
8	56.5	Chicago
17	153	total
	81.000	expected value
	10.392	standard deviation
	1.491	z
	.0679	p-value (one-tailed, upper)

In using the Wilcoxon rank-sum test, you may number the two populations in either order. However, once you have made a choice, W must be the sum of the ranks identified as population 1. If, in the no-show example, the population of Chicago was identified as number 1, the direction of the alternate hypothesis would be changed. The value of z would be the same but have the opposite sign.

H_0: The population distribution of no-shows is the same or larger for Chicago than for Atlanta.

H_1: The population distribution of no-shows is smaller for Chicago than for Atlanta.

The computed value of z is −1.49, found by:

$$z = \frac{W - \dfrac{n_1(n_1 + n_2 + 1)}{2}}{\sqrt{\dfrac{n_1 n_2(n_1 + n_2 + 1)}{12}}} = \frac{56.5 - \dfrac{8(8 + 9 + 1)}{2}}{\sqrt{\dfrac{8(9)(8 + 9 + 1)}{12}}} = -1.49$$

Our conclusion is the same as described earlier. There is no difference in the typical number of no-shows for Chicago and Atlanta.

SELF-REVIEW 16–5

The research director for Top Flite wants to know whether there is a difference in the distribution of the distances traveled by two of the company's golf balls. Eight of its XL-5000 brand and eight of its D2 brand balls were hit by an automatic fairway metal. The distances (in yards) were as follows:

XL-5000:	252, 263, 279, 273, 271, 265, 257, 280
D2:	262, 242, 256, 260, 258, 243, 239, 265

Do not assume the distributions of the distances traveled follow the normal probability distribution. At the .05 significance level, is there a difference between the two distributions?

EXERCISES

15. The eight observations were randomly selected from two populations (population A and population B) that were not necessarily normally distributed. Use the .05 significance level, a two-tailed test, and the Wilcoxon rank-sum test to determine whether there is a difference between the two populations.

Population A	38, 45, 56, 57, 61, 69, 70, 79
Population B	26, 31, 35, 42, 51, 52, 57, 62

16. Nine observations were randomly selected from population A and eight observations were randomly selected from population B. The populations are not necessarily normally distributed. Use the .05 significance level, a two-tailed test, and the Wilcoxon rank-sum test to determine whether there is a difference between the two populations.

Population A	12, 14, 15, 19, 23, 29, 33, 40, 51
Population B	13, 16, 19, 21, 22, 33, 35, 43

17. Tucson State University offers two MBA programs. In the first program, the students meet two nights per week at the university's main campus in downtown Tucson. In the second program, students only communicate online with the instructor. The director of the MBA experience at Tucson wishes to compare the number of hours studied last week by the two groups of students. A sample of 10 on-campus students and 12 online students revealed the following information.

Campus	28, 16, 42, 29, 31, 22, 50, 42, 23, 25
Online	26, 42, 65, 38, 29, 32, 59, 42, 27, 41, 46, 18

Do not assume the two distributions of study times, which are reported in hours, follow a normal distribution. At the .05 significance level, can we conclude the online students study more?

18. In recent times, with mortgage rates at low levels, financial institutions have had to provide more customer convenience. One of the innovations offered by Coastal National Bank and Trust is online entry of mortgage applications. Listed below are the times, in minutes, for eight customers to complete the application process for a 15-year fixed-rate mortgage and the times for nine customers to complete an application for a 30-year fixed-rate mortgage.

15 years, fixed rate	41, 36, 42, 39, 36, 48, 49, 38
30 years, fixed rate	21, 27, 36, 20, 19, 21, 39, 24, 22

At the .05 significance level, is it reasonable to conclude that it takes less time for those customers applying for the 30-year fixed-rate mortgage? Do not assume the distribution times follow a normal distribution for either group.

LO16-5
Test a hypothesis of several independent populations using the Kruskal-Wallis test.

KRUSKAL-WALLIS TEST: ANALYSIS OF VARIANCE BY RANKS

The analysis of variance (ANOVA) procedure discussed in Chapter 12 tests the hypothesis that several population means are equal. The data were interval or ratio level. Also, it was assumed the populations followed the normal probability distribution and their standard deviations were equal. What if the data are ordinal scale and/or the populations do not follow a normal distribution? W. H. Kruskal and W. A. Wallis reported a nonparametric test in 1952 requiring only ordinal-level (ranked) data. No assumptions about the shape of the populations are required. The test is referred to as the **Kruskal-Wallis one-way analysis of variance by ranks.**

For the Kruskal-Wallis test to be applied, the samples selected from the populations must be *independent*. For example, if samples from three groups—executives, staff, and supervisors—are to be selected and interviewed, the responses of one group (say, the executives) must in no way influence the responses of the others.

To compute the Kruskal-Wallis test statistic, (1) all the samples are combined, (2) the combined values are ordered from low to high, and (3) the ordered values are *replaced by ranks, starting with 1 for the smallest value*. An example will clarify the details of the procedure.

EXAMPLE

The Hospital Systems of the Carolinas operate three hospitals in the Greater Charlotte area: St. Luke's Memorial on the west side of the city, Swedish Medical Center to the south, and Piedmont Hospital on the east side of town. The director of administration is concerned about the waiting time of patients with non-life-threatening athletic-type injuries that arrive during weekday evenings at the three hospitals. Specifically, is there a difference in the waiting times at the three hospitals?

SOLUTION

To investigate, the director selected random samples of patients at the three locations and determined the time, in minutes, between entering the particular facility and when treatment was completed. The times in minutes are reported in Table 16–6.

TABLE 16–6 Waiting Times for Emergency Treatment at Hospital Systems of the Carolinas

St. Luke's Memorial	Swedish Medical Center	Piedmont Hospital
56	103	42
39	87	38
48	51	89
38	95	75
73	68	35
60	42	61
62	107	
	89	

From Table 16–6, we observe that the shortest waiting time is 35 minutes for the fifth sampled patient at Piedmont Hospital. The longest waiting time is 107 minutes by the seventh patient at the Swedish Medical Center.

Likely the first thought for comparing the waiting times is to determine whether there is a difference in the mean waiting time at the three hospitals, that is, use the one-way ANOVA described on page 385 of Chapter 12. However, there are three requirements for this test:

1. The samples are from independent populations.
2. The population variances must be equal.
3. The samples are from normal populations.

In this instance, the samples are from independent populations, the three different hospitals. But suppose we do not want to assume equal variance in the waiting times at the three hospitals or that these waiting times follow a normal probability distribution. Failing these two criteria means we do not meet the

ANOVA requirements, and so we cannot use the ANOVA techniques. Instead, we turn to the Kruskal-Wallis test, where these assumptions are not required.

The first step in conducting the Kruskal-Wallis test is to state the null and the alternate hypotheses.

H_0: The population distributions of waiting times are the same for the three hospitals.

H_1: The population distributions are not all the same for the three hospitals.

The director of administration selected the .05 significance level.

The test statistic used for the Kruskal-Wallis test is designated H. Its formula is:

KRUSKAL-WALLIS TEST

$$H = \frac{12}{n(n+1)}\left[\frac{(\Sigma R_1)^2}{n_1} + \frac{(\Sigma R_2)^2}{n_2} + \cdots + \frac{(\Sigma R_k)^2}{n_k}\right] - 3(n+1) \qquad \textbf{[16–5]}$$

with $k - 1$ degrees of freedom (k is the number of populations), where:

$\Sigma R_1, \Sigma R_2, \ldots, \Sigma R_k$ are the sums of the ranks of samples 1, 2, . . . , k, respectively.

$n_1, n_2, \ldots, n_k$ are the sizes of samples 1, 2, . . . , k, respectively.

n is the combined number of observations for all samples.

The distribution of the sample H statistic is very close to the chi-square distribution with $k - 1$ degrees of freedom. We prefer that each sample include at least five observations. We use chi-square to formulate the decision rule. In this example, there are three populations—a population of waiting times for patients at St. Luke's Memorial, another for patients at the Swedish Medical Center, and a third for Piedmont Hospital patients. Thus, there are $k - 1$, or $3 - 1 = 2$ degrees of freedom. Refer to the chi-square table of critical values in Appendix B.7. The critical value for 2 degrees of freedom and the .05 level of significance is 5.991. So our decision rule is: Do not reject the null hypothesis if the computed value of the test statistic H is less than or equal to 5.991. If the computed value of H is greater than 5.991, reject the null hypothesis and accept the alternate hypothesis.

The next step is to determine the value of the test statistic. We replace the waiting times at the three hospitals with the corresponding ranks. Considering the waiting times as a single group, the Piedmont patient with a waiting time of 35 minutes waited the shortest time and hence is given the lowest rank of 1. There are two patients that waited 38 minutes, one at St. Luke's and one at Piedmont. To resolve this tie, each patient is given a rank of 2.5, found by $(2 + 3)/2$. This process is continued for all waiting times. The longest waiting time is 107 minutes, and that Swedish Medical Center patient is given a rank of 21. The scores, the ranks, and the sum of the ranks for each of the three hospitals are given in Table 16–7 on the following page.

Solving for H gives

$$H = \frac{12}{n(n+1)}\left[\frac{(\Sigma R_1)^2}{n_1} + \frac{(\Sigma R_2)^2}{n_2} + \frac{(\Sigma R_3)^2}{n_3}\right] - 3(n+1)$$

$$= \frac{12}{21(21+1)}\left[\frac{58.5^2}{7} + \frac{120^2}{8} + \frac{52.5^2}{6}\right] - 3(21+1) = 5.38$$

Because the computed value of H (5.38) is less than the critical value of 5.991, we do not reject the null hypothesis. There is not enough evidence to conclude that there is a difference among the distributions of waiting times at the three hospitals.

TABLE 16–7 Waiting Times for Emergency Treatment at Hospital Systems of the Carolinas

St. Luke's Memorial		Swedish Medical Center		Piedmont Hospital	
Time	Rank	Time	Rank	Time	Rank
56	9	103	20	42	5.5
39	4	87	16	38	2.5
48	7	51	8	89	17.5
38	2.5	95	19	75	15
73	14	68	13	35	1
60	10	42	5.5	61	11
62	12	107	21		
		89	17.5		
	$\Sigma R_1 = 58.5$		$\Sigma R_2 = 120$		$\Sigma R_3 = 52.5$

Waiting time rank sums

The Kruskal-Wallis procedure can be done using the MegaStat add-in for Excel. Output for the example regarding the hospital waiting time follows. The computed value of H is 5.39 and the p-value is .067. The values are slightly different because of rounding. Based on these results, the decision and conclusion are the same.

Kruskal-Wallis Test

Median	*n*	*Avg. Rank*	
56.00	7	8.36	St. Luke's
88.00	8	15.00	Swedish
51.50	6	8.75	Piedmont
61.00	21		Total
		5.39	H (corrected for ties)
		2	d.f.
		0.067	p-value

Recall from Chapter 12 that, for the analysis of variance technique to apply, we assume (1) the populations are normally distributed, (2) these populations have equal standard deviations, and (3) the samples are selected from independent populations. If these assumptions are met in the hospital waiting time example, we use the F distribution as the test statistic. If these assumptions cannot be met, we apply the distribution-free test by Kruskal-Wallis. To highlight the similarities between the two approaches, we will solve the hospital waiting time example using the ANOVA technique.

To begin, we state the null and the alternate hypotheses for the three hospitals.

H_0: $\mu_1 = \mu_2 = \mu_3$
H_1: The treatment means are not all the same.

For the .05 significance level, with $k - 1 = 3 - 1 = 2$ degrees of freedom in the numerator and $n - k = 21 - 3 = 18$ degrees of freedom in the denominator, the

critical value of F is 3.55. The decision rule is to reject the null hypothesis if the computed value of F is greater than 3.55. The output using Excel follows.

	A	B	C	D	E	F	G	H	I	J	K
1	St. Luke's	Swedish	Piedmont		Anova: Single Factor						
2	56	103	42								
3	39	87	38		SUMMARY						
4	48	51	89		*Groups*	*Count*	*Sum*	*Average*	*Variance*		
5	38	95	75		St. Luke's	7	376	53.714	163.571		
6	73	68	35		Swedish	8	642	80.250	577.357		
7	60	42	61		Piedmont	6	340	56.667	486.667		
8	62	107									
9		89									
10					ANOVA						
11					*Source of Variation*	*SS*	*df*	*MS*	*F*	*P-value*	*F crit*
12					Between Groups	3166.4	2	1583.202	3.822	0.041	3.555
13					Within Groups	7456.26	18	414.24			
14											
15					Total	10622.7	20				

From the previous output, the computed value of F is 3.822 and the p-value is .041. Our decision is to reject the null hypothesis and accept the alternate hypothesis. Using the one-way ANOVA test, we conclude that the treatment means are not the same. That is, the mean waiting times at the three Hospital Systems of the Carolinas hospitals are different.

We have contradictory conclusions on the same data. How can this happen? If we compare the results using p-values, the answers are similar. For the Kruskal-Wallis test, the p-value was .067, which is only slightly more than the significance level of .05, but our decision was not to reject the null hypothesis. The p-value using ANOVA is .041, which is not far beyond the critical value into the rejection region. So, to summarize, we just missed rejecting with the Kruskal-Wallis test, and we were just in the rejection region using ANOVA. The difference in the p-values is .026. Thus, the results are actually quite close in terms of the p-values.

SELF-REVIEW 16–6

The regional bank manager of Statewide Financial Bank is interested in the turnover rate of personal checking accounts at four of the branches. (Turnover rate is the speed at which the money in an account is deposited and withdrawn. An extremely active account may have a rate of 300; if only one or two checks were written, the rate could be about 30.) The turnover rates of the samples selected from the four branch banks are shown in the table below. Using the .01 level and the Kruskal-Wallis test, determine whether there is a difference in the turnover rates of the personal checking accounts among the four branches.

Englewood Branch	West Side Branch	Great Northern Branch	Sylvania Branch
208	91	302	99
307	62	103	116
199	86	319	189
142	91	340	103
91	80	180	100
296			131

EXERCISES

19. Under what conditions should the Kruskal-Wallis test be used instead of analysis of variance?
20. Under what conditions should the Kruskal-Wallis test be used instead of the Wilcoxon rank-sum test?
21. The following sample data were obtained from three populations that did not follow a normal distribution.

Sample 1	Sample 2	Sample 3
50	48	39
54	49	41
59	49	44
59	52	47
65	56	51
	57	

a. State the null hypothesis.
b. Using the .05 level of risk, state the decision rule.
c. Compute the value of the test statistic.
d. What is your decision on the null hypothesis?

22. The following sample data were obtained from three populations where the variances were not equal, and you wish to compare the populations.

Sample 1	Sample 2	Sample 3
21	15	38
29	17	40
35	22	44
45	27	51
56	31	53
71		

a. State the null hypothesis.
b. Using the .01 level of risk, state the decision rule.
c. Compute the value of the test statistic.
d. What is your decision on the null hypothesis?

23. Davis Outboard Motors Inc. recently developed an epoxy painting process for corrosion protection on exhaust components. Bill Davis, the owner, wishes to determine whether the lengths of life for the paint are equal for three different conditions: saltwater, freshwater without weeds, and freshwater with a heavy concentration of weeds. Accelerated-life tests were conducted in the laboratory, and the number of hours the paint lasted before peeling was recorded. Five boats were tested for each condition.

Saltwater	Freshwater	Freshwater with Weeds
167.3	160.6	182.7
189.6	177.6	165.4
177.2	185.3	172.9
169.4	168.6	169.2
180.3	176.6	174.7

Use the Kruskal-Wallis test and the .01 level to determine whether the lasting quality of the paint is the same for the three water conditions.

24. The National Turkey Association wants to experiment with the effects of three different feed mixtures on weight gain in poults. Because no experience exists regarding the three mixtures, no assumptions regarding the population distribution of weights exist. To study the effects of the three mixtures, five poults were given feed A, six were given feed B, and five were given feed C over a three-week time period. Test at the .05 level the hypothesis that there is no effect of feed mixture on weight.

Weight (in pounds)		
Feed Mixture A	Feed Mixture B	Feed Mixture C
11.2	12.6	11.3
12.1	10.8	11.9
10.9	11.3	12.4
11.3	11.0	10.6
12.0	12.0	12.0
	10.7	

LO16-6

Test and interpret a nonparametric hypothesis test of correlation.

RANK-ORDER CORRELATION

In Chapter 13 we described the coefficient of correlation. Recall that it measures the association between two interval- or ratio-scaled variables. For example, the coefficient of correlation reports the association between the salary of executives and their years of experience, or the association between the number of miles a shipment had to travel and the number of days it took to arrive at its destination. The coefficient of correlation is a very versatile measure of association. However, there are several conditions when it is not appropriate or can be misleading. Those conditions include:

1. When the scale of measurement of one of the two variables being considered is ordinal (ranked).
2. When the relationship between the variables is not linear.
3. When one or more of the data points are quite different from the others.

Charles Spearman, a British statistician, introduced a measure of correlation for ranked data. This measure allows us to describe the relationship between sets of ranked data. For example, two staff members in the Office of Research at the University of the Valley are asked to rank 10 faculty research proposals for funding purposes. We want to study the association between the ratings of the two staff members. That is, do the two staff members rate the same proposals as the most worthy and the least worthy of funding?

This coefficient of rank correlation is also applied to conditions 2 and 3 above. Instead of using the actual values in the data set, we rank the sample data and compute a correlation between the ranked values. Like Pearson's coefficient of correlation described in Chapter 13, it can range from −1.00 up to 1.00. Values of −1.00 or 1.00 indicate perfect association between the ranks. A value of 0 indicates no association between the ranks of the two variables. Values of −.84 and .84 both exhibit the same amount of association but −.84 indicates an inverse relationship and .84 a direct relationship. We denote Spearman's coefficient of rank correlation as r_s.

We can use formula (13–1) on page 433 to find the coefficient of rank correlation. However, we use the ranked values in place of the actual values. The values are always ranked from low to high. A simpler method is to use the following, which uses the ranks.

STATISTICS IN ACTION

Manatees are large mammals that like to float just below the water's surface. Because they float just below the surface, they are in danger from powerboat propellers. A study of the correlation between the number of powerboat registrations in coastal Florida counties and the number of accidental manatee deaths revealed a strong positive correlation. As a result, Florida created regions where powerboats are prohibited, so that manatees could thrive.

SPEARMAN'S COEFFICIENT OF RANK CORRELATION

$$r_s = 1 - \frac{6\Sigma d^2}{n(n^2 - 1)} \quad [16\text{–}6]$$

where:

d is the difference between the ranks for each pair.
n is the number of paired observations.

The following example/solution provides the details of computing the coefficient of rank correlation.

EXAMPLE

Recent studies focus on the relationship between the age of online shoppers and the number of minutes spent browsing on the Internet. Table 16–8 shows a sample of 15 online shoppers who actually made a purchase last week. Included is their age and the time, in minutes, spent browsing on the Internet last week.

TABLE 16–8 Age and Browsing Minutes for a Sample of Internet Shoppers

Shopper	Age	Browsing Time (minutes)
Spina, Sal	28	342
Gordon, Ray	50	125
Schnur, Roberta	44	121
Alvear, Jose	32	257
Myers, Tom	55	56
Lyons, George	60	225
Harbin, Joe	38	185
Bobko, Jack	22	141
Koppel, Marty	21	342
Rowatti, Marty	45	169
Monahan, Joyce	52	218
Lanoue, Bernie	33	241
Roll, Judy	19	583
Goodall, Jody	17	394
Broderick, Ron	21	249

1. Draw a scatter diagram; plot age on the horizontal axis and browsing minutes on the vertical axis.
2. What type of association do the sample data suggest? Strong or weak, direct or inverse?
3. Do you see any issues with the relationship between the variables?
4. Find the coefficient of rank correlation.
5. Conduct a test of hypothesis to determine if there is a negative association between the ranks.

SOLUTION

Our first step is to create a scatter diagram, shown in Chart 16–2, to better understand the relationship between the two variables.

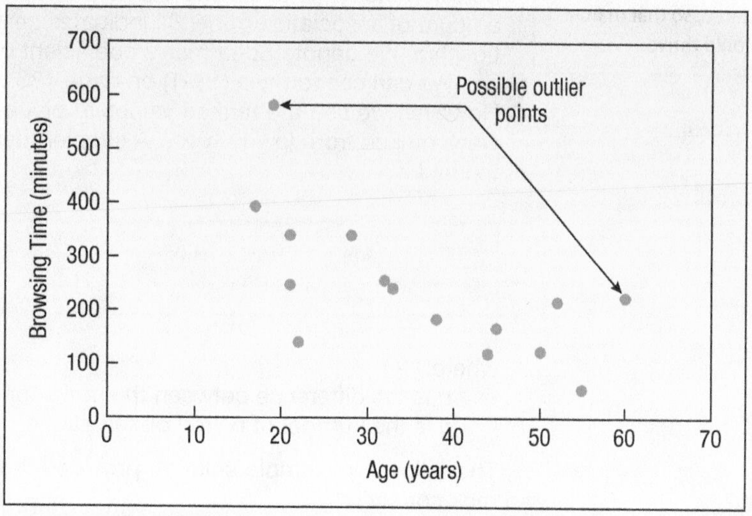

CHART 16–2 Scatter Diagram of Age and Internet Browsing Minutes

There appears to be a fairly strong inverse relationship between the Internet shopper's age and the amount of time spent browsing the Internet. That is, the younger shoppers seem to spend more time browsing. Not surprising. There are a couple of data points that seem quite different than the others. They are identified in Chart 16–2 on the previous page. Because of these points we decide to use the coefficient of rank correlation.

To calculate the coefficient of rank correlation, we first rank the age of the shoppers. The youngest shopper is Jody Goodall, who is 17, so she is ranked 1. The next youngest is Judy Roll, so she is ranked 2. There are two shoppers, Marty Koppel and Ron Broderick, who are 21 years old. This tie is resolved by giving each a rank of 3.5, which is the average of ranks 3 and 4. The oldest shopper in the sample is George Lyons; he is given a rank of 15. The same ranking strategy is used for browsing minutes. Tom Myers spent the fewest minutes browsing the Internet, so he has the rank of 1. Roberta Schnur is next with 141 minutes, so she has a browsing rank of 2. All the ranking data are shown in Table 16–9.

TABLE 16–9 Age, Browsing Time, Ranks, Differences, and Differences Squared

Shopper	Age	Age Rank	Browsing Time (minutes)	Browsing Rank	d	d^2
Spina, Sal	28	6.0	342	12.5	−6.50	42.25
Gordon, Ray	50	12.0	125	3.0	9.00	81.00
Schnur, Roberta	44	10.0	121	2.0	8.00	64.00
Alvear, Jose	32	7.0	257	11.0	−4.00	16.00
Myers, Tom	55	14.0	56	1.0	13.00	169.00
Lyons, George	60	15.0	225	8.0	7.00	49.00
Harbin, Joe	38	9.0	185	6.0	3.00	9.00
Bobko, Jack	22	5.0	141	4.0	1.00	1.00
Koppel, Marty	21	3.5	342	12.5	−9.00	81.00
Rowatti, Marty	45	11.0	169	5.0	6.00	36.00
Monahan, Joyce	52	13.0	218	7.0	6.00	36.00
Lanoue, Bernie	33	8.0	241	9.0	−1.00	1.00
Roll, Judy	19	2.0	583	15.0	−13.00	169.00
Goodall, Jody	17	1.0	394	14.0	−13.00	169.00
Broderick, Ron	21	3.5	249	10.0	−6.50	42.25
					Sum d^2	965.50

The coefficient of rank correlation is −.724, found by using formula (16–6).

$$r_s = 1 - \frac{6\Sigma d^2}{n(n^2 - 1)} = 1 - \frac{6(965.5)}{15(15^2 - 1)} = 1 - 1.724 = -0.724$$

The value of −0.724 indicates a fairly strong negative association between age of the Internet shopper and the minutes spent browsing. The younger shoppers tended to spend more time browsing the Internet.

Testing the Significance of r_s

Next we wish to investigate the question as to whether the degree of association between the ranked variables occurred by chance. You may recall on page 430 in Chapter 13 we investigated this same issue. In that instance, we used interval or ratio data; now we use ranks. In the preceding example/solution we found a rank correlation of −0.724. Is it possible that the correlation of −0.724 is due to chance and that the correlation among the ranks in the population is really 0? We can conduct a test of hypothesis to answer this question.

For a sample of 10 or more, the significance of r_s is determined by computing t using the following formula. The sampling distribution of r_s follows the t distribution with $n - 2$ degrees of freedom.

HYPOTHESIS TEST, RANK CORRELATION $t = r_s\sqrt{\dfrac{n-2}{1-r_s^2}}$ **[16–7]**

The null and the alternate hypotheses are:

H_0: The rank correlation in the population is zero.
H_1: There is a negative association among the ranks.

We use the .05 significance level. The decision rule is to reject the null hypothesis if the computed value is less than −1.771. Go to Appendix B.5 and use a one-tailed test with 15 − 2 = 13 degrees of freedom.

$$t = r_s\sqrt{\frac{n-2}{1-r_s^2}} = -0.724\sqrt{\frac{15-2}{1-(-0.724)^2}} = -3.784$$

The computed value of t is −3.784. The null hypothesis is rejected and the alternate hypothesis is accepted. The computed t of −3.784 is less than −1.771. There is evidence of a negative association between the age of the Internet shopper and the time spent browsing the Internet.

SELF-REVIEW 16–7

A sample of individuals applying for factory positions at Davis Enterprises revealed the following scores on an eye perception test (X) and a mechanical aptitude test (Y):

Subject	Eye Perception	Mechanical Aptitude	Subject	Eye Perception	Mechanical Aptitude
001	805	23	006	810	28
002	777	62	007	805	30
003	820	60	008	840	42
004	682	40	009	777	55
005	777	70	010	820	51

(a) Compute the coefficient of rank correlation between eye perception and mechanical aptitude.
(b) At the .05 significance level, can we conclude that the correlation in the population is different from 0?

EXERCISES

25. Do husbands and wives like the same TV shows? A recent study by Nielsen Media Research asked a young married couple to rank 14 shows from best to worst. A rank of 1 indicates the best-liked show and a rank of 14 the least-liked show. The results for one married couple follow.

Program	Male Rating	Female Rating
60 Minutes	4	5
CSI—New York	6	4
Bones	7	8
SportsCenter	2	7
Late Show with David Letterman	12	11
NBC Nightly News	8	6
Law and Order: Los Angeles	5	3
Miami Medical	3	9
Survivor	13	2
Office	14	10
American Idol	1	1
Grey's Anatomy	9	13
House	10	12
Criminal Minds	11	14

a. Draw a scatter diagram. Place the male rankings on the horizontal axis and the female rankings on the vertical axis.
b. Compute the coefficient of rank correlation between the male and female rankings.
c. At the .05 significance level, is it reasonable to conclude there is a positive association between the two rankings?

26. Far West University offers both day and evening classes in business administration. One question in a survey of students inquires how they perceive the prestige associated with eight careers. A day student was asked to rank the careers from 1 to 8, with 1 having the most prestige and 8 the least prestige. An evening student was asked to do the same. The results follow.

Career	Ranking by Day Student	Ranking by Evening Student	Career	Ranking by Day Student	Ranking by Evening Student
Accountant	6	3	Statistician	1	7
Computer programmer	7	2	Marketing researcher	4	8
Branch bank manager	2	6	Stock analyst	3	5
Hospital administrator	5	4	Production manager	8	1

Find Spearman's coefficient of rank correlation.

27. Ten new sales representatives for Clark Sprocket and Chain, Inc. were required to attend a training program before being assigned to a regional sales office. At the end of the program, the representatives took a series of tests and the scores were ranked. For example, Arden had the lowest test score and is ranked 1; Arbuckle had the highest test score and is ranked 10. At the end of the first sales year, the representatives' ranks based on test scores were paired with their first year sales.

Representative	Annual Sales ($ thousands)	Ranking in Training Program	Representative	Annual Sales ($ thousands)	Ranking in Training Program
Kitchen	319	8	Arden	300	1
Bond	150	2	Crane	280	6
Gross	175	5	Arthur	200	9
Arbuckle	460	10	Keene	190	4
Greene	348	7	Knopf	300	3

a. Compute and interpret the coefficient of rank correlation between first-year sales and class rank after the training program.
b. At the .05 significance level, can we conclude that there is a positive association between first-year sales dollars and ranking in the training program?

28. Suppose Texas A & M University—Commerce has five scholarships available for the women's basketball team. The head coach provided the two assistant coaches with the names of 10 high school players with potential to play at the university. Each assistant coach attended three games and then ranked the 10 players with respect to potential. To explain, the first coach ranked Norma Tidwell as the best player among the 10 scouted and Jeannie Black the worst.

	Rank, by Assistant Coach			Rank, by Assistant Coach	
Player	Jean Cann	John Cannelli	Player	Jean Cann	John Cannelli
Cora Jean Seiple	7	5	Candy Jenkins	3	1
Bette Jones	2	4	Rita Rosinski	5	7
Jeannie Black	10	10	Anita Lockes	4	2
Norma Tidwell	1	3	Brenda Towne	8	9
Kathy Marchal	6	6	Denise Ober	9	8

a. Determine Spearman's rank correlation coefficient.
b. At the .05 significance level, can we conclude there is a positive association between the ranks?

CHAPTER SUMMARY

I. The sign test is based on the sign difference between two related observations.
  A. No assumptions need to be made about the shape of the two populations.
  B. It is based on paired or dependent samples.
  C. For small samples, find the number of + or − signs and refer to the binomial distribution for the critical value.
  D. For a sample of 10 or more, use the standard normal distribution and the following formula.

$$z = \frac{(x \pm .50) - .50n}{.50\sqrt{n}} \qquad \textbf{[16–2] [16–3]}$$

II. The median test is used to test a hypothesis about a population median.
  A. Find μ and σ for a binomial distribution.
  B. The z distribution is used as the test statistic.
  C. The value of z is computed from the following formula, where X is the number of observations above or below the median.

$$z = \frac{(x \pm .50) - \mu}{\sigma} \qquad \textbf{[16–1]}$$

III. The Wilcoxon signed-rank test is a nonparametric test for differences between two dependent populations.
  A. The assumption of normally distributed populations is not required.
  B. The steps to conduct the test are:
    1. Rank absolute differences between the related observations.
    2. Apply the sign of the differences to the ranks.
    3. Sum negative ranks and positive ranks.
    4. The smaller of the two sums is the computed T value.
    5. Refer to Appendix B.8 for the critical value, and make a decision regarding H_0.

IV. The Wilcoxon rank-sum test is used to test whether two independent samples came from equal populations.
  A. The assumption of normally distributed populations is not required.
  B. The data must be at least ordinal scale.
  C. Each sample must contain at least eight observations.
  D. To determine the value of the test statistic W, the sample observations are ranked from low to high as if they were from a single group.
  E. The sum of ranks for each of the two samples is determined.
  F. W is used to compute z, where W is the sum of the ranks for population 1.

$$z = \frac{W - \dfrac{n_1(n_1 + n_2 + 1)}{2}}{\sqrt{\dfrac{n_1 n_2(n_1 + n_2 + 1)}{12}}} \qquad \textbf{[16–4]}$$

  G. The standard normal distribution, found in Appendix B.3, is the test statistic.

V. The Kruskal-Wallis one-way ANOVA by ranks is used to test whether several populations are the same.
  A. The assumption of normally distributed populations is not required.
  B. The samples must be independent and at least ordinal scale.
  C. The sample observations are ranked from smallest to largest as though they were a single group.
  D. The test statistic follows the chi-square distribution, provided there are at least five observations in each sample.
  E. The value of the test statistic is computed from the following:

$$H = \frac{12}{n(n + 1)}\left[\frac{(\Sigma R_1)^2}{n_1} + \frac{(\Sigma R_2)^2}{n_2} + \cdots + \frac{(\Sigma R_k)^2}{n_k}\right] - 3(n + 1) \qquad \textbf{[16–5]}$$

VI. Spearman's coefficient of rank correlation is a measure of the association between two ordinal-scale variables.

A. It can range from −1 up to 1.
   1. A value of 0 indicates there is no association between the variables.
   2. A value of −1 indicates perfect negative correlation, and 1 indicates perfect positive correlation.

B. The value of r_s is computed from the following formula.

$$r_s = 1 - \frac{6\Sigma d^2}{n(n^2 - 1)} \quad \text{[16–6]}$$

C. Provided the sample size is at least 10, we can conduct a test of hypothesis using the following formula:

$$t = r_s \sqrt{\frac{n-2}{1-r_s^2}} \quad \text{[16–7]}$$

   1. The test statistic follows the *t* distribution.
   2. There are $n - 2$ degrees of freedom.

PRONUNCIATION KEY

SYMBOL	MEANING	PRONUNCIATION
$(\Sigma R_1)^2$	Square of the total of the first column ranks	*Sigma R sub 1 squared*
r_s	Spearman's coefficient of rank correlation	*r sub s*

CHAPTER EXERCISES

29. The vice president of programming at NBC is finalizing the prime-time schedule for the fall. She has decided to include a hospital drama but is unsure which of two possibilities to select. She has a pilot called *The Surgeon* and another called *Critical Care*. To help her make a final decision, a sample of 20 viewers from throughout the United States was asked to watch the two pilots and indicate which show they prefer. The results were that 12 liked *The Surgeon,* 7 liked *Critical Care,* and one had no preference. Is there a preference for one of the two shows? Use the .10 significance level.

30. IBM Inc. is going to award a contract for fine-line pens to be used nationally in its offices. Two suppliers, Bic and Pilot, have submitted bids. To determine the preference of office employees, brokers, and others, a personal preference test is to be conducted using a randomly selected sample of 20 employees. The .05 level of significance is to be used.
   a. If the alternate hypothesis states that Bic is preferred over Pilot, is the sign test to be conducted as a one-tailed or a two-tailed test? Explain.
   b. As each of the sample members told the researchers his or her preference, a "+" was recorded if it was Bic and a "−" if it was the Pilot fine-line pen. A count of the pluses revealed that 12 employees preferred Bic, 5 preferred Pilot, and 3 were undecided. What is *n*?
   c. What is the decision rule in words?
   d. What conclusion did you reach regarding pen preference? Explain.

31. Cornwall and Hudson, a large retail department store, wants to handle just one brand of high-quality CD player. The list has been narrowed to two brands: Sony and Panasonic. To help make a decision, a panel of 16 audio experts met. A passage using Sony components (labeled A) was played. Then the same passage was played using Panasonic components (labeled B). A "+" in the following table indicates an individual's preference for the Sony components, a "−" indicates preference for Panasonic, and a 0 signifies no preference.

Expert															
1	2	3	4	5	6	7	8	9	10	11	12	13	14	15	16
+	−	+	−	+	+	−	0	−	+	−	+	+	−	+	−

Conduct a test of hypothesis at the .10 significance level to determine whether there is a difference in preference between the two brands.

32. The Greater Jacksonville, Florida, Real Estate Association claims that the median rental for three-bedroom condominiums is more than $1,200 a month. A random sample of 149 units showed 5 rented for exactly $1,200 a month, and 75 rented for more than $1,200. At the .05 level, can we conclude that the median rental is more than $1,200?
a. State H_0 and H_1.
b. Give the decision rule.
c. Do the necessary calculations, and arrive at a decision.

33. The Citrus Council of America wants to determine whether consumers prefer plain orange juice or juice with some orange pulp in it. A random sample of 212 consumers was selected. Each member of the sample tasted a small, unlabeled cup of one kind and then tasted the other kind. Twelve consumers said they had no preference, 40 preferred plain juice, and the remainder liked the juice with pulp better. Test at the .05 level that the preferences for plain juice and for orange juice with pulp are equal.

34. The objective of a community research project is to determine whether women are more community conscious before marriage or after 5 years of marriage. A test designed to measure community consciousness was administered to a sample of nine women before marriage, and the same test was given to them 5 years after marriage. The test scores are:

Name	Before Marriage	After Marriage	Name	Before Marriage	After Marriage
Beth	110	114	Carol	186	196
Jean	157	159	Lisa	116	116
Sue	121	120	Sandy	160	140
Cathy	96	103	Petra	149	142
Mary	130	139			

Test at the .05 level. H_0 is: There is no difference in community consciousness before and after marriage. H_1 is: There is a difference.

35. Is there a difference in the annual divorce rates in predominantly rural counties among three geographic regions, namely, the Southwest, the Southeast, and the Northwest? Test at the .05 level. Annual divorce rates per 1,000 population for five randomly selected counties in the Southwest, six counties in the Southeast, and 5 counties in the Northwest are:

Southwest:	5.9, 6.2, 7.9, 8.6, 4.6
Southeast:	5.0, 6.4, 7.3, 6.2, 8.1, 5.1
Northwest:	6.7, 6.2, 4.9, 8.0, 5.5

36. The production manager of MPS Audio Systems Inc. is concerned about the idle time of workers. In particular, he would like to know if there is a difference in the idle minutes for workers on the day shift and the evening shift. The information below is the number of idle minutes yesterday for the five day-shift workers and the six evening-shift workers. Use the .05 significance level.

Day Shift	Evening Shift
92	96
103	114
116	80
81	82
89	88
	91

37. Drs. Trythall and Kerns are studying the mobility of executives in selected industries. Their research measures mobility using a score based on the number of times an executive has moved, changed companies, or changed jobs within a company over the last 10 years. The highest number of points is awarded for moving and changing companies; the fewest, for changing jobs within a company and not moving. They randomly sampled five executives in the chemical industry, six in the retail industry, five in the Internet industry, and five in the aerospace industry. The distribution of scores does not follow the normal probability

distribution. Develop an appropriate test to determine if there is a difference in the mobility scores in the four industries. Use the .05 significance level.

Chemical	Retail	Internet	Aerospace
4	3	62	30
17	12	40	38
8	40	81	46
20	17	96	40
16	31	76	21
	19		

38. A series of questions on sports and world events was asked of 14 randomly selected young adult naturalized citizens. The results were translated into sports and world events "knowledge" scores. The scores were:

Citizen	Sports	World Events	Citizen	Sports	World Events
J. C. McCarthy	47	49	L. M. Zaugg	87	75
A. N. Baker	12	10	J. B. Simon	59	86
B. B. Beebe	62	76	J. Goulden	40	61
L. D. Gaucet	81	92	A. A. Fernandez	87	18
C. A. Jones	90	86	A. M. Carbo	16	75
J. N. Lopez	35	42	A. O. Smithy	50	51
A. F. Nissen	61	61	J. J. Pascal	60	61

a. Determine the degree of association between how the citizens ranked with respect to knowledge of sports and how they ranked on world events.

b. At the .05 significance level, is the rank correlation between the sports and world events "knowledge" scores greater than zero?

39. Early in the basketball season, 12 college teams appeared to be outstanding. A panel of sportswriters and a panel of college basketball coaches were asked to rank the 12 teams. Their composite rankings were as follows.

Team	Coaches	Sportswriters	Team	Coaches	Sportswriters
Duke	1	1	Syracuse	7	10
UNLV	2	5	Georgetown	8	11
Indiana	3	4	Villanova	9	7
North Carolina	4	6	LSU	10	12
Louisville	5	3	St. Johns	11	8
Ohio State	6	2	Michigan	12	9

Determine the correlation between the rankings of the coaches and the sportswriters. At the .05 significance level, can we conclude there is a positive correlation between the rankings?

40. Professor Bert Forman believes the students who complete his examinations in the shortest time receive the highest grades and those who take the longest to complete them receive the lowest grades. To verify his suspicion, he assigns a rank to the order of finish and then grades the examinations. The results are shown below:

Student	Order of Completion	Score (50 possible)	Student	Order of Completion	Score (50 possible)
Gromney	1	48	Smythe	7	39
Bates	2	48	Arquette	8	30
MacDonald	3	43	Govito	9	37
Sosa	4	49	Gankowski	10	35
Harris	5	50	Bonfigilo	11	36
Cribb	6	47	Matsui	12	33

Convert the test scores to a rank and find the coefficient of rank correlation between the order of completion and the rank of the test score. At the .05 significance level, can Professor Forman conclude there is a positive association between the order of finish and the test scores?

DATA SET EXERCISES

(The data for these exercises are available at the text website: www.mhhe.com/lind16e.)

41. Refer to the Real Estate data, which report information on homes sold in Goodyear, Arizona, and the surrounding area.

a. Use an appropriate nonparametric test to determine whether there is a difference in the typical selling price of the homes in the several townships. Assume the selling prices are not normally distributed. Use the .05 significance level.

b. Combine the homes with six or more bedrooms into one group and determine whether there is a difference according to the number of bedrooms in the typical selling prices of the homes. Use the .05 significance level and assume the distribution of selling prices is not normally distributed.

c. Assume that the distribution of the distance from the center of the city is positively skewed. That is, the normality assumption is not reasonable. Compare the distribution of the distance from the center of the city of the homes that have a pool with those that do not have a pool. Can we conclude there is a difference in the distributions? Use the .05 significance level.

42. Refer to the Baseball 2012 data, which report information on the 2012 Major League Baseball season.

a. Rank the teams by the number of wins and their total team salary. Compute the coefficient of rank correlation between the two variables. At the .01 significance level, can you conclude that it is greater than zero?

b. Assume that the distributions of team salaries for the American League and National League do not follow the normal distribution. Conduct a test of hypothesis to see whether there is a difference in the two distributions.

c. Rank the 30 teams by attendance and by team salary. Determine the coefficient of rank correlation between these two variables. At the .05 significance level, is it reasonable to conclude the ranks of these two variables are related?

43. Refer to the data on the school buses in the Buena School District.

a. Assume the distribution of the maintenance cost for the three bus manufacturers does not follow a normal distribution. Conduct a test of hypothesis at the .05 significance level to determine whether the distributions differ.

b. Assume the distribution of the maintenance cost for the bus capacities does not follow a normal distribution. Conduct a test of hypothesis at the .05 significance level to determine whether the distributions differ.

c. Assume the distribution of the maintenance cost for the bus types, diesel or gasoline, does not follow a normal distribution. Conduct a test of hypothesis at the .05 significance level to determine whether the distributions differ.

A REVIEW OF CHAPTERS 15–16

In Chapters 15 and 16, we describe statistical methods to study data that are either the nominal or the ordinal scale of measurement. These methods are *nonparametric* or *distribution-free* statistics. They do not require assumptions regarding the shape of the population. Recall, for example, in Chapter 12 when investigating the means of several populations, we assume the populations follow the normal probability distribution.

In Chapter 15, we describe tests for the nominal level of data. We begin by studying one- and two-sample tests of proportions. A proportion is the fraction of individuals or objects that possess a certain characteristic. In a proportion the sampled individual or object either has the characteristic or does not. For example, in a one-sample test of proportions, we study 100 gasoline purchases at the local Kwick Fill station. The individual either purchased regular gasoline or did not. There are only two possible outcomes. In a two-sample test of proportions, we compare the proportion of purchasers who bought regular gasoline at the Corry, PA, Kwick Fill with the proportion of regular gasoline purchases at the Tyrone, PA, Kwick Fill. The test statistic is the standard normal distribution in both the one-sample and the two-sample tests.

We also describe the chi-square distribution. We use this distribution to compare the observed set of frequencies in a random sample with the corresponding set of expected frequencies in the population. The level of measurement is also the nominal

scale. In the previous example, there were only two possible outcomes: the purchaser bought regular gasoline or did not buy it. We use the chi-square distribution to investigate an instance where there are several possible nominal-scale outcomes. A gasoline purchaser can buy regular, midgrade, or premium. Recall that when data are measured at the nominal level, the observations can only be classified according to some label, name, or characteristic.

In Chapter 15, we also explore the relationship between two variables in a contingency table. That is, we observe two characteristics of each sampled individual or object. For example, is there a relationship between the quality of the product (acceptable or unacceptable) and the shift when it was manufactured (day, afternoon, or night)? The chi-square distribution is used as the test statistic.

In Chapter 16, we describe five nonparametric tests of hypothesis and the coefficient of rank correlation. Each of these tests requires at least the ordinal scale of measurement. That is, we are able to rank, or order, the variables of interest.

The *sign test* for dependent samples is based on the sign of the difference between related observations. The binomial distribution is the test statistic. In cases where the sample is greater than 10, the normal approximation to the binomial probability distribution serves as the test statistic.

The first step when using the *median test* is to count the number of observations above (or below) the proposed median. Next, we use the standard normal distribution to determine if this number is reasonable or too large to have occurred by chance.

The *Wilcoxon signed-rank test* requires dependent samples. It is an extension of the sign test in that it makes use of both the direction and the magnitude of the difference between related values. It has its own sampling distribution, which is reported in Appendix B.8.

The *Wilcoxon ranked-sum test* assumes independent populations, but does not require the populations to follow the normal probability distribution. It is an alternative to the *t* test for independent samples described in Chapter 11. When there are at least eight observations in each sample, the test statistic is the standard normal distribution.

The *Kruskal-Wallis test* is an extension of the Wilcoxon ranked-sum test in that it handles more than two populations. It is an alternative to the one-way ANOVA method described in Chapter 12. It does not require the populations to follow the normal probability distribution or that the populations have equal standard deviations.

The statistic *Spearman's coefficient of rank correlation* is a special case of the Pearson coefficient of correlation, described in Chapter 13. It is based on the correlation between the *ranks* of related observations. It may range from −1.00 to 1.00, with 0 indicating no association between the ranks.

PROBLEMS

1. The owner of Beach Front Snow Cones Inc. believes the median number of snow cones sold per day between Memorial Day and Labor Day is 60. Below is the number of snow-cones sold on 20 randomly selected days. Is it reasonable to conclude that the median is actually greater than 60? Use the .05 significance level.

65	70	65	64	66	54	68	61	62	67
65	50	64	55	74	57	67	72	66	65

2. The manufacturer of children's raincoats wants to know if there is a preference among children for blue, red, green, or yellow raincoats. The information below is the color preference for a sample of 50 children between the ages of 6 and 10. Use the .05 significance level to investigate.

Color	Frequency
Blue	17
Red	8
Green	12
Yellow	13

3. Is there a difference (in feet) of the length of suspension bridges in the northeast, southeast, and far west parts of the United States? The following table shows the lengths of seven bridges in the northeast, nine bridges in the southeast, and eight bridges in the far west. Conduct an appropriate test of hypothesis on the following data. Do not assume the bridge lengths follow a normal probability distribution. Use the .05 significance level.

Northeast	Southeast	Far West
3,645	3,502	3,547
3,727	3,645	3,636
3,772	3,718	3,659
3,837	3,746	3,673
3,873	3,758	3,728
3,882	3,845	3,736
3,894	3,940	3,788
	4,070	3,802
	4,081	

4. Research by the First Bank of Illinois revealed that 8% of its customers wait more than 5 minutes for a teller in a bank lobby. Management considers this reasonable and will not add more tellers unless the proportion waiting longer than 5 minutes becomes larger than 8%. The branch manager at the Litchfield Branch believes that the wait is longer than the standard at her branch and requested additional part-time tellers. To support her request, she found that, in a sample of 100 customers, 10 waited more than 5 minutes. At the .01 significance level, is it reasonable to conclude that more than 8% of the customers wait more than 5 minutes?

CASES

A. Century National Bank

Is there a relationship between the location of the branch bank and whether the customer has a debit card? Based on the information available, develop a table that shows the relationship between these two variables. At the .05 significance level, can we conclude there is a relationship between the branch location and whether the customer uses a debit card?

B. Thomas Testing Labs

John Thomas, the owner of Thomas Testing, has for some time done contract work for insurance companies regarding drunk driving. To improve his research capabilities, he recently purchased the Rupple Driving Simulator. This device will allow a subject to take a "road test" and provide a score indicating the number of driving errors committed during the test drive. Higher scores indicate more driving errors. Driving errors would include not coming to a complete stop at a stop sign, not using turning signals, not exercising caution on wet or snowy pavement, and so on. During the road test, problems appear at random and not all problems appear in each road test. These are major advantages to the Rupple Driving Simulator because subjects do not gain any advantage by taking the test several times.

With the new driving simulator, Mr. Thomas would like to study in detail the problem of drunk driving. He begins by selecting a random sample of 25 drivers. He asks each of the selected individuals to take the test drive on the Rupple Driving Simulator. The number of errors for each driver is recorded. Next, he has each of the individuals in the group drink three 16-ounce cans of beer in a 60-minute period and return to the Rupple Driving Simulator for another test drive. The number of driving errors after drinking the beer is also shown.

The research question is: Does alcohol impair the driver's ability and, therefore, increase the number of driving errors?

Mr. Thomas believes the distribution of scores on the test drive does not follow a normal distribution and, therefore, a nonparametric test should be used. Because the observations are paired, he decides to use both the sign test and the Wilcoxon signed-rank test.

	Driving Errors			Driving Errors	
Subject	Without Alcohol	With Alcohol	Subject	Without Alcohol	With Alcohol
1	75	89	14	72	106
2	78	83	15	83	89
3	89	80	16	99	89
4	100	90	17	75	77
5	85	84	18	58	78
6	70	68	19	93	108
7	64	84	20	69	69
8	79	104	21	86	84
9	83	81	22	97	86
10	82	88	23	65	92
11	83	93	24	96	97
12	84	92	25	85	94
13	80	103			

a. Compare the results using these two procedures. Conduct an appropriate test of hypothesis to determine if alcohol is related to driving errors.

b. Write a report that summarizes your findings.

PRACTICE TEST

Part 1—Objective

1. The ________ level of measurement is required for the chi-square goodness-of-fit test. 1. ________
2. Which of the following is *not* a characteristic of the chi-square distribution? (positively skewed, based on degrees of freedom, cannot be negative, at least 30 observations) 2. ________
3. In a contingency table, how many traits are considered for each observation? 3. ________
4. In a contingency table, there are four rows and three columns; hence, there are ________ degrees of freedom. 4. ________
5. In a goodness-of-fit test, the critical value of chi-square is based on ________. (sample size, number of categories, number of variables, none of these) 5. ________
6. In a sign test, are the samples dependent or independent? 6. ________
7. In a sign test of eight paired observations, the test statistic is the ________ distribution. (binomial, *z*, *t*, chi-square) 7. ________
8. What is the major difference between the Kruskal-Wallis test and the Wilcoxon rank-sum test? (one is based on dependent samples and the other independent samples, one is for comparing two independent samples and the other two or more independent samples) 8. ________
9. Under what conditions can the coefficient of rank correlation be less than −1.00? 9. ________
10. The Kruskal-Wallis test is used in place of ANOVA when which two of the following criteria are not met? (normal population, equal standard deviations, more than 12 items in the sample, the populations are independent) 10. ________

Part 2—Problems

Use the standard six-step hypothesis testing procedure.

1. A recent census report indicated that 65% of families have two parents present, 20% have only a mother present, 10% have only a father present, and 5% have no parent present. A random sample of 200 children from a large rural school district revealed the following frequencies of children with two parents, mother only, father only, no parent, and the total of 200.

Two Parents	Mother Only	Father Only	No Parent	Total
120	40	30	10	200

Is there sufficient evidence to conclude that the proportion of families by type of parent present in this particular school district differs from those reported in the recent census?

2. A book publisher wants to investigate the type of books selected for recreational reading by men and women. A random sample of 540 men and 500 women provided the following information regarding their preferences for mystery, romance, or self-help books. At the .05 significance level, should we conclude that gender is related or unrelated to type of book selected?

	Mystery	Romance	Self-Help	Total
Men	250	100	190	540
Women	130	170	200	500

3. An instructor has three sections of basic statistics: 8:00 a.m., 10:00 a.m., and 1:30 p.m. Listed below are the grades on the first exam for each section. Assume that the distributions do not follow the normal probability distribution. At the .05 significance level, is there a difference in the distributions of scores?

8 a.m.	10 a.m.	1:30 p.m.
68	59	67
84	59	69
75	63	75
78	62	76
70	78	79
77	76	83
88	80	86
71		86
		87

4. According to a study in *Health Magazine,* one in three children in the United States is obese or overweight. A health practitioner in Louisiana sampled 500 children and found 210 who were obese or overweight. Does this evidence suggest that the actual proportion of obese or overweight children is more than one out of three? Use the .01 significance level.

17 Index Numbers

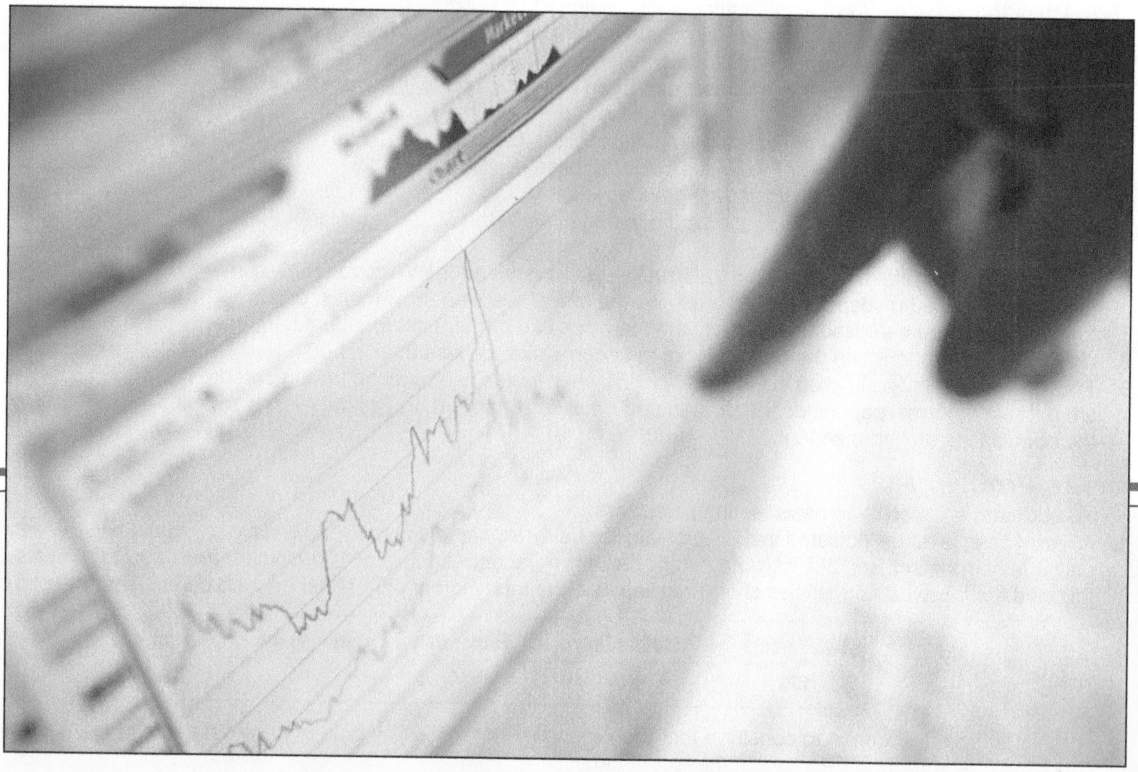

INFORMATION ON PRICES and quantities for margarine, shortening, milk, and potato chips for 2000 and 2013 is provided in Exercise 27. Compute a simple price index for each of the four items, using 2000 as the base period. (See Exercise 27 and LO17-1.)

LEARNING OBJECTIVES

When you have completed this chapter, you will be able to:

LO17-1 Compute and interpret a simple, unweighted index.

LO17-2 Compute and interpret an unweighted aggregate index.

LO17-3 Compute and interpret a weighted aggregate index.

LO17-4 List and describe special-purpose indexes.

LO17-5 Apply the Consumer Price Index.

INTRODUCTION

In this chapter, we will examine a useful descriptive tool called an **index.** An index expresses the relative change in a value from one period to another. No doubt you are familiar with indexes such as the **Consumer Price Index,** which is released monthly by the U.S. Department of Labor. There are many other indexes, such as the **Dow Jones Industrial Average** (DJIA), **NASDAQ, NIKKEI 225,** and **Standard & Poor's 500 Stock Average.** Indexes are published on a regular basis by the federal government, by business publications such as *Bloomberg Businessweek* and *Forbes,* in most daily newspapers, and on the Internet.

Of what importance is an index? Why is the Consumer Price Index so important and so widely reported? As the name implies, it measures the change in the price of a large group of items consumers purchase. The Federal Reserve Board, consumer groups, unions, management, senior citizens organizations, and others in business and economics are very concerned about changes in prices. These groups closely monitor the Consumer Price Index as well as the **Producer Price Index,** which measures price fluctuations at all stages of production. To combat sharp price increases, the Federal Reserve often raises the interest rate to "cool down" the economy. Likewise, the Dow Jones Industrial Average, which is updated continuously during the business day, describes the overall change in common stock prices of 30 large companies.

A few stock market indexes appear daily in the financial section of most newspapers. Many are also reported in real time. Shown below are the Dow Jones Industrial Average, NASDAQ, and other indexes from the Yahoo.com website. (http://financeyahoo.com).

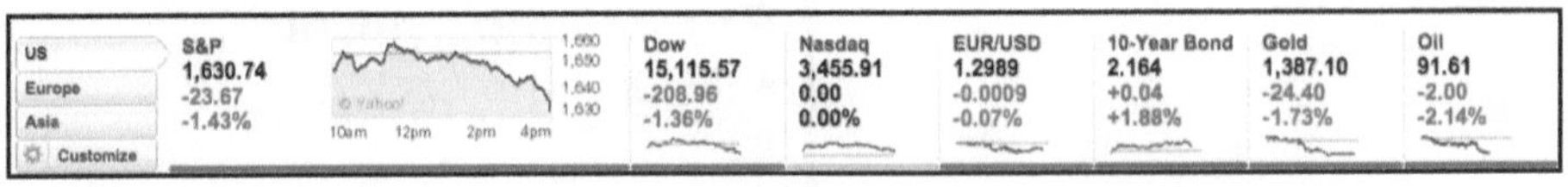

LO17-1
Compute and interpret a simple, unweighted index.

SIMPLE INDEX NUMBERS

What is an index number? An index or index number measures the change in a particular item (typically a product or service) between two time periods.

> **INDEX NUMBER** A number that expresses the relative change in price, quantity, or value compared to a base period.

If the index number is used to measure the relative change in just one variable, such as hourly wages in manufacturing, we refer to this as a simple index. It is the ratio of two variables converted to a percentage. The following four examples illustrate the use of index numbers. As noted in the definition, the main use of an index number in business is to show the percent change in one or more items from one time period to another.

EXAMPLE

According to the Bureau of Labor Statistics, in 2000 the average hourly earnings of production workers was \$14.02. In 2013, it was \$24.92. What is the index of hourly earnings of production workers for 2013 based on 2000 data?

SOLUTION

It is 177.75, found by:

$$P = \frac{\text{Average hourly earnings in 2013}}{\text{Average hourly earnings in 2000}}(100) = \frac{\$24.92}{\$14.02}(100) = 177.75$$

Thus, the hourly earnings in 2013 compared to 2000 were 177.75%. This means there was a 77.75% increase in hourly earnings during the period, found by 177.75 − 100.0 = 77.75.

You can check the latest information on wages, the Consumer Price Indexes, and other business-related values at the Bureau of Labor Statistics (BLS) website, http://www.bls.gov. The following chart shows some statistics from the BLS.

EXAMPLE

An index can also compare one item with another. The population of the Canadian province of British Columbia in 2012 was 4,606,451, and for Ontario it was 13,472,438. What is the population index of British Columbia compared to Ontario?

SOLUTION

The index of population for British Columbia is 34.4, found by:

$$P = \frac{\text{Population of British Columbia}}{\text{Population of Ontario}}(100) = \frac{4{,}606{,}451}{13{,}472{,}438}(100) = 34.2$$

This indicates that the population of British Columbia is 34.2% (about one-third) of the population of Ontario, or the population of British Columbia is 65.8% less than the population of Ontario (100 − 34.2 = 65.8).

EXAMPLE

The following chart shows the number of passengers (in millions) for the 10 busiest airports in the United States in 2011. Use the George Bush Intercontinental Airport in Houston as the base. What is the index for the other airports compared to Houston?

Rank	Airport	Passengers (mil)	Index
1	Hartsfield-Jackson Atlanta International Airport	92.3	230.2
2	O'Hare International Airport (Chicago)	66.7	166.3
3	Los Angeles International Airport	61.9	154.4
4	Dallas-Fort Worth International Airport	57.7	143.9
5	Denver International Airport	52.9	131.9
6	John F. Kennedy International Airport (New York)	47.7	119.0
7	San Francisco International Airport	40.8	101.7
8	Phoenix Sky Harbor International Airport	40.6	101.2
9	McCarran International Airport (Las Vegas)	40.6	101.2
10	George Bush Intercontinental Airport (Houston)	40.1	100.0

Number of Passengers at the Ten Busiest Airports

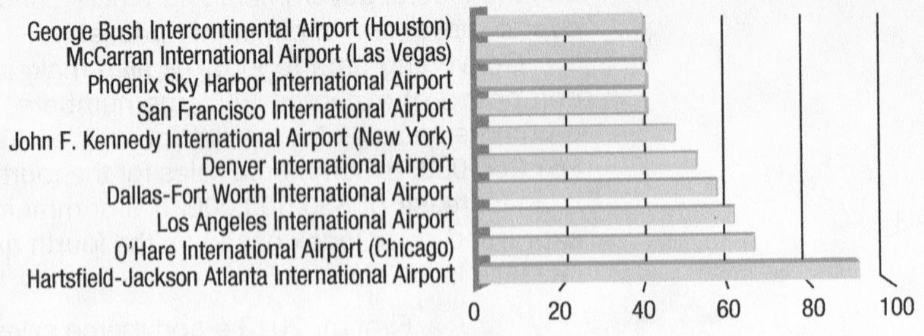

SOLUTION

To find the 10 indexes, we divide the passengers for Houston into the passengers for the other nine airports. So the index for Atlanta is 230.2, found by

(92.3/40.1)*(100). The index for San Francisco International is 101.7, found by (40.8/40.1)*(100). So Atlanta has 130.2% more passengers than Houston and San Francisco has 1.7% more than Houston. The chart on the previous page summarizes the indexes. The chart reveals that Houston, Las Vegas, Phoenix, and San Francisco all served about the same number of passengers in 2011 (all four of the indexes are close to 100) as compared to the George Bush Intercontinental Airport. Atlanta, on the other hand, served more than twice as many passengers in the same year.

Note from the previous discussion that:

1. The index of average hourly earnings of production workers (177.75) is a percentage, but the percent symbol is usually omitted.
2. Indexes have either a **base** or a **base period.** In the example/solution regarding the average hourly earnings of production workers, we used 2000 as the base period. The Consumer Price Index uses 1982–84 as the base period. In contrast, in the example/solution about airport passengers, the George Bush International Airport in Houston was used as the base for comparison.
3. Most business and economic indexes are reported to the nearest whole number, such as 214 or 96, or to the nearest tenth of a percent, such as 83.4 or 118.7.

Why Convert Data to Indexes?

Compiling index numbers is not a recent innovation. An Italian, G. R. Carli, is credited with originating index numbers in 1764. They were incorporated in a report he made regarding price fluctuations in Europe from 1500 to 1750. No systematic approach to collecting and reporting data in index form was evident in the United States until about 1900. The cost-of-living index (now called the Consumer Price Index) was introduced in 1913, and a long list of indexes has been compiled since then.

Why convert data to indexes? An index is a convenient way to express a change in a diverse group of items. The Consumer Price Index (CPI), for example, encompasses 200 categories of items summarized by 8 groups—food and beverages, housing, apparel, transportation, medical care, recreation, education and communication, and other goods and services. The prices of 80,000 goods and services in the 200 categories are collected. Prices are expressed in many different units such as dollars per pound or a dozen eggs. Only by summarizing these prices with an index number can the federal government and others concerned with inflation keep informed of the overall movement of consumer prices.

Converting data to indexes also makes it easier to assess the trend in a series composed of exceptionally large numbers. For example, the estimate of U.S. retail e-commerce sales for the first quarter of 2013, adjusted for seasonal variation, was \$61,200,000. e-Commerce sales for the fourth quarter of 2009 were \$30,700,000. This is an increase of \$30,500,000. If e-commerce sales for the first quarter of 2013 are expressed as an index based on the fourth quarter of 2009, the index is 199.3 and the increase is 99.3%.

$$\text{Index} = \frac{\text{First qtr 2013 e-commerce sales}}{\text{Fourth qtr 2009 e-commerce sales}}(100) = \frac{\$61{,}200{,}000}{\$30{,}700{,}000}(100) = 199.3$$

Construction of Index Numbers

We already discussed the construction of a simple price index. The price in a selected year (such as 2014) is divided by the price in the base year. The base-period price is designated as p_0, and a price other than the base period is often referred to as the

given period or *selected period* and designated p_t. To calculate the simple price index P using 100 as the base value for any given period, use the formula:

SIMPLE INDEX $$P = \frac{p_t}{p_0} \times 100 \qquad [17\text{–}1]$$

Suppose the price of a fall weekend package (including lodging and all meals) at Tryon Mountain Lodge in western North Carolina in 2000 was \$450. The price rose to \$795 in 2013. What is the price index for 2013 using 2000 as the base period and 100 as the base value? It is 176.7, found by:

$$P = \frac{p_t}{p_0}(100) = \frac{\$795}{\$450}(100) = 176.7$$

Interpreting this result, the price of the fall weekend package increased 76.7% from 2000 to 2013.

The base period need not be a single year. Note in Table 17–1 that if we use 2000–01 = 100, the base price for the stapler would be \$21 [found by determining the mean price of 2000 and 2001, (\$20 + \$22)/2 = \$21]. The prices \$20, \$22, and \$23 are averaged if 2000–02 is selected as the base. The mean price would be \$21.67. The indexes constructed using the three different base periods are presented in Table 17–1. (Note that when 2000–02 = 100, the index numbers for 2000, 2001, and 2002 average 100.0, as we would expect.) Logically, the index numbers for 2010 using the three different bases are not the same.

TABLE 17–1 Prices of a Benson Automatic Stapler, Model 3, Converted to Indexes Using Three Different Base Periods

Year	Price of Stapler	Price Index (2000 = 100)	Price Index (2000–01 = 100)	Price Index (2000–02 = 100)
1995	\$18	90.0	$\frac{18}{21} \times 100 = 85.7$	$\frac{18}{21.67} \times 100 = 83.1$
2000	20	100.0	$\frac{20}{21} \times 100 = 95.2$	$\frac{20}{21.67} \times 100 = 92.3$
2001	22	110.0	$\frac{22}{21} \times 100 = 104.8$	$\frac{22}{21.67} \times 100 = 101.5$
2002	23	115.0	$\frac{23}{21} \times 100 = 109.5$	$\frac{23}{21.67} \times 100 = 106.1$
2010	38	190.0	$\frac{38}{21} \times 100 = 181.0$	$\frac{38}{21.67} \times 100 = 175.4$

SELF-REVIEW 17–1

1. Listed below are the top steel-producing countries for the year 2012 (http://www.worldsteel.org). Express the amount produced by China, Japan, India, and Russia as an index, using the United States as a base. What percent more steel does China produce than the United States?

Country	Amount (millions of tons)
China	716.5
Japan	107.2
United States	88.7
India	77.6
Russia	70.4

2. The average hourly earnings of production workers for selected years are given below.

Year	Average Hourly Earnings
1995	$11.65
2000	14.02
2005	16.13
2013	19.97

(a) Using 1995 as the base period and 100 as the base value, determine the indexes for the other years. Interpret the index.
(b) Use the average of 1995 and 2000 as the base and determine indexes for the other years. Interpret the index.

EXERCISES

1. PNC Bank Inc., which has its headquarters in Pittsburgh, reported $17,446 (million) in commercial loans in 1995, $19,989 in 1997, $21,468 in 1999, $21,685 in 2000, $15,922 in 2002, $18,375 in 2004, $54,818 in 2009, and $83,040 in 2012. Using 1995 as the base, develop a simple index of commercial loans for the years 2002, 2004, 2009, and 2012.
2. The table below reports the earnings per share of common stock for Home Depot Inc. for 2003 through 2012. Develop an index, with 2003 as the base, for earnings per share for years 2004 through 2012.

For **DATA FILE**, please visit www.mhhe.com/lind16e

Year	Earnings per Share	Year	Earnings per Share
2003	1.56	2008	2.37
2004	1.88	2009	1.34
2005	2.26	2010	1.57
2006	2.72	2011	2.01
2007	2.79	2012	2.47

3. Listed below are the net sales for a San Francisco–area mail-order retailer for the years 2003 to 2012. Use the mean sales for the earliest three years to determine a base and then find the index for 2011 and 2012. By how much have net sales increased from the base period?

For **DATA FILE**, please visit www.mhhe.com/lind16e

Year	Sales (millions)	Year	Sales (millions)
2003	$486.6	2008	$568.5
2004	506.8	2009	581.9
2005	522.2	2010	496.1
2006	574.6	2011	456.6
2007	580.7	2012	433.3

4. In January 2003, the price for a whole fresh chicken was $1.004 per pound. In January 2013, the price for the same chicken was $1.497 per pound. Use the January 2003 price as the base period and 100 as the base value to develop a simple index. By what percent has the cost of chicken increased?

LO17-2 Compute and interpret an unweighted aggregate index.

UNWEIGHTED INDEXES

In many situations, we wish to combine several items and develop an index to compare the cost of this aggregation of items in two different time periods. For example, we might be interested in an index for items that relate to the expense of operating and maintaining an automobile. The items in the index might include tires, oil changes, and gasoline prices. Or we might be interested in a college student index. This index

might include the cost of books, tuition, housing, meals, and entertainment. There are several ways we can combine the items to determine the index.

Simple Average of the Price Indexes

Table 17–2 reports the prices for several food items for 2003 and 2013. We would like to develop an index for this group of food items for 2013, using the 2003 prices as the base. This is written in the abbreviated code 2003 = 100.

TABLE 17–2 Computation of the Index for Various Food Items, 2003 = 100

Item	2003 Price	2013 Price	Simple Index
Bread, white, cost per pound	$1.042	$1.422	136.5
Eggs, dozen	1.175	1.933	164.5
Milk, gallon, white	2.686	3.526	131.3
Apples, Red Delicious, 1 pound	0.911	1.350	148.2
Orange juice, 12 oz. concentrate	1.848	2.511	135.9
Coffee, 100% ground roast, 1 pound	2.999	5.902	196.8
Total	$10.661	$16.644	

We could begin by computing a **simple average** of the price indexes for each item using 2003 as the base. The simple index for bread is 136.5, found by using formula (17–1).

$$P = \frac{p_t}{p_0}(100) = \frac{1.422}{1.042}(100) = 136.5$$

We compute the simple index for the other items in Table 17–2 similarly. The largest price increase was 96.8% for coffee, and eggs were second at 64.5%.

We can also determine the percentage change in the group of foods by averaging the simple indexes. The formula is:

SIMPLE AVERAGE OF THE PRICE RELATIVES
$$P = \frac{\Sigma P_i}{n} \quad [17\text{–}2]$$

where P_i refers to the simple index for each of the items and n the number of items. In our example, the index is 152.2, found by:

$$P = \frac{\Sigma P_i}{n} = \frac{136.5 + \cdots + 196.8}{6} = \frac{913.2}{6} = 152.2$$

This indicates that the mean price of the group of food items increased 52.2% from 2003 to 2013.

A positive feature of the simple average of price indexes is that we would obtain the same value for the index regardless of the units of measure. In the above index, if apples were priced in tons, instead of pounds, the impact of apples on the combined index would not change. That is, the commodity "apples" represents one of six items in the index, so the impact of the item is not related to the units. A negative feature of this index is that it fails to consider the relative importance of the items included in the index. For example, milk and eggs receive the same weight, even though a typical family might spend far more over the year on milk than on eggs.

Simple Aggregate Index

A second possibility is to sum the prices (rather than the indexes) for the two periods and then determine the index based on the totals. The formula is:

SIMPLE AGGREGATE INDEX $$P = \frac{\Sigma p_t}{\Sigma p_0} \times 100 \quad [17\text{–}3]$$

This is called a **simple aggregate index.** The index for the food items on the previous page is found by dividing the sum of the prices in 2013 by the sum of the prices in 2003. The sum of the prices for the base period is \$10.661 and for the given period it is \$16.644. The simple aggregate index is 156.1. This means that the aggregate group of prices had increased 56.1% in the 10-year period.

$$P = \frac{\Sigma p_t}{\Sigma p_0}(100) = \frac{\$16.644}{\$10.661}(100) = 156.1$$

Because the value of a simple aggregate index can be influenced by the units of measurement, it is not used frequently. In our example, the value of the index would differ significantly if we were to report the price of apples in tons rather than pounds. Also, note the effect of coffee on the total index. For both the current year and the base year, coffee is a significant contributor to the total index, so the current price of coffee will drive the index much more than any other item. Therefore, we need a way to appropriately "weight" the items according to their relative importance.

LO17-3
Compute and interpret a weighted aggregate index.

WEIGHTED INDEXES

Two methods of computing a **weighted price index** are the **Laspeyres** method and the **Paasche** method. They differ only in the period used for weighting. The Laspeyres method uses *base-period weights;* that is, the original prices and quantities of the purchased items are used to find the percent change over a period of time in either price or quantity consumed, depending on the problem. The Paasche method uses *current-year weights*.

Laspeyres Price Index

Etienne Laspeyres developed a method in the latter part of the 18th century to determine a weighted price index using base-period quantities as weights. Applying his method, a weighted price index is computed by:

LASPEYRES PRICE INDEX $$P = \frac{\Sigma p_t q_0}{\Sigma p_0 q_0} \times 100 \quad [17\text{–}4]$$

where:

P is the price index.
p_t is the current price.
p_0 is the price in the base period.
q_0 is the quantity used in the base period.

EXAMPLE

The prices for the six food items from Table 17–2 are repeated on the following page in Table 17–3. Also included is the typical number of units consumed by a family in 2003 and 2013.

TABLE 17–3 Price and Quantity of Food Items in 2003 and 2013

	2003		2013	
Item	**Price**	**Quantity**	**Price**	**Quantity**
Bread, white, cost per pound	$1.042	50	$1.422	55
Eggs, dozen	1.175	26	1.933	20
Milk, gallon, white	2.686	102	3.526	130
Apples, Red Delicious, 1 pound	0.911	30	1.350	40
Orange juice, 12 oz. concentrate	1.848	40	2.511	41
Coffee, 100% ground roast, 1 pound	2.999	12	5.902	12

Determine a weighted price index using the Laspeyres method. Interpret the result.

SOLUTION

First we determine the total amount spent for the six items in the base period, 2003. To find this value, we multiply the base period, 2003, price for bread $1.042 by the base period, 2003, quantity of 50. The result is $52.10. This indicates that a total of $52.10 was spent in the base period on bread. We continue that for all items and total the results. The base period total is $493.86. The current period total is computed in a similar fashion. For the first item, bread, we multiply the quantity in 2003 by the price of bread in 2013, that is, $1.422(50). The result is $71.10. We make the same calculation for each item and total the results. The total is $692.77. Because of the repetitive nature of these calculations, a spreadsheet is very useful for creating the following table.

Laspeyres Index

	2003		03 Price*	2013		13 Price*
Item	**Price**	**Quantity**	**03 Quantity**	**Price**	**Quantity**	**03 Quantity**
Bread, white, cost per pound	$1.042	50	$ 52.10	$1.422	55	$ 71.10
Eggs, dozen	1.175	26	30.55	1.933	20	50.26
Milk, gallon, white	2.686	102	273.97	3.526	130	359.65
Apples, Red Delicious, 1 pound	0.911	30	27.33	1.350	40	40.50
Orange juice, 12 oz. concentrate	1.848	40	73.92	2.511	41	100.44
Coffee, 100% ground roast, 1 pound	2.999	12	35.99	5.902	12	70.82
			$493.86			$692.77
				Index		140.28

The weighted price index for 2013 is 140.28, found by

$$P = \frac{\Sigma p_t q_0}{\Sigma p_0 q_0}(100) = \frac{\$692.77}{\$493.86}(100) = 140.28$$

Based on this analysis, we conclude that the price of this group of items has increased 40.28% in the 10-year period. The advantage of this method over the simple aggregate index is that the weight of each of the items is considered. In the simple aggregate index, coffee had about 40% of the weight in determining the index. In the Laspeyres index, the item with the most weight is milk because the product of the price and the units sold is the largest.

Paasche Price Index

The major disadvantage of the Laspeyres index is it assumes that the base-period quantities are still realistic in the given period. That is, the quantities used for the six items are about the same in 2003 as 2013. In this case, the quantity of eggs purchased declined by 23%, the quantity of milk increased by nearly 28%, and the quantity of apples increased by 33%.

The Paasche index is an alternative. The procedure is similar, but instead of using base-period quantities as weights, we use current-period quantities as weights. We use the sum of the products of the 2003 prices and the 2013 quantities. This has the advantage of using the more recent quantities. If there has been a change in the quantities consumed since the base period, such a change is reflected in the Paasche index.

PAASCHE PRICE INDEX $$P = \frac{\Sigma p_t q_t}{\Sigma p_0 q_t} \times 100 \qquad [17\text{–}5]$$

EXAMPLE

Use the information from Table 17–3 to determine the Paasche index. Discuss which of the indexes should be used.

SOLUTION

The following table shows the calculations to determine the Paasche index. Because of the repetitive calculations, Excel is very useful to compute the index.

Paasche Index

	2003		03 Price*	2013		13 Price*
Item	Price	Quantity	13 Quantity	Price	Quantity	13 Quantity
Bread, white, cost per pound	$1.042	50	$ 57.31	$1.422	55	$ 78.21
Eggs, dozen	1.175	26	23.50	1.933	20	38.66
Milk, gallon, white	2.686	102	349.18	3.526	130	458.38
Apples, Red Delicious, 1 pound	0.911	30	36.44	1.350	40	54.00
Orange juice, 12 oz. concentrate	1.848	40	75.77	2.511	41	102.95
Coffee, 100% ground roast, 1 pound	2.999	12	35.99	5.902	12	70.82
			$578.19	Index	138.9	$803.03

The Paasche index is 138.9, found by

$$P = \frac{\Sigma p_t q_t}{\Sigma p_0 q_t}(100) = \frac{\$803.03}{\$578.19}(100) = 138.9$$

This result indicates that there has been an increase of 38.9% in the price of this "market basket" of goods between 2003 and 2013. That is, it costs 38.9% more to purchase these items in 2013 than it did in 2003.

How do we decide which index to use? When is Laspeyres most appropriate and when is Paasche the better choice?

Laspeyres

Advantages	Requires quantity data from only the base period. This allows a more meaningful comparison over time. The changes in the index can be attributed to changes in the price.
Disadvantages	Does not reflect changes in buying patterns over time. Also, it may overweight goods whose prices increase.

Paasche

Advantages	Because it uses quantities from the current period, it reflects current buying habits.
Disadvantages	It requires quantity data for the current year. Because different quantities are used each year, it is impossible to attribute changes in the index to changes in price alone. It tends to overweight the goods whose prices have declined. It requires the product of prices and quantities to be recomputed each year.

Fisher's Ideal Index

As noted earlier, Laspeyres' index tends to overweight goods whose prices have increased. Paasche's index, on the other hand, tends to overweight goods whose prices have decreased. In an attempt to offset these shortcomings, Irving Fisher, in his book *The Making of Index Numbers,* published in 1922, proposed an index called **Fisher's ideal index.** It is the geometric mean of the Laspeyres and Paasche indexes. We described the geometric mean in Chapter 3. It is determined by taking the kth root of the product of k positive numbers.

$$\text{Fisher's ideal index} = \sqrt{(\text{Laspeyres index})(\text{Paasche index})} \qquad \textbf{[17–6]}$$

Fisher's index seems to be theoretically ideal because it combines the best features of the Laspeyres and Paasche indexes. That is, it balances the effects of the two indexes. However, it is rarely used in practice because it has the same basic set of problems as the Paasche index. It requires that a new set of quantities be determined for each period.

EXAMPLE

Determine Fisher's ideal index for the data in Table 17–3.

SOLUTION

Fisher's ideal index is 139.6.

$$\begin{aligned}\text{Fisher's ideal index} &= \sqrt{(\text{Laspeyres index})(\text{Paasche index})}\\ &= \sqrt{(140.3)(138.9)} = 139.6\end{aligned}$$

SELF-REVIEW 17–2

Construct an index of clothing prices for 2013 based on 2000. The clothing items considered are shoes and dresses. The prices and quantities for both years are given below. Use 2000 as the base period and 100 as the base value.

	2000		2013	
Item	**Price**	**Quantity**	**Price**	**Quantity**
Dress (each)	$75	500	$85	520
Shoes (pair)	40	1,200	45	1,300

(a) Determine the simple average of the price indexes.
(b) Determine the aggregate price index for the two years.
(c) Determine Laspeyres price index.
(d) Determine the Paasche price index.
(e) Determine Fisher's ideal index.

EXERCISES

For exercises 5–8:

a. Determine the simple price indexes.
b. Determine the simple aggregate price index for the two years.
c. Determine Laspeyres price index.
d. Determine the Paasche price index.
e. Determine Fisher's ideal index.

5. Below are the prices of toothpaste (9 oz.), shampoo (7 oz.), cough tablets (package of 100), and antiperspirant (2 oz.) for August 2000 and August 2013. Also included are the quantity purchased. Use August 2000 as the base.

For **DATA FILE**, please visit www.mhhe.com/lind16e

	August 2000		August 2013	
Item	**Price**	**Quantity**	**Price**	**Quantity**
Toothpaste	$2.49	6	$3.35	6
Shampoo	3.29	4	4.49	5
Cough tablets	1.59	2	4.19	3
Antiperspirant	1.79	3	2.49	4

6. Fruit prices and the amounts consumed for 2000 and 2014 are below. Use 2000 as the base.

For **DATA FILE**, please visit www.mhhe.com/lind16e

	2000		2014	
Fruit	**Price**	**Quantity**	**Price**	**Quantity**
Bananas (pound)	$0.23	100	$0.69	120
Grapefruit (each)	0.29	50	1.00	55
Apples (pound)	0.35	85	1.89	85
Strawberries (basket)	1.02	8	3.79	10
Oranges (bag)	0.89	6	2.99	8

7. The prices and the numbers of various items produced by a small machine and stamping plant are reported below. Use 2000 as the base.

For **DATA FILE**, please visit www.mhhe.com/lind16e

	2000		2014	
Item	**Price**	**Quantity**	**Price**	**Quantity**
Washer	$0.07	17,000	$0.10	20,000
Cotter pin	0.04	125,000	0.03	130,000
Stove bolt	0.15	40,000	0.15	42,000
Hex nut	0.08	62,000	0.10	65,000

8. Following are the quantities and prices for the years 2000 and 2014 for Kinzua Valley Geriatrics. Use 2000 as the base period.

For **DATA FILE**, please visit www.mhhe.com/lind16e

	2000		2014	
Item	**Price**	**Quantity**	**Price**	**Quantity**
Syringes (dozen)	$ 6.10	1,500	$ 6.83	2,000
Thermometers	8.10	10	9.35	12
Advil (bottle)	4.00	250	4.62	250
Patient record forms (box)	6.00	1,000	6.85	900
Computer paper (box)	12.00	30	13.65	40

Value Index

A **value index** measures changes in both the price and quantities involved. A value index, such as the index of department store sales, considers the base-year prices, the base-year quantities, the present-year prices, and the present-year quantities for its construction. Its formula is:

VALUE INDEX
$$V = \frac{\Sigma p_t q_t}{\Sigma p_0 q_0} \times 100 \quad [17\text{–}7]$$

EXAMPLE

The prices and quantities sold at the Waleska Clothing Emporium for ties, suits, and shoes for May 2000 and May 2014 are:

	2000		2014	
Item	**Price** p_0	**Quantity** q_0	**Price** p_t	**Quantity** q_t
Ties (each)	$ 1.00	1,000	$ 2	900
Suits (each)	30.00	100	40	120
Shoes (pair)	10.00	500	8	500

What is the index of value for May 2014 using May 2000 as the base period?

SOLUTION

Total sales in May 2014 were $10,600 and the comparable figure for 2000 is $9,000. (See Table 17–4.) Thus, the value index for May 2014 using 2000 = 100 is 117.8. The value of apparel sales in 2014 was 117.8% of the 2000 sales. To put it another way, the value of apparel sales increased 17.8% from May 2000 to May 2014.

$$V = \frac{\Sigma p_t q_t}{\Sigma p_0 q_0}(100) = \frac{\$10{,}600}{\$9{,}000}(100) = 117.8$$

TABLE 17–4 Construction of Value Index for 2014 (2000 = 100)

	2000			2014		
Item	**Price** p_0	**Quantity** q_0	**$** p_0q_0	**Price** p_t	**Quantity** q_t	**$** p_tq_t
Ties (each)	$ 1.00	1,000	$1,000	$ 2.00	900	$ 1,800.00
Suits (each)	30.00	100	3,000	40.00	120	4,800.00
Shoes (pair)	10.00	500	5,000	8.00	500	4,000.00
Total			$9,000	Index = 117.8		$10,600.00

SELF-REVIEW 17–3

The number of items produced by Houghton Products for 2001 and 2013 and the wholesale prices for the two periods are:

Item Produced	Price 2001	Price 2013	Number Produced 2001	Number Produced 2013
Shear pins (box)	$ 3	$4	10,000	9,000
Cutting compound (pound)	1	5	600	200
Tie rods (each)	10	8	3,000	5,000

(a) Find the value index of production for 2013 using 2001 as the base period.
(b) Interpret the index.

EXERCISES

For **DATA FILE**, please visit www.mhhe.com/lind16e

9. The prices and production of grains for 2002 and 2012 (http://www.ers.usda.gov) are listed below.

Grain	2002 Price Per Bushel	2002 Production (millions of bushels)	2012 Price Per Bushel	2012 Production (millions of bushels)
Oats	$1.81	116	$3.8	64
Wheat	3.56	2	7.9	2
Corn	2.32	8,967	6.9	10,780
Barley	2.72	227	6.4	220

Using 2002 as the base period, find the value index of grains produced for August 2012.

For **DATA FILE**, please visit www.mhhe.com/lind16e

10. Johnson Wholesale Company manufactures a variety of products. The prices and quantities produced for April 2000 and April 2013 are:

Product	2000 Price	2013 Price	2000 Quantity Produced	2013 Quantity Produced
Small motor (each)	$23.60	$28.80	1,760	4,259
Scrubbing compound (gallon)	2.96	3.08	86,450	62,949
Nails (pound)	0.40	0.48	9,460	22,370

Using April 2000 as the base period, find the value index of goods produced for April 2013.

LO17-4 List and describe special-purpose indexes.

SPECIAL-PURPOSE INDEXES

Many important indexes are prepared and published by private organizations. J. D. Power & Associates surveys automobile purchasers to determine how satisfied customers are with their vehicle after one year of ownership. This special index is called the *Consumer Satisfaction Index.* Financial institutions, utility companies, and university research centers often prepare indexes on employment, factory hours and wages, and retail sales for the regions they serve. Many trade associations prepare indexes of price and quantity that are vital to their particular area of interest. How are these special indexes prepared? An example, simplified of course, will help to explain some of the details.

EXAMPLE

The Seattle Chamber of Commerce wants to develop a measure of general business activity for the northwest portion of the United States. The director of economic development has been assigned to develop the index. It will be called the *General Business Activity Index of the Northwest.*

SOLUTION

After considerable thought and research, the director concluded that four factors should be considered: the regional department store sales (which are reported in $ millions), the regional employment index (which has a 2005 base and is reported by the State of Washington), the freight car loadings (reported in millions), and exports for the Seattle Harbor (reported in thousands of tons). Table 17–5 shows this information for years 2005, 2010, and 2013.

TABLE 17–5 Data for Computation of the General Business Activity Index of the Northwest

Year	Department Store Sales	Index of Employment	Freight Car Loadings	Exports
2005	20	100	50	500
2010	41	110	30	900
2013	44	125	18	700

After review and consultation, the director assigned weights of 40% to department store sales, 30% to employment, 10% to freight car loadings, and 20% to exports. To develop the General Business Activity Index of the Northwest for 2013 using 2005 = 100, each 2013 value is expressed as a percentage, with the base-period value as the denominator. For illustration, department store sales for 2013 are converted to a percentage by ($44/$20)(100) = 220. This means that department store sales have increased 120% in the period. This percentage is then multiplied by the appropriate weight. For the department store sales, this is (220)(.40) = 88.0. The details of the calculations for the years 2010 and 2013 are shown below.

	2010	2013
Department store sales	[($41)/($20)][100][.40] = 82.0	[($44)/($20)][100][.40] = 88.0
Index of employment	[(110)/(100)][100][.30] = 33.0	[(125)/(100)][100][.30] = 37.5
Freight car loadings	[(30)/(50)][100][.10] = 6.0	[(18)/(50)][100][.10] = 3.6
Experts	[(900)/(500)][100][.20] = 36.0	[(700)/(500)][100][.20] = 28.0
Total	157.0	157.1

The General Business Activity Index of the Northwest for 2010 is 157.0 and for 2013 it is 157.1. Interpreting, business activity has increased 57.0% from 2005 to 2010 and 57.1% from the base period of 2005 to 2013.

As we stated at the start of the section, there are many special-purpose indexes. Here are a few examples.

Consumer Price Index

The U.S. Bureau of Labor Statistics reports this index monthly. It describes the changes in prices from one period to another for a "market basket" of goods and services. We discuss its history in detail and present some applications in the next section. You can access this information by going to http://www.bls.gov, then under

Databases & Tools select **Inflation and Prices,** then select **All Urban Consumers (Current Series), Top Picks,** and then click on **U.S. All items 1982–84 = 100.** You may elect to include different periods. Following is a recent summary report.

UNITED STATES DEPARTMENT OF LABOR

BUREAU OF LABOR STATISTICS

Home ▾ Subject Areas ▾ Databases & Tools ▾ Publications ▾ Economic Releases ▾ Beta ▾

Databases, Tables & Calculators by Subject

Change Output Options: From: 2003 To: 2013 GO

☐ include graphs

Data extracted on: June 3, 2013 (12:35:29 PM)

Consumer Price Index - All Urban Consumers

```
Series Id:    CUUR0000SA0
Not Seasonally Adjusted
Area:         U.S. city average
Item:         All items
Base Period:  1982-84=100
```

Download: .xls

Year	Jan	Feb	Mar	Apr	May	Jun	Jul	Aug	Sep	Oct	Nov	Dec	Annual	HALF1	HALF2
2003	181.7	183.1	184.2	183.8	183.5	183.7	183.9	184.6	185.2	185.0	184.5	184.3	184.0	183.3	184.6
2004	185.2	186.2	187.4	188.0	189.1	189.7	189.4	189.5	189.9	190.9	191.0	190.3	188.9	187.6	190.2
2005	190.7	191.8	193.3	194.6	194.4	194.5	195.4	196.4	198.8	199.2	197.6	196.8	195.3	193.2	197.4
2006	198.3	198.7	199.8	201.5	202.5	202.9	203.5	203.9	202.9	201.8	201.5	201.8	201.6	200.6	202.6
2007	202.416	203.499	205.352	206.686	207.949	208.352	208.299	207.917	208.490	208.936	210.177	210.036	207.342	205.709	208.976
2008	211.080	211.693	213.528	214.823	216.632	218.815	219.964	219.086	218.783	216.573	212.425	210.228	215.303	214.429	216.177
2009	211.143	212.193	212.709	213.240	213.856	215.693	215.351	215.834	215.969	216.177	216.330	215.949	214.537	213.139	215.935
2010	216.687	216.741	217.631	218.009	218.178	217.965	218.011	218.312	218.439	218.711	218.803	219.179	218.056	217.535	218.576
2011	220.223	221.309	223.467	224.906	225.964	225.722	225.922	226.545	226.889	226.421	226.230	225.672	224.939	223.598	226.280
2012	226.665	227.663	229.392	230.085	229.815	229.478	229.104	230.379	231.407	231.317	230.221	229.601	229.594	228.850	230.338
2013	230.280	232.166	232.773	232.531											

Producer Price Index

Formerly called the Wholesale Price Index, it dates back to 1890 and is also published by the U.S. Bureau of Labor Statistics. It reflects the prices of over 3,400 commodities. Price data are collected from the sellers of the commodities, and it usually refers to the first large-volume transaction for each commodity. It is a Laspeyres-type index. To access this information, go to http://www.bls.gov, then **Databases & Tools.** Select **Inflation and Prices,** then select **Commodity Data, Top Picks,** and finally select **Finished Goods.** You may select to include different periods. Below is a recent output.

UNITED STATES DEPARTMENT OF LABOR

BUREAU OF LABOR STATISTICS

Home ▾ Subject Areas ▾ Databases & Tools ▾ Publications ▾ Economic Releases ▾ Beta ▾

Databases, Tables & Calculators by Subject

Change Output Options: From: 2003 To: 2013

☐ include graphs

Data extracted on: June 3, 2013 (12:33:45 PM)

Producer Price Index-Commodities

```
Series Id:   WPUSOP3000
Not Seasonally Adjusted
Group:       Stage of processing
Item:        Finished goods
Base Date:   198200
```

Download: .xls

Year	Jan	Feb	Mar	Apr	May	Jun	Jul	Aug	Sep	Oct	Nov	Dec	Annual
2003	140.8	142.3	144.2	142.1	142.0	143.0	143.0	143.7	144.0	145.5	144.5	144.5	143.3
2004	145.4	145.3	146.3	147.3	148.9	148.7	148.5	148.5	148.7	152.0	151.7	150.6	148.5
2005	151.4	152.1	153.6	154.4	154.3	154.2	155.5	156.3	158.9	160.9	158.3	158.7	155.7
2006	159.9	158.0	159.1	160.7	161.2	161.8	161.7	162.3	160.3	158.9	159.8	160.5	160.4
2007	160.1	161.8	164.1	165.9	167.5	167.2	168.5	166.1	167.4	168.6	171.4	170.4	166.6
2008	172.0	172.3	175.1	176.5	179.8	182.4	185.1	182.2	182.2	177.4	172.0	168.8	177.1
2009	170.4	169.9	169.1	170.3	171.1	174.3	172.4	174.2	173.2	173.8	175.7(R)	176.0	172.5
2010	178.0	177.0	179.1	179.5	179.8	179.0	179.5	179.9	180.0	181.2	181.6	182.6	179.8
2011	184.4	186.6	189.1	191.4	192.5	191.4	192.2	191.7	192.6	191.8	191.7	191.1	190.5
2012	192.0	192.9	194.4	194.9	193.7	192.8	193.2	195.4	196.7	196.3	194.5	193.7	194.2
2013	194.7(P)	196.2(P)	196.6(P)	196.0(P)									

R : Revised

P : Preliminary. All indexes are subject to revision four months after original publication.

Dow Jones Industrial Average (DJIA)

This is an index of stock prices, but perhaps it would be better to say it is an "indicator" rather than an index. It is supposed to be the mean price of 30 specific industrial stocks. However, summing the 30 stock prices and dividing by 30 does not calculate its value. This is because of stock splits, mergers, and stocks being added or dropped. When changes occur, adjustments are made in the denominator used with the average. Today the DJIA is more of a psychological indicator than a representation of the general price movement on the New York Stock Exchange. The lack of representativeness of the stocks on the DJIA is one of the reasons for the development of the **New York Stock Exchange Index.** This index was developed as an average price of *all* stocks on the New York Stock Exchange. More information about the Dow Jones Industrial Average is available by going to the website: http://www.dowjones.com. You can find the current value of the DJIA by going to http://www.marketwatch.com. The default is to show the change in the Dow, NASDAQ, S&P 500, and others for the current day.

	PRICE	1 YEAR CHG	
Dow	15,401	+1822	13.41%
Nasdaq	3,765	+604	19.12%
S&P 500	1,702	+245	16.82%
GlobalDow	2,337	+375	19.08%
Gold	1,327	-450	25.31%
Oil	103.42	+10.85	11.72%

By clicking on **Dow** you can find additional detail on changes. At the bottom center of the chart you can change the horizontal scale to show the changes for a day, 5 days, and so on up to 5 years. In this case we changed the scale to show the changes for a year. Information on the NASDAQ and the S&P 500 is available by clicking on them as well.

On the same page, MarketWatch lists the 30 stocks that make up the Dow and their change today. The change in the stock price for the 10 stocks that had the largest positive change follows.

Index Components

SYMBOL	LAST	CHANGE	% CHANGE
MRK	48.81 ↑	+2.11	+4.52%
INTC	25.19 ↑	+0.91	+3.74%
KO	40.55 ↑	+0.56	+1.40%
HPQ	24.78 ↑	+0.36	+1.45%
BA	100.36 ↑	+1.34	+1.35%
PFE	27.58 ↑	+0.35	+1.29%
MCD	97.50 ↑	+0.93	+0.96%
WMT	75.56 ↑	+0.72	+0.96%
CVX	123.81 ↑	+1.06	+0.86%
MSFT	35.20 ↑	+0.30	+0.86%

The symbol MRK represents Merk & Co., Inc., a pharmaceuticals company. They had the largest increase on this day. The increase was $2.11, or 4.52%. INTC, the market symbol for Intel Corporation, increased $0.91, or 3.74%.

SELF-REVIEW 17–4

As an intern in the Fulton County Economic Development Office, you have been asked to develop a special-purpose index for your county. Three economic series seem to hold promise as the basis of an index. These data are the price of cotton (per pound), the number of new automobiles sold in the county, and the rate of money turnover (published by the local bank). After discussing the project with your supervisor and the director, you decide that money turnover should have a weight of .60, the number of new automobiles sold a weight of .30, and the cotton price a weight of .10. The base period is 2004.

Year	Cotton Price	Automobiles Sold	Money Turnover
2004	$0.20	1,000	80
2009	0.25	1,200	90
2014	0.50	900	75

(a) Construct the index for 2009 and 2014.
(b) Interpret the index for 2009 and 2014.

EXERCISES

11. The index of leading economic indicators, compiled and published by the U.S. National Bureau of Economic Research, is composed of 12 time series, such as the average work hours of production in manufacturing, manufacturers' new orders, and money supply. This index and similar indexes are designed to move up or down before the economy begins to move the same way. Thus, an economist has statistical evidence to forecast future trends.

You want to construct a leading indicator for Erie County in upstate New York. The index is to be based on 2000 data. Because of the time and work involved, you decide to use only four time series. As an experiment, you select these four series: unemployment in the county, a composite index of county stock prices, the County Price Index, and retail sales. Here are the figures for 2000 and 2014.

	2000	2014
Unemployment rate (percent)	5.3	6.8
Composite county stocks	265.88	362.26
County Price Index (1982 = 100)	109.6	125.0
Retail sales ($ millions)	529,917.0	622,864.0

The weights you assign are unemployment rate 20%, stock prices 40%, County Price Index 25%, and retail sales 15%.

a. Using 2000 as the base period, construct a leading economic indicator for 2014.
b. Interpret your leading index.

12. You are employed by the state bureau of economic development. There is a demand for a leading economic index to review past economic activity and to forecast future economic trends in the state. You decide that several key factors should be included in the index: number of new businesses started during the year, number of business failures, state income tax receipts, college enrollment, and the state sales tax receipts. Here are the data for 2000 and 2012.

	2000	2012
New businesses	1,088	1,162
Business failures	627	520
State income tax receipts ($ millions)	191.7	162.6
College student enrollment	242,119	290,841
State sales tax ($ millions)	41.6	39.9

a. Decide on the weights to be applied to each item in the leading index.
b. Compute the leading economic indicator for 2012.
c. Interpret the indexes.

LO17-5
Apply the Consumer Price Index.

CONSUMER PRICE INDEX

Frequent mention has been made of the Consumer Price Index (CPI) in the preceding pages. It measures the change in price of a fixed market basket of goods and services from one period to another. In January 1978, the Bureau of Labor Statistics began publishing CPIs for two groups of the population. One index, called the Consumer Price Index—All Urban Consumers, covers about 87% of the total population. The other index is for urban wage earners and clerical workers and covers about 32% of the population.

The CPI serves several major functions. It allows consumers to determine the degree to which their purchasing power is being eroded by price increases. In that respect, it is a yardstick for revising wages, pensions, and other income payments to keep pace with changes in prices. Equally important, it is an economic indicator of the rate of inflation in the United States.

The index is based on the prices of 80,000 items collected monthly by about 250 agents. Prices are collected from thousands of U.S. retail stores, service establishments, rental units, and doctors' offices (http://stats.bls.gov/cpi/cpifaq.htm). Bread, beer, gasoline, haircuts, mortgage interest rates, physicians' fees, taxes, and operating-room charges are just a few of the items included in what is often termed a "market basket" of goods and services that a typical consumer purchases.

The CPI originated in 1913 and has been published regularly since 1921. The standard reference period (the base period) has been updated periodically. The current base period is 1982–84. The earlier base periods were 1967, 1957–59, 1947–49, 1935–39, and 1925–29. Why is it necessary to change the base? Our purchasing patterns that determine the "market basket" of goods and services change dramatically, and these changes must be reflected in the base period prices.

The CPI is actually not just one index. There are Consumer Price Indexes for New York, Chicago, Seattle, and Atlanta, as well as a number of other large cities. There

STATISTICS IN ACTION

Does it seem that prices only increase? The Consumer Price Index, computed and reported by the U.S. Department of Labor, is a relative measure of price changes. It shows interesting price information for categories of products and services. For example, did you know that the CPI for personal computers and peripheral equipment was 58.045 in April 2013? Using a base of December 2007, this means that relative prices for computers and peripherals have decreased about 42% since December 2007.

are also price indexes for food, apparel, medical care, and other items. A few of them are shown below, 1982–84 = 100, for August 2013.

Item	CPI-U
All items	233.877
Food and beverage	237.348
Apparel	125.767
Transportation	219.217
Medical care	426.866
Housing	228.564

A review of this list shows that a weighted index of all items has increased 133.877% since 1982–84; medical care has increased the most, 326.866%; and apparel went up the least, 25.767%.

Special Uses of the Consumer Price Index

In addition to measuring changes in the prices of goods and services, both consumer price indexes have a number of other applications. The CPI is used to determine real disposable personal income, to deflate sales or other variables, to find the purchasing power of the dollar, and to establish cost-of-living increases. We first discuss the use of the CPI in determining **real income.**

Real Income As an example of the meaning and computation of *real income,* assume the Consumer Price Index is presently 200 with 1982–84 = 100. Also, assume that Ms. Watts earned $20,000 per year in the base period of 1982, 1983, and 1984. She has a current income of $40,000. Note that although her *money income* has doubled since the base period of 1982–84, the prices she paid for food, gasoline, clothing, and other items have also doubled. Thus, Ms. Watts' standard of living has remained the same from the base period to the present time. Price increases have exactly offset an increase in income, so her present buying power (real income) is still $20,000. (See Table 17–6 for computations.) In general:

REAL INCOME

$$\text{Real income} = \frac{\text{Money income}}{\text{CPI}} \times 100 \qquad \textbf{[17–8]}$$

TABLE 17–6 Computation of Real Income for 1982–84 and Present Year

Year	Annual Money Income	Consumer Price Index (1982–84 = 100)	Computation of Real Income	Real Income
1982–84	$20,000	100	$\frac{\$20{,}000}{100}(100)$	$20,000
Present year	40,000	200	$\frac{\$40{,}000}{200}(100)$	20,000

The concept of real income is sometimes called *deflated income,* and the CPI is called the *deflator.* Also, a popular term for deflated income is *income expressed in constant dollars.* Thus, in Table 17–6, to determine whether Ms. Watts' standard of living changed, her money income was converted to constant dollars. We found that her purchasing power, expressed in 1982–84 dollars (constant dollars), remained at $20,000.

SELF-REVIEW 17–5

The take-home pay of Jon Greene and the CPI for 2000 and 2013 are:

Year	Take-Home Pay	CPI (1982–84 = 100)
2000	$25,000	170.8
2013	41,200	229.6

(a) What was Jon's real income in 2000?
(b) What was his real income in 2013?
(c) Interpret your findings.

Deflating Sales A price index can also be used to "deflate" sales or similar money series. Deflated sales are determined by

USING AN INDEX AS A DEFLATOR

$$\text{Deflated sales} = \frac{\text{Actual sales}}{\text{An appropriate index}} \times 100 \qquad [17\text{–}9]$$

EXAMPLE

The sales of Hill Enterprises, a small injection molding company in upstate New York, increased from $875,000 in 1982 to $1,482,000 in 1995, $1,491,000 in 2000, $1,502,000 in 2004, $1,515,000 in 2007, $1,596,000 in 2009, and $1,697,000 in 2013. The owner, Harry Hill, realizes that the price of raw materials used in the process has also increased over the period, so Mr. Hill wants to deflate sales to account for the increase in raw material prices. What are the deflated sales for 1995, 2000, 2004, 2007, 2009, and 2013 based on 1982 dollars? That is, what are sales for 1995, 2000, 2004, 2007, 2009, and 2013 expressed in constant 1982 dollars?

SOLUTION

The Producer Price Index (PPI) is an index released every month and published in the *Monthly Labor Review;* it is also available at the Bureau of Labor Statistics website. The prices included in the PPI reflect the prices the manufacturer pays for the metals, rubber, and other purchased raw materials. So the PPI seems an appropriate index to use to deflate the manufacturer's sales. The manufacturer's sales are listed in the second column of Table 17–7, and the PPI for each year is in the third column. The next column shows sales divided by the PPI. The right-hand column details the calculations.

TABLE 17–7 Calculation of Deflated Sales for Hill Enterprises

Year	Sales	PPI	Constant Dollars	Found by
1982	$ 875,000	100.0	$ 875,000.00	($875,000/100.0)*(100)
1995	1,482,000	127.9	1,158,717.75	($1,482,000/127.9)*(100)
2000	1,491,000	139.0	1,072,661.87	($1,491,000/139.0)*(100)
2004	1,502,000	148.5	1,011,447.81	($1,502,000/148.5)*(100)
2007	1,515,000	166.6	909,363.75	($1,515,000/166.6)*(100)
2009	1,596,000	172.5	925,217.39	($1,596,000/172.5)*(100)
2013	1,697,000	194.2	873,841.40	($1,697,000/194.2)*(100)

Sales increased from 1982 through 2013; in fact, they increased by 93.9% [($1,697,000/$875,000)*100] − 100.0. However, if we compare the sales deflated with the PPI, the constant sales dollars have declined since 1982.

Purchasing Power of the Dollar The Consumer Price Index is also used to determine the *purchasing power of the dollar.*

USING AN INDEX TO FIND PURCHASING POWER

$$\text{Purchasing power of dollar} = \frac{\$1}{\text{CPI}} \times 100 \quad \textbf{[17–10]}$$

EXAMPLE

Suppose the Consumer Price Index this month is 200.0 (1982–84 = 100). What is the purchasing power of the dollar?

SOLUTION

From formula (17–10), it is 50 cents, found by:

$$\text{Purchasing power of dollar} = \frac{\$1}{200.0}(100) = \$0.50$$

The CPI of 200.0 indicates that prices have doubled from the years 1982–84 to this month. Thus, the purchasing power of a dollar has been cut in half. That is, a 1982–84 dollar is worth only 50 cents this month. To put it another way, if you lost \$1,000 in the period 1982–84 and just found it, the \$1,000 could only buy half of what it could have bought in the years 1982, 1983, and 1984.

Cost-of-Living Adjustments The Consumer Price Index (CPI) is also the basis for cost-of-living adjustments, or COLAs, in many management–union contracts. The specific clause in the contract is often referred to as the "escalator clause." About 31 million Social Security beneficiaries, 2.5 million retired military and federal civil service employees and survivors, and 600,000 postal workers have their incomes or pensions pegged to the CPI.

The CPI is also used to adjust alimony and child support payments; attorneys' fees; workers' compensation payments; rentals on apartments, homes, and office buildings; welfare payments; and so on. A retiree receives a pension of \$500 a month and the CPI increases 5 points from 165 to 170. Suppose for each percentage point the CPI increases, the pension benefits increase 1 percent, so the monthly increase in benefits will be \$15.15, found by $[(170 - 165)/165] \times 500$. Now the retiree will receive \$515.15 per month.

SELF-REVIEW 17–6

The Consumer Price Index for the latest month is 195.4 (1982–84 = 100). What is the purchasing power of the dollar? Interpret.

Shifting the Base

If two or more time series have the same base period, they can be compared directly. As an example, suppose we are interested in the trend in the prices of food and beverages, housing, apparel and upkeep, and medical care since the base period, 1982–84. Note in Table 17–8 that all of the consumer price indexes use the same base.

TABLE 17–8 Trend in Consumer Price to 2012 (1982–84 = 100)

Year	All Items	Food and Beverages	Housing	Apparel Upkeep	Medical Care
1982–84	100.0	100.0	100.0	100.0	100.0
1990	130.7	132.1	128.5	124.1	162.8
1995	152.4	148.9	148.5	132	220.5
2000	172.2	168.4	169.6	129.6	260.8
2005	195.3	191.2	195.7	119.5	323.2
2006	201.6	195.7	203.2	119.5	336.2
2010	218.056	219.984	216.256	119.503	388.436
2011	224.939	227.866	219.102	122.111	400.258
2012	229.594	233.67	222.715	126.265	414.924

Table 17–8 shows that the price of all consumer items combined increased 129.594% from the base period (1982–84) to the year 2012. (Beginning with January 2007, the CPI is reported to three decimal places instead of one.) Likewise, food and beverage prices increased 133.67%, housing prices increased 122.715%, apparel and upkeep increased 26.265%, and medical care increased 314.924%.

A problem arises, however, when comparing two or more series that do not have the same base period. The following example compares the two most widely reported stock market indexes, the DJIA and NASDAQ.

EXAMPLE

We want to compare the opening prices of the Dow Jones Industrial Average (DJIA) and the NASDAQ Composite on the first trading day of the year for 2004 through 2013.

	Opening Price	
Date	DJIA	NASDAQ
2-Jan-04	$10,452.74	$2,011.08
3-Jan-05	10,783.75	2,184.75
3-Jan-06	10,718.30	2,216.53
3-Jan-07	12,459.54	2,429.72
2-Jan-08	13,261.82	2,653.91
2-Jan-09	8,772.25	1,578.87
4-Jan-10	10,430.69	2,294.41
3-Jan-11	11,577.43	2,676.65
3-Jan-12	12,221.19	2,657.39
2-Jan-13	13,104.30	3,091.33

SOLUTION

A direct comparison of the DJIA and NASDAQ opening prices is not appropriate. Because we want to compare changes in the opening prices for the two markets, a logical approach is to compute indexes for each market using the 2004 opening price as the base. For the DJIA, the base is $10,452.74, and for the NASDAQ it is $2,011.08.

The calculation of the index for the DJIA in 2013 is:

$$\text{Index} = \frac{\$13,104.30}{\$10,452.74}(100) = 125.4$$

The following table reports the complete set of indexes.

	DJIA		NASDAQ	
Date	Value	Index	Value	Index
2-Jan-04	$10,452.74	100.0	$2,011.08	100.0
3-Jan-05	10,783.75	103.2	2,184.75	108.6
3-Jan-06	10,718.30	102.5	2,216.53	110.2
3-Jan-07	12,459.54	119.2	2,429.72	120.8
2-Jan-08	13,261.82	126.9	2,653.91	132.0
2-Jan-09	8,772.25	83.9	1,578.87	78.5
4-Jan-10	10,430.69	99.8	2,294.41	114.1
3-Jan-11	11,577.43	110.8	2,676.65	133.1
3-Jan-12	12,221.19	116.9	2,657.39	132.1
2-Jan-13	13,104.30	125.4	3,091.33	153.7

We conclude that both indexes have increased over the period. The DJIA has increased 25.4% and the NASDAQ 53.7%.

The following chart shows the DJIA indexes in green and NASDAQ indexes in brown. The graph shows the changes for both indexes starting from the base of January 2, 2004. From this graph we conclude that the NASDAQ reached its high at the start of the year 2013. The high for the Dow was in January 2008. In general, the two indexes seem to mirror each other rather closely. We should point out that if we select different periods as the base, the results may not be exactly the same. One should always be cautious of the base period selected for a chart or a graph.

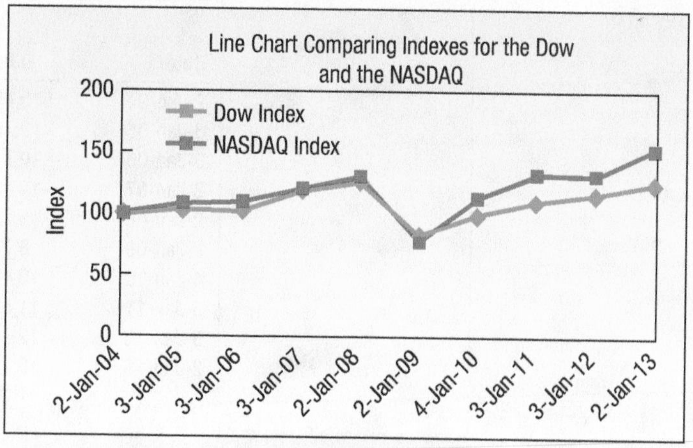

SELF-REVIEW 17–7

The changes in industrial production and in the prices manufacturers paid for raw materials since 1982 are to be compared. Unfortunately, the index of industrial production, which measures changes in production, and the Producer Price Index for raw materials have different base periods. The production index has a 2007 base period and the Producer Price Index uses 1982 as the base period. The following table reports the value of each index at the start of the year. Shift the base to 2010 and make the two series comparable. Interpret the results.

Year	Industrial Production Index (2007 = 100)	Producer Price Index (1982 = 100)
2007	98.16	160.1
2008	100.50	172.0
2009	87.55	170.4
2010	87.96	178.0
2011	92.61	184.4
2012	96.20	192.0
2013	98.06	194.7

EXERCISES

13. In April 2013, the mean salary for a nurse manager with a bachelor's degree was $89,673. The Consumer Price Index for April 2013 was 232.531 (1982–84 = 100). The mean annual salary for a nurse in the base period of 1982–84 was $19,800. What was the real income of the nurse in April 2013? How much had the mean salary increased?
14. The Trade Union Association of Orlando, Florida, maintains indexes on the hourly wages for a number of the trades. Unfortunately, the indexes do not all have the same base periods. Listed below is information on plumbers and electricians. Shift the base periods to 2000 and compare the hourly wage increases for the period from 2000 to 2013.

Year	Plumbers (1995 = 100)	Electricians (1998 = 100)
2000	133.8	126.0
2013	159.4	158.7

15. In 2000, the mean salary of classroom teachers in Tinora School District was $28,650. By 2009, the mean salary increased to $33,972, and further increased in 2013 to $37,382. The American Federation of Classroom Teachers maintains information on the trends throughout the United States in classroom teacher salaries. Its index, which has a base period of 2000, was 122.5 for 2009 and 136.9 for 2013. Compare the Tinora teachers to the national trends.
16. Sam Steward is a freelance Web page designer. Listed below are his yearly wages for several years between 2007 and 2013. Also included is an industry index for Web page designers that reports the rate of wage inflation in the industry. This index has a base period of 1995.

Year	Wage ($000)	Index (1995 = 100)
2007	134.8	160.6
2009	145.2	173.6
2011	156.6	187.9
2013	168.8	203.3

Compute Sam's real income for the selected years during the six-year period. Did his wages keep up with inflation, or did he lose ground?

CHAPTER SUMMARY

I. An index number measures the relative change from one period to another.
   A. The major characteristics of an index are:
      1. It is a percentage, but the percent sign is usually omitted.
      2. It has a base period.
   B. The reasons for computing an index are:
      1. It facilitates the comparison of unlike series.
      2. If the numbers are very large, often it is easier to comprehend the change of the index than the actual numbers.

STATISTICS IN ACTION

In the 1920s, wholesale prices in Germany increased dramatically. In 1920, wholesale prices increased about 80%, in 1921 the rate of increase was 140%, and in 1922 it was a whopping 4,100%! Between December 1922 and November 1923, wholesale prices increased another 4,100%. By that time government printing presses could not keep up, even by printing notes as large as 500 million marks. Stories are told that workers were paid daily, then twice daily, so their wives could shop for necessities before the wages became too devalued.

II. There are two types of price indexes, unweighted and weighted.
  A. In an unweighted index, we do not consider the quantities.
    1. In a simple index, we compare the base period to the given period.

$$P = \frac{p_t}{p_0} \times 100 \qquad \textbf{[17–1]}$$

where p_t refers to the price in the current period and p_0 is the price in the base period.
    2. In the simple average of price indexes, we add the simple indexes for each item and divide by the number of items.

$$P = \frac{\Sigma P_i}{n} \qquad \textbf{[17–2]}$$

    3. In a simple aggregate price index, the price of the items in the group are totaled for both periods and compared.

$$P = \frac{\Sigma p_t}{\Sigma p_0} \times 100 \qquad \textbf{[17–3]}$$

  B. In a weighted index, the quantities are considered.
    1. In the Laspeyres method, the base period quantities are used in both the base period and the given period.

$$P = \frac{\Sigma p_t q_0}{\Sigma p_0 q_0} \times 100 \qquad \textbf{[17–4]}$$

    2. In the Paasche method, current period quantities are used.

$$P = \frac{\Sigma p_t q_t}{\Sigma p_0 q_t} \times 100 \qquad \textbf{[17–5]}$$

    3. Fisher's ideal index is the geometric mean of the Laspeyres and Paasche indexes.

$$\text{Fisher's ideal index} = \sqrt{(\text{Laspeyres index})(\text{Paasche index})} \qquad \textbf{[17–6]}$$

  C. A value index uses both base period and current period prices and quantities.

$$V = \frac{\Sigma p_t q_t}{\Sigma p_0 q_0} \times 100 \qquad \textbf{[17–7]}$$

III. The most widely reported index is the Consumer Price Index (CPI).
  A. It is often used to show the rate of inflation in the United States.
  B. It is reported monthly by the U.S. Bureau of Labor Statistics.
  C. The current base period is 1982–84.
  D. CPI is used to compute "real" income and purchasing power and to adjust pensions and tax brackets.

CHAPTER EXERCISES

For exercises 17 through 22, use the following information taken from Johnson & Johnson annual reports. The principal office of Johnson & Johnson is in New Brunswick, New Jersey. Its common stock is listed on the New York Stock Exchange, using the symbol JNJ.

Year	Domestic Sales ($ million)	International Sales ($ million)	Employees (thousands)
2000	17,316	11,856	100.9
2001	19,825	12,492	101.8
2002	22,455	13,843	108.3
2003	25,274	16,588	110.6
2004	27,770	19,578	109.9
2005	28,377	22,137	115.6
2006	29,775	23,549	122.2
2007	32,444	28,651	119.2
2008	32,309	31,438	118.7
2009	30,889	31,008	115.5
2010	29,437	32,124	114.0
2011	28,907	36,107	117.9
2012	29,832	37,371	118.7

For **DATA FILE**, please visit www.mhhe.com/lind16e

17. Using 2000 as the base period, compute a simple index of domestic sales for each year from 2000 until 2012. Interpret the trend in domestic sales.
18. Using the period 2000–02 as the base period, compute a simple index of domestic sales for each year from 2003 to 2012.
19. Using 2000 as the base period, compute a simple index of international sales for each year from 2001 until 2012. Interpret the trend in international sales.
20. Using the period 2000–02 as the base period, compute a simple index of international sales for each year from 2003 to 2012.
21. Using 2000 as the base period, compute a simple index of the number of employees for each year from 2001 until 2012. Interpret the trend in the number of employees.
22. Using the period 2000–02 as the base period, compute a simple index of the number of employees for each year from 2003 to 2012.

For exercises 23 through 26, use the following information from General Electric Corporation's annual reports.

Year	Revenue ($ million)	Employees (000)	Year	Revenue ($ million)	Employees (000)
2004	134	325	2009	183	323
2005	152	307	2010	149.6	304
2006	157	316	2011	147.3	287
2007	168	319	2012	147.3	301
2008	177	327			

For **DATA FILE**, please visit www.mhhe.com/lind16e

23. Compute a simple index for the revenue of GE. Use 2004 as the base period. What can you conclude about the change in revenue over the period?
24. Compute a simple index for the revenue of GE using the period 2004–06 as the base. What can you conclude about the change in revenue over the period?
25. Compute a simple index for the number of employees for GE. Use 2004 as the base period. What can you conclude about the change in the number of employees over the period?
26. Compute a simple index for the number of employees for GE using the period 2004–06 as the base. What can you conclude about the change in the number of employees over the period?

For exercises 27 through 32, use the following information on food items for the years 2000 and 2013.

	2000		2013	
Item	Price	Quantity	Price	Quantity
Margarine (pound)	$0.81	18	$2.00	27
Shortening (pound)	0.84	5	1.88	9
Milk (½ gallon)	1.44	70	2.89	65
Potato chips	2.91	27	3.99	33

For **DATA FILE**, please visit www.mhhe.com/lind16e

27. Compute a simple price index for each of the four items. Use 2000 as the base period.
28. Compute a simple aggregate price index. Use 2000 as the base period.
29. Compute Laspeyres' price index for 2013 using 2000 as the base period.
30. Compute Paasche's index for 2013 using 2000 as the base period.
31. Determine Fisher's ideal index using the values for the Laspeyres and Paasche indexes computed in the two previous problems.
32. Determine a value index for 2013 using 2000 as the base period.

For exercises 33 through 38, use the following information. Betts Electronics purchases three replacement parts for robotic machines used in its manufacturing process. Information on the price of the replacement parts and the quantity purchased is given below.

	Price		Quantity	
Part	2000	2013	2000	2013
RC-33	$0.50	$0.60	320	340
SM-14	1.20	0.90	110	130
WC50	0.85	1.00	230	250

For **DATA FILE**, please visit www.mhhe.com/lind16e

33. Compute a simple price index for each of the three items. Use 2000 as the base period.
34. Compute a simple aggregate price index for 2013. Use 2000 as the base period.
35. Compute Laspeyres' price index for 2013 using 2000 as the base period.
36. Compute Paasche's index for 2013 using 2000 as the base period.
37. Determine Fisher's ideal index using the values for the Laspeyres and Paasche indexes computed in the two previous problems.
38. Determine a value index for 2013 using 2000 as the base period.

For exercises 39 through 44, use the following price information for selected foods for 2000 and 2013 given in the following table.

	Price		Quantity	
Item	**2000**	**2013**	**2000**	**2013**
Cabbage (pound)	$0.06	$0.05	2,000	1,500
Carrots (bunch)	0.10	0.12	200	200
Peas (quart)	0.20	0.18	400	500
Endive (bunch)	0.15	0.15	100	200

For **DATA FILE**, please visit www.mhhe.com/lind16e

39. Compute a simple price index for each of the four items. Use 2000 as the base period.
40. Compute a simple aggregate price index. Use 2000 as the base period.
41. Compute Laspeyres' price index for 2013 using 2000 as the base period.
42. Compute Paasche's index for 2013 using 2000 as the base period.
43. Determine Fisher's ideal index using the values for the Laspeyres and Paasche indexes computed in the two previous problems.
44. Determine a value index for 2013 using 2000 as the base period.

For exercises 45 through 50, use the following price information for selected items for 1990 and 2013. Production figures for those two periods are also given.

	Price		Quantity	
Item	**1990**	**2013**	**1990**	**2013**
Aluminum (cents per pound)	$ 0.287	$ 0.76	1,000	1,200
Natural gas (1,000 cu. ft.)	0.17	2.50	5,000	4,000
Petroleum (barrel)	3.18	26.00	60,000	60,000
Platinum (troy ounce)	133.00	490.00	500	600

For **DATA FILE**, please visit www.mhhe.com/lind16e

45. Compute a simple price index for each of the four items. Use 1990 as the base period.
46. Compute a simple aggregate price index. Use 1990 as the base period.
47. Compute Laspeyres' price index for 2013 using 1990 as the base period.
48. Compute Paasche's index for 2013 using 1990 as the base period.
49. Determine Fisher's ideal index using the values for the Laspeyres and Paasche indexes computed in the two previous problems.
50. Determine a value index for 2013 using 1990 as the base period.
51. A special-purpose index is to be designed to monitor the overall economy of the Southwest. Four key series were selected. After considerable deliberation, it was decided to weight retail sales 20%, total bank deposits 10%, industrial production in the area 40%, and nonagricultural employment 30%. The data for 1996 and 2013 are:

Year	Retail Sales ($ millions)	Bank Deposits ($ billions)	Industrial Production (1990 = 100)	Employment
1996	1,159.0	87	110.6	1,214,000
2013	1,971.0	91	114.7	1,501,000

Construct a special-purpose index for 2013 using 1996 as the base period and interpret.

52. We are making a historical study of the American economy from 1950 to 1980. Data on prices, the labor force, productivity, and the GNP were collected. Note in the following table that the CPI has a base period of 1967, employment is in millions of persons, and so on. A direct comparison, therefore, is not feasible.
   a. Make whatever calculations are necessary to compare the trend in the four series from 1950 to 1980.
   b. Interpret.

Year	Consumer Price Index (1967 = 100)	Total Labor Force (millions)	Index of Productivity in Manufacturing (1967 = 100)	Gross National Product ($ billions)
1950	72.1	64	64.9	286.2
1967	100.0	81	100.0	789.6
1971	121.3	87	110.3	1,063.4
1975	161.2	95	114.9	1,516.3
1980	246.8	107	146.6	2,626.0

53. The management of Ingalls Super Discount stores, with several stores in the Oklahoma City area, wants to construct an index of economic activity for the metropolitan area. Management contends that, if the index reveals that the economy is slowing down, inventory should be kept at a low level.

   Three series seem to hold promise as predictors of economic activity—area retail sales, bank deposits, and employment. All of these data can be secured monthly from the U.S. government. Retail sales is to be weighted 40%, bank deposits 35%, and employment 25%. Seasonally adjusted data for the first 3 months of the year are:

Month	Retail Sales ($ millions)	Bank Deposits ($ billions)	Employment (thousands)
January	8.0	20	300
February	6.8	23	303
March	6.4	21	297

   Construct an index of economic activity for each of the 3 months, using January as the base period.

54. The following table gives information on the Consumer Price Index and the monthly take-home pay of Bill Martin, an employee at Ford Motor Corporation, from 1982–84 and 2012.

Year	Consumer Price Index (1982–84 = 100)	Mr. Martin's Monthly Take-Home Pay
1982–84	100.0	$ 600
2012	229.594	2,000

   a. What is the purchasing power of the dollar in 2012, based on the period 1982–84?
   b. Determine Mr. Martin's "real" monthly income for 2012.

55. Suppose that the Producer Price Index and the sales of Hoskin's Wholesale Distributors for 1995 and 2012 are:

Year	Producer Price Index	Sales
1995	127.9	$2,400,000
2012	194.5	3,500,000

   What are Hoskin's real sales (also called deflated sales) for the 2 years?

DATA SET EXERCISE

(The data for this exercise is available at the text website: www.mhhe.com/lind16e.)

56. Refer to the Baseball 2012 data, which include information on the 2012 Major League Baseball season. The data also include the mean player salary since 1989.

a. Use the year 2000 salary as the base period and 100 as the base value to develop a simple index for the years since 2000. By what percent has the typical salary increased?

b. The Consumer Price Index values for 2001, 2003, 2011, and 2012 are 177.1, 184.0, 224.94, and 229.594, respectively. What are the average player's real (or deflated) salaries for those years? Describe the trend in the deflated salaries in a few sentences. Compare these results with your reply in part (a).

Time Series and Forecasting

18

TEAM SPORTS INC. sells sporting goods to high schools and colleges via a nationally distributed catalog. Management at Team Sports estimates it will sell 2,000 Wilson Model A2000 catcher's mitts next year. The deseasonalized sales are projected to be the same for each of the four quarters next year. The seasonal factor for the second quarter is 145. Determine the seasonally adjusted sales for the second quarter of next year. (See Exercise 12 and LO18-6.)

LEARNING OBJECTIVES

When you have completed this chapter, you will be able to:

LO18-1 Define and describe the components of a time series.

LO18-2 Smooth a time series by computing a moving average.

LO18-3 Smooth a time series by computing a weighted moving average.

LO18-4 Use regression analysis to fit a linear trend line to a time series.

LO18-5 Use regression analysis to fit a nonlinear time series.

LO18-6 Compute and apply seasonal indexes to make seasonally adjusted forecasts.

LO18-7 Deseasonalize a time series using seasonal indexes.

LO18-8 Conduct a hypothesis test of autocorrelation.

INTRODUCTION

The emphasis in this chapter is on time series analysis and forecasting. A **time series** is a collection of data recorded over a period of time—weekly, monthly, quarterly, or yearly. Two examples of time series are Microsoft Corporation sales by quarter since 1985 and the annual production of sulfuric acid since 1970.

An analysis of history—a time series—is used by management to make current decisions and plans based on long-term forecasting. We usually assume past patterns will continue into the future. Long-term forecasts extend more than 1 year into the future; 2-, 5-, and 10-year projections are common. Long-range predictions are essential to allow sufficient time for the procurement, manufacturing, sales, finance, and other departments of a company to develop plans for possible new plants, financing, development of new products, and new methods of assembling.

Forecasting the level of sales, both short-term and long-term, is practically dictated by the very nature of business organizations in the United States and around the world. Competition for the consumer's dollar, stress on earning a profit for the stockholders, a desire to procure a larger share of the market, and the ambitions of executives are some of the prime motivating forces in business. Thus, a forecast (a statement of the goals of management) is necessary to have the raw materials, production facilities, and staff to meet the projected demand.

This chapter deals with the use of data to forecast future events. First, we look at the components of a time series. Then, we examine some of the techniques used in analyzing data. Finally, we use these techniques to forecast future events.

LO18-1
Define and describe the components of a time series.

COMPONENTS OF A TIME SERIES

There are four components to a time series: the trend, the cyclical variation, the seasonal variation, and the irregular variation.

Secular Trend

The long-term trends of sales, employment, stock prices, and other business and economic series follow various patterns. Some move steadily upward, others decline, and still others stay the same over time. The change over time may be linear and follow a straight line, or it may increase at an exponential rate. The long-run change (or lack of change) is called the trend of the time series or, more precisely, the **secular trend.**

SECULAR TREND The smoothed long-term direction of a time series.

The following are several examples of a secular trend.

- Home Depot, Inc. was founded in 1978 and is the world's largest home improvement retailer. The following chart shows the number of associates working for Home Depot, Inc. You can see the number of associates has increased rapidly over the 15 years from 1993 to 2006. In 1993, there were just over 50,000 associates and by 2006 that number increased to 364,000. Since then, the number of associates fell sharply in 2007, then fell slightly in 2008 and 2009, and remained fairly constant for the past three years.

Year	Associates	Year	Associates
1993	50.6	2003	298.8
1994	67.3	2004	323.1
1995	80.8	2005	344.8
1996	98.1	2006	364.4
1997	124.4	2007	331.0
1998	156.7	2008	322.0
1999	201.4	2009	317.0
2000	227.3	2010	321.0
2001	256.3	2011	331.0
2002	280.9	2012	340.0

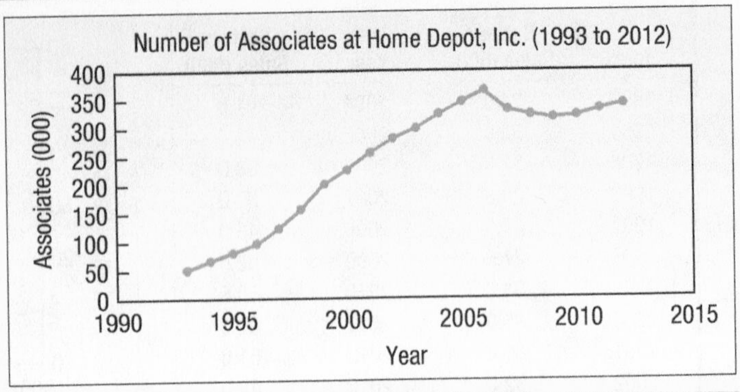

- The average price for a gallon of regular gasoline was about $1.15 through most of the 1990s. Since then, except for a period between 2009 and 2010, it has increased steadily by almost $0.20 per year. This information is shown in the chart below.

Year	Cost/Gallon	Year	Cost/Gallon
1990	$1.30	2002	$1.35
1991	1.10	2003	1.56
1992	1.09	2004	1.85
1993	1.07	2005	2.27
1994	1.08	2006	2.57
1995	1.11	2007	2.80
1996	1.20	2008	3.25
1997	1.20	2009	2.35
1998	1.03	2010	2.78
1999	1.14	2011	3.52
2000	1.48	2012	3.62
2001	1.42		

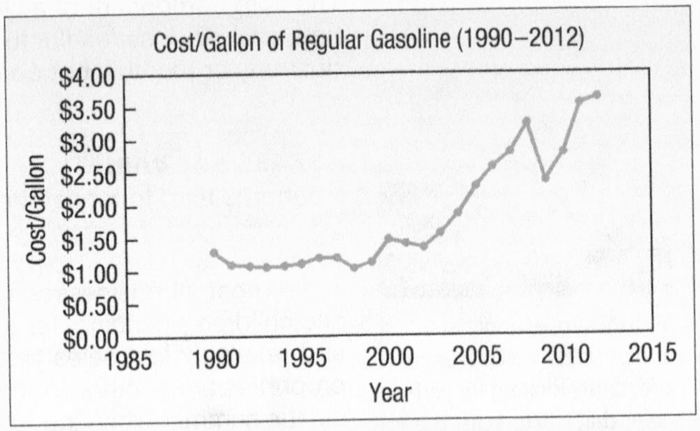

Cyclical Variation

The second component of a time series is **cyclical variation.** A typical business cycle consists of a period of prosperity followed by periods of recession, depression, and then recovery. There are sizable fluctuations unfolding over more than one year in time above and below the secular trend. In a recession, for example, employment, production, the Dow Jones Industrial Average, and many other business and economic series are below the long-term trend lines. Conversely, in periods of prosperity they are above their long-term trend lines.

CYCLICAL VARIATION The rise and fall of a time series over periods longer than 1 year.

Chart 18–1 shows the annual unit sales of batteries sold by National Battery Retailers, Inc. from 1993 through 2013. The cyclical nature of business is highlighted. There are periods of recovery, followed by prosperity, then contraction, and finally the cycle bottoms out with depression.

Year	Battery Sales (000)	Year	Battery Sales (000)
1993	24.0	2004	41.0
1994	30.0	2005	42.0
1995	31.0	2006	38.0
1996	26.5	2007	39.0
1997	27.0	2008	46.0
1998	27.5	2009	52.0
1999	34.0	2010	53.5
2000	35.0	2011	47.0
2001	31.0	2012	51.0
2002	32.0	2013	48.0
2003	35.5		

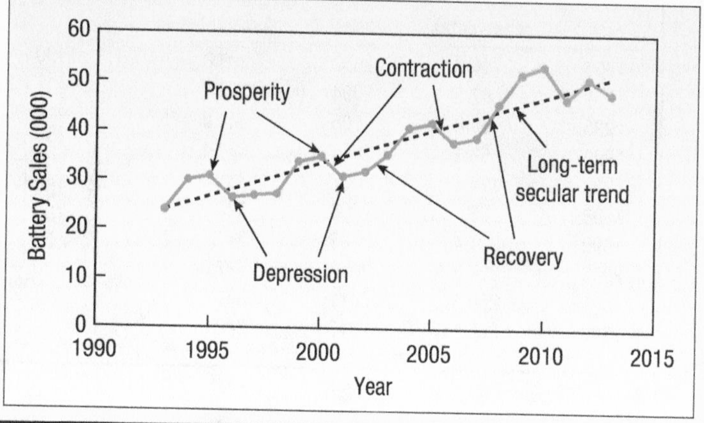

CHART 18–1 Battery Sales for National Battery Retailers, Inc. 1993 to 2013

Seasonal Variation

The third component of a time series is the **seasonal variation.** Many sales, production, and other series fluctuate with the seasons. The unit of time reported is usually quarterly or monthly but could be weekly.

> **SEASONAL VARIATION** Patterns of change in a time series within a year. These patterns tend to repeat themselves each year.

STATISTICS IN ACTION

Statisticians, economists, and business executives are constantly looking for variables that will forecast the country's economy. The production of crude oil, price of gold on world markets, and the Dow Jones average, as well as many published government indexes, are variables that have been used with some success. Variables such as the length of hemlines and the winner of the Super Bowl have also been tried. The variable that seems overall to be the most successful is the price of scrap metal. Why? Scrap metal is the beginning of the manufacturing chain. When its demand increases, this is an indication that manufacturing is also increasing.

Almost all businesses tend to have recurring seasonal patterns. Men's clothing and children's clothing, for example, have extremely high sales just prior to Christmas and relatively low sales just after Christmas and during the summer. Beach rental properties are another example. They have very low rental rates in the winter but during the summer when the temperature is warm, rentals increase significantly. Toy sales are another example with an extreme seasonal pattern. More than half of the business for the year is usually done in the months of November and December. The lawn care business is seasonal in the northeast and north-central states. Many businesses try to even out the seasonal effects by engaging in an offsetting seasonal business. In the Northeast, the operator of a lawn care business will attach a snowplow to the front of a truck in an effort to earn income in the off-season. At ski resorts throughout the country, you will often find golf courses nearby. The owners of the lodges try to rent to skiers in the winter and golfers in the summer. This is an effective method of spreading their fixed costs over the entire year rather than a few months.

Chart 18–2 shows the quarterly sales, in millions of dollars, of Hercher Sporting Goods, Inc. The Chicago-area sporting goods company specializes in selling baseball and softball equipment to high schools, colleges, and youth leagues. It also has several retail outlets in some of the larger shopping malls. There is a distinct seasonal pattern to its business. Most of its sales are in the first and second quarters of the year, when schools and organizations are purchasing equipment for the upcoming season. During the early summer, it keeps busy by selling replacement equipment. It does some business during the holidays (fourth quarter). The late summer (third quarter) is its slow season.

Irregular Variation

Many analysts prefer to subdivide the **irregular variation** into *episodic* and *residual* variations. Episodic fluctuations are unpredictable, but they can be identified. The

Year	Quarter	Code	Sales (mil)
2011	Q_1	1	9.0
	Q_2	2	10.2
	Q_3	3	3.5
	Q_4	4	5.0
2012	Q_1	5	12.0
	Q_2	6	14.1
	Q_3	7	4.4
	Q_4	8	7.3
2013	Q_1	9	16.0
	Q_2	10	18.3
	Q_3	11	4.6
	Q_4	12	8.6

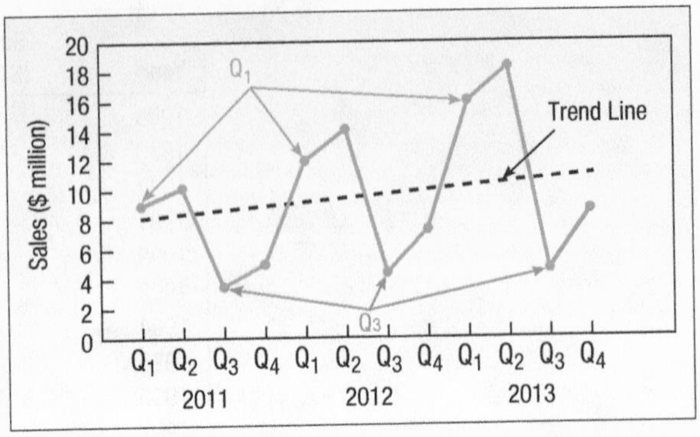

CHART 18–2 Sales of Baseball and Softball Equipment, Hercher Sporting Goods 2011–2013 by Quarter

initial impact on the economy of a major strike or a war can be identified, but a strike or war cannot be predicted. After the episodic fluctuations have been removed, the remaining variation is called the residual variation. The residual fluctuations, often called chance fluctuations, are unpredictable, and they cannot be identified. Of course, neither episodic nor residual variation can be projected into the future.

LO18-2
Smooth a time series by computing a moving average.

A MOVING AVERAGE

A **moving average** is useful in smoothing a time series to see its trend. It is also the basic method used in measuring the seasonal fluctuation, described later in the chapter. In contrast to the least squares method, which expresses the trend in terms of a mathematical equation ($\hat{y} = a + bt$), the moving-average method merely smooths the fluctuations in the data. This is accomplished by "moving" the arithmetic mean values through the time series.

To apply the moving average to a time series, the data should follow a fairly linear trend and have a definite rhythmic pattern of fluctuations (repeating, say, every three years). The data in the following example have three components—trend, cycle, and irregular, abbreviated *T*, *C*, and *I*. There is no seasonal variation because the data are recorded annually. What the moving average accomplishes is to average out *C* and *I*. What is left is the trend.

If the duration of the cycles is constant, and if the amplitudes of the cycles are equal, the cyclical and irregular fluctuations are removed entirely using the moving average. The result is a line. For example, in the following time series, the cycle repeats itself every 7 years, and the amplitude of each cycle is 4; that is, there are exactly four units from the trough (lowest time period) to the peak. The seven-year moving average, therefore, averages out the cyclical and irregular fluctuations perfectly, and the residual is a linear trend.

The first step in computing the seven-year moving average is to determine the seven-year moving totals. The total sales for the first 7 years (1988–94 inclusive) are \$22 million, found by $1 + 2 + 3 + 4 + 5 + 4 + 3$. (See Table 18–1.) The total of \$22 million is divided by 7 to determine the arithmetic mean sales per year. The seven-year total (22) and the seven-year mean (3.143) are positioned opposite the middle year for that group of seven, namely, 1991, as shown in Table 18–1. Then the total sales for the next seven years (1989–95 inclusive) are determined. (A convenient way of doing this is to subtract the sales for 1988 [\$1 million] from the first seven-year total [\$22 million] and add the sales for 1995 [\$2 million], to give the new total of \$23 million.) The mean of this total, \$3.286 million, is positioned opposite the middle year, 1992. The sales data and seven-year moving average are shown graphically in Chart 18–3.

TABLE 18–1 Computation of Seven-Year Moving Average

Year	Sales ($ Mil)	Seven-Year Moving Total	Seven-Year Moving Average
1988	1		
1989	2		
1990	3		
1991	4	22	3.143
1992	5	23	3.286
1993	4	24	3.429
1994	3	25	3.571
1995	2	26	3.714
1996	3	27	3.857
1997	4	28	4.000
1998	5	29	4.143
1999	6	30	4.286
2000	5	31	4.429
2001	4	32	4.571
2002	3	33	4.714
2003	4	34	4.857
2004	5	35	5.000
2005	6	36	5.143
2006	7	37	5.286
2007	6	38	5.429
2008	5	39	5.571
2009	4	40	5.714
2010	5	41	5.857
2011	6		
2012	7		
2013	8		

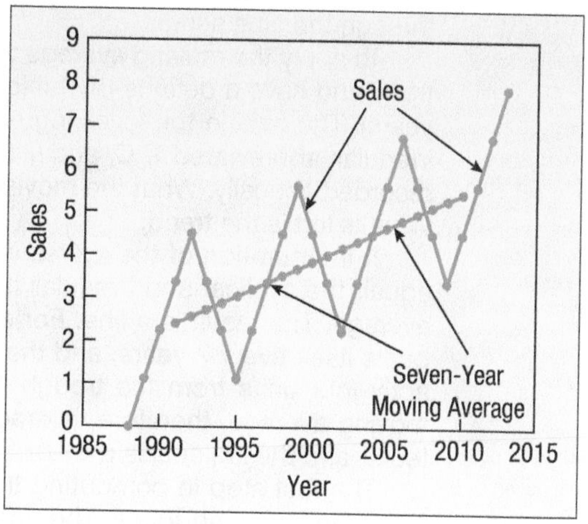

CHART 18–3 Sales and Seven-Year Moving Average

The number of data values to include in a moving average depends on the data collected. If the data are quarterly, then four values is typical because there are four quarters in a year. If the data are daily, then seven values is appropriate because there are 7 days in a week. You might also use trial and error to determine a number that best levels out the chance fluctuations. For example, Table 18–2 and Chart 18–4 show three-year and five-year moving averages for a series of production data.

TABLE 18–2 Production, Three-Year Moving Average, and Five-Year Moving Average

Year	Production y	Three-Year Moving Total	Three-Year Moving Average	Five-Year Moving Total	Five-Year Moving Average
1995	5				
1996	6	19	6.33		
1997	8	24	8.00	34	6.80
1998	10	23	7.67	32	6.40
1999	5	18	6.00	33	6.60
2000	3	15	5.00	35	7.00
2001	7	20	6.67	37	7.40
2002	10	29	9.67	43	8.60
2003	12	33	11.00	49	9.80
2004	11	32	10.67	55	11.00
2005	9	33	11.00	60	12.00
2006	13	37	12.33	66	13.20
2007	15	46	15.33	70	14.00
2008	18	48	16.00	72	14.40
2009	15	44	14.67	73	14.60
2010	11	40	13.33	75	15.00
2011	14	42	14.00	79	15.80
2012	17	53	17.67		
2013	22				

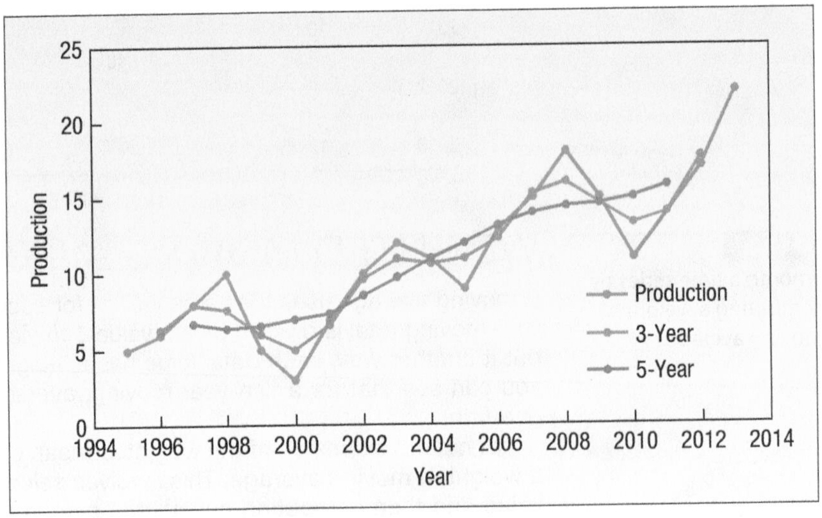

CHART 18–4 Time Series Plot of Production, Three-Year Moving Average, and Five-Year Moving Average

Sales, production, and other economic and business series usually do not have (1) periods of oscillation that are of equal length or (2) oscillations that have identical amplitudes. Thus, in practice, the application of a moving average does not result precisely in a line. For example, the production series in Table 18–2 repeats about every 5 years, but the amplitude of the data varies from one oscillation to another. The trend appears to be upward and somewhat linear. Both moving averages—the three-year and the five-year—seem to adequately describe the trend in production since 1995.

Four-year, six-year, and other even-numbered-year moving averages present one minor problem regarding the centering of the moving totals and moving averages. Note in Table 18–3 below there is no center time period, so the moving totals are positioned *between* two time periods. The total for the first 4 years ($42) is positioned between 2006 and 2007. The total for the next 4 years is $43. The averages of the first four years and the second 4 years ($10.50 and $10.75, respectively) are averaged, and the resulting figure is centered on 2007. This procedure is repeated until all possible four-year averages are computed.

TABLE 18–3 Calculations of a Four-Year Moving Average

Year	Sales	Four-Year Moving Total	Four-Year Moving Average	Centered Moving Average
2005	8			
2006	11			
		42 (8 + 11 + 9 + 14)	10.50 (42/4)	
2007	9			10.625
		43 (11 + 9 + 14 + 9)	10.75 (43/4)	
2008	14			10.625
		42	10.50	
2009	9			10.625
		43	10.75	
2010	10			10.000
		37	9.25	
2011	10			9.625
		40	10.00	
2012	8			
2013	12			

LO18-3
Smooth a time series by computing a weighted moving average.

WEIGHTED MOVING AVERAGE

A moving average uses the same weight for each observation. For example, a three-year moving total is divided by the value 3 to yield the three-year moving average. To put it another way, each data value has a weight of one-third in this case. Similarly, you can see that for a five-year moving, average, each data value has a weight of one-fifth.

A natural extension of the weighted mean discussed in Chapter 3 is to compute a weighted moving average. This involves selecting a different weight for each data value and then computing a weighted average of the most recent *n* values as the smoothed value. In the majority of applications, we use the smoothed value as a forecast of the future. So, the most recent observation receives the most weight, and the weight decreases for older data values. Of course, the sum of the weights must be equal to 1.

Suppose, for example, we compute a two-year weighted moving average for the data in Table 18–3 giving twice as much weight to the most recent value. In other words, give a weight of two-thirds to the last year and one-third to the value immediately before that. Then "forecast" sales for 2007 would be found by (1/3)($8) + (2/3)($11) = $10. The next moving average would be computed as (1/3)($11) + (2/3)($9) = $9.667. Proceeding in the same fashion, the final, or 2014, weighted moving average would be (1/3)($8) + (2/3)($12) = $10.667. To summarize the technique of using moving averages, its purpose is to help identify the long-term trend in a time

series (because it will smooth out short-term fluctuations). It is used to reveal any cyclical and seasonal fluctuations.

EXAMPLE

Cedar Fair operates seven amusement parks and five separately gated water parks. Its combined attendance (in thousands) for the last 20 years is given in the following table. A partner asks you to study the trend in attendance. Compute a three-year moving average and a three-year weighted moving average with weights of 0.2, 0.3, and 0.5 for successive years.

Year	Attendance (000)
1993	5,761
1994	6,148
1995	6,783
1996	7,445
1997	7,405
1998	11,450
1999	11,224
2000	11,703
2001	11,890
2002	12,380
2003	12,181
2004	12,557
2005	12,700
2006	19,300
2007	22,100
2008	22,720
2009	21,136
2010	22,785
2011	23,377
2012	23,300

SOLUTION

The three-year moving average is:

Year	Attendance (000)	3-Year Moving Average	Found by
1993	5,761		
1994	6,148	6,230.7	(5,761.0 + 6,148.0 + 6,783.0)/3
1995	6,783	6,792.0	(6,148.0 + 6,783.0 + 7,445.0)/3
1996	7,445	7,211.0	↑
1997	7,405	8,766.7	
1998	11,450	10,026.3	
1999	11,224	11,459.0	
2000	11,703	11,605.7	
2001	11,890	11,991.0	
2002	12,380	12,150.3	
2003	12,181	12,372.7	
2004	12,557	12,479.3	
2005	12,700	14,852.3	
2006	19,300	18,033.3	
2007	22,100	21,373.3	
2008	22,720	21,985.3	
2009	21,136	22,213.7	
2010	22,785	22,432.7	↓
2011	23,377	23,154.0	(22,785.0 + 23,377.0 + 23,300)/3
2012	23,300		

The three-year weighted moving average is:

Year	Attendance (000)	3-Year Weighted Moving Average	Found by
1993	5,761		
1994	6,148	6,388.1	(.2)(5,761) + (.3)(6,148) + (.5)(6,783)
1995	6,783	6,987.0	(.2)(6,148) + (.3)(6,783) + (.5)(7,445)
1996	7,445	7,292.6	
1997	7,405	9,435.5	
1998	11,450	10,528.0	
1999	11,224	11,508.7	
2000	11,703	11,700.7	
2001	11,890	12,097.6	
2002	12,380	12,182.5	
2003	12,181	12,408.8	
2004	12,557	12,553.3	
2005	12,700	15,971.4	
2006	19,300	19,380.0	
2007	22,100	21,850.0	
2008	22,720	21,804.0	
2009	21,136	22,277.3	
2010	22,785	22,751.2	
2011	23,377	23,220.1	(.2)(22,785) + (.3)(23,377) +(.5)(23,300)
2012	23,300		

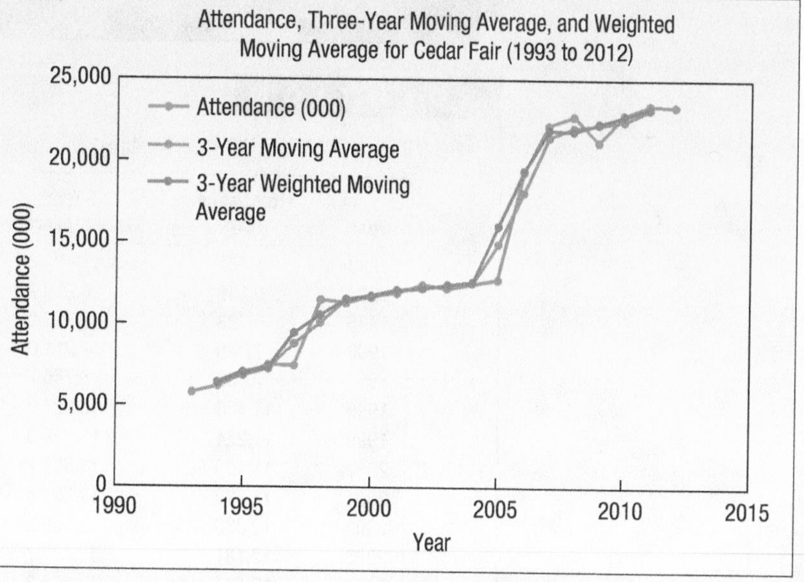

Study the graph carefully. You will see that the attendance trend is evenly upward with approximately 400,000 additional visitors each year. However, there is a "hop" of approximately 3 million per year between 1997 and 1998. That reflects the fact Cedar Fair acquired Knott's Berry Farm (located in Southern California) in late 1997, leading to a boost in attendance. A similar boost occurred in 2006 with the purchase of King's Island near Cincinnati, Ohio. You can also observe the financial crisis in 2009.

The weighted moving average follows the data more closely than the moving average. This reflects the additional influence given to the most recent period. In other words, the weighted method, where the most recent period is given the largest weight, won't be quite as smooth.

SELF-REVIEW 18–1

Determine a three-year moving average for the sales of Waccamaw Machine Tool Inc. Plot both the original data and the moving average.

Year	Number Produced (thousands)	Year	Number Produced (thousands)
2008	2	2011	5
2009	6	2012	3
2010	4	2013	10

EXERCISES

For DATA FILE, please visit www.mhhe.com/lind16e

1. Calculate a four-quarter weighted moving average for the number of shares outstanding for the Boxley Box Company for the nine quarters of data. The data are reported in thousands. Apply weights of .1, .2, .3, and .4, respectively, for the past three quarters and current quarter. In a few words, describe the trend in the number of subscribers.

1st Quarter 2011	28,766
2nd Quarter 2011	30,057
3rd Quarter 2011	31,336
4th Quarter 2011	33,240
1st Quarter 2012	34,610
2nd Quarter 2012	35,102
3rd Quarter 2012	35,308
4th Quarter 2012	35,203
1st Quarter 2013	34,386

For DATA FILE, please visit www.mhhe.com/lind16e

2. Listed below is the number of movie tickets sold at the Library Cinema-Complex, in thousands, for the period from 2001 to 2013. Compute a five-year weighted moving average using weights of .1, .1, .2, .3, and .3, respectively. Describe the trend in yield.

2001	8.61	2008	6.61
2002	8.14	2009	5.58
2003	7.67	2010	5.87
2004	6.59	2011	5.94
2005	7.37	2012	5.49
2006	6.88	2013	5.43
2007	6.71		

LO18-4
Use regression analysis to fit a linear trend line to a time series.

LINEAR TREND

The long-term trend of many business series, such as sales, exports, and production, often approximates a straight line. If so, the equation to describe this growth is:

LINEAR TREND EQUATION $$\hat{y} = a + bt \quad [18\text{–}1]$$

where:

$\hat{y}$, read *y*, hat, is the projected value of the *y* variable for a selected value of *t*.

a is the *y*-intercept. It is the estimated value of *y* when $t = 0$. Another way to put it is: *a* is the estimated value of *y* where the line crosses the *y*-axis when *t* is zero.

b is the slope of the line, or the average change in $\hat{y}$ for each increase of one unit in *t*.

t is any value of time that is selected.

To illustrate the meaning of $\hat{y}$, *a*, *b*, and *t* in a time-series problem, a line is drawn in Chart 18–5 to represent the typical trend of sales. Assume that this company started in business in 2005. This beginning year (2005) has been arbitrarily coded as time period 1. Note that sales increased an average of \$2 million every year; that is, based on the straight line drawn through the sales data, sales increased from \$3 million in 2005 to \$5 million in 2006, to \$7 million in 2007, to \$9 million in 2008, and so on. The slope, or *b*, is therefore 2. The slope is the average change in sales for each unit increase in the time period. Note too that the line intercepts the *y*-axis (when $t = 0$, which is the year 2004) at \$1 million. This point is *a*. Another way of determining *b* is to locate the starting place of the straight line in year 1. It is 3 for 2005 in this example. Then locate the value on the straight line for the last year. It is 19 for 2013.

Time Period	Year	Sales	Trend Line
1	2005	6	3
2	2006	2	5
3	2007	9	7
4	2008	8	9
5	2009	16	11
6	2010	10	13
7	2011	12	15
8	2012	21	17
9	2013	18	19

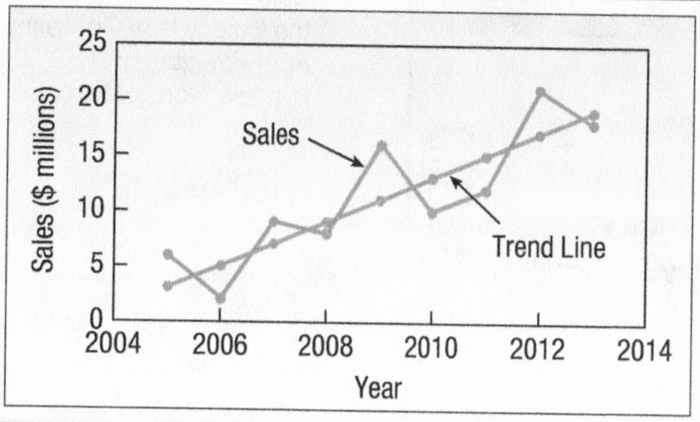

CHART 18–5 A Straight Line Fitted to Sales Data

The equation for the line in Chart 18–5 is:

$$\hat{y} = 1 + 2t$$

where:

$\hat{y}$ is sales in millions of dollars.

1 is the intercept with the *Y*-axis. It is also the sales in millions of dollars for year 0, or 2004.

t is the coded time period for each year.

In Chapter 13, we drew a line through points on a scatter diagram to approximate the regression line. We stressed, however, that this method for determining the regression equation has a serious drawback—namely, the position of the line depends on the judgment of the individual who drew the line. Three people would probably draw three different lines through the scatter plots. Likewise, the line we drew through the sales data in Chart 18–5 might not be the best-fitting line. Because of the subjective judgment involved, this method should be used only when a quick approximation of the straight-line equation is needed, or to check the reasonableness of the least squares line, which is discussed next.

Least Squares Method

In the discussion of simple linear regression in Chapter 13, we showed how the least squares method is used to find the best linear relationship between two variables. In forecasting methods, time is the independent variable and the value of the time series is the dependent variable. Furthermore, we often code the independent variable, time, to make the equations easier to interpret. In other words, we let *t* be 1 for the first year, 2 for the second, and so on. If a time series includes the sales of General Electric for 5 years starting in 2002 and continuing through 2006, we would code the year 2002 as 1, 2003 as 2, and 2006 as 5.

When the least squares method is used to find the trend line for a time series, the errors or residuals are usually correlated and not independent. Therefore, the results of the hypothesis tests for regression analysis presented in Chapter 13 may not be valid

in time series analysis. However, simple linear regression can still be used to find a line of best fit for a time series.

EXAMPLE

The sales of Jensen Foods, a small grocery chain located in southwest Texas, for 2009 through 2013 are:

Year	Time (t)	Sales ($ million)
2009	1	7.0
2010	2	10.0
2011	3	9.0
2012	4	11.0
2013	5	13.0

Determine the regression equation. How much are sales increasing each year? What is the sales forecast for 2015?

SOLUTION

To determine the trend equation, we could use formula (13–4) to find the slope, or b value, and formula (13–5) to locate the intercept, or a value. We would substitute t, the coded values for the year, for X in these equations. Another approach is to use a software package. Chart 18–6 shows the plot of sales and the fitted or trended sales for each year.

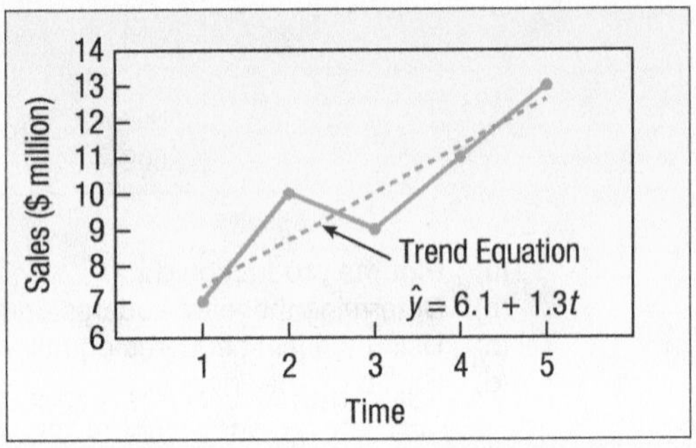

CHART 18–6 Sales and Trend Line for Jensen Foods (2009 to 2013)

From the regression analysis, the trend equation is $\hat{y} = 6.1 + 1.3t$. How do we interpret this equation? The sales are in millions of dollars. So the value 1.3 tells us that sales increased at a rate of 1.3 million dollars per year. The value 6.1 is the estimated value of sales in the year 0. That is the estimate for 2008, which is called the base year. For example, to determine the point on the line for 2012, insert the t value of 4 in the equation. Then $\hat{y} = 6.1 + 1.3(4) = 11.3$.

If sales, production, or other data approximate a linear trend, the equation developed by the least squares technique can be used to estimate future values. It is reasonable that the sales for Jensen Foods follow a linear trend. So we can use the trend equation to forecast future sales.

See Table 18–4. The year 2009 is coded 1, the year 2011 is coded 3, and year 2013 is coded 5. Logically, we code 2015 as 7 and 2016 as 8. So we substitute 7 into the trend equation and solve for $\hat{y}$.

$$\hat{y} = 6.1 + 1.3t = 6.1 + 1.3(7) = 15.2$$

Thus, on the basis of past sales, the estimate for 2015 is $15.2 million.

STATISTICS IN ACTION

Investors frequently use regression analysis to study the relationship between a particular stock and the general condition of the market. The dependent variable is the monthly percentage change in the value of the stock, and the independent variable is the monthly percentage change in a market index, such as the Standard & Poor's 500 Composite Index. The value of b in the regression equation is the particular stock's *beta coefficient,* or just the *beta*. If b is greater than 1, the implication is that the stock is sensitive to market changes. If b is between 0 and 1, the implication is that the stock is not sensitive to market changes.

TABLE 18–4 Calculations for Determining the Points on Trend Line

Year	Sales ($ million)	Code (t)	y	Found by
2009	7.0	1	7.4	6.1 + 1.3(1)
2010	10.0	2	8.7	6.1 + 1.3(2)
2011	9.0	3	10.0	6.1 + 1.3(3)
2012	11.0	4	11.3	6.1 + 1.3(4)
2013	13.0	5	12.6	6.1 + 1.3(5)

In this time series example, there were 5 years of sales data. Based on those five sales figures, we estimated sales for 2016. Many researchers suggest that we do not project sales, production, and other business and economic series more than $n/2$ time periods into the future where n is the number of data points. If, for example, there are 10 years of data, we would make estimates only up to 5 years into the future ($n/2 = 10/2 = 5$). Others suggest the forecast may be for no longer than 2 years, especially in rapidly changing economic times.

SELF-REVIEW 18–2

Annual production of king-size rockers by Wood Products Inc. for 2006 through 2013 follows.

Year	Production (thousands)	Year	Production (thousands)
2006	4	2010	11
2007	8	2011	9
2008	5	2012	11
2009	8	2013	14

(a) Plot the production data.
(b) Determine the least squares equation using a software package.
(c) Using the least squares equation, determine the points on the line for 2006 and 2013.
(d) Based on the linear trend equation, what is the estimated production for 2016?

EXERCISES

For **DATA FILE**, please visit www.mhhe.com/lind16e

3. Listed below is the number of rooms rented at Plantation Resorts of Georgia for the years from 2003 to 2013.

Year	Rental	Year	Rental	Year	Rental
2003	6,714	2007	9,762	2011	6,162
2004	7,991	2008	10,180	2012	6,897
2005	9,075	2009	8,334	2013	8,285
2006	9,775	2010	8,272		

Determine the least squares equation. According to this information, what is the estimated number of rentals for 2014?

For **DATA FILE**, please visit www.mhhe.com/lind16e

4. On the following page is the net sales in $ million for Home Depot Inc. and its subsidiaries from 1993 to 2012.

Year	Net Sales	Year	Net Sales	Year	Net Sales
1993	$ 9,239	2000	$45,738	2007	$77,349
1994	12,477	2001	53,553	2008	71,288
1995	15,470	2002	58,247	2009	66,176
1996	19,535	2003	64,816	2010	67,997
1997	24,156	2004	73,094	2011	70,395
1998	30,219	2005	81,511	2012	74,754
1999	38,434	2006	90,837		

Determine the least squares equation. On the basis of this information, what are the estimated sales for 2014 and 2015?

5. The following table lists the annual amounts of glass cullet produced by Kimble Glass Works Inc. for 2009 through 2013.

For **DATA FILE**, please visit www.mhhe.com/lind16e

Year	Code	Scrap (tons)	Year	Code	Scrap (tons)
2009	1	2	2012	4	5
2010	2	4	2013	5	6
2011	3	3			

Determine the least squares trend equation. Estimate the amount of scrap for the year 2015.

6. The sales by Walker's Milk and Dairy Products in millions of dollars for the period from 2007 to 2013 are reported in the following table.

For **DATA FILE**, please visit www.mhhe.com/lind16e

Year	Code	Sales ($ millions)	Year	Code	Sales ($ millions)
2007	1	17.5	2011	5	24.5
2008	2	19.0	2012	6	26.7
2009	3	21.0	2013	7	27.3
2010	4	22.7			

Determine the least squares regression trend equation. Estimate the sales for 2015.

LO18-5
Use regression analysis to fit a nonlinear time series.

NONLINEAR TRENDS

The emphasis in the previous discussion was on a time series whose growth or decline approximated a straight line. A linear trend equation is used to represent the time series when it is believed that the data are increasing (or decreasing) by *equal amounts,* on the average, from one period to another.

Data that increase (or decrease) by *increasing amounts* over a period of time appear *curvilinear* when plotted on an arithmetic scale. To put it another way, data that increase (or decrease) by *equal percents* or *proportions* over a period of time appear curvilinear. (See Chart 18–7.)

The trend equation for a time series that does approximate a curvilinear trend, such as the one portrayed in Chart 18–7, is computed by using the logarithms of the data and the least squares method. The general equation for the logarithmic trend equation is:

LOG TREND EQUATION $$\log \hat{y} = \log a + \log b(t) \qquad [18\text{–}2]$$

The logarithmic trend equation can be determined for the Gulf Shores Importers data in Chart 18–7 using Excel. The first step is to enter the data, then find the log

Year	Sales ($000)	Year	Sales ($000)
1999	124.2	2007	3,358.2
2000	175.6	2008	4,181.3
2001	306.9	2009	5,388.5
2002	524.2	2010	8,027.4
2003	714.0	2011	10,587.2
2004	1,052.0	2012	13,537.4
2005	1,638.3	2013	17,515.6
2006	2,463.2		

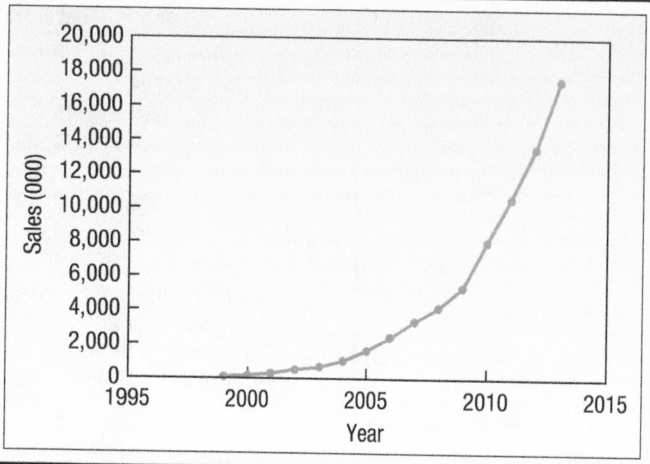

CHART 18–7 Sales for Gulf Shores Importers (1999–2013)

base 10 of each year's imports. Finally, use the regression procedure to find the least squares equation. That is, use the log of each year's data, then use the logs as the dependent variable and the coded year as the independent variable.

Code	Year	Sales ($000)	Log-sales
1	1999	124.2	2.094122
2	2000	175.6	2.244525
3	2001	306.9	2.486997
4	2002	524.2	2.719497
5	2003	714.0	2.853698
6	2004	1052.0	3.022016
7	2005	1638.3	3.214393
8	2006	2463.2	3.391500
9	2007	3358.2	3.526107
10	2008	4181.3	3.621311
11	2009	5388.5	3.731468
12	2010	8027.4	3.904575
13	2011	10587.2	4.024781
14	2012	13537.4	4.131535
15	2013	17515.6	4.243425

SUMMARY OUTPUT

Regression Statistics	
Multiple R	0.994
R Square	0.988
Adjusted R Square	0.987
Standard Error	0.079
Observations	15

ANOVA

	df	*SS*	*MS*	*F*
Regression	1	6.585	6.585	1065.2279
Residual	13	0.080	0.006	
Total	14	6.666		

	Coefficients
Intercept	2.053805
Code	0.153357

Regression Equation
$\hat{y} = 2.053805 + 0.153357t$

The regression equation is $\hat{y} = 2.053805 + 0.153357t$. This equation is the log form. We now have a trend equation in terms of percent of change. That is, the value 0.153357 is the percent of change in $\hat{y}$ for each unit increase in t. This value is similar to the geometric mean described in Chapter 3.

The log of b is 0.153357 and its antilog or inverse is 1.423498. If we subtract 1 from this value, as we did in Chapter 3, the value 0.423498 indicates the geometric mean annual rate of increase from 1999 to 2013. We conclude that imports increased at a rate of 42.35% annually during the period.

We can also use the logarithmic trend equation to make estimates of future values. Suppose we want to estimate the imports in the year 2017. The first step is to determine the code for the year 2017. It is 19. To explain, the year 2013 has a code of 15 and the year 2017 is 4 years later, so 15 + 4 = 19. The log of imports for the year 2017 is

$$\hat{y} = 2.053805 + 0.153357t = 2.053805 + 0.153357(19) = 4.967588$$

To find the estimated imports for the year 2017, we need the antilog of 4.967588. It is 92,809. This is our estimate of the number of imports for 2017. Recall that the data were in thousands of dollars, so the estimate is $92,809,000.

SELF-REVIEW 18–3

Sales at Tomlin Manufacturing from 2009 to 2013 are:

Year	Sales ($ millions)
2009	2.13
2010	18.10
2011	39.80
2012	81.40
2013	112.00

(a) Determine the logarithmic trend equation for the sales data.
(b) Sales increased by what percentage annually from 2009–2013?
(c) What is the projected sales amount for 2014?

EXERCISES

For **DATA FILE**, please visit www.mhhe.com/lind16e

7. Sally's Software Inc. is a rapidly growing supplier of computer software to the Sarasota area. Sales for the last 5 years, 2009 to 2013, are given below.

Year	Sales ($ millions)
2009	1.1
2010	1.5
2011	2.0
2012	2.4
2013	3.1

a. Determine the logarithmic trend equation.
b. By what percent did sales increase, on the average, during the period?
c. Estimate sales for the year 2016.

For **DATA FILE**, please visit www.mhhe.com/lind16e

8. It appears that the imports of carbon black have been increasing by about 10% annually.

Year	Imports of Carbon Black (thousands of tons)	Year	Imports of Carbon Black (thousands of tons)
2006	92.0	2010	135.0
2007	101.0	2011	149.0
2008	112.0	2012	163.0
2009	124.0	2013	180.0

a. Determine the logarithmic trend equation.
b. By what percent did imports increase, on the average, during the period?
c. Estimate imports for the year 2016.

LO18-6
Compute and apply seasonal indexes to make seasonally adjusted forecasts.

SEASONAL VARIATION

We mentioned that *seasonal variation* is another of the components of a time series. Business series, such as automobile sales, shipments of soft-drink bottles, and residential construction, have periods of above-average and below-average activity each year. In the area of production, one of the reasons for analyzing seasonal fluctuations is to have a sufficient supply of raw materials on hand to meet

the varying seasonal demand. The glass container division of a large glass company, for example, manufactures nonreturnable beer bottles, iodine bottles, aspirin bottles, bottles for rubber cement, and so on. The production scheduling department must know how many bottles to produce and when to produce each kind. A run of too many bottles of one kind may cause a serious storage problem. Production cannot be based entirely on orders on hand because many orders are telephoned in for immediate shipment. Since the demand for many of the bottles varies according to the season, a forecast a year or two in advance, by month, is essential to good scheduling.

An analysis of seasonal fluctuations over a period of years can also help in evaluating current sales. The typical sales of department stores in the United States, excluding mail-order sales, are expressed as indexes in Table 18–5. Each index represents the average sales for a period of several years. The actual sales for some months were above average (which is represented by an index over 100.0), and the sales for other months were below average. The index of 126.8 for December indicates that, typically, sales for December are 26.8% above an average month; the index of 86.0 for July indicates that department store sales for July are typically 14% below an average month.

TABLE 18–5 Typical Seasonal Indexes for U.S. Department Store Sales, Excluding Mail-Order Sales

January	87.0	July	86.0
February	83.2	August	99.7
March	100.5	September	101.4
April	106.5	October	105.8
May	101.6	November	111.9
June	89.6	December	126.8

Suppose an enterprising store manager, in an effort to stimulate sales during December, introduced a number of unique promotions, including bands of carolers strolling through the store singing holiday songs, large mechanical exhibits, and clerks dressed in Santa Claus costumes. When the index of sales was computed for that December, it was 150.0. Compared with the typical December sales of 126.8, it was concluded that the promotional program was a huge success.

Determining a Seasonal Index

A typical set of monthly indexes consists of 12 indexes that are representative of the data for a 12-month period. Logically, there are four typical seasonal indexes for data reported quarterly. Each index is a percent, with the average for the year equal to 100.0; that is, each monthly index indicates the level of sales, production, or another variable in relation to the annual average of 100.0. A typical index of 96.0 for January indicates that sales (or whatever the variable is) are usually 4% below the average for the year. An index of 107.2 for October means that the variable is typically 7.2% above the annual average.

Several methods have been developed to measure the typical seasonal fluctuation in a time series. The method most commonly used to compute the typical seasonal pattern is called the **ratio-to-moving-average method.** It eliminates the trend, cyclical, and irregular components from the original data (Y). In the following discussion, T refers to trend, C to cyclical, S to seasonal, and I to irregular variation. The numbers that result are called the *typical seasonal index.*

We will discuss in detail the steps followed in arriving at typical seasonal indexes using the ratio-to-moving-average method. The data of interest might be monthly or

quarterly. To illustrate, we have chosen the quarterly sales of Toys International. First, we will show the steps needed to arrive at a set of typical quarterly indexes. Then we use the MegaStat add-in for Excel to calculate the seasonal indexes.

EXAMPLE

Table 18–6 shows the quarterly sales for Toys International for the years 2008 through 2013. The sales are reported in millions of dollars. Determine a quarterly seasonal index using the ratio-to-moving-average method.

TABLE 18–6 Toys International Quarterly Sales ($ million), 2008 to 2013

Year	Winter	Spring	Summer	Fall
2008	6.7	4.6	10.0	12.7
2009	6.5	4.6	9.8	13.6
2010	6.9	5.0	10.4	14.1
2011	7.0	5.5	10.8	15.0
2012	7.1	5.7	11.1	14.5
2013	8.0	6.2	11.4	14.9

SOLUTION

Chart 18–8 depicts the quarterly sales for Toys International over the six-year period. Notice the seasonal nature of the sales. For each year, the fourth-quarter sales are the largest and the second-quarter sales are the smallest. Also, there is a moderate increase in the sales from one year to the next. To observe this feature, look only at the six fourth-quarter sales values. Over the six-year period, the sales in the fourth quarter increased. You would expect a similar seasonal pattern for 2014.

Year	Quarter	Sales ($ Million)	Year	Quarter	Sales ($ Million)
2008	1	6.7	2011	1	7.0
	2	4.6		2	5.5
	3	10.0		3	10.8
	4	12.7		4	15.0
2009	1	6.5	2012	1	7.1
	2	4.6		2	5.7
	3	9.8		3	11.1
	4	13.6		4	14.5
2010	1	6.9	2013	1	8.0
	2	5.0		2	6.2
	3	10.4		3	11.4
	4	14.1		4	14.9

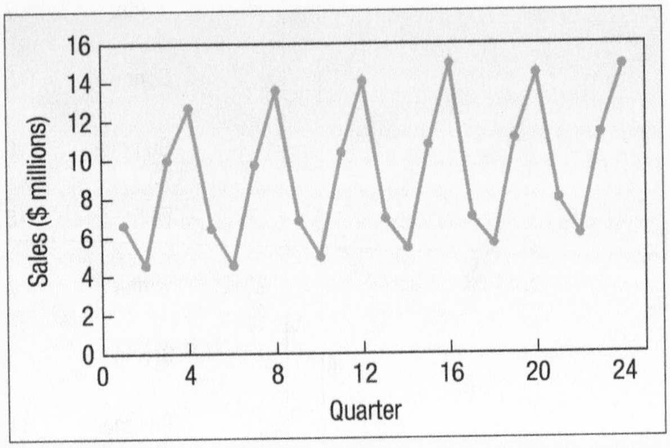

CHART 18–8 Toys International Quarterly Sales in ($ Million), 2008 to 2013

There are six steps to determining the quarterly seasonal indexes.

Step 1: For the following discussion, refer to Table 18–7. The first step is to determine the four-quarter moving total for 2008. Starting with the winter quarter of 2008, we add \$6.7, \$4.6, \$10.0, and \$12.7. The total is \$34.0 (million). The four-quarter total is "moved along" by

TABLE 18–7 Computations Needed for the Specific Seasonal Indexes

Year	Quarter	(1) Sales ($ millions)	(2) Four-Quarter Total	(3) Four-Quarter Moving Average	(4) Centered Moving Average	(5) Specific Seasonal
2008	Winter	6.7				
	Spring	4.6				
			34.0	8.500		
	Summer	10.0			8.475	1.180
			33.8	8.450		
	Fall	12.7			8.450	1.503
			33.8	8.450		
2009	Winter	6.5			8.425	0.772
			33.6	8.400		
	Spring	4.6			8.513	0.540
			34.5	8.625		
	Summer	9.8			8.675	1.130
			34.9	8.725		
	Fall	13.6			8.775	1.550
			35.3	8.825		
2010	Winter	6.9			8.900	0.775
			35.9	8.975		
	Spring	5.0			9.038	0.553
			36.4	9.100		
	Summer	10.4			9.113	1.141
			36.5	9.125		
	Fall	14.1			9.188	1.535
			37.0	9.250		
2011	Winter	7.0			9.300	0.753
			37.4	9.350		
	Spring	5.5			9.463	0.581
			38.3	9.575		
	Summer	10.8			9.588	1.126
			38.4	9.600		
	Fall	15.0			9.625	1.558
			38.6	9.650		
2012	Winter	7.1			9.688	0.733
			38.9	9.725		
	Spring	5.7			9.663	0.590
			38.4	9.600		
	Summer	11.1			9.713	1.143
			39.3	9.825		
	Fall	14.5			9.888	1.466
			39.8	9.950		
2013	Winter	8.0			9.888	0.801
			40.1	10.025		
	Spring	6.2			10.075	0.615
			40.5	10.125		
	Summer	11.4				
	Fall	14.9				

adding the spring, summer, and fall sales of 2008 to the winter sales of 2009. The total is $33.8 (million), found by 4.6 + 10.0 + 12.7 + 6.5. This procedure is continued for the quarterly sales for each of the six years. Column 2 of Table 18–7 shows all of the moving totals. Note that the moving total 34.0 is positioned between the spring and summer sales of 2008. The next moving total, 33.8, is positioned between sales for summer and fall 2008, and so on. Check the totals frequently to avoid arithmetic errors.

Step 2: Each quarterly moving total in column 2 is divided by 4 to give the four-quarter moving average. (See column 3.) All the moving averages are still positioned between the quarters. For example, the first moving average (8.500) is positioned between spring and summer 2008.

Step 3: The moving averages are then centered. The first centered moving average is found by (8.500 + 8.450)/2 = 8.475 and centered opposite summer 2008. The second moving average is found by (8.450 + 8.450)/2 = 8.450. The others are found similarly. Note in column 4 that a centered moving average is positioned on a particular quarter.

Step 4: The **specific seasonal index** for each quarter is then computed by dividing the sales in column 1 by the centered moving average in column 4. The specific seasonal index reports the ratio of the original time series value to the moving average. To explain further, if the time series is represented by *TSCI* and the moving average by *TC*, then, algebraically, if we compute *TSCI*/*TC*, the result is the specified seasonal component *SI*. The specific seasonal index for the summer quarter of 2008 is 1.180, found by 10.0/8.475.

Step 5: The specific seasonal indexes are organized in Table 18–8. This table will help us locate the specific seasonals for the corresponding quarters. The values 1.180, 1.130, 1.141, 1.126, and 1.143 all represent estimates of the typical seasonal index for the summer quarter. A reasonable method to find a typical seasonal index is to average these values in order to eliminate the irregular component. So we find the typical index for the summer quarter by (1.180 + 1.130 + 1.141 + 1.126 + 1.143)/5 = 1.144.

TABLE 18–8 Calculations Needed for Typical Quarterly Indexes

Year	Winter	Spring	Summer	Fall	
2008			1.180	1.503	
2009	0.772	0.540	1.130	1.550	
2010	0.775	0.553	1.141	1.535	
2011	0.753	0.581	1.126	1.558	
2012	0.733	0.590	1.143	1.466	
2013	0.801	0.615			
Total	3.834	2.879	5.720	7.612	
Mean	0.767	0.576	1.144	1.522	4.009
Adjusted	0.765	0.575	1.141	1.519	4.000
Index	76.5	57.5	114.1	151.9	

Step 6: The four quarterly means (0.767, 0.576, 1.144, and 1.522) should theoretically total 4.00 because the average is set at 1.0. The total of the four quarterly means may not exactly equal 4.00 due to rounding. In this problem, the total of the means is 4.009. A *correction factor* is therefore applied to each of the four means to force them to total 4.00.

CORRECTION FACTOR FOR ADJUSTING QUARTERLY MEANS

$$\text{Correction factor} = \frac{4.00}{\text{Total of four means}} \qquad [18\text{–}3]$$

In this example,

$$\text{Correction factor} = \frac{4.00}{4.009} = 0.997755$$

The adjusted winter quarterly index is, therefore, .767(.997755) = .765. Each of the means is adjusted downward so that the total of the four quarterly means is 4.00. Usually indexes are reported as percentages, so each value in the last row of Table 18–8 has been multiplied by 100. So the index for the winter quarter is 76.5 and for the fall it is 151.9. How are these values interpreted? Sales for the fall quarter are 51.9% above the typical quarter, and for winter they are 23.5% below the typical quarter (100.0 − 76.5). These findings should not surprise you. The period prior to Christmas (the fall quarter) is when toy sales are brisk. After Christmas (the winter quarter), sales of the toys decline drastically.

Statistical software can perform these calculations. For example, the output from the MegaStat add-in for Excel is shown below. Use of software will greatly reduce the computational time and the chance of an error in arithmetic, but you should understand the steps in the process, as outlined earlier. There can be slight differences in the answers, due to the number of digits carried in the calculations.

Centered Moving Average and Deseasonalization

t	Year	Quarter	Sales	Centered Moving Average	Ratio to CMA	Seasonal Indexes	Deseasonalized Sales
1	2008	1	6.70			0.765	8.759
2	2008	2	4.60			0.575	8.004
3	2008	3	10.00	8.475	1.180	1.141	8.761
4	2008	4	12.70	8.450	1.503	1.519	8.361
5	2009	1	6.50	8.425	0.772	0.765	8.498
6	2009	2	4.60	8.513	0.540	0.575	8.004
7	2009	3	9.80	8.675	1.130	1.141	8.586
8	2009	4	13.60	8.775	1.550	1.519	8.953
9	2010	1	6.90	8.900	0.775	0.765	9.021
10	2010	2	5.00	9.038	0.553	0.575	8.700
11	2010	3	10.40	9.113	1.141	1.141	9.112
12	2010	4	14.10	9.188	1.535	1.519	9.283
13	2011	1	7.00	9.300	0.753	0.765	9.151
14	2011	2	5.50	9.463	0.581	0.575	9.570
15	2011	3	10.80	9.588	1.126	1.141	9.462
16	2011	4	15.00	9.625	1.558	1.519	9.875
17	2012	1	7.10	9.688	0.733	0.765	9.282
18	2012	2	5.70	9.663	0.590	0.575	9.918
19	2012	3	11.10	9.713	1.143	1.141	9.725
20	2012	4	14.50	9.888	1.466	1.519	9.546
21	2013	1	8.00	9.988	0.801	0.765	10.459
22	2013	2	6.20	10.075	0.615	0.575	10.788
23	2013	3	11.40			1.141	9.988
24	2013	4	14.90			1.519	9.809

Calculation of Seasonal Indexes

	1	2	3	4	
2008			1.180	1.503	
2009	0.772	0.540	1.130	1.550	
2010	0.775	0.553	1.141	1.535	
2011	0.753	0.581	1.126	1.558	
2012	0.733	0.590	1.143	1.466	
2013	0.801	0.615			
Mean:	0.767	0.576	1.144	1.522	4.009
Adjusted:	0.765	0.575	1.141	1.519	4.000

Now we briefly summarize the reasoning underlying the preceding calculations. The original data in column 1 of Table 18–7 contain trend (*T*), cyclical (*C*), seasonal (*S*), and irregular (*I*) components. The ultimate objective is to remove seasonal (*S*) from the original sales valuation.

Columns 2 and 3 in Table 18–7 are concerned with deriving the centered moving average given in column 4. Basically, we "average out" the seasonal and irregular fluctuations from the original data in column 1. Thus, in column 4 we have only trend and cyclical (*TC*).

Next, we divide the sales data in column 1 (*TCSI*) by the centered fourth-quarter moving average in column 4 (*TC*) to arrive at the specific seasonals in column 5 (*SI*). In terms of letters, $TCSI/TC = SI$. We multiply *SI* by 100.0 to express the typical seasonal in index form.

Finally, we take the mean of all the winter typical indexes, all the spring indexes, and so on. This averaging eliminates most of the irregular fluctuations from the specific seasonals, and the resulting four indexes indicate the typical seasonal sales pattern.

SELF-REVIEW 18–4

Teton Village, Wyoming, near Grand Teton Park and Yellowstone Park, contains shops, restaurants, and motels. The village has two peak seasons—winter, for skiing on the 10,000-foot slopes, and summer, for tourists visiting the parks. The number of visitors (in thousands) by quarter for 5 years, 2009 through 2013, follows.

	Quarter			
Year	**Winter**	**Spring**	**Summer**	**Fall**
2009	117.0	80.7	129.6	76.1
2010	118.6	82.5	121.4	77.0
2011	114.0	84.3	119.9	75.0
2012	120.7	79.6	130.7	69.6
2013	125.2	80.2	127.6	72.0

(a) Develop the typical seasonal pattern for Teton Village using the ratio-to-moving-average method.
(b) Explain the typical index for the winter season.

EXERCISES

For **DATA FILE**, please visit www.mhhe.com/lind16e

9. Victor Anderson, the owner of Anderson Belts Inc., is studying absenteeism among his employees. His workforce is small, consisting of only five employees. For the last 3 years, 2011 through 2013, he recorded the following number of employee absences, in days, for each quarter.

	Quarter			
Year	**I**	**II**	**III**	**IV**
2011	4	10	7	3
2012	5	12	9	4
2013	6	16	12	4

Determine a typical seasonal index for each of the four quarters.

For **DATA FILE**, please visit www.mhhe.com/lind16e

10. Appliance Center sells a variety of electronic equipment and home appliances. For the last 4 years, 2010 through 2013, the following quarterly sales (in $ millions) were reported.

Year	Quarter I	II	III	IV
2010	5.3	4.1	6.8	6.7
2011	4.8	3.8	5.6	6.8
2012	4.3	3.8	5.7	6.0
2013	5.6	4.6	6.4	5.9

Determine a typical seasonal index for each of the four quarters.

LO18-7 Deseasonalize a time series using seasonal indexes.

DESEASONALIZING DATA

A set of typical indexes is very useful in adjusting a sales series, for example, for seasonal fluctuations. The resulting sales series is called **deseasonalized sales** or **seasonally adjusted sales.** The reason for deseasonalizing the sales series is to remove the seasonal fluctuations so that the trend and cycle can be studied. To illustrate the procedure, the quarterly sales totals of Toys International from Table 18–6 are repeated in column 1 of Table 18–9.

TABLE 18–9 Actual and Deseasonalized Sales for Toys International

Year	Quarter	(1) Sales	(2) Seasonal Index	(3) Deseasonalized Sales
2008	Winter	6.7	0.765	8.759
	Spring	4.6	0.575	8.004
	Summer	10.0	1.141	8.761
	Fall	12.7	1.519	8.361
2009	Winter	6.5	0.765	8.498
	Spring	4.6	0.575	8.004
	Summer	9.8	1.141	8.586
	Fall	13.6	1.519	8.953
2010	Winter	6.9	0.765	9.021
	Spring	5.0	0.575	8.700
	Summer	10.4	1.141	9.112
	Fall	14.1	1.519	9.283
2011	Winter	7.0	0.765	9.151
	Spring	5.5	0.575	9.570
	Summer	10.8	1.141	9.462
	Fall	15.0	1.519	9.875
2012	Winter	7.1	0.765	9.282
	Spring	5.7	0.575	9.918
	Summer	11.1	1.141	9.725
	Fall	14.5	1.519	9.546
2013	Winter	8.0	0.765	10.459
	Spring	6.2	0.575	10.788
	Summer	11.4	1.141	9.988
	Fall	14.9	1.519	9.809

To remove the effect of seasonal variation, the sales amount for each quarter (which contains trend, cyclical, irregular, and seasonal effects) is divided by the seasonal index for that quarter, that is, $TSCI/S$. For example, the actual sales for the first quarter of 2008 were $6.7 million. The seasonal index for the winter quarter is 76.5%, using the results on page 659. The index of 76.5 indicates that sales for the first quarter are typically 23.5%

below the average for a typical quarter. By dividing the actual sales of \$6.7 million by 76.5 and multiplying the result by 100, we find the *deseasonalized sales* value—that is, removed the seasonal effect on sales—for the first quarter of 2008. It is \$8,758,170, found by (\$6,700,000/76.5)100. We continue this process for the other quarters in column 3 of Table 18–9, with the results reported in millions of dollars. Because the seasonal component has been removed (divided out) from the quarterly sales, the deseasonalized sales value contains only the trend (*T*), cyclical (*C*), and irregular (*I*) components. Scanning the deseasonalized sales in column 3 of Table 18–9, we see that the sales of toys showed a moderate increase over the six-year period. Chart 18–9 shows both the actual sales and the deseasonalized sales. It is clear that removing the seasonal factor allows us to focus on the overall long-term trend of sales. We will also be able to determine the regression equation of the trend data and use it to forecast future sales.

Year	Time	Sales ($ Million)	Deseasonalized Sales ($ Million)	Year	Time	Sales ($ Million)	Deseasonalized Sales ($ Million)
2008	1	6.7	8.759	2011	13	7.0	9.151
	2	4.6	8.004		14	5.5	9.570
	3	10.0	8.761		15	10.8	9.462
	4	12.7	8.361		16	15.0	9.875
2009	5	6.5	8.498	2012	17	7.1	9.282
	6	4.6	8.004		18	5.7	9.918
	7	9.8	8.586		19	11.1	9.725
	8	13.6	8.953		20	14.5	9.546
2010	9	6.9	9.021	2013	21	8.0	10.459
	10	5.0	8.700		22	6.2	10.788
	11	10.4	9.112		23	11.4	9.988
	12	14.1	9.283		24	14.9	9.809

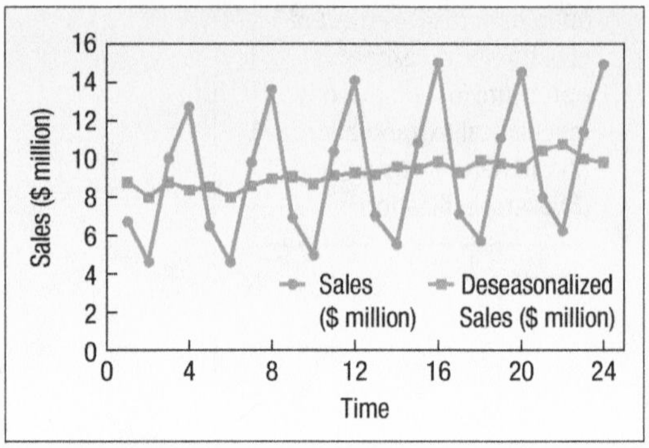

CHART 18–9 Actual and Deseasonalized Sales for Toys International (2008 to 2013)

Using Deseasonalized Data to Forecast

The procedure for identifying trend and the seasonal adjustments can be combined to yield seasonally adjusted forecasts. To identify the trend, we determine the least squares trend equation on the deseasonalized historical data. Then we project this trend into future periods, and finally we adjust these trend values to account for the seasonal factors. The following example will help to clarify.

EXAMPLE

Toys International would like to forecast its sales for each quarter of 2014. Use the information in Table 18–9 to determine the forecast.

SOLUTION

The deseasonalized data depicted in Chart 18–9 seem to follow a straight line. Hence, it is reasonable to develop a linear trend equation based on these data. The deseasonalized trend equation is:

$$\hat{y} = a + bt$$

where:

$\hat{y}$ is the estimated trend value for Toys International sales for the period t.
a is the intercept of the trend line at time 0.
b is the slope of the line.
t is the coded time period.

STATISTICS IN ACTION

Forecasts are not always correct. The reality is that a forecast may just be a best guess as to what will happen. What are the reasons forecasts are not correct? One expert lists eight common errors: (1) failure to carefully examine the assumptions, (2) limited expertise, (3) lack of imagination, (4) neglect of constraints, (5) excessive optimism, (6) reliance on mechanical extrapolation, (7) premature closure, and (8) overspecification.

The winter quarter of 2008 is the first quarter, so it is coded 1, the spring quarter of 2008 is coded 2, and so on. The last quarter of 2013 is coded 24.

We use Excel to find the regression equation. The output follows. The output includes a scatter diagram of the coded time periods and the deseasonalized sales as well as the regression line.

The equation for the trend line is:

$$\hat{y} = 8.11043 + 0.08988t$$

The slope of the trend line is 0.08988. This shows that over the 24 quarters the deseasonalized sales increased at a rate of 0.08988 ($ million) per quarter, or $89,880 per quarter. The value of 8.11043 is the intercept of the trend line on the Y-axis (i.e., for $t = 0$).

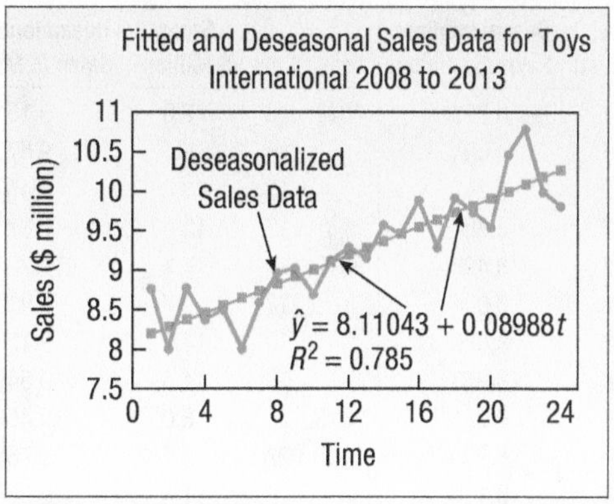

The coefficient of determination is .785. This value is computed using Excel and is shown in the text box on the graph. We can use this value as an indication of the fit of the data. Because this is *not* sample information, technically we should not use R^2 for judging a regression equation. However, it will serve to quickly evaluate the fit of the deseasonalized sales data. In this instance, because R^2 is rather large, we conclude the deseasonalized sales of Toys International are effectively explained by a linear trend equation.

If we assume that the past 24 periods are a good indicator of future sales, we can use the trend equation to estimate future sales. For example, for the winter quarter of 2014 the value of t is 25. Therefore, the estimated sales of that period are 10.35743, found by

$$\hat{y} = 8.11043 + 0.08988t = 8.11043 + 0.08988(25) = 10.35743$$

The estimated deseasonalized sales for the winter quarter of 2014 are $10,357,430. This is the sales forecast, before we consider the effects of seasonality.

We use the same procedure and an Excel spreadsheet to determine a forecast for each of the four quarters of 2014. A partial Excel output follows.

Quarterly Forecast for Toys International 2014

Quarter	Time	Estimated Sales	Seasonal Index	Quarterly Forecast
Winter	25	10.35743	0.765	7.92343
Spring	26	10.44731	0.575	6.00720
Summer	27	10.53719	1.141	12.02293
Fall	28	10.62707	1.519	16.14252

Now that we have the forecasts for the four quarters of 2014, we can seasonally adjust them. The index for a winter quarter is 0.765. So we can seasonally adjust the forecast for the winter quarter of 2014 by 10.35743(.765) = 7.92343. The estimates for each of the four quarters of 2014 are in the right-hand column of the Excel output. Notice how the seasonal adjustments drastically increase the sales estimates for the last two quarters of the year.

SELF-REVIEW 18–5

Westberg Electric Company sells electric motors to customers in the Jamestown, New York, area. The monthly trend equation, based on 5 years of monthly data, is

$$\hat{y} = 4.4 + 0.5t$$

The seasonal factor for the month of January is 120, and it is 95 for February. Determine the seasonally adjusted forecast for January and February of the sixth year.

EXERCISES

11. The planning department of Padget and Kure Shoes, the manufacturer of an exclusive brand of women's shoes, developed the following trend equation, in millions of pairs, based on 5 years of quarterly data.

$$\hat{y} = 3.30 + 1.75t$$

The following table gives the seasonal factors for each quarter.

	Quarter			
	I	II	III	IV
Index	110.0	120.0	80.0	90.0

Determine the seasonally adjusted forecast for each of the four quarters of the sixth year.

12. Team Sports Inc. sells sporting goods to high schools and colleges via a nationally distributed catalog. Management at Team Sports estimates it will sell 2,000 Wilson Model A2000 catcher's mitts next year. The deseasonalized sales are projected to be the same for each of the four quarters next year. The seasonal factor for the second quarter is 145. Determine the seasonally adjusted sales for the second quarter of next year.

13. Refer to Exercise 9 regarding the absences at Anderson Belts, Inc. Use the seasonal indexes you computed to determine the deseasonalized absences. Determine the linear trend equation based on the quarterly data for the 3 years. Forecast the seasonally adjusted absences for 2014.

14. Refer to Exercise 10, regarding sales at Appliance Center. Use the seasonal indexes you computed to determine the deseasonalized sales. Determine the linear trend equation based on the quarterly data for the 4 years. Forecast the seasonally adjusted sales for 2014.

LO18-8
Conduct a hypothesis test of autocorrelation.

THE DURBIN-WATSON STATISTIC

Time series data or observations collected successively over a period of time present a particular difficulty when you use the technique of regression. One of the assumptions traditionally used in regression is that the successive residuals are independent. This means that there is not a pattern to the residuals, the residuals are not highly correlated, and there are not long runs of positive or negative residuals. In Chart 18–10, the residuals are scaled on the vertical axis and the $\hat{y}$ values along the horizontal axis. Notice there are "runs" of residuals above and below the 0 line. If we computed the correlation between successive residuals, it is likely the correlation would be strong.

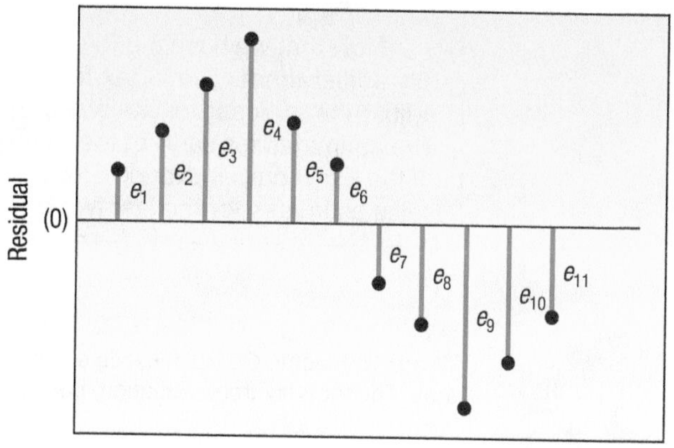

CHART 18–10 Correlated Residuals

This condition is called **autocorrelation** or serial correlation.

> **AUTOCORRELATION** Successive residuals are correlated.

Successive residuals are correlated in time series data because an event in one time period often influences the event in the next period. To explain, the owner of a furniture store decides to have a sale this month and spends a large amount of money advertising the event. We would expect a correlation between sales and advertising expense, but all the results of the increase in advertising are not experienced this month. It is likely that some of the effect of the advertising carries over into next month. Therefore, we expect correlation among the residuals.

The regression relationship in a time series is written

$$Y_t = \alpha + \beta_1 X_t + \varepsilon_t$$

where the subscript t is used in place of i to suggest the data were collected over time.

If the residuals are correlated, problems occur when we try to conduct tests of hypotheses about the regression coefficients. Also, a confidence interval or a prediction interval, where the multiple standard error of estimate is used, may not yield the correct results.

The autocorrelation, reported as r, is the strength of the association among the residuals. The r has the same characteristics as the coefficient of correlation. That is, values close to -1.00 or 1.00 indicate a strong association, and values near 0 indicate no association. Instead of directly conducting a hypothesis test on r, we use the **Durbin-Watson statistic.**

The Durbin-Watson statistic, identified by the letter d, is computed by first determining the residuals for each observation. That is, $e_t = (y_t - \hat{y}_t)$. Next, we compute d using the following relationship.

> **DURBIN-WATSON STATISTIC** $$d = \frac{\sum_{t=2}^{n} (e_t - e_{t-1})^2}{\sum_{t=1}^{n} (e_t)^2} \qquad \textbf{[18–4]}$$

To determine the numerator of formula (18–4), we lag each of the residuals one period and then square the difference between consecutive residuals. This may also be called finding the differences. This accounts for summing the observations from 2, rather than from 1, up to n. In the denominator, we square the residuals and sum over all n observations.

The value of the Durbin-Watson statistic can range from 0 to 4. The value of d is 2.00 when there is no autocorrelation among the residuals. When the value of d is close to 0, this indicates positive autocorrelation. Values beyond 2 indicate negative autocorrelation. Negative autocorrelation seldom exists in practice. To occur, successive residuals would tend to be large, but would have opposite signs.

To conduct a test for autocorrelation, the null and alternate hypotheses are:

H_0: No residual correlation ($\rho = 0$)

H_1: Positive residual correlation ($\rho > 0$)

Recall from the previous chapter that r refers to the sample correlation and that ρ is the correlation coefficient in the population. The critical values for d are reported in Appendix B.9. To determine the critical value, we need α (the significance level), n (the sample size), and k (the number of independent variables). The decision rule for the Durbin-Watson test is altered from what we are used to. As usual, there is a range of values where the null hypothesis is rejected and a range where it is not rejected. However, there is also a range of values where d is inconclusive. That is, in the inconclusive range the null hypothesis is neither rejected nor not rejected. To state this more formally:

- Values less than d_l cause the rejection of the null hypothesis.
- Values greater then d_u will result in the null hypothesis not being rejected.
- Values of d between d_l and d_u yield inconclusive results.

The subscript l refers to the lower limit of d and the subscript u the upper limit.

How do we interpret the various decisions for the test for residual correlation? If the null hypothesis is not rejected, we conclude that autocorrelation is not present. The residuals are not correlated, there is no autocorrelation present, and the regression assumption has been met. There will not be any problem with the estimated value of the standard error of estimate. If the null hypothesis is rejected, then we conclude that autocorrelation is present.

The usual remedy for autocorrelation is to include another predictor variable that captures time order. For example, we might use the square root of y instead of y. This transformation will result in a change in the distribution of the residuals. If the result falls in the inconclusive range, more sophisticated tests are needed, or conservatively, we treat the conclusion as rejecting the null hypothesis.

An example will show the details of the Durbin-Watson test and how the results are interpreted.

EXAMPLE

Banner Rocker Company manufactures and markets rocking chairs. The company developed a special rocker for senior citizens, which it advertises extensively on TV. Banner's market for the special chair is the Carolinas, Florida, and Arizona where there are many senior citizens and retired people. The president of Banner Rocker is studying the association between his advertising expense (X) and the number of rockers sold over the last 20 months (Y). He collected the following data. He would like to create a model to forecast sales, based on the amount spent on advertising, but is concerned that, because he gathered these data over consecutive months, there might be problems with autocorrelation.

Month	Sales (000)	Advertising ($ millions)	Month	Sales (000)	Advertising ($ millions)
1	153	$5.5	11	169	$6.3
2	156	5.5	12	176	5.9
3	153	5.3	13	176	6.1
4	147	5.5	14	179	6.2
5	159	5.4	15	184	6.2
6	160	5.3	16	181	6.5
7	147	5.5	17	192	6.7
8	147	5.7	18	205	6.9
9	152	5.9	19	215	6.5
10	160	6.2	20	209	6.4

Determine the regression equation. Is advertising a good predictor of sales? If the owner were to increase the amount spent on advertising by $1,000,000, how many additional chairs can he expect to sell? Investigate the possibility of autocorrelation.

SOLUTION

The first step is to determine the regression equation.

SUMMARY OUTPUT

Regression Statistics	
Multiple R	0.828
R Square	0.685
Adjusted R Square	0.668
Standard Error	12.347
Observations	20

ANOVA

	df	*SS*	*MS*	*F*
Regression	1	5967.731456	5967.73146	39.1430957
Residual	18	2744.268544	152.459364	
Total	19	8712		

	Coefficients	*Standard Error*	*t Stat*	*P-value*
Intercept	-43.80	34.44	-1.27	0.22
Advertising	35.95	5.75	6.256	0.00

The coefficient of determination is 68.5%. So we know there is a strong positive association between the variables. We conclude that, as we increase the amount spent on advertising, we can expect to sell more chairs. Of course this is what we had hoped.

How many more chairs can we expect to sell if we increase advertising by $1,000,000? We must be careful with the units of the data. Sales are in thousands of chairs and advertising expense is in millions of dollars. The regression equation is:

$$\hat{y} = -43.80 + 35.95x$$

This equation indicates that an increase of 1 in X will result in an increase of 35.95 in y. So an increase of $1,000,000 in advertising will increase sales by 35,950 chairs. To put it another way, it will cost $27.82 in additional advertising expense per chair sold, found by $1,000,000/35,950.

What about the potential issue of autocorrelation? Many software packages will calculate the value of the Durbin-Watson test and output the results. To understand the nature of the test and to see the details of formula (18–4), we use an Excel spreadsheet.

A	B	C	D	E	F	G	H
Month	Sales (000) y	Advertising ($ Millions) x	Predicted Sales $\hat{y}$	Residuals $e_t = y - \hat{y}$	Lagged Residuals e_{t-1}	$(e_t - e_{t-1})^2$	e_t^2
1	153	5.5	153.925	-0.925			0.8556
2	156	5.5	153.925	2.075	-0.925	9.000	4.3056
3	153	5.3	146.735	6.265	2.075	17.556	39.2502
4	147	5.5	153.925	-6.925	6.265	173.976	47.9556
5	159	5.4	150.330	8.670	-6.925	243.204	75.1689
6	160	5.3	146.735	13.265	8.670	21.114	175.9602
7	147	5.5	153.925	-6.925	13.265	407.636	47.9556
8	147	5.7	161.115	-14.115	-6.925	51.696	199.2332
9	152	5.9	168.305	-16.305	-14.115	4.796	265.8530
10	160	6.2	179.090	-19.090	-16.305	7.756	364.4281
11	169	6.3	182.685	-13.685	-19.090	29.214	187.2792
12	176	5.9	168.305	7.695	-13.685	457.104	59.2130
13	176	6.1	175.495	0.505	7.695	51.696	0.2550
14	179	6.2	179.090	-0.090	0.505	0.354	0.0081
15	184	6.2	179.090	4.910	-0.090	25.000	24.1081
16	181	6.5	189.875	-8.875	4.910	190.026	78.7656
17	192	6.7	197.065	-5.065	-8.875	14.516	25.6542
18	205	6.9	204.255	0.745	-5.065	33.756	0.5550
19	215	6.5	189.875	25.125	0.745	594.384	631.2656
20	209	6.4	186.280	22.720	25.125	5.784	516.1984
						2338.570	2744.26858

$\sum_{t=1}^{n}(e_t)^2$

$\sum_{t=2}^{n}(e_t - e_{t-1})^2$

To investigate the possible autocorrelation, we need to determine the residuals for each observation. We find the fitted values—that is, the $\hat{Y}$—for each of the 20 months. This information is shown in the fourth column, column D. Next we find the residual, which is the difference between the actual value and the fitted values. So for the first month:

$$\hat{y} = -43.80 + 35.950x = -43.80 + 35.950(5.5) = 153.925$$

$$e_1 = y_1 - \hat{y}_1 = 153 - 153.925 = -0.925$$

The residual, reported in column E, is slightly different due to rounding in the software. Notice in particular the string of five negative residuals for months 7 through 11. In column F, we lag the residuals one period. In column G, we find the difference between the current residual and the residual in the previous and square this difference. Using the values from the software:

$$(e_t - e_{t-1})^2 = (e_2 - e_{2-1})^2 = [2.075 - (-.925)]^2 = (3.0000)^2 = 9.0000$$

The other values in column G are found the same way. The values in column H are the squares of those in column E.

$$(e_1)^2 = (-0.925)^2 = 0.8556$$

To find the value of *d*, we need the sums of columns G and H. These sums are noted in blue in the spreadsheet.

$$d = \frac{\sum_{t=2}^{n}(e_t - e_{t-1})^2}{\sum_{t=1}^{n}(e_t)^2} = \frac{2338.570}{2744.269} = 0.8522$$

Now to answer the question as to whether there is significant autocorrelation. The null and the alternate hypotheses are stated as follows.

H_0: No residual correlation

H_1: Positive residual correlation

The critical value of d is found in Appendix B.9, a portion of which is shown below. There is one independent variable, so $k = 1$, the level of significance is 0.05, and the sample size is 20. We move to the .05 table, the columns where $k = 1$, and the row of 20. The reported values are $d_l = 1.20$ and $d_u = 1.41$. The null hypothesis is rejected if $d < 1.20$ and not rejected if $d > 1.41$. No conclusion is reached if d is between 1.20 and 1.41.

n	k = 1 d_l	d_u	2 d_l	d_u
15	1.08	1.36	0.95	1.54
16	1.10	1.37	0.98	1.54
17	1.13	1.38	1.02	1.54
18	1.16	1.39	1.05	1.53
19	1.18	1.40	1.08	1.53
20	1.20	1.41	1.10	1.54
21	1.22	1.42	1.13	1.54
22	1.24	1.43	1.15	1.54
23	1.26	1.44	1.17	1.54
24	1.27	1.45	1.19	1.55
25	1.29	1.45	1.21	1.55

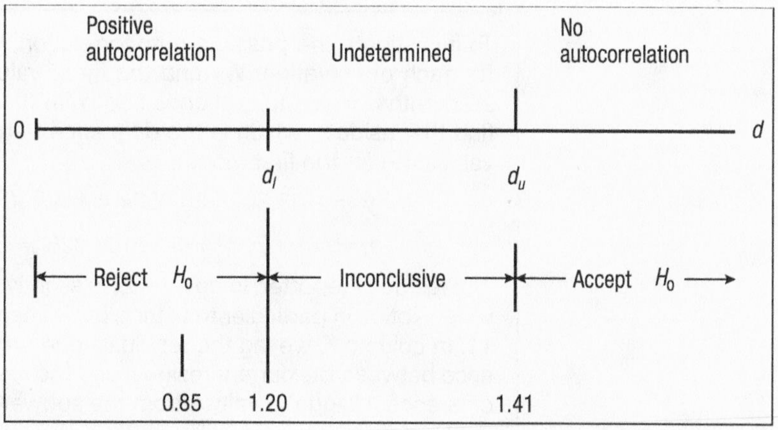

Because the computed value of d is 0.8522, which is less than the d_l, we reject the null hypothesis and accept the alternate hypothesis. We conclude that the residuals are autocorrelated. We have violated one of the regression assumptions. What do we do? The presence of autocorrelation usually means that the regression model has not been correctly specified. It is likely we need to add one or more independent variables that have some time-ordered effects on the dependent variable. The simplest independent variable to add is one that represents the time periods.

EXERCISES

15. Recall Exercise 9 from Chapter 14 and the regression equation to predict job performance. See page 506.
    a. Plot the residuals in the order in which the data are presented.
    b. Test for autocorrelation at the .05 significance level.
16. Consider the data in Exercise 10 from Chapter 14 and the regression equation to predict commissions earned. See page 507.
    a. Plot the residuals in the order in which the data are presented.
    b. Test for autocorrelation at the .01 significance level.

CHAPTER SUMMARY

I. A time series is a collection of data over a period of time.
  A. The trend is the long-run direction of the time series.
  B. The cyclical component is the fluctuation above and below the long-term trend line over a longer period of time.
  C. The seasonal variation is the pattern in a time series within a year. These patterns tend to repeat themselves from year to year for most businesses.
  D. The irregular variation is divided into two components.
    1. The episodic variations are unpredictable, but they can usually be identified. A flood is an example.
    2. The residual variations are random in nature.

II. A moving average is used to smooth the trend in a time series.

III. The linear trend equation is $\hat{y} = a + bt$, where a is the Y-intercept, b is the slope of the line, and t is the coded time.
  A. We use least squares to determine the trend equation.
  B. If the trend is not linear, but rather the increases tend to be a constant percent, the y values are converted to logarithms, and a least squares equation is determined using the logarithms.

IV. The seasonal factor is estimated using the ratio-to-moving-average method.
  A. The six-step procedure yields a seasonal index for each period.
    1. Seasonal factors are usually computed on a monthly or a quarterly basis.
    2. The seasonal factor is used to adjust forecasts, taking into account the effects of the season.

V. The Durbin-Watson statistic [18–4] is used to test for autocorrelation.

$$d = \frac{\sum_{t=2}^{n} (e_t - e_{t-1})^2}{\sum_{t=1}^{n} (e_t)^2} \qquad \textbf{[18–4]}$$

CHAPTER EXERCISES

17. Refer to the following diagram.

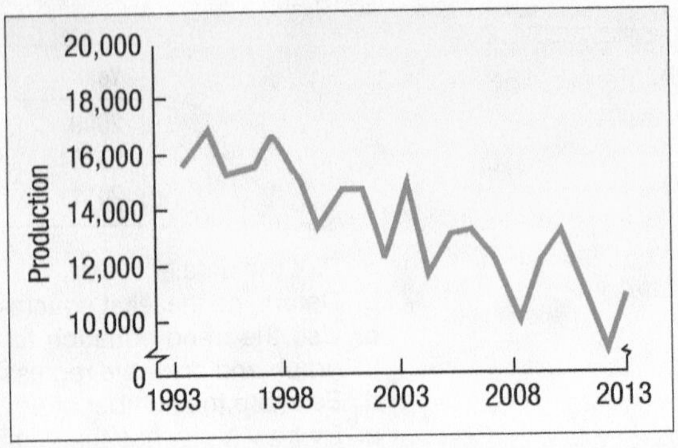

a. Estimate the linear trend equation for the production series by drawing a straight line through the data.
b. What is the average annual decrease in production?
c. Based on the trend equation, what is the forecast for the year 2019?

18. Refer to the following diagram.
a. Estimate the linear trend equation for the personal income series.
b. What is the average annual increase in personal income?

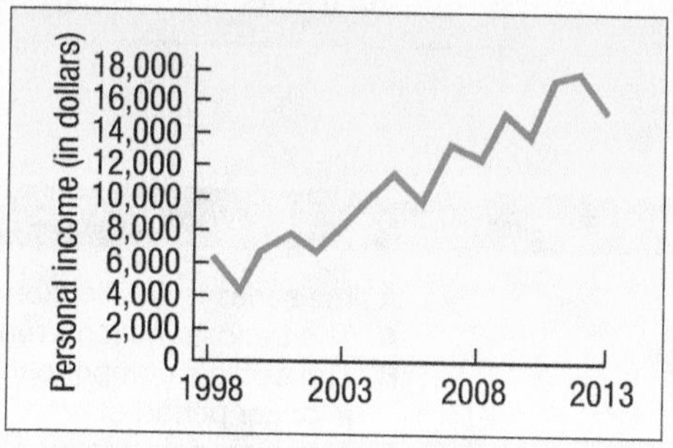

For **DATA FILE**, please visit www.mhhe.com/lind16e

19. The asset turnovers, excluding cash and short-term investments, for RNC Company from 2004 to 2014 are:

2004	2005	2006	2007	2008	2009	2010	2011	2012	2013	2014
1.11	1.28	1.17	1.10	1.06	1.14	1.24	1.33	1.38	1.50	1.65

a. Plot the data.
b. Determine the least squares trend equation.
c. Calculate the points on the trend line for 2007 and 2012, and plot the line on the graph.
d. Estimate the asset turnover for 2019.
e. How much did the asset turnover increase per year, on the average, from 2004 to 2014?

For **DATA FILE**, please visit www.mhhe.com/lind16e

20. The sales, in billions of dollars, of Keller Overhead Door Inc. for 2009 to 2014 are:

Year	Sales	Year	Sales
2009	7.45	2012	7.94
2010	7.83	2013	7.76
2011	8.07	2014	7.90

a. Plot the data.
b. Determine the least squares trend equation.
c. Use the trend equation to calculate the points for 2011 and 2014. Plot them on the graph and draw the regression line.
d. Estimate the net sales for 2017.
e. By how much have sales increased (or decreased) per year on the average during the period?

For **DATA FILE**, please visit www.mhhe.com/lind16e

21. The number of employees, in thousands, of Keller Overhead Door Inc. for the years 2009 to 2014 are:

Year	Employees	Year	Employees
2009	45.6	2012	39.3
2010	42.2	2013	34.0
2011	41.1	2014	30.0

a. Plot the data.
b. Determine the least squares trend equation.
c. Use the trend equation to calculate the points for 2011 and 2014. Plot them on the graph and draw the regression line.
d. Estimate the number of employees in 2017.
e. By how much has the number of employees increased (or decreased) per year, on the average, during the period?

For **DATA FILE**, please visit www.mhhe.com/lind16e

22. Listed below is the selling price for a share of PepsiCo Inc. at the close of each year from 1990 to 2012.

Year	Price	Year	Price	Year	Price	Year	Price
1990	12.9135	1996	29.0581	2002	42.22	2008	54.77
1991	16.8250	1997	36.0155	2003	46.62	2009	60.80
1992	20.6125	1998	40.6111	2004	52.20	2010	65.33
1993	20.3024	1999	35.0230	2005	59.85	2011	66.35
1994	18.3160	2000	49.5625	2006	62.00	2012	68.43
1995	27.7538	2001	48.68	2007	77.51		

a. Plot the data.
b. Determine the least squares trend equation.
c. Calculate the points for the years 1995 and 2000.
d. Estimate the selling price in 2016. Does this seem like a reasonable estimate based on the historical data?
e. By how much has the stock price increased or decreased (per year) on average during the period?

For **DATA FILE**, please visit www.mhhe.com/lind16e

23. If plotted, the following sales series would appear curvilinear. This indicates that sales are increasing at a somewhat constant annual rate (percent). To fit the sales, therefore, a logarithmic equation should be used.

Year	Sales ($ millions)	Year	Sales ($ millions)
2004	8.0	2010	39.4
2005	10.4	2011	50.5
2006	13.5	2012	65.0
2007	17.6	2013	84.1
2008	22.8	2014	109.0
2009	29.3		

a. Determine the logarithmic equation.
b. Determine the coordinates of the points on the logarithmic straight line for 2005 and 2011.
c. By what percent did sales increase per year, on the average, during the period from 2004 to 2014?
d. Based on the equation, what are the estimated sales for 2015?

For **DATA FILE**, please visit www.mhhe.com/lind16e

24. Reported below are the amounts spent on advertising ($ millions) by a large firm from 2004 to 2014.

Year	Amount	Year	Amount
2004	88.1	2010	132.6
2005	94.7	2011	141.9
2006	102.1	2012	150.9
2007	109.8	2013	157.9
2008	118.1	2014	162.6
2009	125.6		

a. Determine the logarithmic trend equation.
b. Estimate the advertising expenses for 2017.
c. By what percent per year did advertising expense increase during the period?

For **DATA FILE**, please visit www.mhhe.com/lind16e

25. Listed below is the selling price for a share of Oracle Inc. stock at the close of the year for 1990 through 2012.

Year	Price	Year	Price	Year	Price	Year	Price
1990	0.1944	1996	4.6388	2002	10.80	2008	17.73
1991	0.3580	1997	3.7188	2003	13.23	2009	24.53
1992	0.7006	1998	7.1875	2004	13.72	2010	31.30
1993	1.4197	1999	28.0156	2005	12.21	2011	26.33
1994	2.1790	2000	29.0625	2006	19.11	2012	34.08
1995	3.1389	2001	13.81	2007	20.23		

a. Plot the data.
b. Determine the least squares trend equation. Use both the actual stock price and the logarithm of the price. Which seems to yield a more accurate forecast?
c. Using the equation with the logarithm of price, calculate the points for the years 1993 and 1998.
d. Using the equation with the logarithm of price, estimate the selling price in 2015. Does this seem like a reasonable estimate based on the historical data?
e. Using the equation with the logarithm of price, how much has the stock price increased or decreased (per year) on average during the period?

26. The production of Reliable Manufacturing Company for 2012 and part of 2013 follows.

Month	2012 Production (thousands)	2013 Production (thousands)	Month	2012 Production (thousands)	2013 Production (thousands)
January	6	7	July	3	4
February	7	9	August	5	
March	12	14	September	14	
April	8	9	October	6	
May	4	5	November	7	
June	3	4	December	6	

a. Using the ratio-to-moving-average method, determine the specific seasonals for July, August, and September 2012.
b. Assume that the specific seasonal indexes in the following table are correct. Insert in the table the specific seasonals you computed in part (a) for July, August, and September 2012, and determine the 12 typical seasonal indexes.

Year	Jan.	Feb.	Mar.	Apr.	May	June	July	Aug.	Sept.	Oct.	Nov.	Dec.
2012							?	?	?	92.1	106.5	92.9
2013	88.9	102.9	178.9	118.2	60.1	43.1	44.0	74.0	200.9	90.0	101.9	90.9
2014	87.6	103.7	170.2	125.9	59.4	48.6	44.2	77.2	196.5	89.6	113.2	80.6
2015	79.8	105.6	165.8	124.7	62.1	41.7	48.2	72.1	203.6	80.2	103.0	94.2
2016	89.0	112.1	182.9	115.1	57.6	56.9						

c. Interpret the typical seasonal index.

27. The sales of Andre's Boutique for 2012 and part of 2013 are:

Month	2012 Sales (thousands)	2013 Sales (thousands)	Month	2012 Sales (thousands)	2013 Sales (thousands)
January	78	65	July	81	65
February	72	60	August	85	61
March	80	72	September	90	75
April	110	97	October	98	
May	92	86	November	115	
June	86	72	December	130	

a. Using the ratio-to-moving-average method, determine the specific seasonals for July, August, September, and October 2012.
b. Assume that the specific seasonals in the following table are correct. Insert in the table the specific seasonals you computed in part (a) for July, August, September, and October 2012, and determine the 12 typical seasonal indexes.

Year	Jan.	Feb.	Mar.	Apr.	May	June	July	Aug.	Sept.	Oct.	Nov.	Dec.
2012							?	?	?	?	123.6	150.9
2013	83.9	77.6	86.1	118.7	99.7	92.0	87.0	91.4	97.3	105.4	124.9	140.1
2014	86.7	72.9	86.2	121.3	96.6	92.0	85.5	93.6	98.2	103.2	126.1	141.7
2015	85.6	65.8	89.2	125.6	99.6	94.4	88.9	90.2	100.2	102.7	121.6	139.6
2016	77.3	81.2	85.8	115.7	100.3	89.7						

c. Interpret the typical seasonal index.

For **DATA FILE**, please visit www.mhhe.com/lind16e

28. The quarterly production of pine lumber, in millions of board feet, by Northwest Lumber for 2010 through 2014 is:

	Quarter			
Year	**Winter**	**Spring**	**Summer**	**Fall**
2010	7.8	10.2	14.7	9.3
2011	6.9	11.6	17.5	9.3
2012	8.9	9.7	15.3	10.1
2013	10.7	12.4	16.8	10.7
2014	9.2	13.6	17.1	10.3

a. Determine the typical seasonal pattern for the production data using the ratio-to-moving-average method.
b. Interpret the pattern.
c. Deseasonalize the data and determine the linear trend equation.
d. Project the seasonally adjusted production for the four quarters of 2015.

For **DATA FILE**, please visit www.mhhe.com/lind16e

29. Work Gloves Corp. is reviewing its quarterly sales of Toughie, the most durable glove it produces. The numbers of pairs produced (in thousands) by quarter for 2009 through 2014 are:

	Quarter			
Year	**I Jan.–Mar.**	**II Apr.–June**	**III July–Sept.**	**IV Oct.–Dec.**
2009	142	312	488	208
2010	146	318	512	212
2011	160	330	602	187
2012	158	338	572	176
2013	162	380	563	200
2014	162	362	587	205

a. Using the ratio-to-moving-average method, determine the four typical quarterly indexes.
b. Interpret the typical seasonal pattern.

For **DATA FILE**, please visit www.mhhe.com/lind16e

30. Sales of roof material, by quarter, for 2007 through 2013, by Carolina Home Construction Inc. are shown below (in $000).

	Quarter			
Year	**I**	**II**	**III**	**IV**
2007	210	180	60	246
2008	214	216	82	230
2009	246	228	91	280
2010	258	250	113	298
2011	279	267	116	304
2012	302	290	114	310
2013	321	291	120	320

a. Determine the typical seasonal patterns for sales using the ratio-to-moving-average method.
b. Deseasonalize the data and determine the trend equation.
c. Project sales for 2014 using the trend equation and seasonally adjust these values to find the predicted sales for each quarter.

For **DATA FILE**, please visit www.mhhe.com/lind16e

31. Blueberry Farms Golf and Fish Club of Hilton Head, South Carolina, wants to find monthly seasonal indexes for package play, nonpackage play, and total play. The package play refers to golfers who visit the area as part of a golf package. Typically, the greens fees, cart fees, lodging, maid service, and meals are included as part of a golfing package. The course earns a certain percentage of this total. The nonpackage play includes play by local

residents and visitors to the area who wish to play golf. The following data, beginning with July 2010 and ending with June 2013, report the package and nonpackage play by month, as well as the total amount, in thousands of dollars.

Year	Month	Package	Local	Total	Year	Month	Package	Local	Total
2010	July	$ 18.36	$43.44	$ 61.80	2012	January	30.60	9.48	40.08
	August	28.62	56.76	85.38		February	63.54	30.96	94.50
	September	101.34	34.44	135.78		March	167.67	47.64	215.31
	October	182.70	38.40	221.10		April	299.97	59.40	359.37
	November	54.72	44.88	99.60		May	173.61	40.56	214.17
	December	36.36	12.24	48.60		June	64.98	63.96	128.94
2011	January	25.20	9.36	34.56		July	25.56	67.20	92.76
	February	67.50	25.80	93.30		August	31.14	52.20	83.34
	March	179.37	34.44	213.81		September	81.09	37.44	118.53
	April	267.66	34.32	301.98		October	213.66	62.52	276.18
	May	179.73	40.80	220.53		November	96.30	35.04	131.34
	June	63.18	40.80	103.98		December	16.20	33.24	49.44
	July	16.20	77.88	94.08	2013	January	26.46	15.96	42.42
	August	23.04	76.20	99.24		February	72.27	35.28	107.55
	September	102.33	42.96	145.29		March	131.67	46.44	178.11
	October	224.37	51.36	275.73		April	293.40	67.56	360.96
	November	65.16	25.56	90.72		May	158.94	59.40	218.34
	December	22.14	15.96	38.10		June	79.38	60.60	139.98

Using statistical software:

a. Develop a seasonal index for each month for the package sales. What do you note about the various months?

b. Develop a seasonal index for each month for the nonpackage sales. What do you note about the various months?

c. Develop a seasonal index for each month for the total sales. What do you note about the various months?

d. Compare the indexes for package sales, nonpackage sales, and total sales. Are the busiest months the same?

For **DATA FILE**, please visit www.mhhe.com/lind16e

32. The following is the number of retirees receiving benefits from the State Teachers Retirement System of Ohio from 1991 until 2012.

Year	Service	Year	Service	Year	Service	Year	Service
1991	58,436	1997	72,601	2003	89,257	2008	106,099
1992	59,994	1998	75,482	2004	92,574	2009	109,031
1993	61,515	1999	78,341	2005	95,843	2010	112,483
1994	63,182	2000	81,111	2006	99,248	2011	117,138
1995	67,989	2001	83,918	2007	102,771	2012	112,136
1996	70,448	2002	86,666				

a. Plot the data.

b. Determine the least squares trend equation. Use a linear equation.

c. Calculate the points for the years 2000 and 2010.

d. Estimate the number of retirees that will be receiving benefits in 2015. Does this seem like a reasonable estimate based on the historical data?

e. By how much has the number of retirees increased or decreased (per year) on average during the period?

For **DATA FILE**, please visit www.mhhe.com/lind16e

33. Ray Anderson, owner of Anderson Ski Lodge in upstate New York, is interested in forecasting the number of visitors for the upcoming year. The following data are available, by quarter, from the first quarter of 2007 to the fourth quarter of 2013. Develop a seasonal index for each quarter. How many visitors would you expect for each quarter of 2014, if Ray projects that there will be a 10% increase from the total number of visitors in 2013? Determine the

trend equation, project the number of visitors for 2014, and seasonally adjust the forecast. Which forecast would you choose?

Year	Quarter	Visitors	Year	Quarter	Visitors
2007	I	86	2011	I	188
	II	62		II	172
	III	28		III	128
	IV	94		IV	198
2008	I	106	2012	I	208
	II	82		II	202
	III	48		III	154
	IV	114		IV	220
2009	I	140	2013	I	246
	II	120		II	240
	III	82		III	190
	IV	154		IV	252
2010	I	162			
	II	140			
	III	100			
	IV	174			

For **DATA FILE**, please visit www.mhhe.com/lind16e

34. The enrollment in the College of Business at Midwestern University by quarter from 2009 to spring 2013 is:

	Quarter			
Year	Winter	Spring	Summer	Fall
2009	2,033	1,871	714	2,318
2010	2,174	2,069	840	2,413
2011	2,370	2,254	927	2,704
2012	2,625	2,478	1,136	3,001
2013	2,803	2,668	—	—

Using the ratio-to-moving-average method:

a. Determine the four quarterly indexes.
b. Interpret the quarterly pattern of enrollment. Does the seasonal variation surprise you?
c. Compute the trend equation, and forecast the 2014 enrollment by quarter.

35. On page 641 at the beginning of this chapter, we presented a graph showing the price per gallon of gasoline from 1990 until 2012. The actual data for each year are given below.

Year	Cost/Gallon	Year	Cost/Gallon
1990	$1.30	2002	$1.35
1991	1.10	2003	1.56
1992	1.09	2004	1.85
1993	1.07	2005	2.27
1994	1.08	2006	2.57
1995	1.11	2007	2.80
1996	1.20	2008	3.25
1997	1.20	2009	2.35
1998	1.03	2010	2.78
1999	1.14	2011	3.52
2000	1.48	2012	3.62
2001	1.42		

Determine the trend line using both linear and nonlinear equations. Which would you suggest? Why? Based on your recommendation as the better equation, what cost per gallon would you estimate for 2013 and 2014?

Use the following information obtained from annual reports of Home Depot to solve Exercises 36, 37, and 38. You will need the help of a software package such as Excel and perhaps a companion package such as MegaStat. For the years 1993 through 2012, the data include a coded time variable (1 through 20), the number of associates in thousands, net sales in millions of dollars, the mean dollar amount per transaction, and the Consumer Price Index (CPI) for each year.

Year	Time	Associates (000)	Net Sales ($ million)	Mean Amount per Transaction	CPI
1993	1	50.6	9,239	39.13	144.500
1994	2	67.3	12,477	41.29	148.200
1995	3	80.8	15,470	41.78	152.400
1996	4	98.1	19,535	42.09	156.900
1997	5	124.4	24,156	43.63	160.500
1998	6	156.7	30,219	45.05	163.000
1999	7	201.4	38,454	47.87	166.000
2000	8	227.3	45,738	48.65	172.200
2001	9	256.3	53,553	48.64	177.100
2002	10	280.9	58,247	49.43	179.900
2003	11	298.8	64,816	51.15	184.000
2004	12	323.1	73,094	54.89	188.900
2005	13	344.8	81,511	57.98	195.300
2006	14	364.4	79,022	58.90	201.600
2007	15	331.0	77,349	57.48	207.342
2008	16	322.0	71,288	55.61	215.303
2009	17	317.0	66,176	51.76	214.537
2010	18	321.0	67,997	51.93	218.056
2011	19	331.0	70,395	53.28	224.939
2012	20	340.0	74,754	54.89	229.594

36. Develop a trend equation for the net sales ($ million) for Home Depot. Consider both a linear trend and a nonlinear trend. Which one would you select and why? Given the trend equation you selected, forecast the net sales for 2014 and 2015.

37. Consider the variable mean amount per transaction in the Home Depot data presented above. This variable indicates, for example, that the average customer spent $39.13 on goods during a store visit in 1993. By 2012 this amount increased to $54.89. During that same period the Consumer Price Index (CPI) as reported by the Bureau of Labor Statistics increased from 144.5 to 229.594. Convert the CPI to a 1993 base, as described on page 640 in the previous chapter, and convert the mean amount per transaction to 1993 dollars. Develop a linear trend equation for the constant 1993 dollars of the mean amount per transaction. Is it reasonable that the trend is linear? Can we conclude that the value of the amount the customer spent is less?

38. Use the variables mean amount per transaction and number of associates to forecast net sales. Are these two independent variables reasonable predictors of net sales? (*Hints:* What is the R^2 value? Is it large? Look at the p-values for each of the independent variables. Is this value less than .05 for each?) Because all of these variables are associated with time, it may be that there is autocorrelation. Conduct the appropriate test of hypothesis to determine if there is autocorrelation present. What is your conclusion? Again, use the .05 significance level.

DATA SET EXERCISE

(The data for this exercise is available at the text website: www.mhhe.com/lind16e.)

39. Refer to the Baseball 2012 data, which include information on the 2012 Major League Baseball season. The data include the mean player salary since 1989. Plot the information and develop a linear trend equation. Write a brief report on your findings.

A REVIEW OF CHAPTERS 17–18

Chapter 17 presents index numbers. An *index number* describes the relative change in value from one period, called the base period, to another called the given period. It is actually a percent, but the percent sign is usually omitted. Indexes are used to compare the change in unlike series over time. For example, a company might wish to compare the change in sales with the change in the number of sales representatives employed over the same period of time. A direct comparison is not meaningful because the units for one set of data are dollars and the other people. Index numbers also facilitate the comparison of very large values, where the amount of change in the actual values is very large and therefore difficult to interpret.

There are two types of price indexes. In an *unweighted price index,* the quantities are not considered. To form an unweighted index, we divide the base period value into the current period (also called the given period) and report the percent change. So if sales were \$12,000,000 in 2008 and \$18,600,000 in 2014, the simple unweighted price index for 2014 is:

$$p = \frac{p_t}{p_0}(100) = \frac{\$18{,}600{,}000}{\$12{,}000{,}000}(100) = 155.0$$

We conclude there is a 55% increase in sales during the six-year period.

In a *weighted price index, quantities* are considered. The most widely used weighted index is the *Laspeyres price index.* It uses the base period quantities as weights to compare changes in prices. It is computed by multiplying the base period quantities by the base period price for each product considered and summing the result. This result is the denominator of the fraction. The numerator of the fraction is the product of the base period quantities and the current price. For example, an appliance store sold 50 computers at \$1,000 and 200 DVDs at \$150 each in year 2008. In 2014, the same store sold 60 computers at \$1,200 and 230 DVDs at \$175. The Laspeyres price index is:

$$p = \frac{\Sigma p_t q_0}{\Sigma p_0 q_0}(100) = \frac{\$1{,}200 \times 50 + \$175 \times 200}{\$1{,}000 \times 50 + \$150 \times 200}(100) = \frac{\$95{,}000}{\$80{,}000}(100) = 118.75$$

Notice the same base period quantities are used as weights in both the numerator and the denominator. The index indicates there has been an 18.75% increase in the value of sales during the six-year period.

The most widely used and reported index is the *Consumer Price Index (CPI).* The CPI is a Laspeyres type index. It is reported monthly by the U.S. Department of Labor and is often used to report the rate of inflation in the prices of goods and services in the United States. The current base period is 1982–84.

In Chapter 18, we studied time series and forecasting. A *time series* is a collection of data over a period of time. The earnings per share of General Electric common stock over the last 10 years is an example of a time series. There are four components to a time series: the trend, cyclic effects, seasonal effects, and irregular effects.

Trend is the long-term direction of the time series. It can be either increasing or decreasing.

The *cyclical component* is the fluctuation above and below the trend line over a period of several years. Economic cycles are examples of the cyclical component. Most businesses shift between relative expansion and reduction periods over a cycle of several years.

Seasonal variation is the recurring pattern of the time series within a year. The consumption of many products and services is seasonal. Beach homes along the Gulf Coast are seldom rented during the winter and ski lodges in Wyoming are not used in the summer months. Hence, we say the rentals of beach front properties and ski lodges are seasonal.

The *irregular component* includes any unpredictable events. In other words, the irregular component includes events that cannot be forecast. There are two types of irregular components. Episodic variations are unpredictable, but can usually be identified. The Nashville flooding in the summer of 2010 is an example. The residual variation is random in nature and not predicted or identified.

The linear trend for a time series is given by the equation $\hat{y} = a + bt$, where $\hat{y}$ is the estimated trend value, a is the intercept with the Y-axis, b is the slope of the trend line (the rate of change), and t refers to the coded values for the time periods. We use the least squares method described in Chapter 13 to determine the trend line. Autocorrelation is often a problem when using the trend equation. Autocorrelation means that successive values of the time series are correlated.

PROBLEMS

1. Listed below are the net sales (in millions of euros) for the Adidas Group from 2008 to 2012.

Year	Net Sales
2008	10,799
2009	10,381
2010	11,990
2011	13,332
2012	14,883

   a. Determine the index for 2012, using 2008 as the base period.
   b. Use the period 2008 to 2010 as the base period and find the index for 2012.
   c. With 2008 as the base year, use the least squares method to find the trend equation. What is the estimated consolidated revenue for 2014? What is the rate of increase per year?

2. The table below shows the unemployment rate and the available workforce for three counties in northwest Pennsylvania for May 2010 and April 2013.

	May 2010		April 2013	
County	Labor Force	Percent Unemployed	Labor Force	Percent Unemployed
Erie	141,800	10.0	140,700	7.5
Warren	22,700	4.7	21,200	6.6
McKean	22,200	4.9	22,000	7.7

   a. In May 2010, the national unemployment rate was 9.7%. For May 2010, compute a simple average unemployment index for the region using the national unemployment rate as the base. Interpret the simple average index.
   b. In April 2013, the national unemployment rate was 7.6%. For April 2013, compute a simple average unemployment index for the region using the national unemployment rate as the base. Interpret the simple average index.
   c. Use the data for this region of northwest Pennsylvania to create a weighted unemployment index using the Laspeyres method. Use May 2010 as the base period. Interpret the index.

3. Based on five years of monthly data (the period from January 2008 to December 2012), the trend equation for a small company is $\hat{y} = 3.5 + 0.7t$. The seasonal index for January is 120 and for June it is 90. What are the seasonally adjusted sales forecasts for January 2013 and June 2013?

PRACTICE TEST

Part 1—Objective

1. To compute an index, the base period is always in the ______. (numerator, denominator, can be in either, always 100) 1. ______
2. A number that measures the relative change from one period to another is called a/an ______. 2. ______
3. In a weighted index, both the price and the ______ are considered. 3. ______
4. In a Laspeyres index, the ______ quantities are used in both the numerator and denominator. (base period, given period, oldest, newest—pick one) 4. ______
5. The current base period for the Consumer Price Index is ______. 5. ______
6. The long-term direction of a time series is called the ______. 6. ______
7. One method used to smooth the trend in a time series is a ______. 7. ______
8. When successive residuals are correlated, this condition is called ______. 8. ______
9. Irregular variation in a time series that is random in nature is called ______. 9. ______
10. In a three-year moving average, the weights given to each period are ______. (the same, oldest year has the most weight, oldest year has the least weight) 10. ______

Part 2—Problems

1. Listed below are the sales at Roberta's Ice Cream Stand for the last 5 years, 2009 through 2013.

Year	Sales
2009	$130,000
2010	145,000
2011	120,000
2012	170,000
2013	190,000

   a. Find the simple index for each year using 2009 as the base year.
   b. Find the simple index for each year using 2009–2010 as the base year.

2. Listed below are the price and quantity of several golf items purchased by members of the men's golf league at Indigo Creek Golf and Tennis Club for 2009 and 2013.

	2009		2013	
	Price	Quantity	Price	Quantity
Driver	$250.00	5	$275.00	6
Putter	60.00	12	75.00	10
Irons	700.00	3	750.00	4

   a. Determine the simple aggregate price index, with 2009 as the base period.
   b. Determine a Laspeyres price index.
   c. Determine the Paasche price index.
   d. Determine a value index.

3. The monthly linear trend equation for the Hoopes ABC Beverage Store is:

$$\hat{y} = 5.50 + 1.25t$$

   The equation is based on 4 years of monthly data and is reported in thousands of dollars. The index for January is 105.0 and for February it is 98.3. Determine the seasonally adjusted forecast for January and February of the fifth year.

19 Statistical Process Control and Quality Management

A BICYCLE MANUFACTURER randomly selects 10 frames each day and tests for defects. The numbers of defective frames found over the last 14 days are 3, 2, 1, 3, 2, 2, 8, 2, 0, 3, 5, 2, 0, and 4. Construct a control chart for this process and comment on whether the process is "in control." (See Exercise 11 and LO19-6.)

LEARNING OBJECTIVES

When you have completed this chapter, you will be able to:

LO19-1 Explain the purpose of quality control in production and service operations.

LO19-2 Define the two sources of process variation and explain how they are used to monitor quality.

LO19-3 Explain the use of charts to investigate the sources of process variation.

LO19-4 Compute control limits for mean and range control charts for a variable measure of quality.

LO19-5 Evaluate control charts to determine if a process is out of control.

LO19-6 Compute control limits of control charts for an attribute measure of quality.

LO19-7 Explain the process of acceptance sampling.

INTRODUCTION

Throughout this text, we present many applications of hypothesis testing. In Chapter 10, we describe methods for testing a hypothesis regarding a single population value. In Chapter 11, we describe methods for testing a hypothesis about two populations. In this chapter, we present another, somewhat different application of hypothesis testing, called **statistical process control** or **SPC.**

Statistical process control is a collection of strategies, techniques, and actions taken by an organization to ensure it is producing a quality product or providing a quality service. SPC begins at the product planning stage, when we specify the attributes of the product or service. It continues through the production stage. Each attribute throughout the process contributes to the overall quality of the product. To effectively use quality control, measurable attributes and specifications are developed against which the actual attributes of the product or service are compared.

LO19-1
Explain the purpose of quality control in production and service operations.

A BRIEF HISTORY OF QUALITY CONTROL

Prior to the 1900s, U.S. industry was largely characterized by small shops making relatively simple products, such as candles or furniture. In these small shops, the individual worker was generally a craftsman who was completely responsible for the quality of the work. The worker could ensure the quality through the personal selection of the materials, skillful manufacturing, and selective fitting and adjustment.

In the early 1900s, factories sprang up where people with limited training were formed into large assembly lines. Products became much more complex. The individual worker no longer had complete control over the quality of the product. A semiprofessional staff, usually called the Inspection Department, became responsible for the quality of the product. The quality responsibility was usually fulfilled by a 100% inspection of all the important characteristics. If there were any discrepancies noted, these problems were handled by the manufacturing department supervisor. In essence, quality was attained by "inspecting the quality into the product."

During the 1920s, Dr. Walter A. Shewhart, of Bell Telephone Laboratories, developed the concepts of statistical quality control. He introduced the concept of "controlling" the quality of a product as it was being manufactured, rather than inspecting the quality into the product after it was manufactured. For the purpose of controlling quality, Shewhart developed charting techniques for controlling in-process manufacturing operations. In addition, he introduced the concept of statistical sample inspection to estimate the quality of a product as it was being manufactured. This replaced the old method of inspecting each part after it was completed in the production operation.

Statistical quality control came into its own during World War II. The need for mass-produced war-related items, such as bomb sights, accurate radar, and other electronic equipment, at the lowest possible cost hastened the use of statistical sampling and quality control charts. Since World War II, these statistical techniques have been refined and sharpened. The use of computers has also widened the use of these techniques.

World War II virtually destroyed the Japanese production capability. Rather than retool their old production methods, the Japanese enlisted the aid of the late Dr. W. Edwards Deming, of the U.S. Department of Agriculture, to help them develop an overall plan. In a series of seminars with Japanese planners, he stressed a philosophy that is known today as Deming's 14 points. These 14 points are listed on the following page. He emphasized that quality originates from improving the process, not from inspection, and that quality is determined by the customers. The manufacturer must be able, via market research, to anticipate the needs of customers. Senior management has the responsibility for long-term improvement. Another of his points, and one that the Japanese strongly endorsed, is that every member of the company must contribute to long-term improvement. To achieve this improvement, ongoing education and training are necessary.

Deming had some ideas that did not mesh with contemporary management philosophies in the United States. Two areas where Deming's ideas differed from U.S. management philosophy were with production quotas and merit ratings. He claimed these two practices, which are both common in the United States, are not productive and should be eliminated. He also pointed out that U.S. managers are mostly interested in good news. Good news, however, does not provide an opportunity for improvement. On the other hand, bad news opens the door for new products and allows for company improvement.

Listed below, in a condensed form, are Dr. Deming's 14 points. He was adamant that the 14 points needed to be adopted as a package in order to be successful. The underlying theme is cooperation, teamwork, and the belief that workers want to do their jobs in a quality fashion.

DEMING'S 14 POINTS

1. Create constancy of purpose for the continual improvement of products and service to society.
2. Adopt a philosophy that we can no longer live with commonly accepted levels of delays, mistakes, defective materials, and defective workmanship.
3. Eliminate the need for mass inspection as the way to achieve quality. Instead, achieve quality by building the product correctly in the first place.
4. End the practice of awarding business solely on the basis of price. Instead, require meaningful measures of quality along with the price.
5. Improve constantly and forever every process for planning, production, and service.
6. Institute modern methods of training on the job for all employees, including managers. This will lead to better utilization of each employee.
7. Adopt and institute leadership aimed at helping people do a better job.
8. Encourage effective two-way communication and other means to drive out fear throughout the organization so that everyone may work more effectively and more productively for the company.
9. Break down barriers between departments and staff areas.
10. Eliminate the use of slogans, posters, and exhortations demanding zero defects and new levels of productivity without providing methods.
11. Eliminate work standards that prescribe quotas for the workforce and numerical goals for people in management. Substitute aids and helpful leadership in order to achieve continual improvement in quality and productivity.
12. Remove the barriers that rob hourly workers and the people in management of their right to pride of workmanship.
13. Institute a vigorous program of education and encourage self-improvement for everyone. What an organization needs is good people and people who are improving with education. Advancement to a competitive position will have its roots in knowledge.
14. Define clearly management's permanent commitment to ever-improving quality and productivity to implement all of these principles.

Deming's 14 points did not ignore statistical quality control, which is often abbreviated as SQC. The objective of statistical quality control is to monitor production through many stages of manufacturing. We use the tools of statistical quality control, such as X-bar and R charts, to monitor the quality of many processes and services. Control charts allow us to identify when a process or service is "out of control," that is, when an excessive number of defective units are being produced.

Interest in quality has accelerated dramatically in the United States since the late 1980s. Turn on the television and watch the commercials sponsored by Ford, Nissan,

and GM to verify the emphasis on quality control on the assembly line. It is now one of the "in" topics in all facets of business. V. Daniel Hunt, a noted American quality control consultant, reports that in the United States 20 to 25% of the cost of production is currently spent finding and correcting mistakes. And, he added, the additional cost incurred in repairing or replacing faulty products in the field drives the total cost of poor quality to nearly 30%. In Japan, he indicated, this cost is about 3%!

In recent years, companies have been motivated to improve quality by the challenge of being recognized for their quality achievements. The Malcolm Baldrige National Quality Award, established in 1988, is awarded annually to U.S. companies that demonstrate excellence in quality achievement and management. The award categories include manufacturing, service, small business, health care, and education. Past winners include Xerox, IBM, the University of Wisconsin–Stout, Ritz-Carlton Hotel Corporation, Federal Express, and Cadillac. The 2012 winners were:

- Lockheed Martin Missiles and Fire Control (MFC) designs, develops, manufactures, and supports advanced combat, missile, rocket, and sensor systems for the U.S. and foreign military. The company's workforce of 10,688 employees produces and delivers more than 100 products through 825 contracts in more than 60 countries. MFC is headquartered in the Dallas, Texas, area with a second major facility in Orlando, Florida. Additional facilities are located in nine U.S. states as well as Japan and the United Kingdom.
- MESA Products, Inc. is a small (139 employees), privately held business that designs, manufactures, and installs cathodic protection systems that control the corrosion of metal surfaces in underground and submerged structures, such as pipelines and tanks. MESA sells products and materials nationwide; technical and installation services are provided regionally. The company's headquarters and production facility are based in Tulsa, Oklahoma. Branch offices are in Fort Worth, Texas; Houston, Texas; Tallahassee, Florida; Huntington Beach, California; Wapakoneta, Ohio; Charleston, South Carolina; and Freeland, Washington. Revenue in 2011 was $45 million and projected to be $55 million in 2012. This is the second Baldrige Award for MESA; the company was a 2006 recipient in the small business category.
- North Mississippi Health Services (NMHS) is a nonprofit, community-owned, and integrated health care delivery system serving 24 rural counties in northeast Mississippi and northwest Alabama. The organization includes six hospitals, four nursing homes, and 34 clinics. It provides preventive and wellness services, hospital-based emergency and acute care services, post-acute care services, and a preferred-provider organization. The NMHS workforce of 6,226 employees and 491 physicians serve at health care facilities located in six Mississippi communities (Tupelo, Baldwyn, Eupora, Iuka, Pontotoc, and West Point) and one Alabama city (Hamilton). Net revenue in 2011 was $730 million. North Mississippi Medical Center (NMMC), the flagship hospital and referral center in the NMHS system, was honored with a health care category Baldrige Award in 2006.
- The City of Irving, located between Dallas and Fort Worth, is the 13th most populous city in Texas and the 94th in the United States. The city, home to approximately 217,700 residents, encompasses an area of 68 square miles, including Dallas–Fort Worth International Airport. Core services provided include law enforcement and compliance, fire protection and emergency medical, water and sewer, refuse collection, street maintenance and traffic management, parks, libraries, recreational and cultural programming, and capital improvements.

You can obtain more information on these and other winners by visiting the website http://www.nist.gov/baldrige.

STATISTICS IN ACTION

Does excellence in quality management lead to higher financial performance? Recent research compared the financial performance of companies that received the Baldrige National Quality Award to similar companies that did not receive the award. The research showed that the companies receiving the award had an average of 39% higher operating income and 26% higher sales, and were 1.22% lower in their cost per sales dollar.

Six Sigma

Many service, manufacturing, and nonprofit organizations are committed to improving the quality of their services and products. "Six Sigma" is a name given to an organizationwide program designed to improve quality and performance throughout an organization. The focus of the program is to reduce the variation in any process used to produce and deliver services and products to customers. Six Sigma programs apply to production processes as well as accounting and other organizational support processes. The ultimate outcomes of a Six Sigma program are to reduce the costs of defects and errors, increase customer satisfaction and sales of products and services, and increase profits.

Six Sigma gets its name from the normal distribution. The term *sigma* means standard deviation, and "plus or minus" three standard deviations gives a total range of six standard deviations. So Six Sigma means that a process should not generate more than 3.4 defects per million for any product or service. Many companies strive for even fewer defects.

To attain this goal, a Six Sigma program trains every organization member in processes to identify sources of process variation that significantly affect quality. The process includes identifying and defining problems, collecting and analyzing data to investigate and become knowledgeable about the problem, making process improvements to reduce process variation, and implementing procedures for improving the process.

Six Sigma uses many statistical techniques to collect and analyze the data needed to reduce process variation. The following are included in this text: histograms, analysis of variation, chi-square test of independence, regression, and correlation.

General Electric, Motorola, and AlliedSignal (now a part of Honeywell) are large companies that have used Six Sigma methods and achieved significant quality improvement and cost savings. Even cities like Fort Wayne, Indiana, have used Six Sigma techniques to improve their operations. The city is reported to have saved $10 million since 2000 and improved customer service at the same time. For example, the city reduced missed trash pickups by 50% and cut the response time to repair potholes from 21 to 3 hours. You can learn more about Six Sigma ideas, methods, and training at http://www.6sigma.us.

LO19-2
Define the two sources of process variation and explain how they are used to monitor quality.

SOURCES OF VARIATION

No two products are *exactly* the same. There is always some variation. The weight of each McDonald's Quarter Pounder is not exactly 0.25 pound. Some will weigh more than 0.25 pound, others less. The standard time for the TARTA (Toledo Area Regional Transit Authority) bus run from downtown Toledo, Ohio, to Perrysburg is 25 minutes. However, each run does not take *exactly* 25 minutes. Some runs take longer. Other times the TARTA driver must wait in Perrysburg before returning to Toledo. In some cases, there is a reason for the bus being late, an accident on the expressway or a snowstorm, for example. In other cases, the driver may not "hit" the green lights or the traffic is unusually heavy and slow for no apparent reason. There are two general sources of variation in a process—chance and assignable.

> **CHANCE VARIATION** Variation that is random in nature. This type of variation cannot be completely eliminated unless there is a major change in the techniques, technologies, methods, equipment, or materials used in the process.

Internal machine friction, slight variations in material or process conditions (such as the temperature of the mold being used to make glass bottles), atmospheric

conditions (such as temperature, humidity, and the dust content of the air), and vibrations transmitted to a machine from a passing forklift are a few examples of sources of chance variation.

If the hole drilled in a piece of steel is too large due to a dull drill, the drill may be sharpened or a new drill inserted. An operator who continually sets up the machine incorrectly can be replaced or retrained. If the roll of steel to be used in the process does not have the correct tensile strength, it can be rejected. These are examples of assignable variation.

ASSIGNABLE VARIATION Variation that is not random. It can be eliminated or reduced by investigating the problem and finding the cause.

There are several reasons why we should be concerned with variation. Two are stated below.

1. It will change the shape, dispersion, and central location of the distribution of the product characteristic being measured.
2. Assignable variation is usually correctable, whereas chance variation usually cannot be corrected or stabilized economically.

LO19-3

Explain the use of charts to investigate the sources of process variation.

DIAGNOSTIC CHARTS

There are a variety of diagnostic techniques available to investigate quality problems. Two of the more prominent of these techniques are **Pareto charts** and **fishbone diagrams.**

Pareto Charts

Pareto analysis is a technique for tallying the number and type of defects that happen within a product or service. The chart is named after a 19-century Italian scientist, Vilfredo Pareto. He noted that most of the "activity" in a process is caused by relatively few of the "factors." His concept, often called the 80–20 rule, is that 80% of the activity is caused by 20% of the factors. By concentrating on 20% of the factors, managers can attack 80% of the problem. For example, Emily's Family Restaurant, located at the junction of Interstates 75 and 70, is investigating "customer complaints." The five complaints heard most frequently are discourteous service, cold food, long wait for seating, few menu choices, and unruly young children. Suppose discourteous service was mentioned most frequently and cold food second. The data show these two factors are more than 85% of the total complaints. Addressing these two complaints first will yield the largest reduction in complaints and the largest increase in customer satisfaction.

To develop a Pareto chart, we begin by tallying the type of defects. Next, we rank the defects in terms of frequency of occurrence from largest to smallest. Finally, we produce a vertical bar chart, with the height of the bars corresponding to the frequency of each defect. The following example illustrates these ideas.

EXAMPLE

The city manager of Grove City, Utah, is concerned with water usage, particularly in single-family homes. She would like to develop a plan to reduce the water usage in Grove City. To investigate, she selects a sample of 100 homes and determines the typical daily water usage for various purposes. These sample results are as follows.

Reasons for Water Usage	Gallons per Day
Laundering	24.9
Watering lawn	143.7
Personal bathing	106.7
Cooking	5.1
Swimming pool	28.3
Dishwashing	12.3
Car washing	10.4
Drinking	7.9

What is the area of greatest usage? Where should she concentrate her efforts to reduce the water usage?

SOLUTION

A Pareto chart is useful for identifying the major areas of water usage and focusing on those areas where the greatest reduction can be achieved. The first step is to convert each of the activities to a percent and then to order them from largest to smallest. The total water usage per day is 339.3 gallons, found by totaling the gallons used in the eight activities. The activity with the largest use is watering lawns. It accounts for 143.7 gallons of water per day, or 42.4% of the amount of water used. The next largest category is personal bathing, which accounts for 31.4% of the water used. These two activities account for 73.8% of the water usage.

Reasons for Water Usage	Gallons per Day	Percent
Laundering	24.9	7.3
Watering lawn	143.7	42.4
Personal bathing	106.7	31.4
Cooking	5.1	1.5
Swimming pool usage	28.3	8.3
Dishwashing	12.3	3.6
Car washing	10.4	3.1
Drinking	7.9	2.3
Total	339.3	100.0

To draw the Pareto chart, we begin by scaling the number of gallons used on the left vertical axis and the corresponding percent on the right vertical axis. Next we draw a vertical bar with the height of the bar corresponding to the activity with the largest number of occurrences. In the Grove City example, we draw a vertical bar for the activity watering lawns to a height of 143.7 gallons. (We call this the count.) We continue this procedure for the other activities, as shown in the Minitab output in Chart 19–1.

Below the chart, we list the activities, their frequency of occurrence, and the percent of the time each activity occurs. In the last row, we list the cumulative percentage. This cumulative row will allow us to quickly determine which set of activities account for most of the activity. These cumulative percents are plotted above the vertical bars. In the Grove City example, the activities of watering lawn, personal bathing, and pools account for 82.1% of the water usage. The city manager can attain the greatest gain by looking to reduce the water usage in these three areas.

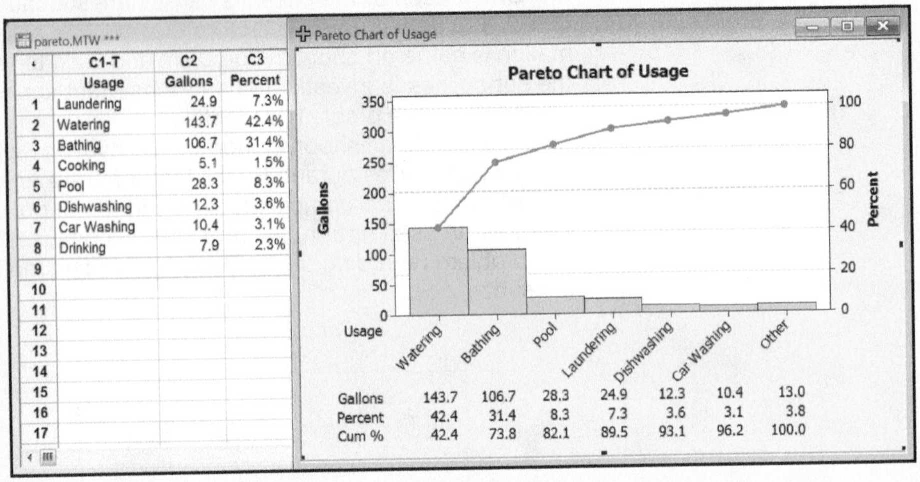

CHART 19–1 Pareto Chart for Water Usage in Grove City, Utah

Fishbone Diagrams

Another diagnostic chart is a **cause-and-effect diagram** or a **fishbone diagram.** It is called a cause-and-effect diagram to emphasize the relationship between an effect and a set of possible causes that produce the particular effect. This diagram is useful to help organize ideas and to identify relationships. It is a tool that encourages open brainstorming for ideas. By identifying these relationships, we can determine factors that are the cause of variability in our process. The name *fishbone* comes from the manner in which the various causes and effects are organized on the diagram. The effect is usually a particular problem, or perhaps a goal, and it is shown on the right-hand side of the diagram. The major causes are listed on the left-hand side of the diagram.

The usual approach to a fishbone diagram is to consider four problem areas, namely, methods, materials, equipment, and personnel. The problem, or the effect, is the head of the fish. See Chart 19–2.

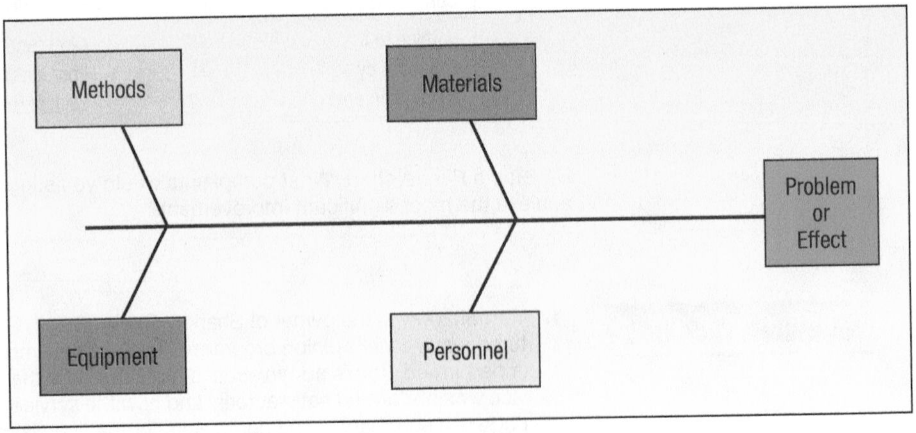

CHART 19–2 Fishbone Diagram

Under each of the possible causes are subcauses that are identified and investigated. The subcauses are factors that may be producing the particular effect. Information is gathered about the problem and used to fill in the fishbone diagram. Each of the subcauses is investigated and those that are not important eliminated, until the real cause of the problem is identified.

To illustrate a fishbone diagram, we investigate the causes of cold food served at Emily's Family Restaurant. Recall that a Pareto Analysis showed that cold food was one of the top two complaints. In Chart 19–3, notice that each of the subcauses is listed as an assumption. Each of these subcauses must be investigated to find the real problem regarding the cold food. In a fishbone diagram, there is no weighting of the subcauses.

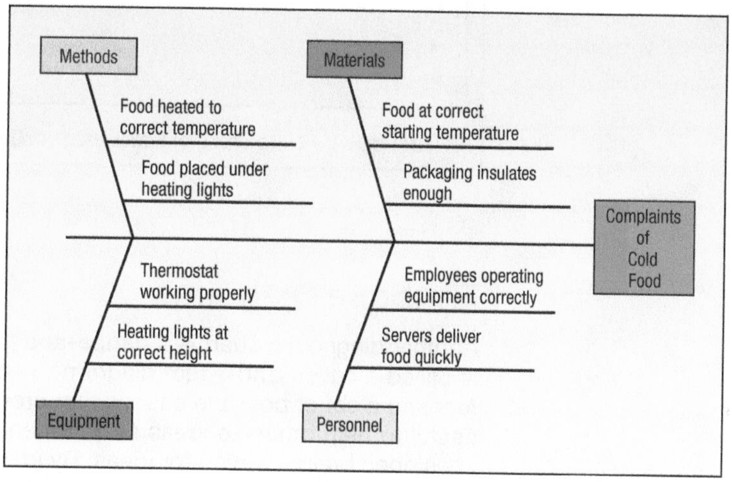

CHART 19–3 Fishbone Diagram for a Restaurant Investigation of Cold Food Complaints

SELF-REVIEW 19–1

The Rouse Home, located on the south side of Chicago, is a mental health facility. Recently there have been complaints regarding conditions at the home. The administrator would like to use a Pareto chart to investigate. When a patient or patient's relative has a complaint, he or she is asked to complete a complaint form. Listed below is a summary of the complaint forms received during the last 12 months.

Complaint	Number	Complaint	Number
Nothing to do	45	Dirty conditions	63
Poor care by staff	71	Poor quality of food	84
Medication error	2	Lack of respect by staff	35

Develop a Pareto chart. What complaints would you suggest the administrator work on first to achieve the most significant improvement?

EXERCISES

1. Tom Sharkey is the owner of Sharkey Chevy, Buick, GMC. At the start of the year, Tom instituted a customer opinion program to find ways to improve service. The day after the service is performed, Tom's administrative assistant calls the customer to find out whether the service was performed satisfactorily and how the service might be improved. Listed on the next page is a summary of the complaints for the first six months. Develop a Pareto chart. What complaints would you suggest that Tom work on to improve the quality of service?

Complaint	Frequency	Complaint	Frequency
Problem not corrected	38	Price too high	23
Error on invoice	8	Wait too long for service	10
Unfriendly atmosphere	12		

2. Out of 110 diesel engines tested, a rework and repair facility found 9 had leaky water pumps, 15 had faulty cylinders, 4 had ignition problems, 52 had oil leaks, and 30 had cracked blocks. Draw a Pareto chart to identify the key problem in the engines.

LO19-4
Compute control limits for mean and range control charts for a variable measure of quality.

PURPOSE AND TYPES OF QUALITY CONTROL CHARTS

Control charts identify when assignable causes of variation or changes have entered the process. For example, Wheeling Company makes vinyl-coated aluminum replacement windows for older homes. The vinyl coating must have a thickness between certain limits. If the coating becomes too thick, it will cause the windows to jam. On the other hand, if the coating becomes too thin, the window will not seal properly. The mechanism that determines how much coating is put on each window becomes worn and begins making the coating too thick. Thus, a change has occurred in the process. Control charts are useful for detecting the change in process conditions. It is important to know when changes have entered the process, so that the cause may be identified and corrected before a large number of unacceptable items are produced.

Control charts are similar to the scoreboard in a baseball game. By looking at the scoreboard, the fans, coaches, and players can tell which team is winning the game. However, the scoreboard can do nothing to win or lose the game. Control charts provide a similar function. These charts indicate to the workers, group leaders, quality control engineers, production supervisor, and management whether the production of the part or service is "in control" or "out of control." If the production is "out of control," the control chart will not fix the situation; it is just a piece of paper with numbers and dots on it. Instead, the person responsible must adjust the machine manufacturing the part or do what is necessary to return production to "in control."

There are two types of control charts. A **variable control chart** portrays measurements, such as the amount of cola in a two-liter bottle or the outside diameter of a piece of pipe. A variable control chart requires the interval or the ratio scale of measurement. An **attribute control chart** classifies a product or service as either acceptable or unacceptable. It is based on the nominal scale of measurement. The Marines stationed at Camp Lejeune are asked to rate the meals served as acceptable or unacceptable; bank loans are either repaid or defaulted.

Control Charts for Variables

To develop control charts for variables, we rely on the sampling theory discussed in connection with the central limit theorem in Chapter 8. Suppose a sample of five pieces is selected each hour from the production process and the mean of each sample computed. The sample means are $\bar{x}_1$, $\bar{x}_2$, $\bar{x}_3$, and so on. The mean of these sample means is denoted as $\bar{\bar{x}}$. We use k to indicate the number of sample means. The overall or grand mean is found by:

GRAND MEAN
$$\bar{\bar{x}} = \frac{\Sigma \text{ of the sample means}}{\text{Number of sample means}} = \frac{\Sigma \bar{x}}{k} \quad [19\text{–}1]$$

The standard error of the distribution of the sample means is designated by $s_{\bar{x}}$. It is found by:

STANDARD ERROR OF THE MEAN $$s_{\bar{x}} = \frac{s}{\sqrt{n}} \qquad [19–2]$$

These relationships allow us to establish limits for the sample means to show how much variation can be expected for a given sample size. These expected limits are called the **upper control limit** (*UCL*) and the **lower control limit** (*LCL*). An example will illustrate the use of control limits and how the limits are determined.

EXAMPLE

Statistical Software Inc. offers a toll-free number where customers can call with problems involving the use of their products from 7 a.m. until 11 p.m. daily. It is impossible to have every call answered immediately by a technical representative, but it is important customers do not wait too long for a person to come on the line. Customers become upset when they hear the message "Your call is important to us. The next available representative will be with you shortly" too many times. To understand its process, Statistical Software decides to develop a control chart describing the total time from when a call is received until the representative answers the call and resolves the issue raised by the caller. Yesterday, for the 16 hours of operation, five calls were sampled each hour and the total time to resolve a customer's problem, in minutes, for each call, was recorded. This information is reported below.

	Sample Number				
Time	**1**	**2**	**3**	**4**	**5**
a.m. 7	8	9	15	4	11
8	7	10	7	6	8
9	11	12	10	9	10
10	12	8	6	9	12
11	11	10	6	14	11
p.m. 12	7	7	10	4	11
1	10	7	4	10	10
2	8	11	11	7	7
3	8	11	8	14	12
4	12	9	12	17	11
5	7	7	9	17	13
6	9	9	4	4	11
7	10	12	12	12	12
8	8	11	9	6	8
9	10	13	9	4	9
10	9	11	8	5	11

Based on this information, develop a control chart for the mean duration of the call. Does there appear to be a trend in the calling times? Is there any period in which it appears that customers wait longer than others?

SOLUTION

A mean chart has two limits, an upper control limit (*UCL*) and a lower control limit (*LCL*). These upper and lower control limits are computed by:

CONTROL LIMITS FOR THE MEAN

$$UCL = \bar{\bar{x}} + 3\frac{s}{\sqrt{n}} \quad \text{and} \quad LCL = \bar{\bar{x}} - 3\frac{s}{\sqrt{n}} \qquad \textbf{[19–3]}$$

where s is an estimate of the standard deviation of the population, σ. Notice that in the calculation of the upper and lower control limits the number 3 appears. It represents the 99.74% confidence limits. The limits are often called the 3-sigma limits. However, other levels of confidence (such as 90 or 95%) can be used.

This application was developed before computers were widely available, and computing standard deviations was difficult. Rather than calculate the standard deviation from each sample as a measure of variation, it is easier to use the range. For fixed-sized samples, there is a constant relationship between the range and the standard deviation, so we can use the following formulas to determine the 99.74% control limits for the mean. It can be demonstrated that the term $3(s/\sqrt{n})$ from formula (19–3) is equivalent to $A_2\bar{R}$ in the following formula.

CONTROL LIMITS FOR THE MEAN

$$UCL = \bar{\bar{x}} + A_2\bar{R} \qquad LCL = \bar{\bar{x}} - A_2\bar{R} \qquad \textbf{[19–4]}$$

where:

A_2 is a constant used in computing the upper and the lower control limits. It is based on the average range, $\bar{R}$. The factors for various sample sizes are available in Appendix B.10. (*Note: n* in this table refers to the number in the sample.) A portion of Appendix B.10 is shown below. To locate the A_2 factor for this problem, find the sample size for n in the left margin. It is 5. Then move horizontally to the A_2 column and read the factor. It is 0.577.

n	A_2	d_2	D_3	D_4
2	1.880	1.128	0	3.267
3	1.023	1.693	0	2.575
4	0.729	2.059	0	2.282
5	0.577	2.326	0	2.115
6	0.483	2.534	0	2.004

$\bar{\bar{x}}$ is the mean of the sample means, computed by $\Sigma\bar{x}/k$, where k is the number of samples selected. In this problem, a sample of five observations is taken each hour for 16 hours, so $k = 16$.

$\bar{R}$ is the mean of the ranges of the sample. It is $\Sigma R/k$. Remember the range is the difference between the largest and the smallest value in each sample. It describes the variability occurring in that particular sample. (See Table 19–1.)

The centerline for the chart is $\bar{\bar{x}}$. It is 9.413 minutes, found by 150.6/16. The mean of the ranges ($\bar{R}$) is 6.375 minutes, found by 102/16. Thus, the upper control limit of the mean chart is:

$$UCL = \bar{\bar{x}} + A_2\bar{R} = 9.413 + 0.577(6.375) = 13.091$$

The lower control limit of the mean chart is:

$$LCL = \bar{\bar{x}} - A_2\bar{R} = 9.413 - 0.577(6.375) = 5.735$$

TABLE 19–1 Sixteen Samples of Call Duration Data for Statistical Software, Inc.

Time	1	2	3	4	5	Mean	Range
a.m. 7	8	9	15	4	11	9.4	11
8	7	10	7	6	8	7.6	4
9	11	12	10	9	10	10.4	3
10	12	8	6	9	12	9.4	6
11	11	10	6	14	11	10.4	8
p.m. 12	7	7	10	4	11	7.8	7
1	10	7	4	10	10	8.2	6
2	8	11	11	7	7	8.8	4
3	8	11	8	14	12	10.6	6
4	12	9	12	17	11	12.2	8
5	7	7	9	17	13	10.6	10
6	9	9	4	4	11	7.4	7
7	10	12	12	12	12	11.6	2
8	8	11	9	6	8	8.4	5
9	10	13	9	4	9	9.0	9
10	9	11	8	5	11	8.8	6
Total						150.6	102

$\bar{\bar{x}}$, *UCL*, *LCL*, and the sample means are portrayed in Chart 19–4. The mean, $\bar{\bar{x}}$, is 9.413 minutes, the upper control limit is located at 13.091 minutes, and the lower control limit is located at 5.735. There is some variation in the duration of the calls, but all sample means are within the control limits. Thus, based on 16 samples of five calls, we conclude that 99.74% of the time the mean length of a sample of five calls will be between 5.735 minutes and 13.091 minutes.

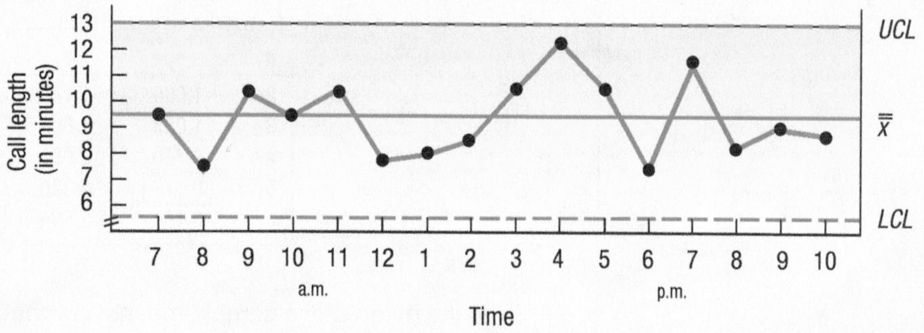

CHART 19–4 Control Chart for Mean Call Duration for Statistical Software Inc.

Because the statistical theory is based on the normality of large samples, control charts should be based on a stable process, that is, a fairly large sample, taken over a long period of time. Before using control charts in practice, at least 25 samples need to be collected to establish control chart limits.

Range Charts

In addition to the central location in a sample, we must also monitor the amount of variation from sample to sample. A **range chart** shows the variation in the sample

ranges. If the points representing the ranges fall between the upper and the lower limits, it is concluded that the operation is in control. According to chance, about 997 times out of 1,000 the range of the samples will fall within the limits. If the range should fall above the limits, we conclude that an assignable cause affected the operation and an adjustment to the process is needed. Why are we not as concerned about the lower control limit of the range? For small samples, the lower limit is often zero. Actually, for any sample of six or less, the lower control limit is 0. If the range is zero, then logically all the parts are the same and there is not a problem with the variability of the operation.

The upper and lower control limits of the range chart are determined from the following equations.

CONTROL CHART FOR RANGES $UCL = D_4\overline{R}$ $LCL = D_3\overline{R}$ **[19–5]**

The values for D_3 and D_4, which reflect the usual three σ (sigma) limits for various sample sizes, are found in Appendix B.10 or in the table on page 693.

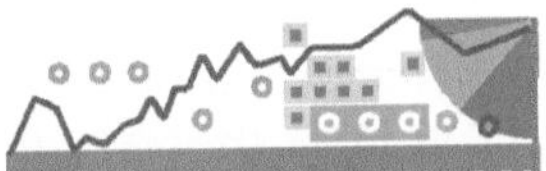

STATISTICS IN ACTION

Control charts were used to help convict a person who bribed jai alai players to lose. Mean and range charts showed unusual betting patterns and that some contestants did not win as much as expected when they made certain bets. A quality control expert was able to identify times when assignable variation stopped, and prosecutors were able to tie those times to the arrest of the suspect.

EXAMPLE

The length of time customers of Statistical Software Inc. waited from the time their call was answered until a technical representative answered their question or solved their problem is recorded in Table 19–1. Develop a control chart for the range. Does it appear that there is any time when there is too much variation in the operation?

SOLUTION

The first step is to find the mean of the sample ranges. The range for the five calls sampled in the 7 a.m. hour is 11 minutes. The longest call selected from that hour was 15 minutes and the shortest 4 minutes; the difference in the lengths is 11 minutes. In the 8 a.m. hour, the range is 4 minutes. The total of the 16 ranges is 102 minutes, so the average range is 6.375 minutes, found by $\overline{R} = 102/16$. Referring to Appendix B.10 or the partial table on page 693, D_3 and D_4 are 0 and 2.115, respectively. The lower and upper control limits are 0 and 13.483.

$$UCL = D_4\overline{R} = 2.115(6.375) = 13.483$$

$$LCL = D_3\overline{R} = 0(6.375) = 0$$

The range chart with the 16 sample ranges plotted is shown in Chart 19–5. This chart shows all the ranges are well within the control limits. Hence, we conclude the variation in the time to service the customers' calls is within normal limits, that is, "in control." Of course, we should be determining the control limits based on one set of data and then applying them to evaluate future data, not the data we already know.

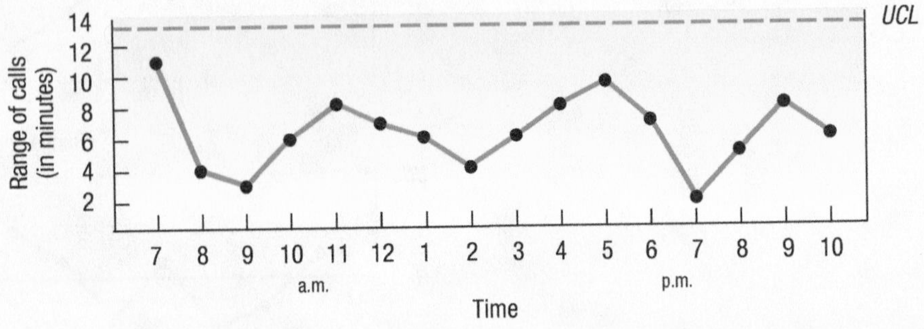

CHART 19–5 Control Chart for Ranges of Length of Customer Calls to Statistical Software Inc.

Minitab will draw a control chart for the mean and the range. Following is the output for the Statistical Software example. The data are in Table 19–1. The minor differences in the control limits are due to rounding.

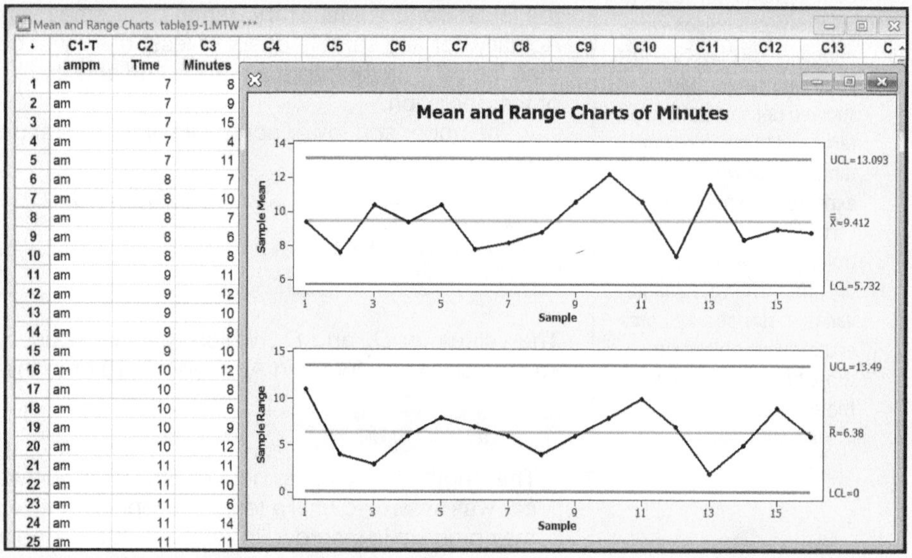

IN-CONTROL AND OUT-OF-CONTROL SITUATIONS

LO19-5
Evaluate control charts to determine if a process is out of control.

Three illustrations of in-control and out-of-control processes follow.

1. The mean chart and the range chart together indicate that the process is in control. Note the sample means and sample ranges are clustered close to the centerlines. Some are above and some below the centerlines, indicating the process is quite stable. That is, there is no visible tendency for the means and ranges to move toward the out-of-control areas.

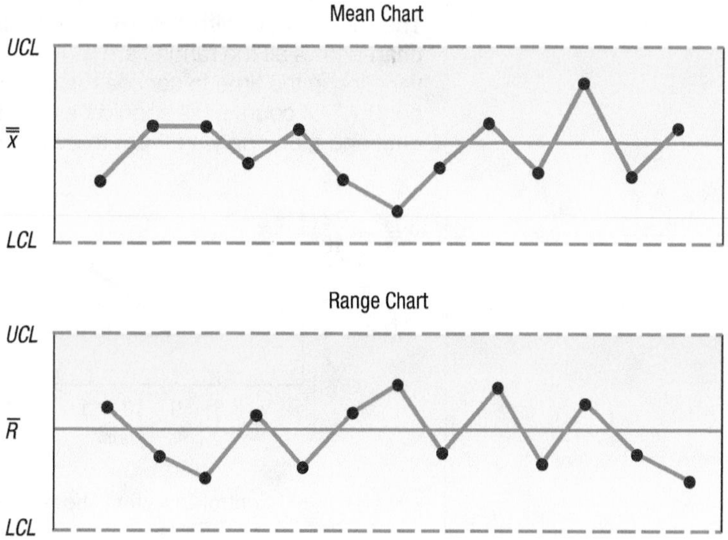

2. The sample means are in control, but the ranges of the last two samples are out of control. This indicates there is considerable variation in the samples. Some sample ranges are large; others are small. An adjustment in the process is probably necessary.

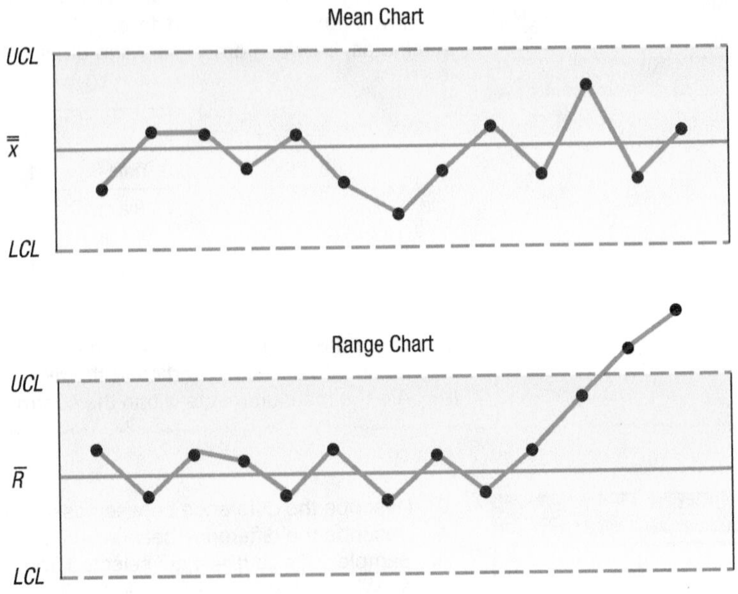

3. The mean is in control for the first samples, but there is an upward trend toward the *UCL*. The last two sample means are out of control. An adjustment in the process is indicated.

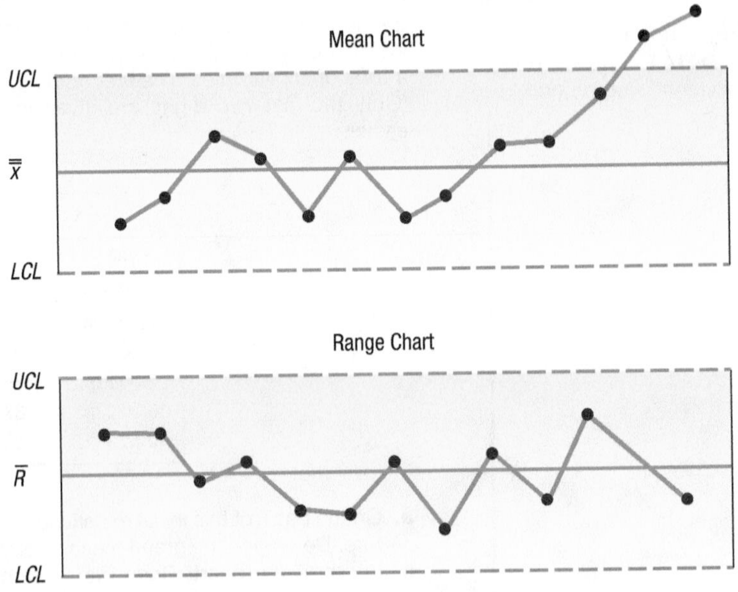

The preceding chart for the mean is an example of a control chart that offers some additional information. Note the direction of the last five observations of the mean. They are all above $\bar{\bar{x}}$ and increasing, and, in fact, the last two observations are out of control. The fact that the sample means were increasing for six consecutive

observations is very improbable and another indication that the process is out of control.

SELF-REVIEW 19–2

The manager of River City McDonald's randomly selects four customers during three hours of the day: 9 a.m., 10 a.m., and 11 a.m. For these selected customers, she determines the time, in minutes, between order entry and order delivery. The results are shown below.

	Sample Times			
Time	**1**	**2**	**3**	**4**
9 a.m.	1	4	5	2
10 a.m.	2	3	2	1
11 a.m.	1	7	3	5

(a) Compute the mean wait and the mean range, and determine the control limits for the mean and the range and chart them.
(b) Are the measurements within the control limits? Interpret the chart.

EXERCISES

3. Describe the difference between assignable variation and chance variation.
4. Describe the difference between an attribute control chart and a variable control chart.
5. Samples of size $n = 4$ are selected from a production line.
   a. What is the value of the A_2 factor used to determine the upper and lower control limits for the mean?
   b. What are the values of the D_3 and D_4 factors used to determine the lower and upper control limits for the range?
6. Samples of size 5 are selected from a manufacturing process. The mean of the sample ranges is .50. What is the estimate of the standard deviation of the population?
7. A new industrial oven has just been installed at Piatt Bakery. To develop experience regarding the oven temperature, an inspector reads the temperature at four different places inside the oven each half hour starting at 8:00 a.m. The last reading was at 10:30 a.m., for a total of six samples. The first reading, taken at 8:00 a.m., was 340 degrees Fahrenheit. (Only the last two digits are given in the following table to make the computations easier.)

For **DATA FILE**, please visit www.mhhe.com/lind16e

	Reading			
Time	**1**	**2**	**3**	**4**
8:00 a.m.	40	50	55	39
8:30 a.m.	44	42	38	38
9:00 a.m.	41	45	47	43
9:30 a.m.	39	39	41	41
10:00 a.m.	37	42	46	41
10:30 a.m.	39	40	39	40

   a. On the basis of this initial experience, determine the control limits for the mean temperature. Determine the grand mean. Plot the experience on a chart.
   b. Interpret the chart. Does there seem to be a time when the temperature is out of control?
8. Refer to Exercise 7.
   a. On the basis of this initial experience, determine the control limits for the range. Plot the experience on a chart.
   b. Does there seem to be a time when there is too much variation in the temperature?

For **DATA FILE**, please visit www.mhhe.com/lind16e

LO19-6
Compute control limits of control charts for an attribute measure of quality.

ATTRIBUTE CONTROL CHARTS

Often the data we collect are the result of counting rather than measuring. That is, we observe the presence or absence of some attribute. For example, the screw top on a bottle of shampoo either fits onto the bottle and does not leak (an "acceptable" condition) or does not seal and a leak results (an "unacceptable" condition), or a bank makes a loan to a customer and the loan is either repaid or not repaid. In other cases, we are interested in the number of defects in a sample. British Airways might count the number of its flights arriving late per day at Gatwick Airport in London. In this section, we discuss two types of attribute charts: the *p*-chart (proportion defective) and the *c*-bar chart (number of defectives per unit).

p-Charts

If the item recorded is the proportion of unacceptable parts made in a larger batch of parts, the appropriate control chart is the **p-chart.** This chart is based on the binomial distribution, discussed in Chapter 6, and proportions, discussed in Chapter 15. The centerline is at p, the mean proportion defective. The p replaces the $\bar{\bar{x}}$ of the variable control chart. The mean proportion defective is found by:

MEAN PROPORTION DEFECTIVE
$$p = \frac{\text{Total number defective}}{\text{Total number of items sampled}} \quad [19\text{–}6]$$

The variation in the sample proportion is described by the standard error of a proportion. It is found by:

STANDARD ERROR OF THE SAMPLE PROPORTION
$$s_p = \sqrt{\frac{p(1-p)}{n}} \quad [19\text{–}7]$$

Hence, the upper control limit (UCL) and the lower control limit (LCL) are computed as the mean proportion defective plus or minus three times the standard error of the proportions. The formula for the control limits is:

CONTROL LIMITS FOR PROPORTIONS
$$LCL, UCL = p \pm 3\sqrt{\frac{p(1-p)}{n}} \quad [19\text{–}8]$$

An example will show the details of the calculations and the conclusions.

EXAMPLE

Jersey Glass Company Inc. produces small hand mirrors. Jersey Glass runs day and evening shifts each weekday. The quality assurance department (QA) monitors the quality of the mirrors twice during the day shift and twice during the evening shift. QA selects and carefully inspects a random sample of 50 mirrors once every four hours. Each mirror is classified as either acceptable or unacceptable. Finally, QA counts the number of mirrors in the sample that do not conform to quality specifications. Listed next are the results of these checks over the last 10 business days.

Date	Number Sampled	Defects	Date	Number Sampled	Defects
10-Oct	50	1	17-Oct	50	7
	50	0		50	9
	50	9		50	0
	50	9		50	8
11-Oct	50	4	18-Oct	50	6
	50	4		50	9
	50	5		50	6
	50	3		50	1
12-Oct	50	9	19-Oct	50	4
	50	3		50	5
	50	10		50	2
	50	2		50	5
13-Oct	50	2	20-Oct	50	0
	50	4		50	0
	50	9		50	4
	50	4		50	7
14-Oct	50	6	21-Oct	50	5
	50	9		50	1
	50	2		50	9
	50	4		50	9

Construct a p-chart for this process. What are the upper and lower control limits? Interpret the results. Does it appear the process is out of control during the period?

SOLUTION

The first step is to determine the overall proportion defective. We use formula (19–6).

$$p = \frac{\text{Total number defective}}{\text{Total number of items sampled}} = \frac{196}{2{,}000} = .098$$

So we estimate that .098 of the mirrors produced during the period do not meet specifications.

Date	Number Sampled	Defects	Proportion Defective	Date	Number Sampled	Defects	Proportion Defective
10-Oct	50	1	0.02	13-Oct	50	2	0.04
	50	0	0.00		50	4	0.08
	50	9	0.18		50	9	0.18
	50	9	0.18		50	4	0.08
11-Oct	50	4	0.08	14-Oct	50	6	0.12
	50	4	0.08		50	9	0.18
	50	5	0.10		50	2	0.04
	50	3	0.06		50	4	0.08

(continued)

Date	Number Sampled	Defects	Proportion Defective	Date	Number Sampled	Defects	Proportion Defective
12-Oct	50	9	0.18	17-Oct	50	7	0.14
	50	3	0.06		50	9	0.18
	50	10	0.20		50	0	0.00
	50	2	0.04		50	8	0.16
18-Oct	50	6	0.12	20-Oct	50	0	0.00
	50	9	0.18		50	0	0.00
	50	6	0.12		50	4	0.08
	50	1	0.02		50	7	0.14
19-Oct	50	4	0.08	21-Oct	50	5	0.10
	50	5	0.10		50	1	0.02
	50	2	0.04		50	9	0.18
	50	5	0.10		50	9	0.18
				Total	2,000	196	

The upper and lower control limits are computed by using formula (19–8).

$$LCL, UCL = p \pm 3\sqrt{\frac{p(1-p)}{n}} = .098 \pm 3\sqrt{\frac{.098(1-.098)}{50}} = .098 \pm .1261$$

From the above calculations, the upper control limit is .2241, found by .098 + .1261. The lower control limit is 0. Why? The lower limit by the formula is .098 − .1261 = −0.0281. However, a negative proportion defective is not possible, so the smallest value is 0. We set the control limits at 0 and 0.2241. Any sample outside these limits indicates the quality level of the process has changed.

This information is summarized in Chart 19–6, which is output from the Minitab system.

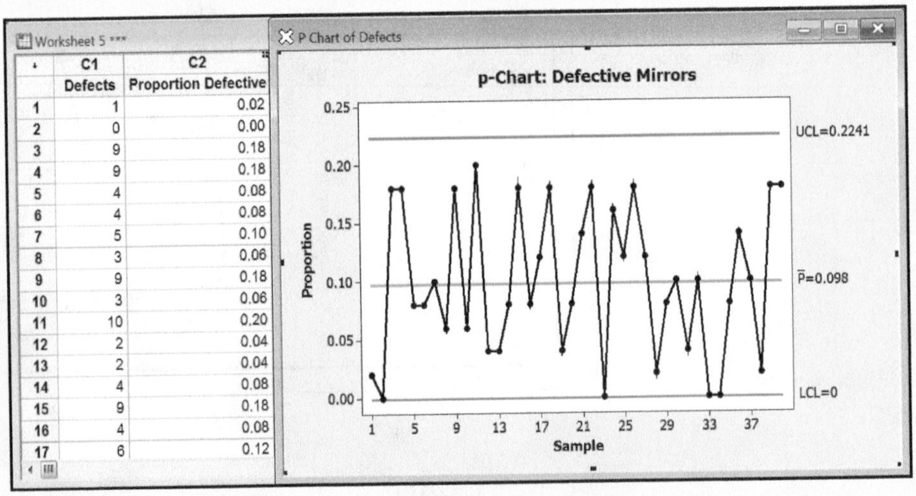

CHART 19–6 p-Chart for Mirrors at Jersey Glass

After establishing the limits, the process is monitored for the next week—five days, two shifts per day—with two quality checks per shift. The results are shown below.

Date	Number Sampled	Defects	Proportion Defective	Date	Number Sampled	Defects	Proportion Defective
24-Oct	50	1	0.02	27-Oct	50	2	0.04
	50	13	0.26		50	1	0.02
	50	10	0.20		50	7	0.14
	50	7	0.14		50	12	0.24
25-Oct	50	4	0.08	28-Oct	50	5	0.10
	50	5	0.10		50	5	0.10
	50	6	0.12		50	10	0.20
	50	10	0.20		50	9	0.18
26-Oct	50	6	0.12				
	50	1	0.02				
	50	8	0.16				
	50	4	0.08				

The process was out of control on two occasions, on October 24 when the proportion of defects was 0.26 and again on October 27 when the proportion of defects was 0.24. QA should report this information to the production department for the appropriate action. The Minitab output follows.

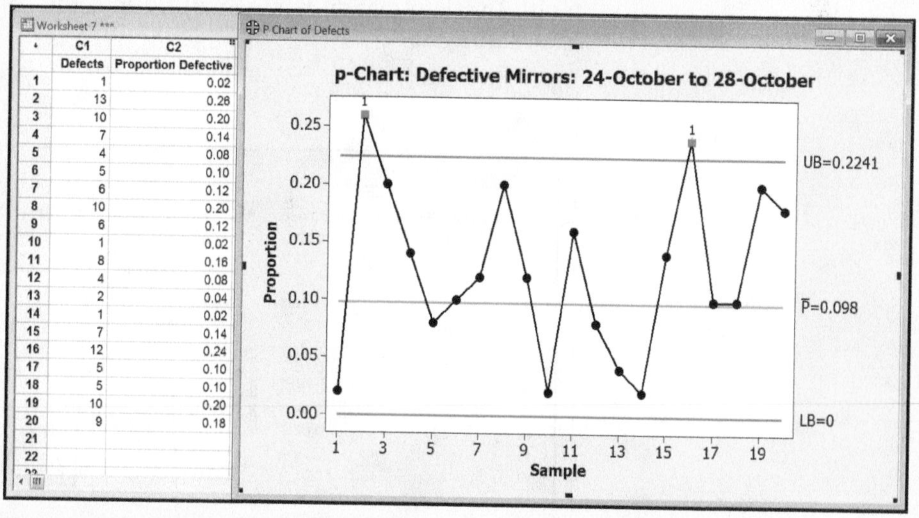

c-Bar Charts

The *c*-bar chart plots the number of defects or failures per unit. It is based on the Poisson distribution discussed in Chapter 6. The number of bags mishandled on a

flight by Southwest Airlines might be monitored by a *c*-bar chart. The "unit" under consideration is the flight. On most flights, there are no bags mishandled. On others, there may be only one, on others two, and so on. The Internal Revenue Service might count and develop a control chart for the number of errors in arithmetic per tax return. Most returns will not have any errors, some returns will have a single error, others will have two, and so on. We let $\bar{c}$ be the mean number of defects per unit. Thus, $\bar{c}$ is the mean number of bags mishandled by Southwest Airlines per flight or the mean number of arithmetic errors per tax return. Recall from Chapter 6 that the standard deviation of a Poisson distribution is the square root of the mean. Thus, we can determine the 3-sigma, or 99.74%, limits on a *c*-bar chart by:

CONTROL LIMITS FOR THE NUMBER OF DEFECTS PER UNIT

$$LCL,\ UCL = \bar{c} \pm 3\sqrt{\bar{c}} \qquad [19\text{–}9]$$

EXAMPLE

The publisher of the *Oak Harbor Daily Telegraph* is concerned about the number of misspelled words in the daily newspaper. In an effort to control the problem and promote the need for correct spelling, a control chart will be used. The numbers of misspelled words found in the final edition of the paper for the last 10 days are 5, 6, 3, 0, 4, 5, 1, 2, 7, and 4. Determine the appropriate control limits and interpret the chart. Were there any days during the period that the number of misspelled words was out of control?

SOLUTION

During the 10-day period, there were a total of 37 misspelled words. The mean number of misspelled words per edition is 3.7. The number of misspelled words per edition follows the Poisson probability distribution. The standard deviation is the square root of the mean.

$$\bar{c} = \frac{\Sigma x}{n} = \frac{5 + 6 + \cdots + 4}{10} = \frac{37}{10} = 3.7 \qquad s = \sqrt{\bar{c}} = \sqrt{3.7} = 1.924$$

To find the upper control limit, we use formula (19–9). The lower control limit is zero.

$$UCL = \bar{c} + 3\sqrt{\bar{c}} = 3.7 + 3\sqrt{3.7} = 3.7 + 5.77 = 9.47$$

The computed lower control limit would be 3.7 − 3(1.924) = −2.07. However, the number of misspelled words cannot be less than 0, so we use 0 as the lower limit. The lower control limit is 0 and the upper limit is 9.47. When we compare each of the data points to the value of 9.47, we see they are all less than the upper control limit; the number of misspelled words is "in control." Of course, newspapers are going to strive to eliminate all misspelled words, but control charting techniques offer a means of tracking daily results and determining whether there has been a change. For example, if a new proofreader was hired, her work could be compared with others. These results are summarized in Chart 19–7, which is output from the Minitab system.

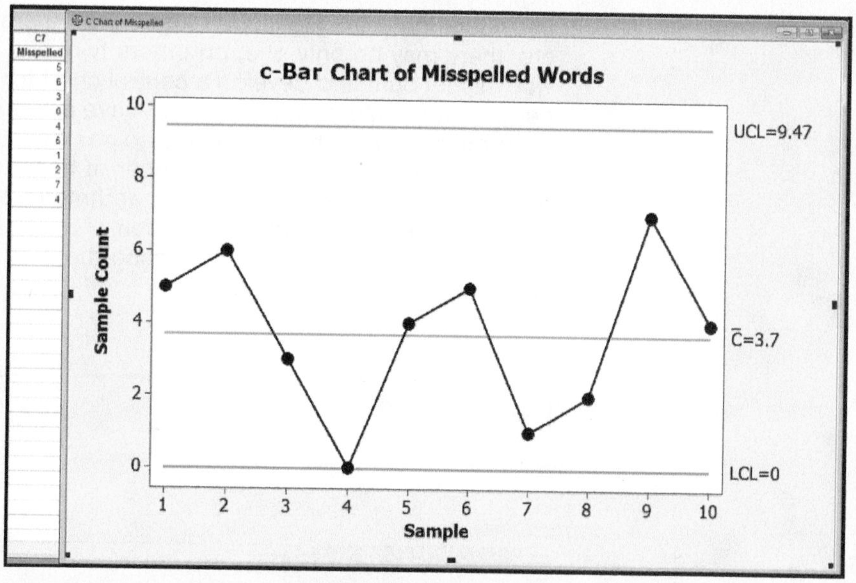

CHART 19–7 c-Bar Chart for Number of Misspelled Words per Edition of the *Oak Harbor Daily Telegraph*

SELF-REVIEW 19–3

Auto-Lite Company manufactures car batteries. At the end of each shift, the quality assurance department selects a sample of batteries and tests them. The numbers of defective batteries found over the last 12 shifts are 2, 1, 0, 2, 1, 1, 7, 1, 1, 2, 6, and 1. Construct a control chart for the process and comment on whether the process is in control.

EXERCISES

9. Below is a p-chart for a manufacturing process.

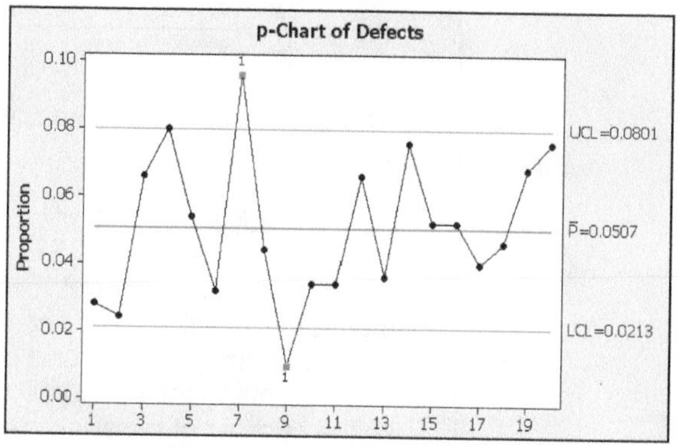

a. What is the mean proportion defective? What are the upper and lower control limits?
b. Are there any sample observations that indicate the process is out of control? Which sample numbers are they?
c. Does there seem to be any trend in the process? That is, does the process seem to be getting better, getting worse, or staying the same?

For **DATA FILE**, please visit www.mhhe.com/lind16e

10. Inter State Moving and Storage Company is setting up a control chart to monitor the proportion of residential moves that result in written complaints due to late delivery, lost items, or damaged items. A sample of 50 moves is selected for each of the last 12 months. The number of written complaints in each sample is 8, 7, 4, 8, 2, 7, 11, 6, 7, 6, 8, and 12.
    a. Design a p-chart and label the mean proportion defective, *UCL*, and *LCL*.
    b. Plot the proportion of written complaints in the last 12 months.
    c. Interpret the chart. Does it appear that the number of complaints is out of control for any of the months?

For **DATA FILE**, please visit www.mhhe.com/lind16e

11. A bicycle manufacturer randomly selects 10 frames each day and tests for defects. The numbers of defective frames found over the last 14 days are 3, 2, 1, 3, 2, 2, 8, 2, 0, 3, 5, 2, 0, and 4. Construct a control chart for this process and comment on whether the process is "in control."
12. During the process of producing toilet paper, Scott Paper randomly selects a toilet paper roll 5 times throughout the day and subjects each roll to a stress test to see how often the paper tears. Over a 3-day period, the testing of 15 rolls found the following number of defectives in each roll: 2, 3, 1, 2, 2, 1, 3, 2, 2, 1, 2, 2, 1, 0, and 0. Construct a control chart for the process and comment on whether the process is "in control."

For **DATA FILE**, please visit www.mhhe.com/lind16e

13. Sam's Supermarkets tests its checkout clerks by randomly examining the printout receipts for scanning errors. The following numbers are the number of errors on each receipt for October 27: 0, 1, 1, 0, 0, 1, 1, 0, 1, 1, 0. Construct a control chart for this process and comment on whether the process is "in control."

For **DATA FILE**, please visit www.mhhe.com/lind16e

14. Dave Christi runs a car wash chain with outlets scattered throughout Chicago. He is concerned that some local managers are giving away free washes to their friends. He decides to collect data on the number of "voided" sales receipts. Of course, some of them are legitimate voids. Would the following data indicate a reasonable number of voids at his facilities: 3, 8, 3, 4, 6, 5, 0, 1, 2, 4? Construct a control chart for this process and comment on whether the process is "in control."

LO19-7
Explain the process of acceptance sampling.

ACCEPTANCE SAMPLING

The previous section was concerned with maintaining the *quality of the product as it is being produced.* In many business situations, we are also concerned with the *quality of the incoming finished product.* What do the following cases have in common?

- Sims Software Inc. purchases DVDs from DVD International. The normal purchase order is for 100,000 DVDs, packaged in lots of 1,000. Todd Sims, president, does not expect each DVD to be perfect. In fact, he has agreed to accept lots of 1,000 with up to 10% defective. He would like to develop a plan to inspect incoming lots, to ensure that the quality standard is met. The purpose of the inspection procedure is to separate the acceptable from the unacceptable lots.
- Zenith Electric purchases magnetron tubes from Bono Electronics for use in its new microwave oven. The tubes are shipped to Zenith in lots of 10,000. Zenith allows the incoming lots to contain up to 5% defective tubes. It would like to develop a sampling plan to determine which lots meet the criterion and which do not.
- General Motors purchases windshields from many suppliers. GM insists that the windshields be in lots of 1,000, and is willing to accept 50 or fewer defects in each lot, that is, 5% defective. They would like to develop a sampling procedure to verify that incoming shipments meet the criterion.

The common thread in these cases is a need to verify that an incoming product meets the stipulated requirements. The situation can be likened to a screen door, which allows the warm summer air to enter the room while keeping the bugs out.

STATISTICS IN ACTION

It was reported during the late 1980s that a Canadian firm ordered some parts from a Japanese company with instructions that there should be "no more than three defective parts per one thousand." When the parts arrived, there was a note attached that said, "Your three defective parts are wrapped separately in the upper left compartment of the shipment." This is a far cry from the days when "Made in Japan" meant cheap but not reliable.

Acceptance sampling lets the lots of acceptable quality into the manufacturing area and screens out lots that are not acceptable.

Of course, the situation in modern business is more complex. The buyer wants protection against accepting lots that are below the quality standard. The best protection against inferior quality is 100% inspection. Unfortunately, the cost of 100% inspection is often prohibitive. Another problem with checking each item is that the test may be destructive. If all lightbulbs were tested until burning out before they were shipped, there would be none left to sell. Also, 100% inspection may not lead to the identification of all defects because boredom might cause a loss of perception on the part of the inspectors. Thus, complete inspection is rarely employed in practical situations.

The usual procedure is to screen the quality of incoming parts by using a statistical sampling plan. According to this plan, a sample of *n* units is randomly selected from the lots of *N* units (the population). This is called **acceptance sampling.** The inspection will determine the number of defects in the sample. This number is compared with a predetermined number called the **critical number** or the **acceptance number.** The acceptance number is usually designated *c.* If the number of defects in the sample of size *n* is less than or equal to *c,* the lot is accepted. If the number of defects exceeds *c,* the lot is rejected and returned to the supplier, or perhaps submitted to 100% inspection.

Acceptance sampling is a decision-making process. There are two possible decisions: accept or reject the lot. In addition, there are two situations under which the decision is made: the lot is good or the lot is bad. These are the states of nature. If the lot is good and the sample inspection reveals the lot to be good, or if the lot is bad and the sample inspection indicates it is bad, then a correct decision is made. However, there are two other possibilities. The lot may actually contain more defects than it should, but it is accepted. This is called **consumer's risk.** Similarly, the lot may be within the agreed-upon limits, but it is rejected during the sample inspection. This is called the **producer's risk.** The following summary table for acceptance decisions shows these possibilities. Notice how this discussion is very similar to the ideas of Type I and Type II errors discussed in Chapter 10.

	States of Nature	
Decision	**Good Lot**	**Bad Lot**
Accept lot	Correct	Consumer's risk
Reject lot	Producer's risk	Correct

To evaluate a sampling plan and determine that it is fair to both the producer and the consumer, the usual procedure is to develop an **operating characteristic curve,** or an **OC curve.** An OC curve reports the percent defective along the horizontal axis and the probability of accepting that percent defective along the vertical axis. A smooth curve is usually drawn connecting all the possible levels of quality. The binomial distribution is used to develop the probabilities for an OC curve.

EXAMPLE

Sims Software, as mentioned earlier, purchases DVDs from DVD International. The DVDs are packaged in lots of 1,000 each. Todd Sims, president of Sims Software, has agreed to accept lots with 10% or fewer defective DVDs. Todd has directed his inspection department to select a random sample of 20 DVDs and

examine them carefully. He will accept the lot if it has two or fewer defectives in the sample. Develop an OC curve for this inspection plan. What is the probability of accepting a lot that is 10% defective?

SOLUTION

This type of sampling is called **attribute sampling** because the sampled item, a DVD in this case, is classified as acceptable or unacceptable. No "reading" or "measurement" is obtained on the DVD. Let π represent the actual proportion defective in the population.

The lot is good if $\pi \leq .10$.
The lot is bad if $\pi > .10$.

Let x be the number of defects in the sample. The decision rule is:

Accept the lot if $x \leq 2$.
Reject the lot if $x \geq 3$.

Here the acceptable lot is one with 10% or fewer defective DVDs. If the lot is acceptable when it has exactly 10% defectives, it would be even more acceptable if it contained fewer than 10% defectives. Hence, it is the usual practice to work with the upper limit of the percent of defectives.

The binomial distribution is used to compute the various values on the OC curve. Recall that for us to use the binomial, there are four requirements:

1. There are only two possible outcomes. Here the DVD is either acceptable or unacceptable.
2. There are a fixed number of trials. In this instance, the number of trials is the sample size of 20.
3. There is a constant probability of success. A success is finding a defective DVD. The probability of success is assumed to be .10.
4. The trials are independent. The probability of obtaining a defective DVD on the third one selected is not related to the likelihood of finding a defect on the fourth DVD selected.

Appendix B.1 gives various binomial probabilities. However, the tables in Appendix B.1 go up to only 15, that is, $n = 15$. For this problem, $n = 20$, so we will use Excel to compute the various binomial probabilities. The following Excel output shows the binomial probabilities for $n = 20$ when π is equal to .05, .10, .15, .20, .25, and .30.

We need to convert the terms used in Chapter 6 to acceptance sampling vocabulary. We let π refer to the probability of finding a defect, c the number of defects allowed, and n the number of items sampled. In this case, we will allow up to two defects, so $c = 2$. This means that we will allow 0, 1, or 2 of the 20 items sampled to be defective and still accept the incoming shipment of DVDs.

To begin, we determine the probability of accepting a lot that is 5% defective. This means that $\pi = .05$, $c = 2$, and $n = 20$. From the Excel output, the likelihood of selecting a sample of 20 items from a shipment that contained 5% defective and finding exactly 0 defects is .358. The likelihood of finding exactly 1 defect is .377, and finding 2 is .189. Hence, the likelihood of 2 or fewer defects is .924, found by .358 + .377 + .189. This result is usually written in shorthand notation as follows (recall that bar "|" means "given that").

$$P(x \leq 2 \mid \pi = .05 \text{ and } n = 20) = .358 + .377 + .189 = .924$$

lot fraction defective.xlsx

Incoming Lot Fraction Defective

Number of Defects	Probability					
	0.05	0.10	0.15	0.20	0.25	0.30
0	0.358	0.122	0.039	0.012	0.003	0.001
1	0.377	0.270	0.137	0.058	0.021	0.007
2	0.189	0.285	0.229	0.137	0.067	0.028
3	0.060	0.190	0.243	0.205	0.134	0.072
4	0.013	0.090	0.182	0.218	0.190	0.130
5	0.002	0.032	0.103	0.175	0.202	0.179
6	0.000	0.009	0.045	0.109	0.169	0.192
7	0.000	0.002	0.016	0.055	0.112	0.164
8	0.000	0.000	0.005	0.022	0.061	0.114
9	0.000	0.000	0.001	0.007	0.027	0.065
10	0.000	0.000	0.000	0.002	0.010	0.031
11	0.000	0.000	0.000	0.000	0.003	0.012
12	0.000	0.000	0.000	0.000	0.001	0.004
13	0.000	0.000	0.000	0.000	0.000	0.001
14	0.000	0.000	0.000	0.000	0.000	0.000
*	*	*	*	*	*	*
20	0.000	0.000	0.000	0.000	0.000	0.000

Continuing, the likelihood of accepting a lot that is actually 10% defective is .677. That is:

$$P(x \leq 2 \mid \pi = .10 \text{ and } n = 20) = .122 + .270 + .285 = .677$$

The complete OC curve in Chart 19–8 shows the smoothed curve for all values of π between 0 and about 30%. There is no need to show values larger than 30% because their probability is very close to 0. The likelihood of accepting lots of selected quality levels is shown in table form on the right-hand side of Chart 19–8. With the OC curve, the management of Sims Software will be able to quickly evaluate the probabilities of various quality levels.

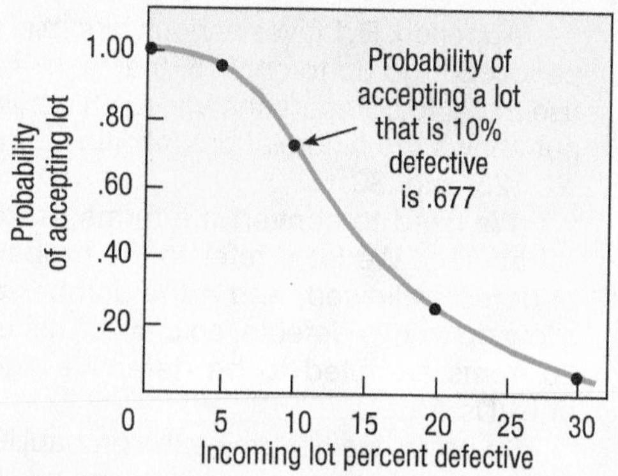

Lot percent defective	Probability of accepting lot
0	1.000
5	.924
10	.677
20	.207
30	.036

CHART 19–8 OC Curve for Sampling Plan ($n = 20, c = 2$)

SELF-REVIEW 19–4

Compute the probability of accepting a lot of DVDs that is actually 30% defective, using the sampling plan for Sims Software.

EXERCISES

15. Determine the probability of accepting lots that are 10%, 20%, 30%, and 40% defective using a sample of size 12 and an acceptance number of 2.

16. Determine the probability of accepting lots that are 10%, 20%, 30%, and 40% defective using a sample of size 14 and an acceptance number of 3.

17. Warren Electric manufactures fuses for many customers. To ensure the quality of the outgoing product, it tests 10 fuses each hour. If no more than one fuse is defective, it packages the fuses and prepares them for shipment. Develop an OC curve for this sampling plan. Compute the probabilities of accepting lots that are 10%, 20%, 30%, and 40% defective. Draw the OC curve for this sampling plan using the four quality levels.

18. Grills Video Products purchases LCDs from Mira Electronics. According to his sampling plan, Art Grills, owner of Grills Video, will accept a shipment of LCDs if 3 or fewer are defective in a sample of 25. Develop an OC curve for these percents defective: 10%, 20%, 30%, and 40%. You will need a statistical software package.

CHAPTER SUMMARY

I. The objective of statistical quality control is to monitor the quality of the product or service as it is being developed.

II. A Pareto chart is a technique for tallying the number and type of defects that happen within a product or service.
- **A.** This chart was named after an Italian scientist, Vilfredo Pareto.
- **B.** The concept of the chart is that 80% of the activity is caused by 20% of the factors.

III. A fishbone diagram emphasizes the relationship between a possible problem cause that will produce the particular effect.
- **A.** It is also called a cause-and-effect diagram.
- **B.** The usual approach is to consider four problem areas: methods, materials, equipment, and personnel.

IV. The purpose of a control chart is to monitor graphically the quality of a product or service.
- **A.** There are two types of control charts.
  - **1.** A variable control chart is the result of a measurement.
  - **2.** An attribute chart shows whether the product or service is acceptable or not acceptable.
- **B.** There are two sources of variation in the quality of a product or service.
  - **1.** Chance variation is random in nature and cannot be controlled or eliminated.
  - **2.** Assignable variation is not due to random causes and can be eliminated.
- **C.** Four control charts were considered in this chapter.
  - **1.** A mean chart shows the mean of a variable, and a range chart shows the range of the variable.
    - **a.** The upper and lower control limits are set at plus and minus 3 standard errors from the mean.
    - **b.** The formulas for the upper and lower control limits for the mean are:

$$UCL = \bar{\bar{x}} + A_2\bar{R} \qquad LCL = \bar{\bar{x}} - A_2\bar{R} \qquad [19\text{–}4]$$

    - **c.** The formulas for the upper and lower control limits for the range are:

$$UCL = D_4\bar{R} \qquad LCL = D_3\bar{R} \qquad [19\text{–}5]$$

  - **2.** A p-chart is an attribute chart that shows the proportion of the product or service that does not conform to the standard.
    - **a.** The mean proportion defective is found by

$$p = \frac{\text{Total number defective}}{\text{Total number of items sampled}} \qquad [19\text{–}6]$$

    - **b.** The control limits for the proportion defective are determined from the equation

$$LCL, UCL = p \pm 3\sqrt{\frac{p(1-p)}{n}} \qquad [19\text{–}8]$$

  - **3.** A c-bar chart refers to the number of defects per unit.
    - **a.** It is based on the Poisson distribution.
    - **b.** The mean number of defects per unit is $\bar{c}$.
    - **c.** The control limits are determined from the following equation.

$$LCL, UCL = \bar{c} \pm 3\sqrt{\bar{c}} \qquad [19\text{–}9]$$

V. Acceptance sampling is a method to determine whether an incoming lot of a product meets specified standards.
- **A.** It is based on random sampling techniques.
- **B.** A random sample of n units is selected from a population of N units.
- **C.** c is the maximum number of defective units that may be found in the sample of n and the lot is still considered acceptable.
- **D.** An OC (operating characteristic) curve is developed using the binomial probability distribution to determine the probability of accepting lots of various quality levels.

PRONUNCIATION KEY

SYMBOL	MEANING	PRONUNCIATION
$\bar{\bar{x}}$	Mean of the sample means	*x double bar*
$s_{\bar{x}}$	Standard error of the mean	*s sub x bar*
A_2	Constant used to determine the upper and lower control limit for the mean	*A sub 2*
$\bar{R}$	Mean of the sample ranges	*R bar*
D_4	Constant used to determine the upper control limit for the range	*D sub 4*
$\bar{c}$	Mean number of defects per unit	*c bar*

CHAPTER EXERCISES

19. The production supervisor at Westburg Electric Inc. noted an increase in the number of electric motors rejected at the time of final inspection. Of the last 200 motors rejected, 80 of the defects were due to poor wiring, 60 contained a short in the coil, 50 involved a defective plug, and 10 involved other defects. Develop a Pareto chart to show the major problem areas.

20. The manufacturer of running shoes conducted a study on its newly developed jogging shoe. Listed below are the type and frequency of the nonconformities and failures found. Develop a Pareto chart to show the major problem areas.

Type of Nonconformity	Frequency	Type of Nonconformity	Frequency
Sole separation	34	Lace breakage	14
Heel separation	98	Eyelet failure	10
Sole penetration	62	Other	16

21. At Rumsey's Old Fashion Roast Beef, cola drinks are filled by an automatic machine whose operation is based on the weight of the drink. When the process is in control, the machine fills each cup so that the grand mean is 10.0 ounces and the mean range is 0.25 for samples of 5.
- **a.** Determine the upper and lower control limits for the process for both the mean and the range.
- **b.** The manager of the I-280 store tested five soft drinks served last hour and found that the mean was 10.16 ounces and the range was 0.35 ounce. Is the process in control? Should other action be taken?

For **DATA FILE**, please visit www.mhhe.com/lind16e

22. A new machine has just been installed to cut and rough-shape large slugs. The slugs are then transferred to a precision grinder. One of the critical measurements is the outside diameter. The quality control inspector randomly selected five slugs each half-hour, measured the outside diameter, and recorded the results. The measurements (in millimeters) for the period 8:00 a.m. to 10:30 a.m. follow.

Time	Outside Diameter (millimeters) 1	2	3	4	5
8:00	87.1	87.3	87.9	87.0	87.0
8:30	86.9	88.5	87.6	87.5	87.4
9:00	87.5	88.4	86.9	87.6	88.2
9:30	86.0	88.0	87.2	87.6	87.1
10:00	87.1	87.1	87.1	87.1	87.1
10:30	88.0	86.2	87.4	87.3	87.8

a. Determine the control limits for the mean and the range.
b. Plot the control limits for the mean outside diameter and the range.
c. Are there any points on the mean or the range chart that are out of control? Comment on the chart.

For **DATA FILE**, please visit www.mhhe.com/lind16e

23. Long Last Tire Company, as part of its inspection process, tests its tires for tread wear under simulated road conditions. Twenty samples of three tires each were selected from different shifts over the last month of operation. The tread wear is reported below in hundredths of an inch.

Sample	Tread Wear			Sample	Tread Wear		
1	44	41	19	11	11	33	34
2	39	31	21	12	51	34	39
3	38	16	25	13	30	16	30
4	20	33	26	14	22	21	35
5	34	33	36	15	11	28	38
6	28	23	39	16	49	25	36
7	40	15	34	17	20	31	33
8	36	36	34	18	26	18	36
9	32	29	30	19	26	47	26
10	29	38	34	20	34	29	32

a. Determine the control limits for the mean and the range.
b. Plot the control limits for the mean tread wear and the range.
c. Are there any points on the mean or the range chart that are "out of control"? Comment on the chart.

For **DATA FILE**, please visit www.mhhe.com/lind16e

24. Charter National Bank has a staff of loan officers located in its branch offices throughout the Southwest. Robert Kerns, vice president of consumer lending, would like some information on the typical amount of loans and the range in the amount of the loans. A staff analyst of the vice president selected a sample of 10 loan officers and from each officer selected a sample of five loans he or she made last month. The data are reported below. Develop a control chart for the mean and the range. Do any of the officers appear to be "out of control"? Comment on your findings.

Officer	Loan Amount ($000) 1	2	3	4	5	Officer	Loan Amount ($000) 1	2	3	4	5
Weinraub	59	74	53	48	65	Bowyer	66	80	54	68	52
Visser	42	51	70	47	67	Kuhlman	74	43	45	65	49
Moore	52	42	53	87	85	Ludwig	75	53	68	50	31
Brunner	36	70	62	44	79	Longnecker	42	65	70	41	52
Wolf	34	59	39	78	61	Simonetti	43	38	10	19	47

25. The producer of a candy bar, called the "King James" Bar, reports on the package that the calorie content is 420 per 2-ounce bar. A sample of five bars from each of the last 10 days is sent for a chemical analysis of the calorie content. The results are shown next. Does it appear that there are any days where the calorie count is out of control? Develop an appropriate control chart and analyze your findings.

Sample	Calorie Count 1	2	3	4	5	Sample	Calorie Count 1	2	3	4	5
1	426	406	418	431	432	6	427	417	408	418	422
2	421	422	415	412	411	7	422	417	426	435	426
3	425	420	406	409	414	8	419	417	412	415	417
4	424	419	402	400	417	9	417	432	417	416	422
5	421	408	423	410	421	10	420	422	421	415	422

For **DATA FILE**, please visit www.mhhe.com/lind16e

26. Early Morning Delivery Service guarantees delivery of small packages by 10:30 a.m. Of course, some of the packages are not delivered by 10:30 a.m. For a sample of 200 packages delivered each of the last 15 working days, the following numbers of packages were delivered after the deadline: 9, 14, 2, 13, 9, 5, 9, 3, 4, 3, 4, 3, 3, 8, and 4.
a. Determine the mean proportion of packages delivered after 10:30 a.m.
b. Determine the control limits for the proportion of packages delivered after 10:30 a.m. Were any of the sampled days out of control?
c. If 10 packages out of 200 in the sample were delivered after 10:30 a.m. today, is this sample within the control limits?

For **DATA FILE**, please visit www.mhhe.com/lind16e

27. An automatic machine produces 5.0-millimeter bolts at a high rate of speed. A quality control program has been initiated to control the number of defectives. The quality control inspector selects 50 bolts at random and determines how many are defective. The numbers of defectives in the first 10 samples are 3, 5, 0, 4, 1, 2, 6, 5, 7, and 7.
a. Design a p-chart. Insert the mean proportion defective, *UCL,* and *LCL.*
b. Plot the proportion defective for the first 10 samples on the chart.
c. Interpret the chart.

For **DATA FILE**, please visit www.mhhe.com/lind16e

28. Steele Breakfast Foods Inc. produces a popular brand of raisin bran cereal. The package indicates it contains 25.0 ounces of cereal. To ensure the product quality, the Steele inspection department makes hourly checks on the production process. As a part of the hourly check, four boxes are selected and their contents weighed. The results for 25 samples are reported below.

Sample	Weights				Sample	Weights			
1	26.1	24.4	25.6	25.2	14	23.1	23.3	24.4	24.7
2	25.2	25.9	25.1	24.8	15	24.6	25.1	24.0	25.3
3	25.6	24.5	25.7	25.1	16	24.4	24.4	22.8	23.4
4	25.5	26.8	25.1	25.0	17	25.1	24.1	23.9	26.2
5	25.2	25.2	26.3	25.7	18	24.5	24.5	26.0	26.2
6	26.6	24.1	25.5	24.0	19	25.3	27.5	24.3	25.5
7	27.6	26.0	24.9	25.3	20	24.6	25.3	25.5	24.3
8	24.5	23.1	23.9	24.7	21	24.9	24.4	25.4	24.8
9	24.1	25.0	23.5	24.9	22	25.7	24.6	26.8	26.9
10	25.8	25.7	24.3	27.3	23	24.8	24.3	25.0	27.2
11	22.5	23.0	23.7	24.0	24	25.4	25.9	26.6	24.8
12	24.5	24.8	23.2	24.2	25	26.2	23.5	23.7	25.0
13	24.4	24.5	25.9	25.5					

Develop an appropriate control chart. What are the limits? Is the process out of control at any time?

For **DATA FILE**, please visit www.mhhe.com/lind16e

29. An investor believes there is a 50–50 chance that a stock will increase on a particular day. To investigate this idea, for 30 consecutive trading days the investor selects a random sample of 50 stocks and counts the number that increase. The number of stocks in the sample that increased is reported below.

14	12	13	17	10	18	10	13	13	14
13	10	12	11	9	13	14	11	12	11
15	13	10	16	10	11	12	15	13	10

Develop p-chart and write a brief report summarizing your findings. Based on these sample results, is it reasonable that the odds are 50–50 that a stock will increase? What percent of the stocks would need to increase in a day for the process to be "out of control"?

For **DATA FILE**, please visit www.mhhe.com/lind16e

30. Lahey Motors specializes in selling cars to buyers with a poor credit history. Listed below is the number of cars that were repossessed from Lahey customers because they did not meet the payment obligations over each of the last 36 months.

6	5	8	20	11	10	9	3	9	9
15	12	4	11	9	9	6	18	6	8
9	7	13	7	11	8	11	13	6	14
13	5	5	8	10	11				

Develop a c-bar chart for the number repossessed. Were there any months when the number was out of control? Write a brief report summarizing your findings.

31. A process engineer is considering two sampling plans. In the first, a sample of 10 will be selected and the lot accepted if 3 or fewer are found defective. In the second, the sample size is 20 and the acceptance number is 5. Develop an OC curve for each. Compare the probability of acceptance for lots that are 5, 10, 20, and 30% defective. Which of the plans would you recommend if you were the supplier?

For **DATA FILE**, please visit www.mhhe.com/lind16e

32. Christina Sanders is a member of the women's basketball team at Windy City College. Last season, she made 55% of her free throw attempts. In an effort to improve this statistic, she attended a summer camp devoted to foul-shooting techniques. The next 20 days she shot 100 foul shots a day. She carefully recorded the number of attempts made each day. The results are reported below.

55	61	52	59	67	57	61	59	69	58
57	66	63	63	63	65	63	68	64	67

To interpret, the first day she made 55 out of 100, or 55%. The last day she made 67 out of 100, or 67%.

a. Develop a control chart for the proportion of shots made. Over the 20 days of practice, what percent of attempts did she make? What are the upper and lower control limits for the proportion of shots made?

b. Is there any trend in her proportion made? Does she seem to be improving, staying the same, or getting worse?

c. Find the percent of attempts made for the last 5 days of practice. Use the hypothesis testing procedure, formula (10–4), to determine if there is an improvement from 55%.

For **DATA FILE**, please visit www.mhhe.com/lind16e

33. Eric's Cookie House sells chocolate chip cookies in shopping malls. Of concern is the number of chocolate chips in each cookie. Eric, the owner and president, would like to establish a control chart for the number of chocolate chips per cookie. He selects a sample of 15 cookies from today's production and counts the number of chocolate chips in each. The results are as follows: 6, 8, 20, 12, 20, 19, 11, 23, 12, 14, 15, 16, 12, 13, and 12.

a. Determine the centerline and the control limits.

b. Develop a control chart and plot the number of chocolate chips per cookie.

c. Interpret the chart. Does it appear that the number of chocolate chips is out of control in any of the cookies sampled?

For **DATA FILE**, please visit www.mhhe.com/lind16e

34. The numbers of "near misses" recorded for the last 20 months at Lima International Airport are 3, 2, 3, 2, 2, 3, 5, 1, 2, 2, 4, 4, 2, 6, 3, 5, 2, 5, 1, and 3. Develop an appropriate control chart. Determine the mean number of misses per month and the limits on the number of misses per month. Are there any months where the number of near misses is out of control?

For **DATA FILE**, please visit www.mhhe.com/lind16e

35. The following numbers of robberies were reported during the last 10 days to the robbery division of the Metro City Police: 10, 8, 8, 7, 8, 5, 8, 5, 4, and 7. Develop an appropriate control chart. Determine the mean number of robberies reported per day and determine the control limits. Are there any days when the number of robberies reported is out of control?

For **DATA FILE**, please visit www.mhhe.com/lind16e

36. Swiss Watches, Ltd. purchases watch stems for their watches in lots of 10,000. Their sampling plan calls for checking 20 stems, and if 3 or fewer stems are defective, the lot is accepted.

a. Based on the sampling plan, what is the probability that a lot of 40% defective will be accepted?

b. Design an OC curve for incoming lots that have zero, 10%, 20%, 30%, and 40% defective stems.

37. Automatic Screen Door Manufacturing Company purchases door latches from a number of vendors. The purchasing department is responsible for inspecting the incoming latches. Automatic purchases 10,000 door latches per month and inspects 20 latches selected at random. Develop an OC curve for the sampling plan if three latches can be defective and the incoming lot is still accepted.

38. At the beginning of each football season, Team Sports, the local sporting goods store, purchases 5,000 footballs. A sample of 25 balls is selected, and they are inflated, tested, and then deflated. If more than two balls are found defective, the lot of 5,000 is returned to the manufacturer. Develop an OC curve for this sampling plan.

a. What are the probabilities of accepting lots that are 10%, 20%, and 30% defective?

b. Estimate the probability of accepting a lot that is 15% defective.

c. John Brennen, owner of Team Sports, would like the probability of accepting a lot that is 5% defective to be more than 90%. Does this appear to be the case with this sampling plan?

An Introduction to Decision Theory 20

BLACKBEARD'S PHANTOM FIREWORKS is considering introducing two new bottle rockets. The company can add both to the current line, neither, or just one of the two. The success of these products depends on consumers' reactions. These reactions can be summarized as good, fair, or poor. The company's revenues are estimated in the payoff table in Exercise 11. Compute the expected monetary value for each decision. (See Exercise 11a and LO20-2.)

LEARNING OBJECTIVES

When you have completed this chapter, you will be able to:

LO20-1 Identify and apply the three components of a decision.

LO20-2 Analyze a decision using expected monetary value.

LO20-3 Analyze a decision using opportunity loss.

LO20-4 Apply maximin, maximax, and minimax regret strategies to make a decision.

LO20-5 Compute and explain the expected value of perfect information.

LO20-6 Apply sensitivity analysis to evaluate a decision subject to uncertainty.

LO20-7 Use a decision tree to illustrate and analyze decision making under uncertainty.

INTRODUCTION

A branch of statistics called **statistical decision theory** that uses probability has been developed since the early 1950s. As the name implies, the focus is on the process of making decisions and explicitly includes the payoffs that may result from selecting a particular decision alternative. In contrast, classical statistics focuses on estimating a parameter, such as the population mean, constructing a confidence interval, or conducting a hypothesis test. Classical statistics does not address the financial consequences.

Statistical decision theory is concerned with determining which decision, from a set of possible alternatives, is optimal for a particular set of conditions. Consider the following examples of decision-theory problems.

- Ford Motor Company must decide whether to purchase assembled door locks for the 2014 Ford F-150 truck or to manufacture and assemble the door locks at its Louisville, Kentucky, plant. If sales of the F-150 truck continue to increase, it will be more profitable to manufacture and assemble the parts. If sales level off or decline, it will be more profitable to purchase the door locks assembled. Should it make or buy the door locks?

- Banana Republic developed a new line of summer rain jackets that are very popular in the cold-weather regions of the country. It would like to purchase commercial television time during the upcoming NCAA basketball final. If both teams that play in the game are from warm parts of the country, it estimates that only a small proportion of the viewers will be interested in the jackets. However, a matchup between two teams who come from cold climates would reach a large proportion of viewers who wear jackets. Should it purchase commercial television time?
- General Electric is considering three options regarding the prices of refrigerators for next year. GE could (1) raise the prices 5%, (2) raise the prices 2.5%, or (3) leave the prices as they are. The final decision will be based on sales estimates and on GE's knowledge of what other refrigerator manufacturers might do.

In each of these cases, the decision is characterized by several alternative courses of action and several factors not under the control of the decision maker. For example, Banana Republic has no control over which teams reach the NCAA basketball final. These cases characterize the nature of decision making. Possible decision alternatives can be listed, possible future events determined, and even probabilities established, but the decisions are *made in the face of uncertainty.*

LO20-1
Identify and apply the three components of a decision.

ELEMENTS OF A DECISION

There are three components to any decision: (1) the choices available, or alternatives; (2) the states of nature, which are not under the control of the decision maker; and (3) the payoffs. These concepts will be explained in the following paragraphs.

The **alternatives,** or **acts,** are the choices available to the decision maker. Ford can decide to manufacture and assemble the door locks in Louisville, or it can decide to purchase them. Banana Republic has two advertising alternatives: to purchase commercial television time or not. GE is considering three pricing alternatives regarding the marketing of refrigerators. To simplify our presentation, we assume the decision maker can select from a rather small number of outcomes. With the help of computers, however, the decision alternatives can be expanded to a large number of possibilities.

The **states of nature** are the uncontrollable future events. The state of nature that actually happens is outside the control of the decision maker. Ford does not know

whether demand will remain high for the F-150. Banana Republic cannot determine whether warm-weather or cold-weather teams will play in the NCAA basketball final. GE does not know how competitors will price refrigerators.

A **payoff** is needed to compare each combination of decision alternative and state of nature. Ford may estimate that if it assembles door locks at its Louisville plant and the demand for F-150 trucks is low, the payoff will be $40,000. Conversely, if it purchases the door locks assembled and the demand is high, the payoff is estimated to be $22,000. Banana Republic needs to estimate the payoffs for purchasing commercial television time given estimates of the potential audience for the rain jacket. GE needs to estimate the payoffs for each pricing alternative given estimates of competitors' pricing.

The main elements of the decision under conditions of uncertainty are identified schematically:

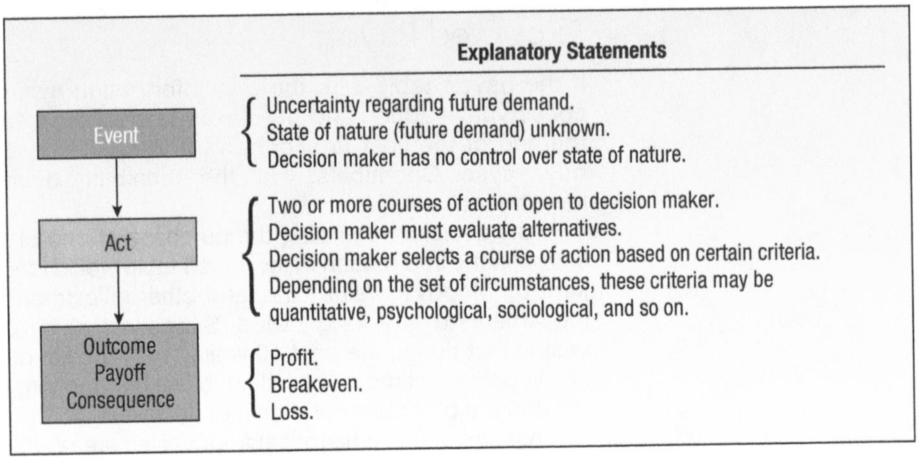

In many cases, we can make better decisions if we establish probabilities for the states of nature. These probabilities may be based on historical data or subjective estimates. Ford may estimate the probability of continued high demand as .70. Banana Republic may estimate a probability of .75 that the commercial will reach the targeted audience. GE may estimate the probability to be .25 that Amana and other manufacturers will raise the prices of their refrigerators.

LO20-2
Analyze a decision using expected monetary value.

DECISION MAKING UNDER CONDITIONS OF UNCERTAINTY

We begin this section with an example of decision making under uncertainty. The purpose of the example is to explain a logical process to evaluate a set of alternatives and select an alternative as the decision. The first step is to set up a payoff table.

Payoff Table

Bob Hill, a small investor, has $1,100 to invest. He has studied several common stocks and narrowed his choices to three, namely, Kayser Chemicals, Rim Homes, and Texas Electronics. He estimated that, if his $1,100 were invested in Kayser Chemicals and a strong bull market developed by the end of the year (that is, stock prices increased drastically), the value of his Kayser stock would more than double, to $2,400. However, if there was a bear market (i.e., stock prices declined), the value of his Kayser stock could conceivably drop to $1,000 by the end of the year. His predictions regarding the value of his $1,100 investment for the three stocks for a bull market and for a bear market are shown in Table 20–1. This table is a **payoff table.**

The various choices are called the **decision alternatives** or the **acts.** There are three in this situation. Let A_1 be the purchase of Kayser Chemicals, A_2 the purchase of Rim Homes, and A_3 the purchase of Texas Electronics. Whether the market turns out

TABLE 20–1 Payoff Table for Three Common Stocks under Two Market Conditions

Purchase	Bull Market, S_1	Bear Market, S_2
Kayser Chemicals (A_1)	$2,400	$1,000
Rim Homes (A_2)	2,200	1,100
Texas Electronics (A_3)	1,900	1,150

to be bear or bull is not under the control of Bob Hill. These uncontrolled future events are the **states of nature.** Let the bull market be represented by S_1 and the bear market by S_2.

Expected Payoff

If the payoff table was the only information available, the investor might take a conservative action and buy Texas Electronics to be assured of at least $1,150 at the end of the year (a slight profit). A speculative venture, however, might be to buy Kayser Chemicals, with the possibility of more than doubling the $1,100 investment.

Any decision regarding the purchase of one of the three common stocks made solely on the information in the payoff table would ignore the valuable historical records kept by Moody's, Value Line, and other investment services relative to stock price movements over a long period. Suppose a study of these investment services revealed that during the past 10 years stock market prices increased six times and declined only four times. According to this information, the probability of a market rise is .60 and the probability of a market decline is .40.

Assuming these historical frequencies are reliable, the payoff table and the probability estimates (.60 and .40) can be combined to arrive at the **expected payoff** of buying each of the three stocks. Expected payoff is also called **expected monetary value,** shortened to EMV. It can also be described as the **mean payoff.** The calculations needed to arrive at the expected payoff for the act of purchasing Kayser Chemicals are shown in Table 20–2.

TABLE 20–2 Expected Payoff for the Act of Buying Kayser Chemicals, EMV (A_1)

State of Nature	Payoff	Probability of State of Nature	Expected Value
Market rise, S_1	$2,400	.60	$1,440
Market decline, S_2	1,000	.40	400
			$1,840

To explain one expected monetary value calculation, note that if the investor had purchased Kayser Chemicals and the market prices declined, the value of the stock would be only $1,000 at the end of the year (from Table 20–1). Past experience, however, revealed that this event (a market decline) occurred only 40% of the time. In the long run, therefore, a market decline would contribute $400 to the total expected payoff from the stock, found by ($1,000)(.40). Adding the $400 to the $1,440 expected under rising market conditions gives $1,840, the "expected" payoff in the long run.

These calculations are summarized as follows.

EXPECTED MONETARY VALUE $$\text{EMV}(A_i) = \Sigma[P(S_j) \cdot V(A_i, S_j)] \quad [20\text{–}1]$$

where:

$EMV(A_i)$ refers to the expected monetary value of decision alternative *i*. There may be many decisions possible. We will let 1 refer to the first decision, 2 to the second, and so on. The lowercase letter *i* represents the entire set of decisions.

$P(S_j)$ refers to the probability of the states of nature. There can be an unlimited number, so we will let *j* represent this possible outcome.

$V(A_i, S_j)$ refers to the value of the payoffs. Note that each payoff is the result of a combination of a decision alternative and a state of nature.

$EMV(A_1)$, the expected monetary value for the decision alternative of purchasing Kayser Chemicals stock, is computed by:

$$EMV(A_1) = [P(S_1) \cdot V(A_1, S_1)] + [P(S_2) \cdot V(A_1, S_2)]$$
$$= .60(\$2,400) + .40(\$1,000) = \$1,840$$

Purchasing Kayser Chemicals stock is only one possible choice. The expected payoffs for the acts of buying Kayser Chemicals, Rim Homes, and Texas Electronics are given in Table 20–3.

TABLE 20–3 Expected Payoffs for Three Stocks

Purchase	Expected Payoff
Kayser Chemicals	$1,840
Rim Homes	1,760
Texas Electronics	1,600

An analysis of the expected payoffs in Table 20–3 indicates that purchasing Kayser Chemicals would yield the greatest expected profit. This outcome is based on (1) the investor's estimated future value of the stocks and (2) historical experience with respect to the rise and decline of stock prices. It should be emphasized that although purchasing Kayser stock represents the best action under the expected-value criterion, the investor still might decide to buy Texas Electronics stock in order to minimize the risk of losing some of the $1,100 investment.

SELF-REVIEW 20–1

Verify the conclusion, shown in Table 20–3, that the expected payoff for the act of purchasing Rim Homes stock is $1,760.

EXERCISES

1. The following payoff table was developed. Let $P(S_1) = .30$, $P(S_2) = .50$, and $P(S_3) = .20$. Compute the expected monetary value for each of the alternatives. What decision would you recommend?

	State of Nature		
Alternative	S_1	S_2	S_3
A_1	$50	$70	$100
A_2	90	40	80
A_3	70	60	90

2. Wilhelms Cola Company plans to market a new lime-flavored cola this summer. The decision is whether to package the cola in returnable or in nonreturnable bottles. Currently, the state legislature is considering eliminating nonreturnable bottles. Tybo Wilhelms, president of Wilhelms Cola Company, has discussed the problem with his state representative and established the probability to be .70 that nonreturnable bottles will be eliminated. The following table shows the estimated monthly profits (in thousands of dollars) if the lime cola is bottled in returnable versus nonreturnable bottles. Of course, if the law is passed and the decision is to bottle the cola in nonreturnable bottles, all profits would be from out-of-state sales. Compute the expected profit for both bottling decisions. Which decision do you recommend?

Alternative	Law Is Passed ($000), S_1	Law Is Not Passed ($000), S_2
Returnable bottle	80	40
Nonreturnable bottle	25	60

LO20-3
Analyze a decision using opportunity loss.

OPPORTUNITY LOSS

Another method to analyze a decision regarding which common stock to purchase is to determine the profit that might be lost because the state of nature (the market behavior) was not known at the time the investor bought the stock. This potential loss is called **opportunity loss** or **regret.** To illustrate, suppose the investor had purchased the common stock of Rim Homes, and a bull market developed. Further, suppose the value of his Rim Homes stock increased from $1,100 to $2,200, as anticipated. But had the investor bought Kayser Chemicals stock and market values increased, the value of his Kayser stock would be $2,400 (from Table 20–1). Thus, the investor missed making an extra profit of $200 by buying Rim Homes instead of Kayser Chemicals. To put it another way, the $200 represents the opportunity loss for not knowing the future state of nature. If market prices did increase, the investor would have *regretted* buying Rim Homes. However, had the investor bought Kayser Chemicals and market prices increased, he would have had no regret, that is, no opportunity loss.

The opportunity losses corresponding to this example are given in Table 20–4. Each amount is the outcome (opportunity loss) of a particular combination of acts and a state of nature, that is, stock purchase and market reaction.

Notice that the stock of Kayser Chemicals would be a good investment choice in a rising (bull) market, Texas Electronics would be the best buy in a declining (bear) market, and Rim Homes is somewhat of a compromise.

TABLE 20–4 Opportunity Losses for Various Combinations of Stock Purchase and Market Movement

	Opportunity Loss	
Purchase	**Market Rise**	**Market Decline**
Kayser Chemicals	$ 0	$150
Rim Homes	200	50
Texas Electronics	500	0

SELF-REVIEW 20–2

Refer to Table 20–4. Verify that the opportunity loss for:
(a) Rim Homes, given a market decline, is $50.
(b) Texas Electronics, given a market rise, is $500.

EXERCISES

3. Refer to Exercise 1. Develop an opportunity loss table. Determine the opportunity loss for each decision.
4. Refer to Exercise 2, involving Wilhelms Cola Company. Develop an opportunity loss table, and determine the opportunity loss for each decision.

Expected Opportunity Loss

The opportunity losses in Table 20–4 again ignore the historical experience of market movements. Recall that the probability of a market rise is .60 and that of a market decline .40. These probabilities and the opportunity losses can be combined to determine the **expected opportunity loss.** These calculations are shown in Table 20–5 for the decision to purchase Rim Homes. The expected opportunity loss is $140.

Interpreting, the expected opportunity loss of $140 means that, in the long run, the investor would lose the opportunity to make an additional profit of $140 if he decided to buy Rim Homes stock. This expected loss would be incurred because the investor was unable to accurately predict the trend of the stock market. In a bull market, he could earn an additional $200 by purchasing the common stock of Kayser Chemicals, but in a bear market an investor could earn an additional $50 by buying Texas Electronics stock. When weighted by the probability of the event, the expected opportunity loss is $140.

TABLE 20–5 Expected Opportunity Loss for the Act of Buying Rim Homes Stock

State of Nature	Opportunity Loss	Probability of State of Nature	Expected Opportunity Loss
Market rise, S_1	$200	.60	$120
Market decline, S_2	50	.40	20
			$140

These calculations are summarized as follows:

EXPECTED OPPORTUNITY LOSS $\text{EOL}(A_i) = \Sigma[P(S_j) \cdot R(A_i, S_j)]$ **[20–2]**

where:

$\text{EOL}(A_i)$ refers to the expected opportunity loss for a particular decision alternative.
$P(S_j)$ refers to the probability associated with the states of nature j.
$R(A_i, S_j)$ refers to the regret or loss for a particular combination of a state of nature and a decision alternative.

$\text{EOL}(A_2)$, the regret, or expected opportunity loss, for selecting Rim Homes, is computed as follows:

$$\begin{aligned}\text{EOL}(A_2) &= [P(S_1) \cdot R(A_2, S_1)] + [P(S_2) \cdot R(A_2, S_2)] \\ &= .60(\$200) + .40(\$50) = \$140\end{aligned}$$

The expected opportunity losses for the three decision alternatives are given in Table 20–6. The lowest expected opportunity loss is $60, meaning that the investor would experience the least regret on average if he purchased Kayser Chemicals.

Appendixes

APPENDIX A: DATA SETS

APPENDIX B: TABLES

APPENDIX C: SOFTWARE COMMANDS

APPENDIX D: ANSWERS TO ODD-NUMBERED CHAPTER EXERCISES & REVIEW EXERCISES & SOLUTIONS TO PRACTICE TESTS

APPENDIX E: ANSWERS TO SELF-REVIEW

A.1 Data Set 1—Goodyear, Arizona, Real Estate Sales Data

Variables

x_1 = Selling price in $000
x_2 = Number of bedrooms
x_3 = Size of the home in square feet
x_4 = Pool (1 = yes, 0 = no)
x_5 = Distance from the center of the city in miles
x_6 = Township
x_7 = Garage attached (1 = yes, 0 = no)
x_8 = Number of bathrooms
105 homes sold

x_1	x_2	x_3	x_4	x_5	x_6	x_7	x_8
263.1	4	2,300	0	17	5	1	2.0
182.4	4	2,100	1	19	4	0	2.0
242.1	3	2,300	1	12	3	0	2.0
213.6	2	2,200	1	16	2	0	2.5
139.9	2	2,100	1	28	1	0	1.5
245.4	2	2,100	0	12	1	1	2.0
327.2	6	2,500	1	15	3	1	2.0
271.8	2	2,100	1	9	2	1	2.5
221.1	3	2,300	0	18	1	0	1.5
266.6	4	2,400	1	13	4	1	2.0
292.4	4	2,100	1	14	3	1	2.0
209.0	2	1,700	1	8	4	1	1.5
270.8	6	2,500	1	7	4	1	2.0
246.1	4	2,100	1	18	3	1	2.0
194.4	2	2,300	1	11	3	0	2.0
281.3	3	2,100	1	16	2	1	2.0
172.7	4	2,200	0	16	3	0	2.0
207.5	5	2,300	0	21	4	0	2.5
198.9	3	2,200	0	10	4	1	2.0
209.3	6	1,900	0	15	4	1	2.0
252.3	4	2,600	1	8	4	1	2.0
192.9	4	1,900	0	14	2	1	2.5
209.3	5	2,100	1	20	5	0	1.5
345.3	8	2,600	1	9	4	1	2.0
326.3	6	2,100	1	11	5	1	3.0
173.1	2	2,200	0	21	5	1	1.5
187.0	2	1,900	1	26	4	0	2.0
257.2	2	2,100	1	9	4	1	2.0
233.0	3	2,200	1	14	3	1	1.5
180.4	2	2,000	1	11	5	0	2.0
234.0	2	1,700	1	19	3	1	2.0
207.1	2	2,000	1	11	5	1	2.0
247.7	5	2,400	1	16	2	1	2.0
166.2	3	2,000	0	16	2	1	2.0
177.1	2	1,900	1	10	5	1	2.0

(continued)

A.1 Data Set 1—Goodyear, Arizona, Real Estate Sales Data (*continued*)

x_1	x_2	x_3	x_4	x_5	x_6	x_7	x_8
182.7	4	2,000	0	14	4	0	2.5
216.0	4	2,300	1	19	2	0	2.0
312.1	6	2,600	1	7	5	1	2.5
199.8	3	2,100	1	19	3	1	2.0
273.2	5	2,200	1	16	2	1	3.0
206.0	3	2,100	0	9	3	0	1.5
232.2	3	1,900	0	16	1	1	1.5
198.3	4	2,100	0	19	1	1	1.5
205.1	3	2,000	0	20	4	0	2.0
175.6	4	2,300	0	24	4	1	2.0
307.8	3	2,400	0	21	2	1	3.0
269.2	5	2,200	1	8	5	1	3.0
224.8	3	2,200	1	17	1	1	2.5
171.6	3	2,000	0	16	4	0	2.0
216.8	3	2,200	1	15	1	1	2.0
192.6	6	2,200	0	14	1	0	2.0
236.4	5	2,200	1	20	3	1	2.0
172.4	3	2,200	1	23	3	0	2.0
251.4	3	1,900	1	12	2	1	2.0
246.0	6	2,300	1	7	3	1	3.0
147.4	6	1,700	0	12	1	0	2.0
176.0	4	2,200	1	15	1	1	2.0
228.4	3	2,300	1	17	5	1	1.5
166.5	3	1,600	0	19	3	0	2.5
189.4	4	2,200	1	24	1	1	2.0
312.1	7	2,400	1	13	3	1	3.0
289.8	6	2,000	1	21	3	1	3.0
269.9	5	2,200	0	11	4	1	2.5
154.3	2	2,000	1	13	2	0	2.0
222.1	2	2,100	1	9	5	1	2.0
209.7	5	2,200	0	13	2	1	2.0
190.9	3	2,200	0	18	3	1	2.0
254.3	4	2,500	0	15	3	1	2.0
207.5	3	2,100	0	10	2	0	2.0
209.7	4	2,200	0	19	2	1	2.0
294.0	2	2,100	1	13	2	1	2.5
176.3	2	2,000	0	17	3	0	2.0
294.3	7	2,400	1	8	4	1	2.0
224.0	3	1,900	0	6	1	1	2.0
125.0	2	1,900	1	18	4	0	1.5
236.8	4	2,600	0	17	5	1	2.0
164.1	4	2,300	1	19	4	0	2.0
217.8	3	2,500	1	12	3	0	2.0
192.2	2	2,400	1	16	2	0	2.5
125.9	2	2,400	1	28	1	0	1.5

(*continued*)

A.1 Data Set 1—Goodyear, Arizona, Real Estate Sales Data (*concluded*)

x_1	x_2	x_3	x_4	x_5	x_6	x_7	x_8
220.9	2	2,300	0	12	1	1	2.0
294.5	6	2,700	1	15	3	1	2.0
244.6	2	2,300	1	9	2	1	2.5
199.0	3	2,500	0	18	1	0	1.5
240.0	4	2,600	1	13	4	1	2.0
263.2	4	2,300	1	14	3	1	2.0
188.1	2	1,900	1	8	4	1	1.5
243.7	6	2,700	1	7	4	1	2.0
221.5	4	2,300	1	18	3	1	2.0
175.0	2	2,500	1	11	3	0	2.0
253.2	3	2,300	1	16	2	1	2.0
155.4	4	2,400	0	16	3	0	2.0
186.7	5	2,500	0	21	4	0	2.5
179.0	3	2,400	0	10	4	1	2.0
188.3	6	2,100	0	15	4	1	2.0
227.1	4	2,900	1	8	4	1	2.0
173.6	4	2,100	0	14	2	1	2.5
188.3	5	2,300	1	20	5	0	1.5
310.8	8	2,900	1	9	4	1	2.0
293.7	6	2,400	1	11	5	1	3.0
179.0	3	2,400	1	8	4	1	2.0
188.3	6	2,100	0	14	2	1	2.5
227.1	4	2,900	1	20	5	0	1.5
173.6	4	2,100	1	9	4	1	2.0
188.3	5	2,300	1	11	5	1	3.0

A.2 Data Set 2—Baseball Statistics, 2012 Season

Variables

x_1 = Team
x_2 = League (American = 1, National = 0)
x_3 = Built (year stadium was built)
x_4 = Size (stadium capacity)
x_5 = Salary (total 2012 team salary, \$ millions)
x_6 = Wins
x_7 = Attendance (total for team in millions)
x_8 = BA (team batting average)
x_9 = ERA (team earned run average)
x_{10} = HR (team home runs)
x_{11} = Errors (team errors)
x_{12} = SB (team stolen bases)
x_{13} = Year
x_{14} = Average player salary (\$)

(continued)

A.2 Data Set 2—Baseball Statistics, 2012 Season (*concluded*)

Team x_1	League x_2	Opened x_3	Capacity Seating x_4	Salary 2012 x_5	Wins x_6	Attendance x_7	BA x_8	ERA x_9	HR x_{10}	Errors x_{11}	SB x_{12}
Arizona Diamondbacks	0	1998	48633	74.3	81	2.18	0.26	3.93	165	90	93
Atlanta Braves	0	1996	49586	83.3	94	2.42	0.25	3.42	149	86	101
Baltimore Orioles	1	1992	45971	81.4	93	2.1	0.25	3.9	214	106	58
Boston Red Sox	1	1912	37495	173.2	69	3.04	0.26	4.7	165	101	97
Chicago Cubs	0	1914	41009	88.2	61	2.88	0.24	4.51	137	105	94
Chicago White Sox	1	1991	40615	96.9	85	1.97	0.26	4.02	211	70	109
Cincinnati Reds	0	2003	42319	82.2	97	2.35	0.25	3.34	172	89	87
Cleveland Indians	1	1994	43429	78.4	68	1.6	0.25	4.78	136	96	110
Colorado Rockies	0	1995	50398	78.1	64	2.63	0.27	5.22	166	122	100
Detroit Tigers	1	2000	41255	132.3	88	3.03	0.27	3.75	163	99	59
Houston Astros	0	2000	40981	60.7	55	1.61	0.24	4.56	146	118	105
Kansas City Royals	1	1973	37903	60.9	72	1.74	0.27	4.3	131	113	132
Los Angeles Angels	1	1966	45957	154.5	89	3.06	0.27	4.02	187	98	134
Los Angeles Dodgers	0	1962	56000	95.1	86	3.32	0.25	3.34	116	98	104
Miami Marlins	0	2012	36742	118.1	69	2.22	0.24	4.09	137	103	149
Milwaukee Brewers	0	2001	41900	97.7	83	2.83	0.26	4.22	202	99	158
Minnesota Twins	1	2010	39504	94.1	66	2.78	0.26	4.77	131	107	135
New York Mets	0	2009	41922	93.4	95	2.24	0.25	4.09	139	101	79
New York Yankees	1	2009	50287	198	74	3.54	0.27	3.85	245	74	93
Oakland Athletics	1	1966	35067	55.4	94	1.68	0.24	3.48	195	111	122
Philadelphia Phillies	0	2004	43651	174.5	81	3.57	0.26	3.83	158	101	116
Pittsburgh Pirates	0	2001	38362	63.4	79	2.09	0.24	3.86	170	112	73
San Diego Padres	0	2004	42691	55.2	76	2.12	0.25	4.01	121	121	155
San Francisco Giants	0	2000	41915	117.6	94	3.38	0.27	3.68	103	115	118
Seattle Mariners	1	1999	47860	82	75	1.72	0.23	3.76	149	72	104
St. Louis Cardinals	0	2006	43975	110.3	88	3.26	0.27	3.71	159	107	91
Tampa Bay Rays	1	1990	34078	64.2	90	1.56	0.24	3.19	175	114	134
Texas Rangers	1	1994	48194	120.5	93	3.46	0.27	3.99	200	85	91
Toronto Blue Jays	1	1989	49260	75.5	73	2.1	0.25	4.64	198	101	123
Washington Nationals	0	2008	41487	81.3	98	2.37	0.26	3.33	194	94	105

Average Salary	
1989	$ 512,930
1990	578,930
1991	891,188
1992	1,084,408
1993	1,120,254
1994	1,188,679
1995	1,071,029
1996	1,176,967
1997	1,383,578
1998	1,441,406
1999	1,720,050
2000	1,988,034
2001	2,264,403
2002	2,383,235
2003	2,555,476
2004	2,486,609
2005	2,632,655
2006	2,866,544
2007	2,944,556
2008	3,154,845
2009	3,240,206
2010	3,297,828
2011	3,305,393
2012	3,440,000

A.3 Data Set 3—Buena School District Bus Data

Variables

x_1 = Bus number
x_2 = Maintenance cost ($)
x_3 = Age
x_4 = Miles
x_5 = Bus type (diesel or gasoline)
x_6 = Bus manufacturer (Bluebird, Keiser, Thompson)
x_7 = Passengers

Bus Number, x_1	Maintenance Cost, x_2	Age, x_3	Miles, x_4	Bus Type, x_5	Bus Manufacturer, x_6	Passengers, x_7
135	329	7	853	Diesel	Bluebird	55
120	503	10	883	Diesel	Keiser	42
200	505	10	822	Diesel	Bluebird	55
40	466	10	865	Gasoline	Bluebird	55
427	359	7	751	Gasoline	Keiser	55
759	546	8	870	Diesel	Keiser	55
10	427	5	780	Gasoline	Keiser	14
880	474	9	857	Gasoline	Keiser	55
481	382	3	818	Gasoline	Keiser	6
387	422	8	869	Gasoline	Bluebird	55
326	433	9	848	Diesel	Bluebird	55
861	474	10	845	Gasoline	Bluebird	55
122	558	10	885	Gasoline	Bluebird	55
156	561	12	838	Diesel	Thompson	55
887	357	8	760	Diesel	Bluebird	6
686	329	3	741	Diesel	Bluebird	55
490	497	10	859	Gasoline	Bluebird	55
370	459	8	826	Gasoline	Keiser	55
464	355	3	806	Gasoline	Bluebird	55
875	489	9	858	Diesel	Bluebird	55
883	436	2	785	Gasoline	Bluebird	55
57	455	7	828	Diesel	Bluebird	55
482	514	11	980	Gasoline	Bluebird	55
704	503	8	857	Diesel	Bluebird	55
989	380	9	803	Diesel	Keiser	55
731	432	6	819	Diesel	Bluebird	42
75	478	6	821	Diesel	Bluebird	55
162	406	3	798	Gasoline	Keiser	55
732	471	9	815	Diesel	Keiser	42
751	444	2	757	Diesel	Keiser	14
600	493	10	1008	Diesel	Bluebird	55
948	452	9	831	Diesel	Keiser	42
358	461	6	849	Diesel	Bluebird	55
833	496	8	839	Diesel	Thompson	55
692	469	8	812	Diesel	Bluebird	55

(continued)

A.3 Data Set 3—Buena School District Bus Data (*concluded*)

Bus Number, x_1	Maintenance Cost, x_2	Age, x_3	Miles, x_4	Bus Type, x_5	Bus Manufacturer, x_6	Passengers, x_7
61	442	9	809	Diesel	Keiser	55
9	414	4	864	Gasoline	Keiser	55
314	459	11	859	Diesel	Thompson	6
396	457	2	815	Diesel	Thompson	55
365	462	6	799	Diesel	Keiser	55
398	570	9	844	Diesel	Thompson	14
43	439	9	832	Gasoline	Bluebird	55
500	369	5	842	Gasoline	Bluebird	55
279	390	2	792	Diesel	Bluebird	55
693	469	9	775	Gasoline	Keiser	55
884	381	9	882	Diesel	Bluebird	55
977	501	7	874	Diesel	Bluebird	55
38	432	6	837	Gasoline	Keiser	14
725	392	5	774	Diesel	Bluebird	55
982	441	1	823	Diesel	Bluebird	55
724	448	8	790	Diesel	Keiser	42
603	468	4	800	Diesel	Keiser	14
168	467	7	827	Gasoline	Thompson	55
45	478	6	830	Diesel	Keiser	55
754	515	14	895	Diesel	Keiser	14
39	411	6	804	Gasoline	Bluebird	55
671	504	8	866	Gasoline	Thompson	55
418	504	9	842	Diesel	Bluebird	55
984	392	8	851	Diesel	Bluebird	55
953	423	10	835	Diesel	Bluebird	55
507	410	7	866	Diesel	Bluebird	55
540	529	4	846	Gasoline	Bluebird	55
695	477	2	802	Diesel	Bluebird	55
193	540	11	847	Diesel	Thompson	55
321	450	6	856	Diesel	Bluebird	6
918	390	5	799	Diesel	Bluebird	55
101	424	4	827	Diesel	Bluebird	55
714	433	7	817	Diesel	Bluebird	42
678	428	7	842	Diesel	Keiser	55
768	494	7	815	Diesel	Bluebird	42
29	396	6	784	Gasoline	Bluebird	55
554	458	4	817	Diesel	Bluebird	14
767	493	6	816	Diesel	Keiser	55
699	475	9	816	Gasoline	Bluebird	55
954	476	10	827	Diesel	Bluebird	42
705	403	4	806	Diesel	Keiser	42
660	337	6	819	Gasoline	Bluebird	55
520	492	10	836	Diesel	Bluebird	55
814	426	4	757	Diesel	Bluebird	55
353	449	4	817	Gasoline	Keiser	55

A.4 Data Set 4—Applewood Auto Group

x_1 = **Age**—the age of the buyer at the time of the purchase
x_2 = **Profit**—the amount earned by the dealership on the sale of each vehicle
x_3 = **Location**—the dealership where the vehicle was purchased
x_4 = **Vehicle type**—SUV, sedan, compact, hybrid, or truck
x_5 = **Previous**—the number of vehicles previously purchased at any of the four Applewood dealerships by the customer

Age x_1	Profit x_2	Location x_3	Vehicle-Type x_4	Previous x_5
21	$1,387	Tionesta	Sedan	0
23	1,754	Sheffield	SUV	1
24	1,817	Sheffield	Hybrid	1
25	1,040	Sheffield	Compact	0
26	1,273	Kane	Sedan	1
27	1,529	Sheffield	Sedan	1
27	3,082	Kane	Truck	0
28	1,951	Kane	SUV	1
28	2,692	Tionesta	Compact	0
29	1,206	Sheffield	Sedan	0
29	1,342	Kane	Sedan	2
30	443	Kane	Sedan	3
30	754	Olean	Sedan	2
30	1,621	Sheffield	Truck	1
31	870	Tionesta	Sedan	1
31	1,174	Kane	Truck	0
31	1,412	Sheffield	Sedan	1
31	1,809	Tionesta	Sedan	1
31	2,415	Kane	Sedan	0
32	1,546	Sheffield	Truck	3
32	2,148	Tionesta	SUV	2
32	2,207	Sheffield	Compact	0
32	2,252	Tionesta	SUV	0
33	1,428	Kane	SUV	2
33	1,889	Olean	SUV	1
34	1,166	Olean	Sedan	1
34	1,320	Tionesta	Sedan	1
34	2,265	Olean	Sedan	0
35	1,323	Olean	Sedan	2
35	1,761	Kane	Sedan	1
35	1,919	Tionesta	SUV	1
36	2,357	Kane	SUV	2
36	2,866	Kane	Sedan	1
37	732	Olean	SUV	1
37	1,464	Olean	Sedan	3
37	1,626	Tionesta	Compact	4
37	1,761	Olean	SUV	1
37	1,915	Tionesta	SUV	2
37	2,119	Kane	Hybrid	1
38	1,766	Sheffield	SUV	0
38	2,201	Sheffield	Truck	2
39	996	Kane	Compact	2
39	2,813	Tionesta	SUV	0
40	323	Kane	Sedan	0
40	352	Sheffield	Compact	0
40	482	Olean	Sedan	1
40	1,144	Tionesta	Truck	0
40	$1,485	Sheffield	Compact	0
40	1,509	Kane	SUV	2
40	1,638	Sheffield	Sedan	0
40	1,961	Sheffield	Sedan	1
40	2,127	Olean	Truck	0
40	2,430	Tionesta	Sedan	1
41	1,704	Sheffield	Sedan	1
41	1,876	Kane	Sedan	2
41	2,010	Tionesta	Sedan	1
41	2,165	Tionesta	SUV	0
41	2,231	Tionesta	SUV	2
41	2,389	Kane	Truck	1
42	335	Olean	SUV	1
42	963	Kane	Sedan	0
42	1,298	Tionesta	Sedan	1
42	1,410	Kane	SUV	2
42	1,553	Tionesta	Compact	0
42	1,648	Olean	SUV	0
42	2,071	Kane	SUV	0
42	2,116	Kane	Compact	2
43	1,500	Tionesta	Sedan	0
43	1,549	Kane	SUV	2
43	2,348	Tionesta	Sedan	0
43	2,498	Tionesta	SUV	1
44	294	Kane	SUV	1
44	1,115	Kane	Truck	0
44	1,124	Tionesta	Compact	2
44	1,532	Tionesta	SUV	3
44	1,688	Kane	Sedan	4
44	1,822	Kane	SUV	0
44	1,897	Sheffield	Compact	0
44	2,445	Kane	SUV	0
44	2,886	Olean	SUV	1
45	820	Kane	Compact	1
45	1,266	Olean	Sedan	0
45	1,741	Olean	Compact	2
45	1,772	Olean	Compact	1
45	1,932	Tionesta	Sedan	1
45	2,350	Sheffield	Compact	0
45	2,422	Kane	Sedan	1
45	2,446	Olean	Compact	1
46	369	Olean	Sedan	1
46	978	Kane	Sedan	1
46	1,238	Sheffield	Compact	1
46	1,818	Kane	SUV	0
46	1,824	Olean	Truck	0
46	1,907	Olean	Sedan	0

(continued)

A.4 Data Set 4—Applewood Auto Group (*concluded*)

Age x_1	Profit x_2	Location x_3	Vehicle-Type x_4	Previous x_5
46	$1,938	Kane	Sedan	0
46	1,940	Kane	Truck	3
46	2,197	Sheffield	Sedan	1
46	2,646	Tionesta	Sedan	2
47	1,461	Kane	Sedan	0
47	1,731	Tionesta	Compact	0
47	2,230	Tionesta	Sedan	1
47	2,341	Sheffield	SUV	1
47	3,292	Olean	Sedan	2
48	1,108	Sheffield	Sedan	1
48	1,295	Sheffield	SUV	1
48	1,344	Sheffield	SUV	0
48	1,906	Kane	Sedan	1
48	1,952	Tionesta	Compact	1
48	2,070	Kane	SUV	1
48	2,454	Kane	Sedan	1
49	1,606	Olean	Compact	0
49	1,680	Kane	SUV	3
49	1,827	Tionesta	Truck	3
49	1,915	Tionesta	SUV	1
49	2,084	Tionesta	Sedan	0
49	2,639	Sheffield	SUV	0
50	842	Kane	SUV	0
50	1,963	Sheffield	Sedan	1
50	2,059	Sheffield	Sedan	1
50	2,338	Tionesta	SUV	0
50	3,043	Kane	Sedan	0
51	1,059	Kane	SUV	1
51	1,674	Sheffield	Sedan	1
51	1,807	Tionesta	Sedan	1
51	2,056	Sheffield	Hybrid	0
51	2,236	Tionesta	SUV	2
51	2,928	Kane	SUV	0
52	1,269	Tionesta	Sedan	1
52	1,717	Sheffield	SUV	3
52	1,797	Kane	Sedan	1
52	1,955	Olean	Hybrid	2
52	2,199	Tionesta	SUV	0
52	2,482	Olean	Compact	0
52	2,701	Sheffield	SUV	0
52	3,210	Olean	Truck	4
53	377	Olean	SUV	1
53	1,220	Olean	Sedan	0

Age x_1	Profit x_2	Location x_3	Vehicle-Type x_4	Previous x_5
53	$1,401	Tionesta	SUV	2
53	2,175	Olean	Sedan	1
54	1,118	Sheffield	Compact	1
54	2,584	Olean	Compact	2
54	2,666	Tionesta	Truck	0
54	2,991	Tionesta	SUV	0
55	934	Sheffield	Truck	1
55	2,063	Kane	SUV	1
55	2,083	Sheffield	Sedan	1
55	2,856	Olean	Hybrid	1
55	2,989	Tionesta	Compact	1
56	910	Sheffield	SUV	0
56	1,536	Kane	SUV	0
56	1,957	Sheffield	SUV	1
56	2,240	Olean	Sedan	0
56	2,695	Kane	Sedan	2
57	1,325	Olean	Sedan	1
57	2,250	Sheffield	Sedan	2
57	2,279	Sheffield	Hybrid	1
57	2,626	Sheffield	Sedan	2
58	1,501	Sheffield	Hybrid	1
58	1,752	Kane	Sedan	3
58	2,058	Kane	SUV	1
58	2,370	Tionesta	Compact	0
58	2,637	Sheffield	SUV	1
59	1,426	Sheffield	Sedan	0
59	2,944	Olean	SUV	2
60	2,147	Olean	Compact	2
61	1,973	Kane	SUV	3
61	2,502	Olean	Sedan	0
62	783	Sheffield	Hybrid	1
62	1,538	Olean	Truck	1
63	2,339	Olean	Compact	1
64	2,700	Kane	Truck	0
65	2,222	Kane	Truck	1
65	2,597	Sheffield	Truck	0
65	2,742	Tionesta	SUV	2
68	1,837	Sheffield	Sedan	1
69	2,842	Kane	SUV	0
70	2,434	Olean	Sedan	4
72	1,640	Olean	Sedan	1
72	1,821	Tionesta	SUV	1
73	2,487	Olean	Compact	4

A.5 Banking Data Set—Century National Bank Case

x_1 = Account balance in \$
x_2 = Number of ATM transactions in the month
x_3 = Number of other bank services used
x_4 = Has a debit card (1 = yes, 0 = no)
x_5 = Receives interest on the account (1 = yes, 0 = no)
x_6 = City where banking is done
60 Accounts

x_1	x_2	x_3	x_4	x_5	x_6
1,756	13	4	0	1	2
748	9	2	1	0	1
1,501	10	1	0	0	1
1,831	10	4	0	1	3
1,622	14	6	0	1	4
1,886	17	3	0	1	1
740	6	3	0	0	3
1,593	10	8	1	0	1
1,169	6	4	0	0	4
2,125	18	6	0	0	2
1,554	12	6	1	0	3
1,474	12	7	1	0	1
1,913	6	5	0	0	1
1,218	10	3	1	0	1
1,006	12	4	0	0	1
2,215	20	3	1	0	4
137	7	2	0	0	3
167	5	4	0	0	4
343	7	2	0	0	1
2,557	20	7	1	0	4
2,276	15	4	1	0	3
1,494	11	2	0	1	1
2,144	17	3	0	0	3
1,995	10	7	0	0	2
1,053	8	4	1	0	3
1,526	8	4	0	1	2
1,120	8	6	1	0	3
1,838	7	5	1	1	3
1,746	11	2	0	0	2
1,616	10	4	1	1	2

x_1	x_2	x_3	x_4	x_5	x_6
1,958	6	2	1	0	2
634	2	7	1	0	4
580	4	1	0	0	1
1,320	4	5	1	0	1
1,675	6	7	1	0	2
789	8	4	0	0	4
1,735	12	7	0	1	3
1,784	11	5	0	0	1
1,326	16	8	0	0	3
2,051	14	4	1	0	4
1,044	7	5	1	0	1
1,885	10	6	1	1	2
1,790	11	4	0	1	3
765	4	3	0	0	4
1,645	6	9	0	1	4
32	2	0	0	0	3
1,266	11	7	0	0	4
890	7	1	0	1	1
2,204	14	5	0	0	2
2,409	16	8	0	0	2
1,338	14	4	1	0	2
2,076	12	5	1	0	2
1,708	13	3	1	0	1
2,138	18	5	0	1	4
2,375	12	4	0	0	2
1,455	9	5	1	1	3
1,487	8	4	1	0	4
1,125	6	4	1	0	2
1,989	12	3	0	1	2
2,156	14	5	1	0	2

APPENDIX B: TABLES

B.1 Binomial Probability Distribution

n = 1

Probability

x	0.05	0.10	0.20	0.30	0.40	0.50	0.60	0.70	0.80	0.90	0.95
0	0.950	0.900	0.800	0.700	0.600	0.500	0.400	0.300	0.200	0.100	0.050
1	0.050	0.100	0.200	0.300	0.400	0.500	0.600	0.700	0.800	0.900	0.950

n = 2

Probability

x	0.05	0.10	0.20	0.30	0.40	0.50	0.60	0.70	0.80	0.90	0.95
0	0.903	0.810	0.640	0.490	0.360	0.250	0.160	0.090	0.040	0.010	0.003
1	0.095	0.180	0.320	0.420	0.480	0.500	0.480	0.420	0.320	0.180	0.095
2	0.003	0.010	0.040	0.090	0.160	0.250	0.360	0.490	0.640	0.810	0.903

n = 3

Probability

x	0.05	0.10	0.20	0.30	0.40	0.50	0.60	0.70	0.80	0.90	0.95
0	0.857	0.729	0.512	0.343	0.216	0.125	0.064	0.027	0.008	0.001	0.000
1	0.135	0.243	0.384	0.441	0.432	0.375	0.288	0.189	0.096	0.027	0.007
2	0.007	0.027	0.096	0.189	0.288	0.375	0.432	0.441	0.384	0.243	0.135
3	0.000	0.001	0.008	0.027	0.064	0.125	0.216	0.343	0.512	0.729	0.857

n = 4

Probability

x	0.05	0.10	0.20	0.30	0.40	0.50	0.60	0.70	0.80	0.90	0.95
0	0.815	0.656	0.410	0.240	0.130	0.063	0.026	0.008	0.002	0.000	0.000
1	0.171	0.292	0.410	0.412	0.346	0.250	0.154	0.076	0.026	0.004	0.000
2	0.014	0.049	0.154	0.265	0.346	0.375	0.346	0.265	0.154	0.049	0.014
3	0.000	0.004	0.026	0.076	0.154	0.250	0.346	0.412	0.410	0.292	0.171
4	0.000	0.000	0.002	0.008	0.026	0.063	0.130	0.240	0.410	0.656	0.815

n = 5

Probability

x	0.05	0.10	0.20	0.30	0.40	0.50	0.60	0.70	0.80	0.90	0.95
0	0.774	0.590	0.328	0.168	0.078	0.031	0.010	0.002	0.000	0.000	0.000
1	0.204	0.328	0.410	0.360	0.259	0.156	0.077	0.028	0.006	0.000	0.000
2	0.021	0.073	0.205	0.309	0.346	0.313	0.230	0.132	0.051	0.008	0.001
3	0.001	0.008	0.051	0.132	0.230	0.313	0.346	0.309	0.205	0.073	0.021
4	0.000	0.000	0.006	0.028	0.077	0.156	0.259	0.360	0.410	0.328	0.204
5	0.000	0.000	0.000	0.002	0.010	0.031	0.078	0.168	0.328	0.590	0.774

(continued)

B.1 Binomial Probability Distribution (*continued*)

n = 6

Probability

x	0.05	0.10	0.20	0.30	0.40	0.50	0.60	0.70	0.80	0.90	0.95
0	0.735	0.531	0.262	0.118	0.047	0.016	0.004	0.001	0.000	0.000	0.000
1	0.232	0.354	0.393	0.303	0.187	0.094	0.037	0.010	0.002	0.000	0.000
2	0.031	0.098	0.246	0.324	0.311	0.234	0.138	0.060	0.015	0.001	0.000
3	0.002	0.015	0.082	0.185	0.276	0.313	0.276	0.185	0.082	0.015	0.002
4	0.000	0.001	0.015	0.060	0.138	0.234	0.311	0.324	0.246	0.098	0.031
5	0.000	0.000	0.002	0.010	0.037	0.094	0.187	0.303	0.393	0.354	0.232
6	0.000	0.000	0.000	0.001	0.004	0.016	0.047	0.118	0.262	0.531	0.735

n = 7

Probability

x	0.05	0.10	0.20	0.30	0.40	0.50	0.60	0.70	0.80	0.90	0.95
0	0.698	0.478	0.210	0.082	0.028	0.008	0.002	0.000	0.000	0.000	0.000
1	0.257	0.372	0.367	0.247	0.131	0.055	0.017	0.004	0.000	0.000	0.000
2	0.041	0.124	0.275	0.318	0.261	0.164	0.077	0.025	0.004	0.000	0.000
3	0.004	0.023	0.115	0.227	0.290	0.273	0.194	0.097	0.029	0.003	0.000
4	0.000	0.003	0.029	0.097	0.194	0.273	0.290	0.227	0.115	0.023	0.004
5	0.000	0.000	0.004	0.025	0.077	0.164	0.261	0.318	0.275	0.124	0.041
6	0.000	0.000	0.000	0.004	0.017	0.055	0.131	0.247	0.367	0.372	0.257
7	0.000	0.000	0.000	0.000	0.002	0.008	0.028	0.082	0.210	0.478	0.698

n = 8

Probability

x	0.05	0.10	0.20	0.30	0.40	0.50	0.60	0.70	0.80	0.90	0.95
0	0.663	0.430	0.168	0.058	0.017	0.004	0.001	0.000	0.000	0.000	0.000
1	0.279	0.383	0.336	0.198	0.090	0.031	0.008	0.001	0.000	0.000	0.000
2	0.051	0.149	0.294	0.296	0.209	0.109	0.041	0.010	0.001	0.000	0.000
3	0.005	0.033	0.147	0.254	0.279	0.219	0.124	0.047	0.009	0.000	0.000
4	0.000	0.005	0.046	0.136	0.232	0.273	0.232	0.136	0.046	0.005	0.000
5	0.000	0.000	0.009	0.047	0.124	0.219	0.279	0.254	0.147	0.033	0.005
6	0.000	0.000	0.001	0.010	0.041	0.109	0.209	0.296	0.294	0.149	0.051
7	0.000	0.000	0.000	0.001	0.008	0.031	0.090	0.198	0.336	0.383	0.279
8	0.000	0.000	0.000	0.000	0.001	0.004	0.017	0.058	0.168	0.430	0.663

(*continued*)

B.1 Binomial Probability Distribution (*continued*)

$n = 9$

Probability

x	0.05	0.10	0.20	0.30	0.40	0.50	0.60	0.70	0.80	0.90	0.95
0	0.630	0.387	0.134	0.040	0.010	0.002	0.000	0.000	0.000	0.000	0.000
1	0.299	0.387	0.302	0.156	0.060	0.018	0.004	0.000	0.000	0.000	0.000
2	0.063	0.172	0.302	0.267	0.161	0.070	0.021	0.004	0.000	0.000	0.000
3	0.008	0.045	0.176	0.267	0.251	0.164	0.074	0.021	0.003	0.000	0.000
4	0.001	0.007	0.066	0.172	0.251	0.246	0.167	0.074	0.017	0.001	0.000
5	0.000	0.001	0.017	0.074	0.167	0.246	0.251	0.172	0.066	0.007	0.001
6	0.000	0.000	0.003	0.021	0.074	0.164	0.251	0.267	0.176	0.045	0.008
7	0.000	0.000	0.000	0.004	0.021	0.070	0.161	0.267	0.302	0.172	0.063
8	0.000	0.000	0.000	0.000	0.004	0.018	0.060	0.156	0.302	0.387	0.299
9	0.000	0.000	0.000	0.000	0.000	0.002	0.010	0.040	0.134	0.387	0.630

$n = 10$

Probability

x	0.05	0.10	0.20	0.30	0.40	0.50	0.60	0.70	0.80	0.90	0.95
0	0.599	0.349	0.107	0.028	0.006	0.001	0.000	0.000	0.000	0.000	0.000
1	0.315	0.387	0.268	0.121	0.040	0.010	0.002	0.000	0.000	0.000	0.000
2	0.075	0.194	0.302	0.233	0.121	0.044	0.011	0.001	0.000	0.000	0.000
3	0.010	0.057	0.201	0.267	0.215	0.117	0.042	0.009	0.001	0.000	0.000
4	0.001	0.011	0.088	0.200	0.251	0.205	0.111	0.037	0.006	0.000	0.000
5	0.000	0.001	0.026	0.103	0.201	0.246	0.201	0.103	0.026	0.001	0.000
6	0.000	0.000	0.006	0.037	0.111	0.205	0.251	0.200	0.088	0.011	0.001
7	0.000	0.000	0.001	0.009	0.042	0.117	0.215	0.267	0.201	0.057	0.010
8	0.000	0.000	0.000	0.001	0.011	0.044	0.121	0.233	0.302	0.194	0.075
9	0.000	0.000	0.000	0.000	0.002	0.010	0.040	0.121	0.268	0.387	0.315
10	0.000	0.000	0.000	0.000	0.000	0.001	0.006	0.028	0.107	0.349	0.599

$n = 11$

Probability

x	0.05	0.10	0.20	0.30	0.40	0.50	0.60	0.70	0.80	0.90	0.95
0	0.569	0.314	0.086	0.020	0.004	0.000	0.000	0.000	0.000	0.000	0.000
1	0.329	0.384	0.236	0.093	0.027	0.005	0.001	0.000	0.000	0.000	0.000
2	0.087	0.213	0.295	0.200	0.089	0.027	0.005	0.001	0.000	0.000	0.000
3	0.014	0.071	0.221	0.257	0.177	0.081	0.023	0.004	0.000	0.000	0.000
4	0.001	0.016	0.111	0.220	0.236	0.161	0.070	0.017	0.002	0.000	0.000
5	0.000	0.002	0.039	0.132	0.221	0.226	0.147	0.057	0.010	0.000	0.000
6	0.000	0.000	0.010	0.057	0.147	0.226	0.221	0.132	0.039	0.002	0.000
7	0.000	0.000	0.002	0.017	0.070	0.161	0.236	0.220	0.111	0.016	0.001
8	0.000	0.000	0.000	0.004	0.023	0.081	0.177	0.257	0.221	0.071	0.014
9	0.000	0.000	0.000	0.001	0.005	0.027	0.089	0.200	0.295	0.213	0.087
10	0.000	0.000	0.000	0.000	0.001	0.005	0.027	0.093	0.236	0.384	0.329
11	0.000	0.000	0.000	0.000	0.000	0.000	0.004	0.020	0.086	0.314	0.569

(*continued*)

B.1 Binomial Probability Distribution (*continued*)

n = 12

	Probability										
x	0.05	0.10	0.20	0.30	0.40	0.50	0.60	0.70	0.80	0.90	0.95
0	0.540	0.282	0.069	0.014	0.002	0.000	0.000	0.000	0.000	0.000	0.000
1	0.341	0.377	0.206	0.071	0.017	0.003	0.000	0.000	0.000	0.000	0.000
2	0.099	0.230	0.283	0.168	0.064	0.016	0.002	0.000	0.000	0.000	0.000
3	0.017	0.085	0.236	0.240	0.142	0.054	0.012	0.001	0.000	0.000	0.000
4	0.002	0.021	0.133	0.231	0.213	0.121	0.042	0.008	0.001	0.000	0.000
5	0.000	0.004	0.053	0.158	0.227	0.193	0.101	0.029	0.003	0.000	0.000
6	0.000	0.000	0.016	0.079	0.177	0.226	0.177	0.079	0.016	0.000	0.000
7	0.000	0.000	0.003	0.029	0.101	0.193	0.227	0.158	0.053	0.004	0.000
8	0.000	0.000	0.001	0.008	0.042	0.121	0.213	0.231	0.133	0.021	0.002
9	0.000	0.000	0.000	0.001	0.012	0.054	0.142	0.240	0.236	0.085	0.017
10	0.000	0.000	0.000	0.000	0.002	0.016	0.064	0.168	0.283	0.230	0.099
11	0.000	0.000	0.000	0.000	0.000	0.003	0.017	0.071	0.206	0.377	0.341
12	0.000	0.000	0.000	0.000	0.000	0.000	0.002	0.014	0.069	0.282	0.540

n = 13

	Probability										
x	0.05	0.10	0.20	0.30	0.40	0.50	0.60	0.70	0.80	0.90	0.95
0	0.513	0.254	0.055	0.010	0.001	0.000	0.000	0.000	0.000	0.000	0.000
1	0.351	0.367	0.179	0.054	0.011	0.002	0.000	0.000	0.000	0.000	0.000
2	0.111	0.245	0.268	0.139	0.045	0.010	0.001	0.000	0.000	0.000	0.000
3	0.021	0.100	0.246	0.218	0.111	0.035	0.006	0.001	0.000	0.000	0.000
4	0.003	0.028	0.154	0.234	0.184	0.087	0.024	0.003	0.000	0.000	0.000
5	0.000	0.006	0.069	0.180	0.221	0.157	0.066	0.014	0.001	0.000	0.000
6	0.000	0.001	0.023	0.103	0.197	0.209	0.131	0.044	0.006	0.000	0.000
7	0.000	0.000	0.006	0.044	0.131	0.209	0.197	0.103	0.023	0.001	0.000
8	0.000	0.000	0.001	0.014	0.066	0.157	0.221	0.180	0.069	0.006	0.000
9	0.000	0.000	0.000	0.003	0.024	0.087	0.184	0.234	0.154	0.028	0.003
10	0.000	0.000	0.000	0.001	0.006	0.035	0.111	0.218	0.246	0.100	0.021
11	0.000	0.000	0.000	0.000	0.001	0.010	0.045	0.139	0.268	0.245	0.111
12	0.000	0.000	0.000	0.000	0.000	0.002	0.011	0.054	0.179	0.367	0.351
13	0.000	0.000	0.000	0.000	0.000	0.000	0.001	0.010	0.055	0.254	0.513

(continued)

B.1 Binomial Probability Distribution (*concluded*)

n = 14
Probability

x	0.05	0.10	0.20	0.30	0.40	0.50	0.60	0.70	0.80	0.90	0.95
0	0.488	0.229	0.044	0.007	0.001	0.000	0.000	0.000	0.000	0.000	0.000
1	0.359	0.356	0.154	0.041	0.007	0.001	0.000	0.000	0.000	0.000	0.000
2	0.123	0.257	0.250	0.113	0.032	0.006	0.001	0.000	0.000	0.000	0.000
3	0.026	0.114	0.250	0.194	0.085	0.022	0.003	0.000	0.000	0.000	0.000
4	0.004	0.035	0.172	0.229	0.155	0.061	0.014	0.001	0.000	0.000	0.000
5	0.000	0.008	0.086	0.196	0.207	0.122	0.041	0.007	0.000	0.000	0.000
6	0.000	0.001	0.032	0.126	0.207	0.183	0.092	0.023	0.002	0.000	0.000
7	0.000	0.000	0.009	0.062	0.157	0.209	0.157	0.062	0.009	0.000	0.000
8	0.000	0.000	0.002	0.023	0.092	0.183	0.207	0.126	0.032	0.001	0.000
9	0.000	0.000	0.000	0.007	0.041	0.122	0.207	0.196	0.086	0.008	0.000
10	0.000	0.000	0.000	0.001	0.014	0.061	0.155	0.229	0.172	0.035	0.004
11	0.000	0.000	0.000	0.000	0.003	0.022	0.085	0.194	0.250	0.114	0.026
12	0.000	0.000	0.000	0.000	0.001	0.006	0.032	0.113	0.250	0.257	0.123
13	0.000	0.000	0.000	0.000	0.000	0.001	0.007	0.041	0.154	0.356	0.359
14	0.000	0.000	0.000	0.000	0.000	0.000	0.001	0.007	0.044	0.229	0.488

n = 15
Probability

x	0.05	0.10	0.20	0.30	0.40	0.50	0.60	0.70	0.80	0.90	0.95
0	0.463	0.206	0.035	0.005	0.000	0.000	0.000	0.000	0.000	0.000	0.000
1	0.366	0.343	0.132	0.031	0.005	0.000	0.000	0.000	0.000	0.000	0.000
2	0.135	0.267	0.231	0.092	0.022	0.003	0.000	0.000	0.000	0.000	0.000
3	0.031	0.129	0.250	0.170	0.063	0.014	0.002	0.000	0.000	0.000	0.000
4	0.005	0.043	0.188	0.219	0.127	0.042	0.007	0.001	0.000	0.000	0.000
5	0.001	0.010	0.103	0.206	0.186	0.092	0.024	0.003	0.000	0.000	0.000
6	0.000	0.002	0.043	0.147	0.207	0.153	0.061	0.012	0.001	0.000	0.000
7	0.000	0.000	0.014	0.081	0.177	0.196	0.118	0.035	0.003	0.000	0.000
8	0.000	0.000	0.003	0.035	0.118	0.196	0.177	0.081	0.014	0.000	0.000
9	0.000	0.000	0.001	0.012	0.061	0.153	0.207	0.147	0.043	0.002	0.000
10	0.000	0.000	0.000	0.003	0.024	0.092	0.186	0.206	0.103	0.010	0.001
11	0.000	0.000	0.000	0.001	0.007	0.042	0.127	0.219	0.188	0.043	0.005
12	0.000	0.000	0.000	0.000	0.002	0.014	0.063	0.170	0.250	0.129	0.031
13	0.000	0.000	0.000	0.000	0.000	0.003	0.022	0.092	0.231	0.267	0.135
14	0.000	0.000	0.000	0.000	0.000	0.000	0.005	0.031	0.132	0.343	0.366
15	0.000	0.000	0.000	0.000	0.000	0.000	0.000	0.005	0.035	0.206	0.463

B.2 Poisson Distribution

	μ								
x	0.1	0.2	0.3	0.4	0.5	0.6	0.7	0.8	0.9
0	0.9048	0.8187	0.7408	0.6703	0.6065	0.5488	0.4966	0.4493	0.4066
1	0.0905	0.1637	0.2222	0.2681	0.3033	0.3293	0.3476	0.3595	0.3659
2	0.0045	0.0164	0.0333	0.0536	0.0758	0.0988	0.1217	0.1438	0.1647
3	0.0002	0.0011	0.0033	0.0072	0.0126	0.0198	0.0284	0.0383	0.0494
4	0.0000	0.0001	0.0003	0.0007	0.0016	0.0030	0.0050	0.0077	0.0111
5	0.0000	0.0000	0.0000	0.0001	0.0002	0.0004	0.0007	0.0012	0.0020
6	0.0000	0.0000	0.0000	0.0000	0.0000	0.0000	0.0001	0.0002	0.0003
7	0.0000	0.0000	0.0000	0.0000	0.0000	0.0000	0.0000	0.0000	0.0000

	μ								
x	1.0	2.0	3.0	4.0	5.0	6.0	7.0	8.0	9.0
0	0.3679	0.1353	0.0498	0.0183	0.0067	0.0025	0.0009	0.0003	0.0001
1	0.3679	0.2707	0.1494	0.0733	0.0337	0.0149	0.0064	0.0027	0.0011
2	0.1839	0.2707	0.2240	0.1465	0.0842	0.0446	0.0223	0.0107	0.0050
3	0.0613	0.1804	0.2240	0.1954	0.1404	0.0892	0.0521	0.0286	0.0150
4	0.0153	0.0902	0.1680	0.1954	0.1755	0.1339	0.0912	0.0573	0.0337
5	0.0031	0.0361	0.1008	0.1563	0.1755	0.1606	0.1277	0.0916	0.0607
6	0.0005	0.0120	0.0504	0.1042	0.1462	0.1606	0.1490	0.1221	0.0911
7	0.0001	0.0034	0.0216	0.0595	0.1044	0.1377	0.1490	0.1396	0.1171
8	0.0000	0.0009	0.0081	0.0298	0.0653	0.1033	0.1304	0.1396	0.1318
9	0.0000	0.0002	0.0027	0.0132	0.0363	0.0688	0.1014	0.1241	0.1318
10	0.0000	0.0000	0.0008	0.0053	0.0181	0.0413	0.0710	0.0993	0.1186
11	0.0000	0.0000	0.0002	0.0019	0.0082	0.0225	0.0452	0.0722	0.0970
12	0.0000	0.0000	0.0001	0.0006	0.0034	0.0113	0.0263	0.0481	0.0728
13	0.0000	0.0000	0.0000	0.0002	0.0013	0.0052	0.0142	0.0296	0.0504
14	0.0000	0.0000	0.0000	0.0001	0.0005	0.0022	0.0071	0.0169	0.0324
15	0.0000	0.0000	0.0000	0.0000	0.0002	0.0009	0.0033	0.0090	0.0194
16	0.0000	0.0000	0.0000	0.0000	0.0000	0.0003	0.0014	0.0045	0.0109
17	0.0000	0.0000	0.0000	0.0000	0.0000	0.0001	0.0006	0.0021	0.0058
18	0.0000	0.0000	0.0000	0.0000	0.0000	0.0000	0.0002	0.0009	0.0029
19	0.0000	0.0000	0.0000	0.0000	0.0000	0.0000	0.0001	0.0004	0.0014
20	0.0000	0.0000	0.0000	0.0000	0.0000	0.0000	0.0000	0.0002	0.0006
21	0.0000	0.0000	0.0000	0.0000	0.0000	0.0000	0.0000	0.0001	0.0003
22	0.0000	0.0000	0.0000	0.0000	0.0000	0.0000	0.0000	0.0000	0.0001

B.3 Areas under the Normal Curve

Example:
If $z = 1.96$, then
$P(0 \text{ to } z) = 0.4750$.

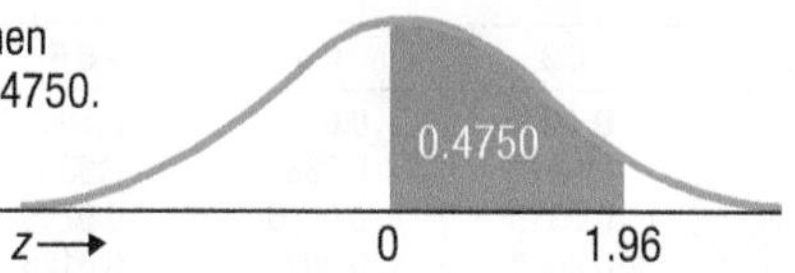

z	0.00	0.01	0.02	0.03	0.04	0.05	0.06	0.07	0.08	0.09
0.0	0.0000	0.0040	0.0080	0.0120	0.0160	0.0199	0.0239	0.0279	0.0319	0.0359
0.1	0.0398	0.0438	0.0478	0.0517	0.0557	0.0596	0.0636	0.0675	0.0714	0.0753
0.2	0.0793	0.0832	0.0871	0.0910	0.0948	0.0987	0.1026	0.1064	0.1103	0.1141
0.3	0.1179	0.1217	0.1255	0.1293	0.1331	0.1368	0.1406	0.1443	0.1480	0.1517
0.4	0.1554	0.1591	0.1628	0.1664	0.1700	0.1736	0.1772	0.1808	0.1844	0.1879
0.5	0.1915	0.1950	0.1985	0.2019	0.2054	0.2088	0.2123	0.2157	0.2190	0.2224
0.6	0.2257	0.2291	0.2324	0.2357	0.2389	0.2422	0.2454	0.2486	0.2517	0.2549
0.7	0.2580	0.2611	0.2642	0.2673	0.2704	0.2734	0.2764	0.2794	0.2823	0.2852
0.8	0.2881	0.2910	0.2939	0.2967	0.2995	0.3023	0.3051	0.3078	0.3106	0.3133
0.9	0.3159	0.3186	0.3212	0.3238	0.3264	0.3289	0.3315	0.3340	0.3365	0.3389
1.0	0.3413	0.3438	0.3461	0.3485	0.3508	0.3531	0.3554	0.3577	0.3599	0.3621
1.1	0.3643	0.3665	0.3686	0.3708	0.3729	0.3749	0.3770	0.3790	0.3810	0.3830
1.2	0.3849	0.3869	0.3888	0.3907	0.3925	0.3944	0.3962	0.3980	0.3997	0.4015
1.3	0.4032	0.4049	0.4066	0.4082	0.4099	0.4115	0.4131	0.4147	0.4162	0.4177
1.4	0.4192	0.4207	0.4222	0.4236	0.4251	0.4265	0.4279	0.4292	0.4306	0.4319
1.5	0.4332	0.4345	0.4357	0.4370	0.4382	0.4394	0.4406	0.4418	0.4429	0.4441
1.6	0.4452	0.4463	0.4474	0.4484	0.4495	0.4505	0.4515	0.4525	0.4535	0.4545
1.7	0.4554	0.4564	0.4573	0.4582	0.4591	0.4599	0.4608	0.4616	0.4625	0.4633
1.8	0.4641	0.4649	0.4656	0.4664	0.4671	0.4678	0.4686	0.4693	0.4699	0.4706
1.9	0.4713	0.4719	0.4726	0.4732	0.4738	0.4744	0.4750	0.4756	0.4761	0.4767
2.0	0.4772	0.4778	0.4783	0.4788	0.4793	0.4798	0.4803	0.4808	0.4812	0.4817
2.1	0.4821	0.4826	0.4830	0.4834	0.4838	0.4842	0.4846	0.4850	0.4854	0.4857
2.2	0.4861	0.4864	0.4868	0.4871	0.4875	0.4878	0.4881	0.4884	0.4887	0.4890
2.3	0.4893	0.4896	0.4898	0.4901	0.4904	0.4906	0.4909	0.4911	0.4913	0.4916
2.4	0.4918	0.4920	0.4922	0.4925	0.4927	0.4929	0.4931	0.4932	0.4934	0.4936
2.5	0.4938	0.4940	0.4941	0.4943	0.4945	0.4946	0.4948	0.4949	0.4951	0.4952
2.6	0.4953	0.4955	0.4956	0.4957	0.4959	0.4960	0.4961	0.4962	0.4963	0.4964
2.7	0.4965	0.4966	0.4967	0.4968	0.4969	0.4970	0.4971	0.4972	0.4973	0.4974
2.8	0.4974	0.4975	0.4976	0.4977	0.4977	0.4978	0.4979	0.4979	0.4980	0.4981
2.9	0.4981	0.4982	0.4982	0.4983	0.4984	0.4984	0.4985	0.4985	0.4986	0.4986
3.0	0.4987	0.4987	0.4987	0.4988	0.4988	0.4989	0.4989	0.4989	0.4990	0.4990

B.4 Table of Random Numbers

02711	08182	75997	79866	58095	83319	80295	79741	74599	84379
94873	90935	31684	63952	09865	14491	99518	93394	34691	14985
54921	78680	06635	98689	17306	25170	65928	87709	30533	89736
77640	97636	37397	93379	56454	59818	45827	74164	71666	46977
61545	00835	93251	87203	36759	49197	85967	01704	19634	21898
17147	19519	22497	16857	42426	84822	92598	49186	88247	39967
13748	04742	92460	85801	53444	65626	58710	55406	17173	69776
87455	14813	50373	28037	91182	32786	65261	11173	34376	36408
08999	57409	91185	10200	61411	23392	47797	56377	71635	08601
78804	81333	53809	32471	46034	36306	22498	19239	85428	55721
82173	26921	28472	98958	07960	66124	89731	95069	18625	92405
97594	25168	89178	68190	05043	17407	48201	83917	11413	72920
73881	67176	93504	42636	38233	16154	96451	57925	29667	30859
46071	22912	90326	42453	88108	72064	58601	32357	90610	32921
44492	19686	12495	93135	95185	77799	52441	88272	22024	80631
31864	72170	37722	55794	14636	05148	54505	50113	21119	25228
51574	90692	43339	65689	76539	27909	05467	21727	51141	72949
35350	76132	92925	92124	92634	35681	43690	89136	35599	84138
46943	36502	01172	46045	46991	33804	80006	35542	61056	75666
22665	87226	33304	57975	03985	21566	65796	72915	81466	89205
39437	97957	11838	10433	21564	51570	73558	27495	34533	57808
77082	47784	40098	97962	89845	28392	78187	06112	08169	11261
24544	25649	43370	28007	06779	72402	62632	53956	24709	06978
27503	15558	37738	24849	70722	71859	83736	06016	94397	12529
24590	24545	06435	52758	45685	90151	46516	49644	92686	84870
48155	86226	40359	28723	15364	69125	12609	57171	86857	31702
20226	53752	90648	24362	83314	00014	19207	69413	97016	86290
70178	73444	38790	53626	93780	18629	68766	24371	74639	30782
10169	41465	51935	05711	09799	79077	88159	33437	68519	03040
81084	03701	28598	70013	63794	53169	97054	60303	23259	96196
69202	20777	21727	81511	51887	16175	53746	46516	70339	62727
80561	95787	89426	93325	86412	57479	54194	52153	19197	81877
08199	26703	95128	48599	09333	12584	24374	31232	61782	44032
98883	28220	39358	53720	80161	83371	15181	11131	12219	55920
84568	69286	76054	21615	80883	36797	82845	39139	90900	18172
04269	35173	95745	53893	86022	77722	52498	84193	22448	22571
10538	13124	36099	13140	37706	44562	57179	44693	67877	01549
77843	24955	25900	63843	95029	93859	93634	20205	66294	41218
12034	94636	49455	76362	83532	31062	69903	91186	65768	55949
10524	72829	47641	93315	80875	28090	97728	52560	34937	79548
68935	76632	46984	61772	92786	22651	07086	89754	44143	97687
89450	65665	29190	43709	11172	34481	95977	47535	25658	73898
90696	20451	24211	97310	60446	73530	62865	96574	13829	72226
49006	32047	93086	00112	20470	17136	28255	86328	07293	38809
74591	87025	52368	59416	34417	70557	86746	55809	53628	12000
06315	17012	77103	00968	07235	10728	42189	33292	51487	64443
62386	09184	62092	46617	99419	64230	95034	85481	07857	42510
86848	82122	04028	36959	87827	12813	08627	80699	13345	51695
65643	69480	46598	04501	40403	91408	32343	48130	49303	90689
11084	46534	78957	77353	39578	77868	22970	84349	09184	70603

B.5 Student's *t* Distribution

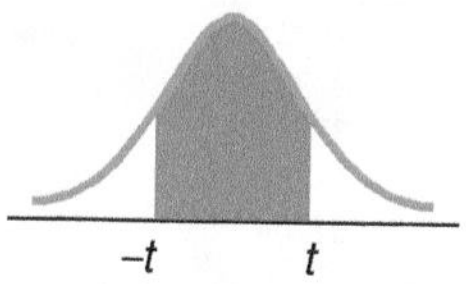

Confidence interval

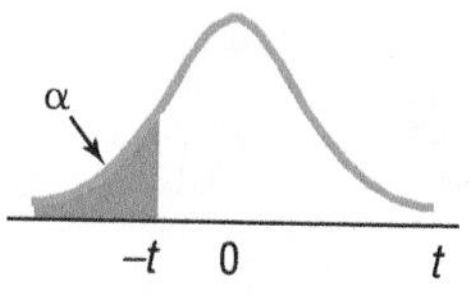

Left-tailed test

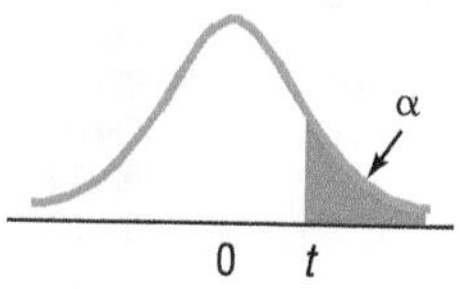

Right-tailed test

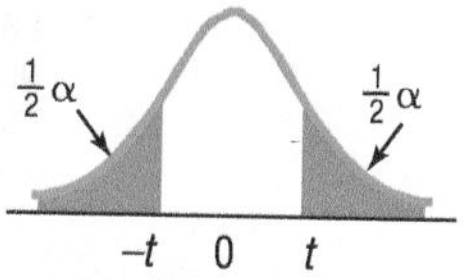

Two-tailed test

	Confidence Intervals, *c*					
	80%	90%	95%	98%	99%	99.9%
	Level of Significance for One-Tailed Test, α					
df	0.10	0.05	0.025	0.01	0.005	0.0005
	Level of Significance for Two-Tailed Test, α					
	0.20	0.10	0.05	0.02	0.01	0.001
1	3.078	6.314	12.706	31.821	63.657	636.619
2	1.886	2.920	4.303	6.965	9.925	31.599
3	1.638	2.353	3.182	4.541	5.841	12.924
4	1.533	2.132	2.776	3.747	4.604	8.610
5	1.476	2.015	2.571	3.365	4.032	6.869
6	1.440	1.943	2.447	3.143	3.707	5.959
7	1.415	1.895	2.365	2.998	3.499	5.408
8	1.397	1.860	2.306	2.896	3.355	5.041
9	1.383	1.833	2.262	2.821	3.250	4.781
10	1.372	1.812	2.228	2.764	3.169	4.587
11	1.363	1.796	2.201	2.718	3.106	4.437
12	1.356	1.782	2.179	2.681	3.055	4.318
13	1.350	1.771	2.160	2.650	3.012	4.221
14	1.345	1.761	2.145	2.624	2.977	4.140
15	1.341	1.753	2.131	2.602	2.947	4.073
16	1.337	1.746	2.120	2.583	2.921	4.015
17	1.333	1.740	2.110	2.567	2.898	3.965
18	1.330	1.734	2.101	2.552	2.878	3.922
19	1.328	1.729	2.093	2.539	2.861	3.883
20	1.325	1.725	2.086	2.528	2.845	3.850
21	1.323	1.721	2.080	2.518	2.831	3.819
22	1.321	1.717	2.074	2.508	2.819	3.792
23	1.319	1.714	2.069	2.500	2.807	3.768
24	1.318	1.711	2.064	2.492	2.797	3.745
25	1.316	1.708	2.060	2.485	2.787	3.725
26	1.315	1.706	2.056	2.479	2.779	3.707
27	1.314	1.703	2.052	2.473	2.771	3.690
28	1.313	1.701	2.048	2.467	2.763	3.674
29	1.311	1.699	2.045	2.462	2.756	3.659
30	1.310	1.697	2.042	2.457	2.750	3.646
31	1.309	1.696	2.040	2.453	2.744	3.633
32	1.309	1.694	2.037	2.449	2.738	3.622
33	1.308	1.692	2.035	2.445	2.733	3.611
34	1.307	1.691	2.032	2.441	2.728	3.601
35	1.306	1.690	2.030	2.438	2.724	3.591
36	1.306	1.688	2.028	2.434	2.719	3.582
37	1.305	1.687	2.026	2.431	2.715	3.574
38	1.304	1.686	2.024	2.429	2.712	3.566
39	1.304	1.685	2.023	2.426	2.708	3.558
40	1.303	1.684	2.021	2.423	2.704	3.551
41	1.303	1.683	2.020	2.421	2.701	3.544
42	1.302	1.682	2.018	2.418	2.698	3.538
43	1.302	1.681	2.017	2.416	2.695	3.532
44	1.301	1.680	2.015	2.414	2.692	3.526
45	1.301	1.679	2.014	2.412	2.690	3.520
46	1.300	1.679	2.013	2.410	2.687	3.515
47	1.300	1.678	2.012	2.408	2.685	3.510
48	1.299	1.677	2.011	2.407	2.682	3.505
49	1.299	1.677	2.010	2.405	2.680	3.500
50	1.299	1.676	2.009	2.403	2.678	3.496
51	1.298	1.675	2.008	2.402	2.676	3.492
52	1.298	1.675	2.007	2.400	2.674	3.488
53	1.298	1.674	2.006	2.399	2.672	3.484
54	1.297	1.674	2.005	2.397	2.670	3.480
55	1.297	1.673	2.004	2.396	2.668	3.476
56	1.297	1.673	2.003	2.395	2.667	3.473
57	1.297	1.672	2.002	2.394	2.665	3.470
58	1.296	1.672	2.002	2.392	2.663	3.466
59	1.296	1.671	2.001	2.391	2.662	3.463
60	1.296	1.671	2.000	2.390	2.660	3.460
61	1.296	1.670	2.000	2.389	2.659	3.457
62	1.295	1.670	1.999	2.388	2.657	3.454
63	1.295	1.669	1.998	2.387	2.656	3.452
64	1.295	1.669	1.998	2.386	2.655	3.449
65	1.295	1.669	1.997	2.385	2.654	3.447
66	1.295	1.668	1.997	2.384	2.652	3.444
67	1.294	1.668	1.996	2.383	2.651	3.442
68	1.294	1.668	1.995	2.382	2.650	3.439
69	1.294	1.667	1.995	2.382	2.649	3.437
70	1.294	1.667	1.994	2.381	2.648	3.435

(continued)

B.5 Student's *t* Distribution (*concluded*)

	Confidence Intervals, *c*					
	80%	90%	95%	98%	99%	99.9%
	Level of Significance for One-Tailed Test, α					
df	0.10	0.05	0.025	0.01	0.005	0.0005
	Level of Significance for Two-Tailed Test, α					
	0.20	0.10	0.05	0.02	0.01	0.001
71	1.294	1.667	1.994	2.380	2.647	3.433
72	1.293	1.666	1.993	2.379	2.646	3.431
73	1.293	1.666	1.993	2.379	2.645	3.429
74	1.293	1.666	1.993	2.378	2.644	3.427
75	1.293	1.665	1.992	2.377	2.643	3.425
76	1.293	1.665	1.992	2.376	2.642	3.423
77	1.293	1.665	1.991	2.376	2.641	3.421
78	1.292	1.665	1.991	2.375	2.640	3.420
79	1.292	1.664	1.990	2.374	2.640	3.418
80	1.292	1.664	1.990	2.374	2.639	3.416
81	1.292	1.664	1.990	2.373	2.638	3.415
82	1.292	1.664	1.989	2.373	2.637	3.413
83	1.292	1.663	1.989	2.372	2.636	3.412
84	1.292	1.663	1.989	2.372	2.636	3.410
85	1.292	1.663	1.988	2.371	2.635	3.409
86	1.291	1.663	1.988	2.370	2.634	3.407
87	1.291	1.663	1.988	2.370	2.634	3.406
88	1.291	1.662	1.987	2.369	2.633	3.405
89	1.291	1.662	1.987	2.369	2.632	3.403
90	1.291	1.662	1.987	2.368	2.632	3.402
91	1.291	1.662	1.986	2.368	2.631	3.401
92	1.291	1.662	1.986	2.368	2.630	3.399
93	1.291	1.661	1.986	2.367	2.630	3.398
94	1.291	1.661	1.986	2.367	2.629	3.397
95	1.291	1.661	1.985	2.366	2.629	3.396
96	1.290	1.661	1.985	2.366	2.628	3.395
97	1.290	1.661	1.985	2.365	2.627	3.394
98	1.290	1.661	1.984	2.365	2.627	3.393
99	1.290	1.660	1.984	2.365	2.626	3.392
100	1.290	1.660	1.984	2.364	2.626	3.390
120	1.289	1.658	1.980	2.358	2.617	3.373
140	1.288	1.656	1.977	2.353	2.611	3.361
160	1.287	1.654	1.975	2.350	2.607	3.352
180	1.286	1.653	1.973	2.347	2.603	3.345
200	1.286	1.653	1.972	2.345	2.601	3.340
∞	1.282	1.645	1.960	2.326	2.576	3.291

B.6A Critical Values of the *F* Distribution ($\alpha = .05$)

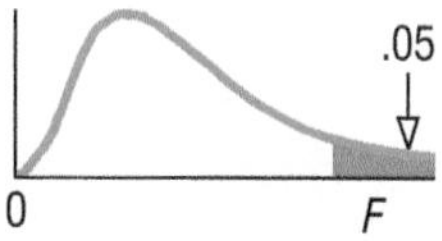

Degrees of Freedom for the Denominator	Degrees of Freedom for the Numerator															
	1	2	3	4	5	6	7	8	9	10	12	15	20	24	30	40
1	161	200	216	225	230	234	237	239	241	242	244	246	248	249	250	251
2	18.5	19.0	19.2	19.2	19.3	19.3	19.4	19.4	19.4	19.4	19.4	19.4	19.4	19.5	19.5	19.5
3	10.1	9.55	9.28	9.12	9.01	8.94	8.89	8.85	8.81	8.79	8.74	8.70	8.66	8.64	8.62	8.59
4	7.71	6.94	6.59	6.39	6.26	6.16	6.09	6.04	6.00	5.96	5.91	5.86	5.80	5.77	5.75	5.72
5	6.61	5.79	5.41	5.19	5.05	4.95	4.88	4.82	4.77	4.74	4.68	4.62	4.56	4.53	4.50	4.46
6	5.99	5.14	4.76	4.53	4.39	4.28	4.21	4.15	4.10	4.06	4.00	3.94	3.87	3.84	3.81	3.77
7	5.59	4.74	4.35	4.12	3.97	3.87	3.79	3.73	3.68	3.64	3.57	3.51	3.44	3.41	3.38	3.34
8	5.32	4.46	4.07	3.84	3.69	3.58	3.50	3.44	3.39	3.35	3.28	3.22	3.15	3.12	3.08	3.04
9	5.12	4.26	3.86	3.63	3.48	3.37	3.29	3.23	3.18	3.14	3.07	3.01	2.94	2.90	2.86	2.83
10	4.96	4.10	3.71	3.48	3.33	3.22	3.14	3.07	3.02	2.98	2.91	2.85	2.77	2.74	2.70	2.66
11	4.84	3.98	3.59	3.36	3.20	3.09	3.01	2.95	2.90	2.85	2.79	2.72	2.65	2.61	2.57	2.53
12	4.75	3.89	3.49	3.26	3.11	3.00	2.91	2.85	2.80	2.75	2.69	2.62	2.54	2.51	2.47	2.43
13	4.67	3.81	3.41	3.18	3.03	2.92	2.83	2.77	2.71	2.67	2.60	2.53	2.46	2.42	2.38	2.34
14	4.60	3.74	3.34	3.11	2.96	2.85	2.76	2.70	2.65	2.60	2.53	2.46	2.39	2.35	2.31	2.27
15	4.54	3.68	3.29	3.06	2.90	2.79	2.71	2.64	2.59	2.54	2.48	2.40	2.33	2.29	2.25	2.20
16	4.49	3.63	3.24	3.01	2.85	2.74	2.66	2.59	2.54	2.49	2.42	2.35	2.28	2.24	2.19	2.15
17	4.45	3.59	3.20	2.96	2.81	2.70	2.61	2.55	2.49	2.45	2.38	2.31	2.23	2.19	2.15	2.10
18	4.41	3.55	3.16	2.93	2.77	2.66	2.58	2.51	2.46	2.41	2.34	2.27	2.19	2.15	2.11	2.06
19	4.38	3.52	3.13	2.90	2.74	2.63	2.54	2.48	2.42	2.38	2.31	2.23	2.16	2.11	2.07	2.03
20	4.35	3.49	3.10	2.87	2.71	2.60	2.51	2.45	2.39	2.35	2.28	2.20	2.12	2.08	2.04	1.99
21	4.32	3.47	3.07	2.84	2.68	2.57	2.49	2.42	2.37	2.32	2.25	2.18	2.10	2.05	2.01	1.96
22	4.30	3.44	3.05	2.82	2.66	2.55	2.46	2.40	2.34	2.30	2.23	2.15	2.07	2.03	1.98	1.94
23	4.28	3.42	3.03	2.80	2.64	2.53	2.44	2.37	2.32	2.27	2.20	2.13	2.05	2.01	1.96	1.91
24	4.26	3.40	3.01	2.78	2.62	2.51	2.42	2.36	2.30	2.25	2.18	2.11	2.03	1.98	1.94	1.89
25	4.24	3.39	2.99	2.76	2.60	2.49	2.40	2.34	2.28	2.24	2.16	2.09	2.01	1.96	1.92	1.87
30	4.17	3.32	2.92	2.69	2.53	2.42	2.33	2.27	2.21	2.16	2.09	2.01	1.93	1.89	1.84	1.79
40	4.08	3.23	2.84	2.61	2.45	2.34	2.25	2.18	2.12	2.08	2.00	1.92	1.84	1.79	1.74	1.69
60	4.00	3.15	2.76	2.53	2.37	2.25	2.17	2.10	2.04	1.99	1.92	1.84	1.75	1.70	1.65	1.59
120	3.92	3.07	2.68	2.45	2.29	2.18	2.09	2.02	1.96	1.91	1.83	1.75	1.66	1.61	1.55	1.50
∞	3.84	3.00	2.60	2.37	2.21	2.10	2.01	1.94	1.88	1.83	1.75	1.67	1.57	1.52	1.46	1.39

B.6B Critical Values of the *F* Distribution ($\alpha = .01$)

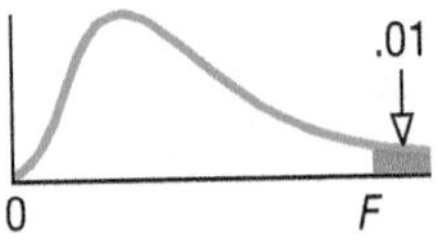

Degrees of Freedom for the Denominator	Degrees of Freedom for the Numerator: 1	2	3	4	5	6	7	8	9	10	12	15	20	24	30	40
1	4052	5000	5403	5625	5764	5859	5928	5981	6022	6056	6106	6157	6209	6235	6261	6287
2	98.5	99.0	99.2	99.2	99.3	99.3	99.4	99.4	99.4	99.4	99.4	99.4	99.4	99.5	99.5	99.5
3	34.1	30.8	29.5	28.7	28.2	27.9	27.7	27.5	27.3	27.2	27.1	26.9	26.7	26.6	26.5	26.4
4	21.2	18.0	16.7	16.0	15.5	15.2	15.0	14.8	14.7	14.5	14.4	14.2	14.0	13.9	13.8	13.7
5	16.3	13.3	12.1	11.4	11.0	10.7	10.5	10.3	10.2	10.1	9.89	9.72	9.55	9.47	9.38	9.29
6	13.7	10.9	9.78	9.15	8.75	8.47	8.26	8.10	7.98	7.87	7.72	7.56	7.40	7.31	7.23	7.14
7	12.2	9.55	8.45	7.85	7.46	7.19	6.99	6.84	6.72	6.62	6.47	6.31	6.16	6.07	5.99	5.91
8	11.3	8.65	7.59	7.01	6.63	6.37	6.18	6.03	5.91	5.81	5.67	5.52	5.36	5.28	5.20	5.12
9	10.6	8.02	6.99	6.42	6.06	5.80	5.61	5.47	5.35	5.26	5.11	4.96	4.81	4.73	4.65	4.57
10	10.0	7.56	6.55	5.99	5.64	5.39	5.20	5.06	4.94	4.85	4.71	4.56	4.41	4.33	4.25	4.17
11	9.65	7.21	6.22	5.67	5.32	5.07	4.89	4.74	4.63	4.54	4.40	4.25	4.10	4.02	3.94	3.86
12	9.33	6.93	5.95	5.41	5.06	4.82	4.64	4.50	4.39	4.30	4.16	4.01	3.86	3.78	3.70	3.62
13	9.07	6.70	5.74	5.21	4.86	4.62	4.44	4.30	4.19	4.10	3.96	3.82	3.66	3.59	3.51	3.43
14	8.86	6.51	5.56	5.04	4.69	4.46	4.28	4.14	4.03	3.94	3.80	3.66	3.51	3.43	3.35	3.27
15	8.68	6.36	5.42	4.89	4.56	4.32	4.14	4.00	3.89	3.80	3.67	3.52	3.37	3.29	3.21	3.13
16	8.53	6.23	5.29	4.77	4.44	4.20	4.03	3.89	3.78	3.69	3.55	3.41	3.26	3.18	3.10	3.02
17	8.40	6.11	5.18	4.67	4.34	4.10	3.93	3.79	3.68	3.59	3.46	3.31	3.16	3.08	3.00	2.92
18	8.29	6.01	5.09	4.58	4.25	4.01	3.84	3.71	3.60	3.51	3.37	3.23	3.08	3.00	2.92	2.84
19	8.18	5.93	5.01	4.50	4.17	3.94	3.77	3.63	3.52	3.43	3.30	3.15	3.00	2.92	2.84	2.76
20	8.10	5.85	4.94	4.43	4.10	3.87	3.70	3.56	3.46	3.37	3.23	3.09	2.94	2.86	2.78	2.69
21	8.02	5.78	4.87	4.37	4.04	3.81	3.64	3.51	3.40	3.31	3.17	3.03	2.88	2.80	2.72	2.64
22	7.95	5.72	4.82	4.31	3.99	3.76	3.59	3.45	3.35	3.26	3.12	2.98	2.83	2.75	2.67	2.58
23	7.88	5.66	4.76	4.26	3.94	3.71	3.54	3.41	3.30	3.21	3.07	2.93	2.78	2.70	2.62	2.54
24	7.82	5.61	4.72	4.22	3.90	3.67	3.50	3.36	3.26	3.17	3.03	2.89	2.74	2.66	2.58	2.49
25	7.77	5.57	4.68	4.18	3.85	3.63	3.46	3.32	3.22	3.13	2.99	2.85	2.70	2.62	2.54	2.45
30	7.56	5.39	4.51	4.02	3.70	3.47	3.30	3.17	3.07	2.98	2.84	2.70	2.55	2.47	2.39	2.30
40	7.31	5.18	4.31	3.83	3.51	3.29	3.12	2.99	2.89	2.80	2.66	2.52	2.37	2.29	2.20	2.11
60	7.08	4.98	4.13	3.65	3.34	3.12	2.95	2.82	2.72	2.63	2.50	2.35	2.20	2.12	2.03	1.94
120	6.85	4.79	3.95	3.48	3.17	2.96	2.79	2.66	2.56	2.47	2.34	2.19	2.03	1.95	1.86	1.76
∞	6.63	4.61	3.78	3.32	3.02	2.80	2.64	2.51	2.41	2.32	2.18	2.04	1.88	1.79	1.70	1.59

B.7 Critical Values of Chi-Square

This table contains the values of χ^2 that correspond to a specific right-tail area and specific number of degrees of freedom.

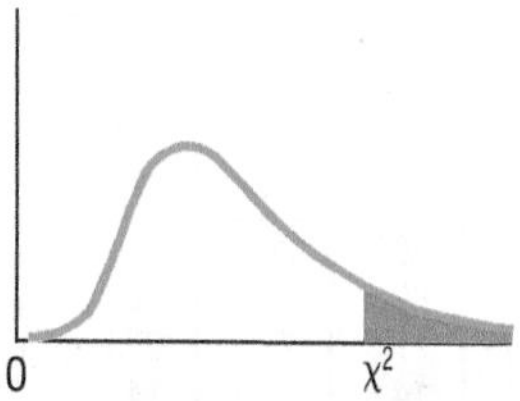

Example: With 17 *df* and a .02 area in the upper tail, $\chi^2 = 30.995$

Degrees of Freedom, *df*	Right-Tail Area			
	0.10	**0.05**	**0.02**	**0.01**
1	2.706	3.841	5.412	6.635
2	4.605	5.991	7.824	9.210
3	6.251	7.815	9.837	11.345
4	7.779	9.488	11.668	13.277
5	9.236	11.070	13.388	15.086
6	10.645	12.592	15.033	16.812
7	12.017	14.067	16.622	18.475
8	13.362	15.507	18.168	20.090
9	14.684	16.919	19.679	21.666
10	15.987	18.307	21.161	23.209
11	17.275	19.675	22.618	24.725
12	18.549	21.026	24.054	26.217
13	19.812	22.362	25.472	27.688
14	21.064	23.685	26.873	29.141
15	22.307	24.996	28.259	30.578
16	23.542	26.296	29.633	32.000
17	24.769	27.587	30.995	33.409
18	25.989	28.869	32.346	34.805
19	27.204	30.144	33.687	36.191
20	28.412	31.410	35.020	37.566
21	29.615	32.671	36.343	38.932
22	30.813	33.924	37.659	40.289
23	32.007	35.172	38.968	41.638
24	33.196	36.415	40.270	42.980
25	34.382	37.652	41.566	44.314
26	35.563	38.885	42.856	45.642
27	36.741	40.113	44.140	46.963
28	37.916	41.337	45.419	48.278
29	39.087	42.557	46.693	49.588
30	40.256	43.773	47.962	50.892

B.8 Wilcoxon *T* Values

	2α						
	.15	.10	.05	.04	.03	.02	.01
	α						
n	.075	.050	.025	.020	.015	.010	.005
4	0						
5	1	0					
6	2	2	0	0			
7	4	3	2	1	0	0	
8	7	5	3	3	2	1	0
9	9	8	5	5	4	3	1
10	12	10	8	7	6	5	3
11	16	13	10	9	8	7	5
12	19	17	13	12	11	9	7
13	24	21	17	16	14	12	9
14	28	25	21	19	18	15	12
15	33	30	25	23	21	19	15
16	39	35	29	28	26	23	19
17	45	41	34	33	30	27	23
18	51	47	40	38	35	32	27
19	58	53	46	43	41	37	32
20	65	60	52	50	47	43	37
21	73	67	58	56	53	49	42
22	81	75	65	63	59	55	48
23	89	83	73	70	66	62	54
24	98	91	81	78	74	69	61
25	108	100	89	86	82	76	68
26	118	110	98	94	90	84	75
27	128	119	107	103	99	92	83
28	138	130	116	112	108	101	91
29	150	140	126	122	117	110	100
30	161	151	137	132	127	120	109
31	173	163	147	143	137	130	118
32	186	175	159	154	148	140	128
33	199	187	170	165	159	151	138
34	212	200	182	177	171	162	148
35	226	213	195	189	182	173	159
40	302	286	264	257	249	238	220
50	487	466	434	425	413	397	373
60	718	690	648	636	620	600	567
70	995	960	907	891	872	846	805
80	1,318	1,276	1,211	1,192	1,168	1,136	1,086
90	1,688	1,638	1,560	1,537	1,509	1,471	1,410
100	2,105	2,045	1,955	1,928	1,894	1,850	1,779

B.9A Critical Values for the Durbin–Watson *d* Statistic ($\alpha = .05$)

	$k = 1$		$k = 2$		$k = 3$		$k = 4$		$k = 5$	
n	$d_{L,.05}$	$d_{U,.05}$	$d_{L,.05}$	$d_{U,.05}$	$d_{L,.05}$	$d_{U,.05}$	$d_{L,.05}$	$d_{U,.05}$	$d_{L,.05}$	$d_{U,.05}$
15	1.08	1.36	0.95	1.54	0.82	1.75	0.69	1.97	0.56	2.21
16	1.10	1.37	0.98	1.54	0.86	1.73	0.74	1.93	0.62	2.15
17	1.13	1.38	1.02	1.54	0.90	1.71	0.78	1.90	0.67	2.10
18	1.16	1.39	1.05	1.53	0.93	1.69	0.82	1.87	0.71	2.06
19	1.18	1.40	1.08	1.53	0.97	1.68	0.86	1.85	0.75	2.02
20	1.20	1.41	1.10	1.54	1.00	1.68	0.90	1.83	0.79	1.99
21	1.22	1.42	1.13	1.54	1.03	1.67	0.93	1.81	0.83	1.96
22	1.24	1.43	1.15	1.54	1.05	1.66	0.96	1.80	0.86	1.94
23	1.26	1.44	1.17	1.54	1.08	1.66	0.99	1.79	0.90	1.92
24	1.27	1.45	1.19	1.55	1.10	1.66	1.01	1.78	0.93	1.90
25	1.29	1.45	1.21	1.55	1.12	1.66	1.04	1.77	0.95	1.89
26	1.30	1.46	1.22	1.55	1.14	1.65	1.06	1.76	0.98	1.88
27	1.32	1.47	1.24	1.56	1.16	1.65	1.08	1.76	1.01	1.86
28	1.33	1.48	1.26	1.56	1.18	1.65	1.10	1.75	1.03	1.85
29	1.34	1.48	1.27	1.56	1.20	1.65	1.12	1.74	1.05	1.84
30	1.35	1.49	1.28	1.57	1.21	1.65	1.14	1.74	1.07	1.83
31	1.36	1.50	1.30	1.57	1.23	1.65	1.16	1.74	1.09	1.83
32	1.37	1.50	1.31	1.57	1.24	1.65	1.18	1.73	1.11	1.82
33	1.38	1.51	1.32	1.58	1.26	1.65	1.19	1.73	1.13	1.81
34	1.39	1.51	1.33	1.58	1.27	1.65	1.21	1.73	1.15	1.81
35	1.40	1.52	1.34	1.58	1.28	1.65	1.22	1.73	1.16	1.80
36	1.41	1.52	1.35	1.59	1.29	1.65	1.24	1.73	1.18	1.80
37	1.42	1.53	1.36	1.59	1.31	1.66	1.25	1.72	1.19	1.80
38	1.43	1.54	1.37	1.59	1.32	1.66	1.26	1.72	1.21	1.79
39	1.43	1.54	1.38	1.60	1.33	1.66	1.27	1.72	1.22	1.79
40	1.44	1.54	1.39	1.60	1.34	1.66	1.29	1.72	1.23	1.79
45	1.48	1.57	1.43	1.62	1.38	1.67	1.34	1.72	1.29	1.78
50	1.50	1.59	1.46	1.63	1.42	1.67	1.38	1.72	1.34	1.77
55	1.53	1.60	1.49	1.64	1.45	1.68	1.41	1.72	1.38	1.77
60	1.55	1.62	1.51	1.65	1.48	1.69	1.44	1.73	1.41	1.77
65	1.57	1.63	1.54	1.66	1.50	1.70	1.47	1.73	1.44	1.77
70	1.58	1.64	1.55	1.67	1.52	1.70	1.49	1.74	1.46	1.77
75	1.60	1.65	1.57	1.68	1.54	1.71	1.51	1.74	1.49	1.77
80	1.61	1.66	1.59	1.69	1.56	1.72	1.53	1.74	1.51	1.77
85	1.62	1.67	1.60	1.70	1.57	1.72	1.55	1.75	1.52	1.77
90	1.63	1.68	1.61	1.70	1.59	1.73	1.57	1.75	1.54	1.78
95	1.64	1.69	1.62	1.71	1.60	1.73	1.58	1.75	1.56	1.78
100	1.65	1.69	1.63	1.72	1.61	1.74	1.59	1.76	1.57	1.78

SOURCE: J. Durbin and G. S. Watson, "Testing for Serial Correlation in Least Squares Regression, II," *Biometrika* 30 (1951), pp. 159–178. Reproduced by permission of the Biometrika Trustees.

B.9B Critical Values for the Durbin–Watson *d* Statistic ($\alpha = .025$)

	$k = 1$		$k = 2$		$k = 3$		$k = 4$		$k = 5$	
n	$d_{L,.025}$	$d_{U,.025}$	$d_{L,.025}$	$d_{U,.025}$	$d_{L,.025}$	$d_{U,.025}$	$d_{L,.025}$	$d_{U,.025}$	$d_{L,.025}$	$d_{U,.025}$
15	0.95	1.23	0.83	1.40	0.71	1.61	0.59	1.84	0.48	2.09
16	0.98	1.24	0.86	1.40	0.75	1.59	0.64	1.80	0.53	2.03
17	1.01	1.25	0.90	1.40	0.79	1.58	0.68	1.77	0.57	1.98
18	1.03	1.26	0.93	1.40	0.82	1.56	0.72	1.74	0.62	1.93
19	1.06	1.28	0.96	1.41	0.86	1.55	0.76	1.72	0.66	1.90
20	1.08	1.28	0.99	1.41	0.89	1.55	0.79	1.70	0.70	1.87
21	1.10	1.30	1.01	1.41	0.92	1.54	0.83	1.69	0.73	1.84
22	1.12	1.31	1.04	1.42	0.95	1.54	0.86	1.68	0.77	1.82
23	1.14	1.32	1.06	1.42	0.97	1.54	0.89	1.67	0.80	1.80
24	1.16	1.33	1.08	1.43	1.00	1.54	0.91	1.66	0.83	1.79
25	1.18	1.34	1.10	1.43	1.02	1.54	0.94	1.65	0.86	1.77
26	1.19	1.35	1.12	1.44	1.04	1.54	0.96	1.65	0.88	1.76
27	1.21	1.36	1.13	1.44	1.06	1.54	0.99	1.64	0.91	1.75
28	1.22	1.37	1.15	1.45	1.08	1.54	1.01	1.64	0.93	1.74
29	1.24	1.38	1.17	1.45	1.10	1.54	1.03	1.63	0.96	1.73
30	1.25	1.38	1.18	1.46	1.12	1.54	1.05	1.63	0.98	1.73
31	1.26	1.39	1.20	1.47	1.13	1.55	1.07	1.63	1.00	1.72
32	1.27	1.40	1.21	1.47	1.15	1.55	1.08	1.63	1.02	1.71
33	1.28	1.41	1.22	1.48	1.16	1.55	1.10	1.63	1.04	1.71
34	1.29	1.41	1.24	1.48	1.17	1.55	1.12	1.63	1.06	1.70
35	1.30	1.42	1.25	1.48	1.19	1.55	1.13	1.63	1.07	1.70
36	1.31	1.43	1.26	1.49	1.20	1.56	1.15	1.63	1.09	1.70
37	1.32	1.43	1.27	1.49	1.21	1.56	1.16	1.62	1.10	1.70
38	1.33	1.44	1.28	1.50	1.23	1.56	1.17	1.62	1.12	1.70
39	1.34	1.44	1.29	1.50	1.24	1.56	1.19	1.63	1.13	1.69
40	1.35	1.45	1.30	1.51	1.25	1.57	1.20	1.63	1.15	1.69
45	1.39	1.48	1.34	1.53	1.30	1.58	1.25	1.63	1.21	1.69
50	1.42	1.50	1.38	1.54	1.34	1.59	1.30	1.64	1.26	1.69
55	1.45	1.52	1.41	1.56	1.37	1.60	1.33	1.64	1.30	1.69
60	1.47	1.54	1.44	1.57	1.40	1.61	1.37	1.65	1.33	1.69
65	1.49	1.55	1.46	1.59	1.43	1.62	1.40	1.66	1.36	1.69
70	1.51	1.57	1.48	1.60	1.45	1.63	1.42	1.66	1.39	1.70
75	1.53	1.58	1.50	1.61	1.47	1.64	1.45	1.67	1.42	1.70
80	1.54	1.59	1.52	1.62	1.49	1.65	1.47	1.67	1.44	1.70
85	1.56	1.60	1.53	1.63	1.51	1.65	1.49	1.68	1.46	1.71
90	1.57	1.61	1.55	1.64	1.53	1.66	1.50	1.69	1.48	1.71
95	1.58	1.62	1.56	1.65	1.54	1.67	1.52	1.69	1.50	1.71
100	1.59	1.63	1.57	1.65	1.55	1.67	1.53	1.70	1.51	1.72

SOURCE: J. Durbin and G. S. Watson, "Testing for Serial Correlation in Least Squares Regression, II," *Biometrika* 30 (1951), pp. 159–178. Reproduced by permission of the Biometrika Trustees.

B.9C Critical Values for the Durbin–Watson *d* Statistic ($\alpha = .01$)

	$k = 1$		$k = 2$		$k = 3$		$k = 4$		$k = 5$	
n	$d_{L,.01}$	$d_{U,.01}$	$d_{L,.01}$	$d_{U,.01}$	$d_{L,.01}$	$d_{U,.01}$	$d_{L,.01}$	$d_{U,.01}$	$d_{L,.01}$	$d_{U,.01}$
15	0.81	1.07	0.70	1.25	0.59	1.46	0.49	1.70	0.39	1.96
16	0.84	1.09	0.74	1.25	0.63	1.44	0.53	1.66	0.44	1.90
17	0.87	1.10	0.77	1.25	0.67	1.43	0.57	1.63	0.48	1.85
18	0.90	1.12	0.80	1.26	0.71	1.42	0.61	1.60	0.52	1.80
19	0.93	1.13	0.83	1.26	0.74	1.41	0.65	1.58	0.56	1.77
20	0.95	1.15	0.86	1.27	0.77	1.41	0.68	1.57	0.60	1.74
21	0.97	1.16	0.89	1.27	0.80	1.41	0.72	1.55	0.63	1.71
22	1.00	1.17	0.91	1.28	0.83	1.40	0.75	1.54	0.66	1.69
23	1.02	1.19	0.94	1.29	0.86	1.40	0.77	1.53	0.70	1.67
24	1.04	1.20	0.96	1.30	0.88	1.41	0.80	1.53	0.72	1.66
25	1.05	1.21	0.98	1.30	0.90	1.41	0.83	1.52	0.75	1.65
26	1.07	1.22	1.00	1.31	0.93	1.41	0.85	1.52	0.78	1.64
27	1.09	1.23	1.02	1.32	0.95	1.41	0.88	1.51	0.81	1.63
28	1.10	1.24	1.04	1.32	0.97	1.41	0.90	1.51	0.83	1.62
29	1.12	1.25	1.05	1.33	0.99	1.42	0.92	1.51	0.85	1.61
30	1.13	1.26	1.07	1.34	1.01	1.42	0.94	1.51	0.88	1.61
31	1.15	1.27	1.08	1.34	1.02	1.42	0.96	1.51	0.90	1.60
32	1.16	1.28	1.10	1.35	1.04	1.43	0.98	1.51	0.92	1.60
33	1.17	1.29	1.11	1.36	1.05	1.43	1.00	1.51	0.94	1.59
34	1.18	1.30	1.13	1.36	1.07	1.43	1.01	1.51	0.95	1.59
35	1.19	1.31	1.14	1.37	1.08	1.44	1.03	1.51	0.97	1.59
36	1.21	1.32	1.15	1.38	1.10	1.44	1.04	1.51	0.99	1.59
37	1.22	1.32	1.16	1.38	1.11	1.45	1.06	1.51	1.00	1.59
38	1.23	1.33	1.18	1.39	1.12	1.45	1.07	1.52	1.02	1.58
39	1.24	1.34	1.19	1.39	1.14	1.45	1.09	1.52	1.03	1.58
40	1.25	1.34	1.20	1.40	1.15	1.46	1.10	1.52	1.05	1.58
45	1.29	1.38	1.24	1.42	1.20	1.48	1.16	1.53	1.11	1.58
50	1.32	1.40	1.28	1.45	1.24	1.49	1.20	1.54	1.16	1.59
55	1.36	1.43	1.32	1.47	1.28	1.51	1.25	1.55	1.21	1.59
60	1.38	1.45	1.35	1.48	1.32	1.52	1.28	1.56	1.25	1.60
65	1.41	1.47	1.38	1.50	1.35	1.53	1.31	1.57	1.28	1.61
70	1.43	1.49	1.40	1.52	1.37	1.55	1.34	1.58	1.31	1.61
75	1.45	1.50	1.42	1.53	1.39	1.56	1.37	1.59	1.34	1.62
80	1.47	1.52	1.44	1.54	1.42	1.57	1.39	1.60	1.36	1.62
85	1,48	1.53	1.46	1.55	1.43	1.58	1.41	1.60	1.39	1.63
90	1.50	1.54	1.47	1.56	1.45	1.59	1.43	1.61	1.41	1.64
95	1.51	1.55	1.49	1.57	1.47	1.60	1.45	1.62	1.42	1.64
100	1.52	1.56	1.50	1.58	1.48	1.60	1.46	1.63	1.44	1.65

SOURCE: J. Durbin and G. S. Watson, "Testing for Serial Correlation in Least Squares Regression, II," *Biometrika* 30 (1951), pp. 159–178. Reproduced by permission of the Biometrika Trustees.

B.10 Factors for Control Charts

Number of Items in Sample, n	Chart for Averages: Factors for Control Limits	Chart for Ranges: Factors for Central Line	Chart for Ranges: Factors for Control Limits	
	A_2	d_2	D_3	D_4
2	1.880	1.128	0	3.267
3	1.023	1.693	0	2.575
4	.729	2.059	0	2.282
5	.577	2.326	0	2.115
6	.483	2.534	0	2.004
7	.419	2.704	.076	1.924
8	.373	2.847	.136	1.864
9	.337	2.970	.184	1.816
10	.308	3.078	.223	1.777
11	.285	3.173	.256	1.744
12	.266	3.258	.284	1.716
13	.249	3.336	.308	1.692
14	.235	3.407	.329	1.671
15	.223	3.472	.348	1.652

SOURCE: Adapted from American Society for Testing and Materials, *Manual on Quality Control of Materials,* 1951, Table B2, p. 115. For a more detailed table and explanation, see J. Duncan Acheson, *Quality Control and Industrial Statistics,* 3d ed. (Homewood, Ill.: Richard D. Irwin, 1974), Table M, p. 927.

APPENDIX C: SOFTWARE COMMANDS

CHAPTER 2

2–1. The Excel commands to use the PivotTable Wizard to create the frequency table, bar chart, and pie chart on page 22 are:

a. Open the Applewood Auto Group data file.

b. Click on a cell somewhere in the data set, such as cell *C5*.

c. Click on the *Insert* menu on the toolbar. Then click *PivotTable* on the far left of the *Ribbon*.

d. The following screen will appear. Click on "*Select a table or range*" to select the data range as shown in the *Table/Range* row. Next, click on "*Existing Worksheet*" and select a cell location, such a *N1,* and click *OK*.

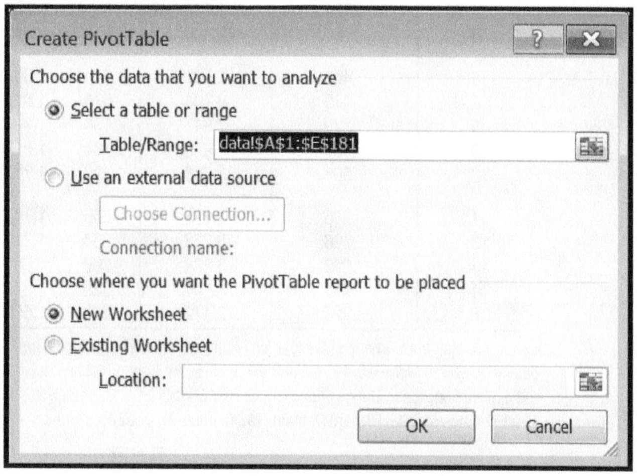

e. On the right-hand side of the spreadsheet, a *PivotTable Field List* will appear with a list of the data set variables. To summarize the "Vehicle-Type" variable, click on the "Vehicle-Type" variable and it will appear in the lower left box called *Row Label*. You will note that the frequency table is started in cell *N1* with the rows labeled with the values of the variable "Vehicle-Type." Next, return to the top box, and select and drag the "Vehicle-Type" variable to the "Σ Values" box. A column of frequencies will be added to the table. Note that you can format the table to center the values and also relabel the column headings as needed.

f. To create the bar chart, select any cell in the PivotTable. Next, select the *Insert* menu from the tool bar and within the *Charts* group, select a bar chart from the *Column* drop-down menu. A bar chart appears. Click on the chart heading and label the chart as needed.

g. To create the pie chart, the frequencies should be converted to relative frequencies. Click in the body of the PivotTable and the *PivotTable Field List* will appear to the right. In the "Σ Values" box, click on the pull-down menu for "Count of Vehicle Type" and select the *Value Field Settings* option. You will see a number of different selections that can be used to summarize the variables in a PivotTable. Click on the tab "*Show Values As*" and, in the pull-down menu, select "*% of Grand Total*." The frequencies will be converted to relative frequencies.

To create the pie chart, select any cell in the PivotTable. Next, select the *Insert* menu from the tool bar, and within the *Charts* group, select a pie chart from the *Column* drop-down menu. A pie chart appears. Click on the chart heading and label the chart as needed. To add the percentages, click on the pie chart and a menu will appear. Click on "Add Data Labels."

2–2. The Excel commands to use the PivotTable Wizard to create the frequency and relative frequency distributions on page 30 and the histogram on page 33 follow.

a. Open the Applewood Auto Group data file.

b. Click on a cell somewhere in the data set, such as cell *C5*.

c. Click on the *Insert* menu on the toolbar. Then click on *PivotTable* on the far left of the *Ribbon*.

d. The following screen will appear. Click on "*Select a table or range*" to select the data range as shown in the *Table/Range* row. Next, click on "*New Worksheet*" and the PivotTable will be created in a new worksheet.

e. On the right-hand side of the spreadsheet, a *PivotTable Field List* will appear with a list of the data set variables. To summarize the "Profit" variable, click on the "Profit" variable and drag it to the "Row Labels" box. Then return to the top box, click on "Profits" again and drag it to the "Σ Values" box. Staying in this box, click on the pull-down menu for "Sum of Profit." You will see a number of different selections that can be used to summarize the variables

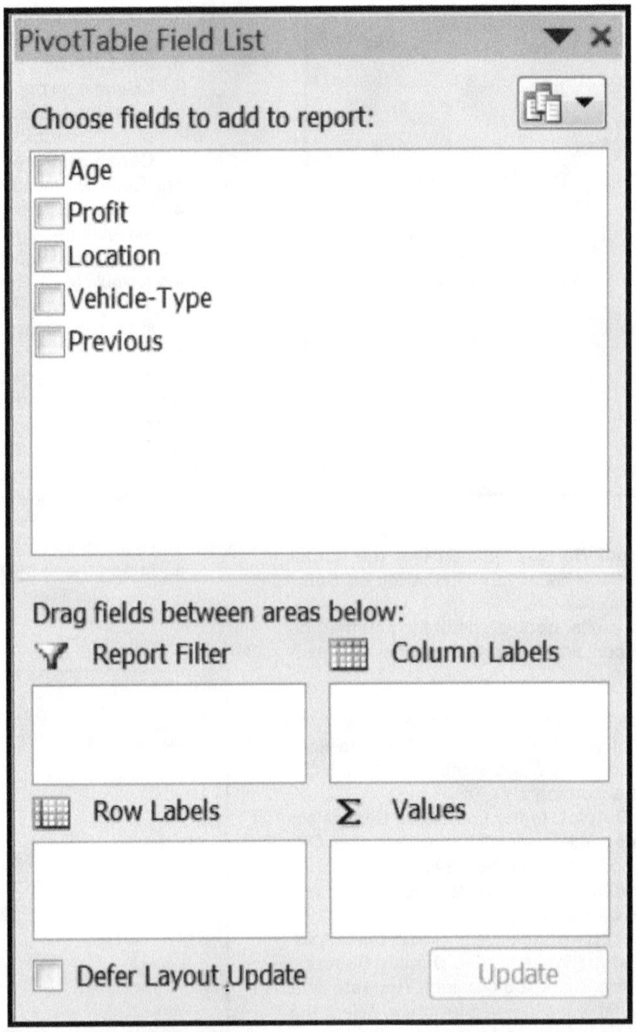

in a PivotTable. In the "*Summarize Values As*" tab, select "Count" to create frequencies for the variable "Profit." A PivotTable will appear in the new worksheet.

f. In the PivotTable, the left column shows each value of the variable "Profit." To create classes for "Profit," select any cell in the column and right-click. A menu appears. Select "Group" from the menu to create the classes. First, uncheck both boxes. Then, in the dialogue box, enter the lower limit of the first class as the "Starting at" value. Enter the upper limit of the last class as the "Ending at" value. Then enter the class interval as the "By" value. Click OK. A frequency distribution appears.

g. To create a relative frequency distribution, point and click on one of the cells in the PivotTable and the "PivotTable Field List" appears to the right. Click and drag the variable "Profits" to the "Σ Values" box. A second "Counts of Profit" appears. In the "Σ Values," click on the second "Counts of Profit" and select the "Value Fields Setting." You will see a number of different selections that can be used to summarize the variables in a PivotTable. Click on the tab "*Show Values As*" and, in the pull-down menu, select "*% of Grand Total.*" The relative frequencies will be added to the table. You can format the table by relabeling the column headings such as "Frequency" and "Relative Frequency."

h. To create a histogram, select a cell in the PivotTable, choose the *Insert* menu from the tool bar, and within the *Charts* group, select a *column* chart from the *Column* drop-down menu. A histogram appears with both "Count of Profit" and "Count of Profit2." On the "Count of Profit2" bubble at the top of the chart, right-click and select "Remove Field." Then the chart and PivotTable only report the frequencies. To eliminate the space between the bars, select the entire chart area, and "PivotChart Tools" will appear at the top. Select "Design." In the "Chart Layouts" choices, select the option that shows no spaces between the bars. The option is illustrated in the figure to the right. To add data labels, select the histogram, right-click, and select "Add Data Labels." Relabel the chart and axes as needed.

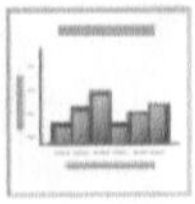

CHAPTER 3

3–1. The Excel Commands for the descriptive statistics on page 63 are:

a. From the website, www.mhhe.com/lind16e, retrieve the Applewood data.

b. From the menu bar, select **Data** and then **Data Analysis.** Select **Descriptive Statistics** and then click **OK.**

c. For the **Input Range,** type *C1:C181,* indicate that the data are grouped by column and that the labels are in the first

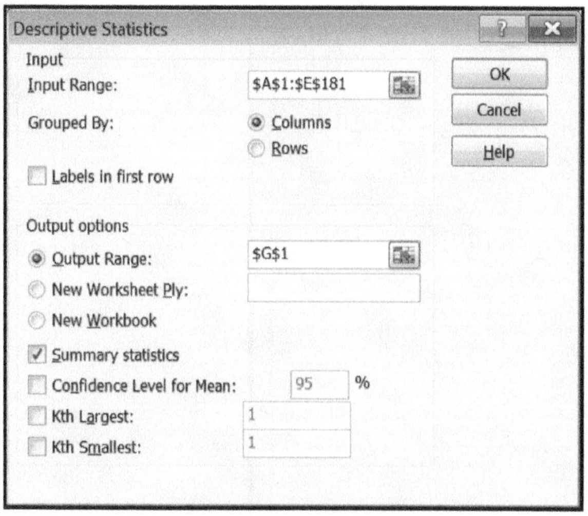

row. Click on **Output Range,** indicate that the output should go in *G1* (or any place you wish), click on **Summary statistics,** then click **OK.**

d. After you get your results, double-check the count in the output to be sure it contains the correct number of items.

CHAPTER 4

4–1. The Minitab commands for the dot plot on page 95 are:

a. Enter the number of vehicles serviced at Tionesta Ford Lincoln Mercury in column *C1* and Sheffield Motors in *C2.* Name the variables accordingly.

b. Select **Graph** and **Dotplot.** In the first dialog box, select **Multiple Y's, Simple** in the lower left corner, and click **OK.** In the next dialog box, select **Tionesta** and **Sheffield** as the variables to **Graph,** click on **Labels,** and write an appropriate title. Then click **OK.**

c. To calculate the descriptive statistics shown in the output, select **Stat, Basic statistics,** and then **Display Descriptive statistics.** In the dialog box, select **Tionesta** and **Sheffield** as the variables, click on **Statistics,** select the desired statistics to be output, and finally click **OK** twice.

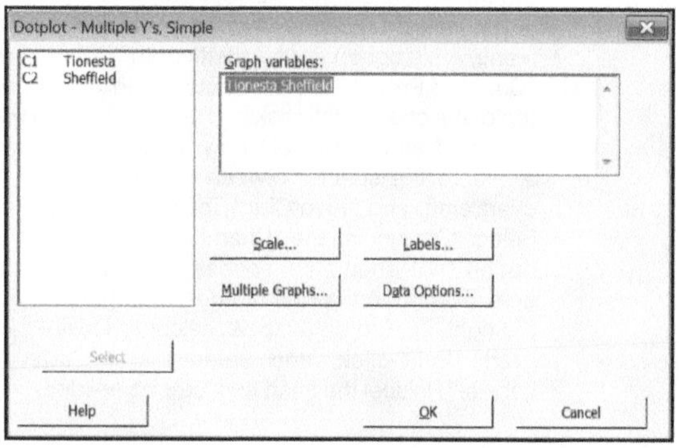

4–2. The Minitab commands for the stem-and-leaf display on page 98 are:

a. Import the data for **Table 4–1** from www.mhhe.com/lind16e.

b. Select **Graph,** and click on **Stem-and-Leaf.**

c. Select the variable **Spots,** enter *10* for the **Increment,** and then click **OK.**

4–3. The Minitab commands for the descriptive summary on page 104 are:

a. Input the data on the Smith Barney commissions from the Example on page 102.

b. From the toolbar, select **Stat, Basic Statistics,** and **Display Descriptive Statistics.** In the dialog box, select **Commissions** as the **Variable,** and then click **OK.**

4–4. The Excel commands for the quartiles on page 104 follow.

a. Input the data on the Smith Barney commissions from the example on page 102 in column A.

If you are using Excel 2010 and wish to compute quartiles using formula (4–1), the steps are:

b. In cell *C3* type **Formula (4–1),** in *C4* write **Quartile 1,** and in *C6* type **Quartile 3.**

c. In cell *D4* type **"=QUARTILE.EXC(A2:A16,1)"** and hit **Enter.** In cell *D6* type **"=QUARTILE.EXC(A2:A16,3)"** and hit **Enter.**

If you are using either Excel 2007 or 2010 and wish to compute quartiles using the Excel Method:

b. In cell *C8* type **Excel Method,** in *C9* write **Quartile 1,** and in *C11* type **Quartile 3.**

c. In cell *D8* type **"=QUARTILE(A2:A16,1)"** and hit **Enter.** In cell *D11* type **"=QUARTILE(A2:A16,3)"** and hit **Enter.**

4–5. The Minitab commands for the box plot on page 107 are:

a. Import the Applewood Auto Group data from www.mhhe.com/lind16e.

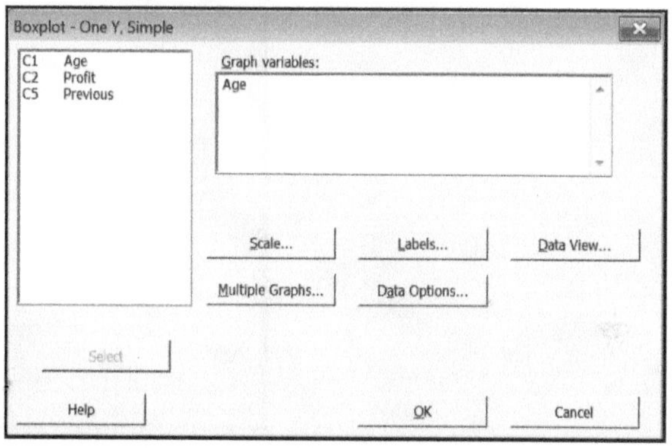

b. Select **Graph** and then **Boxplot.** In the dialog box, select **Simple** in the upper left corner and click **OK.** Select **Age** as the **Graph Variable,** click on **Labels** and include an appropriate heading, and then click **OK.**

4–6. The Minitab commands for the descriptive summary on page 112 are:

a. Enter the data in the first column. In the cell below *C1,* enter the variable *Earnings.*

b. Select **Stat, Basic Statistics,** and then click on **Graphical Summary.** Select **Earnings** as the variable, and then click **OK.**

4–7. The Excel commands for the scatter diagram on page 115 are:

a. Retrieve the Applewood Auto data.

b. Using the mouse, highlight the column of age and profit. Include the first row.

c. Select the **Insert** tab. Select **Scatter** from the **Chart** options. Select the top left option. The scatter plot will appear.

d. With **Chart Tools** displayed at the top, select the **Layout** tab. Select **Chart Title** and type in a title for the plot. Next, under the same **Layout** tab, select **AxisTitles.** Using **Primary Vertical Axis Title,** name the vertical axis *Profit.* Using the **Primary Horizontal Axis Title,** name the horizontal axis *Age.* Next, select **Legend** and select **None.**

CHAPTER 5

5–1. The Excel Commands to determine the number of permutations shown on page 164 are:

a. Click on the **Formulas** tab in the top menu, then, on the far left, select **Insert Function *fx*.**

b. In the **Insert Function** box, select **Statistical** as the category, then scroll down to **PERMUT** in the **Select a function list.** Click **OK.**

c. In the **PERM** box after **Number,** enter *8* and in the **Number_chosen** box enter *3*. The correct answer of *336* appears twice in the box.

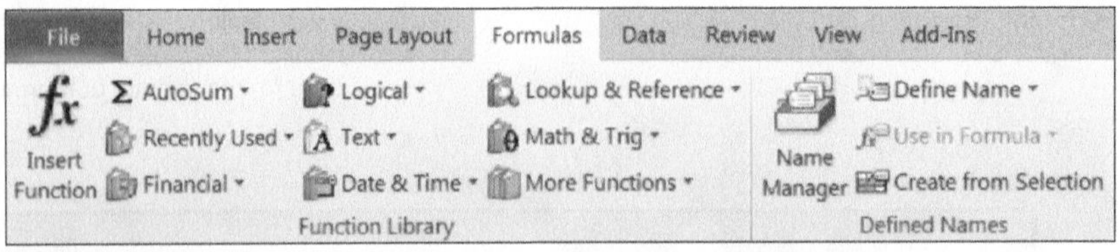

5–2. The Excel Commands to determine the number of combinations shown on page 164 are:

a. Click on the **Formulas** tab in the top menu, then, on the far left, select **Insert Function *fx*.**

b. In the **Insert Function** box, select **Math & Trig** as the category, then scroll down to **COMBIN** in the **Select a function list.** Click **OK.**

c. In the **COMBIN** box after **Number,** enter *7,* and in the **Number_chosen** box enter *3*. The correct answer of *35* appears twice in the box.

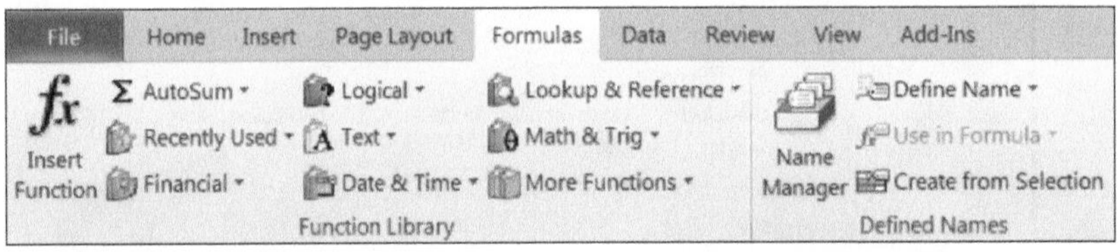

CHAPTER 6

6–1. The Excel commands necessary to determine the binomial probability distribution on page 187 are:

a. On a blank Excel worksheet, write the word *Success* in cell A1 and the word *Probability* in B1. In cells A2 through A17, write the integers *0* to *15*. Click on *B2* as the active cell.

b. Click on the **Formulas** tab in the top menu, then, on the far left, select **Insert Function *fx*.**

c. In the first dialog box, select **Statistical** in the function category and **BINOM.DIST** in the function name category, then click **OK.**

d. In the second dialog box, enter the four items necessary to compute a binomial probability.

1. Enter *0* for the **Number_s.**
2. Enter *40* for the **Trials.**
3. Enter *.09* for the probability of a success.
4. Enter the word *false* or the *0* for **Cumulative** and click on **OK.**
5. Excel will compute the probability of 0 successes in 40 trials, with a .09 probability of success. The result, .02299618, is stored in cell B2.

e. To complete the probability distribution for successes of 1 through 15, double-click on cell **B2.** The binomial function should appear. Replace the **0** to the right of the open parentheses with the cell reference **A2.**

f. Move the mouse to the lower right corner of cell B2 until a solid black + symbol appears, then click and hold and highlight the B column to cell B17. The probability of a success for the various values of the random variable will appear.

6–2. The Excel commands necessary to determine the hypergeometric distribution on page 193 are:

a. On a blank Excel worksheet, write the word *Union Members* in cell A1 and the word *Probability* in B1. In cells A2 through A7, enter the numbers *0* through *5*. Click on cell **B2.**

b. Click the **Formulas** tab in the top menu, then, on the far left, select **Insert Function *fx*.**

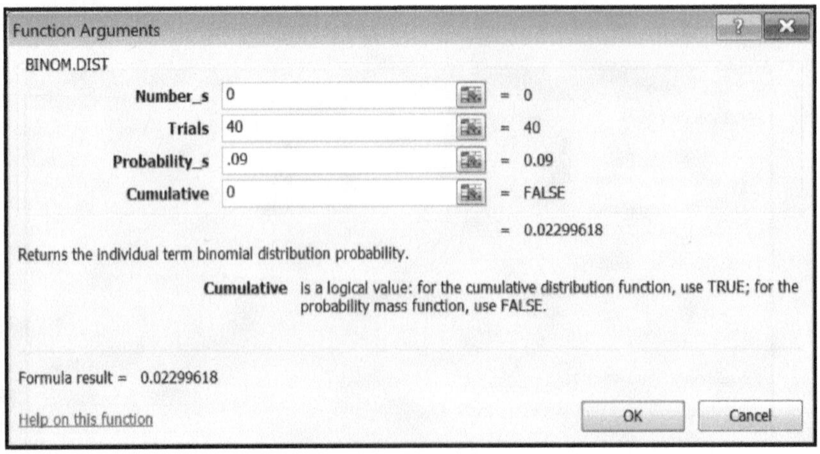

c. In the first dialog box, select **Statistical** and **HYPGEOM.DIST** and then click **OK.**
d. In the second dialog box, enter the four items necessary to compute a hypergeometric probability.
   1. Enter *0* for the **Sample_s.**
   2. Enter *5* for the **Number_sample.**
   3. Enter *40* for the **Population_s.**
   4. Enter *50* for the **Number_pop.**
   5. Enter *0* for the **Cumulative** and click **OK.**
   6. Excel will compute the probability of 0 successes in 5 trials (.000118937) and store that result in cell **B2.**
e. To complete the probability distribution for successes of 1 through 5, double-click on cell **B2.** The hypergeometric function should appear. Replace the **0** to the right of the open parentheses with the cell reference **A2.**
f. Move the mouse to the lower right corner of cell **B2** till a solid black + symbol appears, then click and hold and highlight the **B** column to cell **B7.** The probability of a success for the various outcomes will appear.

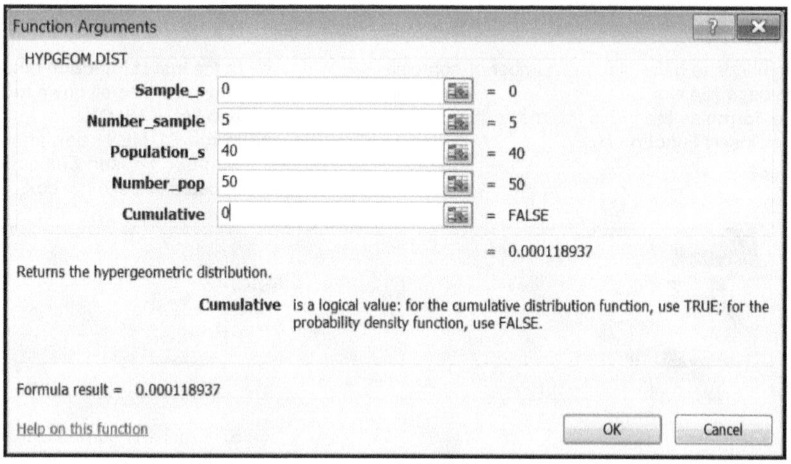

6–3. The Excel commands necessary to determine the Poisson probability distribution on page 196 are:
a. On a blank Excel worksheet, write the word ***Success*** in cell **A1** and the word ***Probability*** in **B1.** In cells **A2** through **A9,** write the integers *0* to *7*. Click on **B2** as the active cell.
b. Click on the **Formulas** tab in the top menu, then, on the far left, select **Insert Function *fx*.**
c. In the first dialog box, select **Statistical** in the function category and **POISSON.DIST** in the function name category, then click **OK.**
d. In the second dialog box, enter the three items necessary to compute a Poisson probability.
   1. Enter *0* for **X.**
   2. Enter *0.3* for the **Mean.**
   3. Enter the word *false* or the number *0* for **Cumulative** and click **OK.**
   4. Excel will compute the probability of 0 successes for a Poisson probability distribution with a mean of 0.3. The result, .74081822, is stored in cell **B2.**
e. To complete the probability distribution for successes of 1 through 7, double-click on cell **B2.** The Poisson function should appear. Replace the **0** to the right of the open parentheses with the cell reference **A2.**
f. Move the mouse to the lower right corner of cell **B2** until a solid black + symbol appears, then click and hold and highlight the **B** column to cell **B9.** The probability of a success for the various values of the random variable will appear.

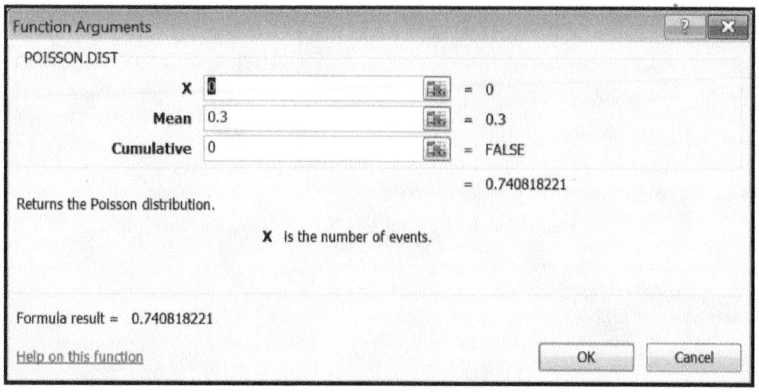

CHAPTER 7

7–1. The Excel commands necessary to produce the output on page 219 are:

- **a.** Click on the **Formulas** tab in the top menu, then, on the far left, select **Insert Function *fx*.** Then from the category box, select **Statistical** and below that **NORM.DIST** and click **OK.**
- **b.** In the dialog box, put *1100* in the box for **X,** *1000* for the **Mean,** *100* for the **Standard_dev,** and *True* in the **Cumulative** box, and click **OK.**
- **c.** The result will appear in the dialog box. If you click **OK,** the answer appears in your spreadsheet.

7–2. The Excel commands necessary to produce the output on page 225 are:

- **a.** Click the **Formulas** tab in the top menu, then, on the far left, select **Insert Function *fx*.** Then from the category box, select **Statistical** and below that **NORM.INV** and click **OK.**
- **b.** In the dialog box, set the **Probability** to *.04,* the **Mean** to *67900,* and the **Standard_dev** to *2050.*
- **c.** The results will appear in the dialog box. Note that the answer is different from page 225 because of rounding error. If you click **OK,** the answer also appears in your spreadsheet.
- **d.** Try entering a **Probability** of *.04,* a **Mean** of *0,* and a **Standard_dev** of *1.* The *z* value will be computed.

CHAPTER 8

8–1. The Excel commands to select a simple random sample from the rental data on page 250 are:

- **a.** Select the **Data** tab on the top of the menu. Then on the far right select **Data Analysis,** then **Sampling** and **OK.**
- **b.** For **Input Range,** insert *B1:B31.* Since the column is named, click the **Labels** box. Select **Random,** and enter the sample size for the **Number of Samples,** in this case *5.* Click on **Output Range** and indicate the place in the spreadsheet where you want the sample information. Note that your sample results will differ from those in the text. Also recall that Excel samples with replacement, so it is possible for a population value to appear more than once in the sample.

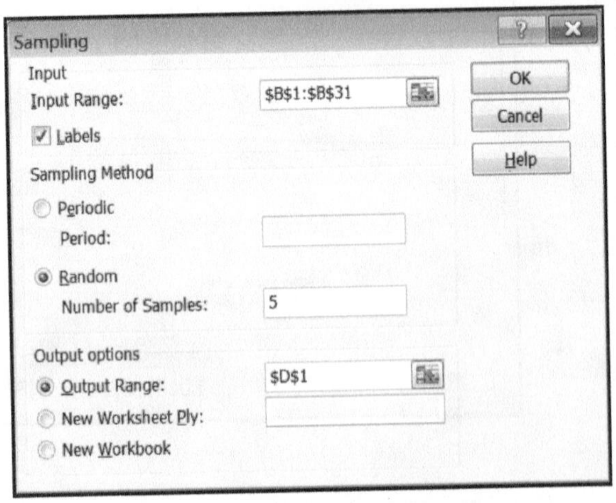

CHAPTER 9

9–1. The Minitab commands for the confidence interval for the amount spent at the Inlet Square Mall on page 294 are:

- **a.** Enter the 20 amounts spent in column **C1** and name the variable *Amount.*
- **b.** On the Toolbar, select **Stat, Basic Statistics,** and click on **1-Sample t.**
- **c.** Select **Samples in columns:** and select **Amount** and click **OK.**

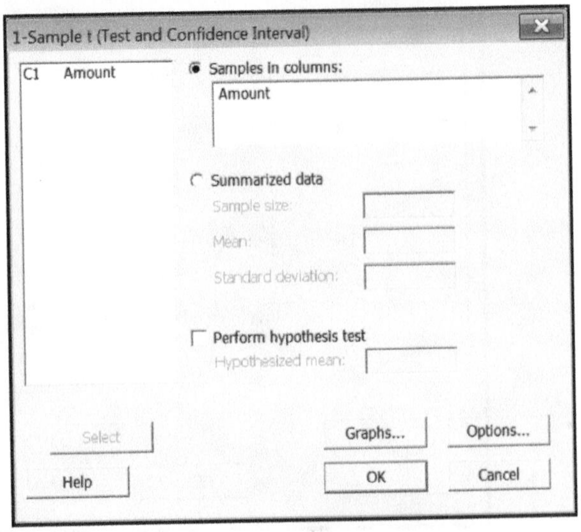

9–2. The Excel commands for the confidence interval for the amounts spent at the Inlet Square Mall on page 295 are:

- **a.** Select the **Data** tab on the top menu. Then, on the far right, select **Data Analysis,** and then **Descriptive Statistics,** and click **OK.**
- **b.** For the **Input Range,** type *A1:A21,* click on **Labels in first row,** type *C1* as the **Output Range,** click on **Summary statistics** and **Confidence Level for Mean,** and then click on **OK.**

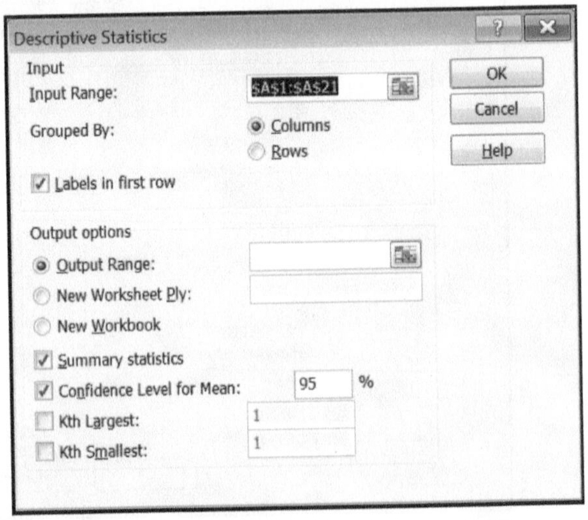

CHAPTER 10

10–1. The Minitab commands for the histogram and the descriptive statistics on page 332 are:

- **a.** Enter the 26 sample observations in column **C1** and name the variable *Cost.*

b. From the menu bar, select **Stat, Basic Statistics,** and **Graphical Summary.** In the dialog box, select **Cost** as the variable and click **OK.**

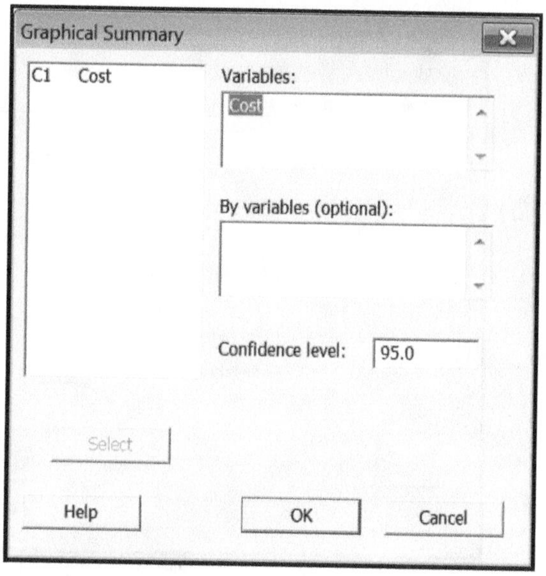

10–2. The Minitab commands for the one-sample *t* test on page 337 are:

a. Enter the sample data into column **C1** and name the variable *Minutes*.

b. From the menu bar, select **Stat, Basic Statistics,** and **1-Sample *t*,** and then hit **Enter.**

c. Select **Minutes** as the variable, select **Perform hypothesized mean,** insert the value *40*. Click **Options.** Under **Alternate,** select **greater than.** Finally, click **OK** twice.

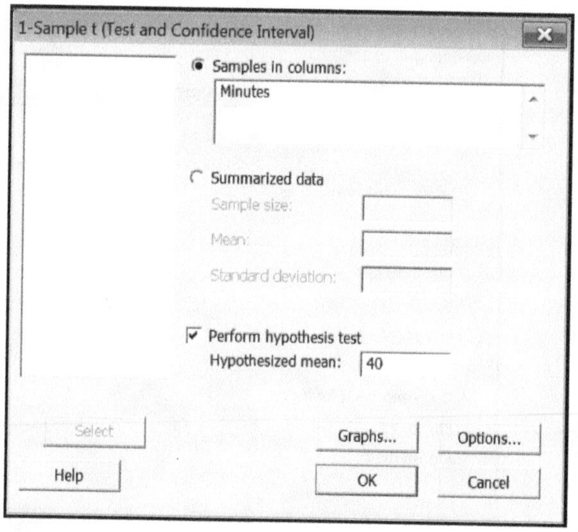

CHAPTER 11

11–1. The Excel commands for the two-sample *t*-test on page 359 are:

a. Enter the data into columns A and B (or any other columns) in the spreadsheet. Use the first row of each column to enter the variable name.

b. Select the **Data** tab on the top menu. Then, on the far right, select **Data Analysis.** Select **t-Test: Two Sample Assuming Equal Variances,** and then click **OK.**

c. In the dialog box, indicate that the range of **Variable 1** is from *A1* to *A6* and **Variable 2** from *B1* to *B7*, the **Hypothesized Mean Difference** is *0*, click **Labels, Alpha** is *0.05*, and the **Output Range** is *D1*. Click **OK.**

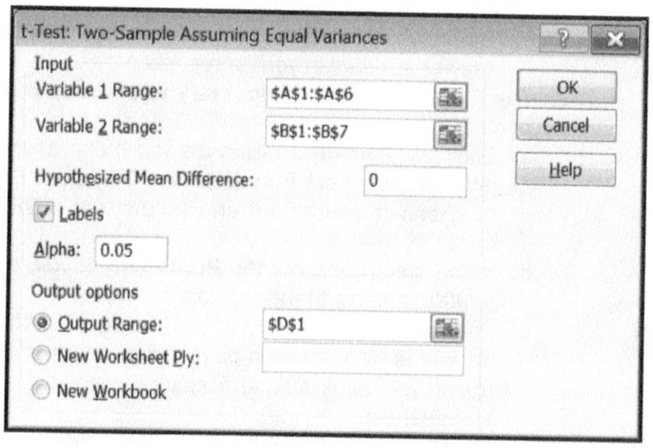

11–2. The Minitab commands for the two-sample *t*-test on page 363 are:

a. Put the amount absorbed by the Store brand in *C1* and the amount absorbed by the Name brand paper towel in *C2*.

b. From the toolbar, select **Stat, Basic Statistics,** and then **2-Sample,** and click **OK.**

c. In the next dialog box, select **Samples in different columns,** select *C1* Store for the **First** column and *C2* Name of the **Second,** click the box next to **Assume equal variances,** and click **OK.**

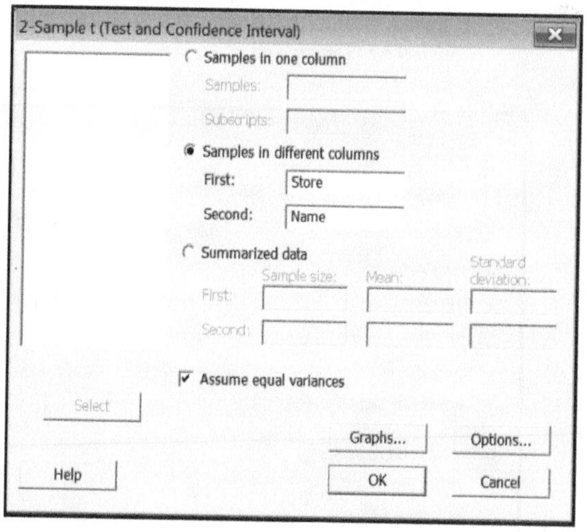

11–3. The Excel commands for the paired *t*-test on page 367 are:

a. Enter the data into columns B and C (or any other two columns) in the spreadsheet, with the variable names in the first row.

b. Select the **Data** tab on the top menu. Then, on the far right, select **Data Analysis.** Select **t-Test: Paired Two Sample for Means,** and then click **OK.**

c. In the dialog box, indicate that the range of **Variable 1** is from *B1* to *B11* and **Variable 2** from *C1* to *C11*, the **Hypothesized Mean Difference** is *0*, click **Labels, Alpha** is *.05*, and the **Output Range** is *E1*. Click **OK.**

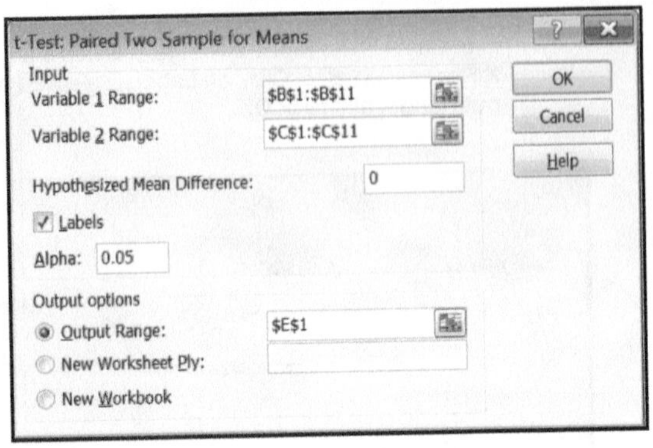

CHAPTER 12

12–1. The Excel commands for the test of variances on page 384 are:

a. Enter the data for U.S. 25 in column A and for I-75 in column B. Label the two columns.

b. Select the **Data** tab on the top menu. Then, on the far right, select **Data Analysis.** Select **F-Test: Two-Sample for Variances,** then click **OK.**

c. The range of the first variable is *A1:A8,* and *B1:B9* for the second. Click on **Labels,** enter *0.05* for **Alpha,** select *D1* for the **Output Range,** and click **OK.**

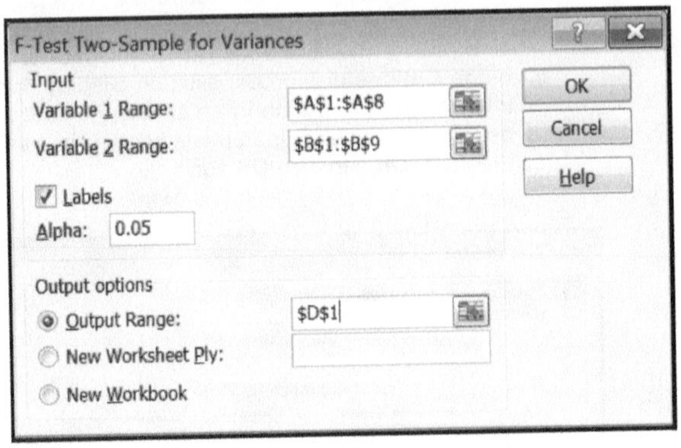

12–2. The Excel commands for the one-way ANOVA on page 393 are:

a. Key in data into four columns labeled *Northern, WTA, Pocono,* and *Branson.*

b. Select the **Data** tab on the top menu. Then, on the far right, select **Data Analysis.** Select **ANOVA: Single Factor,** then click **OK.**

c. In the subsequent dialog box, make the input range *A1:D8,* click on **Grouped by Columns,** click on **Labels in first row,** the **Alpha** text box is *0.05,* and finally select **Output Range** as *F1* and click **OK.**

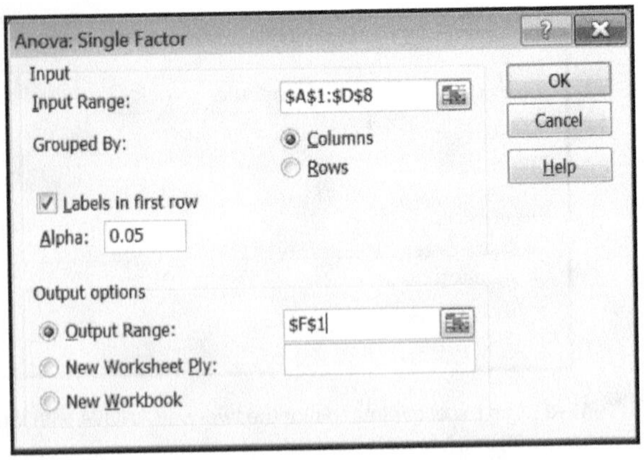

12–3. The Minitab commands for the pairwise comparisons on page 396 are:

a. Input the data into four columns and identify the columns as *Northern, WTA, Pocono,* and *Branson.*

b. Select **Stat, ANOVA,** and **One-way (Unstacked),** select and enter the variable names into the **Responses** box by clicking on the variable names in the following order: *Branson, Pocono, WTA, and Northern.* Then select **Comparisons** and then select **Fisher's, individual error rate.** Then **OK.**

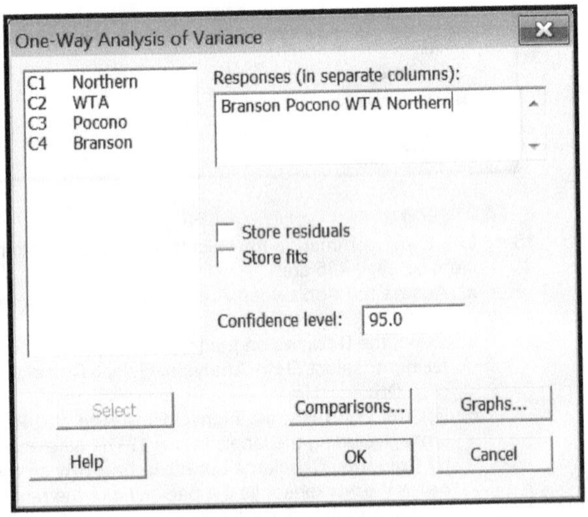

12–4. The Excel commands for the two-way ANOVA on page 400 are:

a. In the first row of the first column, write the word *Driver,* then list the five drivers in the first column. In the first row of the next four columns, enter the names of the routes. Enter the data under each route name.

b. Select the **Data** tab on the top menu. Then, on the far right, select **Data Analysis.** Select **ANOVA: Two-Factor Without Replication,** then click **OK.**

c. In the dialog box, the **Input Range** is *A3:E8,* click on **Labels,** enter *0.05* for **Alpha,** select **G3** for the **Output Range,** and then click **OK.**

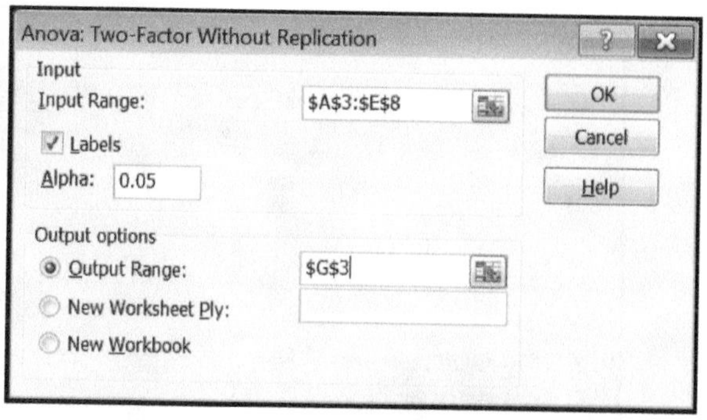

12–5. The Excel commands for the two-way ANOVA with interaction on page 408 are:

a. Enter the data into Excel as shown on page 406.
b. Select the **Data** tab on the top menu. Then, on the far right, select **Data Analysis.** Select **ANOVA: Two-Factor With Replication,** then click **OK.**
c. In the dialog box, for the **Input Range** highlight the entire range for the data including row and column labels, enter **Rows per sample** as *3,* enter *0.05* for **Alpha, Output Range** and cell H1.

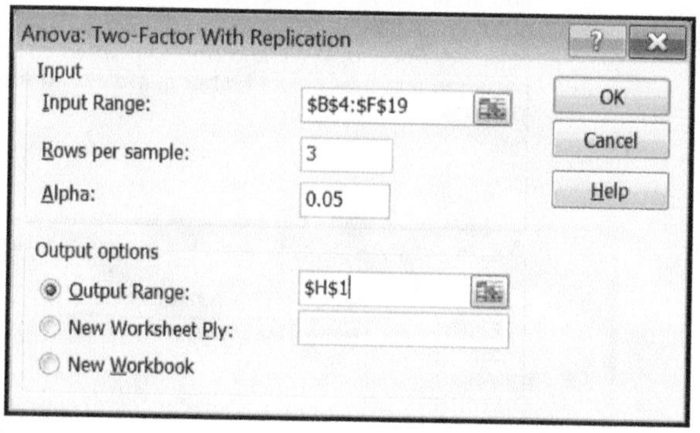

CHAPTER 13

13–1. The Excel commands for calculating the correlation coefficient on page 435 are:

a. Access the Applewood Auto Group dataset (www.mhhe.com/lind16e).
b. Select the **Data** tab on the top of the ribbon. Then, on the far right, select **Data Analysis.** Select **Correlation,** and click **OK.**
c. For the **Input Range,** highlight the **Age** and **Profit** columns, including the labels in row 1. The data are grouped by **Columns.** Check the **Labels in first row** box. Select a cell in the worksheet as the beginning of the range to output the correlation. Click **OK.**

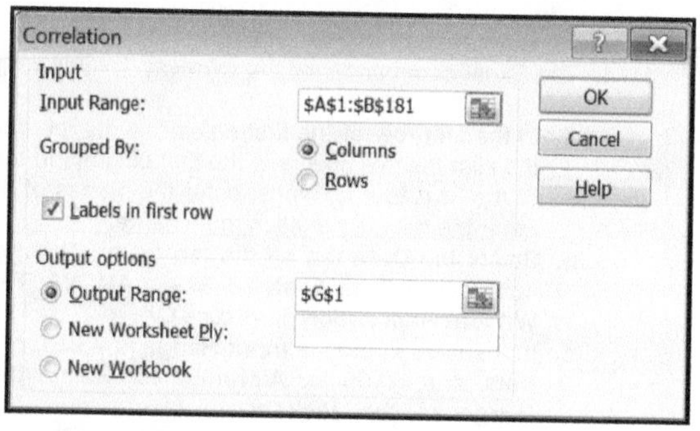

13–2. The computer commands for the Excel output on page 448 are:

a. Enter the variable names in row 1 of columns A, B, and C. Enter the data in rows 2 through 16 in the same columns.
b. Select the **Data** tab on the top of the menu. Then, on the far right, select **Data Analysis.** Select **Regression,** then click **OK.**
c. For our spreadsheet, we have *Calls* in column B and *Sales* in column C. The **Input Y Range** is *C1:C16* and the **Input X Range** is *B1:B16.* Click on **Labels,** select *E1* as the **Output Range,** and click **OK.**

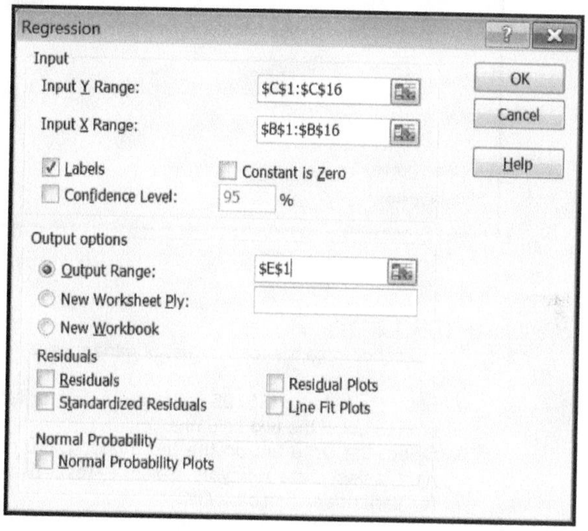

13–3. The Minitab commands to the confidence intervals and prediction intervals on page 458 are:

a. Select **Stat, Regression,** and **Fitted line plot.**
b. In the next dialog box, the **Response (Y)** is *Copiers Sold* and **Predictor (X)** is *Sales Calls.* Select **Linear** for the type of regression model and then click on **Options.**
c. In the **Options** dialog box, click on **Display confidence interval and prediction interval,** use the **95.0 for confidence level,** type an appropriate heading in the **Title** box, then click **OK** and then **OK** again.

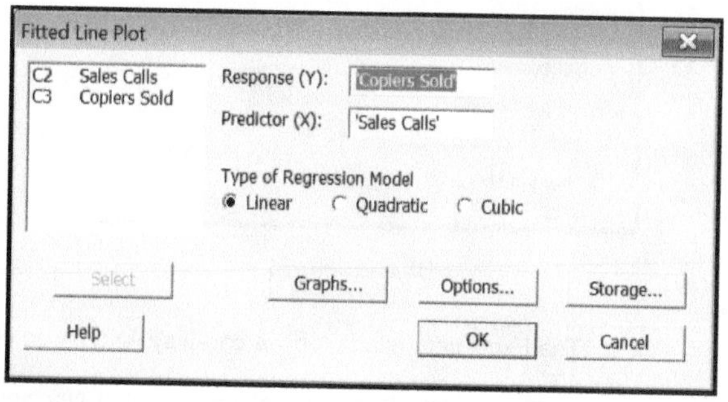

CHAPTER 14

Note: We do not show steps for all the statistical software in Chapter 14. The following shows the basic steps.

14–1. The Excel commands to produce the multiple regression output on page 480 are:

a. Import the data from the text website: www.mhhe.com/lind16e. The file name is **Tbl14.**

b. Select the **Data** tab on the top menu. Then on the far right, select **Data analysis.** Select **Regression** and click **OK.**
c. Make the **Input Y Range** *A1:A21*, the **Input X Range** *B1:D21*, check the **Labels** box, the **Output Range** is *F1*, then click **OK.**

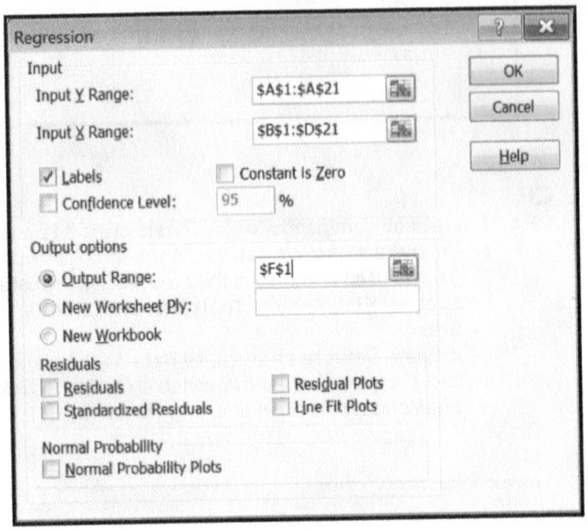

CHAPTER 15

15–1. The MegaStat commands for the two-sample test of proportions on page 541 are:
a. Select **MegaStat** from the **Add-Ins** tab. From the menu, select **Hypothesis Tests,** and then **Compare Two Independent Proportions.**
b. Enter the data. For **Group 1,** enter **x** as *19* and **n** as *100*. For **Group 2,** enter **x** as *62* and **n** as *200*. Select **OK.**

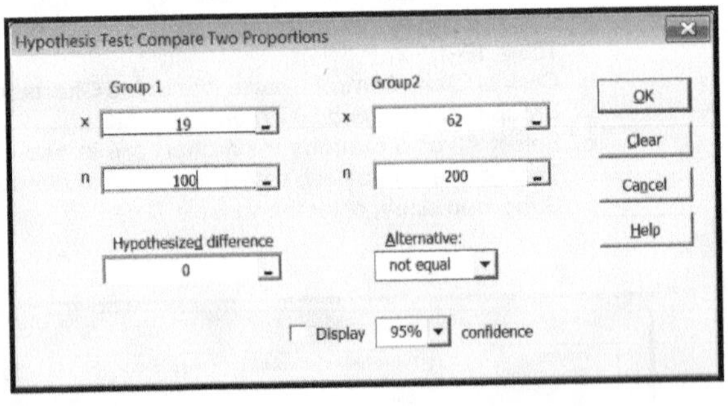

15–2. The MegaStat commands to create the chi-square goodness-of-fit test on page 547 are:
a. Enter the information from Table 15–2 into a worksheet as shown.
b. Select **MegaStat, Chi-Square/Crosstabs,** and **Goodness of Fit Test** and hit **Enter.**
c. In the dialog box, select *B2:B5* as the **Observed values,** *C2:C5* as the **Expected values,** and enter *0* as the **Number of parameters estimated from the data.** Click **OK.**

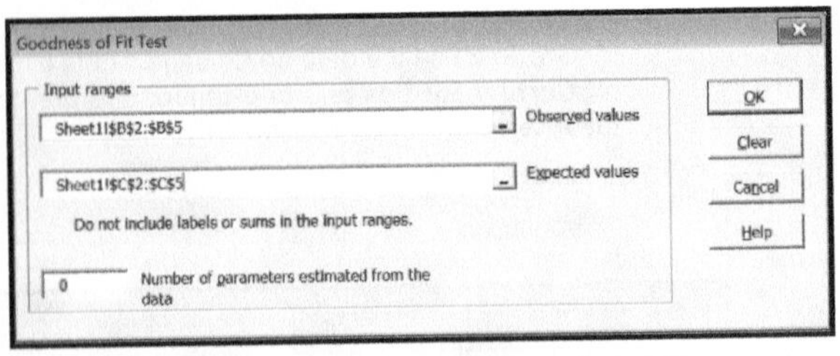

15–3. The MegaStat commands to create the chi-square goodness-of-fit tests on pages 552 and 553 are the same except for the number of items in the observed and expected frequency columns. Only one dialog box is shown.
a. Enter the Levels of Management information shown on page 552.
b. Select **MegaStat, Chi-Square/Crosstabs,** and **Goodness of Fit Test** and hit **Enter.**
c. In the dialog box, select *B1:B7* as the **Observed values,** *C1:C7* as the **Expected values,** and enter *0* as the **Number of parameters estimated from the data.** Click **OK.**

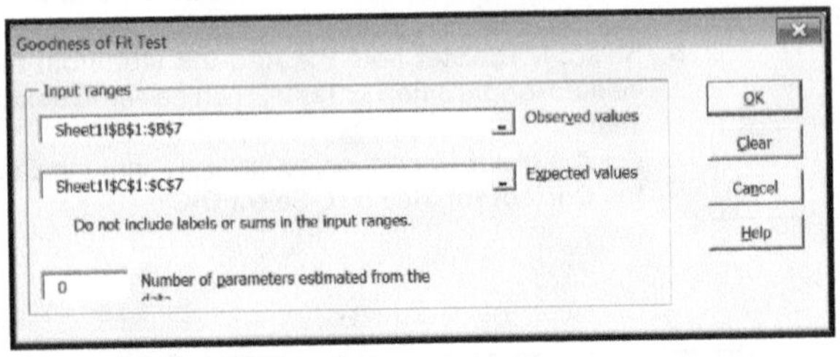

15–4. The MegaStat commands for the contingency table analysis on page 561 are:
a. Enter Table 15–8 on page 559 into cells **A1** through **D3.** Include the row and column labels. DO NOT include the Total column or row.
b. Select **MegaStat** from the **Add-Ins** tab. From the menu select **Chi-square/Crosstab,** then select **Contingency Table.**
c. For the **Input Range,** select cells **A1** through **D3.** Check the **chi-square** and **Expected values** boxes. Select **OK.**

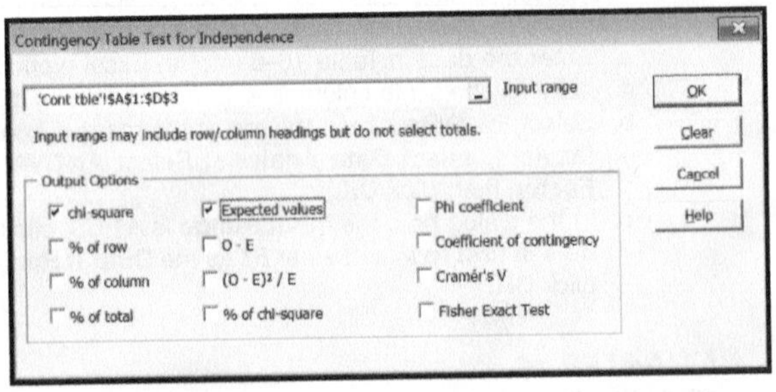

CHAPTER 16

16–1. The MegaStat for Excel commands necessary for the Wilcoxon rank-sum test on page 588 are:
a. Enter the number of no-shows for Atlanta in column A and for Chicago in column B.
b. Select **MegaStat, Nonparametric Tests,** and **Wilcoxon-Mann/Whitney Test,** then hit **Enter.**

c. For **Group 1,** use the data on Atlanta flights (*A1:A9*) and for **Group 2** use the data on Chicago flights (*B1:B8*). Click on **Correct for ties** and **one-tailed,** and *greater than* as the **Alternative,** then click on **OK.**

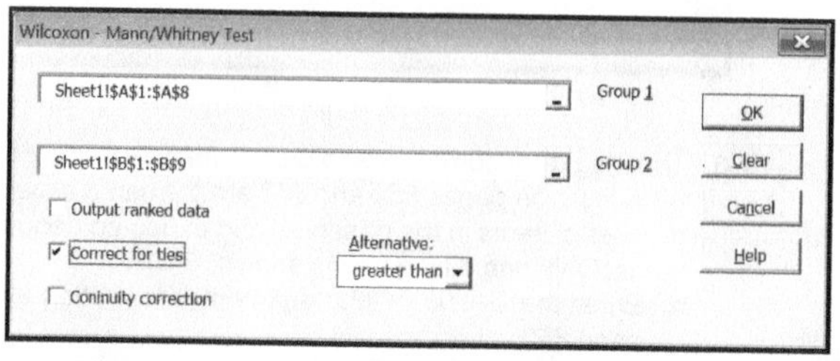

16–2. The MegaStat commands for the Kruskal-Wallis Test on page 592 are:

a. Enter the data in Table 16–6 into an Excel worksheet including labels into columns A, B, and C starting in row 1.

b. Select **MegaStat** from the **Add-Ins** tab. From the menu select **Nonparametric Tests,** then select **Kruskal-Wallis Test.**

c. For the **Input Range,** select cells *A1* through *C9*. Check the **Correct for Ties** box. Select **OK.**

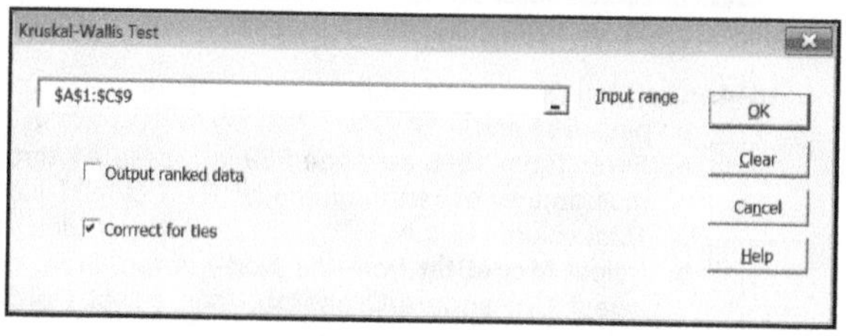

16–3. The Excel commands for the one-way ANOVA on page 593 are:

a. Enter the data in Table 16–6 into an Excel worksheet including labels into columns A, B, and C starting in row 1.

b. Select the **Data** tab on the top of the menu. Then, on the far right, select **Data Analysis.** Select **ANOVA: Single Factor,** then click **OK.**

c. In the dialog box, the **Input Range** is *A1:C9,* click on **Labels in first row,** and enter *E1* as the **Output Range,** then click **OK.**

CHAPTER 18

18–1. The MegaStat commands for creating the seasonal indexes on pages 659 and 660 are:

a. Enter the coded time period and the value of the time series in two columns. You may also want to include information on the years and quarters.

b. Select **MegaStat, Time Series/Forecasting,** and **Deseasonalization,** and hit **Enter.**

c. Input only the range of the sales data, indicate the data are in the first quarter, and click **OK.**

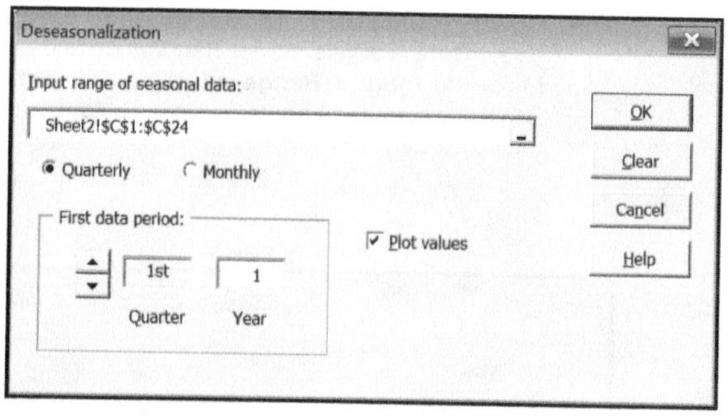

CHAPTER 19

19–1. The Minitab commands for the Pareto chart on page 689 are:

a. Enter the reasons for water usage in column **C1** and the gallons used in **C2.** Give the columns appropriate names.

b. Click on **Stat, Quality Tools, Pareto Chart,** and then hit **Enter.**

c. Indicate **Defects of attribute data** as the variable *Usage* and **Frequencies** as the variable *Gallons*. Click on **Options** and type a chart title, and click **OK.**

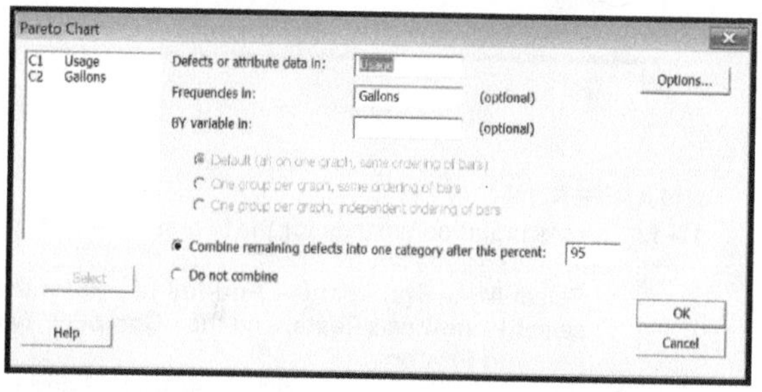

19–2. The Minitab commands for the mean and range charts on page 696 are:

a. Enter the information in Table 19–1 or from the text website, www.mhhe.com/lind16e. The file name is **Table 19–1.**

b. Click on **Stat, Control Charts, Variables Charts for Subgroups, Xbar-R,** and hit **Enter.**

c. Select **All observations for a chart are in one column.** Then in the box below, select the variable **Minutes.** For **Subgroup sizes,** enter the variable *Time*.

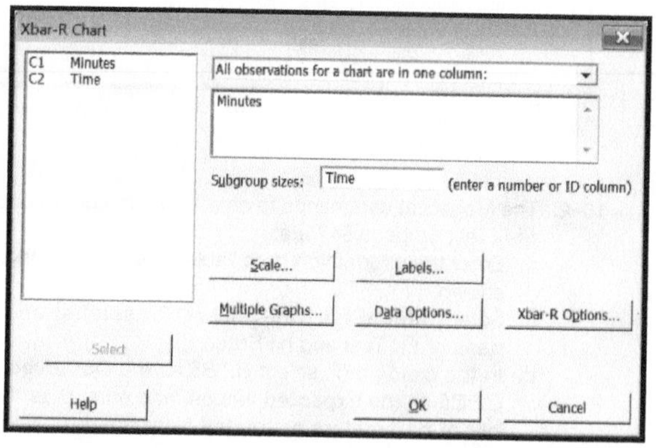

19–3. The Minitab commands for the p-chart on page 701 are:

a. Enter the data on the number of defects from page 700.

b. Click on **Stat, Control Charts, Attribute Charts, P,** and hit **Enter.**

c. Under **Variables,** select *Defects,* then enter *50* for **Subgroup sizes.** Click on **Labels,** type in the title, and click **OK** twice.

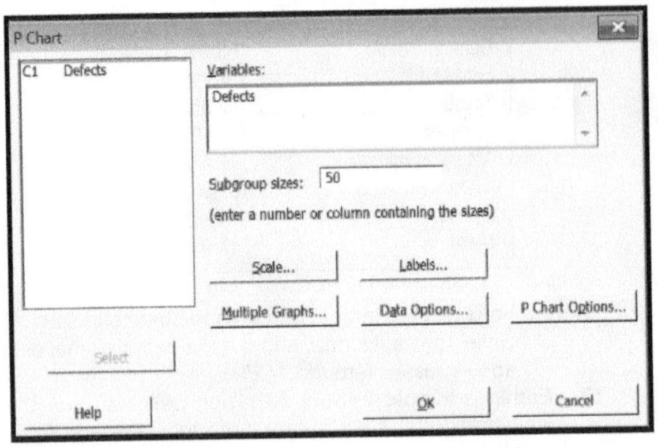

19–4. The Minitab commands for the *c*-bar chart on page 704 are:

a. Enter the data on the number of misspelled words from page 703 .

b. Click on **Stat, Control Charts, Attribute Charts, C,** and hit **Enter.**

c. Select the **Variable** indicating the number of misspelled words, then click on **Labels** and type the title in the space provided, and click **OK** twice.

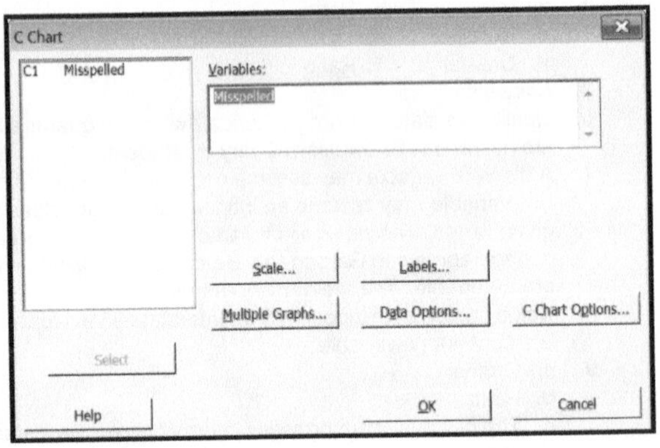

Answers to Odd-Numbered Chapter Exercises

CHAPTER 1

1. **a.** Interval **b.** Ratio
c. Nominal **d.** Nominal
e. Ordinal **f.** Ratio

3. Answers will vary.

5. Qualitative data are not numerical, whereas quantitative data are numerical. Examples will vary by student.

7. A discrete variable may assume only certain values. A continuous variable may assume an infinite number of values within a given range. The number of traffic citations issued each day during February in Garden City Beach, South Carolina, is a discrete variable. The weight of commercial trucks passing the weigh station at milepost 195 on Interstate 95 in North Carolina is a continuous variable.

9. **a.** Ordinal
b. Ratio
c. The newer system provides information on the distance between exits.

11. If you were using this store as typical of all Barnes & Noble stores, then it would be sample data. However, if you were considering it as the only store of interest, then the data would be population data.

13.

	Discrete Variable	Continuous Variable
Qualitative	b. Gender d. Soft drink preference g. Student rank in class h. Rating of a finance professor	
Quantitative	c. Sales volume of MP3 players f. SAT scores i. Number of home computers	a. Salary e. Temperature

	Discrete	Continuous
Nominal	b. Gender	
Ordinal	d. Soft drink preference g. Student rank in class h. Rating of a finance professor	
Interval	f. SAT scores	e. Temperature
Ratio	c. Sales volume of MP3 players i. Number of home computers	a. Salary

15. According to the sample information, 120/300 or 40% would accept a job transfer.

17. **a.** Total sales increased by 736,725, found by 1,886,021 − 1,149,296, which is a 64.1% increase.
b. Market shares through February in 2013 and 2009, respectively, are:

General Motors	22.2%	22.0%
Ford Motor	19.2%	16.2%
Toyota	17.2%	19.7%
Chrysler	13.6%	12.7%
American Honda	10.7%	12.4%
Nissan NA	9.6%	9.4%
Hyundai	5.1%	4.8%
Mazda	2.5%	2.8%

Ford has gained 3.0%, Toyota lost 2.6%, and Honda lost 1.7% of their market share.

c. Percent changes in sales are:

General Motors	165.8%
Ford Motor	197.7%
Toyota	142.9%
Chrysler	175.6%
American Honda	141.4%
Nissan NA	167.0%
Hyundai	174.2%
Mazda	145.4%

Ford had the largest percentage change in sales (197.7%), while Toyota, Honda, and Mazda had the smallest percentage increases (around 142%).

19. Earnings increase about $3 billion per year over the period. However, 2008 sees a very large increase and 2009 sees a large decrease. Perhaps $15 billion of 2008 earnings were somehow "advanced" from the next year or two.

21. **a.** League is a qualitative variable; the others are quantitative.
b. League is a nominal-level variable; the others are ratio-level variables.

CHAPTER 2

1. 25% market share.

3.

Season	Frequency	Relative Frequency
Winter	100	.10
Spring	300	.30
Summer	400	.40
Fall	200	.20
	1,000	1.00

5. **a.** A frequency table.

Color	Frequency	Relative Frequency
Bright White	130	0.10
Metallic Black	104	0.08
Magnetic Lime	325	0.25
Tangerine Orange	455	0.35
Fusion Red	286	0.22
Total	1,300	1.00

b.

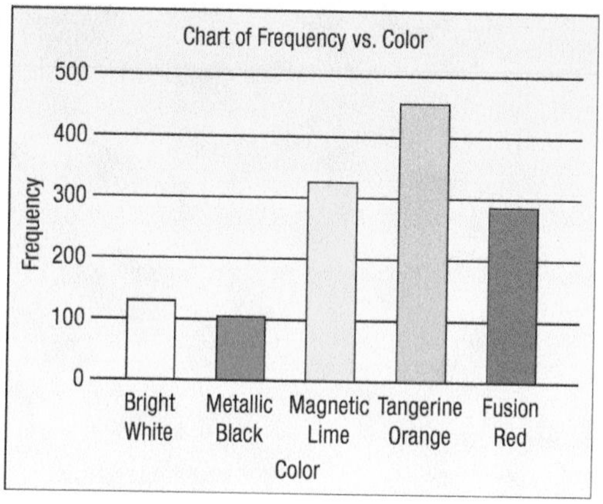

c.

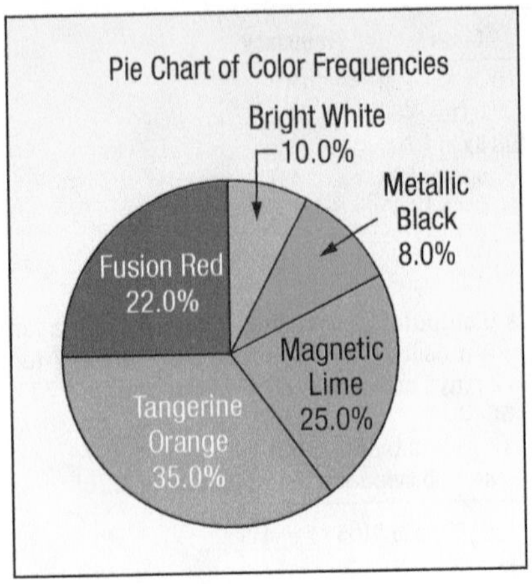

d. 350,000 orange, 250,000 lime, 220,000 red, 100,000 white, and 80,000 black, found by multiplying relative frequency by 1,000,000 production.

7. $2^5 = 32$, $2^6 = 64$, therefore, 6 classes

9. $2^7 = 128$, $2^8 = 256$, suggests 8 classes

$i \geq \frac{\$567 - \$235}{8} = 41$ Class intervals of 45 or 50 would be acceptable.

11. a. $2^4 = 16$ Suggests 5 classes.

b. $i \geq \frac{31 - 25}{5} = 1.2$ Use interval of 1.5.

c. 24

d.

Units	*f*	Relative Frequency
24.0 up to 25.5	2	0.125
25.5 up to 27.0	4	0.250
27.0 up to 28.5	8	0.500
28.5 up to 30.0	0	0.000
30.0 up to 31.5	2	0.125
Total	16	1.000

e. The largest concentration is in the 27.0 up to 28.5 class (8).

13. a.

Number of Visits	*f*
0 up to 3	9
3 up to 6	21
6 up to 9	13
9 up to 12	4
12 up to 15	3
15 up to 18	1
Total	51

b. The largest group of shoppers (21) shop at the BiLo Supermarket 3, 4, or 5 times during a month period. Some customers visit the store only 1 time during the month, but others shop as many as 15 times.

c.

Number of Visits	Percent of Total
0 up to 3	17.65
3 up to 6	41.18
6 up to 9	25.49
9 up to 12	7.84
12 up to 15	5.88
15 up to 18	1.96
Total	100.00

15. a. Histogram
b. 100
c. 5
d. 28
e. 0.28
f. 12.5
g. 13

17. a. 50
b. 1.5 thousand miles, or 1,500 miles.
c.

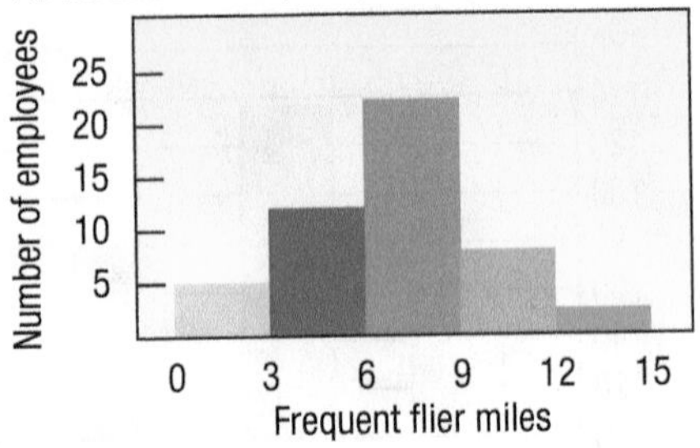

d. $X = 1.5$, $Y = 5$

e.

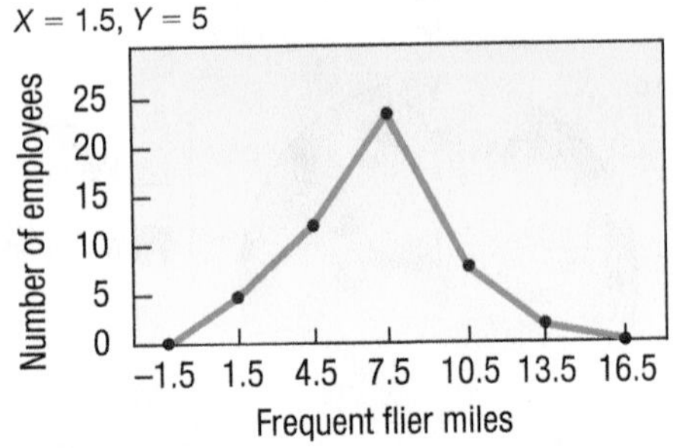

f. For the 50 employees, about half traveled between 6,000 and 9,000 miles. Five employees traveled less than 3,000 miles, and 2 traveled more than 12,000 miles.

19. a. 40
b. 5
c. 11 or 12
d. About $18/hr
e. About $9/hr
f. About 75%

21. a. 5
b.

Miles	*CF*
Less than 3	5
Less than 6	17
Less than 9	40
Less than 12	48
Less than 15	50

c.

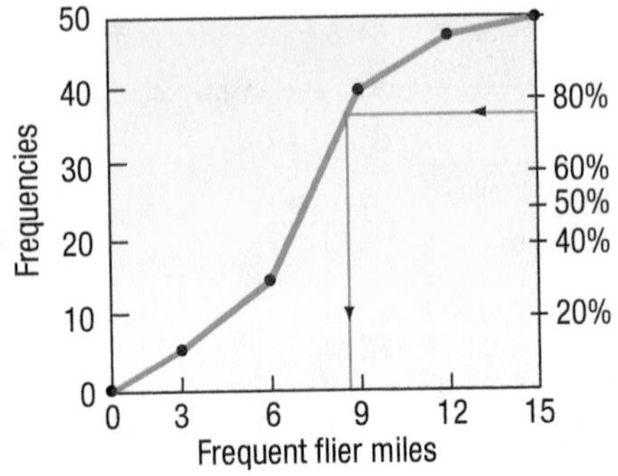

d. About 8.7 thousand miles

23. **a.** A qualitative variable uses either the nominal or ordinal scale of measurement. It is usually the result of counts. Quantitative variables are either discrete or continuous. There is a natural order to the results for a quantitative variable. Quantitative variables can use either the interval or ratio scale of measurement.

b. Both types of variables can be used for samples and populations.

25. **a.** Frequency table

b.

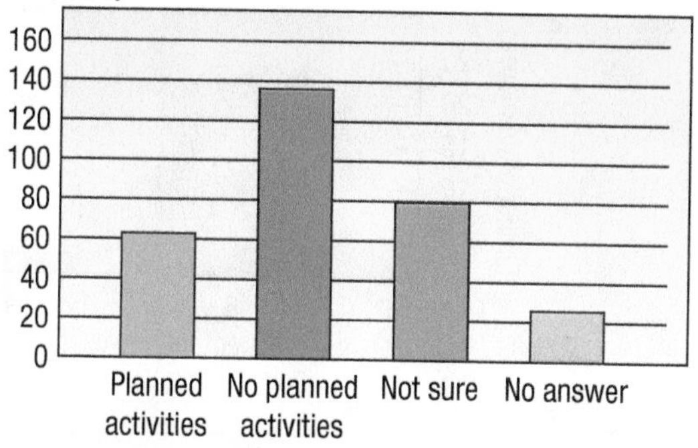

c.

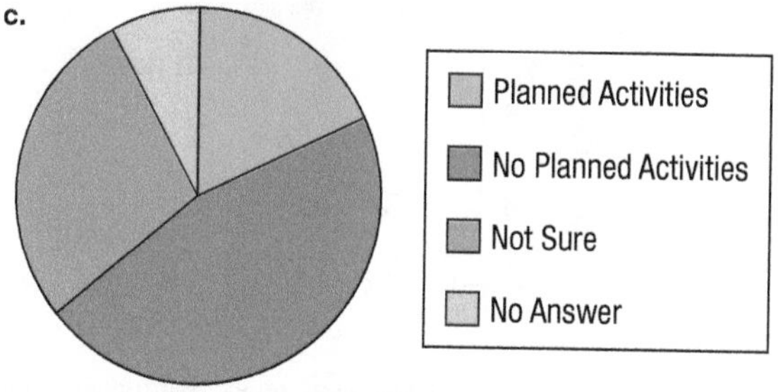

d. A pie chart would be better because it clearly shows that nearly half of the customers prefer no planned activities.

27. $2^6 = 64$ and $2^7 = 128$, suggest 7 classes

29. **a.** 5, because $2^4 = 16 < 25$ and $2^5 = 32 > 25$

b. $i \geq \dfrac{48 - 16}{5} = 6.4$ Use interval of 7.

c. 15

d.

Class	Frequency	
15 up to 22	|||	3
22 up to 29	𝍸 |||	8
29 up to 36	𝍸 ||	7
36 up to 43	𝍸	5
43 up to 50	||	2
		25

e. It is fairly symmetric, with most of the values between 22 and 36.

31. **a.** $2^5 = 32$, $2^6 = 64$, 6 classes recommended.

b. $i = \dfrac{10 - 1}{6} = 1.5$, use an interval of 2.

c. 0

d.

Class	Frequency
0 up to 2	1
2 up to 4	5
4 up to 6	12
6 up to 8	17
8 up to 10	8
10 up to 12	2

e. The distribution is fairly symmetric or bell-shaped with a large peak in the middle of the two classes of 4 up to 8.

33.

Class	Frequency
0 up to 200	19
200 up to 400	1
400 up to 600	4
600 up to 800	1
800 up to 1,000	2

This distribution is positively skewed with a large "tail" to the right or positive values. Notice that the top 7 tunes account for 4,342 plays out of a total of 5,968, or about 73% of all plays.

35. **a.** 56
b. 10 (found by 60 − 50)
c. 55
d. 17

37. **a.** Use $35 because the minimum is ($265 − $82)/6 = $30.5.

b.

$ 70 up to $105	4
105 up to 140	17
140 up to 175	14
175 up to 210	2
210 up to 245	6
245 up to 280	1

c. The purchases range from a low of about $70 to a high of about $280. The concentration is in the $105 up to $140 and $140 up to $175 classes.

39. Bar charts are preferred when the goal is to compare the actual amount in each category.

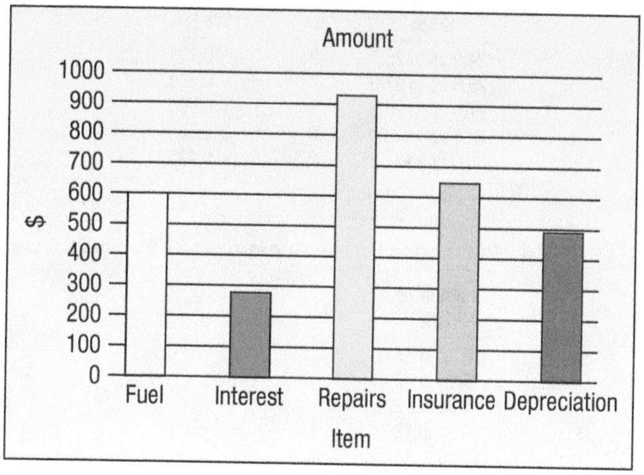

41.

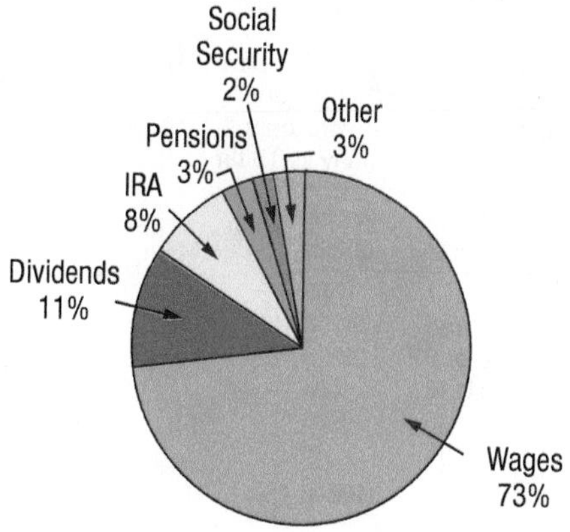

SC Income	Percent	Cumulative
Wages	73	73
Dividends	11	84
IRA	8	92
Pensions	3	95
Social Security	2	97
Other	3	100

By far the largest part of income in South Carolina is wages. Almost three-fourths of the adjusted gross income comes from wages. Dividends and IRAs each contributes roughly another 10%.

43. **a.** Since $2^6 = 64 < 70 < 128 = 2^7$, 7 classes are recommended. The interval should be at least $(1{,}002.2 - 3.3)/7 = 142.7$. Use 150 as a convenient value.

b.

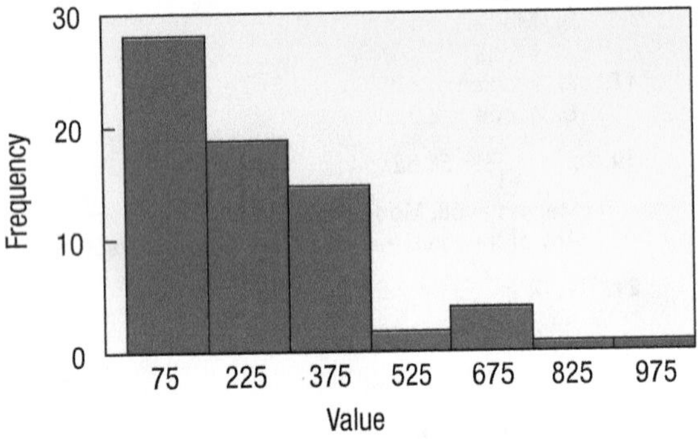

45. **a.** Pie chart
b. 700, found by 0.7(1,000)
c. Yes, $0.70 + 0.20 = 0.90$

47. **a.**

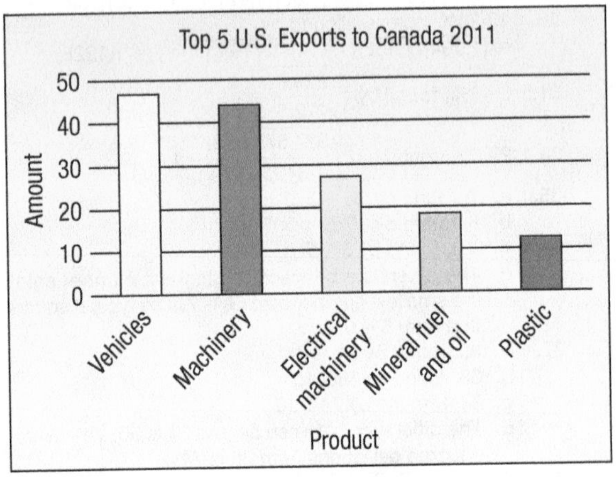

b. 23, found by $(18.4 + 46.9)/281$
c. 44, found by $(18.4 + 46.9)/(46.9 + 44.2 + 27.1 + 18.4 + 12.6)$

49.

Color	Frequency
Brown	130
Yellow	98
Red	96
Blue	52
Orange	35
Green	33
	444

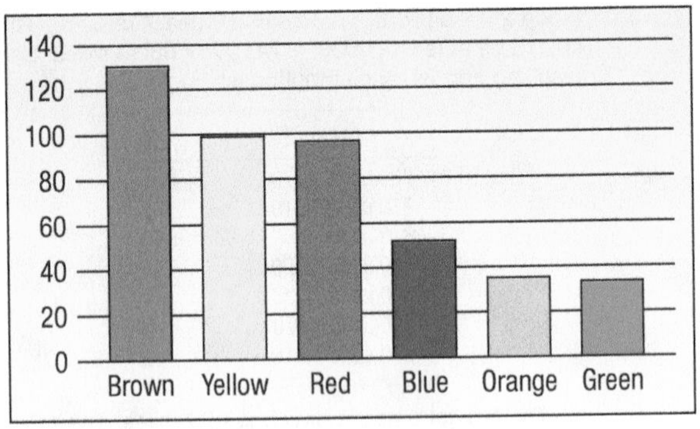

51. $i \geq \dfrac{345.3 - 125.0}{7} = 31.47$ Use interval of 35.

Selling Price	*f*	*CF*
110 up to 145	3	3
145 up to 180	19	22
180 up to 215	31	53
215 up to 250	25	78
250 up to 285	14	92
285 up to 320	10	102
320 up to 355	3	105

a. Most homes (53%) are in the 180 up to 250 range.
b. The largest value is near 355; the smallest, near 110.
c.

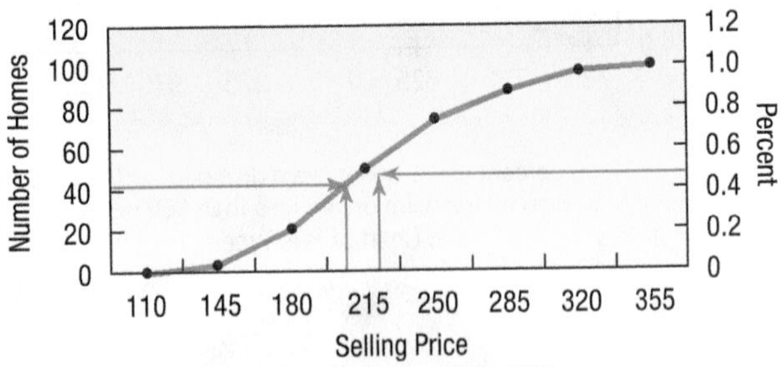

About 42 homes sold for less than 200.
About 55% of the homes sold for less than 220. So 45% sold for more.
Less than 1% of the homes sold for less than 125.

d.

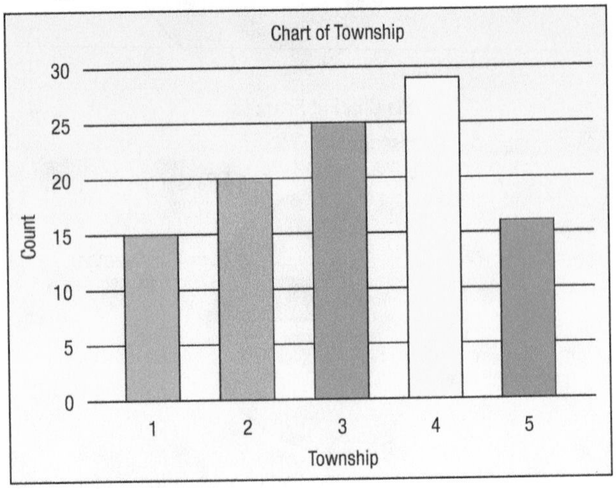

Townships 3 and 4 have more sales than the average and Townships 1 and 5 have somewhat less than the average.

53. Since $2^6 = 64 < 80 < 128 = 2^7$, use 7 classes. The interval should be at least $(1,008 - 741)/7 = 38.14$ miles. Use 40. The resulting frequency distribution is:

Class	f
730 up to 770	5
770 up to 810	17
810 up to 850	37
850 up to 890	18
890 up to 930	1
930 up to 970	0
970 up to 1,010	2

a. The typical amount driven is 830 miles. The range is from 730 up to 1,010 miles.

b. The distribution is "bell shaped" around 830. However, there are two outliers up around 1,000 miles.

c. Cumulative Frequency of Miles Driven per Month

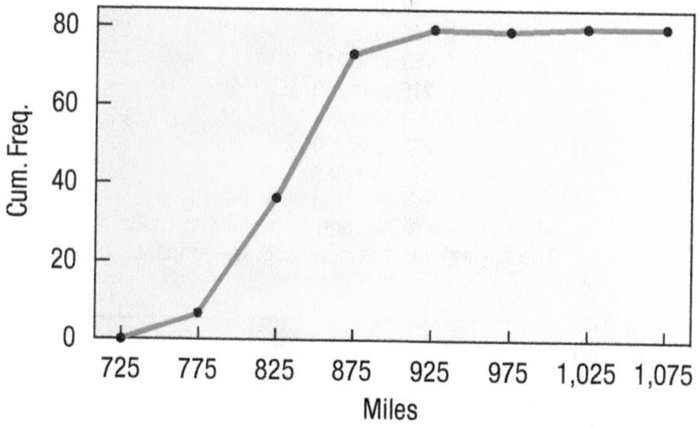

Forty percent of the buses were driven fewer than 820 miles. Fifty-nine buses were driven less than 850 miles.

d. Pie Chart of Bus Type

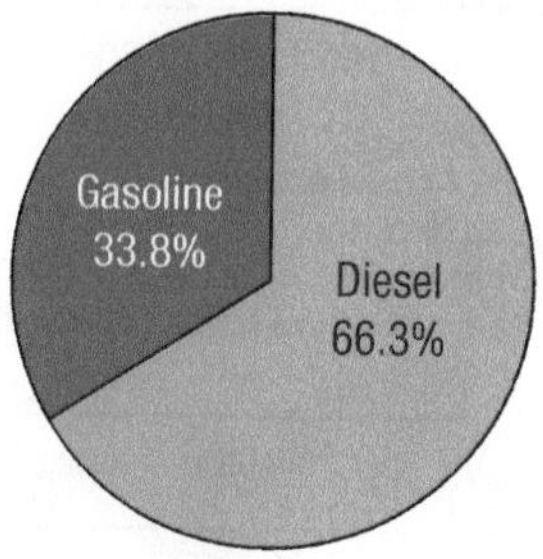

Pie Chart of Seats

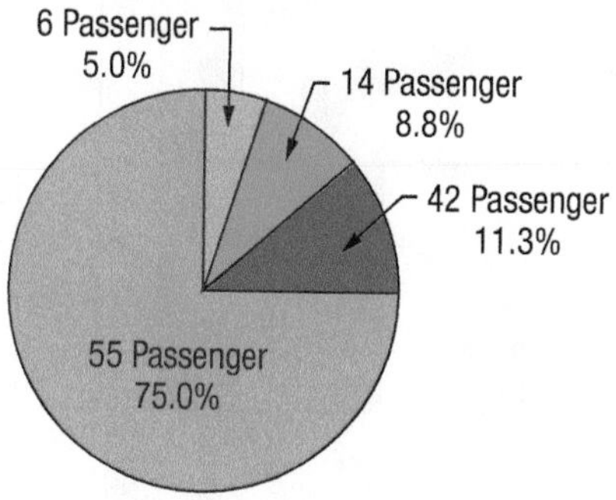

The first chart shows that about two-thirds of the buses are diesel. The second diagram shows that nearly three-fourths of the buses have 55 seats.

CHAPTER 3

1. $\mu = 5.4$, found by $27/5$

3. **a.** $\bar{x} = 7.0$, found by $28/4$

b. $(5 - 7) + (9 - 7) + (4 - 7) + (10 - 7) = 0$

5. $\bar{x} = 14.58$, found by $43.74/3$

7. **a.** 15.4, found by $154/10$

b. Population parameter, since it includes all the salespeople at Midtown Ford

9. **a.** \$54.55, found by \$1,091/20

b. A sample statistic—assuming that the power company serves more than 20 customers

11. $\bar{x} = \frac{\Sigma x}{n}$ so

$\Sigma x = \bar{x} \cdot n = (\$5,430)(30) = \$162,900$

13. **a.** No mode

b. The given value would be the mode.

c. 3 and 4 bimodal

15. **a.** Mean = 3.583

b. Median = 5

c. Mode = 5

17. **a.** Median = 2.9

b. Mode = 2.9

19. $\bar{x} = \frac{647}{11} = 58.82$

Median = 58, Mode = 58

Any of the three measures would be satisfactory.

21. **a.** $\bar{x} = \frac{90.4}{12} = 7.53$

b. Median = 7.45. There are several modes: 6.5, 7.3, 7.8, and 8.7.

c. $\bar{x} = \frac{33.8}{4} = 8.45$,

Median = 8.7

About 1 percentage point higher in winter

23. \$22.91, found by $\frac{300(\$20) + 400(\$25) + 400(\$23)}{300 + 400 + 400}$

25. \$17.75, found by $(\$400 + \$750 + \$2,400)/200$

27. 12.8%, found by $\sqrt[5]{(1.08)(1.12)(1.14)(1.26)(1.05)} = 1.128$

29. 12.28% increase, found by

$\sqrt[5]{(1.094)(1.138)(1.117)(1.119)(1.147)} = 1.1228$

31. 2.43%, found by $\sqrt[12]{\frac{229.6}{172.2}} - 1$

33. 29.0%, found by $\sqrt[27]{\frac{327,577,529}{340,213}} - 1$

35. **a.** 7, found by $10 - 3$

b. 6, found by $30/5$

c. 6.8, found by $34/5$

d. The difference between the highest number sold (10) and the smallest number sold (3) is 7. The typical squared deviation from 6 is 6.8.

37. **a.** 30, found by $54 - 24$

b. 38, found by $380/10$

c. 74.4, found by $744/10$

d. The difference between 54 and 24 is 30. The average of the squared deviations from 38 is 74.4.

39.

State	Mean	Median	Range
California	33.10	34.0	32
Iowa	24.50	25.0	19

The mean and median ratings were higher, but there was also more variation in California.

41. **a.** 5

b. 4.4, found by

$$\frac{(8 - 5)^2 + (3 - 5)^2 + (7 - 5)^2 + (3 - 5)^2 + (4 - 5)^2}{5}$$

43. **a.** \$2.77

b. 1.26, found by

$$\sqrt{\frac{(2.68-2.77)^2+(1.03-2.77)^2+(2.26-2.77)^2+(4.30-2.77)^2+(3.58-2.77)^2}{5}}$$

45. **a.** Range: 7.3, found by 11.6 − 4.3. Arithmetic mean: 6.94, found by 34.7/5. Variance: 6.5944, found by 32.972/5. Standard deviation: 2.568, found by $\sqrt{6.5944}$.

b. Dennis has a higher mean return (11.76 > 6.94). However, Dennis has greater spread in its returns on equity (16.89 > 6.59).

47. **a.** $\bar{x} = 4$

$$s^2 = \frac{(7-4)^2 + \cdots + (3-4)^2}{5-1} = \frac{22}{5-1} = 5.5$$

b. $s = 2.3452$

49. **a.** $\bar{x} = 38$

$$s^2 = \frac{(28-38)^2 + \cdots + (42-38)^2}{10-1}$$

$$= \frac{744}{10-1} = 82.667$$

b. $s = 9.0921$

51. **a.** $\bar{x} = \frac{951}{10} = 95.1$

$$s^2 = \frac{(101-95.1)^2 + \cdots + (88-95.1)^2}{10-1}$$

$$= \frac{1{,}112.9}{9} = 123.66$$

b. $s = \sqrt{123.66} = 11.12$

53. About 69%, found by $1 - 1/(1.8)^2$

55. **a.** About 95%

b. 47.5%, 2.5%

57. Because the exact values in a frequency distribution are not known, the midpoint is used for every member of that class.

59.

Class	f	M	fM	$(M-\bar{x})$	$f(M-\bar{x})^2$
20 up to 30	7	25	175	−22.29	3,477.909
30 up to 40	12	35	420	−12.29	1,812.529
40 up to 50	21	45	945	−2.29	110.126
50 up to 60	18	55	990	7.71	1,069.994
60 up to 70	12	65	780	17.71	3,763.729
	70		3,310		10,234.287

$$\bar{x} = \frac{3{,}310}{70} = 47.29$$

$$s = \sqrt{\frac{10{,}234.287}{70-1}} = 12.18$$

61.

Number of Clients	f	M	fM	$(M-\bar{x})$	$f(M-\bar{x})^2$
20 up to 30	1	25	25	−19.8	392.04
30 up to 40	15	35	525	−9.8	1,440.60
40 up to 50	22	45	990	0.2	0.88
50 up to 60	8	55	440	10.2	832.32
60 up to 70	4	65	260	20.2	1,632.16
	50		2,240		4,298.00

$$\bar{x} = \frac{2{,}240}{50} = 44.8$$

$$s = \sqrt{\frac{4{,}298}{50-1}} = 9.37$$

63. **a.** Mean = 5, found by (6 + 4 + 3 + 7 + 5)/5. Median is 5, found by rearranging the values and selecting the middle value.

b. Population, because all partners were included

c. $\Sigma(x - \mu) = (6-5) + (4-5) + (3-5) + (7-5) + (5-5) = 0$

65. $\bar{x} = \frac{545}{16} = 34.06$

Median = 37.50

67. The mean is 35.675, found by 1,427/40. The median is 36, found by sorting the data and averaging the 20th and 21st observations.

69. $\bar{x}_w = \frac{\$5.00(270) + \$6.50(300) + \$8.00(100)}{270 + 300 + 100} = \$6.12$

71. $\bar{x}_w = \frac{15{,}300(4.5) + 10{,}400(3.0) + 150{,}600(10.2)}{176{,}300} = 9.28$

73. $\text{GM} = \sqrt[21]{\frac{6{,}286{,}800}{5{,}164{,}900}} - 1 = 1.0094 - 1.0 = .0094$

75. **a.** 55, found by 72 − 17

b. 17.6245, found by the square root of 2795.6/9

77. **a.** This is a population because it includes all the public universities in Ohio.

b. The mean is 21,534.

c. The median is 17,529.

d. The range is 54,235.

e. The standard deviation is 13,101.

79. **a.** There were 13 flights, so all items are considered.

b. $\mu = \frac{2{,}259}{13} = 173.77$

Median = 195

c. Range = 301 − 7 = 294

$$s = \sqrt{\frac{133{,}846}{13}} = 101.47$$

81. **a.** The mean is \$717.20, found by \$17,930/25. The median is \$717.00 and there are two modes, \$710 and \$722.

b. The range is \$90, found by \$771 − \$681, and the standard deviation is \$24.87, found by the square root of 14,850/24.

c. From \$667.46 up to \$766.94, found by \$717.20 ± 2(\$24.87)

83. **a.** $\bar{x} = \frac{273}{30} = 9.1$, Median = 9

b. Range = 18 − 4 = 14

$$s = \sqrt{\frac{368.7}{30-1}} = 3.57$$

c. $2^5 = 32$, so suggest 5 classes

$i = \frac{18-4}{5} = 2.8$ Use $i = 3$

Class	M	f	fM	$M-\bar{x}$	$(M-\bar{x})^2$	$f(M-\bar{x})^2$
3.5 up to 6.5	5	10	50	−4	16	160
6.5 up to 9.5	8	6	48	−1	1	6
9.5 up to 12.5	11	9	99	2	4	36
12.5 up to 15.5	14	4	56	5	25	100
15.5 up to 18.5	17	1	17	8	64	64
			270			366

d. $\bar{x} = \frac{270}{30} = 9.0$

$$s = \sqrt{\frac{366}{30-1}} = 3.552$$

The mean and standard deviation from grouped data are estimates of the mean and standard deviations of the actual values.

85. $\bar{x} = 13 = \frac{910}{70}$

$s = 5.228 = \sqrt{1807.5/69}$

87. **a.** The mean team salary is \$98,020,000 and the median is \$85,750,000. Since the distribution is skewed, the median value of \$85,750,000 is more typical.

b. The range is $142,800,000, found by 198,000,000 − 55,200,000. The standard deviation is $36,830,000.
At least 75% of the team salaries are between $24,360,000 and $171,680,000, found by $98,020,000 plus or minus 2($36,830,000).

c. 8.63% per year, found by $\sqrt[23]{\frac{3{,}440{,}000}{512{,}930}} - 1$
Mean team payroll is $104,800,000 and standard deviation is $44,400,000 in the American League. Mean team payroll is $92,090,000 and standard deviation is $28,850,000 in the National League. There is not much difference in the mean payrolls, but there is more dispersion in the American League.

CHAPTER 4

1. In a histogram, observations are grouped so their individual identity is lost. With a dot plot, the identity of each observation is maintained.

3. **a.** Dot plot **b.** 15
c. 1, 7 **d.** 2 and 3

5. **a.** 620 to 629 **b.** 5
c. 621, 623, 623, 627, 629

7. **a.** 25 **b.** One
c. 38,106 **d.** 60, 61, 63, 63, 65, 65, 69
e. No values **f.** 9
g. 9 **h.** 76
i. 16

9.

Stem	Leaves
0	5
1	28
2	
3	0024789
4	12366
5	2

There were a total of 16 calls studied. The number of calls ranged from 5 to 52. Seven of the 16 subscribers made between 30 and 39 calls.

11. Median = 53, found by $(11 + 1)(\frac{1}{2})$ ∴ 6th value in from lowest
Q_1 = 49, found by $(11 + 1)(\frac{1}{4})$ ∴ 3rd value in from lowest
Q_3 = 55, found by $(11 + 1)(\frac{3}{4})$ ∴ 9th value in from lowest

13. **a.** $Q_1 = 33.25$, $Q_3 = 50.25$
b. $D_2 = 27.8$, $D_8 = 52.6$
c. $P_{67} = 47$

15. **a.** 350
b. $Q_1 = 175$, $Q_3 = 930$
c. 930 − 175 = 755
d. Less than 0, or more than about 2,060
e. There are no outliers.
f. The distribution is positively skewed.

17.

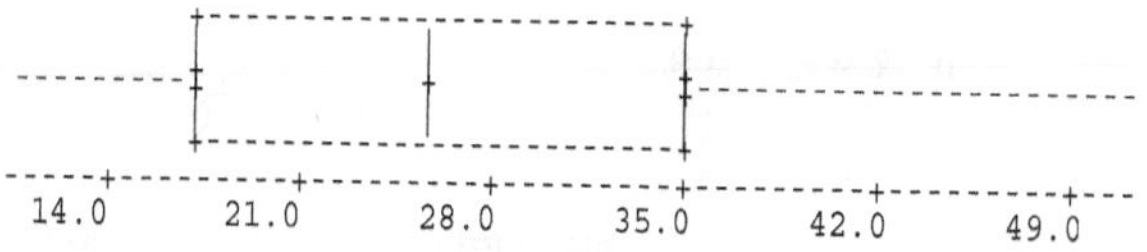

The distribution is somewhat positively skewed. Note that the dashed line above 35 is longer than below 18.

19. **a.** The mean is 30.8, found by 154/5. The median is 31.0, and the standard deviation is 3.96, found by

$$s = \sqrt{\frac{62.8}{4}} = 3.96$$

b. −0.15, found by $\frac{3(30.8 - 31.0)}{3.96}$

c.

Salary	$\left(\frac{x - \bar{x}}{s}\right)$	$\left(\frac{x - \bar{x}}{s}\right)^3$
36	1.313131	2.264250504
26	−1.212121	−1.780894343
33	0.555556	0.171467764
28	−0.707071	−0.353499282
31	0.050505	0.000128826
		0.301453469

0.125, found by [5/(4 × 3)] × 0.301

21. **a.** The mean is 21.93, found by 328.9/15. The median is 15.8, and the standard deviation is 21.18, found by

$$s = \sqrt{\frac{6{,}283}{14}} = 21.18$$

b. 0.868, found by [3(21.93 − 15.8)]/21.18
c. 2.444, found by [15/(14 × 13)] × 29.658

23.

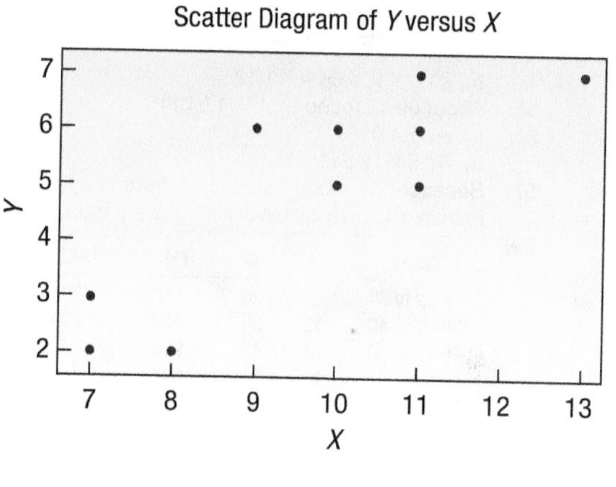

There is a positive relationship between the variables.

25. **a.** Both variables are nominal scale.
b. Contingency table
c. Men are about twice as likely to order a dessert. From the table, 32% of the men ordered dessert, but only 15% of the women.

27. **a.** Dot plot
b. 15
c. 5

29. Stem-and-leaf $N = 23$

3	3	222
5	3	77
11	4	000002
(6)	4	666666
6	5	222222

31. **a.** $L_{50} = (20 + 1)\frac{50}{100} = 10.50$

$$\text{Median} = \frac{83.7 + 85.6}{2} = 84.65$$

$L_{25} = (21)(.25) = 5.25$
$Q_1 = 66.6 + .25(72.9 - 66.6) = 68.175$
$L_{75} = 21(.75) = 15.75$
$Q_3 = 87.1 + .75(90.2 - 87.1) = 89.425$

b. $L_{26} = 21(.26) = 5.46$
$P_{26} = 66.6 + .46(72.9 - 66.6) = 69.498$
$L_{83} = 21(.83) = 17.43$
$P_{83} = 93.3 + .43(98.6 - 93.3)$
$= 95.579$

c.

```
               -------------------------
  ------------I            +   I--------------
               -------------------------

 -------+---------+---------+---------+---------+--------C20
      64.0      72.0      80.0      88.0      96.0
```

33. **a.** $Q_1 = 26.25$, $Q_3 = 35.75$, Median = 31.50

```
              ------------------------
  ------------I           +          I-----------------
              ------------------------

  -----+---------+---------+---------+---------+---------+
     24.5      28.0      31.5      35.0      38.5      42.0
```

b. $Q_1 = 33.25$, $Q_3 = 38.75$, Median = 37.50

```
         --------------------
    -----I                 +  I---------------------
         --------------------

  -----+---------+---------+---------+---------+---------+
     32.5      35.0      37.5      40.0      42.5      45.0
```

c. The median time for public transportation is about 6 minutes less. There is more variation in public transportation. The difference between Q_1 and Q_3 is 9.5 minutes for public transportation and 5.5 minutes for private transportation.

35. The distribution is positively skewed. The first quartile is about \$20 and the third quartile is about \$90. There is one outlier located at \$255. The median is about \$50.

37. **a.**

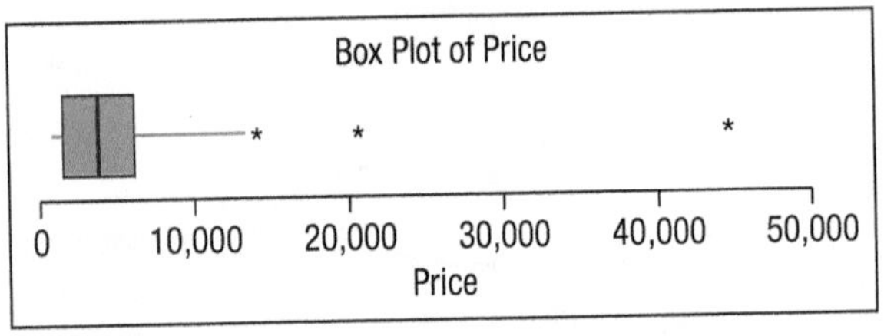

Median is 3,733. First quartile is 1,478. Third quartile is 6,141. So prices over 13,135.5, found by 6,141 + 1.5 × (6,141 − 1,478), are outliers. There are three (13,925; 20,413; and 44,312).

b.

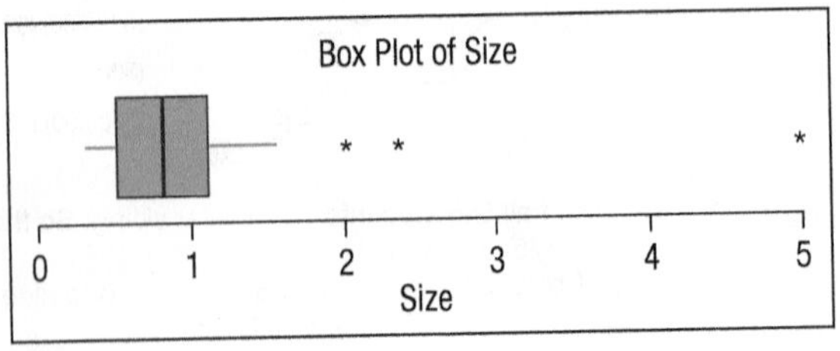

Median is 0.84. First quartile is 0.515. Third quartile is 1.12. So sizes over 2.0275, found by 1.12 + 1.5 (1.12 − 0.515), are outliers. There are three (2.03; 2.35; and 5.03).

c.

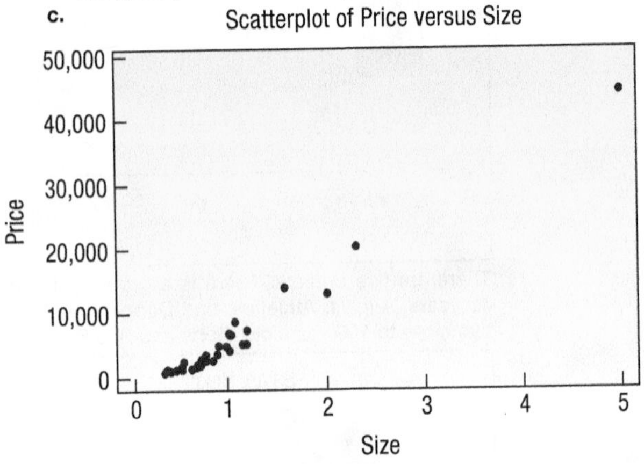

There is a direct association between them. The first observation is larger on both scales.

d.

Shape/ Cut	Average	Good	Ideal	Premium	Ultra Ideal	All
Emerald	0	0	1	0	0	1
Marquise	0	2	0	1	0	3
Oval	0	0	0	1	0	1
Princess	1	0	2	2	0	5
Round	1	3	3	13	3	23
Total	2	5	6	17	3	33

The majority of the diamonds are round (23). Premium cut is most common (17). The Round Premium combination occurs most often (13).

39. $sk = 0.065$ or $sk = \dfrac{3(7.7143 - 8.0)}{3.9036} = -0.22$

41.

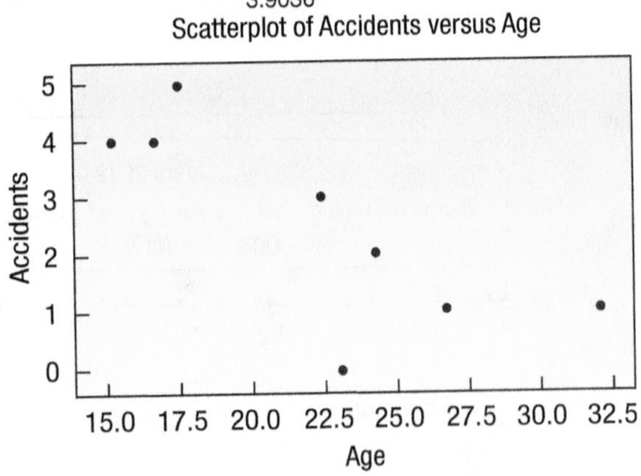

As age increases, the number of accidents decreases.

43. **a.** 139,340,000
b. 5.4% unemployed, found by (7,523/139,340)100
c. Men = 5.64%
Women = 5.12%

45. **a.**

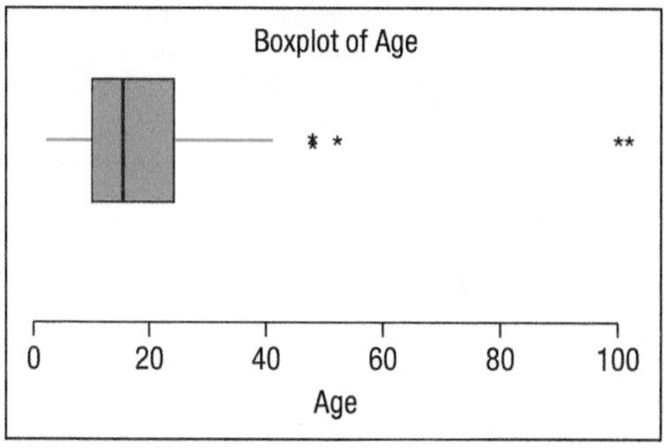

There are five outliers. There is a group of three around 45 years (Angels, Athletics, and Dodgers) and a group of two close to 100 years old (Cubs and Red Sox).

b.

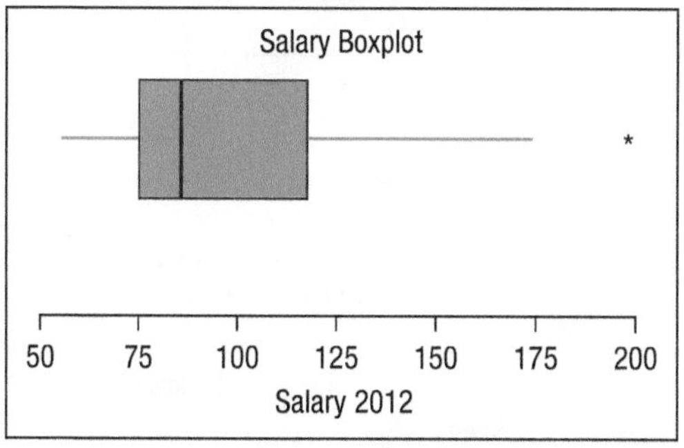

The first quartile is $75,200,000 and the third is $117,720,000. The distribution is positively skewed, with the New York Yankees a definite outlier.

c.

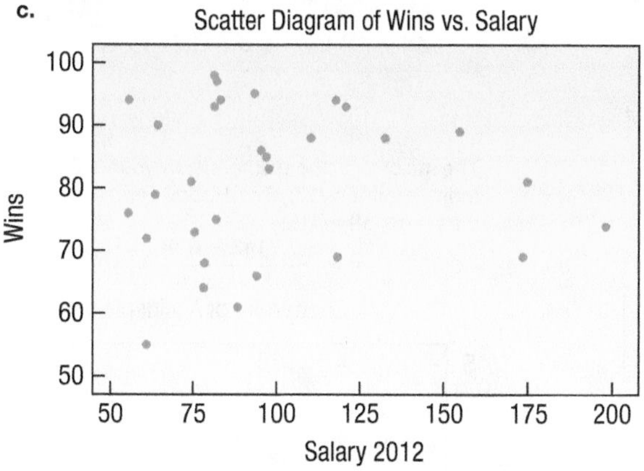

Higher salaries do not necessarily lead to more wins.

d.

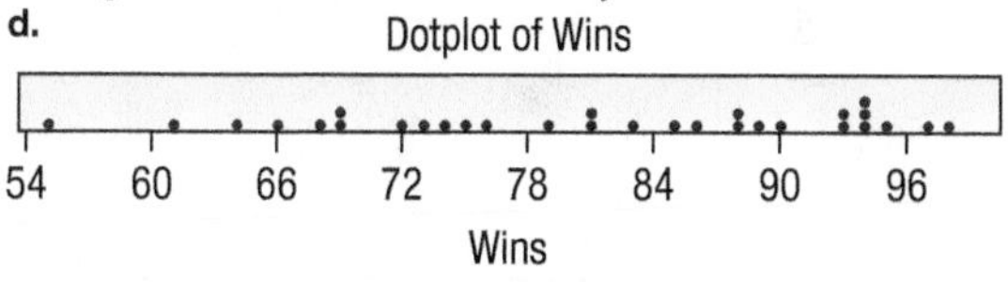

The distribution is fairly uniform between 55 and 98.

CHAPTER 5

1.

	Person	
Outcome	1	2
1	A	A
2	A	F
3	F	A
4	F	F

3. **a.** .176, found by $\frac{6}{34}$ **b.** Empirical

5. **a.** Empirical
b. Classical
c. Classical
d. Empirical, based on seismological data

7. **a.** The survey of 40 people about environmental issues
b. 26 or more respond yes, for example.
c. 10/40 = .25
d. Empirical
e. The events are not equally likely, but they are mutually exclusive.

9. **a.** Answers will vary. Here are some possibilities: 123, 124, 125, 999
b. $(1/10)^3$
c. Classical

11. $P(A \text{ or } B) = P(A) + P(B) = .30 + .20 = .50$
$P(\text{neither}) = 1 - .50 = .50$.

13. **a.** 102/200 = .51
b. .49, found by 61/200 + 37/200 = .305 + .185. Special rule of addition.

15. $P(\text{above } C) = .25 + .50 = .75$

17. $P(A \text{ or } B) = P(A) + P(B) - P(A \text{ and } B) = .20 + .30 - .15 = .35$

19. When two events are mutually exclusive, it means that if one occurs, the other event cannot occur. Therefore, the probability of their joint occurrence is zero.

21. Let *A* denote the event the fish is green and *B* be the event the fish is male.
a. $P(A) = 80/140 = 0.5714$
b. $P(B) = 60/140 = 0.4286$
c. $P(A \text{ and } B) = 36/140 = 0.2571$
d. $P(A \text{ or } B) = P(A) + P(B) - P(A \text{ and } B) = 80/140 + 60/140 - 36/140 = 104/140 = 0.7429$

23. $P(A \text{ and } B) = P(A) \times P(B|A) = .40 \times .30 = .12$

25. .90, found by (.80 + .60) − .5.
.10, found by (1 − .90).

27. **a.** $P(A_1) = 3/10 = .30$
b. $P(B_1|A_2) = 1/3 = .33$
c. $P(B_2 \text{ and } A_3) = 1/10 = .10$

29. **a.** A contingency table
b. .27, found by 300/500 × 135/300
c. The tree diagram would appear as:

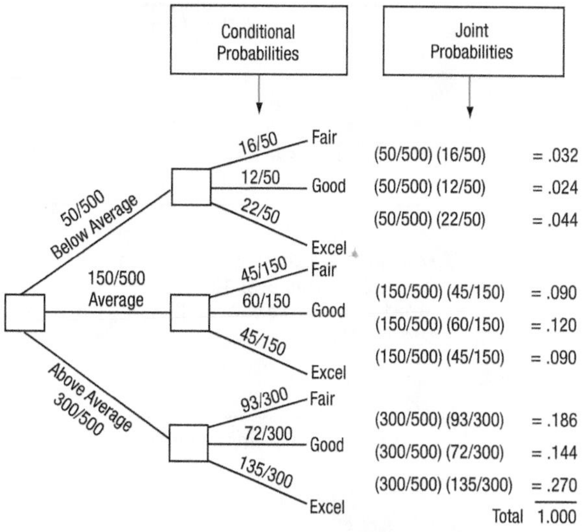

31. **a.** Out of all 545 students, 171 prefer skiing. So the probability is 171/545, or 0.3138.
b. Out of all 545 students, 155 are in junior college. Thus, the probability is 155/545, or 0.2844.

c. Out of 210 four-year students, 70 prefer ice skating. So the probability is 70/210, or 0.3333.
d. Out of 211 students who prefer snowboarding, 68 are in junior college. So the probability is 68/211, or 0.3223.
e. Out of 180 graduate students, 74 prefer skiing and 47 prefer ice skating. So the probability is (74 + 47)/180 = 121/180, or 0.6722.

33. $P(A_1|B_1) = \dfrac{P(A_1) \times P(B_1|A_1)}{P(A_1) \times P(B_1|A_1) + P(A_2) \times P(B_1|A_2)}$

$= \dfrac{.60 \times .05}{(.60 \times .05) + (.40 \times .10)} = .4286$

35. $P(\text{night}|\text{win}) = \dfrac{P(\text{night})P(\text{win}|\text{night})}{P(\text{night})P(\text{win}|\text{night}) + P(\text{day})P(\text{win}|\text{day})}$

$= \dfrac{(.70)(.50)}{[(.70)(.50)] + [(.30)(.90)]} = .5645$

37. $P(\text{cash} \mid >\$50)$

$= \dfrac{P(\text{cash})\ P(>\$50|\text{cash})}{[P(\text{cash})\ P(>\$50|\text{cash}) + P(\text{credit})\ P(>\$50|\text{credit}) + P(\text{debit})\ P(>\$50|\text{debit})]}$

$= \dfrac{(.30)(.20)}{(.30)(.20) + (.30)(.90) + (.40)(.60)} = .1053$

39. a. 78,960,960
b. 840, found by (7)(6)(5)(4). That is 7!/3!
c. 10, found by 5!/3!2!

41. 210, found by (10)(9)(8)(7)/(4)(3)(2)

43. 120, found by 5!

45. 10,897,286,400, found by
$_{15}P_{10}$ = (15)(14)(13)(12)(11)(10)(9)(8)(7)(6)

47. a. Asking teenagers to compare their reactions to a newly developed soft drink.
b. Answers will vary. One possibility is more than half of the respondents like it.

49. Subjective

51. a. 4/9, found by (2/3) · (2/3)
b. 3/4, because (3/4) · (2/3) = 0.5

53. a. .8145, found by $(.95)^4$
b. Special rule of multiplication
c. P(A and B and C and D) = P(A) × P(B) × P(C) × P(D)

55. a. .08, found by .80 × .10
b. No; 90% of females attended college, 78% of males
c.

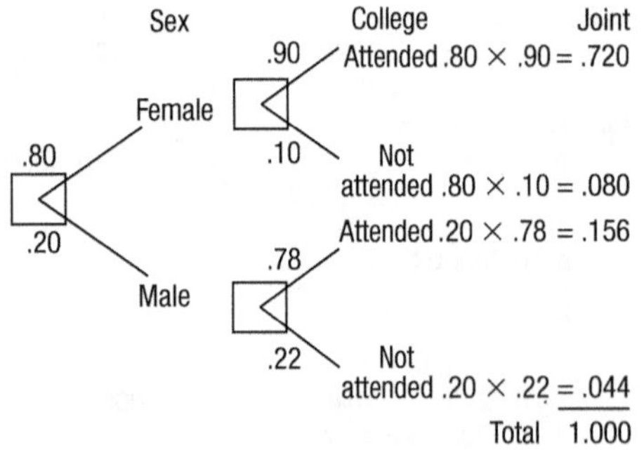

d. Yes, because all the possible outcomes are shown on the tree diagram.

57. a. 0.57, found by 57/100
b. 0.97, found by (57/100) + (40/100)
c. Yes, because an employee cannot be both
d. 0.03, found by 1 − 0.97

59. a. 1/2, found by (2/3)(3/4)
b. 1/12, found by (1/3)(1/4)
c. 11/12, found by 1 − 1/12

61. a. 0.9039, found by $(0.98)^5$
b. 0.0961, found by 1 − 0.9039

63. a. 0.0333, found by (4/10)(3/9)(2/8)
b. 0.1667, found by (6/10)(5/9)(4/8)
c. 0.8333, found by 1 − 0.1667
d. Dependent

65. a. 0.3818, found by (9/12)(8/11)(7/10)
b. 0.6182, found by 1 − 0.3818

67. a. P(S) · P(R|S) = .60(.85) = 0.51
b. P(S) · P(PR|S) = .60(1 − .85) = 0.09

69. a. P(not perfect) = P(bad sector) + P(defective)

$= \dfrac{112}{1{,}000} + \dfrac{31}{1{,}000} = .143$

b. $P(\text{defective}|\text{not perfect}) = \dfrac{.031}{.143} = .217$

71. $P(\text{poor}|\text{profit}) = \dfrac{.10(.20)}{.10(.20) + .60(.80) + .30(.60)}$

$= .0294$

73. a. 0.1 + 0.02 = 0.12
b. 1 − 0.12 = 0.88
c. $(0.88)^3 = 0.6815$
d. 1 − .6815 = 0.3185

75. Yes, 256 is found by 2^8.

77. .9744, found by $1 - (.40)^4$

79. a. .185, found by (.15)(.95) + (.05)(.85)
b. .0075, found by (.15)(.05)

81. a. P(F and >60) = .25, found by solving with the general rule of multiplication:
P(F) · P(>60|F) = (.5)(.5)
b. 0
c. .3333, found by 1/3

83. $26^4 = 456{,}976$

85. 1/3, 628,800

87. a. P(D) = .20(.03) + .30(.04) + .25(.07) + .25(.065)
= .05175

b. $P(\text{Tyson}|\text{defective}) = \dfrac{.20(.03)}{[.20(.03) + .30(.04) + .25(.07) + .25(.065)]} = .1159$

Supplier	Joint	Revised
Tyson	.00600	.1159
Fuji	.01200	.2319
Kirkpatricks	.01750	.3382
Parts	.01625	.3140
	.05175	1.0000

89. 0.512, found by $(0.8)^3$

91. .525, found by $1 - (.78)^3$

93. a.

Winning Season	Attendance			
	Low	Moderate	High	Total
No	4	7	2	13
Yes	3	7	7	17
Total	11	10	9	30

1. 0.5667, found by 17/30
2. 0.5667, found by 17/30 + 9/30 − 9/30 = 17/30
3. 0.7778, found by 7/9
4. 0.1000, found by 3/30

b.

	Losing Season	Winning Season	Total
New	7	8	15
Old	6	9	15
Total	13	17	30

1. 0.5667, found by 17/30
2. 0.2667, found by 8/30
3. 0.8000, found by 17/30 + 15/30 − 8/30 = 24/30

CHAPTER 6

1. Mean = 1.3, variance = .81, found by:

$\mu = 0(.20) + 1(.40) + 2(.30) + 3(.10) = 1.3$

$\sigma^2 = (0 - 1.3)^2(.2) + (1 - 1.3)^2(.4) + (2 - 1.3)^2(.3) + (3 - 1.3)^2(.1) = .81$

3. Mean = 14.5, variance = 27.25, found by:

$\mu = 5(.1) + 10(.3) + 15(.2) + 20(.4) = 14.5$

$\sigma^2 = (5 - 14.5)^2(.1) + (10 - 14.5)^2(.3) + (15 - 14.5)^2(.2) + (20 - 14.5)^2(.4) = 27.25$

5. a.

Calls, x	Frequency	P(x)	xP(x)	$(x - \mu)^2 P(x)$
0	8	.16	0	.4624
1	10	.20	.20	.0980
2	22	.44	.88	.0396
3	9	.18	.54	.3042
4	1	.02	.08	.1058
	50		1.70	1.0100

b. Discrete distribution, because only certain outcomes are possible.

c. $\mu = \Sigma x \cdot P(x) = 1.70$

d. $\sigma = \sqrt{1.01} = 1.005$

7.

Amount	P(x)	xP(x)	$(x - \mu)^2 P(x)$
10	.50	5	60.50
25	.40	10	6.40
50	.08	4	67.28
100	.02	2	124.82
		21	259.00

a. $\mu = \Sigma xP(x) = 21$

b. $\sigma^2 = \Sigma(x - \mu)^2 P(x) = 259$

$\sigma = \sqrt{259} = 16.093$

9. a. $P(2) = \frac{4!}{2!(4-2)!}(.25)^2(.75)^{4-2} = .2109$

b. $P(3) = \frac{4!}{3!(4-3)!}(.25)^3(.75)^{4-3} = .0469$

11. a.

x	P(x)
0	.064
1	.288
2	.432
3	.216

b. $\mu = 1.8$

$\sigma^2 = 0.72$

$\sigma = \sqrt{0.72} = .8485$

13. a. .2668, found by $P(2) = \frac{9!}{(9-2)!2!}(.3)^2(.7)^7$

b. .1715, found by $P(4) = \frac{9!}{(9-4)!4!}(.3)^4(.7)^5$

c. .0404, found by $P(0) = \frac{9!}{(9-0)!0!}(.3)^0(.7)^9$

15. a. .2824, found by $P(0) = \frac{12!}{(12-0)!0!}(.1)^0(.9)^{12}$

b. .3766, found by $P(1) = \frac{12!}{(12-1)!1!}(.1)^1(.9)^{11}$

c. .2301, found by $P(2) = \frac{12!}{(12-2)!2!}(.1)^2(.9)^{10}$

d. $\mu = 1.2$, found by 12(.1)

$\sigma = 1.0392$, found by $\sqrt{1.08}$

17. a. 0.1858, found by $\frac{15!}{2!13!}(0.23)^2(0.77)^{13}$

b. 0.1416, found by $\frac{15!}{5!10!}(0.23)^5(0.77)^{10}$

c. 3.45, found by (0.23)(15)

19. a. 0.296, found by using Appendix B.1 with n of 8, π of 0.30, and x of 2

b. $P(x \leq 2) = 0.058 + 0.198 + 0.296 = 0.552$

c. 0.448, found by $P(x \geq 3) = 1 - P(x \leq 2) = 1 - 0.552$

21. a. 0.387, found from Appendix B.1 with n of 9, π of 0.90, and x of 9

b. $P(x < 5) = 0.001$

c. 0.992, found by 1 − 0.008

d. 0.947, found by 1 − 0.053

23. a. $\mu = 10.5$, found by 15(0.7) and $\sigma = \sqrt{15(0.7)(0.3)} = 1.7748$

b. 0.2061, found by $\frac{15!}{10!5!}(0.7)^{10}(0.3)^5$

c. 0.4247, found by 0.2061 + 0.2186

d. 0.5154, found by 0.2186 + 0.1700 + 0.0916 + 0.0305 + 0.0047

25. $P(2) = \frac{[{}_6C_2][{}_4C_1]}{{}_{10}C_3} = \frac{15(4)}{120} = .50$

27. N is 10, the number of loans in the population; S is 3, the number of underwater loans in the population; x is 0, the number of selected underwater loans in the sample; and n is 2, the size of the sample. Use formula (6–6) to find $P(0) = \frac{({}_7C_2)({}_3C_0)}{{}_{10}C_2} = \frac{21(1)}{45} = 0.4667.$

29. $P(2) = \frac{[{}_9C_3][{}_6C_2]}{[{}_{15}C_5]} = \frac{84(15)}{3003} = .4196$

31. a. .6703

b. .3297

33. a. .0613

b. .0803

35. $\mu = 6$

$P(x \geq 5) = 1 - (.0025 + .0149 + .0446 + .0892 + .1339) = .7149$

37. A random variable is an outcome that results from a chance experiment. A probability distribution also includes the likelihood of each possible outcome.

39. $\mu = \$1{,}000(.25) + \$2{,}000(.60) + \$5{,}000(.15) = \$2{,}200$

$\sigma^2 = (1{,}000 - 2{,}200)^2 .25 + (2{,}000 - 2{,}200)^2 .60 + (5{,}000 - 2{,}200)^2 .15 = 1{,}560{,}000$

41. $\mu = 12(.25) + \cdots + 15(.1) = 13.2$

$\sigma^2 = (12 - 13.2)^2 .25 + \cdots + (15 - 13.2)^2 .10 = 0.86$

$\sigma = \sqrt{0.86} = .927$

43. a. $\mu = 10(.35) = 3.5$

b. $P(x = 4) = {}_{10}C_4 (.35)^4 (.65)^6 = 210(.0150)(.0754) = .2375$

c. $P(x \geq 4) = {}_{10}C_x (.35)^x (.65)^{10-x} = .2375 + .1536 + \cdots + .0000 = .4862$

45. a. 6, found by 0.4 × 15

b. 0.0245, found by $\frac{15!}{10!5!}(0.4)^{10}(0.6)^5$

c. 0.0338, found by 0.0245 + 0.0074 + 0.0016 + 0.0003 + 0.0000

d. 0.0093, found by 0.0338 − 0.0245

47. a. $\mu = 20(0.075) = 1.5$

$\sigma = \sqrt{20(0.075)(0.925)} = 1.1779$

b. 0.2103, found by $\frac{20!}{0!20!}(0.075)^0(0.925)^{20}$

c. 0.7897, found by 1 − 0.2103

49. a. 0.1311, found by $\frac{16!}{4!12!}(0.15)^4(0.85)^{12}$

b. 2.4, found by (0.15)(16)

c. 0.2100, found by 1 − 0.0743 − 0.2097 − 0.2775 − 0.2285

51. 0.2784, found by 0.1472 + 0.0811 + 0.0348 + 0.0116 + 0.0030 + 0.0006 + 0.0001 + 0.0000

53. a.

0	0.0002	7	0.2075
1	0.0019	8	0.1405
2	0.0116	9	0.0676
3	0.0418	10	0.0220
4	0.1020	11	0.0043
5	0.1768	12	0.0004
6	0.2234		

b. $\mu = 12(0.52) = 6.24 \quad \sigma = \sqrt{12(0.52)(0.48)} = 1.7307$
c. 0.1768
d. 0.3343, found by
0.0002 + 0.0019 + 0.0116 + 0.0418 + 0.1020 + 0.1768

55. a. $P(1) = \frac{[_7C_2][_3C_1]}{[_{10}C_3]} = \frac{(21)(3)}{120} = .5250$
b. $P(0) = \frac{[_7C_3][_3C_0]}{[_{10}C_3]} = \frac{(35)(1)}{120} = .2917$
$P(x \geq 1) = 1 - P(0) = 1 - .2917 = .7083$

57. $P(x = 0) = \frac{[_8C_4][_4C_0]}{[_{12}C_4]} = \frac{70}{495} = .141$

59. a. .0498 b. .7746, found by $(1 - .0498)^5$

61. $\mu = 4.0$, from Appendix B.2
a. .0183 b. .1954
c. .6289 d. .5665

63. a. 0.1733, found by $\frac{(3.1)^4 e^{-3.1}}{4!}$
b. 0.0450, found by $\frac{(3.1)^0 e^{-3.1}}{0!}$
c. 0.9550, found by 1 − 0.0450

65. $\mu = n\pi = 23\left(\frac{2}{113}\right) = .407$
$P(2) = \frac{(.407)^2 e^{-.407}}{2!} = 0.0551$
$P(0) = \frac{(.407)^0 e^{-.407}}{0!} = 0.6656$

67. Let $\mu = n\pi = 155(1/3{,}709) = 0.042$
$P(4) = \frac{0.042^4 e^{-0.042}}{4!} = 0.00000012$
Very unlikely!

69. a. $\mu = n\pi = 15(.67) = 10.05$
$\sigma = \sqrt{n\pi(1 - \pi)} = \sqrt{15(.67)(.33)} = 1.8211$
b. $P(8) = {}_{15}C_8(.67)^8(.33)^7 = 6435(.0406)(.000426) = .1114$
c. $P(x \geq 8) = .1114 + .1759 + \cdots + .0025 = .9163$

71. The mean number of home runs per game is 2.0305, found by 4934/[(15)(162)].
a. $P(0) = \frac{2.0305^0 e^{-2.0305}}{0!} = 0.1313$
b. $P(2) = \frac{2.0305^2 e^{-2.0305}}{2!} = 0.2706$
c. $P(x \geq 4) = 0.1484$, found by
1 − (0.1313 + 0.2665 + 0.2706 + 0.1832)

CHAPTER 7

1. a. $b = 10, a = 6$
b. $\mu = \frac{6 + 10}{2} = 8$
c. $\sigma = \sqrt{\frac{(10 - 6)^2}{12}} = 1.1547$
d. $\text{Area} = \frac{1}{(10 - 6)} \cdot \frac{(10 - 6)}{1} = 1$
e. $P(x > 7) = \frac{1}{(10 - 6)} \cdot \frac{10 - 7}{1} = \frac{3}{4} = .75$
f. $P(7 \leq x \leq 9) = \frac{1}{(10 - 6)} \cdot \frac{(9 - 7)}{1} = \frac{2}{4} = .50$

3. a. 0.30, found by (30 − 27)/(30 − 20)
b. 0.40, found by (24 − 20)/(30 − 20)

5. a. $a = 0.5, b = 3.00$
b. $\mu = \frac{0.5 + 3.00}{2} = 1.75$
$\sigma = \sqrt{\frac{(3.00 - .50)^2}{12}} = .72$
c. $P(x < 1) = \frac{1}{(3.0 - 0.5)} \cdot \frac{1 - .5}{1} = \frac{.5}{2.5} = 0.2$
d. 0, found by $\frac{1}{(3.0 - 0.5)} \frac{(1.0 - 1.0)}{1}$
e. $P(x > 1.5) = \frac{1}{(3.0 - 0.5)} \cdot \frac{3.0 - 1.5}{1} = \frac{1.5}{2.5} = 0.6$

7. The actual shape of a normal distribution depends on its mean and standard deviation. Thus, there is a normal distribution, and an accompanying normal curve, for a mean of 7 and a standard deviation of 2. There is another normal curve for a mean of $25,000 and a standard deviation of $1,742, and so on.

9. a. 490 and 510, found by 500 ± 1(10)
b. 480 and 520, found by 500 ± 2(10)
c. 470 and 530, found by 500 ± 3(10)

11. $z_{Rob} = \frac{\$50{,}000 - \$60{,}000}{\$5{,}000} = -2$
$z_{Rachel} = \frac{\$50{,}000 - \$35{,}000}{\$8{,}000} = 1.875$
Adjusting for their industries, Rob is well below average and Rachel well above.

13. a. 1.25, found by $z = \frac{25 - 20}{4.0} = 1.25$
b. 0.3944, found in Appendix B.3
c. 0.3085, found by $z = \frac{18 - 20}{2.5} = -0.5$
Find 0.1915 in Appendix B.3 for $z = -0.5$, then 0.5000 − 0.1915 = 0.3085

15. a. 0.3413, found by $z = \frac{\$24 - \$20.50}{\$3.50} = 1.00$, then find 0.3413 in Appendix B.3 for $z = 1$
b. 0.1587, found by 0.5000 − 0.3413 = 0.1587
c. 0.3336, found by $z = \frac{\$19.00 - \$20.50}{\$3.50} = -0.43$
Find 0.1664 in Appendix B.3, for $z = -0.43$, then 0.5000 − 0.1664 = 0.3336

17. a. 0.8276: First find $z = -1.5$, found by (44 − 50)/4 and $z = 1.25 = (55 - 50)/4$. The area between −1.5 and 0 is 0.4332 and the area between 0 and 1.25 is 0.3944, both from Appendix B.3. Then adding the two areas we find that 0.4332 + 0.3944 = 0.8276.
b. 0.1056, found by 0.5000 − .3944, where $z = 1.25$
c. 0.2029: Recall that the area for $z = 1.25$ is 0.3944, and the area for $z = 0.5$, found by (52 − 50)/4, is 0.1915. Then subtract 0.3944 − 0.1915 and find 0.2029.

19. a. 0.4129: Begin by using formula (7–5) to find the z value for $3,100, which is (3,100 − 3,000)/450, or 0.22. Then see Appendix B.3 to find the area between 0 and 0.22, which is 0.0871. Finally, since the area of interest is beyond 0.22, subtract that probability from 0.5000. The result is 0.5000 − 0.0871, or 0.4129.
b. 0.1929: Use formula (7–5) to find the z value for $3,500, which is (3,500 − 3,000)/450, or 1.11. Then see Appendix B.3 for the area under the standard normal curve. That probability is 0.3665. Since the two points (1.11 and 0.22) are on the same side of the mean, subtract the smaller probability from the larger. The result is 0.3665 − 0.1736 = 0.1929.
c. 0.8190: Use formula (7–5) to find the z value for $2,250, which is −1.67, found by (2,250 − 3,000)/450. The corresponding area is 0.4525. Since 1.11 and −1.67 are on different sides of the mean, add the corresponding probabilities. Thus, we find 0.4525 + 0.3665 = 0.8190.

21. **a.** 0.0764, found by $z = (20 - 15)/3.5 = 1.43$, then $0.5000 - 0.4236 = 0.0764$
b. 0.9236, found by $0.5000 + 0.4236$, where $z = 1.43$
c. 0.1185, found by $z = (12 - 15)/3.5 = -0.86$.
The area under the curve is 0.3051, then $z = (10 - 15)/3.5 = -1.43$. The area is 0.4236. Finally, $0.4236 - 0.3051 = 0.1185$.

23. $x = 56.60$, found by adding 0.5000 (the area left of the mean) and then finding a z value that forces 45% of the data to fall inside the curve. Solving for x: $1.65 = (x - 50)/4$, so $x = 56.60$.

25. \$1,630, found by \$2,100 − 1.88(\$250)

27. **a.** 214.8 hours: Find a z value where 0.4900 of area is between 0 and z. That value is $z = 2.33$. Then solve for x: $2.33 = (x - 195)/8.5$, so $x = 214.8$ hours.
b. 270.2 hours: Find a z value where 0.4900 of area is between 0 and $(-z)$. That value is $z = -2.33$. Then solve for x: $-2.33 = (x - 290)/8.5$, so $x = 270.2$ hours.

29. 41.7%, found by $12 + 1.65(18)$

31. **a.** $\mu = n\pi = 50(0.25) = 12.5$
$\sigma^2 = n\pi(1 - \pi) = 12.5(1 - 0.25) = 9.375$
$\sigma = \sqrt{9.375} = 3.0619$
b. 0.2578, found by $(14.5 - 12.5)/3.0619 = 0.65$.
The area is 0.2422. Then $0.5000 - 0.2422 = 0.2578$.
c. 0.2578, found by $(10.5 - 12.5)/3.0619 = -0.65$.
The area is 0.2422. Then $0.5000 - 0.2422 = 0.2578$.

33. **a.** $\mu = n\pi = 80(0.07) = 5.6 \qquad \sigma = \sqrt{5.208} = 2.2821$
0.3483, found from $z = (6.5 - 5.6)/2.2821 = 0.39$ with the corresponding area of 0.1517, then $0.5000 - 0.1517 = 0.3483$
b. 0.5160, found from $z = (5.5 - 5.6)/2.2821 = -0.04$ with the corresponding area of 0.0160, then $0.5000 + 0.0160 = 0.5160$
c. .1677, found by $.5160 - 0.3483$.

35. **a.** Yes. (1) There are two mutually exclusive outcomes: overweight and not overweight. (2) It is the result of counting the number of successes (overweight members). (3) Each trial is independent. (4) The probability of 0.30 remains the same for each trial.
b. 0.0084, found by
$\mu = 500(0.30) = 150$
$\sigma^2 = 500(.30)(.70) = 105$
$\sigma = \sqrt{105} = 10.24695$
$$z = \frac{x - \mu}{\sigma} = \frac{174.5 - 150}{10.24695} = 2.39$$
The area under the curve for 2.39 is 0.4916.
Then $0.5000 - 0.4916 = 0.0084$.
c. 0.8461, found by $z = \dfrac{139.5 - 150}{10.24695} = -1.02$
The area between 139.5 and 150 is 0.3461.
Adding $0.3461 + 0.5000 = 0.8461$.

37. **a.** 0.3935, found by $1 - e^{[(-1/60)(30)]}$
b. 0.1353, found by $e^{[(-1/60)(120)]}$
c. 0.1859, found by $e^{[(-1/60)(45)]} - e^{[(-1/60)(75)]}$
d. 41.59 seconds, found by $-60 \ln(0.5)$

39. **a.** 0.5654, found by $1 - e^{[(-1/18)(15)]}$,
and 0.2212, found by $1 - e^{[(-1/60)(15)]}$
b. 0.0013, found by $e^{[(-1/18)(120)]}$, and 0.1353, found by $e^{[(-1/60)(120)]}$
c. 0.1821, found by $e^{[(-1/18)(30)]} - e^{[(-1/18)(90)]}$,
and 0.3834, found by $e^{[(-1/60)(30)]} - e^{[(-1/60)(90)]}$
d. 4 minutes, found by $-18 \ln(0.8)$, and 13.4 minutes, found by $-60 \ln(0.8)$

41. **a.** $\mu = \dfrac{11.96 + 12.05}{2} = 12.005$
b. $\sigma = \sqrt{\dfrac{(12.05 - 11.96)^2}{12}} = .0260$
c. $P(x < 12) = \dfrac{1}{(12.05 - 11.96)} \dfrac{12.00 - 11.96}{1} = \dfrac{.04}{.09} = .44$
d. $P(x > 11.98) = \dfrac{1}{(12.05 - 11.96)}\left(\dfrac{12.05 - 11.98}{1}\right)$
$= \dfrac{.07}{.09} = .78$
e. All cans have more than 11.00 ounces, so the probability is 100%.

43. **a.** $\mu = \dfrac{4 + 10}{2} = 7$
b. $\sigma = \sqrt{\dfrac{(10 - 4)^2}{12}} = 1.732$
c. $P(x < 6) = \dfrac{1}{(10 - 4)} \cdot \left(\dfrac{6 - 4}{1}\right) = \dfrac{2}{6} = .33$
d. $P(x > 5) = \dfrac{1}{(10 - 4)} \cdot \left(\dfrac{10 - 5}{1}\right) = \dfrac{5}{6} = .83$

45. **a.** −0.4 for net sales, found by $(170 - 180)/25$. 2.92 for employees, found by $(1{,}850 - 1{,}500)/120$.
b. Net sales are 0.4 standard deviation below the mean. Employees is 2.92 standard deviation above the mean.
c. 65.54% of the aluminum fabricators have greater net sales compared with Clarion, found by $0.1554 + 0.5000$. Only 0.18% have more employees than Clarion, found by $0.5000 - 0.4982$.

47. **a.** 0.5000, because $z = \dfrac{30 - 490}{90} = -5.11$
b. 0.2514, found by $0.5000 - 0.2486$
c. 0.6374, found by $0.2486 + 0.3888$
d. 0.3450, found by $0.3888 - 0.0438$

49. **a.** 0.3015, found by $0.5000 - 0.1985$
b. 0.2579, found by $0.4564 - 0.1985$
c. 0.0011, found by $0.5000 - 0.4989$
d. 1,818, found by $1{,}280 + 1.28(420)$

51. **a.** 90.82%: First find $z = 1.33$, found by $(40 - 34)/4.5$. The area between 0 and 1.33 is 0.4082 hours/week for women. Then add 0.5000 and 0.4082 and find 0.9082, or 90.82%.
b. 78.23%: First find $z = -0.78$, found by $(25 - 29)/5.1$. The area between 0 and (−0.78) is 0.2823. Then add 0.5000 and 0.2823 and find 0.7823, or 78.23%.
c. Find a z value where 0.4900 of the area is between 0 and z. That value is 2.33. Then solve for x: $2.33 = (x - 34)/4.5$, so $x = 44.5$ hours/week for women.
40.9 hours/week for men: $2.33 = (x - 29)/5.1$, so $x = 40.9$ hours/week.

53. About 4,099 units, found by solving for x. $1.65 = (x - 4{,}000)/60$

55. **a.** 15.39%, found by $(8 - 10.3)/2.25 = -1.02$, then $0.5000 - 0.3461 = 0.1539$.
b. 17.31%, found by:
$z = (12 - 10.3)/2.25 = 0.76$. Area is 0.2764.
$z = (14 - 10.3)/2.25 = 1.64$. Area is 0.4495.
The area between 12 and 14 is 0.1731, found by $0.4495 - 0.2764$.
c. On 99.73% of the days, returns are between 3.55 and 17.05, found by $10.3 \pm 3(2.25)$. Thus, the chance of less than 3.55 returns is rather remote.

57. **a.** 0.9678, found by:
$\mu = 60(0.64) = 38.4$
$\sigma^2 = 60(0.64)(0.36) = 13.824$
$\sigma = \sqrt{13.824} = 3.72$
Then $(31.5 - 38.4)/3.72 = -1.85$, for which the area is 0.4678.
Then $0.5000 + 0.4678 = 0.9678$.
b. 0.0853, found by $(43.5 - 38.4)/3.72 = 1.37$, for which the area is 0.4147. Then $0.5000 - 0.4147 = .0853$.
c. 0.8084, found by $0.4441 + 0.3643$
d. 0.0348, found by $0.4495 - 0.4147$

59. 0.0968, found by:
$\mu = 50(0.40) = 20$
$\sigma^2 = 50(0.40)(0.60) = 12$
$\sigma = \sqrt{12} = 3.46$
$z = (24.5 - 20)/3.46 = 1.30$.
The area is 0.4032. Then, for 25 or more, $0.5000 - 0.4032 = 0.0968$.

61. **a.** $1.65 = (45 - \mu)/5$ $\mu = 36.75$
b. $1.65 = (45 - \mu)/10$ $\mu = 28.5$
c. $z = (30 - 28.5)/10 = 0.15$, then $0.5000 + 0.0596 = 0.5596$

63. **a.** 21.19%, found by $z = (9.00 - 9.20)/0.25 = -0.80$, so $0.5000 - 0.2881 = 0.2119$
b. Increase the mean. $z = (9.00 - 9.25)/0.25 = -1.00$, $P = 0.5000 - 0.3413 = 0.1587$.
Reduce the standard deviation. $\sigma = (9.00 - 9.20)/0.15 = -1.33$; $P = 0.5000 - 0.4082 = 0.0918$.
Reducing the standard deviation is better because a smaller percent of the hams will be below the limit.

65. **a.** $z = (60 - 52)/5 = 1.60$, so $0.5000 - 0.4452 = 0.0548$
b. Let $z = 0.67$, so $0.67 = (x - 52)/5$ and $x = 55.35$, set mileage at 55,350
c. $z = (45 - 52)/5 = -1.40$, so $0.5000 - 0.4192 = 0.0808$

67. $\frac{470 - \mu}{\sigma} = 0.25$ $\frac{500 - \mu}{\sigma} = 1.28$ $\sigma = 29{,}126$ and $\mu = 462{,}718$

69. $\mu = 150(0.15) = 22.5$ $\sigma = \sqrt{150(0.15)(0.85)} = 4.37$
$z = (29.5 - 22.5)/4.37 = 1.60$
$P(z > 1.60) = .05000 - 0.4452 = 0.0548$

71. **a.** 0.4262, found by $1 - e^{[(-1/27)(15)]}$
b. 0.1084, found by $e^{[(-1/27)(60)]}$
c. 0.1403, found by $e^{[(-1/27)(30)]} - e^{[(-1/27)(45)]}$
d. 2.84 secs, found by $-27\ \ln(0.9)$

73. **a.** 0.2835, found by $1 - e^{[(-1/300{,}000)(100{,}000)]}$
b. 0.1889, found by $e^{[(-1/300{,}000)(500{,}000)]}$
c. 0.2020, found by $e^{[(-1/300{,}000)(200{,}000)]} - e^{[(-1/300{,}000)(350{,}000)]}$
d. Both the mean and standard deviation are 300,000 hours.

75. **a.** 0.0582, found by $0.5000 - 0.4418$ with $z = (3.500 - 2.495)/0.642 = 1.57$; leads to 1.7 teams, found by 30(0.0582). Two teams actually had attendance of more than 3.5 million, so the estimate is accurate.
b. 0.9032, found by $0.5000 + 0.4032$ with $z = (50 - 98.02)/36.83 = -1.30$; leads to 27.1 teams, found by 30(0.9032). All 30 teams actually had salaries of more than $50 million, so the estimate is not really accurate.

CHAPTER 8

1. **a.** 303 Louisiana, 5155 S. Main, 3501 Monroe, 2652 W. Central
b. Answers will vary.
c. 630 Dixie Hwy, 835 S. McCord Rd, 4624 Woodville Rd
d. Answers will vary.

3. **a.** Bob Schmidt Chevrolet
Great Lakes Ford Nissan
Grogan Towne Chrysler
Southside Lincoln Mercury
Rouen Chrysler Jeep Eagle
b. Answers will vary.
c. Yark Automotive
Thayer Chevrolet Toyota
Franklin Park Lincoln Mercury
Mathews Ford Oregon Inc.
Valiton Chrysler

5. **a.**

Sample	Values	Sum	Mean
1	12, 12	24	12
2	12, 14	26	13
3	12, 16	28	14
4	12, 14	26	13
5	12, 16	28	14
6	14, 16	30	15

b. $\mu_{\bar{X}} = (12 + 13 + 14 + 13 + 14 + 15)/6 = 13.5$
$\mu = (12 + 12 + 14 + 16)/4 = 13.5$
c. More dispersion with population data compared to the sample means. The sample means vary from 12 to 15, whereas the population varies from 12 to 16.

7. **a.**

Sample	Values	Sum	Mean
1	12, 12, 14	38	12.66
2	12, 12, 15	39	13.00
3	12, 12, 20	44	14.66
4	14, 15, 20	49	16.33
5	12, 14, 15	41	13.66
6	12, 14, 15	41	13.66
7	12, 15, 20	47	15.66
8	12, 15, 20	47	15.66
9	12, 14, 20	46	15.33
10	12, 14, 20	46	15.33

b. $\mu_{\bar{X}} = \frac{(12.66 + \cdots + 15.33 + 15.33)}{10} = 14.6$
$\mu = (12 + 12 + 14 + 15 + 20)/5 = 14.6$
c. The dispersion of the population is greater than that of the sample means. The sample means vary from 12.66 to 16.33, whereas the population varies from 12 to 20.

9. **a.** 20, found by ${}_6C_3$
b.

Sample	Cases	Sum	Mean
Ruud, Wu, Sass	3, 6, 3	12	4.00
Ruud, Sass, Flores	3, 3, 3	9	3.00
⋮	⋮	⋮	⋮
Sass, Flores, Schueller	3, 3, 1	7	2.33

c. $\mu_{\bar{X}} = 2.67$, found by $\frac{53.33}{20}$
$\mu = 2.67$, found by $(3 + 6 + 3 + 3 + 0 + 1)/6$.
They are equal.
d.

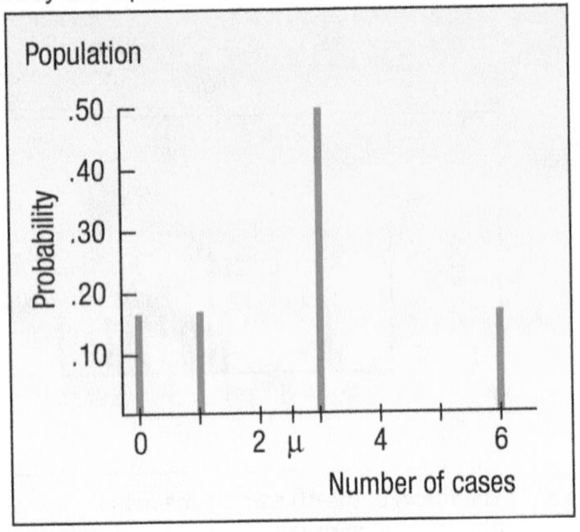

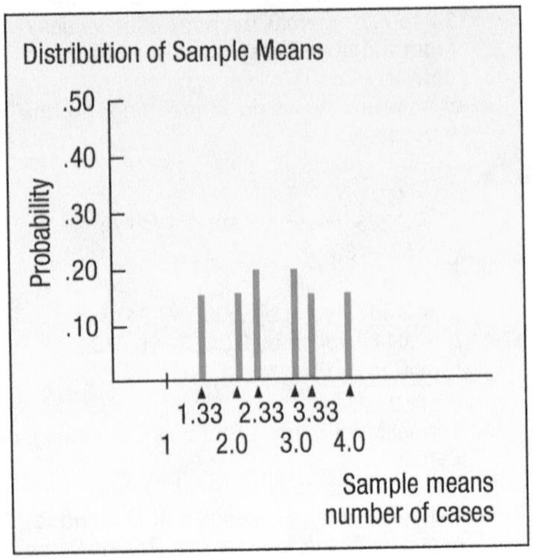

Sample Mean	Number of Means	Probability
1.33	3	.1500
2.00	3	.1500
2.33	4	.2000
3.00	4	.2000
3.33	3	.1500
4.00	3	.1500
	20	1.0000

The population has more dispersion than the sample means. The sample means vary from 1.33 to 4.0. The population varies from 0 to 6.

11. **a.**

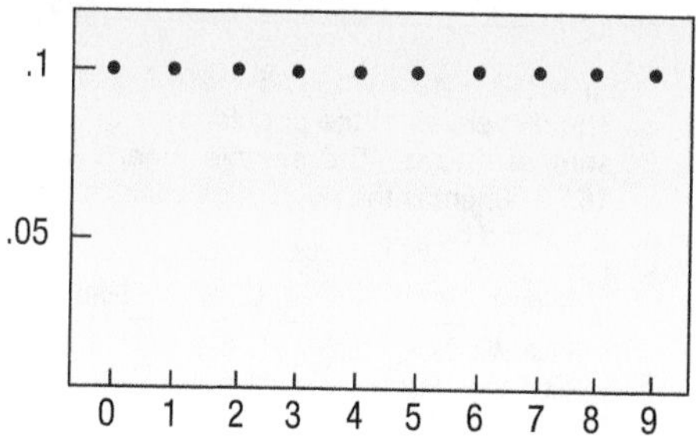

$$\mu = \frac{0 + 1 + \cdots + 9}{10} = 4.5$$

b.

Sample	Sum	$\bar{x}$	Sample	Sum	$\bar{x}$
1	11	2.2	6	20	4.0
2	31	6.2	7	23	4.6
3	21	4.2	8	29	5.8
4	24	4.8	9	35	7.0
5	21	4.2	10	27	5.4

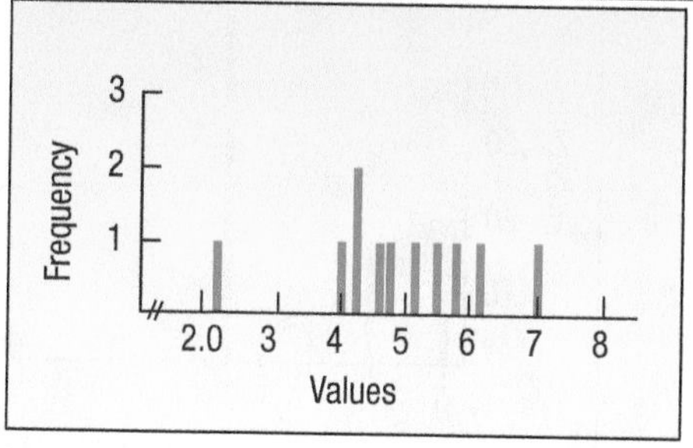

The mean of the 10 sample means is 4.84, which is close to the population mean of 4.5. The sample means range from 2.2 to 7.0, whereas the population values range from 0 to 9. From the above graph, the sample means tend to cluster between 4 and 5.

13. **a.–c.** Answers will vary depending on the coins in your possession.

15. **a.** $z = \dfrac{63 - 60}{12/\sqrt{9}} = 0.75$

$p = .2266$, found by $.5000 - .2734$

b. $z = \dfrac{56 - 60}{12/\sqrt{9}} = -1.00$

$p = .1587$, found by $.5000 - .3413$

c. $p = .6147$, found by $0.3413 + 0.2734$

17. $z = \dfrac{1{,}950 - 2{,}200}{250/\sqrt{50}} = -7.07 \quad p = 1,$ or virtually certain

19. **a.** Formal Man, Summit Stationers, Bootleggers, Leather Ltd., Petries

b. Answers may vary.

c. Elder-Beerman, Frederick's of Hollywood, Summit Stationers, Lion Store, Leather Ltd., Things Remembered, County Seat, Coach House Gifts, Regis Hairstylists

21. **a.**

Samples	Mean	Deviation from Mean	Square of Deviation
1, 1	1.0	−1.0	1.0
1, 2	1.5	−0.5	0.25
1, 3	2.0	0.0	0.0
2, 1	1.5	−0.5	0.25
2, 2	2.0	0.0	0.0
2, 3	2.5	0.5	0.25
3, 1	2.0	0.0	0.0
3, 2	2.5	0.5	0.25
3, 3	3.0	1.0	1.0

b. Mean of sample means is $(1.0 + 1.5 + 2.0 + \cdots + 3.0)/9 = 18/9 = 2.0$. The population mean is $(1 + 2 + 3)/3 = 6/3 = 2$. They are the same value.

c. Variance of sample means is $(1.0 + 0.25 + 0.0 + \cdots + 3.0)/9 = 3/9 = 1/3$. Variance of the population values is $(1 + 0 + 1)/3 = 2/3$. The variance of the population is twice as large as that of the sample means.

d. Sample means follow a triangular shape peaking at 2. The population is uniform between 1 and 3.

23. Larger samples provide narrower estimates of a population mean. So the company with 200 sampled customers can provide more precise estimates. In addition, they are selected consumers who are familiar with laptop computers and may be better able to evaluate the new computer.

25. **a.** We selected 60, 104, 75, 72, and 48. Answers will vary.

b. We selected the third observation. So the sample consists of 75, 72, 68, 82, 48. Answers will vary.

c. Number the first 20 motels from 00 to 19. Randomly select three numbers. Then number the last five numbers 20 to 24. Randomly select two numbers from that group.

27. **a.** 15, found by ${}_6C_2$

b.

Sample	Value	Sum	Mean
1	79, 64	143	71.5
2	79, 84	163	81.5
⋮	⋮	⋮	⋮
15	92, 77	169	84.5
			1,195.0

c. $\mu_{\bar{x}} = 79.67$, found by 1,195/15.
$\mu = 79.67$, found by 478/6.
They are equal.

d. No. The student is not graded on all available information. He/she is as likely to get a lower grade based on the sample as a higher grade.

29. **a.** 10, found by ${}_5C_2$

b.

Number of Shutdowns	Mean	Number of Shutdowns	Mean
4, 3	3.5	3, 3	3.0
4, 5	4.5	3, 2	2.5
4, 3	3.5	5, 3	4.0
4, 2	3.0	5, 2	3.5
3, 5	4.0	3, 2	2.5

Sample Mean	Frequency	Probability
2.5	2	.20
3.0	2	.20
3.5	3	.30
4.0	2	.20
4.5	1	.10
	10	1.00

c. $\mu_{\bar{X}} = (3.5 + 4.5 + \cdots + 2.5)/10 = 3.4$
$\mu = (4 + 3 + 5 + 3 + 2)/5 = 3.4$
The two means are equal.

d. The population values are relatively uniform in shape. The distribution of sample means tends toward normality.

31. a. The distribution will be normal.

b. $\sigma_{\bar{X}} = \frac{5.5}{\sqrt{25}} = 1.1$

c. $z = \frac{36 - 35}{5.5/\sqrt{25}} = 0.91$
$p = 0.1814$, found by $0.5000 - 0.3186$

d. $z = \frac{34.5 - 35}{5.5/\sqrt{25}} = -0.45$
$p = 0.6736$, found by $0.5000 + 0.1736$

e. 0.4922, found by $0.3186 + 0.1736$

33. $z = \frac{\$335 - \$350}{\$45/\sqrt{40}} = -2.11$
$p = 0.9826$, found by $0.5000 + 0.4826$

35. $z = \frac{25.1 - 24.8}{2.5/\sqrt{60}} = 0.93$
$p = 0.8238$, found by $0.5000 + 0.3238$

37. Between 5,954 and 6,046, found by $6{,}000 \pm 1.96\,(150/\sqrt{40})$

39. $z = \frac{900 - 947}{205/\sqrt{60}} = -1.78$
$p = 0.0375$, found by $0.5000 - 0.4625$

41. a. Alaska, Connecticut, Georgia, Kansas, Nebraska, South Carolina, Virginia, Utah

b. Arizona, Florida, Iowa, Massachusetts, Nebraska, North Carolina, Rhode Island, Vermont

43. a. $z = \frac{600 - 510}{14.28/\sqrt{10}} = 19.9$, $P = 0.00$, or virtually never

b. $z = \frac{500 - 510}{14.28/\sqrt{10}} = -2.21$,
$p = 0.4864 + 0.5000 = 0.9864$

c. $z = \frac{500 - 510}{14.28/\sqrt{10}} = -2.21$,
$p = 0.5000 - 0.4864 = 0.0136$

45. a. $\sigma_{\bar{X}} = \frac{2.1}{\sqrt{81}} = 0.23$

b. $z = \frac{7.0 - 6.5}{2.1/\sqrt{81}} = 2.14$, $z = \frac{6.0 - 6.5}{2.1/\sqrt{81}} = -2.14$,
$p = .4838 + .4838 = .9676$

c. $z = \frac{6.75 - 6.5}{2.1/\sqrt{81}} = 1.07$, $z = \frac{6.25 - 6.5}{2.1/\sqrt{81}} = -1.07$,
$p = .3577 + .3577 = .7154$

d. .0162, found by $.5000 - .4838$

47. Mean 2012 attendance is 2.495 million. Likelihood of a sample mean this large or larger is 0.0274, found by $0.5000 - 0.4726$, where $z = \frac{2.495 - 2.25}{\frac{0.70}{\sqrt{30}}} = 1.92$.

CHAPTER 9

1. 51.314 and 58.686, found by $55 \pm 2.58(10/\sqrt{49})$

3. a. 1.581, found by $\sigma_{\bar{x}} = 25/\sqrt{250}$

b. The population is normally distributed and the population variance is known.

c. 16.901 and 23.099, found by 20 ± 3.099

5. a. \$20. It is our best estimate of the population mean.

b. \$18.60 and \$21.40, found by $\$20 \pm 1.96(\$5/\sqrt{49})$. About 95% of the intervals similarly constructed will include the population mean.

7. a. 8.60 gallons

b. 7.83 and 9.37, found by $8.60 \pm 2.58(2.30/\sqrt{60})$

c. If 100 such intervals were determined, the population mean would be included in about 99 intervals.

9. a. 2.201

b. 1.729

c. 3.499

11. a. The population mean is unknown, but the best estimate is 20, the sample mean.

b. Use the t distribution since the standard deviation is unknown. However, assume the population is normally distributed.

c. 2.093

d. Between 19.06 and 20.94, found by $20 \pm 2.093(2/\sqrt{20})$

e. Neither value is reasonable because they are not inside the interval.

13. Between 95.39 and 101.81, found by $98.6 \pm 1.833(5.54/\sqrt{10})$

15. a. 0.8, found by 80/100

b. Between 0.72 and 0.88, found by
$0.8 \pm 1.96\left(\sqrt{\frac{0.8(1 - 0.8)}{100}}\right)$

c. We are reasonably sure the population proportion is between 72 and 88%.

17. a. 0.625, found by 250/400

b. Between 0.563 and 0.687, found by
$0.625 \pm 2.58\left(\sqrt{\frac{0.625(1 - 0.625)}{400}}\right)$

c. We are reasonably sure the population proportion is between 56 and 69%.

19. 97, found by $n = \left(\frac{1.96 \times 10}{2}\right)^2 = 96.04$

21. 196, found by $n = 0.15(0.85)\left(\frac{1.96}{0.05}\right)^2 = 195.9216$

23. 554, found by $n = \left(\frac{1.96 \times 3}{0.25}\right)^2 = 553.19$

25. a. 577, found by $n = 0.60(0.40)\left(\frac{1.96}{0.04}\right)^2 = 576.24$

b. 601, found by $n = 0.50(0.50)\left(\frac{1.96}{0.04}\right)^2 = 600.25$

27. 33.41 and 36.59, found by
$35 \pm 2.030\left(\frac{5}{\sqrt{36}}\right)\sqrt{\frac{300 - 36}{300 - 1}}$

29. 1.683 and 2.037, found by
$1.86 \pm 2.680\left(\frac{0.5}{\sqrt{50}}\right)\sqrt{\frac{400 - 50}{400 - 1}}$

31. 6.13 years to 6.87 years, found by $6.5 \pm 1.989(1.7/\sqrt{85})$

33. a. Between \$313.41 and \$332.59, found by
$323 \pm 2.426\left(\frac{25}{\sqrt{40}}\right)$.

b. \$350 is not reasonable because it is outside of the confidence interval.

35. a. The population mean is unknown.

b. Between 7.50 and 9.14, found by $8.32 \pm 1.685(3.07/\sqrt{40})$

c. 10 is not reasonable because it is outside the confidence interval.

37. a. 65.49 up to 71.71 hours, found by
$68.6 \pm 2.680(8.2/\sqrt{50})$

b. The value suggested by the NCAA is included in the confidence interval. Therefore, it is reasonable.

c. Changing the confidence interval to 95 would reduce the width of the interval. The value of 2.680 would change to 2.010.

39. 61.47, rounded to 62. Found by solving for n in the equation:
$1.96(16/\sqrt{n}) = 4$

41. Between \$13,734 up to \$15,028, found by $14{,}381 \pm 1.711(1{,}892/\sqrt{25})$. 15,000 is reasonable because it is inside the confidence interval.

43. a. \$62.583, found by \$751/12

b. Between \$60.54 and \$64.63, found by
$62.583 \pm 1.796(3.94/\sqrt{12})$

c. \$60 is not reasonable because it is outside the confidence interval.

45. a. 89.4667, found by 1,342/15
b. Between 84.99 and 93.94, found by $89.4667 \pm 2.145(8.08/\sqrt{15})$
c. Yes, because even the lower limit of the confidence interval is above 80.

47. The confidence interval is between 0.011 and 0.059, found by $0.035 \pm 2.576\left(\sqrt{\frac{0.035(1-0.035)}{400}}\right)$. It would not be reasonable to conclude that fewer than 5% of the employees are now failing the test because 0.05 is inside the confidence interval.

49. Between 0.648 and 0.752, found by $0.70 \pm 2.576\left(\sqrt{\frac{0.70(1-0.70)}{500}}\right)\left(\sqrt{\frac{20{,}000-500}{20{,}000-1}}\right)$.
Yes, because even the lower limit of the confidence interval is above 0.500.

51. \$52.51 and \$55.49, found by $\$54.00 \pm 2.032\frac{\$4.50}{\sqrt{35}}\sqrt{\frac{(500-35)}{500-1}}$

53. 369, found by $n = 0.60(1-0.60)(1.96/0.05)^2$

55. 97, found by $[(1.96 \times 500)/100]^2$

57. a. Between 7,849 and 8,151, found by $8{,}000 \pm 2.756(300/\sqrt{30})$
b. 554, found by $n = \left(\frac{(1.96)(300)}{25}\right)^2$

59. a. Between 75.44 and 80.56, found by $78 \pm 2.010(9/\sqrt{50})$
b. 220, found by $n = \left(\frac{(1.645)(9)}{1.0}\right)^2$

61. a. 30, found by $180/\sqrt{36}$
b. \$355.10 and \$476.90, found by $\$416 \pm 2.030\left(\frac{\$180}{\sqrt{36}}\right)$
c. About 1,245, found by $\left(\frac{1.96(180)}{10}\right)^2$

63. a. 708.13, rounded up to 709, found by $0.21(1-0.21)(1.96/0.03)^2$
b. 1,068, found by $0.50(0.50)(1.96/0.03)^2$

65. a. Between 0.156 and 0.184, found by $0.17 \pm 1.96\sqrt{\frac{(0.17)(1-0.17)}{2700}}$
b. Yes, because 18% are inside the confidence interval.
c. 21,682; found by $0.17(1-0.17)[1.96/0.005]^2$

67. Between 12.69 and 14.11, found by $13.4 \pm 1.96(6.8/\sqrt{352})$

69. a. For selling price: 211.99 up to 230.22, found by $221.1 \pm (1.983)(47.11/\sqrt{105}) = 221.1 \pm 9.12$
b. For distance: 13.685 up to 15.572, found by $14.629 \pm (1.983)(4.874/\sqrt{105}) = 14.629 \pm 0.943$
c. For garage: 0.5867 up to 0.7657, found by $0.6762 \pm (1.96)\sqrt{\frac{0.6762(1-0.6762)}{105}} = 0.6762 \pm 0.0895$
d. Answers may vary.

71. a. Between \$438.34 and \$462.24, found by $450.29 \pm 1.99\left(\frac{53.69}{\sqrt{80}}\right)$
b. Between 820.72 and 839.50, found by $830.11 \pm 1.99\left(\frac{42.19}{\sqrt{80}}\right)$
c. Answers will vary.

CHAPTER 10

1. a. Two-tailed
b. Reject H_0 when z does not fall in the region between -1.96 and 1.96.
c. -1.2, found by $z = (49-50)/(5/\sqrt{36}) = -1.2$
d. Fail to reject H_0.
e. $p = .2302$, found by 2(.5000 − .3849). A 23.02% chance of finding a z value this large when H_0 is true.

3. a. One-tailed
b. Reject H_0 when $z > 1.65$.
c. 1.2, found by $z = (21-20)/(5/\sqrt{36})$
d. Fail to reject H_0 at the .05 significance level
e. $p = .1151$, found by .5000 − .3849. An 11.51% chance of finding a z value this large or larger.

5. a. H_0: $\mu = 60{,}000$ H_1: $\mu \neq 60{,}000$
b. Reject H_0 if $z < -1.96$ or $z > 1.96$.
c. -0.69, found by:

$$z = \frac{59{,}500 - 60{,}000}{(5{,}000/\sqrt{48})}$$

d. Do not reject H_0.
e. $p = .4902$, found by 2(.5000 − .2549). Crosset's experience is not different from that claimed by the manufacturer. If H_0 is true, the probability of finding a value more extreme than this is .4902.

7. a. H_0: $\mu \geq 6.8$ H_1: $\mu < 6.8$
b. Reject H_0 if $z < -1.65$
c. $z = \frac{6.2 - 6.8}{1.8/\sqrt{36}} = -2.0$
d. H_0 is rejected.
e. $p = 0.0228$. The mean number of DVDs watched is less than 6.8 per month. If H_0 is true, you will get a statistic this small less than one time out of 40 tests.

9. a. Reject H_0 when $t > 1.833$.
b. $t = \frac{12-10}{(3/\sqrt{10})} = 2.108$
c. Reject H_0. The mean is greater than 10.

11. H_0: $\mu \leq 40$ H_1: $\mu > 40$
Reject H_0 if $t > 1.703$.

$$t = \frac{42-40}{(2.1/\sqrt{28})} = 5.040$$

Reject H_0 and conclude that the mean number of calls is greater than 40 per week.

13. H_0: $\mu \leq 40{,}000$ H_1: $\mu > 40{,}000$
Reject H_0 if $t > 1.833$.

$$t = \frac{50{,}000 - 40{,}000}{10{,}000/\sqrt{10}} = 3.16$$

Reject H_0 and conclude that the mean income in Wilmington is greater than \$40,000.

15. a. Reject H_0 if $t < -3.747$.
b. $\bar{x} = 17$ and $s = \sqrt{\frac{50}{5-1}} = 3.536$

$$t = \frac{17-20}{(3.536/\sqrt{5})} = -1.90$$

c. Do not reject H_0. We cannot conclude the population mean is less than 20.
d. Between .05 and .10, about .065

17. H_0: $\mu \leq 1.4$ H_1: $\mu > 1.4$
Reject H_0 if $t > 2.821$.

$$t = \frac{1.6 - 1.4}{0.216/\sqrt{10}} = 2.93$$

Reject H_0 and conclude that water consumption has increased. The p-value is between 0.01 and 0.005. There is a slight probability (between one chance in 100 and one chance in 200) this rise could have arisen by chance.

19. H_0: $\mu \leq 50$ H_1: $\mu > 50$
Reject H_0 if $t > 1.796$.

$$t = \frac{82.5 - 50}{59.5/\sqrt{12}} = 1.89$$

Reject H_0 and conclude that the mean number of text messages is greater than 50. The p-value is less than 0.05. There is a slight probability (less than one chance in 20) this could happen by chance.

21. 1.05, found by $z = (9{,}992 - 9{,}880)/(400/\sqrt{100})$. Then $0.5000 - 0.3531 = 0.1469$, which is the probability of a Type II error.

23. $H_0: \mu = \$45{,}000$ $\quad H_1: \mu \neq \$45{,}000$
Reject H_0 if $z < -1.65$ or $z > 1.65$.

$$z = \frac{45{,}500 - 45{,}000}{\$3{,}000/\sqrt{120}} = 1.83$$

Reject H_0. We can conclude that the mean salary is not \$45,000. p-value 0.0672, found by $2(0.5000 - 0.4664)$.

25. $H_0: \mu \geq 10$ $\quad H_1: \mu < 10$
Reject H_0 if $z < -1.65$.

$$z = \frac{9.0 - 10.0}{2.8/\sqrt{50}} = -2.53$$

Reject H_0. The mean weight loss is less than 10 pounds. p-value $= 0.5000 - 0.4943 = 0.0057$

27. $H_0: \mu \geq 7.0$ $\quad H_1: \mu < 7.0$
Assuming a 5% significance level, reject H_0 if $t < -1.677$.

$$t = \frac{6.8 - 7.0}{0.9/\sqrt{50}} = -1.57$$

Do not reject H_0. West Virginia students are not sleeping less than 6 hours. p-value is between .05 and .10.

29. $H_0: \mu \geq 3.13$ $\quad H_1: \mu < 3.13$
Reject H_0 if $t < -1.711$

$$t = \frac{2.86 - 3.13}{1.20/\sqrt{25}} = -1.13$$

We fail to reject H_0 and conclude that the mean number of residents is not necessarily less than 3.13.

31. $H_0: \mu \leq 14$ $\quad H_1: \mu > 14$
Reject H_0 if $t > 2.821$.
$\bar{x} = 15.66$ $\quad s = 1.544$

$$t = \frac{15.66 - 14.00}{1.544/\sqrt{10}} = 3.400$$

Reject H_0. The average rate is greater than 14%.

33. $H_0: \mu = 3.1$ $\quad H_1: \mu \neq 3.1$ Assume a normal population.
Reject H_0 if $t < -2.201$ or $t > 2.201$.

$$\bar{x} = \frac{41.1}{12} = 3.425$$

$$s = \sqrt{\frac{4.0625}{12 - 1}} = .6077$$

$$t = \frac{3.425 - 3.1}{.6077/\sqrt{12}} = 1.853$$

Do not reject H_0. Cannot show a difference between senior citizens and the national average. p-value is about 0.09.

35. $H_0: \mu \geq 6.5$ $\quad H_1: \mu < 6.5$ Assume a normal population.
Reject H_0 if $t < -2.718$.
$\bar{x} = 5.1667$ $\quad s = 3.1575$

$$t = \frac{5.1667 - 6.5}{3.1575/\sqrt{12}} = -1.463$$

Do not reject H_0. The p-value is greater than 0.05.

37. $H_0: \mu = 0$ $\quad H_1: \mu \neq 0$
Reject H_0 if $t < -2.110$ or $t > 2.110$.
$\bar{x} = -0.2322$ $\quad s = 0.3120$

$$t = \frac{-0.2322 - 0}{0.3120/\sqrt{18}} = -3.158$$

Reject H_0. The mean gain or loss does not equal 0. The p-value is less than 0.01, but greater than 0.001.

39. $H_0: \mu \leq 100$ $\quad H_1: \mu > 100$ Assume a normal population.
Reject H_0 if $t > 1.761$.

$$\bar{x} = \frac{1{,}641}{15} = 109.4$$

$$s = \sqrt{\frac{1{,}389.6}{15 - 1}} = 9.9628$$

$$t = \frac{109.4 - 100}{9.9628/\sqrt{15}} = 3.654$$

Reject H_0. The mean number with the scanner is greater than 100. p-value is 0.001.

41. $H_0: \mu = 1.5$ $\quad H_1: \mu \neq 1.5$
Reject H_0 if $t > 3.250$ or $t < -3.250$.

$$t = \frac{1.3 - 1.5}{0.9/\sqrt{10}} = -0.703$$

Fail to reject H_0.

43. $H_0: \mu \geq 10$ $\quad H_1: \mu < 10$
Reject H_0 if $t < -1.895$.

$$\bar{x} = \frac{78.3}{8} = 9.7875 \qquad s = \sqrt{\frac{5.889}{8 - 1}} = 0.9172$$

$$t = \frac{9.7875 - 10}{0.9172/\sqrt{8}} = -0.655$$ Do not reject H_0. The cost is not less than \$10,000.

45. **a.** $9.00 \pm 1.645(1/\sqrt{36}) = 9.00 \pm 0.274$.
So the limits are 8.726 and 9.274.

b. $z = \dfrac{8.726 - 8.6}{1/\sqrt{36}} = 0.756$.
$P(z < 0.756) = 0.5000 + 0.2764 = .7764$

c. $z = \dfrac{9.274 - 9.6}{1/\sqrt{36}} = -1.956$.
$P(z > -1.96) = 0.4750 + 0.5000 = .9750$

47. $50 + 2.33\dfrac{10}{\sqrt{n}} = 55 - .525\dfrac{10}{\sqrt{n}}$ $\quad n = (5.71)^2 = 32.6$
Let $n = 33$

49. $H_0: \mu \geq 8$ $\quad H_1: \mu < 8$
Reject H_0 if $t < -1.714$.

$$t = \frac{7.5 - 8}{3.2/\sqrt{24}} = -0.77$$

Do not reject the null hypothesis. The time is not less.

51. **a.** $H_0: \mu = 80$ $\quad H_1: \mu \neq 80$
Reject H_0 if t is not between -2.045 and 2.045.

$$t = \frac{98.02 - 80}{36.83/\sqrt{30}} = 2.68$$ Reject the null.

The mean salary is probably not \$80.0 million.

b. $H_0: \mu \leq 2{,}000{,}000$ $\quad H_1: \mu > 2{,}000{,}000$
Reject H_0 if $t > 1.699$.

$$t = \frac{2{,}495{,}000 - 2{,}000{,}000}{642{,}000/\sqrt{30}} = 4.22$$

Reject the null. The mean attendance was more than 2,000,000.

CHAPTER 11

1. **a.** Two-tailed test
b. Reject H_0 if $z < -2.05$ or $z > 2.05$
c. $z = \dfrac{102 - 99}{\sqrt{\dfrac{5^2}{40} + \dfrac{6^2}{50}}} = 2.59$
d. Reject H_0
e. p-value $= .0096$, found by $2(.5000 - .4952)$

3. **Step 1** $H_0: \mu_1 \geq \mu_2$ $\quad H_1: \mu_1 < \mu_2$
Step 2 The .05 significance level was chosen.
Step 3 Reject H_0 if $z < -1.65$.
Step 4 -0.94, found by:

$$z = \frac{7.6 - 8.1}{\sqrt{\dfrac{(2.3)^2}{40} + \dfrac{(2.9)^2}{55}}} = -0.94$$

Step 5 Fail to reject H_0.
Step 6 Babies using the Gibbs brand did not gain less weight.
p-value = .1736, found by .5000 − .3264.

5. **Step 1** $H_0: \mu_1 \leq \mu_2$ $\quad H_1: \mu_1 > \mu_2$
Step 2 The .05 significance level was chosen.
Step 3 If $z > 1.645$, reject H_0.
Step 4
$$z = \frac{61.4 - 60.6}{\sqrt{\frac{(1.2)^2}{45} + \frac{(1.1)^2}{39}}} = 3.187$$
Step 5 Reject the null.
Step 6 It is reasonable to conclude that those who had a Caesarean section are shorter.
The p-value is virtually zero. That much of a difference could almost never be due to sampling error.

7. **a.** Reject H_0 if $t > 2.120$ or $t < -2.120$. $df = 10 + 8 - 2 = 16$
b. $$s_p^2 = \frac{(10-1)(4)^2 + (8-1)(5)^2}{10 + 8 - 2} = 19.9375$$
c. $$t = \frac{23 - 26}{\sqrt{19.9375\left(\frac{1}{10} + \frac{1}{8}\right)}} = -1.416$$
d. Do not reject H_0.
e. p-value is greater than .10 and less than .20.

9. **Step 1** $H_0: \mu_1 = \mu_2$ $\quad H_1: \mu_1 \neq \mu_2$
Step 2 The .01 significance level was chosen.
Step 3 $df = 12 + 13 - 2 = 23$. Reject H_0 if t is not between −2.807 and 2.807.
Step 4 $$s_p^2 = \frac{(12-1)(7{,}469)^2 + (13-1)(7{,}474)^2}{12 + 13 - 2} = 55{,}825{,}000$$
$$t = \frac{6{,}590 - 5{,}308}{\sqrt{55{,}825{,}000\left(\frac{1}{12} + \frac{1}{13}\right)}} = 0.429$$
Step 5 Do not reject H_0.
Step 6 There is no difference in the mean salaries.

11. **Step 1** $H_0: \mu_s \leq \mu_a$ $\quad H_1: \mu_s > \mu_a$
Step 2 The .10 significance level was chosen.
Step 3 $df = 6 + 7 - 2 = 11$
Reject H_0 if $t > 1.363$.
Step 4 $$s_p^2 = \frac{(6-1)(12.2)^2 + (7-1)(15.8)^2}{6 + 7 - 2} = 203.82$$
$$t = \frac{142.5 - 130.3}{\sqrt{203.82\left(\frac{1}{6} + \frac{1}{7}\right)}} = 1.536$$
Step 5 Reject H_0.
Step 6 The mean daily expenses are greater for the sales staff.
The p-value is between .05 and .10.

13. **a.** $$df = \frac{\left(\frac{25}{15} + \frac{225}{12}\right)^2}{\frac{\left(\frac{25}{15}\right)^2}{15-1} + \frac{\left(\frac{225}{12}\right)^2}{12-1}} = \frac{416.84}{0.1984 + 31.9602}$$
$= 12.96 \rightarrow 12df$
b. $H_0: \mu_1 = \mu_2$ $\quad H_1: \mu_1 \neq \mu_2$
Reject H_0 if $t > 2.179$ or $t < -2.179$.
c. $$t = \frac{50 - 46}{\sqrt{\frac{25}{15} + \frac{225}{12}}} = 0.8852$$
d. Fail to reject the null hypothesis.

15. **a.** $$df = \frac{\left(\frac{697{,}225}{16} + \frac{2{,}387{,}025}{18}\right)^2}{\frac{\left(\frac{697{,}225}{16}\right)^2}{16-1} + \frac{\left(\frac{2{,}387{,}025}{18}\right)^2}{18-1}} = 26.7 \rightarrow 26df$$
b. $H_0: \mu_{Private} \leq \mu_{Public}$ $\quad H_1: \mu_{Private} > \mu_{Public}$
Reject H_0 if $t > 1.706$.
c. $$t = \frac{12{,}840 - 11{,}045}{\sqrt{\frac{2{,}387{,}025}{18} + \frac{697{,}225}{16}}} = 4.276$$
d. Reject the null hypothesis. The mean adoption cost from a private agency is greater than the mean adoption cost from a public agency.

17. **a.** Reject H_0 if $t > 2.353$.
b. $\bar{d} = \frac{12}{4} = 3.00$ $\quad s_d = \sqrt{\frac{2}{3}} = 0.816$
c. $$t = \frac{3.00}{0.816/\sqrt{4}} = 7.35$$
d. Reject H_0. There are more defective parts produced on the day shift.
e. p-value is less than .005 but greater than .0005.

19. $H_0: \mu_d \leq 0$ $\quad H_1: \mu_d > 0$
$\bar{d} = 25.917$
$s_d = 40.791$
Reject H_0 if $t > 1.796$
$$t = \frac{25.917}{40.791/\sqrt{12}} = 2.20$$
Reject H_0. The incentive plan resulted in an increase in daily income. The p-value is about .025.

21. $H_0: \mu_M = \mu_W$ $\quad H_1: \mu_M \neq \mu_W$
Reject H_0 if $t < -2.645$ or $t > 2.645$ ($df = 35 + 40 - 2$).
$$s_p^2 = \frac{(35-1)(4.48)^2 + (40-1)(3.86)^2}{35 + 40 - 2} = 17.3079$$
$$t = \frac{24.51 - 22.69}{\sqrt{17.3079\left(\frac{1}{35} + \frac{1}{40}\right)}} = 1.890$$
Do not reject H_0. There is no difference in the number of times men and women buy take-out dinner in a month. The p-value is between .05 and .10.

23. $H_0: \mu_1 = \mu_2$ $\quad H_1: \mu_1 \neq \mu_2$
Reject H_0 if $z < -1.96$ or $z > 1.96$.
$$z = \frac{4.77 - 5.02}{\sqrt{\frac{(1.05)^2}{40} + \frac{(1.23)^2}{50}}} = -1.04$$
H_0 is not rejected. There is no difference in the mean number of calls. p-value = 2(.5000 − .3508) = .2984.

25. $H_0: \mu_B \leq \mu_A$ $\quad H_1: \mu_B > \mu_A$
Reject H_0 if $t > 1.668$
$$t = \frac{\$61{,}000 - \$57{,}000}{\sqrt{\frac{(\$7{,}100)^2}{30} + \frac{(\$9{,}200)^2}{40}}} = \frac{\$4{,}000.00}{\$1{,}948.42} = 2.05$$
Reject H_0. The mean income is larger for Plan B. The p-value = .5000 − .4798 = .0202.

27. **a.** $$df = \frac{\left(\frac{0.3136}{12} + \frac{0.0900}{12}\right)^2}{\frac{\left(\frac{0.3136}{12}\right)^2}{12-1} + \frac{\left(\frac{0.0900}{12}\right)^2}{12-1}}$$
$$= \frac{0.0011}{0.000062 + 0.0000051} = 16.37 \rightarrow 16df$$
b. $H_0: \mu_a = \mu_w$ $\quad H_1: \mu_a \neq \mu_w$
Reject H_0 if $t > 2.120$ or $t < -2.120$.
c. $$t = \frac{1.65 - 2.20}{\sqrt{\frac{0.3136}{12} + \frac{0.0900}{12}}} = -3.00$$
d. Reject the null hypothesis. There is a difference.

29. Assume equal population standard deviations.
$H_0: \mu_n = \mu_s \quad H_1: \mu_n \neq \mu_s$
Reject H_0 if $t < -2.086$ or $t > 2.086$.

$$s_p^2 = \frac{(10-1)(10.5)^2 + (12-1)(14.25)^2}{10+12-2} = 161.2969$$

$$t = \frac{83.55 - 78.8}{\sqrt{161.2969\left(\frac{1}{10}+\frac{1}{12}\right)}} = 0.874$$

p-value $> .10$. Do not reject H_0. There is no difference in the mean number of hamburgers sold at the two locations.

31. Assume equal population standard deviations.
$H_0: \mu_1 = \mu_2 \quad H_1: \mu_1 \neq \mu_2$
Reject H_0 if $t > 2.819$ or $t < -2.819$.

$$s_p^2 = \frac{(10-1)(2.33)^2 + (14-1)(2.55)^2}{10+14-2} = 6.06$$

$$t = \frac{15.87 - 18.29}{\sqrt{6.06\left(\frac{1}{10}+\frac{1}{14}\right)}} = -2.374$$

Do not reject H_0. There is no difference in the mean amount purchased.

33. Assume equal population standard deviations.
$H_0: \mu_1 \leq \mu_2 \quad H_1: \mu_1 > \mu_2 \quad$ Reject H_0 if $t > 2.567$.

$$s_p^2 = \frac{(8-1)(2.2638)^2 + (11-1)(2.4606)^2}{8+11-2} = 5.672$$

$$t = \frac{10.375 - 5.636}{\sqrt{5.672\left(\frac{1}{8}+\frac{1}{11}\right)}} = 4.28$$

Reject H_0. The mean number of transactions by the young adults is more than for the senior citizens.

35. $H_0: \mu_1 \leq \mu_2 \quad H_1: \mu_1 > \mu_2 \quad$ Reject H_0 if $t > 2.650$.
$\bar{X}_1 = 125.125 \quad s_1 = 15.094$
$\bar{X}_2 = 117.714 \quad s_2 = 19.914$

$$s_p^2 = \frac{(8-1)(15.094)^2 + (7-1)(19.914)^2}{8+7-2} = 305.708$$

$$t = \frac{125.125 - 117.714}{\sqrt{305.708\left(\frac{1}{8}+\frac{1}{7}\right)}} = 0.819$$

H_0 is not rejected. There is no difference in the mean number sold at the regular price and the mean number sold at the reduced price.

37. $H_0: \mu_d \leq 0 \quad H_1: \mu_d > 0 \quad$ Reject H_0 if $t > 1.895$.
$\bar{d} = 1.75 \quad s_d = 2.9155$

$$t = \frac{1.75}{2.9155/\sqrt{8}} = 1.698$$

Do not reject H_0. There is no difference in the mean number of absences. The p-value is greater than .05 but less than .10.

39. $H_0: \mu_1 = \mu_2 \quad H_1: \mu_1 \neq \mu_2$
Reject H_0 if $t < -2.024$ or $t > 2.204$.

$$s_p^2 = \frac{(15-1)(40)^2 + (25-1)(30)^2}{15+25-2} = 1{,}157.89$$

$$t = \frac{150 - 180}{\sqrt{1{,}157.89\left(\frac{1}{15}+\frac{1}{25}\right)}} = -2.699$$

Reject the null hypothesis. The population means are different.

41. $H_0: \mu_d \leq 0 \quad H_1: \mu_d > 0$
Reject H_0 if $t > 1.895$.
$\bar{d} = 3.11 \quad s_d = 2.91$

$$t = \frac{3.11}{2.91/\sqrt{8}} = 3.02$$

Reject H_0. The mean is lower.

43. $H_0: \mu_O = \mu_R, \quad H_1: \mu_O \neq \mu_R$
$df = 25 + 28 - 2 = 51$
Reject H_0 if $t < -2.008$ or $t > 2.008$.
$\bar{X}_O = 86.24,\ s_O = 23.43$
$X_R = 92.04,\ s_R = 24.12$

$$s_p^2 = \frac{(25-1)(23.43)^2 + (28-1)(24.12)^2}{25+28-2} = 566.335$$

$$t = \frac{86.24 - 92.04}{\sqrt{566.335\left(\frac{1}{25}+\frac{1}{28}\right)}} = -0.886$$

Do not reject H_0. There is no difference in the mean number of cars in the two lots.

45. $H_0: \mu_d \leq 0 \quad H_1: \mu_d > 0 \quad$ Reject H_0 if $t > 1.711$.
$\bar{d} = 2.8 \quad s_d = 6.59$

$$t = \frac{2.8}{6.59/\sqrt{25}} = 2.124$$

Reject H_0. There are on average more cars in the US 17 lot.

47. **a.** μ_1 = without pool $\quad \mu_2$ = with pool
$H_0: \mu_1 = \mu_2 \quad H_1: \mu_1 \neq \mu_2$
Reject H_0 if $t > 2.000$ or $t < -2.000$.
$\bar{X}_1 = 202.8 \quad s_1 = 33.7 \quad n_1 = 38$
$\bar{X}_2 = 231.5 \quad s_2 = 50.46 \quad n_2 = 67$

$$s_p^2 = \frac{(38-1)(33.7)^2 + (67-1)(50.46)^2}{38+67-2} = 2{,}041.05$$

$$t = \frac{202.8 - 231.5}{\sqrt{2{,}041.05\left(\frac{1}{38}+\frac{1}{67}\right)}} = -3.12$$

Reject H_0. There is a difference in mean selling price for homes with and without a pool.

b. μ_1 = without attached garage $\quad \mu_2$ = with garage
$H_0: \mu_1 = \mu_2 \quad H_1: \mu_1 \neq \mu_2$
Reject H_0 if $t > 2.000$ or $t < -2.000$.
$\alpha = 0.05 \quad df = 34 + 71 - 2 = 103$
$\bar{X}_1 = 185.45 \quad s_1 = 28.00$
$\bar{X}_2 = 238.18 \quad s_2 = 44.88$

$$s_p^2 = \frac{(34-1)(28.00)^2 + (71-1)(44.88)^2}{103} = 1{,}620.07$$

$$t = \frac{185.45 - 238.18}{\sqrt{1{,}620.07\left(\frac{1}{34}+\frac{1}{71}\right)}} = -6.28$$

Reject H_0. There is a difference in mean selling price for homes with and without an attached garage.

c. $H_0: \mu_1 = \mu_2 \quad H_1: \mu_1 \neq \mu_2$
Reject H_0 if $t > 2.036$ or $t < -2.036$.
$\bar{X}_1 = 196.91 \quad s_1 = 35.78 \quad n_1 = 15$
$\bar{X}_2 = 227.45 \quad s_2 = 44.19 \quad n_2 = 20$

$$s_p^2 = \frac{(15-1)(35.78)^2 + (20-1)(44.19)^2}{15+20-2} = 1{,}667.43$$

$$t = \frac{196.91 - 227.45}{\sqrt{1{,}667.43\left(\frac{1}{15}+\frac{1}{20}\right)}} = -2.19$$

Reject H_0. There is a difference in mean selling price for homes in Township 1 and Township 2.

49. $H_0: \mu_1 = \mu_2 \quad H_1: \mu_1 \neq \mu_2$
If t is not between -1.991 and 1.991, reject H_0.

$$s_p^2 = \frac{(53-1)(52.9)^2 + (27-1)(55.1)^2}{53+27-2} = 2{,}878$$

$$t = \frac{454.8 - 441.5}{\sqrt{2{,}878\left(\frac{1}{53}+\frac{1}{27}\right)}} = 1.05$$

Do not reject H_0. There may be no difference in the mean maintenance cost for the two types of buses.

CHAPTER 12

1. 9.01, from Appendix B.6
3. Reject H_0 if $F > 10.5$, where degrees of freedom in the numerator are 7 and 5 in the denominator. Computed $F = 2.04$, found by:

$$F = \frac{s_1^2}{s_2^2} = \frac{(10)^2}{(7)^2} = 2.04$$

Do not reject H_0. There is no difference in the variations of the two populations.

5. H_0: $\sigma_1^2 = \sigma_2^2$ $\quad H_1$: $\sigma_1^2 \neq \sigma_2^2$
Reject H_0 where $F > 3.10$. (3.10 is about halfway between 3.14 and 3.07.) Computed $F = 1.44$, found by:

$$F = \frac{(12)^2}{(10)^2} = 1.44$$

Do not reject H_0. There is no difference in the variations of the two populations.

7. **a.** H_0: $\mu_1 = \mu_2 = \mu_3$; H_1: Treatment means are not all the same.
b. Reject H_0 if $F > 4.26$.
c & d.

Source	SS	df	MS	F
Treatment	62.17	2	31.08	21.94
Error	12.75	9	1.42	
Total	74.92	11		

e. Reject H_0. The treatment means are not all the same.

9. H_0: $\mu_1 = \mu_2 = \mu_3$; H_1: Treatment means are not all the same. Reject H_0 if $F > 4.26$.

Source	SS	df	MS	F
Treatment	276.50	2	138.25	14.18
Error	87.75	9	9.75	

Reject H_0. The treatment means are not all the same.

11. **a.** H_0: $\mu_1 = \mu_2 = \mu_3$; H_1: Not all means are the same.
b. Reject H_0 if $F > 4.26$.
c. SST = 107.20, SSE = 9.47, SS total = 116.67
d.

Source	SS	df	MS	F
Treatment	107.20	2	53.600	50.96
Error	9.47	9	1.052	
Total	116.67	11		

e. Since 50.96 > 4.26, H_0 is rejected. At least one of the means differs.
f. $(\bar{x}_1 - \bar{x}_2) \pm t\sqrt{MSE(1/n_1 + 1/n_2)}$
$= (9.667 - 2.20) \pm 2.262\sqrt{1.052(1/3 + 1/5)}$
$= 7.467 \pm 1.69$
$= [5.777, 9.157]$
Yes, we can conclude that treatments 1 and 2 have different means.

13. H_0: $\mu_1 = \mu_2 = \mu_3 = \mu_4$; H_1: Not all means are equal. H_0 is rejected if $F > 3.71$.

Source	SS	df	MS	F
Treatment	32.33	3	10.77	2.36
Error	45.67	10	4.567	
Total	78.00	13		

Because 2.36 is less than 3.71, H_0 is not rejected. There is no difference in the mean number of weeks.

15. **a.** H_0: $\mu_1 = \mu_2$; H_1: Not all treatment means are equal.
b. Reject H_0 if $F > 18.5$.
c. H_0: $\mu_1 = \mu_2 = \mu_3$; H_1: Not all block means are equal. H_0 is rejected if $F > 19.0$.
d. SS total $= (46.0 - 36.5)^2 + \cdots + (35 - 36.5)^2 = 289.5$
SST $= 3(42.33 - 36.5)^2 + 3(30.67 - 36.5)^2$
$= 204.167$
SSB $= 2(38.5 - 36.5)^2 + 2(31.5 - 36.5)^2 + 2(39.5 - 36.5)^2 = 8 + 50 + 18 = 76$
SSE $= 289.50 - 204.1667 - 76 = 9.3333$
e.

Source	SS	df	MS	F
Treatment	204.167	1	204.167	43.75
Blocks	76.000	2	38.000	8.14
Error	9.333	2	4.667	
Total	289.5000	5		

f. 43.75 > 18.5, so reject H_0. There is a difference in the treatments. 8.14 < 19.0, so do not reject H_0 for blocks. There is no difference among blocks.

17. For treatment:
H_0: $\mu_1 = \mu_2 = \mu_3$
H_1: Not all means equal
Reject if $F > 4.46$.

For blocks:
H_0: $\mu_1 = \mu_2 = \mu_3 = \mu_4 = \mu_5$
H_1: Not all means equal
Reject if $F > 3.84$.

Source	SS	df	MS	F
Treatment	62.53	2	31.2650	5.75
Blocks	33.73	4	8.4325	1.55
Error	43.47	8	5.4338	
Total	139.73			

There is a difference in shifts, but not by employee.

19.

Source	SS	df	MS	F	P
Size	156.333	2	78.1667	1.98	0.180
Weight	98.000	1	98.000	2.48	0.141
Interaction	36.333	2	18.1667	0.46	0.642
Error	473.333	12	39.444		
Total	764.000	17			

a. Since the p-value (0.18) is greater than 0.05, there is no difference in the Size means.
b. The p-value for Weight (0.141) is also greater than 0.05. Thus, there is no difference in those means.
c. There is no significant interaction because the p-value (0.642) is greater than 0.05.

21. **a.**

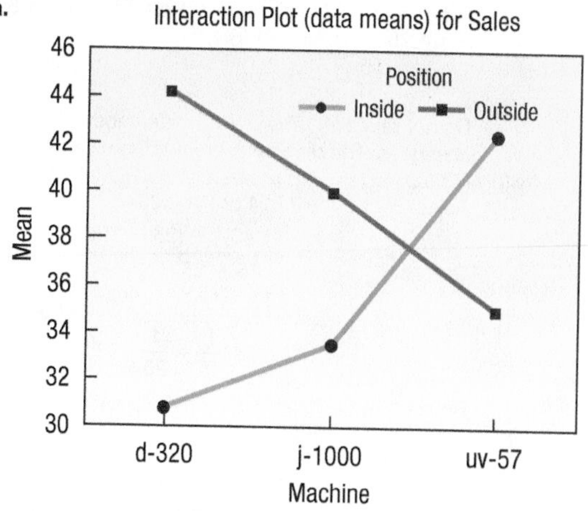

Yes, there appears to be an interaction effect. Sales are different based on machine position, either in the inside or outside position.

b.

Two-way ANOVA: Sales versus Position, Machine

Source	*df*	SS	MS	*F*	P
Position	1	104.167	104.167	9.12	0.007
Machine	2	16.333	8.167	0.72	0.502
Interaction	2	457.333	228.667	20.03	0.000
Error	18	205.500	11.417		
Total	23	783.333			

The position and the interaction of position and machine effects are significant. The effect of machine on sales is not significant.

c.

One-way ANOVA: D-320 Sales versus Position

Source	*df*	SS	MS	*F*	P
Position	1	364.50	364.50	40.88	0.001
Error	6	53.50	8.92		
Total	7	418.00			

One-way ANOVA: J-1000 Sales versus Position

Source	*df*	SS	MS	*F*	P
Position	1	84.5	84.5	5.83	0.052
Error	6	87.0	14.5		
Total	7	171.5			

One-way ANOVA: UV-57 Sales versus Position

Source	*df*	SS	MS	*F*	P
Position	1	112.5	112.5	10.38	0.018
Error	6	65.0	10.8		
Total	7	177.5			

Recommendations using the statistical results and mean sales plotted in part (a): Position the D-320 machine outside. Statistically, the position of the J-1000 does not matter. Position the UV-57 machine inside.

23. H_0: $\sigma_1^2 \leq \sigma_2^2$; H_1: $\sigma_1^2 > \sigma_2^2$. $df_1 = 21 - 1 = 20$; $df_2 = 18 - 1 = 17$. H_0 is rejected if $F > 3.16$.

$$F = \frac{(45{,}600)^2}{(21{,}330)^2} = 4.57$$

Reject H_0. There is more variation in the selling price of oceanfront homes.

25. Sharkey: $n = 7$ $\quad s_s = 14.79$
White: $\quad n = 8$ $\quad s_w = 22.95$
H_0: $\sigma_w^2 \leq \sigma_s^2$; H_1: $\sigma_w^2 > \sigma_s^2$. $df_s = 7 - 1 = 6$; $df_w = 8 - 1 = 7$. Reject H_0 if $F > 8.26$.

$$F = \frac{(22.95)^2}{(14.79)^2} = 2.41$$

Cannot reject H_0. There is no difference in the variation of the monthly sales.

27. **a.** H_0: $\mu_1 = \mu_2 = \mu_3 = \mu_4$
H_1: Treatment means are not all equal.
b. $\alpha = .05$ $\quad$ Reject H_0 if $F > 3.10$.
c.

Source	SS	*df*	MS	*F*
Treatment	50	4 − 1 = 3	50/3	1.67
Error	200	24 − 4 = 20	10	
Total	250	24 − 1 = 23		

d. Do not reject H_0.

29. H_0: $\mu_1 = \mu_2 = \mu_3$; H_1: Not all treatment means are equal. H_0 is rejected if $F > 3.89$.

Source	SS	*df*	MS	*F*
Treatment	63.33	2	31.667	13.38
Error	28.40	12	2.367	
Total	91.73	14		

H_0 is rejected. There is a difference in the treatment means.

31. H_0: $\mu_1 = \mu_2 = \mu_3 = \mu_4$; H_1: Not all means are equal. H_0 is rejected if $F > 3.10$.

Source	SS	*df*	MS	*F*
Factor	87.79	3	29.26	9.12
Error	64.17	20	3.21	
Total	151.96	23		

Because the computed F of $9.12 > 3.10$, the null hypothesis of no difference is rejected at the .05 level.

33. **a.** H_0: $\mu_1 = \mu_2$; H_1: $\mu_1 \neq \mu_2$. Critical value of $F = 4.75$.

Source	SS	*df*	MS	*F*
Treatment	219.43	1	219.43	23.10
Error	114.00	12	9.5	
Total	333.43	13		

b. $$t = \frac{19 - 27}{\sqrt{9.5\left(\frac{1}{6} + \frac{1}{8}\right)}} = -4.806$$

Then $t^2 = F$. That is $(-4.806)^2 = 23.10$.

c. H_0 is rejected. There is a difference in the mean scores.

35. The null hypothesis is rejected because the F statistic (8.26) is greater than the critical value (5.61) at the .01 significance level. The p-value (.0019) is also less than the significance level. The mean gasoline mileages are not the same.

37. H_0: $\mu_1 = \mu_2 = \mu_3 = \mu_4$. $\quad H_1$: At least one mean is different. Reject H_0 if $F > 2.7395$. Since $11.90 > 2.74$, reject H_0. You can also see this from the p-value of $0.000 < 0.05$. Priority mail express is faster than all three of the other classes, and priority mail is faster than either first-class or standard. However, first-class and standard mail may be the same.

39. For color, the critical value of F is 4.76; for size, it is 5.14.

Source	SS	*df*	MS	*F*
Treatment	25.0	3	8.3333	5.88
Blocks	21.5	2	10.75	7.59
Error	8.5	6	1.4167	
Total	55.0	11		

H_0s for both treatment and blocks (color and size) are rejected. At least one mean differs for color and at least one mean differs for size.

41. **a.** Critical value of F is 3.49. Computed F is 0.668. Do not reject H_0.
b. Critical value of F is 3.26. Computed F value is 100.204. Reject H_0 for block means.
There is a difference in homes but not assessors.

43. For gasoline:
H_0: $\mu_1 = \mu_2 = \mu_3$; H_1: Mean mileage is not the same.
Reject H_0 if $F > 3.89$.
For automobile:
H_0: $\mu_1 = \mu_2 = \ldots = \mu_7$; H_1: Mean mileage is not the same.
Reject H_0 if $F > 3.00$.

ANOVA Table

Source	SS	*df*	MS	*F*
Gasoline	44.095	2	22.048	26.71
Autos	77.238	6	12.873	15.60
Error	9.905	12	0.825	
Total	131.238	20		

There is a difference in both autos and gasoline.

45. H_0: $\mu_1 = \mu_2 = \mu_3 = \mu_4 = \mu_5 = \mu_6$; H_1: The treatment means are not equal. Reject H_0 if $F > 2.37$.

Source	SS	*df*	MS	*F*
Treatment	0.03478	5	0.00696	3.86
Error	0.10439	58	0.0018	
Total	0.13917	63		

H_0 is rejected. There is a difference in the mean weight of the colors.

47. a.

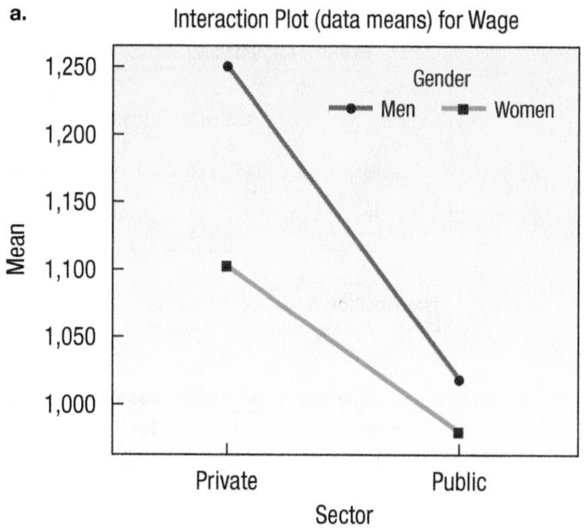

b. Two-way ANOVA: Wage versus Gender, Sector

Source	DF	SS	MS	F	P
Gender	1	44086	44086	11.44	0.004
Sector	1	156468	156468	40.61	0.000
Interaction	1	14851	14851	3.85	0.067
Error	16	61640	3853		
Total	19	277046			

There is no interaction effect of gender and sector on wages. However, there are significant differences in mean wages based on gender and significant differences in mean wages based on sector.

c. One-way ANOVA: Wage versus Sector

Source	DF	SS	MS	F	P
Sector	1	156468	156468	23.36	0.000
Error	18	120578	6699		
Total	19	277046			

s = 81.85   R-Sq = 56.48%   R-Sq(adj) = 54.06%

One-way ANOVA: Wage versus Gender

Source	DF	SS	MS	F	P
Gender	1	44086	44086	3.41	0.081
Error	18	232960	12942		
Total	19	277046			

s = 113.8   R-Sq = 15.91%   R-Sq(adj) = 11.24%

d. The statistical results show that only sector, private or public, has a significant effect on the wages of accountants.

49. a. $H_0: \sigma^2_{np} = \sigma^2_p \quad H_1: \sigma^2_{np} \neq \sigma^2_p$.
Reject H_0 if $F > 2.05$ (estimated).
$df_1 = 67 - 1 = 66$; $df_2 = 38 - 1 = 37$

$$F = \frac{(50.57)^2}{(33.71)^2} = 2.25$$

Reject H_0. There is a difference in the variance of the two selling prices.

b. $H_0: \sigma^2_g = \sigma^2_{ng}$; $H_1: \sigma^2_g \neq \sigma^2_{ng}$.
Reject H_0 if $F > 2.21$ (estimated).

$$F = \frac{(44.88)^2}{(28.00)^2} = 2.57$$

Reject H_0. There is a difference in the variance of the two selling prices.

c.

Source	SS	df	MS	F
Township	13,263	4	3,316	1.52
Error	217,505	100	2,175	
Total	230,768	104		

$H_0: \mu_1 = \mu_2 = \mu_3 = \mu_4 = \mu_5$; H_1: Not all treatment means are equal. Reject H_0 if $F > 2.46$.
Do not reject H_0. There is no difference in the mean selling prices in the five townships.

51. a. $H_0: \mu_1 = \mu_2 = \mu_3 \quad H_1$: Not all treatment means are equal.
Reject H_0 if $F > 4.89$.

Source	SS	df	MS	F
Treatment	28,996	2	14,498	5.62
Error	198,696	77	2,580	
Total	227,692	79		

Reject H_0. The mean maintenance costs are different.

b. $H_0: \mu_1 = \mu_2 = \mu_3 \quad H_1$: Not all treatment means are equal.
Reject H_0 if $F > 3.12$.

Source	SS	df	MS	F
Treatment	5,095	2	2,547	1.45
Error	135,513	77	1,760	
Total	140,608	79		

Do not reject H_0. The mean miles traveled are not different.

c. $(441.81 - 506.75) \pm 1.991\sqrt{2{,}580\left(\frac{1}{47} + \frac{1}{8}\right)}$

This reduces to -64.94 ± 38.68, so the difference is between -103.62 and -26.26. To put it another way, Bluebird is less costly than Thompson by an amount between \$26.26 and \$103.62.

CHAPTER 13

1. $\Sigma(x - \bar{x})(y - \bar{y}) = 10.6$, $s_x = 2.7$, $s_y = 1.3$

$$r = \frac{10.6}{(5 - 1)(2.709)(1.38)} = 0.75$$

3. a. Sales.

b.

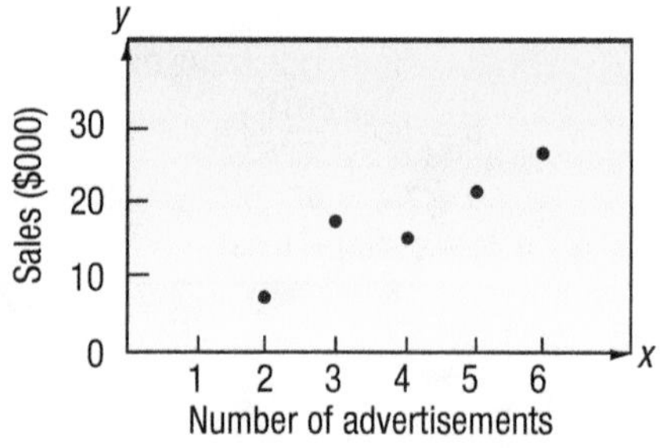

c. $\Sigma(x - \bar{x})(y - \bar{y}) = 36$, $n = 5$, $s_x = 1.5811$, $s_y = 6.1237$

$$r = \frac{36}{(5 - 1)(1.5811)(6.1237)} = 0.9295$$

d. There is a strong positive association between the variables.

5. a. Either variable could be independent. In the scatter plot, police is the independent variable.

b.

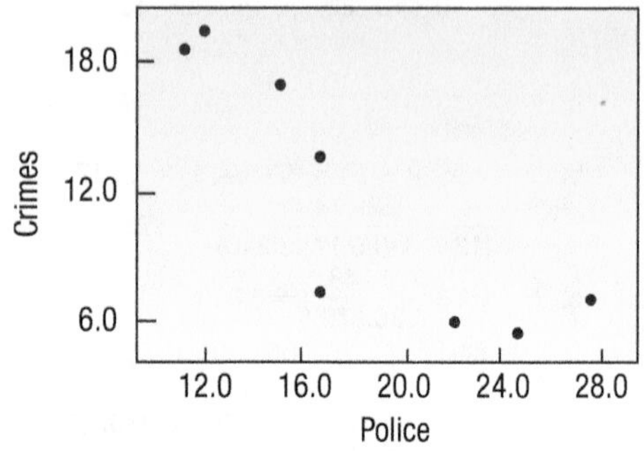

c. $n = 8$, $\Sigma(x - \bar{x})(y - \bar{y}) = -231.75$, $s_x = 5.8737$, $s_y = 6.4462$

$$r = \frac{-231.75}{(8 - 1)(5.8737)(6.4462)} = -0.8744$$

d. Strong inverse relationship. As the number of police increases, the crime decreases or, as crime increases the number of police decrease.

7. Reject H_0 if $t > 1.812$.

$$t = \frac{.32\sqrt{12 - 2}}{\sqrt{1 - (.32)^2}} = 1.068$$

Do not reject H_0.

9. $H_0: \rho \leq 0$; $H_1: \rho > 0$. Reject H_0 if $t > 2.552$. $df = 18$.

$$t = \frac{.78\sqrt{20 - 2}}{\sqrt{1 - (.78)^2}} = 5.288$$

Reject H_0. There is a positive correlation between gallons sold and the pump price.

11. $H_0: \rho \leq 0 \quad H_1: \rho > 0$
Reject H_0 if $t > 2.650$ with df = 13.

$$t = \frac{0.667\sqrt{15 - 2}}{\sqrt{1 - 0.667^2}} = 3.228$$

Reject H_0. There is a positive correlation between the number of passengers and plane weight.

13. a. $\hat{y} = 3.7671 + 0.3630x$

$$b = 0.7522\left(\frac{1.3038}{2.7019}\right) = 0.3630$$

$$a = 5.8 - 0.3630(5.6) = 3.7671$$

b. 6.3081, found by $\hat{y} = 3.7671 + 0.3630(7)$

15. **a.** $\Sigma(x-\bar{x})(y-\bar{y}) = 44.6, s_x = 2.726, s_y = 2.011$

$$r = \frac{44.6}{(10-1)(2.726)(2.011)} = .904$$

$$b = .904\left(\frac{2.011}{2.726}\right) = 0.667$$

$$a = 7.4 - .677(9.1) = 1.333$$

b. $\hat{Y} = 1.333 + .667(6) = 5.335$

17. **a.**

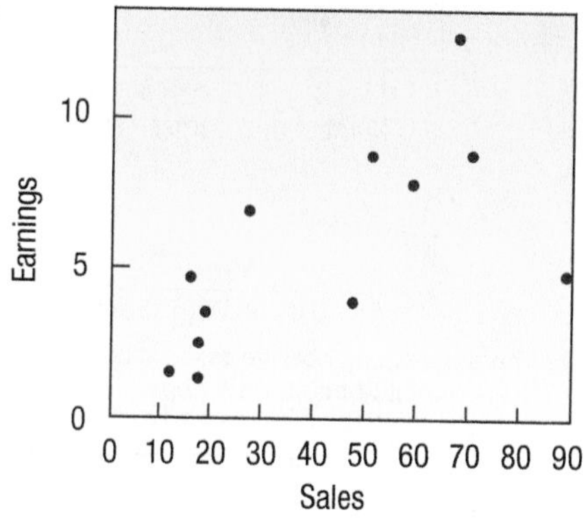

b. $\Sigma(x-\bar{x})(y-\bar{y}) = 629.64, s_x = 26.17, s_y = 3.248$

$$r = \frac{629.64}{(12-1)(26.17)(3.248)} = .6734$$

c. $b = .6734\left(\frac{3.248}{26.170}\right) = 0.0836$

$$a = \frac{64.1}{12} - 0.0836\left(\frac{501.10}{12}\right) = 1.8507$$

d. $\hat{y} = 1.8507 + 0.0836(50.0) = 6.0307$ ($ millions)

19. **a.** $b = -.8744\left(\frac{6.4462}{5.8737}\right) = -0.9596$

$$a = \frac{95}{8} - (-0.9596)\left(\frac{146}{8}\right) = 29.3877$$

b. 10.1957, found by 29.3877 − 0.9596(20)

c. For each policeman added, crime goes down by almost one.

21. $H_0: \beta \geq 0 \quad H_1: \beta < 0 \quad df = n - 2 = 8 - 2 = 6$

Reject H_0 if $t < -1.943$.

$$t = -0.96/0.22 = -4.364$$

Reject H_0 and conclude the slope is less than zero.

23. $H_0: \beta = 0 \quad H_1: \beta \neq 0 \quad df = n - 2 = 12 - 2 = 10$

Reject H_0 if t not between −2.228 and 2.228.

$$t = 0.08/0.03 = 2.667$$

Reject H_0 and conclude the slope is different from zero.

25. The standard error of estimate is 3.378, found by $\sqrt{\frac{68.4814}{8-2}}$.

The coefficient of determination is 0.76, found by $(-0.874)^2$. Seventy-six percent of the variation in crimes can be explained by the variation in police.

27. The standard error of estimate is 0.913, found by $\sqrt{\frac{6.667}{10-2}}$.

The coefficient of determination is 0.82, found by 29.733/36.4. Eighty-two percent of the variation in kilowatt hours can be explained by the variation in the number of rooms.

29. **a.** $r^2 = \frac{1{,}000}{1{,}500} = .6667$

b. $r = \sqrt{.6667} = .8165$

c. $s_{y.x} = \sqrt{\frac{500}{13}} = 6.2017$

31. **a.** $6.308 \pm (3.182)(.993)\sqrt{.2 + \frac{(7-5.6)^2}{29.2}}$

$= 6.308 \pm 1.633$

$= [4.675, 7.941]$

b. $6.308 \pm (3.182)(.993)\sqrt{1 + 1/5 + .0671}$

$= [2.751, 9.865]$

33. **a.** 4.2939, 6.3721

b. 2.9854, 7.6806

35. The correlation between the two variables is 0.298. By squaring x, the correlation increases to .998.

37. $H_0: \rho \leq 0; H_1: \rho > 0$. Reject H_0 if $t > 1.714$.

$$t = \frac{.94\sqrt{25-2}}{\sqrt{1-(.94)^2}} = 13.213$$

Reject H_0. There is a positive correlation between passengers and weight of luggage.

39. $H_0: \rho \leq 0; H_1: \rho > 0$. Reject H_0 if $t > 2.764$.

$$t = \frac{.47\sqrt{12-2}}{\sqrt{1-(.47)^2}} = 1.684$$

Do not reject H_0. There is not a positive correlation between engine size and performance. p-value is greater than .05 but less than .10.

41. **a.** The sales volume is inversely related to their market share.

b. $r = \frac{-299.792}{(13-1)(3.686)(9.808)} = -0.691$

c. $H_0: \rho \geq 0 \quad H_1: \rho < 0 \quad$ Reject H_0 if $t < -2.718 \quad df = 11$

$t = \frac{-0.691\sqrt{13-2}}{\sqrt{1-(-0.691)^2}} = -3.17$ Reject H_0. There is a negative correlation between cars sold and market share.

d. 47.7%, found by $(-0.691)^2$, of the variation in market share is accounted for by variation in cars sold.

43. **a.** $r = -0.393$

b. The coefficient of determination is 0.1544, found by squaring (−0.393).

c. $H_0: \rho \geq 0 \quad H_1: \rho < 0 \quad$ Reject H_0 if $t < -1.697$

$$t = \frac{-0.393\sqrt{32-2}}{\sqrt{1-(-0.393)^2}} = -2.34$$

Reject H_0. There is a negative correlation between points scored and points allowed.

d. For the National conference (NFC): $H_0: \rho \geq 0 \quad H_1: \rho < 0$

Reject H_0 if $t < -1.761$.

$$t = \frac{-0.139\sqrt{16-2}}{\sqrt{1-(-0.139)^2}} = -0.53$$

Do not reject H_0. We *cannot* say there is a negative correlation between points scored and points allowed in the NFC.

For the American conference (AFC): $H_0: \rho \geq 0 \quad H_1: \rho < 0$

Reject H_0 if $t < -1.761$.

$$t = \frac{-0.576\sqrt{16-2}}{\sqrt{1-(-0.576)^2}} = -2.64$$

Reject H_0. We can say there is a negative correlation between points scored and points allowed in the AFC.

45. **a.**

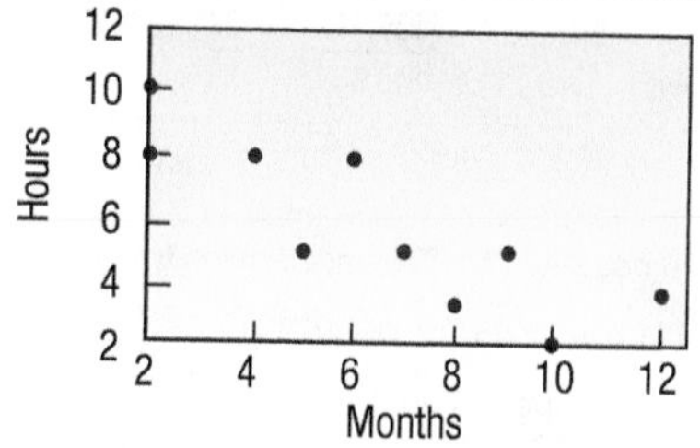

There is an inverse relationship between the variables. As the months owned increase, the number of hours exercised decreases.

b. $r = -0.827$

c. $H_0: \rho \geq 0; H_1: \rho < 0$. Reject H_0 if $t < -2.896$.

$$t = \frac{-0.827\sqrt{10-2}}{\sqrt{1-(-0.827)^2}} = -4.16$$

Reject H_0. There is a negative association between months owned and hours exercised.

47. **a.** Median age and population are directly related.

b. $r = \frac{11.93418}{(10 - 1)(2.207)(1.330)} = 0.452$

c. The slope of 0.272 indicates that for each increase of 1 million in the population, the median age increases on average by 0.272 year.

d. The median age is 32.08 years, found by 31.4 + 0.272(2.5).

e. The *p*-value (0.190) for the population variable is greater than, say, .05. A test for significance of that coefficient would fail to be rejected. In other words, it is possible the population coefficient is zero.

f. H_0: $\rho = 0$ H_1: $\rho \neq 0$ Reject H_0 if *t* is not between −1.86 and 1.86.

$df = 8$ $t = \frac{0.452\sqrt{10 - 2}}{\sqrt{1 - (0.452)^2}} = 1.433$ Do not reject H_0.

There may be no relationship between age and population.

49. **a.** $b = -0.4667$, $a = 11.2358$

b. $\hat{y} = 11.2358 - 0.4667(7.0) = 7.9689$

c. $7.9689 \pm (2.160)(1.114)\sqrt{1 + \frac{1}{15} + \frac{(7 - 7.1333)^2}{73.7333}}$

$= 7.9689 \pm 2.4854$

$= [5.4835, 10.4543]$

d. $R^2 = 0.499$. Nearly 50% of the variation in the amount of the bid is explained by the number of bidders.

51. **a.**

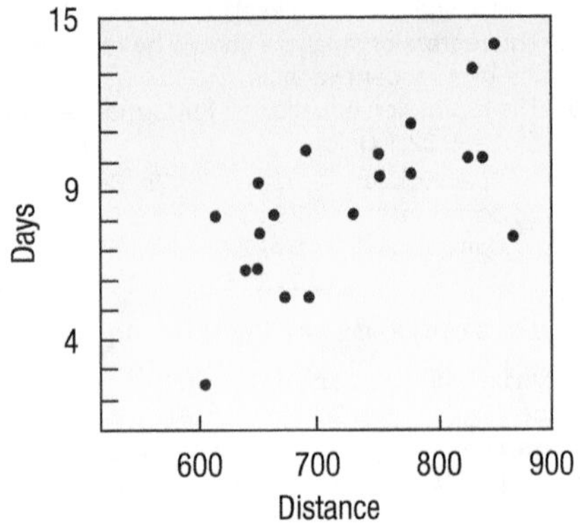

There appears to be a relationship between the two variables. As the distance increases, so does the shipping time.

b. $r = 0.692$

H_0: $\rho \leq 0$; H_1: $\rho > 0$. Reject H_0 if $t > 1.734$.

$$t = \frac{0.692\sqrt{20 - 2}}{\sqrt{1 - (0.692)^2}} = 4.067$$

H_0 is rejected. There is a positive association between shipping distance and shipping time.

c. $R^2 = 0.479$. Nearly half of the variation in shipping time is explained by shipping distance.

d. $s_{y \cdot x} = 2.004$

53. **a.** $b = 2.41$

$a = 26.8$

The regression equation is: Price = 26.8 + 2.41 × Dividend. For each additional dollar of dividend, the price increases by $2.41.

b. To test the significance of the slope, we use $n - 2$, or $30 - 2 = 28$ degrees of freedom. For a 0.05 level of significance, the critical values are −2.048 and 2.048. The *t*-test statistic is $t = \frac{b - 0}{s_b} = \frac{2.408}{0.328} = 7.34$. We reject the null hypothesis that the slope is equal zero.

c. $R^2 = \frac{5,057.6}{7,682.7} = 0.658$ Thus, 65.8% of the variation in price is explained by the dividend.

d. $r = \sqrt{.658} = 0.811$ H_0: $\rho \leq 0$ H_1: $\rho > 0$
At the 5% level, reject H_0 when $t > 1.701$.

$$t = \frac{0.811\sqrt{30 - 2}}{\sqrt{1 - (0.811)^2}} = 7.34$$

Thus, H_0 is rejected. The population correlation is positive.

55. **a.** 35

b. $s_{y \cdot x} = \sqrt{29,778,406} = 5,456.96$

c. $r^2 = \frac{13,548,662,082}{14,531,349,474} = 0.932$

d. $r = \sqrt{0.932} = 0.966$

e. H_0: $\rho \leq 0$, H_1: $\rho > 0$; reject H_0 if $t > 1.692$.

$$t = \frac{.966\sqrt{35 - 2}}{\sqrt{1 - (.966)^2}} = 21.46$$

Reject H_0. There is a direct relationship between size of the house and its market value.

57. **a.** The regression equation is Price = −773 + 1,408 Speed.

b. The second laptop (1.6, 922) with a residual of −557.60, is priced $557.60 below the predicted price. That is a noticeable "bargain."

c. The correlation of Speed and Price is 0.835.
H_0: $\rho \leq 0$ H_1: $\rho > 0$ Reject H_0 if $t > 1.8125$.

$$t = \frac{0.835\sqrt{12 - 2}}{\sqrt{1 - (0.835)^2}} = 4.799$$

Reject H_0. It is reasonable to say the population correlation is positive.

59. **a.** $r = .987$, H_0: $\rho \leq 0$, H_1: $\rho > 0$. Reject H_0 if $t > 1.746$.

$$t = \frac{.987\sqrt{18 - 2}}{\sqrt{1 - (.987)^2}} = 24.564$$

b. $\hat{y} = -29.7 + 22.93x$; an additional cup increases the dog's weight by almost 23 pounds.

c. Dog number 4 is an overeater.

61. **a.**

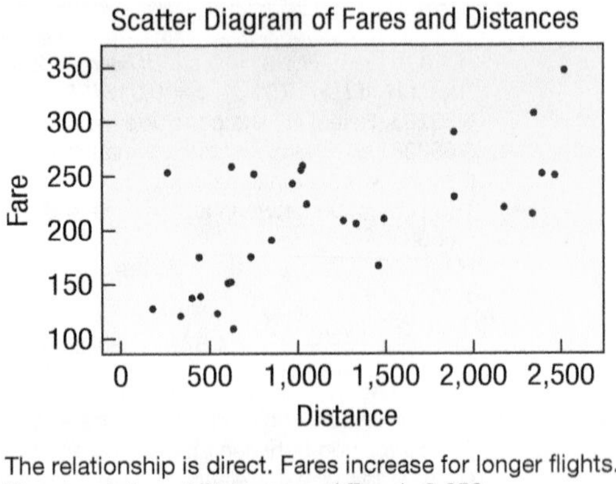

The relationship is direct. Fares increase for longer flights.

b. The correlation of Distance and Fare is 0.656.
H_0: $\rho \leq 0$ H_1: $\rho > 0$ Reject H_0 if $t > 1.701$. $df = 28$

$$t = \frac{0.656\sqrt{30 - 2}}{\sqrt{1 - (0.656)^2}} = 4.599$$

Reject H_0. There is a significant positive correlation between fares and distances.

c. 43%, found by $(0.656)^2$, of the variation in fares is explained by the variation in distance.

d. The regression equation is Fare = 147.08 + 0.05265 Distance. Each additional mile adds $0.05265 to the fare. A 1,500-mile flight would cost $226.06, found by $147.08 + 0.05265(1,500).

e. A flight of 4,218 miles is outside the range of the sampled data, so the regression equation may not be useful.

63. a. There does seem to be a direct relationship between the variables.

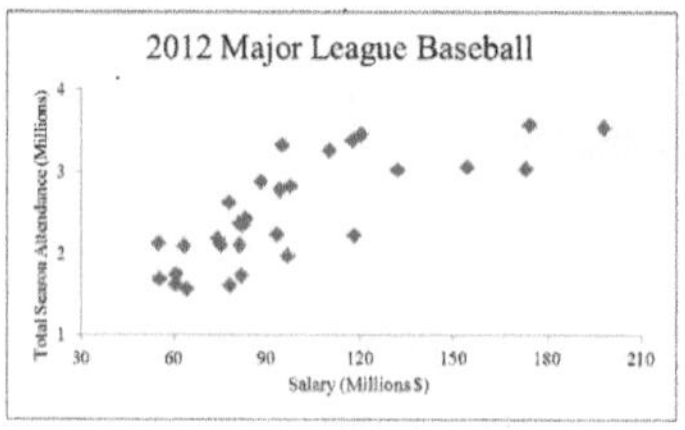

b. Expected attendance with a salary of 80 million is 2.2529 million, found by 1.17855 + 0.01343 (80).

c. Increasing the salary by 30 million will increase attendance by 0.4029 million on average, found by 0.01343 (30). This is also the difference between the expected attendance with a salary of 110 and the expected attendance of 80 million.

d. The regression output from *Excel* is below.

Summary Output

Regression Statistics

Multiple R	0.770317814
R Square	0.593389535
Adjusted R Square	0.578867732
Standard Error	0.416717999
Observations	30

ANOVA

	df	SS	MS	*F*	Significance *F*
Regression	1	7.095841062	7.095841062	40.86197572	6.41022E-07
Residual	28	4.862308938	0.173653891		
Total	29	11.95815			

	Coefficients	Standard Error	*t* Stat	*P*-value
Intercept	1.178554138	0.21954557	5.368152674	1.01455E-05
Salary 2012	0.013429923	0.002100941	6.392337265	6.41022E-07

H_0: $\beta \le 0$ H_1: $\beta > 0$ $df = n - 2 = 30 - 2 = 28$
Reject H_0 if $t > 1.701$ $t = 0.013429923/0.002100941 = 6.39233$. Reject H_0 and conclude the slope is positive.

e. 0.593389 or 59.3389% of the variation in attendance is explained by variation in salary.

f. The correlation between attendance and batting average is 0.6538.

H_0: $\rho \le 0$ H_1: $\rho > 0$ At the 5% level, reject H_0 if $t >$ 1.701.

$$t = \frac{0.6538\sqrt{30-2}}{\sqrt{1-(0.6538)^2}} = 4.573 \qquad \text{Reject } H_0.$$

The batting average and attendance is positively correlated.
The correlation between attendance and ERA is −0.0548.
The correlation between attendance and batting average is stronger than the correlation between attendance and ERA.

H_0: $\rho \ge 0$ H_1: $\rho < 0$ At the 5% level, reject H_0 if $t < -1.701$.

$$t = \frac{-0.0548\sqrt{30-2}}{\sqrt{1-(-0.0548)^2}} = -0.291 \qquad \text{Fail to reject } H_0.$$

The ERA and attendance could have no correlation.

CHAPTER 14

1. a. Multiple regression equation

b. The *y*-intercept

c. $\hat{y} = 64{,}100 + 0.394(796{,}000) + 9.6(6{,}940) - 11{,}600(6.0) = \$374{,}748$

3. a. 497.736, found by
$\hat{y} = 16.24 + 0.017(18) + 0.0028(26{,}500) + 42(3) + 0.0012(156{,}000) + 0.19(141) + 26.8(2.5)$

b. Two more social activities. Income added only 28 to the index; social activities added 53.6.

5. a. $s_{Y\cdot 12} = \sqrt{\dfrac{SSE}{n-(k+1)}} = \sqrt{\dfrac{583.693}{65-(2+1)}}$
$= \sqrt{9.414} = 3.068$
95% of the residuals will be between ±6.136, found by 2(3.068).

b. $R^2 = \dfrac{SSR}{SS\ total} = \dfrac{77.907}{661.6} = .118$
The independent variables explain 11.8% of the variation.

c. $R^2_{adj} = 1 - \dfrac{\dfrac{SSE}{n-(k+1)}}{\dfrac{SS\ total}{n-1}} = 1 - \dfrac{\dfrac{583.693}{65-(2+1)}}{\dfrac{661.6}{65-1}}$
$= 1 - \dfrac{9.414}{10.3375} = 1 - .911 = .089$

7. a. $\hat{y} = 84.998 + 2.391x_1 - 0.4086x_2$

b. 90.0674, found by $\hat{y} = 84.998 + 2.391(4) - 0.4086(11)$

c. $n = 65$ and $k = 2$

d. H_0: $\beta_1 = \beta_2 = 0$ H_1: Not all βs are 0
Reject H_0 if $F > 3.15$.
$F = 4.14$, reject H_0. Not all net regression coefficients equal zero.

e. For x_1 For x_2
H_0: $\beta_1 = 0$ H_0: $\beta_2 = 0$
H_1: $\beta_1 \ne 0$ H_1: $\beta_2 \ne 0$
$t = 1.99$ $t = -2.38$
Reject H_0 if $t > 2.0$ or $t < -2.0$.
Delete variable 1 and keep 2.

f. The regression analysis should be repeated with only x_2 as the independent variable.

9. a. The regression equation is: Performance = 29.3 + 5.22 Aptitude + 22.1 Union

```
Predictor      Coef   SE Coef      T       P
Constant      29.28     12.77   2.29   0.041
Aptitude      5.222     1.702   3.07   0.010
Union        22.135     8.852   2.50   0.028

S = 16.9166 R-Sq = 53.3% R-Sq (adj) = 45.5%

Analysis of Variance
Source           DF      SS       MS      F       P
Regression        2  3919.3   1959.6   6.85   0.010
Residual Error   12  3434.0    286.2
Total            14  7353.3
```

b. These variables are effective in predicting performance. They explain 53.3% of the variation in performance. In particular, union membership increases the typical performance by 22.1.

c. H_0: $\beta_2 = 0$ H_1: $\beta_2 \ne 0$
Reject H_0 if $t < -2.179$ or $t > 2.179$.
Since 2.50 is greater than 2.179, we reject the null hypothesis and conclude that union membership is significant and should be included.

d. When you consider the interaction variable, the regression equation is Performance = 38.7 + 3.80 Aptitude − 0.1 Union + 3.61 x_1x_2

Predictor	Coef	SE Coef	T	P
Constant	38.69	15.62	2.48	0.031
Aptitude	3.802	2.179	1.74	0.109
Union	−0.10	23.14	−0.00	0.997
X_1X_2	3.610	3.473	1.04	0.321

The *t* value corresponding to the interaction term is 1.04. This is not significant. So we conclude there is no interaction between aptitude and union membership when predicting job performance.

11. a. The regression equation is
Price = 3,080 − 54.2 Bidders + 16.3 Age

```
Predictor     Coef   SE Coef       T       P
Constant    3080.1     343.9    8.96   0.000
Bidders     -54.19     12.28   -4.41   0.000
Age         16.289     3.784    4.30   0.000
```

The price decreases 54.2 as each additional bidder participates. Meanwhile the price increases 16.3 as the painting gets older. While one would expect older paintings to be worth more, it is unexpected that the price goes down as more bidders participate!

b. The regression equation is
Price = 3,972 − 185 Bidders + 6.35 Age + 1.46 x_1x_2

Predictor	Coef	SE Coef	T	P
Constant	3971.7	850.2	4.67	0.000
Bidders	−185.0	114.9	−1.61	0.122
Age	6.353	9.455	0.67	0.509
X_1X_2	1.462	1.277	1.15	0.265

The *t* value corresponding to the interaction term is 1.15. This is not significant. So we conclude there is no interaction.

c. In the stepwise procedure, the number of bidders enters the equation first. Then the interaction term enters. The variable age would not be included as it is not significant. Response is Price on 3 predictors, with $N = 25$.

Step	1	2
Constant	4,507	4,540
Bidders	−57	−256
T-Value	−3.53	−5.59
P-Value	0.002	0.000
X_1X_2		2.25
T-Value		4.49
P-Value		0.000
S	295	218
R-Sq	35.11	66.14
R-Sq(adj)	32.29	63.06

13. **a.** $n = 40$

b. 4

c. $R^2 = \dfrac{750}{1{,}250} = .60$

d. $s_{y\cdot 1234} = \sqrt{500/35} = 3.7796$

e. H_0: $\beta_1 = \beta_2 = \beta_3 = \beta_4 = 0$
H_1: Not all the βs equal zero.
H_0 is rejected if $F > 2.65$.

$$F = \frac{750/4}{500/35} = 13.125$$

H_0 is rejected. At least one β_i does not equal zero.

15. **a.** $n = 26$

b. $R^2 = 100/140 = .7143$

c. 1.4142, found by $\sqrt{2}$

d. H_0: $\beta_1 = \beta_2 = \beta_3 = \beta_4 = \beta_5 = 0$
H_1: Not all the βs are 0.
H_0 is rejected if $F > 2.71$.
Computed $F = 10.0$. Reject H_0. At least one regression coefficient is not zero.

e. H_0 is rejected in each case if $t < -2.086$ or $t > 2.086$. x_1 and x_5 should be dropped.

17. **a.** $28,000

b. $R^2 = \dfrac{SSR}{SS\ total} = \dfrac{3{,}050}{5{,}250} = .5809$

c. 9.199, found by $\sqrt{84.62}$

d. H_0 is rejected if $F > 2.97$ (approximately)

$$\text{Computed } F = \frac{1{,}016.67}{84.62} = 12.01$$

H_0 is rejected. At least one regression coefficient is not zero.

e. If computed *t* is to the left of −2.056 or to the right of 2.056, the null hypothesis in each of these cases is rejected. Computed *t* for x_2 and x_3 exceed the critical value. Thus, "population" and "advertising expenses" should be retained and "number of competitors," x_1, dropped.

19. **a.** The strongest correlation is between High School GPA and Paralegal GPA. No problem with multicollinearity.

b. $R^2 = \dfrac{4.3595}{5.0631} = .8610$

c. H_0 is rejected if $F > 5.41$.

$$F = \frac{1.4532}{0.1407} = 10.328$$

At least one coefficient is not zero.

d. Any H_0 is rejected if $t < -2.571$ or $t > 2.571$. It appears that only High School GPA is significant. Verbal and math could be eliminated.

e. $R^2 = \dfrac{4.2061}{5.0631} = .8307$
R^2 has only been reduced .0303.

f. The residuals appear slightly skewed (positive) but acceptable.

g. There does not seem to be a problem with the plot.

21. **a.** The correlation of Screen and Price is 0.893. So there does appear to be a linear relationship between the two.

b. Price is the "dependent" variable.

c. The regression equation is Price = −2,484 + 101 × Screen. For each inch increase in screen size, the price increases $101 on average.

d. Using "dummy" indicator variables for Sharp and Sony, the regression equation is Price = − 2,308 + 94.1 Screen + 15 Manufacturer Sharp + 381 Manufacturer Sony. Sharp can obtain on average $15 more than Samsung and Sony can collect an additional benefit of $381 more than Samsung.

e. Here is some of the output.

Predictor	Coef	SE Coef	T	P
Constant	-2308.2	492.0	-4.69	0.000
Screen	94.12	10.83	8.69	0.000
Manufacturer_Sharp	15.1	171.6	0.09	0.931
Manufacturer_Sony	381.4	168.8	2.26	0.036

The *p*-value for Sharp is relatively large. A test of their coefficient would not be rejected. That means they may not have any real advantage over Samsung. On the other hand, the *p*-value for the Sony coefficient is quite small. That indicates that it did not happen by chance and there is some real advantage to Sony over Samsung.

f. A histogram of the residuals indicates they follow a normal distribution.

g. The residual variation may be increasing for larger fitted values.

23. **a.**

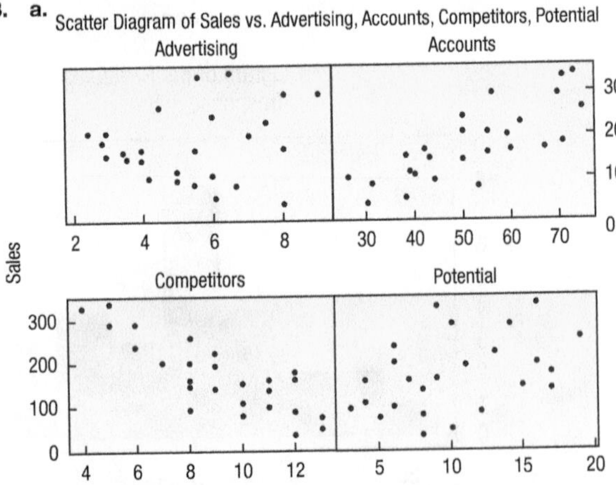

Sales seem to fall with the number of competitors and rise with the number of accounts and potential.

b. Pearson correlations

	Sales	Advertising	Accounts	Competitors
Advertising	0.159			
Accounts	0.783	0.173		
Competitors	−0.833	−0.038	−0.324	
Potential	0.407	−0.071	0.468	−0.202

The number of accounts and the market potential are moderately correlated.

c. The regression equation is:
Sales = 178 + 1.81 Advertising + 3.32 Accounts − 21.2 Competitors + 0.325 Potential

Predictor	Coef	SE Coef	T	P
Constant	178.32	12.96	13.76	0.000
Advertising	1.807	1.081	1.67	0.109
Accounts	3.3178	0.1629	20.37	0.000
Competitors	−21.1850	0.7879	−26.89	0.000
Potential	0.3245	0.4678	0.69	0.495

S = 9.60441 R-Sq = 98.9% R-Sq(adj) = 98.7%

Analysis of Variance

Source	DF	SS	MS	F	P
Regression	4	176777	44194	479.10	0.000
Residual Error	21	1937	92		
Total	25	178714			

The computed F value is quite large. So we can reject the null hypothesis that all of the regression coefficients are zero. We conclude that some of the independent variables are effective in explaining sales.

d. Market potential and advertising have large p-values (0.495 and 0.109, respectively). You would probably drop them.

e. If you omit potential, the regression equation is:
Sales = 180 + 1.68 Advertising + 3.37 Accounts − 21.2 Competitors

Predictor	Coef	SE Coef	T	P
Constant	179.84	12.62	14.25	0.000
Advertising	1.677	1.052	1.59	0.125
Accounts	3.3694	0.1432	23.52	0.000
Competitors	−21.2165	0.7773	−27.30	0.000

Now advertising is not significant. That would also lead you to cut out the advertising variable and report that the polished regression equation is:
Sales = 187 + 3.41 Accounts − 21.2 Competitors

Predictor	Coef	SE Coef	T	P
Constant	186.69	12.26	15.23	0.000
Accounts	3.4081	0.1458	23.37	0.000
Competitors	−21.1930	0.8028	−26.40	0.000

f.

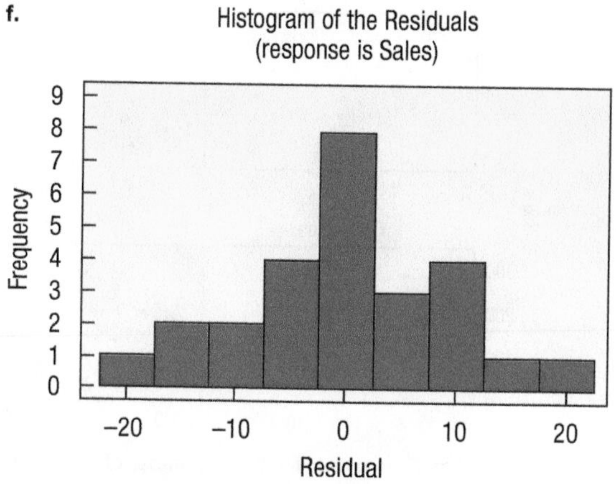

The histogram looks to be normal. There are no problems shown in this plot.

g. The variance inflation factor for both variables is 1.1. They are less than 10. There are no troubles as this value indicates the independent variables are not strongly correlated with each other.

25. The computer output is:

Predictor	*Coef*	*StDev*	*t-ratio*	*p*
Constant	651.9	345.3	1.89	0.071
Service	13.422	5.125	2.62	0.015
Age	−6.710	6.349	−1.06	0.301
Gender	205.65	90.27	2.28	0.032
Job	−33.45	89.55	−0.37	0.712

Analysis of Variance

SOURCE	*DF*	*SS*	*MS*	*F*	*p*
Regression	4	1066830	266708	4.77	0.005
Error	25	1398651	55946		
Total	29	2465481			

a. $\hat{y} = 651.9 + 13.422x_1 - 6.710x_2 + 205.65x_3 - 33.45x_4$

b. $R^2 = .433$, which is somewhat low for this type of study.

c. H_0: $\beta_1 = \beta_2 = \beta_3 = \beta_4 = 0$; H_1: Not all βs equal zero
Reject H_0 if $F > 2.76$.

$$F = \frac{1{,}066{,}830/4}{1{,}398{,}651/25} = 4.77$$

H_0 is rejected. Not all the β_is equal 0.

d. Using the .05 significance level, reject the hypothesis that the regression coefficient is 0 if $t < -2.060$ or $t > 2.060$. Service and gender should remain in the analyses; age and job should be dropped.

e. Following is the computer output using the independent variables service and gender.

Predictor	*Coef*	*StDev*	*t-ratio*	*p*
Constant	784.2	316.8	2.48	0.020
Service	9.021	3.106	2.90	0.007
Gender	224.41	87.35	2.57	0.016

Analysis of Variance

SOURCE	*DF*	*SS*	*MS*	*F*	*p*
Regression	2	998779	499389	9.19	0.001
Error	27	1466703	54322		
Total	29	2465481			

A man earns $224 more per month than a woman. The difference between technical and clerical jobs is not significant.

27. a. $\hat{y} = 29.913 - 5.324x_1 + 1.449x_2$

b. EPS is ($t = -3.26$, p-value = .005). Yield is not ($t = 0.81$, p-value = .431).

c. An increase of 1 in EPS results in a decline of 5.324 in P/E.

d. Stock number 2 is undervalued.

e. Below is a residual plot. It does *not* appear to follow the normal distribution.

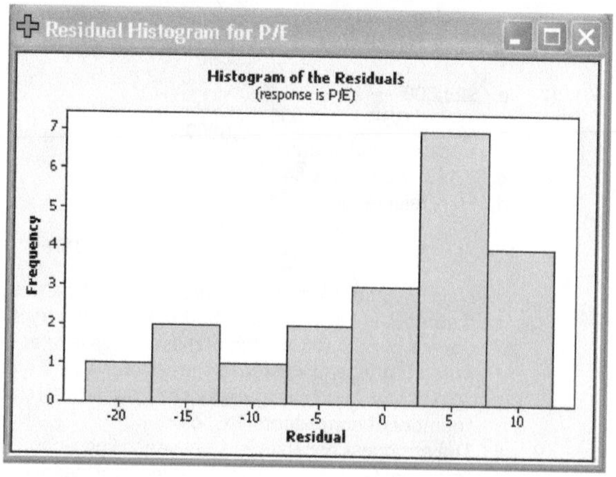

f. There does not seem to be a problem with the plot of the residuals versus the fitted values.

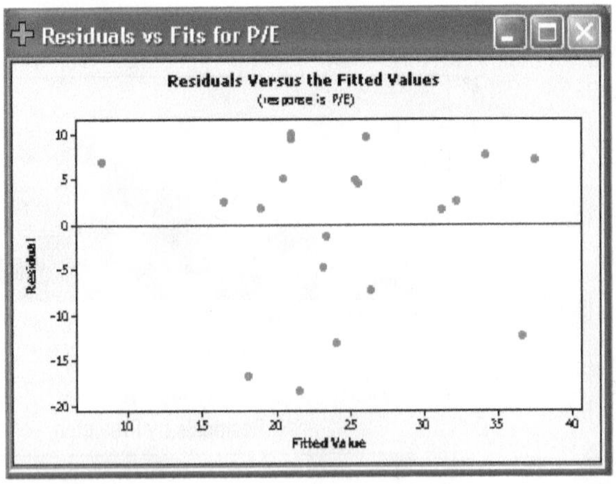

g. The correlation between yield and EPS is not a problem. No problem with multicollinearity.

	P/E	EPS
EPS	−0.602	
Yield	.054	.162

29. a. The regression equation is
Sales (000) = 1.02 + 0.0829 Infomercials

Predictor	Coef	SE Coef	T	P
Constant	1.0188	0.3105	3.28	0.006
Infomercials	0.08291	0.01680	4.94	0.000

Analysis of Variance

Source	DF	SS	MS	F	P
Regression	1	2.3214	2.3214	24.36	0.000
Residual Error	13	1.2386	0.0953		
Total	14	3.5600			

The global test demonstrates there is a relationship between sales and the number of infomercials.

b.

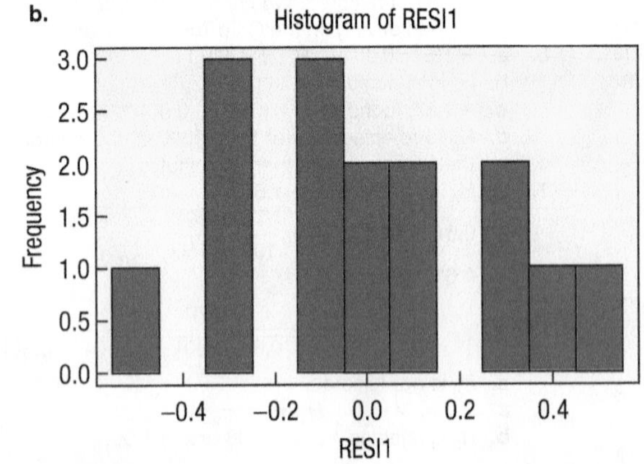

The residuals appear to follow the normal distribution.

31. a. The regression equation is
Auction Price = −118,929 + 1.63 Loan + 2.1 Monthly Payment + 50 Payments Made

Analysis of Variance

Source	DF	SS	MS	F	P
Regression	3	5966725061	1988908354	39.83	0.000
Residual Error	16	798944439	49934027		
Total	19	6765669500			

The computed *F* is 39.83. It is much larger than the critical value 3.24. The *p*-value is also quite small. Thus, the null hypothesis that all the regression coefficients are zero can be rejected. At least one of the multiple regression coefficients is different from zero.

b.

Predictor	Coef	SE Coef	T	P
Constant	−118929	19734	−6.03	0.000
Loan	1.6268	0.1809	8.99	0.000
Monthly Payment	2.06	14.95	0.14	0.892
Payments Made	50.3	134.9	0.37	0.714

The null hypothesis is that the coefficient is zero in the individual test. It would be rejected if *t* is less than −2.120 or more than 2.120. In this case, the *t* value for the loan variable is larger than the critical value. Thus, it should not be removed. However, the monthly payment and payments made variables would likely be removed.

c. The revised regression equation is: Auction Price = −119,893 + 1.67 Loan

33. The computer output is as follows:

Predictor	*Coef*	*SE Coef*	*T*	*P*
Constant	38.71	39.02	.99	.324
Bedrooms	7.118	2.551	2.79	0.006
Size	0.03800	0.01468	2.59	0.011
Pool	18.321	6.999	2.62	0.010
Distance	−0.9295	0.7279	−1.28	0.205
Garage	35.810	7.638	4.69	0.000
Baths	23.315	9.025	2.58	0.011

S = 33.21 R-Sq = 53.2% R-Sq (adj) = 50.3%

Analysis of Variance

SOURCE	*DF*	*SS*	*MS*	*F*	*P*
Regression	6	122676	20446	18.54	0.000
Residual Error	98	108092	1103		
Total	104	230768			

a. Each additional bedroom adds about $7,000 to the selling price, each additional square foot adds $38, a pool adds $18,300 to the value, an attached garage increases the value by $35,800, and each mile the home is from the center of the city reduces the selling price by $929.

b. The *R*-square value is 0.532.

c. The correlation matrix is as follows:

	Price	Bedrooms	Size	Pool	Distance	Garage
Bedrooms	0.467					
Size	0.371	0.383				
Pool	0.294	0.005	0.201			
Distance	−0.347	−0.153	−0.117	−0.139		
Garage	0.526	0.234	0.083	0.114	−0.359	
Baths	0.382	0.329	0.024	0.055	−0.195	0.221

The independent variable *garage* has the strongest correlation with price. Distance is inversely related, as expected, and there does not seem to be a problem with correlation among the independent variables.

d. The results of the global test suggest that some of the independent variables have net regression coefficients different from zero.

e. We can delete *distance*.

f. The new regression output follows.

Predictor	Coef	SE Coef	T	P
Constant	17.01	35.24	.48	.630
Bedrooms	7.169	2.559	2.80	0.006
Size	0.03919	0.01470	−2.67	0.009
Pool	19.110	6.994	2.73	0.007
Garage	38.847	7.281	5.34	0.000
Baths	24.624	8.995	2.74	0.007

S = 33.32 R-Sq = 52.4% R-Sq(adj) = 50.0%

Analysis of Variance

SOURCE	DF	SS	MS	F	P
Regression	5	120877	24175	21.78	0.000
Residual Error	99	109890	1110		
Total	104	230768			

In reviewing the *p*-values for the various regression coefficients, all are less than .05. We leave all the independent variables.

g. & h. Analysis of the residuals, not shown, indicates the normality assumption is reasonable. In addition, there is no pattern to the plots of the residuals and the fitted values of *Y*.

35. a. The regression equation is

$$\text{Maintenance} = 102 + 5.94\text{ Age} + 0.374\text{ Miles} - 11.8\text{ GasolineIndicator}$$

Each additional year of age adds \$5.94 to upkeep cost. Every extra mile adds \$0.374 to maintenance total. Gasoline buses are cheaper to maintain than diesel by \$11.80 per year.

b. The coefficient of determination is 0.286, found by 65,135/227,692. Twenty-nine percent of the variation in maintenance cost is explained by these variables.

c. The correlation matrix is:

	Maintenance	Age	Miles
Age	0.465		
Miles	0.450	0.522	
GasolineIndicator	−0.118	−0.068	0.025

Age and Miles both have moderately strong correlations with maintenance cost. The highest correlation among the independent variables is 0.522 between Age and Miles. That is smaller than 0.70, so multicollinearity may not be a problem.

d.

Analysis of Variance

Source	DF	SS	MS	F	P
Regression	3	65135	21712	10.15	0.000
Residual Error	76	162558	2139		
Total	79	227692			

The *p*-value is zero. Reject the null hypothesis of all coefficients being zero and say at least one is important.

e.

Predictor	Coef	SE Coef	T	P
Constant	102.3	112.9	0.91	0.368
Age	5.939	2.227	2.67	0.009
Miles	0.3740	0.1450	2.58	0.012
GasolineIndicator	−11.80	10.99	−1.07	0.286

The *p*-value of the gasoline indicator is bigger than 0.10. Consider deleting it.

f. The condensed regression equation is

$$\text{Maintenance} = 106 + 6.17\text{ Age} + 0.363\text{ Miles}$$

g.

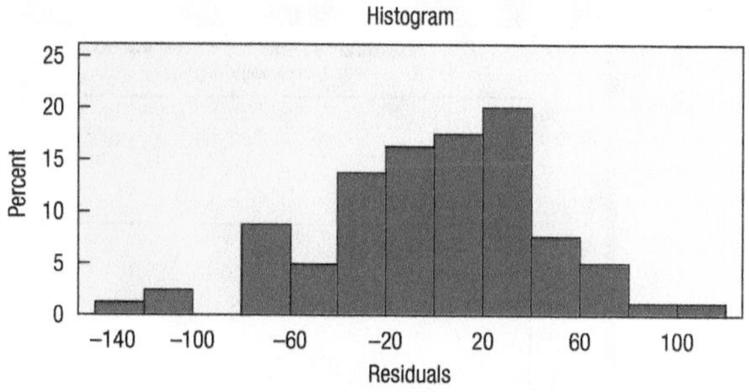

The normality conjecture appears realistic.

h.

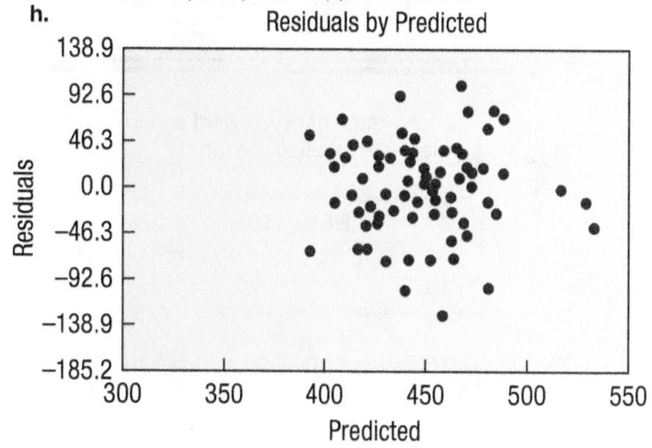

This plot appears to be random and to have a constant variance.

CHAPTER 15

1. a. H_0 is rejected if $z > 1.65$.

b. 1.09, found by $z = (0.75 - 0.70)/\sqrt{(0.70 \times 0.30)/100}$

c. H_0 is not rejected.

3. a. $H_0: \pi \leq 0.52 \quad H_1: \pi > 0.52$

b. H_0 is rejected if $z > 2.33$.

c. 1.62, found by $z = (.5667 - .52)/\sqrt{(0.52 \times 0.48)/300}$

d. H_0 is not rejected. We cannot conclude that the proportion of men driving on the Ohio Turnpike is larger than 0.52.

5. a. $H_0: \pi \geq 0.90 \quad H_1: \pi < 0.90$

b. H_0 is rejected if $z < -1.28$.

c. −2.67, found by $z = (0.82 - 0.90)/\sqrt{(0.90 \times 0.10)/100}$

d. H_0 is rejected. Fewer than 90% of the customers receive their orders in less than 10 minutes.

7. a. H_0 is rejected if $z > 1.65$.

b. 0.64, found by $p_c = \dfrac{70 + 90}{100 + 150}$

c. 1.61, found by

$$z = \frac{0.70 - 0.60}{\sqrt{[(0.64 \times 0.36)/100] + [(0.64 \times 0.36)/150]}}$$

d. H_0 is not rejected.

9. a. $H_0: \pi_1 = \pi_2 \quad H_1: \pi_1 \neq \pi_2$

b. H_0 is rejected if $z < -1.96$ or $z > 1.96$.

c. $p_c = \dfrac{24 + 40}{400 + 400} = 0.08$

d. −2.09, found by

$$z = \frac{0.06 - 0.10}{\sqrt{[(0.08 \times 0.92)/400] + [(0.08 \times 0.92)/400]}}$$

e. H_0 is rejected. The proportion infested is not the same in the two fields.

11. $H_0: \pi_d \leq \pi_r \qquad H_1: \pi_d > \pi_r$
H_0 is rejected if $z > 2.05$.

$$p_c = \frac{168 + 200}{800 + 1{,}000} = 0.2044$$

$$z = \frac{0.21 - 0.20}{\sqrt{\dfrac{(0.2044)(0.7956)}{800} + \dfrac{(0.2044)(0.7956)}{1{,}000}}} = 0.52$$

H_0 is not rejected. We cannot conclude that a larger proportion of Democrats favor lowering the standards. p-value = .3015.

13. **a.** 3
b. 7.815

15. **a.** Reject H_0 if $\chi^2 > 5.991$

b. $\chi^2 = \dfrac{(10 - 20)^2}{20} + \dfrac{(20 - 20)^2}{20} + \dfrac{(30 - 20)^2}{20} = 10.0$

c. Reject H_0. The proportions are not equal.

17. H_0: The outcomes are the same; H_1: The outcomes are not the same. Reject H_0 if $\chi^2 > 9.236$.

$$\chi^2 = \frac{(3 - 5)^2}{5} + \cdots + \frac{(7 - 5)^2}{5} = 7.60$$

Do not reject H_0. Cannot reject H_0 that outcomes are the same.

19. H_0: There is no difference in the proportions.
H_1: There is a difference in the proportions.
Reject H_0 if $\chi^2 > 15.086$.

$$\chi^2 = \frac{(47 - 40)^2}{40} + \cdots + \frac{(34 - 40)^2}{40} = 3.400$$

Do not reject H_0. There is no difference in the proportions.

21. **a.** Reject H_0 if $\chi^2 > 9.210$.

b. $\chi^2 = \dfrac{(30 - 24)^2}{24} + \dfrac{(20 - 24)^2}{24} + \dfrac{(10 - 12)^2}{12} = 2.50$

c. Do not reject H_0.

23. H_0: Proportions are as stated; H_1: Proportions are not as stated. Reject H_0 if $\chi^2 > 11.345$.

$$\chi^2 = \frac{(50 - 25)^2}{25} + \cdots + \frac{(160 - 275)^2}{275} = 115.22$$

Reject H_0. The proportions are not as stated.

25.

Number of Clients	z-values	Area	Found by	f_e
Under 30	Under −1.58	0.0571	0.5000 − 0.4429	2.855
30 up to 40	−1.58 up to −0.51	0.2479	0.4429 − 0.1950	12.395
40 up to 50	−0.51 up to 0.55	0.4038	0.1950 + 0.2088	20.19
50 up to 60	0.55 up to 1.62	0.2386	0.4474 − 0.2088	11.93
60 or more	1.62 or more	0.0526	0.5000 − 0.4474	2.63

The first and last class both have expected frequencies smaller than 5. They are combined with adjacent classes.
H_0: The population of clients follows a normal distribution.
H_1: The population of clients does not follow a normal distribution.
Reject the null if $\chi^2 > 5.991$.

Number of Clients	Area	f_e	f_o	$f_e - f_o$	$(f_o - f_e)^2$	$[(f_o - f_e)^2]/f_e$
Under 40	0.3050	15.25	16	−0.75	0.5625	0.0369
40 up to 50	0.4038	20.19	22	−1.81	3.2761	0.1623
50 or more	0.2912	14.56	12	2.56	6.5536	0.4501
Total	1.0000	50.00	50	0		0.6493

Since 0.6493 is not greater than 5.991, we fail to reject the null hypothesis. These data could be from a normal distribution.

27. H_0: There is no relationship between community size and section read. H_1: There is a relationship. Reject H_0 if $\chi^2 > 9.488$.

$$\chi^2 = \frac{(170 - 157.50)^2}{157.50} + \cdots + \frac{(88 - 83.62)^2}{83.62} = 7.340$$

Do not reject H_0. There is no relationship between community size and section read.

29. H_0: No relationship between error rates and item type.
H_1: There is a relationship between error rates and item type.
Reject H_0 if $\chi^2 > 9.21$.

$$\chi^2 = \frac{(20 - 14.1)^2}{14.1} + \cdots + \frac{(225 - 225.25)^2}{225.25} = 8.033$$

Do not reject H_0. There is not a relationship between error rates and item type.

31. **a.** This is a binomial situation with both the mean number of successes and failures equal to 23.5, found by 0.5(47).

b. $H_0: \pi = 0.50 \qquad H_1: \pi \neq 0.50$

c.

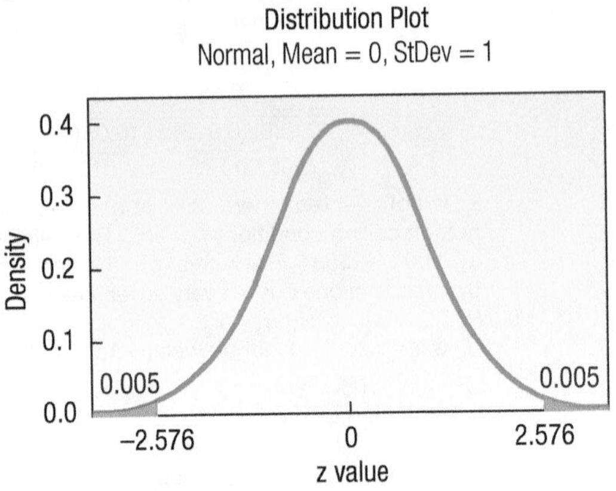

Reject H_0 if z is not between −2.576 and 2.576.

d. $z = \dfrac{\frac{31}{47} - 0.5}{\sqrt{0.5(1 - 0.5)/47}} = 2.19$. We fail to reject the null hypothesis. These data do not prove the coin flip is biased.

e. The p-value is 0.0286, found by 2(0.5000 − 0.4857). A value this extreme will happen about once out of 35 times with a fair coin.

33. $H_0: \pi \leq 0.60 \qquad H_1: \pi > 0.60$
H_0 is rejected if $z > 2.33$.

$$z = \frac{.70 - .60}{\sqrt{\dfrac{.60(.40)}{200}}} = 2.89$$

H_0 is rejected. Ms. Dennis is correct. More than 60% of the accounts are more than three months old.

35. $H_0: \pi \leq 0.44 \qquad H_1: \pi > 0.44$
H_0 is rejected if $z > 1.65$.

$$z = \frac{0.480 - 0.44}{\sqrt{(0.44 \times 0.56)/1.000}} = 2.55$$

H_0 is rejected. We conclude that there has been an increase in the proportion of people wanting to go to Europe.

37. $H_0: \pi \leq 0.20 \qquad H_1: \pi > 0.20$
H_0 is rejected if $z > 2.33$

$$z = \frac{(56/200) - 0.20}{\sqrt{(0.20 \times 0.80)/200}} = 2.83$$

H_0 is rejected. More than 20% of the owners move during a particular year. p-value = 0.5000 − 0.4977 = 0.0023.

39. H_0: $\pi \geq 0.0008$ H_1: $\pi < 0.0008$
H_0 is rejected if $z < -1.645$.

$$z = \frac{0.0006 - 0.0008}{\sqrt{\frac{0.0008\ (0.9992)}{10{,}000}}} = -0.707 \qquad H_0 \text{ is not rejected.}$$

These data do not prove there is a reduced fatality rate.

41. H_0: $\pi_1 \leq \pi_2$ H_1: $\pi_1 > \pi_2$
If $z > 2.33$, reject H_0.

$$p_c = \frac{990 + 970}{1{,}500 + 1{,}600} = 0.63$$

$$z = \frac{.6600 - .60625}{\sqrt{\frac{.63(.37)}{1{,}500} + \frac{.63(.37)}{1{,}600}}} = 3.10$$

Reject the null hypothesis. We can conclude the proportion of men who believe the division is fair is greater.

43. H_0: $\pi_1 \leq \pi_2$ H_1: $\pi_1 > \pi_2$ H_0 is rejected if $z > 1.65$.

$$p_c = \frac{.091 + .085}{2} = .088$$

$$z = \frac{0.091 - 0.085}{\sqrt{\frac{(0.088)\ (0.912)}{5{,}000} + \frac{(0.088)\ (0.912)}{5{,}000}}} = 1.059$$

H_0 is not rejected. There has not been an increase in the proportion calling conditions "good." The p-value is .1446, found by .5000 − .3554. The increase in the percentages will happen by chance in one out of every seven cases.

45. H_0: $\pi_1 = \pi_2$ H_1: $\pi_1 \neq \pi_2$
H_0 is rejected if z is not between −1.96 and 1.96.

$$p_c = \frac{100 + 36}{300 + 200} = .272$$

$$z = \frac{\frac{100}{300} - \frac{36}{200}}{\sqrt{\frac{(0.272)\ (0.728)}{300} + \frac{(0.272)\ (0.728)}{200}}} = 3.775$$

H_0 is rejected. There is a difference in the replies of the sexes.

47. H_0: $\pi_s = 0.50$, $\pi_r = \pi_e = 0.25$
H_1: Distribution is not as given above.
$df = 2$. Reject H_0 if $\chi^2 > 4.605$.

Turn	f_o	f_e	$f_o - f_e$	$(f_o - f_e)^2/f_e$
Straight	112	100	12	1.44
Right	48	50	−2	0.08
Left	40	50	−10	2.00
Total	200	200		3.52

H_0 is not rejected. The proportions are as given in the null hypothesis.

49. H_0: There is no preference with respect to TV stations.
H_1: There is a preference with respect to TV stations.
$df = 3 - 1 = 2$. H_0 is rejected if $\chi^2 > 5.991$.

TV Station	f_o	f_e	$f_o - f_e$	$(f_o - f_e)^2$	$(f_o - f_e)^2/f_e$
WNAE	53	50	3	9	0.18
WRRN	64	50	14	196	3.92
WSPD	33	50	−17	289	5.78
	150	150	0		9.88

H_0 is rejected. There is a preference for TV stations.

51. H_0: $\pi_n = 0.21$, $\pi_m = 0.24$, $\pi_s = 0.35$, $\pi_w = 0.20$
H_1: The distribution is not as given.
Reject H_0 if $\chi^2 > 11.345$.

Region	f_o	f_e	$f_o - f_e$	$(f_o - f_e)^2/f_e$
Northeast	68	84	−16	3.0476
Midwest	104	96	8	0.6667
South	155	140	15	1.6071
West	73	80	−7	0.6125
Total	400	400	0	5.9339

H_0 is not rejected. The distribution of order destinations reflects the population.

53. H_0: The proportions are the same.
H_1: The proportions are not the same.
Reject H_0 if $\chi^2 > 16.919$.

f_o	f_e	$f_o - f_e$	$(f_o - f_e)^2$	$(f_o - f_e)^2/f_e$
44	28	16	256	9.143
32	28	4	16	0.571
23	28	−5	25	0.893
27	28	−1	1	0.036
23	28	−5	25	0.893
24	28	−4	16	0.571
31	28	3	9	0.321
27	28	−1	1	0.036
28	28	0	0	0.000
21	28	−7	49	1.750
				14.214

Do not reject H_0. The digits are evenly distributed.

55.

Hourly Wage	f	M	fM	$M - x$	$(M - x)^2$	$f(M - x)^2$
\$5.50 up to 6.50	20	6	120	−2.222	4.938	98.8
6.50 up to 7.50	24	7	168	−1.222	1.494	35.9
7.50 up to 8.50	130	8	1040	−0.222	0.049	6.4
8.50 up to 9.50	68	9	612	0.778	0.605	41.1
9.50 up to 10.50	28	10	280	1.778	3.161	88.5
Total	270		2220			270.7

The sample mean is 8.222, found by 2,220/270. The sample standard deviation is 1.003, found as the square root of 270.7/269.
H_0: The population of wages follows a normal distribution.
H_1: The population of hourly wages does not follow a normal distribution.
Reject the null if $\chi^2 > 4.605$.

Wage	z-values	Area	Found by	f_e	f_o	$f_e - f_o$	$(f_o - f_e)^2$	$[(f_o - f_e)^2]/f_e$
Under \$6.50	Under −1.72	0.0427	0.5000 − 0.4573	11.529	20	−8.471	71.7578	6.2241
6.50 up to 7.50	−1.72 up to −0.72	0.1931	0.4573 − 0.2642	52.137	24	28.137	791.6908	15.1848
7.50 up to 8.50	−0.72 up to 0.28	0.3745	0.2642 + 0.1103	101.115	130	−28.885	834.3432	8.2514
8.50 up to 9.50	0.28 up to 1.27	0.2877	0.3980 − 0.1103	77.679	68	9.679	93.6830	1.2060
9.50 or more	1.27 or more	0.1020	0.5000 − 0.3980	27.54	28	−0.46	0.2116	0.0077
Total		1.0000		270	270	0		30.874

Since 30.874 is greater than 4.605, we reject the null hypothesis not from a normal distribution.

57. H_0: Gender and attitude toward the deficit are not related.
H_1: Gender and attitude toward the deficit are related.
Reject H_0 if $\chi^2 > 5.991$.

$$\chi^2 = \frac{(244 - 292.41)^2}{292.41} + \frac{(194 - 164.05)^2}{164.05} + \frac{(68 - 49.53)^2}{49.53} + \frac{(305 - 256.59)^2}{256.59} + \frac{(114 - 143.95)^2}{143.95} + \frac{(25 - 43.47)^2}{43.47} = 43.578$$

Since $43.578 > 5.991$, you reject H_0. A person's position on the deficit is influenced by his or her gender.

59. H_0: Whether a claim is filed and age are not related.
H_1: Whether a claim is filed and age are related.
Reject H_0 if $\chi^2 > 7.815$.

$$\chi^2 = \frac{(170 - 203.33)^2}{203.33} + \cdots + \frac{(24 - 35.67)^2}{35.67} = 53.639$$

Reject H_0. Age is related to whether a claim is filed.

61. H_0: $\pi_{BL} = \pi_O = .23$, $\pi_Y = \pi_G = .15$, $\pi_{BR} = \pi_R = .12$. H_1: The proportions are not as given. Reject H_0 if $\chi^2 > 15.086$.

Color	f_o	f_e	$(f_o - f_e)^2/f_e$
Blue	12	16.56	1.256
Brown	14	8.64	3.325
Yellow	13	10.80	0.448
Red	14	8.64	3.325
Orange	7	16.56	5.519
Green	12	10.80	0.133
Total	72		14.006

Do not reject H_0. The color distribution agrees with the manufacturer's information.

63. H_0: Salary and winning are not related H_1: Salary and winning are related Reject H_0 if $\chi^2 > 3.84$.

	Salary		
Winning	Lower Half	Top Half	Total
No	8	5	13
Yes	7	10	17
Total	15	15	

$$\chi^2 = \frac{(8 - 6.5)^2}{6.5} + \frac{(5 - 6.5)^2}{6.5} + \frac{(7 - 8.5)^2}{8.5} + \frac{(10 - 8.5)^2}{8.5} = 1.22$$

Do not reject H_0. Conclude that salary and winning may not be related.

CHAPTER 16

1. **a.** If the number of pluses (successes) in the sample is 9 or more, reject H_0.
b. Reject H_0 because the cumulative probability associated with nine or more successes (.073) does not exceed the significance level (.10).

3. **a.** H_0: $\pi \leq .50$; H_1: $\pi > .50$; $n = 10$
b. H_0 is rejected if there are nine or more plus signs. A "+" represents a loss.
c. Reject H_0. It is an effective program because there were nine people who lost weight.

5. **a.** H_0: $\pi \leq .50$ (There is no change in weight.)
H_1: $\pi > .50$ (There is a loss of weight.)
b. Reject H_0 if $z > 1.65$.
c. $z = \frac{(32 - .50) - .50(45)}{.50\sqrt{45}} = 2.68$
d. Reject H_0. The weight loss program is effective.

7. H_0: $\pi \leq .50$, H_1: $\pi > .50$. H_0 is rejected if $z > 2.05$.

$$z = \frac{42.5 - 40.5}{4.5} = .44$$

Because $.44 < 2.05$, do not reject H_0. No preference.

9. **a.** H_0: Median ≤ \$81,500; H_1: Median > \$81,500
b. H_0 is rejected if $z > 1.65$.
c. $z = \frac{170 - .50 - 100}{7.07} = 9.83$

H_0 is rejected. The median income is greater than \$81,500.

11.

Couple	Difference	Rank
1	550	7
2	190	5
3	250	6
4	−120	3
5	−70	1
6	130	4
7	90	2

Sums: −4, +24. So $T = 4$ (the smaller of the two sums). From Appendix B.8, .05 level, one-tailed test, $n = 7$, the critical value is 3. Since the T of $4 > 3$, do not reject H_0 (one-tailed test). There is no difference in square footage. Professional couples do not live in larger homes.

13. **a.** H_0: The production is the same for the two systems.
H_1: Production using the Mump method is greater.
b. H_0 is rejected if $T \leq 21$, $n = 13$.
c. The calculations for the first three employees are:

Employee	Old	Mump	d	Rank	R^+	R^-
A	60	64	4	6	6	
B	40	52	12	12.5	12.5	
C	59	58	−1	2		2

The sum of the negative ranks is 6.5. Since 6.5 is less than 21, H_0 is rejected. Production using the Mump method is greater.

15. H_0: The distributions are the same. H_1: The distributions are not the same. Reject H_0 if $z < -1.96$ or $z > 1.96$.

A		B	
Score	Rank	Score	Rank
38	4	26	1
45	6	31	2
56	9	35	3
57	10.5	42	5
61	12	51	7
69	14	52	8
70	15	57	10.5
79	16	62	13
	86.5		49.5

$$z = \frac{86.5 - \frac{8(8 + 8 + 1)}{2}}{\sqrt{\frac{8(8)(8 + 8 + 1)}{12}}} = 1.943$$

H_0 is not rejected. There is no difference in the two populations.

17. H_0: The distributions are the same. H_1: The distribution of Campus is to the right. Reject H_0 if $z > 1.65$.

Campus		Online	
Age	**Rank**	**Age**	**Rank**
26	6	28	8
42	16.5	16	1
65	22	42	16.5
38	13	29	9.5
29	9.5	31	11
32	12	22	3
59	21	50	20
42	16.5	42	16.5
27	7	23	4
41	14	25	5
46	19		94.5
18	2		
	158.5		

$$z = \frac{158.5 - \dfrac{12(12 + 10 + 1)}{2}}{\sqrt{\dfrac{12(10)(12 + 10 + 1)}{12}}} = 1.35$$

H_0 is not rejected. There is no difference in the distributions.

19. ANOVA requires that we have two or more populations, the data are interval- or ratio-level, the populations are normally distributed, and the population standard deviations are equal. Kruskal-Wallis requires only ordinal-level data, and no assumptions are made regarding the shape of the populations.

21. **a.** H_0: The three population distributions are equal. H_1: Not all of the distributions are the same.

b. Reject H_0 if $H > 5.991$.

c.

Sample 1 Rank	Sample 2 Rank	Sample 3 Rank
8	5	1
11	6.5	2
14.5	6.5	3
14.5	10	4
16	12	9
64	13	19
	53	

$$H = \frac{12}{16(16 + 1)}\left[\frac{(64)^2}{5} + \frac{(53)^2}{6} + \frac{(19)^2}{5}\right] - 3(16 + 1)$$

$$= 59.98 - 51 = 8.98$$

d. Reject H_0 because $8.98 > 5.991$. The three distributions are not equal.

23. H_0: The distributions of the lengths of life are the same.
H_1: The distributions of the lengths of life are not the same.
H_0 is rejected if $H > 9.210$.

Salt		Fresh		Others	
Hours	**Rank**	**Hours**	**Rank**	**Hours**	**Rank**
167.3	3	160.6	1	182.7	13
189.6	15	177.6	11	165.4	2
177.2	10	185.3	14	172.9	7
169.4	6	168.6	4	169.2	5
180.3	12	176.6	9	174.7	8
	46		39		35

$$H = \frac{12}{15(16)}\left[\frac{(46)^2}{5} + \frac{(39)^2}{5} + \frac{(35)^2}{5}\right] - 3(16) = 0.62$$

H_0 is not rejected. There is no difference in the three distributions.

25. **a.**

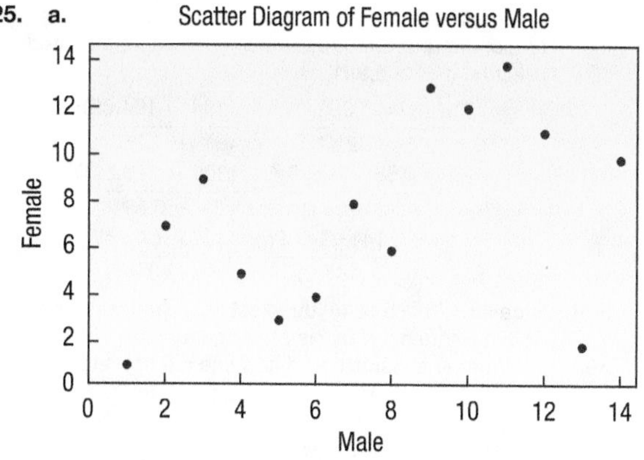

b.

Male	Female	d	d^2
4	5	−1	1
6	4	2	4
7	8	−1	1
2	7	−5	25
12	11	1	1
8	6	2	4
5	3	2	4
3	9	−6	36
13	2	11	121
14	10	4	16
1	1	0	0
9	13	−4	16
10	12	−2	4
11	14	−3	9
		Total	242

$$r_s = 1 - \frac{6(242)}{14(14^2 - 1)} = 0.47$$

c. H_0: No correlation among the ranks.
H_1: A positive correlation among the ranks.
Reject H_0 if $t > 1.782$.

$$t = 0.47\sqrt{\frac{14 - 2}{1 - (0.47)^2}} = 1.84$$

H_0 is rejected. We conclude the correlation in population among the ranks is positive. Husbands and wives generally like the same shows.

27.

Representative	Sales	Rank	Training Rank	d	d^2
1	319	8	8	0	0
2	150	1	2	1	1
3	175	2	5	3	9
4	460	10	10	0	0
5	348	9	7	−2	4
6	300	6.5	1	5.5	30.25
7	280	5	6	1	1
8	200	4	9	5	25
9	190	3	4	1	1
10	300	6.5	3	−3.5	12.25
					83.50

a. $r_s = 1 - \dfrac{6(83.5)}{10(10^2 - 1)} = 0.494$

A moderate positive correlation

b. H_0: No correlation among the ranks. H_1: A positive correlation among the ranks. Reject H_0 if $t > 1.860$.

$$t = 0.494\sqrt{\frac{10 - 2}{1 - (0.494)^2}} = 1.607$$

H_0 is not rejected. The correlation in population among the ranks could be 0.

29. H_0: $\pi = .50$. H_1: $\pi \neq .50$. Use a software package to develop the binomial probability distribution for $n = 19$ and $\pi = .50$. H_0 is rejected if there are either 5 or fewer "+" signs, or 14 or more. The total of 12 "+" signs falls in the acceptance region. H_0 is not rejected. There is no preference between the two shows.

31. H_0: $\pi = .50$ $\quad H_1$: $\pi \neq .50$
H_0 is rejected if there are 12 or more or 3 or fewer plus signs. Because there are only 8 plus signs, H_0 is not rejected. There is no preference with respect to the two brands of components.

33. H_0: $\pi = .50$; H_1: $\pi \neq .50$. Reject H_0 if $z > 1.96$ or $z < -1.96$.

$$z = \frac{159.5 - 100}{7.071} = 8.415$$

Reject H_0. There is a difference in the preference for the two types of orange juice.

35. H_0: Rates are the same; H_1: The rates are not the same. H_0 is rejected if $H > 5.991$. $H = .082$. Do not reject H_0.

37. H_0: The populations are the same. H_1: The populations differ. Reject H_0 if $H > 7.815$. $H = 14.30$. Reject H_0.

39. $$r_s = 1 - \frac{6(78)}{12(12^2 - 1)} = 0.727$$

H_0: There is no correlation between the rankings of the coaches and of the sportswriters.
H_1: There is a positive correlation between the rankings of the coaches and of the sportswriters.
Reject H_0 if $t > 1.812$.

$$t = 0.727\sqrt{\frac{12 - 2}{1 - (.727)^2}} = 3.348$$

H_0 is rejected. There is a positive correlation between the sportswriters and the coaches.

41. **a.** H_0: There is no difference in the distributions of the selling prices in the five townships. H_1: There is a difference in the distributions of the selling prices of the five townships. H_0 is rejected if H is greater than 9.488. The computed value of H is 4.70, so the null hypothesis is not rejected. The sample data do not suggest a difference in the distributions of selling prices.

b. H_0: There is no difference in the distributions of the selling prices depending on the number of bedrooms. H_1: There is a difference in the distributions of the selling prices depending on the number of bedrooms. H_0 is rejected if H is greater than 9.448. The computed value of H is 16.34, so the null hypothesis is rejected. The sample data indicate there is a difference in the distributions of selling prices based on the number of bedrooms. Note: Combine 6 or more into a single group.

c. H_0: There is no difference in the distributions of the distance from the center of the city depending on whether the home had a pool or not. H_1: There is a difference in the distributions of the distances from the center of the city depending on whether the home has a pool or not. H_0 is rejected if H is greater than 3.84. The computed value of H is 3.37, so the null hypothesis is not rejected. The sample data do not suggest a difference in the distributions of the distances.

43. **a.** H_0: The distributions of the maintenance costs are the same for all manufacturers.
H_1: The distributions of the costs are not the same.
H_0 is rejected if $H > 5.991$.

$$H = \frac{12}{80(81)}\left[\frac{(1765)^2}{47} + \frac{(972)^2}{25} + \frac{(503)^2}{8}\right] - 3(81) = 8.29$$

H_0 is rejected. There is a difference in the maintenance cost for the three bus manufacturers.

b. H_0: The distributions of the maintenance costs are the same for bus capacities.
H_1: The distributions of the costs are not the same.
H_0 is rejected if $H > 7.815$.

$$H = \frac{12}{80(81)}\left[\frac{(96.5)^2}{4} + \frac{(332.5)^2}{7} + \frac{(388.5)^2}{9} + \frac{(2422.5)^2}{60}\right] - 3(81) = 2.74$$

H_0 is not rejected. There is no difference in the maintenance cost for the four different capacities.

c. H_0: The distributions are the same.
H_1: The distributions are different.
Reject H_0 if $z < -1.96$ or $z > 1.96$.

$$W = \frac{2{,}252 - \frac{53(53 + 27 + 1)}{2}}{\sqrt{\frac{(53)(27)(53 + 27 + 1)}{12}}} = 1.07$$

We fail to reject H_0. The distributions could be the same.

CHAPTER 17

1. 114.6, found by (\$19,989/\$17,446)(100)
123.1, found by (\$21,468/\$17,446)(100)
124.3, found by (\$21,685/\$17,446)(100)
91.3, found by (\$15,922/\$17,446)(100)
105.3, found by (\$18,375/\$17,446)(100)
314.2, found by (\$54,818/\$17,446)(100)
475.4, found by (\$83,040/\$17,446)(100)

3. The mean sales for the earliest three years is \$(486.6 + 506.8 + 522.2)/3, or \$505.2.
2011: 90.4, found by (456.6/505.2)(100)
2012: 85.8, found by (433.3/505.2)(100)
Net sales decreased by 9.6 and 14.2%, respectively.

5. **a.** $P_t = \frac{3.35}{2.49}(100) = 134.54 \qquad P_s = \frac{4.49}{3.29}(100) = 136.47$

$P_c = \frac{4.19}{1.59}(100) = 263.52 \qquad P_a = \frac{2.49}{1.79}(100) = 139.11$

b. $P = \frac{14.52}{9.16}(100) = 158.52$

c. $$P = \frac{\$3.35(6) + 4.49(4) + 4.19(2) + 2.49(3)}{\$2.49(6) + 3.29(4) + 1.59(2) + 1.79(3)}(100) = 147.1$$

d. $$P = \frac{\$3.35(6) + 4.49(5) + 4.19(3) + 2.49(4)}{\$2.49(6) + 3.29(5) + 1.59(3) + 1.79(4)}(100) = 150.2$$

e. $I = \sqrt{(147.1)(150.2)} = 148.64$

7. **a.** $P_W = \frac{0.10}{0.07}(100) = 142.9 \qquad P_C = \frac{0.03}{0.04}(100) = 75.0$

$P_S = \frac{0.15}{0.15}(100) = 100 \qquad P_H = \frac{0.10}{0.08}(100) = 125.0$

b. $P = \frac{0.38}{0.34}(100) = 111.8$

c.
$$P = \frac{0.10(17{,}000) + 0.03(125{,}000) + 0.15(40{,}000) + 0.10(62{,}000)}{0.07(17{,}000) + 0.04(125{,}000) + 0.15(40{,}000) + 0.08(62{,}000)} \times (100) = 102.92$$

d.
$$P = \frac{0.10(20{,}000) + 0.03(130{,}000) + 0.15(42{,}000) + 0.10(65{,}000)}{0.07(20{,}000) + 0.04(130{,}000) + 0.15(42{,}000) + 0.08(65{,}000)} \times (100) = 103.32$$

e. $I = \sqrt{102.92(103.32)} = 103.12$

9. $$V = \frac{\$3.8(64) + 7.9(2) + 6.9(10{,}780) + 6.4(220)}{\$1.81(116) + 3.56(2) + 2.32(8{,}967) + 2.72(227)}(100) = 351.46$$

11. **a.** $$I = \frac{6.8}{5.3}(0.20) + \frac{362.26}{265.88}(0.40) + \frac{125.0}{109.6}(0.25) + \frac{622{,}864}{529{,}917}(0.15) = 1.263.$$

Index is 126.3.

b. Business activity increased 26.3% from 2000 to 2014.

13. $x = (\$89{,}673)/2.32531 = \$38{,}564$
"Real" salary increased \$38,564 − \$19,800 = \$18,764.

15.

Year	Tinora	Tinora Index	National Index
2000	\$28,650	100.0	100
2009	33,972	118.6	122.5
2013	37,382	130.5	136.9

The Tinora teachers received smaller increases than the national average.

17. The index (2000 = 100) for selected years is:

Year	Index	Year	Index	Year	Index	Year	Index
2001	114.5	2004	160.4	2007	187.4	2010	170.0
2002	129.7	2005	163.9	2008	186.6	2011	166.9
2003	146.0	2006	172.0	2009	178.4	2012	172.3

The domestic sales increased almost 90% between 2000 and 2007 and then decreased about 10 percent over the next five years.

19. The index (2000 = 100) for selected years is:

Year	Index	Year	Index	Year	Index	Year	Index
2001	105.4	2004	165.1	2007	241.7	2010	271.0
2002	116.8	2005	186.7	2008	265.2	2011	304.5
2003	139.9	2006	198.6	2009	261.5	2012	315.2

International sales more than tripled between 2000 and 2012.

21. The index (2000 = 100) for selected years is:

Year	Index	Year	Index	Year	Index	Year	Index
2001	100.9	2004	108.9	2007	118.1	2010	113.0
2002	107.3	2005	114.6	2008	117.6	2011	116.8
2003	109.6	2006	121.1	2009	114.5	2012	117.6

The number of employees increased about 15% between 2000 and 2005 and has remained at the same level since 2012.

23. The index (2004 = 100) for selected years is:

Year	2005	2006	2007	2008	2009	2010	2011	2012
Index	113.4	117.2	125.4	132.1	136.6	111.6	109.9	109.9

Revenue increased about 37% until 2009, then returned to almost 2005 levels.

25. The index (2004 = 100) for selected years is:

Year	2005	2006	2007	2008	2009	2010	2011	2012
Index	94.5	97.2	98.2	100.6	99.4	93.5	88.3	92.6

The number of employees decreased around 7% between 2008 and 2012.

27. $P_{ma} = \frac{2.00}{0.81}(100) = 246.91 \qquad P_{sh} = \frac{1.88}{0.84}(100) = 223.81$

$P_{mi} = \frac{2.89}{1.44}(100) = 200.69 \qquad P_{po} = \frac{3.99}{2.91}(100) = 137.11$

29. $P = \frac{\$2.00(18) + 1.88(5) + 2.89(70) + 3.99(27)}{\$0.81(18) + 0.84(5) + 1.44(70) + 2.91(27)}(100) = 179.37$

31. $I = \sqrt{179.37(178.23)} = 178.80$

33. $P_R = \frac{0.60}{0.50}(100) = 120 \qquad P_S = \frac{0.90}{1.20}(100) = 75.0$

$P_W = \frac{1.00}{0.85}(100) = 117.65$

35. $P = \frac{0.60(320) + 0.90(110) + 1.00(230)}{0.50(320) + 1.20(110) + 0.85(230)}(100) = 106.87$

37. $P = \sqrt{(106.87)(106.04)} = 106.45$

39. $P_C = \frac{0.05}{0.06}(100) = 83.33 \qquad P_C = \frac{0.12}{0.10}(100) = 120$

$P_P = \frac{0.18}{0.20}(100) = 90 \qquad P_E = \frac{.015}{0.15}(100) = 100$

41. $P = \frac{0.05(2{,}000) + 0.12(200) + 0.18(400) + 0.15(100)}{0.06(2{,}000) + 0.10(200) + 0.20(400) + 0.15(100)}(100)$
$= 89.79$

43. $I = \sqrt{(89.79)(91.25)} = 90.52$

45. $P_A = \frac{0.76}{0.287}(100) = 264.81 \qquad P_N = \frac{2.50}{0.17}(100) = 1{,}470.59$

$P_P = \frac{26.00}{3.18}(100) = 817.61 \qquad P_P = \frac{490}{133}(100) = 368.42$

47. $P = \frac{0.76(1{,}000) + 2.50(5{,}000) + 26(60{,}000) + 490(500)}{0.287(1{,}000) + 0.17(5{,}000) + 3.18(60{,}000) + 133(500)} \times$
$(100) = 703.56$

49. $I = \sqrt{(703.56)(686.58)} = 695.02$

51. $I = 100\left[\frac{1{,}971.0}{1{,}159.0}(0.20) + \frac{91}{87}(0.10) + \frac{114.7}{110.6}(0.40) + \frac{1{,}501}{1{,}214}(0.30)\right] = 123.05$

The economy is up 23.05% from 1996 to 2013.

53. February: $I = 100\left[\frac{6.8}{8.0}(0.40) + \frac{23}{20}(0.35) + \frac{303}{300}(0.25)\right] = 99.50$

March: $I = 100\left[\frac{6.4}{8.0}(0.40) + \frac{21}{20}(0.35) + \frac{297}{300}(0.25)\right] = 93.50$

55. For 1995: \$1,876,466, found by \$2,400,000/1.279
For 2012: \$1,799,486, found by \$3,500,000/1.945

CHAPTER 18

1. The weighted moving averages are: 31,584.8, 33,088.9, 34,205.4, 34,899.8, 35,155.0, 34,887.1

3. The regression equation is $\hat{y} = 8{,}842 - 88.1273t$.
For 2014, $t = 12$ and $\hat{y} = 8{,}842 - 88.1273(12) = 7{,}784.47$

5. $\hat{y} = 1.30 + 0.90t$
$\hat{y} = 1.30 + 0.90(7) = 7.6$

7. a. $b = \frac{5.274318 - (1.390087)(15)/5}{55 - (15)^2/5}$
$= \frac{1.104057}{10} = 0.1104057$

$a = \frac{1.390087}{5} - 0.1104057\left(\frac{15}{5}\right) = -0.0531997$

b. 28.95%, found by 1.28945 − 1.0

c. $\hat{y} = -0.0531997 + 0.1104057t$ for 2010, $t = 8$
$\hat{y} = -0.0531997 + 0.1104057(8) = 0.8300459$
Antilog of 0.8300459 = 6.76

9.

Quarter	Average SI Component	Seasonal Index
1	0.6859	0.6911
2	1.6557	1.6682
3	1.1616	1.1704
4	0.4732	0.4768

11.

t	Estimated Pairs (millions)	Seasonal Index	Quarterly Forecast (millions)
21	40.05	110.0	44.055
22	41.80	120.0	50.160
23	43.55	80.0	34.840
24	45.30	90.0	40.770

13. $\hat{y} = 5.1658 + .37805t$. The following are the sales estimates.

Estimate	Index	Seasonally Adjusted
10.080	0.6911	6.966
10.458	1.6682	17.446
10.837	1.1704	12.684
11.215	0.4768	5.343

15. a. The ordered residuals are 2.61, 2.83, −48.50, 15.50, −3.72, 17.17, 6.39, 7.72, −0.41, −16.86, 3.81, 7.25, 8.03, −1.08, and −0.75.

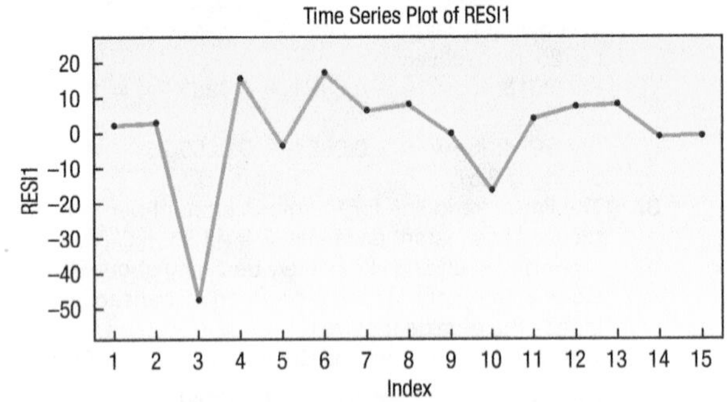

b. There are 2 independent variables (*k*) and the sample size (*n*) is 15. For a significance level of .05, the upper value is 1.54. Since the computed value of the Durbin-Watson statistic is 2.48, which is above the upper limit, the null hypothesis is not rejected. There is no autocorrelation among these residuals.

17. a. $\hat{y} = 18{,}000 - 400t$, assuming the line starts at 18,000 in 1995 and goes down to 10,000 in 2010.
b. 400
c. 8,000, found by 18,000 − 400(25)

19. a.

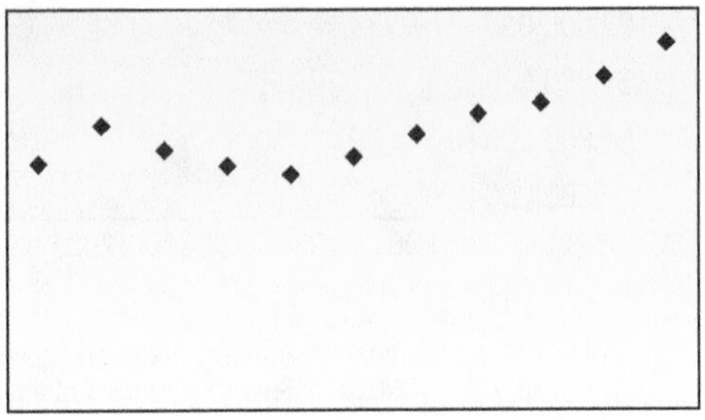

b. $\hat{y} = 1.00455 + 0.04409t$, using $t = 1$ for 2005
c. For 2007, $\hat{y} = 1.18091$, and for 2012, $\hat{y} = 1.40136$
d. For 2019, $\hat{y} = 1.70999$
e. Each asset turned over 0.044 times.

21. a.

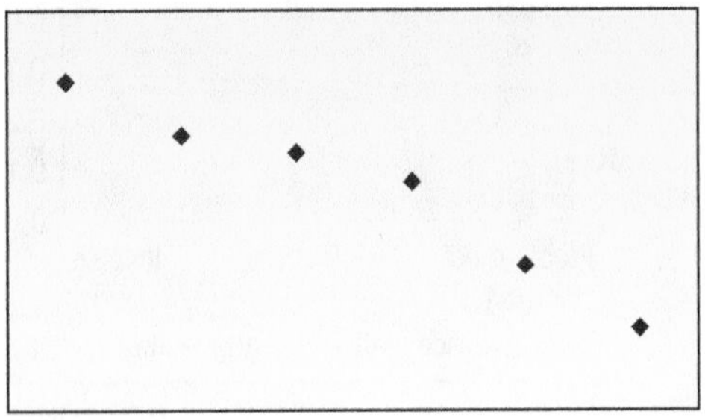

b. $\hat{y} = 49.140 - 2.9829t$
c. For 2011, $\hat{y} = 40.1913$ and for 2014, $\hat{y} = 31.2426$
d. For 2017, $\hat{y} = 22.2939$
e. The number of employees decreases at a rate of 2,983 per year.

23. a. Log $\hat{y} = 0.790231 + .113669t$
b. Log $\hat{y} = 0.9039$, found by 0.790231 + 0.113669(1), antilog is 8.015
Log $\hat{y} = 1.699583$, found by 0.790231 + .113699(8), antilog is 50.071
c. 29.92, which is the antilog of .113669 minus 1
d. Log $\hat{y} = 2.154258$, antilog is 142.65.

25. a.

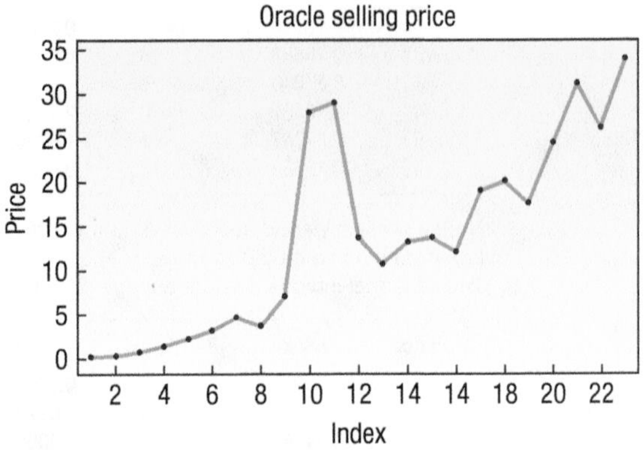

b. The equations are $\hat{y} = -2.58 + 1.37t$ and/or $\log \hat{y} = -0.133 + 0.0831t$.
The equation using the logarithm appears better because R^2 is larger.
c. $\log \hat{y} = -0.133 + 0.0831(4) = 0.1994$, antilog is 1.5827.
$\log \hat{y} = -0.133 + 0.0831(9) = 0.6149$, antilog is 4.12.
d. $\log \hat{y} = -0.133 + 0.0831(26) = 2.0276$, antilog is 106.56. It is reasonable only if the price rises at the historical rate!
e. The annual rate of increase is 21%, found by the antilog of 0.0831 minus 1.

27. a. July 87.5; August 92.9; September 99.3; October 109.1
b.

Month	Total	Mean	Corrected
July	348.9	87.225	86.777
Aug.	368.1	92.025	91.552
Sept.	395.0	98.750	98.242
Oct.	420.4	105.100	104.560
Nov.	496.2	124.050	123.412
Dec.	572.3	143.075	142.340
Jan.	333.5	83.375	82.946
Feb.	297.5	74.375	73.993
March	347.3	86.825	86.379
April	481.3	120.325	119.707
May	396.2	99.050	98.541
June	368.1	92.025	91.552
		1,206.200	

Correction = 1,200/1,206.2 = 0.99486
c. April, November, and December are periods of high sales, while February's sales are lowest.

Note: The solutions to Exercises 29 to 33 may vary due to rounding and the particular software package used.

29. a.

Seasonal Index by Quarter

Quarter	Average SI Component	Seasonal Index
1	0.5014	0.5027
2	1.0909	1.0936
3	1.7709	1.7753
4	0.6354	0.6370

b. Production is the largest in the third quarter. It is 77.5% above the average quarter. The second quarter is also

above average. The first and fourth quarters are well below average, with the first quarter at about 50% of a typical quarter.

31. a. The seasonal indices for package play are shown below. Recall that period 1 is actually July because the data begin with July.

Period	Index	Period	Index
1	0.19792	7	0.26874
2	0.25663	8	0.63189
3	0.87840	9	1.67943
4	2.10481	10	2.73547
5	0.77747	11	1.67903
6	0.18388	12	0.60633

Notice the 4th period (October) and the 10th period (April) are more than twice the average.

b. The seasonal indices for nonpackage play are:

Period	Index	Period	Index
1	1.73270	7	0.23673
2	1.53389	8	0.69732
3	0.94145	9	1.00695
4	1.29183	10	1.13226
5	0.66928	11	0.98282
6	0.52991	12	1.24486

These indices are more constant. Notice the very low values in the 6th (December) and 7th (January) periods.

c. The seasonal indices for total play are:

Period	Index	Period	Index
1	0.63371	7	0.25908
2	0.61870	8	0.65069
3	0.89655	9	1.49028
4	1.86415	10	2.28041
5	0.74353	11	1.48235
6	0.29180	12	0.78876

These indices show both the peaks in October (4th period) and April (10th period) and the valleys in December (6th period) and January (7th period).

d. Package play is relatively highest in April. Nonpackage play is relatively high in July. Since 70% of total play comes from package play, total play is very similar to package play.

33.

Seasonal Index by Quarter		
Quarter	Average SI Component	Seasonal Index
1	1.1962	1.2053
2	1.0135	1.0212
3	0.6253	0.6301
4	1.1371	1.1457

The regression equation is $\hat{y} = 43.611 + 7.21153t$

Period	Visitors	Index	Forecast
29	252.86	1.2053	304.77
30	260.07	1.0212	265.58
31	267.29	0.6301	168.42
32	274.50	1.1457	314.50

In 2013 there were a total of 928 visitors. A 10% increase in 2014 means there will be 1,021 visitors. The quarterly estimates are 1,021/4 = 255.25 visitors per quarter.

Period	Visitors	Index	Forecast
Winter	255.25	1.2053	307.65
Spring	255.25	1.0212	260.66
Summer	255.25	0.6301	160.83
Fall	255.25	1.1457	292.44

The regression approach is probably superior because the trend is considered.

35. The linear trend line is $\hat{y} = 0.469 + 0.114t$ and the logarithmic trend line is $\log \hat{y} = -0.0854 + 0.0255t$.
The equation using the logarithm appears better because R^2 is larger. The years 2013 and 2014 would be coded $t = 24$ and $t = 25$, respectively.
For 2013: $\log \hat{y} = -0.0854 + 0.0255(24) = 0.5266$, and its antilog is 3.36.
For 2014: $\log \hat{y} = -0.0854 + 0.0255(25) = 0.5521$, and its antilog is 3.57.

37. The linear trend line for the mean amount per transaction (expressed in constant dollars) is $\hat{y} = 41.58 - 0.238528t$.
Customer spending is definitely declining about \$0.24 per year. Here is an output for the regression of transactions over time (notice the p-value for time):
The regression equation is CPI = 41.6 − 0.239 Time

```
Predictor       Coef   SE Coef      T      P
Constant      41.583     1.078  38.56  0.000
Time        -0.23853   0.09003  -2.65  0.016
```

39.

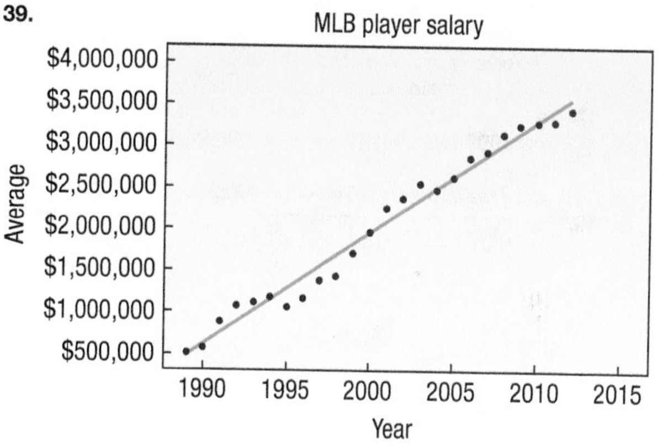

With 1988 as the base year, the regression equation is: $\hat{y} = 352{,}624 + 134{,}221t$. Salary increased at a rate of \$134,221 per year over the period.

CHAPTER 19

1.

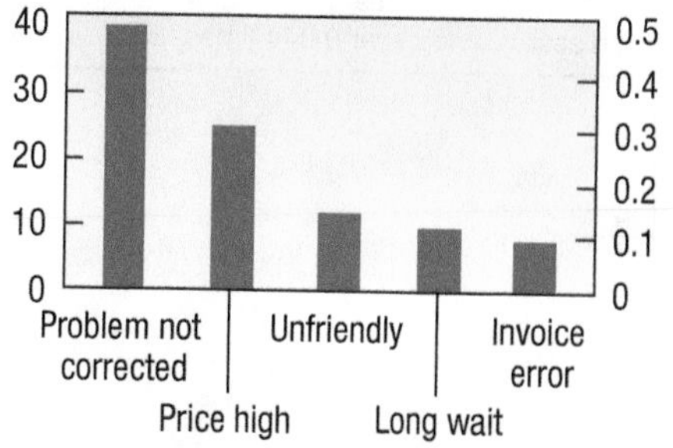

Count	38	23	12	10	8
Percent	42	25	13	11	9
Cum %	42	67	80	91	100

About 67% of the complaints concern the problem not being corrected and the price being too high.

3. Chance variation is random in nature; because the cause is a variety of factors, it cannot be entirely eliminated. Assignable variation is not random; it is usually due to a specific cause and can be eliminated.

5. a. The A_2 factor is 0.729.
   b. The value for D_3 is 0, and for D_4 it is 2.282.

7. a.

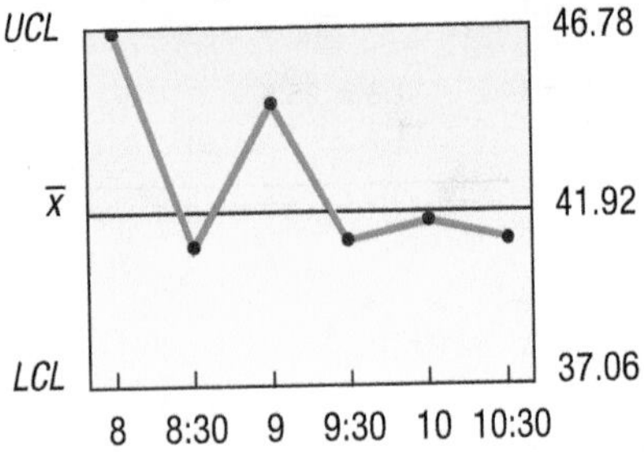

Time	$\overline{X}$, Arithmetic Means	R, Range
8:00 a.m.	46	16
8:30 a.m.	40.5	6
9:00 a.m.	44	6
9:30 a.m.	40	2
10:00 a.m.	41.5	9
10:30 a.m.	39.5	1
	251.5	40

$$\overline{\overline{X}} = \frac{251.5}{6} = 41.92 \qquad \overline{R} = \frac{40}{6} = 6.67$$

$$UCL = 41.92 + 0.729(6.67) = 46.78$$

$$LCL = 41.92 - 0.729(6.67) = 37.06$$

   b. Interpreting, the mean reading was 341.92 degrees Fahrenheit. If the oven continues operating as evidenced by the first six hourly readings, about 99.7% of the mean readings will lie between 337.06 degrees and 346.78 degrees.

9. a. The fraction defective is 0.0507. The upper control limit is 0.0801 and the lower control limit is 0.0213.
   b. Yes, the 7th and 9th samples indicate the process is out of control.
   c. The process appears to stay the same.

11. $\bar{c} = \frac{37}{14} = 2.64$

$2.64 \pm 3\sqrt{2.64}$

The control limits are 0 and 7.5. The process is out of control on the seventh day.

13. $\bar{c} = \frac{6}{11} = 0.545$

$0.545 \pm 3\sqrt{0.545} = 0.545 \pm 2.215$

The control limits are from 0 to 2.760, so there are no receipts out of control.

15.

Percent Defective	Probability of Accepting Lot
10	.889
20	.558
30	.253
40	.083

17. $P(x \leq 1 \mid n = 10, \pi = .10) = .736$
$P(x \leq 1 \mid n = 10, \pi = .20) = .375$
$P(x \leq 1 \mid n = 10, \pi = .30) = .149$
$P(x \leq 1 \mid n = 10, \pi = .40) = .046$

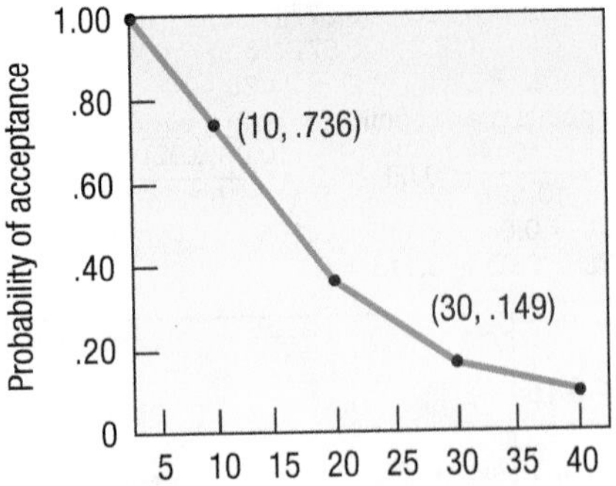

19.

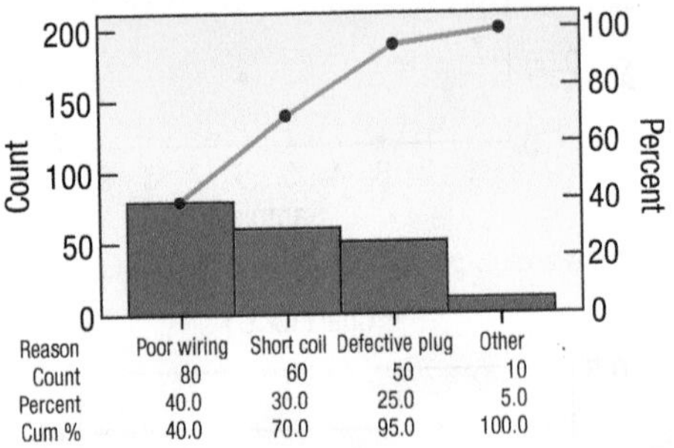

21. a. Mean: $UCL = 10.0 + 0.577(0.25) = 10.0 + 0.14425 = 10.14425$

$LCL = 10.0 - 0.577(0.25) = 10.0 - 0.14425 = 9.85575$

Range: $UCL = 2.115(0.25) = 0.52875$

$LCL = 0(0.25) = 0$

   b. The mean is 10.16, which is above the upper control limit and is out of control. There is too much cola in the soft drinks. The process is in control for variation; an adjustment is needed.

23. a. $\overline{\overline{X}} = \frac{611.3333}{20} = 30.57$

$\overline{R} = \frac{312}{20} = 15.6$

Mean: $UCL = 30.5665 + (1.023)(15.6) = 46.53$

$LCL = 30.5665 - (1.023)(15.6) = 14.61$

Range: $UCL = 2.575(15.6) = 40.17$

   b.

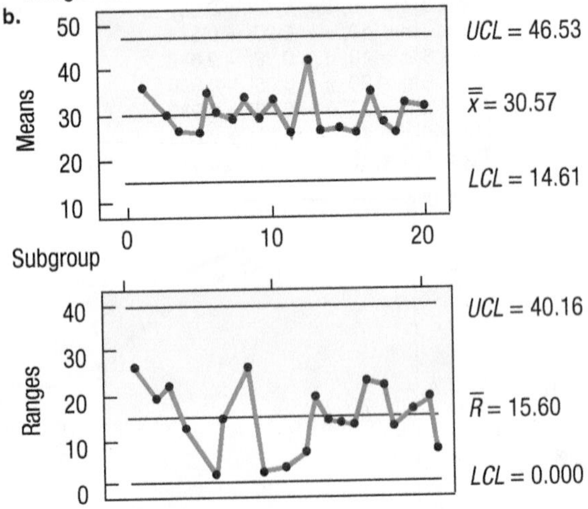

   c. The points all seem to be within the control limits. No adjustments are necessary.

25. $\overline{\overline{X}} = \frac{4,183}{10} = 418.3 \qquad \overline{R} = \frac{162}{10} = 16.2$

Mean: $UCL = 418.3 + (0.577)(16.2) = 427.65$
$LCL = 418.3 - (0.577)(16.2) = 408.95$
Range: $UCL = 2.115(16.2) = 34.26$
All the points are in control for both the mean and the range.

27. **a.** $p = \dfrac{40}{10(50)} = 0.08 \quad 3\sqrt{\dfrac{0.08(0.92)}{50}} = 0.115$
$UCL = 0.08 + 0.115 = 0.195$
$LCL = 0.08 - 0.115 = 0$

b.
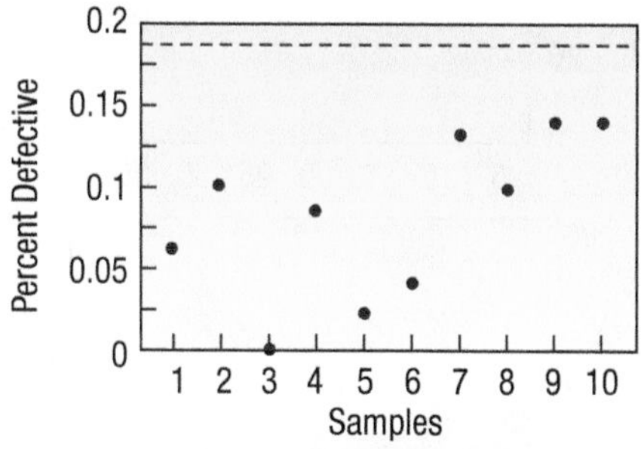

c. There are no points that exceed the limits.

29.
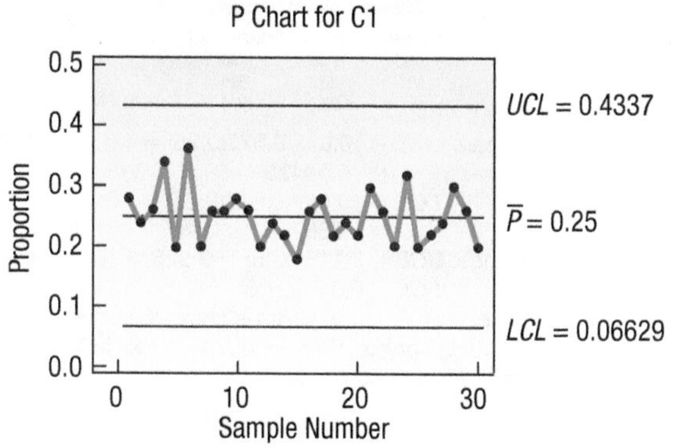

These sample results indicate that the odds are much less than 50-50 for an increase. The percent of stocks that increase is "in control" around 0.25, or 25%. The control limits are 0.06629 and 0.4337.

31. $P(x \le 3 \mid n = 10, \pi = 0.05) = 0.999$
$P(x \le 3 \mid n = 10, \pi = 0.10) = 0.987$
$P(x \le 3 \mid n = 10, \pi = 0.20) = 0.878$
$P(x \le 3 \mid n = 10, \pi = 0.30) = 0.649$
$P(x \le 5 \mid n = 20, \pi = 0.05) = 0.999$
$P(x \le 5 \mid n = 20, \pi = 0.10) = 0.989$
$P(x \le 5 \mid n = 20, \pi = 0.20) = 0.805$
$P(x \le 5 \mid n = 20, \pi = 0.30) = 0.417$

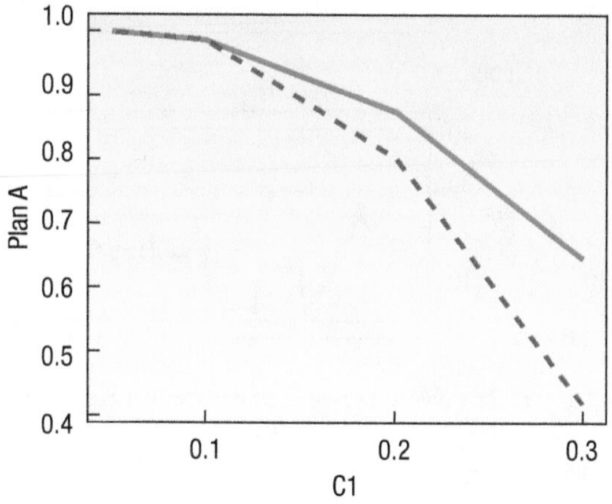

The solid line is the operating characteristic curve for the first plan, and the dashed line, the second. The supplier would prefer the first because the probability of acceptance is higher (above). However, if he is really sure of his quality, the second plan seems higher at the very low range of defect percentages and might be preferred.

33. **a.** $\bar{c} = \dfrac{213}{15} = 14.2; \ 3\sqrt{14.2} = 11.30$
$UCL = 14.2 + 11.3 = 25.5$
$LCL = 14.2 - 11.3 = 2.9$

b.
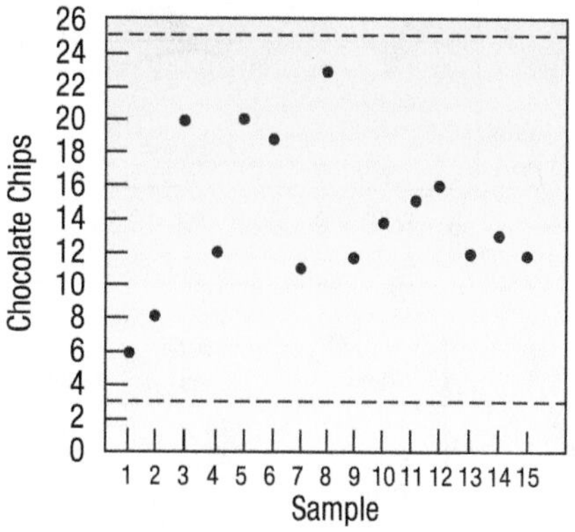

c. All the points are in control.

35. $\bar{c} = \dfrac{70}{10} = 7.0$
$UCL = 7.0 + 3\sqrt{7} = 14.9$
$LCL = 7.0 - 3\sqrt{7} = 0$

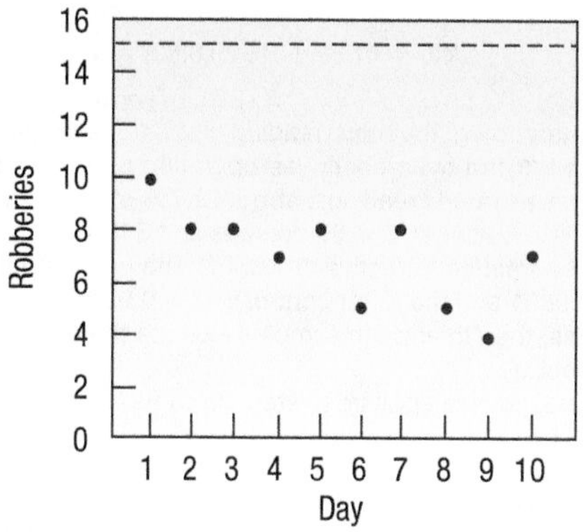

37. $P(x \le 3 \mid n = 20, \pi = .10) = .867$
$P(x \le 3 \mid n = 20, \pi = .20) = .412$
$P(x \le 3 \mid n = 20, \pi = .30) = .108$

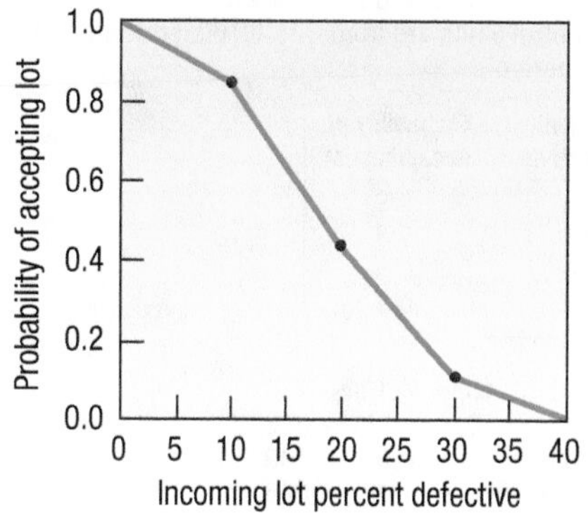

APPENDIX D: ANSWERS

Answers to Odd-Numbered Review Exercises

REVIEW OF CHAPTERS 1–4
PROBLEMS

1. a. Mean is 147.9. Median is 148.5. Standard deviation is 69.24.
   b. The first quartile is 106. The third quartile is 186.25.
   c.

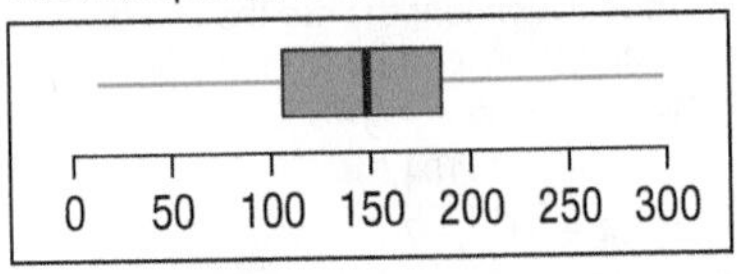

   There are no outliers. The distribution is symmetric. The whiskers and the boxes are about equal on the two sides.

   d. $2^6 = 64$, use 6 classes; $i = \frac{299 - 14}{6} = 47.5$, use $i = 50$.

Amount	Frequency
\$ 0 up to \$ 50	3
50 up to 100	8
100 up to 150	15
150 up to 200	13
200 up to 250	7
250 up to 300	7
Total	50

   e. Answers will vary but include all of the above information.

3. a. Mean is \$35,768. Median is \$34,405. Standard deviation is \$5,992.
   b. The first quartile is \$32,030. The third quartile is 38,994.
   c.

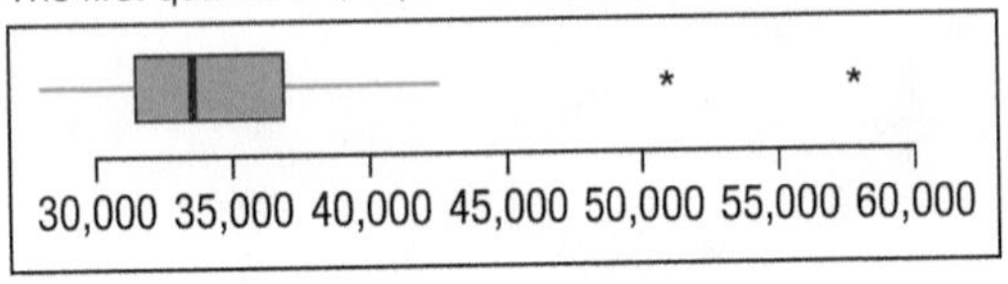

   There are two outliers above \$50,000. The distribution is positively skewed. The whiskers and the boxes on the right are much larger than the ones on the left.

   d.

Amounts	Frequency
\$24,000 up to 30,000	8
30,000 up to 36,000	22
36,000 up to 42,000	15
42,000 up to 48,000	4
48,000 up to 54,000	1
54,000 up to 60,000	1
Total	51

   e. Answers will vary but include all of the above information.

5. a. Box plot.
   b. Median is 48, the first quartile is 24, and the third quartile is 84.
   c. Positively skewed with the long tail to the right.
   d. You cannot determine the number of observations.

REVIEW OF CHAPTERS 5–7
PROBLEMS

1. a. .035
   b. .018
   c. .648

3. a. .0401
   b. .6147
   c. 7,440

5. a. $\mu = 1.10$
   $\sigma = 1.18$
   b. About 550
   c. $\mu = 1.833$

REVIEW OF CHAPTERS 8 AND 9
PROBLEMS

1. $z = \frac{8.8 - 8.6}{2.0/\sqrt{35}} = 0.59$, $.5000 - .2224 = .2776$

3. $160 \pm 2.426 \frac{20}{\sqrt{40}}$, 152.33 up to 167.67

5. $985.5 \pm 2.571 \frac{115.5}{\sqrt{6}}$, 864.27 up to 1,106.73

7. $240 \pm 2.131 \frac{35}{\sqrt{16}}$, 221.35 up to 258.65

   Because 250 is in the interval, the evidence does *not* indicate an increase in production.

9. $n = \left[\frac{1.96(25)}{4}\right]^2 = 150$

11. $n = .08(.92)\left(\frac{2.33}{0.02}\right)^2 = 999$

13. $n = .4(.6)\left(\frac{2.33}{0.03}\right)^2 = 1,448$

REVIEW OF CHAPTERS 10–12
PROBLEMS

1. H_0: $\mu \geq 36$; H_1: $\mu < 36$. Reject H_0 if $t < -1.683$.

$$t = \frac{35.5 - 36.0}{0.9/\sqrt{42}} = -3.60$$

   Reject H_0. The mean height is less than 36 inches.

3. H_0: $\mu_1 = \mu_2$ $\quad H_1$: $\mu_1 \neq \mu_2$
   Reject H_0 if $t < -2.845$ or $t > 2.845$.

$$s_p^2 = \frac{(12 - 1)(5)^2 + (10 - 1)(8)^2}{12 + 10 + 2} = 42.55$$

$$t = \frac{250 - 252}{\sqrt{42.55\left(\frac{1}{12} + \frac{1}{10}\right)}} = -0.716$$

   H_0 is not rejected. There is no difference in the mean strength of the two glues.

5. H_0: $\mu_1 = \mu_2 = \mu_3 = \mu_4$ $\quad H_1$: The means are not all the same
   H_0 rejected if $F > 3.29$.

Source	SS	*df*	MS	*F*
Treatments	20.736	3	6.91	1.04
Error	100.00	15	6.67	
Total	120.736	18		

   H_0 is not rejected. There is no difference in the mean sales.

7. a. From the graph, marketing salaries may be acting differently.
   b. H_0: $\mu_1 = \mu_2 = \mu_3 = \mu_4$
   H_1: At least one mean is different (for four majors)

H_0: $\mu_1 = \mu_2 = \mu_3$
H_1: At least one mean is different (for three years)
H_0: There is no interaction
H_1: There is interaction

c. The p-value (.482) is high. Do not reject the hypothesis of no interaction.

d. The p-value for majors is small (.034 < .05), so there is a difference among mean salaries by major. There is no difference from one year to the next in mean salaries (.894 > .05).

REVIEW OF CHAPTERS 13 AND 14 PROBLEMS

1. a. Profit
   b. $\hat{y} = a + b_1x_1 + b_2x_2 + b_3x_3 + b_4x_4$
   c. $163,200
   d. About 86% of the variation in net profit is explained by the four variables.
   e. About 68% of the net profits would be within $3,000 of the estimates; about 95% would be within 2($3,000), or $6,000, of the estimates; and virtually all would be within 3($3,000), or $9,000, of the estimates.
3. a. 0.9261
   b. 2.0469, found by $\sqrt{83.8/20}$
   c. H_0: $\beta_1 = \beta_2 = \beta_3 = \beta_4 = 0$
      H_1: Not all coefficients are zero.
      Reject if $F > 2.87$; computed $F = 62.697$, found by 162.70/4.19.
   d. Could delete x_2 because t-ratio (1.29) is less than the critical t value of 2.086. Otherwise, reject H_0 for x_1, x_3, and x_4 because all of those t-ratios are greater than 2.086.

REVIEW OF CHAPTERS 15 AND 16 PROBLEMS

1. H_0: Median ≤ 60
   H_1: Median > 60
   $\mu = 20(.5) = 10$
   $\sigma = \sqrt{20(.5)(.5)} = 2.2361$
   H_0 is rejected if $z > 1.65$. There are 16 observations greater than 60.

$$z = \frac{15.5 - 10.0}{2.2361} = 2.46$$

   Reject H_0. The median sales per day are greater than 60.
3. H_0: The population lengths are the same.
   H_1: The population lengths are not the same.
   H_0 is rejected if H is > 5.991.

$$H = \frac{12}{24(24+1)}\left[\frac{(104.5)^2}{7} + \frac{(125.5)^2}{9} + \frac{(70)^2}{8}\right] - 3(24+1)$$
$$= 78.451 - 75 = 3.451$$

   Do not reject H_0. The population lengths are the same.

REVIEW OF CHAPTERS 17 AND 18 PROBLEMS

1. a. 137.8, found by (14,883/10,799)100
   b. 134.6, found by (14,883/11,056.7)100. Note: 11,056.7 is the average for the period 2008 to 2010.
   c. 8,941 + 1,112t and 16,725, found by 8,941 + 1,112(7)
3. 55.44, found by 1.20[3.5 + (0.7)(61)], and 44.73, found by 0.90[3.5 + (0.7)(66)]

APPENDIX D: ANSWERS

Solutions to Practice Tests

PRACTICE TEST (AFTER CHAPTER 4)

Part 1

1. statistics
2. descriptive statistics
3. population
4. quantitative and qualitative
5. discrete
6. nominal
7. nominal
8. zero
9. seven
10. 50
11. variance
12. never
13. median

Part 2

1. $\sqrt[3]{(1.18)(1.04)(1.02)} = 1.0777$, *or* 7.77%
2. **a.** 30 thousands of dollars
   b. 105
   c. 52
   d. 0.19, found by 20/105
   e. 165
   f. 120 and 330
3. **a.** 70
   b. 71.5
   c. 67.8
   d. 28
   e. 9.34
4. $44.20, found by [(200)$36 + (300)$40 + (500)$50]/1,000
5. **a.** pie chart
   b. 11.1
   c. three times
   d. 65%

PRACTICE TEST (AFTER CHAPTER 7)

Part 1

1. never
2. experiment
3. event
4. joint
5. **a.** permutation
   b. combination
6. one
7. three or more outcomes
8. infinite
9. one
10. 0.2764
11. 0.0475
12. independent
13. mutually exclusive
14. only two outcomes
15. bell-shaped

Part 2

1. **a.** 0.0526, found by (5/20)(4/19)
   b. 0.4474, found by 1 − (15/20)(14/19)
2. **a.** 0.2097, found by $16(.15)(.85)^{15}$
   b. 0.9257, found by $1 - (.85)^{16}$
3. 720, found by 6 · 5 · 4 · 3 · 2
4. **a.** 2.2, found by .2(1) + .5(2) + .2(3) + .1(4)
   b. 0.76, found by .2(1.44) + .5(0.04) + .2(0.64) + .1(3.24)
5. **a.** 0.1808. The z value for $2,000 is 0.47, found by (2,000 − 1,600)/850.
   b. 0.4747, found by 0.2939 + 0.1808
   c. 0.0301, found by 0.5000 − 0.4699
6. **a.** contingency table
   b. 0.625, found by 50/80
   c. 0.75, found by 60/80
   d. 0.40, found by 20/50
   e. 0.125, found by 10/80
7. **a.** 0.0498, found by $\frac{3^0 e^{-3}}{0!}$
   b. 0.2240, found by $= \frac{3^3 e^{-3}}{3!}$
   c. 0.1847, found by 1 − [0.0498 + 0.1494 + 0.2240 + 0.2240 + 0.1680]
   d. .0025

PRACTICE TEST (AFTER CHAPTER 9)

Part 1

1. random sample
2. sampling error
3. standard error
4. become smaller
5. point estimate
6. confidence interval
7. population size
8. proportion
9. positively skewed
10. 0.5

Part 2

1. 0.0351, found by 0.5000 − 0.4649. The corresponding $z = \frac{11 - 12.2}{2.3/\sqrt{12}} = -1.81$
2. **a.** The population mean is unknown.
   b. 9.3 years, which is the sample mean
   c. 0.3922, found by $2/\sqrt{26}$
   d. The confidence interval is from 8.63 up to 9.97, found by $9.3 \pm 1.708\left(\frac{2}{\sqrt{26}}\right)$
3. 2,675, found by $.27(1 - .27)\left(\frac{2.33}{.02}\right)^2$
4. The confidence interval is from 0.5459 up to 0.7341, found by $.64 \pm 1.96\sqrt{\frac{.64(1 - .64)}{100}}$

PRACTICE TEST (AFTER CHAPTER 12)

Part 1

1. null hypothesis
2. significance level
3. *p*-value
4. standard deviation
5. normality
6. test statistic
7. split evenly between the two tails
8. range from negative infinity to positive infinity

9. independent
10. three and 20

Part 2

1. H_0: $\mu \leq 90$ H_1: $\mu > 90$ If $t > 2.567$, reject H_0.

$$t = \frac{96 - 90}{12/\sqrt{18}} = 2.12$$

Do not reject the null. The mean time in the park could be 90 minutes.

2. H_0: $\mu_1 = \mu_2$ H_1: $\mu_1 \neq \mu_2$.
$df = 14 + 12 - 2 = 24$
If $t < -2.064$ or $t > 2.064$, then reject H_0.

$$s_p^2 = \frac{(14 - 1)(30)^2 + (12 - 1)(40)^2}{14 + 12 - 2} = 1{,}220.83$$

$$t = \frac{837 - 797}{\sqrt{1{,}220.83\left(\frac{1}{14} + \frac{1}{12}\right)}} = \frac{40.0}{13.7455} = 2.910$$

Reject the null hypothesis. There is a difference in the mean miles traveled.

3. a. three, because there are 2 *df* between groups.
   b. 21, found by the total degrees of freedom plus 1.
   c. If the significance level is .05, the critical value is 3.55.
   d. H_0: $\mu_1 = \mu_2 = \mu_3$ H_1: Treatment means are not all the same.
   e. At a 5% significance level, the null hypothesis is rejected.
   f. At a 5% significance level, we can conclude the treatment means differ.

PRACTICE TEST (AFTER CHAPTER 14)

Part 1

1. vertical
2. interval
3. zero
4. −0.77
5. never
6. 7
7. decrease of .5
8. −0.9
9. zero
10. unlimited
11. linear
12. residual
13. two
14. correlation matrix
15. normal distribution

Part 2

1. a. 30
   b. The regression equation is $\hat{y} = 90.619X - 0.9401$. If x is zero, the line crosses the vertical axis at −0.9401. As the independent variable increases by one unit, the dependent variable increases by 90.619 units.
   c. 905.2499
   d. 0.3412, found by 129.7275/380.1667. Thirty-four percent of the variation in the dependent variable is explained by the independent variable.
   e. 0.5842, found by $\sqrt{0.3412}$ H_0: $\rho \geq 0$ H_1: $\rho < 0$
   Using a significance level of .01, reject H_0 if $t > 2.467$.

$$t = \frac{0.5842\sqrt{30 - 2}}{\sqrt{1 - (0.5842)^2}} = 3.81$$

   Reject H_0. There is a negative correlation between the variables.

2. a. 30
   b. 4
   c. 0.5974, found by 227.0928/380.1667
   d. H_0: $\beta_1 = \beta_2 = \beta_3 = \beta_4 = 0$ H_1: Not all βs are 0.
   Reject H_0 if $F > 4.18$ (using a 1% level of significance).
   Since the computed value of F is 9.27, reject H_0. Not all of the regression coefficients are zero.
   e. Reject H_0 if $t > 2.787$ or $t < -2.787$ (using a 1% level of significance). Drop variable 2 initially and then rerun. Perhaps you will delete variable(s) 1 and/or 4 also.

PRACTICE TEST (AFTER CHAPTER 16)

Part 1

1. nominal
2. at least 30 observations
3. two
4. 6
5. number of categories
6. dependent
7. binomial
8. comparing two or more independent samples
9. never
10. normal populations, equal standard deviations

Part 2

1. H_0: The proportions are as stated.
H_1: The proportions are not as stated.
Using a significance level of .05, reject H_0 if $\chi^2 > 7.815$.

$$\chi^2 = \frac{(120 - 130)^2}{130} + \frac{(40 - 40)^2}{40} + \frac{(30 - 20)^2}{20} + \frac{(10 - 10)^2}{10} = 5.769$$

Do not reject H_0. Proportions could be as declared.

2. H_0: No relationship between gender and book type.
H_1: There is a relationship between gender and book type.
Using a significance level of .01, reject H_0 if $\chi^2 > 9.21$.

$$\chi^2 = \frac{(250 - 197.3)^2}{197.3} + \cdots + \frac{(200 - 187.5)^2}{187.5} = 54.84$$

Reject H_0. There is a relationship between gender and book type.

3. H_0: The distributions are the same.
H_1: The distributions are not the same.
H_0 is rejected if $H > 5.99$.

8:00 a.m. Ranks		10:00 a.m. Ranks		1:30 p.m. Ranks	
68	6	59	1.5	67	5
84	20	59	1.5	69	7
75	10.5	63	4	75	10.5
78	15.5	62	3	76	12.5
70	8	78	15.5	79	17
77	14	76	12.5	83	19
88	24	80	18	86	21.5
71	9			86	21.5
				87	23
Sums	107		56		137
Count	8		7		9

$$H = \frac{12}{24(25)}\left[\frac{107^2}{8} + \frac{56^2}{7} + \frac{137^2}{9}\right] - 3(25) = 4.29$$

H_0 is not rejected. There is no difference in the three distributions.

4. H_0: $\pi \leq 1/3$ H_1: $\pi > 1/3$
At the .01 significance level, the decision rule is to reject H_0 if $z > 2.326$.

$$z = \frac{\left[\frac{210}{500} - \frac{1}{3}\right]}{\sqrt{\frac{\left(\frac{1}{3}\right)\left(1 - \frac{1}{3}\right)}{500}}} = \frac{0.08667}{0.02108} = 4.11$$

Reject the null hypothesis.
The actual proportion of Louisiana children who were obese or overweight is more than one out of three.

PRACTICE TEST (AFTER CHAPTER 18)

Part 1

1. denominator
2. index
3. quantity
4. base period
5. 1982–1984
6. trend
7. moving average
8. autocorrelation
9. residual
10. same

Part 2

1. **a.** 111.54, found by (145,000/130,000) × 100 for 2009
   92.31, found by (120,000/130,000) × 100 for 2010
   130.77, found by (170,000/130,000) × 100 for 2011
   146.15, found by (190,000/130,000) × 100 for 2012
   b. 87.27, found by (120,000/137,500) × 100 for 2010
   126.64, found by (170,000/137,500) × 100 for 2011
   138.18, found by (190,000/137,500) × 100 for 2012
2. **a.** 108.91, found by (1,100/1,010) × 100
   b. 111.18, found by (4,525/4,070) × 100
   c. 110.20, found by (5,400/4,900) × 100
   d. 110.69, found by the square root of (111.18) × (110.20)
3. For January of the fifth year, the seasonally adjusted forecast is 70.0875, found by 1.05 × [5.50 + 1.25(49)].
   For February of the fifth year, the seasonally adjusted forecast is 66.844, found by 0.983 × [5.50 + 1.25(50)].

APPENDIX E: ANSWERS TO SELF-REVIEW

CHAPTER 1

1–1 a. On the basis of the sample of 1,960 consumers, we estimate that, if it is marketed, 60% of all consumers will purchase the chicken dinner: $(1{,}176/1{,}960) \times 100 = 60\%$.

b. Inferential statistics, because a sample was used to draw a conclusion about how all consumers in the population would react if the chicken dinner were marketed.

1–2 a. Age is a ratio-scale variable. A 40-year-old is twice as old as someone 20 years old.

b. Nominal scale. We could arrange the states in any order.

CHAPTER 2

2–1 a. Qualitative data, because the customers' response to the taste test is the name of a beverage.

b. Frequency table. It shows the number of people who prefer each beverage.

c.

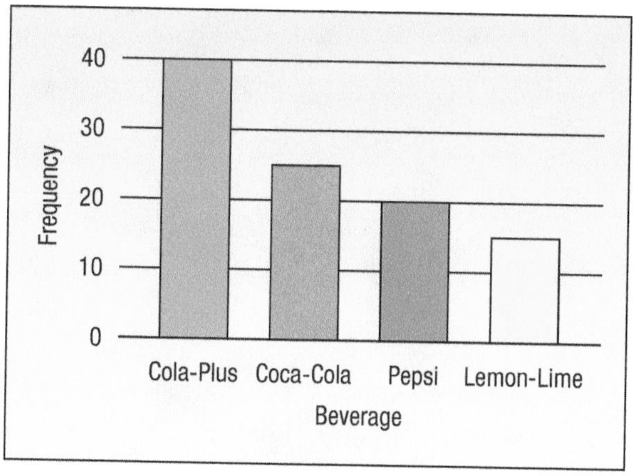

d.

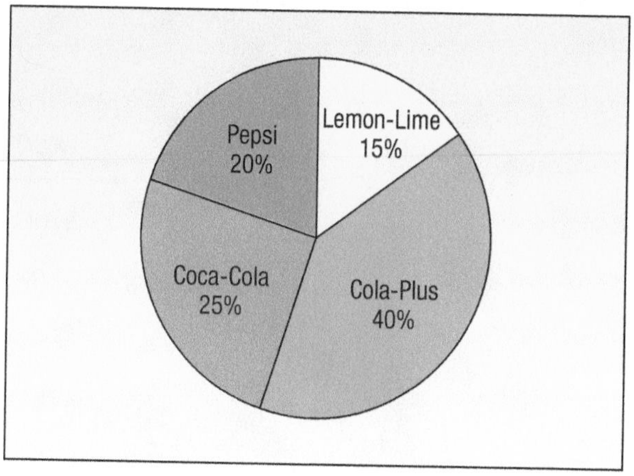

2–2 a. The raw data or ungrouped data.

b.

Commission	Number of Salespeople
\$1,400 up to \$1,500	2
1,500 up to 1,600	5
1,600 up to 1,700	3
1,700 up to 1,800	1
Total	11

c. Class frequencies.

d. The largest concentration of commissions is \$1,500 up to \$1,600. The smallest commission is about \$1,400 and the largest is about \$1,800. The typical amount earned is \$1,550.

2–3 a. $2^6 = 64 < 73 < 128 = 2^7$, so seven classes are recommended.

b. The interval width should be at least $(488 - 320)/7 = 24$. Class intervals of either 25 or 30 are reasonable.

c. Assuming a class interval of 25 and beginning with a lower limit of 300, eight classes are required. If we use an interval of 30 and begin with a lower limit of 300, only 7 classes are required. Seven classes is the better alternative.

Distance Classes	Frequency	Percent
300 up to 330	2	2.7%
330 up to 360	2	2.7
360 up to 390	17	23.3
390 up to 420	27	37.0
420 up to 450	22	30.1
450 up to 480	1	1.4
480 up to 510	2	2.7
Grand Total	73	100.00

d. 17

e. 23.3%, found by 17/73

f. 71.2%, found by $(27 + 22 + 1 + 2)/73$

2–4 a.

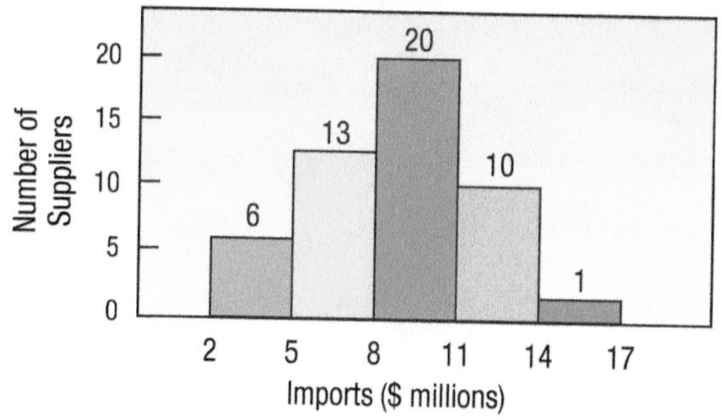

b.

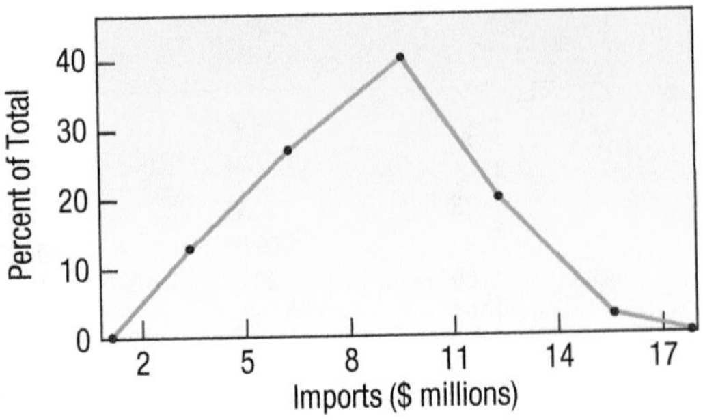

The plots are: (3.5, 12), (6.5, 26), (9.5, 40), (12.5, 20), and (15.5, 2).

c. The smallest annual volume of imports by a supplier is about $2 million, the largest about $17 million. The highest frequency is between $8 million and $11 million.

2–5 **a.** A frequency distribution.

b.

Hourly Wages	Cumulative Number
Less than $8	0
Less than $10	3
Less than $12	10
Less than $14	14
Less than $16	15

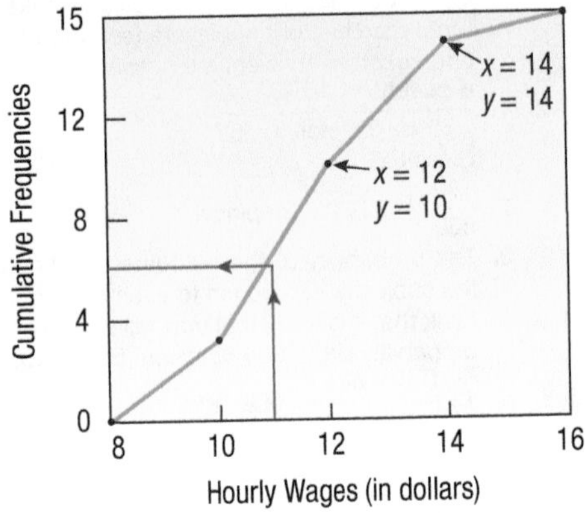

c. About seven employees earn $11.00 or less.

CHAPTER 3

3–1 **1. a.** $\bar{x} = \frac{\Sigma x}{n}$

b. $\bar{x} = \frac{\$267,100}{4} = \$66,775$

c. Statistic, because it is a sample value.

d. $66,775. The sample mean is our best estimate of the population mean.

2. a. $\mu = \frac{\Sigma x}{N}$

b. $\mu = \frac{498}{6} = 83$

c. Parameter, because it was computed using all the population values.

3–2 **1. a.** $878

b. 3, 3

2. a. 7, found by $(6 + 8)/2 = 7$

b. 3, 3

c. 0

3–3 **a.**

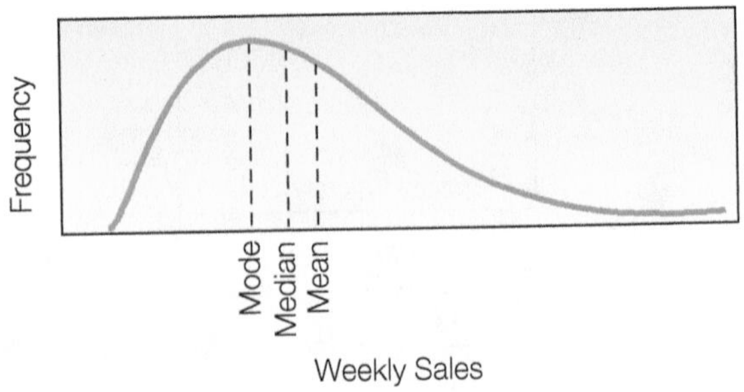

b. Positively skewed, because the mean is the largest average and the mode is the smallest.

3–4 **a.** $237, found by:

$$\frac{(95 \times \$400) + (126 \times \$200) + (79 \times \$100)}{95 + 126 + 79} = \$237.00$$

b. The profit per suit is $12, found by $237 − $200 cost − $25 commission. The total profit for the 300 suits is $3,600, found by 300 × $12.

3–5 **1. a.** About 9.9%, found by $\sqrt[4]{1.458602236}$, then $1.099 - 1.00 = .099$

b. About 10.095%

c. Greater than, because $10.095 > 9.9$

2. 8.63%, found by $\sqrt[20]{\frac{120,520}{23,000}} - 1 = 1.0863 - 1$

3–6 **a.** 22 thousands of pounds, found by 112 − 90

b. $\bar{x} = \frac{824}{8} = 103$ thousands of pounds

c.

x	$(x - x)$	$(x - \bar{x})^2$
95	−8	64
103	0	0
105	2	4
110	7	49
104	1	2
105	2	4
112	9	81
90	−13	169
		Total 373

$$\text{Variance} = \frac{373}{8} = 46.625$$

3–7 **a.** $\mu = \frac{\$16,900}{5} = \$3,380$

b. $\sigma^2 = \frac{(3,536 - 3,380)^2 + \cdots + (3,622 - 3,380)^2}{5}$

$$= \frac{(156)^2 + (-207)^2 + (68)^2 + (-259)^2 + (242)^2}{5}$$

$$= \frac{197,454}{5} = 39,490.8$$

c. $\sigma = \sqrt{39,490.8} = 198.72$

d. There is more variation in the Pittsburgh office because the standard deviation is larger. The mean is also larger in the Pittsburgh office.

3–8 2.33, found by:

$$\bar{x} = \frac{\Sigma x}{n} = \frac{28}{7} = 4$$

x	$x - \bar{x}$	$(x - \bar{x})^2$
4	0	0
2	−2	4
5	1	1
4	0	0
5	1	1
2	−2	4
6	2	4
28	0	14

$$s^2 = \frac{\Sigma(x - \bar{x})^2}{n - 1} = \frac{14}{7 - 1} = 2.33$$

$$s = \sqrt{2.33} = 1.53$$

3–9 **a.** $k = \frac{14.15 - 14.00}{.10} = 1.5$

$k = \frac{13.85 - 14.0}{.10} = -1.5$

$1 - \frac{1}{(1.5)^2} = 1 - .44 = .56$

b. 13.8 and 14.2

3–10 **a.** Frequency distribution.

b.

f	M	fM	$(M - \bar{x})$	$f(M - \bar{x})^2$
1	4	4	−8.2	67.24
4	8	32	−4.2	70.56
10	12	120	−0.2	0.40
3	16	48	3.8	43.32
2	20	40	7.8	121.68
20		244		303.20

$\bar{x} = \frac{\Sigma fM}{M} = \frac{\$244}{20} = \$12.20$

c. $s = \sqrt{\frac{303.20}{20 - 1}} = \$3.99$

CHAPTER 4

4–1 **1. a.** 79, 105

b. 15

c. From 88 to 97; 75% of the stores are in this range.

2.

7	7
8	0013488
9	1256689
10	1248
11	26

a. 8

b. 10.1, 10.2, 10.4, 10.8

c. 9.5

d. 11.6, 7.7

4–2 **a.** 7.9

b. $Q_1 = 7.76$, $Q_3 = 8.015$

4–3 The smallest value is 10 and the largest 85; the first quartile is 25 and the third 60. About 50% of the values are between 25 and 60. The median value is 40. The distribution is positively skewed. There are no outliers.

4–4 **a.** $\bar{x} = \frac{407}{5} = 81.4$, Median = 84

$s = \sqrt{\frac{923.2}{5 - 1}} = 15.19$

b. $sk = \frac{3(81.4 - 84.0)}{15.19} = -0.51$

c.

x	$\frac{x - \bar{x}}{s}$	$\left[\frac{x - \bar{x}}{s}\right]^3$
73	−0.5530	−0.1691
98	1.0928	1.3051
60	−1.4088	−2.7962
92	0.6978	0.3398
84	0.1712	0.0050
		−1.3154

$sk = \frac{5}{(4)(3)}[-1.3154] = -0.5481$

d. The distribution is somewhat negatively skewed.

4–5 **a.** Scatter diagram

b. 16

c. $7,500

d. Strong and direct

CHAPTER 5

5–1 **a.** Count the number who think the new game is playable.

b. Seventy-three players found the game playable. Many other answers are possible.

c. No. Probability cannot be greater than 1. The probability that the game, if put on the market, will be successful is 65/80, or .8125.

d. Cannot be less than 0. Perhaps a mistake in arithmetic.

e. More than half of the players testing the game liked it. (Of course, other answers are possible.)

5–2 **1.** $\frac{\text{4 queens in deck}}{\text{52 cards total}} = \frac{4}{52} = .0769$

Classical.

2. $\frac{182}{539} = .338$ Empirical.

3. The probability of the outcome is estimated by applying the subjective approach to estimating a probability. If you think that it is likely that you will save $1 million, then your probability should be between .5 and 1.0.

5–3 **a. i.** $\frac{(50 + 68)}{2{,}000} = .059$

ii. $1 - \frac{302}{2{,}000} = .849$

b.

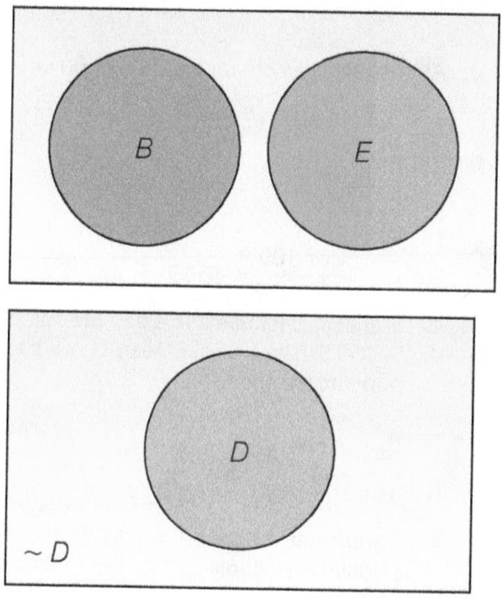

c. They are not complementary, but are mutually exclusive.

5–4 **a.** Need for corrective shoes is event A. Need for major dental work is event B.

$$\begin{aligned} P(A \text{ or } B) &= P(A) + P(B) - P(A \text{ and } B) \\ &= .08 + .15 - .03 \\ &= .20 \end{aligned}$$

b. One possibility is:

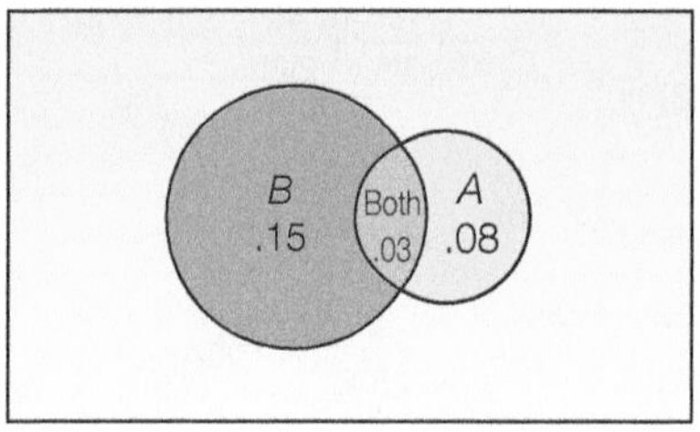

5–5 $(.95)(.95)(.95)(.95) = .8145$

5–6 **a.** .002, found by:

$$\left(\frac{4}{12}\right)\left(\frac{3}{11}\right)\left(\frac{2}{10}\right)\left(\frac{1}{9}\right) = \frac{24}{11{,}880} = .002$$

b. .14, found by:

$$\left(\frac{8}{12}\right)\left(\frac{7}{11}\right)\left(\frac{6}{10}\right)\left(\frac{5}{9}\right) = \frac{1{,}680}{11{,}880} = .1414$$

c. No, because there are other possibilities, such as three women and one man.

5–7 **a.** $P(B_2) = \dfrac{225}{500} = .45$

b. The two events are mutually exclusive, so apply the special rule of addition.

$$P(B_1 \text{ or } B_2) = P(B_1) + P(B_2) = \frac{100}{500} + \frac{225}{500} = .65$$

c. The two events are not mutually exclusive, so apply the general rule of addition.

$$\begin{aligned} P(B_1 \text{ or } A_1) &= P(B_1) + P(A_1) - P(B_1 \text{ and } A_1) \\ &= \frac{100}{500} + \frac{75}{500} - \frac{15}{500} = .32 \end{aligned}$$

d. As shown in the example/solution, movies attended per month and age are not independent, so apply the general rule of multiplication.

$$\begin{aligned} P(B_1 \text{ and } A_1) &= P(B_1)P(A_1 \mid B_1) \\ &= \left(\frac{100}{500}\right)\left(\frac{15}{100}\right) = .03 \end{aligned}$$

5–8 **a.** $P(\text{visited often}) = \dfrac{80}{195} = .41$

b. $P(\text{visited a store in an enclosed mall}) = \dfrac{90}{195} = .46$

c. The two events are not mutually exclusive, so apply the general rule of addition.

P(visited often or visited a Sears in an enclosed mall)
$= P(\text{often}) + P(\text{enclosed mall}) - P(\text{often and enclosed mall})$

$$= \frac{80}{195} + \frac{90}{195} - \frac{60}{195} = .56$$

d. P(visited often | went to a Sears in an enclosed mall)

$$= \frac{60}{90} = .67$$

e. Independence requires that $P(A \mid B) = P(A)$. One possibility is: $P(\text{visit often} \mid \text{visited an enclosed mall}) = P(\text{visit often})$. Does $60/90 = 80/195$? No, the two variables are not independent. Therefore, any joint probability in the table must be computed by using the general rule of multiplication.

f. As shown in part (e), visits often and enclosed mall are not independent, so apply the general rule of multiplication.

$$\begin{aligned} P(\text{often and enclosed mall}) &= P(\text{often})P(\text{enclosed} \mid \text{often}) \\ &= \left(\frac{80}{195}\right)\left(\frac{60}{80}\right) = .31 \end{aligned}$$

g.

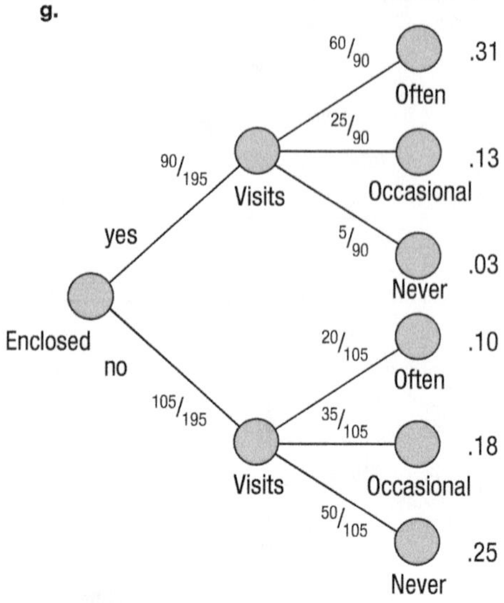

5–9 **a.**

$$P(A_3 \mid B_2) = \frac{P(A_3)P(B_2 \mid A_3)}{P(A_1)P(B_2 \mid A_1) + P(A_2)P(B_2 \mid A_2) + P(A_3)P(B_2 \mid A_3)}$$

b.

$$\begin{aligned} &= \frac{(.50)(.96)}{(.30)(.97) + (.20)(.95) + (.50)(.96)} \\ &= \frac{.480}{.961} = .499 \end{aligned}$$

5–10 **1.** $(5)(4) = 20$

2. $(3)(2)(4)(3) = 72$

5–11 **1.** **a.** 60, found by $(5)(4)(3)$.

b. 60, found by:

$$\frac{5!}{(5-3)!} = \frac{5 \cdot 4 \cdot 3 \cdot \cancel{2 \cdot 1}}{\cancel{2 \cdot 1}}$$

2. 5,040, found by:

$$\frac{10!}{(10-4)!} = \frac{10 \cdot 9 \cdot 8 \cdot 7 \cdot \cancel{6 \cdot 5 \cdot 4 \cdot 3 \cdot 2 \cdot 1}}{\cancel{6 \cdot 5 \cdot 4 \cdot 3 \cdot 2 \cdot 1}}$$

3. **a.** 35 is correct, found by:

$${}_7C_3 = \frac{n!}{r!(n-r)!} = \frac{7!}{3!(7-3)!} = 35$$

b. Yes. There are 21 combinations, found by:

$${}_7C_5 = \frac{n!}{r!(n-r)!} = \frac{7!}{5!(7-5)!} = 21$$

4. **a.** ${}_{50}P_3 = \dfrac{50!}{(50-3)!} = 117{,}600$

b. ${}_{50}C_3 = \dfrac{50!}{3!\,(50-3)!} = 19{,}600$

CHAPTER 6

6–1 a.

Number of Spots	Probability
1	$\frac{1}{6}$
2	$\frac{1}{6}$
3	$\frac{1}{6}$
4	$\frac{1}{6}$
5	$\frac{1}{6}$
6	$\frac{1}{6}$
Total	$\frac{6}{6} = 1.00$

b.

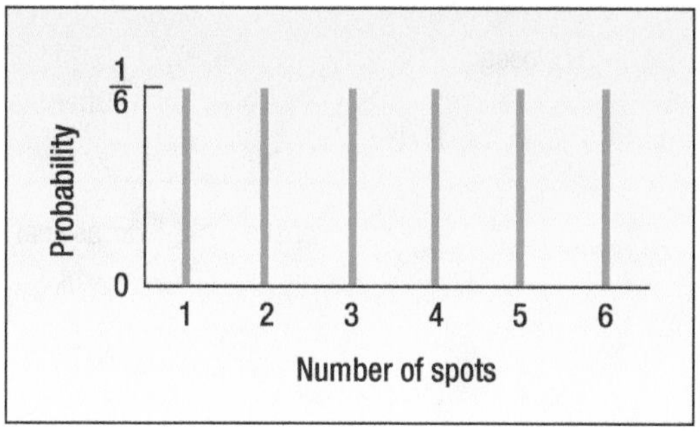

c. $\frac{6}{6}$ or 1.

6–2 a. It is discrete because the values \$0.80, \$0.90, and \$1.20 are clearly separated from each other. Also the sum of the probabilities is 1.00, and the outcomes are mutually exclusive.

b.

x	$P(x)$	$xP(x)$
\$ .80	.30	0.24
.90	.50	0.45
1.20	.20	0.24
		0.93

The mean is 93 cents.

c.

x	$P(x)$	$(x - \mu)$	$(x - \mu)^2 P(x)$
\$0.80	.30	−0.13	.00507
0.90	.50	−0.03	.00045
1.20	.20	0.27	.01458
			.02010

The variance is .02010, and the standard deviation is 14 cents.

6–3 a. It is reasonable because each employee either uses direct deposit or does not; employees are independent; the probability of using direct deposit is 0.95 for all; and we count the number using the service out of 7.

b. $P(7) = {}_7C_7\,(.95)^7\,(.05)^0 = .6983$

c. $P(4) = {}_7C_4\,(.95)^4\,(.05)^3 = .0036$

d. Answers are in agreement.

6–4 a. $n = 8, \pi = .40$

b. $P(x = 3) = .2787$

c. $P(x > 0) = 1 - P(x = 0) = 1 - .0168 = .9832$

6–5 $P(3) = \dfrac{{}_8C_3\,{}_4C_2}{{}_{12}C_5} = \dfrac{\left(\dfrac{8!}{3!5!}\right)\left(\dfrac{4!}{2!2!}\right)}{\dfrac{12!}{5!7!}}$

$= \dfrac{(56)(6)}{792} = .424$

6–6 $\mu = 4{,}000(.0002) = 0.8$

$P(1) = \dfrac{0.8^1 e^{-0.8}}{1!} = .3595$

CHAPTER 7

7–1 a.

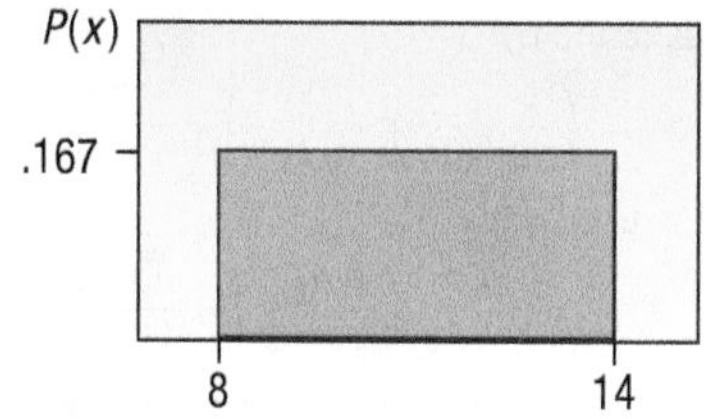

b. $P(x) = \text{(height)(base)}$

$= \left(\dfrac{1}{14 - 8}\right)(14 - 8)$

$= \left(\dfrac{1}{6}\right)(6) = 1.00$

c. $\mu = \dfrac{a + b}{2} = \dfrac{14 + 8}{2} = \dfrac{22}{2} = 11$

$\sigma = \sqrt{\dfrac{(b - a)^2}{12}} = \sqrt{\dfrac{(14 - 8)^2}{12}} = \sqrt{\dfrac{36}{12}} = \sqrt{3}$

$= 1.73$

d. $P(10 < x < 14) = \text{(height)(base)}$

$= \left(\dfrac{1}{14 - 8}\right)(14 - 10)$

$= \dfrac{1}{6}(4)$

$= .667$

e. $P(x < 9) = \text{(height)(base)}$

$= \left(\dfrac{1}{14 - 8}\right)(9 - 8)$

$= 0.167$

7–2 a. $z = (64 - 48)/12.8 = 1.25$. This person's difference of 16 ounces more than average is 1.25 standard deviations above the average.

b. $z = (32 - 48)/12.8 = -1.25$. This person's difference of 16 ounces less than average is 1.25 standard deviations below the average.

7–3 a. \$46,400 and \$48,000, found by \$47,200 ± 1(\$800).

b. \$45,600 and \$48,800, found by \$47,200 ± 2(\$800).

c. \$44,800 and \$49,600, found by \$47,200 ± 3(\$800).

d. \$47,200. The mean, median, and mode are equal for a normal distribution.

e. Yes, a normal distribution is symmetrical.

7–4 **a.** Computing z:

$$z = \frac{154 - 150}{5} = 0.80$$

Referring to Appendix B.3, the area is .2881. So $P(150 < \text{temp} < 154) = .2881$.

b. Computing z:

$$z = \frac{164 - 150}{5} = 2.80$$

Referring to Appendix B.3, the area is .4974. So $P(164 > \text{temp}) = .5000 - .4974 = .0026$

7–5 **a.** Computing the z-values:

$$z = \frac{146 - 150}{5} = -0.80 \quad \text{and} \quad z = \frac{156 - 150}{5} = 1.20$$

$$P(146 < \text{temp} < 156) = P(-0.80 < z < 1.20) = .2881 + .3849 = .6730$$

b. Computing the z-values:

$$z = \frac{162 - 150}{5} = 2.40 \quad \text{and} \quad z = \frac{156 - 150}{5} = 1.20$$

$$P(156 < \text{temp} < 162) = P(1.20 < z < 2.40) = .4918 - .3849 = .1069$$

7–6 85.24 (instructor would no doubt make it 85). The closest area to .4000 is .3997; z is 1.28. Then:

$$1.28 = \frac{x - 75}{8}$$

$$10.24 = x - 75$$

$$x = 85.24$$

7–7 **a.** .0465, found by $\mu = n\pi = 200(.80) = 160$, and $\sigma^2 = n\pi(1 - \pi) = 200(.80)(1 - .80) = 32$. Then,

$$\sigma = \sqrt{32} = 5.66$$

$$z = \frac{169.5 - 160}{5.66} = 1.68$$

Area from Appendix B.3 is .4535. Subtracting from .5000 gives .0465.

b. .9686, found by .4686 + .5000. First calculate z:

$$z = \frac{149.5 - 160}{5.66} = -1.86$$

Area from Appendix B.3 is .4686.

7–8 **a.** .7769, found by:

$$P(\text{Arrival} < 15) = 1 - e^{-\frac{1}{10}(15)} = 1 - .2231 = .7769$$

b. .0821, found by:

$$P(\text{Arrival} > 25) = e^{-\frac{1}{10}(25)} = .0821$$

c. .1410, found by

$$P(15 < x < 25) = P(\text{Arrival} < 25) - P(\text{Arrival} < 15) = .9179 - .7769 = .1410$$

d. 16.09 minutes, found by:

$$.80 = 1 - e^{-\frac{1}{10}(x)}$$

$$-\ln 0.20 = \frac{1}{10}x$$

$$x = -(-1.609)(10) = 1.609(10) = 16.09$$

CHAPTER 8

8–1 **a.** Students selected are Price, Detley, and Molter.

b. Answers will vary.

c. Skip it and move to the next random number.

8–2 The students selected are Berry, Francis, Kopp, Poteau, and Swetye.

8–3 **a.** 10, found by:

$$_5C_2 = \frac{5!}{2!(5-2)!}$$

b.

	Service	Sample Mean
Snow, Tolson	20, 22	21
Snow, Kraft	20, 26	23
Snow, Irwin	20, 24	22
Snow, Jones	20, 28	24
Tolson, Kraft	22, 26	24
Tolson, Irwin	22, 24	23
Tolson, Jones	22, 28	25
Kraft, Irwin	26, 24	25
Kraft, Jones	26, 28	27
Irwin, Jones	24, 28	26

c.

Mean	Number	Probability
21	1	.10
22	1	.10
23	2	.20
24	2	.20
25	2	.20
26	1	.10
27	1	.10
	10	1.00

d. Identical: population mean, μ, is 24, and mean of sample means, $\mu_{\bar{x}}$, is also 24.

e. Sample means range from 21 to 27. Population values go from 20 to 28.

f. No, the population is uniformly distributed.

g. Yes.

8–4 The answers will vary. Here is one solution.

	Sample Number 1	2	3	4	5	6	7	8	9	10
	8	2	2	19	3	4	0	4	1	2
	19	1	14	9	2	5	8	2	14	4
	8	3	4	2	4	4	1	14	4	1
	0	3	2	3	1	2	16	1	2	3
	2	1	7	2	19	18	18	16	3	7
Total	37	10	29	35	29	33	43	37	24	17
$\bar{x}$	7.4	2	5.8	7.0	5.8	6.6	8.6	7.4	4.8	3.4

Mean of the 10 sample means is 5.88.

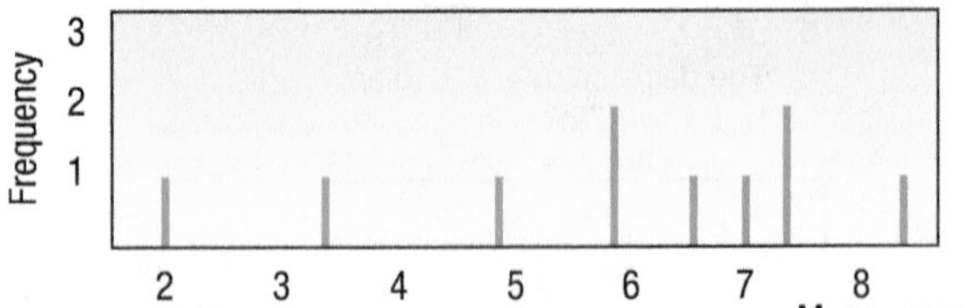

8–5 $z = \frac{31.08 - 31.20}{0.4/\sqrt{16}} = -1.20$

The probability that z is greater than -1.20 is $.5000 + .3849 = .8849$. There is more than an 88% chance the filling operation will produce bottles with at least 31.08 ounces.

CHAPTER 9

9–1 **a.** Unknown. This is the value we wish to estimate.

b. \$20,000, point estimate.

c. $\$20{,}000 \pm 1.960\frac{\$3{,}000}{\sqrt{40}} = \$20{,}000 \pm \$930$

d. The endpoints of the confidence interval are \$19,070 and \$20,930. About 95% of the intervals similarly constructed would include the population mean.

9–2 a. $\bar{x} = \frac{18}{10} = 1.8 \quad s = \sqrt{\frac{11.6}{10 - 1}} = 1.1353$

b. The population mean is not known. The best estimate is the sample mean, 1.8 days.

c. $1.80 \pm 2.262 \frac{1.1353}{\sqrt{10}} = 1.80 \pm 0.81$

The endpoints are 0.99 and 2.61.

d. t is used because the population standard deviation is unknown.

e. The value of 0 is not in the interval. It is unreasonable to conclude that the mean number of days of work missed is 0 per employee.

9–3 a. $p = \frac{420}{1,400} = .30$

b. $.30 \pm 2.576(.0122) = .30 \pm .03$

c. The interval is between .27 and .33. About 99% of the similarly constructed intervals would include the population mean.

9–4 $n = \left(\frac{2.576(.279)}{.05}\right)^2 = 206.6$. The sample should be rounded to 207.

9–5 $.375 \pm 1.96\sqrt{\frac{.375(1 - .375)}{40}}\sqrt{\frac{250 - 40}{250 - 1}} =$

$.375 \pm 1.96(.0765)(.9184) = .375 \pm .138$

CHAPTER 10

10–1 a. H_0: $\mu = 16.0$; H_1: $\mu \neq 16.0$

b. .05

c. $z = \frac{\bar{X} - \mu}{\sigma/\sqrt{n}}$

d. Reject H_0 if $z < -1.96$ or $z > 1.96$.

e. $z = \frac{16.017 - 16.0}{0.15/\sqrt{50}} = \frac{0.0170}{0.0212} = 0.80$

f. Do not reject H_0.

g. We cannot conclude the mean amount dispensed is different from 16.0 ounces.

10–2 a. H_0: $\mu \leq 16.0$; H_1: $\mu > 16.0$

b. Reject H_0 if $z > 1.645$.

c. $z = \frac{16.040 - 16.0}{0.15/\sqrt{50}} = \frac{.0400}{.0212} = 1.89$

d. Reject H_0.

e. The mean amount dispensed is more than 16.0 ounces.

f. p-value $= .5000 - .4706 = .0294$. The p-value is less than α (.05), so H_0 is rejected. It is the same conclusion as in part (d).

10–3 a. H_0: $\mu \leq 305$; H_1: $\mu > 305$

b. $df = n - 1 = 20 - 1 = 19$

The decision rule is to reject H_0 if $t > 1.729$.

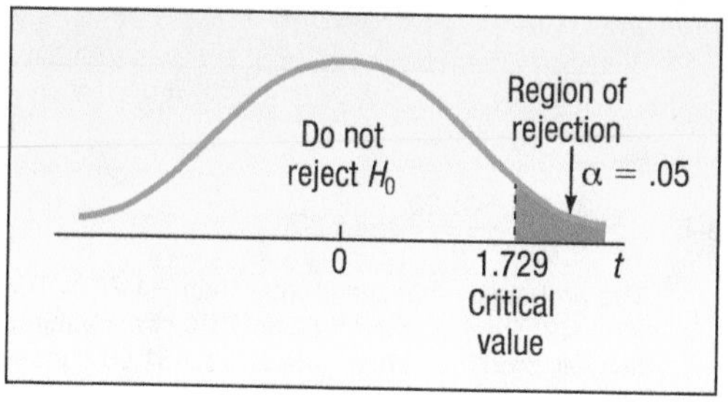

c. $t = \frac{\bar{X} - \mu}{s/\sqrt{n}} = \frac{311 - 305}{12/\sqrt{20}} = 2.236$

Reject H_0 because $2.236 > 1.729$. The modification increased the mean battery life to more than 305 days.

10–4 a. H_0: $\mu \geq 9.0$; H_1: $\mu < 9.0$

b. 7, found by $n - 1 = 8 - 1 = 7$

c. Reject H_0 if $t < -2.998$.

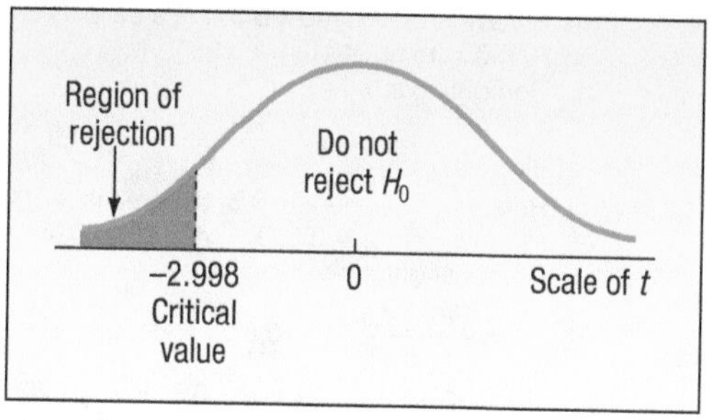

d. $t = -2.494$, found by:

$$s = \sqrt{\frac{0.36}{8 - 1}} = 0.2268$$

$$\bar{x} = \frac{70.4}{8} = 8.8$$

Then

$$t = \frac{8.8 - 9.0}{0.2268/\sqrt{8}} = -2.494$$

Since -2.494 lies to the right of -2.998, H_0 is not rejected. We have not shown that the mean is less than 9.0.

e. The p-value is between .025 and .010.

10–5 .0054, found by determining the area under the curve between 10,078 and 10,180.

$$z = \frac{\bar{X}_c - \mu_1}{\sigma/\sqrt{n}}$$

$$= \frac{10,078 - 10,180}{400/\sqrt{100}} = -2.55$$

The area under the curve for a z of -2.55 is .4946 (Appendix B.3), and $.5000 - .4946 = .0054$.

CHAPTER 11

11–1 a. H_0: $\mu_W \leq \mu_M$ $\quad H_1$: $\mu_W > \mu_M$

The subscript W refers to the women and M to the men.

b. Reject H_0 if $z > 1.645$.

c. $z = \frac{\$1,500 - \$1,400}{\sqrt{\frac{(\$250)^2}{50} + \frac{(\$200)^2}{40}}} = 2.11$

d. Reject the null hypothesis.

e. p-value $= .5000 - .4826 = .0174$

f. The mean amount sold per day is larger for women.

11–2 a. H_0: $\mu_d = \mu_a$ $\quad H_1$: $\mu_d \neq \mu_a$

b. $df = 6 + 8 - 2 = 12$

Reject H_0 if $t < -2.179$ or $t > 2.179$.

c. $\bar{X}_1 = \frac{42}{6} = 7.00 \quad s_1 = \sqrt{\frac{10}{6 - 1}} = 1.4142$

$\bar{X}_2 = \frac{80}{8} = 10.00 \quad s_2 = \sqrt{\frac{36}{8 - 1}} = 2.2678$

$s_p^2 = \frac{(6 - 1)(1.4142)^2 + (8 - 1)(2.2678)^2}{6 + 8 - 2}$

$= 3.8333$

$t = \frac{7.00 - 10.00}{\sqrt{3.8333\left(\frac{1}{6} + \frac{1}{8}\right)}} = -2.837$

d. Reject H_0 because -2.837 is less than the critical value.

e. The p-value is less than .02.

f. The mean number of defects is not the same on the two shifts.

g. Independent populations, populations follow the normal distribution, populations have equal standard deviations.

11–3 **a.** $H_0: \mu_c \geq \mu_a \qquad H_1: \mu_c < \mu_a$

b. $df = \dfrac{[(356^2/10) + (857^2/8)]^2}{\dfrac{(356^2/10)^2}{10-1} + \dfrac{(857^2/8)^2}{8-1}} = 8.93$

so $df = 8$

c. Reject H_0 if $t < -1.860$.

d. $t = \dfrac{\$1,568 - \$1,967}{\sqrt{\dfrac{356^2}{10} + \dfrac{857^2}{8}}} = \dfrac{-399.00}{323.23} = -1.234$

e. Do not reject H_0.

f. There is no difference in the mean account balance of those who applied for their card or were contacted by a telemarketer.

11–4 **a.** $H_0: \mu_d \leq 0, H_1: \mu_d > 0$

b. Reject H_0 if $t > 2.998$.

c.

Name	Before	After	d	$(d - \bar{d})$	$(d - \bar{d})^2$
Hunter	155	154	1	−7.875	62.0156
Cashman	228	207	21	12.125	147.0156
Mervine	141	147	−6	−14.875	221.2656
Massa	162	157	5	−3.875	15.0156
Creola	211	196	15	6.125	37.5156
Peterson	164	150	14	5.125	26.2656
Redding	184	170	14	5.125	26.2656
Poust	172	165	7	−1.875	3.5156
			71		538.8750

$$\bar{d} = \frac{71}{8} = 8.875$$

$$s_d = \sqrt{\frac{538.875}{8-1}} = 8.774$$

$$t = \frac{8.875}{8.774/\sqrt{8}} = 2.861$$

d. Do not reject H_0. We cannot conclude that the students lost weight. The p-value is less than .025 but larger than .01.

e. The distribution of the differences must be approximately normal.

CHAPTER 12

12–1 Let Mark's assemblies be population 1, then $H_0: \sigma_1^2 \leq \sigma_2^2$; $H_1: \sigma_1^2 > \sigma_2^2$; $df_1 = 10 - 1 = 9$; and df_2 also equals 9. H_0 is rejected if $F > 3.18$.

$$F = \frac{(2.0)^2}{(1.5)^2} = 1.78$$

H_0 is not rejected. The variation is the same for both employees.

12–2 **a.** $H_0: \mu_1 = \mu_2 = \mu_3$
H_1: At least one treatment mean is different.

b. Reject H_0 if $F > 4.26$.

c. $\bar{x} = \dfrac{240}{12} = 20$

$$\text{SS total} = (18 - 20)^2 + \cdots + (32 - 20)^2 = 578$$

$$\text{SSE} = (18 - 17)^2 + (14 - 17)^2 + \cdots + (32 - 29)^2 = 74$$

$$\text{SST} = 578 - 74 = 504$$

d.

Source	Sum of Squares	Degrees of Freedom	Mean Square	F
Treatment	504	2	252	30.65
Error	74	9	8.22	
Total	578	11		

e. H_0 is rejected. There is a difference in the mean number of bottles sold at the various locations.

12–3 **a.** $H_0: \mu_1 = \mu_2 = \mu_3$
H_1: Not all means are equal.

b. H_0 is rejected if $F > 3.98$.

c. $\bar{x}_G = 8.86$, $\bar{x}_1 = 11$, $\bar{x}_2 = 8.75$, $\bar{x}_3 = 6.8$
SS total = 53.71
SST = 44.16
SSE = 9.55

Source	Sum of Squares	df	Mean Square	F
Treatment	44.16	2	22.08	25.43
Error	9.55	11	0.8682	
Total	53.71	13		

d. H_0 is rejected. The treatment means differ.

e. $(11.0 - 6.8) \pm 2.201\sqrt{0.8682(\frac{1}{5} + \frac{1}{5})} = 4.2 \pm 1.30 = 2.90$ and 5.50

These treatment means differ because both endpoints of the confidence interval are of the same sign—positive in this problem.

12–4 For types:

$H_0: \mu_1 = \mu_2 = \mu_3$
H_1: The treatment means are not equal.

Reject H_0 if $F > 4.46$.

For months:

$H_0: \mu_1 = \mu_2 = \mu_3 = \mu_4 = \mu_5$
H_1: The block means are not equal.

Reject H_0 if $F > 3.84$.

The analysis of variance table is as follows:

Source	df	SS	MS	F
Types	2	3.60	1.80	0.39
Months	4	31.73	7.93	1.71
Error	8	37.07	4.63	
Total	14	72.40		

The null hypotheses cannot be rejected for either types or months. There is no difference in the mean sales among types or months.

12–5 **a.** There are four levels of Factor A. The p-value is less than .05, so Factor A means differ.

b. There are three levels of Factor B. The p-value is less than .05, so the Factor B means differ.

c. There are three observations in each cell. There is an interaction between Factor A and Factor B means because the p-value is less than .05.

CHAPTER 13

13–1 **a.** Advertising expense is the independent variable, and sales revenue is the dependent variable.

b.

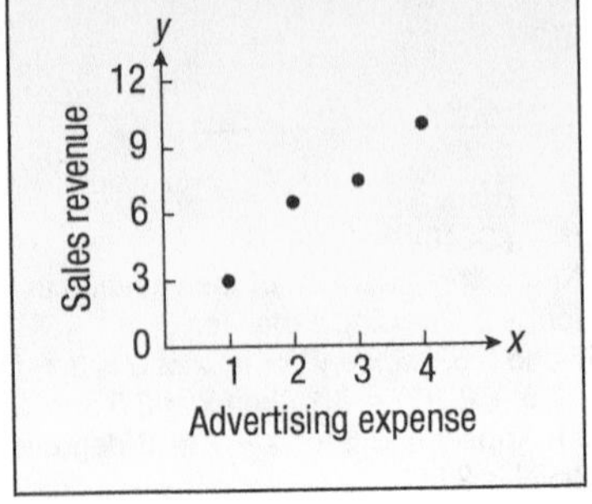

c.

x	y	$(x-\bar{x})$	$(x-\bar{x})^2$	$(y-\bar{y})$	$(y-\bar{y})^2$	$(x-\bar{x})(y-\bar{y})$
2	7	−0.5	.25	0	0	0
1	3	−1.5	2.25	−4	16	6
3	8	0.5	.25	1	1	0.5
4	10	1.5	2.25	3	9	4.5
10	28		5.00		26	11.0

$$\bar{x} = \frac{10}{4} = 2.5 \qquad \bar{y} = \frac{28}{4} = 7$$

$$s_x = \sqrt{\frac{5}{3}} = 1.2910$$

$$s_y = \sqrt{\frac{26}{3}} = 2.9439$$

$$r = \frac{\Sigma(X-\bar{X})(y-\bar{y})}{(n-1)s_x s_y} = \frac{11}{(4-1)(1.2910)(2.9439)}$$
$$= 0.9648$$

d. There is a strong correlation between the advertising expense and sales.

13–2 H_0: $\rho \le 0$, H_1: $\rho > 0$. H_0 is rejected if $t > 1.714$.

$$t = \frac{.43\sqrt{25-2}}{\sqrt{1-(.43)^2}} = 2.284$$

H_0 is rejected. There is a positive correlation between the percent of the vote received and the amount spent on the campaign.

13–3 a. See the calculations in Self-Review 13–1, part (c).

$$b = \frac{rs_y}{s_x} = \frac{(0.9648)(2.9439)}{1.2910} = 2.2$$

$$a = \frac{28}{4} - 2.2\left(\frac{10}{4}\right) = 7 - 5.5 = 1.5$$

b. The slope is 2.2. This indicates that an increase of $1 million in advertising will result in an increase of $2.2 million in sales. The intercept is 1.5. If there was no expenditure for advertising, sales would be $1.5 million.

c. $\hat{Y} = 1.5 + 2.2(3) = 8.1$

13–4 H_0: $\beta_1 \le 0$; H_1: $\beta > 0$. Reject H_0 if $t > 3.182$.

$$t = \frac{2.2 - 0}{0.4243} = 5.1850$$

Reject H_0. The slope of the line is greater than 0.

13–5 a.

y	$\hat{y}$	$(y-\hat{y})$	$(y-\hat{y})^2$
7	5.9	1.1	1.21
3	3.7	−0.7	.49
8	8.1	−0.1	.01
10	10.3	−0.3	.09
			1.80

$$s_{y \cdot x} = \sqrt{\frac{\Sigma(y-\hat{y})^2}{n-2}}$$

$$= \sqrt{\frac{1.80}{4-2}} = .9487$$

b. $r^2 = (.9648)^2 = .9308$

c. Ninety-three percent of the variation in sales is accounted for by advertising expense.

13–6 6.58 and 9.62, since $\hat{y}$ for an x of 3 is 8.1, found by $\hat{y} = 1.5 + 2.2(3) = 8.1$, then $\bar{x} = 2.5$ and $\Sigma(x-\bar{x})^2 = 5$.
t from Appendix B.5 for $4 - 2 = 2$ degrees of freedom at the .10 level is 2.920.

$$\hat{y} \pm t(s_{y \cdot x})\sqrt{\frac{1}{n} + \frac{(x-\bar{x})^2}{\Sigma(x-\bar{x})^2}}$$
$$= 8.1 \pm 2.920(0.9487)\sqrt{\frac{1}{4} + \frac{(3-2.5)^2}{5}}$$
$$= 8.1 \pm 2.920(0.9487)(0.5477)$$
$$= 6.58 \text{ and } 9.62 \text{ (in \$ millions)}$$

CHAPTER 14

14–1 a. $389,500 or 389.5 (in $000); found by
$2.5 + 3(40) + 4(72) - 3(10) + .2(20) + 1(5) = 3{,}895$

b. The b_2 of 4 shows profit will go up $4,000 for each extra hour the restaurant is open (if none of the other variables change). The b_3 of −3 implies profit will fall $3,000 for each added mile away from the central area (if none of the other variables change).

14–2 a. The total degrees of freedom ($n - 1$) is 25. So the sample size is 26.

b. There are 5 independent variables.

c. There is only 1 dependent variable (profit).

d. $S_{Y.12345} = 1.414$, found by $\sqrt{2}$. Ninety-five percent of the residuals will be between −2.828 and 2.828, found by $\pm 2(1.414)$.

e. $R^2 = .714$, found by 100/140. 71.4% of the deviation in profit is accounted for by these five variables.

f. $R^2_{adj} = .643$, found by

$$1 - \left[\frac{40}{(26-(5+1))}\right] \Big/ \left[\frac{140}{(26-1)}\right]$$

14–3 a. H_0: $\beta_1 = \beta_2 = \beta_3 = \beta_4 = \beta_5 = 0$
H_1: Not all of the βs are 0.
The decision rule is to reject H_0 if $F > 2.71$. The computed value of F is 10, found by 20/2. So, you reject H_0, which indicates at least one of the regression coefficients is different from zero.

Based on p-values, the decision rule is to reject the null hypothesis if the p-value is less than .05. The computed value of F is 10, found by 20/2, and has a p-value of .000. Thus, we reject the null hypothesis, which indicates that at least one of the regression coefficients is different from zero.

b. For variable 1: H_0: $\beta_1 = 0$ and H_1: $\beta_1 \ne 0$
The decision rule is to reject H_0 if $t < -2.086$ or $t > 2.086$. Since 2.000 does not go beyond either of those limits, we fail to reject the null hypothesis. This regression coefficient could be zero. We can consider dropping this variable. By parallel logic, the null hypothesis is rejected for variables 3 and 4.

For variable 1, the decision rule is to reject H_0: $\beta_1 = 0$ if the p-value is less than .05. Because the p-value is .056, we cannot reject the null hypothesis. This regression coefficient could be zero. Therefore, we can consider dropping this variable. By parallel logic, we reject the null hypothesis for variables 3 and 4.

c. We should consider dropping variables 1, 2, and 5. Variable 5 has the smallest absolute value of t or largest p-value. So delete it first and compute the regression equation again.

14–4 a. $\hat{y} = 15.7625 + 0.4415x_1 + 3.8598x_2$
$\hat{y} = 15.7625 + 0.4415(30) + 3.8598(1)$
$= 32.87$

b. Female agents make $3,860 more than male agents.

c. H_0: $\beta_3 = 0$
H_1: $\beta_3 \ne 0$
$df = 17$; reject H_0 if $t < -2.110$ or $t > 2.110$

$$t = \frac{3.8598 - 0}{1.4724} = 2.621$$

The t statistic exceeds the critical value of 2.110. Also, the p-value = .0179 and is less than .05. Reject H_0. Gender should be included in the regression equation.

CHAPTER 15

15–1 **a.** Yes, because both $n\pi$ and $n(1 - \pi)$ exceed 5: $n\pi = 200(.40) = 80$, and $n(1 - \pi) = 200(.60) = 120$.

b. $H_0: \pi \geq .40$
$H_1: \pi < .40$

c. Reject H_0 if $z < -2.326$.

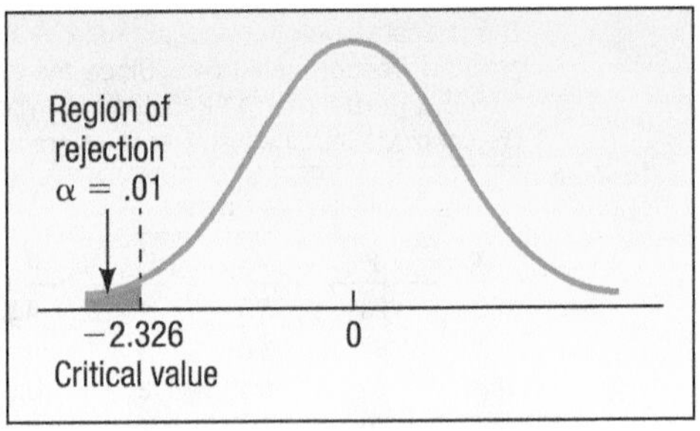

d. $z = -0.87$, found by:

$$z = \frac{.37 - .40}{\sqrt{\frac{.40(1 - .40)}{200}}} = \frac{-.03}{\sqrt{.0012}} = -0.87$$

Do not reject H_0.

e. The p-value is .1922, found by .5000 − .3078.

15–2 **a.** $H_0: \pi_a = \pi_{ch}$
$H_1: \pi_a \neq \pi_{ch}$

b. .10

c. Two-tailed

d. Reject H_0 if $z < -1.645$ or $z > 1.645$.

e. $p_c = \frac{87 + 123}{150 + 200} = \frac{210}{350} = .60$

$p_a = \frac{87}{150} = .58 \quad p_{ch} = \frac{123}{200} = .615$

$$z = \frac{.58 - .615}{\sqrt{\frac{.60(.40)}{150} + \frac{.60(.40)}{200}}} = -0.66$$

f. Do not reject H_0.

g. p-value = 2(.5000 − .2454) = .5092
There is no difference in the proportion of adults and children that liked the proposed flavor.

15–3 **a.** Observed frequencies

b. Six (six days of the week)

c. 10. Total observed frequencies ÷ 6 = 60/6 = 10.

d. 5; $k - 1 = 6 - 1 = 5$

e. 15.086 (from the chi-square table in Appendix B.7).

f. $\chi^2 = \Sigma\left[\frac{(f_o - f_e)^2}{f_e}\right] = \frac{(12 - 10)^2}{10} + \cdots + \frac{(9 - 10)^2}{10} = 0.8$

g. Do not reject H_0.

h. Evidence fails to show a difference in the proportion of absences by day of the week.

15–4 $H_0: P_C = .60$, $P_L = .30$, and $P_U = .10$.
H_1: Distribution is not as above.
Reject H_0 if $\chi^2 > 5.991$.

Category	f_o	f_e	$\frac{(f_o - f_e)^2}{f_e}$
Current	320	300	1.33
Late	120	150	6.00
Uncollectible	60	50	2.00
	500	500	9.33

Reject H_0. The accounts receivable data do not reflect the national average.

15–5 **a.** Contingency table

b. H_0: There is no relationship between income and whether the person played the lottery. H_1: There is a relationship between income and whether the person played the lottery.

c. Reject H_0 if $\chi^2 > 5.991$.

d. $\chi^2 = \frac{(46 - 40.71)^2}{40.71} + \frac{(28 - 27.14)^2}{27.14} + \frac{(21 - 27.14)^2}{27.14}$
$+ \frac{(14 - 19.29)^2}{19.29} + \frac{(12 - 12.86)^2}{12.86} + \frac{(19 - 12.86)^2}{12.86}$
$= 6.544$

e. Reject H_0. There is a relationship between income level and playing the lottery.

CHAPTER 16

16–1 **a.** Two-tailed because H_1 does not state a direction.

b.

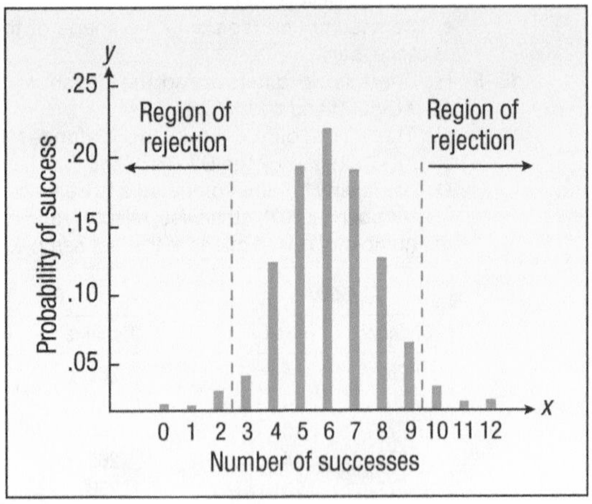

Adding down, .000 + .003 + .016 = .019. This is the largest cumulative probability up to but not exceeding .050, which is half the level of significance. The decision rule is to reject H_0 if the number of plus signs is 2 or less or 10 or more.

c. Reject H_0; accept H_1. There is a preference.

16–2 **a.** $H_0: \pi \leq 0.50$, $H_1: \pi > 0.50$.

b. Reject H_0 if $z > 1.645$.

c. Since 80 is more than $n/2 = 100/2 = 50$, we use:

$$z = \frac{(80 - .50) - .50(100)}{.50\sqrt{100}} = \frac{29.5}{5} = 5.9$$

d. H_0 is rejected.

e. The screening was effective.

16–3 H_0: The median ≤ \$2,505, H_1: The median is more than \$2,505. The decision rule is to reject H_0 if $z > 1.645$.

$$z = \frac{(42 - .50) - 32}{.50\sqrt{64}} = \frac{9.5}{4} = 2.38$$

Reject H_0 because 2.38 is larger than 1.645. The median amount spent is more than \$2,505.

16–4 **a.** $n = 10$ (because there was no change for A. A.)

b.

Before	After	Difference	Absolute Difference	Rank	R^-	R^+
17	18	−1	1	1.5	1.5	
21	23	−2	2	3.0	3.0	
25	22	3	3	5.0		5.0
15	25	−10	10	8.0	8.0	
10	28	−18	18	10.0	10.0	
16	16	—	—	—	—	—
10	22	−12	12	9.0	9.0	
20	19	1	1	1.5		1.5
17	20	−3	3	5.0	5.0	
24	30	−6	6	7.0	7.0	
23	26	−3	3	5.0	5.0	
					48.5	6.5

H_0: Production is the same.
H_1: Production has increased.

The sum of the positive signed ranks is 6.5; the negative sum is 48.5. From Appendix B.8, one-tailed test, $n = 10$, the critical value is 10. Since 6.5 is less than 10, reject the null hypothesis and accept the alternate. New procedures did increase production.

c. No assumption regarding the shape of the distribution is necessary.

16–5 H_0: There is no difference in the distances traveled by the XL-5000 and by the D2.
H_1: There is a difference in the distances traveled by the XL-5000 and by the D2.
Do not reject H_0 if the computed z is between 1.96 and −1.96 (from Appendix B.3); otherwise, reject H_0 and accept H_1. $n_1 = 8$, the number of observations in the first sample.

XL-5000 Distance	XL-5000 Rank	D2 Distance	D2 Rank
252	4	262	9
263	10	242	2
279	15	256	5
273	14	260	8
271	13	258	7
265	11.5	243	3
257	6	239	1
280	16	265	11.5
Total	89.5		46.5

$W = 89.5$

$$z = \frac{89.5 - \dfrac{8(8+8+1)}{2}}{\sqrt{\dfrac{(8)(8)(8+8+1)}{12}}} = \frac{21.5}{9.52} = 2.26$$

Reject H_0; accept H_1. There is evidence of a difference in the distances traveled by the two golf balls.

16–6

Ranks			
Englewood	West Side	Great Northern	Sylvania
17	5	19	7
20	1	9.5	11
16	3	21	15
13	5	22	9.5
5	2	14	8
18			12

$\Sigma R_1 = 89$ $\Sigma R_2 = 16$ $\Sigma R_3 = 85.5$ $\Sigma R_4 = 62.5$
$n_1 = 6$ $n_2 = 5$ $n_3 = 5$ $n_4 = 6$

H_0: The population distributions are identical.
H_1: The population distributions are not identical.

$$H = \frac{12}{22(22+1)}\left[\frac{(89)^2}{6} + \frac{(16)^2}{5} + \frac{(85.5)^2}{5} + \frac{(62.5)^2}{6}\right] - 3(22+1)$$
$$= 13.635$$

The critical value of chi-square for $k - 1 = 4 - 1 = 3$ degrees of freedom is 11.345. Since the computed value of 13.635 is greater than 11.345, the null hypothesis is rejected. We conclude that the turnover rates are not the same.

16–7 a.

x	y	Rank x	Rank y	d	d^2
805	23	5.5	1	4.5	20.25
777	62	3.0	9	−6.0	36.00
820	60	8.5	8	0.5	0.25
682	40	1.0	4	−3.0	9.00
777	70	3.0	10	−7.0	49.00
810	28	7.0	2	5.0	25.00
805	30	5.5	3	2.5	6.25
840	42	10.0	5	5.0	25.00
777	55	3.0	7	−4.0	16.00
820	51	8.5	6	2.5	6.25
				0	193.00

$$r_s = 1 - \frac{6(193)}{10(99)} = -.170$$

b. H_0: $\rho = 0$; H_1: $\rho \neq 0$. Reject H_0 if $t < -2.306$ or $t > 2.306$.

$$t = -.170\sqrt{\frac{10-2}{1-(-0.170)^2}} = -0.488$$

H_0 is not rejected. We have not shown a relationship between the two tests.

CHAPTER 17

17–1 1.

Country	Amount (millions of tons)	Index
China	716.5	807.8
Japan	107.2	120.9
United States	88.7	100.0
India	77.6	87.5
Russia	70.4	79.4

China produced 707.8% more than the United States.

2.

Year	Average Hourly Earnings	(a) Index	(b) Index
1995	$11.65	100.0	90.8
2000	14.02	120.3	109.2
2005	16.13	138.5	125.7
2013	19.97	171.4	155.6

a. Average hourly earnings increased 71.4% from 1995 until 2013.

b. Averaging the hourly earnings for the years 1995 and 2000 and using this as the base shows earnings increased by 55.6%.

17–2 a. $P_1 = (\$85/\$75)(100) = 113.3$
$P_2 = (\$45/\$40)(100) = 112.5$
$P = (113.3 + 112.5)/2 = 112.9$

b. $P = (\$130/\$115)(100) = 113.0$

c. $P = \dfrac{\$85(500) + \$45(1{,}200)}{\$75(500) + \$40(1{,}200)}(100)$

$= \dfrac{\$96{,}500}{85{,}500}(100) = 112.9$

d. $P = \dfrac{\$85(520) + \$45(1{,}300)}{\$75(520) + \$40(1{,}300)}(100)$

$= \dfrac{\$102{,}700}{\$91{,}000}(100) = 112.9$

e. $P = \sqrt{(112.9)(112.9)} = 112.9$

17–3 **a.** $P = \dfrac{\$4(9{,}000) + \$5(200) + \$8(5{,}000)}{\$3(10{,}000) + \$1(600) + \$10(3{,}000)}(100)$

$= \dfrac{\$77{,}000}{60{,}600}(100) = 127.1$

b. The value of sales has gone up 27.1% from 2001 to 2013.

17–4 **a.**

For 2009	
Item	**Weight**
Cotton	($0.25/$0.20)(100)(.10) = 12.50
Autos	(1,200/1,000)(100)(.30) = 36.00
Money turnover	(90/80)(100)(.60) = 67.50
Total	116.00

For 2014	
Item	**Weight**
Cotton	($0.50/$0.20)(100)(.10) = 25.00
Autos	(900/1,000)(100)(.30) = 27.00
Money turnover	(75/80)(100)(.60) = 56.25
Total	108.25

b. Business activity increased 16% from 2004 to 2009. It increased 8.25% from 2004 to 2014.

17–5 **a.** $14,637, found by ($25,000/170.8)(100)

b. $17,944, found by ($41,200/229.6)(100)

c. In terms of the base period, Jon's salary was $14,637 in 2000 and $17,944 in 2013. This indicates that take-home pay increased at a faster rate than the rate price paid for food, transportation, etc.

17–6 $0.51, found by ($1.00/195.4)(100). The purchasing power has declined by $0.49.

17–7 With 2010 as the base period for both series:

Year	IPI	PPI
2007	111.6	89.9
2008	114.3	96.6
2009	99.5	95.7
2010	100.0	100.0
2011	105.3	103.6
2012	109.4	107.9
2013	111.5	109.4

The Industrial Production Index (IPI) increased 11.5% from 2010 until 2013 and the Producer Price Index (PPI) increased 9.4%. The IPI decreased from 2007 to 2010 and by 2013 returned to its 2007 value. The PPI increased steadily from 2007 until 2013.

CHAPTER 18

18–1

Year	Production (thousands)	Three-Year Moving Total	Three-Year Moving Average
2008	2	—	—
2009	6	12	4
2010	4	15	5
2011	5	12	4
2012	3	18	6
2013	10	—	—

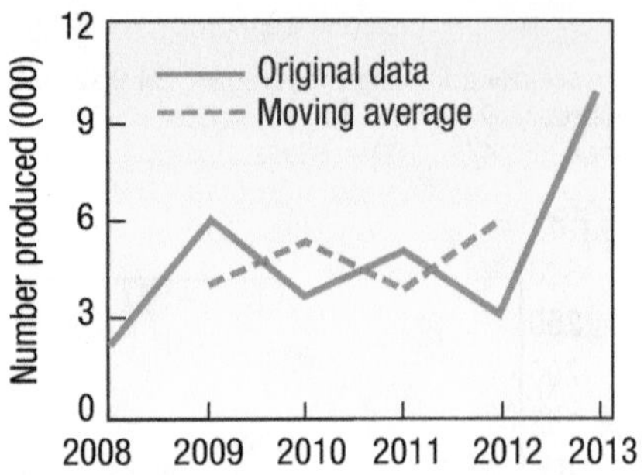

18–2 **a.**

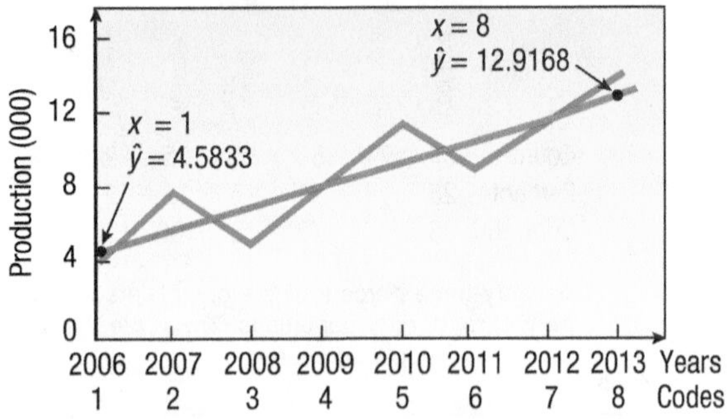

b. $\hat{y} = a + bt = 3.3928 + 1.1905t$ (in thousands)

c. For 2006:

$$\hat{y} = 3.3928 + 1.1905(1) = 4.5833$$

for 2013:

$$\hat{y} = 3.3928 + 1.1905(8) = 12.9168$$

d. For 2016, $t = 11$, so

$$\hat{y} = 3.3928 + 1.1905(11) = 16.4883$$

or 16,488 king-size rockers.

18–3 **a.**

Year	y	$\log y$	t
2009	2.13	0.3284	1
2010	18.10	1.2577	2
2011	39.80	1.5999	3
2012	81.40	1.9106	4
2013	112.00	2.0492	5

$$b = 0.40945$$
$$a = 0.20081$$

b. About 156.7%. The antilog of 0.40945 is 2.567. Subtracting 1 yields 1.567.

c. About 454.5, found by $\hat{y} = 0.20081 + .40945(6) = 2.65751$. The antilog of 2.65751 is 454.5.

18–4 **a.** The following values are from a software package. Due to rounding, your figures might be slightly different.

	Winter	Spring	Summer	Fall
Mean	119.35	81.66	125.31	74.24
Typical seasonal	119.18	81.55	125.13	74.13

The correction factor is 0.9986.

b. Total sales at Teton Village for the winter season are typically 19.18% above the annual average.

18–5 The forecast value for January of the sixth year is 34.9, found by

$$\hat{y} = 4.4 + 0.5(61) = 34.9$$

Seasonally adjusting the forecast, 34.9(120)/100 = 41.88. For February, $\hat{y} = 4.4 + 0.5(62) = 35.4$.
Then, (35.4)95/100 = 33.63.

CHAPTER 19

19–1

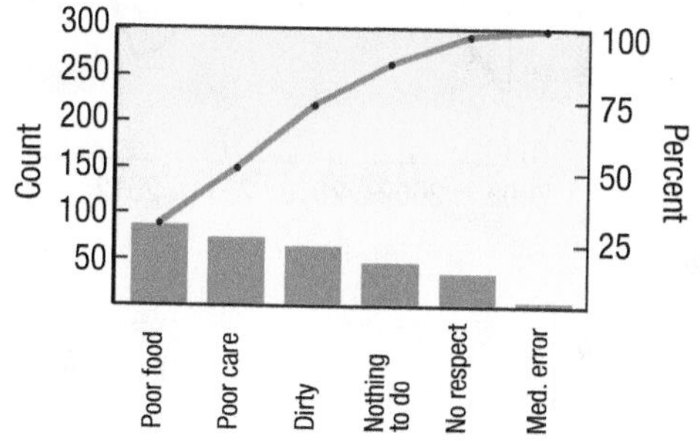

Count	84	71	63	45	35	2
Percent	28	24	21	15	12	0
Cum. %	28	52	73	88	100	100

Seventy-three percent of the complaints involve poor food, poor care, or dirty conditions. These are the factors the administrator should address.

19–2 **a.**

Sample Times 1	2	3	4	Total	Average	Range
1	4	5	2	12	3	4
2	3	2	1	8	2	2
1	7	3	5	16	4	6
					9	12

$$\bar{\bar{x}} = \frac{9}{3} = 3 \qquad \bar{R} = \frac{12}{3} = 4$$

$$UCL \text{ and } LCL = \bar{\bar{x}} \pm A_2\bar{R}$$
$$= 3 \pm 0.729(4)$$

$$UCL = 5.916 \qquad LCL = 0.084$$

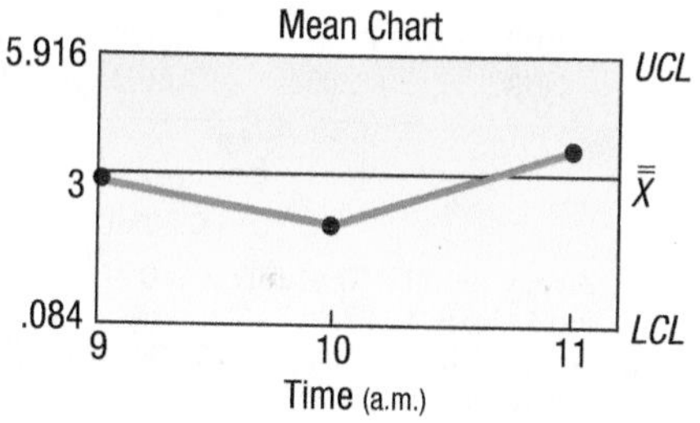

$$LCL = D_3\bar{R} = 0(4) = 0$$
$$UCL = D_4\bar{R} = 2.282(4) = 9.128$$

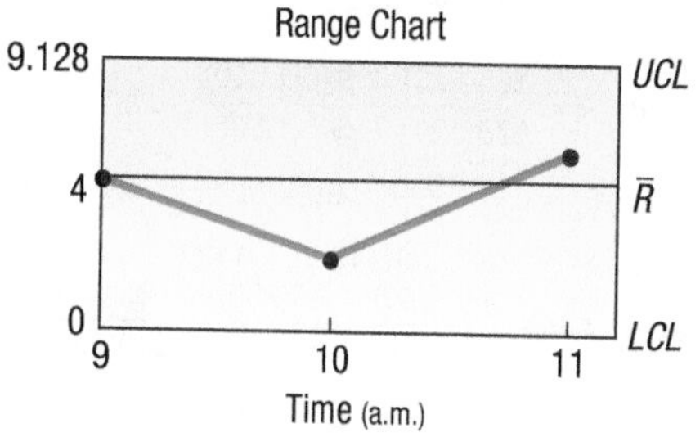

b. Yes. Both the mean chart and the range chart indicate that the process is in control.

19–3 $\bar{c} = \frac{25}{12} = 2.083$

$$UCL = 2.083 + 3\sqrt{2.083} = 6.413$$
$$LCL = 2.083 - 3\sqrt{2.083} = -2.247$$

Because LCL is a negative value, we set $LCL = 0$. The shift with seven defects is out of control.

19–4 $P(x \leq 2 \mid \pi = .30 \text{ and } n = 20) = .036$

CHAPTER 20

20–1

Event	Payoff	Probability of Event	Expected Value
Market rise	$2,200	.60	$1,320
Market decline	1,100	.40	440
			$1,760

20–2 **a.** Suppose the investor purchased Rim Homes stock, and the value of the stock in a bear market dropped to $1,100 as anticipated (Table 20–1). Instead, had the investor purchased Texas Electronics and the market declined, the value of the Texas Electronics stock would be $1,150. The difference of $50, found by $1,150 − $1,100, represents the investor's regret for buying Rim Homes stock.

b. Suppose the investor purchased Texas Electronics stock, and then a bull market developed. The stock rose to $1,900, as anticipated (Table 20–1). However, had the investor bought Kayser Chemicals stock and the market value increased to $2,400 as anticipated, the difference of $500 represents the extra profit the investor could have made by purchasing Kayser Chemicals stock.

20–3

Event	Payoff	Probability of Event	Expected Opportunity Value
Market rise	$500	.60	$300
Market decline	0	.40	0
			$300

20–4 **a.**

Event	Payoff	Probability of Event	Expected Value
Market rise	$1,900	.40	$ 760
Market decline	1,150	.60	690
			$1,450

b.

Event	Payoff	Probability of Event	Expected Value
Market rise	$2,400	.50	$1,200
Market decline	1,000	.50	500
			$1,700

20–5 For probabilities of a market rise (or decline) down to .333, Kayser Chemicals stock would provide the largest expected profit. For probabilities .333 to .143, Rim Homes would be the best buy. For .143 and below, Texas Electronics would give the largest expected profit. Algebraic solutions:

Kayser: $2{,}400p + (1 - p)1{,}000$
Rim: $2{,}200p + (1 - p)1{,}100$

$1{,}400p + 1{,}000 = 1{,}100p + 1{,}100$
$p = .333$

Rim: $2{,}200p + (1 - p)1{,}100$
Texas: $1{,}900p + (1 - p)1{,}150$

$1{,}100p + 1{,}100 = 750p + 1{,}150$
$p = .143$

Glossary

Alpha The probability of a Type I error or the level of significance. Its symbol is the Greek letter α.

Alternate hypothesis The conclusion we accept when we demonstrate that the null hypothesis is false. It is also called the research hypothesis.

Analysis of variance (ANOVA) A technique used to test simultaneously whether the means of several populations are equal. It uses the *F* distribution as the distribution of the test statistic.

Arithmetic mean The sum of the values divided by the number of values. The symbol for the mean of a sample is $\bar{x}$ and the symbol for a population mean is μ.

Assignable variation Variation that is not random. It can be eliminated or reduced by investigating the problem and finding the cause.

Autocorrelation Successive residuals in a time series are correlated.

Bar chart A graph that shows qualitative classes on the horizontal axis and the class frequencies on the vertical axis. The class frequencies are proportional to the heights of the bars.

Bayes' theorem Developed by Reverend Bayes in the 1700s, it is designed to find the probability of one event, *A*, occurring, given that another event, *B*, has already occurred.

Bias A possible consequence if certain members of the population are denied the chance to be selected for the sample. As a result, the sample may not be representative of the population.

Binomial probability distribution A probability distribution based on a discrete random variable. Its major characteristics are:

1. Each outcome can be classified into one of two mutually exclusive categories.
2. The distribution is the result of counting the number of successes.
3. Each trial is independent, meaning that the answer to trial 1 (correct or wrong) in no way affects the answer to trial 2.
4. The probability of a success stays the same from trial to trial.

Block In a two-way ANOVA, a block effect is a second source of variation, in addition to treatments.

Box plot A graphic display that shows the general shape of a variable's distribution. It is based on five descriptive statistics: the maximum and minimum values, the first and third quartiles, and the median.

Central limit theorem As sample size increases, the sampling distribution of the sample mean will approach a normal distribution regardless of the shape of the population.

Chance variation Variation that is random in nature. This type of variation cannot be completely eliminated unless there is a major change in the techniques, technologies, methods, equipment, or materials used in the process.

Charts Special graphical formats used to portray a frequency distribution, including histograms, frequency polygons, and cumulative frequency polygons. Other graphical devices used to portray data are bar charts and pie charts.

Chebyshev's theorem For any set of observations (sample or population), the proportion of the values that lie within *k* standard deviations of the mean is at least $1 - 1/k^2$, where *k* is any value greater than 1.

Chi-square distribution A distribution with these characteristics:

1. Its value can only be positive.
2. There is a family of chi-square distributions, a different one for each different degrees of freedom.
3. The distributions are positively skewed, but as the number of degrees of freedom increases, the distribution approaches the normal distribution.

Chi-square goodness-of-fit test A test with the objective of determining how well an observed set of frequencies fits an expected set of frequencies. It is concerned with one nominal-scale variable, such as the color of a car.

Class The interval in which the data are tallied. For example, \$4 up to \$7 is a class; \$7 up to \$11 is another class.

Class frequency The number of observations in each class. If there are 16 observations in the \$4 up to \$6 class, 16 is the class frequency.

Classical probability Probability based on the assumption we know the number of possible outcomes and that each of the outcomes is equally likely.

Cluster sampling A method often used to lower the cost of sampling if the population is dispersed over a wide geographic area. The area is divided into smaller units (counties, precincts, blocks, etc.) called primary units. Then a few primary units are chosen, and a random sample is selected from each primary unit.

Coefficient of determination The proportion of the total variation in the dependent variable that is explained by the independent variable. It can assume any value between 0 and +1.00 inclusive. This coefficient is computed by squaring the correlation coefficient, *r*.

Coefficient of multiple determination The percent of variation in the dependent variable, *y*, explained by the set of independent variables, $x_1, x_2, x_3, \ldots, x_k$.

Coefficient of skewness A measure of the lack of symmetry in a distribution. For a symmetric distribution, there is no skewness, so the coefficient of skewness is zero. Otherwise, it is either positive or negative, with the limits of ± 3.0.

Collectively exhaustive At least one of the events must occur when an experiment is conducted.

Combination formula A formula to count the number of possible arrangements when the order of the outcomes is not important. For example, the outcome {a, b, c} is considered the same as {c, b, a}.

Conditional probability The likelihood that an event will occur given that another event has occurred.

Confidence interval A range of values constructed from sample data so that the population parameter is likely to occur within that range at a specified probability.

Consumer Price Index An index reported monthly by the U.S. Department of Labor. It describes the change in a market basket of goods and services from the base period of 1982–84 to the present.

Contingency table A table used to classify observations according to two characteristics. If characteristics, such as gender and highest degree earned for a sample of stockbrokers, are cross classified into a table, the result is called a contingency table.

Continuity correction factor Used to improve the accuracy when a continuous distribution is used to estimate a discrete distribution.

Continuous random variable A random variable that may assume an infinite number of values within a given range.

Correlation analysis A group of statistical techniques used to measure the strength of the relationship between two variables.

Correlation coefficient A measure of the strength of association between two variables.

Correlation matrix A listing of all possible simple coefficients of correlation. It consists of the correlations among all the variables.

Critical value A value that is the dividing point between the region where the null hypothesis is not rejected and the region where it is rejected.

Cyclical variation The rise and fall of a time series over periods longer than one year.

Deciles Values of an ordered (minimum to maximum) data set that divide the data into 10 equal parts.

Degrees of freedom The number of items in a sample that are free to vary. Suppose there are two items in a sample, and we know the mean. We are free to specify only one of the two values because the other value is automatically determined (since the two values total twice the mean). Example: If the mean is $6, we are free to choose only one value. Choosing $4 makes the other value $8 because $4 + $8 = 2*($6). So there is 1 degree of freedom in this illustration. We can determine the degrees of freedom by $n - 1 = 2 - 1 = 1$. If n is 4, then there are 3 degrees of freedom, found by $n - 1 = 4 - 1 = 3$.

Dependent samples Dependent samples are characterized by a measurement, then some type of intervention, followed by another measurement. Paired samples are also dependent because the same individual or item is a member of both samples. Example: Ten participants in a marathon were weighed prior to and after competing in the race. We wish to study the mean amount of weight loss.

Dependent variable The variable that is being predicted or estimated.

Descriptive statistics The techniques used to describe the important characteristics of a set of data. This includes organizing the data values into a frequency distribution, computing measures of location, and computing measures of dispersion and skewness.

Discrete random variable A random variable that can assume only certain clearly separated values.

Dot plot A dot plot summarizes the distribution of one variable by stacking dots at points on a number line that shows the values of the variable. A dot plot shows all values.

Dummy variable A qualitative variable. It can assume only one of two possible outcomes.

Empirical probability A concept of probability based on historical information.

Empirical rule For a symmetrical, bell-shaped frequency distribution, approximately 68% of the observations lie within ±1 standard deviation of the mean; about 95% of the observations lie within ±2 standard deviations of the mean; and practically all (99.7%) lie within ±3 standard deviations of the mean.

Episodic variation It is variation that is random in nature, but a cause can be identified.

Event A collection of one or more outcomes of an experiment.

Exhaustive Each observation must fall into one of the categories.

Experiment An activity that is either observed or measured.

Exponential distribution A positively skewed continuous distribution described by the rate parameter, λ.

***F* distribution** It is used as the test statistic for ANOVA problems, as well as others. The major characteristics of the *F* distribution are:

1. It is never negative.
2. It is a continuous distribution approaching the *X*-axis but never touching it.
3. It is positively skewed.
4. It is based on two sets of degrees of freedom.
5. Like the *t* distribution, there is a family of *F* distributions. There is one distribution for 17 degrees of freedom in the numerator and 9 degrees of freedom in the denominator, there is another *F* distribution for 7 degrees of freedom in the numerator and 12 degrees of freedom in the denominator, and so on.

Finite-population correction factor (FPC) When sampling without replacement from a finite population, a correction term is used to reduce the standard error of the mean according to the relative size of the sample to the size of the population. The correction factor is used when the sample is more than 5% of a finite population.

Frequency distribution A grouping of data into classes showing the number of observations in each of the mutually exclusive and collectively exhaustive classes.

Frequency table A grouping of qualitative data into mutually exclusive classes showing the number of observations in each class.

General rule of addition Used to find the probabilities of complex events made up of *A* or *B* when the events are not mutually exclusive.

General rule of multiplication Used to find the probabilities of events *A* and *B* both happening when the events are not independent.

Geometric mean The *n*th root of the product of all the values. It is especially useful for averaging rates of change and index numbers. It minimizes the importance of extreme values. A second use of the geometric mean is to find the mean annual percent change over a period of time.

Global test A test used to determine if any of the set of independent variables has regression coefficients different from zero.

Histogram A graphical display of a frequency or relative frequency distribution. The horizontal axis shows the classes. The vertical height of adjacent bars shows the frequency or relative frequency of each class.

Homoscedasticity The standard error of estimate is the same for all fitted values of the dependent variable.

Hypergeometric distribution A probability distribution based on a discrete random variable. Its major characteristics are a fixed number of trials, only two possible outcomes, and the probability of success is not the same on each trial.

Hypothesis A statement or claim about the value of a population parameter. Examples: 40.7% of all persons 65 years old or older live alone. The mean number of people in a car is 1.33.

Hypothesis testing A statistical procedure, based on sample evidence and probability theory, used to determine whether the statement about the population parameter is reasonable.

Independence The probability of one event has no effect on the probability of another event.

Independent samples The samples chosen at random are not related to each other. We wish to study the mean age of the employees at Google and Yahoo. We select a random sample of 28 employees from Google and a sample of 19 employees from Yahoo. A person cannot be an employee in both companies. The samples are independent, that is, unrelated.

Independent variable A variable that provides the basis for estimation.

Index number A number that expresses the relative change in price, quantity, or value compared to a base period.

Inferential statistics, also called statistical inference This facet of statistics deals with estimating a population parameter based on a sample statistic. For example, if a sample of 10 TI-36X solar calculators revealed 2 to be defective, we might infer that 20% of the production is defective.

Interaction The case in which one independent variable (such as x_2) affects the relationship between another independent variable (x_1) and the dependent variable (y).

Interquartile range The absolute numerical difference between the first and third quartiles. Fifty percent of a distribution's values occur in this range.

Interval estimate The interval within which a population parameter probably lies, based on sample information. Example: According to sample data, the population mean is in the interval between 1.9 and 2.0 pounds.

Interval level of measurement If one observation is greater than another by a certain amount, and the zero point is arbitrary, the measurement is on an interval scale. For example, the difference between temperatures of 70 degrees and 80 degrees is 10 degrees. Likewise, a temperature of 90 degrees is 10 degrees more than a temperature of 80 degrees, and so on.

Irregular variation Variation in a time series that is random in nature and does not regularly repeat itself.

Joint probability A probability that measures the likelihood two or more events will happen concurrently.

Kruskal-Wallis one-way analysis of variance by ranks A test used when the assumptions for parametric analysis of variance (ANOVA) cannot be met. Its purpose is to test whether several populations are the same. The data must be at least ordinal scale.

Law of large numbers Over a large number of trials, the empirical probability of an event will approach its true probability.

Least squares method A technique used to arrive at the regression equation by minimizing the sum of the squares of the vertical distances between the actual *y* values and the predicted *y* values.

Level of significance The probability of rejecting the null hypothesis when it is true.

Linear regression equation A mathematical equation that defines the relationship between two variables. It has the form $y = a + bx$. It is used to predict *y* based on a selected *x* value. *y* is the dependent variable and *x*, the independent variable.

Measure of dispersion A value that shows the spread of a data set. The range, variance, and standard deviation are measures of dispersion.

Measure of location A single value that is typical of the data. It pinpoints the center of a distribution. The arithmetic mean, weighted mean, median, mode, and geometric mean are measures of location.

Median The value of the middle observation after all the observations have been arranged from low to high. For example, if observations 6, 9, 4 are rearranged to read 4, 6, 9, the median is 6, the middle value.

Midpoint The value that divides a class into two equal parts. For the classes $10 up to $20 and $20 up to $30, the midpoints are $15 and $25, respectively.

Mode The value that appears most frequently in a set of data. For grouped data, it is the midpoint of the class containing the largest number of values.

Multicollinearity A condition that occurs in multiple regression analysis if the independent variables are themselves correlated.

Multiple regression equation The relationship in the form of a mathematical equation between several independent variables and a dependent variable. The general form is $\hat{y} = a + b_1x_1 + b_2x_2 + b_3x_3 + \cdots + b_kx_k$. It is used to estimate *y* given *k* independent variables, x_i.

Multiplication formula A formula used to count the number of possible outcomes of an experiment. It states that if there are *m* ways of doing one thing and *n* ways of doing another, there are $(m * n)$ ways of doing both.

Mutually exclusive A property of a set of categories such that an individual, object, or measurement is included in only one category.

Nominal level of measurement The "lowest" level of measurement. Such data can only be classified into categories, and there is no particular order for the categories. For example, it makes no difference whether the categories "male" and "female" are listed in that order, or female first and male second. The categories are mutually exclusive—meaning, in this illustration, that a person cannot be a male and a female at the same time.

Nonparametric or distribution-free tests Hypothesis tests involving nominal- and ordinal-level data. No assumptions need be made about the shape of the population distribution; that is, we do not assume the population is normally distributed.

Normal probability distribution A continuous bell-shaped distribution. It is completely described by its mean and standard deviation. Half the observations are less than the mean.

Null hypothesis A statement about the value of a population parameter that is developed for testing in the face of numerical evidence. It is written as H_0.

One-tailed test Used when the alternate hypothesis states a direction, such as H_1: $\mu > 40$, read "the population mean is greater than 40." Here the rejection region is only in one tail (the right tail).

Ordinal level of measurement Data that can be ranked are referred to as ordinal measures. For example, consumer response to the sound of a new speaker might be excellent, very good, fair, or poor.

Outcome A particular observation or measurement of an experiment.

Outlier A data point that is unusually far from the others. An accepted rule is to classify an observation as an outlier if it is 1.5 times the interquartile range above the third quartile or below the first quartile.

***p*-value** The probability of computing a value of the test statistic at least as extreme as the one found in the sample data when the null hypothesis is true.

Parameter A characteristic of a population.

Percentiles Values of an ordered (minimum to maximum) data set that divide the data into 100 intervals.

Permutation formula A formula to count the number of possible arrangements when the order of the outcomes is important. For example, the outcome {a, b, c} is considered different from {c, b, a}.

Pie chart A chart that shows the proportion or percentage that each class represents of the total number of frequencies.

Point estimate A single value computed from a sample and used to estimate a population parameter. Example: If the sample mean is 1,020, it is the best estimate of the population mean.

Poisson probability distribution A discrete probability distribution often used to approximate binomial probabilities when *n* is large and π is small.

Pooled estimate of the population variance A weighted average of s_1^2 and s_2^2 used to estimate the common variance σ^2 when using small samples to test the difference between two population means.

Population The collection, or set, of all individuals, objects, or measurements whose properties are being studied.

Posterior probability A revised probability based on additional information.

Prior probability The initial probability based on the present level of information.

Probability A value between 0 and 1, inclusive, that reports the likelihood that a specific event will occur.

Probability distribution A listing of all possible outcomes of an experiment and the probability associated with each outcome.

Probability sample A sample of items or individuals chosen so that each member of the population has a chance of being included in the sample.

Proportion A fraction or percentage of a sample or a population having a particular trait. If 5 out of 50 in a sample liked a new cereal, the proportion is 5/50, or .10.

Qualitative variables A nominal-scale variable coded to assume only one nonnumeric outcome or category. For example, a person is considered either employed or unemployed.

Quartiles Values of an ordered (minimum to maximum) data set that divide the data into four intervals.

Random variable A variable defined by a probability distribution. It can have different values with their likelihood determined by its probability distribution.

Random variation The sum of the squared differences between each observation and its treatment mean.

Range A measure of dispersion found by subtracting the minimum value from the maximum value.

Ratio level of measurement If the distance between numbers is a constant size, there is a true zero point, and the ratio of two values is meaningful, then the data are ratio scale. For example, the distance between $200 and $300 is $100, and in the case of money there is a true zero point. If you have zero dollars, there is an absence of money (you have none). Also, the ratio between $200 and $300 is meaningful.

Regression equation An equation that expresses the linear relationship between two variables.

Relative frequency distribution A frequency distribution that shows the fraction or proportion of the total observations in each class.

Residual The difference between the actual value of the dependent variable and the estimated value of the dependent variable, that is, $y - \hat{y}$.

Residual variation It is variation that is random in nature and cannot be identified or predicted.

Sample A portion, or subset, of the population being studied.

Sampling distribution of the sample mean A probability distribution consisting of all possible means of samples of a given size selected from a population.

Sampling error The difference between a sample statistic and the corresponding population parameter. Example: The sample mean income is $22,100; the population mean is $22,000. The sampling error is $22,100 − $22,000 = $100. This error can be attributed to sampling—that is, chance.

Scatter diagram Graphical technique used to show the relationship between two variables measured with interval or ratio scales.

Seasonal variation Patterns of change in a time series within a year. These patterns of change repeat themselves each year.

Secular trend The smoothed long-term direction of a time series.

Sign test A test used for dependent samples. The sign test is used to find whether there is a brand preference for two products or to determine whether performance after an experiment is greater than before the experiment. Also, the sign test is used to test a hypothesis about the median.

Significance level The probability of rejecting the null hypothesis when it is true.

Simple index The value in the given period divided by the value in the base period. The result is usually multiplied by 100 and reported as a percent.

Simple random sampling A sampling scheme such that each member of the population has the same chance of being selected as part of the sample.

Spearman's coefficient of rank correlation A measure of the association between the ranks of two variables. It can range from −1.00 to +1.00. A value of −1.00 indicates a perfect negative association among the ranks and a value of +1.00 means a perfect positive association among the ranks. A value of 0 indicates no association among the ranks.

Special rule of addition A rule used to find the probabilities of events made up of *A* or *B* when the events are mutually exclusive.

Special rule of multiplication A rule used to find the probability of the joint occurrence of independent events.

Standard deviation The square root of the variance.

Standard error of estimate Measures the dispersion of the actual *y* values about the regression line. It is reported in the same units as the dependent variable.

Statistic A characteristic of a sample.

Statistics The science of collecting, organizing, analyzing, and interpreting data for the purpose of making more effective decisions.

Stem-and-leaf display A method to display a variable's distribution using every value. Values are classified by the data's leading digit. For example, if a data set contains values between 13 and 84, eight classes based on the 10s digit would be used for the stems. The 1s digits would be the leaves.

Stepwise regression A step-by-step process for finding the regression equation. Only independent variables with nonzero regression coefficients enter the regression equation. Independent variables are added one at a time to the regression equation.

Stratified random sampling A population is first divided into subgroups called strata. A sample is then chosen from each stratum. If, for example, the population of interest consisted of all undergraduate students, the sample design might call for sampling 62 freshmen, 51 sophomores, 40 juniors, and 39 seniors.

Subjective concept of probability The chance of an event happening based on personal estimates such as hunches, opinions, or rumors.

Systematic random sampling When a population is arranged in some way, such as alphabetically, by height, or in a file drawer, a random starting point is selected, then every *k*th item becomes a member of the sample. If a sample design called for interviewing every ninth household on Main Street starting with 932 Main, the sample would consist of households at 932 Main, 941 Main, 950 Main, and so on.

***t*-distribution** Investigated and reported by William S. Gossett in 1908 and published under the pseudonym Student. It is similar to the standard normal distribution presented in Chapter 7. The major characteristics of *t* are:

1. It is a continuous distribution.
2. It can assume values between minus infinity and plus infinity.
3. It is symmetrical about its mean of zero. However, it is more spread out and flatter at the apex than the standard normal distribution.
4. It approaches the standard normal distribution as *n* gets larger.
5. There is a family of *t* distributions. One *t* distribution exists for a sample of 15 observations, another for 25, and so on.

Test statistic A value, determined from sample information, used to determine whether to reject the null hypothesis.

Total variation The sum of the squared differences between each observation and the overall mean.

Treatment A source of variation. It identifies the several populations being examined.

Treatment variation The sum of the squared differences between each treatment mean and the grand or overall mean.

Two-tailed test Used when the alternate hypothesis does not state a direction, such as H_1: $\mu \neq 75$, read "the population mean is not equal to 75." There is a region of rejection in each tail.

Type I error Occurs when a true H_0 is rejected.

Type II error Occurs when a false H_0 is not rejected.

Uniform distribution A continuous distribution that is rectangular in shape. It is completely described by its minimum and maximum values.

Value of perfect information The difference between the maximum payoff under conditions of certainty and the maximum payoff under uncertainty.

Variance A measure of dispersion based on the average squared differences from the arithmetic mean.

Variance inflation factor A test used to detect correlation among independent variables.

Weighted index The prices in the base period and the given period are multiplied by quantities (weights).

Weighted mean Each value is assigned a relative weight (sometimes a frequency). Each value is multiplied by the weight and then the weighted values are summed. The sum is divided by the sum of the weights.

Wilcoxon rank-sum test A nonparametric test requiring independent samples. The data must be at least ordinal level. That is, the data must be capable of being ranked. The test is used when the assumptions for the parametric Student's *t* test cannot be met. The objective of the test is to find whether two independent samples can be considered as coming from the same population. It is used if the assumptions required for the paired *t* test cannot be met.

***z* value** For a random variable that is approximately normally distributed, it is the distance between a selected value and the mean measured in units of the standard deviation.

Photo Credits

Chapter 1
Page 1: Courtesy Barnes & Noble; p. 2: Gregor Schuster/Getty Images; p. 7: Rachel Epstein/The Image Works.

Chapter 2
Page 17: Jose Luis Pelaez/Getty Images; p. 18: Justin Sullivan/Getty Images; p. 19: Steve Cole/Getty Images.

Chapter 3
Page 50: Andy Lyons/Getty Images; p. 51: Digital Vision/Getty Images; p. 53: Bloomberg via Getty Images; p. 70: Spencer Grant/PhotoEdit.

Chapter 4
Page 93: Randy Faris/Corbis; p. 99: Somos/Veer/Getty Images; p. 103: Ramin Talaie/Getty Images; p. 114: Steve Mason/Getty Images.

Chapter 5
Page 131: Karin Slade/Getty Images; p. 132: Franziska Tetzner/Corbis; p. 141: whiteboxmedia limited/Alamy; p. 143: Tony Arruza/Corbis; p. 157: The McGraw-Hill Companies, Inc./Marker Dierker, photographer.

Chapter 6
Page 173: JGI/Jamie Grill/Getty Images; p. 179: Thinkstock/Jupiterimages; p. 182: David Madison/Digital Vision/Getty Images RF; p. 192: Howard Berman/Getty Images.

Chapter 7
Page 206: Ilene MacDonald/Alamy RF; p. 207: C. Sherburne/PhotoLink/Getty Images; p. 224: Jupiterimages/Getty Images RF; p. 231: zumaamericasseven871062/Newscom.

Chapter 8
Page 247: JB Reed/Landov; p. 249: David Epperson/Getty Images RF.

Chapter 9
Page 279: Jack Hollingsworth/Photodisc/Getty Images RF; p. 281: Andersen Ross/Getty Images; p. 284: Courtesy Del Monte Corporation; p. 294: The McGraw-Hill Companies, Inc./Andrew Resek, photographer; p. 297: Rich Pedroncelli/AP Photo.

Chapter 10
Page 315: Photo Source Hawaii/Alamy; p. 316: Russell Illig/Getty Images; p. 319: Jim Stern/Bloomberg via Getty Images; p. 324: Robert Nicholas/Getty Images; p. 327: Gene J. Puskar/AP Photo.

Chapter 11
Page 348 © JGI/Blend Images LLC RF; p. 349: John Lund/Drew Kelly/Blend Images LLC; p. 352: © Debbie Noda/Modesto Bee/ZUMAPRESS.com/Alamy; p. 365: Photodisc/Getty Images RF.

Chapter 12
Page 379: Photo Illustration by Alexander Hassenstein/Getty Images; p. 381: The McGraw-Hill Companies, Inc./John Flournoy, photographer; p. 382: Daniel Acker/Bloomberg/Getty Images; p. 399: John A. Rizzo/Getty Images RF.

Chapter 13
Page 426: Ingram Publishing/Superstock RF; p. 441: Image Source/Getty Images RF.

Chapter 14
Page 476: Image Source/Getty Images RF.

Chapter 15
Page 533: Najiah Feanny/Corbis; p. 539: Digital Vision/PunchStock RF; p. 544: © Ian Dagnall/Alamy; p. 544: © Blend Images/Getty Images RF.

Chapter 16
Page 570: ITAR-TASS/Landov; p. 571: Photo courtesy of Nestle; p. 575: © Corbis All Rights Reserved RF; p. 580: Blend Images/Getty Images RF.

Chapter 17
Page 608: Steve Cole/Photodisc/Getty Images RF; p. 609: Image Source/Getty Images RF; p. 625: Image Ideas Inc./Picture Quest.

Chapter 18
Page 639: Bob Levey/Getty Images; p. 640: Flying Colours Ltd./Photodisc/Getty Images RF; p. 647: © First Light/Alamy; p. 656: Daniel Belenguer/Alamy; p. 667: Arthur Tilley/Getty Images.

Chapter 19
Page 682: Jerry Lampen/Landov; p. 685: Courtesy of the National Institute of Standards and Technology, Office of Quality Programs, Gaithersburg, MD; p. 691: © Kevpix/Alamy; p. 705: Ingram Publishing.

Chapter 20 (on the website: www.mhhe.com/lind16e)
Page 20-1: Mark Horn/Getty Images; 20-2: Gary C. Knapp/AP Photo.

Index

KEY FORMULAS Lind, Marchal, and Wathen • *Statistical Techniques in Business & Economics*, 16th edition

CHAPTER 3

- Population mean

$$\mu = \frac{\Sigma x}{N} \qquad [3\text{–}1]$$

- Sample mean, raw data

$$\bar{x} = \frac{\Sigma x}{n} \qquad [3\text{–}2]$$

- Weighted mean

$$\bar{x}_w = \frac{w_1x_1 + w_2x_2 + \cdots + w_nx_n}{w_1 + w_2 + \cdots + w_n} \qquad [3\text{–}3]$$

- Geometric mean

$$GM = \sqrt[n]{(x_1)(x_2)(x_3)\cdots(x_n)} \qquad [3\text{–}4]$$

- Geometric mean rate of increase

$$GM = \sqrt[n]{\frac{\text{Value at end of period}}{\text{Value at start of period}}} - 1.0 \qquad [3\text{–}5]$$

- Range

$$\text{Range} = \text{Maximum value} - \text{Minimum value} \qquad [3\text{–}6]$$

- Population variance

$$\sigma^2 = \frac{\Sigma(x - \mu)^2}{N} \qquad [3\text{–}7]$$

- Population standard deviation

$$\sigma = \sqrt{\frac{\Sigma(x - \mu)^2}{N}} \qquad [3\text{–}8]$$

- Sample variance

$$s^2 = \frac{\Sigma(x - \bar{x})^2}{n - 1} \qquad [3\text{–}9]$$

- Sample standard deviation

$$s = \sqrt{\frac{\Sigma(x - \bar{x})^2}{n - 1}} \qquad [3\text{–}10]$$

- Sample mean, grouped data

$$\bar{x} = \frac{\Sigma fM}{n} \qquad [3\text{–}11]$$

- Sample standard deviation, grouped data

$$s = \sqrt{\frac{\Sigma f(M - \bar{x})^2}{n - 1}} \qquad [3\text{–}12]$$

CHAPTER 4

- Location of a percentile

$$L_p = (n + 1)\frac{P}{100} \qquad [4\text{–}1]$$

- Pearson's coefficient of skewness

$$sk = \frac{3(\bar{x} - \text{Median})}{s} \qquad [4\text{–}2]$$

- Software coefficient of skewness

$$sk = \frac{n}{(n - 1)(n - 2)}\left[\Sigma\left(\frac{x - \bar{x}}{s}\right)^3\right] \qquad [4\text{–}3]$$

CHAPTER 5

- Special rule of addition

$$P(A \text{ or } B) = P(A) + P(B) \qquad [5\text{–}2]$$

- Complement rule

$$P(A) = 1 - P(\sim A) \qquad [5\text{–}3]$$

- General rule of addition

$$P(A \text{ or } B) = P(A) + P(B) - P(A \text{ and } B) \qquad [5\text{–}4]$$

- Special rule of multiplication

$$P(A \text{ and } B) = P(A)P(B) \qquad [5\text{–}5]$$

- General rule of multiplication

$$P(A \text{ and } B) = P(A)P(B|A) \qquad [5\text{–}6]$$

- Bayes' Theorem

$$P(A_1|B) = \frac{P(A_1)P(B|A_1)}{P(A_1)P(B|A_1) + P(A_2)P(B|A_2)} \qquad [5\text{–}7]$$

- Multiplication formula

$$\text{Total arrangements} = (m)(n) \qquad [5\text{–}8]$$

- Number of permutations

$$_nP_r = \frac{n!}{(n - r)!} \qquad [5\text{–}9]$$

- Number of combinations

$$_nC_r = \frac{n!}{r!(n - r)!} \qquad [5\text{–}10]$$

CHAPTER 6

- Mean of a probability distribution

$$\mu = \Sigma[xP(x)] \qquad [6\text{–}1]$$

- Variance of a probability distribution

$$\sigma^2 = \Sigma[(x - \mu)^2P(x)] \qquad [6\text{–}2]$$

- Binomial probability distribution

$$P(x) = {_nC_x}\,\pi^x(1 - \pi)^{n - x} \qquad [6\text{–}3]$$

- Mean of a binomial distribution

$$\mu = n\pi \qquad [6\text{–}4]$$

- Variance of a binomial distribution

$$\sigma^2 = n\pi(1 - \pi) \qquad [6\text{–}5]$$

- Hypergeometric probability distribution

$$P(x) = \frac{({_SC_x})({_{N-S}C_{n-x}})}{_NC_n} \qquad [6\text{–}6]$$

- Poisson probability distribution

$$P(x) = \frac{\mu^xe^{-\mu}}{x!} \qquad [6\text{–}7]$$

- Mean of a Poisson distribution

$$\mu = n\pi \qquad [6\text{–}8]$$

CHAPTER 7

- Mean of a uniform distribution

$$\mu = \frac{a + b}{2} \qquad [7\text{–}1]$$

- Standard deviation of a uniform distribution

$$\sigma = \sqrt{\frac{(b - a)^2}{12}} \qquad [7\text{–}2]$$

- Uniform probability distribution

$$P(x) = \frac{1}{b - a} \qquad [7\text{–}3]$$

if $a \leq x \leq b$ and 0 elsewhere

- Normal probability distribution

$$P(x) = \frac{1}{\sigma\sqrt{2\pi}} e^{-\left[\frac{(x-\mu)^2}{2\sigma^2}\right]} \qquad [7\text{–}4]$$

- Standard normal value

$$z = \frac{x - \mu}{\sigma} \qquad [7\text{–}5]$$

- Exponential distribution

$$P(x) = \lambda e^{-\lambda x} \qquad [7\text{–}6]$$

- Finding a probability using the exponential distribution

$$P(\text{Arrival time} < x) = 1 - e^{-\lambda x} \qquad [7\text{–}7]$$

CHAPTER 8

- Standard error of mean

$$\sigma_{\bar{x}} = \frac{\sigma}{\sqrt{n}} \qquad [8\text{–}1]$$

- z-value, μ and σ known

$$z = \frac{\bar{x} - \mu}{\sigma/\sqrt{n}} \qquad [8\text{–}2]$$

CHAPTER 9

- Confidence interval for μ, with σ known

$$\bar{x} \pm z \frac{\sigma}{\sqrt{n}} \qquad [9\text{–}1]$$

- Confidence interval for μ, σ unknown

$$\bar{x} \pm t \frac{s}{\sqrt{n}} \qquad [9\text{–}2]$$

- Sample proportion

$$p = \frac{x}{n} \qquad [9\text{–}3]$$

- Confidence interval for proportion

$$p \pm z\sqrt{\frac{p(1 - p)}{n}} \qquad [9\text{–}4]$$

- Sample size for estimating mean

$$n = \left(\frac{z\sigma}{E}\right)^2 \qquad [9\text{–}5]$$

- Sample size for a proportion

$$n = \pi(1 - \pi)\left(\frac{z}{E}\right)^2 \qquad [9\text{–}6]$$

CHAPTER 10

- Testing a mean, σ known

$$z = \frac{\bar{x} - \mu}{\sigma/\sqrt{n}} \qquad [10\text{–}1]$$

- Testing a mean, σ unknown

$$t = \frac{\bar{x} - \mu}{s/\sqrt{n}} \qquad [10\text{–}2]$$

- Type II error

$$z = \frac{\bar{x}_c - \mu_1}{\sigma/\sqrt{n}} \qquad [10\text{–}3]$$

CHAPTER 11

- Variance of the distribution of difference in means

$$\sigma^2_{\bar{x}_1 - \bar{x}_2} = \frac{\sigma_1^2}{n_1} + \frac{\sigma_2^2}{n_2} \qquad [11\text{–}1]$$

- Two-sample test of means, known σ

$$z = \frac{\bar{x}_1 - \bar{x}_2}{\sqrt{\frac{\sigma_1^2}{n_1} + \frac{\sigma_2^2}{n_2}}} \qquad [11\text{–}2]$$

- Pooled variance

$$s_p^2 = \frac{(n_1 - 1)\, s_1^2 + (n_2 - 1)\, s_2^2}{n_1 + n_2 - 2} \qquad [11\text{–}3]$$

- Two-sample test of means, unknown but equal σ^2s

$$t = \frac{\bar{x}_1 - \bar{x}_2}{\sqrt{s_p^2\left(\frac{1}{n_1} + \frac{1}{n_2}\right)}} \qquad [11\text{–}4]$$

- Two-sample tests of means, unknown and unequal σ^2s

$$t = \frac{\bar{x}_1 - \bar{x}_2}{\sqrt{\frac{s_1^2}{n_1} + \frac{s_2^2}{n_2}}} \qquad [11\text{–}5]$$

- Degrees of freedom for unequal variance test

$$df = \frac{[(s_1^2/n_1) + (s_2^2/n_2)]^2}{\frac{(s_1^2/n_1)^2}{n_1 - 1} + \frac{(s_2^2/n_2)^2}{n_2 - 1}} \qquad [11\text{–}6]$$

- Paired t test

$$t = \frac{\bar{d}}{s_d/\sqrt{n}} \qquad [11\text{–}7]$$

CHAPTER 12

- Test for comparing two variances

$$F = \frac{s_1^2}{s_2^2} \qquad [12\text{–}1]$$

- Sum of squares, total

$$\text{SS total} = \Sigma(x - \bar{x}_G)^2 \qquad [12\text{–}2]$$

- Sum of squares, error

$$SSE = \Sigma(x - \bar{x}_c)^2 \quad [12\text{–}3]$$

- Sum of squares, treatments

$$SST = SS\ total - SSE \quad [12\text{–}4]$$

- Confidence interval for differences in treatment means

$$(\bar{x}_1 - \bar{x}_2) \pm t\sqrt{MSE\left(\frac{1}{n_1} + \frac{1}{n_2}\right)} \quad [12\text{–}5]$$

- Sum of squares, blocks

$$SSB = k\Sigma(\bar{x}_b - \bar{x}_G)^2 \quad [12\text{–}6]$$

- Sum of squares error, two-way ANOVA

$$SSE = SS\ total - SST - SSB \quad [12\text{–}7]$$

CHAPTER 13

- Correlation coefficient

$$r = \frac{\Sigma(x - \bar{x})(y - \bar{y})}{(n - 1)\, s_x s_y} \quad [13\text{–}1]$$

- Test for significant correlation

$$t = \frac{r\sqrt{n - 2}}{\sqrt{1 - r^2}} \quad [13\text{–}2]$$

- Linear regression equation

$$\hat{y} = a + bx \quad [13\text{–}3]$$

- Slope of the regression line

$$b = r\frac{s_y}{s_x} \quad [13\text{–}4]$$

- Intercept of the regression line

$$a = \bar{y} - b\bar{x} \quad [13\text{–}5]$$

- Test for a zero slope

$$t = \frac{b - 0}{s_b} \quad [13\text{–}6]$$

- Standard error of estimate

$$s_{y \cdot x} = \sqrt{\frac{\Sigma(y - \hat{y})^2}{n - 2}} \quad [13\text{–}7]$$

- Coefficient of determination

$$r^2 = \frac{SSR}{SS\ Total} = 1 - \frac{SSE}{SS\ Total} \quad [13\text{–}8]$$

- Standard error of estimate

$$s_{y \cdot x} = \sqrt{\frac{SSE}{n - 2}} \quad [13\text{–}9]$$

- Confidence interval

$$\hat{y} \pm t s_{y \cdot x}\sqrt{\frac{1}{n} + \frac{(x - \bar{x})^2}{\Sigma(x - \bar{x})^2}} \quad [13\text{–}10]$$

- Prediction interval

$$\hat{y} \pm t s_{y \cdot x}\sqrt{1 + \frac{1}{n} + \frac{(x - \bar{x})^2}{\Sigma(x - \bar{x})^2}} \quad [13\text{–}11]$$

CHAPTER 14

- Multiple regression equation

$$\hat{y} = a + b_1x_1 + b_2x_2 + \cdots + b_kx_k \quad [14\text{–}1]$$

- Multiple standard error of estimate

$$s_{y \cdot 123 \ldots k} = \sqrt{\frac{\Sigma(y - \hat{y})^2}{n - (k + 1)}} = \sqrt{\frac{SSE}{n - (k + 1)}} \quad [14\text{–}2]$$

- Coefficient of multiple determination

$$R^2 = \frac{SSR}{SS\ total} \quad [14\text{–}3]$$

- Adjusted coefficient of determination

$$R^2_{adj} = 1 - \frac{\dfrac{SSE}{n - (k + 1)}}{\dfrac{SS\ total}{n - 1}} \quad [14\text{–}4]$$

- Global test of hypothesis

$$F = \frac{SSR/k}{SSE/[n - (k + 1)]} \quad [14\text{–}5]$$

- Testing for a particular regression coefficient

$$t = \frac{b_i - 0}{s_{b_i}} \quad [14\text{–}6]$$

- Variance inflation factor

$$VIF = \frac{1}{1 - R_j^2} \quad [14\text{–}7]$$

CHAPTER 15

- Test of hypothesis, one proportion

$$z = \frac{p - \pi}{\sqrt{\dfrac{\pi(1 - \pi)}{n}}} \quad [15\text{–}1]$$

- Two-sample test of proportions

$$z = \frac{p_1 - p_2}{\sqrt{\dfrac{p_c(1 - p_c)}{n_1} + \dfrac{p_c(1 - p_c)}{n_2}}} \quad [15\text{–}2]$$

- Pooled proportion

$$p_c = \frac{x_1 + x_2}{n_1 + n_2} \quad [15\text{–}3]$$

- Chi-square test statistic

$$\chi^2 = \sum\left[\frac{(f_o - f_e)^2}{f_e}\right] \quad [15\text{–}4]$$

- Expected frequency

$$f_e = \frac{(\text{Row total})(\text{Column total})}{\text{Grand total}} \quad [15\text{–}5]$$

CHAPTER 16

- Sign test, $n > 10$

$$z = \frac{(x \pm .50) - \mu}{\sigma} \quad [16\text{–}1]$$

- Wilcoxon rank-sum test

$$z = \frac{W - \frac{n_1(n_1 + n_2 + 1)}{2}}{\sqrt{\frac{n_1 n_2(n_1 + n_2 + 1)}{12}}} \quad \textbf{[16–4]}$$

- Kruskal-Wallis test

$$H = \frac{12}{n(n+1)}\left[\frac{(\Sigma R_1)^2}{n_1} + \frac{(\Sigma R_2)^2}{n_2} + \cdots + \frac{(\Sigma R_k)^2}{n_k}\right] - 3(n+1) \quad \textbf{[16–5]}$$

- Spearman coefficient of rank correlation

$$r_s = 1 - \frac{6\Sigma d^2}{n(n^2 - 1)} \quad \textbf{[16–6]}$$

- Hypothesis test, rank correlation

$$t = r_s\sqrt{\frac{n-2}{1 - r_s^2}} \quad \textbf{[16–7]}$$

CHAPTER 17

- Simple index

$$P = \frac{p_t}{p_0}(100) \quad \textbf{[17–1]}$$

- Simple average of price relatives

$$P = \frac{\Sigma P_i}{n} \quad \textbf{[17–2]}$$

- Simple aggregate index

$$P = \frac{\Sigma p_t}{\Sigma p_0}(100) \quad \textbf{[17–3]}$$

- Laspeyres' price index

$$P = \frac{\Sigma p_t q_0}{\Sigma p_0 q_0}(100) \quad \textbf{[17–4]}$$

- Paasche's price index

$$P = \frac{\Sigma p_t q_t}{\Sigma p_0 q_t}(100) \quad \textbf{[17–5]}$$

- Fisher's ideal index

$$\sqrt{(\text{Laspeyres' price index})(\text{Paasche's price index})} \quad \textbf{[17–6]}$$

- Value index

$$V = \frac{\Sigma p_t q_t}{\Sigma p_0 q_0}(100) \quad \textbf{[17–7]}$$

- Real income

$$\text{Real income} = \frac{\text{Money income}}{\text{CPI}}(100) \quad \textbf{[17–8]}$$

- Using an index as a deflator

$$\text{Deflated sales} = \frac{\text{Actual sales}}{\text{Index}}(100) \quad \textbf{[17–9]}$$

- Purchasing power

$$\text{Purchasing power} = \frac{\$1}{\text{CPI}}(100) \quad \textbf{[17–10]}$$

CHAPTER 18

- Linear trend

$$\hat{y} = a + bt \quad \textbf{[18–1]}$$

- Log trend equation

$$\log \hat{y} = \log a + \log b(t) \quad \textbf{[18–2]}$$

- Correction factor for adjusting quarterly means

$$\text{Correction factor} = \frac{4.00}{\text{Total of four means}} \quad \textbf{[18–3]}$$

- Durbin-Watson statistic

$$d = \frac{\sum_{t=2}^{n}(e_t - e_{t-1})^2}{\sum_{t=1}^{n} e_t^2} \quad \textbf{[18–4]}$$

CHAPTER 19

- Grand mean

$$\bar{\bar{x}} = \frac{\Sigma \bar{x}}{k} \quad \textbf{[19–1]}$$

- Control limits, mean

$$\text{UCL} = \bar{\bar{x}} + A_2\bar{R} \qquad \text{LCL} = \bar{\bar{x}} - A_2\bar{R} \quad \textbf{[19–4]}$$

- Control limits, range

$$\text{UCL} = D_4\bar{R} \qquad \text{LCL} = D_3\bar{R} \quad \textbf{[19–5]}$$

- Mean proportion defective

$$p = \frac{\text{Total number defective}}{\text{Total number of items sampled}} \quad \textbf{[19–6]}$$

- Control limits, proportion

$$\text{UCL and LCL} = p \pm 3\sqrt{\frac{p(1-p)}{n}} \quad \textbf{[19–8]}$$

- Control limits, c-bar chart

$$\text{UCL and LCL} = \bar{c} \pm 3\sqrt{\bar{c}} \quad \textbf{[19–9]}$$

CHAPTER 20 (ON THE WEBSITE: www.mhhe.com/lind16e)

- Expected monetary value

$$\text{EMV}(A_i) = \Sigma[P(S_j) \cdot V(A_i, S_j)] \quad \textbf{[20–1]}$$

- Expected opportunity loss

$$\text{EOL}(A_i) = \Sigma[P(S_j) \cdot R(A_i, S_j)] \quad \textbf{[20–2]}$$

- Expected value of perfect information

EVPI = Expected value under conditions of certainty
− Expected value of optimal decision under conditions of uncertainty **[20–3]**

Areas under the Normal Curve

Example:
If $z = 1.96$, then
$P(0 \text{ to } z) = 0.4750$.

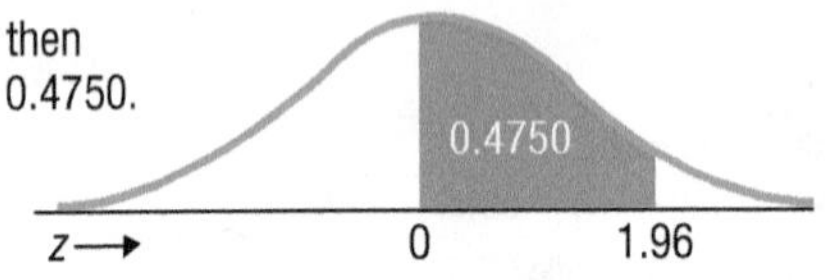

z	0.00	0.01	0.02	0.03	0.04	0.05	0.06	0.07	0.08	0.09
0.0	0.0000	0.0040	0.0080	0.0120	0.0160	0.0199	0.0239	0.0279	0.0319	0.0359
0.1	0.0398	0.0438	0.0478	0.0517	0.0557	0.0596	0.0636	0.0675	0.0714	0.0753
0.2	0.0793	0.0832	0.0871	0.0910	0.0948	0.0987	0.1026	0.1064	0.1103	0.1141
0.3	0.1179	0.1217	0.1255	0.1293	0.1331	0.1368	0.1406	0.1443	0.1480	0.1517
0.4	0.1554	0.1591	0.1628	0.1664	0.1700	0.1736	0.1772	0.1808	0.1844	0.1879
0.5	0.1915	0.1950	0.1985	0.2019	0.2054	0.2088	0.2123	0.2157	0.2190	0.2224
0.6	0.2257	0.2291	0.2324	0.2357	0.2389	0.2422	0.2454	0.2486	0.2517	0.2549
0.7	0.2580	0.2611	0.2642	0.2673	0.2704	0.2734	0.2764	0.2794	0.2823	0.2852
0.8	0.2881	0.2910	0.2939	0.2967	0.2995	0.3023	0.3051	0.3078	0.3106	0.3133
0.9	0.3159	0.3186	0.3212	0.3238	0.3264	0.3289	0.3315	0.3340	0.3365	0.3389
1.0	0.3413	0.3438	0.3461	0.3485	0.3508	0.3531	0.3554	0.3577	0.3599	0.3621
1.1	0.3643	0.3665	0.3686	0.3708	0.3729	0.3749	0.3770	0.3790	0.3810	0.3830
1.2	0.3849	0.3869	0.3888	0.3907	0.3925	0.3944	0.3962	0.3980	0.3997	0.4015
1.3	0.4032	0.4049	0.4066	0.4082	0.4099	0.4115	0.4131	0.4147	0.4162	0.4177
1.4	0.4192	0.4207	0.4222	0.4236	0.4251	0.4265	0.4279	0.4292	0.4306	0.4319
1.5	0.4332	0.4345	0.4357	0.4370	0.4382	0.4394	0.4406	0.4418	0.4429	0.4441
1.6	0.4452	0.4463	0.4474	0.4484	0.4495	0.4505	0.4515	0.4525	0.4535	0.4545
1.7	0.4554	0.4564	0.4573	0.4582	0.4591	0.4599	0.4608	0.4616	0.4625	0.4633
1.8	0.4641	0.4649	0.4656	0.4664	0.4671	0.4678	0.4686	0.4693	0.4699	0.4706
1.9	0.4713	0.4719	0.4726	0.4732	0.4738	0.4744	0.4750	0.4756	0.4761	0.4767
2.0	0.4772	0.4778	0.4783	0.4788	0.4793	0.4798	0.4803	0.4808	0.4812	0.4817
2.1	0.4821	0.4826	0.4830	0.4834	0.4838	0.4842	0.4846	0.4850	0.4854	0.4857
2.2	0.4861	0.4864	0.4868	0.4871	0.4875	0.4878	0.4881	0.4884	0.4887	0.4890
2.3	0.4893	0.4896	0.4898	0.4901	0.4904	0.4906	0.4909	0.4911	0.4913	0.4916
2.4	0.4918	0.4920	0.4922	0.4925	0.4927	0.4929	0.4931	0.4932	0.4934	0.4936
2.5	0.4938	0.4940	0.4941	0.4943	0.4945	0.4946	0.4948	0.4949	0.4951	0.4952
2.6	0.4953	0.4955	0.4956	0.4957	0.4959	0.4960	0.4961	0.4962	0.4963	0.4964
2.7	0.4965	0.4966	0.4967	0.4968	0.4969	0.4970	0.4971	0.4972	0.4973	0.4974
2.8	0.4974	0.4975	0.4976	0.4977	0.4977	0.4978	0.4979	0.4979	0.4980	0.4981
2.9	0.4981	0.4982	0.4982	0.4983	0.4984	0.4984	0.4985	0.4985	0.4986	0.4986
3.0	0.4987	0.4987	0.4987	0.4988	0.4988	0.4989	0.4989	0.4989	0.4990	0.4990

Student's *t* Distribution

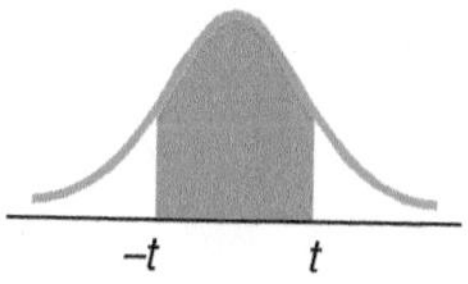

Confidence interval

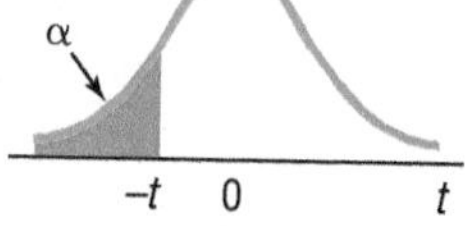

Left-tailed test

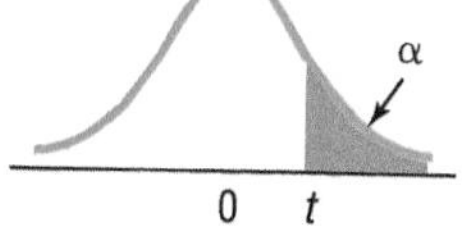

Right-tailed test

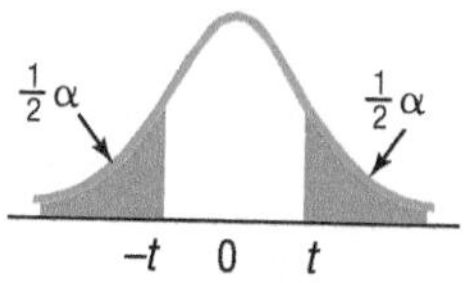

Two-tailed test

df (degrees of freedom)	Confidence Intervals, *c*					
	80%	90%	95%	98%	99%	99.9%
	Level of Significance for One-Tailed Test, α					
	0.10	0.05	0.025	0.01	0.005	0.0005
	Level of Significance for Two-Tailed Test, α					
	0.20	0.10	0.05	0.02	0.01	0.001
1	3.078	6.314	12.706	31.821	63.657	636.619
2	1.886	2.920	4.303	6.965	9.925	31.599
3	1.638	2.353	3.182	4.541	5.841	12.924
4	1.533	2.132	2.776	3.747	4.604	8.610
5	1.476	2.015	2.571	3.365	4.032	6.869
6	1.440	1.943	2.447	3.143	3.707	5.959
7	1.415	1.895	2.365	2.998	3.499	5.408
8	1.397	1.860	2.306	2.896	3.355	5.041
9	1.383	1.833	2.262	2.821	3.250	4.781
10	1.372	1.812	2.228	2.764	3.169	4.587
11	1.363	1.796	2.201	2.718	3.106	4.437
12	1.356	1.782	2.179	2.681	3.055	4.318
13	1.350	1.771	2.160	2.650	3.012	4.221
14	1.345	1.761	2.145	2.624	2.977	4.140
15	1.341	1.753	2.131	2.602	2.947	4.073
16	1.337	1.746	2.120	2.583	2.921	4.015
17	1.333	1.740	2.110	2.567	2.898	3.965
18	1.330	1.734	2.101	2.552	2.878	3.922
19	1.328	1.729	2.093	2.539	2.861	3.883
20	1.325	1.725	2.086	2.528	2.845	3.850
21	1.323	1.721	2.080	2.518	2.831	3.819
22	1.321	1.717	2.074	2.508	2.819	3.792
23	1.319	1.714	2.069	2.500	2.807	3.768
24	1.318	1.711	2.064	2.492	2.797	3.745
25	1.316	1.708	2.060	2.485	2.787	3.725
26	1.315	1.706	2.056	2.479	2.779	3.707
27	1.314	1.703	2.052	2.473	2.771	3.690
28	1.313	1.701	2.048	2.467	2.763	3.674
29	1.311	1.699	2.045	2.462	2.756	3.659
30	1.310	1.697	2.042	2.457	2.750	3.646
31	1.309	1.696	2.040	2.453	2.744	3.633
32	1.309	1.694	2.037	2.449	2.738	3.622
33	1.308	1.692	2.035	2.445	2.733	3.611
34	1.307	1.691	2.032	2.441	2.728	3.601
35	1.306	1.690	2.030	2.438	2.724	3.591

(continued-top right)

(continued)

df (degrees of freedom)	Confidence Intervals, *c*					
	80%	90%	95%	98%	99%	99.9%
	Level of Significance for One-Tailed Test, α					
	0.10	0.05	0.025	0.01	0.005	0.0005
	Level of Significance for Two-Tailed Test, α					
	0.20	0.10	0.05	0.02	0.01	0.001
36	1.306	1.688	2.028	2.434	2.719	3.582
37	1.305	1.687	2.026	2.431	2.715	3.574
38	1.304	1.686	2.024	2.429	2.712	3.566
39	1.304	1.685	2.023	2.426	2.708	3.558
40	1.303	1.684	2.021	2.423	2.704	3.551
41	1.303	1.683	2.020	2.421	2.701	3.544
42	1.302	1.682	2.018	2.418	2.698	3.538
43	1.302	1.681	2.017	2.416	2.695	3.532
44	1.301	1.680	2.015	2.414	2.692	3.526
45	1.301	1.679	2.014	2.412	2.690	3.520
46	1.300	1.679	2.013	2.410	2.687	3.515
47	1.300	1.678	2.012	2.408	2.685	3.510
48	1.299	1.677	2.011	2.407	2.682	3.505
49	1.299	1.677	2.010	2.405	2.680	3.500
50	1.299	1.676	2.009	2.403	2.678	3.496
51	1.298	1.675	2.008	2.402	2.676	3.492
52	1.298	1.675	2.007	2.400	2.674	3.488
53	1.298	1.674	2.006	2.399	2.672	3.484
54	1.297	1.674	2.005	2.397	2.670	3.480
55	1.297	1.673	2.004	2.396	2.668	3.476
56	1.297	1.673	2.003	2.395	2.667	3.473
57	1.297	1.672	2.002	2.394	2.665	3.470
58	1.296	1.672	2.002	2.392	2.663	3.466
59	1.296	1.671	2.001	2.391	2.662	3.463
60	1.296	1.671	2.000	2.390	2.660	3.460
61	1.296	1.670	2.000	2.389	2.659	3.457
62	1.295	1.670	1.999	2.388	2.657	3.454
63	1.295	1.669	1.998	2.387	2.656	3.452
64	1.295	1.669	1.998	2.386	2.655	3.449
65	1.295	1.669	1.997	2.385	2.654	3.447
66	1.295	1.668	1.997	2.384	2.652	3.444
67	1.294	1.668	1.996	2.383	2.651	3.442
68	1.294	1.668	1.995	2.382	2.650	3.439
69	1.294	1.667	1.995	2.382	2.649	3.437
70	1.294	1.667	1.994	2.381	2.648	3.435

(continued)

Student's *t* Distribution (*concluded*)

(*continued*)

df (degrees of freedom)	Confidence Intervals, *c*					
	80%	90%	95%	98%	99%	99.9%
	Level of Significance for One-Tailed Test, α					
	0.10	0.05	0.025	0.01	0.005	0.0005
	Level of Significance for Two-Tailed Test, α					
	0.20	0.10	0.05	0.02	0.01	0.001
71	1.294	1.667	1.994	2.380	2.647	3.433
72	1.293	1.666	1.993	2.379	2.646	3.431
73	1.293	1.666	1.993	2.379	2.645	3.429
74	1.293	1.666	1.993	2.378	2.644	3.427
75	1.293	1.665	1.992	2.377	2.643	3.425
76	1.293	1.665	1.992	2.376	2.642	3.423
77	1.293	1.665	1.991	2.376	2.641	3.421
78	1.292	1.665	1.991	2.375	2.640	3.420
79	1.292	1.664	1.990	2.374	2.640	3.418
80	1.292	1.664	1.990	2.374	2.639	3.416
81	1.292	1.664	1.990	2.373	2.638	3.415
82	1.292	1.664	1.989	2.373	2.637	3.413
83	1.292	1.663	1.989	2.372	2.636	3.412
84	1.292	1.663	1.989	2.372	2.636	3.410
85	1.292	1.663	1.988	2.371	2.635	3.409
86	1.291	1.663	1.988	2.370	2.634	3.407
87	1.291	1.663	1.988	2.370	2.634	3.406
88	1.291	1.662	1.987	2.369	2.633	3.405
89	1.291	1.662	1.987	2.369	2.632	3.403
90	1.291	1.662	1.987	2.368	2.632	3.402
91	1.291	1.662	1.986	2.368	2.631	3.401
92	1.291	1.662	1.986	2.368	2.630	3.399
93	1.291	1.661	1.986	2.367	2.630	3.398
94	1.291	1.661	1.986	2.367	2.629	3.397
95	1.291	1.661	1.985	2.366	2.629	3.396
96	1.290	1.661	1.985	2.366	2.628	3.395
97	1.290	1.661	1.985	2.365	2.627	3.394
98	1.290	1.661	1.984	2.365	2.627	3.393
99	1.290	1.660	1.984	2.365	2.626	3.392
100	1.290	1.660	1.984	2.364	2.626	3.390
120	1.289	1.658	1.980	2.358	2.617	3.373
140	1.288	1.656	1.977	2.353	2.611	3.361
160	1.287	1.654	1.975	2.350	2.607	3.352
180	1.286	1.653	1.973	2.347	2.603	3.345
200	1.286	1.653	1.972	2.345	2.601	3.340
∞	1.282	1.645	1.960	2.326	2.576	3.291

McGraw Hill Education

connect®

BUSINESS STATISTICS

The integrated solutions for Lind/Marchal/Wathen's *Statistical Techniques in Business & Economics*, 16e, have been specifically designed to help you achieve your course goals of improving student readiness, enhancing student engagement, and increasing their comprehension of content.

Connect® Business Statistics provides a wide array of tools and content to improve instructor productivity and student performance. In fact, the aggregated results of 34 *Connect* adoptions showed an 11% improvement in pass rates, a 16% improvement in retention, two times as many students receiving an A, and 77% reduction in instructor grading time.

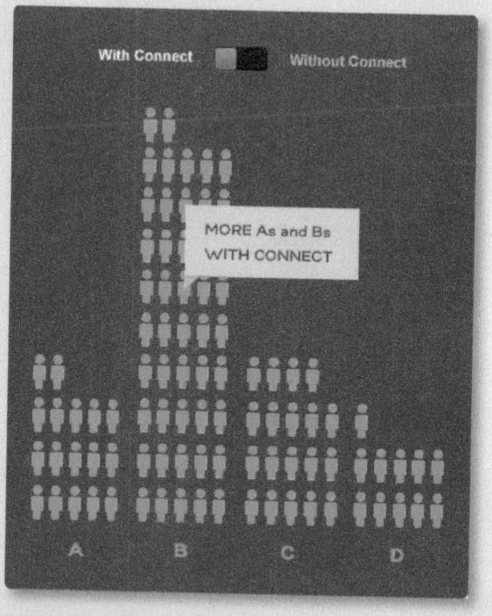

FEATURES

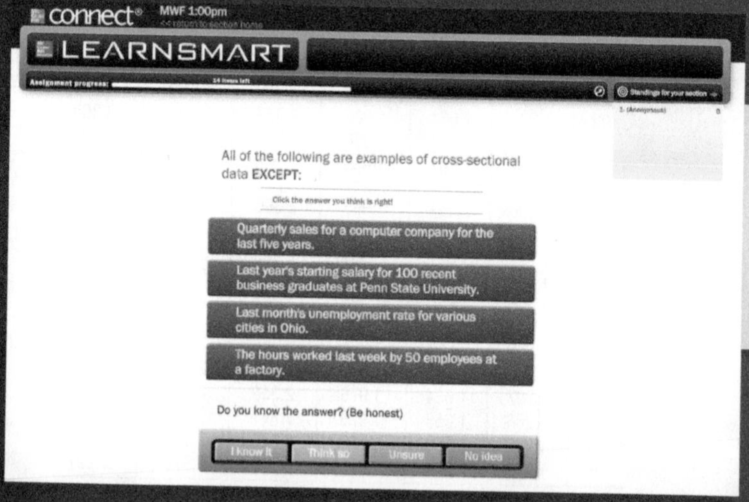

LearnSmart is the most widely used adaptive learning resource in higher education, proven to strengthen concept retention and boost grades—the smartest way to improve student performance.

LearnSmart™

ISBN: 0078020522

Get Connected.

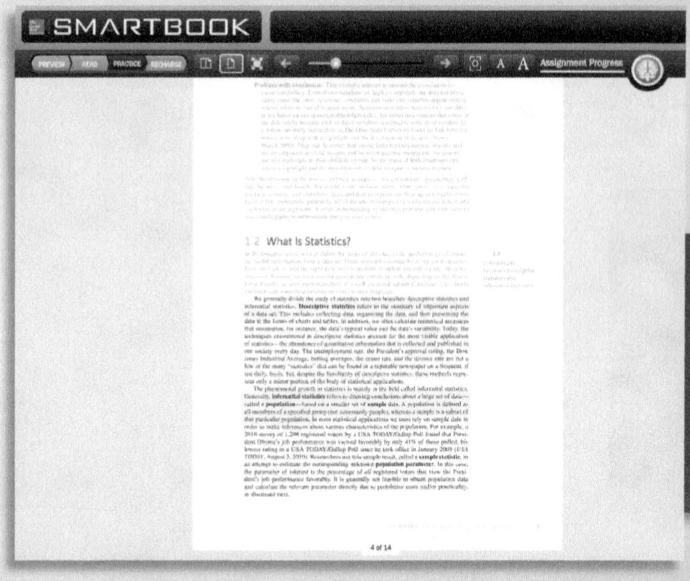

SmartBook™

An extension of *LearnSmart*, ***SmartBook*** is an adaptive eBook that helps students focus their study time more effectively. As the student reads, *SmartBook* assesses comprehension and dynamically highlights where they need to study more.

End-of-Chapter and Test Bank Content

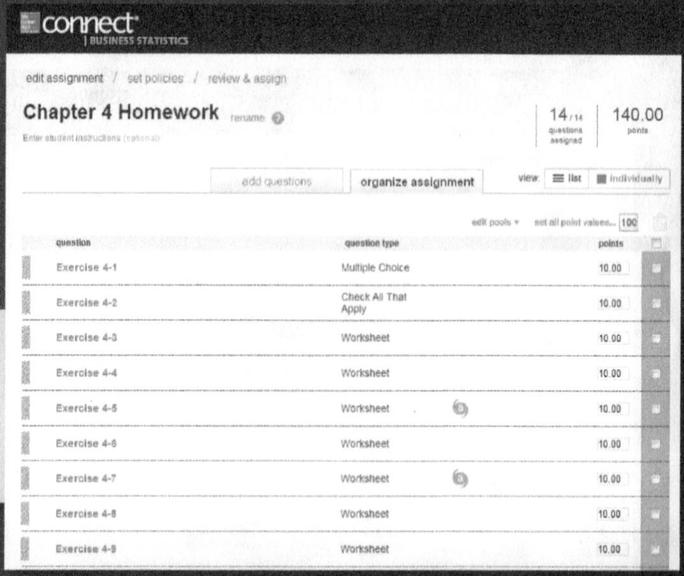

Connect Business Statistics includes both static and algorithmic versions of end-of-chapter problems and test bank questions.

Get Engaged.

Detailed Feedback

Connect Business Statistics helps students learn by providing complete step-by-step solutions for every problem, and you decide when students receive the solutions. These solutions can then be accessed before an exam so students can use them as a study tool for their tests.

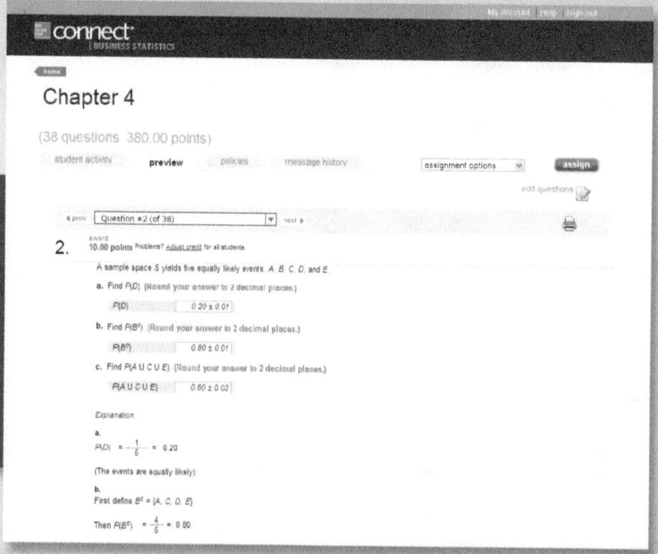

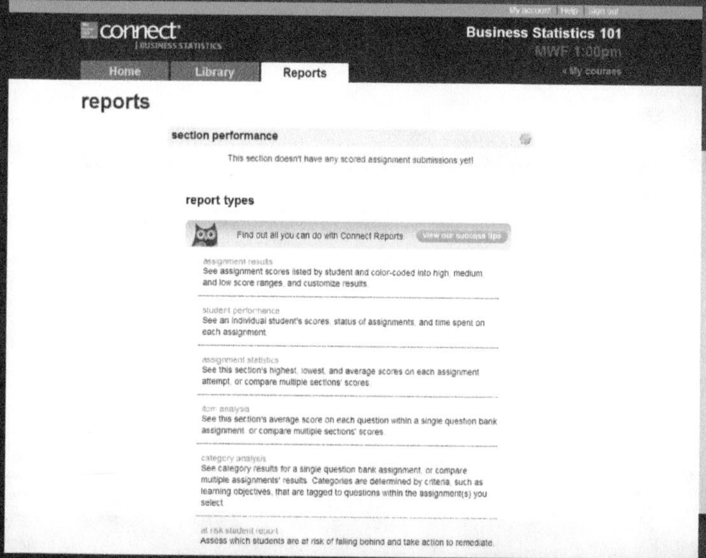

Reporting

Connect Business Statistics generates comprehensive reports and graphs that provide instructors with an instant view of the performance of individual students, a specific section, or multiple sections. Since all content is mapped to learning outcomes, *Connect* reporting is ideal for accreditation or other administrative documentation.

ISBN: 0078020522

Online Supplements

ConnectPlus Business Statistics with LearnSmart Two-Semester Online Access for Statistical Techniques in Business and Economics, 16th Edition

McGraw-Hill ConnectPlus® provides an online eBook and immediate feedback on online assignments, quizzes, and practice tests, providing a learning experience that is personalized for YOU. Study more efficiently and engage with your learning process – Connect with future success!

HOW TO REGISTER

Using a Print Book?
To register and activate your ConnectPlus account, simply follow these easy steps:

1. **Go to the ConnectPlus course web address provided by your instructor or visit the Connect link set up on your instructor's course within your campus learning management system.**
2. **Click on the link to register.**
3. **When prompted, enter the ConnectPlus code found on the inside back cover of your book and click Submit. Complete the brief registration form that follows to begin using Connect.**

Using an eBook?
To register and activate your ConnectPlus account, simply follow these easy steps:

1. **Upon purchase of your eBook, you will be granted automatic access to ConnectPlus.**
2. **Go to the ConnectPlus course web address provided by your instructor or visit the Connect link set up on your instructor's course within your campus learning management system.**
3. **Sign in using the same email address and password you used to register on the eBookstore. Complete your registration and begin using Connect.**

**Note: Access Code is for one use only. If you did not purchase this book new, the access code included in this book is no longer valid.*

Need help? Visit mhhe.com/support

Those instructors without access to a microcomputer, or who prefer not to use one to create tests, can use Irwin's Teletest service. The service provides a toll-free number for instructors to call in a test request. Tests and answer keys are printed on a laser printer according to the specifications provided. Requests are completed the same day they are called in and shipped by first-class mail. Computest 3 and Teletest are provided exclusively by Irwin to make your teaching job easier.

The *Solutions Manual* is complete and incorporates the suggested solutions to professional exam questions. It is organized so that you can easily remove the solution to an individual exercise or case.

TO THE STUDENT

Today, an accounting graduate who lacks an understanding of computers begins a career with a major handicap. Computer-based accounting systems have taken over the routine processes of summarizing and processing accounting information. Accountants now function as the designers, controllers, managers, and users of these systems. Your chances of career success are greater if you understand how to function in these capacities.

Why Study This Text

This text is intended to help you gain the knowledge you need. It is written by authors with many years' experience both in practical accounting and in university-level teaching. Much of the material is not covered in other courses in your business curriculum, so you should master it now.

Previous students' responses to this material have been favorable. They consistently say that "this is what we need to know about how accounting is done in the real world." By the end of this course, you will understand the relevance of an accounting information systems course to your own career.

Objectives of the Text

In developing this text, the authors and editors agreed that it should not simply repeat material covered in courses in management, computer science, or management information systems. We identified the distinct information systems knowledge required by accountants, and then prepared accurate, understandable, thoroughly tested material that addresses those specific needs. We started by recognizing how you, as an accounting graduate, will use your systems knowledge.

This text prepares you for three types of accounting careers. As a *management accountant,* you will use information systems and will participate in project teams that develop them. As an *auditor,* you will evaluate accounting system controls and examine system outputs. As a *consultant,* you will design and implement new accounting systems. In each career, you work with systems using both older technologies and those implementing newer, state-of-the-art methods. Perhaps you do not yet know which direction your accounting career path will follow. With this text, your AIS course will prepare you for any of them.

ACKNOWLEDGMENTS

Permission has been received from the Institute of Certified Management Accountants of the National Association of Accountants to use questions and unofficial answers from past CMA examinations. We are also indebted to the American Institute of Certified Public Accountants and the Institute of Internal Auditors for allowing us to adapt and use material from past CPA and CIA examinations.

Many students made innumerable suggestions and criticisms which greatly improved the book. Special thanks, however, are due to Professor James McInturff, Midwestern State University, and to Professor Patti Golub, University of St. Thomas, for their help in developing the materials. A note of appreciation is also due to Professor Ira Weiss, University of Houston, for his input concerning appropriate content for an AIS course.

Probably we owe the most appreciation to the reviewers who critiqued the book throughout its development. Each of you, as you read the text, can identify your personal contributions to it. The reviewers were:

David Murphy
Oklahoma State University

Gary P. Schneider
Xavier University

Charles E. Carter
University of Missouri/Kansas City

Bill Cummings
Northern Illinois University

Richard V. Calvasina
University of West Florida

Terry J. Nunley
University of North Carolina/Charlotte

Ron Abraham
University of Northern Iowa

Stephen A. McNett
New Mexico State University

Donald V. Saftner
University of Toledo

Jay Holmen
University of Wisconsin/Eau Claire

Howard G. Smith
Southwest Texas State

Richard W. Sapp
Portland State University

Ronald L. Clark
University of Georgia/Athens

Ann Haycock
Kansas State University

A. Faye Borthick
University of Tennessee

Deborah D. Payne
Roosevelt University

W. Ken Harmon
Arizona State University

Eleanor E. Fillebrown
University of New Haven

Frederick G. Davis
University of North Texas

Avi Rushinek
University of Miami

Thanks very, very much to each of you.

Jim Boockholdt
David H. Li

Contents in Brief

PART V
Processing Accounting Transactions

Contents

Part I

Accounting and Systems Concepts

Chapter 1

A Model for Processing Accounting Information

Learning Objectives:

1. To learn the objectives of accounting information systems.
2. To review the steps in the accounting cycle.
3. To review how accounting information systems produce reports for external use.

INTRODUCTION

The study of accounting information systems analyzes how events affecting an organization are recorded, summarized, and reported. These events are recorded using that organization's *system* of human and computer resources, summarized using *accounting* methods and objectives, and reported as *information* to interested persons both within and outside of the organization.

This chapter describes a conceptual model for recording, processing, and reporting these events to external parties. You should be familiar with this model from your introductory accounting course. If so, much of the material in this chapter will be a review. In the next chapter, you will see how this model is adapted for reporting within the organization. The remainder of this book details how this conceptual process is implemented.

Organizations

Accounting information systems exist in many forms of organizations, whether proprietorships, partnerships, corporations, nonprofit foundations, or households. While the complexity of each accounting information system differs, each is similar in three important ways: each contains a similar structure (of human and computer resources), similar processes (the use of accounting methods), and similar purposes (to provide information).

This book, like most accounting textbooks, uses as an example one type of organization: the profit-seeking, publicly owned corporation engaged in manufacturing and selling goods. The structure, processes, and purposes of the accounting information systems are more complex in the manufacturing corporation than in the others. You can readily adapt what you learn about this type of corporation to the circumstances of the other forms listed earlier.

Events Affecting an Organization

The events that affect any organization are a result of its interactions with its environment, which includes economic, social, political, and regulatory entities. Accounting information systems record, summarize, and report events arising from these entities. The events to be processed depend on the scope of the organization's accounting information systems and the nature of the events.

Human and Computer Resources

A system of human and computer resources records, processes, and reports events from the organization's environment. When the system contains only human resources, it is a *manual system*. If it uses only computer resources, it is a *computer system*. When it uses both human and computer resources, it is a *computer-based system*.

Most organizations today use computer-based accounting information systems. This book offers comparisons of manual and computerized methods for recording, processing, and reporting events. However, both methods are important, because each organization's computer-based system has a different mix of computerized and manual methods. Furthermore, many computer and manual systems employ the same procedures. In these cases, understanding manual methods makes it easier to master computerized ones.

ACCOUNTING METHODS AND OBJECTIVES

All accounting information systems record, process, and report events using accounting methods to achieve accounting objectives. These objectives determine the system's scope, which in turn determines the nature of the events and the method of accounting. However, all systems record events in money and use the same conceptual accounting process.

Scope of the System and Nature of the Events

For the publicly held corporation, the accounting information system's scope must comply with generally accepted accounting principles (GAAP). GAAP is necessary to produce financial statements intended for parties external to the organization. With GAAP, any event that has a determinable monetary impact on the organization must be recognized as an accounting *transaction*. A system whose objective is to record, process, and report past transactions in accordance with GAAP is a *financial accounting information system*.

Usually the scope of an organization's system for processing accounting data is broader than that required by GAAP. For example, when an accounting system includes budgetary forecasts, it recognizes future transactions and estimates their monetary impact. Budgeting and other such systems intended primarily for use within the organization constitute *managerial accounting information systems*. The next chapter describes some of them.

Because these systems share objectives and methods, financial accounting information systems are examples of managerial ones. Managerial accounting information systems have both internal and external reporting objectives. For external reporting they use accounting methods required by GAAP; for internal reporting, they use those preferred by management. Management uses the information provided by both systems.

External parties, on the other hand, rely on information provided by financial accounting information systems in accordance with GAAP. Illustration 1–1 shows these relationships graphically.

The Accounting Process

The accounting process begins when an economic event is recognized by an accounting information system, which records the economic event as an accounting transaction. This book illustrates how the system's human and computer components process a transaction.

For financial accounting information systems, the activities that process a transaction constitute the *accounting cycle*. Conceptually, the accounting cycle consists of the following six steps, which you learned in your introductory accounting class:

Journalize. The first step in the accounting cycle is recording the transaction. Someone analyzes the event, determines the accounts it affects, identifies whether each account is debited or credited, and enters the transaction chronologically in a journal.

ILLUSTRATION 1–1 Scope of the Accounting Information Systems

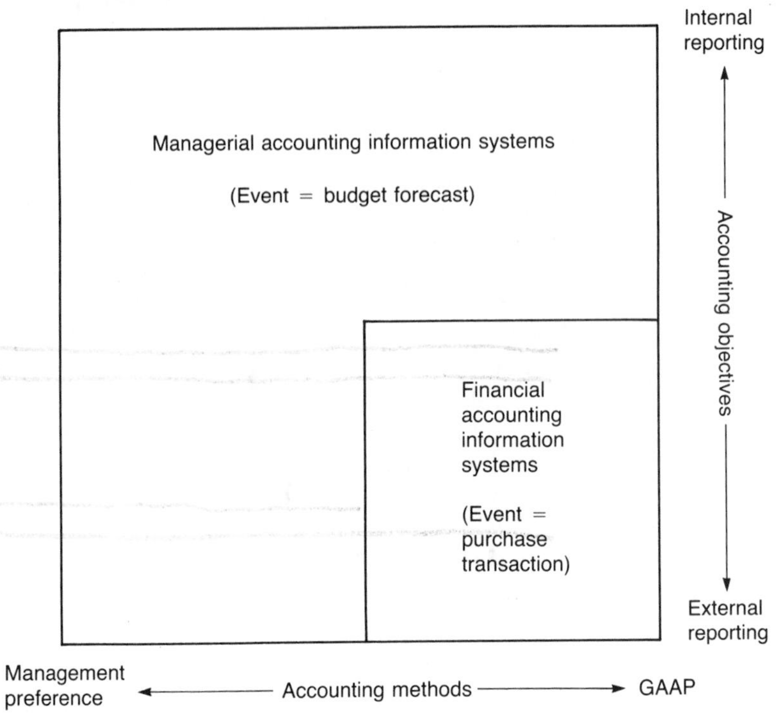

Illustration 1–2 is an example of a general journal whose sample entries reflect some common transactions. Most organizations also use several special journals designed to record specific types of transactions. Common special journals include the cash receipts journal, the cash disbursements journal, the payroll journal, and the sales journal.

Each organization has a *chart of accounts,* which is a list of all account titles maintained in the accounting system. In journalizing an event, the accountant must choose accounts from this list. An analyst establishes this list at the time the accounting information systems are created. Illustration 1–3 contains a sample chart of accounts.

Post. In posting, the second step, an accounting information system transfers journal entries to ledgers. A ledger is a summary, by account, of all transactions affecting that account. Thus after posting, transactions are recorded by account rather than in chronological sequence. This step makes it possible to summarize the effects of all the events affecting the organization. Illustration 1–4 shows a page from a manual system's ledger.

ILLUSTRATION 1–2 A General Journal

GENERAL JOURNAL Page 1

Date		Accounts and Explanation	Ref.	Debit	Credit
Sept.	1	Cash		100,000	
		Capital Stock			100,000
		Issued capital stock for cash.			
	2	Land		20,000	
		Building		60,000	
		Cash			15,000
		Notes Payable			65,000
		Purchased land and building financed in part by a long-term note.			
	3	Equipment		72,000	
		Cash			72,000
		Cash purchase of equipment.			
	4	Supplies Inventories		6,000	
		Accounts Payable			6,000
		Supplies purchased from General Chemical Corporation on account.			
	5	Cash		60,000	
		Services to Be Rendered			60,000
		Advance payment by Delta Aircraft Company for contract signed.			
	8	Accounts Payable		6,000	
		Cash			6,000
		Paid General Chemical Corporation in full.			
	10	Prepaid Insurance		300	
		Cash			300
		Purchased one-year fire insurance policy.			

Most organizations also use subsidiary ledgers, which contain detailed information explaining the general ledger's control account total. Common subsidiary ledgers include the accounts payable subsidiary ledger, the property ledger, and the stockholders' ledger.

Illustration 1–5 shows the results of posting to general ledger accounts the transactions journalized in Illustration 1–2.

ILLUSTRATION 1–3 A Chart of Accounts

Account title	*Account number*
Current assets:	
Cash	11
Accounts Receivable	13
Research Fees Receivable	14
Supplies Inventories	16
Prepaid Insurance	18
Property, plant, and equipment:	
Land	21
Building	22
Accumulated Depreciation—Building	23
Equipment	24
Accumulated Depreciation—Equipment	25
Current liabilities:	
Accounts Payable	31
Income Taxes Payable	33
Salaries Payable	34
Interest Payable	35
Cash Dividends Payable	36
Services to Be Rendered	38
Long-term debt:	
Notes Payable	41
Stockholders' equity:	
Capital Stock	51
Retained Earnings	55
Revenue and Expense Summary	59
Revenue:	
Revenue from Services	61
Expenses:	
Salaries Expense	71
Supplies Expense	72
Depreciation Expense—Equipment	73
Depreciation Expense—Building	81
Insurance Expense	82
Other Administrative Expenses	89
Interest Expense	91
Federal Income Taxes	95

ILLUSTRATION 1–4 The Ledger Page for an Account

			Account Title				*Account Number*
Date	Description	Ref.	Debit	Date	Description	Ref.	Credit

ILLUSTRATION 1–5 Accounts after Posting

Cash 11

Sept. 1 (1)	100,000	Sept. 2 (1)	15,000
5 (1)	60,000	3 (1)	72,000
		8 (1)	6,000
		10 (1)	300

Supplies Inventories 16

Sept. 4 (1)	6,000		

Prepaid Insurance 18

Sept. 10 (1)	300		

Land 21

Sept. 2 (1)	20,000		

Building 22

Sept. 2 (1)	60,000		

Equipment 24

Sept. 3 (1)	72,000		

Accounts Payable 31

Sept. 8 (1)	6,000	Sept. 4 (1)	6,000

Services to Be Rendered 38

		Sept. 5 (1)	60,000

Notes Payable 41

		Sept. 1 (1)	65,000

Capital Stock 51

		Sept. 1 (1)	100,000

Modern organizations produce many kinds of events that result in several different types of transactions. Computer-based systems devote extensive resources to journalizing and posting these transactions. Accounting information systems that concern the journalizing and posting steps constitute the *transaction processing systems*. You will learn how several transaction processing systems work later.

Prepare a Trial Balance. This is step three in the accounting cycle. During any accounting period, accounting information systems journalize and post a large number of transactions. Prior to producing accounting reports, the system summarizes the effect of all the events in a *trial balance*. Illustration 1–6 shows a sample trial balance.

ILLUSTRATION 1–6 A Trial Balance

ALPHA RESEARCH CORPORATION
Trial Balance
September 30, 19XX

Account no.	*Account title*	*Debit*	*Credit*
11	Cash	$ 62,700	
13	Accounts receivable	1,200	
14	Research fees receivable	4,000	
16	Supplies inventories	5,100	
18	Prepaid insurance	275	
21	Land	20,000	
22	Building	60,000	
23	Accumulated depreciation—building		$ 500
24	Equipment	72,000	
25	Accumulated depreciation—equipment		1,200
34	Salaries payable		600
35	Interest payable		314
38	Services to be rendered		55,000
41	Notes payable		65,000
51	Capital stock		100,000
61	Revenue from services		12,200
71	Salaries expense	6,600	
72	Supplies expense	900	
73	Depreciation expense—equipment	1,200	
81	Depreciation expense—building	500	
82	Insurance expense	25	
91	Interest expense	314	
		$234,814	$234,814

Prepare Adjusting Entries. The fourth step in the accounting cycle is the preparation of adjusting entries. When creating an accounting information system, an analyst identifies standard or recurring journal entries, which are adjusting entries made at the end of each reporting period to recognize accruals and deferrals. Sometimes an accountant also proposes adjusting entries to correct previous errors in journalizing transactions. An accountant or bookkeeper prepares adjusting entries, records them in the journal, and posts them to the ledger. These alter the account balances shown in the trial balance.

Prepare Accounting Reports. The fifth step in the accounting cycle is preparing the accounting reports. This task is easier if the system first prepares a second trial balance. Because its debit and credit totals reflect the adjustments made in step four, accountants call it the adjusted trial balance. From the adjusted trial balance, accountants prepare the reports.

Illustrations 1–7 and 1–8 show two reports—the income statement and the balance sheet—that, according to generally accepted accounting principles, must be produced by a financial accounting information system. Managerial accounting information systems, which are broader in scope, produce additional reports. The next chapter describes some of these.

Close the Books. After preparing the accounting reports, accountants prepare the accounting records for the next reporting period. This includes the posting of closing and reversing journal entries.

Closing entries transfer balances from revenue and expense accounts into the Income Summary account. The balance in this account, which equals Net

ILLUSTRATION 1–7 An Income Statement

ALPHA RESEARCH CORPORATION
Income Statement
For Month Ended September 30, 19XX

Revenue from services		$12,200
Expenses:		
Salaries expense	$6,600	
Supplies expense	900	
Depreciation expense—equipment	1,200	
Depreciation expense—building	500	
Insurance expense	25	
Interest expense	314	
Total expenses		9,539
Net income		$ 2,661

ILLUSTRATION 1–8 A Balance Sheet

ALPHA RESEARCH CORPORATION
Balance Sheet
As of September 30, 19XX

Assets			
Current assets:			
Cash			$ 62,700
Accounts receivable			1,200
Research fees receivable			4,000
Supplies inventories			5,100
Prepaid insurance			275
Total current assets			73,275
Property, plant, and equipment:			
Land		$ 20,000	
Building	$60,000		
Less: Accumulated depreciation	500	59,500	
Equipment	72,000		
Less: Accumulated depreciation	1,200	70,800	
			150,300
Total assets			$223,575
Liabilities and Stockholders' Equity			
Current liabilities:			
Notes payable (portion due within year)			$ 10,000
Salaries payable			600
Interest payable			314
Services to be rendered			55,000
Total current liabilities			65,914
Long-term debt:			
Notes payable (portion due after one year: secured by land and building)			55,000
Stockholders' equity:			
Capital stock, par $100, 1,000 shares outstanding		$100,000	
Retained earnings		2,661	
			102,661
Total liabilities and stockholders' equity			$223,575

Income, is then transferred to the Retained Earnings account, leaving zero balances in these accounts in preparation for the next period.

Accountants also post reversing entries, so called because they are the reverse of the accrual and deferral adjusting journal entries made earlier. These reversing entries reset the balances in accrual and deferral accounts at zero and ensure that

ILLUSTRATION 1–9 Steps in the Accounting Cycle

1. **Journalize.** Identify the economic event and record it chronologically as an accounting transaction.
2. **Post.** Transfer transaction totals from the chronological record to summaries maintained by account.
3. **Trial Balance.** Prepare periodically a list of accounts and the balances in them.
4. **Adjusting Entries.** Make journal entries to recognize accruals, record deferrals, or correct errors.
5. **Reports.** Prepare accounting reports from the adjusted trial balance.
6. **Close.** Prepare the accounting records for the next reporting period.

expenses and revenues of the prior period are not included in those of the following period.

Illustration 1–9 summarizes the six steps performed by a financial accounting information system when executing the accounting cycle.

Technology and Accounting Information Systems

You have just reviewed the accounting process in nontechnological terms. In older accounting systems, journals and ledgers are bound volumes in which bookkeepers manually record journal and adjusting entries. An accountant then manually prepares trial balances and reports using a large worksheet.

In modern systems, journals and ledgers take the form of computer files. Computer programs post entries and prepare the accounting reports. Accountants control this process by providing inputs and by determining how these programs work.

Conceptually, the accounting process is identical regardless of the technology employed, which is why your introductory accounting course concentrated on journals and ledgers. This is actually a *technology-independent* view of the accounting process.

As computers have been adapted for accounting, a terminology has evolved that is specific to computerized processing. These terms, introduced in Illustration 1–10, are a *technology-dependent* way of describing the concepts reviewed in this chapter. Your study of accounting information systems will be easier if you become acquainted with these terms now.

Why Study Accounting Information Systems?

In the past few decades the study of accounting information systems has become important for all accountants. Prior to computerized processing, accounting systems used manual technologies that were much easier to understand. Microcomputers, however, have made computers practical for even the smallest organizations. Because almost every organization today uses computers to

ILLUSTRATION 1–10 The Accounting Process Using Computer Technology

The Accounting Concept	*When Implemented on a Computer Is Called*
Journals	**Transaction Files**
General	Journal voucher file
Special	Cash receipts file
	Voucher file
Ledgers	**Master Files**
General	General ledger master file
Subsidiary	Inventory master file
	Property master file
Journalizing	**Data Entry**
Posting	**File Update**

process accounting data, you must understand not only the conceptual process but also the technologies used in the process.

As an accountant, you will work with computerized accounting systems in one of three ways: If you become an auditor, you must know how to review computer-based systems and to plan and execute audit procedures using them. If you become a management accountant, you will work daily with computerized systems and participate in project teams that develop new ones. Many accounting students also become management consultants or systems analysts. These accountants work full time developing new accounting systems. Regardless of your career path, you must understand both the process and the technology. This text makes it easy for you to achieve this understanding.

SUMMARY

The study of accounting information systems concerns events affecting an organization. These events are recognized and recorded by a system of human and computer resources, processed using accounting methods and objectives, and reported as information to interested parties. Most organizations use computer-based accounting information systems, which rely on both manual and computerized processing.

Financial accounting systems are accounting information systems of limited scope. These systems must conform to generally accepted accounting principles for external reporting, and must implement the six steps in the accounting cycle. Financial accounting systems that journalize and post transactions are the transaction processing systems. More broadly defined, accounting information systems also produce reports for internal management purposes.

The accounting cycle, as described in this chapter, is a technology-independent process. The purpose of your study of accounting information systems is to learn how these accounting processes work using computer technology.

KEY TERMS

adjusting entries Accounting entries made at the end of a financial reporting period to record accruals and deferrals and to correct previous errors.

computer-based system An accounting system that uses both human and computer resources when processing transactions.

computer system An accounting system that uses only computer resources when processing transactions.

financial accounting information system An accounting system that records, processes, and reports past transactions in accordance with generally accepted accounting principles.

journalize The process of initially recording a transaction.

managerial accounting information system An accounting system that records, processes, and reports financial information for internal use in accordance with the preferences of management.

manual system An accounting system that uses only human resources when processing transactions.

post The process of transferring information recorded in a journal to a ledger.

transaction The monetary record of an economic event affecting an organization.

trial balance A summary of all the accounts in a general ledger and the balances in those accounts.

QUESTIONS

1–1. How does a transaction differ from an event?

1–2. How does a budgetary accounting information system differ from a historical accounting information system?

1–3. Why is it important for you to understand both the process and the technology associated with accounting information systems?

1–4. The journal is sometimes known as a book of original entry. Could you suggest a reason for the journal's being so known?

1–5. A company paid $3,000 to an attorney retained to render legal services to the company. Under which conditions would each of the following analyses be appropriate?

a.	Legal Expenses	3,000	
	Cash		3,000
b.	Prepaid Legal Fees	3,000	
	Cash		3,000
c.	Accounts Payable	3,000	
	Cash		3,000
d.	Legal Fees Payable	3,000	
	Cash		3,000

1–6. What is the balance of the following T-account?

4,000	2,000
240	330
1,200	150
700	

Is it more likely to be an asset account or a liability account? Which entry is likely to be the first one made?

1–7. What is the balance of the following T-account?

500	400
1,500	500
400	350
	1,500

Is it more likely to be an asset account or a liability account? Can you deduce the order in which these entries were made?

1–8. A sales representative suggests that a copy of the company's annual report be sent to a customer intending to place a large order.
a. What information is generally contained in an annual report of a manufacturing company?
b. What advantages and disadvantages would a company have in allowing its prospective customers to have copies of its annual reports?

1–9. In which order are assets normally listed in the balance sheet of a manufacturing or merchandising company? Why?

1–10. What accounting information might be needed by the following?
a. A newspaper boy who maintains a stand at the corner of Broadway and Main Street, two busy streets in the downtown area.
b. A newspaper girl who has a daily route in her neighborhood.
c. A regional distributor of magazines.

1–11. Would accounting reports become more important when business enterprises are managed by professional management groups?

1–12. What is the purpose of preparing adjusting entries? How often must they be prepared? Could they be made on a daily basis? Under which circumstances would it be desirable to prepare them on a daily basis?

1–13. What are the differences between a manual system, a computer system, and a computer-based system?

1–14. Distinguish between the scope and the objectives of the following accounting information systems:
a. Financial accounting information system
b. Managerial accounting information system
c. Budgetary system
d. Inventory system

EXERCISES AND CASE

1–15. *TRANSACTIONS AND EVENTS*

Sun Belt Market Research, Inc., was incorporated in May 19XX. Selected transactions for the month of May are as follows:

19XX		
May	4	Entered a contract to survey consumer reaction to Pour-Ease Flour for the Lone Star Milling Company. An advance payment of $100,000 was made by the company.
	5	Entered a contract to design a paper tissue box for the Big D Paper Products Corporation.
	15	Completed a research project on consumers' reaction to stainless steel razor blades for the Ever-Clean Corporation. A report was submitted. Cash payment of $20,000 was received for services rendered.
	15	Paid Computer Applications Associates $1,000 for computer time used to analyze data for the report submitted to the Ever-Clean Corporation.
	25	Made a formal presentation of the paper tissue box design to the management of the Big D Paper Products Corporation. The design was accepted. An invoice in the amount of $8,000 was submitted for services rendered.
	31	Paid salaries for the month, $18,000
	31	Received a bill from the telephone company for telephone and telecommunication services for the month, $1,200.
	31	Received payment of $8,000 from the Big D Paper Products Corporation.

Required:

For each of the preceding events,

a. Determine if the event should be recorded as an accounting transaction. If so, identify the journal to be used and show the accounting entry.

b. Determine if the transaction should be posted to a subsidiary ledger. If so, identify the ledger.

1–16. *TRANSACTIONS AND EVENTS*

Citywide Blueprint Service Company was organized in June 19XX. Selected transactions for the month of June are as follows:

19XX		
June	1	Leased a Blueprint-O-Matic from the BOM Corporation. The agreement called for a basic monthly charge of $50 plus 20 cents for each page of blueprint reproduced.

4 Entered a contract to provide blueprint services for the Irving Engineers at a flat fee of $150 per month. The fee for the month of June was collected on signing the contract.
15 Deposited cash of $500 for blueprint services rendered to various customers during the first two weeks of June.
22 Completed a special reproduction assignment for the Oxford Engineering Consultants. The work was delivered. An invoice for $600 was submitted.
30 Paid salaries for the month, $1,000.
30 Reported to the BOM Corporation that 1,500 blueprint reproductions were made during the month.
30 Received payment of $600 from Oxford Engineering Consultants.
30 Received an invoice from Cornerstone Service Station for gasoline and oil used in the delivery truck for the month of June. The amount was $200.
30 Deposited cash of $545 for blueprint services rendered to various customers during the second half of June.

Required:

For each of the preceding events,

a. Determine if the event should be recorded as an accounting transaction. If so, identify the journal to be used and show the accounting entry.
b. Determine if the transaction should be posted to a subsidiary ledger. If so, identify the ledger.

1–17. *ACCOUNTING REPORTS*

The trial balance of the School for the Nineties, Inc., listing their accounts in alphabetical order, follows. The school was organized on September 1, 19XX.

SCHOOL FOR THE NINETIES, INC.
Trial Balance
September 30, 19XX

Accounts payable		$ 100
Accumulated depreciation—classroom equipment		50
Accumulated depreciation—laboratory equipment		200
Capital stock		10,000
Cash	$15,080	
Classroom equipment	6,000	
Depreciation on classroom equipment	50	
Depreciation on laboratory equipment	200	
Instructional supplies expense	50	
Insurance expense	30	
Interest expense	70	
Laboratory equipment	12,000	

Notes payable		$10,000
Prepaid insurance	$ 270	
Prepaid rent	1,200	
Rent expense	400	
Salaries expense	2,800	
Tuition collected in advance		14,000
Tuition earned		4,000
Utilities expense	200	
	$38,350	$38,350

Required:

Close the books and prepare the following reports:

a. An income statement for the month ended September 30, 19XX.
b. A balance sheet as of September 30, 19XX.

1–18. *ACCOUNTING REPORTS*

The Columbus Pioneers Football Club, Inc., was organized on July 1, 19XX, after receiving a franchise from the Transcontinental Professional Football League. The account balances as of September 30, 19XX, follow in alphabetical order:

Accounts payable	$ 10,000
Accumulated depreciation—automobiles	3,000
Administrative expenses	4,000
Advance ticket sales	120,000
Advertising expense	30,000
Automobiles	40,000
Capital stock	600,000
Cash and marketable securities	609,000
Depreciation on automobiles	3,000
Footballs and other supplies on hand	50,000
Footballs and other playing field expense	10,000
Insurance expense	3,000
Players per diem expenses on away games	5,000
Prepaid insurance	9,000
Prepaid rent	40,000
Rent expense	20,000
Revenue from away games	60,000
Revenue from exhibition games	50,000
Revenue from home games	500,000
Salaries expense—office staff	80,000
Salaries expense—professional staff	300,000
Ticket printing expense	15,000
Travel expense	75,000
Visiting teams' share of gate receipts	50,000

Required:

Close the books and prepare the following reports:

a. An income statement for the month ended September 30, 19XX.
b. A balance sheet as of September 30, 19XX.

1–19. *ADJUSTING ENTRIES*

The trial balances related to Data Teleprocessing Service as of October 30, 19XX, follow. The trial balance on the left was prepared before incorporating the effects of adjusting entries for the month of October. The effects of these adjusting entries were included in the trial balance on the right.

DATA TELEPROCESSING SERVICE
Trial Balance
October 30, 19XX

	Before Adjustments		*After Adjustments*	
Cash	$ 50,000		$ 50,000	
Accounts receivable	4,000		4,000	
Notes receivable	1,000		1,000	
Allowance for doubtful accounts		—		$ 190
Office supplies on hand	6,000		4,000	
Land	15,000		15,000	
Building	60,000		60,000	
Accumulated depreciation—building		—		250
Computer	180,000		180,000	
Accumulated depreciation—computer		—		3,000
Accounts payable		$85,000		85,000
Service fees received in advance		22,000		19,000
Taxes payable		—		5,000
Interest payable		—		218
Notes payable		45,000		45,000
Capital stock		30,000		30,000
Additional paid-in capital		80,000		80,000
Retained earnings		40,000		40,000
Revenue from programming consultation		5,000		6,000
Revenue from computer time rental		30,000		32,000
Salaries expense	15,000		15,000	
Maintenance expense	2,000		2,000	

	Before Adjustments		*After Adjustments*	
Telephone and telecommunication expense	$ 1,500		$ 1,500	
Depreciation on computer	—		3,000	
Office supplies expense	—		2,000	
General expense	2,500		2,500	
Depreciation on building	—		250	
Bad debts expense	—		190	
Interest expense	—		218	
Tax expense	—		5,000	
	$337,000	$337,000	$345,658	$345,658

Required:

Prepare adjusting entries as reflected in the changes between the two trial balances.

1–20. ***ADJUSTING ENTRIES***

The trial balance of the Trans-World Storage and Moving Company as of March 31, 19XX, is as follows:

TRANS-WORLD STORAGE AND MOVING COMPANY
Trial Balance
March 31, 19XX

Cash	$11,700	
Prepaid rent	10,000	
Trucks	60,000	
Accumulated depreciation—trucks		$ 2,500
Accounts payable		1,200
Storage fees collected in advance		3,000
Capital stock		70,000
Retained earnings		3,000
Revenue from moving services		11,000
Revenue from storage services		1,000
Salaries expense	7,000	
Gasoline expense	1,000	
Maintenance expense	500	
Utilities and office expense	1,500	
	$91,700	$91,700

Data and information related to adjusting entries for the month ended March 31, 19XX, are as follows:

1. The monthly rent was $1,000.
2. The estimated useful life of trucks was four years.
3. Many clients chose to pay several months' storage fees in advance. Based on individual service records, storage fees earned for the month amounted to $600.

4. Storage fees for some other clients were due on days other than the first of each month. Based on individual service records, storage fees earned from these clients for the month amounted to $1,500.

Required:

a. Prepare adjusting entries for the month ended March 31, 19XX.
b. Deduce the date on which trucks were purchased.

1–21. *JOURNAL ENTRIES AND ADJUSTING ENTRIES*

The Metropolitan Summer Light Opera Festival was organized to stage four musical shows during the summer of 19XX. Each show was to last three weeks, and a three-week accounting period was adopted. Selected transactions during the first weeks of the festival are as follows:

19XX		
June	1	Paid rent for 12 weeks, beginning June 9. The weekly rent was $1,000.
	2	Placed an advertisement in newspapers announcing the dates and programs of the festival. The expense was $200; cash was paid.
	3	Granted Theater Concessions, Inc., the privilege of selling refreshments during the 12-week festival in return for 5 percent of gross receipts payable within three days after the conclusion of each three-week period.
	4	Purchased liability insurance for the 12-week period at a total cost of $600. Payment was to be made when policy was received.
	5	Four "Program Notes," one for each show, were printed at a total cost of $400. Cash was paid.
	7	Season tickets to the festival, totaling $60,000, were sold. The season tickets permitted holders to attend each of the four shows on specified dates.
	9	The first musical show, "The East Side Story," had its premiere. Cash sale of tickets to the performance amounted to $1,400.
	28	The first musical show closed with this performance. Received a report from Theater Concessions, Inc., that total refreshment sales for the three-week period amounted to $20,000.

Required:

For each of the preceding events,

a. Determine if the event should be recorded as an accounting transaction. If so, identify the journal to be used and show the accounting entry.
b. Determine if the transaction should be posted to a subsidiary ledger. If so, identify the ledger.
c. Prepare the proper adjusting journal entry for June 28.

1–22. *THE ACCOUNTING PROCESS*

The following events relate to KQST-TV, a television broadcasting station:

19XX		
July	1	KQST-TV, Incorporated, was organized with the issuance of capital stock for cash, $500,000.
	2	Received a franchise to operate a television broadcasting station from the Federal Communications Commission. The franchise was valid for three years. The cost of acquiring the franchise, mainly attorney's fees, amounted to $3,600. Cash was paid.
	3	Purchased land, valued at $40,000, and office building, valued at $240,000. Cash was paid.
	7	Purchased transmitting and broadcasting equipment at a total cost of $90,000. Cash was paid.
	8	Signed the Adams, Jackson, and Smith Company as the station's national advertising representative. Commission rate was set at 10 percent of revenue generated.
	9	Received a three-year insurance policy, effective July 1. Total premium was $2,400. Cash was paid.
	10	Signed with the Inter-American Broadcasting Company as a member of its network. Cost of such participation was to be determined at the end of each month.
	11	Signed various sponsors of television programs. Advance payments by some sponsors amounted to $100,000. All sponsors were referred by the Adams, Jackson, and Smith Company.
	15	Sold 100 spot announcements at $100 each to the Metropolitan Arrowjet Company to advertise the new Arrowjet food processors. Settlement was to be made at the end of each month. This account was secured by the station's own marketing staff and did not involve the Adams, Jackson, and Smith Company.
	16	The station began broadcasting.
	31	Paid salaries for the month, $50,000.
	31	Received an invoice from the Inter-American Broadcasting Company for program participation for the month of July. The amount was $10,000. Payment was to be made before August 10.

The following data are relevant to adjusting entries for the month ending July 31:

1. The life of the office and broadcasting building was estimated at 10 years.
2. The life of the transmitting and broadcasting equipment was estimated at three years.
3. Of the $100,000 advance payments, services amounting to $80,000 had been rendered.
4. Services amounting to $40,000 had been rendered for those sponsored who signed but did not make advance payments.

5. Eighty spot announcements were made for the Metropolitan Arrowjet Company.
6. Taxes expense was estimated at 50 percent of income before taxes.

Required:

a. Prepare journal entries for the month.
b. Post to accounts.
c. Take a trial balance.
d. Prepare and post adjusting entries for the month.
e. Take an adjusted trial balance.
f. Close the books and prepare an income statement for the month.
g. Prepare a balance sheet as of July 31.

1–23. ***BALANCE SHEET***

On March 1, 19XX, Balboa Bay Cruise, Inc., was organized with the issuance of capital stock to stockholders for cash of $30,000. The company then acquired the assets of the Lido Isle Boating Company for $45,000. The assets consisted of an inland vessel valued at $40,000, a franchise to operate a cruise business valued at $4,000, and office equipment valued at $1,000. In payment for these assets, Balboa Bay Cruise paid cash in the amount of $20,000 and issued a noninterest-bearing note for $25,000. The note was to be paid in five annual installments of $5,000 each. The vessel was put into service on March 18, 19XX, Palm Sunday, the opening of the tourist season.

The season closed on September 3, 19XX, Labor Day. Extremely busy during the season, management did not maintain formal records. All cash received during the day was deposited with the bank the following business day; all bills were paid by check immediately on receipt.

From memorandum notes written on check stubs, it was determined that improvements costing $5,000 were made on the vessel; full payment was made in cash on the completion of each improvement. A portable ticket stand was acquired for $1,000 cash. Two motor boats were also purchased at a total cost of $20,000; settlement was made with $10,000 in cash and $10,000 in a note due one year hence on May 1.

On September 15, after the payment of all bills, the bank balance was $16,000.

Before proceeding further, management decided to prepare a balance sheet as of September 15, 19XX, based on the previous information.

Required:

a. What was the status of assets and liabilities as of March 1, 19XX, after the transaction with the Lido Isle Boating Company was begun?
b. What was the status of assets and liabilities as of September 15?
c. What reservation(s), if any, do you have with respect to amounts carried in the balance sheet as of September 15?

Chapter 2

Responsibility Accounting Systems

Learning Objectives:

1. To discover methods of providing top-down and bottom-up information flows.
2. To learn about the information systems that produce reports for internal use.
3. To understand how account codes are used to produce accounting reports.

INTRODUCTION

In Chapter 1 you learned about the scope of accounting information systems, including managerial and financial ones. You were also introduced to financial components, called transaction processing systems. This chapter describes the managerial accounting information systems that are used for responsibility accounting. These systems provide top-down and bottom-up information flows.

Information Flows

Accounting information systems recognize events, record them, summarize them, and report accounting information. If they use a computer, they are computer-based systems. If they do not, they are manual systems. In both cases, this sequence of activities constitutes a *flow* of data and information. Those who

ILLUSTRATION 2–1 The Flow of Information

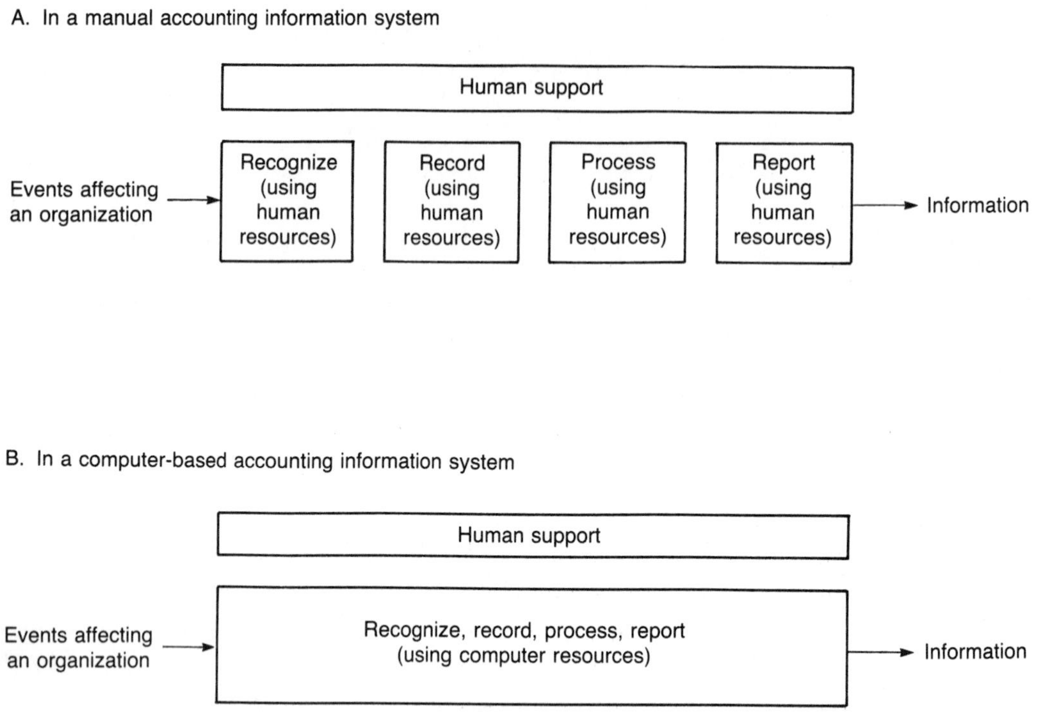

receive this information are parties both internal and external to the organization. They use it for management or investment purposes. Illustration 2–1 depicts this flow of data and information in both manual and computer-based systems.

In managerial accounting information systems, information flows in two directions. A *top-down flow* originates from events that occur at the top management level in an organization. Systems record these events, summarize them, and report them to employees at lower levels. Accounting information systems provide a *bottom-up flow* when events occur at the lower levels. These are recorded, summarized, and reported to top management. The budgeting and responsibility reporting systems provide these flows.

TOP-DOWN INFORMATION FLOW

An organization's budgeting system provides a top-down information flow. This accounting information system produces periodic budgets, which provide managers with quantitative statements of the organization's plans covering the next budgetary period. By establishing and coordinating measurable goals for the organization's segments, budgets help achieve overall organizational objectives.

An effective budgeting system is designed to work within the organization's structure. It requires that top management develop policies concerning the organization's objectives, communicate these policies with policy statements, and set performance goals for the organization.

Organization Structure

An organization's structure provides the environment through which information flows. For the budgeting system to function properly, this environment must have several characteristics: (1) the organization must establish a structure that distinguishes each of its segments; (2) it must issue a clear statement of authority and responsibility for the manager of each segment; (3) each employee should report to only one higher level manager; and (4) top management should clearly define all superior-subordinate relationships among employees. Most corporations adopt a structure that has these characteristics.

Top management communicates the organization's structure by using organization charts and job descriptions. Organization charts identify segments and communicate superior-subordinate relationships. Job descriptions assign responsibility to employees for specific tasks. Illustration 2–2 shows a typical organization chart for a manufacturing corporation.

Another form of top-down information flow is the policy statement used by top management to communicate their responsibilities to employees.

Policy Statements

A company's policy statements identify top management's expectations concerning the behavior of the organization's employees. They provide guidelines for employees on how to carry out specific duties contained in job descriptions. To be effective, policy statements must be both comprehensive and enforceable.

One common policy statement is the code of conduct, a document that describes the ethical standards employees are expected to follow. For example, the code of conduct for one major national corporation establishes ethical policies in six areas:

1. Compliance with laws and regulations, including
   a. antitrust and trade regulation
   b. election campaign laws
   c. securities regulations pertaining to the use of insider information and the trading of securities

ILLUSTRATION 2–2 An Organization Chart

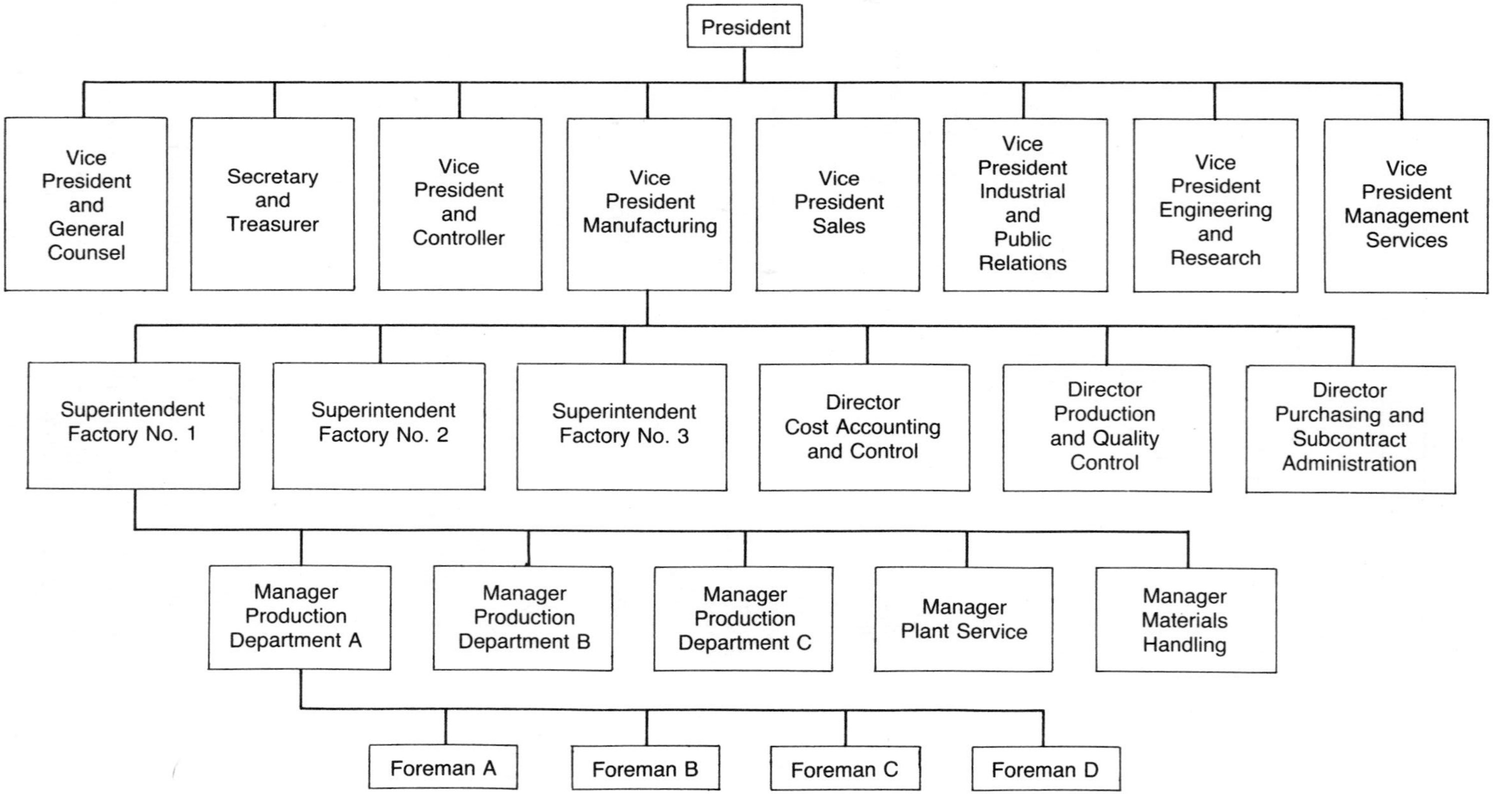

ILLUSTRATION 2–3 The Introductory Section of a Code of Conduct

1. INTRODUCTION AND EXPLANATION

The purpose of this Code is to state the principles of business ethics and conduct which the Board of Directors expects management and other employees to follow in dealings on behalf of the Company with government, the general public, customers, suppliers and fellow employees and to avoid personal activities which might conflict with the Company's interests. These principles relate to compliance with laws and regulations (with special emphasis, because of particular importance to our operations and their complexity which requires constant vigilance to insure compliance, on those relating to antitrust, political activities, relationship with government officials and securities regulation); proper recording of funds, assets and disbursements; conflicts of interest and outside activities; and use of inside information.

These principles are to be strictly adhered to at all times and under all circumstances. The Board of Directors will maintain continuing supervision of compliance with this Code to assure that the Company conducts itself in a manner consistent with its *obligations to society and its stockholders*. This will include the establishment of procedures whereby compliance may be monitored and key employees will periodically affirm in writing that they have adhered to these principles. Violations will result in disciplinary action including, in proper cases, discharge from employment.

Source: Phillips Petroleum Company, *Code of Business Ethics Conduct and Responsibility* (Bartlesville, Okla., n.d.), p. 7. Used with permission.

2. Relationships with government officials
3. Proper recording of funds, assets, and disbursements
4. Outside activities that represent a conflict of interest
5. Subsidiaries and affiliate companies
6. Reports and assurances

In the code of conduct's introduction, this company's top management communicates both the purpose of the code and management's intent to enforce these policies. You can read this introduction to a code of conduct in Illustration 2–3.

Performance Goals

An effective budgeting system requires that management establish performance goals for each segment of the organization. Top management then communicates these goals to managers of the segments by issuing periodic budgets. Such a system, called a *performance budgeting system,* coordinates segment performance goals so that, if each segment meets its goals, then overall organization objectives are met.

Organization Objectives and Department Goals. Many corporations state their objectives using a measure such as residual income or return on invested capital. The performance budgeting system translates these objectives into goals that are meaningful at the subsidiary, division, and department levels. At the lower levels of the organization's structure, performance goals are stated in more detail and become more specific.

As an example, consider a corporation with an invested capital of $17 million. Assume that one of top management's overall company objectives is a return on invested capital of 11.8 percent. One way to achieve this performance goal is with sales of $30 million. In Illustration 2–4 you see how the budget system determines the expenses and working capital needed to achieve this objective. Illustration 2–5 shows how the budget system translates this company objective into performance goals at the vice presidential, regional, and local sales office levels.

Methods of Developing Departmental Goals. When top management establishes departmental goals for lower-level managers, the performance budgeting system is an *authoritative* system. Accountants use this term because the system relies on the authority of top management to motivate employees to achieve the goals.

As an alternative, many companies allow managers at lower levels in the organization to participate in developing their own performance goals. When this occurs, the company uses a *participative* budgeting system. Many accountants believe that when individuals participate in developing their own goals, they are more motivated to achieve them. This means that they work harder and perform better. However, even when participative budgeting is used, lower-level performance goals are established to achieve desired overall company performance. Supervisors and subordinates negotiate these goals to satisfy the objectives of top management.

Organizational structure, policy statements, and performance goals begin at the top management level and are transmitted to lower levels in the company. They represent top-down flows in the communication of accounting information. As this information flows to successively lower levels, it becomes more specific and detailed. This process, called *information amplification*, is shown graphically in Illustration 2–6.

BOTTOM-UP INFORMATION FLOW

Bottom-up information flows originate with events occurring at the lower levels in the organization structure. The system that records these events, processes them, and reports them to managers at higher levels is the *responsibility reporting* system. Often companies implement systems that provide for both

ILLUSTRATION 2–4 Corporate Performance Objectives

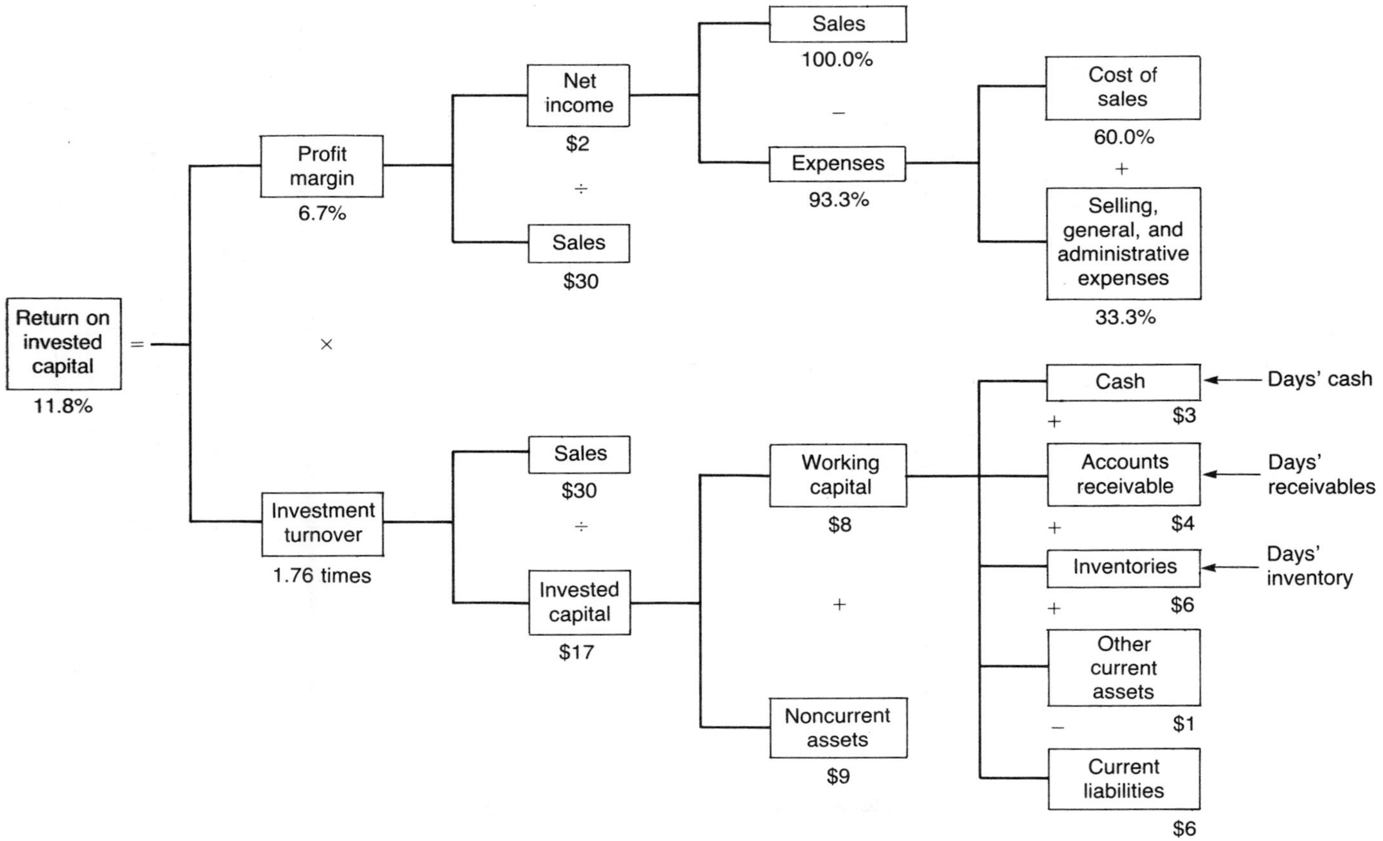

Note: Dollar amounts are in millions of dollars.

Source: Robert N. Anthony and James S. Reece, *Accounting: Text and Cases,* 7th ed. (Homewood, Ill.: Richard D. Irwin, 1983).

ILLUSTRATION 2–5 Top-Down Flow of Performance Goals

Vice President Sales

Automatique Manufacturing Company
Vice President Sales

	X-101	X-102	Y-303	Y-304	Revenue
1. East	x	x	x	x	x
2. Midwest	x	x	x	x	x
3. Southeast	x	x	x	x	x
4. Southwest	x	x	x	x	$ 4,600,000
5. Pacific	x	x	x	x	x
Total	x	x	x	x	$30,000,000

Director Southwest Regional Sales Office

Automatique Manufacturing Company
Southwest Regional Sales Office

	X-101	X-102	Y-303	Y-304	Revenue
1. Denver	x	x	x	x	x
2. Houston	x	x	x	x	x
3. Dallas	x	x	x	x	x
4. Oklahoma City	x	x	x	x	$ 900,000
5. Austin	x	x	x	x	x
Total	x	x	x	x	$4,600,000

Manager Dallas Sales Office

Automatique Manufacturing Company
Dallas Sales Office

	Qty.	Price	Revenue
1. X-101	x	x	x
2. X-102	x	x	x
3. Y-303	x	x	x
4. Y-304	x	x	x
Total			$900,000

responsibility reporting and performance budgeting. In this case, they have *responsibility accounting* systems.

Responsibility reporting systems record performance measures at each segment in the organization. These performance measures may be monetary, such as dollars of revenue or expense, or they may be statistical, such as hours worked or units produced. In a responsibility accounting system, reports compare these performance measures with the performance goals established by the budgeting system. The organization then evaluates its managers by whether actual performance differed from budgeted goals.

ILLUSTRATION 2–6 Information Amplification

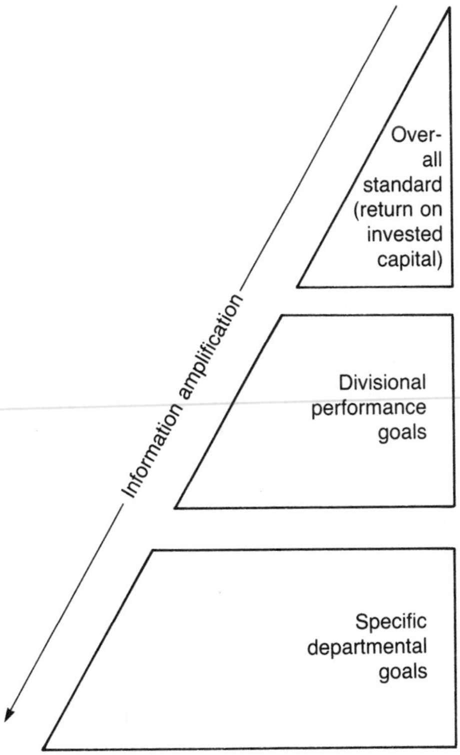

Responsibility Centers

Responsibility accounting systems accumulate performance measures and performance goals at the lowest level in the organizational hierarchy. Accountants refer to these organizational units as *responsibility centers*.

In rare cases, a low-level responsibility center consists of only one person. More frequently, it is a department consisting of a supervisor and several employees. Assume, for example, that the plant service department in Illustration 2–2 consists of a supervisor and 10 service personnel; that supervisor and the 10 personnel together constitute a low-level responsibility center.

Responsibility centers also exist at each higher level in the organizational structure. A higher-level responsibility center consists of a manager and all the responsibility centers reporting to that manager. The organization assigns this manager authority and responsibility over all lower-level responsibility centers below the manager in the organization chart. In Illustration 2–2, the superintendent of factory no. 1 is in charge of a second-level responsibility center. Other higher-level responsibility centers include individual sales regions and the engineering and research division.

Cost, Profit, and Investment Centers

For some responsibility centers, the only existing monetary performance measure is the amount of costs incurred at the center. For example, the manager of production department A controls the costs incurred in that department. Top management evaluates this manager's performance by comparing the actual costs incurred to those budgeted for that month. This department is a type of responsibility center called a *cost center*. Illustration 2–7, parts A and B, shows examples of higher-level cost centers.

Some responsibility centers, such as sales offices, regions, or divisions, generate revenue. In these cases, the responsibility accounting system determines the profit produced by the center by subtracting the costs incurred from the revenue generated. Accountants call such a responsibility center a *profit center*. Illustration 2–7, part C, contains an example. Top management evaluates the performance of a profit center manager by comparing actual profits with those budgeted during each budgetary period.

A responsibility center is known as an *investment center* when its manager not only controls the center's costs and revenues but also helps determine the amount of investment owners make in it. For example, large corporations decide each year how much profit should be reinvested in each subsidiary. If the manager of a subsidiary requests a portion of these retained earnings, then top management evaluates the subsidiary by how well it provides a return on them. At the president's level in the organization chart, the entire company is an investment center.

In designing a responsibility accounting system, an analyst assigns each manager to a responsibility center, each of which is either a cost center, a profit center, or an investment center. The analyst then develops procedures to produce, at the end of each budgeting period, a performance report for every responsibility center.

Performance Reports

All accounting information systems produce information; a responsibility accounting system communicates this information in performance reports. The information disclosed on a performance report depends on the performance measures controlled by the manager.

The manager of a cost center controls its costs; the performance report for that cost center discloses the budgeted and actual costs attained for the budgetary period. Frequently it also shows the difference between these amounts, called a

ILLUSTRATION 2–7 High-Level Responsibility Centers

A. A cost center at the factory level

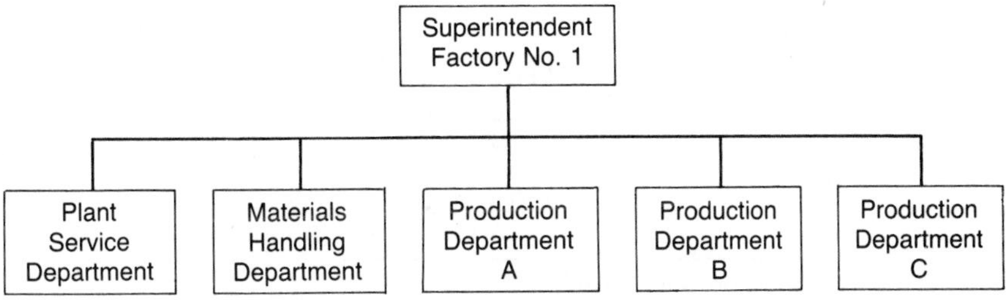

B. A cost center at the vice-presidential level

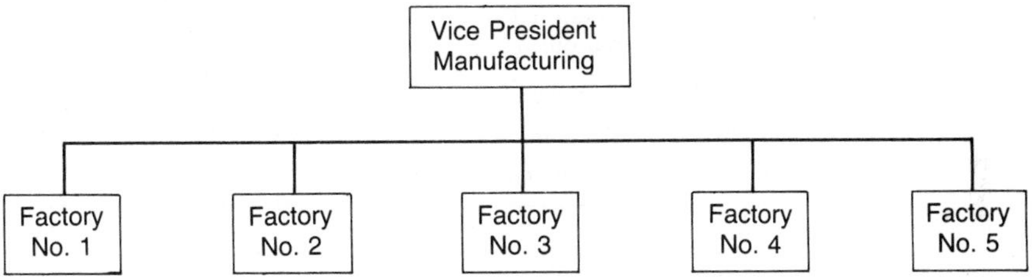

C. A profit center

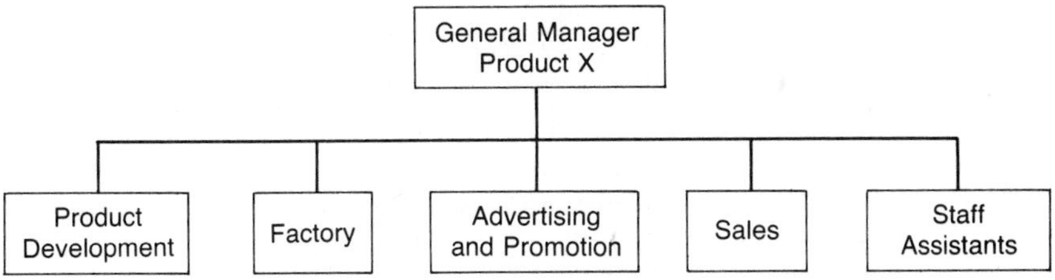

D. An investment center

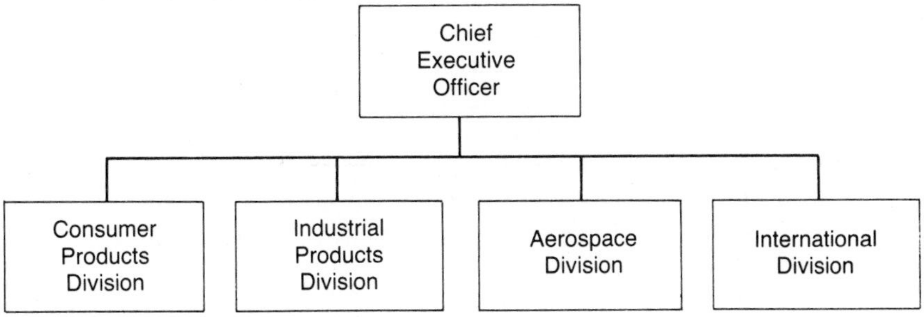

ILLUSTRATION 2–8 A Performance Report

AUTOMATIQUE MANUFACTURING COMPANY
Cost Report—Factory No. 1
Month of _______ 19XX

	Actual Cost	*Budget Allowance*	*Variance*	*Analysis of Variance*
1. Factory supervision				
2. Plant services				
3. Materials handling				
4. Production department A				
5. Production department B				
6. Production department C				
7. Total cost incurred during the period				
8. Unit cost				
9. Number of units budgeted				

budget *variance*. In managerial accounting courses you learn how to analyze this variance to explain its source. Illustration 2–8 contains a sample performance report for a cost center at the factory level.

Sometimes accountants develop budgets that analyze costs into fixed and variable categories. Because this allows the responsibility accounting system to produce *flexible* budgets, accountants call this variance a flexible budget variance. Flexible budgeting is useful for cost centers at the lowest level, where the output of the center is easily measured in nonmonetary terms. Illustration 2–9 shows a cost center performance report for production department B. It discloses budgeted amounts based on fixed and variable costs. This report produces better information for evaluating the manager than does one using a nonflexible, or *static* budget.

A performance report at higher-level cost centers summarizes the budgeted and actual costs of all the centers below it. This shows the costs controlled by the manager of the higher-level cost center. For example, in Illustration 2–8, performance of the superintendent of factory no. 1 is evaluated by the budget variance that incurred in factory supervision, plant services, materials handling, and production departments A, B, and C. The total of these costs is shown on one line in the performance report of the cost center at the next higher level. In Illustration 2–10, the cost total for factory no. 1 is one line on the vice president for manufacturing's performance report.

Performance reports for profit and investment centers are similar. Totals at lower-level centers become line items at the next higher profit or investment

ILLUSTRATION 2–9 A Performance Report with Nonvariable and Variable Budget Components

AUTOMATIQUE MANUFACTURING COMPANY
Cost Performance Report—Production Department B
Month of _______ 19XX

	Budget Components		*Budget Allowance This Month*	*Actual Performance This Month*	*Variance*
	Non-Variable	*Variable*			
0. Equivalent units of production					
1. Supplies and small tools	—	$0.015			
2. Power	—	0.200			
3. Depreciation, taxes, insurance	$1,750	—			
4. Total manufacturing overhead incurred in the department (lines 1, 2, and 3)	1,750	0.215			
5. Labor, direct and indirect	550	2.420			
6. Total processing cost incurred in the department (lines 4 and 5)	$2,300	$2.635			

center. However, for these responsibility centers, the responsibility accounting system discloses four totals: total budgeted revenues, total actual revenues, total budgeted costs, and total actual costs. These may be disclosed on up to four separate performance reports for each center (see Illustration 2–11).

Responsibility accounting systems produce performance reports at each responsibility center in the organization. At a high-level center, the reports summarize budgeted and actual costs and revenues for each center at the next lower level. At each successively higher level, the reports become less detailed, less specific, and more highly summarized. In this way, bottom-up information flow accompanies a process of *data reduction*. Illustration 2–12 shows this process graphically.

ILLUSTRATION 2–10 Responsibility Reporting by Cost Centers

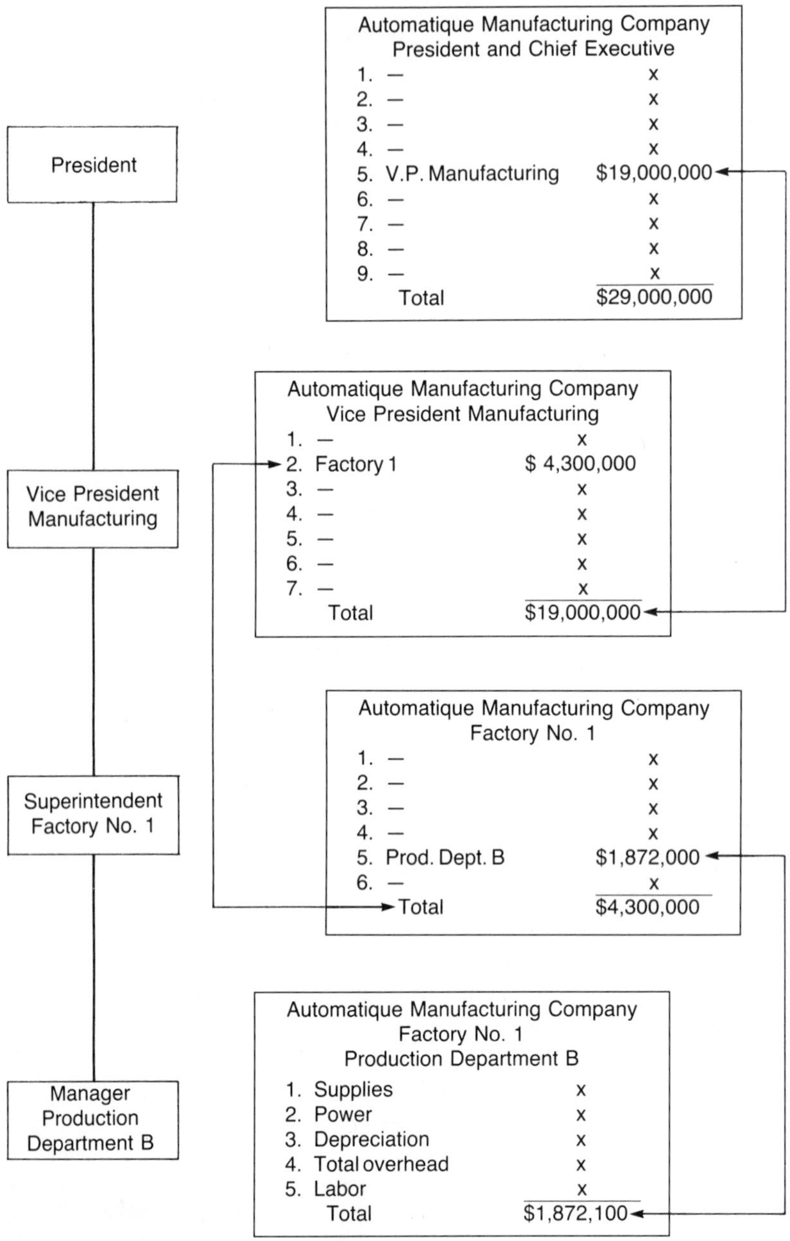

ILLUSTRATION 2–11 Responsibility Reporting by Profit Centers

Vice President Sales

Automatique Manufacturing Company
Vice President Sales

		X-101	X-102	Y-303	Y-304	Revenue
1.	East	x	x	x	x	x
2.	Midwest	x	x	x	x	x
3.	Southeast	x	x	x	x	x
4.	Southwest	x	x	x	x	$ 4,600,000
5.	Pacific	x	x	x	x	x
	Total	x	x	x	x	$30,000,000

Director Southwest Regional Sales Office

Automatique Manufacturing Company
Southwest Regional Sales Office

		X-101	X-102	Y-303	Y-304	Revenue
1.	Denver	x	x	x	x	x
2.	Houston	x	x	x	x	x
3.	Dallas	x	x	x	x	$ 900,000
4.	Oklahoma City	x	x	x	x	x
5.	Austin	x	x	x	x	x
	Total	x	x	x	x	$4,600,000

Manager Dallas Sales Office

Automatique Manufacturing Company
Dallas Sales Revenue

		Qty.	Price	Revenue
1.	X-101	x	x	x
2.	X-102	x	x	x
3.	Y-303	x	x	x
4.	Y-304	x	x	x
	Total			$900,000

ILLUSTRATION 2–12 Data Reduction

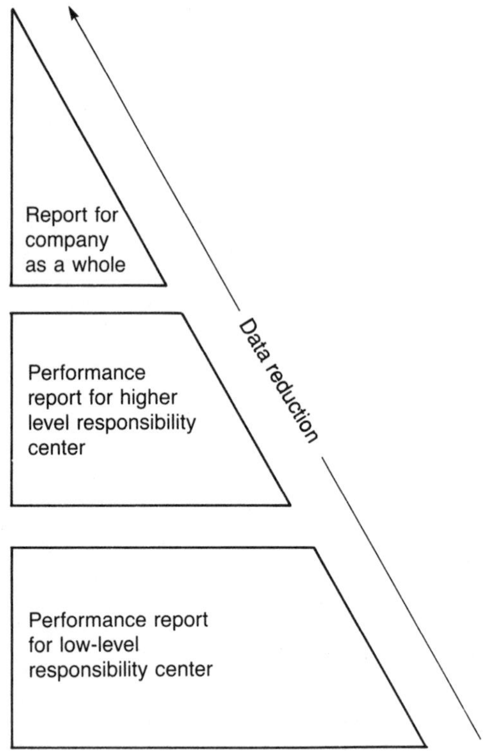

DATA ACCUMULATION

Responsibility accounting systems provide top-down and bottom-up information flows. The system produces a performance report for each responsibility center summarizing budgeted costs and revenues to provide top-down flow, and actual costs and revenues for bottom-up flow.

A system summarizes totals for budgeted costs, budgeted revenues, actual costs, and actual revenues, for each responsibility center and for each month of the year. A large company may have hundreds of responsibility centers, so the system produces a lot of totals. The system accumulates this much data using its responsibility codes.

Responsibility Codes

A responsibility accounting system duplicates the chart of accounts for each responsibility center. When journalizing a transaction, the system debits or credits the appropriate financial statement account, such as Equipment, Raw Materials Purchases, or Salaries and Wages. However, it makes this entry in the account for the center that has control over the event generating the transaction. This is the center responsible for it. The system is able to maintain the large number of totals by assigning a unique code to each responsibility center.

When designing a responsibility accounting system, an analyst develops a coding scheme similar to that in Illustration 2–13. In this example, each responsibility center has a four-digit code. By examining this organization chart carefully, you can see a pattern in how these responsibility codes are assigned.

At the vice president level, each code contains a nonzero digit followed by three zeros. At the factory level, each responsibility center has a code containing two nonzero digits and two zeros. The first of these nonzero digits comes from the code of the higher responsibility center. Thus, the superintendent of factory no. 1, who has a code of 5100, reports to the vice president of manufacturing (code 5000). Furthermore, the manager of production department B, with a code of 5120, reports to the superintendent of factory no. 1 (code 5100), and so on. Using this method, the responsibility center with the most zeros in its code is at the highest level in the organization structure.

Account Codes

In a financial accounting system, each account in the chart of accounts has a unique account code. For example, each account in the chart of Illustration 1–3 contains a two-digit account code. The account code structure in a responsibility accounting system combines a responsibility code with an account code. This structure uniquely identifies each account in the chart of accounts for each responsibility center.

For example, assume that the financial statement account Wages and Salaries has an account code of 571. Using the responsibility codes of Illustration 2–13, any wages paid to employees working for foreman A are debited to account 5111-571. The salaries paid to workers in the office of the manager of production in department A are charged to 5110-571. The salaries of any sales personnel working in the office of the vice president for sales are recorded in account 6000-571, and so on. This is how the responsibility accounting system maintains a separate chart of accounts for each responsibility center.

A chart of accounts is a table of account names and account codes. You could make a similar table containing a list of responsibility centers and responsibility codes. Combining these two tables creates a matrix that shows the coding structure in a responsibility accounting system (see Illustration 2–14).

In Illustration 2–14, each row contains all the account balances for one responsibility center. Each column represents one financial statement account and contains the balances in that account for all responsibility centers. The illustration shows that foreman A controlled total Wages and Salaries expense of $1,850. Wages and salaries of $910 were incurred in office for production department A. In a similar way the responsibility accounting system records

ILLUSTRATION 2–13 Examples of Responsibility Codes

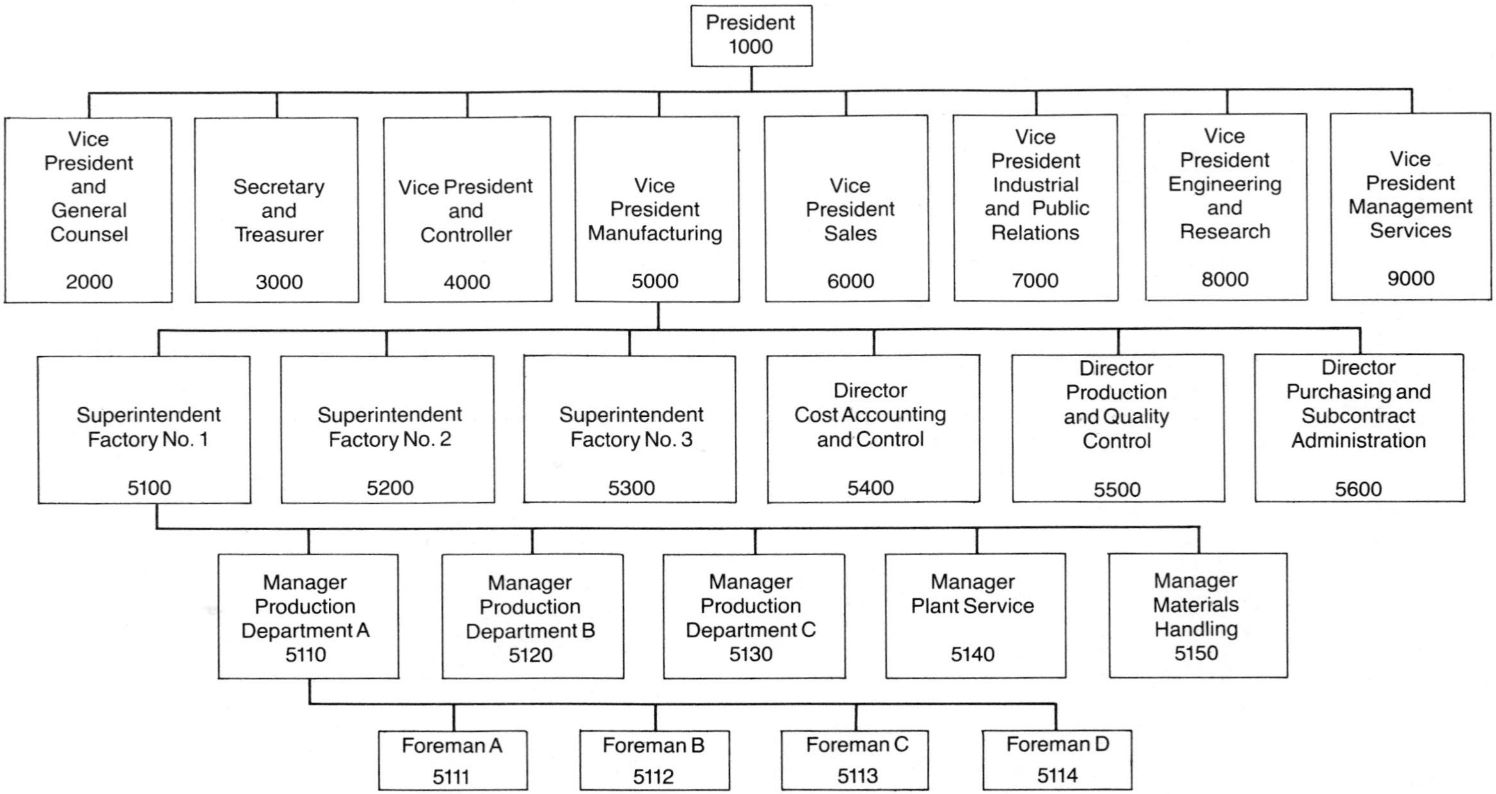

ILLUSTRATION 2–14 Account and Responsibility Code Structure

	—	*571 Salaries and Wages*	—	—	*Total Cost by Responsibility Unit*
1000 President	$x	$ x	$x	$x	$ x
—	x	x	x	x	x
—	x	x	x	x	x
—					
2000 Vice president counsel	x	x	x	x	x
—	x	x	x	x	x
—	x	x	x	x	x
—					
3000 Secretary-treasurer	x	x	x	x	x
—	x	x	x	x	x
—					
4000 Controller	x	x	x	x	x
—					
5000 Vice president manufacturing	x	x	x	x	x
5100 Factory No. 1	x	x	x	x	x
5110 Production department A	x	x	x	x	x
5120 Production department B	x	910	x	x	x
5121 Foreman A	x	1,850	x	x	1,960
—	x	x	x	x	x
—					
5200 Factory No. 2	x	x	x	x	x
—	x	x	x	x	x
—					
6000 Vice president sales	x	x	x	x	x
—	x	x	x	x	x
—	x	x	x	x	x
—					
7000 Vice president industrial relations	x	x	x	x	x
—	x	x	x	x	x
—					
8000 Vice president engineering	x	x	x	x	x
—	x	x	x	x	x
—					
9000 Vice president management services	x	x	x	x	x
—	x	x	x	x	x
—	x	x	x	x	x
—					
Total cost by account	$x	$ x	$x	$x	$ x

revenues under the revenue account codes for a profit center. It records asset purchases under the asset account codes for an investment center.

You have learned how responsibility accounting systems record actual costs and revenues by responsibility centers. Similar procedures are used to record performance goals in a budgeting system.

Budget Codes

A budgeting system records performance goals for each financial statement account at each responsibility center by using budget codes.

When designing the system, an analyst adds one digit to the account code to distinguish between budgeted and actual amounts. For example, assume the digit 0 indicates actual amounts and the digit 9 signifies budgeted amounts. The actual Salaries and Wages expense for production department A is recorded in account 5110-0-571. The budget account, with code 5110-9-571, contains the budgeted Wages and Salaries for this cost center.

Illustration 2–15 shows budgeted costs and revenues as another matrix identical in structure to that used in recording actual transactions. In most accounting information systems, each matrix is a computer file.

Financial Reporting and Responsibility Accounting

The performance reports produced by a responsibility accounting system are useful for managerial purposes. However, their form and content are inadequate for financial accounting because they do not comply with the disclosure requirements of generally accepted accounting principles. An accounting information system must produce financial statements from the data maintained by the responsibility accounting system.

The analyst designing the system identifies each responsibility center account with an income statement or balance sheet classification. In the previous example, Wages and Salaries recorded in the account for foreman A of production department B (account code 5111-0-571) are included in Direct Labor to comply with GAAP. However, Wages and Salaries recorded in account 5120-0-571 are a part of Indirect Labor. These represent costs incurred in the manager's office of production department B, and are not directly related to manufacturing. Illustration 2–16 shows how Wages and Salaries are identified with income statement classifications for several responsibility centers.

A computer program summarizes the amount for each financial statement classification from the responsibility center accounts. Direct Labor expense contains the total of Wages and Salaries from cost centers directly involved in production. Indirect Labor costs are from those cost centers associated with manufacturing but not directly in production. Other Wages and Salaries are

ILLUSTRATION 2–15 Use of Budget Codes

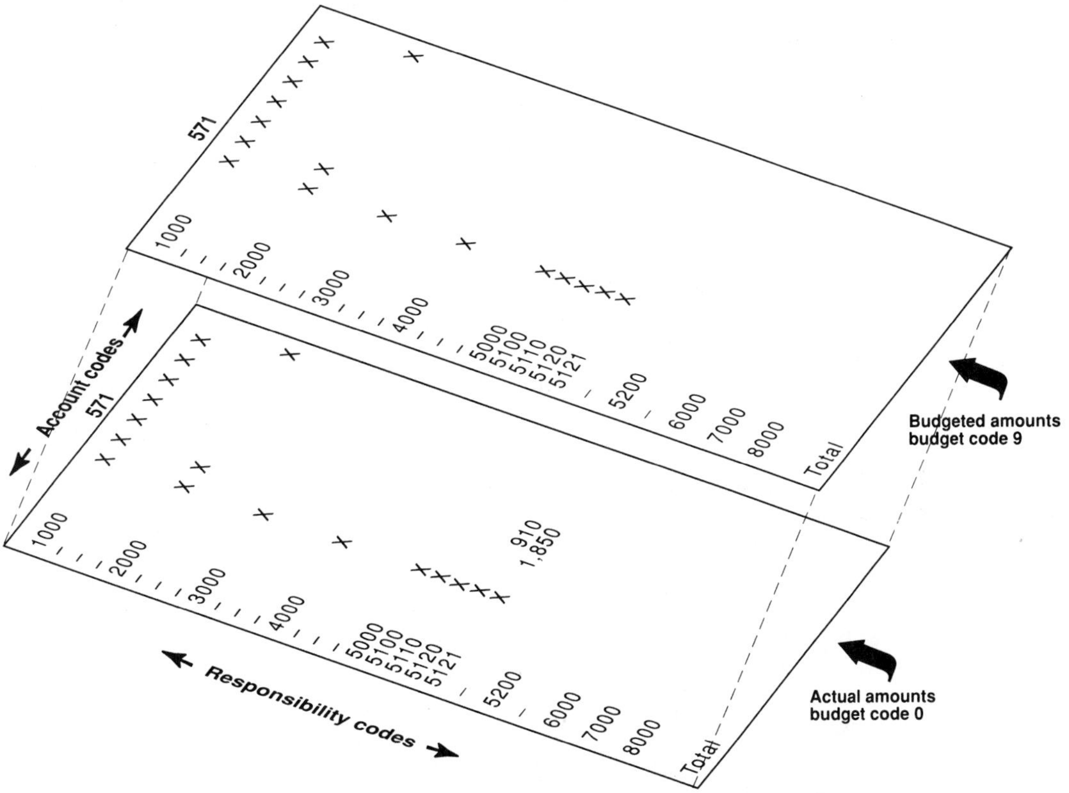

considered Selling and Administrative expenses under GAAP. Illustration 2–17 shows how totals from performance reports produce amounts used on the financial statements.

A responsibility accounting system maintains detailed totals of actual costs, actual revenues, budgeted costs, and budgeted revenues. For each responsibility center in the organization, the system records each total in a separate account identified by a unique account code. At the end of a financial reporting period it classifies the totals in these accounts by financial statement category. This allows the accounting information system to produce information for both managerial and financial reporting purposes.

If you think about the number of individual records processed by such a system, you can appreciate the difficulty of maintaining them on paper in bound journals and ledgers. For this reason, systems like those described in this chapter are most efficient when implemented with computer-based systems.

ILLUSTRATION 2–16 Corresponding Financial and Responsibility Center Accounts

571 Salaries and Wages	*Selling and Administrative General Expenses*	*Direct Labor*	*Indirect Labor*
1000 President	$x		
—	x		
—	x		
2000 Vice president counsel	x		
—	x		
—	x		
3000 Secretary-treasurer	x		
—	x		
—	x		
4000 Controller	x		
—	x		
5000 Vice president manufacturing			$x
5100 Factory No. 1			x
5110 Production department A			x
5120 Production department B			x
5121 Foreman A		$x	x
5122 Foreman B		x	x
5123 Foreman C		x	x
5124 Foreman D		x	x
—			x
5200 Factory No. 2			x
—			x
—			x
6000 Vice president sales	x		
—	x		
—	x		
7000 Vice president industrial relations	x		
—	x		
—	x		
8000 Vice president engineering	x		
—	x		
—	x		
9000 Vice president management services	x		
—	x		
—	x		
Total cost by classification	$x	$x	$x

ILLUSTRATION 2–17 Converting from Performance Reports to Financial Statements

Automatique Manufacturing Company
Vice President Manufacturing

1.	—	x
2.	Factory No. 1	$ 4,300,000
3.	—	x
4.	—	x
5.	—	x
6.	—	x
7.	—	x
	Total	$19,000,000

Automatique Manufacturing Company
Schedule of Cost of Goods
Manufactured and Sold

Beginning finished goods inventory		$ 4,000,000
Manufacturing costs added:		
Direct material	$x	
Direct labor	x	
Factory overhead	x	19,000,000
		23,000,000
Ending finished goods inventory		5,000,000
Cost of goods sold		$18,000,000

Automatique Manufacturing Company
Vice President Sales

		X-101	X-102	Y-303	Y-304	Revenue
1.	East	x	x	x	x	x
2.	Midwest	x	x	x	x	x
3.	Southeast	x	x	x	x	x
4.	Southwest	x	x	x	x	$ 4,600,000
5.	Pacific	x	x	x	x	x
	Total	x	x	x	x	$30,000,000

Automatique Manufacturing Company
Income Statement

Revenue		$30,000,000
Costs and expenses:		
Costs of goods sold	$18,000,000	
Selling and administrative expenses	10,000,000	
		28,000,000
Net income		$ 2,000,000

Automatique Manufacturing Company
President and Chief Executive

1.	—	x
2.	—	x
3.	—	x
4.	—	x
5.	V. P. Manufacturing	$19,000,000
6.	—	x
7.	—	x
8.	—	x
9.	—	x
	Total	$29,000,000

Total costs	$29,000,000
Less: Manufacturing costs	19,000,000
Selling and administrative expenses	$10,000,000

Automatique Manufacturing Company
Balance Sheet

Current assets:		
Cash	$ 3,000,000	
Accounts receivable	4,000,000	
Inventories		
Finished goods	5,000,000	
Raw materials	1,000,000	
Other current assets	1,000,000	
Total current assets		$14,000,000
Property and equipment		9,000,000
Total assets		$23,000,000
Current liabilities		$ 6,000,000
Long-term debt		4,000,000
Stockholders' equity:		
Common stock	6,000,000	
Retained earnings	7,000,000	
		13,000,000
Total liabilities and stockholders' equity		$23,000,000

SUMMARY

Managerial accounting information systems provide both top-down and bottom-up information flows. Organization charts, policy statements, and performance budgeting systems provide a top-down flow. Responsibility reporting systems record performance measures at each level in the organization and summarize them in reports to managers at higher levels. This provides a bottom-up information flow.

An accounting information system that provides both performance budgeting and responsibility reporting is a *responsibility accounting* system. By using a separate chart of accounts for each responsibility center, this system produces performance reports that disclose budgeted and actual performance. Responsibility accounting systems also produce information for financial reporting that complies with generally accepted accounting principles. However, responsibility accounting is practical only in computer-based systems.

KEY TERMS

account code A number uniquely identifying a general ledger account. It enables the accounting system to summarize amounts recorded in that account.

bottom-up information flow Information that originates from events occurring at lower levels in an organization. The information system reports them to people at higher levels.

budget code A number uniquely identifying the budgeted amounts for a responsibility center. It enables the accounting system to disclose comparisons of actual and budgeted amounts on a performance report.

performance budgeting system A managerial accounting information system that communicates budget goals from top management to lower-level managers in the organization.

performance report A report produced by a responsibility accounting system. It discloses financial measures showing the performance of the manager in charge of a responsibility center.

policy statement A written communication from top management that identifies its expectations for the behavior of the organization's employees.

responsibility accounting system A managerial accounting information system that provides both responsibility reporting and performance budgeting.

responsibility center An organizational unit where a manager controls financial measures recorded and reported by a managerial accounting information system. It may be either a cost center, a profit center, or an investment center.

responsibility code A number uniquely identifying a responsibility center. It enables the accounting system to summarize financial measures for the center.

responsibility reporting system A managerial accounting information system that communicates to top management the results of events occurring at lower levels in the organization.

top-down information flow Information that originates from events occurring at the higher levels in an organization. The information system reports them to people at lower levels.

APPENDIX

Coding Structures

This chapter showed how a managerial accounting system uses account and responsibility codes to classify transactions. You may encounter other ways to encode transactions during your career; this appendix discusses them in more detail.

Accountants frequently participate in the development of new accounting systems. When you do this, you help to determine a method for assigning account codes and for coding transaction data. System designers call these methods the coding structures.

Importance of the Coding Structure

An accounting system uses codes to classify, summarize, and retrieve data. For example, when a system records a transaction, it makes debit and credit entries in accounts. Accounting personnel identify the accounts using general ledger account codes. When a payroll system identifies employees to be paid by employee account codes, it records payroll expenses by expense account codes. Accounts receivable systems record and classify sales and customer payment transactions by customer account codes. When systems produce totals, they summarize totals using codes.

The coding structure should be adaptable to changing needs within a company. It should not require replacement as the company grows or as the nature of its business changes. For example, a three-digit employee code becomes inadequate once a company hires more than 999 employees. If a company enters a new industry, it requires new general ledger account codes. Accountants in the company should be able to create them by adding to the old chart of accounts.

The choice of a coding structure is a long-term decision because changes to it are difficult to make. Once employees learn a method, changing to another one requires retraining. Furthermore, producing comparable information from data coded in different ways requires different systems; maintaining redundant systems is expensive and inefficient. For these reasons, accountants participating in system design must choose an appropriate coding structure.

Types of Coding Structures

Many different ways exist of encoding information. The coding structures most commonly used for accounting are sequential codes, block codes, and mnemonic codes.

Sequential Codes. A sequential code assigns unique identifiers to data items in sequence. Accountants commonly assign them to the documents processed by an accounting system. These include checks, sales orders, requisitions, purchase orders, invoices, and receiving reports.

Easy-to-use sequential codes enable an accountant to keep a record of documents on hand and to identify their unauthorized use. These codes are appropriate when the only way to categorize data items is by time. For example, checks issued by a cash disbursement system have unique identifying numbers assigned in increasing sequence. A check with Check No. 10034 was issued immediately before Check No. 10035. Requisition No. 2667 was completed sometime after Requisition No. 2487.

Some people call sequential codes *serial* codes. Although useful in many circumstances, they are less flexible than block codes.

Block Codes. When data items are identified using block (also called *group*) codes, the identifier is segmented into blocks (or groups) of numbers or letters. Each block represents a different characteristic of the data item. The position of the block relative to other blocks identifies it. You see them used commonly as account codes.

Earlier in this chapter you saw a way to encode accounting transactions using block codes. In the example, an account code is of the form: XXXX-X-XXX. Using this structure, the first four digits constitute the first block. They identify the responsibility center controlling the transaction. The second block contains one digit and designates either actual or budgeted amounts. The third block contains three digits and identifies a general ledger account.

Using this method, a transaction coded 5110-0-571 represents an actual expenditure (code 0) for salaries and wages (code 571) in production department A (code 5110).

Block codes are flexible because analysts can readily add or delete blocks when coding a new characteristic is required. Furthermore, a design team can reassign the meaning of a block without affecting other blocks. A person familiar with the structure can interpret the significance of a code from the position of the digits.

Block codes sometimes become long and difficult to remember. Clerks unaccustomed to the block coding structure may make mistakes in recording them. Mnemonic codes avoid this problem.

Mnemonic Codes. Mnemonic coding structures identify data items with combinations of letters and numbers. The design team chooses the combination so that clerks can more easily remember the associated data item. Companies may use them when developing customer or product codes.

For example, to avoid data entry errors by sales clerks, a design team may choose to develop mnemonic codes for customers. The code that identifies each customer is a shortened version of the customer's name. If the code allows six letters or numbers, clerks may assign the code "A&B" to A&B Furniture Company. Merchandise Market, Inc., may have the identifier "MERMKT."

In a proper application, mnemonic codes prevent errors in data entry. If there are many similar data items, however, the mnemonics may also be similar. This would confuse clerks and cause errors. For example, if customers are individuals rather than businesses, different individuals are likely to have similar names. These could produce a set of customer codes that are confusing because of their similarity.

As a part of their daily activities, accounting personnel code accounting transactions and interpret these codes. When the coding structure is logical and easy to use, they are less likely to make errors that produce misleading accounting reports. This is why accountants help to determine the method of coding transactions during the system development process.

QUESTIONS

2–1. Would a well-prepared organizational chart provide answers to each of the following questions?

a. To whom am I accountable?
b. Who has the most seniority?
c. What is the chain of command down to me?
d. What is my position in the organization?
e. Who is responsible to me?

(CIA Adapted)

2–2. In the introductory portion of the policy statement shown in Illustration 2–3:

a. Which groups of employees are covered by the policy statement?
b. Which major areas of employee conduct are discussed?
c. What are the potential consequences of a violation of employee conduct?

2–3. How does a performance budget differ from a cost standard?

2–4. How does the concept of cost controllability vary with the organizational level?

2–5. Why is a return-on-investment figure not usable as a performance standard for a cost responsibility group?

2–6. Ernest R. Breech, former chairman of the board of the Ford Motor Company, once observed: "While many companies believe they have good financial control systems, all too few really do. Many companies confuse a large volume of paperwork and reports with good financial control." What are your views?

2–7. In Illustration 2–10, can you deduce the number of vice presidents who report to the president?

2–8. "A performance budget prepared using the flexible budgeting technique is tantamount to setting standards subsequent to performance. It is not acceptable." Do you agree? What are some of the differences between these two concepts?

2–9. "We have an annual budget, but it is not much help because it is always wrong. Sales do not turn out as expected. Materials go up in cost. Production people work overtime. After only one month our budget is out of date." How could a flexible budget help in a situation like this?

(CIA Adapted)

2–10. A company sets its target volume at 100,000 units for the year. At that level, indirect labor cost is estimated at $150,000, of which $30,000 is nonvariable. Actual volume turns out to be 115,000 units and actual indirect labor cost turns out to be $166,000.

a. How do you evaluate this performance without the benefit of flexible budgeting?

b. How do you evaluate this performance with flexible budgeting?

c. What additional analysis would make information in question *b* even more meaningful?

2–11. "Controllability is relative rather than absolute. In this imperfect world, there are degrees of control. Furthermore, it may often be joint and indivisible." What are the implications of these statements to the analysis of variances disclosed in responsibility reports?

2–12. Standard costs and variance analysis are said to be applications of the principles of management by exception. Why is this so?

EXERCISES AND CASES

2–13. *REPORT OF PROFIT RESPONSIBILITY GROUPS*

Quad-Cities Enterprises is organized on a product basis with profit responsibility. Both product divisions A and B have four departments. During the month of September 19XX, the factory of each product division produced 10,000 units of goods and the sales department of each product division sold 10,000 units of goods. Operating data for the month are as follows:

	Product A	*Product B*
Sales revenue	$40,000	$40,000
Costs and expenses:		
Factory	15,000	12,000
Engineering and research	2,000	5,000
Marketing	10,000	8,000
Staff assistant	1,000	2,000
Divisional manager's office	2,000	3,000

Required:

a. Prepare a profit report for the month of September 19XX for each of the product divisions.

b. Comment on the performance of these divisions.

2–14. *REPORT OF A COST RESPONSIBILITY GROUP*

Harbour Industries is organized on a functional basis with cost responsibility. Its manufacturing division, under the supervision of a production manager, has four service departments and three production departments. Data for these departments and for the production manager's office for the month of November 19XX, a month in which 3,000 units were produced, are as follows:

	Materials	*Labor*	*Manufacturing Overhead*
Production department A	$10,000	$15,000	$ 7,000
Production department B	2,000	18,000	9,000
Production department C	1,000	16,000	8,000
Service department W	—	—	4,000
Service department X	—	—	6,000
Service department Y	—	—	5,000
Service department Z	—	—	10,000
Office of production manager	—	—	11,000

Required:

Prepare a cost responsibility report for the manufacturing division for the month of November 19XX.

2–15. *COST PERFORMANCE REPORT*

The budget components of manufacturing overhead items incurred in production department M of the Homewood Manufacturing Company are as follows:

Supplies		$ 0.20 per unit produced
Power		0.35 per unit produced
Repairs		0.02 per unit produced
	and	200.00 per month
Indirect labor		0.73 per unit produced
	and	600.00 per month
Depreciation and taxes		2,000.00 per month

During the month of September 19XX, the department produced 4,000 units and incurred the following costs:

Supplies	$ 850
Power	1,380
Repairs	320
Indirect labor	3,600
Depreciation and taxes	2,000
	$8,150

Required:

Prepare a cost performance report for the department for the month of September 19XX, with columnar headings similar to those shown as Illustration 2–9.

2–16. *COST PERFORMANCE REPORT*

At the basic research department of Omega Research Corporation, the consumption of research chemicals is found to be $40 per day for the nonvariable portion and $11 for each hour of research activities undertaken. Chemicals consumed and research hours worked during the first week in June 19XX are as follows:

	Chemicals Consumed	*Hours Worked*
June 4, Monday	$ 500	45
June 5, Tuesday	650	55
June 6, Wednesday	800	65
June 7, Thursday	700	58
June 8, Friday	550	47
Total for the week	$3,200	270

Required:

Prepare a report for the manager of Basic Research Department for the week ended June 8, 19XX. Use the following columnar headings:

			Variance	
Day of Week	*Budget Allowance*	*Actual Consumption*	*Favorable for the Day*	*(Unfavorable) Week to Date*

2–17. ***RESPONSIBILITY ACCOUNTING***

The manager of the assembly department of Richardson Manufacturing Company receives a monthly report in the following format:

1. Direct labor	$xxx
2. Material spoilage	xxx
3. Overtime premium	xxx
4. Reassembly	xxx
5. Supplies and small tools	xxx
6. Department manager's salary	xxx
7. Depreciation of plant building	xxx
8. Plant superintendent's office—allocated	xxx
9. Maintenance department cost—allocated	xxx
10. Factory administrative cost—allocated	xxx
Total	xxx

Required:

a. Rearrange the format of this report so that cost items controllable by the manager of the assembly department are separately listed and totaled from those not controllable by that manager.

b. Assume that five departments report to the plant superintendent: machining, assembly, and finishing (production departments), and maintenance and general factory (service departments). Identify those cost items controllable at the level of the plant superintendent that are not controllable by the manager of the assembly department.

2–18. ***RESPONSIBILITY ACCOUNTING***

The manager of production department F of the Wagner Manufacturing Company received the following cost and production report for November 19XX from the accounting department:

WAGNER MANUFACTURING COMPANY
Production Department F
Cost and Production Statistics Report
Month of November 19XX

		Percent of Factory
Production Statistics:		
1. Number of materials requisitions made	250	10%
2. Number of employees in the department	30	12
3. Number of direct labor hours worked	5,000	11

(continued)

		Percent of Factory
4. Square feet of floor space occupied	3,000	20%
5. Number of units produced	4,000	15
Cost Data		
6. Cost of materials requisitioned	$20,000	15
7. Materials handling, allocated on the basis of cost of materials requisitioned	450	
8. Storeroom, allocated on the basis of number of requisitions made	750	
9. Total material cost (lines 6 to 8)	21,200	
10. Total direct labor cost.	11,000	
11. Power	1,000	
12. Building occupancy, allocated on the basis of floor space occupied	1,500	
13. Supplies and small tools	200	
14. Departmental supervision	1,200	
15. Depreciation, insurance, and taxes on machinery	3,000	
16. Factory supervision, allocated on the basis of number of employees	1,800	
17. Inspection, allocated on the basis of number of units inspected (100% inspection)	600	
18. Personnel welfare and first aid, allocated on the basis of direct labor hours worked	275	
19. Total manufacturing overhead (lines 11 to 18)	9,575	
20. Total manufacturing cost (lines 9, 10, and 19)	$41,775	
21. Unit cost of goods manufactured	$10,444	

Required:

a. Deduce the number of service departments involved and establish the departmental cost of each of these departments.

b. Prepare a cost report for production department F for the month of November 19XX with the costs incurred in the department and those allocated to the department clearly labeled and subtotaled.

2–19. ***FLEXIBLE BUDGET***

The Jason Plant of Cast Corporation has been in operation for 15 months. Jason employs a standard cost system for its manufacturing operations. The first six months' performance was affected by the usual problems associated with a new operation. Since that time the operations have been running smoothly. Unfortunately, however, the plant has not been able to produce profits on a consistent basis. As the production requirements to meet sales demand have increased, the profit performance has deteriorated.

During a staff meeting at which the plant general manager, the corporate controller, and the corporate budget director were in attendance, the plant production manager commented that changing production requirements made it more difficult to control manufacturing costs. He further noted that the budget for the plant, included in the company's annual profit plan, was not useful for judging the plant's performance because of the changes in the operating levels. The meeting resulted in a decision to prepare a report that would compare the plant's actual manufacturing cost performance with a budget of manufacturing costs based on actual direct labor-hours in the plant.

The plant production manager and the plant accountant studied the cost patterns for recent months and volume and cost data from other Cast plants. Then they prepared the following flexible budget schedule for a month with 200,000 earned production hours that at standard would result in 50,000 units of output. The corporate controller reviewed and approved the flexible budget.

	Amount	*Per Direct Labor Hour*
Manufacturing costs:		
Variable:		
Indirect labor	$160,000	$0.80
Supplies	26,000	0.13
Power	14,000	0.07
		$1.00
Nonvariable:		
Supervisory labor	64,000	
Heat and light	15,000	
Property taxes	5,000	
	$284,000	

During the month of November 19XX, when 220,000 actual direct labor hours were used in producing 50,500 units, actual cost data were as follows:

Indirect labor	$177,000
Supplies	27,400
Power	16,000
Supervisory labor	65,000
Heat and light	15,500
Property taxes	5,000
	$305,900

Required:

a. Explain the advantages of flexible budgeting over fixed budgeting for cost control purposes.

b. Prepare a cost report, showing variances, for the month of November.

(CMA Adapted)

2–20. *POLICY STATEMENT*

The Leather Corporation plans to offer a one-day course to its management employees in the finance and accounting areas. The topic will be the increased responsibilities of the corporation for the quality and accuracy of its financial information system and the information derived from the system. One of the segments is a review of Leather Corporation's proposed code of professional conduct for corporate financial and accounting personnel; it has been developed as a consequence of recent events.

Required:

Identify and discuss the provisions that probably should be included in Leather Corporation's proposed code of professional conduct regarding the relationship of the corporate financial and accounting personnel with:

a. Other members of corporate management.
b. Shareholders.
c. General public.

(CMA Adapted)

2–21. *DELMARVA COAST HOSPITAL*

The Delmarva Coast Hospital is located in a well-known summer resort area. The area's population doubles during the vacation months (May–August), and hospital activity more than doubles during these months. The hospital is organized into several departments. Although relatively small, its pleasant surroundings have attracted a well-trained and competent medical staff.

An administrator was hired a year ago to improve the business activities of the hospital. Among the new ideas he has introduced is responsibility accounting. This program was announced along with quarterly cost reports supplied to department heads. Previously, cost data were presented to department heads infrequently. Excerpts from the announcement follow:

> The hospital has adopted a "responsibility accounting system." . . . Responsibility accounting means you are accountable for keeping the costs in your department within the budget. The variations from the budget will help you identify what costs are out of line and the size of the variation will indicate which ones are the most important. Your first such report accompanies this announcement.

The first report received by the laundry supervisor is shown as Exhibit 2–1. The annual budget for 19XX was constructed by the new administrator. Quarterly budgets were computed as one fourth of the annual budget. The administrator compiled the budget from analysis of the prior three years' costs. The analysis showed that all costs increased each year, with more rapid increases between the second and third year. He considered establishing the budget at an average of the prior three years' cost hoping that the installation of the system would reduce costs to this level. However, in view of the rapidly increasing prices he finally chose the previous year's costs less 3 percent for the 19XX budget. The budgeted

EXHIBIT 2–1 Case 2–21

DELMARVA COAST HOSPITAL
Performance Report—Laundry Department
July–September 19XX

	Budget	*Actual*	*(Over) Under Budget*	*Percent (Over) Under Budget*
Patient days	9,500	11,900	(2,400)	(25%)
Pounds of laundry processed	125,000	156,000	(31,000)	(25)
Costs:				
Laundry labor	$ 9,000	$ 12,500	$ (3,500)	(39)
Supplies	1,100	1,875	(775)	(70)
Water, water heating, and softening	1,700	2,500	(800)	(47)
Maintenance	1,400	2,200	(800)	(57)
Supervisor's salary	3,150	3,750	(600)	(19)
Allocated administrative costs	4,000	5,000	(1,000)	(25)
Equipment depreciation	1,200	1,250	(50)	(4)
	$ 21,550	$ 29,075	$ (7,525)	(35%)

Administrator's comments: Costs are significantly above budget for the quarter. Particular attention needs to be paid to labor, supplies, and maintenance.

activity level measured by patient days and pounds of laundry processed was set at the previous year's volume, which was approximately equal to the volume of the past three years.

Required:

a. What are your views concerning the method used to construct the budget?

b. What information should be communicated by variations from budget?

c. Does the report effectively communicate the level of efficiency of the laundry department?

(CMA Adapted)

2–22. *PROFIT PLAN REPORT*

Kenbart Company decided to place increased emphasis on profit planning and on analyzing results as compared to its plans. A new computerized profit planning system has been implemented to help in this objective.

The company employs contribution margin reporting for internal reporting purposes and applies the concept of flexible budgeting for estimating variable costs. The following terms were used by Kenbart's executive management when reviewing and analyzing actual results and the profit plan:

- *Original Plan*—Profit plan approved and adopted by management for the year.
- *Revised Plan*—Original plan modified as a consequence of action taken during the year (usually quarterly) by executive management.
- *Flexed Revised Plan*—The most current plan (i.e., either original plan or revised plan, if one has been prepared) adjusted for changes in volume and variable expense rates.
- *YTD Actual Results*—The actual results of operations for the year.
- *Current Outlook*—The summation of the actual year-to-date results of operations plus the flexed revised plan for the remaining months of the year.

Executive management meets monthly to review the actual results as compared to the profit plan. Any assumptions or major changes in the profit plan usually are incorporated on a quarterly basis once the first quarter is completed.

An outline of the basic profit plan report designed by the data processing department is reproduced in Exhibit 2–2. This report is prepared at the end of each month. In addition, this report is generated whenever executive management initiates a change or modification in its plan. Consequently, many different versions of a company profit plan exist which make analysis difficult and confusing.

Several members of executive management have voiced the disapproval of the profit plan report because the Plan column is not well defined and varies in meaning from one report to another. Furthermore, no Current Outlook column is included in the report. Therefore, the accounting department has been asked to work with the data processing department in modifying the report so that users can better understand the information being conveyed and the reference points for comparison of results.

Required:

a. What advantages are there to Kenbart Company having its profit plan system computerized?

b. Redesign the layout of the profit plan report so that it will be more useful to Kenbart's executive management in its task of reviewing results and planning operations. Explain the reason for each modification you make in the report.

c. Which types of data would Kenbart Company be required to capture in its computer-based files to generate the plans and results which executive management reviews and analyzes?

(CMA Adapted)

2–23. *ORGANIZATIONAL CHART*

Thirty years ago four friends started a business which manufactured wooden office furniture. Executive responsibilities were divided among them as shown in Exhibit 2–3.

Their business experienced phenomenal growth and now comprises three product lines, nine factories, and 15 sales offices geographically dispersed throughout the United States. The company has always been departmentized on

EXHIBIT 2–2 Case 2–22

KENBART COMPANY
PROFIT PLAN REPORT
MONTH, YEAR

	MONTH				*YEAR-TO-DATE*			
			OVER/(UNDER)				*OVER/(UNDER)*	
	ACTUAL	*PLAN*	*$*	*%*	*ACTUAL*	*PLAN*	*$*	*%*
SALES								
VARIABLE MANUFACTURING COSTS								
RAW MATERIALS								
DIRECT LABOR								
VARIABLE OVERHEAD								
TOTAL VARIABLE MANUFACTURING COSTS								
MANUFACTURING MARGIN								
VARIABLE SELLING EXPENSES								
CONTRIBUTION MARGIN								
FIXED COSTS								
MANUFACTURING								
SALES								
GENERAL ADMINISTRATION								
INCOME BEFORE TAXES								
INCOME TAXES								
NET INCOME								

EXHIBIT 2–3 Case 2–23

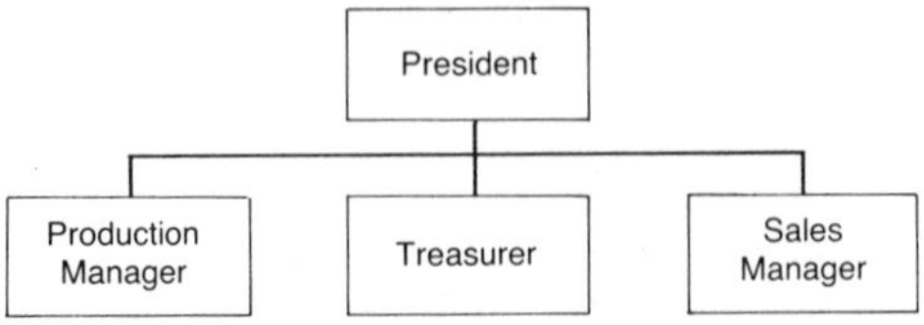

a functional basis. However, the company is now considering a proposal to restructure the organization as reflected in Exhibit 2–4.

Required:

Analyze the proposed organizational chart and answer the following questions:

a. Which type of departmentation is being suggested for:
   1. The entire enterprise at level one?
   2. The manufacturing operation at level two?
   3. The marketing operation at level two?
   4. The marketing operation at level three?
   5. The manufacturing operation at level three?

b. What are the principal advantages of the suggested departmentation plan for the manufacturing operation at:
   1. Level one?
   2. Level two?

c. Why would the departmentation plan suggested for manufacturing at level two be inappropriate for marketing?

d. What are the principal advantages of the suggested departmentation plan for the marketing operation at level two?

e. What rationale supports keeping finance, industrial relations, and market research centralized at level one?

(CIA Adapted)

2–24. ***TRANSACTION CODING***

Ollie Mace has recently been appointed controller of a family-owned manufacturing enterprise. The firm, S. Dilley & Co., was founded by Sam Dilley about 20 years ago, is 78 percent owned by Dilley, and has served the major automotive companies as a parts supplier. The firm's major operating divisions are heat treating, extruding, small parts stamping, and specialized machining. Sales last year from the several divisions ranged from $150,000 to more than $3 million. The divisions are physically and managerially independent except for Dilley's constant surveillance. The accounting system for each division has evolved according to the division's own needs and the abilities of individual accountants or bookkeepers. Mace is the first controller in the firm's history to

EXHIBIT 2–4 Case 2–23

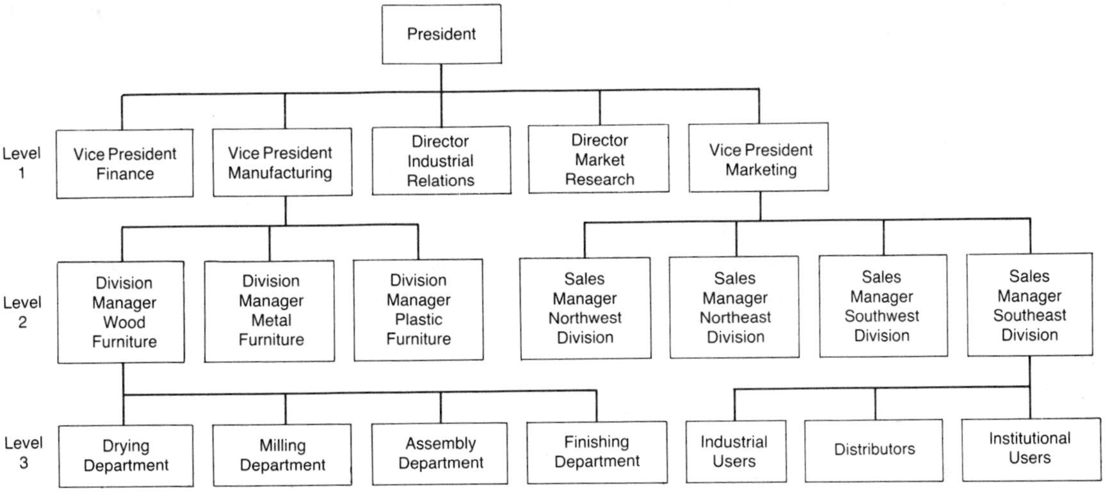

have responsibility for overall financial management. Dilley expects to retire within six years and has hired Mace to improve the firm's accounting system.

Mace decided that he will need to design a new financial reporting system. It should:

1. Give managers uniform, timely, and accurate reports on business activity. Monthly divisional reports should be uniform and available by the 10th of the following month. Companywide financial reports also should be prepared by the 10th.
2. Provide a basis for measuring return on investment by division. Divisional reports should show assets assigned to each division and revenue and expense measurement in each division.
3. Generate meaningful budget data for planning and decision-making purposes. The accounting system should provide for the preparation of budgets recognizing managerial responsibility, controllability of costs, and major product groups.
4. Allow for a uniform basis of evaluating performance and quick access to underlying data. Cost center variances should be measured and reported for both operating and nonoperating units (including headquarters). Also, questions about levels of specific costs should be answerable quickly.

A new chart of accounts, it appears to Mace, is essential before getting started on other critical financial problems. The present account codes used by divisions are not standard.

Mace sees a need to divide asset accounts into six major categories, such as current assets, plant and equipment, and so on. Within each of these categories, he sees a need for a maximum of 10 control accounts. Based on his observations, 100 subsidiary accounts are more than adequate for each control account.

No division now has more than five major product groups. The maximum number of cost centers Mace foresees within any product group is six, including operating and nonoperating groups. He views general divisional costs as a nonrevenue-producing product group. Altogether, Mace estimates that about 44 natural expense accounts plus about 12 specific variance accounts would be adequate.

Mace is planning to implement the new chart of accounts in an environment that includes both manual and computer-based systems. Therefore, the chart of accounts should facilitate the processing of transactions both manually and by machine. Efforts should be made, he believes, to restrict the length of the code for economy in processing and convenience in use.

Required:

a. Design a chart of accounts coding system to meet Ollie Mace's requirements. Your answer should show the number of digits in the coding system and the purpose of each digit. You should explain the coding method you have chosen and the reason for the size of your code elements. Explain your code as it would apply to asset and expense accounts.

b. Use your chart of accounts coding system to illustrate the code needed for the following transactions:

1. In the small parts stamping division, $100 was spent on cleaning supplies expense. The expenditure was requested by Bill Shaw, supervisor in the polishing department of the Door Lever Group.
2. A new motorized sweeper has been purchased for the maintenance department of the Extruding Division. Its cost is $13,450, and it is coded as an asset acquisition.

(CMA Adapted)

Chapter 3

Systems Concepts and Accounting

Learning Objectives:

1. To learn selected concepts from the theory of systems.
2. To apply these selected concepts to the processing of accounting transactions.
3. To learn about those systems that include accounting information systems.
4. To review the systems approach to problem solving.

INTRODUCTION

Accounting processes offer mechanisms for recording and summarizing accounting information, and they provide both top-down and bottom-up information flows. This chapter explores the theoretical basis for these processes. Some relevant concepts from systems theory are described and applied to the processing of accounting information. This will provide a framework for your study of accounting information systems.

SYSTEM THEORY

In your daily activities, you frequently encounter references to many different kinds of *systems:* the public transportation system, the digestive system, the solar system, a high-fidelity stereo system, and communications systems. What is a system? And what do all these systems have in common?

Characteristics of Systems

Because of the wide variety of systems, the concept is a vague one. West Churchman has proposed the following definition: "A *system* is a set of parts coordinated to accomplish a set of goals."[1] According to this definition, any system, whether a computer system or one of those mentioned above, has three characteristics: (1) *component parts,* or those tangible features that can be seen, heard, or felt; (2) *a process,* whereby the parts are coordinated in a defined way; and (3) *goals,* or those objectives toward which the component parts are coordinated. Although the latter two are intangible, they are just as important as the tangible parts. Later you will see how this definition applies to accounting systems.

Subsystems and Supersystems. The definition of a system implies that systems exist at different levels. The parts of a system may themselves be systems with all of a system's characteristics. Lower-level systems are called *subsystems,* each of which also represents a process whereby component parts are coordinated to achieve a set of goals. Although a subsystem's goals are different from those of the higher-level system, they should be consistent with them. A subsystem is also a part of a higher-level *supersystem,* or a system of systems. What constitutes the supersystem, the system, and the subsystem depends on your point of view.

For example, the public transportation system consists of an airline system, a rail system, and a system of highways. An objective of each of these subsystems is to move people or goods using a certain form of technology. These subsystem goals are consistent with the goals of the supersystem, which include movement from one location to another.

Boundaries and Interfaces. Systems are also characterized by the *boundaries* separating them from other systems. The boundaries of subsystems help to identify the system's component parts. In some cases, such as the airline or rail systems, these boundaries are distinct and easy to identify. In others, system boundaries may be imprecise, such as in many business and economic systems. One of the more difficult tasks in designing information systems is identifying the boundaries, or limits, of a new information system.

Whenever subsystem boundaries meet, system *interfaces* are created. An interface occurs where systems or component parts connect. For example, an interface between the highway and airline systems is the airport terminal, which

[1]C. West Churchman, *The Systems Approach* (New York: Dell, 1968), p. 29.

enables a traveler to arrive by auto at the airport, enter the terminal, and then use the airline system. This interface enables the public transportation system to move people from one location to another more efficiently.

Interfaces are often designed to provide decoupling between component parts or subsystems. Therefore, components operate independently, so that the timing of the operations of one component do not rely on the operations of another. For example, air travelers can arrive early for their flights, knowing they will have a comfortable place to wait. The terminal has decoupled arrival by bus from departure by plane.

Accounting system interfaces are designed to provide various degrees of coupling between system components. Many examples are discussed later.

Types of Systems

Although systems have many different forms, they have certain characteristics in common. Systems theory recognizes four basic types of systems. Any system will fit in one of the following categories:

Closed Systems. A *closed* system is totally isolated from its environment. There are no external interfaces, the system has no effects outside of its boundaries, and the environment has no effect on the processes within the system.

The closed system is a theoretical rather than a practical concept, because all systems interact with their environment in some way. Airline and bus systems, for example, are affected by weather, congestion, worker strikes, or accidents.

Relatively Closed Systems. A *relatively closed* system reacts with its environment in a known and controlled way. The system contains interfaces with the environment, and it controls the effects of the environment on its process. The interactions consist of system *inputs* if they flow from the environment to the system; interactions flowing in the opposite direction are called *outputs*.

A well-designed system limits, but does not eliminate, its susceptibility to the environment. Airline companies use radar and other devices to operate in adverse weather and to avoid accidents. Proper scheduling and labor negotiations can limit the effects of congestion and strikes on the airline system.

Open Systems. An *open* system is one in which the system's interaction with the environment is not controlled. Besides having inputs and outputs, an open system has *disturbances,* or uncontrolled inputs, that affect the processes within the system. Disturbances to the airline system, for example, may include icy runways.

Well-designed systems minimize the impact of disturbances. System designers anticipate the things that can go wrong in the environment and create processes and interfaces to control them. For example, to prevent the buildup of ice, airport runways can contain heating elements. In accounting information systems, internal controls protect system processes against disturbances from the environment. An inadequate design is one in which designers gave insufficient thought to potential disturbances, thus producing an open system.

Feedback Control Systems. In *feedback control* systems, a portion of system output is returned as an input to the system. A system may be designed to provide feedback to help the system attain its goals. Automatic guidance systems in airplanes are examples of feedback control systems. They measure the plane's current heading, compare it to a desired heading, and adjust the plane's controls to correct for differences.

Many accounting systems are designed to provide feedback for control purposes. Responsibility reporting systems provide feedback to managers about their performance in achieving organizational objectives. Managers can then make decisions that adjust the inputs to processes, which helps them attain their systems' goals.

Supersystems may have different types of subsystems; for example, a relatively closed system may have component parts that are relatively closed, open, or feedback control systems. The diagrams in Illustration 3–1 represent the four types of systems.

ACCOUNTING INFORMATION SYSTEMS

Now that you have learned some of the basic concepts underlying system theory, you can understand how this theory is applied in processing accounting transactions. The next few pages present the characteristics of an accounting system, the subsystems that make it up, and the supersystems of which it is a part.

Accounting As a System

A well-designed accounting system is an example of a relatively closed system. This system has processes that convert inputs to outputs and utilizes internal controls to limit the effects of its environment on the system.

The inputs to an accounting system are the economic events that become accounting transactions. These include selling goods for cash, selling goods on credit, or incurring an expense. The processes in an accounting system record an economic event as a transaction, journalize and post transactions, and summarize transactions in various reports. The outputs of this system are accounting documents and reports such as financial statements or responsibility reports. Illustration 3–2 shows the accounting system as a relatively closed system.

In the accounting system, internal control measures help to prevent or detect disturbances from the environment. For example, footing and crossfooting is a

ILLUSTRATION 3–1 Types of Systems

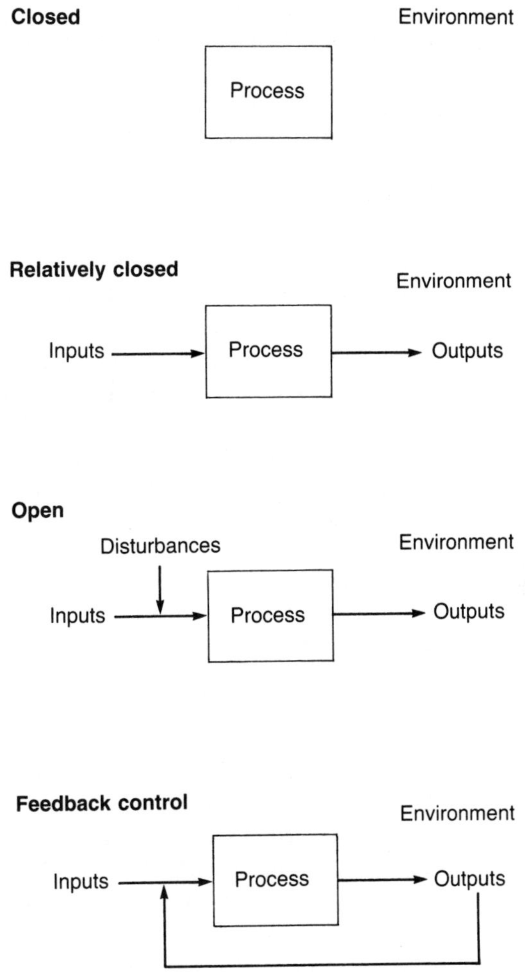

ILLUSTRATION 3–2 The Accounting Process as a Relatively Closed System

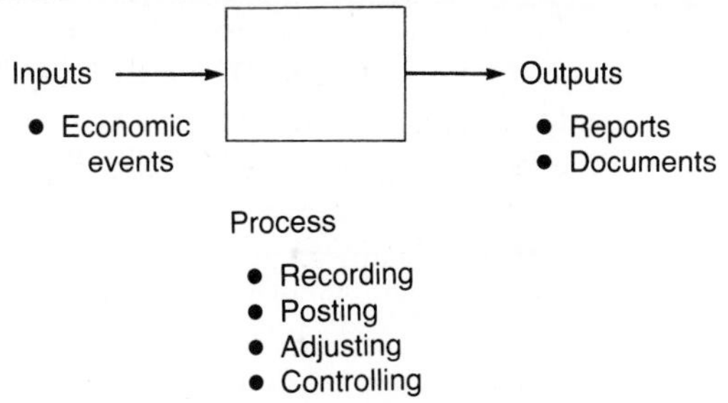

common bookkeeping technique used to disclose arithmetic errors; computerized systems usually require temperature-controlled rooms because they malfunction more frequently when exposed to extremes in temperature; and microcomputer owners often use surge protectors to eliminate the effects of changes in the power source. Many other examples of potential disturbances and the measures necessary to control them are discussed in the chapters about internal control.

Subsystems of the Accounting System. The accounting system has component parts that are themselves systems. Data processing personnel commonly speak of the accounting system as composed of *application systems*. An application system is a set of procedures and computer programs that perform a specific accounting objective. For example, the process of calculating amounts owed to suppliers and then printing checks for those amounts is a *cash disbursements* application.

Many auditors, on the other hand, prefer to think of the accounting system as a set of *transaction cycles*. These auditors identify in a client specific sets of economic events that normally follow each other in a cyclical way. In the expenditure cycle, for example, XYZ Food Company needs a raw material, corn, for its manufacturing process. XYZ locates a grain company that sells the corn on credit. XYZ receives the corn and mails the grain company a check in payment. At the conclusion of this process, the grain company may sell to XYZ Food Company again, producing a cycle of economic events. Each economic event generates an accounting transaction, and this set of transactions forms a transaction cycle. Using transaction cycles enables the auditor to evaluate the effects of internal controls in the accounting system.

As you can see from the preceding example, the cash disbursements application is a part of the expenditure cycle. Any application system is not only a subsystem of the accounting system but also a subsystem of a specific transaction cycle.

Thus, the accounting system is a supersystem consisting of a responsibility accounting system and a transaction processing system. The transaction processing system is composed of transaction cycle subsystems. A transaction cycle is a system composed of subsystems that are application systems. Each is an example of an accounting information system.

Most auditors identify the following four transaction cycles:

1. *Revenue cycle*. Accounting transactions resulting from economic events that produce revenue for the accounting entity.
2. *Expenditure cycle*. Accounting transactions caused by the economic events necessary to acquire material and supplies for the accounting entity.
3. *Conversion cycle*. Accounting transactions recorded when converting purchased inventory into salable finished products.
4. *Financial cycle*. Accounting transactions that record the acquisition of capital from owners and creditors, and the use of that capital to acquire property necessary for generating income.

ILUSTRATION 3–3 The Expenditure Cycle

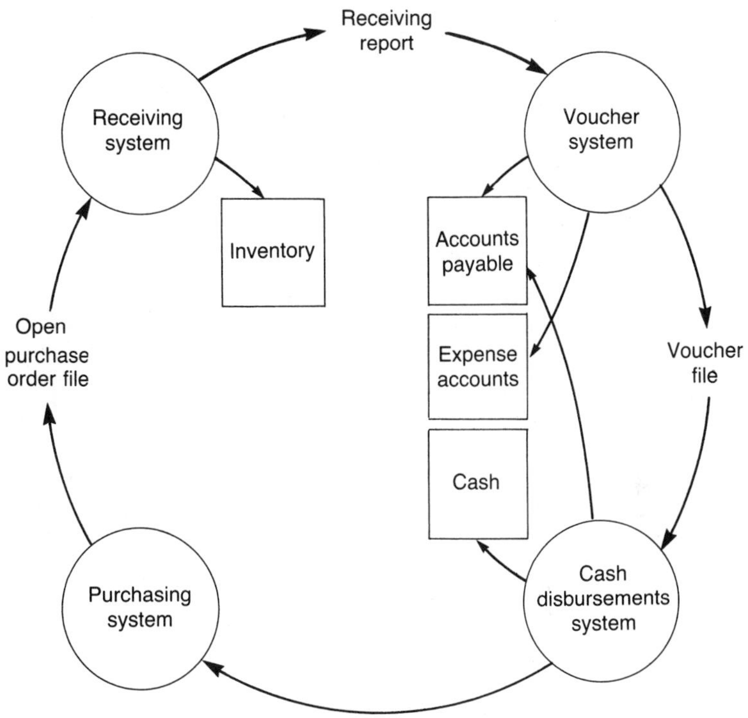

Another chapter describes the application systems that constitute each of these transaction cycles. As an example, the expenditure cycle is shown in Illustration 3–3. This cycle contains four major application systems: purchasing, receiving, voucher, and cash disbursements. These systems impact four major general ledger account categories: cash, inventory, accounts payable, and asset or expense accounts.

Boundaries. Illustration 3–4 shows the boundaries of the accounting transaction processing system in a manufacturing firm. Its boundaries separate this system from the other systems in its environment. Some of these include vendors, employees, customers, and stockholders and creditors who provide capital. Other systems that are also a part of the accounting system include the budgeting system and the responsibility reporting system.

Sometimes the boundaries of a transaction cycle are not clearly defined. Many auditors think that the property application system is a part of the financing cycle; others include it in the conversion cycle. Similarly, some treat the payroll application system as a separate cycle, rather than including it in the expenditure

ILLUSTRATION 3–4 The Accounting Transaction Processing System and Its Cycle Components

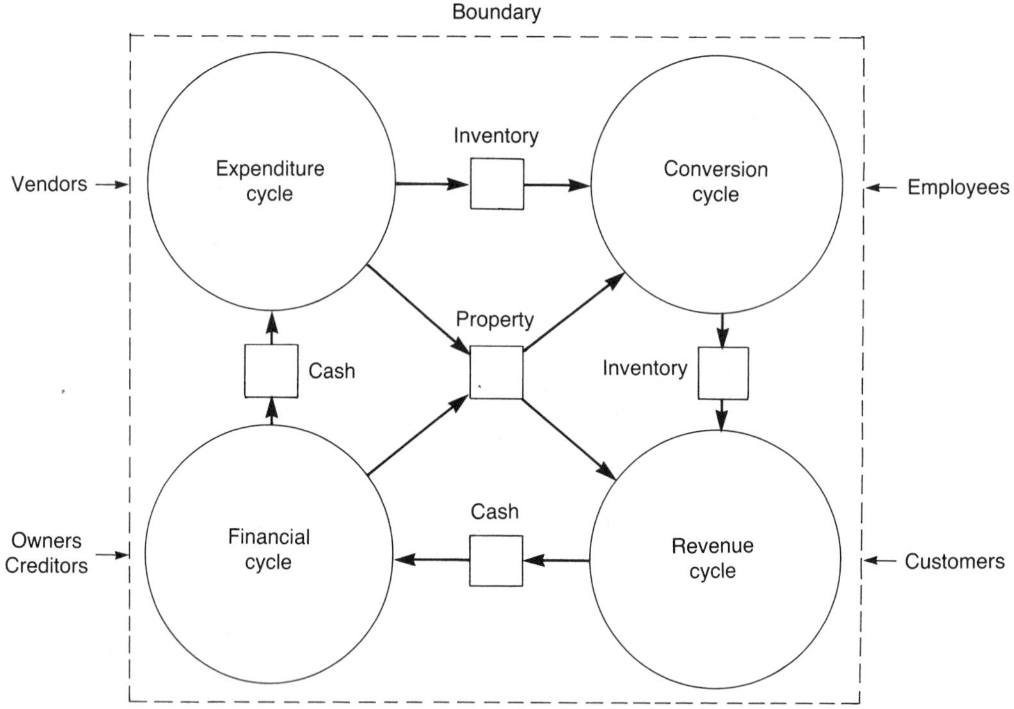

cycle. General ledger accounts that are affected by two cycles or by two or more applications are a part of each cycle or application.

Interfaces. Most systems have interfaces that provide means of interaction with the environment. The interface is a link at which a transaction exits one system and enters another. In the accounting system, an interface can be general ledger accounts, documents, or computer records that contain data flowing between applications. For example, in the expenditure cycle, the receiving report (a document) provides an interface between the receiving system and the voucher system. Illustration 3–3 shows this document used as an interface.

Decoupling. Decoupling is often provided by the files in an accounting system. Decoupling allows individual application systems to operate independently, so that an output of one system does not immediately become an input to another system.

In the expenditure cycle, the purchase order is an interface that provides decoupling between the purchasing and receiving systems. When an order has been placed with a vendor by the purchasing system, information regarding that order is stored in an open purchase order file. This information remains in the file until the merchandise requested in the order is received. At this time the information provides an input to the receiving system. Illustration 3–4 shows how inventory and cash accounts in the general ledger provide decoupling between transaction cycles.

The receiving and voucher systems, on the other hand, are tightly coupled by the receiving report. Whenever a receiving report is issued by the receiving system, it quickly becomes an input to the voucher system.

The designer of an accounting system must decide where decoupling or coupling is useful during development of the system. Too much decoupling between applications, for example, can result in inconsistent data. This can cause the system to produce misleading reports. A later chapter describes how the use of a data base management system can overcome this problem.

The accounting transaction processing system illustrates many of the characteristics identified in systems theory. As you may suspect, accounting information systems are subsystems within a larger supersystem. This supersystem is the organization's management information system (MIS).

ACCOUNTING AS A SUBSYSTEM

An organization's information system has objectives that extend beyond those identified for accounting systems. This section uses systems concepts and terminology to examine the management information system and its subsystems. Also discussed are various goals for a MIS and different information systems needed to achieve these goals. This discussion clarifies the role of accounting information systems in an organization.

Decision-Making Activities

Henry Lucas defined an information system as "a set of organized procedures that, when executed, provides information to support decision making and control in the organization."[2] The goal of any part of the information system, then, is to help the decision-making process. Analyzing decision-making activities helps you to understand the role of the subsystems that make up the information system.

Robert Anthony developed an approach for categorizing the decision-making activities within an organization.[3] Having identified three levels of such

---

[2]Henry C. Lucas, *Information Systems Concepts for Management,* 2nd ed. (New York: McGraw-Hill, 1982), p. 8.

[3]Robert N. Anthony, *Planning and Control Systems: A Framework for Analysis* (Boston: Harvard University Graduate School of Business Administration, 1965), pp. 24–67.

ILLUSTRATION 3–5 Managerial Activity Levels

activities, he stated that decision making differs so significantly between these levels, that different information systems are needed at each level. These levels are strategic planning, management control, and operational control.

> Strategic planning is the process of deciding on the objectives of the organization, on changes in the objectives, on the resources used to obtain these objectives, and on the policies that are to govern the acquisition, use, and disposition of these resources.
>
> Management control . . . is the process by which managers assure that resources are obtained and used effectively and efficiently to accomplish the organization's objective.
>
> Operational control . . . is the process of assuring that specific tasks are carried out effectively and efficiently.

These three levels are often illustrated as a hierarchy of decision-making activities. Management control activities are undertaken to achieve objectives identified during strategic planning. Similarly, the tasks executed at the operational control level are identified with specific management control activities. In this way, operational control information systems support management control information systems, which in turn support those systems used for strategic planning. This hierarchy of decision-making activities is represented by the pyramid in Illustration 3–5.

Strategic Planning. Strategic planning activities are the primary concern of top management, which normally includes the president or chief executive officer and the vice presidents of major divisions of the organization. In their jobs, they identify major markets and product lines for the organization during the long-range planning process. In large corporations, long-range planning staffs advise top management concerning these decisions; top management then communicates these objectives to lower-level managers. Information systems for strategic planning help evaluate possible organization objectives and provide top-down information flows. They are used by top management and those people who advise top management.

Management Control. Management control activities are primarily the concern of an organization's middle management, which includes those men and women in charge of factories, sales regions, and administrative and engineering activities. Middle managers want to operate their segments of the organization efficiently while achieving the objectives identified by top management. The decisions made by middle management are sometimes called *tactical* decisions, because they implement strategy identified at the higher level. Middle managers rely on the budgeting and responsibility reporting systems of the accounting system.

Operational Control. Operational control activities are implemented by department heads and supervisers, the lowest level managers in an organization. Their aim is to achieve those specific tasks assigned to them by middle management. For example, the manager of an accounts payable department may report to a controller or chief accountant in middle management. One task of the accounts payable manager is to pay the organization's bills promptly. In achieving this task, the manager coordinates the activities of several accounts payable clerks. The manager and clerks routinely use the voucher and cash disbursement systems of the accounting transaction processing system.

Decision Problems and the Activity Level

Different activities are performed at various managerial levels in an organization. The managers at each level face different decisions. Those made by top management evaluate many alternatives and require the knowledge and judgment acquired by many years of experience. At lower organizational levels, decision makers face fewer alternatives. These decisions are made within the constraints established at higher levels and affect three categories of problems. Differences in decision problems between levels create differences in the kinds of information systems that are needed.

Unstructured Problems. The problems faced by top management are usually unstructured; many alternatives are available but there is little guidance concerning the best one to pursue. For example, among all the possible new markets or new products, top management must choose those that the organization can deliver successfully within existing human and financial constraints. These decisions impact the long-term success of the organization and may affect decisions at the management control level for 20 years or more. Some activities at the management control and operational control levels are also unstructured, but these are less frequent and less far reaching.

Information systems that solve unstructured problems must have certain characteristics. These systems process data that are largely predictive—long-term forecasts about technology, demographics, and market demand—and that consist of estimates that are relatively inaccurate and highly summarized. The data are obtained mostly from external sources, such as public data bases, economic statistics, and predictions of future trends. Because the decision-making process is unstructured, the information system must be quickly and easily adaptable to new decisions or to new data inputs. Information systems that fit many of these characteristics are sometimes called decision support systems.

Structured Problems. The decisions that managers face at the operational level are significantly different. At this level, managers are assigned specific tasks by middle management and are often given clear directions about how to carry out each task. For example, an accounts payable manager may be instructed to pay all bills when due, but to take purchase discounts whenever they are offered. The problem faced by the manager is a structured one—determining the payment date given the preceding rules. Other structured decision problems are faced by middle and top management, but these become less common at the higher levels.

Information systems needed for structured problems are different because they concentrate on processing historical data from within the organization. These systems are highly detailed and, in that they are both historical and internal, are usually accurate. Since the manager knows in advance what kind of information is necessary to make the decision, a system can be designed to provide what is needed. Data sources for this system can be identified in advance and used repeatedly. The system's adaptability is less important for these structured decision problems than it is for most unstructured ones.

Semistructured Problems. Many decisions management faces cannot easily be classified as structured or unstructured. Middle managers receive a set of objectives, but have some freedom in choosing how to attain them. Thus, middle managers frequently are required to make decisions about semistructured problems. For example, top management may assign production quotas and profit objectives to a middle-level factory manager. The manager must then acquire materials, hire and train workers, and schedule production to meet these objectives. He or she must exercise judgment in selecting the quality of materials, the number of employees, the amount of training, and the proper production schedule. Semistructured decisions also exist at the operational and strategic planning levels.

Information systems used for semistructured decisions tend to combine the characteristics of systems used for structured and unstructured decisions. For example, in selecting the quality of materials to purchase, a factory manager may use both historical data (on the quality of a finished product) and predictive data

ILLUSTRATION 3–6 Decision Problems and Managerial Activity Levels

	Operational control	Management control	Strategic planning
Structured	Accounts payable Cash disbursements	Responsibility accounting	Tanker fleet mix Warehouse and factory location
Semistructured	Inventory control Production scheduling	Budget preparation	Mergers and acquisitions
Unstructured	Cash management	Personnel management	New products R&D planning

(the anticipated sales for a product of low or high quality); he or she may also use externally produced data (purchase prices) as well as data from internal sources (standard quantities of material).

Illustration 3–6 classifies these decision problems by management activity level and provides examples of information subsystems useful in each area. This classification was adapted from a framework for information systems developed by Anthony Gorry and Michael Scott Morton.[4] It provides examples of structured decision problems at the strategic planning level and of unstructured problems at the operational level.

A Spectrum of Management Information Needs

Like all systems, the management information system is composed of many subsystems, each of which is an information system designed to satisfy management's decision-making needs. But each of these systems must be tailored to the structured, semistructured, or unstructured problems faced by a

[4]Reprinted in adapted form from G. Anthony Gorry and Michael S. Scott Morton, "A Framework for Management Information Systems," *Sloan Management Review*, Fall 1971, p. 59, by permission of the publisher.

manager at each of the three levels. You can now draw some conclusions about accounting systems as subsystems of the management information system.

Accounting Information Systems. The three accounting information systems are the transaction processing system, the budgeting system, and the responsibility accounting system. Each is a component of the management information system that provides information for decision making at all levels of an organization.

The *transaction processing system* is the most structured of all those components; it provides information used by clerical and managerial personnel at the operational level. Because it is structured, and because most organizations require transaction processing systems that are similar in nature, we can describe standard processes for these systems. You will learn the details of these systems as you examine the accounting transaction cycles later in this text.

The *budgeting system* allows top management to communicate corporate objectives to all managers in the organization. It provides for the top-down information flows described in Chapter 2. A budgeting system utilizes both internal and external data, is predictive in its nature, and involves estimates that are frequently imprecise. Thus, it is used in semistructured decision processes involving management control activities.

The *responsibility reporting system* summarizes historical data on a periodic basis and provides the bottom-up information flows described in Chapter 2. It is an example of a highly structured information system that is useful for management control.

These three accounting information systems provide information for structured or semistructured decisions at the operational and management control levels. Because accounting systems are more structured, they are more highly developed in most organizations. They are also more standardized across different organizations than other information systems.

Decision Support Systems. Whereas accounting information systems are highly structured and most useful at the lower organizational levels, decision support systems are most useful at the higher levels. At the strategic level decisions are unstructured, and decision styles may differ significantly among managers. Furthermore, a specific decision problem may occur only once. Thus, information systems developed for this level often are decision-specific. Once the decision is made, the information system used for it is no longer applicable in its current form. For subsequent decisions, the system must be modified or discarded, a development that has major implications for the design of information systems.

In considering the nature of decision problems and the management activities at various levels, there is a spectrum of management information needs. At one end of the spectrum are the highly structured, recurring, retrospective needs satisfied by the accounting transaction processing systems. At the other end of the spectrum are the unstructured, nonrecurring, prospective needs that must be

ILLUSTRATION 3–7 The Spectrum of Management Information Needs

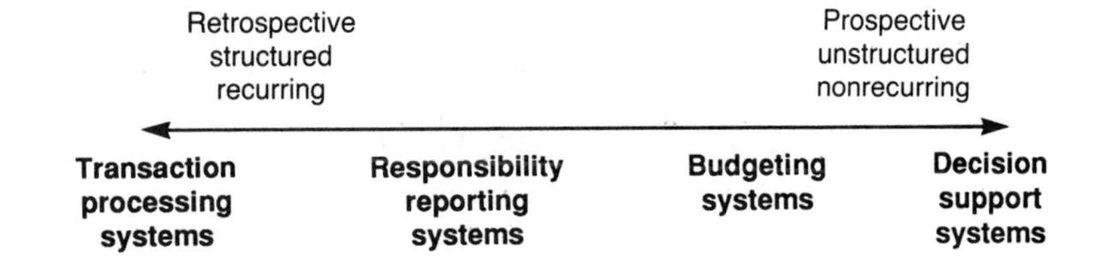

met by decision support systems. All other systems, including those identified in Illustration 3–6, exist somewhere along this spectrum of management information needs, as shown in Illustration 3–7.

THE SYSTEMS APPROACH

The systems approach is a way of approaching a problem that is derived from systems theory. The systems approach recognizes the system-subsystem relationships in any problem situation and provides a structured method for solving the problem. Many organizations use it in the process of designing new information systems. They employ *systems analysts* who apply the systems approach to business problems. You can apply this approach to problems of your own by using these four characteristics:

Define the Objective

First, identify the objective of the system that contains the problem. Frequently, a problem exists because people do not clearly understand the system's objectives.

For example, there are two possible objectives for a customer service department: (1) to aid customers in quickly finding merchandise; or (2) to resolve all customer complaints about product quality or service. If the customer service manager perceives the first as the objective, when the second is the true objective, then problems will arise in resolving customer complaints.

During the information system design process, systems analysts first analyze existing systems to identify the relevant organizational objectives. Then they look for a solution to the information system problem.

Explore Alternative Solutions

Second, consider a range of alternative solutions to your problem. After defining the objective, identify as many ways as possible to achieve it; then carefully consider the advantages, disadvantages, costs, and benefits of each alternative.

Many people mistakenly choose the first solution that occurs to them, when perhaps a better, less obvious solution exists. You can avoid this error by recording each of your alternatives, researching them, and carefully describing your analysis of each. After reflection, you can make an intelligent, objective choice. Professional systems analysts use design tools such as flowcharts, interview notes, and questionnaires to create working papers that help them explore and document alternatives.

Take a Broad Viewpoint

Third, look at the problem and solution alternatives from the viewpoint of the entire system, rather than limiting your perspective to the subsystem presenting the problem. This characteristic of the systems approach recognizes that supersystem and subsystem objectives may differ. An alternative that achieves subsystem objectives may be inadequate from the viewpoint of the larger supersystem. For example, a customer service manager can resolve every complaint by fully satisfying every unhappy customer, but this may be inconsistent with the company's desire to earn a profit and remain in business. A better solution is a compromise that adequately addresses both supersystem and subsystem objectives. Because of their knowledge of business information needs, systems analysts are able to evaluate tradeoffs between the objectives of an organization and those of its subunits.

Use a Project Team

Finally, the systems approach requires the examination of alternatives from several different perspectives. The information system design process accomplishes this using a *project team*. Because the members of a project team have varied backgrounds, each may contribute ideas that would not occur to other team members. Frequently, such a project team is directed by a systems analyst experienced in the use of the systems approach. Other members may include accountants, computer technicians, or internal auditors. The use of a project team accomplishes the same purpose that you accomplish when you ask a friend's advice. Your friend's perspective may give you ideas that would never occur to you otherwise.

SUMMARY

This chapter presented many of the concepts underlying systems theory, and applied these concepts to accounting systems and to management information systems. Systems exist at many different levels; supersystems are made up of components, or subsystems, that are also systems. Each system is defined by a boundary, and interacts with other systems through interfaces at the boundary. Sometimes the interface provides decoupling, which affects the system's operations. Systems are developed by a procedure utilizing the systems approach to problem solving.

Accounting information systems are subsystems of the management information system, and are used to make structured and semistructured decisions at the operational and management control levels. The accounting information systems discussed in this chapter were the transaction processing system, the budgeting system, and the responsibility reporting system. The transaction processing system is composed of four subsystems called transaction cycles. Each transaction cycle is composed of one or more accounting application systems.

KEY TERMS

application system A set of procedures and computer programs that perform a specific accounting objective.

closed system A system totally isolated from its environment.

decision support system An information system that provides information primarily at higher organizational levels to aid decisions that are usually unstructured. Although it may rely on accounting information, a decision support system is ordinarily not an accounting information system.

decoupling A feature that sometimes exists at system interfaces, allowing the systems to operate independently.

feedback control system A system in which a portion of its output is returned as an input.

information system A set of organized procedures that, when executed, provides information to support decision making and control in an organization.

interface The connection between two systems occurring at the boundaries of the systems.

open system A system in which its interaction with its environment is not controlled.

relatively closed system A system that reacts with its environment in a known, controlled way.

subsystem A component part of a system that is itself a system.

system A set of parts coordinated to accomplish a set of goals.

systems approach A way of approaching a problem that recognizes the system-subsystem relationships in any problem situation, and that provides a structured method for solving the problem.

transaction cycle The accounting transactions recording an organization's economic events that normally follow each other in a cyclical way. There are four transaction cycles: the revenue cycle, the expenditure cycle, the conversion cycle, and the financial cycle.

transaction processing system An accounting information system that provides information for structured decisions primarily at the operational level. It also provides information that is summarized and used by other information systems.

QUESTIONS

3–1. What is the definition of a system?

3–2. How does a system differ from a supersystem? From a subsystem?

3–3. Which four systems are recognized by systems theory? Of these, which is the most common in your environment?

3–4. What are the three components of an accounting information system?

3–5. What are the inputs to an accounting information system? The processes? The outputs?

3–6. How does a system boundary differ from a system interface?

3–7. What is the purpose of decoupling?

3–8. What are the levels in management's hierarchy of decision-making activities? What are the distinctions between them?

3–9. How can you characterize the decision problems that commonly face top management? Middle management? Operating management?

3–10. Accounting information systems are more standardized than other information systems. At which decision levels are these systems most useful? Which decision problems do accounting systems address?

3–11. What are the steps in the systems approach to problem solving?

EXERCISES AND CASES

3–12. *SUBSYSTEMS AND SUPERSYSTEMS*

Identify the subsystems and supersystems in each of the following groups of systems:

a. Inventory system, management information system, transaction processing system, accounting information system

b. Solar system, Jupiter, universe, human race, Earth

c. Computer system, information system, central processing unit, computer user, floppy disk drive

d. Air conditioner, electrical system, headlights, radiator, steering system, automobile

3–13. ***APPLYING SYSTEMS CONCEPTS***

Think of one system that has not been discussed in this chapter. For this system,

a. Identify each of the following:
   1. Objectives
   2. Inputs
   3. Processes
   4. Outputs
   5. Levels
   6. Boundaries
   7. Interfaces
   8. Decoupling

b. Which controls can you suggest that would limit the impact of disturbances to this system?

3–14. ***PREVENTIVE AND DETECTIVE CONTROLS***

In a system, controls are used either to prevent or to detect disturbances. Identify each of the following as either a preventive or a detective control:

a. Footing and crossfooting
b. Temperature-controlled computer room
c. Personal computer surge protector
d. Highway speed limit
e. Police radar unit
f. Proctor for an examination

3–15. ***ACCOUNTING ENTRIES AND TRANSACTIONS***

In an introductory accounting course, you learn proper accounting entries for certain transactions. The following accounting transactions produce these entries; for each, identify the transaction cycle of which it is a part.

a. Cash sale
b. Credit sale
c. Obtain long-term bank loan
d. Purchase materials
e. Pay debt
f. Sell stock
g. Manufacture product to inventory
h. Pay employees

3–16. ***MANAGEMENT ACTIVITIES AND DECISION-MAKING LEVELS***

Classify each of the following management activities by decision-making level. Identify each as either strategic planning, management control, or operational control.

a. Assign worker to factory task
b. Develop production schedule
c. Authorize construction of new factory
d. Hire factory personnel
e. Acquire manufacturing subsidiary
f. Select new product for development
g. Bill customer for product

3–17. *JOB POSITIONS AND DECISION LEVELS*

The following positions are typical in a manufacturing company. For each job, decide whether the position's decisions are primarily strategic, tactical, or operational.

a. Corporation president
b. Accounts payable supervisor
c. Controller
d. Chief accountant
e. Factory manager
f. Vice president, manufacturing
g. Shop foreman
h. Product line sales manager
i. District sales manager

3–18. *MANAGEMENT DECISIONS AND DECISION LEVELS*

Look at the following list of typical management decisions. First, classify each decision as either a structured, semistructured, or unstructured decision. Second, suggest the level of the job position that normally makes the decision.

a. Accept an order from a customer
b. Promote an employee
c. Expand sales to an overseas market
d. Allocate capital to divisions for reinvestment
e. Approve an adjusting journal entry
f. Post an adjusting journal entry
g. Approve a purchase order to an existing vendor
h. Terminate an employee

3–19. *PROJECT TEAMS*

Mega-Systems, Inc. is a large company that manufactures and markets office information processing systems. Mega-Systems has consistently been innovative and profitable. From its corporate headquarters and manufacturing facilities in the Midwest, the company has developed a regional system for marketing and servicing its products. The regions are operated as profit centers because regional managers have significant amounts of authority within their territories.

The regional organizations consist of an accounting and budget department, a personnel and training department, and several area offices which market and service the products. The regional organization provides accounting and personnel services for area offices. Each of these offices consists of sales, service, and administrative departments headed by managers who report to the area manager.

The Los Angeles area office has departed from the standard organizational structure by establishing a branch office to market and service the firm's products in the San Diego area. This office is headed by a branch manager who reports to the area manager. Sales and services for the remainder of the Los Angeles territory are handled by the Los Angeles area sales manager and service manager respectively. A partial organization chart showing the relationships among the Western Region, Los Angeles area, and San Diego branch offices is presented in Exhibit 3–1.

The San Diego branch office was opened over a decade ago and was very profitable until the past two years, when it has had declining profits; the most recent two quarters showed losses. The Los Angeles area manager and the Western Region manager have concluded that a project team with people from the regional office, the area office, and the branch office should be established to identify San Diego's problems and make recommendations to correct them. The manager of the Western Region, in consultation with the Los Angeles area manager, appointed the following people to the project team with Richard Moore named chairperson:

Western Region office

John Overton, budget supervisor
Sally Miller, training director

Los Angeles area office

Richard Moore, administrative department manager

San Diego branch

David Alworth, branch manager and sales manager
Tim Smithson, assistant branch manager and service manager
Robert Tishman, salesperson
Harry Bend, serviceperson

Required:

a. A project team, such as the one illustrated for Mega-Systems, Inc., is a group of individuals who contribute their particular skills to accomplish a given objective. Characteristics of members of the group can influence the functioning and effectiveness of it. Identify some of these characteristics.

b. What sources of conflict can you foresee arising among the members of this group because of its composition? Do you think it can achieve its objective?

c. What contribution would a person who holds a position as budget supervisor make in a project team such as this one?

(CMA Adapted)

EXHIBIT 3–1 Case 3–19

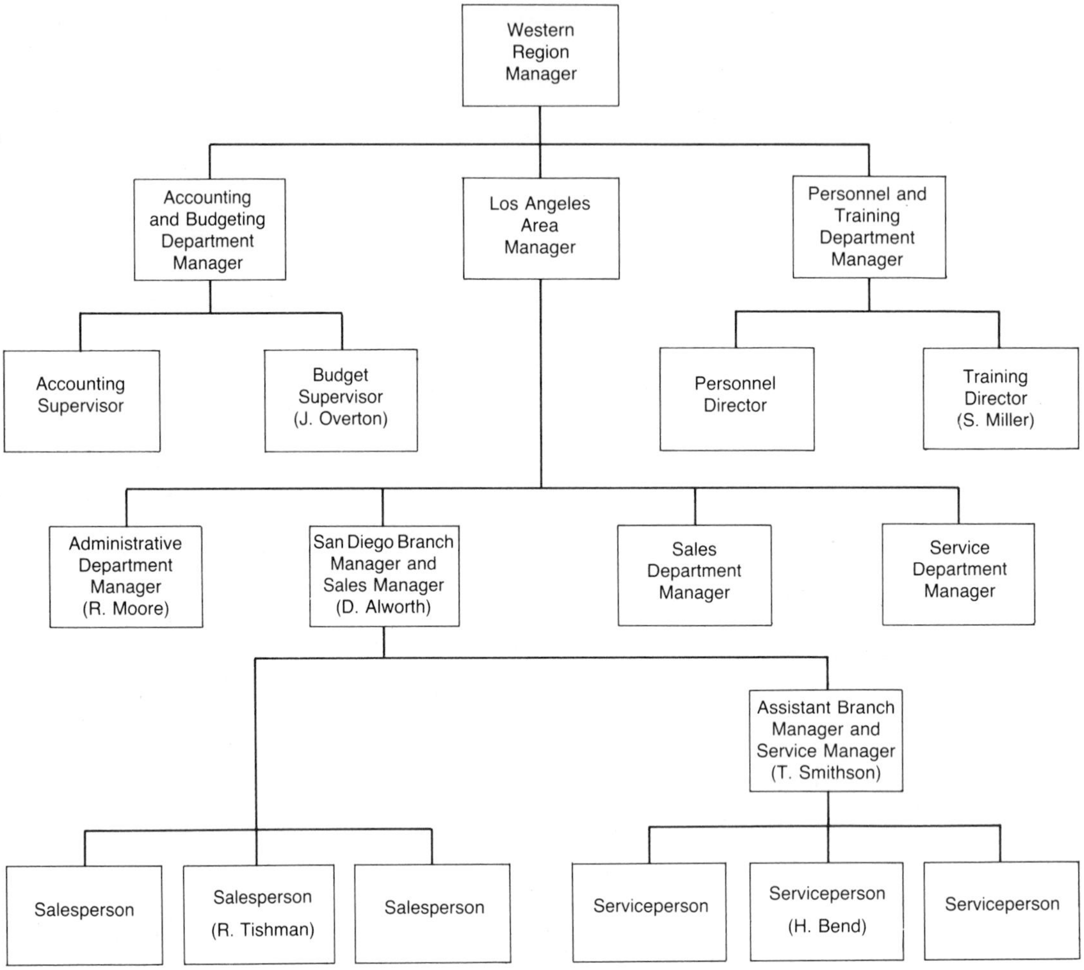

3–20. *A BOOKKEEPING DEPARTMENT*

Linda Fry is the supervisor for the bookkeeping department of Medford Bank and Trust. The department processes 10,000 to 15,000 checks and related items daily. Six clerical employees perform this work under Fry's direct supervision.

The sequence of events in preparing canceled checks for processing by the bookkeeping department is as follows:

1. Checks are processed through the proof department where the dollar amount is microencoded onto the check and a record of the transaction is input to computer records.

2. Computer printouts for the daily check processing activities are printed overnight. The printout, along with the canceled checks, arrives at the bookkeeping department at the beginning of each workday.

Specific operations within the bookkeeping department include the following:

- A sample of payor signatures on the checks is verified for authenticity.
- All checks over $1,000 are examined for an endorsement.
- All check errors are identified and appropriate special handling provisions are completed.
- All stop-payment checks are identified and reversed out of the computer record.
- Insufficient fund checks are identified and reversed out of the computer records. The check is returned to the endorser and appropriate charges are made to the customer's account.
- Questions from customers and creditors concerning check verification, account balance, and collected balance are answered via telephone conversations.

To facilitate control and performance within the bookkeeping department, authority and decision making reside with Fry. She assigns duties and responsibilities to the clerical workers and carefully reviews the performance of her employees. The employees function best when there are specific guidelines and directions for a particular job and when the lines of authority are clear.

Required:

a. How would you characterize Fry's position? At what level of decision-making activity does it exist?

b. Identify the decision problems encountered in the bookkeeping department. Would you say that these are unstructured, semistructured, or structured decisions?

c. Which kind of information system would satisfy the needs for information in her department?

(CMA Adapted)

Chapter 4

Systems Tools

Learning Objectives:

1. To understand some techniques for reviewing, analyzing, and developing accounting information systems.
2. To know how to use some tools for documenting accounting information systems.
3. To acquire some tools for managing accounting information system development projects.
4. To discover some techniques for conducting interviews.

INTRODUCTION

As an accountant, you will participate in project teams that design and implement accounting systems. You will also review these systems when performing internal or independent audits. This chapter presents some useful techniques for performing these tasks, including flowcharts, other forms of system documentation, project management tools, and interviews.

FLOWCHARTING

Charts are widely used by auditors and systems analysts because they concisely summarize ideas that may require many words to express. One of the most useful forms is the flowchart, which describes the relationships among sequential processes. There are a variety of flowcharts, including system, program, and

ILLUSTRATION 4–1 Basic Flowcharting Symbols

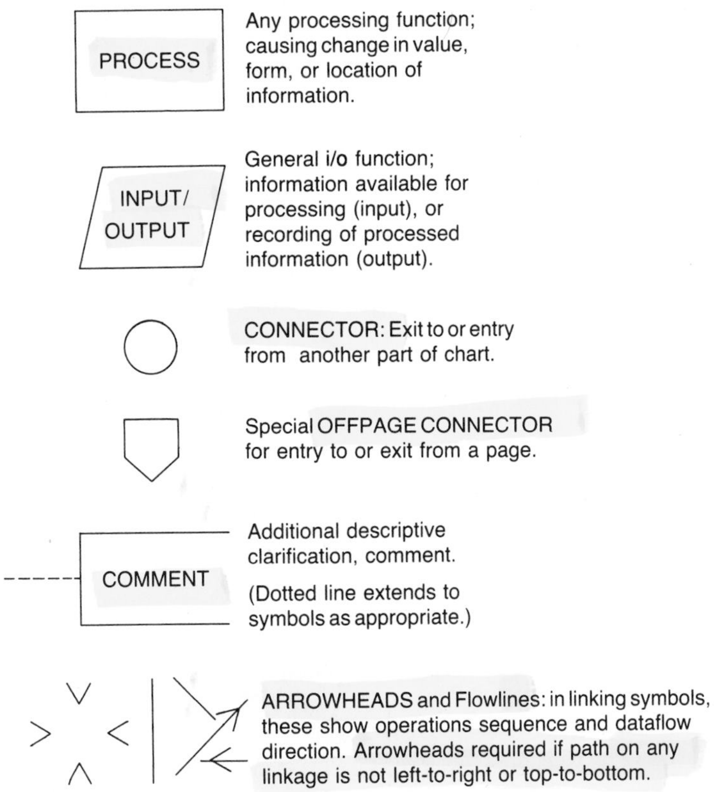

document flowcharts. Before studying some of these, you should first become acquainted with the standard flowchart symbols.

Standard Flowchart Symbols

For most purposes, accountants use standard flowchart symbols recommended by the American National Standards Institute (ANSI), the International Organization for Standardization (ISO), and International Business Machines Corporation (IBM). The symbols are limited in number and yet broad enough to describe most systems. There are three kinds of symbols: basic, programming, and systems.

Basic symbols are flexible in their applications and are important to know because they are used frequently. You can use them with any of the programming or systems symbols. Illustration 4–1 explains the five basic flowchart symbols.

ILLUSTRATION 4–2 Programming Symbols

A decision or switching-type operation that determines which of a number of alternative paths followed.

Instruction modification to change program—set a switch, modify an index register, initialize a routine.

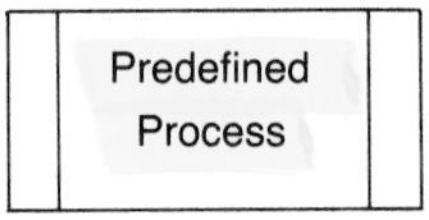

One or more named operations or program steps specified in a subroutine or another set of flowcharts.

A terminal point in a flowchart start, stop, halt, delay or interrupt; may show exit from a closed subroutine.

Illustration 4–2 shows the symbols related to programming. Programmers use them, along with the basic symbols, to describe the logic of computer programs. Accountants see these four programming symbols when reviewing program documentation for accounting systems.

The third kind are systems symbols, which accountants use to document reviews of internal control and to describe the operations of a proposed information system. Although some basic or programming symbols are interchangeable with certain systems symbols, the latter are more specific in their meanings. For example, the *input/output* symbol, a basic symbol, may signify any form of computer output. You may properly use a *document*, a *display*, or a *magnetic tape* systems symbol instead. Good flowcharting technique is to use the more specific representation whenever possible. Illustration 4–3 contains 13 systems symbols.

Study these standard flowchart symbols until you can recognize them. They have many applications throughout this book. The four kinds of flowcharts that accountants use are presented on the following pages.

ILLUSTRATION 4–3 Systems Flowcharting Symbols

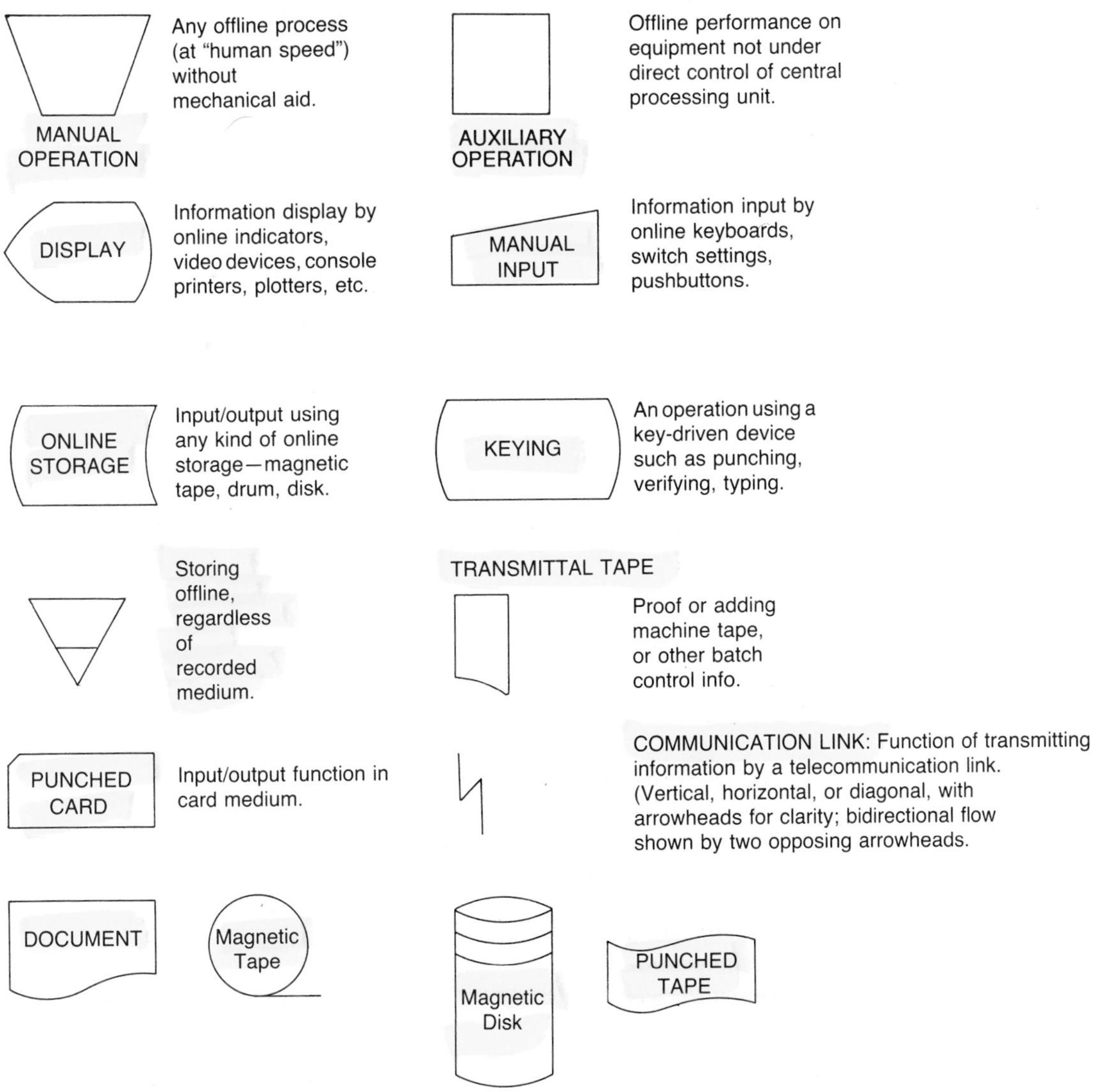

System Flowcharts

A system flowchart is a pictorial representation that shows the relationships between processes. Flowlines represent the sequences of processes, and other symbols represent the inputs and outputs to a process. Accountants use system flowcharts to describe the computerized processes, manual operations, and inputs and outputs of an application system.

A properly drawn system flowchart alternately uses two kinds of symbols. A symbol representing an operation, such as the *process, manual operation,* or *auxiliary operation* symbol, is preceded by a symbol showing the input to the operation. It is followed by another symbol for the output. This output may be an input to another operation. Thus, the system flowchart contains alternate layers of data identification and operation identification. In this way the flowchart specifies each process in the system and the inputs and outputs for the process. The direction of flow in a flowchart should proceed from top to bottom and from left to right.

Illustration 4–4 contains a well-drawn system flowchart that depicts part of an accounts receivable application. It begins with a *manual input* symbol. This shows the input of individual sales transactions to a computer program depicted by a *process* symbol. The output of the process is a computer file represented by the *online storage* symbol. This is the input to the next process. The last process, update customer master file, has two inputs and three outputs.

Program Flowcharts

A system flowchart represents each computer program in an accounting application by the *process* symbol and its accompanying verbal identification. Although this provides a high-level description of a system, it does not describe how individual computer programs work. Computer programmers do this by drawing program flowcharts.

A program flowchart shows in detail each processing step of a computer program. Similar to a system flowchart, a program flowchart uses flowlines to show the sequence of these steps. The lines proceed from top to bottom and left to right across the page. A *terminal* programming symbol both starts and stops the flow. Complete documentation for an accounting system includes program flowcharts for all programs identified on the system flowchart. Often each program consists of several modules, or segments. In this case, there is a flowchart for each module.

Illustration 4–5 shows a flowchart for one program from Illustration 4–4. It is the update customer master file program, which posts sales transactions to customers' accounts in the accounts receivable subsidiary records. This program reads one sales transaction from a transaction file containing records of all sales. It next reads the master file containing customer accounts until it finds the account number of the customer receiving the sale. The program adds the amount of the

ILLUSTRATION 4–4 A System Flowchart

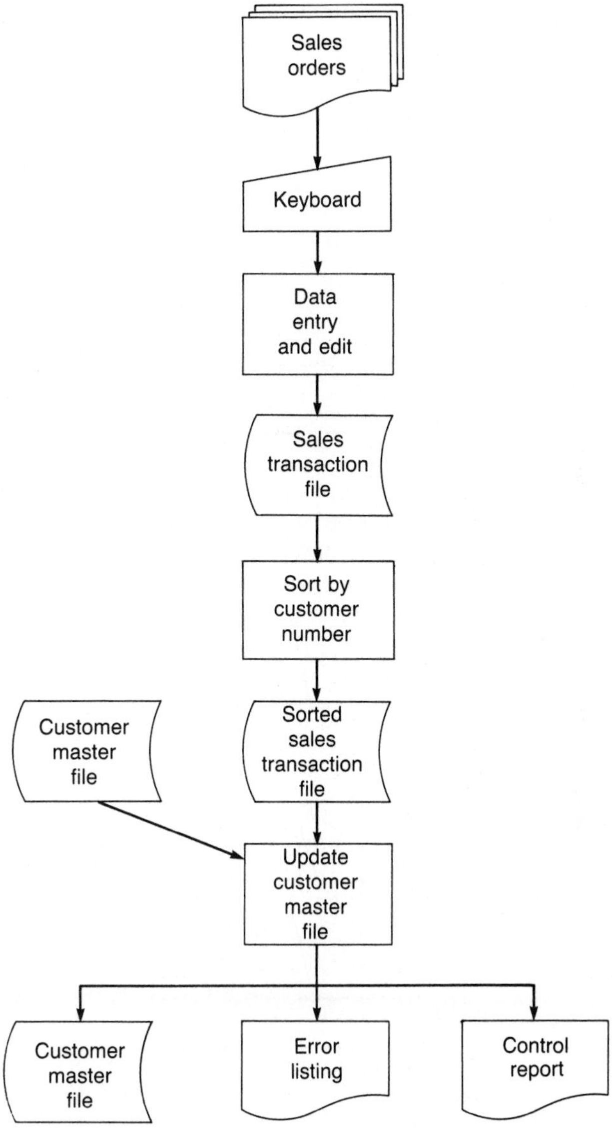

ILLUSTRATION 4–5 A Program Flowchart

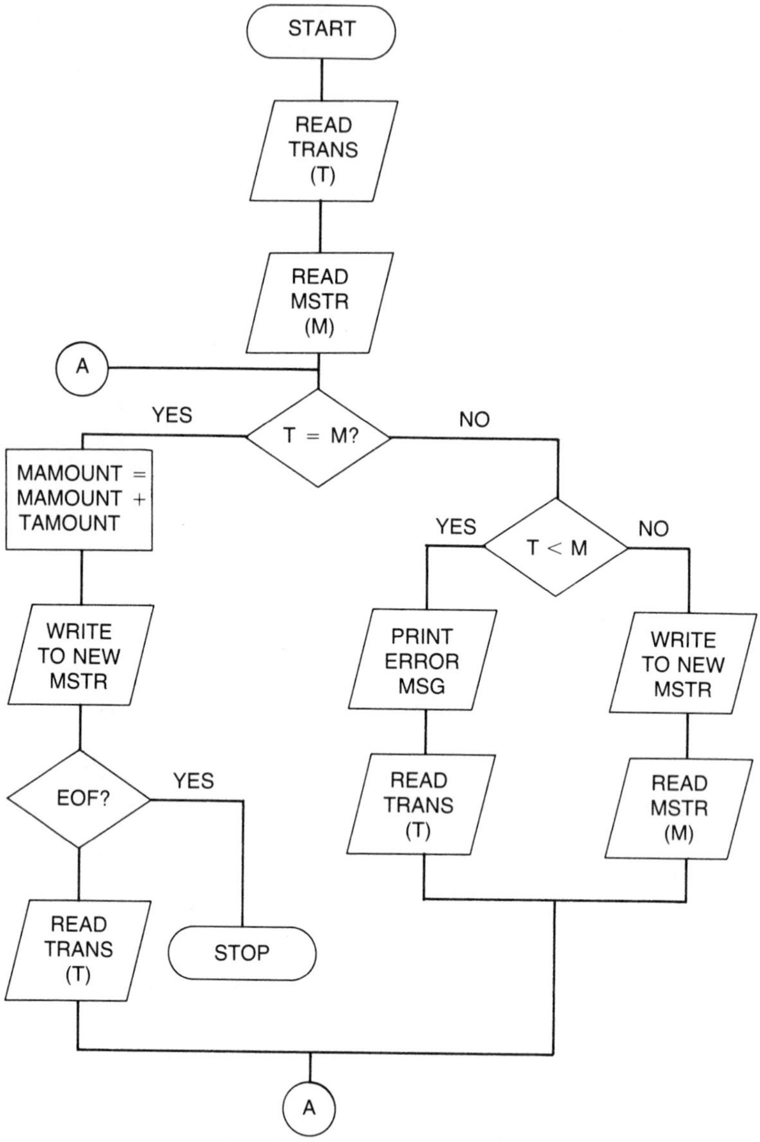

sale to the customer's outstanding balance; then it processes the next sales transaction in the same way. When all transactions are recorded, the program stops.

Accountants may examine program flowcharts when evaluating the internal control of a computer-based system. Sometimes accountants also program a system. In this case, they draw flowcharts to describe how their programs work. Another flowchart accountants use frequently is the document flowchart.

Document Flowcharts

While a system flowchart shows the flow of data between processes, a document flowchart emphasizes the flow of documents between organizational units. Auditors use them when documenting a client's internal control procedures. Systems analysts also use them to describe noncomputerized procedures when designing a new system.

When drawing a document flowchart, divide the page into columns separated by vertical lines. Each column represents an organizational unit, such as a department, office, or employee. An operations symbol within a column indicates that the unit performs an operation. When a document moves from one department to another, the flowchart shows this by a flowline connecting the document symbol in each department. Flowlines start in the upper-left corner of the page and proceed down and to the right.

Illustration 4–6 contains a document flowchart showing procedures to accept and fill a sales request from a customer. The order department receives the customer's order; from it they make four copies of an internal document, the sales order. These are sent to the shipping department, which includes copy 4 as a packing list with the goods when shipped. Copy 2 of the sales order returns to the order department, and copy 3 goes into offline storage. This is usually a filing cabinet. Copy 1 goes to the billing department, which prepares a three-part invoice. Invoice copy 1 is mailed to the customer; invoice copies 2 and 3 go to the accounts receivable department.

A document flowchart is most useful when describing noncomputerized procedures. Both document flowcharts and system flowcharts are necessary to adequately describe a computer-based accounting system. For example, in the sales order entry system of Illustration 4–6, accounts receivable receives two copies of the invoice and records the sale in the customer's account. If they use a noncomputerized system, they record the sale on a ledger page. If they use a computerized system, the system flowchart of Illustration 4–4 describes a possible set of procedures.

OTHER SYSTEMS DOCUMENTATION

Besides flowcharts, accountants use other forms of documentation to describe accounting information systems. They include data flow diagrams, systems charts, structure charts, and decision tables.

Data Flow Diagrams

Data flow diagrams use a small number of simple symbols to represent the flow of data between processes, files, and external destinations. They differ from flowcharts because they emphasize the flow of data rather than the flow of documents or records containing data. In other words, data flow diagrams show

ILLUSTRATION 4–6 A Document Flowchart

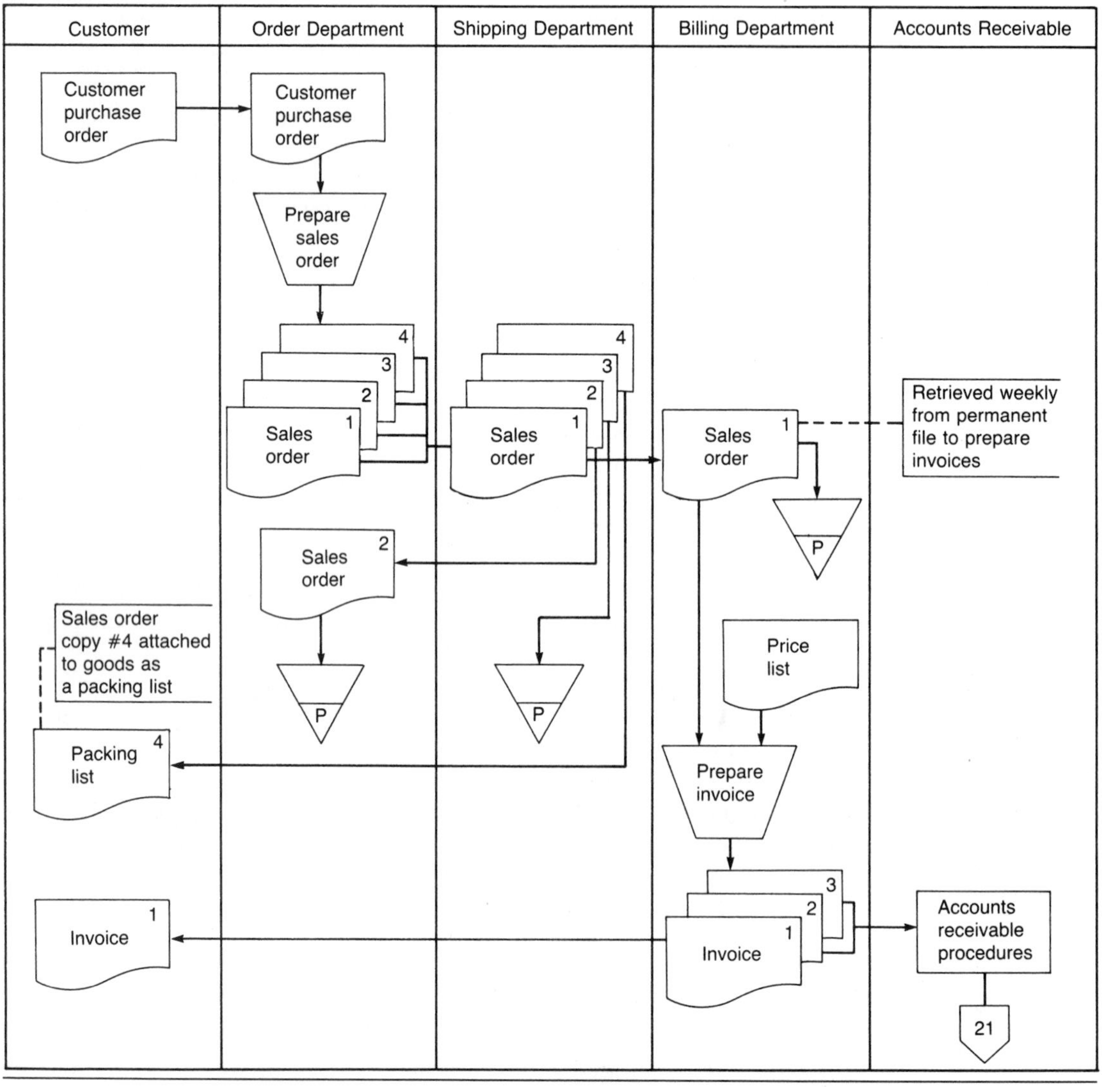

logical rather than physical flows. And because fewer symbols are involved, people using data flow diagrams must be more careful in selecting verbal descriptions to communicate their ideas.

Data flow diagrams are useful for describing data flows at varying levels. For example, a systems analyst using this technique can show data flows between organizational units, between individuals within an unit, between

ILLUSTRATION 4–7 A Data Flow Diagram

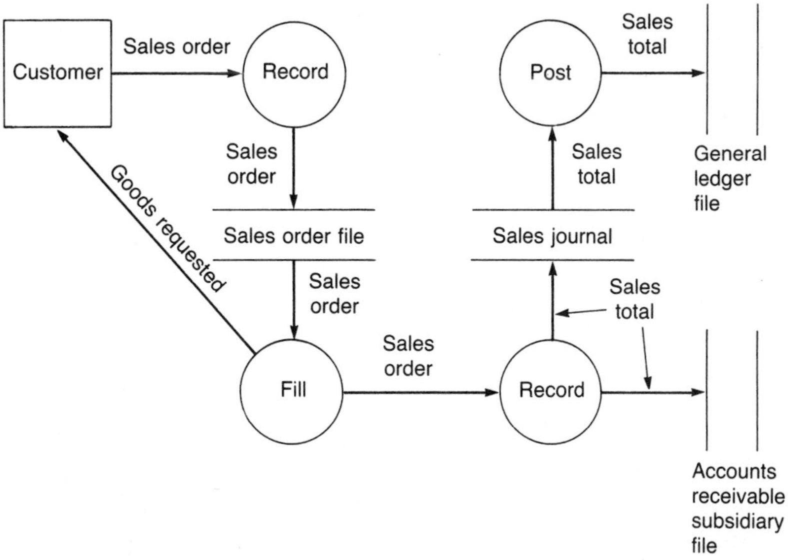

computer programs within a system, or between modules within a computer program.

Data flow diagrams exist in different forms. In the DeMarco-Yourdon symbol set, a circle represents a process, a square indicates an external destination for data (such as a customer, a supplier, or an employee), a rectangle that is open on two sides represents a data file, and arrows represent the flow of data. Each flow begins at a destination or file, goes through a process, and terminates at a destination or file.

Illustration 4–7 shows a data flow diagram for a sales order entry application. In this diagram, a customer's order for goods is recorded in a sales order file. After an order is filled, it is recorded in a sales journal and an accounts receivable subsidiary file. Posting to the general ledger occurs from the sales journal.

Data flow diagrams differ from flowcharts in several ways. Although each uses symbols to represent processes, data flow diagrams do not show the *sequence* of processes, as do flowcharts. Thus a single data flow diagram may show several processes operating in parallel. As seen in Illustration 4–7, recording and filling orders may take place simultaneously.

Furthermore, in a data flow diagram, the arrows connecting processes with destinations or files indicate nothing about the timing of the processes. A single data flow diagram may contain processes that occur daily (such as recording and filling customer orders in Illustration 4–7), or monthly (posting them to a general

ILLUSTRATION 4–8 A System Chart

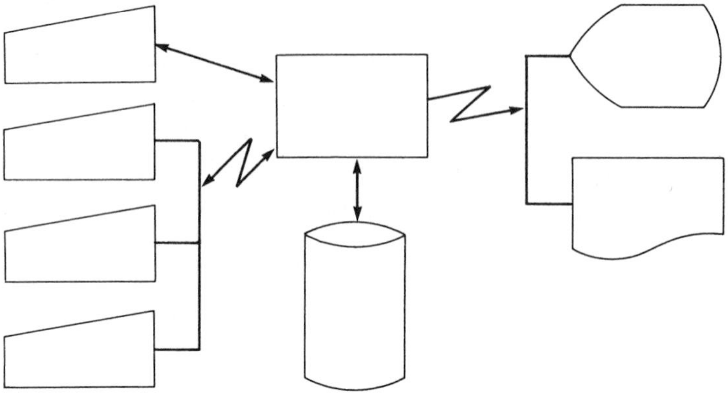

ledger). Finally, because data flow diagrams do not have symbols representing decisions, they cannot explicitly represent the *if* occurrences or looping operations that are common in flowcharts.

System Charts

A system chart provides a graphic representation of the equipment configuration of a computer system. By convention, a system chart shows input devices to the left and output devices to the right. The example in Illustration 4–8 shows input by three remote and one local keyboard data entry devices. The outputs are a video display and the *document* symbol, which indicates a printer. This system chart uses the *process* symbol to represent the central processing unit, and the *magnetic disk* symbol for an information storage device. A system chart for an actual system also contains verbal descriptions of the equipment.

Structure Charts

Many companies develop programs in modules. Each computer program is a module composed of a set of smaller modules. Individuals develop and test each one individually and then test all of them together. When using a modular approach to program development, many organizations use structure charts to document the programs.

A structure chart identifies each of the modules making up the program and shows the hierarchy between them. This hierarchy exists because a high-level module may cause the execution of one or more lower-level modules. On the structure chart, each module is represented by a rectangle. The hierarchical

ILLUSTRATION 4–9 A Structure Chart

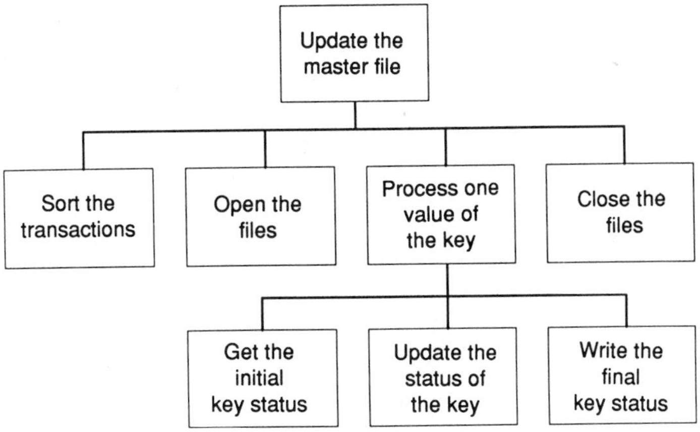

relationship between modules is shown by the levels on the chart. Modules execute in sequence from top to bottom and from left to right. Illustration 4–9 contains an example of a structure chart.

Decision Tables

Another useful systems tool is the preparation of decision tables. These provide a concise way to summarize outcomes of complex decisions. Decision tables offer advantages over flowcharts when there are a large number of alternatives; however, they do not disclose the sequences.

A decision table is a matrix divided into three sections. The left half of the decision table contains two sections, a list of *conditions* and a list of *actions*. The right half contains several columns. Each column represents a *rule*, which is a combination of conditions and actions. Each rule shows the action taken whenever a combination of conditions occurs. An accountant could use a flowchart to show the information contained in a decision table; however, the flowchart is difficult to follow when a large number of conditions and actions are present.

To illustrate the use of decision tables, consider a common decision in an inventory application.[1] In a computer-based system, either a clerk or a computer

[1]James I. Morgan, "Decision Tables," *Management Services,* January–February 1965, pp. 13–18.

decides whether to place an order to replenish inventory. For each inventory item, the following six conditions determine the action taken:

1. Is the current inventory level below the reorder point?
2. Was the item sold during the previous month?
3. Has the inventory reached a critical point below the reorder point?
4. Is the item currently being produced?
5. Will the item be sold in the future?
6. Are sales of the item profitable?

Illustration 4–10 shows a flowchart of this decision. It contains six decision symbols, one representing each condition. It also contains two process symbols, one for each possible action. You can see how awkward the flowchart is; compare it to the decision table in Illustration 4–11.

This decision table shows the six conditions in the upper-left portion, called the *condition stub*. The two actions are in the lower-left portion, the *action stub*. The upper-right portion of the decision table, known as the *condition entry* contains seven rules. For each rule, if a condition is present, the intersection of the row and column contains a Y. If not, it contains an N. The lower-right portion, the *action entry*, shows the action resulting from each condition. Each rule in the decision table corresponds to one logic path through the flowchart.

Within some combinations of conditions, when certain conditions are irrelevant to the decision the condition entries for these combinations are blank. For example, only one condition is relevant to rule 1. Whenever the inventory level exceeds the reorder point, no order is placed regardless of any other condition. The decision table indicates this by leaving blank the rows for the other conditions in the condition entry. By custom, the simplest rule is listed first and the most complex last, producing a triangular shape for the contents of the condition entry.

When should decision tables be used? Whenever there are more than three conditions, a decision table is valuable. It summarizes the logic more clearly and concisely than a flowchart, making it easier for someone to identify errors or omissions. The blanks in the condition entry clearly identify irrelevant combinations of conditions not readily found in a flowchart.

When developing accounting systems, many programmers and analysts use both decision tables and flowcharts. They create the decision table first to ensure that all conditions are considered. They then draw the flowchart showing the sequence in which conditions are evaluated. This approach assures that all possibilities are described in complex situations.

Accountants use flowcharts and decision tables when developing new systems and when reviewing old ones. Systems analysts use data flow diagrams and structure charts when developing systems, and auditors review them during an audit. The next section describes Gantt charts and network diagrams, two tools used to manage large system development projects.

ILLUSTRATION 4–10 Flowchart for an Inventory Decision

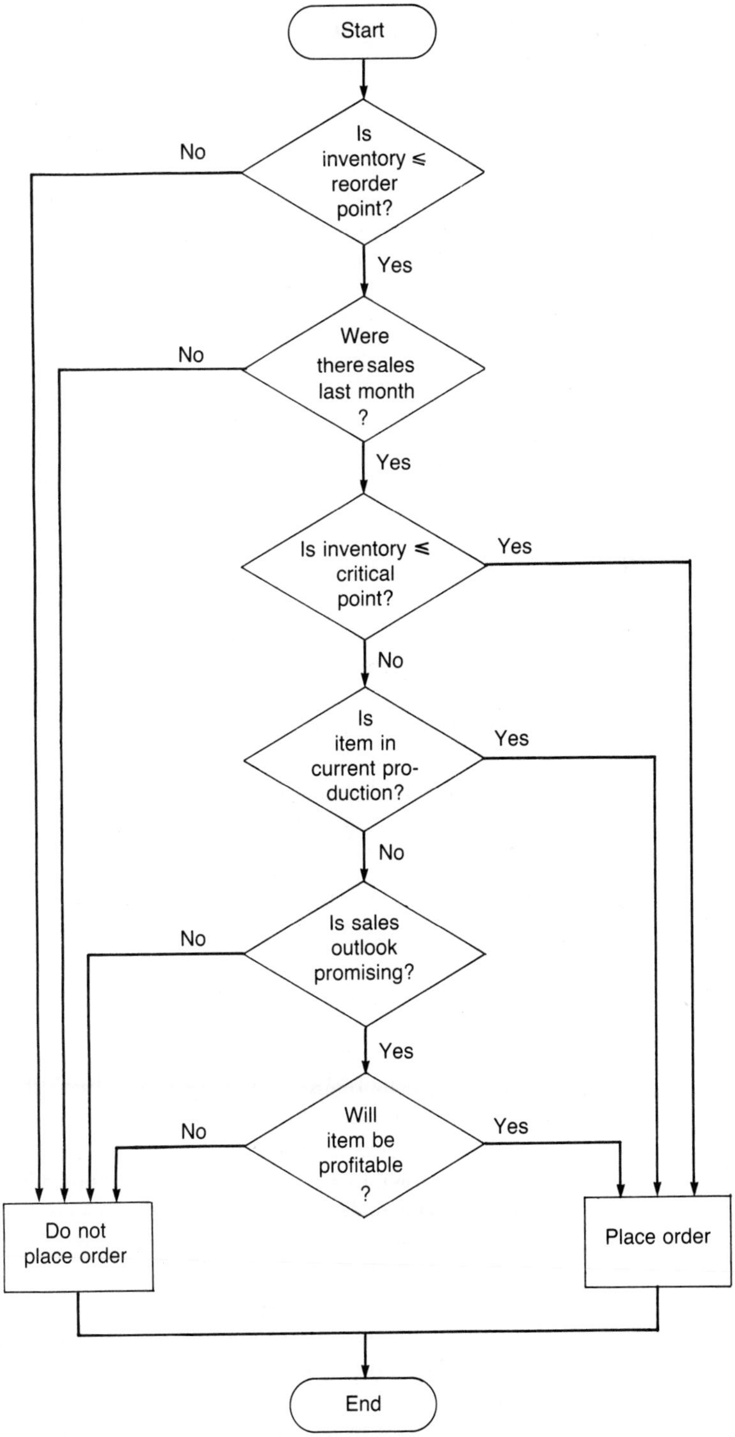

ILLUSTRATION 4–11 A Decision Table

	Inventory-Replenishment Decision Rules						
	Rule 1	*Rule 2*	*Rule 3*	*Rule 4*	*Rule 5*	*Rule 6*	*Rule 7*
Conditions:							
1. Inventory ≤ reorder point	N	Y	Y	Y	Y	Y	Y
2. Sales last month		N	Y	Y	Y	Y	Y
3. Inventory ≤ critical point			Y	N	N	N	N
4. Item currently in production				Y	N	N	N
5. Sales outlook promising					N	Y	Y
6. Profit from sales satisfactory						N	Y
Action:							
1. Place production order			X	X			X
2. Do not place production order	X	X			X	X	

PROJECT MANAGEMENT TOOLS

A successful system is one that is completed within a reasonable period of time. System development projects require from a few months to a few years to complete; they almost always require more time than originally expected. The manager in charge of a development project is evaluated by whether it is implemented on time and within budgeted costs. Project management tools help to accomplish these goals.

Two project management tools that aid in the timely completion of development projects are Gantt charts and network diagrams. The following example project will help you understand how these techniques work.

An Example Project

Developing a new accounting system consists of many different tasks and requires coordinated efforts by many people. Project management techniques are especially helpful in managing this process.

Project management tools require an analyst to divide the project into distinct activities. Each activity has measurable outputs and a clearly defined beginning and end. The analyst also estimates the time required to complete each task, and determines the sequences that they follow. A time budget summarizes this information.

Illustration 4–12 contains a time budget for the activities of the implementation phase of the system development life cycle, which is described in a later chapter. For now, concentrate on learning the project management tools.

This system development project requires 12 implementation activities. Activity A, establish policies, requires an estimated one month from start to

ILLUSTRATION 4–12 Time Budget for Implementation

	Activity	*Estimated Duration in Months*	*Preceding Activity*
A	Establish policies	1	—
B	Select personnel	3	A
C	Prepare user manuals	3	A
D	Train personnel	1½	B, C
E	Develop programming standards	½	A
F	Code programs	5½	E
G	Test systems	1	F, J
H	Convert files	½	G
I	Prepare site	2	A
J	Install equipment	1	I
K	Parallel operations	3	D, H
L	User review and sign-off	½	K

finish. Because it has no preceding activity, it can begin at any time. Activity D, train personnel, requires one and one-half months and cannot begin until activities B and C are complete. Illustration 4–12 shows the estimated times and preceding activities for each of the other 10. Analysts use a Gantt chart to manage the implementation phase of this project.

Gantt Charts

A Gantt chart is a form of graph developed by Henry L. Gantt in the early 1900s. On a Gantt chart, the horizontal axis represents elapsed time and the vertical axis contains a list of activities. A horizontal line connects the beginning and ending times for each activity. The chart schedules the activities so that each begins after the end of all preceding ones.

Illustration 4–13 contains a Gantt chart for the implementation activities of Illustration 4–12. This chart shows that activity A, *establish policies,* is completed before beginning activities B, C, E, and I. The last activity, *user review and sign-off,* ends after 12 months have elapsed.

Gantt charts are easy to develop and to interpret. They show the precedence of activities more clearly than time budgets and indicate the total elapsed time required for the project. For these reasons they are widely used to manage system development projects.

An organization can alter the duration of a project by changing the resources allocated to it. For example, by assigning more programmers to activity F, *code programs,* the project manager decreases the time required for this activity. This

ILLUSTRATION 4–13 A Gantt Chart

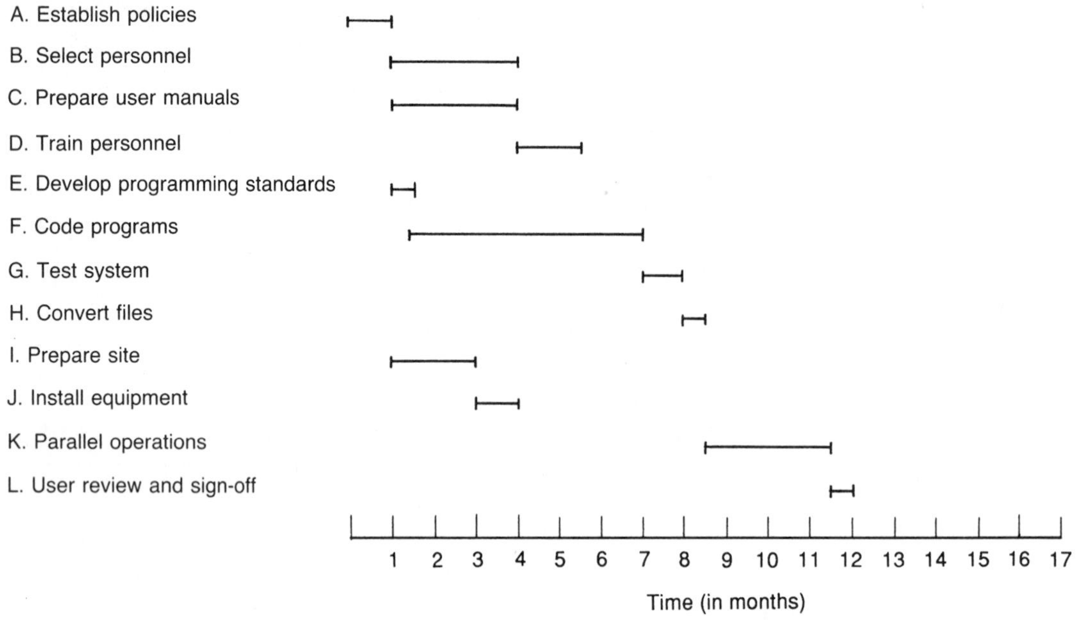

possibly decreases the implementation time for the system. However, from the Gantt chart the manager cannot determine if this would occur. Other project management tools using network techniques provide this information.

Network Diagrams

Widely used network techniques include PERT and CPM. These methods for managing large projects are similar and were developed about the same time. The United States Navy created Program Evaluation and Review Technique (PERT) and first applied it to development of a missile. E. I. duPont de Nemours created Critical Path Method (CPM) to manage the construction of a chemical plant. Many variations of these two techniques now exist, and computer software packages to implement them are widely available.

These approaches represent the project as a network of nodes and arcs. Using PERT, an arc represents an activity of the project and nodes signify the beginning or end of an activity. The sequence of the arcs shows the sequence of the activities. Labels identify durations, starting times, and stopping times for activities. A CPM network is similar, except that nodes represent activities. Illustration 4–14 contains a PERT diagram for the activities of Illustration 4–12.

ILLUSTRATION 4–14 A PERT Network Diagram

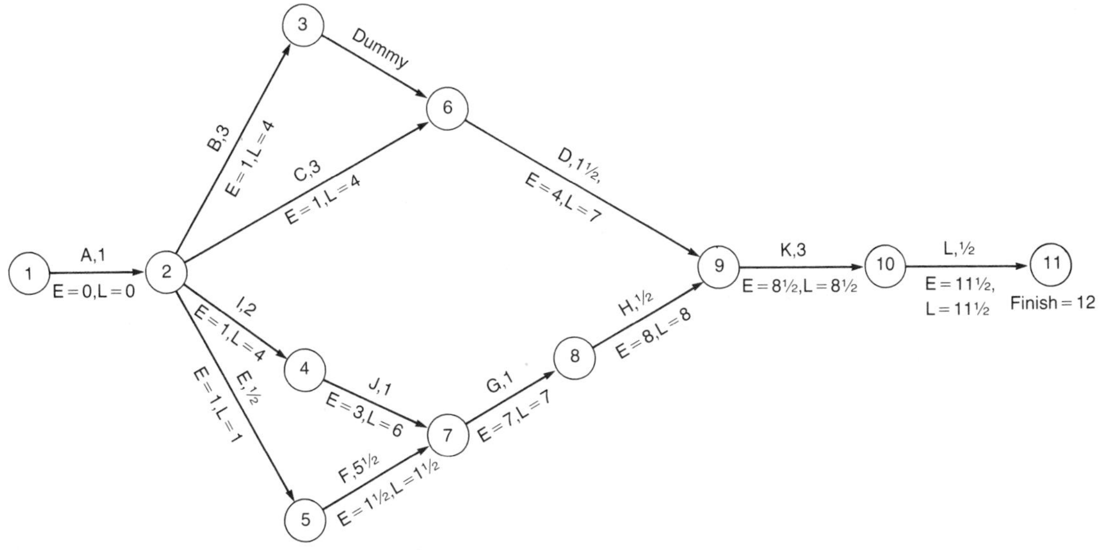

Most computer programs implementing PERT represent each arc as an arrow and identify it by its beginning and ending nodes. They number the nodes so that the node at the point of an arrow is always higher than the one at the tail. This is how you specify the sequence of activities to the PERT program. In Illustration 4–14, the arc representing activity A begins with node 1 and ends at node 2. Its estimated duration is one month.

Label E identifies an activity's earliest possible start time. Label L shows the latest possible start time without delaying the project's completion. For activity D, *train personnel,* the early start time is the fourth month of the project. If this activity begins later than 7 months into the project, the project will not be completed within 12 months.

The difference between the early start time (E) and the late start time (L) for an activity is its *slack*. An activity's slack is the amount of additional time the activity can require without delaying the project. For activity D in Illustration 4–12, the slack is three months. This activity can require up to four and one-half months to complete without delaying the project.

The major advantage of network techniques is that they identify the *critical path,* which is the sequence of project activities that requires the longest elapsed time. These are the activities that determine the duration of the project. If any activity on the critical path is delayed, the entire project is delayed.

You can easily identify the activities on the critical path because they are the ones that have no slack. For these activities, the early start time E equals the late start time L. In the PERT diagram of Illustration 4–14, the critical path contains activities A-E-F-G-H-K-L. The total of the durations for these activities is 12 months, which equals the duration of the project.

Network diagrams are useful in managing system development projects because they enable the project manager to predict the effect of reallocating resources. The manager may transfer resources from an activity with slack to one on the critical path. This often decreases the time required to complete the project. In the implementation phase example, the project manager may reassign personnel from activity D, *train personnel,* to activity F, *code programs.* This decreases the duration for activity F, shortens the critical path, and decreases the time required for the project.

For complex projects, network techniques are difficult to implement without the aid of a computer. Fortunately, software programs that implement them are readily available. Illustration 4–15 shows the output of a PERT computer program used to analyze the project of Illustration 4–12.

INTERVIEWS

Interviewing is an important skill for any accountant to develop; it is especially important for auditors and accountants involved in system development. Auditors interview client employees while conducting reviews during an audit. Members of a development team interview users of the system when evaluating existing systems and when identifying requirements for a new one.

Being a good interviewer requires practice. It is primarily a listening activity, but an interviewer must know when to ask questions, when to politely halt a digression by the person interviewed, and when to encourage the person to talk more. Advance preparation of questions to ask makes the task easier. There are practices you can adopt that will make interviewing easier even if you have not done it before. Illustration 4–16 summarizes some good interview techniques.

SUMMARY

This chapter describes seven techniques for developing and reviewing accounting systems. They are flowcharting, data flow diagrams, system charts, structure charts, decision tables, Gantt charts, and network diagrams.

Flowcharts provide graphic representations of sequential processes. System flowcharts summarize the processes of a system and show their inputs and outputs. Program flowcharts describe in detail how computerized processes work, showing the logic of computer programs or modules. Document flowcharts are useful when describing noncomputerized procedures. A data flow diagram shows flows of data between processes, files, and destinations. A system chart uses flowchart symbols to represent the components of a comput-

ILLUSTRATION 4–15 Output of a PERT Computer Program

PROJECT: System Implementation
DATE: 01-30-1990

No.	Act	Description	Begin Event	End Event	Optimist Time	Likely Time	Pessimist Time
1	A	Establish Policies	1	2	1.00	1.00	1.00
2	B	Select Personnel	2	3	3.00	3.00	3.00
3	C	Prepare User Manuals	2	6	3.00	3.00	3.00
4	E	Develop Prog Stds	2	5	0.50	0.50	0.50
5	I	Prepare Site	2	4	2.00	2.00	2.00
6	M	Dummy Activity	3	6	0.00	0.00	0.00
7	J	Install Equipment	4	7	1.00	1.00	1.00
8	F	Code Programs	5	7	5.50	5.50	5.50
9	D	Train Personnel	6	9	1.50	1.50	1.50
10	G	Test Systems	7	8	1.00	1.00	1.00
11	H	Convert Files	8	9	0.50	0.50	0.50
12	K	Parallel Operations	9	10	3.00	3.00	3.00
13	L	Review & Sign Off	10	11	0.50	0.50	0.50

Project: System Implementation

Act	Description	Expected Time	Early Start	Early Fin.	Last Start	Last Fin.	Slack Time
A	Establish Policies	1.00	0.00	1.00	0.00	1.00	0.00
B	Select Personnel	3.00	1.00	4.00	4.00	7.00	3.00
C	Prepare User Manuals	3.00	1.00	4.00	4.00	7.00	3.00
E	Develop Prog Stds	0.50	1.00	1.50	1.00	1.50	0.00
I	Prepare Site	2.00	1.00	3.00	4.00	6.00	3.00
M	Dummy Activity	0.00	4.00	4.00	7.00	7.00	3.00
J	Install Equipment	1.00	3.00	4.00	6.00	7.00	3.00
F	Code Programs	5.50	1.50	7.00	1.50	7.00	0.00
D	Train Personnel	1.50	4.00	5.50	7.00	8.50	3.00
G	Test Systems	1.00	7.00	8.00	7.00	8.00	0.00
H	Convert Files	0.50	8.00	8.50	8.00	8.50	0.00
K	Parallel Operations	3.00	8.50	11.50	8.50	11.50	0.00
L	Review & Sign Off	0.50	11.50	12.00	11.50	12.00	0.00

CRITICAL PATH
A E F G H K L

Time of critical path
12.00

ILLUSTRATION 4–16 Good Interviewing Techniques

1. Make an appointment for the interview in advance. Employees you wish to interview appreciate this courtesy, and it makes your job easier.
2. Arrive for the interview on time. Thank the other person for taking time to talk to you.
3. Prepare a list of questions in advance. Keep this in front of you during the interview and take notes on the person's answers and comments. Questionnaires are useful for this purpose.
4. Dress appropriately for the interview. If the other person wears a suit, do the same. If he or she is attired for physical work, you should be more casual. Overdressing may intimidate the other person.
5. Ask direct questions and obtain answers to them. Often the person may digress, and you may have to return the discussion to the original question.
6. Be courteous and do not interrupt the other person. Sit at an angle with the person. Sitting directly in front may be interpreted as a confrontational position.
7. When finished, thank the person again. Request permission to ask additional questions later if needed.
8. After the interview, find a quiet place to review your notes. Elaborate on what you wrote, write other comments you remember that the person made, and write your conclusions. Transcribe any abbreviations you used during notetaking. These facts could be hard to remember later.

erized system. A structure chart shows relationships between modules in a computer program.

Decision tables summarize the outcomes of complex decisions involving many alternatives. They enable an auditor or analyst to examine the consequences of all alternatives but do not show sequences. For this reason, decision tables are frequently used with program flowcharts to describe complex situations.

Gantt charts and network diagrams are useful when managing system development projects. Gantt charts are easy to create and read but provide less information than network diagrams. Network methods such as PERT or CPM enable a project manager to reallocate resources to decrease the project's duration. They normally are implemented using computer software packages.

KEY TERMS

data flow diagram A diagram that shows the flow of data between processes, files, and external destinations.

decision table A matrix that summarizes the outcomes of complex decisions. It contains a list of conditions and a list of actions under each condition.

document flowchart A flowchart that emphasizes the flow of documents among organizational units.

flowchart A diagram showing the relationships between sequential processes.

Gantt chart A project management tool that represents a project by a graph. The length of an activity is represented by the length of that activity's line on the graph.

network techniques Project management tools that include PERT and CPM. They represent a project by a network of arcs and nodes. The sequences of the arcs show the sequences of the activities in the project.

program flow diagram A flowchart that shows in detail the logic steps within a computer program.

structure chart A diagram showing the hierarchy of the modules making up a computer program.

system chart A graphic representation of the equipment configuration of a computer system.

system flowchart A flowchart that describes the computerized processes, manual operations, inputs, and outputs of an application system.

APPENDIX

Control Flowcharts

Another tool for describing sequential processes is the control flowchart. It differs from a document flowchart because it emphasizes the internal controls affecting transactions. Like other flowcharts, control flowcharts trace transactions through manual and computerized processes. However, a control flowchart identifies those points in the flow where an internal control practice is applied to the transaction. For this reason, auditors call this technique *control point* flowcharting.

A control flowchart, like other document flowcharts, has a column for each organizational unit. But control flowcharts use a different set of symbols from the standard ones, as Illustration 4–17 shows.

Illustration 4–18 contains a control flowchart describing sales order entry procedures. Following these procedures, the order department receives a customer's request and uses it as a basis for preparing the four-part sales order. It then files the customer's order alphabetically. The four-part sales order goes to the shipping department, which ships the goods to the customer. Sales order copy 4 becomes a packing slip. The shipping department returns copy 2 to the order department, files copy 3 by date, and sends copy 1 to the billing department.

The billing department files the sales order temporarily. Each week it removes sales orders from this file, and for each one prepares a three-part invoice; it sends copy 1 to the customer and copies 2 and 3 to the accounting department.

Comparing this control flowchart with the document flowchart of Illustration 4–6, you see that the procedures are identical. However, examining the control flowchart discloses that all documents are prenumbered. This is an internal control measure that is not disclosed on the standard document flowchart. Control flowcharts for complex systems identify many such internal controls.

ILLUSTRATION 4–17 Control Flowchart Symbols

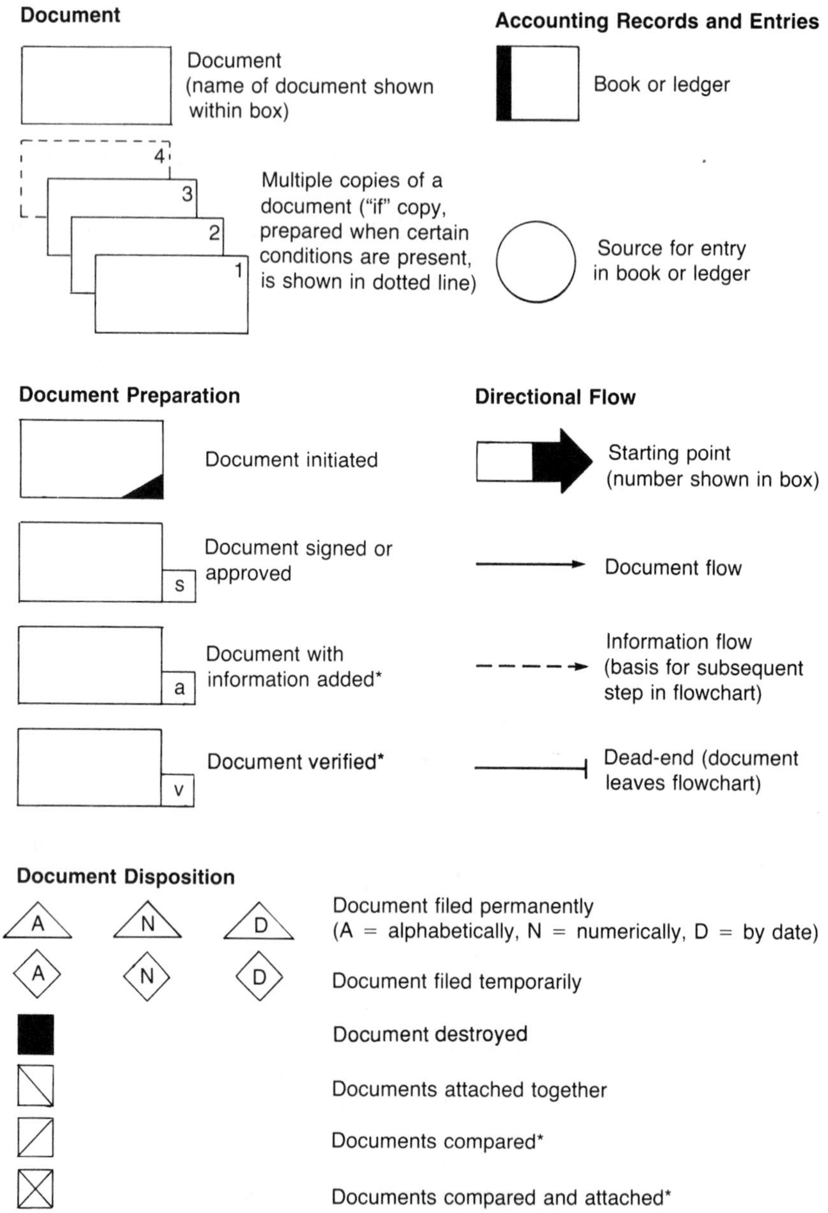

Source: Adapted from R. M. Skinner and R. K. Anderson, *Analytical Auditing: An Outline of the Flow Chart Approach to Audits* (Toronto: Pitman, 1966), except those shown with a * sign, which are extended by David H. Li. Reproduced with permission by the publisher.

ILLUSTRATION 4–18 A Control Flowchart

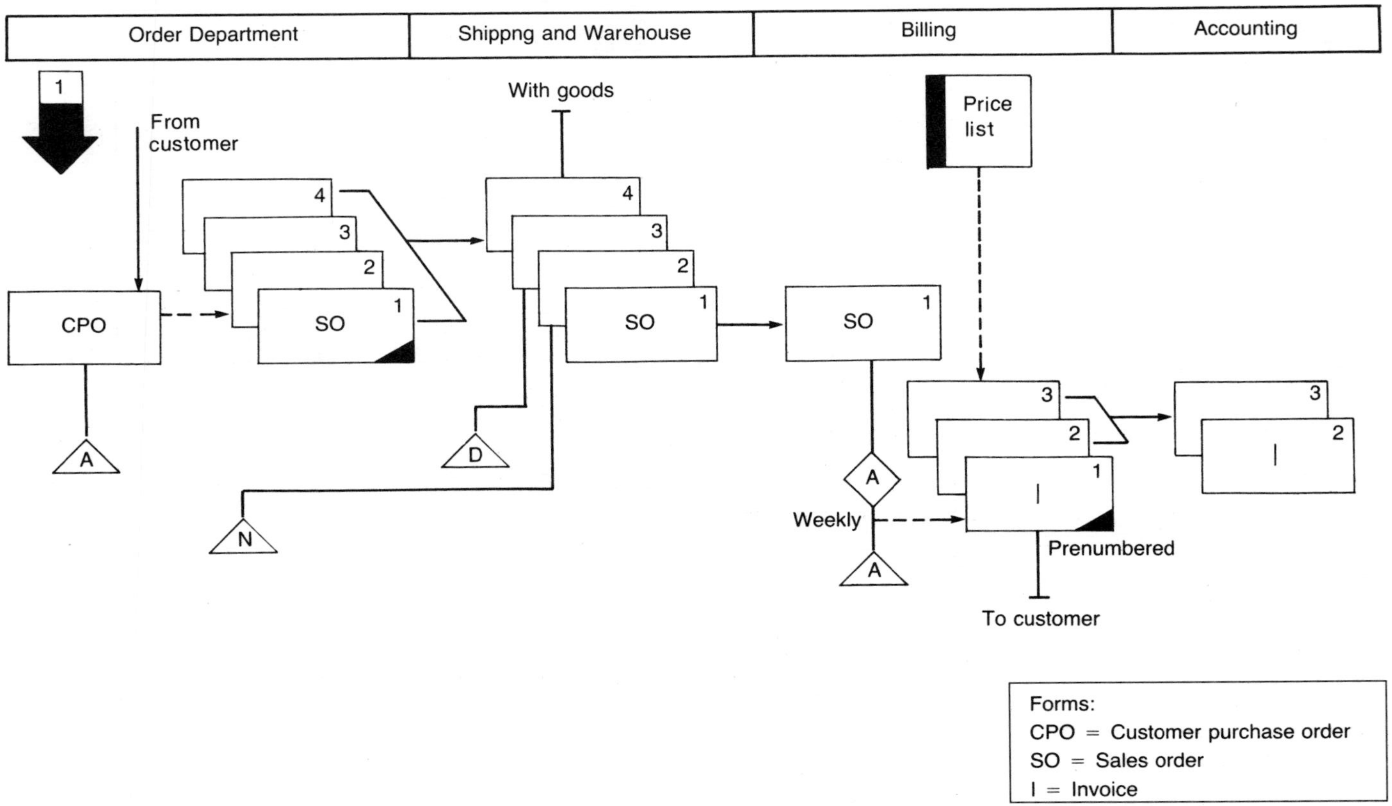

Source: R. M. Skinner and R. K. Anderson, *Analytical Auditing: An Outline of the Flow Chart Approach to Audits* (Toronto: Pitman, 1966), p. 111. Reproduced with permission by the publisher.

Because control flowcharts emphasize the controls in an accounting system, they are popular with auditors. When performing a review, an auditor may develop control flowcharts rather than document flowcharts to describe a client's system. Labeling control points enables the auditor to evaluate more easily the internal control strengths and weaknesses.

QUESTIONS

4–1. What are the distinctions between each of the following?
a. System chart
b. System flowchart
c. Program flowchart
d. Document flowchart
e. Data flow diagram

4–2. What are the alternating layers in a system flowchart?

4–3. The output from one operation has been omitted in Illustration 4–4. Can you identify what it is?

4–4. Why should an accountant know how to read and to draw:
a. A system chart?
b. A system flowchart?
c. A program flowchart?
d. A document flowchart?
e. A data flow diagram?

4–5. What advantages do control flowcharts have over document flowcharts?

4–6. What advantages do decision tables have over program flowcharts? What disadvantages?

4–7. Can you identify the difference between a Gantt chart and a network diagram? What is it?

4–8. How does a PERT network diagram differ from a CPM network diagram?

4–9. What does each of the following symbols represent? Identify each as a basic, a system, or a flowchart symbol.

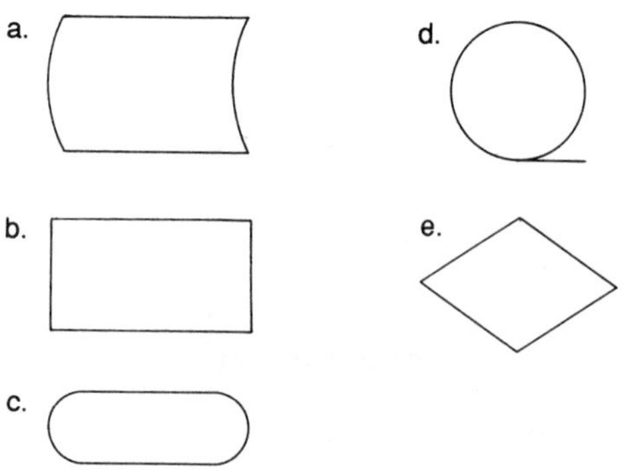

4–10. What are the counterparts of the following four document flowchart symbols using control flowchart symbols?

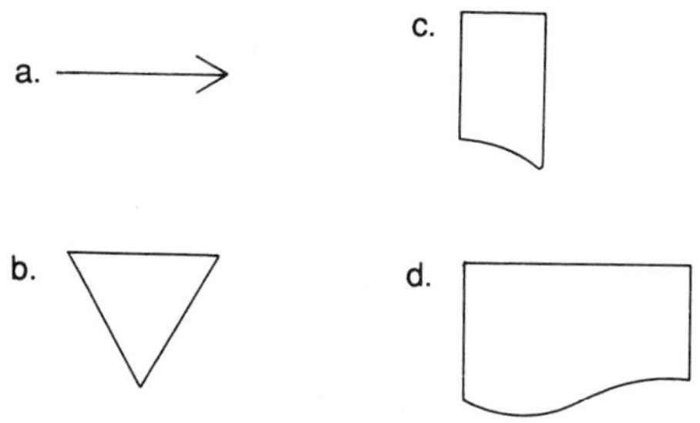

4–11. How do each of the following pairs of control flowchart symbols differ?

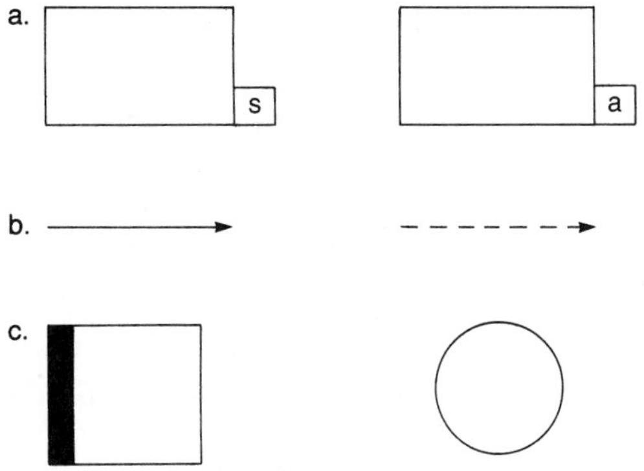

EXERCISES AND CASES

4–12. *SYSTEM FLOWCHART*

Illustration 4–4 contains a system flowchart. Redraw this flowchart using only the basic symbols. Which way of diagramming the process is more descriptive?

4–13. *GANTT CHART*

While reviewing an existing system, an accountant discovers the following document, entitled Project Analysis.

Activity	*Project Analysis Time in Weeks*	*Preceding Activity*
A	3	—
B	3	A
C	7	A
D	4	A
E	2	B
F	4	B
G	1	C,E
H	5	D

Required:

Prepare a Gantt chart for Project Analysis.

4–14. *NETWORK DIAGRAM*

The accountant's supervisor, after reviewing the solution to Exercise 4–13, wants to know how long Project Analysis requires for completion.

Required:

a. With the data given in Exercise 4–13 for Project Analysis, develop a PERT network diagram.
b. What is the earliest completion time for Project Analysis?
c. What is the earliest time that activity G can begin?

(CIA Adapted)

4–15. *SYSTEM FLOWCHART FOR CARD INPUT*

Abacus Corp. has a computer-based sales forecasting system, developed in the 1960s, that uses punch-card data entry. The procedures below are followed in their system:

a. Sales forecasts are submitted by salespersons.
b. Forecasts are keypunched into computer cards.
c. Computer cards are read into the computer and stored in a magnetic tape file.
d. A computer program sorts the forecasts by salesperson, and a sales forecast report is prepared.
e. A computer program sorts the forecasts by product code, and a sales forecast report is prepared.
f. The dollar amount totals produced by Steps d and e are compared.

Required:

Prepare a system flowchart for this sales forecasting system.

4–16. *SYSTEM FLOWCHART FOR TERMINAL INPUT*

Brewster, Inc. employs the following procedures in connection with budgetary control over research activities.

a. Budget projections are entered into a computer at a keyboard and stored on a magnetic disk.
b. Data from expense voucher forms are entered into the computer and stored on a magnetic disk.
c. The computer sorts, or resequences, the budget and expense information by expense account number.
d. Weekly expense transactions, listed by account, are available on inquiry at a computer terminal.
e. A monthly expense summary report is prepared.
f. A monthly budget analysis report is prepared.
g. A year-end budget summary report is prepared comparing actual and budgeted expenses.

Required:

Prepare a system flowchart for this budgeting system.

4–17. ***PROGRAM FLOWCHART***

A program in a payroll system must determine if old age, survivors, and disability insurance (OASDI) should be deducted from employees' pay. One module in the program begins with the employee's gross pay for the current pay period (determined in another module), and calculates the OASDI deduction, if any. This module executes the following procedures:

a. Deduct the employee's gross pay up to the last pay period from $32,400.
b. Test the result. If it is negative or zero, there are no more deductions to be made for the year. The computer transfers to a module that calculates net pay. If the result is positive, proceed to the next step.
c. Compare the result of Step b with the gross pay for the current period and select the smaller of the two amounts as the basis for calculating OASDI.
d. Multiply the amount selected in Step c by 6.7 percent and store the product.
e. Branch to the module that calculates net pay.

Required:

Prepare a program flowchart for the preceding module.

4–18. ***DECISION TABLE***

Prepare a decision table for the program module described in Exercise 4–17.

4–19. ***STRUCTURE CHART***

A program in a cost accounting system must calculate an overhead allocation rate each month. Overhead data and job cost data are stored in separate disk files. The last record in the overhead data file is signified by a dummy record with account code 999. The last record in the job cost file is another dummy record with Job Number ZZ9999. The program executes the following procedures:

a. Read a record from the overhead file.
b. Compare the account code on the record with the number 999. If they are equal, the last overhead data record has been read, and the computer proceeds to Step d. If the account code is not 999, the computer proceeds to Step c.
c. Add the amount on the overhead data record to a total of overhead costs. Return to Step a.
d. Read a record from the job cost file.
e. Compare the job number on the job cost data record to the number ZZ999. If they are equal, the computer branches to Step g. If they are unequal, proceed to Step f.
f. Add the labor hours recorded on the job cost record to a total of labor hours. Then branch to Step d.
g. Divide the total of the overhead data by the total of the labor hours. Print the result.
h. Stop execution.

Required:

Prepare a structure chart for this overhead allocation program.

4–20. ***DOCUMENT FLOWCHART***

Using the customer's purchase order as the authority, the order entry section prepares a six-part prenumbered sales invoice. A seventh part is prepared if it is a special order.

After preparation, the order entry section sends part 5 to the credit department for credit approval and part 6 to the customer as acknowledgment; other parts are temporarily filed numerically.

After approving the credit, the credit department returns part 5 to the order entry section where it is filed numerically. At the same time, parts 1 and 2 are sent to the billing department, part 3 to the warehouse, and part 4 to the shipping department. When a seventh part is prepared, it is sent to the production department.

Required:

Prepare a document flowchart for these procedures.

4–21. ***CONTROL FLOWCHART***

Prepare a control flowchart for the procedures described in Exercise 4–20.

4–22. ***DATA FLOW DIAGRAM***

Prepare a data flow diagram for the procedures described in Exercise 4–20.

4–23. *DOCUMENT FLOWCHART*

At the end of each day, the accounts receivable section prepares a control total showing the total amount debited to various accounts receivable accounts for the general ledger clerk. Independently, the billing clerk summarizes all sales on account during the day and prepares a journal voucher, which is sent to the general ledger clerk.

The general ledger clerk compares the amount shown on the control total with that shown in the journal voucher and attaches the former to the latter. An entry is then made in the sales journal. Finally the journal voucher is filed numerically.

Required:

Prepare a document flowchart for these procedures.

4–24. *CONTROL FLOWCHART*

Prepare a control flowchart for the procedures described in Exercise 4–23.

4–25. *DATA FLOW DIAGRAM*

Prepare a data flow diagram for the procedures described in Exercise 4–23.

4–26. *NETWORK DIAGRAM*

The following data were estimated while planning a system design effort.

Activity	*Duration (in Weeks)*	*Predecessor Activity*
A	10	none
B	8	none
C	30	none
D	12	A
E	15	A
F	14	B
G	15	D
H	20	E,F
I	5	C

Required:

a. Draw a PERT network diagram for this project.
b. Identify the critical path.
c. What is the earliest project completion time?
d. Find the slack time for each activity.
e. Discuss what the project team manager can do if the system design must be completed within 40 weeks.

(CIA Adapted)

4–27. *PROGRAM FLOWCHART*

The Metal Container Corporation was engaged in the manufacture of metal containers for the food industry. Although it began as a regional supplier, swift expansion mostly through acquisitions and mergers made it a national company with several dozen plants from coast to coast. Annual sales were about one quarter of a billion dollars.

Management Problems

Although there were only a few companies in the metal container industry, competition, particularly in customer service, was extremely keen. This generally meant attempting to meet customers' unexpected needs on very short notice and allowing them to cancel orders on the slimmest of pretexts. This policy, coupled with the inherent seasonal nature of the business, meant wide fluctuations in production and, worse yet, a large inventory of slow-moving items. Out of an inventory balance of $50 million, about 20 percent, or $10 million, was judged to be slow moving. Although the controller was fully aware of the situation and prepared monthly reports listing these slow-moving items by plant and by product specifications, his efforts had generated few results. Both the percentage figure and the dollar amount had shown consistent monthly increases during the past several years. Because the company was in need of funds for further expansion, the president's attention was attracted by the sizable inventory. The company's plan to convert to a more sophisticated computer system afforded him the opportunity to ask the advice of a management consultant.

Production Scheduling

In the course of his study, the management consultant came across plant managers' production schedules that reflected each plant's plan to meet expected sales needs for each month of the coming year. Because the plant managers' performance was evaluated mainly on the basis of their ability to service these sales needs, they tended to carry large inventories and to be overcautious about responding to any decreases in sales forecasts. Both factors, of course, contributed to the company's high inventory position and increased its vulnerability to slow-moving items.

Since proper production scheduling provided an attractive avenue to a reduction of inventories, the consultant pursued the matter further. He felt that what top management considered the preferred manner of production scheduling was reflected accurately by the following:

a. Inventory is to be no lower than 50 percent and no higher than 75 percent of the sales forecast for the following month.
b. Production is to be scheduled in such a way that the planned inventory at the end of each month falls within the range just indicated.
c. The normal workload is a five-day, eight-hour-a-day workweek.

d. If the normal workload results in too much inventory, the workweek may be reduced to a four-day, three-day, two-day, or even a one-day workweek.
e. If the normal workload results in inadequate inventory, the workweek may be extended first by working 9, 10, 11, or 12 hours a day for a five-day week, then by working Saturdays, then by working Saturdays and Sundays, and then by working two shifts a day. The extended day options (working 9, 10, 11, or 12 hours a day) are also available to weekend or two-shift operation.
f. If around the clock operation for a month still results in inadequate inventory, the production schedule of the preceding months is to be revised to allow inventory accumulation in these months.

With this set of rules, the consultant prepared some production schedules and compared them with those prepared by plant managers. Invariably, schedules prepared by the consultant showed inventory positions of about 20 percent less than those indicated in plant managers' schedules.

Because of these favorable findings, the consultant suggested that the preparation of production schedules be computerized. He even prepared a program flowchart to be used by the company's programming staff for this task.

Required:

a. How would you have prepared the program flowchart?
b. Would a decision table be useful in this situation?

4–28. *STOCHASTIC NETWORK DIAGRAM*

Whitson Company has just ordered a new computer for its accounting information system. The present computer is fully utilized and no longer adequate for all of the financial applications Whitson would like to implement. The present accounting system applications must all be modified before they can be run on the new computer. Additionally, new applications which Whitson would like to have developed and implemented have been identified and ranked according to priority.

Sally Rose, manager of data processing, is responsible for implementing the new computer system. Rose listed the specific activities to be completed and determined the estimated time to complete each activity. In addition, she prepared a network diagram to help coordinate the activities. The activity list and network diagram are presented in Exhibit 4–1, Case 4–28.

Required:

a. Determine the number of weeks required to fully implement Whitson Company's accounting information system on the new computer.
b. Identify the activities critical to completing the project.
c. Determine the slack time for one activity.
d. Whitson Company's top management would like to reduce the time necessary to begin operation of the system.

EXHIBIT 4–1 Case 4–28

Activity	*Description of Activity*	*Expected Time Required to Complete (in Weeks)*	*Variance in Expected Time (in Weeks)*
AB	Wait for delivery of computer from manufacturer	8	1.2
BC	Install computer	2	.6
CH	General test of computer	2	.2
AD	Complete an evaluation of personnel requirements	2	.8
DE	Hire additional programmers and operators	2	1.6
AG	Design modifications to existing applications	3	1.2
GH	Program modifications to existing applications	4	1.4
HI	Test modified applications on new computer	2	.4
IJ	Revise existing applications as needed	2	.6
JN	Revise and update documentation for existing applications as modified	2	.4
JK	Run existing applications in parallel on new and old computers	2	.4
KP	Implement existing applications as modified on the new computer	1	.6
AE	Design new applications	8	3.2
GE	Design interface between existing and new applications	3	1.8
EF	Program new applications	6	2.6
FI	Test new applications on new computer	2	.8
IL	Revise new applications as needed	3	1.4
LM	Conduct second test of new applications on new computer	2	.6
MN	Prepare documentation for the new applications	3	.8
NP	Implement new applications on the new computer	2	.8

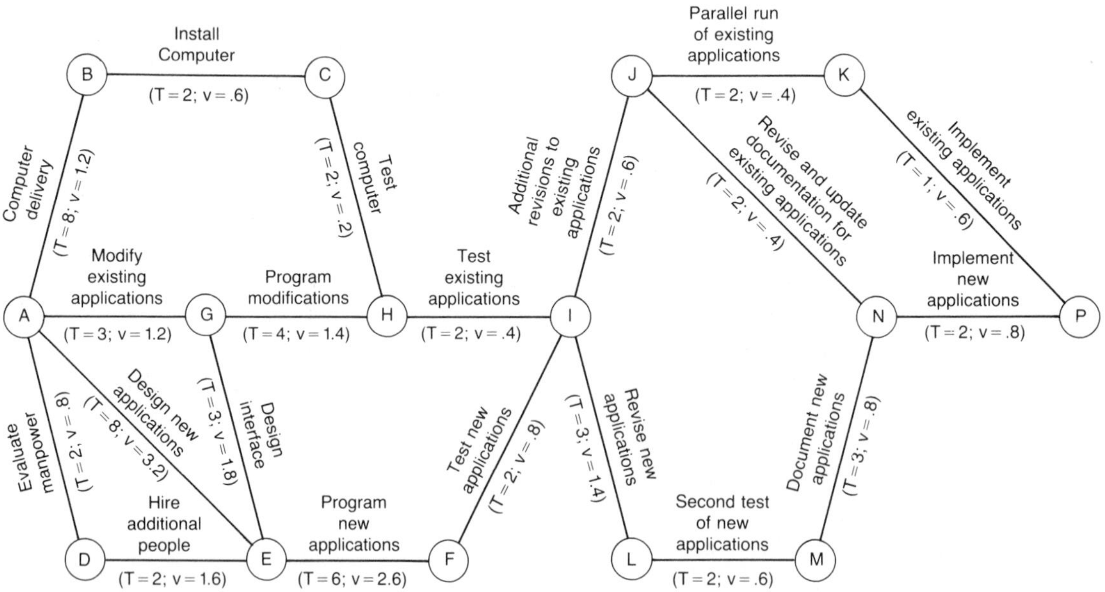

T = Expected time in weeks to complete activity.
V = Variance in expected time in weeks.

1. Which activities should Sally Rose attempt to reduce to implement the system sooner? Explain.
2. Discuss how Sally Rose might proceed to reduce the time of these activities.

e. The general accounting manager would like the existing accounting information system applications to be modified and operational in 22 weeks.

1. Determine the number of weeks required to modify the existing accounting information system applications and make them operational.
2. What is the probability of implementing the existing system applications within 22 weeks? Use the following table in your calculations.

Table of Areas under the Normal Curve

z	*Area*	*z*	*Area*	*z*	*Area*
0.1	.540	1.1	.864	2.1	.982
0.2	.579	1.2	.885	2.2	.986
0.3	.618	1.3	.903	2.3	.989
0.4	.655	1.4	.919	2.4	.992
0.5	.692	1.5	.933	2.5	.994
0.6	.726	1.6	.945	2.6	.995
0.7	.758	1.7	.955	2.7	.997
0.8	.788	1.8	.964	2.8	.997
0.9	.816	1.9	.971	2.9	.998
1.0	.841	2.0	.977	3.0	.999

(CMA Adapted)

Part II

Developing Accounting Systems

Chapter 5

System Development Processes

Learning Objectives:

1. To discover alternative methods for creating accounting information systems.
2. To understand the qualities of a successful information system.
3. To learn the phases that make up the system development life cycle.
4. To understand how prototyping is used to develop information systems.

INTRODUCTION

This chapter introduces you to the systems approach applied to accounting systems, a process that is part of the system development life cycle. Also discussed is a variation on these procedures called prototyping.

Accountants need to know about this process for two reasons. First, they participate in project teams that design accounting systems. Second, auditors review and make suggestions for new systems prior to their implementation. The details of the development process are described more fully in the chapters that follow.

THE OBJECTIVE OF SYSTEM DEVELOPMENT

Unlike systems that occur naturally, accounting information systems must be created. Accountants have been creating accounting systems for hundreds of years; the double-entry system originated in Italy before Columbus discovered

ILLUSTRATION 5–1 Achieving the Qualities of a Successful System

Quality	*Achieved by*
1. Correct information	Have adequate internal control
2. Timely information	Choose a processing method suited to the user's needs
3. Reasonable time for development	*a.* Properly define the scope of the system *b.* Use project management techniques
4. Satisfy the organization's needs	
a. Current	Get steering committee approval for new systems projects
b. Future	Have a long-range systems master plan
5. User satisfaction	*a.* User input in setting policies *b.* User support for projects *c.* Active user participation in projects *d.* User responsibility for the system

America. But the relatively recent adoption of computer technology in accounting has forced accountants to be more attentive to the methods used in developing accounting systems.

In the past 40 years, accountants have had both successes and failures in implementing the double-entry system on computers. Because all accountants are likely to participate in developing a new accounting system, how can one avoid participating in a failure? Which steps are necessary to successfully implement an accounting system? The implementation of a successful system is the objective of any system development process.

The Qualities of a Successful System

No accounting information system is completely successful or totally unsuccessful. In this context, success is a relative quality: a system is successful if it achieves most of the goals set out for it. In general, an accounting information system is successful if it achieves four objectives. First, it should produce correct and timely information. Second, it should be completed within a reasonable amount of time. Third, the system should meet the organization's needs for information. And finally, users should be satisfied with it. These qualities, and some methods of achieving them, are summarized in Illustration 5–1.

Correct and Timely Information. In an accounting system, errors and fraud are the two sources of incorrect information. The double-entry system prevents or detects many of the errors that humans can make in manually processing accounting data. Because of this, double-entry systems are implemented on computers even though computers are less likely to make these kinds of errors. The use of computers, however, creates the possibility of other errors, and makes it easier for a dishonest person to use the accounting system to conceal fraud.

A successful accounting system has *internal controls* that prevent and detect errors and fraud. Accountants and auditors frequently participate in system development processes because they, more than most other professionals who work with computers, are knowledgeable about internal control. Adequate internal control is necessary for implementing a successful accounting information system.

Information is considered *timely* if it is available to its user when needed for decision making. Some of the earlier computerized accounting systems had a serious shortcoming. In these systems, information in computerized ledgers was updated weekly or monthly, even though employees needed current information daily. For example, suppose inventory issues and additions are posted only on Fridays. A customer asks a salesperson about the availability of a particular product on Wednesday. The salesperson can tell the customer that goods were in stock on the previous Friday, but cannot say that the goods are available when the customer wants them. This accounting system provides information that is untimely. More modern processing methods avoid this shortcoming. Timely information is provided by adopting a transaction processing method that meets the needs of the system user.

Time Required for System Development. Another quality of a successful accounting system is that its development should be completed in a reasonable period of time. Many large accounting systems require three or more years to complete. Companies that have used computers for many years can tell horror stories of systems that were never completed. Excessive time for development results in excessive costs that may cause the system's costs to exceed its benefits.

What can be done to avoid this kind of system failure? First, system designers learn to limit the scope of any new system to a size that can be developed within a reasonable time. In the terminology of systems theory, they define the boundaries of the system and limit their efforts to those components within the boundaries. Even though procedures outside the boundaries may need changing, these needs are addressed at a later date. For example, accountants seldom attempt to change an entire transaction cycle. Instead, they identify the application system within the cycle that most needs to be improved. Then they complete a new version of that application system before proceeding to another system within the cycle.

Second, system design teams learn to use project management techniques such as budgets, Gantt charts, and PERT or CPM diagrams. These methods require the designers to identify in advance all activities required by the development effort and the estimated times and costs for each activity. Designers can monitor actual elapsed time and costs, comparing them to those expected. Then they can change either the scope of the system or the resources assigned to the effort before an excessive amount of time elapses.

Satisfy the Organization's Needs. A third quality of a successful system is that it meets the needs of the organization implementing it. The system should provide information that is both meaningful and relevant to its users. Because accounting systems can be expensive and time consuming to develop, they should be useful for many years. Thus, any new system should satisfy not only the current needs of the company but also anticipated future needs. An appropriate system design satisfies the organization's current needs; adequate system planning helps to identify future needs.

Most organizations have management committees that provide short- and medium-range planning for new information systems. Frequently called the *information system steering committee*, this group includes the management information systems (MIS) manager and representatives from all departments that use computer-based applications. The steering committee considers and approves new systems on a project-by-project basis. When approving the final design for a new system, they try to ensure that current information needs will be met.

To produce successful systems, organizations should also engage in long-range systems planning. This type of planning examines information requirements at a broader level than a project-by-project analysis allows. It may be accomplished by members of a corporate long-range planning staff, or by a system planning group within a MIS department. This *long-range systems planning group* identifies long-range information resource requirements and develops a system master plan for new systems. The master plan is based on overall corporate goals, on proposed new products, on new markets the firm will enter, and on future critical tasks within the firm's operations.

Whether a system is intended for a transaction processing application or for aiding in management decisions at a less structured level, adequate system planning is necessary if it is to be considered a success.

User Satisfaction with the System. A system is usually considered to be successful if its users are satisfied. In fact, many systems professionals consider user satisfaction as the strongest indicator of success. The user may be a clerk inputting data into a component of a transaction processing system. Or it may be an operating manager reviewing reports from a responsibility accounting or budgeting system. In either case, user satisfaction indicates that the system provides information that is correct and timely enough to satisfy the user's needs.

Frequently, designers of a new system conduct an evaluation of it months after it starts operation. Major objectives of this *post-implementation review* are to determine if intended users are relying on the system and to find whether they are happy with its operations and outputs. By using surveys and interviews, they can determine if users are satisfied with the system.

Gaining User Acceptance

Often organizations allocate time and money to develop a new system only to find that users are unwilling to use it. In other situations, employees or managers use the new system grudgingly because no other is available. In some cases, users deliberately sabotage a new system, making it inoperable. A system can be technically sound, designed consistently with the organization's needs, and produce correct and timely information. Yet employees may prefer to use an older system, a manual system, or an informal one.

Users may resist a new system for several reasons. Sometimes personnel may feel an economic threat due to the fear of losing a job. In other cases, the threat is simply to the user's ego or status. For example, in the past many managers were unwilling to use computer terminals. Using the keyboard requires typing, which, they believed, was a secretarial task. Sometimes a new system changes an employee's job in an undesirable way. The job may have added complexity or become more rigid due to a time schedule established for the new system. Occasionally a person may feel more insecure because of the formality introduced by using computer-generated reports rather than those humans produce. Many people simply oppose any change in their work routines.

System designers have learned to anticipate these problems, and to take steps during system development to gain users' acceptance of the new system. The right kind of user involvement in the development process encourages user acceptance.

User Input in Setting Policies. The information systems steering committee should involve users. The steering committee should have representatives from top management and from all the major information systems user departments: accounting, marketing, production, engineering, internal audit, and others. Each representative should be a high-ranking manager within a department and may be the head of the department. The manager of the MIS department should also serve on this committee. Large corporations may have several such committees—one at the top management level composed of divisional vice presidents, others within the company's operating divisions or subsidiaries.

The steering committee provides user input into the selection of new systems for development. Just as important, the committee establishes priorities for those system projects that are approved. Every manager thinks that his or her pet project is the most important one! On the steering committee, a manager has to convince other managers of the importance of the project. In a study for the National Association of Accountants, Harold Sollenberger identified the primary responsibilities of a typical steering committee.[1] Illustration 5–2 lists these responsibilities.

User Support for Projects. System designers must enlist user support for development projects in progress. All managers and supervisors should be sold on the project's value to their departments. If the superiors openly support a new system, subordinates will have difficulty resisting it after implementation. In

---

[1]Harold M. Sollenberger, *Management Control of Information System Development* (Montvale, N.J.: National Association of Accountants, 1971), p. 52.

ILLUSTRATION 5–2 Responsibilities of the Information System Steering Committee

1. Review and approve for further study all projects requested by operating departments or the MIS department.
2. Review and approve the MIS department's work program and determine priorities for projects.
3. Review periodic progress reports on active systems projects.
4. Review and approve proposed plans for system implementation.
5. Review periodically the MIS department's budget.

developing a successful accounting system, sales ability and good interpersonal skills are as important as technical skills.

Active User Participation in Projects. Not only should users be sold on the value of a new system project but they should also be active participants in the design process.

A multidisciplinary *project team* handles most projects. Members of the team come from varied backgrounds, and each contributes unique skills to the design process. Accountants usually participate in the design of an accounting system, and so do personnel from the affected operating departments. For example, the design of an order entry system requires someone from sales. The design of a cost accounting system requires input from production. Frequently these personnel are temporarily relieved of their normal duties and assigned full time to the project. Any project team also has people from the MIS department who are experienced in the design and development process. These include systems analysts, programmers, documentation specialists, and technical consultants.

The project team should provide user input to the development process throughout. User representatives should be involved not only in developing specifications for the system but also in coordinating the project, in performing cost-benefit analyses, and in planning the final implementation of a new system.

User Responsibility for the Implemented System. One objective of user involvement throughout a project's life is to have a manager in the affected user area assume responsibility for the implemented system. Ideally, a user representative on the project team is the person with this responsibility. Of all employees in the affected user department, someone from the project team is most likely to feel responsible for the success or failure of the new system.

This manager then becomes the internal advocate for the new system. He or she can help train other users, answer questions or resolve problems in the user department, and serve as a contact person with the MIS department on technical problems.

Relevance for the Accountant

How is this relevant to an accountant? Why is an accountant concerned with the success of a system or the degree of user involvement?

In most organizations, accountants use more computerized information systems than any other professional group. Thus accountants are user representatives on many project teams when older accounting systems are replaced. As the ultimate benefactors of a new accounting system, accountants have a personal concern for its accuracy and efficiency.

Also, accounting systems are pervasive throughout any organization. Actions by all operating departments cause inputs to the accounting transaction processing system. Companies with good budgeting and responsibility reporting systems find that these directly affect the decisions of managers. Often managers hold accountants responsible for inaccuracies or inequities designed into these systems.

Accountants are the auditors of these accounting systems. Auditors want systems that produce accurate, reliable information so that they can rely on them during the audit process. For this reason, internal auditors sometimes participate in developing them.

You can see the importance of the system development process from the accountant's perspective, and now know something about the behavioral concerns in system development. The next section presents some methods for developing successful accounting information systems.

THE SYSTEM DEVELOPMENT LIFE CYCLE

Information systems contribute to management decisions at the strategic planning, management control, and operational levels. As organizations change, managers at all levels face new decisions and acquire new needs for information. Thus, information systems must change to meet these new needs. The evolution of most accounting systems follows a distinct cyclical pattern commonly called the system development life cycle (SDLC). This cycle is evident in accounting systems because these information systems have been in use for a long time.

The system development life cycle describes how an information system progresses from its conception as an idea, through the development process, and into routine operation. Typically, the cycle begins as a manager recognizes a need that existing information systems do not satisfy. This manager may propose a solution or may want a problem studied by someone else who can suggest possible solutions. Management appoints a study team to apply the system study process to the problem. The study team may increase in size and may implement a new information system as a solution to the problem. This solution may be used for many years before another manager recognizes some

ILLUSTRATION 5–3 The System Development Life Cycle

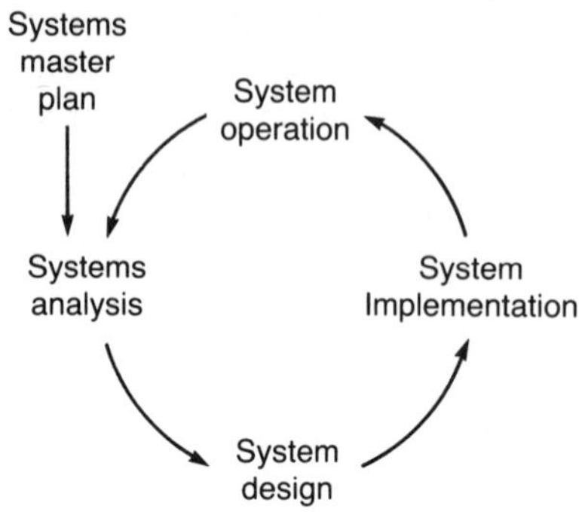

other need for information that the system does not satisfy. Then the cycle begins again.

You can understand the SDLC more clearly by considering its components. Illustration 5–3 shows the cyclical nature of these components, which are important because they are used in the process of developing new information systems.

Components of the SDLC

SDLC components include systems planning, analysis, design, implementation, and operation. Three of the components—analysis, design, and implementation—compose the system development process, and may require from a few months to a few years. The fifth component, operation, may last for decades. For example, one major oil company has used the same payroll accounting system for over 30 years. In the mid-1950s, this system required approximately two years to develop.

Systems Planning. Ideally, systems development takes place within the context of a systems master plan that coordinates new information system development projects with the company's long-range plans.

Many companies employ a staff of strategic planners who advise top management and who identify and suggest long-range goals, such as new markets, new product lines, or new lines of business. If a company is to achieve these goals, its systems must provide relevant information. Members of the strategic planning staff work with senior MIS and accounting personnel to develop the systems master plan. Before beginning new development projects, these people ensure that the new projects are consistent with the master plan.

Systems Analysis. Systems analysis is the process of examining an existing information system and its environment to identify potential improvements.

Systems analysis may begin for a variety of reasons. In some cases, it may be an outgrowth of the systems planning process. A long-range planning group may identify a need for information at some time in the future and may incorporate that need in a systems master plan. The information systems steering committee then appoints a system study team to investigate possible ways of supplying this information. The system study may or may not lead to the development of a new information system.

Many times, systems analysis begins at the request of the manager of a user department. This manager identifies a need for information that is currently not supplied. He or she prepares a proposal for a new or modified information system and submits it to the steering committee. The committee considers the seriousness of the problem, the feasibility of the proposal, the current workload of the MIS development staff, and the relative importance of competing proposals. The steering committee then may decide to appoint a study team to examine the proposal in more detail. The study team may consist of one or more systems analysts and user department representatives.

Systems analysis is initiated for three reasons. The first and most frequent reason is that an existing system is not functioning as required. For example, a small-business accounting system may have been adequate at the time of its acquisition, but the growth of the business now produces bottlenecks in the processing of transactions. In this case, systems analysis begins to *solve a problem* with an existing system.

The second reason a systems study team may be appointed is due to a *new requirement* for information. A new requirement may be identified by a long-range systems planning staff or may result from legal or competitive changes in the business environment. For example, in response to competition, many companies choose to analyze past accounting data on sales by customers to plan future marketing programs. Periodically, changes are made in tax laws that increase reporting requirements to the government by banks, brokerage firms, and publicly held companies. Companies have invested substantial sums in new systems to satisfy these requirements.

Third, sometimes organizations initiate systems analysis to take advantage of a *new technology*. The existing system may be functioning satisfactorily, but since its implementation, technological change introduced new methods that are more efficient. For example, many retailers have attached labels containing computer-readable bar codes to their goods. Cash registers can read the bar codes, and sales are immediately shown in inventory records. In this way, inventory records are kept current. Illustration 5–4 summarizes these reasons for initiating systems analysis.

Sometimes the systems analysis study team concludes that a new information system is a possibility. They stop studying the problem and start to address

ILLUSTRATION 5–4 Reasons for Initiating Systems Analysis

1. *Problem Solving.* An existing system does not meet its objectives.
   Example: A small-business system has been outgrown.
2. *New Requirement.* Information that was not needed before.
   Example: Reporting dividends and interest paid to comply with tax laws.
3. *New Technology.* Better methods are now available.
   Example: Point-of-sale data entry to computer system.

potential solutions that include new forms of technology, new sources for required information, or more efficient procedures. When this occurs, there are two activities in systems analysis: the activity of examining existing systems, the *preliminary survey,* and that of examining potential solutions to the problem, the *feasibility study*. The feasibility study begins the process of developing a new system.

System Design. During system design, the team translates recommendations made in systems analysis into a form that can be implemented.

Usually the study team performs a cost-benefit analysis during systems analysis. If a new system appears cost effective, the MIS manager, with input from the steering committee, appoints a design project team. This team may include members of the original system study team and additional systems analysts and user department personnel. The project team reviews the work of the study team during systems analysis, reexamines their proposed solutions, and begins to define a new system in gradually increasing detail.

In large projects, system design consists of two distinct phases. During *preliminary design*, the first phase, a system is created conceptually. The project team starts with the objectives of the system and identifies the major processes, data, and reports needed to achieve those objectives. At the conclusion of preliminary design, the project team prepares a report for the steering committee. This report describes a proposed new system in general terms.

If authorized by the steering committee, the project team then begins the second phase, *detailed specification* of the new system. During this process, the team identifies in detail how the system will work. The purposes of all computer programs and manual procedures are identified, all documents and reports are designed, all files are described, and the necessary internal controls are identified. Accountants and internal auditors can make significant contributions to the detailed specification of a system because of their training and knowledge in internal control.

By the conclusion of detailed specification, an organization has made a significant commitment in time and money to a new system. A sizable, detailed paper description of the system is created and submitted to the steering committee for approval. Thus, the committee has another opportunity to change the proposed system, or stop it, before additional resources are devoted to the project.

System Implementation. Once the information system's steering committee approves the detailed specifications for the new system, its implementation begins. During implementation, the project team is enlarged to include programmers and clerical personnel from user departments. Many activities occur simultaneously to convert the paper description produced during design into a working information system.

The most time-consuming activity during implementation is computer programming. The programmers assigned to the project team code, debug, and test each computer program that was identified in the system design documentation. Frequently, programs provide inputs to other programs. When this occurs, the programs must be tested together to ensure that interfaces are compatible. System designers call this process *string testing*. When all programs are tested in conjunction with manual procedures, they call it *system testing*.

Some organizations avoid much of the programming by purchasing software packages. Programs are available that perform most accounting transaction processing applications. These can be modified by programmers to suit the organization's needs.

During implementation, personnel are trained in the new system and, if necessary, new personnel are hired. Any required new equipment is acquired and installed. Any new forms or supplies required by the system are ordered.

The entire project team and many user area personnel participate in the final implementation activity, *system conversion*. During this activity, all data stored in the files of the old system are recorded in the form specified by the new system. Operation of the new system then begins.

Many activities can occur during system implementation, but all activities are not necessary for each new system. For example, existing equipment may be adequate so that the purchase of new equipment is unnecessary. Also, many of the activities can take place simultaneously. Frequently, for example, user training begins immediately after the detailed specifications are approved, while programming is taking place.

System Operation. System conversion does not terminate the system development process. Several months after operation of a new system begins, the *post-implementation review* occurs. During this review, members of the design team, frequently with the aid of an internal auditor, examine the operation of the new system. The purpose of the review is to determine if the system meets its objectives. It identifies problems that need correction and provides feedback to the design team concerning the success of the system.

Another activity, *system maintenance*, takes place during the operation phase. These are the tasks that are necessary to correct errors in the system design or to make minor changes to the system because of changes in its environment. System maintenance includes both changes to equipment (hardware maintenance) and changes to computer programs (software maintenance). Although it is not a part of the system development process, system maintenance is necessary for the operation of an information system.

Formal System Development Methodologies

Several formal system development methodologies incorporate the components of the systems development life cycle. These methodologies decompose systems analysis, system design, and system implementation into distinct phases like those previously described. They impose their own design tools and standards on the SDLC.

These methodologies require formal reports to management at the end of each phase. These reports describe the status of the project and show the project team's suggestions for the new system. Usually one or more members of the team make a presentation to the steering committee appraising them of the project's progress.

The end of a phase provides a checkpoint for management; each checkpoint is an opportunity to review and evaluate the proposed system. Management can identify changes to the proposal, stop further consideration of the proposal, or authorize initiation of the next phase.

Structured Systems Analysis and Design. During the 1970s, many organizations adopted formal system development methodologies based on the concepts of *structured analysis* and *structured design*. Several of these differ in the details of their techniques.[2]

Structured analysis techniques rely on the use of data flow diagrams rather than flowcharts. Data flow diagrams force the analyst to focus on the *logical system*, what the system does or should do, rather than the *physical system*, how the system works. Advocates of structured methods argue that this causes the analyst to define more accurately user requirements by not prematurely worrying about technology. This, they believe, improves the creativity of the analyst.

Structured design techniques develop computer programs as a top-down hierarchy of modules. Each module is a segment of computer code that serves only one function. Structure charts (or similar diagrams) describe these programs. Programs developed in this way are more easily written and tested. They also are easier to modify later because they minimize connections between modules.

CASE Tools. Many formal methodologies make extensive use of *computer-aided software engineering* (CASE) tools. These software packages automate many of the processes required during system development. CASE tools serve

---

[2]For a more detailed description of structured techniques, see J. L. Whitten, L. D. Bentley, and V. M. Barlow, *Systems Analysis and Design Methods*, 2d ed. (Homewood, Ill.: Richard D. Irwin, 1989), p. 112.

ILLUSTRATION 5–5 A Phased Approach to System Development

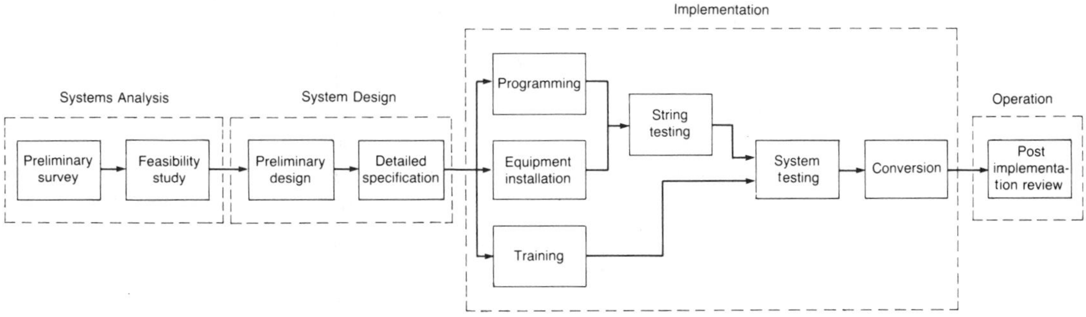

different purposes: they aid in drawing data flow diagrams or flowcharts; they maintain records concerning data files, inputs, and outputs; they provide project management tools; and they maintain system documentation.

CASE tools increase the productivity of personnel assigned to project teams and at the same time improve the quality of the new systems and of their documentation. As a management accountant, you are likely to work with CASE tools when you participate in the development of accounting systems. As an auditor, you are likely to review the documentation produced by them.

Formal system development methodologies impose structure and discipline on the development process and aid in the timely completion of a system. They are most successfully applied in the creation of large transaction processing applications; many organizations consider them a necessity for such a system. Illustration 5–5 presents an example of such a formal, phased approach.

PROTOTYPING

The prototyping approach is an alternative to the phased system development methodology of the SDLC. Prototyping is an iterative process that avoids the structure and the periodic formal approval process of the phased approaches. It relies on the development of a prototype, or working model, of the new system.

A system design team, consisting of a few systems analysts experienced in using the method, is appointed. This team quickly creates a high-level, nondetailed working model of the system. Users are then allowed to repeatedly revise the system, its reports, or its inputs, until they are satisfied with it. Once users are satisfied with the system, the design team creates an actual production system patterned after the prototype.

ILLUSTRATION 5–6 Suggested Steps in Prototyping

1. *Analysis*. Create an incomplete paper model of the system based on preliminary interviews with users.
2. *Data base development*. Create a test data base for use in prototyping. Using a relational data base management system, the prototype can be easily changed.
3. *Menu development*. Describe the menus that will guide the user of the system. A menu identifies functions to be performed.
4. *Function development*. Describe the functional modules that execute the processes in the system. These may include, for example, data entry and report generation.
5. *Prototype iteration*. Using software development tools, create each module. This produces a working model of the system that a user can easily modify. Make changes to the prototype until the user is satisfied.
6. *Detailed specifications*. Refine the system as necessary to make it efficient in creating a production system. Complete the documentation for the system.

Requirements for Successful Prototyping

Prototyping may be used successfully on relatively small transaction processing systems implemented with state-of-the-art technology. These systems have a limited number of users who become closely involved in the design effort. Prototyping is extensively used for developing decision support systems because the prototype can be customized to a decison maker's preferences and decision style.

This approach, however, requires the use of appropriate high-level developmental software tools, discussed in later chapters. They include report generators, display screen generators, fourth-generation languages, and a relational data base management system. Tools of this kind are widely available for use on both desktop and mainframe computers. Prototyping using a conventional procedural language such as COBOL is too cumbersome to be practical. Whereas analysts can create prototypes quickly using high-level developmental tools, creating a prototype in a procedural language is usually too time-consuming and expensive.

An Approach to Prototyping

Any of the many variations on the prototyping approach to system development can be successful whenever the proper software tools are applied to an appropriate application. Illustration 5–6 identifies and describes the suggested steps in one approach.[3] Others minimize the involvement of systems analysts by having the ultimate users of the system learn the tools and create the design.

[3]John Connell and Linda Brice, "Rapid Prototyping," *Datamation*, August 15, 1984, pp. 93–100. Used by permission.

ILLUSTRATION 5–7 Auditor's Role in the Development Process

Systems Analysis Phase

Provide audit reports on systems being examined to the study team.

System Design Phase

Review the proposed design:

1. *Reports*. Identify information needed in reports for control and auditability.
2. *Processing steps*. Suggest control procedures.
3. *Equipment selection*. Ensure that those selected conform to existing company policies.
4. *Data files*. Determine that data will be accurate and complete, and will provide the ability to audit the system.

System Implementation Phase

During system testing, review adequacy of test data and results of tests.

Review plans for conversion to ensure that accurate data is maintained while changing to the new system.

System Operation Phase

During the post-implementation review, assess the adequacy of internal controls in the operational system.

AUDITOR INVOLVEMENT IN SYSTEM DESIGN

Sometimes auditors participate in the system development process. Because of their training and auditing experience, auditors have special skills to contribute to the process of developing an accounting system. Usually these participants are one or two *internal auditors* employed by the company. Internal auditors' other duties include reviewing all the operations of the company and making recommendations to management for improving them. By participating in the SDLC, internal auditors can make suggestions during design, when changes to a system are easier.

Occasionally an *independent auditor* may be asked to participate as well. The independent auditor is a firm of certified public accountants that renders an opinion on the financial statements produced by the accounting information system. The independent auditor may assign this system design duty to a member of its information system consulting staff.

Ideally, most auditor involvement in the SDLC occurs during the system design phase. Auditors review the detailed specifications for the system proposed by the project team. They are also heavily involved in the implementation phase, during system testing and conversion. After completion of the development process, and during the operations phase, auditors participate in reviews of the system. Illustration 5–7 identifies the role of the auditor in each phase of the SDLC.

As this illustration shows, much of the auditors' work in the system development process is concerned with the *auditability* and the *controls* in the system. An audit trail ensures that the system is auditable; controls are the measures adopted to safeguard assets and to ensure accurate and reliable data.

The Audit Trail

Auditors review a system to decide if it provides the information needed to conduct an audit. Called the audit trail, this information is included in the reports produced by the system.

An accounting system records, categorizes, and summarizes transactions to produce reports such as financial statements. The audit trail enables an auditor to begin with a summary balance on the financial statement and trace through the accounting records to the individual transactions that make up the balance. It also allows an auditor to trace from individual transactions to the summary totals. For example, journal entry numbers, posting references, or document numbers are included in reports to provide an audit trail.

The audit trail is important because it enables an auditor to evaluate the accuracy of financial statement amounts and to determine the sources of errors in summary reports.

Controls

The independent auditor relies on controls while examining the financial statements, and the internal auditor evaluates them as a service to management. As a result, auditors are more knowledgeable about controls than are most project team members.

A system that includes good control measures produces accurate, reliable reports. The accounting records stored by such a system are secure from damage or theft. Good internal controls aid in gaining user acceptance and are necessary for a successful system.[4] During the SDLC, auditors review the system design and make suggestions identifying controls that should be included.

SUMMARY

This chapter provided an overview of the processes used in developing accounting information systems. The objective of system development is to create a successful information system. Experience shows that the most

[4]Glenn L. Helms, *An Examination of the Impact of Information System Auditor Involvement in Systems Development on the Quality of New Application Systems*. (Ph.D. diss., University of Houston, 1983).

successful information systems are those created with the right kind of user involvement.

System development is a part of the systems development life cycle. This cycle contains four components that exist in the life of any information system: analysis, design, implementation, and operation. Phased development methodologies attempt to create successful systems by requiring periodic reviews of a project proposal during the development components of the life cycle. An alternative to these methodologies, prototyping, is most useful in the development of smaller systems. Auditors participate in system development by reviewing the controls and the audit trail in proposed systems.

KEY TERMS

audit trail Information, including journal entry numbers, posting references, and document numbers, that are included on the outputs of an accounting system. They allow an auditor to identify the individual transactions that make up an account balance.

information system steering committee A group composed of the MIS manager and managers from computer user departments. Among other duties, this committee considers and approves new information system development projects.

internal controls The features of an accounting system that prevent or detect errors and fraud. They help it to produce accurate information.

project team A group of employees from varying backgrounds that is assigned responsibility for developing a new information system.

prototyping An iterative system development process. A small project team quickly develops a working information system and allows users to modify it until they are satisfied with it.

system design The second phase of the system development life cycle. The process of translating the recommendations made during systems analysis into a form that can be implemented.

system development life cycle A pattern that describes the evolution followed by most accounting systems. It consists of four phases: systems analysis, system design, system implementation, and system operation.

system implementation The third phase of the system development life cycle. The process of converting the description created during system design into a working information system.

system operation The last phase of the system development life cycle. The period of time during which a working information system provides information for decision making and control.

systems analysis The first phase of the system development life cycle. The process of examining an existing information system and its environment for the purpose of identifying potential improvements.

QUESTIONS

5–1. Explain what is meant by a successful information system.

5–2. In a large organization, who performs long-range systems planning? Medium-range? Short-range?

5–3. What can happen when employees refuse to accept a new information system?

5–4. Identify some reasons why employees refuse to accept new systems.

5–5. What can be done to gain user acceptance of a new system?

5–6. Why should an accountant be concerned about the success of an information system?

5–7. Explain why we say that the life of an information system follows a cycle.

5–8. Define the following terms:
a. Systems analysis
b. System design
c. System implementation
d. System operation

5–9. What are some of the reasons for initiating systems analysis within an organization?

5–10. In which ways are the preliminary description and the detailed specification of a new system similar? In which ways do they differ?

5–11. Which activities take place during system implementation?

5–12. What are the advantages of using a formal system development methodology?

(CIA Adapted)

5–13. Why should auditors participate in the system development process? On which features do they concentrate their efforts?

5–14. What is an audit trail? Why is it important?

5–15. When might prototyping be useful in developing an accounting information system?

EXERCISES AND CASES

5–16. ACTIVITIES AND PHASES

Identify in which phase of the system development life cycle each of the following activities is performed:

a. Feasibility study System Analysis
b. Post-implementation review Systems operation
c. System conversion System Implementation
d. Detailed specification System Design

e. Preliminary survey
f. Preliminary design
g. Equipment acquisition

5–17. *SDLC PHASES*

The phases of a system development life cycle project are analysis, design, implementation, and operation. You can identify analogous phases for most projects that you undertake. Identify the activities that occur in each phase for each of the following projects:

a. Writing a term paper.
b. Purchasing a personal computer.
c. Choosing a college to attend.
d. Planning a vacation over spring break.
e. Selecting a job after graduation.

5–18. *STEERING COMMITTEE*

A company president is perplexed by requests for computers from three different areas of the firm. The EDP manager (who reports to the vice president of services) wants $4.5 million to upgrade the mainframe computer. The vice president of engineering wants $500,000 to replace a minicomputer. The vice president of finance wants $100,000 to purchase microcomputers.

The company doubled its sales over the past five years, but profits increased only 50 percent. The added sales volume strained the firm's computer resources. Payroll, accounting, inventory, and engineering functions are computerized; other tasks are manual.

The firm is organized by business functions with vice presidents for manufacturing, marketing, engineering, finance, personnel, and services. The president wonders if an information system steering committee is needed.

Required:

a. Prepare an executive memorandum, to be signed by the president, creating an information systems steering committee. In this memo, you should outline its objectives, responsibilities, and composition.
b. Justify your recommendations concerning its membership and the selection of its chairperson.

(CIA Adapted)

5–19. *PROTOTYPING*

GEM Corp. wants to develop a decision support system to be used in strategic planning through the analysis of varied and often complex alternatives. Potential users have been directed to identify specifically their information requirements in a manner similar to that utilized for recently developed general ledger and accounts payable applications. However, responses to this new request are vague and the project appears to be stalled. Users are having trouble comprehending the tasks required of them in the new system, and the system project team has no experience with systems of this kind.

Because of these problems, GEM's management has concluded that a prototyping approach would be preferable to the system development life cycle approach that was used for the recently developed general ledger and accounts payable applications.

Required:

a. Identify the steps for prototyping an application system.
b. Identify four advantages of prototyping in developing applications that have a high degree of uncertainty as to requirements.
c. Identify two disadvantages of prototyping.
d. Decide whether prototyping should have been used to develop the general ledger and accounts payable applications and explain your response.

(CIA Adapted)

5–20. USER SATISFACTION

Five years ago, Black Motors, an international automaker, contracted with Blue Computer Company for minicomputers to support the data processing for its 30 largest U.S. dealers. Black Motors has 1,400 dealers in the United States. Three years ago, the dealers began using the Blue computers under long-term leases. The Black Motors Computer Support Group (CSG) is responsible for applications software. Altogether, each dealer spends about $5,000 a month on hardware and software rental.

When the Blue systems were first proposed, CSG sent to the dealers specifications of what the systems would and would not do. The dealers were pleased with the proposed capabilities and agreed that the proposed system would serve their needs.

The dealers gradually came to realize, however, that the Blue computer systems did not live up to CSG's promise. At a meeting two years ago, the dealers formed a committee composed of dealer representatives to address the problems. The software problems seem to have begun three years ago when Black Motors moved its corporate staff, including CSG, from the East Coast to the Midwest. Many of its programmers declined to move, impairing CSG's ability to support the Blue systems.

Two years ago, CSG began upgrading the computer systems used by all but the largest 30 dealers with minicomputers from Green Computer Company. To support these systems, most CSG personnel work on software for the Green computers. Software for the Green and Blue computers are incompatible but perform similar functions.

Three months ago, CSG sent the 30 largest dealers a letter assuring support for the Blue systems for the next four years and promising a decision about long-term support. The dealers remained skeptical and have been talking about legal action to force CSG to comply with its original agreement.

Required:

Given the foregoing difficulties, explain what CSG should do to improve computer system support for the 30 largest dealers. Include in your explanation the reasons for the actions you suggest.

(CIA Adapted)

5–21. ***OBTAINING USER ACCEPTANCE***

The B&B Company manufactures and sells chemicals for agricultural and industrial use. The company has grown significantly over the last 10 years but has made few changes in its information gathering and reporting system. Some of the managers have expressed concern that the system is essentially the same as it was when the firm was only half its present size. Others believe that much of the information from the system is not relevant and that more appropriate and timely information should be available.

Dora Hepple, chief accountant, has observed that the actual monthly cost data for most production processes are compared with the actual costs of the same processes for the previous year. Any variance not explained by price changes requires an explanation by the individual in charge of the cost center. She believes that this information is inadequate for good cost control.

George Vector, one of the production supervisors, contends that the system is adequate because it allows an explanation of discrepancies. The current year's costs seldom vary from the previous year's costs (as adjusted for price changes). This indicates that costs are under control.

Vern Hopp, general manager of the Fine Chemical Division, is upset with the current system. He has to request the same information each month regarding recurring operations. This is a problem that he believes should be addressed.

Walter Metts, president, has appointed a committee to review the system. The charge to this System Review Task Force is to determine if the information needs of the internal management of the firm are being met by the existing system. Specific modifications in the existing system or implementation of a new system can be considered only if management's needs are not being met. William Afton, assistant to the president, has been put in charge of the task force.

Shortly after the committee was appointed, Afton overheard one of the cost accountants say, "I've been doing it this way for 15 years, and now Afton and his committee will try to eliminate my job." Another person replied, "That's the way it looks. John and Brownie in general accounting also think that their positions are going to be eliminated or at least changed significantly.'' Over the next few days, Afton overheard a middle-management person saying about the task force, ''That's all this company thinks about—maximizing its profits—not the employees.'' He also overheard a production manager in the mixing department say that he believed the system was in need of revision because the most meaningful information he received came from Brad Cummings, a salesperson. He stated, ''After they have the monthly sales meeting, Brad stops by the office and indicates what the sales plans and targets are for the next few months. This sure helps me in planning my mixing schedules.''

Afton is aware that the problems of paramount importance to be addressed by his task force are (1) to determine management's information needs for cost control and decision-making purposes; and (2) to meet the behavioral needs of the company and its employees.

Required:

a. Discuss the behavioral implications of having an accounting information system that does not appear to meet the needs of management.

b. Identify and explain the specific problems B&B Company appears to have with regard to the perception of B&B's employees concerning:
   1. The accounting information system
   2. The firm

c. Assume that the initial review of the System Review Task Force indicates that a new accounting information system should be designed and implemented.
   1. Identify the concerns B&B employees have about the new system.
   2. For each of these concerns, discuss how B&B's management can address it.

(CMA Adapted)

5–22. *INITIATING SYSTEM DEVELOPMENT*

Kelly Petroleum Company has a large oil and natural gas project in Oklahoma. The project has been organized into two production centers (petroleum production and natural gas production) and one service center (maintenance).

Maintenance Center Activities

Don Pepper, maintenance center manager, has organized his maintenance workers into work crews that serve the two production centers. The maintenance crews perform preventive maintenance and repair equipment both in the field and in the central maintenance shop.

Pepper is responsible for scheduling all maintenance work in the field and at the central shop. Preventive maintenance is performed according to a set schedule established by Pepper and approved by the production center managers. Breakdowns are given immediate priority in scheduling so that downtime is minimized. Thus, preventive maintenance occasionally must be postponed, but every attempt is made to reschedule it within three weeks.

Preventive maintenance work is the responsibility of Pepper. However, if a significant problem is discovered during preventive maintenance, the appropriate production center supervisor authorizes and supervises the repair after checking with Pepper.

When a breakdown in the field occurs, the production centers contact Pepper to initiate the repairs. The repair work is supervised by the production center supervisor. Machinery and equipment sometimes need to be replaced while the original equipment is repaired in the central shop. This procedure is followed only when the time to make the repair in the field would result in an extended interruption of operations. Replacement of equipment is recommended by the maintenance work crew supervisor and approved by a production center supervisor.

Routine preventive maintenance and breakdowns of automotive and mobile equipment used in the field are completed in the central shop. All repairs and maintenance activities taking place in the central shop are under the direction of Pepper.

Pepper has records identifying the work crews assigned to each job in the field, the number of hours spent on the job, and parts and supplies used on the job. In addition, records for the central shop (jobs, labor hours, parts, and supplies) have been maintained. However, this detailed maintenance information is not incorporated into Kelly's accounting system.

Pepper develops the annual budget for the maintenance center by planning the preventive maintenance that will be needed during the year, estimating the number and seriousness of breakdowns, and estimating the shop activities. He then bases the labor, part, and supply costs on his plans and estimates and develops the budget amounts by line item. Because the timing of the breakdowns is impossible to plan, Pepper divides the annual budget by 12 to derive the monthly budget.

All costs incurred by the work crews in the field and in the central shop are accumulated monthly and then allocated to the two production cost centers based on the field hours worked in each production center. This method of cost allocation is used on Pepper's recommendation because he believes that it is easy to implement and to understand. Furthermore, he believes that a better allocation system is impossible to incorporate into the monthly report due to the wide range of salaries paid to maintenance workers and the fast turnover of materials and parts.

The November cost report for the maintenance center provided by the accounting department appears on the next page.

OKLAHOMA PROJECT
Maintenance Center Cost Report
For the Month of November 19XX
(dollars in thousands)

	Budget	*Actual*	*Petroleum Production*	*Natural Gas Production*
Shop hours	2,000	1,800	—	—
Field hours	8,000	10,000	6,000	4,000
Labor—electrical	$ 25.0	$ 24.0	$ 14.4	$ 9.6
Labor—mechanical	30.0	35.0	21.0	14.0
Labor—instruments	18.0	22.5	13.5	9.0
Labor—automotive	3.5	2.8	1.7	1.1
Labor—heavy equipment	9.6	12.3	7.4	4.9
Labor—equipment operation	28.8	35.4	21.2	14.2
Labor—general	15.4	15.9	9.6	6.3
Parts	60.0	86.2	51.7	34.5
Supplies	15.3	12.2	7.3	4.9
Lubricants and fuels	3.4	3.0	1.8	1.2
Tools	2.5	3.2	1.9	1.3
Data processing	1.5	1.5	.9	.6
Total	$ 213.0	$ 254.0	$ 152.4	$ 101.6

Production Center Managers' Concerns

Both production center managers have been upset with the method of cost allocation. Furthermore, they believe the report is virtually useless as a cost control device. Actual costs always seem to deviate from the monthly budget and the proportion charged to each production center varies significantly from month to month. Maintenance costs have increased substantially, and the production managers believe that they have no way to judge whether such an increase is reasonable.

The two production managers, Pepper, and representatives of corporate accounting have met to discuss these concerns. They concluded that a responsibility accounting system could be developed to replace the current system. In their opinion, a responsibility accounting system would alleviate the production managers' concerns and accurately reflect the activity of the maintenance center.

Required:

a. Explain the purposes of a responsibility accounting system, and discuss how such a system could resolve the concerns of the production center managers of Kelly Petroleum Company.

b. Identify the behavioral advantages generally attributed to responsibility accounting systems that the management of Kelly Petroleum Company should expect if the system were effectively introduced for the maintenance center.

c. Discuss the procedures that the production managers should follow to initiate systems analysis for a new responsibility accounting system. What approval processes would the system pass through before being fully implemented?
d. Responsibility reports are created during system design. Describe a report format for the maintenance center that would be based on an effective responsibility accounting system, and explain which, if any, of the maintenance center's costs should be charged to the two production centers.

(CMA Adapted)

5–23. ***PROTOTYPING***

The Super Oil Company has completed a substantial prototyping project in its materials department, resulting in increased efficiency, cost savings, and large numbers of happy users. This project created a tubular information system (TIS) for use in inventory control.[5]

Companies exploring for oil and gas need a lot of tubular goods—steel casing and oil tubing. The casing keeps the well bore clear during drilling, and the tubing conducts the crude oil from the producing formation when the well is completed. Capital investment in inventories of these items can be significant; a single 18,000-foot well, for example, requires about $7 million worth of tubular goods. Inventory management is complicated by fluctuations in both drilling demand and steel availability. Incorrect purchasing decisions result either in excessive inventories tying up unnecessary amounts of capital or out of stock material. Both conditions are costly to Super Oil.

Past materials control at Super had been based on a tubular availability report (TAR). The system producing this report had plenty of limitations: It provided no inquiry capability, its information was out of date, unreliable verbal inputs were used, and it contained no controls or audit trails. This was unsatisfactory to Matthew Seltzer, the materials manager. He discussed the problem with William Cooper, the MIS manager, who agreed to support development of a new system using prototyping methods. They decided to use the old TAR system as an operating prototype.

The design process started with a half-day team effort to create an overall materials system plan tying TIS to the purchasing system. The team consisted of two staffers from MIS and one from the materials department. The plan contained block diagrams of the intended relations among the inventory, purchasing, fixed assets, accounts payable, and general ledger systems. It allowed the design team to draw boundaries around the existing purchasing system and the projected TIS, thereby identifying all interfaces with related systems. The outgrowth of this meeting was a project proposal.

[5] Adapted from T. R. Young, "Superior Prototypes," *Datamation*, May 15, 1984, p. 152. © 1984 by Cahners Publishing Company. Used by permission.

The project proposal called for construction of a production system to manage tubular materials. The system would be constructed by the MIS professional staff in close cooperation with the user's organization. The principal software used would be NATURAL, a high-level language that greatly eases access to the database. A user representative was dedicated full time to the project during system design and implementation. The materials department was particularly motivated—and rightly so—because they regarded the development as their project.

The development process included three stages: The first was initiated by the statement of management objectives covering system boundaries and capabilities. User participation was high during this stage as the specifications for the system are worked out and prototype screens and reports were developed.

To get started, one MIS team member created a number of images of the computer display screens to handle keyboard data input and file inquiry. Users were asked to evaluate the screens and to resolve differences of opinion among themselves. As the users worked with the screens, they realized that certain necessary features had not been included in the initial screen designs. In the course of a day, the entire first draft set of screens was reviewed. The following day, the user group returned and found that a fully revised set of screens had been constructed by the MIS programmers using NATURAL. The revised versions incorporated the new requirements identified during the previous session.

The evolution of screen designs moved quickly along until a set of screens had been developed that satisfied user requirements. The screens' convenience in use, vocabulary, and format was also satisfactory. None of the users had ever experienced such response from the MIS department. The reaction was highly favorable and the materials control users began to warm to the idea of building their own system. Because user involvement was intense, they felt a personal identification with the system being created. As a result, their acceptance of the system was well formed by the end of the first stage.

The second stage primarily consisted of system construction by the supporting MIS organization; user participation dropped back to a consulting capacity. Equipment was selected, programming was completed, and preliminary documentation was produced.

The final stage began with a management review and commitment to system implementation in field operation. A team was formed for implementation, and user involvement accelerated with operational testing of the prototype. When testing was completed, the new system was installed at all field locations. Then work began on Mod II, the inevitable next phase in development that occurs as new needs are discovered through use of the system.

TIS went on-line seven months following the project's start. Management's evaluation of the project indicated that this would have taken approximately 20 months using conventional development methodologies. According to Materials Director Seltzer, TIS contributed directly to inventory reduction of $100 million over a 10-month period. Further savings result from the fact that purchasing a proprietary system would have cost more than twice the price of in-house development. The systems available for purchase were inappropriate for Super Oil's business because they were intended for manufacturing companies and were difficult to adapt to the oil drilling environment. Seltzer was well satisfied with the decision to use prototyping methods for system development. "It went like a train!" he was heard to say.

Required:

a. Who were the users of this information system? Which actions were taken to gain their acceptance of the new system?

b. Would you call this a successful system? Explain why.

c. Which characteristics made the tubular information system a likely candidate for prototyping?

Chapter 6

Systems Analysis

Learning Objectives:

1. To discover which activities take place during the first phase of the system development life cycle.
2. To learn how to conduct a preliminary survey.
3. To know how to perform a feasibility study.
4. To understand the criteria that determine the feasibility of a proposed accounting information system.

INTRODUCTION

The previous chapters provided you with some useful tools for system development and an overview of system development processes. The next chapters go into more detail about the phases that constitute the system development life cycle (SDLC).

The first part of this chapter reviews the relationship between systems analysis and the other phases of the SDLC. Then it describes two systems analysis processes, the preliminary survey and the feasibility study. In the chapters that follow, you learn the activities that take place during the design and implementation of a new information system.

SYSTEMS ANALYSIS

Systems analysis is the process of examining an existing information system and its environment to identify potential improvements. The information systems steering committee begins systems analysis in response to a request from a

ILLUSTRATION 6–1 The Systems Analysis Phase

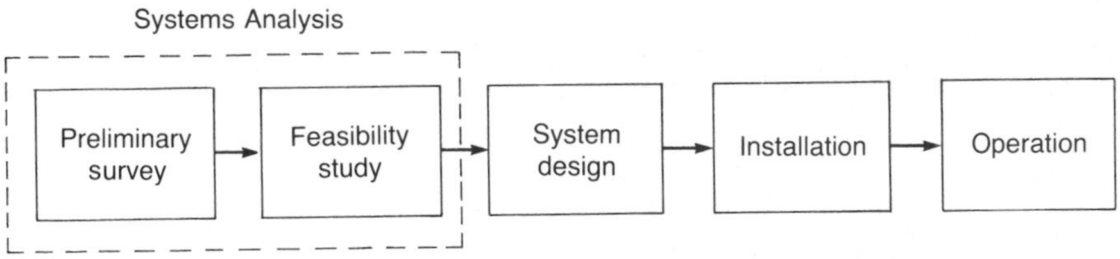

manager or from a long-range systems planning group. As discussed in Chapter 5, systems analysis may begin for three reasons: (1) to solve a problem with an existing system; (2) to satisfy a new requirement for information; or (3) to implement a new form of technology. Illustration 6–1 shows the relationship between systems analysis and the other phases of the SDLC.

In an information systems department, highly skilled employees called *systems analysts* coordinate systems analysis activities. A good systems analyst has a thorough knowledge both of computer processing methods and of business needs for information. A systems analyst is also skillful at applying the *systems approach* to problem solving.

The systems analysis phase of the SDLC represents an application of the systems approach to an organizational problem. During this phase, a multidisciplinary project team examines the problem from the perspective of the entire organization. They sometimes call this process the *preliminary survey*. During their examination, the project team identifies possible solutions to the problem that may, or may not, require the use of a computer. As they explore these alternatives, they may identify this process as the *feasibility study.*

THE PRELIMINARY SURVEY

The preliminary survey consists of an evaluation of an existing system or systems. Performed by a team of analysts from MIS and user departments, it has four objectives:

1. To acquire an understanding of an existing application system.
2. To develop good relationships with users of the system.
3. To collect data that is potentially useful in system design.
4. To identify the nature of the problem being investigated.

The Systems Study Proposal

The information systems steering committee initiates the preliminary survey in response to a system study proposal. Usually this proposal comes from an operating manager. Sometimes it comes from the long-range systems planning group or from top management. If the proposal has merit, the committee appoints a system study team to conduct the survey.

Reasons for the Proposal. Sometimes an operating manager initiates a system study proposal after identifying a problem with an existing system. The manager wants a study team to investigate the problem and to consider the need for changes to the system. Often an organization outgrows an existing system, and because of this growth the system develops *insufficient processing capacity*. You can observe this problem, for example, in noncomputerized accounting systems that develop backlogs of unprocessed accounting transactions. Changes in the organization can also cause *erroneous processing* of transactions. For example, a business may reassign responsibility for entering sales orders from professional to clerical personnel. If the clerical personnel are unfamiliar with the customers or the product line, they may record many sales orders incorrectly. Sometimes a system is simply *not functioning as intended*. For example, a computerized responsibility accounting system may not provide meaningful performance measures for operating supervisors. A manager may submit a study proposal for a new system that provides better information for motivation and control. Finally, many proposals are submitted to correct *processing inefficiency*. In this case, a manager feels that a new system can produce significant cost savings.

Other reasons for initiating a systems study proposal include the existence of new information requirements. These can arise for either *legal* or *competitive* reasons. For example, some companies transact business with governments on a "cost plus" basis. The company's revenues from a government contract are its costs, plus a percentage of costs determined in advance and recorded in the contract. In such a situation, the company is legally obligated to maintain detailed records of its costs of production. Other organizations want to keep detailed cost records for good cost control. This helps them to acquire business from competitors. Additional new information requirements may be identified by a system planning group as a part of long-range strategic planning.

Many times operating managers or long-range planners may submit a system study proposal to implement a new technology. For example, during the 1970s most organizations ceased using punched cards for inputting transactions to computerized systems. On-line computer terminals replaced keypunches because the terminals provide an *improved data entry* method. For the same reason many companies today use cash registers as data entry devices. Accountants call these "point-of-sale" systems because they record the transaction data immediately when the sale occurs.

Another technological development provides *terminal reporting* capability. This allows managers to receive informative reports at terminals or personal computers whenever they desire, rather than when reports are printed as a part of routine processing by older systems. Systems with terminal reporting capability often enable managers to produce ad hoc reports. With ad hoc reporting, managers not only receive the reports at terminals but also can select

ILLUSTRATION 6–2 Reasons for a System Study Proposal

Problems with an Existing System
- Insufficient processing capacity
- Erroneous processing
- Not functioning as intended
- Processing inefficiency

New Requirement for Information
- Legal
- Competitive

Desire for New Technology
- Improved data entry
- Terminal reporting capability
- Ad hoc reporting capability

the information to be reported and rearrange the reports to their own preferences.

Implementing a new technology is an appealing reason to initiate a preliminary survey. However, a system that uses the latest technology is sometimes not cost effective. Costs and benefits of a proposed new technology are evaluated during another activity of systems analysis, the feasibility study. Illustration 6–2 summarizes these reasons for submitting a system study proposal.

Project Initiation. The information systems steering committee consists of the manager of the MIS department and a representative from each user department. A user department is one that uses significant computerized applications. The committee meets on a regular basis, perhaps weekly or monthly, to review and evaluate project proposals. Among these proposals are system study proposals from managers and planners who wish to initiate preliminary surveys.

In deciding which proposals merit further study, the committee establishes priorities for the MIS staff. If the proposal arises from problems with an existing system, the committee evaluates the seriousness of the problem. Processing backlogs or excessive errors may require prompt correction and often require overtime work or temporary clerical help. Less serious problems, such as those represented by minor inefficiencies, may be deferred. A proposal in response to a need for new information requires the committee to evaluate the time frame associated with the need. Frequently, new laws or competitors require prompt action on the part of the committee. Priorities for proposals that implement a new technology depend on the expected costs and benefits associated with the technology. In some cases, potential benefits justify a high priority for a study proposal.

Once the steering committee assigns a priority to each system study proposal, it approves the most important ones for further investigation. The committee then forms a system study team to examine the environment of the problem, the new information requirement, or the new technology.

The System Study Team

A system study team consists of one or more systems analysts and user personnel. An experienced systems analyst is in charge of the team. User personnel may be professional or clerical employees from the affected user department who have some experience or training with the system. These may include engineers or technicians, production managers or supervisors, or sales managers or clerks. For an accounting system, an accountant or experienced accounting clerk may represent the accounting department on the study team.

A common problem in forming a study team is getting adequate user department input. Each user member of a study team has full-time duties within the department. The user member must be relieved of at least some of these duties to participate in any system project. User personnel who are knowledgeable about an existing system's shortcomings are likely to be valuable employees. A manager frequently hesitates to release a valuable subordinate, even temporarily, for assignment to a study team. For example, the production supervisor who best understands the shortcomings of a responsibility accounting system is probably one who uses it. Because of the supervisor's responsibilities in the department, a production manager may resist having this supervisor assigned to a study team. The information system steering committee must ensure that the managers of user departments support the project and allow key personnel to participate.

Scope of the Preliminary Survey

The purposes of the preliminary survey include developing an understanding of existing applications and available resources. This is primarily a fact-gathering process about the way the organization currently operates. In conducting the survey, the system study team determines the following information about the existing system:

Data Flows. The study team gathers facts about the flow of data within the system and across interfaces to other systems. Data flow can take the form of documents, oral communications, or computer records. The study team identifies each of these items used in the system and determines what data is contained on each, who initiates the data, and who receives it.

Effectiveness. The study team evaluates the effectiveness of the existing system. An effective system adequately achieves its goals; to measure effectiveness, the team must first clearly define the goals of the existing system. Then the team gathers data about the system that can be used to measure effectiveness. This data can be objective, such as descriptive statistics on system operations, or subjective, such as users' opinions about the system's usefulness. Often a manager proposes a systems study to investigate a problem with an existing system's effectiveness. During the preliminary survey, the study team can evaluate the source of the manager's dissatisfaction.

3- **Efficiency.** In gathering data about an existing system, the study team looks for ways to improve the system's efficiency. Although efficiency may be difficult to measure, the team can sometimes compute efficiency as the ratio of system outputs to system inputs. At other times, the team calculates a ratio of outputs to cost of inputs. Sometimes the steering committee initiates a system study because of inefficiencies in an existing system; this makes the study team's evaluation of efficiency especially important.

4- **Internal Controls.** The study team also evaluates internal controls in the existing system. Internal controls are the measures taken by the organization to safeguard assets, to ensure accurate data, to promote efficiency, and to encourage compliance with management's policies. Frequently, poor internal control can cause a system to record erroneous transactions and to generate incorrect accounting or management reports. The adequacy of its internal control also influences the system's effectiveness and efficiency. Accountants have special expertise concerning internal control and are assigned to study teams for this reason.

During the preliminary survey, the system study team gathers data on information flows, effectiveness, efficiency, and internal controls in the existing system. In this process, the team identifies both strengths and weaknesses in the existing system. Systems analysis may result in the design and implementation of a new system. If so, the old system's strengths should be retained in the new one. During the system design phase, a project team also corrects any serious weaknesses found during the preliminary survey.

Using System Tools

During the preliminary survey, the study team uses many of the systems tools presented earlier. Members of the team review existing documentation, conduct interviews, and use work measurement techniques to understand how the current system operates. They take notes during these activities and include them in the study team's working papers. They produce flowcharts or data flow diagrams and fill out questionnaires to document their conclusions. They may review reports provided by internal or independent auditors.

Documentation Review. Three kinds of documentation concern the study team: organizational, individual, and processing documentation.

The study team examines documentation describing the organization's structure and accounting procedures. This information includes organization charts, the chart of accounts, and departmental budgets for recent years. Organizational documentation describes the environment of the problem as well as the new requirement or new technology that caused the proposal. Budgets and organization charts may indicate sources of a problem or may affect the feasibility of possible changes to a system. A chart of accounts aids in understanding the budget, and its structure affects the nature of proposed system changes.

The study team also looks at all available documentation concerning how individuals perform their jobs. These include job descriptions, procedures manuals, performance standards, and computer operating instructions. This individual documentation is often highly detailed, and examining it is a tedious process. Yet in this documentation study team members find precise descriptions of individual tasks that may help identify the source of a problem. Frequently a new information requirement or new technology requires changes to these tasks, and gathering data on existing tasks makes later development activities easier.

Another type of documentation examined by the study team is processing documentation. This provides information on interfaces between individual tasks and between these tasks and the computer. Processing documentation shows how computerized and manual procedures interact; it includes flowcharts, example forms, and example reports. By examining flowcharts, the study team identifies the sequence of tasks that make up a system. The sequence, rather than the individual tasks, may require change to correct a problem. Sample forms identify the data that the system collects, and sample reports illustrate the information it provides. Frequently, these must be changed to satisfy a new requirement for information or to implement a new technology.

Illustration 6–3 summarizes the three types of documentation gathered during the preliminary survey. Unfortunately, the study team may find that much of this documentation has become obsolete. For example, if the system under study is old, then existing flowcharts, procedures manuals, and job descriptions may no longer accurately describe the system. An examination of existing documentation provides a way to begin data gathering. This data must be updated by further procedures. These procedures may include interviews, diagrams, questionnaires, and work measurement techniques.

Using Interviews. After collecting documentation, the next step in the preliminary survey of an existing system is conducting interviews. Members of the study team first interview the manager in charge of the affected user department. In this interview, the team not only learns the manager's perspective on the problem but also attempts to gain the manager's enthusiasm and support. The cooperation of all affected user employees is important to the success of the study, and this cooperation is easier to attain if employees realize that their bosses support it. After interviewing the manager, other members of the study team then conduct interviews with key supervisory and clerical personnel.

In conducting interviews, the study team encourages the interviewees—whether managers, supervisors, or clerks—to describe their job functions. This allows the study team to learn how existing documentation is out of date. The team also learns the interviewee's opinions concerning the problem, the

ILLUSTRATION 6–3 Documentation Reviewed during the Preliminary Survey

Organizational Documentation

Organization chart—a diagram showing superior and subordinate relationships.
Chart of accounts—a list of accounts in the general ledger.
Departmental budgets—projected costs and revenues summarized by responsibility centers. These may be compared to actual costs and revenues.

Individual Documentation

Job description—identifies for each clerical and supervisory position the specific tasks, procedures, and responsibilities assigned.
Procedures manual—a document that identifies and describes tasks constituting each noncomputerized procedure required by a system. It also identifies the job description performing each procedure.
Performance standards— Expected measures of efficiency, quality, or quantity for a task or procedure.
Computer operating instructions—a document describing tasks assigned to a computer operator.

Processing Documentation

Flowcharts—a graphic representation of sequential processes.
Sample forms—one of each kind used for data input by the system.
Sample reports—one of each kind produced by the system.

---

information requirement, or the technological change that initiated the study. Even though supervisors or clerks may have limited perspectives on a problem, often they can offer insight regarding its source, its potential solutions, or the difficulties inherent in providing new information or introducing a new technology. While conducting an interview, the study team member may take notes or collect examples of completed forms for later review.

Interviews aid in gaining user acceptance if management decides to introduce a new system later. They also provide the study team with the information needed to understand how an existing system operates. The study team uses diagrams, decision tables, questionnaires, and work measurement techniques to improve their understanding of the system.

Using Flowcharts or Data Flow Diagrams. The system study team uses either flowcharts or data flow diagrams to describe the existing system. A data flow diagram shows the flow of data between processes, files, and external destinations. A flowchart is a graphic representation of sequential processes and may be a system or document flowchart.

The choice between these two diagrams depends on the preferences of the analysts or of the organization employing them. Many companies have adopted structured systems analysis conventions requiring the use of data flow diagrams exclusively. Advocates argue that because data flow diagrams show logical rather than physical flows, they allow analysts more creativity. Analysts are forced to think about *what* is done rather than *how* it is done. This enables them to identify problems easier and develop better solutions.

As an accountant, you may encounter either diagram. Regardless of the approach, the systems study team uses these diagrams for three purposes: summarizing, documenting, and analyzing.

The diagrams are an efficient way to summarize what the study team learns from interviews and documentation reviews. For example, during interviews an analyst accumulates many pages of interview notes. The notes from each interview describe the views of an individual employee. The analyst then summarizes this information into a form that describes operations from the viewpoint of the organization as a whole. Flowcharts or data flow diagrams make this task easier for the analyst.

Diagrams also allow the study team to document how the existing system works. The flowcharts or data flow diagrams produced during the preliminary survey update older documentation that may no longer be correct. If the systems analysis phase is followed by the design of a new system, new diagrams of the old system are useful in design and conversion. New diagrams also demonstrate to management and the steering committee that the study team has adequately examined the existing system.

Flowcharts or data flow diagrams are valuable once the study team has gathered all its data. At this point, the team begins to analyze the existing system to identify problems or potential improvements. A diagram contains a concise description of the processes making up a system. With a diagram, the analyst can see the effects of problems or improvements more easily than when notes, narratives, or other forms of documentation are used. In fact, many experienced analysts find that the process of diagramming itself helps identify problems or produce ideas for new systems.

Using Questionnaires. A study team may also use questionnaires during a preliminary survey. A questionnaire may be used in two ways; either an analyst or user department personnel can complete it.

Sometimes the study team develops a questionnaire for its members to use when conducting interviews. The questionnaire lists facts that should be identified or answers that should be obtained by the analyst during the interview. The analyst uses it as a guide to ensure that all necessary data are gathered. When used in this way, the questionnaire is developed by an experienced systems analyst. Then the study team can use less experienced members to conduct interviews without fear of omitting important information.

At other times, the study team desires information or opinions from a large number of user personnel. The team may allow the users to complete a questionnaire rather than interview each user individually. This approach is efficient when the study team has examined the system and identified specific information requirements. For example, the team may want to gather descriptive statistics concerning user satisfaction or frequency of usage; a questionnaire used in this way may save significant time and cost. However, substituting a questionnaire for interviews may cause the team to omit important information. It does not allow the analyst to ask probing questions, nor does it encourage an interviewee to volunteer information.

Work Measurement. Sometimes the study team uses questionnaires in conjunction with work measurement studies. While other techniques used by the study team identify tasks occurring in the system, a work measurement study determines the magnitude or quantities of these tasks.

For example, an analyst may find through interviews or documentation reviews that an accounts payable clerk prepares a batch control slip. The analyst, however, does not know how frequently this occurs, nor does the analyst know how much time this task requires. The analyst asks the clerk to complete a questionnaire each day showing how much time was required to complete each batch control slip. After several days' questionnaires are available, the analyst computes an average elapsed time for the task. As an alternative, the analyst may choose to time the task over several repetitions using a stopwatch. Industrial engineers refer to this work measurement technique as *time and motion study.*

Another approach to work measurement counts the number of outputs from a task or system, such as forms completed or reports produced. This enables a study team to compute measures of efficiency by the number of outputs per employee or unit of time.

Regardless of the approach taken, the system study team normally undertakes some form of work measurement. This is especially important when the preliminary survey results from problems regarding system efficiency, or when the team uses a cost-benefit analysis to determine the feasibility of developing a new system.

Audit Reports. The study team may choose to examine reports written by auditors prior to the study. These reports may be prepared by internal auditors or by independent auditors.

As part of their duties, internal auditors perform *operational audits* of departments or segments of the organization. In the operational audit, the internal auditor analyzes the operations of the department and identifies weaknesses or potential improvements. At its conclusion, the internal auditor writes a report to management describing them.

The independent auditor writes a *management letter* to top management during the audit of the financial statements. This letter describes weaknesses in internal control that the auditor identified during the audit. The independent auditor provides it as an additional service; the management letter is not a part of the standard independent audit report.

Frequently, an operational audit report or a management letter describes weaknesses and makes suggestions useful to the study team. The auditor may have examined the system under study, and the auditor's evaluation helps the team identify a problem. The auditor's suggestions may be included in the design of a new system.

ILLUSTRATION 6–4 Benefits of the Preliminary Survey

1. *Provides an Objective Evaluation.* A study team may decide that a new system is unnecessary.
2. *Provides Design Information.* Data could be useful in design and implementation, should a new system be authorized.
3. *Aids in Gaining User Acceptance.* Users are involved from the beginning of the system development life cycle.

You have just seen the procedures used during the preliminary survey. The information systems steering committee initiates this activity to gather data about an existing system. However, sometimes the steering committee decides that obtaining this data is unnecessary. By omitting it, the organization fails to receive the benefits of performing a preliminary survey.

Report back to the steering committee

Benefits of the Preliminary Survey

The preliminary survey provides three major benefits. First, it provides an objective evaluation of the situation that produced the system study proposal. Objectivity is attained by appointing to the study team individuals who initiated neither this proposal nor other competing proposals. The study team is directed by a systems analyst who has no daily interaction with the system and is skilled in applying the systems approach. By objectively evaluating the existing system, the system study team may conclude that it is operating satisfactorily. They may decide that a minor modification to the existing system, rather than a new system, is adequate.

A second benefit of the preliminary survey is that it provides necessary information. At the conclusion of systems analysis, the information systems steering committee may decide that a new system is warranted. If this occurs, much of the information gathered during the preliminary survey is useful during the system design and implementation phases. While examining the existing system, the study team determines the resources of personnel and equipment that are available for a new system. The team identifies strengths in the old system that should be retained, and weaknesses that should be eliminated. At the conclusion of the implementation phase, the organization converts from the old system to the new one. The data gathered about the old system's files, procedures, and forms makes this conversion process easier.

And finally, the preliminary survey facilitates gaining user acceptance of a new system. The survey requires significant personal contact between the system study team and user personnel. Knowing that they have provided inputs to the new system, users are more likely to work to make it succeed. Illustration 6–4 summarizes the benefits of performing a preliminary survey.

During the preliminary survey, the study team gathers data concerning the system. After producing working papers to document their conclusions, they begin the process of examining in detail potential changes to the system. This process is the feasibility study.

THE FEASIBILITY STUDY

The preliminary survey consists of an examination of existing systems. In contrast, during the feasibility study the system study team examines alternatives that are potential changes to existing systems. In the feasibility study, the study team specifies the objectives and scope of the system under consideration. Then they examine each alternative in detail and eliminate from consideration those clearly infeasible.

Objectives of the System

Before examining the feasibility of a system change, the study team identifies the objective or objectives of the system. This is necessary if they are to apply the systems approach. The information system steering committee initiates systems analysis because an existing system is not meeting its objectives, or because new objectives have been identified for it. During the preliminary survey, the study team may find that the objectives of an existing system are not clearly defined. During the feasibility study these are specified. Then in determining the feasibility of an alternative, the study team considers whether a proposed change achieves these objectives.

Scope of the System

During the preliminary survey, the system study team examined a problem. They gathered and analyzed data relevant to the problem from throughout the organization. During the feasibility study the problem is known, objectives are identified, and the study team evaluates possible solutions. In doing this, the study team must restrict the limits of their analysis to factors relating to the problem. They define the scope of the system to include only those components relevant to achieving the objectives of the system. In the terminology of systems theory, they establish the boundaries of the system that is to be changed. Then they restrict their efforts only to those components within these boundaries.

This is frequently a difficult task. During a preliminary survey, a study team may find many problems that need correction or many opportunities for technological improvement. They may wish to correct all the problems or make all the improvements immediately. Such a major system development effort is unlikely to be completed within a reasonable time period and will probably be unsuccessful. An experienced systems analyst recognizes the need to select the most critical needs and implement solutions to them first. Another study team can address less critical needs later.

Defining System Scope—An Example

This example can help you understand how to define the scope of a system. XYZ Company is considering a contract to produce 10,000 widgets for the government. The selling price for the widgets is equal to their production cost, plus 10 percent. The latter provides XYZ's profit on the transaction. However, XYZ must improve its cost accounting system to comply with government requirements.

XYZ appoints a study team to evaluate the existing cost accounting system and to identify the changes needed. The team determines that the system's objectives are to record costs for the direct material and direct labor used in producing the widgets and to allocate to the widgets their share of factory overhead. XYZ's payroll system is a manual one and can provide data concerning direct labor costs for the widgets. However, purchases of materials and supplies are recorded by a computerized accounts payable system that is inadequate for cost accounting purposes. The accounts payable system is incapable of recording the costs of material for the widgets separately from the costs of material for other products. The study team concludes that a new cost accounting system would be unsuccessful without a new accounts payable system. The company cannot develop two major systems simultaneously with the resources currently available to it.

How should the study team proceed? They should first identify the system that has the most critical need. Then they should define the scope of their study to include only this system and identify alternative ways to satisfy this need. The most critical system is the accounts payable system because it must be changed before the cost accounting system can provide accurate information. Once an adequate accounts payable system is functioning, another project team can develop a job costing system that complies with government cost accounting standards. At some later date, XYZ Company may decide to computerize its payroll system to increase processing efficiency.

This example illustrates the interactions that occur between the components of the accounting transaction processing system. These interactions require that, as accounting systems evolve, study teams carefully define boundaries for these components before implementing improvements. Once the study team determines the scope of a system, it then considers the feasibility of changes to it.

Determining Feasibility

During the preliminary survey, the study team identifies a problem and possible solutions to it. These solutions may include minor changes, major changes, or completely new systems. After establishing limits to the scope of its efforts, the study team evaluates the feasibility of solution alternatives. For an alternative to progress beyond the systems analysis phase, it must be feasible in four ways: technical, operating, time, and economic.

Technical Feasibility. This feasibility criterion concerns the state of technology in the computer industry and the technological capabilities of the organization. In evaluating technical feasibility, the study team determines whether computer software and equipment that allow implementation are available from manufacturers.

This is the easiest feasibility criterion to evaluate. MIS representatives on a study team usually are knowledgeable about the capabilities of available equipment. Their knowledge can be supplemented by advice from outside consultants. Technical and trade journals keep team members up to date regarding the state of technology.

Predicting the success of a technology in an organization is more difficult. This requires evaluation of a second feasibility criterion, the operating feasibility.

Operating Feasibility. In considering the operating feasibility of an alternative, the study team determines if a proposed system change could enable the system to meet its operating objectives. An alternative that fails to do so is discarded.

Technological change often occurs faster than employees can adapt to it. Sometimes a system alternative is unsuccessful if employees feel threatened by the new technology, or if they feel that it makes their jobs less important or enjoyable. In other cases, a new technology may require capabilities that existing personnel lack. For example, using a computer keyboard requires typing skills that some factory workers may be unwilling to learn.

A significant factor in determining operating feasibility is user satisfaction. If users are dissatisfied with a system, it does not meet its objectives. When users are dissatisfied with a system, they fail to use it. Or, even worse, they may sabotage it, making it ineffective or inoperable. Thus, when a study team performs the feasibility study, they must consider any behavioral or social implications of a system change on the people who work with it.

Another issue examined by the study team is the expected performance of the system alternative. Many system studies are initiated to overcome problems with processing backlogs, or to implement a new technology that improves performance. For example, a new system may complete the accounting cycle more quickly than an old one and thus eliminate the backlog. It may allow more data entry operators to use it simultaneously. The study team compares the performance of a system alternative to that desired. A system that does not meet performance expectations is eliminated from further consideration.

Time Feasibility. In evaluating this feasibility criterion, the study team determines if the alternative can be implemented within a reasonable length of time. They compare the time needed to implement it with the company's needs for the system. If the company started a system study to implement a new

ILLUSTRATION 6–5 Evaluating System Feasibility

Technical Feasibility. Can it be implemented?
Operating Feasibility. Will it achieve its objectives?
Time Feasibility. Within a reasonable length of time?
Economic Feasibility. Are the benefits worth the costs?

technology, it may be willing to go through a lengthy development process, maybe two or three years, to gain the technology. If the study resulted from a critical problem with an existing system or an immediate need for information, the company wants an alternative that can be implemented quickly.

In determining time feasibility, the study team predicts the time needed to design and implement the new system. This time frame is affected by four factors: (1) The team estimates the equipment delivery time. Sometimes purchasers wait from several months to a year for the delivery of equipment. (2) The team must project the software delivery time. If computer programs are available for purchase, the system can be implemented much more quickly than if programs must be written. The team also estimates (3) the training time for users and (4) the time for conversion to the new system. These will be longer if the system requires a major technological change than if it requires only a minor change to an existing system. The study team considers these factors and compares implemention time to the time allowed by the company.

Economic Feasibility. In analyzing this criterion, the study team determines if the proposed change will benefit the organization financially. Their objective in evaluating economic feasibility is to find out if the change is worth making. Many system development projects last from two to three years and cost millions of dollars to implement. During the feasibility study the team makes preliminary calculations to determine that the benefits received are worth the costs.

Before a study team recommends initiation of system design, the proposed system or system change must satisfy all four feasibility criteria. If an alternative is infeasible on any of these grounds, then the alternative is not considered further. Illustration 6–5 summarizes the four criteria for feasibility.

Determining Economic Feasibility

The system study team determines the economic feasibility of a system by comparing the projected costs of a system change with its projected benefits. Estimating economic feasibility is useful during systems analysis even though at this stage all costs are approximate. If the steering committee decides to proceed with the development project, the team formed for system design develops a more accurate appraisal of costs and benefits later.

In estimating economic feasibility, the study team distinguishes between *annual* costs or benefits and those which occur only once, the *onetime* costs or benefits. Annual costs include the costs of operating the system, such as operating salaries, supplies, and utilities. Onetime costs include equipment and salaries of the system development team. A new system may produce an annual cost savings or annual additional revenue; this becomes the annual benefit.

Determining Costs. The expected costs of an alternative can be projected in advance with some accuracy. Members of the study team who worked on previous development projects use past costs as guidelines. Actual costs of developing previous systems are modified to reflect differences between the old one and the proposed one. Modifications are made based on differences in scope, differences in technology used, the experience of project team members, and inflation. Everyone involved recognizes the inaccuracy of such a cost projection. However, an estimate may be off by 100 percent or more and still be usable. Such an estimate is better than no estimate at all.

What if no one on the study team has experience with a system similar to the proposed one? When a proposed application or technology is unfamiliar to the study team, the wisest and safest course is to engage a consultant. Many accounting firms, for example, employ specialists in this area. They have wide ranges of experience and their advice can easily be worth the cost of obtaining it. The costs of implementing a successful system are high, but these costs produce benefits; the costs of producing an unsuccessful system are equally high but may produce no benefits. The wise study team recognizes its limitations.

Determining Benefits. Before an information systems steering committee proceeds with a development project, members want to know that its benefits justify its costs. Usually benefits can be identified easily in qualitative terms. The study team can state with confidence that a new system will, for example, eliminate a backlog, improve the company's competitive position, or improve decision making. However, such vague statements are insufficient during the SDLC. The study team must estimate in monetary terms the financial benefits from the new system or system change.

The nature of the system application determines the accuracy of this benefit estimate. The financial benefits of certain systems can be projected quite accurately, while for other systems the projection may be little more than a guess. You can understand these differences if you relate them to the three levels of decision-making activity.

Strategic Planning. At the strategic planning level, top management makes decisions about the organization's objectives and the policies necessary to achieve them. Information systems aid in decisions about the introduction of future products or product lines, the entrance into future markets, and the acquisition of factories, subsidiaries, or companies. The payoff from these decisions may be from 5 to 25 years or more in the future. Furthermore, these payoffs are affected by future events that a study team cannot anticipate in the present. When the team evaluates the economic feasibility of these information systems, their estimates of financial benefits are very inaccurate.

Management Control. Decisions at this level are made to accomplish the organization's objectives effectively and efficiently. Information systems used in management control include responsibility accounting and budgeting systems, and systems used in personnel management. Some of these provide benefits that are difficult to quantify; nevertheless, estimation is easier than at the strategic planning level. The benefits from these systems occur from one to five years after implementation. Because fewer unexpected events occur during this time period, the study team can predict the financial benefits of such a system more accurately.

Operational Control. Decisions at the operational control level ensure that specific tasks are carried out properly. Examples of information systems at this level include accounting transaction processing, inventory control, and cash management systems. For these applications, benefits often result from cost savings that are easily projected. Their payoffs may be immediate and can be estimated with accuracy. In many organizations, the largest and most expensive systems are developed at the operational control level. Organizations make these investments because they feel confident that the projected financial benefits can be attained.

Determining Financial Benefits—An Example. XYZ Company is considering the development of a computerized inventory control system to replace its current manual one. The average cost of finished goods inventory during the most recent year was $10 million. A consultant has determined that a computerized system would allow inventories to decrease to an average of $8 million while maintaining the same level of customer service. XYZ finances its inventories with a line of credit at its bank, which charges an interest rate of 10 percent per year. What are the expected financial benefits to XYZ Company from the computerized inventory system?

This proposed operational control system allows XYZ to reduce its inventory level by $2 million. The inventory carrying cost for XYZ Company is 10 percent. The financial benefit resulting from the computerized system is as follows:

Current average inventory	$10,000,000
Possible average inventory with the new system	8,000,000
Decrease in average inventory	2,000,000
Inventory carrying cost	× .10
Annual savings in inventory carrying costs	$ 200,000

XYZ Company could save $200,000 per year by implementing the computerized inventory control system. This savings constitutes interest that XYZ does not pay due to excessive inventory.

Comparing Costs and Benefits. The study team evaluates the economic feasibility of a new system or system change by comparing its costs with its benefits. In many cases, such as the previous example, these costs and benefits can be estimated accurately. The next step is to compare the costs with the benefits by using one of three methods: net cost or benefit, return on investment, or discounted cash flow.

Net Cost or Benefit. The simplest way to compare costs and benefits is to subtract one from the other. When benefits exceed costs, the study team calculates the net benefit. If benefits are less than costs, the result is a net cost. Many people refer to this calculation as *cost-benefit analysis*.

This form of analysis is appropriate when the study team is comparing annual costs with annual benefits, or onetime costs with onetime benefits. However, the method may produce incorrect conclusions if, for example, onetime costs are subtracted from annual benefits. Doing so ignores the time value of money; discounted cash flow methods are better for this comparison.

Return on Investment. Some companies evaluate economic feasibility using return on investment (ROI). One way of computing ROI is to divide annual benefits from a system by the onetime costs of developing it. If there are annual costs, these should be subtracted from the annual benefits first.

$$\text{ROI} = \frac{\text{Annual Benefits} - \text{Annual Costs}}{\text{Onetime Development Costs}}$$

ROI is a popular measure but, like cost-benefit analysis, it ignores the time value of money. Discounted cash flow methods overcome this disadvantage.

Discounted Cash Flow Methods. These methods of comparing costs and benefits recognize the importance of the *timing* of cash flows as well as their *magnitudes*. Many new systems require a major onetime investment of cash during development and produce smaller annual benefits over many years. The value to an organization of the annual benefit received this year is greater than an identical annual benefit received 10 years in the future. Because of this, the money saved or received over an extended period of time has *time value*. In other accounting courses you learn methods of evaluating projects, such as investments in new systems, that are called capital budgeting models. These methods consider the time value of money and include such techniques as the internal rate of return, the net present value, and the present value index.[1] Illustration 6–6 shows calculations of the net benefit, ROI, and net present value for the XYZ Company example.

---

[1] W. M. Liao and J. L. Boockholdt, *Cost Accounting for Managerial Planning, Decision Making and Control*, 3d ed.(Houston: Dame, 1989) pp. 575–90.

ILLUSTRATION 6–6 Example of Comparing Costs and Benefits for a New System

Example: XYZ Company estimates that a computerized inventory control system produces an annual savings of $200,000. The system will be used for eight years. XYZ's cost of capital is 10 percent. Projected costs for the system are as follows:

Annual cost:	Salaries	$ 70,000
	Utilities	20,000
	Supplies	10,000
	Total	$100,000
Onetime development costs:	Equipment	$100,000
	Computer programs	350,000
	Conversion costs	50,000
	Total	$500,000

Net benefit =

Annual benefits	$200,000	
Less: Annual costs	100,000	
Net annual benefit	$100,000	

Return on investment =

Net annual benefits	$100,000	
Investment	500,000	
ROI (100,000/500,000)	20%	

Net present value =

Present value of benefits:		
$200,000 × 5.335		$1,067,000
Less: Present value of costs:		
Annual $100,000 × 5.335	533,500	
Onetime	500,000	
Total		1,033,500
Net present value		$ 33,500

Report to Management

At the conclusion of the feasibility study, the system study team prepares a report describing its findings. This system study report may vary in length from a few pages to a bound volume. The study team submits this report to the information systems steering committee and may provide copies to interested parties in top management, the long-range systems planning group, and user departments.

The form of the system study report varies depending on the preferences of company management. Some managers like to see elaborate detailed analysis in the report, which they can skim or read in depth if necessary. Other managers prefer to have an executive summary in the first two or three pages, followed by pages of thorough analysis. With this approach, a busy manager quickly determines the study team's conclusions and has detailed information available to answer questions. Regardless of the form of the system study report, it should contain the information summarized in Illustration 6–7.

The system study report begins by describing the impetus for the study. This

ILLUSTRATION 6–7 Contents of a System Study Report

1. Describe the problem, information need, or desired technology.
2. State the objective of the system study.
3. Describe procedures followed in the preliminary survey.
4. Identify the constraints on the problem solution.
5. Discuss the two or three best system alternatives:
   - Identify the solution, its objectives, and its scope.
   - Describe advantages and disadvantages.
   - Summarize financial costs and benefits.
   - State major assumptions.
6. Make a recommendation.

information is contained in the original system study proposal written by a manager and submitted to the steering committee. Because several months may have elapsed between the proposal and the report, the description is repeated. The impetus for the study may have been a problem with an existing system, a new requirement for information, or the desire to implement a new technology. The system study report then restates the objective of the study as it was identified by the steering committee.

The report also describes briefly the procedures followed in the preliminary survey. It identifies the departments and existing systems that were reviewed, and discusses how tools such as questionnaires or work measurement techniques were employed. The report then provides a concise statement of the problem identified by the study team. It also includes a description of the constraints, or limitations, on possible solutions to the problem.

Most of a system study report is devoted to discussions of alternative solutions to the problem. In the report, the team identifies the two or three most promising solutions and describes them in detail. These solutions may include minor changes to existing systems, major overhauls of existing systems, or replacing an old system with a completely new one. The discussion lists the advantages, disadvantages, costs, and benefits of each solution. It also contains a summary of the major assumptions made by the study team in evaluating the alternatives.

Most important, the system study report contains the study team's final recommendation, which may be to implement one of the alternatives, to take no further action, or to delay action until some time in the future.

Frequently, members of the system study team present their findings to the steering committee and members of top management. Their presentation is an oral summary of the information contained in the system study report. It may include numerous graphs, charts, and other visual aids. This gives the managers an opportunity to ask questions about the study and to evaluate the competence of the study team. At the conclusion of this presentation, the steering committee makes a decision regarding the team's recommendations.

ILLUSTRATION 6–8 Possible Outcomes of Systems Analysis

Do Nothing—problem is not serious or resources are unavailable.

Modify Existing System—a less costly solution that may provide satisfactory results.

Design a New System—existing systems cannot solve the problem.

Outcomes of Systems Analysis

The systems analysis phase has three possible outcomes. The outcome is selected by the steering committee with input from top management. It is based on the recommendations of the study team.

Do Nothing. The information system steering committee may decide that no further action is warranted. Perhaps the problem is not as serious as originally thought, the need for new information no longer exists, or the new technology is not cost efficient. Often the committee will simply delay further action until some time in the future when more resources are available. Any change to information systems requires a commitment of MIS and user department personnel. The committee must allocate existing analysts and programmers to the needs that are currently most critical.

Modify an Existing System. The committee may decide that a satisfactory solution can be attained by modifying an existing application system. This outcome may be chosen because it requires fewer resources and can be accomplished more quickly than developing a new system. It often represents a compromise; although not ideal, this solution is satisfactory and can be implemented at lower cost.

Design a New System. Sometimes the committee concludes that the problem or need is serious enough to require a completely new system. This occurs when the committee believes that an existing system is outdated and that a modification would be unsatisfactory or not worth the cost. A new system is desired to solve the problem. They then authorize the formation of a system design team which creates a paper description of a new system. This marks the beginning of the system design phase of the system development life cycle. Illustration 6–8 summarizes the outcomes of the systems analysis phase.

SUMMARY

Systems analysis is the first phase in the system development life cycle. An application of the systems approach, it is the process of evaluating existing systems and identifying recommendations for improvement.

Systems analysis begins with a system study proposal submitted by a manager to the information system steering committee. The steering committee appoints a system study team to investigate the need identified in the proposal. The study team conducts a preliminary survey of existing systems and identifies problems in them. Then in the feasibility study, the team evaluates alternative solutions to the problems.

The study team prepares a system study report for management that summarizes the results of its analysis. The report may be accompanied by an oral presentation of recommendations. Based on the study team's report, the steering committee may decide to appoint a design team and begin the system design phase.

KEY TERMS

economic feasibility A feasibility criterion that concerns whether or not the benefits from a system alternative are worth its costs.

feasibility study A systems analysis activity during which a study team examines alternatives that are potential improvements to an existing system.

operating feasibility A feasibility criterion that concerns whether or not a proposed system alternative can meet its objectives.

operational audit A study performed by internal auditors to analyze the operations of a department and to identify improvements.

preliminary survey A systems analysis activity during which a study team evaluates existing systems.

systems analyst An employee who participates in system development project teams. This employee is skilled in computer processing methods, recognizes business needs for information, and understands the systems approach to problem solving.

system study proposal A written request from a manager asking that a study team be formed to analyze a system problem.

system study report A report submitted to top management and the information systems steering committee summarizing the results of systems analysis.

system study team One or more systems analysts and computer user personnel who are responsible for conducting systems analysis.

technical feasibility A feasibility criterion that concerns whether or not a system alternative can be implemented given the technical capabilities of the organization.

time feasibility A feasibility criterion that concerns whether or not a system alternative can be implemented within a reasonable time.

work measurement study A study intended to determine the magnitude or quantities of tasks performed in an existing system.

QUESTIONS

6–1. What are the steps in the systems approach to problem solving discussed in Chapter 3? How are they applied during systems analysis?

6–2. How does the preliminary survey differ from the feasibility study?

6–3. What are the objectives of a preliminary survey?

6–4. Who initiates a system study proposal? For which reasons?

6–5. A preliminary survey is a process of gathering data about certain features of an existing system. What are these features?

6–6. Why is it sometimes difficult to get adequate user input on a system study team?

6–7. Which procedures does the system study team use in conducting a preliminary survey?

6–8. What are the advantages of conducting a preliminary survey?

6–9. What is the first step in performing a feasibility study?

6–10. In a feasibility study, a system study team evaluates possible solutions to an information system problem. What forms can these solutions take? Which of these forms requires a continuation of the system development process?

6–11. Can you distinguish between the four feasibility criteria? Which do you think is the easiest to determine? The hardest?

6–12. Discuss the advantages and disadvantages of three ways to compare costs and benefits of a proposed system solution.

6–13. Describe the contents of a report to management prepared at the conclusion of systems analysis.

EXERCISES AND CASE

6–14. ECONOMIC BENEFITS AND DECISION LEVELS

Using the following three levels of decision-making activity, identify some possible financial benefits from a new information system that provides information at each level. Classify each as either easy or difficult to determine.

a. Operational control
b. Management control
c. Strategic planning

6–15. SYSTEM STUDY TEAM

A systems analysis study team frequently includes representatives from user departments in the organization. These employees provide knowledge to the team about how the existing system operates. Identify by job positions which employees might be assigned to a system study team that conducts a preliminary survey on:

a. A payroll system.
b. An accounts receivable system.
c. An inventory system.
d. A cost accounting system.

6–16. *PRELIMINARY SURVEY*

What are the possible shortcomings of studying an existing system before designing a new one to replace it?

6–17. *ACTIVITIES IN SYSTEMS ANALYSIS*

Each of the following activities may be performed during the development of a new system. Which are done as a part of the systems analysis phase?

a. Interviews are conducted with operating people and managers.
b. The complete documentation of the system is obtained and reviewed.
c. Measures of processing volume are obtained for each operation.
d. Equipment sold by various computer manufacturers is evaluated for its capability, cost, and availability.
e. Work measurement studies are conducted to determine the time required to complete various tasks or jobs.

(CMA Adapted)

6–18. *DETERMINING FEASIBILITY*

The following five conclusions were drawn by a system study team as part of a feasibility study. For each conclusion, determine which of the four kinds of feasibility is being evaluated.

a. A proposed system is attainable, given the existing technology.
b. The MIS manager is able to coordinate and control the activities of the MIS department.
c. An adequate computer site exists for the proposed computer system.
d. The proposed system could produce economic benefits that exceed its costs.
e. The system could be effectively used within the operating environment of the organization.

(CMA Adapted)

6–19. *ECONOMIC FEASIBILITY*

Newton Enterprises has no experience with computer-based systems. When considering the acquisition of a new computer, they gathered the following information as part of a feasibility study:

Total initial cost for acquiring a computer system	$150,000
Annual operating costs when computerized	60,000
Annual operating costs for the existing system	90,000
Discount factor	30%
Estimated useful life of a computer-based system	3 years

Required:

Evaluate the economic feasibility of the proposed computer-based system.

6–20. *SYSTEM FLOWCHART* (Document Flowchart)

After a shipment is prepared, the shipping department prepares a three-part shipping notice form. The first copy is included with the goods sent to the customer as a packing slip. The second copy is forwarded to the billing department. The third copy is sent to the accountant. When the billing department receives the second copy of the shipping order, it uses that information to prepare a two-part sales invoice. The second copy of the shipping order is then filed in the billing department. The first copy of the sales invoice is sent to the customer. The second copy of the sales invoice is forwarded to the accountant. Periodically, the accountant matches the copy of the shipping order with the copy of the sales invoice and files them alphabetically by customer. Before doing so, however, the accountant uses the copy of the sales invoice to post the sales entry in the subsidiary accounts receivable ledger.

Required:

Prepare a system flowchart summarizing these procedures.

(CIA Adapted)

6–21. *DATA FLOW DIAGRAM*

Prepare a data flow diagram for the procedures described in Exercise 6–20.

6–22. *SYSTEM FLOWCHART*

The Alaska branch of Far Distributing Company has substantial annual sales, which are billed and collected locally. Its procedures for handling cash receipts are as follows:

Cash collections on over-the-counter sales and COD sales are received from customers or the delivery service by the cashier. On receipt of cash, the cashier stamps the sales ticket "paid" and files a copy for future reference. The only record of COD sales is a copy of the sales ticket given to the cashier to hold until the cash is received from the delivery service.

Mail is opened by the secretary to the credit manager, and remittances are given to the credit manager for his review. The credit manager then places the remittances in a tray on the cashier's desk. At the daily deposit cutoff time the cashier delivers the checks and cash on hand to the assistant credit manager. She prepares remittance lists, makes up the bank deposit, and takes the deposit to the bank. The assistant credit manager also posts remittances to the accounts receivable ledger cards and verifies the cash discount allowable.

Required:

Prepare a system flowchart summarizing these procedures.

(AICPA Adapted)

6–23. ***DATA FLOW DIAGRAM***

Prepare a data flow diagram summarizing the procedures described in Exercise 6–22.

6–24. ***STEERING COMMITTEE***

Information system steering committees composed of high-level personnel have come into increasing use in many organizations for making key decisions regarding data processing.

Required:

a. List four responsibilities of a steering committee for data processing.

b. Give two reasons why it is desirable for a steering committee to perform these responsibilities rather than the MIS manager.

(CIA Adapted)

6–25. ***SYSTEMS SURVEY AND ANALYSIS***

Business organizations are required to modify or replace a portion or all of their accounting information systems to keep pace with growth and to take advantage of improved information technology. The process involved in modifying or replacing an information system, especially if computer equipment is involved, requires a substantial commitment of time and resources. When an organization undertakes a change in its information system, a series of steps or phases is taken. The steps or phases included in a systems study are:

Survey of the existing system.

Analysis of information collected in the survey and development of recommendations for corrective action.

Design of a new or modified system.

Equipment study and acquisition.

Implementation of a new or modified system.

These steps or phases tend to overlap rather than to be separate and distinct. In addition, the effort required in each step or phase varies from one system change to another, depending on such factors as extent of the changes or the need for different equipment.

Required:

a. Explain the purpose and reasons for surveying an organization's existing system.

b. Identify and explain the activities and techniques commonly used during the systems survey and analysis steps for an accounting information system.

c. The systems survey and analysis steps are often carried out by a project team composed of a systems analyst, a management accountant, and other persons in the company who would be knowledgeable and helpful in the system study. What would be the role of the management accountant in these steps for an accounting information system study?

(CMA Adapted)

6–26. CORPORATE CONSOLIDATION SYSTEM— PART I

Several years ago at R. J. Reynolds Industries, Inc. (RJR), the corporate accounting group, which is responsible for developing consolidated and line-of-business financial statements, was facing difficulties in developing the financial information reported to the corporation's stockholders and executive management.[2] Management concluded that the accounting system being used to consolidate the financial information from the operating companies for reports to management and stockholders was rapidly becoming inadequate because of RJR's internal growth and expansion and the increasing requirements of public reporting.

The Environment

R. J. Reynolds Industries, Inc., is a diversified, worldwide corporation with 1977 consolidated net sales and revenues of $6.4 billion. It serves as the parent company for seven subsidiaries each of which is a major line of business. Because RJR deals in a multicountry and multi-industry environment, any actions taken by financial management that might affect the corporation as a whole must reflect consideration of not only the current lines of business but also the possibility of future growth and acquisition.

The old consolidation system was a converted autocoder general ledger program built around a series of card sorts. The system could no longer handle RJR's growth nor generate financial reports in the time frame and manner required in the 1970s. Also, the addition of new reporting entities resulting from acquisitions was an extremely time-consuming process that entailed preparing a series of new header cards for the various card sorts.

---

[2] This case, and its continuation in Chapters 7 and 8, is adapted from James H. Wood, "How RJR Put Its New MIS On-Line," *Management Accounting*, April 1979, p. 17. Copyright by National Association of Accountants (1979), Montvale, N.J. 07645.

Another problem grew out of the increase in public reporting requirements from expanded Securities and Exchange Commission (SEC) regulations and accounting pronouncements issued by the Financial Accounting Standards Board (FASB). The growth in reporting requirements is illustrated by comparing R. J. Reynolds' 1968 and 1977 annual reports. In 1968 the annual report had 28 pages, including 6 pages of financial statements and notes. The notes to the financial statements were confined to one half page. In 1977 the report had been expanded to 64 pages with financial statements covering 17 pages and 14 pages of notes. Overall, the accounting information requirements both within and outside of RJR had grown tremendously over the past years. The corporate accounting staff was being asked to respond to questions faster and to make the financial information more useful to management and stockholders.

In recognition of the growth of the corporation and the changing public reporting environment, the corporate accounting group undertook a study to develop a response to the growing financial information requirements. The study resulted in the installation of a general ledger system in corporate headquarters to handle consolidation accounting and reporting. The general ledger system, when installed in corporate accounting, was named the corporate consolidation system (CCS).

The New System

CCS was designed to allow the corporate accounting department to keep its analysis records on the computer, to handle routine transactions automatically and systematically, to produce and change reports without systems assistance, and to maintain a data base that can be accessed by other systems and departments. It processes the financial statements and selected account analyses of each of the reporting entities and consolidates them into the total corporate statements, with statements of earnings and balance sheets for each individual reporting company in a line of business. In addition, certain selected schedules for SEC Form 10-K are prepared using the statistical capabilities of CCS.

The system contains a variable report writer which gives a user in the accounting department the ability to request, design, and implement required reports, including budgeting and exception reports. CCS has an allocation feature for financial and statistical accounts which can support recurring journal entries, budgeting, consolidations, and distributions. Capability is provided for data entry and inquiry from terminals. Automatic consolidations and support for unlike charts of accounts are provided by CCS. Multiple regional user groups for the general ledger cover both domestic and international markets.

Justification

To justify CCS, the corporate accounting group had to estimate what its payout would be. The project team identified time savings as the principal justification for providing analytical capabilities at user terminals.

During closing in consolidation accounting, managers need to focus their attention on account fluctuations, and at the same time to have the capacity to research backup data while a question is still current. Commonly an accounting staff member is asked a question, provides an answer, and immediately is asked a second question. Terminal access capability gave the accounting staff the power to handle this iterative questioning process. Its short response time allows accountants to verify input and output several times before presenting finished financial statements to management.

By using this terminal input and display feature, technical corrections and last-minute input of corrections are immediately processed and errors corrected. The accountant receives an immediate response to coding errors and usually can correct them on the spot.

Additionally, multiple users have access to the same updated financial data base at the same time. As an example, someone within the financial organization may ask a question concerning the balances with the CCS data base. An accountant at a terminal can give the answer, with assurance that all other users have access to the same financial data. Corporate accounting no longer had to type, copy, and distribute a financial statement every time a question was asked.

Required:

a. What were the changes that initiated this system study?

b. What were the objectives of the corporate consolidation system?

Chapter 7

System Design

Learning Objectives:

1. To learn the activities that take place during the second phase of the system development life cycle.
2. To discover how to create a preliminary system design.
3. To understand how to develop the detailed specifications for an accounting information system.
4. To learn how auditors participate in the system design process.

INTRODUCTION

The previous chapter described the activities taking place during the systems analysis phase of the system development life cycle (SDLC). At the conclusion of systems analysis, a system study team makes a recommendation to the information systems steering committee.

If the decision is to continue the development project, the steering committee appoints a project team to begin the system design phase. This design team consists of the systems analysis study team supplemented by accountants and systems analysts.

The system design team begins by identifying the major features of the new system. Then, after receiving the steering committee's approval, they specify in detail the system's characteristics. These activities are called preliminary system design and detailed specification. Following these activities, the design team begins the implementation phase. Illustration 7–1 shows the relationship of the system design phase to the other phases in the SDLC.

ILLUSTRATION 7–1 The System Design Phase

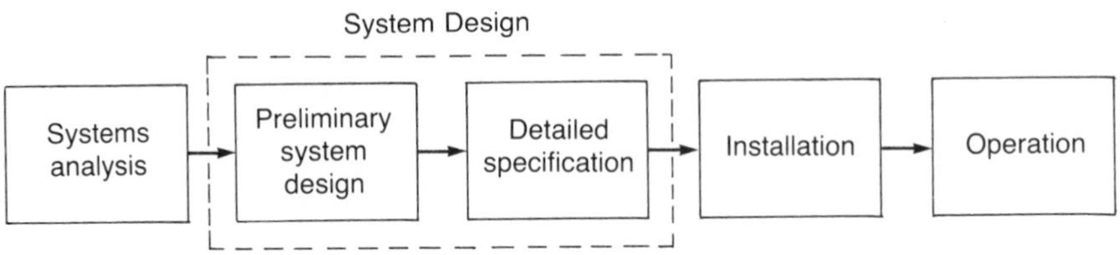

Importance of System Design

System design is the process of developing specifications for a proposed new system from the recommendations made during systems analysis. During the design phase, the project team produces working papers containing these specifications. The documentation contained in the working papers provides management with descriptions of the inputs, outputs, and processes of the proposed system.

Performing a thorough system design provides two significant benefits: First, it gives management and the information systems steering committee opportunities to approve or disapprove the system before proceeding with implementation. During design the team can make changes or stop development of the system. Second, the design documentation provides the project team with an overview of how the system works. Careful attention to design allows the project team to identify inefficiencies in processing, inconsistencies with other systems, weaknesses in internal control, or other problems. Changes are much easier to make while the system is still in the design phase. Substantial effort devoted to design usually pays off later with easier implementation and a more successful system.

PRELIMINARY SYSTEM DESIGN

System design is a process of starting with a set of objectives, identifying general methods of achieving those objectives, and gradually making those methods more specific and more concrete. Many organizations choose to break this process into two activities separated by a management decision point. The first of these activities is preliminary system design.

A study team identifies system objectives in the systems analysis phase. During preliminary system design, a design team develops a logical description of the proposed system. This gives management the opportunity to determine if the proposed system meets its objectives prior to detailed specification. The team creates a documentation package that identifies the scope, the system requirements, and the resource requirements of the proposed system.

Statement of Scope

During preliminary design, the project team first defines the scope of the new system. This process is sometimes simply a restatement of the scope established during systems analysis. In that phase, however, the study team defines system scope for purposes of estimating feasibility. During preliminary system design, the project team defines scope for the purpose of creating a new system. The design team defines boundaries by identifying the interfaces between the proposed new system and other systems in its environment. They may have to redefine the boundaries of the system to avoid changes to other existing systems.

The new system's boundaries must be comprehensive enough to achieve the system's objectives. Yet if boundaries are set too broadly, the system development project becomes so large that it is difficult to implement successfully. One way to determine the limits of the current design project is to identify procedures that do not change when the new system is implemented. Any procedures that are not subject to change are beyond the boundaries of the new system.

System Requirements

During preliminary design, the design team identifies features necessary for the system to achieve its objectives. These are the requirements that the proposed system must provide, and include outputs, data, processes, inputs, and policies.

Outputs. The design team first determines the outputs that the system should produce. They address two issues: (1) the information content of the outputs, and (2) the form of the outputs. When the proposed system must provide new or different information, the design team must determine both the form and the information content of the outputs. When the information content does not change, the team determines only the form of the outputs.

Information Content. A new system is proposed for one of three reasons: to satisfy a new information requirement, to solve a problem with an existing system, or to implement a new technology. When a new system is developed to satisfy a new reporting requirement, the information it provides is unavailable from existing systems. The design team ensures that the new system's outputs provide information to satisfy the requirement. For example, in designing a cost accounting system, the team may decide that an output should summarize the costs of production for a specific batch of widgets produced under government contract.

If a proposed system is to solve a problem with an existing system, the information content of system outputs may change to correct the problem. For example, a billing system may provide an inadequate audit trail. In creating a new billing system, the design team includes new information on its outputs that allows an auditor to trace individual transactions into the accounts. If the reason for the system is to implement a new technology, the information content of its outputs need not change. In this case, the outputs may take a new form.

Form. When selecting the form of the outputs, the design team decides how the information should be presented. This may be in the form of reports printed routinely, or it may be a computer terminal display that a clerk uses for data entry. Sometimes the team creates a system that produces reports or displays on an ad hoc, or as needed, basis. The system does not provide outputs routinely, but rather allows a manager or user to obtain them on request. For a routine output, the study team must decide how frequently to produce it. They give each report or display a unique name and identifying number and decide who in the organization receives it. When the purpose of system development is to implement a new technology, the form of system output sometimes changes even though its information content does not.

Data. The system's data records provide the information contained in reports or displays. After determining the information content of system outputs, the design team identifies the data items necessary to produce them. Data items include account numbers, quantities, amounts, names, addresses, and pay rates. At this point in the SDLC, the design team makes preliminary decisions about which data files are required, which storage medium to use, and how to organize the data in each file. Each file is assigned a unique name and identifying number.

Processes. The working papers produced during preliminary system design identify the processes required by the system. These processes may be manual procedures or computer programs.

In some organizations, the design team develops system flowcharts to show the sequence of the processes and how they produce the reports and displays from source documents and data records. However, when the organization uses a structured design methodology, they use data flow diagrams rather than flowcharts. This allows the design team to concentrate on the logical processes independent of the technology used in implementing them. The design team also determines those measures necessary to provide good internal control in the proposed system.

Inputs. Inputs to the system provide the sources of the data contained in system files. Commonly used inputs include forms such as sales orders, requisitions, and payroll timecards. System users record on these forms information describing accounting transactions. The system converts this information into computer readable form and summarizes it in data files. Systems analysts call these forms *source documents* because they provide the source for all data items used by the system. Sometimes transactions are entered directly into a system without using a document. This occurs, for example, when a computer terminal is also a cash register in a point-of-sale system.

During preliminary system design, the project team identifies each source document with a name and form number, determines where it originates, estimates its volume, and decides how its information is converted into computer readable form. They may also identify methods of data entry that do not use source documents.

Policies. Sometimes a new system requires that management adopt new policies for it to be successful. For example, manual system users have flexibility in deciding when to perform many of their job tasks. However, if the manual system is replaced by a computerized one, user activities are constrained by the computer operating schedule. Management may adopt policies that dictate when users perform their duties so the computerized system can operate efficiently.

If new policies are required by a proposed system, management wants to know about them before authorizing the system's development. Policies may have a detrimental effect on employee morale and turnover. Management considers these effects when evaluating the costs and benefits of a system.

At this stage, the design team develops descriptions of outputs, data files, inputs, processing steps, and policies without attention to specific detail. Their purpose is to identify only the essential features of the system. The preliminary system design allows the design team to assess more accurately the resources required to implement the proposed system and the benefits it could provide. Illustration 7–2 summarizes the system requirements determined during preliminary system design.

Resource Requirements

During preliminary system design, the design team identifies the financial resources required to successfully implement and operate the system. They determine the additional computer software and equipment that are necessary. They estimate the costs to complete development of the system and produce a schedule for completion. They estimate the ongoing costs to operate the system after implementation is complete. Because system requirements have been specified, these estimates are more accurate than those prepared during the feasibility study. The design team then performs another evaluation of the proposed system's costs and benefits and summarizes their conclusions in a report to management.

Software Resources. Software is the set of programs that control the operations performed by the computer equipment. Once the design team identifies the necessary features for the system, they choose one of four alternative sources for the software.

ILLUSTRATION 7–2 System Requirements Identified during Preliminary System Design

Outputs. Reports and terminal displays
- Name and number
- Information content
- Form
- Frequency
- Receiving person

Data items. Manual and computer files
- Name and number
- Storage medium
- Content
- Data organization method

Inputs. Source documents and direct data entry
- Document name and number
- Originating person
- Volume estimate
- Conversion method

Processes. Procedures and computer programs
- Files accessed
- Outputs produced
- Internal controls

Policies. Established by top management

In-House Development. With this alternative, the organization's own employees write the computer programs required by the system. A large system contains many programs, and numerous users or programmers are added to the design team to complete in-house development.

Sometimes the MIS manager also uses *contract programmers*. Contract programmers are employees of another firm who work for the organization only for the duration of the project. Using them is sometimes an efficient way to supplement the MIS programming staff.

In-house development has the advantage that the project team controls development of the programs. Thus, the programs specifically meet the organization's needs, and the system is more acceptable to the users who work with it. However, for accounting applications other sources are ordinarily less expensive.

Software Development Companies. Some companies are in the business of producing and selling software packages. These packages are computer programs that provide commonly needed applications, such as payroll, inventory, or general ledger applications. Software development companies employ systems analysts and programmers to develop packages, and a sales staff to market them. They may sell software directly to a MIS department or through computer stores or software brokers.

Packages are designed to satisfy the needs of many organizations, so any package probably is less acceptable to users than a system developed in-house. Because a package may be sold to hundreds or thousands of buyers, each shares in its development costs. Thus the cost of obtaining a package is much less than the costs of in-house development.

Computer Manufacturers. Most manufacturers of computer equipment also produce and sell software. This software is intended for use on the manufacturer's product line, and includes both application programs and system software. System software provides basic functions that control the computer and its peripheral devices. It includes operating systems that schedule the operations of the computer, file management programs that control data storage, and utility programs that perform frequently needed functions, such as sorting or printing files. In some cases, systems software is available only from a manufacturer, while the manufacturer's applications software competes with that of software development companies. Some systems software is necessary for the equipment to function; its costs are part of the initial acquisition costs of the system.

Users' Groups. A users' group is a club formed by individuals and organizations that own a particular brand of equipment or software. Members of the group exchange software at low cost, exchange advice, and frequently publish newsletters or operate computerized bulletin boards. A computerized bulletin board consists of an operating computer connected to a telephone line. Anyone can call the telephone number of the bulletin board on a computer modem and leave or receive messages. Members frequently exchange programs in this way.

In the early days of management information systems, users' groups were valuable as a source of business application programs. Today, users' groups primarily benefit users of small computers. If you own a personal computer, joining a users' group provides you with an inexpensive source of programs and advice.

Internal and External Sources. The possible sources for the programs in a new system are in-house development, software development companies, computer manufacturers, and users' groups. During preliminary system design, the design team chooses between in-house development and buying a software package from a source external to the organization. This is an example of the make-or-buy decision that you study in managerial and cost accounting courses.

Illustration 7–3 summarizes five considerations in choosing between in-house development or an external software package. Normally, gaining user acceptance is easier and fewer modifications are required when programs are written internally. However, installation time and costs are less when a package is

ILLUSTRATION 7–3 Considerations in the Make-or-Buy Decision for Software

User acceptance
In-House. Programs customized to users' preferences.
External package. Users adapt to requirements of externally written programs.

Required modifications
In-House. No modifications required.
External package. Modifications may be necessary to make software acceptable.

Installation time
In-House. Measured in months or years.
External package. Measured in weeks or months.

Quality of instruction manuals
In-House. Time pressures may discourage preparation of good documentation
External package. Documentation available for review prior to purchase.

Installation Cost
In-House. Costly; all costs absorbed by one system.
External package. Less costly; developmental costs absorbed by many systems.

purchased. Furthermore, with an external package, the design team can review the quality of its instruction manuals prior to purchase. If this documentation is inadequate, the team does not select the package.

Equipment Resources. After determining system requirements, the design team evaluates the need for computer equipment. In some cases, a new computerized system can be implemented without acquiring additional hardware. This is true when excess capacity exists on current equipment, and no new technology is needed by the new system. Where hardware is needed, the design team identifies a source for it during preliminary system design. The five alternative ways an organization can acquire computer equipment follow.

Purchase. Organizations frequently choose to purchase the additional equipment required by a new system. An organization with existing equipment may have a preferred manufacturer and may be knowledgeable about equipment that is available. Because of this knowledge and experience, the firm is willing to make the investment required by a purchase. Purchasing may provide tax benefits to profit-making businesses. However, this alternative requires a large initial cash outlay. Furthermore, in later years the equipment may become obsolete and the organization may have difficulty selling it.

Lease or Rental. Many organizations choose to rent or lease computer equipment. A lease is a rental of the equipment for a length of time fixed by a lease contract. The acquiring organization contracts with a bank or leasing company that provides the equipment in return for a monthly rental fee. Computer equipment leases commonly extend from two to five years. By leasing or renting, the acquiring organization avoids the initial large cash outlay of a purchase. However, the total of the lease or rental payments over several years exceeds the purchase cost of the same equipment. Leasing or renting allows the organization to avoid many risks of technological obsolescence that a purchaser incurs.

Service Bureau. A service bureau is a business that provides computer services to other organizations for a fee. The service bureau owns its computer equipment and provides programs for many accounting transaction processing applications. An organization records accounting events on its own source documents and then delivers them to the service bureau. The service bureau converts the transactions into computer readable form, processes them, and returns them along with accounting reports to the organization. A service bureau is a good alternative for an organization that has no experience with computerized data processing. It can obtain many of the advantages of computerization without establishing a MIS department. However, the organization is restricted to only those applications that the service bureau provides. And if the number of transactions is large, using a service bureau is an expensive alternative.

Remote Batch. Remote batch processing results from a modification of the procedures used by a service bureau. With remote batch, the organization installs equipment at its own location that converts accounting transactions into computer readable form. Its employees accumulate transactions into batches, convert them into computer files, and transmit these files over telephone lines to a computer at another location. The company that owns the computer then processes them and returns system outputs over telephone lines to a printer. This process is faster than using a service bureau, but the organization must employ data entry personnel and operate computer equipment. Many organizations first use a service bureau and then progress to remote batch processing. Later they establish a MIS department and lease, rent, or purchase their own equipment.

Timesharing. Timesharing services are provided by companies that own large computers accessible by telephone lines. To use a timesharing service, an organization acquires terminals at its location and connects them to telephone lines with modems. This enables the organization to use the computers at a remote location as if they were located in the same building. A user at a terminal dials the telephone number of the computer to connect with it. The user can write and debug computer programs, enter data from source documents, or execute programs on the remote computer. Use of a timesharing service provides access to a computer just as if the organization owned it. The organization can develop its own applications, provide its own data entry, and control its own processing. Furthermore, the organization avoids the risk of obsolescence of the computer. However, extensive use of a timesharing service is expensive. For processing many transactions, owning or leasing a computer is usually less costly.

Economic Resources. After identifying the equipment and computer software needed for the proposed new system, the design team estimates the costs to acquire them. Because the system's requirements have been identified, this cost estimate is more accurate than that developed during the feasibility study. The design team more accurately projects the benefits from it as well.

Costs. Costs associated with a computer system include both the initial cost of development and the annual recurring costs of operation. After preliminary system design, the initial costs include the computer system (equipment and software), computer housing (air conditioning and special wiring), and the remaining costs of development (detailed system specification, implementation, and the post-implementation review). Annual recurring costs include salaries of MIS personnel, hardware maintenance, software maintenance, computer supplies, and utilities.

Benefits. Benefits vary depending on the nature of the system. Salary reductions for clerical personnel, decreases in inventory carrying costs, and decreases in interest expense are easily quantifiable. Benefits that are more difficult to estimate may include better customer service and more informative management reports.

Illustration 7–4 shows an evaluation of the costs and benefits for a proposed computer system to replace a manual one. Using both return on investment and net present value measures, the change is a desirable one.

The design team may consider the alternative of leasing the equipment rather than purchasing it. Illustration 7–5 shows an economic analysis of this alternative. In this example leasing is more desirable than either purchasing a computer or retaining the existing system.

Report to Management

At the conclusion of preliminary system design, the design team describes its recommendation in a report to management. The report consists of an executive summary and the documentation package created by the design team. They submit it to the information system steering committee. They may also submit it or present it orally to top management.

The executive summary begins with a statement of the objectives and scope of the system. This is followed by a concise description of the system using system flowcharts. The report then details economic analyses similar to those in Illustrations 7–4 and 7–5. Next comes a description of any anticipated policy changes or implementation difficulties. Finally, the design team states its recommendation either to halt further design efforts or to proceed with detailed specification of the system.

DETAILED SPECIFICATION

The system design phase of the SDLC consists of two activities: The first of these, preliminary system design, provides a high-level, conceptual description of how the system should work. At its conclusion the steering committee

ILLUSTRATION 7–4 Costs and Benefits for a Proposed Computer Purchase

Return on investment analysis

Initial cost:	
Probable purchase price of equipment	$180,000
Installation, including air conditioning and cabling, estimated 6% of price	12,000
Software, estimated at 40% of price	72,000
Training, estimated at 20% of price	36,000
Total initial cost	$300,000
Annual operating costs:	
Salaries of MIS personnel	$104,000
Power, supplies, repairs, estimated at 20% of personnel cost	21,000
Facilities maintenance, estimated at 7½% of purchase price	14,000
Total annual operating cost	$139,000
Less salaries of clerical workers displaced by computer	267,000
Annual savings	$128,000
ROI ($128,000/$300,000)	43%

Present value analysis

(Assume five-year life and cost of capital = 20%)

Year	*Annual Savings*	*Discount Factor*	*Present Value of Savings*
1	$128,000	.833	$ 106,624
2	128,000	.694	88,832
3	128,000	.579	74,112
4	128,000	.482	61,696
5	128,000	.402	51,456
Present value of benefits			$ 382,720
Present value of costs			(300,000)
Net present value			$ 82,720

evaluates the proposed system. During the second activity, detailed specification, the design team creates a detailed description of the system on paper. Auditors review these specifications and suggest needed changes to internal control measures and to the audit trail. Finally, the design team submits the specifications to the steering committee for review and approval.

Activities in Detailed Specification

Three major functions occur during detailed specification. The design team specifically defines the requirements for the system. These requirements identified during preliminary system design include outputs, data, inputs, and

ILLUSTRATION 7–5 Costs and Benefits for a Proposed Computer Lease

Return on investment analysis

Initial cost:	
Installation	$ 12,000
Software	72,000
Training	36,000
Total initial costs	$120,000
Annual operating costs:	
Salaries of MIS personnel	$104,000
Power, supplies, repairs	21,000
Computer rental	43,200
Total annual operating costs	$168,200
Less salaries of clerical workers displaced by computer	267,000
Annual savings	$ 98,800
ROI ($98,800/$120,000)	82%

Present value analysis

(Assume five-year lease and cost of capital = 20%)

Year	*Annual Savings*	*Discount Factor*	*Present Value of Savings*
1	$98,800	.833	$ 82,300
2	98,800	.694	68,567
3	98,800	.579	57,205
4	98,800	.484	47,819
5	98,800	.402	39,718
Present value of benefits			$295,609
Present value of costs			120,000
Net present value			$175,609

processing steps. After these activities are complete, the team is ready to select a source for the software. If additional computer equipment is required, the design team selects a source for the equipment and orders it.

Equipment Selection

During preliminary system design, the design team identifies the computer equipment necessary to implement the proposed system. During system specification, they select a source for this equipment. They identify possible suppliers by studying trade journals and subscription services. Then they evaluate these vendors as possible sources for the equipment.

Subscription Services. Subscription services provide an efficient way to determine the kinds of equipment available. These services come from companies that monitor changes in the computer industry. They maintain contact with equipment and software suppliers and gather information when new products are released. These services then compile this information into loose-leaf notebooks; subscribers to the service purchase notebooks, and receive updates whenever information on a new product becomes available. Different subscription services exist for different products. Some services describe large computer systems; others cover small business computers, peripheral equipment used with a computer, and software.

Subscription services summarize many equipment sources in a way that makes comparisons easy. The study team reviews the equipment specifications described in the notebook and identifies the models most suitable for the proposed system. Then they contact equipment sellers directly to negotiate prices and delivery dates.

Evaluation of Equipment Vendors. Two common approaches exist for evaluating vendors. In one approach, the design team establishes a minimum configuration for the hardware required by the system. They identify the quantity and specifications of all the computers and peripheral equipment needed. They summarize this in a *request for quotation* (RFQ) mailed to potential vendors. In the RFQ, the design team asks the vendor to quote a price for this configuration. This approach relies on the expertise of the design team.

Using the second approach, the design team establishes performance specifications for the proposed system. They describe these in a *request for proposal* (RFP) that goes to vendors. Each vendor then proposes a configuration for the hardware that meets these specifications and quotes a price for it. This approach is useful when the design team lacks the experience or time to develop its own configuration. However, because a vendor sometimes overstates the capabilities of its equipment, the second approach may result in inadequate configurations.

Criteria for Equipment Evaluation. The design team considers five concerns in evaluating equipment sources and examining proposals from vendors: equipment performance, adaptability, vendor support, availability, and cost. Illustration 7–6 summarizes these criteria.

Equipment Performance. The design team wants to acquire equipment that performs adequately. During system specification, they may compare performance of equipment from alternative vendors. Unfortunately, making meaningful predictions of equipment performance in a particular application is difficult. Manufacturers publish performance specifications for each model they manufacture. For example, computers are described by a MIPS number, the number of millions of instructions per second that they can process. For magnetic disk drives, manufacturers specify the *mean access time* to retrieve data stored on it.

ILLUSTRATION 7–6 Criteria for Equipment Evaluation

Equipment performance. Difficult to measure properly

Adaptability. Includes expandability and compatability

Vendor support. Quality of technical help

Availability. Affects the implementation schedule

Cost. Tangible costs of installation and operation

In determining these numbers, manufacturers assume operating conditions for the equipment that may be unrepresentative of an accounting application. Manufacturers' performance specifications are useful in comparing equipment, but they do not reflect expected performance in practice.

Sometimes a *benchmark* is used as a measure of performance. A benchmark is a computer program written to represent a typical application, such as computing payroll. The design team runs a benchmark program on two or more different computers and compares execution times. The system that requires the least time is the better performer. Data provided by benchmarking is useful whenever the benchmark program is similar to those in the proposed system.

Adaptability. Organizations investing thousands or millions of dollars in systems want them to be useful for many years and adaptable to changing needs. As the organization grows, the system must be able to grow; thus, adaptability of the system requires expandability for the equipment. The system should also be compatible with other equipment and software that may become available later.

Many medium-sized computers are not expandable into faster, more powerful systems. Some purchasers have found that although their performance is adequate at the time of acquisition, these computers cannot add memory, terminals, or other peripheral equipment when needed. Similarly, purchasers of less popular brands of computers have few sources for software or peripheral equipment. As a result, costs are higher and the selection is smaller. A wise design team purchases a brand compatible with a variety of other brands.

Vendor Support. Most organizations that acquire new computer equipment require technical help from the manufacturer. A design team should select a vendor that has the ability and desire to provide this help. Adequate vendor support facilitates the activities performed during the implementation phase of the SDLC.

Vendor support reflects both the capabilities and the desires of the seller. A computer equipment manufacturer with technicians in the local area can provide more help than one who must bring in technicians from some other region. Some vendors make backup computers available or service equipment at the data center, while others do not. A supplier who wants to maintain good customer relations can be relied on to keep promises and to aid customers in resolving implementation problems.

Evaluating vendor support is a subjective task. A design team does it by talking to each vendor's current customers and relying on their experience.

Availability. The design team must choose a supplier that can provide the equipment at the time it is needed. Some new or popular models of computers are difficult to get and may be unavailable for several months. This can delay many activities of the implementation phase and be costly to the organization.

Sometimes a purchaser inserts a penalty clause in the purchase contract. This entitles the purchaser to a discount if equipment is not delivered on time. If a vendor refuses to accept such a clause, the purchaser should interpret this as an admission of uncertainty regarding the delivery date.

Cost. A final factor in the selection of computer equipment is its cost, not only the initial cost of purchase and installation, but also the ongoing costs of operation. Equipment that requires special air conditioning, piped water for internal cooling, and raised floors for cables is more expensive than equipment that is simply plugged into a source of electricity. Although the design team always considers these tangible costs, they are seldom the only criterion for equipment selection.

The other four criteria for equipment evaluation have implied costs that are difficult to estimate. There are costs for slow performance, for lack of adaptability, for poor vendor support, and for waiting on equipment that is unavailable. Usually a design team makes no attempt to estimate these costs. Instead, they identify equipment sources that are adequate in each of these areas; then they select equipment from these sources that is available at the lowest cost.

Requirements Definition

During preliminary system design, the design team identifies the logical requirements for the proposed system. Prior to implementation, outputs, data, processes, and inputs must be specified in detail. The design team does this during requirements definition, the second major function of detailed specification.

Output Specification. Outputs are the display screens and reports produced by the system. In preliminary system design, the design team identifies them by name and number and determines their information content. During detailed specification, the design team decides how each screen or report looks. They produce sample screens and reports, called *screen layouts* and *report layouts,* and include these examples in the documentation package for the proposed system. Users have the opportunity to examine them and suggest improvements prior to implementation. Illustrations 7–7 and 7–8 contain sample screen and report layouts.

ILLUSTRATION 7–7 A Display Screen Layout

SECTION: CORRECTION TRANSACTIONS INPUT/UPDATE	NUMBER: 5.1
SUBJECT: Screen: Suspended Batch Master Batch Identification Inquiry	DATE ISSUED:

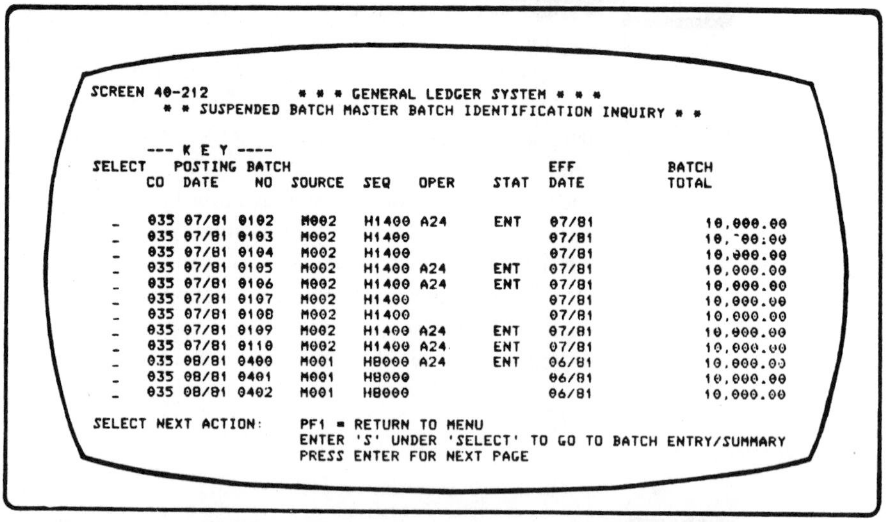

SCREEN 40-212 * * * GENERAL LEDGER SYSTEM * * *

* * SUSPENDED BATCH MASTER BATCH IDENTIFICATION INQUIRY * *

SELECT	--- K E Y ---- CO	POSTING DATE	BATCH NO	SOURCE	SEQ	OPER	STAT	EFF DATE	BATCH TOTAL
_	035	07/81	0102	M002	H1400	A24	ENT	07/81	10,000.00
_	035	07/81	0103	M002	H1400			07/81	10,-00:00
_	035	07/81	0104	M002	H1400			07/81	10,000.00
_	035	07/81	0105	M002	H1400	A24	ENT	07/81	10,000.00
_	035	07/81	0106	M002	H1400	A24	ENT	07/81	10,000.00
_	035	07/81	0107	M002	H1400			07/81	10,000.00
_	035	07/81	0108	M002	H1400			07/81	10,000.00
_	035	07/81	0109	M002	H1400	A24	ENT	07/81	10,000.00
_	035	07/81	0110	M002	H1400	A24	ENT	07/81	10,000.00
_	035	08/81	0400	M001	H8000	A24	ENT	06/81	10,000.00
_	035	08/81	0401	M001	H8000			06/81	10,000.00
_	035	08/81	0402	M001	H8000			06/81	10,000.00

SELECT NEXT ACTION: PF1 = RETURN TO MENU

ENTER 'S' UNDER 'SELECT' TO GO TO BATCH ENTRY/SUMMARY

PRESS ENTER FOR NEXT PAGE

SUSPENDED BATCH MASTER BATCH IDENTIFICATION INQUIRY SCREEN

List of Suspended Batches

ILLUSTRATION 7–8 A Report Layout

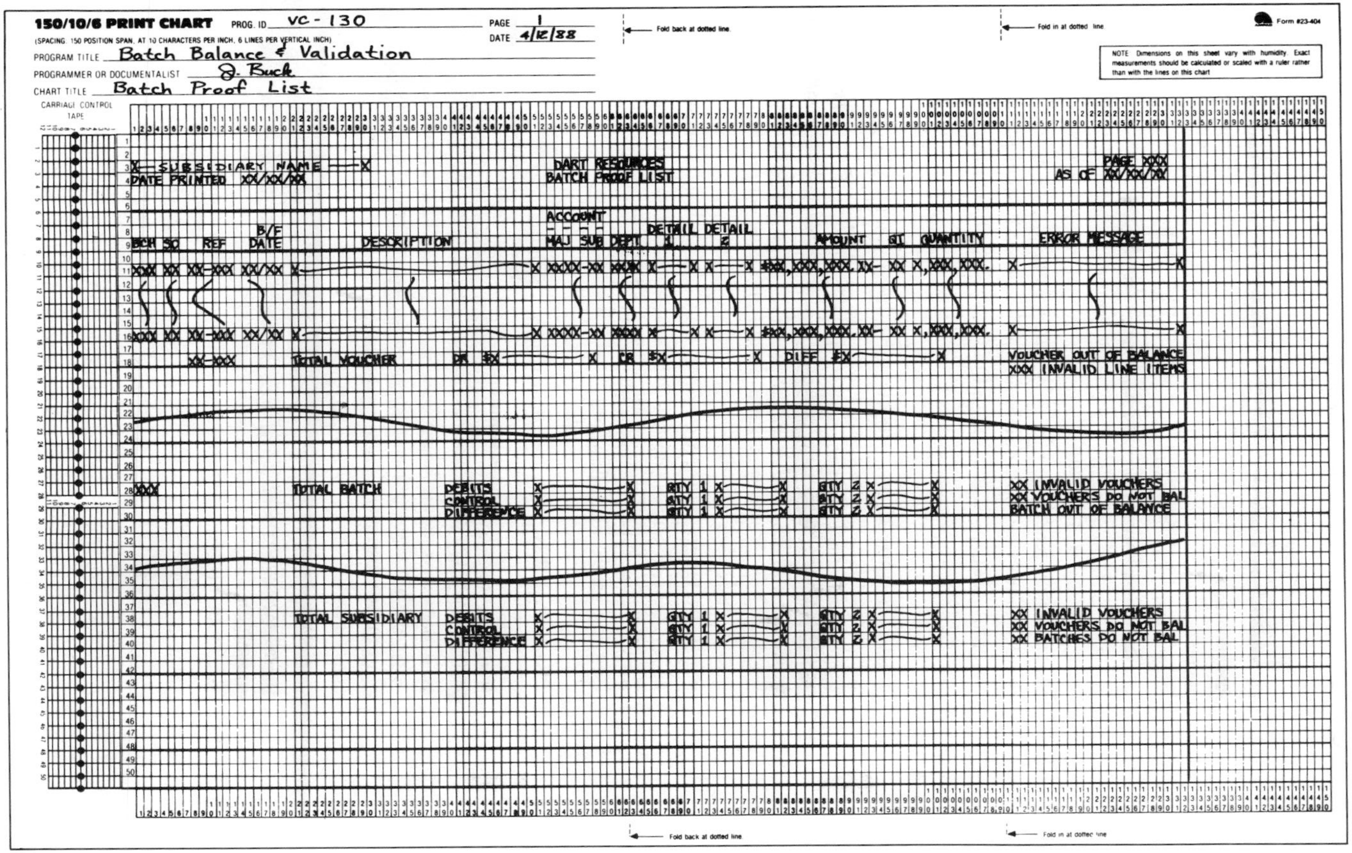

Data Specification. Data records contain the data summarized and presented in reports and display screens. Manual files in cabinets or desks store data on records made of paper. Computer files store data in records written magnetically on computer disks or tape.

During detailed specification, the design team describes each data record in detail, listing its purpose, the data items it contains, and the way the data are organized. For computerized records, this includes producing a record layout showing the arrangement of all its data items.

For each data record, the design team estimates its number of occurrences and specifies retention and backup procedures. Retention procedures identify how long a copy of the data must be maintained for tax and audit purposes. Backup procedures describe how frequently backup, or spare, copies of the data are made. They are internal control measures that prevent loss of data when the original record is accidentally destroyed. Illustration 7–9 contains a sample record layout.

Input Specification. Inputs include the source documents and magnetic media on which data are initially recorded by the system. During preliminary system design, the design team identifies each input and its source and estimates its volume. During system specification, they determine how each source document looks. They produce sample documents that show the arrangement of the data and include these in the design documentation. Users review these samples and suggest changes to them prior to implementation. For magnetic data input, such as in point-of-sale systems, the design team decides how the data are converted into a magnetic record. Illustration 7–10 contains a sample form produced during system specification.

Computer Program Specification. Prior to detailed specification, the design team identifies each process and shows its relationship to other processes with system flowcharts or data flow diagrams. In requirements definition, a systems analyst from the team produces a programming work package containing a written description of each program. A programmer uses this package later when coding the program. The work package contains a description of the program's logic, its inputs, and its outputs.

Program Narratives. In some organizations, the work package contains a program narrative describing the program's purpose, how frequently it executes, the computer data records that it accesses, and the inputs and outputs of the program. Inputs are magnetic computer records; outputs may be computer records, reports, or display screens. The narrative also describes the internal control measures to be coded into the program. You see an example of a program narrative in Illustration 7–11. If the program is complex, the narrative may be accompanied by a program flowchart.

When the organization uses a structured design methodology, the design team does not use flowcharts. Instead, the programming work package contains

ILLUSTRATION 7–9 A Computer File Record Layout

SECTION: FILE DOCUMENTATION	NUMBER:
SUBJECT: Record Layout, Journal Entry Transaction Record	DATE ISSUED:

SYSTEM NAME	On-Line General Ledger
FILE NAME	Journal Entry Transaction File
FILE DESCRIPTION	Contains all detail transactions to be posted to the General Ledger
STORAGE MEDIA	Disk - 3380
FILE ORGANIZATION	Indexed-sequential
FILE KEYS:	
PRIMARY	Group Number
SECONDARY	None
MODULE NAMES WHERE USED	ADD001, CHG001, DEL001, RPT001, RPT002

```
         11111111112222222222333333333344444444445555555555666666666677777777778
12345678901234567890123456789012345678901234567890123456789012345678901234567890

9999XXXXXXXXXXXXXXXXXXXXXXXXXS9999999.99XXMM/DD/YY9999XXXXXXXXXXXXXXXXXXXXXXXXXX
|   |                        |           |DR/|        |    |                          |
|ACCOUNT|<---- ACCOUNT DESCRIPTION ---->|<-- AMOUNT -->|CR |<-TRANSACTION->|<-GRP->|<---------- FILLER ---------->|
|NUMBER |                        |           |CODE   DATE  | NUM |                    |
```

DATA NOTATION:
- 9 - Numeric
- P - Packed Numeric
- X - Alphanumeric
- C - Character
- S - Sign (+ or -)
- N - Null Surpression
- MM - Month
- DD - Day
- YY - Year

DART RESOURCES

ILLUSTRATION 7–10 A Sample Input Form

SECTION: COMPUTER SYSTEM INPUTS	NUMBER: 9.1
SUBJECT: Input Form: On-line Operator Authorization Form	DATE ISSUED:

GENERAL LEDGER SYSTEM

ON-LINE OPERATOR AUTHORIZATION FORM

TRANS CODE [O, P] (1–2) OPERATOR CODE (3–6)

RECORD TYPE [1] (7) ACTION (A,C,D) (8) OPERATOR NAME (Initial & Last Name) (9, 11–29)

AUTHORIZED ON-LINE FUNCTIONS

[2] (7) (8) (9)

1–POSTING TRANSACTIONS INPUT/UPDATE

2–CORRECTION TRANSACTIONS INPUT/UPDATE

3–MAINTENANCE TRANSACTIONS INPUT/UPDATE

4–SUBMISSION OF BATCH JOBS

5–GENERAL LEDGER INQUIRIES

AUTHORIZED COMPANIES

[3] (7) (8) (9–36)
[3] (7) (8) (9–36)
[3] (7) (8) (9–36)
[3] (7) (8) (9–36)
[3] (7) (8) (9–36)
[3] (7) (8) (9–36)
[3] (7) (8) (9–36)
[3] (7) (8) (9–36)
[3] (7) (8) (9–36)
[3] (7) (8) (9–36)

PREPARED BY ______________________ DATE ________

APPROVED BY ______________________ DATE ________

IMPLEMENTED BY ______________________ DATE ________

ON-LINE OPERATOR AUTHORIZATION FORM

Form Number C-3

DART RESOURCES

ILLUSTRATION 7–11 A Program Narrative

SECTION: VALIDATION	NUMBER: VC-130
SUBJECT: Batch Balance & Validation	DATE ISSUED: 5/88

PURPOSE: Balance batches and vouchers within entities and balance forward dates. Check the basic validity of certain fields. Print Batch Proof List.

LOGIC OUTLINE:

I. Balancing
   A. By batch:
      1. Control on: debits
         Quantity 1
         Quantity 2
      2. Balance debits and credits for entire batch
      3. Require separate batches for each:
         - Company
         - Source
         - Balance Forward Date
         Assume new batch if one of these changes within an input batch.

II. Basic Validation
   A. Batch No. - numeric
   B. Reference - numeric, first two digits between 1 and 12 inclusive (first two digits signify month)
   C. Source - numeric, valid within B/F Date. Source must be for an accounting transaction to be posted to current or prior months. If source is for a budget transaction it can only be posted to a future period.
   D. Line Item Number - numeric
   E. B/F Date - numeric and valid first 2 digits between 1 and 12 inclusive. B/F Date must remain constant within a voucher. If it changes or is invalid, generate an error message for each line item in the voucher. This will cause the entire voucher to be rejected in VC-190.
   F. Trans-Date - numeric and possible date
   G. Amount - numeric or blank
   H. Quantity Type - 1 or 2
   I. Quantity Fields - numeric or blank

III. Other Processing
   A. If Amount is coded = blank, make it 0 so that it can be added in subsequent programs.
   B. Print Batch Proof List report (see Report Layout for details).

DART RESOURCES

structure charts and logic specifications. One effective way of specifying program logic uses pseudocode.

Structure Charts. Structured methodologies utilize structure charts to describe a program. A structure chart identifies each of the modules making up the program and shows the hierarchy among them. This hierarchy exists because a high-level module may cause the execution of one or more lower-level modules. On the structure chart, each module is represented by a rectangle. The hierarchical relationship between modules is shown by the levels on the chart. Not only is the structure chart useful in specifying the logic of a program but it is also a good form of documentation after programming is complete. Illustration 7–12 contains a structure chart for a program that prints a report.

Pseudocode. Sometimes a project team uses pseudocode to describe modules. Pseudocode is an informal language that uses English-like statements representing the actions performed by computer language instructions after the module is programmed. Pseudocode allows a programmer to describe how the module works without paying attention to the syntax of a computer language. Later the pseudocode statements are translated into a language understandable by the computer. Pseudocode facilitates the development of the logic; it also enables another person to understand more readily how the program works. Illustration 7–13 provides a sample of pseudocode.

Manual Procedures. Virtually all systems, even technologically advanced ones, require processes performed by people. Members of the design team identify these manual procedures for a proposed system during preliminary system design. During detailed specification they record each procedure in a procedures manual, usually a loose-leaf notebook containing a one-page narrative description of each procedure.

The procedure description, written by an analyst on the design team, identifies the job category of the person who performs the procedure. It lists the documents prepared and the reports or display screens used, as well as the steps necessary to carry out the procedure. The analyst estimates the frequency of the procedure and may illustrate it with a document flowchart. After reviewing this procedure description, users may suggest changes to it. Illustration 7–14 provides an example of a procedure description.

In requirements definition, the design team specifies the contents of all data records, manual procedures, and computer programs. They also decide how all forms, display screens, and reports should look, recording these decisions in their working papers. Users, managers, and steering committee members review these working papers, identify problems they expect with the system design, and suggest possible improvements. At the conclusion of requirements definition, a thorough description of the proposed system exists on paper. The design team then selects the computer programs required by the system.

ILLUSTRATION 7–12 A Structure Chart

SECTION: PROGRAM DOCUMENTATION	NUMBER:
SUBJECT: Structure Chart, A-100-UPDATE-MASTER module	DATE ISSUED:

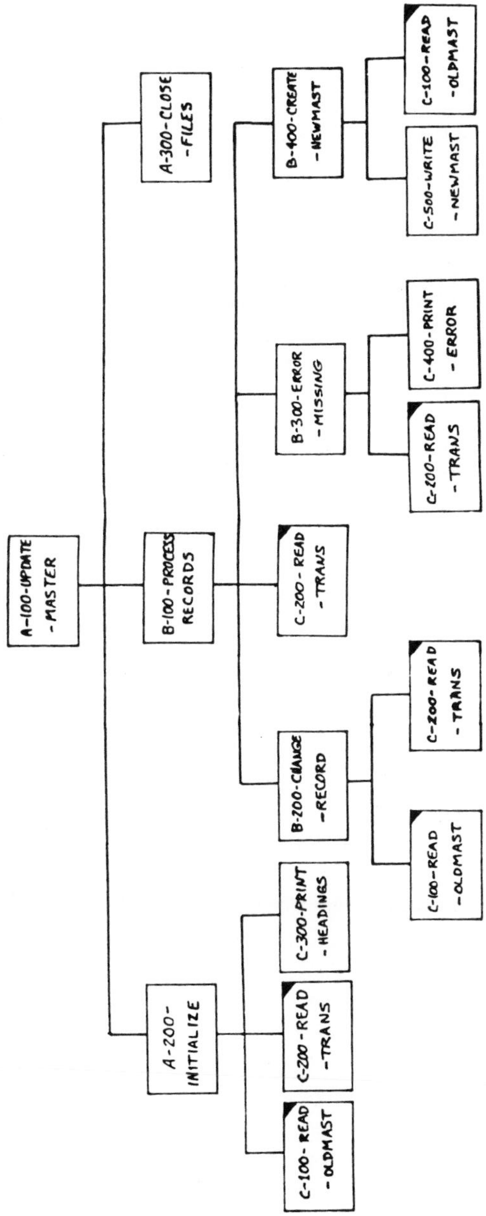

DART RESOURCES

ILLUSTRATION 7–13 Pseudocode

SECTION: PROGRAM DOCUMENTATION	NUMBER:
SUBJECT: Pseudocode, B-100-PROCESS-RECORDS module	DATE ISSUED:

```
IF Oldmaster account number = Transaction account number
     PERFORM Change Masterrecord Module
     ENDPERFORM
     PERFORM Read Transactionfile Module
     ENDPERFORM
     GO TO EXIT
ENDIF
IF Oldmaster account number > Transaction account number
     PERFORM Missing Masterrecord Error Module
     ENDPERFORM
     PERFORM Read Transactionfile Module
     ENDPERFORM
     GO TO EXIT
ENDIF
IF Oldmaster account number < Transaction account number
     MOVE Oldmaster record to Newmaster record
     PERFORM Create Masterrecord Module
     ENDPERFORM
ENDIF
EXIT
```

DART RESOURCES

ILLUSTRATION 7–14 A Procedure Description

SECTION: CORRECTION TRANSACTIONS INPUT/UPDATE	NUMBER: 5.2
SUBJECT: Screen: Batch Entry/Summary for Correction Transaction	DATE ISSUED:

I. PURPOSE

The purpose of this procedure is to describe the Batch Entry/Summary for Correction Transactions screen - Screen 40-212

II. GENERAL FUNCTIONS

A. Display Function. This function displays a suspended batch header and suspended line items (posting transactions). In addition, any corrections to the batch header information or to the line items information is also displayed.

B. Input Function. This function edits correction data to the suspended batch header information and edits correction data to suspended line items' data. If the correction data is valid, this function creates a correction transaction.

C. Update Function. This function edits changes to a previously input correction to the suspended batch header's data and edits changes to previously input corrections to line items' information. If the changes are valid, this function updates the correction transactions.

D. Finalize Function. This function finalizes a batch of correction transactions. A finalized batch is ready to be processed into a Batch Front-End Edit and Validation Job. After it has been successfully processed into a Batch Front-End Job, it is deleted from the On-line Transaction File. Neither the batch header correction data nor the correction transaction data of a finalized batch can be updated; however, a finalized batch can be un-finalized.

E. Un-finalize Function. This function un-finalizes a previously finalized batch. An un-finalized batch will not be processed into the Batch Front-End Job until it is finalized again. An un-finalized batch's corrections to header data can be updated, its corrections to line items can be updated or deleted, and new line items can be added.

F. Delete Function. This function deletes a correction transaction to a suspended line item.

G. Transfer Function. This function transfers to the following screens at the operator's request:

1. Main Menu screen,
2. Suspended Batch Master Batch Identification Inquiry screen,

Software Specification

During preliminary system design, the design team evaluates possible sources for computer software. These are either custom programs written in-house or an external software package. Some organizations prefer a hybrid approach, in which they purchase a package written by another company but modify it to suit their own needs.

During detailed specification, the design team makes a final decision concerning the source of the software. If they choose in-house development, they must create a software development plan. If they choose to purchase an external software package, they must select the package and then plan to make any necessary modifications.

Planning Software Development. When the programming for a new system is done in-house, it is likely to be the most time-consuming and most expensive undertaking in the implementation phase. Adequate planning for software development enables the design team to avoid excessive costs during programming, to ensure its timely completion, and to achieve a more orderly system conversion. A software development plan contains estimates of time requirements, assigns personnel to programming tasks, and describes software standards.

Estimate Time Requirements. After the programs have been described in detail, the design team can estimate the time required to develop each one. In developing a program, the programmer writes the code, debugs it, develops data to test the program, tests it, and produces documentation for it. In some cases the programmer also determines the logic of the program. In a language such as COBOL or BASIC, this requires periods of time varying from a few days for a simple program to a few weeks for a complex one. The design team categorizes programs according to their complexity and then estimates the time required to develop each program. From these estimates, the team calculates the total time required for programming.

Assign Personnel. During the implementation phase, the MIS department assigns programmers to the project team. These programmers may be employees in the MIS department, or they may be consultants or contract programmers from outside the organization. The design team estimates the number of programmers needed and arranges to have them assigned to the project. Some organizations create programmer teams, with each team led by a chief programmer. Other personnel such as data entry clerks, documentation specialists, and technicians may also be needed during implementation. The design team identifies these people and schedules their services as well.

Software Standards. The MIS manager adopts a set of rules for programmers to follow in coding their programs. These software standards ensure consistency in programming style between programmers working on different systems. This aids in debugging the programs and makes later changes to them easier. Software standards describe acceptable ways to structure programs and to name variables and segments of programs.

Usually organizations adopt standards that provide for *modularity* in program structure. This divides each program into segments, or modules, with standardized ways of passing data between modules. Individuals on a programmer team are assigned different modules; more experienced programmers work on the more complex ones. Modularity aids later changes to the system because changes are restricted to one or a few modules. You may have learned *structured programming,* which is a popular approach to achieving modularity. It is described in more detail in the next chapter.

Software Acquisition. During detailed specification, the design team defines the requirements for the proposed system. Most accounting transaction processing systems have similar requirements. For example, the requirements for a wholesaler's inventory control system are probably very much like those for any other wholesaler. The requirements for a cash disbursements application are identical for most businesses. Thus, the design team may find that an existing software package meets most of the requirements for the proposed system. A cost effective alternative is to purchase the package and then, if necessary, modify it. The design team follows a seven-step procedure in selecting a package for acquisition. If you own a personal computer, you will find this procedure useful in buying your own software.

Review the Requirements. The design team first reviews the requirements specified during requirements definition. These include reports, display screens, files, and manual procedures for the proposed system. The package chosen by the team contains as many of these requirements as possible. Reports and display screens provide the information needed for management control and operational decisions, so a software package should produce the essential information content of these outputs. The files store data not only for the proposed system but also for other systems; therefore, their content and storage methods must be consistent with these other systems. Manual procedures show the capabilities of personnel who work with the system. Any proposed software package should require similar capabilities. After reviewing the requirements, the design team gathers data about existing software packages.

Identify Available Packages. The design team identifies the software packages currently being marketed for this application. Subscription services are useful sources of information concerning available packages. The design team also may contact consultants and computer stores or talk to software development companies directly. Trade publications routinely publish descriptions of newly released software packages, and some publish surveys summarizing the features of those available for a particular application. Others survey their readers and summarize users' experiences with software. Reviewing these information sources provides the design team with a list of software packages that could possibly satisfy the requirements of the proposed system.

Narrow the Choice. By eliminating clearly unsuitable packages, the design team narrows the list to three to five serious candidates. Many packages on the list likely do not execute on the computer hardware selected for the system.

Others do not provide the essential information requirements defined by the design team. Still others are not compatible with existing application systems or software and are rejected from further consideration. The design team then evaluates the remaining candidates in detail.

Perform Detailed Comparisons. The design team contacts the companies that sell the remaining packages. They may request that vendor sales representatives make presentations concerning each package. They obtain as much detailed information as possible about each, including user's manuals, installation instructions, other documentation, and copies of purchase or lease contracts. They then perform a detailed examination of this documentation to identify the advantages for each alternative.

For example, some software vendors provide the programs in a high-level language such as COBOL or BASIC. This *source code* version of the programs enables the design team to modify the software to suit the requirements. Other vendors provide software only in *object code,* the computer's machine language that cannot be easily changed. Some vendors agree to aid in the installation process or to make changes desired by the design team. Other vendors provide a toll-free telephone number where purchasers can receive technical advice. Some vendors only sell their packages, while others lease them or finance a sale. The design team considers these factors before making a software acquisition decision. The design team also solicits the opinions of current users of the packages.

Talk to Users. Someone from the design team should contact MIS managers at other organizations that use the package. This provides an objective appraisal of the package's strengths and weaknesses. In this way the design team learns of weaknesses or installation difficulties not evident from documentation. An external user can also evaluate the quality of the vendor's help.

If the design team knows no current user of the package, they ask the vendor for a list of current customers. A member of the team then contacts parties selected from the list. The design team realizes that users from a vendor-provided list may not be objective.

Conduct Benchmark Tests. If possible, the design team conducts benchmark tests of the software. As mentioned earlier, benchmarks are used to evaluate equipment. In evaluating software, the team borrows a copy of each software package. They execute each, using copies of actual data files on computer equipment similar to that proposed for the system. Any package that completes processing in significantly less time is a preferred one. In this way the design team sees how the package performs under conditions similar to those during operations.

In practice, conducting benchmark tests may be impracticable. Identical equipment may be unavailable, or actual files may not exist for the system. Benchmarks conducted with different equipment or different files may be misleading and the design team cannot rely on them. Whenever they are

ILLUSTRATION 7–15 Steps in Software Acquisition

1. **Review the requirements.** Define these requirements during detailed system specification.
2. **Identify available packages.** Identify packages being marketed for this application.
3. **Narrow the choices.** Eliminate those not satisfying system requirements.
4. **Perform a detailed comparison.** Evaluate thoroughly the features of each package.
5. **Talk to users.** Interview people experienced with the package.
6. **Conduct benchmark tests.** Execute the package on the actual computer equipment.
7. **Select a package.** Make a choice based on features, interviews, and tests.

or choose inhouse procedures

appropriate, benchmarks may provide conclusive evidence for the software acquisition decision.

Select a Package. After considering the detailed comparison of advantages, the discussions with users, and the results of benchmark tests, the design team selects a package. Frequently a single software package appears clearly preferable. In other cases, the design team makes subjective evaluations between two or more packages with contrasting advantages. By following this procedure, the design team conducts a thorough evaluation of available packages.

Illustration 7–15 summarizes the steps in software acquisition. Organizations frequently find that, for proposed accounting systems, this is a desirable alternative. Even when modifications are necessary, a software package is less costly than in-house development. Furthermore, a package with many current users has had most of its problems discovered and eliminated. With in-house programming, the project team almost always encounters difficulties during implementation requiring last-minute changes to programs. When an organization's requirements are unusual, or users cannot be satisfied by existing packages, then in-house development is necessary. Each alternative is considered by the design team during detailed specification.

Report to Management

At the conclusion of detailed specification, the design team prepares another report to management. This report is similar to that produced at the end of preliminary system design. It contains an executive summary that describes the objectives, scope, and major features of the system. It also contains a copy of the documentation package created during detailed specification.

This report differs from the earlier one because of the amount of detail it provides. At the end of detailed specification, descriptions of the outputs, processing, files, and inputs to the system are specified exactly. The design team has identified the necessary computer equipment and programs, and sources for them are selected. Costs of installing and operating the system are known with accuracy, so this report contains a better projection of costs and benefits for the system.

The information systems steering committee and interested members of top management review the report. They may request an oral presentation of recommendations by the design team. After considering these recommendations, they may halt further development efforts, suggest changes in the design, or appoint a project team to proceed with the implementation phase.

AUDITOR INVOLVEMENT IN SYSTEM DESIGN

Many design teams obtain auditor involvement in the design process. Auditors are skilled in evaluating the auditability and controls in a system, and provide an independent appraisal of it. Auditors' suggestions that are difficult to implement in an existing system are more easily designed into a new one. Usually internal auditors participate, although sometimes independent auditors or consultants from the audit firm participate as well.

Auditors are normally not members of the design team, but rather conduct a detailed review of the system during the system design phase. Auditors perform two major functions: they evaluate the detailed specifications of the system to recommend improvements, and they consider how to introduce audit modules into the system's programs.

Specifications Review

Auditors review the detailed specifications of the new system to evaluate the adequacy of its audit trail and of its internal controls.

The audit trail is produced by information contained in the reports and files of the system. It provides the ability to trace an individual transaction through the system into a financial statement amount, or to trace from an amount in the financial statements to the transactions making it up. When a report discloses a journal entry number, a posting reference, or a document number, it is creating an audit trail. Good bookkeepers produce an audit trail in a manual accounting system; similar procedures are needed in a computerized one. Because systems analysts and programmers are not experts concerning these procedures, an auditors' review of system specifications is important.

A new system should also have adequate internal controls. In a computerized system, these include the measures taken to prevent or detect erroneous data and to secure data from theft or unauthorized change. In reviewing controls, auditors examine the proposed procedures for file backup, file retention, and for correcting erroneous transactions detected by the system. These are important to provide accurate and secure accounting data.

When reviewing system specifications, auditors examine in detail the reports, the processing steps, and the data files described during requirements definition. They also review the computer equipment that was selected by the design team.

Reports. Auditors examine the proposed reports to verify that they include information needed for auditability and control. Each report that produces summary totals should identify the sources of the detailed amounts. For example, a report that discloses journalized transactions should identify document numbers for all the transactions. A printout of a ledger should indicate a source for all journal postings making up the ledger balance. These enable an auditor to trace from a ledger total to an individual transaction. Batch and control totals should also be included on many reports to ensure that no transactions are omitted during processing.

Processing Steps. In the design documentation package, program narratives and procedures manuals describe the processing steps. After reviewing these, auditors suggest control procedures to add to them. For example, auditors may suggest that a clerk accumulate transactions into batches, and take an adding machine total of all transaction amounts in the batch. This batch total is input to all computer programs that process the batch. The programs are coded so that, in addition to normal processing, they compute control totals of all transactions in the batch. Each program compares the batch total to its control total, and discloses any difference in a control report.

Data Files. Auditors also review the data file specifications for the new system. They evaluate the control measures ensuring the security and accuracy of the data and verify that data items included in the file provide an audit trail. They determine that specified backup procedures allow reconstruction of each data file should one be destroyed. They ensure that retention procedures satisfy audit and legal requirements.

Equipment Selection. In reviewing the equipment selected by the design team, auditors provide an independent appraisal. They examine equipment choices to ensure that the hardware selected can fulfill management's desires. They evaluate the capacity of the equipment and determine if it is sufficient—but not excessive—for the needs of the system. In some organizations, MIS quality assurance personnel rather than auditors perform this function.

Audit Modules

Many modern systems do not contain the kind of audit trail that auditors prefer. Some of these systems enter a transaction into the system and immediately post it to a ledger, with no record on paper of intermediate processing steps. Thus, auditors cannot establish reliance on the system by simply examining evidence provided in its reports by the audit trail. To determine that such a system is producing accurate data, auditors must introduce audit modules into the system's programs.

An *audit module* is a segment of an accounting application program that enables auditors to examine transactions as they are processed in magnetic form by the program. An audit module may, for example, examine transactions for a special characteristic such as a high monetary value. Transactions that have this characteristic are summarized in a file for later review by an auditor. The use of audit modules is discussed further in the chapter on data security and integrity.

Audit modules are difficult to add to programs in operational systems. However, if created during system design, they can be implemented at reasonable cost. During the review of design documentation, auditors look for opportunities to embed audit modules into the system's programs.

SUMMARY

System design is a process of starting with a set of system objectives and selecting ways to achieve those objectives. It is an outgrowth of the recommendations made at the end of systems analysis. As design proceeds, the features of the proposed system are gradually refined and made more specific.

The system design phase of the systems development life cycle contains two activities: During the first, preliminary system design, the design team identifies the outputs, processes, inputs, and files for the system in a high-level, conceptual form. In the second, detailed specification, the design team defines these precisely. Each activity terminates with a report to users and management. These reports give them opportunities to suggest changes to the proposed system, or to halt further system development. If the information systems steering committee wishes to proceed with system development, they appoint a project team for the implementation phase of the SDLC.

Auditors become involved in system design near the end of the design phase. They review the documentation created by the design team and suggest ways to improve auditability and control in the proposed system. They also may include audit modules in the system's programs.

KEY TERMS

ad hoc report A system output produced as needed at irregular intervals rather than periodically.

benchmark A test of the performance of either computer hardware or software.

detailed specification An activity performed during system design in which a project team creates on paper a detailed description of how an information system should work.

preliminary system design An activity performed during system design in which a project team develops a conceptual description of a proposed system.

request for quotation (RFQ) A letter prepared by a design project team that identifies a computer configuration and requests a cost estimate from a vendor. If the vendor is asked to specify the configuration, it is called a request for proposal (RFP).

requirements definition A detailed specification activity during which the design project team describes the outputs, data, inputs, and processing steps of the system.

service bureau A company that owns and operates computer hardware and software and provides data processing services to other organizations.

source document A form used in an accounting system to serve as the initial record of data for later processing.

subscription service A newsletter published at regular intervals by companies who monitor and evaluate available computer hardware and software.

QUESTIONS

7–1. Which two major benefits accrue from performing a thorough system design?

7–2. How is the product of detailed specification different from that of preliminary system design? How are they similar?

7–3. Distinguish between the outputs of preliminary system design and the outputs of detailed specification when describing:
a. Outputs
b. Data
c. Inputs
d. Processes

7–4. The following list of documents is produced during the system design phase. Which component of a computer-based system does each describe?
a. Record layout
b. Procedures manual
c. Program narrative
d. Screen layout

7–5. Application software may be either purchased or developed in-house. State three possible advantages and three possible disadvantages of purchasing software.

(CIA Adapted)

7–6. Which procedures should be followed when selecting a software package for acquisition?

7–7. What are the alternative ways of acquiring computer equipment?

7–8. Name and describe the three major activities that occur during detailed specification.

7–9. How can you use a subscription service during detailed specification? What advantages does one provide?

7–10. Should you always acquire the lowest-cost computer equipment? Which other factors affect the decision?

7–11. What does the auditor look for when conducting a specifications review during the system design phase?

7–12. It has been said that system design is a creative act and that creativity cannot be taught. To what extent do you agree with this statement? Why?

EXERCISES AND CASES

7–13. DEFINITIONS

Define each of the following terms:

a. Source document
b. Ad hoc report
c. RFQ
d. RFP
e. Hardware configuration
f. Software standards
g. Benchmark

7–14. LEASE OR PURCHASE

A study team at Oceanographic Enterprises has gathered the following information for a proposed information system:

Purchase price of computer equipment	$200,000
Annual rental of same equipment under a lease contract	$ 48,000
Initial cost:	
Installation	12,000
Programming	80,000
Training and conversion	40,000
Total	$132,000
Annual operating cost:	
MIS salaries	$115,200
Utilities and supplies	23,040

Facilities maintenance	$ 15,000
Total	$153,240
Present annual operating costs	260,000
Discount factor	20%
Estimated useful life of computer	5 years

Required:

Analyze the economic feasibility of the computerized system assuming the equipment is

a. Purchased.

b. Leased.

7–15. ***SYSTEM DEVELOPMENT LIFE CYCLE***

Curtis Company operates in a five-county industrial area. The company employs a manual system for all its recordkeeping except payroll; the payroll is processed by a local service bureau. Other applications have not been computerized because previously they could not be cost justified.

The company's sales have grown at an increasing rate over the past years. With this substantial growth rate, a computer-based system seemed more practical. Consequently, Curtis Company engaged the management consulting department of their public accounting firm to conduct a feasibility study for converting their recordkeeping systems to a computer-based system. The accounting firm reported that a computer-based system would improve the company's recordkeeping system and still provide material cost savings.

Therefore, Curtis Company decided to develop a computer-based system for their records. Curtis hired a person with experience in systems development as manager of systems and data processing. His responsibilities are to oversee the entire systems operations with special emphasis on the development of the new system.

Required:

Describe the major steps in developing and implementing Curtis Company's new computer-based system.

(CMA Adapted)

7–16. ***BUDGET SYSTEM***

Small Company wants to implement a budget system. A computer file containing budget data must contain, at a minimum, the following data items: An account number, an account description, and a budgeted amount. The actual amount in the account may be obtained from another computer file containing the general ledger. A computer program reads the budget data from the budget file, the actual data from the general ledger file, and prints a budget report.

Required:

a. Design a budget report that compares actual and budgeted amounts for each account.
b. Prepare a system flowchart for this budgeting system.
c. Draw a program flowchart for this computerized process.

7–17. *STRUCTURED METHODOLOGIES*

For the budget system described in Exercise 7–16:

a. Design a budget report that compares actual and budgeted amounts for each account.
b. Prepare a data flow diagram.
c. Develop logic specifications using pseudocode.

7–18. *RETAIL INVENTORY SYSTEM*

Megamarket Food Stores attempts to maintain its competitive position by keeping operating costs as low as possible. Megamarket managers are considering installing an optical character reader at each grocery checkout stand. The reader uses a laser beam to read the Universal Product Code printed in black ink on the label of each item that Megamarket sells.

When a customer brings an item to a checkout stand, the clerk scans its label with the reader. The reader notifies a computer elsewhere in the store that the item has been sold.

The store's computer maintains a computer file of all items sold during the day. At night, this data is transferred to a larger computer at corporate headquarters. The corporate computer deducts each sale from the quantities shown in the inventory records and places orders to replenish inventory levels at each store. Megamarket's management believes that this system can lower labor costs and minimize investment in inventory.

Required:

a. Suggest two daily reports and one monthly report that such a system would produce. What would be the purpose of each report?
b. Identify the data items that this system would use in the inventory records at
   1. Each store computer
   2. The corporate computer
c. Develop a system flowchart for this system.

7–19. *STRUCTURED METHODOLOGIES*

For the inventory system described in Exercise 7–18:

a. Suggest two daily reports and one monthly report that such a system would produce. What would be the purpose of each report?

b. Identify the data items that this system would use in the inventory records at
  1. Each store computer.
  2. The corporate computer.

c. Develop a data flow diagram.

7–20. ***PERSONNEL SYSTEM***

Wagner Wagons, Inc. uses a computer-based personnel system in calculating payroll for hourly employees. The system maintains one entry for each hourly employee in a computerized personnel file. Each entry, a computer record, contains the following data items:

1. Social security number (9 characters)
2. Employee last name (12 characters)
3. Employee first name (12 characters)
4. Employee middle initial (1 character)
5. Street address (15 characters)
6. City (12 characters)
7. State (2 characters)
8. Zip code (9 characters)
9. Department (4 characters)
10. Hourly pay rate (5 characters)
11. Job skill code (4 characters)
12. Job skill description (12 characters).

Required:

Develop a record layout for this personnel file.

7–21. ***BILLING SYSTEM***

Huge Lighting & Power Company (HL&P) is developing a computer-based billing system to improve its processing of accounts receivable. Once a month an employee reads the electric meter at each service location and enters the meter number and meter reading into a hand-held computer. At the end of the day the employee plugs the hand-held computer into the HL&P corporate mainframe computer.

The mainframe executes a data entry program that posts the reading at each meter to a computer file called the AR master file. The AR master file contains, for each meter number, the customer name, address, previous meter reading, the total amount owed from previous billing cycles, and a billing code. Residential, business, industrial, nonprofit, and government customers all have different billing codes, allowing them to be charged for usage at different rates. The data entry program determines the quantity of electricity used at a meter by subtracting the previous reading from the current one.

The data entry program then calculates the charge for the electricity used. It looks up the customer's billing code in a computerized unit charge file. This file contains the cost in dollars per unit of electricity for each billing code. The data entry program then multiplies the unit charge by the quantity of electricity used to get the current amount owed.

Once this amount is known, the data entry program prints a statement that is mailed to the customer.

Required:

a. Identify the data items that should be disclosed on HL&P's monthly statement.

b. Identify the data items that are contained in each file processed by the data entry program.

c. Draw a system flowchart for this billing system. You may represent all computer files by the ONLINE STORAGE symbol.

d. The system as designed has a major shortcoming. Although a monthly statement is produced for each customer, the system keeps no record either of the quantity or of the amount that is invoiced on a statement. Describe how you would correct this design flaw in the system.

7–22. ***SALES ANALYSIS SYSTEM***

Universal Floor Covering is a manufacturer and distributor of carpet and vinyl floor coverings. The home office is located in Charlotte, North Carolina. Carpet mills are located in Dalton, Georgia, and Greenville, South Carolina; a floor covering manufacturing plant is in High Point, North Carolina. Total sales last year were just over $250 million.

The company manufactures more than 200 different varieties of carpet. The carpet is classified as commercial or residential and is sold under five brand names with up to five lines under each brand. The lines indicate different quality grades measured by type of tuft and number of tufts per square inch. Each line of carpet can have up to 15 different color styles.

Almost 200 varieties of vinyl floor covering are manufactured for either commercial or residential use. The four separate brand names are distinguished by type of finish, eight different patterns for each brand, and eight color styles for each pattern.

Ten different grades of padding are manufactured. The padding is usually differentiated by intended use, either commercial or residential, and by thickness and composition of materials.

Universal serves more than 2,000 regular wholesale customers. Retail showrooms are the primary customers. Many major corporations are direct buyers of Universal's products. Large construction companies have contracts with Universal to purchase carpet and floor covering at reduced rates for use in newly constructed homes and commercial buildings. In addition, Universal produces a line of residential carpet for a large national retail chain. Sales to these customers range from $10,000 to $1 million annually.

Company-owned retail outlets at each plant carry overruns, seconds, and discontinued items. This is Universal's only retail sales function.

The company has divided the sales market into seven territories, with the majority of these concentrated on the East Coast. The market segments are New England, New York, Mid-Atlantic, Carolinas, South, Midwest, and West. Each sales territory is divided into 5 to 10 districts with a salesperson assigned to each district.

The current accounting system has been adequate for monitoring sales by product. However, there are limitations to the system because specific information is sometimes not available. The accounting department has been asked to design a sales analysis system. The system should permit Universal to prepare sales analysis reports that would reflect the characteristics of the company's business. The first step in designing this system is to develop a method of coding sales transactions when they are recorded.

Required:

a. Identify and describe the factors that must be considered before a method of coding can be designed and implemented for an organization.

b. Develop a coding system for Universal Floor Covering that would assign sales analysis codes to sales transactions. This coding system should enable Universal to perform market analysis on past sales data. For each portion of the code:

1. Explain the meaning and purpose of the position.
2. Identify and justify the number of digits required.

(CMA Adapted)

7–23. ***CORPORATE CONSOLIDATION SYSTEM—PART II***

R. J. Reynolds Industries, Inc., is a diversified worldwide corporation with consolidated net sales measured in billions of dollars. It serves as parent company for seven subsidiaries each of which is a major line of business. These are: R. J. Reynolds Tobacco Co.; Del Monte Corp. (processed foods and fresh fruits); R. J. Reynolds Tobacco International, Inc.; Aminoil USA, Inc. (energy); Sea-Land Service, Inc. (containerized shipping); RJR Foods, Inc. (convenience foods and beverages); and RJR Archer, Inc. (packaging).

As a result of corporate growth and of increased public reporting requirements, the corporate accounting group at R. J. Reynolds undertook a systems study during the mid-1970s. The study resulted in the selection and installation of a general ledger software package in corporate headquarters. The general ledger system, when installed, was named the corporate consolidation system (CCS). It processed the financial statements and selected account analysis of each of the reporting entities and consolidated them into the total corporate statements, with statements of earnings and balance sheets for each individual reporting company in a line of business. In addition, certain selected Form 10-K schedules were prepared using the statistical capabilities of the general ledger package.

Choosing the Software Package

When designing the system, the corporate accounting team examined in detail a number of alternatives and visited several companies that had installed this package, or other packages, to handle their consolidation accounting. The project team developed a set of criteria to evaluate each package on the market that possibly could meet the information requirements of RJR.

They categorized the criteria into "musts" and "desires." The musts were necessary before RJR would consider the system, and the desires included those elements the company hoped the system would have. The must criteria included:

1. A report writer to easily design and implement required reports.
2. Account analysis for 10-K and 10-Q reporting.
3. Multiple consolidation paths to handle multiples of business consolidation accounting.
4. Intercompany account eliminations.
5. Package provided in COBOL source code.
6. The capability of extending the system to other companies and other operating computer facilities as a general ledger package.

The four desired criteria were:

1. Five years of history.
2. Capability to provide a cash flow statement.
3. Ability to convert from one currency to another.
4. Terminal input and reporting capabilities.

After evaluating the various packages on the market, the corporate accounting team recommended a specific package which had been used at a large number of sites for several years. Additionally, it met all of the must criteria and most of the desired ones with slight modifications. In selecting the package, however, the team noted certain disadvantages:

1. Corporate accounting would have to write the 10-K report modules.
2. Corporate accounting would have to add any currency conversion routines.
3. The system was a generalized general ledger system and not a consolidation ledger system.

Why didn't RJR write the package in-house with its own MIS department? The answer was that the immediate purchase of proven experience tested by many companies in the software market was preferable to attempting to write a new consolidation accounting system in-house. It has been estimated that RJR saved a minimum of three calendar years of development effort by a project team by purchasing a package instead of attempting to write this application in-house.

Consolidation Accounting

In the consolidation process, corporate accounting is required to prepare financial statements and analyses on the individual reporting entities, to consolidate these entities by lines of business, and to prepare consolidated R. J. Reynolds Industries statements. Two major problems facing the team in the new system effort were the inflexibility of the old account code structure and the accurate and rapid elimination of intercompany accounts.

The old system would, for example, collect total property, plant, and equipment, and accumulate depreciation from each reporting entity. But the team wanted to collect the details behind such summary accounts so the analysis statements could be developed on the computer instead of by hand. By collecting the necessary level of detail and having the computer do the work, the accounting department would be able to devote more of its efforts to analyzing the financial information instead of just adding and footing work sheets. Also, the various operating companies have many intercompany relationships, such as intercompany sales, receivables, payables, and investments. These accounts must be handled quickly and accurately in the consolidation process to develop the financial statements quickly. Accounts have to be handled on an "intra" basis among companies within a line of business and on an "inter" basis between companies in different lines of business. In addition, the elimination process should be consistent from period to period and provide a good audit trail for review by both internal and external auditors.

Using the Package

After evaluating the old consolidation chart of accounts and the accounting systems used by the operating companies in light of the two major problems of consolidation, the team decided to develop a completely new set of accounts. Criteria for the new account structure required that it be as small as possible yet flexible enough to meet all anticipated accounting changes from the FASB and SEC and possible corporate acquisitions. As a result, the team chose a 13-position account code.

The first four positions are the identifier designators—the first position indicating the line of business and the next three positions indicating the company within that particular line of business. This four-position identifier provided enough flexibility so that the operating companies can be consolidated into entities other than the lines of business used for public reporting. For example, different reporting might be necessary for legal reasons or due to management's desires. The fifth position indicated the statement type; that is, statement of earnings, balance sheet, or 10-K account analysis. The sixth through the ninth are four-digit prime account codes. These use codes 0000-4999 for the balance sheet and codes 5000-9999 for the statement of earnings. Positions 10 through 13 are subaccount codes used in intercompany accounting and account analysis.

The designation "99" was chosen to indicate the consolidation of a group of similar reporting entities. Thus, the code 1199 indicated the consolidation of information for companies in line of business 11. The team took this consolidation point approach one step further by creating a complete company at each level of consolidation. Amounts posted at the operating company level automatically are combined with the other operating companies in that group's consolidation company. This system also provided an opportunity for possible adjustments at each account within a consolidation company. When requesting a specific amount, such as notes payable for a line of business, management addresses the notes payable account in the consolidation company. Because of the relationship between operating and consolidation companies, this account contains the sum of the notes payable for all companies in that line of business, plus any adjustments. In this way, the user does not have to add the amounts for each company in the line of business to determine the total.

One of the most difficult problems in consolidation accounting is the elimination of intercompany balances. The new account code and the operating consolidation company relationships provided the tools necessary to greatly speed up the intercompany accounting process. With the four position identifier in the new code, each individual reporting company within the corporation could be identified specifically with its own identifier code and line of business code. This code is used in handling intercompany relationships because it enables a particular company to report its intercompany balances with any other company. It does this by using that company's unique identifier in the subaccount positions in conjunction with the proper general ledger account. For example, company 0004's intercompany receivable from company 1135 should have a contra payable of company 1135 to company 0004.

By relating the intra-accounts receivable accounts to the intra-accounts payable accounts at a consolidation level, the intra-accounts within a line of business are eliminated at the consolidated line of business level. This eliminating relationship feature permits an accountant to use the report writer feature of the package to create a report showing how the intercompany accounts have been reported. The report developed is used as a working document by the accountant and makes it easy to determine whether or not the intercompany balances reconcile.

Required:

a. Why did RJR Industries choose to purchase and modify a software package, rather than develop a consolidation system in-house?

b. What procedure did the project team use in selecting a software package?

c. The package chosen was a general ledger package rather than a consolidation package. How did the project team adapt it to the problems of consolidation accounting?

7–24. *CORPORATE CONSOLIDATION SYSTEM—PART III*

In developing the account structure for the CCS, RJR's corporate accounting team used the statistical accounting capabilities of the package to develop certain critical information. The statistical account feature was used to develop a separate level of accounting information within the financial statements; such information is normally not available within a standard general ledger chart of

Exhibit 7–1 Case 7–24

Standard Profit and Loss Statement

		Current Year	*Prior Year*
Sales and operating revenues	XXXX-A-5000-0000[b]		
Cost of products sold-OPR EXP	XXXX-A-6000-0000		
Selling, advertising, G&A	XXXX-A-7400-0000		
Earnings from operations[a]	XXXX-A-7500-0000		
Outside interest and debt	XXXX-A-8000-0000		
Intercompany interest expense	XXXX-A-8100-0000		
Intercompany interest (income)	XXXX-A-8200-0000		
Other financial (inc)/exp	XXXX-A-8300-0000		
Realized foreign exchange	XXXX-A-8400-0000		
Unrealized foreign exchange	XXXX-A-8420-0000		
Earnings before income taxes[a]	XXXX-A-8500-0000		
Provision for income taxes	XXXX-A-8800-0000		
Net earnings/(loss)[a]	XXXX-A-9000-0000		
Net loss will print in brackets			

[a]The variable report writer calculates these amounts by totaling the accounts listed above. This total is compared with the statistical account on file, and an error message is printed if the two do not agree. The double-check insures the accuracy of the reports.
[b]The four position would indicate a specific line of business and company within that line of business.

accounts. This was accomplished by developing relationships to a given set of standard accounts designated as prime management information accounts. These accounts were established at each reporting entity as well as at each consolidation level. The profit and loss statement was established to contain 13 prime codes for all operating companies and consolidation levels. All of the sales and expense categories collected from each of the operating companies are eventually summarized into these standard 13 accounts. Exhibit 7–1 contains this standard profit and loss statement.

In addition, a three-way comparison is developed (current period compared to the same period last year, current year-to-date compared to last year-to-date, current period compared to previous period) using these standard accounts for evaluation during closings. Exhibit 7–2 shows how various accounts collected from the operating companies can be related to these standard accounts so that reports which are the same across company lines can be generated for management.

One requirement of consolidation accounting is to determine the changes in the balance sheet position from the end of last year to the current reporting period. This analysis forms the basis for certain schedules required in the annual 10-K report, such as the analysis of property, plant, and equipment. The data for developing the analysis is collected from the operating companies using statistical accounts within the general ledger system. For the statistical accounts,

Exhibit 7–2 Case 7–24

Standard Account Relationships *

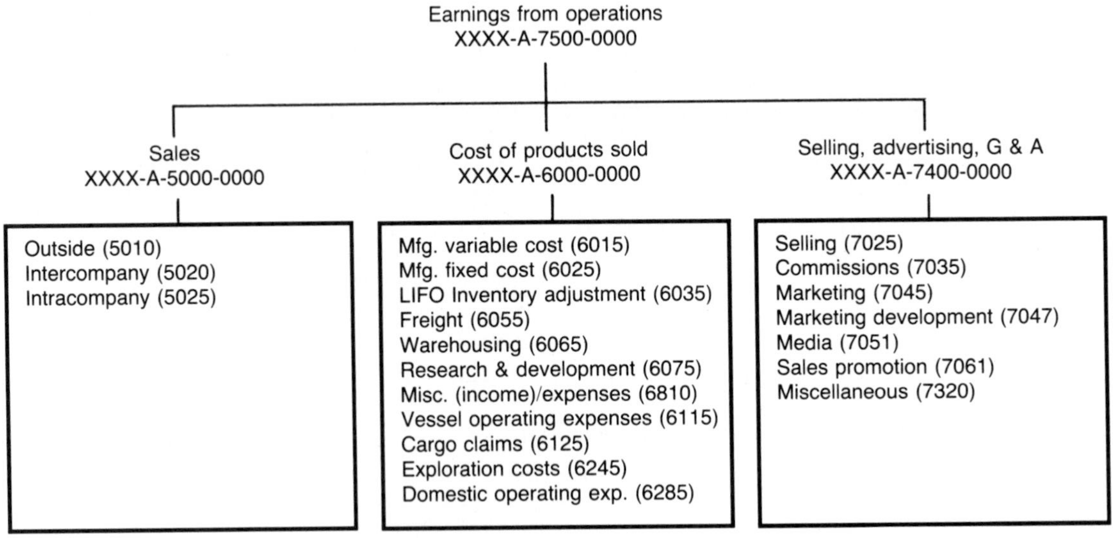

*Accounts are from different companies to show how different accounts could be related to the standard accounts. There can be other posting accounts which relate to a particular account illustrated.

strict debit equals credit accounting procedures are not required. The prior year-end balance is already within the data base from the prior year-end closing, and the current period balance has been input as part of the current closing activities.

Subaccount codes are recorded in the last four positions of the 13-digit account code. To collect the changes, a set of standard change codes are used in the subaccount positions. Each of the change codes on an account is related to a cross-check account that contains the sum of the changes to an account. The variable report writer program performs the analysis by first checking to see if the balance in the cross-check account equals the differences between the prior year-end balance and the current period balance. If the balances agree, then the program prints out the changes in an account. Again, through use of the consolidation company approach, changes posted for an operating company are automatically reflected in the appropriate consolidation level. Exhibit 7–3 illustrates how this occurs. By using the statistical account features and the report writer, the team was able to develop successfully an analysis on property, plant, and equipment, accumulated depreciation, and other long-term account analyses needed for both the 10-K and the 10-Q schedules.

Exhibit 7–3 Case 7–24

Variable Report Writer Program (dollars in thousands)

Run date XX/XX/XX *Property, plant and equipment periods ended XXXX 30, 19XX* *Schedule X*

	Prior Year Ending Balance	*Capital Expenditures*	*Retirements*	*Transfers out of CIP*	*Other Changes*	*Inter-company Transfers*	*Current Period Balance*
	(a)	0068	0058	0036	0032	0022	
Machinery and Equipment							
004[b]	$175,328	$18,201	(2,003)	331	(23)	(347)	$191,487
005	424	75	(1)	—	(18)	20	500
006	19	—	(19)	—	—	—	—
007	325,858	18,652	(205)	652	—	(454)	344,503
008	2,976	202	(50)	—	—	—	3,128
Total[c]	$504,605	$37,130	(2,278)	983	(41)	(781)	$539,618[d]

[a]Standard change codes for this analysis of machinery and equipment.
[b]List of companies in this line of business report.
[c]Totals for this line of business report.
[d]The cross-check account does not print unless there is an error. Then the account and an error message will print.

Required:

a. The project team designed a 13-digit account code for RJR's chart of accounts. Identify the significance of each digit in this account code.

b. How did the project team modify the package to provide statistical information beyond that required for the basic financial statements?

c. CCS was designed by a project team containing members from corporate accounting department. Do you think a team of nonaccountants could have designed this system?

Chapter 8

System Implementation and Operation

Learning Objectives:

1. To discover which activities take place during the third and fourth phases of the system development life cycle.
2. To know how auditors participate in system implementation.
3. To understand how to do a post-implementation review.
4. To learn how to properly account for the costs of an accounting information system.

INTRODUCTION

In the previous chapters you learned about the first two phases of the system development life cycle (SDLC). In this chapter you will learn about the last two phases of the SDLC, system implementation and system operation.

In the implementation phase, a project team creates a working system from the design specifications. The operations phase consists of the time period that the system is used to process accounting data. It represents the objective of the system development process.

SYSTEM IMPLEMENTATION

The implementation phase is the period of time during which a working system is produced and placed in operation. Implementation begins when the informa-

ILLUSTRATION 8–1 System Implementation and Operation

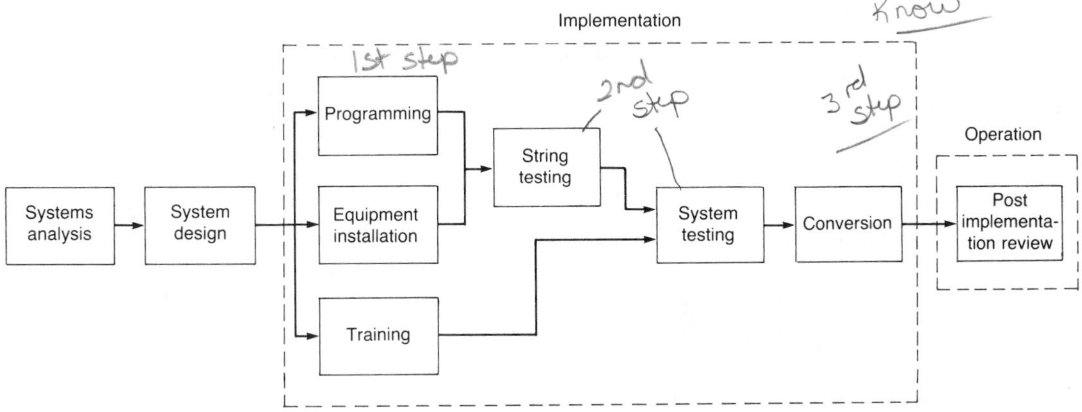

tion systems steering committee accepts the detailed specifications produced during system design. It ends with the acceptance of the system by management as an operational success. The information systems steering committee appoints a project team to complete implementation. This project team consists of members of the design team, programmers, documentation specialists, and data entry clerks.

Five major activities take place during the implementation phase: equipment installation, programming, training, testing, and conversion. Unlike those in the system design phase, some of these activities may occur simultaneously. Auditors participate in implementation by reviewing two of the activities. Illustration 8–1 shows the relationship between implementation and the other phases in the SDLC.

Equipment Installation

Frequently a new system requires the acquisition of additional computer equipment and software. The design team selects their sources during the system design phase and places orders for them. The implementation project team then installs the equipment and software so that testing and conversion activities can occur. Sometimes the team must prepare a site for the equipment before installing it.

For a personal computer, *site preparation* may simply be clearing a desk, identifying a nearby electrical outlet, and installing a surge protector. For a mainframe computer, site preparation is much more extensive. For example, some computers are cooled by water, so plumbing must be installed at the site. Most computers require special wiring for electrical power, air conditioning for cooling, and cabling to connect the computer with other equipment. If the project team decides to run this cabling under the floor, special raised floors must be installed at the site. The team may also choose to install fireproof storage areas, a fire alarm and extinguishing system, and an emergency power supply. It must provide adequate space to locate all the additional equipment.

Next the project team installs any software packages that have been purchased. This allows programmers to verify that the equipment and packages work, and to make any desired modifications. If the design team decided to develop programs in-house, the programming activity begins.

Programming

If programs are developed in-house, the project team devotes significant resources to programming. Modern programming techniques require that programmers concentrate on producing code that not only executes correctly but also is self-documenting and easy to understand. This makes changes to the programs easier during the operations phase.

The project team performs four tasks during this activity. For each program identified during system design, the team develops its logic and then codes it, debugs it, and creates documentation for it.

Develop Program Logic. The design team prepares specifications for each program during detailed specification. It identifies the purpose of the program, its internal controls, and the data records, inputs, and outputs it processes. In developing the logic of a program, members of the project team determine the code necessary for the program to accomplish these things.

Programmer Teams. Many companies find that programmers work efficiently in teams of three to six members. The project manager assigns each program to a programmer team. The team leader then assigns each module to a member of the team. A *module* is a segment of the program that performs only one function within the program, such as printing the column headings for a report.

Sometimes the project manager uses the *chief programmer team* approach. With this approach, each programmer on the team has a special function such as documenting, editing, or testing modules. This type of team also includes a librarian who organizes the program documentation.

Structured Programming. When developing programs in-house, many organizations adopt standards requiring structured programming. This is a modular approach that provides a standardized way of coding a computer program. The structured approach calls for developing a program's logic prior to coding. Structured programs need less time to debug and test, and changes to these programs are easier to make during the operations phase.

Structured programming has two basic requirements. First, each module has only one entry point and one exit point. Second, only three logic constructs are allowed: the sequence, the selection, and the iteration constructs. Once a programmer learns how to code using these constructs, the programming task becomes easier. Illustration 8–2 presents these constructs using standard program flowchart symbols.

ILLUSTRATION 8–2 Logic Constructs Used in Structured Programming

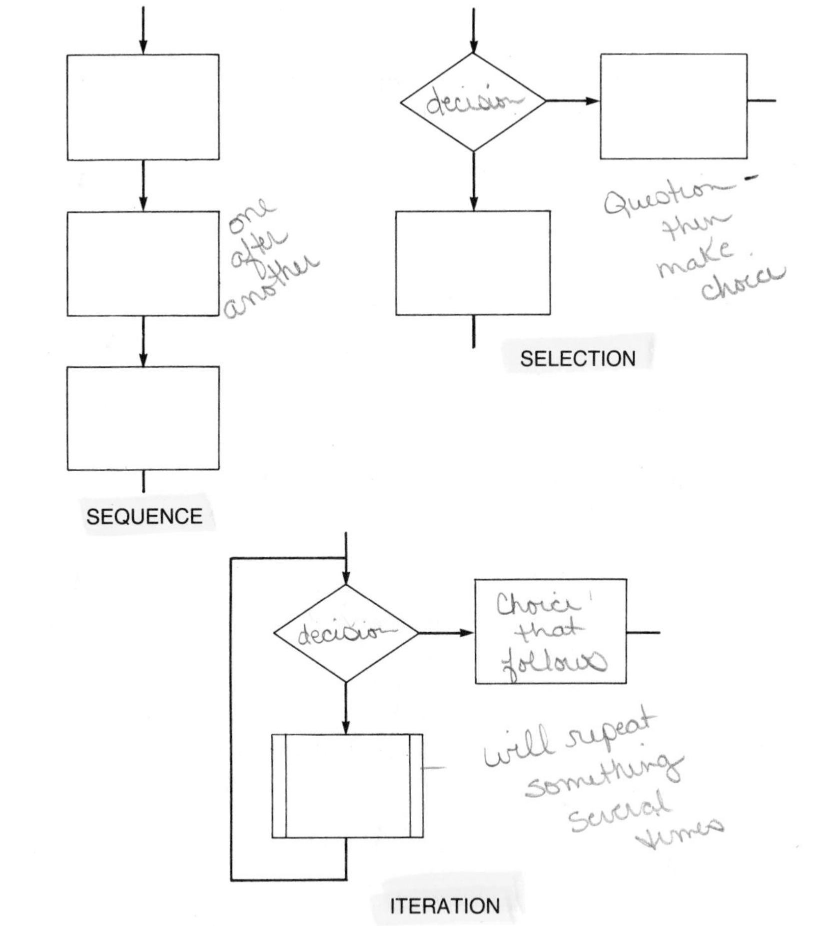

Code the Program. Once the programmers on the team develop the logic for all the modules constituting a program, they begin to code the program. A *Programming Standards Manual* describes how this is done. In addition to structured programming, good standards require top-down coding and internal documentation.

Top-Down Coding. The "top-down" in this expression refers to the structure chart of the program. The programming team first codes the module at the highest level shown on the chart, normally called the *mainline module*. Once this module is functioning properly, the team proceeds to the second level, then the third, and so on. This approach is most useful when a team of programmers is coding a long program with many modules. It simplifies the process of locating errors in such a program because an error is known to be within a certain module.

If you code programs in a programming course, top-down programming may not be as beneficial, because usually the programs written while learning a computer language are relatively short.

Internal Documentation. Good programming standards also require that programs contain internal documentation. These are verbal descriptions included in a program's code that describe what the program is doing. Internal documentation separates and identifies each module within a program, and describes the data names or variables used in the module. Because another programmer can quickly ascertain what the module is doing, internal documentation facilitates debugging the program and making changes to it.

Debug the Program. Program "bugs" are errors in the logic or syntax of the code that cause the program to malfunction.[1] Thus when programmers "debug" a module, they are removing the errors from a module they have coded. Structured programming and top-down coding both make debugging easier. Structured walk-throughs are also commonly used for this purpose.

Structured Walk-throughs. These are useful in large projects that employ programming teams. A structured walk-through is a review of an individual programmer's work by the other programmers on the team. In conducting this review, the team examines the design of each module to ensure that it conforms to standards and satisfies the needs of users. It also reviews the adequacy of the documentation, the internal controls, and the testing procedures for the module. The team produces a list of defects and gives a copy to each team member. This process may be repeated several times during the development of a module. Frequently a programmer's coworkers spot problems the programmer would never see. It is easy for a programmer, engrossed in the complexity of the code, to "lose sight of the forest for the trees." Structured walk-throughs prevent this occurrence.

Test the Program. After all modules are complete, the programming team tests the program. When top-down coding is used, the team normally uses top-down testing. A programmer tests each module as it is completed. After the last module is finished, the entire program should function according to design specifications. Later each program is tested in operation with the other programs in the system.

To test a program or a module, the programmer prepares test data. Sometimes programmers use computer software packages, called *test data generators,* for this purpose. Test data should be simple enough that the purpose of the test is evident, and yet comprehensive enough to test all possible real occurrences of the data. The programmer includes in the program documentation a working paper summarizing the expected results for each test data item and the actual results produced by the program or module. The programmer team reviews this working paper during a structured walk-through. Illustration 8–3 presents an example of such a working paper.

---

[1]Grace Hopper, the developer of the COBOL computer language, first applied this term to program errors. She was working on an early model computer and kept having errors. The cause of the error was a dead moth caught in one of the components—a "bug" in the program.

ILLUSTRATION 8–3 A Working Paper Showing the Design of Test Data and Analysis of Results

			Expected Results			*Actual Results*		
Test Transaction Number	*Condition Tested*	*Description of Test Data*	*Description of Master File Condition Before Test*	*Expected Master File Condition After Test*	*Expected Error Type Out*	*Computer Output Number*	*Computer Output*	*Further Action Needed*
1	. . .	. . .	. . .	. . .	. . .			
2	. . .	. . .	. . .	. . .	. . .			
3	Out of limit	Earnings for 3245 at $200	$5,200.35	$5,400.35	No			
4	Out of limit	Earnings for 3382 at $972	6,311.00	6,311.00	Yes			
⋮	⋮	⋮	⋮	⋮	⋮			
25	Illogical relation	Employee 3735 in Department 3 with earnings of $180	5,832.00	6,012.00	No			
26	Illogical relation	Employee 3862 in Department 5 with earnings of $200	6,431.00	6,431.00	Yes			
⋮	⋮	⋮	⋮	⋮	⋮			

ILLUSTRATION 8–4 A Warnier-Orr Diagram

```
*******************************************************************************************
*                                                                                         *
* <Determine 1099 Amounts>                                                                *
*                                                                                         *
* Prepared By:                         | Reviewed By:                                     *
*                                      |                                                  *
* Date:                                | Date:                                            *
*                                                                                         *
* Program Name       : Determine 1099 Amounts                                             *
*                                                                                         *
* Frequency          :                                                                    *
*                                                                                         *
* Program Hierarchy  :                                                                    *
*                                                 ________                                *
*                                                 | OPEN FILES                            *
*                          ________________       | CALL DATE ROUTINE                     *
*                          | OPEN ROUTINE   ______| WRITE REPORT HEADINGS                 *
*                          |                      | READ RECORD                           *
*                          |                      |________                               *
*                          |                      ________                   ________     *
*                          |                      | SELECT 1099 RECORDS ______| SELECT CASH HIST PAYABLE TYPE
*                          |                      |                           | SELECT RECORDS FROM PREVIOUS
*                          |                      |                           |      CALENDAR YEAR
*                          |                      |                           |________   *
*                          |                      |                           ________    *
*                          |                      |                           | DETERMINE IF NEW CO, GS, OWNER
*                          |                      |                           | ADD AMOUNTS TO CO, GS, OWNER TOTAL
*                          |                      | SUMMARIZE BY GOVT ID ______| DETERMINE IF NEW GOVT ID
*                          |                      |                           | ADD AMOUNTS TO GOVT ID TOTAL
* DETERMINE 1099  ________ | PROCESS PAYMENT  ____|                           |________   *
* AMOUNTS                  | HISTORY INFORMATION  |                           ________    *
*                          |                      |                           | OBTAIN N & A INFORMATION
*                          |                      |                           | CHECK PAGING
*                          |                      | OUTPUT ROUTINE      ______| FORMAT CO, GS, OWNER TOTAL LINE
*                          |                      |                           | PRINT 1099 LISTING REPORT LINE
*                          |                      |                           | DETERMINE IF GOVT ID TOTAL > $600
*                          |                      |                           |     (OWNER SHOULD RECEIVE 1099)
*                          |                      |                           | FORMAT IRS FORM 1099 RECORDS
*                          |                      |                           | WRITE RECORD TO 1099 FILE
*                          |                      |                           |________   *
*                          |                      | NEXT RECORD                           *
*                          |                      |________                               *
*                          |                      ________                                *
*                          |                      | WRITE REPORT TRAILER                  *
*                          | CLOSE ROUTINE  ______| CLOSE FILES                           *
*                          |________________      |________                               *
*                                                                                         *
*******************************************************************************************
*                                                                                         *
*     This program will contain a module to select all payment history for each owner for the calendar year to be
* processed.  These records should then be summarized by government ID, gathering system, and owner number.  A grand total
* for the government ID should also be produced.  Two outputs should be generated: a report indicating all owners and
* their 1099 totals, and a file containing the summarized records for owners who received more than $600 in payments over the
* course of the year.                                                                     *
*                                                                                         *
*******************************************************************************************
```

Document the Program. In the process of defining the logic of a program, the programming team creates several types of documentation. These include structure charts, pseudocode, memos produced during structured walk-throughs, and the working papers produced during testing. Once satisfied that the program works properly, the team also produces a listing of the program in its source language. The source language is the high-level computer language used in coding the program. Other methods of documentation sometimes are used with structured programming. For example, many programmer teams use *Warnier-Orr Diagrams* to describe how a module works. Such a diagram looks like a structure chart turned on its side containing pseudocode. Illustration 8–4 contains an example.

At the conclusion of programming, the project team prepares a *Computer Operations Manual*. This document contains instructions for computer operators

ILLUSTRATION 8–5 Equipment Installation and Programming Tasks

Equipment installation

Site preparation. Complexity depends on equipment.
Acceptance test. Find out if it works.

Programming

Define program logic. Should be modular.
Code. Use structured program constructs.
Debug. Use structured walk-throughs.
Test. Verify all logic paths.
Document. Important for changes, reviews, training.

and describes the requirements for executing the programs in the system. For each program, the computer operations manual specifies the operating schedule, the files accessed, the equipment used, the kind of paper required on the printer, and internal control, security, and file retention requirements. It also describes any necessary procedures for stopping and restarting the program should erroneous conditions occur.

Importance of Documentation. In the early days of computerized accounting, programmers were primarily concerned with the size and efficiency of their programs. Today, most project teams consider the adequacy of documentation to be a more serious concern. A programming team is required to produce good documentation for three reasons.

First, documentation makes easier any changes to programs that may be required later. At some time in the operations phase, most programs require minor changes requested by system users or caused by errors in the original programs. Called *program maintenance,* these changes are usually made by a programmer who did not participate in the original programmer team. Good documentation is necessary for the maintenance programmer to make these changes efficiently.

Second, documentation facilitates the reviews of the programs by the project team and auditors. These reviews are needed to ensure that the system functions as intended. If the documentation is incomplete or not understandable, reviews may be difficult. This increases the costs of the development project during implementation and the costs of an audit during operations.

Third, programming and system documentation provide the basis for training personnel in the new system. Sometimes organizations use flowcharts, sample inputs and outputs, the *Procedures Manual,* and the *Computer Operations Manual* for this purpose. Some organizations develop other training materials from these forms of documentation. Training is difficult without accurate and complete documentation.

You have learned the four tasks that occur during the development of a computer program and some of the preferred techniques for completing them. Illustration 8–5 summarizes the tasks performed during equipment installation and programming. Another activity during implementation is training, which often occurs at the same time.

Training

In some system development projects, training begins as soon as a preliminary system design is completed, and may continue into the operations phase. Most training, however, occurs after the completion of the design phase and prior to testing of the system. The two groups of employees who benefit from training are the users and the computer operations personnel.

User Training. Users include the managers, supervisors, and clerks who receive outputs from the system or provide inputs to it. Members of the system design team have primary responsibility for user training, although they may receive help from supervisors or outside consultants. User training relies heavily on the descriptions contained in the *Procedures Manual*. Members of the design team teach users the noncomputerized tasks required by the new system. They describe procedures for data entry and give instruction on the use of outputs from the system.

The design team sometimes provides training in a classroom, with lectures and discussion. At other times team members use computerized tutorials or training manuals that allow employees to work at their own pace. Developing training materials is often a major task for members of the design team during the implementation phase. In some projects, the team completes development of the *Procedures Manual* at this time. Many tasks, such as data entry at a terminal, cannot be described in detail until after programming is complete.

Operations Training. The project manager provides operations training for employees directly involved with running the computer equipment. They include data entry clerks, computer operators, technical support personnel, and data control clerks. Data entry clerks are the people who convert accounting transactions into a magnetic form readable by the computer; computer operators work at a data center and physically operate the computer and its file storage devices; technical support personnel make repairs to equipment or software when it malfunctions; data control clerks distribute to users the reports produced at the data center. During operations training these employees learn how to use the equipment and software included in the system.

Members of the design team conduct operations training using classroom instruction, computerized tutorials, and training manuals. They use the *Computer Operations Manual* to train data entry clerks, computer operators, and data control clerks. Frequently, however, technical topics are taught by equipment and software vendors. Some vendors provide videotaped instruction courses; others offer regularly scheduled classes for their customers at which vendor personnel conduct operations training. Sometimes the best way to acquire adequate technical knowledge is through on-the-job training. As a result, management frequently chooses to hire technical support personnel rather than to train them.

Testing

Another activity during the implementation phase is testing. This activity follows programming and must precede conversion, but may proceed at the same time as some training tasks. Programmer teams test individual programs as a part of programming; during the testing activity two other tests occur: string and system testing.

String Testing. In many accounting applications, the output of one program provides an immediate input to another program. For example, one program may resequence a batch of accounting transactions. This sorted batch of transactions is then an input to another program that prints a report listing them. Next, another program posts each transaction to a ledger. In systems terminology, these programs are tightly coupled. It is not enough to know that each program works properly; the project team must also determine that the entire *string,* or series of programs, functions as intended.

During string testing, the project team produces test data for the first of a series of programs. Team members then execute each program in the series and examine the validity of the last program's output. String testing ensures that the outputs produced by each program are consistent with the input requirements of the program that follows it. It is most important in those accounting systems that apply each computerized process to a batch of transactions before allowing the batch to proceed to the next process.

System Testing. In contrast to string testing, which evaluates only computerized procedures, system testing allows the project team to evaluate noncomputerized ones as well. System testing includes tests of procedures used to capture data, to convert it into computer readable form, and to produce the outputs of the system. It concerns user and operations personnel involved in the system's routine operations.

The project team creates sample transactions representing a full range of both valid and invalid data. User and data entry personnel enter these transactions into the system. Computer operators execute on the actual equipment the computer programs to process the transactions. The project team then compares the outputs from processing with those expected.

During system testing, the project team's main concern is the system's capabilities. Team members determine that the system has the capacity to process transactions correctly without creating backlogs. They also verify that it does not produce excessive erroneous transactions, or allow erroneous data to enter data files. System testing sometimes alerts the project team to errors made during system design. Such errors must be corrected before conversion. In that activity, the project team uses the system to process actual transactions.

Conversion

Conversion is the process of changing from the old system to the new one. During the conversion activity, the project team tests the new system under actual operating conditions. Conversion provides the team with the opportunity to make final modifications to the system before the organization relies on it for processing accounting transactions. The project team completes three tasks during conversion: file conversion, volume testing, and system changeover.

File Conversion. The first task in conversion is to change the way data are stored. The objective in file conversion is to maintain the accuracy and completeness of existing files while creating new ones required by the new system. The method for doing this depends on the technology used by the old system.

Sometimes, the project team converts from a noncomputerized system to a computerized one. In this case, the data used by the old system are recorded on paper in journals, ledgers, documents, and reports, which are stored in filing cabinets. The project team changes this data into a form that can be interpreted by the computer equipment. The method of organizing the data files in the new system is consistent with the file specifications created during system design.

This conversion process can be time-consuming and expensive. Frequently, the project team hires temporary data entry clerks to complete the task. Because of the length of this type of conversion, the project team may decide to begin the process immediately after detailed specification, when the new file formats are known.

When the change is from one computerized system to another, the process of file conversion is usually quicker. The project team writes computer programs to change data files from the old format to the new one. The team in this case verifies that the programs create the new data files without losing computer records or altering their contents.

From an internal control standpoint, file conversion is critical. Data contained in a new file may come from a variety of sources in the old system, and some may be computerized while others are not. Thus, the process may be a complex one. The project team concentrates on ensuring that all data are transcribed correctly. Even a seemingly insignificant error in file conversion can cause a new system to produce inaccurate reports. This can occur regardless of how carefully the system was designed, and the results of the error may be difficult to identify and eliminate. File conversion requires thorough planning and careful attention to detail.

Volume Testing. In a volume test, the project team executes the system using actual inputs for a typical processing period. This may be the number of transactions representing one day's, one week's, or one month's processing. These transactions are posted to copies of the actual data files created during file conversion. The test produces all outputs required by the system.

The purpose of volume testing is to determine how well the system works under an actual processing load. Often an inefficiency that appears minor during system testing may create serious problems when a new system attempts to handle a realistic number of transactions. During a volume test the project team discovers these inefficiencies and corrects them before the organization becomes dependent on the new system. A project team may repeat the volume test several times before all problems in the system are discovered and corrected.

Changeover. After the new system has passed volume testing, the project team makes it operational. They call this task system changeover. The four alternative approaches to changeover are the direct approach, a pilot system, parallel operations, and system phase-in.

Direct Changeover. Using this approach, the project team places the new system in operation and immediately ceases operating the old one. Direct changeover avoids the costs and inconvenience of the other approaches. It is a viable alternative for noncritical systems that involve simple processes and few people.

In most cases, however, unexpected problems surface during changeover. If this occurs with direct changeover, the old system is not available as a backup. The organization must function without the system until the problems with the new one are corrected. Because an organization cannot afford to do this for most accounting applications, the approach is seldom used.

Pilot System. The project team may decide to implement the system first within a limited segment of the organization, such as a department, sales region, or a subsidiary. Referring to this as a pilot system, the team members correct the unexpected problems in this system before introducing it throughout the organization. In this way, the unexpected problems affect only a portion of the organization.

However, a system that works well in one department or region may not work as well in others. Furthermore, the high transaction volume of organization-wide implementation may produce problems that do not exist in the more limited pilot system. In some cases, a pilot system is a useful approach when used with parallel operation.

Parallel Operation. Using parallel operation, the project team independently processes actual data on both the old system and the new one. Team members then compare the results from both systems and reconcile any differences. If differences arise because the new system functions improperly, they correct it before the organization becomes reliant on it. The old system continues to operate as a backup.

Because parallel operation is the safest approach to system changeover, it is also a common one. But this alternative requires that all operations be performed twice: once using the old documents, procedures, and programs, and once using the new ones. Often employees dread parallel operation because it doubles their workloads. If they are already working at near capacity, parallel operation may require extended overtime work. For this reason, the organization may choose to hire temporary workers to help the full-time employees.

Phase-in. In some situations, the project team may choose to phase in the new system. With phase-in, team members implement portions of the new system one at a time until the entire new system is functioning properly. For example, they may decide to implement data-entry procedures first. When all problems with data entry have been eliminated, they change to the new procedures for ad hoc reporting. Finally, after this works well, they use the procedures and programs for generating routine reports. This produces a working system acceptable to the users.

Phase-in limits the problems that can arise during changeover to those associated with the current portion of the system. This makes it easier to correct problems and it helps control their impact. However, the characteristics of many systems do not allow phase-in. For example, the design of the system may dictate that data entry, ad hoc reporting, and routine reporting change simultaneously. In these cases, the design team must convert all procedures at the same time.

User Sign-off

Of the four alternatives to system changeover, parallel operation is the most common. It may continue for a period of several weeks to several months. The design team continues parallel operation until the two systems produce consistent outputs over a number of processing cycles. Once the design team and users are satisfied with the new system, a manager in the affected user department signs an agreement accepting the system. This agreement, called *user sign-off,* indicates that the users are satisfied with the system. It marks the end of the system development project. Illustration 8–6 summarizes the tasks performed during training, testing, and conversion.

Auditor Involvement in Implementation

Auditors devote more time to the implementation phase than to systems analysis, but less than to system design. They perform critical tasks during two implementation activities.

ILLUSTRATION 8–6 Training, Testing, and Conversion Tasks

Training

User training. Rely on written procedures.

Operations training. Operations manual and vendor training.

Testing

String testing. Execute a series of programs.

System testing. All computerized and noncomputerized procedures.

Conversion

File conversion. Accuracy is critical.

Volume testing. With a normal processing volume.

Changeover. Safest approach is parallel operation.

During *system testing*, auditors review the adequacy of the test data and the results of the tests. Their primary concern is that the test data adequately evaluate the internal controls in the system. If system test documentation does not show that control measures are functioning properly, auditors may produce their own test data to evaluate these controls. If the controls are not functioning, auditors insist on modifications to the system before proceeding with conversion.

In the *conversion* activity, auditors ensure the adequacy of file conversion procedures. They review the plans for conversion prior to its start, and they determine that these plans will maintain accurate data during changeover. After file conversion is complete, auditors satisfy themselves that data in the new files is complete and consistent with that contained in the old ones. Because accurate file conversion is so critical to the accuracy of accounting reports, the project team usually appreciates this independent check on their activities.

This review of the file conversion procedures and results does not terminate the auditors' involvement in a new system. Auditors are again involved during reviews that they make in the operations phase of the SDLC.

SYSTEM OPERATIONS

now becomes Annual Cost

The operations phase is the period of time during which the system functions as a provider of accounting information. As the last phase in the SDLC, it is the objective of the system development process. A well-designed accounting system, requiring six months to three years to develop, typically operates from 5 to 10 years before being replaced. As an accountant you will be involved in three activities during the operations phase: post-implementation review, system maintenance, and accounting for systems costs.

Post-Implementation Review

The post-implementation review follows the completion of a system development project. This analysis and appraisal of the new system usually occurs about six months after conversion. Its purpose is to determine if the new system meets the objectives established for it during systems analysis.

Responsibility for the Review. The information systems steering committee appoints a review team to conduct the post-implementation review. The review team normally consists of one or two systems analysts who participated in the development process from systems analysis through implementation. It should also include someone impartial, who did not work on the development project. Sometimes the committee appoints an internal auditor to the review team for this reason.

These systems analysts know the assumptions made when designing the system and understand how the system was intended to work. Thus, during the review they center their attention on appraising the system rather than on learning about its design. The auditor adds an expertise in auditability and controls to the review team. The review provides the auditor with an opportunity to learn about the system from analysts who designed it. This knowledge is valuable when the auditor conducts periodic operational audits throughout the operations phase.

Procedures in the Review. In its review, the team evaluates the outcome of the system design project. Its members estimate the costs and benefits of the system and compare them to those predicted during development. They identify the source of differences between actual and predicted costs. They determine the adequacy of the documentation provided by the design team and the implementation project team. The review team also evaluates user satisfaction with the system, and the adequacy of its internal controls.

Costs and Benefits. The first step in the review is to estimate the costs and benefits of the system. The review team calculates the initial costs of developing the system. Because it has operated for several months, it also develops accurate estimates of ongoing costs and savings. The review team calculates these and compares them to the costs and benefits projected during systems analysis. This provides the analysts on the team with feedback concerning the accuracy of the cost-benefit analysis that they performed when determining economic feasibility. This feedback aids them when performing another feasibility analysis for a later project. Illustration 8–7 contains such an evaluation of the cost-benefit analysis.

The review team then determines why actual costs differ from predicted costs. Differences sometimes arise from uncontrollable sources such as unexpected price changes, policy changes, or changes in the economic environment of the organization. In other cases, differences originate from controllable sources that include inaccurate estimates or inefficiencies in the development process. The review team learns by identifying these sources and is able to correct for them in future projects.

ILLUSTRATION 8–7 Evaluation of Cost-Benefit Analysis

	Estimated	*Actual*
Initial cost:		
Installation	$ 12,000	$ 20,000
Initial programming	72,000	85,800
Training and parallel systems cost	36,000	45,000
Total initial cost	$120,000	$150,800
Annual operating costs and savings:		
Salaries of computer personnel	$104,000	$120,000
Power and supplies	21,000	22,000
Computer rental	43,200	45,000
Total	168,200	187,000
Less: Salary savings	267,000	230,000
Net cost savings	$ 98,800	$ 43,000

ILLUSTRATION 8–8 Comparison of Estimated and Actual Programming Costs

	Estimated	*Actual*
Number of instructions to be written	7,200	7,800
Weekly salary of programmers	$ 500	$ 572
Average number of instructions written per programmer per week	50	52
Average cost per instruction	$ 10	$ 11
Total initial programming cost	$72,000	$85,800

Illustration 8–8 identifies one source for the difference between the estimated and actual development costs in Illustration 8–7. Illustration 8–9 shows how to apply variance analysis techniques learned in managerial accounting courses to further isolate the causes for this difference.

Documentation. During the post-implementation review, the review team evaluates the adequacy of the documentation for the new system. Preparing adequate documentation during a project is important because auditors review documentation as a part of operational and financial audits. Adequate documentation also aids systems analysts when they investigate future problems with the system. Furthermore, an examination of documentation is an efficient way to begin the other procedures in the post-implementation review.

In studying the phases of the SDLC, you have learned about three types of documentation: *design documentation* includes the working papers produced by the design team when developing detailed specifications for the system; *user documentation* describes the features of the system user personnel need to know to perform their jobs; *operations documentation* provides similar information for

ILLUSTRATION 8–9 Variance Analysis of Programming Costs

A. Variance caused by volume

$$\text{Volume variance} = \left(\text{Actual volume} - \text{Estimated volume}\right) \times \text{Estimated cost per instruction}$$
$$= (7{,}200 - 7{,}800) \times \$10$$
$$= \$6{,}000 \text{ unfavorable}$$

B. Variance caused by price

$$\text{Price variance} = \left(\text{Actual volume} \div \text{Estimated production per week}\right) \times \left(\text{Actual salary per week} - \text{Estimated salary per week}\right)$$
$$= (7{,}800 \div 50) \times (\$572 - \$500)$$
$$= \$11{,}232 \text{ unfavorable}$$

C. Variance caused by efficiency

$$\text{Efficiency variance} = \left[\left(\text{Actual volume} \div \text{Actual production per week}\right) - \left(\text{Actual volume} \div \text{Estimated production per week}\right)\right] \times \text{Actual salary per week}$$
$$= [(7{,}800 \div 52) - (7{,}800 \div 50)] \times \$572$$
$$= \$3{,}432 \text{ favorable}$$

D. Summary of variances

Estimated initial programming cost	$72,000	
Actual initial programming cost	85,800	
Variance	$13,800	unfavorable
Causes of variances:		
Variance caused by volume	$ 6,000	unfavorable
Variance caused by price	11,232	unfavorable
Variance caused by efficiency	3,432	favorable
Total variances	$13,800	unfavorable

personnel in the MIS department. Illustration 8–10 describes the contents of an adequate documentation package.

The team may use checklists to guide its review of the system documentation package. Checklists are an efficient approach because once developed, they may be used repeatedly during later system reviews. A checklist identifies the desired contents of a documentation package and provides spaces to indicate whether the contents are present. It is designed in such a way that a "yes" answer indicates the presence of a desired form of documentation. Illustration 8–11 shows a sample checklist for program documentation.

User Satisfaction. The objective of a post-implementation review is to determine whether a new system meets its objectives. An effective way of doing this is find out users' reactions to the system. In many cases, users initiated the development process. Such a system cannot be considered a success unless these users think that the objectives of the system have been met.

ILLUSTRATION 8–10 A System Documentation Package

Development Documentation

- Existing system description (from preliminary survey)
- Cost-benefit analysis (from feasibility study)
- System specifications, including:
  - Sample outputs
  - Sample inputs
  - Description of data storage methods
  - Program documentation, including:
    - Programming standards manual
    - Program narratives
    - Structure charts
    - Pseudocode
    - Test data and test runs
    - Program listings
- Acceptance test descriptions
- Conversion results, including:
  - File conversion procedures
  - Volume testing results
  - Changeover schedule
- User sign-off agreement

User Documentation

- Procedures manual
- Training manuals

Operations Documentation

- Operations manual, including a program operating schedule. For each program:
  - Files accessed
  - Equipment required
  - Special requirements for printing, security, and file retention

Commonly the review team determines user satisfaction by conducting interviews with key users or supervisors within the user departments. If there are many users, the team may develop questionnaires for this purpose.

Input from users during the review identifies shortcomings in the system design that are to be avoided in later projects. Additionally, the team may identify problems that can be corrected easily by changes to the system's programs or procedures.

Internal Control. Frequently, the review team includes an auditor to evaluate the effectiveness of internal control in the new system. Auditors evaluate controls as a part of their routine operational and financial audits. However, by examining them during the post-implementation review, an auditor identifies material control weaknesses before they have a widespread effect on the accuracy of the accounting records.

ILLUSTRATION 8–11 Checklist for Program Documentation

	Yes	No
Programming administration:		
1. Is there a standards manual?		
2. Is the use of flowchart symbols standardized?		
3. Is the procedure for systems documentation standardized?		
4. Is the use of programming language standardized?		
5. Is the use of programming techniques such as initialization routines standardized?		
6. Are there established procedures for program testing?		
7. Are there established procedures for program changes?		
8. Is the procedure for compiling a program operations manual standardized?		
Program operations manual:		
1. Is there a program operations manual?		
2. Is documentation adequate as to:		
a. Program identification.		
b. Program background.		
c. Systems description.		
d. Program description.		
e. Program listing.		
f. Program test data.		
g. Program change record.		
3. Is information in the operator's manual adequate as to:		
a. Program objective.		
b. Control data format.		
c. Run priority.		
d. Console operations.		
e. Tape requirements.		
f. Output distribution.		

The review team pays special attention to the *error correction procedures* in the new system. Errors may be introduced into accounting data either on input, as transactions are recorded in computer readable form, or during processing by computer programs. Many control measures, called *detective controls,* are included in accounting systems to identify these erroneous transactions before they are posted to a ledger. Error correction procedures provide a method of correcting these erroneous transactions and reentering them into computer processing.

In reviewing error correction procedures, the team looks for either of two possible occurrences. Sometimes these procedures may identify excessive erroneous transactions, which indicates to the auditor that additional *preventive controls* are needed in the system to stop these errors. On the other hand, the system may identify few errors, which may indicate that additional detective controls are needed. Error correction procedures provide the auditor with an accurate indicator of the adequacy of internal control.

Reasons for Performing the Review. A post-implementation review may seem unnecessary. After all, at this time the system is completed, the project team disbanded, and users have signed off indicating acceptance of the system. Nevertheless, there are four benefits from conducting a post-implementation review.[2]

First, the review provides information to the design team that could improve future projects. It identifies shortcomings that can be avoided in future designs and improves the abilities of analysts to estimate costs and benefits. Second, the review occurs soon after conversion. If the system has serious shortcomings, these can be corrected promptly before excessive costs result. Third, the knowledge that a review will be performed motivates the members of the design and project teams. They are more thorough in their tasks knowing that a review team will later examine their work. Finally, the review provides another opportunity to evaluate the performance of MIS personnel. The success of future design projects depends on how effectively their skills are utilized.

Although the procedures of the post-implementation review consist of an examination of past actions, the focus of the review is on the future. A review is successful and worthwhile when it benefits future system development projects.

System Maintenance

An activity that takes place throughout the life of a system is the maintenance of both computer equipment and computer software.

Equipment maintenance is an ongoing activity performed by technical personnel. Usually the MIS department employs technical specialists for this purpose. Sometimes the organization enters into contracts with vendors to maintain selected pieces of equipment for a monthly fee. Accountants are only indirectly concerned with equipment maintenance.

Accountants and other users frequently initiate *program maintenance*. These are the inevitable minor changes to existing systems during the operations phase. Users submit requests for program maintenance whenever they identify improvements for the inputs, programs, or outputs of a system. Program maintenance also occurs when a malfunction in an accounting system requires unplanned changes.

---

[2]H. M. Sollenberger, "Assessing Information Systems Projects," *Management Accounting*, September 1973, p. 41.

Planned System Improvements. Users' needs for information change rapidly, and accounting systems must adapt to new information needs. As users identify potential improvements, they submit program change requests to the MIS manager, who refers the requests to the information systems steering committee. If they think a change has merit, they assign an analyst to conduct a preliminary survey. If the user's change is a minor one, however, the manager assigns it to a maintenance programmer for implementation.

As you can see, the difference between a change that requires a new system and one that requires only system maintenance is a matter of degree. A major change requires a development project; a minor change requires maintenance. As a guideline, system maintenance changes are those small enough to be accomplished by one person rather than by a project team.

Unplanned Changes. During the implementation phase the project team tests each individual program and then tests all the programs operating together. Ideally, they test every logic path in every program and every possible type of transaction. In reality, complete testing is difficult to achieve.

Sometimes the project team overlooks a possible combination of events, or an unusual type of transaction, and the system is incapable of processing it. When this occurs, a program in the system terminates abnormally and the system does not produce the desired output. Computer operators then call a maintenance programmer to modify the program. This unplanned maintenance is common in new systems; occasionally it is necessary even after a system has been operational for many years.

Controlling System Maintenance. Because software maintenance is unavoidable, an organization must adopt measures to control it. Anytime a programmer changes an accounting program, there is a risk that the change may be improper, or that the change will not be recorded in program documentation. For example, an unscrupulous programmer may make a program change that is intended to defraud the organization. Such a change would be difficult for anyone else to discover.

When changes are made, the maintenance programmer should enter them in a *program change record.* This record is usually a form included in the program documentation. It shows the date and nature of the change, the name of the programmer making it, and the approval of a supervisor. A supervisor signs the program change record indicating approval only after reviewing the change with the programmer and examining the updated program documentation. Auditors sometimes review the program change records for critical programs when studying internal control for a system.

Another good procedure is to refer all planned system improvements to the steering committee. The committee reviews the change and considers its impact on all users before they authorize a programmer or project team to implement it.

Unplanned changes are more difficult to control. Usually they occur in an emergency when there is insufficient time for review by the steering committee or MIS manager. Typically, all computer processing is halted while the maintenance programmer consults program documentation and attempts to isolate the cause of the problem. Once the cause is found, the programmer's main objective is to get the program working properly as quickly as possible. Unplanned maintenance presents the greatest risks and should always be reviewed later by the MIS manager and approved by the steering committee.

System maintenance consists of equipment maintenance, planned system improvements, and unplanned program changes. Accountants are involved in the last two forms. They often originate requests for system improvements, and auditors review approvals for program changes when studying internal control. Another activity in the operations phase that involves accountants is accounting for systems costs.

Accounting for Systems Costs

Developing and operating computerized information systems are costly activities; many organizations use responsibility accounting systems to control these costs. They trace the costs to a responsibility center and hold the manager of the center responsible for them. Accountants participate in deciding how this is done. The two kinds of systems costs are the initial costs of developing and implementing the system, and the ongoing costs of operating it. A responsibility accounting system charges each to responsibility centers.

Development Costs. Development costs include supplies, equipment, and salaries of personnel working in a system development project. These costs may vary from a few thousand to a few million dollars, depending on the size of the project. In accounting for these costs, the organization must choose between two alternatives: allocating them to specific user departments or including them in general overhead. Each approach may be appropriate in certain circumstances.

Allocate Development Costs. A fair method of accounting for development costs recognizes that the departments benefiting from a system should bear its costs. Thus, many organizations choose to assign development costs to specific user departments. The most common approach is to allocate these costs to the responsibility center of the manager who submits the project proposal. This gives the manager a personal interest in the success of the project and motivates the manager to cooperate with the project team. The manager is more willing to assign personnel to it and wants to see the project completed on schedule. Furthermore, the manager cannot propose a project unless it produces enough benefits for the responsibility center to recover its costs.

This is a reasonable approach for those systems that clearly benefit a single department; however, in many cases this department may not be able to afford the system. Even though a proposed system is beneficial for the organization, a manager may reject it rather than absorb its costs in the department's budget. For this reason, some organizations simply include development costs as general overhead.

Development Costs as General Overhead. Advocates of this approach recognize that an improved system in any department or division benefits the entire organization. They argue that the costs of a new system should be included in general overhead.

With this approach, the costs of a new system are traced to a high-level responsibility center, such as at the organization or plant level. They are then allocated to all lower-level responsibility centers. In this way the costs are borne by all departments. This approach avoids the possibility that a manager might reject a beneficial system because of its effect on a departmental budget.

The disadvantage of including development costs in general overhead is that this approach offers individual managers no incentive to control development costs. Because the user department is not charged for these costs, its manager may propose projects that are unnecessary or unprofitable. Furthermore, the manager may not actively support the project because cost overruns do not adversely impact his or her performance reports.

Many organizations adopt a combination of these two methods of accounting for system development costs. Some allow the information system steering committee to select a method for each individual project. Before selecting an accounting method, the committee evaluates the user managers' support for the project, the department's ability to pay for it, and its benefits to the entire organization. Other organizations establish a consistent policy in which all systems analysis costs are included in general overhead, and design and implementation costs are allocated to the proposing manager's responsibility center. This compromise approach provides the manager with incentives for cost control while not burdening the user department with all of the costs of development. It decreases, but does not eliminate, the disadvantages of each method.

Operational Costs. Operational costs are the ongoing costs of using the system during the operations phase. These include expenditures for utilities, supplies, equipment repairs, software maintenance, and salaries for operations personnel.

Most organizations consider these costs a form of overhead and allocate them to user departments based on consumption of services. A computerized application system called a *charge-out system* measures the services provided to different departments. It multiplies these quantities of services by predetermined rates to assess the total charges. The organization adopts a *charging algorithm* for this purpose. The predetermined rates may be calculated as cost-based, market, or standard rates.

Cost-based Rates. When using cost-based rates, the charge-out system determines the actual expenditures for operating the MIS department. These actual costs are then allocated to user departments using the charging algorithm. User departments absorb these costs as part of their departmental overhead.

This method is an obvious one to most accountants, who are accustomed to recording and allocating other overhead costs. It requires the recovery of all MIS operating costs by revenue-producing departments. Each department absorbs its share of MIS expenditures based on its consumption of MIS services.

However, the use of cost-based rates may produce undesirable effects in user departments. The magnitude of the expenditures for MIS operations affects the costs allocated to each user department. The level of these expenditures may vary significantly from month to month or year to year. Because user managers have no control over these expenditures, they may react unfavorably to a responsibility accounting system that includes uncontrollable costs on their performance reports. They sometimes blame excessive overhead not on their department's consumption of MIS services, but rather on the level of expenditures in the MIS department.

Adverse effects occur in the MIS department as well. Because all of its costs are recovered, the MIS manager has little incentive to minimize them. The use of market rates overcomes these shortcomings.

Market Rates. In many cases, the services provided by a MIS department can also be provided by a service bureau or a time-sharing service. When charging for their services, these businesses establish a market for MIS services. Some organizations choose to include these market rates in the charging algorithm for internally provided MIS services.

Market rates provide an objective measure of the value of MIS services. The costs allocated to a user department by the charging algorithm are approximately equal to the costs incurred if an external source were used. The manager of a user department cannot reasonably blame the MIS department for the magnitude of these costs. Furthermore, if the user department's manager has the authority to use a service bureau or time-sharing service, the MIS department is motivated to limit its costs to compete with these external businesses.

This method is useful in many circumstances and is frequently adopted by companies who previously experimented unsuccessfully with cost-based rates. Many large organizations establish subsidiaries that provide MIS services not only within the organization but also to outside companies. However, the use of market rates may result in some MIS costs not being recovered. When user department managers purchase MIS services from outside, the organization's overall profitability is decreased. Services required by a user department may be unavailable from outside businesses, or a lack of competition may produce rates that are unreasonable. For these reasons, some organizations establish standard rates for MIS services.

Standard Rates. Standard rates are set by negotiation between MIS and user department managers who agree to rates that provide recovery of reasonable MIS operating costs averaged over an extended period. MIS costs should be approximately equal to market rates when the latter are available.

Organizations with highly developed standard costing and budgeting systems frequently adopt this method. Standard rates encourage MIS managers to limit operating costs, so that actual expenditures are within those assumed in setting the charge-out rates. In this case, all MIS department costs are recovered by charges to user departments. With standard rates, charges to user departments are solely based on their consumption of services. Thus, any variation in a user

ILLUSTRATION 8–12 A Charging Algorithm

$$\text{Cost/Job} = A_0 + F_1 \left[\sum_{n=1}^{n=n} [A_1(\Theta_{CPU-X} + 1.5\ \Theta_{CPU-Y}) + A_2\Theta_{I/O} + A_3(\Theta_{CPU-X} + 1.5\ \Theta_{CPU-Y} + \Theta_{I/O})\ (B)\ (.80 + .001B)] \right] + F_1 \left[\sum_{n=1}^{n=n} (A_4\ T_{nr} + A_5 D_{nr} + A_6 C_{nr}) \right]$$

$$\text{Cost/Month} = A_7 D_r + A_8 C_r$$

where

A_0, A_1, A_2, A_3, A_4, A_5, A_6, A_7, A_8, and A_9, are charging rates

F_1	= Factor dependent on priority requested
n	= Job step number
$\Theta_{CPU\text{-}X}$	= CPU time in hours on Model X
$\Theta_{CPU\text{-}Y}$	= CPU time in hours on Model Y
$\Theta_{I/O}$	= Input-output time
B	= Core requested in thousands of bytes
T_{nr}	= Number nonresident tape data sets used
D_{nr}	= Number nonresident disk data sets used
C_{nr}	= Number nonresident data cell data sets used
D_r	= Thousands of bytes of disk resident storage
C_r	= Thousands of bytes of data cell resident storage

department's MIS overhead charge results from changes in its activity, not from changes in expenditure level within the MIS department. These are controllable by the user department's manager.

Standard rates overcome the disadvantages of cost-based rates and are usable when market rates do not exist; however, setting them requires skill and effort. Managers with different objectives and perspectives must agree, and like standard costs for material, labor, and factory overhead, rates must be revised periodically.

The three methods for determining costs included in a charging algorithm are cost-based, market, or standard rates. The charging algorithm multiplies these rates by measures of system usage, such as time or computer memory used. These algorithms may become very complex; Illustration 8–12 shows the charging algorithm from an actual company.[3] Illustration 8–13

[3]H. M. Sollenberger, *Management Control of Information Systems Development* (Montvale, N.J.: National Association of Accountants 1971), p. 135.

ILLUSTRATION 8–13 Accounting for System Costs

DEVELOPMENT COSTS. May choose to

1. *Allocate to user department proposing the system*
   Provides incentive to limit development costs.
   Provides incentive to avoid unprofitable systems.
   May prevent development of beneficial systems.
2. *Include in general overhead*
   Recognizes the system's benefits to entire organization.
   Provides little user department incentive to limit developmental costs.

OPERATIONAL COSTS. Allocate to user departments based on

1. *Cost-based rates*
   All MIS expenditures are borne by those departments consuming MIS services.
   Allocated costs are uncontrollable in user departments.
2. *Market rates*
   Allocated costs are objectively determined.
   Provides incentive to limit MIS expenditures.
   A market rate for equivalent services may not exist.
3. *Standard rates*
   Provides recovery of MIS expenditures over long term.
   Provides incentive to limit MIS expenditures.
   May be difficult to set.

summarizes the advantages and disadvantages of the methods of accounting for system costs.

SUMMARY

This chapter describes the last two phases of the system development life cycle. During the implementation phase, a project team produces a working system from design specifications, and places this system in operation. The operation phase is the period of time during which the system functions as a provider of accounting information; it may last for many years.

Five activities take place during the implementation phase: equipment installation, programming, training, testing, and conversion. During this phase, the project team completes a documentation package for the system. Good documentation facilitates later changes and reviews of the system and provides a source of training materials for users and operations personnel. Auditors participate in implementation by reviewing the project team's tests of internal control and its file conversion procedures. The end of this phase occurs when a user department manager signs off, indicating acceptance of the system.

This chapter describes three activities that involve accountants during the operations phase. They are the post-implementation review, system maintenance, and accounting for systems costs. A later chapter describes a fourth activity—conducting reviews of the computerized system.

KEY TERMS

charge-out system A system used to measure the information system services provided to user departments and to allocate to them their share of ongoing operational costs.

conversion The implementation phase process of changing from using the old system to using the new one.

installation The implementation phase process of putting in place the equipment and software required for a new system.

parallel operation The most common form of system changeover in which both old and new systems operate simultaneously for a period of time.

post-implementation review An analysis and appraisal of a new system conducted by a review team several weeks after conversion to determine if the new system meets its objectives.

program maintenance The planned or unplanned changes to computer programs made during the operations phase.

programming The implementation phase process of developing program logic, and of coding, debugging, testing, and documenting computer programs.

pseudocode An informal language that uses English-like statements to represent the actions performed by a computer program.

structured programming A modular approach to writing computer programs. It allows only one entry and one exit point to each module and permits only three logic constructs.

structured walk-through A review of an individual programmer's work by the others on a programming team.

testing A system implementation activity that determines if modules, programs, and systems work properly.

training A system implementation activity of training both user and operations personnel.

user sign-off A written agreement between the managers of the project design team and the user department marking the end of the implementation phase and of the system development project.

QUESTIONS

8–1. Which actions begin and end the system implementation phase? Can you name five activities that occur between them?

8–2. Why is it important for programmers to produce code that is easy to understand? How do they accomplish this?

8–3. What is a computer operations manual? What are its contents?

8–4. When in the system development process does training occur? What is involved in training?

8–5. Identify four kinds of testing that occur prior to file conversion. Who performs each kind?

8–6. How is file conversion accomplished? Why is it important?

8–7. Distinguish between four approaches to system changeover. Which is the most common?

8–8. How is the auditor involved during the implementation phase of the system development life cycle?

8–9. Who performs the post-implementation review? Why? Which procedures are followed?

8–10. What is a program change record? How is it used?

8–11. Identify the ways of accounting for:

a. System development costs.

b. Computer system operational costs.

8–12. It has been said that a system design is never completely finished. What are the reasons for this statement?

EXERCISES AND CASES

8–13. DEFINITIONS

Define each of the following terms:

a. Detective control
b. Preventive control
c. Pseudocode
d. Acceptance test
e. Chief programmer team
f. Charge-out system
g. Volume testing

8–14. PROJECT TEAMS

Project teams are used during all four phases of the system development life cycle. Which personnel are assigned to the project team during:

a. Systems analysis?
b. System design?
c. Implementation?
d. Post-implementation review?

8–15. ***PERT DIAGRAM***

Site preparation for a computer installation may consist of the following activities:

a. Select site.
b. Prepare site plan.
c. Approve site plan.
d. Install electrical wiring.
e. Add false floor.
f. Install air conditioning (may be done after event *d* is completed).
g. Install air ducts and cooling water pipes.
h. Add overhead racks.
i. Complete building inspection (to be done after events *d*, *e*, *f*, *g* and *h* are completed).
j. Clean site.

Required:

Prepare a PERT network diagram for the activities involved in site preparation.

8–16. ***PERT DIAGRAM***

Equipment installation for a new computer system may be described by the following activities:

a. Review site.
b. Select software package.
c. Receive equipment.
d. Inspect equipment.
e. Install equipment.
f. Test equipment (to be done after activities *b* and *e* are completed).
g. Accept equipment.

Required:

Prepare a PERT network diagram for the activities involved in equipment installation.

8–17. ***DOCUMENTATION***

Look at the two columns that follow. The left one lists 6 categories of documentation produced during system design and implementation. The right column lists 18 elements of documentation related to the categories.

Categories

a. System documentation
b. Program documentation
c. Operations documentation
d. User documentation
e. Library documentation
f. Data entry documentation

Elements

1. Flowcharts showing the flow of information
2. Procedures needed to balance, reconcile, and maintain overall control
3. Storage instructions
4. Contents and format of data to be captured
5. Constants, codes, and tables
6. Verification procedures
7. Program flow diagrams and decision tables
8. Report distribution instructions
9. Messages and programmed halts
10. Procedures for backup files
11. Retention times
12. Source listings
13. Instructions to show proper use of each document
14. A complete history from planning through installation
15. Restart and recovery procedures
16. Rules for handling blank spaces
17. Instructions to ensure the proper completion of all input forms
18. List of programs in a system

Required:

Match each of the elements of documentation with the category in which it should be found. Use every element only once.

(CIA Adapted)

8–18. ***DOCUMENTATION***

The documentation of data processing applications is an important step in the design and implementation of any computer-based system. Documentation provides a complete record of data processing applications. However, documentation is a phase of systems development that often is neglected. Even though documentation can be tedious and time-consuming, the lack of proper documentation can be very costly for an organization.

Required:

a. Identify and explain briefly the purposes proper documentation can serve.
b. Discuss briefly the basic types of information that should be included in the documentation of a data processing application.

(CMA Adapted)

8–19. ***POST-IMPLEMENTATION REVIEW***

During a post-implementation review of a new system at Wilcox Corporation, a team member gathered the following data:

	Estimated	*Actual*
Computer rental	$ 42,000	$ 45,000
Programming	70,000	90,000
Installation	10,000	15,000
Power and supplies	20,000	21,000
Salaries of MIS personnel	100,000	120,000
Salaries of displaced workers	240,000	210,000
Training and parallel operations costs	35,000	44,000

Required:

Prepare a statement that computes the estimated and actual costs and cost savings.

8–20. ***POST-IMPLEMENTATION REVIEW***

An accountant on the review team at Wilcox Corporation (see Exercise 8–19) developed the following schedule during the post-implementation review:

	Volume	*Price*	*Efficiency*
Computer rental	$ —	$ (3,000)	$ —
Programming	(15,000)	(4,000)	(1,000)
Installation	(2,000)	(1,800)	(1,200)
Power and supplies	(1,000)	—	—
Salaries of MIS personnel	(6,000)	(14,000)	—
Salaries of displaced workers	(20,000)	(20,000)	10,000
Training and parallel operations costs	(2,000)	(1,000)	(6,000)

Required:

Prepare an analysis of estimated and actual costs and cost savings to show probable causes for any variances.

8–21. ***POST-IMPLEMENTATION REVIEW***

A post-implementation review team at Rogers Enterprises is evaluating the performance of the programmers on a recent system development project. They have gathered the following data concerning the programs written:

	Estimated	*Actual*
Number of instructions	10,000	11,000
Average weekly salaries of programming personnel	$ 500	$ 550
Average number of instructions written per programmer per week	50	51

Required:

Prepare an analysis of Rogers Enterprises's data that shows the programming cost variance and identifies probable causes for it.

8–22. ***POST-IMPLEMENTATION REVIEW***

A new accounting information system was recently developed in-house at Dolly Corporation. While conducting a post-implementation review, an analyst determined the following:

	Estimated	*Actual*
Number of instructions	8,000	7,000
Average weekly salaries of programming personnel	$ 500	$ 550
Average number of instructions written per programmer per week	50	45

Required:

Prepare a report that measures programmers' performance and discloses probable causes for it.

8–23. ***CONVERSION***

Since its inception one year ago, Instantware, Inc., a discount microcomputer software house, has used manual procedures to account for its receivables, payables, and inventory. The company receives most orders by telephone, billing customers' bank charge card accounts. Some customers order by mail, enclosing checks or money orders in payment. Instantware ships immediately on receiving certified checks or money orders but waits for personal checks to clear the bank before shipping software. Five sales representatives prepare order forms for telephone and walk-in customers, open mail orders, and complete those order forms as time permits.

Normally, a sales representative is preparing orders for several customers at the same time. The sales representatives give personal checks enclosed with mail orders to the accounting clerk. When personal checks clear, the accounting clerk tells the sales representative who then prepares the order form. The sales representatives, all in their late twenties, are proud of their relationships with customers, many of whom place reorders with the same sales representatives.

The owner suspects that Instantware has outgrown its accounting and inventory procedures and also believes that using manual accounting and inventory procedures is a poor advertisement for a software house. Therefore, the owner has decided to install computer-based accounting and inventory systems.

Required:

a. The owner intends to convert from a manual to a computer-based system. What should be done before the conversion activity begins?

b. Which steps should be taken to ensure that data is transcribed correctly from manual to computer readable form?
c. How might the sales representatives' current level of autonomy affect the conversion?

(CIA Adapted)

8–24. *AUDITOR INVOLVEMENT*

A savings and loan association has decided to undertake the development of an in-house computer system to replace the processing it currently purchases from a time-sharing service. The auditors have suggested that the system development process be planned in accordance with the system development life cycle concept.

The following nine items are major system development activities that must be undertaken:

1. System test
2. User specifications
3. Conversion
4. System planning study
5. Technical specifications
6. Post-implementation review
7. Implementation planning
8. User procedures and training
9. Programming

Required:

a. Arrange these nine items in the sequence in which they should logically occur.
b. One major activity that occurs during system implementation is the conversion of data files from the old system to the new system. Indicate three types of documentation for a file conversion work plan that would be of particular interest to an auditor.
c. List the major steps taken by an auditor who participates in the system development process.

(CIA Adapted)

8–25. *ALLOCATING MIS DEPARTMENT COSTS*

The Independent Underwriters Insurance Co. (IUI) established a MIS department two years ago to implement and operate its own data processing systems. IUI believed that its own system would be more cost effective than the service bureau it had been using.

IUI's three departments—claims, records, and finance—have different requirements for hardware, other capacity-related resources, and operating resources. The system was designed to recognize these differing requirements. In addition, the system was designed to meet IUI's long-term capacity needs. The excess capacity designed into the system would be sold to outside users until needed by IUI. The estimated resource requirements used to design and implement the system are shown in the following schedule:

	Hardware and Other Capacity Related Resources	*Operating Resources*
Records	30%	60%
Claims	50	20
Finance	15	15
Expansion	5	5
Total	100%	100%

IUI currently sells the equivalent of its expansion capacity to a few outside clients.

At the time the system became operational, management decided to redistribute total expenses of the MIS department to the user departments based on actual computer time used. The actual costs for the first quarter of the current fiscal year were distributed to the user departments as follows:

Department	*Percentage Utilization*	*Amount*
Records	60%	$330,000
Claims	20	110,000
Finance	15	82,500
Outside	5	27,500
Total	100%	$550,000

The three departments have complained about the cost distribution method since the MIS department was established. The records department's monthly costs have been as much as three times the costs experienced with the service bureau. The finance department is concerned about the cost distributed to the outside user category because these allocated costs form the basis for fees billed to the outside clients.

James Dale, IUI's controller, decided to review the distribution method by which the MIS department's costs have been allocated for the past two years. The additional information he gathered for his review is reported in Exhibits 8–1, 8–2, and 8–3.

Dale has concluded that the method of cost distribution should be changed to reflect more directly the actual benefits received by the departments. He believes that the hardware and capacity-related costs should be allocated to the user departments in proportion to the planned, long-term needs. Any difference

EXHIBIT 8–1 Systems Department Costs and Activity Levels

	Annual Budget		First Quarter Budget		First Quarter Actual	
	Hours	*Dollars*	*Hours*	*Dollars*	*Hours*	*Dollars*
Hardware and other capacity-related costs	—	$ 600,000	—	$150,000	—	$155,000
Software development	18,750	562,500	4,725	141,750	4,250	130,000
Operations						
Computer related	3,750	750,000	945	189,000	920	187,000
Input/output related	30,000	300,000	7,560	75,600	7,900	78,000
		$2,212,500		$556,350		$550,000

EXHIBIT 8–2 Historical Utilization by Users

	Hardware and Other Capacity Needs	Software Development		Operations: Computer		Operations: Input/Output	
		Range	*Average*	*Range*	*Average*	*Range*	*Average*
Records	30%	0–30%	12%	55–65%	60%	10–30%	20%
Claims	50	15–60	35	10–25	20	60–80	70
Finance	15	25–75	45	10–25	15	3–10	6
Outside	5	0–25	8	3–8	5	3–10	4
	100%		100%		100%		100%

EXHIBIT 8–3 Utilization of Systems Department's Services in Hours (First Quarter)

	Software development	Operations: Computer related	Operations: Input/output
Records	425	552	1,580
Claims	1,700	184	5,530
Finance	1,700	138	395
Outside	425	46	395
Total	4,250	920	7,900

between actual and budgeted hardware costs would not be allocated to the departments but would remain with the MIS department.

The remaining costs for software development and operations would be charged to the user departments based on actual hours used. A predetermined hourly rate based on the annual budget data would be used. The hourly rates for the current fiscal year are as follows:

Function	*Hourly rate*
Software development	$ 30
Operations:	
Computer related	200
Input/output related	10

Dale plans to use first-quarter activity and cost data to illustrate his recommendations. The recommendations will be presented to the MIS department and the user departments for their comments and reactions. He then expects to present his recommendation to management for approval.

Required:

a. Calculate the amount of data processing costs that would be included in the claims department's first-quarter budget according to the method James Dale has recommended.

b. Prepare a schedule to show how the actual first-quarter costs of the MIS department would be charged to the users if James Dale's recommended method were adopted.

c. Explain whether James Dale's recommended system for charging costs to user departments will:

1. Improve cost control in the MIS department.
2. Improve planning and cost control in the user departments.
3. Be a more equitable basis for charging costs to user departments.

(CMA Adapted)

8–26. *CORPORATE CONSOLIDATION SYSTEM—PART IV*

In response to corporate growth and to increased public reporting requirements, R. J. Reynolds Industries, Inc., developed the Corporate Consolidation System (CCS), a computer-based system for consolidation accounting. A project team from the corporate accounting department created CCS from a general ledger package purchased from a software house. Using the package's report writer feature, the team modified its outputs to meet RJR's specific needs. Besides maintaining the corporate general ledger, CCS consolidates the financial statements of all the companies making up RJR's seven major lines of business. It also generates statistical data required for SEC reporting.

User Acceptance

Completing the new system was a high-priority project in the corporate accounting department. Nevertheless, during implementation all team members performed their normal departmental duties at the same time. In this way other members of the department could participate in the development of the system, and all had a vested interest in the system's success. Although the team relied heavily on the systems department for technical support, the team was responsible for the account structure and the reports generated by the system.

After CCS was completed three years ago, the corporate accounting department successfully completed a year-end closing the following year. The department established two criteria for the system's success. First, CCS had to generate detailed results that were consistent with summary results produced by the old system in two actual closings. Second, the system had to undergo a complete year-end audit by RJR's independent auditor.

To ensure the accuracy of the new system, a phased approach to system changeover was selected. This approach first developed the statement of earnings, then the balance sheet, and finally the statistical analysis for the SEC reports. Each phase had to be virtually complete before work could begin on the next phase. Although time-consuming to implement, this approach provided accuracy and control and fostered the gradual acceptance of the new system by the staff. Their positive response was vital to the success of the project. Also, this phased approach minimized the impact of the new system on the reporting entities.

Extensions

After successful performance by CCS for two successive years, a decision was made to extend the system to the operating companies. The Winston-Salem-based companies use a common computer site, so they were chosen to be the first to adopt CCS. When completely installed, CCS allowed these companies' general ledgers to interface automatically with the consolidation system of the parent corporation. When this phase was completed, the system demonstrated the flexibility and capabilities necessary to handle multiple lines of business and the analysis needed by R. J. Reynolds Industries. However, because of new accounting pronouncements, reorganizations, and acquisitions, the system is constantly being modified to reflect changes in the environment.

Required:

a. Who constituted the project team for implementing the Corporate Consolidation System? Which benefits did this provide?

b. Which approach to system changeover did RJR use? What were the advantages and disadvantages of this approach?

Part III

Technology of Accounting Systems

Chapter 9

Computer Hardware and Software

LEARNING OBJECTIVES:

1. To review the components of a computer system.
2. To review the forms that computer hardware can take.
3. To review the kinds of software used by a computer.
4. To understand the alternative configurations for a computer system.

INTRODUCTION

In this part of the text you will learn about the technology used in computer-based accounting systems. This chapter discusses the software and hardware devices that are the components of a computer system. Some of what you will read is a review, but there are also some new topics. To begin, you will review the components of a computer system.

COMPONENTS OF A COMPUTER SYSTEM

Any system consists of its component parts, a process that coordinates these parts in a defined way, and goals toward which the component parts are coordinated. For a computer system, a project team identifies goals during

ILLUSTRATION 9–1 Components of the Central Processing Unit

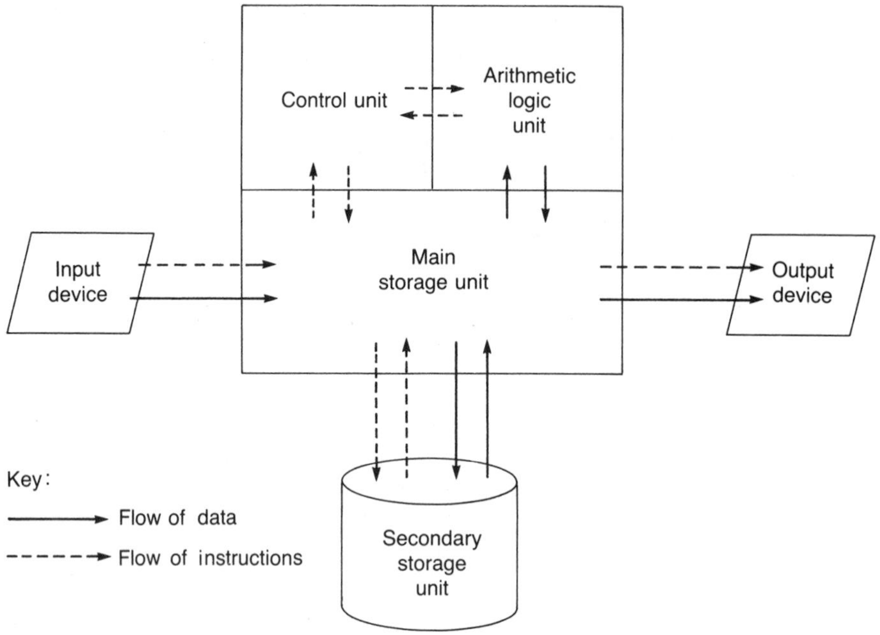

system design and creates software that determines the system's process. Component parts include the computer hardware and software used by the system.

Computer Hardware

People who have worked with personal computers know that the computer consists of several different devices located at various distances apart. These devices consist of a central processing unit (CPU) and several peripheral devices. In a personal computer system, the CPU and some of the peripheral devices are located within a single computer chassis. In a large system, these devices are usually housed separately.

Central Processing Unit. The heart of a computer system is its central processing unit, which consists of three other devices: the control unit, the arithmetic-logic unit, and the main storage unit. Each of these devices is a separate electronic circuit. Illustration 9–1 shows how data and instructions flow between these circuits and the peripheral devices.

Main Storage. The main storage unit of the CPU fulfills two functions: it provides a place to store the executable instructions making up a computer program and it provides areas for storing data processed by the program.

The size of main storage is an indicator of the computer's power and usefulness. Size is measured in *kilobytes;* one kilobyte is 1,024 characters of storage. For a small, special-purpose computer, main storage may be as small as eight or ten kilobytes. (For convenience, we say that this CPU has 8 or 10K of main storage.) A general-purpose computer used for scientific or business applications may have main storage measured in megabytes (thousands of K) or gigabytes (millions of K). It is capable of storing millions of characters of data and instructions.

Main storage is also called *primary storage* or *main memory.* In modern computers, main storage is made of circuits such as the RAM used in microcomputers. In older processors, main storage was made from thousands of magnetic cores, each about the size of a pinhead. For this reason, it is occasionally called *core storage.*

Control Unit. The control unit is a circuit that interprets the instructions contained in an executable computer program and directs the operations of the computer system. An instruction contains codes identifying one operation to be performed, and designating data to be used in the operation. Each instruction is copied in sequence from main storage into the control unit. The control unit then reads the operation code of the instruction and carries out the operation on data contained in main storage. The time needed for the CPU to process an operation is its execution time, which is one of the factors determining the speed of the computer system.

Arithmetic-Logic Unit. The arithmetic-logic unit, or ALU, executes the operation identified by the control unit. This circuit is designed to perform two operations, addition and comparison. All other arithmetic and logic operations that it performs are combinations of these two. For example, multiplication is repeated addition, subtraction is addition in reverse, and division is repeated subtraction. Logic operations include determining whether two quantities are equal, whether a quantity is positive, or which of two quantities is larger.

The ALU, the control unit, and main storage are all made up of electronic circuits. In the oldest, or *first-generation* computers, these circuits contained vacuum tubes. Illustration 9–2 shows one of the earliest computers, called ENIAC, built at the University of Pennsylvania in 1945. In *second-generation* computers the vacuum tubes were replaced by much smaller transistors. *Third-generation* computers used integrated circuits which contained, in a small package, the equivalent of hundreds of transistors and other components. *Fourth-generation* computers use very large-scale integration (VLSI) circuits, in which the components are reduced even further. Illustration 9–3 contrasts the four primary components of each computer generation: a vacuum tube, a transistor, an integrated circuit, and a VLSI circuit. This shrinkage in component size has allowed computers to become as small as they are today.

ILLUSTRATION 9–2 ENIAC, One of the First Electronic Computers

Completed at the University of Pennsylvania in 1945, ENIAC occupied 15,000 square feet. Here technicians work inside *it to maintain its 30 tons of hardware, which included 18,000 vacuum tubes. Photograph courtesy of University of Pennsylvania, Office of Publications.*

Peripheral Devices. Peripheral devices in a computer system are those pieces of equipment outside of the central processor. They include secondary storage devices, input devices, output devices, and devices that perform both input and output. Illustration 9–4 lists many of these devices.

Secondary Storage. Regardless of the size of main storage, it is inadequate for storing all the records maintained by a computer-based information system. The system stores this information in files contained in secondary, or *mass storage,* devices. Whenever accounting data from these files is required for processing, the CPU transfers it from a secondary storage device into main storage. Then the control unit can transfer it into the arithmetic-logic unit and perform an operation on it.

Secondary storage also contains copies of computer programs when they are not being used. Before being executed, the program must be transferred into main storage; then the instructions are copied into the control unit one by one and executed.

ILLUSTRATION 9–3 Electronic Components Used in Four Generations of Computers

Virtual storage systems allow transfer of segments of a program, rather than the entire program, into main storage. Each segment of a program, called a *page*, contains only those instructions needed for current execution. When other instructions are needed later, another page of the program is transferred into main storage. In this way, virtual storage systems can execute very large programs without using up a lot of main storage. The CPU uses the remainder of main storage for data or pages of other programs. When more than one program is in main storage for execution at the same time, the system is called a *multiprogramming* system. In these systems, the computer functions so rapidly that it appears to execute multiple programs simultaneously.

When a secondary storage device such as a magnetic disk can interact with the CPU without human intervention, it is said to be *on-line*. Modern business

ILLUSTRATION 9–4 Peripheral Devices Used in Computer Systems

Secondary storage devices
- Magnetic disk
- Magnetic tape
- Magnetic drum
- Data cell devices
- Optical disk

Input devices
- Terminal
- Magnetic tape drive
- Magnetic disk drive
- Console
- Card reader
- Key to disk device
- Key to tape device
- Magnetic ink character reader
- Optical scanner
- Audio input unit

Output devices
- Terminal
- Magnetic tape drive
- Magnetic disk drive
- Printer
- Computer output on microfilm
- Graphics plotter
- Voice response unit
- Card punch
- Paper tape punch

computer systems provide the ability to store many millions of characters of data in on-line secondary storage devices. Removable storage media, such as magnetic tape, provide storage that is *off-line*. For example, computer operators store a magnetic tape in a nearby tape library until the data on it is needed. Then the operator retrieves the tape, mounts it on a magnetic tape drive, and the data on it becomes available for transfer into the CPU. Off-line storage creates virtually unlimited secondary storage capacity.

The time needed for the CPU to gain access to instructions or data on a secondary storage device is the device's *access time*. It is another factor in determining the speed of the computer system. When data are stored on-line, access time is ordinarily much faster than when it is off-line. This is why modern computer-based systems rely primarily on magnetic disk storage. Systems today primarily use off-line storage, such as tapes, for making spare copies called *backup files*. Computer operators use backup files to recreate on-line files when an accident destroys them in the on-line device.

Input Devices. Input devices are the communications links between the computer and its users. They provide the means to convert accounting data from a form understood by people to one understood by a computer.

The earliest input devices were punched card readers and paper tape readers. A keypunch operator, for example, operated a machine that encoded accounting transactions by punching holes in a card. The input device, a card reader, sensed the location of the holes in the card and translated this data into electronic pulses

ILLUSTRATION 9–5 The Punched Card, an Early Form of Data Entry

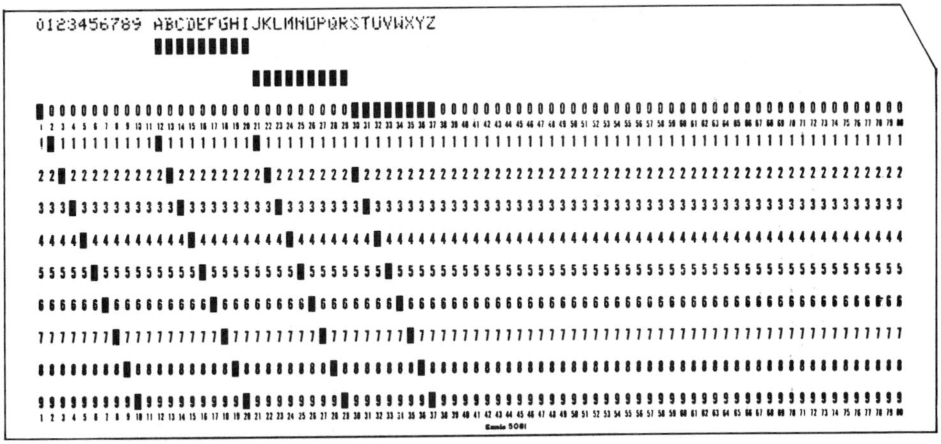

recorded on magnetic tape. Punched card data entry was common in the 1950s and the 1960s, but now is seldom used. Illustration 9–5 shows one of these cards.

Modern computer systems use terminals as the primary form of data entry; these are faster and easier to use than keypunch machines. The standard terminal consists of a keyboard and a cathode ray tube (CRT) display. This allows the data entry clerk who enters data at the keyboard to see on the CRT the data received by the computer. The clerk can then correct input errors promptly before any further processing occurs. This is an example of *on-line processing,* because the clerk is in direct communication with the central processor. When the terminal also contains some main storage and can be programmed to perform simple tasks, it is an *intelligent terminal.*

Business computer applications are characterized by the input of large numbers of transactions. Thus, efficient systems are those that allow rapid, accurate input of data. Computer manufacturers devote a great deal of developmental effort to creating more efficient forms of data entry.

This has led to the use of optical character readers (OCR), magnetic ink character recognition (MICR), and point-of-sale (POS) devices to improve data entry. Optical character readers use a light to read data written on paper by a data entry clerk. Students use OCR input whenever they take standardized tests, such as the Scholastic Aptitude Test or the American College Test. Banks use MICR in processing canceled checks; the bank number, account number, check number, and amount are printed at the bottom of the check in special ink that can be read by the MICR input device. Point-of-sale data entry uses a cash register as a computer terminal; when a sales clerk rings up a sale at a cash register, the register records the transaction in magnetic form for processing by a computer. Other popular devices to ease data entry include the optical scanner used in supermarkets and the audio input unit that allows data input from a touch-tone telephone.

Output Devices. The most common output device, the printer, translates electronic impulses into reports that can be read by people. Frequently a personal computer uses a dot matrix, laser, or daisy wheel printer with output rates measured in characters per second. These are slow in comparison to the high-speed printers used in corporate data centers, which can produce reports at a rate of several pages per second. Nevertheless, many accounting applications are *printer bound;* that is, their speed of processing is limited by the rate at which a printer can produce the reports.

The accounting information systems of a business produce reports that must be retained for several years for tax and audit purposes. Rather than produce all of these reports on a printer, many organizations acquire computer output on microfilm (COM) devices. These produce reports directly on a piece of transparent plastic a few square inches in size; such reports are easier to store than those printed on paper.

Many devices provide both inputs to and outputs from the computer system. Because this describes magnetic disk drives, magnetic tape drives, and terminals, they are called *input/output devices.* In one application of an input-output device, a computer user enters data at an on-line terminal. The system immediately posts the data to computer files so that the results of processing are immediately available for the user at the terminal. This is a *real-time* system.

Real-time systems always use on-line devices, but on-line devices do not necessarily signify real-time systems. Many payroll systems, for example, allow entry of payroll data from a keyboard directly into a computer file. This is on-line data entry. However, because this data is posted to ledgers at a later date and the outputs from posting are not immediately available to the user, such processing is not considered real-time.

Equally as important as the hardware component of a computer system is computer software. Computer software consists of computer programs, the executable instructions that control how the hardware devices function.

Computer Software Computer software controls the activities of today's hardware. However, computers have not always used software. Early computers were programmed by painstakingly wiring pegboards or setting scores of individual switches. This made computers difficult to adapt to varying applications.

In 1946 a German mathematician, John Von Neuman, proposed the idea of storing an entire set of instructions in the computer hardware. The operations of the hardware could be changed simply by changing these instructions. This concept, the *stored program computer,* marked the beginning of computer

ILLUSTRATION 9–6 Functions of an Operating System

Job control. Keeping track of jobs submitted for processing.

Job scheduling. Assessing the priority of jobs awaiting processing and assigning them to a queue.

Library Management. Making available various applications and systems programs needed in executing individual jobs.

Memory management. Keeping track of main memory usage and allocating it to individual jobs for storing their instructions and data.

Peripheral management. Keeping track of input and output devices in use, and assigning output to them as it is produced by the CPU.

systems as we know them today. For this reason, computer scientists refer to programmable computers as Von Neuman computers.

Computers used for accounting purposes rely on two basic categories of software: systems and application. Any organization with a computer-based information system uses many different programs in each category.

Systems Software. These are programs intended to execute on a specific make and model of computer. The MIS department usually obtains systems software from the computer manufacturer or from independent software vendors. Although the users of accounting systems are frequently unaware of systems software, it is necessary for any accounting program to function properly. Systems software includes the operating system, utility programs, language translators, and data management software.

Operating System. The operating system is a set of computer programs that directs the operations of the entire computer system. When starting the system, a computer operator copies the operating system software from a secondary storage device into main storage. The operating system then takes control of the CPU and all of its peripherals. Sometimes the operating system allows other programs to control the CPU temporarily, but control always returns to the operating system. Illustration 9–6 summarizes the five basic functions of an operating system.

Programmers control the activities of the operating system by communicating with it using a *job control language* (JCL). Using JCL, for example, they identify the peripheral devices to be used for input, for output, and for secondary storage by accounting programs. The operating system is a powerful, complex piece of software; without it the computer hardware is useless.

Utility Programs. Computer manufacturers normally provide utility software. A utility program performs a specialized function such as sorting files, printing out the contents of main storage or of a computer file, or copying files

ILLUSTRATION 9–7 An Instruction in Procedure-Oriented, Assembly, and Machine Languages

Procedure-oriented languages

COBOL:	MOVE ZERO TO TOT-AMT.
FORTRAN:	B = 0
BASIC:	LET B = 0

IBM 360/370 assembly language

MVI 100(3),0

IBM 360/370 machine language

10010010000000000011000001100100

from one device to another. A utility program may be useful in many different accounting applications. A programmer executes a utility program and directs its activities using job control language.

Language Translation Programs. Language translation programs convert application programs written in a form understood by humans into a form that the CPU's control unit can interpret.

Most people prefer computer languages that resemble either English sentences or mathematical equations. Procedure-oriented languages, such as COBOL, FORTRAN, or BASIC, have this characteristic. The CPU, however, requires instructions written in a binary form or *machine language*. These instructions are difficult for people to interpret, so we usually write them in a symbolic form called *assembly language*. Illustration 9–7 shows how one instruction looks in procedure-oriented, assembly, and machine languages. This should make you appreciate those languages you learned in programming courses. Imagine having to write even a simple program in machine language!

Programmers use software packages called *compilers* to translate a program from a procedure-oriented language into machine language. The procedure-oriented version of the program is the *source program;* the machine language version is the *object program*. Some languages, such as BASIC, also have interpreters. An *interpreter* translates procedure-oriented language instructions one at a time, rather than translating the entire program at once. Although avoiding compilation makes it easier for users to debug a program, it slows the program's execution. For this reason, professional programmers normally use compilers rather than interpreters in developing accounting systems.

In the early days of computers, programs were frequently written in assembly language. Today some programmers use assembly language whenever they develop programs for a new kind of computer or when they want the fastest possible execution speed. Software called an *assembler* translates from the symbolic assembly language into machine language.

During the 1980s software development companies began marketing packages they call *fourth-generation languages*. These make it much easier to generate

ILLUSTRATION 9–8 FOCUS, a Fourth-Generation Language

Contents of a computer file containing sales data

Data Item	*Meaning*
REGION	Marketing region code
SITE	Store code
PONUM	Customer's purchase order number
DATE	Date of customer order
NAME	Customer's name
AMOUNT	Total amount of order
FILLCODE	Indicator of shipment status
PRODUCT	Product number of item ordered
UNITS	Quantity ordered

Nonprocedural language instructions

```
TABLE FILE SALES
PRINT NAME AND AMOUNT AND DATE
BY REGION BY SITE
IF AMOUNT GT 1000
ON REGION SKIP-LINE
END
```

Report displayed and printed

Page 1

Region	*Site*	*Name*	*Amount*	*Date*
MA	NEWK	ELIZABETH GAS	$ 2,877.30	90 JAN
	NEWY	KOCH CONSTRUCTION	$ 6,086.23	90 APR
		LASSITER STORES	$ 1,210.34	90 MAR
	PHIL	ROSS, INC.	$ 3,980.11	90 JAN
MW	CHIC	NORTHSHORE, INC.	$ 5,678.23	90 MAY
		ROPER BROTHERS	$ 2,879.54	90 JUN
	CLEV	BOXEY PARTS	$ 6,454.10	90 JUL
		ERIE TOOLS	$ 1,556.78	89 DEC
SE	ATL	RICH STORES, INC.	$ 1,345.18	90 FEB
	NASH	MUSIC CITY CO.	$ 1,195.23	89 DEC

FOCUS is a product of Information Builders, Inc., 1250 Broadway, New York, NY 10001.

reports from accounting data files. A user of the package, such as a manager or a programmer, specifies in a nonprocedural language the files and the data to be displayed or printed. The language translation package interprets these commands, formats the report, displays it at a terminal, and prints it on a printer. Illustration 9–8 shows how one such language translator, called FOCUS, works.

Data Management Software. When learning a programming language, you were taught to use input and output commands such as READ and WRITE. These commands identify to the computer system the procedure you want executed, and the system figures out how to do it. Programmers of first-generation computers were required to specify in programs not only the desired procedure but also how the procedure was to be carried out. This made programming these machines complex and time-consuming. Because computer systems use these procedures so frequently, computer manufacturers developed data management software.

Data management software determines how to locate desired data when it is transferred from a secondary storage device to main storage. It also determines where to record data transferred from main to secondary storage. This software allows a user to execute the foregoing simple commands without being concerned about the mechanics of input and output. This greatly eases the task of programming a new system.

When designing a system, a project team selects for each computer file in the system a method of accessing the data in the file. Each method requires that the system have a data management program to implement it. On large computers, these programs have names such as QSAM, VSAM, and ISAM. Many systems use another form of data management software called a *data base management system* (DBMS).

The four kinds of systems software just described are important because they make using computers much easier. However, the real purpose for having a computer system is to apply it to problems in accounting, management, or science. Applications software accomplishes this purpose.

Applications Software. In an earlier chapter, you learned that an accounting information system is composed of application systems such as the payroll and billing systems. In a computer-based system, these application systems rely on computerized processes to accomplish their goals. The computer programs used in these systems are examples of applications software. There are two kinds of applications software: transaction processing software (i.e., payroll and billing programs), and decision support software (i.e., computer models).

Transaction Processing Software. Most transaction processing software automates procedures that have been performed manually for centuries. It is easy to identify the manual accounting procedures you learn in introductory accounting courses with those procedures performed in computerized systems. Although these procedures may vary between organizations—depending on the technology used and the preferences of management—even these variations are predictable.

For this reason, few organizations today choose to develop in-house programs for processing general ledger, accounts receivable, accounts payable, or payroll. They find it quicker and less costly to purchase this application software from software development companies. Frequently they modify these packages to suit the preferences of their management.

When an organization chooses to develop its own application software, it may choose to do so using an *application generator,* which is a computer program that writes other programs. Members of the implementation project team specify to the application generator the files, inputs, and outputs of the application program. The software package then produces a source program in COBOL, or some other procedural language, that satisfies these specifications.

Because application generators are more difficult to use than fourth-generation languages, they are seldom used by managers to produce ad hoc reports. However, their use is quicker than programming in a procedural language. Furthermore, the programs generated operate more efficiently than those written in a fourth-generation language.

Decision Support Software. A second classification of application software consists of those computer programs used in decision support systems. These programs are created to help managers make decisions. Decision support software includes computer models and most expert systems.

Managers use computer models to evaluate alternatives in both structured and unstructured decisions. *Optimization models,* such as linear programming formulations, are useful when making repetitive decisions in structured situations. You may, for example, have seen linear programming used in determining an optimal product mix. Managers frequently use *simulation models* in unstructured situations. These models rely on data estimates and require the evaluation of numerous "what if" scenarios.

Probably the most commonly used simulation model is the financial model, which is similar to a computerized budget. To create a financial model, a programmer decribes in equations the relationships between income—a dependent variable—and several independent variables such as sales volume and costs. A manager executes the model to determine how net income would be affected by different decision alternatives. Several nonprocedural languages make it easy for managers to create their own financial models. Some fourth-generation languages provide this modeling capability.

Computer models are useful in describing decisions that can be analyzed as algorithmic processes, whose relationships can be described by equations in a computer program. The inputs to the decision can be stated as inputs to the equations, and the results of the decision can be predicted by solving the equations. Many management decisions, however, do not have these characteristics, and are better served by a form of decision support software known as the expert system.

Expert Systems. Expert systems are a practical result of research in a branch of computer science called artificial intelligence. An expert system is an on-line, real-time system that uses computer programs and the knowledge of a human expert to mimic the expert's decision-making processes. It serves as an advisor to less-experienced managers who make decisions in the expert's field. Expert systems have applications in many areas, including medicine, computer system design, equipment maintenance, accounting, and auditing.

Expert systems can be written in procedural languages such as BASIC, Pascal, or LISP. However, implementing them is easier using an expert system *shell,* which is a software package designed for this purpose. An analyst, or *knowledge engineer,* customizes the shell to a specific decision-making application. The knowledge engineer uses the shell to create the components of the expert system:

ILLUSTRATION 9–9 Components of an Expert System

Component	*Description*	*Purpose*
Knowledge base	Facts and rules encoded as data for the system	Provides a source for the knowledge obtained from a human expert
Inference engine	Computer program that processes data in the knowledge base	Creates a chain of inferences leading to a final conclusion
User interface	Computer program that handles on-line communication with system user	Requests information and displays explanations or conclusions
Explanation facility	Optional feature of the user interface	Explains why the expert system draws its conclusions

a knowledge base, an inference engine, a user interface, and an explanation facility. Illustration 9–9 summarizes these components.

The *knowledge base* consists of facts about a specific field and a set of rules for using those facts. These may describe objects, identify relationships, explain procedures, or encode rules of thumb that an expert has gained through experience. Typically each rule contains a condition and an action of the form "if X, then Y." This means that whenever condition X is true, then the expert concludes action Y . The knowledge engineer determines these facts and rules by interviewing the expert and encodes them as required by the expert system shell.

The *user interface* is a computer program that provides communication between the inference engine and the expert system user. Using the interface, the expert system conversationally asks the user for facts related to conditions in the knowledge base. The user interface also communicates the system's conclusions to the user. Some expert systems do not have a distinct user interface; the inference engine performs that function.

The *inference engine* is a computer program that uses the data contained in the knowledge base. It first identifies information desired from the expert system user and then combines this information with a rule from the knowledge base to develop a temporary conclusion. From this temporary conclusion, the inference engine formulates another question that is communicated to the user via the user interface. This process continues, forming a chain of rules that eventually lead to a final conclusion. Most inference engines are backward chaining; that is, they start with a final conclusion and look for rules that establish facts to support it. A forward chaining inference engine starts with elementary data and develops a collection of facts leading to the final conclusion.

Not all expert systems have an *explanation facility,* but many of the most successful ones do. This component uses the user interface to explain to the user why the expert system reaches its conclusions. It increases the user's confidence in the system's conclusions and educates the user in how the expert approaches the decision. A similar situation occurs when an instructor returns an exam. You want to know why you received the grade you did. This shows why your grade is a fair one and helps you to decide how to prepare for the next exam.

Hardware and software components make up a computer system. Hardware consists of the central processing unit and its peripheral devices. Software consists of the instructions which, when converted to machine language and stored in main storage, direct the activities of the hardware. All computer systems contain these components, but not all systems combine them in the same way. How they are combined depends on the configuration of the computer system. A project team determines system configuration during the system design process.

COMPUTER SYSTEM CONFIGURATIONS

The configuration describes how a specific organization combines hardware devices to support the applications required by its computer system. A large number of different configurations are possible, and in the course of a career an accountant is exposed to many of them. In this section, you will learn about some of the more popular ones. We begin by discussing the alternative kinds of central processors available. Then a section on computer networks explains how these processors communicate with each other.

Processors

The central processor is the heart of any computer system. Choosing an inappropriate processor may prevent applications software from satisfactorily achieving system objectives. Because processors come in a wide range of sizes and speeds, a system development project team can easily become confused when comparing them. For this reason, the computer industry has developed schemes for classifying processors; this aids in identifying which processor is appropriate for an organization's specific needs.

The computer industry's categories are not clearly defined. Different experts frequently disagree about how to classify the same model computer. Furthermore, some experts prefer to identify many categories while others use just a few. A simple classification scheme identifies three processor sizes: the mainframe computer, the minicomputer, and the microcomputer.

Mainframe Computers. Mainframes are also known as large-scale computers or general purpose computers. They are large, fast, powerful, and flexible in what they can do. Accountants often encounter mainframes in the data centers of large organizations. Mainframes are useful not only for accounting and management purposes but also for scientific and engineering applications.

ILLUSTRATION 9–10 A Mainframe Computer Configuration

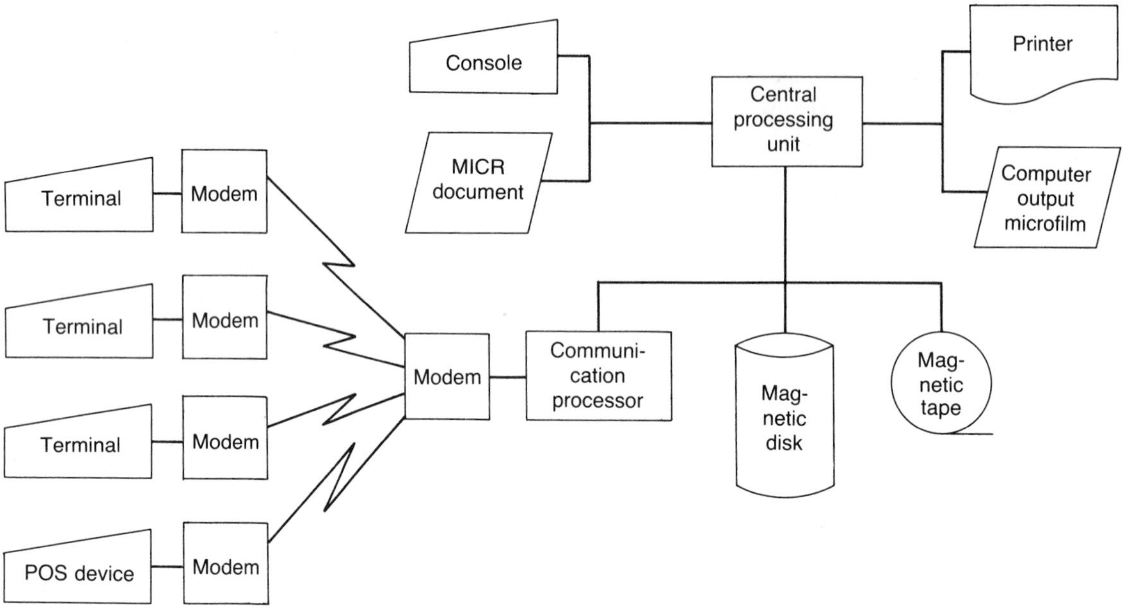

A configuration built around a mainframe may include dozens of tape and disk drives, hundreds of terminals, and several high-speed printers. If the system includes terminals at a remote site, such as in another room or building, it may include a *communications processor.* This smaller processor controls communication by the central processor with remote terminals. The cost of a mainframe system usually totals millions of dollars.

Illustration 9–10 contains a typical mainframe computer configuration. It shows input devices to the left of the CPU, secondary storage devices below it, and output devices to the right.

Often companies configure their systems to include two or more identical central processors operating together. All applications can execute on either CPU because each has access to the peripherals of the entire system. This is a *multiprocessor* system. If the organization has many applications that execute at the same time, a multiprocessor configuration speeds up use of the computer system considerably.

You have probably read about supercomputers—large, expensive mainframes specially designed to perform calculations very, very fast. Although definitely useful for scientific and engineering applications, companies seldom use supercomputers for accounting or management purposes.

Minicomputers. Minicomputers are so called because they are smaller than mainframes. In that they tend to be somewhat slower, companies use them for applications that do not require a lot of calculations. Minicomputers are adequate for business applications in medium-sized companies. In spite of the name, many of these are not mini in size or cost.

A configuration built around a minicomputer typically includes one or a few disk drives, one or a few tape drives, and one or two high-speed printers. It may also have one or two dozen terminals for input and output. The cost of a minicomputer system is measured in hundreds of thousands of dollars.

The distinctions between large minicomputers and small mainframes, and between small minis and large microcomputers, are often unclear. For example, the specifications of a large mini (sometimes called a maximini) and a small mainframe are very similar. The specifications of a ''minimini'' are also similar to those of a ''supermicro.'' This is why there is disagreement concerning how to categorize processors.

Microcomputers. Microcomputers are characterized by the use of an integrated circuit, a *microprocessor,* as a CPU. This circuit contains the equivalent of thousands of discrete electronic components forming both a control unit and an arithmetic-logic unit. Main storage for a microcomputer usually consists of other integrated circuits (*random access memory,* or RAM) mounted on the same board, called the *motherboard.* Many microcomputers have peripherals such as disk or tape drives included in the chassis with the motherboard. Sometimes people also connect these peripherals externally.

A typical microcomputer configuration contains a motherboard, a floppy disk drive, a hard disk, a CRT display, and a printer. Its cost is measured in thousands of dollars.

Businesses use microcomputers in two ways, as stand-alone computers and in networks. The most common applications for stand-alone microcomputers are word processing, spreadsheet analysis, and small business program execution. In addition to these applications, many large or medium-sized businesses connect micros in a network with a mainframe or a minicomputer. Users can then transfer data from the larger computer to the microcomputer for use in electronic spreadsheet software.

This is just one of many applications of computer networks that have made them very popular. Because you are certain to encounter them, you should know something about how computer networks work.

Computer Networks

Most large organizations adopt a computer system configuration that utilizes a data communication network. A network employs devices at different locations connected by a communication link. Devices transfer data and programs between each other across a communication link that may be as simple as a twisted pair of wires, coaxial cable, or a telephone line. Or the link may be as complex as fiber-optic cable, a laser beam, a series of microwave transmission towers, or a communications satellite.

The oldest form of computer network is the teleprocessing network using a single centralized processor. Newer forms with multiple processors are called distributed processing networks.

Teleprocessing Networks. Teleprocessing networks connect peripheral devices at remote locations with a single central processor. They allow data entry at remote locations, such as in a different building or at a branch office in a different city. This data moves across the communication link to the central processor at a data center where an application program processes it. Outputs from processing, such as CRT displays or reports for printing, may move from the CPU to the remote site. Outputs also may be printed or stored in secondary storage files at the data center.

Many companies use the telephone lines intended for carrying voice signals as communications links in a teleprocessing network. When they do this, they must add modems to the network to translate digital signals coming from the remote device into an audible signal appropriate for the telephone line. They add another modem at the central processor to translate from the audible signal back to digital. Technical people say that the modem *mo*dulates and then *dem*odulates the signal at each end of the telephone line; thus the origin of the name.

The three configurations for linking devices in a teleprocessing network are point-to-point, multidrop, and multiplexed networks. Illustration 9–11 contrasts these methods graphically.

Point-to-Point. In a point-to-point network, a communication link connects each remote device to the central processor. Therefore, each terminal user is constantly on-line with the CPU and usually gets rapid response from the system. This network requires more communication lines than the other methods, making it more expensive to install and operate. Furthermore, a point-to-point network does not use the links efficiently. Because the computer equipment can encode and transmit messages much faster than a human user can enter the message, the link is seldom used.

For example, many teleprocessing networks use telephone systems as communications links. When a point-to-point network does this, each remote device is assigned its own incoming telephone line. Each line is in use only for a fraction of a second whenever data is moving across it. For a system that uses many remote terminals, the monthly telephone bill for this configuration is very expensive. Similar inefficiencies and excessive costs result when an organization uses other forms of point-to-point communication links. For this reason, most companies use a different configuration.

Multidrop. The multidrop approach connects several remote devices to the central processor with a single communication link; that is, a single link is "dropped" to multiple devices. This requires fewer communication links than a point-to-point network, and each is used more efficiently. Because each device must contend with other devices for the use of the link, a multidrop teleprocessing network provides poorer service to users of the remote devices.

ILLUSTRATION 9–11 Teleprocessing Network Configurations

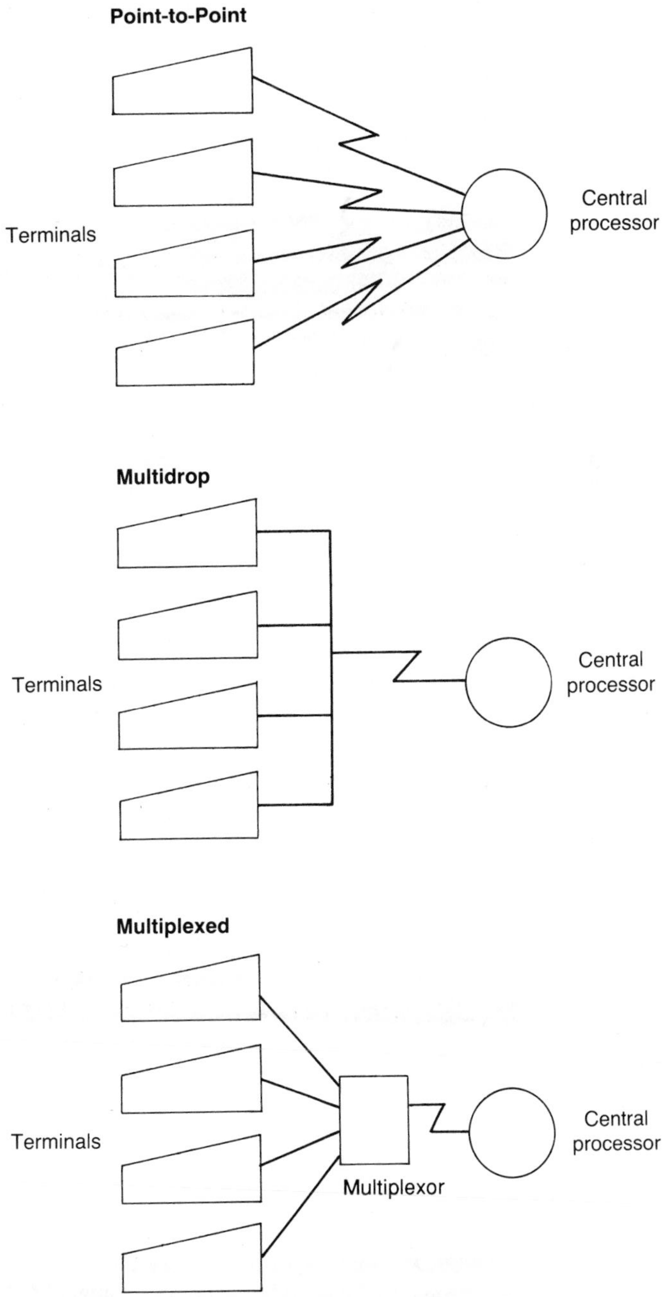

Continuing the previous example, a district sales office may contain 20 terminals where clerks enter sales orders for transmission to a processor at another location. Rather than install 20 telephone lines for the clerks to use, the sales manager may install 5 lines and attach four terminals to each line. No clerk can use a terminal while another on the same line is using one, so each must schedule usage around three other people. However, the monthly telephone costs are only a fraction of point-to-point communication; and each line is in use a greater percentage of the time.

Multiplexed. A multiplexed configuration exploits the fact that computer devices operate at much faster speeds than do their human users. Similar to a multidrop network, this configuration attaches several remote devices to a single communication link. However, a *multiplexor* interfaces the other remote devices with the link and schedules transmissions from each device so that they do not conflict.

In the telephone link example, the sales manager can install five multiplexors. Each multiplexor connects four terminals to a telephone line. Even when all four terminals on a line are used at the same time, the people operating them never have to wait more than a few seconds to use the computer at the data center. The multiplexor schedules data transfer so that while one user is thinking about what to enter at a terminal, another user's data is being transferred. Initially, this alternative is more expensive than a multidrop configuration because the manager must buy the multiplexors. However, it is less expensive and more efficient than point-to-point communication.

In practice, most companies connect many more than four devices to a multiplexor; as more and more devices are added, the response time for an individual user slows. When response time decreases enough to affect users, these companies add another communication link with another multiplexor.

In telecommunication networks, the devices attached to the network are usually CRT terminals, remote job entry terminals, or printers. Many companies have created a different network—a distributed processing network—by adding other processors at remote locations.

Distributed Systems. A distributed processing network contains two or more processors connected by data communications links. Thus, the processing done by the system is distributed between two or more remote locations. Some systems use a single large mainframe computer connected to several minicomputers or microcomputers. Others utilize several processors of approximately equal size and speed. Each processor may have its own peripheral equipment, or they may share peripherals.

Advantages and Disadvantages. Why have companies adopted distributed processing systems? The first and probably most significant reason is that distributed systems are more *adaptable* to the needs of users. Managers at remote sites control their own processing and do not have to rely on a distant centralized processor as in a teleprocessing system. Because each site has its own system, each site can customize or develop its own applications. Second, in most cases distributed systems *decrease costs* of data communication. For example, local processing of accounting applications avoids transferring large numbers of transactions across the communication link. A third advantage is *reliability.* A distributed system has multiple processors, each of which serves as a backup processor for the others; when one processor malfunctions, another can execute its applications. And finally, another advantage is the *flexibility* of the distributed system. The processing capability of the network can be increased by expanding the number of its processors. This is much easier than upgrading a centralized system by replacing its processor with a larger one.

Distributed systems have disadvantages as well. *Control* of the system is more difficult because managers at remote locations can make unauthorized changes to their systems. Sometimes these managers decide that internal control measures are unnecessary and cease to implement them. This may introduce incorrect data into the network. Adequate *security* for the system is more difficult to achieve because security procedures must be implemented at numerous sites. However, companies that implement distributed networks conclude that their advantages outweigh the disadvantages.

Distributed Network Configurations. Three configurations are common for distributed processing networks. Illustration 9–12 shows these graphically.

The *star network* uses a single, central computer as a switch that transfers data among all other computers in the network. Physically, however, the network is not shaped like the star in Illustration 9–12. Some of the peripheral processors may be very close to the central computer while others may be hundreds of miles away. Each peripheral processor connects directly only to the central processor using a single data communication link. This allows use of a diagram showing communication links radiating out from the central processor.

For example, many star networks use a mainframe computer as the central processor with minis or micros as peripheral processors. Each peripheral processor executes a single application during the day, and at night transfers journal entries summarizing the results of processing to the mainframe. An application on the mainframe then posts these journal entries to the general ledger. Point-of-sale retail systems usually work this way. Other systems may use a small processor at the center. It functions only as a switch, transferring data among larger peripheral processors.

The *tree network* is sometimes identified as a *hierarchical network* because it contains a hierarchy of processors. The one at the top, the root of the upside-down tree, is the most important and is usually a mainframe computer. The processors at lower levels may be smaller mainframes, minicomputers, or microcomputers. Processors at the second level transfer data among lower levels and the high-level mainframe.

Organizations sometimes use a *ring network* when all the processors are of approximately equal size and speed. Each processor is connected only to two other processors, and each may be dedicated to processing only one or a few related applications.

For example, processor A may be used to process accounts receivable, processor B for payroll, processor C for inventory, and processor D maintains the general ledger. When the network transfers journal entries representing sales to

ILLUSTRATION 9–12 Distributed Processing Network Configurations

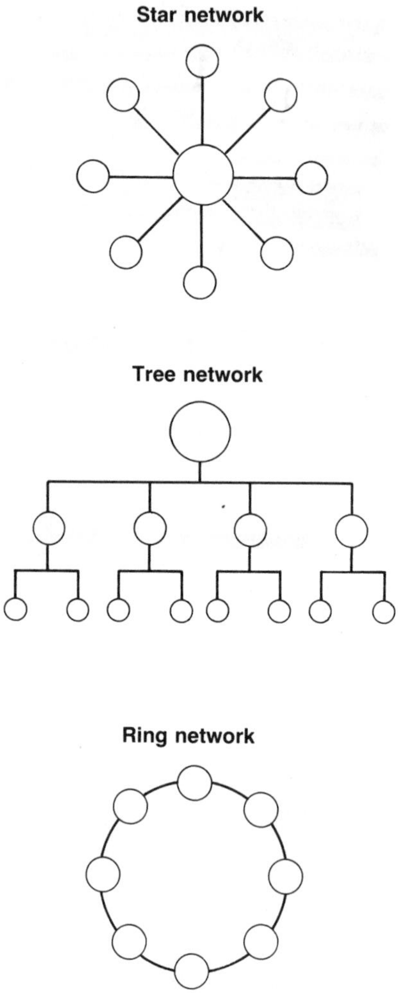

processor D, processor A formats the entry into a packet of data addressed to processor D. Other processors then pass this packet around the ring until it reaches processor D. The receiving processor decodes the journal entry from the packet and enters it in the general ledger.

Distributed Data Bases. When a system design team decides to use distributed processing, it must select not only a configuration for the processing but also a way of distributing the data—either by replication or by partitioning.

When data is *replicated,* copies of all data are maintained at each processor location. This produces a system with faster response but increases the communication required between processors. Whenever a processor posts a journal entry to the general ledger, for example, that same entry must be posted at each processor. Otherwise, different processors in the system produce conflicting information.

With *partitioned* data, the design team assigns each data file to only one processor in the network. For example, the accounts receivable records may be stored at processor A. When a user at processor E wants to record a credit sale, the user enters the journal entry for the sale at processor E which transfers it to processor A. This avoids the problem of conflicting data, but may result in some processors that are very busy while others are hardly used.

In most cases, organizations adopt a distributed data base that is neither replicated nor partitioned, but some combination of the two. For example, the general ledger may be replicated at all processors that produce journal entries for it. Other files, such as those for accounts receivable, may be partitioned and kept only at those processors that use them frequently.

Local Area Networks. When distributed processing is applied within a limited geographic area, such as within a single building or office, the system is a local area network (LAN). LANs are frequently implemented using microcomputers connected by coaxial or fiber-optic cables. A single LAN may have several processors and peripheral devices attached to it. A LAN may, in turn, be a part of a larger network of other LANs, minicomputers, or mainframes.

A local area network usually contains four components: a workstation, file server, print server, and a communications server. Whether the LAN has one or more *workstations,* each workstation may include a microcomputer, a keyboard, a CRT display, a disk storage device, and a printer. A network user enters data, executes accounting application software, and receives output at a workstation. The LAN also contains a *file server.* This is a processor connected to a high-speed on-line form of secondary storage such as a magnetic disk drive. All workstations on the LAN may place files on the file server. A *print server* is a high-speed printer connected to the network that can also be used by all workstations. The *communications server* is a processor in the LAN that handles communications with other systems or networks outside of the LAN. It provides an interface between the LAN and other processors in a distributed network.

Baseband and broadband are two standard technologies used in local area networks. Using *baseband* technology, a workstation forms data into packets. The LAN transfers data one packet at a time over the communication link very much like in a teleprocessing network. This is less expensive to implement but is less flexible than the other approach.

With *broadband* technology, a workstation broadcasts messages onto the link very much like a radio transmitter broadcasts into the air. Different devices can broadcast at different frequencies, so that many can use the communication link at the same time. Voice and video signals can be transmitted on a broadband LAN along with digitized data from workstations. Although more flexible, broadband technology is more expensive to implement.

SUMMARY

The components of a computer system are the hardware, consisting of the central processing unit and its peripherals, and computer software for systems or applications. Systems software are programs controlling the activities of the hardware. Applications software programs accomplish specific business or scientific purposes. Transaction processing applications programs may be coded, purchased, or produced with an application generator. Decision support software includes computer models and expert systems.

The configuration of a computer system describes how its components are arranged. Many system configurations use a central mainframe computer in a teleprocessing network; the mainframe transfers data across communications links to devices at remote locations. Other configurations combine multiple processors, including mainframes, minicomputers, and microcomputers, in a distributed processing network. The selection of a configuration is an important decision in the design of a computer system.

KEY TERMS

applications software Computer software used to achieve a specific accounting or managerial objective. When used to process accounting transactions, it is transaction processing software.

central processing unit The computer hardware component that controls the operations of the entire computer. It consists of main storage, the control unit, and the arithmetic-logic unit.

configuration A description of how a specific organization combines hardware devices to support the applications required by its computer system.

data management software System software that determines the location on secondary storage of data transferred between secondary and main storage.

distributed network A computer configuration in which two or more processors are connected by data communication links allowing the transfer of data between them. The network may be shaped as a star, a tree, or a ring.

expert system Applications software that incorporates the knowledge of a human expert and can be used to mimic the expert's decision-making processes.

local area network A distributed network, usually composed of microcomputers, and used within a limited geographical area such as a building.

main storage A component of the central processing unit in which executable instructions are stored. It also provides temporary storage for data while the CPU is in use.

operating system System software that controls the operations of the entire computer.

peripheral devices Components of computer hardware that are external to the central processing unit. They include input devices, output devices, and secondary storage devices.

secondary storage Computer hardware components used to store accounting data and programs while not in use.

teleprocessing network A computer configuration connecting peripheral devices at remote locations by communications links with a central computer. It may be a point-to-point, a multidrop, or a multiplexed network.

QUESTIONS

9–1. Can you name the parts of the hardware component of a computer system? The software components?

9–2. What is the purpose of each of the following?
a. Control unit
b. Arithmetic-logic unit
c. Main storage

9–3. Why are peripheral devices given this name? Name three kinds of peripheral devices.

9–4. Why is an operating system important to a computer system? What are its functions?

9–5. Computers use several kinds of language translation software. Distinguish between each of the following language translators:
a. Compiler
b. Interpreter
c. Assembler
d. Fourth-generation language
e. Application generator

9–6. What is the difference between a source program and an object program?

9–7. Name the components of an expert system and explain what each component does.

9–8. What distinguishes each of the following types of processors?
a. Central processor
b. Peripheral processor
c. Communications processor
d. Microprocessor

9–9. Which advantages do multiplexed teleprocessing networks offer over point-to-point and multidrop networks?

9–10. Describe the differences among the three common configurations of distributed processing networks.

9–11. What are the components of a local area network?

EXERCISES AND CASES

9–12. *SIGNIFICANT TERMS*

For each of the following sets, distinguish between the terms listed:

a. Main storage, secondary storage, and virtual storage
b. Execution time and access time
c. Instructions and data
d. On-line storage and off-line storage
e. On-line processing and real-time processing
f. Operating system and utility program
g. Terminal and intelligent terminal

9–13. *COMPUTER COMPONENTS*

Two columns of peripheral devices follow. Under certain circumstances, each device in column A has an advantage over the device of the same number in column B. In other circumstances, the device in column B has an advantage over the one in A.

A	*B*
1. Magnetic tape storage	1. Magnetic disk storage
2. MICR reader	2. CRT terminal
3. Printer	3. COM device

Required:

a. For each number identify the advantage the device in column A has over the one in column B and indicate when it occurs.
b. For each number identify the advantage the device in column B has over the one in column A and indicate when it occurs.

(CIA Adapted)

9–14. *ON-LINE REAL-TIME SYSTEM*

Executive management of Continental Incorporated, a rapidly expanding manufacturing company, has been reviewing a proposal prepared by the manager of the data processing department to update the computer equipment now in use. The present equipment includes a central processing unit, tape drives, a card reader, and a printer.

The MIS manager suggests that new equipment should be acquired to provide on-line real-time capability for inventory control and more efficient operations.

Required:

a. Briefly describe the function of each item of equipment now in use.
b. Identify two types of equipment not mentioned that would be required for the proposed on-line real-time application.

(CIA Adapted)

9–15. *DISTRIBUTED PROCESSING*

Megapolis Bank and Trust offers a wide range of financial services through a network of regional offices. The firm's present information system is highly concentrated, with a large centralized mainframe computer providing services to individual offices through the use of remote data entry terminals.

Megapolis's information system steering committee proposes a major change in the configuration of the system. It recommends that each office be equipped with a minicomputer that can communicate with the other minicomputers and with the firm's mainframe.

Required:

a. What are the potential advantages of the system proposed by the steering committee?

b. Which system configuration would you recommend for Megapolis?

9–16. *MINICOMPUTERS*

Minicomputers are small, programmable digital computers. The term *microcomputer* describes a computer of even smaller dimensions, but the distinction between minicomputers and microcomputers has become blurred due to advancements in technology. Consequently, minicomputer in this exercise refers to both categories of computer systems.

A typical minicomputer system consists of a central processing unit, input devices, output devices, memory, and software. Minicomputers are used extensively in business, both in networks with a larger computer and as small but complete data processing systems.

Required:

a. List and discuss the advantages and limitations generally associated with minicomputer systems.

b. Identify and explain the factors a business should consider before it decides to use a minicomputer.

(CMA Adapted)

9–17. *POINT-OF-SALE SYSTEMS*

Pinta Company is a regional discount chain selling general merchandise in the Southwest. The company is considering acquiring a point-of-sale (POS) system for use in its stores.

Currently, three types of firms primarily use POS systems: large retailers, grocery stores, and fast-food chains. Pinta would probably employ cash registers that use light pens to read the universal product code (UPC) printed on the packages.

Cindy Brenski, president of Pinta, knows that the equipment is very expensive. She has asked her controller to prepare a report on POS systems including a survey describing the companies employing POS systems and why they have adopted them.

Required:

a. Explain briefly how a POS system operates.

b. Describe the potential advantages and disadvantages of a POS system for a company's operations and recordkeeping system.

c. Identify and explain the special control problems that a POS system could present to Pinta Company's personnel.

(CMA Adapted)

9–18. ***EXPERT SYSTEMS***

You are a consultant with a major CPA firm and have been engaged by a client, Kindly Cat Kennels, Inc., to develop an expert system. You know that any expert system includes a knowledge base and that the knowledge base consists of a set of rules in the form:

IF *condition,* THEN *action.*

As the knowledge engineer on this engagement, you identify a set of questions. The expert system presents these questions one at a time to the system user. From the answers to these questions, the system determines which conditions are present. For each condition, you encode in the knowledge base the action to be taken next.

Your client wants the expert system to aid its employees in deciding if an animal is a cat.

Required:

a. Prepare a list of questions which, when answered, aid in determining if an animal is a cat.

b. Assuming a yes answer to each question in part *a,* identify the appropriate action. (Hint: Your actions are either [1] to ask another question, or [2] to conclude that the animal is a cat, or [3] to conclude that the animal is not a cat.)

c. From your answers to parts *a* and *b,* formulate a set of rules for this knowledge base.

d. Develop a chain from these rules that allows you to decide that an animal is a cat.

9–19. ***SYSTEM CONFIGURATION***

While attending college, Simple Simon studied finance and dabbled in the stock market. Since graduating, he has begun offering financial planning services to his friends and business associates. These are primarily small businesses and working people of modest means who rely on Simon for assistance in investment planning. He helps them in purchasing stocks and bonds and in setting up pension, profit sharing, and retirement plans.

Simon attempts to track the performance of thousands of different stock and bond issues. He also tries to keep up to date on economic trends and investment opportunities to advise his clients effectively. Additionally, he sometimes performs complex calculations when setting up profit-sharing and pension plans.

Simon has read of computerized data bases that provide financial market and economic information on-line. He would like to get access to this information.

Required:

Configure a computer system that satisfies Simon's information processing needs.

9–20. ***SYSTEM CONFIGURATION***

Rex, Finney & Co. is a law firm specializing in personal injury litigation. The firm's five partners and eight associates are each involved in litigating and settling claims regarding product liability, automobile accidents, and job related injuries. As a result, they daily prepare and update legal briefs, pleadings, and correspondence with clients, litigants, and other attorneys.

At any time, Rex Finney has dozens of cases pending. Law clerks research cases, prepare legal briefs, summarize points of law, and look up other documents. Partners review all of this material before it leaves the office. As a result, a document undergoes many changes and revisions before reaching its final form. The firm must be able to make changes to documents literally up to the final minute before an attorney leaves for a courtroom.

All these documents are prepared by a staff of legal secretaries using typewriters. Workloads for the secretarial staff change from periods of idleness to periods of continuous rush jobs. Frequently attorneys present to secretaries last-minute work requests that conflict with each other. Several have complained about being late for engagements and court appearances as a result.

Rex Finney has a small computer which they use for accounts receivable and payroll. The partners wonder if it can be used in some way to correct some of their problems.

Required:

Configure a computer system that meets the information processing needs of Rex, Finney & Co.

9–21. ***SYSTEM CONFIGURATION***

Highsmith Auto Parts is an auto parts distributor headquartered in North Carolina. During the past 20 years the company has expanded to include 5 distribution centers and 48 retail outlets throughout the southeastern part of the country.

For many years Highsmith relied on a centralized management information system. This included two large centralized computers operating as multiprocessors and terminals in each store and distribution center. Terminals communicated with the central processors using high-speed data communication links provided by the telephone company. Using these terminals, employees at remote locations were able to access credit, sales, and inventory data stored on the mainframes. The mainframes also are used at company headquarters for executing general ledger, accounts payable, accounts receivable, and payroll applications.

Although the system worked well, it was expensive to operate because it relied on expensive high-speed communications circuits. Recently Highsmith has begun to encounter problems with processor reliability. When the system goes down, it effectively halts data processing throughout the entire organization. Highsmith would like to find a way to eliminate these problems.

Required:

Configure a system to satisfy the information processing needs of Highsmith Auto Parts.

9–22. ***EXPERT SYSTEMS***

Tax accrual involves calculating deferred income tax and explaining the difference between statutory and effective tax rates. Audit staff accountants usually gather information needed for tax accrual by completing questionnaires. Frequently they give little attention to the significance of this information for tax planning, even though this may be important to the client.[1]

Coopers & Lybrand has developed an expert system called ExperTAX^{sm} to actively guide audit and tax staff accountants through the process of gathering information necessary for tax accrual and planning. At the same time, ExperTAX^{sm} has the ability to point out the importance of the information being requested. It can be a very effective training and education tool, providing the professional with the experts' reasons for requesting specific information.

Developed in a programming language called Common LISP, ExperTAX^{sm} is intended to run on a microcomputer equipped with a hard disk and an attached printer. Coopers & Lybrand developed the system by encoding the expertise of more than 30 of its senior tax and audit professionals.

ExperTAX^{sm} consists of three modules: the expert system shell (called QShell), the knowledge base, and the knowledge base maintenance system. The latter facilitates modification of the contents of the knowledge base as tax laws and experts' opinions change.

The Expert System Shell

QShell is rule based and designed specifically to accommodate the requirements of the tax accrual and planning process at Coopers & Lybrand. Although it was designed for ExperTAX^{sm} in particular, QShell has also been used as a flexible

[1]Adapted from *An Introduction to Artificial Intelligence and Expert Systems*. Copyright © 1987 by American Institute of CPAs. Used by permission.

EXHIBIT 9–1 Case 9–22 ExperTAX^{sm} Display

ARTIFICIAL COMPANY SEPTEMBER 3, 19XX
Coopers & Lybrand—ExperTAX(sm)—
Tax Accrual & Planning Expert System Inventory

Any inventory: Yes

Does the client include any of the following items in inventory for TAX purposes?
Real Estate
Materials and supplies not held for sale (e.g., office supplies)
Deferred cost under the Completed Contract method
Consigned goods to which the client does not have title

Summary: Noninventory items
QB3 Answer one of: (Y N) Y
The items mentioned above may be treated as inventory items for BOOK purposes, but may not be treated as inventory items for TAX purposes (Ref. Atlantic Coast Realty v. Comm., Rev Rul 59–329, Reg. 1.471–1)

F1—Note F2—Skip F3—More WHY

programming tool for other expert systems. Its two main components are the inference engine and the user interface.

The *inference engine* controls the logic search through the knowledge base by executing the appropriate rules, tracking the inference process, and communicating with the user through the user interface. The *user interface* controls the screen display and keyboard used to communicate with the user and issues printer commands to format and print reports.

The layout of a CRT display has three distinct horizontal portions. The top portion of the display shows information identifying the section being analyzed. The middle portion displays the questions being asked, the condition that caused the current question, and the possible valid answers. The lower portion presents explanatory messages. It also allows the user to enter either notes desired by the user or information requested by the system. Exhibit 9–1 shows a sample display.

The user operates the user interface through a system of nested menus. The information it displays comes directly from the knowledge base. Responses to its questions direct its search processes and improve the intelligibility of its output. The printed reports generated by the user interface include lists of all issues identified by ExperTAX^{sm}, lists of all questions asked and answers received, notes entered during the session, and special forms. These forms are completed by the professional staff to provide additional documentation. Exhibit 9–2 is a sample report.

EXHIBIT 9–2 Case 9–22 ExperTAX[sm] Report

Coopers & Lybrand

ExperTAX[sm]
Planning Issues and Ideas

April 8, 19XX

The practitioner should review the following planning ideas and issues to determine their applicability to the client.

Inventory

- Section 1.471–2(c) allows obsolete goods to be written down to bona fide selling price less direct cost of disposition. Such write-downs reduce taxable income. However, excess inventory does not come under this provision. See Thor Power v. Comm.*
- LIFO inventory may not be valued for tax purposes using the lower-of-cost-or-market method! The IRS may terminate the taxpayer's LIFO election if LIFO inventory is valued at the lower of cost or market. See Rev. Proc. 79–23. In limited situations, a taxpayer may be able to change to the cost method and preclude the IRS from terminating its LIFO election. See Rev. Proc. 84–74. Market write-downs are required to be included in income under the provisions of Sec. 472(d) when LIFO is elected.

*These issues require a change in accounting method for which IRS approval must be requested within 180 days of the beginning of the taxable year.

EXHIBIT 9–3 Case 9–22 ExperTAX^{sm} Question Frame

Coopers & Lybrand—ExperTAX(sm)—Tax Accrual & Planning Expert System

Question:

What is client's bad-debt write-off method for TAX purposes?
S—Specific charge-off
R—Reserve method

Possible Answers:
S—Specific charge-off
(Clarifying explanation required)
R—Reserve method
Follow-up Questions:
QA19—Bad-debt reserve method
QA20—Difference between BOOK and TAX reserve
QA21—Bad-debt recoveries to reserve

WHY message:

In a typical environment, the Reserve method over time will result in larger tax deductions than the Specific charge-off method.

The Knowledge Base

The knowledge base contains several thousand frames, rules, and facts that constitute the system's expertise. It makes these available to the inference engine and to the user interface.

Each frame in the knowledge base contains information on how and when it is used, what should happen next, and what to display or print. A frame can include several rules. The two kinds of frames are question and issue frames.

The *question frames* include the following:

1. Questions.
2. Conditions. These appear as antecedents, and if true, cause the questions to be asked.
3. Rules. These control the structure of the session and of the outputs.
4. Explanatory messages.

Exhibit 9–3 contains an example of a question frame.

The *issue frames* are simpler than the question frames. They include only a rule and a display. The inference engine tests the rule in the frame, and if it is true, the display appears on the CRT or in a printed report. Exhibit 9–4 is an example of an issue frame.

EXHIBIT 9–4 Case 9–22 ExperTAX^{sm} Issue Frame

Coopers & Lybrand—ExperTAX(sm)—Tax Accrual & Planning Expert System

Rule:

(QB6 IS L): Inventory valuing IS Lower of cost or market
AND
(QB14 IS L): Method of accounting for inventory IS LIFO
OR
(QB14 IS B): Method of accounting for inventory IS Both LIFO and FIFO

Display:

LIFO inventory may not be valued for tax purposes using the lower-of-cost-or-market method!! The IRS may terminate the taxpayer's LIFO election if LIFO inventory is valued at lower-of-cost-or-market. See Rev Proc 79–23. In limited situations, a taxpayer may be able to change to the Cost method and preclude the IRS from terminating its LIFO election. See Rev Proc 84–74. Market write-downs are required to be included in income under the provisions of SEC. 472(d) when LIFO is elected.

Required:

a. What motivated this large CPA firm to create this expert system? What financial justification can you suggest for their investment in it?

b. Which other possible applications can you suggest for expert systems in accounting and auditing?

9–23. *APPLICATION GENERATORS*

Hamilton Brothers Oil Company developed a comprehensive accounting and financial information system under an extremely difficult schedule.[2] A key ingredient in the success of this project was the use of an application generator to satisfy the programming requirements. An application generator is a software package that anticipates standard user requirements in a functional area such as accounting and finance. It provides data management facilities, automates common functions, and has a specialized language for coding.

Project Background

Hamilton Brothers's senior management decided in January 19XX to terminate its service bureau computer support and to implement an in-house financial

[2]Adapted from J. H. Waldrop, "Application Generators: A Case Study," *Proceedings of the 1982 National Computer Conference,* Houston, Texas, p. 363. Reprinted with the permission of the American Federation of Information Processing Societies, all rights reserved.

reporting system (FRS). This system consists of five integrated subsystems: accounts payable, accounts receivable, general ledger, joint interest billing, and budget. After a thorough four-month evaluation of 19 vendors, management determined that Hamilton Brothers's requirements could best be met by making significant modifications to an existing software package. In addition to customizing the software, the company had to establish and staff a complete medium-size computer installation. The data in the new system would require a complex conversion effort from the previous service bureau environment. The target date for implementation of the new system was 20 months from the beginning of the project.

This project required completion of several phases. First, a project team issued requests for proposals (RFPs) to software package vendors. They evaluated the resulting proposals based on four criteria: ability of the package to address user requirements, its utilization of the most current software architecture, maximum software flexibility, and the financial and technical reputation of the vendor. After two months, a software package was selected. In the second phase, a system concept definition was performed to refine the general requirements presented in the RFP. This phase also required two months. Next, the project teams developed a general design for the system, requiring six months.

At this point, the project team had only 10 months remaining to accomplish detailed specification, programming, testing, and conversion. They began to examine techniques to maximize efficiency during programming, testing, and conversion. This led to their decision to use an application generator to perform the custom development work.

Project Goals

As with any new system, this project's ultimate goal was to provide a sound system meeting the user's requirements. The project team identified three ancillary goals in order to achieve this with FRS.

First, the new system must be user friendly. To accomplish this, the project team decided to provide on-line processing and user report development with minimal support from the data processing staff. They also wanted an architecture that provides flexible data modification by users. Second, the system must be capable of easy technical modification, thus providing a solid base for future expansion. This required a structured development methodology and self-documenting code. Third, the system development process must take advantage of development productivity tools. These required on-line program development, simple report writers, on-line screen generators, a data dictionary, and a project management plan.

The Completed System

The use of an application generator contributed to the achievement of the project's goals and its timely implementation. The following summary describes the completed system and provides insight into the magnitude of the project. The project entailed:

- 1,300 pages of preliminary design narrative
- 6,000 persondays to complete the entire project
- 25 people assigned full time at the peak of the project
- 3,000 pages of automated technical documentation in a data dictionary
- 1,320 data items
- 285 programs, most of them developed using the application generator
- 157 reports
- 53 on-line screens
- 132 data files
- 48 input forms

The project team both encountered problems and achieved benefits from the use of an application generator. All in all, the package was less flexible than a procedural language in how it accomplished specific tasks. This required some adaptation by programmers accustomed to coding in COBOL. However, its structured architecture and selected keywords enforced programmer standardization. It also provided an excellent technique for developing common code used in many programs. The generator allowed the use of identical data names for multiple fields, thus minimizing unique data names. These characteristics reduced the amount of code that would have been required using a procedural language such as COBOL.

A major benefit provided by this application generator is an automatic transaction suspense processing facility. On input, transactions reside in a holding file awaiting subsequent processing. After processing, transactions rejected because of invalid fields or account numbers are retained in this holding file until corrected. Valid transactions proceed through the remainder of the processing cycle. This feature eliminates the effort required to code programs to apply these procedures with transaction and master files.

The application generator supported several general housekeeping functions that directly contributed to improved programmer productivity both in the coding and the testing stages. The use of selected application-unique keywords such as REJECT-BATCH or REJECT-DOCUMENT eliminated the need to code and test these types of routines. Other unique keywords such as POST or GENERATE offered no productivity gains but did relate the function (WRITE) to the application-oriented terminology (POST).

The on-line screen generation provided the greatest increase in programmer productivity. Fourteen of the 16 programmers on the project team had never developed a teleprocessing system and, therefore, had no experience in generating on-line screens. The application generator screen facility provided each programmer with an easy-to-learn tool to perform this function.

Perhaps the best measure of the productivity gains provided by this application generator was the relatively brief time required to develop the code through program testing. The elapsed time for this task was approximately three months, certainly a significant testimony to the potential value of an application generator.

Future Uses of Application Generators

The project team identified several factors that affect future decisions to use an application generator. Perhaps the most important is the size and complexity of the project. A complex system requiring unique access methods, specialized processing techniques, and sophisticated on-line requirements may not be suitable for development using an application generator. For less complex systems, the benefits from the time saved during coding and testing may make use of a generator worthwhile.

Whenever a project team decides to use an application generator, they should carefully evaluate its technical capabilities. Application generators are inherently oriented to specific functional areas. The selection of an appropriate generator for a given functional area is necessary for the success of the project. Furthermore, the design of the system must be consistent with the technical capabilities of the software. The project team must develop an understanding of the capabilities and constraints of the application generator and be willing to live within those constraints.

Conclusions

Hamilton Brothers's use of this application generator provided several key benefits. It did, however, introduce inefficiencies into the design process that could have been avoided with a COBOL-based system. How effective was the project team in meeting the goals of FRS as outlined earlier?

The user friendliness is superior to that of the old system. The application generator provides extremely flexible data file modifications, allowing users to change most edit criteria without programmer intervention. With the report development facility, selected users can create simple reports with minimal MIS support. However, more complex reporting requires direct programmer help.

Future modifications can easily be made to FRS if the new code is developed with the same application generator. The benefits of the generator's structured coding requirements were somewhat offset by the limitations in its flexibility.

The benefits of development productivity tools such as on-line program development, report writers, screen generators, a data dictionary, and project management planning exceeded original expectations. They were critical factors in the success achieved by the project team.

In conclusion, the use of application generators is a technique for improving the quality of a system and the timeliness of its development. The package used at Hamilton Brothers offers a good tool for accounting applications. Its potential for use in other application areas is, by design, limited.

Required:

a. Which source for computing services had Hamilton Brothers used prior to developing the new financial reporting system?

b. How long did the project team require to develop FRS? How much time was needed to create the code? How do you think this would have changed had the team used a procedural language such as COBOL?

c. What are the key considerations in the decision to use an application generator?

Chapter 10

Data Storage and Processing Methods

Learning Objectives:

1. To review how a computer stores data in electronic devices.
2. To compare two alternative approaches to organizing accounting data in computer systems.
3. To understand four approaches to processing data stored in an accounting information system.

INTRODUCTION

In the previous chapter you learned about the components of a computer system, including secondary storage devices. A computer system stores accounting records on secondary storage devices until needed. Then system software transfers accounting data into main storage for processing by application software.

This chapter explains how secondary storage devices store accounting information. The last part of the chapter describes four ways of implementing procedures to process this data.

DATA REPRESENTATION

The devices in a computer system record data by changing the *state* of the circuits and magnetic devices constituting the peripherals. A circuit or magnetic component can be in either of two states: either magnetized or energized one way

ILLUSTRATION 10–1 Methods of Binary Encoding

Decimal:	941		
Binary:	1110101101		
EBCDIC:	11111001	11110100	11110001
	9	4	1
ASCII:	01011001	01010100	01010001
	9	4	1

or the opposite way. When data is transferred across a data communication link, an electronic pulse is either present or absent. Technicians use *binary notation* to describe the state of a circuit, a magnetic device, or a communication link.

Binary Encoding

In writing, the binary numbering system denotes the state of the component. This system uses the digit 1 to represent the existence of a pulse on a data communication link, or one way of energizing a circuit or device. The digit 0 represents the other way. In this manner, technicians can describe the contents of the computer system without concern for the specific device or circuit in use. The most elementary amount of information in a pulse or circuit utilizes one *bi*nary digi*t* when written; thus, these devices transfer or store information in *bits.*

Storing information in pure binary form is awkward and difficult to interpret. Consequently, computer manufacturers developed easier ways of encoding information using the digits 1 and 0. The two methods for encoding information are called EBCDIC and ASCII. Illustration 10–1 shows how each method encodes numbers. They encode letters of the alphabet, punctuation marks, and other characters similarly.

Computers use ASCII codes for transferring data over communications links. Most computer manufacturers also use ASCII to store data internally on devices. However, mainframe computers that use IBM operating systems employ EBCDIC.

Data Hierarchy

A data hierarchy describes how binary codes combine to provide meaningful information. Furthermore, there are two views of this hierarchy. One is the view of the computer hardware and the other is that of the human user.

ILLUSTRATION 10–2 Fields and Their Data Names

Data Name	*Length*	*Contents*	*Example*
DEPARTMENT	10	Alphanumeric	ASSEMBLY-1
SOCIAL-SECURITY-NUMBER	9	Numeric	361267091
HOURS-WORKED	2	Numeric	40

From the View of the Computer. When designing computer hardware, manufacturers select either EBCDIC or ASCII as a way of digitally encoding data. The circuits required to store one human readable character in each method is called one *byte* of storage. A storage device that contains 1 million bytes can store this number of characters readable by a human. Large storage capacity indicates a powerful computer that can execute large programs and store large amounts of data.

Another measure of the processing power of a computer is its word length. A computer *word* is the minimum amount of storage that can be addressed, or specifically identified as to location, by the CPU. Depending on the computer, the length of a word may be 1, 2, 4, 8, or 16 bytes. A modern computer with a large word length can store and process larger numbers, and it can store small numbers more accurately than can an older computer with a smaller word length. It can also execute larger programs.

From the View of the User. Although computers process data in the form of bits, bytes, and computer words, we as humans have difficulty thinking in these terms. To us, the most elemental form of data is the character. Usually this is either a number, a letter, or a punctuation mark. When we process data, we combine these characters to form data fields.

A *field* represents a single item of data needed by an accounting application, and it contains one or more characters. Unlike byte or word lengths fixed by computer manufacturers, the length of a field is determined by the designer of the application software. The designer also decides which characters compose the field and selects a *data name* to uniquely identify the field. Illustration 10–2 contains some accounting data fields.

Most accounting systems initially record data on documents. One type of document contains all the data needed to record a sales order from a customer; another type records data showing an obligation to pay a supplier for goods received. Data recorded on these documents constitute a logically related set of data items. When an accounting system converts all the data from a document into computer readable form, it stores this set of data fields in a *logical record.* The application software designer decides not only how to store each data item in a data field but also how to combine these in the logical record.

For example, application software in an inventory system maintains perpetual inventory data. A logical record for an inventory application might contain the following seven fields:

INVENTORY-NUMBER	REORDER-QUANTITY
INVENTORY-DESCRIPTION	VENDOR-CODE
STANDARD-COST	QUANTITY-ON-HAND
REORDER-POINT	

In this example, the INVENTORY-NUMBER field is the primary key field for the record. The record's *primary key field* is a data field that uniquely identifies it. In an inventory application, the primary key contains a number that uniquely identifies the product or inventory item described by the contents of the record. In an accounts receivable record, the primary key is a customer number that uniquely identifies the customer with a receivables balance.

Some records also contain secondary (or generic) keys. A *secondary key field* is a field that identifies a record but is not unique to the record. For example, VENDOR-CODE in the preceding record identifies the supplier for the inventory item. The same vendor may supply numerous items; thus a vendor code may appear in numerous inventory records.

You have seen how characters combine to form data fields, and how fields combine to form records. A collection of similar data records form a *data file*. Humans commonly maintain data files in filing cabinets; these collections of similar documents may be a file of old credit card bills, a file of old accounting exams, or the like. Each old document is a record in these manually processed files.

A computer file is a collection of similar computer records. Computers maintain their files on secondary storage devices. For example, a computerized inventory file might contain thousands of computer records, one for each item in inventory. Each record contains the data items identified earlier.

All the data used by an organization and stored on secondary storage devices constitute the organization's *data base*. In older systems, the data base is simply a collection of computer data files. Illustration 10–3 shows the data hierarchy in such a system.

In many newer systems, data records are maintained in the data base by a system software package, the data base management system (DBMS). In all systems, the computer and its human users have two alternative views of how data is stored in a computer. Illustration 10–4 summarizes these.

Whenever a DBMS is used, the application software designer is unconcerned with how the data fields are arranged on secondary storage. The DBMS allows the computer application to access the data items it needs regardless of how they are stored.

ILLUSTRATION 10–3 Data Hierarchy

a. Bit
1 a bit showing a yes-state

b. Byte
11010011 an 8-bit byte representing an L in EBCDIC

c. Field
CUSTOMER-NAME

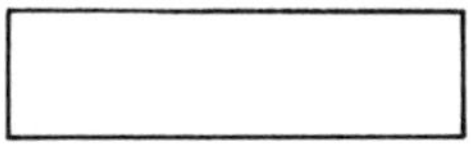

a 15-byte field with the data name of CUSTOMER-NAME

d. Record

CUSTOMER-NUMBER CUSTOMER-NAME

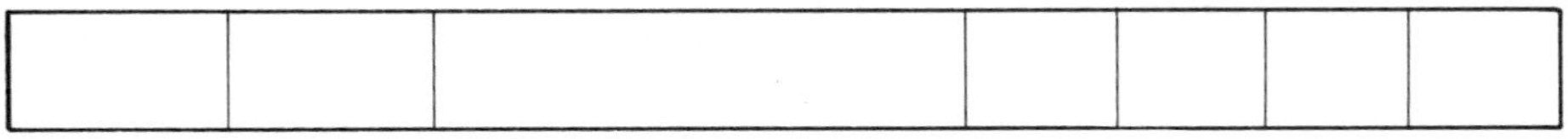

A record with CUSTOMER-NUMBER as its key and CUSTOMER-NAME as one of its fields

e. File

RECORD RECORD RECORD RECORD

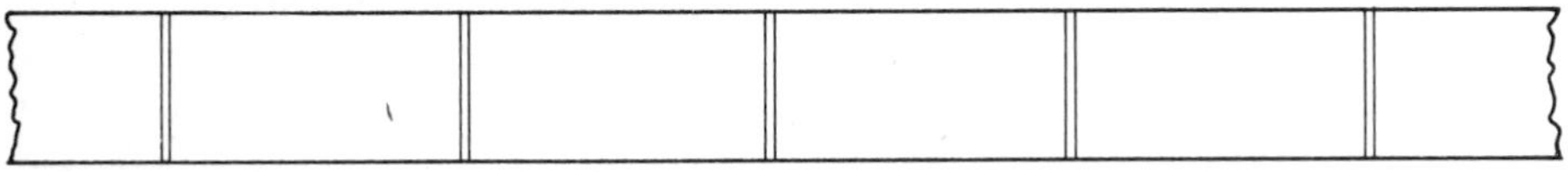

A segment of a file, on magnetic tape, showing four records. The little strip between records is known as interrecord gap.

f. Data base
All files or records in the system.

ILLUSTRATION 10–4 Alternative Views of Data Storage

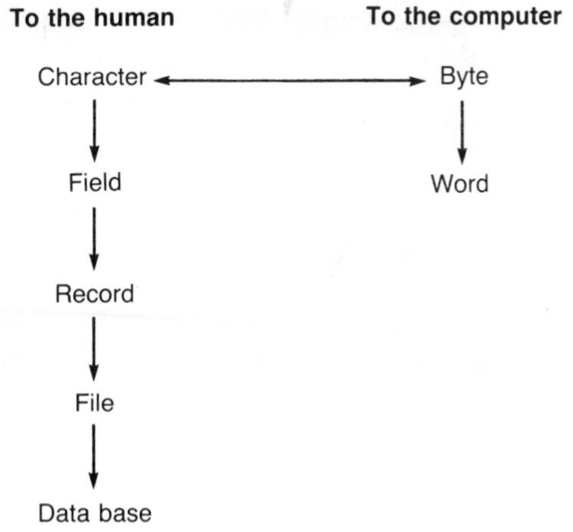

APPROACHES TO DATA ORGANIZATION

Two approaches exist for organizing data in a data base. The first represents a modification of early manual procedures. The second was developed to overcome deficiencies with the first. However, both are common in today's business environment. In this text, we will refer to them as the traditional data file approach and the data base management approach. Accountants encounter both approaches as they develop and audit computer systems.

Traditional Data File Organization

From your perspective as a computer user, accounting data are stored in groups of logically related fields called records. In noncomputerized systems, these records are documents. Accountants collect groups of similar documents in files and store them in filing cabinets.

When businesses first computerized the accounting process, they created a computer file for each manual file and a computer record for each document. Computerized procedures replaced manual procedures when processing these records and files. In this way a computer application created and maintained its own data files independent of other applications. Even though these applications have expanded and improved over the years, many businesses still use this traditional approach to organizing data.

Characteristics. With traditional data file organization, each application maintains its own accounting files. Each file consists of a collection of data records. Other applications may process records containing similar data items, but those applications store these records in different files. Thus the company's data base contains many different data files and each is processed independently.

The three common methods of arranging records within a data file use sequential, direct access, and indexed sequential files.

Sequential. A sequential file contains records that are physically arranged in sequence by the key field of the record. Thus, in a sequential customer file, the record containing the balance for customer number 12034 is located immediately prior to that for customer number 12035.

A computer program locates a record in a sequential file by searching through the entire file, record by record, from the first one until it finds the desired key field. All magnetic tape files are sequential, but magnetic disks allow this method as well.

Direct Access. With direct access, data management software accesses a record directly; it computes a physical location on a secondary storage device from the key field of a record. The software then stores the record at that location. Whenever a program must use the record, the data management software again computes the location and copies it from the device into main storage. The most common device used for direct access files is a magnetic disk, an example of a *direct access storage device*. Magnetic tapes cannot be used with this method.

Indexed Sequential. Indexed sequential files are so named because they contain an index to records in the file. The index shows the key field and the location of the record for some (but not all) records. The records themselves are physically located in sequence by key field.

A program reads a record from an indexed sequential file by either simply searching sequentially through the file until it finds the desired key, or looking up the key field in the index. If the key field is not there, it finds the next lowest key field in the index and locates this record on the secondary storage device. The software then searches sequentially from the location of this record until the record containing the desired key field is found. Indexed sequential files must be stored on direct access devices, such as magnetic disks.

The way data management software uses a file index is similar to the way you use an index to a book. You look up a topic in the book's index and then read sequentially from the page number shown until you find the information you want.

Example Manual Procedures. Consider, for example, the manual accounts receivable procedures for Acme Company. When Acme sells on account to customers, a clerk records these transactions in the general ledger by making debit entries in the Accounts Receivable account and credit entries in the Sales Revenue account. An accounts receivable clerk receives copies of sales invoices that show the amounts each customer owes. The clerk records these in the accounts receivable subsidiary ledger with entries to the customers' accounts. Each account consists of a ledger card arranged in alphabetical sequence. The clerk then stores the sales invoice copies by invoice number sequence in a filing cabinet. The accounts receivable clerk uses one document and two files when processing each transaction. The document is the sales invoice copy, the files are the sales invoice file, and the accounts receivable subsidiary ledger, a card file.

Example Computerized Procedures. After Acme computerizes this procedure, a computer program in the general ledger application posts the sale to the general ledger accounts. Another program in the accounts receivable application posts the sale to the customer's account. In processing this transaction, the accounts receivable program uses two computer records and two computer files. They are the sales invoice record, the customer master record, the sales invoice file, and the customer master file. The sales invoice file is organized sequentially by invoice number. The customer master file is organized sequentially by customer number. Illustration 10–5 shows the similarities between manual and traditional file processing in this example.

ILLUSTRATION 10–5 Accounts Receivable Procedures

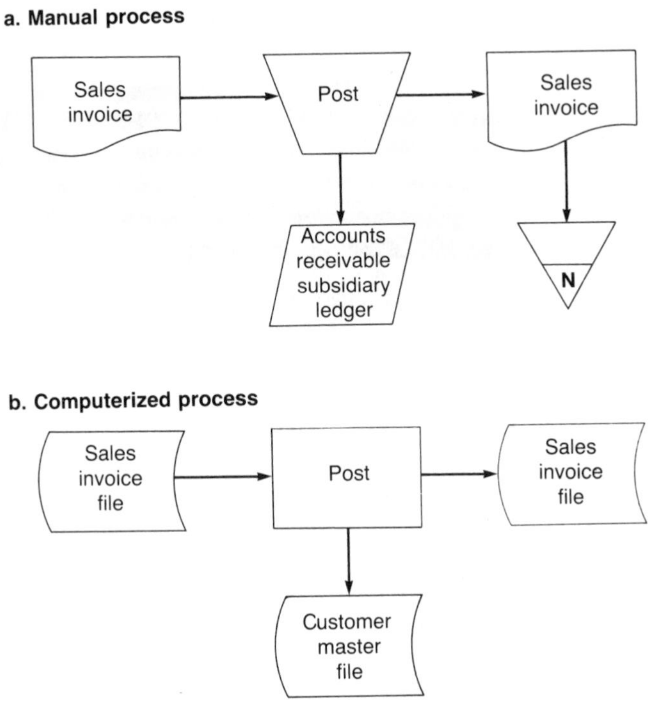

This accounts receivable application maintains two files. No other application uses them; thus many people say that the accounts receivable application "owns" the sales invoice and customer master files.

Deficiencies. Companies adopted traditional data file organization as their manual systems evolved to computer-based ones. After using traditional methods for several years, however, they recognized deficiencies with this way of structuring their data bases. These deficiencies exist because of *data redundancy.* Different computer files, maintained by several applications in the same computer-based system, store records containing the same data items. Three deficiencies result from data redundancy: inefficient use of storage, conflicting data, and the difficulty of making changes to the applications software.

Inefficient Use of Storage. When a computer system stores the same data item in multiple locations on a secondary storage device, the system wastes storage capacity. The system requires less storage capacity if it records each data item only once.

For example, both billing and inventory systems maintain files containing data on quantities of products sold. Billing systems use this data to calculate amounts due from customers. Inventory systems subtract quantities sold from the QUANTITY-ON-HAND data item in the file containing perpetual inventory records. A record in a file of billing transactions and a record in a file of inventory transactions contain the same data item.

Although this is possibly the most obvious deficiency of traditional file processing, it is the least serious. Most computer systems have adequate secondary storage capacity, and this usually can be increased by adding devices. The storage capacity inefficiencies introduced by duplicate data fields are small.

Conflicting Data. A more serious problem arising from duplicate data fields is the possibility of conflicting data. When the same data item exists in two or more files, the contents of these data fields may differ. Reports printed from these files show conflicting information and cause managers to question the validity of all reports produced by the system. Conflicting data may indicate errors. Or it may occur simply because different applications may follow different processing schedules.

Consider again the preceding example. Suppose that the billing system executes daily, but the inventory system executes only once a week on Friday. And suppose that each system produces on Wednesday a report showing quantities sold by inventory item. These two reports will contain conflicting information; the report produced by the inventory system contains data three days older than that of the billing system.

When conflicting data occurs in systems using traditional file organization, as in this example, there is usually a valid explanation. Furthermore, by careful system design a project team can avoid producing reports that contain conflicting information. In this example, both the billing and the inventory systems can produce reports using the most current data item, that from the billing system. However, this solution to the problem of conflicting data creates another deficiency of traditional data file organization.

Difficulty of System Change. Many organizations corrected the problems arising from duplicate and conflicting data by allowing different application systems to share data files. With shared files, each data item is recorded only once in a file. This file is used by several different programs in different applications. Accountants call such a system an *integrated information system.*

Because they avoid many data inconsistencies, integrated information systems provide better accounting information. However, their use creates an even more serious deficiency—they make it difficult to change the applications.

Each program accessing a shared data file contains code describing the data processed by the program. Any change to one program that requires a change in data format also requires changes to all other programs that access the file. Thus, what seems to be a relatively small change may become far reaching and expensive. Furthermore, changes to existing programs may produce unintended consequences.

As an example, in 1981 the U.S. Social Security Administration decided to change its programs to allow benefit checks to be printed in excess of $999.99. Superficially, this was a simple change, requiring an increase in an amount field

ILLUSTRATION 10–6 Deficiencies of Traditional Data File Organization

Inefficient
Duplicate storage on peripheral devices
The least serious problem

Conflicting data
May occur due to different operating schedules
Can be avoided by using shared data files

Difficult changes
A result of shared data files
Can be avoided by separating data storage from the use of the data

from five to six characters. However, this change was required in over 600 programs and cost about $500,000 to make. Furthermore, the altered systems then produced unexpected errors, such as issuing checks for incorrect amounts. In a large system like this one, a systems analyst or programmer cannot anticipate every possible effect of such a change.

Illustration 10–6 summarizes these deficiencies. How can they be avoided? By separating two processes performed by most accounting programs. Using the data base management organization, modern systems separate the process of accessing data from the process of using data to produce outputs. They accomplish this using a form of system software called a data base management system.

Data Base Management Organization

This approach to structuring a data base relies on system software to manage the data. This software, a *data base management system* (DBMS), is a set of computer programs that maintain centralized control of the data base. Whenever an application program or a user wants data from the data base, it requests the data from the DBMS. The DBMS locates the data on a secondary storage device and transfers it into main storage in a form that can be used by the application. A DBMS uses on-line secondary storage devices.

By eliminating redundancy, a DBMS overcomes the deficiencies of traditional data file organization. The DBMS stores data for use by all applications, so they are not required to maintain their own data files.

Characteristics. Computer systems using data base management systems store data in ways unknown to users of the computer. When application programs request data from DBMS software, system software determines data locations on secondary storage and makes this data accessible to the applications. This

ILLUSTRATION 10–7 A Data Manipulation Language Statement

A COBOL request for data using IBM's DL/I:

CALL 'CBLTDLI' USING *call function, pcb-name,*
i-o-area, label.

where

Call function identifies what is to be done with the data record. This includes INSERT data, DELETE data, or GET NEXT data.
Pcb-name and *i-o-area* provide parameters needed by the operating system.
Label identifies the desired subschema of the data base.

illustrates one of the major advantages of the data base management approach—data independence.

Data Independence. With a DBMS, the method of storing and organizing the data is independent of the computer programs that use it. Application programs requesting data neither specify its location nor describe its structure. Rather they identify it to the DBMS using a request such as that in Illustration 10–7. This is an example of a command in a *data manipulation language* (DML). A DML consists of a small set of commands included in the procedural language of the application program. The actual structure of the data base, the location of the data, or how the fields combine to form records in the data base are irrelevant to the application program.

When changes to a system occur that require altering the format of a data item, these changes affect only application programs using this data item. A traditional file system would require changes to all programs using the entire data record. This entails many more changes.

A simple example illustrates this characteristic. With a DBMS, if management decides to add another field to a record because of a new application, no previously existing programs require changes. Naturally, the data records in the data base change, but only the DBMS software is concerned with this.

How does the DBMS achieve this data independence? It provides a different view of the data to each application program. Each view is called a subschema.

The Data Base Administrator. Organizations using a data base management system employ a data base administrator (DBA). Illustration 10–8 shows this person's major responsibilities, one of which is to identify the data items needed by each application using the data base. The DBA then specifies to the data base software a label for this set of data items. The application program uses this label when requesting the data.

The DBA also specifies to the project team developing the application a *subschema* for the data. This is a restricted view of the data, that describes how it looks when the DBMS provides it to the application program. In this way, the application program knows the size and type of the data fields it will process. The

ILLUSTRATION 10–8 Responsibilities of the Data Base Administrator

1. Define the schema, the data to be included in the data base, and the logical manner in which it will be stored.
2. Define the subschemas, the subsets of data to be made available to users and application programs.
3. Maintain the data dictionary. Assign unique data names to all data items in the data base.
4. Assign passwords and user access codes to control access to the data base.
5. Monitor usage of the data base to:
   - eliminate inefficiencies,
   - identify possible improvements,
   - uncover unauthorized access to data.
6. Educate users and publish procedures for accessing the data base.
7. Reorganize the data base when necessary.

subschema is usually different for each application. A billing system, for example, uses a different subschema from that used by an inventory system.

The data base administrator also determines a *schema* for the data base. This is a logical view of data records as they are stored by the DBMS software. The DBA communicates this to the data base software using the software's *data definition language* (DDL). Each subschema defines a subset of the data fields contained in the schema.

Illustration 10–9 shows examples of schema and subschema for a simple data base. Two applications use the customer records in it. An order entry application requires data necessary to check a customer's credit limit and send an order acknowledgment to the customer. A sales analysis application requires data to report periodically total sales by customer and by sales division. The two subschemas shown provide this data.

Using subschema, the DBMS separates the way application programs use the data base from the way it is actually structured. This greatly eases the way application programmers use the data. Most data base management systems also provide easy access to data for nonprogrammer users of the computer system. They obtain this access using a query language.

Query Languages. A query language is a nonprocedural language similar to a fourth-generation language. It is composed of high-level commands that the DBMS software interprets and executes. Managers enter commands into a terminal identifying the data they wish to see. In response, the DBMS retrieves the data from the data base and displays it at the terminal.

Query languages allow managers to access information in the data base independently of application programs. Managers see ad hoc reports showing only the data they want to see, at the time they want to see it. This kind of easy access to data is difficult to obtain with traditional data file organization.

A data base management system provides a single source for all the accounting data of a company. This eliminates the problems of data duplication and

ILLUSTRATION 10–9 Example Schema and Subschema

Schema for a Customer Record

ACCOUNT-NUMBER
CUSTOMER-NAME
CUSTOMER-ADDRESS
SALES-DIVISION
CREDIT-LIMIT
BALANCE
CREDIT-TERMS
TOT-YEARS-SALES
DATE-RECENT-SALE

Subschema for a Sales Order Entry Application

ACCOUNT-NUMBER
CUSTOMER-NAME
CUSTOMER-ADDRESS
CREDIT-LIMIT
BALANCE
CREDIT-TERMS

Subschema for a Sales Analysis Application

ACCOUNT-NUMBER
CUSTOMER-NAME
CUSTOMER-ADDRESS
SALES-DIVISION
TOT-YEARS-SALES

conflicting data in traditional file systems. To do this, DBMSs use a data dictionary.

Data Dictionary. A data dictionary is a computer file containing standardized names and formats for all data items included in the data base. It ensures that applications programmers and managers use the correct name to identify any data item required by a program or a query language inquiry. The data base administrator uses data dictionary software to keep this file up to date. Illustration 10–10 contains a data dictionary entry for a CUSTOMER-NAME data field.

ILLUSTRATION 10–10 Entry in a Data Dictionary

Description	*Entry*
Data name	CUSTOMER-NAME
Meaning of data name	Customer name
Format	25 alphanumeric characters
Date originated	10–13–19XX
Programs in which the data names are used	ORDER-ENTRY, SALES-ANALYSIS

In Illustration 10–10, CUSTOMER-NAME is a 25-character alphanumeric data field containing the name of a customer. Two programs, ORDER-ENTRY and SALES-ANALYSIS, use this data field. Because the data dictionary identifies all programs using each data item, the data base administrator knows immediately which programs must be changed if the format of the data field changes. This simplifies making changes to systems when the schema of the data base changes.

Because data base management software always requires the use of a data dictionary, it includes the software to maintain the dictionary. However, use of a data dictionary eliminates conflicting data names and formats in a traditional file system as well. For this reason, many companies implement a data dictionary in that environment also.

Logical Data Structures. Data base management systems separate the way users view the data from the way the data is actually stored on the device. In addition, they distinguish between its physical arrangement and its logical arrangement.

The *physical* arrangement of data, which describes how data are recorded on the device, is determined by data management software. The *logical* arrangement, called the data structure, describes how the DBMS searches through the data base to identify and retrieve a desired record. Different DBMS packages use different data structures; the choice is important because each has its strengths and weaknesses. Three data structures common among accounting systems are tree, network, and relational.

Tree. The first widely adopted DBMS packages utilized a tree structure, also called a hierarchical data structure. With this approach, the data base consists of a set of "trees," each of which is a collection of data records associated in some way. A record in the tree can be located only through a single record, the "root" of the tree. A user must specify the key field of the root to locate any information in the tree.

For example, an individual customer's record may be the root of a tree consisting of several other records representing past sales to the customer, invoices outstanding with the customer, and products purchased by the customer. To find out if the customer has paid a specific invoice, you give the DBMS the customer account number and the invoice number. The DBMS locates the root (with the customer number) and then searches the tree for the record containing the invoice number you specified.

Tree structures are popular because they execute rapidly in transaction-processing applications. However, because data is only accessible through the root, trees are less flexible than other structures in the reports they produce. They are inefficient for producing ad hoc reports.

Network. Software companies developed network structured packages to overcome the inflexibility of the tree structure. The data base consists of sets of related data similar to trees. In the network structure, however, each set of data has multiple entry points. So the network structure is similar to a tree structure with multiple roots.

For example, a data set may have two entry points: the customer record, discussed earlier, and the salesperson record. Users can find out the amount of a specific invoice if they know either the customer number or the number of the salesperson making the sale.

Network structures make it easier to develop ad hoc reports because they are much more flexible than hierarchical ones. However, they are more difficult to create and they execute more slowly in transaction-processing applications.

Relational. A DBMS using the relational data structure views the data as if they were organized in tables. Each table contains a set of identically structured rows.

It is easiest to view a relational data base as if it were equivalent to a file. One row in the table contains all the data in the record of a file, and a column in the table shows the same data field for all records. However, with a relational DBMS these records may not actually exist; this is just the human way of viewing the data. The DBMS software determines how the data are actually stored on the secondary storage device.

You may wonder why a relational DBMS is better than a file system if a file is equivalent to a table. A relational DBMS is better because it allows operations on the data that cannot be performed either in a traditional file system or using another kind of DBMS. With either approach to organizing data, users can identify specific records in a file (e.g., by customer and invoice number) and look at specific fields (such as an amount) within these records. However, with a relational DBMS, users can also (with one command) combine two or more tables. This creates a new table containing only those data fields they want to see. In a traditional data file system, this is equivalent to creating a totally new file—a complex and time-consuming operation. You can learn more about relational operations in the chapter on data base management systems.

Relational DBMSs are much more flexible than traditional file systems or tree and network-structured DBMSs. They make it easier for managers to produce ad hoc reports that are virtually impossible with other methods of data organization. They are less efficient, however, in many transaction-processing applications. File-oriented, tree, and network systems process transactions in large quantities more quickly because the DBA structures them specifically for that purpose.

A data base management system is a software package that separates managers, clerks, and applications programs from the actual physical structure of the data base. These users always access data by requesting it from the DBMS. In this way, a DBMS avoids the problems of storage inefficiency and conflicting data inherent in a traditional file system. It also lessens the difficulty of change that accompanies integrated systems.

Illustration 10–11 shows graphically the function of a data base management system. The DBMS software provides an interface between the DBA, human

ILLUSTRATION 10–11 Function of a Data Base Management System

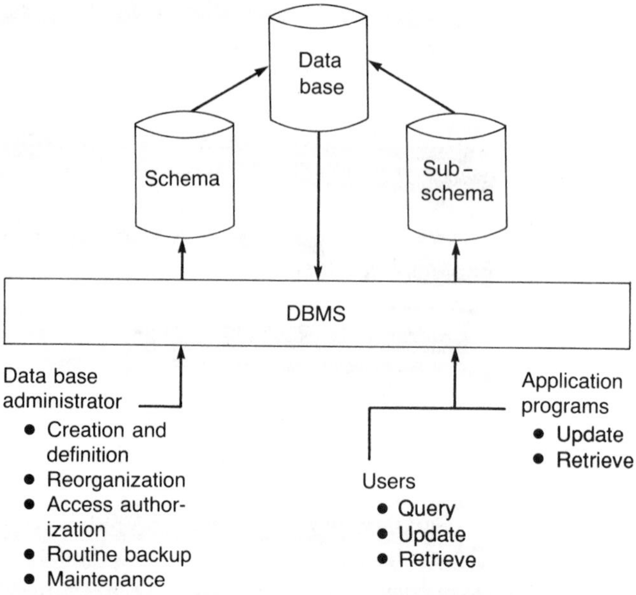

users, application programs, and the data base. Application programs may update or retrieve data. In addition, managers may use the query language to produce ad hoc reports. When users and applications programs access data, they do so using the subschema. When the DBA defines the data in the data base, the DBA creates the schema. The DBMS provides users and applications programs with data from the data base.

You have learned two approaches to organizing the data in an accounting system. When an organization uses traditional data file organization, its applications process sequential files, direct access files, or indexed sequential files. When the organization uses a data base management system, users and applications are unconcerned with how the data are physically stored. The choice of an approach affects the method they use in processing the data.

APPROACHES TO DATA PROCESSING

There are four approaches to processing the data stored in an accounting system. Although some approaches use older forms of technology, many companies still use them for certain applications. Most organizations have accounting systems using all of them. The four approaches to data processing are manual systems, batch systems, batch systems with on-line inquiry, and on-line real-time systems.

ILLUSTRATION 10–12 A Manual System

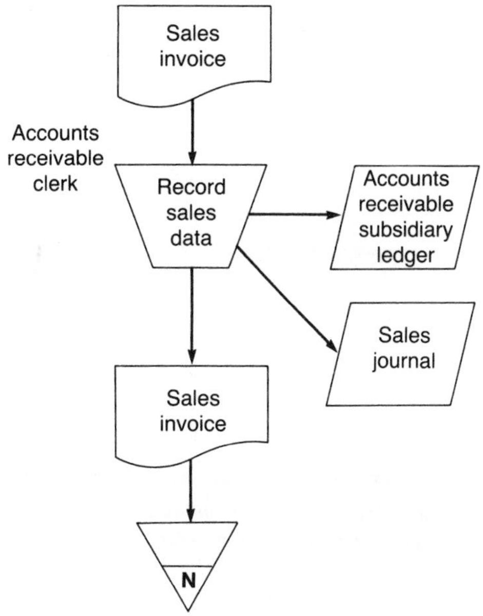

Manual Systems

Manual systems do not use a computer in processing the accounting data base. Several decades ago all systems were manual ones; today, most accounting systems are a combination of manual and computerized processes.

Humans execute the processes performed in manual systems. In large manual systems of the 1930s and 1940s, hundreds of clerks recorded transactions on documents, transferred documents between departments, and recorded these transactions in human readable journals and ledgers. Mechanical punch-card processing equipment sometimes aided in this process. Accountants stored these documents, punch cards, and accounting records sequentially in filing cabinets and books.

Today companies sometimes process transactions manually using *one-write systems*. A one-write system uses a pegboard with specially printed documents, pages, and ledger cards treated with a layer of black ink on one side. When a clerk records a transaction on a document by hand, the layer of ink transfers the information onto other pages or cards aligned behind it on the pegboard. The clerk writes the information only once, rather than copying it several times onto each document.

Illustration 10–12 shows how a one-write system records a sales transaction. The accounts receivable clerk receives a copy of an invoice. The clerk aligns a sales journal page (with a layer of ink on its back) above the customer's ledger card from the accounts receivable subsidiary ledger. In this way the clerk simultaneously records the data in both the sales journal and the accounts receivable subsidiary ledger.

Batch Sequential Processing Systems

The earliest computer-based systems used batch processing methods. Early systems relied on punched-card data entry; this approach was an efficient way to control the keypunch process. After companies quit using punched cards, they recorded transactions directly in magnetic form with on-line data entry. However, because of its efficiency, many companies continued to use the batch processing computer programs they had developed. Many still use the approach for accounting transaction processing. For example, there is little reason to process a payroll application any other way.

With a batch sequential processing application, clerks write down the data necessary for recording accounting transactions. They then accumulate data in batches of, for example, 50 documents per batch and deliver these batches to data entry clerks who convert them into computer-readable form. With older punched-card systems, each batch of documents resulted in a deck of computer cards. In modern systems with on-line data entry, each batch becomes a computer transaction file. After data entry, computer programs process the transactions an entire batch at a time. Data control clerks in the MIS department monitor this processing to ensure that each batch stays intact. No transactions should be lost or be added to any batch.

Illustration 10–13 contains a flowchart of a typical application. It shows how the manual accounts receivable process of the previous illustration might be performed using batch processing. This system consists of four computer programs. The *validation* program examines each transaction in a batch for obvious recording or data conversion errors. It also verifies that the total of the debit entries equals the total of the credit entries in the batch. (Sometimes these programs are called *edit* programs.) The *sort* program, normally a utility program, resequences the batch of transactions into ascending customer number order. The *print* program produces a list of the transactions called the sales journal. And finally, the *update* program posts each sales transaction to the computer file containing the accounts receivable subsidiary ledger.

Batch sequential processing systems are conceptually simple, and it is relatively easy to convert to this form of processing from a manual system. Although Illustration 10–13 shows that all computer files are on magnetic tape, this is seldom the case. Most files in batch sequential systems are recorded in on-line devices.

Batch sequential processing systems also have disadvantages. First, the information they produce may not be current. Usually transactions are gathered into batches for a day, a week, or a month at a time. The system then posts many

ILLUSTRATION 10–13 A Batch Processing System Using Sequential Files

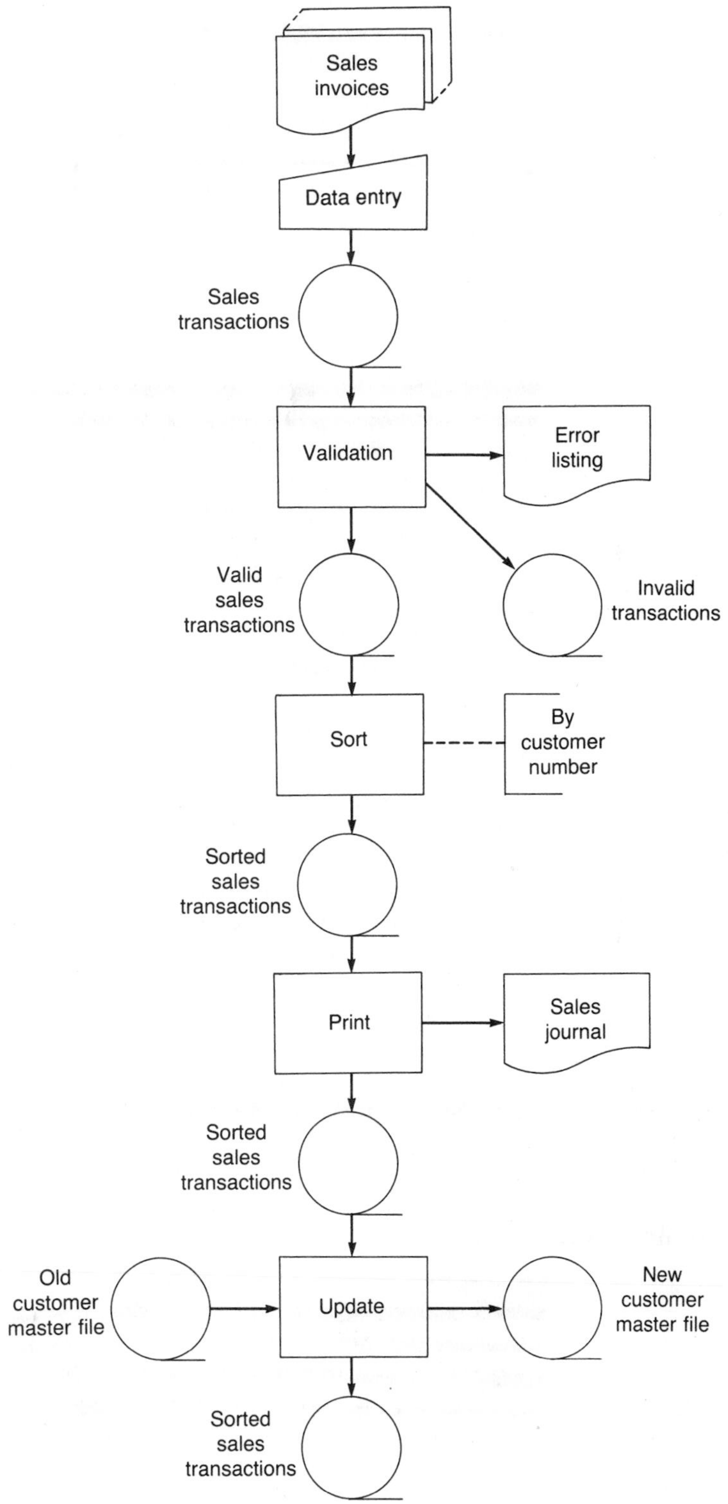

batches at once, either daily, weekly, or monthly. This means that the contents of a computerized data file are usually out of date in a batch system. Contents are current only when no transactions have occurred after the last execution of the update program. Second, batch sequential systems are inflexible. They are unable to produce ad hoc reports, or provide information in any form other than that coded into the system's print programs. Other processing methods overcome these disadvantages.

Batch Systems with On-Line Inquiry

When many companies replaced magnetic tape files with on-line devices in batch processing systems, they made significant improvements in them without replacing the systems. They did this by providing on-line inquiry capability.

This capability means that a user at a terminal can retrieve data from an accounting data file located in an on-line device. For example, a sales clerk may want to know if a customer has exceeded a credit limit. In a system with on-line inquiry, the clerk accesses the computerized accounts receivable subsidiary ledger using a query program to find the customer's balance. The clerk then decides whether or not to sell on credit to the customer. If the sale is made, the system posts the transaction to the computerized ledger using batch processing procedures.

Illustration 10–14 contains a batch processing system with on-line inquiry. It shows how the accounts receivable system in the previous illustration could provide ad hoc information for credit granting purposes. In systems of this kind, all data files are on-line.

Batch systems with on-line inquiry are popular in accounting applications using *indexed sequential* files. They achieve the efficiencies of batch sequential processing but are more flexible in how they produce their outputs. In a batch sequential system, a sales clerk wanting to check a customer's credit limit must consult a computer printed report. With on-line inquiry, this information is available at a terminal.

However, in each of these systems the information may not be current. This is because the data in the file was updated at the last posting, and this may be yesterday, last week, or last month. On-line real-time systems overcome this disadvantage.

On-Line Real-Time Systems

When it is important that clerks and managers have access to data that is current, companies implement on-line real-time systems. A batch system applies a single processing step, such as validate, sort, print, or update, to an entire batch of transactions before proceeding to the next step. An on-line real-time system applies all processes to a single transaction before proceeding to the next

ILLUSTRATION 10–14 A Batch System with On-Line Inquiry Using Indexed Sequential Files

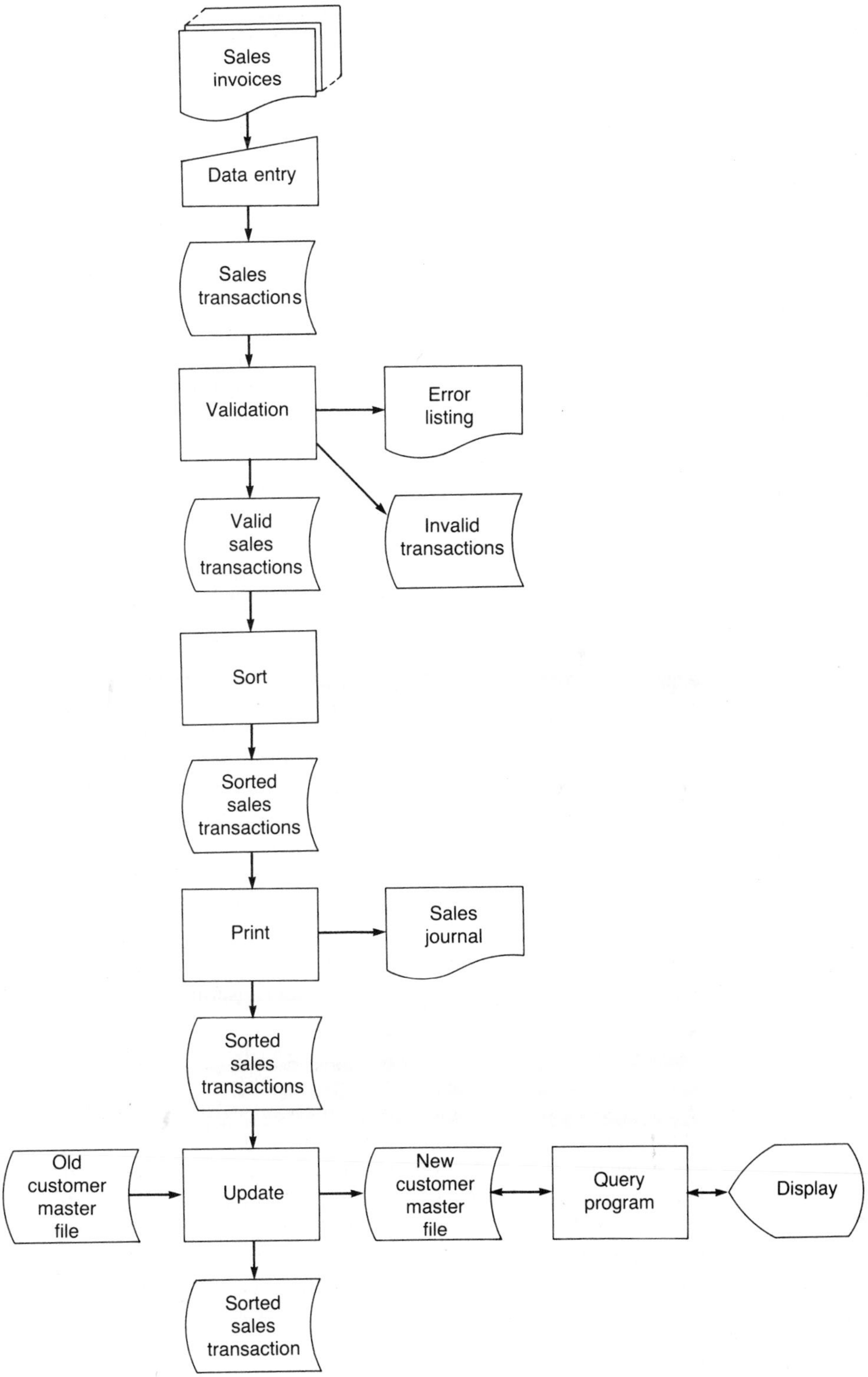

ILLUSTRATION 10–15 An On-Line Real-Time System Using Direct Access Files

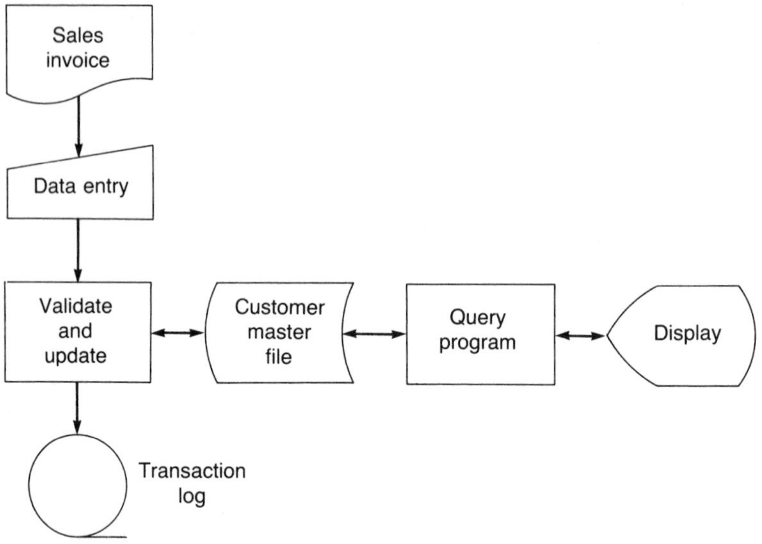

transaction. This means that the results of processing are immediately available to the clerk or manager entering the data into the system.

On-line systems are invaluable for management purposes such as recording airline reservations. Many companies use them in accounting systems as well. An on-line accounts receivable system allows a sales clerk to determine a customer's current balance; an on-line inventory system allows the same clerk to determine if the product requested by the customer is currently in stock.

Illustration 10–15 shows an on-line real-time accounts receivable system. A single program validates and updates each transaction as it is entered. This program also guides the user in entering the data. It may prompt the user with questions, provide a menu, or display on the terminal a replica of the source document. Because the CPU interacts with the user in one of these ways, this is an example of an *interactive system.*

On-line real-time systems frequently provide no printed record of transactions. For this reason they make magnetic records of them on a *transaction log.* This allows reconstruction of the computer file containing the receivables records should the file accidentally be erased or destroyed.

On-line real-time systems provide current data because the results of processing are immediately available. They are frequently used with data base management systems so users can easily produce ad hoc reports from the data base. They are more complex to develop and maintain than the other approaches, however, and more expensive to implement. They use direct access files that are frequently less efficient for processing accounting transactions. Because they have no visible audit trail, an erroneous transaction entered into an on-line real-time system may create incorrect account balances that are difficult to detect and correct.

SUMMARY

In this chapter you have learned how accounting data are stored and processed in computer-based systems. As humans, we think of data as consisting of characters, fields, records, files, and the data base. Some accounting systems do not use files; instead they use a data base management system to store and locate data records. You have learned some advantages and disadvantages of each approach.

There are four approaches to processing the data base. Many accounting systems contain elements of all four. They are manual systems, batch sequential processing systems, batch systems with on-line inquiry, and on-line real-time systems. You have learned how each works, and which advantages each provides.

KEY TERMS

batch sequential processing system An approach to processing accounting data. Transactions are accumulated in batches and a processing step is completed on the entire batch before beginning another processing step.

batch system with on-line inquiry An approach to processing accounting data. Transactions are accumulated in batches when changes are made to the data base. However, the data in individual data records can be read one at a time.

data base management organization An approach to organizing data in which a set of computer programs, called a data base management system, maintains data for all applications.

direct access An approach to organizing traditional data files. Data management software computes from the key field of a record the storage location for it on a secondary storage device.

indexed sequential An approach to organizing traditional data files. The records are physically located in sequence by key field. An index shows the locations on secondary storage of some of the records in the file.

logical data structure A logical view of how data is organized by a data base management system. It describes how the software searches through a data base to locate a data item.

on-line real-time system An approach to processing accounting data. All processes are applied to one transaction before proceeding to the next transaction.

query language A nonprocedural language that enables accountants and managers to retrieve easily data that are stored by a data base management system.

schema A logical view of data records as they are stored by a data base management system.

sequential An approach to organizing traditional data files in which records are physically arranged in sequence by primary key field.

subschema A restricted view of data records maintained by a data base management system. Each application program has its own subschema.

traditional data file organization An approach to organizing data in which application software maintain data files independent of those maintained by other applications.

QUESTIONS

10–1. Why did computer manufacturers develop ways to encode numbers, letters, and punctuation marks in binary form?

10–2. How are accounting data stored in a computer from the viewpoint of the computer? Of the human user?

10–3. What is the difference between a logical record and a physical record?

10–4. What is the difference between a primary key and a generic key?

10–5. A customer master file contains one record for each customer. A field in the record shows the amount that the customer owes. How does a computer program locate the amount owed by customer number 43056 if the file is:

a. Sequential?
b. Direct access?
c. Indexed sequential?

10–6. What are the deficiencies of the traditional data file organization? Which is the least serious? Which is the most serious? How does a data base management organization overcome them?

10–7. What is a data base management system?

10–8. How does a subschema differ from a schema?

10–9. What do each of the following have in common? How do they differ?

a. Data definition language
b. Data manipulation language
c. Query language

10–10. Describe the purpose of a data dictionary.

10–11. A data base consists of a set of related records. What is the difference between the physical arrangement of those records and their logical arrangement?

10–12. For which reporting situations is each of the following data structures best suited?
a. Tree
b. Network
c. Relational

10–13. What is a one-write system? When would one be most useful?

10–14. A batch processing system is so named because it processes transactions in batches. Which forms can these batches of transactions take?

10–15. How do batch processing systems that provide on-line inquiry differ from those that do not?

10–16. What distinguishes an on-line real-time system?

10–17. In which system do you find a transaction log? What does it look like? What is its purpose?

EXERCISES AND CASES

10–18. PROCESSING METHODS

For each of the following application systems, suggest which kind of processing method is best.

a. Airline reservations
b. Sales order entry
c. Cash disbursements
d. Inventory
e. Cash receipts

10–19. PROCESSING METHODS

Why do you think that most payroll applications use batch processing?

10–20. DATA STORAGE

Following are seven components of data as they are stored in a computer. For each component, identify the other component(s) of which it is a part.

a. Record
b. Data base
c. Field
d. Word
e. Bit
f. Byte
g. File

EXHIBIT 10–1 Exercises 10–21 and 10–22

Record Type 1: Master File Vendor Name record

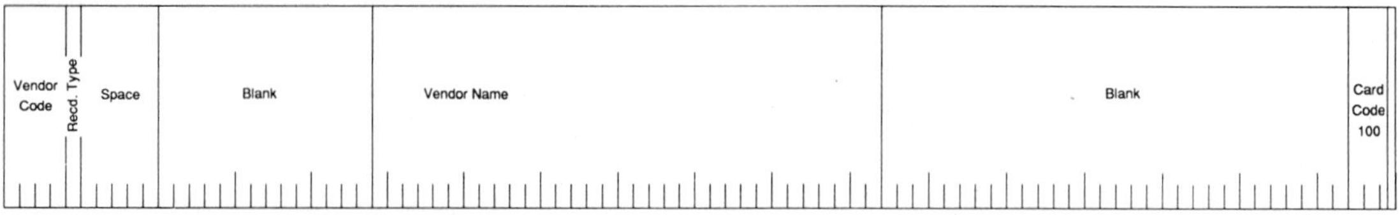

Record Type 2: Master File Vendor Address record

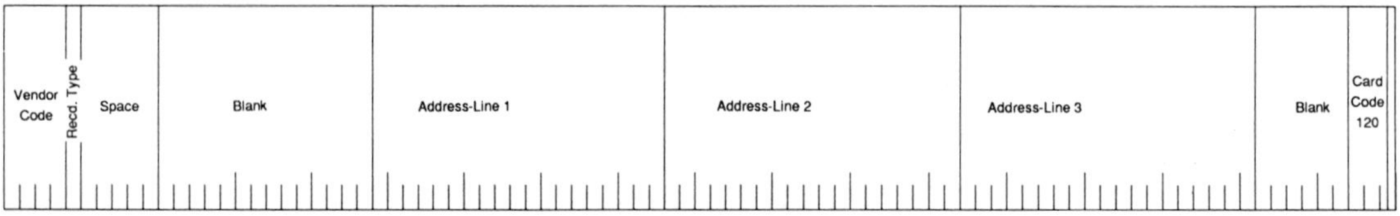

Record Type 3: Transaction File Expense Detail record

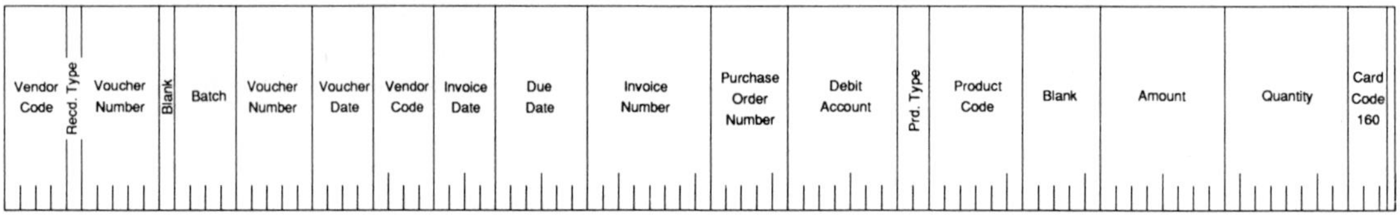

10–21. *DATA STORAGE*

Exhibit 10–1 contains three different record layouts. After examining them, answer each of the following questions.

a. How many characters are in the VENDOR NAME field?
b. What is the primary key of record type 3, the transaction file expense detail record?
c. What is the primary key of record type 2, the master file vendor address record?
d. Identify one generic key in this system.
e. How many digits are in a purchase order number?
f. What is the largest quantity that this system can process? The largest amount?

10–22. *SHARED DATA ITEMS*

The records in Exhibit 10–1 are from an accounts payable application. Identify four data items in these records that would be used in other applications. For each, suggest an application that would use it.

10–23. *STORAGE AND PROCESSING METHODS*

A sales analysis application can be valuable for decision makers in a marketing department. Such a system generates reports allowing a sales manager to analyze the results of sales promotions, evaluate salepersons' performance, and identify successful products or important customers.

Often, data for sales analysis reports come from the billing system in an organization. This system uses an invoice transaction file that includes as a minimum the following fields: customer number, sales division code, shipment date, customer purchase order number, product number, quantity shipped, and unit price.

Required:

a. Of the four methods of processing, which would be most appropriate for a sales analysis application?

b. Assume that you are designing a sales analysis system using the traditional data file approach. Which routine reports would you want this system to provide?

c. Assume that you are a divisional sales manager and that the system uses the data base management approach. Which ad hoc reports would you want to produce using a query language?

10–24. *DATA BASE MANAGEMENT SYSTEMS*

Progress in the design and development of computer-based management information systems has been impressive. Traditionally, computer-based data processing systems were arranged by departments and applications. Computers were applied to single, large-volume applications such as inventory control or customer billing. Other applications were added once the first applications were operating smoothly.

As more applications were added, problems in data management developed. Businesses looked for ways to integrate the data processing systems to make them more comprehensive and to have shorter response times. As a consequence, the data base systems composed of the data base itself, the data base management system, and the individual application programs were developed.

Required:

a. Explain the differences between the traditional approach to data processing and the use of data base management systems in:
   1. File structure
   2. Processing of data

b. Identify and discuss the unfavorable issues which a company should consider before implementing a data base management system.

10–25. *STORAGE AND PROCESSING METHODS*

The controller of Kensler Company has been working with the MIS department to revise part of the company's financial reporting system. A study is underway on how to develop and implement a data entry and data retention system for key computer files used by various departments responsible to the controller. The departments involved and details on their data processing activities are as follows:

General Accounting

- Daily processing of journal entries submitted by various departments.
- Weekly updating of file balances with subsystem data from areas such as payroll, accounts receivable, and accounts payable.
- Sporadic requests for account balances during the month with increased activity at month-end.

Accounts Receivable

- Daily processing of receipts for payments on account.
- Daily processing of sales to customers.
- Daily checks to be sure that the maximum credit limit of $200,000 per customer is not exceeded and to identify orders in excess of $20,000 per customer.
- Daily requests for customer credit status regarding payments and account balances.
- Weekly reporting to general accounting file.

Accounts Payable

- Processing of payments to vendors three times a week.
- Weekly expense distribution reporting to general accounting file.

Budget Planning and Control

- Updating of flexible budgets on a monthly basis.
- Quarterly rebudgeting based on sales forecast and production schedule changes.
- Monthly inquiry requests for budget balances.

The MIS manager has explained the concepts of the following processing techniques to the controller's staff and the appropriate members of the affected departments:

Batch processing.
On-line real-time processing.
Batch processing with on-line inquiry.

The MIS manager has indicated to the controller that batch processing is the least expensive processing technique and that a rough estimate of the cost of the other techniques would be as follows:

Technique	*Cost in Relation to Batch Processing*
On-line real-time processing	2.5 times
Batch with on-line inquiry	1.5 times

Required:

a. Define and discuss the major differences between the input options of the following processing techniques:
1. Batch processing
2. Batch processing with on-line inquiry
3. On-line real-time processing

b. Identify and explain the input technique and the file inquiry that probably should be employed by Kensler Company for each of the four departments responsible to the controller. Assume that the volume of transactions is not a key variable in these decisions.
1. General accounting
2. Accounts receivable
3. Accounts payable
4. Budget planning and control

(CMA Adapted)

10–26. ***PROCESSING METHODS***

Weekender Corporation owns and operates 15 large departmentalized retail hardware stores in major metropolitan areas of the southwest United States. The stores carry a wide variety of merchandise but their major thrust is toward the weekend do-it-yourselfer. The company has been successful in this field, and the number of stores in the chain has almost doubled in the past 10 years.

Each retail store acquires its merchandise from the company's centrally located warehouse. Consequently, the warehouse must maintain an up-to-date and well-stocked inventory ready to meet the demands of the individual stores.

The company wishes to hold its competitive position with similar stores of other companies in its marketing area. Therefore, Weekender Corporation must improve its purchasing and inventory procedures. The company's stores must have the proper goods to meet customer demand, and the warehouse in turn must have the goods available. The number of company stores, the number of inventory items carried, and the volume of business all are providing pressure to change from basically manual data processing routines to mechanized data processing procedures. Recently, the company has been investigating two different approaches to computerization, batch processing and real-time processing. No decision has been reached on the approach to be followed.

Top management has determined that the following items should have high priority in the new system procedures:

1. Rapid ordering to replenish warehouse inventory stocks with as little delay as possible.
2. Quick filling and shipping of merchandise to the stores (this involves determining if sufficient stock exists).
3. Some indication of inventory activity.
4. Perpetual records to determine quickly inventory level by item number.

A description of the current warehousing and purchasing procedures follows:

Warehouse Procedures

Stock is stored in bins and located by an inventory number. The numbers are listed sequentially on the bins to facilitate locating items for shipment; frequently this system is not followed, and, as a result, some items are difficult to locate.

Whenever a retail store needs merchandise, it completes a three-part merchandise request form. One copy is kept by the store and two copies are mailed to the warehouse the next day. If the merchandise requested is on hand, the goods are delivered to the store accompanied by the third copy of the request. The second copy is filed at the warehouse.

If the quantity of goods on hand is not sufficient to fill the order, the warehouse sends the quantity available and notes the quantity shipped on the request form. Then a purchase memorandum for the shortage is prepared by the warehouse. At the end of each day, all three memos are sent to the purchasing department.

When ordered goods are received, they are checked at the receiving area, and a receiving report is prepared. One copy of the receiving report is retained at the receiving area, one is forwarded to accounts payable, and one is filed at the warehouse with the purchase memorandum.

Purchasing Department Procedures

When the purchase memoranda are received from the warehouse, purchase orders are prepared. Vendor catalogs are used to select the best source for the requested goods, and the purchase order is prepared and mailed. Copies of the order are sent to accounts payable and the receiving area; one copy is retained in the purchasing department.

When the receiving report arrives in the purchasing department, it is compared with the purchase order on file. The receiving report is also checked with the invoice before forwarding the invoice to accounts payable for payment.

The purchasing department strives periodically to evaluate the vendors for financial soundness, reliability, and trade relationships. However, because the volume of requests received from the warehouse is so great, currently this activity does not have a high priority.

Each week a report of the open purchase orders is prepared to determine if any action should be taken on overdue deliveries. This report is prepared manually from scanning the file of outstanding purchase orders.

Required:

a. Of the possible methods of processing, which one would best meet the needs of Weekender?

b. To implement the system you recommend in your answer to part *a,* which computer hardware must Weekender acquire?

(CMA Adapted)

Chapter 11

File Processing Methods

Learning Objectives:

1. To understand how accounting data files are processed when using the traditional data file approach.
2. To recognize the types of files used in accounting information systems.
3. To identify the operations that accounting information systems use when processing files.
4. To discover how batch processing systems use sequential files.
5. To find out how batch systems with on-line inquiry use indexed sequential files.
6. To learn how on-line real-time systems use direct access files.

INTRODUCTION

Organizations use two approaches when organizing the data in their data bases: the traditional data file approach and the data base management approach. In this chapter you will learn more about traditional data file organization. The chapter discusses the different forms that files can take, and explains the three methods used for organizing data files. You will learn how these methods work and the advantages and disadvantages of each.

TYPES OF FILES

A *file* is a collection of information stored so that it can be retrieved for later use. Computer-based accounting systems use files in many forms. Most accounting records are contained in one type of file, the data file. However, other forms are employed as a system processes data files. Before understanding how systems retrieve information from data files, you should know about the file types. All files are classified by the technology used and by their content.

Classifying Files by Technology

When classified by technology, files are either manual files or computer files. A *manual* file stores information that can be retrieved, read, and used by people. A *computer* file stores information for retrieval by the systems software of the computer. It cannot be read by humans without additional computer processing.

Manual Files. Companies have used manual files for hundreds of years. The procedures for manual files have much in common with those used in computerized files. Reviewing some examples of manual files makes it easier to understand how the computer processes its files.

Manual Storage Devices. Most manual files in accounting systems use filing cabinets as the storage device. Clerks frequently combine similar documents in file folders within the cabinets. A label on the outside of each cabinet drawer identifies the file folders in that drawer. Within a filing cabinet, a clerk may sequence folders alphabetically, such as by customer name, or numerically by invoice number. Documents within a file folder may also follow alphabetical, date, or numerical sequence.

Other storage devices used for manual files include a box to hold a card file or a bound volume containing a ledger or journal. For example, a perpetual inventory system may be kept in a card file with one card for each item in inventory. The inventory clerk files cards either alphabetically by description or numerically by item number. Early accounting systems used bound ledgers. One page in the ledger summarized transactions for one account. The bookkeeper creating the ledger sequenced the pages alphabetically by account name within the volume.

Manual Storage and Retrieval. Regardless of the storage device, these manual systems use the same method of arranging the records they contain. Each system arranges the records sequentially by some key field. The key field is the customer name, invoice number, item description, item number, or account name used in determining the filing sequence. These manual systems, then, are all examples of *sequential* files.

ILLUSTRATION 11–1 Record Storage and Retrieval in Manual Systems

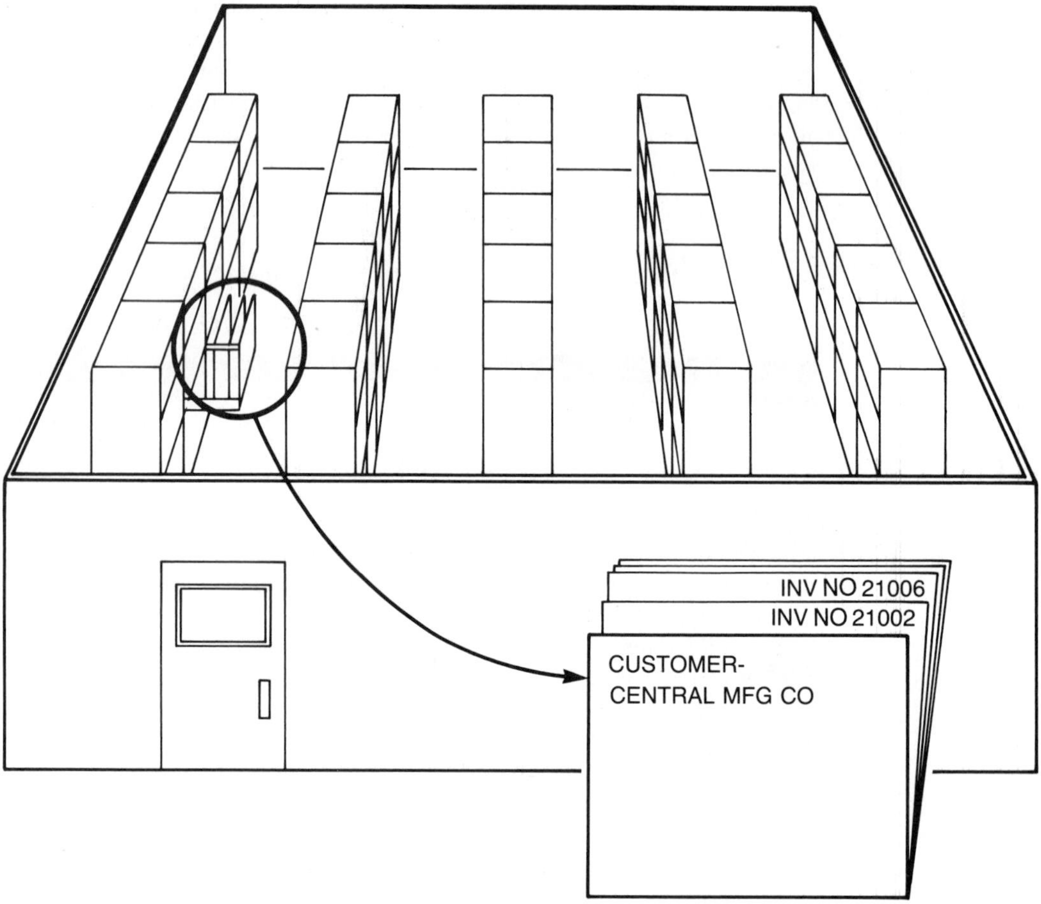

How do clerks retrieve information from files in a manual system? Different clerks do this different ways, even when working with the same system. An inexperienced clerk may start with the first filing cabinet and look in sequence at the label on each file drawer until finding the desired one. An experienced clerk, knowing that the customers whose names begin with the letter *C* start in the second drawer of the second cabinet, would begin a sequential search there. A large file room may have a map posted at its door showing the locations of various files within the room. Illustration 11–1 shows how information storage and retrieval may occur in such a manual system.

Manual systems are flexible in how a user retrieves information from them. Different clerks may use various methods, and their preferences may change as the amount of data grows. In this case, the method of information retrieval may change without changing the system's method of storage.

Computer systems do not have this advantage. The system design team determines the method of information retrieval for a computer file when the system is created. Changes to this method require changes to the system itself.

Computer Files. Most modern accounting systems use both manual and computer files. Although each uses different recording techniques, they share similar methods for organizing data.

Computer Storage Devices. The most common storage devices for computer files are magnetic disks, magnetic tapes, and floppy disks (or diskettes). Peripheral devices magnetically encode characters, fields, and records on these devices. Data management software places records on the device at locations it can identify. When a computer program requires a specific record, the software determines the location of the record on the device and retrieves the record for the program.

Computer Storage and Retrieval. Just as a file room contains a fixed number of filing cabinet drawers, a magnetic storage device contains a fixed number of storage locations. On a diskette, for example, locations exist for each combination of a sector and a track. A *sector* is a segment of the disk radiating outward from its center at a specified angle from a reference point on the diskette. A *track* is an imaginary ring at a constant radius from the center. Data management software assigns to each sector-track combination an *address* that uniquely identifies it. Illustration 11–2 shows how a sector and a track identifies an addressable location on a diskette. Other direct access storage devices work similarly.

Each direct access storage device also contains a *directory* written magnetically on it. This directory is equivalent to the file room map in Illustration 11–1, because it guides the data management software to the locations of specific data on the device. For example, a diskette contains a directory track about halfway outward from its center. Whenever a user saves a new file on the diskette, data management software records the name of the file and the location of its first data record (along with other information) on this directory track.

A magnetic tape lacks addressable locations on its recording surface. For this reason, data management software always stores and retrieves records sequentially when using this device. A *header record* precedes the first data in the file and marks the beginning of the file; a *trailer record* after the last data marks its end. To locate a specific record in a tape file, a computer program first locates the header record for the file. It then reads each data record until it finds the desired one. This is similar to the way a clerk locates a specific invoice copy in a file folder of invoices. Illustration 11–3 shows how data are stored and retrieved using magnetic tape.

Now that you know how records are stored in both manual and computer files, you should not be surprised that similar methods are used. After all, when accountants first began to use computers, they did so by simply converting

ILLUSTRATION 11–2 Record Storage and Retrieval on Direct Access Devices

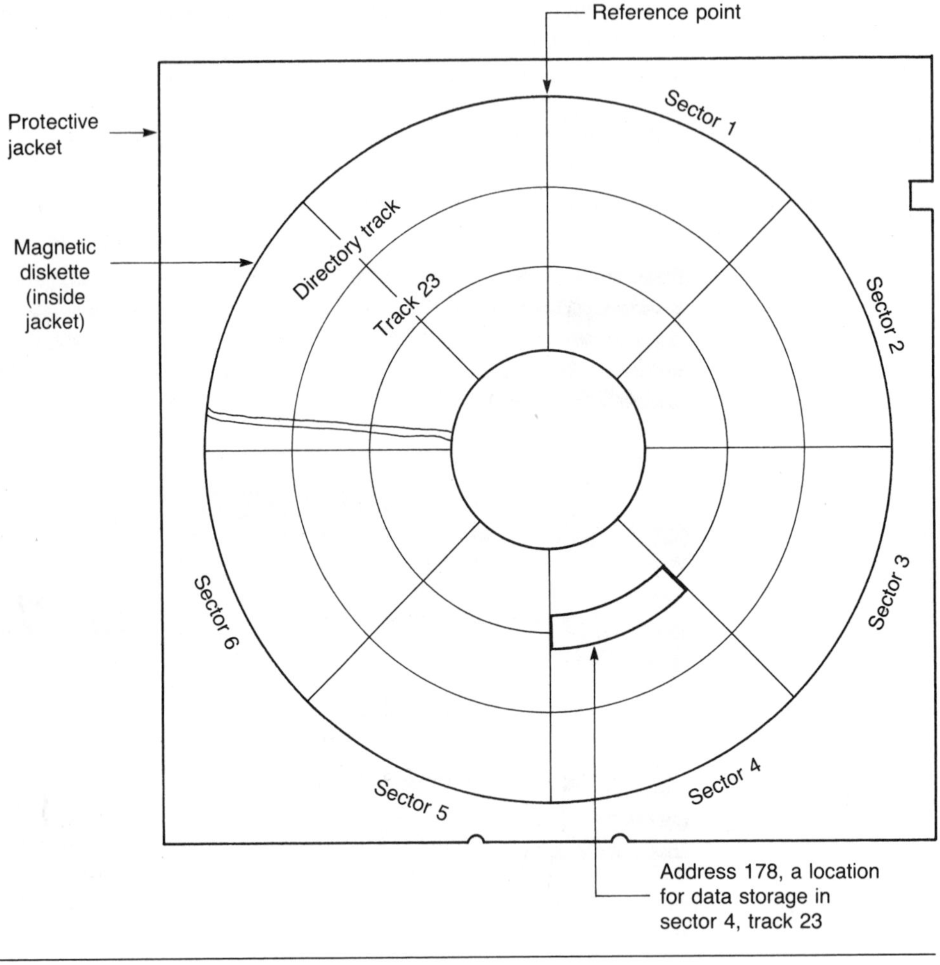

ILLUSTRATION 11–3 Data Storage and Retrieval on Magnetic Tape

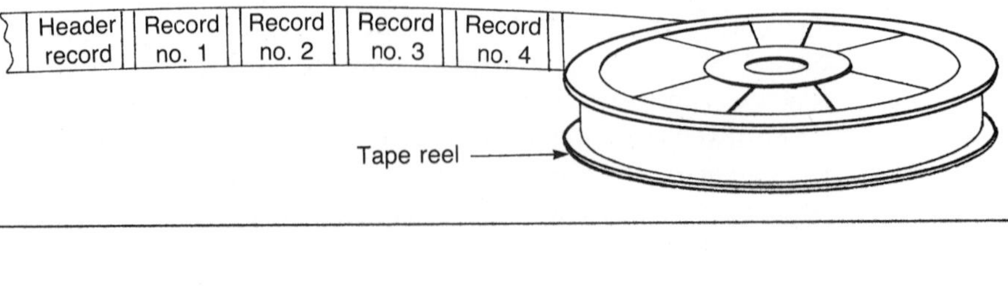

ILLUSTRATION 11–4 Accounting Data Files

Master file. Contains relatively permanent records that are added and deleted infrequently during file maintenance; balance data are changed during file update.

Transaction file. Records are removed from the file after posting; balance data change a master record during file update.

Backup file. A duplicate copy of another file that enables recreating the original file if lost or destroyed.

Archive file. A file kept for many years as a record for historical or reference purposes.

Scratch file. A file used temporarily by computer programs.

existing methods to a new recording medium. Later in this chapter you will study similarities in file processing, but first you should learn how to classify files by their content.

Classifying Files by Content

All files used in a computer system are either program files or data files. The operating system deals with each type of file in a different way.

A *program file*'s records contain instructions that are executable by the computer. Program files include not only application programs but also system programs such as utilities. Most program files seldom change during the routine operation of an accounting system.

A *data file* contains records that are nonexecutable. These records are used for some purpose by program files and may be changed many times during the operation of a system. Data files include text files used by word processing software, index files used by data management software, and parameter files used by many kinds of system software. However, the data files of most concern to accountants are those containing accounting data. The five types of accounting data files are master, transaction, backup, archive, and scratch files. Illustration 11–4 summarizes these types of files.

Master Files. All accounting systems use master files. A master file is the computer-readable equivalent of a ledger in a manual system. Each record in a master file typically contains a collection of data fields relating to a specific account. Although contents of these fields may change, the records are added or deleted from the file infrequently. Master file records consist of data fields containing both reference and balance data.

For example, a general ledger master file contains one record for each account in the chart of accounts. *Reference data* in a record include those fields that seldom change, such as account numbers and account titles. Each record also contains *balance data,* the amounts or quantities that change each time a

ILLUSTRATION 11–5 Reference and Balance Data in Master Files

Example	*Reference Data*	*Balance Data*
General ledger master file	Account number Account description	Account balance
Inventory master file	Item number Item description Reorder point Order quantity	Quantity on hand Quantity on order
Customer master file	Customer number Name and address Credit limit	Balance owed
Vendor master file	Vendor number Name and address Discount policy	Year-to-date purchases
Payroll master file	Employee number Name and address Personal data Deductions code Withholding code	Year-to-date earnings and withholdings amounts

transaction is posted to the account. Other common master files include the inventory master file, containing one record for each item maintained in inventory, and the customer master file, with one record for each approved customer. Illustration 11–5 shows typical reference and balance data for these and some other master files.

Transaction Files. Batch processing systems use transaction files. In these systems, clerks accumulate source documents—each representing one accounting transaction of a certain type—into batches prior to processing. Data entry clerks then convert each document into computer-readable form, producing a transaction file. The file thus contains one record for each transaction. The system applies each processing step to all transactions in the transaction file before proceeding to the next step. One process in many systems is posting the transactions in the transaction file to a master file.

For example, a computerized payroll system collects employees' timecards prior to payday on Friday. A payroll clerk sorts these cards into batches, one for each department. The clerk then enters the data from the timecards at a terminal, creating a file of payroll transactions. This file contains one record for each employee for whom a weekly paycheck is due. The system applies each processing step first to all the transaction records in a batch, and then to all batches in the transaction file, before proceeding to the next step. During a posting step, the system adds the gross pay for each employee to the year-to-date earnings field in that employee's payroll master file record.

ILLUSTRATION 11–6 Data in Typical Transaction File Records

Example	*Data Field*	*Type*
Journal voucher transaction file	Account number	Reference
	Date	Reference
	Debit or credit code	Reference
	Description	Reference
	Amount	Balance
	Source number	Reference
Payroll transaction file	Employee number	Reference
	Regular hours	Balance
	Overtime hours	Balance
	Vacation time	Balance
	Sick time	Balance
Sales order transaction file	Customer number	Reference
	Salesperson number	Reference
	Purchase order number	Reference
	Item number	Reference
	Quantity	Balance
	Price	Reference

A transaction record contains both reference and balance data. At a minimum, each record contains two fields: the primary key field identifying the master record affected by the transaction and an amount or quantity. Illustration 11–6 summarizes the data typically contained in three types, a journal voucher transaction file, a payroll transaction file, and a sales order transaction file.

Accountants use transaction files because they are an efficient way to process a large number of transactions of the same type. However, on-line real-time systems process transaction records individually. They post a transaction record to a master record without first creating a file of transaction records.

Backup Files. A backup file is a duplicate copy of another file. Computer operators make backup copies of files for use in case the original is accidentally damaged or erased. Mainframe system users commonly record the backup copies on magnetic tape. Those with personal computers may use tape or disks.

Most organizations make backup copies of all program files and store them away from the processing facility. If a fire, flood, or other disaster damages the facility, the organization avoids loss of its computer programs.

They also make periodic backup copies of all master files. This allows re-creation of the file as of the last backup date. Backups of certain master files, such as a customer master file, are very important. The records in this file show the balances owed by customers. Many of these balances would never be collected if the organization lost its record of them.

Organizations frequently do not make backups of transaction files. Instead, they keep the original documents on hand for a reasonable period of time. They use these to re-create the transaction file when this is necessary. A magnetic tape copy of the transaction log serves as a backup in an on-line real-time system.

If you have a personal computer, it is important that you learn to make routine backup copies of all your files. Many business files created on personal computers are irreplaceable. People never appreciate the importance of this backup procedure until they accidentally lose a file containing hours of hard work!

Archive Files. Archive files are copies of master files and transactions maintained for historical or reference purposes. In the United States, tax laws require maintenance of documentation supporting taxable income for a specified period of time. Auditors are frequently concerned with account balances up to five years in the past. They may consult archive files as part of their audits.

Scratch Files. A scratch file contains the computer readable equivalent of a piece of scratch paper. Some utility programs, such as sort programs, require that the computer operator make a scratch file available to the program. The program then records data records in the scratch file temporarily while executing. At the conclusion of execution, the scratch file is no longer needed.

You have learned about five types of files used in both manual and computer systems. You have also seen the similarities that exist between these two recording methods in how data are stored and retrieved from files. The next section discusses some operations performed on computer files when storing and retrieving data.

FILE OPERATIONS

Computerized accounting systems routinely use certain procedures when processing computer files. Conceptually they are similar to the operations used in manual systems. However, the terminology describing them may be new. Knowing these concepts is important before learning how files are processed. Four common operations on computer files are updating, maintenance, sorting, and merging.

File Update

In a file update operation, a computer program changes the balance data in a master file record. This is the computerized equivalent of posting to a ledger in a manual system. You have seen the term *posting* used with a computer system already in this text, so the concept is familiar. When a system posts transactions, it also updates a master file. Both terms identify one of the procedures that the computer system applies to a transaction when processing it.

In a batch processing system, the update process uses an old master file and a transaction file containing batches of transactions for posting. For each record in

ILLUSTRATION 11–7 File Update Processes

a. In a batch processing system

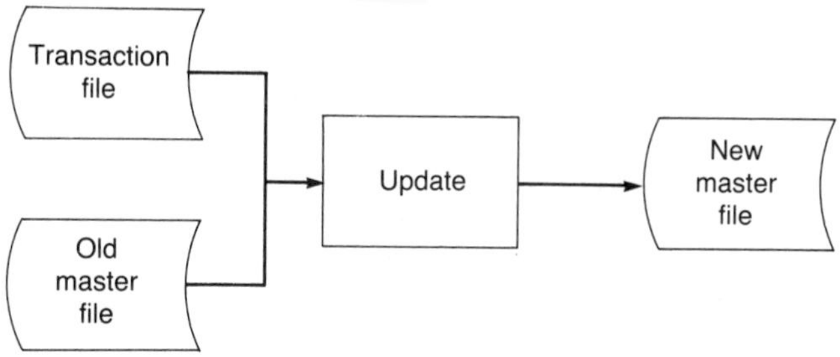

b. In an on-line real-time system

the transaction file, a computer program adds the balance data to the record having the same key field in the master file. This creates a new master file with updated balance data. The accounting system may then apply other processes to the new master file. Illustration 4–5 contains a program flowchart of the update process in a batch processing system.

An on-line real-time system applies all processes to an individual transaction before it begins processing the next transaction. A computer user enters the transaction at a terminal. The data entry program examines the transaction for obvious errors. If there are none, the program updates an on-line master file with the balance data from the transaction. The program then copies the transaction onto the transaction log, and the user enters the next transaction. Illustration 11–7 contains system flowcharts contrasting the update process in batch processing and on-line real-time systems.

File Maintenance

In a file maintenance operation, a computer program changes the reference data in a master file, adds records to the master file, or deletes them. In this way, the computer program maintains the reference data in the file.

For example, the reference data in a customer master file includes fields containing the customer's address. A file maintenance program changes the contents of this field whenever the address changes. When the company acquires a new customer, the file maintenance program adds a new record to the master file.

In batch processing systems, file maintenance routinely occurs prior to a file update. This avoids attempting to update a new master record that is awaiting addition to the master file.

In an on-line real-time system, a clerk executes the file maintenance program at an on-line terminal. The clerk makes changes one at a time to the master file.

Sort

In a sort operation, a computer program resequences the records in a data file. This produces a file in which all records are physically arranged on a secondary storage device in a sequence determined by one of the fields in each record. In accounting applications, this is frequently the primary key field.

Batch processing systems routinely apply a sort operation to transaction files prior to performing an update. The update procedure flowcharted in Illustration 4–5 requires that both transaction and master files occur in the same sequence. The master file ordinarily stays in sequence by primary key field. However, the records in a transaction file are in random order. This is why the system sorts this file into order of ascending primary key prior to executing the update program.

Illustration 11–8 contains a flowchart of a batch system requiring a sort operation. In this example, a program sorts the transaction file of sales orders into customer number order before updating a customer master file.

A utility program usually executes the sort operation. On-line real-time systems require sorts less often because they process individual transactions rather than transaction files.

Merge

A merge operation combines two sequential files into a third file of the same sequence. The program performing this operation therefore merges two files into one. Some batch processing systems routinely merge two transaction files into a third one prior to updating. Merging is efficient whenever two conditions occur: (1) transactions are entered into a transaction file more frequently than the update occurs; and (2) the transaction files are large.

To understand why the merge operation is useful, consider the example shown in the sales order entry system of Illustration 11–9. In this system, a clerk enters sales into the computer daily, creating a daily sales transaction file. The system sorts the daily transactions and merges them with those entered and sorted earlier in the week. It posts the sorted sales transaction file to the customer master file on Friday evening.

ILLUSTRATION 11–8 Sort Operation in Batch Processing

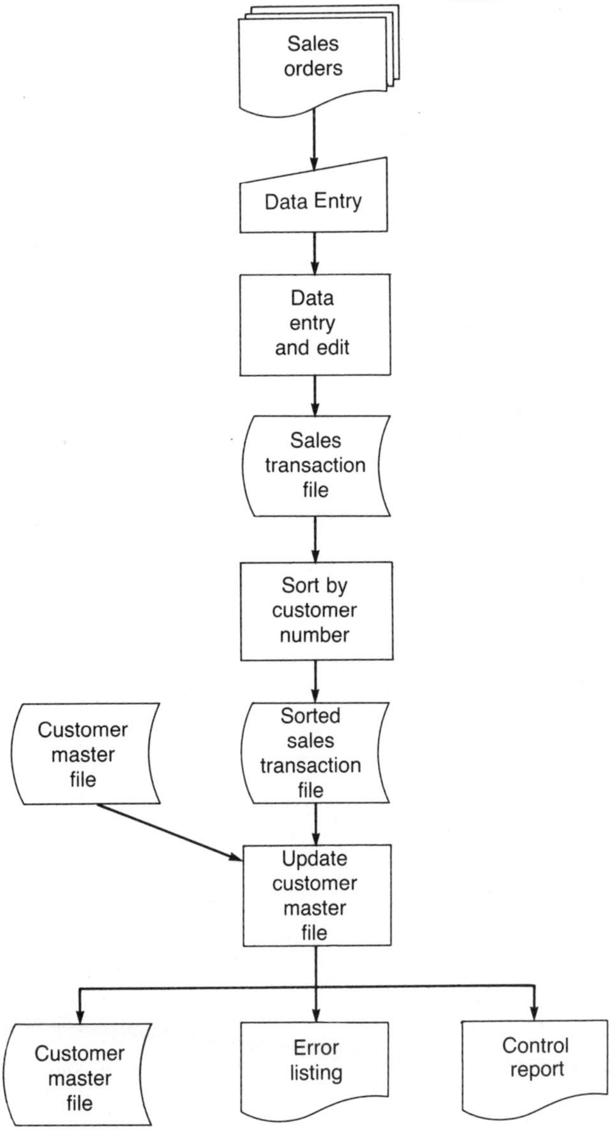

Why did the clerk use a merge operation rather than sort all the transactions each day? If only a few transactions are involved, the clerk can simply add the daily transactions to those recorded earlier in the week and then sort them. However, if there are a large number of transactions, the sort would be much slower than using a merge. Merging two sorted files daily occupies the

ILLUSTRATION 11–9 Merge Operation in Batch Processing

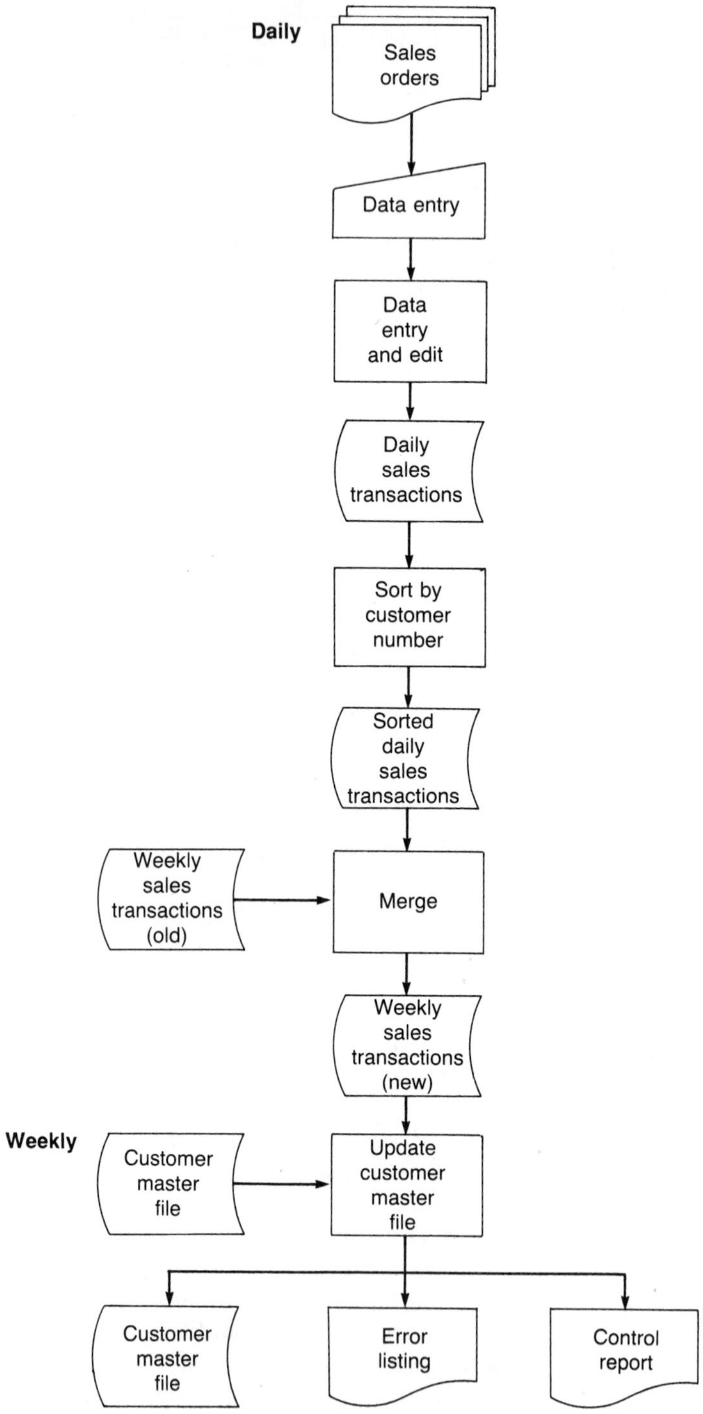

central processor for much less time than would sorting an entire week's transactions.

You have learned about the different types of files in a computer system and the major operations applied to them. Next we discuss how these files are organized and processed in a system using traditional data file organization.

FILE ORGANIZATION METHODS

Traditional data file systems use three forms of file organization. One form, sequential data organization, computerizes methods used in previous manual systems. Although more expensive to implement, the other approaches—direct access and indexed sequential file organization—overcome some disadvantages of using sequential files.

Sequential Files

Sequential files contain data records physically located in primary key field sequence. Thus, records with successively higher keys are stored at successively higher addresses on a device. A program processing a sequential file writes and retrieves records in this physical sequence. Each time this type of file is processed, the records are retrieved in sequence starting with the first one. Sequential data organization is useful for data files in which most of the records are updated each time the file is used.

Processing Sequential Files. Companies developed sequential file processing techniques for mechanical systems using card sorters. They later adapted them to electronic computers using tape storage. Now they apply similar procedures to processing sequential files on direct access storage devices. This approach requires three separate sequential files, a transaction file, an old master file, and a new master file. Illustration 14–16 diagrams the update process. A file update program reads records in sequence from the transaction and master files and compares key fields of the records. If the keys are equal, the program adds amounts or quantities to the equivalent fields in the master record. If the transaction key is greater than the master key, the program reads additional master records in sequence until it finds matching keys. If the transaction key is less than the master key, the program prints an error message on a report. This alerts accounting personnel to add the proper master record by performing file maintenance.

This program creates the new master file, record by record, as it retrieves the records in the old master file. Changes to the master file are complete when the program reaches the end of the transaction file. It then copies all remaining records from the old master file to the new one. Usually the old master file is retained as a backup file.

ILLUSTRATION 11–10 Sequential File Processing

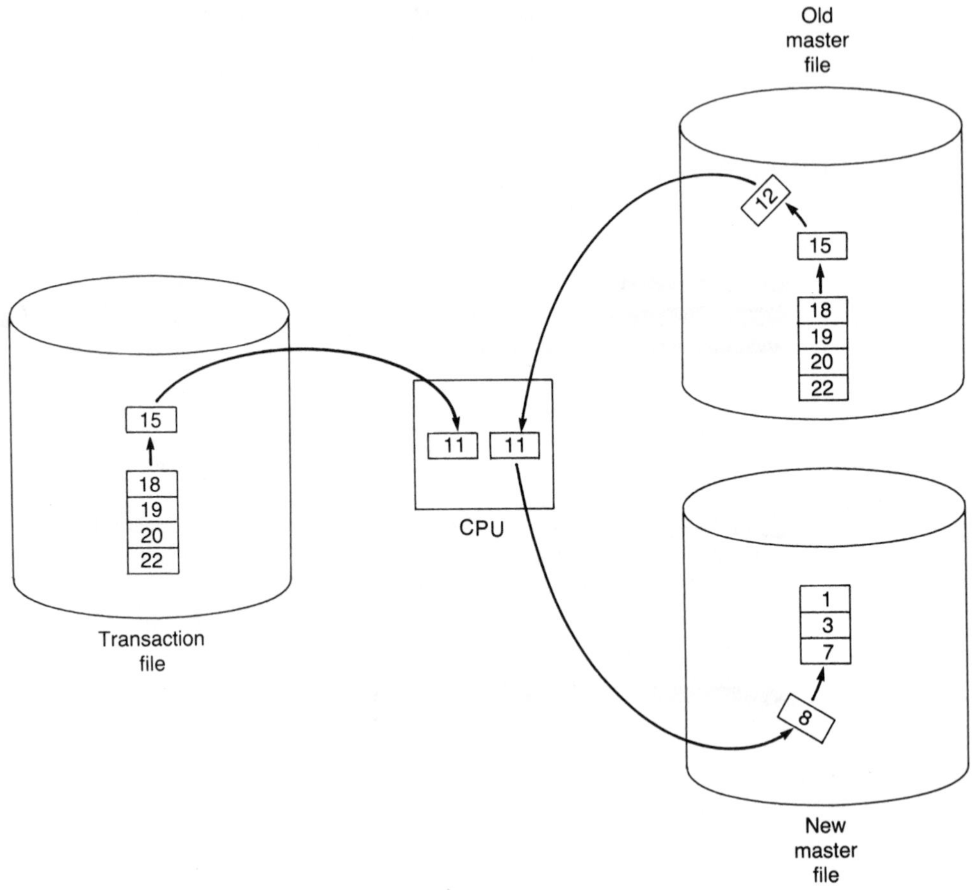

Occasionally this is described as father-son sequential processing.[1] The term applies because the process uses the old master file, the *father,* to create the new master file, the *son.* Because the transactions in the transaction file are usually batched, people also call them *batch sequential* systems.

Illustration 11–10 shows how a central processing unit (CPU) processes sequential files when executing an application program. It reads transactions in sequence from the transaction and old master files. It compares their key fields (shown by the numbers in the boxes), takes the proper action described earlier, and writes the master record to the new master file.

[1]Some people prefer to call this parent-child processing.

In this illustration, the CPU has copied the transaction record with a key field of 11 into main storage. It also has copied the master record with a key field of 11 into main storage, and is changing the contents of this record. After the change is complete, it copies the changed master record to the new master file. It next processes the transaction and old master records with key fields containing the number 15.

Sequential processing requires that the application program search through every record in the file. In a manual system, this is like having a clerk search in sequence through every file in a file room. It is inefficient if the clerk needs only one document, but if the clerk must process a high percentage of the documents, it is an appropriate approach. This illustrates the major advantage of sequential files.

Advantages and Disadvantages. Sequential processing is efficient for applications in which a relatively high percentage of master file records change during one pass through the file. The storage device requires only a short time to locate the next record in the file because the next record is physically located next to the last one processed. When a report printed from the files requires a listing in key field order, printing is faster because the files are already in the desired sequence. If the master file is massive, it can be processed without the entire file being on-line. This saves hardware costs. Sequential processing allows the use of magnetic tape files that are ordinarily less expensive.

When a relatively low percentage of master file records are required, however, sequential processing is inefficient. This is because the update program must copy all records in the old master file to the new one even if they are not used. For this reason, sequential processing is not used when on-line inquiry is desired. Furthermore, all files must be sorted in the same sequence prior to file update or file maintenance.

Direct Access Files

Direct access files are used on direct access storage devices, such as a magnetic disk. Rather than storing data physically in sequence, direct access files contain records stored at randomly chosen addresses throughout the device.

To store a record, data management software reads the primary key and with a *hashing algorithm* computes an address. (A hashing algorithm is a complex equation that distributes records evenly throughout the external storage device.) Later, when an application program wants to change the contents of the record, it recomputes this address to locate the record. If the hashing algorithm works properly, it always calculates the same address from any specific key field.

Designers for this data management software would like to develop algorithms that produce a unique storage address for each record in a file. This is practically impossible, so instead they develop routines that minimize the number of times more than one record receives the same address. These duplicate addresses,

ILLUSTRATION 11–11 Direct Access File Processing

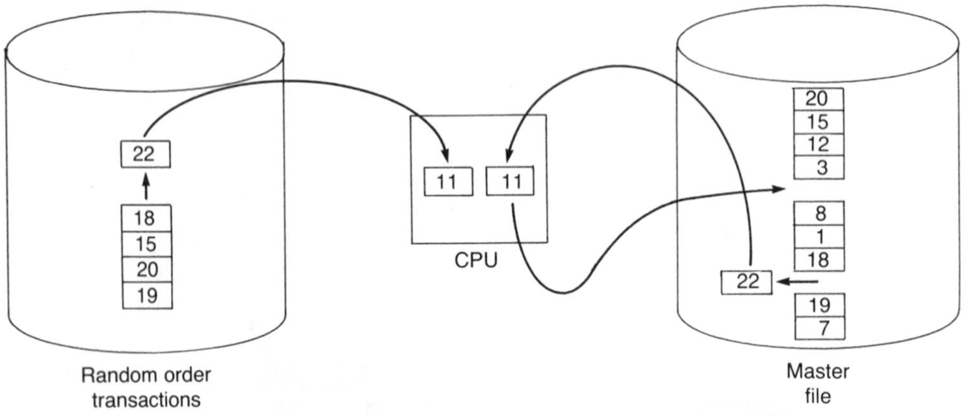

called *synonyms,* are difficult to avoid. Designers provide for synonyms by using either buckets or overflow areas.

A *bucket* is an area on the device, defined in size by a programmer, containing one or more records. When key fields of two different records produce the same device address, the software places both records, in no particular order, in the bucket at that address. To retrieve a record, the software again executes the algorithm originally used to store the data. It then searches the bucket at the resulting address to find the record with the proper key.

An *overflow area* is a section on the direct access device where data management software places all synonyms. When retrieving a synonym, it must search the overflow area sequentially.

Processing Direct Access Files. An application system using direct access files processes transactions in any order. The application program provides the primary key of the desired record to the data management software. This software locates the record and transfers it into main storage.

Illustration 11–11 shows this process. In this illustration, both the transactions and the master file are in no specified sequence. The CPU examines the key field of a transaction, currently the number 11. From this, it computes the address on secondary storage of the master record with the number 11 as its key field. It then transfers record number 11 from the device into main storage. After processing master record number 11, the CPU rewrites it in its original location on the device. Then it processes the next transaction record which has a key field of 22.

This is equivalent to a manual system in which a clerk reads a customer's name on an invoice. Knowing that this customer's file is in the third drawer of the fifth filing cabinet, the clerk goes directly there to file the invoice.

Advantages and Disadvantages. Direct access files require retrieval of only the desired record. This gives them the fastest response of any file organization method to on-line inquiries. In fact, they are an efficient way to structure data in any low-activity file because direct access processing requires no sorting of files. This explains the usefulness of this organization method in on-line real-time systems.

If the address calculation algorithm is inadequate, data records are distributed unevenly throughout the direct access device. This causes inefficient use of file storage area and may result in excessive equipment costs.

Furthermore, the system must sort the direct access file when printing reports requiring a certain sequence. In applications where a relatively high percentage of master file records are retrieved during a single execution, processing direct access files is slower than for sequential ones.

Indexed Sequential Files

Indexed sequential files utilize an index that permits both rapid direct access of individual records and rapid sequential processing of all records in a file. This method physically stores each master file record in primary key field sequence. It also requires a reserved storage area either in memory or on the device for the index. Each entry in the index consists of two elements: the primary key of the indexed record and its address on the device. The index allows file processing as if it were a direct access file without reading the entire file as in a sequential process.

Ideally, the index is stored in main storage; reading from it is much faster than from secondary storage. But this is usually impractical, so the index is normally located on a direct access storage device. Some kinds of data management software use two indexes, a small one in main storage and a more precise one on the device.

The index can be as detailed as the applications using the file require. It need not contain an entry for each record, but fewer entries increase the time required to retrieve a record. Periodically a programmer redefines the index to develop a level of detail appropriate for the contents of the file.

Processing Indexed Sequential Files. The usefulness of indexed sequential files is due to the flexibility allowed in processing them. Application programs may process them either sequentially or using direct access. Either way utilizes the index to locate records on a direct access device.

An application program provides the primary key to data management software. While searching in the index, if the software is unable to find the key, it selects the next lower key and locates the associated address on the direct access device. The data management software examines the record at this address and all records at successively higher addresses, until it finds the record

ILLUSTRATION 11–12 Sequential Processing of Indexed Sequential Files

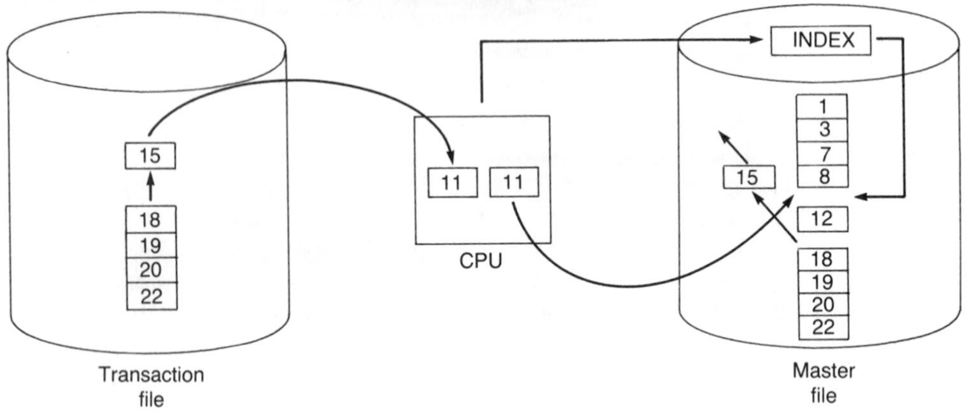

containing the desired key field. It transfers this record into main storage. After the application program changes the record, data management software writes it at its original address on the device. (In a manual system, this is equivalent to a clerk consulting the map on a file room door to locate the desired filing cabinet.)

Sequential Processing. With sequential updating of an indexed sequential master file, the transaction file is first sorted in the same sequence as the master file. Data management software finds a desired record quickly because the next master record it seeks is always near the previous one. Illustration 11–12 depicts sequential processing of an indexed sequential file.

With sequential processing of indexed sequential files, both the transaction file and the master file are in ascending key field sequence. The CPU executing an application program reads the key field of a transaction and identifies the key field to the data management software. It finds the key in the index which gives the location of the master record. The CPU then retrieves the master record, changes its amounts or quantities, and copies it onto the secondary storage device.

In Illustration 11–12, the CPU has copied the transaction record with the key field containing the number 11 into main storage from the transaction file. It has looked up in the index the location of the master record containing this key field, and transferred this record into main storage. After processing master record number 11, it again looks up its location in the index and copies the changed record into that location. Next it processes transaction and master records with key fields containing the number 12.

As you learned earlier, a program updating a sequential file reads each master record into main storage, regardless of whether a transaction existed for the

ILLUSTRATION 11–13 Direct Access Processing of Indexed Sequential Files

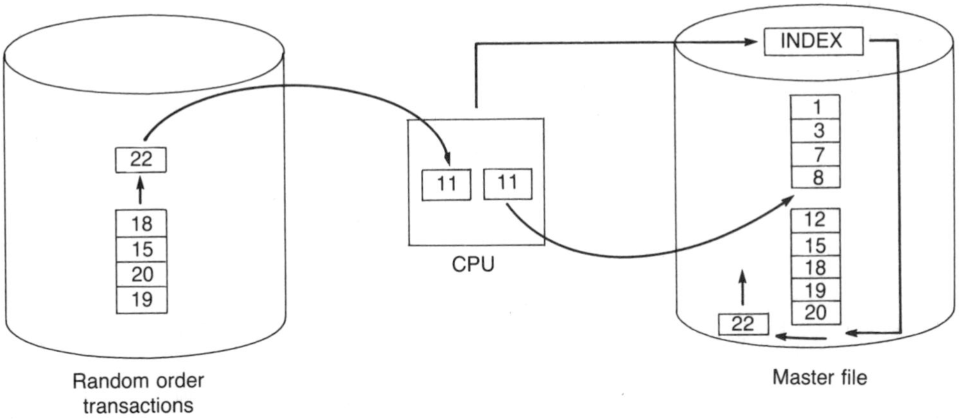

master record. If only a few master records in a file require changing, this process wastes processor time and is inefficient. A program sequentially updating an indexed sequential file avoids this problem. It reads into main storage only those master records for which there are transactions.

Direct Access Processing. With direct access processing of an indexed sequential master file, transactions are not sorted. Because data management software processes them in the random order in which they occur, this approach requires more time to locate a set of transactions than does sequential processing. Illustration 11–13 shows how this works. Data management software has copied transaction record number 11 into main storage. It has also looked up key field number 11 in the index and retrieved the master record with this key. After processing these records, it again determines the address of master record number 11 in the index and copies it into that location. Next it looks up the address of record number 22 and copies it into main storage.

As you can see, direct access processing of an indexed sequential file differs from sequential processing only by the sequence in which transactions are processed.

Because it is slower than sequential processing, you may wonder why systems use direct access processing of this kind of file. In many applications, sorting transactions in advance is impractical. For example, a sales clerk may wish to check if a customer has exceeded a credit limit before charging a sale to a credit card. The clerk uses a terminal to interrogate an indexed sequential customer master file. The sales clerk queries the file as customers arrive. This occurs in random order and requires direct access processing.

Once the sale has been authorized and the clerk records it on a credit card charge slip, the system may exploit the efficiency of sequential processing. The

ILLUSTRATION 11–14 Summary of File Organization Methods

Characteristic	*Method*			
	Sequential	*Direct Access*	*Indexed Sequential*	
Processing method	Sequential	Direct	Sequential	Direct
Transaction input	Sorted file	Random transaction	Sorted file	Random transaction
Master file	Sorted order	Random order	Sorted order	Sorted order
Record location technique	Physical search	Hashing algorithm	Search an index	Search an index
Master record retrieval	Retrieve every record	Retrieve affected records	Retrieve affected records	Retrieve affected records

clerk batches the charge slips, a data entry clerk creates a transaction file from them, and the system sorts the file and posts these transactions sequentially to the customer master file.

Advantages and Disadvantages. The major advantage of indexed sequential file organization is the flexibility it provides. These files achieve the efficiency of sequential processing when there are a large number of transactions, while providing prompt responses to on-line queries. Only the desired master records are retrieved by the data management software, rather than all of them as with sequential files. Because the master file is sorted in key field sequence, printing many kinds of reports from this file is quicker than with a direct access file.

Each of these files, however, requires an index. When an application program accesses a record, the data management software conducts two searches of the direct access device, first of the index and then for the data record. In contrast, direct access files only require one search of the device. Thus, accessing an indexed sequential file is almost always slower than accessing a direct access file. In applications where most of the master records are updated, processing an indexed sequential file is slower than processing a sequential one.

As you can see from this discussion, no one file organization method is best for all applications. The system design team selects a method based on its appraisal of the needs at the time an application is developed. Sequential files are best when capacity on direct access devices is limited, when most records are changed at each update of the file, or when no need exists to retrieve individual data records. Direct access files are best when the quickest possible response is required. To some extent, indexed sequential files provide the advantages of each of the other methods. Illustration 11–14 summarizes the major characteristics of the sequential, direct access, and indexed sequential file organization methods.

SUMMARY

In this chapter you have learned how accounting data are structured when organizations use the traditional data file approach. Early accounting systems used manual files. When computers were adapted to accounting, procedures for processing older manual files were applied to computer files. You now know that computer files are actually structured in a way similar to those manual ones.

Computers process program files and data files. Accounting application programs are stored in program files; accounting records are stored in data files. An accounting data file may be a master, transaction, backup, archive, or scratch file.

Accounting systems commonly perform four file operations. A file update is equivalent to posting in a manual system and refers to changing the balance data in a master file. File maintenance refers to changes to the reference data in a master file. Batch sequential processing systems also rely on file sorts and merges.

Three common methods of file organization are sequential, direct access, and indexed sequential. Each has advantages over the others in certain kinds of accounting applications.

KEY TERMS

archive file A copy of a data file kept for historical or reference purposes.

backup file A duplicate copy of a file kept in case the original is lost or destroyed.

balance data The data items in a record that represent amounts or quantities.

data file A file containing data records that are not executable by the computer.

direct access storage device A form of secondary storage capable of recording direct access files, such as a magnetic disk.

file A collection of information stored so that it can be retrieved for later use.

file maintenance A file operation in which a computer program changes the reference data in a master file.

file organization method The way that records are physically arranged in a data file. It may be sequential, direct access, or indexed sequential.

file update A file operation in which a computer program changes the balance data in a master file.

master file A data file whose records contain data relating to a specific account.

merge A file operation in which a computer program combines two sequential files to produce a third file in the same sequence.

program file A file containing instructions executable by the computer.

reference data The data items in a record that identify or describe the record.

sort A file operation in which a computer program resequences the records in a data file.

transaction file A data file in which each record represents an accounting transaction.

QUESTIONS

11–1. Do you think a system that processes manual files is more flexible than one processing computerized files? Explain your answer.

11–2. How does data management software identify addresses on a magnetic diskette?

11–3. How does data management software identify the beginning of a magnetic tape file? The end?

11–4. What is the distinction between a program file and a data file? How does an accountant use each type?

11–5. Name and describe five types of accounting data files.

11–6. What distinguishes a transaction file from a master file? Which file organization methods use transaction files?

11–7. What is the distinction between an archive file and a backup file?

11–8. Distinguish between the file update operation and the file maintenance operation. In any system, which operation should be performed first?

11–9. In which systems are the sort and merge operations used?

11–10. What is meant by father-son processing? What is the father in this approach? The son?

11–11. When is sequential data organization the most efficient method? When is direct access organization most efficient?

11–12. Describe two ways that indexed sequential files are processed.

11–13. What advantages and disadvantages do indexed sequential files have in comparison to the other two methods?

EXERCISES AND CASES

11–14. *TYPES OF DATA*

The following are data fields commonly processed by accounting systems. Determine whether each field contains balance or reference data.

a. General ledger master file posting reference.
b. Sales order transaction file date of sale.
c. Inventory master file economic order quantity.
d. Customer master file year-to-date sales to the customer.
e. Payroll master file employee pay rate.
f. Payroll transaction file gross pay.

11–15. ***MANUAL FILES***

The following files are human-readable and may be processed manually. For each file, identify its key field and its method of organizing data. The method may be sequential, indexed sequential, or direct access.

a. A general ledger used by a bookkeeping machine. Each account is recorded on a ledger card stored in a rack, and arranged by account number.
b. A card catalog in a library.
c. An address book containing the addresses of your friends alphabetically by last name.
d. A filing cabinet. A label on each file drawer identifies the contents of the drawer. File folders in a drawer contain documents arranged by date.
e. An unabridged dictionary.

11–16. ***SEQUENTIAL FILE UPDATE***

The first of the following tables contains a customer master file with eleven records. The second contains six records representing sales transactions for the week of June 28, 19XX. The key field for each record is the four-digit customer number.

Customer Master File		
1047	Gimlet Corp.	1,006.00
2110	ABC Manufacturing Co.	812.00
2132	Wixson Widgets Inc.	45.00
2448	J. B. Sampson	18.00
2919	Bach Music Co.	219.00
3042	College Bookstores, Inc.	2,120.00
3166	Alpha Retail Co.	781.00
3529	Ma & Pa Grocery Co.	186.00
3584	J. Smith, CPA	7.00
4262	Expert TV Repair	68.00
4375	Big Donut Co.	333.00

Sales Transaction File—Week of June 28		
3584	June 28, 19XX	10.00
2132	June 29, 19XX	35.00
3166	June 29, 19XX	21.00
3148	June 30, 19XX	4.00
2132	July 1, 19XX	8.00
4262	July 2, 19XX	20.00

Required:

a. Sort the transactions in the sales transaction file into the correct order.

b. Following the flowchart in Illustration 4–5, post each transaction to the master file. Show the updated balance in each master file record.

c. What is the nature of the error message referred to in the flowchart of Illustration 4–5?

11–17. ***SEQUENTIAL FILE UPDATE***

The following table shows the content of the sales transaction file produced during the week of July 5, 19XX. Use these transactions, together with the files provided in Exercise 11–16, to complete the requirements.

Sales Transaction File—Week of July 5		
4375	July 5, 19XX	16.00
2132	July 5, 19XX	37.00
3584	July 7, 19XX	14.00
1047	July 8, 19XX	11.00
2919	July 8, 19XX	26.00
3166	July 9, 19XX	8.00

Required:

a. Sort the records in the transaction file for the week of July 5 into the correct order.

b. Sort the records in the transaction file for the week of June 28 (given in 11–16) into the correct order.

c. Merge the two sorted transaction files (from parts *a* and *b*) into another transaction file in the correct order.

d. Post sales transactions for these two weeks to the customer master file given in Exercise 11–16. (Disregard any answer you may have obtained to Exercise 11–16.)

11–18. ***DIRECT ACCESS FILES***

One possible algorithm for computing an address on a direct access device is:

$$\text{address} = [25 * \text{Key}]_{\text{mod}1000}.$$

Using this algorithm, data management software reads the key field of a record. It multiplies this key value by 25 thus obtaining a product. The last three digits of the product are the address where the record is stored.

The following five numbers represent key fields in the records of a vendor master file:

1. 10018
2. 10060
3. 10093
4. 10140
5. 10178

Required:

a. Using the preceding algorithm, calculate the address of the location for each vendor master record.
b. Identify the records in the list that produce synonyms.
c. Suggest how the algorithm could be changed to produce fewer synonyms.

11–19. ***INDEXED SEQUENTIAL FILE MAINTENANCE***

Whirlwind Corp. maintains its employee records in an indexed sequential file. Employees are identified to the personnel benefits system by four-digit employee numbers. The following index for the employee master file contains personnel and payroll data.

Index to Employee Master File	
1006	860
1014	246
1017	119
1018	201
1124	747
1129	831
1146	226
1183	661
1201	483
1222	780

During June 19XX, the following changes took place in the work force:

1. Employees terminated: 1124
   1201
2. Employees added: 1019
   1136
   1211
3. Employees acquiring additional dependents: 1017
4. Employees receiving pay increases: 1006
   1017
   1129

Required:

Show how the index changes in response to the file maintenance required for the preceding work force changes.

11–20. ***FILE ORGANIZATION METHODS***

Each of the following identifies a master file that is updated by an information system. In each case, describe the contents of a record and identify the most appropriate file organization method.

a. A university student file. The file is used to produce fee statements at the beginning of each semester and for on-line registration.
b. A file used by a hotel chain for its reservation system.
c. A file of retirees. A pension fund uses this file to produce retirement checks at the beginning of each month.
d. The customer file of a retail chain.
e. The customer file of an electric utility.
f. A file containing perpetual inventory records of a wholesaler.

11–21. ***DATA FILES FOR THE REVENUE CYCLE***

Ivy Real Estate Company owns four apartment complexes in a college town. Because these complexes cater to the students at the college, tenant turnover is relatively high. In the spring students generally want to select apartments for the following fall from those Ivy has to offer. Occasionally Ivy encounters undesirable students who move out without paying all the rent that is due.

Ivy is developing a computerized system to maintain records regarding its rentals. It would like the system to show which apartments are available, which are rented, how much each rents for, and whether or not a tenant is behind in rent.

Required:

a. Describe the contents of a master file and suggest a file organization method for this application.
b. For your master file, which events initiate:
  1. File updates?
  2. File maintenance?
c. Which routine management reports should be produced from this file? Suggest an appropriate sequence for printing the items in each report you identify.

11–22. ***DATA FILES FOR THE REVENUE CYCLE***

Metropolis Life Insurance Company (Metro) is considering a computer-based system for maintaining data about its policyholders and for processing premium payments from them. Metro currently has about 15,000 life insurance policies in force. Policyholders may pay premiums annually, semiannually, or monthly. Although all payments are due on the first day of each month, experience shows that Metro can expect to receive premiums throughout the month. Because cash should be deposited quickly, the computerized cash receipts system must process premium payments promptly regardless of when they are received.

Each month Metro makes numerous changes to the data regarding policyholders. These include new policies, policy lapses, name and address changes for the policyholders, and beneficiary changes. The proposed system must be able to process these as well.

Required:

a. Identify the fields Metro needs for its:
   1. Policyholder master file.
   2. Cash receipts transaction file.

b. Which file organization and file processing methods do you recommend for this application?

c. Draw a system flowchart describing this process assuming that:
   1. The policyholder master file is updated daily.
   2. A merge operation is used and the master file is updated monthly.

11–23. *DATA FILES FOR THE CONVERSION CYCLE*

Finley Foundry has used a manual cost accounting system for decades. However, business volume has increased to the point where Finley is now computerizing this system. A cost accountant working in the factory office operates the present manual system.

The cost accountant maintains three files in a filing cabinet: a file folder of job cost sheets, another of time reporting sheets, and a third folder of materials requisitions. When the factory begins a new job, the cost accountant prepares a job cost sheet for it. The job cost sheet summarizes the total costs incurred on the job through its completion.

At the end of each day supervisors turn in time reporting sheets that the cost accountant uses to record labor costs on the appropriate job cost sheets. Also daily the warehouse foreman turns in materials requisitions, from which the accountant determines and records the costs of materials used in each job. The cost accountant allocates factory overhead to jobs daily based on labor used the previous day. When the job is completed, the cost accountant computes the total costs of the job and sends the completed job cost sheet to the chief accountant.

Required:

a. Describe the master file for this computerized cost accounting system. For the file, identify:
   1. Data fields.
   2. File organization method.
   3. File processing method.

b. Identify the transaction data used by this system. Suggest a preferred method for entering this transaction data into the system so it can be posted to the master file.

c. What file maintenance does this system require?

11–24. *DATA FILES FOR DECISION SUPPORT*

Superway Grocery Stores, Inc., is a local grocery chain in a midwestern city. To compete with the national chains, they advertise special discounts on selected inventory items. The items selected for discount change each week based on expected competition and the overall budgeted profit margin. Discounted items are selected by a pricing specialist at company headquarters.

From estimates of sales volumes, the pricing specialist develops a weekly markdown plan which identifies the items for discount. First, the specialist computes the normal selling price for each item in inventory. This is the item's cost plus the normal markup, currently 20 percent. The specialist then identifies candidate items for discount and proposes a discount on them. Using sales volume estimates based on previous weeks' data, the specialist projects total sales revenue and gross profit on sales for the week. The specialist then adds or eliminates discounts to achieve weekly budgeted profit goals.

For example, the specialist may propose a special discount of 10 percent on a loaf of bread. If the cost of a loaf is $1.00 and the normal markup is 20 percent, the normal selling price for a loaf is $1.20. A 10 percent discount reduces the selling price to a markdown value of $1.08. If sales of 1,000 loaves are expected, then projected sales revenue from this item is $1,080 for the week. To reflect the discounted price, the pricing specialist normally adjusts the previous week's sales volume upward when projecting new volume.

Currently Superway has a computerized inventory system. Inventory quantities are updated nightly from sales volumes recorded for each item during the day at computerized checkout stands. The pricing specialist determines the markdown plan manually using reports from this inventory system. Superway would like to develop a computerized system to aid the pricing specialist.

Required:

a. Describe the inventory master file for the existing system. Identify:
   1. Data fields in each record.
   2. File organization method.
   3. Method of file processing.

b. Describe the reports from this file needed by the pricing specialist to develop a markdown plan manually.

c. Assuming that a computerized system is developed to aid the pricing specialist, identify the following for this new system:
   1. Additional data fields required for records in the inventory master file.
   2. Master file organization method.
   3. Method of processing the master file.
   4. Additional reports that the new system can produce to aid the pricing specialist.

11–25. *FILE OPERATIONS*

Guaranty Bank of Lafayette, Louisiana, with assets in excess of $600 million, ranks in the 10 largest banks in the state. Faced with rapid growth and a competitive environment, its management decided to establish an in-house data processing department to provide accurate, timely information.[2]

The system Guaranty developed processes over 100,000 accounts and an average of 95,000 transactions during a single nightly production run. Each day's processing requires about 14 hours; this is expected to increase as the bank grows and adds new systems.

The Problem

Computerized systems automate the majority of Guaranty's deposit, loan, and financial departments. Application systems used by these departments include demand deposits, savings, commercial loans, mortgage loans, installment loans, and payroll. Each is a purchased software package maintained through maintenance agreements with vendors. Additionally, Guaranty uses a general ledger software package obtained from a different vendor.

Because each application system is a separate package and most are from different vendors, data files produced by them are incompatible. For most applications, this is not a serious operational problem. However, the general ledger system requires inputs from most of the other applications. After acquisition of the general ledger package, management realized the need to interface it with the others. They appointed a project team to develop a computerized system to extract data from the other applications and to provide it as inputs to the general ledger system.

Objectives of the General Ledger Interface

The project team identified four objectives for the general ledger/application system interface. They were to:

1. Provide data from the application systems using account codes consistent with the general ledger chart of accounts. This creates greater flexibility in reporting and allows daily balancing procedures between application system totals and general ledger totals.

2. Provide the general ledger system with access to nonfinancial as well as financial information. This increases flexibility in producing reports for management. Internal management reports utilize nonfinancial data such as the number of IRA accounts, the number of personnel by department and by function, aging reports of loans and of certificates of deposit, and maturity schedules of loans and of certificates of deposit.

3. Provide the ability to reverse incorrectly run application data that has been posted to the general ledger without reprocessing the general ledger system.

---

[2]Adapted from Bobby L. Doxey and Jean Chambers, "Making the Most of Bank Information Systems," *Management Accounting*, February 1983, pp. 58–61. Copyright by National Association of Accountants (1983), Montvale, N.J. 07645.

4. Allow the data processing manager to bypass the processing of an application system one day, followed by processing multiple runs of the application the following day.

5. Establish controls that guarantee data integrity without creating excessive processing overhead. These include backup copies of all disk files made on magnetic tape at strategic points in processing. They also include control reports that allow manual comparison of information generated by application systems with totals submitted to the general ledger system.

Extract Procedures

Each day an extract program accesses each application system file and extracts data to build an interface data file. The data in this file is taken from the application systems' daily transactions and accruals and changed into the format required by the general ledger system. The interface data file then provides inputs to the general ledger system; the application data files produce reports for the application. Used in this way, interface data extraction provides consistent data for all systems.

After all application system extracts are completed, the computer operator makes backup copies of all interface data files. Each backup file contains one day's transactions for one application and provides protection against loss of the original data file before processing is completed. Exhibit 11–1 shows a system flowchart of these extract procedures.

Multiple Run Processing

Multiple run processing provides the ability to combine two days' data from an application system into a single interface data file. The previous day's extracted data is first copied into the multiple run interface data file. Then the current day's application extracts are handled normally. This allows the receipt of multiple run data and normal application data as a single input to the general ledger system.

The system generates a control listing of multiple run data. This provides the accounting department with a list of erroneous transactions for correction. A copy also goes to the data control group in the data processing department. They compare the count of the records in the application data files with those in the interface data files to ensure that no transactions are lost in processing.

Reversal Processing

The computer operator executes a reversal program when the accounting department determines that an application system's data have significant errors after posting them to the general ledger. This program reverses all entries produced from the application data. Inputs to the program come from the merged interface data backup tape produced during the previous general ledger file update. Outputs are contained in a reversal data file that becomes an input to the

EXHIBIT 11–1 Case 11–25 General Ledger Interface System Extract Procedures

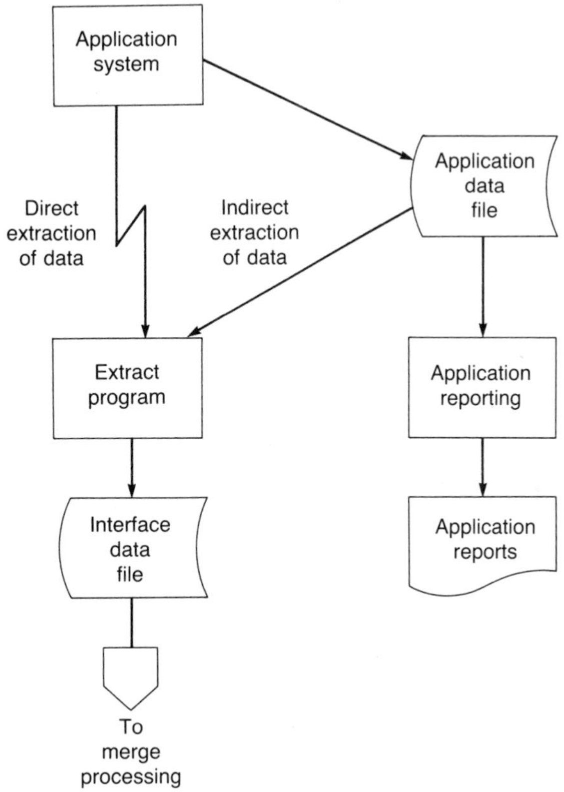

current day's processing. These reversal entries contain the same data as the original entry but are distinguished within the general ledger system by a special code.

The reversal program produces a control listing used as in multiple run processing. Use of the reversal program allows the accounting department to avoid making manual adjustments to the general ledger. It is followed by multiple run processing to introduce the corrected data into the system. The computer operator makes a backup copy of the reversal data file. Exhibit 11–2 contains a system flowchart of these reversal procedures.

Merge Processing

Merge processing takes place after multiple run and reversal backup files have been made. A merge program consolidates data from the application interface data file, the multiple run data file, and the reversal data file into a merged

EXHIBIT 11–2 Case 11–25 General Ledger Interface System Reversal Procedures

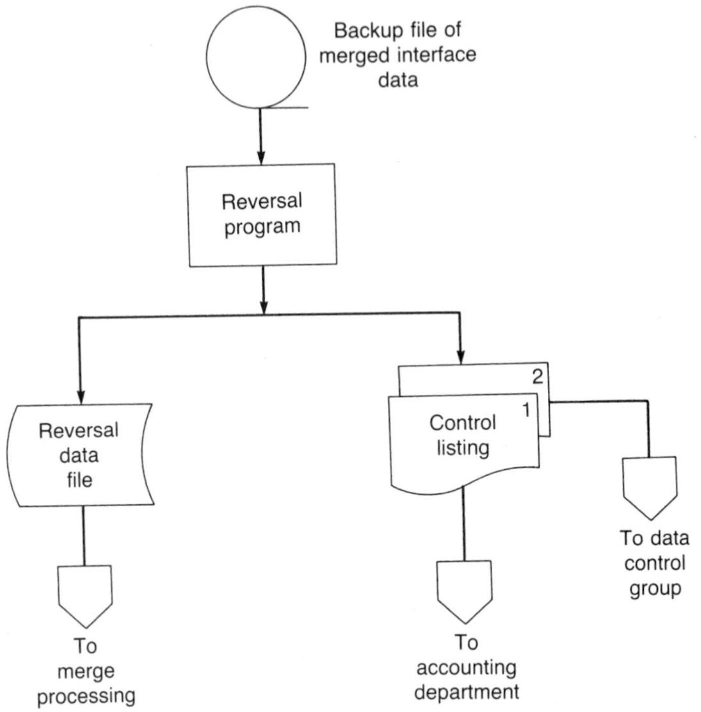

interface data file. This is the input file to the general ledger system. This program has several control checks coded into it. If it detects an erroneous condition, it halts processing for corrective action. The computer operator can enter commands to exclude application data if this is necessary to complete processing.

The merge program produces two reports. The control listing provides an error report for the accounting department and a record count for the data control group. The invalid and unpostable transactions report is sent to the accounting department for correction and reentry of these transactions. The backup tape of the merged interface data is used both for system backup and, when required, as an input to reversal processing.

After merge processing has been completed, the application interface data files, multiple run data files, and reversal data files are cleared of data in preparation for the next day's processing. Exhibit 11–3 shows the procedures used in merge processing.

Implementation of the general ledger system interface has been a success at Guaranty Bank. Besides producing accurate and consistent data for accounting

EXHIBIT 11–3 Case 11–25 General Ledger Interface System Merge Procedures

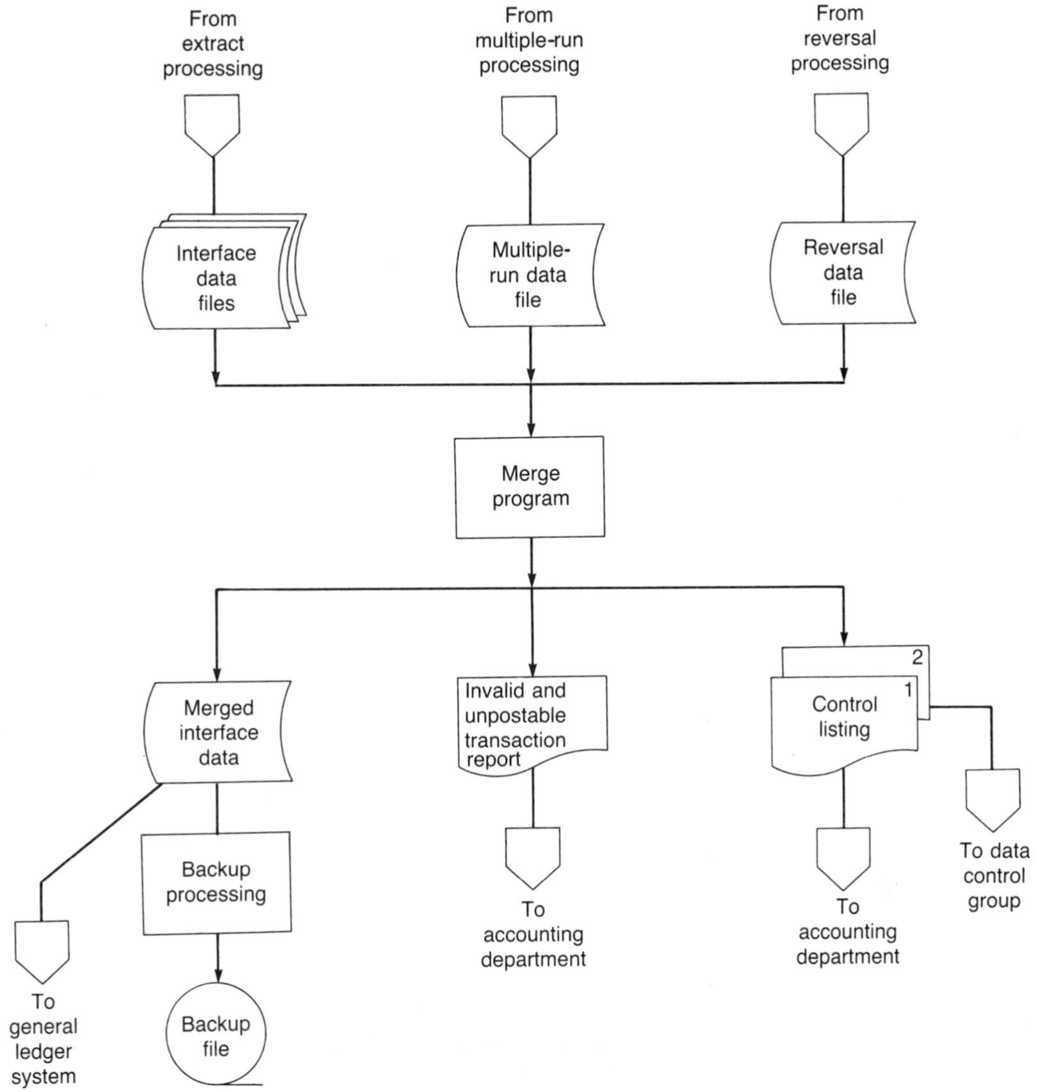

reports, it supplies management with information on market conditions so it can make short-term decisions and plan for the future.

Required:

a. In this system, which manual procedures are performed by:
   1. The accounting department?
   2. The data control group of the data processing department?

b. What is the purpose of the merge operation in Guaranty's general ledger interface system?

c. The case does not describe the methods of file organization used in this system. Based on the descriptions given, which method do you think is used for the general ledger master file? The master files in the other application systems? Why?

d. Guaranty created this system because its applications systems produce files containing records incompatible with the general ledger system. Based on what you learned in the previous chapter, can you suggest another way of correcting this problem?

Chapter 12

Data Base Management Systems

Learning Objectives:

1. To discover how accounting data are processed using the data base management system approach.
2. To learn how a data base management system maintains data relationships.
3. To understand the three alternative structural models for data.

INTRODUCTION

Chapter 10 describes two ways of organizing data in computer-based systems: traditional data files and data base management systems (DBMSs). In that chapter, you learned the advantages and disadvantages of each approach. In Chapter 11, you learned the details of organizing and processing accounting data using traditional data files. This chapter describes how data base management systems work and shows you how to choose the DBMS that best satisfies the needs of users in accounting and management.

A DBMS is a set of computer programs that maintains an organization's data base. The method of storing data in the data base is independent of the application programs using it. Users of the data are unconcerned with how data are physically organized on secondary storage devices. A DBMS stores data more efficiently, eliminates conflicting data, and allows easier changes to applications than does a traditional data file system.

A data base management system works most efficiently when it implements a data structure recognizing the logical relationships in the data base. Identifying the data structure and selecting the software is a responsibility of the project team that implements the DBMS.

IMPLEMENTING A DBMS

In implementing a data base management system, the project team performs two functions: First, it determines the content of the data base. This includes defining the data elements and the relationships between them. Second, the project team identifies an appropriate structural model for the data and selects a DBMS software package to implement it.

Defining the Data Base

During systems design, systems analysts identify reports and displays produced by the system. The contents of these outputs summarize the *data elements* maintained in the data base. A data element is equivalent to a data field in a traditional data file system. For example, a report disclosing customers' current unpaid balances contains information from three data elements. They are the customer's account number, name, and unpaid balance.

The relationships between data elements are as important as the elements themselves—for example, knowing an unpaid balance is useless unless you know which customer has the balance. A system not only records the customer name, number, and unpaid balance but also links them in some way to maintain their relationships. The developer of a DBMS programs the software to maintain not only the data elements but also the relationships between them.

Types of Relationships

The four possible relationships between data elements are:

One-to-one.

One-to-many.

Many-to-one.

Many-to-many.

The terms *one* and *many* in these descriptions refer to the number of related data elements. If a data element is related to only one occurrence of another element, the relationship is one-to-one. If an element is related to many occurrences, the relationship is one-to-many.

ILLUSTRATION 12–1 Factory Employees

Employee Number	*Name*	*Factory*	*Department*	*Job Code*	*Employ Date*	*Pay Rate*
11	Smith, A.	3	2	4	19X9	10.00
14	Garcia, B.	3	2	2	19X8	10.00
27	Wong, C.	3	1	3	19X9	10.00
29	Riley, D.	3	2	4	19X8	10.00
33	O'Hara, E.	3	1	1	19X9	20.00
36	Weiss, F.	3	1	1	19X8	20.00
41	Abbott, G.	3	1	3	19X9	20.00
45	Powski, H.	3	2	4	19X8	20.00

Department codes
1—Factory office
2—Assembly

Job codes
1—clerk
2—machinist
3—accountant
4—laborer

In the previous accounts receivable example, there is only one occurrence of an unpaid balance for a customer. Thus, there is a one-to-one relationship between the data element customer name and the data element unpaid balance. However, an unpaid balance may represent many sales transactions to the customer. Some accounts receivable systems record not only the total unpaid balance but also the individual sales amounts making up the balance. In this case, there is a one-to-many relationship between the customer name and the sales amount. There are many occurrences of the sales amount element for each occurrence of the unpaid balance element.

In accounting application systems, one-to-one and one-to-many relationships are common. Other types of relationships are frequently needed for producing management reports. To see how they may be used, consider the list of employees in Illustration 12–1. It contains the portion of an employee data base applicable to factory number 3.

In this example, factory number 3 consists of two departments, employs people in four jobs, and has two different pay rates. It employs clerks and accountants in the factory office, and uses machinists and laborers in the assembly department. This list contains eight occurrences of seven data elements. Illustration 12–2 shows examples of the four kinds of relationships in this list.

In Illustration 12–1, there is a distinct employee number for each name and thus a one-to-one relationship. Each department may have two kinds of jobs, so there is a one-to-many relationship between these data elements. Because many employees work in each department, the data elements employee name and department have a many-to-one relationship. A many-to-many relationship exists

ILLUSTRATION 12–2 Data Relationships

Relationship	*Example*
One-to-one	Employee number to name
One-to-many	Department code to job code
Many-to-one	Employee name to department
Many-to-many	Job code to pay rate

between jobs and pay rates because employees in each job may receive one of two pay rates.

If a manager wishes to know which employees work in the assembly department, the manager must use the many-to-one relationship inherent in the data. When a payroll clerk uses a laborer's employee number to encode a payroll transaction, the clerk utilizes the one-to-one relationship between employee name and employee number.

As you can see from these examples, relationships are inherent in the data. If a system is to produce meaningful outputs, it must record not only the data but also the relevant relationships. When system designers identify relationships, they determine the "logical structure" of the data. This is different from their physical arrangement of the data, called its "physical structure."

A traditional data file system maintains relationships by physically recording related data fields adjacent to each other. Programmers code application programs to recognize this relationship. With a DBMS, the physical location of the data is independent of the application programs. A DBMS achieves this independence by separating the physical structure of the data from its logical structure. The DBMS records relationships by linking logically related data using a method other than physical location.

Maintaining Relationships in a Data Base

The way a DBMS physically stores data differs from the way application programs use it. The DBMS's *schema* describes the data in the data base and its relationships. An application program uses only a portion of this data, defined by the application's *subschema*. When designing the data base, MIS professionals use special terminology to describe how the DBMS stores data.

DBMS Terminology. When creating a schema, system designers combine two or more related data elements to form a data *segment*. A segment is a set of elements stored together on a secondary storage device. Multiple occurrences of a type of segment form a *data set*. The DBMS then combines many different data sets to form the data base.

ILLUSTRATION 12–3 Similarities in Data Storage

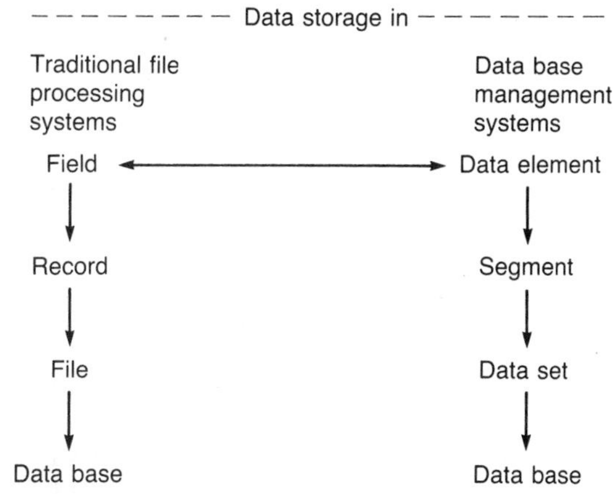

Illustration 12–3 shows the analogy between the physical structure in a traditional data file system and the schema of a DBMS. Data fields are analogous to data elements, data records are analogous to segments, and data files are analogous to data sets. You may also hear people refer to fields and records when using DBMSs. In this case, they describe the application's logical view of the data rather than how the data are stored.

With a DBMS, application programs process records formed from a restricted view of the data, the application's subschema. The data contained in a subschema may be stored within different segments of the data base. The application program is unaware of this; the DBMS locates the appropriate data elements and makes them available to the program in the way defined by the subschema.

Illustration 12–4 shows data dictionary descriptions for a data set formed from the list of employees in Illustration 12–1. It demonstrates how the DBMS eliminates and rearranges elements from a schema to form subschemas for human resources and payroll application systems.

When an organization uses a DBMS, its data base consists of many different data sets. Each segment in a data set is one occurrence of a group of logically related data elements. A data set may contain many such occurrences. For the example in Illustrations 12–1 and 12–4, there are eight occurrences in the data set. Illustration 12–5 shows these segments as if they were stored at random locations on a secondary storage device.

In a DBMS, related data elements may be physically located at different addresses on the device. The DBMS must record data relationships in some way other than physical location. Most DBMSs use pointers and chains to link related data segments.

ILLUSTRATION 12–4 Schema and Subschema

Schema for the Employee Data Set

Data Element	*Data Name*	*Data Format*
Employee number	EMP NO	2 bytes numeric
Employee name	EMP NAME	15 bytes character
Factory code	FAC	1 byte numeric
Department code	DEPT	1 byte numeric
Job code	JOB	1 byte numeric
Employment date	EMP DATE	6 bytes numeric
Pay rate	PAY RATE	6 bytes numeric

Subschema for the Human Resources Application System

Data Element	*Data Name*	*Data Format*
Employee number	EMP NO	2 bytes numeric
Employee name	EMP NAME	15 bytes character
Job code	JOB	1 byte numeric
Employment date	EMP DATE	6 bytes numeric

Subschema for the Payroll Application System

Data Element	*Data Name*	*Data Format*
Employee number	EMP NO	2 bytes numeric
Employee name	EMP NAME	15 bytes character
Factory code	FAC	1 byte numeric
Department code	DEPT	1 byte numeric
Pay rate	PAY RATE	6 bytes numeric

Pointers, Chains, and Lists. A *pointer* is a data element added to a segment by the DBMS. The DBMS inserts information into this element that identifies another segment containing related data. Sometimes a DBMS copies the location of another segment into the pointer. Other DBMS packages copy the primary key of the other segment instead, and data management software computes its location from this key. In either case, this element points to another related record. Pointers create the links that maintain data relationships in a DBMS.

When pointers connect several related segments in succession, the segments form a *chain*. The segments connected by one or more chains form a *list*. DBMSs use four kinds of lists to maintain relationships in a data set: simple, ring, multithreaded, and inverted. When a project team selects a DBMS software package, they are choosing to maintain data relationships in one or more of these ways.

Simple Lists. In a simple list, all segments but one contain pointers that indicate the next segment in the data set. The last segment in the list, however, contains no pointer; instead, it has a data element containing an end-of-chain marker. To retrieve data, the DBMS first determines from the application program the beginning record in the list. It then searches linearly from the

ILLUSTRATION 12–5 An Employee Data Set on a Direct Access Device

Emp. No.	Name	Fac.	Dept.	Job	Emp. Date	Pay Rate
11	Smith, A.	3	2	4	19 x 9	1000
14	Garcia, B.	3	2	2	19 x 8	1000
27	Wong, C.	3	1	3	19 x 9	1000
29	Riley, D.	3	2	4	19 x 8	1000
33	O'Hara, E.	3	1	1	19 x 9	2000
36	Weiss, F.	3	1	1	19 x 8	2000
41	Abbott, G.	3	1	3	19 x 9	2000
45	Powski, H.	3	2	4	19 x 8	2000

beginning of the list to its end. (For this reason, it is sometimes called a *linear* list.) A DBMS commonly uses simple lists to form more complex data structures described later.

Illustration 12–6 shows how the employee data set in Illustration 12–5 is linked using a simple list. In this diagram, the additional element in each segment is its pointer. An arrow shows the direction of the pointer. This list contains one chain that connects the segments in employee number sequence.

Ring Lists. A ring list is similar to a simple list. The DBMS searches linearly through a data set to retrieve a specific segment. In a ring list, however,

ILLUSTRATION 12–6 A Simple List

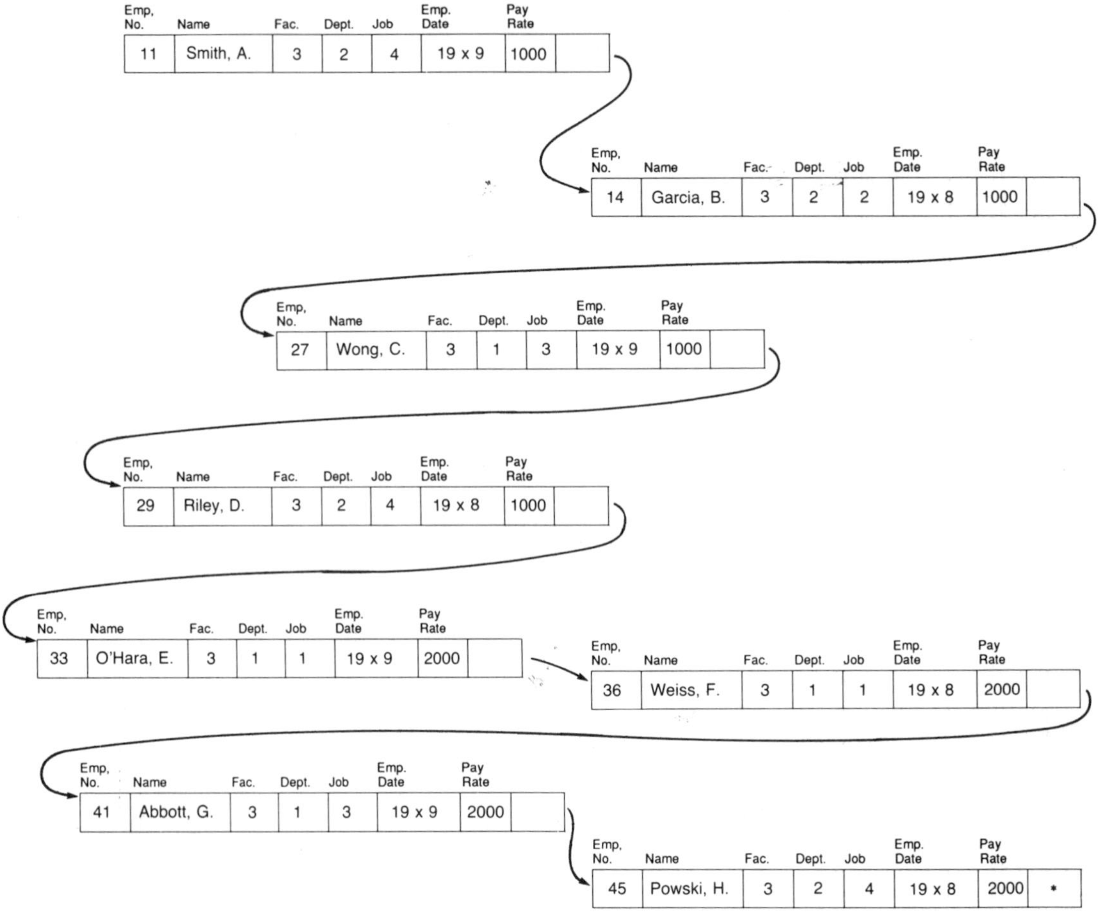

*End of chain marker.

the last record in a data set contains a pointer to the first record in the set. In this way a search through the data set completes a ring after leaving the last segment.

Illustration 12–7 shows how to link the employee data set of Illustration 12–5 in a ring list. This list consists of one chain sequenced by employee number.

Multithreaded Lists. Many times organizations wish to access data in different sequences. In traditional data file systems, this is done by sorting the records in a file into different orders. This procedure changes the physical sequence in which the records are located. With a data base management system, physical sorts of data are unnecessary if the data set is structured as a multithreaded list.

ILLUSTRATION 12–7 A Ring List

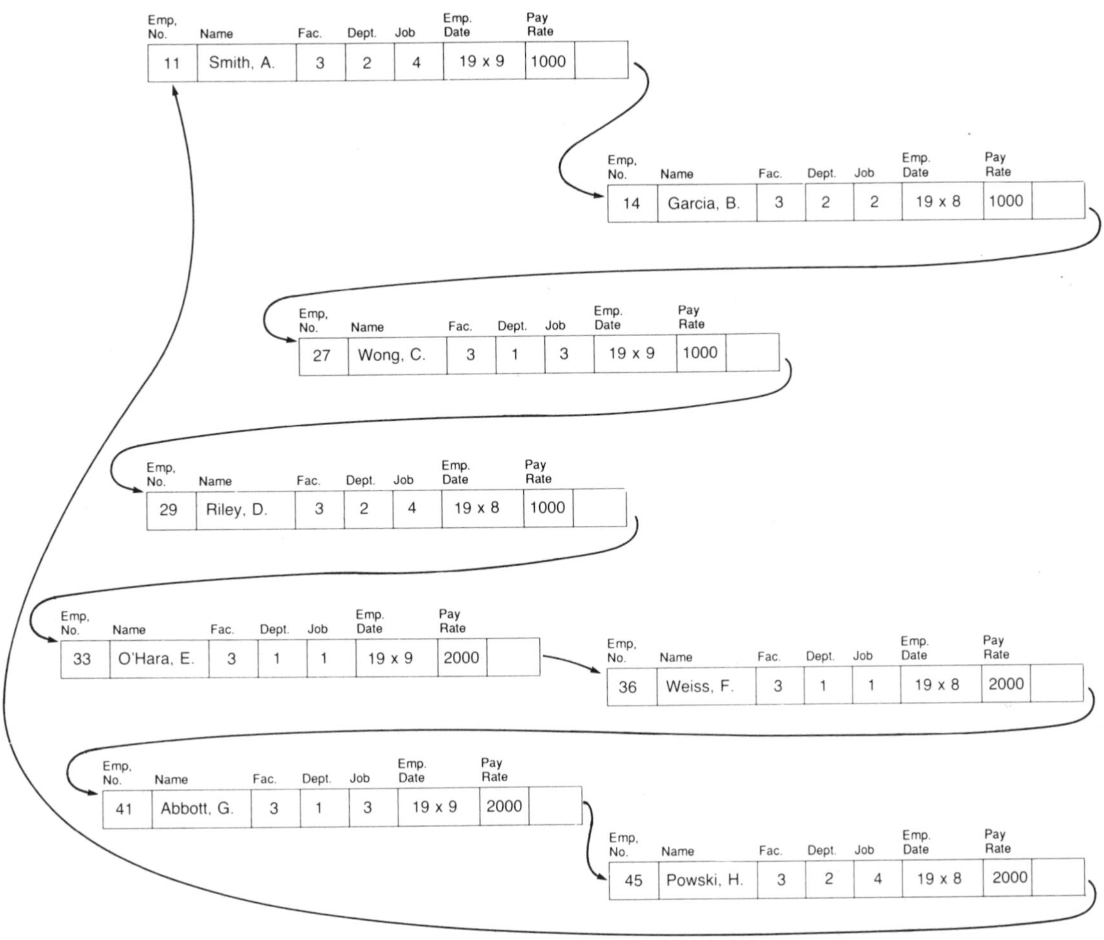

In a multithreaded list, a segment contains a separate pointer for each way of organizing the data. Thus, the data set contains a separate chain for each desired sequence. Pointers enable a segment to be in a different position in each chain. A multithreaded list has multiple entry and terminal points.

In the employee data set in Illustration 12–5, a payroll application may need to access the data in employee number sequence. Then each segment must contain a pointer, and these pointers form a chain that connects all segments in ascending employee number order. A manager evaluating employees for promotion, on the other hand, may wish to obtain a list of employees in alphabetical order. A second pointer must be added to each segment to record this relationship. These form an alphabetical chain of segments. Illustration 12–8 shows the chains formed in such a list for the employee data set.

ILLUSTRATION 12–8 A Multithreaded List

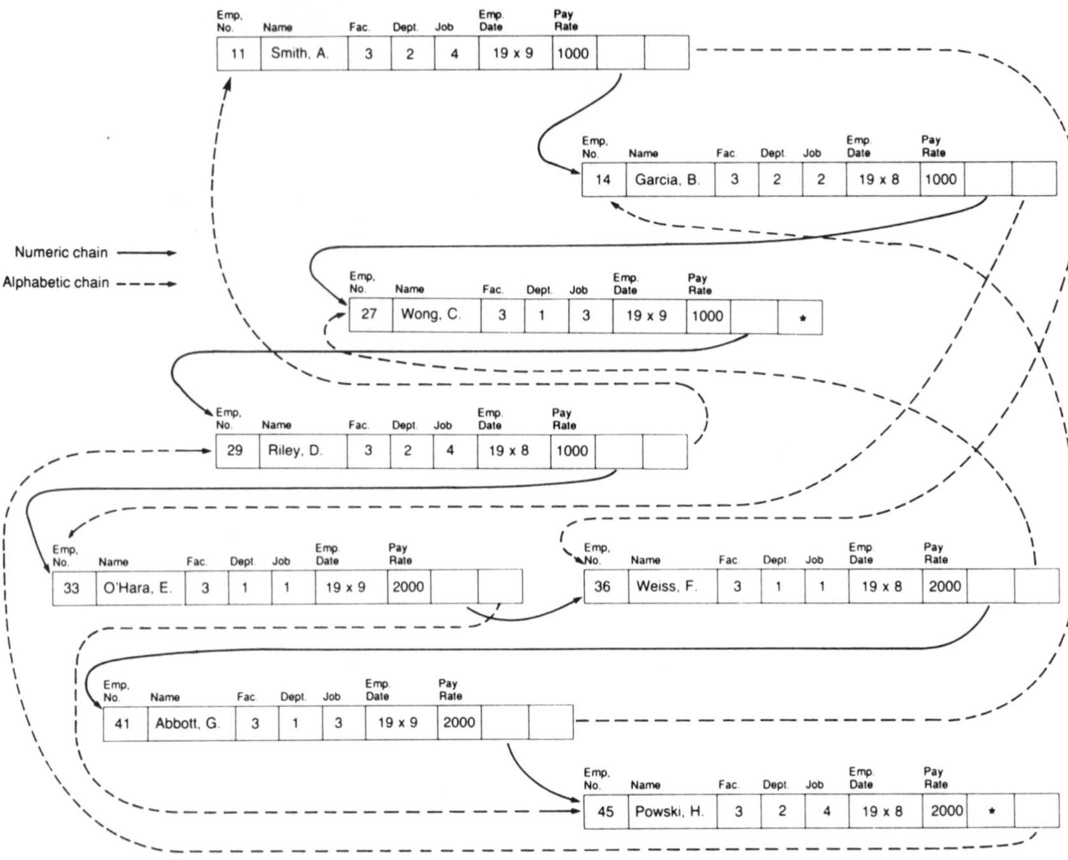

*End of chain marker.

The data base administrator (DBA) must anticipate these information needs when implementing the data base and must structure the data to satisfy them. As you see in Illustration 12–8, a multithreaded list can be very complex. Added complexity causes the DBMS to respond more slowly to requests for data.

Inverted Lists. Rather than chains, the inverted list uses an *index* (or *directory*). The index contains an entry for each segment in the data set. An entry contains the key field of a segment and a pointer to the location of the segment.

An inverted list requires a separate index for each way of ordering the data. When the DBMS searches a data set for a segment, it first searches the proper index sequentially for the key of the desired segment. Then it uses the pointer to

ILLUSTRATION 12–9 An Inverted List

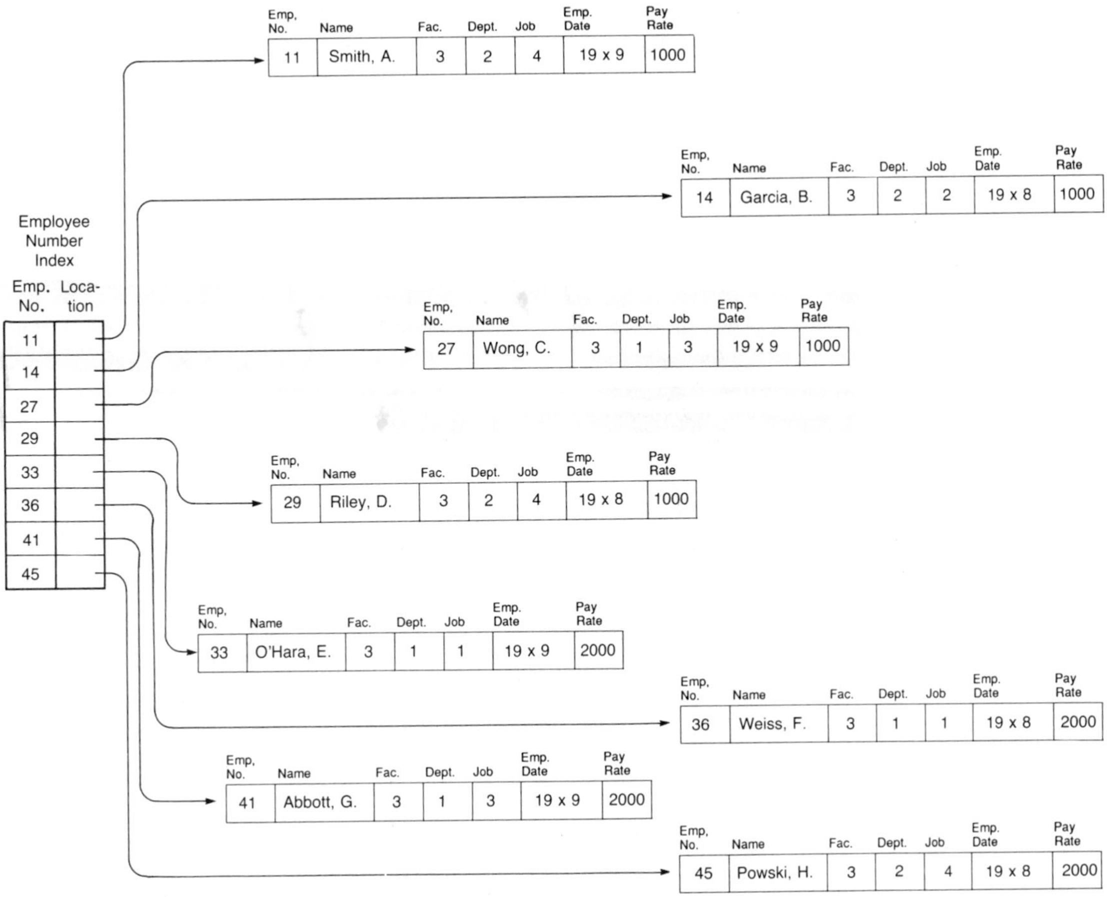

identify the proper location on the direct access device. You can see how this works for the employee data set by examining Illustration 12–9.

A DBMS using an inverted list provides prompt response to queries of the data base because it searches the index rather than the data itself. When segments are added or deleted, however, the DBMS must change both the index and the data. Furthermore, it may become inefficient with a very large data set or when it uses many different indexes.

You have learned about four kinds of lists used by DBMSs to maintain the relationships in a data set. Simple, ring, multithreaded, and inverted lists are the components that maintain relationships in a DBMS data base. In practice, few DBMS packages use one of these components exclusively. The designers of a DBMS combine these components to form more complex structural models.

STRUCTURAL MODELS FOR DATA

Accounting systems use DBMS software that implements one of three structural models for data: the tree, the network, or the relational structure. Each model maintains certain relationships more efficiently than the others. Each offers some advantages over the others in certain kinds of accounting applications.

Tree Structures

One of the earliest structural models used in data base management systems is the *tree* (or *hierarchical*) structure. This structure links segments in a data set so that they form a hierarchy resembling an inverted tree. At the top of the hierarchy is the root segment of the tree. The DBA defines the root when creating the data set. A user or an application program accesses any data element in the set by identifying the root segment to the DBMS.

An Example of Tree Structure. You can see why this data structure is so named by examining Illustration 12–10. This illustration shows the hierarchy of data within a tree structure for the employee data set of Illustration 12–5.

This data set contains two *subtrees,* one for each department. The DBA created three root segments, one for the tree and one for each subtree. To obtain a data element for any employee, you must identify to the DBMS both the factory number (the root of the tree) and the department number (the root of a subtree) for the employee. This is easy to do if each employee has a four-digit identifier of the form:

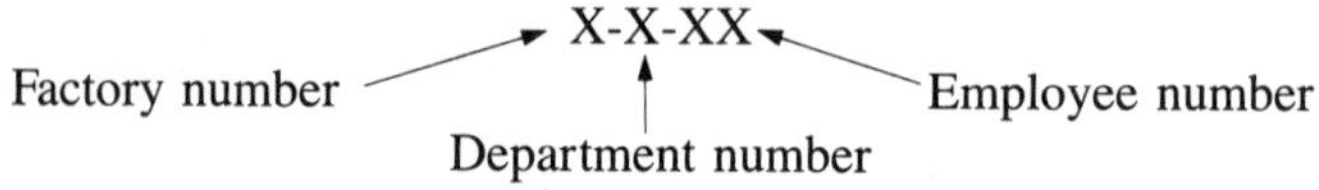

Illustration 12–11 shows how to link the segments in this data set using ring lists. The employee data set contains three ring lists, one for department 1, one for department 2, and a multithreaded ring list for the departments in the factory. Illustration 12–11 shows two of these lists. The DBMS adds one pointer to each segment for each ring containing the segment.

In Illustrations 12–10 and 12–11 you can see one characteristic of tree structures, the "parent-child" relationship between segments. Each segment has only one other segment, its parent, immediately above it in the hierarchy. Each parent, however, can have numerous children immediately below it. A DBMS user identifies a child segment by first identifying its parent in much the same way as you are identified by the family name of your parent.

Advantages and Disadvantages. Tree structures are useful for organizing data in which one-to-one or one-to-many relationships are important. Because

ILLUSTRATION 12–10 A Tree Structure

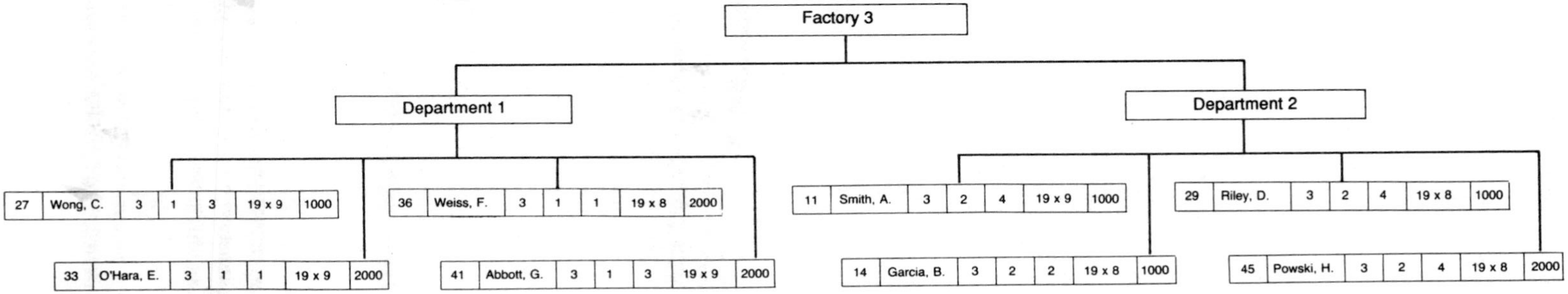

ILLUSTRATION 12–11 Implementation of a Tree Structure Using Ring Lists

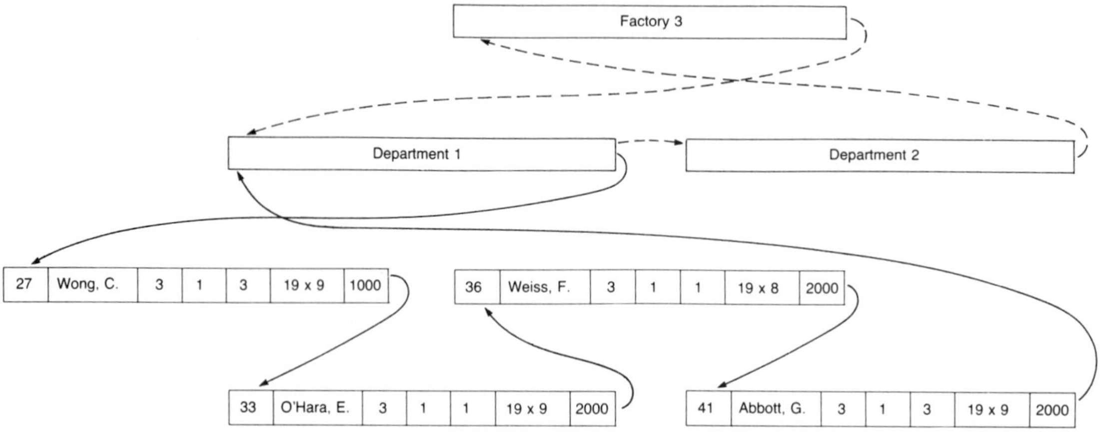

many accounting applications process data of this type, organizations have used DBMSs based on tree structures for many years in processing accounting transactions. They are more efficient than other structures for many such systems.

However, tree structures are less flexible than the other forms. Because they allow only one parent per child, they cannot describe many-to-one or many-to-many relationships. A tree-structured DBMS identifies data elements only through the root of the tree containing them.

In Illustration 12–10, you can quickly obtain information about an employee if you know the factory, department, and employee numbers. However, if you want to know, for example, all the employees in the factory who are machinists, the DBMS would be very slow in providing this information. The DBMS must search through each segment in the data set and compile a separate list of employees who are machinists. Because of this kind of inefficiency, software development companies created a second data structure, the network structure.

Network Structures

A *network* structure, also called a *plex* structure, overcomes many of the shortcomings of the tree. A DBMS using this structure is able to maintain all four relationships that may occur within a data set. It allows multiple entry points into the data and requires multiple pointers in each segment.

It is easiest to think of the network structure as a set of multiple trees within the same data. The network contains one tree for each way of organizing the data segments. Thus, in a network structure, a child segment has multiple parents—

one for each way of organizing the data. This maintains many-to-one and many-to-many relationships.

An Example of Network Structure. Suppose you want to access the data in the employee data set both by employee number and by job code. This allows a payroll application program to determine an employee's pay rate by providing an employee number. It also allows a manager to promptly answer questions of the kind, "How many laborers are employed in factory 3?"

Illustration 12–12 shows a network structure that provides both kinds of information efficiently. In it you can visualize two trees, one with its root at the top and another with its root at the bottom. The top tree in the network maintains relationships by department number; the bottom tree maintains relationships by job code. Each employee segment has two parents, one representing the department and one representing the job code.

What if a manager wishes to know which employees are laborers? The DBMS obtains this information for the manager using the lower tree of Illustration 12–12. Using a query language statement such as "LIST EMPLOYEES IN FACTORY 3 WITH JOB CODE 4," the manager identifies to the DBMS what he or she wants. The DBMS searches the employee data set, entering at the root of the subtree for job code 4.

Illustration 12–13 shows how a chain of pointers allows this search when the data is structured using multithreaded lists. For simplicity, this illustration shows only two lists. However, the DBMS must maintain a separate list for each department and each job code.

Advantages and Disadvantages. By maintaining many-to-one and many-to-many relationships, a DBMS using the network structure is more flexible than a tree structure in the kinds of information it provides. A network structure allows multiple ways of entering the data set and, thus, allows the DBMS to maintain several different relationships at the same time. When organized properly, it can be efficient both in processing accounting transactions and in providing information in response to managerial requests.

However, the data base administrator must anticipate all the desired relationships between data elements when creating the schema. The DBA then creates the required entry segments for the data and causes the DBMS to establish the pointers and chains. If the DBA has not done this in advance, a manager or application program cannot access the data in the desired way.

Furthermore, maintaining the lists in a network structure can be very complex. Consider, for example, what Illustration 12–13 would look like if it showed *all* chains that exist in the data set! In practice, a DBMS may maintain data sets containing thousands of segments. The DBMS changes a chain each time it adds or deletes a segment from a data set. These housekeeping procedures constitute overhead for the system, become time-consuming, and cause the DBMS to respond to requests more slowly. As the complexity of a network structure increases, the speed, responsiveness, and efficiency of the DBMS decreases.

ILLUSTRATION FOR 12–12 A Network Structure

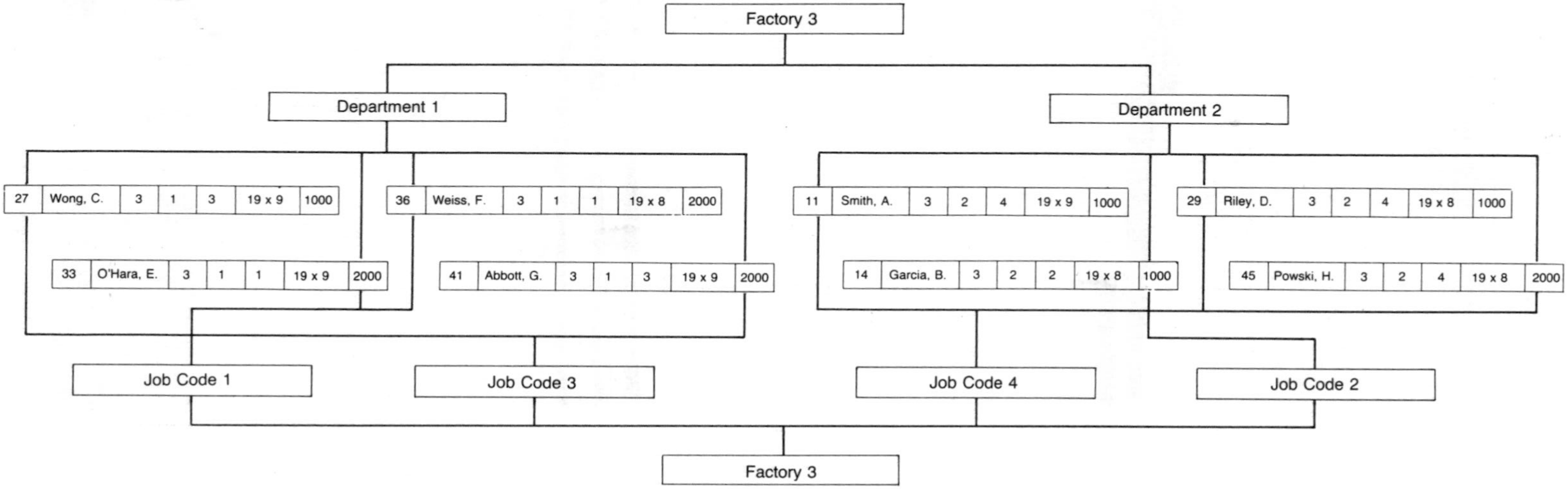

ILLUSTRATION 12–13 Implementation of a Network Structure Using Simple Lists

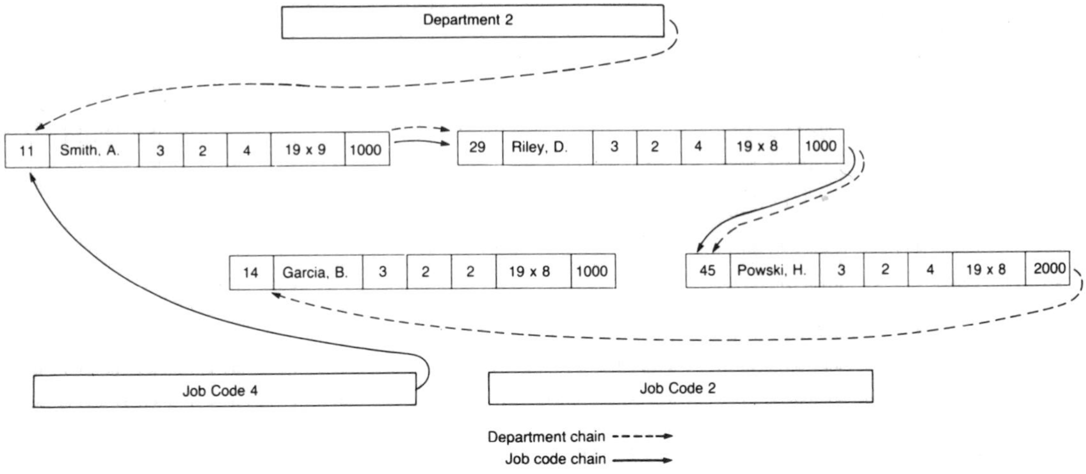

Whenever the number of levels in the parent-child hierarchy exceeds two or three, or when the DBMS maintains more than a few relationships, a network structure becomes inefficient. A third data structure, the relational structure, overcomes some of these disadvantages.

Relational Structures

The structural model that provides the greatest flexibility to users is the relational structure. A DBMS using this structure does not organize data in trees or networks; rather it views data elements as if they were organized in tables.

Each table contains a set of data elements that are related in some way. For this reason, MIS professionals refer to each table as a *relation*. A relation, similar to a table, contains rows (called *tuples*) and columns (called *attributes*). Each row in a table represents an occurrence of two or more logically related data elements. Illustration 12–14 shows the data set of Illustration 12–5 in the form of a relation.

Comparison to Data Files. Logically, the content of a relation is no different than the content of a file in a traditional data file system. A row is equivalent to a record, and a column is equivalent to a data field. Thus, one tuple in a relation contains two or more attributes, just as one record in a file contains two or more fields. A relation is a collection of similar tuples just as a file is a collection of similar records. Illustration 12–15 summarizes these similarities.

ILLUSTRATION 12–14 A Relation

Attributes (columns) / Tuples (rows)

11	Smith, A.	3	2	4	19x9	10.00
14	Garcia, B.	3	2	2	19x8	10.00
27	Wong, C.	3	1	3	19x9	10.00
29	Riley, D.	3	2	4	19x8	10.00
33	O'Hara, E.	3	1	1	19x9	20.00
36	Weiss, F.	3	1	1	19x8	20.00
41	Abbott, G.	3	1	3	19x9	20.00
45	Powski, H.	3	2	4	19x8	20.00

You may wonder why a relational DBMS is advantageous if its contents are equivalent to a traditional file. Its advantage arises because relations, similar to trees and networks, describe *logical* views of the data. Even though users may view a relation as a data set arranged in a table, the DBMS stores data differently on a direct access device. The DBMS software separates the physical arrangement of the data from the user's view. In other words, it separates the logical structure of the data from the physical structure. A file description in a traditional data file system, on the other hand, identifies both the user's view of the data and how the data are physically arranged on the device.

One way of physically storing the data in a relation uses one inverted list for each relation. Illustration 12–9 shows an inverted list for the data in the relation of Illustration 12–14.

Relational Operations. A relational DBMS allows users to perform data operations unavailable in a traditional data file system. These operations allow a manager to examine specific rows or columns in a table, or to combine two or more tables producing another one. They provide the flexibility that makes relational DBMSs popular for producing ad hoc reports and answering unusual

ILLUSTRATION 12–15 Similarities between Relational DBMSs and Traditional Files

Relational DBMS	*Traditional File*
Relation (a table)	Data file
Tuple (a row)	Data record
Attribute (a column)	Data field
Key attribute	Key field

ILLUSTRATION 12–16 Data Operations in a Relational DBMS

SELECT.	Extract one or more tuples (rows) from a relation (table).
PROJECT.	Extract one or more domains (columns) from a relation (table).
JOIN.	Combine two or more separate relations (tables) producing a new relation (table). The new relation (table) contains only specified attributes (columns) from the original ones.

queries. Illustration 12–16 summarizes the major operations; these are illustrated by examples later in this chapter.

The data base administrator establishes the relations used by a relational DBMS. To work most efficiently, the relations should possess certain characteristics:

1. Each table represents only one relationship. For example, a table shows the relationship between employees and their pay rates, or employees and where they work. The table in Illustration 12–14 contains both of these relationships. A DBMS could not perform operations efficiently on this relation.
2. Each row in the table is unique. This means that no two rows in a relation contain exactly the same data. In accounting applications, each row usually contains a primary key that identifies it and makes it unique. The table in Illustration 12–14 has this characteristic.
3. All data elements in any column represent the same attribute. For example, all data elements in the first column of Illustration 12–14 are employee numbers.
4. The data elements contained in any column are not duplicated in other columns. This means that the columns are independent. This is not the case in the example. If you know an employee's department, you also know that the employee has one of the two jobs assigned to that department. These columns are not independent.

MIS professionals say that when a relation has these characteristics, it is *normalized*. The table in Illustration 12–14 does not have all of these characteristics. The example that follows shows how to establish a data base which contains them.

An Example of Relational Structure. Assume that the DBA wishes to maintain the employee data set of Illustration 12–5 using a relational DBMS. The DBA identifies four important relationships among the data elements: (1) the department of an employee, (2) the pay rate of an employee, (3) the job of an employee, and (4) the jobs assigned to a department.

ILLUSTRATION 12–17 Relations in the Employee Data Base

An employee relation

EMP NO	NAME	JOB
11	Smith, A.	4
14	Garcia, B.	2
27	Wong, C.	3
29	Riley, D.	4
33	O'Hara, E.	1
36	Weiss, F.	1
41	Abbott, G.	3
45	Powski, H.	4

A job/department relation

JOB	DEPT
1	1
2	2
3	1
4	2

A pay-rate relation

EMP NO	EMP DATE	PAY RATE
11	19 x 9	10.00
14	19x 8	10.00
27	19 x 9	10.00
29	19x 8	10.00
33	19 x 9	20.00
36	19x 8	20.00
41	19 x 9	20.00
45	19x 8	20.00

The DBA then establishes data sets containing the three relations shown in Illustration 12–17. The employee relation identifies the job of each employee. The pay-rate relation identifies an employee's pay rate, and the job/department relation shows which jobs are assigned to a department.

Why did the DBA not establish a fourth relation showing the department of each employee? A manager can obtain this information from the other relations using relational operations. The department attribute is not independent of the job attribute.

Illustration 12–18 shows how users employ the SELECT operation to obtain data from this data base. Suppose, for example, a manager wishes to know the job performed by employee G. Abbott. The manager uses a query language command applying the SELECT operation to the employee relation. This selects the row of the relation for this employee and displays it at the manager's terminal. The illustration shows a command and the results of the operation.

In Illustration 12–19, you see the results of a PROJECT operation. A payroll clerk issues this command to obtain a list of the pay rates of all employees in the factory. The DBMS produces the list from the pay-rate relation.

ILLUSTRATION 12–18 The SELECT Operation

Query language command: SELECT ABBOTT OF EMPLOYEE
DISPLAY EMP NAME AND JOB

	11	Smith, A.	4
	14	Garcia, B.	2
	27	Wong, C.	3
	29	Riley, D.	4
	33	O'Hara, E.	1
	36	Wiess, F.	1
SELECT →	41	Abbott, G.	3
	45	Powski, H.	4

CRT display:

NAME	JOB
Abbott, G.	3

ILLUSTRATION 12–19 The PROJECT Operation

Query language command: PROJECT EMP NO AND PAY RATE
OF PAY-RATE

PROJECT (arrows to first and third columns)

11	19 x 9	10.00
14	19 x 8	10.00
27	19 x 9	10.00
29	19 x 8	10.00
33	19 x 9	20.00
36	19 x 8	20.00
41	19 x 9	20.00
45	19 x 8	20.00

CRT display:

EMP NO	PAY RATE
11	10.00
14	10.00
27	10.00
29	10.00
33	20.00
36	20.00
41	20.00
45	20.00

What if the manager wishes to know the departments to which all employees are assigned? To find the answer, the manager uses the JOIN operation. The DBMS combines the employee relation and the job/department relation into a table. A query language command selects from this table only the information of interest to the manager. Illustration 12–20 shows this.

ILLUSTRATION 12–20 The JOIN Operation

Query Language Command: JOIN EMPLOYEE WITH JOB/DEPT
DISPLAY DEPT AND NAME

11	Smith, A.	4
14	Garcia, B.	2
27	Wong, C.	3
29	Riley, D.	4
33	O'Hara, E.	1
36	Weiss, F.	1
41	Abbott,G.	3
45	Powski, H.	4

1	1
2	2
3	1
4	2

JOIN

11	Smith, A.	4	2
14	Garcia, B.	2	2
27	Wong, C.	1	1
29	Riley, D.	4	2
33	O'Hara, E.	1	1
36	Weiss, F.	1	1
41	Abbott, G.	3	1
45	Powski, H.	4	2

CRT display :

DEPT	NAME
2	Smith, A.
2	Garcia, B.
1	Wong, C.
2	Riley, D.
1	O'Hara, E.
1	Weiss,F.
1	Abbott, G.
2	Powski, H.

Advantages and Disadvantages. A relational DBMS is much more flexible than those using tree and network structures. With a relational structure, a user or application program accesses data from the data base using the key attribute of a relation. Users can find answers to specific questions without help from MIS personnel.

Accountants are accustomed to using data in tabular form, so the relational view of data is a more natural one than that provided by the other structures. Accountants readily learn relational operations and query language commands. This enables them to exploit the flexibility of the DBMS software package.

In transaction processing applications, a relational DBMS may perform more slowly than DBMSs using tree and network structures. Transaction processing applications use only one point of entry into the data base—the key field of the application's data records. With tree and network structures, the DBA logically arranges the data to process specific transactions efficiently. A relational DBMS, structured for flexibility rather than efficiency, may require more time to process them.

Adding or deleting data, however, may be faster in a relational system than in a complex network DBMS. In a relational DBMS using an inverted list, all pointers are in the index. To delete a data segment, the DBMS only changes the index of the inverted list. To add a segment, it changes the index and adds the segment in an unused location on the disk. The DBMS does not change existing data segments as it does in a tree or network.

SUMMARY

A data base management system (DBMS) is a set of computer programs that controls access to the data base by users and by applications programs. This separates the way data are physically stored on a secondary storage device from the way users and applications view the data. The DBMS maintains not only the data itself but also the relationships between the data. In accounting applications, data may have four kinds of relationships.

Each DBMS software package assumes a structural model for the data. The data base administrator (DBA) creates data sets on secondary storage devices that are consistent with this structural model. A DBMS uses simple, ring, multi-threaded, and inverted lists to implement its structural model.

Three structural models for data are common: tree, network, and relational structures. Each has advantages over the others. Tree structures are fastest in large transaction-processing applications, but they are inflexible and make it difficult to obtain ad hoc reports. Network structures are more flexible because they allow access of the data using multiple key fields, yet they are slower and more complex to set up than trees. The flexibility and tabular format of the relational structure makes it popular with accountants, but it may be slower than the others in transaction processing applications.

KEY TERMS

data base management system (DBMS) A set of computer programs that maintains a data base independent of the application programs using it.

data element The most elemental form of data stored in a DBMS, equivalent to a data field in a traditional data file system.

data segment Two or more related data elements stored together on a direct access device, equivalent to a record in a traditional data file system.

data set Multiple occurrences of a data segment. For example, payroll records for all employees stored in multiple data segments constitute a payroll data set.

inverted list A data set that has an index containing an entry for each segment. The index entry contains a pointer to the segment.

list Two or more data segments linked by pointers. Each segment has a pointer to the next segment in the data set.

network structure A structural model for data allowing multiple entry points for a data set. This provides multiple ways of accessing the data. It is also called a plex structure.

pointer A data element added to a segment by the DBMS linking the segment to other related segments.

relational operations With a relational DBMS, processes that a user can apply to a data set using query language commands. They make a relational DBMS very flexible in how its data can be accessed. Relational operations are SELECT, PROJECT, and JOIN.

relational structure A structural model for data arranging a data set as a table. A row in the table contains a data segment and a column represents one data element.

tree structure A structural model for data requiring one data segment designated as the root. This root segment provides the only way to enter the data set. It is also called a hierarchical structure.

QUESTIONS

12–1. What advantages does a data base management system (DBMS) offer over a traditional file processing system? What disadvantages?

12–2. What four types of relationships exist among data?

12–3. When used by a DBMS, how does a data segment differ from a data record?

12–4. Explain the contents of a data dictionary description of a schema.

12–5. What is a pointer? What information is contained in a pointer?

12–6. A DBMS stores relationships explicitly using pointers. Why is this not required in a traditional data file system?

12–7. A DBMS uses chains of pointers to form lists. What are four kinds of lists?

12–8. Identify three structural models for data, and the types of relationships each can describe.

12–9. What are the advantages of each structural model? The disadvantages?

12–10. In a relational DBMS, how is a relation similar to a file? In what way is it different?

12–11. What are the characteristics that relations should have if a relational DBMS is to work efficiently?

12–12. Which operations are available to the user of a relational DBMS? Describe each.

EXERCISES AND CASES

12–13. *DEFINITIONS*

Define each of the following terms:

a. Data element.
b. Segment.
c. Data set.
d. Pointer.
e. Root of a tree.
f. Parent-child relationship.

12–14. *RELATIONSHIPS*

In the following list of comparisons between two items identify the relationship between each pair. It may be one-to-one (1:1), one-to-many (1:M), many-to-one (M:1), or many-to-many (M:M).

a. County to state.
b. Composer to musical work.
c. Orchestra to musical instrument.
d. Chapter number to chapter title.
e. Chapter number to book.
f. Chapter number to chapter subheading.

12–15. *RELATIONSHIPS*

In the following list of comparisons between two data elements identify the relationship between each pair. It may be one-to-one (1:1), one-to-many (1:M), many-to-one (M:1), or many-to-many (M:M).

a. Employee number to employee name.
b. Employee number to net pay.
c. Customer address to customer name.
d. Sales amount to customer name.
e. Product number to customer name.
f. Product number to component part number.

12–16. *LISTS*

Distinguish between each of the following lists:

a. Simple list.
b. Ring list.
c. Multithreaded list.
d. Inverted list.

12–17. *STRUCTURAL MODELS*

Each of the following block diagrams represents a structural model for data. Identify the structural model represented by each.

a.

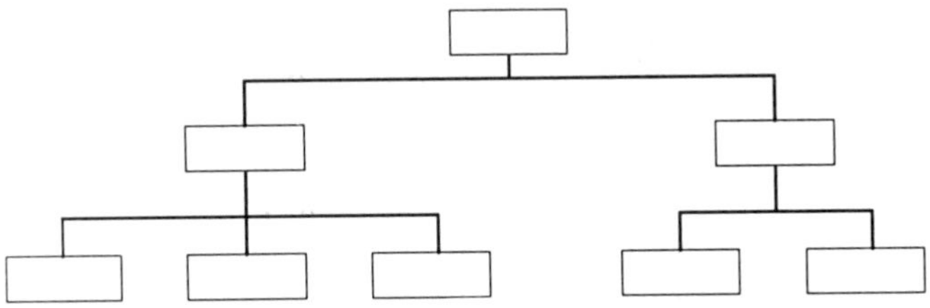

b.

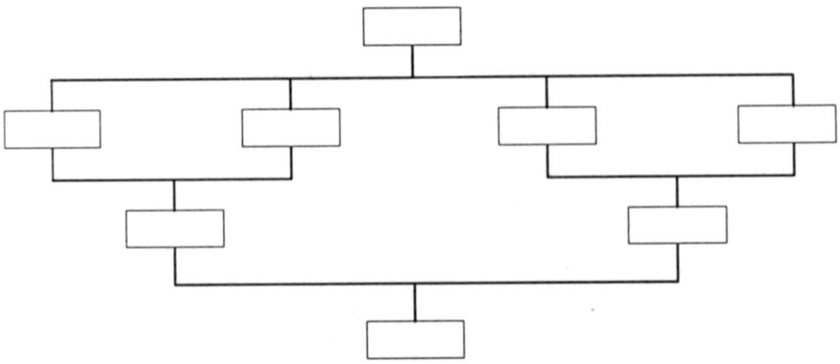

c.

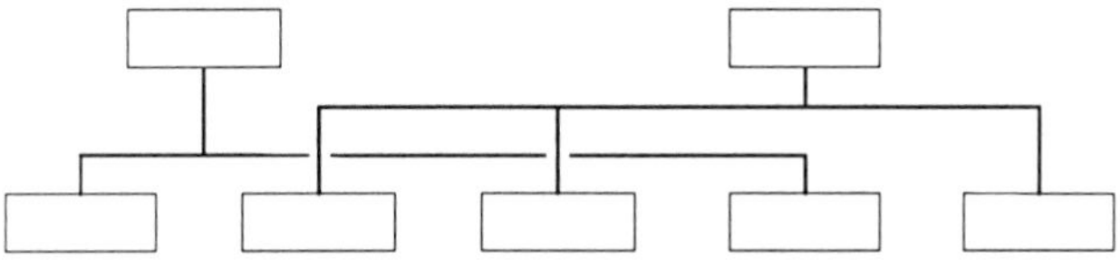

d.

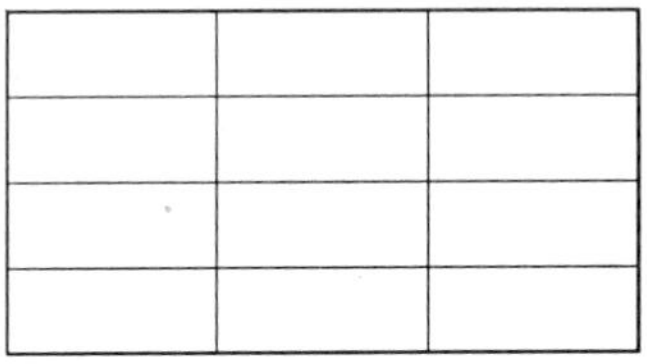

12–18. ***MULTITHREADED LIST***

Climax Corp. is a manufacturing company that uses a DBMS to maintain its bill of materials information. A bill of materials shows the component parts contained in each product manufactured by Climax. The following diagram shows data sets associated with two of its products.

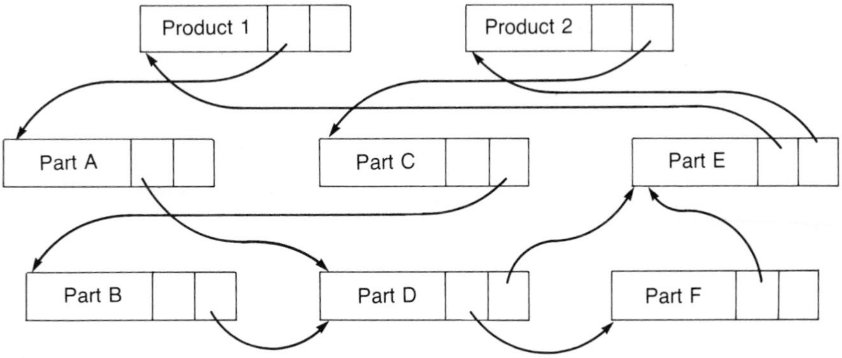

Required:

a. Identify the component parts used in product 1.
b. Identify the component parts used in product 2.
c. Which structural model is used for this data? Explain your answer.

12–19. *SIMPLE AND RING LISTS*

The following segments are from a tree structured data base that contains accounts receivable information. You wish to link these segments so that a receivables clerk can determine the invoices outstanding and the unpaid balance for each customer.

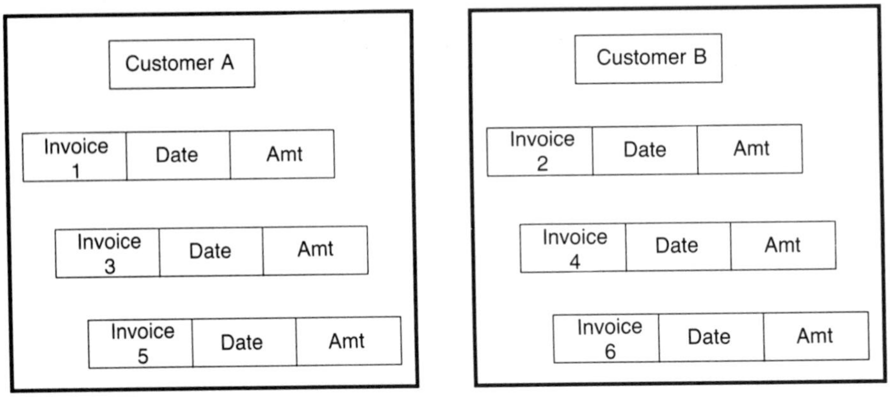

Required:

a. Show how to link the segments in the data set for customer A using a simple list.

b. Show how to link the segments in the data set for customer B using a ring list.

12–20. *NETWORK STRUCTURE*

Wrigley Manufacturing Co. uses a job cost system. Workers obtain component parts required for manufacturing by listing them on a materials requisition and submitting the requisition to an inventory clerk. Wrigley uses a network DBMS to maintain its production cost records.

The data base contains segments representing jobs, material requisitions, and component parts issued for each job. The diagram on the next page shows the data sets for Job No. 101 and Job No. 102.

In this diagram, the number encircled at the beginning of each segment is the physical address of that segment on a disk. The numbers in squares at the end of a segment are pointers to another location.

Required:

Using the diagram on the next page, answer each of the following questions.

a. Which material requisitions were issued for Job No. 102?

b. List the parts issued for Material Requisition No. 34.

c. Which job(s) required Part No. 205?

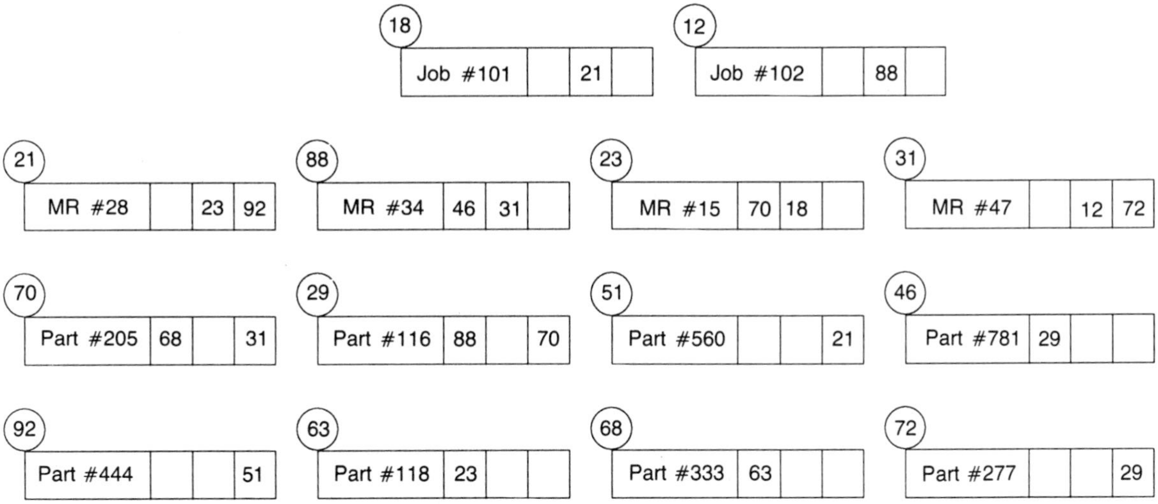

12–21. ***TREE AND NETWORK STRUCTURES***

ABC Wholesale Inc. maintains its accounts receivable records using a DBMS. These records show the outstanding invoices for each customer and all line items listed on an invoice. Each line item represents one product ordered from inventory; a maximum of three line items appear on each invoice. A customer may have any number of invoices outstanding.

The data base contains four segments: customer, invoice, line item, and product segments.

Required:

a. Assume the DBMS uses a tree structure. Users must be able to identify the invoices for each customer and the line items for each invoice. Draw a diagram showing how to link segments providing this information. It is unnecessary to show pointers.

b. Assume the DBMS uses a network structure. In addition to the preceding information, users want to be able to associate customers with the products they purchase. Draw a diagram showing how to link segments to provide this information. (Hint: Your answer should be based on your answer to part *a*.)

12–22. ***RELATIONAL STRUCTURE***

Ample Assets Co. uses a relational DBMS to maintain its accounting records. The following four relations are from its accounting data base. Using the information in these relations, answer these questions:

Customer Relation		
Cust No.	*Name*	*Address*
12	Able	Tulsa, OK
15	Baker	Seattle, WA
23	Charlie	Boston, MA
28	Delta	Chicago, IL
36	Easy	Cleveland, OH

Product Relation		
Product no.	*Description*	*Unit price*
123	Widget	3.00
456	Bearing	10.00
789	Sleeve	7.00
432	Lubricant	4.00
765	Cleaner	5.00

Invoice Relation	
Invoice no.	*Cust no.*
A1111	12
A2222	15
B3333	36
D4444	12
E5555	28

Line Item Relation			
Invoice no.	*Line item no.*	*Product no.*	*Quantity*
A1111	1	765	10
A2222	1	456	2
A2222	2	765	5
B3333	1	123	7
D4444	1	123	1
D4444	2	789	3

Required:

a. What products were billed to the customer on Invoice No. B3333?
b. What is the total amount due from Invoice No. A2222?
c. Which invoice(s) represents sales to customer Baker in Seattle?
d. How much is owed to Ample Assets by customer Able in Tulsa? (Assume that the invoice relation contains only unpaid invoices.)

12–23. ***RELATIONAL OPERATIONS***

Pixel Products is a job shop manufacturing company. The following three relations are from its data base. The job relation identifies each job currently in work-in-process inventory. The product relation shows, for each product in Pixel's product line, the standard quantity of each material required. The material relation contains the standard cost for each kind of material in raw material inventory.

Job Relation

Job no.	*Customer no.*	*Product no.*	*Quantity*	*Due date*
101	1234	216	10	12/12/XX
102	2345	218	30	10/31/XX
103	3456	217	5	11/30/XX

Product Relation

Product no.	*Raw material*	*Standard quantity*
216	A	1
216	R	2
216	Q	1
217	B	4
218	R	3
218	X	2

Material Relation

Raw material	*Standard cost per unit*
A	5.00
B	11.00
Q	2.00
R	4.00
X	10.00

Required:

a. Show the result of performing the JOIN operation on the PRODUCT and MATERIAL relations. Call the result PROD/MATL.

b. Show the result of performing the JOIN operation on the JOB and PROD/MATL relations. (The latter is your result from part *a.*) Call the result from this JOIN operation JOBCOST.

c. Show the result of performing the SELECT operation on JOBCOST for Job No. 101.

d. From your answer to part *c*, determine the total standard material cost for Job No. 101.

e. Which operation can you use to simplify the display resulting from part *c* and yet enable an answer to part *d?*

12–24. ***ON-LINE REAL-TIME DBMS***

American Airlines anticipated a lot of disasters that could disrupt its Sabre Passenger Services System, but it did not foresee the glitch that brought the reservation system down for 13 hours one weekend.[1] Located in an underground storeroom, Sabre computers are protected from tornadoes, plane crashes, and power outages. But they were not isolated from an internal error that erased internal labels on 1,080 disk drives. This forced reservations clerks and travel agents to rely on printed flight schedules and to write out tickets by hand.

"Our reaction was one of absolute horror, it was our worst nightmare," said Jim Jackson, vice president of systems engineering for American's Sabre Computer Services Division. He had learned of the problem after being awakened by an emergency telephone call on Friday night. "Even if we had intended to do this damage, it would have been extremely difficult to duplicate."

The massive computer crash started just before midnight on Friday. It happened while Sabre technicians were reformatting the disk drives during an expansion project. This would have extended support from Sabre's operating system to a total of 1,260 disk drives.

"We had a program that was changed erroneously and did something that we never intended for it to do," said Jackson. The erroneous program stripped away the digital labels on each disk volume, making it impossible for the operating system to address any of Sabre's disk drives. Although only about 2,500 records were destroyed, this made it impossible to access about 1 million bytes of data.

"The field that was changed was a control field in the formatter utility," he explained. "The operating system, overwhelmed by its inability to address the disk drives, collapsed nearly instantaneously." Sabre technicians had to restart the crashed system, relabel each disk drive, and reset the pointers that indicate where passenger data is located. The pointers are critical because the information on just one ticket is scattered across multiple disk drives. This process took 100 programmers and systems engineers more than 10 hours.

The system was restarted just before 7:00 A.M. on Saturday and reformatting was complete by 11:00 A.M. Then, due to pent-up demand, American's technicians had to gradually restart Sabre, slowly admitting more traffic from 27 front-end communications processors. American Airlines officials would not comment on the amount of revenue lost because of the problem.

---

[1]Adapted from "Runaway Program Gores Sabre," *Computerworld*, May 22, 1989, p. 1. Used by permission.

Said one travel agent, ''We could have booked the American flights on a competing reservations system, but we could not be certain the space was available. Without Sabre, the seats and the discounted fares could not be confirmed until flight time.'' Their 35 employees had to handwrite most tickets until 2:30 P.M. on Saturday. ''We were picking up the phone and calling like in the old days,'' he said. ''We really didn't catch up with the paperwork until Monday morning.''

Required:

a. How were pointers used to link the data in this on-line real-time applications system?

b. Which procedures, implemented routinely at the data center, could have prevented this error?

c. Which routine procedures could have made recovery of the data base easier?

Part IV

Controls

Chapter 13

Internal Control Structure

Learning Objectives:

1. To understand the components of an organization's internal control structure.
2. To know the objectives and limitations of internal control.
3. To discover which characteristics of a control environment promote accurate and reliable data.
4. To learn which characteristics of an accounting system promote accurate and reliable data.
5. To describe good control procedures.

INTRODUCTION

Accounting systems provide information for people both internal and external to an organization. The users of this information rely on the accuracy of the system's reports and displays. Organizations adopt policies and procedures, or system controls, to maintain accurate information and reliable operation of the system. These policies and procedures are a part of the overall internal control structure of the organization.

In this chapter you will learn about the components of an organization's internal control structure, its limitations, and some basic policies and procedures.

ILLUSTRATION 13–1 Internal Controls

Type	*Objective*	*Example Procedure*
Accounting controls	Safeguard assets.	A bank locks cash in its vault.
	Ensure accurate and reliable accounting data.	Point-of-sale cash register terminals eliminate data entry errors.
Administrative controls	Promote operational efficiency.	A standard cost materials variance measures wasted material.
	Encourage adherence to management's policies.	A performance report discloses whether a department meets its budget goals.

INTERNAL CONTROLS

An organization's internal control structure consists of the policies and procedures established by management to achieve organizational objectives. Although this structure may include a wide variety of actions directed toward many objectives, accountants commonly recognize these four major ones:

1. Safeguard the organization's assets.
2. Verify the accuracy and reliability of accounting data.
3. Promote operational efficiency.
4. Encourage employees in the organization to follow management's policies.

Many accountants make a distinction between two categories of internal controls.[1] *Accounting controls* are those policies and procedures directed toward the first two objectives, safeguarding assets and ensuring accurate and reliable accounting data. *Administrative controls* serve the second two objectives, promoting operational efficiency and adherence to management's policies. Illustration 13–1 contrasts these types of controls and provides examples.

Accountants consider accounting controls important because they have a direct impact on the accuracy of accounting information. For example, if money is stolen from a bank vault, the bank's balance sheet is misleading because it overstates the amount of cash in the vault. If a sales transaction is recorded at an incorrect amount, the financial statements misstate both the Sales and Accounts Receivable accounts.

---

[1]The distinction between these categories of internal controls was for many years a part of auditing standards. They were eliminated by Statement on Auditing Standards No. 55. The terms are, however, still in common use and students should be familiar with them.

ILLUSTRATION 13–2 Threats to the Accuracy of Accounting Information

Errors.	Accidental misstatements. Errors from *carelessness*—due to inattention or fatigue. Errors in *judgment*—due to lack of knowledge or inadequate training.
Irregularities.	Intentional misstatements. *Defalcation*—theft of an asset. *Management fraud*—management deliberately distorts financial information.

From the perspective of the organization, administrative controls are equally as important; however, these have a less direct impact on the accuracy of accounting information. For example, one administrative control is employee training. Well-trained accounting personnel work more efficiently and follow management's policies more closely. This indirectly produces more accurate accounting information because trained employees make fewer errors.

Entering erroneous data into an accounting system is just one threat to the accuracy of accounting information. Accountants identify two major sources of such threats.

Threats to the Accuracy of Accounting Data

Accountants recognize that misleading accounting information results both from errors and from irregularities. Errors are accidental, while irregularities are intentional. Top management creates an internal control structure to detect or prevent errors and irregularities. Illustration 13–2 summarizes these threats to the accuracy of accounting information.

Errors. An error may be due to *carelessness* or it may arise from a *lack of knowledge*. For example, an error from carelessness occurs when a sales clerk unintentionally hits the wrong key and enters an incorrect amount into a cash register. Lack of knowledge causes an error when the clerk unknowingly codes the transaction incorrectly as a cash sale rather than a credit sale. Appropriate control procedures detect these errors when they occur. For the preceding examples, most cash registers display the sales amount to the customer, and most retailers daily compare total cash in a register to its recorded cash sales.

Irregularities. Irregularities also occur in two forms. *Management fraud* occurs when a manager intentionally misstates financial information. Managers sometimes do this to overstate earnings. In this way they may increase the size of their bonuses, or increase the selling price of stock they own. A *defalcation* is a theft of assets from the organization. For example, a sales clerk may remove cash from a cash register and use the cash for personal purposes. Because this theft is unrecorded in the accounting records, the theft causes them to overstate the balance in the cash account.

Control procedures also prevent or detect defalcations. A retailer who reconciles cash in the register with recorded sales at the end of each day can detect theft by sales clerks. Many forms of management fraud, however, are undetectable by an organization's internal control structure. Often the internal control structure cannot prevent or detect management fraud at reasonable cost.

Reasonable Assurance

Top management chooses an organization's internal controls by implementing policies, procedures, and a structure appropriate to achieve the organization's objectives. However, most managers are unwilling to implement controls that are more costly than the benefits they provide. Thus, errors or irregularities may be undetected simply because the cost of preventing or detecting them exceeds the potential loss from them.

For example, a sales clerk may steal cash from a cash register and immediately leave the country. A supervisor may not discover this theft until the cash in the register is reconciled at the end of the day. One way to prevent this defalcation is to hire another employee to constantly watch the sales clerk. However, because this defalcation is unlikely, most managers think the cost of hiring the second employee exceeds the benefits. Managers require a daily reconciliation of the cash in the register because it is a cost-effective way to detect and prevent the most likely errors and irregularities concerning cash sales.

Accountants refer to this implied cost-benefit analysis of internal controls as the concept of reasonable assurance. Internal control policies and procedures are intended to provide *reasonable, but not absolute, assurance* that management's objectives are attained. Reasonable controls are those for which the benefits exceed the costs. Providing absolute assurance of no errors or irregularities cannot be achieved at a reasonable cost, and few organizations attempt it.

When selecting an internal control structure, most managers consider it unreasonable to establish policies and procedures that absolutely prevent three kinds of threats. These constitute the three major limitations of a good internal control structure.

Limitations of Internal Control

It is seldom cost effective to select controls that are absolutely effective in detecting errors from carelessness or in preventing collusion between employees. And because management establishes them, no internal control structure prevents management from violating its own policies and procedures. Accountants call this management override of internal controls.

Errors. Everyone occasionally becomes distracted from a task at hand. Employees may be inattentive due to fatigue, to outside interruptions, or to overwork. This inattention may cause them to become careless and make errors. Even though well-trained and conscientious employees make fewer errors, most managers recognize that even the best employees sometimes make mistakes. They consider it unreasonable to develop an internal control structure that prevents or detects every such error. Rather, they attempt to hire good employees and to adopt policies and procedures preventing or detecting the most likely or most serious errors.

Collusion. Collusion occurs when two or more employees conspire to commit a theft from their employer. For example, a sales clerk and a sales supervisor may agree to steal cash from a cash register and to cover the theft by falsifying the daily reconciliation for that register. By colluding in this way, they may succeed in perpetrating a defalcation.

Although it is possible to adopt policies and procedures that detect theft where collusion occurs, most managers consider the costs of doing so excessive. Instead, they try to hire honest employees and to keep them satisfied with their jobs. This minimizes the desire to steal and makes collusion unlikely. Accountants and managers recognize, however, that if collusion occurs, the existing control structure will be ineffective in preventing it.

Management Override. Managers in the organization have more authority than production or clerical personnel. This causes control policies and procedures that are effective at lower levels in an organization to become ineffective at higher ones.

For example, a store manager may steal cash from the day's receipts after the daily cash reconciliation at each register is complete. The manager can then simply misstate the amount of cash received in reports to superiors in the organization. The reconciliation procedure, although effective at the sales clerk level, is ineffective in preventing or detecting these irregularities at a higher level. The store manager overrides this control procedure.

Management override, similar to collusion, is preventable. In most situations the costs of designing an internal control structure to prevent or detect management override exceeds the benefits. Instead, organizations try to employ honest managers and to compensate them adequately for good performance. The possibility of management override is a limitation to any well-designed internal control structure.

This section describes some objectives and some limitations of internal control. Management selects an internal control structure based on the concept of reasonable assurance. The next section discusses the elements, or components, of an internal control structure.

COMPONENTS OF AN INTERNAL CONTROL STRUCTURE

The three components to an organization's internal control structure are the control environment, the accounting system, and control procedures.[2]

The Control Environment

The control environment—those circumstances surrounding an organization's accounting system—either improves or limits the effectiveness of control procedures. It consists of many factors subject to management's control and some that are not. These factors determine how effectively control procedures achieve the objectives set out for them. The following discussion identifies some of the factors in the control environment.

Management's Philosophy and Operating Style. These include management's approach to taking business risks, attitudes toward the accuracy of accounting data, and emphasis on meeting budget and operating goals.

A management prone to taking risks is less likely to be concerned with measures taken to secure assets and maintain accurate accounting records. This increases the likelihood of errors and irregularities. When top management insists that managerial employees show continued improvement at all costs, managers are more likely to attempt management fraud to meet budget goals. These characteristics have a significant influence on the accuracy of the accounting records and the effectiveness of control procedures.

Organizational Structure. The organizational structure provides an overall framework for the planning and controlling activities performed by management. Objectives are more easily achieved in an organization whose structure reflects its management functions and that assigns authority and responsibility appropriately.

Audit Committee. An audit committee consists of several of the organization's directors who are not employed by it in another capacity. If the audit committee takes an active role in overseeing accounting policies and practices, the accounting system and control procedures are more effective in achieving control objectives. The audit committee can alert the entire board of directors to problems before they become serious.

Methods of Assigning Authority and Responsibility. These may be either formally described in writing or informally assigned. They may reflect either a centralized or a decentralized approach to management.

---

[2]The following discussion is adapted from "Consideration of the Internal Control Structure in a Financial Statement Audit," Statement on Auditing Standards No. 55, AICPA, New York, 1988.

ILLUSTRATION 13–3 Good Personnel Policies and Practices

Training. Employees who understand their jobs are less likely to make errors.

Recognition for work well done. Encourages employees to prevent errors and irregularities.

Adequate pay. Fairly compensated employees are less likely to steal.

Investigate employees before hiring. A potential employee may have a history of carelessness or dishonesty.

Job rotation. Require employees to change jobs periodically. Then an employee cannot continue to conceal an error or irregularity made in the past.

Required vacations. An employee filling in for an employee on vacation may discover an error or irregularity made in the past.

Bonding. A bond is a contract whereby a surety company agrees to reimburse the employer for loss if an employee commits theft. The surety company thoroughly investigates the background of the bonded employee before issuing the bond.

With a centralized approach, top management makes most major decisions affecting the organization. With a decentralized one, they delegate decision-making authority and responsibility to middle- and lower-level managers. Authority and responsibility affect such matters as acceptable business practices, conflicts of interest, and codes of conduct.

When these methods are formally assigned and centrally controlled by an effective accounting system, there are fewer opportunities for errors and irregularities in the organization.

Management Control Methods. Control methods are used by top management to monitor performance by lower-level managers. They affect top management's ability to control the exercise of authority delegated to others. They include systems for planning, budgeting, and performance reporting as well as the internal audit function. Effective management control methods provide an environment less prone to errors and irregularities than ineffective ones.

Personnel Policies and Practices. Personnel policies affect the organization's ability to employ enough capable people to accomplish its objectives. These policies describe how the organization hires, trains, evaluates, promotes, and compensates employees.

Ultimately, the effectiveness of any internal control structure relies on the honesty and the abilities of the employees. Honest employees are less likely to commit defalcations, and capable ones are less likely to make errors. Adequate personnel policies and practices ensure that the organization hires capable people, trains them properly, treats them fairly, and compensates them adequately. Such policies and practices make errors and irregularities less likely. Illustration 13–3 contains some internal control practices that encourage a work force of honest and capable employees.

ILLUSTRATION 13–4 Factors Affecting the Control Environment

Management's philosophy and operating style
Organizational structure
Audit committee
Methods of assigning authority and responsibility
Management control methods
Personnel policies and practices
External influences

External Influences. Many parties outside the organization affect the environment in which the accounting system and control procedures function. External influences include requirements imposed by governmental agencies, creditors, and owners.

These external influences are normally not under the control of management. They may affect management's attitudes toward ensuring proper conduct, maintaining accurate accounting data, and establishing specific internal control policies and procedures. Illustration 13–4 summarizes the factors affecting the control environment of an organization.

The Accounting System

A second component of an organization's internal control structure is the accounting system. It consists of the methods and records used to identify accounting transactions, assemble them, and analyze, classify, and report them. The accounting system also maintains accountability for the organization's assets and liabilities.

Modern accounting systems implement double-entry accounting methods. A double-entry system includes several features that prevent and detect errors and irregularities. These are debit and credit analysis, a chart of accounts, standard journal vouchers, a trial balance, and control accounts.

Debit and Credit Analysis. When an accounting system records a transaction, it records the effects of that transaction in at least two accounts. Half of the journal entry is a debit, and the other half is a credit. And, as you learned in your first accounting course, the total of the accounts debited must equal the total of the accounts credited. This simple feature detects many errors and detects or prevents many irregularities.

How does the double-entry accounting system detect errors? Any accounting transaction contains entries in two or more accounts. An incorrect entry in one account must be compensated for by an equal error in another account. Otherwise, the entry does not balance and a clerk easily detects the error.

ILLUSTRATION 13–5 Characteristics of a Well-Designed Chart of Accounts

Responds to organization's needs. Accounts included in a chart of accounts should meet both management's needs for control of operations and financial accounting requirements for external reporting.

Facilitates report preparation. Accounts in the chart of accounts should be listed in their order of appearance in the financial statements and should be compatible with the organizational structure.

Provides adequate description. A description of each account and its contents should be provided. This guidance to the accounting staff enables consistent use of the accounts.

Account titles provide clear distinctions. Account titles should be chosen to minimize ambiguities concerning the contents of an account.

Control accounts. When cost effective, the chart of accounts should incorporate control accounts.

For example, when an organization purchases inventory, the system records a debit to the Inventory account and a credit to the Accounts Payable account. To go undetected an error must be repeated twice, once in Inventory and again in Accounts Payable. Two equal errors are more unlikely, and much easier to detect, than a single error would be if debit and credit analysis were not required.

The double-entry system also makes detecting defalcations easier. If an employee steals inventory, then the inventory on hand does not equal the recorded balance in the accounting records. An auditor or supervisor can easily detect the theft by counting the inventory. An employee wishing to cover the theft must make fraudulent entries in two accounts rather than one. This doubles the chance of detection.

Chart of Accounts. The chart of accounts is a list of all the account names and account codes used by the organization. An employee may use only those accounts listed when making debit and credit entries. This restricts the opportunity for employees to make errors or commit irregularities when recording transactions.

For example, when an employee steals cash, the employee may attempt to cover the theft by crediting the Cash account and debiting an expense account. If there are only a limited number of expense accounts in the chart of accounts, any prolonged use of this scheme produces excessive expense account balances. Management would question the cause of these excessive expenses, and discover the defalcation.

A properly designed chart of accounts also minimizes errors. Illustration 13–5 shows some characteristics of a well-designed chart of accounts.

Standard Journal Vouchers. A standard journal voucher is a document on which an accountant makes a standard journal entry.

Accountants repeat many adjusting entries each time the closing process occurs in the accounting cycle. Fewer errors occur if a project team, when designing the system, creates a *standard journal entry* for each of these repeated adjustments. Then during closing, the accountant records the standard journal entry on a standard journal voucher printed to show the proper accounts to debit and credit. An accountant determines the appropriate amounts and records them on the standard journal voucher. In this way the accountant does not make entries in incorrect accounts.

For example, at each closing an accountant makes an adjusting entry accruing unpaid wages as of the closing date. If the design project team creates a standard journal voucher for this adjustment, it contains a debit to Wages Expense and a credit to Wages Payable. They print a set of standard journal vouchers for this entry. At closing the accountant determines the amount of the accrual, fills in the amount on a standard journal voucher form, obtains proper approvals, and enters the adjustment in the records.

Illustration 13–6 shows an example of a standard journal voucher. For this company, Journal Voucher No. 29 is used to write off the accounts receivable balance of a customer. A credit manager initiates this document after reviewing an aged trial balance of accounts receivable. The treasurer initials approval of it after verifying that the debt is uncollectable. The chief accountant or controller reviews it for correctness before an accounting clerk enters it in the computer system.

Trial Balance. Accountants prepare a trial balance as one step in the accounting cycle. Preparation of the trial balance provides an opportunity to determine if the system has recorded transactions erroneously.

Because each transaction is recorded as a combination of equal debits and credits, the total of the debits must equal the total of the credits on the trial balance. An inequality is evidence of an error in recording transactions.

Common errors disclosed on the trial balance include transposition and misfooting. A transposition error occurs when a clerk records the amount of an entry but interchanges two of its digits. For example, the clerk may intend to write 456, but instead writes 465. Misfooting occurs when the clerk adds numbers incorrectly.

Accountants also review the trial balance for abnormal account balances. An abnormal account balance may indicate errors either in posting or during debit and credit analysis. Asset and expense accounts normally have debit balances. Liability, Capital, and Revenue accounts normally have credit balances. If a different balance is noted when reviewing the trial balance, the accountant investigates to determine its cause.

Control Accounts. A control account in the general ledger summarizes the contents of many accounts in a subsidiary ledger. Organizations commonly use them when recording accounts receivable, inventory, fixed assets, and common stock. An accounts receivable control account, for example, summarizes the

ILLUSTRATION 13–6 A Standard Journal Voucher

SUNLIGHT MANUFACTURING COMPANY JV No. 4 -29
105 Red Hot Road
Dallas TX 75248

STANDARD JOURNAL VOUCHER

For the month of April 19 XX

	Account Title	Debit	Credit
106	Allowance for Doubtful Accounts	255.15	
105	Accounts Receivable/RST Company		255.15

EXPLANATION

To write off accounts receivable from RST Company, declared bankruptcy; see attached documents.

Prepared by	Approved by	Reviewed by	Entered by
D. Li			
Date 4/28/XX	Date	Date	Date

amounts owed by those customers with outstanding balances in the accounts receivable subsidiary ledger. In a computerized system, this subsidiary ledger is the customer master file.

When a transaction produces an entry in a control account, the accounting system also records the transaction in the proper account in the subsidiary ledger. At the end of a reporting period, the total of the debits (or credits) in the control account should equal the total of the debits (or credits) in the subsidiary ledger. An inequality alerts an accountant to the existence of a recording error.

The second component of an organization's internal control structure is its accounting system. A double-entry accounting system implements practices that

ILLUSTRATION 13–7 Good Procedures for Processing Transactions

Prompt recording. Employees record transactions immediately as they occur. This decreases opportunities for errors and irregularities regarding the transactions.

Visual checking. An employee recording the transaction visually confirms that all data is complete and correct.

Balancing. An employee determines that the total debit entries equal the total credit entries for the transaction.

Batch controls. Employees accumulate transactions into batches. They total the amount of the transactions in each batch and attach this total to the batch. In each later processing step, this total is recalculated and compared to the original batch total. This verifies that no transactions are lost from the batch.

prevent or detect many errors and irregularities. Management may adopt many other practices as part of the internal control structure whenever the benefits of these control procedures exceed their costs.

Control Procedures

Control procedures are the third component of an organization's internal control structure. Management adopts them to provide reasonable assurance that the organization achieves its objectives. When the objectives are safeguarding assets and assuring accurate and reliable accounting data, accountants call them *internal accounting* control procedures. The first of the five categories of internal accounting control procedures concerns the methods of authorizing transactions and the activities that process transactions.

Proper Procedures for Transactions. Management implements procedures for authorizing transactions and prescribes activities for processing them. The proper way to process transactions differs for each class of accounting transaction. For example, good procedures for processing cash disbursements transactions in the expenditure cycle differ from procedures for processing cash receipts in the revenue cycle. Yet good procedures in different transaction cycles have many characteristics in common. Illustration 13–7 summarizes some of these. Employees should record all transactions promptly and examine their records for obvious inaccuracies. Batch controls and balancing procedures help to discover errors.

Proper procedures for authorizing transactions likewise depend on the kind of transaction. Management authorizes transactions in two ways, using general and specific authorizations.

General Authorization. Management's general authorization relates to a whole class of transactions. A general authorization describes conditions under which employees may initiate, record, and process one kind of transaction. When these conditions are met, an employee is authorized to carry out these actions without further consultation with management.

For example, management of a retail store approves a sales price for certain merchandise. Whenever a customer arrives who wants that merchandise and has the cash to pay for it, employees are authorized to initiate, record, and process the sales transaction.

Specific Authorization. Management's specific authorization applies only to a single, specific transaction. Management normally requires specific authorization for large dollar amount transactions or those that represent high potential for fraud. Before an employee initiates a transaction of this kind, the employee consults with management and obtains approval specifically for it.

Transactions for larger amounts require specific authorization at higher organizational levels than smaller transactions. For example, if a customer wishes to purchase merchandise but wants to pay by check rather than currency, management may require a sales clerk to obtain specific approval of the transaction from a supervisor. If a manager wishes to initiate a transaction to purchase a new factory building, the manager obtains specific authorization for this transaction from the board of directors.

Procedures for processing transactions are the first of five categories of control procedures. A second category concerns security for assets and records.

Security for Assets and Records. Management should implement adequate safeguards to protect assets and records. Safeguards include fixing responsibility for them and providing physical security.

Physical Security. Management implements procedures to provide physical security for inventory, cash, property, plant, equipment, and for the records of these assets.

Inventory and cash are easily stolen and should be locked up; access should be limited to authorized employees. Thieves are sometimes able to steal other property and equipment, so these require safeguards as well. Many organizations attach nonremovable labels to each item of equipment. The label assigns an identifying number to the item. A property master file—a subsidiary ledger for the property account in the general ledger—lists each item by identifying number.

In a computer-based system, records include documents, filing cabinets, and computer files. When an employee steals an asset, the accounting records concerning the asset are overstated. To cover up a theft of assets, the thief must alter the accounting records for the asset. Adequate security over records prevents this and allows detection of the theft.

For example, if a clerk steals something from the inventory warehouse, the inventory records show more on hand than actually exists. If the thief cannot gain access to inventory records, a supervisor or internal auditor may discover the theft by comparing the inventory records to the quantity on hand. Adequate physical security prevents unauthorized access to inventory records as well as inventory itself. Physical security, however, is only effective when management fixes responsibility for it with specific individuals.

Fixed Responsibility. Management assigns responsibility for specific assets and records to specific job positions. Then if an error or irregularity occurs, management holds the individual in that job position responsible.

For example, management appoints an employee to the position of inventory clerk and gives that employee responsibility for physical security of inventory. If inventory is stolen, the inventory clerk is held responsible. Even if the inventory clerk did not commit the theft, the clerk was responsible for protecting the inventory and failed in that responsibility.

Internal control is better when management summarizes and communicates responsibilities in writing. During system implementation, a project team creates a procedures manual for this purpose. When it clearly fixes responsibility in this way, management encourages employees to do their jobs accurately and honestly.

A third category of control procedures concerns separation of responsibilities, or segregation of duties.

Segregation of Duties. Management should assign responsibility in order to attain adequate segregation of duties. This means that no employees have the opportunity both to carry out and conceal errors and irregularities in the normal course of their duties. Management assigns duties so that different people perform three duties affecting an asset. Different employees are responsible for *authorizing* transactions in an asset, for *recording* transactions in an asset, and for *maintaining custody* of the asset.

For example, inventory is an asset that is easily stolen. In applying the principle of segregation of duties to inventory, management assigns responsibility for the custody of the inventory to an inventory clerk. When the records indicate that inventory is missing, management holds the inventory clerk responsible.

An accounting clerk maintains the inventory records, and a shop supervisor authorizes issuance of inventory by signing a materials requisition. These individuals do not have access to the inventory warehouse. In this way neither the inventory clerk, the accounting clerk, nor the shop supervisor is in a position to steal inventory and then conceal the theft by altering the inventory records. At least two of these employees must collude to commit and successfully hide a theft of inventory.

Accountants say that having custody of an asset, authorizing transactions in the same asset, and keeping the records regarding the asset are *incompatible functions*. Management should design the organization's structure and assign responsibilities so that no employee performs functions that are incompatible. Although this is often difficult to do in a small organization, in such firms management can more closely monitor the actions of employees.

The fourth category of control procedures concerns the kinds of documents and records used in the accounting system.

Adequate Documents and Records. Management should require the use of accounting documents and records that ensure proper recording of transactions and events. You have learned how a double-entry accounting system helps achieve this objective. Controlling blank forms and prenumbering documents do so as well.

Forms Control. When filled out, the forms used in an organization provide authorization for transactions or for the transfer of assets. An employee can cover up a theft of assets by stealing a document and falsifying it to alter the accounting records. For this reason, an individual employee should be assigned responsibility for each type of blank form. This employee maintains custody of the form and assures its physical security.

For example, an unscrupulous employee may steal a materials requisition form from a shop supervisor. The employee fills out the form, forges the supervisor's signature, receives the inventory from the inventory clerk, and sells the inventory to a nonemployee. Nothing in the accounting records discloses this theft because the records agree with the quantity of inventory on hand. When checking for missing requisitions, the supervisor will discover the theft.

Management should review each form periodically and change it if necessary. A review may disclose that the form collects data no longer used or that it could easily collect data useful for management purposes if other lines were added. Management may also decide to change the number of copies produced or their distribution. Many organizations establish a policy that each form is reviewed every few years. A form has the date of its last review printed in small letters somewhere on it, so management can easily see when it is time for another review.

Prenumbered Documents. Adequate forms control is much easier when each copy of a form has a unique identifying number added by the printer. Then a supervisor can periodically check the quantity on hand of each prenumbered document and verify that none are missing. If one is missing, the supervisor can determine its number and prevent a thief from using it to falsify a transaction.

Documents that should be prenumbered and controlled include blank checks, check requests, purchase orders, receiving reports, invoices, materials and purchase requisitions, journal vouchers, and credit memos. Any of these, when stolen, can be falsified and used to cover the theft of an asset.

Once a form has been filled out, it becomes a completed document. Completed documents must be controlled just like blank forms, because thieves use them to falsify transactions as well.

For example, an unscrupulous employee may steal a completed materials requisition—documenting an issue of material earlier in the year—from the filing

ILLUSTRATION 13–8 Independent Checks on Performance

Check	*Example*
Clerical checks	A shop worker fills out a materials requisition. The shop supervisor reviews it before signing it.
Reconciliations	A shop supervisor examines the sequence of completed material requisitions to assure that none are missing.
Comparison of assets with records	An internal auditor and an inventory clerk count the physical inventory. The auditor compares the count totals with quantities shown in accounting records.
Computer programmed controls	A computer program checks calculations on a material requisition after the data is entered into the computer.
Management review of accounts	A factory manager investigates the cause of an excessive materials quantity variance.
User review of computer reports	An inventory clerk reviews a list of material requisitions to look for duplicate processing of the same requisition.

cabinet in the factory office. The employee alters the requisition by changing its date, submits the requisition, receives the inventory from the inventory clerk, and sells the inventory to a nonemployee. Again the accounting records agree with the inventory on hand, so reconciling them does not disclose the theft. However, while periodically checking the sequence of the completed requisitions stored in the filing cabinet, the supervisor would discover the theft of one of them. The supervisor can then search for the missing requisition and, perhaps, catch the thief.

Many organizations prevent defalcations of this kind by defacing documents once they have been used. They may punch small holes in the document forming the word "paid," or they may ink stamp it with the word "cancelled." This control procedure indicates to all employees that the document should not be used again.

The effectiveness of many control procedures depends on actions by supervisors or internal auditors. These are examples of the fifth category, independent verification of performance.

Independent Verification of Performance. Management should authorize independent checks on the performance of employees and on the accuracy of the accounting records. These include clerical checks, reconciliations, comparing assets on hand with the accounting records, control procedures carried out by computer programs, management review of summaries of changes in account balances, and review by users of computer reports. Illustration 13–8 contains examples of each of these.

When verification procedures are independent, someone who did not originally process the transaction performs the procedure. This may be another employee, a supervisor, a manager at a higher level, or an auditor. Auditors provide an objective form of verification because they have no superior-subordinate relationship with employees processing the transaction. Both independent auditors and internal auditors perform verification procedures.

Independent Auditors. Independent auditors are employees of a firm of certified public accountants. They may perform verification procedures as a part of their annual audits of the financial statements. Because they are not employees of the organization being audited, their examination provides the most objective form of verification.

Independent auditors examine only those control procedures important for the independent audit. Standards for independent auditing require them to obtain an understanding of the internal control structure sufficient to plan the audit. Yet they ordinarily do not examine control procedures related to each account or each class of transaction. They may omit verification procedures that are not relevant to their objectives. Management relies on internal auditors to verify performance in these areas.

Internal Auditors. Internal auditors are staff people employed by the organization. Frequently they have backgrounds in accounting, although they may come from other disciplines such as management information systems. As a service to management, the internal audit staff reviews the operations of the organization and makes recommendations for improving them.

Internal auditors make periodic reviews, called *operational audits,* of each department in the organization. A part of these reviews is to carry out verification procedures appropriate for the department. For example, as part of a review of inventory procedures, an internal auditor may supervise the count of physical inventory in the warehouse. The internal auditor then reconciles the inventory on hand with the accounting records for inventory. This verifies the performance of those employees involved in authorizing and recording transactions in inventory and those who have custody of it.

Operational audits are most effective when internal auditors are completely independent of the department being audited. An internal audit staff that reports to the controller would be independent of the inventory function in a production department. It would not be independent of the accounting department, however, because the controller has a superior-subordinate relationship with both accounting and internal audit. For maximum independence, the internal audit staff should report as high in the organizational hierarchy as possible. The internal audit staff should always have direct access to the audit committee of the board of directors.

Control procedures are the third component of an organization's internal control structure. The five categories of control procedures concern proper procedures for processing transactions, security for assets and records, segregation of duties, adequate documents and records, and independent verification of performance. Illustration 13–9 summarizes these categories of control procedures.

ILLUSTRATION 13–9 Control Procedures Categories

1. **Procedures for authorizing and processing transactions**
   General authorization
   Specific authorization
2. **Security for assets and records**
   Physical security
   Fixed responsibility
3. **Segregation of duties**
   Different employees *(a)* authorize transactions in an asset, *(b)* record those transactions, and *(c)* have custody of the asset.
4. **Adequate documents and records**
   Prenumbered documents
   Control of blank forms and completed documents
5. **Independent verification of performance**
   Managers and supervisors
   Internal and independent auditors

SUMMARY

An organization's internal control structure consists of the policies and procedures established by management to achieve the organization's objectives. When these objectives are safeguarding assets and ensuring accurate and reliable accounting data, accountants call the policies and procedures internal accounting controls.

The threats to accurate accounting data include accidental errors and intentional irregularities. Internal controls provide reasonable, but not absolute, assurance that the objectives will be obtained. As a result, any internal control structure is limited by the possibilities of errors from carelessness, collusion, or management override.

The components of an internal control structure are the control environment, the accounting system, and control procedures. The control environment consists of those circumstances surrounding the accounting system that improves or limits the effectiveness of control procedures. The accounting system consists of the methods used to identify, assemble, analyze, classify, and report accounting transactions. Control procedures are other policies and procedures established by management to achieve the organization's objectives. There are five categories of control procedures.

KEY TERMS

accounting system The methods and records used to identify, assemble, analyze, classify, and report accounting transactions.

collusion Two or more people conspiring to steal from an organization.

control environment Those circumstances surrounding an organization's accounting system that either improve or limit the effectiveness of control procedures.

control procedures Procedures adopted by management to provide reasonable assurance that the organization achieves its objectives.

control structure An organization's control environment, its accounting system, and its control procedures.

defalcation The theft of assets from an organization.

general authorization Management's authorization in advance for a class of transactions.

internal controls Policies and procedures established by management to achieve the organization's objectives.

irregularity An intentional act, such as defalcation or management fraud, that may misstate accounting data.

management override The ability of managers to overcome control policies or procedures that are effective with operations level employees.

reasonable assurance A concept applied to internal controls stating that the costs of a control policy or procedure should not exceed its benefits.

segregation of duties Management should assign responsibility so that no individual performs any two of three functions: custody of an asset, recordkeeping regarding the asset, and authorizing transactions in the asset.

specific authorization Management's authorization for a single, specific transaction.

standard journal voucher A document used to record a standard journal entry. It shows the proper accounting entry for a common transaction, and minimizes the likelihood of recording it incorrectly.

APPENDIX

The Foreign Corrupt Practices Act

In 1977 the United States Congress enacted the Foreign Corrupt Practices Act (FCPA). It was in response to scandals during the early 1970s involving bribery to foreign officials. Congress was concerned that such activities could occur without the knowledge of top management and without detection by auditors. The act had two main provisions, one relating to illegal foreign payments and another to internal control.

Illegal Foreign Payments

It is a criminal offense for any U.S. business to pay, to promise to pay, or to authorize payment of anything of value to officials of other governments to maintain a business relationship. A business violating this provision may be fined up to $1 million; its managers may be fined up to $10,000, imprisoned up to five years, or both.

This provision of the FCPA is an effective deterrent against bribes by businesses in the United States. The provision of most interest to accountants, however, is that concerning internal control.

Internal Control Provisions

These provisions apply only to companies required to file reports with the U.S. Securities and Exchange Commission (SEC). The provisions require that these companies maintain books, records, and accounts accurately recording their transactions. The FCPA also requires that these companies:

> devise and maintain a system of internal accounting controls sufficient to provide reasonable assurance that
>
> (i) transactions are executed in accordance with management's general and specific authorization;
>
> (ii) transactions are recorded as necessary (I) to permit preparation of financial statements, and (II) to maintain accountability for assets;
>
> (iii) access to assets is permitted only in accordance with management's general or specific authorization; and
>
> (iv) the recorded accountability for assets is compared with the existing assets at reasonable intervals and appropriate action is taken with respect to any differences.[3]

The SEC has responsibility for monitoring compliance with these provisions.

Thus, management must establish an adequate internal control structure not only to fulfill its obligations to owners of the business but also to comply with the FCPA. Because accountants are the experts in internal control, in most organizations top management relies heavily on them in satisfying these provisions.

QUESTIONS

13–1. Which four objectives do accountants recognize for an internal control structure?

13–2. What is the distinction between accounting controls and administrative controls?

13–3. What are the two threats to accurate and reliable accounting data? Describe and distinguish between them.

---

[3]Sec. 102 of the Foreign Corrupt Practices Act of 1977 (PL 95–213).

13–4. What is meant by the following statement: "Internal control policies and procedures are intended to provide reasonable, but not absolute, assurance that management's objectives are attained"?

13–5. Which kinds of errors and irregularities can occur even in an organization having a good internal control structure?

13–6. What are the components of an internal control structure?

13–7. Identify seven factors that affect an organization's control environment.

13–8. Which features of a double-entry accounting system prevent and detect errors and irregularities?

13–9. How does debit and credit analysis aid in preventing and detecting errors? Irregularities?

13–10. What is a standard journal voucher? Why is it a good control practice?

13–11. What are five categories of control procedures?

13–12. Describe the difference between general authorization and specific authorization.

EXERCISES AND CASES

13–13. CONTROL PROCEDURES

The following is a list of control procedures discussed in this chapter. Identify to which of the five categories each belongs.

a. Balancing.
b. Operational audits.
c. Prenumbered documents.
d. Prompt recording.
e. Locks.
f. Fixing responsibility to avoid incompatible functions.

13–14. CONTROL PROCEDURES

Describe how each control policy, practice, or procedure in the following list either prevents or detects errors and irregularities.

a. Training.
b. Locking up blank forms.
c. Bonding.
d. Chart of accounts.
e. Job rotation.
f. Batch controls.

13–15. *INCOMPATIBLE FUNCTIONS*

The following list contains pairs of job functions. From this list identify the pairs that are incompatible. Explain your answer.

a. Inventory clerk and shop supervisor.
b. Inventory clerk and payroll clerk.
c. Shop supervisor and payroll clerk.
d. Factory superintendent and shop supervisor.
e. Chief accountant and controller.
f. Treasurer and controller.

13–16. *CHART OF ACCOUNTS*

The following chart of accounts is that of Summertime Patio Furniture, a small retail store which rents space in a shopping center.

Current Assets (100–199)
101 Cash in Bank
102 Prepaid Rent
105 Petty Cash

Other Assets (200–299)
200 Delivery Truck
201 Accumulated Depreciation—Delivery Truck
210 Office Equipment
211 Accumulated Depreciation—Office Equipment
220 Merchandise Inventory

Liabilities and Equity (300–499)
310 Accounts Payable
320 Loan from Bank
400 Pat Summertime, Capital
410 Pat Summertime, Drawings

Revenue and Expenses (500–999)
501 Cash Sales
502 Sales on Account
610 Salaries Expense
620 Supplies Expense
699 Other Expenses
999 Income and Expense Summary

Required:

a. Suggest five account titles that should be added to make Summertime's chart of accounts internally consistent.
b. Renumber two accounts so that the account title sequence makes the preparation of accounting reports easier.

13–17. ***CHART OF ACCOUNTS***

The chart of accounts of Dobson Distributors, Inc., a manufacturers' representative, follows:

Current Assets (10–19)
- 10 Cash in Bank
- 11 Petty Cash
- 12 Inventories
- 15 Supplies
- 17 Prepaid Rent

Property (20–25)
- 20 Land
- 25 Office Machines

Other Assets (26–29)
- 28 Organizational Costs

Liabilities and Equity (30–59)
- 31 Accounts Payable
- 33 Notes Payable
- 40 Bonds Payable
- 50 Capital Stock
- 51 Retained Earnings

Revenue (60–69)
- 60 Sales from Showroom Displays
- 61 Sales from Direct Shipments

Expenses (70–89)
- 71 Salaries
- 72 Power
- 73 Supplies
- 75 Rent

Other Revenue and Expenses (90–99)
- 99 Income and Expense Summary

Required:

a. Suggest five account titles that should be added to make the Dobson's chart of accounts internally consistent.

b. Suggest account titles that are not needed in their chart of accounts.

13–18. ***STANDARD JOURNAL VOUCHERS***

The following entries are routinely recorded by accounting systems. Identify those appropriate for standard journal vouchers. Explain your choices.

a. Record wages payable.

b. Record cash sales.

c. Record purchase of inventory.
d. Record prepaid insurance.
e. Record supplies expense.
f. Record depreciation expense.

13–19. ***INCOMPATIBLE FUNCTIONS***

The Mid-Cities Company has three clerical employees who must perform the following functions:

a. Maintain general ledger.
b. Maintain accounts payable ledger.
c. Maintain accounts receivable ledger.
d. Prepare checks for signature.
e. Maintain disbursements journal.
f. Issue credits on returns and allowances.
g. Handle and deposit cash receipts.
h. Reconcile the bank account.

Of the eight functions, items *f* and *h* take a negligible amount of time; all other functions require an equal amount of time. All three employees are equally capable; they perform no other accounting functions than those listed. Accounting functions not listed are performed by others.

Required:

a. Distribute the functions among the three employees in a way that provides the best internal control.
b. List four possible unsatisfactory combinations of these functions.

(AICPA Adapted)

13–20. ***INCOMPATIBLE FUNCTIONS***

The following list contains functions to be performed by personnel of the Metroplex Paint Company, a small wholesaler. Each function marked by an asterisk (*) takes about the same amount of time. These should be assigned equally to employees A and B, who have the same training and competence. The president of the company, C, is unwilling to perform any function marked with an asterisk, but is willing to assume two of the other functions.

* *a.* Assemble supporting documents for disbursements and prepare checks for signature.
* *b.* Sign general disbursement checks.
* *c.* Record checks written in the cash disbursements and payroll journal.
d. Mail disbursement checks to suppliers.
e. Cancel supporting documents to prevent their reuse.

* *f*. Approve credit for customers.
* *g*. Bill customers and record the invoices in the sales journal and subsidiary ledger.
* *h*. Open the mail and prepare a prelisting of cash receipts.
* *i*. Record cash receipts in the cash journal and subsidiary ledger.
* *j*. Prepare daily cash deposits.
* *k*. Deliver daily cash deposits to the bank.
* *l*. Assemble the payroll timecards and prepare the paychecks.
* *m*. Sign paychecks.
n. Post the journals to the general ledger.
o. Reconcile the accounts receivable subsidiary ledger with the control account.
p. Prepare monthly statements for customers by copying the subsidiary ledger accounts.
q. Reconcile the monthly statements from vendors with the subsidiary accounts payable accounts.
r. Reconcile the bank account.

Required:

Divide the above duties among A, B, and C.

(AICPA Adapted)

13–21. *REASONABLE ASSURANCE*

Sally Jones, CPA, has been engaged to examine the financial statement of Ajax, Inc. Jones is about to undertake a study of Ajax's internal control structure and is aware of the inherent limitations that should be considered.

Required:

a. Which objectives do accountants recognize for an internal control structure?
b. What is meant by the concept of reasonable assurance?
c. When considering the potential effectiveness of any internal control structure, which inherent limitations should be recognized?

(AICPA Adapted)

13–22. *ACCOUNTING AND ADMINISTRATIVE CONTROLS*

The division manager of a large firm was preparing for an operational audit by the firm's internal audit department. In a preaudit conference, the manager was told that although the audit would examine accounting controls, the emphasis of the upcoming audit would be on administrative controls. As part of the preparation for the audit, the manager was asked to assemble materials that would indicate the degree of control in the plan of organization.

Required:

a. Define accounting control and administrative control.

b. List three documents used by a company to describe its plan of organization. For each, describe at least two characteristics that would be of interest to the auditor. (Hint: You may refer to Chapters 4 and 7.)

(CIA Adapted)

13–23. ***SEGREGATION OF DUTIES***

As the internal auditor for a large savings and loan association, you are concerned about segregation of duties for a wholly owned real estate investment subsidiary. The subsidiary, despite its $10 million in assets, operates out of the main office of the parent. The parent company administers all purchasing, payroll, and personnel functions. The subsidiary's board of directors consists entirely of selected officers of the parent.

The real estate investment subsidiary's activities consist primarily of buying, developing, and selling real estate, with some development projects involving joint ventures with contractors. Day-to-day operations are handled by the president and two vice presidents. The president also acts as liaison with the parent; each vice president has additional projects to manage.

All invoices and itemized statements requiring direct payment or reimbursement to contractors or vendors are delivered to one of the two vice presidents for review and approval. After approval, the staff accountant prepares checks and then obtains the signature of one of the vice presidents on the checks. After signing, the checks are returned to the staff accountant for mailing, and supporting documents are filed. All blank checks are kept by the staff accountant.

All customer payments on notes and accounts receivable originating from the sale of real estate are sent to one of the two vice presidents and then forwarded to the staff accountant who records the payment and prepares the deposit slip. The deposit may be given to the parent's accounting department or to a teller of the parent.

If the subsidiary experiences a cash shortage, a promissory note is prepared by the staff accountant and signed by the president or one of the vice presidents. The staff accountant submits the promissory note to the parent and awaits receipt of the funds. The staff accountant is responsible for billing customers and advising management when payments are due. The staff accountant reconciles the bank statement once a month on receipt.

The staff accountant prepares monthly financial statements, including the accrual of interest receivable and the capitalization of certain interest charges. These financial statements are prepared to reflect the substance of both joint ventures and subsidiary operations. The board of directors reviews the financial statements.

Required:

Identify specific areas in which segregation of duties is inadequate.

(CIA Adapted)

13–24. *FOREIGN CORRUPT PRACTICES ACT*

The home office of GHP Insurance Company has a formal statement on policies and procedures for the expense reimbursement of agents. A description of these policies and procedures follows.

Agents are to obtain an expense report form at the beginning of each week. The completed forms are submitted to the branch manager at the end of each week. The branch manager looks over the expense report to determine if (1) the expenses qualify for reimbursement under the company's expense reimbursement policy statement; and (2) the amounts are reasonable. Agents are asked to explain any questionable expense item and to show documentation supporting the amounts. Any single expenditure that is expected to exceed $100 should be approved by the branch manager in advance.

The branch manager approves each expense report by signing it and forwards the report to the accounting department at the home office. The accounting department makes the appropriate journal entries and posts to the general ledger accounts and agent subsidiary records. A check is prepared by the cash disbursements office to each agent to whom an amount is owed. These expense reimbursement checks are sent to the branch manager, who then distributes them to the agents.

Agents may receive cash advances for expenses by completing a cash advance approval form. The branch manager reviews these forms and gives approval by signing the forms. One copy of the form goes to the accounting department at the home office for recording in the general ledger accounts and agent subsidiary records. A second copy of the form is given to the agent who submits it to the branch office cashier and obtains the cash.

At the end of the month, the internal auditing department at the home office adds the total dollar amounts on the expense reports from each branch, subtracts the sum of the dollar totals on each branch's cash advance approval form, and compares the net amount to the sum of the expense reimbursement checks issued to agents. Any differences are investigated.

The Foreign Corrupt Practices Act of 1977 has identified five general control objectives related to transactions or accounts-authorization, recording, safeguarding, reconciliation, and valuation. To evaluate internal control effectively, these general objectives must be related to specific internal control procedures for each aspect of a system.

Required:

a. Define and discuss each of the five internal control objectives identified in the Foreign Corrupt Practices Act of 1977 (FCPA).

b. Discuss whether GHP Insurance Company's internal control system for the reimbursement of agent expenses satisfies the first four objectives—authorization, recording, safeguarding, and reconciliation—identified in the FCPA.

(CMA Adapted)

13–25. ***CONTROL PROCEDURES***

Bertly Company was organized in 1935. Management has always recognized that a well-designed accounting system provides many benefits including reliable financial records for decision making and a control system that increases the probability of preventing or detecting errors or irregularities. Thus Bertly has developed an adequate internal control structure.

Bertly's internal audit department periodically reviews the company's accounting records to determine if the internal accounting control system is functioning effectively. The internal audit director believes such reviews are important because inconsistencies or discrepancies can serve as a warning that something is amiss.

The following seven conditions were detected by Bertly's internal audit staff during a routine examination of accounting records:

1. Daily bank deposits do not always correspond with cash receipts.
2. Bad checks from customers are consistently approved by the same employee.
3. Physical inventory counts sometimes differ from perpetual inventory records, and there have been alterations to physical counts and perpetual records.
4. There is a high percentage of customer refunds and credits.
5. There is an excessive use of substitute documents because originals are lost or missing.
6. An unexplained and unexpected decrease in gross profit percentage has occurred.
7. Many documents are not countersigned.

Required:

For each of the seven conditions detected by Bertly Company's internal audit staff,

a. Describe a possible cause of the condition.
b. Recommend actions to be taken and/or controls to be implemented that would correct the condition.

(CMA Adapted)

13–26. ***DOUBLE-ENTRY SYSTEM***

On November 9, Leslie Young, president of the High Sierra Development Company, received a letter from the Redwood Lumber Company saying that a check for $1,500 issued to Redwood in payment of lumber purchased was returned by the bank marked ''insufficient funds.'' Redwood asked whether an error had been made and whether the check could be redeposited. Young was surprised at this; according to its records the company had an ample cash balance at the bank to cover the check.

Young was a ski enthusiast and a frequent visitor to Mamouth, California, a well-known ski resort. On the way home during one of many trips, Young noted a ranch for sale. Young persuaded several friends to join in acquiring the property, and the High Sierra Development Company was organized. It was agreed that the amount of initial capital contribution should be at a minimum.

Accordingly, the capitalization of the company was set initially at $20,000. Payment for this amount was received on November 1.

In acquiring the property valued at $80,000 for the land and $20,000 for the building, the company paid only a cash down payment of $18,000; the balance was financed by a noninterest-bearing note, payable in five equal annual installments, beginning a year from November 2, the date at which the transaction took place.

Young made a careful review of the records of High Sierra Development Company. No error could be found. To further ensure correctness, Young prepared a trial balance as of November 9; it was in balance. Puzzled, Young came to you for assistance. The journal on which analyses are made is shown in Exhibit 13–1. The ledger accounts are in Exhibit 13–2, and the trial balance in Exhibit 13–3.

EXHIBIT 13–1 Case 13–26

GENERAL JOURNAL Page 1

Date		Accounts and Explanation	Ref.	Debit	Credit
Nov.	1	Cash	1	20,000	
		Capital Stock	9		20,000
		Issued capital stock for cash.			
	2	Land	3	80,000	
		Building	4	20,000	
		Cash	1		18,000
		Notes Payable	8		82,000
		Purchased ranch as investment. Note is payable in five annual installments and bears no interest.			
	3	Building	4	1,500	
		Accounts Payable	7		1,500
		Purchased lumber for building innovation. Amount is to be paid in 10 days.			
	4	Prepaid Insurance	2	600	
		Accounts Payable	7		600
		Purchased one-year insurance policy, paying cash.			
	5	Building	4	400	
		Accounts Payable	7		400
		Purchased paint for building innovation, paying cash.			
	6	Accounts Payable	7	1,500	
		Cash	1		1,500
		Paid lumber purchased on account.			

EXHIBIT 13–2 Case 13–26 Ledger Accounts

Cash 1

Nov. 1 (1)	30,000	Nov. 2 (1)	18,000
		6 (1)	1,500

Prepaid Insurance 2

Nov. 4 (1)	600		

Land 3

Nov. 2 (1)	80,000		
5 (1)	400		

Building 4

Nov. 2 (1)	20,000		
3 (1)	1,500		

Accounts Payable 7

Nov. 6 (1)	1,500	Nov. 3 (1)	1,500
		4 (1)	600
		5 (1)	400

Notes Payable 8

		Nov. 2 (1)	82,000

Capital Stock 9

		Nov. 1 (1)	30,000

EXHIBIT 13–3 Case 13–26

HIGH SIERRA DEVELOPMENT COMPANY
Trial Balance
November 9, 19XX

Cash	$ 10,500	
Prepaid insurance	600	
Land	80,400	
Building	21,500	
Accounts payable		$ 1,000
Notes payable		82,000
Capital stock		30,000
	$113,000	$113,000

Required:

a. What comments do you have in regard to records kept by Leslie Young?
b. What is the proper cash balance as of November 9?
c. Why is the trial balance unable to disclose the errors you have located?

13–27. INTERNAL CONTROL STRUCTURE

Days Inns of America, Inc., is the sixth largest lodging company in the United States, with a total revenue of $306 million during a recent year. Being privately owned, Days Inns is not subject to regulations of the Securities and Exchange Commission concerning financial activities or the adequacy of internal controls. Nevertheless, corporate management believes that sound internal control is a prerequisite to sound managerial accountability. As a result, it launched an improved managerial control (IMC) project in July after a presentation by its independent auditors on management's responsibility for internal control.

Task Force

In approving the IMC project, the company's president appointed a task force composed of senior executive vice presidents for finance, operations, and administration, the three top officials below the company's chief executive. Their participation underlined the executive support for the project and its broad coverage of all areas of corporate activity. Others named to the task force were the senior vice president for human relations, the director of internal audit, and the director of systems, standards, and procedures.

The executive vice president for finance was designated task force leader with responsibility for calling meetings and presiding and approving the agenda. The director of systems, standards, and procedures was named project coordinator, responsible for planning, organizing, directing, and controlling staff activities, and for periodically reporting results. The director of internal audit was made responsible for conducting specific internal control reviews, eventual systematic monitoring of the overall internal control structure, and served as the task force's secretary.

Objective and Action Plan

The task force agreed on an action plan, shown as Exhibit 13–4, and immediately initiated the project. The plan set forth the following as the project's primary objective:

> To establish and maintain a control environment and internal managerial and accounting controls adequate to safeguard the company's resources and assure their efficient and effective utilization.

EXHIBIT 13–4 Case 13–27 Phases of the IMC Action Plan

Phase 1. Strengthening the management control environment

Objective: To evaluate, strengthen, and maintain a control environment within the company to stimulate honesty, integrity, ethical behavior, accountability, self-discipline, supervisory review, and adherence to corporate policies, standards, and procedures among all personnel.

Time frame: August 19XX to March 19XX.

Focus: Developing, documenting, and communicating most important corporate policies and organizational responsibilities, stimulating control consciousness, and evaluating employees' integrity and potential risks.

Responsibility: Systems, standards, and procedures department in collaboration with executive management.

Phase 2. Strengthening internal accounting controls

Objective: To permit management to reach a conclusion about the overall effectiveness of the total structure in achieving the broad objectives of internal accounting control *at fiscal year-end* in order to make a public statement of management's unqualified opinion in its annual report.

Time frame: October 19XX to September 19XX (corporate fiscal year).

Focus: Developing and evaluating achievement of control objectives, identifying high risks, and improving specific internal accounting controls.

Responsibility: Systems, standards, and procedures department and internal audit department in cooperation with all management levels.

Phase 3. Monitoring and reporting on internal accounting control with auditor's opinion

Objective: To annually and systematically reach a conclusion about the overall effectiveness of the total structure in achieving the broad objectives of internal accounting control *during the entire fiscal year,* to include a statement of management's unqualified opinion in each annual report, and to obtain and publish the unqualified opinion of the company's independent auditors regarding management's representations.

Time frame: Annually for each fiscal year after September 30, 19XX.

Focus: Correcting immediately any material weaknesses, reported by the independent auditors, continuous monitoring by internal auditors, and eliminating control weaknesses based on informal risk or cost-benefit analysis.

Responsibility: Internal audit department in collaboration with all levels of management.

Preliminary Assessment

In preparing the action plan, the task force made a preliminary assessment of the company's control environment. This did not involve an in-depth review because management was already aware of the need for many improvements; indeed, several improvements in the control environment were already in progress. Instead, the assessment consolidated reports of the internal and independent auditors into a brief analysis of basic needs. The assessment resulted in including "strengthening the management control environment" as phase one of the action plan.

To simplify departmental contacts, one person in each of the company's 20 departments was appointed to serve as internal control coordinator. The role of these coordinators was to assist the project in obtaining information and documenting policies and procedures.

Other important actions taken at the beginning of the project included determining documentation requirements and defining the role of the company's independent auditors.

Actions during Phase One

The first step during phase one was to draft and issue three basic corporate policy statements.

Statement No. 1, *General Corporate Policy,* contains many policies covering corporate responsibilities to customers, employees, franchisees, management, and stockholders; these had been observed but never committed to writing.

Statement No. 2, *Standards of Corporate and Personal Conduct,* provides guidance to officers and employees about legal areas, accounting and internal control requirements, conflicts of interest, and so on. Possible violations are to be reported to the director of internal audit who sets procedures for appropriate review and for reporting to responsible corporate officers.

Statement No. 3, *Internal Audit,* prescribes responsibilities for the internal audit function and for taking corrective actions based on internal audit findings.

A high-quality brochure presenting these policy statements was printed for distribution to all Days Inns' employees and franchisees.

Other activities in phase one included developing the internal audit follow-up procedures under the new policies, completing the internal managerial policy framework, assuring adequate policy communication, publishing an organization manual, improving employee integrity and risk evaluation, and evaluating forms and reports in current use.

Actions during Phase Two

At the outset, the task force decided to use the transaction cycle approach to monitor internal accounting control. Cycles were defined according to the nature of the company's business, and control objectives tailored to these cycles were then developed.

During phase two, achievement of each objective was evaluated; results were documented and included in working papers. The work in this phase was done primarily by staff members in the systems, standards, and procedures department. They were responsible for following through from the initial interview to installing new procedures, controls, and even systems. They were assigned this task because the implementation responsibility might impair the independence of internal auditors.

During this phase, standard procedures to be followed in the review of functions were also developed. These are shown in Exhibit 13–5. The flowchart for reviewing internal accounting controls within a specific function is shown in Exhibit 13–6.

Required:

a. How would you characterize the control environment in this company? Why?

b. What observations do you have concerning the company's approach to studying its internal controls?

EXHIBIT 13–5 Case 13–27 Procedures for Organizing and Controlling Implementation of the IMC Project

IMC Phase 2—Review of Functions

1. Obtain all readily available information relative to the function. Prepare a preliminary review program and/or control evaluation questionnaire indicating procedures and scope of the review to conduct. Contact the department head responsible for the function in advance of a request for an initial appointment.
2. Meet with the department head and briefly discuss the objectives, scope, and nature of the review. Inquire about improvements under consideration and about actual or anticipated problems. Arrange to meet with the supervisor of (or individual primarily responsible for) the function.
   The time length and depth of discussion depend on the department head's interest and availability. Care must be taken to avoid tying up top executives with minute details. Where appropriate, steps 1 and 2 may be combined into a single interview with both department head and supervisor.
3. Meet with the supervisor and:
   a. Indicate review objectives, scope, and nature.
   b. Determine the objective(s) of the function and related existing policies. If policies are not in writing, note the principal existing policies and practices.
   c. Ask what other specific persons or units are involved directly with the function or interface with it.
   d. Discuss current procedures, making notes on the logical sequence of tasks.
4. Observe the tasks being performed and make sufficient inquiries to have a general understanding of the function and its tasks. Obtain copies of all forms and reports, determining origin, number of copies, recipients, and so on.
   This work varies depending on the complexity of the function and number of persons involved. It is essential to note existing controls as well as opportunities for improvements. Under no circumstances should the preliminary review

EXHIBIT 13–5 Case 13–27 *(continued)*

interfere with the normal work process, especially if the work provides key services to others. You may find it necessary to conduct one- or two-hour interviews separated by periods for performing regular duties.

5. (Optional) After the preliminary review (steps 1–4), the department head may ask for a conference to discuss the work completed. Take care to discuss only the conditions observed without giving conclusions or recommendations at this time. Alternate actions may be discussed without making any commitment regarding a final position.
6. Review all notes and documents and prepare either a brief general narrative description of the work flow or a high-level flowchart that includes only highlights and leaves out such details as copies and files.
7. Assess the effectiveness of the general corporate control environment as it relates to the specific function.
8. Develop specific control objectives applicable to the function and consistent with the overall cycle control objectives. Furnish copies of the first draft to persons interviewed for their comments and suggestions. Obtain their acceptance of the final objectives. Identify "material," "high-risk," or significant "potential-saving" areas within the function by considering:
   a. Areas in which errors or irregularities could involve large dollar amounts because of volume or significance of transactions.
   b. Areas where there are significant changes in circumstances.
   c. Areas that management recognizes as having poor controls or a history of "surprises."
   d. Areas pointed out by internal or external auditors in reports or management letters.
9. Document all control techniques applied in the function, especially those related to step 8.
10. Determine whether the specific control objectives are being met through the control techniques in step 9 by evaluating the specific control environment, potential risks, and the internal accounting controls surrounding each area.
11. Identify and evaluate any specific internal accounting control objectives not achieved due to weaknesses. Discuss their significance with the internal and external auditors. Identify those functional components where policies and procedures are lacking, inadequate, or obsolete. (Some of these may not bear directly on internal accounting control but should be identified to eventually perfect the full structure of company policies and procedures.)
12. (Optional) Confirm the evaluation in step 11 by preparing and executing a program to test compliance with controls considered most likely to achieve the internal accounting control objectives. (These tests, which show whether the internal control system is actually functioning as intended, may be unnecessary at this point if weaknesses are significant, obvious, or admitted.)
13. Tentatively formulate conclusions regarding control weaknesses, developing one or more alternative control techniques proposals for overcoming them.

EXHIBIT 13–5 Case 13–27 *(concluded)*

14. Draft those tentative policies and procedures considered necessary to properly operate and document the function:
    a. Furnish advanced copies or drafts to the supervisor.
    b. Discuss the proposed alternate control techniques and drafts of policies and procedures with the supervisor. Obtain suggestions, and if possible, acceptance of any modifications.
    c. Finalize the proposals and discuss them with the department head. Obtain suggestions and, if possible, acceptance of any modifications. (Steps *b* and *c* may be combined, but subordinates are sometimes reluctant to speak up in the presence of a superior. Discussions with higher-echelon executives should be limited to policy decisions and a general outline of procedural controls without great detail to save time.)
15. When all matters and actions to take are agreed on, prepare a summary to include in the monthly progress report to the task force. Include review results, recommendations, actions taken, and decisions not to act. (The latter should be a normal situation.)
16. (Optional) If you have failed to reach agreement on specific actions, it may be appropriate to apply informal cost-benefit analysis with a relatively nontechnical approach to obtain a more concrete estimate of the risks involved. By weighing the benefits against the costs of introducing new control techniques and then comparing these with the risks of not introducing new techniques, a convincing argument in their favor is possible. Conversely, a decision to withdraw or modify proposed control techniques may be justified. (This step may be applied as an option after step 11, step 14 *b* or *c*, or at the request of the task force after step 17. The decision whether and when to apply it should be based on the importance of the proposed control techniques and the degree of resistance encountered.)
17. In cases of a department head's rejection, resistance, or reluctance to accept suggested control techniques and/or significant policy content, refer the matter to the next higher managerial level. If acceptance is still not forthcoming and the matter is considered significant, present it to the IMC task force in a brief, specific report outlining results of the review, proposed alternatives, and why the department head disagrees. At this point, further action rests with the task force, which will likely discuss the matter directly with the department head.
18. Once a final decision is made, issue or modify the related policies and/or procedures.

EXHIBIT 13–6 Case 13–27 Flowchart for Review of Internal Accounting Control within a Specific Function

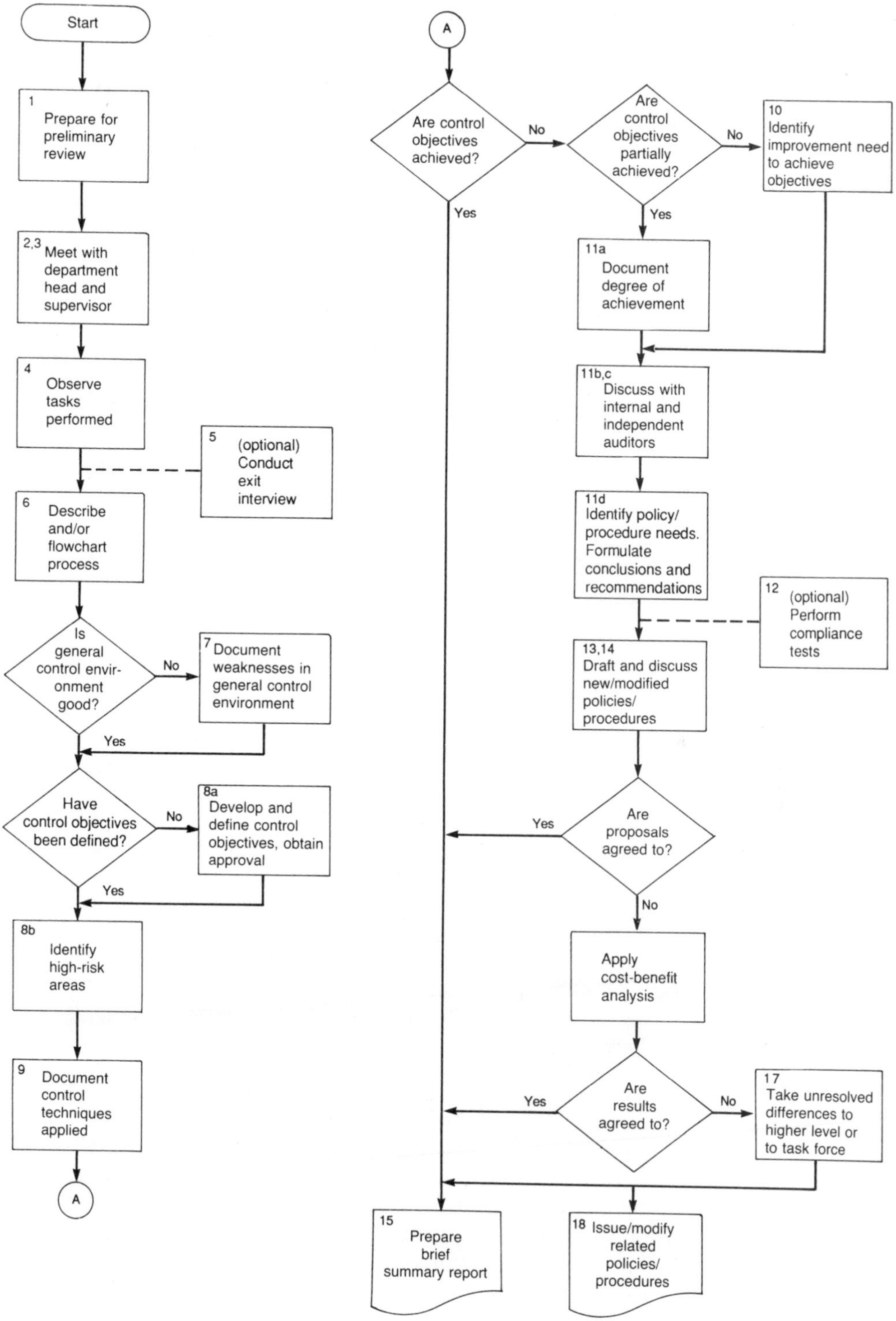

Chapter 14

System Controls

Learning Objectives:

1. To understand the control policies, practices, and procedures that are important in computer-based accounting systems.
2. To learn the three objectives for system controls.
3. To categorize control policies, practices, and procedures by their scope.
4. To describe practices that control the input, processing, and output of application systems.

INTRODUCTION

An organization's internal control structure includes the measures adopted by management to achieve the organization's objectives. Two objectives important to accountants are safeguarding assets and ensuring accurate and reliable accounting data. Accountants call the policies, practices, and procedures directed toward these objectives *internal accounting controls*, or more simply *internal controls*.

Those internal controls implemented in a computer-based accounting system are *system controls*. This chapter describes many important ones. From these, management selects and implements system controls to provide reasonable assurance that the objectives are achieved.

Because accountants are responsible for providing accounting information, they have a professional interest in maintaining adequate system controls. As auditors, accountants evaluate system controls to determine their effects on the accuracy of accounting information. An understanding of system controls is vital for any competent accountant.

VIEWS OF SYSTEM CONTROLS

Accountants may view an organization's system controls in different ways. Some prefer to categorize them by objective, while others categorize them by scope. Each view is correct; each represents a different perspective on the same set of policies, practices, and procedures. This chapter presents both views.

Categorizing Controls by Objective

Management implements internal controls either to prevent or to detect errors and irregularities. An error is an accidental misstatement of accounting information, while an irregularity is an intentional one.

Procedures adopted to achieve the first objective, preventing errors and irregularities, are *preventive controls*. These are valuable because they do not allow certain errors and irregularities to occur. The use of standard journal vouchers in a double-entry accounting system is a preventive control. They prevent bookkeepers from making entries to improper accounts.

Procedures adopted to achieve the second objective, detecting errors and irregularities, are *detective controls*. These procedures identify errors and irregularities after they have occurred. For example, a double-entry accounting system summarizes account balances in a trial balance. Bookkeepers detect the existence of errors in the general ledger whenever the debit and credit totals on the trial balance are unequal. The trial balance provides a detective control.

Usually management prescribes procedures to correct errors and irregularities after detection. These are *corrective controls*. As a corrective control, management may establish a policy requiring an adjusting journal entry to correct an error found on the trial balance. Because a detective control is always accompanied by a corrective one, some accountants do not distinguish between them. These accountants classify as detective controls those procedures used both to find and to correct errors and irregularities.

One way of classifying controls in a system is by objective. Using this method, accountants describe control policies, practices, and procedures as either preventive, detective, or corrective controls.

Categorizing Controls by Scope

Other accountants prefer to classify controls by the scope of the systems they affect. Policies, practices, and procedures that prevent or detect errors and irregularities for all accounting systems are *general controls*. They affect all transaction cycles and all application systems in each transaction cycle. For example, locking those rooms that contain computer terminals affects all applications of the computer, and is a general control.

Other policies, practices, and procedures affect only a specific application system, such as the cash receipts system or the inventory system. Accountants call these *application controls*. For example, many companies use an application system to process charges to credit cards. A sales clerk inserts the credit card into a terminal and connects the terminal to a computer by a telephone line. Then a computer program verifies the account number on the card before authorizing a charge to it. If the program determines that the account number is invalid, the system rejects the sales transaction. This system uses an application control called a check digit to verify the account number.

Applications systems frequently differ in the quality of the system controls they contain. One on-line system with very good controls may be reliable and produce accurate information. Another on-line system using the same hardware and system software may lack adequate controls and produce erroneous information. Inadequate application controls in a system is frequently a justification for initiating the system development process.

Within any transaction cycle, the combination of general controls and application controls determines whether or not system controls are effective. Both categories affect the ability of the applications systems to prevent or detect errors and irregularities. A strength in applications controls may compensate for a weakness in general controls.

For example, a credit card charge system may have terminals in thousands of locations in retail stores all over the country. Security for these terminals may be quite weak, allowing easy access to them by unauthorized users. Yet an application control that verifies the validity of an account number effectively compensates for this weakness in general controls. It prevents charges to fraudulent credit card accounts.

Accountants view system controls in different ways. The remaining discussion in this chapter is structured around the second view, which categorizes system controls by scope. As you read about specific system controls, you can determine if they are preventive, detective, or corrective controls. The chapter describes the five types of general controls next, giving the most important examples of them.

GENERAL CONTROLS

General controls are the system controls that affect all applications of the computer in the organization. Illustration 14–1 summarizes the five types of

ILLUSTRATION 14–1 Categories of General Controls

Organization of the MIS activity
Procedures for system and program changes
Hardware controls
Access controls
Other data and procedural controls

general controls. The first concerns the organization of the management information systems (MIS) activity.

Organization of the MIS Activity

The MIS activity is the segment of the organization that provides computer services to other segments. In a large company, the MIS activity may be a subsidiary or a division headed by a vice president. In a medium-sized company, it is frequently a separate department headed by a manager of MIS reporting to the controller. In a small company, it may be a few employees who operate a microcomputer in addition to performing other accounting duties. Illustration 14–2 contains an organizational chart showing two possible locations for the MIS activity.

Incompatible Functions. Before organizations used computers in their accounting systems, employees performed all processes manually. Organizations achieved adequate segregation of duties by assigning responsibility to people so that no one had incompatible duties. Firms assigned custody of an asset, record keeping for the asset, and authorizing transactions in the asset to separate people.

Then organizations purchased computers to perform many routine accounting processes. They centralized in the computer those incompatible functions previously assigned to separate individuals. Any employee who could control

ILLUSTRATION 14–2 Two Locations for the MIS Activity

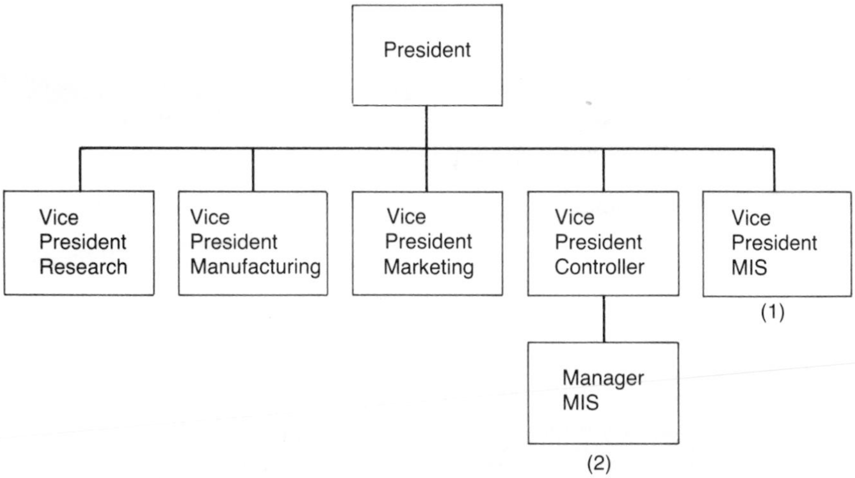

(1) In a large company, as a subsidiary reporting to a vice president of MIS.
(2) In a smaller company, as a department reporting to a manager of MIS.

ILLUSTRATION 14–3 Proper Organization in an MIS Department

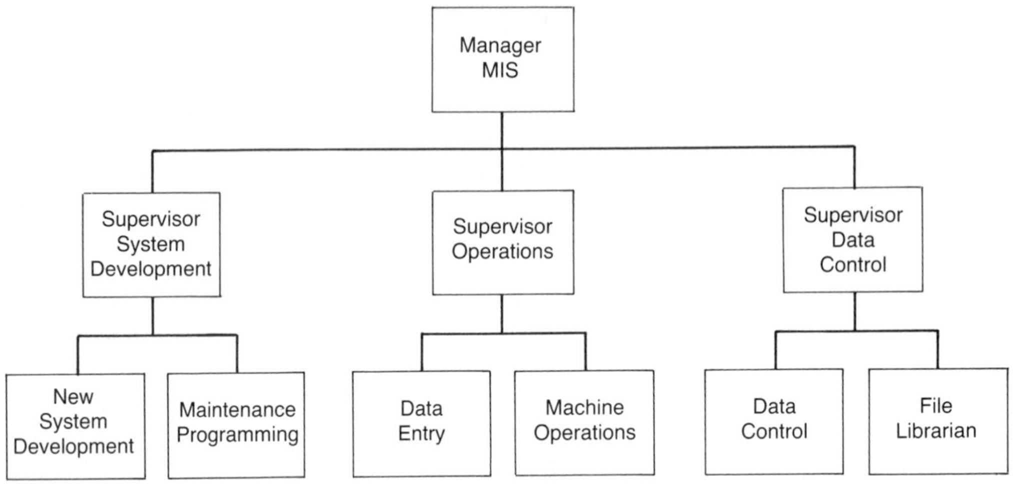

the actions of the computer could commit an error or irregularity and conceal it.

For example, most organizations use computers to print paychecks. The computer operator executing a payroll program has access to the asset cash. If the operator can gain access to payroll records stored in the computer, the operator can cause it to produce a paycheck for a nonexistent employee. The operator can then steal the paycheck and falsify the payroll records to cover the theft. Management prevents such irregularities by properly organizing the MIS activity.

Segregation of Duties. Proper organization requires that critical functions performed in the MIS activity should be separate. These critical functions are systems analysis and programming, computer operations, and maintaining the library of computer files. Illustration 14–3 shows an organization chart that separates these critical functions for the MIS department in a medium-sized company.

Systems Analysis and Programming. Systems analysts and programmers participate in the projects that develop accounting systems. Some organizations also assign to certain programmers the duty of program maintenance. Rather than working on new systems, maintenance programmers correct coding errors or make minor changes to existing programs.

Systems analysts and programmers are more knowledgeable than anyone else about how accounting systems work. If given access to the production program files used in processing accounting transactions, they could easily alter them to carry out and conceal thefts of assets. For this reason, organizations with good general controls ensure that systems analysts and developmental programmers never gain access to production program files. When changes to existing programs are needed, maintenance programmers make them after authorization from the MIS manager.

Computer Operations. Computer operations personnel include those involved in data entry and in machine operations. Data entry personnel convert data from the human readable form recorded on a document to machine readable form. They commonly do this using computer terminals. Sometimes data entry personnel work in user departments rather than in the MIS department.

Machine operators physically operate the computer equipment. They communicate with the operating system at the computer console, mount magnetic tapes on tape drives, and respond to malfunctions of hardware.

Data entry personnel have the opportunity to enter fraudulent transactions into an accounting system. Because they have access to computer hardware while it executes production programs, machine operators can make unauthorized changes to them. Fortunately, few data entry clerks or machine operators know enough about the programs they work with to do this successfully.

Organizations with good general controls ensure that data entry clerks and machine operators have no access to program documentation, including source code. This information would give them the knowledge they need to both carry out and conceal a theft. Many accountants believe that the most important segregation of duties in an MIS activity should be between systems development and computer operations. No individual should have job responsibilities in both areas, even if one of the jobs is part time.

Data Control and Librarian. The data control group takes custody of reports produced by the computer system. They scan them to ensure they are free of obvious errors and distribute them to appropriate personnel. They have custody of checks printed by the computer and have access to sensitive or proprietary information.

In a traditional data file system, the librarian has custody of computer files, and thus also of the accounting records. When files are stored on magnetic tape, the librarian may be a person who maintains the tape library and issues tapes to operators when needed by a program. With on-line files, the librarian may be a computer program that keeps records of every attempted file access and prevents access by unauthorized personnel or programs. An employee monitors the actions of this computer program to detect unauthorized attempts to access records.

When an organization uses a data base management system (DBMS), the DBMS software maintains custody of the accounting records and prevents unauthorized changes to them. The data base administrator (DBA) determines which users gain access to accounting records and monitors the data base to detect attempts at unauthorized access.

The data control group and the librarian have access to assets and to records. Organizations with good general controls restrict their access to the computer when it executes production programs. This minimizes their opportunities to commit irregularities.

Small Businesses. In small organizations, the MIS activity is also small, which makes proper segregation of duties impractical. If, for example, a small business keeps its accounting records on a microcomputer, only one or two people may operate it. It is impossible to assign duties so that a person cannot commit an error or fraud using the computer. In these organizations, management must be aware of this control weakness and closely supervise the work of these employees.

Even though a computer-based system combines incompatible functions in the computer, proper organization of the MIS activity prevents employees from both causing and concealing an error or irregularity. The next section describes a second type of general control, the procedures for documenting, reviewing, testing, and approving systems and programs or changes to them.

Procedures for System and Program Changes

Adequate procedures for system and program changes are preventive controls. They minimize errors and irregularities introduced by new systems or changes to existing systems.

An organization should have procedures requiring *formal review and authorization* for any new system before implementing it. This prevents implementation of many systems that are inefficient, ineffective, or unable to meet the organization's needs. Many organizations use an information systems steering committee to review and recommend information system project proposals for this purpose.

All manual and computerized procedures should have *adequate documentation* enabling programmers and analysts to understand existing procedures before changing them. This may prevent changes that have an unforeseen effect or that may produce inaccurate or unreliable data. Documentation also provides auditors with the information needed to perform an effective review of controls in the system.

A project team or programmer should adequately test each new system or change to an existing system before implementing it. This prevents many systems from creating inaccurate data. It also enables the project team or programmer to detect inefficiencies in processing, or to select areas for improving the design. During the system development life cycle, a project team that correctly uses program or module testing, string testing, and system testing has tested the system adequately.

The organization should have *required procedures for authorizing and documenting changes* to existing programs and systems. Many organizations require the inclusion of a program change record in the documentation package for a computer program. Whenever a programmer makes a change to the production version of a program (the version used during routine processing), the MIS manager requires the programmer to list the change in the program change record. The programmer includes a more thorough description of the change

ILLUSTRATION 14–4 Procedures for Changes to Systems and Programs

- Formal review and authorization for each new system (as by an information system steering committee)
- Adequate documentation for manual and programmed procedures
- A plan for adequately testing each new system
- Authorization and documentation for changes to existing systems

elsewhere in the documentation. The MIS manager then reviews the change and its documentation. This procedure prevents a change that would cause errors or irregularities.

You have seen some desirable procedures for controlling and documenting changes to systems and programs. Illustration 14–4 summarizes these. Another category of general controls is hardware controls.

Hardware Controls

Hardware controls are capabilities designed into computer equipment by manufacturers to prevent or detect errors that could misstate data during processing. Errors of this kind result from malfunctioning electronic circuits, from power fluctuations, or from interference by other electronic devices in the vicinity.

Hardware controls on modern computer equipment make errors from these sources rare. Because of this, accountants seldom evaluate hardware controls when reviewing a system or when participating in system development. Illustration 14–5 summarizes some frequently used hardware controls.

A third category of general controls includes those limiting access to computer equipment and files.

Access Controls

Access controls restrict a person's ability to retrieve or modify data and to gain unauthorized use of computer equipment. They ensure that all changes to accounting records are properly authorized. Management implements access controls by establishing segregation of duties in the MIS activity, by requiring identification and authentication procedures, and by providing physical security for computer equipment.

Segregation of Duties. By properly assigning duties in the MIS activity, management minimizes the opportunities for employees to alter computer programs or records to cover the theft of an asset. This requires segregation of

ILLUSTRATION 14–5 Hardware Controls

Control	*Example*
Parity check	A terminal adds an extra binary digit (the parity bit) to the character when transmitting it to a CPU. This bit is set to 0 or 1 to maintain an odd number of 1s in the character (in an odd parity system). When the CPU receives the character, it counts the number of 1s contained in it. If this is an even number, the CPU has detected an error in data transfer. (Some hardware uses a similar even parity system.)
Dual read	When transferring data from a magnetic disk, the CPU reads each character twice. The CPU compares the results of each transfer. If the results differ, the CPU has detected an error in data transfer.
Read after write	Following the transfer of data to a magnetic disk, the CPU reads the character just recorded on the disk. If the character read differs from the character written, the CPU has detected an error in data transfer.
Echo check	A CPU directs a printer to print a specific character by transmitting the character to the printer. Prior to printing, the printer echoes the character back to the CPU. If the CPU detects a difference between the echoed character and the transmitted one, it retransmits. This prevents printing an incorrect character.

duties between system development, operations, data control, and library personnel.

For example, the librarian or DBA controls access to accounting records and to the computer files containing production programs. They allow computer operators access to these files only on a predetermined operating schedule. Computer operators have no access to program documentation. This prevents them from making changes to production programs or files because they lack the knowledge of them. System development personnel who have adequate knowledge have no access to production programs and are prevented from making unauthorized changes.

Maintenance programmers have access to production programs and data files, and are able to make unauthorized changes. However, a MIS manager who reviews all program maintenance after it occurs can detect any inappropriate changes to program or data files.

Identification and Authentication Procedures. In modern computer-based systems, system software implements identification and authentication procedures. This system software may be the operating system software, or it may be a computer security software package used in conjunction with the operating system.

System Access. Before allowing anyone to use a computer system, the software requires the user to identify himself or herself to the system. Management may assign account numbers or userids for this purpose. The software then consults an authorization file containing authentication information for that individual. After requesting authentication information, the system compares the information provided by the user with that recorded in the computer file.

For example, the system may ask the user to provide a password for access to the system. The software then looks up in the authorization file that user's password. If the password and the authorization file agree, the user is logged on the system. If they differ, the software does not allow the user access to the system.

Some systems that allow dial-up access by telephone use an automatic callback procedure. A user calls the telephone number of the computer's automatic switchboard. The computer answers the call, accepts the user's password, and then disconnects. The computer looks up in a file the telephone number of the user listed for this password, and calls the user back at that number. This makes unauthorized access by telephone more difficult.

Passwords are effective in preventing unauthorized system access only if used properly; all passwords should be changed periodically and selected from a random combination of letters and digits. Too often employees select as a password a familiar name which is easy for an unauthorized user to guess. Some people even write down their passwords and tape them to desks or terminals. These actions make passwords less effective as control procedures.

Userids and passwords known by the user are common forms of identification and authentication. Some systems use other forms such as badges, keys, fingerprints, or voiceprints. Software uses all of these as methods of identification and authentication to prevent unauthorized system access.

Data Access. The authorization file identifies not only system passwords but also passwords for individual files stored by the system. It shows all the files a user is authorized to access, a password for each file, and a file permission.

The *file permission* shows the kind of access authorized for the user. It tells whether the user can only see the contents of the file (read permission), can change its contents (write permission), or can both read and change the file (read/write permission). Illustration 14–6 shows how an authorization file stores this information.

Many organizations employ a data security officer to maintain the authorization file. When properly used, this file prevents many unauthorized changes to data and program files. The data security officer assigns write permission only to those employees and applications that must update or maintain files. Other employees and applications, which only need to see the information contained in them, receive read permission.

ILLUSTRATION 14–6 Using an Authorization File to Control Data Access

Userid	Name	System Password	File Name	File Password	File Permission
1122	J. Thomas	9898	all	1776	R/W
2233	I. Watts	steam	inv sales credit	vapor water ice	R W R
3232	T. Edison	wizard	product inv	87654 light	R/W R
4321	L. Pasteur	germ	vendor voucher Purchase Gen Led	germ wheat virus vaccine	R W R R/W
5112	L. Pacioli	quill	Gen Led	ink	W

For example, an accounts receivable clerk may have both read and write permission in a customer master file. This allows the clerk to perform file maintenance, such as changing customer names and addresses. A salesperson may have only read permission, allowing the salesperson to see the balance of the customer's account but not to change it. Application programs in the cash receipts system, which records cash payments from customers, require only write permission.

Physical Security. Another way management limits access to data and equipment is by providing physical security. Management implements policies and procedures to secure both the organization's data center and its remote computer devices.

Security for the Data Center. A data center is the location of a mainframe computer and its peripherals. Frequently the data control group, the tape library, and various input devices are in the data center. It is the physical storage location for accounting records in a computer-based system.

Management should restrict routine access to the data center to those employees whose jobs require such access. Entry by others, such as accountants, systems development personnel, or visitors, should require special authorization. Entrances should be locked at all times.

Security for Remote Devices. Remote devices include terminals, minicomputers, desktop computers, and remote job entry terminals. Such devices create two threats: the improper use of the device and theft of the device.

When connected to a mainframe by a communication link, remote devices allow access to data files on the mainframe. Employees can use them to gain unauthorized access to accounting records. Many of these devices are small enough to be easily stolen. And because remote devices are located in user areas throughout the organization, limiting physical access to them is more difficult than restricting access to devices at a data center.

Data security software packages on the mainframe can help control access to the mainframe from remote devices. Such a package monitors communication between them and restricts the access that is made available. A security package may allow access from specific devices only to specific data files or schemas, or it may allow access only during specified hours of the day.

For example, company policy may specify that all cash receipts are to be processed from 9:00 A.M. to 12:00 noon each day. The accounts receivable department uses a remote job entry terminal for this purpose. Data security software restricts access from this terminal to accounts receivable files from 9:00 A.M. to 12:00 noon. Similarly, the software can limit access from desktop terminals or smaller computers to normal working hours. During these hours, supervisors monitor physical access to them.

Often sensitive data are accessed on desktop computers not connected to the mainframe. Management must assign responsibility for these computers and for the accuracy of the data on them to individual employees. Computers should be physically attached to the desk and locked up when not in use. If a computer is stolen, or if unauthorized people gain access to data stored in a desktop computer, the individual is responsible.

Access controls prevent unauthorized access to accounting records and prevent theft of remote devices. A fifth category of general controls contains policies, practices, and procedures not included in the first four categories.

Other Data and Procedural Controls

Other data and procedural controls affect all the applications in a computer-based system; they are general controls that do not fit in the other four categories. They include file backup procedures and contingency plans.

File Backup Procedures. Accounting systems process many master files and transaction files each day. Occasionally, when an event occurs that destroys one or more of these files, file backup procedures can prevent the loss of accounting data.

Using File Backups. For example, a power fluctuation sometimes causes a disk drive to malfunction, destroying the disk and making the information on the disk inaccessible. Floods, lightning, temperature extremes, vandalism, or mistakes by a computer operator may also destroy accounting files. For this reason, computer operators routinely make *backup copies* of all computer files. The backup copy is a duplicate of the original that is stored at a different location. If an unusual occurrence destroys the original, the computer operator recreates it from the backup copy.

Management establishes control policies that describe file backup procedures. For accounting master files, backup copies are cost beneficial, and management establishes policies requiring routine periodic backups. These policies describe procedures for making copies of the file, for storing them separately from the original, and for reconstructing the master file if it is destroyed. The nature of these procedures depends on the processing method used by the accounting system.

The four approaches to processing accounting data are manual processing, batch processing, batch processing with on-line inquiry, and on-line real-time systems. In manual systems, backup files are human readable records and documents that require no special procedures. Good backup procedures for systems using the second approach, batch processing, are identical to those for the third approach, batch processing with on-line inquiry. Good backup procedures for on-line real-time systems differ significantly from these.

File Backup in Batch Processing Systems. A batch processing system applies all processing steps to batches of transactions. A data entry program converts each transaction in a batch to computer readable form. Another program then examines each transaction in the batch, looking for obvious errors. An update program then posts each transaction in the batch to a master file. When processing of a batch is complete, then processing of the next batch begins. The standard method for backing up files in a batch processing system, or a batch system with on-line update, uses the *grandfather-father-son* technique.[1] It requires the MIS activity to have available at all times three ''generations'' of each master file. The most recent version of the master file is the ''son.'' Employees use this generation in daily processing, and it requires a backup copy. The previous generation master file, the ''father,'' is the version that was updated to produce the current one. If the current file is destroyed, computer operators can recreate it from the father. The ''grandfather'' is the version that was updated to produce the father. Computer operators can use it to recreate both the father and the son.

In the application of the grandfather-father-son technique in Illustration 14–7, a computer program daily updates a master file with a transaction file. Although this illustration shows tape files, the method works equally well with direct access devices.

In this example, the computer operators maintain three generations of the master file after Wednesday's file update. They are the master file from Wednesday (the current file, or son), and the master files from Tuesday (the father) and Monday (the grandfather). On Thursday the system updates Wednesday's master file with Thursday's transaction file, producing Thursday's master file. The operators use Thursday's master file (the son) for current processing. They save as backups Wednesday's master file (now the father), and Tuesday's master file (now the grandfather). Monday's master file is no longer needed and the operators do not save it. After Friday's file update, Tuesday's master file is no longer required.

---

[1]Some people prefer to call this the grandparent-parent-child technique.

ILLUSTRATION 14–7 The Grandfather-Father-Son Technique

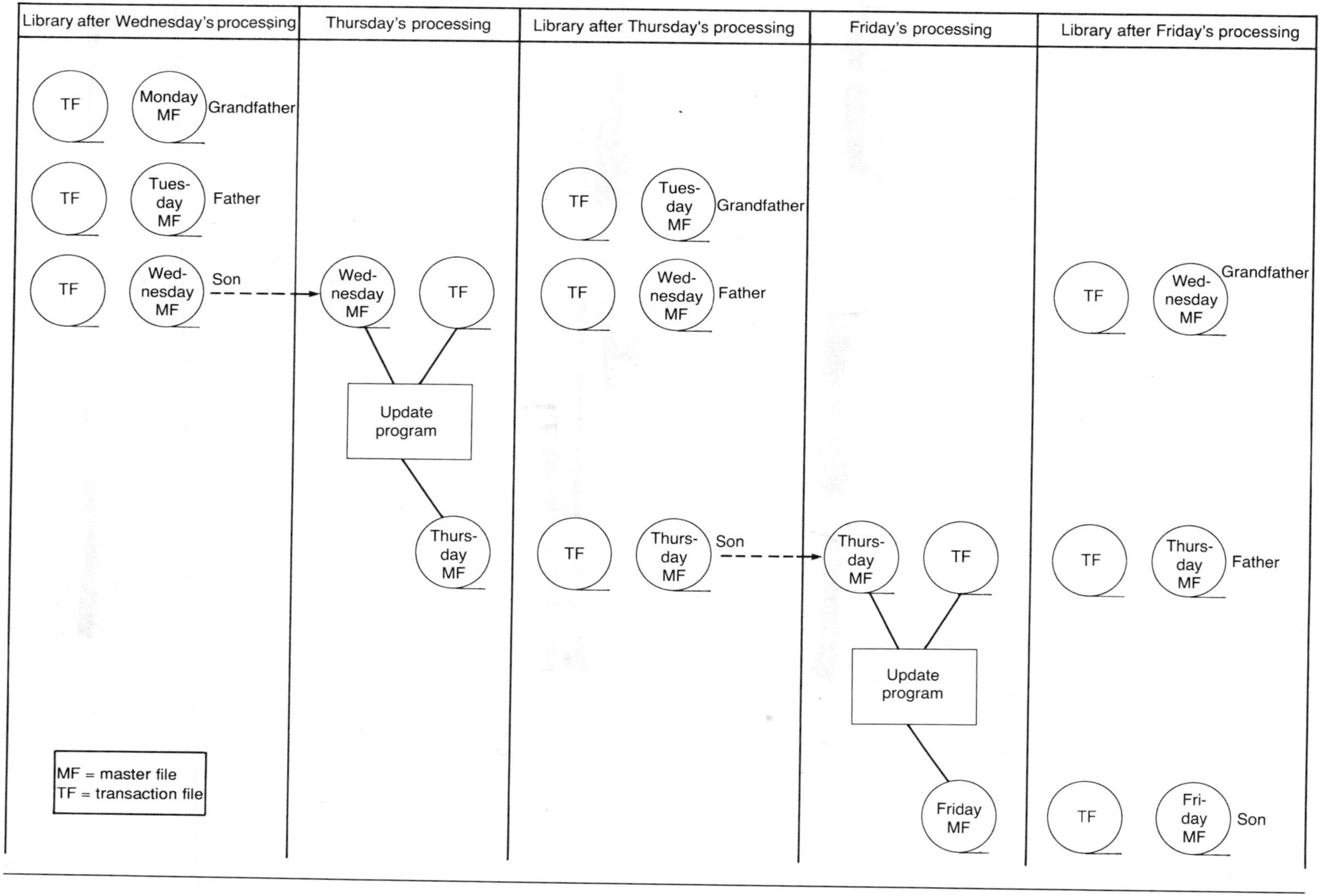

Most managers do not consider it cost effective to require backups of transaction files. When they are maintained, however, they can be used to recreate a current master file. An alternative is to keep for a specified period of time copies of the original documents recording the transactions. If a transaction file is destroyed, the MIS activity recreates it from these documents.

The grandfather-father-son technique works well in batch processing systems because these systems update master files daily, weekly, or monthly. An on-line real-time system, on the other hand, updates its master files continually. For them, the technique is not cost effective.

File Backup in On-Line Real-Time Systems. In an on-line real-time system, users at terminals enter transactions as they occur. A computer program controls entry of the data fields in a transaction, examines them for obvious errors, posts the transaction to a master file, and then proceeds to the next transaction. All processing of a transaction occurs at once, and the results of processing immediately change the master file. The standard method of file backup in on-line real-time systems uses a transaction log with periodic master file dumps.

A *file dump* occurs when the computer operator copies the contents of an on-line master file to a removable device, such as a magnetic tape. This serves as a backup of the master file in case the original on-line copy is destroyed. Management establishes policies that determine how frequently file dumps should occur, but commonly they are done once or twice each day.

The file dump provides a backup file as of the time of the dump, but because transactions occur continually in an on-line real-time system, the backup file quickly becomes out of date. As a result, the computer operator also maintains a *transaction log*. This file contains a copy of all transactions posted to the master file since the last file dump. While posting a transaction to the master file, the system also copies it to the transaction log. If the on-line master file is accidently destroyed, the operator recreates it from the transaction log and the most recent file dump.

Illustration 14–8 shows how file backups work in on-line real-time systems. In this example, the master files are on a magnetic disk, and the backup files and transaction logs are on magnetic tapes.

During Wednesday's processing, data entry clerks continuously enter transactions. The system posts these transactions to the master file and copies them to the transaction log. On Wednesday night at midnight the computer operator dumps the master file to magnetic tape. This produces the backup master file for use on Thursday. During Thursday's processing, the system again creates a transaction log as file updates occur. If the master file is accidently destroyed sometime Thursday, the operator can recreate it as of the moment of destruction. The operator does this by updating Thursday's backup master file with Thursday's transaction log.

File backup procedures are a form of general control that prevent the loss of data; another data and procedural control involves contingency plans.

ILLUSTRATION 14–8 File Backup Procedures in On-Line Real-Time Systems

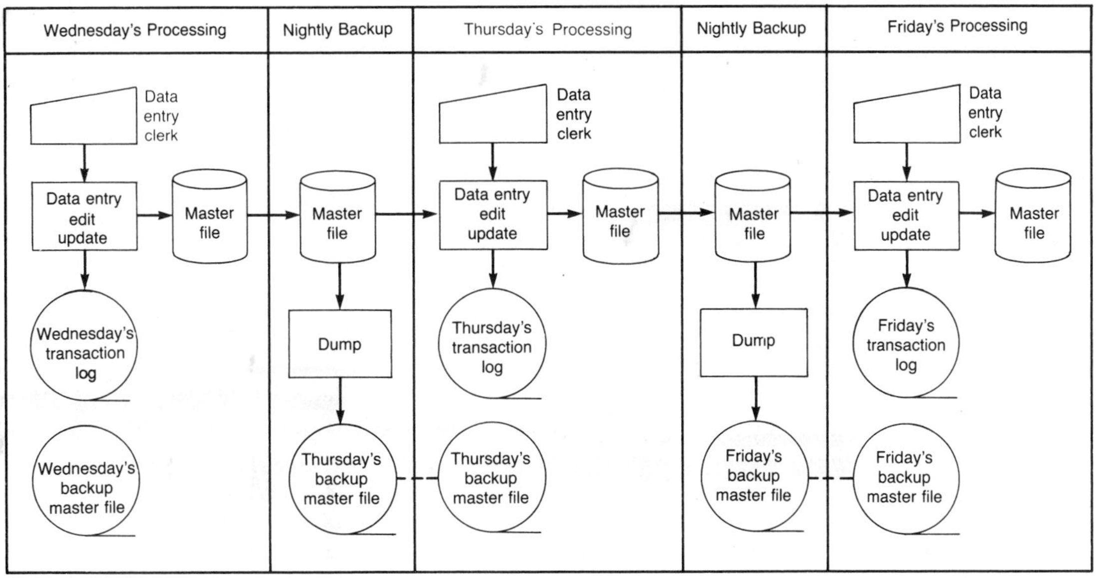

Contingency Plans. A contingency plan is a formal document that describes procedures should a catastrophe occur at the data center. Catastrophes, such as fires, explosions, floods, or tornadoes, are unlikely, yet when one occurs, it can completely destroy an entire mainframe computer facility. If all accounting records are destroyed as well, it would be difficult to collect receivables and determine how much the organization owes to vendors and employees.

The contingency plan should provide adequate insurance coverage, designate alternative locations for processing and data storage, identify vital applications, and assign responsibility for recovery procedures.

Provide Adequate Insurance Coverage. Periodically, management should review the insurance coverage for the data center. Insurance should be adequate to replace equipment and software destroyed by a catastrophe. Management should also purchase business loss insurance. This compensates the organization for the costs of reconstructing the data base and for any revenues lost due to computer downtime.

Designate an Alternative Processing Location. If a data center is destroyed, the MIS activity may require many months to place it in operation again. Because some applications are vital for its continued existence, the organization must identify another computer that it can use during reconstruction.

As an alternative processing site, many companies designate another of its data centers at a different location. Smaller organizations may reach a reciprocal alternative processing agreement with others that have similar equipment. Or they may arrange to use a service bureau or timesharing service. The alternative site must have enough unused processing capacity to process all vital applications.

Identify Vital Applications. Vital applications are those the organization requires to continue operating. If a data center is destroyed, the MIS activity must implement these applications first at an alternative processing location. Management must identify vital applications and ensure that they can be implemented quickly at the alternative site.

Accounts receivable, accounts payable, and payroll are vital applications to most organizations. Other applications are vital in specific industries. For example, an airline reservations system is vital to an airline, and a computerized typesetting system is vital to a newspaper. These companies cannot function if management fails to reimplement them promptly.

Vital applications require an off-site storage location.

Designate an Off-site Storage Location. Management should designate a place, away from the data center, to store items necessary to continue operating the vital applications. These include copies of system software, programs, backup data files, documentation, and operating instructions. Management should establish policies ensuring that these items are current.

Some organizations use the alternative processing site for this purpose. Others use a warehouse that is convenient, secure, safe from environmental hazards, and has controlled access.

Assign Responsibility. Management should assign responsibility to an individual for maintaining and implementing an up-to-date contingency plan. This includes acquiring an adequate alternative processing site, selecting a satisfactory off-site storage location, keeping current backup files at that location, and testing the plan. Someone should be designated in advance as responsible for beginning recovery procedures if a catastrophe occurs. The plan should also identify and assign other responsibilities necessary to begin operation at the alternative site.

Assigning responsibility in advance minimizes delays at a time when top management is preoccupied with things other than the information system.

A contingency plan prevents the sizable financial losses an organization could incur if an information system were destroyed. Illustration 14–9 summarizes its contents. Because a contingency plan affects several vital accounting applications, it is a general control.

Illustration 14–10 summarizes the five types of general controls. Other policies, practices, and procedures may affect only one application. Accountants call these applications controls.

APPLICATIONS CONTROLS

Applications controls affect an individual application, such as the sales order entry, cash receipts, or payroll application. A project team develops them during design and implementation of the application system. Accountants identify three

ILLUSTRATION 14–9 Contents of a Contingency Plan

1. **Adequate insurance coverage.** For lost equipment, software, and business
2. **Location of the alternative processing site.** Another organization or data center with similar equipment
3. **Vital applications.** The applications necessary for the organization to function
4. **Location of off-site storage.** The alternative processing site or a warehouse; maintain current records necessary to begin operation at the alternative site
5. **Responsibility assignments.** Person responsible for beginning recovery procedures; other responsibilities necessary to resume operation at the alternative site; person responsible for maintaining a current contingency plan

ILLUSTRATION 14–10 Summary of General Controls

Organization of the MIS activity. Separate:
1. systems analysis and programming.
2. computer operations.
3. data control and librarian.

Procedures for system and program changes. Require formal authorization and approval.

Hardware controls. Provided by computer manufacturers.

Access controls. Limit access to equipment, programs, and files.

Other data and procedural controls. Establish file backup procedures and contingency plans.

ways that applications controls prevent or detect errors and irregularities. Input controls prevent or detect errors when the system converts data from human to computer readable form. Processing controls detect errors during computer processing, and output controls detect them after processing is complete.

Input Controls

Input controls are concerned with converting data into computer readable form and with preventing or detecting errors while inputting data. Four forms of input controls common in accounting systems are check digits, data validation, control totals, and direct data entry procedures.

Check Digits. A check digit is a digit added to an account number. An algorithm determines how to calculate the correct value of the check digit from the other digits in the account number.

A computer program uses the algorithm to verify the account number of a transaction. If, using the algorithm, it calculates a check digit that is different from the one in the transaction's account number, the system knows that the account number is invalid. In this way, it detects data entry errors. Almost all major credit card companies use check digits in their credit card account numbers. When an account number contains a check digit, it is referred to as a *self-checking number*.

Illustration 14–11 shows one way to calculate a check digit. Known as the modulus 11 method, it is both simple and effective in detecting errors and preventing irregularities. Companies use a method similar to this one to calculate the check digit when assigning account numbers.

Illustration 14–12 shows how an application system verifies an account number that contains a check digit. It again uses the modulus 11 method. However, when verifying the account number, the procedures are slightly different from those used when computing the check digit.

In practice, people seldom calculate check digits as shown in these illustrations. Programs in application systems calculate them to assign account numbers and also to verify a transaction's account number before posting the transaction. The project team selects an algorithm during system design, and a programmer codes it into a program during system implementation.

Check digits are a common method of verifying account numbers before posting transactions to a master file. Application systems also use data validation procedures to identify invalid transactions before posting.

Data Validation. Data validation procedures detect erroneous data as it enters an application system and prevent the system from posting the invalid data to a master file. They also provide for the data's correction and reentry. You may see different forms of data validation, depending on the approach to data processing.

Data Validation in Batch Processing Systems. In batch processing systems, and in batch systems with on-line inquiry, a separate computer program performs data validation. This program, an *input edit* program,

ILLUSTRATION 14–11 Calculating a Check Digit

1. Take a customer number	6 7 3 5 5
2. Multiply each digit by a weight equaling its position plus 1 (here, the number has 5 digits; the most significant digit is thus multiplied by 6; the next one, by 5; and so on)	6 5 4 3 2
3. Add the product	36 + 35 + 12 + 15 + 10 = 108
4. Subtract the total from the next higher multiple of 11 to get the self-checking digit	110 − 108 = 2
5. Include the self-checking digit as the last digit of the customer's account	673552

ILLUSTRATION 14–12 Using a Check Digit to Verify an Account Number

	Example A	*Example B*
1. Take the customer's number	6 7 3 5 5 2	6 3 7 5 5 2
2. Multiply each digit by a weight equaling its position	6 5 4 3 2 1	6 5 4 3 2 1
3. Add the product	36 + 35 + 12 + 15 + 10 + 2 = 110	36 + 15 + 28 + 15 + 10 + 2 = 106
4. Divide the total by 11 and establish the remainder	110 ÷ 11 = 10 remainder 0	106 ÷ 11 = 9 remainder 7
5. Accept the number if the remainder is 0; reject it if it is not	Valid	Invalid

examines data fields in each transaction record and identifies those transactions that have fields containing obvious errors. The program prints a listing of transactions containing errors and removes these transactions from the transaction file. In this way, the application system does not post these erroneous transactions to a master file.

Many application systems add erroneous transactions to a computer file called a *suspense file*. The system suspends further processing of each of these transactions until someone reviews the error listing, corrects the error in the transaction, removes it from the suspense file, and reenters it in the system. The project team determines these error correction procedures during design of the application.

The project team also determines the actions of the edit program during system design. They select the fields in a transaction record for examination and decide which kinds of errors should be detected. An input edit program would not find all possible errors in transactions, but a well-designed program could find most of the common ones. Illustration 14–13 shows some common validation procedures performed by edit programs.

Data Validation in On-Line Real-Time Systems. On-line real-time applications apply all processes to a transaction before beginning to process the next transaction. Usually a single program converts data into computer readable form, performs validation checks on certain fields in the transaction, copies it to the transaction log, and then posts the transaction to a master file. The program may also add the transaction to a file. The system later prints the contents of this file in the form of a journal.

Many on-line real-time systems use data entry clerks to enter transactions at terminals. Data entry programs apply validation procedures, such as those in Illustration 14–13, to data fields as the clerk enters them. If the validation procedure identifies a field as erroneous, the program does not accept the

ILLUSTRATION 14–13 Common Data Validation Procedures

1. *Field check.* Verify that fields which should contain only numeric data contain no nonnumeric characters. Also verify that fields which should contain only alphabetic data contain no nonalphabetic characters.
2. *Validity check.* Determine that a field that should contain only characters from a limited set contains no improper characters. For example, assume a transaction contains a RECORD TYPE field and there are only two record types, Record Type 1 and Record Type 2. A transaction with a Record Type of 3 is invalid.
3. *Sign check.* Determine if a field contains data of the proper sign, either positive or negative.
4. *Limit (reasonableness) check.* Determine that a field does not contain an excessive amount. For example, an HOURS WORKED field in a weekly payroll program should not contain numbers greater than 168.
5. *Sequence check.* The key field of the current transaction should be greater than that of the transaction previously processed.
6. *Self-checking account number.* Use the modulus 11 method (or some other method) to verify that a check digit is correct.
7. *Completeness check.* Determine that a critical field in a record has not been left blank. If the field is blank, the record is not processed.
8. *Default values.* Determine if a field in a record is blank. If it is blank, the program assumes a value; this is the default value.

transaction until the clerk corrects it. In this way these systems avoid suspense files, error listings, and delayed reentry of many transactions.

Validation procedures enable the computer to prevent or detect erroneous data before it affects a master file. Another source of errors for a master file is lost or added data. Control totals are useful in detecting errors from this source.

Control Totals. A control total is the sum, taken from all transactions in a batch, of a numeric data field that exists in each transaction. For example, a clerk may form a batch of sales transactions from all the sales orders accepted on Wednesday. The clerk calculates a control total by summing the gross sales amounts from each sales order.

When a control total is taken on a batch of documents such as this, accountants also call it a *batch total.* In an on-line real-time system, where transactions are not batched, it is simply a control total.

Control totals ensure that no transactions are lost or added during processing. For example, assume you are entering cash receipts transactions in a batch order entry system. After inputting Wednesday's receipts, you enter the control total. At the conclusion of each succeeding processing step, a computer program recalculates the control total. It compares the most recent calculation with the control total you entered at data entry. If these differ, the program has detected an error in processing. If you are using an on-line real-time system, a computer program compares your control total with the total changes in the balances of the cash and accounts receivable accounts.

Control totals are most useful in detecting lost or added transactions; they include amount or quantity totals and hash totals. Another similar device is the record count.

Amount or Quantity Totals. A control total taken on amount fields produces an amount control total. The total of all gross sales amounts from a batch of sales transactions, as described above, is an example. The total of all quantities issued from inventory of an item is an example of a quantity total.

Amount or quantity totals have significance for decision making as well as for control purposes. A sales manager may wish to know the total gross sales for Wednesday to evaluate the performance of sales personnel. When a performance report discloses this amount, the manager uses it for decision making. The data control group of the MIS activity may also use this control total to detect errors in the report.

Hash Totals. A hash total is a form of control total that has no significance for decision making. It is useful only for control purposes.

For example, rather than summing the gross sales amounts for all sales orders accepted on Wednesday, the clerk may sum the customer account numbers. This produces a total that has no significance for decision making. The clerk enters this hash total in the system during data entry, and computer programs may recalculate it during later processing steps. The data control group can compare hash totals at the conclusion of each processing step to ensure that no transactions are lost or added. For control purposes, the hash total functions like an amount control total. Yet it serves no other purpose.

Record Counts. A record count is simply a total of the number of transactions in a batch. Similar to a hash total, it is useful only for control purposes.

For example, a clerk may count the number of sales orders accepted on Wednesday. After entering the data from these transactions into the computer-based system, the clerk enters the number of transactions. During each subsequent processing step, a computer program counts the number of transaction records and compares it to that entered during data entry. If they differ, a transaction has been lost or added.

Because a record count is not obtained from a field in each transaction, it is not really a control total. Yet record counts are used like control totals, so most accountants consider them to be equivalent. In fact, many batch processing systems detect lost or added data using both a control total and a record count.

Illustration 14–14 summarizes the forms a control total can take. Another input control utilizes procedures for direct data entry.

Direct Data Entry Procedures. Many application systems prevent errors by using direct data entry. With this kind of procedure, data enters a file in a

ILLUSTRATION 14–14 Control Totals

Distinguishing Characteristic	Example
Batch total	
A control total of a batch in a batch processing system	Total of gross sales from the documents in a batch of written sales orders
Amount or quantity total	
A control total useful for decision making as well as for control purposes	Total of gross sales from the transactions in a file of sales transactions
Hash total	
A control total that has no significance for decision making	Total of customer account numbers from the transactions in a file of sales transactions
Record count	
The total number of transactions to be processed	The number of sales transaction records processed in one day by a sales order entry system

computer-based system directly from its source. Human intervention is not required to convert the data from human readable to computer readable form. These systems avoid errors originating from human fatigue, inattention, or mistakes in judgment during data entry.

For example, many sales order entry systems require that salespersons complete written sales orders. They send the sales orders to a data entry clerk, who enters the data from the orders in the system at a terminal. The data entry clerk occasionally makes errors that are not detected by the validation procedures of the system. If the salesperson completes the written sales order on a document that can be read directly by a computer, the system avoids these errors.

There are many forms of direct data entry. These include source input documents, turnaround documents, and point-of-sale data entry.

Source Input Documents. When a salesperson records sales data on a form that a computer input device can read, that form is a source input document. An *optical character reader* scans the form and creates a transaction record from the data it contains.

Students use one form of source input document when they take standardized college entrance examinations. They mark their answers on the form in the appropriate places using a pencil. When grading each exam, the optical character reader senses these marks and a computer program interprets the answers according to where the marks are on the form.

Source input documents provide fast and accurate ways to enter data into an application system. However, because they require special equipment, they may be more expensive to develop than systems using terminal data entry.

Turnaround Documents. A turnaround document is an output from a computerized process that later becomes an input to another process. When producing the document, a computer program records data on it needed by another application. By recording data that an input device can read, it avoids human input errors.

For example, many utility bills contain turnaround documents. The utility's billing application produces a remittance advice that is mailed to the customer. Recorded on the remittance advice in magnetic ink is the customer's account number and amount owed. The customer returns the remittance advice with the payment, and it becomes an input to the cash receipts application. An input device called a magnetic ink character reader reads the account number and amount owed and records it in a transaction record. This prevents erroneous account numbers because people do not enter them in the system.

Point-of-Sale Data Entry. Retailers use this form of direct data entry when recording sales. In point-of-sale systems, the cash register is also a computer terminal.

When a sales clerk punches buttons to record the addition of cash to the register, the clerk also produces a sales transaction record for a transaction file. Later, perhaps at night after the store closes, a centralized computer posts these transactions to a master file. Because it does not use written sales tickets or data entered at a terminal, this system prevents many errors.

Source input documents, turnaround documents, and point-of-sale data entry are input controls because they prevent errors during data input. Other application controls are processing controls.

Processing Controls

Processing controls monitor the accuracy of accounting data during computer processing. If an application system is tested adequately during system development, errors due to its hardware or software are rare. However, errors arising from human intervention during processing are more common. Certain control procedures used during processing detect errors arising from these sources.

Sequence Checks. Batch processing systems require that records in data files are in the proper sequence. If they are not, the system does not function properly. Sequence checks verify that records are in the proper sequence.

For example, batch processing file update programs require two input files, a transaction file, and a master file. The records in these files must be sorted in the same sequence. If a transaction is out of sequence, the update program produces an error message rather than posting it to the master file. To prevent this, a programmer codes a program to check the sequence of records in data files prior to posting. Rather than posting it, the program adds to a suspense file any record that is out of sequence.

ILLUSTRATION 14–15 Run-to-Run Controls

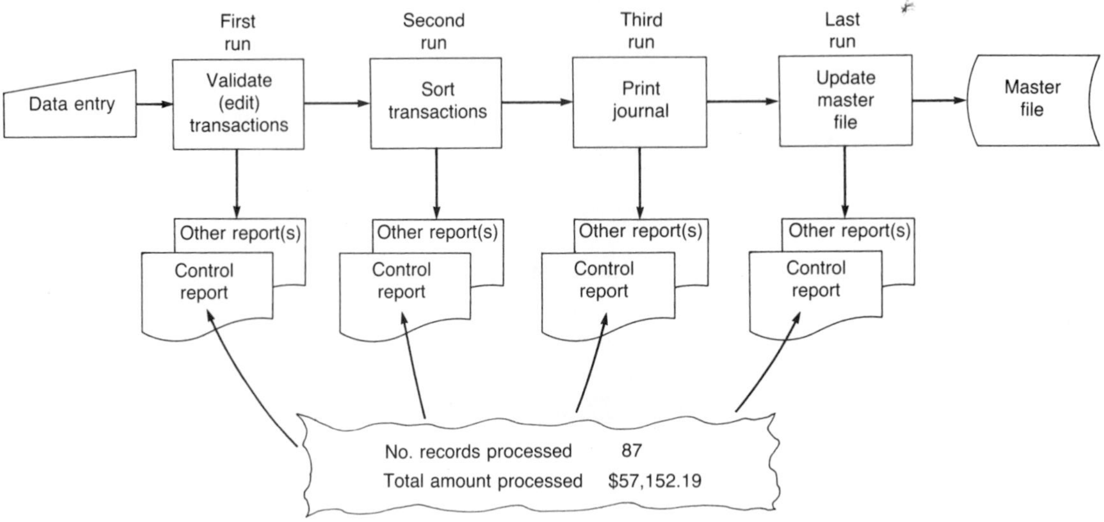

System designers also include sequence checks in programs that print reports. Many reports contain listings of data in a desired sequence. Sequence checks ensure that these are printed properly. For example, a payroll register is a list of all paychecks issued for a pay period. When printed, these checks should be sequenced by employee number.

Run-to-Run Controls. Accountants use control totals to detect lost or added records. With a batch processing system, they become processing controls called *run-to-run controls*.

In these systems, a computer program applies a processing step to all transactions before beginning the next step. In information systems terminology, a processing step is a *run*. In each run, the computer prints a report disclosing control totals. A clerk from the data control group compares control totals from successive runs. If the totals are identical, the clerk knows that no transactions were lost or added during processing.

Sometimes the program adds control totals to a report containing other data, such as a list of transactions. In other cases, the program prints a special *control report* that discloses only the control totals.

Illustration 14–15 shows how a batch processing system uses run-to-run controls. A data entry clerk enters transactions at a keyboard. An edit program validates each transaction as it is entered, and creates from them a transaction file. Subsequent processing steps in this example consist of a program that sorts the transactions, one that prints a listing of them, and one that posts them to a master file. Each step produces a report containing amount totals and a record count. These are control reports because they disclose only control totals.

Physical File Identification. Sometimes during processing computer operators erroneously mount the incorrect tape, disk pack, or diskette. This applies a processing step to the incorrect file and produces incorrect data. Physical file identification prevents this occurrence.

Physical file identification comes in two forms. The computer operator attaches *external file labels* to identify the proper tape, disk pack, or diskette to insert on the equipment. Devices also contain *internal file labels* read by the computer's operating system. Internal file labels include header and trailer records on magnetic tape and volume labels on magnetic disks and diskettes. If a mainframe operating system encounters a file with an improper internal label, it prints a message on the system console alerting the operator.

Programmed Controls. During system design, the project team determines the computerized processing steps for the application system. In accounting applications, they identify control procedures, or *programmed controls,* to be performed by computer programs.

Programmed controls sometimes duplicate the error-detection procedures performed by a bookkeeper in a manual system. For example, a bookkeeper may foot and crossfoot the columns of numbers on a schedule to detect arithmetic errors. A programmer may code a computer program to do the same thing. This is a *crossfooting check.* A bookkeeper looks at numbers in manual accounting records and verifies that they are of reasonable magnitude, or of the proper sign. Computer programs use limit checks and sign checks to accomplish these objectives.

Output Controls

Output controls apply to the output of a computer-based accounting system. They include those policies, practices, and procedures that ensure the accuracy of the results of processing. These controls also ensure that only authorized personnel receive the reports produced by an application system.

Implementing output controls are a major responsibility of the *data control group.* Members of this group scan reports produced by this system. When a report is clearly erroneous or illegible, they alert the computer operator to the problem. They reconcile control totals on reports with those totals established at the beginning of processing. In this way, they detect the loss or addition of data. The data control group distributes reports to authorized users, which prevents exposure of sensitive information against company policy. They maintain an output distribution log, which is a record of the reports produced and the disposition of those reports.

You have seen many control procedures that accountants include in computerized application systems. These prevent or detect errors and irregularities at the input of data, during its processing, and at its output. Accountants devote the most attention to data input. Input controls prevent and detect the most common errors—those concerned with transcription into computer readable form. Pro-

ILLUSTRATION 14–16 Summary of Application Controls

Input Controls
- Check digits
- Data validation
- Control totals
- Direct data entry

Processing Controls
- Sequence checks
- Run-to-run controls
- Physical file identification
- Programmed controls

Output Controls
- Data control group reviews and distributes reports

cessing controls detect errors primarily when people intervene in processing. Output controls are a final check on the accuracy of accounting information. Illustration 14–16 summarizes these application controls.

SUMMARY

Policies, practices, and procedures adopted to prevent or detect errors and irregularities in a computer-based system are system controls. Those system controls that affect all applications in a computer-based system are general controls. Management establishes policies and adopts procedures to implement them. System controls that affect only a specific application are application controls. A project team identifies application controls during the design of the application system.

There are five categories of general controls and three categories of applications controls. A strength in application controls may compensate for a weakness in general controls. Management selects combinations of general and application controls to provide reasonable assurance that assets are safeguarded and accounting records are accurate.

KEY TERMS

application controls Policies, practices, and procedures that prevent or detect errors and irregularities within a specific accounting application system, such as payroll.

check digit A digit in an account number that is calculated from the other digits in the number. It is used to detect erroneous account numbers.

contingency plan A formal document that describes procedures for processing accounting data should a catastrophe occur to the data center.

control total The sum, taken from all transactions in a batch, of a numeric data field in each transaction. It may be an amount total, a quantity total, a hash total, or a record count.

corrective controls Procedures adopted by management to correct misstated records after an error or irregularity has occurred.

data control group An organizational unit in the MIS department that reviews and distributes reports printed by the computer system. In some organizations, they also review inputs to the system and reconcile inputs with outputs.

data validation The process of examining accounting transactions for erroneous data. Also called data editing, it is frequently performed by a computer program.

detective controls Procedures adopted by management to identify errors and irregularities after they have occurred.

file dump The process of copying the contents of a master file onto a removable device. This creates a backup copy.

general controls Policies, practices, and procedures that prevent or detect errors and irregularities for all accounting application systems.

grandfather-father-son technique The standard file backup policy in batch processing systems using sequential files. It maintains three generations of each master file.

preventive controls Procedures adopted by management to prevent errors and irregularities.

transaction log In an on-line real-time system, a computer file containing copies of all transactions posted to a master file since the last master file dump. It serves as a backup copy of the transactions.

QUESTIONS

14–1. How are system controls categorized:
   a. By objective?
   b. By scope?

14–2. How are incompatible functions combined in a computer-based accounting system?

14–3. What is the objective of providing adequate segregation of duties? How is this done within an MIS activity?

14–4. How is custody of accounting records maintained in:
   a. A traditional file processing system?
   b. A data base management system?

14–5. What are appropriate procedures for authorizing and approving:
a. Implementation of a new accounting system?
b. Changes to an existing computer program?

14–6. How does segregation of duties in the MIS activity control access to accounting records?

14–7. Why are file backup procedures needed? How do these differ between batch processing and on-line real-time systems?

14–8. What are the contents of a contingency plan?

14–9. What is the purpose of data validation procedures? How do they differ between batch processing and on-line real-time systems?

14–10. Which system control procedures are classified as both input and processing controls?

14–11. Distinguish between three kinds of control totals.

14–12. How do direct data entry procedures prevent errors?

14–13. Who in the MIS activity is primarily responsible for output controls? Which functions do they perform?

EXERCISES AND CASES

14–14. CHECK DIGITS

Calculate a check digit for each of the following account numbers using the modulus 11 method.

a. 666335
b. 62779
c. 1234
d. 10102

14–15. SELF-CHECKING NUMBERS

Each of the following is an account number. The last digit is a check digit calculated using the modulus 11 method. Identify the invalid account number(s).

a. 66635
b. 6661
c. 666774
d. 770701

14–16. SYSTEM CONTROL OBJECTIVES

Controls over system activities can be classified as either preventive or detective controls.

Required:

a. Briefly define these classifications of controls and give two examples of each.
b. Cite two examples of controls which may be used either as a preventive control or as a detective control.

(CIA Adapted)

14–17. ***ACCESS TO DATA***

The Ultimate Life Insurance Company recently established a data base management system. The company is now planning to provide its branch offices with terminals that have on-line access to the central computer facility.

Required:

a. Briefly discuss three security steps to safeguard the data base from improper access through terminals.
b. Briefly describe four steps to control the completeness and accuracy of data transmitted through terminals to the data base.

(CIA Adapted)

14–18. ***ACCESS TO DOCUMENTATION***

The documentation of data processing applications is an important step in the design and implementation of any computer-based system. Documentation provides a complete record of data processing applications.

Required:

Describe policies to regulate access to documentation data for each of the following groups of company employees.

a. Computer operators.
b. Internal auditors.
c. Production planning analysts.
d. Systems analysts.

(CMA Adapted)

14–19. ***SEGREGATION OF DUTIES***

The following questions are often asked on internal control questionnaires:

a. Is there controlled access to computerized data files?
b. Are computer programmers and computer operators prohibited from correcting errors and reconciling control totals appearing on computer generated reports?

Required:

For each of these questions, identify two risks or exposures which could exist if the related internal control procedure is not followed.

(CIA Adapted)

14–20. *APPLICATION CONTROLS*

Looking at the following columns, the left one lists six procedural controls often found in accounting information systems. The right column lists 10 explanations of various types of procedural controls.

Procedural Controls	*Explanation*
1. Default option	A. Rekeying incorrect data detected on a CRT display
2. Hash total	B. A test of specified amount fields against stipulated high or low limits of acceptability
3. Completeness check	C. A test of characters in a coded field against an acceptable set of values, patterns, formats, subcodes, or character values
4. Visual verification	D. A test to determine that data entries are made in fields that cannot be processed in a blank state
5. Validity check	E. The automatic utilization of a predetermined value in situations where input transactions having certain values are left blank
6. Limit check	F. Internally initiated processing in a predetermined manner unless specific input transactions are received that specify processing with different values or in a different manner
	G. The immediate return of input information to the sender for comparison and approval
	H. Provides a control total for comparison with accumulated counts or values of records processed
	I. A meaningless but useful value developed from the accumulated numerical amounts of nonmonetary information
	J. Any type of control total or count applied to a specific number of transactions documents or to the transaction documents that arrive within a specified period of time

Required:

For each procedural control, identify the explanation that best applies to it. (Each procedural control has only one explanation.)

(CIA Adapted)

14–21. *APPLICATION CONTROLS*

A well-designed computer-based information system includes methods of assuring that the data are accurate and appropriate for the situation.

Required:

a. Describe procedures that would assure that the input data are accurate and appropriate.
b. Describe procedures that would assure that all data were processed and processed properly.
c. Describe procedures that would assure that the output data are accurate and appropriate.

(CMA Adapted)

14–22. *SYSTEM CONTROLS*

A small local bakery has expanded its operations into a regional area. Expansion has increased the business information needs in all areas including distribution (truck routes), fixed assets (including tracking mobile equipment), inventory, order processing, and accounting (general ledger, accounts payable, payroll, etc.) These factors have required a change from a manual to a computerized environment.

Required:

Identify control procedures that the internal auditor, as a member of the system design project team, should suggest for the following activities:

a. Transaction origination.
b. Data communication.
c. Computer processing.
d. Data storage and retrieval.
e. Output processing.

(CIA Adapted)

14–23. *GENERAL CONTROLS*

As an auditor, you conducted a review of a client's computer-based information system and observed the following:

1. The MIS manager reports to the director of accounting who, in turn, reports to the controller. The controller reports to the treasurer, who is one of several vice presidents of the company. The MIS manager has made several unsuccessful requests to the director of accounting for another printer.
2. There is no written charter for the MIS function, but the MIS manager tells you that the primary objective is to get the accounting reports out on time.
3. Transaction tapes are used daily to update the master file and then are retired to the scratch tape area.

4. A new computer with large disk capacity was installed three years ago. The MIS activity previously used an older computer, and many of the programs written for that computer are used on the present equipment by means of an emulator. (The emulator is a computer program that translates code from the form required by the old computer to that required by the new one.)
5. You observe that the output from the computer runs is written on tape for printing at a later time. Some output tapes from several days' runs are waiting to be printed.
6. The MIS manager states that the central processing unit could handle at least twice the work currently being processed.

Required:

a. Identify the defect inherent in each of the six preceding conditions.

b. Briefly describe the probable effect if the condition is permitted to continue.

(CIA Adapted)

14–24. ***DATA VALIDATION***

Talbert Corporation hired an independent computer programmer to develop a simplified payroll application for its computer. The programmer developed an on-line, DBMS-based microcomputer system that minimized the level of knowledge required by the operator. It required a user to type answers to input cues that appeared on the terminal's viewing screen. Examples of these cues follow:

Access routine

1. Operator access number to payroll file?
2. Are there new employees?

New employees routine

1. Employee name?
2. Employee number?
3. Social security number?
4. Rate per hour?
5. Single or married?
6. Number of dependents?
7. Account distribution?

Current payroll routine

1. Employee number?
2. Regular hours worked?
3. Overtime hours worked?
4. Total employees this payroll period?

The auditor is attempting to verify that certain input validation (edit) checks exist to ensure that errors resulting from omissions, invalid entries, or other inaccuracies would be detected during the typing of answers to the input cues.

Required:

Identify the various types of input validation (edit) checks the auditor would expect to find in the system. Describe the assurances provided by each validation check you identify.

(AICPA Adapted)

14–25. *SMALL BUSINESS SYSTEMS*

A typical small computer system consists of a central processing unit, input devices, output devices, memory, and software. These systems are being used extensively in small businesses as small but complete data processing systems.

Required:

Discuss the internal control considerations for a small company using such a system.

(CMA Adapted)

14–26. *MINICOMPUTERS*

Your company has procured a number of minicomputers for use in various locations and applications. One of these has been installed in the stores department which has the responsibility for disbursing stock items and maintaining stores records. In this department a competent employee trained in computer applications receives the requisitions for stores, reviews them for completeness and for the propriety of approvals, disburses the stock, maintains the records, operates the computer, and authorizes adjustments to the total amounts of stock accumulated by the computer.

You have discussed the applicable controls with the department manager. The manager states that because the minicomputer is assigned exclusively to that department it does not require the same types of controls applicable to large computer systems.

Required:

Comment on the manager's contentions. Discuss briefly five controls that would apply to this application.

(CIA Adapted)

14–27. *SYSTEM CONTROL OBJECTIVES*

A bank provides services such as money transfers, letters of credit, and foreign exchange for its customers who maintain minimum balances in demand deposit accounts (DDAs). Earnings on DDA balances compensate the bank for the services and contribute to income. The amount of income earned by DDA balances, however, is a function of variable interest rates. These are beyond the bank's control, and the bank cannot continually change minimum balance requirements as interest rates fluctuate.

The bank uses a spreadsheet model on a desktop computer to help it plan changes in minimum balances. The spreadsheet model projects operating results for different minimum balances. As interest rates fall, larger balances are required to produce the same income. The costs of the services include fixed costs and variable costs which are linear functions of volume.

Required:

For this application, identify three preventive controls, three detective controls, and three corrective controls. For each one, indicate the risk of errors or irregularities it is intended to control.

(CIA Adapted)

14–28. ***SYSTEM CONTROLS***

The state department of taxation is developing a new computer system for processing state income tax returns. The new system features on-line input and inquiry capability. Identification of taxpayers is provided by the social security number for individuals and federal identification number for corporations. The new system should be fully implemented in time for the next tax season. The new system will serve the following three primary purposes:

1. Data entry clerks will input data from tax returns using cathode ray tube (CRT) terminals at the department's central headquarters.
2. The returns will be processed using the main computer facilities at headquarters. Processing includes:
   a. Verification of mathematical accuracy.
   b. Auditing the reasonableness of deductions and tax due through the use of edit routines. These routines also include a comparison of the current year's data with the prior year's data.
   c. Identification of returns which should be considered for audit by revenue agents of the department.
3. Inquiry service will be provided taxpayers on request through the assistance of tax department personnel at five regional offices. A total of 50 CRT terminals will be placed at the regional offices. Taxpayers will be allowed to determine the status of their returns or get information from the last three years' returns by calling or visiting one of the department's regional offices.

The state commissioner of taxation is concerned about data security during input and processing. This includes both protection against the loss or damage of data during input or processing and the improper input or processing of data. In addition, the tax commissioner and the state attorney general have discussed the general problem of data confidentiality which may arise from the nature and operation of the new system. Both individuals want to have all potential problems identified before the system is fully developed and implemented so that the proper controls can be incorporated into the new system.

Required:

a. Describe the potential risks that could arise in each of the following three areas of processing. Recommend corrective action(s) to minimize the risks.
   1. Data input.
   2. Processing of returns.
   3. Data inquiry.

b. The state tax commission wants to incorporate controls to provide security against the loss, damage, or improper input or use of data during data input and processing. Identify the potential problems (other than natural hazards such as fire or floods) for which the state department of taxation should develop controls and recommend the possible controls for each problem identified.

(CMA Adapted)

14–29. ***SEGREGATION OF DUTIES***

Robinson Industries is a loosely knit conglomerate that offers centralized data processing services to its affiliated companies.[2] To improve the attractiveness of its services, this past year the data processing department introduced on-line service. Several affiliates have become, or are becoming, users of this service. It has resulted in a reorganization of the department, although a new organization chart for it has yet to be prepared.

The data processing department now consists of 25 persons reporting to the president through the director of data processing. In addition to these data employees, key committees perform important roles as do the internal and independent auditors for the company.

Committees

Selected functions of key committees important to the management and control of the data processing department are as follows:

Data Processing Committee. The data processing committee, composed of three members of the board of directors, meets as required to review and evaluate major changes in the data processing area and to review approval of all pricing of services offered. Their responsibilities also include a review of major agreements with hardware and software vendors.

Audit Committee. In its oversight of the audit function, this committee of the board of directors is directly concerned with the quality of the records and reports processed by the department and the controls employed.

---

[2]Adapted from a case prepared by Professors Frederick L. Neumann and Richard J. Boland, University of Illinois, through a grant by the Touche Ross Foundation.

Users' Groups. Users' groups consist of representatives from on-line users within a specific geographical area. They meet periodically throughout the year to discuss common areas of interest, possible enhancements, and current problems related to the on-line system. The results of these group meetings are reported directly to the data processing committee through a user advisory committee.

Data Processing Department

Data processing department management consists of five managers who report to the director through an assistant director. The department management meets weekly to review the status of projects, customer service levels, and any problems. Weekly status reports are then prepared and distributed to each level of line management. Formal meetings with Robinson's president are held quarterly, or more often if required, to review future plans and past performance.

Each of the following five sections in the department is under the direction of a manager:

1. *On-line Services*
   a. *On-line technical staff.* The on-line technical staff conducts all user training, conversions, and parameter definitions necessary to set up a new user. Training classes are conducted at the data processing center. Conversion assistance is provided to the user prior to the initiation of on-line services. If conversion programs are required, these are defined by the on-line services section to the on-line analyst programmers for program preparation. During the first month after conversion of a new user, calls are directed to on-line services; thereafter, user calls are directed to the user liaison section.
   b. *Applications coordinator.* The applications coordinator is responsible for coordinating the approval of user and data processing department project requests, assisting in the requirements definition of a systems maintenance project, monitoring ongoing projects, and approving project test results.
2. *Operations*
   a. *Data communications coordinator.* The coordinator of data communications monitors all service levels and response time related to the communications network and terminals. The coordinator receives all user calls regarding communications problems, logs these calls, identifies the nature of the problem, and reports the status of the problems until they are corrected.
   b. *Computer operators.* Operators, supervisors, and librarians in this section execute, review, and service the daily computer production runs, special computer runs, and program compilations and tests. The operations are scheduled on a 24-hour basis for six days a week. Shift supervisors review all on-line operations and prepare written documentation of each problem encountered.

c. Scheduler. The scheduler is responsible for setting up the computer job runs and adjusting them for one-time special requests.

d. User liaison. User liaison staff consists of four persons who receive, log, and report all questions or potential problems, other than communications problems, by on-line users. User input is obtained through telephone calls, letters, and on-line messages over the communications network and notes from users' group meetings.

e. On-line reports control. The on-line reports control staff is responsible for the distribution of all hardcopy output to all users. Microfiche are sent directly to users from the outside processing vendor. Logs are maintained where appropriate to control distribution and to reconcile items such as check numbers and dividend totals.

3. *Systems and Programming*

   a. On-line analyst programmers. On-line analyst programmers are responsible for all of the applications and system software programming required for the on-line system. Systems analysis and programming consists primarily of maintenance to existing computer programs, correction of problems, and enhancements to the current applications.

   b. In-house analyst programmers. In-house analyst programmers are responsible for all applications and system software programming not on-line.

4. *Research and Development*

   The research and development staff evaluates and conducts preliminary investigations into new applications.

5. *Marketing*

   The marketing staff responds to requests for information regarding the services provided by the data processing department. Once a new user signs an on-line service agreement, that member is turned over to on-line services for training and conversion.

Required:

a. Prepare an organization chart of the data processing department and of its relationship to the rest of the organization.

b. From a controls standpoint, how could organizational independence be improved?

Chapter 15

Data Security and Integrity

Learning Objectives:

1. To distinguish between data security and data integrity in computer-based accounting systems.
2. To understand data security risks and their sources.
3. To learn methods of detecting fraud.
4. To discover how auditors evaluate data security and integrity in computer-based accounting systems.

INTRODUCTION

Management adopts an organization's internal control structure. It selects control policies, practices, and procedures for its accounting systems to provide reasonable assurance of preventing or detecting errors and irregularities. These help to safeguard assets and to ensure accurate and reliable accounting data.

Those control policies, practices, and procedures that ensure accurate and reliable data provide *data integrity.* Because computers contain records and authorize transactions regarding assets, the controls that safeguard computer files also safeguard assets. These controls provide *data security.*

In this chapter, you will learn about the risks associated with data security and integrity, the sources of those risks, and an approach to detecting fraud. You will also learn how auditors evaluate the security and integrity in a computer-based system.

SECURITY IN COMPUTER-BASED SYSTEMS

Criminals who gain unauthorized access to computerized accounting records may alter data to defraud the organization. Security features prevent unauthorized access and thereby safeguard the organization's assets. A computer-based system that safeguards its data from risk is one that provides adequate data security.

Sources of Security Risk

Weaknesses in data security allow risks from three sources: internal, external, and collusive.[1]

Internal Sources. Internal sources of risk are employees who might exploit weaknesses in data security. They include managers and operations level employees.

Operations Level Employees. Operations level employees include accounting clerks, sales clerks, and factory workers. Because these employees have routine access to the assets of the organization, they have opportunities to steal these assets. They have, however, only limited access to computerized records concerning assets.

When the organization implements good segregation of duties, no one has both custody of an asset and access to the records concerning that asset. This restricts the ability of operations level employees to both steal an asset and conceal the theft by altering computerized records.

Managers. Managerial and supervisory employees have greater access to records, but fewer opportunities to steal assets. Although they can more easily falsify records to cover a theft, it is difficult for managers to steal an asset without the knowledge of others in the organization. They may, however, bypass restrictions by threatening to dismiss operations level employees who know of their thefts.

External Sources. External sources of risk include business contacts and potential criminals who have opportunities to steal the organization's assets.

---

[1]For a different treatment of this subject, see Michael J. Comer, *Corporate Fraud* (London: McGraw-Hill, 1985).

Business Contacts. Several kinds of business contacts have the opportunity to commit a computer-related crime. Two major sources of risk are customers and vendors. Because they process transactions with the organization, the employees of customers and vendors have indirect access to assets and to records. The greatest risk occurs when their employees act in conjunction with one of the organization's employees. Acting together, they may commit a theft and conceal it by entering fraudulent transactions in the computer-based system.

Former employees also constitute a risk to an accounting system. Frequently they have intimate knowledge of the system and its control weaknesses. If they hold a grudge against their former employer, they may attempt to exploit weaknesses to commit computer-related crimes.

Another source of risk is business competitors who may seek competitive advantage by gaining access to confidential data stored in computer files.

Unknown Criminals. Other criminals may also become sources of risk to computerized records. ''Hackers'' attempt to bypass system security features using access by telephone. Usually the challenge, rather than theft, is the motive for these criminals. Nevertheless, they can do extensive damage to an organization's data base. Organized crime may also exploit weaknesses in data security to defraud an organization of its assets.

Collusive Sources. Collusive sources of risk exist when two or more individuals conspire to defraud an organization and to conceal the theft by altering computerized records. All organizations, even those with adequate segregation of duties, are subject to frauds from this source. For this reason, accountants must be aware of these sources and adopt procedures to prevent or detect them. Collusive sources exist in two forms: internal collusion and external collusion.

Internal Collusion. Internal collusion occurs when two or more employees of the organization cooperate to bypass its control policies, practices, or procedures. For example, internal collusion occurs when an operations employee steals an asset and a manager or another employee conceals the theft by falsifying records. Effective segregation of duties may not prevent frauds of this kind.

External Collusion. External collusion exists when an employee acts with a nonemployee to defraud the organization. The nonemployee may simply be an acquaintance or an employee of one of the organization's business contacts.

For example, a vendor's employee mails a fraudulent invoice to the organization. A clerk in the accounts payable department uses it to support issuing a check to the vendor. The vendor's employee intercepts the check, cashes it, and shares the proceeds with the accounts payable clerk. Good cash disbursements procedures prevent this form of external collusion; however, other forms are more difficult to prevent or detect.

In organizations with sound control policies, practices, and procedures, managers and collusive sources are the primary sources of risk. Without good internal control, risks exist from all sources. Illustration 15–1 summarizes the sources of risk arising from weaknesses in data security.

ILLUSTRATION 15–1 Sources of Data Security Risks

Internal

Operations employees. They have direct access to assets, but limited access to records.

Managers and supervisors. They may bypass control policies, practices, and procedures.

External

Business contacts. Includes competitors, employees of customers, and employees of vendors.

Other criminals. Includes hackers and organized crime.

Collusive

Internal collusion. Two or more employees. This source is not prevented by most control practices and procedures.

External collusion. An employee and a nonemployee. This source is difficult to detect.

Risks

Just as you must know the sources of risk due to weaknesses in data security, you must also understand the four risks: destruction, espionage, invasion of privacy, and fraud.[2]

Destruction of Data. Even though all accounting data are important because they provide the basis for internal and external reporting, certain data files are vital to the operation of any organization. These, including accounts receivable and accounts payable detail records, are difficult to reconstruct accurately if destroyed.

Destruction of data may be accidental or it may be intentional. The MIS department minimizes the risk of accidental destruction by employing trained computer operators, by having a computer operations manual that describes procedures for safeguarding files, and by following standard file backup policies. They prevent intentional destruction by having security procedures that eliminate the possibility of unauthorized access to data files.

Intentional data destruction usually arises from one of two sources. Disgruntled employees or former employees may gain unauthorized access to the employer's system and destroy files as a form of revenge. Hackers destroy files as a form of sport, to demonstrate their ability to bypass the security features of the system.

Illustration 15–2 describes a computer-related crime that details the risk of data destruction. In this example, a former employee was able to commit a crime because of inadequate controls over access to the system.

---

[2]Adapted from Donn C. Parker, *Crime by Computer* (New York: Scribner, 1976).

ILLUSTRATION 15–2 An Example of Data Destruction

In September 19XX, a Texas jury convicted Jean Burley, a former employee of an insurance and brokerage firm, on a felony charge of harmful access to a computer. Burley faced up to 10 years in prison.

Burley had been fired on September 18. Three days later, at about 3 A.M., she broke into her old office and sat down at her old terminal. She signed on with a password that allowed her to perform her old job, that of data security officer. She then erased 168,000 records in the company's payroll system. Burley also activated a "time bomb" program intended to erase these records on a monthly basis.

"She was having continual conflict with the company and anticipated being fired," said the district attorney. "Burley created the time bomb in a new program beginning with the letter Q. This is the same letter that begins program names provided in the operating system software, so the program would go undetected. Burley then tied this program, which was intended to erase files, to legitimate files and put in it a time switch." The company made a cursory check of the accounts after Burley was fired but did not find the hidden program file.

Saturday morning, after Burley's break-in, a programmer came to the office to figure out how a new bonus system would affect the company's payroll. Every time the programmer executed the system, the payroll came up with zeros. This led the company to shut down the computer for two days to cleanse the system, and allowed discovery of the time bomb.

Damages were about $12,000, including computer downtime and the cost to fix the payroll accounts. "In the scheme of things, it was not a large loss. But 550 people did not get their checks for a week or two. And if the program had gone off as planned, it would have created havoc," said the district attorney.

(Adapted from "Computer Time Bomb Defused; Felon Nailed," *Computerworld*, September 26, 1988. Used by permission.)

Espionage. Managers are continually concerned with the actions and plans of competing companies. They can acquire much useful information about competitors by gaining access to computerized data files.

For example, lists of customers from accounts receivable records are useful to a competitor's sales force. Competitors can learn proprietary manufacturing processes by accessing certain production files. They may learn pricing strategies by accessing sales or cost accounting records. Budget files disclose plans for future operations and capital expenditures. Payroll files reveal information on pay rates a competitor may use to lure away key employees.

Espionage is primarily an external threat. However, a competitor may also gain access to sensitive data by collusion with an employee. Illustration 15–3 contains a description of how a company used data gained from espionage for a competitive advantage. In this case, inadequate access controls allowed the crime to occur.

Invasion of Privacy. Computerized data files contain much personal information about individuals. Disclosure of this information is an invasion of privacy.

ILLUSTRATION 15–3 An Example of Data Espionage

On February 7, 19XX, a Florida news reporter was arrested and charged with 14 felony counts of breaking into a computer system. Each count carries a maximum sentence of 15 years and a $10,000 fine.

Michelle Shaffer, an assistant news director at WTSP-TV (Channel 10), allegedly broke into a rival station's system on at least six occasions to steal sensitive news information. The missing files contained information about news stories in progress or being planned, rundowns of how stories were to be handled during midday and evening news broadcasts, and planned format changes and special projects.

The accused news director was formerly employed by WTVT-TV (Channel 13) as an assignment manager. There she had participated in the installation of a system about six months earlier and had been made responsible for administering it. Shaffer had recently left Channel 13 for its crosstown rival. Although computer users and system administrators at the station routinely change computer system access codes and passwords when employees leave, a few ''slipped through'' when Shaffer left, according to a Channel 13 official.

The first theft was discovered on January 12 when the morning producer came to work and discovered a number of confidential and sensitive files missing. Channel 13 managers contacted the Florida Department of Law Enforcement, which began investigating and tracing calls to the station's computers. Phone records showed that Shaffer was making calls from her residence and from a personal computer in her office. A search warrant was obtained, and law enforcement officials seized a personal computer, 200 floppy disks, and operating manuals for the system. Shaffer was subsequently fired from her job at Channel 10.

(Adapted from ''Newsman Faces Tamper Charge,'' *Computerworld,* February 13, 1989, p. 4, and from ''TV News Execs Ousted after Hacking Charges from Rival,'' *Computerworld,* March 20, 1989, p. 16. Used by permission.)

For example, many employees object to release of data concerning their pay rates, ages, pension records, or home addresses. Customers expect confidentiality concerning current balances, credit ratings, and payment histories. In the United States, laws protect individuals from release of personal information contained in data files. These laws require organizations to maintain adequate security for personal data.[3]

Threats to privacy come from hackers and from employees. Hackers enjoy examining the contents of computer files simply to learn about other people or to demonstrate their ability to bypass data security. Employees may gain unauthorized access to pay rates, for example, when dissatisfied with their own pay.

---

[3]In the United States, the Privacy Act of 1974 and several state statutes establish these requirements for federal, state, and local governments and for regulated industries. For a discussion of their provisions, see Porter and Perry, *EDP Controls and Auditing,* 5th ed. (Boston: Kent Publishing Co., 1987), p. 188.

Fraud. Fraud is the risk that affects the accuracy of the accounting records. Frauds result in misstatements of assets and expenses in the financial statements. Major frauds also endanger the ability of an organization to continue its operations.

A fraud against an organization consists of three acts: theft of assets, conversion of those assets, and concealment of the theft.[4]

Theft. An organization entrusts its employees with its assets so they can perform their duties. A fraud begins when someone steals assets. This causes the overstatement of asset accounts in the accounting records.

Because of its liquidity, the most desirable asset to a thief is currency. Most organizations implement controls making a theft of currency difficult to commit and conceal. Therefore, most frauds involve stealing other assets such as checks, inventory, or equipment. These require a second fraudulent act, conversion of the assets.

Conversion. When a criminal steals an asset other than currency, usually the asset itself is not valuable to the criminal. So the criminal attempts to convert the asset into currency. This occurs, for example, when a thief sells stolen inventory or equipment or cashes a stolen check.

Conversion does not affect the accuracy of the accounting records, but it does provide opportunities to detect a theft. Furthermore, making conversion difficult is an effective way to discourage theft.

Concealment. A thief who has an ongoing relationship with an organization, such as an employee or business contact, usually attempts to conceal the theft. This either prevents or delays recognition of it or prevents identification of the thief. Concealment provides additional opportunities to steal and can result in an ongoing fraud.

To conceal a theft, the criminal must alter the records concerning the stolen asset. For example, if inventory is stolen, the thief must alter the inventory records. Otherwise, an auditor or superviser could discover the theft when performing a routine inventory count.

Alterations to the records require fraudulent accounting entries that produce misstated account balances. In a computer-based system, they require that the thief bypass those system controls limiting access to data. The case history in Illustration 15–4 shows how an employee bypassed controls to commit fraud.

One well-known type of fraud is a *lapping* fraud. It occurs in companies lacking adequate segregation of duties over accounts receivable. In a lapping fraud, an accounts receivable clerk intercepts and steals a check mailed by a customer in payment of the customer's account. Conversion occurs when the clerk endorses the check and cashes it. Because the customer's account is not credited for the payment, the customer would eventually complain, causing a supervisor to discover the theft. So to conceal the theft, the clerk intercepts a later check from a second customer and credits it to the first customer's account.

---

[4]For an extended discussion of this topic, see Comer, *Corporate Fraud*.

ILLUSTRATION 15–4 An Example of Fraud

Samuel Stanford didn't worry too much about getting caught by his fellow employees. "Most people just don't want to know much about computers," he said in a deposition to investigators. "When they saw that I was doing something, they would just turn and leave. They would say, 'That turkey, that technician, all he ever does is talk his buzz words . . . we can't talk to him.' " So Stanford was left alone to steal from the State of Washington.

Stanford was the employee who developed the software through which Washington's Division of Vocational Rehabilitation authorized payments to injured loggers and others requiring retraining. One-armed since a childhood accident, he was an expert programmer and was trusted even more because of his handicap. He used the system to authorize payments of nearly $17,000 to himself and two friends. Using the computer he prepared records that the state required to issue the payments. Following their issue, he erased the records. He also capitalized on people's tendency to ignore small computer errors—he had the computer make out the checks to Samuel Tanford. No bank ever questioned the missing S in his last name.

He was arrested after the daughter of one of his friends tipped police to the crime. A search of the paper records turned up the name Tanford, and the searcher recognized Stanford's address. He eventually pleaded guilty.

Stanford claimed he never kept a dime for himself, but rather gave the money to friends who were down on their luck. He called himself the "one-armed bandit" and liked to think of himself as a Robin Hood. The judge didn't accept this view of the crime and sentenced Stanford to 10 years in prison.

(Adapted from "Computers Turn Out to Be Valuable Aid in Employee Crime." Reprinted by permission of *The Wall Street Journal,* Dow Jones & Company, Inc., 1985. All rights reserved.

To conceal the second theft, the clerk must intercept a third check and credit it to the second customer's account. This requires a third false credit, followed by a fourth one, and so on. The clerk must continue to intercept payments and make false entries to conceal the theft.

Lapping may be prevented by separating responsibilities for handling cash receipts from those for maintaining accounts receivable records. Firms that mail monthly statements enable their customers to detect lapping. Illustration 15–5 summarizes the sources and risks to data security in a computer-based accounting system.

Fraud Detection

Any fraud requires three acts: theft, conversion, and concealment. Each act provides an opportunity to detect the fraud. Accountants may detect one when performing their routine duties, or auditors may detect fraud while conducting an audit.

ILLUSTRATION 15–5 Data Security Risks and Their Sources

	Risks			
Sources	*Destruction*	*Espionage*	*Invasion of Privacy*	*Fraud*
Internal				
Employees	x		x	x
Managers	x		x	x
External				
Business contacts	x	x	x	x
Other criminals	x	x	x	x
Collusive				
Internal			x	x
External		x	x	x

Detecting Theft. Accountants detect thefts by periodically reconciling asset records with assets on hand. If records indicate that assets are missing, the accountant alerts management at least one level higher than the employee responsible for the assets. For example, accountants and auditors routinely reconcile bank accounts, count the physical inventory, and verify property and equipment records to detect theft.

Detecting Conversion. Conversion occurs when a thief converts a stolen asset into currency. Many forms of asset conversion are difficult to detect from within the organization. The sale of stolen inventory or equipment, for example, is more likely to be detected by the police than by accountants. In their audits of cash disbursements, however, auditors perform procedures to uncover fraudulent check endorsements. These disclose the conversion of stolen or fraudulent checks into currency.

Detecting Concealment. Accountants and auditors use their understanding of the accounting system to detect the concealment of a theft. To conceal a theft, the criminal must record an entry that keeps the recorded assets equal to the actual assets on hand. Because assets have been taken, the thief must make a fraudulent credit entry to an asset account. For example, to conceal a theft of inventory, an employee must make a credit entry to an inventory account.

At the same time, a double-entry accounting system requires that the thief falsify a debit entry. Commonly thieves conceal a theft by debiting an expense account such as bad debts expense or miscellaneous expense. As an alternative, they may debit an asset account that is less carefully controlled than that of the asset stolen. For example, the thief may make a debit entry in a goodwill or prepaid asset account. Accountants or auditors discover the theft by identifying the fraudulent debit entry.

Experienced accountants learn the most likely ways to commit and conceal frauds in transaction processing applications, and they establish control procedures to detect these schemes. Auditors develop audit procedures to detect material frauds. If accountants and auditors lack this experience, management may engage a *forensic accountant* as a consultant. This accountant's specialty is detecting fraud. Many organizations also hire a *data security officer* whose primary responsibility is maintaining adequate data security and integrity.

You have seen examples of how auditors implement procedures to detect fraud. Fraud detection is not the primary objective of most audit engagements, however; the primary objective depends on the nature of the engagement. All auditors evaluate data security and integrity as a part of their audits.

EVALUATING SECURITY AND INTEGRITY

Management relies on auditors to evaluate the security and integrity of a computer-based system. They hire internal auditors whose objectives are to review and appraise operations as a service to management. They also engage independent auditors to evaluate the fairness of the financial statements. Each auditor is responsible for evaluating data security and integrity and reporting weaknesses to management.

Auditors' Responsibilities

Management is responsible for establishing policies, practices, and procedures that provide adequate data security. Auditors review these policies, practices, and procedures in conjunction with the evaluation of other internal controls.

Internal Auditors. Internal auditors evaluate computer security during their reviews of operating departments. They identify security risks and report them to management in the reports containing their recommendations. They may also recommend methods of improving data security; however, whether or not management implements these recommendations depends on management's evaluation of their costs and benefits. Internal auditors fulfill their responsibility to management by communicating risks to them.

Independent Auditors. Independent auditors also evaluate computer security while studying and evaluating internal control. They provide recommendations to management in the form of a management letter. In this letter they describe, as a service to management, security and other control weaknesses observed during the audit. The responsibility of independent auditors extends beyond this advisory one, however; they use their evaluation of internal control as a basis for determining which procedures are necessary in their audit.

Weaknesses in data security increase the risk that errors and irregularities may cause material misstatements in the financial statements. Generally accepted auditing standards require that independent auditors design their audits to provide reasonable assurance of detecting material irregularities, such as fraud. Weaknesses, then, require independent auditors to extend audit procedures to obtain this assurance. By creating additional risks, weaknesses in data security affect the scope of the independent audit.

The methods used by auditors to evaluate security and integrity include reviews and tests of controls. When testing controls, auditors frequently implement computer-assisted audit techniques.

System Reviews

Auditors conduct periodic reviews of computer-based accounting systems to gain an understanding of the accounting system prior to conducting tests of controls. These reviews also allow auditors to evaluate certain controls, such as segregation of duties, that are not documented by the system's records. Independent auditors conduct reviews as a part of their annual audit. Internal auditors review systems when they examine the MIS department, or as a part of examinations of departments that use the information system.

Methods of Conducting Reviews. A system review is a survey of those activities in a department that the auditors consider important. The accounting system and internal controls primarily concern the independent auditors. In addition to these, internal auditors evaluate the efficiency and effectiveness of the department. They use three methods in conducting reviews: interviews, walk-throughs, and questionnaires.

Interviews. An auditor begins the review of a department by first interviewing the manager of the department. The purpose of this interview is to meet the manager, gain an overview of the functions of the department, and gain the manager's support for the auditor's other activities during the review. An auditor then interviews other employees to understand their functions in the department. While conducting interviews, the auditor takes notes on the discussions. Later the auditor may refer to these notes when developing flowcharts of the system.

Interviews are valuable while conducting a review because they allow the auditor to request the specific information needed. They also provide an opportunity for the auditor to gain the confidence of client personnel. This helps to establish a good working relationship and may make later audit tests easier. Interviews are difficult to conduct, however, and require practice. Another method sometimes used in conjunction with interviews is the walk-through.

Walk-throughs. In a walk-through, an auditor traces a transaction through the department from the time it enters until the time it leaves or is recorded in a journal or ledger. This gives the auditor an understanding of the sequence of activities performed in the department.

ILLUSTRATION 15–6 Summary of Methods Used in Reviews

Interviews. To acquaint employees with the purpose of the review and to learn the function of each job position.

Walk-throughs. To learn the sequence of the activities performed in the department.

Questionnaires. To identify internal control weaknesses in the department.

Many auditors prefer to conduct interviews during the walk-through. When the auditor identifies the next step in the sequence of activities, a person supervising or performing that step becomes the next person to interview. At the conclusion of a walk-through, the auditor draws flowcharts documenting the flow of transactions.

Walk-throughs are beneficial in smaller departments or clients where they can be conducted in a reasonable length of time. They allow the auditor to obtain evidence by direct observation concerning how the client functions. However, the operations of large clients may be so widespread or diverse that a walk-through for certain kinds of transactions is impractical. Also, in highly computerized systems there may be no visible evidence of how transactions are processed. In these situations, walk-throughs are impossible.

When a purpose of the review is to evaluate internal control, auditors use questionnaires to guide them in conducting interviews and walk-throughs.

Questionnaires. An internal control questionnaire is a set of questions developed from a list of desirable control practices, policies, and procedures. Auditors use them in reviews of both general controls and application controls.

An experienced auditor develops the questionnaire to ensure that it contains all important controls. A less experienced auditor then determines answers to each question during the review. Questions are worded so that a ''no'' answer indicates a weakness in internal control. In this way, the questionnaire clearly identifies control weaknesses.

Use of an internal control questionnaire guides the auditor in conducting the review, ensures that a complete review is performed, and documents its results. It allows a less experienced auditor to benefit from the knowledge of one more experienced. In this way, a less experienced auditor can perform the review. However, a thorough questionnaire is difficult to develop. If it is developed inadequately, the reviews performed using it will be inadequate. Furthermore, some users may learn that ''yes'' answers are more desirable and may answer affirmatively without seriously considering the question. Illustration 15–6 summarizes the methods used in conducting reviews.

Reviews of General Controls. General controls are those practices, policies, and procedures that affect all application systems. Auditors review general controls during an examination of the MIS department.

A review of general controls emphasizes the organization and operation of the MIS department. Auditors examine evidence for proper segregation of duties, adequate access controls over data files and equipment, routine backup of data files, and the existence of a contingency plan. Illustration 15–7 shows a portion of an internal control questionnaire covering these topics.

Weaknesses in general controls, considered alone, may not concern the auditor. A strength in applications controls may, in certain circumstances, compensate for a general controls weakness. For this reason, auditors also review applications controls.

Reviews of Applications Controls. Applications controls are the control practices, policies, and procedures included in specific application systems during their design. They include input, processing, and output controls.

Auditors use internal control questionnaires during the review of input controls. Illustration 15–8 contains a questionnaire for a batch processing system. Illustration 15–9 shows one for an on-line real-time system.

Computer software executes processing controls. Because auditors cannot observe them directly, they must evaluate them by examining the results of computer processing. They use *tests of controls* for this purpose.

The data control group implements the output controls in an application system. The auditor evaluates the performance of this group during the review of the MIS and operating departments.

During system reviews, auditors hold interviews, conduct walk-throughs, and complete questionnaires. From these procedures, auditors document how the control structure should function within the department. However, auditors obtain little assurance from a review that control policies are being followed, or that control practices and procedures are implemented properly. To determine these things, auditors conduct tests of controls.

Tests of Controls

Auditors perform tests of controls to determine that employees routinely follow control policies, practices, and procedures. In the past accountants called these tests *compliance tests,* because they show whether employees are complying with the policies, practices, and procedures established by management.[5] Because auditors cannot read computer files or see computerized processes, they cannot determine if many computerized controls function properly by observing them. As a result, they use computer-assisted techniques to evaluate controls.

Auditors employ computer-assisted audit techniques (CAATs) whenever they examine on-line real-time systems. They also may use them when auditing batch processing systems because they are an efficient way to obtain reliable evidence.

[5]The Auditing Standards Board of the American Institute of Certified Public Accountants replaced the term *compliance tests* with the term *tests of controls* when it issued Statement on Auditing Standards No. 55.

ILLUSTRATION 15–7 Questionnaire for a General Controls Review

	Yes	No
Organizational control		
1. Is there an organizational chart for this group? Is the chart current?		
2. Is the computer operations group independent of operating units in the organization structure?		
3. Is there a division of functions among systems and programming, data processing, and data control?		
4. Is there a standards manual? Is the manual current?		
Administrative control		
1. Are systems and programming personnel not allowed to operate computers during processing runs?		
2. Is access to the computer center limited to authorized personnel?		
3. Is access to the data control area limited to data control personnel?		
4. Is proper record kept of library usage?		
5. Is output properly reviewed by data control personnel before releasing?		
6. Is there a definite procedure for following up on errors and their corrections?		
7. Are standard file backup procedures followed?		
User relations		
1. Is there a designated person to receive and follow up on users' comments?		
2. Are runs properly logged?		
3. Is turnaround time consistent with job priority?		
4. Are users satisfied with computer service charges?		
General emergency preparedness		
1. Is there a procedures manual covering emergency preparedness?		
2. Is the manual current?		
3. Have these procedures been tested?		
Alternative processing facilities		
1. Is there an arrangement for use of others' computer facilities? Is the arrangement in writing?		
2. Are these facilities compatible? Have they been tested?		
3. Is the location of the facilities readily accessible?		
4. Is there documentation concerning the use of the facilities?		
5. Has the contingency plan been tested?		
Data security		
1. Is the physical protection accorded programs, files, and data against heat, fire, water, and other hazards adequate?		
2. Is the file-retention procedure adequate for reconstructing files?		
3. Is access to on-line terminals limited to authorized personnel? Are levels of access identified?		
4. Are user identification and passwords in use? Are they changed frequently?		
5. Is there off-site storage of programs, files, and data?		

ILLUSTRATION 15–8 Questionnaire for an Input Controls Review in a Batch Processing System

	Yes	No
1. Are documents reviewed and batched at the originating location?		
2. Are documents prenumbered?		
3. Are control counts forwarded in duplicate, with the original sent separately?		
4. Are there positive methods for discovering a loss of source documents?		
5. Are source documents edited before being entered?		
6. Are there several types of batch controls, such as the number of documents, dollar totals, hash totals?		
7. Is each document's batch number entered on the document?		
8. Are records maintained of the data entry clerks who process each batch?		
9. Are error experience charts maintained for data entry clerks?		
10. What is the disposition of documents rejected by data entry clerks due to illegibility or errors?		
11. What is the method for entering batch controls into the computer system?		
12. Are documents held until computer processing has been completed and cleared? Who holds and controls the documents?		

ILLUSTRATION 15–9 Questionnaire for an Input Controls Review in an On-Line Real-Time System

	Yes	No
1. Are persons authorized to activate input/output devices provided with special keys or code numbers?		
2. Are employee numbers a part of input data transmitted for processing?		
3. Are source documents or management approvals needed before one activates input/output devices? Are such documents maintained for a reasonable period of time? Are they reviewed?		
4. Are programmed checks designed to control input data adequate?		
5. Are invalid input data tabulated? Are such tabulations controlled? Are they followed up?		
6. Are machine-initiated transactions tabulated? Are these tabulations reviewed by responsible personnel?		
7. Does the system appear to be able to handle peak loads with ease?		
8. Are inputs in queue protected until processing to avoid accidental loss?		
9. Are backup equipment available to receive input data during machine breakdowns?		
10. Are there tabulations of input data received and/or processed? Are they controlled? Are they reviewed?		
11. Are actions taken to protect the system when a person authorized to activate input/output devices leaves the employ of the company?		

ILLUSTRATION 15–10 Auditors' Use of Test Data

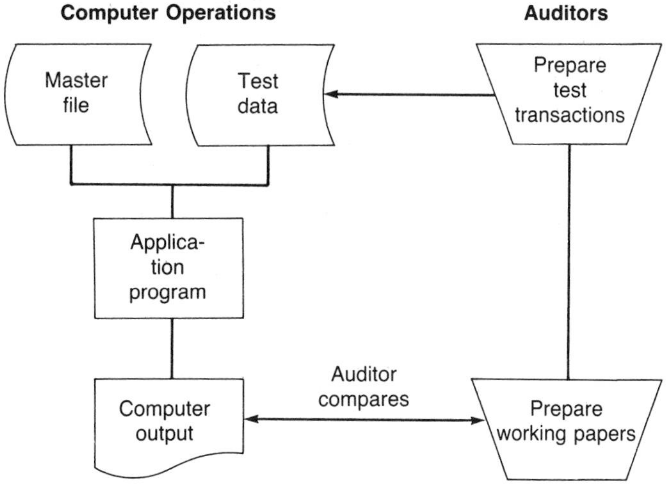

There are many kinds of CAATs; four that auditors use to evaluate data integrity are test data, parallel simulation, an integrated test facility, and embedded audit modules.

Test Data. The use of test data in auditing is similar to its use in program and system testing. Auditors develop a file of simulated input transactions for the program to be tested. They also prepare working papers showing how each transaction should be processed if the program functions properly.

Auditors execute the program using this test data and examine the output. If actual output differs from that expected, auditors identify the source of the difference. This may occur because of program logic errors or because a programmed control is ineffective.

The file of test data contains both valid and invalid transactions. Auditors create an invalid transaction to test each application control procedure of interest. Such transactions should be detected by input or processing controls; if they are, auditors know that these controls function as intended. Using valid test transactions shows that the program produces desired reports accurately.

At one time auditors keypunched a file of test data, producing a deck of computer cards. For this reason, sometimes this technique is called "test decks." Although the method of data entry has changed, the technique is still useful. Illustration 15–10 shows how the auditor uses test data.

Auditors encounter two problems when using test data. First, they must ensure that the application program they test is the one used during normal processing of accounting transactions. Second, the auditors must take steps to avoid recording the test transactions in the actual accounting records. Parallel simulation is a technique that lacks these problems.

ILLUSTRATION 15–11 Auditors' Use of Parallel Simulation

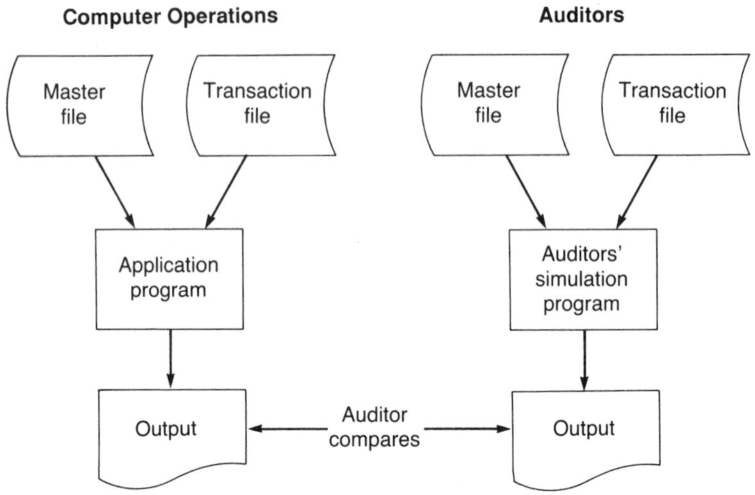

Parallel Simulation. Using parallel simulation, auditors write a computer program that performs the major functions of a client's application program. The auditors execute this simulation program for a representative time period using the client's data. The auditors then compare the output of the simulation program with the output produced by the client's application program during the same time period. Differences may indicate that the application program processes data erroneously.

You can see how this technique got its name in Illustration 15–11. The auditors' simulation program executes in parallel to the client's application program because each uses identical transaction and master file data.

Parallel simulation allows auditors to avoid the limitations of test data; however, developing an adequate simulation program requires significant computer skills. The auditors must understand the application program and be proficient enough in a computer language to program a simulation of it. Because the auditors never test the application program directly, they obtain no assurance about how it processes erroneous or unusual transactions.

A technique that overcomes the latter disadvantage is the integrated test facility.

Integrated Test Facility. The integrated test facility (ITF) is an effective technique. Although it takes other forms, most commonly it is a dummy cost center created for use by auditors.

To use it, auditors first create test transactions for the controls they wish to test. They create working papers showing the expected results of processing with these test transactions; then they enter the test transactions in the application program. The program processes these transactions along with actual ones during a routine reporting period. Auditors examine the results of processing the test transactions, comparing them to the expected results. This allows the auditors to verify that the application program functions properly.

Because test transactions are processed along with real ones, auditors know that they are testing the client's production programs. And because the auditors create test transactions, they can develop both valid and invalid ones and thoroughly test application controls. If left in the data files, the test transactions would produce inaccurate information; therefore, auditors must either take steps to prevent their posting to master files, or post adjusting journal entries to eliminate them.

Because ITF entities are integrated into master files, auditors create them most efficiently during the development of the application system. Once developed, auditors use them routinely to provide assurance that controls function as desired. Illustration 15–12 shows how an ITF works.

In large companies, the dummy cost center may be coded as a subsidiary company. In these circumstances, auditors call this the minicompany approach.

Using an integrated test facility requires changes to the client's master files. In contrast, embedded audit modules require changes to the client's application programs.

Embedded Audit Modules. Auditors sometimes create small programs, or modules, and include them in an application program. As the application program executes, a module performs functions of interest to the auditors. Embedded audit modules allow auditors to monitor the actions of the application program as actual transactions are processed.

Auditors use embedded audit modules for many purposes. With a technique known as *real-time notification,* the module identifies transactions of special interest and displays them at an auditor's terminal. The module may, for example, identify cash disbursements transactions intended for a vendor suspected of fraud.

In another technique, called *tagging,* the module marks a specified data field for certain transaction records. This tag identifies the transaction as one of special interest to the auditor. For example, the auditor may tag all transactions for very large amounts, or transactions in accounts subject to fraud. An audit module copies tagged transactions to a computer file or prints a report listing them for later examination by auditors.

Sometimes tagging is used in conjunction with the *snapshot* technique. The snapshot is a report showing the contents of main storage. An audit module produces this report immediately before processing a tagged transaction (called a ''beforeimage'') and immediately after (producing an ''afterimage''). The auditors then compare the changes produced with those expected. Auditors sometimes use the snapshot technique to identify logic errors that produce erroneous data in master files. An application program may use several snapshots; the example in Illustration 15–13 produces three of them.

ILLUSTRATION 15–12 Auditors' Use of an Integrated Test Facility

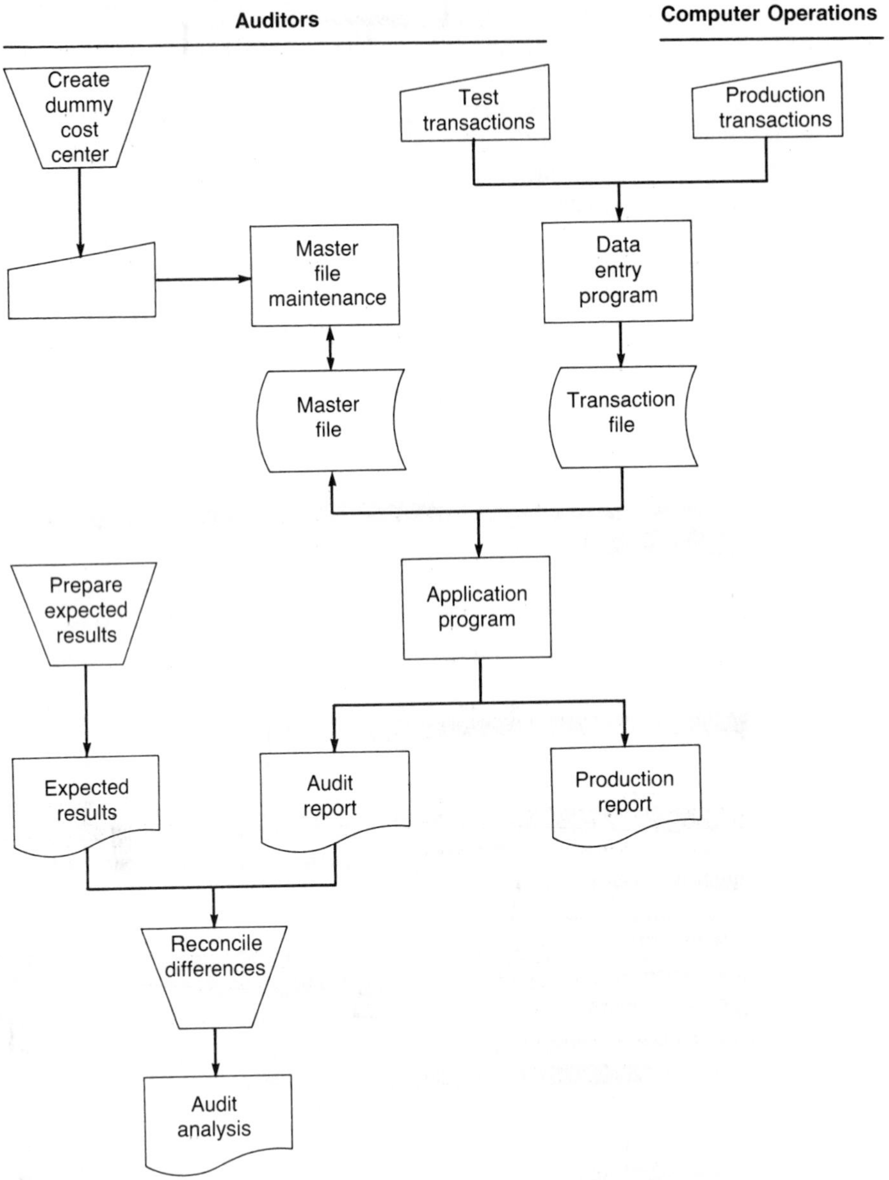

ILLUSTRATION 15–13 Auditors' Use of Snapshots

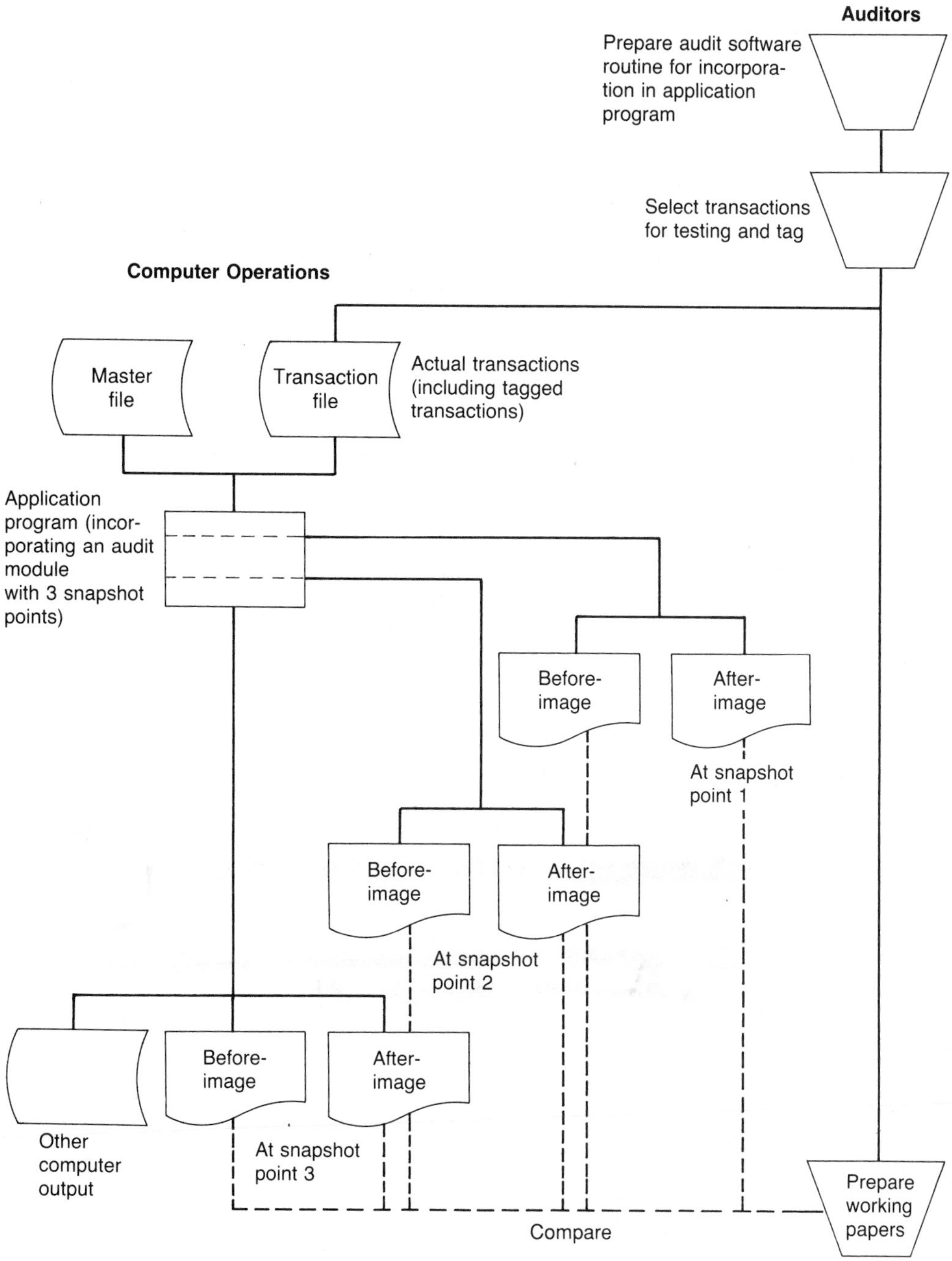

ILLUSTRATION 15–14 Applications of Computer-Assisted Audit Techniques

	Application		
Technique	*Audit Objective*	*Audit Test*	*Auditor Concludes*
Test data	Auditor wants to determine if a validation program correctly calculates a check digit.	Auditor creates several transactions containing both valid and invalid account numbers, and enters them in the validation program.	Auditor concludes that the program does (or does not) calculate the check digit correctly.
Parallel simulation	Auditor wants to determine if a validation program properly performs completeness tests.	Auditor codes a program to perform the test and executes it using a client transaction file containing errors.	Auditor concludes that the program does (or does not) correctly perform the completeness test.
Integrated test facility	Auditor wants to determine if all expenditures are recorded in proper expense accounts.	Auditor creates test expenditure transactions for a dummy cost center. A data entry clerk enters them along with real transactions.	Auditor concludes that the expenditures are (or are not) recorded in the proper accounts.
Embedded audit module	Auditor wants to determine that all large dollar value paychecks are not fraudulent.	Auditor creates a module to tag all payroll transactions for more than $5,000. The module copies all such transactions into a file.	Auditor examines payroll transactions in the file and identifies questionable ones for further investigation.

Another technique sometimes used with tagged transactions is *tracing*. A trace is a computer report that describes the path followed by a transaction through the logic of an application program during execution. Utility software and some computer languages provide the ability to produce traces. Auditors use this software to record execution steps for specific transactions tagged for the purpose. This allows the auditor to identify the logic errors that produce erroneous data in an application program.

As you can see, embedded audit modules can be complex and difficult to develop. Because they require changes to application programs, auditors create them most easily during the development of the application system. When auditors attempt to detect fraud or to correct problems with existing systems, they may add audit modules to existing programs. Developing and using audit modules is expensive, and auditors require significant computer skills to use them successfully.

Illustration 15–14 gives applications for the four computer-assisted audit techniques just discussed. Each requires auditor proficiency in computer technology and computer programming. Achieving adequate programming proficiency is easier when the auditor uses a generalized audit software package.

Generalized Audit Software

Most auditors use generalized audit software (GAS) during their evaluations of computer-based systems. GAS is a software package developed by auditors to aid in performing common audit tasks. GASs can be purchased from software development companies, and some large CPA firms have their own. GAS packages are different from the other computer-assisted audit techniques described earlier. Auditors seldom use GAS programs to test controls; instead, they use them to mechanize the gathering of evidence. The use of GAS replaces manual operations performed by auditors with computerized operations controlled by the GAS programs.

How GAS Works. Each GAS package has its own programming language that auditors use to write programs. The software package interprets the program and from it produces instructions that are executable by the CPU. Auditors can perform most operations in the GAS language that are possible in general purpose languages such as BASIC or COBOL.

Auditors program in the language by entering parameters on specification sheets. Each line in a specification sheet becomes one instruction in the GAS program. In this way, the specification sheet makes it easy for the auditor to encode correctly the commands required by the GAS language. An auditor then enters the instructions into a computer file that becomes an input to the GAS package. Illustration 15–15 contains a GAS specification sheet.

What Can GAS Do? GAS packages make it easy for auditors to perform commonly used audit functions. GAS programs access data in computer files, manipulate the data, perform calculations and comparisons, and print reports. Illustration 15–16 shows some common applications of GAS in an audit. GAS also provides an efficient way to write programs used in parallel simulation.

Advantages of GAS. Auditors use GAS to perform many audit procedures that would be performed manually without the package. Using GAS the computer performs the procedure more quickly, more thoroughly, and with greater accuracy than would be done by a person. In this way, GAS increases both the efficiency and the effectiveness of the audit.

GAS also improves the auditors' independence. It allows auditors to examine the contents of a client's data files without using the client's software. Whenever the auditor uses client programs, there is a possibility that an employee has modified them in a way unknown to the auditors. This modification could misstate accounting data or conceal a theft.

ILLUSTRATION 15–15 A Generalized Audit Software Specification Sheet

P PARAMETER — REPORT PRINT LINE

PARAM CODE (1)	TAG (2–4) ƀ = NONE (XXX)	INPUT: FIELD SIZE (5–7)	AREA CODE (8)	FIELD LOCATION F = FORMULA DERIVED FIELD (9–12)	DECIMALS (13)	DATA TYPE (14)	PRINTED OUTPUT: PRINT FIELD SIZE (NNN) ƀ = USE I/P OR EDIT SIZE (15–17)	FIXED LOCATION: AREA (18)	PRINT POSITION ƀ = COMPOSE TAG = ALIGN (nnn) = FIXED POS (19–22)	DECIMALS (N) (23)	EDIT CODE (24)	ROUND X YES (25)	JUSTIFY ② (26)	CAUSE BREAK ① (27)	TOTAL FIELD (28)	DETAIL (29)	PRINT AT CONTROL BREAK MINOR → MAJOR 1 (30)	2 (31)	3 (32)	4 (33)	5 (34)	6 (35)	7 (36)	MULTI-LINE CONTROL: LINE NO ƀ = 1 (37–38)	SPACE AFT PRINT ƀ = 1 ③ (39–40)	CONTROL (41)	COLUMN HEADINGS, LITERALS, FORMULAS & COMMENTS (42–71)	SEQUENCE NUMBER (73–80)
P	A	2	A	1										2		S		X									'REGION	REPT2Ø31
P		2	A	3										1		S	X										'WHSE	2
P		3	A	5	Ø	P				Ø	Z					X											PRODUCT'CODE	3
P		25	A	16												X											'PRODUCT DESCRIPTION	4
P	B	5	A	77	Ø	P				Ø	E					X											'QUANTITY	5
P		3	A	13												X											UNIT OF MEASURE	6
P		4	A	82	Ø	P	12			Ø	E				X	X	X	X	X								ENDING'INVENTORY	7
P		23							B								X									V	WHSE ENDING INVENTORY	8
P		23							B									X								V	REGION ENDING INVENTORY	9
P		23							B										X							V	TOTAL ENDING INVENTORY	1Ø
P		29							A										X							V	NUMBER OF ITEMS PROCESSED	1
P			U	1	Ø	N			A+3Ø	Ø	E				X		X	X	X							*	ITEM COUNT	2
P		8	U	EDT					11Ø																	*	RUN DATE	
P		13	U	LPG					111Ø																	*	PAGE	
P																												
P																												
P																												
P																												
P																												
P																												

PRINT CONTROL: ƀ = NO PRINT; X = PRINT; P = PRINT PRIOR; S = PRINT IF CHG

EXAMPLES:
FORMULA (41) F (42) A = B + 3 2/6 — Determine Field A by adding 3 2 to field B and divide the result by 6
COLUMN HEADING (41) ƀ (42) GROSS' AMOUNT — PRINTED GROSS AMOUNT
NOTE COLUMN HEADINGS ARE SEPARATED BY (')

AREA CODES (I/P)
ƀ = A INPUT
B, C, D = INPUT AREAS
J, K, L, M = WORK AREAS
U = USER AREA
R = REFORMAT AREA

DATA TYPE
ƀ = CHAR
P = PACKED
B = BINARY
N = NUMERIC ZONED

AREA CODES
ƀ = NORMAL PRINT LINE AREA
1—9 = TITLE LINE AREA

EDIT CODES
ƀ = NONE OR UNPACK DATA IF PACKED
E = FULL EDIT
Z = ZERO SUPRESS
D = DATE EDIT (MM/DD/YY)
S = SOC SEC

TOTAL THIS FIELD
ƀ = NO TOTAL
X = TOTAL THIS FIELD
(N) = 1—7, ACCUM TOTAL THRU LEVEL GIVEN

CONTROL
D = FIELD NOT PRINTED—BREAK FIELD OR USED IN FORMULA
F = COLUMNS 42—71 CONTAIN FORMULA
L = PRINTED FIELD WITH LEFT JUSTIFIED COLUMN HEADINGS
R = PRINTED FIELD WITH RIGHT JUSTIFIED COLUMN HEADINGS
ƀ = PRINTED FIELD WITH NO COLUMN HEADINGS, OR CENTER JUSTIFY COLUMN HEADINGS IF COLUMNS 42—71 NON-BLANK
* = PRINTED FIELD WITH COLUMNS 42—71 CONTAINING COMMENTS NOT COLUMN HEADING
V = PRINTED FIELD IS LITERAL CONTAINED IN COLUMNS 42-71

① BREAK
ƀ = FIELD DOESN'T CAUSE CONTROL BREAK
(N) = 1—6, BREAK AT LEVEL GIVEN
LINE SPACING ON BREAKS GIVEN IN COLS 16—29 OF R PARAM

② JUSTIFY
ƀ = CENTER
L = LEFT
R = RIGHT

③ SPACE AFTER CONTROLS
FOR LINES 2 & UP
01—99 = SPACE LINES
EJ = EJECT

Coding in the GAS language is much quicker than writing a program in a general purpose language. Auditors can execute in twenty lines of GAS code a program that would require hundreds of lines of code in COBOL. Their ease of programming allows auditors to use the computer to perform audit tests that would be too costly if done in a general purpose language.

A GAS language is also easier to learn than a general purpose language. As an auditor, you learn how to complete the dozen or so types of specification sheets used by a GAS language. Specification sheets replace rules of syntax so there are few rules to master. In two or three weeks you can learn the GAS language and how to use it during an audit.

ILLUSTRATION 15–16 Functions Performed by Generalized Audit Software Programs

1. Scan computer files to:
   a. Count records.
   b. Verify contents for:
      Completeness.
      Arithmetic accuracy.
      Consistency.
   c. Retrieve records of significance to auditors.
   d. Summarize contents.
2. Print contents of files.
3. Select samples from files.
4. Perform arithmetic operations.
5. Compare contents of two files.
6. Sort and merge files.
7. Print reports, such as:
   Aging schedules.
   Audit sample listings.
8. Print confirmations.
9. Calculate parameters for statistical samples.

Disadvantages of GAS. If GAS is quicker and easier than general purpose languages, why not always use it rather than, say, COBOL? In most cases, GAS is less efficient than a general purpose language. GAS programs require more main storage and execute more slowly, so they are not used for routine transaction processing. In most cases these limitations are unimportant to auditors.

GAS is also less flexible. Auditors have designed GAS commands to make it easy to perform common audit tasks. However, the limited variety of commands makes GAS awkward for complex procedures.

Its developers design a GAS package to execute on a specific brand of computer using a limited set of operating systems. A specific GAS package does not work on all brands of computers, and for some brands no GAS packages are available. Additionally, most GAS packages are awkward to use with data base management systems.

Generalized audit software packages enable auditors to perform audit tests rapidly and thoroughly and to utilize audit techniques that would be impractical without the assistance of a computer. Modern accounting systems require the use of a computer in an audit, so you will probably encounter one of these packages sometime in your career. Illustration 15–17 summarizes the advantages and disadvantages of using generalized audit software.

ILLUSTRATION 15–17 Advantages and Disadvantages of Using Generalized Audit Software

ADVANTAGES

1. *Speed.* With GAS, a computer performs audit procedures that would otherwise be done manually. A computer is much faster.
2. *Accuracy.* A computer performing audit procedures directed by GAS makes fewer mistakes than people performing the same procedures.
3. *Thoroughness.* Because of the speed of a computer using GAS, many more records can be examined than could be done by a person.
4. *Ease of use.* An auditor can code a program in a GAS language faster than in a general purpose language.
5. *Ease of learning.* An auditor can learn how to code in a GAS language faster than in a general purpose language.

DISADVANTAGES

1. *Execution efficiency.* Programs written in a GAS language require more main storage and more time when executing than those in a general purpose language.
2. *Flexibility.* GAS packages are intended to perform audit procedures. Using them for other procedures, such as calculations, is awkward.
3. *Transportability.* A GAS package is intended for use on specific makes of hardware and software. For some computers, GAS is unavailable.

SUMMARY

An accounting system that implements good control policies, practices, and procedures maintains data security and integrity. Data security procedures safeguard assets, while data integrity procedures provide accurate and reliable accounting data.

Data security risks come from three sources and take four forms. Fraud is the threat that both deprives the organization of assets and misstates its accounting records. Accountants must understand the sources of fraud and develop procedures to detect or undermine them.

Auditors use reviews and tests of controls to evaluate the data security and integrity of a computer-based system. Reviews rely on interviews, walk-throughs, and questionnaires. Tests of controls allow auditors to see how well computerized processes maintain the integrity of data. Computer-assisted audit techniques and generalized audit software aid the auditor in examining computerized processes.

KEY TERMS

concealment Hiding a theft by falsifying accounting records. This causes the recorded assets to be consistent with the assets on hand and allows a fraud to continue.

conversion Changing into cash proceeds from the theft of inventory, checks, or equipment.

data integrity An objective of internal control. Data has integrity when it is accurate, reliable, and safe from improper changes.

data security An objective of internal control. Data is secure when it is safeguarded from theft or unauthorized access.

embedded audit modules As part of client application programs, these small programs perform tasks of interest to the auditor including real-time notification, tagging, tracing, and snapshots.

generalized audit software A software package that makes it easy for auditors to perform common audit tasks on data stored in computer files

integrated test facility A computer-assisted audit technique. The auditor enters simulated and actual transactions for processing by client programs and verifies that these are processed properly.

lapping fraud A fraud in which an employee steals and cashes a customer's check. To conceal the theft, the employee falsifies a credit to the customer's account by applying a subsequent payment from another customer. The clerk must continue this process to conceal the crime.

parallel simulation A computer-assisted audit technique. The auditor processes actual client data with an auditor-written program and compares the outputs with those produced by client programs.

review A survey in which an auditor evaluates a department's data security and integrity.

test data A computer-assisted audit technique. The auditor creates a file of simulated data, processes it with client accounting programs, and verifies that the programs work properly.

tests of controls Audit procedures to determine whether or not employees are complying with the control policies, practices, and procedures established by management. They are used to evaluate data security and integrity.

QUESTIONS

15–1. What are the primary sources of risks to security in organizations with:
a. Good internal control?
b. Poor internal control?

15–2. Can you name four data security risks? Who are the sources of each of these risks?

15–3. What are three ways that auditors detect frauds involving a computer-based system? Can you give an example of each?

15–4. What are the objectives of the two types of auditors who evaluate data security and integrity?

15–5. What is the difference between data integrity and data security?

15–6. Which methods do auditors use in conducting a review? Distinguish between each.

15–7. Why do auditors use computer-assisted audit techniques when conducting tests of controls?

15–8. What are the limitations of the following computer-assisted audit techniques when auditing a computer-based accounting system?

a. Test data.

b. Parallel simulation.

c. Integrated test facility.

d. Embedded audit modules.

15–9. When are auditors likely to use embedded audit modules?

15–10. How does generalized audit software improve the effectiveness and efficiency of an audit?

15–11. Why does an auditor use generalized audit software rather than writing programs in a general purpose computer language?

15–12. What are the auditors' responsibilities for evaluating computer security?

EXERCISES AND CASES

15–13. *COMPUTER-ASSISTED AUDIT TECHNIQUES*

Management has requested a special audit of the recently established electronic controls system division because the last three quarterly profit reports seem to be inconsistent with the division's cash flow. The division sells customized control systems on a contract basis. A work-in-process record is established for each contract on the work-in-process master file, a sequential file on a magnetic disk. Contract charges for material, labor, and overhead are entered in batches by terminal and processed by the work-in-process computer program to maintain the work-in-process master file and to provide billing information.

An audit review revealed that not all costs have been charged against the work-in-process records. Thus when contracts are closed, reported profits have been overstated. It is now necessary to determine the reasons for this loss of data integrity.

Required:

a. What computer-assisted audit technique would be most appropriate to evaluate the accuracy of the computer program posting transactions to the work-in-process master file?

b. How could the auditor most efficiently determine the contents of the work-in-process master file?

c. How could the auditor most effectively evaluate the overall business and systems environment of this computerized work-in-process system?

(CIA Adapted)

15–14. *GENERALIZED AUDIT SOFTWARE*

You decide to use a newly acquired audit software package in auditing accounts payable. The accounts payable system has been computerized for several years, and the transaction records are stored on magnetic tape.

Required:

Briefly describe how the generalized audit software package should be used to audit accounts payable.

(CIA Adapted)

15–15. *COMPUTER-ASSISTED AUDIT TECHNIQUES*

The following flowchart was drawn by an auditor and included in the audit working papers.

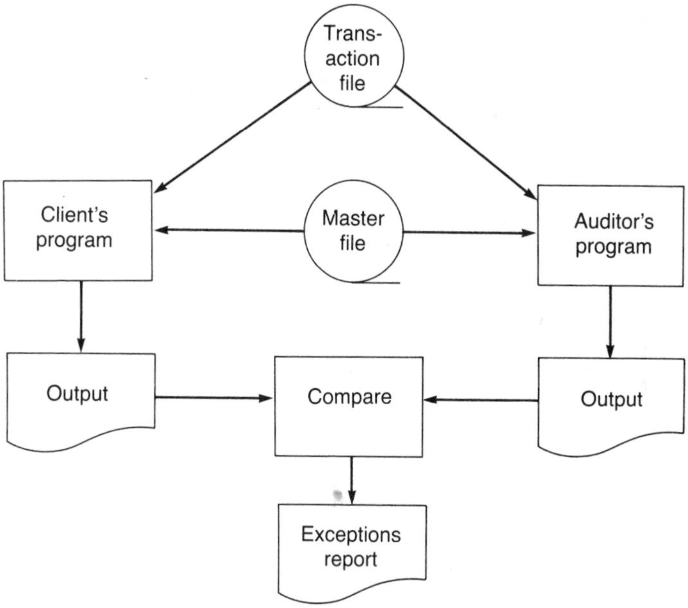

Required:

Which computer-assisted audit technique does this flowchart represent? Explain how the technique is used.

(AICPA Adapted)

15–16. *COMPUTER-ASSISTED AUDIT TECHNIQUES*

A company processes its payroll through a data center that features a large mainframe computer. Payroll data are processed in weekly batches input to the computer via magnetic tape. The auditor is considering testing the controls over payroll using the computer.

Required:

a. Identify three distinct approaches to using the computer in an audit. Discuss the relative advantages of each.

b. Identify three situations which would lead an auditor to conclude that using the computer in an audit is inappropriate.

(CIA Adapted)

15–17. *TEST DATA*

You are an auditor about to test controls in Bennett Company's computerized sales order entry system. In this system, outside salepersons take orders from customers and record them on a sales order form. Completed forms are returned to the district sales office where data entry clerks enter each sales transaction into the system at a terminal.

From the data dictionary you obtain the following description of a sales transaction record:

Data name	*Length*	*Contents*
Customer-number	9	Numeric
Customer-name	30	Alphanumeric
Customer-PO-number	12	Alphanumeric
Product-number	9	Numeric
Product-description	20	Alphanumeric
Quantity	5	Numeric
Unit-price	9	Numeric
Extended-amount	9	Numeric

By examining system documentation, you find that the data entry program should perform the following checks to validate the data:

1. Determines that the customer number is a valid one by calculating its check digit using the modulus 11 method (a validity test).
2. Determines that the quantity is a numeric and a positive number (a field test and a sign test).
3. Verifies that the extended amount does not exceed $10,000 (a limit or reasonableness test).
4. Verifies that the customer purchase order number is not omitted (a completeness test).

Required:

Develop a set of test data to determine if each of the preceding input controls works properly.

15–18. *INTEGRATED TEST FACILITY*

The internal audit department of Abacus Corp. has created an integrated test facility for evaluating certain of its accounting application systems. Abacus uses a responsibility accounting system which assigns a four-digit code to each responsibility center. The code for the internal audit department is 4210.

As an auditor, you wish to test the controls in Abacus's accounts payable system. In this system, payables clerks enter expenditure transactions in the system by creating voucher transaction records. Examining the documentation for this system, you determine that a transaction record contains the following fields.

Data name	*Length*	*Contents*
Voucher-number	7	Numeric
Vendor-number	5	Numeric
Vendor-invoice-no	12	Alphanumeric
Vendor-invoice-date	6	Numeric
Vendor-due-date	6	Numeric
Gen-ledger-account	4	Numeric
Responsibility-code	4	Numeric
Amount	9	Numeric

A batch processing program performs the following validation procedures:

1. Determines that the voucher number is not omitted (a completeness test).
2. Determines that the vendor number is numeric (a field test).
3. Verifies that the amount of the voucher does not exceed $200,000 (a limit or reasonableness test).

Required:

a. Develop test transactions that enable you to evaluate these validation procedures using the integrated test facility.

b. Assume that the test is complete and that the validation procedures work satisfactorily. What must you do next?

15–19. *GENERALIZED AUDIT SOFTWARE*

Boos & Baumkirchner, Inc., is a medium-sized manufacturer of products for the leisure-time activities market (camping equipment, scuba gear, bows and arrows, etc.). Boos maintains its inventory records in a sequential file stored on magnetic disk. Each record in the inventory master file contains the following information:

Item or part number

Description

Size

Unit of measure code

Quantity on hand

Cost per unit

Total value of inventory on hand, at cost

Date of last sale or usage

Quantity used or sold this year

Economic order quantity

Code number of major vendor

Code number of secondary vendor

In preparation for the year-end inventory count, Boos has prepared two identical sets of preprinted inventory count cards. One set is for Boos's counts and the other is for the auditors' use in making audit test counts. The following information is printed on each card:

Item or part number

Description

Size

Unit of measure code

In taking the year-end inventory, Boos's personnel write the actual counted quantity on the face of each card. When all counts are completed, the counted quantity is entered into a computer program. This program processes the counted quantities against the inventory master file and adjusts the quantity on hand numbers to reflect the actual count. A computer listing shows any missing inventory count cards and all quantity adjustments of more than $100 in value. These items can be investigated by client personnel and all required adjustments can be made. When adjustments are complete, the final year-end balances are computed and posted to the general ledger. You, as the auditor, use generalized audit software that executes on Boos's computer.

Required:

List and describe at least five ways a generalized audit software package can assist in the audit of inventory at Boos & Baumkirchner, Inc.

(AICPA Adapted)

15–20. ***GENERALIZED AUDIT SOFTWARE***

You plan to use generalized audit software during your examination of the accounts payable system of Solt Manufacturing Company. Solt's EDP manager has agreed to prepare special tapes of data from company records for your use with generalized audit software programs. The following information is applicable to your examination:

1. The formats of the pertinent files are shown in Exhibit 15–1.
2. You wish to prepare the following audit reports using GAS:
   a. Cash disbursements by check number.
   b. Outstanding payables.

EXHIBIT 15–1 Exercise 15–20 File Formats

Master File — Vendor Name

Vendor code	Recd type	Space	Blank	Vendor name	Blank	Card code 100

Master File — Vendor Address

Vendor code	Recd type	Space	Blank	Address — line 1	Address — line 2	Address — line 3	Blank	Card code 120

Transaction File — Expense Detail

Vendor code	Recd type	Voucher number	Blank	Batch	Voucher number	Voucher date	Vendor code	Invoice date	Due date	Invoice number	Purchase order number	Debit account	Prd type	Product code	Blank	Amount	Quantity	Card code 160

Transaction File — Payment Detail

Vendor code	Recd type	Voucher number	Blank	Batch	Voucher number	Voucher date	Vendor code	Invoice date	Due date	Invoice number	Purchase order number	Check number	Check date	Blank	Amount	Blank	Card code 170

c. Purchase transactions arranged by:
   i. account debited
   ii. vendor
3. Vouchers and supporting invoices, receiving reports, and purchase order copies are filed by vendor code. Purchase orders and checks are filed numerically.
4. Company records are maintained in sequential files on a magnetic disk.

Required:

a. Prepare instructions for the MIS manager outlining the data that should be included on the special tape. These instructions should state:
   1. Client file from which the item should be extracted.
   2. Name of the item of data.

b. Describe the controls that you, as an auditor, should maintain over:
   1. Preparing the special tape.
   2. Processing the special tape with generalized audit software programs.

(AICPA Adapted)

15–21. *EMBEDDED AUDIT MODULES*

In December 19XX, Jack Brown was arrested and charged with theft, forgery, and tampering with records in connection with a fraud committed against his employer.[6]

Employed by Girard Bank in Philadelphia, Brown's job was to examine computer printouts of transactions at automatic teller machines (ATMs) looking for suspicious withdrawals. Brown's department also received automatic teller cards returned as undeliverable by the U.S. Postal Service and issued the personal identification numbers that made these cards useful.

On December 6, Brown made a fake $5,000 deposit in the account of a man whose bank card had been returned. (Police and bank officials refused to reveal how he did it.) Because of this entry, the bank's files showed that this account contained more money than it actually did. Brown also used his terminal to raise the withdrawal limit on this ATM card from the usual $200 daily ceiling to $4,500 a day.

The card was then used to make 13 withdrawals totaling $2,500 from a teller machine. The following day Brown faked another deposit. The card was again used to withdraw money. Then, by computer, Brown returned the withdrawal limit to its proper level. Fortunately, an audit program was monitoring Brown's maneuvers and provided evidence for the discovery of his theft.

Required:

a. Which weaknesses in system controls allowed this fraud to occur?

b. How could an embedded audit module aid in detecting Brown's actions?

---

[6]Adapted from "Computers Turn Out to be Valuable Aid in Employee Crime." Reprinted by permission of *The Wall Street Journal,* © Dow Jones & Company, Inc., 1985. All rights reserved.

15–22. *THREATS FROM MANAGERS*

After deliberating for two hours, a Florida jury found A. B. Crocker, former chief financial officer at Golden Eagle Group, Inc., guilty of extortion and denying computer access with intent to defraud.[7] These are second-degree felonies carrying up to 15 years in prison. Crocker was arrested on May 6.

During a three-day trial, Crocker testified that he created a secret password for a computer billing system that he developed and considered his. Crocker said that company officials failed to respond to his request for a $5,000 a year raise. In a letter of resignation, Crocker threatened to withhold the password if certain demands were not met.

He resigned on May 6, leaving the billing system inoperable because its files could not be accessed. On May 11 company employees succeeded in determining the password; however, the search had delayed a $400,000 monthly billing. According to Crocker, the password, "WGACA," stood for "What goes around comes around."

Required:

a. Which control procedures could have prevented this crime?
b. Would you consider this accounting data vital? Why or why not?

15–23. *THREATS FROM HACKERS*

Richard Marsh, a 24-year-old former computer science graduate student, pleaded innocent to felony charges before a U.S. court in New York.[8] He had earlier been indicted by a federal grand jury on one felony count of violating the Computer Fraud and Abuse Act of 1986. He was charged with gaining access to university and military computers without authorization, preventing authorized access to those computers, and causing losses of $1,000 or more. If convicted, Marsh could receive up to a five-year sentence and a $250,000 fine.

Marsh was allegedly the author of a "worm," a computer program that copied itself into processors connected to the Internet computer network. Once the program entered a processor, it continued to replicate itself uncontrollably until it clogged the memory of the computer and caused its shutdown. It caused substantial damage at many computer centers resulting from the loss of computer services and the expense of halting the program and correcting its effects. It entered as many as 6,200 computers, including those at the National Aeronautics and Space Administration's Ames Research Center, Wright-Patterson Air Force Base, the University of California at Berkeley, and Purdue University.

---

[7]Adapted from "Man Convicted of Holding Firm's Computer Hostage," *Houston Chronicle*, October 24, 1987. Copyright 1987 by Associated Press. Used by permission.

[8]Adapted from articles in *Computerworld*, dated July 31, 1989, p. 8, and August 7, 1989, p. 8.

According to Marsh, the program was created to point out weaknesses in computer security on Internet. However, a flaw in the program caused it to multiply and spread uncontrollably.

Required:

a. What risk to security is posed by a hacker such as Marsh? Explain your answer.

b. Do you consider Marsh's actions unethical? Do you consider them criminal? Explain your answer.

15–24. *DESTRUCTION OF DATA*

Paul Louis, a 23-year-old former employee of a large Los Angeles accounting firm, was placed on three-year probation and given a five-month jail sentence after his conviction for computer fraud.[9] Louis pleaded no contest to charges that he illicitly used a San Francisco-based system belonging to U.S. Leasing International, Inc. He was also convicted of physically breaking into Pacific Telephone Company's local computing center and stealing sensitive documents, including password lists and computer manuals.

After swiping this material, Louis publicized the material through various electronic bulletin boards. From there other hackers used the information to change the phone company's billing data, enter fake stop orders, and otherwise wreak systems havoc.

"From what I know, their ultimate goal was to shut down the entire phone system in Southern California," said the prosecuting attorney. "Phone freaks don't like Ma Bell, and they enjoy harrassing the firm whenever they can."

Louis's crime spree began two years earlier when he and a woman companion used a terminal in her home to gain unauthorized access to U.S. Leasing's computer. After bypassing the processor's security safeguards, the two used the remote terminal to delete information from files belonging to one of the company's subsidiaries. The destruction occurred in the files that tell the subsidiary where its rented equipment is located and when it will become available for future leasing.

By destroying the files, Louis seriously impeded the company's business. "When U.S. Leasing was contacted by a customer and asked for a piece of equipment, the company was unable to say where it was located or when it would become available," said the attorney. Louis also used the terminal to create his own program files on the system. One was designed to inform him whenever U.S. Leasing changed its passwords. In addition, Louis peppered the company's data files with messages, including "some very foul language" according to the prosecuting attorney.

---

[9]Adapted from " 'Phone Freak' Going to Jail for Two Schemes," *Computerworld,* June 28, 1982. Used by permission.

"In at least one of his inserts, Louis boasted openly of his sabotage and threatened to do further damage. He was very proud of being able to get into someone else's system and was eager to tell other people about his activities," the attorney said.

Required:

a. What did Louis gain from these activities? What did the victims lose?
b. Do you consider Louis a criminal? Why or why not?

15–25. COMPUTER-RELATED FRAUD

A Louisiana man was convicted of stealing more than $100,000 in money orders from a minicomputer system that he helped to develop.[10] Nowell Norris, 30, faces up to 10 years in prison and a $3,000 fine for the theft from National Bonded Money Orders Corp.

Norris was an employee of a systems development company that provided the packaged system to National. The systems development company fired Norris shortly after the applications programs were completed. Norris was then hired by Charles Carrs, National's office manager and a close personal friend, to "help work some of the remaining bugs out of the system."

National later began to notice excessively large losses of paper and engaged an auditor to investigate. During this investigation, National was burglarized and the computer printout records and money order code numbers were stolen. A probe of the investigation revealed that more than 1,000 money orders had been stolen throughout the preceding months and that the system was programmed not to reveal the losses.

The investigation led to Norris who admitted his guilt. Norris had also altered programs so that money orders he wrote to fictitious people and cashed himself were ignored by the system after they were returned.

"We know that he was using some of the stolen money orders to pay off his VISA charge card, among other things," said the assistant district attorney. Those other things included gambling debts and an investment in a small business.

Required:

a. In this fraud, identify the:
   1. Theft.
   2. Conversion.
   3. Concealment.
b. How was this fraud detected?
c. Which control procedures could have prevented it?

---

[10]Adapted from "CPU Programmed to Hide Theft," *Computerworld,* June 8, 1981. Used by permission.

15–26. ***COMPUTER-RELATED FRAUD***

A federal grand jury indicted three people for conspiracy, making and receiving false government securities, fraudulent use of a government computer, stealing money from the United States, and mail fraud, in connection with the fraudulent issuance of a government check.[11]

Adell Adams, 31, was a customer relations clerk at the Defense Contract Administration Services (DCAS) region in Los Angeles. DCAS, a branch of the U.S. Department of Defense, administers ongoing U.S. defense contracts.

Adams accessed the DCAS computer to alter the name and address of a legitimate contractor, Tasker Systems Division. She then submitted false paperwork, with Tasker's valid contract number, to another clerk showing a $9.5 million check was due. As a result a check was issued on February 19 to Fortress Indemnity. Adams then changed the computer files so that all later checks would be issued to Tasker as usual.

Fortress Indemnity was a fictitious company set up by Bob Baker, 31, of Los Angeles, and Cecil Carlson, 35, of Seattle. The check was mailed to a Los Angeles address provided by Carlson, who picked it up and mailed it to Baker in Seattle. Baker tried to deposit the check at Northwest Commercial Bank on February 23, but suspicious bank officials called federal agents. Baker was arrested on February 25 when he returned to the bank to collect the proceeds of the check. When confronted, Baker disclosed the identities of the other two defendants.

Required:

a. In this fraud, identify the:
   1. theft.
   2. conversion.
   3. concealment.

b. How was the fraud detected?

c. Which control procedures could have prevented it?

15–27. ***REVIEWS***

Mark Tick is an internal auditor employed by the Highlight Corp. Tick's supervisor has assigned him to perform a general controls review of Highlight's data center.[12]

As Tick drove up, he was welcomed by a neon sign on the roof of the building indicating the data center's presence. The data center was in the

---

[11]Adapted from "Three Indicted in Computer Contract Fraud," *Houston Chronicle,* October 25, 1987. Reprinted with the permission of United Press International, Inc. Used by permission. Copyright 1988.

[12]Reprinted from *EDPACS* (New York: Auerbach Publishers). © 1974 Warren, Gorham & Lamont, Inc. Used with permission.

basement of the corporate headquarters building on the river side, four inches below flood level.

Tick donned his dark glasses, combed his hair, checked his supply of red lead pencils, and entered the building. He approached the receptionist and asked for the data center manager. Without questioning Tick's identity or his reason for being there, she informed him that the manager was away from the data center for a few minutes and told him to wait in the computer room.

''We have all our visitors wait there. They seem to be infatuated with the twinkling little lights on the console,'' she said.

''What's a console?'' asked Tick.

''It's the thing next to the 10-gallon gas-fired coffee urn,'' was her reply.

Tick walked toward the data center, down a hallway crowded with employees on their way to the cafeteria. On both sides of the hall he noticed, without interest, open racks of magnetic tapes labeled neatly with such titles as ''accounts receivable master file,'' ''YTD payroll master,'' ''stockholder records,'' and ''general ledger summary.'' He paused for a moment to watch a pickup game of ring toss, noting that the lunch crowd had obtained the rings from the sides of magnetic tape reels.

''Ingenious people,'' he thought, ''finding use for those worthless little rings.''

As Tick walked through the data entry room, he noticed employees drifting into the room and dumping loose source documents into a box labeled ''Input.'' The data entry operators were taking out handfuls of the documents and entering them at terminals. Tick, ever alert, recognized the documents were selected in conformity with the generally accepted ''random LIFO'' method.

Entering the computer room, Tick waved to the sole occupant, a machine operator who was hastily punching up cards and inserting them in a deck labeled ''payroll source code.''

''Obviously a valuable employee,'' mused Tick. ''It's good to see someone putting forth some extra effort.''

Tick poured a cup of coffee, and as he started to count petty cash, placed it on top of the 4-foot-high stack of dust-covered disk packs. He wondered if the small amount of coffee he spilled would stain the floor as it drained through the disks.

Tick noticed that the machine operator, having run the unnumbered payroll checks through the check signer, was separating the carbons from the checks. The fourth copy of the checks passed neatly into the fiberboard wastebasket as the machine hummed smoothly, giving the operator a chance to have a smoke and discuss with two mailboys, who had just entered, how much the various vice presidents were being paid. Tick was impressed with the operator's concern for neatness—he even ran the console log sheets through the shredder as soon as he finished the payroll run. Tick drew an appreciative smile from the operator as he quipped, ''Nobody could make anything out of the gobblygook the typewriter just printed, so better to destroy it than get buried under it.''

Tick saw a box in the corner labeled ''To Contingency File'' and inquired, ''What's this for?''

The operator explained that the maintenance department's foreman allowed the data center to store copies of important programs in the bottom of his locker.

"What type of programs?" asked Tick.

"Well, as far as I know, the only program over there is the one which causes the printer to use millions of little X's to form a cartoon character saying 'Merry Christmas,' " was the reply.

Tick glanced at the bulletin board and immediately got an indication of how well organized the data center manager was and that he was nobody's fool. The three signs that impressed him most read:

Fairness is our motto. All input is processed on a first come, first served basis.

This is a data processing operation, not a delivery service. All output for the current week will be placed on the big table in the cafeteria before 4 P.M. each Friday. Help yourself!

To expedite processing and cut down on unnecessary paper shuffling, all documents rejected by the computer because of out-of-balance controls or invalid data will be immediately corrected and reentered by machine operators.

The data center manager came in, introduced himself to Tick, and apologized for being away so long. He explained that he had a difficult time finding a garden hose long enough to reach into the data center through a hole in the plywood partition separating it from the adjacent boiler room.

"Good idea," Tick said approvingly. "A lot cheaper than buying fire extinguishers for the data center."

"Well, how does the place look?" the manager asked, perspiring slightly in the heat.

"Great!" said Tick. "There will be only one item in my report. There is the serious matter of the 47 cent unexplained shortage in your $5.00 petty cash fund. Now, as soon as you buy me lunch, I can be off on my next assignment."

Required:

If you had conducted this review, what would you have included in your report?

15–28. ***INTERVIEWS***

Mike Kess, a senior auditor for the regional accounting firm Sanders and McDonald, was assigned to audit the Rayo Corporation.[13] He was to conduct a review of the general controls over systems and programming. Kess has already identified the current applications used in the accounting system (described in Exhibit 15–2) and is about to start on system maintenance.

---

[13]Adapted from a case prepared by Professors Frederick L. Neumann and Richard J. Boland of the University of Illinois, with a grant from the Touche Ross Foundation.

EXHIBIT 15–2 Case 15–28

CLIENT RAYO CORPORATION AUDIT DATE ____________

GENERAL INFORMATION

	Yes	No	N/A
1. Provide a copy of the EDP department organization chart including names and titles of all personnel assigned to the department.	X		
2. Is there a written plan for this year's new applications and changes?		X	

a. If yes, attach a copy of the plan or a summary.

b. If no, list any changes in financial or accounting applications expected to be implemented prior to year-end.

None planned this year

3. Indicate whether the following applications have been significantly modified since the prior audit. ("Significantly modified" means additions or deletions of reports, changes in the types of data input as stored on the files, modifications in calculations or decision criteria, etc.)

	Yes	No	N/A
a. Payroll		X	
b. Accounts payble		X	
c. Accounts receivable		X	
d. General ledger		X	

4. List below, or on a separate schedule, a summary of the significant financial and accounting applications now in use.

Application	Name or nature of principal reports or other output	Brief description of application, impact on other applications, comments, etc.
Payroll	Weekly batch run updating payroll and providing reports.	
Accounts payable	Batch system with online inquiry, providing daily status reports.	
Accounts receivable	Both online processing of A/R and batch reporting.	
General ledger	Online system to post G/L and provide all cash flow, operating and statement of condition reports.	

EXHIBIT 15–2 Case 15–28 (*concluded*)

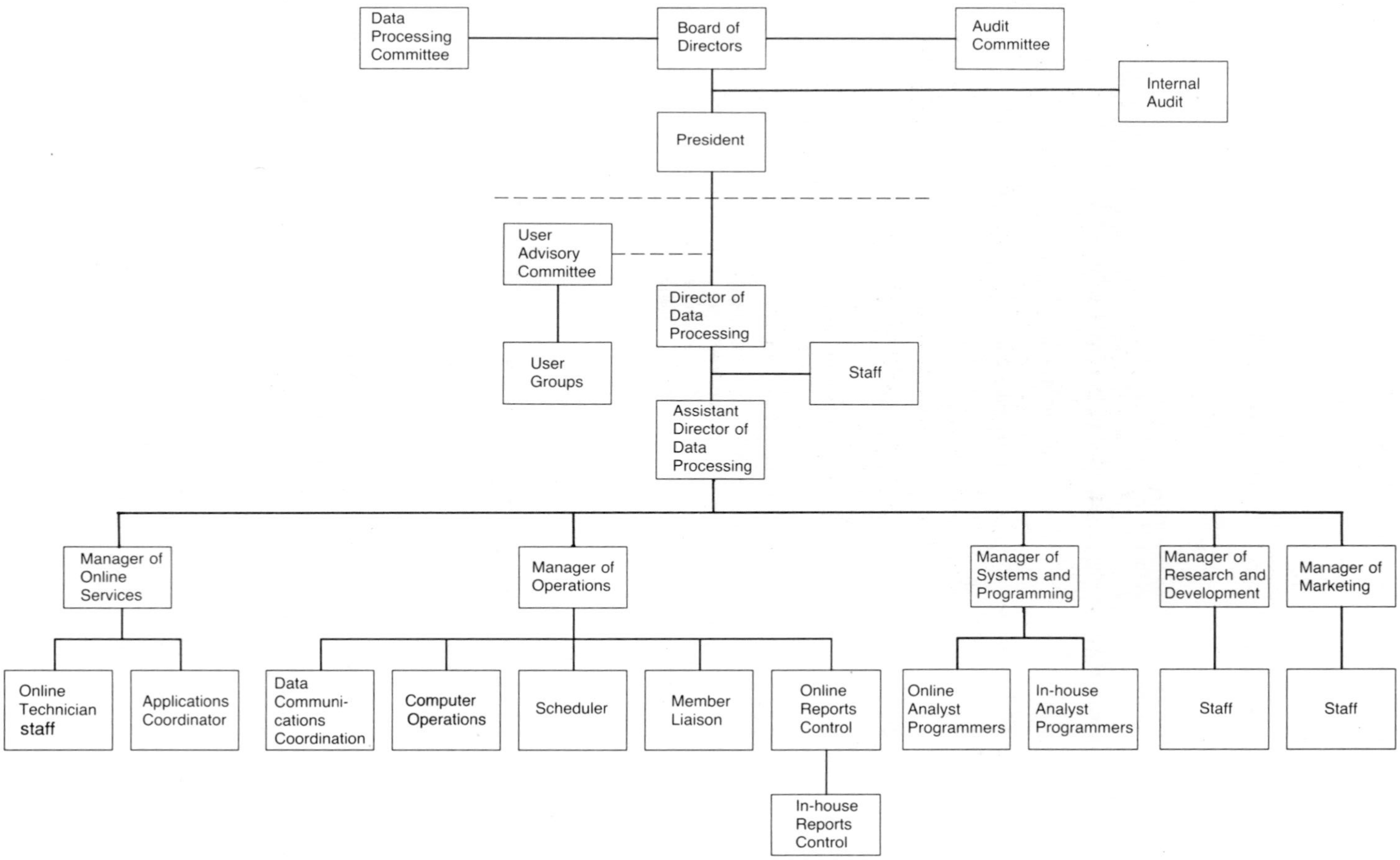

Kess contacted Jim Stram, the manager of systems and programming in the MIS department, and requested an interview. A summary of their conversation follows:

Kess:

How are system maintenance projects initiated and developed?

Stram:

All potential projects are sent to a member of my staff, called an application coordinator, for analysis. We do all our systems and programming work in-house. If a programming change is required for a project, the application coordinator prepares a revision request form. These revision request forms must be approved by both the manager of operations and me. The director of data processing and the internal auditor receive copies of each revision request form for information purposes.

Kess:

How does the application coordinator keep track of the revision request form and any change that might be made to it?

Stram:

The revision request forms are numbered in different series depending on the nature of the change requested. The application coordinator assigns the next number in the sequence and records in a master log each request he prepares. Changes in revision requests, from whatever source, are prepared on request forms just as initial requests are. Each change request is given the same basic number with a suffix indicating it is an amendment, and there is a place for recording amendments in the master log.

Kess:

What is the distribution of an approved request form?

Stram:

It goes to one of my systems supervisors for design, programming, and testing. The primary effort is usually performed by a programmer who has responsibility over the area of the application or the specific programs to be changed.

Kess:

But how are projects controlled?

Stram:

At the beginning of each programming project, estimated start and completion dates are assigned and entered on the request form and the master log. The system supervisor keeps on top of the projects assigned to him, and the application coordinator also monitors the open requests. The system supervisor files written status reports with the applications coordinator twice a month and briefs me on any problems. However, I'm usually aware of any difficulties long before then.

During the programming and testing phase, I think we have good control over the project. None of the compiles made during this phase changes any production source code for the existing computer programs. Also, all test object programs are identified by a strictly enforced naming convention that clearly distinguishes them from production programs. So far this has been successful in inhibiting their use in processing production. If a programmer has specific questions or problems on a project, the systems supervisor is generally available to give advice.

Kess:

Are there written guidelines to direct this activity? If so, how detailed are they?

Stram:

Only informal procedures exist to provide any uniformity to the programs and the coding changes made to a program. Formal standards do exist to define which documentation should be present for a system and for the programs within a system. These apply to program changes as well and again are strictly enforced. There is a periodic management review to see that we comply. We just had one about a month ago and got a clean bill of health.

Kess:

Are adequate tests and reviews made of changes before they are implemented?

Stram:

The application coordinator, the systems supervisor, and the individual programmer informally discuss the necessary tests for a specific project. Sometimes I get involved, too, but our guidelines are pretty good in this area and provide a fairly thorough approach to test design. After the tests have been completed to the systems supervisor's satisfaction, the applications coordinator reviews and approves the test results. This must be done on all revision requests before they are implemented into production. I usually review the programmers' work to see that all authorized changes are made correctly and are adequately tested and documented.

Kess:

How does implementation take place and which controls are exercised over it?

Stram:

After the test results for a revision request have been approved by the applications coordinator, it is the responsibility of the programmer to implement the changes into production. Before putting a program change into production, a programmer must update the source code of the production program version. The programmer is required to give the program name and compile date for all changed programs to the system supervisor. The programmer also has the responsibility for updating the systems and programming documentation. The system supervisor is supposed to review this and certify completion to the applications coordinator who then completes the log entry.

Kess:

Are post-implementation reviews undertaken on systems maintenance projects?

Stram:

Once the project is implemented, the applications coordinator reviews the output from the first few production runs of the changed program. The coordinator also questions users to see if any problem areas can be identified. A documented audit trail is provided by the completed project file maintained by the application coordinator for each request number. This file contains all the required documentation, including test results. A copy of the final summary goes to the department which originally submitted the request. A table in the computer is updated to provide listings of the most current compile dates for each set of production object code within the system. Before any program is implemented it is checked against this table.

Kess:

Well, that seems to be it. I think I have all that I need for now, but I'll probably be back to take a look at the files and records. I may have more questions for you then. Thanks very much for your time and thoughtful answers. I really appreciate your help.

Stram:

That's quite all right. If I can be of any more help, just let me know.

Required:

a. Which additional questions would you have asked Jim Stram if you had been in Mike Kess's place?

b. What are some weaknesses in internal control that you identified from the interview?

c. Based on the interview, attempt to fill in the questionnaire contained in Exhibit 15–3.

EXHIBIT 15–3 Case 15–28

CLIENT RAYO CORPORATION AUDIT DATE ______

SYSTEMS AND PROGRAMMING

	Yes	No	N/A
1. Are there systems and programming standards in the following areas:			
a. Applications design	___	___	___
b. Programming conventions and procedures?	___	___	___
c. Systems and program documentation?	___	___	___
d. Applications control?	___	___	___
e. Project planning and management?	___	___	___
2. Does the normal documentation for an application include the following:			
Application documentation:			
a. *Narrative description?*	___	___	___
b. Systems flowchart?	___	___	___
c. Definition of input data and source format?	___	___	___
d. Description of expected output data and format?	___	___	___
e. A listing of all valid transactions and other codes and abbreviations and master file fields affected?	___	___	___

EXHIBIT 15–3 Case 15–28 (*continued*)

f. File definition or layouts? ___ ___ ___

g. Instructions for preparing input? ___ ___ ___

h. Instructions for correcting errors? ___ ___ ___

i. Backup requirements? ___ ___ ___

j. Description of test data? ___ ___ ___

Program documentation:

a. Program narrative? ___ ___ ___

b. Flowchart of each program? ___ ___ ___

c. Current source listing of each program ___ ___ ___

Operations documentation:

a. Data entry instructions, including verification? ___ ___ ___

b. Instructions for control personnel, including batching? ___ ___ ___

c. Instructions for the tape librarian? ___ ___ ___

d. Operator's run manual? ___ ___ ___

e. Reconstruction procedure? ___ ___ ___

3. Is there a periodic management review of documentation to insure that it is current and accurate? ___ ___ ___

   If yes, when and by whom was it last performed? ________________

   ____

4. Is all systems and programming work done in-house? ___ ___ ___

   If not, is it done:

   a. By computer manufacturer's personnel? ___ ___ ___

   b. By contract programming? ___ ___ ___

   c. Other? Describe ______________________________ ___ ___ ___

   ____

5. Are all changes programmed by persons other than those assigned to computer operations? ___ ___ ___

6. Are program changes documented in a manner that preserves an accurate chronological record of the applications? ___ ___ ___

   If yes, describe ______________________________

   ____

   ____

EXHIBIT 15–3 Case 15–28 (*concluded*)

7. Do the users participate in the development of new applications or modifications of existing applications through frequent reviews of work performed? ___ ___ ___

   If yes, are the results of reviews documented? ___ ___ ___

8. Are testing procedures and techniques standardized? ___ ___ ___

9. Are program revisions tested as stringently as new programs? ___ ___ ___

10. Are tests designed to uncover weaknesses in the links between programs, as well as within programs? ___ ___ ___

11. Are users involved in the testing process, i.e., do they use the application as it is intended during the testing process? ___ ___ ___

12. Do user departments perform the final review and signoff on projects before acceptance? ___ ___ ___

13. What departments and/or individuals have the authority to authorize an operator to put a new or modified program into production? ___

    ____

    ____

14. What supervisory or management approval is necessary for the conversion of files? ______________________________

    ____

    ____

Chapter 16

Cost-Benefit Analysis of Internal Accounting Controls

Learning Objectives:

1. To understand the concept of reasonable assurance when it is applied to internal accounting controls.
2. To distinguish between the loss exposure and the risk exposure due to omitting a control procedure.
3. To learn how to apply cost-benefit analysis to control policies, practices, and procedures.

INTRODUCTION

Management establishes an internal control structure to achieve management's objectives. These objectives include safeguarding the organization's assets and ensuring accurate and reliable accounting data. Accountants call the control policies, practices, and procedures directed toward these objectives *internal accounting* controls. Internal accounting controls provide reasonable, but not absolute, assurance that these objectives will be attained.

In this chapter you will learn how accountants evaluate the reasonableness of a control policy, practice, or procedure. Some of the concepts in this chapter originated in auditing standards that are no longer in effect. Nevertheless, the concepts are still valid and in the United States are a part of law. The procedures presented in this chapter are useful in evaluating controls and in complying with the law.

THE CONCEPT OF REASONABLE ASSURANCE

The term *reasonable assurance* is from the codified auditing standards published in 1973 by the American Institute of Certified Public Accountants (AICPA).[1] In that codification, the AICPA clarified the concept of reasonable assurance as follows:

> The establishment and maintenance of a system of internal control is an important responsibility of management. The basic concepts implicit in the definition of accounting control are discussed in the context of that responsibility. . . .
>
> The definition of accounting control comprehends reasonable, but not absolute, assurance that the objective expressed in it will be accomplished by the system. The concept of reasonable assurance recognizes that the cost of internal control should not exceed the benefits expected to be derived. . . .[2]

Thus accountants have long recognized the concept of reasonable assurance: The cost of internal accounting controls should not exceed the benefits expected from them. Stated differently, when management implements a control procedure in its accounting system, that procedure must be justified by a cost-benefit analysis. Furthermore, any control procedure whose cost is determined to exceed its benefits should be omitted from the accounting system.

USING COST-BENEFIT ANALYSIS

To use cost-benefit analysis, accountants must estimate the costs and benefits of a control procedure. Then accountants compare the costs and benefits and make a recommendation to management concerning its implementation. Costs are usually relatively easy to project; estimating benefits is more difficult.

Estimating Benefits

Which benefits are associated with a control procedure? According to the AICPA, "the benefits consist of reduction in the risk of failing to achieve the

---

[1]In the United States, the Foreign Corrupt Practices Act of 1977 requires companies "to devise and maintain a system of internal accounting controls." These must be sufficient to provide reasonable assurance that the execution of transactions, recording of transactions, gaining access to assets, and accountability for assets are done in accordance with management's general or specific authorization.

[2]*Statement on Auditing Standards No. 1: Codification of Standards and Procedures* (New York: AICPA, 1973), p. 21. This section has been superseded by Statement on Auditing Standards #55.

objectives'' of the control procedure.[3] In addition, ''the benefits to be considered often may include not only quantifiable benefits, such as reduction in exposure to theft of assets, but also qualitative benefits, such as reputation of the company and its management.''[4]

Thus the benefits of a control procedure are both qualitative and quantitative. Qualitative benefits are subjective and may be difficult to estimate when performing cost-benefit analysis. They include, as examples, the advantages of making better decisions because of more accurate information, and improved employee morale because the system works and produces fewer errors. Quantitative benefits are tangible and easier to establish. They include decreases in insurance premiums due to better segregation of duties and improvements in cash flow due to prompt customer billing procedures.

Probabilistic Estimates

Sometimes the benefits from correcting a control weakness must be estimated using probabilities. Some threats to the integrity and security of data are unlikely. Yet if these threats occur, the cost of recovering from them is substantial. For example, the chance that a fire would completely destroy a data center is improbable. Yet if this occurs, the cost of replacing equipment and recreating data files may be large. Management must consider controls to protect the firm from these threats.

To make probabilistic estimates, compute the *expected value*. The expected value of a cost or benefit is its monetary value multiplied by the probability of its occurrence. To estimate the probabilities, use past experience or your own judgment.

For example, by consulting with your insurance company you determine that there is a 2 percent probability of a fire in the data center. You also estimate that if a fire occurs, replacing data and equipment would cost \$1 million. Then the *loss exposure* from the threat of fire, the amount of your loss if it occurs, is \$1 million. The expected value of this cost is $.02 \times \$1,000,000$, or \$20,000. This expected value is your *risk exposure* from the threat.

Estimating probabilities is sometimes difficult and always approximate; because the risk exposure is determined from estimates, it also is approximate. However, using an approximate risk exposure is better than ignoring the likelihood of the threat. In the preceding example, another person may estimate the threat of a fire at only 1 percent, while a third person may estimate it at 10 percent. In each case, calculating the risk exposure allows a more informed decision than ignoring the possibility of a \$1 million loss.

Probabilistic estimates are valuable when performing cost-benefit analysis. They allow consideration of risks that are unlikely, but too large to be ignored. Calculating expected values allows you to evaluate quantitatively control procedures that, without probability estimates, must be considered qualitatively.

---

[3]AICPA, *Statement on Auditing Standards No. 1.*

[4]*Federal Register,* May 4, 1979, p. 26704.

Incremental Costs and Benefits

Usually benefits are associated with increases in revenues and decreases in costs. In accounting terminology, they are *incremental* benefits because they exist with the control procedure and do not exist without it. In performing cost-benefit analysis, accountants compare these incremental benefits with the incremental costs of attaining them. Costs and benefits that do not change when the control procedure is adopted do not affect the decision.

STEPS IN COST-BENEFIT ANALYSIS

The steps in performing a cost-benefit analysis of an internal accounting control are

1. Estimate the potential loss from a threat to the accounting system. From an estimate of its likelihood, compute the risk exposure.
2. Determine a control procedure that, if implemented, reduces the risk.
3. Identify incremental costs of the control procedure.
4. Determine the reduction in risk exposure resulting from the control procedure.
5. Compare the incremental costs with the reduction in risk exposure.
6. Consider qualitative benefits (those difficult to state in financial terms) and the accuracy of your estimates.
7. Decide whether or not to implement the control procedure.
8. Document the decision.

This chapter describes how to apply these steps by using several examples. They show how to evaluate the costs and benefits for both computerized and noncomputerized control procedures.

EXAMPLES OF COST-BENEFIT ANALYSIS

Now you will see how to apply these concepts to some important system controls. A computer-based accounting system contains both computerized and noncomputerized (or manual) control procedures. The form of technology used in implementing a control procedure affects its costs.

Costs and Benefits of Manual Control Procedures

For noncomputerized control procedures, the major costs are usually salaries, wages, and related costs. Benefits arise from improved asset utilization and improved accountability. Qualitative considerations may override the results of cost-benefit analysis and affect the desirability of a control. Illustration 16–1 shows some costs and benefits of manual internal control procedures.

ILLUSTRATION 16–1 Costs and Benefits of Manual Control Procedures

Costs:

One time:
1. Installation of partitions and other security devices.
2. Initial design and printing cost of new forms.

Recurring:
1. Salaries of additional employees to be hired and their related fringe benefits.
2. Operating costs such as office supplies and postage.

Opportunity:
1. Interest forgone as a result of investment in capital project.

Benefits:

Improving asset utilization:
1. Interest savings from reduction in billing delays.
2. Interest savings from reduction in accounts receivable balances.

Reducing asset shrinkages:
1. Reduction in bad debts.
2. Reduction in inventory shortages.
3. Reduction in frequency of customers' underbilling.

Other costs (not easily quantifiable):
1. Possible loss of gross profit due to rejection of sale to prospective customers judged to be not creditworthy.
2. Increase in employees' workload not significant enough to result in adding new positions.

Other benefits (not easily quantifiable):
1. Savings in employees' workload not significant enough to result in elimination of positions.
2. Improved customer relations or communications.
3. Reduction in time spent in answering and following up on customer's inquiries regarding their account balances.

An Accounts Receivable System. To see how to estimate the costs and benefits of manual control procedures, consider the example of an accounts receivable system.

In this system, sales personnel accept orders from customers. A shipping clerk removes the ordered goods from the warehouse, packages them for shipment, and transfers them to a freight line. A billing department prepares an invoice for the goods and mails it to the customer. The accounting department then records the sale by debiting the accounts receivable control and subsidiary accounts and crediting the sales account in the general ledger.

The auditors have identified five possible organizational and procedural changes to this system, as shown in Illustration 16–2. You wish to evaluate these proposed changes to determine whether their costs exceed their benefits. If the benefits of a control procedure exceed its costs, you will include it in a list of proposed changes you prepare for management.

ILLUSTRATION 16–2 Proposed Control Procedures for an Accounts Receivable System

1. Separate warehousing function from the shipping function.
2. Change system to use a six-part sales invoice, rather than a sales order and a three-part sales invoice.
3. Require approval of sales by a credit manager prior to shipment.
4. Assign an employee to verify bills before they are sent to customers.
5. Prepare monthly statements for customers.

Illustration 16–3 contains information useful in performing this cost-benefit analysis. As you can see, the company has experienced higher percentages of bad debts and greater inventory shortages than are common in its industry. These are a result of the internal control weaknesses identified by auditors.

The first proposed change is to separate the warehousing function from the shipping function. The company hires a warehouse clerk and assigns to this clerk responsbility for custody of inventory. The warehouse clerk removes goods from inventory only when authorized to do so by the sales department. This organizational change makes the theft of goods from inventory more difficult.

Illustration 16–4 contains an analysis of the costs and benefits of this proposed change. Because its projected benefits exceed its projected costs, you recommend this proposal to management.

ILLUSTRATION 16–3 Data for Cost-Benefit Analysis in the Accounts Receivable System

Average weekly sales on account	$ 50,000		
Balance in Accounts Receivable account	305,000		
Average ratio of bad debts to credit sales:			
Industry average		2.4%	
Company experience of bad debts written off	112,500		
Industry average of days in receivables			35 days
Average error rate in billing:			
As experienced, as percentage of credit sales		0.2%	
Expected to achieve, with billing verification		0.05%	
Inventory shortage:			
Shortages as experienced	78,000		
Expected normal inventory shortage, with improved control		1.1%	
Balance in Inventories account	1,200,000		
Fringe benefits as a percentage of base pay		30%	
Interest rate		18%	

ILLUSTRATION 16–4 Cost-Benefit Analysis of the First Proposed Control

Separation of warehousing and shipping

Preliminary suggestion: Separate the warehousing function from shipping function to improve accountability of goods in stock.

Cost-benefit analysis:	
Calculation of costs:	
Costs associated with hiring a warehouse clerk:	
Salary	$18,000
Fringe benefits, 30%	5,400
Costs associated with installing partitions to separate the warehouse from the shipping area, $10,000.	
Interest on $10,000 for first year, at 18%	1,800
Depreciation, based on five-year life	2,000
Total cost	27,200
Calculation of benefits:	
Total amount of goods in stock: $1,200,000.	
Unaccounted for inventory shortage last year, $78,000, or 6.5%.	
Estimated normal inventory shortage, 1.1%, or $13,200 on inventories of $1,200,000.	
Benefit: Reduction in inventory shortage ($78,000 − $13,200)	64,800
Excess of benefits over costs, first year	$37,600
Decision	Include in final list of suggestions

The second proposal is to change invoicing procedures. Currently the company uses two different documents, a sales order and an invoice. Auditors suggest changing the procedures to use just an invoice prepared in six copies rather than the three used in the old procedure. Because one less form is required, the change could save costs of printing and of using the extra form. Illustration 16–5 shows a cost-benefit analysis of this change.

The third proposal is to employ a credit manager to approve all sales prior to shipment. The credit manager would evaluate the creditworthiness of customers and refuse to authorize shipments to those with poor payment records. This change should reduce the company's bad debts expense. Illustration 16–6 contains the projected costs and benefits of this control procedure.

Illustrations 16–7 and 16–8 contain cost-benefit analyses of the two remaining proposals. Proposal number four, having an employee verify bills before mailing them, is cost-effective and recommended. For proposal number five,

ILLUSTRATION 16–5 Cost-Benefit Analysis of the Second Proposed Control

Use of six-part sales invoice

Preliminary suggestion: Use a six-part sales invoice to replace the present (1) four-part sales order and (2) three-part invoice so that prebilling may be done by the order-entry department, allowing the billing department to do billing on a daily, instead of weekly, basis.

Cost-benefit analysis:	
Calculation of costs:	
Initial cost of printing sales invoices	$2,000
Calculation of benefits:	
Average weekly sales on account: $50,000.	
Reduction in billing delay from weekly to daily, an average of two days, or $20,000 (= $50,000 ÷ 5 × 2).	
Benefit: annual interest savings on $20,000 at 18%	3,600
Excess of benefits over cost, first year	$1,600
Additional benefits (not quantified):	
Savings of 20 hours per week for a billing clerk due to prebilling work being done by the order-entry department (not quantified as there is no reduction in outflow of resources).	
Decision	Include in final list of suggestions

ILLUSTRATION 16–6 Cost-Benefit Analysis of the Third Proposed Control

Addition of credit approval

Preliminary suggestion: Seek credit approval from credit manager who can (1) check prospective customers' creditworthiness and (2) follow up on slow-paying customers.

Cost-benefit analysis:		
Costs associated with hiring a credit manager:		
Salary		$30,000
Fringe benefits, 30%		9,000
Other related costs (telephone, travel, etc.)		3,000
Total costs		42,000
Calculation of benefits:		
A. Company's bad debts last year: $112,500.		
Company's bad debts as a percentage of credit sales of $2,600,000 (= $50,000 per week × 52 weeks): 4.3%		
Industry average ratio of bad debts to credit sales, 2.4%, or $62,400 on credit sales of $2,600,000.		
Benefit: Annual savings in bad debts ($112,500 − $62,400)	$50,100	

ILLUSTRATION 16–6 *(concluded)*

B. Company's number of days in receivable last year: 42.8 days (= Accounts receivable balance of \$305,000 ÷ \$2,600,000 × 365).		
Industry average number of days in receivable, 35 days, or \$249,300 on credit sales of \$2,600,000.		
Benefit: Annual savings in interest of \$55,700 (= \$305,000 − \$249,300) at 18%	\$10,000	
Total benefits		\$60,100
Excess of benefits over costs, per year		\$18,100
Other considerations (not quantified):		
Possible loss of gross profit due to sales not made		
Decision		Include in final list of suggestions

ILLUSTRATION 16–7 Cost-Benefit Analysis of the Fourth Proposed Control

Verification of billing

Preliminary suggestion: Have bills verified before they are sent out.

Cost-benefit analysis:	
Calculation of costs:	
Estimated time of 12 hours per week for a billing clerk (no net cost is established, since time has been made available from 20 hours per week savings in the sales invoice preparation step; no outflow of resources).	
Calculation of benefits:	
Estimated error in billing, at 0.2% of credit sales of \$2,600,000, or \$5,200.	
Estimated error in billing, with verification step added, at 0.05%, or \$1,300.	
Benefit: Reduction in errors in billing (\$5,200 − \$1,300)	\$3,900
Excess of benefits over costs, per year	\$3,900
Additional benefits (not quantified):	
1. Reduction in customers' inquiries due to errors in billing.	
2. Improved customer relations.	
Decision (based on quantified cost-benefit analysis)	Include in final list of suggestions

mailing monthly statements, the costs approximately equal the benefits. Thus you should evaluate qualitative considerations before making a recommendation. These include improved communication that reduces inquiries about accounts from individual customers. You decide to include this proposal in the final list of suggestions you submit to management.

ILLUSTRATION 16–8 Cost-Benefit Analysis of the Fifth Proposed Control

Mailing of monthly statements to customers
Preliminary suggestion: Prepare monthly statements for mailing to customers.

Cost-benefit analysis:	
Calculation of costs:	
Cost of printing monthly statement forms, being the same as accounts receivable record	$ 1,100
Other stationery costs	100
Mailing cost:	
Average number of customers: 600.	
Percentage with activity during month or balance at month-end, 90%.	
Postage cost, at 25¢ per letter (= 600 × 90% × 12 × 25¢)	1,620
Total cost	2,820
Calculation of benefits:	
Estimated further collection of accounts receivable speedier by one day, from industry average of 35 days to 34 days, or from $249,300 average balance of accounts receivable to $242,200	
Benefit: Annual savings in interest, at 18%, of $7,100 (= $249,300 − $242,200)	1,300
Excess of benefits over costs, per year	$(1,520)
Other benefits (not quantified):	
1. Improved customer communications, allowing the marketing department to include special sale announcements with monthly statements.	
2. Reduction in customers' inquiries concerning their account balances.	
Decision (based on cost-benefit analysis, but also considering other benefits)	Include in final list of suggestions

Cost-benefit analyses of manual control procedures are concerned primarily with the labor-related costs. A cost-benefit analysis of computerized procedures, on the other hand, considers primarily the costs of computer equipment and software modification.

Cost and Benefits of Computerized Control Procedures

Computerized control procedures are performed by computer hardware and software systems rather than by people. They include processing controls such as sequence, crossfooting, and limit checks, and software verification of internal file identification. Because a computer performs these control procedures in a fraction of a second, their incremental costs are negligible. However, adding these procedures to an existing system can be expensive. They should be included in the system during its development. This is why a system design team should include someone, such as an accountant or auditor, who is knowledgeable about controls.

When computerized control procedures require additional equipment or the modification of existing programs, however, you must compare costs and benefits to determine if the costs are reasonable. Illustration 16–9 contains such an example.

ILLUSTRATION 16–9 Cost-Benefit Analysis of Computerized Controls

Calculation of costs:	
One time	
Costs of installing a security system (written procedures for authorized access, coded employee badges, system of locks, etc.) to ensure access to the computer room and tape library by authorized personnel only	$ 5,000
Cost of buying duplicate tapes, 144 tapes (for storing 12 months' information, at 12 tapes per month), at $15	2,400
Cost of processing 144 tapes on computer, at $25 each	3,600
Total one-time costs	$ 11,000
Recurring	
Cost to maintain the security system	$ 500
Cost to update 144 tapes (oldest month's tapes erased and data for current month duplicated)	3,600
Cost related to off-site storage	2,000
Total recurring costs	$ 6,100
Calculation of benefits:	
Estimated personnel costs to recreate the information stored on tapes:	
5,000 worker-hours at $6.50	$ 32,500
Taxes and fringe benefits, at 20%	6,500
200 computer-hours, at $25	5,000
Estimated costs related to the delay in recreating or inability to recreate certain accounts receivable information:	
Slower collections assuming 10% of the accounts are collected 30 days later than normal ($5,000,000 at 9% × 30 days)	37,000
Lost collections ($50,000,000 × 0.02%)	100,000

ILLUSTRATION 16–9 *(concluded)*

Estimated costs to conduct a special physical inventory:		
2,000 worker-hours at $6.50		$ 13,000
Taxes and fringe benefits, at 20%		2,500
20 computer-hours, at $25		500
Quantifiable risk per occurrence, the loss exposure		$197,000
Estimated annual probability of occurrence:		
Without controls	5%	
With controls	—	5%
Annual benefit of risk elimination, the risk exposure		$ 9,850

Other risks (not easily quantified):
- Interruption of business.
- Inability to operate the business efficiently.
- Possible cover-up of embezzlement or fraud.
- Possible effects on employees' attitude and productivity because of delay in processing payroll.

Decision:

The quantifiable annual risk is $9,850 and the unquantifiable risks are substantial. On the other hand, the estimated identifiable costs of the controls to significantly reduce the risks of loss are approximately $11,000 of one-time costs and $6,100 of recurring costs. Balancing the two, controls probably should be installed.

Source: Arthur Young & Company, *Evaluating Accounting Controls: A Systematic Approach* (New York: 1980), pp. 63–64. Used by permission.

The analysis in Illustration 16–9 evaluates procedures to improve general controls at a data center. In it, management considers the reasonableness of two improvements. The first is to install a system that improves the physical security of the data center. The second provides for routine backup on magnetic tape of all data files and for off-site storage of them.

The incremental costs of these proposals include both one time and recurring costs of the equipment required. The benefits are more difficult to determine because the company benefits from them only if accounting data files are destroyed. Although the probability of this is small, the potential cost is large. To quantify the benefits, you must identify the amount of risk exposure that is reduced by implementation of the control.

Without these controls, the data center is exposed to the threat of lost accounts receivable and inventory data. The loss exposure arising from the control weakness is the cost of recreating these files should the threat occur, or $197,000. The estimated risk of the loss is 5 percent, so the risk exposure is the expected value of this loss, or $9,850. Management compares these expected benefits to the costs and considers qualitative risks before deciding to implement the control procedures.

A Comprehensive Application

In these examples, you saw cost-benefit analysis applied to commonly used control procedures. Accountability for inventory, independent credit approval, physical security, and routine file backup procedures are controls that address specific weaknesses identified by an auditor.

Sometimes accountants wish to evaluate the reasonableness of safeguarding the entire computer-based information system. To do this, they identify all the threats to data and apply cost-benefit analysis to the controls that prevent or detect them. Illustration 16–10 shows such a comprehensive application.

In Illustration 16–10, accountants identify seven categories of threats to data integrity and security. They also estimate the risk exposure, the amount of expected loss per year, from each threat category. They determine a threat's risk exposure by multiplying the estimated loss from that threat by the probability of its occurrence. Because there are many possible threats in each category, separate calculations may be necessary to determine risk exposure. Illustration 16–11 shows how to calculate the risk exposure for the fraud category.[5]

Ilustration 16–12 shows how accountants summarize the effect of appropriate control procedures in the system. For each control this schedule shows the affected threat category and the effect on risk of implementing the control. In this

ILLUSTRATION 16–10 Risk Exposures in a Computer-Based System

Threat Category Number	*Exposure to Hazards*	*Average Expected Loss Per Year*
E1	Malfunctions and human errors	$39,825
E2	Fraud	14,000
E3	Power and communications failures ...	12,500
E4	Fire	10,535
E5	Sabotage and riot	9,030
E6	Natural disasters	5,475
E7	General hazards	2,505
	Total average expected loss	$93,870

[5]This example is adapted from IBM Corporation, *Data Security and Data Processing* (White Plains, N.Y.: 1974). Used by permission.

ILLUSTRATION 16–11 Risk Exposure to Fraud

	Probability (percent) Hazard Will Occur	*Loss Range*	*Loss Range Weighted by Probability*
Embezzlement	5%	$ 10,000–$100,000	$ 500–$ 5,000
File confiscation	10	10,000– 100,000	1,000– 10,000
Tapping	5	10,000– 100,000	500– 5,000
Program changes	20	5,000– 25,000	1,000– 5,000
Subtotal			$ 3,000–$25,000
Average			$14,000

Source: Adapted from IBM Corporation, *Data Security and Data Processing* (White Plains, N.Y.: 1974). Used by permission.

ILLUSTRATION 16–12 Controls Reducing Risk Exposure

Control Number	*Description of Control*	*Exposures Protected*	*Probability That Control Fails*
C1	Administrative, operational, documentation	E1, E2	.01
C2	Backup	E3	.02
C3	Fire detection and extinguishing system	E4	.03
C4	Various security controls	E5, E6, E7	.01

example, these controls may fail to prevent or detect a threat from 1 to 3 percent of the time. This simplified example shows four controls; in fact an actual system may require dozens of them.

Illustration 16–13 contains the estimated costs of each control. Accountants use this information in the cost-benefit analysis shown in Illustration 16–14. Based on this analysis, you would include in your recommendations to management that controls C1, C2, and C3 be implemented. Control C4 would not be included in your recommendations.

ILLUSTRATION 16–13 Cost of Controls

Control Number	*Cost to Implement*	*Operating Cost Per Year*
C1	$ 10,000	$ 3,000
C2	6,000	500
C3	2,000	1,000
C4	22,000	15,500

ILLUSTRATION 16–14 Comparison of Costs and Benefits

Control Number	*Exposure(s) Protected*	*Incremental Cost (from Illustration 16–13)*	*Incremental Benefits (from Illustrations 16–10 and 16–12)*	*Decision*
C1	E1, E2	$13,000	($39,825 + $14,000) × (1 − .01) = $53,287	Include
C2	E3	6,500	$12,500 × (1 − .02) = $12,250	Include
C3	E4	3,000	$10,535 × (1 − .03) = $10,219	Include
C4	E5, E6, E7	37,500	($9,030 + $5,475 + $2,505) × (1 − .01) = $16,840	Exclude

SUMMARY

Internal accounting controls are intended to provide reasonable assurance that accounting records are accurate and reliable and that assets are safeguarded. The concept of reasonable assurance recognizes that the costs of an internal accounting control policy, practice, or procedure should not exceed the benefits from it.

The benefits from a control procedure consist of a reduction in risk exposure. This is the expected value of loss that the control procedure prevents or detects. Costs of a control procedure consist of both one-time and recurring costs.

Cost-benefit analysis requires comparison of the incremental costs and benefits of a control procedure. Qualitative costs and benefits are difficult to quantify and should be considered whenever quantitative ones are approximately equal.

KEY TERMS

cost-benefit analysis The process of comparing the costs of performing a control procedure with the expected benefits.

expected value The monetary value of an event multiplied by the probability of the event's occurrence.

incremental cost (or benefit) A cost (or benefit) that exists due to a control procedure and does not exist without the procedure.

internal accounting controls Policies, practices, and procedures adopted by management to safeguard the organization's assets and to ensure accurate and reliable accounting data.

loss exposure The monetary loss that might occur due to the absence of a control procedure.

reasonable assurance The concept that the cost of internal accounting controls should not exceed the benefits expected from them.

risk exposure The expected value of the monetary loss from a control weakness. It equals the loss exposure multiplied by the probability of the loss.

QUESTIONS

16–1. The concept of reasonable assurance includes the principle that the cost of control should not exceed the benefits to be derived. In the process of analyzing the costs and benefits related to a particular control, which of the following factors should be considered?
   a. The maximum monetary loss the organization could conceivably incur without the control.
   b. The frequency and monetary values of specific losses that could conceivably be sustained without the control.
   c. The availability and feasibility of alternate controls closely related to the same control objective(s).
   d. The effects of the control on employee productivity and morale.

16–2. Control procedures are intended to provide reasonable, but not absolute, assurance. Suggest some characteristics of an accounting information system intended to provide absolute assurance.

16–3. How does loss exposure differ from risk exposure?

16–4. What are qualitative benefits? Cite several examples. How would including them affect cost-benefit analysis of internal accounting controls?

16–5. In cost-benefit analyses, how is the incremental approach different from the total approach?

16–6. In cost-benefit analyses of controls in a manual system, which types of cost are likely to be involved? Which types of benefits are likely to be expected?

16–7. In cost-benefit analyses of controls in a computerized system, why is attention mainly directed at general controls rather than at application controls?

16–8. What role does probability play in cost-benefit analyses?

EXERCISES AND CASE

16–9. *FOREIGN CORRUPT PRACTICES ACT*

The Foreign Corrupt Practices Act of 1977 was an outgrowth of public hearings and investigations conducted by the U.S. Congress and the Securities and Exchange Commission (SEC) regarding questionable activities and payments by U.S. corporations in foreign countries and markets. Although the subject of this act is primarily foreign bribery, the act also has provisions dealing with internal accounting controls. These provisions affect virtually all public companies whether or not they have business abroad.

Required:

Explain which criterion the SEC has identified as important in determining how extensive an internal control system needs to be to comply with the Foreign Corrupt Practices Act of 1977.

(CMA Adapted)

16–10. *REASONABLE ASSURANCE*

Since its enactment in December 1977, the Foreign Corrupt Practices Act (FCPA) has been the subject of much discussion among boards of directors, management, internal auditors, independent accountants, and lawyers. Much of this discussion relates to the accounting provisions of the FCPA.

Required:

Briefly explain the concept of reasonable assurance as it applies to the FCPA.

(CIA Adapted)

16–11. *COST-BENEFIT ANALYSIS*

The following data have been gathered for the purpose of performing cost-benefit analysis of internal accounting controls.[6]

Level of Controls	*Total Annual Cost of Controls*	*Probability of Event*	*Consequences of Event (total loss)*	*Expected Loss*
1	$ —	0.5	$200,000	$100,000
2	20,000	0.3	200,000	60,000
3	40,000	0.15	200,000	30,000
4	60,000	0.06	200,000	12,000
5	80,000	0.01	200,000	2,000

In the preceding tabulation, the levels of controls are cumulative—that is, level 2 control is built on top of level 1 control, level 3 control is built on top of level 2, and so forth. These levels of controls are intended to respond to the same event, such as the loss of inventories. As the level of controls increases (such as adding inventory clerks at each level), the probability of an event drops, thus the expected loss drops.

---

[6]Michael W. Maher, ''Costs and Benefits of the Foreign Corrupt Practices Act,'' in *Internal Control in U.S. Corporations: The State of the Art,* ed. Robert K. Mautz, Walter G. Kell, Michael W. Maher, Alan G. Merten, Raymond R. Reilly, Dennis G. Severance, and Bernard J. White (New York: Financial Executives Foundation, 1980), pp. 313–21. Used by permission.

Required:

a. Prepare a cost-benefit analysis.
b. Identify the appropriate level of controls based on this analysis.

16–12. COST-BENEFIT ANALYSIS

Refer to the preceding exercise. Suppose the probability of an event for each level of controls is as follows:

Level of Controls	*Probability of Event*
1	0.45
2	0.29
3	0.18
4	0.05
5	0.005

Other data remain unchanged.

Required:

a. Prepare a cost-benefit analysis.
b. Identify the appropriate level of controls based on this analysis.

16–13. COST-BENEFIT ANALYSIS

The following data for exposures and controls were developed for performing cost-benefit analysis:[7]

Data for Exposure:

Threat	*Loss Exposure*	*Probability of Loss*	*Risk Exposure*
E1	$50,833	0.05	$2,542
E2	46,667	0.03	1,400
E3	21,833	0.10	2,183
			$6,125

Data for Controls:

Control	*Affected Threat*	*Probability of Control Failure*	*Implementation Cost*	*Annual Cost*	*Expected Life of Control*
C1	E1	0.01	$ 500	$ 100	7
C2	E2	0.10	2,000	1,000	5
C3	E3	0.05	4,000	1,000	10

Required:

a. Prepare a cost-benefit analysis.
b. Identify which controls, if any, should be included.

[7] Michael J. Cerullo and Fred A. Shelton, "Analyzing the Cost-Effectiveness of Computer Controls and Security," *Internal Auditor* (October 1981), pp. 30–37. Used by permission.

16–14. COST-BENEFIT ANALYSIS

Refer to the preceding exercise. Suppose the probability of loss for each threat and the probability of control failure for each control were as follows:

Threat	*Probability of Loss*	*Control*	*Probability of Control Failure*
E1	0.06	C1	0.02
E2	0.04	C2	0.03
E3	0.24	C3	0.04

Other data remain unchanged.

Required:

a. Prepare a cost-benefit analysis.
b. Identify which controls, if any, should be included.

16–15. COST-BENEFIT ANALYSIS

The following data have been gathered to evaluate whether the Richardson Company should use a lockbox to process its cash receipts from customers.

Cost of renting a lockbox	$200 per year
Cost of processing checks by bank	$0.10 per check
Cost of copying check for transmittal to bank's customer (in cases where checks are not accompanied by remittance advices)	$0.25 per check
Average daily total cash receipts arriving in mail ...	$15,000
Average amount per check	$ 75
Percentage of customers' checks not accompanied by remittance advices	10%

Richardson Company is located in Richardson, a suburb of Dallas, Texas. Checks mailed to Richardson Company are normally deposited intact in the bank on the business day following their receipt. The bank is able to credit the collection to the company's loan account the same day. The interest rate on the loan account is 18 percent.

Required:

Prepare a cost-benefit analysis and evaluate whether the company should use a lockbox. Suggest some intangible benefits.

16–16. COST-BENEFIT ANALYSIS

Refer to the preceding exercise. Assume that the Richardson Company is located in a small town in northeast Texas but still maintains its banking relationship with a Dallas bank. This means that checks received by Richardson Company in the mail are deposited, intact, by mail, to the bank in Dallas. The bank normally receives mailed-in deposits three days later, instead of one day later as in the preceding exercise. Assume also that the average amount per check is $750, instead of $75 as in the preceding exercise. Other data are unchanged.

Required:

Prepare a cost-benefit analysis and evaluate whether the company should use a lockbox. Suggest some intangible benefits.

16–17. *COST-BENEFIT ANALYSIS*

The Madison Company's vendor payment system processes approximately 390,000 invoices per year.[8] Management estimates that about 1 percent of these invoices contain errors and that the average error per erroneous invoice is $100. In 50 percent of the cases, vendors notify the company of errors, even when no controls have been put into the system. Each time the vendor notifies the company of the error, the company has to investigate the original payment, verify amounts with receiving, and reprocess payment. This is estimated to cost $40 per correction. Based on these estimates, the total cost per erroneous invoice is set at $70, computed as follows: $100 × 50% + $40 × 50%. Using this figure, management estimates the exposure of the system at $273,000, computed as follows: $70 × 390,000 × 1%.

Proposed control alternatives

Data processing proposes the three control alternatives shown in Exhibit 16–1, along with their estimated reliability and cost. Management raises two questions. First, which controls are optimal? Second, are controls justified based on costs and benefits?

EXHIBIT 16–1 Case 16–17 Control Alternatives for Vendor Payments

		Reliability	*Cost*
C_1	Random sample verification: A random sample of input documents is pulled and compared with the keyed-in data.	0.55	$20,000
C_2	Sight verification: The dollar amount input is visually displayed to the operator before system acceptance.	0.60	20,000
C_3	Batch control totals: Invoices are grouped in batches prior to entry, and control totals are computed on key fields for later comparison with input data.	0.95	40,000

[8]Larry E. Rittenberg and Donald L. Miner, "Performing Cost/Benefit Analysis of Internal Controls," *Internal Auditor* (February 1981), pp. 56–64. Used by permission.

Decision Rules

Because the alternatives involve multiple controls, management establishes decision rules to simplify analysis. Under these decision rules, controls or control combinations that provide less benefit are systematically eliminated from consideration. These decision rules are shown as Exhibit 16–2.

Ranking Control Alternatives

Using these decision rules, management first ranks the three control alternatives. These are shown in columns 1 and 2 of Exhibit 16–3.

Applying the second decision rule criterion eliminates alternatives B, D, and F because other combinations provide greater reliability for less or equal cost. For each of the remaining alternatives, management computes the benefit, which is the reduction in exposure.

For example, including control C2, with a reliability of 0.60, reduces the exposure to \$109,200 (= Total exposure of \$273,000 × (1 − 0.60)). The benefit of C2, therefore, is \$163,800 (= \$273,000 − \$109,200). These figures are shown in columns 3 and 4 of Exhibit 16–3.

The next step is to calculate the net benefit, which is the difference between benefit and the cost of the control or control combination. For C2, with benefit at \$163,800 and cost at \$20,000, management calculates the net benefit at \$143,800. This figure is entered in column 5 of Exhibit 16–3. The exposures, benefits, and net benefits of other controls or control combinations are similarly calculated and entered in the proper columns of Exhibit 16–3.

Required:

How would you have answered the management's two questions?

EXHIBIT 16–2 Case 16–17 Decision Rules Involving Multiple Control Situations

1. Rank the individual controls and control combinations in ascending order (*a*) by cost and (*b*) by reliability in reducing exposure when costs are equal.
2. Eliminate from consideration any individual control with lower reliability and greater or equal cost than other single controls.
3. Eliminate from consideration any control combinations with lower reliability and greater or equal cost than other individual or combined controls.
4. Calculate the net benefit for all control combinations still being considered.
5. Select, subject to outside constraints, the control or control combination with the greater positive benefit.

EXHIBIT 16–3 Case 16–17 Banking control alternatives

Alternative		Control	(1) Reliability	(2) Cost	(3) Remaining Exposure	(4) Benefit	(5) Net Benefit
(A)		No controls		-0-	$273,000		
(B)	C_1	Random sampling	0.55	$20,000	†	†	†
(C)	C_2	Sight verification	0.60	20,000	109,200	$163,800	$143,800
(D)	C_1 C_2	Random sampling and sight verification	0.82*	40,000	†	†	†
(E)	C_3	Batch controls	0.95	40,000	13,650	259,350	219,350
(F)	C_1 C_3	Random sampling and batch controls	0.9775*	60,000	†	†	†
(G)	C_2 C_3	Sight verification and batch controls	0.98*	60,000	5,460	267,540	207,540
(H)	C_1 C_2 C_3	Random sampling, sight verification, and batch controls	0.991*	80,000	2,457	270,543	190,543

*Reliability is computed as $1 - (1 - R_1)(1 - R_2). \ldots (1 - R_n)$; for combination C_1 C_2 = $1 - (0.45)(0.40) = 0.82$; for C_1 C_3 = $1 - (0.45)(0.05) = 0.9775$; for C_2 C_3 = $1 - (0.4)(0.05) = 0.98$; and for C_1 C_2 C_3 = $1 - (0.45)(0.40)(0.05) = 0.991$.
†Not considered.

Part V

Processing Accounting Transactions

Chapter 17

Accounting Transaction Cycles

Learning Objectives:

1. To recognize those economic activities in which all organizations engage.
2. To understand how economic events are recorded as accounting transactions.
3. To find out the transaction cycles that make up an accounting transaction processing system.
4. To learn the application systems constituting each transaction cycle.

INTRODUCTION

The preceding chapters describe the technology that accounting information systems use and the system controls that prevent and detect errors and threats to these systems. The last part of this book describes how this technology and these controls are used when processing specific accounting transactions.

To make it easier to understand these procedures, they are structured by accounting transaction cycle. This chapter explains four transaction cycles and provides you with an overview of the detailed descriptions of them in later chapters.

Different accountants describe transaction cycles in different ways. The cycles described in this chapter represent just one way of looking at them. As you work with accounting information systems, you may encounter accountants who use five or even six transaction cycles. These are not incorrect; they are simply different ways of viewing the economic events that make up an organization's activities.

ECONOMIC EVENTS

We live in a complex society. It contains many organizations engaging in different activities for both profit and nonprofit objectives. Accounting systems are designed to record, to summarize, and to report the results of economic events for a wide range of organizations. How can you begin to understand or structure this variety of economic events? How could the designer of an accounting system hope to anticipate all the possible events that can occur? Designing such a system is easier than you think if you first consider the basic activities of all businesses.

The Cycle of Business Activities

Even though businesses differ in their operations, all of them engage in a cycle of basic activities. Each activity has certain economic events common to most; these economic events produce accounting transactions that must be processed by the accounting system. By examining these economic events, you can identify a small number of accounting processes appropriate for most organizations. Illustration 17–1 summarizes these basic business activities.

Capital Investment. The cycle of business activities begins when capital is invested in a business. Generally accepted accounting principles (GAAP) require recognizing the business as an entity separate from the sources of this capital.

ILLUSTRATION 17–1 The Cycle of Basic Business Activities

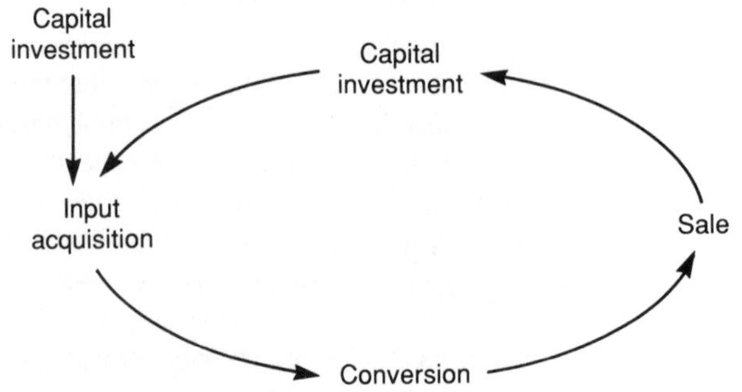

These sources may be the owners of the business or they may be creditors. If the source is from owners, then the investment is owners' equity. If the source is from borrowing, the investment is either long-term debt or current liabilities. In many businesses, most of the capital is used to purchase long-term productive assets. The business uses the productive assets to increase its capital. Periodically, the business reports the results of its operations to the sources of its capital.

The capital investment component of the business activity cycle has two significant economic events: raising capital and using capital to acquire productive assets. Another event occurring during this activity is not economic in the sense of the other two: Periodically the business reports to its sources of capital. This is necessary to maintain those sources when additional capital is needed later.

The final chapter in this text describes how these events are recorded by the accounting system.

Input Acquisition. The second component of the cycle of business activities is the acquisition of materials and overhead items such as supplies. These inputs are used to increase the capital of the business. The exact way they are used is not important at this point; they are used differently for different businesses.

Most organizations operate on credit; that is, when a business purchases inputs, it receives the inputs in return for a promise to pay for them. The business records an obligation to pay, and pays for them at a later date. So, the activity of input acquisition has these four economic events: ordering of inputs, receiving the inputs, recording an obligation to pay for them, and paying for the inputs.

Conversion. The next step in the cycle of activities is the conversion of inputs into goods or services. The business sells these to increase its capital. The conversion process is different for different businesses.

Manufacturing companies buy raw material inventories, apply labor and overhead to them, and produce an output different from the material purchased. Service companies convert inputs that are predominantly labor into outputs in the form of services. In contrast, the conversion process of merchandising companies (retailers and wholesalers) uses relatively little labor. These organizations purchase inventories of goods, repackage them, and then market them. All three businesses use inventories of supplies in their conversion processes.

One economic event taking place during conversion is the consumption of labor, materials, and overhead to produce a salable product or service.

Sales. The final component in the cycle of basic business activities is the sale of the goods or services that were outputs of the conversion process. When these are sold at a profit, the capital investment of the business increases. Additional cash is available for reinvestment, or for making payments to the sources of capital in the form of dividends and interest. By providing a source of additional capital, the sales component completes the cycle of business activities.

ILLUSTRATION 17–2 Events in the Business Activity Cycle

Business Cycle Activity	*Events*
Capital investment	Raise capital Use capital to acquire property Periodic reporting
Input acquisition	Request inputs to the conversion process Receive inputs Record obligation to pay Pay for inputs
Conversion	Consume labor, material, and overhead
Sales	Receive request for goods or services Deliver to customer Request payment Receive payment

The sale of goods or services consists of four economic events: receive a customer order, deliver goods to the customer, request payment for the goods, and receive payment. Illustration 17–2 summarizes the economic events in the cycle of business activities.

ECONOMIC EVENTS AND ACCOUNTING TRANSACTIONS

A normal business's operation consists of a series of economic events. This series results from the cycle of business activities that describes how all accounting entities operate.

An accounting system records economic events in the form of accounting transactions, summarizes those transactions, and reports them in some useful way. Thus you can consider business activities as cycles of accounting transactions. In fact, the study of *transaction cycles* is a convenient way to understand how most accounting systems work.

Transaction Cycles

A transaction cycle is a set of accounting transactions that occur in a normal sequence. They record the economic events of a component in the cycle of business activities. For example, a sales transaction is normally followed by a shipping transaction, a billing transaction, and a cash receipts transaction. These constitute a cycle.

Illustration 17–1 shows the four basic business activities. From them you can identify four accounting transaction cycles: the financial cycle, the expenditure cycle, the conversion cycle, and the revenue cycle.

ILLUSTRATION 17–3 The Financial Cycle

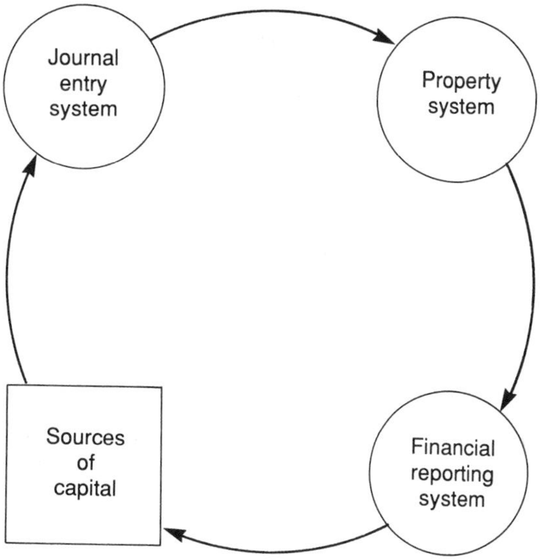

Early in this text you were introduced to these cycles as subsystems of the accounting transaction processing system. At that time you learned that the transaction cycles consist of subsystems called application systems. Now you can see in detail how these subsystems record common business economic events.

Financial Cycle. The financial cycle consists of those accounting transactions that record the acquisition of capital from owners and creditors, the use of that capital to acquire productive assets, and the reporting to them on how it is used. The two significant economic events in the financial cycle are raising capital and the use of that capital to acquire property, plant, and equipment. A third event—not really an economic one—is periodic reporting to the sources of capital.

The basic financial statements provide periodic reporting. These statements include the balance sheet, the income statement, and the statement of cash flows. The summaries in these statements come from the general ledger. Periodic reporting to the sources of capital enables a business to raise additional capital. For this reason, you can view the series of transactions as a cycle.

The three accounting application systems that record the events in the financial cycle are the property, the journal entry, and the financial reporting systems.[1] Illustration 17–3 depicts the relationships among these application systems and the sources of capital.

[1]Many accountants refer to the journal entry and financial reporting systems together as the general ledger system. However, it is easier to understand how they work if you learn them as separate systems.

ILLUSTRATION 17–4 The Expenditure Cycle

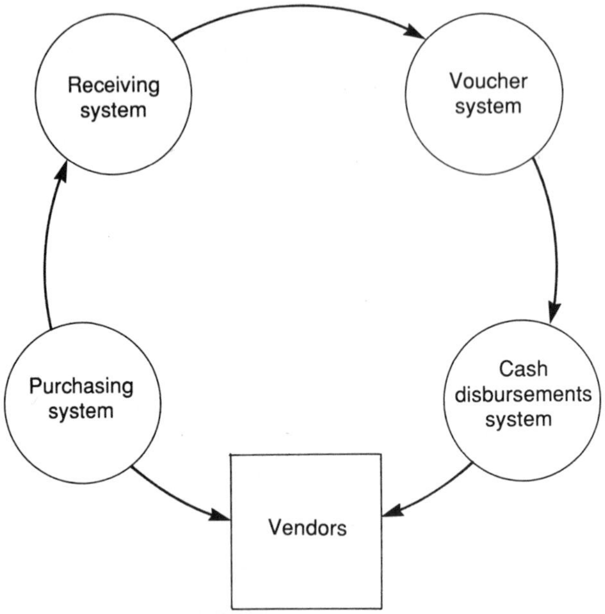

Expenditure Cycle. The expenditure cycle consists of those transactions incurred to acquire material and overhead items for the conversion process of the business. This cycle processes transactions representing the following economic events: requesting the items, receiving the items, recording the obligation to pay for the items, and paying for them.

Most businesses use a purchasing department to acquire materials and supplies. A purchasing agent orders material from a vendor who ships the material and mails an invoice. The business uses the invoice to record the payable and later pays the vendor. When the vendor is paid according to the terms of the sale, the vendor again sells items to the business. This causes the sequence of transactions to form a cycle.

The application systems in the expenditure cycle execute these transactions. They include the purchasing, receiving, voucher, and the cash disbursements systems.[2] Illustration 17–4 shows the relationships among vendors and the systems in the expenditure cycle.

Revenue Cycle. The revenue cycle includes the accounting transactions that record the generation of revenue from the outputs of the conversion process. As

[2]Many accountants consider the voucher and cash disbursements systems as one, called the accounts payable system. Again, it is easier to learn them as separate processes.

ILLUSTRATION 17–5 The Revenue Cycle

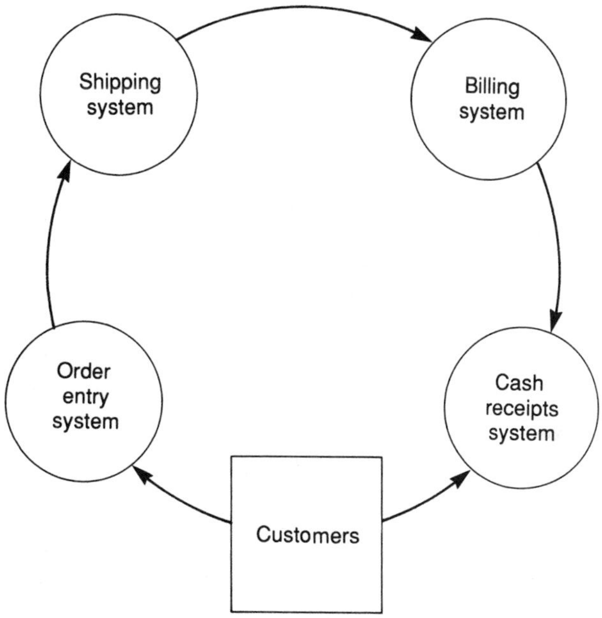

mentioned earlier, these four economic events generate revenue: receiving an order from a customer, delivering goods or services to the customer, requesting payment from the customer, and receiving the payment.

Whenever companies sell goods or services on credit, each of these events produces a transaction. Each transaction may occur at separate times. If the sale is a cash sale, then ordering, delivery, request, and payment occur at the same time. In this case, accounting systems ordinarily record these four events with one transaction. When a customer pays and the accounting system records the cash receipt, the business is willing to sell again to the customer. This causes the cycle of transactions to repeat.

Companies that sell on credit use four application systems in the revenue cycle. They are the order entry, shipping, billing, and the cash receipts systems.[3] Companies that sell on a cash basis frequently use a point-of-sale system that combines the four economic events in one transaction. Illustration 17–5 provides a graphic description of the transactions in the revenue cycle.

Conversion Cycle. The conversion cycle contains those transactions incurred when inputs are converted into salable goods or services. One economic event

[3]The billing and cash receipts systems are called the accounts receivable system. As before, it is easier to learn them separately.

exists in the conversion cycle. Materials, labor, and overhead are consumed in the conversion process.

In manufacturing and service companies, either actual or standard material and labor costs are recorded in a cost ledger as conversion occurs. Overhead costs are allocated in the cost ledger, usually based on the amount of labor used. These costs become associated with the products and are matched with revenue when the products are sold. In merchandising companies, costs of conversion are recorded when incurred and matched against revenue in the same period.

Depending on the type of organization, the conversion cycle contains either two or three application systems. Manufacturing and service companies use the cost accounting system to record material, labor, and overhead costs. All types of organizations use the payroll system. It ensures that employees are paid for their labor. Manufacturing and merchandising companies use the inventory system to maintain records of inventory on hand.

In merchandising and manufacturing companies, the systems of the conversion cycle provide interfaces between the expenditure and revenue cycles. Because it contains only one event, the conversion cycle cannot be represented as a circle as can the other cycles.

For example, a merchandising company maintains a merchandise inventory for sale. The expenditure cycle adds to this inventory and the revenue cycle takes from it. The inventory system records the associated transactions. The payroll system in a merchandising company compensates sales and administrative personnel for their work. Illustration 17–6 shows the interfaces between the expenditure and revenue cycles and the inventory and payroll systems in such a company.

A manufacturing company has raw materials, work in process, and finished goods inventories. The production process converts raw material into finished goods. Raw materials are acquired in the expenditure cycle and finished goods are sold in the revenue cycle. In this way, these inventory accounts are a part of two cycles. The cost accounting, payroll, and inventory systems provide interfaces by recording transactions during the production process. Illustration 17–7 shows a graphic representation of the conversion cycle in a manufacturing company.

Cycles and Applications

Basic business activities were used to identify four transaction cycles common to all businesses. These transaction cycles differ in various businesses.

For example, in large corporations, the financial cycle is complex. In a small business, there are fewer sources and uses of capital so the cycle is much simpler. In manufacturing companies, the conversion cycle may contain a highly developed cost accounting system that is unnecessary in a merchandising company. Service companies may also use inventory and cost accounting systems, but they are simpler because these companies do not have raw material inventories.

ILLUSTRATION 17–6 The Conversion Cycle in a Merchandising Company

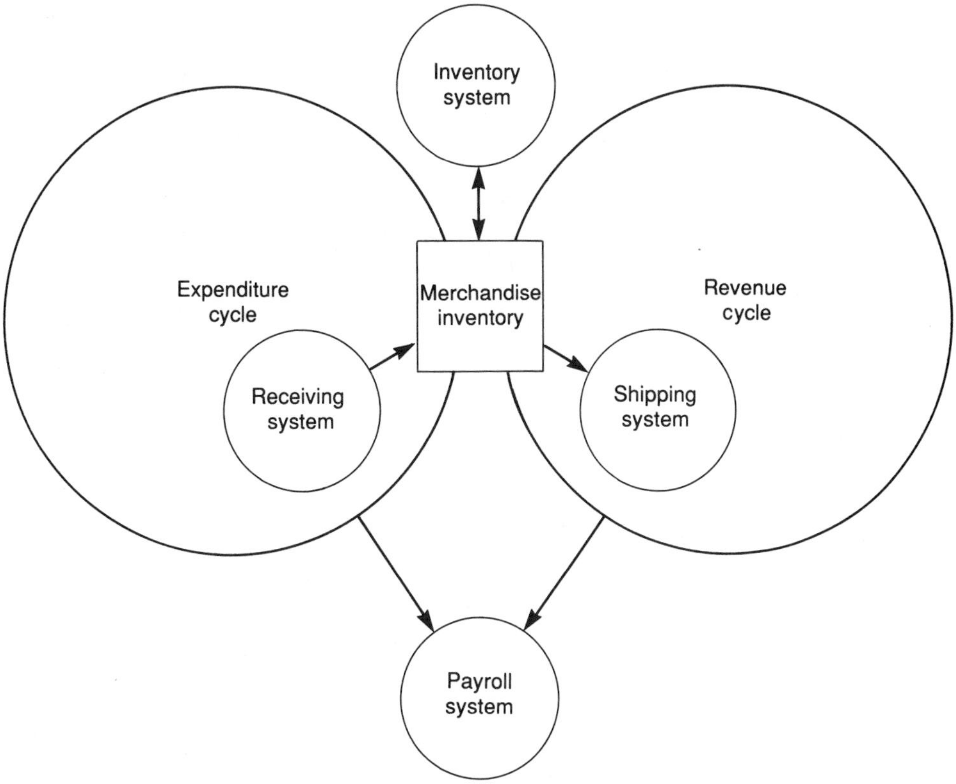

The diversity among companies is significant. Although they engage in basically the same activities and their accounting transactions record the same economic events, all companies cannot use identical application systems. Large companies have a greater number of computerized application systems, and these systems are more sophisticated than those in smaller companies. Older application systems are less complex than newer ones, even within the same company. Some applications are much more important in some industries than in others. Illustration 17–8 suggests the relative significance of various accounting applications in different industries.

While learning how accounting information systems process transactions, you are learning different ways of recording the same economic event. As a practicing accountant, you will be working with systems of varying complexity and technology. The systems described in this book are typical transaction processing methods with *good internal control;* however, these examples are not the only ways a business can operate.

ILLUSTRATION 17–7 The Conversion Cycle in a Manufacturing Company

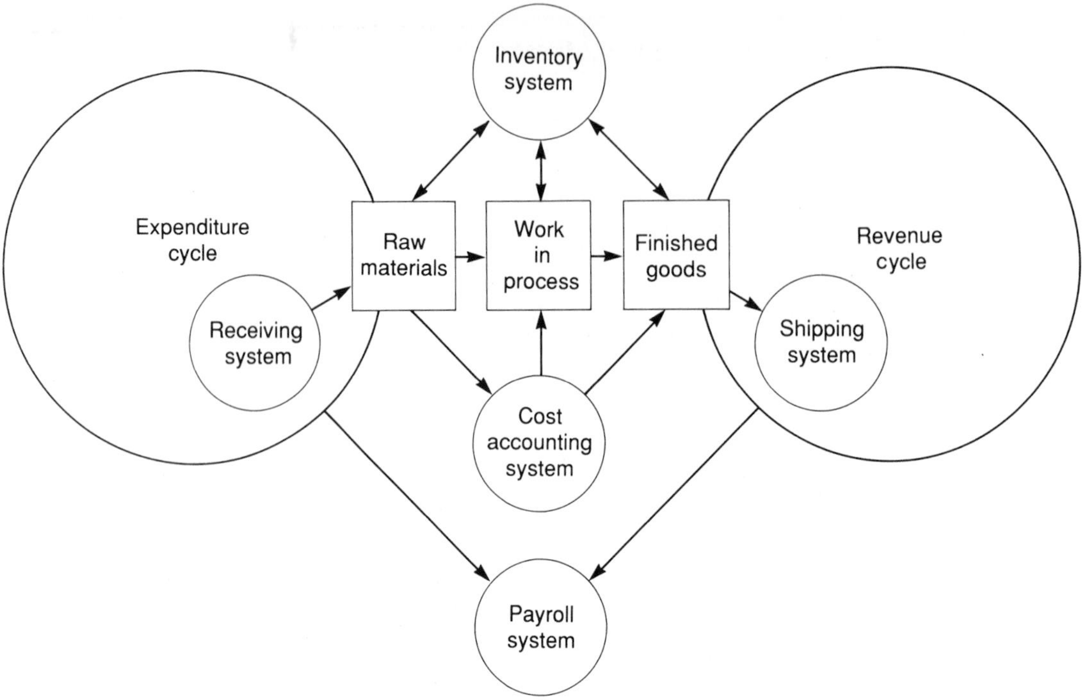

ILLUSTRATION 17–8 Relative Significance of Accounting Applications by Industry

Industry	*Shipping*	*Purchasing*	*Receiving*	*Cost Accounting*	*Inventory*
Agriculture	Maj	Maj	Maj		Min
Banking		Min	Min	Min	Min
Construction		Maj	Maj	Maj	Maj
Health care		Maj	Maj	Min	Maj
Insurance		Min	Min	Min	Min
Manufacturing	Maj	Maj	Maj	Maj	Maj
Merchandising	Maj	Maj	Maj		Maj
Mining	Maj	Maj	Maj		Min
Transportation		Min	Min		Min
Utility		Maj	Maj	Maj	Min

Legend: Maj—indicates that the application is a major one in the industry
Min—indicates that the application is a minor one in the industry
Blank—indicates that the application is not used in the industry

Note: The following applications are not shown because they are major ones in most industries: billing, cash receipts, voucher, cash disbursements, property, payroll, order entry, journal entry, and financial reporting.

ILLUSTRATION 17–9 Economic Events and Application Systems that Process Them

Transaction Cycle	*Economic Event*	*Application System*
Financial	Raise capital	Journal entry
	Consume capital	Property
	Periodic reporting	Financial reporting
Expenditure	Request inputs	Purchasing
	Receive inputs	Receiving
	Obligation to pay	Voucher
	Payment	Cash disbursements
Conversion	Consume labor, material, overhead	Cost accounting, payroll, and inventory
Revenue	Receive request	Order entry
	Deliver	Shipping
	Request payment	Billing
	Receive payment	Cash receipts

Just as accounting transaction cycles were identified with basic business activities, accounting application systems can be identified with economic events, as shown in Illustration 17–9. This illustration identifies 14 application systems which the following chapters describe.

Advantages of Using Transaction Cycles

Why learn about transaction cycles? How does understanding the cyclical nature of transaction processing help you as a student and as an accountant? There are several benefits to your study of transaction cycles.

Transaction cycles emphasize the continuous nature of all business and accounting processes. You learned accounting by thinking of journals and ledgers, debits and credits, and their effect on accounts in a general ledger. Because of this, you may think of the accounting process as static, as something that happens at the end of a month or a year. In fact, accounting activities occur constantly, just as do the activities of the business in which the accounting system operates.

Transaction cycles also demonstrate how events early in a transaction cycle affect events and records later in the cycle. A weakness in internal control affecting a transaction may mean that records created later in that same cycle are misstated. For example, a purchase from a fraudulent vendor is possible due to poor internal control in the purchasing system of the expenditure cycle. Although this might cause excessive expenses in the voucher system of the same cycle, transactions in the other cycles are not affected. These questions greatly concern auditors, who must evaluate the effects of internal control weaknesses in determining audit tests.

Many modern organizations use highly computerized accounting systems with records maintained in a unified data base. In these integrated systems, it is often difficult to distinguish the processes applied to accounting transactions. Analyzing these processes by transaction cycle makes it easier to understand these systems.

Finally, accounting information systems process many kinds of accounting transactions, and in so doing, generate a variety of documents and reports. Many files are processed using both manual and computerized methods. Transaction cycles provide a framework for the study of these processing methods that emphasizes the similarities among them. Thus the use of transaction cycles makes easier your study of accounting information systems.

SUMMARY

In this chapter you learned the structure that underlies the processing of accounting transactions. Analyzing the cycle of basic business activities revealed the origin of the transaction cycles that make up the accounting transaction processing system. They are the financial, expenditure, conversion, and revenue cycles. The economic events that occur in each of the basic business activities have an accounting application system associated with each of them.

KEY TERMS

application systems The components of a transaction cycle.

capital investment The first component in the cycle of business activities. It concerns acquiring money to generate products and services and produce revenue.

conversion The third component in the cycle of business activities. Inputs of labor, material, and overhead are converted into salable goods or services.

conversion cycle Those transactions incurred when inputs to the conversion process are converted into salable goods or services.

cycle of business activities A series of activities in which all businesses engage.

economic event An action by a business affecting its assets, liabilities, and owners' equity; the accounting system records it as a transaction.

expenditure cycle Those accounting transactions recording the acquisition of material and overhead items for the conversion process of the business.

financial cycle Those accounting transactions recording the acquisition of capital from owners and creditors and reporting to them on how it is used.

input acquisition The second component in the cycle of business activities. It is concerned with the acquisition of materials and overhead.

revenue cycle The accounting transactions recording the generation of revenue from the outputs of the conversion process.

sales The fourth component in the cycle of business activities. Goods or services are sold, producing revenue and income for the business.

transaction cycle A set of accounting transactions occurring in a normal sequence and used to record economic events.

QUESTIONS

17–1. What are the components of the cycle of business activities?

17–2. Describe the conversion processes that take place in:
a. Manufacturing companies.
b. Service companies.
c. Merchandising companies.

17–3. Which economic events occur during each of the following components of the business cycle?
a. Capital investment.
b. Input acquisition.
c. Conversion.
d. Sales.

17–4. What is a transaction cycle?

17–5. What are the four transaction cycles?

17–6. How do the events in the financial cycle make it different from the others?

17–7. Which application systems are in each of the following transaction cycles?
a. Financial cycle.
b. Expenditure cycle.
c. Conversion cycle.
d. Revenue cycle.

17–8. How can the same transaction cycle differ significantly between different businesses, even if they are in the same industry?

17–9. What are the major accounting applications in companies in the following industries?
a. Agriculture.
b. Construction.
c. Health care.
d. Transportation.

17–10. What are the advantages of using transaction cycles to understand how accounting information systems work?

EXERCISES AND CASE

17–11. *APPLICATION SYSTEMS*

In the following columns, the left one contains transaction cycles and the right column lists application systems.

a. Revenue	1. Cost accounting
b. Expenditure	2. Order entry
c. Conversion	3. Cash disbursements
d. Financial	4. Cash receipts
	5. Shipping
	6. Journal entry
	7. Property
	8. Voucher
	9. Billing
	10. Receiving
	11. Payroll
	12. Inventory

Required:
Match each application system with the transaction cycle to which it belongs.

17–12. *ECONOMIC EVENTS*

The following left column contains transaction cycles. In the right column are economic events common in organizations.

a. Revenue	1. Request inputs to production.
b. Expenditure	2. Deliver goods to customer.
c. Conversion	3. Raise capital.
d. Financial	4. Use property in production.
	5. Recognize obligation to pay.
	6. Receive request from customer.
	7. Consume material and labor.
	8. Periodic reporting.
	9. Receive inputs to production.
	10. Receive payment from customers.

Required:
Match each economic event with the transaction cycle to which it belongs.

17–13. *ACCOUNTING ENTRIES*

The following list contains economic events common in organizations:

a. Receive material for use in production.
b. Ship goods to customers.

c. Receive a loan from a bank.
d. Pay employees.
e. Receive cash from customers.
f. Consume equipment in production.

Required:

Show the accounting entries for each of these economic events.

17–14. *BUSINESS ACTIVITIES*

Each of the activities in the following list is commonly performed by the employees of a business.

a. Mail an invoice to a customer.
b. Issue stock.
c. Manufacture a product.
d. Acquire equipment.
e. Provide a service for a customer.
f. Complete a timecard.
g. Fill out a receiving report.

Required:

Identify the transaction cycle in which the accounting system records each activity.

17–15. *DOCUMENTS*

The economic events in the following list are common in organizations:

a. Receive material for use in production.
b. Ship goods to customers.
c. Receive a loan from a bank.
d. Pay employees.
e. Receive cash from customers.
f. Consume equipment in production.

Required:

Identify the documents used by an accounting system to record each economic event.

17–16. *DATA FILES*

The data files in the following are maintained by accounting application systems:

a. Property master file.
b. General ledger master file.
c. Customer master file.
d. Vendor master file.

e. Open purchase order file.
f. Inventory master file.

Required:

For each file above, determine the transaction cycle or cycles that affect it.

17–17. DOCUMENTS

The documents in the following list are commonly used by accounting applications:

a. Material requisition.
b. Sales order.
c. Timecard.
d. Job cost sheet.
e. Standard journal voucher.
f. Receiving report.

Required:

Identify the transaction cycle of each document in the preceding list.

17–18. CONVERSION CYCLE

Mom's Cookie Company employs 17 people and produces 11 varieties of cookies for sale in local supermarkets. The firm purchases ingredients from a wholesale grocery company and stores them in a refrigerated storage area next to the bakery.

When a batch of cookies is started, an assistant baker blends into dough the appropriate ingredients for that particular cookie. A machine squirts dough onto oversize cookie sheets that the assistant baker inserts into ovens for baking. When done, a packing machine scrapes cookies, sold by weight rather than count, into bags. A packer then assembles them into cartons of 20 bags for delivery to supermarkets.

Required:

a. What are the inputs and outputs of this conversion process?
b. Which activities does the conversion process contain?
c. Which documents and records are needed to record the economic events in this conversion cycle?

17–19. CONVERSION CYCLE

Tiny TV Repair Co. has been in existence for two years. The owner and sole employee, Jo Wizard, works out of a shop in a building adjacent to her home. In this shop she stores tools and test equipment, as well as any televisions requiring major service that cannot be performed in owners' homes.

Because of the size of her business, Jo operates on a cash basis. When repairing a set, Jo's terms are strictly cash on delivery. The charges include an hourly rate plus the cost of any repair parts required. She maintains a charge account at a local electronic part supply house where she obtains repair supplies. Jo pays this account in full on a monthly basis.

Required:

a. What are the inputs and outputs of this conversion process?
b. Which activities does the conversion process contain?
c. Which documents and records are needed to record the economic events in this conversion cycle?

17–20. ***CONVERSION CYCLE***

Howell's Ready to Wear has been selling men's clothing in the same location for over 40 years. The founder, Henry Howell, has achieved stability and growth because of a reputation for service and fair dealing. The company now employs 12 sales personnel, an office administrator, and a bookkeeper. The business has a loyal clientele, in part because of Howell's record of community service and philanthropic activities.

Howell's avoids fashion fads, thereby minimizing the risk of obsolescence in the items it carries. As a result, sales are never held and profit margins are adequate on all items. Howell's maintains a sizable inventory of traditional styles in a wide range of selections and sizes. Sales personnel provide personal service of a kind seldom found in the larger chain stores, which constitute Howell's primary competition.

Required:

a. What are the inputs and outputs of this conversion process?
b. Which activities does the conversion process contain?
c. Which documents and records are needed to record the economic events in this conversion cycle?

17–21. ***TRANSACTION CYCLES***

Abacus Manufacturing Company operates a job shop producing a variety of heavy exercise equipment. These include stationary cycles, rowing machines, exercise machines, and barbell equipment. Customers are primarily chains of sporting goods stores scattered throughout the Midwest.

Abacus accepts orders for its products in lots of six or more items, producing to the specifications in the order. Prior to accepting an order from a customer, the sales manager prepares a quotation for the cost of the lot. He mails the quotation to the customer who signs it and returns a copy to the sales manager indicating acceptance of the terms. The sales manager then forwards the customer's order to the shop foreman and the quotation to the invoicing clerk.

Raw materials include steel bars, sheets, tubing, and angles; plastic foam padding; and plastic sheets. Abacus purchases these items in bulk from warehouse distributors and fabricates them into finished products.

When the shop foreman receives the customer's order, he verbally notifies the purchasing agent of the material needed for the job. The purchasing agent prepares a purchase order for the material and mails it to the supplier. When the material arrives, the supervisor at the loading dock prepares a receiving report and carries it to the accounting office. As soon as the invoice arrives from the supplier, the bookkeeper in the accounting office prepares and mails a check to the supplier in payment.

When manufacture of the lot is complete, all items in it are transferred to the loading dock. The loading supervisor then calls a truck line and arranges for delivery to the customer. The loading supervisor prepares a bill of lading in duplicate. One copy goes to the truck line and the other to the invoicing clerk, indicating that shipment has taken place. From it and the original quotation, the invoicing clerk prepares an invoice and mails it to the customer.

Required:

a. Draw a flowchart showing the events and documents just described in the revenue cycle at Abacus Manufacturing Company.

b. Draw a flowchart showing the events and documents used in the expenditure cycle of Abacus.

Chapter 18

Revenue Cycle Applications

Learning Objectives:

1. To review the accounting entries recorded in the revenue cycle.
2. To learn which documents, reports, and records are used in the revenue cycle.
3. To understand how accounting transactions are processed by the application systems in the revenue cycle.
4. To see how control practices and procedures are applied in the revenue cycle.

INTRODUCTION

An accounting system records the activities of a business using four transaction cycles. In this chapter, you learn how accounting systems record those activities that generate revenue. These activities are a part of the revenue cycle.

In this transaction cycle, the accounting system records four economic events. First, the organization receives a request for goods or services. Computer-based systems use an order entry application system to record these requests. Second, the organization delivers the goods or services. When goods are involved, a shipping application system records this event. Third, the organization requests payment for the goods or services; this economic event is processed by the billing system. An organization uses a cash receipts application system to record the fourth economic event, the receipt of cash in payment from the customer. Sometimes the billing and cash receipts applications together are called the accounts receivable system.

Illustration 18–1 shows the relationships among the application systems in the revenue cycle. In this diagram, circles represent application systems, the large square represents an external entity, and small squares stand for general ledger accounts. The interfaces between the systems contain accounting data and may take the form of the documents or computer records. You will learn about them in this chapter.

DOCUMENTS, RECORDS, AND REPORTS

An accounting system records economic events in the form of accounting transactions. In an introductory accounting course, you described this process conceptually by making journal entries. Very few organizations actually record transactions that way today. This chapter explains how application systems record the entries that you learned earlier. An application system captures transaction data on source documents, enters this data in the subsidiary accounting records, and discloses the transactions in reports.

ILLUSTRATION 18–1 Application Systems in the Revenue Cycle

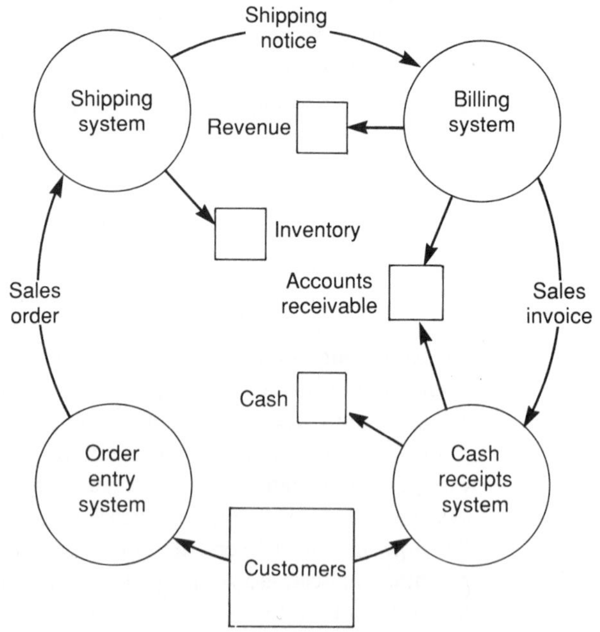

ILLUSTRATION 18–2 Revenue Cycle Transactions and Related Documents

Type of transaction	*Related documents*
Credit sale	Sales order Shipping notice Sales invoice
Cash sale	Sales ticket
Cash receipt	Remittance advice
Sales return	Credit memo
Sales allowance	Credit memo
Bad debt writeoff	Memo and aged accounts receivable trial balance Journal voucher

Revenue Cycle Transactions and Documents

This chapter discusses five transactions that occur routinely in the revenue cycle. Illustration 18–2 summarizes these transactions and shows the documents used by the accounting system in recording them.

Credit Sales. Most businesses sell to their customers on credit. The general ledger entry recording such a sale is

Dr.	Accounts Receivable	xxx	
Cr.	Sales		xxx

An accounting system records a credit sale in general and subsidiary ledgers using three documents. The sales department records the customer's request for merchandise or services on a *sales order.* The shipping department records shipment of merchandise on a *shipping notice*. (Sometimes a copy of the bill of lading, a document provided for the transportation company and completed by the shipping department, serves as a shipping notice.) The accounting department prepares a *sales invoice* and mails it to the customer requesting payment for the merchandise. From the sales invoice, the system records these entries in both the general ledger and the accounts receivable subsidiary record.

Illustrations 18–3, 18–4, and 18–5 contain examples of these documents. Their format and contents vary from company to company and from industry to industry. When designing the system, the design team ensures that these documents capture the data necessary to record properly the transaction in the accounting records and to produce management reports.

Usually when the customer is another business, the customer mails to the sales department a document called a *purchase order.* A sales clerk receives the purchase order and records its number and date on the sales order. This number then is recorded on all other records relating to that sales transaction, enabling

ILLUSTRATION 18–3 A Sales Order

Garage Repair Order

No. 10001

Quan.	Part No. And Description	Price
	Accessories	
	Sublet	

Name	Date
Address	City

Phone When Ready Yes ☐ No ☐	Res. Phone	Bus. Phone	Promised
License No.	Year	Make / Model	Mileage
Serial No.	Motor No.		Written by

Labor	√	Amount
Lubricate		
Change Oil		
Change Lub Trans ☐ Diff ☐		
Replace Oil Filter		
Clean Air Filter		
Repack Front Wheels		
Adj. Brakes		
Rotate Tires		
Wash ☐ Polish ☐		
Tune Motor		

I hereby authorize the above repair work to be done along with necessary materials. You and your employees may operate above vehicle for purposes of testing, inspection or delivery at my risk. An express mechanic's lien is acknowledged on above vehicle to secure the amount of repairs thereto. You will not be held responsible for loss or damage to vehicle or articles left in vehicle in case of fire, theft, accident or any other cause beyond your control.

Authorized By

	Total Labor
Gal. Gas @	Total Parts
Qts. Oil @	Total Accessories
Lbs. Grease @	Total Sublet
	Total Gas-Oil-Grease
	Tax
Total	Total

the customer and seller to identify the order in later correspondence. The next chapter describes the use of purchase orders in more detail.

Some organizations record sales not only by customer but also by product, salesperson, or district. They do so by maintaining subsidiary records for each. In a computerized system, the coding structure allows salesclerks to code transactions by product, salesperson, and district. A nonaccounting application system, the *sales analysis system,* summarizes these transactions and produces sales analysis reports for use by marketing personnel.

Cash Receipts. Businesses receive cash in return for their goods or services from two sources: credit sales and cash sales.

Cash Receipts from Credit Sales. The accounting entry recording a customer's payment for a sale made on credit is

ILLUSTRATION 18–4 A Shipping Notice

S H I P P I N G M E M O

TO: ______________________

ADDRESS: ______________________

DATE: __________

EMP # __________

PAGE # __________

MEMO # B-12286

I M P O R T A N T: ALL CREDIT MEMOS OR CORRESPONDENCE REGARDING MERCHANDISE SHIPPED TO YOU MUST BEAR OUR SHIPPING MEMO NUMBER AND DATE.

MFG. STYLE #		SIZE	UNITS	COST

TOTAL UNITS:

TOTAL COST:

Dr. Cash	xxx	
Cr. Accounts Receivable		xxx

Businesses ask customers to return a document called a *remittance advice* with their payments. The remittance advice shows the customer's account number and the amount paid, and is the system's source of data for making the entry in the accounts receivable subsidiary record.

Illustration 18–6, a remittance advice, shows the amount included and identifies the customer's account number. Accounts receivable procedures credit the customer's account from this document. Whenever a customer mails a cash

ILLUSTRATION 18–5 A Sales Invoice

INVOICE

T. L. James Enterprises
57 Executive Park Drive
Suite 200
Atlanta, Ga. 30329

INVOICE NUMBER 000017
INVOICE DATE 06/30/91
PAGE 1

SOLD TO
LINDSEY & LOVE FURNITURE
6104 ELLIOT STREET
TUCKER, GA 30341

SHIP TO
LINDSEY & LOVE FURNITURE
6104 ELLIOT STREET
TUCKER, GA 30341

SHIP VIA:
SHIP DATE: 05/30/91
DUE DATE: 06/30/91
TERMS: 0-30-30

CUST. I.D.: L L
P.O. NUMBER:
P.O. DATE: 04/30/91
OUR ORDER NO.:
SALESMAN:

PRODUCT I.D.	DESCRIPTION	ORDERED	SHIPPED	U M	UNIT PRICE	AMOUNT	TX
MIS10000VAS	VASE, ORIENTAL	1.00	1.00	EA	22.50	22.50	*
					NET AMOUNT:	22.50	
					TAX:	1.34	*
					TOTAL DUE:	23.84	

payment without including a remittance advice, a mail room employee must prepare one on a preprinted form prior to further processing.

Cash Receipts from Cash Sales. The required accounting entry to record a cash sale is

Dr.	Cash	xxx	
Cr.	Sales		xxx

When businesses make a cash sale, they safeguard the cash by placing it in a cash register. A salesclerk enters the amount of the sale either on a sales ticket or in an internal record maintained by the register. A sales supervisor reconciles these with the cash in the register at least once daily. The register also produces a receipt so the customer can verify that the transaction was recorded at the proper amount. This occurs each time you purchase from a retailer.

Sales Returns. A third transaction in the revenue cycle is the sales return. This occurs when a customer returns merchandise to the seller. Sometimes the customer is dissatisfied with the quality of the merchandise, or at other times the

ILLUSTRATION 18–6 A Remittance Advice

Southwestern Bell Telephone

** RETURN PAGE **

FEB 17 90 PAGE 1

DUE DATE MAR 15 | AMOUNT DUE 11.79

** PLEASE MAIL THIS PAGE WITH YOUR PAYMENT **

CAR-RT SORT **CR13
J L BOOCKHOLDT S67
3440 ARLINGTON
HOUSTON TX 77008

03 17

MAKE CHECKS PAYABLE TO:
SOUTHWESTERN BELL TELEPHONE

P.O. BOX 1550
HOUSTON TX 77097-0047

99 67 7136630098 632 0416 0430 510010 000000000 000001179 05

See Reverse THANK YOU FOR PAYING BY MAIL

Courtesy of Southwestern Bell Telephone Company.

seller ships a quantity in excess of that desired. In either case, the seller usually subtracts the cost of the returned items from the balance owed by the customer. The entry recording a sales return is

Dr.	Sales Returns	xxx	
Cr.	Accounts Receivable		xxx

The accounting system documents a sales return with a *credit memo*. The credit memo shows the customer's name, account number, and the amount for the entry. The billing department attaches it to a memo from the customer and a receiving report from the receiving department showing the quantity of the items returned. These documents allow the treasurer to authorize the entry.

Illustration 18–7 shows a credit memo which the system prepares in two copies. The billing department uses one to record the credit in the subsidiary ledger; the other records the transaction in the general ledger.

Because the credit memo also records a fourth transaction, the sales allowance, some companies call it a *sales return and allowance memo*.

Sales Allowances. A sales allowance occurs when the sales department agrees to give the customer credit for items that were not returned. For example, if defective merchandise was shipped, the sales department may authorize a deduction from the customer's balance without requiring return of the merchandise. The entry for a sales allowance is

ILLUSTRATION 18–7 A Credit Memo

SUNLIGHT MANUFACTORY COMPANY
105 Red Hot Road
Dallas, Texas 75248

CM no. B6941

To:

Date:

Your memo number	Your memo date	Credit	Customer number	Salesperson number

Product code	Product description	Quantity returned	Unit price	Total

1. Billing

2. General Ledger

Dr.	Sales Allowances	xxx	
Cr.	Accounts Receivable		xxx

The sales department prepares a memo explaining why the credit to the customer's account is justified. This initiates the preparation of a credit memo by the billing system to record this entry in the accounts receivable subsidiary records.

Sometimes a thief attempts to make a fraudulent entry in the sales allowances account to cover the theft of merchandise. For this reason, all credit memos should be approved by a manager or supervisor who has no access to the merchandise.

Bad Debts Write-Off. When a business determines that the cash from a credit sale will never be received, management may choose to give up efforts at collecting it and assume that it is a bad debt. The entry to record a bad debt write-off is

Dr.	Allowance for Doubtful Accounts	xxx	
Cr.	Accounts Receivable		xxx

The credit department usually initiates a bad debts write-off after efforts to collect from the customer have failed. The credit manager documents the inability to collect the account in a memo. The treasurer authorizes the write-off by approving the memo, and the accounting department prepares a journal voucher to record it in the general ledger. The billing system removes the bad debt from the accounts receivable subsidiary records.

The documents in the revenue cycle generate the accounting entries produced from the data on these documents. Accounting systems enter this data in the accounting records and summarize it to produce reports.

Revenue Cycle Reports

Application systems in the revenue cycle produce three kinds of reports: control reports, registers, and special purpose reports.

Control Reports. Accounting systems produce control reports whenever they process multiple changes to a file. Control reports may disclose the transactions posted, the total number or amount of these transactions, or list changes made during file maintenance. In computer-based systems, control reports disclose record counts, control totals, and hash totals. Data control clerks review control reports, comparing these totals to verify that all changes were made properly.

Illustration 18–8 contains a control report prepared by a billing application; it shows the entries produced by the system for posting to the general ledger. Most systems prepare a similar control report when entering the other changes.

Registers. A register is a listing of all the transactions of a certain type that were processed during a single processing period. For example, if the accounting system requires preparation of invoices each day, then it produces a daily *invoice register* showing all sales invoices prepared during the day. This register, as shown in Illustration 18–9, also summarizes the total credit sales entries made during the day.

The revenue cycle produces other registers as well; an accounting system usually has a cash receipts register and a credit memo register. In a manual system, the register is the journal in which transactions are initially recorded. In computerized systems, registers are frequently identified as "journals" for this reason.

Registers are important components in accounting systems because they provide an audit trail. They allow auditors to link the documents recording transactions with the general ledger account balance summarizing them.

ILLUSTRATION 18–8 A Control Report

RUN DATE 06/30/91 T.L. JAMES ENTERPRISES PAGE 1
Accounts Receivable
Create G/L Journal Entries CONTROL REPORT
SELECTION: REPORT ONLY

ACCT.	SC	REF.	DESC.	DATE	DEBIT	CREDIT	NET
11100	R	000024		06/15/91	3120.00	0.00	3120.00
11100	R	000025		06/15/91	3439.49	0.00	3439.49
11100	R	000025		06/15/91	143.31	0.00	143.31
11100	R	000034		06/15/91	263.68	0.00	263.68
11100	R	000029		06/15/91	1942.98	0.00	1942.98
11100	R	000029		06/15/91	124.02	0.00	124.02
11100	R	000036		06/15/91	1477.77	0.00	1477.77
11100	R	000036		06/15/91	61.57	0.00	61.57
11100	R	000030		06/15/91	2476.83	0.00	2476.83
11100	R	000031		06/15/91	185.40	0.00	185.40
11100	R	000032		06/15/91	1469.78	0.00	1469.78
11100	R	000032		06/15/91	61.24	0.00	61.24
11100	R	000033		06/15/91	676.00	0.00	676.00
11100	R	000035		06/15/91	380.07	0.00	380.07
11100	R	000028		06/15/91	4602.94	0.00	4602.94
11100	R	000028		06/15/91	191.79	0.00	191.79
				ACCOUNT TOTAL	20616.87	0.00	20616.87
30104	R	000034		06/15/91	0.00	263.68-	263.68-
30104	R	000032		06/15/91	0.00	1469.78-	1469.78-
				ACCOUNT TOTAL	0.00	1733.46-	1733.46-

Special Purpose Reports. Most systems require three special purpose accounting reports in the revenue cycle. They are the customer statement, the aged accounts receivable trial balance, and the remittance list. In addition, systems may produce sales analysis reports for evaluating management performance.

Customer Statement. A customer statement is a list of all transactions in a customer's account during a specified time period. Many businesses mail a monthly statement to each active customer. It shows the sales made to the customer since the last statement, the payments received, and the balance still owed by the customer.

Monthly statements are beneficial for two reasons: First, they enable the customers to monitor transactions in their accounts. This may disclose errors or irregularities undetected by the control procedures in the accounting system. Second, they remind customers about outstanding balances, which sometimes encourages customers to pay their accounts more promptly. Illustration 18–10 shows a monthly statement.

ILLUSTRATION 18–9 A Register

RUN DATE 06/30/91 — T. L. JAMES ENTERPRISES — PAGE 1

Invoicing

REPORT DATE 06/30/91 — Product Invoice Register

INVOICE NUMBER	INVOICE DATE	CUST. ID	CUSTOMER NAME	TERMS	MERCHANDISE	OTHER CHARGES	FREIGHT	SALES TAX	INVOICE TOTAL
000045	06/30/91	123456	BETTY'S HOME INTERIORS	0-60-60	5.00	0.00	0.00	0.20	5.20
000046	06/30/91	ABE	ABE APPLIANCE & FURNITURE	2/10, NET 30	1199.97	0.00	0.00	48.00	1247.97
000047	06/30/91	BOWERS	BOWER'S FURNITURE MART	2/10, NET 30	1100.00	0.00	0.00	0.00	1100.00
000048	06/30/91	HABERS	HABERSHAM'S INTERIORS	2/10, NET 30	274.00	0.00	0.00	0.00	274.00
000049	06/30/91	MERMKT	MERCHANDISE MARKET, THE	2/10, NET 30	455.97	0.00	0.00	0.00	455.97
000050	06/30/91	SOFAS	SOFAS & STUFF	2/10, NET 30	1599.97	0.00	0.00	0.00	1599.97
000051	06/30/91	123456	BETTY'S HOME INTERIORS	0-60-60	391.96	0.00	0.00	15.68	407.64
NO. OF ITEMS LISTED: 7				TOTALS	5026.87	0.00	0.00	63.88	5090.75

REPORT SUMMARY TOTALS

	TAXABLE	NON-TAXABLE	GROSS
SALES :	1596.93	3429.94	5026.87
MISC. DEBITS :	0.00	0.00	0.00
RETURNS :	0.00	0.00	0.00
MISC. CREDITS :	0.00	0.00	0.00
FREIGHT :	0.00	0.00	0.00
SUB-TOTALS :	1596.93	3429.94	5026.87
CREDITS :	0.00	0.00	0.00
PAYMENTS :	0.00	0.00	0.00
ADJUSTMENTS :	0.00	0.00	0.00
SERVICE CHARGES :	0.00	0.00	0.00

TAXES:	SALES TAXES	TAX REFUNDS	GROSS
STATE :	47.91	0.00	47.91
COUNTY :	15.97	0.00	15.97
CITY :	0.00	0.00	0.00
SUB-TOTAL TAXES :	63.88	0.00	63.88
REPORT TOTAL :			5090.75

*** END OF INVOICE REGISTER ***

ILLUSTRATION 18–10 A Customer Statement

STATEMENT

T. L. James Enterprises
57 Executive Park Drive
Suite 200
Atlanta, Ga. 30329

STATEMENT DATE 06/30/91

ACCOUNT NUMBER 123456

PAGE 1

BETTY'S HOME INTERIORS
2435 WILDWOOD BLVD.
MARIETTA, GA 43434
ATTN: BETTY SCHMIDT

AMOUNT REMITTED

$ ________________

RETURN THIS PORTION OF STATEMENT
WITH YOUR PAYMENT

INVOICE	DATE	TERMS OF SALE	CODE	DEBITS	CREDITS	BALANCE
000021	04/01/91		MD	671.82		671.82
				671.82	0.00	671.82

CURRENT	1-30	31-60
0.00	0.00	0.00
OVER 60	**TOTAL**	**OPEN CR**
671.82	671.82	0.00

TOTAL DUE 671.82

ILLUSTRATION 18–11 An Aged Accounts Receivable Trial Balance

RUN DATE 06/30/91 T.L. JAMES ENTERPRISES PAGE 1
REPORT DATE 06/30/91 Accounts Receivable
AGEING DATE 06/30/91 Detailed Aged Receivables Report

CUST.ID	CUSTOMER NAME	PHONE	INVOICE	DUE DATE	CURRENT	1 - 30 PAST DUE	31 - 60 PAST DUE	OVER 60 PAST DUE	OPEN CR	TOTAL
123456	BETTY'S HOME INTERIORS	404-234-2343	000021	05/31/91		671.82				671.82
A B	A&B FURNITURE & TV SALES	404/366-1567	000018	04/30/91				900.14		900.14
			000024	07/15/91	3120.00					3120.00
					3120.00	0.00	0.00	900.14	0.00	4020.14
MERMKT	MERCHANDISE MARKET, THE	404/653-8945	000036	07/15/91	1539.34					1539.34
SOFAS	SOFAS & STUFF	404/958-4562	000030	07/15/91	2476.83					2476.83
	TOTALS				13617.49	1789.77	0.00	900.14	0.00	23874.62

*** END OF Detailed Aged Receivables Report ***

Aged Accounts Receivable Trial Balance. An accounts receivable trial balance is a list of all customers and the balances they owe at a specified date. When this trial balance is *aged,* each customer balance is categorized according to how long it has existed. Usually an aged accounts receivable trial balance discloses for each customer the amounts less than 30 days old, and those 30 to 60, 60 to 90, and more than 90 days old. Illustration 18–11 contains an aged accounts receivable trial balance.

Many businesses produce aged accounts receivable trial balances each month. Credit managers review them to identify customer accounts that are unpaid for excessive lengths of time. They also use these documents to determine when customers' accounts should be written off as uncollectible. Accountants use these trial balances to determine the adequacy of the Allowance for Doubtful Accounts.

Remittance List. A remittance list enumerates all currency and checks received during one day. It establishes a control total over cash receipts, prevents theft, and ensures that no receipts are lost before being credited to a customer's account. Illustration 18–12 shows a remittance list.

ILLUSTRATION 18–12 A Remittance List

SUNLIGHT MANUFACTORY COMPANY
105 Red Hot Road
Dallas, Texas 75248

Remittance list

No. ________

Date ________

Check no.	Customer name	Amount	Check here if remittance advice is attached
4123	ABC Company	123.29	✓
816	H. Jackson	19.56	✓
2803	Betty's Home Interiors	228.00	✓
666	I.M. Able	26.00	
	Total	4,012.20	

In many companies, customers' payments for credit sales arrive in the mail. These companies assign the responsibility for opening the mail to a mail room clerk who also prepares the remittance list. One copy accompanies the checks which go to the company cashier, and the other goes with the remittance advices to the accounting department.

This procedure implements segregation of duties over cash receipts because the cashier has custody of the checks while the accounting department has the records regarding them. The use of a remittance list allows an auditor or manager to determine that no remittance advice has been removed to cover the theft of a check.

Sales Analysis Reports. From the accounting files maintained in the revenue cycle, the sales analysis application produces various management performance reports. These summarize sales revenue, costs, and profit margin by customer, product, salesperson, or by sales district. They enable marketing management to evaluate the profitabilty of products, the performance of sales personnel, or the effects of special advertising campaigns or promotions.

The revenue cycle produces three kinds of reports: Control reports ensure that changes are made correctly, registers provide an audit trail, and special purpose reports provide management information. Application systems in the other cycles produce these kinds of reports as well.

Accounting systems capture transaction data in documents and disclose this data in reports. They produce these reports from data contained in the accounting records.

Revenue Cycle Accounting Records

Accounting systems maintain records in journals, ledgers, and filing cabinets for manual processes, and in computer files and data bases for computerized ones. Although the forms of the records differ, their contents are similar.

Noncomputerized Records. Manual journals and ledgers may be in the form of books or card files. In the revenue cycle, the accounting records consist of three special journals and one subsidiary ledger.

The subsidiary ledger is the accounts receivable subsidiary ledger. It contains one page or card for each customer. This page shows debit and credit postings from the journals to the account of that customer and the balance the customer owes.

The special journals are the sales journal, the credit memo journal, and the cash receipts journal. Accounting clerks enter transactions chronologically in these journals from documents. Then daily, weekly, or monthly, totals from these journals are transferred to the general ledger and the accounts receivable subsidiary ledger.

Illustration 18–13 shows how these records look.

Computerized Records. Accounting records kept by computerized processes are in the form of computer files and data bases. In a traditional data file system, revenue cycle applications use two master files and as many as six transaction files.

If data base management system (DBMS) software is used, the applications do not maintain separate files. Instead, they store data in the data base and each application has access to this data determined by the application's subschema. The subschema contains the same data fields provided by the files in a traditional data file system.

Master Files. Applications in the revenue cycle routinely update the *customer master file*. This file has one record for each credit customer and contains data on the customer's address, credit limit, credit terms, and balance owed. During system design, the design team determines that this record contains data required to maintain the accounting records and produce management reports.

Illustration 18–14 shows the contents of a record. By comparing these contents with Illustration 18–13, you can see that the customer master file is the computerized equivalent of the accounts receivable subsidiary ledger in a manual system.

The shipping application also updates the *inventory master file* which contains perpetual inventory records. It has one record for each item kept in the inventory

ILLUSTRATION 18–13 Noncomputerized Accounting Records

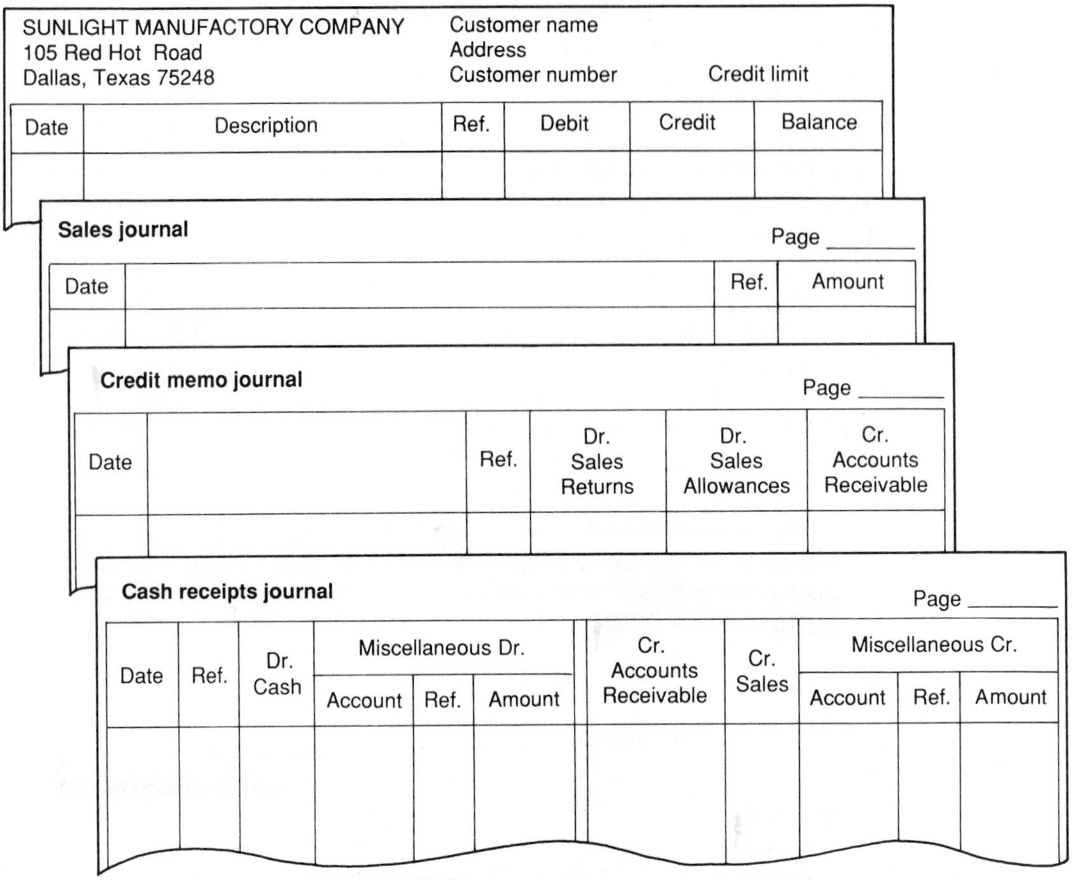

ILLUSTRATION 18–14 Contents of a Customer Master Record

1. CUSTOMER-NUMBER*
2. CUSTOMER-NAME
3. BILLING-ADDRESS
4. SHIPPING-ADDRESS
5. CREDIT-LIMIT
6. CREDIT-TERMS
7. STATEMENT-DATE
8. STATEMENT-BALANCE
9. CURRENT-BALANCE

*Designates the primary key.

Inv Master File

ILLUSTRATION 18–15 Contents of an Invoice Detail Record

1. INVOICE-NUMBER*
2. TRANSACTION-CODE*
3. CUSTOMER-NUMBER**
4. TRANSACTION-DATE
5. SALES-ORDER-NUMBER
6. SHIPPING-NOTICE-NUMBER
7. SALES-TERMS
8. RESPONSIBILITY-CODE
9. PRODUCT-CODE
10. PRODUCT-PRICE
11. PRODUCT-QUANTITY
12. TRANSACTION-AMOUNT

*Designates the primary key.
**Designates a secondary key.

warehouse. When merchandise is shipped, the billing application subtracts the quantity shipped from the quantity on hand in the inventory master file. A later chapter on conversion cycle applications describes its other contents.

Transaction Files. Different companies process revenue cycle transactions in various ways. Businesses relying on noncomputerized processes use fewer transaction files than highly computerized firms. With noncomputerized processes, data flows between departments on documents rather than on computer records. Depending on the extent of computerization, a computer-based system may have as many as six transaction files.

The *invoice detail* file contains one record for each sales invoice mailed to a customer. The billing application adds a record to this file when a sales invoice is mailed, and the cash receipts application removes the record when the invoice is paid. Illustration 18–15 shows the contents of a record in this file; as you can see, it is the same data contained on a sales invoice.

The RESPONSIBILITY-CODE field identifies the salesperson and sales division producing the sale. The responsibility accounting system uses this field to summarize sales transactions by responsibility center on performance reports. The TRANSACTION-CODE field contains a code identifying this as a record representing a sales invoice. Illustration 18–16 contains an example set of transaction codes.

Computerized systems may also have a sales order detail file and a shipments file. The *sales order detail* file contains one record for each customer sales order that has been accepted, and contains the data shown on a customer sales order. It is created by the order entry application and provides inputs to the shipping application. The *shipments* file contains one record for each shipment made to a customer, and contains the data shown on the shipping notice. After the shipping application creates it, the record is an input to the billing application.

The *cash receipts detail* file contains the transactions processed by the cash receipts application. A data entry clerk adds a transaction record to this file for each remittance advice received from a customer. The cash receipts application then identifies the transaction with an unpaid invoice record from the invoice detail file, deletes the invoice record, and posts the cash receipt to the customer

Invoice Master File

ILLUSTRATION 18–16 Transaction Codes

12	Cash collection from customers' payment on account
27	Sales on account
72	Sales returns
82	Sales allowances
92	Write-off of accounts receivable

master file. Illustration 18–17 shows the contents of a record in the cash receipts detail file.

The *accounts receivable change log* file provides an audit trail and allows preparation of monthly customer statements. It contains one record for each change to a customer's balance since the date of the last statement. The billing and cash receipts applications add a record to this file for each invoice detail record and cash receipts detail record they process. When customer statements are printed, a program in the billing application converts the accounts receivable change log file into an archival file. The MIS department keeps this file on tape for use by the auditors. Illustration 18–18 shows the contents of a record.

Revenue cycle applications also provide inputs to another file, the *general ledger batch summary* file. After producing all records for the accounts receivable change log file, the billing application prepares a transaction record containing the general ledger entry summarizing the transactions. Similarly, the cash receipts application adds a transaction record to this file summarizing all cash receipts transactions. Throughout the month these and other application systems add transaction records to the general ledger batch summary file. Then during the monthly closing process, the general ledger application posts these records to the general ledger master file. The general ledger batch summary file is also discussed in the chapters describing the other transaction cycles.

ILLUSTRATION 18–17 Contents of a Cash Receipts Detail Record

1. INVOICE-NUMBER*
2. TRANSACTION-CODE*
3. CUSTOMER-NUMBER**
4. TRANSACTION-DATE
5. CUSTOMER-CHECK-NUMBER
6. DATE-RECEIVED
7. AMOUNT

*Designates the primary key.
**Designates a secondary key.

ILLUSTRATION 18–18 Contents of an Accounts Receivable Change Log Record

1. CUSTOMER-NUMBER*
2. DATE*
3. TRANSACTION-CODE*
4. TRANSACTION-AMOUNT
5. INVOICE/CM-NUMBER

*Designates the primary key.

Types of Accounts Receivable Systems. A computerized system maintains accounts receivable records in the customer master file and the invoice detail file. Depending on how much data is kept in these files, they are categorized as balance only, balance forward, or open item systems.

Balance Only Systems. In a balance only system, the customer master file contains only the current balance of the customer. The system uses no invoice detail file. Detailed data on customers' purchases and payments is available only from manual files containing copies of the original documents.

Some older credit card and department store credit sale applications use the balance only approach. Their monthly statements disclose only the current amount owed by the customer. They include copies of the documents with the monthly statement mailed to customers to support the balance due.

Balance Forward Systems. In a balance forward system, the record in the customer master file shows both the customer's current balance and the balance as of the last statement date. The invoice detail file contains records for all invoices prepared since that date. The system routinely deletes old records for the customer from the invoice detail file when it prints the customer's monthly statement. This system uses prior customer statements to obtain detail data supporting balances more than one month old.

Newer credit card and department store systems are of the balance forward type. Your credit card statements probably show your unpaid balance at the beginning of the billing cycle, the transactions in your account since then, and the resulting balance at the billing date.

Open Item Systems. An open item system is similar to a balance forward one except that it has a larger invoice detail file. In an open item system, this file contains a record for each unpaid invoice. The system deletes records from the file when the invoice is paid.

When customers make payments, they may not identify specific invoices for them. Instead, they may pay either a fixed amount or the amount on their statements. An open item system must be able to accept such payments and treat them as partial payments on invoices. This is called an *automatic cash application* feature.

Businesses that sell to other businesses use open item systems. They frequently establish discounting policies that encourage customers to pay specific invoices promptly.

The revenue cycle can use both computerized and manual accounting records. As you can see, the contents of the records in the two recording media are similar. In many respects, the methods of processing them are also similar.

TRANSACTION PROCESSING

In an introductory accounting course you studied the procedures for recording transactions in journals and ledgers. In a large company these procedures may be performed by different people. A computer-based accounting system implements many of these procedures using computer programs. These computer programs, together with documents, reports, records, and manual procedures, constitute a computer application system.

Manual Processes

Before the development of computers, companies processed transactions manually; today, few have manual systems. Instead, most companies use a combination of computerized and manual procedures. For this reason, you should understand noncomputerized as well as computerized processes.

Credit Sales. Illustration 18–19 shows manual procedures for processing credit sales transactions. The sales department initiates the transaction by completing a customer sales order. Once the credit department approves credit for this customer, the shipping department obtains the merchandise from the warehouse and ships it. The shipping department sends a shipping notice to the billing department, which initiates preparation of a sales invoice.

Illustration 18–20 depicts the manual procedures for processing sales returns, sales allowances, and bad debt write-offs. The sales department initiates returns and allowances, while the credit department initiates the write-off of an account as uncollectible. The treasurer approves each transaction before the accounting department enters it in the accounting records. The receiving department completes a receiving report to document the return of goods.

Cash Receipts. Illustration 18–21 contains manual procedures for processing cash receipts. The mail room receives customers' payments from credit sales, while the sales department receives them from cash sales. All cash goes directly to the cashier for deposit in the bank, while remittance advices and sales tickets go to the accounting department for entry in the accounting records.

ILLUSTRATION 18–19 Manual Procedures for Credit Sales

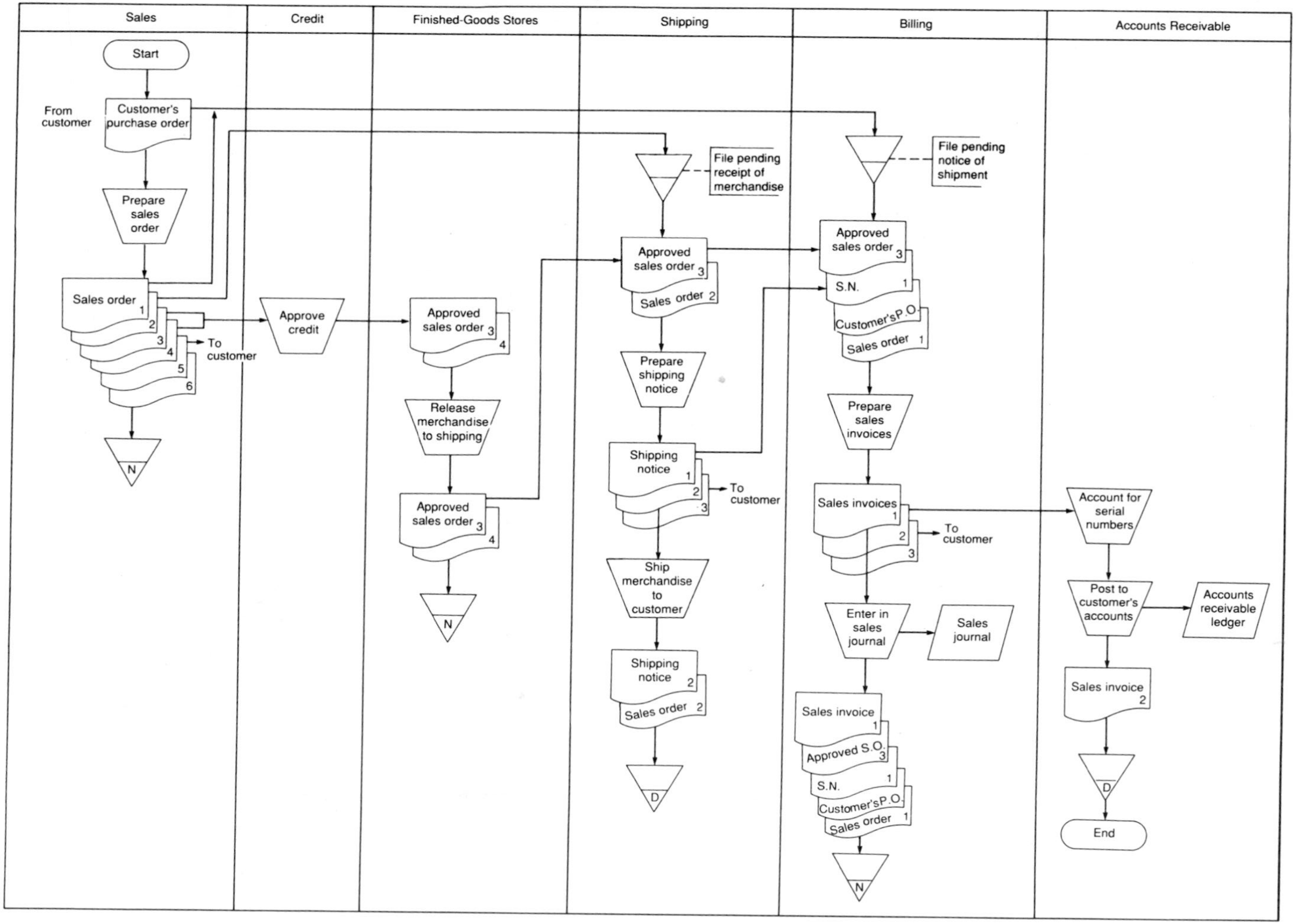

ILLUSTRATION 18–20 Manual Procedures for Sales Returns, Allowances, and Bad Debt Write-Offs

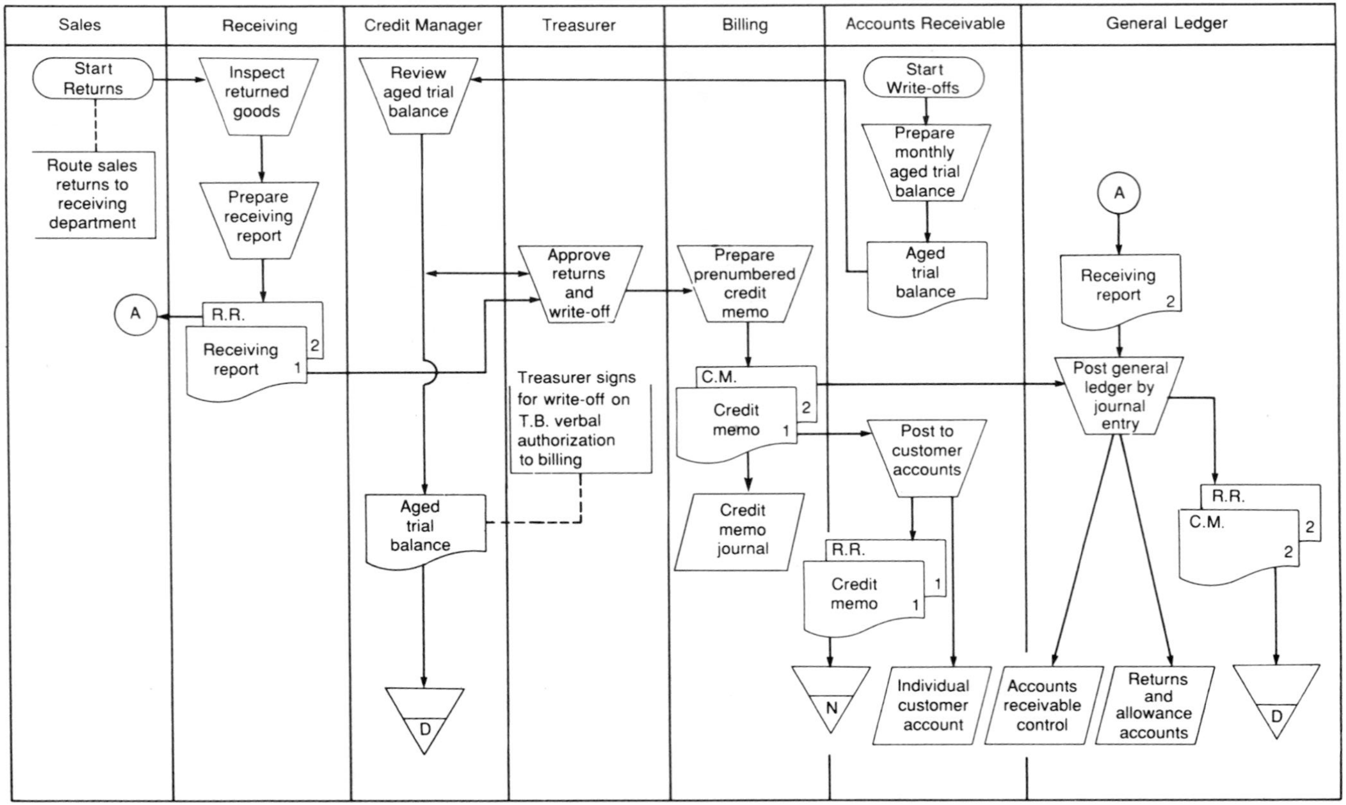

ILLUSTRATION 18–21 Manual Procedures for Cash Receipts

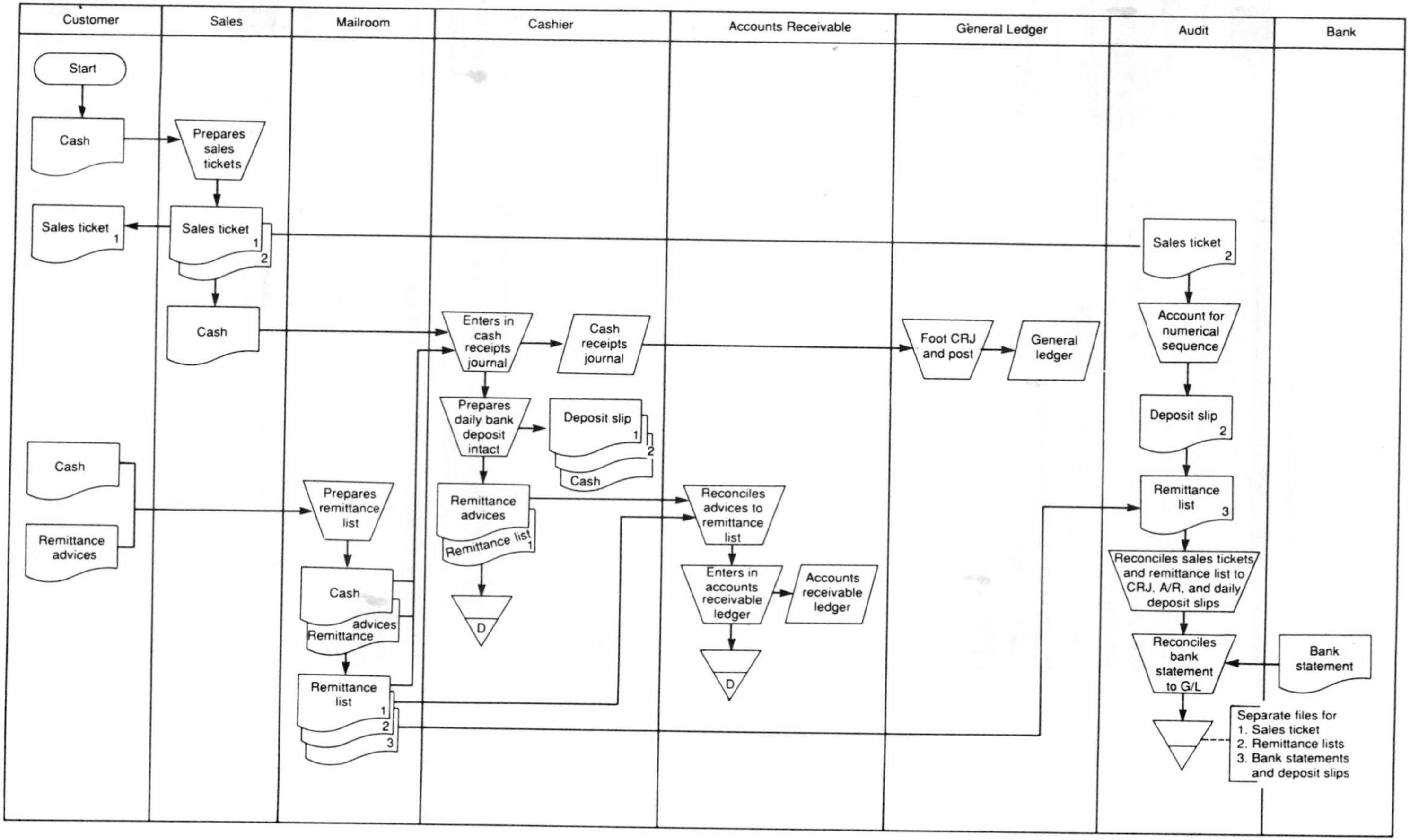

Control Procedures. Manual procedures for processing transactions should provide adequate segregation of duties and should implement other good control practices. The chapter on internal control structure describes these practices. Segregation of duties requires separation of three functions: custody of the asset, recordkeeping for the asset, and authorizing transactions in the asset.

Credit Sales. The sales order entry personnel and the credit department authorize credit sales transactions. Inventory warehouse and shipping personnel have physical custody of inventory prior to shipment. Accounts receivable and general ledger clerks keep the records regarding credit sales. Thus segregation of duties requires that these functions are assigned to different individuals.

Most companies also assign duties so that order entry is separate from credit approval, inventory warehouse is separate from shipping, and maintaining accounts receivable detail records is separate from maintaining the general ledger. These divisions not only provide improved control by allowing employees to verify the actions of others but also improve efficiency by allowing specialization.

For example, the credit department verifies that sales personnel do not accept a sales order from a customer unable to pay for it. Because credit department employees work full time evaluating the creditworthiness of customers, they become skilled at making these decisions.

Sales Returns and Allowances. Usually a customer service department and a credit department authorize sales returns and allowances transactions. A receiving department and personnel in the inventory warehouse have custody of returned goods. Accounts receivable and general ledger clerks maintain records regarding these transactions. A company that maintains these distinctions implements adequate segregation of duties over sales returns and allowances.

As with credit sales transactions, companies frequently further divide responsibilities to improve control and efficiency.

Bad Debts Write-Off. Segregation of duties over a credit transaction prevents an employee from intercepting a payment from a customer, stealing the check, and then writing off the debt as uncollectible. Someone in the treasurer's department, such as a cashier, has custody of cash when it is received. Accounts receivable and general ledger personnel keep the records regarding cash and bad debts. In most companies a credit manager authorizes a bad debt write-off and the treasurer approves it. With good segregation of duties, these positions are separate.

Illustration 18–22 summarizes good internal control measures for credit sales, sales returns, sales allowances, and bad debt write-off transactions. The upper part of the illustration identifies the duties that should be segregated for good internal control. The lower part identifies good control practices over the documents and records used to process the transaction.

For example, the upper left column identifies good segregation of duties over credit sales transactions. These require that order entry and credit granting procedures are assigned to different people. Furthermore, custody of the inventory in the warehouse should be separate from the shipping function, and

ILLUSTRATION 18–22 Controls for Billing Transactions

Credit sales	*Sales returns sales allowances*	*Bad debts write-off*
	Segregation of duties	
1. Order entry and credit 2. Warehouse and shipping 3. Accounts receivable and general ledger	1. Customer service and credit 2. Receiving and warehouse 3. Accounts receivable and general ledger	1. Credit and treasurer 2. Cashier 3. Accounts receivable and general ledger
	Control practices	
1. Sales invoice	1. Sales returns and allowance memo	1. Write-off memorandum
a. Prepared only on receipt of customer purchase order	*a*. Prepared only on receipt of goods and/or customer advice	*a*. Prepared only with proper documentation
b. Prenumbered	*b*. Prenumbered	*b*. Approved
c. Credit approved	*c*. Return or allowance approved	*c*. Approved by a second officer if amount is over certain limit
d. Checked against current price list	*d*. Price checked against sales invoice	
e. Verified before sent to customer	*e*. Verified before sent to customer	
2. Goods	2. Returned goods	
a. Order filled only with approved sales invoice	*a*. Sales returns and allowance memo prepared only on receipt of goods	
b. Quantity independently counted	*b*. Quantity independently counted	
c. Shipped to customer only on receipt of sales invoice from order entry		
3. Accounts receivable	3. Accounts receivable	2. Accounts receivable
a. Posted daily	*a*. Posted daily	
b. Control total established daily	*b*. Control total established daily	*a*. Control total established
c. Customer statement sent monthly		
d. Aged accounts receivable trial balance prepared monthly		
4. General ledger	4. General ledger	3. General ledger
a. Standard journal voucher used	*a*. Standard journal voucher used	*a*. Standard journal voucher used
b. Control total compared daily	*b*. Control total compared daily	*b*. Control total compared
c. Journal entry made daily	*c*. Journal entry made daily	

employees who maintain accounts receivable detail records should not also maintain the general ledger. The lower left column in Illustration 18–22 shows proper control practices for the sales invoice, the goods sold, the accounts receivable detail records, and the general ledger.

Customer Payments on Account. These transactions represent cash receipts received in the mail. Mail room personnel and the cashier have custody of these assets each day. These duties should be separate from those of people maintaining accounts receivable and general ledger records.

Separating accounts receivable processing from that for the general ledger makes falsifying accounts receivable records more difficult. If an accounts receivable clerk creates a false entry, perhaps to cover the theft of a customer's payment, the clerk must also falsify a general ledger entry. This is examined by a general ledger clerk who may detect it as a fraudulent entry. Otherwise, a supervisor or auditor detects the theft when reconciling the accounts receivable detail records with the general ledger control account.

Cash Sales. Sales personnel and the cashier have custody of the assets arising from these transactions. Accountability for cash is established by recording each cash sale in a cash register or terminal and providing each customer with a receipt. Customers verify that the amount of the sale on the receipt and recorded in the register is correct. This creates records for the asset summarized in the general ledger. Illustration 18–23 applies segregation of duties and good control practices to cash receipts.

Computerized Processes

A computer-based accounting system uses both computerized and manual processes. In the revenue cycle, a computer-based system used four application systems: the order entry, shipping, billing, and cash receipts applications.

Order Entry Application. The purpose of the order entry application is to record a customer's request for goods or services, to obtain credit approval for the customer, and to ensure that the order is filled.

Procedures for credit approval usually require the credit department to establish a credit limit for each customer. This credit limit is the maximum unpaid balance the customer is allowed to have. Whenever an order is received from a customer, the order entry system determines if the order would cause the outstanding balance to exceed the credit limit. If so, the customer's order is disapproved.

Illustration 18–24 contains flowcharts of batch and on-line real-time order entry systems. Each produces an *order acknowledgment* that is mailed to the customer to confirm acceptance of the order. Each also produces a sales register and a sales order detail file.

ILLUSTRATION 18–23 Controls for Cash Receipts Transactions

Customers' payment on account	*Cash sales*
Segregation of duties	
1. Mail room and cashier	1. Counter sales and cashier
2. Mail room and accounts receivable	
3. Cashier and accounts receivable	
4. Cashier and general ledger	2. Cashier and general ledger
5. Accounts receivable and general ledger	
Control practices	
1. Initial documentation	1. Initial documentation
a. Remittance list prepared by the mail room as soon as mail is opened	*a.* Prepared before asking customer to pay
b. Remittance list is prenumbered	*b.* Prenumbered
	c. Tendered to customer as a matter of course
	d. Control total established for each shift
2. Cash receipts	2. Cash receipts
a. Deposited intact daily	*a.* Deposited intact daily
b. Authenticated deposit slip secured	*b.* Authenticated deposit slip secured
3. Accounts receivable	3. Sales
a. Posted daily	
b. Control total established daily	*a.* Control total established daily
c. Customer statement sent monthly	
4. General ledger	4. General ledger
a. Standard journal voucher used	*a.* Standard journal voucher used
b. Control total compared daily	*b.* Control total compared daily
c. Journal entry made daily	*c.* Journal entry made daily

The batch system contains a validation program that examines transactions and lists errors. The sales department must correct these errors and reenter the transactions. In the on-line real-time system, the program controlling data entry performs validation procedures.

On-line real-time systems provide query capability, allowing users to examine the contents of specific records in the file. In this order entry application, a sales clerk may query the customer master file to determine a customer's balance, credit limit, or terms of sale. The clerk may also query the order entry detail file to determine the status of a past order.

ILLUSTRATION 18–24 An Order Entry Application

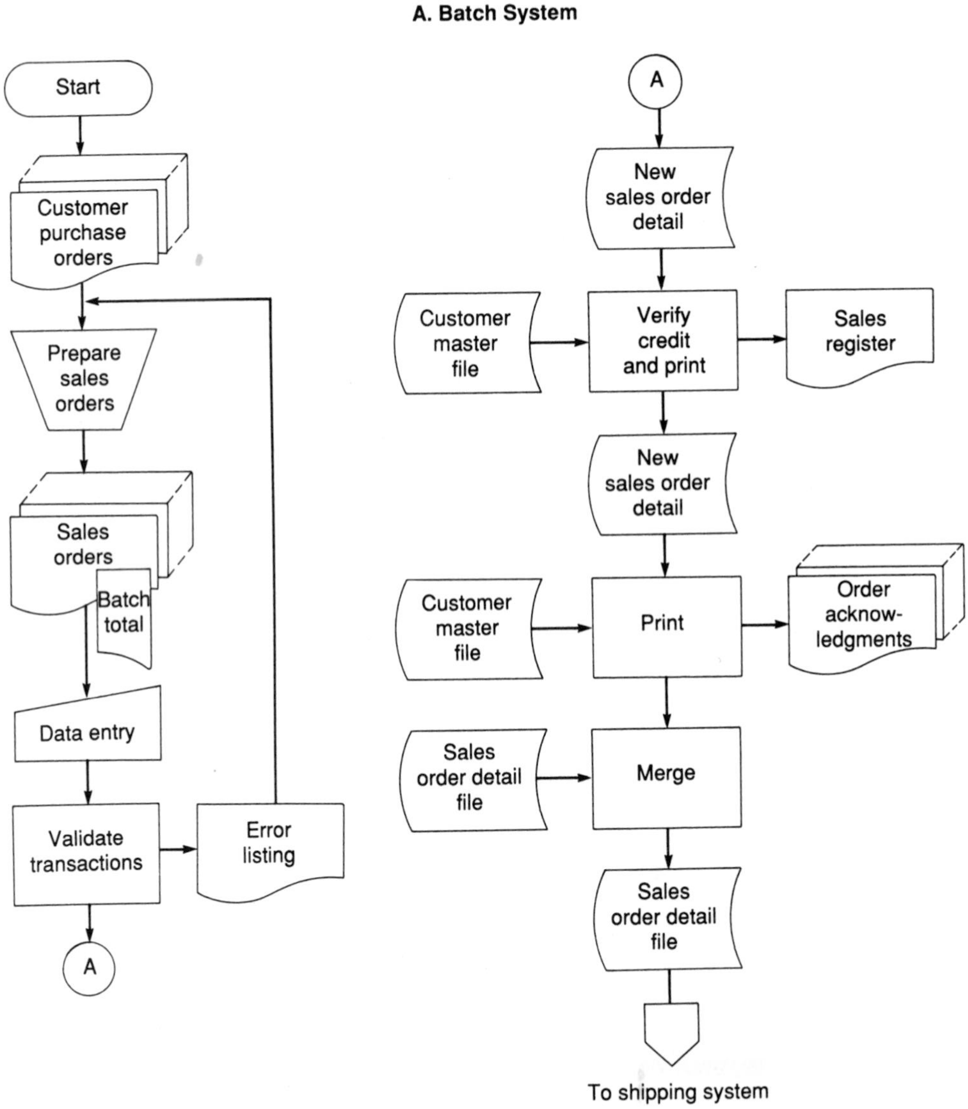

Shipping Application. The purposes of the shipping application are to ensure that merchandise is shipped prior to the date desired by the customer and that the customer is promptly billed for the merchandise. Illustration 18–25 shows batch and on-line real-time shipping systems.

The batch system sorts the sales order detail file to get it in sequence by due date. A shipping clerk identifies to the system those sales orders due for

ILLUSTRATION 18–25 *(concluded)*

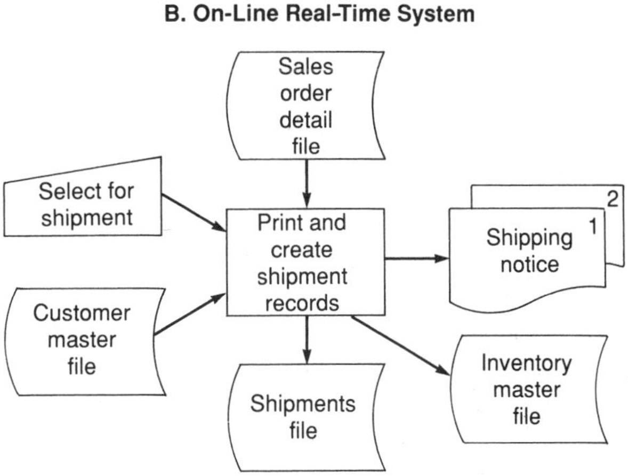

Monthly, the system prints customer statements and an aged trial balance. Many companies practice *cycle billing,* which means they print and mail statements to a different portion of their customers each day of the month. This avoids the difficulties of producing all customer statements at the month's end.

Cash Receipts Application. The purpose of the cash receipts application is to record payments made by customers for credit sales. It also deletes paid invoice records from the invoice detail file. Illustration 18–27 shows these procedures.

In the batch cash receipts system, a cash receipts clerk creates transaction records from remittance advices. A validation program prints an error listing for correction by the clerk and produces the cash receipts detail file. An invoice matching program identifies each cash receipt record in this file with the appropriate invoice detail record in the invoice detail file. It deletes the invoice detail record and prints a register of deleted invoices. Another program prints the cash receipts register, and an accounts receivable posting program then records each cash receipt in the proper customer record in the customer master file. It also adds each cash receipt record to the accounts receivable change log file and produces a record summarizing these transactions for the general ledger batch summary file. In the on-line real-time system, a single program performs these processes on each cash receipts transaction.

File Maintenance. During file maintenance, a computer application system adds or deletes a master record or makes changes to the reference data in an existing master record. In the revenue cycle, file maintenance is necessary when the organization obtains a new customer; loses an old customer; or the name,

ILLUSTRATION 18–26 A Billing Application

A. Batch System

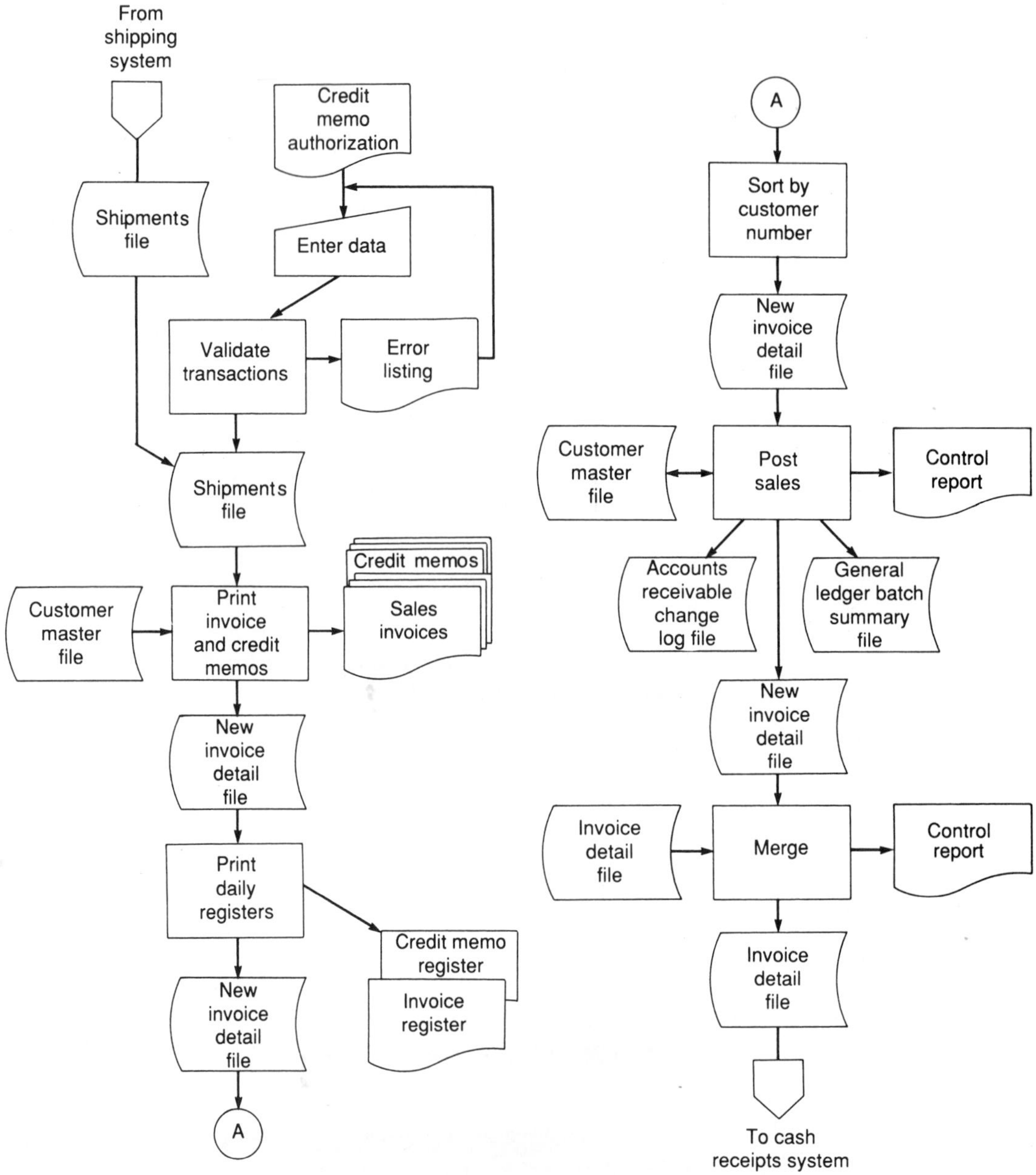

ILLUSTRATION 18–26 *(concluded)*

B. On-Line Real-Time System

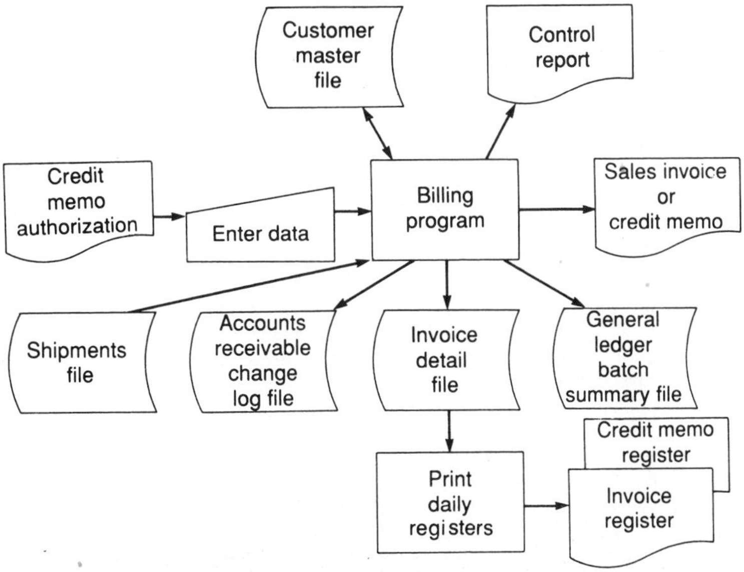

C. Monthly Processing

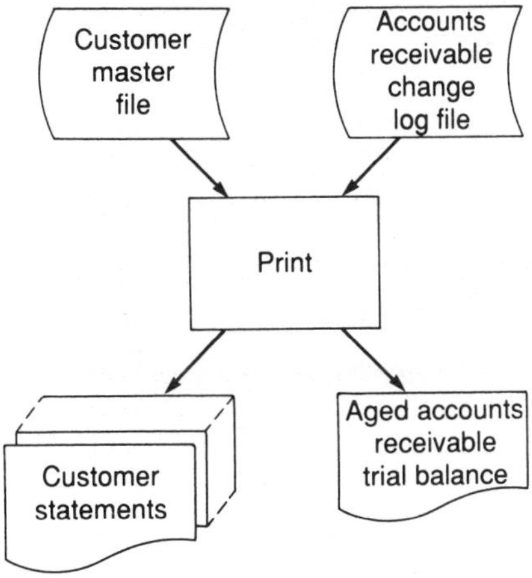

address, credit limits, or credit terms of an existing customer change. These require changes to a customer master record.

The sales department initiates these changes by recording them on a file maintenance form. In an on-line real-time system, the clerk enters changes from these forms at a terminal. In a batch processing system, a clerk batches file

ILLUSTRATION 18–27 A Cash Receipts Application

A. Batch System

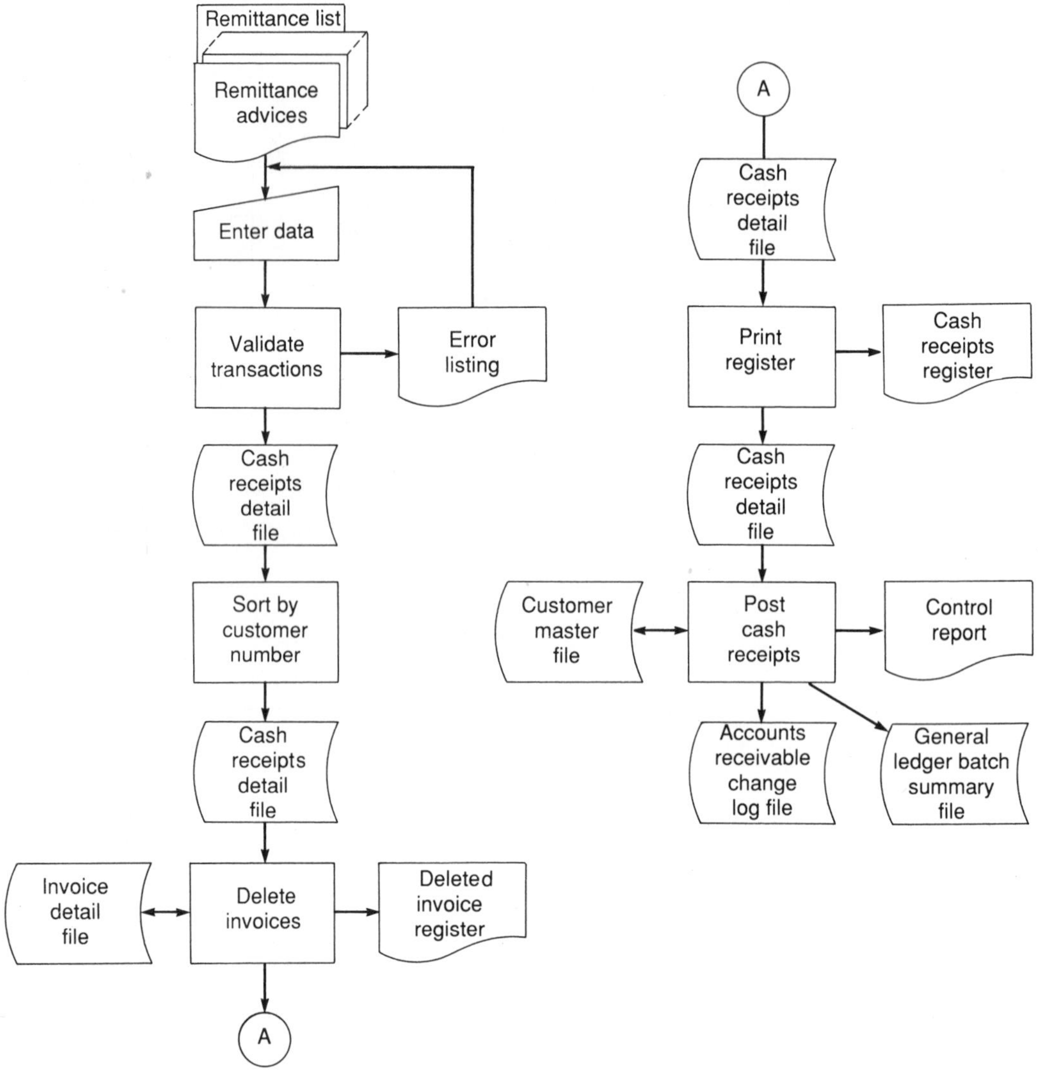

maintenance changes, a data entry clerk converts them to computer readable form, and a file maintenance program makes the changes prior to execution of the order entry application. This ensures that master records exist for all approved customers and that customer data is current prior to processing sales transactions. The credit department should approve any master record changes adding new customers or any changes to existing credit limits and credit terms.

ILLUSTRATION 18–27 *(concluded)*

B. On-Line Real Time System

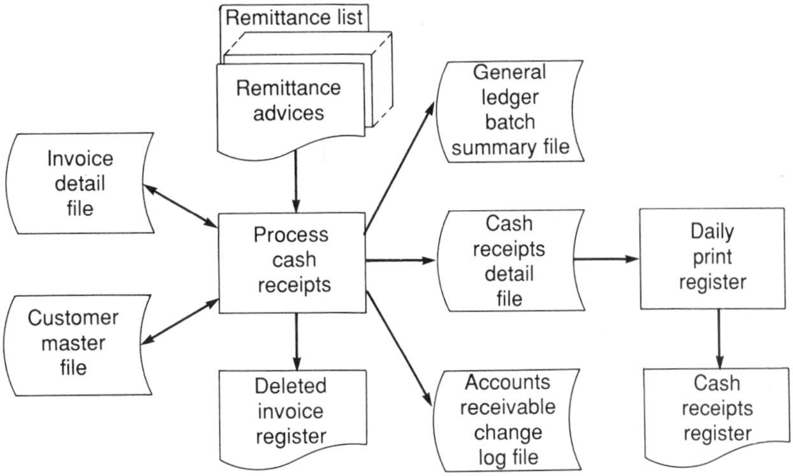

Application Controls. The designers of a computer-based system include application controls when an individual application is developed. Application controls may be input controls, processing controls, and output controls.

Input Controls. Input controls prevent or detect errors on the input of data. They ensure that data entry clerks accurately convert data from the human readable form on a document to a form readable by the computer. Most computer systems implement input controls using validation procedures. Validity tests, completeness tests, and control totals are examples of control procedures used for data validation. Illustration 18–28 shows how to employ these procedures in the application systems of the revenue cycle.

Processing Controls. Processing controls prevent or detect erroneous processing by computer programs. They are procedures coded into the programs during the development of the application system. Frequently programs reconcile the transactions read by the program with the number produced, or reconcile the total amounts on the input transactions with the amounts processed. Accountants call these control totals and record counts; other programs may use limit and reasonableness checks. Illustration 18–29 applies these control procedures to the application systems of the revenue cycle.

Output Controls. Output controls prevent and detect erroneous outputs from computer processing. In many companies, the data control group implements them; other companies assign clerks in user areas these responsibilities. Output controls compare record counts and control totals from successive computer runs to verify that all transactions were processed correctly. They also scan output

ILLUSTRATION 18–28 Input Controls in the Revenue Cycle

System	*Program*	*Control procedure*
Order entry	Validate transactions	**Validity test.** Program computes a check digit for the field CUSTOMER-NUMBER. **Completeness test.** Program verifies that each input record contains data in the following fields: TRANSACTION-CODE, TRANSACTION-DATE, SALES-ORDER-NUMBER, SALES-TERMS, PRODUCT-CODE, PRODUCT-PRICE, PRODUCT-QUANTITY, TRANSACTION-AMOUNT. **Control total.** In the batch system, the data control group compares to a batch total the total of the TRANSACTION-AMOUNT fields for all transactions.
Shipping	Create shipping record	**Validity test.** Program verifies that cutoff date is of the form AA-BB-CCCC, where AA < 13, BB < 32, and CCCC is numeric.
Billing	Validate transactions	**Validity test.** Program computes a check digit for the field CUSTOMER-NUMBER. **Completeness test.** Program verifies that each input record contains data in the following fields: TRANSACTION-CODE, TRANSACTION-DATE, SALES-ORDER-NUMBER, SALES-TERMS, PRODUCT-CODE, PRODUCT-PRICE, PRODUCT-QUANTITY, TRANSACTION-AMOUNT. **Control total.** In the batch system, the data control group compares total of the TRANSACTION-AMOUNT fields for all transactions to the batch total.
Cash receipts	Validate transactions	**Validity test.** Program computes a check digit for the field CUSTOMER-NUMBER. **Completeness test.** Program verifies that each input record contains all data fields. **Control total.** In the batch system, the data control group compares the total of the TRANSACTION-AMOUNT fields for all transactions to the batch total on the remittance list.

ILLUSTRATION 18–29 Processing Controls in the Revenue Cycle

System	*Program*	*Control Procedure*
Order entry	Credit verification	**Limit test.** Program verifies that sale does cause customer to exceed credit limit.
Shipping	Create shipment records	**Completeness test.** Program verifies that each record contains SHIPPING-NOTICE-NUMBER. **Record count.** In the batch system, the program verifies that the number of records in the input sales order detail file = number of records in output sales order detail file + number of records in the shipments file.
Billing	Print invoices and credit memos	**Completeness test.** Program verifies that each record contains INVOICE-NUMBER. **Reasonableness test.** Program verifies that on a document, TRANSACTION-AMOUNT < $99,999.
	Post sales	**Control total.** Program verifies that total postings to the customer master file = total amounts in the accounts receivable change log file = total debits and total credits in general ledger batch summary file. **Control total.** In batch system, program verifies that total postings to customer master file = total of TRANSACTION-AMOUNT fields in new invoice detail file.
	Merge	**Control total.** In batch system, total of TRANSACTION-AMOUNT fields in input files = total of TRANSACTION-AMOUNT fields in output file. **Record count.** In batch system, number of records in input files = number of records in output file.
Cash receipts	Post cash receipts	**Control total.** Program verifies that total postings to the customer master file = total amounts in the accounts receivable change log file = total debits and total credits in general ledger batch summary file. **Control total.** In batch system, program verifies that total postings to customer master file = total of TRANSACTION-AMOUNT fields in cash receipts detail file.
Shipping, billing, cash receipts	Sort	**Control total.** In batch systems, total of TRANSACTION-AMOUNT fields in input file = total of TRANSACTION-AMOUNT fields in output file. **Record count.** In batch systems, the number of records in input file = number of records in output file.

ILLUSTRATION 18–30 Output Controls in the Revenue Cycle

System	*Program*	*Control Procedure*
Order entry	Print order acknowledgment	**Visual verification.** Data control group examines documents for proper preparation. **Record count.** Data control group verifies that number of order acknowledgments = the number of valid sales order transactions shown on the error listing.
Shipping	Create shipment records	**Record count.** Data control group verifies that the number of shipping notices = number of records in shipments file shown on shipments register.
Billing	Print daily registers	**Record count.** Data control group verifies that the number of credit memos and invoices printed are the numbers shown on the credit memo and invoice registers.
	Print invoices and credit memos	**Visual verification.** Data control group examines invoices and credit memos for proper preparation.
Cash receipts	Print cash receipts register	**Control total.** Data control group verifies that total amount of listings on deleted invoice register = total listings on cash receipts register.
All batch systems	Successive programs	**Run-to-run controls.** Data control group reconciles control totals and record counts on registers and control reports produced by each pair of programs executed in succession.

documents and reports to identify obvious errors in their preparation. Illustration 18–30 lists the procedures that the data control group performs in the revenue cycle.

You now see how a system design team includes application controls in the application systems of the revenue cycle. Perhaps you can identify some other control procedures that would be useful as well in these applications.

SUMMARY

The revenue cycle processes accounting transactions that record four economic events: the request for goods or services by a customer, the delivery of those goods or services, the request for payment, and the receipt for payment.

Accounting systems in the revenue cycle must be able to process five types of transactions. The data for these transactions are recorded on documents, entered into accounting records, and summarized in reports. Documents in this transaction cycle are the sales order, the shipping notice, the sales invoice, the credit memo, and the remittance advice. Reports include control reports, registers, customer statements, the aged accounts receivable trial balance, and the remittance list.

Manual systems in this cycle process three special journals and the accounts receivable subsidiary ledger. Computer-based systems include the order entry, shipping, billing, and cash receipts applications. They post sales and cash receipts transactions to the customer master file and provide inputs to the general ledger system. When a data base management system is used, these applications access the data using their subschemas.

KEY TERMS

accounts receivable change log file A file containing one record for each transaction in a customer's account since the last statement. It is used to print a monthly statement.

accounts receivable system A name sometimes applied to a combination of the billing and cash receipts applications.

balance forward system An accounts receivable system that maintains records of transactions since the last statement date. Detail on older transactions are deleted.

balance only system A type of accounts receivable system that records only the current balance owed by a customer. Detail concerning that balance must be obtained from documents.

customer master record A record for each customer showing reference data, a credit limit, and balances owed.

customer statement A list of all transactions in a customer's account during a specified time period, usually a month. It is mailed to the customer.

cycle billing The practice of mailing customer statements to a different group of customers each day of the month.

general ledger batch summary file A file containing records produced by revenue cycle applications that are to be posted to the general ledger master file.

open item system An accounts receivable system that maintains records showing all transactions making up the customer's unpaid balance.

remittance advice A document returned by customers with their payments.

remittance list A list of all currency and checks received during one day.

sales invoice A document mailed to customers, informing them of the amount due from them because of shipments.

sales order A document on which the sales department records an order from a customer.

shipping notice A document completed by the shipping department to notify the billing department that a shipment has been made.

APPENDIX

Control Flowcharts for Revenue Cycle Transactions

Control Flowchart 18–1 Receipts from Credit Sales

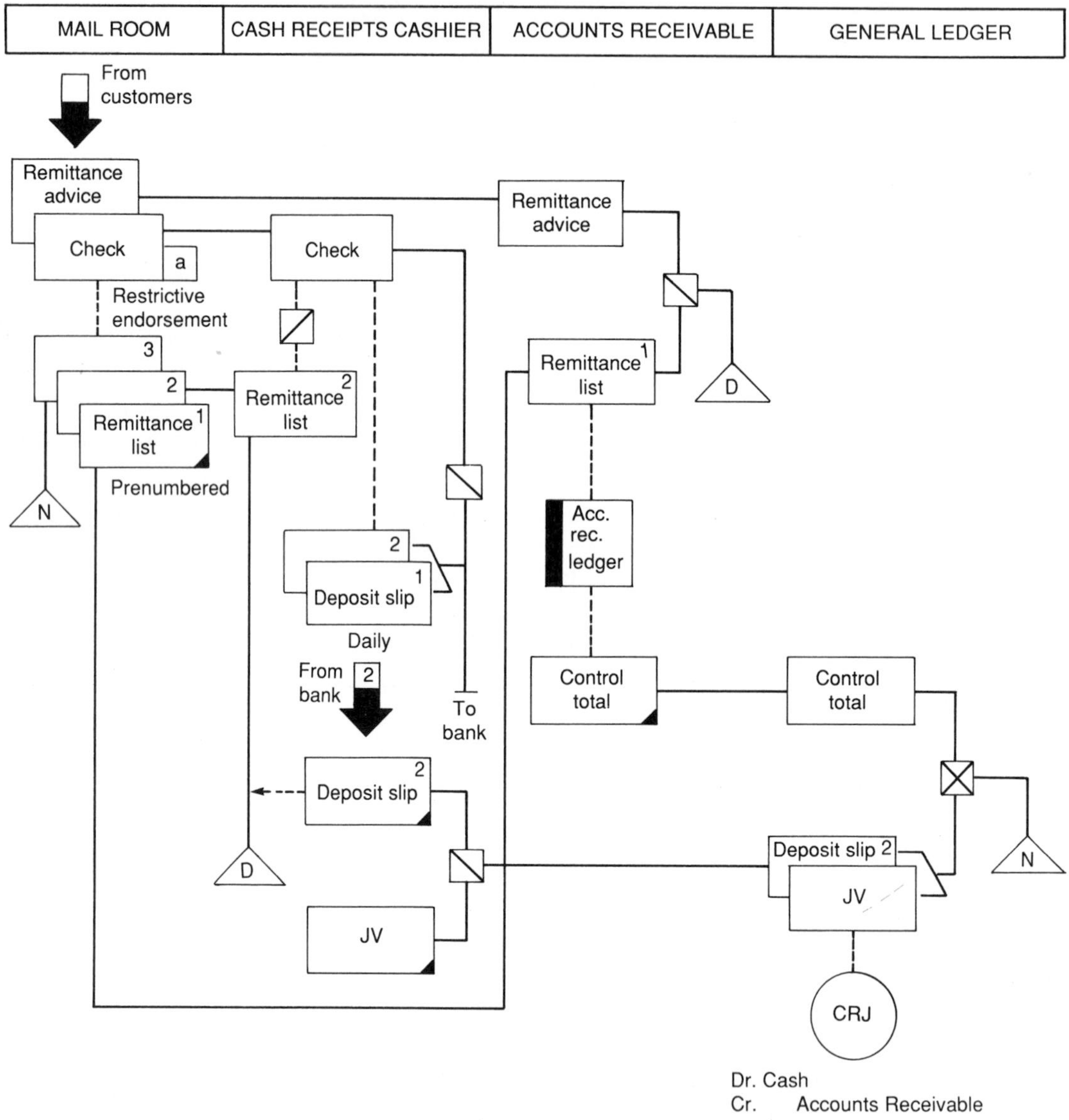

Control Flowchart 18–2 Credit Sales

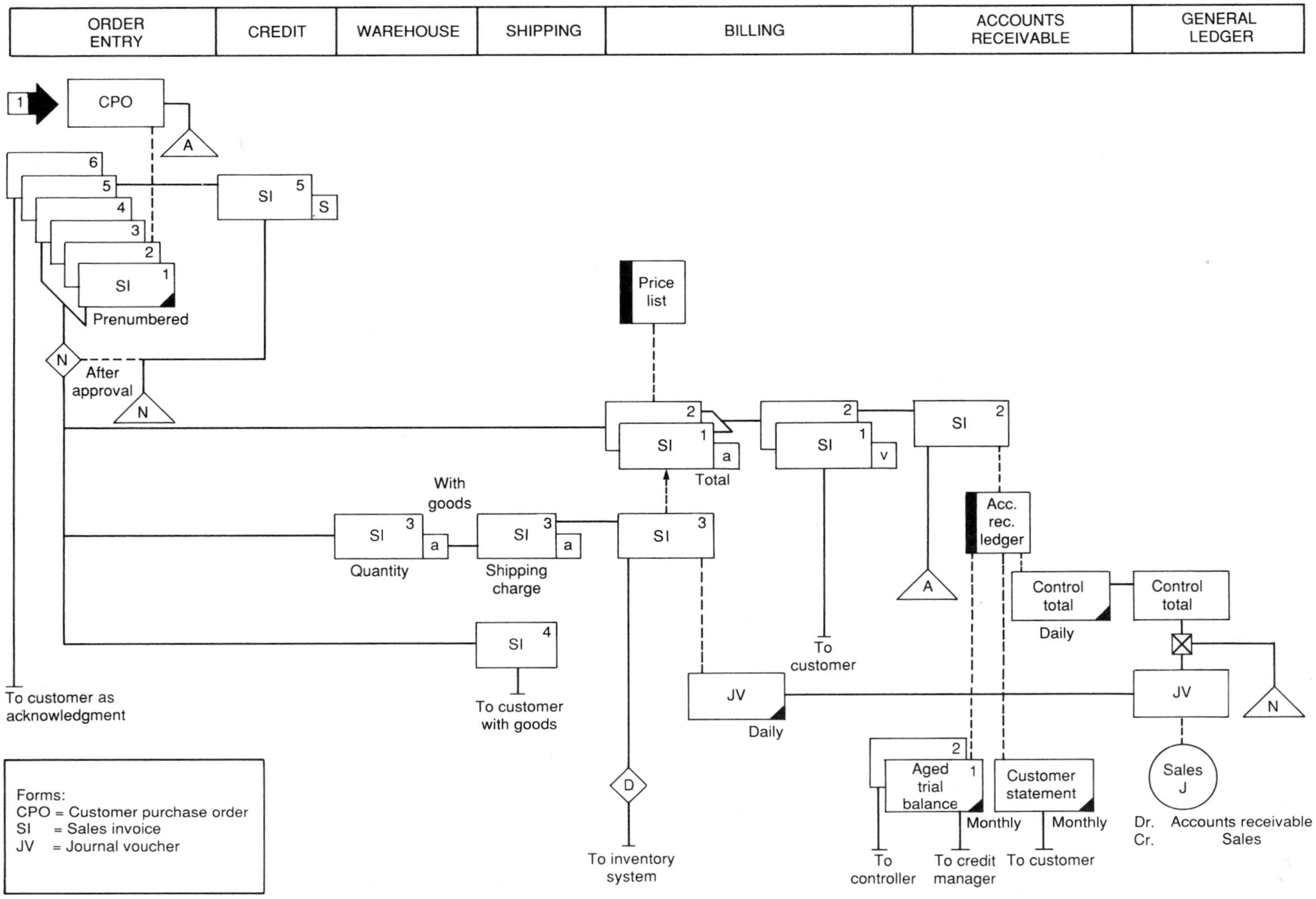

Control Flowchart 18–3 Sales Returns and Allowances

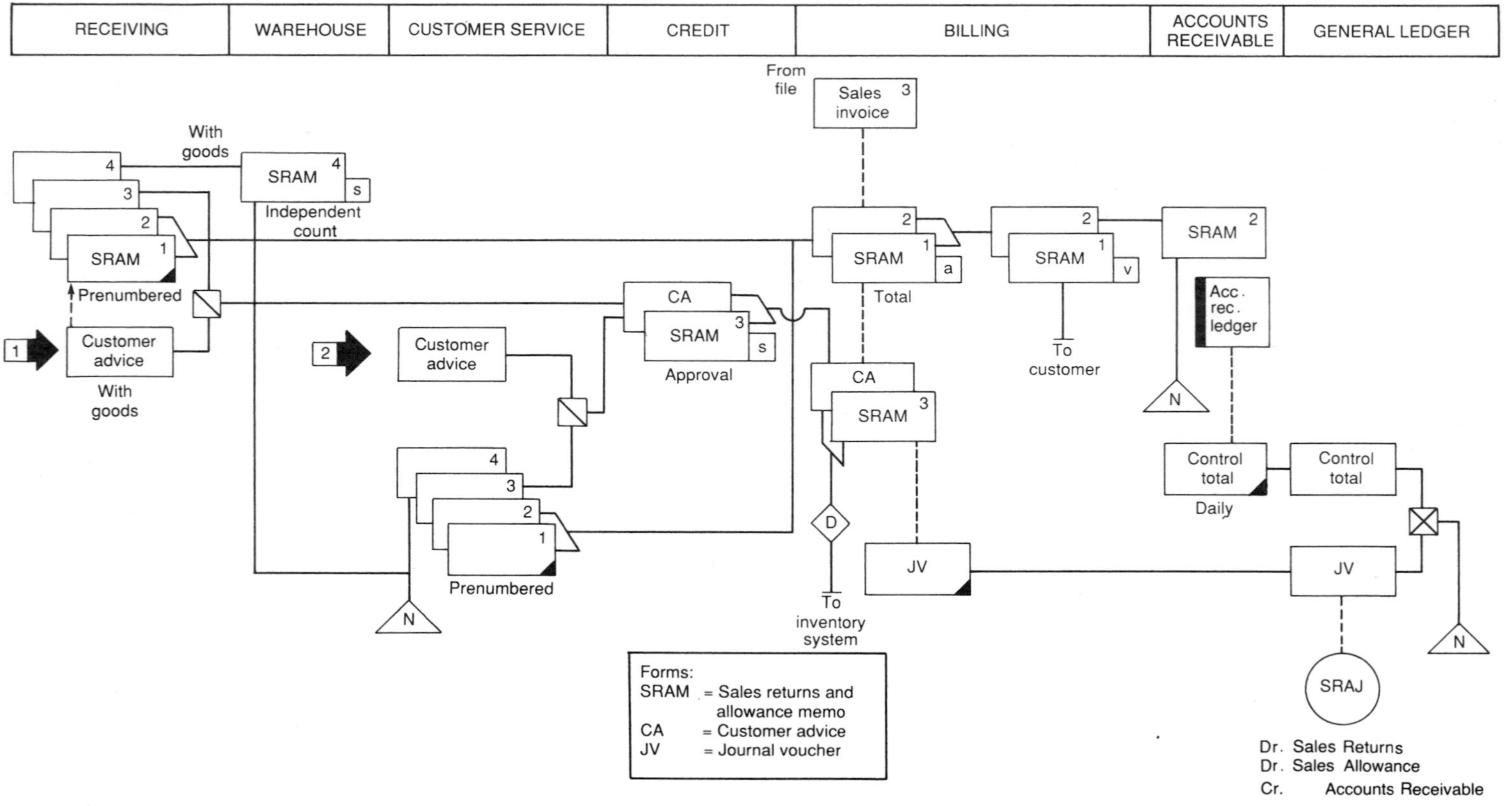

Control Flowchart 18–4 Bad Debts Write-Offs

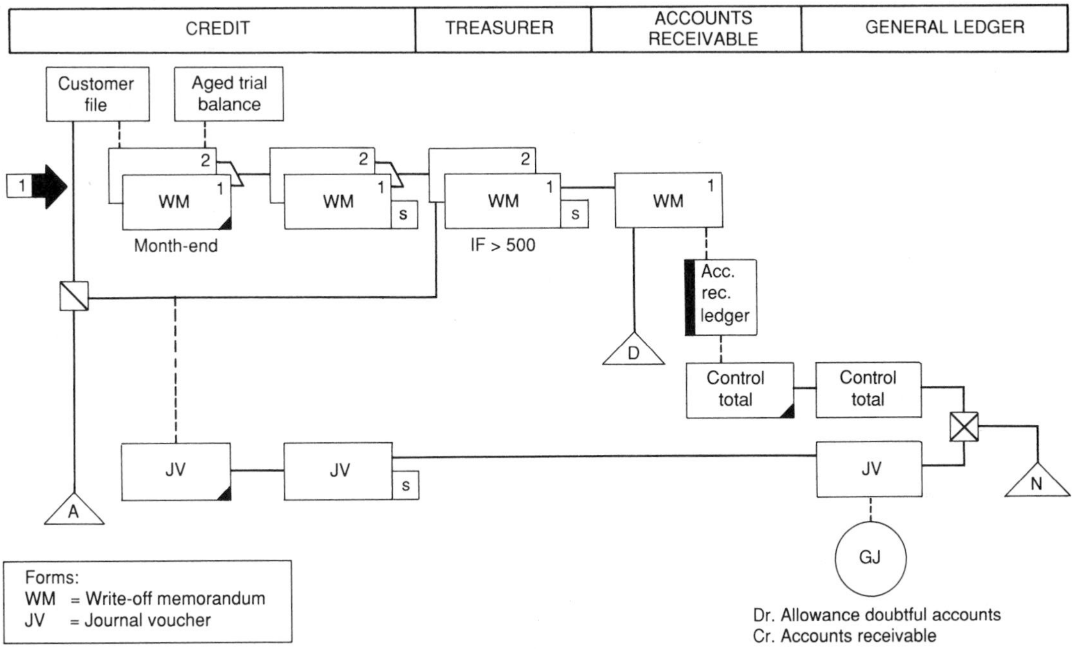

Control Flowchart 18–5 Receipts from Credit Sales Using a Lockbox

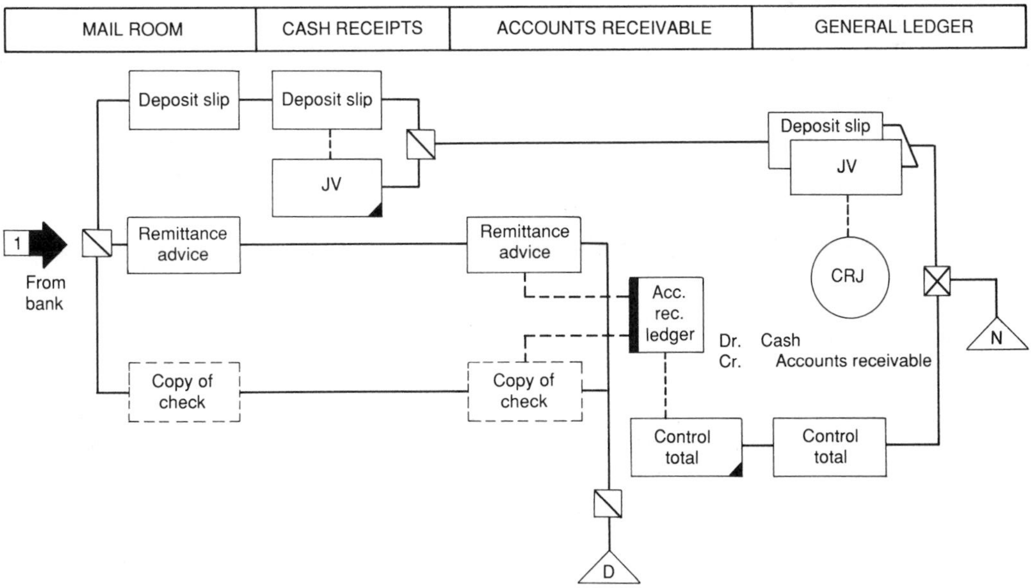

Control Flowchart 18–6 Receipts from Cash Sales

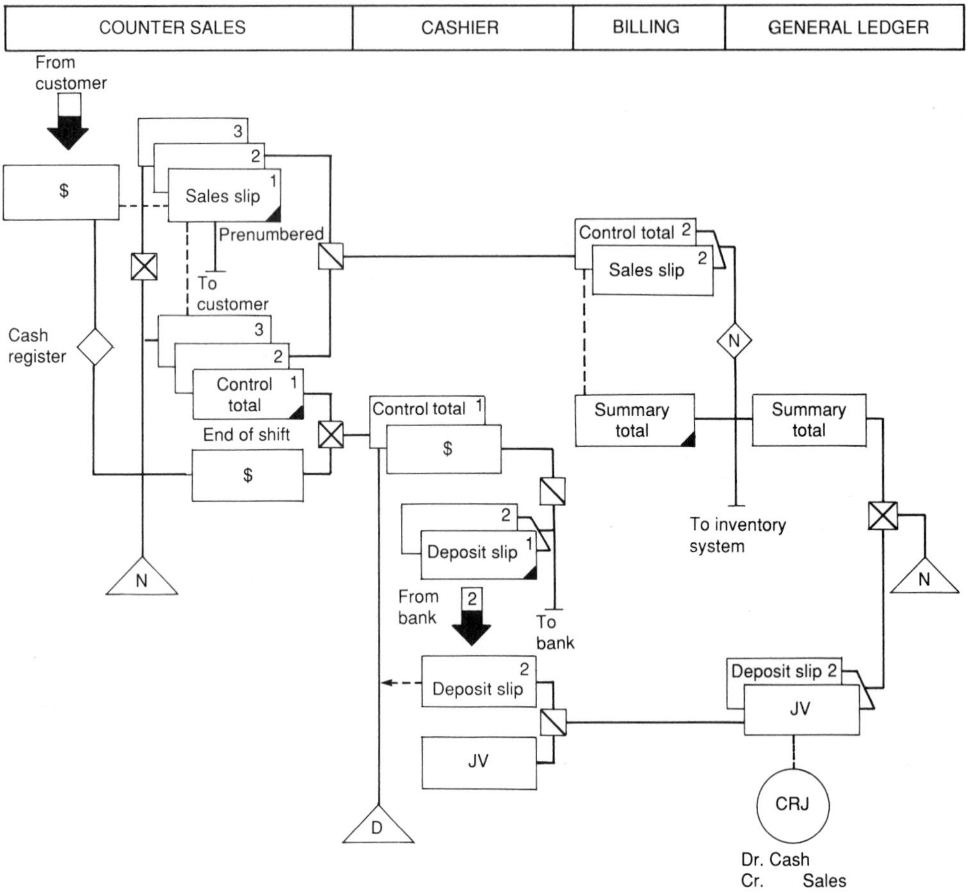

QUESTIONS

18–1. Which economic events produce transactions in the revenue cycle?

18–2. Which five types of transactions do accounting systems record in the revenue cycle?

18–3. What is the purpose of each of the following documents?

a. Sales order

b. Shipping notice

c. Sales invoice
d. Credit memo

18–4. When is a control report used? What is its function?

18–5. Which information is disclosed in a register? Why is it important to accountants?

18–6. Describe three special purpose reports produced in the revenue cycle.

18–7. What form do noncomputerized records take in the revenue cycle?

18–8. In a computerized accounting system, which data files are used in the revenue cycle? Can you identify the purpose of each file?

18–9. Describe each of the three kinds of accounts receivable systems and distinguish among them.

18–10. In a computer-based accounting system, what are the applications in the revenue cycle? What is the purpose of each?

18–11. The following system flowchart illustrates a credit sales and cash receipts system. What does the symbol X represent?

(AICPA Adapted)

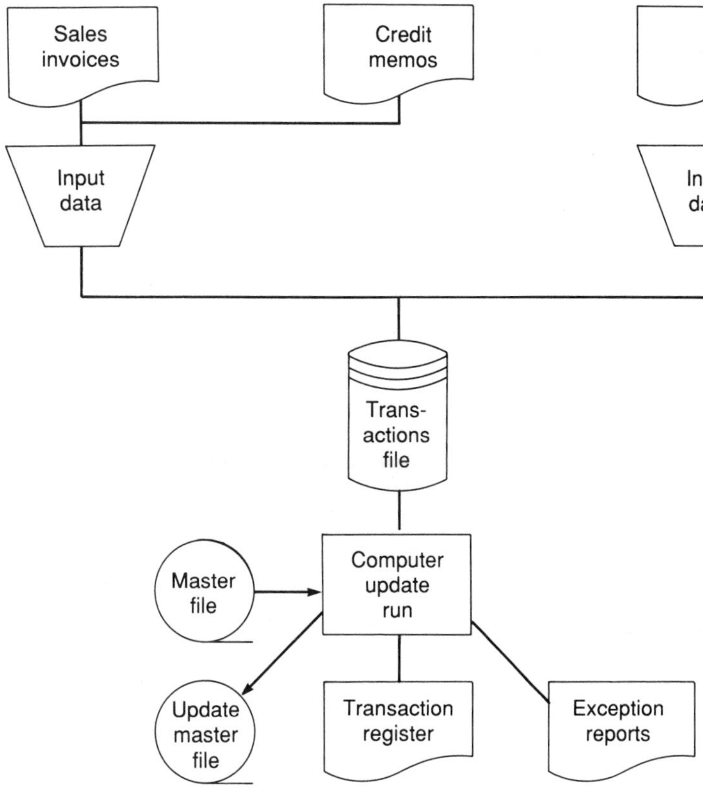

EXERCISES AND CASES

18–12. TRANSACTIONS AND DOCUMENTS

The column on the left lists accounting transactions processed in the revenue cycle. In the right column is a list of documents and reports. For each transaction, identify the document(s) and report(s) associated with it.

Transaction	*Document or report*
a. Cash sale	1. Sales invoice
b. Credit sale	2. Credit memo
c. Bad debt write-off	3. Remittance advice
d. Sales return	4. Aged trial balance
e. Sales allowance	5. Sales ticket
f. Payment on account	6. Sales order

18–13. TRANSACTIONS AND APPLICATIONS

The column on the left lists accounting transactions. In the right column is a list of application systems used in the revenue cycle. For each transaction, identify the application system that processes it.

a. Cash sale	1. Order entry
b. Credit sale	2. Shipping
c. Sales return	3. Billing
d. Sales allowance	4. Cash receipts
e. Payment on account	

18–14. FRAUD

Consider the following situations involving fraud in the revenue cycle.

1. Cash receipts for discount sales to employees were misappropriated as a result of inadequate control over, and accounting for, special sales invoices used to document them. A clerk who knew of the lack of control over the invoices stole over $20,000 during a two-year period.
2. A company had given employees unlimited authority to issue customer cash sales adjustments under a specified dollar amount without a supervisor's approval. An employee made over $10,000 of false adjustments to cash sales and kept the money.
3. Substantial amounts were collected daily from cash sales. A single trusted employee recorded the cash receipts, made the bank deposits, reconciled the cash accounts, and posted accounts receivable. External auditors had previously noted inadequate segregation of duties even though extensive audit tests had revealed no shortages. Internal auditors then discovered that over an eight-year period, the trusted employee had embezzled over $100,000.

Required:

For each situation just described:

a. Which conditions allowed the fraud?

b. What could a manager or auditor have done to detect the fraud?

(CIA Adapted)

18–15. ***CREDIT SALES***

After a shipment is prepared, the shipping department completes a three-part shipping notice form. The first copy is included with the goods sent to the customer as a packing slip. The second copy is forwarded to the billing department. The third copy is sent to the accountant. When the billing department receives the second copy of the shipping order, it uses the information on it to prepare a two-part sales invoice. The second copy of the shipping order is then filed in the billing department. The first copy of the sales invoice is sent to the customer. The second copy of the sales invoice is forwarded to the accountant. Periodically, the accountant matches the copy of the shipping order with the copy of the sales invoice and files them alphabetically by customer name. Before doing so, however, the accountant uses the copy of the sales invoice to post the sales entry in the subsidiary accounts receivable ledger.

Required:

a. Prepare a document flowchart showing the preceding steps.

b. Identify the internal control deficiencies and omissions in the foregoing procedures.

(CIA Adapted)

18–16. ***SALES RETURNS***

Customers return goods—usually with a copy of the original sales invoice—to Wilson & Company's customer service department. Using the information on these original invoices, the department prepares a prenumbered, three-part sales return slip. In instances where the returned goods are not accompanied by an original invoice, the customer service department uses the company's current sales price lists to prepare sales return slips.

After mailing the customer the original sales return slip, the customer service department sends copies two and three to the inventory control department, along with the returned goods. After noting the quantity of goods returned on the slip, the inventory control department uses copy three to post to the perpetual inventory records. It then sends a control total, along with copy two of the sales return slip, to the accounts receivable department. Copy three is then filed by date.

On receipt of copy two of the sales return slip, the accounts receivable department posts to customers' accounts. At the end of posting, the accounts receivable department verifies the control total supplied by the inventory control department. Then accounts receivable forwards the total to the general ledger department where a journal entry is made.

Required:

a. Prepare a document flowchart showing the steps just described.
b. Identify the internal control deficiencies and omissions in these procedures.

18–17. ***DATA FILE DESIGN***

A department store, Sanger Harris, accepts all charges incurred on credit cards issued by that store. Exhibit 18–1 shows a copy of a monthly customer statement.

Required:

Assume that you are developing a system that produces the customer statement in Exhibit 18–1. Design record layouts for the following files:

a. Customer master file.
b. Invoice detail file.
c. Cash receipts detail file.
d. Accounts receivable change log file.

18–18. ***ON-LINE REAL-TIME CONTROLS***

In Exhibit 18–2 a flowchart depicts a section of an open item accounts receivable system. The system is 1 of 10 computerized on-line real-time systems installed at a large manufacturing company. At 11 control points in the cash application segment of this system, control practices are applied.

Required:

a. Identify the 11 control points in Exhibit 18–2.
b. Explain how each control point aids in preventing or detecting errors and irregularities.

(CIA Adapted)

18–19. ***CASH RECEIPTS FROM CREDIT SALES***

Procedures for handling the cash receipts of the Alaska branch of the Far Distributing Company are as follows: The branch's substantial annual sales are billed and collected locally. Cash collections on over-the-counter sales and COD sales are received from the customer or delivery service by the cashier. On receipt of cash, the cashier stamps the sales ticket "paid" and files a copy for future reference. The only record of COD sales is the copy of the sales ticket the cashier holds until the cash is received from the delivery service.

EXHIBIT 18–1 Exercise 18–17

SangerHarris

66555310007350000073500

--	--	DR & MRS DAVID H LI
--	--	7707 QUEENSFERRY LANE
	--	DALLAS, TX
		75248

PLEASE SHOW AMOUNT PAID ______________

ACCOUNT NUMBER	ACCOUNT TYPE	NEW BALANCE	PAYMENT NOW DUE
6-6555-3-1	30 DAY ACCOUNT	73.50	73.50

PLEASE DETACH AND RETURN THIS PORTION WITH YOUR PAYMENT

CHECK BOX FOR CREDIT CARD REQUEST(S) OR ADDRESS CHANGE AND COMPLETE OTHER SIDE ☐

DATE	STORE LOC • CODE	REFERENCE NUMBER	DEPT	DESCRIPTION	PURCHASES AND OTHER CHARGES	PAYMENTS RETURNS AND OTHER CREDITS
06-19	09	9008001491	446	LINGERIE	15.75	
06-29	13	1344004270	171	HANDBAGS	57.75	
07-12		10217690		PAYMENT--THANK YOU		17.84

THIS MONTH S BILL CLOSING DATE	SANGER HARRIS ACCOUNT NUMBER	NEXT MONTH S BILL CLOSING DATE	PAYMENT NOW DUE •
JULY 16, 1991	6-6555-3-1	AUG. 16, 1991	73.50

PREVIOUS BALANCE		**FINANCE CHARGE**		PURCHASES AND OTHER CHARGES		PAYMENTS RETURNS AND OTHER CREDITS		NEW BALANCE
17.84	+	NONE	+	73.50	–	17.84	=	73.50

To avoid a Finance Charge on your next statement we must receive the New Balance in full on or before your Next Month s Bill Closing Date

TERMS CHANGE DATE	OLD PREVIOUS BALANCE •	NEW PREVIOUS BALANCE •
N/A	N/A	N/A

***NOTICE:** SEE REVERSE SIDE FOR IMPORTANT INFORMATION

CRBAL CREDIT BALANCE

EXHIBIT 18–2 Exercise 18–18

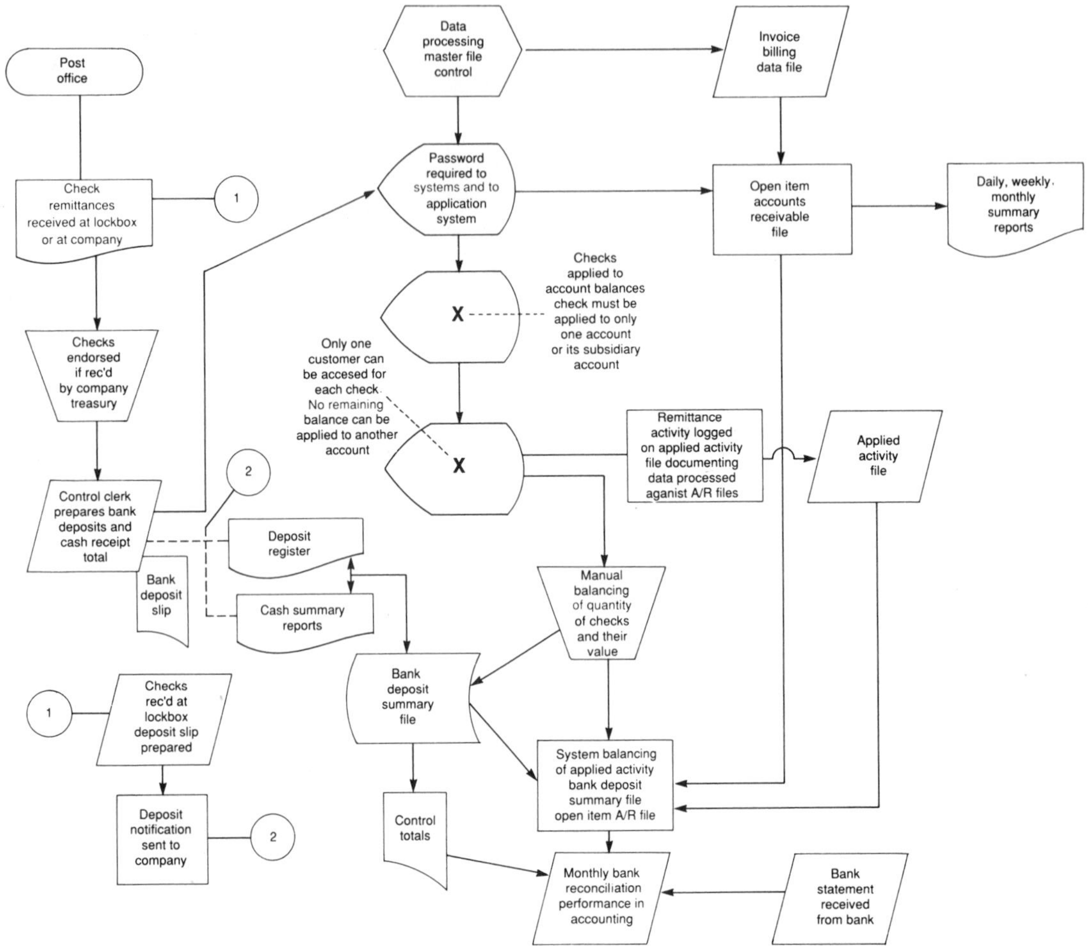

Mail is opened by the credit manager's secretary who gives remittances to the credit manager for her review. The credit manager then places the remittances in a tray on the cashier's desk. At the daily deposit cutoff time the cashier delivers the checks and cash on hand to the assistant credit manager. He prepares remittance lists, makes up the bank deposit, and takes the deposit to the bank. The assistant credit manager also posts remittances to the accounts receivable ledger cards and verifies the cash discount allowable.

To write off uncollectible accounts, the credit manager obtains approval from the executive office of Far Distributing Company in Chicago. The credit manager has retained in her custody, as of the end of the fiscal year, some remittances that were received on various days during the month.

Required:

a. Describe the irregularities that might occur under the procedures now in effect for handling cash collections and remittances.
b. Identify procedures that you would recommend to improve internal control over cash collections and remittances.

(AICPA Adapted)

18–20. *REVENUE CYCLE PROCEDURES*

While auditing the Top Manufacturing Corporation, the auditor prepared the flowchart of credit sale activities shown in Exhibit 18–3. In this flowchart, the letter *A* represents CUSTOMER.

Required:

Identify what is represented by the letters *B* through *P*.

(AICPA Adapted)

18–21. *CASH RECEIPTS*

The town of Oaks Park operates a private parking lot near the railroad for the benefit of town residents. The guard on duty issues annual prenumbered parking stickers to residents who submit an application form and show evidence of residency. A sticker affixed to the auto allows a resident to park anywhere in the lot for 12 hours if four quarters are placed in the parking meter. Applications are maintained in the guard office on the lot. The guard checks to see that only residents are using the lot and that no resident has parked without paying the required meter fee.

Once a week the guard on duty, who has a master key for all meters, takes the coins from the meters and places them in a locked steel box. The guard delivers the box to the town storage building, where it is opened and the coins are manually counted by a storage department clerk who records the total cash counted on a weekly cash report. This report is sent to the town accounting department. The storage clerk puts the cash in a safe; on the following day the cash is picked up by the town's treasurer, who manually recounts the cash, prepares the bank deposit slip, and delivers the deposit to the bank. The deposit slip, authenticated by the bank teller, is sent to the accounting department where it is filed with the weekly cash report.

Required:

a. Describe internal control weaknesses in these procedures.
b. For each weakness, recommend at least one way to improve internal control over parking lot cash receipts.

(AICPA Adapted)

EXHIBIT 18–3 Exercise 18–20

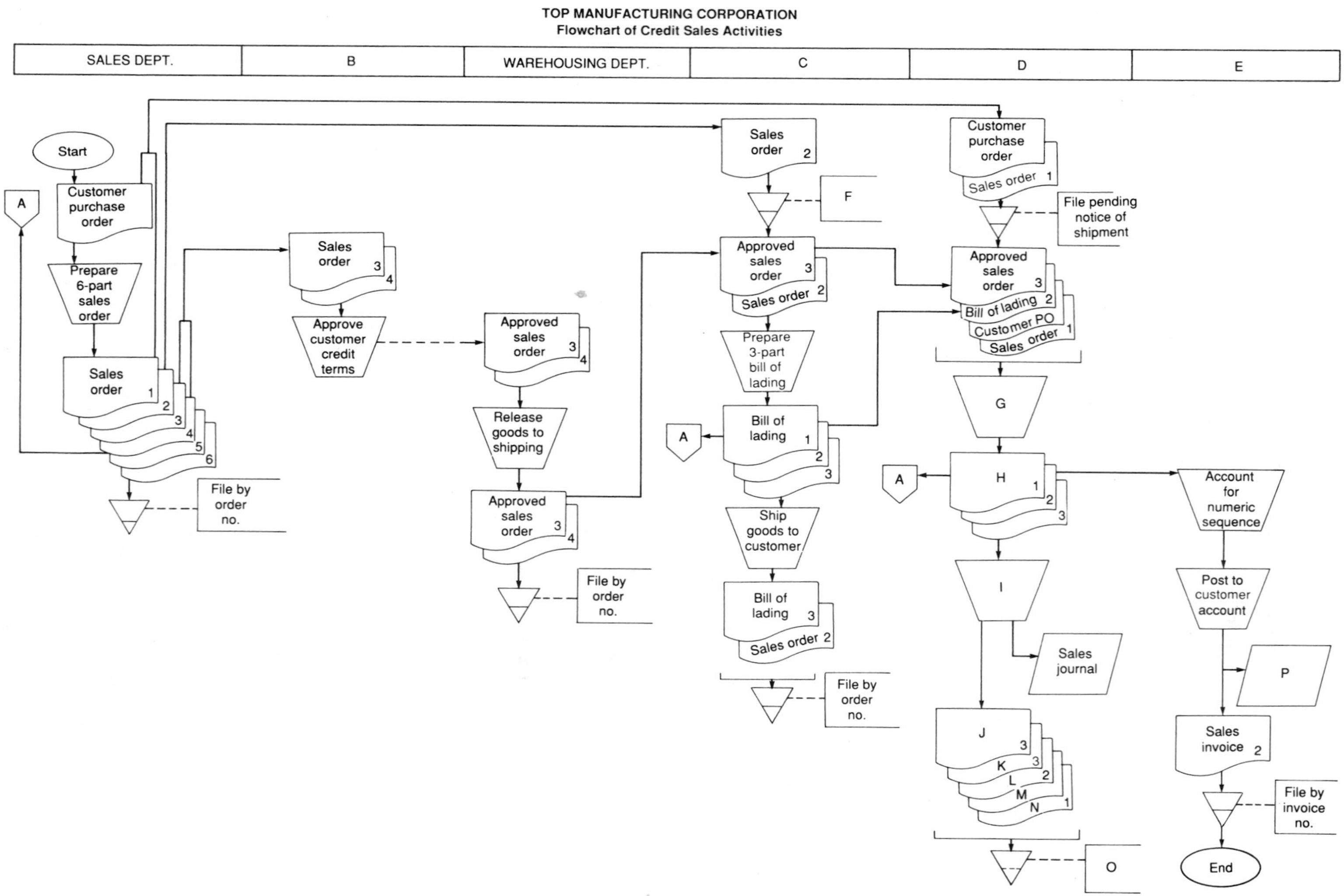

18–22. *CONTROL PROCEDURES AND DOCUMENTS*

A partially completed flowchart for credit sales appears in Exhibit 18–4. The flowchart depicts the activities of the Bottom Manufacturing Corporation.

When a customer's purchase order is received, a six-part sales order is prepared from it. The six copies are initially distributed as follows:

Copy 1—to billing department

Copy 2—to shipping department

Copy 3—to credit department

Copy 4—to credit department

Copy 5—to customer

Copy 6—file in sales order department

When a copy of the sales order reaches its destination, it initiates specific control procedures and related documents. Some of the procedures and documents are indicated on the flowchart. Others are labeled with letters *a* to *r*.

Required:

List the control procedures and documents represented by letters *a* through *r* in the flowchart of Bottom Manufacturing Corporation's credit sales system.

(AICPA Adapted)

18–23. *GENERAL AND APPLICATION CONTROLS*

Ajax, Inc. recently installed a new computer-based system to process more efficiently the shipping, billing, and accounts receivable records. During a review, an auditor determined the following information concerning the new system.

Each major application—that is, shipping, billing, cash receipts, and so forth—is permanently assigned to a specific computer operator responsible for making program changes, running the program, and reconciling the computer log. Responsibility for the custody and control over tape files and system documentation is randomly rotated among the computer operators on a monthly basis to prevent any one person from having access to the tapes and documentation at all times. Each computer programmer and computer operator has access to the computer room via a magnetic card containing an individual digital code. The systems analyst and the supervisor of the computer operators do not have access to the computer room.

The system documentation consists of the following items: program listing, error listing, logs, and record layouts. To increase efficiency, batch totals and processing controls are omitted from the system.

Ajax ships its products directly from two warehouses which forward shipping notices to general accounting. There, the billing clerk enters the price of the item and accounts for the numerical sequence of the shipping notices. The billing

EXHIBIT 18–4 Exercise 18–22

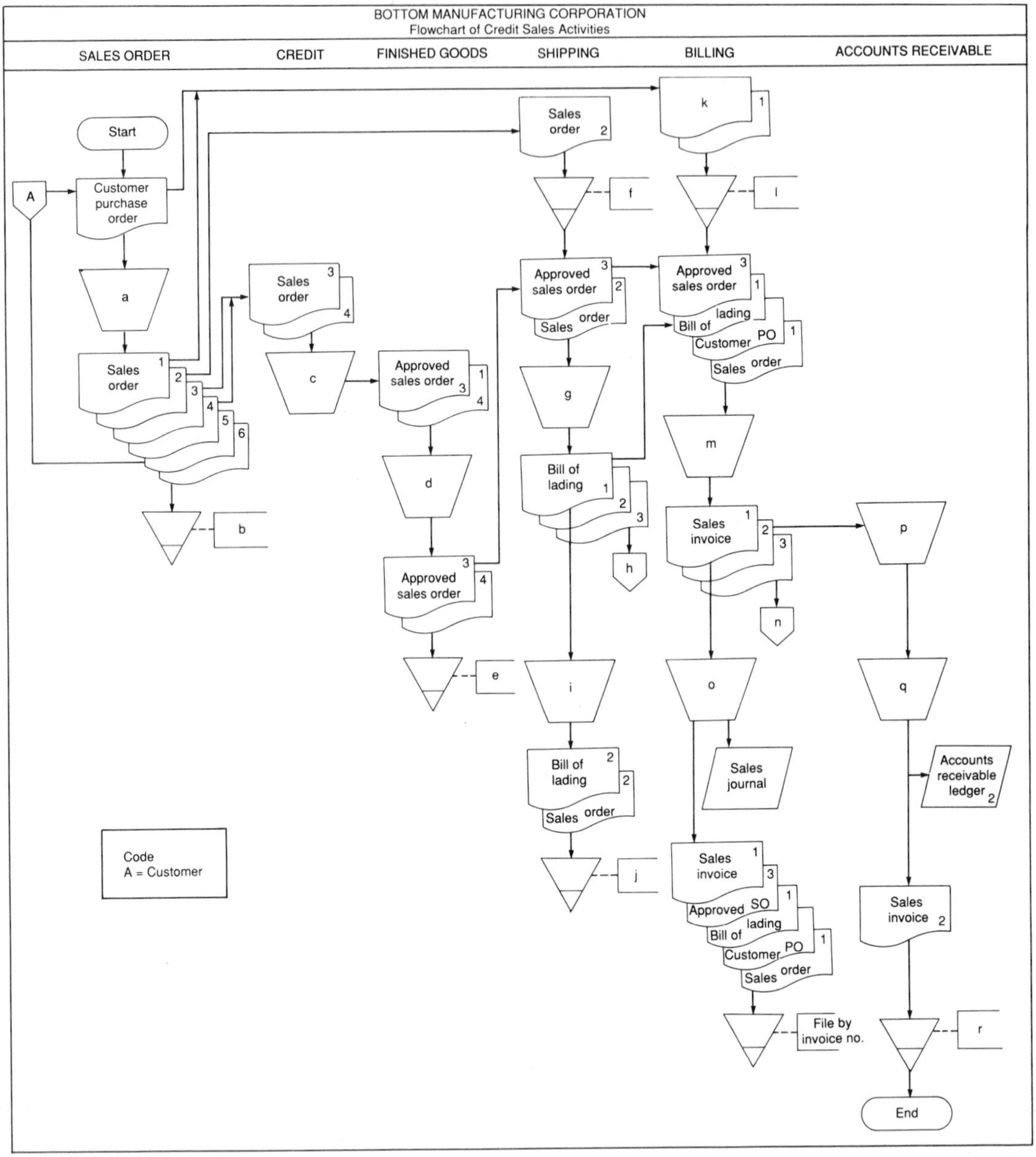

clerk also prepares daily adding machine tapes of the units shipped and the sales amounts. Shipping notices and adding machine tapes are forwarded to the computer department for processing. The computer output consists of:

- A three-part sales invoice that is forwarded to the billing clerk.
- A daily sales register showing the aggregate totals of units shipped and sales amounts that the computer operator compares to the adding machine tapes.

The billing clerk mails two copies of each invoice to the customer and retains the third copy in an open invoice file that serves as a detail accounts receivable record.

Required:

Describe one specific recommendation for correcting each control weakness in the new system and for correcting each weakness or inefficiency in the procedures for processing and controlling shipping notices and sales invoices.

(AICPA Adapted)

18–24. ***CONTROL WEAKNESSES***

The document flowchart in Exhibit 18–5 depicts the revenue cycle activities of Smallco Lumber, Inc.

Required:

For each of the following job functions, identify the control weakness related to its activities.

a. Warehouse clerk
b. Bookkeeper 1
c. Bookkeeper 2
d. Collection clerk

(AICPA Adapted)

18–25. ***CASH RECEIPTS AND SALES***

Charting, Inc., processes its sales and cash receipts documents in the following manner:

Cash Receipts

The mail is opened each morning by a mail clerk in the sales department. The mail clerk prepares a remittance advice (showing the customer and amount paid) if one is not received. The checks and remittance advices are then forwarded to the sales department supervisor, who reviews each check and forwards the checks and remittance advices to the accounting department supervisor. The accounting department supervisor, who also functions as the credit manager, reviews all checks for payments of past-due accounts and then forwards the

EXHIBIT 18–5 Exercise 18–24

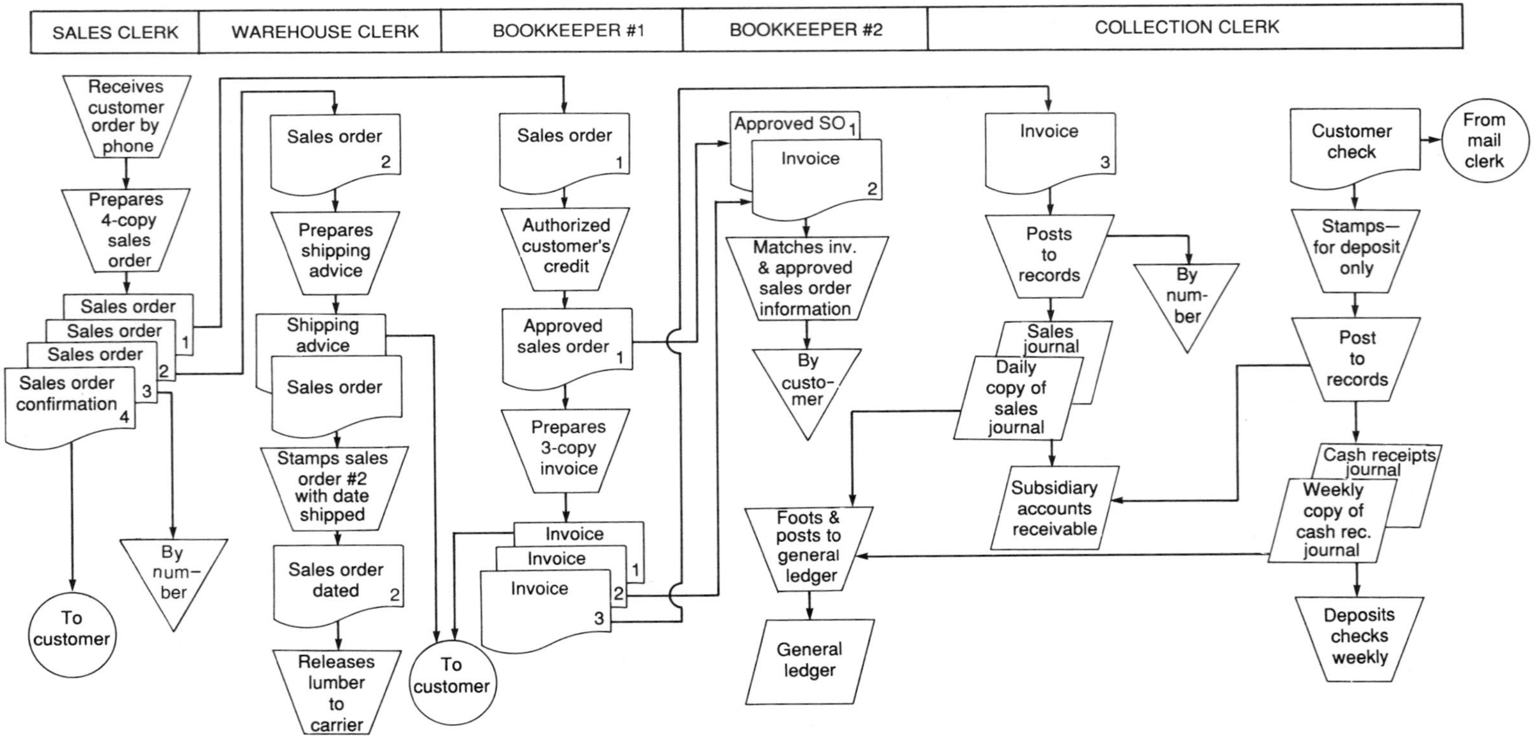

checks and remittance advices to the accounts receivable clerk, who arranges the advices in alphabetical order. The remittance advices are posted directly to the accounts receivable ledger cards. The checks are endorsed by stamp and totaled. The total is posted to the cash receipts journal. The remittance advices are filed chronologically.

After receiving the cash from the preceding day's cash sales, the accounts receivable clerk prepares the daily deposit slip in triplicate. The third copy of the deposit slip is filed by date, and the second copy and the original accompany the bank deposit.

Sales

Salesclerks prepare the sales invoices in triplicate. The original and the second copy are presented to the cashier, while the third copy is retained by the salesclerk in the sales book. When the sale is for cash, the customer pays the salesclerk, who presents the money to the cashier with the invoice copies.

A credit sale is okayed by the cashier using an approved credit list after the salesclerk prepares the three-part invoice. After receiving the cash or approving the invoice, the cashier validates the original copy of the sales invoice and gives it to the customer. At the end of each day the cashier recaps the sales and cash received and forwards the cash and the second copy of all sales invoices to the accounts receivable clerk. The accounts receivable clerk balances the cash received with cash sales invoices and prepares a daily sales summary. The credit sales invoices are posted to the accounts receivable ledger, and then all invoices are sent to the inventory control clerk in the sales department for posting to the inventory control catalog. After posting, the inventory control clerk files all invoices numerically. The accounts receivable clerk posts the daily sales summary to the cash receipts journal and sales journal and files the sales summaries by date.

The cash from cash sales is combined with the cash received on account; this constitutes the daily bank deposit.

Bank Deposits

The bank validates the deposit slip and returns the second copy to the accounting department, where it is filed by date by the accounts receivable clerk. Monthly bank statements are reconciled promptly by the accounting department supervisor and filed by date.

Required:

a. Prepare a document flowchart covering the preceding narrative.

b. Identify potential internal control weaknesses in the Charting, Inc., procedures.

(AICPA Adapted)

18–26. *PROPOSED SYSTEM DESIGN*

Tunefork, Inc., is a large wholesaler of sheet music, music books, musical instruments, and other music-related supplies. The company acquired a medium-sized, tape-oriented computer system last year, and an inventory control system has been implemented already. Now the systems department is developing a new accounts receivable system.

The flowchart in Exhibit 18–6 is a diagram of the accounts receivable system proposed by the design project team. The objectives of the new system are to produce current and timely information that can be used to control bad debts, to provide information to the sales department regarding customers whose accounts are delinquent, to produce monthly statements for customers, and to produce notices to customers regarding a change in the status of their charge privileges.

Input data for the system are taken from four source documents: approved credit applications, sales invoices, cash payment remittances, and credit memoranda. The accounts receivable file is maintained on magnetic tape by customer account number. The record for each customer contains identification information, last month's balance, current month's transactions (detailed), and current balance. The following output items are some of those generated from the system:

Accounts receivable register (weekly). A listing of all customers and account balances included in the accounts receivable file.

Aging schedule (monthly). A schedule of all customers with outstanding balances detailing the amount owed by age classifications: 0–30 days, 30–60 days, 60–90 days, and more than 90 days old.

Delinquency and write-off registers (monthly). Two reports, one listing those accounts which are delinquent and a second listing those customer accounts which have been closed and written off. Related notices are prepared and sent to these customers.

Required:

a. Which system controls should be instituted with the new system? When appropriate, describe the location in the flowchart where the control should be introduced.

b. The credit manager has indicated that the department receives frequent telephone inquiries from customers regarding their accounts. The manager has asked if the department could have a cathode ray tube (CRT) terminal connected to the main computer. Can a CRT terminal be used with the new accounts receivable system as proposed to satisfy the needs of the credit manager?

(CMA Adapted)

18–27. *DESIGNING FILES AND REPORTS*

Value Clothing is a large distributor of all types of clothing acquired from buy-outs, overstocks, and factory seconds. All sales are on account with terms of net 30 days from date of monthly statement. The number of delinquent

EXHIBIT 18–6 Exercise 18–26

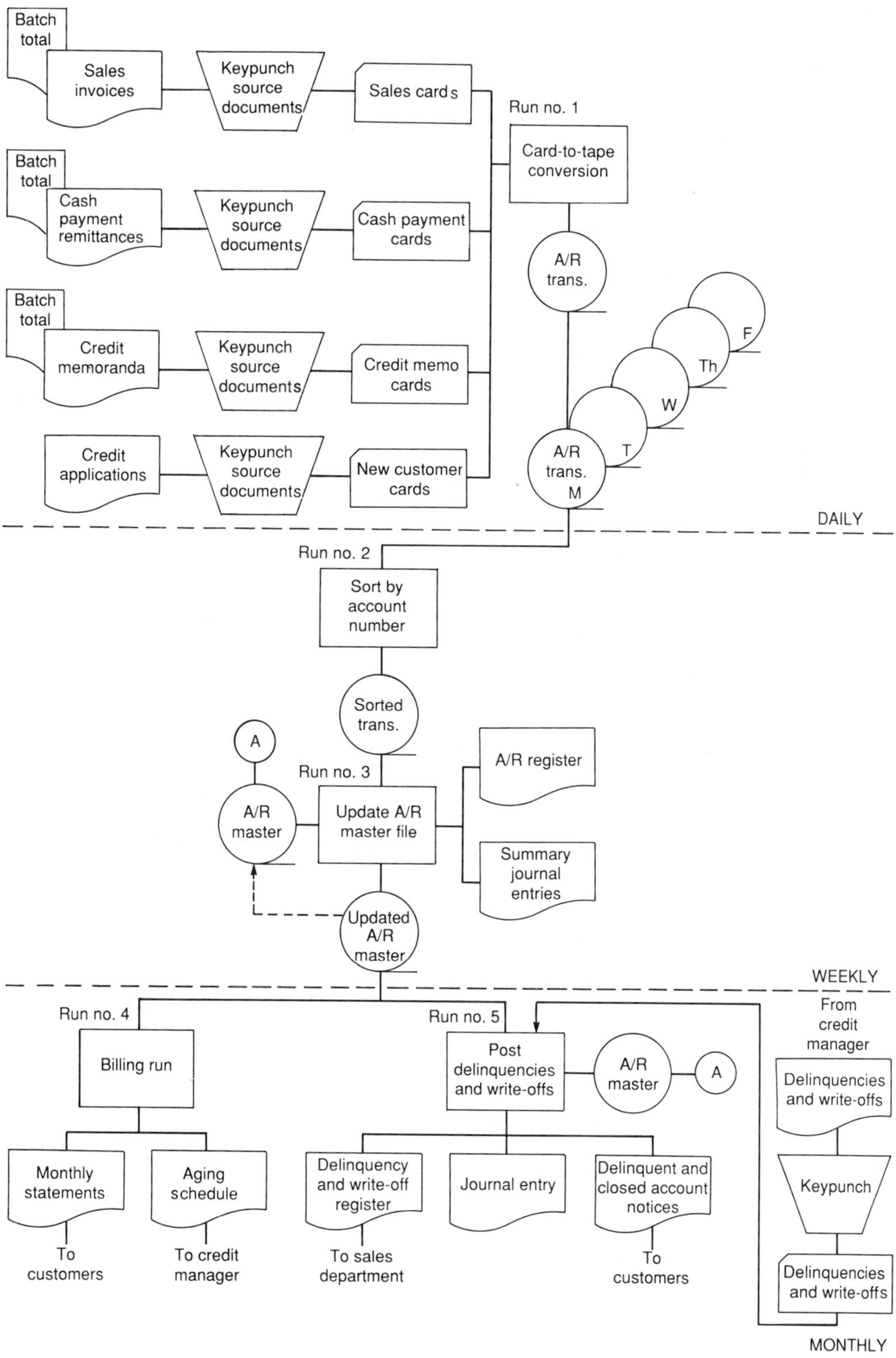

accounts and uncollectible accounts have increased significantly during the last 12 months. Management has determined that the information generated from the present accounts receivable system is inadequate and untimely. In addition, customers frequently complain of errors in their accounts.

The current accounts receivable system has not been changed since Value Clothing started its operations. A new computer was acquired 18 months ago but no attempt has been made to revise the accounts receivable application because other applications were considered more important. Recently the IS Steering Committee has authorized the formation of a design project team to develop a new accounts receivable system. Top management has requested that the new system satisfy the following objectives:

1. Produce current and timely reports regarding customers; these reports would provide useful information to:
   a. Aid in controlling bad debts.
   b. Notify the sales department of customer accounts which are delinquent (accounts which should lose charge privileges).
   c. Notify the sales department of customers whose accounts are considered uncollectible (accounts which should be closed and written off).
2. Produce timely notices to customers regarding:
   a. Amounts owed to Value Clothing.
   b. A change of status of their accounts (loss of charge privileges, account closed).
3. Incorporate the necessary procedures and controls to minimize the chance for errors in customers' accounts.

Input data for the system would be taken from four source documents: credit applications, sales invoices, cash payment remittances, and credit memoranda. The accounts receivable master file would be maintained on a machine-readable file by customer account number. The preliminary design of the new accounts receivable system has been completed by the project team who also put together this brief description of the proposed reports and other output generated by the system:

1. *Accounts Receivable Register.* A daily alphabetical listing of all customers' accounts showing balances as of the last statement, activity since the last statements, and current account balances.
2. *Customer Statements.* Monthly statements for customers showing activity since the last statements and the new account balances. The top portion of the statement is returned with the payment and serves as a remittance advice.
3. *Aging Schedule for All Customers.* A monthly schedule of all customers with outstanding balances displaying the total amounts owed with the amounts classified into age groups: 0–30 days, 30–60 days, 60–90 days, and more than 90 days. The schedule includes totals and percentages for each age category.
4. *Aging Schedule for Past-Due Customers.* A schedule prepared monthly of only those customers whose accounts are past due; that is, over 30 days

outstanding, classified by age. The credit manager uses this schedule to decide which customers receive delinquent notices or temporary suspension of their charge privileges or have their accounts closed.

5. *Activity Reports.* Monthly reports that show:
   a. Customers who have not purchased any merchandise for 90 days.
   b. Customers whose account balance exceeds their credit limit.
   c. Customers whose accounts are delinquent yet they have current sales on account.
6. *Delinquency and Write-Off Register.* A monthly alphabetical listing of customers' accounts which are (*a*) delinquent and (*b*) closed. The listings show names, account numbers, and balances; related notices are prepared and sent to these customers.
7. *Summary of Journal Entries.* Entries are prepared monthly to record write-offs to the accounts receivable file.

Required:

a. Identify the data which should be captured and stored in the computer records for each customer.

b. Review the proposed reports to be generated by the new accounts receivable system.
   1. Discuss whether the proposed reports would be adequate to satisfy the objectives listed.
   2. Recommend changes, if any, which should be made in the proposed reporting structure generated by the new accounts receivable system.

(CMA Adapted)

18–28. ***DESIGNING AN ON-LINE SYSTEM***

Until recently, Consolidated Electricity Company employed a batch processing system for recording the receipt of customers' payments. The following narrative and the flowchart of Exhibit 18–7 describe the procedures involved in this system.

The customer's payment and punched card remittance advice are received in the treasurer's office. An accounts receivable clerk in the treasurer's office keypunches the cash receipt into the remittance advice and forwards the card to the MIS department. The cash receipt is added to a control tape listing and then filed for deposit later in the day. When the deposit slips are received from MIS at approximately 2:30 P.M. each day, the cash receipts are removed from the file and deposited with the original deposit slip. Before the deposit is made, the second copy of the deposit slip and the control tape are compared for accuracy and then filed together.

In the MIS department, the remittance advices received from the treasurer's office are held until 2:00 P.M. daily. At that time the customers' payments are processed to update the records on magnetic tape and to prepare a deposit slip in triplicate. During the update process, data are read from the master accounts receivable tape, processed, and then recorded on a new master tape. The original

EXHIBIT 18–7 Case 18–28

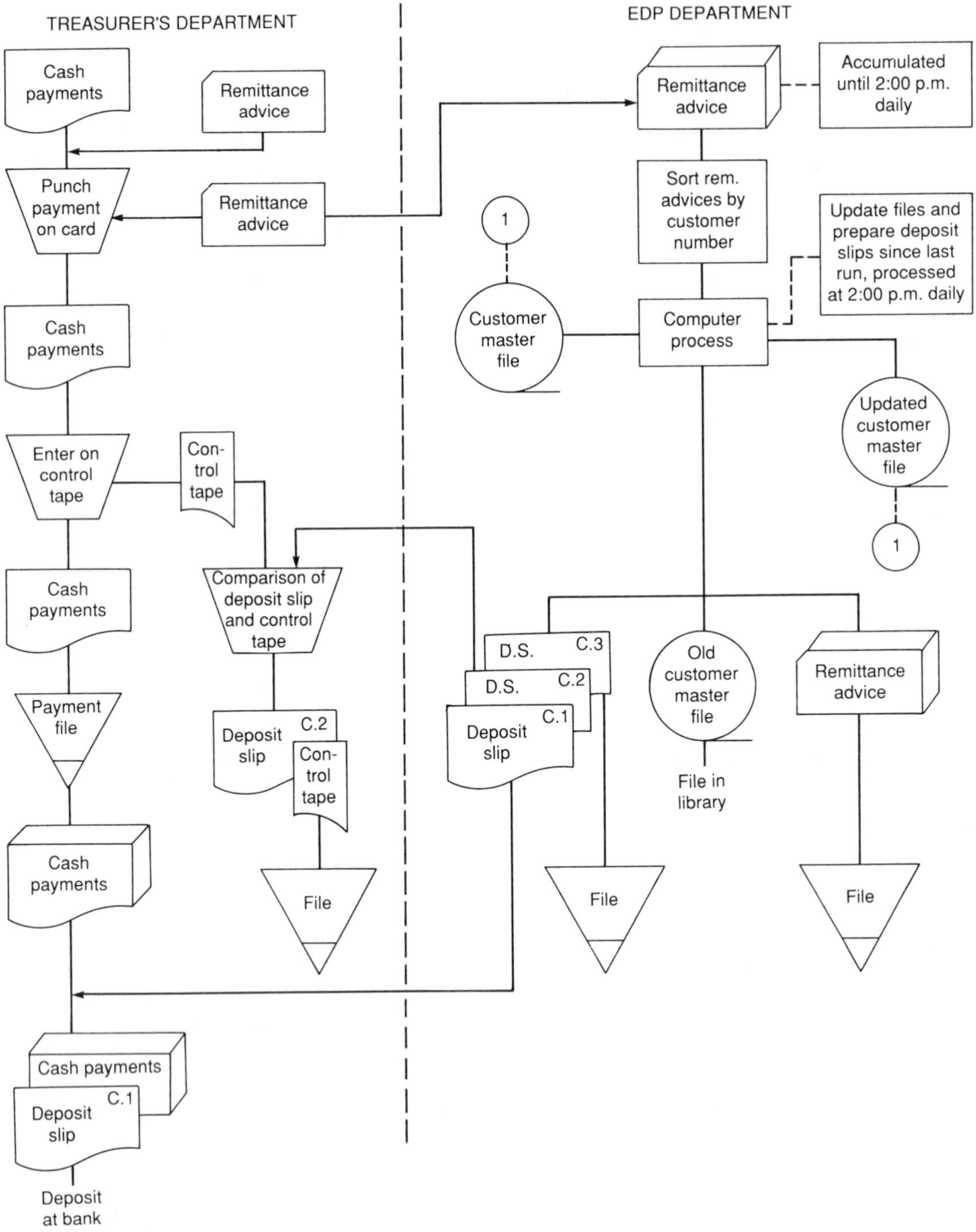

and second copy of the deposit slip are forwarded to the treasurer's office. The old master tape (former accounts receivable file), the remittance advices (in customer number order), and the third copy of the deposit slip are stored and filed in a secure place. The updated accounts receivable master tape is maintained in the system for processing the next day.

Consolidated Electricity Company has revised and redesigned its computer system so that it has on-line capabilities. The new cash receipts procedures, described next, are designed to take advantage of the new system.

The customer's payment and remittance advice are received in the treasurer's office as before. A cathode ray tube terminal is located in the treasurer's office to enter the cash receipts. An operator keys in the customer's number and payment from the remittance advice and checks. The cash receipt is entered into the system once the operator has confirmed that the proper account and amount are displayed on the screen. The payment is then processed on-line against the accounts receivable file maintained on magnetic disk. The cash receipts are filed for deposit later in the day. The remittance advices are filed in the order they are processed. These cards are kept until the next working day and then destroyed. The computer prints out a deposit slip in duplicate at 2:00 P.M. for all cash receipts since the last deposit. The deposit slips are forwarded to the treasurer's office. The cash receipts are removed from the file and deposited with the original deposit slip; the duplicate deposit slip is filed for further reference. At the close of business hours (5:00 P.M.) each day, the EDP department prepares a record of the current day's cash receipts activity on a magnetic tape. This tape is then stored in a secure place in the event of a system malfunction; after 10 working days the tape is released for further use.

Required:

Prepare a system flowchart of the company's new on-line cash receipts system.

(CMA Adapted)

18–29. ***SYSTEM CONVERSION***

Delmo, Inc., is an automotive parts wholesale distributor serving customers east of the Mississippi River. The company has grown during the last 25 years from a small regional distributorship to its present size.

The states are divided into eight separate territories to service Delmo customers adequately. Delmo salespersons regularly call on current and prospective customers in each of the territories. Delmo customers are of four general types: automotive parts stores, hardware stores with an automotive parts section, independent garage owners, and buying groups for garages and filling stations.

Because Delmo must stock such a large variety and quantity of automotive parts to accommodate its customers, the company acquired its own computer system very early and implemented an inventory system first. Other applications such as cash receipts and disbursements, sales analysis, accounts receivable, payroll, and accounts payable have since been added.

Delmo's inventory system consists of an integrated purchase ordering and perpetual inventory system. Each item of inventory is identified by an inventory code number identifying both the product line and the item itself. When the quantity on hand for an item falls below the specified stock level, a purchase order is automatically generated by the computer. After approval by the purchasing manager, the purchase order is sent to the vendor. All receipts, issues, and returns are entered into the computer daily. A printout of all inventory items within product lines showing receipts, issues, and current balance is prepared weekly. However, current status for a particular item carried in the inventory can be obtained daily if it is desired.

Sales orders are filled within 48 hours of receipt. Sales invoices are prepared by the computer the same day that the merchandise is shipped. At the end of each month, several reports are produced that summarize the monthly sales. The current month's and year-to-date sales by product line, territory, and customer class are compared with the same figures from the previous year. In addition, reports showing only the monthly figures for product lines within each territory and customer class within each territory are prepared. In all cases, the reports provide summarized data; that is, detailed data, such as sales by individual customers or product, are not listed. Terms of 2/10, net 30 are standard for all of Delmo's customers.

Customers' accounts receivable are updated daily for sales, sales returns and allowances, and payments on account. Monthly statements are computer prepared and mailed following completion of entries for the last day of the month. Each Friday a schedule is prepared showing the total amount of accounts receivable outstanding by age: Current accounts (0–30 days), slightly past-due accounts (30–90 days), and long overdue accounts (more than 90 days).

Delmo, Inc., recently acquired Wenrock Company, a wholesale distributor of tools and light equipment. In addition to servicing the same type of customers as Delmo, Wenrock also sells to equipment rental shops. Wenrock's sales region is not as extensive as Delmo's but the Delmo management has encouraged Wenrock to expand the distribution of its product to all of Delmo's sales territories.

Wenrock Company uses a computer service bureau to aid in its accounting functions. For example, certain inventory activities are recorded by the service bureau. Each item carried by Wenrock is assigned a product code number identifying the product and the product line. Data regarding shipments received from manufacturers, shipments to customers (sales), and any other physical inventory changes are delivered to the service bureau daily, and the service bureau updates Wenrock's inventory records. A weekly inventory listing showing beginning balance, receipts, issues, and ending balance for each item in the inventory is provided to Wenrock on Monday morning.

Wenrock furnishes the service bureau with information about each sale of merchandise to a customer. The service bureau prepares a five-part invoice and records the sales in its records. This processing is done at night, and all copies of each invoice are delivered to Wenrock the next morning. At the end of the month, the service bureau provides Wenrock with a sales report classified by product line showing the sales in units and dollars for each item sold. Wenrock's sales terms are 2/10, net 30.

The accounts receivable function is still handled by Wenrock's bookkeeper. Two copies of the invoice are mailed to each customer. Two of the remaining copies are filed, one numerically and the other alphabetically by customer. The alphabetic file represents the accounts receivable file. When a customer's payment is received, the invoice is marked ''paid'' and placed in a paid invoice file in alphabetical order. The bookkeeper mails monthly statements according to the following schedule:

10th of the month: A–G

20th of the month: H–O

30th of the month: P–Z.

The final copy of the invoice is included with the merchandise when it is shipped.

Wenrock has continued to use its present accounting system and supplies Delmo management with monthly financial information developed from this system. However, management is anxious to have Wenrock use Delmo's computer and its information system because that would reduce accounting and computer costs, make the financial reports of Wenrock more useful to Delmo management, and provide Wenrock personnel with better information to manage the company.

At the time Delmo acquired Wenrock, it also hired a new marketing manager with experience in both product areas. The new manager wants Wenrock to organize its sales force using the same territorial distribution as Delmo to facilitate the management of the two sales forces.

The new manager also believes that more useful sales information should be provided to individual salespersons and to the department. Even though the monthly sales reports currently prepared provide adequate summary data, the manager would like additional details to aid the sales personnel.

The acquisition of Wenrock Company and expansion of its sales to a larger geographic area has created a cash strain on Delmo, Inc., particularly in the short run. Consequently, cash management has become much more important than in prior years. A weekly report which presents a reliable estimate of daily cash receipts is needed. The treasurer heard that a local company had improved its cash forecasting system by studying the timing of customers' payments on account to see if a discernible payment pattern existed. The model payment pattern was applied to outstanding invoices to estimate the daily cash receipts for the next week. The treasurer thinks this is a good approach and wonders if it can be done at Delmo.

Required:

a. Which additional data must Wenrock Company collect and furnish to use the Delmo data processing system? Which data currently accumulated by Wenrock would no longer be needed due to the conversion to the Delmo system?

b. Using only the data currently available from the Delmo data processing system, which additional reports could be prepared that would be useful to the marketing manager and to the individual salespersons? How would each report be useful to the sales personnel?

(CMA Adapted)

18–30. *MANUAL SYSTEM*

Pat Clark, an obstetrician/gynecologist, began her solo practice two years ago. Currently, she has a case load of about 500 patients. An average of one new patient a day is being added to the case load. She sees between 10 and 12 patients each day.

Organization

The physician employs a registered nurse who provides clinical support to the practice. An office manager is also employed to handle most of the administrative responsibilities, including financial functions and maintenance of medical records.

As a result of this small staff, the majority of the tasks associated with billing and collections are performed by the office manager. No office functions are automated; a one-write pegboard accounting system is used.

Billing

Three main documents are used in the billing process: (1) a patient communication sheet is completed for each patient visit; (2) a daily business summary records all of the transactions for a two- or three-day period (when patient volume increases it will be used daily); and (3) a patient ledger card is an ongoing record of each patient's individual account.

When a patient comes to the office for medical services, the office manager initiates a patient communication sheet (PCS), which is on three-part NCR paper. Using the one-write pegboard system, the patient's name, previous balance, and PCS serial number are entered on the PCS and on one line of the daily business summary. The PCS is then attached to the medical record and sent to the examination room. After providing services, the physician checks the appropriate boxes on the PCS indicating which procedures were performed.

The PCS is returned to the office manager who enters the charges for each of the procedures performed. The patient ledger card is pulled. The procedure codes and total charges are entered on copy three of the PCS as well as on the patient ledger card and the daily business summary using the one-write pegboard. If the patient makes any payment, or if the physician authorizes any adjustments, the payments and/or adjustments are also written on the PCS, the ledger card, and the daily business summary. Finally, the new balance is entered.

At this point, the PCS contains this information: patient name, procedures performed, previous balance, charges, payments, adjustments, and current balance. Identical information has also been entered on one line of the daily business summary and on the patient ledger card.

Copy three of the PCS is given to the patient. Copy one is filed numerically by PCS serial number. Copy two is used for insurance claims. If any hospitalization has taken place, copy two is put in a folder for filing insurance claims. If no hospitalization occurred, it is given to the patient along with copy three. Each patient has to file her own insurance claim.

Cash Receipts

The cash receipts are received by the office manager, either at the time of the visit, during a later visit, or through the mail. If the payment is received at the time of a visit, it is entered as previously described on the PCS, the patient ledger card, and the daily business summary. If payment is received through the mail, the office manager enters the credit on the patient ledger card and the daily business summary.

Cash and checks are kept in a locked drawer until the end of each day when they are put into a locked box in the office. The checks are endorsed immediately by the office manager using a rubber stamp indicating the bank account number and ''For Deposit Only.'' Every few days deposit slips are prepared and deposits are made by the office manager.

Aging of Accounts Receivable

At the end of the day, the office manager reviews all ledger cards pulled that day and color codes them according to the month in which the oldest unpaid charge was incurred. A colored tab is attached to the top of the ledger card indicating whether an account is 30, 60, 90, 120, or more than 120 days old. Accounts with zero balances have no tabs on the ledger card. The ledger cards are then filed in one of two alphabetical files, one for zero balances and one for patients owing money.

Balancing of the Daily Business Summary

Every two or three days, totals for the daily business summary are calculated. Control totals are run to do a proof of posting, an accounts receivable control, an accounts receivable proof, and a cash control. The proof of posting verifies that the total current balances on the daily business summary equal the total previous balances plus charges minus payments minus adjustments. The accounts receivable control takes the previous day's total accounts receivable, adds charges, subtracts payments and adjustments, and produces a current total for accounts receivable. The accounts receivable proof takes accounts receivable at the beginning of the month, adds month-to-date charges, subtracts month-to-date payments and adjustments, and compares the result to the current total for accounts receivable. The cash control provides a current total for cash on hand by taking the beginning cash on hand, adding receipts, subtracting cash paid out and bank deposits, and verifying that against an actual cash count. The daily business summary is then filed by date.

Monthly Accounts Receivable Statement

Once a month all patient ledger cards with debit balances are pulled. For each patient who owes money, an entry is made on the monthly accounts receivable statement listing the date, name, present balance, aging of the account (30, 60, 90, 120, or more than 120 days), and a notation if an insurance claim has been filed. From this accounts receivable statement, the office manager prepares monthly statements and mails them to the patients. Accounts that are more than 120 days past due are reviewed by the physician and turned over to a collection agency.

The physician totals the balances on the ledger cards and compares this total with the total on the monthly accounts receivable statement and with the accounts receivable total on the daily business summary. The accounts receivable statement is then filed by date.

Required:

a. What observations do you have with regard to Dr. Clark's billing and collection system?

b. Prepare a flowchart covering the preceding narrative.

18–31. *CONTROL FLOWCHART*

The following control flowchart covers procedures related to sales order entry, accounts receivable, and shipping of the Floyd Company.

Required:

Suggest areas where internal control may be strengthened.

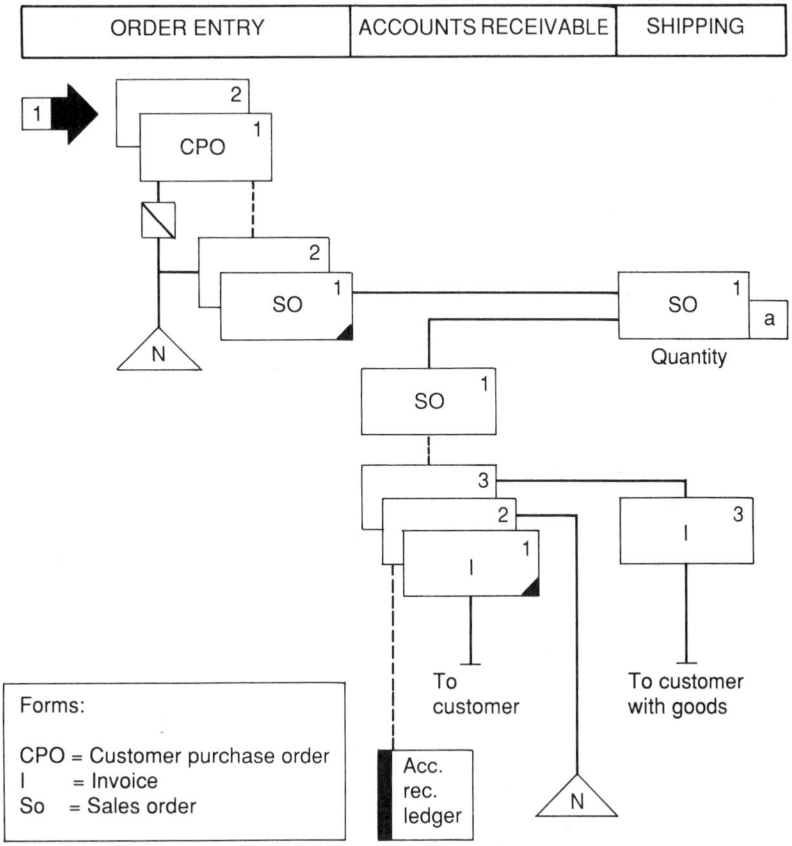

18–32. ***CONTROL FLOWCHART***

The control flowchart on the next page covers procedures related to writing off of accounts receivable of the Sterling Company.

Required:

Suggest areas where internal control may be strengthened.

18–33. ***CONTROL FLOWCHART***

The customer billing function of the Campbell Company, a small paint manufacturer, is attended to by a receptionist, an accounts receivable clerk, and a secretary who also serves as a cashier. The company's paint products are sold to wholesalers and retail stores. The following describes *all* of the procedures performed by the employees of the Campbell Company pertaining to customer billings:

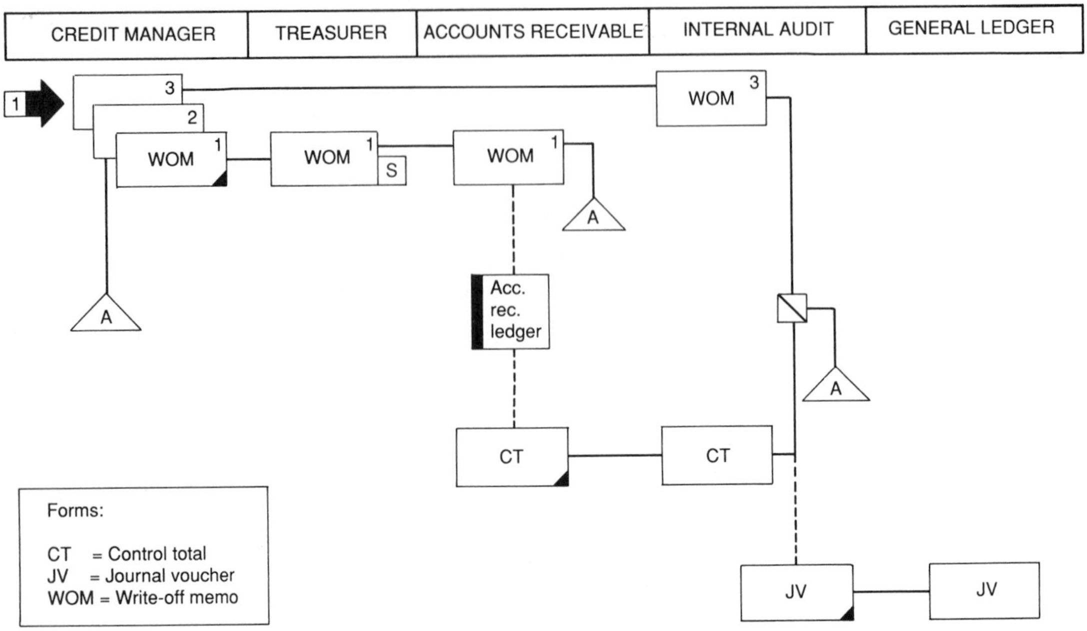

a. The mail is opened by the receptionist, who gives the customers' purchase orders to the accounts receivable clerk. Fifteen to twenty orders are received each day. Under instructions to expedite the shipment of orders, the accounts receivable clerk at once prepares a five-copy sales invoice form, which is distributed as follows:

Copy one is the customer billing copy and is held by the accounts receivable clerk until notice of shipment is received.

Copy two is the accounts receivable department copy and is held for ultimate posting of the accounts receivable records.

Copies three and four are sent to the shipping department.

Copy five is sent to the storeroom as authority for release of the goods to the shipping department.

b. After the paint order has been moved from the storeroom to the shipping department, the shipping department prepares the bills of lading and labels the cartons. Sales invoice copy four is inserted in a carton as a packing slip. After the trucker has picked up the shipment, the customer's copy of the bill of lading and copy three, on which are noted any undershipments, are returned to the accounts receivable clerk. The company does not back order in the event of undershipments; customers are expected to reorder the merchandise. The Campbell Company's copy of the bill of lading is filed by the shipping department.

c. When copy three and the customer's copy of the bill of lading are received by the accounts receivable clerk, copies one and two are completed by numbering them and inserting quantities shipped, unit price, extensions, discounts, and totals. The accounts receivable clerk then mails copy one and the copy of the bill of lading to the customer. Copies two and three are stapled together.

d. The individual accounts receivable ledger cards are posted by the accounts receivable clerk by a bookkeeping machine procedure whereby the sales register is prepared as a carbon copy of the postings. Postings are made from copy two, which is then filed, along with staple-attached copy three, in numerical order. Monthly, the general ledger clerk summarizes the sales register for posting to the general ledger accounts.

Required:

a. Prepare a control flowchart covering the procedures just presented.

b. Discuss the internal control weaknesses in the Campbell Company's procedures concerning customer billings and related accounting.

c. Suggest changes to overcome internal control weaknesses listed in *b*.

(AICPA Adapted)

18–34. *CONTROL FLOWCHART*

The following procedures relate to the Black Biscuit Company, which is privately owned by two brothers. One of the brothers serves as the president (in charge of sales and finance); the other, vice president (in charge of production).

Sales orders (prenumbered)

Sales orders are prepared in quadruplicate by salespersons, showing shipping and billing instructions. Quantities are shown under the *ordered* section, opposite a printed list of biscuits and packagings. Unit prices are also marked by salespersons. Three copies are mailed to the company.

The president reviews the orders and checks with the collection department concerning questionable credit risks, or asks the secretary-treasurer for a credit rating on new accounts. He approves the orders and turns them over to the order department to verify unit prices. The order department retains one copy and turns two copies over to the finished goods, stores, and shipping department.

Goods are prepared for shipment and the quantities are entered under the *shipped* section of the order, one copy of which is included with the merchandise as a shipping memo. The other copy is entered on a daily summary sheet which forms the basis for deductions from the stock cards in the finished goods, stores, and shipping department.

The order department prepares a back-order form in quadruplicate, if necessary. One copy is sent to the salesperson.

A calculator operator extends and adds the completed orders, which are turned over to the billing machine operator.

Telephone orders are handled in the same manner, with a copy mailed to the salesperson.

Contacts with institutions are handled by the president. He, or his secretary, calls the institutions and advises them of items that are available and agrees on a price, if there is an excessive supply that the president believes has to be reduced more than 10 percent in price. The president has these orders written up in triplicate and at the same time prepares the invoice. He retains one copy of the order, sending two to the finished goods, stores, and shipping department.

Invoices

Regular invoices are prepared in quadruplicate on prenumbered invoice forms by a billing machine operator whose automatic calculations must agree with the calculator operator's figures. Three copies are returned to the calculator operator, and the remaining copy is filed in a tray under customer's name (one tray for each salesperson). These trays are the accounts receivable ledgers. The operator keeps control sheets for each tray on which she lists the total debits and credits each day. Each tray contains about 100 active accounts. Trays are locked when the operator is not there, and nothing can be extracted from a tray without her making a record on her control.

Copies of invoices to institutions that are prepared in the president's office are filed in a separate accounts receivable tray by the operator.

The calculator operator compares regular invoices with orders for typographical errors, sends the original to the mailing department, and sends one copy to the statistical department. The third copy is added; the total for the day is entered in a sales summary that forms the basis of the posting to the general ledger and is then filed in numerical order with the related order form attached.

The statistical department puts its copy of the invoice, by salespersons, on pegboards. Quantities, packagings, and values are cross-added and entered on sales summaries that balance with the total determined by the calculator operator in the order department. Invoices are then filed by customers; the total dollar value for each customer is determined monthly and agreed in total with the sales summary. The former are the basis of commission calculations, and the latter of rebate calculations.

Credit memos

The receiving department prepares *returned goods* slips in quadruplicate. These are approved by the superintendent after the returned goods are inspected, and are then sent to the order department. The order, billing, and statistical departments handle receiving slips and credit memos in the same manner as orders and invoices.

Required:

a. Prepare a control flowchart covering procedures related to the return of goods and issuance of credit memos.

b. Give your comments on the existing internal control related to the return of goods and issuance of credit memos.

(AICPA Adapted)

Chapter 19

Expenditure Cycle Applications

Learning Objectives:

1. To review the accounting entries recorded in the expenditure cycle.
2. To learn which documents, reports, and records are used in the expenditure cycle.
3. To understand how accounting transactions are processed by the application systems in the expenditure cycle.
4. To see how control practices and procedures are applied in the expenditure cycle.

INTRODUCTION

An accounting system records the activities of a business using four transaction cycles. In this chapter, you will learn how accounting systems record those activities that acquire goods and services. These activities are part of the expenditure cycle.

In this transaction cycle, the accounting system records four economic events. First, organizations request goods or services. Computer-based systems use purchasing systems to record these requests. Second, organizations receive the goods or services. When goods are involved, a receiving system records this event. Third, organizations recognize an obligation to pay for the goods or services. This economic event is processed by the voucher system. Finally,

ILLUSTRATION 19–1 Application Systems in the Expenditure Cycle

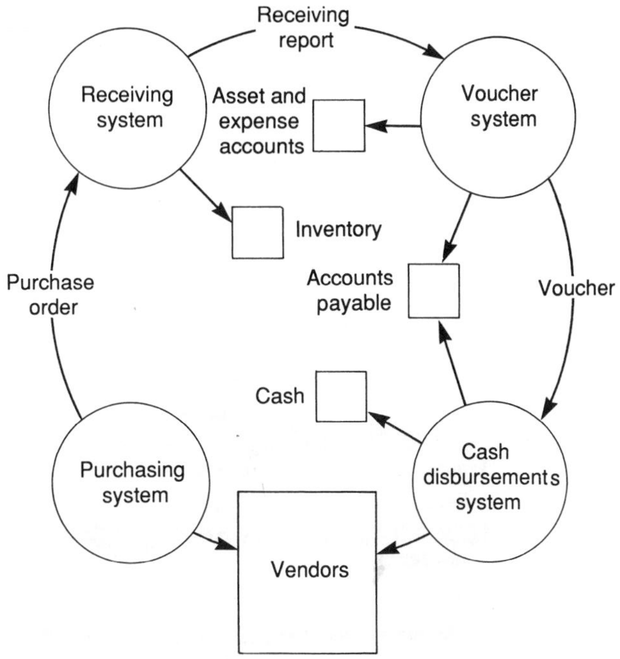

organizations use cash disbursements systems to record the fourth economic event, payment for the goods or services. The voucher and cash disbursements systems together are called the *accounts payable* system.

Illustration 19–1 shows the relationships between the application systems in the expenditure cycle. The circles in this diagram represent application systems, the large square is the external entity, and the small squares stand for general ledger accounts. The accounts interface these systems with those in other transaction cycles. The interfaces shown between these systems may take the form of documents or data records.

DOCUMENTS, REPORTS, AND RECORDS

In an introductory accounting course you studied entries for recording transactions that provide a conceptual representation of how accounting systems work. Few organizations record transactions in that way now. However, this chapter reviews those entries so you can relate what you learned in introductory accounting to how modern organizations record transactions.

In practice, an accounting system records transaction data in documents, accumulates the data in accounting records, and discloses the data in reports. To understand the accounting system, you must know how manual and computerized procedures process these documents, records, and reports.

Expenditure Cycle Transactions and Documents

Three types of transactions occur routinely in the expenditure cycle: credit purchases, cash disbursements, and purchase returns. Illustration 19–2 summarizes these transactions and shows the documents used by the accounting system in recording them.

Credit Purchases. An organization with a good credit rating makes most of its purchases on credit. To initiate a credit purchase, someone in the organization recognizes the need for goods or services. An authorized person such as a supervisor requests them on a *purchase requisition.* A copy of this document goes to the purchasing department, where a purchasing agent approves the purchase, selects a vendor, prepares a *purchase order,* and mails it to the vendor. The purchase order, when accepted by the vendor, becomes a legally binding contract.

When the vendor provides the goods or services, a *receiving report* documents their receipt in the receiving department. After receiving a copy of the receiving report, an invoice from the vendor, and a copy of the purchase order, the accounts payable department prepares a *voucher* showing which asset or expense account to debit. Accountants call this the "account distribution." Accounts payable then attaches the invoice, receiving report, and purchase order to the voucher and submits it to the treasurer for approval.

The accounting entry recording a credit purchase in the general ledger is

Dr.	Asset or expense account	xxx	
Cr.	Accounts payable		xxx

ILLUSTRATION 19–2 Expenditure Cycle Transactions and Related Documents

Type of Transaction	*Related Documents*
Credit purchase	Purchase requisition Purchase order Receiving report Voucher
Cash disbursement	Check
Purchase return	Debit memo

ILLUSTRATION 19–3 A Purchase Requisition

```
                         *********************************
                         *OFFICIAL TEXTBOOK REQUISITION *
                         *********************************
UNIV. OF HOUSTON BOOKSTORE                                   RETURN THIS FORM BY : 10/01/88
CALL : 748-XXXX              TXT. MGR

              SIGNATURE DEPT CHAIR
              SIGNATURE INSTRUCTOR
              PRINT OR TYPE INSTRUCTOR NAME             INSTRUCTOR PHONE #

INFORMATION FOR TERM : S89    CLASS :                          FILL IN DATA BELOW :
DEPARTMENT CONTACT :                     PHONE :

AUTHOR    :                                                REQUIRED      ? : YES / NO
TITLE     :                              EDITION :         ENROLLMENT      :
PUBLISHER :              COVER :                           SECTION NUMBERS:
                         ISBN  :                           INSTRUCTOR      :

AUTHOR    :                                                REQUIRED      ? : YES / NO
TITLE     :                              EDITION :         ENROLLMENT      :
PUBLISHER :              COVER :                           SECTION NUMBERS:
                         ISBN  :                           INSTRUCTOR      :

AUTHOR    :                                                REQUIRED      ? : YES / NO
TITLE     :                              EDITION :         ENROLLMENT      :
PUBLISHER :              COVER :                           SECTION NUMBERS:
                         ISBN  :                           INSTRUCTOR      :

REQUIRED SUPPLIES :
```

Illustration 19–3 contains a purchase requisition. Illustration 19–4 shows a purchase order, and Illustration 19–5, a receiving report. During system design, the design team determines their contents and layouts. These documents must capture the data required for the accounting and management reports produced by the systems in the expenditure cycle.

Vouchers exist in different forms. Sometimes the voucher is a large envelope containing the other documents and showing the expense distribution on the outside. Other companies use a rubber stamp applied to the vendor invoice. Regardless of its form, the voucher should show the general ledger accounts to be debited, the amounts, the name and address of the vendor, and the due date for payment.

Illustration 19–6 shows a common approach. This voucher is a prenumbered form that is fastened to the other documents.

Cash Disbursements. After a voucher is attached to the associated invoice, receiving report, and purchase order, these documents remain filed in the accounts payable department until the date payment is due. On the due date, this

ILLUSTRATION 19–4 A Purchase Order

UNIVERSITY OF HOUSTON BOOKSTORE

UNIVERSITY PARK
4800 CALHOUN RD
(713) 749-1301

UNIVERSITY CENTER
HOUSTON, TX 77004
EASYLINK 62025399

STORE NO. 613

PURCHASE ORDER

SAN # 100-6134

BILL TO:

SHIP TO:

PURCHASE ORDER NUMBER
2178863
PURCHASE ORDER DATE

THIS NUMBER MUST ACCOMPANY ALL SHIPMENTS WITH PACKING LIST SHOWING LIST PRICES AND DISCOUNTS.

SPECIAL INSTRUCTIONS
SEND INVOICE TO "SHIP TO" ADDRESS
SHIP LATEST EDITION UNLESS OTHERWISE SPECIFIED

SHIP VIA:

QUANTITY REC'D	QUANTITY ORD	AUTHOR	TITLE	EDITION	COVER	SUB-PUB	ISBN	DEPARTMENT COURSE

OPERATOR INITIALS: CRTN RCVD: DATE: BY: INVOICE NO. AUTHORIZED PER:
50-00141 (3/85)

ILLUSTRATION 19–5 A Receiving Report

STORE #	DATE REC'D	VENDOR	CTNS.	INVOICE #	CLASS	TOTAL COST	TOTAL RETAIL	KEY-REC NO	BARNES NOBLE
								177788	

P.O. # | CARRIER | B/L # | INVOICE DATE | ACTUAL FREIGHT CHARGES ______

FROM FREIGHT BILL OR POSTAGE CHARGES

OVER / SHORT / INFORMATION
(ONLY IF REQUIRED)

CLASS	NUMBER OVER	NUMBER SHORT	BARNES & NOBLE TOTAL RETAIL

RETAIL INFORMATION (WHEN REQUIRED)

CLASS	DISC %	COST	FREIGHT	RETAIL

RECEIVED BY ______
DATE ______
APPROVED BY ______
DATE ______
COMMENTS ______

KEY-REC

177788 **1 - ACCOUNTS PAYABLE**

ILLUSTRATION 19–6 A Voucher

SUNLIGHT MANUFACTORY COMPANY
105 Red Hot Road
Dallas, Texas 75248

Voucher No. 175324
Date ____________

Vendor invoice date	Vendor invoice number	Amount	Discount	Return and allowance	Net	Account distribution

Detach Here

SUNLIGHT MANUFACTORY COMPANY
105 Red Hot Road
Dallas, Texas 75248

Check No. ____________
Date ____________

Pay to the order of ________________________________ $ ____________

____

First National Bank of
Far North Dallas
Box 7707
Dallas, Texas 75248

____

____

Prepared by	Verified by	Entered by	Filed	Due date

voucher package goes to the treasurer's department where it is approved for payment. This department then mails a check in payment.

Some vendors offer discounts from the invoice price in return for prompt payment. For example, a common discount policy is 2/10, n/30, read as "two ten, net thirty." This means that a buyer paying the invoice within 10 days of its mailing is entitled to a 2 percent discount from the amount shown on the invoice. Otherwise, the buyer should pay the total, or net, amount within 30 days.

When an organization takes discounts of this kind, it records the amount of the discount in a special account. The accounting entry recording the cash disbursement transaction is

Dr. Accounts Payable	xxx	
Cr. Purchase Discounts		xxx
Cr. Cash		xxx

Illustration 19–7 contains a check with a check stub attached showing the specific invoices paid by the check. This allows the vendor to record the payment properly in the vendor's accounts receivable records. It also shows the dates of these invoices and any discounts claimed by the buyer.

ILLUSTRATION 19–7 A Check

T.L. JAMES ENTERPRISES

001693

EVANS AUTO SUPPLY CO.
6078 PIEDMONT RD. NE
ATLANTA, GA. 30324

DATE
08/31/91

CHECK NUMBER
1010

INVOICE NO.	DATE	AMOUNT	DISCOUNT	NET AMT.
46	05/01	68.34	0.00	68.34
#1258	06/16	10250.00	0.00	10250.00
#1264	06/20	5000.00	0.00	5000.00
#1287	06/30	2005.36	0.00	2005.36
#1287	06/30	4436.73	0.00	4436.73
1201	08/01	450.00	0.00	450.00
	06/30	-111.00	0.00	111.00
1201	08/01	-50.00	0.00	-50.00
		TOTAL =		$22049.43

NEGATIVE AMOUNTS ARE CREDITS APPLIED ON THIS PAYMENT

T.L. JAMES ENTERPRISES
1710 MY STREET
YOUR CITY, STATE 04444

NATIONAL STATE BANK
DOWNTOWN OFFICE
YOUR CITY, STATE 12345

001693
1010

**** TWENTY TWO THOUSAND FORTY NINE & 43/100 DOLLARS

DATE 08/31/91 AMOUNT ****$22,049.43

PAY TO THE ORDER OF EVANS AUTO SUPPLY CO.
6078 PIEDMONT RD. NE
ATLANTA, GA. 30324

SAMPLE - VOID
FORM 1015
COMPATIBLE ENVELOPE E500

⑈001693⑈ ⑆028001489⑆ 045-05507 6⑈

Purchase Returns. This transaction occurs when an organization returns to the vendor an item purchased on credit. This may occur because the purchaser received unrequested items, an excessive number of items, or items of inferior quality. Along with the returned goods, the purchaser sends a request that the vendor credit the purchaser's account (containing a debit balance in the vendor's accounting records) for the cost of the return. The document used by the purchaser to make this request is a *debit memo* as shown in Illustration 19–8. They use this name because of the accounts payable entry recording the purchase return:

Dr. Accounts payable	xxx	
Cr. Asset or expense account		xxx

You are now familiar with the documents used in the expenditure cycle and with the accounting entries produced from the data on these documents. Next you will see the reports produced in this transaction cycle.

ILLUSTRATION 19–8 A Debit Memo

SUNLIGHT MANUFACTORY COMPANY
105 Red Hot Road
Dallas, Texas 75248

Debit
Memo no. 643

To: Date:

Debit

We return the items indicated below and debit your account by the amount shown.

Item	Description	Quantity	Unit Price	Amount

Remarks:

Goods shipped by Date	Goods shipped via	Debit memo prepared by Date	

Expenditure Cycle Reports

Just as in the revenue cycle, application systems in the expenditure cycle produce three kinds of reports: control reports, registers, and special purpose reports. However, these disclose different data from those in the other cycle.

Control Reports. A control report summarizes the changes made to a file. Accountants use a control report to determine when changes were made improperly or to ensure that no transactions were omitted during processing. With a computer-based system, data control clerks examine control reports. They compare control totals, hash totals, and record counts to detect improper processing.

Illustration 19–9 contains a control report that lists the vendor invoices received and added to a file of pending vendor invoices by an on-line real-time system. It allows the data entry clerk to ensure that all invoices were properly added by the system.

ILLUSTRATION 19–9 A Control Report

RUN DATE 08/24/91 — T.L. JAMES COMPANY — PAGE 1

Accounts Payable

ENTER INVOICES CONTROL REPORT

VENDOR ID	INVOICE NUMBER / DATE	AMOUNT DUE / DATE DUE	DISCOUNT AMOUNT / DATE	ACCOUNT	AMOUNT	ACCOUNT	AMOUNT	ACCOUNT	AMOUNT	PRE-PAID	ACCT C/AP
EVANS	1201 08/01/91	$450.00 08/31/91	$0.00 08/24/91	51200	$400.00	51600	$50.00		$0.00		1 / 1
MARSH	003187 08/31/91	$10,000.00 09/30/91	$200.00 09/10/91	53000	$5,000.00	53100	$5,000.00		$0.00		1 / 1
COX PR	1 AUTO INVOICE 08/30/91	$2,000.00 08/30/91	$0.00 08/30/91	51100	$2,000.00		$0.00		$0.00		1 / 1
GAPOWR	2 AUTO INVOICE 08/10/91	$1,000.00 08/10/91	$0.00 08/10/91	51400	$1,000.00		$0.00		$0.00		1 / 1
	RUN TOTALS	$13,450.00	$200.00								

*** END OF Enter Invoices ***

Registers. A register contains a list of transactions of a certain type recorded during a processing period, such as a day, a week, or a month. Registers contain detail data supporting summary entries in accounting ledgers, so they provide an audit trail for account balances.

A register in a manual system is a special purpose journal. For this reason, a register in a computer-based system is sometimes identified as a journal.

Illustration 19–10 contains a check register that shows a list of checks issued in payment of vendor invoices. Other registers produced in the expenditure cycle include purchase order, receipts, and voucher registers.

Special Purpose Reports. Special purpose reports in the expenditure cycle help managers schedule payments to vendors. They include the open voucher report, the voucher aging report, and the cash requirements report. An on-line real-time system may also produce a vendor query report.

Open Invoices Report. An open invoices report lists unpaid vendor invoices as of the date of the report. It lists the invoices received from each vendor and the amounts owed on each invoice, as shown in Illustration 19–11.

ILLUSTRATION 19–10 A Register

RUN DATE: 08/24/91

T.L. JAMES COMPANY
Accounts Payable
Check Register

PAGE 1

VENDOR ID	VENDOR NAME	CHECK NUMBER	CHECK DATE	AMOUNT	DISCOUNT	NET / TOTAL
BANKAM	BANK OF AMERICA	804	08/26/91	$1,205.67	$0.00	$1,205.67
FICA	NATIONAL BANK OF ATLANTA	805	08/26/91	$5,773.15	$0.00	$5,773.15
GAPOWR	GAINESVILLE POWER CO.	806	08/26/91	$1,387.21	$0.00	$1,387.21

NUMBER OF CHECKS WRITTEN: 3

TOTAL GROSS	=	$8,366.03
TOTAL DISCOUNT	=	$0.00
TOTAL NET	=	$8,366.03

*** END OF Check Register ***

ILLUSTRATION 19–11 An Open Invoices Report

RUN DATE 08/24/91 | T.L. JAMES COMPANY | PAGE 1

Accounts Payable

Open Invoices Report

A/P ACCOUNT CODE : 1 20100

VENDOR ID	ENTRY DATE	INVOICE NUMBER	INVOICE DATE	DUE AMOUNT	DUE DATE	DISCOUNT AMOUNT	DISCOUNT DATE	NET	PAY?
ALLEN	05/01/90	016	04/10/90	$305.00	05/10/90			$305.00	YES
	08/24/91	OPEN CREDIT	08/24/91	-$75.00	08/24/91			-$75.00	YES
				$230.00		$0.00		$230.00	
ATLGAS	05/01/90	45	05/13/90	$302.00	06/12/90			$302.00	YES
	06/05/90	01177	06/15/90	$250.00	07/15/90			$250.00	YES
				$552.00		$0.00		$552.00	
PETWAY	06/10/90	4	03/22/90	$65.00	04/21/90			$65.00	YES
	06/05/90	030795	06/08/90	$170.00	07/08/90			$170.00	YES
				$235.00		$0.00		$235.00	
				$30,046.05		$0.00		$30,046.05	

TOTAL OPEN INVOICES = 18

*** END OF Open Invoices Report ***

Voucher Aging Report. A voucher aging report summarizes vouchers by how long they have existed. Vendor invoices that remain unpaid for an excessive length of time may damage a firm's business relationship with the vendor. They may also harm the firm's credit rating, making it difficult to purchase on credit. Frequently, old unpaid invoices are a result of disagreements with the vendor. The voucher aging report, as shown in Illustration 19–12, alerts the accounts payable department to the existence of such problems.

Cash Requirements Report. A cash requirements report lists vouchers by the date they are due to be paid. It aids the accounts payable department in planning cash flows and in identifying which invoices should be paid promptly to receive discounts and maintain good relations with vendors. This report also shows the effect of paying these invoices on the cash balance. Illustration 19–13 contains a cash requirements report.

Query Vendors. An on-line real-time system allows users to query the data base for current information. In the expenditure cycle, accounts payable clerks often need to know the status of a specific vendor's account. They obtain this

ILLUSTRATION 19–12 A Voucher Aging Report

RUN DATE: 08/24/91 T.L. JAMES COMPANY PAGE 1
Accounts Payable
Ageing Report

AGEING DATE: 08/24/91
A/P ACCOUNT CODE : 1 20100

VENDOR	CURRENT	1 TO 30	31 TO 60	61 TO 90	OVER 90	CREDITS	TOTAL NET DUE
ALLEN	$0.00	$0.00	$0.00	$0.00	$305.00	$75.00	$230.00
ATLMAG	$0.00	$0.00	$0.00	$0.00	$552.00	$0.00	$552.00
BANKAM	$0.00	$0.00	$0.00	$0.00	$1,205.67	$0.00	$1,205.67
EVANS	$450.00	-$50.00	$0.00	$0.00	$21,760.43	$111.00	$22,049.43
FICA	$0.00	$0.00	$0.00	$0.00	$5,773.15	$0.00	$5,773.15
MARSH	$10,000.00	$0.00	$0.00	$0.00	$152.09	$0.00	$10,152.09
SOBELL	$0.00	$0.00	$0.00	$0.00	$45.00	$0.00	$45.00
TOTAL=	$10,450.00	$950.00	$0.00	$0.00	$42,137.05	$186.00	$53,351.05

TOTAL VENDORS LISTED = 16

** END OF - Ageing Report **

from a query vendors report, shown in Illustration 19–14. Many systems allow users the option of printing the report or displaying it on a terminal.

Four special purpose reports are produced by the applications in the expenditure cycle. The application systems in this cycle use registers and control reports to summarize the information from data maintained in the accounting records.

Expenditure Cycle Accounting Records

Accounting systems maintain records for manual processes on paper journals, ledgers, and in filing cabinets. For computerized processes, journals and ledgers are in computer readable form and contain master records and transaction records. Although their forms differ, their contents are similar.

Noncomputerized Records. Manual systems maintain accounting records in the form of books, cards, and filing cabinets. The expenditure cycle uses two special journals and several manual files.

ILLUSTRATION 19–13 A Cash Requirements Report

RUN DATE 08/24/91 — T.L. JAMES COMPANY — PAGE 1

Accounts Payable

Cash Requirements Report

** DATA SORTED BY DUE DATE

** CASH ACCOUNT : 1 10200

DUE DATE	VENDOR	INVOICE NUMBER	INV. DATE	AMOUNT	DISCOUNT	NET	DAILY TOTAL	REQ. TO DATE
03/10/90	HARLEN	56	02/16/90	$32.19	$0.00	$32.19	$32.19	$32.19
04/17/90	MARSH	70	03/10/90	$52.09	$0.00	$52.09	$52.09	$84.28
04/21/90	PRTWAY	4	03/22/90	$65.80	$0.00	$65.80	$65.80	$150.08
05/01/90	FICA	MAY	05/01/90	$273.15	$0.00	$273.15	$273.15	$423.23
05/10/90	ALLEN	016	04/10/90	$305.00	$0.00	$305.00	$305.00	$728.23
05/12/90	MARSH	345	04/12/90	$100.00	$0.00	$100.00	$100.00	$828.23
OPEN CR.	EVANS		06/30/90	-$111.00	$0.00	-$111.00		
	ALLEN	OPEN CREDIT	08/24/91	-$75.00	$0.00	-$75.00	-$186.00	$53,201.85
SPEC.CR.	EVANS	1201	08/01/91	-$50.00	$0.00	-$50.00	-$50.00	$53,151.85
	$0.00	$53,151.85						

*** END OF Cash Requirements Report ***

In a manual system, the voucher register and the check register are special journals. Accounts payable clerks record vouchers in the voucher register as they prepare vendor invoices for payment. Cash disbursements clerks record checks in the check register as they prepare them. These, similar to all registers, provide an audit trail by showing the sources of entries in the general and subsidiary ledgers. Additionally, they serve as methods of initially recording the transactions creating the entries. Illustration 19–15 shows the contents of these journals.

Computerized Records. In computerized systems, accounting records are kept in computer files and data bases. In a traditional data file system, applications in the expenditure cycle use one master file and seven transaction files.

A data base management system (DBMS) stores data in a data base rather than in files. The difference between how traditional data file systems and how DBMSs store data has no effect on how application systems process the data. The difference only affects how the system retrieves the data from the secondary storage device.

ILLUSTRATION 19–14 A Vendor Query Report

```
RUN DATE: 08/24/91                                T.L. JAMES COMPANY
                                                  Accounts Payable
                                                   Query Vendors

VENDOR
  ID        NAME / ADDRESS           PHONE             AMOUNTS              LAST CHECK
------ -------------------------- ------------- ------------------------ -----------------
GAPOWR GAINESVILLE POWER CO.                     YTD PURCH:    $8,226.75 NO. :    806
       27 GAINESVILLE RD.                        YTD PAYMT:    $7,226.75 AMT.:    $1,307.21
       GAINESVILLE, GA. 30776                    CURR. BAL:    $1,307.21 DATE:  08/26/91


     INVOICE         AMOUNT DUE      DISCOUNT                                                                     DISC.
  NUMBER / DATE     / DATE DUE    AMOUNT / DATE  ACCOUNT - AMOUNT   ACCOUNT - AMOUNT   ACCOUNT - AMOUNT  TAKEN PAY
----------------  -------------  -------------  ---------------------------------------------------------- ----- ---
4443                   $307.21          $0.00  51400      $307.21 0            $0.00 0             $0.00 NO  NH
  05/01/90            05/31/90                 0            $0.00 0            $0.00 0             $0.00
                                                   CASH ACCOUNT  1 A/P ACCOUNT  1

2  AUTO INVOICE      $1,000.00          $0.00  51400    $1,000.00 0            $0.00 0             $0.00 NO  NH
  08/10/91            08/10/91       08/10/91  0            $0.00 0            $0.00 0             $0.00
                                                   CASH ACCOUNT  1 A/P ACCOUNT  1

CK. NO. 806         -$1,307.21          $0.00  0            $0.00 0            $0.00 0             $0.00 NO  VC
  08/26/91            08/26/91       08/26/91  0            $0.00 0            $0.00 0             $0.00
                                                   CASH ACCOUNT  1 A/P ACCOUNT  1
```


ILLUSTRATION 19–15 Noncomputerized Records in the Expenditure Cycle

A voucher register

Page ______

Date	Voucher Number	Date Paid	Check Number	Cr. Vouchers Payable	Miscellaneous Cr.			Dr. Inventory	Dr. Accounts Payable	Expense Ledger Dr.			Miscellaneous Dr.		
					Account	Ref.	Amount			Account	Ref.	Amount	Account	Ref.	Amount

A check register

Page ______

Date	Check No.	Voucher No.	Name of Payee	Amount

This means that if you learn how a traditional file system arranges data in files, you will understand how the DBMS software maintains relationships in the data base. The record layout for an application in a traditional file system identifies the subschema required by that application with a DBMS.

Master Files. The *vendor master file* contains one record for each approved supplier of goods and services. The key field for this record is the vendor number. The record contains the vendor's name, address, discount terms, and payment terms. In some systems the vendor master record also contains data summarizing past transactions with the supplier. This file constitutes the list of suppliers from whom employees are authorized to purchase goods and services.

Good internal control requires that a manager screen and approve all additions to the vendor master file. This prevents employees from creating a nonexistent vendor and then creating false documentation to cause issue of payments to that vendor. Purchasing agents should be allowed to acquire goods or services from other suppliers only with special approval.

Transaction Files. Depending on the design of the system, applications in the expenditure cycle use as many as seven transaction files. On-line real-time systems, because they process transactions one at a time rather than in batches, require fewer computerized transaction files.

Some systems create a *requisitions* file containing one record for each item that requires purchasing. This file is an input to the purchasing application. Other systems enter data into the purchasing system directly from a manual file containing purchase requisitions. From the data in the requisitions file, a purchasing agent creates files containing the data required for printing purchase orders. Two files, the open purchase order and purchase order detail files, contain this data.

The *open purchase order* file has one record for each purchase order that has been mailed; its key field is the purchase order number. Most purchase orders authorize the vendor to ship several different products. The purchase order shows each one on a separate line, and each is called a line item. The purchasing application uses a *purchase order detail* file to record line item data. It contains one record for each line on the purchase order, and its key field is the purchase order number and line item number combined. Illustration 19–16 shows the contents of the two purchasing files.

Some systems create a computerized *receipts* file containing one record for each item received from vendors. This record shows the purchase order and line item numbers authorizing receipt, the date, and the quantity received. The receiving system produces this file as an input to the voucher system. Other systems use a manual file of receiving reports for this purpose.

A similar transaction file is the *pending invoice* file. Its records contain data on vendor invoices that have arrived in the mail prior to receipt of the goods. The voucher system matches a pending invoice record with one or more receipts records before producing a record for the voucher file. Some systems replace the pending invoice file with a manual file of vendor invoices.

ILLUSTRATION 19–16 Contents of Purchasing Records

Open Purchase Order File	*Purchase Order Detail File*
PURCHASE-ORDER-NUMBER*	PURCHASE-ORDER-NUMBER*
VENDOR-NUMBER**	LINE-ITEM-NUMBER*
PURCHASE-ORDER-DATE	REQUISITION-NUMBER
DELIVERY-DUE-DATE	REQUISITION-DATE
PURCHASING-AGENT-NAME	INVENTORY-ITEM-NUMBER
	VENDOR-PRODUCT-NUMBER
	ITEM-DESCRIPTION
	ITEM-QUANTITY
	ITEM-UNIT-PRICE

*Designates a primary key.
**Designates a secondary key.

The *voucher* file contains one record for each unpaid voucher. A fully computerized voucher system creates a voucher record when it finds matching purchase order, pending invoice, and receipts records in those files. In other systems, an accounts payable clerk matches the purchase order, vendor invoice, and receiving report. The clerk then prepares the voucher documents and enters data from the document in the voucher system. Each voucher produces a record in the voucher file. The cash disbursements application removes the record from the voucher file when the invoice is paid.

Illustration 19–17 shows the contents of a voucher record in a traditional data file system. It shows two fields, GENERAL-LEDGER-ACCOUNT and GENERAL-LEDGER-AMOUNT, repeating six times. This allows each voucher record to represent debit entries in up to six accounts. As an example, three debits are required when a single vendor's invoice requests payment for raw materials inventory, supplies inventory, and freight.[1]

The voucher system adds records to the *general ledger batch summary* file summarizing the transactions processed by these systems. These record a credit entry in Accounts Payable, and debit entries to several asset and expense accounts. Each record also shows the responsibility code of the department that requested the expenditure. The general ledger batch summary file accumulates summary records from many application systems. The general ledger system posts the records in this file to the general ledger and produces performance reports.

[1]With a data base management system having normalized relations, each debit account requires a separate voucher record. The primary key field for the record is a combination of two fields, VOUCHER-NUMBER and GENERAL-LEDGER-ACCOUNT. In such a system, a single vendor invoice may produce multiple voucher records.

ILLUSTRATION 19–17 Contents of a Voucher Record

VOUCHER-NUMBER*
VOUCHER-DATE
PURCHASE-ORDER-NUMBER
REQUISITION-NUMBER
RESPONSIBILITY-CODE
VENDOR-NUMBER**
VENDOR-INVOICE-NUMBER
VENDOR-INVOICE-DATE
GROSS-AMOUNT
DISCOUNT-DATE
PAYMENT-DUE-DATE
GENERAL-LEDGER-ACCOUNT } repeats six times
GENERAL-LEDGER-AMOUNT }
⋮

*Designates a primary key.
**Designates a secondary key.

As you can see, the expenditure cycle records maintained in a computerized system are similar to those maintained in a manual system. Most systems combine both computerized and noncomputerized processing. Frequently, on-line real-time systems enter data directly from source documents and maintain transaction files of the documents rather than of computer records. The next section describes another way that applications in this cycle vary between organizations.

Types of Accounts Payable Systems. Applications in the revenue cycle, described in the previous chapter, maintain a computerized subsidiary ledger for the general ledger accounts receivable account. The computer files just described have no equivalent subsidiary ledger for the Accounts Payable account because the system described in this chapter is a pure voucher system. Other systems use a subsidiary ledger instead of vouchers, while still others use both vouchers and an accounts payable subsidiary ledger.

Voucher Systems. A voucher system assigns a unique identifying number to each invoice received from a vendor. The system accounts for all vouchers and voucher numbers. In this way, it prevents lost vendor invoices and omitted payments. Once a check is issued in payment of the voucher, an accounts payable clerk stamps the voucher and all supporting documents as "paid." This prevents a dishonest employee from using the documents to cause the issue of a second check and then stealing and cashing the check.

Many companies use voucher systems because they provide good control over vendor invoices. However, these systems require the preparation of voucher documentation for each cash payment, which may be inconvenient or difficult. For example, often receiving reports documenting the receipt of services do not exist. Special documentation must be prepared showing receipt of the services.

Furthermore, pure voucher systems make it difficult to determine the total amount owed to a vendor. To produce the vendor query report, for example, a person or a computer program must search the entire voucher file for invoices from the desired vendor. Locating this information is easier when the system maintains a subsidiary ledger for the Accounts Payable account.

Systems with a Subsidiary Ledger. In a manual system, an accounts payable subsidiary ledger is a book or card file containing one page or card for each approved vendor. In a computerized system, the subsidiary data is kept in the vendor master file.

With this system, a vendor's record in the vendor master file contains a field showing the balance owed to that vendor. When a vendor invoice and a receiving report are received, the system adds the amount of the invoice to this balance and adds a record to the pending invoice file. When a check is issued to the vendor, the amount of the check (including the discount) is deducted and the pending invoice record removed. With data base management system software, the vendor master record is linked with its invoice records.

An accounts payable subsidiary ledger enables the system to determine the balance owed to a vendor more easily. However, it requires more recordkeeping. With a manual system, management may consider the costs of a subsidiary ledger excessive. In a computerized system, where the added recordkeeping is performed by computer programs, management often considers it worthwhile to use both vouchers and vendor master records containing payable totals.

You have seen the documents and records used in the expenditure cycle by both manual and computerized systems. These records can take a variety of forms. A similar variety exists in the way systems process these documents and records.

TRANSACTION PROCESSING

Most organizations today use a combination of computerized and manual processes to keep their records. The way these processes combine differs from one organization to the next. Because many combinations are possible, few companies process an accounting transaction in exactly the same way. This is why you should understand both manual and computerized processes. Fortunately, the concepts underlying the procedures are the same regardless of the method of implementation.

Manual Processes

Illustration 19–18 contains a document flowchart showing manual procedures for purchasing and cash disbursements transactions. With these procedures, the purchasing department receives a purchase requisition, identifies a vendor, and

ILLUSTRATION 19–18 Manual Procedures for Purchases and Cash Disbursements

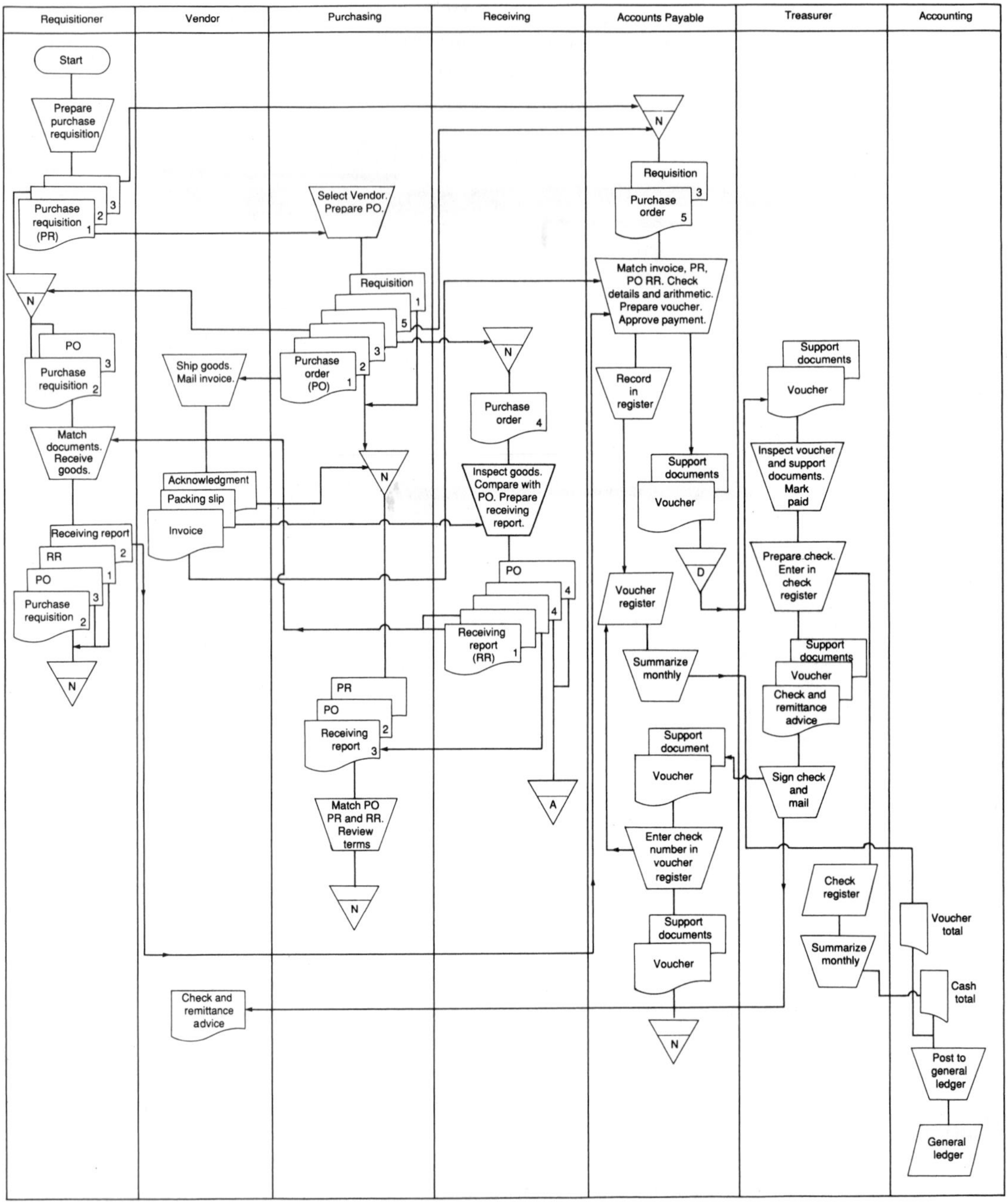

mails a copy of the purchase order. A second purchase order copy alerts the receiving department to expect a shipment of goods, and a third goes to accounts payable. When the vendor invoice arrives in accounts payable, the clerk files it until a receiving report indicates that the goods have arrived. Then accounts payable prepares the voucher that supports approval and issue of a check by the treasurer's department.

Control Procedures. The accounting system includes control procedures in the systems that process purchase transactions. Some practices, such as segregation of duties, are appropriate regardless of whether the system uses computerized or manual processes. Other control procedures, called application controls, relate specifically to computerized processes.

Illustration 19–19 summarizes appropriate control procedures for purchase transactions. It shows the procedures appropriate for the documents, the goods or services, and for the voucher package itself. Effective segregation of duties requires the separation of asset custody (in the warehouse and receiving departments) from records custody (in inventory records and accounts payable). The receiving department should be separate from the inventory warehouse. The purchasing function that authorizes transactions in the asset should also be separate from accounts payable.

Illustration 19–20 shows good segregation of duties and control practices for cash disbursements transactions. The most important segregation of duties is between accounts payable personnel, who maintain records, and cash disbursements personnel, who prepare checks and thus have access to the asset. These should be separate from the general ledger personnel who maintain the control accounts for cash and accounts payable. A later section in this chapter describes the applications controls in these systems.

Computerized Processes

In the expenditure cycle, a computer-based accounting system uses four applications: the purchasing, receiving, voucher, and cash disbursements systems.

Purchasing Application. The purposes of the purchasing application are to identify materials, supplies, and equipment for acquisition; to select a supplier for these items; and to ensure that the items are requested and received.

A purchase requisition initiates a purchases transaction in a manual system. Computerized systems use this document as well; however, inputs to a computerized purchasing system may also come from computerized applications in other transaction cycles.

A computerized inventory system maintains an inventory master file, which contains one record for each item held in inventory and shows the quantity of that item on hand. Many such systems also identify a *reorder point* and an *order*

ILLUSTRATION 19–19 Controls for Purchases Transactions

Purchase of Inventories	*Purchase of Services*	*Purchase Returns*
	Segregation of duties	
1. Purchasing and accounts payable 2. Inventory records and warehouse 3. Receiving and warehouse	1. Purchasing and accounts payable	1. Purchasing and accounts payable 2. Inventory records and warehouse 3. Receiving and warehouse
	Control practices	
1. Purchase requisition *a.* Based on reorder point and reorder quantity *b.* Approved if a special order	1. Purchase requisition *a.* Initiated by user department *b.* Approved	
2. Purchase order *a.* Prepared only on receipt of purchase requisition *b.* Prenumbered *c.* Vendor selected from approved vendor list *d.* Checked for vendor price, terms	2. Purchase order *a.* Prepared only on receipt of purchase requisition *b.* Prenumbered *c.* Vendor selected from approved vendor list *d.* Checked for vendor price, terms	1. Debit memo *a.* Prepared only by purchasing department *b.* Prenumbered
3. Goods *a.* Receiving report prepared as goods are received *b.* Receiving report is prenumbered *c.* Quantity counted at time of receipt *d.* Quantity independently counted	3. Services *a.* Copy of purchase order acknowledged as services are received	2. Return of goods *a.* Released only on receipt of copy of debit memo *b.* Shipped only on receipt of copy of debit memo *c.* Quantity returned is independently counted
4. Voucher package *a.* Invoice sent directly to accounts payable *b.* Prenumbered *c.* Supported by purchase requisition, purchase order, receiving report, and original invoice *d.* Verified	4. Voucher package *a.* Invoice sent directly to accounts payable *b.* Prenumbered *c.* Supported by purchase requisition, purchase order, acknowledged copy of purchase order, and original invoice *d.* Verified	3. New voucher package *a.* Debit memo sent to accounts payable *b.* Prenumbered *c.* Supported by original voucher package and debit memo *d.* Verified

ILLUSTRATION 19–20 Controls for Cash Disbursements Transactions

Cash Disbursements

Segregation of Duties

1. Accounts payable and cash disbursements
2. Cash disbursements and general ledger
3. Accounts payable and general ledger

Control Practices

1. Initial documentation
   a. Reviewed for completeness of voucher package, particularly original invoice
   b. Canceled immediately after check is signed
2. Checks
   a. Prepared only based on properly prepared voucher package
   b. Prenumbered
   c. Signed only if properly prepared
   d. Signed by two officials when amount reaches a predetermined figure
   e. Mailed out by persons other than check preparer
   f. Voided checks kept
3. Accounts payable
   a. Posted daily
4. General ledger
   a. Journal entry made daily

quantity for the item. Whenever the quantity on hand drops below the reorder point, the inventory system generates a computer record requesting the issue of a purchase order to replenish inventory. This record is an input to the purchasing system, and the quantity shown in the record is the item's order quantity.

Other inputs to the purchasing system may come from a computerized production control system. Some such systems, called *material requirements planning* (MRP) systems, compute the quantities of raw materials needed for production from a production schedule for finished products. An MRP system then generates computer records requesting the purchase of this material. This record is another input to the purchasing application.

Some mail order merchandising companies stock little inventory. Instead, when a customer requests an item they promptly acquire the item from a supplier. If such a company has a computerized order entry system, it may generate a record as input to the purchasing application. This record requests the purchase of the item needed for resale.

Illustration 19–21 shows these sources for inputs to both batch and on-line real-time computerized purchasing systems. Purchase requisitions and computer record inputs from other applications add to the requisitions file. Purchasing agents review this file, assign vendors, and adjust order quantities based on their knowledge of the business. The system prints a purchase order register, the

ILLUSTRATION 19–21 A Purchasing Application

A. Batch Processing System

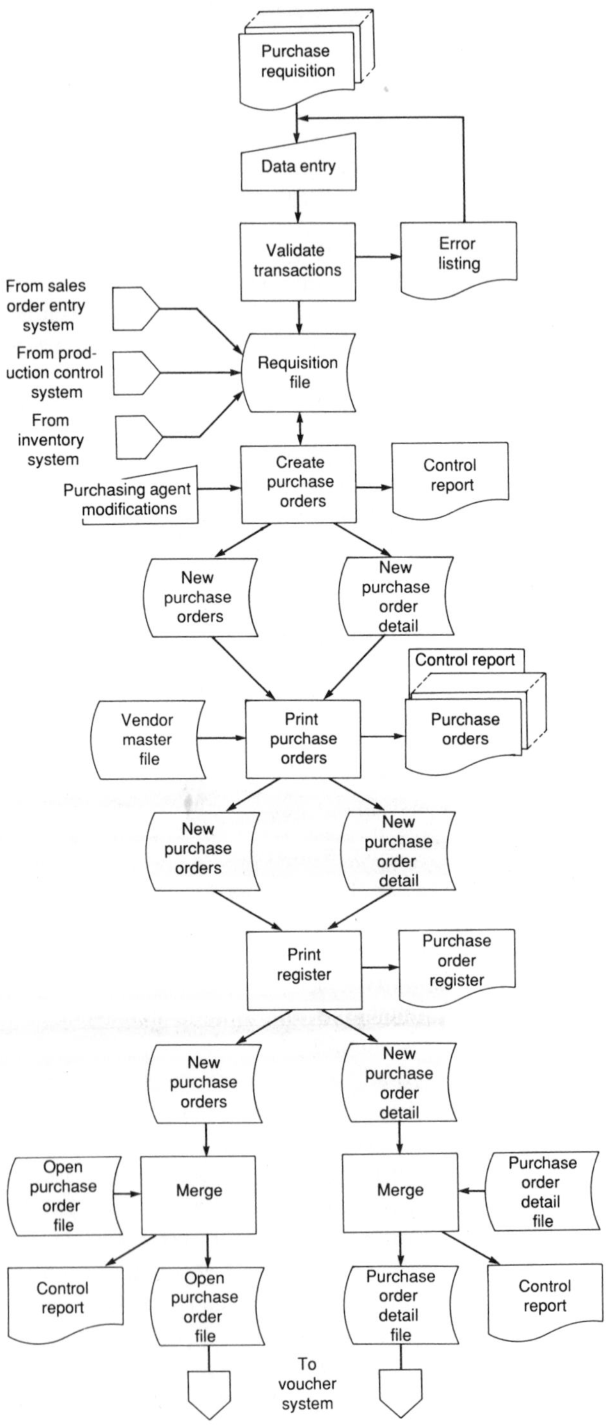

ILLUSTRATION 19–21 *(concluded)*

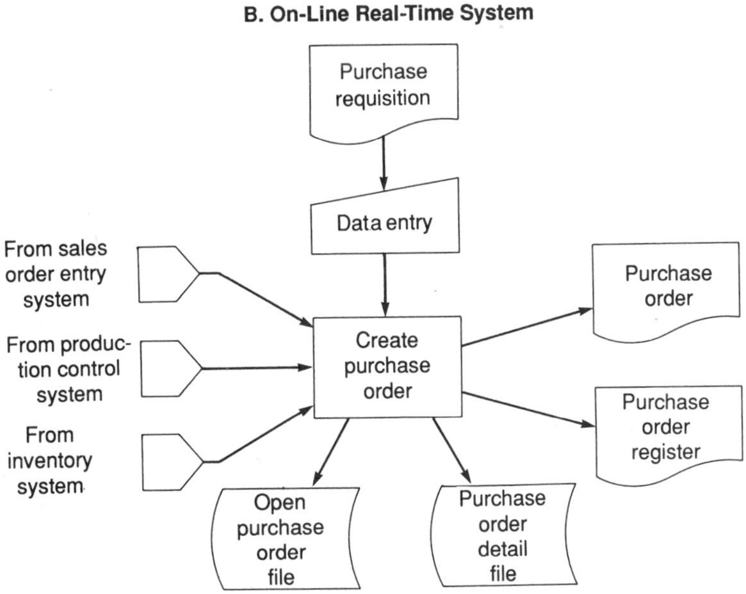

purchase orders, and adds records to the open purchase order and purchase order detail files. These files are inputs to the voucher application.

Receiving Application. The purposes of the receiving application are to ensure that all receipts of material, supplies, and equipment are authorized, and to record their receipt in the accounting records. System flowcharts of batch and on-line real-time receiving systems are shown in Illustration 19–22.

When a transportation company brings items to the receiving department, a clerk first locates the purchase order authorizing the shipment in the purchase order file.

In the batch system, the purchase order is in a manual file. The clerk examines the contents of the shipment and verifies the quantity shown on the purchase order copy and on the vendor's packing list. The clerk then prepares a receiving report and attaches the purchase order copy to it. From a batch of these documents a data entry clerk creates additional records in the receipts file.

In the on-line real-time system, the receiving clerk locates the shipment in the purchase order detail file. A computer program prints the receiving report and creates a record for the receipts file. Each system prints a receipts register to provide an audit trail and provides the receipts file as an input to the voucher system.

ILLUSTRATION 19–22 A Receiving Application

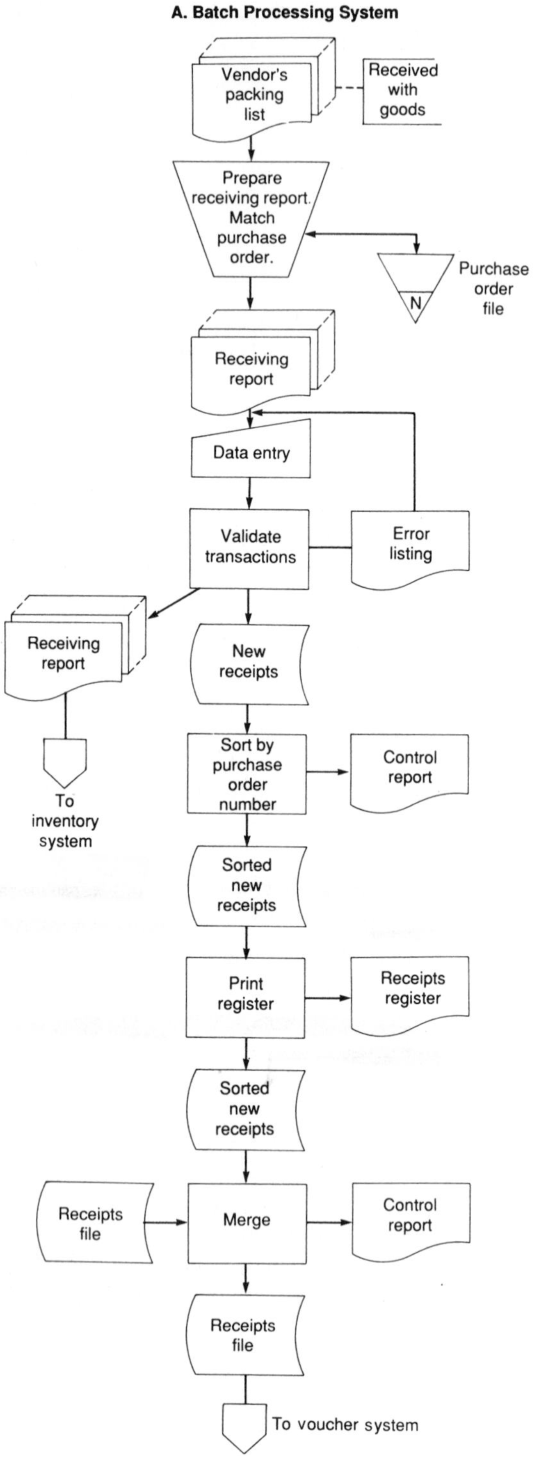

ILLUSTRATION 19–22 *(concluded)*

B. On-Line Real-Time System

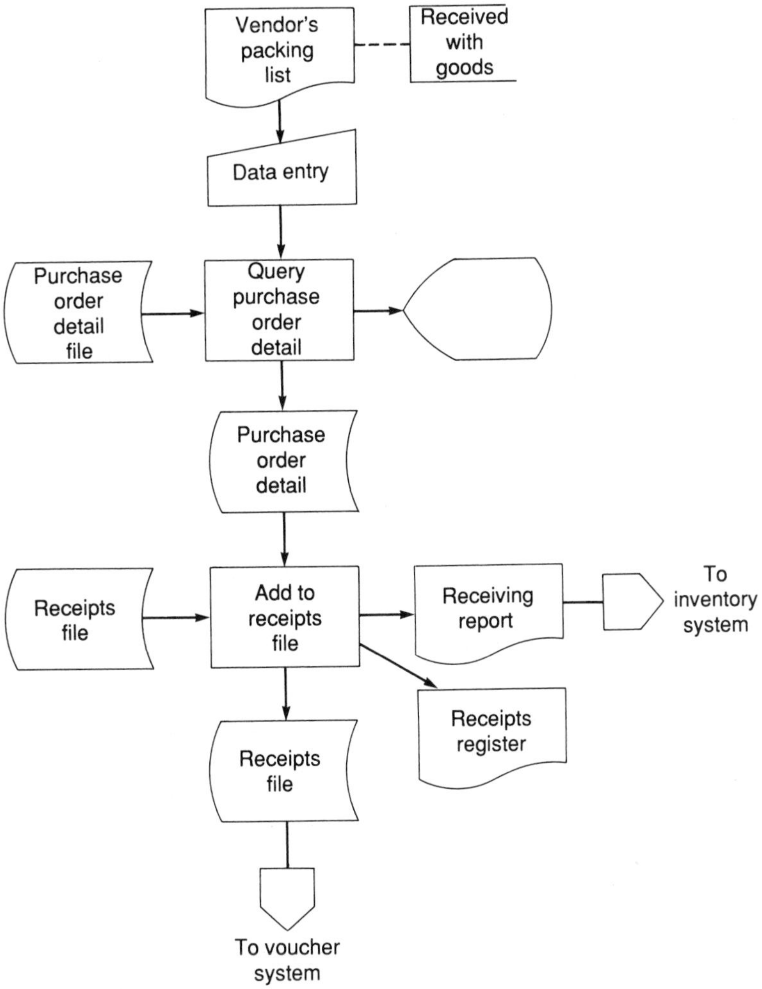

Voucher Application. The purpose of the voucher application is to record the obligation to pay a supplier. Inputs to this system are vendor invoices and records from the receipts, open purchase order, and purchase order detail files. Illustration 19–23 shows the procedures in a voucher system.

In the batch system, a mail clerk batches vendor invoices and a data entry clerk enters them in the system. In the on-line real-time system, the clerk enters invoices one at a time. The system adds a new invoice record to the pending

ILLUSTRATION 19–23 A Voucher Application

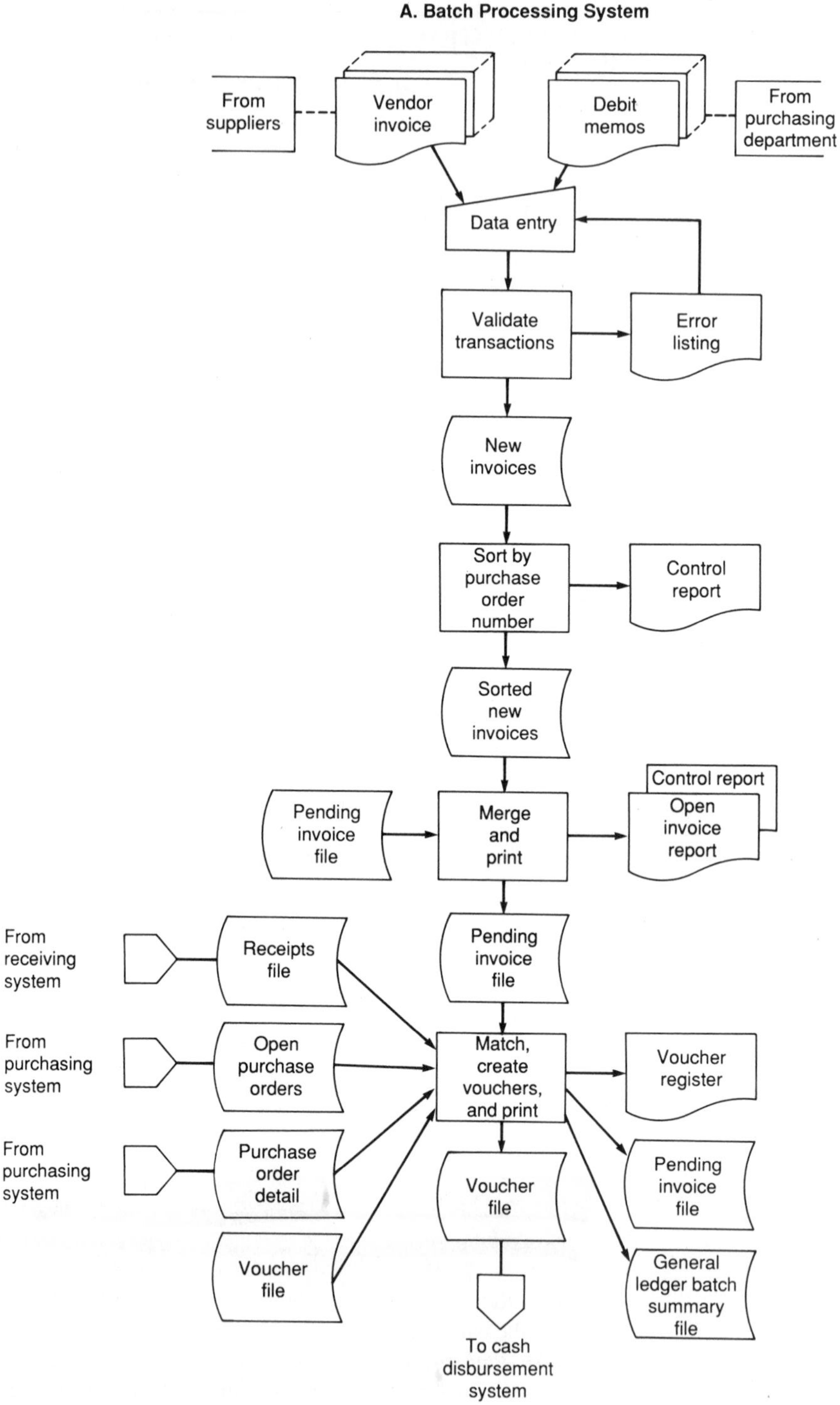

ILLUSTRATION 19–23 *(concluded)*

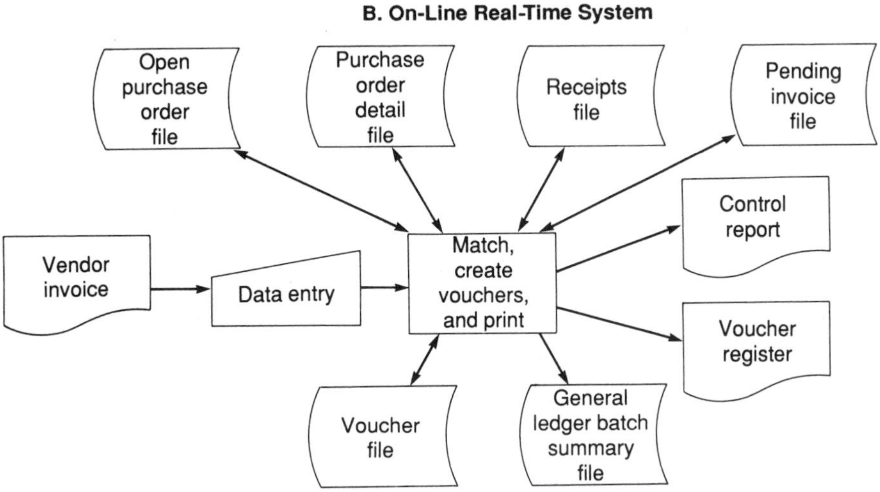

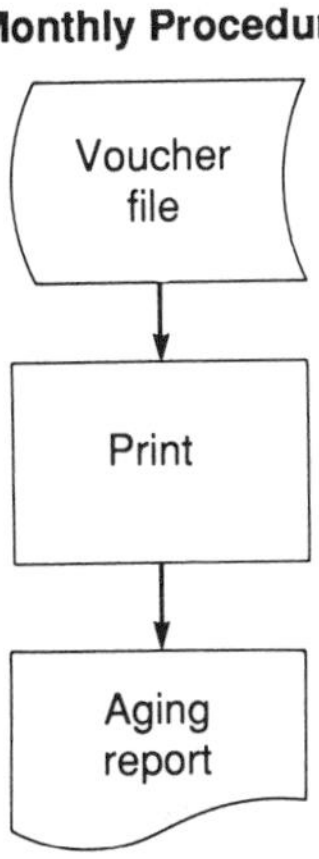

invoice file for each invoice received. It then matches records in this file with those in the receipts and purchasing files. When it locates a receipts record and a purchase order record for the invoice, it creates a record in the voucher file and assigns it a voucher number. This program prints a voucher register and provides the voucher file as input to the cash disbursements application. It also generates summary records for the general ledger batch summary file.

Cash Disbursements Application. The purpose of this application system is to ensure that payments are made to vendors in the proper amount and at the proper time. Illustration 19–24 shows a flowchart for such a system. The inputs to this system are records from the voucher file.

This system first sorts the voucher file by due date and then prints the cash requirements report. A cash manager or clerk in the treasurer's department identifies the vouchers to be paid and enters the cutoff date. From this point, the

ILLUSTRATION 19–24 A Cash Disbursements Application

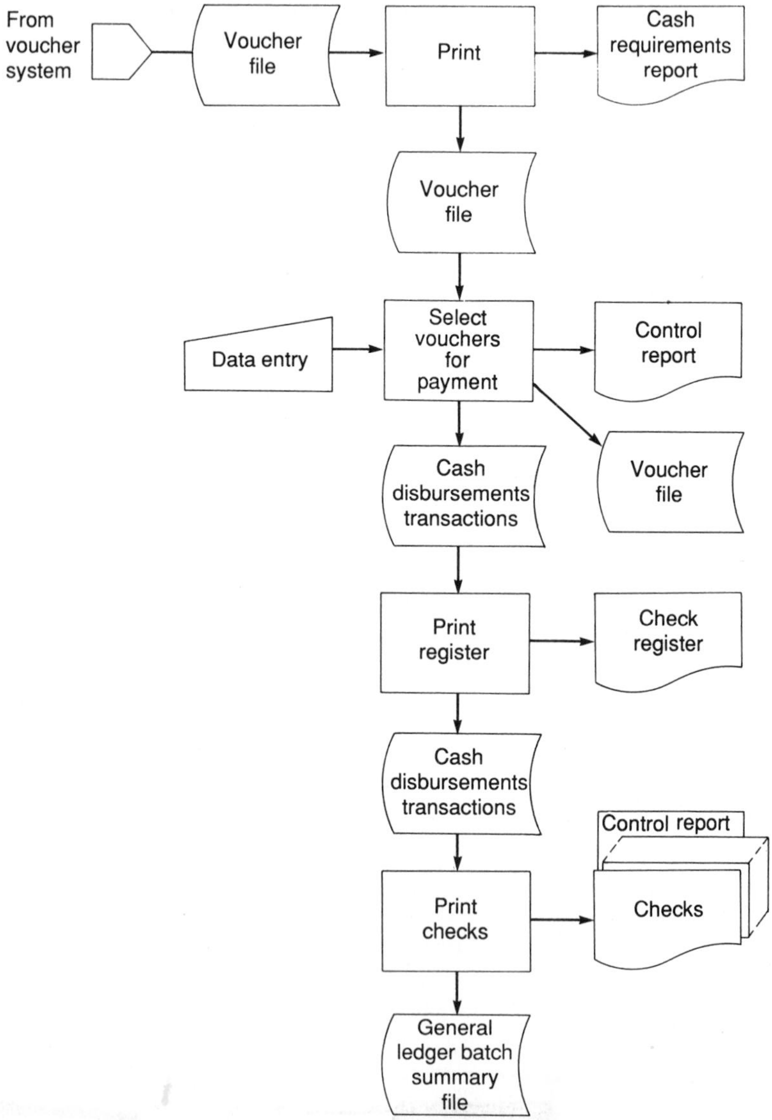

remainder of the processing is done in batch mode. The system establishes control totals for the vouchers to be paid and maintains those totals until the checks are mailed. This prevents a dishonest employee from concealing the theft of a check during later processing.

The system removes all vouchers due prior to the cutoff date from the voucher file and creates from them a file of cash disbursements transactions. From these, computer programs print the check register and checks and create records for the general ledger batch summary file.

Application Controls. The system design team creates application controls when developing the application systems of the expenditure cycle. They may be input controls, processing controls, and output controls.

Input Controls. Input controls prevent or detect errors as data are converted from human readable to computer readable form. Most computer systems implement input controls using validation procedures. Validity tests, completeness tests, and control totals are examples of control procedures that can be used for data validation.

Illustration 19–25 shows how to employ these procedures in the application systems of the expenditure cycle. The system design team may implement these procedures when designing the system.

Processing Controls. Processing controls prevent or detect erroneous processing by computer programs. These controls are coded into the programs during the development of the application system. Batch processing systems make extensive use of record counts and control or hash totals. Sometimes these totals are useful in on-line real-time systems as well. Illustration 19–26 applies processing controls to the applications in the expenditure cycle.

Output Controls. Output controls prevent and detect erroneous outputs from computer processing. In many companies, the data control group of the MIS department implements these controls. Other companies may assign these responsibilities to clerks in user departments. In batch processing systems, these clerks compare record counts and control totals from successive computer runs to verify that all transactions were processed correctly. Accountants call these "run-to-run controls." The data control group also scans output documents and reports to identify obvious errors in their preparation. Illustration 19–27 shows example output controls that are performed in the expenditure cycle.

ILLUSTRATION 19–25 Input Controls in the Expenditure Cycle

System	*Program*	*Control Procedure*
Purchasing	Validate transactions	**Completeness test.** Program verifies existence of REQUISITION-NUMBER, INVENTORY-ITEM-NUMBER, ITEM-DESCRIPTION, ITEM-QUANTITY, DELIVERY-DUE-DATE.
	Create purchase order	**Completeness test.** Purchasing agent enters VENDOR-NUMBER, PURCHASING-AGENT-NAME, VENDOR-PRODUCT-NUMBER, ITEM-UNIT-PRICE. **Validity test.** Program computes check digit on VENDOR-NUMBER.
Receiving	Validate transactions	**Completeness test.** Program verifies existence of PURCHASE-ORDER-NUMBER, RECEIVED-QUANTITY, ITEM-NUMBER, ITEM-DESCRIPTION, VENDOR-NAME.
Voucher	Validate transactions	**Completeness test.** Program verifies existence of PURCHASE-ORDER-NUMBER, VENDOR-INVOICE-NUMBER, VENDOR-INVOICE-DATE, GROSS-AMOUNT, DISCOUNT-DATE, NET-AMOUNT, PAYMENT-DUE-DATE, GENERAL-LEDGER-ACCOUNT, GENERAL-LEDGER-AMOUNT. **Consistency test.** Program verifies that total of GENERAL-LEDGER-AMOUNT fields equals NET-AMOUNT field. **Validity test.** Program verifies that dates are of the form AA-BB-CCCC, where AA<13, BB<32, and CCCC is numeric.

ILLUSTRATION 19–26 Processing Controls in the Expenditure Cycle

System	*Program*	*Control Procedure*
Purchasing	Create purchase orders	**Record count.** Program verifies that the number of new purchase orders = number of purchase requisitions + number of records from order entry, production control, and inventory systems.
Receiving	Sort	**Record count.** Program verifies that the number of transactions in the input file = the number of transactions in the output file.
Voucher	Match, create vouchers and print	**Record count.** Program verifies that the decrease in the number of open purchase order records = increase in the number of pending invoice records. **Record count.** Program verifies that the decrease in the number of receipts records = the increase in the number of pending invoice records. **Record count.** Program verifies that the number of records in the old pending invoice file = number of records in the new pending invoice file + number of new voucher records.
Cash disbursements	Select vouchers for payment	**Record count.** Program verifies that the number of records in the old voucher file = number of records in the new voucher file + number of cash disbursement transaction records.

ILLUSTRATION 19–27 Output Controls in the Expenditure Cycle

System	*Program*	*Control Procedure*
Purchasing	Print purchase orders	**Record count.** Program verifies that the number of new records in purchase order detail file = number of line items on purchase orders.
	Create POs Print POs Print register	**Run-to-run controls.** In the batch system, the data control group compares hash totals of purchase order numbers disclosed on control reports and purchase order register.
Receiving	Print register	**Record count.** Program verifies that the number of lines on the report = the number of receipts in transaction records.
	Sort Print register	**Run-to-run controls.** In the batch system, the data control group compares hash totals of purchase order numbers disclosed on the control report and the receipts register.
Voucher	Match, create vouchers and print	**Record count.** Program verifies that the number of lines on the voucher register = the number of records added to the voucher file.
	Validate Sort, Merge and print	**Run-to-run controls.** In the batch system, the data control group compares hash totals of purchase order numbers disclosed on the error listing, control report, and open invoice report.
Cash disbursements	Print register	**Record count.** Number of lines on check register = number of cash disbursement transaction records. **Limit test.** Program flags for review by data control group those transactions with amount > $100,000.
	Select vouchers Print register Print checks	**Run-to-run controls.** Data control group verifies that total amount of checks = total amounts of vouchers disclosed on control reports and check register.

SUMMARY

The expenditure cycle processes accounting transactions that record four economic events. They are the request for goods or services from a supplier, their delivery, recognition of the obligation to pay for them, and payment.

Accounting systems in the expenditure cycle must be able to process three transactions: credit purchases, purchase returns, and cash disbursements. The documents that record these transactions are the purchase requisition, the purchase order, the receiving report, the voucher, and the check. Reports that disclose the results of processing include control reports, registers, the open voucher report, the accounts payable aging report, the cash requirements report, and the vendor query report.

Manual systems in this cycle utilize two special journals and files containing documents. Computer-based systems include the purchasing, receiving, voucher, and cash disbursements applications. They make changes to the open purchase order, the purchase order detail, the voucher, and the vendor master files. If data base management software is used, these applications access the data base using their subschema.

KEY TERMS

accounts payable system A name sometimes applied to a combination of the voucher and cash disbursements applications.

purchase order A document prepared in the purchasing department and mailed to a vendor requesting that the vendor sell goods or services on credit.

purchase requisition A document prepared by someone in an organization requesting that the purchasing department acquire goods or services.

receiving report A document prepared in the receiving department to record the receipt of goods from a vendor.

vendor master record Contains data concerning an approved vendor, from which a purchasing agent is authorized to acquire goods or services.

voucher A document prepared in the accounts payable department to record an accounts payable and showing the proper account to debit.

voucher system An accounts payable system that assigns a unique identifying number to each vendor invoice.

APPENDIX

Control Flowcharts for Expenditure Cycle Transactions

CONTROL FLOWCHART 19–1 Cash Disbursements

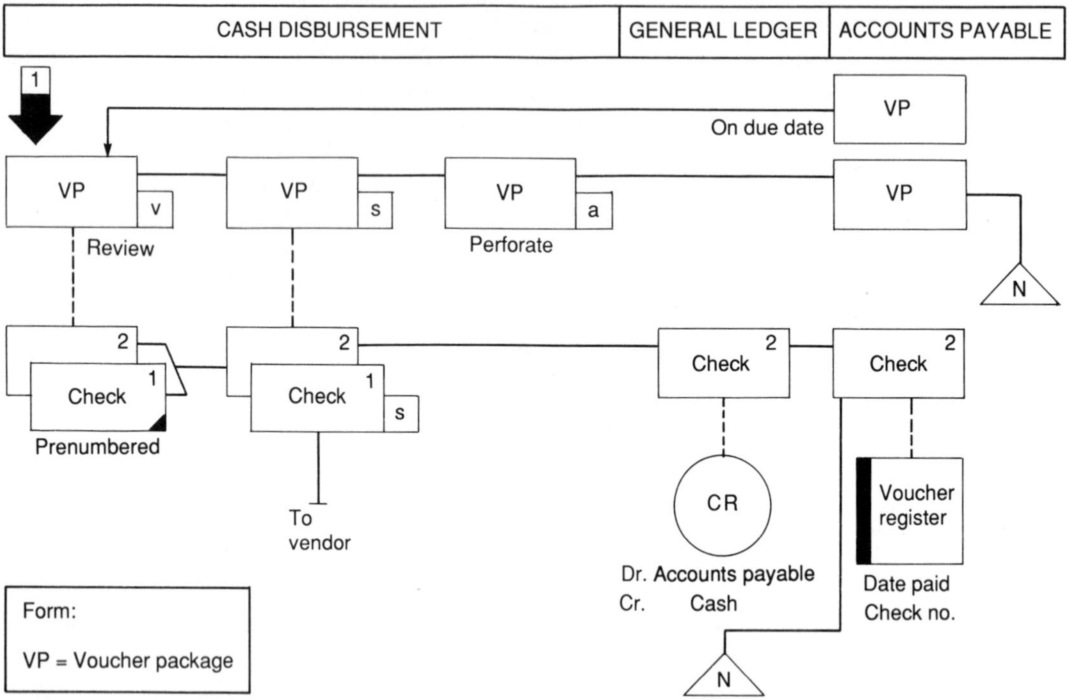

CONTROL FLOWCHART 19–2 Purchases for Inventories

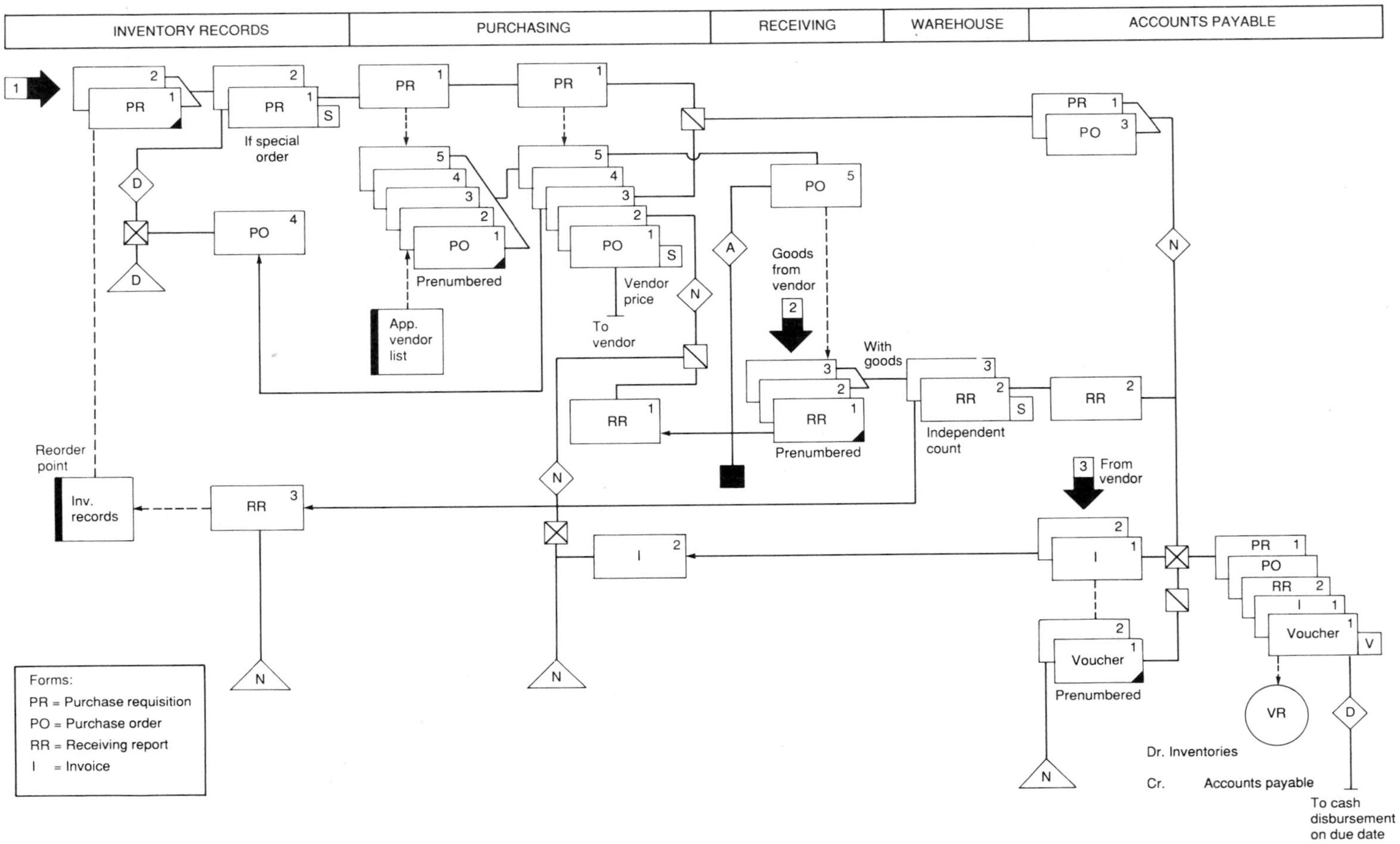

CONTROL FLOWCHART 19–3 Purchases of Services

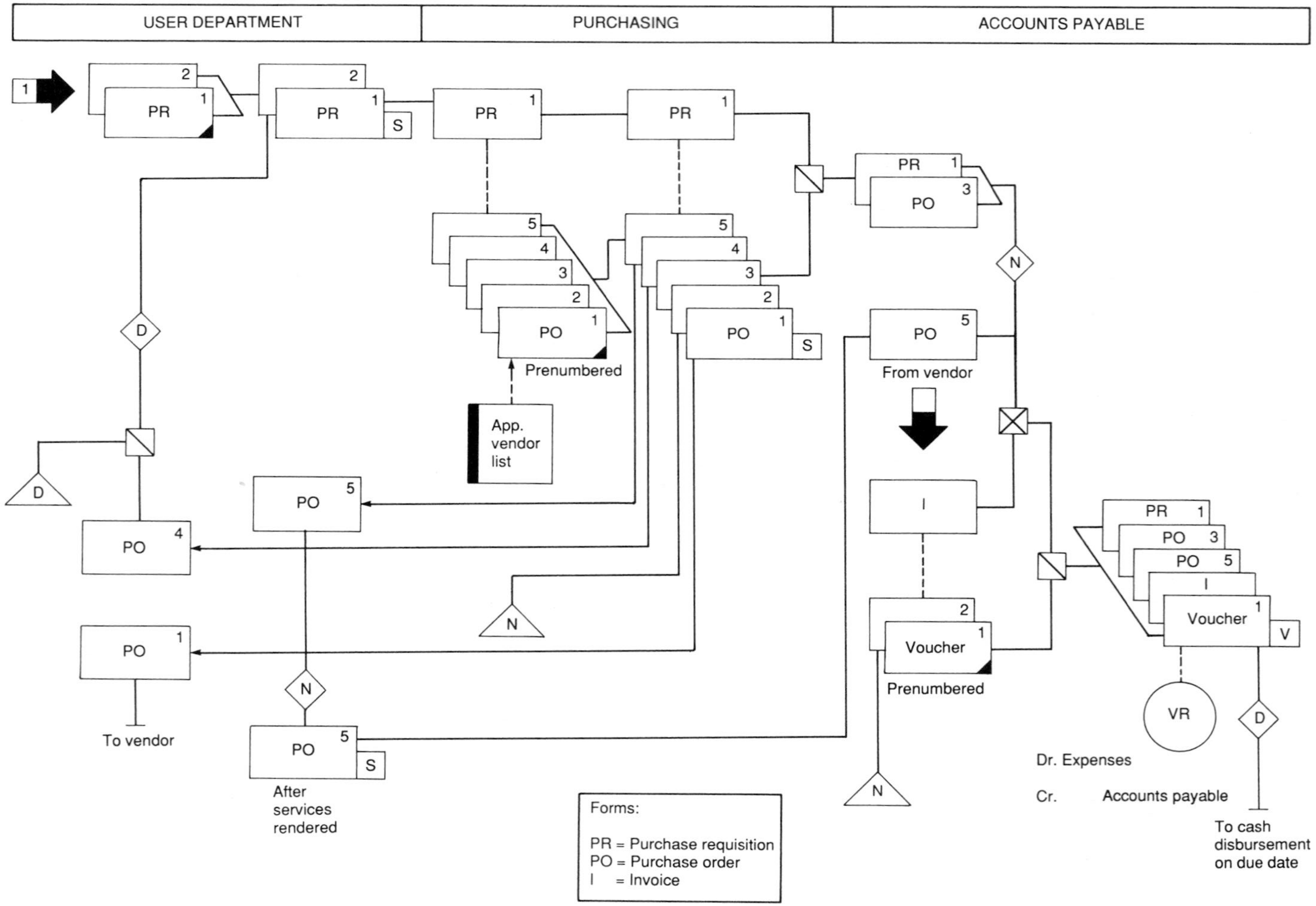

CONTROL FLOWCHART 19–4 Purchase Returns

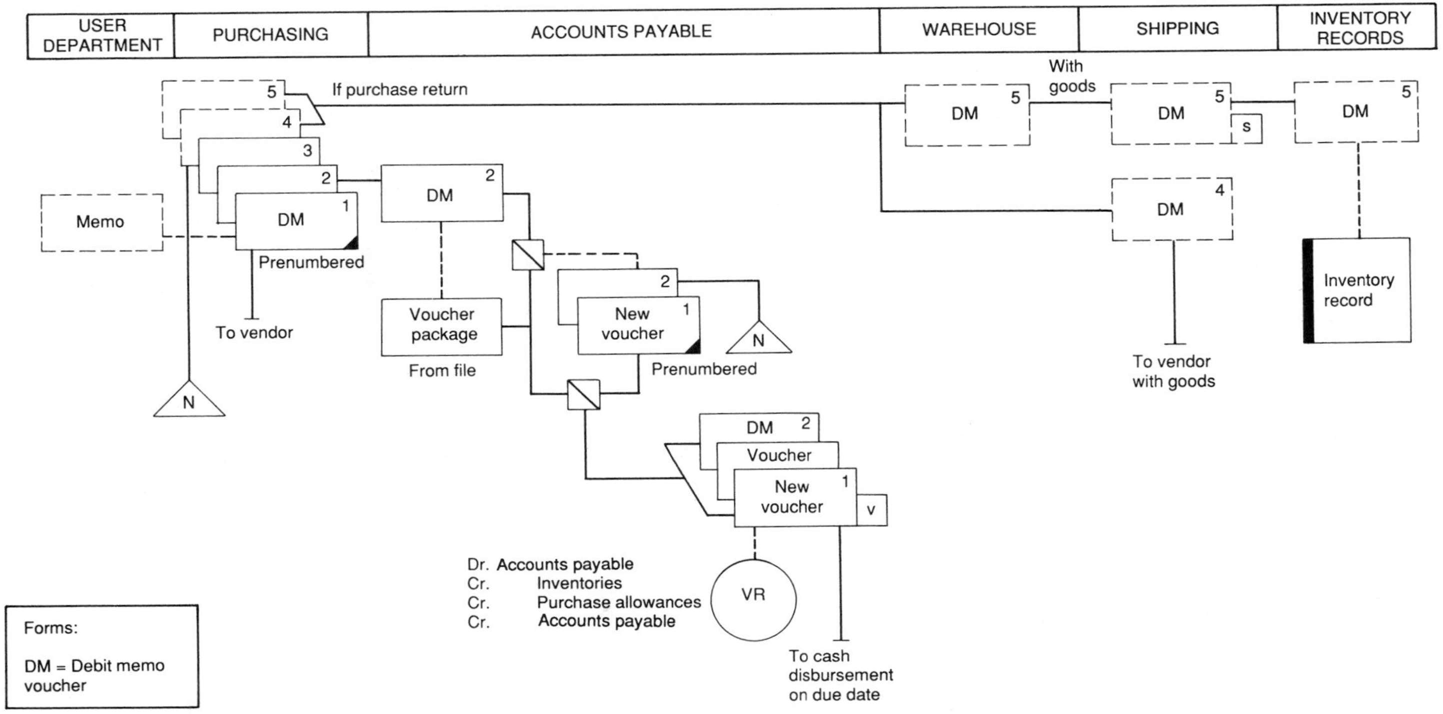

QUESTIONS

19–1. Which economic events produce transactions in the expenditure cycle?

19–2. Which three types of transactions do accounting systems record in the expenditure cycle?

19–3. What is the purpose of each of the following documents?
a. Purchase order
b. Vendor invoice
c. Voucher
d. Debit memo

19–4. When is a control report used? What is its function?

19–5. Which information is disclosed in a register? Why is it important to accountants?

19–6. Describe three special purpose reports produced in the expenditure cycle.

19–7. What form do noncomputerized records take in the expenditure cycle?

19–8. In a computerized accounting system, which data files are used in the expenditure cycle? Can you identify the purpose of each file?

19–9. Describe two types of accounts payable systems and distinguish between them.

19–10. In a computer-based accounting system, what are the applications in the expenditure cycle? What is the purpose of each?

19–11. How does use of a data base management system affect the way application systems process accounting records?

EXERCISES AND CASES

19–12. TRANSACTIONS AND DOCUMENTS

The following column on the left lists accounting transactions processed in the expenditure cycle. The right column lists documents and reports. For each transaction, identify the document(s) and report(s) associated with it.

Transaction	*Document or report*
a. Credit purchase	1. Vendor invoice
b. Cash payment	2. Debit memo
c. Purchase return	3. Receiving report
	4. Purchase order
	5. Check

19–13. TRANSACTIONS AND APPLICATIONS

The following column on the left lists accounting transactions. The right column lists application systems used in the expenditure cycle. For each transaction, identify the application system that processes it.

Transaction	*Document or report*
a. Credit purchase	1. Voucher
b. Cash payment	2. Receiving
c. Purchase return	3. Cash disbursements

19–14. ***RECEIVING PROCEDURES***

To strengthen internal control, some have suggested that information on quantity should be omitted from the copy of a purchase order going to the receiving department.

Required:

a. What are some advantages of omitting quantity information from this copy?
b. What are some disadvantages?
c. Considering your answers to *a* and *b,* which approach do you favor?

19–15. ***CREDIT PURCHASE PROCEDURES***

The Witt Company is engaged in manufacturing. When materials are ordered, a duplicate of the purchase order is sent to the receiving department. When the materials are received, the receiving clerk records the receipt on the copy of the order, which is then sent to the accounting department to support the entry to accounts payable and material purchases. The materials are then taken to stores where the quantity is entered on bin records.

Required:

a. Identify any control deficiencies in these procedures.
b. Explain which errors or manipulations might occur as a result of each weakness.
c. Recommend changes in procedures that could be made to correct each weakness.

(AICPA Adapted)

19–16. ***PURCHASING PROCEDURES***

Wooster Company is a beauty and barber supply and equipment distributorship servicing a five-state area. Management generally has been pleased with the overall operations to date. However, the present purchasing system, which evolved through practice rather than having been formally designed, is inadequate and needs to be redesigned.

A description of the present purchasing system is as follows: Whenever the quantity of an item is low, the inventory supervisor phones the purchasing department with the item description and quantity to be ordered. A purchase order is prepared in duplicate in the purchasing department. The original is sent to the vendor, and the copy is retained in the purchasing department filed in numerical order. When the shipment arrives, the inventory supervisor sees that each item received is checked off on the packing slip which accompanies the shipment. The packing slip is then forwarded to the accounts payable department. When the invoice arrives, the packing slip is compared with the invoice in the accounts payable department. Once any differences between the packing slip and the invoice are reconciled, a check is drawn for the appropriate amount and is mailed to the vendor with a copy of the invoice. The packing slip is attached to the invoice and filed alphabetically in the paid invoice file.

Required:

Wooster Company intends to redesign its purchasing system from the point when an item needs to be ordered until payment is made. The system should be designed to ensure that all of the proper controls are incorporated into the system.

a. Identify the internally and externally generated documents that would satisfy the minimum requirements of a basic system and indicate how many copies of each document would be needed.

b. Explain how all of these documents should interrelate and flow among Wooster's various departments including the final destination or file for each copy.

(CMA Adapted)

19–17. ***CONTROLS AND FRAUD***

In each of the following situations, companies suffered the loss of assets as a consequence of employee fraud:

Situation No. 1. Although most bills are sent to the corporate office for payment, each manufacturing plant maintains a petty cash fund to pay small, routine purchases. While reviewing the accounts payable at one of the plants, an auditor discovered that a trusted employee had embezzled $152,000 during the past 10 years. Using the petty cash fund, the employee had processed and paid fictitious freight bills by using copies of authentic shipments for support. The employee had pocketed the duplicate payments.

Situation No. 2. While examining a random sample of employee expense reports, an auditor found that altered receipts and duplicate receipts were being routinely submitted for reimbursement by members of the sales force.

Situation No. 3. The company had a contract with a tire manufacturer to supply tires for company vehicles at favorable discounts. As a courtesy, company employees were allowed to purchase tires at discounted prices by placing an order with the office manager, who ordered the tires in the company name. When the bill arrived, the office manager asked employees to make checks payable to him. The invoices were processed for payment through the company's accounts payable system. As a consequence, 37 tires were billed to the company and the office manager deposited the employees' checks to his own account.

Required:

For each of the three situations:

a. Identify the concept of internal control that was violated.

b. Recommend a specific control that would prevent or detect future occurrences.

(CIA Adapted)

19–18. *SYSTEM FLOWCHART*

Flowcharts are frequently used to represent an activity graphically. These flowcharts allow identification of the physical flow of documents through the accounting system.

Required:

Given the flowchart in Exhibit 19–1:

a. Identify the activity taking place and the document(s) involved at each numbered symbol when applicable.

b. Describe control procedures you would expect to find in practice at symbols 1, 6, 7, and 10.

(CIA Adapted)

19–19. *RECEIVING PROCEDURES*

Dunbar Camera Manufacturing, Inc., is a manufacturer of high-priced precision motion picture cameras in which the specifications of component parts are vital to the manufacturing process. Dunbar buys valuable camera lenses and large quantities of sheet metal and screws. The screws and lenses ordered by Dunbar are billed by the vendors on a unit basis. Sheet metal ordered by Dunbar is billed by the vendors on the basis of weight. The receiving clerk is responsible for documenting the quality and quantity of merchandise received. A review indicates that these internal control procedures are being followed:

Receiving Report. Properly approved purchase orders, which are prenumbered, are filed numerically. The copy sent to the receiving clerk is an exact duplicate of the copy sent to the vendor. Receipts of merchandise are recorded on the duplicate copy by the receiving clerk.

Sheet metal. The company receives sheet metal by railroad. The railroad independently weighs the sheet metal and records the weight and date of receipt on a bill of lading (waybill) that accompanies all deliveries. The receiving clerk only checks the weight on the waybill to the purchase order.

Screws. The receiving clerk opens cartons containing screws, then inspects and weighs the contents. The weight is converted to the number of units by means of conversion charts. The receiving clerk then checks the computed quantity against the purchase order.

Camera Lens. Each camera lens is delivered in a separate corrugated carton. Cartons are counted by the receiving clerk when they arrive; the total is checked against purchase orders.

Required:

Explain why the control procedures applying to receiving reports and to receipts of sheet metal, screws, and camera lenses are adequate or inadequate.

(AICPA Adapted)

EXHIBIT 19–1 Exercise 19–18

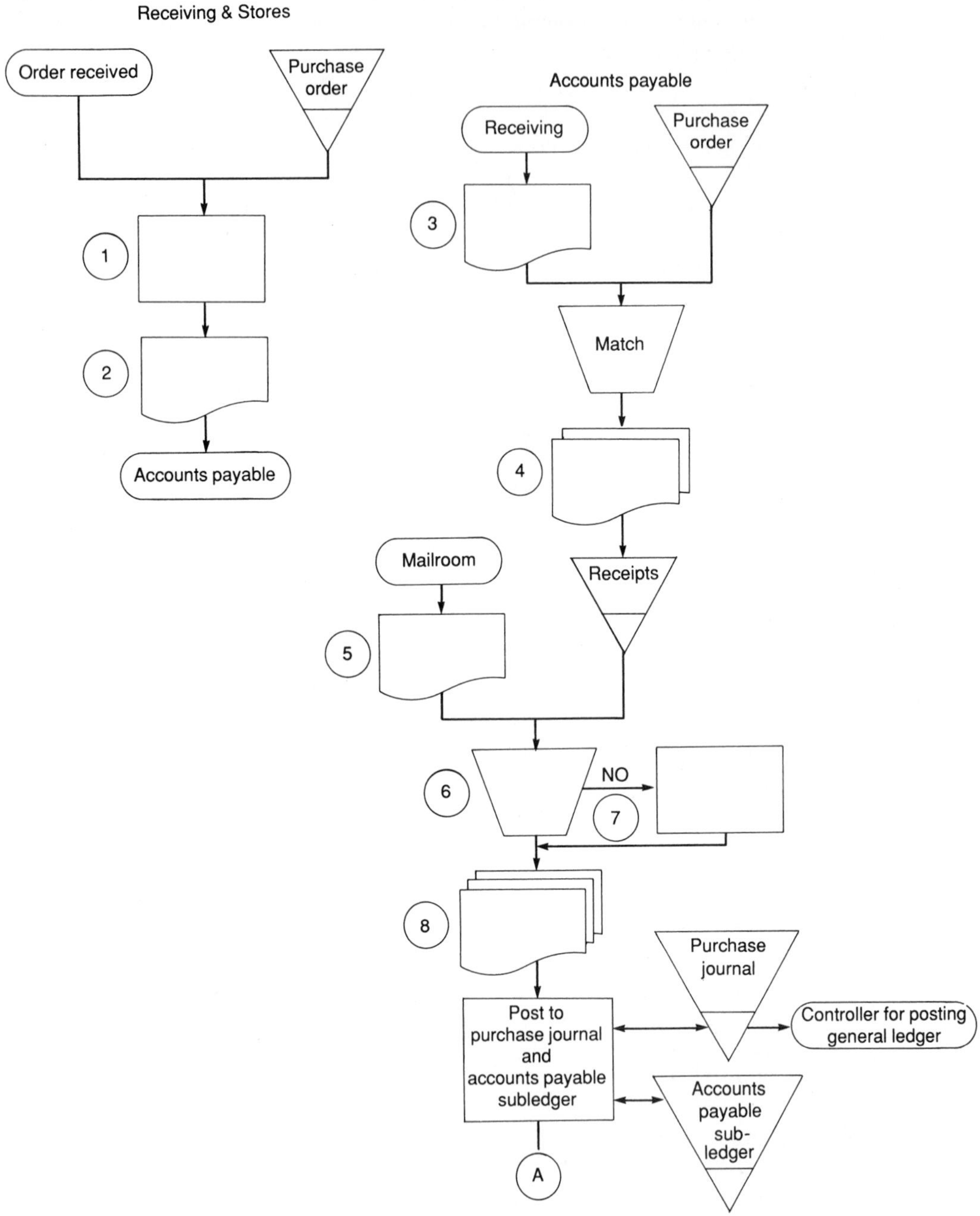

EXHIBIT 19–1 Exercise 19–18 *(concluded)*

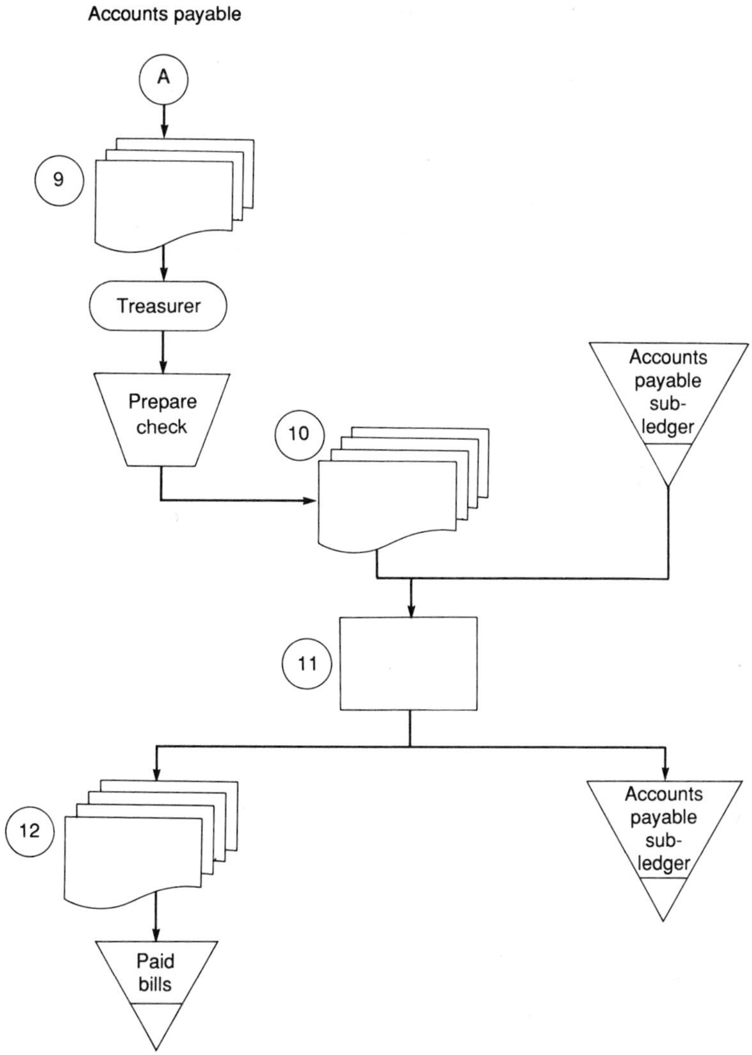

19–20. *COMPUTERIZED PURCHASING PROCEDURES*

Peabock Company is a wholesaler of soft goods. The inventory is composed of approximately 3,500 different items. The company employs a computerized batch processing system to maintain its perpetual inventory records. The system is run each weekend so that the inventory reports are available on Monday morning for management use. The system has been functioning satisfactorily for the past 15 months, providing the company with accurate records and timely reports.

The preparation of purchase orders has been automatic as a part of the inventory system to ensure that the company maintains enough inventory to meet customer demand. When an item of inventory falls below a predetermined level, a record of the inventory item is written. This record is used in conjunction with the vendor file to prepare purchase orders.

Exception reports are prepared during the update of the inventory and the preparation of the purchase orders. These reports identify any errors or exceptions found during the processing. In addition, the system provides for management approval of all purchase orders exceeding a specified amount. Any exceptions or items requiring management approval are handled by supplemental runs on Monday morning and combined with the weekend results.

A system flowchart of Peabock Company's inventory and purchase order procedures appears in Exhibit 19–2.

The flowchart was prepared before the system was fully operational. Several steps important to the successful operation of the system were inadvertently omitted from the chart. Now that the system is operating effectively, management wants the system documentation to be complete and would like the flowchart corrected.

Required:

a. Describe the steps which have been omitted and indicate where the omissions occurred. The flowchart does not need to be redrawn.

b. Describe the type of control procedures Peabock Company would use in its system and indicate where these procedures should be placed.

c. Design the contents of each master record required by the system flowchart in Exhibit 19–2.

(CMA Adapted)

19–21. *PURCHASING FRAUD*

A dead child, a love triangle, and a computer scheme all contributed to the swindling of some \$155,000 from Magnum Products, Inc. (MPI), a subsidiary of Consolidated Corp. in Chicago.[2]

According to the district attorney assigned to the case, in May Betty X. Tipps was transferred into MPI's accounts payable department. After the transfer, she discussed with her boyfriend, Robert Katz, the possibility of stealing money from MPI using a bogus company set up for the purpose.

Tipps and Katz went to a local graveyard and learned the name of a child who had died shortly after birth. They then obtained the birth certificate of the

[2]Adapted from ''Love and Death Figure in \$155,000 DP Scam,'' *Computerworld,* May 3, 1982, p. 20. Used by permission.

EXHIBIT 19–2 Exercise 19–20

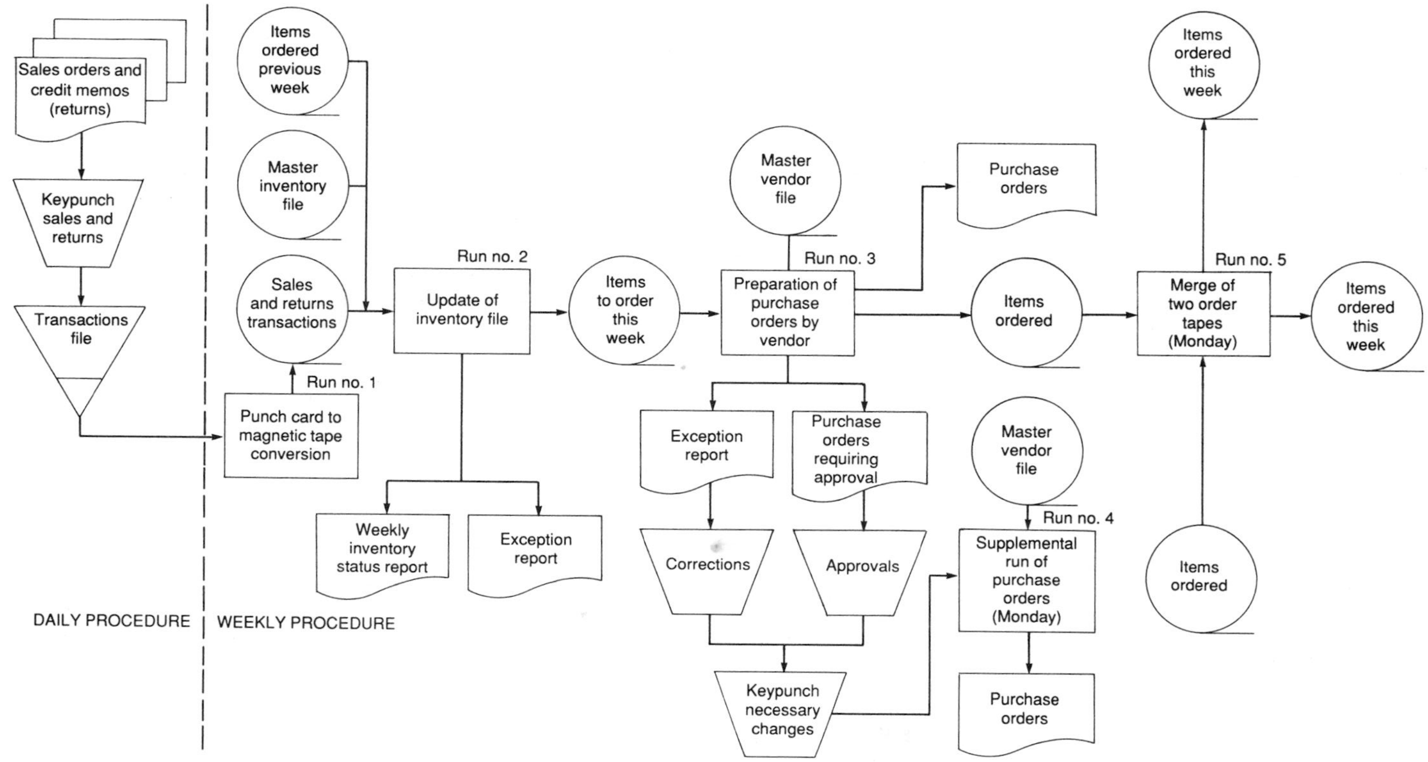

deceased child, Larry Robert Gandalf, from the Cook County Government Center. With the birth certificate, they opened a bank account, obtained picture identification for Katz, and established an address for L. R. Gandalf Co. at an answering and mailing service.

Tipps then obtained legitimate receiving documents that came from companies supplying MPI with parts and materials. She altered these documents to make it appear that L. R. Gandalf Co. was supplying parts to MPI for which payment was required. Five checks totaling $155,000 were received by the false company in August and September. These checks were deposited into the L. R. Gandalf savings account, from which both Tipps and Katz could make withdrawals. Around the time the last check was received, Tipps terminated her employment with MPI.

According to investigators, the couple traveled to Costa Rica, Panama, Florida, California, and Arizona, invested in gold coins, and bought three cars—one each for Tipps and Katz and one for his former wife. While the couple was in Florida they had a bad fight, and the police were called.

How was the crime discovered? ''He assaulted her,'' the district attorney said. ''He had a three-way love triangle going with Tipps and his ex-wife. Tipps just turned herself in. I guess she just had enough.'' The couple is awaiting sentencing, and each faces up to 10 years in prison and a $10,000 fine.

Required:

Which control procedures would have prevented this crime?

19–22. ***RECORD LAYOUTS***

Exhibit 19–3 contains layouts for two master file and two transaction file records used by applications in the expenditure cycle.

Required:

a. Identify the files that contain these records.

b. Based on the information contained in these record layouts, identify reports obtained from these files that would be useful to company management.

(AICPA Adapted)

19–23. ***PURCHASES AND CASH DISBURSEMENTS***

Exhibit 19–4 contains a document flowchart describing manual procedures for processing purchases and cash disbursements transactions.

Required:

Indicate what each of the letters *A* through *L* in Exhibit 19–4 represent.

(AICPA Adapted)

EXHIBIT 19–3 Exercise 19–22

Master File — Vendor Name

Vendor code	Recd type	Space	Blank	Vendor name	Blank	Card code 100

Master File — Vendor Address

Vendor code	Recd type	Space	Blank	Address — line 1	Address — line 2	Address — line 3	Blank	Card code 120

Transaction File — Expense Detail

Vendor code	Recd type	Voucher number	Blank	Batch	Voucher number	Voucher date	Vendor code	Invoice date	Due date	Invoice number	Purchase order number	Debit account	Prd type	Product code	Blank	Amount	Quantity	Card code 160

Transaction File — Payment Detail

Vendor code	Recd type	Voucher number	Blank	Batch	Voucher number	Voucher date	Vendor code	Invoice date	Due date	Invoice number	Purchase order number	Check number	Check date	Blank	Amount	Blank	Card code 170

EXHIBIT 19–4 Exercise 19–23

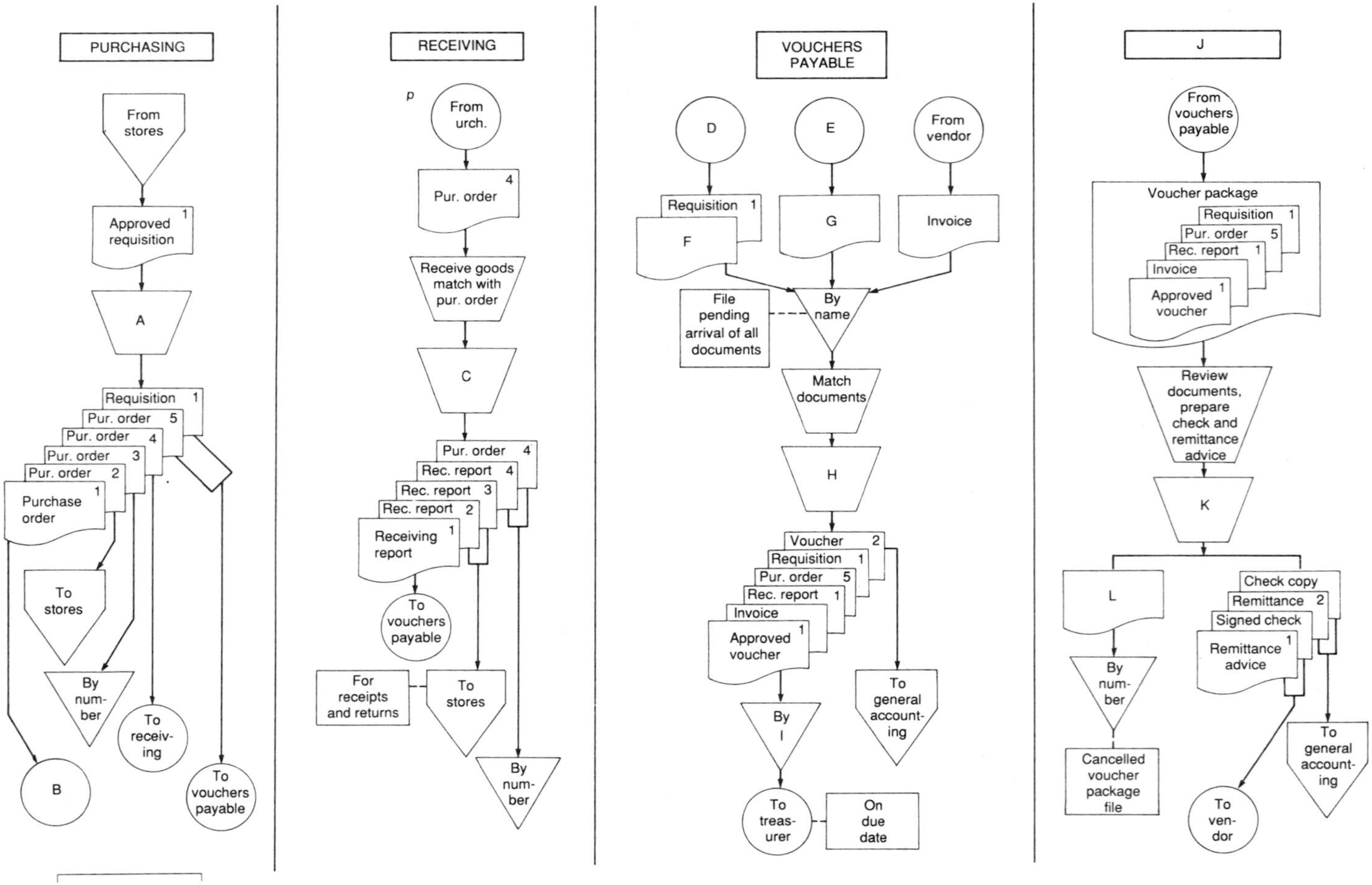

19–24. *MANUAL PURCHASES SYSTEM*

One of the functions of the Office of Sponsored Research at the Southwest State University is to administer grants and research funds obtained by professors, researchers, and students. Administration of purchases to be paid from grants and research funds is a part of the office's responsibilities.

Purchase Requisitions

The purchasing process begins with the initiation of a purchase requisition by either a principal investigator or a research assistant. The office maintains a list of persons authorized to initiate or approve purchase requisitions for each active research project. A copy of this list is sent to the university's purchasing department regularly.

The purchase requisitions are prenumbered by department. The form provides spaces for the description and specification of each desired item, its quantity, and the suggested supplier. The requisitioner submits the purchase requisition to the Office of Sponsored Research, where the availability of funds is checked. Two copies of each approved requisition are sent to the purchasing department. The third copy is filed by a clerk in the office, and the last copy is sent back to the requisitioner.

Purchase Orders

Using the purchase requisitions, the purchasing department prepares purchase orders in 12 copies. Two are sent to the vendor, with the request that one be returned as an acknowledgment. Five copies (numbered 3 through 7) are forwarded to the receiving section. Two copies (11 and 12) are filed in the purchasing department. Other copies are sent to the Office of Sponsored Research (copy 8), accounts payable (copy 9), and the requisitioner (copy 10).

The purchasing department records the receipt of acknowledgments from vendors in the open purchase order file. It also follows up on orders for which no acknowledgment has been received or for which delivery is overdue. In the event that items received are damaged, incomplete, or do not meet quality standards (as indicated on receiving reports), the purchasing department is responsible for contacting the vendor for appropriate adjustments.

In placing orders, buyers in the purchasing department must observe the regents' rules governing conflicts of interest. With respect to the purchasing policy, these rules state:

> Purchases are not permitted from any officer or employee of the university, or from a company or firm owned or partially owned by an officer or employee of the university unless the following conditions are met: (*a*) the relationship between the intended purchaser and any officer or employee is disclosed, (*b*) the cost is less than that from any other source, and (*c*) the purchase is approved by the vice president for business affairs, the president, or the board of regents as appropriate.

Generally, it takes about 15 days to process a routine purchase requisition. In many instances, however, the interval between making a requisition and placing a purchase order is longer. When this occurs, purchase orders have to be canceled or changed due to vendors' running out of stock or their inability to deliver on time. This results in dissatisfaction from researchers, who complain that they have been promised on-time delivery by these vendors when they prepared purchase requisitions.

The purchasing department's explanation is that often purchase requisitions have not been properly filled out, causing unnecessary delays. Another source of delay cited by the purchasing department is the poor intercampus mail delivery service.

Receiving Reports

Clerks in the receiving section file purchase orders numerically. When items are presented to the receiving section for acceptance, receiving personnel use copies of purchase orders on file as receiving reports. Separate receiving reports are prepared only when they receive a partial shipment.

After examining items for quantity and quality, the receiving section indicates acceptance or rejection on copies of purchase orders. One copy (number 3) is routed to the purchasing department for posting in its open purchase order file. Other copies are sent to the requisitioner (copy 4), accounts payable (copy 5), and Office of Sponsored Research (copy 6). Copy 7 is filed numerically in the receiving section.

Accounts Payable

The accounts payable department receives vendors' invoices in triplicate. Before approving these invoices for payment, accounts payable clerks check each invoice against its corresponding purchase order and receiving report. They also verify the accuracy of extensions on invoices. Once these steps are completed, a voucher is prepared authorizing cash disbursements in payment of the invoice. A copy of this voucher is sent to the office of sponsored research where the amount is subtracted from available balances for that project.

At the end of each month, the accounting department produces a monthly expense summary report. A copy of this summary report is sent to the Office of Sponsored Research. Another copy is sent to the principal investigators of all active research projects.

Required:

a. What are some of the strengths of the expenditure cycle procedures just described?
b. What are some of the weaknesses?
c. Which recommendations would you make to remedy these weaknesses?
d. Prepare a flowchart describing the foregoing procedures.

19–25. ***MANUAL VOUCHER SYSTEM***

ConSport Corporation is a regional wholesaler of sporting goods. The system flowchart in Exhibit 19–5 and the following description present ConSport's cash distribution system:

1. The accounts payable department approves for payment all invoices (I) for the purchase of inventory. Invoices are matched with purchase requisitions (PR), purchase orders (PO), and receiving reports (RR). Accounts payable clerks focus on vendors' names and skim the documents when they are combined.
2. When all the documents for an invoice are assembled, a two-copy disbursement voucher (DV) is prepared and the transaction is recorded in the voucher register (VR). The disbursement voucher and supporting documents are then filed alphabetically by vendor.
3. A two-copy journal voucher (JV) that summarizes each day's entries in the voucher register is prepared daily. The first copy is sent to the general ledger department, and the second copy is filed in the accounts payable department by date.
4. The vendor file is searched daily for the disbursement vouchers of invoices due to be paid. Both copies of disbursement vouchers due are sent to the treasury department along with the supporting documents. The cashier prepares a check for each vendor, signs the check, and records it in the check register (CR). Copy one of the disbursement voucher is attached to the check copy and filed by check number in the treasury department. Copy two and the supporting documents are returned to the accounts payable department and filed alphabetically by vendor.
5. A two-copy journal voucher that summarizes each day's checks is prepared. Copy one is sent to the general ledger department and copy two is filed in the treasury department by date.
6. The cashier receives the monthly bank statement with cancelled checks and prepares the bank reconciliation (BR). If an adjustment is required as a consequence of the bank reconciliation, a two-copy journal voucher is prepared. Copy one is sent to the general ledger department. Copy two is attached to copy one of the bank reconciliation and filed by month in the treasury department. Copy two of the bank reconciliation is sent to the internal audit department.

Required:

ConSport Corporation's cash disbursement system has some weaknesses. Review the cash disbursement system and for each weakness:

a. Identify where the weakness exists by using the reference number that appears to the left of each symbol.
b. Describe the nature of the weakness.
c. Make a recommendation about how to correct the weakness.

(CMA Adapted)

EXHIBIT 19–5 Exercise 19–25

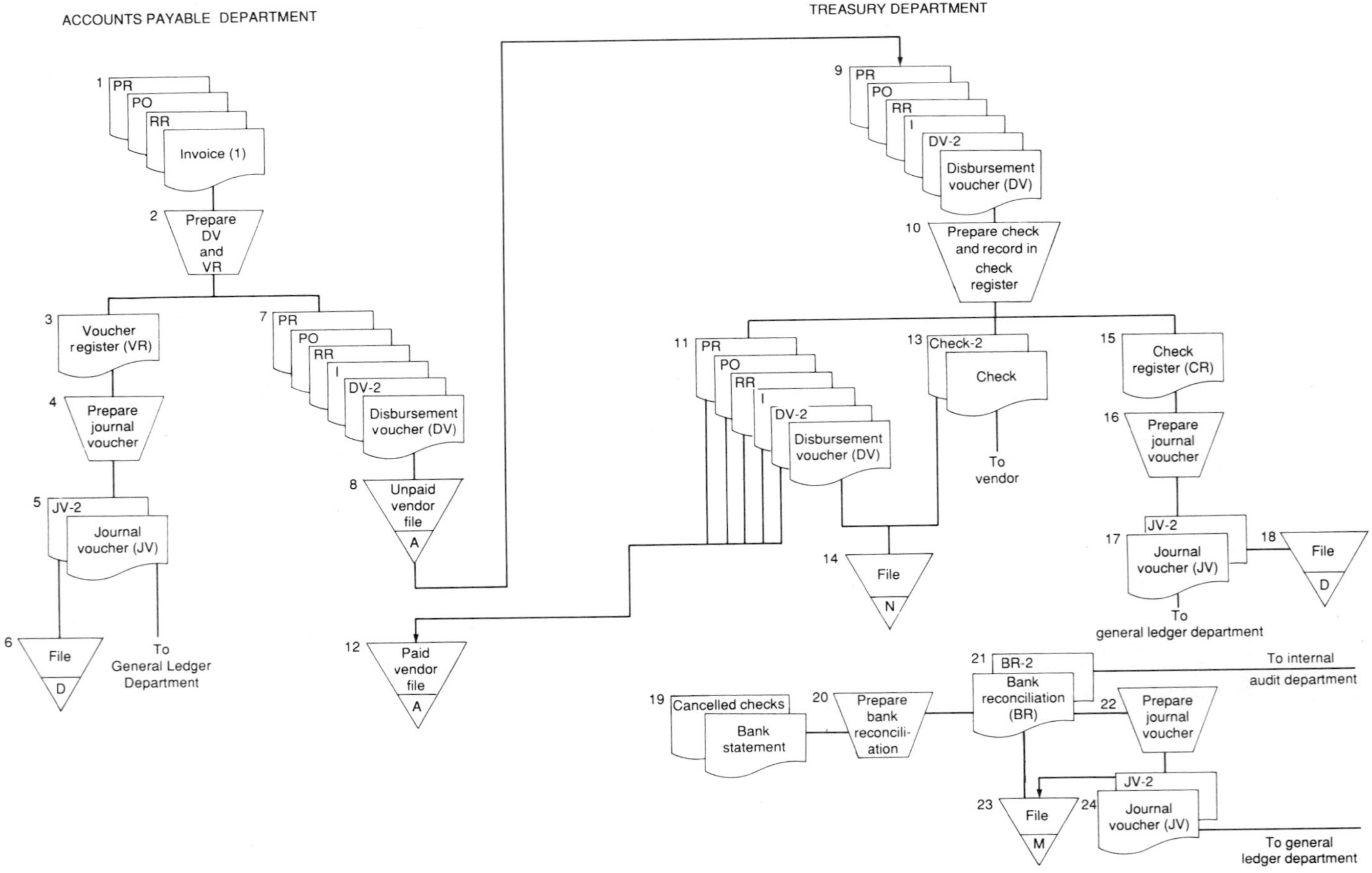

19–26. *CASH DISBURSEMENTS*

The King Company manufactures and distributes duplicating machines and related supplies.[3] The company has grown rapidly since its formation by the merger of two smaller manufacturing companies in 1983. Sales last year reached $80 million. This growth has been particularly due to a management policy emphasizing high product quality and fast, responsive customer service.

Initially, the duplicating machines were manufactured entirely in King Company factories. The rapid growth in machine sales, however, has forced the company to buy an increasing number of subassemblies rather than produce and assemble all the parts itself. All duplicating supplies, however, are purchased from outside vendors.

King's four manufacturing plants and 13 warehouses in the midwest and western states are managed from corporate headquarters in Des Moines, Iowa. Sales are made through local sales agents who place orders with the nearest warehouse.

To provide greater flexibility in meeting local needs, purchases of parts, subassemblies, materials, and supplies are made by the individual plants and warehouses. Each manufacturing plant purchases raw materials and subassemblies for its own production requirements. Warehouses order machines from the factories and purchase duplicating supplies from the best local vendors. Corporate headquarters does not interfere with this decentralized purchasing function unless a plant or warehouse is not providing an adequate return on investment or shows other signs of difficulty. All cash disbursements for purchases, however, are centralized in the headquarters at Des Moines.

Processing at Purchase Locations

Purchases by manufacturing plants and warehouses are made with prenumbered purchase orders issued by a separate purchasing section. One copy of each purchase order goes to accounting which also gets and date stamps a copy of each receiving report and all copies of vendors' invoices. The accounting department keeps track of purchase order numbers and matches their detail to the receiving reports and vendors' invoices. The latter are also checked for clerical accuracy.

When all the details agree, a prenumbered disbursement voucher is prepared by accounting summarizing the detailed information of each purchase. These disbursement vouchers, together with supporting documents, are reviewed and approved for payment by plant controllers or warehouse office managers. The vouchers, together with the supporting documents, are then turned over to the approver's secretary who holds the vouchers, cancels the supporting documents, and returns them to accounting for filing. Periodically, the secretary batches the

---

[3]Adapted from a case prepared by Professors Frederick L. Neumann and Robert J. Boland, of the University of Illinois, under a grant from the Touche Ross Foundation.

approved disbursement vouchers, attaches a transmittal slip indicating the number of vouchers in the batch, and forwards them to Des Moines for payment.

The corporate office at Des Moines distributes to each plant and warehouse a report listing the checks prepared that week, cross-referenced to the disbursement vouchers submitted. At each of the four manufacturing plants, the controller's office compares the checks listed to a retained copy of the disbursement voucher. The warehouse accounting offices are severely understaffed and do not perform this reconciliation. Vendor statements and inquiries about unpaid bills are replied to by the purchase location if invoices have not yet been forwarded for payment. Otherwise, inquiries are sent to Des Moines for a response.

Cash Disbursement Processing

Corporate headquarters in Des Moines processes each disbursement voucher using the combination of manual and computer data processing activities flowcharted in Exhibit 19–6 and described as follows:

Group	*Activity Performed*
Input	Open the mail containing approved disbursement vouchers and transmittal slips from the manufacturing plants and warehouses. Make test counts of disbursement vouchers against transmittal slips and forward both for further processing.
Vendor code	File transmittal slips. Sort disbursement vouchers alphabetically by vendor. Scan vouchers for completeness; check vendor's code, name, address, and terms against the vendor master file. Initiate changes or additions to vendor master file if warranted. Forward acceptable vouchers for further processing.
Batching	Scan vouchers for missing data and check calculations. Group acceptable vouchers by type, in batches of approximately 50. Create batch control totals on dollars and hash totals on quantities. Forward batches and control totals for processing.
Control desk	Scan batches for missing data and recalculate control totals. Assign control numbers to batches. Log them in with their control totals. Forward batches with control numbers and totals for further processing.
Data entry	Keypunch and key verify data. Send batched documents to control desk for cancellation and return to accounting department for filing. Create tape transfer status report. Convert cards to tape. Forward tape with control and summary cards for processing.
Data center	Perform program edits for completeness and reasonableness as well as appropriate limit and validity checks. Process acceptable data against vendor master file and transaction history file. Mechanically sign resulting prenumbered checks. Forward signed checks, reports, and unresolved rejects to control desk.
Control desk	Log and reconcile data center totals. Distribute data center output as appropriate. Foot, balance, and mail checks. Correct errors and otherwise resolve rejects.

EXHIBIT 19–6 Case 19–26

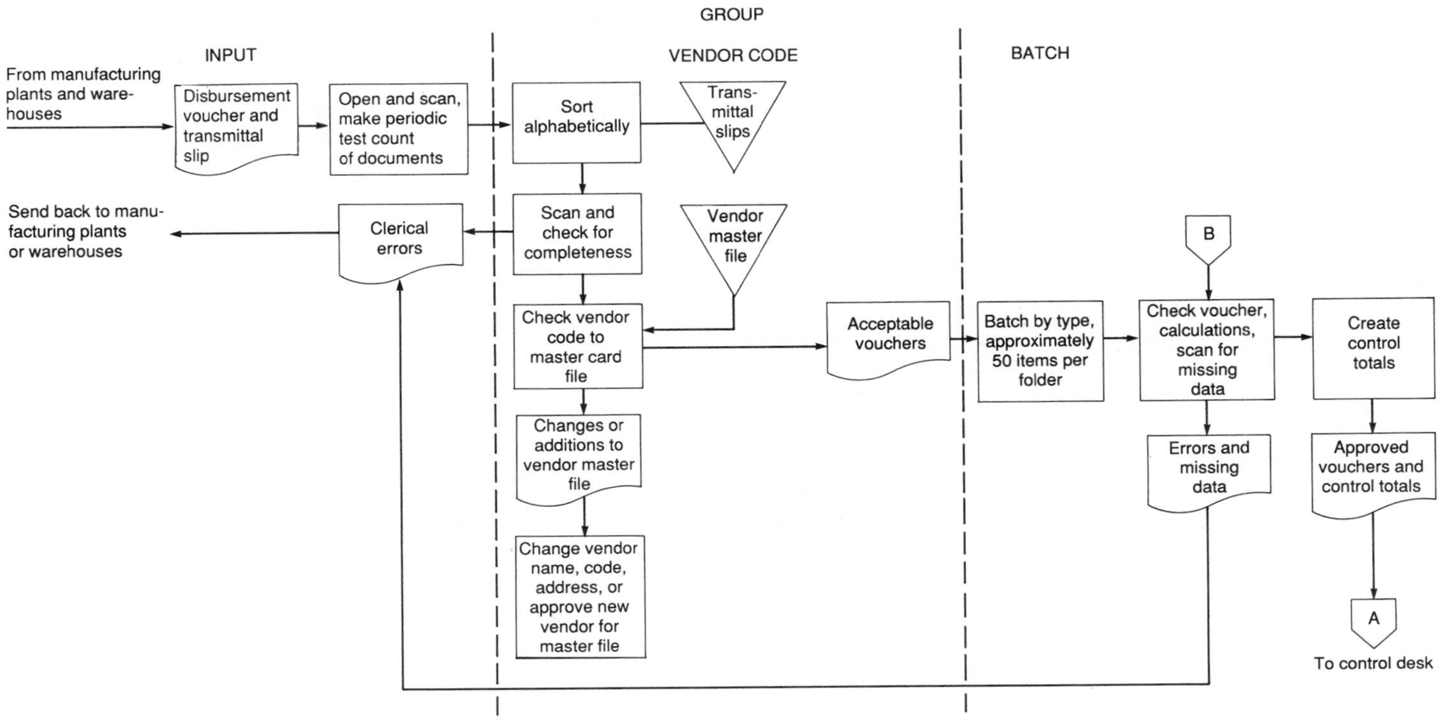

EXHIBIT 19–6 Case 19–26 (*concluded*)

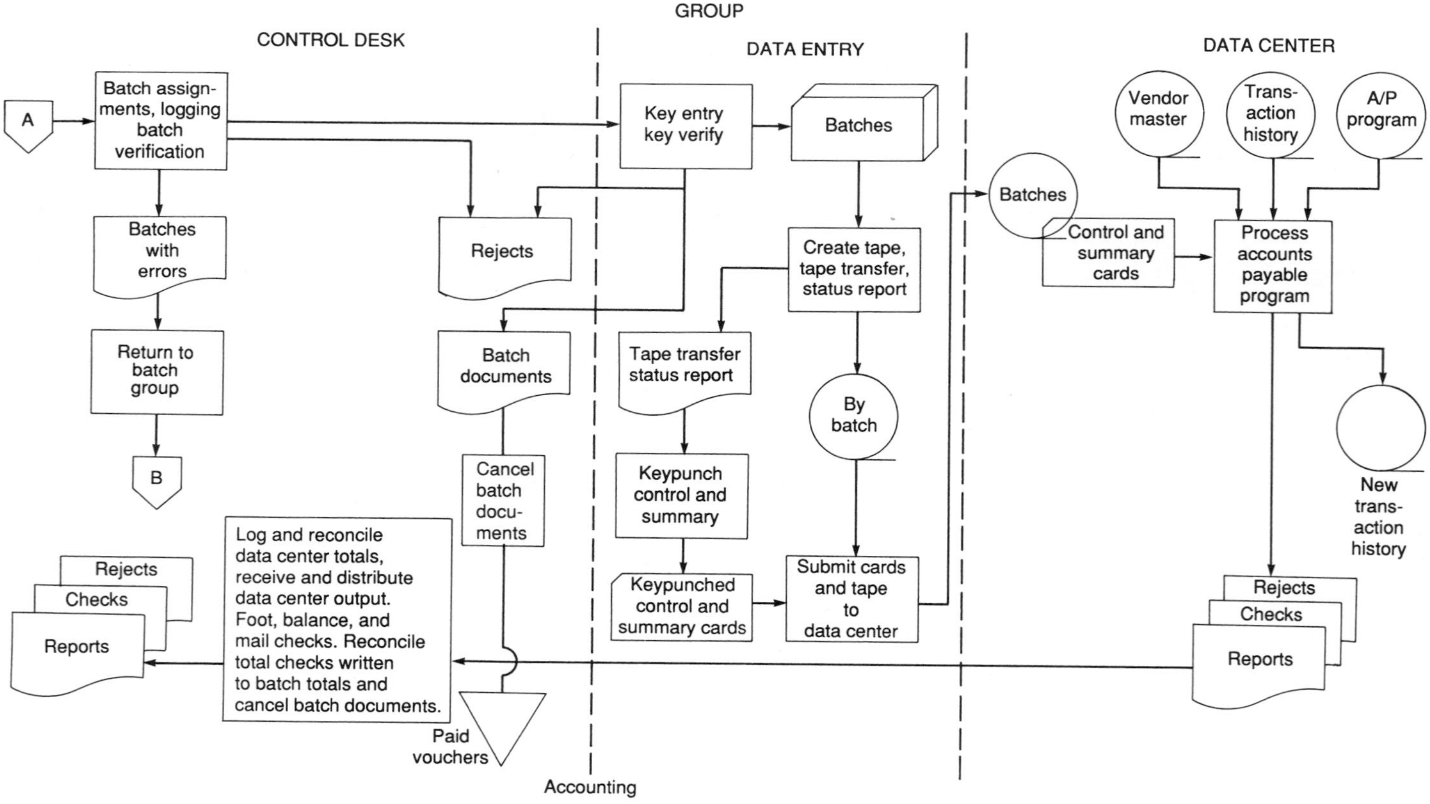

Required:

a. What additional information would you like to obtain before making your evaluation of the cash disbursements system?
b. What are the objectives of the cash disbursements system?
c. How are these objectives accomplished in this system and what controls are available to assist?
d. What recommendations would you make to King Company management about the internal control over their centralized disbursement system?

19–27. *APPLICATION CONTROLS*

Ziegler Cosmetics is a rapidly growing manufacturer of women's and men's fragrances.[4] Its success is due to its founder's discovery of a means to help perfumes and colognes retain their fragrances longer.

Computer Conversion

This rapid growth has prompted the company's decision to put its accounting system on a computer. Cash disbursements have already been successfully converted. A flowchart of the proposed accounts payable system appears in Exhibit 19–7. The system begins with the procedure of matching purchase orders to receiving reports and invoices. The processing of the documents would update the accounts payable file and produce three output files.

One output, a payment file, would produce the checks, a check register, and a payment report. Processing the report file would produce several reports including an aged listing of unmatched documents. The distribution file would also produce several reports including the list of accounts to be debited. The list is subdivided between matched and unmatched documents. The latter amount would be reversed at the start of the following period.

Document Format

A standard format, which has been developed for processing each of the three major input documents, includes the following fields:

			Document		
Fields	*Size*	*Content*	*PO*	*RR*	*INV*
Vendor number	5	numeric and first digit nonzero	x	x	x
Purchase order number	6	first 3 alpha, last 3 numeric	x	x	x

(continued)

[4]Adapted from a case prepared by Professors Frederick L. Neumann and Richard J. Boland, of the University of Illinois, under a grant from the Touche Ross Foundation.

EXHIBIT 19–7 Case 19–27

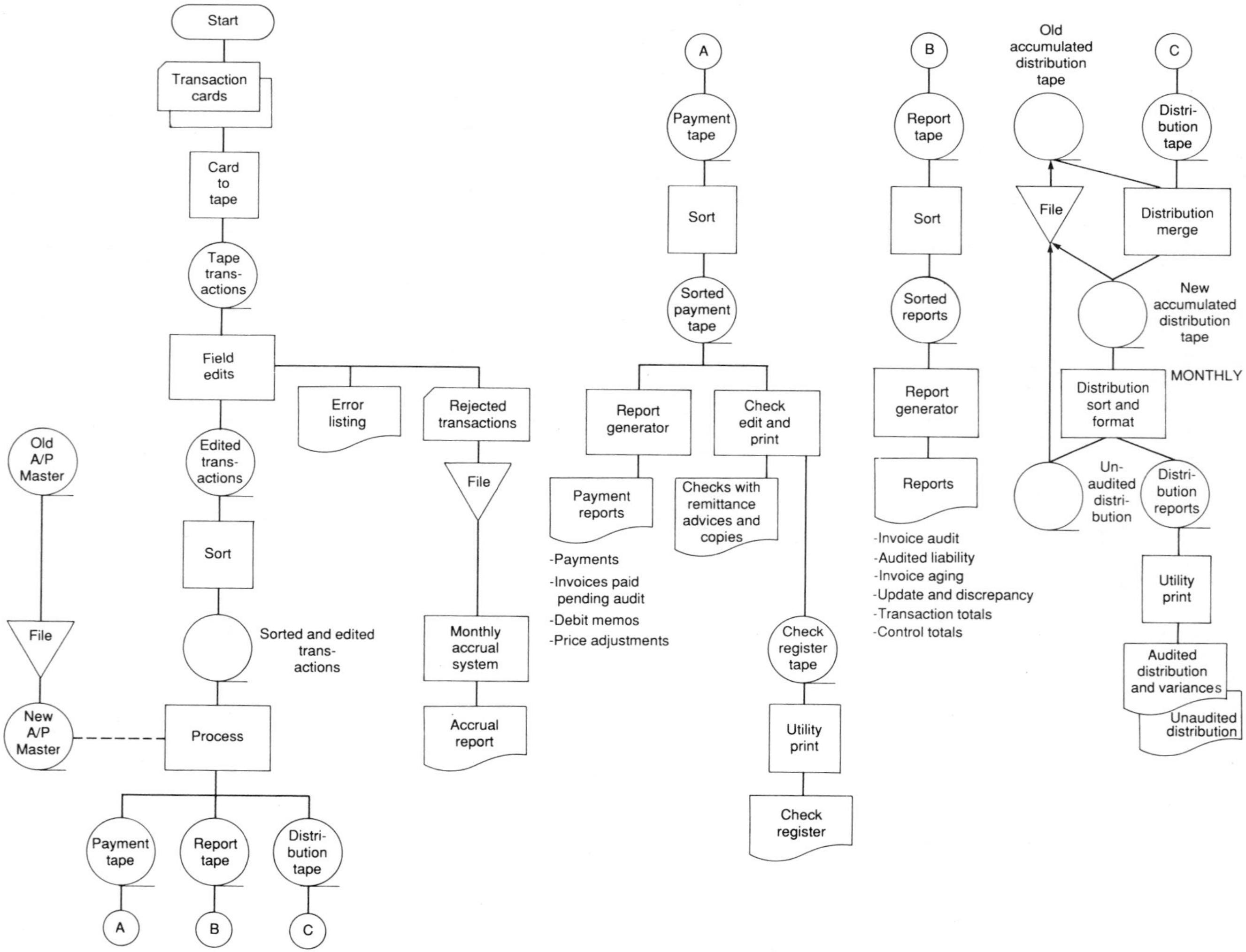

Fields	*Size*	*Content*	*Document* *PO*	*RR*	*INV*
Item number/name	16	alpha/numeric	x	x	x
Terms code	2	first alpha, second numeric	x		
Tax code	2	numeric	x		
Effective date	4	year: 0–9, month: 1–9 and A-C day: 1–31	x		
Expiration date	4	year: 0–9, month: 1–9 and A-C day: 1–31	x		
Freight code	1	A-X or blank	x	x	
Unit of measure	2	01–50		x	x
Receiving report number	7	numeric		x	
Shipping date	3	month: 1–9 and A-C day: 1–31		x	x
Quantity	6	numeric		x	x
Receiving date	3	month: 1–9 and A-C day: 1–31		x	
Invoice gross amount	8	numeric			x
Type of material code	1	1–6 and A-C	x	x	x
PO type code	1	1–4	x		

The proposed programmed edit controls for each document are listed in Exhibits 19–8, 19–9, and 19–10. They are defined as follows:

Format Check. Determines that data are entered in the proper mode, either alphabetic, numeric, or alphanumeric, within designated fields of a record.

Completeness Check. Assures that data entries are made in fields that cannot be processed in a blank state.

Reasonableness Check. Tests various fields of data through comparison with other information available within the transaction or master records.

Limit Check. Tests specified amount fields against stipulated high or low limits of acceptability.

Validity Check. Examines characters constituting a field for a defined pattern format, legitimate subcode, or character values using logic and arithmetic rather than tables.

Legitimate Code. Matches the characters in a coded field to an acceptable set of values in a table. Only transactions with matching codes are acceptable.

The proposed edit controls for each document, by field, are listed on Exhibits 19–8 (purchase order), 19–9 (receiving report), and 19–10 (vendor invoice).

Required:

How would you evaluate the appropriateness and expected effectiveness of the proposed controls?

a. By field

b. By source document

EXHIBIT 19–8 Case 19–27

Examination of: Acquisition system	As of:	Exam. no.	W/P no. ______
Function: Purchasing			Prepared by ______
Activity: Purchase order			Date ______

Controls

What can go wrong?	Format check	Completeness check	Reasonableness check	Limit check	Validity check	Legitimate code
Vendor no. (numeric, first position nonzero)	X	X				X
PO no. (first 3 characters alpha, rest numeric)	X	X		X		
Item no./name (numeric/alpha)	X	X				X
Terms, code (first character alpha, second numeric)	X	X				X
Tax, code (numeric)	X	X				X
(0-9) (1-9/A-C) (0-9) Effective Date (4 characters: year, month day)	X	X		X	X	
(0-9) (1-9A-C) (0-9) Expiration Date (4 characters: year, month, day)	X	X		X	X	
Freight, code (A-X or blank)	X					X
Type of material code (1-8/A-C)	X	X				X
Purchase order type, code (1-4)	X	X				X

EXHIBIT 19–9 Case 19–27

Examination of: Acquisition system	As of:	Exam no.	W/P no. ______
Function: Material receipt			Prepared by ______
Activity: Receiving report			Date ______

Controls

What can go wrong?	Format check	Completeness check	Reasonableness check	Limit check	Validity check	Legitimate code
Vendor no. (numeric, first position nonzero)	X	X				X
PO no. (first 3 characters alpha, rest numeric)	X	X		X		
Item no./name (numeric/alpha)	X	X				X
Unit of measure	X	X				X
Receiving report no. (all numeric)	X	X		X		
Shipping date (month 1-9/A-C, day no.)	X	X		X	X	
Freight, code (A-X or blank)	X					X
Quantity (numeric)	X	X				
Received date (month 1-9/A-C, day no.)	X	X		X	X	
Type of material, code (1-8/A-C)	X	X				X

EXHIBIT 19–10 Case 19–27

Examination of: Acquisition system | As of: | Exam no. | W/P no. ______

Function: Accounts payable | Prepared by ______

Activity: Vendor invoices | Date ______

Controls

What can go wrong?	Format check	Legitimate code	Reasonableness	Limit check	Validity check	Legitimate code	
Vendor no. (numeric, first position nonzero)	X	X				X	
PO no. (first 3 characters alpha, rest numeric)	X	X		X			
Item no./name (numeric/alpha)	X	X				X	
Unit of measure	X	X				X	
Shipping date (month 1-9/A-C, day no.)	X	X		X	X		
Quantity (numeric)	X	X					
Invoice gross amount (numeric)	X	X		X	X		
Type of material, code (1-8/A-C)	X	X				X	

19–28 ***CONTROL FLOWCHART***

The flowchart on page 704 shows selected aspects of Maylou Corporation's procedures related to purchase requisitions and purchase orders. The flowchart is incomplete.

Required:

Identify procedures that should be incorporated in Maylou's system if its internal accounting control over purchases is to be effective. Assume that the separation of duties, as reflected in the flowchart, cannot be changed. An example of the needed answers follows.

1. Purchase orders are prepared only after receipt of properly prepared purchase requisitions.

(AICPA Adapted)

19–29. ***CONTROL FLOWCHART***

The following procedures relate to purchasing and receiving activities of the Black Biscuit Company. The company is privately owned by two brothers, with

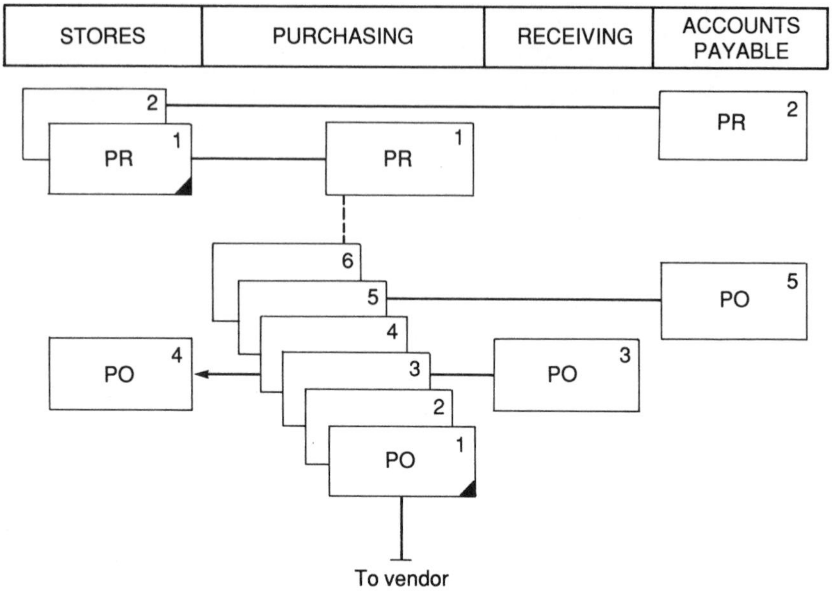

one serving as president (in charge of sales and finance) and the other as vice president (in charge of production).

Purchase requisitions (prenumbered)

These are prepared by the stores department heads, plant superintendent, or office, and approved by the vice president.

Purchase orders (prenumbered)

These are prepared in quadruplicate (last copy without prices). The original is mailed to the supplier, a copy goes to the accounting department, a copy without prices to the receiving department, and one copy is filed by suppliers in the purchasing department.

Receiving slips (prenumbered)

These are prepared in duplicate in the receiving department. One copy goes to the accounting department and one copy to the stores department.

Purchase invoices (prenumbered)

Suppliers are requested to use the invoice form supplied with the purchase order and to send an original and a copy. Most suppliers comply. The accounting department marks the distribution. The original is matched with the receiving slip and purchase order, and then sent to the purchasing department head for approval. Purchasing department retains the order and receiving slip, which are filed numerically. All numbers of the order and of the slip must be accounted for.

Original invoices form the basis of direct posting to the general ledger and to the voucher part of the check. Invoices and checks are filed in trays, by suppliers, under classification of due dates.

The second copy of the invoice is sent to the cost department for individual machine posting to perpetual inventory cards and for total posting to the cost ledger. It is then filed in that department, under names of suppliers.

Where a supplier does not use the specified invoice form, the president must approve payment. He prepares memos to serve in lieu of the invoice form.

Salesmen's expense advances, commissions, and other disbursements are recorded on *cash disbursement* forms in duplicate. The original is approved by the president, numbered consecutively with invoices, and posted in the same manner. The duplicate is filed alphabetically in the accounting department.

Credit memos from suppliers

Credit memos follow the same procedures as invoices.

Required:

a. Prepare a control flowchart covering procedures related to purchases.
b. Give your comments on the existing internal control related to purchases.

(AICPA Adapted)

Chapter 20

Conversion Cycle Applications

Learning Objectives:

1. To review the accounting entries recorded in the conversion cycle.
2. To learn the documents, reports, and records used in the conversion cycle.
3. To understand how accounting transactions are processed by the application systems in the conversion cycle.
4. To see how control practices and procedures are applied in the conversion cycle.

INTRODUCTION

This chapter discusses the conversion cycle—one of the four transaction cycles used by accounting systems to record the activities of a business. This cycle differs depending on whether the organization is a manufacturing, merchandising, or service firm.

In the conversion cycle, the accounting system records one economic event—the consumption of labor, material, and overhead to produce a salable product or service. In service organizations, this cycle consists of the payroll and the cost accounting systems. In merchandising companies, it contains the payroll and inventory systems. In manufacturing companies, the conversion cycle

ILLUSTRATION 20–1 Application Systems in the Conversion Cycle

System	*Purpose*	*Type of Organization*
Payroll	To calculate the pay due employees, to print paychecks, and to maintain cumulative earnings records	Service Merchandising Manufacturing
Inventory	To maintain inventory records and to notify managers when the inventory level of a specific item requires replenishing	Merchandising Manufacturing
Cost accounting	To determine the costs of products manufactured or services provided, and to record those costs in the accounting records	Service Manufacturing

includes all three systems. Illustration 20–1 shows the application systems in the conversion cycle for each of these organizations.

Application systems in the conversion cycle process five types of transactions. Systems in the revenue and expenditure cycles also process two of these types. Illustration 20–2 summarizes these transactions and the documents recording them.

ILLUSTRATION 20–2 Conversion Cycle Applications and Related Documents

Type of Transaction	*Related Documents*
Purchase of inventory*	Purchase order Receiving report Voucher
Sale of inventory**	Sales order Shipping notice Sales invoice
Transfer of material, labor, and overhead into production	Material requisition Job ticket
Transfer of work in process into finished goods	Completed production order
Payroll	Timecard Salary authorization Other documents

*This transaction is processed in the expenditure cycle.
**This transaction is processed in the revenue cycle.

INVENTORY SYSTEMS

The inventory system maintains inventory records and notifies managers when the inventory level of a specific item requires replenishing. Manufacturing companies use inventory systems to control the levels of raw materials and finished goods inventories. Merchandising companies use them to ensure that goods are available for resale. Although service organizations maintain supplies inventories, most do not use a formal system to control them. They simply purchase supplies inventories as necessary and expense their costs.

Inventory System Transactions and Documents

An inventory system processes two types of transactions that originate in the revenue and expenditure cycles. These transactions are the purchase and sale of inventory.

Purchase of Inventory. The expenditure cycle processes this type of transaction. However, the entry made to record the transaction depends on the method used for inventory accounting. The two methods are the periodic method and the perpetual method.

Periodic Method. A company using this method maintains no ongoing record of the amount of inventory on hand. Instead, it records the acquisition of inventory in a general ledger account entitled Purchases. The company determines beginning and ending inventory values by physical count. Periodically, it calculates Cost of Goods Sold from the Beginning and Ending Inventories and the Purchases account balance. The entry recording the acquisition of inventory is

Dr.	Purchases	xxx	
Cr.	Accounts Payable		xxx

Merchandising companies used this method for many years. They have many transactions in inventory during each day, and implementing the perpetual method manually was impractical. Now, however, computerized inventory systems using the perpetual method are practical even for the smallest retailer.

Perpetual Method. With this method, a company maintains an ongoing count of the inventory on hand. When it acquires inventory, it increases the quantity and cost of inventory. When inventory is sold, the company decreases quantity and cost. At any time it knows how much of each inventory item is available for sale. This allows the company to replenish inventory prior to completely depleting it.

Manufacturing companies use the perpetual method because they need to know if sufficient inventory is on hand for their manufacturing processes. Most merchandising companies with computer-based systems also use this method.

A company using the perpetual method has one or more inventory accounts in the general ledger. When inventory is acquired, it records the transaction by debiting the proper inventory account. For example, when a manufacturing company purchases raw material inventory for use in its factory, it makes the following entry:

Dr.	Raw Material Inventory	xxx	
Cr.	Accounts Payable		xxx

Because a merchandising company does not carry raw materials, it makes the debit in an account simply entitled Inventory. If the material is not to be resold, the debit is to the Supplies Inventory account.

The same documents record the purchase of inventory using both the periodic and the perpetual methods. They are purchase orders, receiving reports, and vouchers. A voucher documents the credit entry in Accounts Payable.

Sale of Inventory. A company records the cost of inventory sold in the general ledger account entitled Cost of Goods Sold. How the firm determines this amount depends on the inventory method used.

With the periodic method, no entry is made at the time of the sale. Cost of Goods Sold is determined by adding the amount of the Purchases to the cost of the Beginning Inventory. This tells the cost of the goods available for sale. Subtracting from this amount the cost of the Ending Inventory gives the cost of the inventory sold.

With the perpetual method, the company records the sale by crediting an inventory account and debiting the Cost of Goods Sold account. At the end of a reporting period, the total in this account is the cost of the inventory that was sold during the period. In a manufacturing company, the credit entry is to an account containing the cost of all products manufactured during the period:

Dr.	Cost of Goods Sold	xxx	
Cr.	Finished Goods Inventory		xxx

The documents used in the revenue cycle to record the sale are sales orders, shipping notices, and sales invoices.

Illustration 20–3 compares the periodic and perpetual methods of accounting for inventories. This example shows how a perpetual system implements better internal control for inventories. When reported to management, the perpetual system discloses a $50 shortage in Ending Inventory. Management can take action to keep it from occurring again. The periodic method conceals the shortage.

Inventory System Reports

Like other applications, the inventory system produces control reports and registers. In addition, there are four special purpose reports: inventory status reports, query reports, reorder reports, and physical inventory reports.

ILLUSTRATION 20–3 Periodic and Perpetual Inventory Methods

Data:

Beginning inventory balance (at cost of $10 per unit) .... 80 units

Physical movements during the period (in units, at cost):

Transaction no.	1	2	3	4	5	6	7	8	9	10	11	12
Receipts				60					60			
Shipments	10	20	15		12	15	20	10		25	12	14

Ending inventory balance (based on a physical inventory) .... 42 units

Periodic Method

A. As Analyzed in the Journal

1. At the time of purchase:

Dr.	Purchases	xxx	
Cr.	Accounts Payable		xxx

2. At the time of sale:

Dr.	Accounts Receivable	xxx	
Cr.	Sales		xxx

B. As Reflected in the Ledger

Inventories

Debit		Credit	
(beg.)	800		

Purchases

Debit		Credit	
(4)	600		
(9)	600		

Accounts Payable

Debit		Credit	
		(4)	600
		(9)	600

Perpetual Method

A. As Analyzed in the Journal

1. At the time of purchase:

Dr.	Inventories	xxx	
Cr.	Accounts Payable		xxx

2. At the time of sale:

Dr.	Accounts Receivable	xxx	
Cr.	Sales		xxx
Dr.	Cost of Goods Sold	xxx	
Cr.	Inventories		xxx

B. As Reflected in the Ledger

Inventories

Debit		Credit	
(beg.)	800	(1)	100
(4)	600	(2)	200
(9)	600	(3)	150
		(5)	120
		(6)	150
		(7)	200
		(8)	100
		(10)	250
		(11)	120
		(12)	140

Accounts Payable

Debit		Credit	
		(4)	600
		(9)	600

Cost of Goods Sold

Debit		Credit	
(1)	100		
(2)	200		
(3)	150		
(5)	120		
(6)	150		
(7)	200		
(8)	100		
(10)	250		
(11)	120		
(12)	140		

ILLUSTRATION 20–3 *(concluded)*

Periodic Method

C. Inventory Ledger Is Not Used.

Perpetual Method

C. As Recorded in Inventory Ledger

Item: XYZ						Reorder point: 40 Reorder quantity: 60		
Received			Issued			Balance		
Qty.	Pr.	Amt.	Qty.	Pr.	Amt.	Qty.	Pr.	Amt.
						80	10	800
			10	10	100	70	10	700
			20	10	200	50	10	500
			15	10	150	35	10	350
60	10	600				95	10	950
			12	10	120	83	10	830
			15	10	150	68	10	680
			20	10	200	48	10	480
			10	10	100	38	10	380
60	10	600				98	10	980
			25	10	250	73	10	730
			12	10	120	61	10	610
			14	10	140	47	10	470

D. As Reported to Management (Periodic Method)

Cost of goods sold:	
Beginning inventory	$ 800
Purchases	1,200
	2,000
Ending inventory	420
Cost of goods sold	$1,580

D. As Reported to Management (Perpetual Method)

Cost of goods sold:		
Cost of goods sold, per books		$1,530
Add: Inventory shortage:		
Ending book inventory	$470	
Ending physical inventory	420	50
Adjusted cost of goods sold		$1,580

Inventory Status Report. An inventory status report lists all items normally kept in inventory, the quantity on hand of each item, and the cost. It provides detail explaining the inventory amount shown on the balance sheet. A batch processing system prints this report daily or weekly. Employees use it to determine quantities that were available at the time of the most recent printing. Illustration 20–4 contains an inventory status report.

ILLUSTRATION 20–4 An Inventory Status Report

RUN DATE 04/30/91 T. L. James Enterprises PAGE 3
Inventory Control
REPORT DATE 04/30/91 INVENTORY STATUS REPORT
DEPARTMENT BDR

ITEM NUMBER	DESCRIPTION	BEGINNING BALANCE	SALES	RETURNS	RECEIPTS	ADJMTS.	CURRENT BALANCE	CURRENT AVG. COST	TOTAL VALUATION
BDR-10000TWI	TWIN MATTRESS	5.00	1.00	0.00	0.00	2.00	6.00	40.000	240.00
BDR-10010TWI	TWIN FOUNDATION	4.00	0.00	2.00	0.00	0.00	6.00	45.000	270.00
BDR-10020TWI	TWIN SET	2.00	1.00	0.00	0.00	0.00	1.00	80.000	80.00
BDR-10040FUL	FULL MATTRESS	9.00	1.00	0.00	0.00	0.00	8.00	50.000	400.00
BDR-10050FUL	FULL FOUNDATION	10.00	0.00	0.00	0.00	0.00	10.00	50.000	500.00
BDR-10060FUL	FULL SET	2.00	0.00	0.00	0.00	0.00	2.00	95.000	190.00
BDR-10070QUE	QUEEN SET	5.00	2.00	0.00	0.00	0.00	3.00	150.000	450.00
BDR-10080KIN	KING SET	2.00	0.00	0.00	0.00	0.00	2.00	200.000	400.00
BDR-10090EX-	EX-LONG TWIN SET	1.00	0.00	0.00	0.00	0.00	1.00	100.000	100.00
BDR-11000BED	BED FRAME	16.00	2.00	0.00	0.00	0.00	14.00	29.990	419.86
	DEPARTMENT BDR TOTALS		NUMBER OF ITEMS:			10.00	53.00	57.545	3,049.86
	GRAND TOTALS		NUMBER OF ITEMS:			40.00	389.00	147.465	57,363.75

*** END OF INVENTORY STATUS REPORT ***

Query Inventory Items. On-line real-time systems allow an employee to determine quantities on hand at the time of inquiry. A report such as that shown in Illustration 20–5 provides this information. Many systems provide employees the option of either printing the report or displaying it at a terminal.

Reorder Report. A reorder report identifies items in inventory that should be replenished. When the quantity on hand decreases to the reorder point, the inventory control system includes the item on this report. A purchasing agent uses the reorder report, such as that in Illustration 20–6, to identify items for purchase. In a manufacturing company, a report of this type may identify items for manufacture.

Physical Inventory Report. Periodically organizations physically count the number of each inventory item on hand. Called "taking the physical inventory," this process allows computation of cost of goods sold when the periodic method is used. With the perpetual method, it allows the organization to correct errors in the inventory records.

A report such as that in Illustration 20–7 makes the process easier. This physical inventory report lists all items maintained in inventory and, with the

ILLUSTRATION 20–5 An Inventory Query Report

```
                      T. L. JAMES ENTERPRISE                              PAGE  1
                             Inventory
                        Query Inventory Items

DEPARTMENT: APP                         PTD BEG. QTY ON HAND..:         14.00
ITEM......: 10000STO
       STOVE, ELECTRIC                  PTD ACTIVITY
PRODUCT CODE.....: A                        # SOLD............:         5.00
SELLING UNIT.....: EA                       # RECEIVED........:         1.00
VENDOR ID........: FRIGID                   # RETURNED........:         1.00
VENDOR ITEM #....: LMP-3467                 # ADJUSTED........:         0.00
CURRENT AVG. COST:      344.7600000
LAST COST/ITEM...:      344.76          CURRENT QTY ON HAND...:         11.00
SELLING PRICES
    PRICE A......:      700.00          YTLP # SOLD...........:         24.00
    PRICE B......:      675.00
    PRICE C......:      599.99          PROFITABILITY              PTD          YTLP
REORDER LEVEL....:        8.00              SALES.........:     2775.00     16324.00
REORDER QUANTITY.:        8.00              COST OF SALES.:     1379.04      8274.24
ON REORDER REPORT: 01/01/00                 PROFIT %......:      101.23        97.29
```


perpetual method, the quantities on hand. An employee reconciles these quantities with item counts made by other employees in the inventory warehouse.

Inventory System Records

Noncomputerized Records. In a manual system, a company using the perpetual inventory method requires an inventory ledger. It contains one page in a book, or one card in a card file, for each item maintained in inventory. The information contained on a page in this ledger is shown in Illustration 20–3c.

A clerk records changes on the proper page or card each time items are added to or removed from inventory. The clerk also calculates the cost of the remaining quantity of the items after each transaction. The inventory ledger is a subsidiary ledger for the Inventory account in the general ledger.

Computerized Records. Computerized records in a traditional data file system are similar to noncomputerized records in a manual system. They consist

ILLUSTRATION 20–6 An Inventory Reorder Report

RUN DATE 04/30/91 T. L. James Enterprises PAGE 1
Inventory Control
REPORT DATE 04/30/91 REORDER REPORT

VENDOR	VENDOR ITEM	YOUR ITEM ID	P C	DESCRIPTION	BALANCE	REORDER LEVEL	WEEKS BELOW R/O LEVEL	REORDER QUANTITY	DATE ORDERED	FIRST TIME?
BASSET	EAM510	DNR-10010MOB	D	MOBILE SERVER	1.00	2.00	3	2.00	--------	
BROYHL	752DN	DNR-10040OVA	D	OVAL TABLE	2.00	4.00	3	2.00	--------	
BROYHL	772DN	DNR-10050PED	D	PEDESTAL TABLE	4.00	4.00	2	4.00	--------	
DREW	798062	LVR-10000SOF	L	SOFA	9.00	12.00	3	12.00	--------	
DREW	798064	LVR-10020CHA	L	CHAIR	10.00	18.00	2	18.00	--------	
DREW	798065	LVR-10030OTT	L	OTTOMAN	8.00	10.00	3	10.00	--------	
DREXEL	1-1234S	ABC-2500S	B	SOFA, FLORAL	3.00	4.00	0	5.00	--------	*****
FRIGID	RMP-2398	APP-10010REF	A	REFRIG, 22 CU. FT.	8.00	8.00	3	6.00	--------	
FRIGID	OMP-5782	APP-10030OVE	A	OVEN, MICROWAVE	6.00	6.00	4	6.00	--------	
FRIGID	DMP-6742	APP-10040DIS	A	DISHWASHER	4.00	8.00	2	8.00	--------	
HICKRY	H8120	DNR-10070CAN	D	CANE BACK CHAIR	10.00	12.00	1	12.00	--------	
SEALY	S80658	BDR-10020TWI	B	TWIN SET	1.00	1.00	4	2.00	--------	
SEALY	S80636	BDR-10070QUE	B	QUEEN SET	3.00	4.00	3	4.00	--------	
SEALY	S80605	BDR-10090EX-	B	EX-LONG TWIN SET	1.00	1.00	2	1.00	--------	
SINGER	S0667TB	LVR-10040END	L	END TABLE	2.00	6.00	4	6.00	--------	

TOTAL ITEMS BELOW REORDER LEVEL = 15

*** END OF REORDER REPORT ***

of both master files and transaction files. A data base management system (DBMS) maintains the same data and provides it to application programs as a subschema. However, the DBMS stores this data independently of the subschema.

The computerized equivalent of the inventory ledger is the *inventory master file*. It contains one record for each item maintained in inventory. Illustration 20–8 shows the contents of this record. If the company uses a DBMS, this illustration shows its subschema.

Inventory System Transaction Processing

Computerized Procedures. Illustration 20–9 shows batch and on-line real-time system flowcharts of an inventory application. In the batch processing system, the receiving department accumulates receiving reports in batches and daily sends them to data entry. The inventory warehouse prepares batches of

ILLUSTRATION 20–7 A Physical Inventory Report

RUN DATE 04/30/91

T. L. James Enterprises
Inventory Control
PHYSICAL INVENTORY REPORT

PAGE 5

DEPARTMENT LVR

ITEM NUMBER	P C	DESCRIPTION	VENDOR ID	VENDOR ITEM #	UNIT	BALANCE CALCULATED	BALANCE ACTUAL	COMMENTS
LVR-10000SOF	L	SOFA	DREW	798062	EA	9.00	----------	----------------------------------
LVR-10010LOV	L	LOVESEAT	DREW	798063	EA	4.00	----------	----------------------------------
LVR-10020CHA	L	CHAIR	DREW	798064	EA	10.00	----------	----------------------------------
LVR-10030OTT	L	OTTOMAN	DREW	798065	EA	8.00	----------	----------------------------------
LVR-10040END	L	END TABLE	SINGER	S0667TB	EA	2.00	----------	----------------------------------
LVR-10050COC	L	COCKTAIL TABLE	SINGER	S0675T	EA	17.00	----------	----------------------------------
LVR-10060SOF	L	SOFA TABLE	SINGER	S0683T	EA	4.00	----------	----------------------------------
LVR-10070SPI	L	SPICE JAR LAMP	LITECO	704457	EA	16.00	----------	----------------------------------
LVR-10080FLO	L	FLOOR LAMP	LITECO	706161	EA	47.00	----------	----------------------------------

DEPARTMENT TOTALS TOTAL ITEMS: 9 TOTAL UNITS: 117

GRAND TOTALS TOTAL ITEMS: 40 TOTAL UNITS: 389

*** END OF PHYSICAL INVENTORY REPORT ***

ILLUSTRATION 20–8 Contents of an Inventory Master Record

ITEM-NUMBER*
ITEM-DESCRIPTION
UNIT-COST**
REORDER-POINT
REORDER-QUANTITY
VENDOR-FIRST
VENDOR-SECOND
VENDOR-THIRD
QUANTITY-ON-HAND
QUANTITY-ON-ORDER

*Designates the primary key.
**If a standard costing system is used, this is replaced by STANDARD-COST.

ILLUSTRATION 20–9 An Inventory Application

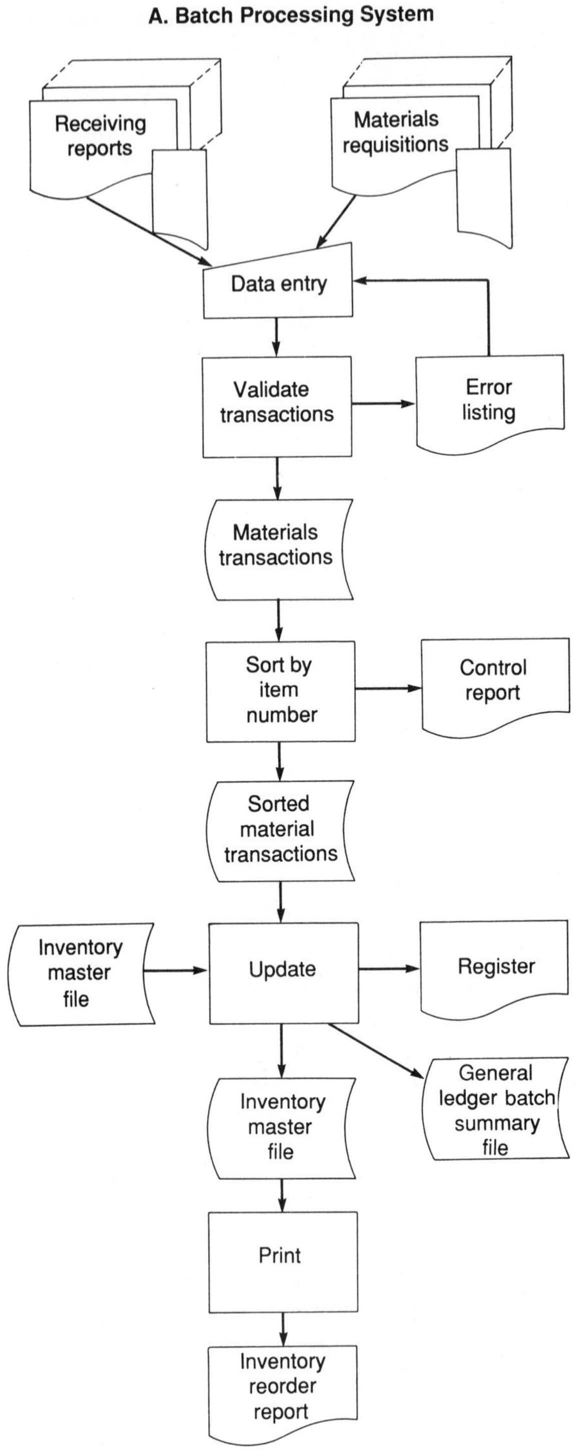

ILLUSTRATION 20–9 *(concluded)*

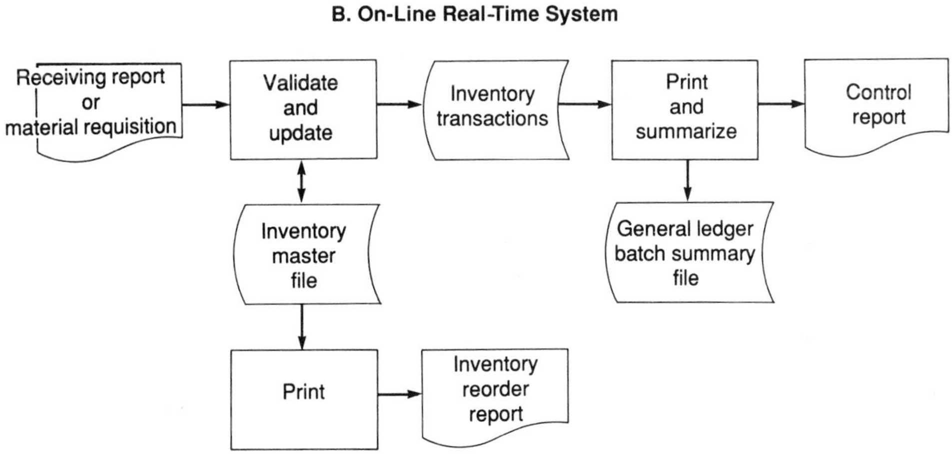

materials requisitions that are also forwarded to data entry. These are converted to computer records and form a materials transaction file.

A validation program examines each transaction for errors. A file update program then posts these transactions to the inventory master file, prints a materials transaction register, and adds summary records to the general ledger batch summary file. Another program then prints the inventory reorder report. Prior to the physical inventory count, a program prints the physical inventory report.

The on-line real-time system processes transactions individually. Rather than printing a register, such a system prints a control report showing control totals and record counts.

Application Controls. Illustration 20–10 shows how input, processing, and output controls are implemented with an inventory system. The examples shown here consist of completeness and validity tests, record counts, and run-to-run controls.

COST ACCOUNTING SYSTEMS

The purpose of a cost accounting system is to determine the costs of products manufactured or services provided and to record those costs in the accounting records.

ILLUSTRATION 20–10 Application Controls in an Inventory System

Type	*Program*	*Control Procedure*
Input	Validate transactions	**Completeness tests.** Verify existence of item number and quantity on receiving report transactions. Verify existence of item number, quantity, and general ledger account number on materials requisition transactions. **Validity test.** In the on-line real-time system, verify that the item number on a transaction exists in the inventory master file.
Processing	Update	**Record counts.** Program verifies that the number of debits to the inventory account = number of receiving reports. Program verifies that the number of credits = number of materials requisitions.
Output	Validate, Update	**Run-to-run controls.** In batch system, data control group verifies that total on register = total transactions shown on error listing.

Cost Accounting Transactions and Documents

In a manufacturing company, a cost accounting system records two transactions in addition to those recorded in the inventory system. They are the transfer of material, labor, and overhead into production, and the transfer of completed production into finished goods inventory.

Transfer of Material, Labor, and Overhead. A manufacturing company purchases raw material inventory and adds labor and overhead to it. This produces units of product that are in process. After the units are completed, it sells the finished products.

The cost accounting system accumulates production costs—including those of material, labor, and overhead—in an inventory account called Work in Process. Labor costs include the pay earned by all workers directly involved in the process. Overhead costs include those required for manufacturing but not directly associated with the products. Examples are factory power, factory heating, manufacturing supplies, and pay for factory supervisors. Most companies allocate to products their fair share of these costs.

The entry recording this transaction is

Dr.	Work in Process Inventory	xxx	
Cr.	Raw Material Inventory		xxx
Cr.	Direct Labor		xxx
Cr.	Factory Overhead		xxx

ILLUSTRATION 20–11 A Materials Requisition

<table>
<tr><td colspan="4">MATERIALS REQUISITION</td><td colspan="2">No. 6-1054</td></tr>
<tr><td>Date</td><td colspan="2">Production order no.</td><td colspan="3">Materials to</td></tr>
<tr><td rowspan="2">Item number</td><td rowspan="2">Description</td><td rowspan="2">Date issued</td><td rowspan="2">Quantity</td><td colspan="2">For office use</td></tr>
<tr><td>Cost per unit</td><td>Amount</td></tr>
<tr><td></td><td></td><td></td><td></td><td></td><td></td></tr>
<tr><td>Prepared by</td><td colspan="2">Materials received by</td><td colspan="2">Cost data by</td><td>Posted to work in process record by</td></tr>
</table>

A manufacturing company uses a *materials requisition* to document the use of raw material in the process. A factory worker completes the requisition and submits it to the inventory warehouse. The inventory clerk accepts the requisition, issues the materials, and records on the requisition the cost of the materials issued. This is the source of the amount of the credit entry in the Direct Raw Material account. Illustration 20–11 shows a materials requisition.

On a *job ticket* employees record the hours of labor devoted to manufacturing each kind of product. Daily or weekly employees give their job tickets to a cost accountant, who computes the cost of their labor based on their pay rates. This becomes the source of the amount of the credit entry in the Direct Labor account. Illustration 20–12 shows a job ticket. Periodically, someone reconciles all job tickets with the timecards used in calculating payroll.

ILLUSTRATION 20–12 A Job Ticket

<table>
<tr><td colspan="5">JOB TICKET</td><td>No. B0248</td></tr>
<tr><td>Production order no.</td><td colspan="2">Employee name</td><td colspan="2">Employee no.</td><td>Date</td></tr>
<tr><td rowspan="2">Time stopped</td><td rowspan="2">Time started</td><td colspan="4">For office use</td></tr>
<tr><td>Elapsed time</td><td colspan="2">Rate</td><td>Amount</td></tr>
<tr><td>Employee</td><td>Foreman approval</td><td>Time accoun-
ted for by</td><td colspan="2">Cost compu-
ted by</td><td>Posting to labor summary by</td></tr>
</table>

Newer systems replace job tickets with automated data collection techniques. A case at the end of this chapter explores one such technique—the use of magnetically encoded badges.

Most companies determine the amount of the credit entry to Factory Overhead from a predetermined allocation rate. The rate may be stated as the dollars of overhead allocated per labor hour worked or per machine hour worked. In a standard costing system, the rate is in dollars per unit produced. (A cost accounting course would teach you how to calculate and use this rate.)

Transfer of Completed Goods. In a manufacturing company, when the production process is completed workers transfer products to the inventory warehouse. The costs of these products are no longer associated with the units in process. Accountants transfer the cost of completed goods out of the Work in Process account with the entry:

Dr.	Finished Goods Inventory	xxx	
Cr.	Work in Process Inventory		xxx

Companies determine the amount of this entry in different ways; some use a *job costing system,* in which they identify products by job or batch number. They accumulate costs for the job, and these constitute the amount of the entry that is recorded when the job is complete.

Other companies, for example those that employ assembly lines, use a *process costing system.* They accumulate costs incurred in the factory and transfer these costs monthly to the Finished Goods account.

With either system, a *completed production order* documents the completion of the products. A cost accountant or computerized cost accounting system calculates the amount of the entry. Illustration 20–13 shows a production order that a cost accountant could use to record and calculate these costs.

This section described the accounting entries made by the cost accounting system and the documents that record the data for these entries. The next section describes typical cost accounting reports.

Cost Accounting System Reports

Cost accounting systems produce control reports and various production cost reports.

Control Reports. Illustration 20–14 shows a control report in the conversion cycle. A job costing system uses it to summarize all jobs, or batches of products, completed and removed from the Work in Process Inventory account. These jobs have been purged from the system.

Production Cost Reports. Cost accounting systems produce several different production cost reports. Some disclose total and unit costs by production cost center. Others disclose these for specific jobs. When a company uses a standard costing system, these reports compare actual costs with those budgeted.

Batch processing systems produce periodic reports showing costs incurred up to the date of printing for all jobs or cost centers. Illustration 20–15 contains a job cost summary report that summarizes the costs of all active jobs for a construction company. In a manufacturing company, this report provides detail supporting the balance in the Work in Process Inventory account.

In an on-line real-time system, employees can display at a terminal or print a report showing current costs recorded for a specific job or cost center. This provides better information for controlling costs than is available from a manual or batch processing system. Illustration 20–16 shows such a job inquiry report produced by a job costing system.

Three kinds of reports used in the cost accounting system are discussed here; in practice, you will see many others. This system frequently produces reports specially designed to suit management's preferences. The next section shows the accounting records needed to produce these reports.

ILLUSTRATION 20–13 A Production Order

For: ______________________ Production order no. A1282

Item: ______________________ Quantity desired ______

Material			Direct labor			Factory overhead
Date	Material requisition no.	Amount	Pay period ended	Hours	Amount	Amount

Date received ______

Date delivery promised ______

Date order completed ______

Quantity produced ______

Cost summary:

	Standard	*Variance*	*Total*
Material			
Labor			
Factory overhead			

ILLUSTRATION 20–14 A Control Report

RUN DATE 06/30/91 T. L. JAMES ENTERPRISES PAGE 1
Job Cost
JOB PURGE CONTROL REPORT

JOB NUMBER	JOB DESCRIPTION	CLOSED DATE	PURGE TYPE	DATE RANGE BEGIN	DATE RANGE END
8121	PEACHTECH EDUCATION BLDG.	11/11/88	CLOSED		
8130	RIVERDALE OFFICE PARK	04/30/88	CLOSED		
8202	CHATTAHOOCHEE APTS.	07/01/89	CLOSED		
8205	PEACHWOOD DENTAL BLDG.	07/01/89	CLOSED		
8206	PEACHTREE CONDOMINIUMS	10/31/89	CLOSED		

*** END OF Purge Job Cost Files ***

Cost Accounting System Records

Manual accounting systems use books, card files, and filing cabinets to record and store accounting data. Computer-based systems replace books and cards with magnetic media such as disks and tapes. Although the data maintained by each form of technology are similar, computer-based systems use this data to produce more management reports than manual systems can generate.

Noncomputerized Records. Manufacturing and service companies use a *production cost ledger.* It serves as a subsidiary ledger for the general ledger Work in Process Inventory account and exists in different forms in various industries.

If the company uses a job costing system, this ledger contains one page for each active job. If the company uses a process costing system, it contains one page for each cost center. A file of production orders, such as the one in Illustration 20–13, is an efficient production cost ledger.

Computerized Records. Computerized records in a traditional data file system are similar to the noncomputerized records in a manual system. They

ILLUSTRATION 20–15 A Job Cost Summary Report

RUN DATE 04/30/90 — T. L. James Enterprises — PAGE 1

Job Cost System

JOB COST SUMMARY REPORT

JOB NUMBER	JOB DESCRIPTION	REVISED PRICE	% COM	DUE DATE	BILLINGS TOTAL	BILLINGS %	PAYMENTS TOTAL	PAYMENTS %	COSTS TOTAL	COSTS %	MARGIN TOTAL	MARGIN %
8121	PEACHTECH EDUCATION BLDG.	2125921.00	50	11/11/90	1058460.50	50	952614.50	45	354649.41	17	1771271.59	83
8130	RIVERDALE OFFICE PARK	6394500.00	100	05/31/90	6394500.00	100	3242300.00	51	1657880.00	26	4736620.00	74
8202	CHATTAHOOCHEE APTS.	1173363.00	10	07/01/91	0.00	0	0.00	0	615802.91	52	557560.09	48
8205	PEACHWOOD DENTAL BLDG.	885411.00	10	07/01/91	0.00	0	0.00	0	0.00	0	885411.00	100
8206	PEACHTREE CONDOMINIUMS	5548347.00	0	10/31/91	0.00	0	0.00	0	0.00	0	5548347.00	100
OFFICE	GENERAL & ADMINISTRATIVE	0.00	0	01/01/00	0.00	0	0.00	0	0.00	0	0.00	0
OVER	JOB OVERHEAD	0.00	0	01/01/00	0.00	0	0.00	0	0.00	0	0.00	0
	REPORT TOTAL	16127542.00			7452960.50	46	4194914.50	26	2628332.32	16	13499209.68	84

*** END OF Print Job Cost Summary Report ***

consist of both master files and transaction files. A DBMS maintains the same data and provides it to application programs as a subschema. However, the DBMS stores this data independently of the subschema.

In manufacturing companies, the cost accounting system processes those transactions that record the transfer of goods into or out of Work in Process Inventory. The computerized equivalent of a cost ledger in a manual system is a production cost file. Depending on the industry, this may exist in two forms.

A company that uses a process costing system establishes a *cost center file* containing one record for each factory cost center. The cost accounting system records in this file the costs of material, labor, and allocated factory overhead for the cost center during each month. From this data, the system calculates the cost of the units completed and the cost of the Work in Process Inventory in that cost center at the end of the month. Illustration 20–17 shows the contents of a cost center record.

A company that uses a job costing system establishes a *job cost file* containing one record for each job. In this record, the cost accounting system posts the costs of material, labor, and factory overhead for the job. Whenever the production

ILLUSTRATION 20–16 A Job Inquiry Report

```
RUN DATE 06/30/90          T. L. JAMES ENTERPRISES                  PAGE    1
                                  Job Cost
                             JOB INQUIRY REPORT

JOB NUMBER 8080    BROADVIEW HIGH SCHOOL
SUPERVISOR         WILLIAM PERRY                    COMPLETION %          10
CUSTOMER # L L     STATE GOVERNMENT                 CHANGE ORDERS          1
                                                    ORIGINAL PRICE  2964564.00
  BILLINGS           0.00        START 01/10/90     REVISED PRICE   2965064.00
  PAYMENTS           0.00        DUE   05/31/91     TOTAL JOB COST        0.00
   0 % DUE           0.00        CLOSE 01/01/00       100 % MARGIN  2965064.00

PHASE COST   ESTIMATED   ACTUAL   %     ESTIMATED       ACTUAL
CODE..CODE.....UNITS.... UNITS...DIF....DOLLARS......DOLLARS....DIFFERENCE..%.

LABOR          33000.00     0.00 100-   495000.00         0.00 495000.00-100-
MATERIAL       77870.00     0.00 100-   176280.00         0.00 176280.00-100-
EQUIPMENT          0.00     0.00   0    100000.00         0.00 100000.00-100-
SUBCONTRACT        0.00     0.00   0    180000.00         0.00 180000.00-100-
OTHER              0.00     0.00   0     80000.00         0.00  80000.00-100-
               ========  ========     ===========  ===========  =========
JOB TOTAL     110870.00     0.00 100-  1031280.00         0.00 1031280.00-100-

                  *** END OF Display/Print Job Inquiry ***
```


control manager issues a new production order, the system creates a record in this file for it and assigns a job number. When production is complete and the products are transferred to the inventory warehouse, the system removes the job cost record. Illustration 20–18 shows its contents.

A batch processing system creates transaction files containing the data found on materials requisitions and job tickets. These transaction files contain records that the system posts to the inventory master, cost center and job cost files. An on-line real-time system posts these transactions individually when they enter the system. Illustration 20–19 summarizes the contents of material requisition and job ticket records.

Similar to certain other application systems, a cost accounting system produces records for the general ledger batch summary file. These records summarize the transfers of material, labor, and overhead costs into work in process inventory. Other records summarize the transfer of completed units into finished goods inventory. The general ledger system posts the records in this transaction file to the general ledger master file during the closing process.

ILLUSTRATION 20–17 Contents of a Cost Center Record

RESPONSIBILITY-CODE*
COST-CENTER-NAME
COST-CENTER-MANAGER
LABOR-COST-ACTUAL
LABOR-HOURS-ACTUAL
LABOR-RATE-STANDARD**
STANDARD-HOURS-ALLOWED**
MATERIAL-COST-ACTUAL
MATERIAL-COST-STANDARD**
VARIABLE-OVERHEAD-ACTUAL
VARIABLE-OVERHEAD-BUDGET**
FIXED-OVERHEAD-ACTUAL
FIXED-OVERHEAD-BUDGET**

*Designates the primary key.
**Required with a standard costing system.

ILLUSTRATION 20–18 Contents of a Job Cost Record

PRODUCTION-ORDER-NUMBER*
ITEM-NUMBER
ITEM-DESCRIPTION
ORDER-SOURCE
ORDER-QUANTITY
ORDER-COMPLETION-DATE
LABOR-COST-ACTUAL
LABOR-COST-STANDARD**
MATERIALS-COST-ACTUAL
MATERIALS-COST-STANDARD**
LABOR-HOURS-ACTUAL
LABOR-HOURS-STANDARD**
TOTAL-VARIABLE-OVERHEAD**
TOTAL-FIXED-OVERHEAD**
TOTAL-COST
SALES-PRICE
MARGIN

*Designates the primary key.
**Required with a standard costing system.

ILLUSTRATION 20–19 Contents of Materials Requisition and Job Ticket Records

Materials Requisition Record	*Job Ticket Record*
MATERIALS-REQUISITION-NUMBER*	JOB-TICKET-NUMBER*
TRANSACTION-CODE	TRANSACTION-CODE
RESPONSIBILITY-CODE	RESPONSIBILITY-CODE
GENERAL-LEDGER-ACCOUNT	GENERAL-LEDGER-ACCOUNT
PRODUCTION-ORDER-NUMBER	PRODUCTION-ORDER-NUMBER
DATE	DATE
ACTUAL-QUANTITY	ACTUAL-HOURS
STANDARD-QUANTITY**	STANDARD-HOURS**
ACTUAL-UNIT-COST	ACTUAL-RATE
STANDARD-UNIT-COST**	STANDARD-RATE**

*Designates the primary key.
**Required in a standard costing system.

This is how organizations record accounting data in both manual and computerized cost accounting systems. These records are similar even though the methods of recording them differ. The next section describes how this system processes transactions.

Cost Accounting Transaction Processing

Manual Processes. Illustration 20–20 contains a document flowchart describing manual cost accounting procedures.

Using these procedures, a production control manager initiates the process by scheduling a specific item for production. Many companies produce to order, meaning they schedule a product for manufacture when they receive a request for the product from a customer. In other companies, the production control manager may schedule production because an inventory reorder report indicates that a certain item needs replenishing. In either case, the manager prepares a production order.

A copy of this document, a production cost sheet, goes to cost accounting where a clerk files it in the production cost ledger. When factory workers need material, they complete a materials requisition and exchange it for the material at the inventory warehouse. This document goes to cost accounting, where a clerk records the material on the production cost sheet. As work proceeds on the products, workers complete job tickets. A production supervisor forwards these to cost accounting daily or weekly, where a clerk records labor costs on the production cost sheet.

When production is complete in a job costing system, a cost accountant computes the unit cost of the goods and records the transfers of materials, labor, overhead, and Work in Process on journal vouchers. The accountant does this monthly for each cost center in a process costing system.

ILLUSTRATION 20–20 Manual Procedures for Cost Accounting

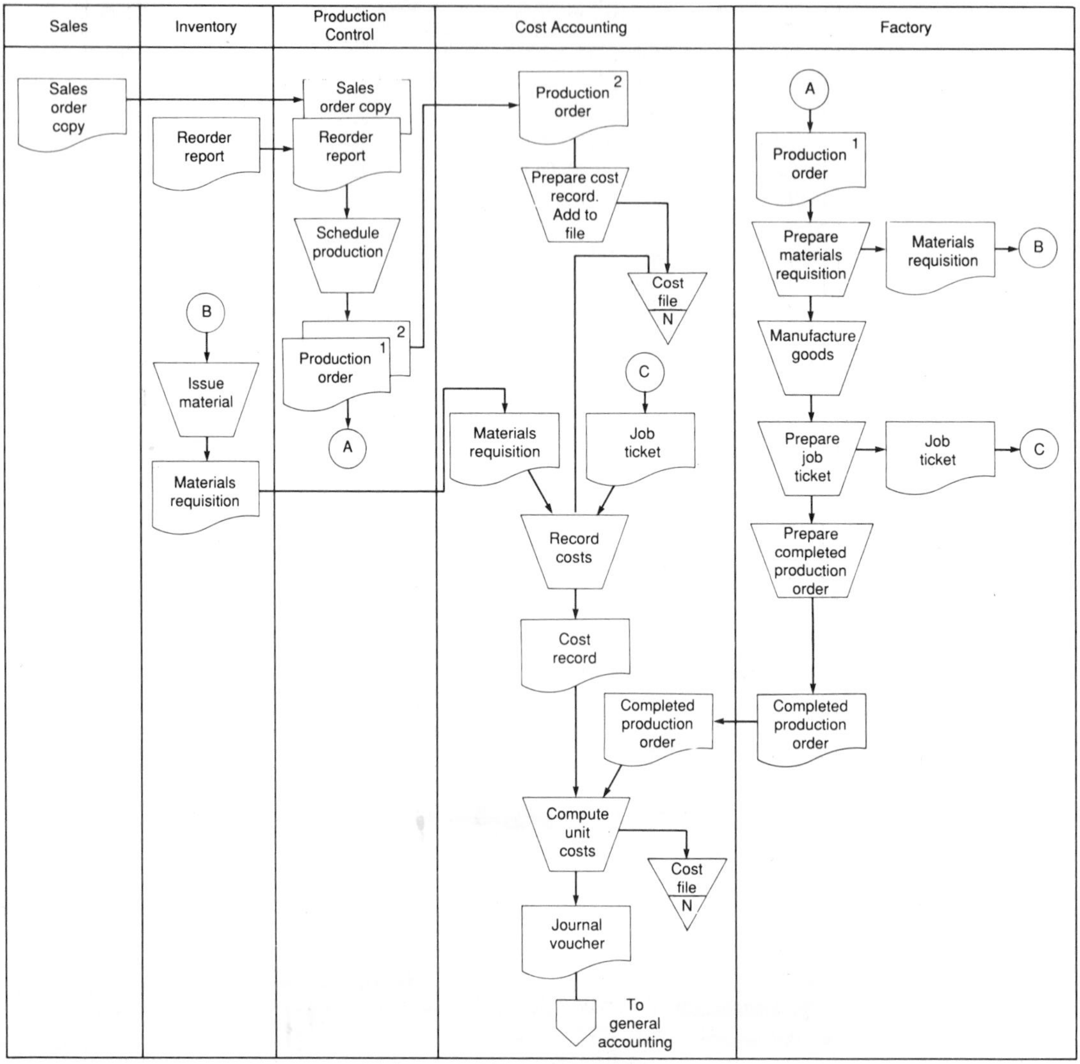

Control Procedures. An adequate internal control structure requires proper segregation of duties and good control practices over transactions. Illustration 20–21 shows how to implement them in a cost accounting system. It summarizes the control practices that should be applied to the documents and records just described.

Effective segregation of duties requires separating the custody of assets from recordkeeping regarding them. This means that the employees keeping inventory

ILLUSTRATION 20–21 Controls for Cost Accounting Transactions

Accounting for Materials	*Accounting for Labor*	*Accounting for Transfer from Work in Process to Finished Goods*
	Segregation of Duties	
1. Factory and production control	1. Timekeeping and payroll	
2. Inventory records and warehouse	2. Factory and timekeeping	1. Inventory records and warehouse
3. Cost accounting and general accounting	3. Cost accounting and general accounting	2. Cost accounting and general accounting
	4. Payroll and personnel	
	Control Practices	
1. Production order request *a.* Based on reorder point and reorder quantity, or based on special customer order		
2. Production order *a.* Issued only on the basis of a production order request *b.* Prenumbered		1. Finished goods report *a.* Issued as soon as production process is completed *b.* Prenumbered
3. Raw materials *a.* Initial quantity based on bill of materials *b.* Released only on receipt of material requisitions	1. Labor time *a.* Allowed time based on operations list *b.* Job ticket prepared with each assignment *c.* Data on job ticket and clock card compared	2. Finished goods *a.* Transfer based on finished goods report
4. Job cost record *a.* Initiated only on receipt of production order *b.* Posted daily *c.* Control total established at month-end	2. Labor cost *a.* Updated employee list and pay rates provided by personnel department *b.* Posted with each pay period *c.* Control total established at month-end	3. Job cost record *a.* Removed from work in process records only on receipt of finished goods report *b.* Control total established at month-end
5. Inventory record *a.* Numerical sequence of material requisitions accounted for *b.* Control total established at month-end		4. Inventory record *a.* Numerical sequence of finished goods report accounted for *b.* Control total established at month-end
6. General ledger *a.* Cost accounting integrated into financial accounting *b.* Control total from inventory records and cost accounting compared	3. General ledger *a.* Control total for direct labor compared to payroll total	5. General ledger *a.* Cost accounting integrated into financial accounting *b.* Control total from inventory records and cost accounting compared

records should not have access to the warehouse, and that employees performing timekeeping should not aid in preparing paychecks. Separating cost accounting functions from those of general accounting allows cost accountants to become more specialized and helps to prevent errors.

Computerized Processes. Illustration 20–22 shows how computer-based job costing systems work. Process costing systems are simpler because transactions representing costs are posted only to a cost center file.

Data entry clerks create a new job cost record for each production order received from the production control manager. The system merges the new job cost records with the existing job cost file.

Each day data entry clerks create transaction records from materials requisitions and job tickets. In a batch system, these form transaction files. An on-line real-time system processes each transaction one at a time. The system records these material and labor transactions in the proper job cost record.

When production is complete, a factory supervisor records the number of units produced on the production order and sends it to cost accounting. Here clerks execute a program that calculates unit costs for the job, produces summary records for the general ledger batch summary file, purges the completed job from the job cost file, and prints a job cost report. It also records in the inventory master file the transfer to work in process and finished goods inventory.

Application Controls. Application controls prevent or detect errors and irregularities in an application system. They do this during input of data, during processing of data by the computer, and with the outputs from processing. Illustration 20–23 shows how a system design team implements input, processing, and output controls for the cost accounting system. These controls include completeness tests, control totals, and record counts.

PAYROLL SYSTEMS

The purposes of a payroll application are to calculate the pay due employees, to print paychecks, and to maintain cumulative earnings records. In theory, an organization could process payroll transactions by the cash disbursements application in the expenditure cycle. In practice, however, most process them by a separate payroll system for two reasons.

First, payroll systems must withhold amounts for deductions and taxes and summarize these in cumulative earnings reports. Such withholding and reporting are unnecessary when processing purchases transactions in the expenditure cycle. Second, payroll systems produce paychecks made out to employees. This makes fraud in payroll systems easier to conceal than in those systems that produce checks for vendors. Establishing a separate system for payroll allows greater control over these transactions.

ILLUSTRATION 20–22 A Cost Accounting Application

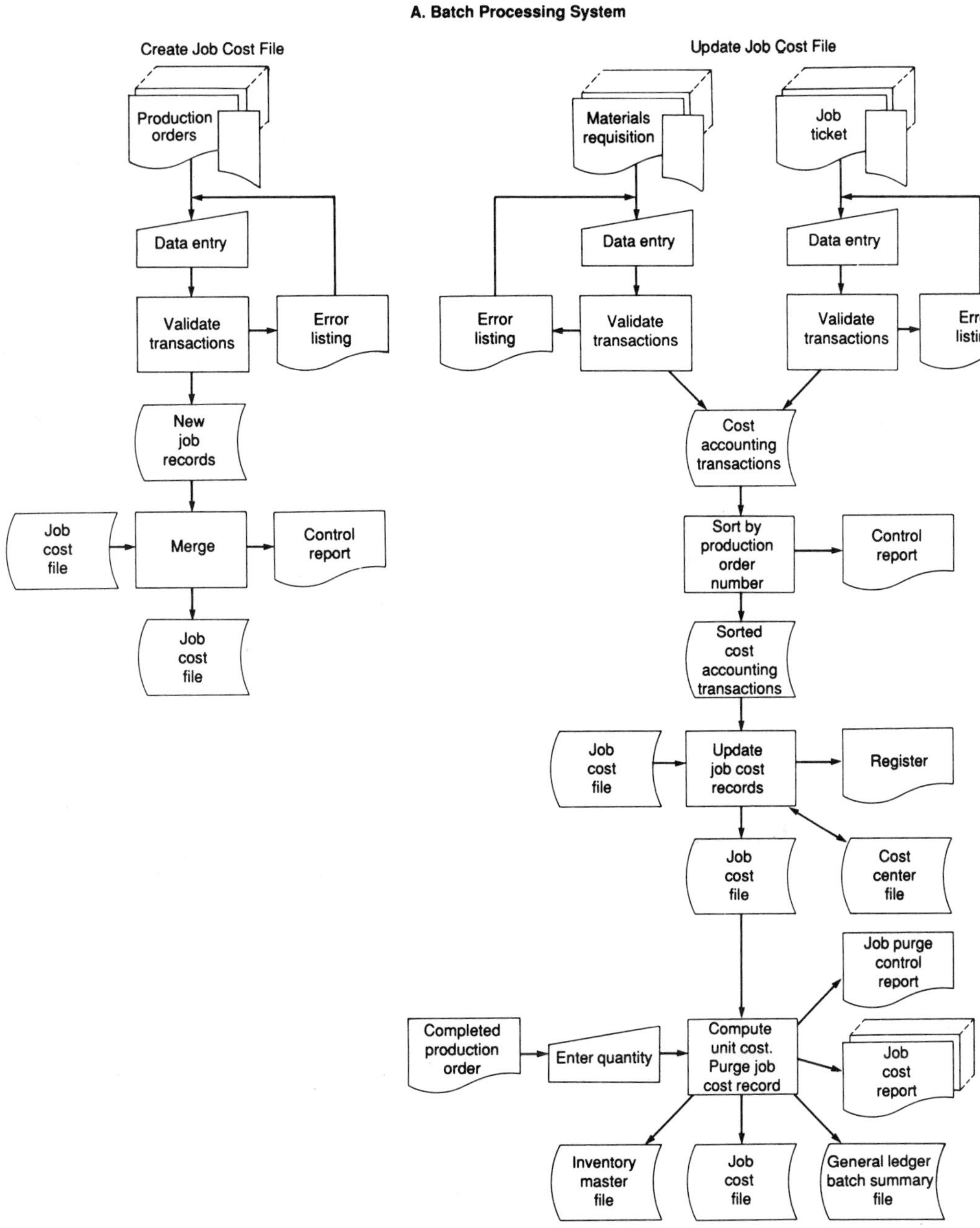

ILLUSTRATION 20–22 (*concluded*)

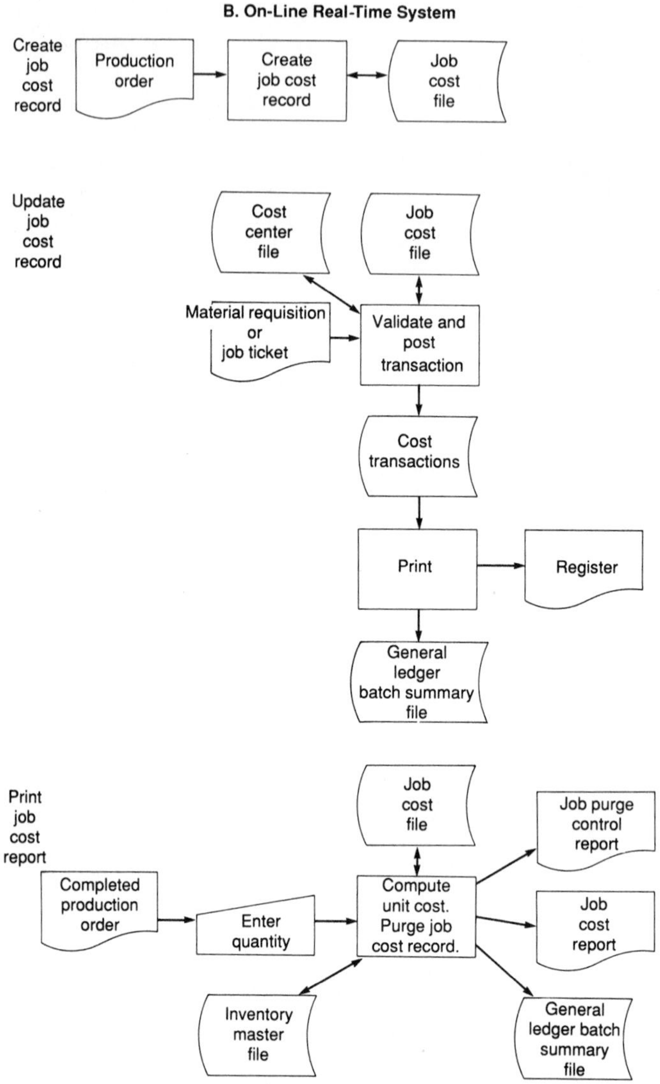

ILLUSTRATION 20–23 Application Controls in the Cost Accounting System

Type	*Program*	*Control Procedure*
Input	Validate transactions	**Completeness tests.** Verify that all fields exist in the materials transaction and labor transaction records.
Processing	Compute and Purge	**Control total.** Program verifies that total credits to work in process = total debits to finished goods.
	Validate and Post	**Control total.** In the on-line real-time system, program verifies that total costs recorded in job cost file = total costs recorded in cost center file.
	Merge	**Record count.** Verify that the number of new job records + number of records in the old job cost file = number of records in the new job cost file.
Output	Compute and Purge	**Control totals.** Data control group verifies that total cost of jobs on job purge control report = total of job cost reports.
	Post to cost records Validate	**Run-to-run controls.** In batch system, data control group verifies that total on register = total transactions disclosed on error listings.

Payroll Transactions and Documents

Payroll systems use different documents for hourly employees and salaried employees. Some companies also pay employees by other methods using specialized documents. Each document serves as authorization for the issue of a *paycheck*.

Hourly Employees. Employers pay hourly employees a fixed rate per hour. Each day each employee records on a *timecard* the number of hours worked. Depending on the system, the employee may either enter the number by hand or insert the card into a clock that imprints it. A supervisor signs the timecard, verifying the total hours worked and authorizing issue of the paycheck by the payroll department. Illustration 20–24 shows a timecard. Fully computerized systems capture this data in magnetic form using terminals.

Salaried Employees. Employers pay salaried employees a fixed amount per biweekly or monthly pay period. For them, the employer authorizes the preparation of paychecks when employees are hired. The personnel department completes an *employment form* that documents the hiring and sends a copy to the

ILLUSTRATION 20–24 A Timecard

EMPLOYEE NAME NUMBER

DATE TIME BEGINS: ________ DATE TIME ENDS: ________

STORE	DAY	DATE		IN	OUT	HOURS WORKED	ABSENT EXPLAIN BY CODE
		1	16				
		2	17				
		3	18				
		4	19				
		5	20				
		6	21				
		7	22				
		8	23				
		9	24				
		10	25				
		11	26				
		12	27				
		13	28				
		14	29				
		15	30				
			31				
TOTAL HOURS WORKED							

CODE:
O-DAY OFF
S-SUNDAY
H-HOLIDAY
I-ILL
V-VACATION
P-PERSONAL
ANY OTHER EXPLAIN

OT HOURS WORKED ________ APPROVED BY ________

I HEREBY CERTIFY THAT THE ABOVE IS CORRECT

____
EMPLOYEE SIGNATURE

APPROVED BY: ________

payroll department which prepares salaried paychecks. Different organizations give different names to this form, such as a "personnel action request," a "salary authorization," or some other name. Illustration 20–25 shows an employment form.

Other Pay Methods. Some organizations use incentives, such as piecework rates or commissions, to determine employees' pay. For these employees, other forms of documentation are used to support the payroll calculations. For example, a production supervisor may approve a production count card for a factory worker. A payroll clerk then computes the worker's pay based on the number of units produced rather than the hours worked. A payroll system may calculate a salesperson's commissions based on gross sales recorded in a sales order entry system.

ILLUSTRATION 20–25 A Salary Authorization

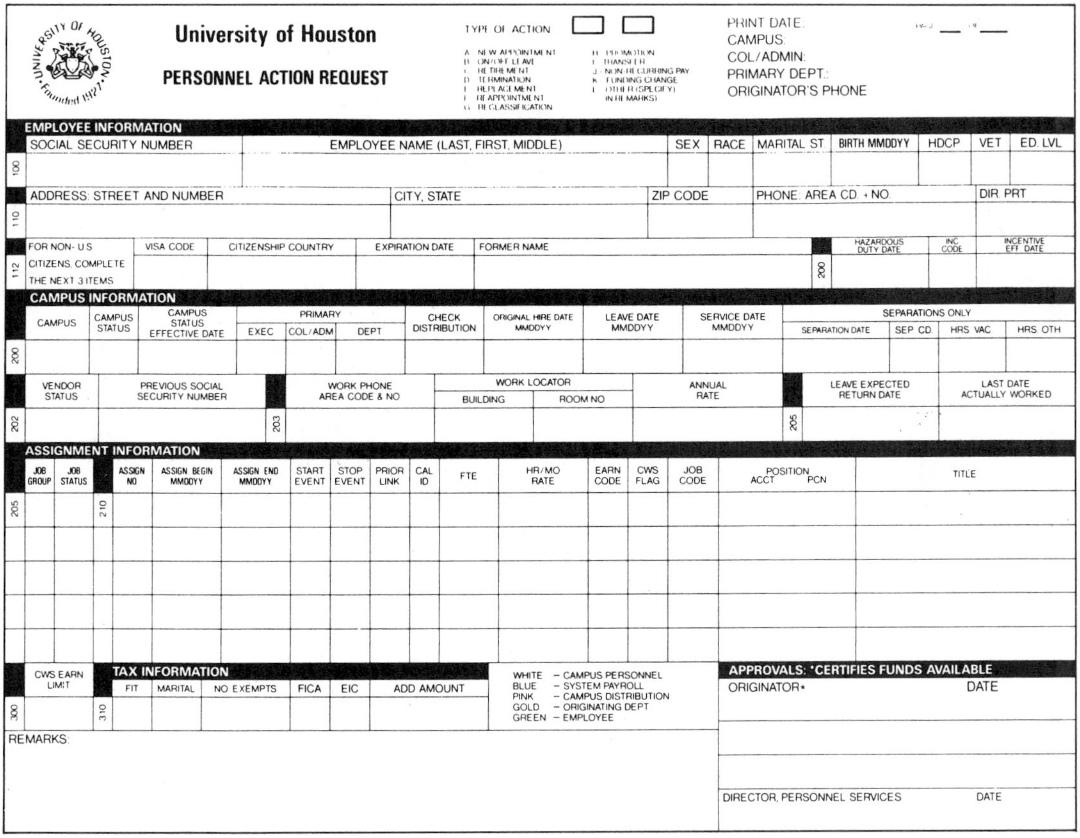
University of Houston
PERSONNEL ACTION REQUEST

TYPE OF ACTION

A NEW APPOINTMENT
B ON/OFF LEAVE
C RETIREMENT
D TERMINATION
E REPLACEMENT
F REAPPOINTMENT
G RECLASSIFICATION
H PROMOTION
I TRANSFER
J NON-RECURRING PAY
K FUNDING CHANGE
L OTHER (SPECIFY IN REMARKS)

PRINT DATE:
CAMPUS:
COL/ADMIN:
PRIMARY DEPT.:
ORIGINATOR'S PHONE

EMPLOYEE INFORMATION

100	SOCIAL SECURITY NUMBER	EMPLOYEE NAME (LAST, FIRST, MIDDLE)	SEX	RACE	MARITAL ST	BIRTH MMDDYY	HDCP	VET	ED. LVL

110	ADDRESS: STREET AND NUMBER	CITY, STATE	ZIP CODE	PHONE: AREA CD. + NO.	DIR. PRT

112	FOR NON-U.S. CITIZENS, COMPLETE THE NEXT 3 ITEMS	VISA CODE	CITIZENSHIP COUNTRY	EXPIRATION DATE	FORMER NAME	200	HAZARDOUS DUTY DATE	INC CODE	INCENTIVE EFF DATE

CAMPUS INFORMATION

200	CAMPUS	CAMPUS STATUS	CAMPUS STATUS EFFECTIVE DATE	PRIMARY EXEC	PRIMARY COL/ADM	PRIMARY DEPT	CHECK DISTRIBUTION	ORIGINAL HIRE DATE MMDDYY	LEAVE DATE MMDDYY	SERVICE DATE MMDDYY	SEPARATIONS ONLY: SEPARATION DATE	SEP CD	HRS VAC	HRS OTH

202	VENDOR STATUS	PREVIOUS SOCIAL SECURITY NUMBER	203	WORK PHONE AREA CODE & NO	WORK LOCATOR BUILDING	WORK LOCATOR ROOM NO	ANNUAL RATE	205	LEAVE EXPECTED RETURN DATE	LAST DATE ACTUALLY WORKED

ASSIGNMENT INFORMATION

205	JOB GROUP	JOB STATUS	210	ASSIGN NO	ASSIGN BEGIN MMDDYY	ASSIGN END MMDDYY	START EVENT	STOP EVENT	PRIOR LINK	CAL ID	FTE	HR/MO RATE	EARN CODE	CWS FLAG	JOB CODE	POSITION ACCT	POSITION PCN	TITLE

300	CWS EARN LIMIT	310	TAX INFORMATION: FIT	MARITAL	NO. EXEMPTS	FICA	EIC	ADD AMOUNT

WHITE – CAMPUS PERSONNEL
BLUE – SYSTEM PAYROLL
PINK – CAMPUS DISTRIBUTION
GOLD – ORIGINATING DEPT
GREEN – EMPLOYEE

APPROVALS: *CERTIFIES FUNDS AVAILABLE
ORIGINATOR* DATE

DIRECTOR, PERSONNEL SERVICES DATE

REMARKS:

Used by permission of the University of Houston System.

Illustration 20–26 shows a paycheck. During system design, the design team determines how the check and its attached paycheck stub should look. The check itself must comply with the requirements of the banks that process it. The stub contains information to show the employee how the amount on the check was determined. It shows the calculations for determining gross pay, lists all deductions, and discloses net pay. Frequently it also shows these amounts accumulated for the year to date.

Accounting Entries. The accounting entry recording payroll transactions recognizes the classifications of labor expenses in the chart of accounts. For most companies, the chart of accounts distinguishes between sales salaries, administrative salaries, indirect labor, and direct labor. It may make further distinctions if management wishes. The entry distributes total labor costs among these

ILLUSTRATION 20–26 A Paycheck

J. C. MORRISON CO.

EMP NO /DEPT	EMPLOYEE NAME	SOCIAL SECURITY NO	PERIOD BEG	PERIOD END	CHECK NO	
CCC 02	CATHY C. CASWELL	583-78-6324	04/01/91	04/30/91	2224	1829

EARNINGS	HRS/UNITS	CURRENT AMOUNT	YEAR TO DATE	DEDUCTIONS	CURRENT AMOUNT	YEAR TO DATE
SALARY		2000.00	8000.00	FICA	134.00	870.42
COMMISSIONS		0.00	3991.30	FEDERAL WH.	380.42	3466.20
OVERTIME 1		0.00	0.00	ALABAMA	69.31	735.13
OVERTIME 2		0.00	0.00	INSUR.	12.50	50.00
EXP REIM		0.00	1013.91	COFFEE	2.00	8.00
BONUS		0.00	1000.00	PENSION	45.00	180.00

PAY RATE	CURRENT EARNINGS	CURRENT DEDUCTIONS	NET PAY	Y T D EARNINGS	Y T D DEDUCTIONS	Y T D NET PAY
24000.000	2000.00	643.23	1356.77	14005.21	5309.75	8695.46

CHECK 2224 1829

J. C. MORRISON CO.
1765 SHERIDAN DR.
YOUR CITY, U.S.A. 10083

NATIONAL STATE BANK
YOUR CITY, STATE 12345
00-6789/2345

04/30/91 ****$1,356.77
DATE AMOUNT

PAY **** ONE THOUSAND THREE HUNDRED FIFTY SIX & 77 /100 DOLLARS

TO THE ORDER OF
CATHY C. CASWELL
1234 WHITEHALL DRIVE
APT. 201
HUNTSVILLE, ALABAMA 35805

SAMPLE VOID
STYLE 1000

⑈0000 1829⑈ ⑆23456789⑆ 12345678⑈

accounts and also among responsibility center accounts. For this reason, accountants call this entry the labor expense distribution. An accounting entry recording payroll is

Dr.	Sales Salaries	xxx	
Dr.	Administrative Salaries	xxx	
Dr.	Indirect Labor	xxx	
Dr.	Direct Labor	xxx	
Cr.	Wages and Salaries Payable		xxx

The following entry records the issue of paychecks:

Dr.	Wages and Salaries Payable	xxx	
Cr.	Cash		xxx
Cr.	Payroll Taxes Payable		xxx
Cr.	Other deductions payable		xxx

In this entry, the Payroll Taxes Payable account records the withholdings from the employee's salary for taxes. Amounts may also be voluntarily withheld for such items as insurance, contributions, or union dues.

Payroll Reports

Payroll systems produce three reports: the payroll register, control reports for paychecks, and various cumulative earnings reports.

Payroll Register. Payroll systems produce a payroll register prior to printing paychecks. The register lists all employees for whom paychecks are due. For each employee, it shows the gross pay, lists all deductions, and shows the net pay.

Producing the payroll register is an important control practice. A payroll supervisor reviews the payroll register for errors before printing paychecks. Then a clerk corrects errors prior to printing the checks. This avoids printing erroneous checks that could be stolen and cashed. Illustration 20–27 contains a computer-printed payroll register.

ILLUSTRATION 20–27 A Computer-Printed Payroll Register

```
RUN DATE 06/30/91                          T. L. James Enterprises                                      PAGE  1
                                              PAYROLL REGISTER                              PERIOD ENDING 06/30/91
DEPARTMENT 00
                        REGULAR    DISB.   NON-DISB   VOL.                                                    CHECK
CODE      NAME         EARNINGS MISC.INC  MISC.INC  DEDUCT.  FED.WH.    FICA   TAX #1   TAX #2   TAX #3   TAX #4 NUMB   NET PAY
------ ------------- --------- --------- --------- -------- -------- -------- -------- -------- -------- -------- ------ ----------
00666 GLORIA G. GAI   1500.00      0.00      0.00    14.50   227.07   107.25    65.67     0.00     0.00     0.00  2244   1085.51

                      --------- --------- --------- -------- -------- -------- -------- -------- -------- --------        ---------
                        1500.00      0.00      0.00    14.50   227.07   107.25    65.67     0.00     0.00     0.00         1085.51

BREAKDOWN OF MISCELLANEOUS INCOME AND TAX CODES FOR DEPARTMENT 00

DRAW           1500.00         GEORGIA    WH.    65.67          CURRENT DEF. DEDUCT.        0.00
COMMISSION        0.00                                          CURRENT ALLOC. DEDUCT.      0.00
TIPS              0.00
EXP REIM          0.00
MHDSE   #         0.00
BONUS             0.00
EIC               0.00

COMPANY TOTALS          3866.65      0.00      0.00    77.34   625.98   276.47   144.01     0.00     0.00     0.00         2742.85
BREAKDOWN OF MISCELLANEOUS INCOME AND TAX CODES FOR COMPANY

DRAW           1500.00         GEORGIA    WH.    65.67          CURRENT DEF. DEDUCT.      0.00
COMMISSION        0.00         ALABAMA    WH.    78.34          CURRENT ALLOC. DEDUCT.    0.00
TIPS              0.00
EXP REIM          0.00
MHDSE   #         0.00
BONUS             0.00
EIC               0.00
                                        *** END OF PAYROLL REGISTER ***
```

Print Checks Control Report. Because paychecks can easily be stolen or falsified, the system must control their preparation. The print checks control report aids in detecting missing or unauthorized checks.

The computer program that prints checks also produces this control report showing the number of checks printed and the total amount of these checks. The data control group compares these control totals with the checks. A payroll supervisor reconciles these amounts with those shown on the payroll register. Illustration 20–28 shows such a control report.

Cumulative Earnings Reports. In the United States, employers are required to withhold taxes from employees' paychecks; quarterly they send these taxes to the government. Payroll systems aid in this process by producing several kinds of cumulative earnings reports, which summarize the gross pay and tax withheld for an employee during each quarter of the year. A report produced at year-end discloses this data for the entire year.

ILLUSTRATION 20–28 A Control Report for Printing Paychecks

RUN DATE 06/30/91 T. L. James Enterprises PAGE 1
Print Checks

CHECK DATE: 06/30/91 PERIOD ENDING DATE: 06/30/91

STARTING CHECK NUMBER: 2244 LAST CHECK NUMBER: 2246 TOTAL: 3

REPRINT: NO

TOTAL REGULAR HOURS	:	44.00
TOTAL OVERTIME 1 HOURS	:	0.00
TOTAL OVERTIME 2 HOURS	:	0.00
TOTAL EARNINGS	:	3,866.65
TOTAL NON-DISB. EARNINGS	:	0.00
TOTAL DEFERRED DEDUCTIONS	:	0.00
TOTAL ALLOCATED DEDUCTIONS	:	0.00
TOTAL DEDUCTIONS	:	1,123.80-
TOTAL NET PAY	:	2,742.85

Payroll System Records

Noncomputerized Records. Manual payroll systems maintain data in a filing cabinet about each individual employee. Payroll clerks use data in this file to calculate gross pay and to determine the amounts of deductions. They also record in this file cumulative earnings information for individual employees. Other files hold documents during or after processing them.

Noncomputerized systems use a journal called the *payroll register,* in which a payroll clerk records the calculations for gross pay, deductions, and net pay. The payroll register provides an audit trail for the amounts shown on the paychecks. Illustration 20–29 shows the contents of a noncomputerized payroll register. Its contents are similar to those of the computer-printed payroll register.

Computerized Records. Computerized payroll systems update a master file called the *employee master file*. This file contains one record for each current or past employee, and contains data necessary for determining payroll deductions and submitting earnings information required in government reports. Illustration 20–30 shows contents of an employee master record.

For hourly employees, the input to the payroll system is the file of timecards. For employees paid on piecework or commissions, payroll clerks create files of other documents. These are converted into computer readable form and constitute the *payroll transaction* file. The system adds records to this file for any salaried employees whose paychecks are due during the pay period. The payroll system produces one paycheck from each record in this file.

ILLUSTRATION 20–29 A Manual Payroll Register

Page ______

Employee		Name of Employee	Hours Worked	Base Rate	Earnings			Deductions				Net Pay
Dept.	Number				Regular	Over-time	Other	FICA	Income Tax With-held	Insur-ance	Other	

ILLUSTRATION 20–30 Contents of an Employee Master Record

EMPLOYEE-NUMBER*
EMPLOYEE-NAME
EMPLOYEE-ADDRESS
SOCIAL-SECURITY-NUMBER
MARITAL-STATUS
NUMBER-EXEMPTIONS
DEPARTMENT-CODE**
PAY-RATE
HOURLY/SALARY-CODE
INSURANCE-DEDUCTION
OTHER-DEDUCTION
DATE-EMPLOYED
DATE-TERMINATED
EARNINGS-DATA-CURRENT-PERIOD
  HOURS-WORKED
  REGULAR-EARNINGS
  OVERTIME-PREMIUM
  OTHER
  FICA-DEDUCTION
  INCOME-TAX-WITHHELD
  DEDUCTED-INSURANCE
  DEDUCTED-OTHER
EARNINGS-DATA-THIS-QUARTER
  HOURS-WORKED
  REGULAR-EARNINGS
  OVERTIME-PREMIUM
  OTHER
  FICA-DEDUCTION
  INCOME-TAX-WITHHELD
  DEDUCTED-INSURANCE
  DEDUCTED-OTHER
EARNINGS-DATA-THIS-YEAR
  HOURS-WORKED
  REGULAR-EARNINGS
  OVERTIME-PREMIUM
  OTHER
  FICA-DEDUCTION
  INCOME-TAX-WITHHELD
  DEDUCTED-INSURANCE
  DEDUCTED-OTHER

*Designates a primary key.
**Designates a secondary key.

The payroll system adds records to the *general ledger batch summary* file summarizing the transactions. Records placed in this file from the payroll system record a credit entry in Wages Payable, and debits to various labor expense accounts. The general ledger batch summary file accumulates summary records from many application systems. The general ledger system posts the records in this file to the general ledger.

Payroll Transaction Processing

Noncomputerized Procedures. Illustration 20–31 contains a document flowchart showing manual payroll procedures. The personnel department screens applicants, authorizes the employee's initial pay rate, and creates the manual employment record. For salaried employees, this record authorizes a periodic paycheck.

During each pay period, hourly employees complete timecards. A supervisor approves these timecards and sends them to the payroll department, where clerks compute paycheck amounts and complete payroll records. The cash disbursements section in the treasurer's department prepares and distributes paychecks.

Imprest Accounts. To improve control over payroll transactions, many organizations establish a separate bank checking account for the payroll system. All paycheck disbursements, but no other withdrawals, are made from this special bank account. Usually the payroll bank account is an *imprest* account, meaning that the balance in the account is always kept at a predetermined amount. This amount is usually sufficient to cover paychecks of all employees terminated between pay periods.

For example, suppose your company seldom fires more than one or two employees per month, and no employee makes more than $5,000 in a month. You decide to create a payroll bank account separate from the regular account used for disbursements to suppliers. You decide to make the payroll bank account an imprest account and to maintain its balance at $10,000. When paychecks are written on this account, the payroll department determines their total amount. Then they request a cash disbursements check, drawn on the regular bank account, to reimburse the payroll account for the amount of the payroll. This maintains the payroll bank account balance at $10,000.

Why do organizations follow this procedure? Having a separate checking account for payroll makes reconciling this account easier. It also makes detecting certain frauds easier because all checks drawn on the payroll account should be payable to employees. Because checks payable to employees from the regular account are infrequent, they are examined closely. Also, should a dishonest employee find a way to embezzle from the payroll account, the employee's theft is limited to the imprest amount.

ILLUSTRATION 20–31 Manual Procedures for Payroll

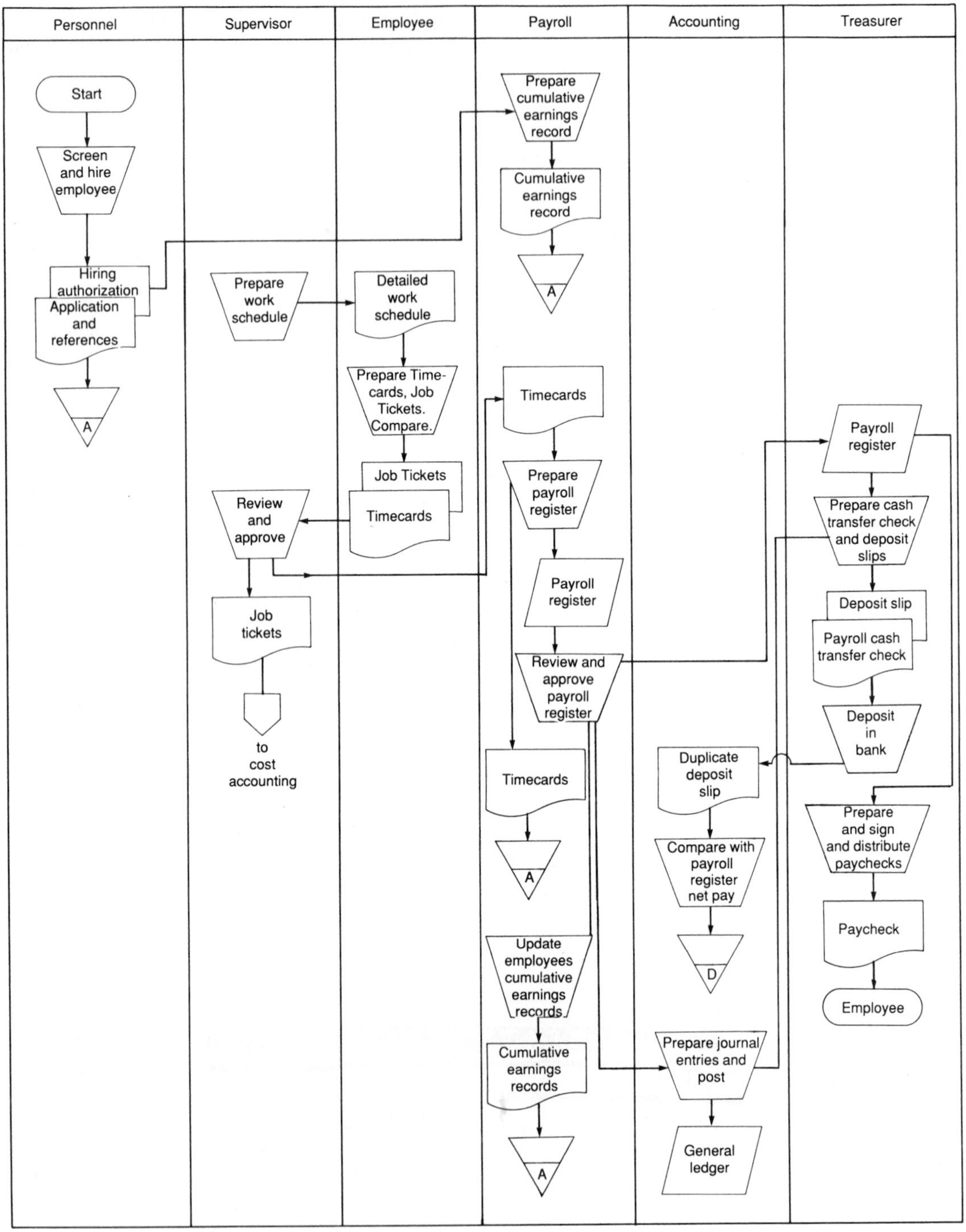

Control Procedures. The use of imprest accounts is a procedure that prevents and detects errors and irregularities in payroll systems. It is appropriate regardless of whether the system uses computerized or manual processes. Other control procedures, called application controls, relate specifically to computerized processes.

Payroll registers, control reports, and imprest accounts improve control over payroll transactions. Illustration 20–32 summarizes effective segregation of duties and control practices applied to the documents for payroll transactions.

Adequate segregation of duties requires that the timekeeping and personnel departments, which authorize paychecks and pay rates, are separate from the payroll department that prepares paychecks. As discussed earlier, payroll employees and procedures should be separate from those used to process other cash disbursements checks.

Computerized Procedures. Illustration 20–33 contains a system flowchart of a payroll system. Similar to the cash disbursements system, the payroll application uses batch processing.

In this system, a supervisor approves timecards for payment, batches them, and establishes a control total over the total hours worked in a batch. A data entry clerk enters the timecard data in a computer file. Some systems validate each data

ILLUSTRATION 20–32 Controls for Payroll Transactions

Payroll Transactions

Segregation of Duties

1. Timekeeping and payroll
2. Payroll and cash disbursements
3. Payroll and personnel

Control Practices

1. Initial documentation
   a. Updated employee list and pay rates provided by personnel department
   b. Timecards reviewed
   c. Payroll preparation reviewed
2. Paychecks
   a. Prepared only based on properly prepared payroll register
   b. Prenumbered
   c. Signed only if properly prepared
   d. Imprest bank account used
   e. Distributed by persons not involved in payroll process
   f. Voided checks kept
   g. Unclaimed checks listed

ILLUSTRATION 20–33 A Payroll Application

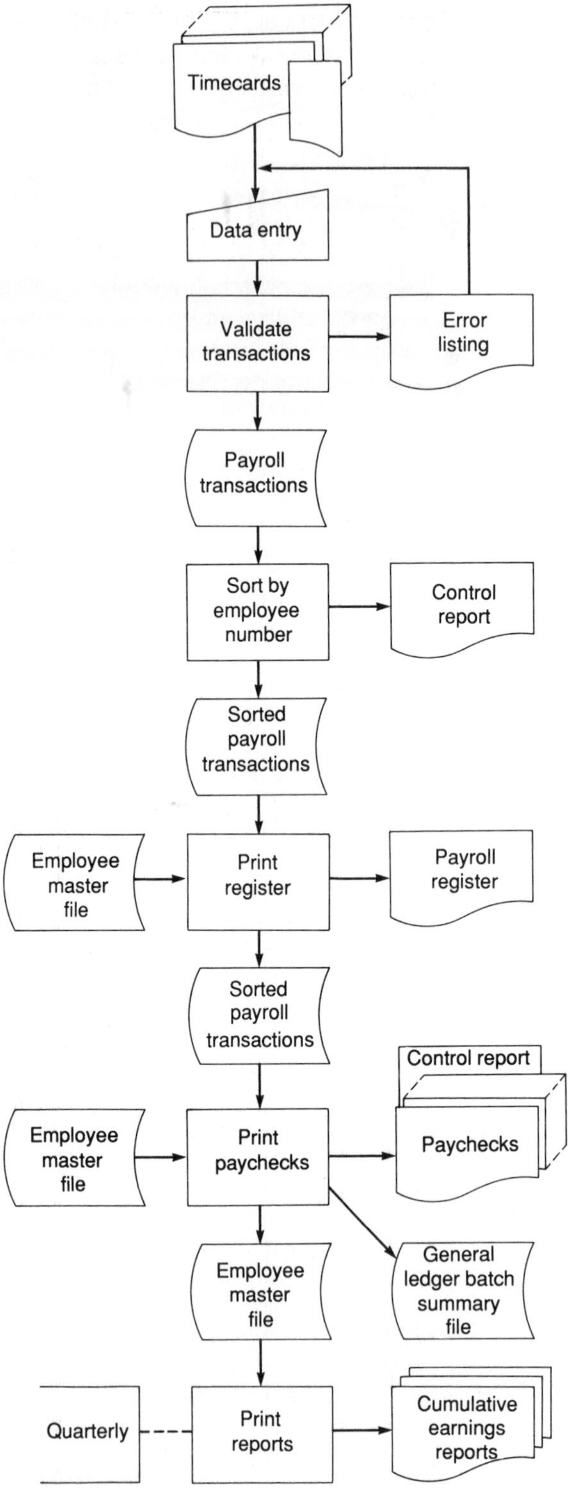

record during its data entry. Others create the transaction file and then validate them a batch at a time, producing an error listing.

The validation program produces a payroll transaction file which the system sorts into employee number sequence. A program calculates pay and deductions, updates the cumulative earnings data in the employee master file, and prints the payroll register. After payroll clerks have reviewed the register for errors, another program prints paychecks and creates records for the general ledger batch summary file.

Application Controls. Input, processing, and output controls help to prevent or detect errors when processing payroll transactions. Because most payroll systems use batch sequential processing, the data control group uses run-to-run controls to verify the total amounts for each pay period. Illustration 20–34 shows

ILLUSTRATION 20–34 Application Controls in the Payroll System

Type	*Program*	*Control Procedure*
Input	Validate transactions	**Completeness test.** Program verifies existence of EMPLOYEE-NUMBER, EMPLOYEE-NAME, HOURS-WORKED.
		Control total. Program verifies that total number of hours on batch transmittal form = total number of hours on valid payroll transactions + total number of hours on erroneous payroll transactions.
Processing	Sort	**Record count.** Number of input transaction records = number of output transaction records.
		Control total. Total hours in input file = total hours in output file.
Output	Print register	**Record count.** Program verifies that the number of lines on the register = the number of payroll transaction records.
		Limit test. Program flags for review by data control group those transactions with amounts > $10,000.
	Print paychecks	**Record count.** Program verifies that the number of paychecks = number of payroll transaction records.
		Control total. Program verifies that total amount of paychecks = total debits to general ledger accounts = total credits to general ledger accounts.
	Print register Print paychecks	**Run-to-run controls.** Data control group compares control totals taken on paycheck amounts and disclosed on control report and payroll register.

how record counts, control totals, and other validation procedures can be used in the payroll system.

NONACCOUNTING APPLICATIONS

Companies with more advanced computer-based systems use computer applications in the conversion cycle to aid in controlling the production process. Although these systems do not process accounting transactions, they affect these transactions. Three such systems are production scheduling systems, material requirements planning systems, and just in time systems.[1]

Production Scheduling Systems

In the system just described, a production control manager schedules jobs for production and authorizes them with production orders. Many manufacturing companies now use an on-line real-time computer-based system that replaces written production orders with computer records.

Such a system maintains two files, a *work order* file and a *work order detail* file. The work order file contains a record for each production order and shows its priority and desired completion date. A computer program schedules production by ranking active work orders by priority and date and disclosing this ranking on a computer report.

For each work order, there are several associated records in the work order detail file. Each represents one manufacturing operation required for production. As the factory completes operations, employees use terminals to record cost accounting data in the detail record. When production is complete, the cost accounting system summarizes costs using data in the work order detail file.

MRP Systems

A material requirements planning (MRP) system is actually a production information system rather than an accounting system. Its purpose is to minimize investment in inventory while ensuring that parts are available for production. This computerized system schedules not only finished products for production but also component parts and subassemblies.

---

[1]For a description of computerized production scheduling and MRP systems, see J. E. Gessford, *Modern Information Systems Designed for Decision Support* (Reading, Mass.: Addison-Wesley, 1980), pp. 393–424. For a discussion of the JIT concept, see A. T. Sadhwani and M. H. Sarhan, "The Impact of Just-in-Time Inventory Systems on Small Businesses," *Journal of Accountancy,* January 1987, pp. 119–28.

When developing an MRP system, the design team creates a *bill of materials* file. This file contains one record for each product manufactured in the factory. This record shows all the components for the product and the quantities of each component needed.

The system uses this information to schedule not only finished products but also the components for production. It arranges the production schedule so that all manufactured components are available when needed for producing the finished product. When the component must be purchased rather than produced, the MRP system produces a purchase requisition for the purchasing application system. It generates this requisition far enough in advance that the purchased material arrives shortly before it is needed for production.

Because a company with an MRP system produces or purchases components only when they are needed, the company avoids carrying inventories of these components. This decreases the financial investment in inventory and lowers storage and spoilage costs.

JIT Systems

The purposes of just in time (JIT) systems are to minimize work in process inventory and to eliminate raw materials inventories. This system expands the MRP concept by altering the production process to minimize inventory investments.

A JIT system schedules deliveries of raw materials so that they arrive just in time for the beginning of the production process. A truck delivering raw materials arrives at a receiving dock and unloads the material. Workers immediately move it to the factory and place it into production. In this way, a company using a JIT system avoids costs of carrying and storing raw material. This system requires close coordination between the company implementing JIT and its suppliers.

When a company implements a just-in-time system, its accounting application systems function differently from those you have learned about thus far. Procedures differ in the purchasing, receiving, and cost accounting applications.

Purchasing with JIT. Many times, companies issue blanket purchase orders to suppliers. These identify the goods requested and create for the purchaser a legal obligation to pay for the goods. However, they do not specify quantities as do individual purchase orders. Instead, the purchasing company must specify quantities required, usually daily, in some other way.

Sometimes purchasing agents inform vendors of the desired quantity by telephone. Other companies use *electronic data interchange* (EDI) systems; these computer networks link their computerized purchasing systems to the computerized sales order entry systems of their suppliers. Rather than mailing individual purchase orders, the purchasing company transmits purchase order records to the supplier. The supplier's system is programmed to read this record and create from it a sales order detail record. This initiates the procedures in the supplier's order entry system. Usually with such systems, the supplier agrees to fill orders within a few hours of receipt.

Receiving with JIT. When a company uses JIT, it does not use a single receiving dock. Instead, the company has multiple receiving points near the production facilities that use the material. The supplier must deliver the material not only at the proper time but also to the proper receiving point.

The supplier packages goods to speed the process of counting them on receipt. Usually the receiving personnel do not need to perform inspections because the supplier agreed to maintain certain quality standards prior to becoming an approved vendor. If the supplier does not meet these standards, the purchasing company finds another supplier.

Accounting with JIT. Frequently, companies that use JIT find that their labor costs decrease. They may cease to report labor costs daily or weekly, but instead provide monthly reports.

The company designs its assembly lines to produce one product, so production orders and job cost sheets may become unnecessary. Instead, the company calculates its costs at the end of a month from the quantities of finished goods produced. Since there are few raw materials inventories, the company combines the costs of purchased materials with those of units that are in process.

Similar to MRP, JIT systems are production rather than accounting systems. Yet their existence affects how accounting systems process transactions. A case at the end of this chapter explores the implications of JIT for the cost accounting system.

SUMMARY

The conversion cycle processes accounting transactions that record one economic event—the consumption of labor, material, and overhead to produce a salable product or service. This process is different depending on whether it occurs in a service, merchandising, or manufacturing organization.

The economic events in the conversion cycle are recorded by five types of transactions. Two of these, purchase and sale of inventory, are recorded in other transaction cycles. The other transactions are the transfer of material, labor, and overhead into production; the transfer of work in process into finished goods; and payroll.

There are three application systems in this cycle. The inventory system maintains perpetual inventory records and notifies managers when items require replenishing. The cost accounting system determines the costs of goods or services produced. The payroll system calculates the pay due employees, prints paychecks, and maintains cumulative earnings records. This chapter has explored methods of implementing segregation of duties and applying control practices in these systems.

KEY TERMS

cost center record A record for a cost center containing data that identifies the cost center and recording costs incurred during a reporting period.

employee master record Contains data on each current and past employee that is used in determining payroll deductions and when preparing government reports.

imprest account A bank checking account kept at a predetermined balance and frequently used for writing paychecks.

inventory master record A record in a perpetual system for each item maintained in inventory. It shows reference data and the quantity on hand.

job costing system A cost accounting system that accumulates production costs by job or batch number.

job cost record In a job costing system, a record that exists for each job. It contains data identifying the job and recording the costs incurred on that job.

job ticket A document used by factory employees to record the number of hours of their labor devoted to manufacturing each kind of product.

materials requisition A document that, when completed by a production worker or supervisor, documents the issue of materials for use in production.

periodic method A method of accounting for inventory that relies on a periodic physical inventory count to determine Cost of Goods Sold and ending inventories.

perpetual method A method of accounting for inventory in which an organization maintains an ongoing count of each inventory item on hand.

process costing system A cost accounting system that accumulates production costs by department or cost center.

timecard A document on which employees record their hours worked. It is the basis for computing their pay.

APPENDIX

Control Flowcharts for the Conversion Cycle

CONTROL FLOWCHART 20–1 Inventories

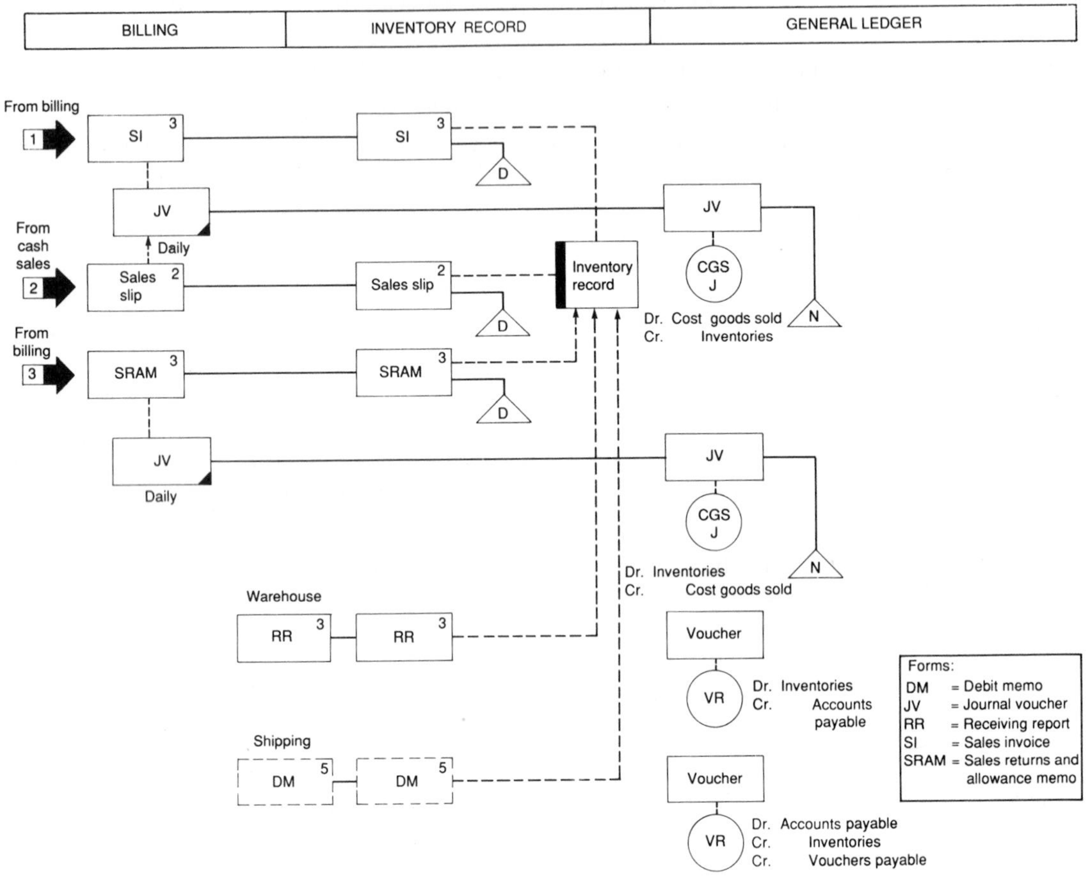

CONTROL FLOWCHART 20–2 Transferring Materials to Work in Process

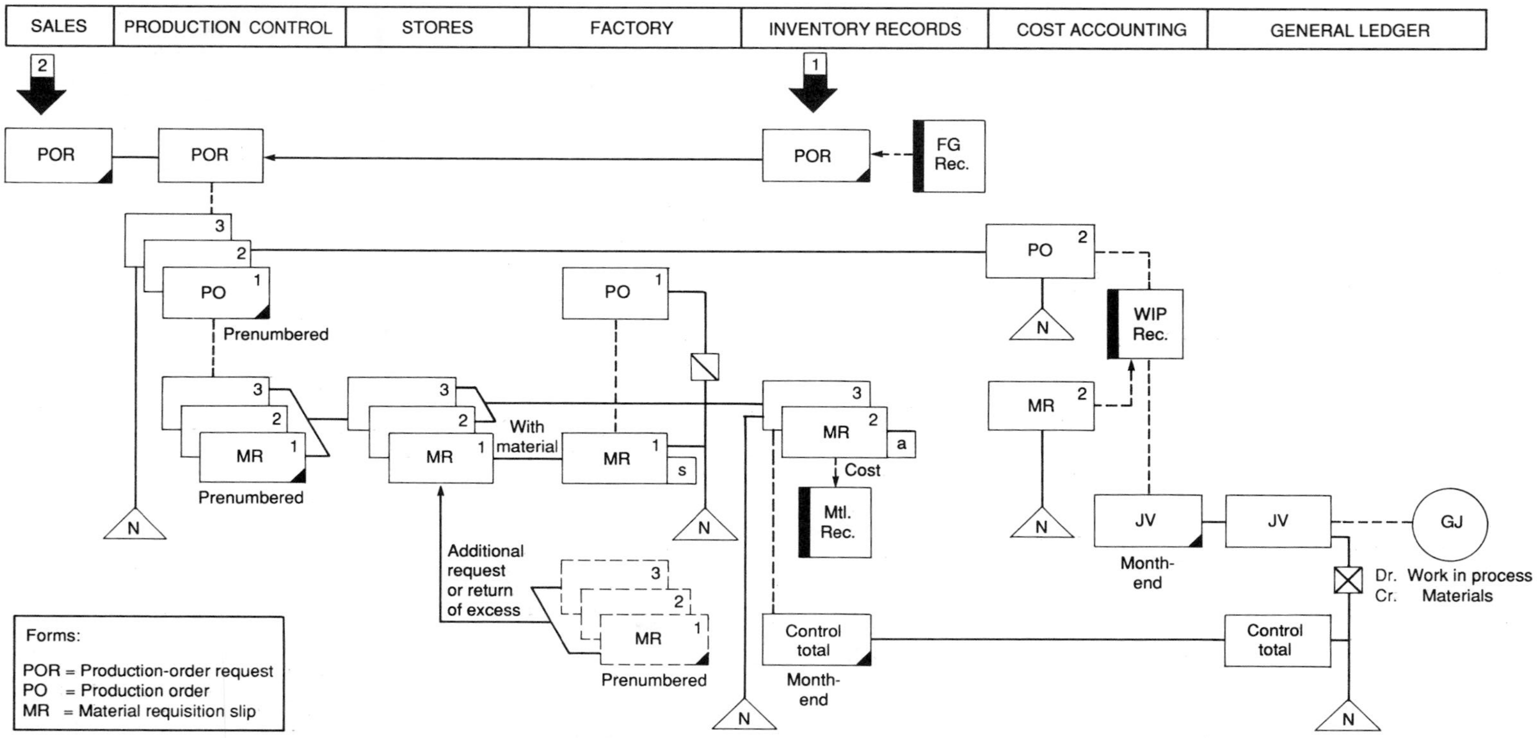

CONTROL FLOWCHART 20–3 Transferring Labor to Work in Process

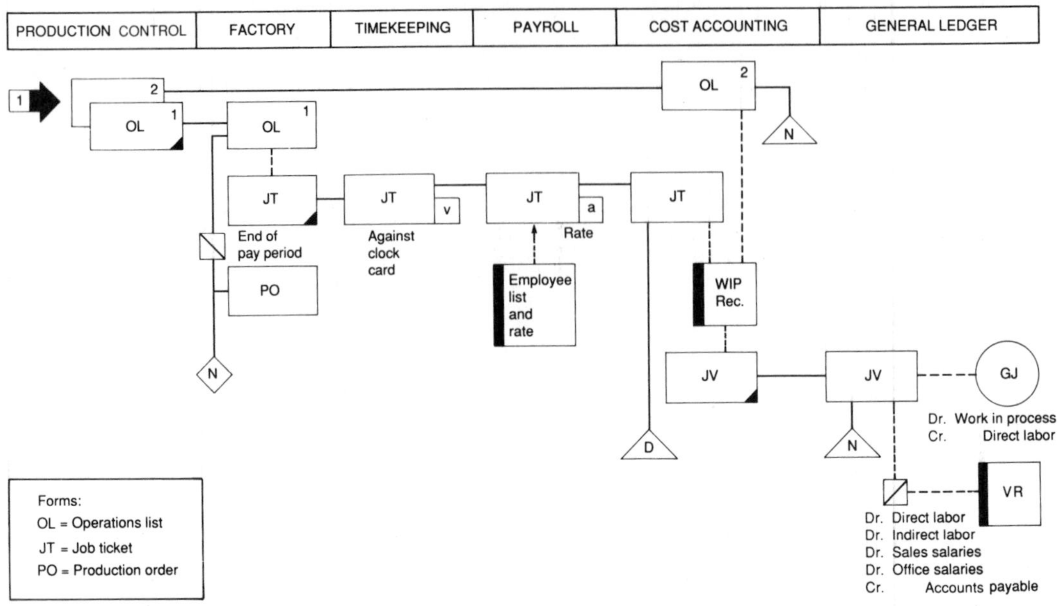

CONTROL FLOWCHART 20–4 Accounting for Factory Overhead

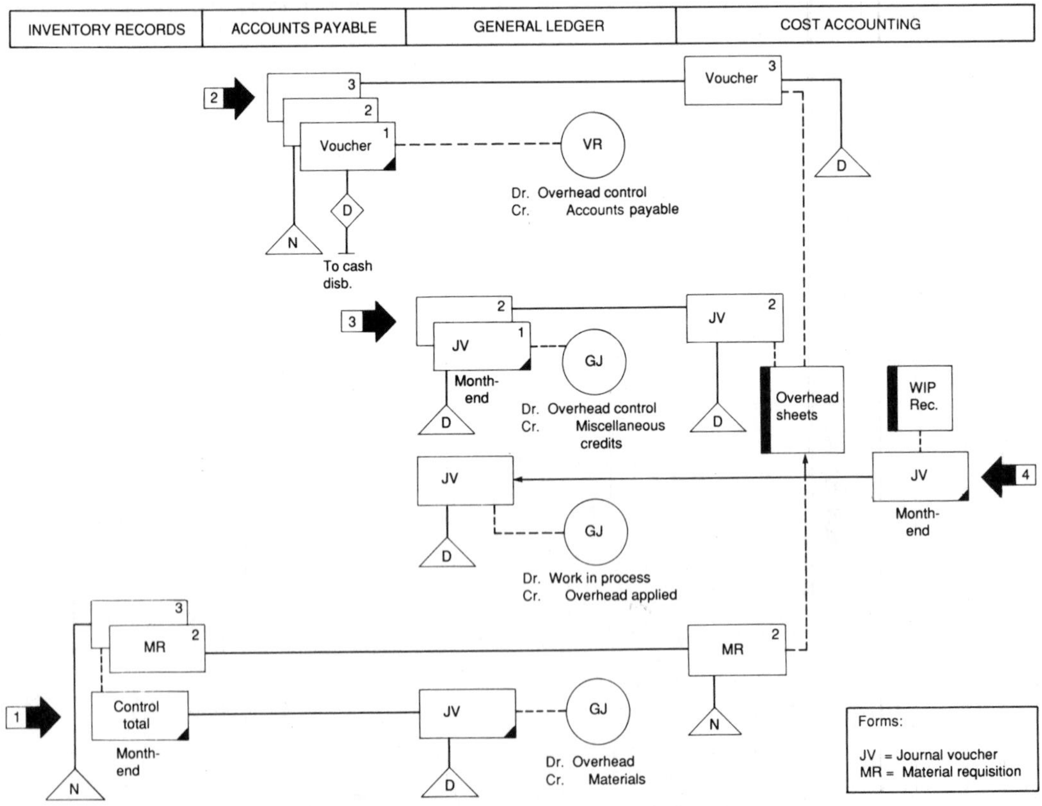

CONTROL FLOWCHART 20–5 Transferring Work in Process to Finished Goods

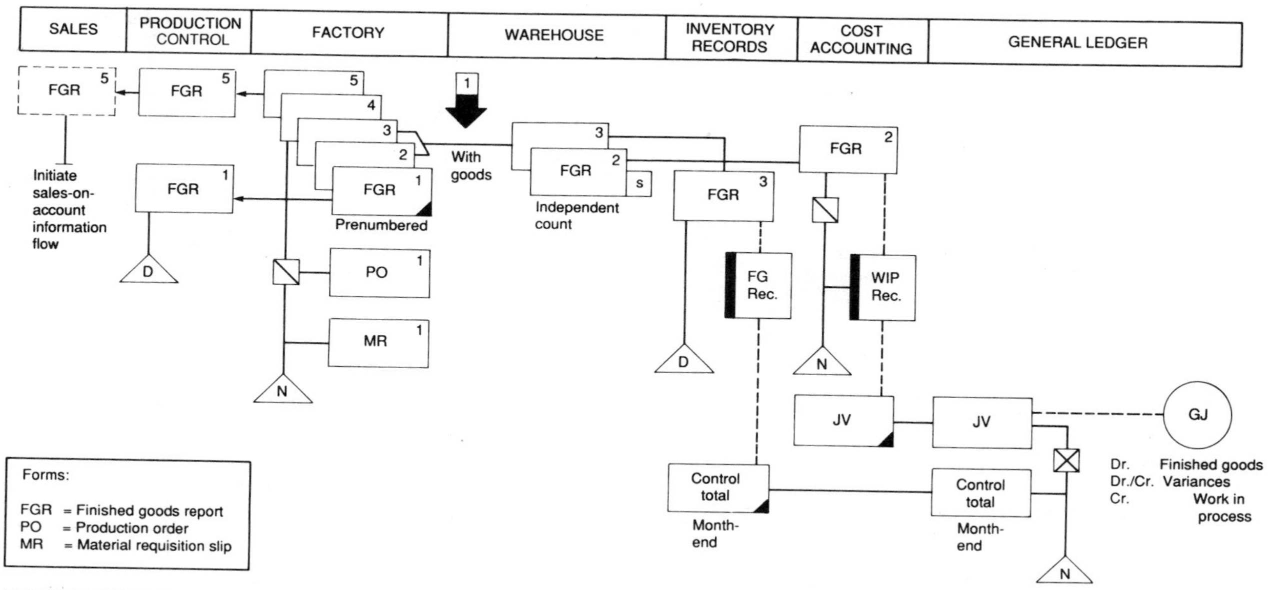

CONTROL FLOWCHART 20–6 Payroll

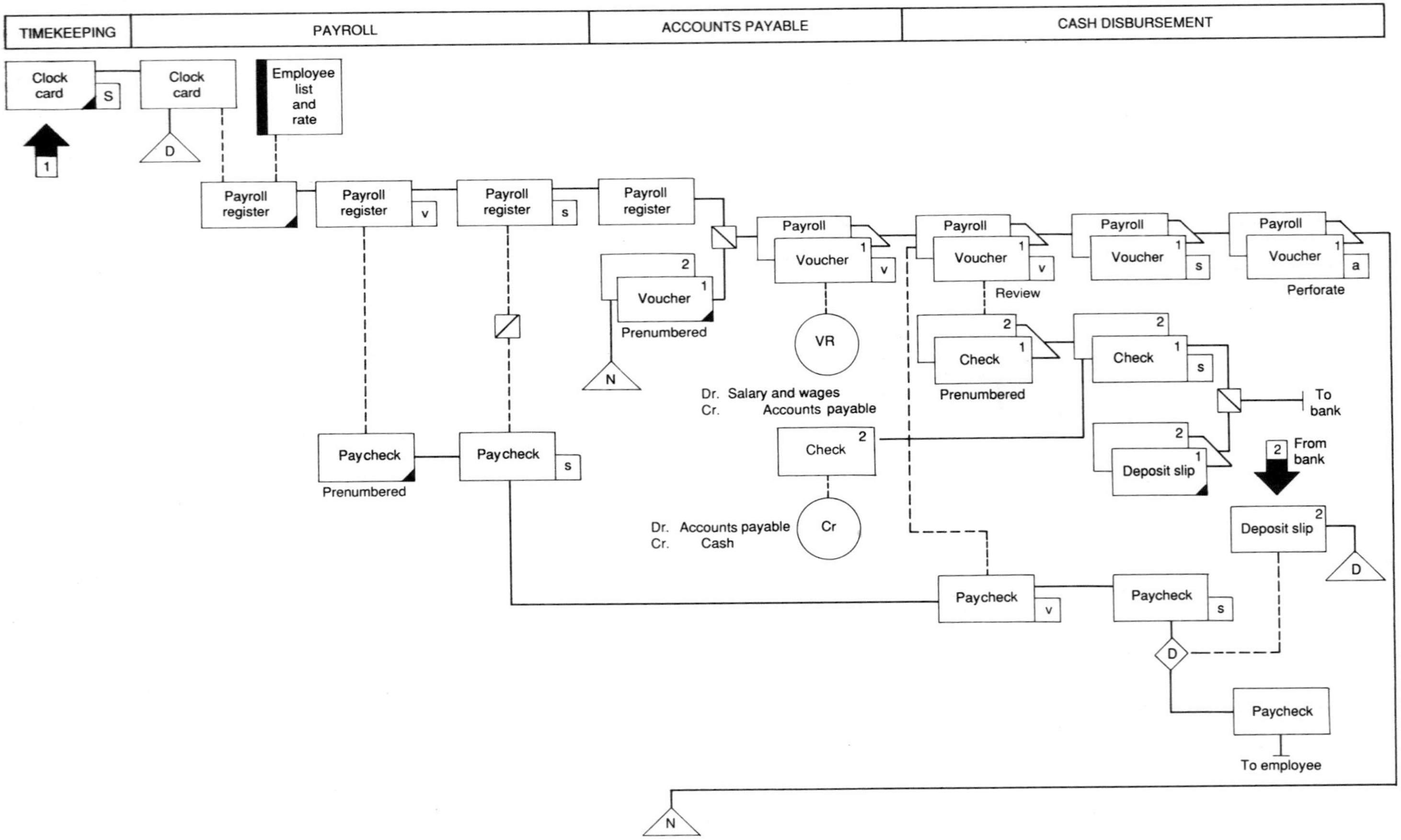

QUESTIONS

20–1. Which economic events produce transactions in the conversion cycle?

20–2. Which types of transactions affect the accounting records in the conversion cycle? Which of them are processed in this cycle?

20–3. What is the purpose of each of the following documents?
a. Material requisition
b. Job ticket
c. Timecard
d. Salary authorization
e. Production order

20–4. What are the two methods of accounting for inventory? Which is most likely in a computer-based system?

20–5. What are two ways of calculating the cost of finished goods inventory? How do they differ?

20–6. Describe five special-purpose reports produced in the conversion cycle.

20–7. Which forms do noncomputerized records take in the conversion cycle?

20–8. In a computerized accounting system, which data files are used in the conversion cycle? Identify the purpose of each file.

20–9. In a computer-based accounting system, what are the applications in the conversion cycle? What is the purpose of each?

20–10. Identify three nonaccounting computerized systems that affect the accounting applications in the conversion cycle.

EXERCISES AND CASES

20–11. *TRANSACTIONS AND DOCUMENTS*

The column on the left lists accounting transactions that affect the conversion cycle. The right column lists documents and reports. For each transaction, identify the document(s) and report(s) associated with it.

Transaction	*Document or report*
a. Purchase inventory	1. Journal voucher
b. Sale of inventory	2. Timecard
c. Transfer of material and labor	3. Purchase requisition
d. Transfer of completed goods	4. Job ticket
e. Payroll	5. Completed production order
	6. Sales order
	7. Material requisition

20–12. *TRANSACTIONS AND APPLICATIONS*

The following column on the left lists accounting transactions. The right column lists application systems used in the conversion cycle. For each transaction, identify the application system associated with it.

Transaction	*Application system*
a. Purchase inventory	1. Cost accounting
b. Sale of inventory	2. Payroll
c. Transfer of material, labor, and overhead	3. Inventory
d. Transfer of completed goods	
e. Paycheck	

20–13. ***TAKING PHYSICAL INVENTORY***

A company maintains its detailed inventory records and its general ledger inventory account on a perpetual basis. Thus, the cost of materials entering into production and the cost of inventory on hand for financial statement purposes can be readily determined. Nevertheless, the company takes periodic physical inventories.

Required:

State four reasons why the company should make periodic physical inventory counts.

(CIA Adapted)

20–14. ***PERPETUAL INVENTORY METHOD***

The year-end physical inventory of a large wholesaler of automotive parts has just been completed. The internal auditor reviewed the inventory taking instructions before the start of the physical inventory, made and recorded test counts, and observed the controls over the inventory taking process. No significant exceptions to the process were observed. After completion of the inventory count, the auditor compared quantities shown on count sheets with those listed on the physical inventory report. There were numerous discrepancies.

Required:

a. List five likely causes of such discrepancies.
b. List five inappropriate management actions that might have been taken as a result of relying on incorrect perpetual inventory data.

(CIA Adapted)

20–15. ***PURCHASE OF MATERIALS***

Exhibit 20–1 contains a document flowchart. It shows the raw materials purchasing procedures for Medium-Sized Manufacturing Company, from preparation of initial documents through vouching of invoices for payment in accounts payable.

EXHIBIT 20–1 Exercise 20–15

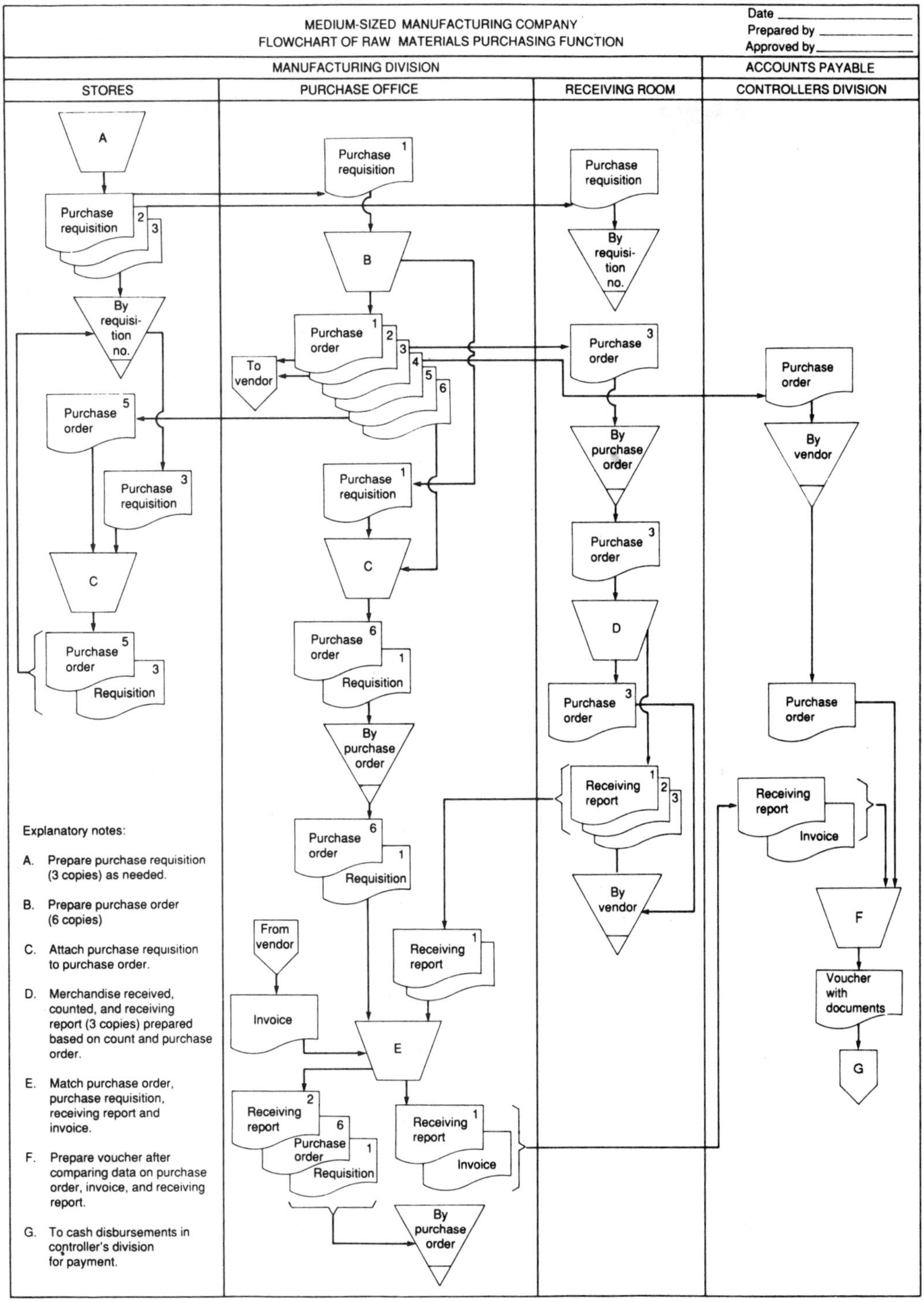

Required:

Identify and explain the systems and control weaknesses evident from the flowchart. Include the internal control weaknesses resulting from activities performed or not performed. All documents are prenumbered.

(AICPA Adapted)

20–16. ***INVENTORY CONTROL***

Alex Corporation manufactures several lines of machine tools for the automotive industry. As a consequence of the high demand for its products, the firm currently operates three shifts, five days a week. Maintenance work is done on the weekends unless breakdowns require immediate attention.

The production supervisors have complained that many times the maintenance work is not completed because parts have not been available in the storeroom. In reviewing the operating and accounting procedures of the maintenance crew and storerooms, the internal audit staff has identified the following procedures:

The maintenance crew consists of three persons, each of whom works 12 hours on most Saturdays and Sundays. Two of the three are on call during the week for breakdowns. Each person on the maintenance crew reports directly to the production supervisor. At the end of the week, the production supervisor leaves a list of maintenance work to be completed. At the end of the weekend, the maintenance crew leaves the list for the supervisor indicating with a check mark the completed jobs and giving a reason for those not completed.

Maintenance parts and supplies are stored in a separate locked room. Many of the parts and supplies are very small in size and monetary value. However, a large number are very expensive and quite portable. The production supervisor, the receiving supervisor, and all maintenance crew members have keys to this room.

Perpetual inventory cards are maintained for all parts and supplies in the maintenance storeroom; the inventory cards are kept in the maintenance storeroom. When ordered parts and supplies are received, the receiving supervisor places them in the storeroom and records the receipt on the proper perpetual inventory card. The maintenance crew members record deductions on the inventory cards when they take parts and supplies. Parts and supplies are ordered by the receiving supervisor based on notes from the maintenance crew members indicating that quantities are low or depleted.

The accounting department uses the perpetual inventory cards at the end of the month to determine the value of the maintenance parts and supplies inventory. The balances indicated on the inventory cards are multiplied by the most recent prices to determine the carrying value of the maintenance inventory.

Required:

Identify the internal control weaknesses and recommend improvements regarding the operating and accounting procedures of Alex Corporation's maintenance crew and storeroom.

(CMA Adapted)

20–17. *PURCHASING AND INVENTORY CONTROL*

At Alden, Inc., raw materials consist mainly of high-cost electronic components kept in a locked storeroom. Storeroom personnel include a supervisor and four clerks. All are well trained, competent, and adequately bonded. Raw materials are removed from the storeroom only on written or oral authorization of one of the production supervisors.

There are no perpetual inventory records, so the storeroom clerks do not keep records of goods received or issued. To compensate for the lack of perpetual records, a physical inventory count is taken monthly by the storeroom clerks, who are well supervised. Appropriate procedures are followed in making the inventory count.

After the physical inventory count, the storeroom supervisor matches quantities counted against a predetermined reorder level. If the count for a given part is below the reorder level, the supervisor enters the part number on a materials requisition list and sends this list to the accounts payable clerk. The accounts payable clerk prepares a purchase order for the predetermined reorder quantity for each part and mails the purchase order to the vendor from whom the part was last purchased.

When ordered materials arrive at Alden, they are received by the storeroom clerks. The clerks count the items and compare the counts to the shipper's bill of lading. All vendors' bills of lading are initialed, dated, and filed in the storeroom to serve as receiving reports.

Required:

Describe the weaknesses in internal control and recommend improvements in Alden's procedures for purchase, receipt, storage, and issue of raw materials.

(AICPA Adapted)

20–18. *COST ACCOUNTING SYSTEM*

The Phillips Foundry Company, a family-owned company in the greater Chicago area, is engaged in the manufacture of iron castings like barstool bases. It employs about 120 people and has annual sales of $1 million.

The production process for iron castings is composed of four steps: molding, casting, machining, and assembly. The company produces both to customer specifications and to inventory for several selected standard products. In either case, a production order is prepared showing the quantity and specifications of castings to be produced. A job order cost sheet is created to accumulate cost related to each production order. Costs are accumulated in the following manner:

Direct Material. Materials requisition slips are filled out by supervisors when materials are needed. At the end of each month, requisitions are sorted by production order number and posted to job order cost sheets.

Direct Labor. Employees are required to indicate on their timecards the production order numbers on which they have worked. These labor hours are converted to labor cost, summarized by production order number, and posted to job order cost sheets at the end of each month.

Factory Overhead. Actual factory overhead incurred in the plant is totaled at the end of each month. An overhead costing rate is then established by dividing the total factory overhead by labor cost for the month. Concurrent with the posting of labor cost to job order cost sheets, factory overhead, computed by multiplying labor cost with the overhead costing rate, is entered in each job order cost sheet.

Unit Costs. When posting to job order cost sheets at the end of the month, sheets marked "JOB COMPLETED" are removed and the costs of material, labor, and factory overhead posted on them are totaled. Unit costs are derived by dividing these total costs by the number of castings produced in these production orders.

During a slow period in April, Johnston Phillips, president and principal owner of the company, was scanning completed job order cost sheets for the past year or so to gain some understanding of the type of castings being produced by the company. He noted that production orders for Bar Stool X135 in lots of 100 came up most frequently. In an attempt to establish the total number of Bar Stool X135 produced during the past year, he pulled out its job order cost sheets. While pulling these sheets, Phillips was puzzled that none showed the same unit cost and that unit costs differed by as much as 60 percent between April and September. Unable to find an answer, he asked one of his golfing friends, management consultant Ronald Thompson, to come to his plant and take a look.

Required:

a. Make recommendations to Johnston Phillips as if you were Ronald Thompson. Present these recommendations in the form of a short letter.

b. In your letter, suggest several reasons why unit costs may differ by as much as 60 percent for the same product produced in different months.

20–19. ***PAYROLL PROCEDURES***

The Kowal Manufacturing Company employs about 50 production workers and has the following payroll procedures:

The factory supervisor interviews applicants, and on the basis of the interview, either hires or rejects them. An applicant who is hired prepares a W-4 form (Employee's Withholding Exemption Certificate) and gives it to the supervisor. The supervisor writes the hourly rate of pay for the new employee in the corner of the W-4 form and then gives the form to a payroll clerk as notice that the worker has been employed. The supervisor verbally advises the payroll department of rate adjustments.

A supply of blank timecards is kept in a box near the entrance to the factory. Each worker takes a weekly timecard on Monday morning, fills in the name, and notes in pencil daily arrival and departure times. At the end of the week, the workers drop their timecards in a box near the door to the factory.

The completed timecards are taken from the box on Monday morning by a payroll clerk. Two payroll clerks divide the cards alphabetically, one taking the A to L section and the other the M to Z section. Fully responsible for a section of the payroll, each clerk computes the gross pay, deductions, and net pay; posts the details to the employee's earnings records; and prepares and numbers the payroll checks. Employees are automatically removed from the payroll when they fail to turn in timecards.

The payroll checks are manually signed by the chief accountant and given to the supervisor. The supervisor distributes the checks to the workers in the factory and arranges for the delivery of the checks to absent workers. The payroll bank account is reconciled by the chief accountant, who also prepares the various quarterly and annual payroll tax reports.

Required:

List suggestions for improving the Kowal Manufacturing Company's internal control procedures for factory hiring and payroll.

(AICPA Adapted)

20–20. *TIMEKEEPING*

Olympia Manufacturing Company accounts for all production using job orders. All employees are paid hourly wages, with time and one half for overtime. The company's direct labor hour input process for payroll and job cost determination is summarized in the system flowchart of Exhibit 20–2.

Steps A and C are performed in timekeeping, step B in the factory operating departments, step D in payroll, step E in data entry, and step F in computer operations.

Required:

a. For each processing step, A through F, list the possible errors or discrepancies that may occur.
b. Cite the corresponding control procedure that should be in effect for each error or discrepancy.

(AICPA Adapted)

20–21. *INVENTORY SYSTEM*

Beccan Company is a discount tire dealer that operates 25 retail stores in the Seattle metropolitan area. Both private brand and name brand tires are sold by Beccan. The company operates a centralized purchasing and warehousing facility and employs a perpetual inventory system. All purchases of tires and related supplies are placed through the company's central purchasing department to take advantage of quantity discounts. The tires and supplies are received at the central warehouse and distributed to the retail stores as needed. The perpetual inventory system at the central facility maintains current inventory records, designated reorder points, optimum order quantities, and continuous stocktakings for each type of tire and other related supplies.

The following documents are employed by Beccan in their inventory control system:

Retail stores requisition. This document is submitted by the retail stores to the central warehouse whenever tires or supplies are needed at the stores. The

EXHIBIT 20–2 Exercise 20–20

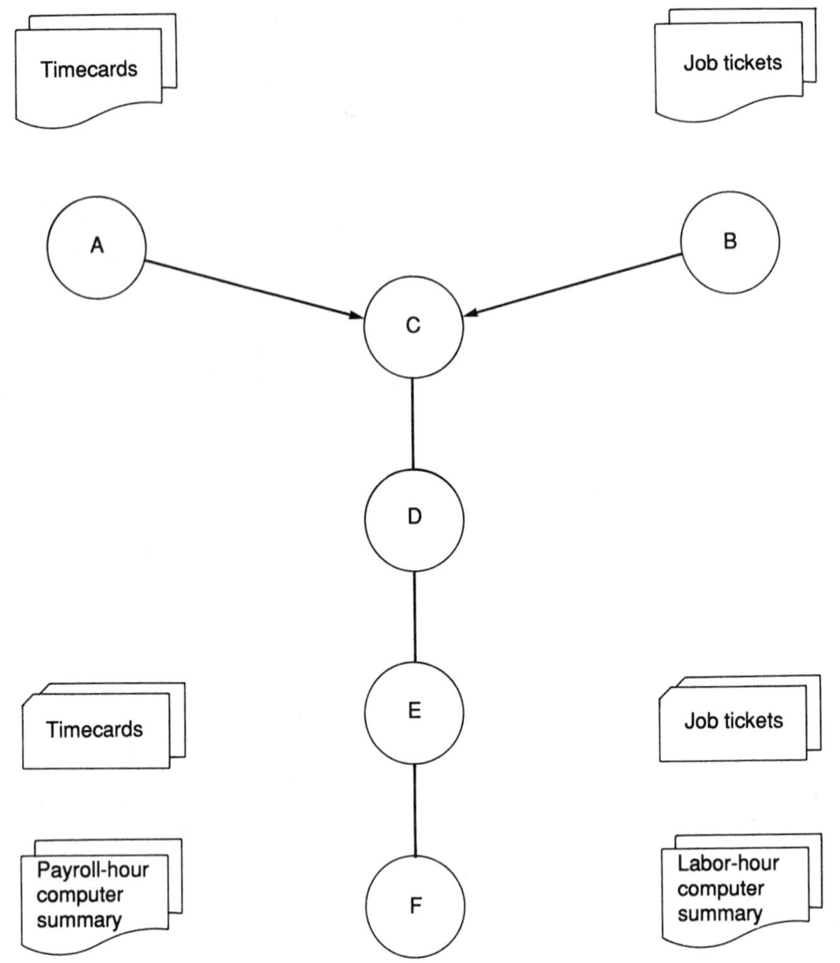

shipping clerks in the warehouse department fill the orders from inventory and have them delivered to the stores.

Purchase requisition. The inventory control clerk in the inventory control department prepares this document when the quantity on hand for an item falls below the designated reorder point. The document is forwarded to the purchasing department.

Purchase order. The purchasing department prepares this document when items need to be ordered. The document is submitted to an authorized vendor.

Receiving report. The warehouse department prepares this document when ordered items are received from vendors. The receiving clerk completes the document by indicating the vendor's name, the date the shipment is received, and the quantity of each item received.

Invoice. An invoice is received from the vendors specifying the amounts owed by Beccan.

The following departments are involved in Beccan's inventory control system:

Inventory control department. The inventory control department is responsible for the maintenance of all perpetual inventory records for all items carried in inventory. This includes current quantity on hand, reorder point, optimum order quantity, and quantity on order for each item carried.

Warehouse department. The warehouse department maintains the physical inventory of all items carried in inventory. All orders from vendors are received by a receiving clerk, and all distributions to retail stores are filled by shipping clerks in this department.

Purchasing department. The purchasing department places all orders for items needed by the company.

Accounts payable department. Accounts payable maintains all open accounts with vendors and other creditors. All payments are processed in this department.

Required:

a. Prepare a document flowchart showing how these documents should be used to provide adequate internal control over receipt, issue, replenishment, and payment.

b. Assume that Beccan plans to computerize its operations.
   1. Design the content of each master record required by your system.
   2. Prepare a system flowchart describing how these operations would occur in a computer-based system.
   3. Describe the control procedures Beccan would use in its system and indicate where these procedures would be placed.

(CMA Adapted)

20–22. ***COST ACCOUNTING SYSTEM***

Valpaige Company is an industrial machinery and equipment manufacturer with several production departments. The company employs automated and heavy equipment in its production departments. Consequently, Valpaige has a large repair and maintenance department (R&M) for servicing this equipment.

The operating efficiency of the R&M department has decreased over the past two years. Further, repair and maintenance costs seem to be climbing more rapidly than other department costs. The assistant controller has reviewed the operations of the R&M department and has concluded that the administrative procedures used since the early days of the department are outmoded due in part to the growth of the company. The two major causes for the decrease, in the opinion of the assistant controller, are an antiquated scheduling system for repair and maintenance work and the actual cost system to distribute the R&M department's costs to the production departments. The actual costs of the R&M

department are allocated monthly to the production departments on the basis of the number of service calls made during each month.

The assistant controller has proposed that a formal work order system be implemented for the R&M department. The production departments would submit a service request to the R&M department for the maintenance, including a suggested time for having the work done. The supervisor of the R&M department would prepare a cost estimate on the service request for the work required (labor and materials) and indicate a suggested time for completing the work on the service request. The R&M department supervisor would return the request to the production department that initiated the request. Once the production department okays the work by returning a copy of the service request, the R&M supervisor would prepare a repair and maintenance work order and schedule the job. This work order provides the repair worker with the details of the work to be done and is used to record the actual maintenance hours worked and the materials and supplies used.

Production departments would be charged for actual labor hours worked at a predetermined standard rate for the type of work required. The parts and supplies used would be charged to the production departments at cost.

The assistant controller believes that only two documents are required in this new system. These are a maintenance service request initiated by the production departments, and a maintenance work order initiated by the R&M department. These documents would be used to request maintenance work, to charge the production departments for completed work, and to evaluate the performance of the R&M department.

Required:

a. Which data items should be included on the maintenance work order?

b. How many copies of the maintenance work order would be required? How should each copy be distributed?

c. Prepare a document flowchart showing how the maintenance service request and the maintenance work order would be used.

d. Assume that Valpaige decides to develop a computer-based system for processing work orders. Design the record format for the:

1. Maintenance work order master record.
2. Maintenance service request record.

(CMA Adapted)

20–23. *AUTOMATED DATA ENTRY*

After a series of production level increases, the management of a division of ITT Space Communications decided to introduce automated data collection techniques for the payroll and cost accounting systems at one of its plants.[2]

---

[2]Adapted from an article by Quentin L. Karchner, Jr., "How One Plant Automated Its Collection of Data," *Management Accounting*, September 1980, pp. 45–48. Copyright by the National Association of Accountants (1980), Montvale, N.J. 07645. Used by permission.

With this system, attendance and payroll records are automatically generated, edited, and summarized without the use of timecards. The system provides information for employee appraisals, unemployment insurance claims, and occasional disciplinary actions. It required changes to the existing manual systems in three areas: data entry, time and absence reporting, and transaction editing and error corrections.

Data Entry

Each employee authorized to use the system is issued a plastic badge encoded with his or her employee number. This badge allows the employee access to the remote terminals used for data entry.

These terminals at various stations on the manufacturing floor are connected to a central processing unit (CPU) that is dedicated to this application. The dedicated CPU operates independently of the plant's main computer. During the day, the CPU accumulates data in a file. These transactions are off-loaded to the main computer at night. The main computer then produces labor distribution and efficiency reports.

A program executing on the dedicated CPU controls data entry at a terminal. It provides a display shown in Exhibit 20–3. As specific data input is required, individual blocks light up on the terminal. This tells the employee which data should be entered next. As employees became familiar with the operations at the terminals, they developed the ability to bypass the instructions on the screen and enter data without prompts. This greatly speeded up the recording of transactions.

When the CPU recognizes an attempt to enter erroneous data, the red REPEAT button lights up. The employee then presses the REPEAT button and reenters the data. An employee who continues to have trouble can consult with a supervisor who refers to a user's guide. The user's guide describes the procedure in a simple step-by-step format.

Transactions reported through the terminals are time attendence (clocking out and in), standard labor at the completion of each operation, multisequence standard labor (multiple operations against one part number), auxiliary direct labor, project orders (those for a nonstandard part number), transfer of labor to other departments, rework, and engineering change orders.

Time and Attendance Reporting

All time and attendance transactions are recorded in the attendance master file. It contains records similar to those in the payroll master file but omits the pay data. The attendance master file contains one record for each employee and shows such data as the employee number, the employee's supervisor's number, shift, lunch hours, and department number. This allows updating the system about an individual employee more frequently than is done with the payroll system. Production supervisors are responsible for updating the attendance master file each day.

EXHIBIT 20–3 Case 20–23

Table 1
Sample Terminal Display

Idle T/A	Badge	Keyboard entry	Offline software
STD labor	Job card long card	Sequence number	Department number
Multi-Seq std-labor		Exception program ID	Shift
Adl project orders		Date mm/dd/y	Overtime hours xx.x
Transfers		Supervisor number	Time xxxx
Rework and expense	Short card	Job code 3	Continue 1 = Yes 2 = No
Eco		Code ID Status code override code	Charge department quantity
		Employee number	Expense number

The terminal illuminates the individual blocks as data input is required. In this manner, the employee is guided through the proper data entry steps

The attendance file provides up-to-date information to both the manufacturing and accounting departments in the plant. To ensure its accuracy, timekeeping personnel are available to advise production supervisors and to review updates to the file. When timekeepers find discrepancies in the attendance master file, they report them to the cost accounting supervisor for correction.

Daily Reports. Twenty minutes after the start of each shift, the system produces the daily absentee report. This report identifies each absent employee, which shift the employee normally works, and the employee's current status (active, medical leave, vacation, etc.).

If an employee is shown as unaccounted for, the production supervisor determines the reason and reports it to timekeeping using the codes printed at the top of the report. Timekeeping personnel enter this information into the system and it is reflected in future reports. The system produces monthly and year-to-date reports showing employees' attendance history for use by management.

A daily labor hours worked report is generated and forwarded the next day to the production supervisor. This report discloses for each employee the number of hours worked, the time in, the time out, and the number of authorized overtime hours.

The system also produces daily efficiency reports. These show the supervisor how an employee performed on each different operation during the previous day. This makes the supervisor aware of any employee/job mismatches, unrealistic standards, special assembly problems, and high or low individual performance. The supervisor can take action to correct problems when they occur, rather than speculating about what happened a month later.

Editing Procedures

The system employs both expense editing and work in process editing procedures.

Expense Editing. The expense coding file is the basis for the expense editing. It consists of lists and tables of all acceptable expense and department numbers that can be entered at a terminal. This file is changed whenever changes are made to the direct labor procedures. Expense editing verifies the propriety of transaction expense accounts by comparing codes entered by an employee with codes in this file.

Work in Process Editing. Work in process editing procedures also verify the validity of transactions applied to a work order by employees. The edit program, for example, causes the system to reject a transaction that charges labor to a work order that is closed.

The edit program also determines the reasonableness of the production quantities entered at a terminal. It does this by maintaining a record of the quantity of items processed by the prior operation applied to the work order. If, for a current operation, a worker enters a quantity greater than that shown for the prior one, the transaction is rejected. This procedure also provides exact unit counts for all parts in production under a work order.

By extending these counts at the standard cost for each part, the system calculates the total cost of the work in process inventory located in each production department. When these totals are adjusted for known exceptions such as floor stock, they greatly aid in the process of taking a physical inventory.

Error Correction Procedures. Because of the possibility of errors in data entry, the system provides procedures for their correction. Examples of errors normally encountered include (1) an employee who failed to clock in; (2) an employee who inadvertently clocked out while entering a labor transaction; (3) an employee who clocked out twice; and (4) the failure to clock in or out at lunch hour.

Error correction procedures are called the daily review routine. Production supervisors record corrections on the form shown in Exhibit 20–4. They submit this form to timekeeping personnel who enter the corrections in the system. The form is flexible enough, and contains sufficient explanation, so that supervisors find error corrections easy to make.

Benefits of the System

The elapsed time for the development of the system, from initial concept to implementation, was almost a year. Even during parallel operation with the previous manual system, the benefits of the new system began to appear.

During parallel operation, analysts noted differences between the outputs of the automated and the manual systems. These were investigated, and in most cases the manual system was faulty. Invalid shop orders were charged, labor was reported in error, and so forth. Thus the new system was probably producing more accurate results than the old manual one.

The automated collection system has provided more accurate information from the shop floor, reduced paperwork, increased productivity, reduced costs, and provided a means of integrating production data with other management information systems. It has been able to handle significantly higher production volume than the manual system with no increase in timekeeping personnel. Management has estimated that the benefits gained from this system paid for the cost of implementation in less than one year.

In addition, there were intangible benefits—better control of procedures for clocking in and out, error checks as data is entered at its source, daily attendance monitoring, and timely and accurate portrayal of operations.

Required:

What observations do you have concerning the company's automated data collection system?

20–24. ***PAYROLL SYSTEM***

The Vane Corporation is a manufacturing concern that has been in business for the past 18 years. During this period, the company has grown from a very small family-owned operation to a medium-sized manufacturing concern with several departments. Despite this growth, a substantial number of the procedures employed by Vane Corporation have been in effect since the business was started. Just recently, Vane Corporation has computerized its payroll operations.

The payroll function operates in the following manner: Blank timecards are kept near the factory entrance. After picking up their weekly timecards on Monday morning, workers write in their names and identification numbers. Each day they write on the timecards the time of their arrivals and departures. On the following Monday, the factory foremen collect the completed timecards for the previous week and send them to data processing.

EXHIBIT 20–4 Case 20–23

Table 2
Corrections to Weekly T & A Records

Date:______________

Sample Input Form

Employee number	Date	Hours worked	Shift	Clock time In	Clock time Out	Optional clock In	Optional clock Out	Optional clock In	Optional clock Out	Shift time Start	Shift time Stop	Optional lunch Start	Optional lunch Stop	Day code	Act code	Log day
1-5	10-14	19-22	22	32-35	36-39	40-43	44-47	48-51		56-59	60-63	64-67	68-71	80	81	85

Action codes
A = Add to file
C = Change file
D = Delete from file
BLANK = Original

Day code
J = Monday-Friday
K = Saturday
L = Sunday

Logical day
Monday = 1
Tuesday = 2
Wednesday = 3
Thursday = 4
Friday = 5
Saturday = 6
Sunday = 7

INSTRUCTIONS

Employee number
An employee number is required for all transactions

Date
A date is required for all transactions, i.e.,
10037
Month Day Year

Hours worked
Hours are required for all action codes except "D" and "F." Three digits are required, i.e., 02.5
tenths
hours

Shift
All transactions require a shift except a "D" and "F" action code

Clock time
Time should be shown in military time, i.e., 0750, 1600. Not required for "D" and "F" action codes.

Optional clock
To be used when additional clock-in and clock-out is required. Not required for "D" and "F" action codes

Shift time
Required for "A," "C" and blank action codes.

Optional lunch
Must be completed if lunch is to be taken out. If employee does not take lunch do not show hours. Hours should be in military time, i.e., 0850, 1740 Not required for "D" and "F" action codes.

Day code
J, K, or L code is required for all transactions.

Action code
A = Addition to file
C = Change file
D = Delete from file
BLANK = Data entered as terminal input
F = Flush (for timekeeping use only)

Logical day
Required for all transactions.

In data processing the timecards are used to prepare the weekly timefile. This file is processed with the master payroll file that is maintained in a sequential file according to worker identification numbers. The checks are written by the computer on the regular checking account and imprinted with the treasurer's signature. After the payroll file is updated and the checks are prepared, the checks are sent to the foremen who distribute them to the workers or hold them for absent workers to pick up later.

The foremen notify data processing of new employees and terminations. Any changes in hourly pay rate or any other changes affecting payroll are usually communicated to data processing by the foremen. The workers also complete a job time ticket for each individual job they work on each day. The job time tickets are collected daily and sent to cost accounting where they are used to prepare a cost distribution analysis.

Further analysis of the payroll function reveals the following:

a. A worker's gross wages never exceed $300 per week.
b. Raises never exceed $0.55 per hour for the factory workers.
c. No more than 20 hours of overtime are allowed each week.
d. The factory employs 150 workers in 10 departments.

The payroll function has not been operating smoothly for some time, but even more problems have surfaced since the payroll was computerized. The foremen have indicated that they would like a weekly report indicating worker tardiness, absenteeism, and idle time so they can determine the amount of productive time lost and the reason for the lost time.

Required:

a. Identify the control weaknesses in the payroll procedures.
b. Suggest which application controls could be designed into Vane Corporation's payroll processing programs.

(CMA Adapted)

20–25. ***JUST IN TIME SYSTEMS***

Just in time (JIT) systems refer to a class of manufacturing systems that attempt to minimize inventories of raw and partially finished products.[3] When successfully implemented, such a system improves productivity by linking all production operations together in a smooth, uninterrupted flow.

Hewlett-Packard Company (HP) implemented a JIT system, which it calls repetitive manufacturing, in one of its plants recently. This system required significant changes to its methods of accounting for production costs.

---

[3]Adapted from "Kanban, ZIPS, and Cost Accounting: A Case Study," by B. R. Neumann and P. R. Jaouen. *Journal of Accountancy,* August 1986, pp. 132–41. Copyright © 1986 by American Institute of CPAs. Used by permission.

JIT at Hewlett-Packard

Prior to developing the system, Hewlett-Packard management identified five goals for it: total quality control, reduction of inventory, cooperation with vendors, 100 percent on time deliveries, and emphasis on cost reduction while maintaining employee satisfaction. No employees were unionized, none were paid on an incentive basis, and each was eligible for an annual bonus depending on overall company profits.

Production Control. As a new facility involved in the production of data storage devices, the plant's layout was designed to implement JIT concepts. The production line was set up in a U-shaped cell, so that one unit at a time would pass along the line. Exhibit 20–5 shows its arrangement.

In this diagram, the squares represent the physical locations of bins, racks, or pallets near each worker. They provide a visible signal indicating when a given employee may pass a unit to the next worker.

If an employee's outgoing square is filled, the employee may either complete the unit being worked on, sit idle, or help another employee. However, he or she may not begin work on another unit. When a quality or production problem occurs, the entire line shuts down and a flashing red light attracts help from a supervisor, other employees, or engineers.

EXHIBIT 20–5 Case 20–25

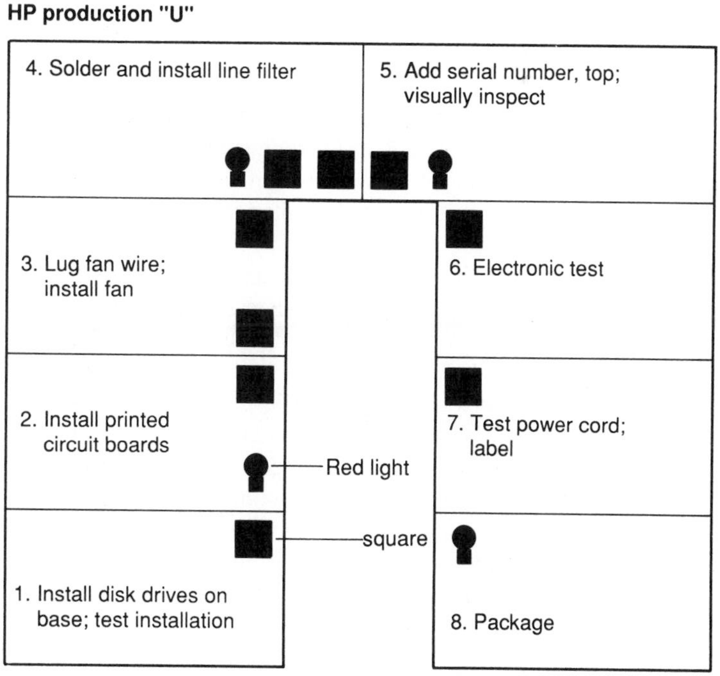

At all times the slowest work station is being analyzed to make it faster. As soon as it improves, the next slowest station is analyzed, and so on. The result is a continual process of upgrading quality and making production a smooth process. The goal is to make the physical material ''flow like water'' through the production line.

Inventory Control. HP management desires to manage inventory on a real-time basis and minimize their investment in it. Inventory reduction is achieved by having many raw materials delivered straight to production lines, bypassing the storeroom. They use monthly rolling forecasts, long-term contracts, and a commitment to work together with vendors. This has resulted in vendors supplying 100 parts with a two-week lead time and daily deliveries.

Annual physical counts of inventory are no longer sufficient. These have been replaced by one-minute monthly physical inventories or perpetual cycle counts. The ultimate goal is to function in such a way that no physical verification is needed at year-end.

Because of these policies, warehouse space has been reduced by 50 percent and units produced per square foot have doubled. The total inventory supply decreased from 2.8 months to 1.3 months within a six-month period. The number of vendors has decreased from 50 to 24 and there has been a 30 percent reduction in raw material inspections.

Cost Accounting Procedures

Historically, the cost accounting system used by HP had been a work-order-based job costing system. With this approach, labor, materials, and overhead were assigned to work orders and average unit costs were calculated for each work order.

With JIT, work orders have been eliminated and specific unit costs are deemphasized. The resulting cost accounting system is a hybrid containing some elements of both job and process costing. In addition, many of the traditional job and process cost accounts are eliminated.

Accounting for Material. After implementing JIT, Hewlett-Packard eliminated work orders and work in process inventory accounts. Unlike traditional manufacturing systems, at HP parts buildups are limited within each work station. Therefore, the parts component of work in process is relatively immaterial. HP has combined it with the much reduced raw materials inventories, creating a new account called raw and in process inventory (RIP).

To account for manufacturing costs without requisitions or work orders, HP uses a postmanufacturing deduction procedure. Raw materials costs (in RIP) are transferred to finished goods inventories when the unit is completed. Material usage variances are recognized after they are incurred by the use of a manual tracking system based on quantities of scrap.

Accounting for Labor. Prior to implementing JIT, management recognized that excessive resources were used to account for direct labor costs. Although simplicity was being emphasized in the manufacturing process, this had not translated into simplicity in the accounting records. Detailed records were kept assigning worker time to products, inspection, and training. These were no longer consistent with the team concept used in the manufacturing process.

Direct labor accounted for approximately 2.8 percent of total production costs and less than 1 percent of total inventory costs. So HP accountants decided to cease charging direct labor to manufacturing processes and to quit tracking them through the inventory accounts. Instead, they expense direct labor and overhead on a monthly basis. They also maintain in the RIP and finished goods inventory accounts a base level of labor and overhead costs.

Direct labor costs are still identified with groups of major products by summarizing the total direct labor costs and the number of units produced in each department. Accountants analyze direct labor costs quarterly or as needed, but unitary labor costs are not used to transfer costs between manufacturing processes.

Accounting for Overhead. In a traditional cost accounting system, overhead costs are allocated to products based on a direct labor activity measure such as hours or costs. HP determined that in this plant about half its overhead costs are more closely related to materials procurement and manufacturing support than to direct labor time. (Materials procurement activities include purchasing, receiving, stockroom, materials planning, and materials engineering. Manufacturing support entails manufacturing engineering, quality assurance, manufacturing management, and central EDP.) Using direct labor time as an allocation basis would, therefore, penalize departments with many small or inexpensive parts, but whose production line is longer than departments with relatively large parts but shorter production times.

Because of this, HP accountants identified three separate overhead allocation bases. For costs related to procurement activities, they allocate overhead according to department material costs. They allocate indirect overhead using total direct costs. Production overhead costs are allocated using estimated cycle times. The cycle time is the time to process one unit, and equals the total time for production, waiting in squares, testing, and machine operation.

For accounting purposes, labor and overhead costs are lumped together. At the same time, detailed standards and actual costs are maintained for groups of products such that data is available for inventory valuation, performance measurement, and pricing decisions.

Results of JIT at HP

Because the data storage unit was never produced at this plant under a different manufacturing system, it is difficult to generalize about JIT's effects on reducing costs. However, accountants have been able to develop some specific comparisons concerning costs and efficiency.

Effects on Costs. The actual cost per unit for direct material, ignoring inflation, decreased by 33 percent over the first 18-month period. Because some additional investments were required, there has been no change in labor and overhead costs per unit. Period expenses, which include material scrap and rework, have decreased 39 percent per unit. This may have had a small impact on material usage.

Additional investments include those in training and in emphasizing teamwork on the production floor. In this environment, teamwork is essential so HP holds team meetings to discuss stress, quality, and line balancing issues. Educating employees about why HP converted to JIT has also been emphasized.

The per unit factory labor and overhead cost did not significantly improve during this first 18-month period. With a 500 percent increase in quantity produced, one would expect a per unit decrease. Failure to reduce factory overhead was due to the addition of new factory floor space and additional manufacturing, engineering, and support staff.

Effects on Efficiency. HP's JIT system has resulted in numerous benefits in other areas. Warehouse space has been reduced by 50 percent, while units produced per square foot have doubled. There has been a 48 percent reduction in the number of vendors, and 30 percent reduction in incoming inspection. This accompanies a 300 percent increase in volume and a 10 percent increase in personnel.

Another positive result is the 60 percent reduction in raw material accounting transactions at this plant each month. This significant saving eliminates the collection and processing of work orders. Both product and raw material inventories have also been reduced. Although actual production time per unit has remained relatively constant, warranty costs are significantly below the average for all plants manufacturing this product.

Conclusions

Although HP has evolved many innovative techniques for cost accounting in a repetitive manufacturing environment, the evolution is not complete.

Undeniably, a major benefit of this system is the accounting time saved by reducing the number of transactions. The characteristics of repetitive manufacturing have led to simplified accounting. As physical material flows are smoothed, accounting material flows are streamlined. Production variances are recognized more through manufacturing process control techniques and less through accounting systems.

JIT has significantly affected cost accounting at HP. Nevertheless, this cost accounting system retains its basic objectives of providing information for inventory valuation, performance measurement, and pricing and operating decisions.

Required:

a. How do the inventory control and cost accounting systems at this factory differ from a traditional factory's systems?

b. Are the cost accounting methods described in this case consistent with generally accepted accounting principles? Why or why not?

20–26. ***CONTROL FLOWCHART***

Refer to Exercise 20–16 concerning Alex Corporation's maintenance crew and supplies.

Required:

a. Prepare a control flowchart depicting the existing procedures described in the narrative.

b. Prepare a control flowchart to show the procedures that Alex should follow concerning maintenance crew and supplies. This system should overcome weaknesses in the existing system.

Chapter 21

Financial Cycle Applications

Learning Objectives:

1. To learn the kinds of transactions processed in the financial cycle.
2. To find out which reports and records are produced in the financial cycle.
3. To understand how accounting transactions are processed by the application systems in the financial cycle.
4. To see how control practices and procedures are applied in the financial cycle.

INTRODUCTION

The first chapter of this text presented a conceptual model describing how accounting systems work. You reviewed the basic records in an accounting system and how to use the accounting cycle. For simplicity, this model assumed that all accounting records were in human readable form. This chapter presents the activities in the accounting cycle with a computer-based system. These activities are a part of the financial cycle.

In this transaction cycle, the accounting system records two economic events. First, the business raises capital from owners and creditors. A journal entry system processes these and other infrequent transactions. Second, the business uses this capital to acquire the productive assets used to generate revenue. A property system records these transactions.

ILLUSTRATION 21-1 The Financial Cycle

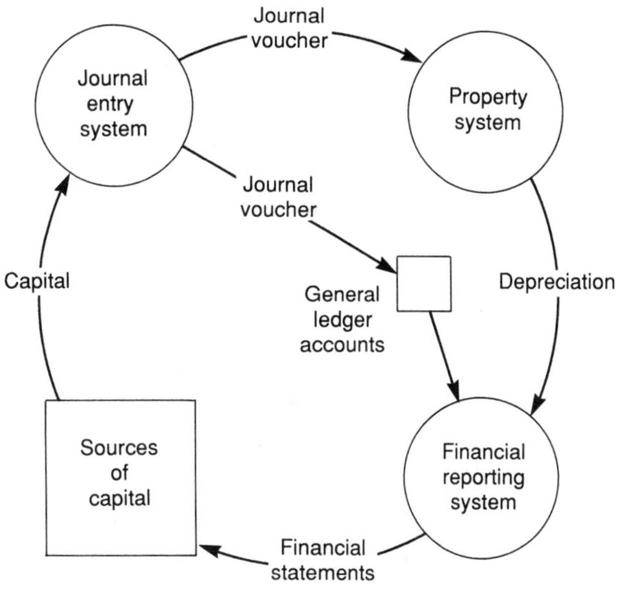

This transaction cycle also performs a third function that is not really an economic event—the financial reporting function. The financial cycle reports to the sources of capital and to managers concerning the results of its operations. A financial reporting system reports to external entities by summarizing accounting data and presenting them in financial statements. Sometimes it includes a responsibility accounting system that reports budgeted and actual costs to individual managers. The journal entry and financial reporting applications are sometimes called the components of a *general ledger* system. Illustration 21-1 summarizes the components of the financial cycle.

DEBT AND EQUITY CAPITAL

Sources of an organization's capital include its owners and its creditors. The organization receives cash from these sources and invests this cash in productive assets. The journal entry system, described later in this chapter, processes the accounting transactions that record these events.

Capital Transactions

Organizations engage in three forms of capital transactions: bank loans, bond issues, and issues of capital stock.

Bank Loans. Small organizations receive most of their debt financing in the form of bank loans. These may be medium- or long-term loans secured by mortgages on property, or they may be unsecured short-term loans. Large organizations usually rely on bank loans for short- or medium-term financing. If the organization has a good credit rating, these may be unsecured or they may be secured by mortgages. The journal entry system records bank loans in the Notes Payable account.

Bond Issues. Large organizations acquire medium- and long-term capital by issuing bonds. When an organization issues bonds, it creates a contractual obligation to pay a fixed amount of interest to purchasers of the bonds at intervals specified in the contract. Ordinarily, the contract, or *bond indenture,* requires interest payments twice a year and repayment of the principal amount to the purchaser in 5 to 30 years.

The journal entry system records each bond issue in a separate long-term liability account. The balance sheet summarizes them under the heading Bonds Payable.

Stock Issues. Corporations issue common and preferred stock in return for capital. Each share of stock represents an ownership interest in the corporation. A share of stock always has a *par* or *stated* value which is commonly an even amount, such as $1 or $10 per share. The corporate charter and bylaws, legal documents created at incorporation, state the quantities, par or stated values, and classes of stock that the corporation may issue.

Corporations maintain different Capital Stock accounts for each class of stock. They record the par or stated value of issued shares in Common Stock and Preferred Stock accounts. They record amounts received that exceed the par or stated values in one or more accounts called Paid-in-Capital in Excess of Par.

Accounting Records for Debt and Equity Capital

Organizations keep separate subsidiary records for the Notes Payable, Bonds Payable, and Capital Stock accounts. When they are noncomputerized, accountants call them subsidiary ledgers; when computerized, they are master files.

Notes Payable Ledger. If an organization has many notes outstanding, it may have a notes payable ledger. This ledger (or master file) is the subsidiary ledger for the Notes Payable account. It contains one page or record for each note outstanding. The record identifies the note, its holder, its maturity, its interest rate, and the original and current balance.

Bondholders Ledger. The bondholders ledger maintains records of all the individuals or organizations that have purchased bonds. These records show their names and addresses, the bond certificate number, and the face value of the bonds they own. They provide the information necessary to issue interest checks.

A company with one outstanding bond issue has only one bondholders ledger. A large company has a separate bondholders ledger for each bond issue. Each is a subsidiary ledger for one Bonds Payable account. Frequently an organization employs a bank, called the *independent trustee,* to maintain the bondholders ledger.

Stockholders Ledger. This file maintains data on all individuals or organizations who have purchased stock. It contains their names, addresses, the stock certificate number, the date the certificate was issued, and the number of shares. The stockholders ledger contains the information necessary to issue dividend checks.

A company maintains a separate stockholders ledger for each class of capital stock. Small corporations that issue only common stock have only one stockholders ledger. Larger companies may have multiple ledgers. Companies whose stock is traded on stock exchanges employ banks to maintain their stockholders ledgers. A bank performing this service is a *stock transfer agent.*

Controls for Debt and Equity Transactions

The most important control policies and procedures affecting debt and equity transactions concern authorization procedures for the transactions and segregation of duties over them.

Controls for Bank Loans. An organization should have formal procedures for authorizing bank loans. The level of required management approval depends on the organization and the amount of the loan. Written company policies specify the level of approval required for loans of different amounts and durations.

Most organizations allow an appropriate officer, such as a treasurer, to authorize short-term loans. The board of directors should authorize large or long-term loans. The controller, as head of the accounting department, is responsible for recording the transactions.

Controls for Bond Issues. The best control for bond issues is the use of an independent trustee. The trustee, a large bank, is experienced in handling these transactions. It has employees trained in processing bonds efficiently and safely. Most organizations that issue bonds consider the use of an independent trustee cost-beneficial.

An independent trustee performs four functions: It maintains the bondholders ledger, changing the records as bonds are sold, traded, or recalled. It has custody of bond certificates, issues new ones, and cancels old ones. It issues checks to bondholders representing interest payments and payments of principal at maturity. During the life of the bonds, the independent trustee represents the bondholders, ensuring that the borrowing organization complies with the terms of the bond indenture. The board of directors should authorize any new bond issue and the selection of the independent trustee.

Controls for Stock Issues. Large corporations usually employ an independent registrar and a stock transfer agent. Large banks provide these services which are similar to those that independent trustees provide for bond issues. A single bank may serve in both capacities.

The independent registrar represents the interest of the stockholders. It monitors stock issues and determines that they do not exceed the quantities allowed by the corporate charter or bylaws. It verifies that all transactions in capital stock have been properly authorized by the board of directors or by vote of the stockholders.

The stock transfer agent maintains the stockholders ledger. It records changes in stock ownership, maintains custody of blank stock certificates, issues certificates to new owners, and cancels certificates when shares are sold. It also issues dividend checks to stockholders.

Smaller companies often do not use independent registrars and transfer agents. These companies should assign responsibilities so that no one individual has custody of blank stock certificates, signs the certificates, and maintains the stockholders ledger. The person who maintains the stockholders ledger should not sign dividend checks. All stock certificates and dividend checks should be prenumbered.

Often the treasurer of a small company maintains the stock certificates and signs dividend checks. The president signs stock certificates and the controller maintains the stockholders ledger.

Because debt and equity transactions are relatively infrequent and represent large amounts, top management usually monitors them closely. Illustration 21–2 summarizes controls over these transactions.

ILLUSTRATION 21–2 Controls over Debt and Equity Transactions

Bank Loans	*Bond Issues*	*Stock Issues*
	Segregation of Duties	
1. Authorization for bank loans separate from recordkeeping	1. Independent trustee	1. Independent registrar and stock transfer agent 2. Custody of certificates, signing certificates, and maintain stockholders ledger 3. Sign dividend checks and maintain stockholders ledger
	Control Practices	
1. Written, formal authorization procedures 2. Higher-level approvals for larger or longer-term loans	1. Board of directors' authorization	1. Board of directors' or stockholders' approval for all transactions 2. Board of directors authorizes all dividends 3. Prenumbered certificates

PROPERTY SYSTEMS

The purpose of a property system is to maintain an accurate record of all depreciable property, plant, and equipment. It also maintains records of annual and accumulated depreciation on this property.

Property System Transactions and Documents

A property system records three types of transactions: the acquisition, depreciation, and disposition of property.

Acquisition of Property. Companies use buildings and equipment when generating revenue. The expenditure cycle processes the transactions acquiring the property. Because of its long life, accountants treat property as an investment of capital. They record the acquisition of property in Property, Plant, and Equipment accounts. An example entry is:

Dr.	Buildings	xxx	
Cr.	Accounts Payable		xxx

Property acquisitions may represent significant amounts; thus, most organizations establish policies governing them. These policies require approval of all purchases; larger purchases require approvals at higher levels in the organization. For example, purchases of less than $10,000 may require a department head's approval. Those between $10,000 and $100,000 may require approval of an officer, and larger expenditures must be approved by the board of directors. Employees request the asset's acquisition and document its approval on a *capital acquisition request,* as shown in Illustration 21–3.

Sometimes companies construct property and equipment themselves. In this case, a *capital work order,* approved by top management or the board of directors, authorizes construction. Material requisitions and job tickets document the costs of construction. The completed capital work order documents the preceding journal entry.

Depreciation. Accountants use depreciation to approximate the consumption of property, plant, and equipment as the firm produces goods or services. For financial reporting, organizations compute depreciation using a method allowable by Generally Accepted Accounting Principles. For computing their U.S. federal income tax, they use a method allowable by law. Accountants add each year's depreciation expense to an account called Accumulated Depreciation with an entry such as:

Dr.	Depreciation Expense	xxx	
Cr.	Accumulated Depreciation–Buildings		xxx

Accountants usually make this entry at year-end while closing the books. A *journal voucher,* frequently a standard journal voucher, documents the entry.

ILLUSTRATION 21–3 A Capital Acquisition Request

Proposed acquisition ________	Probable amount $ ________
Nature: ☐ replacement ☐ addition ☐ modernization ☐ new project	☐ Proposed vendor(s): ________ ________ ☐ competitive bidding
Justification for proposed acquisition (submit supporting data and specifications as needed)	Return on investment analysis (for additions and new projects over $50,000) *Year* *Return* *Discount rate* *Discounted cash flow* Net cash flow ________ Profitability index ________

Prepared by ________ Date ________
Departmental approval ________ ________
Divisional approval ________ ________
Group approval ________ ________
Board approval ________ ________

Disposition of Property. Ultimately a business disposes of all of its revenue producing property. If the property has value they sell it; otherwise, they abandon it. The accounting entry recording this transaction may take several forms. The simplest form occurs when an asset is sold for its net book value:

Dr.	Cash	xxx	
Dr.	Accumulated Depreciation–Buildings	xxx	
Cr.	Buildings		xxx

More frequently, the organization records a gain or loss on the sale. In some cases, no cash is received; these require different accounting entries.

Because entries of this kind can take many different forms, accountants document them on journal vouchers. Many organizations authorize the disposition of property on a *retirement work order*. This document, which must be approved by top management, prevents employees from falsifying an entry on a journal voucher to cover the theft of an asset.

Property System Reports

Control Reports and Registers. A system produces control reports to allow employees to monitor the actions of the system. By reviewing a control report, an accountant or data control clerk determines that a data entry clerk entered the proper number or amounts of transactions in a file or that a computer program executed correctly.

Illustration 21–4 shows a control report used in a property system. It lists all deletions from property records made by a clerk and allows verification that these were made properly.

A register is a report listing the transactions of a specific type processed during a reporting period. It provides an audit trail by showing the changes that occurred in an account balance during the period. It also allows an accountant to review changes made to computer files by a program.

Illustration 21–5 contains a register used in the property system. Called an asset acquisition schedule, it shows the assets added to the Office Furniture account during the fiscal year. A similar register shows additions to other

ILLUSTRATION 21–4 A Property System Control Report

```
RUN DATE 08/25/91          T.L.JAMES ENTERPRISES                    PAGE  1
                                Fixed Assets
                         ASSET PURGE CONTROL REPORT

    CLASS:  DPEQP   DATA PROCESSING EQUIPMENT

    ASSET                                        ACQ          DIS
    CODE       DESCRIPTION/SERIAL NO             DATE         DATE
    ------     -------------------------       --------     --------

    4959       OKIDATA PRINTER                 04/01/82     07/01/87
               TSI32A

    TOTAL ASSETS PURGED        1

RUN DATE 08/25/91          T.L.JAMES ENTERPRISES                    PAGE  3
                                Fixed Assets
                         ASSET PURGE CONTROL REPORT

    TOTAL ASSETS PURGED        2

           *** END OF - ASSET PURGE CONTROL REPORT ***
```

ILLUSTRATION 21–5 A Property System Register

RUN DATE 08/25/91 — T.L.JAMES ENTERPRISES — PAGE 1
CLASS: FURN — Fixed Assets
OFFICE FURNITURE — Asset Acquisition Schedule — FOR FISCAL YEAR ENDING 12/31/90

CODE	DESCRIPTION/SERIAL NO	DEPT N/U	ACQ/DIS DATE	SALES PRICE	BOOK	METHOD/ ITC RATE	LIFE/ TEFRA	OPT SV	RBC ST-L	ORIG COST/ ACCUM DEP	SEC 179/ TEFRA ADJ	SALVAGE VAL
001356	SOFA	0	04/15/86	0.00	TAX	ACRS	10.0		0	1500.00	100.00	0.00
		N				10	1		0	0.00	70.00	
					FIN	ST-L	10.0		0	1500.00	100.00	100.00
	VENDOR IVAN ALLEN					10	0		0	0.00	0.00	
	LOCATION RECEPTIO				OPT	ACRS	10.0		0	1500.00	100.00	0.00
						10	1		0	0.00	70.00	
CLASS: OFFICE FURNITURE				0.00				TAX		9000.00	600.00	0.00
TOTALS										0.00	420.00	
NUMBER OF ASSETS: 2								FIN		9000.00	100.00	600.00
										0.00	0.00	
								OPT		9000.00	600.00	0.00
										0.00	420.00	
REPORT				0.00				TAX		9000.00	600.00	0.00
TOTALS										0.00	420.00	
NUMBER OF ASSETS: 2								FIN		9000.00	100.00	600.00
										0.00	0.00	
								OPT		9000.00	600.00	0.00
										0.00	420.00	

*** END OF - Asset Acquisition Schedule ***

property, plant, and equipment accounts. Property systems also produce asset disposition schedules that show disposals of property, plant, and equipment.

Special Purpose Reports. Property systems produce two special purpose reports: property listings and depreciation schedules.

Property Listing. The property listing identifies the location of all property, plant, and equipment. Employees produce this report periodically and use it when conducting a physical count of property. A property listing provides detail that supports the balances in Property, Plant, and Equipment accounts. Illustration 21–6 contains a property listing.

Depreciation Schedule. The depreciation schedule shows annual depreciation amounts for items of property. In a manual system, an accountant prepares this report for each item when it is acquired. Periodically a batch processing system prints this schedule for all property. In an on-line real-time system, an employee can obtain this information for a specific item of interest and display it on a terminal or print it in a report.

The depreciation schedule allows an accountant or computer program to determine the proper amount of annual depreciation each year without recalculating it. Illustration 21–7 shows a depreciation schedule.

ILLUSTRATION 21–6 A Property Listing

T.L.JAMES ENTERPRISES
Fixed Assets
PROPERTY CONTROL REPORT

LOCATION RANGE HILL S TO TLJ

LOCATION	ASSET CODE	ASSET DESCRIPTION	SERIAL NUMBER	VENDOR NAME	GL DEPT	ACQ DATE
HILL ST	6423	[illegible] RESIDENTIAL OFFICE PARK		HOLMES & JONES	0	01/10/83
RECEPTIO	001356	SOFA		IVAN [illegible]	0	04/15/86
TLJ	000034	1985 CADILLAC SEVILLE	J371421	JONES CADILLAC	0	12/01/84
TLJ	000036	1987 TOYOTA CELICA SUPRA	J10535	[illegible] TOYOTA	0	03/01/89
TLJ	000047	1991 MERCURY GRAN MARQUIS	[illegible]10773	[illegible] LINC-MERC	0	01/01/91
TLJ	6100	TLJ OFFICE BUILDING		JS SMITH & ASSC	0	02/01/81

*** END OF - PROPERTY CONTROL REPORT ***

Property System Records

Noncomputerized Records. A noncomputerized property system maintains a *property ledger* containing one page or card for each depreciable asset owned by the business. It is a subsidiary ledger for the Property, Plant, and Equipment account in the general ledger. Each page discloses an identifying number for the asset, its description, location, date of acquisition, and cost. A depreciation schedule for the asset is usually on this page.

Computerized Records. In a computerized system, the equivalent of the property ledger is the *property master file,* which contains one record for each depreciable asset. Illustration 21–8 shows the contents of a property master record.

The system's designers develop a coding structure that assigns to each piece of property a unique identifying number, the ASSET-ID-NUMBER. It allows the property system to distinguish this asset from others and improves control over assets. The master record also shows the cost center that is assigned responsibility for the asset and the account classification code for the asset in the general ledger.

ILLUSTRATION 21–7 A Depreciation Schedule

```
RUN DATE 08/25/91                       T.L.JAMES ENTERPRISES                                     PAGE  1
CLASS:  BUILD                                Fixed Assets
        BUILDINGS                    EXPANDED DEPRECIATION SCHEDULE          FOR FISCAL YEAR ENDING 12/31/90

--------------ASSET--------------  B/  ACQ/DIS               SALVAGE VAL/   SECTION   TEFRA BASIS   ORIGINAL   METH/
CODE        DESCRIPTION            U    DATE     ORIG COST   SALES PRICE      179     ADJUSTMENT     BASIS      LF
------  -------------------------  -  --------  ----------  -----------  ----------  ----------  ----------  -----

6100    TLJ OFFICE BUILDING        B  02/01/81  400000.00         0.00        0.00    14000.00   386000.00  AST-L
                                                                  0.00                                       35.0

    YR...AMOUNT...  YR...AMOUNT...  YR...AMOUNT...  YR...AMOUNT...  YR...AMOUNT...  YR...AMOUNT...  YR...AMOUNT...
    81   11500.00   82   11500.00   83   11500.00   84   11500.00   85   11500.00   86   11500.00   87   11500.00
    88   11500.00   89   11500.00   90   11500.00   91   11500.00   92   11500.00   93   11500.00   94   11500.00
    95   11500.00   96   11500.00   97   11500.00   98   11500.00   99   11500.00   00   11500.00   01   11500.00
    02   11500.00   03   11500.00   04   11500.00   05   11500.00   06   11500.00   07   11500.00   08   11500.00
    09   11500.00   10   11500.00   11    7720.00   12    7720.00   13    7720.00   14    7720.00   15    7720.00

--------------ASSET--------------  B/  ACQ/DIS               SALVAGE VAL/   SECTION   TEFRA BASIS   ORIGINAL   METH/
CODE        DESCRIPTION            U    DATE     ORIG COST   SALES PRICE      179     ADJUSTMENT     BASIS      LF
------  -------------------------  -  --------  ----------  -----------  ----------  ----------  ----------  -----

6423    DOW RESIDENTIAL OFFICE PARK B  01/10/83  250000.00        0.00        0.00        0.00   250000.00  ACRS
                                                                  0.00                                       15.0

    YR...AMOUNT...  YR...AMOUNT...  YR...AMOUNT...  YR...AMOUNT...  YR...AMOUNT...  YR...AMOUNT...  YR...AMOUNT...
    83   30000.00   84   25000.00   85   22500.00   86   20000.00   87   17500.00   88   15000.00   89   15000.00
    90   15000.00   91   15000.00   92   12500.00   93   12500.00   94   12500.00   95   12500.00   96   12500.00
    97   12500.00

                            *** END OF - EXPANDED DEPRECIATION SCHEDULE ***
```


ILLUSTRATION 21–8 Contents of a Property Master Record

ASSET-ID-NUMBER*
ASSET-DESCRIPTION
RESPONSIBILITY-CODE
CUSTODIAN
LOCATION
GENERAL-LEDGER-CLASS
ACQUISITION-DATE
COST
DEPRECIATION-METHOD
DEPRECIATION-RATE
SALVAGE-VALUE
USEFUL-LIFE
ACCUMULATED-DEPRECIATION
VENDOR

*Denotes the primary key.

Property Transaction Processing

Manual Processes. Illustration 21–9 shows a document flowchart of manual procedures for a property system.

When property is acquired, an accounting clerk adds a page recording it to the property ledger. Either a voucher or a completed capital work order documents the acquisition. The clerk records its cost and depreciation method and calculates

ILLUSTRATION 21–9 Manual Procedures for Property

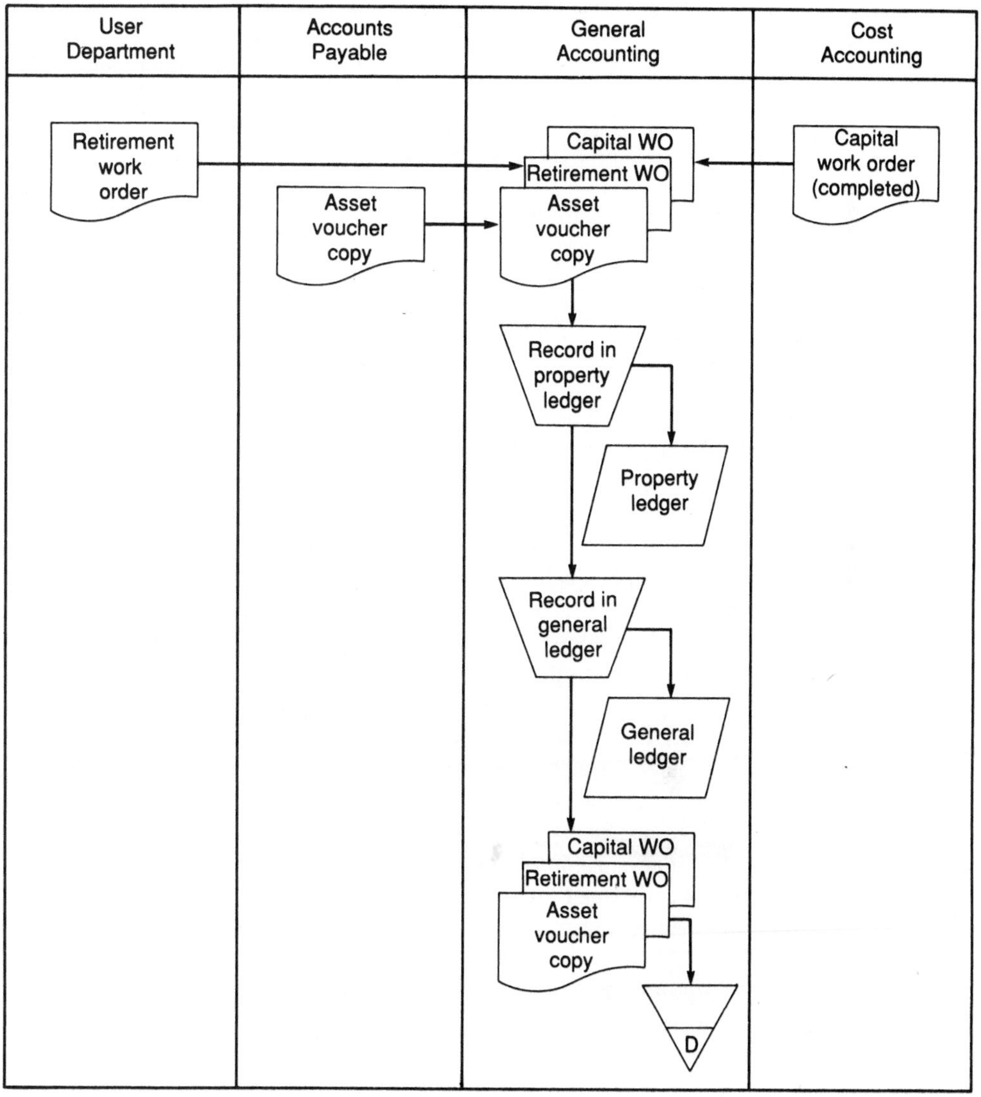

ILLUSTRATION 21–10 Property System Control Procedures

Property System Controls

Segregation of Duties

1. Purchasing and accounts payable

Control Practices

1. Request for capital asset acquisition
   a. Initiated by user department
   b. Approved
   c. Approved by higher-level management as needed
2. Purchase order
   a. Prepared only on receipt of request for capital asset acquisition
   b. Prenumbered
   c. Vendor based on competitive bidding, if new project
   d. Checked for price, specifications, terms
3. Capital asset
   a. Receiving/inspection report prepared as asset is received
   b. Receiving report is prenumbered
   c. Accepted by user department
4. Voucher package
   a. Invoice sent directly to accounts payable
   b. Prenumbered
   c. Supported by request for capital asset acquisition, purchase order, receiving/inspection report, and original invoice
   d. Verified

the depreciation schedule. The clerk then prepares a journal voucher recording the acquisition in the general ledger.

A retirement work order documents the disposition of property, which a clerk records in the property and general ledgers.

Control Procedures. Illustration 21–10 summarizes the important control procedures for a property system. These procedures are similar to controls over purchase transactions in the expenditure cycle. However, for the purchase of property, a capital acquisition request (rather than a purchase requisition) initiates the procedures. As with other purchases, the important segregation of duties is between the purchasing department, which authorizes the transaction, and the accounts payable department, which maintains the accounting records.

Computerized Processes. Illustration 21–11 contains system flowcharts showing a batch property system. In this system, accounts payable clerks code

ILLUSTRATION 21–11 A Property Application

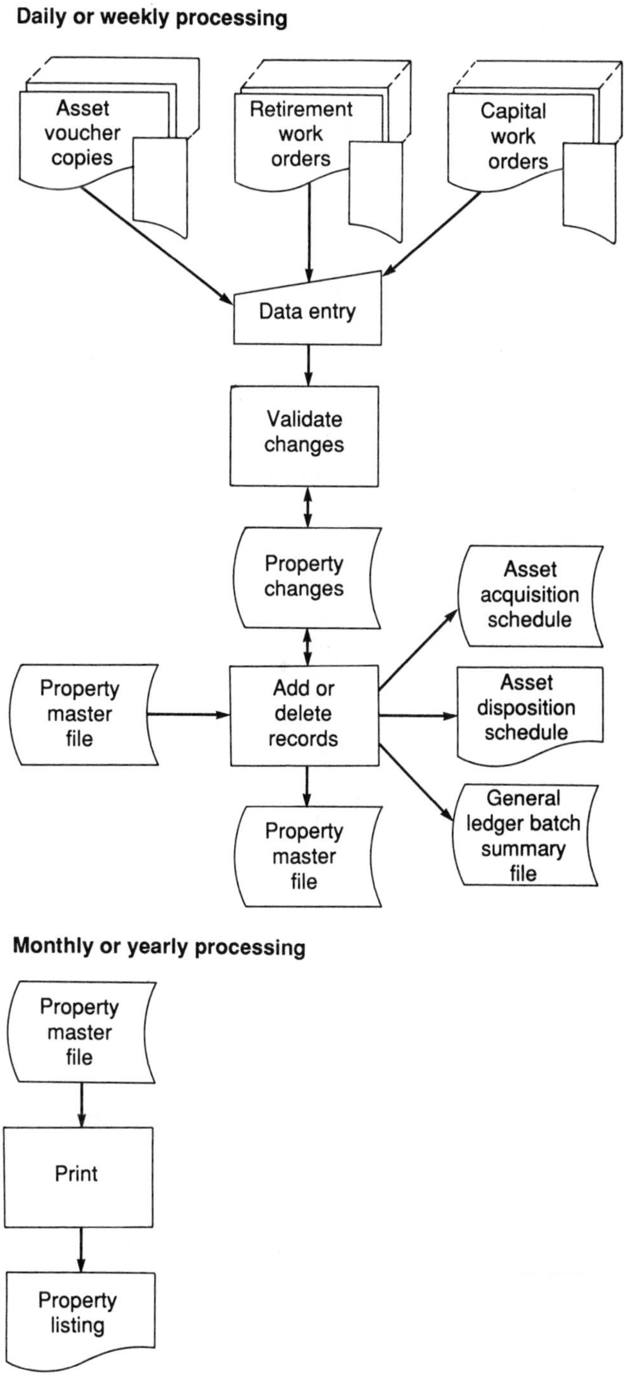

vouchers for depreciable assets with the proper account numbers. They forward batched copies of these vouchers to data entry. Employees complete capital work orders for constructed assets. These and retirement work orders constitute the transaction file that provides inputs to the system. The system posts these transactions to the property master file, produces asset transaction registers, and produces summary records for the general ledger batch summary file. Annually or monthly, another program prints the property listing.

Many computerized systems receive inputs from the voucher system in the form of voucher records rather than documents. A program in the voucher system examines records added to the voucher file and identifies those recording debits to property accounts. The program places copies of these records in a batch file that is an input to the property system. This system is more reliable than one requiring human intervention.

Application Controls. These include control procedures applied to the input, the processing, and the output of computerized procedures. Illustration 21–12 shows application controls in the property system. They include completeness and validity tests, control totals, and run-to-run controls.

ILLUSTRATION 21–12 Application Controls in the Property System

Type	*Program*	*Control Procedure*
Input	Validate transactions	**Completeness test.** Verify that all master file fields are completed on the voucher or capital work order records. **Validity test.** Verify that an account number represents a valid asset account.
Processing	Add or delete records	**Record count.** Program verifies that the number of changes to the property master file = number of vouchers + number of retirement orders + number of capital work orders. **Control total.** Program verifies that total debits to general ledger batch summary file = batch total of vouchers + batch total of capital work orders. **Control total.** Program verifies that total credits to general ledger batch summary file = total of retirement work orders.
Output	Add or delete records	**Control total.** Data control group verifies that total on asset acquisition schedule = total of vouchers + total of capital work orders. **Control total.** Data control group verifies that total on asset disposition schedule = total of retirement work orders.

THE JOURNAL ENTRY AND FINANCIAL REPORTING SYSTEMS

The purpose of the journal entry system is to post to the general ledger transactions that are not processed by other application systems. These include transactions recording the acquisition of capital from the issue of stocks and bonds, obtaining cash from bank loans, and the acquisition and disposition of property.

The purpose of the financial reporting system is to close the general ledger and to produce financial statements and performance reports. It uses the journal entry system to record adjustments made to the accounts during the closing process. This is why some accountants identify the two systems together as the *general ledger system*.

Journal Entry and Financial Reporting Transactions

Businesses record transactions in the general ledger using three types of accounting entries: summaries of high-volume transactions, low-volume transactions, and closing entries.

Summaries of High-Volume Transactions. High-volume transactions are those a business has many times each day; they include sales, purchases, and manufacturing transactions. The accounting system records each of these with an accounting entry.

In computer-based systems, application systems process these high-volume transactions. For example, the application systems in the revenue cycle process sales transactions. These application systems are the order entry, shipping, billing, and cash receipts systems. Application systems in the expenditure cycle process purchases transactions, and those in the conversion cycle process those related to manufacturing. Illustration 21–13 lists the applications in these cycles that produce summaries of high-volume transactions.

ILLUSTRATION 21–13 Applications that Produce Summaries of High-Volume Transactions

Transaction Type	*Transaction Cycle*	*Applications*
Sale	Revenue	Billing Cash receipts
Purchase	Expenditure	Voucher Cash disbursement
Production	Conversion	Inventory Cost accounting
Payroll	Conversion	Payroll

In a manual system, the equivalents of application systems are the special journals and subsidiary ledgers. Each day a bookkeeper totals the accounting entries made in special journals and posts these summaries to a ledger. In a computer-based system, an application system summarizes the results of its transactions in computer records daily and adds these records to the *general ledger batch summary* file. Then a journal entry system creates journal entries from these records and posts them to the computerized general ledger.

Low-Volume Transactions. Low-volume transactions include those incurred to record changes in debt and equity capital, to dispose of depreciable property, and to pay taxes. They also include accruals and deferrals made as part of the closing process. These include interest accruals, bad debt accruals, and accruals for warranty expenses.

Because a low-volume transaction occurs infrequently, accountants do not develop special journals or application systems for them. Instead, in a manual system they make these entries in the general journal. In a computer-based system, they make them using the journal entry system.

Accountants record a low-volume transaction on a journal voucher. A data entry clerk enters data from the journal voucher in the journal entry system. For repetitive low-volume transactions such as accruals, accountants create standard journal vouchers.

Illustration 21–14 shows a journal voucher. A clerk codes one entry on each line of the form. Each line contains space for an account description, an account code, a responsibility code, and an amount. With this system, credits to an account are shown by placing the amount in parentheses. Other systems use an entry code to designate debits and credits. This journal voucher form also has space for a data control clerk to enter a batch number for the set of transactions.

Closing Entries. Accountants make closing entries when preparing the financial statements. In a manual system, bookkeepers use a general ledger account called Income Summary. They credit each expense account, producing a zero balance, and debit Income Summary for equal amounts. They also debit each revenue account and credit Income Summary. After this procedure, the balance in Income Summary is Net Income.

In a computer-based system, a computer program in the financial reporting system makes this entry and uses the balances in the general ledger to produce financial statements. It transfers balances from revenue and expense accounts into the general ledger income summary account. In many systems, it also calculates and records depreciation, allocates overhead to responsibility centers, and posts final adjustments to the general ledger.

Another function of the financial reporting system is to prepare the general ledger for the next reporting period. Many computerized general ledgers record

ILLUSTRATION 21–14 A Journal Voucher

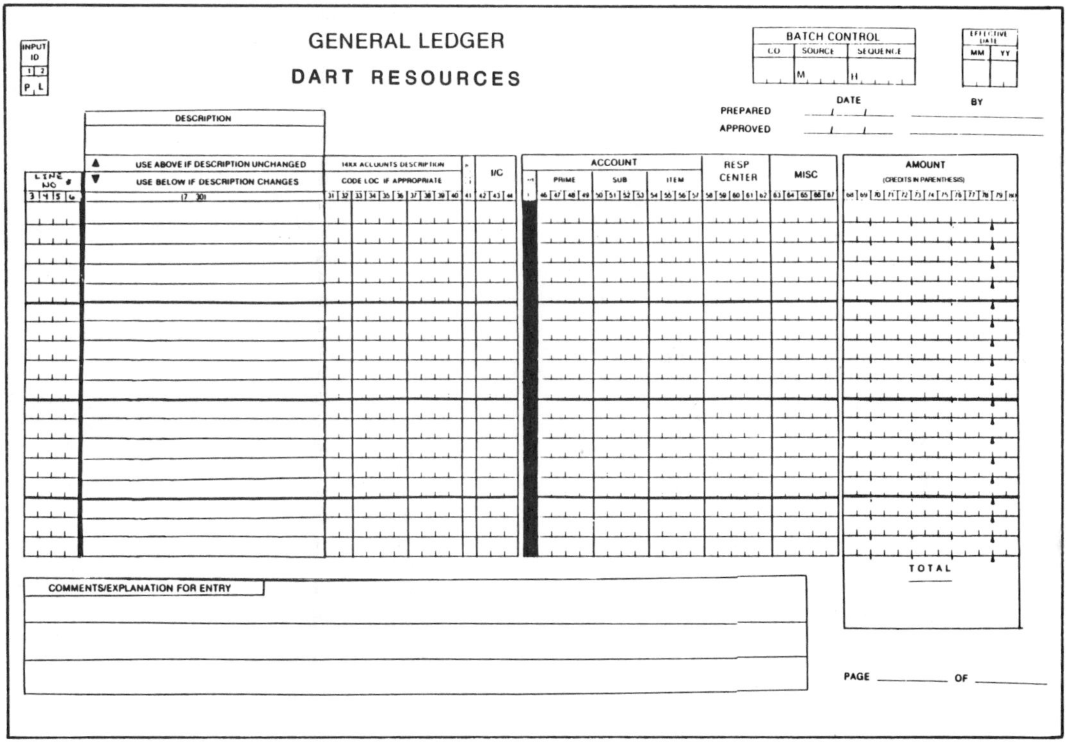

balances for both the current period and the prior period. In these, the financial reporting system transfers current period balances to the prior period fields. This system also may make reversing journal entries for accrual and deferral accounts.

Journal Entry and Financial Reports

Journal entry and financial reports include control reports, registers, financial statements, and performance reports.

Control Reports and Registers. Illustration 21–15 contains a control report produced by a journal entry system. It lists the summary entries from other applications contained in a general ledger batch summary file. An accounting clerk reviews it to ensure that the system properly summarized these entries.

ILLUSTRATION 21–15 A Control Report

RUN DATE 06/30/86 T. L. James Enterprises PAGE 1
General Ledger
BATCH: 38 Transfer Summary Journals Control Report

ACCOUNT	DESCRIPTION	REFERENCE	SC	DATE	AMOUNT	ACTION
11100			R	06/30/86	21,184.71	*** TRANSFERRED ***
21400			R	06/30/86	903.11-	*** TRANSFERRED ***
30101			R	06/30/86	3,701.00-	*** TRANSFERRED ***
30102			R	06/30/86	16,031.60-	*** TRANSFERRED ***
30104			R	06/30/86	549.00-	*** TRANSFERRED ***

TOTAL TRANSACTIONS ENTERED = 5
TOTAL DEBITS = 21,184.71
TOTAL CREDITS = 21,184.71-

DIFFERENCE = 0.00

*** END OF - Transfer Summary Journals Control Report ***

Illustration 21–16 shows a transaction register that lists all transactions posted to general ledger account number 102 during a reporting period. Using this, an accountant or auditor can explain the changes in the account balance during the period.

Financial Statements. The reports in the financial reporting cycle are the trial balance, the balance sheet, the income statement, and the statement of cash flows. Examples of some of these familiar reports are in Illustrations 21–17, 21–18, and 21–19.

Performance Reports. Performance reports disclose performance measures for managers in the organization. Usually these performance measures include those revenues and costs that a manager can control. Performance reports disclose actual amounts, budgeted amounts, and their difference (called a variance). When the organization uses responsibility accounting, the financial reporting system produces performance reports for each responsibility center. (Chapter 2 contains several examples of these reports.)

ILLUSTRATION 21–16 A Register

RUN DATE — T. L. James Enterprises — PAGE 1

General Ledger

Transaction Register

SC	BATCH	REF	DATE	DESCRIPTION	ACCOUNT	AMOUNT
1	3	1554	06/09/86	HARWICK ASSOC.	102	625.42
1	1	501	06/05/86	JOHN MOODY	102	625.00
1	1	502	06/05/86	S.W. WELLS & SONS	102	582.40
1	1	503	06/05/86	DANIEL B. JOHNSON	102	3,640.98
1	1	6342	06/05/86	SALE - JAMES WILSON	102	765.00
1	3	643	06/09/86	SALE - C. D. JAMES & CO.	102	2,678.90

SOURCE TRANSACTIONS LISTED = 12
SOURCE DEBITS = 13,619.10
SOURCE CREDITS = 0.00

DIFFERENCE = 13,619.10

*** CONTROL TOTALS ***	CONTROL	ACTUAL
TRANSACTION COUNT	69	69
TRANSACTION TOTAL	0.00	0.00

*** END OF - Transaction Register ***

ILLUSTRATION 21–17 A Trial Balance

RUN DATE — T. L. James Enterprises — PAGE 1

General Ledger

DETAIL TRIAL BALANCE — PERIOD ENDING 08/30/86

ACCOUNT NUMBER	ACCOUNT DESCRIPTION	BEGINNING BALANCE	TRANSACTION DESCRIPTION	DATE	S	REFERENCE	AMOUNT	ENDING BALANCE
102	CASH OPERATING	19,320.99						
			JOHN MOODY	06/05	1	501	625.00	
			S.W. WELLS & SONS	06/05	1	502	582.40	
			DANIEL B. JOHNSON	06/05	1	503	3,640.98	
			SALE - JAMES WILSON	06/05	1	6342	765.00	
			SALE - BAKER HARDWARE	06/05	1	7940	1,256.80	
			SALE - P. J. YOUNG	06/09	1	96	635.00	
			SALE - C. D. JAMES & CO.	06/09	1	643	2,678.90	
			SALE - REYNOLDS & BAXTER	06/09	1	823	215.60	
			ALLEN & JONES	06/09	1	866	1,565.00	
			HARWICK ASSOC.	06/09	1	1554	625.42	
			DEPT 2 SALARIES 6/15/86	06/14	2	758-762	2,200.00-	
			DEPT 1 SALARIES 6/15/86	06/14	2	752-757	2,600.00-	
							4,153.54 *	23,474.53 *
109	CASH ON HAND	459.15					0.00 *	459.15 *
	TOTAL DEBITS	226,589.31					39,890.26	266,479.57
	TOTAL CREDITS	226,589.31-					39,890.26-	266,479.57-
	*** DIFFERENCE	0.00-**					0.00 **	0.00-**

*** CONTROL TOTALS ***	CONTROL	ACTUAL
TRANSACTION COUNT	69	69
TRANSACTION TOTAL	0.00	0.00

ILLUSTRATION 21–18 A Balance Sheet

RUN DATE — T. L. James Enterprises — General Ledger — BALANCE SHEET — AS OF 06/30/86 — PAGE 1

	** THIS MONTH THIS YEAR **			** THIS MONTH LAST YEAR **		
ASSETS						
CURRENT ASSETS						
CASH	24,051.12			14,670.10		
ACCOUNTS RECEIVABLE	52,605.18			22,331.80		
PREPAID EXPENSES	616.10			310.00		
INVENTORY	25,020.99			18,495.33		
TOTAL CURRENT ASSETS		102,293.39			55,807.23	
FIXED ASSETS						
FURNITURE & EQUIPMENT	4,307.87			2,445.00		
ACCUMULATED DEPRECIATION	1,686.00-			150.00-		
DEPOSITS	750.00			575.00		
TOTAL FIXED ASSETS		3,371.87			2,870.00	
TOTAL ASSETS			105,665.26			58,677.23
LIABILITIES & CAPITAL						
CURRENT LIABILITIES						
ACCOUNTS PAYABLE	31,606.52			13,205.40		
TAXES PAYABLE	971.74-			1,190.11		
TOTAL CURRENT LIABILITIES		30,634.78			14,395.51	
LONG TERM LIABILITIES						
NOTE PAYABLE-BANK	1,400.00			2,600.00		

ILLUSTRATION 21–19 An Income Statement

RUN DATE — T. L. James Enterprises — General Ledger — INCOME STATEMENT — FOR PERIOD ENDED 06/30/86 — PAGE 1

	THIS YEAR				BUDGET	LAST YEAR	
RATIO: INCOME	THIS MONTH	RATIO	4 MONTHS	RATIO	4 MONTHS	THIS MONTH	4 MONTHS
INCOME							
SALES	19,284.34	99.7	148,523.70	102.3	135,600.00-	18,194.90	104,719.61
SERVICE	60.00	0.3	2,133.00	1.5	9,704.00-	60.00	9,114.43
RETURNS & ALLOWANCES	0.00	0.0	5,500.00-	3.8-	1,880.00-	0.00	1,397.51-
NET SALES	19,344.34	100.0	145,156.70	100.0	147,184.00-	18,254.90	112,436.53
UTILITIES	[illegible]	[illegible]	[illegible]	[illegible]	[illegible]	[illegible]	[illegible]
ADVERTISING	4,742.00	24.5	55,964.04	38.6	65,440.00	4,742.00	46,484.92
INSURANCE	[illegible]	[illegible]	5,229.00	3.6	3,000.00	239.00	3,541.75
PROFESSIONAL FEES	100.00	0.5	[illegible]	8.1	15,400.00	0.00	1,244.10
DEPRECIATION	150.00	0.8	1,360.80	[illegible]			
INTEREST EXPENSE	0.00	0.0	214.00	0.1	[illegible]	13,273.90	61,165.76
MISC. EXPENSES	0.00	0.0	10.32	0.0	140.00		[illegible]
TOTAL EXPENSES	7,682.56	39.7	58,849.92	40.5	28,888.00	7,682.56	44,310.69
INCOME BEFORE TAXES	6,680.78	34.5	13,357.22	9.2	259,912.00-	5,591.34	16,855.07
INCOME TAXES	0.00	0.0	3,500.00	2.4	0.00	0.00	2,000.00
NET INCOME	6,680.78	34.5	9,857.22	6.8	259,912.00-	5,591.34	14,855.07

The journal entry and financial reporting systems process three types of transactions and produce various reports. The next section describes the forms taken by the accounting records.

Journal Entry and Financial Reporting Records

Manual systems keep accounting records in books, card files, and filing cabinets. In addition, computer-based systems use computer files or a data base management system.

Noncomputerized Records. A manual system keeps its records entirely in noncomputerized form. The general journal, any special journals, the general ledger, and any subsidiary ledgers are books or card files. Chapter 1 of this text reviews these records.

Computerized Records. A computer-based system keeps accounting records in computer readable form. These consist of five computer files.

General Ledger Master File. The general ledger master file is the computerized equivalent of the general ledger, containing one record for each account in the chart of accounts. The record key is the account number, and the record shows the current balance in the account. In some systems, the record also shows a budgeted balance, a balance for the previous reporting period, and a balance for the same period in the previous year.

Illustration 21–20 shows the contents of a general ledger master record. When a data base management system is used, this illustration shows the contents of the subschema for the journal entry and financial reporting applications.

General Ledger Batch Summary File. The general ledger batch summary file is a sequential file. It contains transactions that, after further processing, are posted to the general ledger master file.

ILLUSTRATION 21–20 Contents of a General Ledger Master Record

ACCOUNT-CODE*
ACCOUNT-NAME
BALANCE-CURRENT-MONTH
BALANCE-CURRENT-QUARTER
BALANCE-CURRENT-YEAR
BALANCE-LAST-YEAR-JANUARY
BALANCE-LAST-YEAR-FEBRUARY
⋮
BALANCE-LAST-YEAR-DECEMBER

*Denotes the primary key.

The transactions in this file are summaries of high-volume transactions processed in other application systems. For example, many companies close their books monthly. In this case, the file contains one record summarizing sales transactions in each responsibility center for each workday during the month. It also contains summary transactions produced daily by other applications in the revenue, expenditure, and conversion cycles.

Illustration 21–21 shows the contents of this file. In a general ledger batch summary record, the TRANSACTION-CODE identifies the application system producing the record. The record contains two amount fields. TOTAL-AMOUNT is a control total that shows the total of the debits or credits for the summary transaction. POSTING-AMOUNT shows the amount of the entry in the account identified by ACCOUNT-CODE. At least two records should be in this file for each transaction code, date, and total amount. These records show each debit entry and each credit entry associated with the summary transaction.

Journal Voucher File. This transaction file contains one record for each transaction affecting the general ledger. Each contains the data field TRANSACTION-CODE that identifies its source.

Systems analysts designate transaction codes when creating the journal entry and financial reporting application systems. They identify each transaction code with a standard journal entry. For example, they may designate a transaction code of 1 to represent a billing transaction. Then a journal voucher record with a transaction code of 1 indicates a summary transaction recorded in the billing system. It causes the journal entry system to make general ledger entries of the form:

Dr.	Accounts Receivable	xxx	
Cr.	Sales		xxx
Dr.	Cost of Goods Sold	yyy	
Cr.	Inventory		yyy

The journal entry system creates the journal voucher file from two sources. An accountant may input them manually, or the system may create them from the records in the general ledger batch summary file. Illustration 21–22 shows the contents of a journal voucher record.

ILLUSTRATION 21–21 Contents of a General Ledger Batch Summary Record

TRANSACTION-CODE*
DATE*
TOTAL-AMOUNT
ACCOUNT-CODE
RESPONSIBILITY-CODE
POSTING-AMOUNT

*Denotes the primary key.

ILLUSTRATION 21–22 Contents of a Journal Voucher and Detail Posting Records

Journal Voucher Record	*Detail Posting Record*
JOURNAL-VOUCHER-NUMBER*	JOURNAL-VOUCHER-NUMBER*
DATE	ACCOUNT-CODE*
TOTAL-AMOUNT	DR-CR-CODE
TRANSACTION-CODE	POSTING-AMOUNT

*Denotes the primary key.

A journal voucher record contains only one amount—the total of the debits or credits in the transaction. The journal entry system uses this field as a control total. Another file, the detail posting file, contains records showing the amounts of entries in individual accounts.

Detail Postings File. The detail postings file contains data records showing the detailed entries in general ledger accounts. Each journal voucher record has associated with it two or more detail posting records. The journal entry system produces the records in this file from manual input or from the summary transactions in the general ledger batch summary file.

In the previous example, the journal entry system produces one journal voucher record and four detail posting records. It produces one detail posting record for each line in the journal entry. Illustration 21–22 shows the contents of a detail posting record. It contains data fields showing the account for the entry, its amount, and whether the entry is a debit or a credit.

Standard Postings File. Systems analysts create the standard postings file when developing the journal entry system. It shows the standard journal entries provided by the system; a transaction code identifies each standard journal entry.

For each transaction code, the standard postings file shows the required debit and credit accounts. The journal entry system reads a journal voucher record, identifies its transaction code, and then locates the code in the standard postings file. This file tells the journal entry system how many records to read from the detail postings file, which accounts these records affect, and whether to enter them as debits or credits in the account. The journal entry system then locates these detail posting records and posts their amounts to the general ledger master file.

Illustration 21–23 shows a standard postings file. This is how a computer-based system uses the transaction codes contained in the general ledger batch summary records.

You may wonder why a design team creates a separate standard postings file. After all, they could code this data as a table in a computer program and avoid using the file. However, using a standard postings file makes system changes simpler. If later an accountant decides to create another standard journal entry, the accountant creates another transaction code and adds this code and entry to the file. This avoids changes to the programs in the journal entry system.

ILLUSTRATION 21–23 A Standard Postings File

Transaction Code	*Transaction Type*	*Posting Instruction* *Dr/Cr*	*Account Code*	*Account Name*
1	Billing	Dr	xxxx	Accounts Receivable
		Cr	xxxx	Sales
		Dr	xxxx	Cost of Goods Sold
		Cr	xxxx	Finished Goods Inventory
2	Cash receipts	Dr	xxxx	Cash
		Cr	xxxx	Accounts Receivable
3	Issue material	Dr	xxxx	Work in Process Inventory
	to production	Cr	xxxx	Raw Material Inventory
4	Production	Dr	xxxx	Work in Process Inventory
	labor	Cr	xxxx	Wages Payable
5	Apply factory	Dr	xxxx	Work in Process Inventory
	overhead	Cr	xxxx	Factory Overhead
6	Complete	Dr	xxxx	Finished Goods Inventory
	production	Cr	xxxx	Work in Process Inventory
7	Receive vendor	Dr	——	asset or expense
	invoice	Cr	xxxx	Accounts Payable
8	Pay vendor	Dr	xxxx	Accounts Payable
	invoice	Cr	xxxx	Cash
0	Journal	Dr	——	any account
	voucher	Cr	——	any account

xxxx Indicates a general ledger account code from the chart of accounts. It is included in the standard postings file entry.
—— Indicates an account code that is not included in the standard postings file entry. The journal entry system obtains it from the general ledger batch summary record.

For accounting records used by computer-based applications in the financial cycle, a DBMS does not maintain these records in separate files. Instead, it places them in the data base at main storage locations known only to the DBMS software. It links a journal voucher record with its associated detail posting records. In a relational DBMS, each of these files is a separate relation.

Journal Entry and Financial Reporting Processing

Chapter 1 discusses how journal entry and financial reporting systems process transactions manually. In computerized systems, the same conceptual process is followed; however, procedures differ because different media are used to record the data.

Journal Entry System Processing. The journal entry system updates the general ledger master file with low-volume transactions and with summaries of high-volume transactions. Illustration 21–24 shows a journal entry system that allows on-line data entry by an accounting clerk.

In this system, a computer program uses the information in the standard posting file to match the records in the general ledger batch summary file into accounting transactions. For each transaction, this program creates a record in the journal voucher file, creates two or more records in the detail postings file, and removes the associated records from the general ledger batch summary file.

Unmatched summary records remain in the general ledger batch summary file and are reported on an error listing. A clerk in the general accounting department corrects these erroneous entries before producing financial statements.

An accountant enters low-volume transactions from journal vouchers at a terminal. The data entry program validates each journal voucher before adding records for it to the journal voucher and detail postings files. An update program posts the journal voucher transactions to the general ledger master file and produces a transaction register.

An organization usually executes the journal entry system monthly. This precedes execution of the second system in this transaction cycle, the financial reporting system.

Financial Reporting System Processing. Companies execute this application system only when they wish to produce financial statements. This may be monthly, quarterly, or annually, but it always follows execution of the journal entry system. Illustration 21–25 contains a system flowchart of a financial reporting system.

In a procedure many accountants call the first closing, the system prints a preliminary trial balance from the updated general ledger master file. Accountants then review this trial balance.

The accountants examine the account balances and identify inconsistencies or incorrect amounts for correction. They also identify necessary accruals or deferrals and create journal vouchers documenting these changes.

Accountants or data entry clerks enter these journal vouchers, creating new journal voucher and detail posting files. A computer program posts these to the general ledger master file. Then in the second closing, the system produces a final trial balance and the financial statements. Finally, the system prepares the general ledger master file for the next reporting period.

Recording Depreciation

Accountants define depreciation as a systematic allocation of an asset's cost over its useful life. It is intended to represent the consumption of the asset during the conversion process. For this reason, many accountants consider depreciation to be a part of the conversion cycle.

ILLUSTRATION 21–24 A Journal Entry System

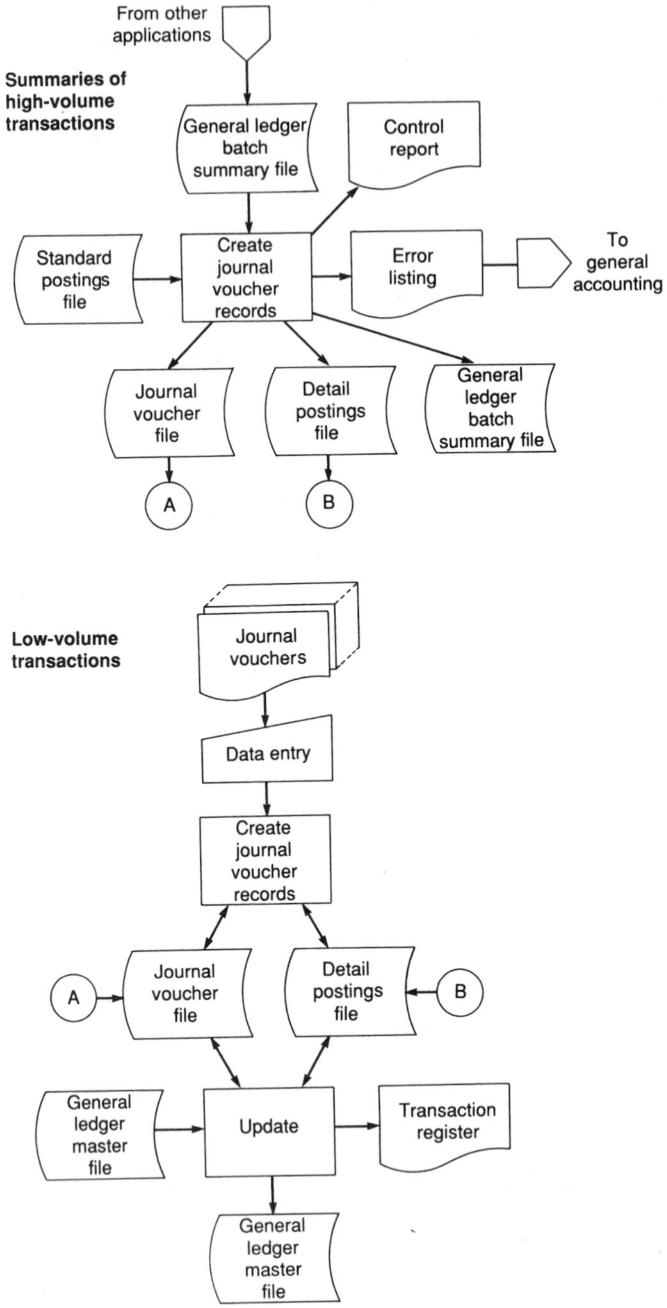

ILLUSTRATION 21–25 A Financial Reporting System

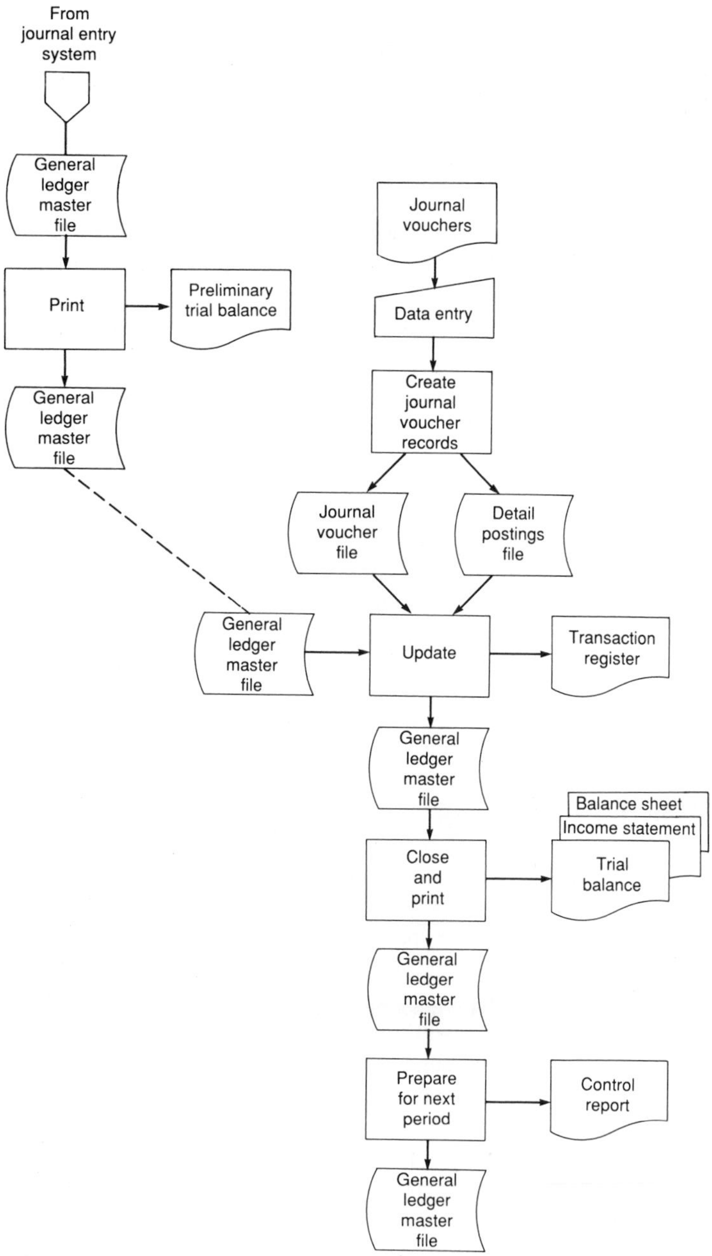

Most computer-based accounting systems record depreciation, not as this consumption occurs, but rather immediately prior to the closing process.

Manual Systems. In manual systems, accountants determine the amount of depreciation for each asset from the property ledger. They total this amount for each class of assets and create a journal voucher recording these totals in the general ledger. They also post the accumulated depreciation to individual records in the property ledger.

Computerized Systems. With a computerized system, a depreciation program performs these procedures. The program calculates depreciation expense for each asset, totals these for each asset class, and records this additional accumulated depreciation in the property master file. It then generates summary records for the general ledger batch summary file. These record depreciation expense in the general ledger master file.

Application Controls

Application controls are those control procedures that the design team places in an application system during its development. They prevent or detect errors when processing transactions. Illustration 21–26 shows how application controls are used in the financial cycle. These examples include completeness tests, consistency tests, record counts, and run-to-run controls.

Responsibility Accounting

Many organizations implement a financial reporting system that produces not only financial statements but also performance reports for responsibility centers. These responsibility accounting systems associate costs and revenues with the responsibility center that best controls them. They produce monthly reports comparing controllable revenues and costs with those budgeted for each responsibility center.

A financial reporting system that provides responsibility accounting uses two additional files and two added sets of computerized procedures.

Files. The files required by a responsibility accounting system are the general ledger batch summary file, the responsibility center file, and the budget file.

General Ledger Batch Summary File. The journal entry system uses this file that contains summary entries for the general ledger created by other application systems. These entries identify not only general ledger accounts but also the codes of the responsibility centers that create them. This allows the

ILLUSTRATION 21–26 Application Controls in the Journal Entry and Financial Reporting Systems

Type	*Program*	*System*	*Control Procedure*
Input	Create journal vouchers	Journal entry and financial reporting	**Completeness test.** Input program determines that all fields are provided. **Consistency test.** For any journal voucher, sum of debits = sum of credits.
Processing	Create journal vouchers	Journal entry	**Record count.** Number of records from input general ledger batch summary file = number of records in detail postings file + number of records in output general ledger batch summary file.
	Update	Journal entry and financial reporting	**Consistency test.** For each transaction, sum of debits = sum of credits.
Output	Create journal vouchers, Update	Journal entry	**Run-to-run control.** Data control group reconciles totals on control report, error listing, and transaction register.
	Print, Update, Close and Print	Financial reporting	**Run-to-run control.** Data control group uses transaction register to reconcile difference between first and second trial balances.

responsibility accounting system to summarize revenues and expenses by center.

Responsibility Center File. The responsibility center file contains one record for each center. During design of the system, analysts determine the data required on the performance report for each center and add a record to this file containing fields that accumulate this data. Data from general ledger batch summary records update these fields.

Budget File. The budget file is similar to the responsibility center file because it contains one record for each responsibility center. Likewise it contains, in the budget record, a field for each revenue and expense category on that responsibility center's performance report. The only difference is that these fields contain budgeted rather than actual amounts. Budgetary accountants enter these budgeted amounts following the development of the annual budget.

Computerized Processes. Processes in the responsibility accounting system include performance budgeting procedures and responsibility reporting procedures.

Performance Budgeting Procedures. Performance budgeting procedures translate overall organizational objectives into goals for each responsibility center. In this way, they provide a top-down information flow. They include the procedures to develop budget goals and those used to enter them in the budget file.

Managerial accounting courses discuss typical procedures for developing budget goals. Nonaccounting managers take part in this process. Some companies implement *participative* budgeting, in which individual managers take part in setting goals for their responsibility centers. Others use *authoritative* budgeting whereby top management sets all budget goals. Regardless of the procedures used to develop them, budgetary accountants summarize the goals in a budgetary document and enter them in the budget file.

The system design team creates special data entry programs that create budgetary transactions. Fields in these records identify the budgeted amount, the general ledger account, and the responsibility center. A transaction code identifies them as budgetary transactions. An update program posts these transactions to the budget file.

Responsibility Reporting Procedures. Responsibility reporting procedures summarize actual controllable revenues and costs by responsibility center and disclose them on performance reports. They provide a bottom-up information flow. Illustration 21–27 shows computerized responsibility reporting procedures.

The system sorts the general ledger batch summary records into responsibility code sequence. It then posts transactions from this file to the responsibility center file. Other programs then print performance reports by obtaining actual revenues and expenses from the responsibility center file and budgeted ones from the budget file. In this way, the system produces reports that compare actual and budgeted amounts for each responsibility center.

SUMMARY

This chapter describes how computer-based accounting systems process transactions in the financial cycle. This cycle processes two economic events, the acquisition of capital and the use of that capital to acquire property. The financial cycle also performs the financial reporting function.

The three application systems in the financial cycle are the property system, the journal entry system, and the financial reporting system. The property system processes transactions recording the acquisition of property. The journal entry system records the acquisition of capital, depreciation, and the disposition of property.

The journal entry and financial reporting systems process three types of transactions. They are summary transactions from other application systems,

ILLUSTRATION 21–27 Responsibility Reporting Procedures

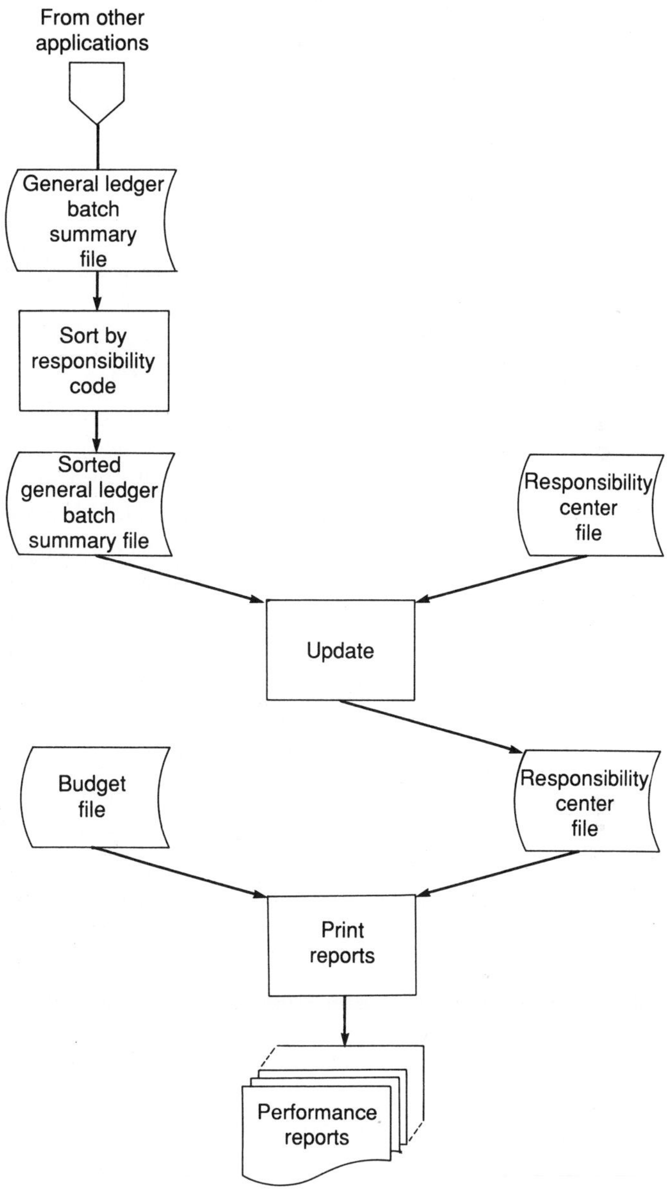

low-volume transactions documented by journal vouchers, and closing entries. The files used by these systems are the general ledger master file, the general ledger batch summary file, the journal voucher file, the detailed postings file, and the standard postings file.

With a responsibility accounting system, the financial reporting system uses responsibility center and budget files to produce performance reports.

KEY TERMS

bondholders ledger A subsidiary record containing data on all bondholders of an organization.

depreciation A systematic allocation of the costs of property, plant, and equipment over their useful lives. It is recorded by a journal entry made in the financial cycle.

first closing The process of printing a first trial balance; it occurs prior to the final accrual and deferral adjusting journal entries.

general ledger batch summary file A computer file that accumulates summary transactions from the revenue, expenditure, and conversion cycles for posting to the general ledger.

general ledger master record A record that exists for each account in the general ledger. It records the account number, description, and the balance in the account.

general ledger system A name applied by many people to the combination of the journal entry and financial reporting application systems.

high-volume transactions Accounting transactions that are processed by application systems in the revenue, expenditure, and conversion cycles. They are summarized by these applications for posting to the general ledger.

low-volume transactions Accounting transactions recorded by the journal entry system. They include the acquisition of capital, the disposal of property, the accrual of revenues and expenses, and the payment of taxes.

property master record A type of record that exists for each item of property, plant, and equipment in the organization. It identifies the property and serves as a record of its cost and accumulated depreciation.

retirement work order A document used to authorize and record the disposition of property.

second closing The process of printing a second trial balance and the financial statements after posting all adjusting journal entries.

standard postings file A computer file containing all the standard journal entries that have been defined for an accounting system.

stockholders ledger A subsidiary record containing information on all stockholders of a corporation.

Control Flowchart 21–1 Purchases of Property

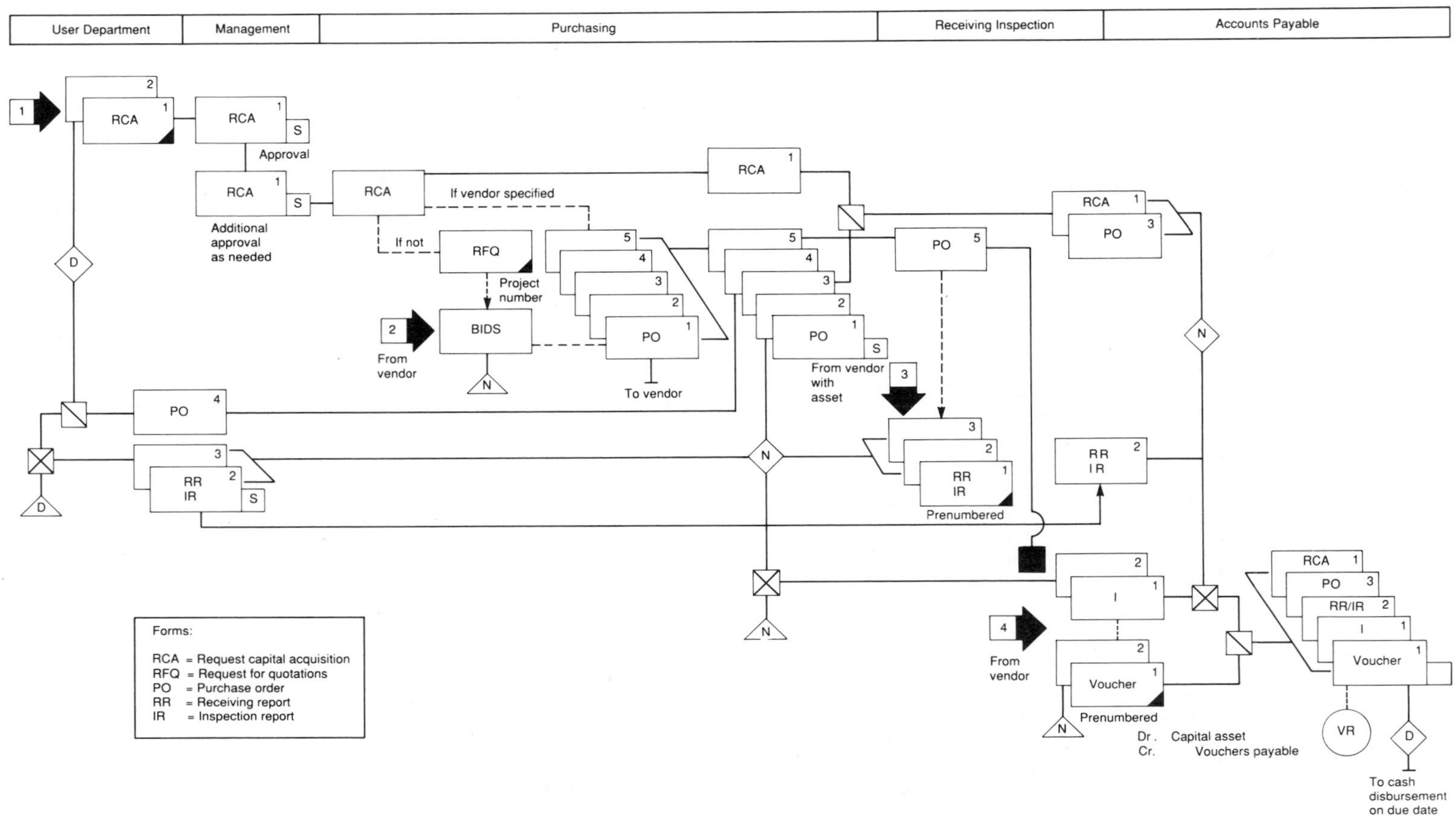

QUESTIONS

21–1. Which economic events produce transactions in the financial cycle?

21–2. Which three types of transactions are processed in the financial cycle?

21–3. Which applications systems not in this cycle are sources of summary entries for the financial cycle?

21–4. What is the purpose of a journal voucher? How is it used by applications in the financial cycle?

21–5. What are the purposes of these property system reports?
a. Control reports
b. Registers

21–6. What are some sources of the low-volume transactions processed in the financial cycle?

21–7. In a computerized accounting system, which data files are used in the financial cycle? Identify the purpose of each file.

21–8. Why do computerized systems use a separate file that contains standard journal entries?

21–9. In a computer-based system, which application systems are in the financial cycle? What is the purpose of each system?

21–10. What is depreciation? How is it recorded in an accounting system?

EXERCISES AND CASE

21–11. *LOW- AND HIGH-VOLUME TRANSACTIONS*

Application systems in the financial cycle process both low-volume transactions and summaries of high-volume transactions. Classify each accounting transaction in the following list as a low-volume or high-volume transaction:

a. Cash sale
b. Credit sale
c. Increase Allowance for Doubtful Accounts
d. Sell common stock
e. Acquire equipment
f. Receive bank loan
g. Reimburse payroll imprest account

21–12. *SUMMARY TRANSACTIONS*

Other application systems provide summaries of transactions to the applications in the financial cycle. The following application systems are described in this text. For each one, identify the accounts debited and credited by its summary transactions. (Hint: Refer to the transactions described in Chapters 18–20.)

a. Cash receipts
b. Cash disbursements
c. Cost accounting
d. Billing
e. Voucher

21–13. *STANDARD JOURNAL ENTRIES*

Standard journal entries are controls that prevent errors when recording transactions. Show how a standard journal entry would look for each of the following accounting transactions:

a. Record depreciation on a building.
b. Accrue wages owed for factory direct labor, but unpaid at year-end.
c. Write-off of an account receivable.
d. Summary transaction for one day's credit sales.
e. Pay dividends.

21–14. *JOURNAL VOUCHERS*

Of the transactions processed by a general ledger system, some originate from other application systems and some originate on a journal voucher. For each of the following transactions, decide if it originates with this document. If not, identify the application system that originates it.

a. Payment of property taxes.
b. Repayment of bank loan.
c. Payment of vendor invoice.
d. Sale of a piece of machinery.
e. Customer payment on account.

21–15. *TRANSACTION RECORDS*

Pine & Apple Company, a retailer, uses a computerized general ledger system. On July 15, 19xx, P&A had credit sales of $1,710. Its markup on inventory cost is 20 percent. The following account codes are from its chart of accounts.

Code	*Account name*
1100	Cash
1300	Accounts Receivable
1400	Inventory
2400	Equipment
3100	Accounts Payable
6100	Sales
7000	Cost of Goods Sold

Required:

Show the contents of all the following records that are necessary to make the preceding entry in P&A's computerized general ledger.

a. General ledger batch summary records
b. Journal voucher records
c. Detail posting records

21–16. ***TRANSACTION RECORDS***

IPL, Inc. is a manufacturing company with a computerized general ledger. On April 21, IPL received vendor invoices for material totaling $2,467. The material had been properly ordered and has been received. The following accounts are a part of IPL's chart of accounts.

Code	*Account name*
1100	Cash
1300	Accounts Receivable
1400	Raw Material Inventory
2400	Equipment
3100	Accounts Payable
6100	Sales
7000	Cost of Goods Sold

Required:

Show the contents of all the following records that are necessary to record the preceding transaction in IPL's general ledger:

a. General ledger batch summary records
b. Journal voucher records
c. Detail posting records

21–17. ***APPLICATION CONTROLS***

Illustration 21–26 shows some application controls that can be used in the journal entry and financial reporting systems of Illustrations 21–24 and 21–25. There are other application controls that can be used in these systems.

Required:

Identify one input control, one processing control, and one output control that can be used in these systems, in addition to those shown in Illustration 21–26.

21–18. ***SYSTEM FLOWCHART***

Illustration 21–24 contains a system flowchart of a journal entry system. This system shows on-line data entry and validation; that is, transactions are entered and validated one at a time.

Required:

Using standard flowchart symbols, show how the flowchart of the journal entry system would change if the system used batch processing data entry procedures.

21–19. ***PROPERTY SYSTEM***

Superior Company manufactures automobile parts for sale to the major U.S. automakers. You have been asked to review the internal controls over machinery and equipment and make recommendations for improvements where appropriate. You have obtained the following information:

Requests to purchase machinery and equipment are normally initiated by the supervisor in need of the asset. The supervisor discusses the proposed acquisition with the plant manager. A purchase requisition is submitted to the purchasing department when the plant manager is satisfied that the request is reasonable and that there is a remaining balance in the plant's share of the total corporate budget for capital acquisitions.

On receiving a purchase requisition for machinery or equipment, the purchasing department manager looks through the records for an appropriate supplier. A formal purchase order is then completed and mailed. When the machine or equipment is received, it is immediately sent to the user department for installation. This allows the economic benefits from the acquisition to be realized as early as possible.

The property, plant, and equipment ledger control accounts are supported by depreciation schedules organized by year of acquisition. These depreciation schedules are used to compute depreciation as a unit for all assets of a given type acquired in the same year. Standard rates, depreciation methods, and salvage values are used for each major type of fixed asset. These rates, methods, and salvage values were set 10 years ago during the company's initial year of operation.

When machinery or equipment is retired, the plant manager notifies the accounting department so that the appropriate entries can be made in the accounting records.

Since the company began operation there has been no reconciliation between the accounting records and the machinery and equipment on hand.

Required:

Identify the internal control weaknesses and recommend improvements in the property system of Superior Company.

(CMA Adapted)

21–20. ***STANDARD POSTINGS FILE***

The Metropolitan Summer Light Opera Festival was organized to stage four musical shows during the summer. Each show was to last three weeks, and a three-week accounting period was adopted. Selected transactions during the first weeks of the festival were as follows:

June 1 Paid rent for 12 weeks, beginning June 9. The weekly rent was $1,000.

2 Placed an advertisement in newspapers announcing the dates and programs of the festival. The expense was $200. Invoices were paid as received.

3 Granted the Theater Concessions, Inc., the privilege of selling refreshments during the 12-week festival in return for 5 percent of gross receipts payable within three days after the conclusion of each three-week period.

4 Purchased liability insurance for the 12-week period at a total cost of $600. Payment is to be made when the policy is received.

5 Four *Program Notes*, one for each show, were printed at a total cost of $400. Cash was paid.

7 Season tickets to the festival totaling $60,000 were sold. The season tickets permitted holders to attend each of the four shows on specified dates.

9 The first musical show, *The East Side Story*, had its premier. Cash sale of tickets to the performance amounted to $1,400.

28 The first musical show closed with this performance. Received a report from Theater Concessions, Inc., that total refreshment sales for the three-week period amounted to $20,000.

Required:

a. Assume that the festival uses a computerized accounting system. Decide whether each of the preceding transactions should be recorded:
   1. By an application system, or
   2. By a journal voucher in the general ledger system.

b. Design a standard postings file appropriate for the festival's system.

21–21. ***DEVELOPING A SYSTEM***

Two years ago, East Coast Utility Co. (ECUCO) concluded that its manual general ledger system was no longer meeting the needs of its users.[1] Management decided to develop a new computerized general ledger system that would improve the accuracy and control of ECUCO's accounting data. This system was to provide a base for a more comprehensive computerized accounting system encompassing other applications.

---

[1]Adapted from D. P. Lubas, ''Developing a Computerized General Ledger System,'' *Management Accounting,* May 1976, pp. 53–56. Copyright by National Association of Accountants (1976), Montvale, N.J. 07645. Used by permission.

Defining Inputs

The first step in developing this system was to identify the data elements necessary to support the general ledger system. The design team asked users to prepare lists of all the data they would like to see as outputs from this system. The team found that a number of the data items were processed by other systems, such as accounts payable, accounts receivable, and payroll. For this reason, they did not include them in this system. After repeated discussions with users, a list of general ledger system inputs was finally compiled.

Defining Outputs

The second step was to define the reports required from the system. After discussions with users, the design team determined that the system should produce a total of six reports. Four of these would be produced monthly; the remaining two would be produced after each execution of the system. These two reports allowed the accounting department to monitor the system and to maintain adequate system controls. The following is a brief description of these reports:

General Ledger. The general ledger is normally produced at month-end, but it can be produced during the month if necessary. The design team decided that, in keeping with traditional general ledger layouts, each general ledger account and its detail would start on a new page. When the general ledger account is supported by a subsidiary ledger (or subledger), only totals appear in the general ledger. All details supporting the general ledger balance appear in the subledger.

The last page of the general ledger contains total debits for the month, total credits for the month, and trial balance figures. These figures can be reconciled with the most current summary control report printed prior to the printing of the general ledger. At year-end the system produces a pile up general ledger, disclosing totals for all months rather than those for an individual month.

Exhibit 21–1 contains a schematic of the general ledger system showing how it captures data from both manual and mechanized sources, feeds summary data, and produces reports for top management.

Subledgers. Similar to the general ledger, the subledgers are normally produced monthly; however, they can be produced at other times if necessary.

Each subledger account and its detail starts on a new page and contains two types of information. First, the page contains a functional department breakdown by month and year. This shows each department that incurs a charge in that account. Second, it provides totals by charge classification (payroll, depreciation, taxes, and so forth).

Subledger Summary. The system prints the subledger summary at the end of each subledger. It contains the total debits and total credits for the account code range contained in the subledger. The accounting department reconciles these figures with the controlling general ledger account. The subledger summary also

EXHIBIT 21–1 Case 21–21

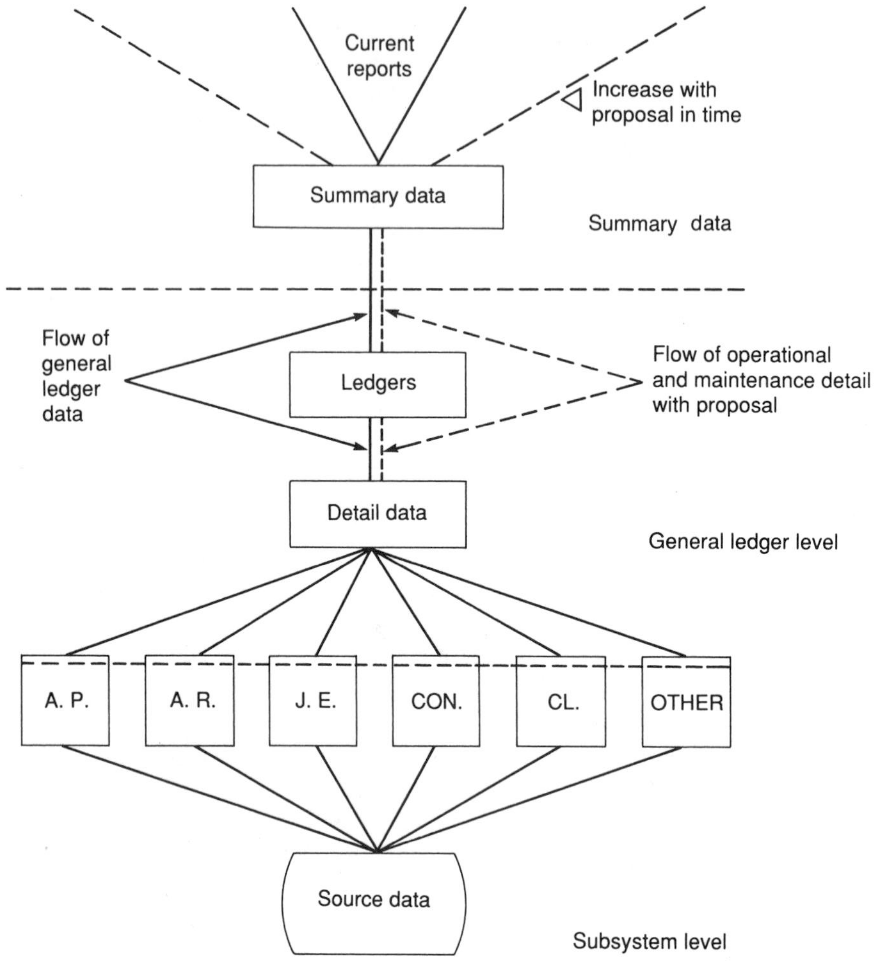

contains a functional department summary that lists, by department, totals for each charge classification by month and by year.

Operation and Maintenance Work Order Summary. An operation and maintenance work order identifies individual construction projects, types of project, or classes of expense. The system produces it monthly after the subledgers are printed. This summary contains detail totals by account for each operation and maintenance work order. It also contains a classification summary that lists monthly and year-to-date totals by charge classification.

Summary Control Report. The summary control report is printed at the end of each execution of the batch validation program. The report shows month-to-date totals for all accounts with subledgers and for all other accounts selected by the user. Frequently accountants use this to obtain a listing of totals for classification codes of interest to them. The report also shows total debits, total credits, trial balance amounts, and the amounts in any contra accounts.

Journal Register and Error List. The system produces these reports whenever transactions are submitted to the system. These reports list both valid and erroneous transactions. The error list identifies each erroneous transaction by printing the contents of the transaction and a description of the error.

The journal register and error list disclose both record counts and control totals. The record counts are provided when the batch is accepted as correct and added to the accepted records file.

System Procedures

The third step in the development of this general ledger system was determining how to collect and process the data. The design team identified methods for data collection, process flow, and procedures for data validation and correction.

Data Collection. Users record the data in one of three forms: manual input transactions, computerized interface input, and system control input.

Manual Input Transactions. Manual input transactions are all general journal entries. The accounts payable and accounts receivable entries are manual for two classes of users. Some do not have computerized systems, while others have computerized systems that are not interfaced with the new general ledger system. Management plans to integrate some of these systems with the new general ledger at some time in the future.

Computerized Interface Transactions. Computerized interface transactions consist of data passed automatically from the existing computerized system to the general ledger system for processing.

System Control Input. System control data is generated both manually by users and by computerized systems. Although individual users are responsible for submitting correct transactions, a central data control group coordinates their efforts.

Each user department maintains a control log of transaction batches that the control group reconciles with the journal register and error list. Batch control for computerized interface transactions are created automatically by the system; therefore, a control log is not required for these entries.

Processing Flow. After defining how data are gathered, the design team developed the processing flow. Source documents—including journal entries, accounts payable vouchers, and accounts receivable documents—are grouped by batch. Each batch contains documents of one source type and is numbered in sequence and then forwarded to data processing for data entry.

Batches are first processed by a validation program. Any number of batches can be submitted to one validation run, and all types of batches can be submitted simultaneously. Computerized entries from other systems are also validated; however, these maintain their original identity to simplify error correction procedures.

Data Validation and Correction. Batches submitted to the validation program pass sequentially through validity and compatibility checks. Records found to be in error are flagged with a descriptive error message and all records of the batch are written to an error file. Erroneous records are assigned an identification key to enable the accounting clerk to locate them quickly.

Batches that have no errors are then processed by a control program that accumulates data and prints account totals on the summary control report.

Users correct their errors with a separate error correction program. They use identification keys to locate erroneous records in the error file. They correct the erroneous records and then reprocess the entire error file through the validation program as if the errors were normal batch entries. Even when the erroneous transaction was produced by one of the computerized systems, the transaction is corrected by the general ledger system in this way.

Users execute the validation program whenever desired. On the last validation run of a month, however, the error file must be cleared of transactions. The system executes no general ledger or subledger programs if error records remain in this file. This is important because the system holds an entire batch in suspense whenever an error occurs in any record in the batch. Omitting an entire batch when printing the general ledger could seriously affect the accuracy of reported financial data.

System Controls

While the design team was developing processing flow, users requested numerous controls. After considering these requests, the design team developed controls in three basic areas: manual controls, automatic computerized controls, and manually initiated computerized controls.

Manual Controls. The design team instituted the following manual controls intended to ensure accurate submission of data and proper and complete acceptance of data by the system:

Single Source Document. All manual input, including corrections to the system, are in one standard format on a standard form. This simplifies submitting data, auditing the system, and eliminates errors arising from multiple forms and transactions.

Control Totals per Batch. The control total is calculated by totaling the amounts while ignoring their signs. Using this total ensures that all transactions in a batch are entered in the system.

Month-to-Date Controls. Each user location maintains month-to-date totals of amounts processed at that location. They reconcile these totals with those on the control report produced by the system.

Review of Output Reports. Both daily and monthly reports are reviewed. By reviewing key reports, users discover errors undetected by the system validation program. An example is recording a transaction in an incorrect expense account.

Automatic Computerized Controls. The system uses these controls during validation, updating, and in numerous other programs throughout the general ledger system.

Detail Element Validation. The system checks individual data elements for accuracy. These elements include the voucher number, accounting month, improper blanks, and alphabetic or numeric characters.

Amount Verification. Computer programs determine that debits equal credits on all input transactions. Also, the total amounts of all transactions in a batch must equal the control totals submitted for the batch.

Control File. The control file contains current month totals by account code and by work order qualifier. From it, the system produces a monthly control report. Users verify the totals on this report to assess the accuracy of computerized procedures.

Journal Register and Error List. The system produces these reports whenever transactions enter it. They identify errors submitted to the system and suspense account entries created to eliminate the errors. The journal register provides a complete list of data submitted for validation and enables users to identify missing journal entries.

Manually Initiated Computerized Controls. Manual procedures provide audit capability and provide greater assurance of accuracy. They are initiated on request.

These control procedures check the various files of the system to ensure that they are in balance. All transactions processed are copied to a backup file. The total of all transactions in the backup file underlying a control file balance are checked against the total in the control file. These totals are also compared to the balance in the control accounts in the general ledger file.

Users initiate these procedures daily. They not only verify the accuracy of control file and general ledger file totals but also ensure accurate backup of the current day's transactions.

Responsibilities

The final step in the development of the general ledger system was establishing responsibilities. Two important job positions identified by the design team were those of site controller and system coordinator.

Site Controller. Management decided that users' groups would be responsible for the timely submission of transactions from their own departments or companies. To monitor and control system processing properly, each department and company was required to appoint a site controller.

The site controller accumulates and verifies transactions, develops batch totals, enters these batch totals on a transmittal form, and submits the batches for data entry. The site controller also reviews the journal register and error list and either corrects errors or initiates activity to resolve them. In addition, he or she reviews general and subledger reports.

System Coordinator. Although the system relies on data submitted by various locations, management desired a single, common accounting system using standardized procedures. For this reason, they appointed a system coordinator. This person reviews and approves policies and procedures and further coordinates processing between users' groups. The system coordinator is also responsible for reconciling system outputs with each users' group's site controller and serves as a centralized communication point for resolving inquiries regarding the system.

Conclusion

This computerized general ledger system makes standardized accounting information available throughout ECUCO. Besides enabling easier analysis and better decision making throughout the company, it eliminates manual preparation of many schedules, reports, and ledgers. It maintains system control while providing for future expansion of the computerized system into other application areas.

Required:

a. For this general ledger system identify:
   1. Its objectives
   2. Its outputs

b. Describe the use of registers and control reports in this application.

c. Identify the following application controls in this system:
   1. Input controls
   2. Processing controls
   3. Output controls

d. Draw a system flowchart showing the system's data validation and error correction procedures.

Index

I

J

L

M

N

O

P

Q